SCOTT®

[redacted]

2010 STANDARD POSTAGE STAMP CATALOGUE

ONE HUNDRED AND SIXTY-SIXTH EDITION IN SIX VOLUMES

VOLUME 2
COUNTRIES OF THE WORLD
C-F

EDITOR	James E. Kloetzel
ASSOCIATE EDITOR	William A. Jones
ASSISTANT EDITOR /NEW ISSUES & VALUING	Martin J. Frankevicz
ASSISTANT EDITOR	Charles Snee
VALUING ANALYST	Steven R. Myers
ADMINISTRATIVE ASSISTANT/IMAGE COORDINATOR	Beth L. Brown
DESIGN MANAGER	Teresa M. Wenrick
ADVERTISING	Phyllis Stegemoller
CIRCULATION / PRODUCT PROMOTION MANAGER	Tim Wagner
VICE PRESIDENT/EDITORIAL AND PRODUCTION	Steve Collins
PRESIDENT	William Fay

Released May 2009

Includes New Stamp Listings through the May 2009 *Scott Stamp Monthly* Catalogue Update

Scott Publishing Co.

911 Vandemark Road, Sidney, OH 45365-0828

A division of AMOS PRESS, INC., publishers of *Scott Stamp Monthly, Linn's Stamp News, Coin World* and *Coin World's Coin Values.*

Table of Contents

See Volume 1 for United States, United Nations and Countries of the World A-B
See Volume 3 through 6 for Countries of the World, G-Z.

Volume 3: G-I
Volume 4: J-O
Volume 5: P-Sl
Volume 6: So-Z

ISBN 0-89487-439-X

Library of Congress Card No. 2-3301

Vol. 2 Number Additions, Deletions & Changes

Number in 2009 Catalogue	Number in 2010 Catalogue
Cameroun	
new	21a
new	22a
Canada	
new	1737f
new	2006b
new	2201a
new	2235a
Castellorizo	
new	2a
new	35a
new	35b
new	37a
new	54b
new	58a
Cilicia	
new	99d
new	99e
Cochin China	
new	3a
new	4d
new	4e
Comoro Islands	
800Cf	deleted
800Ij	deleted
Croatia	
new	100b
Djibouti	
new	C233a
new	C234a
Dominica	
new	1a
France	
96a	96b
96b	96a
new	162c
162c	162d
162d	162e
162e	162f
new	166b
new	169a
new	172b
new	173b
new	176a
new	198a-201a
French Congo	
8c	deleted
10b	deleted
French Equatorial Africa	
new	80a
new	81a
new	82a
new	83a
new	83b
new	84a
new	85a

Number in 2009 Catalogue	Number in 2010 Catalogue
French Equatorial Africa	
new	86a
new	87a
new	88a
new	89a
new	90a
new	91a
new	93a
new	94b
new	C10a
new	C10b
new	C12a
new	C13a
French Guiana	
new	1a
new	1b
1b	1c
2a	2b
new	2a
new	4a
new	4b
new	5a
new	5b
new	5c
new	6a
new	6b
new	6c
new	7a
new	7b
new	11a
new	11b
new	12a
new	17c
new	22b
new	25a
new	25b
new	27a
new	30a
new	31a
new	31b
new	31c
new	52a
new	78a
new	84a
new	94a
new	95b
new	95c
new	96b
new	100a
new	100b
new	109a
new	110a
new	115a
new	124a
new	126a
new	J1a
new	J7a
French Guinea	
new	66a
new	68a
new	71a
new	116a
new	118a
new	119a

Number in 2009 Catalogue	Number in 2010 Catalogue
French Morocco	
11a	deleted
new	122a

Scott Publishing Co.

SCOTT 911 VANDEMARK ROAD, SIDNEY, OHIO 45365 937-498-0802

Dear Scott Catalogue User:

A time of uncertainty.

We all know that economies worldwide are weak. As part of that situation, demand for most products is soft. From all information we can gather, it appears that the market for stamps is a bit stronger than most, and for that we can be grateful. However, let's be honest. Unless you have the rarest of the rare or the highest possible grade of a stamp, the market is not lively. Most stamps are holding their own, but just barely.

As a result of these circumstances, collectors and dealers will find that many fewer values have changed in this 2010 Volume 2 edition of the *Scott Standard Postage Stamp Catalogue* compared to the record number of changes that were seen in last year's edition. There are certainly value changes, almost 18,000 of them, but this is many fewer than were made last year.

Where are the value changes in the 2010 Volume 2?

There are more than 5,000 value changes in the group of French-area countries running from French Colonies to French West Africa, with French Morocco leading the way in this group with 1,163 changes. Canada shows 2,100 value changes, followed by Cuba (1,183), Reunion (1,173), Costa Rica (1,008), People's Republic of China (764), Cameroun (727) and Estonia (603).

With certain exceptions, stamp values in Canada are holding steady. A minor exception in the classic period is the 1852 3p Beaver, Scott 4, which drops slightly in used condition to $225 from $240 in the 2009 Volume 2. The dollar-value Victoria Jubilees of 1897, Scott 61-65, also drop in value slightly in all three conditions of unused, mint never hinged, and used. There is minor slippage in the values of comparatively very few stamps from the late-1930s to mid-1950s, then relative stability in the late-1950s to 1970s issues. However, starting in the late 1970s and continuing to the current new issues, the weakness of the Canadian dollar is evident in the general lowering of values for mint never hinged stamps.

Despite this slight lowering of selected Canada values, there are signs of strength in some areas. Some classic issues rise in value, such as the 1857 7½p green Victoria, which takes a healthy jump to $10,000 unused from $8,500 last year. Some other earlier issues show modest increases in value, and the first three sets of postage dues, Scott J1-J14, also see healthy value gains.

Value changes in the People's Republic of China are scattered, but the changes are upward where they occur.

In Costa Rica, a thorough review has resulted in more than a thousand value changes, and these changes are almost always to higher values, sometimes significantly higher. Two of the most noteworthy increases are seen for the strips of five pre-Columbian art stamps issued in 1986, Scott 375 and 376, which jump to $5.25 and $9.75 in mint never-hinged condition, from just $1.75 and $3.25, respectively, in last year's Volume 2. A number of other increases of this size appear in the modern issues, though most increases are of a smaller size.

A significant number of early Cuba stamps show modest increases of 10 percent to 15 percent both unused and used. There are few changes throughout most of the 20th century, but the period 1998 to the present shows an interesting pattern of selected increases and decreases in values. The value changes in the back-of-the-book stamps of Cuba are quite scattered, but where there is movement it is to modestly higher levels.

Values for Estonia stamps trend higher, often by 20 percent in the earlier issues, with smaller increases in later issues. The 1928-40 1s-80s Arms set, Scott 90-104, moves to $73.95 unused and $125.00 mint never hinged, from $58.80 unused and $85.00 mint never hinged last year.

Also trending higher are the values for the various French areas. A somewhat typical example is the attractive 1c-20fr definitives scenes issue of 1933-34 from French Morocco, Scott 124-147, which rises to $96.90 unused from $74.80 unused in the 2009 Volume 2. While other singles and sets throughout all these French areas may not show the same percentage increases, the overall trend is clear.

We are close to completing our all-color image project.

Collectors may remember that color images began appearing in the Scott catalogs for the first time in October 2004, when the 2005 *Scott Specialized Catalogue of United States Stamps and Covers* was published for the first time in color. That was followed by the *Scott Classic Specialized Catalogue* of 2005. Then, with the 2006 Standard catalogues, Volumes 1-6, the entire Scott catalogue line appeared in color.

We began scanning stamps from the Scott reference collection in early 2001, and these images (in black and white) started appearing in the 2002 catalogues. Later in 2001 we were blessed by the appearance of a philatelic angel who loaned us, during a period of many months, his entire 400-volume collection of worldwide mint stamps. That angel was Dr. Hsien-ming Meng, an Ohio collector within easy driving distance from our Sidney, Ohio, offices. Between the Scott reference collection and Dr. Meng's collection, we soon approached 90 percent to 100 percent completion in color scans for country after country.

Many other collectors and dealers have helped in the last few years, to the point to where we now show close to 100 percent of the stamps in the catalogues in full color. Those who have helped with this project have sent color scans or the actual stamps that were needed. We want to thank once again George Holschauer of Colonial Stamp Co., who has loaned Scott several hundred valuable and seldom-seen stamps from the British Commonwealth and also from many non-British countries. These stamps were scanned, and they have replaced black and white images or used stamps previously shown in color, or they have been added as new, previously unpictured stamps. We wish to express our deep appreciation to Mr. Holschauer for his generous support of our color image project.

And we thank all the others who continue to send in scans or stamps. Remember, if you see a Scott image of a stamp in black and white, we probably need a color scan. Any help you can provide will be appreciated. Just call or write us for details concerning what must be done.

We now have begun a new project of replacing images of stamps that are not in an appropriate condition for the catalogues or are in need of color correction. Hundreds of scans already have been replaced, and many more will be in coming years.

Final thoughts.

On the editorial side, there are numerous new minor-number listings added in fifteen different countries, and there are a very few minor numbers deleted from the catalogue. See the Volume 2 Number Additions, Deletions & Changes listing on page 4A of the introduction for these changes.

Especially in uncertain economic times such as these, a hobby is a great gift. Happy collecting.

James E. Kloetzel

James E. Kloetzel/Catalogue Editor

Acknowledgments

Our appreciation and gratitude go to the following individuals who have assisted us in preparing information included in this year's Scott Catalogues. Some helpers prefer anonymity. These individuals have generously shared their stamp knowledge with others through the medium of the Scott Catalogue.

Those who follow provided information that is in addition to the hundreds of dealer price lists and advertisements and scores of auction catalogues and realizations that were used in producing the catalogue values. It is from those noted here that we have been able to obtain information on items not normally seen in published lists and advertisements. Support from these people goes beyond data leading to catalogue values, for they also are key to editorial changes.

A special acknowledgment to Liane and Sergio Sismondo of The Classic Collector for their extraordinary assistance and knowledge sharing that has aided in the preparation of this year's Standard and Classic Specialized Catalogues.

A. R. Allison (Orange Free State Study Circle)
Roland Austin
Robert Ausubel (Great Britain Collectors Club)
Jack Hagop Barsoumian (International Stamp Co.)
Tim Bartshe
William Batty-Smith
Jules K. Beck (Latin American Philatelic Society)
Vladimir Berrio-Lemm
John Birkinbine II
John D. Bowman (Carriers and Locals Society)
Bernard Bujnak
Timothy Bryan Burgess
Mike Bush (Joseph V. Bush, Inc.)
Tina & John Carlson (JET Stamps)
Carlson Chambliss
Richard A. Champagne (Richard A. Champagne, Inc.)
Henry Chlanda
Richard Clever
Leroy P. Collins III (United Postal Stationery Society)
Laurie Conrad
Frank D. Correl
Tony L. Crumbley (Carolina Coin & Stamp, Inc.)
Stephen R. Datz
Tony Davis
Charles Deaton
Bob Dumaine
Sister Theresa Durand
Mark Eastzer (Markest Stamp Co.)
Esi Ebrani (Iran Philatelic Study Circle)
Paul G. Eckman
Marty Farber
Leon Finik (Loral Stamps)
Henry Fisher
Robert A. Fisher
Jeffrey M. Forster
Ken Fowler
Robert S. Freeman
Ernest E. Fricks (France & Colonies Philatelic Society)
Michael A. Goldman (Regency Superior, Ltd.)
Daniel E. Grau
Andy Green
Jan E. Gronwall
Joe Hahn (Associated Collectors of El Salvador)
Bruce Hecht (Bruce L. Hecht Co.)
Clifford O. Herrick (Fidelity Trading Co.)
Peter Hoffman
George W. Holschauer (Colonial Stamp Company)
Armen Hovsepian
Philip J. Hughes (Croatian Philatelic Society)
Doug Iams
N. M. Janoowalla
Stephen Joe (International Stamp Service)
John Kardos (The Stamp Gallery)
Allan Katz (Ventura Stamp Co.)
Stanford M. Katz
Patricia A. Kaufmann
William V. Kriebel
Dr. Ingert (Ihor) Kuzych-Berlzovsky
Michael Lenard
John R. Lewis (The William Henry Stamp Co.)
William A. Litle
Pedro Llach (Filatelia Llach S.L.)
George Luzitano
Dennis Lynch
Robert L. Markovits (Quality Investors, Ltd.)
Marilyn R. Mattke
William K. McDaniel
Mark S. Miller (India Study Circle)
Allen Mintz (United Postal Stationery Society)
William E. Mooz
Gary M. Morris (Pacific Midwest Co.)
Peter Mosiondz, Jr.
Bruce M. Moyer (Moyer Stamps & Collectibles)
Gary Nelson
Dr. Marwan Nusair
Robert Odenweller (AIEP)
Albert Olejnik
Dr. Everett L. Parker
Mark Parren
John E. Pearson (Pittwater Philatelic Service)
John Pedneault
Michael O. Perry
Donald J. Peterson (International Philippine Philatelic Society)
Stanley M. Piller (Stanley M. Piller & Associates)
Todor Drumev Popov
Peter W. W. Powell
Stephen Radin (Albany Stamp Co.)
Siddique Mahmudur Rahman
Dr. Reuben A. Ramkissoon
Ghassan D. Riachi
Peter A. Robertson
Omar Rodriquez
Michael Rogers (Michael Rogers, Inc.)
Michael Ruggiero
Mehrdad Sadri (Persiphila)
Richard H. Salz
Alex Schauss (Schauss Philatelics)
Jacques C. Schiff, Jr. (Jacques C. Schiff, Jr., Inc.)
Bernard Seckler (Fine Arts Philatelists)
Guy Shaw
Charles F. Shreve (Spink Shreves Galleries)
Sergio & Liane Sismondo (The Classic Collector)
Jay Smith
Frank J. Stanley, III
Philip & Henry Stevens (postalstationery.com)
Jerry Summers
Scott R. Trepel (Siegel Auction Galleries)
Steve Unkrich
Philip T. Wall
Kristian Wang
Richard A. Washburn
Giana Wayman
William R. Weiss, Jr. (Weiss Philatelics)
Ed Wener (Indigo)
Hans A. Westphal
Don White (Dunedin Stamp Centre)
Kirk Wolford (Kirkís Stamp Company)
Robert F. Yacano (K-Line Philippines)
Ralph Yorio
Val Zabijaka
Michal Zika
John P. Zuckerman (Siegel Auction Galleries)
Alfonsa G. Zulueta, Jr.

Addresses, Telephone Numbers, Web Sites, E-Mail Addresses of General & Specialized Philatelic Societies

Collectors can contact the following groups for information about the philately of the areas within the scope of these societies, or inquire about membership in these groups. Aside from the general societies, we limit this list to groups that specialize in particular fields of philately, particular areas covered by the Scott Standard Postage Stamp Catalogue, and topical groups. Many more specialized philatelic society exist than those listed below. These addresses are updated yearly, and they are, to the best of our knowledge, correct and current. Groups should inform the editors of address changes whenever they occur. The editors also want to hear from other such specialized groups not listed.

Unless otherwise noted all website addresses begin with http://

American Philatelic Society
100 Match Factory Place
Bellefonte PA 16823-1367
Ph: (814) 933-3803
www.stamps.org
E-mail: apsinfo@stamps.org

American Stamp Dealers Association, Inc.
Matthew Hansen
3 School St. Suite #205
Glen Cove NY 11542
Ph: (516) 759-7000
www.asdaonline.com
E-mail: asda@erols.com

National Stamp Dealers Association
Dick Keiser, president
2916 NW Bucklin Hill Rd #136
Silverdale WA 98383-8514
Ph: (800) 875-6633
www.nsdainc.org
E-mail: gail@nsdainc.org

International Society of Worldwide Stamp Collectors
Joanne Berkowitz, MD
PO Box 19006
Sacramento CA 95819
www.iswsc.org
E-mail: executivedirector@iswsc.org

Royal Philatelic Society
41 Devonshire Place
London, United Kingdom, W1G 6JY
www.rpsl.org.uk
E-mail: secretary@rpsl.org.uk

Royal Philatelic Society of Canada
PO Box 929, Station Q
Toronto, ON, Canada, M4T 2P1
Ph: (888) 285-4143
www.rpsc.org
E-mail: info@rpsc.org

Young Stamp Collectors of America
Janet Houser
100 Match Factory Place
Bellefonte PA 16823-1367
Ph: (814) 933-3820
www.stamps.org/ysca/intro.htm
E-mail: ysca@stamps.org

Groups focusing on fields or aspects found in worldwide philately (some may cover U.S. area only)

American Air Mail Society
Stephen Reinhard
PO Box 110
Mineola NY 11501
www.americanairmailsociety.org
E-mail: sreinhard1@optonline.net

American First Day Cover Society
Douglas Kelsey
PO Box 16277
Tucson AZ 85732-6277
Ph: (520) 321-0880
www.afdcs.org
E-mail: afdcs@aol.com

American Revenue Association
Eric Jackson
PO Box 728
Leesport PA 19533-0728
Ph: (610) 926-6200
www.revenuer.org
E-mail: eric@revenuer.com

American Topical Association
Ray E. Cartier
PO Box 57
Arlington TX 76004-0057
Ph: (817) 274-1181
americantopicalassn.org
E-mail: americantopical@msn.com

Christmas Seal & Charity Stamp Society
John Denune
234 East Broadway
Granville OH 43023
Ph: (740) 587-0276
http://cscss.home.att.net
E-mail: jdenune@roadrunner.com

Errors, Freaks and Oddities Collectors Club
Stan Raugh
4217 Eighth Ave.
Temple PA 19560
Ph: (717) 445-9420 Nor. Am. Phone No.
www.efocc.org
E-mail: ddprice98@hotmail.com

First Issues Collectors Club
Clark Buchi
P.O. Box 453
Brentwood TN 37024-0453
www.firstissues.org
E-mail: orders@firstissues.org

International Society of Reply Coupon Collectors
Peter Robin
PO Box 353
Bala Cynwyd PA 19004
E-mail: peterrobin@verizon.net

The Joint Stamp Issues Society
Pascal LeBlond
60-600 Rue Cormier
Gatineau, QC, Canada, J9H 6B4
jointissues.ovh.org
E-mail: jointissues@yahoo.com

National Duck Stamp Collectors Society
Anthony J. Monico
PO Box 43
Harleysville PA 19438-0043
www.ndscs.org
E-mail: ndscs@hwcn.org

No Value Identified Club
Albert Sauvanet
Le Clos Royal B, Boulevard des Pas Enchantes
St. Sebastien-sur Loire, France, 44230
E-mail: alain.vailly@irin.univ nantes.fr

The Perfins Club
Jerry Hejduk
PO Box 490450.
Leesburg FL 34749-0450
Ph: (352) 326-2117
E-mail: flprepers@comcast.net

Postage Due Mail Study Group
John Rawlins
13, Longacre
Chelmsford
United Kingdom, CM1 3BJ
E-mail: john.rawlins2@ukonline.co.uk.

Post Mark Collectors Club
Beverly Proulx
7629 Homestead Drive
Baldwinsville NY 13027
Ph: (315) 638-0532
www.postmarks.org
E-mail: stampdance@tweny.rr.com

Postal History Society
Kalman V. Illyefalvi
869 Bridgewater Drive
New Oxford PA 17350-8206
Ph: (717) 624-5941
www.stampclubs.com
E-mail: kalphyl@juno.com

Precancel Stamp Society
Jerry Hejduk
PO Box 490450.
Leesburg FL 34749-0450
Ph: (352) 326-2117
www.precancels.com
E-mail: psspromosec@comcast.net

United Postal Stationery Society
Stuart Leven
1445-50 Foxworthy Ave. #187
San Jose, CA 95118-1119
www.upss.org
E-mail: poststat@gmail.com

Groups focusing on U.S. area philately as covered in the Standard Catalogue

Canal Zone Study Group
Richard H. Salz
60 27th Ave.
San Francisco CA 94121-1026

Carriers and Locals Society
John D. Bowman
PO Box 74
Grosse Ile MI 48138
www.pennypost.org
E-mail: jbowman@stx.rr.net

Confederate Stamp Alliance
Gen. Francis J. Crown
PO Box 278
Capshaw AL 35742-0278
Ph. (302) 422-2656
www.csalliance.org
E-mail: csaas@knology.net

Hawaiian Philatelic Society
Kay H. Hoke
PO Box 10115
Honolulu HI 96816-0115
Ph: (808) 521-5721

Plate Number Coil Collectors Club
Ronald E. Maifeld
PO Box 54622
Cincinnati OH 45254-0622
Ph: (513) 231-4208
www.pnc3.org
E-mail: president@pnc3.org

Ryukyu Philatelic Specialist Society
Laura Edmonds, Secy.
PO Box 240177
Charlotte NC 28224-0177
Ph: (704) 519-5157
www.ryukyustamps.org
E-mail: secretary@ryukyustamps.org

United Nations Philatelists
Blanton Clement, Jr.
P.O. Box 146
Morrisville PA 19067-0146
www.unpi.com
E-mail: bclemjr@yahoo.com

United States Stamp Society
Executive Secretary
PO Box 6634
Katy TX 77491-6631
www.usstamps.org
E-mail: webmaster@usstamps.org

U.S. Cancellation Club
Roger Rhoads
6160 Brownstone Ct.
Mentor OH 44060
www.geocities.com/athens/2088/uscchome.htm
E-mail: rrrhoads@aol.com

U.S. Philatelic Classics Society
Rob Lund
2913 Fulton
Everett WA 98201-3733
www.uspcs.org
E-mail: membershipchairman@uspcs.org

United States Possessions Philatelic Society
Geoffrey Brewster
6453 E. Stallion Rd.
Paradise Valley AZ 85253
Ph: (480) 607-7184

Groups focusing on philately of foreign countries or regions

Aden & Somaliland Study Group
Gary Brown
PO Box 106
Briar Hill, Victoria, Australia, 3088
E-mail: garyjohn951@optushome.com.au

American Society of Polar Philatelists (Antarctic areas)
Alan Warren
PO Box 39
Exton PA 19341-0039
Ph: (847) 421-7655
www.polarphilatelists.org
E-mail: cjenner00@yahoo.com

Andorran Philatelic Study Circle
D. Hope
17 Hawthorn Dr.
Stalybridge, Cheshire, United Kingdom, SK15 1UE
http://apsc.free.fr
E-mail: apsc@free.fr

Australian States Study Circle of The Royal Sydney Philatelic Club
Ben Palmer
GPO 1751
Sydney, N.S.W., Australia, 2001

Austria Philatelic Society
Ralph Schneider
PO Box 23049
Belleville IL 62223
Ph: (618) 277-6152
www.austriaphilatelicsociety.com
E-mail: rsstamps@aol.com

American Belgian Philatelic Society
Edward de Bary
11 Wakefield Dr. Apt. 2105
Asheville NC 28803
E-mail: belgam@charter.net

Bechuanalands and Botswana Society
Neville Midwood
69 Porlock Lane
Furzton, Milton Keynes, United Kingdom, MK4 1JY
www.nevsoft.com
E-mail: bbsoc@nevsoft.com

Bermuda Collectors Society
Thomas J. McMahon
PO Box 1949
Stuart FL 34995
www.bermudacollectorssociety.org
E-mail: science29@comcast.net

Brazil Philatelic Association
William V. Kriebel
1923 ManningSt.
Philadelphia PA 19103-5728
Ph: (215) 735-3697
E-mail: kriebewv@drexel.edu

British Caribbean Philatelic Study Group
Dr. Reuben A. Ramkissoon
3011 White Oak Lane
Oak Brook IL 60523-2513
Ph: (630) 963-1439
www.bcpsg.com
E-mail: rramkissoon@juno.com

The King George VI Collectors Society (British Commonwealth)
John Shaw
17 Balcaskie Road, Eltham
London, United Kingdom, SE9 1HQ
www.kg6.info

British North America Philatelic Society (Canada & Provinces)
H. P. Jacobi
6-2168 150A St.
Surrey, B.C., Canada, V4A 9W4
www.bnaps.org
E-mail: pjacobi@shaw.ca

British West Indies Study Circle
W. Clary Holt
PO Drawer 59
Burlington NC 27216
Ph: (336) 227-7461

Burma Philatelic Study Circle
Michael Whittaker
1, Ecton Leys, Hillside
Rugby, Warwickshire, United Kingdom, CV22 5SL
E-mail: whittaker2004@ntlworld.com

Ceylon Study Group
R. W. P. Frost
42 Lonsdale Road, Cannington
Bridgewater, Somerset, United Kingdom, TA5 2JS
E-mail: rodney.frost@tiscali.co.uk

Channel Islands Specialists Society
Moira Edwards
86, Hall Lane, Sandon,
Chelmsford, United Kingdom, CM2 7RQ
www.ciss1950.org.uk
E-mail: am012e5360@blueyonder.co.uk

China Stamp Society
Paul H. Gault
PO Box 20711
Columbus OH 43220
www.chinastampsociety.org
E-mail: secretary@chinastampsociety.org

Colombia/Panama Philatelic Study Group (COPAPHIL)
Thomas P. Myers
7411 Old Post Road #1
Lincoln NE 68506
www.copaphil.org
E-mail: tpmphil@hotmail.com

Association Filatelic de Costa Rica
Giana Wayman
c/o Interlink 102, PO Box 52-6770
Miami, FL 33152
E-mail: scotland@racsa.co.cr

Society for Costa Rica Collectors
Dr. Hector R. Mena
PO Box 14831
Baton Rouge LA 70808
www.socorico.org
E-mail: hrmena@aol.com

Cuban Philatelic Society of America
Ernesto Cuesta
PO Box 34434
Bethesda MD 20827
www.philat.com/cpsa
E-mail: ecuesta@philat.com

Cyprus Study Circle
Colin Dear
10 Marne Close, Wem
Shropshire, United Kingdom, SY4 5YE
www.cyprusstudycircle.org/index.htm
E-mail: colindear@talktalk.net.

Society for Czechoslovak Philately
Phil Rhoade
905 E. Oakside St.
South Bend IN 46614
www.csphilately.org
E-mail: philip.rhoade@mnsu.edu

Danish West Indies Study Unit of the Scandinavian Collectors Club
Arnold Sorensen
7666 Edgedale Drive
Newburgh IN 47630
Ph: (812) 853-2653
dwistudygroup.com
E-mail: valbydwi@hotmail.com

East Africa Study Circle
Jonathan Smalley
1 Lincoln Close
Tweeksbury, United Kingdom, B91 1AE
easc.org.uk
E-mail: jpasmalley@tiscali.co.uk

Egypt Study Circle
Mike Murphy
109 Chadwick Road
London, United Kingdom, SE15 4PY
Dick Wilson: North American Agent
egyptstudycircle.org.uk
E-mail: egyptstudycircle@hotmail.com

Estonian Philatelic Society
Juri Kirsimagi
29 Clifford Ave.
Pelham NY 10803
Ph: (914) 738-3713

Ethiopian Philatelic Society
Ulf Lindahl
21 Westview Place
Riverside CT 06878
Ph: (203) 866-3540
home.comcast.net/~fbheiser/ethiopia5.htm
E-mail: ulindahl@optonline.net

Falkland Islands Philatelic Study Group
Carl J. Faulkner
Williams Inn, On-the-Green
Williamstown MA 01267-2620
www.fipsg.org.uk
Ph: (413) 458-9371

Faroe Islands Study Circle
Norman Hudson
28 Enfield Road
Ellesmere Port, Cheshire, United Kingdom, CH65 8BY
www.faroeislandssc.org.
E-mail: jntropics@hotmail.com

Former French Colonies Specialist Society
BP 628
75367 Paris, Cedex 08, France
www.colfra.com
E-mail: clubcolfra@aol.com

France & Colonies Philatelic Society
Edward Grabowski
111 Prospect St., 4C
Westfield NJ 07090
www.drunkenboat.net/frandcol/
E-mail: edjjg@alum.mit.edu

Germany Philatelic Society
PO Box 6547
Chesterfield MO 63006
www.gps.nu

Gibraltar Study Circle
David R. Stirrups
34 Glamis Drive
Dundee, United Kingdom, DD2 1QP
E-mail: drstirrups@dundee.ac.uk

Great Britain Collectors Club
Timothy Bryan Burgess
3547 Windmill Way
Concord CA 94518
www.gbstamps.com/gbcc
E-mail: Pennyred@earthlink.net

International Society of Guatemala Collectors
Jaime Marckwordt
449 St. Francis Blvd.
Daly City CA 94015-2136
www.guatemalastamps.com

Hellenic Philatelic Society of America (Greece and related areas)
Dr. Nicholas Asimakopulos
541 Cedar Hill Ave.
Wyckoff NJ 07481
Ph: (201) 447-6262
E-mail: nick1821@aol.com

Haiti Philatelic Society
Ubaldo Del Toro
5709 Marble Archway
Alexandria VA 22315
www.haitiphilately.org
E-mail: u007ubi@aol.com

Hong Kong Stamp Society
Dr. An-Min Chung
3300 Darby Rd. Cottage 503
Haverford PA 19041-1064

Society for Hungarian Philately
Robert Morgan
2201 Roscomare Rd.
Los Angeles CA 90077-2222
www.hungarianphilately.org
E-mail: h.alan.hoover@hungarianphilately.org

India Study Circle
John Warren
PO Box 7326
Washington DC 20044
Ph: (202) 564-6876
www.indiastudycircle.org
E-mail: warren.john@epa.gov

Indian Ocean Study Circle
Mrs. S. Hopson
Field Acre, Hoe Benham
Newbury, Berkshire, United Kingdom, RG20 8PD

Society of Indo-China Philatelists
Ron Bentley
2600 North 24th Street
Arlington VA 22207
www.sicp-online.org
E-mail: ron.bentley@verizon.net

Iran Philatelic Study Circle
Mehdi Esmaili
PO Box 750096
Forest Hills NY 11375
www.iranphilatelic.org
E-mail: m.esmaili@earthlink.net

Eire Philatelic Association (Ireland)
David J. Brennan
PO Box 704
Bernardsville NJ 07924
eirephilatelicassoc.org
E-mail: brennan704@aol.com

Society of Israel Philatelists
Paul S. Aufrichtig
300 East 42nd St.
New York NY 10017

Italy and Colonies Study Circle
Andrew DíAnneo
1085 Dunweal Lane
Calistoga CA 94515
www.icsc.pwp.blueyonder.co.uk
E-mail: audanneo@napanet.net

International Society for Japanese Philately
Kenneth Kamholz
PO Box 1283
Haddonfield NJ 08033
www.isjp.org
E-mail: isjp@isjp.org

Korea Stamp Society
John E. Talmage
PO Box 6889
Oak Ridge TN 37831
www.pennfamily.org/KSS-USA
E-mail: jtalmage@usit.net

Latin American Philatelic Society
Jules K. Beck
30 1/2 Street #209
St. Louis Park MN 55426-3551

Liberian Philatelic Society
William Thomas Lockard
PO Box 106
Wellston OH 45692
Ph: (740) 384-2020
E-mail: tlockard@zoomnet.net

Liechtenstudy USA (Liechtenstein)
Paul Tremaine
PO Box 601
Dundee OR 97115-0601
Ph: (503) 538-4500
www.liechtenstudy.org
E-mail: editor@liechtenstudy.org

Lithuania Philatelic Society
John Variakojis
3715 W. 68th St.
Chicago IL 60629
Ph: (773) 585-8649
www.withgusto.org/lps/index.htm
E-mail: variakojis@earthlink.net

Luxembourg Collectors Club
Gary B. Little
7319 Beau Road
Sechelt, BC, Canada, VON 3A8
http://lcc.luxcentral.com
E-mail: gary@luxcentral.com

Malaya Study Group
David Tett
PO Box 34
Wheathampstead, Herts, United Kingdom, AL4 8JY
www.m-s-g/org/uk
E-mail: davidtett@aol.com

Malta Study Circle
Alec Webster
50 Worcester Road
Sutton, Surrey,
United Kingdom, SM2 6QB
E-mail: alecwebster50@hotmail.com

Mexico-Elmhurst Philatelic Society International
David Pietsch
PO Box 50997
Irvine CA 92619-0997
E-mail: mepsi@msn.com

Society for Moroccan and Tunisian Philately
206, bld. Pereire
75017 Paris, France
members.aol.com/Jhaik5814
E-mail: splm206@aol.com

Natal and Zululand Study Circle
Dr. Guy Dillaway
PO Box 181
Weston MA 02493
www.nzsc.demon.co.uk

Nepal & Tibet Philatelic Study Group
Roger D. Skinner
1020 Covington Road
Los Altos CA 94024-5003
Ph: (650) 968-4163
fuchs-online.com/ntpsc/
E-mail: colinhepper@hotmail.co.uk

American Society for Netherlands Philately
Hans Kremer
50 Rockport Ct.
Danville CA 94526
Ph: (925) 820-5841
www.angelfire.com/ca2/asnp
E-mail: hkremer@usa.net

New Zealand Society of Great Britain
Keith C. Collins
13 Briton Crescent
Sanderstead, Surrey, United Kingdom, CR2 0JN
www.cs.stir.ac.uk/~rgc/nzsgb
E-mail: rgc@cs.stir.ac.uk

Nicaragua Study Group
Erick Rodriguez
11817 S.W. 11th St.
Miami FL 33184-2501
clubs.yahoo.com/clubs/nicaraguastudygroup
E-mail: nsgsec@yahoo.com

Society of Australasian Specialists/ Oceania
Henry Bateman
PO Box 4862
Monroe LA 71211-4862
Ph: (800) 571-0293 members.aol.com/stampsho/saso.html
E-mail: hbateman@jam.rr.com

Orange Free State Study Circle
J. R. Stroud
28 Oxford St.
Burnham-on-sea, Somerset, United Kingdom, TA8 1LQ
orangefreestatephilately.org.uk
E-mail: richardstroudph@gofast.co.uk

Pacific Islands Study Circle
John Ray
24 Woodvale Avenue
London, United Kingdom, SE25 4AE
www.pisc.org.uk
E-mail: info@pisc.org.uk

Pakistan Philatelic Study Circle
Jeff Siddiqui
PO Box 7002
Lynnwood WA 98046
E-mail: jeffsiddiqui@msn.com

Centro de Filatelistas Independientes de Panama
Vladimir Berrio-Lemm
Apartado 0823-02748
Plaza Concordia Panama, Panama
E-mail: panahistoria@gmail.com

Papuan Philatelic Society
Steven Zirinsky
PO Box 49, Ansonia Station
New York NY 10023
Ph: (718) 706-0616
www.communigate.co.uk/york/pps
E-mail: szirinsky@cs.com

International Philippine Philatelic Society
Donald J. Peterson
7408 Alaska Ave., NW
Washington DC 20012
Ph: (202) 291-6229
www.theipps.info
E-mail: dpeterson@comcast.net

Pitcairn Islands Study Group
Dr. Everett L. Parker
719 Moosehead Lake Rd.
Greenville ME 04441-3626
Ph: (336) 475-4558
www.pisg.net
E-mail: nalweller@aol.com

Plebiscite-Memel-Saar Study Group of the German Philatelic Society
Clay Wallace
100 Lark Court
Alamo CA 94507
E-mail: claywl@sbcglobal.net

Polonus Philatelic Society (Poland)
Chris Kulpinski
9350 E. Palm Tree Dr.
Scottsdale AZ 85255
Ph: (480) 585-7114
www.polonus.org
E-mail: ctk@kulpinski.net

International Society for Portuguese Philately
Clyde Homen
1491 Bonnie View Rd.
Hollister CA 95023-5117
www.portugalstamps.com
E-mail: cjh1491@sbcglobal.net

Rhodesian Study Circle
William R. Wallace
PO Box 16381
San Francisco CA 94116
www.rhodesianstudycircle.org.uk
E-mail: bwall8rscr@earthlink.net

Rossica Society of Russian Philately
Edward J. Laveroni
P.O. Box 320997
Los Gatos CA 95032-0116
www.rossica.org
E-mail: ed.laveroni@rossica.org

St. Helena, Ascension & Tristan Da Cunha Philatelic Society
Dr. Everett L. Parker
719 Moosehead Lake Rd.
Greenville ME 04441-3626
Ph: (207) 695-3163
ourworld.compuserve.com/homepages/ ST_HELENA_ASCEN_TDC
E-mail: eparker@hughes.net

St. Pierre & Miquelon Philatelic Society
James R. (Jim) Taylor
2335 Paliswood Rd. SW
Calgary, AB, T2V 3P6, Canada

Associated Collectors of El Salvador
Joseph D. Hahn
1015 Old Boalsburg Rd. Apt G-5
State College PA 16801-6149
www.elsalvadorphilately.org
E-mail: joehahn2@yahoo.com

Fellowship of Samoa Specialists
Donald Mee
23 Leo Street
Christchurch, 8051, New Zealand
www.samoaexpress.org
E-mail: donanm@xtra.co.nz

Sarawak Specialistsí Society
Stu Leven
PO Box 24764
San Jose CA 95154-4764
Ph: (408) 978-0193
www.britborneostamps.org.uk
E-mail: stulev@ix.netcom.com

Scandinavian Collectors Club
Donald B. Brent
PO Box 13196
El Cajon CA 92020
www.scc-online.org
E-mail: dbrent47@sprynet.com

Slovakia Stamp Society
Jack Benchik
PO Box 555
Notre Dame IN 46556

Philatelic Society for Greater Southern Africa
Alan Hanks
34 Seaton Drive
Aurora, ON, L4G 2KI, Canada
Ph: (905) 727-6993
www.psgsa.thestampweb.com
Email: alan.hanks@sympatico.ca

Spanish Philatelic Society
Robert H. Penn
1108 Walnut Drive
Danielsville PA 18038
Ph: (610) 767-6793

Sudan Study Group
c/o North American Agent
Richard S. Wilson
53 Middle Patent Road
Bedford NY 10506
www.sudanphilately.co.uk
E-mail: dadu1@verizon.net

American Helvetia Philatelic Society (Switzerland, Liechtenstein)
Richard T. Hall
PO Box 15053
Asheville NC 28813-0053
www.swiss-stamps.org
E-mail: secretary2@swiss-stamps.org

Tannu Tuva Collectors Society
Ken Simon
513 Sixth Ave. So.
Lake Worth FL 33460-4507
Ph: (561) 588-5954
www.tuva.tk
E-mail: yurttuva@yahoo.com

Society for Thai Philately
H. R. Blakeney
PO Box 25644
Oklahoma City OK 73125
E-mail: HRBlakeney@aol.com

Transvaal Study Circle
J. Woolgar
PO Box 379
Gravesend, DA11 9EW, United Kingdom
www.transvaal.org.uk

Ottoman and Near East Philatelic Society (Turkey and related areas)
Bob Stuchell
193 Valley Stream Lane
Wayne PA 19087
www.oneps.org
E-mail: rstuchell@msn.com

Ukrainian Philatelic & Numismatic Society
George Slusarczuk
PO Box 303
Southfields NY 10975-0303
www.upns.org
E-mail: Yurko@frontiernet.net

Vatican Philatelic Society
Sal Quinonez
1 Aldersgate, Apt. 1002
Riverhead NY 11901-1830
Ph: (516) 727-6426
www.vaticanphilately.org

British Virgin Islands Philatelic Society
Giorgio Migliavacca
PO Box 7007
St. Thomas VI 00801-0007
www.islandsun.com/FEATURES/bviphil9198.html
E-mail: issun@candwbvi.net

West Africa Study Circle
Dr. Peter Newroth
Suite 603
5332 Sayward Hill Crescent
Victoria, BC, Canada, V8Y 3H8
www.wasc.org.uk/

Western Australia Study Group
Brian Pope
PO Box 423
Claremont, Western Australia, Australia, 6910

Yugoslavia Study Group of the Croatian Philatelic Society
Michael Lenard
1514 North 3rd Ave.
Wausau WI 54401
Ph: (715) 675-2833
E-mail: mjlenard@aol.com

Topical Groups

Americana Unit
Dennis Dengel
17 Peckham Rd.
Poughkeepsie NY 12603-2018
www.americanaunit.org
E-mail: info@americanaunit.org

Astronomy Study Unit
John Budd
29203 Coharie Loop
San Antonio FL 33576-4643
Ph: (978) 851-8283
E-mail: jwgbudd@earthlink.net

Bicycle Stamp Club
Norman Batho
358 Iverson Place
East Windsor NJ 08520
Ph: (609) 448-9547
members.tripod.com/~bicyclestamps
E-mail: normbatho@worldnet.att.net

Biology Unit
Alan Hanks
34 Seaton Dr.
Aurora, ON, Canada, L4G 2K1
Ph: (905) 727-6993

Bird Stamp Society
Graham Horsman
23 A East Main Street
Blackburn West Lothian
Scotland, EH47 7QR, United Kingdom
www.bird-stamps.org/bss
E-mail: graham_horsman7@msn.com

Canadiana Study Unit
John Peebles
PO Box 3262, Station ìAî
London, ON, Canada, N6A 4K3
E-mail: john.peebles@sympatico.ca

Captain Cook Study Unit
Brian P. Sandford
173 Minuteman Dr.
Concord MA 01742-1923
www.captaincooksociety.com
E-mail: US@captaincooksociety.com

Casey Jones Railroad Unit
Donald Kesler
709 NW 35th Place
Lawton OK 73505-5121
www.uqp.de/cjr/index.htm
E-mail: normaned@rochester.rr.com

Cats on Stamps Study Unit
Mary Ann Brown
3006 Wade Rd.
Durham NC 27705
www.catsonstamps.org
E-mail: mabrown@nc.rr.com

Chemistry & Physics on Stamps Study Unit
Dr. Roland Hirsch
20458 Water Point Lane
Germantown MD 20874
www.cpossu.org
E-mail: rfhirsch@cpossu.org

Chess on Stamps Study Unit
Anne Kasonic
7625 County Road #153
Interlaken NY 14847
E-mail: akasonic@capital.net

Christmas Philatelic Club
Linda Lawrence
312 Northwood Drive
Lexington KY 40505
www.hwcn.org/link/cpc
E-mail: stamplinda@aol.com

Christopher Columbus Philatelic Society
Donald R. Ager
PO Box 71
Hillsboro NH 03244-0071
http://ccps.maphist.nl/
Ph: (603) 464-5379
E-mail: meganddon@tds.net

Collectors of Religion on Stamps
Verna Shackleton
425 North Linwood Avenue #110
Appleton WI 54914
www://my.vbe.com/~cmfourl/coros1.htm
E-mail: corosec@sbcglobal.net

Dogs on Stamps Study Unit
Morris Raskin
202A Newport Rd.
Monroe Township NJ 08831
Ph: (609) 655-7411
www.dossu.org
E-mail: mraskin@cellurian.com

Earthís Physical Features Study Group
Fred Klein
515 Magdalena Ave.
Los Altos CA 94024
epfsu.jeffhayward.com

Ebony Society of Philatelic Events and Reflections (African-American topicals)
Manuel Gilyard
800 Riverside Drive, Ste 4H
New York NY 10032-7412
www.esperstamps.org
E-mail: gilyardmani@aol.com

Europa Study Unit
Donald W. Smith
PO Box 576
Johnstown PA 15907-0576
www.europanews.emperors.net
E-mail: eunity@aol.com or donsmith65@msn.com

Fine & Performing Arts
Deborah L. Washington
6922 So. Jeffery Boulevard
#7 - North
Chicago IL 60649
E-mail: brasslady@comcast.net

Fire Service in Philately
Brian R. Engler, Sr.
726 1/2 W. Tilghman St.
Allentown PA 18102-2324
Ph: (610) 433-2782
www.firestamps.com

Gay & Lesbian History on Stamps Club
Joe Petronie
PO Box 190842
Dallas TX 75219-0842
www.glhsc.org
E-mail: glhsc@aol.com

Gems, Minerals & Jewelry Study Unit
George Young
PO Box 632
Tewksbury MA 01876-0632
Ph: (978) 851-8283
www.rockhounds.com/rockshop/gmjsuapp.txt
E-mail: george-young@msn.com

Graphics Philately Association
Mark H Winnegrad
PO Box 380
Bronx NY 10462-0380
www.graphics-stamps.org
E-mail: indybruce1@yahoo.com

Journalists, Authors & Poets on Stamps
Ms. Lee Straayer
P.O. Box 6808
Champaign IL 61826
E-mail: lstraayer@dcbnet.com

Lighthouse Stamp Society
Dalene Thomas
8612 West Warren Lane
Lakewood CO 80227-2352
Ph: (303) 986-6620
www.lighthousestampsociety.org
E-mail: dalene@lighthousestampsociety.org

Lions International Stamp Club
John Bargus
108-2777 Barry Rd. RR 2
Mill Bay, BC, Canada, V0R 2P2
Ph: (250) 743-5782

Mahatma Gandhi On Stamps Study Circle
Pramod Shivagunde
Pratik Clinic, Akluj
Solapur, Maharashtra, India, 413101
E-mail: drnanda@bom6.vsnl.net.in

Mask Study Unit
Carolyn Weber
1220 Johnson Drive, Villa 104
Ventura CA 93003-0540
E-mail: cweber@venturalink.net

Masonic Study Unit
Stanley R. Longenecker
930 Wood St.
Mount Joy PA 17552-1926
Ph: (717) 653-1155
E-mail: natsco@usa.net

Mathematical Study Unit
Estelle Buccino
5615 Glenwood Rd.
Bethesda MD 20817-6727
Ph: (301) 718-8898
www.math.ttu.edu/msu/
E-mail: m.strauss@ttu.edu

Medical Subjects Unit
Dr. Frederick C. Skvara
PO Box 6228
Bridgewater NJ 08807
E-mail: fcskvara@optonline.net

Mourning Stamps and Covers Club
John Hotchner
PO Box 1125
Falls Church VA 22041-0125
E-mail: jmhstamp@ix.netcom.com

Napoleonic Age Philatelists
Ken Berry
7513 Clayton Dr.
Oklahoma City OK 73132-5636
Ph: (405) 721-0044
www.nap-stamps.org
E-mail: krb2@earthlink.net

Old World Archeological Study Unit
Caroline Scannel
11 Dawn Drive
Smithtown NY 11787-1761
www.owasu.org
E-mail: editor@owasu.org

Petroleum Philatelic Society International
Dr. Chris Coggins
174 Old Bedford Road
Luton, England, LU2 7HW, United Kingdom
E-mail: WAMTECH@Luton174.fsnet.co.uk

Philatelic Computing Study Group
Robert de Violini
PO Box 5025
Oxnard CA 93031-5025
www.pcsg.org
E-mail: dviolini@adelphia.net

Philatelic Lepidopteristsí Association
Alan Hanks
34 Seaton Dr.
Aurora, ON, Canada, L4G 2K1
Ph: (905) 727-6933
E-mail: alan.hanks@sympatico.ca

Rotary on Stamps Unit
Gerald L. Fitzsimmons
105 Calla Ricardo
Victoria TX 77904
rotaryonstamps.org
E-mail: glfitz@suddenlink.net

Scouts on Stamps Society International
Lawrence Clay
PO Box 6228
Kennewick WA 99336
Ph: (509) 735-3731
www.sossi.org
E-mail: rfrank@sossi.org

Ships on Stamps Unit
Les Smith
302 Conklin Avenue
Penticton, BC, Canada, V2A 2T4
Ph: (250) 493-7486
www.shipsonstamps.org
E-mail: lessmith440@shaw.ca

Space Unit
Carmine Torrisi
PO Box 780241
Maspeth NY 11378
Ph: (718) 386-7882
stargate.1usa.com/stamps/
E-mail: ctorrisi1@nyc.rr.com

Sports Philatelists International
Margaret Jones
5310 Lindenwood Ave.
St. Louis MO 63109-1758
www.sportstamps.org

Stamps on Stamps Collectors Club
Alf Jordan
156 West Elm Street
Yarmouth ME 04096
www.stampsonstamps.org
E-mail: ajordan1@maine.rr.com

Textile Unit
John C. Monson
1062 Bramblewood Dr.
Castle Rock CO 80108-3643
www.caratex.com
E-mail: textilerama@mindspring.com

Windmill Study Unit
Walter J. Hollien
PO Box 346
Long Valley NJ 07853-0346
Ph: (862) 812-0030
E-mail: whollien@earthlink.net

Wine On Stamps Study Unit
Bruce L. Johnson
115 Raintree Drive
Zionsville IN 46077
www.wine-on-stamps.org
E-mail: indybruce@yahoo.com

Women on Stamps Study Unit
Hugh Gottfried
2232 26th St.
Santa Monica CA 90405-1902
E-mail: hgottfried@adelphia.net

Zeppelin Collectors Club
Cheryl Ganz
PO Box 77196
Washington DC 20013
www.americanairmailsociety.org

Expertizing Services

The following organizations will, for a fee, provide expert opinions about stamps submitted to them. Collectors should contact these organizations to find out about their fees andrequirements before submiting philatelic material to them. The listing of these groups here is not intended as an endorsement by Scott Publishing Co.

General Expertizing Services

American Philatelic Expertizing Service (a service of the American Philatelic Society)
100 Match Factory Place
Bellefonte PA 16823-1367
Ph: (814) 237-3803
Fax: (814) 237-6128
www.stamps.org
E-mail: ambristo@stamps.org
Areas of Expertise: Worldwide

B. P. A. Expertising, Ltd.
PO Box 137
Leatherhead, Surrey, United Kingdom KT22 0RG
E-mail: sec.bpa@tcom.co.uk
Areas of Expertise: British Commonwealth, Great Britain, Classics of Europe, South America and the Far East

Philatelic Foundation
70 West 40th St., 15th Floor
New York NY 10018
Ph: (212) 221-6555
Fax: (212) 221-6208
www.philatelicfoundation.org
E-mail:philatelicfoundation@verizon.net
Areas of Expertise: U.S. & Worldwide

Professional Stamp Experts
PO Box 6170
Newport Beach CA 92658
Ph: (877) STAMP-88
Fax: (949) 833-7955
www.collectors.com/pse
E-mail: pseinfo@collectors.com
Areas of Expertise: Stamps and covers of U.S., U.S. Possessions, British Commonwealth

Royal Philatelic Society Expert Committee
41 Devonshire Place
London, United Kingdom W1N 1PE
www.rpsl.org.uk/experts.html
E-mail: experts@rpsl.org.uk
Areas of Expertise: All

Expertizing Services Covering Specific Fields Or Countries

China Stamp Society Expertizing Service
1050 West Blue Ridge Blvd
Kansas City MO 64145
Ph: (816) 942-6300
E-mail: hjmesq@aol.com
Areas of Expertise: China

Confederate Stamp Alliance Authentication Service
Gen. Frank Crown, Jr.
PO Box 278
Capshaw AL 35742-0396
Ph: (302) 422-2656
Fax: (302) 424-1990
www.csalliance.org
E-mail: csaas@knology.net
Areas of Expertise: Confederate stamps and postal history

Errors, Freaks and Oddities Collectors Club Expertizing Service
138 East Lakemont Dr.
Kingsland GA 31548
Ph: (912) 729-1573
Areas of Expertise: U.S. errors, freaks and oddities

Estonian Philatelic Society Expertizing Service
39 Clafford Lane
Melville NY 11747
Ph: (516) 421-2078
E-mail: esto4@aol.com
Areas of Expertise: Estonia

Hawaiian Philatelic Society Expertizing Service
PO Box 10115
Honolulu HI 96816-0115
Areas of Expertise: Hawaii

Hong Kong Stamp Society Expertizing Service
PO Box 206
Glenside PA 19038
Fax: (215) 576-6850
Areas of Expertise: Hong Kong

International Association of Philatelic Experts
United States Associate members:

Paul Buchsbayew
119 W. 57th St.
New York NY 10019
Ph: (212) 977-7734
Fax: (212) 977-8653
Areas of Expertise: Russia, Soviet Union

William T. Crowe
(see Professional Stamp Experts)
Areas of Expertise: United States

John Lievsay
(see American Philatelic Expertizing Service and Philatelic Foundation)
Areas of Expertise: France

Robert W. Lyman
P.O. Box 348
Irvington on Hudson NY 10533
Ph and Fax: (914) 591-6937
Areas of Expertise: British North America, New Zealand

Robert Odenweller
P.O. Box 401
Bernardsville, NJ 07924-0401
Ph and Fax: (908) 766-5460
Areas of Expertise: New Zealand, Samoa to 1900

Alex Rendon
P.O. Box 323
Massapequa NY 11762
Ph and Fax: (516) 795-0464
Areas of Expertise: Bolivia, Colombia, Colombian States

Sergio Sismondo
10035 Carousel Center Dr.
Syracuse NY 13290-0001
Ph: (315) 422-2331
Fax: (315) 422-2956
Areas of Expertise: British East Africa, Camerouns, Cape of Good Hope, Canada, British North America

International Society for Japanese Philately Expertizing Committee
32 King James Court
Staten Island NY 10308-2910
Ph: (718) 227-5229
Areas of Expertise: Japan and related areas, except WWII Japanese Occupation issues

International Society for Portuguese Philately Expertizing Service
PO Box 43146
Philadelphia PA 19129-3146
Ph: (215) 843-2106
Fax: (215) 843-2106
E-mail: s.s.washburne@worldnet.att.net
Areas of Expertise: Portugal and Colonies

Mexico-Elmhurst Philatelic Society International Expert Committee
PO Box 1133
West Covina CA 91793
Areas of Expertise: Mexico

Ukrainian Philatelic & Numismatic Society Expertizing Service
30552 Dell Lane
Warren MI 48092-1862
Ph: (810) 751-5754
Areas of Expertise: Ukraine, Western Ukraine

V. G. Greene Philatelic Research Foundation
P.O. Box 204, Station Q
Toronto, ON, Canada M4T 2M1
Ph: (416) 921-2073
Fax: (416) 921-1282
E-mail: vggfoundation@on.aibn.com
www.greenefoundation.ca
Areas of Expertise: British North America

Information on Catalogue Values, Grade and Condition

Catalogue Value

The Scott Catalogue value is a retail value; that is, an amount you could expect to pay for a stamp in the grade of Very Fine with no faults. Any exceptions to the grade valued will be noted in the text. The general introduction on the following pages and the individual section introductions further explain the type of material that is valued. The value listed for any given stamp is a reference that reflects recent actual dealer selling prices for that item.

Dealer retail price lists, public auction results, published prices in advertising and individual solicitation of retail prices from dealers, collectors and specialty organizations have been used in establishing the values found in this catalogue. Scott Publishing Co. values stamps, but Scott is not a company engaged in the business of buying and selling stamps as a dealer.

Use this catalogue as a guide for buying and selling. The actual price you pay for a stamp may be higher or lower than the catalogue value because of many different factors, including the amount of personal service a dealer offers, or increased or decreased interest in the country or topic represented by a stamp or set. An item may occasionally be offered at a lower price as a "loss leader," or as part of a special sale. You also may obtain an item inexpensively at public auction because of little interest at that time or as part of a large lot.

Stamps that are of a lesser grade than Very Fine, or those with condition problems, generally trade at lower prices than those given in this catalogue. Stamps of exceptional quality in both grade and condition often command higher prices than those listed.

Values for pre-1900 unused issues are for stamps with approximately half or more of their original gum. Stamps with most or all of their original gum may be expected to sell for more, and stamps with less than half of their original gum may be expected to sell for somewhat less than the values listed. On rarer stamps, it may be expected that the original gum will be somewhat more disturbed than it will be on more common issues. Post-1900 unused issues are assumed to have full original gum. From breakpoints in most countries' listings, stamps are valued as never hinged, due to the wide availability of stamps in that condition. These notations are prominently placed in the listings and in the country information preceding the listings. Some countries also feature listings with dual values for hinged and never-hinged stamps.

Grade

A stamp's grade and condition are crucial to its value. The accompanying illustrations show examples of Very Fine stamps from different time periods, along with examples of stamps in Fine to Very Fine and Extremely Fine grades as points of reference. When a stamp seller offers a stamp in any grade from fine to superb without further qualifying statements, that stamp should not only have the centering grade as defined, but it also should be free of faults or other condition problems.

FINE stamps (illustrations not shown) have designs that are quite off center, with the perforations on one or two sides very close to the design but not quite touching it. There is white space between the perforations and the design that is minimal but evident to the unaided eye. Imperforate stamps may have small margins, and earlier issues may show the design just touching one edge of the stamp design. Very early perforated issues normally will have the perforations slightly cutting into the design. Used stamps may have heavier than usual cancellations.

FINE-VERY FINE stamps will be somewhat off center on one side, or slightly off center on two sides. Imperforate stamps will have two margins of at least normal size, and the design will not touch any edge. For perforated stamps, the perfs are well clear of the design, but are still noticeably off center. *However, early issues of a country may be printed in such a way that the design naturally is very close to the edges. In these cases, the perforations may cut into the design very slightly.* Used stamps will not have a cancellation that detracts from the design.

VERY FINE stamps will be just slightly off center on one or two sides, but the design will be well clear of the edge. The stamp will present a nice, balanced appearance. Imperforate stamps will be well centered within normal-sized margins. *However, early issues of many countries may be printed in such a way that the perforations may touch the design on one or more sides. Where this is the case, a boxed note will be found defining the centering and margins of the stamps being valued.* Used stamps will have light or otherwise neat cancellations. This is the grade used to establish Scott Catalogue values.

EXTREMELY FINE stamps are close to being perfectly centered. Imperforate stamps will have even margins that are slightly larger than normal. Even the earliest perforated issues will have perforations clear of the design on all sides.

Scott Publishing Co. recognizes that there is no formally enforced grading scheme for postage stamps, and that the final price you pay or obtain for a stamp will be determined by individual agreement at the time of transaction.

Condition

Grade addresses only centering and (for used stamps) cancellation. *Condition* refers to factors other than grade that affect a stamp's desirability.

Factors that can increase the value of a stamp include exceptionally wide margins, particularly fresh color, the presence of selvage, and plate or die varieties. Unusual cancels on used stamps (particularly those of the 19th century) can greatly enhance their value as well.

Factors other than faults that decrease the value of a stamp include loss of original gum, regumming, a hinge remnant or foreign object adhering to the gum, natural inclusions, straight edges, and markings or notations applied by collectors or dealers.

Faults include missing pieces, tears, pin or other holes, surface scuffs, thin spots, creases, toning, short or pulled perforations, clipped perforations, oxidation or other forms of color changelings, soiling, stains, and such man-made changes as reperforations or the chemical removal or lightening of a cancellation.

Grading Illustrations

On the following two pages are illustrations of various stamps from countries appearing in this volume. These stamps are arranged by country, and they represent early or important issues that are often found in widely different grades in the marketplace. The editors believe the illustrations will prove useful in showing the margin size and centering that will be seen on the various issues.

In addition to the matters of margin size and centering, collectors are reminded that the very fine stamps valued in the Scott catalogues also will possess fresh color and intact perforations, and they will be free from defects.

Examples shown are computer-manipulated images made from single digitized master illustrations.

Stamp Illustrations Used in the Catalogue

It is important to note that the stamp images used for identification purposes in this catlaogue may not be indicative of the grade of stamp being valued. Refer to the written discussion of grades on this page and to the grading illustrations on the following two pages for grading information.

Fine-Very Fine

SCOTT CATALOGUES VALUE STAMPS IN THIS GRADE

Very Fine

Extremely Fine

Fine-Very Fine

SCOTT CATALOGUES VALUE STAMPS IN THIS GRADE

Very Fine

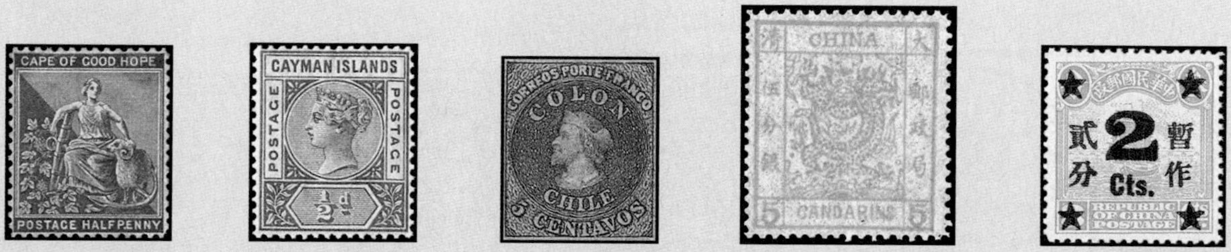

Extremely Fine

Fine-Very Fine →

SCOTT CATALOGUES VALUE STAMPS IN THIS GRADE

Very Fine →

Extremely Fine →

Fine-Very Fine →

SCOTT CATALOGUES VALUE STAMPS IN THIS GRADE

Very Fine →

Extremely Fine →

For purposes of helping to determine the gum condition and value of an unused stamp, Scott Publishing Co. presents the following chart which details different gum conditions and indicates how the conditions correlate with the Scott values for unused stamps. Used together, the Illustrated Grading Chart on the previous pages and this Illustrated Gum Chart should allow catalogue users to better understand the grade and gum condition of stamps valued in the Scott catalogues.

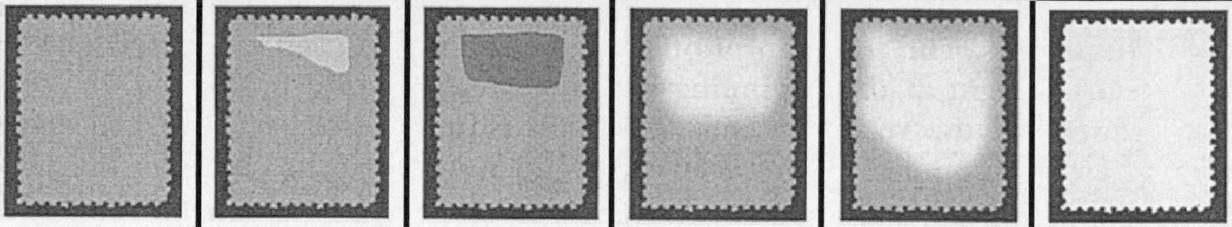

Gum Categories:	**MINT N.H.**	**ORIGINAL GUM (O.G.)**				**NO GUM**
	Mint Never Hinged *Free from any disturbance*	**Lightly Hinged** *Faint impression of a removed hinge over a small area*	**Hinge Mark or Remnant** *Prominent hinged spot with part or all of the hinge remaining*	**Large part o.g.** *Approximately half or more of the gum intact*	**Small part o.g.** *Approximately less than half of the gum intact*	**No gum** *Only if issued with gum*
Commonly Used Symbol:	★★	★	★	★	★	(★)
Pre-1900 Issues (Pre-1881 for U.S.)	*Very fine pre-1900 stamps in these categories trade at a premium over Scott value*			Scott Value for "Unused"		Scott "No Gum" listings for selected unused classic stamps
From 1900 to breakpoints for listings of never-hinged stamps	Scott "Never Hinged" listings for selected unused stamps	Scott Value for "Unused" (Actual value will be affected by the degree of hinging of the full o.g.)				
From breakpoints noted for many countries	Scott Value for "Unused"					

Never Hinged (NH; ★★): A never-hinged stamp will have full original gum that will have no hinge mark or disturbance. The presence of an expertizer's mark does not disqualify a stamp from this designation.

Original Gum (OG; ★): Pre-1900 stamps should have approximately half or more of their original gum. On rarer stamps, it may be expected that the original gum will be somewhat more disturbed than it will be on more common issues. Post-1900 stamps should have full original gum. Original gum will show some disturbance caused by a previous hinge(s) which may be present or entirely removed. The actual value of a post-1900 stamp will be affected by the degree of hinging of the full original gum.

Disturbed Original Gum: Gum showing noticeable effects of humidity, climate or hinging over more than half of the gum. The significance of gum disturbance in valuing a stamp in any of the Original Gum categories depends on the degree of disturbance, the rarity and normal gum condition of the issue and other variables affecting quality.

Regummed (RG; (★)): A regummed stamp is a stamp without gum that has had some type of gum privately applied at a time after it was issued. This normally is done to deceive collectors and/or dealers into thinking that the stamp has original gum and therefore has a higher value. A regummed stamp is considered the same as a stamp with none of its original gum for purposes of grading.

Understanding the Listings

On the opposite page is an enlarged "typical" listing from this catalogue. Below are detailed explanations of each of the highlighted parts of the listing.

1 Scott number — Scott catalogue numbers are used to identify specific items when buying, selling or trading stamps. Each listed postage stamp from every country has a unique Scott catalogue number. Therefore, Germany Scott 99, for example, can only refer to a single stamp. Although the Scott catalogue usually lists stamps in chronological order by date of issue, there are exceptions. When a country has issued a set of stamps over a period of time, those stamps within the set are kept together without regard to date of issue. This follows the normal collecting approach of keeping stamps in their natural sets.

When a country issues a set of stamps over a period of time, a group of consecutive catalogue numbers is reserved for the stamps in that set, as issued. If that group of numbers proves to be too few, capital-letter suffixes, such as "A" or "B," may be added to existing numbers to create enough catalogue numbers to cover all items in the set. A capital-letter suffix indicates a major Scott catalogue number listing. Scott uses a suffix letter only once. Therefore, a catalogue number listing with a capital-letter suffix will not also be found with the same letter (lower case) used as a minor-letter listing. If there is a Scott 16A in a set, for example, there will not also be a Scott 16a. However, a minor-letter "a" listing may be added to a major number containing an "A" suffix (Scott 16Aa, for example).

Suffix letters are cumulative. A minor "b" variety of Scott 16A would be Scott 16Ab, not Scott 16b.

There are times when a reserved block of Scott catalogue numbers is too large for a set, leaving some numbers unused. Such gaps in the numbering sequence also occur when the catalogue editors move an item's listing elsewhere or have removed it entirely from the catalogue. Scott does not attempt to account for every possible number, but rather attempts to assure that each stamp is assigned its own number.

Scott numbers designating regular postage normally are only numerals. Scott numbers for other types of stamps, such as air post, semi-postal, postal tax, postage due, occupation and others have a prefix consisting of one or more capital letters or a combination of numerals and capital letters.

2 Illustration number — Illustration or design-type numbers are used to identify each catalogue illustration. For most sets, the lowest face-value stamp is shown. It then serves as an example of the basic design approach for other stamps not illustrated. Where more than one stamp use the same illustration number, but have differences in design, the design paragraph or the description line clearly indicates the design on each stamp not illustrated. Where there are both vertical and horizontal designs in a set, a single illustration may be used, with the exceptions noted in the design paragraph or description line.

When an illustration is followed by a lower-case letter in parentheses, such as "A2(b)," the trailing letter indicates which overprint or surcharge illustration applies.

Illustrations normally are 70 percent of the original size of the stamp. An effort has been made to note all illustrations not illustrated at that percentage. Virtually all souvenir sheet illustrations are reduced even more. Overprints and surcharges are shown at 100 percent of their original size if shown alone, but are 70 percent of original size if shown on stamps. In some cases, the illustration will be placed above the set, between listings or omitted completely. Overprint and surcharge illustrations are not placed in this catalogue for purposes of expertizing stamps.

3 Paper color — The color of a stamp's paper is noted in italic type when the paper used is not white.

4 Listing styles — There are two principal types of catalogue listings: major and minor.

Major listings are in a larger type style than minor listings. The catalogue number is a numeral that can be found with or without a capital-letter suffix, and with or without a prefix.

Minor listings are in a smaller type style and have a small-letter suffix or (if the listing immediately follows that of the major number) may show only the letter. These listings identify a variety of the major item. Examples include perforation, color, watermark or printing method differences, multiples (some souvenir sheets, booklet panes and se-tenant combinations), and singles of multiples.

Examples of major number listings include 16, 28A, B97, C13A, 10N5, and 10N6A. Examples of minor numbers are 16a and C13Ab.

5 Basic information about a stamp or set — Introducing each stamp issue is a small section (usually a line listing) of basic information about a stamp or set. This section normally includes the date of issue, method of printing, perforation, watermark and, sometimes, some additional information of note. *Printing method, perforation and watermark apply to the following sets until a change is noted.* Stamps created by overprinting or surcharging previous issues are assumed to have the same perforation, watermark, printing method and other production characteristics as the original. Dates of issue are as precise as Scott is able to confirm and often reflect the dates on first-day covers, rather than the actual date of release.

6 Denomination — This normally refers to the face value of the stamp; that is, the cost of the unused stamp at the post office at the time of issue. When a denomination is shown in parentheses, it does not appear on the stamp. This includes the non-denominated stamps of the United States, Brazil and Great Britain, for example.

7 Color or other description — This area provides information to solidify identification of a stamp. In many recent cases, a description of the stamp design appears in this space, rather than a listing of colors.

8 Year of issue — In stamp sets that have been released in a period that spans more than a year, the number shown in parentheses is the year that stamp first appeared. Stamps without a date appeared during the first year of the issue. Dates are not always given for minor varieties.

9 Value unused and Value used — The Scott catalogue values are based on stamps that are in a grade of Very Fine unless stated otherwise. Unused values refer to items that have not seen postal, revenue or any other duty for which they were intended. Pre-1900 unused stamps that were issued with gum must have at least most of their original gum. Later issues are assumed to have full original gum. From breakpoints specified in most countries' listings, stamps are valued as never hinged. Stamps issued without gum are noted. Modern issues with PVA or other synthetic adhesives may appear ungummed. Unused self-adhesive stamps are valued as appearing undisturbed on their original backing paper. Values for used self-adhesive stamps are for examples either on piece or off piece. For a more detailed explanation of these values, please see the "Catalogue Value," "Condition" and "Understanding Valuing Notations" sections elsewhere in this introduction.

In some cases, where used stamps are more valuable than unused stamps, the value is for an example with a contemporaneous cancel, rather than a modern cancel or a smudge or other unclear marking. For those stamps that were released for postal and fiscal purposes, the used value represents a postally used stamp. Stamps with revenue cancels generally sell for less.

Stamps separated from a complete se-tenant multiple usually will be worth less than a pro-rated portion of the se-tenant multiple, and stamps lacking the attached labels that are noted in the listings will be worth less than the values shown.

10 Changes in basic set information — Bold type is used to show any changes in the basic data given for a set of stamps. These basic data categories include perforation gauge measurement, paper type, printing method and watermark.

11 Total value of a set — The total value of sets of three or more stamps issued after 1900 are shown. The set line also notes the range of Scott numbers and total number of stamps included in the grouping. The actual value of a set consisting predominantly of stamps having the minimum value of twenty cents may be less than the total value shown. Similary, the actual value or catalogue value of se-tenant pairs or of blocks consisting of stamps having the minimum value of twenty cents may be less than the catalogue values of the component parts.

A6

King George VI
A7

1938-44 **Engr.** **Perf. 12½**

54	A6	½p	green	.20	*1.50*
54A	A6	½p	dk brown ('42)	.20	*2.00*
55	A6	1p	dark brown	1.75	.35
55A	A6	1p	green ('42)	.20	*.90*
56	A6	1½p	dark carmine	3.00	*4.50*
56A	A6	1½p	gray ('42)	.20	*5.75*
57	A6	2p	gray	4.00	1.25
57A	A6	2p	dark car ('42)	.20	*2.00*
58	A6	3p	blue	.50	.50
59	A6	4p	rose lilac	1.50	1.25
60	A6	6p	dark violet	2.00	1.25
61	A6	9p	olive bister	2.00	*3.25*
62	A6	1sh	orange & blk	1.75	*2.00*

Typo.
Perf. 14
Chalky Paper

63	A7	2sh	ultra & dl vio, *bl*	7.00	*11.00*
64	A7	2sh6p	red & blk, *bl*	8.00	*13.00*
65	A7	5sh	red & grn, *yel*	25.00	22.50
a.		5sh	dk red & dp grn, *yel* ('44)	55.00	*80.00*
66	A7	10sh	red & grn, *grn*	35.00	*45.00*

Wmk. 3

67	A7	£1	blk & vio, *red*	22.50	*32.50*
			Nos. 54-67 (18)	115.00	*150.50*
			Set, never hinged	200.00	

1 SCOTT NUMBER

2 ILLUS. NUMBER

3 PAPER COLOR

4 LISTING STYLES — MAJORS, MINORS

5 BASIC INFORMATION ON STAMP OR SET

6 DENOMINATION

7 COLOR OR OTHER DESCRIPTION

8 YEAR OF ISSUE

9 CATALOGUE VALUES — UNUSED, USED

10 CHANGES IN BASIC SET INFORMATION

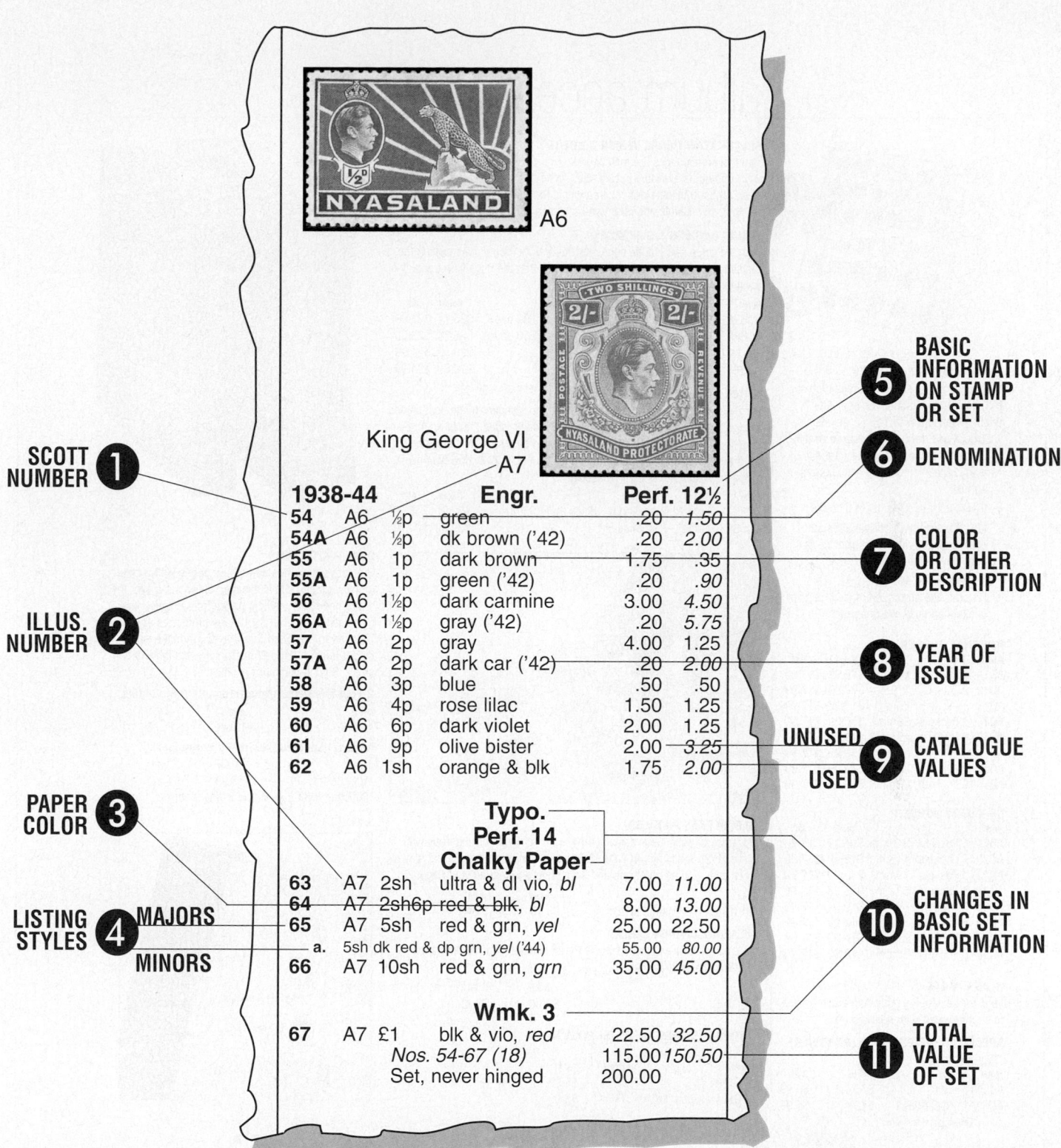

11 TOTAL VALUE OF SET

album accessories

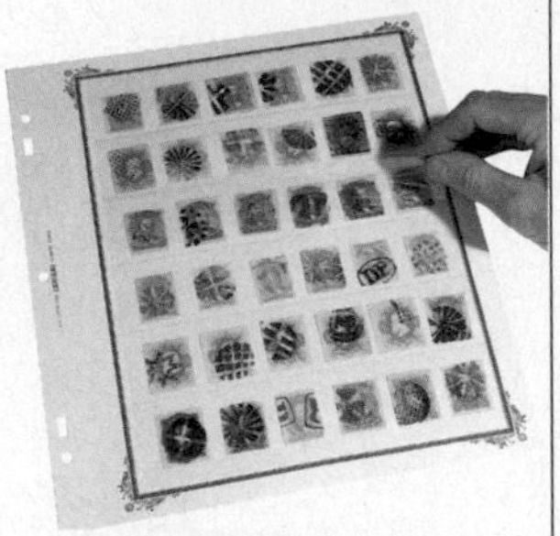

ADVANTAGE STOCK SHEETS

Advantage stock sheets fit directly in your 2-post or 3-ring National or Specialty album. Available with 1 to 8 pockets.

Sheets are sold in packages of 10.

- Stock sheets match album pages in every respect, including size, border, and color.
- Punched to fit perfectly in binder.
- Ideal for storing minor varieties and collateral material. A great place to keep new issues until the next supplement is available.
- Provides the protection of clear acetate pockets on heavyweight pages.

NATIONAL BORDER

Item			*Retail*	*AA**
AD11	1 Pocket	242mm	$19.99	$17.99
AD12	2 Pockets	119mm	$19.99	$17.99
AD13	3 Pockets	79mm	$19.99	$17.99
AD14	4 Pockets	58mm	$19.99	$17.99
AD15	5 Pockets	45mm	$19.99	$17.99
AD16	6 Pockets	37mm	$19.99	$17.99
AD17	7 Pockets	34mm	$19.99	$17.99
AD18	8 Pockets	31mm	$19.99	$17.99

SPECIALTY BORDER

Item			*Retail*	*AA**
AD21	1 Pocket	242mm	$19.99	$17.99
AD22	2 Pockets	119mm	$19.99	$17.99
AD23	3 Pockets	79mm	$19.99	$17.99
AD24	4 Pockets	58mm	$19.99	$17.99
AD25	5 Pockets	45mm	$19.99	$17.99
AD26	6 Pockets	37mm	$19.99	$17.99
AD27	7 Pockets	34mm	$19.99	$17.99
AD28	8 Pockets	31mm	$19.99	$17.99

BLANK PAGES

Ideal for developing your own album pages to be integrated with your album.

SPECIALTY SERIES PAGES (BORDER A)

(20 per pack)

Item	*Retail*	*AA**
ACC110	$7.74	$5.99
ACC111 Quadrille*	$7.74	$5.99

** Graph pattern printed on page.*

SPECIALTY/NATIONAL SERIES BINDERS

National series pages are punched for 3-ring and 2-post binders. The 3-ring binder is available in two sizes. The 2-post binder comes in one size. All Scott binders are covered with a tough green leatherette material that is washable and reinforced at stress points for long wear.

3-RING BINDERS & SLIPCASES

With the three ring binder, pages lay flat and the rings make turning the pages easy. The locking mechanism insure that the rings won't pop open even when the binder is full.

Item			*Retail*	*AA**
ACBR01	Small 3-Ring Binder	Holds up to 100 pages	$36.74	$29.99
ACBR03	Large 3-Ring Binder	Holds up to 250 pages	$36.74	$29.99
ACSR01	Small 3-Ring Slipcase.		$29.99	$24.99
ACSR03	Large 3-Ring Slipcase.		$29.99	$24.99

LARGE 2-POST BINDER & SLIPCASE

For the traditional Scott collector, we offer the standard hinge post binder. Scott album pages are punched with rectangular holes that fit on rectangular posts. The posts and pages are held by a rod that slides down from the top. With the post binder pages do not lie flat. However, filler strips are available for a minimal cost.

Item			*Retail*	*AA**
ACBS03	Large 2-Post Binder	Holds up to 250 pages	$52.99	$45.99
ACSS03	Large 2-Post Slipcase		$29.99	$24.99

ALBUM PAGE DIVIDERS

Postage, air post, semi-postals; they're all right at your fingertips with National/Specialty Album Page Dividers. The dividers are a great way to keep your albums organized and save wear and tear on your pages.

Item		*Retail*	*AA**
ACC145	Package of 10	$4.49	$3.49

NATIONAL DIVIDER LABELS

35 clear, pressure sensitive labels for all categories of United States issues in the National Album.

Item	*Retail*	*AA**
ACC146	$4.49	$3.49

NATIONAL SERIES PAGES (BORDER B)

(20 per pack)

Item	*Retail*	*AA**
ACC120	$7.74	$5.99
ACC121 Quadrille*	$7.74	$5.99

PAGE PROTECTORS

Protect your stamps and album pages with a clear archival quality plastic sleeve. Sleeves fits over the entire page and protects pages from creases, fingerprints and tears. Scott Page protectors are pvc free and thin enough that they won't make your binder bulge. Page Protectors are available in two sizes. Sold in packages of 25.

2-Post Minuteman/International Pg Protectors

Item	*Retail*	*AA**
ACC165	$13.99	$11.75

National/Specialty Series Pg Protectors*

Item	*Retail*	*AA**
ACC166	$13.99	$11.75

*Punched to fit 2-post and 3-ring binder.

To Order Call 1-800-572-6885

www.amosadvantage.com

AMOS ADVANTAGE

1. AA* prices apply to paid subscribers of *Scott Stamp Monthly* and *Linn's*.
2. Prices, terms and product availability subject to change.
3. **Shipping & Handling:**
   United States: 10% of order total. Minimum charge $5.99 Maximum charge $40.00.
   Canada: 15% of order total. Minimum charge $14.99 Maximum charge $45.00.
   Foreign orders are shipped via DHL and billed actual freight. Credit cards only.

Catalogue Listing Policy

It is the intent of Scott Publishing Co. to list all postage stamps of the world in the *Scott Standard Postage Stamp Catalogue*. The only strict criteria for listing is that stamps be decreed legal for postage by the issuing country and that the issuing country actually have an operating postal system. Whether the primary intent of issuing a given stamp or set was for sale to postal patrons or to stamp collectors is not part of our listing criteria. Scott's role is to provide basic comprehensive postage stamp information. It is up to each stamp collector to choose which items to include in a collection.

It is Scott's objective to seek reasons why a stamp should be listed, rather than why it should not. Nevertheless, there are certain types of items that will not be listed. These include the following:

1. Unissued items that are not officially distributed or released by the issuing postal authority. If such items are officially issued at a later date by the country, they will be listed. Unissued items consist of those that have been printed and then held from sale for reasons such as change in government, errors found on stamps or something deemed objectionable about a stamp subject or design.

2. Stamps "issued" by non-existent postal entities or fantasy countries, such as Nagaland, Occusi-Ambeno, Staffa, Sedang, Torres Straits and others. Also, stamps "issued" in the names of legitimate, stamp-issuing countries that are not authorized by those countries.

3. Semi-official or unofficial items not required for postage. Examples include items issued by private agencies for their own express services. When such items are required for delivery, or are valid as prepayment of postage, they are listed.

4. Local stamps issued for local use only. Postage stamps issued by governments specifically for "domestic" use, such as Haiti Scott 219-228, or the United States non-denominated stamps, are not considered to be locals, since they are valid for postage throughout the country of origin.

5. Items not valid for postal use. For example, a few countries have issued souvenir sheets that are not valid for postage. This area also includes a number of worldwide charity labels (some denominated) that do not pay postage.

6. Intentional varieties, such as imperforate stamps that look like their perforated counterparts and are usually issued in very small quantities. Also, other egregiously exploitative issues such as stamps sold for far more than face value, stamps purposefully issued in artificially small quantities or only against advance orders, stamps awarded only to a selected audience such as a philatelic bureau's standing order customers, or stamps sold only in conjunction with other products. All of these kinds of items are usually controlled issues and/or are intended for speculation. These items normally will be included in a footnote.

7. Items distributed by the issuing government only to a limited group, club, philatelic exhibition or a single stamp dealer or other private company. These items normally will be included in a footnote.

The fact that a stamp has been used successfully as postage, even on international mail, is not in itself sufficient proof that it was legitimately issued. Numerous examples of so-called stamps from non-existent countries are known to have been used to post letters that have successfully passed through the international mail system.

There are certain items that are subject to interpretation. When a stamp falls outside our specifications, it may be listed along with a cautionary footnote.

A number of factors are considered in our approach to analyzing how a stamp is listed. The following list of factors is presented to share with you, the catalogue user, the complexity of the listing process.

Additional printings — "Additional printings" of a previously issued stamp may range from an item that is totally different to cases where it is impossible to differentiate from the original. At least a minor number (a small-letter suffix) is assigned if there is a distinct change in stamp shade, noticeably redrawn design, or a significantly different perforation measurement. A major number (numeral or numeral and capital-letter combination) is assigned if the editors feel the "additional printing" is sufficiently different from the original that it constitutes a different issue.

Commemoratives — Where practical, commemoratives with the same theme are placed in a set. For example, the U.S. Civil War Centennial set of 1961-65 and the Constitution Bicentennial series of 1989-90 appear as sets. Countries such as Japan and Korea issue such material on a regular basis, with an announced, or at least predictable, number of stamps known in advance. Occasionally, however, stamp sets that were released over a period of years have been separated. Appropriately placed footnotes will guide you to each set's continuation.

Definitive sets — Blocks of numbers generally have been reserved for definitive sets, based on previous experience with any given country. If a few more stamps were issued in a set than originally expected, they often have been inserted into the original set with a capital-letter suffix, such as U.S. Scott 1059A. If it appears that many more stamps than the originally allotted block will be released before the set is completed, a new block of numbers will be reserved, with the original one being closed off. In some cases, such as the U.S. Transportation and Great Americans series, several blocks of numbers exist. Appropriately placed footnotes will guide you to each set's continuation.

New country — Membership in the Universal Postal Union is not a consideration for listing status or order of placement within the catalogue. The index will tell you in what volume or page number the listings begin.

"No release date" items — The amount of information available for any given stamp issue varies greatly from country to country and even from time to time. Extremely comprehensive information about new stamps is available from some countries well before the stamps are released. By contrast some countries do not provide information about stamps or release dates. Most countries, however, fall between these extremes. A country may provide denominations or subjects of stamps from upcoming issues that are not issued as planned. Sometimes, philatelic agencies, those private firms hired to represent countries, add these later-issued items to sets well after the formal release date. This time period can range from weeks to years. If these items were officially released by the country, they will be added to the appropriate spot in the set. In many cases, the specific release date of a stamp or set of stamps may never be known.

Overprints — The color of an overprint is always noted if it is other than black. Where more than one color of ink has been used on overprints of a single set, the color used is noted. Early overprint and surcharge illustrations were altered to prevent their use by forgers.

Se-tenants — Connected stamps of differing features (se-tenants) will be listed in the format most commonly collected. This includes pairs, blocks or larger multiples. Se-tenant units are not always symmetrical. An example is Australia Scott 508, which is a block of seven stamps. If the stamps are primarily collected as a unit, the major number may be assigned to the multiple, with minors going to each component stamp. In cases where continuous-design or other unit se-tenants will receive significant postal use, each stamp is given a major Scott number listing. This includes issues from the United States, Canada, Germany and Great Britain, for example.

Special Notices

Classification of stamps

The *Scott Standard Postage Stamp Catalogue* lists stamps by country of issue. The next level of organization is a listing by section on the basis of the function of the stamps. The principal sections cover regular postage, semi-postal, air post, special delivery, registration, postage due and other categories. Except for regular postage, catalogue numbers for all sections include a prefix letter (or number-letter combination) denoting the class to which a given stamp belongs. When some countries issue sets containing stamps from more than one category, the catalogue will at times list all of the stamps in one category (such as air post stamps listed as part of a postage set).

The following is a listing of the most commonly used catalogue prefixes.

Prefix... Category
C .... Air Post
M....... Military
P........ Newspaper
N .... Occupation - Regular Issues
O .... Official
Q .... Parcel Post
J......... Postage Due
RA ..... Postal Tax
B........ Semi-Postal
E........ Special Delivery
MR .... War Tax

Other prefixes used by more than one country include the following:
H .... Acknowledgment of Receipt
I......... Late Fee
CO.... Air Post Official
CQ..... Air Post Parcel Post
RAC... Air Post Postal Tax
CF...... Air Post Registration
CB ..... Air Post Semi-Postal
CBO... Air Post Semi-Postal Official
CE ..... Air Post Special Delivery
EY...... Authorized Delivery
S .... Franchise
G .... Insured Letter
GY ..... Marine Insurance
MC .... Military Air Post
MQ.... Military Parcel Post
NC..... Occupation - Air Post
NO..... Occupation - Official
NJ ...... Occupation - Postage Due
NRA... Occupation - Postal Tax
NB ..... Occupation - Semi-Postal
NE ..... Occupation - Special Delivery
QY ..... Parcel Post Authorized Delivery
AR ..... Postal-fiscal
RAJ .... Postal Tax Due
RAB ... Postal Tax Semi-Postal
F......... Registration
EB...... Semi-Postal Special Delivery
EO ..... Special Delivery Official
QE ..... Special Handling

New issue listings

Updates to this catalogue appear each month in the *Scott Stamp Monthly* magazine. Included in this update are additions to the listings of countries found in the *Scott Standard Postage Stamp Catalogue* and the *Specialized Catalogue of United States Stamps*, as well as corrections and updates to current editions of this catalogue.

From time to time there will be changes in the final listings of stamps from the *Scott Stamp Monthly* to the next edition of the catalogue. This occurs as more information about certain stamps or sets becomes available.

The catalogue update section of the *Scott Stamp Monthly* is the most timely presentation of this material available. Annual subscriptions to the *Scott Stamp Monthly* are available from Scott Publishing Co., Box 828, Sidney, OH 45365-0828.

Number additions, deletions & changes

A listing of catalogue number additions, deletions and changes from the previous edition of the catalogue appears in each volume. See Catalogue Number Additions, Deletions & Changes in the table of contents for the location of this list.

Understanding valuing notations

The *minimum catalogue value* of an individual stamp or set is 20 cents. This represents a portion of the cost incurred by a dealer when he prepares an individual stamp for resale. As a point of philatelic-economic fact, the lower the value shown for an item in this catalogue, the greater the percentage of that value is attributed to dealer mark up and profit margin. In many cases, such as the 20-cent minimum value, that price does not cover the labor or other costs involved with stocking it as an individual stamp. The sum of minimum values in a set does not properly represent the value of a complete set primarily composed of a number of minimum-value stamps, nor does the sum represent the actual value of a packet made up of minimum-value stamps. Thus a packet of 1,000 different common stamps — each of which has a catalogue value of 20-cents — normally sells for considerably less than 200 dollars!

The *absence of a retail value* for a stamp does not necessarily suggest that a stamp is scarce or rare. A dash in the value column means that the stamp is known in a stated form or variety, but information is either lacking or insufficient for purposes of establishing a usable catalogue value.

Stamp values in *italics* generally refer to items that are difficult to value accurately. For expensive items, such as those priced at $1,000 or higher, a value in italics indicates that the affected item trades very seldom. For inexpensive items, a value in italics represents a warning. One example is a "blocked" issue where the issuing postal administration may have controlled one stamp in a set in an attempt to make the whole set more valuable. Another example is an item that sold at an extreme multiple of face value in the marketplace at the time of its issue.

One type of warning to collectors that appears in the catalogue is illustrated by a stamp that is valued considerably higher in used condition than it is as unused. In this case, collectors are cautioned to be certain the used version has a genuine and contemporaneous cancellation. The type of cancellation on a stamp can be an important factor in determining its sale price. Catalogue values do not apply to fiscal, telegraph or non-contemporaneous postal cancels, unless otherwise noted.

Some countries have released back issues of stamps in canceled-to-order form, sometimes covering as much as a 10-year period. The Scott Catalogue values for used stamps reflect canceled-to-order material when such stamps are found to predominate in the marketplace for the issue involved. Notes frequently appear in the stamp listings to specify which items are valued as canceled-to-order, or if there is a premium for postally used examples.

Many countries sell canceled-to-order stamps at a marked reduction of face value. Countries that sell or have sold canceled-to-order stamps at *full* face value include United Nations, Australia, Netherlands, France and Switzerland. It may be almost impossible to identify such stamps if the gum has been removed, because official government canceling devices are used. Postally used copies of these items on cover, however, are usually worth more than the canceled-to-order stamps with original gum.

Abbreviations

Scott Publishing Co. uses a consistent set of abbreviations throughout this catalogue to conserve space, while still providing necessary information.

COLOR ABBREVIATIONS

amb	amber	crim	crimson	ol	olive
anil	aniline	cr	cream	olvn	olivine
ap	apple	dk	dark	org	orange
aqua	aquamarine	dl	dull	pck	peacock
az	azure	dp	deep	pnksh	pinkish
bis	bister	db	drab	Prus	Prussian
bl	blue	emer	emerald	pur	purple
bld	blood	gldn	golden	redsh	reddish
blk	black	grysh	grayish	res	reseda
bril	brilliant	grn	green	ros	rosine
brn	brown	grnsh	greenish	ryl	royal
brnsh	brownish	hel	heliotrope	sal	salmon
brnz	bronze	hn	henna	saph	sapphire
brt	bright	ind	indigo	scar	scarlet
brnt	burnt	int	intense	sep	sepia
car	carmine	lav	lavender	sien	sienna
cer	cerise	lem	lemon	sil	silver
chlky	chalky	lil	lilac	sl	slate
cham	chamois	lt	light	stl	steel
chnt	chestnut	mag	magenta	turq	turquoise
choc	chocolate	man	manila	ultra	ultramarine
chr	chrome	mar	maroon	Ven	Venetian
cit	citron	mv	mauve	ver	vermilion
cl	claret	multi	multicolored	vio	violet
cob	cobalt	mlky	milky	yel	yellow
cop	copper	myr	myrtle	yelsh	yellowish

When no color is given for an overprint or surcharge, black is the color used. Abbreviations for colors used for overprints and surcharges include: "(B)" or "(Blk)," black; "(Bl)," blue; "(R)," red; and "(G)," green.

Additional abbreviations in this catalogue are shown below:

Adm.	Administration
AFL	American Federation of Labor
Anniv.	Anniversary
APS	American Philatelic Society
Assoc.	Association
ASSR	Autonomous Soviet Socialist Republic
b.	Born
BEP	Bureau of Engraving and Printing
Bicent.	Bicentennial
Bklt.	Booklet
Brit.	British
btwn.	Between
Bur.	Bureau
c. or ca.	Circa
Cat.	Catalogue
Cent.	Centennial, century, centenary
CIO	Congress of Industrial Organizations
Conf.	Conference
Cong.	Congress
Cpl.	Corporal
CTO	Canceled to order
d.	Died
Dbl.	Double
EKU	Earliest known use
Engr.	Engraved
Exhib.	Exhibition
Expo.	Exposition
Fed.	Federation
GB	Great Britain
Gen.	General
GPO	General post office
Horiz.	Horizontal
Imperf.	Imperforate
Impt.	Imprint
Intl.	International
Invtd.	Inverted
L	Left
Lieut., lt.	Lieutenant
Litho.	Lithographed
LL	Lower left
LR	Lower right
mm	Millimeter
Ms.	Manuscript
Natl.	National
No.	Number
NY	New York
NYC	New York City
Ovpt.	Overprint
Ovptd.	Overprinted
P	Plate number
Perf.	Perforated, perforation
Phil.	Philatelic
Photo.	Photogravure
PO	Post office
Pr.	Pair
P.R.	Puerto Rico
Prec.	Precancel, precanceled
Pres.	President
PTT	Post, Telephone and Telegraph
Rio	Rio de Janeiro
Sgt.	Sergeant
Soc.	Society
Souv.	Souvenir
SSR	Soviet Socialist Republic, see ASSR
St.	Saint, street
Surch.	Surcharge
Typo.	Typographed
UL	Upper left
Unwmkd.	Unwatermarked
UPU	Universal Postal Union
UR	Upper Right
US	United States
USPOD	United States Post Office Department
USSR	Union of Soviet Socialist Republics
Vert.	Vertical
VP	Vice president
Wmk.	Watermark
Wmkd.	Watermarked
WWI	World War I
WWII	World War II

Examination

Scott Publishing Co. will not comment upon the genuineness, grade or condition of stamps, because of the time and responsibility involved. Rather, there are several expertizing groups that undertake this work for both collectors and dealers. Neither will Scott Publishing Co. appraise or identify philatelic material. The company cannot take responsibility for unsolicited stamps or covers sent by individuals.

All letters, E-mails, etc. are read attentively, but they are not always answered due to time considerations.

How to order from your dealer

When ordering stamps from a dealer, it is not necessary to write the full description of a stamp as listed in this catalogue. All you need is the name of the country, the Scott catalogue number and whether the desired item is unused or used. For example, "Japan Scott 422 unused" is sufficient to identify the unused stamp of Japan listed as "422 A206 5y brown."

Basic Stamp Information

A stamp collector's knowledge of the combined elements that make a given stamp issue unique determines his or her ability to identify stamps. These elements include paper, watermark, method of separation, printing, design and gum. On the following pages each of these important areas is briefly described.

Paper

Paper is an organic material composed of a compacted weave of cellulose fibers and generally formed into sheets. Paper used to print stamps may be manufactured in sheets, or it may have been part of a large roll (called a web) before being cut to size. The fibers most often used to create paper on which stamps are printed include bark, wood, straw and certain grasses. In many cases, linen or cotton rags have been added for greater strength and durability. Grinding, bleaching, cooking and rinsing these raw fibers reduces them to a slushy pulp, referred to by paper makers as "stuff." Sizing and, sometimes, coloring matter is added to the pulp to make different types of finished paper.

After the stuff is prepared, it is poured onto sieve-like frames that allow the water to run off, while retaining the matted pulp. As fibers fall onto the screen and are held by gravity, they form a natural weave that will later hold the paper together. If the screen has metal bits that are formed into letters or images attached, it leaves slightly thinned areas on the paper. These are called watermarks.

When the stuff is almost dry, it is passed under pressure through smooth or engraved rollers - dandy rolls - or placed between cloth in a press to be flattened and dried.

Stamp paper falls broadly into two types: wove and laid. The nature of the surface of the frame onto which the pulp is first deposited causes the differences in appearance between the two. If the surface is smooth and even, the paper will be of fairly uniform texture throughout. This is known as *wove paper*. Early papermaking machines poured the pulp onto a continuously circulating web of felt, but modern machines feed the pulp onto a cloth-like screen made of closely interwoven fine wires. This paper, when held to a light, will show little dots or points very close together. The proper name for this is "wire wove," but the type is still considered wove. Any U.S. or British stamp printed after 1880 will serve as an example of wire wove paper.

Closely spaced parallel wires, with cross wires at wider intervals, make up the frames used for what is known as *laid paper*. A greater thickness of the pulp will settle between the wires. The paper, when held to a light, will show alternate light and dark lines. The spacing and the thickness of the lines may vary, but on any one sheet of paper they are all alike. See Russia Scott 31-38 for examples of laid paper.

Batonne, from the French word meaning "a staff," is a term used if the lines in the paper are spaced quite far apart, like the printed ruling on a writing tablet. Batonne paper may be either wove or laid. If laid, fine laid lines can be seen between the batons.

Quadrille is the term used when the lines in the paper form little squares. *Oblong quadrille* is the term used when rectangles, rather than squares, are formed. See Mexico-Guadalajara Scott 35-37 for examples of oblong quadrille paper.

Paper also is classified as thick or thin, hard or soft, and by color if dye is added during manufacture. Such colors may include yellowish, greenish, bluish and reddish.

Brief explanations of other types of paper used for printing stamps, as well as examples, follow.

Pelure — Pelure paper is a very thin, hard and often brittle paper that is sometimes bluish or grayish in appearance. See Serbia Scott 169-170.

Native — This is a term applied to handmade papers used to produce some of the early stamps of the Indian states. Stamps printed on native paper may be expected to display various natural inclusions that are normal and do not negatively affect value. Japanese paper, originally made of mulberry fibers and rice flour, is part of this group. See Japan Scott 1-18.

Manila — This type of paper is often used to make stamped envelopes and wrappers. It is a coarse-textured stock, usually smooth on one side and rough on the other. A variety of colors of manila paper exist, but the most common range is yellowish-brown.

Silk — Introduced by the British in 1847 as a safeguard against counterfeiting, silk paper contains bits of colored silk thread scattered throughout. The density of these fibers varies greatly and can include as few as one fiber per stamp or hundreds. U.S. revenue Scott R152 is a good example of an easy-to-identify silk paper stamp.

Silk-thread paper has uninterrupted threads of colored silk arranged so that one or more threads run through the stamp or postal stationery. See Great Britain Scott 5-6 and Switzerland Scott 14-19.

Granite — Filled with minute cloth or colored paper fibers of various colors and lengths, granite paper should not be confused with either type of silk paper. Austria Scott 172-175 and a number of Swiss stamps are examples of granite paper.

Chalky — A chalk-like substance coats the surface of chalky paper to discourage the cleaning and reuse of canceled stamps, as well as to provide a smoother, more acceptable printing surface. Because the designs of stamps printed on chalky paper are imprinted on what is often a water-soluble coating, any attempt to remove a cancellation will destroy the stamp. *Do not soak these stamps in any fluid.* To remove a stamp printed on chalky paper from an envelope, wet the paper from underneath the stamp until the gum dissolves enough to release the stamp from the paper. See St. Kitts-Nevis Scott 89-90 for examples of stamps printed on this type of chalky paper.

India — Another name for this paper, originally introduced from China about 1750, is "China Paper." It is a thin, opaque paper often used for plate and die proofs by many countries.

Double — In philately, the term double paper has two distinct meanings. The first is a two-ply paper, usually a combination of a thick and a thin sheet, joined during manufacture. This type was used experimentally as a means to discourage the reuse of stamps.

The design is printed on the thin paper. Any attempt to remove a cancellation would destroy the design. U.S. Scott 158 and other Banknote-era stamps exist on this form of double paper.

The second type of double paper occurs on a rotary press, when the end of one paper roll, or web, is affixed to the next roll to save time feeding the paper through the press. Stamp designs are printed over the joined paper and, if overlooked by inspectors, may get into post office stocks.

Goldbeater's Skin — This type of paper was used for the 1866 issue of Prussia, and was a tough, translucent paper. The design was printed in reverse on the back of the stamp, and the gum applied over the printing. It is impossible to remove stamps printed on this type of paper from the paper to which they are affixed without destroying the design.

Ribbed — Ribbed paper has an uneven, corrugated surface made by passing the paper through ridged rollers. This type exists on some copies of U.S. Scott 156-165.

Various other substances, or substrates, have been used for stamp manufacture, including wood, aluminum, copper, silver and gold foil, plastic, and silk and cotton fabrics.

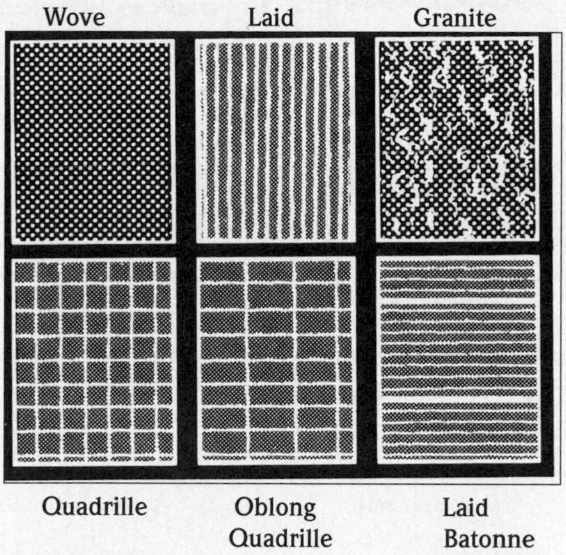

Watermarks

Watermarks are an integral part of some papers. They are formed in the process of paper manufacture. Watermarks consist of small designs, formed of wire or cut from metal and soldered to the surface of the mold or, sometimes, on the dandy roll. The designs may be in the form of crowns, stars, anchors, letters or other characters or symbols. These pieces of metal - known in the paper-making industry as "bits" - impress a design into the paper. The design sometimes may be seen by holding the stamp to the light. Some are more easily seen with a watermark detector. This important tool is a small black tray into which a stamp is placed face down and dampened with a fast-evaporating watermark detection fluid that brings up the watermark image in the form of dark lines against a lighter background. These dark lines are the thinner areas of the paper known as the watermark. Some watermarks are extremely difficult to locate, due to either a faint impression, watermark location or the color of the stamp. There also are electric watermark detectors that come with plastic filter disks of various colors. The disks neutralize the color of the stamp, permitting the watermark to be seen more easily.

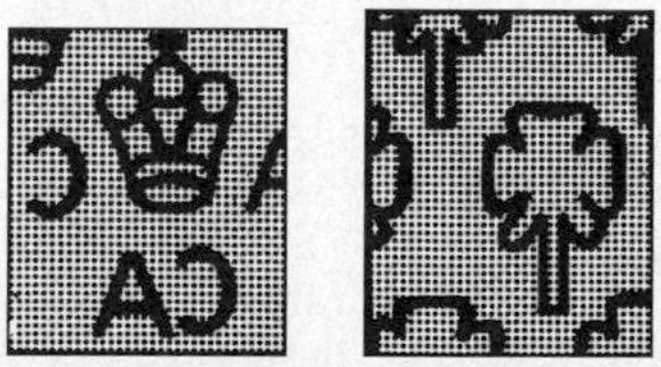

Multiple watermarks of Crown Agents and Burma

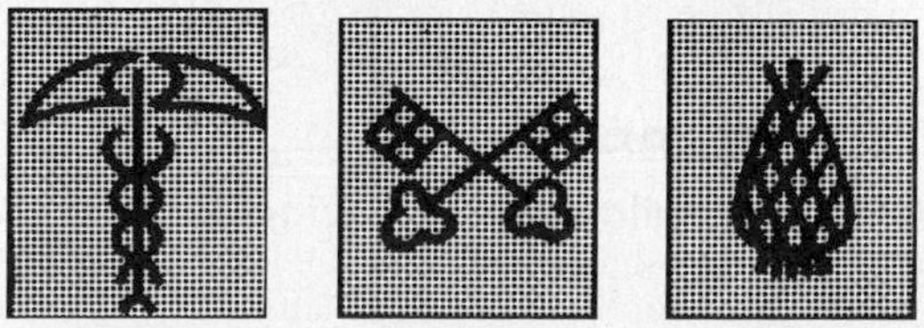

Watermarks of Uruguay, Vatican City and Jamaica

WARNING: Some inks used in the photogravure process dissolve in watermark fluids (Please see the section on Soluble Printing Inks). Also, see "chalky paper."

Watermarks may be found normal, reversed, inverted, reversed and inverted, sideways or diagonal, as seen from the back of the stamp. The relationship of watermark to stamp design depends on the position of the printing plates or how paper is fed through the press. On machine-made paper, watermarks normally are read from right to left. The design is repeated closely throughout the sheet in a "multiple-watermark design." In a "sheet watermark," the design appears only once on the sheet, but extends over many stamps. Individual stamps may carry only a small fraction or none of the watermark.

"Marginal watermarks" occur in the margins of sheets or panes of stamps. They occur on the outside border of paper (ostensibly outside the area where stamps are to be printed). A large row of letters may spell the name of the country or the manufacturer of the paper, or a border of lines may appear. Careless press feeding may cause parts of these letters and/or lines to show on stamps of the outer row of a pane.

Soluble Printing Inks

WARNING: Most stamp colors are permanent; that is, they are not seriously affected by short-term exposure to light or water. Many colors, especially of modern inks, fade from excessive exposure to light. There are stamps printed with inks that dissolve easily in water or in fluids used to detect watermarks. Use of these inks was intentional to prevent the removal of cancellations. Water affects all aniline inks, those on so-called safety paper and some photogravure printings - all such inks are known as *fugitive colors. Removal from paper of such stamps requires care and alternatives to traditional soaking.*

Separation

"Separation" is the general term used to describe methods used to separate stamps. The three standard forms currently in use are perforating, rouletting and die-cutting. These methods are done during the stamp production process, after printing. Sometimes these methods are done on-press or sometimes as a separate step. The earliest issues, such as the 1840 Penny Black of Great Britain (Scott 1), did not have any means provided for separation. It was expected the stamps would be cut apart with scissors or folded and torn. These are examples of imperforate stamps. Many stamps were first issued in imperforate formats and were later issued with perforations. Therefore, care must be observed in buying single imperforate stamps to be certain they were issued imperforate and are not perforated copies that have been altered by having the perforations trimmed away. Stamps issued imperforate usually are valued as singles. However, imperforate varieties of normally perforated stamps should be collected in pairs or larger pieces as indisputable evidence of their imperforate character.

PERFORATION

The chief style of separation of stamps, and the one that is in almost universal use today, is perforating. By this process, paper between the stamps is cut away in a line of holes, usually round, leaving little bridges of paper between the stamps to hold them together. Some types of perforation, such as hyphen-hole perfs, can be confused with roulettes, but a close visual inspection reveals that paper has been removed. The little perforation bridges, which project from the stamp when it is torn from the pane, are called the teeth of the perforation.

As the size of the perforation is sometimes the only way to differentiate between two otherwise identical stamps, it is necessary to be able to accurately measure and describe them. This is done with a perforation gauge, usually a ruler-like device that has dots or graduated lines to show how many perforations may be counted in the space of two centimeters. Two centimeters is the space universally adopted in which to measure perforations.

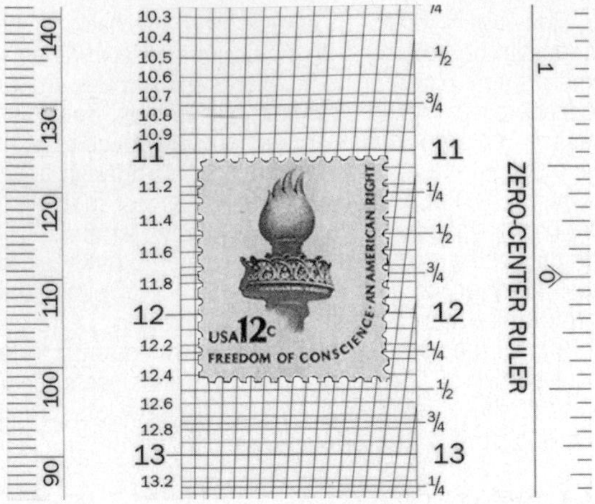

Perforation gauge

To measure a stamp, run it along the gauge until the dots on it fit exactly into the perforations of the stamp. If you are using a graduated-line perforation gauge, simply slide the stamp along the surface until the lines on the gauge perfectly project from the center of the bridges or holes. The number to the side of the line of dots or lines that fit the stamp's perforation is the measurement. For example, an "11" means that 11 perforations fit between two centimeters. The description of the stamp therefore is "perf. 11." If the gauge of the perforations on the top and bottom of a stamp differs from that on the sides, the result is what is known as *compound perforations*. In measuring compound perforations, the gauge at top and bottom is always given first, then the sides. Thus, a stamp that measures 11 at top and bottom and 10 1/2 at the sides is "perf. 11 x 10 1/2." See U.S. Scott 632-642 for examples of compound perforations.

Stamps also are known with perforations different on three or all four sides. Descriptions of such items are clockwise, beginning with the top of the stamp.

A perforation with small holes and teeth close together is a "fine perforation." One with large holes and teeth far apart is a "coarse perforation." Holes that are jagged, rather than clean-cut, are "rough perforations." *Blind perforations* are the slight impressions left by the perforating pins if they fail to puncture the paper. Multiples of stamps showing blind perforations may command a slight premium over normally perforated stamps.

The term *syncopated perfs* describes intentional irregularities in the perforations. The earliest form was used by the Netherlands from 1925-33, where holes were omitted to create distinctive patterns. Beginning in 1992, Great Britain has used an oval perforation to help prevent counterfeiting. Several other countries have started using the oval perfs or other syncopated perf patterns.

A new type of perforation, still primarily used for postal stationery, is known as microperfs. Microperfs are tiny perforations (in some cases hundreds of holes per two centimeters) that allows items to be intentionally separated very easily, while not accidentally breaking apart as easily as standard perforations. These are not currently measured or differentiated by size, as are standard perforations.

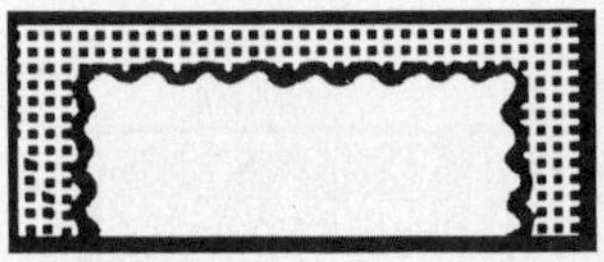

perce en arc

perce en lignes

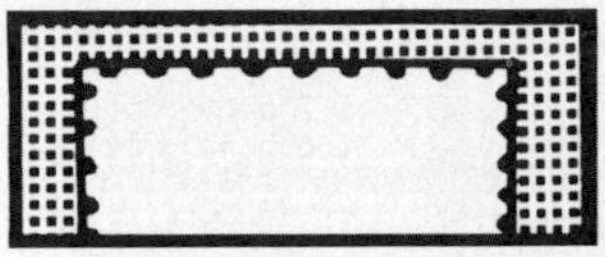

perce en points

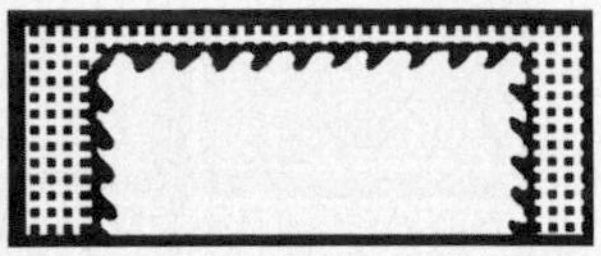

oblique roulette

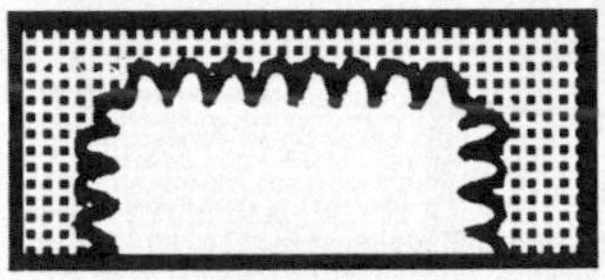

perce en scie

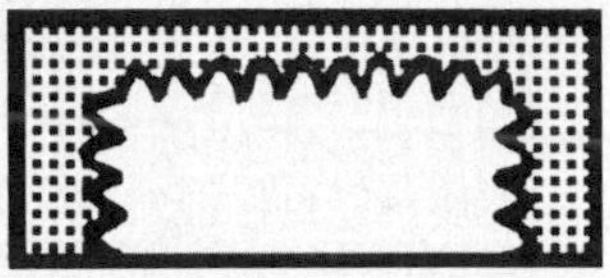

perce serpentin

ROULETTING

In rouletting, the stamp paper is cut partly or wholly through, with no paper removed. In perforating, some paper is removed. Rouletting derives its name from the French roulette, a spur-like wheel. As the wheel is rolled over the paper, each point makes a small cut. The number of cuts made in a two-centimeter space determines the gauge of the roulette, just as the number of perforations in two centimeters determines the gauge of the perforation.

The shape and arrangement of the teeth on the wheels varies. Various roulette types generally carry French names:

Perce en lignes - rouletted in lines. The paper receives short, straight cuts in lines. This is the most common type of rouletting. See Mexico Scott 500.

Perce en points - pin-rouletted or pin-perfed. This differs from a small perforation because no paper is removed, although round, equidistant holes are pricked through the paper. See Mexico Scott 242-256.

Perce en arc and *perce en scie* - pierced in an arc or saw-toothed designs, forming half circles or small triangles. See Hanover (German States) Scott 25-29.

Perce en serpentin - serpentine roulettes. The cuts form a serpentine or wavy line. See Brunswick (German States) Scott 13-18.

Once again, no paper is removed by these processes, leaving the stamps easily separated, but closely attached.

DIE-CUTTING

The third major form of stamp separation is die-cutting. This is a method where a die in the pattern of separation is created that later cuts the stamp paper in a stroke motion. Although some standard stamps bear die-cut perforations, this process is primarily used for self-adhesive postage stamps. Die-cutting can appear in straight lines, such as U.S. Scott 2522, shapes, such as U.S. Scott 1551, or imitating the appearance of perforations, such as New Zealand Scott 935A and 935B.

Printing Processes

ENGRAVING (Intaglio, Line-engraving, Etching)

Master die — The initial operation in the process of line engraving is making the master die. The die is a small, flat block of softened steel upon which the stamp design is recess engraved in reverse.

Master die

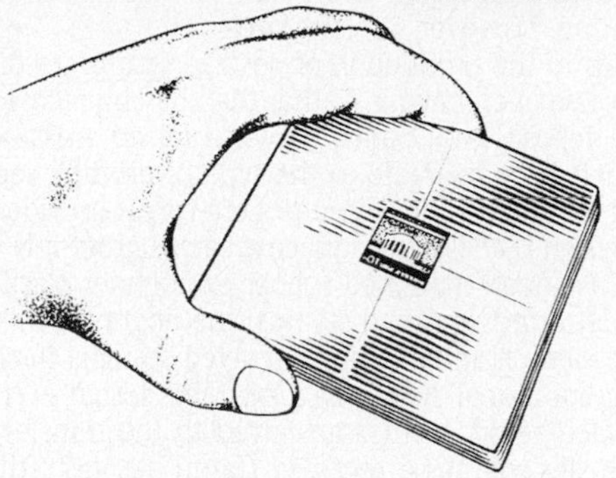

Photographic reduction of the original art is made to the appropriate size. It then serves as a tracing guide for the initial outline of the design. The engraver lightly traces the design on the steel with his graver, then slowly works the design until it is completed. At various points during the engraving process, the engraver hand-inks the die and makes an impression to check his progress. These are known as progressive die proofs. After completion of the engraving, the die is hardened to withstand the stress and pressures of later transfer operations.

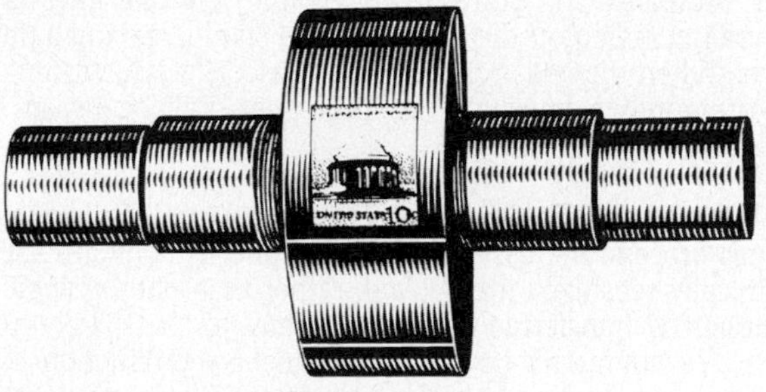

Transfer roll

Transfer roll — Next is production of the transfer roll that, as the name implies, is the medium used to transfer the subject from the master die to the printing plate. A blank roll of soft steel, mounted on a mandrel, is placed under the bearers of the transfer press to allow it to roll freely on its axis. The hardened die is placed on the bed of the press and the face of the transfer roll is applied to the die, under pressure. The bed or the roll is then rocked back and forth under increasing pressure, until the soft steel of the roll is forced into every engraved line of the die. The resulting impression on the roll is known as a "relief" or a "relief transfer." The engraved image is now positive in appearance and stands out from the steel. After the required number of reliefs are "rocked in," the soft steel transfer roll is hardened.

Different flaws may occur during the relief process. A defective relief may occur during the rocking in process because of a minute piece of foreign material lodging on the die, or some other cause. Imperfections in the steel of the transfer roll may result in a breaking away of parts of the design. This is known as a relief break, which will show up on finished stamps as small, unprinted areas. If a damaged relief remains in use, it will transfer a repeating defect to the plate. Deliberate alterations of reliefs sometimes occur. "Altered reliefs" designate these changed conditions.

Plate — The final step in pre-printing production is the making of the printing plate. A flat piece of soft steel replaces the die on the bed of the transfer press. One of the reliefs on the transfer roll is positioned over this soft steel. Position, or layout, dots determine the correct position on the plate. The dots have been lightly marked on the plate in advance. After the correct position of the relief is determined, the design is rocked in by following the same method used in making the transfer roll. The difference is that this time the image is being transferred from the transfer roll, rather than to it. Once the design is entered on the plate, it appears in reverse and is recessed. There are as many transfers entered on the plate as there are subjects printed on the sheet of stamps. It is during this process that double and shifted transfers occur, as well as re-entries. These are the result of improperly entered images that have not been properly burnished out prior to rocking in a new image.

Modern siderography processes, such as those used by the U.S. Bureau of Engraving and Printing, involve an automated form of rocking designs in on preformed cylindrical printing sleeves. The same process also allows for easier removal and re-entry of worn images right on the sleeve.

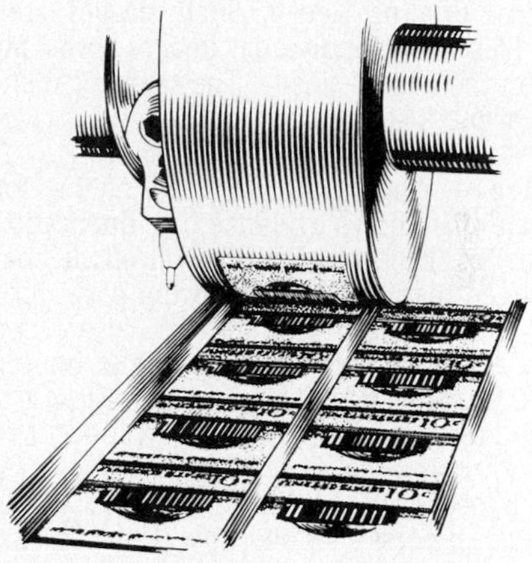

Transferring the design to the plate

Following the entering of the required transfers on the plate, the position dots, layout dots and lines, scratches and other markings generally are burnished out. Added at this time by the siderographer are any required *guide lines, plate numbers* or other *marginal markings.* The plate is then hand-inked and a proof impression is taken. This is known as a plate proof. If the impression is approved, the plate is machined for fitting onto the press, is hardened and sent to the plate vault ready for use.

On press, the plate is inked and the surface is automatically wiped clean, leaving ink only in the recessed lines. Paper is then forced under pressure into the engraved recessed lines, thereby receiving the ink. Thus, the ink lines on engraved stamps are slightly raised, and slight depressions (debossing) occur on the back of the stamp. Prior to the advent of modern high-speed presses and more advanced ink formulations, paper had to be dampened before receiving the ink. This sometimes led to uneven shrinkage by the time the stamps were perforated, resulting in improperly perforated stamps, or misperfs. Newer presses use drier paper, thus both *wet* and *dry printings* exist on some stamps.

Rotary Press — Until 1914, only flat plates were used to print engraved stamps. Rotary press printing was introduced in 1914, and slowly spread. Some countries still use flat-plate printing.

After approval of the plate proof, older *rotary press plates* require additional machining. They are curved to fit the press cylinder. "Gripper slots" are cut into the back of each plate to receive the "grippers," which hold the plate securely on the press. The plate is then hardened. Stamps printed from these bent rotary press plates are longer or wider than the same stamps printed from flat-plate presses. The stretching of the plate during the curving process is what causes this distortion.

Re-entry — To execute a re-entry on a flat plate, the transfer roll is re-applied to the plate, often at some time after its first use on the press. Worn-out designs can be resharpened by carefully burnishing out the original image and re-entering it from the transfer roll. If the original impression has not been sufficiently removed and the transfer roll is not precisely in line with the remaining impression, the resulting double transfer will make the re-entry obvious. If the registration is true, a re-entry may be difficult or impossible to distinguish. Sometimes a stamp printed from a successful re-entry is identified by having a much sharper and clearer impression than its neighbors. With the advent of rotary presses, post-press re-entries were not possible. After a plate was curved for the rotary press, it was impossible to make a re-entry. This is because the plate had already been bent once (with the design distorted).

However, with the introduction of the previously mentioned modern-style siderography machines, entries are made to the preformed cylindrical printing sleeve. Such sleeves are dechromed and softened. This allows individual images to be burnished out and re-entered on the curved sleeve. The sleeve is then rechromed, resulting in longer press life.

Double Transfer — This is a description of the condition of a transfer on a plate that shows evidence of a duplication of all, or a portion of the design. It usually is the result of the changing of the registration between the transfer roll and the plate during the rocking in of the original entry. Double transfers also occur when only a portion of the design has been rocked in and improper positioning is noted. If the worker elected not to burnish out the partial or completed design, a strong double transfer will occur for part or all of the design.

It sometimes is necessary to remove the original transfer from a plate and repeat the process a second time. If the finished re-worked image shows traces of the original impression, attributable to incomplete burnishing, the result is a partial double transfer.

With the modern automatic machines mentioned previously, double transfers are all but impossible to create. Those partially doubled images on stamps printed from such sleeves are more than likely re-entries, rather than true double transfers.

Re-engraved — Alterations to a stamp design are sometimes necessary after some stamps have been printed. In some cases, either the original die or the actual printing plate may have its "temper" drawn (softened), and the design will be re-cut. The resulting impressions from such a re-engraved die or plate may differ slightly from the original issue, and are known as "re-engraved." If the alteration was made to the master die, all future printings will be consistently different from the original. If alterations were made to the printing plate, each altered stamp on the plate will be slightly different from each other, allowing specialists to reconstruct a complete printing plate.

Dropped Transfers — If an impression from the transfer roll has not been properly placed, a dropped transfer may occur. The final stamp image will appear obviously out of line with its neighbors.

Short Transfer — Sometimes a transfer roll is not rocked its entire length when entering a transfer onto a plate. As a result, the finished transfer on the plate fails to show the complete design, and the finished stamp will have an incomplete design printed. This is known as a "short transfer." U.S. Scott No. 8 is a good example of a short transfer.

TYPOGRAPHY (Letterpress, Surface Printing, Flexography, Dry Offset, High Etch)

Although the word "Typography" is obsolete as a term describing a printing method, it was the accepted term throughout the first century of postage stamps. Therefore, appropriate Scott listings in this catalogue refer to typographed stamps. The current term for this form of printing, however, is "letterpress."

As it relates to the production of postage stamps, letterpress printing is the reverse of engraving. Rather than having recessed areas trap the ink and deposit it on paper, only the raised areas of the design are inked. This is comparable to the type of printing seen by inking and using an ordinary rubber stamp. Letterpress includes all printing where the design is above the surface area, whether it is wood, metal or, in some instances, hardened rubber or polymer plastic.

For most letterpress-printed stamps, the engraved master is made in much the same manner as for engraved stamps. In this instance, however, an additional step is needed. The design is transferred to another surface before being transferred to the transfer roll. In this way, the transfer roll has a recessed stamp design, rather than one done in relief. This makes the printing areas on the final plate raised, or relief areas.

For less-detailed stamps of the 19th century, the area on the die not used as a printing surface was cut away, leaving the surface area raised. The original die was then reproduced by stereotyping or electrotyping. The resulting electrotypes were assembled in the required number and format of the desired sheet of stamps. The plate used in printing the stamps was an electroplate of these assembled electrotypes.

Once the final letterpress plates are created, ink is applied to the raised surface and the pressure of the press transfers the ink impression to the paper. In contrast to engraving, the fine lines of letterpress are impressed on the surface of the stamp, leaving a debossed surface. When viewed from the back (as on a typewritten page), the corresponding line work on the stamp will be raised slightly (embossed) above the surface.

PHOTOGRAVURE (Gravure, Rotogravure, Heliogravure)

In this process, the basic principles of photography are applied to a chemically sensitized metal plate, rather than photographic paper. The design is transferred photographically to the plate through a halftone, or dot-matrix screen, breaking the reproduction into tiny dots. The plate is treated chemically and the dots form depressions, called cells, of varying depths and diameters, depending on the degrees of shade in the design. Then, like engraving, ink is applied to the plate and the surface is wiped clean. This leaves ink in the tiny cells that is lifted out and deposited on the paper when it is pressed against the plate.

Gravure is most often used for multicolored stamps, generally using the three primary colors (red, yellow and blue) and black. By varying the dot matrix pattern and density of these colors, virtually any color can be reproduced. A typical full-color gravure stamp will be created from four printing cylinders (one for each color). The original multicolored image will have been photographically separated into its component colors.

Modern gravure printing may use computer-generated dot-matrix screens, and modern plates may be of various types including metal-coated plastic. The catalogue designation of Photogravure (or "Photo") covers any of these older and more modern gravure methods of printing.

For examples of the first photogravure stamps printed (1914), see Bavaria Scott 94-114.

LITHOGRAPHY (Offset Lithography, Stone Lithography, Dilitho, Planography, Collotype)

The principle that oil and water do not mix is the basis for lithography. The stamp design is drawn by hand or transferred from engraving to the surface of a lithographic stone or metal plate in a greasy (oily) substance. This oily substance holds the ink, which will later be transferred to the paper. The stone (or plate) is wet with an acid fluid, causing it to repel the printing ink in all areas not covered by the greasy substance.

Transfer paper is used to transfer the design from the original stone or plate. A series of duplicate transfers are grouped and, in turn, transferred to the final printing plate.

Photolithography — The application of photographic processes to lithography. This process allows greater flexibility of design, related to use of halftone screens combined with line work. Unlike photogravure or engraving, this process can allow large, solid areas to be printed.

Offset — A refinement of the lithographic process. A rubber-covered blanket cylinder takes the impression from the inked lithographic plate. From the "blanket" the impression is *offset* or transferred to the paper. Greater flexibility and speed are the principal reasons offset printing has largely displaced lithography. The term "lithography" covers both processes, and results are almost identical.

EMBOSSED (Relief) Printing

Embossing, not considered one of the four main printing types, is a method in which the design first is sunk into the metal of the die. Printing is done against a yielding platen, such as leather or linoleum. The platen is forced into the depression of the die, thus forming the design on the paper in relief. This process is often used for metallic inks.

Embossing may be done without color (see Sardinia Scott 4-6); with color printed around the embossed area (see Great Britain Scott 5 and most U.S. envelopes); and with color in exact registration with the embossed subject (see Canada Scott 656-657).

HOLOGRAMS

For objects to appear as holograms on stamps, a model exactly the same size as it is to appear on the hologram must be created. Rather than using photographic film to capture the image, holography records an image on a photoresist material. In processing, chemicals eat away at certain exposed areas, leaving a pattern of constructive and destructive interference. When the phororesist is developed, the result is a pattern of uneven ridges that acts as a mold. This mold is then coated with metal, and the resulting form is used to press copies in much the same way phonograph records are produced.

A typical reflective hologram used for stamps consists of a reproduction of the uneven patterns on a plastic film that is applied to a reflective background, usually a silver or gold foil. Light is reflected off the background through the film, making the pattern present on the film visible. Because of the uneven pattern of the film, the viewer will perceive the objects in their proper three-dimensional relationships with appropriate brightness.

The first hologram on a stamp was produced by Austria in 1988 (Scott 1441).

FOIL APPLICATION

A modern tecnique of applying color to stamps involves the application of metallic foil to the stamp paper. A pattern of foil is applied to the stamp paper by use of a stamping die. The foil usually is flat, but it may be textured. Canada Scott 1735 has three different foil applications in pearl, bronze and gold. The gold foil was textured using a chemical-etch copper embossing die. The printing of this stamp also involved two-color offset lithography plus embossing.

COMBINATION PRINTINGS

Sometimes two or even three printing methods are combined in producing stamps. In these cases, such as Austria Scott 933 or Canada 1735 (described in the preceding paragraph), the multiple-printing technique can be determined by studying the individual characteristics of each printing type. A few stamps, such as Singapore Scott 684-684A, combine as many as three of the four major printing types (lithography, engraving and typography). When this is done it often indicates the incorporation of security devices against counterfeiting.

INK COLORS

Inks or colored papers used in stamp printing often are of mineral origin, although there are numerous examples of organic-based pigments. As a general rule, organic-based pigments are far more subject to varieties and change than those of mineral-based origin.

The appearance of any given color on a stamp may be affected by many aspects, including printing variations, light, color of paper, aging and chemical alterations.

Numerous printing variations may be observed. Heavier pressure or inking will cause a more intense color, while slight interruptions in the ink feed or lighter impressions will cause a lighter appearance. Stamps printed in the same color by water-based and solvent-based inks can differ significantly in appearance. This affects several stamps in the U.S. Prominent Americans series. Hand-mixed ink formulas (primarily from the 19th century) produced under different conditions (humidity and temperature) account for notable color variations in early printings of the same stamp (see U.S. Scott 248-250, 279B, for example). Different sources of pigment can also result in significant differences in color.

Light exposure and aging are closely related in the way they affect stamp color. Both eventually break down the ink and fade colors, so that a carefully kept stamp may differ significantly in color from an identical copy that has been exposed to light. If stamps are exposed to light either intentionally or accidentally, their colors can be faded or completely changed in some cases.

Papers of different quality and consistency used for the same stamp printing may affect color appearance. Most pelure papers, for example, show a richer color when compared with wove or laid papers. See Russia Scott 181a, for an example of this effect.

The very nature of the printing processes can cause a variety of differences in shades or hues of the same stamp. Some of these shades are scarcer than others, and are of particular interest to the advanced collector.

Luminescence

All forms of tagged stamps fall under the general category of luminescence. Within this broad category is fluorescence, dealing with forms of tagging visible under longwave ultraviolet light, and phosphorescence, which deals with tagging visible only under shortwave light. Phosphorescence leaves an afterglow and fluorescence does not. These treated stamps show up in a range of different colors when exposed to UV light. The differing wavelengths of the light activates the tagging material, making it glow in various colors that usually serve different mail processing purposes.

Intentional tagging is a post-World War II phenomenon, brought about by the increased literacy rate and rapidly growing mail volume. It was one of several answers to the problem of the need for more automated mail processes. Early tagged stamps served the purpose of triggering machines to separate different types of mail. A natural outgrowth was to also use the signal to trigger machines that faced all envelopes the same way and canceled them.

Tagged stamps come in many different forms. Some tagged stamps have luminescent shapes or images imprinted on them as a form of security device. Others have blocks (United States), stripes, frames (South Africa and Canada), overall coatings (United States), bars (Great Britain and Canada) and many other types. Some types of tagging are even mixed in with the pigmented printing ink (Australia Scott 366, Netherlands Scott 478 and U.S. Scott 1359 and 2443).

The means of applying taggant to stamps differs as much as the intended purposes for the stamps. The most common form of tagging is a coating applied to the surface of the printed stamp. Since the taggant ink is frequently invisible except under UV light, it does not interfere with the appearance of the stamp. Another common application is the use of phosphored papers. In this case the paper itself either has a coating of taggant applied before the stamp is printed, has taggant applied during the papermaking process (incorporating it into the fibers), or has the taggant mixed into the coating of the paper. The latter method, among others, is currently in use in the United States.

Many countries now use tagging in various forms to either expedite mail handling or to serve as a printing security device against counterfeiting. Following the introduction of tagged stamps for public use in 1959 by Great Britain, other countries have steadily joined the parade. Among those are Germany (1961); Canada and Denmark (1962); United States, Australia, France and Switzerland (1963); Belgium and Japan (1966); Sweden and Norway (1967); Italy (1968); and Russia (1969). Since then, many other countries have begun using forms of tagging, including Brazil, China, Czechoslovakia, Hong Kong, Guatemala, Indonesia, Israel, Lithuania, Luxembourg, Netherlands, Penrhyn Islands, Portugal, St. Vincent, Singapore, South Africa, Spain and Sweden to name a few.

In some cases, including United States, Canada, Great Britain and Switzerland, stamps were released both with and without tagging. Many of these were released during each country's experimental period. Tagged and untagged versions are listed for the aforementioned countries and are noted in some other countries' listings. For at least a few stamps, the experimentally tagged version is worth far more than its untagged counterpart, such as the 1963 experimental tagged version of France Scott 1024.

In some cases, luminescent varieties of stamps were inadvertently created. Several Russian stamps, for example, sport highly fluorescent ink that was not intended as a form of tagging. Older stamps, such as early U.S. postage dues, can be positively identified by the use of UV light, since the organic ink used has become slightly fluorescent over time. Other stamps, such as Austria Scott 70a-82a (varnish bars) and Obock Scott 46-64 (printed quadrille lines), have become fluorescent over time.

Various fluorescent substances have been added to paper to make it appear brighter. These optical brightners, as they are known, greatly affect the appearance of the stamp under UV light. The brightest of these is known as Hi-Brite paper. These paper varieties are beyond the scope of the Scott Catalogue.

Shortwave UV light also is used extensively in expertizing, since each form of paper has its own fluorescent characteristics that are impossible to perfectly match. It is therefore a simple matter to detect filled thins, added perforation teeth and other alterations that involve the addition of paper. UV light also is used to examine stamps that have had cancels chemically removed and for other purposes as well.

Gum

The Illustrated Gum Chart in the first part of this introduction shows and defines various types of gum condition. Because gum condition has an important impact on the value of unused stamps, we recommend studying this chart and the accompanying text carefully.

The gum on the back of a stamp may be shiny, dull, smooth, rough, dark, white, colored or tinted. Most stamp gumming adhesives use gum arabic or dextrine as a base. Certain polymers such as polyvinyl alcohol (PVA) have been used extensively since World War II.

The *Scott Standard Postage Stamp Catalogue* does not list items by types of gum. The *Scott Specialized Catalogue of United States Stamps* does differentiate among some types of gum for certain issues.

Reprints of stamps may have gum differing from the original issues. In addition, some countries have used different gum formulas for different seasons. These adhesives have different properties that may become more apparent over time.

Many stamps have been issued without gum, and the catalogue will note this fact. See, for example, United States Scott 40-47. Sometimes, gum may have been removed to preserve the stamp. Germany Scott B68, for example, has a highly acidic gum that eventually destroys the stamps. This item is valued in the catalogue with gum removed.

Reprints and Reissues

These are impressions of stamps (usually obsolete) made from the original plates or stones. If they are valid for postage and reproduce obsolete issues (such as U.S. Scott 102-111), the stamps are *reissues.* If they are from current issues, they are designated as *second, third,* etc., *printing.* If designated for a particular purpose, they are called *special printings.*

When special printings are not valid for postage, but are made from original dies and plates by authorized persons, they are *official reprints. Private reprints* are made from the original plates and dies by private hands. An example of a private reprint is that of the 1871-1932 reprints made from the original die of the 1845 New Haven, Conn., postmaster's provisional. *Official reproductions* or imitations are made from new dies and plates by government authorization. Scott will list those reissues that are valid for postage if they differ significantly from the original printing.

The U.S. government made special printings of its first postage stamps in 1875. Produced were official imitations of the first two stamps (listed as Scott 3-4), reprints of the demonetized pre-1861 issues (Scott 40-47) and reissues of the 1861 stamps, the 1869 stamps and the then-current 1875 denominations. Even though the official imitations and the reprints were not valid for postage, Scott lists all of these U.S. special printings.

Most reprints or reissues differ slightly from the original stamp in some characteristic, such as gum, paper, perforation, color or watermark. Sometimes the details are followed so meticulously that only a student of that specific stamp is able to distinguish the reprint or reissue from the original.

Remainders and Canceled to Order

Some countries sell their stock of old stamps when a new issue replaces them. To avoid postal use, the *remainders* usually are canceled with a punch hole, a heavy line or bar, or a more-or-less regular-looking cancellation. The most famous merchant of remainders was Nicholas F. Seebeck. In the 1880s and 1890s, he arranged printing contracts between the Hamilton Bank Note Co., of which he was a director, and several Central and South American countries. The contracts provided that the plates and all remainders of the yearly issues became the property of Hamilton. Seebeck saw to it that ample stock remained. The "Seebecks," both remainders and reprints, were standard packet fillers for decades.

Some countries also issue stamps *canceled-to-order (CTO),* either in sheets with original gum or stuck onto pieces of paper or envelopes and canceled. Such CTO items generally are worth less than postally used stamps. In cases where the CTO material is far more prevalent in the marketplace than postally used examples, the catalogue value relates to the CTO examples, with postally used examples noted as premium items. Most CTOs can be detected by the presence of gum. However, as the CTO practice goes back at least to 1885, the gum inevitably has been soaked off some stamps so they could pass as postally used. The normally applied postmarks usually differ slightly from standard postmarks, and specialists are able to tell the difference. When applied individually to envelopes by philatelically minded persons, CTO material is known as *favor canceled* and generally sells at large discounts.

Cinderellas and Facsimiles

Cinderella is a catch-all term used by stamp collectors to describe phantoms, fantasies, bogus items, municipal issues, exhibition seals, local revenues, transportation stamps, labels, poster stamps and many other types of items. Some cinderella collectors include in their collections local postage issues, telegraph stamps, essays and proofs, forgeries and counterfeits.

A *fantasy* is an adhesive created for a nonexistent stamp-issuing authority. Fantasy items range from imaginary countries (Occusi-Ambeno, Kingdom of Sedang, Principality of Trinidad or Torres Straits), to non-existent locals (Winans City Post), or nonexistent transportation lines (McRobish & Co.'s Acapulco-San Francisco Line).

On the other hand, if the entity exists and could have issued stamps (but did not) or was known to have issued other stamps, the items are considered *bogus* stamps. These would include the Mormon postage stamps of Utah, S. Allan Taylor's Guatemala and Paraguay inventions, the propaganda issues for the South Moluccas and the adhesives of the Page & Keyes local post of Boston.

Phantoms is another term for both fantasy and bogus issues.

Facsimiles are copies or imitations made to represent original stamps, but which do not pretend to be originals. A catalogue illustration is such a facsimile. Illustrations from the Moens catalogue of the last century were occasionally colored and passed off as stamps. Since the beginning of stamp collecting, facsimiles have been made for collectors as space fillers or for reference. They often carry the word "facsimile," "falsch" (German), "sanko" or "mozo" (Japanese), or "faux" (French) overprinted on the face or stamped on the back. Unfortunately, over the years a number of these items have had fake cancels applied over the facsimile notation and have been passed off as genuine.

Forgeries and Counterfeits

Forgeries and counterfeits have been with philately virtually from the beginning of stamp production. Over time, the terminology for the two has been used interchangeably. Although both forgeries and counterfeits are reproductions of stamps, the purposes behind their creation differ considerably.

Among specialists there is an increasing movement to more specifically define such items. Although there is no universally accepted terminology, we feel the following definitions most closely mirror the items and their purposes as they are currently defined.

Forgeries (also often referred to as *Counterfeits*) are reproductions of genuine stamps that have been created to defraud collectors. Such spurious items first appeared on the market around 1860, and most old-time collections contain one or more. Many are crude and easily spotted, but some can deceive experts.

An important supplier of these early philatelic forgeries was the Hamburg printer Gebruder Spiro. Many others with reputations in this craft included S. Allan Taylor, George Hussey, James Chute, George Forune, Benjamin & Sarpy, Julius Goldner, E. Oneglia and L.H. Mercier. Among the noted 20th-century forgers were Francois Fournier, Jean Sperati and the prolific Raoul DeThuin.

Forgeries may be complete replications, or they may be genuine stamps altered to resemble a scarcer (and more valuable) type. Most forgeries, particularly those of rare stamps, are worth only a small fraction of the value of a genuine example, but a few types, created by some of the most notable forgers, such as Sperati, can be worth as much or more than the genuine. Fraudulently produced copies are known of most classic rarities and many medium-priced stamps.

In addition to rare stamps, large numbers of common 19th- and early 20th-century stamps were forged to supply stamps to the early packet trade. Many can still be easily found. Few new philatelic forgeries have appeared in recent decades. Successful imitation of well-engraved work is virtually impossible. It has proven far easier to produce a fake by altering a genuine stamp than to duplicate a stamp completely.

Counterfeit (also often referred to as *Postal Counterfeit* or *Postal Forgery*) is the term generally applied to reproductions of stamps that have been created to defraud the government of revenue. Such items usually are created at the time a stamp is current and, in some cases, are hard to detect. Because most counterfeits are seized when the perpetrator is captured, postal counterfeits, particularly used on cover, are usually worth much more than a genuine example to specialists. The first postal counterfeit was of Spain's 4-cuarto carmine of 1854 (the real one is Scott 25). Apparently, the counterfeiters were not satisfied with their first version, which is now very scarce, and they soon created an engraved counterfeit, which is common. Postal counterfeits quickly followed in Austria, Naples, Sardinia and the Roman States. They have since been created in many other countries as well, including the United States.

An infamous counterfeit to defraud the government is the 1-shilling Great Britain "Stock Exchange" forgery of 1872, used on telegraph forms at the exchange that year. The stamp escaped detection until a stamp dealer noticed it in 1898.

Fakes

Fakes are genuine stamps altered in some way to make them more desirable. One student of this part of stamp collecting has estimated that by the 1950s more than 30,000 varieties of fakes were known. That number has grown greatly since then. The widespread existence of fakes makes it important for stamp collectors to study their philatelic holdings and use relevant literature. Likewise, collectors should buy from reputable dealers who guarantee their stamps and make full and prompt refunds should a purchased item be declared faked or altered by some mutually agreed-upon authority. Because fakes always have some genuine characteristics, it is not always possible to obtain unanimous agreement among experts regarding specific items. These students may change their opinions as philatelic knowledge increases. More than 80 percent of all fakes on the philatelic market today are regummed, reperforated (or perforated for the first time), or bear forged overprints, surcharges or cancellations.

Stamps can be chemically treated to alter or eliminate colors. For example, a pale rose stamp can be re-colored to resemble a blue shade of high market value. In other cases, treated stamps can be made to resemble missing color varieties. Designs may be changed by painting, or a stroke or a dot added or bleached out to turn an ordinary variety into a seemingly scarcer stamp. Part of a stamp can be bleached and reprinted in a different version, achieving an inverted center or frame. Margins can be added or repairs done so deceptively that the stamps move from the "repaired" into the "fake" category.

Fakers have not left the backs of the stamps untouched either. They may create false watermarks, add fake grills or press out genuine grills. A thin India paper proof may be glued onto a thicker backing to create the appearance an issued stamp, or a proof printed on cardboard may be shaved down and perforated to resemble a stamp. Silk threads are impressed into paper and stamps have been split so that a rare paper variety is added to an otherwise inexpensive stamp. The most common treatment to the back of a stamp, however, is regumming.

Some in the business of faking stamps have openly advertised foolproof application of "original gum" to stamps that lack it, although most publications now ban such ads from their pages. It is believed that very few early stamps have survived without being hinged. The large number of never-hinged examples of such earlier material offered for sale thus suggests the widespread extent of regumming activity. Regumming also may be used to hide repairs or thin spots. Dipping the stamp into watermark fluid, or examining it under longwave ultraviolet light often will reveal these flaws.

Fakers also tamper with separations. Ingenious ways to add margins are known. Perforated wide-margin stamps may be falsely represented as imperforate when trimmed. Reperforating is commonly done to create scarce coil or perforation varieties, and to eliminate the naturally occurring straight-edge stamps found in sheet margin positions of many earlier issues. Custom has made straight-edged stamps less desirable. Fakers have obliged by perforating straight-edged stamps so that many are now uncommon, if not rare.

Another fertile field for the faker is that of overprints, surcharges and cancellations. The forging of rare surcharges or overprints began in the 1880s or 1890s. These forgeries are sometimes difficult to detect, but experts have identified almost all. Occasionally, overprints or cancellations are removed to create non-overprinted stamps or seemingly unused items. This is most commonly done by removing a manuscript cancel to make a stamp resemble an unused example. "SPECIMEN" overprints may be removed by scraping and repainting to create non-overprinted varieties. Fakers use inexpensive revenues or pen-canceled stamps to generate unused stamps for further faking by adding other markings. The quartz lamp or UV lamp and a high-powered magnifying glass help to easily detect removed cancellations.

The bigger problem, however, is the addition of overprints, surcharges or cancellations - many with such precision that they are very difficult to ascertain. Plating of the stamps or the overprint can be an important method of detection.

Fake postmarks may range from many spurious fancy cancellations to a host of markings applied to transatlantic covers, to adding normally appearing postmarks to definitives of some countries with stamps that are valued far higher used than unused. With the increased popularity of cover collecting, and the widespread interest in postal history, a fertile new field for fakers has come about. Some have tried to create entire covers. Others specialize in adding stamps, tied by fake cancellations, to genuine stampless covers, or replacing less expensive or damaged stamps with more valuable ones. Detailed study of postal rates in effect at the time a cover in question was mailed, including the analysis of each handstamp used during the period, ink analysis and similar techniques, usually will unmask the fraud.

Restoration and Repairs

Scott Publishing Co. bases its catalogue values on stamps that are free of defects and otherwise meet the standards set forth earlier in this introduction. Most stamp collectors desire to have the finest copy of an item possible. Even within given grading categories there are variances. This leads to a controversial practice that is not defined in any universal manner: stamp *restoration.*

There are broad differences of opinion about what is permissible when it comes to restoration. Carefully applying a soft eraser to a stamp or cover to remove light soiling is one form of restoration, as is washing a stamp in mild soap and water to clean it. These are fairly accepted forms of restoration. More severe forms of restoration include pressing out creases or removing stains caused by tape. To what degree each of these is acceptable is dependent upon the individual situation. Further along the spectrum is the freshening of a stamp's color by removing oxide build-up or the effects of wax paper left next to stamps shipped to the tropics.

At some point in this spectrum the concept of *repair* replaces that of restoration. Repairs include filling thin spots, mending tears by reweaving or adding a missing perforation tooth. Regumming stamps may have been acceptable as a restoration or repair technique many decades ago, but today it is considered a form of fakery.

Restored stamps may or may not sell at a discount, and it is possible that the value of individual restored items may be enhanced over that of their pre-restoration state. Specific situations dictate the resultant value of such an item. Repaired stamps sell at substantial discounts from the value of sound stamps.

Terminology

Booklets — Many countries have issued stamps in small booklets for the convenience of users. This idea continues to become increasingly popular in many countries. Booklets have been issued in many sizes and forms, often with advertising on the covers, the panes of stamps or on the interleaving.

The panes used in booklets may be printed from special plates or made from regular sheets. All panes from booklets issued by the United States and many from those of other countries contain stamps that are straight edged on the sides, but perforated between. Others are distinguished by orientation of watermark or other identifying features. Any stamp-like unit in the pane, either printed or blank, that is not a postage stamp, is considered to be a *label* in the catalogue listings.

Scott lists and values booklet panes. Modern complete booklets also are listed and valued. Individual booklet panes are listed only when they are not fashioned from existing sheet stamps and, therefore, are identifiable from their sheet stamp counterparts.

Panes usually do not have a used value assigned to them because there is little market activity for used booklet panes, even though many exist used and there is some demand for them.

Cancellations — The marks or obliterations put on stamps by postal authorities to show that they have performed service and to prevent their reuse are known as cancellations. If the marking is made with a pen, it is considered a "pen cancel." When the location of the post office appears in the marking, it is a "town cancellation." A "postmark" is technically any postal marking, but in practice the term generally is applied to a town cancellation with a date. When calling attention to a cause or celebration, the marking is known as a "slogan cancellation." Many other types and styles of cancellations exist, such as duplex, numerals, targets, fancy and others. See also "precancels," below.

Coil Stamps — These are stamps that are issued in rolls for use in dispensers, affixing and vending machines. Those coils of the United States, Canada, Sweden and some other countries are perforated horizontally or vertically only, with the outer edges imperforate. Coil stamps of some countries, such as Great Britain and Germany, are perforated on all four sides and may in some cases be distinguished from their sheet stamp counterparts by watermarks, counting numbers on the reverse or other means.

Covers — Entire envelopes, with or without adhesive postage stamps, that have passed through the mail and bear postal or other markings of philatelic interest are known as covers. Before the introduction of envelopes in about 1840, people folded letters and wrote the address on the outside. Some people covered their letters with an extra sheet of paper on the outside for the address, producing the term "cover." Used airletter sheets, stamped envelopes and other items of postal stationery also are considered covers.

Errors — Stamps that have some major, consistent, unintentional deviation from the normal are considered errors. Errors include, but are not limited to, missing or wrong colors, wrong paper, wrong watermarks, inverted centers or frames on multicolor printing, inverted or missing surcharges or overprints, double impressions, missing perforations, unintentionally omitted tagging and others. Factually wrong or misspelled information, if it appears on all examples of a stamp, are not considered errors in the true sense of the word. They are errors of design. Inconsistent or randomly appearing items, such as misperfs or color shifts, are classified as freaks.

Color-Omitted Errors — This term refers to stamps where a missing color is caused by the complete failure of the printing plate to deliver ink to the stamp paper or any other paper. Generally, this is caused by the printing plate not being engaged on the press or the ink station running dry of ink during printing.

Color-Missing Errors — This term refers to stamps where a color or colors were printed somewhere but do not appear on the finished stamp. There are four different classes of color-missing errors, and the catalog indicates with a two-letter code appended to each such listing what caused the color to be missing. These codes are used only for the United States' color-missing error listings.

FO = A *foldover* of the stamp sheet during printing may block ink from appearing on a stamp. Instead, the color will appear on the back of the foldover (where it might fall on the back of the selvage or perhaps on the back of the stamp or another stamp). FO also will be used in the case of foldunders, where the paper may fold underneath the other stamp paper and the color will print on the platen.

EP = A piece of *extraneous paper* falling across the plate or stamp paper will receive the printed ink. When the extraneous paper is removed, an unprinted portion of stamp paper remains and shows partially or totally missing colors.

CM = A misregistration of the printing plates during printing will result in a *color misregistration*, and such a misregistraion may result in a color not appearing on the finished stamp.

PS = A *perforation shift* after printing may remove a color from the finished stamp. Normally, this will occur on a row of stamps at the edge of the stamp pane.

Measurements – When measurements are given in the Scott catalogues for stamp size, grill size or any other reason, the first measurement given is always for the top and bottom dimension, while the second measurement will be for the sides (just as perforation gauges are measured). Thus, a stamp size of 15mm x 21mm will indicate a vertically oriented stamp 15mm wide at top and bottom, and 21mm tall at the sides. The same principle holds for measuring or counting items such as U.S. grills. A grill count of 22x18 points (B grill) indicates that there are 22 grill points across by 18 grill points down.

Overprints and Surcharges — Overprinting involves applying wording or design elements over an already existing stamp. Overprints can be used to alter the place of use (such as "Canal Zone" on U.S. stamps), to adapt them for a special purpose ("Porto" on Denmark's 1913-20 regular issues for use as postage due stamps, Scott J1-J7) or to commemorate a special occasion (United States Scott 647-648).

A *surcharge* is a form of overprint that changes or restates the face value of a stamp or piece of postal stationery.

Surcharges and overprints may be handstamped, typeset or, occasionally, lithographed or engraved. A few hand-written overprints and surcharges are known.

Personalized Stamps — In 1999, Australia issued stamps with se-tenant labels that could be personalized with pictures of the customer's choice. Other countries quickly followed suit, with some offering to print the selected picture on the stamp itself within a frame that was used exclusively for personalized issues. As the picture used on these stamps or labels vary, listings for such stamps are for *any* picture within the common frame (or any picture on a se-tenant label), be it a "generic" image or one produced especially for a customer, almost invariably at a premium price.

Precancels — Stamps that are canceled before they are placed in the mail are known as precancels. Precanceling usually is done to expedite the handling of large mailings and generally allow the affected mail pieces to skip certain phases of mail handling.

In the United States, precancellations generally identified the point of origin; that is, the city and state. This information appeared across the face of the stamp, usually centered between parallel lines. More recently, bureau precancels retained the parallel lines, but the city and state designations were dropped. Recent coils have a service inscription that is present on the original printing plate. These show the mail service paid for by the stamp. Since these stamps are not intended to receive further cancellations when used as intended, they are considered precancels. Such items often do not have parallel lines as part of the precancellation.

In France, the abbreviation *Affranchts* in a semicircle together with the word *Postes* is the general form of precancel in use. Belgian precancellations usually appear in a box in which the name of the city appears. Netherlands precancels have the name of the city enclosed between concentric circles, sometimes called a "lifesaver." Precancellations of other countries usually follow these patterns, but may be any arrangement of bars, boxes and city names.

Precancels are listed in the Scott catalogues only if the precancel changes the denomination (Belgium Scott 477-478); if the precanceled stamp is different from the non-precanceled version (such as untagged U.S. precancels); or if the stamp exists only precanceled (France Scott 1096-1099, U.S. Scott 2265).

Proofs and Essays — Proofs are impressions taken from an approved die, plate or stone in which the design and color are the same as the stamp issued to the public. Trial color proofs are impressions taken from approved dies, plates or stones in colors that vary from the final version. An essay is the impression of a design that differs in some way from the issued stamp. "Progressive die proofs" generally are considered to be essays.

Provisionals — These are stamps that are issued on short notice and intended for temporary use pending the arrival of regular issues. They usually are issued to meet such contingencies as changes in government or currency, shortage of necessary postage values or military occupation.

During the 1840s, postmasters in certain American cities issued stamps that were valid only at specific post offices. In 1861, postmasters of the Confederate States also issued stamps with limited validity. Both of these examples are known as "postmaster's provisionals."

Se-tenant — This term refers to an unsevered pair, strip or block of stamps that differ in design, denomination or overprint.

Unless the se-tenant item has a continuous design (see U.S. Scott 1451a, 1694a) the stamps do not have to be in the same order as shown in the catalogue (see U.S. Scott 2158a).

Specimens — The Universal Postal Union required member nations to send samples of all stamps they released into service to the International Bureau in Switzerland. Member nations of the UPU received these specimens as samples of what stamps were valid for postage. Many are overprinted, handstamped or initial-perforated "Specimen," "Canceled" or "Muestra." Some are marked with bars across the denominations (China-Taiwan), punched holes (Czechoslovakia) or back inscriptions (Mongolia).

Stamps distributed to government officials or for publicity purposes, and stamps submitted by private security printers for official approval, also may receive such defacements.

The previously described defacement markings prevent postal use, and all such items generally are known as "specimens."

Tete Beche — This term describes a pair of stamps in which one is upside down in relation to the other. Some of these are the result of intentional sheet arrangements, such as Morocco Scott B10-B11. Others occurred when one or more electrotypes accidentally were placed upside down on the plate, such as Colombia Scott 57a. Separation of the tete-beche stamps, of course, destroys the tete beche variety.

Currency Conversion

Country	Dollar	Pound	S Franc	Yen	HK $	Euro	Cdn $	Aus $
Australia	1.4237	2.1595	1.2780	0.0158	0.1835	1.9123	1.1956	—
Canada	1.1908	1.8062	1.0689	0.0132	0.1535	1.5995	—	0.8364
European Union	0.7445	1.1293	0.6683	0.0083	0.0960	—	0.6252	0.5229
Hong Kong	7.7567	11.765	6.9629	0.0860		10.419	6.5139	5.4483
Japan	90.236	136.87	81.002	—	11.633	121.20	75.778	63.381
Switzerland	1.1140	1.6897	—	0.0123	0.1436	1.4963	0.9355	0.7825
United Kingdom	0.6593	—	0.5918	0.0073	0.0850	0.8855	0.5536	0.4631
United States	—	1.5168	0.8977	0.0111	0.1289	1.3432	0.8398	0.7024

Country	Currency	U.S. $ Equiv.
Cambodia	riel	.0002
Cameroun	Community of French Africa (CFA) franc	.0021
Canada	dollar	.8398
Cape Verde	escudo	.0123
Cayman Islands	dollar	1.2195
Central African Republic	CFA franc	.0021
Chad	CFA franc	.0021
Chile	peso	.0016
China (Taiwan)	dollar	.0301
China (Peopleís Republic)	yuan	.1463
Christmas Island	Australian dollar	.7024
Cocos Island	Australian dollar	.7024
Colombia	peso	.0004
Comoro Islands	franc	.0027
Congo Republic	CFA franc	.0021
Cook Islands	New Zealand dollar	.5902
Costa Rica	colon	.0018
Croatia	kuna	.1833
Cyprus	euro	1.3432
Czech Republic	koruna	.0505
Denmark	krone	.1802
Djibouti	franc	.0057
Dominica	East Caribbean dollar	.3724
Dominican Republic	peso	.0283
Ecuador	US dollar	1.00
Egypt	pound	.1816
Equatorial Guinea	CFA franc	.0021
Eritrea	nakfa	.0610
Estonia	kroon	.0858
Ethiopia	birr	.0961
Falkland Islands	pound	1.5168
Faroe Islands	krone	.1802
Fiji	dollar	.5681
Finland	euro	1.3432
Aland Islands	euro	1.3432
France	euro	1.3432
French Polynesia	Community of French Pacific (CFP) franc	.0112
French So. & Antarctic Terr.	euro	1.3432

*Source: **Wall Street Journal** Jan. 12, 2009. Figures reflect values as of Jan. 9, 2009.*

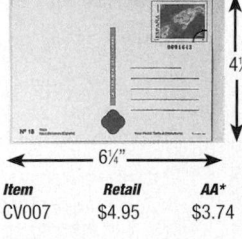

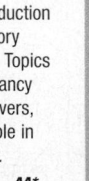

COMMON DESIGN TYPES

Pictured in this section are issues where one illustration has been used for a number of countries in the Catalogue. Not included in this section are overprinted stamps or those issues which are illustrated in each country.

EUROPA

Europa, 1956

The design symbolizing the cooperation among the six countries comprising the Coal and Steel Community is illustrated in each country.

Belgium	496-497
France	805-806
Germany	748-749
Italy	715-716
Luxembourg	318-320
Netherlands	368-369

Europa, 1958

"E" and Dove — CD1

European Postal Union at the service of European integration.

1958, Sept. 13

Belgium	527-528
France	889-890
Germany	790-791
Italy	750-751
Luxembourg	341-343
Netherlands	375-376
Saar	317-318

Europa, 1959

6-Link Enless Chain — CD2

1959, Sept. 19

Belgium	536-537
France	929-930
Germany	805-806
Italy	791-792
Luxembourg	354-355
Netherlands	379-380

Europa, 1960

19-Spoke Wheel CD3

First anniversary of the establishment of C.E.P.T. (Conference Europeenne des Administrations des Postes et des Telecommunications.) The spokes symbolize the 19 founding members of the Conference.

1960, Sept.

Belgium	553-554
Denmark	379
Finland	376-377
France	970-971
Germany	818-820
Great Britain	377-378
Greece	688
Iceland	327-328
Ireland	175-176
Italy	809-810
Luxembourg	374-375
Netherlands	385-386
Norway	387
Portugal	866-867
Spain	941-942
Sweden	562-563
Switzerland	400-401
Turkey	1493-1494

Europa, 1961

19 Doves Flying as One — CD4

The 19 doves represent the 19 members of the Conference of European Postal and Telecommunications Administrations C.E.P.T.

1961-62

Belgium	572-573
Cyprus	201-203
France	1005-1006
Germany	844-845
Great Britain	383-384
Greece	718-719
Iceland	340-341
Italy	845-846
Luxembourg	382-383
Netherlands	387-388
Spain	1010-1011
Switzerland	410-411
Turkey	1518-1520

Europa, 1962

Young Tree with 19 Leaves CD5

The 19 leaves represent the 19 original members of C.E.P.T.

1962-63

Belgium	582-583
Cyprus	219-221
France	1045-1046
Germany	852-853
Greece	739-740
Iceland	348-349
Ireland	184-185
Italy	860-861
Luxembourg	386-387
Netherlands	394-395
Norway	414-415
Switzerland	416-417
Turkey	1553-1555

Europa, 1963

Stylized Links, Symbolizing Unity — CD6

1963, Sept.

Belgium	598-599
Cyprus	229-231
Finland	419
France	1074-1075
Germany	867-868
Greece	768-769
Iceland	357-358
Ireland	188-189
Italy	880-881
Luxembourg	403-404
Netherlands	416-417
Norway	441-442
Switzerland	429
Turkey	1602-1603

Europa, 1964

Symbolic Daisy — CD7

5th anniversary of the establishment of C.E.P.T. The 22 petals of the flower symbolize the 22 members of the Conference.

1964, Sept.

Austria	738
Belgium	614-615
Cyprus	244-246
France	1109-1110
Germany	897-898
Greece	801-802
Iceland	367-368
Ireland	196-197
Italy	894-895
Luxembourg	411-412
Monaco	590-591
Netherlands	428-429
Norway	458
Portugal	931-933
Spain	1262-1263
Switzerland	438-439
Turkey	1628-1629

Europa, 1965

Leaves and "Fruit" CD8

1965

Belgium	636-637
Cyprus	262-264
Finland	437
France	1131-1132
Germany	934-935
Greece	833-834
Iceland	375-376
Ireland	204-205
Italy	915-916
Luxembourg	432-433
Monaco	616-617
Netherlands	438-439
Norway	475-476
Portugal	958-960
Switzerland	469
Turkey	1665-1666

Europa, 1966

Symbolic Sailboat — CD9

1966, Sept.

Andorra, French	172
Belgium	675-676
Cyprus	275-277
France	1163-1164
Germany	963-964
Greece	862-863
Iceland	384-385
Ireland	216-217
Italy	942-943
Liechtenstein	415
Luxembourg	440-441
Monaco	639-640
Netherlands	441-442
Norway	496-497
Portugal	980-982
Switzerland	477-478
Turkey	1718-1719

Europa, 1967

Cogwheels CD10

1967

Andorra, French	174-175
Belgium	688-689
Cyprus	297-299
France	1178-1179
Germany	969-970
Greece	891-892
Iceland	389-390
Ireland	232-233
Italy	951-952
Liechtenstein	420
Luxembourg	449-450
Monaco	669-670
Netherlands	444-447
Norway	504-505
Portugal	994-996
Spain	1465-1466
Switzerland	482
Turkey	B120-B121

Europa, 1968

Golden Key with C.E.P.T. Emblem CD11

1968

Andorra, French	182-183
Belgium	705-706
Cyprus	314-316
France	1209-1210
Germany	983-984
Greece	916-917
Iceland	395-396
Ireland	242-243
Italy	979-980
Liechtenstein	442
Luxembourg	466-467
Monaco	689-691
Netherlands	452-453
Portugal	1019-1021
San Marino	687
Spain	1526
Turkey	1775-1776

Europa, 1969

"EUROPA" and "CEPT" CD12

Tenth anniversary of C.E.P.T.

1969

Andorra, French	188-189
Austria	837
Belgium	718-719
Cyprus	326-328
Denmark	458
Finland	483
France	1245-1246
Germany	996-997
Great Britain	585
Greece	947-948
Iceland	406-407
Ireland	270-271
Italy	1000-1001
Liechtenstein	453
Luxembourg	474-475
Monaco	722-724
Netherlands	475-476
Norway	533-534
Portugal	1038-1040
San Marino	701-702
Spain	1567
Sweden	814-816

Switzerland	500-501
Turkey	1799-1800
Vatican	470-472
Yugoslavia	1003-1004

Europa, 1970

Interwoven Threads CD13

1970

Andorra, French	196-197
Belgium	741-742
Cyprus	340-342
France	1271-1272
Germany	1018-1019
Greece	985, 987
Iceland	420-421
Ireland	279-281
Italy	1013-1014
Liechtenstein	470
Luxembourg	489-490
Monaco	768-770
Netherlands	483-484
Portugal	1060-1062
San Marino	729-730
Spain	1607
Switzerland	515-516
Turkey	1848-1849
Yugoslavia	1024-1025

Europa, 1971

"Fraternity, Cooperation, Common Effort" CD14

1971

Andorra, French	205-206
Belgium	803-804
Cyprus	365-367
Finland	504
France	1304
Germany	1064-1065
Greece	1029-1030
Iceland	429-430
Ireland	305-306
Italy	1038-1039
Liechtenstein	485
Luxembourg	500-501
Malta	425-427
Monaco	797-799
Netherlands	488-489
Portugal	1094-1096
San Marino	749-750
Spain	1675-1676
Switzerland	531-532
Turkey	1876-1877
Yugoslavia	1052-1053

Europa, 1972

Sparkles, Symbolic of Communications CD15

1972

Andorra, French	210-211
Andorra, Spanish	62
Belgium	825-826
Cyprus	380-382
Finland	512-513
France	1341
Germany	1089-1090
Greece	1049-1050
Iceland	439-440
Ireland	316-317
Italy	1065-1066
Liechtenstein	504
Luxembourg	512-513
Malta	450-453
Monaco	831-832
Netherlands	494-495
Portugal	1141-1143
San Marino	771-772
Spain	1718
Switzerland	544-545
Turkey	1907-1908
Yugoslavia	1100-1101

Europa, 1973

Post Horn and Arrows CD16

1973

Andorra, French	219-220
Andorra, Spanish	76
Belgium	839-840
Cyprus	396-398
Finland	526
France	1367
Germany	1114-1115
Greece	1090-1092
Iceland	447-448
Ireland	329-330
Italy	1108-1109
Liechtenstein	528-529
Luxembourg	523-524
Malta	469-471
Monaco	866-867
Netherlands	504-505
Norway	604-605
Portugal	1170-1172
San Marino	802-803
Spain	1753
Switzerland	580-581
Turkey	1935-1936
Yugoslavia	1138-1139

Europa, 2000

CD17

2000

Albania	2621-2622
Andorra, French	522
Andorra, Spanish	262
Armenia	610-611
Austria	1814
Azerbaijan	698-699
Belarus	350
Belgium	1818
Bosnia & Herzegovina (Moslem)	358
Bosnia & Herzegovina (Serb)	111-112
Croatia	428-429
Cyprus	959
Czech Republic	3120
Denmark	1189
Estonia	394
Faroe Islands	376
Finland	1129
Aland Islands	166
France	2771
Georgia	228-229
Germany	2086-2087
Gibraltar	837-840
Great Britain (Guernsey)	805-809
Great Britain (Jersey)	935-936
Great Britain (Isle of Man)	883
Greece	1959
Greenland	363
Hungary	3699-3700
Iceland	910
Ireland	1230-1231
Italy	2349
Latvia	504
Liechtenstein	1178
Lithuania	668
Luxembourg	1035
Macedonia	187
Malta	1011-1012
Moldova	355
Monaco	2161-2162
Poland	3519
Portugal	2358
Portugal (Azores)	455
Portugal (Madeira)	208
Romania	4370
Russia	6589
San Marino	1480
Slovakia	355
Slovenia	424
Spain	3036
Sweden	2394
Switzerland	1074
Turkey	2762
Turkish Rep. of Northern Cyprus	500
Ukraine	379
Vatican City	1152

The Gibraltar stamps are similar to the stamp illustrated, but none have the design shown above. All other sets listed above include at least one stamp with the design shown, but some include stamps with entirely different designs. Bulgaria Nos. 4131-4132 and Yugoslavia Nos. 2485-2486 are Europa stamps with completely different designs.

PORTUGAL & COLONIES
Vasco da Gama

Fleet Departing CD20

Fleet Arriving at Calicut — CD21

Embarking at Rastello CD22

Muse of History CD23

San Gabriel, da Gama and Camoens CD24

Archangel Gabriel, the Patron Saint CD25

Flagship San Gabriel — CD26

Vasco da Gama — CD27

Fourth centenary of Vasco da Gama's discovery of the route to India.

1898

Azores	93-100
Macao	67-74
Madeira	37-44
Portugal	147-154
Port. Africa	1-8
Port. Congo	75-98
Port. India	189-196
St. Thomas & Prince Islands	170-193
Timor	45-52

Pombal
POSTAL TAX
POSTAL TAX DUES

Marquis de Pombal — CD28

Planning Reconstruction of Lisbon, 1755 — CD29

Pombal Monument, Lisbon — CD30

Sebastiao Jose de Carvalho e Mello, Marquis de Pombal (1699-1782), statesman, rebuilt Lisbon after earthquake of 1755. Tax was for the erection of Pombal monument. Obligatory on all mail on certain days throughout the year. Postal Tax Dues are inscribed "Multa."

1925

Angola	RA1-RA3, RAJ1-RAJ3
Azores	RA9-RA11, RAJ2-RAJ4
Cape Verde	RA1-RA3, RAJ1-RAJ3
Macao	RA1-RA3, RAJ1-RAJ3
Madeira	RA1-RA3, RAJ1-RAJ3
Mozambique	RA1-RA3, RAJ1-RAJ3
Nyassa	RA1-RA3, RAJ1-RAJ3
Portugal	RA11-RA13, RAJ2-RAJ4
Port. Guinea	RA1-RA3, RAJ1-RAJ3
Port. India	RA1-RA3, RAJ1-RAJ3
St. Thomas & Prince Islands	RA1-RA3, RAJ1-RAJ3
Timor	RA1-RA3, RAJ1-RAJ3

Vasco da Gama
CD34

Mousinho de Albuquerque
CD35

Dam
CD36

Prince Henry the Navigator
CD37

Affonso de Albuquerque
CD38

Plane over Globe
CD39

1938-39

Angola 274-291, C1-C9
Cape Verde 234-251, C1-C9
Macao.......................289-305, C7-C15
Mozambique 270-287, C1-C9
Port. Guinea 233-250, C1-C9
Port. India....................439-453, C1-C8
St. Thomas & Prince Islands ... 302-319, 323-340, C1-C18
Timor 223-239, C1-C9

Lady of Fatima

Our Lady of the Rosary, Fatima, Portugal — CD40

1948-49

Angola 315-318
Cape Verde 266
Macao..336
Mozambique 325-328
Port. Guinea 271
Port. India......................................480
St. Thomas & Prince Islands..........351
Timor 254

A souvenir sheet of 9 stamps was issued in 1951 to mark the extension of the 1950 Holy Year. The sheet contains: Angola No. 316, Cape Verde No. 266, Macao No. 336, Mozambique No. 325, Portuguese Guinea No. 271, Portuguese India Nos. 480, 485, St. Thomas & Prince Islands No. 351, Timor No. 254. The sheet also contains a portrait of Pope Pius XII and is inscribed "Encerramento do Ano Santo, Fatima 1951." It was sold for 11 escudos.

Holy Year

Church Bells and Dove
CD41

Angel Holding Candelabra
CD42

Holy Year, 1950.

1950-51

Angola 331-332
Cape Verde 268-269
Macao......................................339-340
Mozambique 330-331
Port. Guinea 273-274
Port. India................ 490-491, 496-503
St. Thomas & Prince Islands ...353-354
Timor 258-259

A souvenir sheet of 8 stamps was issued in 1951 to mark the extension of the Holy Year. The sheet contains: Angola No. 331, Cape Verde No. 269, Macao No. 340, Mozambique No. 331, Portuguese Guinea No. 275, Portuguese India No. 490, St. Thomas & Prince Islands No. 354, Timor No. 258, some with colors changed. The sheet contains doves and is inscribed 'Encerramento do Ano Santo, Fatima 1951.' It was sold for 17 escudos.

Holy Year Conclusion

Our Lady of Fatima — CD43

Conclusion of Holy Year. Sheets contain alternate vertical rows of stamps and labels bearing quotation from Pope Pius XII, different for each colony.

1951

Angola 357
Cape Verde 270
Macao...352
Mozambique 356
Port. Guinea 275
Port. India.......................................506
St. Thomas & Prince Islands..........355
Timor 270

Medical Congress

CD44

First National Congress of Tropical Medicine, Lisbon, 1952. Each stamp has a different design.

1952

Angola 358
Cape Verde 287
Macao...364
Mozambique 359
Port. Guinea 276
Port. India.......................................516
St. Thomas & Prince Islands..........356
Timor 271

Postage Due Stamps

CD45

1952

Angola J37-J42
Cape Verde J31-J36
Macao.......................................J53-J58
Mozambique J51-J56
Port. Guinea J40-J45
Port. India.................................J47-J52
St. Thomas & Prince Islands ...J52-J57
Timor J31-J36

Sao Paulo

Father Manuel da Nobrega and View of Sao Paulo — CD46

Founding of Sao Paulo, Brazil, 400th anniv.

1954

Angola 385
Cape Verde 297
Macao...382
Mozambique 395
Port. Guinea 291
Port. India.......................................530
St. Thomas & Prince Islands..........369
Timor 279

Tropical Medicine Congress

CD47

Sixth International Congress for Tropical Medicine and Malaria, Lisbon, Sept. 1958. Each stamp shows a different plant.

1958

Angola 409
Cape Verde 303
Macao...392
Mozambique 404
Port. Guinea 295
Port. India.......................................569
St. Thomas & Prince Islands..........371
Timor 289

Sports

CD48

Each stamp shows a different sport.

1962

Angola 433-438
Cape Verde 320-325
Macao......................................394-399
Mozambique 424-429
Port. Guinea 299-304
St. Thomas & Prince Islands...374-379
Timor 313-318

Anti-Malaria

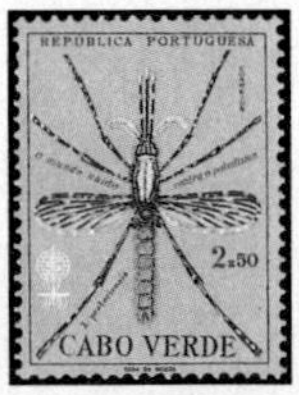

Anopheles Funestus and Malaria Eradication Symbol — CD49

World Health Organization drive to eradicate malaria.

1962

Angola 439
Cape Verde 326
Macao...400
Mozambique 430
Port. Guinea 305
St. Thomas & Prince Islands..........380
Timor 319

Airline Anniversary

Map of Africa, Super Constellation and Jet Liner — CD50

Tenth anniversary of Transportes Aereos Portugueses (TAP).

1963

Angola 490
Cape Verde 327
Mozambique 434
Port. Guinea 318
St. Thomas & Prince Islands..........381

National Overseas Bank

Antonio Teixeira de Sousa — CD51

Centenary of the National Overseas Bank of Portugal.

1964, May 16

Angola 509
Cape Verde 328
Port. Guinea 319
St. Thomas & Prince Islands..........382
Timor 320

ITU

ITU Emblem and the Archangel Gabriel — CD52

International Communications Union, Cent.

1965, May 17

Angola 511
Cape Verde 329
Macao...402
Mozambique 464
Port. Guinea 320
St. Thomas & Prince Islands..........383
Timor 321

National Revolution

CD53

40th anniv. of the National Revolution. Different buildings on each stamp.

1966, May 28

Angola 525
Cape Verde 338
Macao...403
Mozambique 465
Port. Guinea 329
St. Thomas & Prince Islands..........392
Timor 322

Navy Club

CD54

Centenary of Portugal's Navy Club. Each stamp has a different design.

1967, Jan. 31

Angola	527-528
Cape Verde	339-340
Macao	412-413
Mozambique	478-479
Port. Guinea	330-331
St. Thomas & Prince Islands	393-394
Timor	323-324

Admiral Coutinho

CD55

Centenary of the birth of Admiral Carlos Viegas Gago Coutinho (1869-1959), explorer and aviation pioneer. Each stamp has a different design.

1969, Feb. 17

Angola	547
Cape Verde	355
Macao	417
Mozambique	484
Port. Guinea	335
St. Thomas & Prince Islands	397
Timor	335

Administration Reform

Luiz Augusto Rebello da Silva — CD56

Centenary of the administration reforms of the overseas territories.

1969, Sept. 25

Angola	549
Cape Verde	357
Macao	419
Mozambique	491
Port. Guinea	337
St. Thomas & Prince Islands	399
Timor	338

Marshal Carmona

CD57

Birth centenary of Marshal Antonio Oscar Carmona de Fragoso (1869-1951), President of Portugal. Each stamp has a different design.

1970, Nov. 15

Angola	563
Cape Verde	359
Macao	422
Mozambique	493
Port. Guinea	340
St. Thomas & Prince Islands	403
Timor	341

Olympic Games

CD59

20th Olympic Games, Munich, Aug. 26-Sept. 11. Each stamp shows a different sport.

1972, June 20

Angola	569
Cape Verde	361
Macao	426
Mozambique	504
Port. Guinea	342
St. Thomas & Prince Islands	408
Timor	343

Lisbon-Rio de Janeiro Flight

CD60

50th anniversary of the Lisbon to Rio de Janeiro flight by Arturo de Sacadura and Coutinho, March 30-June 5, 1922. Each stamp shows a different stage of the flight.

1972, Sept. 20

Angola	570
Cape Verde	362
Macao	427
Mozambique	505
Port. Guinea	343
St. Thomas & Prince Islands	409
Timor	344

WMO Centenary

WMO Emblem — CD61

Centenary of international meterological cooperation.

1973, Dec. 15

Angola	571
Cape Verde	363
Macao	429
Mozambique	509
Port. Guinea	344
St. Thomas & Prince Islands	410
Timor	345

FRENCH COMMUNITY

Upper Volta can be found under Burkina Faso in Vol. 1

Madagascar can be found under Malagasy in Vol. 3

Colonial Exposition

People of French Empire CD70

Women's Heads CD71

France Showing Way to Civilization CD72

"Colonial Commerce" CD73

International Colonial Exposition, Paris.

1931

Cameroun	213-216
Chad	60-63
Dahomey	97-100
Fr. Guiana	152-155
Fr. Guinea	116-119
Fr. India	100-103
Fr. Polynesia	76-79
Fr. Sudan	102-105
Gabon	120-123
Guadeloupe	138-141
Indo-China	140-142
Ivory Coast	92-95
Madagascar	169-172
Martinique	129-132
Mauritania	65-68
Middle Congo	61-64
New Caledonia	176-179
Niger	73-76
Reunion	122-125
St. Pierre & Miquelon	132-135
Senegal	138-141
Somali Coast	135-138
Togo	254-257
Ubangi-Shari	82-85
Upper Volta	66-69
Wallis & Futuna Isls.	85-88

Paris International Exposition Colonial Arts Exposition

"Colonial Resources" CD74 CD77

Overseas Commerce CD75

Exposition Building and Women CD76

"France and the Empire" CD78

Cultural Treasures of the Colonies CD79

Souvenir sheets contain one imperf. stamp.

1937

Cameroun	217-222A
Dahomey	101-107
Fr. Equatorial Africa	27-32, 73
Fr. Guiana	162-168
Fr. Guinea	120-126
Fr. India	104-110
Fr. Polynesia	117-123
Fr. Sudan	106-112
Guadeloupe	148-154
Indo-China	193-199
Inini	41
Ivory Coast	152-158
Kwangchowan	132
Madagascar	191-197
Martinique	179-185
Mauritania	69-75
New Caledonia	208-214
Niger	72-83
Reunion	167-173
St. Pierre & Miquelon	165-171
Senegal	172-178
Somali Coast	139-145
Togo	258-264
Wallis & Futuna Isls.	89

Curie

Pierre and Marie Curie CD80

40th anniversary of the discovery of radium. The surtax was for the benefit of the Intl. Union for the Control of Cancer.

1938

Cameroun	B1
Cuba	B1-B2
Dahomey	B2
France	B76
Fr. Equatorial Africa	B1
Fr. Guiana	B3
Fr. Guinea	B2
Fr. India	B6
Fr. Polynesia	B5
Fr. Sudan	B1
Guadeloupe	B3
Indo-China	B14
Ivory Coast	B2
Madagascar	B2
Martinique	B2
Mauritania	B3
New Caledonia	B4
Niger	B1
Reunion	B4
St. Pierre & Miquelon	B3
Senegal	B3
Somali Coast	B2
Togo	B1

Caillie

Rene Caillie and Map of Northwestern Africa — CD81

Death centenary of Rene Caillie (1799-1838), French explorer. All three denominations exist with colony name omitted.

1939

Dahomey	108-110
Fr. Guinea	161-163
Fr. Sudan	113-115
Ivory Coast	160-162
Mauritania	109-111
Niger	84-86
Senegal	188-190
Togo	265-267

New York World's Fair

Natives and New York Skyline CD82

1939

Cameroun	223-224
Dahomey	111-112
Fr. Equatorial Africa	78-79
Fr. Guiana	169-170
Fr. Guinea	164-165
Fr. India	111-112
Fr. Polynesia	124-125
Fr. Sudan	116-117
Guadeloupe	155-156
Indo-China	203-204
Inini	42-43
Ivory Coast	163-164
Kwangchowan	121-122
Madagascar	209-210
Martinique	186-187
Mauritania	112-113
New Caledonia	215-216
Niger	87-88
Reunion	174-175
St. Pierre & Miquelon	205-206
Senegal	191-192
Somali Coast	179-180
Togo	268-269
Wallis & Futuna Isls.	90-91

French Revolution

Storming of the Bastille CD83

French Revolution, 150th anniv. The surtax was for the defense of the colonies.

1939

Cameroun	B2-B6
Dahomey	B3-B7
Fr. Equatorial Africa	B4-B8, CB1
Fr. Guiana	B4-B8, CB1
Fr. Guinea	B3-B7
Fr. India	B7-B11
Fr. Polynesia	B6-B10, CB1
Fr. Sudan	B2-B6
Guadeloupe	B4-B8
Indo-China	B15-B19, CB1
Inini	B1-B5
Ivory Coast	B3-B7
Kwangchowan	B1-B5
Madagascar	B3-B7, CB1
Martinique	B3-B7
Mauritania	B4-B8
New Caledonia	B5-B9, CB1
Niger	B2-B6
Reunion	B5-B9, CB1
St. Pierre & Miquelon	B4-B8
Senegal	B4-B8, CB1
Somali Coast	B3-B7
Togo	B2-B6
Wallis & Futuna Isls.	B1-B5

Plane over Coastal Area CD85

All five denominations exist with colony name omitted.

1940

Dahomey	C1-C5
Fr. Guinea	C1-C5
Fr. Sudan	C1-C5
Ivory Coast	C1-C5
Mauritania	C1-C5
Niger	C1-C5
Senegal	C12-C16
Togo	C1-C5

Defense of the Empire

Colonial Infantryman — CD86

1941

Cameroun	B13B
Dahomey	B13
Fr. Equatorial Africa	B8B
Fr. Guiana	B10
Fr. Guinea	B13
Fr. India	B13
Fr. Polynesia	B12
Fr. Sudan	B12
Guadeloupe	B10
Indo-China	B19B
Inini	B7
Ivory Coast	B13
Kwangchowan	B7
Madagascar	B9
Martinique	B9
Mauritania	B14
New Caledonia	B11
Niger	B12
Reunion	B11
St. Pierre & Miquelon	B8B
Senegal	B14
Somali Coast	B9
Togo	B10B

Wallis & Futuna Isls.	B7

Colonial Education Fund

CD86a

1942

Cameroun	CB3
Dahomey	CB4
Fr. Equatorial Africa	CB5
Fr. Guiana	CB4
Fr. Guinea	CB4
Fr. India	CB3
Fr. Polynesia	CB4
Fr. Sudan	CB4
Guadeloupe	CB3
Indo-China	CB5
Inini	CB3
Ivory Coast	CB4
Kwangchowan	CB4
Malagasy	CB5
Martinique	CB3
Mauritania	CB4
New Caledonia	CB4
Niger	CB4
Reunion	CB4
St. Pierre & Miquelon	CB3
Senegal	CB5
Somali Coast	CB3
Togo	CB3
Wallis & Futuna	CB3

Cross of Lorraine & Four-motor Plane CD87

1941-5

Cameroun	C1-C7
Fr. Equatorial Africa	C17-C23
Fr. Guiana	C9-C10
Fr. India	C1-C6
Fr. Polynesia	C3-C9
Fr. West Africa	C1-C3
Guadeloupe	C1-C2
Madagascar	C37-C43
Martinique	C1-C2
New Caledonia	C7-C13
Reunion	C18-C24
St. Pierre & Miquelon	C1-C7
Somali Coast	C1-C7

Transport Plane CD88

Caravan and Plane CD89

1942

Dahomey	C6-C13
Fr. Guinea	C6-C13
Fr. Sudan	C6-C13
Ivory Coast	C6-C13
Mauritania	C6-C13
Niger	C6-C13
Senegal	C17-C25
Togo	C6-C13

Red Cross

Marianne CD90

The surtax was for the French Red Cross and national relief.

1944

Cameroun	B28
Fr. Equatorial Africa	B38
Fr. Guiana	B12
Fr. India	B14
Fr. Polynesia	B13
Fr. West Africa	B1
Guadeloupe	B12
Madagascar	B15
Martinique	B11
New Caledonia	B13
Reunion	B15
St. Pierre & Miquelon	B13
Somali Coast	B13
Wallis & Futuna Isls.	B9

Eboue

CD91

Felix Eboue, first French colonial administrator to proclaim resistance to Germany after French surrender in World War II.

1945

Cameroun	296-297
Fr. Equatorial Africa	156-157
Fr. Guiana	171-172
Fr. India	210-211
Fr. Polynesia	150-151
Fr. West Africa	15-16
Guadeloupe	187-188
Madagascar	259-260
Martinique	196-197
New Caledonia	274-275
Reunion	238-239
St. Pierre & Miquelon	322-323
Somali Coast	238-239

Victory

Victory — CD92

European victory of the Allied Nations in World War II.

1946, May 8

Cameroun	C8
Fr. Equatorial Africa	C24
Fr. Guiana	C11
Fr. India	C7
Fr. Polynesia	C10
Fr. West Africa	C4
Guadeloupe	C3
Indo-China	C19
Madagascar	C44
Martinique	C3
New Caledonia	C14
Reunion	C25
St. Pierre & Miquelon	C8
Somali Coast	C8
Wallis & Futuna Isls.	C1

Chad to Rhine

Leclerc's Departure from Chad — CD93

Battle at Cufra Oasis — CD94

Tanks in Action, Mareth — CD95

Normandy Invasion — CD96

Entering Paris — CD97

Liberation of Strasbourg — CD98

"Chad to the Rhine" march, 1942-44, by Gen. Jacques Leclerc's column, later French 2nd Armored Division.

1946, June 6

Cameroun	C9-C14
Fr. Equatorial Africa	C25-C30
Fr. Guiana	C12-C17
Fr. India	C8-C13
Fr. Polynesia	C11-C16
Fr. West Africa	C5-C10
Guadeloupe	C4-C9
Indo-China	C20-C25
Madagascar	C45-C50
Martinique	C4-C9
New Caledonia	C15-C20
Reunion	C26-C31
St. Pierre & Miquelon	C9-C14
Somali Coast	C9-C14
Wallis & Futuna Isls.	C2-C7

UPU

French Colonials, Globe and Plane — CD99

Universal Postal Union, 75th anniv.

1949, July 4

Cameroun	C29
Fr. Equatorial Africa	C34
Fr. India	C17
Fr. Polynesia	C20
Fr. West Africa	C15
Indo-China	C26
Madagascar	C55
New Caledonia	C24
St. Pierre & Miquelon	C18
Somali Coast	C18
Togo	C18
Wallis & Futuna Isls.	C10

Tropical Medicine

Doctor Treating Infant CD100

The surtax was for charitable work.

1950

Cameroun	B29
Fr. Equatorial Africa	B39
Fr. India	B15
Fr. Polynesia	B14
Fr. West Africa	B3
Madagascar	B17
New Caledonia	B14
St. Pierre & Miquelon	B14
Somali Coast	B14
Togo	B11

Military Medal

Medal, Early Marine and Colonial Soldier — CD101

Centenary of the creation of the French Military Medal.

1952

Cameroun	332
Comoro Isls.	39
Fr. Equatorial Africa	186
Fr. India	233
Fr. Polynesia	179
Fr. West Africa	57
Madagascar	286
New Caledonia	295
St. Pierre & Miquelon	345
Somali Coast	267
Togo	327
Wallis & Futuna Isls.	149

Liberation

Allied Landing, Victory Sign and Cross of Lorraine — CD102

Liberation of France, 10th anniv.

1954, June 6

Cameroun	C32
Comoro Isls.	C4
Fr. Equatorial Africa	C38
Fr. India	C18
Fr. Polynesia	C22
Fr. West Africa	C17
Madagascar	C57
New Caledonia	C25
St. Pierre & Miquelon	C19
Somali Coast	C19
Togo	C19
Wallis & Futuna Isls.	C11

FIDES

Plowmen CD103

Efforts of FIDES, the Economic and Social Development Fund for Overseas Possessions (Fonds d' Investissement pour le Developpement Economique et Social). Each stamp has a different design.

1956

Cameroun	326-329
Comoro Isls.	43
Fr. Equatorial Africa	189-192
Fr. Polynesia	181
Fr. West Africa	65-72
Madagascar	292-295
New Caledonia	303
St. Pierre & Miquelon 350	
Somali Coast	268
Togo	331

Flower

CD104

Each stamp shows a different flower.

1958-9

Cameroun	333
Comoro Isls.	45
Fr. Equatorial Africa	200-201
Fr. Polynesia	192
Fr. So. & Antarctic Terr.	11
Fr. West Africa	79-83
Madagascar	301-302
New Caledonia	304-305
St. Pierre & Miquelon	357
Somali Coast	270
Togo	348-349
Wallis & Futuna Isls.	152

Human Rights

Sun, Dove and U.N. Emblem CD105

10th anniversary of the signing of the Universal Declaration of Human Rights.

1958

Comoro Isls.	44
Fr. Equatorial Africa	202
Fr. Polynesia	191
Fr. West Africa	85
Madagascar	300
New Caledonia	306
St. Pierre & Miquelon	356
Somali Coast	274
Wallis & Futuna Isls.	153

C.C.T.A.

CD106

Commission for Technical Cooperation in Africa south of the Sahara, 10th anniv.

1960

Cameroun	335
Cent. Africa	3
Chad	66
Congo, P.R.	90
Dahomey	138
Gabon	150
Ivory Coast	180
Madagascar	317
Mali	9
Mauritania	117
Niger	104
Upper Volta	89

Air Afrique, 1961

Modern and Ancient Africa, Map and Planes — CD107

Founding of Air Afrique (African Airlines).

1961-62

Cameroun	C37
Cent. Africa	C5
Chad	C7
Congo, P.R.	C5
Dahomey	C17
Gabon	C5
Ivory Coast	C18
Mauritania	C17
Niger	C22
Senegal	C31
Upper Volta	C4

Anti-Malaria

CD108

World Health Organization drive to eradicate malaria.

1962, Apr. 7

Cameroun	B36
Cent. Africa	B1
Chad	B1
Comoro Isls.	B1
Congo, P.R.	B3
Dahomey	B15
Gabon	B4
Ivory Coast	B15
Madagascar	B19
Mali	B1
Mauritania	B16
Niger	B14
Senegal	B16
Somali Coast	B15
Upper Volta	B1

Abidjan Games

CD109

Abidjan Games, Ivory Coast, Dec. 24-31, 1961. Each stamp shows a different sport.

1962

Chad	83-84
Cent. Africa	19-20
Congo, P.R.	103-104
Gabon	163-164, C6
Niger	109-111
Upper Volta	103-105

African and Malagasy Union

Flag of Union CD110

First anniversary of the Union.

1962, Sept. 8

Cameroun	373
Cent. Africa	21
Chad	85
Congo, P.R.	105
Dahomey	155
Gabon	165
Ivory Coast	198
Madagascar	332
Mauritania	170
Niger	112
Senegal	211
Upper Volta	106

Telstar

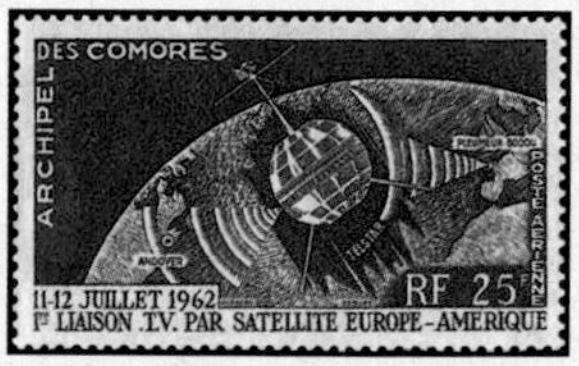

Telstar and Globe Showing Andover and Pleumeur-Bodou — CD111

First television connection of the United States and Europe through the Telstar satellite, July 11-12, 1962.

1962-63

Andorra, French	154
Comoro Isls.	C7
Fr. Polynesia	C29
Fr. So. & Antarctic Terr.	C5
New Caledonia	C33
Somali Coast	C31
St. Pierre & Miquelon	C26
Wallis & Futuna Isls.	C17

Freedom From Hunger

World Map and Wheat Emblem CD112

U.N. Food and Agriculture Organization's "Freedom from Hunger" campaign.

1963, Mar. 21

Cameroun	B37-B38
Cent. Africa	B2
Chad	B2
Congo, P.R.	B4
Dahomey	B16
Gabon	B5
Ivory Coast	B16
Madagascar	B21
Mauritania	B17
Niger	B15
Senegal	B17
Upper Volta	B2

Red Cross Centenary

CD113

Centenary of the International Red Cross.

1963, Sept. 2

Comoro Isls.	55

Fr. Polynesia	205
New Caledonia	328
St. Pierre & Miquelon	367
Somali Coast	297
Wallis & Futuna Isls.	165

African Postal Union, 1963

UAMPT Emblem, Radio Masts, Plane and Mail
CD114

Establishment of the African and Malagasy Posts and Telecommunications Union.

1963, Sept. 8

Cameroun	C47
Cent. Africa	C10
Chad	C9
Congo, P.R.	C13
Dahomey	C19
Gabon	C13
Ivory Coast	C25
Madagascar	C75
Mauritania	C22
Niger	C27
Rwanda	36
Senegal	C32
Upper Volta	C9

Air Afrique, 1963

Symbols of Flight — CD115

First anniversary of Air Afrique and inauguration of DC-8 service.

1963, Nov. 19

Cameroun	C48
Chad	C10
Congo, P.R.	C14
Gabon	C18
Ivory Coast	C26
Mauritania	C26
Niger	C35
Senegal	C33

Europafrica

Europe and Africa Linked — CD116

Signing of an economic agreement between the European Economic Community and the African and Malagasy Union, Yaounde, Cameroun, July 20, 1963.

1963-64

Cameroun	402
Chad	C11
Cent. Africa	C12
Congo, P.R.	C16
Gabon	C19
Ivory Coast	217
Niger	C43
Upper Volta	C11

Human Rights

Scales of Justice and Globe
CD117

15th anniversary of the Universal Declaration of Human Hights.

1963, Dec. 10

Comoro Isls.	58
Fr. Polynesia	206
New Caledonia	329
St. Pierre & Miquelon	368
Somali Coast	300
Wallis & Futuna Isls.	166

PHILATEC

Stamp Album, Champs Elysees Palace and Horses of Marly
CD118

Intl. Philatelic and Postal Techniques Exhibition, Paris, June 5-21, 1964.

1963-64

Comoro Isls.	60
France	1078
Fr. Polynesia	207
New Caledonia	341
St. Pierre & Miquelon	369
Somali Coast	301
Wallis & Futuna Isls.	167

Cooperation

CD119

Cooperation between France and the French-speaking countries of Africa and Madagascar.

1964

Cameroun	409-410
Cent. Africa	39
Chad	103
Congo, P.R.	121
Dahomey	193
France	1111
Gabon	175
Ivory Coast	221
Madagascar	360
Mauritania	181
Niger	143
Senegal	236
Togo	495

ITU

Telegraph, Syncom Satellite and ITU Emblem
CD120

Intl. Telecommunication Union, Cent.

1965, May 17

Comoro Isls.	C14
Fr. Polynesia	C33
Fr. So. & Antarctic Terr.	C8
New Caledonia	C40
New Hebrides	124-125
St. Pierre & Miquelon	C29
Somali Coast	C36
Wallis & Futuna Isls.	C20

French Satellite A-1

Diamant Rocket and Launching Installation — CD121

Launching of France's first satellite, Nov. 26, 1965.

1965-66

Comoro Isls.	C15-C16
France	1137-1138
Fr. Polynesia	C40-C41
Fr. So. & Antarctic Terr.	C9-C10
New Caledonia	C44-C45
St. Pierre & Miquelon	C30-C31
Somali Coast	C39-C40
Wallis & Futuna Isls.	C22-C23

French Satellite D-1

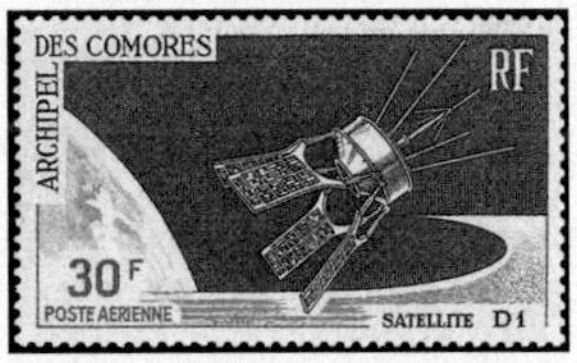

D-1 Satellite in Orbit — CD122

Launching of the D-1 satellite at Hammaguir, Algeria, Feb. 17, 1966.

1966

Comoro Isls.	C17
France	1148
Fr. Polynesia	C42
Fr. So. & Antarctic Terr.	C11
New Caledonia	C46
St. Pierre & Miquelon	C32
Somali Coast	C49
Wallis & Futuna Isls.	C24

Air Afrique, 1966

Planes and Air Afrique Emblem — CD123

Introduction of DC-8F planes by Air Afrique.

1966

Cameroun	C79
Cent. Africa	C35
Chad	C26
Congo, P.R.	C42
Dahomey	C42
Gabon	C47
Ivory Coast	C32
Mauritania	C57
Niger	C63
Senegal	C47
Togo	C54
Upper Volta	C31

African Postal Union, 1967

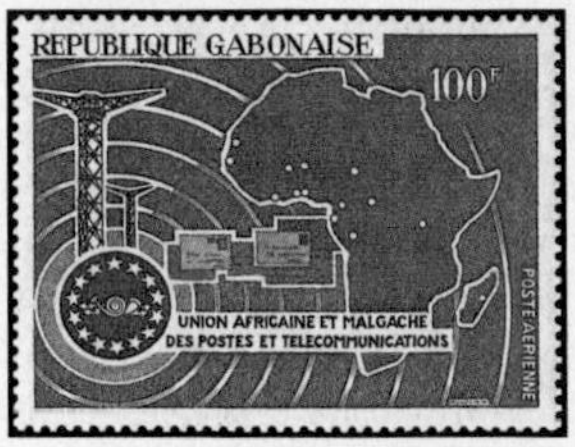

Telecommunications Symbols and Map of Africa — CD124

Fifth anniversary of the establishment of the African and Malagasy Union of Posts and Telecommunications, UAMPT.

1967

Cameroun	C90
Cent. Africa	C46
Chad	C37
Congo, P.R.	C57
Dahomey	C61
Gabon	C58
Ivory Coast	C34
Madagascar	C85
Mauritania	C65
Niger	C75
Rwanda	C1-C3
Senegal	C60
Togo	C81
Upper Volta	C50

Monetary Union

Gold Token of the Ashantis, 17-18th Centuries — CD125

West African Monetary Union, 5th anniv.

1967, Nov. 4

Dahomey	244
Ivory Coast	259
Mauritania	238
Niger	204
Senegal	294
Togo	623
Upper Volta	181

WHO Anniversary

Sun, Flowers and WHO Emblem
CD126

World Health Organization, 20th anniv.

1968, May 4

Afars & Issas	317
Comoro Isls.	73
Fr. Polynesia	241-242
Fr. So. & Antarctic Terr.	31
New Caledonia	367
St. Pierre & Miquelon	377
Wallis & Futuna Isls.	169

Human Rights Year

Human Rights Flame — CD127

1968, Aug. 10

Afars & Issas	322-323

Comoro Isls. 76
Fr. Polynesia............................243-244
Fr. So. & Antarctic Terr. 32
New Caledonia...............................369
St. Pierre & Miquelon.....................382
Wallis & Futuna Isls. 170

2nd PHILEXAFRIQUE

CD128

Opening of PHILEXAFRIQUE, Abidjan, Feb. 14. Each stamp shows a local scene and stamp.

1969, Feb. 14

Cameroun.................................... C118
Cent. Africa C65
Chad... C48
Congo, P.R.................................... C77
Dahomey C94
Gabon.. C82
Ivory Coast C38-C40
Madagascar.................................. C92
Mali... C65
Mauritania...................................... C80
Niger.. C104
Senegal C68
Togo.. C104
Upper Volta.................................... C62

Concorde

Concorde in Flight CD129

First flight of the prototype Concorde supersonic plane at Toulouse, Mar. 1, 1969.

1969

Afars & Issas................................ C56
Comoro Isls. C29
France... C42
Fr. Polynesia.................................. C50
Fr. So. & Antarctic Terr. C18
New Caledonia.............................. C63
St. Pierre & Miquelon.................... C40
Wallis & Futuna Isls. C30

Development Bank

Bank Emblem — CD130

African Development Bank, fifth anniv.

1969

Cameroun.......................................499
Chad..217
Congo, P.R..............................181-182
Ivory Coast 281
Mali..127-128
Mauritania......................................267
Niger..220
Senegal 317-318
Upper Volta....................................201

ILO

ILO Headquarters, Geneva, and Emblem — CD131

Intl. Labor Organization, 50th anniv.

1969-70

Afars & Issas.................................337
Comoro Isls. 83
Fr. Polynesia............................251-252
Fr. So. & Antarctic Terr. 35
New Caledonia...............................379
St. Pierre & Miquelon.....................396
Wallis & Futuna Isls. 172

ASECNA

Map of Africa, Plane and Airport CD132

10th anniversary of the Agency for the Security of Aerial Navigation in Africa and Madagascar (ASECNA, Agence pour la Securite de la Navigation Aerienne en Afrique et a Madagascar).

1969-70

Cameroun.......................................500
Cent. Africa 119
Chad..222
Congo, P.R.....................................197
Dahomey 269
Gabon...260
Ivory Coast 287
Mali..130
Niger..221
Senegal 321
Upper Volta.....................................204

U.P.U. Headquarters

CD133

New Universal Postal Union headquarters, Bern, Switzerland.

1970

Afars & Issas.................................342
Algeria 443
Cameroun...............................503-504
Cent. Africa 125
Chad...225
Comoro Isls. 84
Congo, P.R.....................................216
Fr. Polynesia............................261-262
Fr. So. & Antarctic Terr. 36
Gabon...258
Ivory Coast 295
Madagascar....................................444
Mali..134-135
Mauritania......................................283
New Caledonia...............................382
Niger.......................................231-232
St. Pierre & Miquelon..............397-398
Senegal 328-329
Tunisia 535
Wallis & Futuna Isls. 173

De Gaulle

CD134

First anniversary of the death of Charles de Gaulle, (1890-1970), President of France.

1971-72

Afars & Issas..........................356-357
Comoro Isls. 104-105
France...............................1322-1325
Fr. Polynesia............................270-271
Fr. So. & Antarctic Terr. 52-53
New Caledonia........................393-394
Reunion 377, 380
St. Pierre & Miquelon..............417-418
Wallis & Futuna Isls. 177-178

African Postal Union, 1971

UAMPT Building, Brazzaville, Congo — CD135

10th anniversary of the establishment of the African and Malagasy Posts and Telecommunications Union, UAMPT. Each stamp has a different native design.

1971, Nov. 13

Cameroun.................................... C177
Cent. Africa C89
Chad... C94
Congo, P.R.................................. C136
Dahomey C146
Gabon.. C120
Ivory Coast C47
Mauritania.................................... C113
Niger.. C164
Rwanda C8
Senegal C105
Togo.. C166
Upper Volta.................................... C97

West African Monetary Union

African Couple, City, Village and Commemorative Coin — CD136

West African Monetary Union, 10th anniv.

1972, Nov. 2

Dahomey 300
Ivory Coast 331
Mauritania......................................299
Niger..258
Senegal 374
Togo...825
Upper Volta.....................................280

African Postal Union, 1973

Telecommunications Symbols and Map of Africa — CD137

11th anniversary of the African and Malagasy Posts and Telecommunications Union (UAMPT).

1973, Sept. 12

Cameroun.......................................574
Cent. Africa 194
Chad...294
Congo, P.R.....................................289
Dahomey 311
Gabon...320
Ivory Coast 361
Madagascar....................................500
Mauritania......................................304
Niger...287
Rwanda 540
Senegal 393
Togo...849
Upper Volta.....................................297

Philexafrique II — Essen

CD138

CD139

Designs: Indigenous fauna, local and German stamps. Types CD138-CD139 printed horizontally and vertically se-tenant in sheets of 10 (2x5). Label between horizontal pairs alternately commemoratives Philexafrique II, Libreville, Gabon, June 1978, and 2nd International Stamp Fair, Essen, Germany, Nov. 1-5.

1978-1979

Benin C285-C286
Central Africa C200-C201
Chad................................. C238-C239
Congo Republic................. C245-C246
Djibouti.............................. C121-C122
Gabon................................ C215-C216
Ivory Coast C64-C65
Mali.................................... C356-C357
Mauritania.......................... C185-C186
Niger.................................. C291-C292
Rwanda C12-C13
Senegal C146-C147

BRITISH COMMONWEALTH OF NATIONS

The listings follow established trade practices when these issues are offered as units by dealers. The Peace issue, for example, includes only one stamp from the Indian state of Hyderabad. The U.P.U. issue includes the Egypt set. Pairs are included for those varieties issues with bilingual designs se-tenant.

Silver Jubilee

Windsor Castle and King George V CD301

Reign of King George V, 25th anniv.

1935

Antigua 77-80
Ascension 33-36
Bahamas 92-95
Barbados 186-189
Basutoland.....................................11-14
Bechuanaland Protectorate......117-120
Bermuda 100-103
British Guiana............................223-226
British Honduras........................108-111
Cayman Islands.............................81-84
Ceylon 260-263
Cyprus 136-139
Dominica..90-93
Falkland Islands 77-80
Fiji..110-113
Gambia 125-128
Gibraltar.....................................100-103
Gilbert & Ellice Islands....................33-36

Gold Coast 108-111
Grenada 124-127
Hong Kong 147-150
Jamaica 109-112
Kenya, Uganda, Tanganyika 42-45
Leeward Islands 96-99
Malta 184-187
Mauritius 204-207
Montserrat 85-88
Newfoundland 226-229
Nigeria 34-37
Northern Rhodesia 18-21
Nyasaland Protectorate 47-50
St. Helena 111-114
St. Kitts-Nevis 72-75
St. Lucia 91-94
St. Vincent 134-137
Seychelles 118-121
Sierra Leone 166-169
Solomon Islands 60-63
Somaliland Protectorate 77-80
Straits Settlements 213-216
Swaziland 20-23
Trinidad & Tobago 43-46
Turks & Caicos Islands 71-74
Virgin Islands 69-72

The following have different designs but are included in the omnibus set:

Great Britain 226-229
Offices in Morocco 67-70, 226-229, 422-425, 508-510
Australia 152-154
Canada 211-216
Cook Islands 98-100
India 142-148
Nauru 31-34
New Guinea 46-47
New Zealand 199-201
Niue 67-69
Papua 114-117
Samoa 163-165
South Africa 68-71
Southern Rhodesia 33-36
South-West Africa 121-124

249 stamps

Coronation

Queen Elizabeth and King George VI CD302

1937

Aden 13-15
Antigua 81-83
Ascension 37-39
Bahamas 97-99
Barbados 190-192
Basutoland 15-17
Bechuanaland Protectorate 121-123
Bermuda 115-117
British Guiana 227-229
British Honduras 112-114
Cayman Islands 97-99
Ceylon 275-277
Cyprus 140-142
Dominica 94-96
Falkland Islands 81-83
Fiji 114-116
Gambia 129-131
Gibraltar 104-106
Gilbert & Ellice Islands 37-39
Gold Coast 112-114
Grenada 128-130
Hong Kong 151-153
Jamaica 113-115
Kenya, Uganda, Tanganyika 60-62
Leeward Islands 100-102
Malta 188-190
Mauritius 208-210
Montserrat 89-91
Newfoundland 230-232
Nigeria 50-52
Northern Rhodesia 22-24
Nyasaland Protectorate 51-53
St. Helena 115-117
St. Kitts-Nevis 76-78
St. Lucia 107-109
St. Vincent 138-140
Seychelles 122-124
Sierra Leone 170-172
Solomon Islands 64-66
Somaliland Protectorate 81-83
Straits Settlements 235-237
Swaziland 24-26
Trinidad & Tobago 47-49
Turks & Caicos Islands 75-77
Virgin Islands 73-75

The following have different designs but are included in the omnibus set:

Great Britain 234
Offices in Morocco 82, 439, 514
Canada 237
Cook Islands 109-111
Nauru 35-38
Newfoundland 233-243
New Guinea 48-51
New Zealand 223-225
Niue 70-72
Papua 118-121
South Africa 74-78
Southern Rhodesia 38-41
South-West Africa 125-132

202 stamps

Peace

King George VI and Parliament Buildings, London CD303

Return to peace at the close of World War II.

1945-46

Aden 28-29
Antigua 96-97
Ascension 50-51
Bahamas 130-131
Barbados 207-208
Bermuda 131-132
British Guiana 242-243
British Honduras 127-128
Cayman Islands 112-113
Ceylon 293-294
Cyprus 156-157
Dominica 112-113
Falkland Islands 97-98
Falkland Islands Dep. 1L9-1L10
Fiji 137-138
Gambia 144-145
Gibraltar 119-120
Gilbert & Ellice Islands 52-53
Gold Coast 128-129
Grenada 143-144
Jamaica 136-137
Kenya, Uganda, Tanganyika 90-91
Leeward Islands 116-117
Malta 206-207
Mauritius 223-224
Montserrat 104-105
Nigeria 71-72
Northern Rhodesia 46-47
Nyasaland Protectorate 82-83
Pitcairn Island 9-10
St. Helena 128-129
St. Kitts-Nevis 91-92
St. Lucia 127-128
St. Vincent 152-153
Seychelles 149-150
Sierra Leone 186-187
Solomon Islands 80-81
Somaliland Protectorate 108-109
Trinidad & Tobago 62-63
Turks & Caicos Islands 90-91
Virgin Islands 88-89

The following have different designs but are included in the omnibus set:

Great Britain 264-265
Offices in Morocco 523-524
Aden
Kathiri State of Seiyun 12-13
Qu'aiti State of Shihr and Mukalla 12-13
Australia 200-202
Basutoland 29-31
Bechuanaland Protectorate 137-139
Burma 66-69
Cook Islands 127-130
Hong Kong 174-175
India 195-198
Hyderabad 51
New Zealand 247-257
Niue 90-93
Pakistan-Bahawalpur O16
Samoa 191-194
South Africa 100-102
Southern Rhodesia 67-70
South-West Africa 153-155
Swaziland 38-40
Zanzibar 222-223

164 stamps

Silver Wedding

King George VI and Queen Elizabeth
CD304 CD305

1948-49

Aden 30-31
Kathiri State of Seiyun 14-15
Qu'aiti State of Shihr and Mukalla 14-15
Antigua 98-99
Ascension 52-53
Bahamas 148-149
Barbados 210-211
Basutoland 39-40
Bechuanaland Protectorate 147-148
Bermuda 133-134
British Guiana 244-245
British Honduras 129-130
Cayman Islands 116-117
Cyprus 158-159
Dominica 114-115
Falkland Islands 99-100
Falkland Islands Dep. 1L11-1L12
Fiji 139-140
Gambia 146-147
Gibraltar 121-122
Gilbert & Ellice Islands 54-55
Gold Coast 142-143
Grenada 145-146
Hong Kong 178-179
Jamaica 138-139
Kenya, Uganda, Tanganyika 92-93
Leeward Islands 118-119
Malaya
Johore 128-129
Kedah 55-56
Kelantan 44-45
Malacca 1-2
Negri Sembilan 36-37
Pahang 44-45
Penang 1-2
Perak 99-100
Perlis 1-2
Selangor 74-75
Trengganu 47-48
Malta 223-224
Mauritius 229-230
Montserrat 106-107
Nigeria 73-74
North Borneo 238-239
Northern Rhodesia 48-49
Nyasaland Protectorate 85-86
Pitcairn Island 11-12
St. Helena 130-131
St. Kitts-Nevis 93-94
St. Lucia 129-130
St. Vincent 154-155
Sarawak 174-175
Seychelles 151-152
Sierra Leone 188-189
Singapore 21-22
Solomon Islands 82-83
Somaliland Protectorate 110-111
Swaziland 48-49
Trinidad & Tobago 64-65
Turks & Caicos Islands 92-93
Virgin Islands 90-91
Zanzibar 224-225

The following have different designs but are included in the omnibus set:

Great Britain 267-268
Offices in Morocco 93-94, 525-526
Bahrain 62-63
Kuwait 82-83
Oman 25-26
South Africa 106
South-West Africa 159

138 stamps

U.P.U.

Mercury and Symbols of Communications — CD306

Plane, Ship and Hemispheres — CD307

Mercury Scattering Letters over Globe CD308

U.P.U. Monument, Bern CD309

Universal Postal Union, 75th anniversary.

1949

Aden 32-35
Kathiri State of Seiyun 16-19
Qu'aiti State of Shihr and Mukalla 16-19
Antigua 100-103
Ascension 57-60
Bahamas 150-153
Barbados 212-215
Basutoland 41-44
Bechuanaland Protectorate 149-152
Bermuda 138-141
British Guiana 246-249
British Honduras 137-140
Brunei 79-82
Cayman Islands 118-121
Cyprus 160-163
Dominica 116-119
Falkland Islands 103-106
Falkland Islands Dep. 1L14-1L17
Fiji 141-144
Gambia 148-151
Gibraltar 123-126
Gilbert & Ellice Islands 56-59
Gold Coast 144-147
Grenada 147-150
Hong Kong 180-183
Jamaica 142-145
Kenya, Uganda, Tanganyika 94-97
Leeward Islands 126-129
Malaya
Johore 151-154
Kedah 57-60
Kelantan 46-49
Malacca 18-21
Negri Sembilan 59-62
Pahang 46-49
Penang 23-26
Perak 101-104
Perlis 3-6
Selangor 76-79
Trengganu 49-52
Malta 225-228
Mauritius 231-234
Montserrat 108-111
New Hebrides, British 62-65
New Hebrides, French 79-82
Nigeria 75-78
North Borneo 240-243
Northern Rhodesia 50-53
Nyasaland Protectorate 87-90
Pitcairn Islands 13-16
St. Helena 132-135
St. Kitts-Nevis 95-98
St. Lucia 131-134
St. Vincent 170-173

Sarawak.....176-179
Seychelles.....153-156
Sierra Leone.....190-193
Singapore.....23-26
Solomon Islands.....84-87
Somaliland Protectorate.....112-115
Southern Rhodesia.....71-72
Swaziland.....50-53
Tonga.....87-90
Trinidad & Tobago.....66-69
Turks & Caicos Islands.....101-104
Virgin Islands.....92-95
Zanzibar.....226-229

The following have different designs but are included in the omnibus set:

Great Britain.....276-279
Offices in Morocco.....546-549
Australia.....223
Bahrain.....68-71
Burma.....116-121
Ceylon.....304-306
Egypt.....281-283
India.....223-226
Kuwait.....89-92
Oman.....31-34
Pakistan-Bahawalpur 26-29, O25-O28
South Africa.....109-111
South-West Africa.....160-162

319 stamps

University

Arms of University College CD310

Alice, Princess of Athlone CD311

1948 opening of University College of the West Indies at Jamaica.

1951

Antigua.....104-105
Barbados.....228-229
British Guiana.....250-251
British Honduras.....141-142
Dominica.....120-121
Grenada.....164-165
Jamaica.....146-147
Leeward Islands.....130-131
Montserrat.....112-113
St. Kitts-Nevis.....105-106
St. Lucia.....149-150
St. Vincent.....174-175
Trinidad & Tobago.....70-71
Virgin Islands.....96-97

28 stamps

Coronation

Queen Elizabeth II — CD312

1953

Aden.....47
Kathiri State of Seiyun.....28
Qu'aiti State of Shihr and Mukalla.....28
Antigua.....106
Ascension.....61
Bahamas.....157
Barbados.....234
Basutoland.....45
Bechuanaland Protectorate.....153
Bermuda.....142
British Guiana.....252
British Honduras.....143
Cayman Islands.....150
Cyprus.....167
Dominica.....141
Falkland Islands.....121
Falkland Islands Dependencies.....1L18
Fiji.....145
Gambia.....152
Gibraltar.....131
Gilbert & Ellice Islands.....60
Gold Coast.....160
Grenada.....170
Hong Kong.....184
Jamaica.....153
Kenya, Uganda, Tanganyika.....101
Leeward Islands.....132
Malaya
Johore.....155
Kedah.....82
Kelantan.....71
Malacca.....27
Negri Sembilan.....63
Pahang.....71
Penang.....27
Perak.....126
Perlis.....28
Selangor.....101
Trengganu.....74
Malta.....241
Mauritius.....250
Montserrat.....127
New Hebrides, British.....77
Nigeria.....79
North Borneo.....260
Northern Rhodesia.....60
Nyasaland Protectorate.....96
Pitcairn.....19
St. Helena.....139
St. Kitts-Nevis.....119
St. Lucia.....156
St. Vincent.....185
Sarawak.....196
Seychelles.....172
Sierra Leone.....194
Singapore.....27
Solomon Islands.....88
Somaliland Protectorate.....127
Swaziland.....54
Trinidad & Tobago.....84
Tristan da Cunha.....13
Turks & Caicos Islands.....118
Virgin Islands.....114

The following have different designs but are included in the omnibus set:

Great Britain.....313-316
Offices in Morocco.....579-582
Australia.....259-261
Bahrain.....92-95
Canada.....330
Ceylon.....317
Cook Islands.....145-146
Kuwait.....113-116
New Zealand.....280-284
Niue.....104-105
Oman.....52-55
Samoa.....214-215
South Africa.....192
Southern Rhodesia.....80
South-West Africa.....244-248
Tokelau Islands.....4

106 stamps

Royal Visit 1953

Separate designs for each country for the visit of Queen Elizabeth II and the Duke of Edinburgh.

1953

Aden.....62
Australia.....267-269
Bermuda.....163
Ceylon.....318
Fiji.....146
Gibraltar.....146
Jamaica.....154
Kenya, Uganda, Tanganyika.....102
Malta.....242
New Zealand.....286-287

13 stamps

West Indies Federation

Map of the Caribbean CD313

Federation of the West Indies, April 22, 1958.

1958

Antigua.....122-124
Barbados.....248-250
Dominica.....161-163
Grenada.....184-186
Jamaica.....175-177
Montserrat.....143-145
St. Kitts-Nevis.....136-138
St. Lucia.....170-172
St. Vincent.....198-200
Trinidad & Tobago.....86-88

30 stamps

Freedom from Hunger

Protein Food CD314

U.N. Food and Agricultural Organization's "Freedom from Hunger" campaign.

1963

Aden.....65
Antigua.....133
Ascension.....89
Bahamas.....180
Basutoland.....83
Bechuanaland Protectorate.....194
Bermuda.....192
British Guiana.....271
British Honduras.....179
Brunei.....100
Cayman Islands.....168
Dominica.....181
Falkland Islands.....146
Fiji.....198
Gambia.....172
Gibraltar.....161
Gilbert & Ellice Islands.....76
Grenada.....190
Hong Kong.....218
Malta.....291
Mauritius.....270
Montserrat.....150
New Hebrides, British.....93
North Borneo.....296
Pitcairn.....35
St. Helena.....173
St. Lucia.....179
St. Vincent.....201
Sarawak.....212
Seychelles.....213
Solomon Islands.....109
Swaziland.....108
Tonga.....127
Tristan da Cunha.....68
Turks & Caicos Islands.....138
Virgin Islands.....140
Zanzibar.....280

37 stamps

Red Cross Centenary

Red Cross and Elizabeth II CD315

1963

Antigua.....134-135
Ascension.....90-91
Bahamas.....183-184
Basutoland.....84-85
Bechuanaland Protectorate.....195-196
Bermuda.....193-194
British Guiana.....272-273
British Honduras.....180-181
Cayman Islands.....169-170
Dominica.....182-183
Falkland Islands.....147-148
Fiji.....203-204
Gambia.....173-174
Gibraltar.....162-163
Gilbert & Ellice Islands.....77-78
Grenada.....191-192
Hong Kong.....219-220
Jamaica.....203-204
Malta.....292-293
Mauritius.....271-272
Montserrat.....151-152
New Hebrides, British.....94-95
Pitcairn Islands.....36-37
St. Helena.....174-175
St. Kitts-Nevis.....143-144
St. Lucia.....180-181
St. Vincent.....202-203
Seychelles.....214-215
Solomon Islands.....110-111
South Arabia.....1-2
Swaziland.....109-110
Tonga.....134-135
Tristan da Cunha.....69-70
Turks & Caicos Islands.....139-140
Virgin Islands.....141-142

70 stamps

Shakespeare

Shakespeare Memorial Theatre, Stratford-on-Avon — CD316

400th anniversary of the birth of William Shakespeare.

1964

Antigua.....151
Bahamas.....201
Bechuanaland Protectorate.....197
Cayman Islands.....171
Dominica.....184
Falkland Islands.....149
Gambia.....192
Gibraltar.....164
Montserrat.....153
St. Lucia.....196
Turks & Caicos Islands.....141
Virgin Islands.....143

12 stamps

ITU

ITU Emblem CD317

Intl. Telecommunication Union, cent.

1965

Antigua.....153-154
Ascension.....92-93
Bahamas.....219-220
Barbados.....265-266
Basutoland.....101-102
Bechuanaland Protectorate.....202-203
Bermuda.....196-197
British Guiana.....293-294
British Honduras.....187-188
Brunei.....116-117
Cayman Islands.....172-173
Dominica.....185-186
Falkland Islands.....154-155
Fiji.....211-212
Gibraltar.....167-168
Gilbert & Ellice Islands.....87-88
Grenada.....205-206
Hong Kong.....221-222
Mauritius.....291-292
Montserrat.....157-158
New Hebrides, British.....108-109
Pitcairn Islands.....52-53
St. Helena.....180-181
St. Kitts-Nevis.....163-164
St. Lucia.....197-198
St. Vincent.....224-225
Seychelles.....218-219
Solomon Islands.....126-127
Swaziland.....115-116
Tristan da Cunha.....85-86
Turks & Caicos Islands.....142-143
Virgin Islands.....159-160

64 stamps

Intl. Cooperation Year

ICY Emblem CD318

1965

Antigua 155-156
Ascension 94-95
Bahamas 222-223
Basutoland 103-104
Bechuanaland Protectorate 204-205
Bermuda 199-200
British Guiana 295-296
British Honduras 189-190
Brunei 118-119
Cayman Islands 174-175
Dominica 187-188
Falkland Islands 156-157
Fiji 213-214
Gibraltar 169-170
Gilbert & Ellice Islands 104-105
Grenada 207-208
Hong Kong 223-224
Mauritius 293-294
Montserrat 176-177
New Hebrides, British 110-111
New Hebrides, French 126-127
Pitcairn Islands 54-55
St. Helena 182-183
St. Kitts-Nevis 165-166
St. Lucia 199-200
Seychelles 220-221
Solomon Islands 143-144
South Arabia 17-18
Swaziland 117-118
Tristan da Cunha 87-88
Turks & Caicos Islands 144-145
Virgin Islands 161-162

64 stamps

Churchill Memorial

Winston Churchill and St. Paul's, London, During Air Attack CD319

1966

Antigua 157-160
Ascension 96-99
Bahamas 224-227
Barbados 281-284
Basutoland 105-108
Bechuanaland Protectorate 206-209
Bermuda 201-204
British Antarctic Territory 16-19
British Honduras 191-194
Brunei 120-123
Cayman Islands 176-179
Dominica 189-192
Falkland Islands 158-161
Fiji 215-218
Gibraltar 171-174
Gilbert & Ellice Islands 106-109
Grenada 209-212
Hong Kong 225-228
Mauritius 295-298
Montserrat 178-181
New Hebrides, British 112-115
New Hebrides, French 128-131
Pitcairn Islands 56-59
St. Helena 184-187
St. Kitts-Nevis 167-170
St. Lucia 201-204
St. Vincent 241-244
Seychelles 222-225
Solomon Islands 145-148
South Arabia 19-22
Swaziland 119-122
Tristan da Cunha 89-92
Turks & Caicos Islands 146-149
Virgin Islands 163-166

136 stamps

Royal Visit, 1966

Queen Elizabeth II and Prince Philip CD320

Caribbean visit, Feb. 4 - Mar. 6, 1966.

1966

Antigua 161-162
Bahamas 228-229
Barbados 285-286
British Guiana 299-300
Cayman Islands 180-181
Dominica 193-194
Grenada 213-214
Montserrat 182-183
St. Kitts-Nevis 171-172
St. Lucia 205-206
St. Vincent 245-246
Turks & Caicos Islands 150-151
Virgin Islands 167-168

26 stamps

World Cup Soccer

Soccer Player and Jules Rimet Cup CD321

World Cup Soccer Championship, Wembley, England, July 11-30.

1966

Antigua 163-164
Ascension 100-101
Bahamas 245-246
Bermuda 205-206
Brunei 124-125
Cayman Islands 182-183
Dominica 195-196
Fiji 219-220
Gibraltar 175-176
Gilbert & Ellice Islands 125-126
Grenada 230-231
New Hebrides, British 116-117
New Hebrides, French 132-133
Pitcairn Islands 60-61
St. Helena 188-189
St. Kitts-Nevis 173-174
St. Lucia 207-208
Seychelles 226-227
Solomon Islands 167-168
South Arabia 23-24
Tristan da Cunha 93-94

42 stamps

WHO Headquarters

World Health Organization Headquarters, Geneva — CD322

1966

Antigua 165-166
Ascension 102-103
Bahamas 247-248
Brunei 126-127
Cayman Islands 184-185
Dominica 197-198
Fiji 224-225
Gibraltar 180-181
Gilbert & Ellice Islands 127-128
Grenada 232-233
Hong Kong 229-230
Montserrat 184-185
New Hebrides, British 118-119
New Hebrides, French 134-135
Pitcairn Islands 62-63
St. Helena 190-191
St. Kitts-Nevis 177-178
St. Lucia 209-210
St. Vincent 247-248
Seychelles 228-229
Solomon Islands 169-170
South Arabia 25-26
Tristan da Cunha 99-100

46 stamps

UNESCO Anniversary

"Education" — CD323

"Science" (Wheat ears & flask enclosing globe). "Culture" (lyre & columns). 20th anniversary of the UNESCO.

1966-67

Antigua 183-185
Ascension 108-110
Bahamas 249-251
Barbados 287-289
Bermuda 207-209
Brunei 128-130
Cayman Islands 186-188
Dominica 199-201
Gibraltar 183-185
Gilbert & Ellice Islands 129-131
Grenada 234-236
Hong Kong 231-233
Mauritius 299-301
Montserrat 186-188
New Hebrides, British 120-122
New Hebrides, French 136-138
Pitcairn Islands 64-66
St. Helena 192-194
St. Kitts-Nevis 179-181
St. Lucia 211-213
St. Vincent 249-251
Seychelles 230-232
Solomon Islands 171-173
South Arabia 27-29
Swaziland 123-125
Tristan da Cunha 101-103
Turks & Caicos Islands 155-157
Virgin Islands 176-178

84 stamps

Silver Wedding, 1972

Queen Elizabeth II and Prince Philip — CD324

Designs: borders differ for each country.

1972

Anguilla 161-162
Antigua 295-296
Ascension 164-165
Bahamas 344-345
Bermuda 296-297
British Antarctic Territory 43-44
British Honduras 306-307
British Indian Ocean Territory 48-49
Brunei 186-187
Cayman Islands 304-305
Dominica 352-353
Falkland Islands 223-224
Fiji 328-329
Gibraltar 292-293
Gilbert & Ellice Islands 206-207
Grenada 466-467
Hong Kong 271-272
Montserrat 286-287
New Hebrides, British 169-170
Pitcairn Islands 127-128
St. Helena 271-272
St. Kitts-Nevis 257-258
St. Lucia 328-329
St.Vincent 344-345
Seychelles 309-310
Solomon Islands 248-249
South Georgia 35-36
Tristan da Cunha 178-179
Turks & Caicos Islands 257-258
Virgin Islands 241-242

60 stamps

Princess Anne's Wedding

Princess Anne and Mark Phillips — CD325

Wedding of Princess Anne and Mark Phillips, Nov. 14, 1973.

1973

Anguilla 179-180
Ascension 177-178
Belize 325-326
Bermuda 302-303
British Antarctic Territory 60-61
Cayman Islands 320-321
Falkland Islands 225-226
Gibraltar 305-306
Gilbert & Ellice Islands 216-217
Hong Kong 289-290
Montserrat 300-301
Pitcairn Island 135-136
St. Helena 277-278
St. Kitts-Nevis 274-275
St. Lucia 349-350
St. Vincent 358-359
St. Vincent Grenadines 1-2
Seychelles 311-312
Solomon Islands 259-260
South Georgia 37-38
Tristan da Cunha 189-190
Turks & Caicos Islands 286-287
Virgin Islands 260-261

44 stamps

Elizabeth II Coronation Anniv.

CD326

CD327

CD328

Designs: Royal and local beasts in heraldic form and simulated stonework. Portrait of Elizabeth II by Peter Grugeon. 25th anniversary of coronation of Queen Elizabeth II.

1978

Ascension 229
Barbados 474
Belize 397
British Antarctic Territory 71
Cayman Islands 404
Christmas Island 87
Falkland Islands 275
Fiji 384
Gambia 380
Gilbert Islands 312
Mauritius 464
New Hebrides, British 258
St. Helena 317
St. Kitts-Nevis 354
Samoa 472

Solomon Islands....368
South Georgia....51
Swaziland....302
Tristan da Cunha....238
Virgin Islands....337

20 sheets

Queen Mother Elizabeth's 80th Birthday

CD330

Designs: Photographs of Queen Mother Elizabeth. Falkland Islands issued in sheets of 50; others in sheets of 9.

1980

Ascension....261
Bermuda....401
Cayman Islands....443
Falkland Islands....305
Gambia....412
Gibraltar....393
Hong Kong....364
Pitcairn Islands....193
St. Helena....341
Samoa....532
Solomon Islands....426
Tristan da Cunha....277

12 stamps

Royal Wedding, 1981

Prince Charles and Lady Diana — CD331

CD331a

Wedding of Charles, Prince of Wales, and Lady Diana Spencer, St. Paul's Cathedral, London, July 29, 1981.

1981

Antigua....623-625
Ascension....294-296
Barbados....547-549
Barbuda....497-499
Bermuda....412-414
Brunei....268-270
Cayman Islands....471-473
Dominica....701-703
Falkland Islands....324-326
Falkland Islands Dep....1L59-1L61
Fiji....442-444
Gambia....426-428
Ghana....759-761
Grenada....1051-1053
Grenada Grenadines....440-443
Hong Kong....373-375
Jamaica....500-503
Lesotho....335-337
Maldive Islands....906-908
Mauritius....520-522
Norfolk Island....280-282
Pitcairn Islands....206-208
St. Helena....353-355
St. Lucia....543-545
Samoa....558-560
Sierra Leone....509-517
Solomon Islands....450-452
Swaziland....382-384
Tristan da Cunha....294-296
Turks & Caicos Islands....486-488
Caicos Island....8-10
Uganda....314-316
Vanuatu....308-310
Virgin Islands....406-408

Princess Diana

CD332

CD333

Designs: Photographs and portrait of Princess Diana, wedding or honeymoon photographs, royal residences, arms of issuing country. Portrait photograph by Clive Friend. Souvenir sheet margins show family tree, various people related to the princess. 21st birthday of Princess Diana of Wales, July 1.

1982

Antigua....663-666
Ascension....313-316
Bahamas....510-513
Barbados....585-588
Barbuda....544-546
British Antarctic Territory....92-95
Cayman Islands....486-489
Dominica....773-776
Falkland Islands....348-351
Falkland Islands Dep....1L72-1L75
Fiji....470-473
Gambia....447-450
Grenada....1101A-1105
Grenada Grenadines....485-491
Lesotho....372-375
Maldive Islands....952-955
Mauritius....548-551
Pitcairn Islands....213-216
St. Helena....372-375
St. Lucia....591-594
Sierra Leone....531-534
Solomon Islands....471-474
Swaziland....406-409
Tristan da Cunha....310-313
Turks and Caicos Islands....530A-534
Virgin Islands....430-433

250th anniv. of first edition of Lloyd's List (shipping news publication) & of Lloyd's marine insurance.

CD335

Designs: First page of early edition of the list; historical ships, modern transportation or harbor scenes.

1984

Ascension....351-354
Bahamas....555-558
Barbados....627-630
Cayes of Belize....10-13
Cayman Islands....522-525
Falkland Islands....404-407
Fiji....509-512
Gambia....519-522
Mauritius....587-590
Nauru....280-283
St. Helena....412-415
Samoa....624-627
Seychelles....538-541
Solomon Islands....521-524
Vanuatu....368-371
Virgin Islands....466-469

Queen Mother 85th Birthday

CD336

Designs: Photographs tracing the life of the Queen Mother, Elizabeth. The high value in each set pictures the same photograph taken of the Queen Mother holding the infant Prince Henry.

1985

Ascension....372-376
Bahamas....580-584
Barbados....660-664
Bermuda....469-473
Falkland Islands....420-424
Falkland Islands Dep....1L92-1L96
Fiji....531-535
Hong Kong....447-450
Jamaica....599-603
Mauritius....604-608
Norfolk Island....364-368
Pitcairn Islands....253-257
St. Helena....428-432
Samoa....649-653
Seychelles....567-571
Solomon Islands....543-547
Swaziland....476-480
Tristan da Cunha....372-376
Vanuatu....392-396
Zil Elwannyen Sesel....101-105

Queen Elizabeth II, 60th Birthday

CD337

1986, April 21

Ascension....389-393
Bahamas....592-596
Barbados....675-679
Bermuda....499-503
Cayman Islands....555-559
Falkland Islands....441-445
Fiji....544-548
Hong Kong....465-469
Jamaica....620-624
Kiribati....470-474
Mauritius....629-633
Papua New Guinea....640-644
Pitcairn Islands....270-274
St. Helena....451-455
Samoa....670-674
Seychelles....592-596
Solomon Islands....562-566
South Georgia....101-105
Swaziland....490-494
Tristan da Cunha....388-392
Vanuatu....414-418
Zambia....343-347
Zil Elwannyen Sesel....114-118

Royal Wedding

Marriage of Prince Andrew and Sarah Ferguson CD338

1986, July 23

Ascension....399-400
Bahamas....602-603
Barbados....687-688
Cayman Islands....560-561
Jamaica....629-630
Pitcairn Islands....275-276
St. Helena....460-461
St. Kitts....181-182
Seychelles....602-603
Solomon Islands....567-568
Tristan da Cunha....397-398
Zambia....348-349
Zil Elwannyen Sesel....119-120

Queen Elizabeth II, 60th Birthday

Queen Elizabeth II & Prince Philip, 1947 Wedding Portrait — CD339

Designs: Photographs tracing the life of Queen Elizabeth II.

1986

Anguilla....674-677
Antigua....925-928
Barbuda....783-786
Dominica....950-953
Gambia....611-614
Grenada....1371-1374
Grenada Grenadines....749-752
Lesotho....531-534
Maldive Islands....1172-1175
Sierra Leone....760-763
Uganda....495-498

Royal Wedding, 1986

CD340

Designs: Photographs of Prince Andrew and Sarah Ferguson during courtship, engagement and marriage.

1986

Antigua....939-942
Barbuda....809-812
Dominica....970-973
Gambia....635-638
Grenada....1385-1388
Grenada Grenadines....758-761
Lesotho....545-548
Maldive Islands....1181-1184
Sierra Leone....769-772
Uganda....510-513

Lloyds of London, 300th Anniv.

CD341

Designs: 17th century aspects of Lloyds, representations of each country's individual connections with Lloyds and publicized disasters insured by the organization.

1986

Ascension....454-457
Bahamas....655-658
Barbados....731-734
Bermuda....541-544
Falkland Islands....481-484
Liberia....1101-1104
Malawi....534-537
Nevis....571-574
St. Helena....501-504
St. Lucia....923-926
Seychelles....649-652
Solomon Islands....627-630

South Georgia..........................131-134
Trinidad & Tobago....................484-487
Tristan da Cunha.....................439-442
Vanuatu...................................485-488
Zil Elwannyen Sesel................146-149

Moon Landing, 20th Anniv.

CD342

Designs: Equipment, crew photographs, spacecraft, official emblems and report profiles created for the Apollo Missions. Two stamps in each set are square in format rather than like the stamp shown; see individual country listings for more information.

1989

Ascension Is...........................468-472
Bahamas.................................674-678
Belize......................................916-920
Kiribati....................................517-521
Liberia.................................1125-1129
Nevis.......................................586-590
St. Kitts...................................248-252
Samoa.....................................760-764
Seychelles...............................676-680
Solomon Islands......................643-647
Vanuatu...................................507-511
Zil Elwannyen Sesel................154-158

Queen Mother, 90th Birthday

CD343

CD344

Designs: Portraits of Queen Elizabeth, the Queen Mother. See individual country listings for more information.

1990

Ascension Is...........................491-492
Bahamas.................................698-699
Barbados.................................782-783
British Antarctic Territory..........170-171
British Indian Ocean Territory........106-107
Cayman Islands.......................622-623
Falkland Islands......................524-525
Kenya.......................................527-528
Kiribati....................................555-556
Liberia.................................1145-1146
Pitcairn Islands.......................336-337
St. Helena...............................532-533
St. Lucia.................................969-970
Seychelles...............................710-711
Solomon Islands......................671-672
South Georgia.........................143-144
Swaziland...............................565-566
Tristan da Cunha.....................480-481
Zil Elwannyen Sesel................171-172

Queen Elizabeth II, 65th Birthday, and Prince Philip, 70th Birthday

CD345

CD346

Designs: Portraits of Queen Elizabeth II and Prince Philip differ for each country. Printed in sheets of 10 + 5 labels (3 different) between. Stamps alternate, producing 5 different triptychs.

1991

Ascension Is...........................505-506
Bahamas.................................730-731
Belize......................................969-970
Bermuda..................................617-618
Kiribati....................................571-572
Mauritius.................................733-734
Pitcairn Islands.......................348-349
St. Helena...............................554-555
St. Kitts...................................318-319
Samoa.....................................790-791
Seychelles...............................723-724
Solomon Islands......................688-689
South Georgia.........................149-150
Swaziland...............................586-587
Vanuatu...................................540-541
Zil Elwannyen Sesel................177-178

Royal Family Birthday, Anniversary

CD347

Queen Elizabeth II, 65th birthday, Charles and Diana, 10th wedding anniversary: Various photographs of Queen Elizabeth II, Prince Philip, Prince Charles, Princess Diana and their sons William and Henry.

1991

Antigua................................1446-1455
Barbuda................................1229-1238
Dominica...............................1328-1337
Gambia..................................1080-1089
Grenada................................2006-2015
Grenada Grenadines...........1331-1340
Guyana..................................2440-2451
Lesotho...................................871-875
Maldive Islands...................1533-1542
Nevis.......................................666-675
St. Vincent...........................1485-1494
St. Vincent Grenadines...........769-778
Sierra Leone.........................1387-1396
Turks & Caicos Islands...........913-922
Uganda...................................918-927

Queen Elizabeth II's Accession to the Throne, 40th Anniv.

CD348

CD349

Various photographs of Queen Elizabeth II with local Scenes.

1992 - CD348

Antigua................................1513-1518
Barbuda................................1306-1309
Dominica...............................1414-1419
Gambia..................................1172-1177
Grenada................................2047-2052
Grenada Grenadines...........1368-1373
Lesotho...................................881-885
Maldive Islands...................1637-1642
Nevis.......................................702-707
St. Vincent...........................1582-1587
St. Vincent Grenadines...........829-834
Sierra Leone.........................1482-1487
Turks and Caicos Islands.........978-987
Uganda...................................990-995
Virgin Islands...........................742-746

1992 - CD349

Ascension Islands...................531-535
Bahamas.................................744-748
Bermuda..................................623-627
British Indian Ocean Territory........119-123
Cayman Islands.......................648-652
Falkland Islands......................549-553
Gibraltar..................................605-609
Hong Kong..............................619-623
Kenya.......................................563-567
Kiribati....................................582-586
Pitcairn Islands.......................362-366
St. Helena...............................570-574
St. Kitts...................................332-336
Samoa.....................................805-809
Seychelles...............................734-738
Solomon Islands......................708-712
South Georgia.........................157-161
Tristan da Cunha.....................508-512
Vanuatu...................................555-559
Zambia....................................561-565
Zil Elwannyen Sesel................183-187

Royal Air Force, 75th Anniversary

CD350

1993

Ascension.................................557-561
Bahamas.................................771-775
Barbados.................................842-846
Belize....................................1003-1008
Bermuda..................................648-651
British Indian Ocean Territory........136-140
Falkland Is..............................573-577
Fiji...687-691
Montserrat...............................830-834
St. Kitts...................................351-355

Royal Air Force, 80th Anniv.

Design CD350 Re-inscribed

1998

Ascension.................................697-701
Bahamas.................................907-911
British Indian Ocean Terr.........198-202
Cayman Islands.......................754-758
Fiji...814-818
Gibraltar..................................755-759
Samoa.....................................957-961
Turks & Caicos Islands........1258-1265
Tuvalu.....................................763-767
Virgin Islands......................... 879-883

End of World War II, 50th Anniv.

CD351

CD352

1995

Ascension.................................613-617
Bahamas.................................824-828
Barbados.................................891-895
Belize....................................1047-1050
British Indian Ocean Territory........163-167
Cayman Islands.......................704-708
Falkland Islands......................634-638
Fiji...720-724
Kiribati....................................662-668
Liberia.................................1175-1179
Mauritius.................................803-805
St. Helena...............................646-654
St. Kitts...................................389-393
St. Lucia...............................1018-1022
Samoa.....................................890-894
Solomon Islands......................799-803
South Georgia & S. Sandwich Is.........198-200
Tristan da Cunha.....................562-566

UN, 50th Anniv.

CD353

1995

Bahamas.................................839-842
Barbados.................................901-904
Belize....................................1055-1058
Jamaica...................................847-851
Liberia.................................1187-1190
Mauritius.................................813-816
Pitcairn Islands.......................436-439
St. Kitts...................................398-401
St. Lucia...............................1023-1026
Samoa.....................................900-903
Tristan da Cunha.....................568-571
Virgin Islands...........................807-810

Queen Elizabeth, 70th Birthday

CD354

1996

Ascension.................................632-635
British Antarctic Territory..........240-243
British Indian Ocean Territory........176-180
Falkland Islands......................653-657
Pitcairn Islands.......................446-449
St. Helena...............................672-676
Samoa.....................................912-916
Tokelau...................................223-227
Tristan da Cunha.....................576-579
Virgin Islands...........................824-828

Diana, Princess of Wales (1961-97)

CD355

1998

Ascension 696
Bahamas 901A-902
Barbados 950
Belize 1091
Bermuda 753
Botswana 659-663
British Antarctic Territory 258
British Indian Ocean Terr. 197
Cayman Islands 752A-753
Falkland Islands 694
Fiji 819-820
Gibraltar 754
Kiribati 719A-720
Namibia 909
Niue 706
Norfolk Island 644-645
Papua New Guinea 937
Pitcairn Islands 487
St. Helena 711
St. Kitts 437A-438
Samoa 955A-956
Seycelles 802
Solomon Islands 866-867
South Georgia & S. Sandwich Islands 220
Tokelau 252B-253
Tonga 980
Niuafo'ou 201
Tristan da Cunha 618
Tuvalu 762
Vanuatu 719
Virgin Islands 878

Wedding of Prince Edward and Sophie Rhys-Jones

CD356

1999

Ascension 729-730
Cayman Islands 775-776
Falkland Islands 729-730
Pitcairn Islands 505-506
St. Helena 733-734
Samoa 971-972
Tristan da Cunha 636-637
Virgin Islands 908-909

1st Manned Moon Landing, 30th Anniv.

CD357

1999

Ascension 731-735
Bahamas 942-946
Barbados 967-971
Bermuda 778
Cayman Islands 777-781
Fiji 853-857
Jamaica 889-893
Kirbati 746-750
Nauru 465-469
St. Kitts 460-464
Samoa 973-977
Solomon Islands 875-879
Tuvalu 800-804
Virgin Islands 910-914

Queen Mother's Century

CD358

1999

Ascension 736-740
Bahamas 951-955
Cayman Islands 782-786
Falkland Islands 734-738
Fiji 858-862
Norfolk Island 688-692
St. Helena 740-744
Samoa 978-982
Solomon Islands 880-884
South Georgia & South Sandwich Islands 231-235
Tristan da Cunha 638-642
Tuvalu 805-809

Prince William, 18th Birthday

CD359

2000

Ascension 755-759
Cayman Islands 797-801
Falkland Islands 762-766
Fiji 889-893
South Georgia and South Sandwich Islands 257-261
Tristan da Cunha 664-668
Virgin Islands 925-929

Reign of Queen Elizabeth II, 50th Anniv.

CD360

2002

Ascension 790-794
Bahamas 1033-1037
Barbados 1019-1023
Belize 1152-1156
Bermuda 822-826
British Antarctic Territory 307-311
British Indian Ocean Territory 239-243
Cayman Islands 844-848
Falkland Islands 804-808
Gibraltar 896-900
Jamaica 952-956
Nauru 491-495
Norfolk Island 758-762
Papua New Guinea 1019-1023
Pitcairn Islands 552
St. Helena 788-792
St. Lucia 1146-1150
Solomon Islands 931-935
South Georgia & So. Sandwich Is. 274-278
Swaziland 706-710
Tokelau 302-306
Tonga 1059
Niuafo'ou 239
Tristan da Cunha 706-710
Virgin Islands 967-971

Queen Mother Elizabeth (1900-2002)

CD361

2002

Ascension 799-801
Bahamas 1044-1046
Bermuda 834-836
British Antarctic Territory 312-314
British Indian Ocean Territory 245-247
Cayman Islands 857-861
Falkland Islands 812-816
Nauru 499-501
Pitcairn Islands 561-565
St. Helena 808-812
St. Lucia 1155-1159
Seychelles 830
Solomon Islands 945-947
South Georgia & So. Sandwich Isls. 281-285
Tokelau 312-314
Tristan da Cunha 715-717
Virgin Islands 979-983

Head of Queen Elizabeth II

CD362

2003

Ascension 822
Bermuda 865
British Antarctic Territory 322
British Indian Ocean Territory 261
Cayman Islands 878
Falkland Islands 828
St. Helena 820
South Georgia & South Sandwich Islands 294
Tristan da Cunha 731
Virgin Islands 1003

Coronation of Queen Elizabeth II, 50th Anniv.

CD363

2003

Ascension 823-825
Bahamas 1073-1075
Bermuda 866-868
British Antarctic Territory 323-325
British Indian Ocean Territory 262-264
Cayman Islands 879-881
Jamaica 970-972
Kiribati 825-827
Pitcairn Islands 577-581
St. Helena 821-823
St. Lucia 1171-1173
Tokelau 320-322
Tristan da Cunha 732-734
Virgin Islands 1004-1006

Prince William, 21st Birthday

CD364

2003

Ascension 826
British Indian Ocean Territory 265
Cayman Islands 882-884
Falkland Islands 829
South Georgia & South Sandwich Islands 295
Tokelau 323
Tristan da Cunha 735
Virgin Islands 1007-1009

British Commonwealth of Nations

Dominions, Colonies, Territories, Offices and Independent Members

Comprising stamps of the British Commonwealth and associated nations.

A strict observance of technicalities would bar some or all of the stamps listed under Burma, Ireland, Kuwait, Nepal, New Republic, Orange Free State, Samoa, South Africa, South-West Africa, Stellaland, Sudan, Swaziland, the two Transvaal Republics and others but these are included for the convenience of collectors.

1. Great Britain

Great Britain: Including England, Scotland, Wales and Northern Ireland.

2. The Dominions, Present and Past

AUSTRALIA

The Commonwealth of Australia was proclaimed on January 1, 1901. It consists of six former colonies as follows:

New South Wales
Queensland
South Australia
Victoria
Tasmania
Western Australia

The following islands and territories are, or have been, administered by Australia: Australian Antarctic Territory, Christmas Island, Cocos (Keeling) Islands, Nauru, New Guinea, Norfolk Island, Papua.

CANADA

The Dominion of Canada was created by the British North America Act in 1867. The following provinces were former separate colonies and issued postage stamps:

British Columbia and
 Vancouver Island
New Brunswick
Newfoundland
Nova Scotia
Prince Edward Island

FIJI

The colony of Fiji became an independent nation with dominion status on Oct. 10, 1970.

GHANA

This state came into existence Mar. 6, 1957, with dominion status. It consists of the former colony of the Gold Coast and the Trusteeship Territory of Togoland. Ghana became a republic July 1, 1960.

INDIA

The Republic of India was inaugurated on January 26, 1950. It succeeded the Dominion of India which was proclaimed August 15, 1947, when the former Empire of India was divided into Pakistan and the Union of India. The Republic is composed of about 40 predominantly Hindu states of three classes: governor's provinces, chief commissioner's provinces and princely states. India also has various territories, such as the Andaman and Nicobar Islands.

The old Empire of India was a federation of British India and the native states. The more important princely states were autonomous. Of the more than 700 Indian states, these 43 are familiar names to philatelists because of their postage stamps.

CONVENTION STATES

Chamba
Faridkot
Gwalior
Jhind
Nabha
Patiala

NATIVE FEUDATORY STATES

Alwar
Bahawalpur
Bamra
Barwani
Bhopal
Bhor
Bijawar
Bundi
Bussahir
Charkhari
Cochin
Dhar
Duttia
Faridkot (1879-85)
Hyderabad
Idar
Indore
Jaipur
Jammu
Jammu and Kashmir
Jasdan
Jhalawar
Jhind (1875-76)
Kashmir
Kishangarh
Las Bela
Morvi
Nandgaon
Nowanuggur
Orchha
Poonch
Rajpeepla
Sirmur
Soruth
Travancore
Wadhwan

NEW ZEALAND

Became a dominion on September 26, 1907. The following islands and territories are, or have been, administered by New Zealand:

Aitutaki
Cook Islands (Rarotonga)
Niue
Penrhyn
Ross Dependency
Samoa (Western Samoa)
Tokelau Islands

PAKISTAN

The Republic of Pakistan was proclaimed March 23, 1956. It succeeded the Dominion which was proclaimed August 15, 1947. It is made up of all or part of several Moslem provinces and various districts of the former Empire of India, including Bahawalpur and Las Bela. Pakistan withdrew from the Commonwealth in 1972.

SOUTH AFRICA

Under the terms of the South African Act (1909) the self-governing colonies of Cape of Good Hope, Natal, Orange River Colony and Transvaal united on May 31, 1910, to form the Union of South Africa. It became an independent republic May 3, 1961.

Under the terms of the Treaty of Versailles, South-West Africa, formerly German South-West Africa, was mandated to the Union of South Africa.

SRI LANKA (CEYLON)

The Dominion of Ceylon was proclaimed February 4, 1948. The island had been a Crown Colony from 1802 until then. On May 22, 1972, Ceylon became the Republic of Sri Lanka.

3. Colonies, Past and Present; ControlledTerritory and Independent Members of the Commonwealth

Aden
Aitutaki
Antigua
Ascension
Bahamas
Bahrain
Bangladesh
Barbados
Barbuda
Basutoland
Batum
Bechuanaland
Bechuanaland Prot.
Belize
Bermuda
Botswana
British Antarctic Territory
British Central Africa
British Columbia and
 Vancouver Island
British East Africa
British Guiana

Papilio Oeacus A56

Butterflies: 4r, Papilio agamenon. 8r, Danaus plexippus.

1969, Oct. 10 Engr. *Perf. 13*

210 A56 3r lilac, blk & yel 5.00 1.25
211 A56 4r ver, blk & grn 8.50 2.00
212 A56 8r yel grn, dk brn & org 11.50 3.00
Nos. 210-212 (3) 25.00 6.25

Map of Cambodia and Diesel Engine A57

Various railroad stations and trains.

1969, Nov. 27 Engr. *Perf. 13*

213 A57 3r multicolored 1.00 .75
214 A57 6r slate grn & lt brn 2.00 1.50
215 A57 8r black 3.25 2.25
216 A57 9r dk green & blue 3.75 2.40
Nos. 213-216 (4) 10.00 6.90

Issued to publicize the new rail link between Phnom Penh and Sihanoukville.

Fish — A58

1970, Jan. 29 Photo. *Perf. 13*

217 A58 3r Tripletail 2.40 1.40
218 A58 7r Sleeper goby 4.50 2.40
219 A58 9r Snakehead 5.25 3.00
Nos. 217-219 (3) 12.15 6.80

Wat Maniratanaram — A59

Monasteries: 2r, Wat Tepthidaram, vert. 6r, Wat Patumavati. 8r, Wat Unnalom.

1970, Apr. 29 Photo. *Perf. 13*

220 A59 2r multicolored .35 .30
221 A59 3r multicolored .40 .30
222 A59 6r multicolored .85 .35
223 A59 8r multicolored 1.60 .45
Nos. 220-223 (4) 3.20 1.40

UPU Headquarters and Monument, Bern — A60

1970, May 20

224 A60 1r green & multi .30 .20
225 A60 3r scarlet & multi .50 .20
226 A60 4r dp blue & multi .60 .20
227 A60 10r brown & multi 1.10 .40
Nos. 224-227 (4) 2.50 1.00

New UPU Headquarters in Bern.

Open Book and Satellite Earth Receiving Station — A61

1970, May 17 Photo. *Perf. 13*

228 A61 3r dk vio bl & multi .25 .20
229 A61 4r sl grn & multi .35 .25
230 A61 9r brn ol & multi .85 .35
Nos. 228-230 (3) 1.45 .80

World Telecommunications Day.

Nelumbium Speciosum A62

Flowers: 4r, Eichhornia crassipes. 13r, Nymphea lotus.

1970, Aug. 17 Photo. *Perf. 13*

231 A62 3r multicolored .60 .30
a. Cambodian and Arabic 3's transposed 15.00 20.00
232 A62 4r multicolored 1.40 .45
233 A62 13r multicolored 2.50 .70
Nos. 231-233 (3) 4.50 1.45

Elephant God, Bas relief at Banteay Srei — A63

1970, Sept. 21 Engr. *Perf. 13*

234 A63 3r lil rose & dp grn .25 .25
235 A63 4r bl grn, grn & lil rose .55 .25
236 A63 7r bl grn, dk brn & grn .80 .40
Nos. 234-236 (3) 1.60 .90

Issued for World Meteorological Day.

Khmer Republic

Globe, Rocket, Dove and UN Emblem A64

1970, Nov. 9 Photo. *Perf. 12½x12*

237 A64 3r black & multi .30 .20
238 A64 5r brown red & multi .45 .25
239 A64 10r dp violet & multi .90 .50
Nos. 237-239 (3) 1.65 .95

25th anniversary of the United Nations.

Education Year Emblem A65

1970, Nov. 9 Engr. *Perf. 13x12½*

240 A65 1r blue .25 .20
241 A65 3r brt rose lilac .30 .20
242 A65 8r blue green .70 .45
Nos. 240-242 (3) 1.25 .85

Issued for International Education Year.

Chuon-Nath — A66

1971, Jan. 27 Photo. *Perf. 13*

243 A66 3r ol grn & multi .30 .20
244 A66 8r purple & multi .65 .35
245 A66 9r violet & multi .90 .55
Nos. 243-245 (3) 1.85 1.10

In memory of Chuon-Nath (1883-1969), Cambodian language expert.

For surcharge see No. 322.

Soldiers in Battle A67

1971, Mar. 18 Photo. *Perf. 13*

246 A67 1r gray & multi .50 .20
247 A67 3r bister & multi .50 .40
248 A67 10r blue & multi 4.00 .75
Nos. 246-248 (3) 5.00 1.35

National territorial defense.

For overprint see No. 321.

UN Emblem, Men of Four Races A68

1971, Mar. 21

249 A68 3r blue & multi .30 .20
250 A68 7r green & multi .45 .30
251 A68 8r brt rose & multi 1.00 .50
Nos. 249-251 (3) 1.75 1.00

Intl. year against racial discrimination.

General Post Office, Phnom Penh — A69

1971, Apr. 19

252 A69 3r blue & multi .20 .20
253 A69 9r lilac rose & multi .55 .35
254 A69 10r black & multi .70 .40
Nos. 252-254 (3) 1.45 .95

Symbolic Globe and Waves A70

Design: 7r, 8r, ITU emblem and waves.

1971, May 17 Photo. *Perf. 13*

255 A70 3r green, blk & bl .25 .20
256 A70 4r yellow & multi .25 .20
257 A70 7r lilac, blk & red .35 .25
258 A70 8r sal pink, blk & red .50 .30
Nos. 255-258 (4) 1.35 .95

3rd World Telecommunications Day.

Erythrina Indica A71

Wild Flowers: 3r, Bauhinia variegata. 6r, Butea frondosa. 10r, Lagerstroemia floribunda, vert.

1971, July 5 *Perf. 13x12½, 12½x13*

259 A71 2r lt ultra & multi .45 .45
260 A71 3r yel grn & multi .55 .55
261 A71 6r blue & multi 1.10 1.10
262 A71 10r brown & multi 1.40 1.40
Nos. 259-262 (4) 3.50 3.50

Khmer Coat of Arms — A72

Flag and Square of the Republic — A73

1971, Oct. 9 Engr. *Perf. 13*

263 A72 3r brt grn & bis .20 .20
264 A73 3r purple & multi .20 .20
265 A73 4r dp claret & multi .25 .20
266 A72 8r orange & bis .45 .25
267 A72 10r lt brn & bis .70 .30
a. Souv. sheet of 3, #263, 266-267 2.75 2.75
268 A73 10r slate grn & multi .70 .35
a. Souv. sheet of 3, #264-265, 268 2.75 2.75
Nos. 263-268 (6) 2.50 1.50

Republic, 1st anniv.

#267a sold for 25r, #268a for 20r.

For overprints and surcharges see Nos. 301-302, B13-B14.

UNICEF Emblem — A74

1971, Dec. 11

269 A74 3r black brown .30 .20
270 A74 5r ultra .40 .25
271 A74 9r dk pur & brn red .80 .45
Nos. 269-271 (3) 1.50 .90

25th anniv. of UNICEF.

This set and others exist with overprint "RPK," both with and without frame. Status has not been determined.

Book Year Emblem A75

1972, Feb. 7 Engr.

272 A75 3r blue, grn & vio .40 .20
273 A75 8r violet, grn & bl .60 .30
274 A75 9r emerald & multi 1.00 .50
a. Souvenir sheet of 3, #272-274 2.25 2.25
Nos. 272-274 (3) 2.00 1.00

Intl. Book Year. No. 274a sold for 23r.

Lion of St. Mark A76

Designs: 5r, Waves engulfing St. Mark's Basilica. 10r, Bridge of Sighs, vert.

1972, Feb. 7 Engr. *Perf. 13*

275 A76 3r lil rose & org brn .50 .20
276 A76 5r yel grn & org brn .75 .25
277 A76 10r org brn, bl & yel grn 1.25 .45
a. Souvenir sheet of 3, #275-277 3.00 3.00
Nos. 275-277 (3) 2.50 .90

UNESCO campaign to save Venice. No. 277a sold for 23r.

UN Emblem
A77

1972, Mar. 28

278 A77 3r deep carmine .30 .20
279 A77 6r deep blue .50 .25
280 A77 9r deep orange .70 .45
a. Souvenir sheet of 3, #278-280 2.00 2.00
Nos. 278-280 (3) 1.50 .90

25th anniv. UN Economic Commission for Asia and the Far East (ECAFE). No. 280a sold for 23r.

Dancing Apsarases — A78

"UIT"
A79

1972, May 5 **Engr.** ***Perf. 13***

281 A78 1r golden brn .20 .20
282 A78 3r violet .30 .20
283 A78 7r rose claret .40 .30
284 A78 8r olive brn .50 .30
285 A78 9r blue grn .60 .30
286 A78 10r ultra .90 .30
287 A78 12r purple 1.10 .30
288 A78 14r Prus blue 1.40 .45
Nos. 281-288 (8) 5.40 2.35

1972, May 17 **Litho.**

289 A79 3r blk, yel & grnsh bl .30 .20
290 A79 9r blk, dp lil rose & bl grn .65 .30
291 A79 14r blk, brn & bl grn .95 .45
Nos. 289-291 (3) 1.90 .95

4th World Telecommunications Day.

"Human Environment" — A80

1972, June 5 **Engr.**

292 A80 3r org, plum & grn .35 .20
293 A80 12r brt grn & plum .50 .30
294 A80 15r plum & brt grn .75 .40
a. Souvenir sheet of 3, #292-294 3.25 3.25
Nos. 292-294 (3) 1.60 .90

UN Conf. on Human Environment, Stockholm, June 5-16. No. 294a sold for 35r.
For overprints and surcharges see Nos. 304-305, B15, B17.

Javan Rhinoceros
A81

1972, Aug. 1 **Engr.** ***Perf. 13***

295 A81 3r shown .45 .20
296 A81 4r Serow .55 .20
297 A81 6r Malayan sambar 1.00 .30
298 A81 7r Banteng 1.50 .30
299 A81 8r Water buffalo 1.75 .50
300 A81 10r Gaur 2.25 .60
Nos. 295-300 (6) 7.50 2.10

Nos. 263, 267, 134, 293, 294 Overprinted in Red

1972, Sept. 9 **Engr.** ***Perf. 13***

301 A72 3r brt grn & bister .75 .30
302 A72 10r orange & bister 1.50 .60
303 A34 12r multicolored 1.50 .75
304 A80 12r brt grn & plum 1.60 .75
305 A80 15r plum & brt grn 2.10 .90
Nos. 301-305 (5) 7.45 3.30

20th Olympic Games, Munich, 8/26-9/11.

Raising Khmer Flag — A82

1972, Oct. 9 **Photo.** ***Perf. 12½x13***

306 A82 3r multicolored .20 .20
307 A82 5r brt rose & multi .40 .30
308 A82 9r yel grn & multi .90 .30
Nos. 306-308 (3) 1.50 .80

2nd anniversary of the establishment of the Khmer Republic.
For surcharge see No. 323.

Stupa and Crest — A83

Apsaras — A84

1973, May 12 **Engr.** ***Perf. 13***

309 A83 3r ocher & multi .30 .20
310 A83 12r yel grn & multi .30 .20
311 A83 14r blue & multi .50 .20
a. Souvenir sheet of 3, #309-311 2.50 2.50
Nos. 309-311 (3) 1.10 .60

New Constitution. No. 311a sold for 34r.

1973, July 23 **Engr.** ***Perf. 13***

Sculptures from Angkor Wat: 8r, 10r, Devata, diff.

312 A84 3r brown black .60 .25
313 A84 8r Prus green 1.00 .30
314 A84 10r olive bister 1.50 .45
a. Souvenir sheet of 3, #312-314 2.50 2.25
Nos. 312-314 (3) 3.10 1.00

No. 314a sold for 25r.

INTERPOL Emblem — A85

Marshal Lon Nol — A86

1973, Oct. 2 **Engr.** ***Perf. 13***

315 A85 3r green & multi .35 .20
316 A85 7r red brn & multi .45 .20
317 A85 10r olive & multi .60 .30
a. Souvenir sheet of 3, #315-317 2.75 2.75
Nos. 315-317 (3) 1.40 .70

50th anniv. of the Intl. Criminal Police Org. No. 317a sold for 30r.

1973, Oct. 9

318 A86 3r lt grn, blk & brn .40 .20
319 A86 8r brown, ol & blk .60 .30
320 A86 14r black & brn 1.00 .40
a. Souvenir sheet of 3 4.25 4.25
Nos. 318-320 (3) 2.00 .90

Marshal Lon Nol, 1st pres. of the Republic. No. 320a contains stamps similar to Nos. 318-320 in changed colors. Sold for 50r.

Nos. 248, 243 and 307 Surcharged with New Value, 2 Bars and Overprinted in Red or Silver: "4th ANNIVERSAIRE/DE LA REPUBLIQUE"

1974 **Photo.** ***Perf. 13, 12½x13***

321 A67 10r multi (R) 1.00 .50
322 A66 50r on 3r multi 2.00 1.00
323 A82 100r on 5r multi 7.00 3.50
Nos. 321-323 (3) 10.00 5.00

4th anniversary of the Republic.

Copernicus and "Nerva" — A87

Copernicus, various spacecraft and events.

1974, Sept. 10 **Litho.** ***Perf. 13***

324 A87 1r shown
325 A87 5r Mariner II
326 A87 10r Apollo
327 A87 25r Telstar
328 A87 50r Space walk
329 A87 100r Moon landing
330 A87 150r Separation of spaceship and module
Nos. 324-330 (7) *45.00*
Nos. 324-330, C46-C47 (9) *55.00*

500th anniversary of the birth of Nicolaus Copernicus (1473-1543), Polish astronomer.

Carrier Pigeon and UPU Emblem — A88

Design: 60r, Sailing ship and UPU emblem.

1974, Nov. 2

331 A88 10r multicolored .25 .20
332 A88 60r multicolored .75 .20
Nos. 331-332,C50 (3) 11.00 10.40

Cent. of UPU. A souvenir sheet containing one No. 332 exists.

A set of 8 stamps picturing musical instruments, overprinted and surcharged for use by the Khmer Republic just before the fall of the government in Apr. 1975, exists. Value, $1,100. Value for same set without surcharge, $500.

A89

1976 Summer Olympic Games, Montreal — A90

1r, 18th cent. swordsmen. 5r, Modern fencers. 10r, Ancient Olympic runner. 25r, Modern runner. 50r, Ancient rowers. 100r, Modern kayakers. 150r, Ancient horseman. 200r, Modern equestrian competitor. 250r, Buildings, Olympic flame.

1975, Jan. 2 **Litho.** ***Perf. 13½***

333-341 A89 Set of 9 15.00

Litho. & Embossed

342 A90 1200r gold & multi *35.00*

Souvenir Sheets

343 A89 200r silver & multi *7.50*
344 A89 250r silver & multi *7.50*

Nos. 337-344 are airmail.
A number has been reserved for another souvenir sheet released with this set.

A91

1974 World Cup Soccer Championships — A92

Soccer players and arms of: 1r, Hamburg. 5r, Gelsenkirchen. 10r, Dortmund. 25r, Stuttgart. 50r, Dusseldorf. 100r, Hannover. 150r, Frankfurt. 200r, Munich. 250r, Berlin.

Litho. (#346-354, 356-357)
Litho. & Embossed (#355, 358)

1975, Feb. 13

346-354 A91 Set of 9 7.50
355 A92 1200r gold & multi *37.50*

Souvenir Sheets

356 A91 200r gold & multi *6.00*
357 A91 250r gold & multi *6.00*
358 A92 1200r gold & multi *13.00*

Nos. 350-358 are airmail. Nos. 346-354 exist in imperforate souvenir sheets.

UPU, Cent. — A93

Designs: 15r, Letter carrier, pack mule. 20r, Biplane. 70r, Post coach. 160r, Biplane, Concorde. 180r, Steam-powered wagon. 235r, Postrider, tail of mailplane. 500r, Railway mail car. 1000r, Airship. 2000r, Caravel.

1975, Apr. 12
359-367 A93 Set of 9 10.00
366a Souvenir sheet of 1 *10.00*
367a Souvenir sheet of 1 *10.00*

Nos. 365-367 are airmail. Nos. 366a and 367a exist imperf. Values, each $25.

People's Republic of Kampuchea

Soldiers — A94

Designs, horiz.: 20c, People, flag. 50c, Fishermen. 1r, Soldiers passing flag.

1980, Apr. 10 Litho. *Perf. 11*
368-371 A94 Set of 4 45.00 45.00

Soviet Union, 60th Anniv. — A95

Designs: 50c, Globe, Kremlin. 1r, Buildings, map of USSR.

1982, Dec. 30 *Perf. 12x12½*
372-373 A95 Set of 2 .75 .40

People's Republic of Kampuchea, 4th Anniv. — A96

Designs: 50c, Natl. arms, vert. 1r, shown. 3r, Map, stylized figures, vert. 6r, Temple, vert.

1983, Jan. 7 Litho. *Perf. 13*
374-376 A96 Set of 3 3.50 1.10

Souvenir Sheet

377 A96 6r multicolored 4.75 2.25

1984 Summer Olympic Games, Los Angeles A97

Designs: 20c, Runner with torch. 50c, Javelin. 80c, Pole vault. 1r, Discus. 1.50r, Relay race. 2r, Swimming. 3r, Basketball.
20c-1r, 3r are vert.

1983, Jan. 20 Litho. *Perf. 13*
378-384 A97 Set of 7 7.00 1.50

Souvenir Sheet

385 A97 6r Soccer 5.00 3.00

No. 385 contains one 32x40mm stamp.

Butterflies — A98

20c, Salatura genutia. 50c, Euploea althaea. 80c, Byasa polyeuctes. 1r, Stichophthalma howqua. 1.50r, Kallima inachus. 2r, Precis orithya. 3r, Catopsilia pomona.
20c, 50c, 1.50r, 2r, 3r are vert.

1983, Feb. 18 Litho. *Perf. 13*
386-392 A98 Set of 7 8.00 2.00

Khmer Culture A99

Designs: 20c, Ruins, Srah Srang. 50c, Temple, Bakong. 80c, Ta Son. 1r, North Gate, Angkor Thom. 1.50r, Two winged figures. 2r, Apsara, Angkor. 3r, Statue of Banteai Srei.
80c-3r are vert.

1983, Mar. 15
393-399 A99 Set of 7 6.00 1.75

Folk Dances A100

Various dances. Denominations 50c, 1r, 3r.

1983, Apr. 17 Litho. *Perf. 13*
400-402 A100 Set of 3 3.75 1.25

Souvenir Sheet

403 A100 6r Native, "buffalo" 6.50 1.40

No. 403 contains one 32x40mm stamp.

Raphael (1483-1520) — A101

Parnassus (details): #404, 20c, Dante, Ennius, Homer. #406, 80c, Horace, Ovid, others. #409, 2r, The Muses. #410, 3r, Alcaeus, Petrarch, others.
School at Athens (details): #407, 1r, Euclid, disciples. #408, 1.50r, Telange, Pythagoras.
Details from: #405, 50c, Mass of Bolsena). 6r, Angels from Dispute of the Holy Sacrament, horiz.

1983, May 10 Litho. *Perf. 12½x13*
404-410 A101 Set of 7 6.50 2.25

Souvenir Sheet

Perf. 13

411 A101 6r multicolored 5.00 1.40

No. 411 contains one 40x32mm stamp.

1st Hot Air Balloon Ascension, Bicent. A102

Designs: 20c, Montgolfier. 30c, Ville d'Orleans. 50c, Hydrogen balloon. 1r, Blanchard & Jeffries, 1785. 1.50r, Ascension in Arctic. 2r, Stratosphere balloon. 3r, Balloon race. 6r, Balloons over town.

1983, June 3 *Perf. 12½*
412-418 A102 Set of 7 5.50 2.00

Souvenir Sheet

Perf. 13

419 A102 6r multicolored 5.50 1.50

Reptiles — A103

Designs: 20c, Iguana. 30c, Cobra. 80c, Trionyx turtle. 1r, Chameleon. 1.50r, Boa constrictor. 2r, Crocodile. 3r, Turtle.
30c, 1r, 1.50r are vert.

1983, June 28
420-426 A103 Set of 7 6.00 2.00

Birds A104

Designs: 20c, Lorikeet. 50c, Swallow. 80c, Eagle. 1r, Vulture. 1.50r, Turtle dove. 2r, Magpie. 3r, Hornbill.
20c-50c, 2r-3r are vert.

1983, Sept. 20
427-433 A104 Set of 7 6.00 2.00

Flowers — A105

20c, Sunflower. 50c, Caprifoliacae. 80c, Bougainvillea. 1r, Renonculacae. 1.50r, Nyctaginaceae. 2r, Cockscomb. 3r, Roses.

1983, Oct. 18 *Perf. 13*
434-440 A105 Set of 7 5.00 1.75

1984 Winter Olympic Games, Sarajevo — A106

Designs: 1r, Luge. 2r, Biathlon. 4r, Ski jumping. 5r, Two-man bobsled. 7r, Hockey.

1983, Nov. 10 *Perf. 12½*
441-445 A106 Set of 5 8.50 2.75

Souvenir Sheet

446 A106 6r Cross-country skiing 4.50 1.75

No. 446 contains one 40x32mm stamp.

Fish A107

20c, 1.50r, 2r, 3r, Various Cyprinidae. 50c, Trout. 80c, Catfish. 1r, Moray eel.

1983, Nov. 16 *Perf. 13*
447-453 A107 Set of 7 7.00 2.00

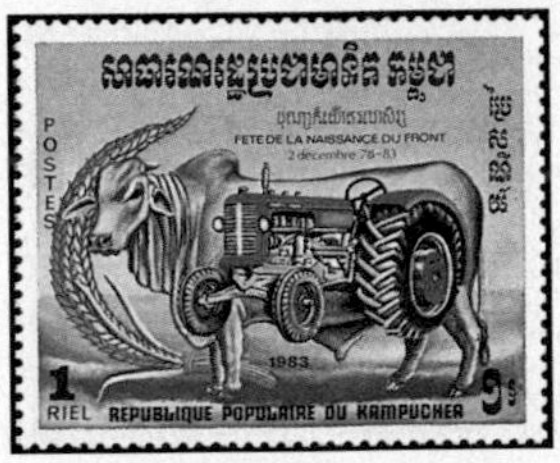

Festival of Rebirth — A108

50c, Factory. 1r, Bull, tractor. 3r, Bridge, ship, train. 6r, Radio antenna. 50c, 3r, 6r vert.

Perf. 12½x13, 13x12½
1983, Dec. 2 Litho.
454-456 A108 Set of 3 3.25 1.00

Souvenir Sheet

457 A108 6r multicolored 4.25 1.40

No. 457 contains one 32x40mm stamp.

People's Republic of Kampuchea, 5th Anniv. — A109

Designs: 50c, Red Cross. 1r, Soldiers. 3r, People celebrating. 6r, Man carrying water.

1984, Jan. 7 Litho. *Perf. 13*
458-460 A109 Set of 3 3.75 1.25

Souvenir Sheet

461 A109 6r multicolored 4.50 1.50

No. 461 contains one 32x40mm stamp.
For surcharges see Nos. 775-776.

1984 Winter Olympics, Sarajevo A110

Designs: 20c, Speed skating. 50c, Hockey. 80c, Slalom skiing. 1r, Ski jumping. 1.50r, Biathlon. 2r, Cross-country skiing. 3r, Pairs figure skating. 6r, Women's figure skating.

1984, Jan. 6 Litho. *Perf. 13*
462-468 A110 Set of 7 6.00 2.00

Souvenir Sheet

469 A110 6r multicolored 4.50 1.40

No. 469 contains one 32x40mm stamp.

Birds — A111

Designs: 10c, Bubulcus ibis. 40c, Lanius schach. 80c, Psittacula himalayana. 1r, Chloropsis aurifrons. 1.20r, Clamator coromandus. 2r, Motacilla cinerea. 2.50r, Dendronanthus indicus.

1984, Feb. 2
470-476 A111 Set of 7 9.00 3.00

Intl. Peace in Southeast Asia Forum — A112

Background color: 50c, Green. 1r, Blue. 3r, Violet.

1984, Feb. 25 *Perf. 13x12½*
477-479 A112 Set of 3 3.75 1.00

Space Exploration — A113

Designs: 10c, Luna 1. 40c, Luna 2. 80c, Luna 3. 1r, Soyuz 6. 1.20r, Soyuz 7. 2r, Soyuz 8. 2.50r, Book, rocket, S.P. Koralev. 6r, Salyut space station.
1r-2.50r are vert.

1984, Mar. 8 *Perf. 12½*
480-486 A113 Set of 7 6.00 2.00

Souvenir Sheet

487 A113 6r multicolored 5.00 1.75

No. 487 contains one 40x32mm stamp.

1984 Summer Olympic Games, Los Angeles A114

Designs: 20c, Discus. 50c, Long jump. 80c, Hurdles. 1r, Relay race. 1.50r, Pole vault. 2r, Javelin. 3r, High jump. 6r, Sprint race.

1984, Apr. 20 *Perf. 13*
488-494 A114 Set of 7 5.00 2.00

Souvenir Sheet

495 A114 6r multicolored 5.00 2.00

No. 495 contains one 32x40mm stamp.

Souvenir Sheet

ESPAÑA '84, Madrid — A115

1984, Apr. 24 *Perf. 12½*
496 A115 5r 1933 Hispano-Suiza K6 5.00 1.50

Wild Animals A116

Designs: 10c, Canis latrans. 40c, Canis dingo. 80c, Lycaon pictus. 1r, Canis aureus. 1.20r, Vulpes vulpes. 2r, Chrysocyon brachyurus, vert. 2.50r, Canis lupus.

1984, May 5 *Perf. 13*
497-503 A116 Set of 7 6.00 1.60

Locomotives — A117

Designs: 10c, BB-1002, France, 1966. 40c, BB-1052, France, 1966. 80c, Franco-Belgian, 1945. 1r, #231-505, Franco-Belgian, 1929. 1.20r, #803, Germany, 1968. 2r, BDE-405, France, 1957. 2.50r, DS-01, France, 1979.

1984, June 15 Litho. *Perf. 12½*
504-510 A117 Set of 7 5.50 1.75

Flowers A118

Designs: 10c, Magnolia. 40c, Plumeria. 80c, Himenoballis. 1r, Peltophorum roxburghii. 1.20r, Couroupita guianensis. 2r, Lagerstroemia. 2.50r, Thevetia perubiana.

1984, July 10 Litho. *Perf. 13*
511-517 A118 Set of 7 6.00 2.00

Classic Automobiles — A119

Designs: 20c, Mercedes-Benz. 50c, Bugatti. 80c, Alfa Romeo. 1r, Franklin. 1.50r, Hispano-Suiza. 2r, Rolls Royce. 3r, Tatra. 6r, Mercedes Benz, diff.

1984, Sept. 15 *Perf. 13x12½*
518-524 A119 Set of 7 6.00 1.50

Souvenir Sheet

Perf. 12½

525 A119 6r multicolored 5.00 1.25

No. 525 contains one 40x32mm stamp.

Musical Instruments — A120

Designs: 10c, Sra Lai. 40c, Skor drum. 80c, Skor thom. 1r, Thro khmer. 1.20r, Raneat ek. 2r, Raneat kong. 2.50r, Thro khe.
10c, 80c are vert.

1984, Oct. 10 *Perf. 13*
526-532 A120 Set of 7 5.25 1.50

Wild Animals A121

Designs: 10c, Gazelle. 40c, Capreolus capreolus. 80c, Lepus. 1r, Cervus elaphus. 1.20r, Elephas maximus. 2r, Genet. 2.50r, Bibos sauveli.
10c-40c, 1r-1.20r are vert.

1984, Nov. 11 *Perf. 13*
533-539 A121 Set of 7 6.00 1.75

Correggio (1489-1534) — A122

Details from paintings: 20c, Rest on Flight into Egypt. 50c, Martyrdom of the Four Saints. 80c, Mystic Marriage of St. Catherine with Saints Francis and Dominic. 1r, Madonna & Child with Saints John the Baptist, Geminian, Peter Martyr and George. 1.50r, Mystic Marriage of St. Catherine. 2r, The Deposition. 2.50r, The Deposition, diff. 6r, Virgin Crowned by Christ.

1984, Dec. 10 *Perf. 12½x13*
540-546 A122 Set of 7 4.25 1.00

Souvenir Sheet

Perf. 12½

547 A122 6r multicolored 4.25 1.00

No. 547 contains one 40x32mm stamp.

Natl. Festival — A123

50c, Oxcart. 1r, Horse-drawn cart. 3r, Elephants. 6r, Oxcart with passengers, vert.

1985, Jan. 5 *Perf. 12½x12*
548-550 A123 Set of 3 4.25 1.00

Souvenir Sheet

Perf. 12½

551 A123 6r multicolored 4.25 1.00

No. 551 contains one 32x40mm stamp.

1986 World Cup Soccer Championships, Mexico — A124

Various soccer players; 20c, vert. 50c, vert. 80c, vert. 1r. 1.50r. 2r, vert. 3r, vert.

1985, Feb. 4 *Perf. 13*
552-558 A124 Set of 7 4.25 1.25

Souvenir Sheet

559 A124 6r multicolored 4.25 1.00

No. 559 contains one 40x32mm stamp.

Motorcycles — A125

20c, 1939 Eska-Mofa. 50c, 1939 Wanderer. 80c, 1929 Premier. 1r, 1939 Ardie. 1.50r, 1932 Jawa. 2r, 1983 Simson. 3r, 1984 CZ-125.

1985, Mar. 8 Litho. *Perf. 13*
560-566 A125 Set of 7 4.00 1.50

Souvenir Sheet

567 A125 6r 1984 MBA 4.00 1.50

No. 567 contains one 40x32mm stamp.

Mushrooms — A126

Designs: 20c, Gymnopilus spectabilis. 50c, Coprinus micaceus. 80c, Amanita panterina. 1r, Hebelona crustuliniforme. 1.50r, Amanita muscaria. 2r, Coprinus comatus. 3r, Amanita caesarea.
Nos. 569-574 are vert.

1985, Apr. 4 *Perf. 13*
568-574 A126 Set of 7 5.75 1.40

Soviet Space Achievements — A127

Designs: 20c, Sputnik. 50c, Yuri Gagarin, rocket. 80c, Valentina Tereshkova, Vostok 6. 1r, Cosmonaut walking in space. 1.50r, Soyuz 4 docked with Soyuz 5. 2r, Lunar rover. 3r, Apollo-Soyuz mission. 6r, Soyuz capsule.

1985, Apr. 12 *Perf. 13*
575-581 A127 Set of 7 4.25 1.25

Souvenir Sheet

582 A127 6r multicolored 4.25 1.00

No. 582 contains one 40x32mm stamp.

Traditional Dances — A128

Designs: 50c, Four dancers. 1r, Three dancers. 3r, One dancer, vert.

1985, Apr. 13 Litho. *Perf. 12½*
583-585 A128 Set of 3 3.25 1.00

End of World War II, 40th Anniv. A129

Designs: 50c, Soldiers celebrating. 1r, Victory parade, Moscow. 3r, Tank battle.

1985, May 9 Litho. *Perf. 12x12½*
586-588 A129 Set of 3 4.25 1.50

Cats — A130

Various cats: 20c, 50c, 80c, 1r, 1.50r, 2r, 3r.

1985, May 16 Litho. *Perf. 12x12½*
589-595 A130 Set of 7 6.00 1.25

Flowers — A131

20c, Lilium Black Dragon. 50c, Iris delavayi. 80c, Crocus aureus. 1r, Cyclamen persicum, wild form. 1.50r, Primula malacoides. 2r, Viola tricolor. 3r, Crocus purpureus.

1985, June 5 Litho. *Perf. 13*
596-602 A131 Set of 7 4.25 1.25

Intl. Music Year — A132

Paintings: 20c, Mezzetin, by Watteau. 50c, St. Cecilia and the Angel, by Saraceni. 80c, Still Life with Violin, Flute and Guitar, by Oudry, horiz. 1r, Three Musicians, by F. Leger. 1.50r, Opera Orchestra, by Degas. 2r, St. Cecilia, by Schedoni. 3r, Young Harlequin with Violin, by Caillard. 6r, The Fifer, by Manet.

1985, June 13 *Perf. 13*
603-609 A132 Set of 7 3.50 1.00

Souvenir Sheet

610 A132 6r multicolored 3.25 1.00

No. 610 contains one 32x40mm stamp.

Lenin (1870-1924) A133

1r, Portrait. 3r, Lenin standing, map of Soviet Union.

1985, June 20 Litho. *Perf. 13*
611-612 A133 Set of 2 3.50 .75

ARGENTINA '85 — A134

Birds: 20c, Xanthopsar flavus. 50c, Sicalis flaveola. 80c, Thraupis bonariensis. 1r, Amblyramphus holosericeus. 1.50r, Chiloroceryle amazona. 2r, Ramphastos toco. 3r, Turdus rufiventris.
20c-80c, 1.50r-2r are vert.

1985, July 5 Litho. *Perf. 12½*
613-619 A134 Set of 7 6.00 2.00

Ships A135

Designs: 10c, River boat, 1942. 40c, River boat, 1948. 80c, Tugboat, Japan, 1913. 1r, Dredge. 1.20r, Tugboat, US. 2r, Freighter. 2.50r, Tanker, Panama.

1985, Aug. 8
620-626 A135 Set of 7 4.25 1.25

ITALIA 85 — A136

Paintings: 20c, The Flood, by Michelangelo. 50c, Virgin & St. Margaret, by Il Parmigianino (Filippo Mazzola). 80c, Martyrdom of St. Peter Martyr, by Domenichino. 1r, Spring, by Botticelli. 1.50r, Sacrifice of Abraham, by Veronese. 2r, Meeting of St. Joachim and St. Anne, by Giotto. 3r, Bacchus, by Caravaggio.
6r, Early train.

1985, Oct. 25
627-633 A136 Set of 7 4.00 1.10

Souvenir Sheet

634 A136 6r multicolored 3.75 1.10

No. 634 contains one 32x40mm stamp.

Son Ngoc Minh — A137

1985, Dec. 2 Litho. *Perf. 12x12½*
635-637 A137 Set of 3, 50c, 1r, 3r 3.50 1.25

Fish A138

20c, Barbus tetrazona. 50c, Ophiocephalus micropeltes. 80c, Carassius auratus. 1r, Trichogaster leeri. 1.50r, Puntius hexazona. 2r, Betta splendens. 3r, Datnioides microlepis.

1985, Dec. 28 Litho. *Perf. 13*
638-644 A138 Set of 7 4.25 1.25

1986 World Cup Soccer Championships, Mexico — A139

Various soccer players: 20c, 50c, 80c, 1r, 1.50r, 2r, 3r.

1986, Jan. 29
645-651 A139 Set of 7 4.00 1.10

Souvenir Sheet

652 A139 6r multicolored 3.50 .90

No. 652 contains one 32x40mm stamp.

Horses A140

Designs: 20c, Cob. 50c, Arabian. 80c, Australian pony. 1r, Appaloosa. 1.50r, Quarter horse. 2r, Vladimir heavy draft. 3r, Andalusian.

1986, Feb. 15
653-659 A140 Set of 7 4.50 1.50

27th Soviet Communist Party Congress A141

Designs: 50c, Space capsules. 1r, Lenin. 5r, Statue, rocket lift-off.

1986, Feb. 25 *Perf. 12x12½*
660-662 A141 Set of 3 3.25 1.00

Prehistoric Animals — A142

Designs: 20c, Edaphosaurus, horiz. 50c, Sauroctonus, horiz. 80c, Mastodonsaurus, horiz. 1r, Rhamphorhynchus. 1.50r, Brachiosaurus. 2r, Tarbosaurus. 3r, Indricotherium.

1986, Mar. 20 *Perf. 12½*
663-669 A142 Set of 7 8.00 3.00

Manned Space Flight, 25th Anniv. — A143

10c, Luna 16. 40c, Luna 3. 80c, Vostok. 1r, Alexei Leonov walking in space. 1.20r, Apollo-Soyuz mission. 2r, Soyuz capsule docking with Salyut station. 2.50r, Yuri Gagarin.

1986, Apr. 12 *Perf. 12½*
670-676 A143 Set of 7 6.00 2.00

Khmer Culture — A144

20c, Temple. 50c, Head of Buddha. 80c, Temple entrance. 1r, 1.50r, 2r, 3r, Various fans.

1986, Apr. 12 *Perf. 13*
677-683 A144 Set of 7 4.50 1.60

Mercedes-Benz Automobiles — A145

20c, 1885 3-wheel. 50c, 1935 sedan. 80c, 1907 open touring car. 1r, 1920 convertible. 1.50r, 1932 cabriolet. 2r, 1938 2-door. 3r, 1985 sedan.

1986, May 14 *Perf. 13x12½*
684-690 A145 Set of 7 4.50 1.25

Butterflies A146

Designs: 20c, Danaus genutia. 50c, Graphium amtiphates. 80c, Papilio demoleus. 1r, Danaus sita. 1.50r, Idea blanchardi. 2r, Papilio polytes. 3r, Dabasa payeni.

1986, June 19 ***Perf. 13***
691-697 A146 Set of 7 5.50 1.75

Ships A147

20c, English cog. 50c, Cog. 80c, Nile barge. 1r, Galley. 1.50r, Viking long ship. 2r, Two-masted lateen-rigged ship. 3r, Cog, diff.

1986, July 7 ***Perf. 13***
698-704 A147 Set of 7 4.25 1.50

Halley's Comet — A148

Designs: 10c, Solar system, Copernicus, Galileo, Brahe. 20c, Comet above Adoration of the Magi in painting by Giotto. 50c, Comet, observatory. 80c, Edmond Halley. 1.20r, Giotto probe. 1.50r, Vega probe. 2r, Computer-enhanced images of comet. 6r, Vega probe, diff.

1986, July 21 Litho. ***Perf. 12x12½***
705-711 A148 Set of 7 3.50 1.25

Souvenir Sheet

Perf. 13

712 A148 6r multicolored 3.00 1.00

No. 712 contains one 32x40mm stamp.

STOCKHOLMIA 86 — A149

Chess masters: 20c, Ruy Lopez. 50c, Francois Philador. 80c, Adolph Anderssen. 1r, Wilhelm Steinetz. 1.50r, Emanuel Lasker. 2r, José Capablanca. 3r, Alexander Alekhine.
6r, Chess pieces.

1986, Aug. 28 Litho. ***Perf. 12½***
713-719 A149 Set of 7 4.00 1.10

Souvenir Sheet

Perf. 13

720 A149 6r multicolored 3.75 1.00

No. 720 contains one 40x32mm stamp.

Cactus — A150

Fruit — A151

20c, Parodia maasii. 50c, Rebutia marsoneri. 80c, Melocactus evae. 1r, Gymnocalycium valnicekianum. 1.50r, Discocactus silichromus. 2r, Neochilenia simulans. 3r, Weingartia chiqichuquensis.

1986, Sept. 25 ***Perf. 13***
721-727 A150 Set of 7 4.25 1.25

1986, Oct. 4 ***Perf. 12½***

Designs: 10c, Bananas. 40c, Papayas. 80c, Mangos. 1r, Breadfruit. 1.20r, Litchi. 2r, Pineapple. 2.50r, Grapefruit, horiz.

728-734 A151 Set of 7 3.25 1.25

Aircraft — A152

20c, Concorde. 50c, DC-10. 80c, 747. 1r, IL-62. 1.50r, IL-86. 2r, AN-124. 3r, A-300.
Illustration reduced.

1986, Nov. 21
735-741 A152 Set of 7 4.25 1.25

Silverware — A153

Designs: 50c, Elephant, containers. 1r, Covered bowl. 3r, Serving dish.

1986, Dec. 2 ***Perf. 13***
742-744 A153 Set of 3 4.00 1.40

World Wildlife Fund A154

Designs: No. 745, 20c, Kouprey. No. 746, 20c, Gaur. 80c, Banteng. 1.50r, Buffalo.

1986, Dec. 30 Litho. ***Perf. 13***
745-748 A154 Set of 4 *17.00* 2.75

Tou Samouth A155

Denominations and background colors: 50c, green. 1r, blue, 3r, yellow.

1987, Jan. 7 Litho. ***Perf. 13***
749-751 A155 Set of 3 3.00 1.00

1988 Winter Olympic Games, Calgary — A156

Designs: 20c, Biathlon. 50c, Women's figure skating. 80c, Speed skating. 1r, Hockey. 1.50r, Luge. 2r, Two-man bobsled. 3r, Cross-country skiing. 6r, Slalom skiing.

1987, Jan. 14 ***Perf. 13x12½***
752-758 A156 Set of 7 3.25 1.10

Souvenir Sheet

Perf. 12½

759 A156 6r multicolored 2.75 .90

No. 759 contains one 40x32mm stamp.

1988 Summer Olympic Games, Seoul — A157

Designs: 20c, Weight lifting, vert. 50c, Archery. 80c, Fencing. 1r, Gymnastics, vert. 1.50r, Discus. 2r, Javelin, vert. 3r, Hurdles. 6r, Wrestling.

1987, Feb. 2 ***Perf. 12½x13, 13x12½***
760-766 A157 Set of 7 3.50 1.25

Souvenir Sheet

Perf. 13

767 A157 6r multicolored 3.00 1.00

No. 767 contains one 40x32mm stamp.

Dogs A158

Designs: 20c, shown. 50c, Greyhound. 80c, Great Dane. 1r, Doberman pinscher. 1.50r, Samoyed. 2r, Borzoi. 3r, Collie.

1987, Mar. 3 ***Perf. 13***
768-774 A158 Set of 7 4.75 1.50

Nos. 458, 463 Surcharged

1987, Mar. Litho. ***Perf. 13***
775 A110 35r on 50c #463 5.00
776 A109 50r on 50c #458 5.00

Soviet Spacecraft A159

Designs: 20c, Sputnik. 50c, Weather satellite. 80c, Proton. 1r, Vostok 1. 1.50r, Electron-2. 2r, Kosmos. 3r, Luna 2. 6r, Electron-4.

1987, Apr. 12 Litho. ***Perf. 13***
777-783 A159 Set of 7 4.00 1.40

Souvenir Sheet

784 A159 6r multicolored 3.25 1.00

No. 784 contains one 40x32mm stamp.

Silverware — A159a

Designs: 50c, Long-necked pot, vert. 1r, Box. 1.50r, Tea set. 3r, Sword.

1987, Apr. 13 ***Perf. 13***
785-788 A159a Set of 4 3.00 .90

CAPEX 87 — A160

Birds: 20c, Merops nubicus. 50c, Upupa epops. 80c, Balearica pavonina. 1r, Tyto alba. 1.50r, Halcyon leucocephala. 2r, Pycnonotus jocosus. 3r, Ardea purpurea. 6r, Terpsiphone paradisi.
50c-1.50r, 3r are vert.

1987, May 5 ***Perf. 13***
789-795 A160 Set of 7 4.00 1.25

Souvenir Sheet

796 A160 6r multicolored 3.50 1.25

No. 796 contains one 32x40mm stamp.

Early Aircraft Designs A161

Designs by: 20c, Horatio F. Phillips, 1893. 50c, John Stringfellow, 1848. 80c, Thomas Moy, 1875. 1r, Leonardo da Vinci, 1490. 1.50r, Sir George Cayley, 1840. 2r, Sir Hiram Maxim, 1894. 3r, William S. Henson, 1842. 6r, Da Vinci, diff.

1987, Aug. 7 ***Perf. 13***
797-803 A161 Set of 7 4.00 1.40

Souvenir Sheet

Perf. 12½

804 A161 6r multicolored 3.00 1.00

No. 804 contains one 32x40mm stamp.

Reptiles
A162

Designs: 20c, Testudo gigantea. 50c, Uromastix acanthinuros. 80c, Cyclura macleayi. 1r, Phrynosoma coronatum. 1.50r, Sauromalus obesus. 2r, Ophisaurus apodus. 3r, Thamnophis sirtalis.

1987, Sept. 9 *Perf. 13*
805-811 A162 Set of 7 5.00 1.50

HAFNIA 87 — A163

Helicopters: 20c, Kamov KA-15. 50c, Kamov KA-18. 80c, Westland Lynx WG-13. 1r, Sud Aviation Gazelle. 1.50r, Sud Aviation Puma. 2r, Boeing CH-47 Chinook. 3r, Boeing UTTAS. 6r, Fairey Rotodyne.

1987, Oct. 16 *Perf. 12½x12*
812-818 A163 Set of 7 4.00 1.40

Souvenir Sheet

Perf. 13

819 A163 6r multicolored 3.00 1.00

No. 819 contains one 40x32mm stamp.

Russian October Revolution, 70th Anniv.
A164

1987	**Litho.**	*Perf. 12x12¼*	
820 A164	2r Soldiers, horse	1.25	.30
821 A164	3r Soldiers	1.75	.45
822 A164	5r Lenin, aides	3.50	.80

Two additional stamps were issued in this set. The editors would like to examine them.

Fire Trucks
A165

1987, Nov. 24 **Litho.** *Perf. 13*
823-829 A165 20c, 50c, 80c, 1r, 1.50r, 2r, 3r, set of 7 6.50 2.00

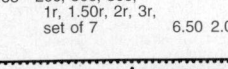

Telecommunications — A166

50c, Dish antenna, vert. 1r, Broadcast center, vert. 3r, Dish antenna, broadcast center.

Perf. 13x12½, 12x12½, 12½x12

1987, Dec. 2
830-832 A166 Set of 3 3.00 1.00

No. 830 is 29x40mm. No. 831 is 28x44mm. No. 832 printed with se-tenant label.

1988 Winter Olympic Games, Calgary
A167

Designs: 20c, Speed skating. 50c, Hockey. 80c, Downhill skiing. 1r, Ski jumping. 1.50r, Biathlon. 2r, Pairs figure skating. 3r, Cross-country skiing. 6r, Four-man bobsled.

1988, Jan. 7 *Perf. 12½*
833-839 A167 Set of 7 3.00 1.00

Souvenir Sheet

Perf. 13

840 A167 6r multicolored 2.50 .75

No. 840 contains one 32x40mm stamp.

Water Projects
A168

Designs: 50c, Canal. 1r, Dam under construction. 3r, Dam, bridge.

1988, Jan. 7 **Litho.** *Perf. 13*
841-843 A168 Set of 3 4.00 1.25

1988 Summer Olympic Games, Seoul — A169

Designs: 20c, Balance beam, vert. 50c, Uneven bars. 80c, Rhythmic gymnastics ribbon, vert. 1r, Rhythmic gymnastics hoop, vert. 1.50r, Rhythmic gymnastics clubs, vert. 2r, Rhythmic gymnastics ball. 3r, Floor exercise.

Perf. 12½x13, 13x12½

1988, Feb. 2 **Litho.**
844-850 A169 Set of 7 4.00 1.50

Souvenir Sheet

Perf. 12½

851 A169 6r Rhythmic gymnastics, diff. 3.00 1.50

No. 851 contains one 32x40mm stamp.

JUVALUX 88
A170

Various cats. Denominations: 20c, 50c, 80c, 1r, 1.50r, 2r, 3r. Nos. 853-854, 856-858 are vert.

1988, Mar. 15 *Perf. 12½*
852-858 A170 Set of 7 4.00 1.25

Souvenir Sheet

Perf. 13

859 A170 6r multicolored 4.00 1.25

No. 859 contains one 40x32mm stamp.

ESSEN 88 — A171

Ships: 20c, Passenger liner. 50c, Passenger liner, diff. 80c, Research ship. 1r, Communications ship. 1.50r, Tanker. 2r, Hydrofoil. 3r, Hovercraft.

1988, Apr. 14 **Litho.** *Perf. 12½*
860-866 A171 Set of 7 3.50 1.25

Souvenir Sheet

Perf. 13

867 A171 6r Hydrofoil 3.25 1.10

Satellites — A172

Various satellites. Denominations: 20c, 50c, 80c, 1r, 1.50r, 2r, 3r. Nos. 868-870 are vert.

1988, Apr. 24 *Perf. 12½x13, 13x12½*
868-874 A172 Set of 7 4.00 1.50

Souvenir Sheet

Perf. 13

875 A172 6r multicolored 6.00 2.25

No. 875 contains one 40x32mm stamp.

FINLANDIA 88 — A173

Fish: 20c, Xiphophorus helleri. 50c, Hemigrammus ocellifer. 80c, Macropodus opercularis. 1r, Carassius auratus. 1.50r, Hyphessobrycon inesi. 2r, Corynopoma riisei. 3r, Mollienisia latipinna.
6r, Pterophyllum scalare.

1988, Jun 10 **Litho.** *Perf. 13x12½*
876-882 A173 Set of 7 4.25 1.50

Souvenir Sheet

Perf. 12½

883 A173 6r multicolored 4.00 1.25

No. 883 contains one 32x40mm stamp.

Shells — A174

Designs: 20c, Helicostyla florida. 50c, Helicostyla marinduquensis. 80c, Helicostyla fulgens. 1r, Helicostyla woodiana. 1.50r, Chloraea sirena. 2r, Helicostyla mirabilis. 3r, Helicostyla limansauensis.

1988, Aug. 5 **Litho.** *Perf. 13x12½*
884-890 A174 Set of 7 4.25 1.50

Insects A175

Designs: 20c, Coccinellidae. 50c, Zonabride geminata. 80c, Carabus auronitens. 1r, Apis mellifera. 1.50r, Praying mantis. 2r, Odonata. 3r, Malachius aeneus.

1988, Sept. 6 *Perf. 13x12½*
891-897 A175 Set of 7 4.75 1.40

Orchids
A176

Designs: 20c, Cattleya aclandiae. 50c, Odontoglossum Royal Sovereign. 80c, Cattleya labiata. 1r, Ophrys apifera. 1.50r, Laelia anceps. 2r, Laelia pumila. 3r, Stanhopea tigrina, horiz.

1988, Oct. 10 *Perf. 12½x13, 13x12½*
898-904 A176 Set of 7 5.50 1.75

Reptiles — A177

Designs: 20c, Naja haje, vert. 50c, Iguana iguana, vert. 80c, Dryophis nasuta. 1r, Terrapene carolina. 1.50r, Cyclura macleayi. 2r, Bothrops bicolor. 3r, Naja naja, with hood spread, vert.

1988, Nov. 7 *Perf. 12x12½, 12½x12*
905-911 A177 Set of 7 5.50 1.75

Dance of the Peacock
A178

50c, 3 dancers, vert. 1r, shown. 3r, 2 dancers.

1988, Dec. 2 *Perf. 13*
912-914 A178 Set of 3 4.00 1.25

For surcharges see Nos. 1195-1196.

Bridges — A179

1989 *Perf. 13x12½*
915-917 A179 50c, 1r, 3r, set of 3 3.00 1.00

Decade of Progress — A180

3r, Telecommunications station. 12r, Central Electrical Plant No. 4. 30r, Cement plant, vert.

1989
918-920 A180 Set of 3 3.50 1.25

1990 World Cup Soccer Championships, Italy — A181

Various soccer players. Denominations: 2r, 3r, 5r, 10r, 15r, 20r, 35r.

1989 ***Perf. 12½x13***
921-927 A181 Set of 7 4.50 1.50

Souvenir Sheet

Perf. 13

928 A181 45r multicolored 3.00 1.00

No. 928 contains one 32x40mm stamp.

Trains A182

Various locomotives. Denominations: 2r, 3r, 5r, 10r, 15r, 20r, 35r.

1989 ***Perf. 13***
929-935 A182 Set of 7 4.25 1.50

Souvenir Sheet

Perf. 12½

936 A182 45r multicolored 3.25 1.00

No. 936 contains one 40x32mm stamp.

A183

A184

1989 ***Perf. 13***
937 A183 12r red & black 1.00 .35

Cuban Revolution, 30th anniv.

1989

Birds: 20c, Ara macao. 80c, Kakatoe galerita. 3r, Psittacula krameri. 6r, Ara ararauna. 10r, Poicephalus robustus. 15r, Amazona aestiva. 25r, Pionus senilis, horiz.
45r, Cyanoramphus novaezelandiae.

938-944 A184 Set of 7 4.25 1.25

Souvenir Sheet

Perf. 12½

945 A184 45r multicolored 3.25 1.00

No. 945 contains one 40x32mm stamp.

1992 Winter Olympic Games, Albertville A185

2r, Slalom skiing. 3r, Biathlon. 5r, Cross-country skiing. 10r, Ski jumping. 15r, Speed skating. 20r, Hockey. 35r, Bobsled. 45r, Pairs figure skating.

1989, Mar. 30 ***Perf. 13***
946-952 A185 Set of 7 4.50 1.50

Souvenir Sheet

Perf. 12½

953 A185 45r multicolored 2.75 .90

No. 953 contains one 32x40mm stamp.

Water Lilies A186

20c, Nymphaea capensis (pink). 80c, Nymphaea capensis (purple). 3r, Nymphaea lotus. 6r, Nymphaea Dir. Geo. T. Moore. 10r, Nymphaea Sunrise. 15r, Nymphaea Escarboncie. 25r, Nymphaea Cladstoniana. 45r, Nymphaea Paul Hariot.

1989 ***Perf. 12½x13***
954-960 A186 Set of 7 4.25 1.25

Souvenir Sheet

Perf. 12½

961 A186 45r multicolored 3.25 1.00

No. 961 contains one 32x40mm stamp.

1992 Summer Olympic Games, Barcelona — A187

Designs: 2r, Wrestling. 3r, Pommel horse, vert. 5r, Shot put. 10r, Running, vert. 15r, Fencing. 20r, Canoeing, vert. 35r, Steeplechase, vert. 45r, Weight lifting, vert.

1989 ***Perf. 13***
962-968 A187 Set of 7 4.50 1.50

Souvenir Sheet

Perf. 12½

969 A187 45r multicolored 4.00 1.50

No. 969 contains one 32x40mm stamp.

Mushrooms A188

Designs: 20c, Xerocomus subtomentosus. 80c, Inocybe patouillardii. 3r, Armillaria mellea. 6r, Agaricus campestris. 10r, Paxillus involutus. 15r, Coprinus comatus. 25r, Lepiota procera.

1989 ***Perf. 12½x13***
970-976 A188 Set of 7 4.00 1.10

Horses — A189

Designs: 2r, Shire. 3r, Brabant. 5r, Bolounais. 10r, Breton. 15r, Vladimir heavy draft. 20r, Italian heavy draft. 35r, Freiberger. 45r, Horse-drawn cart.

1989 ***Perf. 12½***
977-983 A189 Set of 7 4.25 1.50

Souvenir Sheet

984 A189 45r multicolored 3.25 1.10

Nos. 977-983 printed with se-tenant label. No. 984 contains one 40x32mm stamp.

Angkor Wat — A190

Denominations: 35r, 50r, 80r, 100r.

1989, May 15 **Litho.** ***Perf. 13¼***
985-988 A190 Set of 4 *75.00 75.00*

Cambodia

PHILEXFRANCE 89 — A191

Mail coaches: 2r, 17th cent. 3r, Paris-Lyon, 1720. 5r, 1793. 10r, 1805. 15r, Royal Mail. 20r, 1843. 35r, Paris-Lille, 1837, vert. 45r, 1815, vert.

1989 **Litho.** ***Perf. 13***
989-995 A191 Set of 7 4.50 1.50

Souvenir Sheet

Perf. 12½

996 A191 45r multicolored 3.00 1.50

No. 996 contains one 23x40mm stamp.

BRASILIANA 89 — A192

Butterflies: 2r, Papilio zagreus. 3r, Morpho catenarius. 5r, Morpho aega. 10r, Callithea sapphira. 15r, Catagramma sorana. 20r, Pierella nereis. 35r, Papilio brasiliensis. 45r, Thacia marsyas, horiz.

1989 ***Perf. 13***
997-1003 A192 Set of 7 5.00 1.50

Souvenir Sheet

1004 A192 45r multicolored 5.00 1.50

No. 1004 contains one 40x32mm stamp.

Khmer Boats A193

Various pirogues. Denominations: 3r, 12r, 30r.

1989, Dec. 2 **Litho.** ***Perf. 12½***
1005-1007 A193 Set of 3 3.50 1.25

Natl. Organizations — A194

3r, Youth, vert. 12r, Labor. 30r, Natl. Front.

1990, Jan. 7 **Litho.** ***Perf. 13***
1008-1010 A194 Set of 3 3.50 .90

1990 World Cup Soccer Championships, Italy — A195

Various soccer players. Denominations: 2r, 3r, 5r, 10r, 15r, 20r, 35r.

1990, Jan. 5 **Litho.** ***Perf. 13***
1011-1017 A195 Set of 7 4.00 1.50

Souvenir Sheet

1018 A195 45r multicolored 2.75 1.00

No. 1018 contains one 32x40mm stamp.
For surcharges see Nos. 1072, 1075.

STAMPWORLD LONDON 90 — A196

Various mail coaches. Denominations: 2r, 3r, 5r, 10r, 15r, 20r, 35r.
45r, Single horse van for rural deliveries.

1990 ***Perf. 12½x12***
1019-1025 A196 Set of 7 4.00 1.25

Souvenir Sheet

Perf. 13

1026 A196 45r multicolored 2.50 .90

Nos. 1019-1025 are printed with se-tenant label. No. 1026 contains one 40x32mm stamp.

Rice — A197

Designs: 3r, Woman, rice. 12r, People hauling rice, horiz. 30r, Women threshing rice.

1990, June 19 **Litho.** ***Perf. 13***
1027-1029 A197 Set of 3 3.50 1.25

1992 Winter Olympic Games, Albertville A198

2r, 4-man bobsled. 3r, Speed skating. 5r, Pairs figure skating. 10r, Hockey. 15r, Biathlon. 20r, Luge. 35r, Ski jumping. 45r, Hockey goalie.

1990 **Litho.** ***Perf. 13***
1030-1036 A198 Set of 7 4.50 1.50

Souvenir Sheet

1037 A198 45r multicolored 2.50 .90

No. 1037 contains one 32x40mm stamp.

1992 Summer Olympic Games, Barcelona A199

Designs: 2r, Shooting. 3r, Shot put. 5r, Weight lifting. 10r, Boxing. 15r, Pole vault. 20r, Basketball. 35r, Fencing. 45r, Rhythmic gymnastics.

1990
1038-1044 A199 Set of 7 4.50 1.50

Souvenir Sheet

1045 A199 45r multicolored 2.50 .75

No. 1045 contains one 32x40mm stamp.

Khmer Culture A200

Designs: 3r, Facade, Bantey Srei. 12r, Relief. 30r, Ruins, Banon.

Perf. 12½, 12½x13 (#1048)

1990, Dec. 2 **Litho.**
1046-1048 A200 Set of 3 3.00 1.25

No. 1048 is 36x21mm.

Dogs A201

20c, Poodle. 80c, Shetland. 3r, Samoyed. 6r, Springer spaniel. 10r, Fox terrier. 15r, Afghan. 25r, Dalmatian. 45r, Bernese.

1990 **Litho.** ***Perf. 13***
1049-1055 A201 Set of 7 4.00 1.25

Souvenir Sheet

1056 A201 45r multicolored 3.00 1.00

No. 1056 contains one 40x32mm stamp.

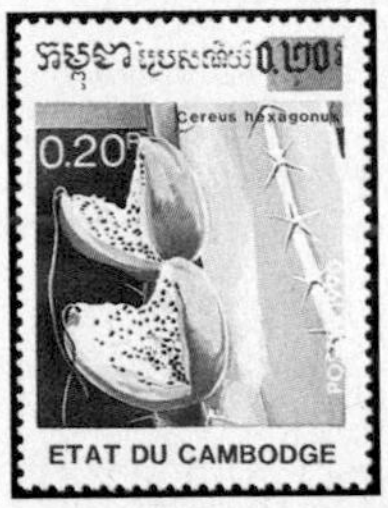

Cacti — A202

Designs: 20c, Cereus hexagonus. 80c, Arthrocereus rondonianus. 3r, Matucana multicolor. 6r, Hildewintera aureispina. 10r, Opuntia retrosa. 15r, Erdisia tenuicula. 25r, Mamillaria yaquensis.

1990
1057-1063 A202 Set of 7 4.00 1.50

NEW ZEALAND 90 — A203

Butterflies: 2r, Zizina oxleyi. 3r, Cupha prosope. 5r, Heteronympha merope. 10r, Dodonidia helmsi. 15r, Argirophenga antipodum. 20r, Tysonotis danis. 35r, Pyrameis gonnarilla. 45r, Pyrameis itea.

1990 ***Perf. 13***
1064-1070 A203 Set of 7 5.00 1.50

Souvenir Sheet

Perf. 12½

1071 A203 45r multicolored 3.25 1.00

No. 1071 contains one 40x32mm stamp.

Nos. 1012, 1013, 1015, 1016 Surcharged in Red

1990 **Litho.** ***Perf. 13***
1072 A195 200r on 3r #1012
1073 A195 300r on 5r multi
1075 A195 800r on 15r multi
1076 A195 1000r on 20r multi

Nos. are reserved for additions to this set.

Intl. Literacy Year — A204

Denominations: 3r, 12r, 30r.

1990 **Litho.** ***Perf. 13***
1077-1079 A204 Set of 3 3.50 1.25

Ships A205

Designs: 20c, English, 1200. 80c, Spanish galloon, 16th cent. 3r, Dutch ship, 1627. 6r, La Couronne, 1638. 10r, L'Astrolabe, 1826. 15r, French packet, Louisiana, 1864. 25r, Clipper ship, 1900, vert. 45r, Merchant ship, 1800.

1990 **Litho.** ***Perf. 13***
1080-1086 A205 Set of 7 4.25 1.50

Souvenir Sheet

Perf. 12½

1087 A205 45r multicolored 3.00 1.00

No. 1087 contains one 32x40mm stamp.

Natl. Building Campaign — A206

3r, Railroad. 12r, Cargo ship, Kampong Som. 30r, Fishing boats, Kampong Som.

1990 **Litho.** ***Perf. 13***
1088-1090 A206 Set of 3 3.25 1.25

PARIS 90 — A207

Chess pieces and: 2r, Sacré Coeur. 3r, Equestrian statue. 5r, Winged Victory of Samothrace. 10r, Chateau, Azay le Riddeau. 15r, Sculpture, "The Dance." 20r, Eiffel Tower. 35r, Arc de Triomphe.
45r, Chess pieces, horiz.

1990, Nov. 15 **Litho.** ***Perf. 13***
1091-1097 A207 Set of 7 6.50 2.00

Souvenir Sheet

1098 A207 45r multicolored 4.25 1.50

No. 1098 contains one 40x32mm stamp.

Space Day — A208

Designs: 2r, Vostok. 3r, Soyuz. 5r, Artificial satellite. 10r, Luna 10. 15r, Mars 1. 20r, Venus 3. 35r, Mir. 45r, Energia, Buran.

1990 **Litho.** ***Perf. 13***
1099-1105 A208 Set of 7 4.75 1.50

Souvenir Sheet

1106 A208 45r multicolored 3.00 1.00

No. 1106 contains one 32x40mm stamp.
For surcharges see Nos. 1145-1151.

Discovery of America, 500th Anniv. (in 1992) — A209

Designs: 2r, Columbus. 3r, Queen Isabella's jewelry chest. 5r, Queen Isabella. 10r, Santa Maria. 15r, Juan de la Cosa. 20r, Columbus Monument. 35r, Pyramid, Yucatan.
45r, Columbus, diff.

1990, Oct. 12 **Litho.** ***Perf. 13***
1107-1113 A209 Set of 7 6.00 2.00

Souvenir Sheet

1114 A209 45r multicolored 3.75 1.25

No. 1114 contains one 32x40mm stamp.

Natl. Festival A210

Designs: 100r, Tire production. 300r, Rural infirmary. 500r, Fisherman, vert.

Perf. 12½, 13 (#1117)

1991, Jan. 7 **Litho.**
1115-1117 A210 Set of 3 4.50 1.25

No. 1117 is 28x40mm.

1994 World Cup Soccer Championships, US — A211

Various soccer players. Denominations: 5r, 25r, 50r, 100r, 200r, 400r, 1000r.

1991, Feb. 15 **Litho.** ***Perf. 13***
1118-1124 A211 Set of 7 5.50 1.75

Souvenir Sheet

1125 A211 900r multicolored 3.00 1.10

No. 1125 contains one 32x40mm stamp.

1992 Winter Olympic Games, Albertville A212

Designs: 5r, Speed skating. 25r, Slalom skiing. 70r, Hockey. 100r, Bobsled. 200r, Freestyle skiing. 400r, Pairs figure skating. 1000r, Downhill skiing.
900r, Ski jumping.

1991, Mar. 30 **Litho.** ***Perf. 12½***
1126-1132 A212 Set of 7 6.00 2.00

Souvenir Sheet

Perf. 13

1133 A212 900r multicolored 3.00 1.00

No. 1133 contains one 32x40mm stamp.

Khmer Culture A213

Statues: 100r, Garuda, 10th cent. 300r, Torso of Vishnu reclining, 11th cent. 500r, Reclining Nandin, 7th cent.

1991, Apr. 13 **Litho.** *Perf. 12½*
1134-1136 A213 Set of 3 3.50 1.25

1992 Summer Olympic Games, Barcelona A214

Designs: 5r, Pole vault. 25r, Table tennis. 70r, Women's running. 100r, Wrestling. 200r, Women's gymnastics. 400r, Tennis. 1000r, Boxing.
900r, Balance beam.

1991, Apr. 25 **Litho.** *Perf. 12½x13*
1137-1143 A214 Set of 7 5.00 1.50

Souvenir Sheet

Perf. 13

1144 A214 900r multicolored 3.25 1.00

No. 1144 contains one 32x40mm stamp.

Nos. 1099-1103, 1105 Surcharged in Red

1991 **Litho.** *Perf. 13*
1145 A208 100r on 2r #1099
1146 A208 150r on 3r #1100
1147 A208 200r on 5r #1101
1148 A208 300r on 10r #1102
1149 A208 500r on 15r #1103
1151 A208 2000r on 35r #1105

Number is reserved for surcharge on No. 1104.

Aircraft — A215

Designs: 5r, DC-10-30. 25r, MD-11. 70r, IL-96-300. 100r, A-310. 200r, YAK-42. 400r, TU-154. 1000r, DC-9

1991, June 15 **Litho.** *Perf. 13x12½*
1152-1158 A215 Set of 7 5.25 1.75

ESPAMER 91 — A216

Pre-Columbian pottery: 5r, Catamarca. 25r, Catamarca, vert. 70r, Tucuman, vert. 100r, Santiago del Estero. 200r, Santiago del Estero, diff. 400r, Tucuman, diff., vert. 1000r, Catamarca, diff.
900r, Catamarca, diff.

1991, July 10 *Perf. 13*
1159-1165 A216 Set of 7 6.00 2.00

Souvenir Sheet

Perf. 12½

1166 A216 900r multicolored 4.00 1.25

No. 1166 contains one 40x32mm stamp.

Discovery of America, 500th Anniv. (in 1992) — A217

Designs: 5r, Pinta, vert. 25r, Niña, vert. 70r, Santa Maria, vert. 100r, Landing of Columbus. 200r, Encountering new cultures. 400r, First European settlement in Americas. 1000r, Native village.
900r, Columbus.

1991, Oct. 12 *Perf. 12½x13, 13x12½*
1167-1173 A217 Set of 7 6.00 2.00

Souvenir Sheet

Perf. 12½

1174 A217 900r multicolored 3.25 1.10

No. 1174 contains one 40x32mm stamp.

PHILANIPPON 91 — A218

Butterflies: 5r, Neptis pryeri. 25r, Papilio xuthus. 70r, Cyrestis thyodamas. 100r, Argynnis anadiomene. 200r, Lethe marginalis. 400r, Artopoetes pryeri. 1000r, Danaus chrysippus.
900r, Ochlodes subhyalina.

1991, Nov. 16 *Perf. 13*
1175-1181 A218 Set of 7 6.00 2.00

Souvenir Sheet

Perf. 12½

1182 A218 900r multicolored 4.00 1.25

No. 1182 contains one 40x32mm stamp.

Natl. Building Campaign A219

Designs: 100r, Fishing port. 300r, Preparing palm sugar, vert. 500r, Harvesting peppers.

1991, Dec. 2 **Litho.** *Perf. 12½*
1183-1185 A219 Set of 3 4.50 1.25

Natl. Festival — A220

Traditional costumes: 150r, Chakdomuk. 350r, Longvek. 1000r, Angkor.

1992, Jan. 7 *Perf. 13*
1186-1188 A220 Set of 3 3.75 1.25

1992 Summer Olympic Games, Barcelona A221

5r, Wrestling. 15r, Soccer. 80r, Weight lifting. 400r, Archery. 1500r, Balance beam.
1000r, Equestrian.

1992, Jan. **Litho.** *Perf. 13*
1189-1193 A221 Set of 5 3.75 1.25

Souvenir Sheet

Perf. 12½

1194 A221 1000r multicolored 2.50 .80

No. 1194 contains one 32x40mm stamp.

Nos. 913-914 Surcharged in Red

1992, Jan. **Litho.** *Perf. 13*
1195 A178 200r on 3r #914
1196 A178 300r on 1r #913

Fish A222

Designs: 5r, Hyphessobrycon innesi. 15r, Betta splendens. 80r, Nematobrycon palmen. 400r, Colisa lalia. 1500r, Hoplosternum thoracatum.
1000r, Pterophyllum scalare.

1992, Feb. 8 **Litho.** *Perf. 12½*
1197-1201 A222 Set of 5 4.50 1.50

Souvenir Sheet

1202 A222 1000r multicolored 2.75 1.00

No. 1202 contains one 40x32mm stamp.

1994 World Cup Soccer Championships, US — A223

Various soccer plays. Denominations: 5r, 15r, 80r, 400r, 1500r. Nos. 1203, 1205-1207 are vert.

1992, Mar. 6 **Litho.** *Perf. 12½*
1203-1207 A223 Set of 5 4.25 1.50

Souvenir Sheet

1208 A223 1000r multicolored 2.75 .90

No. 1208 contains one 40x32mm stamp.

Khmer Culture — A224

19th cent. structures: 150r, Monument. 350r, Stupa. 1000r, Library of Mandapa.

1992, Apr. 13 **Litho.** *Perf. 12½*
1209-1211 A224 Set of 3 4.25 1.40

Leonardo da Vinci (1452-1519) — A225

Designs: 5r, Automobile. 15r, Container ship. 80r, Helicopter. 400r, Scuba gear. 1500r, Parachute, vert.
1000r, Portrait.

1992, Apr. 15 **Litho.** *Perf. 12x12½*
1212-1216 A225 Set of 5 4.50 1.50

Souvenir Sheet

Perf. 13

1217 A225 1000r multicolored 2.75 .80

Nos. 1212-1216 each printed with se-tenant labels showing Da Vinci's conceptions of the items shown on the stamps. No. 1217 contains one 32x40mm stamp.

EXPO 92, Seville A226

Inventors, builders: 5r, De la Cierva, autogyro. 15r, Edison, electric light bulb. 80r, Morse, telegraph. 400r, Monturiol, submarine. No. 1222, 1500r, Bell, telephone.
No. 1223, 1500r, Fulton, steamship.

1992, Apr. 23 *Perf. 12½*
1218-1222 A226 Set of 5 4.00 1.25

Souvenir Sheet

Perf. 13

1223 A226 1000r pink & black 2.75 .80

No. 1223 contains one 32x40mm stamp.

1992 Summer Olympic Games, Barcelona — A227

Designs: 5r, Weight lifting. 15r, Boxing. 80r, Basketball. 400r, Sprints. 1500r, Water polo.
1000r, Women's gymnastics.

1992, May 15 *Perf. 13*
1224-1228 A227 Set of 5 8.00 1.75

Souvenir Sheet

Perf. 12½

1229 A227 1000r multicolored 4.00 1.25

No. 1229 contains one 40x32mm stamp.

Environmental Protection — A228

Designs: 5r, Women filling water jars. 15r, Pagoda. 80r, Palm trees. 400r, Boy riding water buffalo. 1500r, Lake, swimmers.
1000r, Angkor Wat.

1992, June 16 **Litho.** *Perf. 12½*
1230-1234 A228 Set of 5 6.00 1.75

Souvenir Sheet

Perf. 13

1235 A228 1000r multicolored 5.00 1.25

No. 1235 contains one 42x32mm stamp.

GENOA 92 — A229

Explorers, ship: 5r, Bougainville, Boudeuse. 15r, Cook, Endeavour. 80r, Darwin, Beagle. 400r, Cousteau, Calypso. 1500r, Heyerdahl, Kon Tiki.
1000r, Columbus.

1992, Aug. 1 Litho. *Perf. 12x12½*
1236-1240 A229 Set of 5 4.50 1.50

Souvenir Sheet
Perf. 12½

1241 A229 1000r multicolored 2.75 .80

No. 1241 contains one 32x40mm stamp.

Mushrooms A230

Designs: 5r, Albatrellus confluens. 15r, Boletus calopus. 80r, Stropharia aeruginosa. 400r, Telamonia armillata. 1500r, Cortinarius traganus.

1992, Sept. 25 *Perf. 13*
1242-1246 A230 Set of 5 5.00 1.50

Seaplanes — A231

Designs: 5r, Bellanca Pacemaker, 1930. 15r, Canadair CL-215, 1965. 80r, G-21A Goose, 1937. 400r, Sealand SA-6, 1947. 1500r, Short S-23, 1936.
1000r, G-44 Widgeon, 1940.

1992, Oct. 16 *Perf. 12½x12*
1247-1251 A231 Set of 5 4.00 1.25

Souvenir Sheet
Perf. 13

1252 A231 1000r multicolored 2.75 .90

No. 1252 contains one 32x40mm stamp.

Natl. Development A232

Designs: 150r, Dish antenna. 350r, Dish antenna, flags. 1000r, Hotel Cambodiana.

1992, Dec. 2 Litho. *Perf. 12½*
1253-1255 A232 Set of 3 4.00 1.25

Natl. Festival A233

Designs: 50r, Sociological Institute. 450r, Motel Cambodiana. 1000r, Theater.

1993, Jan. 7 Litho. *Perf. 12½*
1256-1258 A233 Set of 3 4.25 1.25

Dolphin, Bathyscaph — A234

Fauna, machine: 150r, shown. 200r, Falcon, jet fighter. 250r, Beaver, dam. 500r, Bat, satellite. 900r, Hummingbird, helicopter.

1993, Feb. 5 Litho. *Perf. 13*
Without Gum
1259-1263 A234 Set of 5 4.25 1.25

Flowers — A235

Designs: 150r, Datura suaveolens. 200r, Convolvulus tricolor. 250r, Hippeastrum hybrid. 500r, Camellia hybrid. 900r, Lilium speciosum.
1000r, Datura suaveolens, camellia, lilium speciosum.

1993, Mar. 15 *Perf. 13*
Without Gum
1264-1268 A235 Set of 5 5.00 1.25

Souvenir Sheet
Perf. 12½

1269 A235 1000r multicolored 2.50 .85

No. 1269 contains one 40x32mm stamp.

Khmer Culture A236

Designs: 50r, Statue of a Nandin. 450r, Temple Vihear. 1000r, Man with offerings.

1993, Apr. 13 Litho. *Perf. 12½*
1270-1272 A236 Set of 3 4.00 1.25

Wildlife — A237

150r, Cynocephalus volans. 200r, Petuarista petuarista. 250r, Ptychozoon homalocephalum. 500r, Rhacophorus nigropalmatus. 900r, Draco volans.

1993, May 4 Litho. *Perf. 12½x12*
Without Gum
1273-1277 A237 Set of 5 4.25 1.25

BRASILIANA 93 — A238

Butterflies: 250r, Symbrenthia hypselis. 350r, Sithon nedymond. 600r, Geitoneura minyas. 800r, Argyreus hyperbius. 1000r, Argyrophenga antipodum
1500r, Pararge schakra.

1993, June 15 *Perf. 12½x12*
Without Gum
1278-1282 A238 Set of 5 6.00 1.50

Souvenir Sheet
Perf. 12½

1283 A238 1500r multicolored 4.00 1.25

No. 1283 contains one 40x32mm stamp.

UN Transitional Authority in Cambodia (UNTAC) Pacification Program A239

150r, Cambodian soldiers approaching UN base. 200r, Cambodians entering camp. 250r, Cambodians surrendering weapons to UN. 500r, Vocational training. 900r, Cambodians re-entering society.
1000r, Returning to homes and family.

1993, Aug. 4 Litho. *Perf. 12½*
1284-1288 A239 Set of 5 5.50 1.50

Souvenir Sheet
Perf. 13

1289 A239 1000r blue & black 3.75 1.25

No. 1289 contains one 32x40mm stamp.

Ships A240

150r, Venetian caravel. 200r, Phoenician galley. 250r, Egyptian merchantman. 500r, Genoese merchantman. 900r, English merchantman.

1993, Aug. 27 Litho. *Perf. 13*
Without Gum
1290-1294 A240 Set of 5 4.25 1.25

Alberto Santos-Dumont (1873-1932) — A241

Designs: 150r, Portrait, Balloon, Eiffel Tower, vert. 200r, 14-bis, 1906. 250r, Demoiselle. 500r, EMB-201A. 900r, EMB-111.

1993, Sept. 10 *Perf. 13*
Without Gum
1295-1299 A241 Set of 5 4.25 1.25

1994 World Cup Soccer Championships, US — A242

Various soccer plays. Denominations: 250r, 350r, 600r, 800r, 1000r, vert.

1993, Sept. 23 Litho. *Perf. 12½*
1300-1304 A242 Set of 5 5.25 1.75

Souvenir Sheet

1305 A242 1500r multicolored 4.50 1.50

No. 1305 contains one 40x32mm stamp.

BANGKOK 93 — A243

Ducks: 250r, Anas penelope. 350r, Anas formosa. 600r, Aix galericulata. 800r, Aix sponsa. 1000r, Histrionicus histrionicus.
1500r, Head of Air galericulata.

1993, Oct. 1 Litho. *Perf. 13*
Without Gum
1306-1310 A243 Set of 5 5.50 1.75

Souvenir Sheet

1311 A243 1500r multicolored 3.25 1.10

No. 1311 contains one 40x32mm stamp.

Vertical Take-Off Aircraft — A244

Designs: 150r, First helicopter model, France, 1784, vert. 200r, Steam helicopter model, 1863, vert. 250r, New York-Atlanta-Miami autogyro flight, 1927. 500r, Sikorsky helicopter, 1943. 900r, French VTOL jet.
1000r, Juan de la Cierva's autogyro C-4, 1923.

Perf. 12x12½, 12½x12
1993, Nov. 6 Without Gum
1312-1316 A244 Set of 5 4.25 1.25

Souvenir Sheet
Perf. 12½

1317 A244 1000r multicolored 2.50 .90

No. 1317 contains one 40x32mm stamp.

Insects — A245

Designs: 50r, Cnaphalocrosis medinalis. 450r, Cicadelle brune. 500r, Scirpophaga incertulas. No. 1321, 1000r, Diopsis macrophthlalma.
No. 1322, Leptocorisa oratorius.

1993, Dec. 2 *Perf. 13*
1318-1321 A245 Set of 4 3.50 1.25

Souvenir Sheet
Perf. 12½

1322 A245 1000r multicolored 3.00 .80

Issued without gum.
No. 1322 contains one 32x40mm stamp.

Independence, 40th Anniv. — A246

Designs: 300r, Ministry of Posts and Telecommunications. 500r, Independence Monument, 1953, vert. 700r, Natl. flag.

1993 **Litho.** ***Perf. 12½***
1323-1325 A246 Set of 3 3.00 1.00

Hummel Figurines A247

Designs: 50r, Boy riding pony. 100r, Girl with baby carriage. 150r, Girl bathing doll. 200r, Girl holding doll. 250r, Boys playing. 300r, Girls pulling boy in cart. 350r, Girls playing ring-around-the-rosie. 600r, Boys with stick and drum.

1993 **Litho.** ***Perf. 12½***
1326-1333 A247 Set of 8 5.00 1.50

1994 Winter Olympic Games, Lillehammer — A248

150r, Women's figure skating, vert. 250r, Two-man luge. 400r, Downhill skiing. 700r, Biathlon. 1000r, Speed skating, vert.
1500r, Curling, vert.

1994, Jan. 23 ***Perf. 13***
1334-1338 A248 Set of 5 5.75 1.50

Souvenir Sheet

1339 A248 1500r multicolored 3.50 1.25

No. 1339 contains one 32x40mm stamp.

Classic Automobiles — A249

Designs: 150r, 1924 Opel. 200r, 1901 Mercedes. 250r, 1927 Model T Ford. 500r, 1907 Rolls Royce. 900r, 1908 Hutton.
1000r, 1931 Duesenberg.

1994, Feb. 20 ***Perf. 13***
1340-1344 A249 Set of 5 5.00 1.50

Souvenir Sheet

1345 A249 1000r multicolored 3.00 .90

No. 1345 contains one 32x40mm stamp.

1996 Summer Olympic Games, Atlanta — A250

Designs: 150r, Women's gymnastics. 200r, Soccer. 250r, Javelin. 300r, Canoeing. 600r, Running. 1000r, Diving, horiz.
1500r, Equestrian.

1994, Mar. 20 ***Perf. 13***
1346-1351 A250 Set of 6 5.00 1.50

Souvenir Sheet

1352 A250 1500r multicolored 4.50 1.25

No. 1352 contains one 32x40mm stamp.

Khmer Statues — A251

Designs: 300r, Siva and Uma. 500r, Vishnu. 700r, King Jayavarman VII.

1994, Apr. 13
1353-1355 A251 Set of 3 5.00 1.50

Intl. Olympic Committee, Cent. — A252

Designs: 100r, Olympic Flag. 300r, Flag, Torch. 600r, Flag, Baron de Coubertin.

1994, Apr. 23 ***Perf. 12½***
1356-1358 A252 Set of 3 3.00 1.00

Prehistoric Animals — A253

150r, Mesonyx. 250r, Doedicurus. 400r, Mylodon. 700r, Uintatherium. 1000r, Hyrachyus.

1994, May 10 ***Perf. 12½***
1359-1363 A253 Set of 5 5.00 1.50

1994 World Cup Soccer Championships, U.S. — A254

Various soccer plays. Denominations: 150r, 250r, 400r, 700r, 1000r.

1994, June 17 ***Perf. 12½***
1364-1368 A254 Set of 5 5.00 1.50

Souvenir Sheet

1369 A254 1500r multicolored 3.50 1.25

No. 1369 contains one 32x40mm stamp.

Statues A255

Designs: 300r, shown. 500r, Soldiers in combat, vert. 700r, Lions, vert.

1994 ***Perf. 13***
1370-1372 A255 Set of 3 3.75 1.25

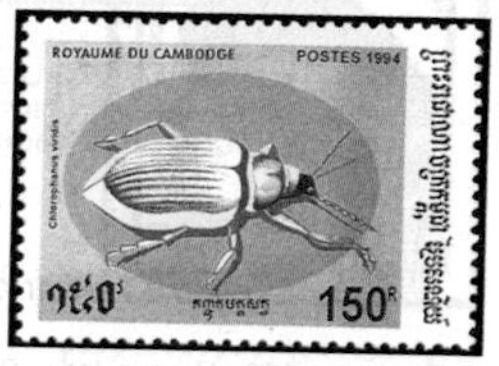

Beetles A256

Designs: 150r, Chlorophanus viridis. 200r, Chrysochroa fulgidissima. 250r, Lytta vesicatoria. 500r, Purpuricenus kaehleri. 900r, Dynastes hercules.
1000r, Timarcha tenebricosa.

1994, July 7 ***Perf. 12½***
1373-1377 A256 Set of 5 4.50 1.25

Souvenir Sheet

1378 A256 1000r multicolored 2.50 .90

No. 1378 contains one 40x32mm stamp.

Submarines — A257

Designs: 150r, Halley's diving bell, 1690, vert. 200r, Gimnote, 1886. 250r, Peral, 1888. 500r, Nuclear-powered Nautilus, 1954. 900r, Bathyscaphe Trieste, 1953.
1000r, Ictineo, 1885.

1994, Aug. 12 ***Perf. 13***
1379-1383 A257 Set of 5 5.00 1.50

Souvenir Sheet

Perf. 12½

1384 A257 1000r multicolored 3.00 1.00

No. 1384 contains one 40x32mm stamp.

Chess Champions — A258

Designs: 150r, Francois-André Philador, 1795. 200r, Louis de la Bourdonnais, 1821. 250r, Adolph Anderssen, 1851. 500r, Paul Morphy, 1858. 900r, Wilhelm Steinitz, 1866.
1000r, Emanuel Lasker, 1894.

1994, Sept. 20 ***Perf. 13***
1385-1389 A258 Set of 5 4.50 1.50

Souvenir Sheet

1390 A258 1000r multicolored 3.00 1.00

No. 1390 contains one 32x40mm stamp.

Aircraft A259

Designs: 150r, Sikorsky S-42 flying boat. 200r, Vought-Sikorsky VS-300A helicopter. 250r, Sikorsky S-37 biplane. 500r, Sikorsky S-35 biplane. 900r, Sikorsky S-43 amphibian.
1000r, 1st 4-engine bomber, Ilya Mourometz.

1994, Oct. 6 ***Perf. 13***
1391-1395 A259 Set of 5 4.50 1.50

Souvenir Sheet

Perf. 12½

1396 A259 1000r multicolored 3.00 1.00

No. 1396 contains one 40x32mm stamp.

Birds A260

Designs: 150r, Remiz pendulinus, vert. 250r, Panurus biarmicus. 400r, Emberiza rustica. 700r, Emberiza schoeniclus. 1000r, Regulus regulus.
1500r, Pitta angolensis.

1994, Nov. 20 ***Perf. 12½***
1397-1401 A260 Set of 5 6.00 1.50

Souvenir Sheet

Perf. 13

1402 A260 1500r multicolored 4.00 1.25

No. 1402 contains one 32x40mm stamp.

Independence Festival — A261

Designs: 300r, Postal Service float. 500r, Soldiers marching. 700r, Army unit marching.

1994, Dec. 9 ***Perf. 13***
1403-1405 A261 Set of 3 5.00 1.50

Natl. Development — A262

Designs: 300r, Chruoi Changwar Bridge. 500r, Olympic Commercial Center. 700r, Sakamony Chedei Temple.

1994, Dec. 10
1406-1408 A262 Set of 3 5.00 1.50

Prehistoric Animals — A263

Pelé and Team — AP61

1970, Oct. 14 Photo. *Perf. 12½*

Designs: 50fr, Aztec Stadium, Mexico City, horiz. 100fr, Mexican soccer team, horiz.

C150 AP61 50fr multi .90 .25
C151 AP61 100fr multi 2.00 .50
C152 AP61 200fr multi 3.50 1.00
Nos. C150-C152 (3) 6.40 1.75

9th World Soccer Championships for the Jules Rimet Cup, Mexico City, May 30-June 21, and the final victory of Brazil over Italy.

Ludwig van Beethoven (1770-1827), Composer AP62

1970, Nov. 23 Engr. *Perf. 13*

C153 AP62 250fr multi 5.75 1.00

Christ at Emmaus, by Rembrandt — AP63

150fr, The Anatomy Lesson, by Rembrandt.

1970, Dec. 5 Photo. *Perf. 12x12½*

C154 AP63 70fr grn & multi 1.40 .25
C155 AP63 150fr multi 2.75 .60

Charles Dickens — AP64

Designs: 50fr, Scenes from David Copperfield. 100fr, Dickens holding quill.

1970, Dec. 22 *Perf. 13*

C156 AP64 40fr blk & rose .95 .20
C157 AP64 50fr bis & multi 1.00 .20
C158 AP64 100fr rose & multi 2.00 .40
a. Strip of 3, #C156-C158 5.00 1.00

Charles Dickens (1812-1870), English novelist.

De Gaulle Type of 1970 Overprinted

Charles de Gaulle

1971, Jan. 15 Engr. *Perf. 13*

C159 100fr vio bl, emer & brn red 2.75 .40
C160 200fr brn red, emer & vio bl 5.75 .80
a. AP60 Pair, #C159-C160 + label 9.00 1.40

In memory of Gen. Charles de Gaulle (1890-1970), President of France.

Timber Storage, Douala — AP65

Industrialization: 70fr, ALUCAM aluminum plant, Edea, vert. 100fr, Mbakaou Dam.

1971, Feb. 14 Engr. *Perf. 13*

C161 AP65 40fr dk red, bl grn & ol brn .55 .20
C162 AP65 70fr ol brn, sl grn & brt bl 1.10 .25
C163 AP65 100fr Prus bl, yel grn & red brn 1.75 .40
Nos. C161-C163 (3) 3.40 .85

Relay Race — AP66

50fr, Torch bearer, vert. 100fr, Discus.

1971, Apr. 24 Engr. *Perf. 13*

C164 AP66 30fr dk brn, ver & ind .65 .20
C165 AP66 50fr blk, bl & choc .80 .25
C166 AP66 100fr multi 1.75 .35
Nos. C164-C166 (3) 3.20 .80

75th anniv. of revival of Olympic Games.

Fishing Trawler — AP67

Designs: 40fr, Local fishermen, Northern Cameroun. 70fr, Fishing harbor, Douala. 150fr, Shrimp boats, Douala.

1971, May 14 Engr. *Perf. 13*

C167 AP67 30fr lt brn, bl & grn .70 .20
C168 AP67 40fr sl grn, bl & dk brn .90 .20
C169 AP67 70fr dk brn, bl & red org 2.00 .25
C170 AP67 150fr multi 4.25 .60
Nos. C167-C170 (4) 7.85 1.25

Cameroun fishing industry.

Cameroun No. 123 and War Memorial, Yaoundé — AP68

Designs (Cameroun Stamps): 25fr, No. C33 and Jamot memorial. 40fr, No. 431 and government buildings, Yaoundé. 50fr, No. 19 and Imperial German postal emblem. 100fr, No. 101 and World War II memorial.

1971, Aug. 1 Engr. *Perf. 13*

C171 AP68 20fr grn, ocher & dk brn .35 .20
C172 AP68 25fr dk brn, vio bl & sl grn .55 .20
C173 AP68 40fr grn, mar & sl .70 .20
C174 AP68 50fr dk brn, blk & ver 1.00 .20
C175 AP68 100fr mar, sl grn & org 1.75 .40
Nos. C171-C175 (5) 4.35 1.20

PHILATECAM 1971 Philatelic Exhibition.

Cameroun Flag, Pres. Ahidjo and Reunification Highway — AP69

Typographed, Silk Screen, Embossed

1971, Oct. 1 *Perf. 12½*

C176 AP69 250fr gold & multi 5.75 2.00

PHILATECAM Philatelic Exhibition, Yaoundé-Douala.

African Postal Union Issue, 1971

Common Design Type

1971, Nov. 13 Photo. *Perf. 13x13½*

C177 CD135 100fr bl & multi 2.00 .40

Annunciation, by Fra Angelico — AP71

Christmmas (Paintings): 45fr, Virgin and Child, by Andrea del Sarto. 150fr, Christ Child with Lamb, detail from Holy Family, by Raphael, vert.

1971, Dec. 19 *Perf. 13x13½, 13½x13*

C178 AP71 40fr multi .55 .20
C179 AP71 45fr multi .70 .20
C180 AP71 150fr multi 3.25 .60
Nos. C178-C180 (3) 4.50 1.00

Cameroun Airlines Emblem AP72

1972, Feb. 2 Photo. *Perf. 12½x12*

C181 AP72 50fr lt bl & multi .80 .20

Inauguration of Cameroun Airlines.

Doge's Palace, by Ippolito Caffi AP73

100fr, 200fr, Details from "Regatta on the Grand Canal," by School of Canaletto.

1972 Photo. *Perf. 13*

C182 AP73 40fr gold & multi .70 .20
C183 AP73 100fr gold & multi 1.75 .40
C184 AP73 200fr gold & multi 3.75 .80
Nos. C182-C184 (3) 6.20 1.40

UNESCO campaign to save Venice.

Cosmonauts Patsayev, Dobrovolsky and Volkov — AP74

1972, May 1 Photo. *Perf. 13x13½*

C185 AP74 50fr multi 1.00 .20

Salute-Soyuz 11 space mission, and in memory of the Russian cosmonauts Victor I. Patsayev, Georgi T. Dobrovolsky and Vladislav N. Volkov, who died during Soyuz 11 space mission, June 6-30, 1971.

UN Headquarters, Chinese Flag and Gate of Heavenly Peace — AP75

1972, May 19 *Perf. 13*

C186 AP75 50fr blk, scar & gold 3.25 .20

Admission of People's Republic of China to UN.

United Republic

Olympic Rings, Swimming AP76

Designs (Olympic Rings and): No. C188, Boxing, vert. 200fr, Equestrian.

1972, Aug. 1 Engr. *Perf. 13*

C187 AP76 50fr lake & slate grn .90 .20
C188 AP76 50fr choc & slate .90 .20
C189 AP76 200fr cl, gray & dk brn 3.50 .70
a. Min. sheet of 3 5.75 2.25
Nos. C187-C189 (3) 5.30 1.10

20th Olympic Games, Munich, Aug. 26-Sept. 11. No. C189a contains stamps similar to Nos. C187-C189, but in changed colors. The 50fr (swimming) is Prussian blue, violet & brown; the 50c (boxing) lilac, Prussian blue & brown; the 200fr, Prussian blue & brown.

Nos. C187-C189 Overprinted in Red or Black

a

b

c

1972, Oct. 23 **Engr.** ***Perf. 13***

C190 AP76(a) 50fr (R) .90 .20
C191 AP76(b) 50fr .90 .20
C192 AP76(c) 200fr 3.50 .80
Nos. C190-C192 (3) 5.30 1.20

Gold Medal Winners in 20th Olympic Games: Mark Spitz, US, swimming (#C190); Dieter Kottysch, West Germany, light middle-weight boxing (#C191); Richard Meade, Great Britain, 3-day equestrian (#C192).

Madonna with Angels, by Cimabue AP77

Christmas: 140fr, Madonna of the Rose Arbor, by Stefan Lochner.

1972, Dec. 21 **Photo.** ***Perf. 13***

C193 AP77 45fr gold & multi 1.00 .20
C194 AP77 140fr gold & multi 2.75 .45

St. Teresa, the Little Flower — AP78

100fr, Lisieux Cathedral and St. Teresa.

1973, Jan. 2 **Engr.**

C195 AP78 45fr vio bl, pur & mar .70 .20
C196 AP78 100fr mag, ultra & brn 1.75 .40

Centenary of the birth of St. Teresa of Lisieux (1873-1897), Carmelite nun.

African Unity Hall, Addis Ababa and Emperor Haile Selassie — AP79

1973, Mar. 14 **Photo.** ***Perf. 13***

C197 AP79 45fr yellow & multi 1.00 .20

80th birthday of Emperor Haile Selassie of Ethiopia.

Corn, Grain, Healthy and Starving People — AP80

1973, Apr. 10 **Typo.** ***Perf. 13***

C198 AP80 45fr multi .80 .20

World Food Program, 10th anniversary.

Hearts and Blood Vessels — AP81

Scout Emblem and Flags — AP82

1973, May 5 **Engr.**

C199 AP81 50fr dk car rose & dk vio bl 1.00 .20

"Your Heart is Your Health" and for the 25th anniv. of the WHO.

Type of Regular Issue

Designs: 45fr, Map of Cameroun, Pres. Ahidjo and No. C176. 70fr, National colors and commemorative inscriptions.

1973, May 20 **Engr.** ***Perf. 13***

C200 A128 45fr grn & multi .80 .20
C201 A128 70fr red & multi 1.00 .25

1973, July 31 **Typo.** ***Perf. 13***

C202 AP82 40fr multi 1.00 .20
C203 AP82 45fr multi 1.25 .20
C204 AP82 100fr multi 3.25 .40
Nos. C202-C204 (3) 5.50 .80

Cameroun's admission to the World Scout Conference, Mar. 26, 1971.

African Weeks Issue

Head and City Hall, Brussels — AP83

1973, Sept. 17 **Engr.** ***Perf. 13***

C205 AP83 40fr dp brn & rose claret .80 .20

African Weeks, Brussels, Sept. 15-30.

Map of Africa with Cameroun — AP84

1973, Sept. 29 **Engr.** ***Perf. 13***

C206 AP84 40fr blk, red & grn .80 .20

Help for handicapped children.

Zamengoe Radar Station AP85

1973, Dec. 8 **Engr.** ***Perf. 13***

C207 AP85 100fr bl, lt brn & grn 1.50 .40

Chancellor Rolin Madonna, by Van Eyck AP86

Christmas: 140fr, Nativity, by Federigo Barocei.

1973, Dec. 11 **Photo.** ***Perf. 13***

C208 AP86 45fr gold & multi 1.00 .20
C209 AP86 140fr gold & multi 2.75 .70

Zebu Type of 1974

1974, June 1 **Litho.** ***Perf. 13***

C210 A140 45fr Zebu herd 1.40 .20

Churchill and Union Jack AP87

1974, July 10 **Engr.** ***Perf. 13***

C211 AP87 100fr blk, bl & red 1.60 .40

Winston Churchill (1874-1965).

Soccer, Arms of Frankfurt, Dortmund, Gelsenkirchen and Stuttgart — AP88

100fr, Soccer & arms of Berlin, Hamburg, Hanover & Düsseldorf. 200fr, Soccer cup & game.

1974, Aug. 5 **Photo.** ***Perf. 13***

C212 AP88 45fr gray, sl & org .65 .20
C213 AP88 100fr gray, sl & org 1.25 .40
C214 AP88 200fr org, slate & bl 2.50 .65
a. Strip of 3, Nos. C212-C214 5.00 1.40

World Cup Soccer Championship, Munich, June 13-July 7.

Nos. C212-C214 Overprinted in Dark Blue

1974, Sept. 16 **Photo.** ***Perf. 13***

C215 AP88 45fr multi .65 .20
C216 AP88 100fr multi 1.25 .40
C217 AP88 200fr multi 2.40 .80
a. Strip of 3, Nos. C215-C217 5.50 1.50

World Cup Soccer Championship, 1974, victory of German Federal Republic.

UPU Type of 1974

100fr, Cameroun #503. 200fr, Cameroun #C29.

1974, Oct. 8 **Engr.** ***Perf. 13***

C218 A142 100fr blue & multi 1.75 .30
C219 A142 200fr red & multi 3.25 .60

Copernicus and Planets Circling Sun — AP89

1974, Oct. 15 **Engr.** ***Perf. 13***

C220 AP89 250fr multi 3.50 1.00

500th anniversary of the birth of Nicolaus Copernicus (1473-1543), Polish astronomer.

21st Chess Olympiad, Nice, France, June 6-30 — AP90

1974, Nov. 3 **Photo.** ***Perf. 13x12½***

C221 AP90 100fr Chess pieces 5.25 1.00

Mask and ARPHILA Emblem — AP91

1974, Nov. 30 **Engr.** ***Perf. 13***

C222 AP91 50fr choc & magenta .80 .25

ARPHILA 75, Paris, June 6-16, 1975.

Presidents and Flags of Cameroun, CAR, Gabon and Congo — AP92

1974, Dec. 8 **Photo.**

C223 AP92 100fr gold & multi 2.40 .40

See note after No. 595.

No. 78 Surcharged in Blue or Violet

A32a

A32b

1899, Jan. 5

88B	A32a 1(c) on ⅓ of 3c, on cover (Bl)		7,750.	
88C	A32b 2(c) on ⅔ of 3c, on cover (V)		7,750.	

Nos. 88B-88C were prepared and used at Port Hood, Nova Scotia, without official authorization.

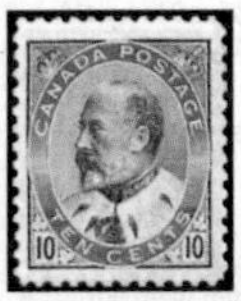
King Edward VII — A34

1903-08 **Engr.**

89	A34	1c green	35.00	.20
		Never hinged	87.50	
90	A34	2c carmine	37.50	.20
		Never hinged	95.00	
b.		Booklet pane of 6	1,600.	*1,250.*
		Never hinged	*2,750.*	
91	A34	5c blue, *blue*	225.00	4.50
		Never hinged	550.00	
92	A34	7c olive bister	225.00	4.50
		Never hinged	550.00	
93	A34	10c brown lilac	400.00	10.00
		Never hinged	1,000.	
94	A34	20c olive green	675.00	40.00
		Never hinged	1,700.	
95	A34	50c purple ('08)	850.00	150.00
		Never hinged	2,100.	
		Nos. 89-95 (7)	2,447.	209.40
		Nos. 89-95, never hinged	6,020.	

Values for Nos. 94 and 95 used are for examples with contemporaneous circular datestamps. Stamps with heavy cancellations or parcel cancellations sell for much less.

Issued: 1c-10c, 7/1/03; 20c, 9/27/04; 50c, 11/19/08.

Imperf., Pairs

89a	A34	1c	725.00	
90a	A34	2c	45.00	45.00
		Never hinged	75.00	
c.		As No. 90b, imperf, 2 panes tete beche	*14,500.*	
91a	A34	5c	1,200.	
92a	A34	7c	800.00	
93a	A34	10c	1,200.	

All imperfs except No. 90a made without gum.

No. 90a issued to the public with gum; also made without gum from different plates distinguishable by experts. Value without gum, $350 with certificate of authenticity.

Quebec Tercentenary Issue

Prince and Princess of Wales, 1908 — A35

Jacques Cartier and Samuel de Champlain A36

Queen Alexandra and King Edward A37

Champlain's Home in Quebec A38

Generals Montcalm and Wolfe — A39

View of Quebec in 1700 — A40

Champlain's Departure for the West — A41

Arrival of Cartier at Quebec A42

1908, July 16

96	A35	½c black brown	6.00	5.00
		Never hinged	15.00	
97	A36	1c blue green	22.50	4.50
		Never hinged	55.00	
98	A37	2c carmine	32.50	2.00
		Never hinged	82.50	
99	A38	5c dark blue	75.00	55.00
		Never hinged	190.00	
100	A39	7c olive green	150.00	100.00
		Never hinged	375.00	
101	A40	10c dark violet	190.00	140.00
		Never hinged	475.00	
102	A41	15c red orange	225.00	130.00
		Never hinged	550.00	
103	A42	20c yel brn	250.00	175.00
		Never hinged	625.00	
		Nos. 96-103 (8)	951.00	611.50
		Nos. 96-103, never hinged	2,367.	

Imperf., Pairs

96a	A35	½c	650.00
		Never hinged	1,150.
97a	A36	1c	650.00
		Never hinged	1,150.
98a	A37	2c	650.00
		Never hinged	1,150.
99a	A38	5c	650.00
		Never hinged	1,150.
100a	A39	7c	650.00
		Never hinged	1,150.
101a	A40	10c	650.00
		Never hinged	1,150.
102a	A41	15c	650.00
		Never hinged	1,150.
103a	A42	20c	650.00
		Never hinged	1,150.

100 pairs of imperfs made, 50 with gum and 50 without. Due to demand, pairs without gum generally sell for 90-95% of the unused hinged price.

King George V — A43

Two dies of 1c.
Die I — The "N" of "ONE" is separated from the oval above it.
Die II — The "N" of "ONE" almost touches the oval above it.

Two dies of 3c carmine.
Die I — The "R" of "THREE" is separated from the oval above it. The bottom line of the vignette does not touch the heavy diagonal stroke at right.
Die II — The "R" of "THREE" almost touches the oval above it. The bottom horizontal line of the vignette touches the heavy diagonal stroke at right.

1911-25

104	A43	1c green	18.00	.20
		Never hinged	45.00	
a.		Booklet pane of 6	32.50	*35.00*
		Never hinged	65.00	
105	A43	1c org yel (I) ('22)	18.00	.20
		Never hinged	45.00	
a.		Booklet pane of 4 + 2 labels	55.00	*55.00*
		Never hinged	110.00	
b.		Booklet pane of 6	62.50	*62.50*
		Never hinged	125.00	
d.		1c orange yellow (II)	15.00	.20
		Never hinged	37.50	
106	A43	2c carmine	18.00	.20
		Never hinged	45.00	
a.		Booklet pane of 6	40.00	40.00
		Never hinged	80.00	
b.		2c pink	140.00	18.00
		Never hinged	350.00	
c.		2c rose carmine	18.00	.20
		Never hinged	45.00	
d.		As "c," booklet pane of 6	160.00	160.00
		Never hinged	320.00	
107	A43	2c yel green ('22)	16.00	.20
		Never hinged	40.00	
a.		Thin paper ('24)	16.00	2.50
		Never hinged	40.00	
b.		Booklet pane of 4 + 2 labels ('22)	65.00	*70.00*
		Never hinged	130.00	
c.		Booklet pane of 6 ('22)	300.00	*325.00*
		Never hinged	550.00	
108	A43	3c brown ('18)	16.00	.20
		Never hinged	40.00	
a.		Booklet pane of 4 + 2 labels	90.00	*95.00*
		Never hinged	180.00	
109	A43	3c car (I) ('23)	16.00	.20
		Never hinged	40.00	
a.		Booklet pane of 4 + 2 labels	70.00	*75.00*
		Never hinged	140.00	
c.		Die II ('24)	35.00	.20
		Never hinged	90.00	
110	A43	4c ol bis ('22)	50.00	3.25
		Never hinged	125.00	
111	A43	5c dk bl ('12)	135.00	1.00
		Never hinged	340.00	
112	A43	5c violet ('22)	35.00	.75
		Never hinged	87.50	
a.		Thin paper ('24)	30.00	7.50
		Never hinged	75.00	
113	A43	7c yel ocher ('12)	47.50	3.25
		Never hinged	120.00	
114	A43	7c red brown ('24)	22.50	11.00
		Never hinged	57.50	
115	A43	8c blue ('25)	35.00	11.00
		Never hinged	87.50	
116	A43	10c plum ('12)	275.00	3.00
		Never hinged	690.00	
117	A43	10c blue ('22)	47.50	2.25
		Never hinged	120.00	
118	A43	10c bis brn ('25)	42.50	2.25
		Never hinged	105.00	
119	A43	20c olive grn ('12)	110.00	2.00
		Never hinged	275.00	
120	A43	50c blk brn ('25)	85.00	3.00
		Never hinged	210.00	
a.		50c black ('12)	210.00	9.00
		Never hinged	525.00	
122	A43	$1 orange ('23)	100.00	10.00
		Never hinged	250.00	
		Nos. 104-122 (18)	1,087.	53.95
		Nos. 104-122, never hinged	2,705.	

For type A43 perforated 12x8 see No. 184.
For surcharges see Nos. 139-140.
Issued: #104, #106, 12/22/11; #105, 6/7/22; #108, 8/6/18; #109, 12/18/23; 4c, 7/7/22; #111, 1/17/12; #112, 2/2/22; #113, 116, 1/12/12; #114, 12/12/24; 8c, 9/1/25; #117, 2/20/22; #118, 8/1/25; 20c, 1/23/12; 50c, 1/26/12; $1, 7/22/23.

Imperf., Panes

105c	As No. 105b, imperf, 2 panes tete beche	*12,500.*
107d	As No. 107c, imperf, 2 panes tete beche	*12,500.*
109b	As No. 109a, imperf, 2 panes tete beche	*12,500.*

Imperf., Pairs

110a	A43	4c	2,000.
		Never hinged	3,600.
112b	A43	5c	2,000.
		Never hinged	3,600.
114a	A43	7c	2,000.
		Never hinged	3,600.
115a	A43	8c	2,000.
		Never hinged	3,600.
118a	A43	10c	2,000.
		Never hinged	3,600.
119a	A43	20c	2,000.
		Never hinged	3,600.
120b	A43	50c	2,400.
		Never hinged	4,250.
122a	A43	$1	2,000.
		Never hinged	3,600.

Nos. 105c and 109b made without gum, others with gum. About half of the No. 120b pairs have creases; value thus $500.

Coil Stamps

1912 ***Perf. 8 Horizontally***

123	A43	1c dark green	105.00	65.00
		Never hinged	250.00	
124	A43	2c carmine	105.00	65.00
		Never hinged	250.00	

1912-24 ***Perf. 8 Vertically***

125	A43	1c green	25.00	2.00
		Never hinged	50.00	
126	A43	1c orange yellow (II) ('23)	12.00	7.50
		Never hinged	24.00	
a.		Block of 4 (II)	60.00	50.00
		Never hinged	90.00	
b.		1c orange yellow (I)	25.00	11.00
		Never hinged	50.00	
c.		Block of 4 (I)	450.00	
		Never hinged	750.00	
127	A43	2c carmine	35.00	2.00
		Never hinged	70.00	
128	A43	2c green ('22)	16.00	1.10
		Never hinged	32.50	
a.		Block of 4	60.00	60.00
		Never hinged	90.00	
129	A43	3c brown ('18)	27.50	1.30
		Never hinged	55.00	
130	A43	3c carmine (I) ('24)	70.00	9.00
		Never hinged	140.00	
a.		Block of 4 (I)	950.00	750.00
		Never hinged	1,500.	
b.		Die II	85.00	10.00
		Never hinged	170.00	
		Nos. 125-130 (6)	185.50	22.90
		Nos. 125-130, never hinged	399.00	

Nos. 126a and 128a were issued to the public. Nos. 126c and 130a were issued "by favor" as were the various other imperf and part-perfs of this era.
Beware of fakes of No. 130a made from No. 138.

1915-24 ***Perf. 12 Horizontally***

131	A43	1c dark green	7.50	6.50
		Never hinged	15.00	
132	A43	2c carmine	27.50	8.00
		Never hinged	55.00	
133	A43	2c yellow grn ('24)	75.00	60.00
		Never hinged	150.00	
134	A43	3c brown ('21)	11.00	6.50
		Never hinged	22.00	
		Nos. 131-134 (4)	121.00	81.00
		Nos. 131-134, never hinged	242.00	

"The Fathers of Confederation" — A44

1917, Sept. 15 ***Perf. 12***

135	A44	3c brown	47.50	1.25
		Never hinged	120.00	
a.		Imperf., pair	600.00	

50th anniv. of the Canadian Confederation.
Imperfs. are without gum.

1924 ***Imperf.***

136	A43	1c orange yellow	35.00	35.00
		Never hinged	65.00	
		Pair	75.00	75.00
		Never hinged	135.00	
137	A43	2c green	35.00	35.00
		Never hinged	65.00	
		Pair	75.00	75.00
		Never hinged	135.00	
138	A43	3c carmine (I)	17.50	17.50
		Never hinged	32.50	
		Pair	37.50	37.50
		Never hinged	67.50	
		Nos. 136-138 (3)	87.50	87.50
		Nos. 136-138, never hinged	110.00	

No. 109 Surcharged:

a

b

1926 ***Perf. 12***

139	A43(a)	2c on 3c car (I)	55.00	55.00
		Never hinged	90.00	
a.		Pair, one without surcharge	350.00	
b.		Double surcharge	225.00	
		Never hinged	350.00	
c.		Die II	700.00	
		Never hinged	1,150.	
140	A43(b)	2c on 3c carmine	25.00	22.50
		Never hinged	42.50	
a.		Double surcharge	225.00	
		Never hinged	350.00	
b.		Triple surcharge	225.00	
		Never hinged	350.00	
c.		Double surch., one invtd.	350.00	

Sir John A. Macdonald
A45

Sir Wilfrid Laurier
A48

"The Fathers of Confederation" — A46

Parliament Building at Ottawa
A47

Map of Canada
A49

1927, June 29

141	A45	1c orange	3.50	1.30
		Never hinged	6.50	
142	A46	2c green	1.90	.20
		Never hinged	3.50	
143	A47	3c brown carmine	10.00	6.50
		Never hinged	18.00	
144	A48	5c violet	4.50	3.50
		Never hinged	8.25	
145	A49	12c dark blue	25.00	6.50
		Never hinged	45.00	
		Nos. 141-145 (5)	44.90	18.00
		Nos. 141-145, never hinged	81.25	

60th year of the Canadian Confederation.
Nos. 141-145 exist partly perforated.

Imperf., Pairs

141a	A45	1c	125.00
		Never hinged	180.00
142a	A46	2c	125.00
		Never hinged	180.00
143a	A47	3c	125.00
		Never hinged	180.00
144a	A48	5c	125.00
		Never hinged	180.00
145a	A49	12c	125.00
		Never hinged	180.00

Thomas d'Arcy McGee — A50

Laurier and Macdonald A51

Robert Baldwin and Sir Louis Hypolyte Lafontaine A52

1927, June 29

146	A50	5c violet	4.00	3.00
		Never hinged	7.25	
147	A51	12c green	10.00	5.50
		Never hinged	18.00	
148	A52	20c brown carmine	27.50	6.50
		Never hinged	50.00	
		Nos. 146-148 (3)	41.50	15.00
		Nos. 146-148, never hinged	75.25	

Nos. 146-148 were to have been issued in July, 1926, as a commemorative series, but were withheld and issued June 29, 1927. They exist partly perforated.

Imperf., Pairs

146a	A50	5c	125.00
		Never hinged	180.00
147a	A51	12c	125.00
		Never hinged	180.00
148a	A52	20c	125.00
		Never hinged	180.00

King George V — A53

Mt. Hurd from Bell-Smith's Painting "The Ice-crowned Monarch of the Rockies" A54

Quebec Bridge — A55

Harvesting Wheat A56

Schooner "Bluenose" A57

Parliament Building A58

1928-29

149	A53	1c orange	3.50	.35
		Never hinged	6.50	
	a.	Booklet pane of 6	25.00	20.00
		Never hinged	35.00	
150	A53	2c green	1.90	.20
		Never hinged	3.50	
	a.	Booklet pane of 6	25.00	20.00
		Never hinged	35.00	
151	A53	3c dk carmine	32.50	12.50
		Never hinged	60.00	
152	A53	4c bister ('29)	27.50	6.00
		Never hinged	50.00	
153	A53	5c dp violet	16.00	3.00
		Never hinged	30.00	
	a.	Booklet pane of 6	200.00	140.00
		Never hinged	280.00	
154	A53	8c blue	19.00	7.50
		Never hinged	35.00	
155	A54	10c green	22.50	2.50
		Never hinged	42.50	
156	A55	12c gray ('29)	45.00	7.50
		Never hinged	85.00	
157	A56	20c dk car ('29)	60.00	12.00
		Never hinged	110.00	
158	A57	50c dk blue ('29)	220.00	65.00
		Never hinged	440.00	
159	A58	$1 olive grn ('29)	300.00	80.00
		Never hinged	600.00	
		Nos. 149-159 (11)	747.90	196.55
		#149-159, never hinged	1,463.	

Nos. 149 to 159 exist partly perforated.

Imperf., Panes

149c	As No. 149a, imperf, 2 panes tete beche	1,050.
	Never hinged	1,550.
150c	As No. 150a, imperf, 2 panes tete beche	1,050.
	Never hinged	1,550.
153c	As No. 153a, imperf, 2 panes tete beche	1,050.
	Never hinged	1,550.

Imperf., Pairs

149b	A53	1c	100.00
		Never hinged	140.00
150b	A53	2c	100.00
		Never hinged	140.00
151a	A53	3c	120.00
		Never hinged	170.00
152a	A53	4c	120.00
		Never hinged	170.00
153b	A53	5c	100.00
		Never hinged	140.00
154a	A53	8c	120.00
		Never hinged	170.00
155a	A54	10c	200.00
		Never hinged	280.00
156a	A55	12c	200.00
		Never hinged	280.00
157a	A56	20c	200.00
		Never hinged	280.00
158a	A57	50c	800.00
		Never hinged	1,150.
159a	A58	$1	725.00
		Never hinged	1,050.

Coil Stamps

1929 ***Perf. 8 Vertically***

160	A53	1c orange	40.00	22.50
		Never hinged	75.00	
		Precanceled		17.50
161	A53	2c green	35.00	3.50
		Never hinged	65.00	

King George V A59

Library of Parliament A60

The Citadel at Quebec A61

Harvesting Wheat A62

Museum at Grand Pré and Monument to Evangeline A63

Mt. Edith Cavell A64

Two dies of 1c.
Die I — 3 thick and one thin colored lines between "P" at right and ornament above it.
Die II — 4 thick colored lines. Curved line in ball of ornament at right is longer than in die I.

Two dies of 2c.
Die I — The top of the letter "P" encloses a tiny dot of color.
Die II — The top of the "P" encloses a larger spot of color than in die I. The "P" appears almost like a "D."

1930-31 ***Perf. 11***

162	A59	1c orange	1.30	.60
		Never hinged	2.75	
163	A59	1c deep green (II)	2.25	.25
		Never hinged	4.75	
	a.	Booklet pane of 4 + 2 labels (II)	120.00	110.00
		Never hinged	180.00	
	b.	Die I	2.25	.20
		Never hinged	4.75	
	c.	Booklet pane of 6 (I)	22.50	20.00
		Never hinged	35.00	
164	A59	2c dull green (I)	1.20	.20
		Never hinged	2.60	
	a.	Booklet pane of 6	32.50	32.50
		Never hinged	47.50	
165	A59	2c deep red (I)	1.70	.20
		Never hinged	3.60	
	a.	Die II	2.25	.20
		Never hinged	4.75	
	b.	Booklet pane of 6 (I)	25.00	25.00
		Never hinged	37.50	
166	A59	2c dk brn (II) ('31)	2.25	.20
		Never hinged	4.75	
	a.	Booklet pane of 4 + 2 labels (II)	130.00	130.00
		Never hinged	200.00	
	b.	Die I	5.00	4.25
		Never hinged	10.50	
	c.	Booklet pane of 6 (I)	57.50	57.50
		Never hinged	87.50	
167	A59	3c deep red ('31)	3.50	.25
		Never hinged	7.50	
	a.	Booklet pane of 4 + 2 labels	40.00	40.00
		Never hinged	60.00	
168	A59	4c yel bister	14.00	7.50
		Never hinged	28.00	
169	A59	5c dull violet	8.50	5.00
		Never hinged	17.00	
170	A59	5c dull blue	5.50	1.25
		Never hinged	11.00	
171	A59	8c dark blue	27.50	13.50
		Never hinged	55.00	
172	A59	8c red orange	6.50	5.50
		Never hinged	13.00	
173	A60	10c olive green	14.00	1.30
		Never hinged	28.00	
174	A61	12c gray black	27.50	6.50
		Never hinged	55.00	
175	A62	20c brown red	42.50	1.40
		Never hinged	85.00	
176	A63	50c dull blue	200.00	14.00
		Never hinged	400.00	
177	A64	$1 dk ol green	200.00	27.50
		Never hinged	400.00	
		Nos. 162-177 (16)	558.20	85.15
		Nos. 162-177, never hinged	1,108.	

No. 169 was printed from both flat and rotary press plates.
See No. 201. For surcharge see No. 191. For overprint see No. 203.

Imperf., Pairs

163d	A59	1c (II)	1,600.
		Never hinged	2,400.
173a	A60	10c	1,600.
		Never hinged	2,400.
174a	A61	12c	725.
		Never hinged	1,050.
175a	A62	20c	725.
		Never hinged	1,050.
176a	A63	50c	1,000.
		Never hinged	1,500.
177a	A64	$1	1,000.
		Never hinged	1,500.

Coil Stamps

1930-31 ***Perf. 8½ Vertically***

178	A59	1c orange	15.00	9.00
		Never hinged	30.00	
179	A59	1c deep green	9.00	5.75
		Never hinged	18.00	
180	A59	2c dull green	6.00	3.00
		Never hinged	12.00	
181	A59	2c deep red	25.00	2.50
		Never hinged	50.00	
182	A59	2c dark brown ('31)	12.00	.70
		Never hinged	24.00	
183	A59	3c deep red ('31)	18.00	.70
		Never hinged	36.00	
		Nos. 178-183 (6)	85.00	21.65
		Nos. 178-183, never hinged	170.00	

George V Type of 1912-25

1931, June 24 ***Perf. 12x8***

184	A43	3c carmine	8.00	4.50
		Never hinged	20.00	

Sir Georges Etienne Cartier — A65

1931, Sept. 30 ***Perf. 11***

190	A65	10c dark green	14.00	.20
		Never hinged	30.00	
	a.	Imperf., pair	500.00	
		Never hinged	750.00	

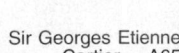

Nos. 165, 165a Surcharged

1932, June 21

191	A59	3c on 2c dp red (II)	1.40	.20
		Never hinged	2.25	
	a.	Die I	2.75	1.90
		Never hinged	4.50	

King George V — A66

Edward, Prince of Wales — A67

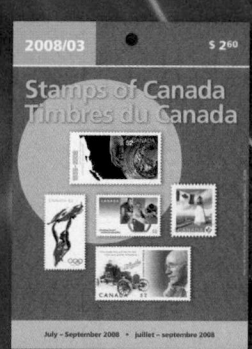

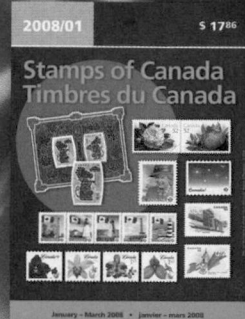

Allegory of British Empire A68

1932, July 12

No.	Type	Description	Unused	Used
192	A66	3c deep red	1.25	.20
		Never hinged	2.50	
193	A67	5c dull blue	7.00	3.00
		Never hinged	14.00	
194	A68	13c deep green	10.00	7.00
		Never hinged	20.00	
		Nos. 192-194 (3)	18.25	10.20
		Nos. 192-194, never hinged	36.50	

Imperial Economic Conference, Ottawa.

Type of 1930 and

King George V — A69

Two dies of 3c.

Die I — Upper left tip of "3" level with horizontal line to its left.

Die II — Raised "3"; upper left tip of "3" is above horizontal line.

1932, Dec. 1

No.	Type	Description	Unused	Used
195	A69	1c dark green	1.25	.20
		Never hinged	2.50	
a.		Booklet pane of 4 + 2 labels	80.00	80.00
		Never hinged	120.00	
b.		Booklet pane of 6	47.50	47.50
		Never hinged	72.50	
196	A69	2c black brown	1.40	.20
		Never hinged	2.80	
a.		Booklet pane of 4 + 2 labels	110.00	110.00
		Never hinged	165.00	
b.		Booklet pane of 6	70.00	70.00
		Never hinged	105.00	
197	A69	3c deep red (I)	1.40	.20
		Never hinged	2.80	
a.		Booklet pane of 4 + 2 labels	45.00	40.00
		Never hinged	67.50	
c.		Die II	1.40	.20
		Never hinged	2.80	
d.		As "a," die II	37.50	37.50
		Never hinged	57.50	
198	A69	4c ocher	50.00	7.00
		Never hinged	100.00	
199	A69	5c dark blue	14.00	.50
		Never hinged	28.00	
a.		Horiz. pair, imperf. vert.	1,600.	
		Never hinged	2,250.	
200	A69	8c red orange	45.00	3.50
		Never hinged	90.00	
201	A61	13c dull violet	42.50	3.50
		Never hinged	85.00	
		Nos. 195-201 (7)	155.55	15.10
		Nos. 195-201, never hinged	311.40	

Type A66 has at the foot of the stamp "OTTAWA-CONFERENCE 1932". This inscription does not appear on the stamps of type A69.

Imperf., Pairs

No.	Type	Description	Value
195c	A69	1c	240.00
		Never hinged	360.00
196c	A69	2c	240.00
		Never hinged	360.00
197b	A69	3c (I)	240.00
		Never hinged	360.00
197e	A69	3c (II)	*2,000.*
198a	A69	4c	240.00
		Never hinged	360.00
199b	A69	5c	240.00
		Never hinged	360.00
200a	A69	8c	240.00
		Never hinged	360.00
201a	A61	13c	800.00
		Never hinged	1,200.

No. 197e exists as one unused block of 4.

Government Buildings, Ottawa — A70

1933, May 18 *Perf. 11*

No.	Type	Description	Unused	Used
202	A70	5c dark blue	10.00	3.75
		Never hinged	18.50	
a.		Imperf., pair	625.00	
		Never hinged	950.00	

Meeting of the Executive Committee of the UPU at Ottawa, May and June, 1933.

No. 175 Overprinted in Blue

1933, July 24

No.	Type	Description	Unused	Used
203	A62	20c brown red	45.00	14.00
		Never hinged	80.00	
a.		Imperf., pair	625.00	
		Never hinged	950.00	

World's Grain Exhibition and Conference at Regina.

Steamship Royal William — A71

1933, Aug. 17

No.	Type	Description	Unused	Used
204	A71	5c dark blue	10.00	3.75
		Never hinged	18.50	
a.		Imperf., pair	625.00	
		Never hinged	950.00	

Centenary of the linking by steam of the Dominion, then a colony, with Great Britain, the mother country. The Royal William's 1833 voyage was the first Trans-Atlantic passage under steam all the way.

George V Type of 1932

Coil Stamps

1933 *Perf. 8½ Vertically*

No.	Type	Description	Unused	Used
205	A69	1c dark green	14.00	3.00
		Never hinged	24.00	
206	A69	2c black brown	17.50	1.10
		Never hinged	30.00	
207	A69	3c deep red	14.00	.40
		Never hinged	24.00	
		Nos. 205-207 (3)	45.50	4.50
		Nos. 205-207, never hinged	78.00	

Cartier's Arrival at Quebec — A72

1934, July 1 *Perf. 11*

No.	Type	Description	Unused	Used
208	A72	3c blue	4.50	1.40
		Never hinged	9.00	
a.		Imperf., pair	625.00	
		Never hinged	950.00	

Landing of Jacques Cartier, 400th anniv.

Group from Loyalists Monument, Hamilton, Ontario A73

1934, July 1

No.	Type	Description	Unused	Used
209	A73	10c olive green	28.00	7.50
		Never hinged	52.50	
a.		Imperf., pair	1,400.	
		Never hinged	2,100.	

Emigration of the United Empire Loyalists from the US to Canada, 150th anniv.

Seal of New Brunswick — A74

1934, Aug. 16

No.	Type	Description	Unused	Used
210	A74	2c red brown	3.25	2.25
		Never hinged	6.00	
a.		Imperf., pair	675.00	
		Never hinged	1,100.	

150th anniv. of the founding of the Province of New Brunswick.

Princess Elizabeth A75

Duke of York A76

King George V and Queen Mary — A77

Prince of Wales — A78

Windsor Castle A79

Royal Yacht Britannia A80

1935, May 4 *Perf. 12*

No.	Type	Description	Unused	Used
211	A75	1c green	.65	.35
		Never hinged	1.00	
212	A76	2c brown	1.00	.20
		Never hinged	1.50	
213	A77	3c carmine	2.00	.20
		Never hinged	3.25	
214	A78	5c blue	5.25	3.00
		Never hinged	8.50	
215	A79	10c green	8.00	3.00
		Never hinged	13.00	
216	A80	13c dark blue	9.00	6.50
		Never hinged	15.00	
		Nos. 211-216 (6)	25.90	13.25
		Nos. 211-216, never hinged	40.70	

25th anniv. of the accession to the throne of George V.

Imperf., Pairs

No.	Type	Description	Value
211a	A75	1c	275.00
		Never hinged	425.00
212a	A76	2c	275.00
		Never hinged	425.00
213a	A77	3c	275.00
		Never hinged	425.00
214a	A78	5c	275.00
		Never hinged	425.00
215a	A79	10c	275.00
		Never hinged	425.00
216b	A80	13c	275.00
		Never hinged	425.00

King George V — A81

Royal Canadian Mounted Police — A82

Confederation Conference at Charlottetown, 1864 — A83

Niagara Falls — A84

Parliament Buildings, Victoria, B.C. — A85

Champlain Monument, Quebec A86

1935, June 1 *Perf. 12*

No.	Type	Description	Unused	Used
217	A81	1c green	.30	.20
		Never hinged	.40	
a.		Booklet pane of 4 + 2 labels	70.00	70.00
		Never hinged	105.00	
b.		Booklet pane of 6	55.00	55.00
		Never hinged	32.50	
218	A81	2c brown	.45	.20
		Never hinged	.65	
a.		Booklet pane of 4 + 2 labels	70.00	70.00
		Never hinged	105.00	
b.		Booklet pane of 6	55.00	55.00
		Never hinged	82.50	
219	A81	3c dk carmine	.60	.20
		Never hinged	.90	
a.		Booklet pane of 4 + 2 labels	40.00	40.00
		Never hinged	60.00	
c.		Printed on gummed side	475.00	
220	A81	4c yel org	2.50	.55
		Never hinged	3.75	
221	A81	5c blue	3.25	.35
		Never hinged	5.00	
a.		Horiz. pair, imperf. vert.	225.00	
		Never hinged	340.00	
222	A81	8c dp orange	3.00	2.25
		Never hinged	4.50	
223	A82	10c car rose	7.00	.20
		Never hinged	10.50	
224	A83	13c violet	8.00	.75
		Never hinged	12.00	
225	A84	20c olive green	20.00	.75
		Never hinged	30.00	
226	A85	50c dull violet	30.00	6.00
		Never hinged	45.00	
227	A86	$1 deep blue	65.00	11.00
		Never hinged	100.00	
		Nos. 217-227 (11)	140.10	22.45
		Nos. 217-227, never hinged	212.70	

Imperf., Pairs

No.	Type	Description	Value
217c	A81	1c	150.00
		Never hinged	220.00
218c	A81	2c	150.00
		Never hinged	220.00
219b	A81	3c	150.00
		Never hinged	220.00
220a	A81	4c	150.00
		Never hinged	220.00
221b	A81	5c	150.00
		Never hinged	220.00
222a	A81	8c	150.00
		Never hinged	220.00
223a	A82	10c	225.00
		Never hinged	340.00
224a	A83	13c	225.00
		Never hinged	340.00
225a	A84	20c	225.00
		Never hinged	340.00
226a	A85	50c	225.00
		Never hinged	340.00
227a	A86	$1	300.00
		Never hinged	450.00

Coil Stamps

1935 *Perf. 8 Vertically*

No.	Type	Description	Unused	Used
228	A81	1c green	15.00	3.25
		Never hinged	22.50	
229	A81	2c brown	19.00	1.00
		Never hinged	28.00	
230	A81	3c dark carmine	15.00	.60
		Never hinged	22.50	
		Nos. 228-230 (3)	49.00	4.85
		Nos. 228-230, never hinged	73.00	

George VI — A87

George VI and Queen Elizabeth
A88

1937 *Perf. 12*

231 A87 1c green .25 .20
Never hinged .40
a. Booklet pane of 4 + 2 labels 20.00 *25.00*
Never hinged 30.00
b. Booklet pane of 6 7.50 *20.00*
Never hinged 11.50
232 A87 2c brown .65 .20
Never hinged 1.00
a. Booklet pane of 4 + 2 labels 20.00 *22.50*
Never hinged 30.00
b. Booklet pane of 6 12.00 *15.00*
Never hinged 18.00
233 A87 3c carmine .65 .20
Never hinged 1.00
a. Booklet pane of 4 + 2 labels 7.00 *14.00*
Never hinged 10.50
234 A87 4c yellow 2.75 .20
Never hinged 4.00
235 A87 5c blue 3.50 .20
Never hinged 5.00
236 A87 8c orange 2.75 .45
Never hinged 4.00
Nos. 231-236 (6) 10.55 1.45
Nos. 231-236, never hinged 15.40

Imperf., Pairs

231c A87 1c 300.00
Never hinged 450.00
232c A87 2c 300.00
Never hinged 450.00
233b A87 3c 300.00
Never hinged 450.00
234a A87 4c 300.00
Never hinged 450.00
235a A87 5c 300.00
Never hinged 450.00
236a A87 8c 300.00
Never hinged 450.00

1937, May 10

237 A88 3c carmine .25 .20
Never hinged .35
a. Imperf., pair 625.00
Never hinged 950.00

Coronation of King George VI and Queen Elizabeth.

George VI Types of 1937
Coil Stamps

1937 *Perf. 8 Vertically*

238 A87 1c green 2.40 1.10
Never hinged 3.60
239 A87 2c brown 4.00 .40
Never hinged 6.00
240 A87 3c carmine 7.50 .20
Never hinged 11.50
Nos. 238-240 (3) 13.90 1.70
Nos. 238-240, never hinged 21.10

Memorial Chamber, Parliament Building, Ottawa — A89

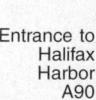

Entrance to Halifax Harbor
A90

Fort Garry Gate, Winnipeg
A91

Vancouver Harbor
A92

Chateau de Ramezay, Montreal
A93

1938 *Perf. 12*

241 A89 10c dk carmine 9.00 .20
Never hinged 13.50
a. 10c carmine rose 9.00 .20
Never hinged 13.50
242 A90 13c deep blue 12.00 .60
Never hinged 18.00
243 A91 20c red brown 16.00 .45
Never hinged 24.00
244 A92 50c green 40.00 6.00
Never hinged 60.00
245 A93 $1 dull violet 80.00 7.75
Never hinged 120.00
a. Vert. pair, imperf., horiz. *4,750.*
Nos. 241-245 (5) 157.00 15.00
Nos. 241-245, never hinged 235.50

Imperf., Pairs

241b A89 10c dark carmine 450.00
Never hinged 675.00
241c A89 10c carmine rose 450.00
Never hinged 675.00
242a A90 13c 450.00
Never hinged 675.00
243a A91 20c 450.00
Never hinged 675.00
244a A92 50c 450.00
Never hinged 675.00
245b A93 $1 600.00
Never hinged 900.00

Princess Elizabeth and Princess Margaret Rose — A94

War Memorial, Ottawa — A95

King George VI and Queen Elizabeth
A96

Unwmk.

1939, May 15 **Engr.** *Perf. 12*

246 A94 1c green & black .25 .20
Never hinged .30
247 A95 2c brown & black .25 .20
Never hinged .30
248 A96 3c dk car & black .25 .20
Never hinged .30
Nos. 246-248 (3) .75 .60
Nos. 246-248, never hinged .90

Visit of George VI and Queen Elizabeth to Canada and the US.

Imperf., Pairs

246a A94 1c 550.00
Never hinged 800.00
247a A95 2c 550.00
Never hinged 800.00
248a A96 3c 550.00
Never hinged 800.00

A97

A98

King George VI
A99

Grain Elevators
A100

Farm Scene
A101

Parliament Buildings
A102

"Ram" Tank — A103

Corvette
A104

Munitions Factory
A105

Destroyer
A106

1942-43 **Engr.** *Perf. 12*

249 A97 1c green .30 .20
Never hinged .40
a. Booklet pane of 4 + 2 labels 3.50 *3.75*
Never hinged 5.25
b. Booklet pane of 6 5.00 *5.50*
Never hinged 7.50
c. Booklet pane of 3 2.50 *5.00*
Never hinged 3.75
250 A98 2c brown .40 .20
Never hinged .60
a. Booklet pane of 4 + 2 labels 7.00 *8.00*
Never hinged 10.50
b. Booklet pane of 6 10.50 *11.50*
Never hinged 16.00
d. Vert. strip of 3, imperf. horiz. *5,000.*
251 A99 3c dk carmine .60 .20
Never hinged .90
a. Booklet pane of 4 + 2 labels 4.25 *5.25*
Never hinged 6.50
252 A99 3c rose violet ('43) .40 .20
Never hinged .60
a. Booklet pane of 4 + 2 labels 3.25 *4.50*
Never hinged 5.00
b. Booklet pane of 3 3.25 *4.50*
Never hinged 4.75
c. Booklet pane of 6 3.50 *4.00*
Never hinged 5.25
253 A100 4c greenish black 1.25 .60
Never hinged 1.90
254 A98 4c dk car ('43) .60 .20
Never hinged .90
a. Booklet pane of 6 5.25 *10.00*
Never hinged 8.00
b. Booklet pane of 3 3.25 *4.50*
Never hinged 4.75
255 A97 5c deep blue 1.20 .20
Never hinged 1.80
256 A101 8c red brown 1.60 .50
Never hinged 2.40
257 A102 10c brown 4.50 .20
Never hinged 6.75
258 A103 13c dull green 5.00 3.60
Never hinged 7.50
259 A103 14c dull grn ('43) 7.00 .35
Never hinged 10.50
260 A104 20c chocolate 9.00 .20
Never hinged 13.50
261 A105 50c violet 30.00 1.75
Never hinged 45.00
262 A106 $1 deep blue 65.00 7.50
Never hinged 100.00
Nos. 249-262 (14) 126.85 15.90
Nos. 249-262, never hinged 192.75

Canada's contribution to the war effort of the Allied Nations.

No. 250d totally imperf horiz. is unique. Beware of strips with blind perfs; these sell for much less.

For overprints see Nos. O1-O4.

Imperf., Pairs

249d A97 1c 300.00
Never hinged 450.00
250c A98 2c 300.00
Never hinged 450.00
251b A99 3c 300.00
Never hinged 450.00
252d A99 3c 300.00
Never hinged 450.00
253a A100 4c 300.00
Never hinged 450.00
254c A98 4c 300.00
Never hinged 450.00
255a A97 5c 300.00
Never hinged 450.00
256a A100 8c 300.00
Never hinged 450.00
257a A102 10c 450.00
Never hinged 675.00
258a A103 13c 450.00
Never hinged 675.00
259a A103 14c 450.00
Never hinged 675.00
260a A104 20c 450.00
Never hinged 675.00
261a A105 50c 450.00
Never hinged 675.00
262a A106 $1 450.00
Never hinged 675.00

Types of 1942
Coil Stamps

1942-43 *Perf. 8 Vertically*

263 A97 1c green ('43) 1.30 .55
Never hinged 2.00
264 A98 2c brown 2.00 1.10
Never hinged 3.00
265 A99 3c dark carmine 2.00 1.10
Never hinged 3.00
266 A99 3c rose violet ('43) 3.25 .40
Never hinged 5.00
267 A98 4c dk carmine ('43) 5.00 .30
Never hinged 7.50
Nos. 263-267 (5) 13.55 3.45
Nos. 263-267, never hinged 20.50

See Nos. 278-281.

Catalogue values for unused stamps in this section, from this point to the end of the section, are for Never Hinged items.

Farm Scene, Ontario
A107

Great Bear Lake, Mackenzie
A108

Hydroelectric Station, Saint Maurice River
A109

Combine
A110

Logging, British Columbia
A111

Train Ferry, Prince Edward Island
A112

1946, Sept. 16 **Engr.** *Perf. 12*

268 A107 8c red brown 1.80 .60
269 A108 10c olive 2.40 .20
270 A109 14c black brown 4.00 .20
271 A110 20c slate black 5.50 .20
272 A111 50c dk blue green 24.00 1.50
273 A112 $1 red violet 47.50 3.00
Nos. 268-273 (6) 85.20 5.70

For overprints see Nos. O6-O10, O21-O23, O25.

Alexander Graham Bell — A113

1947, Mar. 3

274 A113 4c deep blue .30 .20

Birth centenary of Alexander Graham Bell.

Citizen of Canada — A114

1947, July 1

275 A114 4c deep blue .30 .20

Issued on the 80th anniv. of the Canadian Confederation, to mark the advent of Canadian Citizenship.

Princess Elizabeth — A115

1948, Feb. 16

276 A115 4c deep blue .25 .20

Marriage of Princess Elizabeth to Lieut. Philip Mountbatten, R. N., on Nov. 20, 1947.

Parliament Buildings Ottawa A116

1948, Oct. 1

277 A116 4c gray .25 .20

Centenary of Responsible Government.

George VI Types of 1942

Coil Stamps

1948 ***Perf. 9½ Vertically***

278 A97 1c green 6.00 2.00
279 A98 2c brown 20.00 8.50
280 A99 3c rose violet 11.50 2.00
281 A90 4c dark carmine 17.00 2.25
Nos. 278-281 (4) 54.50 14.75

John Cabot's Ship "Matthew" A117

1949, Apr. 1 **Engr.** ***Perf. 12***

282 A117 4c deep green .25 .20

Entry of Newfoundland into confederation with Canada.

"Founding of Halifax, 1749" A118

1949, June 21 **Unwmk.**

283 A118 4c purple .25 .20

200th anniv. of the founding of Halifax, Nova Scotia.

A119

A120

A121

A122

A123

1949, Nov. 15

284 A119 1c green .25 .20
a. Booklet pane of 3 ('50) .60 *1.25*
285 A120 2c sepia .30 .20
286 A121 3c rose violet .35 .20
a. Booklet pane of 3 ('50) 2.50 *6.50*
b. Booklet pane of 4 + 2 labels ('50) 3.25 *3.75*
287 A122 4c dk carmine .60 .20
a. Booklet pane of 3 ('50) 12.50 12.50
b. Booklet pane of 6 ('50) 18.00 18.00
288 A123 5c deep blue 1.25 .30
Nos. 284-288 (5) 2.75 1.10

Stamps from booklet panes of 3 are imperf. on 2 or 3 sides.

"POSTES POSTAGE" Omitted

1950, Jan. 19

289 A119 1c green .25 .20
290 A120 2c sepia .30 .20
291 A121 3c rose violet .30 .20
292 A122 4c dark carmine .30 .20
293 A123 5c deep blue 1.40 1.00
Nos. 289-293 (5) 2.55 1.80

See Nos. 295-300, 305-306, 309-310. For overprints see Nos. O12-O20.

Oil Wells, Alberta A124

1950, Mar. 1 **Engr.** ***Perf. 12***

294 A124 50c dull green 9.00 1.40

Development of oil wells in Canada. For overprints see Nos. O11, O24.

Types of 1949

Coil Stamps

"POSTES POSTAGE" Omitted

1950 ***Perf. 9½ Vertically***

295 A119 1c green .70 .30
296 A121 3c rose violet 1.10 .60

With "POSTES POSTAGE"

Perf. 9½ Vertically

297 A119 1c green .40 .20
298 A120 2c sepia 3.25 1.30
299 A121 3c rose violet 2.00 .20
300 A122 4c dark carmine 16.00 .70
Nos. 297-300 (4) 21.65 2.40

See note after No. 288.

Indians Drying Skins on Stretchers A125

1950, Oct. 2 ***Perf. 12***

301 A125 10c black brown .90 .20

Canada's fur resources. For overprint see No. O26.

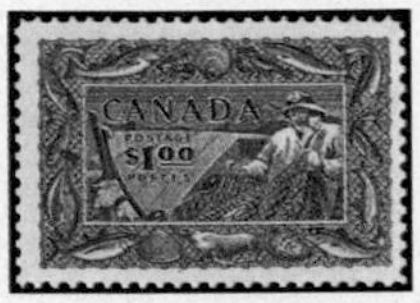

Fishing A126

1951, Feb. 1 **Unwmk.**

302 A126 $1 bright ultra 45.00 10.00

Canada's fish resources. For overprint see No. O27.

Sir Robert Laird Borden A127

William L. Mackenzie King A128

1951, June 25 ***Perf. 12***

303 A127 3c turquoise green .25 .20
304 A128 4c rose pink .30 .20

George VI Types of 1949

1951 ***Perf. 12***

305 A120 2c olive green .20 .20
306 A122 4c orange vermilion .25 .20
a. Booklet pane of 3 5.25 2.75
b. Booklet pane of 6 5.00 5.00

For overprints see Nos. O28-O29.

Coil Stamps

Perf. 9½ Vertically

309 A120 2c olive green 1.40 .60
310 A122 4c orange vermilion 2.75 .70

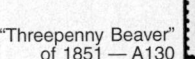

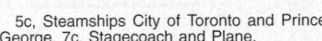

Trains of 1851 and 1951 — A129

"Threepenny Beaver" of 1851 — A130

5c, Steamships City of Toronto and Prince George. 7c, Stagecoach and Plane.

1951, Sept. 24 **Unwmk.** ***Perf. 12***

311 A129 4c dark gray .60 .20
312 A129 5c purple 1.80 1.25
313 A129 7c deep blue 1.10 .30
314 A130 15c bright red 1.20 .30
Nos. 311-314 (4) 4.70 2.05

Centenary of British North American postal administration.

Princess Elizabeth and Duke of Edinburgh A131

1951, Oct. 26 **Engr.**

315 A131 4c violet .20 .20

Visit of Princess Elizabeth, Duchess of Edinburgh and the Duke of Edinburgh to Canada and the US.

Symbols of Newsprint Paper Production A132

1952, Apr. 1 **Unwmk.** ***Perf. 12***

316 A132 20c gray 1.70 .20

Canada's paper production. For overprint see No. O30.

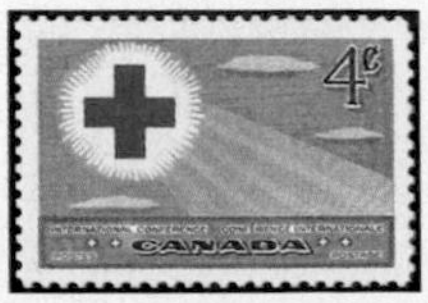

Red Cross on Sun — A133

1952, July 26 **Engr. and Litho.**

317 A133 4c blue & red .20 .20

18th Intl. Red Cross Conf., Toronto, July 1952.

Sir John J. C. Abbott A134

Alexander Mackenzie A135

1952, Nov. 3 **Engr.**

318 A134 3c rose lilac .20 .20
319 A135 4c orange vermilion .25 .20

Canada Goose A136

1952, Nov. 3

320 A136 7c blue .40 .20

For overprint see No. O31.

Pacific Coast Indian House and Totem Pole — A137

1953, Feb. 2

321 A137 $1 gray 7.00 .90

For overprint see No. O32.

Natl. Wildlife Week — A138

1953, Apr. 1

322 A138 2c Polar bear .20 .20
323 A138 3c Moose .25 .20
324 A138 4c Bighorn sheep .25 .20
Nos. 322-324 (3) .70 .60

Elizabeth II — A139

1953, May 1

325 A139 1c violet brown .20 .20
a. Booklet pane of 3 1.40 1.40
326 A139 2c green .20 .20
327 A139 3c carmine rose .20 .20
a. Booklet pane of 3 1.90 1.50
b. Booklet pane of 4 + 2 labels 1.40 *1.75*
328 A139 4c violet .25 .20
a. Booklet pane of 3 1.90 1.75
b. Booklet pane of 6 1.60 1.60
329 A139 5c ultramarine .25 .20
Nos. 325-329 (5) 1.10 1.00

Stamps from booklet panes of 3 are imperf. on 2 or 3 sides.

See Nos. 331-333. For overprints see Nos. O33-O37.

Coronation Issue

Queen Elizabeth II — A140

1953, June 1
330 A140 4c violet .20 .20

Coil Stamps

1953 ***Perf. 9½ Vertically***
331 A139 2c green 1.40 .90
332 A139 3c carmine rose 1.40 .90
333 A139 4c violet 3.25 1.40
Nos. 331-333 (3) 6.05 3.20

See note after No. 329.
Issued: 2c, 7/30; 3c, 7/27; 4c, 9/3.

Bobbin, Cloth and Spinning Wheel A141

1953, Nov. 2 ***Perf. 12***
334 A141 50c light green 3.25 .25

For overprint see No. O38.

Walrus A142

Beaver A143

1954, Apr. 1
335 A142 4c gray .30 .20
336 A143 5c ultramarine .35 .20
a. Booklet pane of 5 + label 1.75 1.50

National Wildlife Week, 1954.

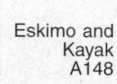

Elizabeth II A144

Gannet A145

1954-61
337 A144 1c violet brn .20 .20
a. Booklet pane of 5 + label ('56) 1.10 1.10
338 A144 2c green .20 .20
a. Pane of 25 ('61) 3.75 3.75
339 A144 3c carmine rose .20 .20
a. Horiz. pair, imperf. vert. *1,500.*
340 A144 4c violet .25 .20
a. Booklet pane of 5 + label ('56) 1.50 1.50
b. Booklet pane of 6 ('55) 3.00 3.00
341 A144 5c bright blue .25 .20
a. Booklet pane of 5 + label 1.20 1.20
b. Pane of 20 (5 x 4) ('61) 7.00 7.00
c. Horiz. pair, imperf. vert. *6,000.*
342 A144 6c orange .50 .20
343 A145 15c gray 1.50 .20
Nos. 337-343 (7) 3.10 1.40

Panes of 20 and 25 are imperf. on 4 sides.
Issued: 5c, 15c, 4/1; others, 6/10.
For overprints see Nos. O40-O44.

Luminescence

The overprinting of regular stamps with vertical luminescent bands began experimentally in 1962 when Nos. 337p-341p were released at Winnipeg. The bands are of varying number, position and chemical content.

Tagged varieties of stamps which were issued both untagged and with luminescent overprint are listed with suffix letter "p".

Tagged

1962, Jan. 13
337p A144 1c violet brown 1.30 .95
338p A144 2c green 1.30 .95
339p A144 3c carmine rose 1.30 .95
340p A144 4c violet 3.75 3.25
341p A144 5c bright blue 4.25 2.25
Nos. 337p-341p (5) 11.90 8.35

Coil Stamps

1954 ***Perf. 9½ Vertically***
345 A144 2c green .55 .20
347 A144 4c violet 1.60 .25
348 A144 5c bright blue 2.25 .20
Nos. 345-348 (3) 4.40 .65

Issued: 2c, 9/9; 3c, 8/23; 4c, 7/6.

Sir John Sparrow David Thompson A146

Sir Mackenzie Bowell A147

1954, Nov. 1 ***Perf. 12***
349 A146 4c violet .35 .20
350 A147 5c bright blue .35 .20

Eskimo and Kayak A148

1955, Feb. 21
351 A148 10c violet brown .40 .20

For overprint see No. O39.

Musk Ox — A149

Whooping Cranes A150

1955, Apr. 4
352 A149 4c purple .35 .20
353 A150 5c blue .40 .20

National Wildlife Week, April 10-16.

Torch, Dove and Maple Leaves — A151

1955, June 1 **Unwmk.**
354 A151 5c light blue .40 .20

ICAO, 10th anniversary.

Pioneer Settlers A152

1955, June 30 ***Perf. 12***
355 A152 5c ultramarine .40 .20

50th anniv. of the founding of the provinces of Alberta and Saskatchewan.

Globe and Scout Emblem A153

1955, Aug. 20 **Engr.**
356 A153 5c green & org brown .40 .20

8th Boy Scout World Jamboree, Niagara-on-the-Lake, Ont.

Richard Bedford Bennett A154

Sir Charles Tupper A155

1955, Nov. 8
357 A154 4c violet .35 .20
358 A155 5c ultramarine .35 .20

Ice Hockey Players A156

1956, Jan. 23
359 A156 5c ultramarine .35 .20

Issued to publicize Canada's most popular winter sport.

Caribou A157

Mountain Goat A158

1956, Apr. 12
360 A157 4c deep violet .40 .20
361 A158 5c ultramarine .40 .20

National Wildlife Week, 1956.

"Paper Industry" A159

"Chemical Industry" — A160

1956, June 7 **Engr.**
362 A159 20c green 1.40 .20
363 A160 25c red 1.50 .20

For overprint see No. O45.

House on Fire — A161

1956, Oct. 9 **Unwmk.** ***Perf. 12***
364 A161 5c gray & red .35 .20

Issued to emphasize the needless waste caused by preventable fires.

Canada's Outdoor Recreation Facilities A162

1957, Mar. 7
365 A162 5c Fishing .40 .20
366 A162 5c Swimming .40 .20
367 A162 5c Hunter and dog .40 .20
368 A162 5c Skiing .40 .20
a. Block of 4, #365-368 1.60 1.10

All four designs are printed alternating in sheet of 50, with various combinations possible.

Loon — A163

1957, Apr. 10 ***Perf. 12***
369 A163 5c black .35 .20

David Thompson and Map of Western Canada A164

1957, June 5 **Unwmk.**
370 A164 5c ultramarine .35 .20

David Thompson (1770-1857), explorer and geographer.

Parliament Building, Ottawa — A165

Post Horn and Globe A166

1957, Aug. 14 ***Perf. 12***
371 A165 5c dark blue .35 .20
372 A166 15c dark blue 2.10 1.90

UPU, 14th Congress, Ottawa, Aug. 1957.

Miner With Pneumatic Drill — A167

1957, Sept. 5
373 A167 5c black .30 .20

Canada's mining industry; 6th Commonwealth Mining and Metallurgical Congress, Vancouver, Sept. 8-Oct. 8.

Elizabeth II and Prince Philip — A168

1957, Oct. 10 **Unwmk.**
374 A168 5c black .30 .20

Visit of Queen Elizabeth II and Prince Philip to Canada, Oct. 12-16.

Newspapers and Symbols of Industry A169

1958, Jan. 22 **Engr.**
375 A169 5c black .35 .20

Canadian press; the importance of a free press.

Microscope and Globe — A170

1958, Mar. 5 ***Perf. 12***
376 A170 5c blue .35 .20

Intl. Geophysical Year, 1957-1958.

Miner Panning Gold — A171

1958, May 8 **Unwmk.**
377 A171 5c bluish green .35 .20

Province of British Columbia, cent.

La Verendrye A172

1958, June 4 ***Perf. 12***
378 A172 5c bright ultra .35 .20

Pierre Gaultier de Varenne, Sieur de la Verendrye, 18th century French explorer of Western Canada.

Champlain and View of Quebec A173

1958, June 26
379 A173 5c dk green & bis brn .35 .20

Founding of Quebec, 350th anniv.

Nurse — A174

1958, July 30 **Engr.**
380 A174 5c rose lilac .35 .20

Importance of health, both to the individual and to the nation.

Kerosene Lamp and Refinery — A175

1958, Sept. 10 ***Perf. 12***
381 A175 5c olive & red .35 .20

Centennial of Canada's oil industry.

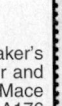

Speaker's Chair and Mace A176

1958, Oct. 2
382 A176 5c slate blue .35 .20

Bicentennial of the meeting of the first House of Representatives in Canada, Halifax, Oct. 2, 1758.

"Silver Dart" and Delta Wing Planes A177

1959, Feb. 23 ***Perf. 12***
383 A177 5c blue & black .35 .20

50th anniv. of the 1st airplane flight in Canada near Baddeck, N. S., with J. A. D. McCurdy as pilot.

Globe and Dove — A178

1959, Apr. 2
384 A178 5c violet blue .35 .20

NATO, 10th anniversary.

Woman Tending Tree — A179

1959, May 13
385 A179 5c apple green & blk .35 .20

Associated Country Women of the World.

Elizabeth II — A180

1959, June 18
386 A180 5c dark carmine .35 .20

Visit of Queen Elizabeth and Prince Philip to Canada, June 18-Aug. 1.

Great Lakes, Maple Leaf and Eagle Emblems A181

1959, June 26 **Engr.**
387 A181 5c red & blue .35 .20
a. Center inverted 12,000. 10,000.

Opening of the St. Lawrence Seaway, June 26, 1959.
See United States No. 1131.

British Lion, Fleur-de-Lis and Maple Leaves A182

1959, Sept. 10 ***Perf. 12***
388 A182 5c crim rose & dk green .35 .20

Bicentenary of the Battle of the Plains of Abraham.

Girl Guide Emblem — A183

1960, Apr. 20 **Unwmk.**
389 A183 5c brown org & ultra .35 .20

Canadian Girl Guides Assoc., 50th anniv.

Dollard des Ormeaux and Battle Scene — A184

1960, May 19
390 A184 5c ultra & bis brown .35 .20

Battle of the Long Sault, 300th anniv.

Compass Rose, Earth Mover and Surveyor A185

Emily Pauline Johnson A186

1961, Feb. 8 **Engr.** ***Perf. 12***
391 A185 5c green & vermilion .35 .20

Development of Canada's Northland.

1961, Mar. 10
392 A186 5c green & red .35 .20

Emily Pauline Johnson (1861-1913), Mohawk princess and poet.

Arthur Meighen — A187

1961, Apr. 19
393 A187 5c ultramarine .35 .20

Arthur Meighen, Prime Minister of Canada, (1920-21, 1926).

Power Plant and Men Holding Blueprint A188

1961, June 28 **Unwmk.** ***Perf. 12***
394 A188 5c lt red brn & blue .35 .20

10th anniv. of the Colombo Plan, initiated to assist underdeveloped countries by providing trained manpower and resources.

Natural Resources and Hands Holding Cogwheel — A189

1961, Oct. 12 **Engr.** ***Perf. 12***
395 A189 5c brown & blue grn .35 .20

Canada's "Resources for Tomorrow Program" and to publicize the close link between industry and the country's renewable natural resources.

Young Adults and Education Symbols — A190

1962, Feb. 28 **Unwmk.** ***Perf. 12***
396 A190 5c black & lt red brn .35 .20
a. Light red brown (symbols) omitted

Issued to stimulate public awareness of the importance of education.

Scottish Settler and Lord Selkirk A191

1962, May 3 ***Perf. 12***
397 A191 5c lt green & vio brn .35 .20

150th anniv. of the Red River Settlement in Western Canada (Prairie Provinces).

Jean Talon Presenting Gifts to Young Farm Couple — A192

1962, June 13 **Unwmk.** ***Perf. 12***
398 A192 5c dark blue .35 .20

Jean Talon, administrator of New France (Canada), 1665-1668.

British Columbia Legislative Building and Stamp of 1860 — A193

1962, Aug. 22 **Engr.** ***Perf. 12***
399 A193 5c black & rose .35 .20

Centenary of Victoria as incorporated city.

Arms of the Provinces A194

1962, Aug. 31

400 A194 5c brown orange & black .35 .20

Official opening of the Trans-Canada Highway, Rogers Pass, Glacier National Park, Sept. 4.

Queen Elizabeth II and Wheat — A195

Designs (Symbol in upper left corner): 1c, Mineral crystals. 2c, Tree. 3c, Fish. 4c, Electric high tension tower.

1962-63 Engr. *Perf. 12*

401 A195 1c dp brn ('63) .20 .20
a. Booklet pane of 5 + label ('63) 3.00 3.00
402 A195 2c green ('63) .20 .20
a. Pane of 25 ('63) 8.00 8.00
403 A195 3c purple ('63) .20 .20
404 A195 4c carmine ('63) .20 .20
a. Booklet pane of 5 + label ('63) 3.00 3.00
b. Pane of 25 ('63) 12.00 12.00
405 A195 5c violet blue .25 .20
a. Booklet pane of 5 + label ('63) 3.00 3.00
b. Pane of 20 ('63) 14.00 14.00
c. Imperf., pair (#405b) *3,500.*
d. Vert. pair, imperf. horiz. *4,000.* *575.00*
Nos. 401-405 (5) 1.05 1.00

Nos. 402a, 404b, and 405b are imperf. on four sides.

Used examples of No. 405d are canceled "Gonor, MB." Beware of examples with traces of blind perfs; a certificate of authenticity is recommended.

Issued: 5c, 10/3; 1c, 4c, 2/4/63; 2c, 3c, 5/2/63.

For overprints see Nos. O46-O49.

Tagged

1963

401p A195 1c deep brown .20 .20
402p A195 2c green .20 .20
403p A195 3c purple .25 .20
404p A195 4c carmine .80 .50
405p A195 5c violet blue .50 .25
q. Pane of 20 42.50 42.50
Nos. 401p-405p (5) 1.95 1.35

See note after No. 343.

Coil Stamps

1962-63 *Perf. 9½ Horiz.*

406 A195 2c green 4.25 2.25
407 A195 3c purple 3.00 1.75
408 A195 4c carmine 4.25 2.25
a. Pair, imperf between *3,000.*
409 A195 5c violet blue 4.25 .90
Nos. 406-409 (4) 15.75 7.15

No. 408a is valued in the grade of fine. Beware of dangerous fakes; a certificate of authenticity is necessary.

Issued: 5c, 10/3; 4c, 2/4/63; 2c, 3c, 5/2/63.

Sir Casimir Stanislaus Gzowski (1813-98), Engineer, Soldier and Educator — A196

1963, Mar. 5 Unwmk. *Perf. 12*

410 A196 5c rose lilac .30 .20

Export Crate and Mercator Map — A197

1963, June 14 Unwmk. *Perf. 12*

411 A197 $1 rose carmine 10.00 2.00

Sir Martin Frobisher (1535-1594), Explorer and Discoverer of Frobisher Bay — A198

1963, Aug. 21 Engr.

412 A198 5c ultramarine .30 .20

Postrider and First Land Mail Routes A199

1963, Sept. 25

413 A199 5c green & red brn .30 .20

Bicentennial of the 1st regular postal service between Quebec, Three Rivers & Montreal.

Jet at Ottawa Airport — A200

Canada Geese — A201

1963-64

414 A200 7c blue ('64) .50 .40
415 A201 15c deep ultra 1.80 .20

See No. 436. For surcharge see No. 430.

"Peace on Earth" — A202

1964, Apr. 8 Engr. & Litho.

416 A202 5c grnsh blue, Prus bl & ocher .30 .20

Issued to promote world peace.

Three-Maple-Leaf Emblem (Canadian Unity) — A203

White Trillium and Arms of Ontario A204

#419, White garden lily and arms of Quebec. #420, Mayflower (trailing arbutus) and arms of Nova Scotia. #421, Purple violet and arms of New Brunswick. #422, Prairie crocus and arms of Manitoba. #423, Dogwood and arms of British Columbia. #424, Lady's slipper and arms of Prince Edward Island. #425, Prairie lily and arms of Saskatchewan. #426, Wild rose and arms of Alberta. #427, Pitcher plant and arms of Newfoundland. #428, Fireweed and arms of Yukon. #429, Mountain avens and arms of Northwest Territories. #429A, Maple leaf and arms of Canada.

1964-66 Engr. & Litho. *Perf. 12*

417 A203 5c lt blue & dk car .25 .20
418 A204 5c red brn, buff & green .25 .20
419 A204 5c grn, yel & org .25 .20
420 A204 5c blue, pink & grn .25 .20
421 A204 5c car, green & vio .25 .20
422 A204 5c red brn, lil & dl grn .25 .20
423 A204 5c lilac, grn & bis .25 .20
424 A204 5c vio, grn & dp rose .25 .20
425 A204 5c sepia, org & grn .25 .20
426 A204 5c dl grn, yel & car .25 .20
427 A204 5c black, grn & car .25 .20
428 A204 5c dk bl, rose & grn .25 .20
429 A204 5c ol, yel & green .25 .20
429A A204 5c dk blue & dp red .25 .20
Nos. 417-429A (14) 3.50 2.80

Issued: #417, 5/14/64; #418-419, 6/30/64; #420-421, 2/3/65; #422-423, 4/28/65; #424, 7/21/65; #425-426, 1/19/66; #427, 2/23/66; #428-429, 3/23/66; #429A, 6/30/66.

No. 414 Surcharged

1964, July 15 Engr.

430 A200 8c on 7c blue .45 .25
a. Pair, one without surcharge *12,000.*
b. Surcharge on reverse, inverted *4,000.*

Nos. 430a and 430b are each unique.

Fathers of Confederation Memorial, Charlottetown — A205

1964, July 29 Engr.

431 A205 5c black .30 .20

Centenary of the Charlottetown, P.E.I., Conference, Sept. 1-9, 1864, which led to the creation of the Canadian nation in 1867.

Maple Leaf and Hand Holding Quill Pen — A206

1964, Sept. 9 Unwmk. *Perf. 12*

432 A206 5c dark brown & rose .30 .20

Centenary of the Quebec Conference, Oct. 10-27, 1864, which led to the creation of the Canadian nation.

Elizabeth II A207

Family and Star of Bethlehem A208

1964, Oct. 5 Engr.

433 A207 5c claret .25 .20

Queen Elizabeth's visit, Oct. 6-13.

1964, Oct. 14 *Perf. 12*

434 A208 3c red .20 .20
a. Pane of 25 8.00 8.00
p. Tagged .70 .35
q. As "a," tagged 12.50 12.50
435 A208 5c blue .25 .20
p. Tagged 1.20 .40

Panes of 25 are imperf. on four sides.

Jet Type of 1964

1964, Nov. 18 Unwmk. *Perf. 12*

436 A200 8c blue .40 .20

Maple Leaf and ICY Emblem A209

1965, Mar. 3 Engr. *Perf. 12*

437 A209 5c slate green .25 .20

International Cooperation Year.

Sir Wilfred Grenfell at Wheel of Hospital Ship Strathcona II A210

1965, June 9 Engr. *Perf. 12*

438 A210 5c Prussian blue .25 .20

Sir Wilfred Grenfell, author, medical missionary and founder of the Grenfell Mission, birth cent.

Canada's Maple Leaf Flag, 1965 A211

1965, June 30 Unwmk.

439 A211 5c blue & red .25 .20

Winston Churchill — A212

1965, Aug. 12 Litho. *Perf. 12*

440 A212 5c brown .25 .20

Sir Winston Spencer Churchill (1874-1965).

Peace Tower, Ottawa — A213

1965, Sept. 8 Engr. *Perf. 12*

441 A213 5c slate green .25 .20

Meeting of the Inter-Parliamentary Union, Ottawa, Sept. 8-17.

Parliament and Ottawa River A214

1965, Sept. 8

442 A214 5c brown .25 .20

Centenary of the final selection of Ottawa as national capital.

Gifts of the Wise Men — A215

1965, Oct. 13 **Engr.**

443 A215 3c olive .20 .20
a. Pane of 25 6.50 6.50
p. Tagged .25 .20
q. As "a," tagged 8.75 8.75
444 A215 5c violet blue .20 .20
p. Tagged .35 .20

Christmas. Panes of 25 are imperf. on four sides.

Alouette II Orbiting Globe — A216

1966, Jan. 5 **Unwmk.** ***Perf. 12***

445 A216 5c dark violet blue .25 .20

Launching (in California) of the Canadian satellite Alouette II, Nov. 28, 1965, as part of the Canadian-American program of space research.

La Salle, Map of 17th Century Canada, Ship, Canoe, Spyglass and Compass — A217

1966, Apr. 13 **Engr.** ***Perf. 12***

446 A217 5c blue green .25 .20

Tercentenary of the arrival in Canada of Rene Robert Cavelier, Sieur de La Salle (1643-1687).

Traffic Signs — A218

1966, May 2

447 A218 5c black, blue & yel .25 .20

Issued to publicize traffic safety.

House of Commons, Thames River and Canadian Delegates A219

1966, May 26

448 A219 5c brown .25 .20

Centenary of the London Conf., Dec. 4, 1866, which resulted in the British North America Act.

Atomic Reactor, Heavy Water Atom Symbol and Microscope A220

1966, July 27 **Engr.** ***Perf. 12***

449 A220 5c deep ultra .25 .20

Peaceful uses of atomic power. The design shows a stylized view of the Douglas Point Nuclear Power Station, Lake Huron, Ontario.

Parliamentary Library, Ottawa — A221

Praying Hands, by Albrecht Dürer — A222

1966, Sept. 8 **Engr.** ***Perf. 12***

450 A221 5c plum .25 .20

12th General Conf. of the Commonwealth Parliamentary Assoc., Ottawa, Sept. 8-Oct. 5.

1966, Oct. 12 **Engr.** ***Perf. 12***

451 A222 3c carmine rose .20 .20
a. Pane of 25 4.00 4.00
p. Tagged .20 .20
q. As "a," tagged 5.00 5.00
452 A222 5c orange .20 .20
p. Tagged .45 .25

Christmas. Panes of 25 are imperf. on four sides.

Canadian Flag over Globe and Centennial Emblem — A223

1967, Jan. 11 **Engr.** ***Perf. 12***

453 A223 5c blue & red .25 .20
p. Tagged .35 .30

Canada's centenary as a nation.

Northern Lights and Dog Team — A224

"Alaska Highway" by A. Y. Jackson A225

Two types of 6c black:

Type I

Type II

Designs: 2c, Totem pole (Pacific Area). 3c, Combine and oil rig (Prairie Region). 4c, Ship in lock (Central Canada). 5c, Lobster traps and boat (Atlantic Provinces). 6c, Transportation means. 10c, "The Jack Pine" by Tom Thomson. 15c, "Bylot Island" by Lawren Harris. 20c, "The Ferry, Quebec" by James Wilson Morrice. 25c, "The Solemn Land" by J. E. H. MacDonald. 50c, "Summer's Stores" by John Ensor (grain elevators). $1, Oilfield near Edmonton, by H. G. Glyde.

1967-72 **Engr.** ***Perf. 12***

454 A224 1c brown .20 .20
a. Booklet pane of 5 + label .45 .45
b. Bklt. pane, 1 #454d, 4 #459 + label, perf. 10 ('68) 3.00 2.50
c. Bklt. pane, 5 #454d + 5 #457d, perf. 10 ('68) 1.75 1.75
d. Perf. 10 ('68) .25 .20
e. Perf. 12½x12 ('71) .20 .20
f. Printed on gummed side *925.00*
455 A224 2c green .20 .20
a. Bklt. pane, 4 #455, 4 #456 with gutter btwn. ('70) 1.60 1.60
456 A224 3c dull purple .20 .20
a. Perf. 12½x12 ('71) .75 .30
457 A224 4c car rose .20 .20
a. Booklet pane of 5 + label 1.10 1.10
b. Pane of 25 (5x5) 25.00 22.50
c. Booklet pane of 25 + 2 labels, perf. 10 ('68) 8.00 7.50
d. Perf. 10 .50 .20
458 A224 5c blue .20 .20
a. Booklet pane of 5 + label 5.25 5.25
b. Pane of 20 35.00 32.50
c. Bklt. pane of 20, perf. 10 ('68) 8.00 8.00
d. Perf. 10 .60 .20
459 A224 6c org, perf. 10 .25 .20
a. Bklt. pane of 25 + 2 labels, perf. 10 ('68) 8.00 8.00
b. Perf. 12½x12 ('69) .25 .20
460 A224 6c black (I), perf. 12½x12 .20 .20
a. Bklt. pane of 25 + 2 labels (I), perf. 10 ('70) 12.00 8.00
b. As "a," perf. 12½x12 16.00 13.00
c. Type II, perf. 12½x12 .40 .20
d. As "c," booklet pane of 4 3.50 3.25
e. As "d," perf. 10 ('70) 11.00 6.50
f. Type II, perf. 12 ('72) .40 .20
g. Type I, perf. 10 1.60 .30
h. Type II, perf. 10 2.00 .65
i. As "f," printed on gummed side 20.00
461 A225 8c violet brown .25 .20
462 A225 10c olive green .25 .20
463 A225 15c dull purple .50 .20
464 A225 20c dark blue .55 .20
465 A225 25c slate green 1.60 .20
465A A225 50c brown org 3.75 .20
465B A225 $1 carmine rose 6.00 .75
Nos. 454-465B (14) 14.35 3.35

Nos. 454d, 454e, 456a, 457d, 458d, 460c, 460g and 460h are from booklet panes.

Issued: #459, 11/1/68; #460, 1/7/70; others, 2/8/67.

See Nos. 543-544, 549-550.

Tagged

454p A224 1c brown .25 .20
ep. Perf. 12½x12 ('71) .30 .20
455p A224 2c green .25 .20
456p A224 3c dull purple .20 .20
457p A224 4c car rose .60 .20
458p A224 5c blue .60 .20
bp. Pane of 20 60.00 50.00
459p A224 6c org, perf. 10 .60 .20
bp. Perf. 12½x12 ('69) .75 .30
460p A224 6c black (I), perf. 12½x12 .35 .20
cp. Type II ('70) .45 .50
fp. As "cp," perf. 12 ('72) .25 .20
462p A225 10c olive green .90 .35
463p A225 15c dull purple .90 .35
464p A225 20c dark blue 1.60 .55
465p A225 25c slate green 7.00 2.00
Nos. 454p-465p (11) 13.25 4.65

Nos. 454ep and 460cp are from booklet panes Nos. 544q-544s.

Issued: 1c-5c, 2/8/67; #459p, 11/1/68; #460p, 1/7/70; others, 12/9/69.

See note after No. 343.

Coil Stamps

1967-70 ***Perf. 9½ Horiz.***

466 A224 3c dull purple 3.75 .85
467 A224 4c carmine rose 1.10 .50
468 A224 5c blue 2.25 .65

Perf. 10 Horiz.

468A A224 6c orange .50 .20
c. Imperf., pair 325.00
468B A224 6c black, die II .45 .20
d. Imperf., pair 2,750.
Nos. 466-468B (5) 8.05 2.40

Horizontal pairs or blocks of Nos. 468A and 468B may be found with a fine vertical score line between the stamps. These sell for little more than vertical pairs or strips.

Issued: #468A, 1/69; #468B, 8/70; others, 2/8/67.

EXPO '67 Emblem and Canadian Pavilion A226

1967, Apr. 28 **Engr.** ***Perf. 12***

469 A226 5c blue & red .25 .20

EXPO '67, Intl. Exhib., Montreal, Apr. 28-Oct. 27.

Symbolic Woman and Ballot — A227

1967, May 24 **Litho.** ***Perf. 12***

470 A227 5c black & rose lilac .25 .20

50th anniversary of woman suffrage.

Elizabeth II — A228

1967, June 30 **Engr.** ***Perf. 12***

471 A228 5c deep org & purple .25 .20

Centennial Year visit of Queen Elizabeth II and the Duke of Edinburgh.

Runner A229

1967, July 19 **Engr.** ***Perf. 12***

472 A229 5c red .25 .20

Pan-American Games, Winnipeg, Manitoba, July 22-Aug. 7.

Globe and Flash A230

1967, Aug. 31 **Unwmk.**

473 A230 5c deep ultra .25 .20

50th anniv. of the Canadian Press, news gathering and distributing service.

Georges Philias Vanier A231

Engr. & Litho.

1967, Sept. 15 ***Perf. 12***

474 A231 5c black .25 .20

Georges Philias Vanier (1888-1967), Governor General of Canada, 1959-1967.

Toronto in 1967 and Citizens of 1867 — A232

1967, Sept. 28 **Engr.**

475 A232 5c sl grn & sal pink .25 .20

Centenary of Toronto as capital of Ontario.

Singing Children and Peace Tower, Ottawa — A233

1967, Oct. 11 **Engr.** ***Perf. 12***

476 A233 3c carmine .20 .20
a. Pane of 25 4.00 4.00
p. Tagged .20 .20
q. As "a" tagged 4.50 4.50
477 A233 5c green .20 .20
p. Tagged .30 .20

Christmas. Panes of 25 are imperf. on four sides.

Gray Jays — A234

1968, Feb. 15 **Litho.**
478 A234 5c green, blk & red .45 .20

Weather Map and Composite of Instruments A235

1968, Mar. 13 ***Perf. 11***
479 A235 5c dk & lt blue, yel & red .25 .20

200th anniv. of Canada's first long-term fixed point weather observations at Fort Prince of Wales, Churchill, by William Wales and Joseph Dymond.

Male Narwhal A236

1968, Apr. 10 **Litho.** ***Perf. 11***
480 A236 5c multicolored .30 .20

Weighing Rain Gauge, World Map and Maple Leaf A237

1968, May 8 **Litho.** ***Perf. 11***
481 A237 5c multicolored .25 .20

Intl. Hydrological Decade, 1965-74.

The Nonsuch A238

Photo. & Engr.
1968, June 5 ***Perf. 10***
482 A238 5c dk blue & multi .25 .20

300th anniv. of the voyage of the Nonsuch which opened the way to Canada's West through the fur trade.

Contemporary and Indian Lacrosse Players — A239

1968, July 3 **Photo. & Engr.**
483 A239 5c yel, black & red .25 .20

George Brown, "Globe" Front Page and Legislature, Prince Edward Island A240

1968, Aug. 21 ***Perf. 10***
484 A240 5c multicolored .25 .20

George Brown (1818-1880), founder of Toronto "Globe" and political leader.

Henri Bourassa and Newspaper Page — A241

Canadian Memorial, Near Vimy, France — A242

Litho. & Engr.
1968, Sept. 4 ***Perf. 12***
485 A241 5c ver, buff & black .25 .20

Henri Bourassa (1868-1952), jounalist and statesman.

1968, Oct. 15 **Engr.** ***Perf. 12***
486 A242 15c slate 1.90 1.10

50th anniv. of the Armistice which ended WWI. The stamp shows "The Defenders and the Breaking of the Sword," a detail from the memorial designed by W. S. Allward.

John McCrae and "Flanders Fields" A243

1968, Oct. 15 **Litho. & Engr.**
487 A243 5c multicolored .25 .20

50th death anniv. of Lt. Col. John McCrae (1872-1918), author of "In Flanders Fields."

Eskimo Family, Carving — A244

1968, Nov. **Photo.** ***Perf. 12***

Eskimo soapstone carving: 6c, Mother and infant, by Munamee of Cape Dorset.

488	A244 5c brt blue & black	.20	.20
a.	Booklet pane of 10	3.25	3.25
p.	Tagged	.20	.20
q.	As "a," tagged	4.00	4.00
489	A244 6c dp bister & black	.20	.20
p.	Tagged	.25	.20

Christmas. Issued: 5c, Nov. 1; 6c, Nov. 15.

Curling A245

Photo. & Engr.
1969, Jan. 15 ***Perf. 10***
490 A245 6c black, brt blue & car .20 .20

Vincent Massey — A246

Litho. & Engr.
1969, Feb. 20 ***Perf. 12***
491 A246 6c yel olive & dk brn .25 .20

Vincent Massey (1887-1967), 1st Canadian-born Gov. General of Canada, 1952-59.

Return from the Harvest Field, by Aurele de Foy Suzor-Cote A247

1969, Mar. 14 **Photo.**
492 A247 50c multicolored 3.25 2.25

Aurele de Foy Suzor-Cote (1869-1937), painter.

Globe and Tools of Various Trades A248

1969, May 21 **Engr.** ***Perf. 12x12½***
493 A248 6c dk olive green .25 .20

50th anniv. of the ILO.

Vickers Vimy, 1919, and Map of the Atlantic A249

1969, June 13 **Photo. and Engr.**
494 A249 15c red brn, yel grn & lt ultra 1.75 1.50

50th anniv. of the first non-stop Atlantic flight from Newfoundland to Ireland of Capt. John Alcock and Lt. Arthur Whitten Brown.

Sir William Osler — A250

Ipswich Sparrow A251

1969, June 23 ***Perf. 12½x12***
495 A250 6c dk blue & lt red brn .25 .20

Osler (1849-1919), physician, professor of physiology and pathology in Canada, US and England.

1969, July 23 **Litho.** ***Perf. 12***

Birds: 6c, White-throated sparrows, vert. 25c, Hermit thrush.

496	A251 6c multicolored	.35	.20
497	A251 10c ultra & multi	.70	.40
498	A251 25c black & multi	1.75	1.50
	Nos. 496-498 (3)	2.80	2.10

Map of Prince Edward Island A252

Photo. & Engr.
1969, Aug. 15 ***Perf. 12x12½***
499 A252 6c ultra, org brn & black .25 .20

Bicentenary of Charlottetown as capital of Prince Edward Island.

Flags of Summer and Winter Canada Games — A253

Litho. & Engr.
1969, Aug. 15 ***Perf. 12***
500 A253 6c ultra, brt green & red .25 .20

1st Canada Summer Games, Halifax and Dartmouth, N.S., Aug. 16-24.

Sir Isaac Brock and Memorial Queenston Heights — A254

1969, Sept. 12 **Litho. and Engr.**
501 A254 6c yel brown, brn & pale sal .25 .20

Major General Sir Isaac Brock (1769-1812), administrator of Upper Canada and leader in the war of 1812.

Children of Various Races — A255

1969, Oct. 8 **Litho.** ***Perf. 12***

502	A255 5c blue & multi	.20	.20
a.	Booklet pane of 10	3.00	3.00
p.	Tagged	.25	.20
q.	As "a" tagged	4.00	
503	A255 6c red & multi	.20	.20
a.	Black (inscriptions & frame line) omitted	2,250.	1,750.
p.	Tagged	.25	.20

Christmas.

Stephen Leacock, Comedy Mask and Mariposa View A256

Photo. & Engr.
1969, Nov. 12 ***Perf. 12x12½***
504 A256 6c multicolored .25 .20

Stephen Butler Leacock (1869-1944), humorist, historian and economist.

Manitoba, Crossroads of Canada A257

1970, Jan. 27 Litho. *Perf. 12*

505 A257 6c violet blue & multi .25 .20
p. Tagged .35 .20

Centenary of the province of Manitoba.

Enchanted Owl, by Kenojuak — A258

1970, Jan. 27 Engr. *Perf. 12*

506 A258 6c dark red & black .25 .20

Centenary of Nortwest Territories.

Microscopic View of Inside of Leaf A259

1970, Feb. 18 Photo. & Engr.

507 A259 6c green, lt org & blue .25 .20

Canada's participation in the Intl. Biological Program, 1967-1972.

Emblems of EXPO '67 and '70 — A260

EXPO '70 Emblem and Dogwood, British Columbia A261

Designs: No. 510, EXPO '70 emblem and white garden lily, Quebec. No. 511, EXPO '70 emblem and white trillium, Ontario.

1970, Mar. 18 Litho. *Perf. 12*

508 A260 25c red emblem 2.00 2.00
p. Tagged 2.25 2.25
509 A261 25c violet emblem 2.00 2.00
p. Tagged 2.25 2.25
510 A261 25c green emblem 2.00 2.00
p. Tagged 2.25 2.25
511 A261 25c blue emblem 2.00 2.00
p. Tagged 2.25 2.25
a. Block of 4, #508-511 8.00 8.00
b. As "a," tagged 10.00 10.00
Nos. 508-511 (4) 8.00 8.00

EXPO '70 Intl. Exhibition, Osaka, Japan, Mar. 15-Sept. 13. Nos. 508-511 printed se-tenant in sheets of 50 (5x10), with various combinations possible.

Henry Kelsey A262

Photo. & Engr.

1970, Apr. 15 *Perf. 12x12½*

512 A262 6c multicolored .25 .20

300th birth anniv. of Henry Kelsey, explorer of Canada's western plains.

"A Divided World, with Energy Focused on Unification..." — A263

1970, May 13 Litho. *Perf. 11*

513 A263 10c blue .70 .55
p. Tagged .85 .85
514 A263 15c lilac & dk red 1.10 .70
p. Tagged 1.50 1.50

25th anniversary of the United Nations.

Louis Riel A264

Mackenzie Rock, Dean Channel A265

1970, June 19 Photo. *Perf. 12½x12*

515 A264 6c red & brt blue .25 .20

Louis Riel (1844-1885), Metis leader who became president of the Council of Assiniboin in 1870.

1970, June 25 Engr. *Perf. 12*

516 A265 6c brown .25 .20

Sir Alexander Mackenzie (1764-1820), Scottish explorer who in 1793 completed the first crossing of the North American continent north of Mexico.

Sir Oliver Mowat and Parliament, Ottawa A266

Photo. & Engr.

1970, Aug. 12 *Perf. 12x12½*

517 A266 6c red & black .25 .20

Sir Oliver Mowat (1820-1903), government leader and a Father of Confederation.

Isle of Spruce, by Arthur Lismer A267

1970, Sept. 18 Litho. *Perf. 11*

518 A267 6c multicolored .25 .20

50th anniv. of "The Group of Seven," Canadian landscape artists.

Santa Claus — A268

Christ Child — A269

Child in the Manger and Star-studded Sky — A270

Christmas: Designs by Canadian School Children.

1970, Oct. 7 Litho. *Perf. 12*

519 A268 5c Santa Claus .30 .20
520 A268 5c Horse-drawn Sleigh .30 .20
521 A268 5c Nativity .30 .20
522 A268 5c Children Skiing .30 .20
523 A268 5c Snowmen and Christmas Tree .30 .20
a. Strip of 5, #519-523 2.75 2.25
524 A269 6c Christ Child .40 .20
525 A269 6c Christmas Tree and Children .40 .20
526 A269 6c Toy Store .40 .20
527 A269 6c Santa Claus .40 .20
528 A269 6c Church .40 .20
a. Strip of 5, #524-528 3.25 2.50
529 A270 10c Christ Child .40 .35
530 A270 15c Snowmobile and Trees .90 .90
Nos. 519-530 (12) 4.80 3.25

Tagged

519p A268 5c multicolored .35 .25
520p A268 5c multicolored .35 .25
521p A268 5c multicolored .35 .25
522p A268 5c multicolored .35 .25
523p A268 5c multicolored .35 .25
ap. Strip of 5, #519p-523p 3.25 2.75
524p A269 6c multicolored .40 .25
525p A269 6c multicolored .40 .25
526p A269 6c multicolored .40 .25
527p A269 6c multicolored .40 .25
528p A269 6c multicolored .40 .25
ap. Strip of 5, #524p-528p 4.50 3.00
529p A270 10c multicolored .50 .50
530p A270 15c multicolored 1.10 1.10
Nos. 519p-530p (12) 5.35 4.10

Christmas.

The sheets of 100 of both 5c and 6c contain all 5 designs, generally alternating, and arranged to permit vertical and horizontal pairs of each design in the two center vertical and horizontal rows. The center block of 4 is entirely of No. 522 (5c) and 525 (6c). The sheet may also be broken to provide 20 strips of 5, each stamp of different design.

Sir Donald Alexander Smith — A271

1970, Nov. 4 Litho. *Perf. 12*

531 A271 6c dk grn, yel & black .25 .20

Smith (1820-1914), railroad builder and Canadian High Commissioner, 1896-1914.

Big Raven, by Emily Carr — A272

1971, Feb. 12 Litho. *Perf. 12*

532 A272 6c multicolored .25 .20

Emily Carr (1871-1945), painter and writer.

Laboratory Equipment Used for Insulin Discovery — A273

1971, Mar. 3 Litho. *Perf. 11*

533 A273 6c multicolored .25 .20

Discovery of insulin by Dr. Frederick G. Banting and Dr. Charles H. Best, 50th anniversary.

A274

1971, Mar. 24 Litho. *Perf. 11*

534 A274 6c red, org & black .25 .20

Sir Ernest Rutherford (1871-1937), physicist, developer of theory of spontaneous disintegration of the atom.

Spring, Winged Maple Seed A275

Louis Joseph Papineau A276

1971 Litho. *Perf. 11*

535 A275 6c shown .25 .20
a. Imperf., pair *950.00*
536 A275 6c Summer .25 .20
537 A275 7c Autumn .25 .20
538 A275 7c Winter .25 .20
Nos. 535-538 (4) 1.00 .80

Issue dates: No. 535, Apr. 14; No. 536, June 16; No. 537, Sept. 3; No. 538, Nov. 19.

Litho. & Engr.

1971, May 7 *Perf. 12½x12*

539 A276 6c multicolored .25 .20

Louis Joseph Papineau (1786-1871), member of Legislative Assembly and leader of French Canadian Patriote party.

Map of Copper Mine River Basin A277

1971, May 7 *Perf. 12x12½*

540 A277 6c buff, red & brown .25 .20

Bicentenary of Samuel Hearne's expedition to the Copper Mine River.

Maple Leaves A278

1971, June 1

541 A278 15c blk, red org & yel 1.60 1.10
p. Tagged 2.25 2.25

Inauguration of new transmitters for Radio Canada International.

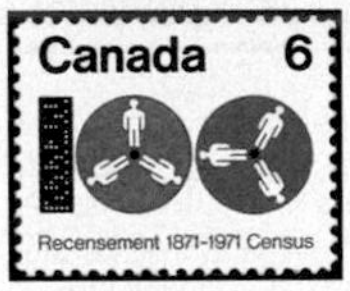

Computer Tape and Reels — A279

1971, June 1

542 A279 6c black, ultra & red .25 .20

Centenary of measured progress through census.

Migrating Phosphor

Canada's "Ottawa/General" tagging of engraved stamps printed March-October, 1972, used a phosphor which migrates onto or through other stamps, booklet covers and album pages. It fluoresces yellow under ultraviolet light.

This bleeding, contaminating "OP4" phosphor can be somewhat contained in mounts or envelopes of acetate, glassine or polyethylene, but it may leak or penetrate.

The migrating phosphor is found on all copies of Nos. 560p-561p, and on some of Nos. 544p, 544q, 544r, 544s, 562p-565p and 594-598.

Transportation Means — A280

Design: 8c, Library of Parliament.

1971-72 Engr. *Perf. 12½x12*
543 A280 7c slate green .35 .20
a. Booklet pane of 5 + label (#454e, #456a + 3#543) 4.25 2.25
b. Booklet pane of 20 (4 #454e, 4 #456a, 12 #543) 8.00 7.00
p. Tagged .60 .25
544 A280 8c slate .25 .20
a. Booklet pane of 6 (3 #454e, 1 #460c, 2 #544) 1.75 .80
b. Booklet pane of 18 (6 #454e, 1 #460c, 11 #544) 5.25 3.50
c. Booklet pane of 10 (4 #454e, 1 #460c, 5 #544 ('72) 2.25 2.25
p. Tagged .35 .20
q. As "a," tagged 2.00 2.00
r. As "b," tagged 4.00 4.00
s. As "c," tagged 2.00 2.00

Coil Stamps

1971 *Perf. 10 Horiz.*
549 A280 7c slate green .40 .20
a. Imperf, pair 1,200.
550 A280 8c slate .35 .20
a. Imperf, pair 600.00
p. Tagged .50 .20
q. As "p," imperf, pair 1,100.

See note below No. 468B.
Issued: 7c, 6/30/71; 8c, 12/30/71.

Abstract "BC" A282

1971, July 20 Litho. *Perf. 12*
552 A282 7c multicolored .25 .20

Centenary of British Columbia's entry into Canadian Confederation.

Indian Encampment on Lake Huron, by Kane — A283

1971, Aug. 11 *Perf. 12½*
553 A283 7c multicolored .40 .20

Paul Kane (1810-1871), painter.

Snowflake A284

Pierre Laporte A285

1971, Oct. 6 Engr. *Perf. 12*
Size: 24x30mm
554 A284 6c dark blue .20 .20
p. Tagged .20 .20
a. All color omitted (from foldover) 2,000.
b. Printed on gummed side (from foldover) 1,100.
555 A284 7c bright green .20 .20
p. Tagged .30 .20

Litho. and Engr.
Size: 30x30mm
556 A284 10c dp car & silver .35 .30
p. Tagged .45 .30
557 A284 15c lt ultra, dp car & silver .70 .65
p. Tagged .90 .75
Nos. 554-557 (4) 1.45 1.35

Christmas.

1971, Oct. 20 Engr. *Perf. 12½x12*
558 A285 7c black .25 .20

Pierre Laporte (1921-1970), Minister of Labor, kidnapped and killed.

Figure Skating — A286

1972, Mar. 1 Litho. *Perf. 12*
559 A286 8c deep red lilac .25 .20

World Figure Skating Championships, Calgary, Alberta, Mar. 6-12.

"Your Heart is your Health" A287

1972, Apr. 7 Engr. *Perf. 12x12½*
560 A287 8c red .30 .20
p. Tagged .55 .35

World Health Day, Apr. 7.

Frontenac, by Philippe Hébert and Fort Saint Louis, Quebec A288

Photo. and Engr.
1972, May 17 *Perf. 12x12½*
561 A288 8c red brown & multi .25 .20
p. Tagged .65 .55

Tercentenary of the appointment of Louis de Buade, Count of Frontenac and Palluau (1622-1698), as Governor of New France.

Indians of Canada

Buffalo Chase, by George Catlin A289

Thunderbird, Assiniboin Pattern — A290

In Nos. 562-581, the first two and last two stamps of each annual set are printed checkerwise in same sheet of 50.

1972 Litho. *Perf. 12x12½*
562 A289 8c shown .40 .20
p. Tagged .55 .30
563 A289 8c Plains Indian artifacts .40 .20
p. Tagged .55 .30
a. Pair, #562-563 .80 .50
b. As "a," tagged 1.10 .75

Perf. 12½x12
Photo. & Engr.
564 A290 8c shown .40 .20
p. Tagged .55 .30
565 A290 8c Ceremonial sun dance costume .40 .20
p. Tagged .55 .30
a. Pair, #564-565 .80 .50
b. As "a," tagged 1.10 .75

Plains Indians of Canada.
Issued: #562-563, July 6; #564-565, Oct. 4.

Tagged (Nos. 566-581)

1973 Litho. *Perf. 12x12½*
566 A289 8c Algonkian artifacts .35 .20
567 A289 8c "Micmac Indians" .35 .20
a. Pair, #566-567 .70 .50

Perf. 12½x12
Photo. & Engr.
568 A290 8c Thunderbird and belt .35 .20
569 A290 8c Algonkian man and woman .35 .20
a. Pair, #568-569 .70 .50

Algonkian-speaking Indians of Canada (Malecite, Micmac, Montagnais, Algonquin and Ojibwa).
Issued: #566-567, 2/21; #568-569, 11/28.

1974 Litho. *Perf. 12x12½*
570 A289 8c Nootka Sound, house, inside .35 .20
571 A289 8c Artifacts .35 .20
a. Pair, #570-571 .70 .50

Perf. 12½x12
Photo. & Engr.
572 A290 8c Chief wearing Chilkat blanket .35 .20
573 A290 8c Thunderbird from Kwakiutl house .35 .20
a. Pair, #572-573 .70 .50

Pacific Coast Indians of Canada (Haida, Salish, Tsimshian, Chilkat and Kwakiutl).
Issued: #570-571, 1/16; #572-573, 2/22.

1975, Apr. 4 Litho. *Perf. 13½*
574 A289 8c Montagnais-Naskapi artifacts .25 .20
575 A289 8c Dance of the Kutcha-Kutchin .25 .20
a. Pair, #574-575 .50 .50
b. As "a," imperf. between *900.00*

Perf. 12½
576 A290 8c Kutchin ceremonial costume .25 .20

Litho. and Embossed
577 A290 8c Ojibwa thunderbird and Naskapi pattern .25 .20
a. Pair, #576-577 .50 .50

Subarctic Indians.

1976, Sept. 17 Litho. *Perf. 13½*
578 A289 10c Cornhusk mask, artifacts .25 .20
579 A289 10c Iroquoian Encampment, by George Heriot .25 .20
a. Pair, #578-579 .50 .50

Perf. 12½
Litho. & Embossed
580 A290 10c Iroquoian thunderbird .25 .20

Litho.
581 A290 10c Iroquoian man, woman .25 .20
a. Pair, #580-581 .50 .50
Nos. 562-581 (20) 6.40 4.00

Iroquois (Mohawk, Cayuga, Seneca, Oneida, Onondaga and Tuscarora).

Geological Fault — A291

1972, Aug. 2 *Perf. 12*
582 A291 15c shown 1.75 1.60
p. Tagged 2.25 2.25
583 A291 15c Bird's eye view of town 1.75 1.60
p. Tagged 2.25 2.25
584 A291 15c Aerial map photography 1.75 1.60
p. Tagged 2.25 2.25
585 A291 15c Contour lines 1.75 1.60
p. Tagged 2.25 2.25
a. Block of 4, #582-585 7.00 7.00
b. As "a," tagged 9.00 9.00
Nos. 582-585 (4) 7.00 6.40

Earth sciences: 24th Intl. Geological Cong. (#582); 22nd Intl. Geographical Cong. (#583); 12th Cong. of Intl. Soc. of Photogrammetry (#584); 6th Cong. of Intl. Cartographic Assoc. (#585).

Sir John A. Macdonald A292

Elizabeth II A292a

Forest, Central Canada — A293

Vancouver, B.C. — A294

Designs: 2c, Sir Wilfrid Laurier. 3c, Sir Robert L. Borden. 4c, William Lyon Mackenzie King. 5c Richard Bedford Bennett. 6c, Lester B. Pearson. 7c, Louis St. Laurent. 15c, Mountain sheep, Western Canada. 20c, Grain fields, Prairie. 25c, Polar bears, North. 50c, Seashore. $2, Quebec.

1972-76 Engr. *Perf. 12x12½*
Tagged
586 A292 1c orange ('73) .20 .20
a. Booklet pane, 3 #586, 1 #591, 2 #593 ('74) 1.20 1.00
b. Bklt. pane, 6 #586, 1 #591, 11 #593 ('75) 1.60 1.60
c. Bklt. pane, 2 #586, 4 #587, 4 #593Ac ('76) 1.20 1.00
d. Printed on gummed side 600.00
587 A292 2c green ('73) .20 .20
588 A292 3c brown ('73) .20 .20
589 A292 4c black ('73) .20 .20
590 A292 5c lilac ('73) .20 .20
591 A292 6c dk red ('73) .20 .20
a. Printed on gummed side 200.00
592 A292 7c dk brn ('74) .20 .20
593 A292a 8c ultra ('73) .20 .20
b. Perf. 13x13½ ('76) .65 .20

Perf. 13x13½
593A A292a 10c dk car ('76) .20 .20
c. Perf. 12x12½ .35 .20

Perf. 12½x12
Photo. & Engr.
594 A293 10c multicolored .30 .20
595 A293 15c multicolored .45 .20
596 A293 20c multicolored .45 .20
597 A293 25c multicolored .50 .20
598 A293 50c multicolored 1.10 .20
599 A294 $1 multi ('73) 2.50 .50

Perf. 11
Litho. & Engraved
600 A294 $1 multicolored 5.75 1.60
601 A294 $2 multicolored 4.50 2.25
Nos. 586-601 (17) 17.35 7.15

No. 599 has engraved shading added in some areas.

Plates 1 and 2 of the scenic 10c differ in impression and colors. Plate 1 has distinct crosshatching of "Canada" background. On plate 2, released in 1974, this area appears solidly inked.

A 1976 printing of the 15c shows the blue trees on the hillside as solid color, while the 1972 printing shows clear detail on the trees.

A 1974 printing of the 50c has darker shading and a deeper tone for the dark blue areas of the photogravure impression.

Nos. 600 and 601 are untagged.

1976-77 Photo. & Engr. *Perf. 13½*
594a A293 10c multicolored .30 .20
595a A293 15c multicolored .45 .20
596a A293 20c multicolored .60 .20
597a A293 25c multicolored .65 .20
598a A293 50c multicolored 1.75 .20
599a A294 $1 multi ('77) 2.50 .30
Nos. 594a-599a (6) 6.25 1.30

Coil Stamps

1974-76 Engr. *Perf. 10 Vert.*
604 A292a 8c ultramarine .25 .20
a. Imperf., horiz. pair 160.00
605 A292a 10c dk carmine ('76) .35 .20
a. Imperf., horiz. pair 175.00

See note below No. 468B. No. 604 also exists in vertical multiples without score line.

Candles — A295

Candles and Fruit A296

Christmas: 8c, Like 6c. 15c, Candles, 15th century prayer book, boxes and brass vase.

1972, Nov. 1 Litho. ***Perf. 12½x12***

606	A295 6c red & multi	.20	.20
p.	Tagged	.30	.25
607	A295 8c vio blue & multi	.20	.20
p.	Tagged	.35	.25

Perf. 11

608	A296 10c green & multi	.45	.35
p.	Tagged	.65	.55
609	A296 15c yel bister & multi	.65	.65
p.	Tagged	1.20	1.20
	Nos. 606-609 (4)	1.50	1.40

"The Blacksmith's Shop," by Krieghoff — A297

1972, Nov. 29 Litho. ***Perf. 12½***

610	A297 8c multicolored	.30	.20
p.	Tagged	.35	.20

Cornelius Krieghoff (1815-1872), painter.

Tagged

From No. 611 onward, all stamps are tagged unless otherwise noted.

Monsignor de Laval — A298

1973, Jan. 31 Litho. ***Perf. 11***

611 A298 8c silver, ultra & gold .20 .20

Francois-Xavier de Montmorency-Laval de Montigny (1623-1708), 1st Bishop of Quebec and founder of many educational institutions; one of the builders of New France.

Commissioner G. A. French and Map of 1874 Trek — A299

10c, Spectrograph. 15c, R.C.M.P. Musical Ride.

1973, Mar. 9 Litho. ***Perf. 11***

612	A299 8c dk brn, org & red	.20	.20
613	A299 10c dk blue & multi	.35	.30
614	A299 15c yel grn & multi	.75	.50
a.	Imperf., pair	500.00	
	Nos. 612-614 (3)	1.30	1.00

Royal Canadian Mounted Police, cent.

Imperfs of No. 614 with a double impression and examples with 15c printed on 10c are from printer's waste.

Jeanne Mance A300

1973, Apr. 18

615 A300 8c multicolored .20 .20

Jeanne Mance (1606-1673), first secular nurse in North America and founder of first hospital, the Hôtel-Dieu in Montreal settlement.

Joseph Howe — A301

1973, May 16

616 A301 8c gold & black .20 .20

Joseph Howe (1804-1873), journalist, poet and Lieutenant-Governor of Nova Scotia.

Mist Fantasy, by James MacDonald A302

1973, June 8 ***Perf. 12½***

617 A302 15c multicolored .55 .50

Centenary of the birth of James E. H. MacDonald (1873-1932), painter.

Oaks on Shore A303

Photo. & Engr.

1973, June 22 ***Perf. 12x12½***

618 A303 8c orange & red brn .20 .20

Centenary of Prince Edward Island's entry into Confederation.

Scottish Settlers and "Hector" A304

1973, July 20 Litho. ***Perf. 12x12½***

619 A304 8c multicolored .20 .20

Bicentenary of arrival of Scottish settlers at Pictou, N.S.

Queen Elizabeth II — A305

1973, Aug. 2 Photo. and Engr.

620	A305 8c silver & multi	.20	.20
621	A305 15c gold & multi	.60	.55

Visit to Ottawa of Elizabeth II and the Duke of Edinburgh, July 31-Aug. 4, and meeting of Commonwealth Heads of Government, Ottawa, Aug. 2-10.

Nellie McClung — A306

1973, Aug. 29 Litho. ***Perf. 10½x11***

622 A306 8c multicolored .20 .20

Nellie McClung (1873-1951), leader of women's suffrage movement, social reformer and writer.

Montreal Olympic Games — A307

1973, Sept. 20 ***Perf. 12x12½***

Size: 26x44mm

623	A307 8c silver & multi	.20	.20
624	A307 15c gold & multi	.55	.45

21st Olympic Games, Montreal, 1976.

See Nos. B1-B3.

Ice Skate — A308

Santa Claus — A309

1973, Nov. 7 Litho. ***Perf. 12½x12***

625	A308 6c shown	.20	.20
626	A308 8c Dove	.20	.20

Perf. 10½

627	A309 10c shown	.25	.25
628	A309 15c Shepherd and star	.55	.55
	Nos. 625-628 (4)	1.20	1.20

Christmas.

Children Diving from Dock — A310

1974, Mar. 22 Engr. ***Perf. 12***

629	A310 8c shown	.40	.20
630	A310 8c Joggers	.40	.20
631	A310 8c Bicycling family	.40	.20
632	A310 8c Hikers	.40	.20
a.	Block of 4, #629-632	1.60	.85

"Keep Fit." 21st Summer Olympic Games, Montreal, 1976. When stamps are observed at an angle the Montreal Olympic Games' emblem can be seen.

Main St. and Portage Ave., Winnipeg, 1872 — A311

Litho. & Engr.

1974, May 3 ***Perf. 12x12½***

633 A311 8c multicolored .20 .20

Winnipeg's incorporation as a city, cent.

Postmaster A312

1974, June 11 Litho. ***Perf. 13½x13***

634	A312 8c shown	.35	.30
635	A312 8c Mail collector and truck	.35	.30
636	A312 8c Mail handler	.35	.30
637	A312 8c Mail sorters	.35	.30
638	A312 8c Mailman	.35	.30
639	A312 8c Rural mail delivery	.35	.30
a.	Block of 6, #634-639	2.25	2.25

Centenary of letter carrier delivery service. Printed in sheets of 50 (5x10).

Agricultural Education A313

1974, July 12 ***Perf. 12½x12***

640 A313 8c multicolored .20 .20

Ontario Agricultural College centenary.

Pedestal, Gallows Frame and Contempra Telephones A314

1974, July 26 ***Perf. 12½***

641	A314 8c multicolored	.20	.20
a.	Imperf., pair	*1,600.*	

Centenary of the idea for the telephone by Alexander Graham Bell while visiting Brantford, Canada.

Bicycle Wheel and Cycling Emblem A315

Photo. & Engr.

1974, Aug. 7 ***Perf. 12x12½***

642 A315 8c black, red & silver .20 .20

World Cycling Championships, Montreal, Aug. 14-25.

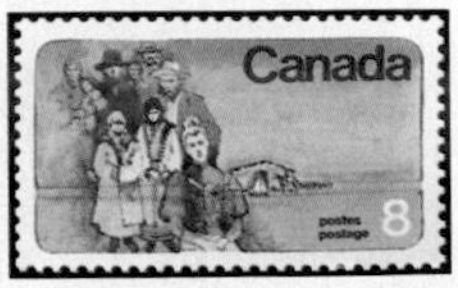

Mennonite Settlers A316

1974, Aug. 28 Litho. ***Perf. 12x12½***

643 A316 8c multicolored .20 .20

Centenary of arrival of Mennonite settlers in Manitoba.

Snowshoeing
A317

1974, Sept. 23 Engr. *Perf. 13½*

644 A317 8c shown	.35	.20
645 A317 8c Skiing	.35	.20
646 A317 8c Skating	.35	.20
647 A317 8c Curling	.35	.20
a. Block of 4, #644-647	1.40	1.40
b. Block or strip of 4, printed on gummed side	3,000.	

"Keep Fit." 1976 Winter Olympic Games. When the stamps are observed at an angle the Montreal Olympic Games' emblem can be seen.

Warning: No. 647b must show each design; blocks exist that contain 2 No. 645 but no example of No. 647.

Mercury with Winged Horses, UPU Emblem
A318

Photo. & Engr.

1974, Oct. 9 *Perf. 12x12½*

648 A318 8c violet, red & blue	.20	.20
649 A318 15c violet, red & blue	.85	.70

Centenary of Universal Postal Union.

Nativity, by Jean Paul Lemieux
A319

Skaters at Hull, by Henri Masson — A320

Christmas (Paintings): 10c, The Ice Cone, Montmorency Falls, by Robert C. Todd. 15c, Village in the Laurentian Mountains, by Clarence A. Gagnon.

1974, Nov. 1 Litho. *Perf. 13½*

650 A319 6c multicolored	.20	.20
651 A320 8c multicolored	.20	.20
652 A319 10c multicolored	.35	.30
653 A319 15c multicolored	.65	.55
Nos. 650-653 (4)	1.40	1.25

Marconi and St. John's, Newfoundland, from Signal Hill — A321

1974, Nov. 15 *Perf. 13*

654 A321 8c multicolored	.20	.20

Guglielmo Marconi (1874-1937), Italian electrical engineer and inventor.

Merritt and Welland Canal
A322

Litho. & Engr.

1974, Nov. 29 *Perf. 13x13½*

655 A322 8c multicolored	.20	.20

Sesquicentennial of the start of construction of the Welland Canal between Lakes Ontario and Erie, a project conceived and supervised by William Hamilton Merritt (1793-1862). Portrait by Robert Whale.

The Sprinter — A323

The Plunger — A324

Designs: Sculptures by Robert Tait McKenzie, M.D. (1867-1938), and Montreal Olympic Games' emblem.

Perf. 12½x12, 12x12½

1975, Mar. 14 Litho.; Embossed

656 A323 $1 multicolored	2.25	2.25
657 A324 $2 multicolored	4.50	3.50

21st Olympic Games, Montreal, July 17-Aug. 1, 1976.

A325

No. 658, Anne of Green Gables. No. 659, Maria Chapdelaine.

1975, May 15 Litho. *Perf. 13*

658 8c blue & multi	.20	.20
659 8c brown & multi	.20	.20
a. A325 Pair, #658-659	.40	.30

Birth centenary of Lucy Maud Montgomery (1874-1942), writer and author of "Anne of Green Gables"; Louis Hémon (1880-1913), writer and author of "Maria Chapdelaine." Nos. 658-659 printed checkerwise.

Marguerite Bourgeoys
A327

Alphonse Desjardins
A328

1975, May 30 Litho. *Perf. 12½x12*

660 A327 8c red & multi	.20	.20
661 A328 8c red & multi	.20	.20

Marguerite Bourgeoys (1620-1700), founder of the Congrégation de Notre-Dame, Montreal, first girls' school in New France; Alphonse Desjardins (1854-1920), journalist, founder of first credit union in North America.

A329

No. 662, Samuel Dwight Chown (1853-1933), Methodist minister, leader of temperance movement, founder of United Church. No. 663, Dr. John Cook (1805-92), 1st Moderator of the United Presbyterian Church in Canada.

Nos. 662-663 printed checkerwise.

Photo. & Engr.

1975, May 30 *Perf. 12x12½*

662 8c dk brown, yel & buff	.20	.20
663 8c dk brown, yel & buff	.20	.20
a. A329 Pair, #662-663	.40	.40

Pole Vaulting — A331

Hurdling — A332

Design: 25c, Marathon running and Montreal Olympic Games' emblem.

1975, June 11 Litho. *Perf. 12x12½*

664 A331 20c dk blue & multi	.55	.45
665 A331 25c maroon & multi	.65	.50
666 A332 50c green & multi	1.40	1.00
Nos. 664-666 (3)	2.60	1.95

21st Olympic Games, Montreal, July 17-Aug. 1, 1976.

"Untamed" (Wild Horse Race)
A333

1975, July 3

667 A333 8c gray & multi	.20	.20

Centenary of the founding of Calgary.

Female Symbol
A334

"Justice," by Walter S. Allward
A335

Photo. & Engr.

1975, July 14 *Perf. 13*

668 A334 8c dp yel, gray & black	.20	.20

International Women's Year.

1975, Sept. 2 Litho. *Perf. 12½*

669 A335 8c multicolored	.20	.20

Supreme Court of Canada, centenary.

"Wm. D. Lawrence"
A336

Photo. & Engr.

1975, Sept. 24 *Perf. 13*

670 A336 8c shown	.35	.30
671 A336 8c "Beaver"	.35	.30
672 A336 8c "Neptune"	.35	.30
673 A336 8c "Quadra"	.35	.30
a. Block of 4, #670-673	1.40	1.40

Coastal ships.

Santa Claus — A337

Child — A338

Trees — A339

Designs by Canadian School Children: "What Christmas Means to Me."

1975, Oct. 22 Litho. *Perf. 13½*

674 A337 6c shown	.20	.20
675 A337 6c Skater	.20	.20
a. Pair, #674-675	.40	.30
676 A338 8c shown	.20	.20
677 A338 8c Family and Christmas tree	.20	.20
a. Pair, #676-677	.40	.35
678 A338 10c Gift box	.25	.20
679 A339 15c shown	.45	.45
Nos. 674-679 (6)	1.50	1.45

Christmas. Stamps of same denomination printed checkerwise.

Legion Emblem and Bugle
A340

Photo. & Engr.

1975, Nov. 10 *Perf. 13*
680 A340 8c gray & multi .20 .20

Royal Canadian Legion, 50th anniversary.

Olympic Torch Ignited by Satellite in Canada A341

Communication Arts — A342

High-rise Tower, Notre Dame Church, Montreal, and Games' Emblem — A343

Snowflake, Winter Olympics' Emblem — A344

Montreal Olympic Games' Emblem and: 20c, Canadian athletes carrying Olympic flag. 25c, Women athletes receiving Olympic medals.

1976, June 18 **Litho.** *Perf. 13*
681 A341 8c black & multi .20 .20
682 A341 20c black & multi .60 .55
683 A341 25c black & multi .80 .60
Nos. 681-683 (3) 1.60 1.35

1976 Olympic Games ceremonies.

1976, Feb. 6 **Photo.** *Perf. 12x12½*

25c, Handicraft tools. 50c, Performing arts.

684 A342 20c gray & multi 1.10 .50
685 A342 25c ocher & multi 1.40 .65
686 A342 50c blue & multi 2.00 1.10
Nos. 684-686 (3) 4.50 2.25

Olympic Fine Arts and Cultural Program.

Photo. & Engr.

1976, Mar. 12 *Perf. 13*

Design: $2, Olympic Stadium, Velodrome, flags and emblem.

687 A343 $1 silver & multi 3.25 2.25
688 A343 $2 gold & multi 5.25 4.25

Nos. 681-688 were issued in commemoration of, or in connection with the 21st Olympic Games, Montreal, July 17-Aug. 1. Nos. 687-688 were issued in panes of 8.

Photo. and Embossed

1976, Feb. 6 *Perf. 12½*
689 A344 20c multicolored .85 .65

12th Winter Olympic Games, Innsbruck, Austria, Feb. 4-15.

Flower Growing from City — A345

1976, May 12 **Litho.** *Perf. 12x12½*
690 A345 20c multicolored .50 .45

Habitat, UN Conference on Human Settlements, Vancouver, May 31-June 11.

Franklin and Map of North America, 1776 A346

Litho. & Engr.

1976, June 1 *Perf. 13*
691 A346 10c multicolored .35 .20

American Bicentennial; Benjamin Franklin (1706-1790), deputy postmaster general for the colonies (1753-1774).
See US No. 1690.

Royal Military College, Kingston, Ont., Cent. — A347

No. 692, Color Parade, Memorial Arch. No. 693, Wing Parade, Mackenzie Building.

1976, June 1 **Litho.** *Perf. 12*
692 8c red & multi .20 .20
693 8c red & multi .20 .20
a. A347 Pair, #692-693 .40 .30
b. As "a," imperf. *2,250.*
c. Block of 4, imperf. horiz. *650.00*
d. As "a," double impression *4,000.*

A few used singles exist of Nos. 692-693 with double impression. Very rare.

Archer in Wheelchair A349

1976, Aug. 3 *Perf. 12x12½*
694 A349 20c green & multi .60 .50

Olympiad for the Physically Disabled (25th Stoke Mandeville Games), Toronto, Aug. 3-11.

A350

No. 695, The Cremation of Sam McGee. No. 696, The Outlander.

1976, Aug. 17 *Perf. 13½*
695 8c multicolored .20 .20
696 8c multicolored .20 .20
a. A350 Pair, #695-696 .40 .30

Robert W. Service (1874-1958), author of poem "The Cremation of Sam McGee"; Germaine Guevremont, author of "Le Survenant" (The Outlander).

Nativity, St. Michael's, Toronto — A352

Stained-glass windows: 10c, Nativity, St. Jude, London, Ontario. 20c, Nativity, by Yvonne Williams.

1976, Nov. 3 **Litho.** *Perf. 13½*
697 A352 8c multicolored .20 .20
698 A352 10c multicolored .20 .20
699 A352 20c multicolored .40 .40
Nos. 697-699 (3) .80 .80

Christmas.

Inland Vessels A353

Litho. & Engr.

1976, Nov. 19 *Perf. 12*
700 A353 10c Northcote .35 .30
701 A353 10c Passport .35 .30
702 A353 10c Chicora .35 .30
703 A353 10c Athabasca .35 .30
a. Block of 4, #700-703 1.40 1.25

Elizabeth II A354

Litho. and Typo.

1977, Feb. 4 *Perf. 12½x12*
704 A354 25c silver & multi .65 .50

25th anniv. of the reign of Elizabeth II.

Bottle Gentian A355

Elizabeth II A356

Parliament, Ottawa A357

Trembling Aspen A358

Main Street, Prairie Town — A359

Fundy National Park — A359a

Designs: 2c, Western columbine. 3c, Canada lily. 4c, Hepatica. 5c, Shooting star. 10c, Franklin's lady's-slipper. No. 712, Jewelweed. No. 715, Parliament, Ottawa. No. 716, Queen Elizabeth II. 20c, Douglas fir. 25c, Maple. 30c, Red oak. 35c, White pine. 60c, Street scene, Ontario City. 75c, Old houses, eastern City Street. 80c, Street leading to the sea, Eastern Maritime Provinces. $2 Kluane National Park.

Litho. & Engr.

1977-82 *Perf. 12x12½*
705 A355 1c multicolored .20 .20
a. Printed on gummed side, precanceled 950.00
707 A355 2c multicolored .20 .20
a. Printed on gummed side 950.00
708 A355 3c multicolored .20 .20
709 A355 4c multicolored .20 .20
a. Printed on gummed side 300.00
710 A355 5c multicolored .20 .20
711 A355 10c multicolored .20 .20
a. Perf. 13x13½ ('78) .20 .20

Photo. & Engr.

Perf. 13x13½

712 A355 12c multi ('78) .30 .20
713 A356 12c blue & multi .25 .20
a. Perf. 12x12½ .35 .20

Engraved

Perf. 13x13½

714 A357 12c blue .25 .20
a. Printed on gummed side 300.00
715 A357 14c red ('78) .30 .20
a. Printed on gummed side 37.50
b. All color omitted 400.00

Photo. & Engr.

Perf. 13x13½

716 A356 14c red & blk ('78) .30 .20
a. Perf. 12x12½ .30 .20
b. As "a," booklet pane of 25 + 2 labels ('78) 6.00
c. Red omitted *1,600.*

Perf. 13½

717 A358 15c multi .40 .20
718 A358 20c multi .40 .20
719 A358 25c multi .50 .20
720 A358 30c multi ('78) .60 .20
721 A358 35c multi ('79) .70 .20
723 A359 50c multi ('78) 1.10 .20
723A A359 50c multi, litho. & engr. ('78) 1.00 .20
b. Brown (all inscriptions, etc.) omitted *2,250.*
723C A359 60c multi, litho. ('82) 1.20 .20
724 A359 75c multi ('78) 1.50 .25
725 A359 80c multi ('78) 1.60 .35

Lithographed and Engraved

726 A359a $1 multi ('79) 1.75 .55
a. Untagged 2.75 .65
b. As "a," blk inscriptions omitted 750.00 600.00
727 A359a $2 multi ('79) 3.50 1.40
a. Silver inscriptions omitted 550.00
Nos. 705-727 (23) 16.85 6.35

On No. 715b, a strong embossed impression from the plate, without color, is evident.
On No. 723A license plate on yellow car reads "1978."
See Nos. 781-806, 934-937, 1084.

Coil Stamps

1977-78 **Engr.** *Perf. 10 Vert.*
729 A357 12c blue .25 .20
a. Imperf., pair 160.00
730 A357 14c red ('78) .30 .20
a. Imperf., pair 175.00

See note below No. 468B.

Eastern Cougar A360

1977, Mar. 30 **Litho.** *Perf. 12½*
732 A360 12c multicolored .25 .20

Wildlife protection.

April in Algonquin Park, by Thomson — A361

#734, Autumn Birches, by Tom Thomson.

1977, May 26 *Perf. 12*
733 A361 12c black & multi .25 .20
734 A361 12c ocher & multi .25 .20
a. Pair, #733-734 .50 .40

Tom Thomson (1877-1917), landscape painter, birth centenary. Nos. 733-734 printed checkerwise.

Names of Governors General and Standard A362

1977, June 30 *Perf. 12½*
735 A362 12c vio blue & multi .25 .20

Honoring Canadian-born Governors General: Vincent Massey, Georges Philias Vanier, Daniel Roland Michener and Jules Léger.

Order of Canada A363

Litho. & Embossed
1977, June 30
736 A363 12c multicolored .25 .20

Order of Canada, 10th anniversary.

Peace Bridge, Canadian, US and UN Flags A364

1977, Aug. 4 **Litho.**
737 A364 12c blue & multi .25 .20

50th anniversary of the Peace Bridge, connecting Fort Erie, Ontario, with Buffalo, N.Y.

Joseph E. Bernier, CGS Arctic A365

Sandford Fleming, Railroad Bridge A366

1977, Sept. 16 **Engr.** *Perf. 13*
738 A365 12c dark blue .25 .20
739 A366 12c brown .25 .20
a. Pair, #738-739 .50 .40

Joseph-Elzéar Bernier (1852-1934), explorer; Sandford Fleming (1827-1915), mapped route for Intercolonial Railway and designed Canada's first stamp.

Nos. 738-739 printed checkerwise.

Peace Tower, Parliament, Ottawa A367

1977, Sept. 19 **Litho.** *Perf. 12½*
740 A367 25c multicolored .70 .60

23rd Commonwealth Parliamentary Conference, Ottawa, Sept. 19-25.

Hunters Following Star — A368

Christmas: 12c, Angelic choir in northern light. 25c, Christ Child in Ring of Glory blessing chiefs from afar. Illustrations for Canada's first Christmas carol, written by Father Brébeuf, 1649.

1977, Oct. 26 *Perf. 13½*
741 A368 10c multicolored .20 .20
a. Horiz. pair, imperf between *1,250.*
b. Printed on gummed side 700.00
742 A368 12c multicolored .20 .20
a. Left margin block of 4, left vert. pair imperf, right pair part perf *1,900.*
743 A368 25c multicolored .50 .35
Nos. 741-743 (3) .90 .75

Pinky A369

Designs: Canadian sailing ships.

Litho. and Engr.
1977, Nov. 18 *Perf. 12x12½*
744 A369 12c shown .25 .20
745 A369 12c Tern schooner .25 .20
746 A369 12c 5-masted schooner .25 .20
747 A369 12c Mackinaw boat .25 .20
a. Block of 4, #744-747 1.00 .90
b. As "a," #745, 747 imperf, #744, 746 part perf *3,500.*

See Nos. 776-779.

Seal Hunter, Soapstone Sculpture A370

Disguised Caribou Hunter, Print — A371

Inuit Art: #749, Spear fishing. #751, Walrus hunt. #749-751 are after stonecut prints.

1977, Nov. 18 **Litho.** *Perf. 12x12½*
748 A370 12c multicolored .25 .20
749 A371 12c multicolored .25 .20
a. Pair, #748-749 .50 .40
b. As "a," gray (inscriptions) omitted on No. 749 *2,400.*
750 A371 12c multicolored .25 .20
751 A371 12c multicolored .25 .20
a. Pair, #750-751 .50 .40
Nos. 748-751 (4) 1.00 .80

Inuit hunting. Nos. 748-749 and Nos. 750-751 printed se-tenant checkerwise.

Peregrine Falcon A372

1978, Jan. 18
752 A372 12c multicolored .25 .20

Endangered wildlife.

Canada No. 3, 1851 — A373

1978 **Photo. & Engr.** *Perf. 13½*
753 A373 12c shown .20 .20
754 A373 14c No. 7 .25 .20
755 A373 30c No. 8 .55 .30
756 A373 $1.25 No. 2 2.25 1.00
a. Souvenir sheet of 3 3.25
Nos. 753-756 (4) 3.25 1.70

CAPEX '78, Canadian Intl. Phil. Exhib., Toronto, June 9-18 (cent. of Canada's admission to UPU).

No. 756a contains one each of Nos. 754-756 ($1.25 untagged). Value of No. 756 untagged, $2.75.

Issue dates: 12c, Jan. 18; others, June 10.

Games' Emblem A374

Stadium A375

Design: 30c, Badminton.

1978, Mar. 31 **Litho.** *Perf. 12½*
757 A374 14c silver & multi .30 .20
758 A374 30c silver & multi .60 .45

1978, Aug. 3

#760, Running. #761, Alberta Legislature building, Edmonton. #762, Lawn bowling.

759 A375 14c silver & multi .25 .20
760 A375 14c silver & multi .25 .20
a. Pair, #759-760 .50 .40
761 A375 30c silver & multi .60 .50
762 A375 30c silver & multi .60 .50
a. Pair, #761-762 1.20 1.10
Nos. 759-762 (4) 1.70 1.40

Nos. 757-762 commemorate 11th Commonwealth Games, Edmonton, Aug. 3-12.
#760a, 762a printed checkerwise.

A376

No. 763, Capt. Cook, by Nathaniel Dance. No. 764, Nootka Sound, by John Webber.

1978, Apr. 26 *Perf. 13*
763 14c multicolored .25 .20
764 14c multicolored .25 .20
a. A376 Pair, #763-764 .50 .40

Capt. James Cook (1728-1779), explorer of Canada's East and West Coasts and bicentenary of his anchorage near Anchorage, June 1, 1778. Nos. 763-764 printed checkerwise.

Silver Mine, Cobalt Lake A378

Stripmining, Athabasca Tar Sands A379

1978, May 19 *Perf. 12½*
765 A378 14c multicolored .25 .20
766 A379 14c multicolored .25 .20
a. Pair, #765-766 .50 .40

Development of national resources. Nos. 765-766 printed checkerwise.

Prince's Gate A380

1978, Aug. 16
767 A380 14c multicolored .25 .20

Canadian National Exhibition, centenary.

Mère d'Youville and Miracle of Food — A381

1978, Sept. 21 *Perf. 13x13½*
768 A381 14c multicolored .25 .20

Marguerite d'Youville (1701-1771), founder of the Gray Nuns, beatified 1959.

Woman Walking, by Pitseolak A382

Migration, Soapstone by Joe Talurinili A383

Works by Eskimo Artists: No. 771, Plane over village, stonecut and stencil print by Pudlo. No. 772, Dogteam and sled, ivory sculpture by Abraham Kingmeatook.

1978, Sept. 27 *Perf. 13½*
769 A382 14c multicolored .25 .20
770 A383 14c multicolored .25 .20
a. Pair, #769-770 .50 .40
771 A382 14c multicolored .25 .20
772 A383 14c multicolored .25 .20
a. Pair, #771-772 .50 .40
Nos. 769-772 (4) 1.00 .80

Travels of the Inuit. Printed checkerwise.

Madonna of the Flowering Pea, Cologne School — A384

Renaissance Paintings in National Gallery of Canada: 14c, Virgin and Child, by Hans Memling. 30c, Virgin and Child, by Jacopo Di Cione.

1978, Oct. 20 *Perf. 12½*
773 A384 12c multicolored .20 .20
774 A384 14c multicolored .30 .20
a. Black omitted *1,200.*
775 A384 30c multicolored .60 .25
Nos. 773-775 (3) 1.10 .65

Christmas.

Sailing Ships Type of 1977
Litho. & Engr.
1978, Nov. 15 *Perf. 13*
776 A369 14c "Chief Justice Robinson," 1842 .30 .25
777 A369 14c "St. Roch," 1928 .30 .25
778 A369 14c "Northern Light," 1928 .30 .25
779 A369 14c "Labrador," 1954 .30 .25
a. Block of 4, #776-779 1.25 1.10

Ice vessels.

Quebec Carnival — A386

1979, Feb. 1 Litho. *Perf. 13½*
780 A386 14c multicolored .25 .20

Flower, Queen & Parliament Types

1c, Bottle gentian. 2c, Western columbine. 3c, Canada lily. 4c, Hepatica. 5c, Shooting star. 10c, Franklin's lady's-slipper. 15c, Canada violet. No. 789, Elizabeth II. No. 790, Parliament, Ottawa.

Photo. & Engr., Engr. (#790)

1977-83 *Perf. 13x13½*
781 A355 1c multi ('79) .20 .20
a. Perf. 12x12½ ('77) .20 .20
b. Bklt. pane, 2 #781a, 4 #713a 1.50
782 A355 2c multi ('79) .20 .20
a. Bklt. pane, 4 #782, 3 #716a + label 1.00
b. Perf. 12x12½ ('78) .20 .20
783 A355 3c multi ('79) .20 .20
784 A355 4c multi ('79) .20 .20
785 A355 5c multi ('79) .20 .20
786 A355 10c multi ('79) .20 .20
787 A355 15c multi ('79) .30 .20
789 A356 17c green & blk ('79) .30 .20
a. Perf. 12x12½ .30 .20
b. Bklt. pane of 25 + 2 labels 7.00
c. Horiz. pair, imperf. btwn. and at left and bottom *2,000.*
d. Black inscriptions omitted *1,000.*
790 A357 17c slate green ('79) .30 .20
a. Printed on gummed side 37.50
791 A356 30c multi ('82) .55 .20
792 A356 32c multi ('83) .60 .20
Nos. 781-792 (11) 3.25 2.20

Nos. 781a, 782b, 789a are from booklet panes. No. 782b has one straight edge, others one or two.

No. 789d also shows the horiz. perfs. shifted.

Parliament Type of 1977

Booklet Stamps

1979, Mar. 28 Engr. *Perf. 12x12½*
797 A357 1c slate blue .50 .20
a. Bklt. pane, 1 #797, 3 #800, 2 #789a 1.40
800 A357 5c violet brown .25 .20

#797 has one straight edge, #800 has one or two.

Coil Stamp

1979, Mar. 8 *Perf. 10 Vert.*
806 A357 17c slate green .30 .20
a. Imperf., pair 150.00

Endangered Wildlife A392

1979, Apr. 10 Litho. *Perf. 12½*
813 A392 17c Soft-shelled turtle .35 .20
814 A392 35c Bowhead whale .70 .35

Ribbon Around Woman's Finger — A393

No. 816, String around man's finger.

1979, Apr. 10
815 A393 17c multicolored .30 .20
816 A393 17c multicolored .30 .20
a. Pair, #815-816 .60 .55

Use postal code. Printed checkerwise.

Fruits of the Earth, by F. P. Grove A394

The Golden Vessel, by Emile Nelligan A395

1979, May 3 *Perf. 13x13½*
817 A394 17c multicolored .30 .20
818 A395 17c multicolored .30 .20
a. Pair, #817-818 .60 .55
c. As "a," left margin block of 4, left vert. pair imperf, right pair part perf *2,000.* —

Frederick Philip Grove (1879-1948), teacher and writer; Emile Nelligan (1879-1941), French-Canadian poet. Nos. 817-818 printed checkerwise.

Warning: horizontal pairs exist of No. 818a that appear to be imperforate. These actually are pairs made from No. 818c with normal perforations trimmed off the right edge.

A396

1979, May 11 *Perf. 13½*
819 17c De Salaberry .30 .20
820 17c John By .30 .20
a. A396 Pair, #819-820 .60 .55

Charles-Michel d'Irumberry de Salaberry (1778-1829), and John By (1779-1836), Canadian colonels. Printed checkerwise.

Flag of Ontario A398

Designs: Provincial and Territorial flags.

1979, June 15 Litho. *Perf. 13½*
821 A398 17c shown .35 .25
822 A398 17c Quebec .35 .25
823 A398 17c Nova Scotia .35 .25
824 A398 17c New Brunswick .35 .25
825 A398 17c Manitoba .35 .25
826 A398 17c British Columbia .35 .25
827 A398 17c Prince Edward Island .35 .25
828 A398 17c Saskatchewan .35 .25
829 A398 17c Alberta .35 .25
830 A398 17c Newfoundland .35 .25
831 A398 17c Northwest Territories .35 .25
832 A398 17c Yukon Territory .35 .25
a. Pane of 12, #821-832 4.50 4.00

White Water Kayak Race A399

1979, July 3 *Perf. 12½*
833 A399 17c multicolored .35 .20

Canoe-Kayak (Slalom and Wild Water) World Championships, Jonquière and Desbiens, Quebec, June 30-July 8.

Women's Field Hockey A400

1979, Aug. 16
834 A400 17c multicolored .35 .20

Women's Field Hockey Championship, Vancouver, B.C., Aug. 16-30.

Summer Tent, Print by Kiakshuk A401

Eskimos Building Igloo, by Abraham of Povungnituk A402

Works by Eskimo Artists: No. 837, The Dance, print by Kalvak of Holman Island. No. 838, Two soapstone figures from Repulse Bay, by Madeleine Isserkut and Jean Mapsalak.

1979, Sept. 13 Litho. *Perf. 13½*
835 A401 17c multicolored .30 .20
836 A402 17c multicolored .30 .20
a. Pair, #835-836 .60 .55
837 A401 17c multicolored .30 .20
838 A402 17c multicolored .30 .20
a. Pair, #837-838 .60 .55
Nos. 835-838 (4) 1.20 .80

Inuit shelters and community. Printed checkerwise.

Painted Wooden Train A403

Antique Toys: 17c, Horse, pull toy. 35c, Knitted doll, vert.

1979, Oct. 17 Litho. *Perf. 13*
839 A403 15c multicolored .30 .20
840 A403 17c multicolored .35 .20
841 A403 35c multicolored .70 .30
a. Gold (and tagging) omitted *1,400.*
Nos. 839-841 (3) 1.35 .70

Christmas.

Girl Watering Tree of Life — A404

1979, Oct. 24
842 A404 17c multicolored .30 .20

International Year of the Child.

Curtiss HS-2L A405

1979, Nov. 15 Litho. *Perf. 12½*
843 A405 17c shown .35 .20
844 A405 17c Canadair CL-215 .35 .20
a. Pair, #843-844 .70 .55
845 A405 35c Vickers Vedette .70 .55
846 A405 35c Consolidated Canso .70 .55
a. Pair, #845-846 1.40 1.25
Nos. 843-846 (4) 2.10 1.50

Map of Canada Showing Arctic Islands A406

1980, Jan. 23 Litho. *Perf. 13½*
847 A406 17c multicolored .30 .20

Acquisition of the Arctic Islands, centenary.

Downhill Skiing A407

1980, Jan. 23
848 A407 35c multicolored .70 .30

13th Winter Olympic Games, Lake Placid, NY, Feb. 12-24.

Meeting of the School Trustees, by Robert Harris A408

Royal Canadian Academy of Arts Centenary: No. 850, Inspiration, bronze sculpture, by Louis-Philippe Hebert (1850-1917). No. 851, Parliament Buildings, by Thomas Fuller (1822-1919). No. 852, Sunrise on the Saguenay, by Lucius O'Brien (1832-99).

1980, Mar. 6 Litho.
849 A408 17c multicolored .35 .20
850 A408 17c multicolored .35 .20
a. Pair, #849-850 .70 .55
851 A408 35c multicolored .70 .55
852 A408 35c multicolored .70 .55
a. Pair, #851-852 1.40 1.25
Nos. 849-852 (4) 2.10 1.50

Printed checkerwise.

Atlantic Whitefish A409

Endangered wildlife. No. 854, Greater prairie chicken.

1980, May 6 Litho. *Perf. 12½*
853 A409 17c multicolored .35 .20
854 A409 17c multicolored .35 .20

Garden — A410

1980, May 29 Litho. *Perf. 13½*
855 A410 17c multicolored .30 .20

Intl. Flower Show, Montreal, May 17-Sept. 1.

Helping Hands — A411

Litho. & Embossed

1980, May 29 *Perf. 12½*

856 A411 17c ultra & gold .30 .20

14th World Congress of Rehabilitation International, Winnipeg, June 22-27.

"O Canada" Opening Bars A412

Composers Lavallee, Routhier, Weir A413

1980, June 6 **Litho.** *Perf. 12½*

857 A412 17c multicolored .30 .20
858 A413 17c multicolored .30 .20
a. Pair, #857-858 .60 .55

"O Canada" centenary. Printed checkerwise in sheets of 16.

John George Diefenbaker (1895-1979), Prime Minister, 1956-63 — A414

1980, June 20 **Engr.** *Perf. 13½*

859 A414 17c dark blue .30 .20

Emma Albani (1847-1930), Soprano — A415

#861, Healey Willan (1880-1968), organist, composer. Printed checkerwise.

1980, July 4 **Litho.** *Perf. 13½*

860 A415 17c multicolored .30 .20
861 A415 17c multicolored .30 .20
a. Pair, #860-861 .60 .55

Ned Hanlan (1855-1908), Oarsman A416

1980, July 4 **Litho.**

862 A416 17c multicolored .30 .20

Wheat Fields, Saskatchewan A417

No. 864, Strip mining and town, Alberta.

1980, Aug. 27 **Litho.** *Perf. 13½*

863 A417 17c multicolored .30 .20
864 A417 17c multicolored .30 .20

75th anniversary of Saskatchewan's and Alberta's creation as Provinces.

Uraninite Molecular Structure A418

1980, Sept. 3

865 A418 35c multicolored .70 .50
a. Printed on gummed side 800.00

Discovery of uranium in Canada, 80th anniversary.

Sedna, by Ashoona Kiawak A419

Return of the Sun, Print by Kenojouak A420

Works by Eskimo Artists: No. 868, Bird Spirit, by Doris Hagiolok. No. 869, Shaman, print by Simon Tookoome.

1980, Sept. 25 **Litho.** *Perf. 13½*

866 A419 17c multicolored .30 .20
867 A420 17c multicolored .30 .20
a. Pair, #866-867 .60 .55
868 A419 35c multicolored .65 .55
869 A420 35c multicolored .65 .55
a. Pair, #868-869 1.30 1.25
Nos. 866-869 (4) 1.90 1.50

Inuit spirits. Printed checkerwise.

Christmas Morning, by Frank Charles Hennessey — A421

Christmas (Greeting Cards, 1931): 17c, Sleigh Ride, by Joseph Sydney Hallam. 35c, McGill Cab Stand, by Kathleen Morris.

1980, Oct. 22 **Litho.** *Perf. 12½x12*

870 A421 15c multicolored .25 .20
871 A421 17c multicolored .30 .20
872 A421 35c multicolored .60 .35
Nos. 870-872 (3) 1.15 .75

Avro Canada CF-100, 1950 A422

Military Aircraft: No. 874, Avro Lancaster, 1941. No. 875, Curtiss JN-4 Canuck. No. 876, Hawker Hurricane, 1935.

1980, Nov. 10 *Perf. 13x13½*

873 A422 17c multicolored .35 .20
874 A422 17c multicolored .35 .20
a. Pair, #873-874 .70 .55
875 A422 35c multicolored .70 .55
876 A422 35c multicolored .70 .55
a. Pair, #875-876 1.40 1.25
Nos. 873-876 (4) 2.10 1.50

Printed checkerwise.

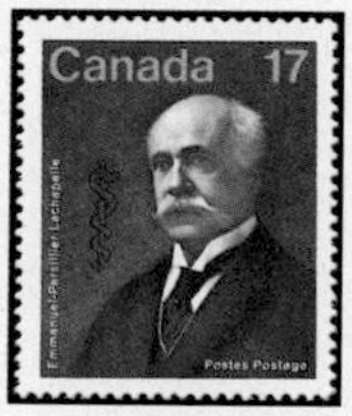

Emmanuel-Persillier Lachapelle, Caduceus — A423

1980, Dec. 5 *Perf. 13½*

877 A423 17c multicolored .35 .20

Lachapelle (1845-1918), physician, founded Notre Dame Hospital, Montreal, 1880.

Mandora, 18th Century A424

1981, Jan. 19 **Litho.** *Perf. 12½*

878 A424 17c multicolored .30 .20

"The Look of Music" rare musical instrument exhibition, Vancouver, Nov. 2, 1980-Apr. 5, 1981.

No. 878 exists printed on gummed side with gold color and tagging omitted, from printer's waste.

Emily Stowe (1831-1903) and Toronto General Hospital — A425

Designs: No. 880, Louise McKinney, (1868-1931) Alberta legislative building. No. 881, Idola Saint-Jean, (1875-1945) Quebec legislative building. No. 882, Henrietta Edwards, (1849-1931) clubwomen.

1981, Mar. 4 **Litho.** *Perf. 13x13½*

879 A425 17c multicolored .35 .20
880 A425 17c multicolored .35 .20
881 A425 17c multicolored .35 .20
882 A425 17c multicolored .35 .20
a. Block of 4, #879-882 1.40 1.40

Vancouver Island Marmot, by Michael Dumas A426

Endangered Wildlife: 35c, Wood bison, by Robert Bateman.

1981, Apr. 6 **Litho.**

883 A426 17c multicolored .35 .20
884 A426 35c multicolored .70 .60

Kateri Tekakwitha ("Lily of the Mohawks"), by Emile Brunet — A427

Brunet Sculpture: #886, Marie de L'Incarnation.

1981, Apr. 24 *Perf. 12½*

885 A427 17c brown & pale grn .30 .20
886 A427 17c lt blue & ultra .30 .20
a. Pair, #885-886 .60 .55

Beatification of Kateri Tekakwitha (1656-1680), first North American Indian saint, and Marie De L'Incarnation (1599-1672), founder of Ursuline Order.

At Baie Saint-Paul, by Marc-Aurele Fortin (1888-1970) — A428

Paintings: No. 888, Self-portrait, by Frederick H. Varley (1881-1969). 35c, Untitled No. 6, by Paul-Emile Borduas (1905-60).

1981, May 22 **Litho.** *Perf. 12½*

887 A428 17c multi .30 .20
888 A428 17c multi, vert. .30 .20
a. Imperf, pair *1,600.*

Photo.

Perf. 13

889 A428 35c multi, vert. .70 .60
Nos. 887-889 (3) 1.30 1.00

Map of Canada Showing Provincial Boundaries, 1867 — A429

1981, June 30 **Litho.** *Perf. 13½*

890 A429 17c shown .35 .20
891 A429 17c 1873 .35 .20
892 A429 17c 1905 .35 .20
893 A429 17c 1949 .35 .20
a. Strip of 4, #890-893 1.40 1.40

Canada Day.

Frere Marie-Victorin (1885-1944) Botanist — A430

Botanists: #895, John Macoun (1831-1920).

1981, July 22 **Litho.** *Perf. 12½*

894 A430 17c multicolored .30 .20
895 A430 17c multicolored .30 .20
a. Pair, #894-895 .60 .50

Montreal Rose — A431

1981, July 22 *Perf. 13½*

896 A431 17c multicolored .30 .20

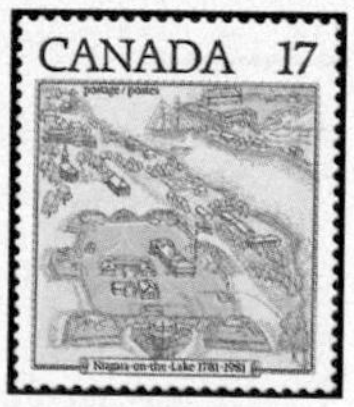

A432

Photo. & Engr.

1981, July 31 *Perf. 13½*

897 A432 17c multicolored .30 .20

Niagara-on-the-Lake (1st capital of Upper Canada).

A433

1981, Aug. 14 **Litho.**
898 A433 17c multicolored .30 .20

Acadian Congress centenary.

A434

1981, Sept. 8
899 A434 17c multicolored .30 .20

Aaron Mosher (1881-1959), Labor Congress founder.

A435

1981, Nov. 16 **Litho.** ***Perf. 13½***
900 A435 15c 1781 .25 .20
901 A435 15c 1881 .25 .20
902 A435 15c 1981 .25 .20
Nos. 900-902 (3) .75 .60

Christmas; bicentenary of 1st illuminated Christmas tree in Canada.

Canadair CL-41 Tutor A436

1981, Nov. 24 **Litho.** ***Perf. 12½***
903 A436 17c shown .35 .20
904 A436 17c de Havilland Tiger Moth .35 .20
a. Pair, #903-904 .70 .55
905 A436 35c Avro Canada C-102 .70 .55
906 A436 35c de Havilland Canada Dash-7 .70 .55
a. Pair, #905-906 1.40 1.25
Nos. 903-906 (4) 2.10 1.50

A437

1981, Dec. 29 **Engr.** ***Perf. 13x13½***
907 A437 (30c) red .85 .20
a. Printed on gummed side 800.00

Coil Stamp

Perf. 10 Vert.

908 A437 (30c) red .75 .20
a. Imperf., pair 400.00

See Nos. 923-924, 940, 943-946, 950-951.

CANADA '82 Intl. Philatelic Youth Exhibition, Toronto, May 20-24 — A438

1982 **Litho.** ***Perf. 13½***
909 A438 30c No. 1 .55 .20
910 A438 30c No. 102 .55 .20
911 A438 35c No. 223 .65 .50
912 A438 35c No. 155 .65 .50
913 A438 60c No. 158 1.10 .75
a. Souvenir sheet of 5, #909-913 3.75 3.50
Nos. 909-913 (5) 3.50 2.15

Issued: #909, 911, 3/11; others, 5/20.

Jules Leger (1913-1980), 26th Governor General — A439

1982, Apr. 2 **Litho.** ***Perf. 13½***
914 A439 30c multicolored .55 .20

Terry Fox (1958-1981), Marathon of Hope — A440

1982, Apr. 13 ***Perf. 12½***
915 A440 30c multicolored .55 .20

1982 Constitution — A441

1982, Apr. 16 **Litho.** ***Perf. 12x12½***
916 A441 30c multicolored .55 .20

Types of 1979-81 and

Decoy A442

Parliament (Library) A443

Parliament (West Block) — A444

Parliament (East Block) — A445

Elizabeth II — A446

Designs: Artifacts, 18th and 19th cent.

1982-87 **Litho.** ***Perf. 14x13½***
917 A442 1c shown .20 .20
a. Perf. 13x13½ ('85) .20 .20
918 A442 2c Fishing spear .20 .20
a. Perf. 13x13½ ('84) .20 .20
b. Bottom margin block of 4, bottom pair imperf, top pair part perf 2,250.
c. As "a," printed on gummed side 60.00
919 A442 3c Stable lantern .20 .20
a. Perf. 13x13½ ('85) .20 .20
920 A442 5c Bucket .20 .20
a. Perf. 13x13½ ('84) .20 .20
921 A442 10c Weathercock .20 .20
a. Perf. 13x13½ ('85) .30 .20
922 A442 20c Ice skates .40 .20
a. Brown omitted 400.00

Photo. & Engr.

Perf. 13x13½

923 A437 30c lt blue, bl, & red .55 .20
a. Bklt. pane of 20, perf. 12x12½ 13.00
b. Perf. 12x12½ .65 .20
924 A437 32c beige, red & brn .60 .20
a. Bklt. pane of 25, perf. 12x12½ 13.00
b. Perf. 12x12½ .65 .20
c. As #924, beige (and tagging) omitted 1,200.

Litho.

Perf. 13½x13

925 A443 34c multi .65 .20
a. Booklet pane of 25 13.00
b. Perf. 13½x14 ('86) .65 .20
c. Bklt. pane of 25, perf. 13½x14 13.00

Photo. & Engr.

Perf. 13x13½

926 A446 34c lt bl & int bl .70 .20
926A A446 36c plum 3.00 2.50

Perf. 13½x13

926B A443 36c multi .65 .20
c. Booklet pane of 10 #926Be 6.50
d. Booklet pane of 25 #926Be 17.50
e. Perf. 13½x14 ('87) .80 .20
f. Left margin block of 4, left vert. pair imperf, right pair part perf 1,600.

Litho. ***Perf. 12x12½***

Size A442: 26x20mm

927 A442 37c Wooden plow .70 .20
928 A442 39c Settle-bed .75 .20
929 A442 48c Cradle .85 .30
930 A442 50c Sleigh .90 .25
932 A442 64c Wood stove 1.15 .40
933 A442 68c Spinning wheel 1.25 .35

Litho. & Engr.

Perf. 13½

934 A359a $1 Glacier Natl. Park 1.80 .45
a. Blue inscriptions omitted 1,000.
b. Imperf., pair 2,400.
935 A359a $1.50 Waterton Lakes Natl. Park 3.50 .55
a. Black omitted 2,400.
936 A359a $2 Moraine Lake, Banff Park 3.75 1.10
a. Bluish green inscriptions omitted 1,200.
937 A359a $5 Point Pelee Natl. Park 10.00 2.25
Nos. 917-937 (22) 32.20 10.75

Issued:1c-20c, 10/19; 30c, 5/11; $1.50, 6/18; $5, 1/10/83; 32c, 2/10/83; 37c, 48c, 64c, 4/8/83; $1, 8/15/84; #925, $2, 6/21/85; #926, 7/12/85; 39c, 50c, 68c, 8/1/85; #926B, 3/30/87; #926A, 10/1/87.

For former No. 931, see new No. 723C.

Booklet Stamps

Perf. 12x12½ (A437), 12½x12

Engr.

938 A445 1c sage green ('87) .20 .20
939 A444 2c myrtle grn ('85) .20 .20
a. 2c slate green ('89) .20 .20
940 A437 5c deep claret .20 .20
941 A445 5c dp brown ('85) .25 .20
942 A444 6c henna brn ('87) .20 .20
943 A437 8c dk blue ('83) .45 .20
944 A437 10c dark green .40 .25
945 A437 30c red .75 .30
a. Bklt. pane of 4 + 2 labels (2 #940, 944, 945) 1.20 1.40
946 A437 32c brown ('83) .65 .20
b. Bklt. pane of 4 + 2 labels (2 #940, 943, 946) 1.20 1.40
947 A443 34c dp slate bl ('85) 1.10 .55
a. Bklt. pane of 6 (3 #939, 2 #941, #947) 1.75 1.25
948 A443 36c dark lil rose ('87) 1.25 .55
a. Bklt. pane of 5 + label (2 #938, 2 #942, #948) 1.75 1.25

Issued: #940, 10c, 30c, 3/1; 8c, 32c, 2/15/83; #941, 30c, 6/21/85; 1c, 6c, 36c, 3/30/87.

Coil Stamps

Engr. ***Perf. 10 Vert.***

950 A437 30c red .95 .20
a. Imperf., pair 350.00
951 A437 32c brown ('83) .65 .20
a. Imperf., pair 175.00

Perf. 10 Horiz.

952 A443 34c dull red brn ('85) .70 .20
a. Imperf., pair 160.00
953 A443 36c dark red ('87) .75 .20
a. Imperf., pair 300.00

Issued: 30c, 5/11; 32c, 2/10/83; 34c, 8/1/85; 36c, 5/19/87.

See #1080-1083, 1186-1188, 1194-1194A.

Centenary of Salvation Army in Canada A457

1982, June 25 **Litho.** ***Perf. 13***
954 A457 30c multicolored .55 .20

Canada Day A458

Paintings: No. 955, The Highway near Kluana Lake, by A.Y. Jackson. No. 956, Montreal Street Scene, by Adrien Hebert. No. 957, Breakwater, by Christopher Pratt. No. 958, Along Great Slave Lake, by Rene Richard. No. 959, Tea Hill, by Molly Lamb. No. 960, Family and Rainstorm, by Alex Colville. No. 961, Brown Shadows, by Dorothy Knowles. No. 962, The Red Brick House, by David Milne. No. 963, Campus Gates, by Bruno Bobak. No. 964, Prairie Town—Early Morning, by Illingworth Kerr. No. 965, Totems at Ninstints, by Joe Plaskett. No. 966, Doc Snider's House, by Lionel LeMoine FitzGerald.

1982, June 30 ***Perf. 12½x12***
955 A458 30c multicolored .65 .65
956 A458 30c multicolored .65 .65
957 A458 30c multicolored .65 .65
958 A458 30c multicolored .65 .65
959 A458 30c multicolored .65 .65
960 A458 30c multicolored .65 .65
961 A458 30c multicolored .65 .65
962 A458 30c multicolored .65 .65
963 A458 30c multicolored .65 .65
964 A458 30c multicolored .65 .65
965 A458 30c multicolored .65 .65
966 A458 30c multicolored .65 .65
a. Min. sheet of 12, #955-966 8.00 8.00

Regina Centenary A459

1982, Aug. 3 ***Perf. 13½x13***
967 A459 30c multicolored .55 .20

Centenary of Royal Canadian Henley Regatta, St. Catharines, Aug. 4-8 — A460

1982, Aug. 4
968 A460 30c multicolored .55 .20

Fairchild FC-2W1
A461

1982, Oct. 5 Litho. *Perf. 12½*

969 A461 30c shown .65 .20
970 A461 30c De Havilland Canada Beaver .65 .20
a. Pair, #969-970 1.30 1.00
971 A461 60c Noorduyn Norseman 1.20 .75
972 A461 60c Fokker Super Universal 1.20 .75
a. Pair, #971-972 2.40 1.90
Nos. 909-972 (4) 3.70 1.90

Christmas
A462

Designs: Creche figures.

1982, Nov. 3 *Perf. 13½*

973 A462 30c Holy Family .55 .20
a. All colors except black omitted *12,000.*
b. Printed on gummed side, black omitted *12,000.*
974 A462 35c Shepherds .65 .45
975 A462 60c Three Kings 1.10 .75
Nos. 973-975 (3) 2.30 1.40

Nos. 973a and 973b are each unique and were caused by a paper foldover.

World Communications Year — A463

1983, Mar. 10 Litho. *Perf. 12x12½*

976 A463 32c multicolored .60 .20

Commonwealth Day — A464

1983, Mar. 14

977 A464 $2 multicolored 8.50 3.50

Scene from Angeline de Montbrun, by Laure Conan (1845-1924), Painted by Rene Milot — A465

Design: No. 979, Sea Gulls, by Edwin John Pratt (1882-1966), woodcut by Claire Pratt.

1983, Apr. 22 Litho. *Perf. 13½*

978 A465 32c multicolored .60 .20
979 A465 32c multicolored .60 .20
a. Pair, #978-979 1.20 1.00
b. As "a," all color missing *4,000.*

No. 979b resulted from an extraneous piece of paper receiving the colors. After removal, the issued pane shows two vertical pairs without color plus six other stamps with only partial color.

St. John Ambulance Centenary
A466

1983, June 3 *Perf. 13½*

980 A466 32c Emblem .60 .20

World University Games, Edmonton, July 1-11 — A467

1983, June 28 *Perf. 13½*

981 A467 32c multicolored .60 .20
a. Printed on gummed side 1,000.
982 A467 64c multicolored 1.20 .65

Canada Day — A468

#983, Fort Henry, Ontario. #984, Fort William, Ontario. #985, Fort Rodd Hill, British Columbia. #986, Fort Wellington, Ontario. #987, Fort Prince of Wales, Manitoba. #988, Halifax Citadel, Nova Scotia. #989, Fort Chambly, Quebec. #990, Fort No. 1, Point Levis, Quebec. #991, Fort at Coteau-du-Lac, Quebec. #992, Fort Beausejour, New Brunswick. Sizes: #983, 988: 44x22mm; #984-985, 989-990, 36x22mm; #986-987, 991-992, 28x22mm.

1983, June 30 *Perf. 12½x13*

Booklet Stamps

983 A468 32c multicolored .75 .65
984 A468 32c multicolored .75 .65
985 A468 32c multicolored .75 .65
986 A468 32c multicolored .75 .65
987 A468 32c multicolored .75 .65
988 A468 32c multicolored .75 .65
989 A468 32c multicolored .75 .65
990 A468 32c multicolored .75 .65
991 A468 32c multicolored .75 .65
992 A468 32c multicolored .75 .65
a. Booklet pane of 10, #983-992 7.50 7.50

Scouting Year — A469

1983, July 6 *Perf. 13½*

993 A469 32c multicolored .60 .20

Church Council Emblem — A470

1983, July 22 Litho.

994 A470 32c tan & green .60 .20

6th World Council of Churches Assembly, Vancouver, July 24-Aug. 10.

Humphrey Gilbert — A471

1983, Aug. 3 Litho.

995 A471 32c multicolored .60 .20

400th anniv. of discovery of Newfoundland by Sir Humphrey Gilbert (1537-1583).

Centenary of Discovery of Nickel, Sudbury, Ontario
A472

Litho. & Typo.

1983, Aug. 12 *Perf. 13*

996 A472 32c multicolored .65 .20
a. Silver (and tagging) omitted *850.00*

Beware of forgeries of No. 996a. A certificate of authenticity is mandatory.

Josiah Henson (1789-1883), Preacher — A473

1983, Sept. 16 Litho. *Perf. 13x13½*

997 A473 32c multicolored .60 .20

Antoine Labelle (1833-1891), Deputy Minister for Settlement
A474

1983, Sept. 16 *Perf. 13½*

998 A474 32c multicolored .60 .20

Locomotives — A475

1983, Oct. 3 *Perf. 12½x13*

999 A475 32c Toronto 4-4-0, 1853 .60 .30
1000 A475 32c Dorchester 0-4-0, 1836 .60 .30
a. Pair, #999-1000 1.20 .90
1001 A475 37c Samson 0-6-0, 1838 .75 .60
1002 A475 64c Adam Brown 4-4-0, 1860 1.20 1.10
Nos. 999-1002 (4) 3.15 2.30

Dalhousie Law School Centenary
A476

1983, Oct. 28 *Perf. 13*

1003 A476 32c Arms .60 .20

Christmas
A477

1983, Nov. 3 Litho. *Perf. 13½*

1004 A477 32c Urban church .60 .20
1005 A477 37c Family going to church .70 .45
1006 A477 64c Rural church 1.20 .75
Nos. 1004-1006 (3) 2.50 1.40

Army Regiments, Centenaries
A478

19th Cent. Uniforms: No. 1007, Royal Canadian Regiment, British Columbia Regiment. No. 1008, Royal Winnipeg Rifles, Royal Canadian Dragoons.

1983, Nov. 10 *Perf. 13½x13*

1007 A478 32c shown .60 .20
1008 A478 32c multicolored .60 .20
a. Pair, #1007-1008 1.20 1.00

Yellowknife, 50th Anniv. — A479

1984, Mar. 15 Litho. *Perf. 13½*

1009 A479 32c Gold mine .60 .20

50th Anniv. of Montreal Symphony Orchestra
A480

1984, Mar. 24 Litho. *Perf. 12½*

1010 A480 32c multicolored .60 .20

450th Anniv. of Cartier's Landing in Quebec
A481

1984, Apr. 20 Photo. & Engr.

1011 A481 32c multicolored .60 .20

See France No. 1923.

Voyage of Tall Ships, Saint-Malo, France, to Quebec City — A482

1984, May 18 Litho. *Perf. 12x12½*

1012 A482 32c multicolored .60 .20

450th anniv. of Cartier's landing in Quebec.

Canadian Red Cross Society, 75th Anniv. — A483

1984, May 28 Litho. *Perf. 13*

1013 A483 32c Meritorious Service Medal .60 .20

New Brunswick, Bicentenary A484

Photo. & Engr.

1984, June 18 *Perf. 13*

1014 A484 32c Galleys .60 .20

St. Lawrence Seaway, 25th Anniv. — A485

1984, June 26 Litho. *Perf. 13*

1015 A485 32c Seaway, Lake Superior .60 .20

Canada Day A486

Provincial Landscapes by Jean Paul Lemieux (b. 1904).

1984, June 29 *Perf. 13*

1016	A486	32c	New Brunswick	.65	.35
1017	A486	32c	British Columbia	.65	.35
1018	A486	32c	Yukon Territory	.65	.35
1019	A486	32c	Quebec	.65	.35
1020	A486	32c	Manitoba	.65	.35
1021	A486	32c	Alberta	.65	.35
1022	A486	32c	Prince Edward Island	.65	.35
1023	A486	32c	Saskatchewan	.65	.35
1024	A486	32c	Nova Scotia, vert.	.65	.35
1025	A486	32c	Northwest Territories	.65	.35
1026	A486	32c	Newfoundland	.65	.35
1027	A486	32c	Ontario, vert.	.65	.35
a.			Min. sheet of 12, #1016-1027	8.00	8.00

Nos. 1018 and 1025 incorrectly inscribed. No. 1018 shows Northwest Territories landscape; No. 1025, Yukon Territory church.

Loyalists, British Flag (1606-1801) — A487

1984, July 3

1028 A487 32c multicolored .60 .20

United Empire Loyalists, American colonists who remained loyal to British throne and emigrated to Canada during American Revolution.

Roman Catholic Church in Newfoundland A488

1984, Aug. 17 Litho. *Perf. 13½*

1029 A488 32c St. John's Basilica .60 .20

Papal Visit A489

1984, Aug. 31 Litho. *Perf. 12½*

1030 A489 32c multicolored .60 .20
1031 A489 64c multicolored 1.20 .60

Lighthouses — A490

1984, Sept. 21 Litho. *Perf. 12½*

1032	A490	32c	Louisbourg, 1734	.65	.20
1033	A490	32c	Fisgard, 1860	.65	.20
1034	A490	32c	Ile Verte, 1809	.65	.20
1035	A490	32c	Gibraltar Point, 1808	.65	.20
a.			Block of 4, #1032-1035	2.60	1.30

Steam Locomotives — A491

1984, Oct. 25 Litho. *Perf. 12½x13*

1036	A491	32c	Scotia	.60	.20
1037	A491	32c	Countess of Dufferin	.60	.20
a.			Pair, #1036-1037	1.20	1.00
1038	A491	37c	Grand Trunk Class E3	.75	.65
1039	A491	64c	Canadian Pacific D10a	1.30	1.10
a.			Souvenir sheet	3.25	3.25
			Nos. 1036-1039 (4)	3.25	2.15

#1039a contains #1036-1039 in changed colors.

See #1071-1074, 1118-1121.

Christmas A492

Paintings: 32c, The Annunciation, by Jean Dallaire. 37c, The Three Kings, by Simone Mary Bouchard. 64c, Snow in Bethlehem, by David Milne.

1984, Nov. 2 Litho. *Perf. 13*

1040	A492	32c	multicolored	.60	.20
1041	A492	37c	multicolored	.70	.50
1042	A492	64c	multicolored	1.20	.65
			Nos. 1040-1042 (3)	2.50	1.35

Royal Canadian Air Force — A493

1984, Nov. 9 Litho. *Perf. 12x12½*

1043 A493 32c Pilots .60 .20

Cent. of La Presse — A494

1984, Nov. 16 Litho. *Perf. 13x13½*

1044 A494 32c Treffle Berthiaume .60 .20

International Youth Year — A495

1985, Feb. 8 Litho. *Perf. 12½*

1045 A495 32c Heart, arrow, jeans .60 .20

Canadians in Space — A496

1985, Mar. 15 Litho. *Perf. 13½*

1046 A496 32c Astronaut .65 .20

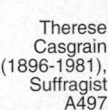

Therese Casgrain (1896-1981), Suffragist A497

Emily Murphy (1868-1933), Writer A498

1985, Apr. 17 Litho.

1047	A497	32c	multicolored	.60	.20
1048	A498	32c	multicolored	.60	.20
a.			Pair, #1047-1048	1.20	1.10

Gabriel Dumont (1837-1906), Metis Leader — A499

1985, May 6 Litho. *Perf. 13*

1049 A499 32c multicolored .60 .20

Centenary of the Northwest Rebellion.

Canada Day — A500

#1050, Lower Ft. Garry, Manitoba. #1051, Ft. Anne, Nova Scotia. #1052, Ft. York, Ontario. #1053, Castle Hill, Newfoundland. #1054, Ft. Whoop Up, Alberta. #1055, Ft. Erie, Ontario. #1056, Ft. Walsh, Saskatchewan. #1057, Ft. Lennox, Quebec. #1058, York Redoubt, Nova Scotia. #1059, Ft. Frederick, Ontario. Sizes: #1050, 1055: 48x26mm. #1051-1052, 1056-1057: 40x26mm. #1053-1054, 1058-1059, 32x26mm.

1985, June 28 Litho. *Perf. 12½x13*

Booklet Stamps

1050	A500	34c	multicolored	1.00	.65
1051	A500	34c	multicolored	1.00	.65
1052	A500	34c	multicolored	1.00	.65
1053	A500	34c	multicolored	1.00	.65
1054	A500	34c	multicolored	1.00	.65
1055	A500	34c	multicolored	1.00	.65
1056	A500	34c	multicolored	1.00	.65
1057	A500	34c	multicolored	1.00	.65
1058	A500	34c	multicolored	1.00	.65
1059	A500	34c	multicolored	1.00	.65
a.			Bklt. pane of 10, #1050-1059	10.00	12.00

Intl. Pharmaceutical Federation Congress — A501

Design: Louis Hebert (1575-1627), 1st French Apothecary in North America.

1985, Aug. 30 Litho. *Perf. 12½*

1060 A501 34c multicolored .60 .20

Interparliamentary Union '85, Ottawa — A502

1985, Sept. 3 *Perf. 13½*

1061 A502 34c multicolored .60 .20

A503

1985, Sept. 12 Photo. *Perf. 13½x13*

1062 A503 34c Guide, brownie saluting .60 .20

Natl. Girl Guides movement, cent.

Lighthouses A504

1985, Oct. 3 Litho. *Perf. 13½*

1063	A504	34c	Sisters Islets	.75	.30
1064	A504	34c	Pelee Passage	.75	.30
1065	A504	34c	Haut-fond Prince	.75	.30

1066 A504 34c Rose Blanche .75 .30
a. Block of 4, #1063-1066 3.00 2.25
b. Souv. sheet of 4, #1063-1066 4.50 4.50

Santa Claus Parade A505

Paintings by Barbara Carroll.

1985, Oct. 23 Litho. *Perf. 13½*
1067 A505 34c Santa Claus .60 .20
1068 A505 39c Horse-drawn coach .80 .50
1069 A505 68c Christmas tree 1.35 1.00

Perf. 13½ on 3 Sides

1070 A505 32c Polar float 1.00 .50
a. Booklet pane of 10 10.00
Nos. 1067-1070 (4) 3.75 2.20

No. 1070 printed in booklets only.

Locomotives Type of 1984

1985, Nov. 7 *Perf. 12½x13*
1071 A491 34c Grand Trunk K2 .70 .20
1072 A491 34c Canadian Pacific P2a .70 .20
a. Pair, #1071-1072 1.40 1.00
1073 A491 39c Canadian North-ern O10a .80 .70
1074 A491 68c Canadian Govt. Railways H4D 1.35 1.10
Nos. 1071-1074 (4) 3.55 2.20

1910 Gunner's Mate, World War II Officer, 1985 Woman Recruit — A507

1985, Nov. 8 *Perf. 13½x13*
1075 A507 34c multicolored .60 .20

Royal Canadian Navy, 75th anniv.

Old Holton House, Sherbrooke Street, Montreal, by James Wilson Morrice (1865-1924) A508

1985, Nov. 15 *Perf. 13½*
1076 A508 34c multicolored .60 .20

Montreal Museum of Fine Arts, 120th anniv.

Southwestern Alberta, Computer Design Map — A509

1986, Feb. 13 Litho. *Perf. 12½x13*
1077 A509 34c multicolored .60 .20

1988 Winter Olympics, Calgary, Alberta, Feb. 13-28.

EXPO '86, Vancouver, May 2-Oct. 13 — A510

1986, Mar. 7 Photo. & Engr.
1078 A510 34c Canada Pavilion .60 .20
1079 A510 39c Communications .80 .60

Heritage Artifacts Type of 1982

1987, May 6 Litho. *Perf. 14x13½*
1080 A442 25c Butter stamp .50 .30

Size: 20x26mm

Perf. 12x12½

1081 A442 42c Linen chest 1.10 .20
1082 A442 55c Iron kettle 1.45 .30
1083 A442 72c Hand-drawn cart 1.75 .40
Nos. 1080-1083 (4) 4.80 1.20

Park Type of 1979

Litho. & Engr.

1986, Mar. 14 *Perf. 13½*
1084 A359a $5 La Mauricie Natl. Park 9.50 2.25
a. Dark blue inscriptions omitted *2,750. 1,600.*

No. 1084a is valued in the grade of fine as all known examples are centered thus.

Philippe Aubert de Gaspe (1786-1871), Novelist A511

Molly Brant (1736-1796), Iroquois Leader and Loyalist A512

1986, Apr. 14 Litho. *Perf. 12½*
1090 A511 34c multicolored .60 .20

Perf. 13½

1091 A512 34c multicolored .60 .20

EXPO '86 — A513

Photo. & Engr.

1986, Apr. 28 *Perf. 13x13½*
1092 A513 34c Expo Center, Vancouver .60 .20
1093 A513 68c Transportation, horiz. 1.20 .65

Canadian Forces Postal Service, 75th Anniv. A514

1986, May 9 Litho. *Perf. 13½*
1094 A514 34c multicolored .60 .20

Indigenous Birds — A515

1986, May 22
1095 A515 34c Great blue heron .70 .30
1096 A515 34c Snow goose .70 .30
1097 A515 34c Great horned owl .70 .30
1098 A515 34c Spruce grouse .70 .30
a. Block of 4, #1095-1098 2.80 2.00

19th Intl. Ornithological Congress, Ottawa, June 22-29.

Canada Day — A516

Invention blueprints.

1986, June 27 Litho.
1099 A516 34c Rotary snowplow, 1869 .70 .25
1100 A516 34c Canadarm, 1986 .70 .25
1101 A516 34c Anti-gravity flight suit, 1938 .70 .25
1102 A516 34c Variable pitch propeller, 1923 .70 .25
a. Block of 4, #1099-1102 2.80 2.00

Canadian Broadcasting Corp., 50th Anniv. — A517

1986, July 23 Litho. *Perf. 12½*
1103 A517 34c Emblem, map .65 .20

Exploration of Canada A518

#1104, Siberian Indians discover and inhabit America, 10,000 B.C. #1105, Viking settlement, A.D. 1000. #1106, John Cabot lands, 1498. #1107, Henry Hudson pioneers Hudson Strait and Bay, 1610.

1986, Aug. 29 Litho. *Perf. 12½x13*
1104 A518 34c multicolored .65 .30
1105 A518 34c multicolored .65 .30
1106 A518 34c multicolored .65 .30
1107 A518 34c multicolored .65 .30
a. Block of 4, #1104-1107 2.60 2.25
b. Souv. sheet of 4, #1104-1107 3.25 2.75

No. 1107b issued Oct. 1 for CAPEX '87.
See #1126-1129, 1199-1202, 1233-1236.

Peacemakers of the Frontier, 1870s — A519

Designs: No. 1108, Crowfoot (1830-1890), Blackfoot Indian chief. No. 1109, James F. Macleod (1836-1894), asst. commissioner of Northwest Mounted Police.

1986, Sept. 5 *Perf. 13x13½*
1108 A519 34c scar, gray & ind .60 .25
1109 A519 34c ind, gray & scar .60 .25
a. Pair, #1108-1109 1.20 1.10

Intl. Peace Year — A520

Litho. & Embossed

1986, Sept. 16 *Perf. 13½*
1110 A520 34c multicolored .60 .20

1988 Calgary Winter Olympics — A521

1986, Oct. 15 Litho. *Perf. 13½x13*
1111 A521 34c Ice hockey .60 .20
1112 A521 34c Biathlon .60 .20
a. Pair, #1111-1112 1.20 1.00

See #1130-1131, 1152-1153, 1195-1198.

Christmas Angels — A522

1986, Oct. 29 Litho. *Perf. 12½*
1113 A522 34c multicolored .60 .20
1114 A522 39c multicolored .75 .60
1115 A522 68c multicolored 1.20 .80

Booklet Stamps

Size: 72x26mm

Perf. 13½ Horiz.

1116 A522 29c multicolored 1.50 1.10
a. Booklet pane of 10 15.00 14.00
b. Perf. 12½ horiz. 8.00 3.25
c. Bklt. pane of 10, #1116b 80.00 70.00
Nos. 1113-1116 (4) 4.05 2.70

No. 1116 has bar code at left, for use on covers with printed postal code matrix.

John Molson (1763-1836), Entrepreneur — A523

1986, Nov. 4
1117 A523 34c multicolored .60 .20

Locomotives Type of 1984

Locomotives, 1925-1945.

1986, Nov. 21 *Perf. 12½x13*
1118 A491 34c CN V1a .70 .25
1119 A491 34c CP T1a .70 .25
a. Pair, #1118-1119 1.40 1.10
1120 A491 39c CN U2a .85 .75
1121 A491 68c CP H1c 1.40 1.10
Nos. 1118-1121 (4) 3.65 2.35

CAPEX '87 — A524

1987 Litho. & Engr. *Perf. 13x13½*
1122 A524 34c 1st Toronto P.O. .60 .20
1123 A524 36c Nelson-Miramichi P.O. .70 .25
1124 A524 42c Saint Ours P.O. .80 .70
1125 A524 72c Battleford P.O. 1.30 1.10
Nos. 1122-1125 (4) 3.40 2.25

Souvenir Sheet

Yellow Green Inscription

1125A Sheet of 4 3.50 3.50
b. A524 36c like #1122 .65 .65
c. A524 36c like #1123 .65 .65
d. A524 42c like #1124 .80 .80
e. A524 72c like #1125 1.25 1.25

Issue dates: 34c, Feb. 16; others, June 12.

Exploration Type of 1986

Pioneers of New France: #1126, Etienne Brule (c. 1592-1633), 1st European to see the Great Lakes. #1127, Pierre Esprit Radisson (c. 1636-1710) & Medard Chouart des Groseilliers (1625-98), British expedition to Hudson Bay, 1668. #1128, Louis Jolliet (1645-1700) & Fr. Jacques Marquette (1637-75) discovering the Mississippi River, 1673. #1129, Recollet wilderness mission, 1615.

1987, Mar. 13 Litho. *Perf. 12½x13*

1126 A518 34c multicolored .65 .30
1127 A518 34c multicolored .65 .30
1128 A518 34c multicolored .65 .30
1129 A518 34c multicolored .65 .30
a. Block of 4, #1126-1129 2.60 2.25

Olympics Type of 1986

1987, Apr. 3 *Perf. 13½x13*

1130 A521 36c Speed skating .60 .20
1131 A521 42c Bobsledding .75 .50

Volunteers Week — A525

1987, Apr. 13 *Perf. 12½x13*

1132 A525 36c multicolored .65 .20

Law Day — A526

1987, Apr. 15 *Perf. 14x13½*

1133 A526 36c Coat of arms .65 .20
a. Imperf, pair *1,600.*

Canadian Charter of Rights and Freedoms, 5th anniv.

Engineering Institute of Canada, Cent. — A527

1987, May 19 *Perf. 12½x13*

1134 A527 36c multicolored .65 .20

Canada Day — A528

Inventors & communications innovations: #1135, Reginald Aubrey Fessenden (1866-1932), AM radio, 1900. #1136, Charles Fenerty, newsprint, 1838. #1137, Georges-Edouard Desbarats and William Leggo, halftone engraving, 1869. #1138, Frederick Newton Gisborne, No. America's 1st undersea cable, 1852, New Brunswick-Prince Edward Island.

1987, June 25 Litho. *Perf. 13½*

1135 A528 36c multicolored .65 .30
1136 A528 36c multicolored .65 .30
1137 A528 36c multicolored .65 .30
1138 A528 36c multicolored .65 .30
a. Block of 4, #1135-1138 2.60 2.40

Steamships A529

1987, July 20 *Perf. 13½x13*

1139 A529 36c Segwun, 1887 .65 .30

51x22mm

1140 A529 36c Princess Marguerite, 1948 .65 .30
a. Pair, #1139-1140 1.30 1.10

Shipwrecks A530

1987, Aug. 7

1141 A530 36c Hamilton & Scourge, 1813 .65 .30
1142 A530 36c San Juan, 1565 .65 .30
1143 A530 36c Breadalbane, 1853 .65 .30
1144 A530 36c Ericsson, 1892 .65 .30
a. Block of 4, #1141-1144 2.60 2.40

Air Canada, 50th Anniv. — A531

1987, Sept. 1 *Perf. 13½*

1145 A531 36c multicolored .65 .20

2nd Intl. Francophone Summit, Quebec, 9/2-4 — A532

1987, Sept. 2 *Perf. 13x12½*

1146 A532 36c multicolored .65 .20

9th Commonwealth Meeting, Vancouver, Oct. 13-17 — A533

1987, Oct. 13

1147 A533 36c multicolored .65 .20

Christmas A534

1987, Nov. 2 Litho. *Perf. 13½*

1148 A534 36c Poinsettia .65 .20
1149 A534 42c Holly wreath .80 .65
1150 A534 72c Mistletoe, Christmas tree 1.30 1.00

Size: 39x25mm

1151 A534 31c Gifts, Christmas tree .70 .70
a. Booklet pane of 10 7.00 *9.00*
Nos. 1148-1151 (4) 3.45 2.55

No. 1151 has bar code at left, for use on covers with printed postal code matrix. Issued in booklets only.

Olympics Type of 1986

1987, Nov. 13 *Perf. 13½x13*

1152 A521 36c Cross-country skiing .65 .25
1153 A521 36c Ski jumping .65 .25
a. Pair, #1152-1153 1.30 .75

75th Grey Cup, Vancouver, Nov. 29 — A535

1987, Nov. 20 *Perf. 12½*

1154 A535 36c multicolored .65 .20

Types of 1982 and

Elizabeth II A536

Mammals A538

Parliament (Center Block) A537 A539

Architecture — A540

Flag and Clouds A541

Flag A542

Natl. Flag, Deciduous Forest A543

Flag and Mountains A544

1987-91 Litho. *Perf. 13x13½*

Sizes Vary on A536, A538

1155 A538 1c Flying squirrel .20 .20
a. Perf. 13x12½ *4.00* .85
1156 A538 2c Prickly porcupine .20 .20
1157 A538 3c Muskrat .20 .20
1158 A538 5c Varying hare .20 .20
a. Imperf, pair *1,500.*
1159 A538 6c Red fox .20 .20
a. Horiz. pair, imperf *2,400.*
1160 A538 10c Skunk .20 .20
a. Perf. 13x12½ 4.00 .40
1161 A538 25c Beaver .45 .20

Perf. 13½x13

1162 A536 37c multicolored .75 .20
1163 A537 37c multicolored .75 .20
a. Bklt. pane of 10, #1163c 7.50
b. Bklt. pane of 25, #1163c 19.00
c. Perf. 13½x14 .75 .20

Perf. 13x12½

1164 A536 38c multicolored .75 .20
a. Perf. 13x13½ .75 .25
b. As "a," bklt. pane of 10 + 2 labels 7.50
c. Vert. block of 10, middle pair imperf, 2nd and 4th pairs part perf 1,200.
d. As "a," horiz. pair, imperf btwn. *1,000.*
e. Bottom margin horiz. pair, imperf —

Perf. 13x13½ on 3 or 4 Sides

1165 A539 38c multicolored .75 .20
a. Bklt. pane of 10 + 2 labels 7.50
b. Bklt. pane of 25 + 2 labels 19.00
c. Printed on gummed side 120.00
d. Double impression of all litho colors except black 275.00

Perf. 13½x13

1166 A541 39c multicolored .80 .20
a. Bklt. pane of 10 + 2 labels 8.00
b. Bklt. pane of 25 + 2 labels 22.50
c. Perf. 12½x13 12.00 .75

Perf. 13x13½

1167 A536 39c multicolored .80 .20
a. Bklt. pane of 10 + 2 labels 8.00
b. Perf. 13 10.00 .75
1168 A536 40c multicolored .80 .20
a. Bklt. pane of 10 + 2 labels 8.00

Perf. 13½x13

1169 A544 40c multicolored .80 .20
a. Bklt. pane of 25 + 2 labels 27.50
b. Bklt. pane of 10 + 2 labels 8.00

Perf. 12x12½

1170 A538 43c Lynx 1.10 .40

Perf. 14½x14

1171 A538 44c Walrus 1.60 .20
a. Perf. 12½x13 2.75 1.50
b. As "a," bklt. pane of 5 + label 12.50 12.00
c. Perf. 13½x13 450.00 47.50
1172 A538 45c Pronghorn .90 .25
b. As "f," bklt. pane of 5 + label 13.00 11.00
d. Perf. 13 22.50 1.10
f. Perf. 12½x13 2.60 .50
h. Imperf., pair *950.00*

Perf. 13

1172A A538 46c Wolverine .95 .25
c. Perf. 12½x13 1.25 .50
e. As "c," bklt. pane of 5 + label 6.50 6.00
g. Perf. 14½x14 5.50 .40

Perf. 12x12½

1173 A538 57c Killer whale 1.15 .35

Perf. 14½x14

1174 A538 59c Musk-ox 1.30 .35
a. Perf. 13 12.00 7.00
1175 A538 61c Timber wolf 1.25 .40
a. Perf. 13 77.50 5.75
1176 A538 63c Harbor porpoise 3.00 .40
a. Perf. 13 12.50 4.75

Perf. 12x12½

1177 A538 74c Wapiti 1.90 .70

Perf. 14½x14

1178 A538 76c Grizzly bear 2.00 .55
a. Perf. 12½x13 3.00 2.50
b. As "a," bklt. pane of 5 + label 15.00 15.00
c. Perf. 13 37.50 16.00
1179 A538 78c Beluga whale 2.40 .65
a. As "c," bklt. pane of 5 15.00 15.00
b. Perf. 13 35.00 6.00
c. Perf. 12½x13 3.00 2.60
d. Imperf, pair *950.00*

Perf. 13

1180 A538 80c Peary caribou 1.90 .70
a. Perf. 12½x13 3.00 1.10
b. As "a," bklt. pane of 5 + label 15.00 15.00
c. Perf. 14½x14 6.00 2.25

Perf. 13½

Litho. & Engr.

1181 A540 $1 Runnymede Library, Toronto 1.80 .55
a. Engr. inscriptions inverted *12,000.*
b. Imperf, pair *1,600.*
1182 A540 $2 McAdam Railway Station 3.75 1.00
a. Imperf., pair *1,200.*
1183 A540 $5 Bonsecours Market, Montreal 8.00 2.25
Nos. 1155-1183 (30) 40.85 12.00

A later printing of No. 1182 has more intense and clearly defined green shading on the roofline and the deep orange background extends closer to the roofline.

Imperfs exist of Nos. 1155-1157 and 1160, from printer's waste.

Issued: 1c, 2c, 3c, 5c, 6c, 10c, 25c, 10/3/88; 37c, 12/30/87; 38c, 12/29/88; 43c, 57c, 74c, 1/18/88; 44c, 59c, 76c, 1/18/89; $1, $2, 5/5/89; #1166, 12/28/89; 45c, 61c, 78c, #1167, 1/12/90; $5, 5/28/90; 40c, 46c, 63c, 80c, 12/28/90.

Booklet Stamps
Perf. 13½x14 on 3 Sides
Litho.

1184 A542 1c shown .20 .20
a. Perf. 12½x13 12.00 12.00
1185 A542 5c multi .20 .20
a. Perf. 12½x13 8.00 8.00

Perf. 12½x12 on 2 or 3 sides
Engr.

1186 A445 6c dark purple .65 .30
1187 A443 37c dark blue .90 .75
a. Bklt. pane of 4 + 2 labels (#938, 2 #942, #1187) 1.25 1.25
1188 A443 38c dark blue .80 .35
a. Bklt. pane of 5 (3 #939a, #1186, #1188) 1.00 1.00

Perf. 13½x14 on 3 Sides
Litho.

1189 A542 39c multi .90 .35
a. Bklt. pane of 4 (#1184, 2 #1185, #1189) 1.10 1.10
b. Perf. 12½x13 16.00 16.00
c. As "a," perf. 12½x13 45.00 45.00
1190 A542 40c multi 1.60 .50
a. Bklt. pane of 4 (2 #1184, #1185, #1190) 1.80 1.25
b. As "a," imperf *1,600.*

Nos. 1190a, 1190c sold for 50c.

Issued: #1187, 2/3/88; #1188, 1/18/89; #1186, 1989; #1184-1185, 1189, 1/12/90; #1190, 12/28/90.

Self-Adhesives
Die Cut
Booklet Stamps

1191 A543 38c multicolored 1.50 .70
a. Booklet of 12 18.00
b. Blue omitted *2,000.*
c. Yellow omitted *1,000.*
1192 A543 39c Flag, field 1.25 .70
a. Booklet of 12 15.00
1193 A543 40c Flag, seacoast 1.25 .70
a. Booklet of 12 15.00

Issued: 38c, 6/30/89; 39c, 2/8/90; 40c, 1/11/91.

Issued on peelable paper backing serving as booklet cover. Nos. 1191a, 1192a sold for $5, No. 1193a for $5.25.

Coil Stamps
Perf. 10 Horiz.
Engr.

1194 A443 37c dark blue .75 .20
d. Imperf., pair 175.00
1194A A443 38c dark green 1.10 .20
e. Imperf., pair 400.00
1194B A542 39c violet .80 .20
f. Imperf., pair 200.00
1194C A542 40c blue gray .80 .20
g. Imperf., pair 300.00

Issued: 37c, 2/22/88; 38c, 2/1/89; 39c, 2/8/90; 40c, 12/28/90.

See #1356-1362, 1375-1376, 1388, 1394-1396, 1682-1683, 1687, 1703, 1705.

Olympics Type of 1986

1988, Feb. 12 Litho. *Perf. 12x12½*

1195 A521 37c Alpine skiing .70 .25
1196 A521 37c Curling .70 .25
a. Pair, #1195-1196 1.40 1.00
1197 A521 43c Figure skating .80 .70
1198 A521 74c Luge 1.30 1.00
Nos. 1195-1198 (4) 3.50 2.20

Exploration Type of 1986

18th Cent. explorers of the western territories: No. 1199, Anthony Henday, who traveled the Prairies in 1754 from the Hayes River to Red Deer, Alberta. No. 1200, George Vancouver (1757-1798), who circumnavigated Vancouver Is. and explored the Pacific Coast, 1792-94. No. 1201, Simon Fraser (1776-1862), fur trader who discovered and navigated the Fraser River. No. 1202, John Palliser (1807-1887), geographer who determined the topographical boundary between Canada and the US from Lake Superior to the Pacific Coast.

1988, Mar. 17 Litho. *Perf. 12½x13*

1199 A518 37c multicolored .65 .35
1200 A518 37c multicolored .65 .35
1201 A518 37c multicolored .65 .35
1202 A518 37c multicolored .65 .35
a. Block of 4, #1199-1202 2.60 2.40

The Young Reader, by Ozias Leduc A546

Photo. & Engr. with Foil Application
1988, May 20 *Perf. 13x13½*

1203 A546 50c multicolored 1.10 1.00

Masterpieces of Canadian art. Printed in sheets of 16.

See Nos. 1241, 1271, 1310, 1419, 1466, 1516, 1545, 1602, 1635, 1754, 1800, 1863, 1916.

Wildlife and Habitat Conservation A547

1988, June 1 Litho. *Perf. 13x13½*

1204 A547 37c Duck landing .65 .30
1205 A547 37c Moose at water hole .65 .30
a. Pair, #1204-1205 1.30 1.00

Grey Owl, born Archibald Belaney, (b. 1888), conservationist; Ducks Unlimited Canada, 50th anniv.

Science and Technology — A548

Inventions: No. 1206, Kerosene, invented by Abraham Gesner (1797-1864), patented in 1854. No. 1207, Marquis wheat, developed in 1908 by Charles Saunders. No. 1208, Electron microscope, developed in 1938 at the University of Toronto by James Hillier and Albert Prebus under the supervision of Eli Burton. No. 1209, Cobalt cancer therapy, introduced by Dr. Harold Johns and Atomic Energy of Canada, Ltd., in 1951.

1988, June 17 *Perf. 12½x13*

1206 A548 37c multicolored .65 .35
1207 A548 37c multicolored .65 .35
1208 A548 37c multicolored .65 .35
1209 A548 37c multicolored .65 .35
a. Block of 4, #1206-1209 2.60 2.50

Intl. Entomology Congress, Vancouver A549

1988, July 4 Litho. *Perf. 12*

1210 A549 37c Short-tailed swallowtail .65 .35
1211 A549 37c Northern blue .65 .35
1212 A549 37c Macoun's Arctic .65 .35
1213 A549 37c Canadian tiger swallowtail .65 .35
a. Block of 4, #1210-1213 2.60 2.50

St. John's, Newfoundland, Cent. of Incorporation — A550

1988, July 22 *Perf. 13½x13*

1214 A550 37c Harbor entrance, skyline .65 .20

Canadian 4-H Council, 75th Anniv. A551

1988, Aug. 5

1215 A551 37c Motto, farm, young scientists .65 .20

Les Forges Du St. Maurice (1738-1883), Canada's 1st Industrial Complex — A552

Litho. & Engr.
1988, Aug. 19 *Perf. 13½*

1216 A552 37c multicolored .65 .20

Canadian Kennel Club, Cent. A553

1988, Aug. 26 *Perf. 12½x12*

1217 A553 37c Tahltan bear dog 1.00 .40
1218 A553 37c Nova Scotia duck-tolling retriever 1.00 .40
1219 A553 37c Canadian Eskimo dog 1.00 .40
1220 A553 37c Newfoundland 1.00 .40
a. Block of 4, #1217-1220 4.00 3.00

A554

1988, Sept. 14 Litho. *Perf. 13½x13*

1221 A554 37c multicolored .65 .20

Sesquicentennial of the 1st baseball game played in Canada, June 4, 1838 at Beachville, Upper Canada.

A555

1988, Oct. 27 Litho. *Perf. 13½*

Christmas (Icons of the Eastern Church): 32c, Nativity. 37c, Conception. 43c, Virgin and Child. 74c, Virgin and Child, diff.

1222 A555 37c multicolored .75 .20
1223 A555 43c multicolored .85 .65
1224 A555 74c multicolored 1.50 1.00

Booklet Stamp
Size: 35½x21mm
Perf. 12½x13½

1225 A555 32c multicolored 1.00 .75
a. Booklet pane of 10 10.00
Nos. 1222-1225 (4) 4.10 2.60

Millennium of Christianity in the Ukraine. No. 1225 has bar code at left; for use on covers with printed postal code matrix.

Inglis and Anglican Church A556

1988, Nov. 1 *Perf. 12½x12*

1226 A556 37c multicolored .65 .25

Charles Inglis (1734-1816), Canada's 1st Anglican bishop and founder of the Kings-Edgehill School, Nova Scotia, and the University of King's College at Halifax, bicent.

Hopkins and *Canoe Manned by Voyageurs* A557

1988, Nov. 18 *Perf. 13½x13*

1227 A557 37c multicolored .65 .25

Frances Ann Hopkins (1838-1918), painter.

The Bluenose and Capt. Walters — A558

1988, Nov. 18 *Perf. 13½*

1228 A558 37c multicolored .70 .25

Angus Walters (1882-1968), mariner.

Small Craft A559

1989, Feb. 1 Litho. *Perf. 13½x13*

1229 A559 38c Chipewyan canoe .70 .35
1230 A559 38c Haida canoe .70 .35
1231 A559 38c Inuit kayak .70 .35
1232 A559 38c Micmac canoe .70 .35
a. Block of 4, #1229-1232 2.80 2.40

See Nos. 1266-1269, 1317-1320.

Exploration Type of 1986

Explorers of the North: No. 1233, Matonabbee (c. 1737-1782), Indian guide who led 1st overland European expedition to the Arctic Ocean. No. 1234, Relics of expedition led by Sir John Franklin (1786-1847) that proved the existence of the Northwest Passage. No. 1235, Relics of the discovery of the Alberta fossil bed by geologist Joseph Burr Tyrrell (1858-1957). No. 1236, Vilhjalmur Stefansson (1879-1962), American ethnologist who discovered the last uncharted islands in the Arctic Archipelago.

1989, Mar. 22 Litho. *Perf. 12½x13*

1233 A518 38c multicolored .70 .35
1234 A518 38c multicolored .70 .35
1235 A518 38c multicolored .70 .35
1236 A518 38c multicolored .70 .35
a. Block of 4, #1233-1236 2.80 2.40

Photography in Canada, Sesquicentennial — A560

Photographers and their work: No. 1237, William Notman (1826-1891). No. 1238, W. Hanson Boorne (1859-1945). No. 1239, Alexander Henderson (1831-1913). No. 1240, Jules-Ernest Livernois (1851-1933).

1989, June 23 Litho. *Perf. 12½x12*

1237 A560 38c multicolored .70 .35
1238 A560 38c multicolored .70 .35
1239 A560 38c multicolored .70 .35
1240 A560 38c multicolored .70 .35
a. Block of 4, #1237-1240 2.80 2.40

Art Type of 1988

Ceremonial Frontlet (headpiece) Worn by Tsimshian Indian Chiefs, Early 20th Cent.

Litho. with Foil Application

1989, June 29 *Perf. 12½x13*

1241 A546 50c multicolored 1.10 .85

Masterpieces of Canadian Art and opening of the Museum of Civilization.

Poets — A562

1989, July 7 Litho. *Perf. 13½*

1243 A562 38c Louis Frechette (1839-1908) .70 .35
1244 A562 38c Archibald Lampman (1861-1899) .70 .35
a. Pair, #1243-1244 1.40 1.00

Mushrooms A563

1989, Aug. 4

1245 A563 38c *Clavulinopsis fusiformis* .70 .35
1246 A563 38c *Boletus mirabilis* .70 .35
1247 A563 38c *Cantharellus cinnabarinus* .70 .35
1248 A563 38c *Morchella esculenta* .70 .35
a. Block of 4, #1245-1248 2.80 2.40

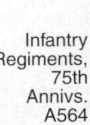

Infantry Regiments, 75th Annivs. A564

#1249, Princess Patricia's Canadian Light Infantry. #1250, Royal 22nd Regiment.

Litho. & Engr.

1989, Sept. 8 *Perf. 13*

1249 A564 38c multicolored .80 .40
1250 A564 38c multicolored .80 .40
a. Pair, #1249-1250 1.60 1.50

Intl. Trade A565

1989, Oct. 2 Litho. *Perf. 13½x13*

1251 A565 38c multicolored .70 .30

Performing Arts — A566

1989, Oct. 4 *Perf. 13x13½*

1252 A566 38c Dancers .70 .35
1253 A566 38c Musicians .70 .35
1254 A566 38c Camera, director .70 .35
1255 A566 38c Youth and adult entertainers .70 .35
a. Block of 4, #1252-1255 2.80 2.40

Royal Winnipeg Ballet 50th anniv. (No. 1252), Vancouver Opera 30th anniv. (No. 1253), Natl. Film Board 50th anniv. (No. 1254), and Confederation Center of the Arts, Charlottetown, P.E.I., 25th anniv. (No. 1255).

A566a

A567

Winter landscapes: 33c, *Champ-de-Mars, Winter,* 1892, by William Brymner (1855-1925). 38c, *Bend in the Gosselin River, Arthabaska,* c. 1906, by Marc-Aurele de Foy Suzor-Cote (1869-1937). 44c, *Snow II,* 1915, by Lawren S. Harris (1885-1970). 76c, *Ste. Agnes,* c. 1925-30, by Albert H. Robinson (1881-1956). Nos. 1256-1258 vert.

1989, Oct. 26 Litho. *Perf. 13x13½*

Size of 44c, 76c: 25x31mm

1256 A566a 38c multicolored .70 .30
a. Bklt. pane of 10, #1256b 47.50
b. Perf. 13x12½ 4.75

Perf. 13½

1257 A566a 44c multicolored .90 .65
a. Booklet pane of 5 + label 16.00 16.00
1258 A566a 76c multicolored 1.50 1.00
a. Booklet pane of 5 + label 30.00 30.00

Booklet Stamp

Size: 35x21mm

Perf. 12½x13½

1259 A567 33c shown 1.25 1.25
a. Booklet pane of 10 12.50
b. Horiz. pair, imperf btwn. *2,400.*
Nos. 1256-1259 (4) 4.35 3.20

Christmas. No. 1259 has bar code at left; for use on covers with printed postal code matrix. Booklet panes separate easily.

Declaration of War, 1939 — A568

Political and military actions taken by Canada at the outbreak of World War II.

1989, Nov. 10 *Perf. 13½*

1260 A568 38c shown .80 .55
1261 A568 38c Army mobilization .80 .55
1262 A568 38c Navy convoy system .80 .55
1263 A568 38c Commonwealth Air Training Plan .80 .55
a. Block of 4, #1260-1263 3.20 2.50

See Nos. 1298-1301, 1345-1348, 1448-1451, 1503-1506, 1537-1544.

Norman Bethune (1890-1939), Surgeon — A569

Litho. & Engr.

1990, Mar. 2 *Perf. 13x13½*

1264 A569 39c In Canada 1.00 .35
1265 A569 39c In China 1.00 .35
a. Pair, #1264-1265 2.00 1.25

See People's Republic of China Nos. 2263-2264.

Small Craft Type of 1989

1990, Mar. 15 Litho. *Perf. 13½x13*

1266 A559 39c Dory .75 .35
1267 A559 39c Pointer .75 .35
1268 A559 39c York boat .75 .35
1269 A559 39c North canoe .75 .35
a. Block of 4, #1266-1269 3.00 2.50

Multicultural Heritage of Canada A570

Litho. & Engr.

1990, Apr. 5 *Perf. 13*

1270 A570 39c multicolored .75 .20
a. Black (inscriptions) omitted *1,200.*

Art Type of 1988

Painting: *The West Wind,* by Tom Thomson.

Litho. with Foil Application

1990, May 3 *Perf. 12½x13*

1271 A546 50c multicolored 1.10 1.00

Masterpieces of Canadian Art.

Mail Trucks
A571 A572

1990, May 3 Litho. *Perf. 13½*

Booklet Stamps

1272 A571 39c multicolored .90 .70
1273 A572 39c multicolored .90 .70
a. Bklt. pane of 8+printed margin (4 each #1272-1273) 7.25
b. Bklt. pane of 9+3 labels, printed margin (5 #1272, 4 #1273) 12.50

Dolls A573

1990, June 8 Litho. *Perf. 12½x12*

1274 A573 39c Native .80 .35
1275 A573 39c Settlers .80 .35
1276 A573 39c 4 Commercial .80 .35
1277 A573 39c 5 Commercial .80 .35
a. Block of 4, #1274-1277 3.20 2.75

Natl. Flag, 25th Anniv. — A574

1990, June 29 *Perf. 13x12½*

1278 A574 39c Flag, fireworks .70 .20
a. Silver (inscriptions) omitted *2,000.*

Printed in sheets of 16.

Prehistoric Life A575

Litho. & Engr.

1990, July 12 *Perf. 13x13½*

1279 A575 39c Trilobite .80 .35
1280 A575 39c Sea scorpion .80 .35
1281 A575 39c Fossil algae .80 .35
1282 A575 39c Soft invertebrate .80 .35
a. Block of 4, #1279-1282 3.20 2.75

See Nos. 1306-1309.

Canadian Forests A576

1990, Aug. 7 Litho. *Perf. 12½x13*

1283 A576 39c Acadian .80 .30
a. Sheet of 4 10.00 8.00
1284 A576 39c Great Lakes-St. Lawrence .80 .30
a. Sheet of 4 10.00 8.00
1285 A576 39c Coast .80 .30
a. Sheet of 4 10.00 8.00
1286 A576 39c Boreal .80 .30
a. Block of 4, #1283-1286 3.20 2.75
b. Sheet of 4 10.00 8.00

Sheets of four sold for $1 each through Petro-Canada gas stations, and for full face value through the philatelic bureau. Issue date: Sept. 7.

Weather Observations in Canada, 150th Anniv. — A577

1990, Sept. 5 Litho. *Perf. 12½x13½*

1287 A577 39c multicolored .70 .20

The left and right margin singles of No. 1287 differ slightly in design from stamps from columns 2-4, due to the nature of the continuous cloud design across the pane.

Intl. Literacy Year — A578

1990, Sept. 7 *Perf. 13½x13*

1288 A578 39c multicolored .70 .20

Legendary Creatures A579

1990, Oct. 1 Litho. *Perf. 12½x13½*

1289 A579 39c Sasquatch .90 .75
1290 A579 39c Kraken .90 .75
1291 A579 39c Werewolf .90 .75

1292 A579 39c Ogopogo .90 .75
a. Block of 4, #1289-1292 3.60 3.00
b. As "a," imperf. *2,000.*

Perf. 12½x12

1289a A579 39c 12.00 4.00
1290a A579 39c 12.00 4.00
1291a A579 39c 12.00 4.00
1292c A579 39c 12.00 4.00
d. Block of 4, #1289a-1292c 50.00 30.00

Agnes Campbell Macphail (1890-1954), First Woman Member of Parliament — A580

1990, Oct. 9 Litho. ***Perf. 13x13½***
1293 A580 39c multicolored .70 .20

Virgin Mary with Christ Child and St. John the Baptist by Norval Morrisseau A581

Rebirth by Jackson Beardy A582

Indian Art: 45c, Sculpture of Mother and Child by an Inuit artist. 78c, Children of the Raven by Bill Reid.

1990, Oct. 25 Litho. ***Perf. 13½***
1294 A581 39c multicolored .80 .20
a. Booklet pane of 10 8.00
1295 A581 45c multicolored .90 .70
a. Bklt. pane of 5 + label 4.50 4.50
1296 A581 78c multicolored 1.60 1.10
a. Bklt. pane of 5 + label 8.00 7.00

Booklet Stamp

Perf. 12½x13 on 2 or 3 Sides

1297 A582 34c multicolored .85 .40
a. Booklet pane of 10 8.50
Nos. 1294-1297 (4) 4.15 2.40

Christmas. No. 1297 has bar code at left; for use on covers with printed postal code matrix.

World War II Type of 1989

1990, Nov. 9 ***Perf. 12½x12***
1298 A568 39c Home front .90 .60
1299 A568 39c Communal war efforts .90 .60
1300 A568 39c Food production .90 .60
1301 A568 39c Science and war .90 .60
a. Block of 4, #1298-1301 3.60 3.25

A583

Physicians: No. 1302, Jennie Trout (1841-1921), first licensed Canadian woman physician. No. 1303, Wilder Penfield (1891-1976), neurosurgeon. No. 1304, Sir Frederick Banting (1891-1941), discoverer of insulin. No. 1305, Harold Griffith (1894-1985), anesthesiologist.

1991, Mar. 15 Litho. ***Perf. 13½***
1302 A583 40c multicolored .80 .35
1303 A583 40c multicolored .80 .35
1304 A583 40c multicolored .80 .35
1305 A583 40c multicolored .80 .35
a. Block of 4, #1302-1305 3.20 2.75

Prehistoric Life Type of 1990

1991, Apr. 5 Litho. ***Perf. 12½x13½***
1306 A575 40c Microfossils .80 .35
1307 A575 40c Early tree .80 .35
1308 A575 40c Early fish .80 .35
1309 A575 40c Land reptile .80 .35
a. Block of 4, #1306-1309 3.20 2.75

Art Type of 1988

Forest, British Columbia by Emily Carr.

Litho. with Foil Application

1991, May 7 ***Perf. 12½x13***
1310 A546 50c multicolored 1.10 .90

Masterpieces of Canadian Art.

A584

1991, May 22 Litho. ***Perf. 13x12½***

Public Gardens: #1311, Butchart Gardens, Victoria, B.C. #1312, Intl. Peace Garden, Boissevain, Manitoba. #1313, Royal Botanical Gardens, Hamilton, Ontario. #1314, Montreal Botanical Gardens. #1315, Halifax Public Gardens, Nova Scotia.

Booklet Stamps

1311 A584 40c multicolored .85 .40
1312 A584 40c multicolored .85 .40
1313 A584 40c multicolored .85 .40
1314 A584 40c multicolored .85 .40
1315 A584 40c multicolored .85 .40
a. Strip of 5, #1311-1315 4.25 3.75
b. Bklt. pane, 2 each #1311-1315 8.50

Canada Day — A585

1991, June 28 ***Perf. 13½x13***
1316 A585 40c multicolored .80 .20

Small Craft Type of 1989

1991, July 18
1317 A559 40c Verchere rowboat .80 .35
1318 A559 40c Touring kayak .80 .35
1319 A559 40c Sailing dinghy .80 .35
1320 A559 40c Cedar strip canoe .80 .35
a. Block of 4, #1317-1320 3.20 2.75

Canadian Rivers — A586

1991, Aug. 20 ***Perf. 13x12½***

Booklet Stamps

1321 A586 40c South Nahanni .85 .35
1322 A586 40c Athabasca .85 .35
1323 A586 40c Boundary Waters-Voyageur Waterway .85 .35
1324 A586 40c Jacques Cartier .85 .35
1325 A586 40c Main .85 .35
a. Strip of 5, #1321-1325 4.25 3.25
b. Bklt. pane, 2 each #1321-1325 8.50

See #1408-1412, 1485-1489, 1511-1515.

Arrival of Ukrainians, Cent. — A587

Paintings by William Kurelek.

1991, Aug. 29 ***Perf. 13½x13***
1326 A587 40c Leaving homeland .80 .35
1327 A587 40c Winter in Canada .80 .35
1328 A587 40c Clearing land .80 .35
1329 A587 40c Growing wheat .80 .35
a. Block of 4, #1326-1329 3.20 2.75

Dangerous Public Service Occupations A588

1991, Sept. 23 ***Perf. 13½***
1330 A588 40c Ski Patrol 1.10 .35
1331 A588 40c Police 1.10 .35
1332 A588 40c Fire fighters 1.10 .35
1333 A588 40c Search & Rescue 1.10 .35
a. Block of 4, #1330-1333 4.40 2.75

Folktales A589

1991, Oct. 1 Litho. ***Perf. 13½x12½***
1334 A589 40c Witched Canoe .80 .35
1335 A589 40c Orphan Boy .80 .35
1336 A589 40c Chinook Wind .80 .35
1337 A589 40c Buried Treasure .80 .35
a. Block of 4, #1334-1337 3.20 2.75

Queen's University, Kingston, Ont., Sesqui. — A590

1991, Oct. 16 Litho. ***Perf. 13x12½***
1338 A590 40c multicolored .80 .55
a. Bklt. pane of 10 + 2 labels 8.00

A591

Santa Claus A592

1991, Oct. 23 ***Perf. 13½***
1339 A591 40c At fireplace .80 .20
a. Booklet pane of 10 8.00
1340 A591 46c With white horse, tree .90 .50
a. Bklt. pane of 5 + label 4.50 3.50
1341 A591 80c Sinterklaas, girl 1.50 1.00
a. Bklt. pane of 5 + label 7.50 7.50

Booklet Stamp

Perf. 12½x13 on 2 or 3 Sides

1342 A592 35c With punchbowl .80 .25
a. Booklet pane of 10 8.00
Nos. 1339-1342 (4) 4.00 1.95

Christmas. No. 1342 has bar code at left; for use on covers with printed postal code matrix.

Basketball, Cent. — A593

1991, Oct. 25 ***Perf. 13x13½***
1343 A593 40c multicolored .80 .20

Souvenir Sheet

1344 Sheet of 3 5.25 5.25
a. A593 40c like #1343 1.20 1.20
b. A593 46c Player shooting, diff. 1.60 1.60
c. A593 80c Player dribbling 2.40 2.40

No. 1344a has 3-line inscription.

World War II Type of 1989

1991, Nov. 8 ***Perf. 13½***
1345 A568 40c Women's Armed Forces .80 .55
1346 A568 40c War industry .80 .55
1347 A568 40c Cadets and veterans .80 .55
1348 A568 40c Defense of Hong Kong .80 .55
a. Block or strip of 4, #1345-1348 3.20 2.75

Types of 1987-91 and

Edible Berries — A594

Hills — A595

Prairie A596

Building A597

Trees — A598

1991-98 Litho. ***Perf. 13x13½***
1349 A594 1c Blueberry .20 .20
1350 A594 2c Wild strawberry .20 .20
1351 A594 3c Black crowberry .20 .20
1352 A594 5c Rose hip .20 .20
1353 A594 6c Black raspberry .20 .20
1354 A594 10c Kinnikinnick .20 .20
a. Horiz. pair, imperf at sides and bottom *1,000.*
1355 A594 25c Saskatoon berry .45 .20

Perf. 13½x13

1356 A595 42c multicolored .85 .20
a. Booklet pane of 10 8.50
b. Bklt. pane of 50 + 2 labels 95.00 80.00
c. Bklt. pane of 25 + 2 labels 21.00 16.00
d. Vert. pair, imperf between *1,000.*

Perf. 13x13½

1357 A536 42c multicolored .85 .20
a. Booklet pane of 10 8.50 7.50
1358 A536 43c multicolored 1.00 .20
a. Booklet pane of 10 10.00 9.00

Perf. 13½x13

1359 A596 43c multicolored .90 .20
a. Booklet pane of 10 9.00 7.50
b. Bklt. pane of 25 + 2 labels 22.50
c. Perf. 14½ 1.10 .20
d. As "c," bklt. pane of 10 11.00 9.00
e. As "c," bklt. pane of 25 + 2 labels 27.50 25.00

f. Vert. pair, imperf between (from #1359e) 900.00

Perf. 13x13½

1360 A536 45c multicolored .85 .20
a. Booklet pane of 10 8.50 7.50
Complete booklet, #1360a 9.00

Perf. 14½

1361 A597 45c multicolored .85 .20
a. Booklet pane of 10 8.50
Complete booklet, #1361a 9.00
b. Bklt. pane of 25+2 labels 30.00
Complete booklet, #1361b 30.00
c. Perf. 13½x13 .85 .20
d. As "c," bklt. pane of 10 8.50
Complete booklet, #1361d 9.00
e. As "c," bklt. pane of 25 + 2 labels 20.00
Complete booklet, #1361e 20.00

Perf. 13x13½
Size: 16x20mm

1362 A597 45c multicolored .80 .30
a. Booklet pane of 10 8.00
Complete booklet, #1362a 8.50
b. Booklet pane of 30 27.50
Complete booklet, #1362b 27.50

No. 1361 is 17x21mm.

Perf. 13

1363 A598 48c McIntosh apple .95 .25
a. Perf. 14½x14 on 3 sides 1.60 .40
b. As "a," bklt. pane of 5 + label 8.00 7.00
1364 A598 49c Delicious apple 1.00 .25
a. Perf. 14½x14 2.75 .35
b. As "a," bklt. pane of 5 + 1 label 14.00 6.50
c. Booklet pane of 5 + label 13.00 11.00
1365 A598 50c Snow apple 1.00 .30
a. Booklet pane of 5 + label 7.00 5.75
b. Perf. 14½x14 2.50 .45
c. As "b," bklt. pane of 5 + label 14.00 12.50
1366 A598 52c Gravenstein apple 1.50 .40
a. Booklet pane of 5+label 7.50 6.00
Complete booklet, #1366a 8.00
b. Perf. 14½x14 2.50 .60
c. As "b," bklt. pane of 5 + label 12.50 11.00
Complete booklet, #1366c 13.00
1367 A598 65c Black walnut 1.20 .40
1368 A598 67c Beaked hazelnut 1.20 .40
1369 A598 69c Shagbark hickory 1.30 .35
1370 A598 71c American chestnut 1.25 .35
a. Perf. 14½x14 55.00 .85
1371 A598 84c Stanley plum 1.60 .40
a. Perf. 14½x14 on 3 sides 2.50 .60
b. As "a," bklt. pane of 5 + label 12.50 10.00
1372 A598 86c Bartlett pear 1.80 .60
a. Perf. 14½x14 3.00 1.50
b. As "a," bklt. pane of 5 + 1 label 15.00 12.50
c. Booklet pane of 5 + label 17.50 16.00
1373 A598 88c Westcot apricot 1.60 .55
a. Booklet pane of 5 + label 11.00 8.00
b. Perf. 14½x14 4.25 2.25
c. As "b," bklt. pane of 5 + label 22.50 15.00
1374 A598 90c Elberta peach 1.80 .45
a. Booklet pane of 5+label 10.00 8.00
Complete booklet, #1374a 10.50
b. Perf. 14½x14 4.00 1.60
c. As "b," bklt. pane of 5+label 20.00 14.00
Complete booklet, #1374c 21.00

Size: 48x40mm
Litho. & Engr.
Perf. 14½x14

1375 A540 $1 Court House, Yorkton 2.00 .60
a. Dk bl (inscriptions) omitted 1,350.
b. Perf 13½x13 2.00 .60
c. As "b," dk bl (inscriptions) omitted 1,350.
1376 A540 $2 Provincial Normal School, Truro 4.00 1.10
a. Dk grn (inscriptions) omitted 1,200.
b. Engr. inscriptions inverted 9,000.
c. Perf. 13½x13 4.00 1.10
d. As "c," dk grn (inscriptions) omitted 1,400.

Perf. 13½x13

1378 A540 $5 Carnegie Public Library, Victoria 9.00 2.50
Nos. 1349-1378 (29) 38.95 11.80

Self-Adhesive
Die Cut
Imperf
Booklet Stamps

1388 A543 42c Flag, mountains 1.20 .80
a. Booklet of 12 16.00
1389 A543 43c Flag, estuary shore 1.20 .60
a. Booklet pane of 12 16.00

Nos. 1388a, 1389a issued on peelable paper backing serving as booklet cover and sold for $5.25.

Coil Stamps
Perf. 10 Horiz.
Engr.

1394 A542 42c red .80 .20
a. Imperf., pair 180.00
1395 A542 43c olive green .80 .20
a. Imperf., pair 160.00
1396 A542 45c blue green .85 .20
a. Imperf., pair 160.00
Nos. 1394-1396 (3) 2.45 .60

Nos. 1349-1363 are known imperf from printer's waste. Items exist imperf in wrong colors and with wrong denominations. These may be essays or printer's waste.

Issued: 1c-25c, 8/5/92; #1356-1357, 1394, 48c, 65c, 84c, 12/27/91; #1388, 1/28/92; #1358-1359, 1364, 1368, 1372, 1395, 12/30/92; #1389, 2/15/93; #1359c-1359e, 1/18/94; #1364c, 1372c, 1/7/94; 50c, 69c, 88c, 2/25/94; $1, $2, 2/21/94; #1375b, 1376c, 2/20/95; #1365c, 1373c, 3/27/95; #1360-1361, 1396, 52c, 71c, 90c, 7/31/95; $5, 2/29/96; #1362, 2/2/98.

1992 Winter Olympics, Albertville A601

1992, Feb. 7 Litho. ***Perf. 12½x13***

Booklet Stamps

1399 A601 42c Ski jumping .85 .40
1400 A601 42c Pairs figure skating .85 .40
1401 A601 42c Hockey .85 .40
1402 A601 42c Bobsledding .85 .40
1403 A601 42c Alpine skiing .85 .40
a. Strip of 5, #1399-1403 4.25 3.75
b. Bklt. pane, 2 each #1399-1403 8.50 8.50

See Nos. 1414-1418.

City of Montreal, 350th Anniv. — A602

Designs: No. 1404, City of Montreal, modern times. No. 1405, Early settlement of Montreal (Ville-Marie). 48c, Jacques Cartier's chart of Canada, snowshoe, ship's mast. 84c, World map, nocturnal and Aztec calendar stone.

1992, Mar. 25 ***Perf. 13½***

1404 A602 42c multicolored .75 .35
1405 A602 42c multicolored .75 .35
a. Pair, #1404-1405 1.50 .90
1406 A602 48c multicolored .85 .75
1407 A602 84c multicolored 1.40 1.00
a. Souvenir sheet of 4, #1404-1407 4.00 4.00
Nos. 1404-1407 (4) 3.75 2.45

Discovery of America, 500th anniv. (#1407).

Nos. 1404-1405 printed checkerwise. No. 1407a with engraved signatures in margin was produced in limited quantities for World Philatelic Youth Exhibition catalogue which sold for $12.

Canadian Rivers Type of 1991

1992, Apr. 22 ***Perf. 12½***

Booklet Stamps

1408 A586 42c Margaree .85 .40
1409 A586 42c West (Eliot) .85 .40
1410 A586 42c Ottawa .85 .40
1411 A586 42c Niagara .85 .40
1412 A586 42c South Saskatchewan .85 .40
a. Strip of 5, #1408-1412 4.25 3.75
b. Bklt. pane, 2 each #1408-1412 8.50

Nos. 1408-1412 are horiz.

Alaska Highway, 50th Anniv. — A603

1992, May 15 ***Perf. 13½***

1413 A603 42c multicolored .75 .25

1992 Olympic Games Type

1992, June 15 Litho. ***Perf. 12½x13***

1414 A601 42c Gymnastics .80 .40
1415 A601 42c Running .80 .40
1416 A601 42c Diving .80 .40
1417 A601 42c Cycling .80 .40
1418 A601 42c Swimming .80 .40
a. Strip of 5, #1414-1418 4.00 4.00
b. Bklt. pane, 2 each #1414-1418 8.00

1992 Summer Olympics, Barcelona.

Stamps in bottom row of #1418b are in different sequence than those in #1418a.

Art Type of 1988

Painting: Red Nasturtiums, by David Milne.

Litho. with Foil Application

1992, June 29 ***Perf. 12½x13***

1419 A546 50c multicolored 1.00 .75

Masterpieces in Canadian Art.

Miniature Sheet

Canada Day A604

1992, June 29 Litho. ***Perf. 12½x13***

1420 A604 42c Nova Scotia 1.60 1.60
1421 A604 42c Ontario 1.60 1.60
1422 A604 42c Prince Edward Island 1.60 1.60
1423 A604 42c New Brunswick 1.60 1.60
1424 A604 42c Quebec 1.60 1.60
1425 A604 42c Saskatchewan 1.60 1.60
1426 A604 42c Manitoba 1.60 1.60
1427 A604 42c Northwest Territories 1.60 1.60
1428 A604 42c Alberta 1.60 1.60
1429 A604 42c British Columbia 1.60 1.60
1430 A604 42c Yukon 1.60 1.60
1431 A604 42c Newfoundland 1.60 1.60
a. Sheet of 12, #1420-1431 + 13 labels 20.00 21.00

Canadian Folklore — A605

Legendary heroes: No. 1432, Jerry Potts, guide, interpreter. No. 1433, Captain William Jackman, rescuer. No. 1434, Laura Secord, patriot. No. 1435, Jos Monferrand, lumberjack.

1992, Sept. 8 Litho. ***Perf. 12½***

1432 A605 42c multicolored .80 .35
1433 A605 42c multicolored .80 .35
1434 A605 42c multicolored .80 .35
1435 A605 42c multicolored .80 .35
a. Block of 4, #1432-1435 3.20 2.50

Minerals A606

1992, Sept. 21 ***Perf. 12½***

1436 A606 42c Copper 1.00 .40
1437 A606 42c Sodalite 1.00 .40
1438 A606 42c Gold 1.00 .40
1439 A606 42c Galena 1.00 .40
1440 A606 42c Grossular 1.00 .40
a. Strip of 5, #1436-1440 5.00 4.50
b. Bklt. pane, 2 each #1436-1440 10.00

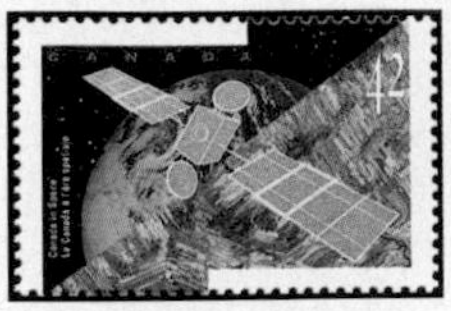

Canada in Space A607

1992, Oct. 1 Litho. ***Perf. 13***

1441 A607 42c Anik E2 satellite .80 .80
a. Silver omitted 3,000. 2,000.

Size: 32x26mm

1442 A607 42c Earth, space shuttle 1.10 1.10
a. Pair, #1441-1442 2.00 2.00
b. As "a," hologram omitted on #1442 2,000.

No. 1442 has a holographic image. Soaking in water may affect the hologram.

Natl. Hockey League, 75th Anniv. A608

Designs: No. 1443, Skates, stick, puck, photograph from the early years (1917-1942). No. 1444, Photograph, team emblems from the six-team years (1942-1967). No. 1445, Goalie's mask, gloves, photograph from the expansion years (1967-1992).

1992, Oct. 9 Litho. ***Perf. 13x12½***

Booklet Stamps

1443 A608 42c multicolored .80 .25
a. Bklt. pane of 8 + 4 labels 6.50
1444 A608 42c multicolored .80 .25
a. Bklt. pane of 8 + 4 labels 6.50
1445 A608 42c multicolored .80 .25
a. Bklt. pane of 9 + 3 labels 7.25
Nos. 1443-1445 (3) 2.40 .75

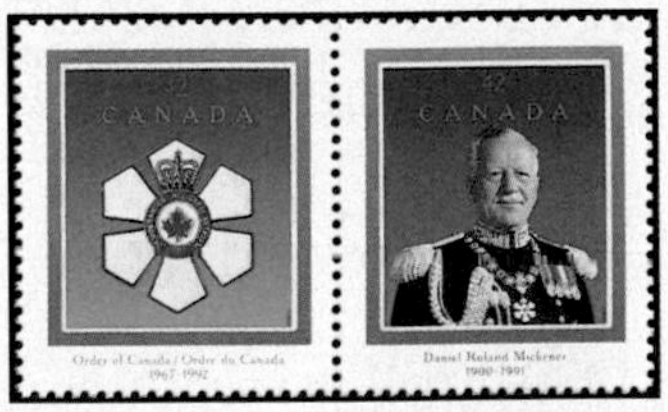

A609

No. 1446, Order of Canada, 25th anniv. No. 1447, Daniel Roland Michener (1900-1991), Governor General.

1992, Oct. 21 ***Perf. 12½***

1446 42c multicolored .80 .25
1447 42c multicolored .80 .35
a. A609 Pair, #1446-1447 1.60 1.00

Nos. 1446-1447 printed in sheets of 25 containing 16 #1446 and 9 #1447.

World War II Type of 1989

1992, Nov. 10 Litho. ***Perf. 13½***

1448 A568 42c War reporting .80 .45
1449 A568 42c Newfoundland air bases .80 .45
1450 A568 42c Raid on Dieppe .80 .45
1451 A568 42c U-boats offshore .80 .45
a. Block or strip of 4, #1448-1451 3.20 2.50

A611

Santa Claus A612

1992, Nov. 13 Litho. *Perf. 12½*

1452 A611 42c Jouluvana .75 .20
a. Perf. 13½ 1.00 .25
b. As "a," booklet pane of 10 10.00 6.00

Perf. 13½

1453 A611 48c La Befana 1.10 .75
a. Booklet pane of 5 + label 5.50 4.50
1454 A611 84c Weihnachtsmann 1.70 .75
a. Booklet pane of 5 + label 8.50 6.50

Booklet Stamp

Perf. 12½x13

1455 A612 37c Santa Claus .75 .75
a. Booklet pane of 10 7.50
Nos. 1452-1455 (4) 4.30 2.45

Christmas. No. 1455 has bar code at left; for use on covers with printed postal code matrix.

A613

Canadian Women: No. 1456, Adelaide Sophia Hoodless (1857-1910), founder of Victorian Order of Nurses. No. 1457, Marie-Josephine Gerin-Lajoie (1890-1971), founder of Notre-Dame du Bon Conseil Institute. No. 1458, Pitseolak Ashoona (c. 1904-83), Inuit graphic artist. No. 1459, Helen Alice Kinnear (1894-1970), first woman appointed King's Counsel and first federally appointed woman judge.

1993, Mar. 8 Litho. *Perf. 12½*

1456 A613 43c multicolored .80 .35
1457 A613 43c multicolored .80 .35
1458 A613 43c multicolored .80 .35
1459 A613 43c multicolored .80 .35
a. Block or strip of 4, #1456-1459 3.20 2.50

Natl. Council of Women of Canada (NCWC), and Natl. office of YWCA, cent.

Stanley Cup, Cent. — A614

1993, Apr. 16 Litho. *Perf. 13½*

1460 A614 43c multicolored .85 .25

Handcrafted Textiles — A615

#1461, Coverlet, New Brunswick. #1462, Pieced quilt, Ontario. #1463, Doukhobor bedcover, Saskatchewan. #1464, Kwakwaka'wakw ceremonial robe, British Columbia. #1465, Boutonne coverlet, Quebec.

Perf. 13x12½ on 3 Sides

1993, Apr. 30

Booklet Stamps

1461 A615 43c multicolored .85 .40
1462 A615 43c multicolored .85 .40
1463 A615 43c multicolored .85 .40
1464 A615 43c multicolored .85 .40
1465 A615 43c multicolored .85 .40
a. Strip of 5, #1461-1465 4.25 3.50
b. Bklt. pane, 2 ea #1461-1465 8.50

Stamps in bottom row of #1465b are in different sequence than those in #1465a.

Art Type of 1988

Painting: Drawing for The Owl, by Kenojuak Ashevak.

Litho. with Foil Application

1993, May 17 *Perf. 12½x13½*

1466 A546 86c multicolored 1.60 1.10

Intl. Year of Indigenous People.

Historic Canadian Pacific Railway Hotels A616

#1467, Empress, Victoria, B.C. #1468, Banff Springs, Banff, Alberta. #1469, Royal York, Toronto, Ont. #1470, Chateau Frontenac, Quebec. #1471, Algonquin, St. Andrews, N.B.

Perf. 13½ on 3 Sides

1993, June 14 Litho.

Booklet Stamps

1467 A616 43c multicolored .90 .55
1468 A616 43c multicolored .90 .55
1469 A616 43c multicolored .90 .55
1470 A616 43c multicolored .90 .55
1471 A616 43c multicolored .90 .55
a. Strip of 5, #1467-1471 4.50 3.50
b. Booklet pane, 2 #1471a 9.00

Opening of Chateau Frontenac, cent.

Miniature Sheet

Canada Day A617

Provincial and Territorial Parks: No. 1472, Algonquin, Ontario. No. 1473, De la Gaspesie, Quebec. No. 1474, Cedar Dunes, Prince Edward Island. No. 1475, Cape St. Mary's Seabird Ecological Reserve, Newfoundland. No. 1476, Mount Robson, British Columbia. No. 1477, Writing-On-Stone, Alberta. No. 1478, Spruce Woods, Manitoba. No. 1479, Herschel Island, Yukon. No. 1480, Cypress Hills, Saskatchewan. No. 1481, The Rocks, New Brunswick. No. 1482, Blomidon, Nova Scotia. No. 1483, Katannilik, Northwest Territories.

1993, June 30 Litho. *Perf. 13*

1472 A617 43c multicolored 1.10 1.00
1473 A617 43c multicolored 1.10 1.00
1474 A617 43c multicolored 1.10 1.00
1475 A617 43c multicolored 1.10 1.00
1476 A617 43c multicolored 1.10 1.00
1477 A617 43c multicolored 1.10 1.00
1478 A617 43c multicolored 1.10 1.00
1479 A617 43c multicolored 1.10 1.00
1480 A617 43c multicolored 1.10 1.00
1481 A617 43c multicolored 1.10 1.00
1482 A617 43c multicolored 1.10 1.00
1483 A617 43c multicolored 1.10 1.00
a. Sheet of 12, #1472-1483 13.50 13.50

Algonquin Park, centennial.

City of Toronto, Bicent. — A618

1993, Aug. 6 Litho. *Perf. 13½x13*

1484 A618 43c multicolored .85 .25

Canadian Rivers Type of 1991

1993, Aug. 10 *Perf. 13x12½*

Booklet Stamps

1485 A586 43c Fraser .80 .40
1486 A586 43c Yukon .80 .40
1487 A586 43c Red .80 .40
1488 A586 43c St. Lawrence .80 .40
1489 A586 43c St. John .80 .40
a. Strip of 5, #1485-1489 4.00 3.50
b. Bklt. pane, 2 each #1485-1489 8.00

Miniature Sheet

Historic Automobiles — A619

a, 1867 H.S. Taylor Steam Buggy. b, 1908 Russell Model L Touring Car. c, 1914 Ford Model T Open Touring Car. d, 1950 Studebaker Champion Deluxe Starlight Coupe. e, 1928 McLaughlin-Buick Model 28-496 Special Car. f, 1923-24 Gray-Dort 25-SM Luxury Sedan.

1993, Aug. 23 Litho. *Perf. 12½x13*

1490 A619 Sheet of 6 7.50 7.50
a.-b. 43c any single, 35x22mm .85 .85
c.-d. 49c any single, 43x22mm 1.00 1.00
e.-f. 86c any single, 51x22mm 1.70 1.70

See Nos. 1527, 1552, 1604-1605.

Folk Songs A620

Designs: No. 1491, The Alberta Homesteader, Alberta. No. 1492, Les Raftmans, Quebec. No. 1493, I'se the B'y That Builds the Boat, Newfoundland. No. 1494, Onkwa:ri tenhanonniahkwe, Kanien'kehaka (Mohawk).

1993, Sept. 7 Litho. *Perf. 12½*

1491 A620 43c multicolored .80 .35
1492 A620 43c multicolored .80 .35
1493 A620 43c multicolored .80 .35
1494 A620 43c multicolored .80 .35
a. Block of 4, #1491-1494 3.20 2.50

Dinosaurs — A621

1993, Oct. 1 Litho. *Perf. 13½*

1495 A621 43c Massospondylus .80 .35
1496 A621 43c Styracosaurus .80 .35
1497 A621 43c Albertosaurus .80 .35
1498 A621 43c Platecarpus .80 .35
a. Block or strip of 4, #1495-1498 3.20 2.50

See Nos. 1529-1532.

A622

Santa Claus A623

1993, Nov. 4 Litho. *Perf. 13½*

1499 A622 43c Swiety Mikolaj .80 .20
a. Booklet pane of 10 8.00 5.50
b. Horiz. pair, imperf between *1,750.*
1500 A622 49c Ded Moroz .85 .45
a. Booklet pane of 5 + label 4.25 4.50
1501 A622 86c Father Christmas, Australia 1.70 .55
a. Booklet pane of 5 + label 8.50 7.00

Booklet Stamp

Perf. 13

1502 A623 38c Santa Claus .80 .60
a. Booklet pane of 10 8.00
Nos. 1499-1502 (4) 4.15 1.80

Christmas. No. 1502 has bar code at left; for use on covers with printed postal code matrix.

World War II Type of 1989

1993, Nov. 8 Litho. *Perf. 13½*

1503 A568 43c Aid to Allies .85 .50
1504 A568 43c Bomber forces .85 .50
1505 A568 43c Battle of the Atlantic .85 .50
1506 A568 43c Italian campaign .85 .50
a. Block or strip of 4, #1503-1506 3.40 3.00

Greetings — A624

Design: No. 1508, "Canada" at right.

1994, Jan. 28 Litho. *Die Cut*

1507 A624 43c multicolored 1.00 .70
1508 A624 43c multicolored 1.00 .70
a. Bklt pane, 5 ea #1507-1508 10.00

No. 1508a also contains 35 self-adhesive greetings labels in seven designs that complete the design when placed in the central circle of Nos. 1507-1508.
See Nos. 1568-1569, 1600-1601.

Jeanne Sauve (1922-93), Governor General — A625

1994, Mar. 8 Litho. *Perf. 12½x13*

1509 A625 43c + label, multi .80 .30
a. Block or horiz. strip of 4 + 4 labels 3.20 2.75

No. 1509 issued se-tenant with label in sheets of 20 + 20 labels in four designs. In alternating rows, labels appear on left or right side of stamp.

T. Eaton Company, 125th Anniv. — A626

1994, Mar. 17 Litho. *Perf. 13½x13*
1510 A626 43c multicolored .80 .30
a. Booklet pane of 10 + 2 labels 8.00

Canadian Rivers Type of 1991

1994, Apr. 22 *Perf. 13½*

Booklet Stamps

1511 A586 43c Saguenay 1.00 .50
1512 A586 43c French 1.00 .50
1513 A586 43c Mackenzie 1.00 .50
1514 A586 43c Churchill 1.00 .50
1515 A586 43c Columbia 1.00 .50
a. Strip of 5, #1511-1515 5.00 4.00
b. Bklt. pane, 2 ea #1511-1515 10.00 9.00

Art Type of 1988

Vera, by Frederick H. Varley (1881-1969).

Litho. with Foil Application

1994, May 6 *Perf. 14x14½*
1516 A546 88c multicolored 1.60 1.20

XV Commonwealth Games, Victoria, BC — A627

1994 Litho. *Perf. 14*
1517 A627 43c Lawn bowls .80 .25
1518 A627 43c Lacrosse .80 .25
a. Pair, #1517-1518 1.60 1.00
1519 A627 43c Wheelchair marathon .80 .25
1520 A627 43c High jump .80 .25
a. Pair, #1519-1520 1.60 1.00
1521 A627 50c Diving 1.00 .75
a. Gold ("CANADA 50") omitted *1,600.*
1522 A627 88c Cycling 1.60 1.00
a. Gold ("CANADA 88") omitted *2,000.*
Nos. 1517-1522 (6) 5.80 2.75

Certificates of authenticity recommended for Nos. 1521a and 1522a.
Issued: #1517-1518, 5/20; #1519-1522, 8/5.

Souvenir Sheet

Intl. Year of the Family — A628

Designs: a, Mother and infant. b, Adults, children playing. c, Elderly woman, child. d, Adults, children in class. e, Judge, health care worker, child.

1994, June 2 Litho. *Perf. 14*
1523 A628 Sheet of 5 4.25 4.25
a.-e. 43c any single .85 .55

Canada Day A629

Maple trees: a, Big leaf. b, Sugar. c, Silver. d, Striped. e, Norway. f, Manitoba. g, Black. h, Douglas. i, Mountain. j, Vine. k, Hedge. l, Red.

1994, June 30 Litho. *Perf. 13x13½*
1524 A629 Sheet of 12 10.00 10.00
a.-l. 43c any single .80 .80

Billy Bishop (1894-1956), Fighter Ace — A630

Design: No. 1526, Mary Travers, "La Bolduc" (1894-1941), folk singer.

1994, Aug. 12 *Perf. 13*
1525 A630 43c multicolored .80 .35
1526 A630 43c multicolored .80 .35
a. Pair, #1525-1526 1.60 1.10

Historic Vehicles Type of 1993

Miniature Sheet

Designs: a, 1942 Ford F60L-AMB military ambulance. b, 1925 REO Speed Wagon Police Wagon. c, 1927 Sicard Snow Remover/Snowblower. d, 1936 Bickle Chieftain Fire Engine. e, 1894 Ottawa Car Company Streetcar. f, 1950 Motor Coach Industries Courier 50 Skyview bus.

1994, Aug. 19 Litho. *Perf. 12½x13*
1527 Sheet of 6 7.50 7.50
a.-b. A619 43c any single .85 .85
c.-d. A619 50c any single 1.00 1.00
e.-f. A619 88c any single 1.75 1.75

ICAO, 50th Anniv. A632

1994, Sept. 16 Litho. *Perf. 13*
1528 A632 43c multicolored 1.00 .25

Dinosaur Type of 1993

Prehistoric animals: No. 1529, Coryphodon. No. 1530, Megacerops. No. 1531, Short-faced bear. No. 1532, Woolly mammoth.

1994, Sept. 26
1529 A621 43c multicolored .80 .30
1530 A621 43c multicolored .80 .30
1531 A621 43c multicolored .80 .30
1532 A621 43c multicolored .80 .30
a. Block or strip of 4, #1529-1532 3.20 2.50

Family Singing Carols A633

Soloist A634

1994, Nov. 3 Litho. *Perf. 13½*
1533 A633 43c multicolored .88 .20
a. Booklet pane of 10 8.00
1534 A633 50c Choir, vert. .90 .55
a. Booklet pane of 5 + label 4.50 4.25
1535 A633 88c Caroling, vert. 1.60 1.00
a. Booklet pane of 5 + label 8.00 7.00

Booklet Stamp

Perf. 13

1536 A634 38c multicolored .80 .45
a. Booklet pane of 10 8.00
Nos. 1533-1536 (4) 4.18 2.20

Christmas. No. 1536 has bar code at left; for use on covers with printed postal code matrix.
Examples exist of 52c and 90c denominations with the same designs as Nos. 1534 (52c) and 1535 (90c). These were prepared in advance in anticipation of a rate increase that was not approved. Virtually all were destroyed, but a small quantity are known in private hands. None were regularly issued or sold at post offices.

World War II Type of 1989

1994, Nov. 7 Litho. *Perf. 13½*
1537 A568 43c D-Day beachhead .90 .35
1538 A568 43c Artillery-Normandy .90 .35
1539 A568 43c Tactical Air Forces .90 .35
1540 A568 43c Walcheren and the Scheldt .90 .35
a. Block or strip of 4, #1537-1540 3.60 2.50

1995, Mar. 20 Litho. *Perf. 13½*
1541 A568 43c Veterans return home .90 .35
1542 A568 43c Freeing the POW .90 .35
1543 A568 43c Liberation of civilians .90 .35
1544 A568 43c Crossing the Rhine .90 .35
a. Block or strip of 4, #1541-1544 3.60 2.50

Art Type of 1988

Painting: Floraison, by Alfred Pellan (1906-88).

Litho. with Foil Application

1995, Apr. 21 *Perf. 13*
1545 A546 88c multicolored 1.75 1.10
a. Gold foil omitted *1,600.*

Flag Over Lake — A635

1995, May 1 Litho. *Perf. 13½x13*
1546 A635 (43c) multicolored .90 .25

No. 1546 was valued at the first class domestic letter rate on day of issue.

Fortress of Louisbourg, 275th Anniv. — A636

#1547, Louisbourg Harbor, ships near Dauphin Gate. #1548, Walls, streets, buildings of Louisbourg. #1549, Museum behind King's Bastion. #1550, Drawing of King's Garden, Convent, Hospital and barracks. #1551, Partially eroded fortifications.

1995, May 5 *Perf. 12½x13*
1547 A636 (43c) 48x32mm .85 .40
1548 A636 (43c) 32x32mm .85 .40
1549 A636 (43c) 40x32mm .85 .40
1550 A636 (43c) 56x32mm .85 .40
1551 A636 (43c) 48x32mm .85 .40
a. Strip of 5, #1547-1551 4.25 3.75
b. Booklet pane, 2 #1551a 8.50
Complete booklet, #1551b 8.75

Nos. 1547-1551 were valued at the first class domestic letter rate on day of issue. No. 1551a is a continuous design.

Historic Vehicles Type of 1993

Miniature Sheet

Farm, frontier vehicles: a, 1950 Cockshutt "30" farm tractor. b, 1970 Bombardier Ski-Doo Olympique 335 snowmobile. c, 1948 Bombardier B-12 CS multi-passenger snowmobile. d, 1924 Gotfredson model 20 farm truck. e, 1962 Robin-Nodwell RN 110 tracked carrier. f, 1942 Massey-Harris No. 21 self-propelled combine.

1995, May 26 Litho. *Perf. 12½x13*
1552 Sheet of 6 7.50 7.50
a.-b. A619 43c any single, 35x22mm .85 .85
c.-d. A619 50c any single, 43x22mm 1.00 1.00
e.-f. A619 88c any single, 43x22mm 1.75 1.75

Golf in Canada A637

Designs: No. 1553, Banff Springs Golf Club. No. 1554, Riverside Country Club. No. 1555, Glen Abbey Golf Club. No. 1556, Victoria Golf Club. No. 1557, Royal Montreal Golf Club.

Perf. 13½x13 on 3 Sides

1995, June 6

Booklet Stamps

1553 A637 43c multicolored 1.00 .40
1554 A637 43c multicolored 1.00 .40
1555 A637 43c multicolored 1.00 .40
1556 A637 43c multicolored 1.00 .40
1557 A637 43c multicolored 1.00 .40
a. Strip of 5, #1553-1557 5.00 4.00
b. Booklet pane, 2 #1557a 10.00
Complete booklet, #1557b 10.50

Nat. Golf Week. Canadian Amateur Golf Championship, cent. Royal Canadian Golf Assoc., cent.

Lunenburg Academy, Cent. — A638

1995, June 29 Litho. *Perf. 13*
1558 A638 43c multicolored .80 .25

Souvenir Sheets

Group of Seven — A639

Painting, original members: No. 1559a, October Gold, by Franklin Carmichael. b, From the North Shore, Lake Superior, by Lawren Harris. c, Evening, Les Eboulements, Quebec, by A.Y. Jackson.
No. 1560a, Serenity, Lake of the Woods, by Frank H. Johnston. b, A September Gale, Georgian Bay, by Arthur Lismer. c, Falls, Montreal River, by J.E.H. MacDonald. d, Open Window, by Frederick Horsman Varley.
Painting, new members: No. 1561a, Mill Houses, by Alfred J. Casson. b, Pembina Valley, by Lionel LeMoine FitzGerald. c, The Lumberjack, by Edwin Headley Holgate.

1995, June 29
1559 A639 Sheet of 3 3.00 3.00
a.-c. 43c any single 1.00 1.00
1560 A639 Sheet of 4 4.00 4.00
a.-d. 43c any single 1.00 1.00
1561 A639 Sheet of 3 3.00 3.00
a.-c. 43c any single 1.00 1.00

Manitoba's Entry Into Confederation, 125th Anniv. — A640

1995, July 14 *Perf. 13½x13*
1562 A640 43c multicolored .80 .30

Migratory Wildlife — A641

1995, Aug. 15 Litho. *Perf. 13x12½*
1563 A641 45c Monarch butterfly .85 .25
1564 A641 45c Belted kingfisher .85 .40
1565 A641 45c Northern pintail .85 .25
1566 A641 45c Hoary bat .85 .25
a. Block or strip of 4, #1563-1566 3.40 2.50

No. 1564 with Revised Inscription

1995, Sept. 26

1567 A641 45c like #1564 1.10 .90
a. Block or strip of 4, #1563, 1565-1567 3.75 3.75

#1564 inscribed "aune," #1567 "Faune." See Mexico #1924.

Greetings Type of 1994

Designs: No. 1568, "Canada" at left. No. 1569, "Canada" at right.

1995, Sept. 1 ***Die Cut***

Self-Adhesive

Size: 46x22mm

1568 A624 45c green & multi 1.00 .75
1569 A624 45c green & multi 1.00 .75
a. Bklt. pane, 5 ea #1568-1569 10.00

By its nature, No. 1569a is a complete booklet. The peelable backing serves as a booklet cover.

No. 1569a also contains 15 self-adhesive greetings labels in four designs that complete the design when placed in the central circle of Nos. 1568-1569.

No. 1569a exists with special cover and labels commemorating the Canadian Memorial Chiropractic College, Toronto, 50th anniv.

Bridges A642

#1570, Quebec Bridge, Quebec. #1571, Highway 403-401-410 interchange, Ontario. #1572, Hartland Covered Wooden Bridge, New Brunswick. #1573, Alex Fraser Bridge, British Columbia.

1995, Sept. 1 ***Perf. 12½x13***

1570 A642 45c multicolored .85 .30
1571 A642 45c multicolored .85 .30
1572 A642 45c multicolored .85 .30
1573 A642 45c multicolored .85 .30
a. Block or strip of 4, #1570-1573 3.40 2.50

Canadian Arctic A643

#1574, Polar bear, caribou. #1575, Arctic poppy, cargo canoe. #1576, Inuk man, igloo, sled dogs. #1577, Dog-sled team, ski plane. No. 1578, Children.

1995, Sept. 15 ***Perf. 13x12½***

Booklet Stamps

1574 A643 45c multicolored .85 .30
1575 A643 45c multicolored .85 .30
1576 A643 45c multicolored .85 .30
1577 A643 45c multicolored .85 .30
1578 A643 45c multicolored .85 .30
a. Strip of 5, #1574-1578 4.25 3.50
b. Bklt. pane, 2 #1578a 8.50
Complete booklet, #1578b 9.00

Stamps in bottom row of #1578b are in different sequence.

Comic Book Characters A644

1995, Oct. 2 **Litho.** ***Perf. 13x12½***

Booklet Stamps

1579 A644 45c Superman 1.10 .40
1580 A644 45c Johnny Canuck 1.10 .40
1581 A644 45c Nelvana 1.10 .40
1582 A644 45c Captain Canuck 1.10 .40
1583 A644 45c Fleur de Lys 1.10 .40
a. Strip of 5, #1579-1583 5.50 5.00
b. Booklet pane, 2 #1583a 11.00
Complete booklet, #1583b 11.50

Stamps in the bottom row of No. 1583b are in different sequence.

UN, 50th Anniv. A645

1995, Oct. 24 **Litho.** ***Perf. 13½***

1584 A645 45c blue & multi 1.25 .25

No. 1584 printed in sheets of 10 with top label equal to 10 stamps. Label shows details of Canadian participation in UN activities. UN emblem on No. 1584 is stamped in blue foil.

Capital Sculptures, by Emile Brunet (1893-1977), Sainte-Anne-de-Deaupre Basilica — A646

Holly A647

1995, Nov. 2 **Litho.** ***Perf. 13½***

1585 A646 45c The Nativity .80 .20
a. Booklet pane of 10 8.00
Complete booklet, #1585a 8.50
1586 A646 52c The Annunciation .90 .50
a. Booklet pane of 5 + label 4.50 4.50
Complete booklet, #1586a 4.75
1587 A646 90c Flight to Egypt 1.50 .60
a. Booklet pane of 5 + label 7.50 7.00
Complete booklet, #1587a 8.00

Booklet Stamp

Perf. 12½x13

1588 A647 40c multicolored .80 .80
a. Booklet pane of 10 8.00 10.00
Complete booklet, #1588a 8.25
Nos. 1585-1588 (4) 4.00 2.10

Christmas. No. 1588 has bar code at left; for use on covers with printed postal code matrix.

La Francophonie's Agency for Cultural and Technical Cooperation, 25th Anniv. — A648

1995, Nov. 6 ***Perf. 13x13½***

1589 A648 45c multicolored .80 .25

End of the Holocaust, 50th Anniv. — A649

1995, Nov. 9 ***Perf. 12½x13***

1590 A649 45c multicolored .80 .25

Birds A650

#1591, American kestrel. #1592, Atlantic puffin. #1593, Pileated woodpecker. #1594, Ruby-throated hummingbird.

1996, Jan. 9 **Litho.** ***Perf. 13½***

1591 A650 45c multicolored .80 .30
1592 A650 45c multicolored .80 .30
1593 A650 45c multicolored .80 .30
1594 A650 45c multicolored .80 .30
a. Strip of 4, Nos. 1591-1594 3.20 2.75

Issued in panes of 12 stamps, printed checkerwise, and in uncut sheets of 5 panes.

See Nos. 1631-1634, 1710-1713, 1770-1777, 1839-1846, 1886-1889.

High Technology Industries — A651

Designs: No. 1595, Ocean technology. No. 1596, Aerospace technology. No. 1597, Information technology. No. 1598, Biotechnology.

Perf. 13½ on 3 Sides

1996, Feb. 15 **Litho.**

Booklet Stamps

1595 A651 45c multicolored 1.00 .35
1596 A651 45c multicolored 1.00 .35
1597 A651 45c multicolored 1.00 .35
1598 A651 45c multicolored 1.00 .35
a. Booklet pane of 12, 3 each Nos. 1595-1598 12.00 8.00
Complete booklet, No. 1598a 12.50
Nos. 1595-1598 (4) 4.00 1.40

Greetings Type of 1994

"Canada": #1600, at L. #1601, at R.

1996, Jan. 15 **Litho.** ***Die Cut***

Self-Adhesive

Size: 51x25mm

1600 A624 45c green & multi 1.50 1.00
1601 A624 45c green & multi 1.50 1.00
a. Booklet pane, 5 ea #1600-1601 15.00
b. As "a," die cutting omitted *3,250.*

By its nature No. 1601a is a complete booklet. The peelable backing serves as a booklet cover.

No. 1601a also contains 35 self-adhesive greetings labels in seven designs that complete the design when placed in the central circle of Nos. 1600-1601.

Art Type of 1988

Sculpture: The Spirit of Haida Gwaii, by Bill Reid.

Litho. with Foil Application

1996, Apr. 30 ***Perf. 12½x13***

1602 A546 90c multicolored 1.60 1.00

AIDS Awareness — A652

1996, May 8 **Litho.** ***Perf. 13½***

1603 A652 45c multicolored .80 .20

Historic Vehicles Type of 1993

#1604: a, 1899 Still Motor Co. Ltd. Electric Van. b. 1914 Waterous Engine Works Road Roller. c, 1938 International D-35 Delivery Truck. d, 1936 Champion Road Grader. e, 1947 White Model WA 122 Tractor Trailer. f, 1975 Hayes HDX 45-115 Logging Truck.

#1605: a, like #1490a. b, like #1490b. c, like 1527a. d, like #1527b. e, like #1552b. f, like #1604a. g, like #1604b, h, like #1552a. i, like #1604c. j, like 1604d. k, like #1527e. l, like #1527f. m, like #1604e. n, like #1604f. o, like #1490c. p, like #1490d. q, like #1527d. r, like #1490e. s, like #1490f. t, like #1527c. u, like #1552c. v, like #1552d. w, like #1552e. x, like #1552f. y, 1975 Bricklin SV-1 Sports car.

1996 **Litho.** ***Perf. 12½x13***

1604 A619 Sheet of 6 7.25 7.25
a.-b. 45c any single .90 .90
c.-d. 52c any single 1.00 1.00
e.-f. 90c any single 1.70 1.70
1605 A619 Sheet of 25 9.00 9.00
a.-j. 5c any single .20 .20
k.-n. 10c any single .35 .35
o.-x. 20c any single .45 .45
y. 45c multicolored 1.00 1.00

Nos. 1604e-1604f, 1605k-1605n, 1605y are 51x22mm. Nos. 1605o-1605x are 43x21mm.

Yukon Gold Rush, Cent. A653

Designs: a, "Skookum" Jim Mason's discovery on Rabbit (Bonanza) Creek, 1896. b, Miners trekking to gold fields, boats on Lake Laberge. c, Supr. Sam Steele, North West Mounted Police, Alaska-Yukon border. d, Dawson, boom town, city of entertainment. e, Klondike gold fields.

1996, June 13 ***Perf. 13½***

1606 Strip of 5 5.50 4.75
a.-e. A653 45c any single 1.10 .60

CAPEX '96. #1606 was issued in sheets of 10 stamps.

Canada Day — A654

1996, June 28 **Litho.** ***Die Cut***

Self-Adhesive

1607 A654 45c multicolored .80 .25
a. Pane of 12 10.00

Canadian Olympic Gold Medalists A655

#1608, Ethel Catherwood, high jump, 1928. #1609, Etienne Desmarteau, 56 lb. weight throw, 1904. #1610, Fanny Rosenfeld, 100m, 400m relay, 1928. #1611, Gerald Ouellette, smallbore rifle, prone, 1956. #1612, Percy Williams, 100m, 200m, 1928.

Litho. & Typo.

1996, July 8 ***Perf. 13x12½***

Booklet Stamps

1608 A655 45c gold, sep & silver 1.10 .55
1609 A655 45c gold, sep & silver 1.10 .55
1610 A655 45c gold, sep & silver 1.10 .55
1611 A655 45c gold, sep & silver 1.10 .55
1612 A655 45c gold, sep & silver 1.10 .55
a. Strip of 5, #1608-1612 5.50 3.75
b. Booklet pane, 2 #1612a 11.00
Complete booklet, #1612b 11.50

British Columbia's Entry Into Confederation, 125th Anniv. — A656

1996, July 19

1613 A656 45c multicolored .80 .25

A657

1996, Aug. 19 Litho. *Perf. 12½x12*

1614	A657 45c Canadian Heraldry	.80	.25

Motion Pictures, Cent. — A658

Film strips from motion pictures: No. 1615a, L'arrivée d'un train en gare, Lumière cinematography, 1896. b, Back to God's Country, Nell & Ernest Shipman, 1919. c, Hen Hop, Norman McLaren, 1942. d, Pour la suite du monde, Pierre Perrault, Michel Brault, 1963. e, Goin' Down the Road, Don Shebib, 1970.

No. 1616a, Mon oncle Antoine, Claude Jutra, 1971. b, The Apprenticeship of Duddy Kravitz, Ted Kotcheff, 1974. c, Les Ordres, Michel Brault, 1974. d, Les Bons Débarras, Francis Mankiewiez, 1980. e, The Grey Fox, Philip Borsos, 1982.

1996, Aug. 22 *Die Cut*

Self-Adhesive

1615	A658 Sheet of 5	4.00	4.00
a.-e.	45c Any single	.80	.75
1616	A658 Sheet of 5	4.00	4.00
a.-e.	45c Any single	.80	.75

Edouard Montpetit (1881-1954), Educator A659

1996, Sept. 26 Litho. *Perf. 12½*

1617	A659 45c multicolored	.80	.25

Winnie the Pooh A660

Designs: No. 1618, Winnie, Lt. Colebourne, 1914. No. 1619, Winnie, Christopher Robin, 1925. No. 1620, Milne and Shepard's Winnie the Pooh, 1926. No. 1621, Winnie the Pooh at Walt Disney World, 1996.

1996, Oct. 1 Litho. *Perf. 12½x13*

1618	A660 45c multicolored	.80	.40
1619	A660 45c multicolored	.80	.40
1620	A660 45c multicolored	.80	.40
1621	A660 45c multicolored	.80	.40
a.	Block of 4, #1618-1621	3.20	2.50
b.	Souv. sheet of 4, #1618-1621	8.00	7.50
c.	Booklet pane of 16, 4 each #1618-1621	13.00	
	Complete booklet, #1621c	13.50	

No. 1621c was issued with the halves of the booklet pane printed tete-beche. The booklet pane of 16 was used as a cover for a souvenir story booklet.

Walt Disney World, 25th anniv.

Authors — A661

#1622, Margaret Laurence (1926-87). #1623, Donald G. Creighton (1902-79). #1624, Gabrielle Roy (1909-83). #1625, Felix-Antoine Savard (1896-1982). #1626, Thomas C. Haliburton (1796-1865).

Perf. 13½x13 on 3 Sides

1996, Oct. 10 Litho. & Engr.

Booklet Stamps

1622	A661 45c multicolored	1.10	.40
1623	A661 45c multicolored	1.10	.40
1624	A661 45c multicolored	1.10	.40
1625	A661 45c multicolored	1.10	.40
1626	A661 45c multicolored	1.10	.40
a.	Strip of 5, #1622-1626	5.50	4.50
b.	Booklet pane, 2 #1626a	11.00	11.00
	Complete booklet, #1626b	11.50	

A662

Christmas: 45c, Children on snowshoes, sled. 52c, Santa Claus skiing. 90c, Children skating.

Perf. 13½ (#1627, 1629a), 12¾x12¼ (#1628, 1629), 13½x13 (#1627a, 1628a)

1996, Nov. 1 Litho.

1627	A662 45c multicolored	.80	.20
a.	Booklet pane of 10	8.00	8.00
	Complete booklet, #1627a	8.50	
1628	A662 52c multicolored	.90	.25
a.	Booklet pane of 5 + label	4.50	4.50
	Complete booklet, #1628a	4.75	
1629	A662 90c multicolored	1.60	.50
a.	Booklet pane of 5 + label	8.00	8.00
	Complete booklet, #1629a	8.50	

UNICEF, 50th anniv.

New Year 1997 (Year of the Ox) — A663

1997, Jan. 7 Litho. *Perf. 13x12½*

1630	A663 45c multicolored	.90	.25
a.	Souvenir sheet of 2	2.75	2.75
b.	As No. 1630, gold omitted	*4,000.*	

No. 1630a is fan shaped.

No. 1630a with Hong Kong 97 overprint was sold as a limited edition only at the show. Value $8.

Bird Type of 1996

#1631, Mountain bluebird. #1632, Western grebe. #1633, Northern gannet. #1634, Scarlet tanager.

1997, Jan. 10 Litho. *Perf. 12½x13*

1631	A650 45c multicolored	.80	.30
1632	A650 45c multicolored	.80	.30
1633	A650 45c multicolored	.80	.30
1634	A650 45c multicolored	.80	.30
a.	Block or strip of 4, #1631-1634	3.20	2.50

Nos. 1631-1634 were issued in sheets of 20, 5 each, printed checkerwise to contain 4 complete blocks or 5 strips.

Art Type of 1988

Painting: York Boat on Lake Winnipeg, by Walter J. Phillips.

Litho. with Foil Application

1997, Feb. 17 *Perf. 12½x13*

1635	A546 90c gold & multi	1.90	1.10

Canadian Tire, 75th Anniv. A664

1997, Mar. 3 Litho. *Perf. 13x13½*

1636	A664 45c multicolored	.80	.25

Father Charles-Emile Gadbois (1906-81), Musicologist A665

1997, Mar. 20 *Perf. 13½x13*

1637	A665 45c multicolored	.80	.25

Québec en Fleurs 97, Intl. Horticultural Exhibition A666

Perf. 13x12½ on 3 Sides

1997, Apr. 4 Litho.

Booklet Stamp

1638	A666 45c Blue poppy	.80	.25
a.	Booklet pane of 12	9.75	
	Complete booklet, #1638a	10.25	

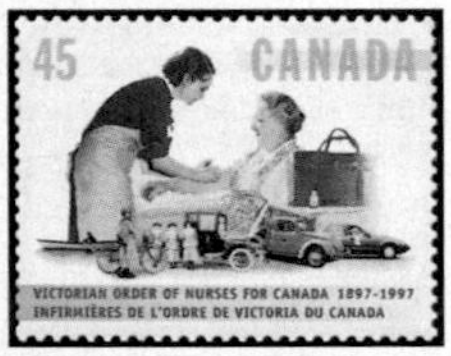
Victorian Order of Nurses for Canada, Cent. A667

1997, May 12 Litho. *Perf. 12½x13*

1639	A667 45c multicolored	.80	.25

Law Society of Upper Canada, Bicent. — A668

1997, May 23 *Perf. 13½x13*

1640	A668 45c multicolored	.80	.25

Salt Water Fish A669

#1641, Great white shark. #1642, Pacific halibut. #1643, Atlantic sturgeon. #1644, Bluefin tuna.

1997, May 30 Litho. *Perf. 12½x13*

1641	A669 45c multicolored	.80	.30
1642	A669 45c multicolored	.80	.30
1643	A669 45c multicolored	.80	.30
1644	A669 45c multicolored	.80	.30
a.	Block or strip of 4, #1641-1644	3.20	2.50

Opening of the Confederation Bridge — A670

1997, May 31

1645	A670 45c Lighthouse, bridge	.80	.25
1646	A670 45c Bridge, bird	.80	.25
a.	Pair, #1645-1646 + label	1.60	1.00

Gilles Villeneuve (1950-82), Formula One Race Car Driver — A671

45c, Villeneuve winning race in Ferrari T-4. 90c, Close-up, racing in Number 12 Ferrari T-3.

1997, June 12

1647	A671 45c multicolored	.80	.25
1648	A671 90c multicolored	1.60	1.00
a.	Pair, #1647-1648	2.40	2.25
b.	Sheet of 4 #1648a	9.75	9.00

John Cabot's Voyage to Canada, 500th Anniv. A672

1997, June 24 Litho. *Perf. 12½x13*

1649	A672 45c multicolored	.80	.25

See Italy No. 2162.

Scenic Canadian Highways — A673

Designs: No. 1650, Sea to Sky Highway, British Columbia. No. 1651, The Cabot Trail, Nova Scotia. No. 1652, The Wine Route, starting in Ontario. No. 1653, The Big Muddy, Saskatchewan.

1997, June 30 *Perf. 12½x13*

1650	A673 45c multicolored	.80	.50
1651	A673 45c multicolored	.80	.50
1652	A673 45c multicolored	.80	.50
1653	A673 45c multicolored	.80	.50
a.	Block or strip of 4, #1650-1653	3.20	2.50

See Nos. 1739-1742, 1780-1783.

Canadian Industrial Design — A674

1997, July 23

1654	A674 45c multicolored	.80	.25

No. 1654 was issued with se-tenant label in sheets of 24 + 24 labels. The 12 different labels each appear twice in different colors. In alternating rows, labels appear on left or right side of stamp.

Association of Canadian Industrial Designers, 50th anniv. and 20th Intl. Congress of Intl. Council of Societies of Industrial Design.

Highland Games, Maxville, Ontario — A675

1997, Aug. 1

1655	A675 45c multicolored	.80	.25

Knights of Columbus in Canada, Cent. — A676

1997, Aug. 5 *Perf. 13*

1656	A676 45c multicolored	.80	.25

28th World Congress of Postal, Telegraph and Telephone Intl. Labor Union, Montreal A677

1997, Aug. 18 Litho. *Perf. 13*

1657	A677 45c multicolored	.80	.25

Asia Pacific Year A678

1997, Aug. 25 *Perf. 13½*

1658	A678 45c multicolored	.80	.25

Canada-USSR Ice Hockey "Series of the Century," 25th Anniv. — A679

Designs: No. 1659, Canadian players, Paul Henderson, Yvan Cournoyer (No. 12), after scoring winning goal in final game. No. 1660, Canadian team members celebrating victory.

1997, Sept. 20 Litho. *Perf. 14x13*

Booklet Stamps

1659	A679 45c multicolored	.80	.30
1660	A679 45c multicolored	.80	.30
a.	Bklt. pane, 5 ea #1659-1660	8.00	
	Complete booklet, #1660a	8.50	

Famous Politicians A680

#1661, Martha Black (1866-1957). #1662, Lionel Chevrier (1903-87). #1663, Judy LaMarsh (1924-80). #1664, Réal Caouette (1917-76).

1997, Sept. 26 *Perf. 13½x13*

1661	A680 45c multicolored	.80	.35
1662	A680 45c multicolored	.80	.35
1663	A680 45c multicolored	.80	.35
1664	A680 45c multicolored	.80	.35
a.	Block or strip of 4, #1661-1664	3.20	2.50

Supernatural — A681

1997, Oct. 1 *Perf. 13x12½*

1665	A681 45c Vampire	.80	.30
1666	A681 45c Werewolf	.80	.30
1667	A681 45c Ghost	.80	.30
1668	A681 45c Goblin	.80	.30
a.	Block of 4, #1665-1668	3.20	2.50

Christmas — A682

Stained glass windows: 45c, "Our Lady of the Rosary," Holy Rosary Cathedral, Vancouver. 52c, "Nativity Scene," United Church, Leith, Ontario. 90c, Madonna and Child, St. Stephen's Ukrainian Byzantine Rite Roman Catholic Church, Calgary.

1997, Nov. 3 Litho. *Perf. 12½x13*

1669	A682 45c multicolored	.80	.20
a.	Booklet pane of 10	8.00	8.00
	Complete booklet, #1669a	8.50	
1670	A682 52c multicolored	.90	.25
a.	Booklet pane of 5	4.50	4.50
	Complete booklet, #1670a	4.75	
1671	A682 90c multicolored	1.60	.50
a.	Booklet pane of 5	8.00	8.00
	Complete booklet, #1671a	8.50	
	Nos. 1669-1671 (3)	3.30	.95

75th Royal Agriculture Winter Fair, Toronto A683

1997, Nov. 6

1672	A683 45c multicolored	.80	.25

Types of 1987-98 and:

Traditional Handiwork A684

Maple Leaf A685

Loon A686

Moose — A687

Flag and Inukshuk — A688

1997-2005 Litho. *Perf. 13x13½*

1673	A684 1c Bookbinding	.20	.20
1674	A684 2c Ironwork	.20	.20
1675	A684 3c Glass blowing	.20	.20
1676	A684 4c Oyster farmer	.20	.20
1677	A684 5c Weaving	.20	.20
1678	A684 9c Quilting	.20	.20
1679	A684 10c Artistic woodworking	.20	.20
a.	Imperf, single	—	
b.	Block of 4, top two stamps imperf (cut between)	—	
1680	A684 25c Leatherworking	.45	.20

Perf. 13

1681	A536 46c Queen Elizabeth II	.80	.30
1682	A541 46c Flag over Icebergs	.80	.30
a.	Booklet pane of 10	8.00	
	Complete booklet, #1682a	8.50	

Perf. 13¼x13

1683	A536 47c multi	.85	.30
a.	Imperf, pair	*725.00*	

Perf. 13

1684	A685 55c multicolored	1.10	.35
a.	Booklet pane of 5 + label	5.50	5.00
	Complete booklet, #1684a	5.75	
1685	A685 73c multicolored	1.30	.50
1686	A685 95c multicolored	1.90	.65
a.	Booklet pane of 5 + label	9.50	9.00
	Complete booklet, #1686a	10.00	

Litho. & Engr.

1687	A686 $1 Loon	1.80	.50
1688	A686 $1 White-tailed deer ('05)	1.80	.60
1689	A686 $1 Atlantic walrus ('05)	1.80	.60
a.	Pair, #1688-1689	3.60	2.50
b.	Souvenir sheet, 2 each #1688-1689	6.50	6.50
1690	A686 $2 Polar bear	3.50	1.00
1691	A686 $2 Peregrine falcons ('05)	3.50	1.00
1692	A686 $2 Sable Island horses ('05)	3.50	1.00
a.	Pair, #1691-1692	7.00	5.00
b.	Souvenir sheet, 2 each #1691-1692	14.00	14.00

Size 63x48mm

Perf. 12½x13

1693	A687 $5 Moose	9.00	2.00
a.	Engraved colors (Moose, etc.) omitted	*6,000.*	
1694	A687 $8 Grizzly bear	14.00	4.50
	Nos. 1673-1694 (22)	47.50	15.20

Coil Stamp

Engr.

Perf. 10 Horiz.

1695	A542 46c red	.80	.30
a.	Imperf, pair	175.00	

Booklet Stamps

Self-Adhesive

Die Cut

1696	A685 45c multicolored	1.40	1.50
a.	Booklet pane of 18	25.00	

Typo. & Embossed

Die Cut Perf. 13

Self-adhesive

1697	A685 45c multicolored	1.10	.65

Litho.

Die Cut

1698	A541 46c Flag over Icebergs	.90	.65
a.	Booklet pane of 30	27.00	
b.	Imperf, pair	*325.00*	
1699	A685 46c multicolored	2.75	2.25
a.	Booklet pane of 18	50.00	
1700	A688 47c multi	.85	.20
a.	Booklet of 10	8.50	
b.	Booklet of 30	26.00	

Nos. 1698a-1699a are complete booklets. The peelable backing serves as a booklet cover.

Issued: #1681, 1682, 1685-1687, 1695, 1698-1699, 12/28/98; $8, 10/15/97; Nos. 1690-1691, 4/14/98. No. 1688, $2, 10/27/98; 1c-25c, 4/29/99; 47c, 12/28/00; Nos. 1689-1690, 10/20/05; Nos. 1692-1693, 12/19/05.

The peelable paper backing of No. 1696a serves as a booklet cover.

No. 1697 does not have the "POSTAGE / POSTES" and copyright inscriptions found in No. 1696. The gold on No. 1697 is embossed and brighter than that on No. 1696.

See Nos. 1928-1930.

New Year 1998 (Year of the Tiger) A690

1998, Jan. 8 Litho. *Perf. 13x12½*

1708	A690 45c multicolored	.80	.25
a.	Souvenir sheet of 2	1.60	1.25

No. 1708a overprinted exists. Value $2.50.

Provincial Leaders A691

Designs: a, John P. Robarts (1917-82), Ontario. b, Jean Lesage (1912-80), Quebec. c, John B. McNair (1889-1968), New Brunswick. d, Tommy Douglas (1904-86), Saskatchewan. e, Joseph R. Smallwood (1900-91), Newfoundland. f, Angus L. MacDonald (1890-1954), Nova Scotia. g, W.A.C. Bennett (1900-79), British Columbia. h, Ernest C. Manning (1908-95), Alberta. i, John Bracken (1883-1969), Manitoba. j, J. Walter Jones (1878-1954), Prince Edward Island.

1998, Feb. 18 Litho. *Perf. 13½*

1709	A691 Sheet of 10	11.00	7.50
a.-j.	45c any single	1.10	.40

Bird Type of 1996

#1710, Hairy woodpecker. #1711, Great crested flycatcher. #1712, Eastern screech owl. #1713, Gray-crowned rosy-finch.

1998, Mar. 13 Litho. *Perf. 13x13½*

1710	A650 45c multicolored	.80	.30
1711	A650 45c multicolored	.80	.30
1712	A650 45c multicolored	.80	.30
1713	A650 45c multicolored	.80	.30
a.	Block or strip of 4, #1710-1713	3.20	2.50

Nos. 1710-1713 were issued in sheets of 20, 5 each, printed checkerwise to contain 4 complete blocks or 5 strips.

Fly Fishing in Canada — A693

Lure, type of fish: No. 1715, Coquihalla orange, steelhead trout. No. 1716, Steelhead bee, steelhead trout. No. 1717, Dark Montreal, brook trout. No. 1718, Lady Amherst, Atlantic salmon. No. 1719, Coho blue, coho salmon. No. 1720, Cosseboom special, Atlantic salmon.

1998, Apr. 16 *Perf. 12½x13*

1715	A693 45c multicolored	1.00	.45
1716	A693 45c multicolored	1.00	.45
1717	A693 45c multicolored	1.00	.45
1718	A693 45c multicolored	1.00	.45
1719	A693 45c multicolored	1.00	.45
1720	A693 45c multicolored	1.00	.45
a.	Vertical strip of 6, #1715-1720	6.00	5.00
b.	Bklt. pane, 2 ea #1715-1720	12.00	
	Complete booklet, #1720a	12.50	

Canadian Institute of Mining, Metallurgy and Petroleum, Cent. — A694

1998, May 4 Litho. *Perf. 12½*

1721 A694 45c multicolored .80 .25

Imperial Penny Post, Cent. A695

St. Edward's Crown, #86, Sir William Mulock.

1998, May 29 *Perf. 12½x13*

1722 A695 45c multicolored .80 .25

#1722 was issued in sheets of 14 + 1 label.

Sumo Wrestling Tournament, Vancouver — A696

Rising sun, mapleleaf and: No. 1723, Two wrestlers. No. 1724, Sumo champion performing bow twirling ceremony.

1998, June 5 Litho. & Embossed

1723 A696 45c multicolored .80 .25
1724 A696 45c multicolored .80 .25
a. Horiz. or Vert. Pair, #1723-1724 + 4 labels 1.60 1.20
b. Souvenir sheet, #1723-1724 4.00 4.00

Nos. 1723-1724 were printed checkerwise in sheets of 20, 10 each, plus 40 labels.

Canals of Canada — A697

#1725, St. Peters Canal, Nova Scotia. #1726, St. Ours Canal, Quebec. #1727, Port Carling Lock, Ontario. #1728, Locks, Rideau Canal, Ontario. #1729, Peterborough lift lock, Trent-Severn Waterway, Ontario. #1730, Chambly Canal, Quebec. #1731, Lachine Canal, Quebec. #1732, Ice skating on Rideau Canal, Ottawa. #1733, Boat on Big Chute Marine Railway, Trent-Severn Waterway. #1734, Sault Ste. Marie Canal, Ontario.

1998, June 17 Litho. *Perf. 12½*
Booklet Stamps

1725 A697 45c multicolored 1.10 .60
1726 A697 45c multicolored 1.10 .60
1727 A697 45c multicolored 1.10 .60
1728 A697 45c multicolored 1.10 .60
1729 A697 45c multicolored 1.10 .60
1730 A697 45c multicolored 1.10 .60
1731 A697 45c multicolored 1.10 .60
1732 A697 45c multicolored 1.10 .60
1733 A697 45c multicolored 1.10 .60
1734 A697 45c multicolored 1.10 .60
a. Bklt. pane, #1725-1734 + 10 labels 14.00
Complete booklet, #1734a 15.00

Health Professionals A698

Litho. & Embossed with Foil Application

1998, June 25 *Perf. 12½*

1735 A698 45c multicolored .80 .25

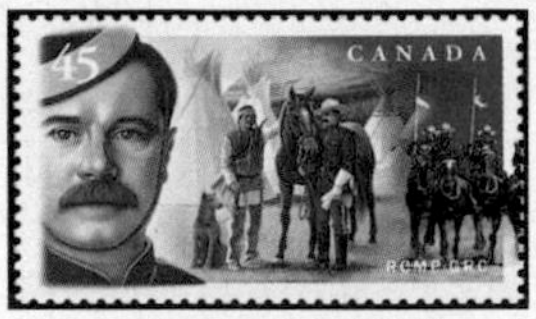

Royal Canadian Mounted Police, 125th Anniv. — A699

#1736, Male mountie, native, horse. #1737, Female mountie, helicopter, cityscape.

1998, July 3 Litho. *Perf. 12½x13*

1736 A699 45c multicolored .80 .25
1737 A699 45c multicolored .80 .25
a. Pair, #1736-1737 + 2 labels 1.60 1.25
b. Souvenir sheet, #1736-1737 + 1 label 1.60 1.60
c. As "b," with signature 3.25 3.25
d. As "b," with Portugal 98 emblem 4.00 4.00
e. As "b," with Italia 98 emblem 4.00 4.00
f. As "d," gold embossed emblem omitted *800.00*

#1737c-1737e have added inscriptions in gold. Issued: #1737c, 7/3; #1737d, 9/4; #1737e, 10/23.

William James Roué (1879-1970), Naval Architect — A700

Litho. & Engr.

1998, July 24 *Perf. 13*

1738 A700 45c multicolored .80 .25

Scenic Highway Type of 1997

Designs: No. 1739, Dempster Highway, Yukon. No. 1740, Dinosaur Trail, Alberta. No. 1741, River Valley Scenic Drive, New Brunswick. No. 1742, Blue Heron Route, Prince Edward Island.

1998, July 28 Litho. *Perf. 12½x13*

1739 A673 45c multicolored .80 .30
1740 A673 45c multicolored .80 .30
1741 A673 45c multicolored .80 .30
1742 A673 45c multicolored .80 .30
a. Block or strip of 4, #1739-1742 3.20 2.50

Publication of "Refus Global" by The Automatistes, 50th Anniv. — A701

Painting, artist: No. 1743, "Peinture," Jean-Paul Riopelle. No. 1744, "La dernière campagne de Napoléon," Fernand Leduc. No. 1745, "Jet fuligineux sur noir torturé," Jean-Paul Mousseau. No. 1746, "Le fond du garde-robe," Pierre Gauvreau. No. 1747, "Joie lacustre," Paul-Emile Borduas. No. 1748, "Syndicat des gens de mer," Marcelle Ferron. No. 1749, "Le tumulte á la machoire crispée," Marcel Barbeau.

1998, Aug. 7 *Die Cut*
Self-Adhesive
Booklet Stamps

1743 A701 45c multicolored 1.20 1.10
1744 A701 45c multicolored 1.20 1.10
1745 A701 45c multicolored 1.20 1.10
1746 A701 45c multicolored 1.20 1.10
1747 A701 45c multicolored 1.20 1.10
1748 A701 45c multicolored 1.20 1.10
1749 A701 45c multicolored 1.20 1.10
a. Booklet pane, #1743-1749 8.50

No. 1746 is 34x48mm. No. 1749a is a complete booklet. The peelable paper backing serves as a booklet cover.

Legendary Canadians A702

#1750, Napoléon-Alexandre Comeau (1848-1923), outdoorsman, "King of the North Shore." #1751, Phyllis Munday (1894-1990), mountaineer, community service worker. #1752, Bill Mason (1929-88), film maker, canoe enthusiast. #1753, Harry "Red" Foster (1905-1985), founder of Canadian Special Olympics, sports enthusiast.

1998, Aug. 15 *Perf. 13½*

1750 A702 45c multicolored .80 .30
1751 A702 45c multicolored .80 .30
1752 A702 45c multicolored .80 .30
1753 A702 45c multicolored .80 .30
a. Block or strip of 4, #1750-1753 3.20 2.50

Art Type of 1988

Painting: The Farmer's Family (detail), by Bruno Bobak.

Litho. with Foil Application

1998, Sept. 8 *Perf. 12½x13*

1754 A546 90c gold & multi 1.60 1.10

Housing in Canada A703

a, Native peoples. b, Settler. c, Regional. d, Heritage preservation. e, Multiple unit. f, Prefabricated. g, Veterans. h, Planned community. i, Innovative.

1998, Sept. 23

1755 Sheet of 9 11.00 11.00
a.-i. A703 45c Any single 1.10 1.00

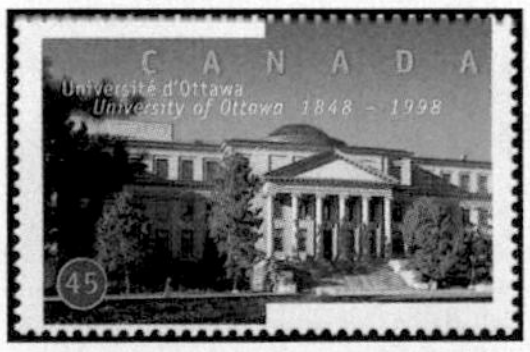

University of Ottawa, 150th Anniv. — A704

1998, Sept. 25 *Perf. 13*

1756 A704 45c multicolored .80 .25

The Circus — A705

Various circus clowns and: No. 1757, Elephant, bear performing tricks. No. 1758, Woman standing on horse, aerial act. No. 1759, Lion tamer. No. 1760, Contortionists, acrobats.

Perf. 13 on 3 Sides

1998, Oct. 1 Litho.
Booklet Stamps

1757 A705 45c multicolored .80 .30
1758 A705 45c multicolored .80 .30
1759 A705 45c multicolored .80 .30
1760 A705 45c multicolored .80 .30
a. Bklt. pane, 3 ea #1757-1760 9.75 9.75
Complete booklet, #1760a 10.25
b. Souvenir sheet, #1757-1760 4.75 4.50

Stamps in No. 1760b are perforated on all four sides.

John Peters Humphrey (1905-95), Author of Universal Declaration of Human Rights A706

1998, Oct. 7 *Perf. 13*

1761 A706 45c multicolored .80 .25

Canadian Naval Reserve, 75th Anniv. — A707

1998, Nov. 4 Litho. *Perf. 12½x13*

1762 A707 45c HMCS Sackville .80 .25
1763 A707 45c HMCS Shawinigan .80 .25
a. Pair, #1762-1763 1.60 1.40

Christmas — A708

Sculpted wooden angels: 45c, "Angel of Last Judgment" blowing trumpet. 52c, "Adoring Angel" raising hand. 90c, "Adoring Angel, Kneeling," by Thomas Baillairgé.

1998, Nov. 6 *Perf. 13*

1764 A708 45c multicolored .90 .25
a. Booklet pane of 10 35.00 35.00
Complete booklet, #1764a 37.50
b. Perf 13x13½ 400.00 16.00
c. As "b," booklet pane of 10 14.00
Complete booklet, #1764c 15.00

The values for No. 1764b are for singles perfed on all four sides from sheet format. These are extremely scarce. Single stamps from booklet pane No. 1764c have a straight edge on one side. Value, booklet single, unused $1.60, used $.30.

Perf. 13x13½

1765 A708 52c multicolored .90 .30
a. Booklet pane of 5 + label 19.00 17.50
Complete booklet, #1765a 20.00
b. Perf 13 1.10 .50
c. As "b," booklet pane of 5 + label 5.50 5.00
Complete booklet, #1765c 6.00
1766 A708 90c multicolored 1.60 .60
a. Booklet pane of 5 + label 30.00 25.00
Complete booklet, #1766a 32.50
b. Perf 13 1.60 .90
c. As "b," booklet pane of 5 + label 8.00 7.00
Complete booklet, #1766c 8.50
Nos. 1764-1766 (3) 3.40 1.15

New Year 1999 (Year of the Rabbit) A709

1999, Jan. 8 Litho. *Perf. 13½*
1767 A709 46c multicolored .80 .25

Souvenir Sheet

Perf. 12½x13
1768 A709 95c Sheet of 1 2.50 2.25
a. Single stamp 1.75 1.25

No. 1768 with China 99 overprint was sold only at the show. Value same as unoverprinted sheet.

Le Theatre du Rideau Vert, 50th Anniv. — A710

1999, Feb. 17 Litho. *Perf. 13x12½*
1769 A710 46c multicolored .80 .30

Bird Type of 1996

Designs: No. 1770, Northern goshawk. No. 1771, Red-winged blackbird. No. 1772, American goldfinch. No. 1773, Sandhill crane.

1999, Feb. 24 Litho. *Perf. 12½x13*
1770 A650 46c multicolored .80 .30
1771 A650 46c multicolored .80 .30
1772 A650 46c multicolored .80 .30
1773 A650 46c multicolored .80 .30
a. Block or strip of 4, #1770-1773 3.20 1.75

Booklet Stamps

Self-Adhesive

Die Cut Perf. 11½
1774 A650 46c like #1770 1.00 .30
1775 A650 46c like #1771 1.00 .30
1776 A650 46c like #1772 1.00 .30
1777 A650 46c like #1773 1.00 .30
a. Booklet pane, 2 each #1774-1775, 1 each #1776-1777 6.00
b. Booklet pane, 2 each #1776-1777, 1 each #1774-1775 6.00
Complete booklet, #1777a, #1777b 12.00

Nos. 1770-1773 were issued in sheets of 20, 5 each, printed checkerwise to contain 4 complete blocks or strips.
The peelable paper backing of Nos. 1777a, 1777b serves as the booklet cover.

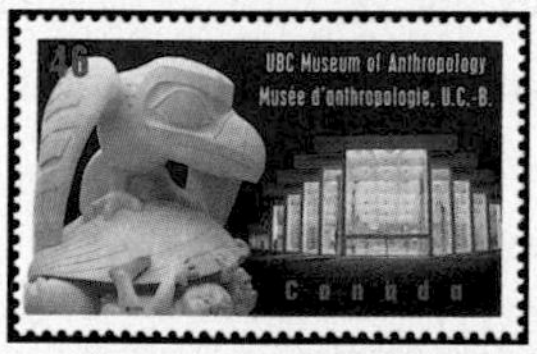

Univ. of British Columbia's Museum of Anthropology, 50th Anniv. — A711

1999, Mar. 9 Litho. *Perf. 13½*
1778 A711 46c multicolored .80 .25

Sailing Ship Marco Polo — A712

1999, Mar. 19 Litho. *Perf. 13x12½*
1779 A712 46c multicolored .80 .25
a. Sheet of 2, #1779 perf. 13, Australia #1631 perf. 13½ 3.25 3.25

Australia '99 World Stamp Expo. See Australia #1631a.

Scenic Highway Type of 1997

#1780, Gaspé Peninsula, Highway 132, Quebec. #1781, Yellowhead Highway (PTH 16), Manitoba. #1782, Dempster Highway 8, Northwest Territories. #1783, Discovery Trail, Route 230N, Newfoundland.

1999, Mar. 31 *Perf. 12½x13*
1780 A673 46c multicolored .80 .30
1781 A673 46c multicolored .80 .30
1782 A673 46c multicolored .80 .30
1783 A673 46c multicolored .80 .30
a. Block or strip of 4, #1780-1783 3.20 2.50

Creation of the Nunavut Territory — A713

1999, Apr. 1
1784 A713 46c multicolored .80 .25

Intl. Year of Older Persons — A714

1999, Apr. 12 Litho. *Perf. 13½*
1785 A714 46c multicolored .80 .25

A715

A716

1999, Apr. 19 *Perf. 13*
1786 A715 46c multicolored 1.00 .35

Baisakhi, Religious Holiday of Sikh Canadians, 300th Anniv.

1999, Apr. 27 *Perf. 13x12½*

Paintings (Canadian Orchids): No. 1787, Arethusa bulbosa, by Poon-Kuen Chow. No. 1788, Amerorchis rotundifolia, by Yakman Lai. No. 1789, Platanthera psycodes, by Lai. No. 1790, Cypripedium pubescens, by Chow.

Booklet Stamps
1787 A716 46c multicolored .90 .30
1788 A716 46c multicolored .90 .30
1789 A716 46c multicolored .90 .30
1790 A716 46c multicolored .90 .30
a. Bklt. pane, 3 ea #1787-1790 11.00
Complete booklet, #1790a 11.50
b. Souvenir sheet, #1787-1790 3.75 3.75

China '99 World Philatelic Exhibition, Beijing. Designs of some stamps contained in No. 1790a extend into selvage of booklet pane.
Issued: No. 1790b, 8/21/99.

Horses A717

#1791, Northern Dancer, thoroughbred race horse. #1792, Kingsway Skoal, bucking horse. #1793, Big Ben, show horse. #1794, Armbro Flight, harness race horse.

1999, June 2 Litho. *Perf. 13x13½*
1791 A717 46c multicolored 1.00 .35
1792 A717 46c multicolored 1.00 .35
1793 A717 46c multicolored 1.00 .35
1794 A717 46c multicolored 1.00 .35
a. Block or strip of 4, #1791-1794 4.00 3.00

Booklet Stamps

Self-Adhesive

Serpentine Die Cut 11½
1795 A717 46c like #1791 1.25 .35
1796 A717 46c like #1792 1.25 .35
1797 A717 46c like #1793 1.25 .35
1798 A717 46c like #1794 1.25 .35
a. Block of 4, #1795-1798 5.00
b. Complete booklet, 3 each #1795-1798 15.00

Nos. 1791-1794 were issued in sheets of 16, 4 each, printed checkerwise to contain 4 complete blocks or strips.

Quebec Bar Assoc., 150th Anniv. — A718

1999, June 3 *Perf. 13½*
1799 A718 46c multicolored .80 .25

Art Type of 1988

Coq Licorne, by Jean Dallaire (1916-65).

Litho. with Foil Application

1999, July 3 *Perf. 12½x13¼*
1800 A546 95c multicolored 1.75 1.10
a. Silver omitted *1,300.*

1999 Pan American Games, Winnipeg A719

Designs: No. 1801, Track & field. No. 1802, Cycling, weight lifting, gymnastics. No. 1803, Swimming, sailboarding, kayaking. No. 1804, Soccer, tennis, medal winners.

1999, July 12 *Perf. 13¼*
1801 A719 46c multicolored .80 .30
1802 A719 46c multicolored .80 .30
1803 A719 46c multicolored .80 .30
1804 A719 46c multicolored .80 .30
a. Block of 4, #1801-1804 3.20 2.50

Issued in sheets of 16 stamps.

23rd World Rowing Championships, St. Catherines, Ont. — A720

1999, Aug. 22 Litho. *Perf. 12½x13*
1805 A720 46c multicolored .80 .25

UPU, 125th Anniv. — A721

1999, Aug. 26
1806 A721 46c multicolored .80 .25

Airplanes — A722

No. 1807: a, Fokker DR-1, CT-114 Tutors. b, Tutors, H101 Salto sailplane. c, De Havilland DH100 Vampire MKIII. d, Stearman A-75.
No. 1808: a, De Havilland Mosquito FBVI. b, Sopwith F1 Camel. c, De Havilland Canada DHC-3 Otter. d, De Havilland Canada CC-108 Caribou. e, Canadair CL-28 Argus MK 2. f, North American F-86 Sabre 6. g, McDonnell Douglas CF-18 Hornet. h, Sopwith SF-1 Dolphin. i, Armstrong Whitworth Siskin IIIA. j, Canadian Vickers (Northrop) Delta II. k, Sikorsky CH-124A Sea King helicopter. l, Vickers-Armstrong Wellington MKII. m, Avro Anson MKI. n, Canadair (Lockheed) CF-104G Starfighter. o, Burgess-Dunne seaplane. p, Avro 504K.
Illustration reduced.

1999, Sept. 4 Litho. *Perf. 12½x13*
1807 A722 Sheet of 4 5.00 5.00
a.-d. 46c any single 1.25 1.00
1808 A722 Sheet of 16 16.00 16.00
a.-p. 46c any single 1.00 1.00

Canadian Intl. Air Show, 50th anniv. (#1807). Royal Canadian Air Force, 75th anniv. (#1808). Nos. 1808a-1808p are each 56x28mm.

NATO, 50th Anniv. — A723

1999, Sept. 21 Litho. *Perf. 12½x13*
1809 A723 46c multicolored .80 .25

Frontier College, 100th Anniv. A724

1999, Sept. 24 Litho. *Perf. 13x13½*
1810 A724 46c multicolored .80 .25

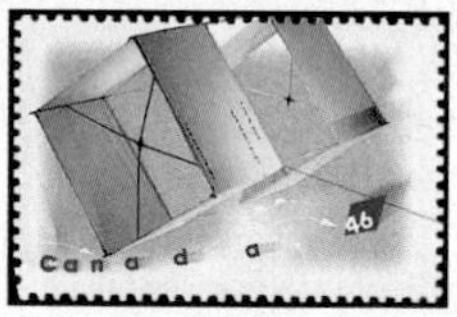

Kites A725

Designs: a, Master Control, sport kite by Lam Hoac (triagular). b, Indian Garden Flying Carpet, edo kite by Skye Morrison (trapezoidal). c, Gibson Girl, manufactured box kite (rectangular). d, Dragon centipede kite by Zhang tian Wei (oval).

Die cut in various patterns

1999, Oct. 1 Litho.

Self-Adhesive
1811 Complete booklet, 2 each #a.-d. 9.00
a.-d. A725 46c any single 1.10 .35

A726

A727

Millennium
A728

1999, Oct. 12 Holography *Die Cut*
Self-Adhesive (46c)

1812	A726 46c silver	1.00	.40
	Pane of 4	4.00	4.00

Litho.
Perf. 13¼

1813	A727 55c multicolored	1.00	.75
	Pane of 4	4.00	4.00

Engr.
Perf. 12¾

1814	A728 95c brown	1.80	1.50
	Pane of 4	7.25	7.25
	Nos. 1812-1814 (3)	3.80	2.65

Nos. 1812-1814 each exist in souvenir sheets of 1 with decorative border.

Christmas — A729

1999, Nov. 4 Litho. *Perf. 13¼*

1815	A729 46c Angel, drum	.80	.25
a.	Booklet pane of 10	8.00	8.00
	Complete booklet	8.50	
1816	A729 55c Angel, toys	.90	.35
a.	Booklet pane of 5 + label	4.50	4.50
	Complete booklet	5.00	
1817	A729 95c Angel, candle	1.60	.75
a.	Booklet pane of 5 + label	8.00	8.00
	Complete booklet	8.50	
	Nos. 1815-1817 (3)	3.30	1.35

Souvenir Sheets

Millennium — A730

No. 1818 — Media Technologies: a, IMAX movies. b, Softimage animation software. c, Ted Rogers, Sr. (1900-39) and radio tube. d, Invention of radio facsimile device for transmission of photographs for publishing by Sir William Stephenson (1896-1989).

No. 1819 — Canadian Entertainment: a, Calgary Stampede. b, Performers from Cirque du Soleil. c, Hockey Night in Canada. d, La Soiree du Hockey.

No. 1820 — Entertainers: a, Portia White (1911-68), singer. b, Glenn Gould (1932-82), pianist. c, Guy Lombardo (1902-77), band leader. d, Félix Leclerc (1914-88), singer, guitarist.

No. 1821 — Fostering Canadian Talent: a, Royal Canadian Academy of Arts (men viewing painting). b, Canada Council (sky, musical staff, "A"). c, National Film Board of Canada. d, Canadian Broadcasting Corporation.

No. 1822 — Medical Innovators: a, Sir Frederick Banting (1891-1941), co-discoverer of insulin, syringe and dog. b, Dr. Armand Frappier (1904-91), microbiologist, holding flask. c, Dr. Hans Selye (1907-82), endocrinologist, and molecular diagram. d, Maude Abbott (1869-1940), pathologist, and roses.

No. 1823 — Social Progress: a, Nun, doctor, hospital. b, Statue of woman holding decree. c, Alphonse Desjardins (1854-1920) and wife Dorimène (1858-1932), credit union founders, and credit union emblem. d, Father Moses Coady (1882-1959), educator of adults.

No. 1824 — Charity: a, Canadian International Development Agency (hands and tools). b, Dr. Lucille Teasdale (1929-96), hospital administrator in Uganda. c, Marathon of Hope inspired by Terry Fox (1958-81). d, Meals on Wheels program.

No. 1825 — Humanitarians and Peacekeepers: a, Raoul Dandurand (1861-1942), b, Pauline Vanier (1898-1991), Red Cross volunteer, and Elizabeth Smellie (1884-1968), head of various nursing services. c, Lester B. Pearson (1897-1972), prime minister, and Nobel Peace Prize winner, and dove. d, Amputee and shadow (Ottawa Convention on Land Mines).

No. 1826 — Canada's First People: a, Chief Pontiac (c. 1720-69). b, Tom Longboat (1887-1949), marathon runner. c, Inuit sculpture of shaman. d, Medicine man.

No. 1827 — Canada's Cultural Fabric: a, Norse boat, L'Anse aux Meadows. b, Immigrants on Halifax's Pier 21. c, Neptune Theater, Halifax (head of Neptune). d, Stratford Festival (actor and theater).

No. 1828 — Literary Legends: a, W. O. Mitchell (1914-98), novelist, and prairie scene. b, Gratien Gélinas (1909-99), actor and playwright, and stars. c, Le Cercle du Livre de France book club. d, Harlequin paperback books.

No. 1829 — Great Thinkers: a, Marshall McLuhan (1911-80), philosopher, and television set. b, Northrop Frye (1912-91), literary critic, and word "code." c, Roger Lemelin (1919-92), novelist, and cast of "The Plouffe Family" TV series. d, Hilda Marion Neatby (1904-75), historian, and farm scene.

No. 1830 — A Tradition of Generosity: a, Hart Massey (1823-96), Hart House, University of Toronto. b, Dorothy (1899-1965) and Izaak Killam (1885-1955), philantropists, and molecular model. c, Eric Lafferty Harvie (1892-1975), philantropist, and mountain scene. d, Macdonald Stewart Foundation.

No. 1831 — Engineering and Technological Marvels: a, Map of Rogers Pass, locomotive, tunnel diggers. b, Manic Dams. c, Canadian satellites, Remote Manipulator Arm. d, CN Tower.

No. 1832 — Fathers of Invention: a, George Klein (1904-92), gearwheels. b, Abraham Gesner (1797-1864), beaker of kerosene and lamp. c, Alexander Graham Bell (1847-1922), passenger-carrying kite, hydrofoil. d, Joseph-Armand Bombardier (1907-64), snowmobile.

No. 1833 — Food: a, Sir Charles Saunders (1867-1937), Marquis wheat. b, Pablum. c, Dr. Archibald Gowanlock Huntsman (1883-1973), marketer of frozen fish. d, Products of McCain Foods, Ltd., tractor.

No. 1834 — Enterprising Giants: a, Hudson's Bay Company (Colonist, Indian, canoe). b, Bell Canada Enterprises (earth, satellite, string of binary digits). c, Vachon Co. snack cakes. d, George Weston Limited (Baked goods, eggs).

1999-2000 Litho. *Perf. 13¼*

1818	A730 Sheet of 4	6.00	6.00
a.-d.	46c any single	1.40	.60
1819	A730 Sheet of 4	6.00	6.00
a.-d.	46c any single	1.40	.60
1820	A730 Sheet of 4	6.00	6.00
a.-d.	46c any single	1.40	.60
1821	A730 Sheet of 4	6.00	6.00
a.-d.	46c any single	1.40	.60
1822	A730 Sheet of 4	6.00	6.00
a.-d.	46c any single	1.40	.60
1823	A730 Sheet of 4	6.00	6.00
a.-d.	46c any single	1.40	.60
1824	A730 Sheet of 4	6.00	6.00
a.-d.	46c any single	1.40	.60
1825	A730 Sheet of 4	6.00	6.00
a.-d.	46c any single	1.40	.60
1826	A730 Sheet of 4	6.00	6.00
a.-d.	46c any single	1.40	.60
1827	A730 Sheet of 4	6.00	6.00
a.-d.	46c any single	1.40	.60
1828	A730 Sheet of 4	6.00	6.00
a.-d.	46c any single	1.40	.60
1829	A730 Sheet of 4	6.00	6.00
a.-d.	46c any single	1.40	.60
1830	A730 Sheet of 4	6.00	6.00
a.-d.	46c any single	1.40	.60
1831	A730 Sheet of 4	6.00	6.00
a.-d.	46c any single	1.40	.60
1832	A730 Sheet of 4	6.00	6.00
a.-d.	46c any single	1.40	.60
1833	A730 Sheet of 4	6.00	6.00
a.-d.	46c any single	1.40	.60
1834	A730 Sheet of 4	6.00	6.00
a.-d.	46c any single	1.40	.60
	Nos. 1818-1834 (17)	102.00	102.00

Issued: #1818-1821, 12/17; #1822-1825, 1/17/00; #1826-1830, 2/17/00; #1831-1834, 3/17/00.

Stamps similar to these were printed in a hardcover book produced by Canada Post Sept. 15, 1999 that sold for $59.99. Stamps from souvenir sheets show a distinct upward turn of the tails of the nines in the small 1999 date at upper left. The tails of the nines on stamps from the book are flat.

Millennium — A731

2000, Jan. 1 Litho. *Perf. 13x12½*

1835	A731 46c multicolored	.80	.25

New Year 2000 (Year of the Dragon) — A732

Litho. & Embossed
2000, Jan. 5 *Perf. 12½x12¾*

1836	A732 46c multicolored	.80	.25

Souvenir Sheet
Perf. 13¾x13¼

1837	A732 95c multicolored	1.90	1.90
a.	Orange and tagging omitted	*1,600.*	

No. 1837 has rounded corners and contains one 56x29mm stamp.

50th National Hockey League All-Star Game A733

Famous NHL players: a, Wayne Gretzky (Oilers jersey No. 99). b, Gordie Howe (Red Wings jersey No. 9). c, Maurice Richard (red, white and blue Canadiens jersey No. 9). d, Doug Harvey (Canadiens jersey No. 2). e, Bobby Orr (Bruins jersey No. 4). f, Jacques Plante (Canadiens jersey No. 1).

2000, Feb. 5 Litho. *Perf. 12¾*

1838	A733 Sheet of 6	5.00	5.00
a.-f.	46c any single	.80	.40

Bird Type of 1996

Designs: Nos. 1839, 1843, Canada warbler. Nos. 1840, 1844, Osprey. Nos. 1841, 1845, Pacific loon. Nos. 1842, 1846, Blue jay.

2000, Mar. 1 Litho. *Perf. 12½x13¼*

1839	A650 46c multi	1.00	.35
1840	A650 46c multi	1.00	.35
1841	A650 46c multi	1.00	.35
1842	A650 46c multi	1.00	.35
a.	Block or strip of 4	4.00	2.50

Booklet Stamps
Self-Adhesive
Die Cut 11½x11¼

1843	A650 46c multi	1.00	.35
1844	A650 46c multi	1.00	.35
1845	A650 46c multi	1.00	.35
1846	A650 46c multi	1.00	.35
a.	Booklet pane, 2 each #1843-1844, 1 each #1845-1846	6.00	
b.	Booklet pane, 2 each #1845-1846, 1 each #1843-1844	6.00	
	Complete bklt., #1846a, 1846b	12.00	

Nos. 1839-1842 were issued in sheets of 20, 5 each printed checkerwise to contain 4 complete blocks or strips.

Supreme Court, 125th Anniv. A734

2000, Apr. 10 Litho. *Perf. 12½x13¼*

1847	A734 46c multi	.80	.25

Ritual of the Calling of an Engineer, 75th Anniv. — A735

2000, Apr. 25

1848	A735 46c multi	.80	.25
a.	Tete-beche pair	1.60	1.20
b.	Silver ("CANADA 46") omitted	*2,400.*	

Decorated Rural Mailboxes — A736

Mailboxes with: No. 1849, Ship, fish, house designs. No. 1850, Flower, cow and church designs. No. 1851, Tractor design. No. 1852, Goose head, house designs.

Perf. 12½x13¼ on 3 sides
2000, Apr. 28
Booklet Stamps

1849	A736 46c multi	1.00	.30
1850	A736 46c multi	1.00	.30
1851	A736 46c multi	1.00	.30
1852	A736 46c multi	1.00	.30
a.	Block of 4, #1849-1852	4.00	3.50
b.	Bklt. pane, 3 ea #1849-1852	12.00	
	Complete booklet, #1852a	12.50	

Picture Frame A737

Serpentine Die Cut 11½
2000, Apr. 28 Litho.
Self-Adhesive

1853	A737 46c multi	1.00	.30
a.	Booklet pane of 5 + 5 different labels	5.00	
	Complete booklet, #1853a	5.50	
b.	Pane of 25	*45.00*	

No. 1853b sold for $24.95 each for one or two sheets, and $22.95 for three to ten sheets. Twenty-five self-adhesive, die cut address labels and reproductions of a photo sent in by the customer are on the reverse of No. 1853b. These panes were not available at post offices or through the philatelic bureau, but special orders from the printer, Ashton-Potter. The front cover of the booklet containing No. 1853a served as the order blank for No. 1853b.

See No. 1882.

A738

A739

A740

A741

A742

A743

A744

A745

A746

Fresh Waters — A747

Serpentine Die Cut 2½ Horiz.

2000, Feb. 23 **Litho.**

Self-Adhesive

1854 Complete booklet, #a.-e. 7.50
a. A738 55c multi 1.50 .90
b. A739 55c multi 1.50 .90
c. A740 55c multi 1.50 .90
d. A741 55c multi 1.50 .90
e. A742 55c multi 1.50 .90
1855 Complete booklet, #a.-e. 8.75
a. A743 95c multi 1.75 1.40
b. A744 95c multi 1.75 1.40
c. A745 95c multi 1.75 1.40
d. A746 95c multi 1.75 1.40
e. A747 95c multi 1.75 1.40

Queen Mother (b. 1900) A748

2000, May 23 **Litho.** ***Perf. 13x13¼***
1856 A748 95c multi 1.60 1.00

Boys and Girls Clubs of Canada, Cent. — A749

2000, June 1 ***Perf. 13***
1857 A749 46c multi .80 .25

World Session of Seventh Day Adventist Church, Toronto A750

2000, June 29 ***Perf. 13½x13¼***
1858 A750 46c multi .80 .25

Stampin' the Future Children's Stamp Design Contest Winners A751

Designs: No. 1859, Rainbow, space vehicle, astronauts, flag, by Rosalie Anne Nardelli. No. 1860, Three children in space vehicle, three children on ground, by Sarah Lutgen. No. 1861, Children and map of Canada, by Christine Weera. No. 1862, Two astronauts in space vehicle, planets, by Andrew Wright.

2000, July 1 ***Perf. 13¼***
1859 A751 46c multi .80 .30
1860 A751 46c multi .80 .30
1861 A751 46c multi .80 .30
1862 A751 46c multi .80 .30
a. Block or strip, #1859-1862 3.20 2.75
b. Souvenir sheet, #1859-1862 3.20 3.20

Art Type of 1988

The Artist at Niagara, by Cornelius Krieghoff.

Litho. with Foil Application

2000, July 7 ***Perf. 12½x13¼***
1863 A546 95c multi 1.60 .65

Tall Ships in Halifax Harbor — A752

Various ships: No. 1864, Denomination at L. No. 1865, Denomination at R.

Serpentine Die Cut 4¾x5

2000, July 19 **Litho.**

Booklet Stamps

Self-Adhesive

1864 A752 46c multi 1.00 .40
1865 A752 46c multi 1.00 .40
a. Pair, #1864-1865 2.00
b. Booklet, 5 #1864a 10.00

Dept. of Labor, Cent. — A753

2000, Sept. 1 **Litho.** ***Perf. 12½x13¼***
1866 A753 46c multi .80 .30

Petro-Canada, 25th Anniv. — A754

2000, Sept. 13 **Litho.** ***Die Cut***

Self-Adhesive

Booklet Stamp

1867 A754 46c multi 1.00 .40
a. Booklet pane of 12 12.00
Booklet, #1867a 12.50
b. Die cutting inverted (2 points jut at T, L) 8.50 8.50

No. 1867a is the cover of an informational booket about Petro-Canada. No. 1867b was issued in collector packs.

Cetaceans — A755

#1868, Monodon monoceros. #1869, Balaenoptera musculus. #1870, Balaena mysticetus. #1871, Delphinapterus leucas.

2000, Oct. 2 ***Perf. 12½x13***
1868 A755 46c multi .80 .30
1869 A755 46c multi .80 .30
1870 A755 46c multi .80 .30
1871 A755 46c multi .80 .30
a. Block of 4, #1868-1871 3.20 2.50

Christmas A756

Serpentine Die Cut 11¾

2000, Oct. 5

Booklet Stamp

Self-Adhesive

1872 A756 46c multi 1.00 .80
a. Booklet pane of 5 + 5 labels 5.00
Booklet, #1872a 5.50

See No. 1882e.

Christmas A757

Designs: 46c, Adoration of the shepherds. 55c, Creche. 95c Flight into Egypt.

2000, Nov. 3 **Litho.** ***Perf. 13¼***
1873 A757 46c multi .80 .25
a. Booklet pane of 10 8.00 8.00
Booklet, #1873a 8.50
1874 A757 55c multi 1.00 .35
a. Booklet pane of 6 6.00 6.00
Booklet, #1874a 6.50
1875 A757 95c multi 1.60 .70
a. Booklet pane of 6 9.75 9.75
Booklet, #1875a 10.25
Nos. 1873-1875 (3) 3.40 1.30

Regiments A758

No. 1876, Lord Strathcona's Horse Regiment. No. 1877, Les Voltigeurs de Quebec.

2000, Nov. 11 ***Perf. 13¼x13***
1876 A758 46c multi .80 .30
1877 A758 46c multi .80 .30
a. Pair, #1876-1877 1.60 .85

Maple Leaves A759

Animals A760

Serpentine Die Cut 8½ Horiz.

2000, Dec. 28 **Litho.**

Coil Stamps

Self-Adhesive

1878 A759 47c multi .85 .20
1879 A760 60c Red fox 1.10 .25
a. Booklet pane of 6 11.00
1880 A760 75c Gray wolf 1.20 .40
1881 A760 $1.05 White-tailed deer 2.00 .65
a. Booklet pane of 6 12.00
Nos. 1878-1881 (4) 5.15 1.50

Nos. 1879a and 1881a are complete booklets. See No. 1927.

Frame Type of 2000

No. 1882: a, Silver. b, Like #1853. c, Mahogany. d, Love (roses). e, Christmas.

Serpentine Die Cut 11¾

2000, Dec. 28 **Litho.**

Booklet Stamps

Self-Adhesive

1882 Bklt. pane of 5+5 labels 5.00
a.-e. A737 47c Any single 1.00 1.00
Booklet, #1882 5.50

New Year 2001 (Year of the Snake) A761

Litho. & Embossed

2001, Jan. 5 ***Perf. 13¼***
1883 A761 47c green & multi .95 .25
a. Gold omitted 1,600.

Souvenir Sheet

1884 A761 $1.05 brown & multi 2.50 2.50

National Hockey League Stars A762

No. 1885: a, Jean Beliveau (Montreal Canadiens jersey No. 4). b, Terry Sawchuk (goalie in Detroit Red Wings uniform). c, Eddie Shore (Boston Bruins jersey No. 2). d, Denis Potvin (Islanders jersey No. 5). e, Bobby Hull (Chicago Black Hawks jersey No. 9). f, Syl Apps, Sr. (Toronto Maple Leafs jersey).

Perf. 12½x13 on 3 sides

2001, Jan. 18 **Litho.**
1885 Sheet of 6 + 3 labels 5.25 5.25
a.-f. A762 47c Any single .85 .50

Bird Type of 1996

Designs: Nos. 1886, 1890, Golden eagle. Nos. 1887, 1891, Arctic tern. Nos. 1888, 1892, Rock ptarmigan. Nos. 1889, 1893, Lapland longspur.

2001, Feb. 1 Litho. ***Perf. 12½x13***

1886 A650 47c multi .85 .30
1887 A650 47c multi .85 .30
1888 A650 47c multi .85 .30
1889 A650 47c multi .85 .30
a. Block or strip of 4, #1886-1889 3.40 2.75

Booklet Stamps
Self-Adhesive
Die Cut Perf 11½x11¼

1890 A650 47c multi 1.00 .35
1891 A650 47c multi 1.00 .35
1892 A650 47c multi 1.00 .35
1893 A650 47c multi 1.00 .35
a. Booklet pane, 2 each #1890-1891, 1 each #1892-1893 6.00
b. Booklet pane, 2 each #1892-1893, 1 each #1890-1891 6.00
Booklet, #1893a, 1893b 12.00

Nos. 1886-1889 were issued in sheets of 20, 5 each printed checkerwise to contain 4 complete blocks or strips.

Games of La Francophonie, Ottawa and Hull — A763

2001, Feb. 28 ***Perf. 13¼***

1894 A763 47c High jumper .85 .30
1895 A763 47c Dancer .85 .30
a. Horiz. pair, #1894-1895 1.70 1.00

World Figure Skating Championships, Vancouver — A764

Designs: No. 1896, Pairs. No. 1897, Ice dancing. No. 1898, Men's singles. No. 1899, Women's singles.

2001, Mar. 19 Litho. ***Perf. 13x12½***

1896 A764 47c shown .85 .30
1897 A764 47c multi .85 .30
1898 A764 47c multi .85 .30
1899 A764 47c multi .85 .30
a. Block of 4, #1896-1899 3.40 2.50

First Canadian Postage Stamps, 150th Anniv. — A765

Litho. & Engr.

2001, Apr. 6 ***Perf. 13***

1900 A765 47c multi .85 .30

Toronto Blue Jays Baseball Team, 25th Anniv. A766

2001, Apr. 9 Litho. ***Die Cut***

Self-Adhesive

1901 A766 47c multi 1.00 .30
a. Booklet pane of 8 8.00

No. 1901a is a complete booklet.

Summit of the Americas, Quebec — A767

2001, Apr. 20 ***Perf. 13¼x13***

1902 A767 47c multi .85 .30

Tourist Attractions — A768

No. 1903: a, Butchart Gardens, British Columbia. b, Apple Blossom Festival, Nova Scotia. c, White Pass and Yukon Route. d, Sugar bushes, Quebec. e, Niagara-on-the-Lake, Ontario.

No. 1904: a, The Forks, Manitoba. b, Barkerville, British Columbia. c, Canadian Tulip Festival, Ontario. d, Auyuittuq National Park, Nunavut. e, Signal Hill National Historic Site, Newfoundland.

Die Cut Perf. 11x11¼

2001, May 11 Litho.

Self-Adhesive

1903 Booklet of 5 5.00
a.-e. A768 60c Any single 1.00 .75
1904 Booklet of 5 8.75
a.-e. A768 $1.05 Any single 1.75 1.25

Armenian Church, 1,700th Anniv. — A769

2001, May 16 Litho. ***Perf. 13x12½***

1905 A769 47c multi .85 .30

Royal Military College of Canada, 125th Anniv. — A770

2001, June 1 ***Perf. 12½x13***

1906 A770 47c multi .85 .30

Eighth Intl. Amateur Athletic Federation World Championships, Edmonton A771

Perf. 12¾x12½

2001, June 25 Litho.

1907 A771 47c Pole vault .85 .30
1908 A771 47c Runner .85 .30
a. Pair, #1907-1908 1.70 1.00

Pierre Elliott Trudeau (1919-2000), Prime Minister — A772

2001, July 1 ***Perf. 13x12½***

1909 A772 47c multi .85 .30
a. Souvenir sheet of 4 3.40 3.40

Roses — A773

Designs: Nos. 1910a, 1911, Morden Centennial. Nos. 1910b, 1912, Agnes. Nos. 1910c, 1913, Champlain. Nos. 1910d, 1914, Canadian White Star.

Illustration reduced.

2001, Aug. 1 Litho. ***Perf. 12½x13***

Souvenir Sheet

1910 Sheet of 4 5.00 5.00
a.-d. A773 47c Any single 1.25 .75

Booklet Stamps
Die Cut

1911 A773 47c multi .90 .30
1912 A773 47c multi .90 .30
1913 A773 47c multi .90 .30
1914 A773 47c multi .90 .30
a. Booklet pane, #1911-1914 3.60
Booklet, 3 #1914a 11.00

Phila Nippon '01, Japan (No. 1910). Die cutting on Nos. 1911-1914 has "thorn" at the center of each side, pointing outward at top and left and toward the design at bottom and right.

Great Peace of Montreal, 300th Anniv. — A774

2001, Aug. 3 ***Perf. 12½x13***

1915 A774 47c multi .85 .30

Art Type of 1988

Design: The Space Between Columns #21 (Italian), by Jack Shadbolt.

Litho. with Foil Application

2001, Aug. 24 ***Perf. 13x13¼***

1916 A546 $1.05 multi 1.75 1.00

Shriners — A775

2001, Sept. 19 Litho. ***Perf. 13¼x13***

1917 A775 47c multi .85 .30

Frame Type of 2000 Inscribed "Domestic Lettermail / Poste-lettres du régime intérieur"

No. 1918: a, Like #1882a. b, Like #1882b. c, Baby toys and flowers. d, Like #1882d. e, Like #1882e.

Serpentine Die Cut 11¾

2001, Sept. 21

Self-Adhesive

1918 Bklt. pane of 5 + 5 labels 5.00
a.-e. A737 (47c) Any single 1.00 1.00
Booklet, #1918 5.50

Theater Anniversaries — A776

Designs: No. 1919, Théatre du Nouveau Monde, Montreal, 50th anniv. No. 1920, Grand Theater, London, Ont., cent.

2001, Sept. 28 ***Perf. 12½x12¾***

1919 A776 47c multi .85 .30
1920 A776 47c multi .85 .30
a. Horiz. pair, #1919-1920 1.70 1.00

Hot Air Balloons A777

Background colors: a, Green. b, Blue violet. c, Red violet. d, Olive.

2001, Oct. 1 ***Die Cut***

Self-Adhesive

1921 Booklet, 2 each #a-d 8.00
a.-d. A777 47c Any single 1.00 .35

Christmas A778

Illuminated trees and: 47c, Horse-drawn sleigh. 60c, Skaters. $1.05, Children making snowman.

2001, Nov. 1 Litho. ***Perf. 12½x13¼***

1922 A778 47c multi .85 .25
a. Booklet pane of 10 8.50
Booklet, #1922a 9.00
1923 A778 60c multi 1.00 .40
a. Booklet pane of 6 6.00
Booklet, #1923a 6.50
1924 A778 $1.05 multi 1.75 .65
a. Booklet pane of 6 10.50
Booklet, #1924a 11.00

YMCA in Canada, 150th Anniv. — A779

2001, Nov. 8 Litho. *Perf. 13¼*

1925 A779 47c multi .85 .30

Royal Canadian Legion, 75th Anniv. — A780

2001, Nov. 11 *Perf. 12½x13*

1926 A780 47c multi .85 .30

Maple Leaves Type of 2000, Traditional Handiwork Type of 1999 and

Flag and Canada Post Headquarters, Ottawa — A781

Designs: 65c, Jewelry making, horiz. 77c, Basket weaving, horiz. $1.25, Sculpture, horiz.

Serpentine Die Cut 8½ Horiz.

2002, Jan. 2 Litho.

Self-Adhesive

Coil Stamps

1927 A759 48c multi .85 .20
1928 A684 65c multi 1.10 .40
a. Booklet of 6 6.75
1929 A684 77c multi 1.25 .40
1930 A684 $1.25 multi 2.00 .65
a. Booklet of 6 12.00

Booklet Stamp

Serpentine Die Cut 8½

1931 A781 48c multi .85 .20
a. Booklet of 10 8.50
b. Booklet of 30 26.00
Nos. 1927-1931 (5) 6.05 1.85

By separating the booklet along the columns of rouletting, No. 1931b could be broken up into three separately obtainable examples of No. 1931a. See No. 1991.

Reign of Queen Elizabeth II, 50th Anniv. A782

2002, Jan. 2 Litho. *Perf. 13¼x12½*

1932 A782 48c multi .85 .30
a. Imperf, pair *1,500.*

New Year 2002 (Year of the Horse) — A783

Horse and: 48c, Bamboo leaves. $1.25, Peach blossoms.

Litho. & Embossed With Foil Application

2002, Jan. 3 *Perf. 13¼*

1933 A783 48c multi .85 .30

Souvenir Sheet

1934 A783 $1.25 multi 2.50 2.50

National Hockey League Stars A784

No. 1935: a, Tim Horton (Toronto Maple Leafs jersey No. 7). b, Guy Lafleur (Montreal Canadiens jersey No. 10). c, Howie Morenz (Canadiens jersey, with brown gloves). d, Glenn Hall (Chicago Black Hawks jersey No. 1). e, Red Kelly (Maple Leafs jersey No. 4). f, Phil Esposito (Boston Bruins jersey no. 7).

Perf. 12½x13 on 3 Sides

2002, Jan. 12 Litho.

1935 Sheet of 6 + 3 labels 6.00 6.00
a.-f. A784 48c Any single 1.00 .65

2002 Winter Olympics, Salt Lake City — A785

Designs: No. 1936, Short track speed skating. No. 1937, Curling. No. 1938, Freestyle aerial skiing. No. 1939, Women's hockey.

2002, Jan. 25 Litho. *Perf. 13¼x13*

1936 A785 48c multi .85 .35
1937 A785 48c multi .85 .35
1938 A785 48c multi .85 .35
1939 A785 48c multi .85 .35
a. Block or strip of 4, #1936-1939 3.40 3.00

Appointment of First Canadian Governor General, 50th Anniv. A786

2002, Feb. 1 Litho. *Perf. 13¼x12½*

1940 A786 48c multi .85 .30

Universities — A787

Design: No. 1941, University of Manitoba, 125th anniv. No. 1942, Laval University, 150th anniv. No. 1943, University of Trinity College, 150th anniv. No. 1944, Saint Mary's University, Halifax, 200th anniv.

2002 Litho. *Perf. 13½*

Booklet Stamp

1941 A787 48c multi .85 .30
a. Booklet pane of 8 7.75 —
Booklet, #1941a 8.25
1942 A787 48c multi .85 .30
a. Booklet pane of 8 6.75 —
Booklet, #1942a 7.25
1943 A787 48c multi .85 .30
a. Booklet pane of 8 6.75 —
Booklet, #1943a 7.25
1944 A787 48c multi .85 .30
a. Booklet pane of 8 6.75 —
Booklet, #1944a 7.25
Nos. 1941-1944 (4) 3.40 1.20

Issued: No. 1941, 2/28. No. 1942, 4/4. No. 1943, 4/30. No. 1944, 5/27.

Art Type of 1988

Design: Church and Horse, by Alex Colville.

Litho. with Foil Application

2002, Mar. 22 *Perf. 12½x13*

1945 A546 $1.25 multi 2.00 1.10
a. Foil only (all other colors and tagging omitted) *1,600.*
b. Imperf, pair *1,500.*

Tulips — A788

Tulip varieties: a, City of Vancouver. b, Monte Carlo. c, Ottawa. d, The Bishop.

2002, May 3 *Die Cut*

Self-Adhesive

1946 Booklet pane of 4 3.40
a.-d. A788 48c Any single .85 .30
Booklet, 2 #1946 7.25

Tulips Type of 2002

Souvenir Sheet

No. 1947: a, Like #1946a. b, Like #1946b. c, Like #1946c. d, Like #1946d.

2002, Aug. 30 Litho. *Perf. 13x12½*

1947 Sheet of 4 3.40 3.40
a.-d. A788 48c Any single .85 .80

Dendronepthea Giagantea and Dendronepthea Corals — A789

Tubastrea and Echinogorgia Corals — A790

North Atlantic Pink Tree, Pacific Orange Cup and North Pacific Horn Corals A791

North Atlantic Giant Orange Tree and Black Corals A792

2002, May 19 Litho. *Perf. 12½x13*

1948 A789 48c multi .85 .35
1949 A790 48c multi .85 .35
1950 A791 48c multi .85 .35
1951 A792 48c multi .85 .35
a. Block of 4, #1948-1951 3.40 3.00
b. Souvenir sheet, #1948-1951, perf. 13¼x13 3.40 4.00

See Hong Kong Nos. 979-982.

Tourist Attractions Type of 2001

No. 1952: a, Yukon Quest, Yukon Territory. b, Icefields Parkway, Alberta. c, Agawa Canyon, Ontario. d, Old Port of Montreal, Quebec. e, Kings Landing, New Brunswick.

No. 1953: a, Northern Lights, Northwest Territories. b, Stanley Park, Vancouver, British Columbia. c, Head-Smashed-In Buffalo Jump, Alberta. d, Saguenay Fjord, Quebec. e, Peggy's Cove, Nova Scotia.

2002, June 1 *Die Cut Perf. 11x11¼*

Self-Adhesive

1952 Booklet of 5 6.00
a.-e. A768 65c Any single 1.20 .75
1953 Booklet of 5 10.00
a.-e. A768 $1.25 Any single 2.00 1.10

Sculpture — A793

Designs: No. 1954, Embacle, by Charles Daudelin. No. 1955, Lumberjacks, by Leo Mol.

2002, June 10 Litho. *Perf. 13¼*

1954 A793 48c multi .85 .30
1955 A793 48c multi .85 .30
a. Horiz. or vert. pair, #1954-1955 1.70 1.00

Canadian Postmasters and Assistants Association, Cent. — A794

2002, July 5 *Perf. 13¼x12½*

1956 A794 48c multi .85 .30

Printed in sheets of 16 stamps + 12 labels.

17th World Youth Day, Toronto — A795

2002, July 23 Litho. *Die Cut*

Booklet Stamp

Self-Adhesive

1957 A795 48c multi .85 .30
a. Booklet of 8 7.00

Public Services International World Congress, Ottawa — A796

2002, Sept. 4 Litho. *Perf. 12½x13*

1958 A796 48c multi .85 .30

Public Pensions, 75th Anniv. — A797

2002, Sept. 10 *Perf. 13¼*

1959 A797 48c multi .85 .30

Souvenir Sheet

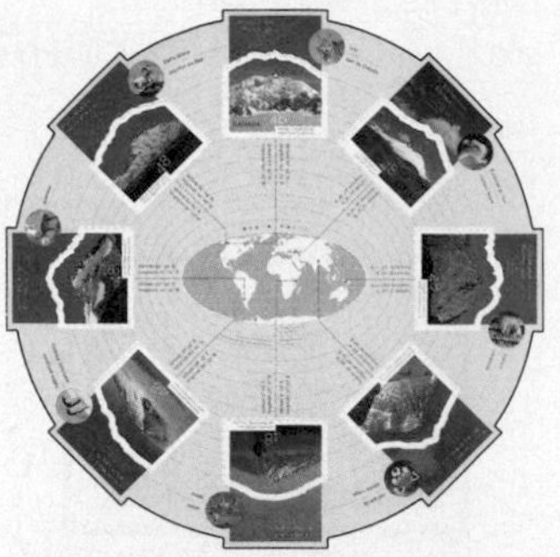

Intl. Year of Mountains — A798

No. 1960: a, Mt. Logan, Canada. b, Mt. Elbrus, Russia. c, Puncak Jaya, Indonesia. d, Mt. Everest, Nepal and China. e, Mt. Kilimanjaro, Tanzania. f, Vinson Massif, Antarctica. g, Mt. Aconcagua, Argentina. h, Mt. McKinley, Alaska.

2002, Oct. 1 Litho. *Die Cut*
Self-Adhesive

1960 A798 Sheet of 8 + 8 labels 8.00 8.00
a.-h. 48c Any single 1.00 1.00

World Teachers' Day — A799

2002, Oct. 4 Litho. *Perf. 12½x13*
1961 A799 48c multi .85 .30

Toronto Stock Exchange, 150th Anniv. — A800

2002, Oct. 24 Litho. *Perf. 12½x13*
1962 A800 48c multi .85 .30

Communication Technology Centenaries — A801

Part of map of North America and: No. 1963, Sir Sandford Fleming (1827-1915), cable-laying ship . No. 1964, Guglielmo Marconi (1874-1937), radio and transmission towers.

2002, Oct. 31 Litho. *Perf. 13x12½*
1963 48c multi .85 .30
1964 48c multi .85 .30
a. A801 Horiz. pair, #1963-1964 1.70 1.20

Cent. of first telegraph message sent over transpacific cable (#1963); first transatlantic radio message (#1964).

Christmas A802

Art by aboriginals: 48c, Genesis, by Daphne Odjig. 65c, Winter Travel, by Cecil Youngfox. $1.25, Mary and Child, sculpture by Irene Katak Angutitaq.

2002, Nov. 4 *Perf. 12½x13*
1965 A802 48c multi .85 .25
a. Booklet pane of 10 8.50
Booklet, #1965a 9.00
1966 A802 65c multi 1.05 .40
a. Booklet pane of 6 6.50
Booklet, #1966a 7.00
1967 A802 $1.25 multi 2.00 .75
a. Booklet pane of 6 12.00
Booklet, #1967a 12.50
Nos. 1965-1967 (3) 3.90 1.40

Quebec Symphony Orchestra, Cent. A803

2002, Nov. 7
1968 A803 48c multi .85 .30

New Year 2003 (Year of the Ram) — A804

Litho. & Embossed with Foil Application

2003, Jan. 3 *Perf. 13*
1969 A804 48c shown .85 .30
a. Gold omitted *475.00*

Souvenir Sheet
Perf. 13¼

1970 A804 $1.25 Ram, diff. 2.50 2.50

No. 1970 contains one 33x58mm stamp. Slits replace perforations on the vertical sides of the stamps between the point of the acute angle made with the curving perforations and the point perpendicular to where the perforations on the opposite side form the obtuse angle with the curving perforations.

National Hockey League Stars A805

Designs: Nos. 1971a, 1972a, Frank Mahovlich (orange panel). Nos. 1971b, 1972b, Raymond Bourque (lilac panel). Nos. 1971c, 1972c, Serge Savard (blue panel). Nos. 1971d, 1972d, Stan Mikita (red violet panel). Nos. 1971e, 1972e, Mike Bossy (bright pink panel). Nos. 1971f, 1972f, Bill Durnan (green panel).

Perf. 12½x13¼ on 3 Sides
2003, Jan. 18 Litho.

1971 Sheet of 6 + 3 labels 15.00 —
a.-f. A805 48c Any single 2.50 2.00

Self-Adhseive
Die Cut

1972 Pane of 6 57.50 —
a.-f. A805 48c Any single 7.00 2.00

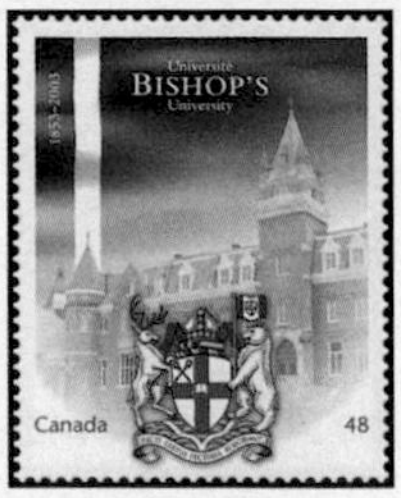

Universities A806

Design: No. 1973, Bishop's University, Lennoxville, Quebec, 150th anniv. No. 1974, University of Western Ontario, London, Ont., 125th anniv. No. 1975, St. Francis Xavier University, Antigonish, N. S., 150th Anniv. No. 1976, Macdonald Institute, Guelph, Ont., cent. No. 1977, University of Montreal, 125th anniv.

2003 Litho. *Perf. 13¼x13½*
Booklet Stamps

1973 A806 48c multi .85 .30
a. Booklet pane of 8 6.50 —
Booklet, #1973a 7.00
1974 A806 48c multi .85 .30
a. Booklet pane of 8 7.00 —
Booklet, #1974a 7.50
1975 A806 48c multi .85 .30
a. Booklet pane of 8 7.00 —
Complete booklet, #1975a 7.50
1976 A806 48c multi .85 .30
a. Booklet pane of 8 7.00 —
Complete booklet, #1976a 7.50
1977 A806 48c multi .85 .30
a. Booklet pane of 8 7.00 —
Complete booklet, #1977a 7.50

Issued: No. 1973, 1/28. No. 1975, 4/4. No. 1976, 6/20. No. 1977, 9/4. No. 1974, 3/19.
See Nos. 2033-2034.

Bird Paintings by John James Audubon — A807

Designs: No. 1979, Leach's storm petrel. No. 1980, Brant. No. 1981, Great cormorant. No. 1982, Common murre. 65c, Gyrfalcon, vert.

Perf. 13¼x12½
2003, Feb. 21 Litho.

1979 A807 48c multi .85 .35
1980 A807 48c multi .85 .35
1981 A807 48c multi .85 .35
1982 A807 48c multi .85 .35
a. Block of 4, #1979-1982 3.40 2.75

Booklet Stamp
Self-Adhesive
Die Cut

1983 A807 65c multi 1.20 .65
a. Booklet pane of 6 7.25
Nos. 1979-1983 (5) 4.60 2.05

Canadian Rangers — A808

2003, Mar. 3 *Perf. 12½x13¼*
1984 A808 48c multi .85 .30

American Hellenic Educational Progressive Association In Canada, 75th Anniv. — A809

Perf. 12½x13¼
2003, Mar. 25 Litho.
1985 A809 48c multi .85 .30

Volunteer Firefighters A810

2003, May 30 Litho. *Perf. 13¼*
1986 A810 48c multi .85 .30

Coronation of Queen Elizabeth II, 50th Anniv. A811

2003, June 2 *Perf. 13x12½*
1987 A811 48c multi .85 .30

Quebec City, Seal of Sovereign Council of New France, Signature of Pedro da Silva — A812

2003, June 6 *Perf. 13x12¾*
1988 A812 48c multi .85 .30

Pedro da Silva, first courier in New France, 50th anniv. of Portuguese immigration to Canada.

Tourist Attractions Type of 2001

No. 1989: a, Wilberforce Falls, Nunavut. b, Inside Passage, B. C. c, Royal Canadian Mounted Police Depot Division, Regina, Sask. d, Casa Loma, Toronto, Ont. e, Gatineau Park, Que.

No. 1990: a, Dragon boat races, Vancouver, B. C. b, Polar bear watching, Man. c, Niagara Falls, Ont. d, Magdalen Islands, Que. e, Charlottestown, P. E. I.

2003, June 12 *Die Cut Perf. 11¼*
Self-Adhesive

1989 Booklet of 5 6.50
a.-e. A768 65c Any single 1.30 .60
1990 Booklet of 5 12.50
a.-e. A768 $1.25 Any single 2.50 1.10

Flag and Canada Post Headquarters Type of 2002 With "Vancouver / 2010" Added in Red
Serpentine Die Cut 8½
2003, July 11 Litho.
Booklet Stamp
Self-Adhesive

1991 A781 48c multi 1.60 1.20
a. Booklet of 10 16.00
b. Booklet of 30 47.50
c. Die cutting omitted, pair *800.00*

Selection of Vancouver as site of 2010 Winter Olympics. By separating the booklet along the columns of rouletting, No. 1991b could be broken up into three separately obtainable examples of No. 1991a.

Canada-Alaska Cruise Scenes — A813

Mountains and: No. 1991C, Totem pole. No. 1991D, Whale's tail.

2003, July 19 Litho. *Die Cut*
Self-Adhesive

1991C A813 ($1.25) multi 8.00 8.00
1991D A813 ($1.25) multi 8.00 8.00
e. Horiz. pair, #19901C-1991D 16.00

Nos. 1991C-1991D were printed in sheets of 10 containing five of each stamp. The blank spaces in each stamp and the three stamp-like vignettes at the left of the sheet that lack die cutting and "Postage Paid / Port Payé" inscription could be personalized on cruise ships. Personalized sheets sold for $19.95 in US currency, while unpersonalized sheets sold for $12.50.

Lutheran World Federation, 10th Assembly, Winnipeg A814

2003, July 21 Litho. *Perf. 12½x13*
1992 A814 48c multi .85 .30

Korean War Armistice Agreement, 50th Anniv. — A815

2003, July 25 *Perf. 12¾*
1993 A815 48c multi .85 .30

Authors A816

Designs: No. 1994, Anne Hébert (1916-2000). No. 1995, Hector de Saint-Denys Garneau (1912-43). No. 1996, Morley Callaghan (1903-90). No. 1997, Susanna Moodie (1803-85), and Catharine Parr Traill (1802-99).

2003, Sept. 8 Litho. *Perf. 13¼x12½*
Booklet Stamps

1994 A816 48c multi .85 .35
1995 A816 48c multi .85 .35
1996 A816 48c multi .85 .35
1997 A816 48c multi .85 .35
a. Block of 4, #1994-1997 3.40 2.75
b. Booklet pane, 2 #1997a 7.00 —
Complete booklet, #1997b 7.50

2003 Road Cycling World Championships, Hamilton, Ont. — A817

2003, Sept. 10 Litho. *Perf. 12½x13*
Booklet Stamp

1998 A817 48c multi .85 .55
a. Booklet pane of 8 7.00 —
Complete booklet, #1998a 7.50

Canadian Astronauts A818

No. 1999: a, Marc Garneau. b, Roberta Bondar. c, Steve MacLean. d, Chris Hadfield. e, Robert Thirsk. f, Bjarni Tryggvason. g, Dave Williams. h, Julie Payette.

Litho. With Foil Application
2003, Oct. 1 *Die Cut*
Self-Adhesive

1999 Sheet of 8 9.00
a.-h. A818 48c Any single .85 .75

Trees of Canada and Thailand — A819

Designs: No. 2000, Acer saccharum leaves (Canada). No. 2001, Cassia fistula (Thailand).

2003, Oct. 4 Litho. *Perf. 12¾x12½*
2000 A819 48c multi .85 .30
2001 A819 48c multi .85 .30
a. Pair, #2000-2001 1.70 .80
b. Souvenir sheet, #2000-2001 1.70 .80
c. As "a," imperf *1,000.*
d. As "b," imperf *1,600.*

Bangkok 2003 Intl. Philatelic Exhibition (#2001b).
See Thailand No. 2090.

L'Hommage à Rosa Luxemburg, by Jean-Paul Riopelle — A820

Painting details — No. 2002; a, Red and blue dots between birds at LR. b, Bird with yellow beak at center. c, Three birds in circle at R. d, Sun at UR. e, Birds with purple outlines at L. f, Bird with red outline in circle at R. $1.25, Pink bird in red circle at R.

2003, Oct. 7 Litho. *Perf. 12½x13*
2002 A820 Sheet of 6 8.50 8.50
a.-f. 48c Any single 1.40 1.00

Souvenir Sheet
Perf. 12¾
2003 A820 $1.25 multi 3.00 3.00

Christmas A821

Gift boxes and: 48c, Ice skates. 65c, Teddy bear. $1.25, Toy duck.

2003, Nov. 4 *Die Cut*
Booklet Stamps
Self-Adhesive

2004 A821 48c multi .85 .35
a. Booklet pane of 6 5.25
Complete booklet, 2 #2004a 10.50
b. Pair, die cutting omitted 400.00
2005 A821 65c multi 1.10 .50
a. Booklet pane of 6 6.75
b. As "a," die cutting omitted 1,500.
2006 A821 $1.25 multi 2.00 1.00
a. Booklet pane of 6 12.00
b. Die cutting omitted, pair 350.00
Nos. 2004-2006 (3) 3.95 1.85

Maple Leaf and Samara A822

Maple Leaf on Twig A823

Flag Over Edmonton, Alberta A824

Queen Elizabeth II A825

2003, Dec. 19 *Perf. 12½x13*
Coil Stamps
Litho.
Self-Adhesive
Serpentine Die Cut 8 Horiz.

2008 A822 49c multi .85 .20

Serpentine Die Cut 8 Vert.

2009 A823 80c red & multi 1.40 .40
2010 A823 $1.40 grn & multi 2.50 .55

Booklet Stamps
Die Cut

2011 A824 49c multi .85 .20
a. Booklet pane of 10 8.50
b. Die cutting omitted, pair 160.00
2012 A825 49c multi .85 .20
a. Booklet pane of 10 8.50
2013 A823 80c red & multi 1.60 .35
a. Booklet pane of 6 9.50
2014 A823 $1.40 grn & multi 2.60 .65
a. Booklet pane of 6 16.00
Nos. 2008-2014 (7) 10.65 2.55

New Year 2004 (Year of the Monkey) — A826

Scenes from Chinese story *Journey to the West*: 49c, Monkey King. $1.40, Monkey King, Xuan Zang, Sandy, Pigsy and horse.

Litho. & Embossed with Foil Application
2004, Jan. 8 *Perf. 13x12½*
2015 A826 49c multi .85 .30

Souvenir Sheet

2016 A826 $1.40 multi 3.25 3.25
a. As No. 2016, with 2004 Hong Kong Stamp Expo ovpt. in margin 4.00 4.00

No. 2016 has rouletted tab at right showing bar code.

National Hockey League Stars A827

Designs: Nos. 2017a, 2018a, Larry Robinson (blue background). Nos. 2017b, 2018b, Marcel Dionne (orange background). Nos. 2017c, 2018c, Ted Lindsay (red background). Nos. 2017d, 2018d, Johnny Bower (green background). Nos. 2017e, 2018e, Brad Park (brown background). Nos. 2017f, 2018f, Milt Schmidt (purple background).

Perf. 12½x13¼ on 3 Sides
2004, Jan. 24 Litho.
2017 Sheet of 6 + 3 labels 6.00 6.00
a.-f. A827 49c Any single .85 .60

Self-Adhesive
Die Cut

2018 Pane of 6 6.00 6.00
a.-f. A827 49c Any single .85 .55

Tourist Attractions Type of 2001

Design: No. 2019, Quebec Winter Carnival; No. 2020, St. Joseph's Oratory, Montreal, Quebec; No. 2021, International Jazz Festival, Montreal. No. 2022, Traversée Internationale du Lac St. Jean Swimming Marathon, Quebec; No. 2023, Canadian National Exhibition, Toronto.

2004, Jan. 29 Litho. *Die Cut*
Self-Adhesive
Booklet Stamp

2019 A768 49c multi .85 .35
a. Booklet of 6 5.25
2020 A768 49c multi .85 .35
a. Booklet of 6 5.25
2021 A768 49c multi .85 .35
a. Booklet of 6 5.25
2022 A768 49c multi .85 .35
a. Booklet of 6 5.25
2023 A768 49c multi .85 .35
a. Booklet of 6 5.25

Issued: No. 2019, 1/29; No. 2020, 4/2; No. 2021, 6/1; No. 2022, 6/18; No. 2023, 7/19.

Governor General Ramon John Hnatyshyn (1934-2002) — A828

2004, Mar. 16 Litho. *Perf. 12½x13*
2024 A828 49c multi .85 .25

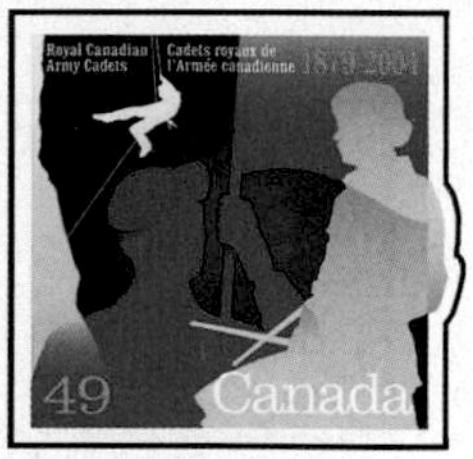

Royal Canadian Army Cadets, 125th Anniv. A829

2004, Mar. 26 Litho. *Die Cut*
Booklet Stamp
Self-Adhesive

2025 A829 49c multi .85 .30
a. Booklet pane of 4 3.50
Complete booklet, 2 #2025a 7.00

The Fram, Ship of Otto Sverdrup (1854-1930), Arctic Explorer — A830

Litho. & Engr.
2004, Mar. 26 *Perf. 13¼*
2026 A830 49c multi .85 .30

Souvenir Sheet

2027 A830 $1.40 multi + 2 labels 3.25 3.25

See Greenland No. 426, Norway Nos. 1398-1399.

Urban Transit and Light Rail Systems — A831

Train cars, station names and system emblems of: No. 2028, Toronto Transit Commission. No. 2029, TransLink SkyTrain, Vancouver. No. 2030, Société de Transport de Montreal. No. 2031, Calgary Transit Light Rail.

2004, Mar. 30 Litho. *Perf. 12½x13*

2028	A831 49c multi		.85	.30
2029	A831 49c multi		.85	.30
2030	A831 49c multi		.85	.30
2031	A831 49c multi		.85	.30
a.	Vert. strip of 4, #2028-2031		3.40	2.75

Home Hardware, 40th Anniv. — A832

Die Cut Perf. 11

2004, Apr. 19 Litho.

Self-Adhesive

Booklet Stamp

2032 A832 49c multi		.85	.20
a. Booklet pane of 10 + label		8.50	
Complete booklet, #2032a		9.00	

No. 2032a is the inside front cover of the complete booklet. Fifteen self-adhesive seals are on the inside back cover of the complete booklet.

Universities Type of 2003

Designs: No. 2033, Sherbrooke University, Sherbrooke, Quebec, 50th anniv. No. 2034, University of Prince Edward Island, Charlottetown, bicent.

2004 Litho. *Perf. 13¼x13½*

Booklet Stamps

2033 A806 49c multi	.85	.30
a. Booklet pane of 8	7.00	—
Complete booklet, #2033a	7.50	
2034 A806 49c multi	.85	.30
a. Booklet pane of 8	7.00	—
Complete booklet, #2034a	7.50	

Issued: No. 2033, 5/4; No. 2034, 5/8.

Montreal Children's Hospital, Cent. — A833

2004, May 6 *Die Cut Perf. 9½x10¾*

Self-Adhesive

Booklet Stamp

2035 A833 49c multi	.85	.35
a. Booklet pane of 4	3.40	
Complete booklet, 2 #2035a	7.00	

Bird Paintings by John James Audubon A834

Designs: No. 2036, Ruby-crowned kinglet. No. 2037, White-winged crossbill. No. 2038, Bohemian waxwing. No. 2039, Boreal chickadee. 80c, Lincoln's sparrow.

2004, May 14 *Perf. 12½x13*

2036 A834 49c multi	.85	.35
2037 A834 49c multi	.85	.35
2038 A834 49c multi	.85	.35
2039 A834 49c multi	.85	.35
a. Block of 4, #2036-2039	3.40	2.75

Self-Adhesive

Booklet Stamp

Die Cut

2040 A834 80c multi	1.30	.40
a. Booklet pane of 6	8.00	
Nos. 2036-2040 (5)	4.70	1.80

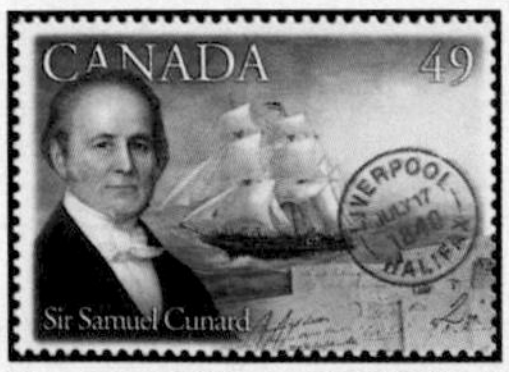

Pioneers of Transatlantic Mail Service — A835

Designs: No. 2041, Sir Samuel Cunard (1787-1865). No. 2042, Sir Hugh Allan (1810-82).

2004, May 28 Litho. *Perf. 13¼x12½*

Self-Adhesive

2041 A835 49c multi	.85	.30
2042 A835 49c multi	.85	.30
a. Horiz. pair, #2041-2042	1.70	1.20

D-Day, 60th Anniv. A836

2004, June 6 Litho. *Perf. 13x12½*

2043 A836 49c multi	.85	.30

Pierre Dugua de Mons, Leader of First French Settlement in Acadia, and Ship A837

Litho. & Engr.

2004, June 26 *Perf. 13x12½*

2044 A837 49c multi	.85	.30

See France No. 3032.

Butterfly and Flower A838

Children on Beach A839

Rose A840

Dog A841

Serpentine Die Cut 11¾

2004, June Litho.

Self-Adhesive

Booklet Stamps

2045 A838 (49c) multi	10.00	10.00
a. Booklet pane of 2	20.00	
Complete booklet, #2045a + phonecard in greeting card	26.00	
2046 A839 (49c) multi	10.00	10.00
a. Booklet pane of 2	20.00	
Complete booklet, #2046a + phonecard in greeting card	26.00	
2047 A840 (49c) multi	10.00	10.00
a. Booklet pane of 2	20.00	
Complete booklet, #2047a + phonecard in greeting card	26.00	
2048 A841 (49c) multi	10.00	10.00
a. Booklet pane of 2	20.00	
Complete booklet, #2048a + phonecard in greeting card	26.00	
Nos. 2045-2048 (4)	40.00	40.00

Nos. 2045-2048, have a frame like No. 1918a, and are similarly inscribed "Domestic Lettermail" and "Poste-lettres du régime intérieur," but Nos. 2045-2048 have the vignettes printed on the stamps, while any vignettes found on No. 1918a are affixed stickers. Nos. 2045a-2048a are affixed to the insides of greeting cards that contain detachable phonecards valid for 15 minutes calling time on any touchtone phone in Canada or the United States. The stamps were available only in the greeting card, which sold for $5.99 along with a blank envelope for sending the greeting card.

2004 Summer Olympics, Athens — A842

Olympic rings and: No. 2049, Spyros Louis, 1896 Marathon gold medalist, diagram of track, "Athens" in Greek, and stylized runner. No. 2050, Soccer net inscribed "Canada," girls playing soccer.

2004, July 28 *Perf. 12½x13¼*

2049 A842 49c multi	.85	.30
2050 A842 49c multi	.85	.30
a. Horiz. pair, #2049-2050	1.70	1.25

Canadian Open Golf Championship, Cent. — A843

Crowd, trophy and golfer: No. 2051, Finishing swing. No. 2052, Ready to putt.

Litho. & Embossed With Foil Application

2004, Aug. 12 *Serpentine Die Cut*

Self-Adhesive

2051 A843 49c multi	.85	.30
2052 A843 49c multi	.85	.30

Nos. 2051-2052 were issued in a sheet containing four of each stamp.

Maple Leaf Types of 2003

2004, Aug. 18 Litho. *Die Cut*

Self-Adhesive

Coil Stamps

2053 A822 49c multi	.85	.20

Serpentine Die Cut 8¼ Horiz.

2054 A823 80c red & multi	1.80	.50
2055 A823 $1.40 grn & multi	3.25	.75
a. Die cutting omitted, pair	—	
Nos. 2053-2055 (3)	5.90	1.45

Die cut gauges on Nos. 2054-2055 vary widely within the roll, from 8¼-8¾. Gauge 8¼ is the most common.

Montreal Heart Institute, 50th Anniv. — A844

Die Cut Perf. 13½

2004, Sept. 15 Litho.

Self-Adhesive

Booklet Stamp

2056 A844 49c multi	.85	.30
a. Booklet pane of 4	3.40	
Complete booklet, 2 #2056	7.00	

Pets A845

2004, Oct. 1 Litho. *Die Cut*

Self-Adhesive

Booklet Stamps

2057 A845 49c Fish	.85	.35
2058 A845 49c Cats	.85	.35
2059 A845 49c Rabbit	.85	.35
2060 A845 49c Dog	.85	.35
a. Booklet pane, #2057-2060	3.40	
Complete booklet, 2 #2060a	7.00	

Nobel Laureates in Chemistry — A846

Designs: No. 2061, Gerhard Herzberg, 1971 laureate, and molecular structures. No. 2062, Michael Smith, 1993 laureate, and DNA double helix.

2004, Oct. 4 *Perf. 12½x13*

2061 A846 49c multi	.85	.30
2062 A846 49c multi	.85	.30
a. Pair, #2061-2062	1.70	1.20

Ribbon Frame A847

Picture Album Frame A848

Serpentine Die Cut 12¾x13

2004, Oct. 8 Litho.

Self-Adhesive

2063 A847 (49c) multi	.85	.75
2064 A848 (49c) multi	.85	.75

Nos. 2063 and 2064 were each printed in sheets of 21 that sold for $9.80. These sheets were split by a row of rouletting in the center, with 20 stamps on one side and one on the other side. Sheets of 21 with vignettes that could be personalized by the customer were available for $24.95. Sheets of 40 stamps with personalized vignettes were also available for $39.95.

Victoria Cross, 150th Anniv. — A849

Designs: No. 2065, Victoria Cross. No. 2066, Design for Canadian Victoria Cross, approved with Queen Elizabeth II's signature.

Litho. & Embossed

2004, Oct. 21 *Perf. 13x12½*

2065 A849 49c multi .85 .30

Litho.

2066 A849 49c multi .85 .30
a. Pair, #2065-2066 1.70 1.20

Paintings by Jean Paul Lemieux — A850

Designs: 49c, Self-portrait. 80c, A June Wedding, horiz. (53x35mm). $1.40, Summer, horiz. (64x31mm).

2004, Oct. 22 Litho. *Perf. 13x13¼*

2067 A850 49c multi .85 .35
a. Perf. 13 1.60 1.60

Souvenir Sheet

Perf. 13

2068 Sheet, #2067a, 2068a, 2068b 5.25 5.25
a. A850 80c multi 1.60 1.60
b. A850 $1.40 multi 2.50 2.50

Christmas — A851

Santa Claus and: 49c, Sleigh. 80c, Automobile. $1.40, Train.

Serpentine Die Cut 7¼ Horiz.

2004, Nov. 2

Booklet Stamps

Self-Adhesive

2069 A851 49c multi .85 .20
a. Booklet pane of 6 5.25
Complete booklet, 2 #2069a 11.00
2070 A851 80c multi 1.30 .50
a. Booklet pane of 6 8.00
2071 A851 $1.40 multi 2.25 .75
a. Booklet pane of 6 13.50

Queen Type of 2003 and

Red Calla Lilies A852

Flag and Saskatoon, Saskatchewan A853

Flag and Durrell, Newfoundland A854

Flag and Shannon Falls, British Columbia A855

Flag and Mont-Saint-Hilaire, Quebec — A856

Flag and Toronto — A857

Designs: 85c, Yellow calla lily. $1.45, Dutch iris.

Serpentine Die Cut 6½-8¾ Horiz.

2004-05 Litho.

Self-Adhesive

Coil Stamps

2072 A852 50c multi .85 .20
a. Serpentine die cut 6¾ horiz. ('05) .85 .20
2073 A852 85c multi 1.35 .30
a. Serpentine die cut 6¾ horiz. ('05) 1.35 .30
2074 A852 $1.45 multi 2.30 .65
a. Serpentine die cut 6¾ horiz. ('05) 4.00 1.60

The die cutting gauge on Nos. 2072-2074a will vary between stamps on a roll and between stamps on one roll and other rolls.

Issued: Nos. 2072, 2073, 2074, 12/20/04. Nos. 2072a, 2073a, 2074a, 2/2005. Die cuttings on these issues are variable. The editors are obtaining additional strips of the coils. Die cutting notes may change.

Booklet Stamps

Die Cut

2075 A825 50c multi .85 .20
a. Booklet pane of 10 8.50
2076 A853 50c multi .85 .20
2077 A854 50c multi .85 .20
2078 A855 50c multi .85 .20
2079 A856 50c multi .85 .20
2080 A857 50c multi .85 .20
a. Booklet pane, 2 each #2076-2080 8.50
2081 A852 85c multi 1.70 .40
a. Booklet pane of 6 10.50
b. As "a," black inscriptions omitted *800.00*
2082 A852 $1.45 multi 2.30 .50
a. Booklet pane of 6 14.00
Nos. 2072-2082 (11) 13.60 3.25

New Year 2005 (Year of the Cock) — A858

Rooster with: 50c, Red tail feathers. $1.45, Gold tail feathers.

Litho. & Embossed with Foil Application

2005, Jan. 7 *Perf. 13¼*

2083 A858 50c multi .85 .30

Souvenir Sheet

Perf. 12½x13

2084 A858 $1.45 multi 2.25 2.25
a. With dates, Canadian and Chinese flags added in sheet margin 3.50 3.50

Canada — People's Republic of China diplomatic relations, 35th anniv. (#2084a). No. 2084 contains one 40x40mm stamp.

National Hockey League Stars A859

Designs: Nos. 2085a, 2086a, Henri Richard (blue background). Nos. 2085b, 2086b, Grant Fuhr (orange background). Nos. 2085c, 2086c, Allan Stanley (red background). Nos. 2085d, 2086d, Pierre Pilote (green background). Nos. 2085e, 2086e, Bryan Trottier (purple background). Nos. 2085f, 2086f, John Bucyk (yellow background).

Perf. 12½x13¼ on 3 Sides

2005, Jan. 29 Litho.

2085 Sheet of 6 + 3 labels 5.25 5.25
a.-f. A859 50c Any single .85 .50

Self-Adhesive

Die Cut

2086 Pane of 6 5.25
a.-f. A859 50c Any single .85 .50

Fishing Flies — A860

Designs: Nos. 2087a, 2088a, Alevin. Nos. 2087b, 2088b, Jock Scott. Nos. 2087c, 2088d, P. E. I. Fly. Nos. 2087d, 2088c, Mickey Finn.

2005, Feb. 4 *Perf. 12½x13¼*

2087 A860 Sheet of 4 5.75 5.75
a.-d. 50c Any single 1.40 1.20

Self-Adhesive

Serpentine Die Cut 10 Syncopated

2088 A860 Booklet pane of 4 3.50
a.-d. 50c Any single .85 .35
Complete booklet, 2 #2088 7.00

Universities Type of 2003

Design: Nova Scotia Agricultural College, cent.

Die Cut Perf. 12¾x13¼

2005, Feb. 14 Litho.

Booklet Stamp

Self-Adhesive

2089 A806 50c multi .85 .35
a. Booklet pane of 4 3.50
Complete booklet, 2 #2089a 7.00

Expo 2005, Aichi, Japan — A861

2005, Mar. 4 Litho. *Perf. 13½*

2090 A861 50c multi .85 .35

Daffodils A862

Designs: Nos. 2091a, 2092, Yellow daffodils, green and yellow background. Nos. 2091b, 2093, White daffodils, red orange and yellow background.

2005, Mar. 10 Litho. *Perf. 13x13¼*

Souvenir Sheet

2091 Sheet of 2 2.40 2.40
a.-b. A862 50c Either single 1.20 .80

Booklet Stamps

Self-Adhesive

Die Cut Perf. 10

2092 A862 50c multi .85 .35
2093 A862 50c multi .85 .35
a. Booklet pane, 5 each #2092-2093 + 10 stickers 8.50

Pacific Explore 2005 World Stamp Expo, Sydney, Australia (#2091).

TD Bank Financial Group, 150th Anniv. — A863

2005, Mar. 18 *Die Cut Perf. 11¼*

Self-Adhesive

Booklet Stamp

2094 A863 50c multi .85 .35
a. Booklet pane of 10 8.50
Complete booklet, #2094a 12.50

The booklet pane of 10 is the inside front cover of the booklet. Fifteen stickers are on inside back cover.

Bird Paintings by John James Audubon — A864

Designs: No. 2095, Horned lark. No. 2096, Piping plover. No. 2097, Stilt sandpiper. No. 2098, Willow ptarmigan. 85c, Double-crested cormorant.

2005, Mar. 23 *Perf. 12½x13¼*

2095 A864 50c multi .85 .35
2096 A864 50c multi .85 .35
2097 A864 50c multi .85 .35
2098 A864 50c multi .85 .35
a. Block of 4, #2095-2098 3.40 2.75

Booklet Stamp

Self-Adhesive

Size: 48x39mm

Die Cut

2099 A864 85c multi 1.20 .50
a. Booklet pane of 6 7.25

Bridges — A865

Designs: No. 2100, Jacques Cartier Bridge, Quebec. No. 2101, Souris Swinging Bridge, Manitoba. No. 2102, Angus L. Macdonald Bridge, Nova Scotia. No. 2103, Canso Causeway, Nova Scotia.

2005, Apr. 2 Litho. *Perf. 12½x13*

Self-Adhesive

2100 A865 50c multi .85 .35
2101 A865 50c multi .85 .35
2102 A865 50c multi .85 .35
2103 A865 50c multi .85 .35
a. Block or strip of 4, #2100-2103 3.40 2.75

Maclean's Magazine, Cent. A866

2005, Apr. 12

2104 A866 50c multi .85 .30

Biosphere Reserves in Canada and Ireland — A867

Designs: No. 2105, Saskatoon berries, Waterton Lakes National Park, Canada. No. 2106, Deer, Killarney National Park, Ireland.

2005, Apr. 22

2105	A867	50c multi	.85	.30
2106	A867	50c multi	.85	.30
a.		Pair, #2105-2106	1.70	1.25
b.		Souvenir sheet, #2106a	2.50	2.50

See Ireland Nos. 1611-1612.

Battle of the Atlantic, World War II — A868

2005, Apr. 29

2107 A868 50c multi .85 .35

Opening of Canadian War Museum, Ottawa — A869

Serpentine Die Cut 8x8½ Syncopated

2005, May 6 **Litho.**

Self-Adhesive

Booklet Stamp

2108	A869	50c multi	.85	.35
a.		Booklet pane of 4	3.40	
		Complete booklet, 2 #2108a	7.00	

Paintings by Homer Watson (1855-1936) — A870

Designs: 50c, Down in the Laurentides. 85c, The Flood Gate (54x40mm)

2005, May 27 **Litho.** ***Perf. 13¼x13***

2109	A870	50c multi	.85	.35
a.		Perf. 13½x13	1.60	1.60

Souvenir Sheet

Perf. 13½x13

2110		Sheet, #2109a, 2110a	5.50	5.50
a.		A870 85c multi	3.25	3.25

Miniature Sheet

Search and Rescue — A871

No. 2111: a, Rescuer and dog at plane crash. b, Rescuers at shipwreck. c, Helicopter, airplane and rescuers. d, Mountainside rescuers.

2005, June 13 ***Perf. 13x13¼***

2111	A871	Sheet, 2 each #a-d	6.75	6.75
a.-d.		50c Any single	.85	.50

No. 2111 contains two horizontal strips, one of which is inverted, so that a tete-beche pair of No. 2111c and two tete-beche pairs containing Nos. 2111b and 2111d can be created.

Ellen Fairclough (1905-2004), First Female Cabinet Minister — A872

2005, June 21 ***Perf. 13x12½***

2112 A872 50c multi .85 .35

Diver A873

Swimmer A874

2005, July 5 **Litho.** ***Perf. 13¼***

2113	A873	50c multi	.85	.40
2114	A874	50c multi	.85	.40
a.		Horiz. pair, #2113-2114	1.70	1.00

9th FINA World Championships, Montreal. In No. 2114a, the denomination for one stamp is on the opposite side of the pair from that of the other stamp.

Founding of Port-Royal, Nova Scotia, 400th Anniv. A875

Litho. & Engr.

2005, July 16 ***Perf. 13x12½***

2115 A875 50c multi .85 .35

Province of Alberta, Cent. — A876

2005, July 21 **Litho.** ***Perf. 12½x13***

Self-Adhesive

2116 A876 50c multi .85 .35

Printed in panes of 8 with each stamp having a different design on the backing.

Province of Saskatchewan, Cent. — A877

2005, Aug. 2 **Litho.** ***Perf. 13x12½***

2117 A877 50c multi .85 .35

Oscar Peterson, Pianist, 80th Birthday — A878

2005, Aug. 15

2118	A878	50c multi	.85	.35
a.		Souvenir sheet of 4	3.40	3.40

No. 176 and Acadian Flag A879

2005, Aug. 15 **Litho.** ***Perf. 13x12½***

2119 A879 50c multi .85 .35

Acadian Deportation, 250th anniv.

Children Playing and Leg Braces — A880

2005, Sept. 2 ***Perf. 12½x13***

2120 A880 50c multi .85 .35

Mass polio vaccinations in Canada, 50th anniv.

Youth Sports — A881

No. 2121: a, Wall climbing. b, Skateboarding. c, Mountain biking. d, Snowboarding.

2005, Oct. 1 **Litho.** ***Die Cut***

Self-Adhesive

2121		Complete booket, 2 each #a-d	6.75	
a.-d.		A881 50c Any single	.85	.35

Wild Cats A882

Designs: No. 2122, Puma concolor. No. 2123, Panthera pardus orientalis.

Perf. 13½x13¼ Syncopated

2005, Oct. 13

2122	A882	50c multi	.85	.35
2123	A882	50c multi	.85	.35
a.		Horiz. pair, #2122-2123	1.70	1.00
b.		Souvenir sheet, #2123a	2.00	2.00

Diplomatic relations with People's Republic of China, 35th anniv. (#2123b). The perforation column between the two stamps, which gauges perf. 13½, has a maple leaf shaped syncopation.

See People's Republic of China Nos. 3458-3459.

Snowman — A883

Litho. with Hologram Applied

Serpentine Die Cut 8¼ Horiz.

2005, Nov. 2

Booklet Stamp

Self-Adhesive

2124	A883	50c multi	.85	.35
a.		Booklet pane of 6	5.00	
		Complete booklet, 2 #2124a	10.00	

A884

A885

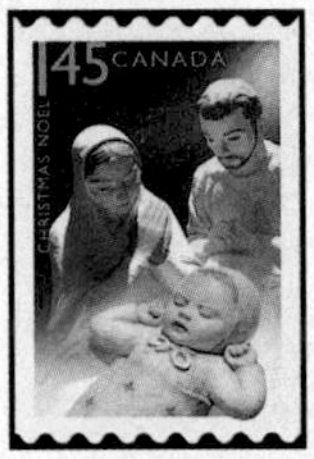

Creche Figures, St. Joseph's Oratory, Montreal — A886

Serpentine Die Cut 6¾ Horiz.

2005, Nov. 2 **Litho.**

Booklet Stamps

Self-Adhesive

2125	A884	50c multi	.85	.35
a.		Booklet pane of 6	5.00	
		Complete booklet, 2 #2125a	10.00	

Serpentine Die Cut 6½ Horiz.

2126	A885	85c multi	1.40	.50
a.		Booklet pane of 6	8.50	

Serpentine Die Cut 6¾ Horiz.

2127	A886	$1.45 multi	2.40	1.20
a.		Booklet pane of 6	14.50	

Flowers — A887

Designs: 51c, Red bergamot. 89c, Yellow lady's slipper. $1.05, Pink fairy slipper. $1.49, Himalayan blue poppy.

Serpentine Die Cut 7 to 7¾ Horiz.

2005, Dec. 19 **Litho.**

Coil Stamps

Self-Adhesive

2128	A887	51c multi	.85	.20
2129	A887	89c multi	1.40	.35
2130	A887	$1.05 multi	1.70	.60
2131	A887	$1.49 multi	2.40	.90

Booklet Stamps

Die Cut

2132	A887	89c multi	1.60	.40
a.		Booklet pane of 6	9.75	
2133	A887	$1.05 multi	2.00	.65
a.		Booklet pane of 6	12.00	

2134 A887 $1.49 multi 2.40 .90
a. Booklet pane of 6 14.50
Nos. 2128-2134 (7) 12.35 4.00

Flag and Houses, New Glasgow, Prince Edward Island A888

Flag and Bridge, Bouctouche, New Brunswick A889

Flag and Windmills, Pincher Creek, Alberta A890

Flag and Lower Fort Garry, Manitoba A891

Flag and Dogsled, Yukon Territory — A892

2005, Dec. 19 *Die Cut*

Booklet Stamps

Self-Adhesive

2135 A888 51c multi .85 .20
2136 A889 51c multi .85 .20
2137 A890 51c multi .85 .20
2138 A891 51c multi .85 .20
2139 A892 51c multi .85 .20
a. Booklet pane, 2 each #2135-2139 8.50
Nos. 2135-2139 (5) 4.25 1.00

New Year 2006 (Year of the Dog) — A893

Litho. & Embossed With Foil Application

2006, Jan. 6 *Perf. 13¼*
2140 A893 51c shown .85 .35

Souvenir Sheet

2141 A893 $1.49 Dog and pup 2.40 2.40

Queen Elizabeth II, 80th Birthday A894

Serpentine Die Cut 10
2006, Jan. 12 **Litho.**

Booklet Stamp

Self-Adhesive

2142 A894 51c multi .85 .30
a. Booklet pane of 10 8.50

See No. 2150.

2006 Winter Olympics, Turin, Italy A895

Designs: No. 2143, Team pursuit speed skating. No. 2144, Skeleton.

2006, Feb. 3 **Litho.** ***Perf. 12½x13***
2143 A895 51c multi .85 .30
2144 A895 51c multi .85 .30
a. Horiz. pair, #2143-2144 1.70 1.00

Gardens — A896

No. 2145: a, Shade garden and black-throated blue warbler. b, Flower garden and American painted lady butterfly. c, Water garden and green darner dragonfly. d, Rock garden and blue-spotted salamander.

Serpentine Die Cut 10
2006, Mar. 8 **Litho.**

Self-Adhesive

2145 Complete booklet, 2 each #a-d 6.75
a.-d. A896 51c Any single .85 .45

Party Balloons A897

Serpentine Die Cut 6¾ Horiz.
2006, Apr. 3 **Litho.**

Self-Adhesive

Booklet Stamp

2146 A897 51c multi .85 .35
a. Booklet pane of 6 5.00

Paintings by Dorothy Knowles — A898

Designs: 51c, The Field of Rapeseed. 89c, North Saskatchewan River, vert. (42x51mm).

2006, Apr. 7 ***Perf. 13¼x12½***
2147 A898 51c multi .85 .35
a. Perf. 12¾x12½ 1.60 1.60

Souvenir Sheet

Perf. 13

2148 Sheet, #2147a, 2148a 4.00 4.00
a. A898 89c multi 2.25 2.25

Canadian Labor Congress, 50th Anniv. — A899

2006, Apr. 20 ***Perf. 13½x13¼***
2149 A899 51c multi .85 .35

Queen Elizabeth II, 80th Birthday Type of 2006

Souvenir Sheet

2006, Apr. 21 **Litho.** ***Perf. 12½x13***
2150 Sheet of 2 #2150a 5.00 5.00
a. A894 149c multi, 36x28mm 2.50 2.50

McClelland & Stewart Publishing House, Cent. — A900

2006, Apr. 26 ***Die Cut Perf. 11¼x11***

Self-Adhesive

Booklet Stamp

2151 A900 51c slate grn & sil .85 .35
a. Booklet pane of 4 + 4 stickers 3.40
Complete booklet, 2 #2151a 6.75

Northwest Coast Transformation Mask and Northwest Coast Exhibit — A901

Serpentine Die Cut 8 Horiz. Syncopated
2006, May 11

Self-Adhesive

Booklet Stamp

2152 A901 89c multi 1.40 .80
a. Booklet pane of 4 5.75
Complete booklet, 2 #2152a 11.50

Canadian Museum of Civilization, 150th anniv.

Canadians in Hollywood A903

Actors and actresses: Nos. 2153a, 2154a, John Candy (1950-94). Nos. 2153b, 2154c, Fay Wray (1907-2004). Nos. 2153c, 2154d, Lorne Greene (1915-87). Nos. 2153d, 2154b, Mary Pickford (1893-1979).

2006, May 26 ***Perf. 13x12½***
2153 Souvenir sheet of 4 4.75 4.75
a.-d. A903 51c Any single 1.20 1.00

Self-Adhesive

Serpentine Die Cut 9¾x10

2154 Booklet pane of 4 + 4 stickers 3.40
a.-d. A903 51c Any single .85 .40
Complete booklet, 2 #2154 6.75

Complete booklets were issued with four different covers depicting the featured actors or actresses.

A904

Exploration of Eastern Coast by Samuel de Champlain, 400th Anniv. — A905

Litho. & Engr.

2006, May 28 ***Perf. 13x12½***
2155 A904 51c multi .85 .35

Souvenir Sheet

2156 A905 Sheet, 2 #2156a, 2 US #4074a 6.00 6.00
a. A904 51c multi, perf. 11 1.50 1.50

Washington 2006 World Philatelic Exhibition (#2156). No. 2156, sold only by Canada Post for $2, has bar code in sheet margin at lower left. United States No. 4074, sold only by the United States Postal Service, lacks this bar code.

Vancouver Aquarium, 50th Anniv. — A906

Serpentine Die Cut 9½
2006, June 15 **Litho.**

Self-Adhesive

Booklet Stamp

2157 A906 51c multi .85 .35
a. Booklet pane of 5 4.25
Complete booklet, 2 #2157a 8.50

Canadian Forces Snowbirds Aerobatics Team — A907

Designs: No. 2158, Pilot in cockpit, two airplanes. No. 2159, Three airplanes.

Perf. 12½x13¼
2006, June 28 **Litho.**
2158 A907 51c multi .85 .35
2159 A907 51c multi .85 .35
a. Horiz. pair, #2158-2159 1.70 1.25
b. Souvenir sheet, #2159a 2.50 2.50

James White, Dividers and Map of Canada — A908

2006, June 30 ***Perf. 13¼x12½***
2160 A908 51c multi .85 .35

Atlas of Canada, cent. Printed in sheets of 16 + 4 labels.

World Lacrosse Championships, London, Ontario — A909

Serpentine Die Cut 11¾ Horiz.

2006, July 6

Self-Adhesive

Booklet Stamp

2161 A909 51c multi .85 .35
a. Booklet pane of 8 6.75

Alpine Club of Canada, Cent. — A910

2006, July 19 *Die Cut Perf. 12½x13*

Self-Adhesive

Booklet Stamp

2162 A910 51c multi .85 .35
a. Booklet pane of 8 6.75

Ducks and Duck Decoys A911

Designs: No. 2163, Barrow's goldeneyes. No. 2164, Mallards. No. 2165, American black ducks. No. 2166, Redbreasted mergansers.

2006, Aug. 3 Litho. *Perf. 13¼x12½*

2163 A911 51c blue & multi .85 .40
2164 A911 51c yel & multi .85 .40
2165 A911 51c red & multi .85 .40
2166 A911 51c grn & multi .85 .40
a. Block of 4, #2163-2166 3.40 2.50
b. Souvenir sheet, #2163-2166 4.00 4.00

Society of Graphic Designers of Canada, 50th Anniv. — A912

2006, Aug. 16 *Perf. 12½x13*

2167 A912 51c multi .85 .35

Canadian Wines A913

Canadian Cheeses A914

Designs: No. 2168, Three glasses of wine. No. 2169, Wine taster, barrels. No. 2170, Various cheeses. No. 2171, Woman with tray of cheeses and fruit.

2006, Aug. 23 Litho. *Die Cut*

Booklet Stamps

Self-Adhesive

2168 A913 51c multi .85 .35
2169 A913 51c multi .85 .35
2170 A914 51c multi .85 .35
2171 A914 51c multi .85 .35
a. Booklet pane, 2 each #2168-2171 6.75
Nos. 2168-2171 (4) 3.40 1.40

Universities Type of 2003

Design: Macdonald College, Sainte-Anne-de-Bellevue, Quebec, cent.

Die Cut Perf. 12¾x13¼

2006, Sept. 26

Booklet Stamp

Self-Adhesive

2172 A806 51c multi .85 .35
a. Booklet pane of 4 3.40
Complete booklet, 2 #2172a 6.75

Endangered Animals — A915

Designs: Nos. 2173a, 2174, Newfoundland marten. Nos. 2173b, 2175, Blotched tiger salamander. Nos. 2173c, 2176, Blue racer snake. Nos. 2173d, 2177, Swift fox.

2006, Sept. 29 Litho. *Perf. 13¼*

2173 Sheet of 4 + 4 labels 4.00 4.00
a.-d. A915 51c Any single 1.00 1.00

Booklet Stamps

Self-Adhesive

Size: 47x24mm

Die Cut

2174 A915 51c multi .85 .40
2175 A915 51c multi .85 .40
2176 A915 51c multi .85 .40
2177 A915 51c multi .85 .40
a. Block of 4, #2174-2177 3.40
b. Booklet pane, 2, #2177a 6.75

Opera Singers — A916

Designs: No. 2178, Maureen Forrester. No. 2179, Raoul Jobin (1906-74). No. 2180, Léopold Simoneau (1916-2006) and Pierrette Alarie. No. 2181, Jon Vickers. No. 2182, Edward Johnson (1878-1959).

2006, Oct. 17 Litho. *Perf. 13½x13*

2178 A916 51c multi .85 .40
2179 A916 51c multi .85 .40
2180 A916 51c multi .85 .40
2181 A916 51c multi .85 .40
2182 A916 51c multi .85 .40
a. Vert. strip of 5, #2178-2182 4.25 4.25

Madonna and Child, by Antoine-Sébastien Falardeau A917

Christmas Card Art A918

Designs: No. 2184, Snowman, by Yvonne McKague Housser. 89c, Winter Joys, by J. E. Sampson. $1.49, Contemplation, by Edwin Holgate.

2006, Nov. 1 Litho. *Die Cut*

Booklet Stamps

Self-Adhesive

2183 A917 51c multi .85 .25
a. Booklet pane of 12 10.00

Serpentine Die Cut 13¼ Horiz.

2184 A918 51c multi .85 .25
a. Booklet pane of 12 10.00
2185 A918 89c multi 1.40 .50
a. Booklet pane of 6 8.50
2186 A918 $1.49 multi 2.40 .90
a. Booklet pane of 6 14.50
Nos. 2183-2186 (4) 5.50 1.90

Spotted Coralroot A919

Queen Elizabeth II A920

Flag and Sirmilik Natl. Park, Nunavut A921

Flag and Cliff Near Chemainus, British Columbia A922

Flag and Polar Bears Near Churchill, Manitoba A923

Flag and Bras d'Or Lake, Nova Scotia A924

Flag and Tuktut Nogait Natl. Park, Northwest Territories — A925

2006, Nov. 16 Litho.

Coil Stamp

Self-Adhesive

Serpentine Die Cut 7½-9 Horiz.

2187 A919 P multi 1.25 .20

Booklet Stamps

Die Cut

2188 A920 P multi .85 .20
a. Booklet pane of 10 8.50
2189 A921 P multi .85 .20
2190 A922 P multi .85 .20
2191 A923 P multi .85 .20
2192 A924 P multi .85 .20
2193 A925 P multi .85 .20
a. Booklet pane, 2 each #2189-2193 8.50
b. Booklet pane, 6 each #2189-2193 25.00
Nos. 2187-2193 (7) 6.35 1.40

Nos. 2187-2193 each sold for 51c on day of issue. On Nos. 2188a, 2193a and 2193b, adjacent stamps that are on both sides of the booklet fold have rouletting rather than die cutting between them. No. 2193b is sold folded into thirds. Each of the thirds has selvage surrounding the ten stamps on it, unlike No. 2193a.

Spotted Coralroot Type of 2006 and

Flat-leaved Bladderwort — A926

Designs: $1.10, Marsh skullcap. $1.55, Little larkspur.

2006, Dec. 19 Litho. *Perf. 13¼x13*

2194 Souvenir sheet of 4 7.00 7.00
a. A919 P multi 1.00 .60
b. A926 93c multi 1.60 1.10
c. A926 $1.10 multi 1.75 1.30
d. A926 $1.55 multi 2.50 2.00

Self-Adhesive

Coil Stamps

Serpentine Die Cut 7½-9

2195 A926 93c multi 1.50 .40
2196 A926 $1.10 multi 1.75 .60
2197 A926 $1.55 multi 2.50 .65

Booklet Stamps

Die Cut

2198 A926 93c multi 1.60 .50
a. Booklet pane of 6 9.50
2199 A926 $1.10 multi 1.90 .75
a. Booklet pane of 6 11.50
2200 A926 $1.55 multi 2.50 1.00
a. Booklet pane of 6 15.00
Nos. 2195-2200 (6) 11.75 3.90

No. 2194a sold for 51c on day of issue.

New Year 2007 (Year of the Pig) A927

Pig facing: 52c, Left. $1.55, Right.

Litho. & Embossed with Foil Application

2007, Jan. 5 *Perf. 13½x13*

2201 A927 52c red & multi .85 .35
a. Gold foil omitted —

Souvenir Sheet

2202 A927 $1.55 grn & multi 2.60 2.60

Confetti and Streamers A928

Serpentine Die Cut 6¾ Horiz.

2007, Jan. 15 Litho.

Booklet Stamp

Self-Adhesive

2203 A928 52c multi .85 .35
a. Booklet pane of 6 5.00

International Polar Year — A929

Designs: No. 2204, Somateria spectabilis. No. 2205, Crossota millsaeare.

Perf. 13½ Syncopated

2007, Feb. 12 Litho.

2204 A929 52c multi .85 .35
2205 A929 52c multi .85 .35
a. Horiz. pair, #2204-2205 1.70 1.00
b. Souvenir sheet, #2205a 2.25 2.25

Lilacs — A930

Color of lilacs: Nos. 2206a, 2207, White. Nos. 2206b, 2208, Purple.

2007, Mar. 1 Litho. *Perf. 12¾*

Souvenir Sheet

2206 A930 Sheet of 2 2.40 2.40
a.-b. 52c Either single 1.20 .75

Booklet Stamps
Self-Adhesive
Die Cut

2207 A930 52c multi .85 .35
2208 A930 52c multi .85 .35
a. Booklet pane of 10, 5 each #2207-2208 8.50

Universities Type of 2003

Design: No. 2209, HEC Montreal, cent. No. 2210, University of Saskatchewan, cent.

2007 Litho. *Die Cut Perf. 12¾x13¼*
Booklet Stamp
Self-Adhesive

2209 A806 52c multi .85 .35
a. Booklet pane of 4 3.40
Complete booklet, 2 #2209a 6.75
2210 A806 52c multi .85 .35
a. Booklet pane of 4 3.40
Complete booklet, 2 #2210a 6.75

Issued: No. 2209, 3/12. No. 2210, 4/3.

Art by Mary Pratt — A931

Designs: 52c, Jelly Shelf. $1.55 Iceberg in the North Atlantic (58x36mm).

2007, Mar. 15 Litho. *Perf. 13x12½*
2211 A931 52c multi .85 .35

Souvenir Sheet

2212 Sheet, #2211, 2212a 3.75 3.75
a. A931 $1.55 multi 2.60 2.60

Selection of Ottawa as National Capital, 150th Anniv. — A932

Litho., Litho & Embossed with Foil Application (#2213b)

2007, May 3 *Perf. 13¼*
2213 Sheet of 2 3.75 3.75
a. A932 52c multi 1.20 1.00
b. A932 $1.55 multi 2.40 2.25

Booklet Stamp
Self-Adhesive
Serpentine Die Cut 7¼ Horiz.

2214 A932 52c multi .85 .35
a. Booklet pane of 4 3.40
Complete booklet, 2 #2214a 6.75

Royal Architectural Institute of Canada, Cent. — A933

Buildings: No. 2215, University of Lethbridge, by Arthur Erickson. No. 2216, St. Mary's Church, by Douglas Cardinal. No. 2217, Ontario Science Centre, by Raymond Moriyama. No. 2218, National Gallery of Canada, by Moshe Safdie.

2007, May 9 Litho. *Perf. 13*
2215 A933 52c multi + label .85 .45
2216 A933 52c multi + label .85 .45
2217 A933 52c multi + label .85 .45
2218 A933 52c multi + label .85 .45
a. Vert. strip of 4, #2215-2218, + 4 labels 3.40 2.50

Nos. 2215-2218 were printed in sheets containing two of each stamp. Labels flank the stamps, with labels on the left showing drawings of the buildings and the labels on the right showing the architect.

Capt. George Vancouver (1757-98), Explorer — A934

Litho. & Embossed

2007, June 22 *Perf. 13x12½*
2219 A934 $1.55 multi 2.40 1.00
a. Souvenir sheet of 1, perf. 13 2.40 2.40

FIFA Under-20 World Soccer Championships, Canada — A935

2007, June 26 Litho. *Perf. 12½x13*
2220 A935 52c multi .85 .35

Popular Singers — A936

Designs: Nos. 2221a, 2222a, Gordon Lightfoot. Nos. 2221b, 2222b, Joni Mitchell. Nos. 2221c, 2222c, Anne Murray. Nos. 2221d, 2222d, Paul Anka.

2007, June 29 *Perf. 12½x13*
2221 A936 Sheet of 4 3.40 3.40
a.-d. 52c Any single .85 .75

Self-Adhesive
Serpentine Die Cut 13½

2222 A936 Booklet pane of 4 3.40
a.-d. 52c Any single .85 .45
Complete booklet, 2 #2222 6.75

Complete booklets were issued with four different covers depicting the featured singers.

National Parks — A937

Designs: No. 2223, Terra Nova National Park, Newfoundland, 50th anniv. No. 2224, Jasper National Park, Alberta, cent.

2007 *Serpentine Die Cut 13¼*
Booklet Stamps
Self-Adhesive

2223 A937 52c multi .85 .35
a. Booklet pane of 5 4.25
Complete booklet, 2 #2223a 8.50
2224 A937 52c multi .85 .35
a. Booklet pane of 5 4.25
Complete booklet, 2 #2224a 8.50
b. Gutter pane, 5 each #2223-2224 10.00

Issued: No. 2223, 7/6; No. 2224, 7/20.

Scouting, Cent. A938

2007, July 25 Litho.
Booklet Stamp
Self-Adhesive

2225 A938 52c multi .85 .35
a. Booklet pane of 4 + 4 labels 3.40
Complete booklet, 2 #2225a 6.75

Henri Membertou, Grand Chief of Mi'kmaq Tribe — A939

2007, June 26 Engr. *Perf. 13x12½*
2226 A939 52c multi .85 .35

Law Society of Saskatchewan, Cent. — A940

2007, Sept. 13 Litho. *Perf. 13*
2227 A940 52c multi .85 .35

Printed in sheets of 8 + 8 labels.

Law Society of Alberta, Cent. A941

2007, Sept. 13 *Perf. 12½x13*
2228 A941 52c multi .85 .35

Endangered Animals Type of 2006

Designs: Nos. 2229a, 2230, North Atlantic right whale. Nos. 2229b, 2231, Northern cricket frog. Nos. 2229c, 2232, White sturgeon. Nos. 2229d, 2233, Leatherback turtle.

2007, Oct. 1 Litho. *Perf. 13¼*
2229 Sheet of 4 + 4 labels 3.40 3.40
a.-d. A915 52c Any single .85 .75

Booklet Stamps
Self-Adhesive
Size: 47x24mm
Die Cut

2230 A915 52c multi .85 .35
2231 A915 52c multi .85 .35
2232 A915 52c multi .85 .35
2233 A915 52c multi .85 .35
a. Block of 4, #2230-2233 3.40
b. Booklet pane, 2 #2233a 6.75

Beneficial Insects — A942

Designs: 1c, Convergent lady beetle (Hippodamia convergens). 3c, Golden-eyed lacewing (Chrysopa oculata). 5c, Northern bumblebee (Bombus polaris). 10c, Canada darner (Aeshna canadensis). 25c, Cecropia moth (Hyalophora cecropia).

No. 2235 

 No. 2235a

2007, Oct. 12 Litho. *Perf. 13¼x13*
2234 A942 1c multi .20 .20
2235 A942 3c multi .20 .20
a. "Canada" shifted to right, touching "Oculata" (pos. 11-14) .45 .25
2236 A942 5c multi .20 .20
2237 A942 10c multi .20 .20
2238 A942 25c multi .40 .20
a. Souvenir sheet, #2234-2238 .80 .80
Nos. 2234-2238 (5) 1.20 1.00

No. 2235a occurs four times on each pane of 50.

Christmas
A943 A944

Designs: No. 2239, Reindeer and snowflakes. No. 2240, Holy Family. 93c, Angel over town. $1.55, Dove.

Litho. With Hologram Affixed
Serpentine Die Cut 8¼ Horiz.
2007, Nov. 1
Booklet Stamps
Self-Adhesive

2239 A943 (52c) multi .85 .20
a. Booklet pane of 6 5.00
Complete booklet, 2 #2239a 10.00

Litho.
Serpentine Die Cut 13½

2240 A944 (52c) multi .85 .20
a. Booklet pane of 6 5.00
Complete booklet, 2 #2240a 10.00
2241 A944 93c multi 1.50 .45
a. Booklet pane of 6 9.00
2242 A944 $1.55 multi 2.50 .60
a. Booklet pane of 6 15.00
Nos. 2239-2242 (4) 5.70 1.45

Flowers Type of 2006 and

Odontioda Island Red Orchid — A945

Queen Elizabeth II — A946

Flag and Sambro Island Lighthouse, Nova Scotia A947

Flag and Point Clark Lighthouse, Ontario A948

Flag and Cap-des-Rosiers Lighthouse, Quebec — A949

Flag and Warren Landing Lighthouse, Manitoba
A950

Flag and Pachena Point Lighthouse, British Columbia
A951

Flag and Pachena Point Lighthouse, British Columbia — A951a

Designs: 96c, Potinara Janet Elizabeth "Fire Dancer" orchid. $1.15, Laeliocattleya Memoria Evelyn Light orchid. $1.60, Masdevallia Kaleidoscope "Conni" orchid.

2007, Dec. 27 Litho. ***Perf. 13¼x13***

2243 Sheet of 4 7.00 7.00
a. A945 P multi 1.00 .65
b. A926 96c multi 1.60 1.20
c. A926 $1.15 multi 1.80 1.40
d. A926 $1.60 multi 2.40 2.00

Self-Adhesive

Coil Stamps

Serpentine Die Cut 8½-9 Horiz.

2244 A945 P multi .85 .20
a. Horiz. coil pair, serpentine die cut 9.1 horiz. 2.25
2245 A926 96c multi 1.50 .30
2246 A926 $1.15 multi 1.80 .50
2247 A926 $1.60 multi 2.60 .65
Nos. 2244-2247 (4) 6.75 1.65

Booklet Stamps

Serpentine Die Cut 13¼

2248 A946 P multi .85 .20
a. Booklet pane of 10 8.50
2249 A947 P multi .85 .20
2250 A948 P multi .85 .20
2251 A949 P multi .85 .20
2252 A950 P multi .85 .20
2253 A951 P multi .85 .20
a. Booklet pane of 10, 2 each #2249-2253 8.50

Serpentine Die Cut 13¼

2253B A951a P multi 1.10 .55
c. Booklet pane of 10, 2 each #2249-2252, 2253B 11.00
d. Booklet pane of 30, 6 each #2249-2252, 2253B 33.00

Die Cut

2254 A926 96c multi 1.60 .30
a. Booklet pane of 6 9.50
2255 A926 $1.15 multi 2.00 .45
a. Booklet pane of 6 12.00
2256 A926 $1.60 multi 2.60 .65
a. Booklet pane of 6 15.50
Nos. 2248-2256 (10) 12.40 3.15

Nos. 2243a, 2244, 2248-2253 each sold for 52c on day of issue.

No. 2244a issued 2/1/08. Stamps in pairs of No. 2244a are not adjacent. Pairs of No. 2244 have stamps that are vertically adjacent.

No. 2253B issued 5/1/08. No. 2253Bd was separated into thirds by two rows of rouletting. The separated thirds of this booklet have the same contents as No. 2253Bc, but have different selvage markings.

New Year 2008 (Year of the Rat) — A952

Designs: 52c, Rat with umbrella. $1.60, Rat with fan.

Litho. & Embossed With Foil Application

2008, Jan. 8 ***Perf. 13***

2257 A952 52c multi .85 .30

Souvenir Sheet

2258 A952 $1.60 multi 2.60 2.60

No. 2257 printed in sheets of 25 + 20 labels.

Fireworks
A953

Serpentine Die Cut 13½ Horiz.

2008, Jan. 15 Litho.

Self-Adhesive

Booklet Stamp

2259 A953 P multi .85 .30
a. Booklet pane of 6 5.00

No. 2259 sold for 52c on day of issue.

Peonies
A954

Peony color: Nos. 2260a, 2261, Pink. Nos. 2260b, 2262, Red.

2008, Mar. 3 Litho. ***Perf. 13¼***

2260 Sheet of 2 2.25 2.25
a.-b. A954 52c Either single 1.10 .55

Booklet Stamps

Self-Adhesive

Serpentine Die Cut 13¼

2261 A954 52c multi 1.10 .55
2262 A954 52c multi 1.10 .55
a. Pair, #2261-2262 2.20
b. Booklet pane, 5 each #2261-2262, + 10 stickers 11.00

The country name and denomination are closer to the flowers on Nos. 2261-2262 than on Nos. 2260a-2260b.

Universities
A955

Designs: No. 2263, University of Alberta, cent. No. 2264, University of British Columbia, cent.

Serpentine Die Cut 13¼

2008, Mar. 7

Booklet Stamps

Self-Adhesive

2263 A955 52c multi 1.10 .55
a. Booklet pane of 8 9.00
2264 A955 52c multi 1.10 .55
a. Booklet pane of 8 9.00
b. Gutter pane, 4 each #2263-2264 9.00

2008 Intl. Ice Hockey Federation Championships, Halifax and Quebec — A956

Serpentine Die Cut 13½

2008, Apr. 3 Litho.

Booklet Stamp

Self-Adhesive

2265 A956 52c multi 1.10 .55
a. Booklet pane of 10 11.00

No. 2265a was printed with two different booklet covers.

Guide Dog
A957

Serpentine Die Cut 13½x13

2008, Apr. 21 Litho. & Embossed

Booklet Stamp

Self-Adhesive

2266 A957 52c multi 1.10 .55
a. Booklet pane of 10 11.00

Montreal Association for the Blind, cent.

Oil and Gas Anniversaries — A958

Designs: No. 2267, Welder welding Trans-Canada Pipeline. No. 2268, James M. Williams, Charles Tripp, Oil Springs, Ontario oil field.

Serpentine Die Cut 13¼

2008, May 2 Litho.

Booklet Stamps

Self-Adhesive

2267 A958 52c multi 1.10 .55
2268 A958 52c multi 1.10 .55
a. Booklet pane of 10, 5 each #2267-2268 11.00

Trans-Canada Pipeline, 50th anniv., First commercial oil well in Canada, 150th anniv.

Quebec City, 400th Anniv.
A959

Litho. & Engr.

2008, May 16 ***Perf. 13x12½***

2269 A959 52c multi 1.10 .55

See France No. 3437. A souvenir sheet containing No. 2269 and France No. 3437 sold for $4.99.

Photographic Portraits by Yousuf Karsh (1908-2008)
A960

Designs: 52c, Self-portrait, 1952. 96c, Audrey Hepburn, 1956. $1.60, Sir Winston Churchill, 1941.

2008, May 21 Litho. ***Perf. 13x12½***

2270 A960 52c multi 1.10 .55

Souvenir Sheet

2271 Sheet of 3, #2270, 2271a, 2271b 6.25 6.25
a. A960 96c multi 1.90 .95
b. A960 $1.60 multi 3.25 1.60

Booklet Stamps

Self-Adhesive

2272 A960 96c multi 1.90 .95
a. Booklet pane of 4 7.75 —
Complete booklet, 2 #2272a 15.50
2273 A960 $1.60 multi 3.25 1.60
a. Booklet pane of 4 13.00 —
Complete booklet, 2 #2273a 26.00
b. Gutter pane, #2272a, 2273a 21.00

No. 2270 printed in sheets of 16 + 4 labels.

1908 Fifty-cent Coin — A961

Litho. & Embossed

2008, June 4 ***Perf. 13x13¼***

2274 A961 52c multi 1.10 .55

Royal Canadian Mint, cent. Printed in sheets of 16 + 4 labels.

Canadian Nurses Association, Cent. — A962

Serpentine Die Cut 13¼

2008, June 16 Litho.

Booklet Stamp

Self-Adhesive

2275 A962 52c multi 1.10 .55
a. Booklet pane of 10 11.00

Publication of *Anne of Green Gables*, by Lucy Maud Montgomery, Cent. — A963

Designs: Nos. 2276a, 2277, Anne holding buttercups. Nos. 2276b, 2278, Green Gables House.

Perf. 13½ Syncopated

2008, June 20

Souvenir Sheet

2276 A963 Sheet of 2 2.25 2.25
a.-b. 52c Either single 1.10 .55

Booklet Stamps

Self-Adhesive

Serpentine Die Cut 13¼x13

2277 A963 52c multi 1.10 .55
2278 A963 52c multi 1.10 .55
a. Booklet pane of 10, 5 each #2277-2278 + 10 stickers 11.00

See Japan No. 3028.

Canadians in Hollywood Type of 2006

Actors and actresses: Nos. 2279a, 2280c, Norma Shearer (1902?-83). Nos. 2279b, 2280b, Chief Dan George (1899-1981). Nos. 2279c, 2280a, Marie Dressler (1868-1934). Nos. 2279d, 2280d, Raymond Burr (1917-93).

2008, June 30 ***Perf. 13x12½***

2279 Souvenir sheet of 4 4.50 4.50
a.-d. A903 52c Any single 1.10 .55

Self-Adhesive

Serpentine Die Cut 13½x13¼

2280 Booklet pane of 4 + 4 stickers 4.50
a.-d. A903 52c Any single 1.10 .55
Complete booklet, 2 #2280 9.00

Complete booklets were issued with four different covers depicting the featured actors or actresses. The order of the stamps and labels in the booklet pane differed in the four booklets.

2008 Summer Olympics, Beijing — A964

Serpentine Die Cut 13½

2008, July 18

Booklet Stamp

Self-Adhesive

2281 A964 52c multi 1.10 .55
a. Booklet pane of 10 11.00

Lifesaving Society, Cent. A965

Serpentine Die Cut 13¼x12¾

2008, July 25 **Litho.**

Booklet Stamp

Self-Adhesive

2282 A965 52c multi 1.10 .55
a. Booklet pane of 10 11.00

British Columbia, 150th Anniv. — A966

2008, Aug. 1 ***Perf. 12½x13***

Self-Adhesive

2283 A966 52c multi 1.10 .55

R. Samuel McLaughlin (1871-1972), Automobile Manufacturer, and Buick Automobile — A967

2008, Sept. 8 **Litho.** ***Perf. 12½x13***

2284 A967 52c multi 1.00 .50

Endangered Animals Type of 2006

Designs: Nos. 2285a, 2286, Prothonotary warbler. Nos. 2285b, 2287, Taylor's checker-spot butterfly. Nos. 2285c, 2288, Roseate tern. Nos. 2285d, 2289, Burrowing owl.

2008, Oct. 1 **Litho.** ***Perf. 13¼***

2285 Sheet of 4 + 4 labels 4.00 4.00
a.-d. A915 52c Any single 1.00 .50

Booklet Stamps

Self-Adhesive

Size: 48x24mm

Die Cut

2286 A915 52c multi 1.00 .50
2287 A915 52c multi 1.00 .50
2288 A915 52c multi 1.00 .50
2289 A915 52c multi 1.00 .50
a. Block of 4, #2286-2289 4.00
b. Booklet pane, 2 #2289a 8.00

12th Francophone Summit, Quebec — A968

2008, Oct. 15 **Litho.** ***Perf. 12½x13¼***

2290 A968 52c multi .90 .45

A969

Christmas — A970

Child: Nos. 2291a, 2293, Making snow angel. Nos. 2291b, 2294, Skiing. Nos. 2291c, 2295, Tobogganing.

2008, Nov. 3 ***Perf. 13½***

Souvenir Sheet

2291 Sheet of 3 5.25 5.25
a. A969 P multi .90 .45
b. A969 96c multi 1.60 .80
c. A969 $1.60 multi 2.75 1.40

Booklet Stamps

Self-Adhesive

Serpentine Die Cut 13¼

2292 A970 P multi .90 .45
a. Booklet pane of 6 5.50
Complete booklet, 2 #2292a 11.00

Serpentine Die Cut 13¾

2293 A969 P multi .90 .45
a. Booklet pane of 6 5.50
Complete booklet, 2 #2293a 11.00
2294 A969 96c multi 1.60 .80
a. Booklet pane of 6 9.75
2295 A969 $1.60 multi 2.75 1.40
a. Booklet pane of 6 16.50
b. Gutter pane, #2294a, 2295a 26.50
Nos. 2292-2295 (4) 6.15 3.10

Nos. 2291a, 2292 and 2293 each sold for 52c on day of issue.

A971

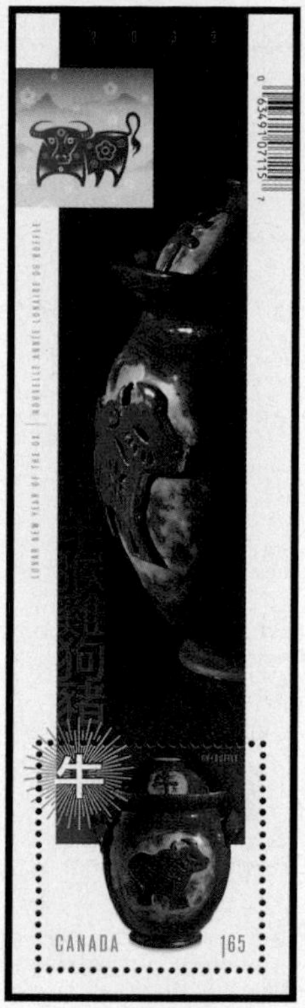

New Year 2009 (Year of the Ox) A972

Litho. & Embossed With Foil Application

2009, Jan. 8 ***Perf. 12½***

2296 A971 P multi .90 .45

Souvenir Sheet

2297 A972 $1.65 multi 2.75 2.75
a. With China 2009 emblem over-printed in gold in sheet margin 2.75 2.75

No. 2296 sold for 54c on day of issue.

Queen Elizabeth II — A973

Serpentine Die Cut 13½x13¼

2009, Jan. 12 **Litho.**

Booklet Stamp

Self-Adhesive

2298 A973 P multi .90 .45
a. Booklet pane of 10 9.00

No. 2298 sold for 54c on day of issue.

Sports of the Winter Olympics and Paralympics
A974 A975

Designs: Nos. 2299a, 2303, Curling. Nos. 2299b, 2302, Bobsledding. Nos. 2299c, 2304, Snowboarding. Nos. 2299d, 2300, Freestyle skiing. Nos. 2299e, 2301, Ice-sled hockey.

2009, Jan. 12 **Litho.** ***Perf. 13¼x13***

2299 Sheet of 5 4.50 4.50
a.-d. A974 P Any single .90 .45
e. A975 P multi .90 .45

Booklet Stamps

Self-Adhesive

Serpentine Die Cut 13¼x13½

2300 A974 P multi .90 .45
2301 A975 P multi .90 .45
2302 A974 P multi .90 .45
2303 A974 P multi .90 .45
2304 A974 P multi .90 .45
a. Booklet pane of 10, 2 each #2300-2304 9.00

On day of issue, Nos. 2299a-2299e, 2300-2304 each sold for 54c.

Celebration A981

Serpentine Die Cut 13½ Horiz.

2009, Feb. 2 **Litho.**

Booklet Stamp

Self-Adhesive

2314 A981 P multi .90 .45
a. Booklet pane of 6 5.50

No. 2314 sold for 54c on day of issue.

Rosemary Brown (1930-2003) — A982

Abraham Doras Shadd (1801-82) A983

2009, Feb. 2 ***Perf. 13x12½***

2315 A982 54c multi .90 .45
2316 A983 54c multi .90 .45
a. Pair, #2315-2316 1.80 .90

Black History Month. Brown and Shadd were the first black woman and man elected to public office in Canada.

SEMI-POSTAL STAMPS

Catalogue values for unused stamps in this section are for Never Hinged items.

Olympic Type of 1973 and

SP1

SP2

1974, Apr. 17 **Litho.** ***Perf. 12½***

Size: 20x36mm

B1 A307 8c + 2c multi .40 .40
B2 A307 10c + 5c multi .60 .60
B3 A307 15c + 5c multi .80 .80
Nos. B1-B3 (3) 1.80 1.80

1975, Feb. 5 **Litho.** ***Perf. 13***

B4 SP1 8c + 2c Swimming .40 .40
B5 SP1 10c + 5c Rowing .60 .60
B6 SP1 15c + 5c Sailing .80 .80
Nos. B4-B6 (3) 1.80 1.80

1975, Aug. 6 Litho. *Perf. 13*

B7 SP2 8c + 2c Fencing .40 .40
B8 SP2 10c + 5c Boxing .60 .60
B9 SP2 15c + 5c Judo .80 .80
Nos. B7-B9 (3) 1.80 1.80

1976, Jan. 7

B10 SP2 8c + 2c Basketball .40 .40
B11 SP2 10c + 5c Vaulting .60 .60
B12 SP2 20c + 5c Soccer 1.00 1.00
Nos. B10-B12 (3) 2.00 2.00

21st Olympic Games, Montreal, July 17-Aug. 1. The surtax was for the Canadian Olympic Committee.

Literacy — SP3

1996, Sept. 9 Litho. *Perf. 13x12½*

B13 SP3 45c +5c multi 1.10 .40
a. Booklet pane of 10 11.00
Complete booklet 11.50

No. B13 has die cut opening in center to represent missing puzzle piece.

Surcharge donated to ABC CANADA literacy organization.

Mental Health — SP4

Serpentine Die Cut 13¼

2008, Oct. 6 Litho.

Booklet Stamp

Self-Adhesive

B14 SP4 P +10c multi 1.10 1.10
a. Booklet pane of 10 11.00

No. B14 had a franking value of 52c on day of issue. Surtax for Canada Post Foundation for Mental Health.

AIR POST STAMPS

Allegory of Flight — AP1

Unwmk.

1928, Sept. 21 Engr. *Perf. 12*

C1 AP1 5c brown olive 16.00 4.75
Never hinged 30.00
a. Imperf., pair 275.00
Never hinged 375.00

No. C1 is known imperforate horizontally and imperforate vertically.

For surcharge see No. C3.

Allegory-Air Mail Circles Globe AP2

1930, Dec. 4 *Perf. 11*

C2 AP2 5c olive brown 85.00 27.50
Never hinged 140.00

For surcharge see No. C4.

No. C1 Surcharged

1932, Feb. 22 *Perf. 12*

C3 AP1 6c on 5c brown olive 12.50 3.75
Never hinged 22.00
a. Inverted surcharge 200.00
Never hinged 280.00
b. Double surcharge 675.00
Never hinged 950.00
c. Triple surcharge 400.00
Never hinged 550.00
d. Pair, one without surcharge 950.00
Never hinged 1,350.

Counterfeit surcharges exist.

No. C3b is valued in the grade of fine.

No. C2 Surcharged in Dark Blue

1932, July 12 *Perf. 11*

C4 AP2 6c on 5c olive brown 40.00 12.50
Never hinged 70.00

Daedalus AP3

1935, June 1 Engr. *Perf. 12*

C5 AP3 6c red brown 4.25 1.25
Never hinged 6.00
a. Horiz. pair, imperf. vert. *6,000.*
b. Imperf., pair 650.00
Never hinged 1,000.

No. C5a is believed to be unique and is the result of a pre-perforating paper foldover.

For information on imperforate and part-perforate varieties, see note following No. 47a.

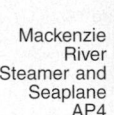

Mackenzie River Steamer and Seaplane AP4

1938, June 15

C6 AP4 6c blue 3.75 .40
Never hinged 5.25
a. Imperf., pair 650.00
Never hinged 950.00

Planes and Student Flyers AP5

1942-43

C7 AP5 6c deep blue 5.25 1.20
Never hinged 7.50
a. Imperf., pair 650.00
Never hinged 950.00

C8 AP5 7c deep blue ('43) 1.00 .20
Never hinged 1.40
a. Imperf., pair 650.00
Never hinged 950.00

Canada's contribution to the war effort of the Allied Nations.

Catalogue values for unused stamps in this section, from this point to the end of the section, are for Never Hinged items.

Canada Geese in Flight — AP6

1946, Sept. 16

C9 AP6 7c deep blue 1.10 .20
a. Booklet pane of 4 3.25 3.25

For overprints see Nos. CO1, CO2.

AIR POST SPECIAL DELIVERY STAMPS

Trans-Canada Airplane and Aerial View of a City — APSD1

1942-43 Unwmk. Engr. *Perf. 12*

CE1 APSD1 16c bright ultra 2.50 2.00
Never hinged 3.50
a. Imperf., pair 650.00
Never hinged 950.00
CE2 APSD1 17c brt ultra ('43) 3.25 3.00
Never hinged 4.75
a. Imperf., pair 650.00
Never hinged 950.00

Canada's contribution to the war effort of the Allied Nations.

Catalogue values for unused stamps in this section, from this point to the end of the section, are for Never Hinged items.

DC-4 Transatlantic Mail Plane Over Quebec — APSD2

1946, Sept. 16

CE3 APSD2 17c bright ultra 6.00 4.25

Circumflex accent on second "E" of "EXPRES."

Corrected Die

1946, Dec. 3

CE4 APSD2 17c bright ultra 6.00 4.25

Grave accent on the 2nd "E" of "EXPRES."

AIR POST OFFICIAL STAMPS

Catalogue values for unused stamps in this section are for Never Hinged items.

No. C9 Overprinted in Black

1949 Unwmk. *Perf. 12*

CO1 AP6 7c deep blue 12.00 4.75
a. No period after "S" 100.00 60.00

Same Overprinted

1950

CO2 AP6 7c deep blue 17.50 15.00

SPECIAL DELIVERY

SD1

Unwmk.

1898, June 28 Engr. *Perf. 12*

E1 SD1 10c blue green 110.00 11.00
Never hinged 300.00

SD2

1922, Aug. 21

E2 SD2 20c carmine 100.00 9.00
Never hinged 220.00

Five Stages of Mail Transportation SD3

1927, June 29

E3 SD3 20c orange 27.50 17.50
Never hinged 55.00
a. Imperf., pair 200.00
Never hinged 275.00

No. E3 forms part of the Confederation Commemorative issue. It is known imperforate vertically and imperforate horizontally.

SD4

1930, Sept. 2 *Perf. 11*

E4 SD4 20c henna brown 65.00 15.00
Never hinged 125.00

SD5

1933, Dec. 24

E5 SD5 20c henna brown 60.00 16.00
  Never hinged 115.00
  a. Imperf., pair 650.00
  Never hinged 950.00

Allegory of Progress — SD6

1935, June 1 *Perf. 12*

E6 SD6 20c dark carmine 12.50 7.50
  Never hinged 20.00
  a. Imperf., pair 650.00
  Never hinged 950.00

Arms of Canada — SD7

1938-39

E7 SD7 10c dk green ('39) 6.00 3.25
  Never hinged 8.75
  a. Imperf., pair 650.00
  Never hinged 950.00
E8 SD7 20c dark carmine 30.00 25.00
  Never hinged 47.50
  a. Imperf., pair 650.00
  Never hinged 950.00

No. E8 Surcharged in Black

1939, Mar. 1

E9 SD7 10c on 20c dk car 7.50 6.50
  Never hinged 11.00

Coat of Arms and Flags SD8

1942, July 1 **Engr.**

E10 SD8 10c green 2.75 2.00
  Never hinged 3.75
  a. Imperf., pair 650.00
  Never hinged 950.00

Canada's contribution to the war effort of the Allied Nations.

Catalogue values for unused stamps in this section, from this point to the end of the section, are for Never Hinged items.

Arms of Canada — SD9

1946, Sept. 16

E11 SD9 10c green 3.25 1.10

The laurel and olive branches symbolize Victory and Peace.

For overprints see Nos. EO1, EO2.

SPECIAL DELIVERY OFFICIAL STAMPS

Catalogue values for unused stamps in this section are for Never Hinged items.

No. E11 Overprinted in Black

1950 **Unwmk.** *Perf. 12*

EO1 SD9 10c green 17.50 15.00

Same Overprinted

EO2 SD9 10c green 25.00 20.00

REGISTRATION STAMPS

R1

1875-88 **Unwmk.** **Engr.** *Perf. 12*

F1 R1 2c orange 115.00 5.75
  Never hinged 225.00
  a. 2c vermilion 170.00 15.00
  Never hinged 290.00
  b. 2c rose carmine 340.00 110.00
  Never hinged 625.00
  c. As "a," imperf., pair —
  d. Perf. 12x11½ 525.00 100.00
  Never hinged 950.00
F2 R1 5c dark green 150.00 6.00
  Never hinged 300.00
  a. 5c blue green ('88) 160.00 6.00
  Never hinged 325.00
  b. 5c yellow green 240.00 7.50
  Never hinged 475.00
  c. Imperf., pair 1,200.
  d. Perf. 12x11½ 1,300. 240.00
  Never hinged 1,700.
F3 R1 8c blue 500.00 350.00
  Never hinged 875.00
  Nos. F1-F3 (3) 765.00 361.75

POSTAGE DUE STAMPS

D1

D2

1906-28 **Unwmk.** **Engr.** *Perf. 12*

J1 D1 1c violet 20.00 4.75
  Never hinged 32.50
  a. Thin paper ('24) 40.00 7.50
  Never hinged 72.50
  b. Imperf., pair 400.00
J2 D1 2c violet 20.00 1.00
  Never hinged 32.50
  a. Thin paper ('24) 40.00 11.00
  Never hinged 72.50
  b. Imperf., pair 400.00
J3 D1 4c violet ('28) 65.00 22.50
  Never hinged 110.00
J4 D1 5c violet 20.00 2.00
  Never hinged 32.50
  a. Thin paper 17.50 7.50
  Never hinged 30.00
  b. Imperf., pair 400.00
J5 D1 10c violet ('28) 85.00 14.00
  Never hinged 160.00
  Nos. J1-J5 (5) 210.00 44.25
  Nos. J1-J5, never hinged 367.50

In 1924 there was a printing of Nos. J1, J2 and J4 on thin semi-transparent paper. Imperf pairs are without gum.

1930-32 *Perf. 11*

J6 D2 1c dark violet 12.50 4.25
  Never hinged 22.50
J7 D2 2c dark violet 7.00 1.10
  Never hinged 12.50
J8 D2 4c dark violet 20.00 5.50
  Never hinged 35.00
J9 D2 5c dark violet 25.00 6.50
  Never hinged 35.00
J10 D2 10c dark violet ('32) 110.00 10.00
  Never hinged 200.00
  a. Vert. pair, imperf. horiz. 2,000. —
  Never hinged 3,000.
  Nos. J6-J10 (5) 174.50 27.35
  Nos. J6-J10, never hinged 305.00

No. J10a is valued in the grade of fine.

D3

D4

1933-34

J11 D3 1c dark violet ('34) 12.50 6.50
  Never hinged 22.50
  a. Imperf., pair 400.00
  Never hinged 575.00
J12 D3 2c dark violet 7.00 1.25
  Never hinged 12.00
J13 D3 4c dark violet 13.00 8.00
  Never hinged 22.50
J14 D3 10c dark violet 27.50 6.50
  Never hinged 45.00
  Nos. J11-J14 (4) 60.00 22.25
  Nos. J11-J14, never hinged 102.00

Catalogue values for unused stamps in this section, from this point to the end of the section, are for Never Hinged items.

1935-65 *Perf. 12*

J15 D4 1c dark violet .30 .20
  a. Imperf., pair 200.00
J16 D4 2c dark violet .30 .20
  a. Imperf., pair 200.00
J16B D4 3c dark vio ('65) 2.00 1.50
J17 D4 4c dark violet .35 .20
  a. Imperf., pair 200.00
J18 D4 5c dark vio ('48) .40 .35
J19 D4 6c dark vio ('57) 2.25 1.75
J20 D4 10c dark violet .40 .20
  a. Imperf., pair 200.00
  Nos. J15-J20 (7) 6.00 4.40

D5

1967, Feb. 8 **Litho.** *Perf. 12*

Size: 20x17mm

J21 D5 1c carmine rose .20 .20
J22 D5 2c carmine rose .20 .25
J23 D5 3c carmine rose .20 .25
J24 D5 4c carmine rose .25 .25
J25 D5 5c carmine rose 1.50 1.50
J26 D5 6c carmine rose .25 .25
J27 D5 10c carmine rose .40 .30
  Nos. J21-J27 (7) 3.00 3.00

1969-78 *Perf. 12*

Size: 20x15¾mm

J28 D5 1c car rose ('70) .45 .30
  a. Perf. 12½x12 ('77) .20 .20
J29 D5 2c car rose ('72) .25 .20
J30 D5 3c car rose ('74) .25 .20
J31 D5 4c carmine rose .40 .30
  a. Perf. 12½x12 ('77) .20 .20
J32 D5 5c car rose, perf. 12½x12 ('77) .20 .20
  a. Perf. 12 16.00 12.50
J33 D5 6c car rose ('72) .20 .20
J34 D5 8c carmine rose .20 .20
  a. Perf. 12½x12 ('78) .40 .30
J35 D5 10c carmine rose .55 .20
  a. Perf. 12½x12 ('77) .25 .20
J36 D5 12c carmine rose .75 .60
  a. Perf. 12½x12 ('77) 1.50 .70
J37 D5 16c carmine rose ('74) .40 .25

Perf. 12½x12

J38 D5 20c carmine rose ('77) .55 .40
J39 D5 24c carmine rose ('77) .65 .40
J40 D5 50c carmine rose ('77) 1.00 .75
  Nos. J28-J40 (13) 5.85 4.20

WAR TAX STAMPS

WT1

WT2

Unwmk.

1915, Mar. 25 **Engr.** *Perf. 12*

MR1 WT1 1c green 25.00 .20
  Never hinged 60.00
MR2 WT1 2c carmine 25.00 .25
  Never hinged 60.00

In 1915 postage stamps of 5, 20 and 50 cents were overprinted "WAR TAX" in two lines. These stamps were intended for fiscal use, the war tax on postal matter being 1 cent. A few of these stamps were used to pay postage.

1916

TWO DIES:

Die I — There is a colored line between two white lines below the large letter "T."

Die II — The right half of the colored line is replaced by two short diagonal lines and five small dots.

MR3 WT2 2c + 1c car (I) 35.00 .20
  Never hinged 87.50
  a. 2c + 1c carmine (II) 175.00 4.50
  Never hinged 400.00
MR4 WT2 2c + 1c brn (II) 20.00 .20
  Never hinged 50.00
  a. 2c + 1c brown (I) 600.00 10.00
  Never hinged 1,100.
  b. Imperf., pair (I) 200.00
  c. Imperf., pair (II) 1,600.

#MR4b-MR4c were made without gum.

Perf. 12x8

MR5 WT2 2c + 1c car (I) 65.00 30.00
  Never hinged 140.00

Coil Stamps

Perf. 8 Vertically

MR6 WT2 2c + 1c car (I) 150.00 9.00
  Never hinged 320.00
MR7 WT2 2c + 1c brn (II) 35.00 1.10
  Never hinged 75.00
  a. 2c + 1c brown (I) 175.00 7.50
  Never hinged 400.00

OFFICIAL STAMPS

With Perforated Initials O H M S

On March 28, 1939 the Treasury Board ruled that on and after June 30, 1939 all stamps used by government departments throughout the country should be perforated O H M S (On His Majesty's Service) and that "the Post Office Department is to make arrangements required to provide that all stamps sold to Government Departments are perforated with the letters O H M S." The sale of such perforated stamps was discontinued in 1948.

For listings see the *Scott Classic Specialized Catalogue.*

Catalogue values for unused stamps in this section are for Never Hinged items.

Nos. 249, 250, 252 and 254 Overprinted in Black

1949-50		Unwmk.	Perf. 12	
O1	A97	1c green	2.00	1.75
a.		No period after "S"	90.00	65.00
O2	A98	2c brown	10.00	7.50
a.		No period after "S"	90.00	65.00
O3	A99	3c rose violet	2.25	1.25
O4	A98	4c dark carmine	2.75	.75

Nos. 269 to 273 Overprinted in Black

O6	A108	10c olive	3.50	.60
a.		No period after "S"	65.00	60.00
O7	A109	14c black brown	4.00	2.25
a.		No period after "S"	100.00	75.00
O8	A110	20c slate black	16.00	3.25
a.		No period after "S"	110.00	75.00
O9	A111	50c dk blue grn	200.00	110.00
a.		No period after "S"	600.00	500.00
O10	A112	$1 red violet	70.00	35.00
a.		No period after "S"	*2,250.*	*1,750.*
		Nos. O1-O4,O6-O10 (9)	310.50	162.35

It is recommended that a certificate of authenticity be acquired for O10a.

Same Overprint on No. 294

1950				
O11	A124	50c dull green	40.00	25.00

Nos. 284 to 288 Overprinted in Black

1950				
O12	A119	1c green	.40	.30
O13	A120	2c sepia	1.10	.75
O14	A121	3c rose violet	1.10	.50
O15	A122	4c dark carmine	1.10	.20
b.		No period after "S"	65.00	55.00
O15A	A123	5c deep blue	2.25	1.50
c.		No period after "S"	65.00	55.00
		Nos. O12-O15A (5)	5.95	3.25

Stamps of 1946-1950 Overprinted in Black

a

b

c

1950				
O16	A119(a)	1c grn (#284)	.50	.20
O17	A120(a)	2c sepia (#285)	1.30	.90
O18	A121(a)	3c rose vio (#286)	1.30	.20
O19	A122(a)	4c dk car (#287)	1.30	.20
O20	A123(a)	5c dp bl (#288)	1.60	.90
O21	A108(b)	10c olive	2.50	.50
O22	A109(b)	14c black brn	6.50	2.00
O23	A110(b)	20c slate blk	14.00	1.00
O24	A124(b)	50c dull green	10.00	5.50
O25	A112(b)	$1 red violet	105.00	80.00
		Nos. O16-O25 (10)	144.00	91.40

Nos. 301-302 Overprinted Type "b"

1950-51				
O26	A125	10c black brown	1.30	.20
a.		Pair, one without "G"	775.00	650.00
O27	A126	$1 brt ultra ('51)	100.00	90.00

It is recommended that a certificate of authenticity be acquired for No. O26a.

Nos. 305-306 Overprinted Type "a"

1951-52		Unwmk.	Perf. 12	
O28	A120	2c olive green	.60	.20
O29	A122	4c orange ver ('52)	.95	.20

No. 316 Overprinted Type "b"

1952				
O30	A132	20c gray	2.25	.20

Nos. 320-321 Overprinted Type "b"

1952-53				
O31	A136	7c blue	4.00	1.25
O32	A137	$1 gray ('53)	15.00	8.00

Same Overprints on #325-329, 334

1953-61				
O33	A139(a)	1c violet brown	.35	.20
O34	A139(a)	2c green	.35	.20
O35	A139(a)	3c carmine rose	.35	.20
O36	A139(a)	4c violet	.45	.20
O37	A139(a)	5c ultramarine	.45	.20
O38	A141(b)	50c light green	5.00	1.20
a.		Overprinted type "c" ('61)	5.00	2.00
		Nos. O33-O38 (6)	6.95	2.20

No. 351 Overprinted Type "b"

1955-62				
O39	A148	10c violet brown	.90	.20
a.		Overprinted type "c" ('62)	1.90	1.25

#337-338, 340-341 Ovptd. Type "a"

1955-56				
O40	A144	1c vio brown ('56)	.35	.30
O41	A144	2c green ('56)	.35	.20
O43	A144	4c violet ('56)	1.00	.20
O44	A144	5c bright blue	.60	.20
		Nos. O40-O44 (4)	2.30	.90

No. 362 Overprinted Type "b"

1956-62				
O45	A159	20c green	1.75	.20
a.		Overprinted type "c" ('62)	7.00	.50

#401-402, 404-405 Ovptd. Type "a"

1963, May 15		Engr.	Perf. 12	
O46	A195	1c deep brown	.75	.70
a.		Double overprint	750.00	
O47	A195	2c green	.75	.70
a.		Pair, one without "G"	750.00	
O48	A195	4c carmine	.80	.70
O49	A195	5c violet blue	.50	.50
		Nos. O46-O49 (4)	2.80	2.60

CAPE JUBY

'kāp 'jü-bē

LOCATION — Northwest coast of Africa in Spanish Sahara
GOVT. — Spanish administration
AREA — 12,700 sq. mi.
POP. — 9,836
CAPITAL — Villa Bens (Cape Juby)

By agreement with France, Spain's Sahara possessions were extended to include Cape Juby and in 1916 Spanish troops occupied the territory. It was attached for administrative purposes to Spanish Sahara.

100 Centimos = 1 Peseta

Stamps of Rio de Oro, 1914 Surcharged in Violet, Red or Green

1916 Unwmk. *Perf. 13*

No.	Type	Description	Unused	Used
1	A6	5c on 4p rose (V)	175.00	19.00
2	A6	10c on 10p dl vio (R)	40.00	19.00
2E	A6	10c on 10p dl vio (V)	125.00	72.50
2G	A6	10c on 10p dl vio (B)	125.00	72.50
3	A6	15c on 50c dk brn (G)	52.50	30.00
4	A6	15c on 50c dk brn (R)	37.50	19.00
5	A6	40c on 1p red vio (G)	77.50	35.00
6	A6	40c on 1p red vio (R)	65.00	26.00
		Nos. 1-6 (8)	697.50	293.00
		Set, never hinged	1,150.	

For type II, inverted and double surcharges, see the *Scott Classic Catalogue*.

Very fine examples of Nos. 1-6 will be somewhat off center. Well centered examples are uncommon and will sell for more.

Stamps of Spain, 1876-1917, Overprinted in Red or Black

1919 *Imperf.*

No.	Type	Description	Unused	Used
7	A21	¼c bl grn (R)	.30	.30

Perf. 13x12½, 14

No.	Type	Description	Unused	Used
8	A46	2c dk brn (Bk)	.30	.30
a.		Double overprint	19.00	16.00
b.		Double overprint (Bk + R)	60.00	52.50
9	A46	5c grn (R)	.60	.60
a.		Double overprint	19.00	16.00
b.		Inverted overprint	30.00	*47.50*
10	A46	10c car (Bk)	.70	.70
a.		Double overprint (Bk + R)	60.00	52.50
11	A46	15c ocher (Bk)	3.00	3.00
b.		Double overprint	19.00	16.00
c.		Red control #	6.00	3.75
d.		As "c," inverted overprint	13.00	
12	A46	20c ol grn (R)	16.00	16.00
13	A46	25c dp bl (R)	3.00	3.00
a.		Double overprint	19.00	16.00
14	A46	30c bl grn (R)	3.00	3.00
15	A46	40c rose (Bk)	3.25	3.25
16	A46	50c sl bl (R)	3.50	3.50
17	A46	1p lake (Bk)	10.00	8.50
18	A46	4p dp vio (R)	37.50	32.50
19	A46	10p org (Bk)	52.50	42.50
		Nos. 7-19 (13)	133.65	117.15
		Set, never hinged	240.00	

Nos. 8-19 have blue control number on back. For imperfs, see the *Scott Classic Catalogue*.

Same on Stamps of Spain, 1920-21

1922 *Imperf.*

No.	Type	Description	Unused	Used
20	A47	1c blue green (R)	25.00	14.00
		Never hinged	42.50	

Engr. *Perf. 13x12½*

Blue Control Number on Back

No.	Type	Description	Unused	Used
23	A46	20c violet	140.00	40.00
		Never hinged	200.00	

A 2c and a 15c exist, values $400 and $10, respectively, for unused, hinged copies, $600 and $15 for never hinged.

Same on Stamps of Spain, 1922-23

1925 *Perf. 13½x13*

No.	Type	Description	Unused	Used
25	A49	5c red vio	5.00	3.50
26	A49	10c bl grn	12.50	3.50
28	A49	20c violet	26.50	10.00
		Nos. 25-28 (3)	44.00	17.00
		Set, never hinged	65.00	

Exists on Spain No. 331, 2c olive green. Value $350 unused hinged and $600 never hinged.

Seville-Barcelona Exposition Issue

CABO JUBY

Stamps of Spain, 1929, Overprinted in Red or Blue

1929 *Perf. 11*

No.	Type	Description	Unused	Used
29	A52	5c rose lake (Bl)	.45	.45
30	A53	10c green (R)	.45	.45
31	A50	15c Prus bl (R)	.45	.45
32	A51	20c pur (R)	.45	.45
33	A50	25c brt rose (Bl)	.45	.45
34	A52	30c blk brn (Bl)	.45	.45
35	A53	40c dk bl (R)	.45	.45
36	A51	50c dp org (Bl)	.80	.80
37	A52	1p bl blk (R)	22.50	22.50
38	A53	4p dp rose (Bl)	29.00	29.00
39	A53	10p brn (Bl)	29.00	29.00
		Nos. 29-39 (11)	84.45	84.45
		Set, never hinged	125.00	

Stamps of Spanish Morocco, 1928-33, Overprinted in Black or Red

1934 *Perf. 14*

No.	Type	Description	Unused	Used
40	A7	1c brt rose (Bk)	.50	.50
41	A2	2c dk vio (R)	4.50	4.50
42	A2	5c dp bl (R)	5.00	5.00
43	A2	10c dk grn (Bk)	10.00	10.00
43A	A10	10c dk grn (R)	3.00	3.00
44	A2	15c org brn (Bk)	25.00	25.00
45	A7	20c sl grn (R)	8.75	8.75
46	A3	25c cop red (Bk)	4.75	4.75
47	A10	30c red brn (Bk)	8.75	8.75
48	A13	40c dp bl (R)	32.50	32.50
49	A13	50c red org (Bk)	60.00	60.00
50	A4	1p yel grn (Bk)	50.00	50.00
51	A5	2.50p red vio (Bk)	100.00	100.00
52	A6	4p ultra (R)	125.00	125.00

No. 43A and 1c, 20c, 30c, 40c, 50c, with control numbers.

Same Overprint in Black on Stamp of Spanish Morocco, 1932

No.	Type	Description	Unused	Used
53	A2	1c car rose ("Ct")	2.10	2.10
		Nos. 40-53 (15)	439.85	439.85
		Set, never hinged	750.00	

Stamps of Spanish Morocco, 1933-35, Overprinted in Black, Blue or Red

1935-36

No.	Type	Description	Unused	Used
54	A8	2c grn (R)	.95	.95
55	A9	5c mag (Bk)	3.00	3.00
55A	A10	10c dk grn (R) ('36)	19.00	19.00
56	A11	15c yel (Bl)	7.50	7.50
57	A12	25c crim (Bk)	85.00	85.00
58	A8	1p sl blk (R)	11.50	11.50
59	A9	2.50p brn (Bl)	45.00	45.00
60	A11	4p yel grn (R)	77.50	77.50
61	A12	5p blk (R)	65.00	65.00
		Nos. 54-61 (9)	314.45	314.45
		Set, never hinged	500.00	

Same Overprint in Black or Red on Stamps of Spanish Morocco, 1935

1935 *Perf. 13½*

No.	Type	Description	Unused	Used
62	A14	25c vio (R)	4.00	4.00
63	A15	30c crim (Bk)	4.00	4.00
64	A14	40c org (Bk)	5.25	5.25
65	A15	50c brt bl (R)	9.50	9.50
66	A14	60c dk bl grn (R)	11.50	11.50
67	A15	2p brn lake (Bk)	62.50	62.50

Same Overprint on Stamps of Spanish Morocco, 1933

Perf. 13½, 14

No.	Type	Description	Unused	Used
68	A7	1c brt rose (Bk)	.30	.30

Perf. 14

No.	Type	Description	Unused	Used
69	A7	20c slate grn (R)	4.50	4.50
		Nos. 62-69 (8)	101.55	101.55
		Set, never hinged	160.00	160.00

Same Overprint on Stamps of Spanish Morocco, 1937

1937 *Perf. 13½*

No.	Type	Description	Unused	Used
70	A21	1c dk bl (Bk)	.45	.45
71	A21	2c org brn (Bk)	.45	.45
72	A21	5c cer (Bk)	.45	.45
73	A21	10c emer (Bk)	.45	.45
74	A21	15c brt bl (Bk)	.45	.45
75	A21	20c red brn (Bk)	.45	.45
76	A21	25c mag (Bk)	.45	.45
77	A21	30c red org (Bk)	.45	.45
78	A21	40c org (Bk)	1.10	1.10
79	A21	50c ultra (R)	1.10	1.10
80	A21	60c yel grn (Bk)	1.10	1.10
81	A21	1p bl vio (Bk)	1.10	1.10
82	A21	2p Prus bl (Bk)	70.00	70.00
83	A21	2.50p gray blk (R)	70.00	70.00
84	A21	4p dk brn (Bk)	70.00	70.00
85	A22	10p vio blk (R)	70.00	70.00
		Nos. 70-85 (16)	288.00	288.00
		Set, never hinged	475.00	

1st Year of the Revolution.

Same Overprint in Black on Types of Spanish Morocco, 1939

Designs: 5c, Spanish quarter. 10c, Moroccan quarter. 15c, Street scene, Larache. 20c, Tetuan.

1939 Photo. *Perf. 13½*

No.	Type	Description	Unused	Used
86	A25	5c vermilion	.50	.50
87	A25	10c deep green	.50	.50
88	A25	15c brown lake	.50	.50
89	A25	20c bright blue	.50	.50
		Nos. 86-89 (4)	2.00	2.00
		Set, never hinged	2.75	

Same Overprint in Black or Red on Stamps of Spanish Morocco, 1940

1940 *Perf. 11½x11*

No.	Type	Description	Unused	Used
90	A26	1c dk brn (Bk)	.25	.25
91	A27	2c ol grn (R)	.25	.25
92	A28	5c dk bl (R)	.25	.25
93	A29	10c dk red lil (Bk)	.25	.25
94	A30	15c dk grn (R)	.25	.25
95	A31	20c pur (R)	.25	.25
96	A32	25c blk brn (R)	.25	.25
97	A33	30c brt grn (Bk)	.30	.30
98	A34	40c slate grn (R)	.60	.60
99	A35	45c org ver (Bk)	.60	.60
100	A36	50c brn org (Bk)	.65	.65
101	A37	70c saph (R)	1.90	1.90
102	A38	1p ind & brn (Bk)	4.00	4.00
103	A39	2.50p choc & dk grn (Bk)	10.00	10.00
104	A40	5p dk cer & sep (Bk)	10.50	10.50
105	A41	10p dk ol grn & brn org (Bk)	26.00	26.00
		Nos. 90-105 (16)	56.30	56.30
		Set, never hinged	85.00	

Imperfs exist. Value, set $275.

Stamps of Spanish Morocco, 1944, Overprinted in Black or Red

1944, Oct. 2 Unwmk. *Perf. 12½*

No.	Type	Description	Unused	Used
106	A47	1c choc & lt bl	.25	.25
107	A48	2c slate grn & lt grn	.25	.25
108	A49	5c choc & grnsh blk (R)	.25	.25
109	A50	10c brt ultra & red org	.25	.25
110	A51	15c sl grn & lt grn	.25	.25
111	A52	20c dp cl & blk (R)	.25	.25
112	A53	25c lt bl & choc	.25	.25
113	A47	30c yel grn & brt ultra (R)	.25	.25
114	A48	40c choc & red vio	.25	.25
115	A49	50c brt ultra, & red brn	.25	.25
116	A50	75c yel grn & brt ultra (R)	1.25	1.25
117	A51	1p brt ultra & choc	1.40	1.40
118	A52	2.50p blk & brt ultra (R)	3.25	3.25
119	A53	10p sal & gray blk (R)	25.00	25.00
		Nos. 106-119 (14)	33.40	33.40
		Set, never hinged	52.50	

Same Overprint on Stamps of Spanish Morocco, 1946

1946, Mar. *Perf. 10½x10*

No.	Type	Description	Unused	Used
120	A54	1c pur & brn	.25	.25
121	A55	2c dk Prus grn & vio blk (R)	.25	.25
122	A54	10c dp org vio bl	.25	.25
123	A55	15c dk bl & bl grn	.25	.25
124	A54	25c yel grn & ultra	.25	.25
125	A56	40c dk bl & brn (R)	.30	.30
126	A55	45c blk & rose	.45	.45
127	A57	1p dk Prus grn & dp bl	1.60	1.60
128	A58	2.50p dp org & grnsh gray (R)	4.75	4.75
129	A59	10p dk bl & gray (R)	13.50	13.50
		Nos. 120-129 (10)	21.85	21.85
		Set, never hinged	30.00	

Same Overprint in Carmine, Black or Brown on Stamps of Spanish Morocco, 1948

1948, Jan. 1 *Perf. 10, 10x10½*

No.	Type	Description	Unused	Used
130	A64	2c pur & brn	.40	*1.00*
131	A65	5c dp claret & vio	.25	.25
132	A66	15c brt ultra & bl grn (Bk)	.25	.25
133	A67	25c blk & Prus grn	.25	.25
134	A65	35c brt ultra & gray blk	.25	.25
135	A68	50c red & vio (Br)	.25	.25
136	A66	70c dk gray grn & ultra (Bk)	.25	.25
137	A67	90c cer & dk gray grn (Bk)	.30	.30
138	A68	1p brt ultra & vio (Br)	.45	.45
139	A64	2.50p vio brn & sl grn	1.60	1.60
140	A69	10p blk & dp ultra	3.00	3.00
		Nos. 130-140 (11)	7.25	7.85
		Set, never hinged	12.00	

SEMI-POSTAL STAMPS

Types of Semi-Postal Stamps of Spain, 1926, Overprinted

1926 Unwmk. *Perf. 12½, 13*

No.	Type	Description	Unused	Used
B1	SP1	1c orange	12.50	12.50
B2	SP2	2c rose	12.50	12.50
B3	SP3	5c blk brn	3.50	3.50
B4	SP4	10c dk grn	1.60	1.60
B5	SP1	15c dk vio	1.10	1.10
B6	SP4	20c vio brn	1.10	1.10
B7	SP5	25c dp car	1.10	1.10
B8	SP1	30c ol grn	1.10	1.10
B9	SP3	40c ultra	.45	.45
B10	SP2	50c red brn	.45	.45
B11	SP4	1p vermilion	.45	.45
B12	SP3	4p bister	1.60	1.60
B13	SP5	10p lt vio	3.50	3.50
		Nos. B1-B13 (13)	40.95	40.95
		Set, never hinged	65.00	

Nos. B12-B13 surcharged "Alfonso XIII" and new value are listed as Spain Nos. B68-B69. See Spain No. B6a.

AIR POST STAMPS

Spanish Morocco, Nos. C1 to C10 Overprinted "CABO JUBY" as on #54-61

1938, June 1 Unwmk. *Perf. 13½*

No.	Type	Description	Unused	Used
C1	AP1	5c brown	.25	.25
C2	AP1	10c brt grn	.25	.25
C3	AP1	25c crimson	.25	.25
C4	AP1	40c light blue	2.10	2.10
C5	AP2	50c brt mag	.25	.25
C6	AP2	75c dk bl	.25	.25
C7	AP1	1p sepia	.25	.25
C8	AP1	1.50p dp vio	1.90	1.90
C9	AP1	2p dp red brn	2.75	2.75
C10	AP1	3p brn blk	7.25	7.25
		Nos. C1-C10 (10)	15.50	15.50
		Set, never hinged	25.00	

Moroccan Views — AP3

Designs: 5c, Ketama landscape. 10c, Mosque, Tangier. 15c, Velez. 90c, Sanjurjo. 5p, Strait of Gibraltar

1942, Apr. 1 Photo. *Perf. 12½*

C11 AP3 5c deep blue .25 .25
C12 AP3 10c org brn .25 .25
C13 AP3 15c grnsh blk .25 .25
C14 AP3 90c dk rose .50 .50
C15 AP3 5p black 1.75 1.75
Nos. C11-C15 (5) 3.00 3.00

SPECIAL DELIVERY STAMPS

Special Delivery Stamp of Spain Ovptd. "CABO JUBY" as on #7-28

1919 Unwmk. *Perf. 14*

E1 SD1 20c red (Bk) 3.25 3.25
b. Double overprint 27.50 13.00

Spanish Morocco #E4 Overprinted "CABO JUBY" as on #40-52 in Red

1934

E2 SD2 20c black 10.00 10.00

Spanish Morocco No. E5 Overprinted "CABO JUBY" as on Nos. 54-61

1935

E3 SD3 20c vermilion 3.50 3.50

Same Ovpt. on Spanish Morocco #E6

1937 *Perf. 13½*

E4 SD4 20c bright carmine 1.10 1.10

1st Year of the Revolution.

Same Ovpt. on Spanish Morocco #E8

1940 *Perf. 11½x11*

E5 SD5 25c scarlet .55 .55

SEMI-POSTAL SPECIAL DELIVERY STAMP

Type of Semi-Postal Special Delivery Stamp of Spain, 1926, Overprinted "CABO-JUBY" as on Nos. B1-B13

1926 Unwmk. *Perf. 12½, 13*

EB1 SPSD1 20c ultra & black 3.50 3.50

CAPE OF GOOD HOPE

'kāp əv 'gud 'hōp

LOCATION — In the extreme southern part of South Africa
GOVT. — Former British Colony
AREA — 276,995 sq mi. (1911)
POP. — 2,564,965 (1911)
CAPITAL — Cape Town

Cape of Good Hope joined with Natal, the Transvaal and the Orange River Colony in 1910, forming the Union of South Africa.

12 Pence = 1 Shilling

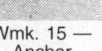

Watermarks

Wmk. 15 — Anchor

Wmk. 16 — Anchor

"Hope" Seated
A1

Printed by Perkins, Bacon & Co.
Wmk. 15

1853, Sept. 1 Engr. *Imperf.*
Bluish Paper

1 A1 1p brick red, bluish paper 3,500. 240.
a. 1p pale brick red, deeply blued paper 4,500. 350.
b. 1p deep brick red, deeply blued paper 10,500. 390.
2 A1 4p deep blue, lightly blued paper 1,750. 130.
a. 4p deep blue, deeply blued paper 3,500. 190.
b. 4p blue, bluish paper 3,250. 175.

Counterfeits exist.

1855-58
White Paper

3 A1 1p rose ('57) 600.00 240.00
a. 1p dull red 775.00 300.00
b. 1p brick red 6,000. 1,050.
4 A1 4p blue 575.00 60.00
a. Half used as 3p on cover *42,000.*
b. 4p deep blue 775.00 60.00
e. 4p bright blue 775.00 60.00
5 A1 6p pale lilac ('58) 950.00 240.00
a. 6p rose lilac 2,500. 350.00
b. 6p grayish lilac on bluish paper 5,000. 540.00
c. 6p slate purple on bluish paper 4,150. 1,200.
d. Half used as 3p on cover —
6 A1 1sh yellow grn ('58) *3,250.* 210.00
a. 1sh dark green 325.00 *600.00*
b. Half used as 6p on cover —

Nos. 3-6 are known rouletted unofficially.
Counterfeits exist.
No. 4 was reproduced by the collotype process in an unwatermarked souvenir sheet distributed at the London Intl. Stamp Exhib. 1950.

A2

Printed by Saul Solomon & Co.

1861 Laid Paper Unwmk. Typo.

7 A2 1p vermilion *16,500.* 2,650.
a. 1p carmine *42,500.* 4,000.
b. 1p red *45,000.* 5,000.
c. 1p milky blue (error) 175,000. *32,500.*
d. 1p pale blue (error) *36,000.*
9 A2 4p milky blue *40,000.* 3,000.
a. 4p pale blue *42,000.* 3,250.
b. 4p blue *45,000.* 3,500.
c. 4p dark blue *112,500.* 5,750.
d. Right corner retouched 7,750.
f. 4p vermilion (error) *177,500.* *65,000.*
g. 4p carmine (error) *112,500.*

Nos. 7 and 9 are usually called Wood Blocks. The plates were made locally and composed of clichés mounted on wood. The errors were caused by a cliché of each value being mounted in the plate of the other value.

In 1883 plate proofs of both values on white paper, usually called "reprints," were made. The 1p is in dull orange red; the 4p in dark blue. These are known canceled, as a few were misused as stamps. The proofs do not include the errors.

Counterfeits exist.

Printed by De La Rue & Co.

1863-64 Wmk. 15 Engr.

12 A1 1p dark carmine 200.00 *270.00*
a. 1p reddish brown 450.00 300.00
b. 1p brown red 450.00 275.00
13 A1 4p dark blue 200.00 65.00
a. 4p slate blue 2,400. 600.00
14 A1 6p purple 275.00 *540.00*
15 A1 1sh emerald 475.00 *540.00*
a. 1sh pale emerald 1,200. —

Nos. 12-15 can be distinguished from Nos. 3-6 not only by colors but because Nos. 12-15 often appear in a granular ink or with the background lightly printed in whole or part.

No. 12a, Wmk. 1, is believed to be a proof. Value $29,000.

Counterfeits exist.

"Hope" and Symbols of Colony
A3 A6
Frame Line Around Stamp

1864-65 Typo. Wmk. 1 *Perf. 14*

16 A3 1p rose ('65) 95.00 30.00
17 A3 4p blue ('65) 120.00 4.25
a. 4p pale blue 120.00 4.25
b. 4p dull ultramarine 300.00 65.00
c. 4p deep blue ('72) 175.00 4.50
18 A3 6p bright violet 150.00 1.75
a. 6p dull violet 240.00 8.25
b. 6p pale lilac 130.00 26.00
19 A3 1sh yellow green 130.00 4.50
a. 1sh blue green 145.00 5.75
Nos. 16-19 (4) 495.00 40.50

Imperf. stamps are believed to be proofs.
For surcharges see Nos. 20-21, N3.
For types A3 and A6 with manuscript surcharge of 1d or overprints "G. W." or "G," see Griqualand West listings.

Stamps of 1864 Surcharged in Red or Black:

a

b

1868-74 Red Surcharge

20 A3(a) 4p on 6p 300.00 19.00
a. "Peuce" for "Pence" 2,150. 900.00
b. "Fonr" for "Four" 850.00
21 A3(b) 1p on 6p ('74) 600.00 115.00
a. "E" of PENNY omitted 1,200.

Space between words and bars varies from 12½-16mm on #20, and 16½-18mm on #21.

1876 Black Surcharge

22 A3 (b) 1p on 1sh green 100.00 65.00

Without Frame Line Around Stamp

1871-81 *Perf. 14*

23 A6 ½p gray black ('75) 24.00 10.00
24 A6 1p rose ('72) 42.50 .70
25 A6 3p lilac rose ('80) 225.00 31.00
26 A6 3p claret ('81) 135.00 3.25
27 A6 4p blue ('76) 120.00 .90
a. 4p ultramarine 240.00 60.00
28 A6 5sh orange 425.00 19.00
Nos. 23-28 (6) 971.50 64.85

For surcharges see Nos. 29-32, 39, 55.

No. 27 Surcharged in Red

1879

29 A6 3p on 4p blue 120.00 2.40
a. "THE.EE" 2,400. 350.00
b. "PENCB" 2,000. 275.00
c. Double surcharge *10,750.* *3,900.*
d. As "a," double surcharge — —

Type of 1871 Surcharged in Black

1880

30 A6 3p on 4p lilac rose 82.50 2.40

No. 25 Surcharged in Black

e

f

31 A6(e) 3p on 3p lil rose 225.00 9.00
a. Inverted surcharge 9,500. 1,200.
32 A6(f) 3p on 3p lil rose 90.00 2.10
a. Inverted surcharge 1,100. 47.50

1882-83 Wmk. 2

33 A6 ½p gray black 27.50 3.00
34 A6 1p rose 72.50 2.00
35 A6 2p bister 115.00 .90
36 A6 3p claret 9.00 1.50
37 A3 6p bright violet 105.00 1.00
38 A6 5sh orange ('83) 950.00 275.00

For overprint see Rhodesia No. 49.

Nos. 26 and 36 Surcharged in Black

1882 Wmk. 1

39 A6 ½p on 3p claret 8,000. 150.00
a. Hyphen omitted *3,750.*

Wmk. 2

40 A6 ½p on 3p claret 36.00 4.75
a. "ENNY" 2,400. 825.00
b. "PENN" 1,200. *725.00*
c. Hyphen omitted 775.00 425.00

1884-98 Wmk. 16

41 A6 ½p gray black ('86) 6.50 .20
42 A6 ½p yel grn ('96) 1.80 .60
43 A6 1p rose ('85) 7.75 .20
44 A6 2p bister 7.25 .20
45 A6 2p choc brown ('97) 2.35 1.20
46 A6 3p red violet ('98) 12.00 1.20
47 A6 4p blue ('90) 15.50 .60
48 A6 4p pale ol grn ('97) 6.00 3.00
49 A3 6p violet 14.00 .25
50 A3 1sh dull bluish green ('89) 115.00 .60

51 A6 1sh blue grn ('94) 77.50 6.00
52 A6 1sh yel buff ('96) 13.00 2.00
53 A6 5sh orange ('87) 115.00 7.25
54 A6 5sh brown org ('96) 90.00 4.25
Nos. 41-54 (14) 483.65 27.55

For surcharges see Nos. 58, 162, 165-166. For overprints see Rhodesia Nos. 43, 45-48.

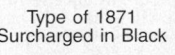

Type of 1871 Surcharged in Black

1891, Mar.
55 A6 2½p on 3p dp mag 5.00 .25
a. "1" of "½" has straight serif 65.00 37.50

Hope Seated — A13

1892-96
56 A13 2½p sage green 15.50 .20
57 A13 2½p ultra ('96) 7.25 .20

For surcharge see No. N4. For overprint see Orange River Colony No. 55.

No. 44 Surcharged in Black

1893, Mar.
58 A6 1p on 2p bister 4.25 .60
a. Double surcharge 500.00
b. No period after "PENNY" 65.00 15.50

Hope Standing A15

Table Mountain and Bay; Coat of Arms A16

1893-1902
59 A15 ½p green ('98) 4.25 .20
60 A15 1p rose 1.50 .20
61 A15 3p red violet ('02) 5.25 2.00
Nos. 59-61 (3) 11.00 2.40

For surcharges see Nos. 163-164, N2. For overprints see Orange River Colony #54, 56, Rhodesia #44, Transvaal #236-236A.

1900, Jan.
62 A16 1p carmine rose 4.25 .25

King Edward VII — A17

Various frames.

1902-04 **Wmk. 16**
63 A17 ½p emerald 2.75 .20
64 A17 1p car rose 2.40 .20
65 A17 2p brown ('04) 15.50 .95
66 A17 2½p ultra ('04) 3.25 *7.75*
67 A17 3p red violet ('03) 9.50 1.20
68 A17 4p ol green ('03) 13.00 .80
69 A17 6p violet ('03) 21.00 .60
70 A17 1sh bister 16.50 .95
71 A17 5sh brown org ('03) 110.00 22.50
Nos. 63-71 (9) 193.90 35.15

Imperf. stamps are proofs.

ISSUED IN MAFEKING

Excellent forgeries of Nos. 162-180 are known.

Stamps of Cape of Good Hope Surcharged

1900, Mar. 24
162 A6 1p on ½p grn 240. 77.50
163 A15 1p on ½p grn 300. 90.00
164 A15 3p on 1p rose 275. 60.00
165 A6 6p on 3p red vio *42,500.* 300.00
166 A6 1sh on 4p pale ol green 8,000. 425.00

Stamps of Bechuanaland Protectorate Surcharged

1900 **Wmk. 30**
167 A54 1p on ½p ver 240. 77.50
a. Inverted surcharge — 6,500.
168 A40 3p on 1p lilac 1,000. *105.*
a. Double surcharge *30,000.*
169 A56 6p on 2p grn & car 2,250. 90.
170 A58 6p on 3p vio, *yel* 16,500. 325.
a. Inverted surcharge — *36,000.*
b. Double surcharge — —

The lettering of "Mafeking Besieged" shows varying breaks in various letters, and may have either a period or no punctuation after "Mafeking."

On Stamps of Bechuanaland
Wmk. 29
171 A1 6p on 3p violet & black 450. 80.
Wmk. 30
172 A59 1sh on 4p brn & grn 1,650. 95.
a. Double surch., one inverted — *27,500.*
b. Triple surcharge — *25,000.*
c. Inverted surcharge — —
d. Double surcharge — *25,000.*

Stamps of Bechuanaland Protectorate Surcharged

173 A40 3p on 1p lilac 1,050. 90.
a. Double surcharge — *10,750.*
174 A56 6p on 2p grn & car 1,300. 90.
175 A62 1sh on 6p vio, *rose* 7,250. 105.

On Stamps of Bechuanaland
176 A62 1sh on 6p vio, *rose* *55,000.* 900.
177 A65 2sh on 1sh green *14,500.* 500.

Sgt. Major Goodyear M1

Gen. Robert S. S. Baden-Powell M2

Wmk. OCEANA FINE
Photographic Print
1900, Apr. ***Perf. 12***
Laid Paper
178 M1 1p blue, *blue* 1,000. *425.00*
a. Imperf, pair 21,500.
179 M2 3p blue, *blue*, 18½mm wide 1,400. 425.00
a. Horiz. pair, imperf btwn. — *77,500.*
b. Double impression — *20,000.*
c. Reversed design *77,500.* *45,000.*
180 M2 3p blue, *blue*, 21mm wide 10,750. 1,500.

The color of the paper varies from pale to deep blue.

OCEANA FINE is a sheet watermark and does not appear on every stamp.

Imperfs of No. 178 are proofs.

There is one used pair of No. 179a privately owned. There are 2 unused and 6 used examples of No. 179c privately owned.

Issued: #179, Apr. 6; #178, 180, Apr. 10.

ISSUED IN VRYBURG

Under Boer Occupation

Cape of Good Hope Stamps of 1884-96 Surcharged

Two Types of Surcharge:

Type I — Surcharge 10mm high. Space between lines 5½mm.

Type II — Surcharge 12mm high. Space between lines 7½mm.

1899, Nov. **Wmk. 16** ***Perf. 14***
N1 A6 ½p on ½p emer (I) 240. 95.
a. Type II 2,000. 825.
N2 A15 1p on 1p rose (I) 275. 120.
a. Double surcharge —
b. Type II 2,250. 950.
N3 A3 2p on 6p vio (II) 2,500. 600.
N4 A13 2½p on 2½p ultra (I) 2,000. 500.
a. Type II *12,000.* *5,000.*

"Z.A.R." stands for Zuid Afrikaansche Republiek (South African Republic).

Under British Occupation

Transvaal Stamps of 1895-96 Handstamped

1900 **Unwmk.** ***Perf. 12½***
N5 A13 ½p green — *3,250.*
N6 A13 1p rose & grn *10,750.* *5,000.*
N7 A13 2p brown & grn — *36,000.*
N8 A13 2½p ultra & grn — *36,000.*

CAPE VERDE

'kāp 'vərd

LOCATION — A group of 10 islands and five islets in the Atlantic Ocean, about 500 miles due west of Senegal.
GOVT. — Republic
AREA — 1,557 sq. mi.
POP. — 405,748 (1999 est.)
CAPITAL — Praia

The Portuguese territory of Cape Verde became independent on July 5, 1975.

1000 Reis = 1 Milreis
100 Centavos = 1 Escudo (1913)

Catalogue values for unused stamps in this country are for Never Hinged items, beginning with Scott 268 in the regular postage section, Scott J31 in the postage due section, and Scott RA6 in the postal tax section.

Crown of Portugal — A1

King Luiz — A2

Perf. 12½, 13½
1877 **Unwmk.** **Typo.**
1 A1 5r black 2.75 1.25
2 A1 10r yellow 40.00 7.00
3 A1 20r bister 2.50 1.00
4 A1 25r rose 1.40 .85
5 A1 40r blue 67.50 20.00
b. Cliche of Mozambique in Cape Verde plate, in pair with #5 1,500. 1,100.
6 A1 50r green 125.00 65.00
7 A1 100r lilac 5.50 1.90
8 A1 200r orange 3.50 2.25
9 A1 300r brown 4.00 2.75
Nos. 1-9 (9) 252.15 102.00

For expanded treatment of Nos. 1-9, see the *Scott Classic Catalogue.*

1881-85
10 A1 10r green 1.75 1.25
11 A1 20r carmine ('85) 3.50 2.00
12 A1 25r violet ('85) 2.75 1.60
13 A1 40r yellow buff 1.75 1.00
a. Imperf. 1.00
b. Cliche of Mozambique in Cape Verde plate, in pair with #13 70.00 62.50
c. As "b," imperf. 35.00
14 A1 50r blue 4.50 2.50
Nos. 10-14 (5) 14.25 8.35

Reprints of the 1877-85 issues are on smooth white chalky paper, ungummed, and on thin white paper with shiny white gum. They are perf 13½.

For expanded treatment of Nos. 10-14, see the *Scott Classic Catalogue.*

1886 **Embossed** ***Perf. 12½, 13½***
Chalk-Surfaced Paper
15 A2 5r black 3.75 1.60
16 A2 10r green 4.00 1.75
17 A2 20r carmine 5.00 2.75
18 A2 25r violet 4.50 3.25
19 A2 40r chocolate 6.50 2.00
20 A2 50r blue 5.50 2.00
21 A2 100r yel brown 5.50 2.75
22 A2 200r gray lilac 11.00 6.00
23 A2 300r orange 17.00 8.75
Nos. 15-23 (9) 62.75 30.85

The 25r, 50r and 100r have been reprinted in aniline colors with clean-cut Perf. 13½.

For expanded treatment of Nos. 15-19, see the *Scott Classic Catalogue.*

For surcharges see Nos. 59-67, 184-187.

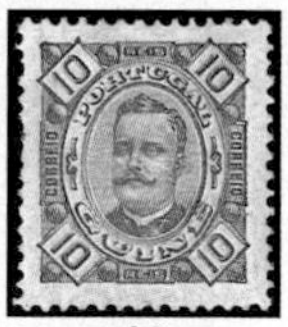
A3

King Carlos — A4

1894-95 **Typo.** ***Perf. 11½, 12½, 13½***
24 A3 5r orange .90 .75
25 A3 10r redsh violet .90 .75
26 A3 15r chocolate 2.25 1.50
a. Perf. 12½ 90.00 67.50
27 A3 20r lavender 2.25 1.50
28 A3 25r dp green 1.90 1.40
a. Perf. 12½ 3.50 2.75
29 A3 50r lt blue 1.90 1.40
a. Perf. 13½ 8.00 3.00
30 A3 75r carmine ('95) 6.50 3.50
a. Perf. 13½ 17.50 10.50
31 A3 80r yel grn ('95) 7.75 4.50
a. Perf. 13½ 25.00 19.00
32 A3 100r brn, *buff* ('95) 5.50 2.75
a. Perf. 12½ 40.00 18.00
33 A3 150r car, *rose* ('95) 18.00 15.00
a. Perf. 12½ 110.00 90.00
b. Perf. 11½ 45.00 30.00
34 A3 200r dk blue, *lt blue* ('95) 18.00 15.00
a. Perf. 12½ 90.00 70.00
35 A3 300r dk blue, *sal* ('95) 20.00 9.50
Nos. 24-35 (12) 85.85 57.55

For surcharges see Nos. 68-78, 137, 189-193, 201-205.

1898-1903 *Perf. 11½*

Name and Value in Black except 500r

36	A4	2½r gray	.25	.20
37	A4	5r orange	.30	.20
38	A4	10r lt green	.40	.20
39	A4	15r brown	3.25	1.10
40	A4	15r gray grn ('03)	1.00	.75
41	A4	20r gray violet	1.00	.50
42	A4	25r sea green	2.00	.70
a.		Perf. 12½	35.00	20.00
43	A4	25r carmine ('03)	.60	.30
44	A4	50r dark blue	2.25	.80
45	A4	50r brown ('03)	2.00	1.40
46	A4	65r slate blue ('03)	50.00	*40.00*
47	A4	75r rose	4.75	2.00
48	A4	75r lilac ('03)	1.75	1.25
49	A4	80r violet	4.75	2.25
50	A4	100r dk blue, *blue*	1.75	1.00
51	A4	115r org brn, *pink* ('03)	12.00	*13.50*
52	A4	130r brn, *straw* ('03)	12.00	*13.50*
53	A4	150r brown, *straw*	8.00	6.75
54	A4	200r red vio, *pnksh*	2.50	1.60
55	A4	300r dk blue, *rose*	8.00	3.00
56	A4	400r dull blue, *straw* ('03)	10.00	6.00
57	A4	500r blk & red, *blue* ('01)	9.00	3.00
58	A4	700r vio, *yelsh* ('01)	16.00	10.00
		Nos. 36-58 (23)	153.55	110.00

For overprints and surcharges see Nos. 80-99, 139, 200.

Regular Issues Surcharged in Red or Black

Two spacing types of surcharge. See note above Angola No. 61.

On Issue of 1886

1902, Dec. 1 *Perf. 12½, 13½*

59	A2	65r on 5r black (R)	4.00	2.50
60	A2	65r on 200r gray lilac	4.00	2.50
61	A2	65r on 300r orange	4.00	2.50
62	A2	115r on 10r green	4.00	2.50
63	A2	115r on 20r rose	4.00	2.50
a.		Perf. 13½	27.50	19.00
64	A2	130r on 50r blue	4.00	2.50
65	A2	130r on 100r brown	4.00	2.50
66	A2	400r on 25r violet	2.00	1.50
67	A2	400r on 40r choc	4.00	2.25
a.		Perf. 13½	27.50	22.50

On Issue of 1894

Perf. 11½, 12½, 13½

68	A3	65r on 10r red violet	4.75	2.75
69	A3	65r on 20r lavender	4.50	2.50
70	A3	65r on 100r brown, *buff*	5.00	3.00
a.		Perf 12½	15.00	13.50
71	A3	115r on 5r orange	2.75	1.90
a.		Inverted surcharge	45.00	45.00
72	A3	115r on 25r blue grn	2.75	1.75
a.		Perf. 11½	45.00	25.00
73	A3	115r on 150r car, *rose*	4.75	3.75
a.		Perf. 13½	20.00	12.00
74	A3	130r on 75r car	2.75	2.00
a.		Perf. 13½	45.00	42.50
75	A3	130r on 80r yel grn	2.25	1.75
76	A3	130r on 200r dk blue, *blue*	3.00	1.75
77	A3	400r on 50r lt blue	3.25	2.25
a.		Inverted surcharge	65.00	55.00
b.		Perf. 13½	55.00	55.00
78	A3	400r on 300r dk blue, *sal*	1.75	1.10

On Newspaper Stamp of 1893

79	N1	400r on 2½r brown	1.25	1.10
a.		Inverted surcharge	27.50	
b.		Perf. 12½	45.00	42.50
		Nos. 59-79 (21)	72.75	46.85

Reprints of Nos. 59, 66, 67, and 77 have shiny white gum and clean-cut perforation 13½.

For overprint and surcharges see #137, 205-206.

Overprinted in Black On Nos. 39, 42, 44, 47

1902-03 *Perf. 11½*

80	A4	15r brown	1.50	.80
81	A4	25r sea green	1.50	.80
82	A4	50r blue ('03)	1.75	1.00
83	A4	75r rose ('03)	2.25	1.40
a.		Inverted overprint	42.50	42.50
		Nos. 80-83 (4)	7.00	4.00

For overprint see No. 139.

No. 46 Surcharged in Black

1905, July 1

84	A4	50r on 65r slate blue	2.50	1.75

Stamps of 1898-1903 Overprinted in Carmine or Green

1911, Aug. 20

85	A4	2½r gray	.20	.20
86	A4	5r orange	.20	.20
87	A4	10r lt green	.60	.50
88	A4	15r gray green	.35	.20
89	A4	20r gray violet	.65	.65
90	A4	25r carmine (G)	.65	.30
91	A4	50r brown	4.00	2.75
92	A4	75r red lilac	.85	.50
93	A4	100r dk blue, *blue*	.85	.60
94	A4	115r org brn, *pink*	.45	*1.25*
95	A4	130r brown, *straw*	.45	*1.25*
96	A4	200r red vio, *pnksh*	3.25	3.25
97	A4	400r dull bl, *straw*	1.25	1.25
98	A4	500r blk & red, *bl*	1.50	1.00
99	A4	700r violet, *straw*	1.50	1.10
		Nos. 85-99 (15)	16.75	15.00

King Manuel II — A5

Overprinted in Carmine or Green

1912 *Perf. 11½x12*

100	A5	2½r violet	.20	*1.25*
101	A5	5r black	.20	.20
102	A5	10r gray grn	.20	.20
103	A5	20r carmine (G)	1.25	.70
104	A5	25r vio brown	.25	.20
105	A5	50r dk blue	2.00	1.60
106	A5	75r bister brn	.45	.35
107	A5	100r brown, *lt grn*	.45	.35
108	A5	200r dk green, *sal*	.70	.60
109	A5	300r black, *azure*	.70	.60

Perf. 14½x15

110	A5	400r black & blue	2.00	1.60
111	A5	500r ol grn & vio brn	2.00	1.60
		Nos. 100-111 (12)	10.40	9.25

Common Design Types pictured following the introduction.

Vasco da Gama Issue of Various Portuguese Colonies

Common Design Types CD20-CD27 Surcharged

On Stamps of Macao

1913, Feb. 13 *Perf. 12½ to 16*

112	CD20	¼c on ½a blue grn	1.25	.75
113	CD21	½c on 1a red	.85	.75
114	CD22	1c on 2a red violet	.85	.75
115	CD23	2½c on 4a yel grn	.85	.75
116	CD24	5c on 8a dk blue	4.00	3.00
117	CD25	7½c on 12a vio brn	3.25	2.00
118	CD26	10c on 16a bister brn	1.40	1.25
119	CD27	15c on 24a bister	3.50	2.50
		Nos. 112-119 (8)	15.95	11.75

On Stamps of Portuguese Africa

Perf. 14 to 15

120	CD20	¼c on 2½r bl grn	.65	.55
121	CD21	½c on 5r red	.65	.55
122	CD22	1c on 10r red vio	.65	.55
123	CD23	2½c on 25r yel grn	.65	.55
124	CD24	5c on 50r dk blue	1.25	.90
125	CD25	7½c on 75r vio brn	1.90	1.60
126	CD26	10c on 100r bis brn	1.25	1.10
127	CD27	15c on 150r bister	1.75	1.50
		Nos. 120-127 (8)	8.75	7.30

On Stamps of Timor

128	CD20	¼c on ½a bl grn	.85	.75
129	CD21	½c on 1a red	.85	.75
130	CD22	1c on 2a red vio	.85	.75
131	CD23	2½c on 4a yel grn	.85	.75
132	CD24	5c on 8a dk blue	4.00	3.00
133	CD25	7½c On 12a vio brn	3.50	2.50
134	CD26	10c on 16a bis brn	1.40	1.25
135	CD27	15c on 24a bister	2.75	1.50
		Nos. 128-135 (8)	15.05	11.25
		Nos. 112-135 (24)	39.75	30.30

For surcharges see Nos. 197-198.

No. 75 Overprinted in Red

1913 *Perf. 11½, 12½, 13½*

137	A3	130r on 80r yel grn	3.25	2.50

Nos. 73 and 76 overprinted but not issued. Values, $15, $20.

Same Overprint on No. 83 in Green

1914 *Perf. 12*

139	A4	75r rose	3.25	2.50
a.		"PROVISORIO" double (G and R)	45.00	40.00

Ceres — A6

Perf. 11½, 12x11½, 15x14

1914-26 **Typo.**

Name and Value in Black

144	A6	¼c olive brn	.20	.20
a.		Imperf.		
145	A6	½c black	.20	.20
146	A6	1c blue grn	.85	.75
147	A6	1c yel grn ('22)	.20	.20
148	A6	1½c lilac brown	.20	.20
149	A6	2c carmine	.20	.20
150	A6	2c gray ('26)	.25	*5.00*
151	A6	2½c lt violet	.20	.20
152	A6	3c org ('22)	.30	.25
153	A6	4c rose ('22)	.20	*1.60*
154	A6	4½c gray ('22)	.20	*5.00*
155	A6	5c deep blue	.75	.45
156	A6	5c brt blue ('22)	.20	.20
157	A6	6c lilac ('22)	.20	*2.75*
158	A6	7c ultra ('22)	.20	*2.75*
159	A6	7½c yel brn	.20	*1.00*
160	A6	8c slate	.40	.30
161	A6	10c orange brn	.20	.20
162	A6	12c blue grn ('22)	.35	.25
163	A6	15c plum	4.00	3.00
164	A6	15c brn rose ('22)	.25	.20
165	A6	20c yel grn	.20	.20
166	A6	24c ultra ('26)	1.50	*1.40*
167	A6	25c choc ('26)	1.50	1.40
168	A6	30c brown, *grn*	3.00	3.00
169	A6	30c gray grn ('22)	.75	.25
170	A6	40c brown, *pink*	3.00	3.00
171	A6	40c turq blue ('22)	1.75	.25
172	A6	50c orange, *sal*	3.00	3.00
173	A6	50c violet ('26)	1.75	.30
174	A6	60c dk blue ('22)	1.75	.45
175	A6	60c rose ('26)	1.75	.45
176	A6	80c brt rose ('22)	2.00	1.10
177	A6	1e green, *blue*	3.00	3.00
178	A6	1e rose ('22)	7.00	2.25
179	A6	1e dp blue ('26)	9.00	1.50
180	A6	2e dk violet ('22)	10.00	4.00
181	A6	5e buff ('26)	25.00	12.00
182	A6	10e pink ('26)	90.00	40.00
183	A6	20e pale turq ('26)	125.00	50.00
		Nos. 144-183 (40)	300.70	152.45

For surcharge see No. 214.

Provisional Issue of 1902 Overprinted in Carmine

1915 *Perf. 11½, 12½, 13½*

184	A2	115r on 10r green	2.50	2.00
a.		Perf. 13½	15.00	15.00
185	A2	115r on 20r rose	2.00	1.25
a.		Perf. 13½	15.00	15.00
186	A2	130r on 50r blue	2.00	1.10
187	A2	130r on 100r brown	1.50	.70
188	A3	115r on 5r orange	1.25	.40
a.		Inverted overprint	30.00	
189	A3	115r on 25r blue grn	1.50	.65
a.		Perf. 11½	15.00	15.00
190	A3	115r on 150r car, *rose*	1.00	.40
191	A3	130r on 75r carmine	2.00	.90
192	A3	130r on 80r yel grn	1.50	.70
a.		Inverted overprint	30.00	
193	A3	130r on 200r bl, *bl*	2.00	.90
a.		Perf. 12½	40.00	32.50
		Nos. 184-193 (10)	17.25	9.00

War Tax Stamps of Portuguese Africa Surcharged

1921, Feb. 3 *Perf. 15x14, 11½*

194	WT1	¼c on 1c green	.25	.25
195	WT1	½c on 1c green	.40	.30
a.		"1/2" instead of "½" as shown	10.00	10.00
196	WT1	1c green	.40	.30

Nos. 127 and 126 Surcharged

Perf. 14 to 15

197	CD27	2c on 15c on 150r	1.00	1.00
198	CD26	4c on 10c on 100r	1.25	1.00
a.		On No. 118 (error)	150.00	150.00

The 4c surcharge also exists on No. 134. Value, $500.

No. 50 Surcharged

Perf. 12

200	A4	6c on 100r dk bl, *bl*	1.25	1.25
a.		No accent on "U" of surcharge	12.50	8.00
		Nos. 194-200 (6)	4.55	4.10

No. 200 has an accent on the "U" of the surcharge.

Stamps of 1913-15 Surcharged

1922, Apr. *Perf. 11½, 12½, 13½*

On No. 137

201	A3	4c on 130r on 80r	1.25	1.25

On Nos. 191-193

202	A3	4c on 130r on 75r	1.60	1.60
203	A3	4c on 130r on 80r	1.25	1.25
204	A3	4c on 130r on 200r	.90	.60
a.		Perf. 12½	15.00	15.00
		Nos. 201-204 (4)	5.00	4.70

Surcharge of Nos. 201-204 with smaller $ occurs once in sheet of 28. Value eight times normal.

Nos. 78-79 Surcharged

1925 *Perf. 13½, 11½*

205	A3	40c on 400r on 300r	.60	.55
206	N1	40c on 400r on 2½r	.60	.45

No. 176 Surcharged

1931, Nov. ***Perf. 12x11½***

214	A6	70c on 80c brt rose	2.75	1.40

Ceres — A7

1934, May 1 **Wmk. 232**

215	A7	1c	bister	.20	*.20*
216	A7	5c	olive brown	.20	.20
217	A7	10c	violet	.20	.20
218	A7	15c	black	.20	.20
219	A7	20c	gray	.20	.20
220	A7	30c	dk green	.20	.20
221	A7	40c	red org	.20	.20
222	A7	45c	brt blue	1.40	.60
223	A7	50c	brown	.65	.45
224	A7	60c	olive grn	.65	.45
225	A7	70c	brown org	.65	.45
226	A7	80c	emerald	.65	.45
227	A7	85c	deep rose	3.00	1.90
228	A7	1e	maroon	2.10	.35
229	A7	1.40e	dk blue	2.75	2.40
230	A7	2e	dk violet	3.25	1.90
231	A7	5e	apple green	14.50	3.75
232	A7	10e	olive bister	24.00	14.00
233	A7	20e	orange	45.00	18.00
			Nos. 215-233 (19)	100.00	46.10

For surcharge see No. 256.

Vasco da Gama Issue
Common Design Types

1938 **Unwmk.** ***Perf. 13½x13***

Name and Value in Black

234	CD34	1c	gray green	.20	*.20*
235	CD34	5c	orange brn	.20	*.20*
236	CD34	10c	dk carmine	.20	.20
237	CD34	15c	dk vio brn	.70	.65
238	CD34	20c	slate	.35	.20
239	CD35	30c	rose vio	.35	.20
240	CD35	35c	brt green	.35	.20
241	CD35	40c	brown	.35	.20
242	CD35	50c	brt red vio	.35	.20
243	CD36	60c	gray blk	.35	.20
244	CD36	70c	brown vio	.35	.20
245	CD36	80c	orange	.30	.20
246	CD36	1e	red	.50	.20
247	CD37	1.75e	blue	1.25	.55
248	CD37	2e	dk blue grn	2.50	1.50
249	CD37	5e	ol grn	5.75	1.50
250	CD38	10e	blue vio	9.75	2.00
251	CD38	20e	red brown	30.00	4.00
			Nos. 234-251 (18)	53.80	12.60

For surcharges see #255, 271-276, 288-292.

Outline Map of Africa — A8

1939, June 23 **Litho.** ***Perf. 11½x12***

252	A8	80c vio, *pale rose*	4.00	2.75
253	A8	1.75e blue, *pale bl*	32.50	25.00
254	A8	20e brown, *buff*	70.00	22.50
		Nos. 252-254 (3)	106.50	50.25

Visit of the President of Portugal in 1939.

Nos. 239 and 221 Surcharged with New Value and Bars in Black

1948 **Unwmk.** ***Perf. 13½x13***

255	CD35	10c on 30c rose violet	1.25	*.70*

Perf. 12x11½
Wmk. 232

256	A7	25c on 40c red orange	1.25	*.70*

Machado Pt., Sao Vicente — A9

Brava Creek, Sao Nicoláo — A10

Designs: 10c, Ribeira Grande. 1e, Harbor, Sao Vicente. 1.75e, Mindelo, distant view. 2e, Joao de Evora Beach. 5e, Mindelo. 10e, Volcano, Fire Island. 20e, Mt. Paul.

Perf. 14½

1948, Oct. 1 **Litho.** **Unwmk.**

257	A9	5c	vio brn & bis	.25	.20
258	A9	10c	ol grn & pale grn	.25	.20
259	A10	50c	mag & lil rose	.45	.20
260	A10	1e	brn vio & rose lil	1.60	.70
261	A10	1.75e	ultra & grnsh bl	2.00	1.10
262	A10	2e	dk brn & buff	4.50	1.25
263	A10	5e	ol grn & yel	9.00	2.50
264	A10	10e	red & cream	15.00	8.50
265	A10	20e	dk vio & bis	37.50	16.00
			Nos. 257-265 (9)	70.55	30.65

Lady of Fatima Issue
Common Design Type

1948, Dec.

266	CD40	50c dark blue	6.50	4.50

UPU Symbols — A10a

1949, Oct. ***Perf. 14***

267	A10a	1e red vio & pink	5.00	2.50

UPU, 75th anniversary.

Catalogue values for unused stamps in this section, from this point to the end of the section, are for Never Hinged items.

Holy Year Issue
Common Design Types

1950, May ***Perf. 13x13½***

268	CD41	1e orange brown	.90	.45
269	CD42	2e slate	3.50	1.75

Holy Year Conclusion Issue
Common Design Type

1951, Oct. **Unwmk.** ***Perf. 14***

270	CD43	2e purple & lilac + label	1.40	1.25

Stamps without labels sell for less.

Nos. 240, 244-245, 247, 250 Surcharged with New Value and Bars

Perf. 13½x13

1951, May 21 **Unwmk.**

271	CD35	10c on 35c	.70	.55
272	CD36	20c on 70c	.90	.65
273	CD36	40c on 70c	1.10	.65
274	CD36	50c on 80c	1.10	.65
275	CD37	1e on 1.75e	1.25	.65
276	CD38	2e on 10e	5.75	2.00
a.		1e on 10e	200.00	125.00
		Nos. 271-276 (6)	10.80	5.15

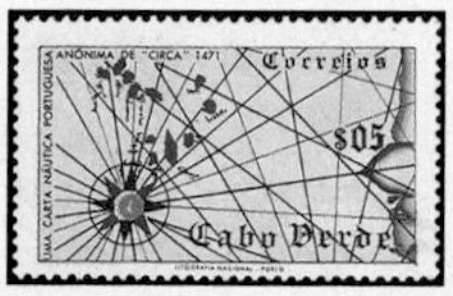

Map of Cape Verde Islands, 1502 — A11

Vicente Dias and Gonçalo de Cintra — A12

Portraits: 30c, Diogo Alfonso and Alvaro Fernandes. 50c, Lançarote and Soeiro da Costa. 1e, Diogo Gomes and Antonio da Nola. 2e, Prince Fernando and Prince Henry the Navigator. 3e, Antao Gonçalves and Dinis Dias. 5e, Alfonso Goncalves Baldaia and Joao Fernandes. 10e, Dinis Eanes da Gra and Alvaro de Freitas. 20e, Map of Cape Verde Islands, 1502.

1952, Feb. 24 ***Perf. 14***

277	A11	5c	multicolored	.20	.20
278	A12	10c	multicolored	.20	.20
279	A12	30c	multicolored	.20	.20
280	A12	50c	multicolored	.20	.20
281	A12	1e	multicolored	.20	.20
282	A12	2e	multicolored	1.25	.20
283	A12	3e	multicolored	10.50	1.50
284	A12	5e	multicolored	3.50	.70
285	A12	10e	multicolored	7.00	1.75
286	A11	20e	multicolored	12.50	2.40
			Nos. 277-286 (10)	35.75	7.55

Medical Congress Issue
Common Design Type

Design: Hypodermic Injection.

1952, June ***Perf. 13½***

287	CD44	20c ol grn & dk brn	.70	.50

No. 247 Surcharged with New Values and "X" in Black

1952, Jan. 25 ***Perf. 13½x13***

288	CD37	10c	on 1.75e	2.00	1.10
289	CD37	20c	on 1.75e	2.00	1.10
290	CD37	50c	on 1.75e	8.00	5.00
291	CD37	1e	on 1.75e	1.00	.25
292	CD37	1.50e	on 1.75e	1.00	.25
			Nos. 288-292 (5)	14.00	7.70

Facade of Jeronymos Convent — A13

Perf. 13½

1953, Jan. **Unwmk.** **Litho.**

293	A13	10c brown & pale olive	.20	.20
294	A13	50c purple & fawn	.90	.40
295	A13	1e dark green & fawn	2.10	1.10
		Nos. 293-295 (3)	3.20	1.70

Exhibition of Sacred Missionary Art held at Lisbon in 1951.

Stamp of Portugal and Arms of Colonies — A13a

1953 **Photo.**

296	A13a	50c multicolored	1.75	1.10

Centenary of Portuguese stamps.

Sao Paulo Issue
Common Design Type

1954 **Litho.** ***Perf. 13½***

297	CD46	1e green, cream & gray	.70	.60

Belem Tower, Lisbon, and Colonial Arms — A14

Arms of Praia — A15

1955, May 15 **Litho.** ***Perf. 13½***

298	A14	1e multicolored	.50	.25
299	A14	1.60e buff & multi	.75	.60

Visit of Pres. Francisco H. C. Lopes.

1958, June 14 ***Perf. 12x11½***

300	A15	1e multicolored	.65	.45
301	A15	2.50e pink & multi	1.10	.90

Centenary of city of Praia.

Fair Emblem, Globe and Arms — A15a

1958 ***Perf. 12x11½***

302	A15a	2e multicolored	.90	.40

World's Fair, Brussels, Apr. 17-Oct. 19.

Tropical Medicine Congress Issue
Common Design Type

1958, Sept. 5 ***Perf. 13½***

303	CD47	3e Aloe vera	5.50	2.10

Prince Henry — A16

Antonio da Nola — A17

1960, June 25 **Litho.** ***Perf. 13½***

304	A16	2e multicolored	.50	.25

500th anniv. of the death of Prince Henry the Navigator.

1960, Oct. **Unwmk.** ***Perf. 14½***

Design: 2.50e, Diogo Gomes.

305	A17	1e multicolored	.75	.45
306	A17	2.50e multicolored	2.50	1.00

Discovery of Cape Verde, 500th anniv.

School Children — A18

1960

307	A18	2.50e multicolored	1.25	.65

10th anniv. of the Commission for Technical Cooperation in Africa South of the Sahara (C.C.T.A.).

Arms of Praia — A19

Arms of various cities & towns of Cape Verde.

1961, July **Litho.** ***Perf. 13½***

308	A19	5c	shown	.25	.20
309	A19	15c	Nova Sintra	.25	.20
310	A19	20c	Ribeira Brava	.25	.20
311	A19	30c	Assomada	.25	.20
312	A19	1e	Maio	.65	.20
313	A19	2e	Mindelo	.65	.20
314	A19	2.50e	Santa Maria	1.00	.20
315	A19	3e	Pombas	1.60	.50
316	A19	5e	Sal-Rei	1.60	.50
317	A19	7.50e	Tarrafal	1.75	.90
318	A19	15e	Maria Pia	2.40	.90
319	A19	30e	San Felipe	6.50	2.50
			Nos. 308-319 (12)	17.15	6.70

Sports Issue
Common Design Type

Sports: 50c, Javelin. 1e, Discus. 1.50e, Cricket. 2.50e, Boxing. 4.50e, Hurdling. 12.50e, Golf.

1962, Jan. 18 *Perf. 13½*

320 CD48	50c lt brown	.25	.20
321 CD48	1e lt green	.75	.25
322 CD48	1.50e lt blue grn	7.00	2.00
323 CD48	2.50e pale vio bl	.75	.35
324 CD48	4.50e orange	1.10	.75
325 CD48	12.50e beige	2.40	1.60
	Nos. 320-325 (6)	12.25	5.15

Anti-Malaria Issue
Common Design Type

Design: Anopheles pretoriensis.

1962 **Litho.** *Perf. 13½*
326 CD49 2.50e multicolored 1.40 .90

Airline Anniversary Issue
Common Design Type

1963, Oct. **Unwmk.** *Perf. 14½*
327 CD50 2.50e gray & multi 1.10 .70

National Overseas Bank Issue
Common Design Type

Design: 1.50e, Jose da Silva Mendes Leal.

1964, May 16 *Perf. 13½*
328 CD51 1.50e multicolored 1.10 .75

ITU Issue
Common Design Type

1965, May 17 **Litho.** *Perf. 14½*
329 CD52 2.50e buff & multi 2.10 1.40

Militia Drummer, 1806 — A20

Designs: 1e, Soldier, Militia, 1806. 1.50e, Grenadier officer, 1833. 2.50e, Grenadier, 1833. 3e, Cavalry officer, 1834. 4e, Grenadier, 1835. 5e, Artillery officer, 1848. 10e, Drum major, infantry, 1856.

1965, Dec. 1 **Litho.** *Perf. 14½*

330 A20	50c multicolored	.25	.25
331 A20	1e multicolored	.45	.25
332 A20	1.50e multicolored	.45	.40
333 A20	2.50e multicolored	1.25	.35
334 A20	3e multicolored	2.50	.55
335 A20	4e multicolored	1.10	.55
336 A20	5e multicolored	1.25	.55
337 A20	10e multicolored	2.75	1.75
	Nos. 330-337 (8)	10.00	4.65

National Revolution Issue
Common Design Type

1e, Dr. Adriano Moreira School & Health Center.

1966, May 28 **Litho.** *Perf. 12*
338 CD53 1e multicolored .60 .45

Navy Club Issue
Common Design Type

Designs: 1e, Capt. Fontoura da Costa and gunboat Mandovy. 1.50e, Capt. Carvalho Araujo and minesweeper Augusto Castilho.

1967, Jan. 31 **Litho.** *Perf. 13*
339 CD54 1e multicolored .75 .50
340 CD54 1.50e multicolored 1.25 .90

Virgin Mary Statue — A21

Pres. Rodrigues Thomaz — A22

1967, May 13 **Litho.** *Perf. 12½x13*
341 A21 1e multicolored .35 .25

50th anniv. of the apparition of the Virgin Mary to 3 shepherd children at Fatima.

1968, Feb. 9 **Litho.** *Perf. 13½*
342 A22 1e multicolored .35 .25

Issued to commemorate the 1968 visit of Pres. Americo de Deus Rodrigues Thomaz.

Cabral Issue

Pedro Alvares Cabral — A23

1e, Cantino's world map, 1502, horiz.

1968, Apr. 22 **Litho.** *Perf. 14*
343 A23 1e multicolored .85 .70
344 A23 1.50e multicolored 1.40 .75

See note after Angola No. 545.
For overprint see No. 365.

Sao Vicente Harbor — A24

Physic Nut — A25

Designs: 1.50e, Peanut plant. 2.50e, Castor-oil plant. 3.50e, Yams. 4e, Date palm. 4.50e, Guavas. 5e, Tamarind. 10e, Bitter cassava. 30e, Woman carrying fruit baskets.

1968, Oct. 15 **Litho.** *Perf. 14*

345 A24	50c multicolored	.25	.20
346 A25	1e multicolored	.40	.25
347 A25	1.50e multicolored	.40	.25
348 A25	2.50e multicolored	.40	.25
349 A25	3.50e multicolored	.45	.25
350 A25	4e multicolored	.45	.25
351 A25	4.50e multicolored	.70	.25
352 A25	5 multicolored	1.00	.30
353 A25	10e multicolored	1.25	.60
354 A25	30e multicolored	3.00	2.50
	Nos. 345-354 (10)	8.30	5.10

For overprint see No. 372.

Admiral Coutinho Issue
Common Design Type

Adm. Coutinho & map showing route of 1st flight from Lisbon to Rio de Janeiro.

1969, Feb. 17 **Litho.** *Perf. 14*
355 CD55 30c multi, vert. .35 .25

For surcharge see No. 388.

Vasco da Gama — A26

King Manuel I — A27

Vasco da Gama Issue

1969, Aug. 29 **Litho.** *Perf. 14*
356 A26 1.50e multicolored .35 .25

Vasco da Gama (1469-1524), navigator.

Administration Reform Issue
Common Design Type

1969, Sept. 25 **Litho.** *Perf. 14*
357 CD56 2e multicolored .35 .25

King Manuel I Issue

1969, Dec. 1 **Litho.** *Perf. 14*
358 A27 3e multicolored .55 .35

500th anniv. of the birth of King Manuel I.

Marshal Carmona Issue
Common Design Type

Design: 2.50e, Antonio Oscar Carmona in marshal's uniform.

1970, Nov. 15 **Litho.** *Perf. 14*
359 CD57 2.50e multi .55 .35

Galleons on Sanaga River — A28

1972, May 25 **Litho.** *Perf. 13*
360 A28 5e lilac rose & multi .65 .30

4th centenary of the publication of The Lusiads by Luiz Camoens.

Olympic Games Issue
Common Design Type

4e, Basketball & boxing, Olympic emblem.

1972, June 20 *Perf. 14x13½*
361 CD59 4e multicolored .65 .30

For surcharge see No. 371.

Lisbon-Rio de Janeiro Flight Issue
Common Design Type

Design: "Lusitania" landing at San Vicente.

1972, Sept. 20 **Litho.** *Perf. 13½*
362 CD60 3.50e multi .65 .30

WMO Centenary Issue
Common Design Type

1973, Dec. 15 **Litho.** *Perf. 13*
363 CD61 2.50e ultra & multi .65 .30

For overprint see No. 387.

Mindelo Desalination Plant — A29

1974 **Litho.** *Perf. 13½*
364 A29 4e multicolored 1.25 .85

Opening of the Mindelo desalination plant.
For surcharge see No. 371A.

Republic

No. 343 Overprinted:
"INDEPENDENCIA / 5-Julho-75"

1975, Dec. 19 **Litho.** *Perf. 14*
365 A23 1e multicolored .35 .25

Proclamation of Independence.

Amilcar Cabral, Flag and Crowd — A30

1976, Jan. 20
366 A30 5e multicolored .55 .25

3rd anniv. of the assassination of Amilcar Cabral (1924-73), revolutionary leader.

Rising Sun, Coat of Arms, Liberated People — A31

1976, July 5 **Litho.** *Perf. 14*

367 A31	50c multicolored	.25	.20
368 A31	3e multicolored	.90	.20
369 A31	15e multicolored	2.00	.35
370 A31	50e multicolored	6.25	1.25
a.	Miniature sheet, #367-370	*16.00*	*16.00*
	Nos. 367-370 (4)	9.40	2.00

First anniversary of independence.

Nos. 351, 361, 364 Overprinted with Row of Stars and: "REPUBLICA / DE"

1976 **Litho.** *Perf. 14*

371	CD59	4e multi	—	
371A	A29	4e multi	*37.50*	*27.50*
372	A25	4.50e multi	4.25	2.25

Amilcar Cabral, Map and Flag of Cape Verde A32

1976, Sept. 19 *Perf. 14*
373 A32 1e multicolored .45 .25

Party of Intl. Action (PAICC), 20th anniv.

Electronic Tree and ITU Emblem — A33

Ashtray — A34

1977, May 17 Litho. *Perf. 13½x13*

374	A33	5.50e multi	.45	.25

World Telecommunications Day.

1977, July 5 Litho. *Perf. 14*

Carved Coconut Shells: 30c, Bell on stand. 50c, Lamp with Adam and Eve. 1e, Hollow shell with Nativity. 1.50e, Desk lamp. 5e, Jar. 10e, Jar with hinged cover. 20e, Tobacco jar with palms. 30e, Stringed instrument.

375	A34	20c	lilac & multi	.25	.20
376	A34	30c	rose & multi	.25	.20
377	A34	50c	salmon & multi	.25	.20
378	A34	1e	lt green & multi	.35	.25
379	A34	1.50e	orange yel & multi	.35	.25
380	A34	5e	gray & multi	.75	.35
381	A34	10e	lt blue & multi	1.25	.55
382	A34	20e	yellow & multi	2.00	1.25
383	A34	30e	rose lilac & multi	3.25	1.40
			Nos. 375-383 (9)	8.70	4.65

Cape Verde No. 1 and Coat of Arms — A35

Congress Emblem — A36

1977, Sept. 12 Litho. *Perf. 13½*

384	A35	4e blue & multi	.40	.25
385	A35	8e lilac & multi	.80	.35

Centenary of Cape Verde stamps.

1977, Nov. 15 *Perf. 14*

386	A36	3.50e multi	.60	.25

African Party of Independence of Guinea-Bissau and Cape Verde (PAIGC), 3rd cong., Nov. 15-20.

No. 363 Overprinted

1978, May 1 *Perf. 12*

387	CD61	2.50e ultra & multi	.60	.25

No. 355 Surcharged with New Value and Bars

1978, May 1 *Perf. 14*

388	CD55	3e on 30c multi	2.25	.35

Antenna and ITU Emblem — A37

1978, May 17 Litho. *Perf. 14*

389	A37	3.50e silver & multi	.55	.25

10th World Telecommunications Day.

Freighter Cabo Verde — A38

1978, June 25 Litho. *Perf. 14*

391	A38	1e multicolored	.70	.20

First ship of Cape Verde merchant marine.

Map of Africa and Equality Emblem — A39

1978, June 21

392	A39	4.50e multi	.55	.25

Anti-Apartheid Year.

Human Rights Emblem — A40

1978, Dec. 10 Litho. *Perf. 14*

393	A40	1.50e multicolored	.35	.25
394	A40	2e multicolored	.55	.35

Universal Declaration of Human Rights, 30th anniversary.

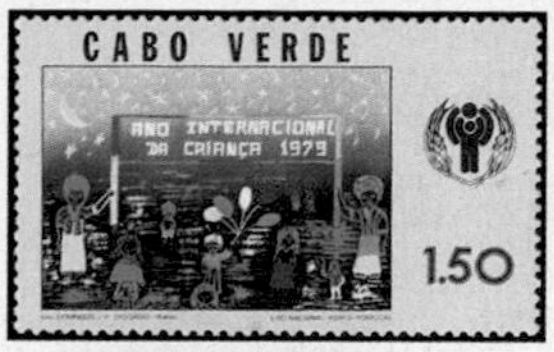

Children and Balloons, IYC Emblem — A41

IYC Emblem and Child's Drawing: 3.50e, Children and flowers.

1979, June 1 Litho. *Perf. 14*

395	A41	1.50e multi	.65	.25
396	A41	3.50e multi	1.10	.35

International Year of the Child.

Pindjiguiti Massacre Monument — A42

Natl. Youth Week — A42a

1979, Aug. 3 *Perf. 13*

397	A42	4.50e multi	2.10	.25

Massacre of Pindjiguiti, 20th anniversary.

1979, Sept. 1 Litho. *Perf. 14*

397A	A42a	3.50e Poster	1.10	.25

Centenary of Mindelo — A43

1980, Apr. 23 Litho. *Perf. 12½*

398	A43	4e multicolored	.70	.25

Flag of Cape Verde — A44

Stylized Bird, "V" — A45

1980 Litho. *Perf. 12½*

399	A44	4e	multicolored	1.25	.25
400	A45	4e	multicolored	.45	.25
401	A45	7e	multicolored	.80	.35
402	A45	11e	multicolored	1.10	.45
			Nos. 399-402 (4)	3.60	1.30

5th anniversary of independence.
Issued: No. 399, June 1; others July 5.

A45a

A46

1980, May 13

402A	A45a	3.50e multi	.55	.25
402B	A45a	4.50e multi	.70	.25

1980 Natl. census.

1980, June 6

403	A46	1e	Running	.20	.20
404	A46	2.50e	Boxing	.25	.20
405	A46	3e	Basketball	.35	.25
406	A46	4e	Volleyball	.50	.30
407	A46	20e	Swimming	1.40	.90
408	A46	50e	Tennis	4.00	1.75
			Nos. 403-408 (6)	6.70	3.60

Souvenir Sheet

Perf. 13

409	A46	30e	Soccer, horiz.	*18.00*	*18.00*

22nd Summer Olympic Games, Moscow, July 19-Aug. 3.

Thunnus Alalunga A47

1980, Nov. 11 Litho. *Perf. 13*

410	A47	50c	shown	.25	.20
411	A47	4.50e	Trachurus trachurus	.40	.20
412	A47	8e	Muraena helena	.65	.25
413	A47	10e	Corvina nigra	.75	.35
414	A47	12e	Katsuwonus pelamis	1.10	.60
415	A47	50e	Prionace glauca	4.00	1.90
			Nos. 410-415 (6)	7.15	3.50

Lochnera Rosea — A48

1980, Dec. 29

416	A48	50c	shown	.25	.20
417	A48	4.50e	Poinciana regia-bojer	.30	.25
418	A48	8e	Mirabilis jalapa	.75	.35
419	A48	10e	Nerium oleander	.95	.45
420	A48	12e	Bougainvillia litoralis	1.10	.55
421	A48	30e	Hibiscus	2.60	1.50
			Nos. 416-421 (6)	5.95	3.30

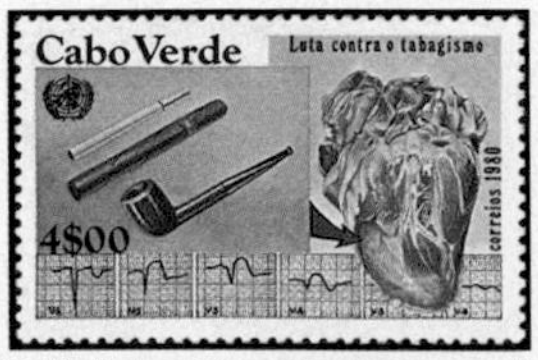

WHO Anti-smoking Campaign — A48a

1980, Sept. 19 *Perf. 12½*

421A A48a 4e multicolored .50 .25
421B A48a 7e multicolored 1.10 .35

Arca Verde A49

1980, Nov. 30 Litho. *Perf. 12½x12*

422 A49 3e shown .30 .20
423 A49 5.50e Ilha do Maio .50 .25
424 A49 7.50e Ilha de Komo .95 .55
425 A49 9e Boa Vista 1.25 .75
426 A49 12e Santo Antao 1.40 .55
427 A49 30e Santiago 3.25 1.40
Nos. 422-427 (6) 7.65 3.70

Hand-woven Bag, Map — A49a

Various hand-woven articles. 10e, vert.

1978, May 21 Litho. *Perf. 14*

427A A49a 50c multi .25 .20
427B A49a 1.50e multi .25 .20
427C A49a 2e multi .55 .25
427D A49a 3e multi .55 .30
427E A49a 10e multi 1.40 .70
Nos. 427A-427E (5) 3.00 1.65

Desert Erosion Prevention Campaign — A50

1981, Mar. 30 Litho. *Perf. 13*

428 A50 4.50e multi .60 .25
429 A50 10.50e multi 1.25 .50

6th Anniv. of Constitution A51

1981, Apr. 15

430 A51 4.50e multicolored .60 .25

Souvenir Sheet

Austria No. B336 A52

1981, May 18

431 A52 50e multicolored 6.50 6.50

WIPA '81 Philatelic Exhibition, Vienna, Austria, May 22-31.

Antenna — A53

1981, Aug. 25 Litho. *Perf. 12½*

432 A53 4.50e shown .65 .25
433 A53 8e Dish antenna .95 .40
434 A53 20e Dish antenna, diff. 2.00 .95
Nos. 432-434 (3) 3.60 1.60

Intl. Year of the Disabled A54

1981, Dec. 25 Litho. *Perf. 12½*

435 A54 4.50e multicolored .65 .35

Purple Gallinule A55

1981, Dec. 30

436 A55 1e Egret, vert. .60 .20
437 A55 4.50e Barn owl, vert. 1.25 .40
438 A55 8e Passerine, vert. 2.75 .55
439 A55 10e shown 3.00 .65
440 A55 12e Guinea fowl 3.75 .75
Nos. 436-440 (5) 11.35 2.55

Souvenir Sheet

Perf. 13

441 A55 50e Razo Isld. lark 9.50 9.50

No. 441 contains 31x39mm one stamp.

CILSS Congress, Praia, Jan. 17 — A56

1982, Jan. 17 *Perf. 13x12½*

442 A56 11.50e multicolored 1.40 .65

Amilcar Cabral Soccer Championship — A57

Designs: Soccer players and flags.

1982, Feb. 10 Litho. *Perf. 12½*

443 A57 4.50e multicolored .55 .25
444 A57 7.50e multicolored .85 .40
445 A57 11.50e multicolored 1.40 .70
Nos. 443-445 (3) 2.80 1.35

1982 World Cup — A58

Designs: Soccer players and ball.

1982, Apr. 25

446 A58 1.50e multi .25 .20
447 A58 4.50e multi .50 .25
448 A58 8e multi .85 .35
449 A58 10.50e multi 1.00 .45
450 A58 12e multi 1.25 .55
451 A58 20e multi 2.25 .90
Nos. 446-451 (6) 6.10 2.70

Souvenir Sheet

452 A58 50e multi 6.25 6.25

First Anniv. of Women's Organization — A59

1982, Apr. 15 Litho. *Perf. 12½x12*

453 A59 4.50e Marching .55 .25
454 A59 8e Farming 1.10 .40
455 A59 12e Child care 1.60 .70
Nos. 453-455 (3) 3.25 1.35

Estaleiros Navais Port, St. Vincent A59a

1982, July 5 Litho. *Perf. 13x12½*

455A A59a 10.50e multi 1.75 .60

Natl. independence, 7th anniv.

Return of Barque Morrissey-Ernestina — A60

1982, July 5 Litho. *Perf. 13*

456 A60 12e multi 1.40 .80

Butterflies — A61

1982, July 27 **Litho.**

457 A61 2e Hypolimnas misippus .35 .20
458 A61 4.50e Melanitis lede .70 .25
459 A61 8e Catopsilia florella 1.10 .25
460 A61 10.50e Colias electo 1.50 .40
461 A61 11.50e Danaus chrysippus 1.60 .60
462 A61 12e Papilio demodecus 2.75 .70
Nos. 457-462 (6) 8.00 2.40

Francisco Xavier da Cruz (1905-1958), Composer — A62

14e, Eugenio Tavares (1867-1930), poet.

1983, Feb. 20 Litho. *Perf. 13*

463 A62 7e multi .45 .30
464 A62 14e multi 1.90 .80

World Communications Year — A63

1983, Oct. 10 **Litho.**

465 A63 13e multicolored 1.60 .80

Local Seashells — A64

1983, Nov. 30 *Perf. 13½*

466 A64 50c Conus ateralbus .25 .20
467 A64 1e Conus decoratus .25 .20
468 A64 3e Conus salreiensis .35 .20
469 A64 10e Conus verdensis 1.50 .55
470 A64 50e Conus cuneolus 5.00 2.75
Nos. 466-470 (5) 7.35 3.90

40th Anniv. of Intl. Civil Aviation Org. A65

Airplanes: 50c, Ogma-Auster D5/160, 1966. 2e, De Havilland DH-104 Dove, 1945. 10e, Hawker Siddeley 748-200, 1972. 13e, De Havilland Dragon Rapide, 1945. 20e, De Havilland Twin Otter, 1977. 50e, Britten-Norman Islander, 1971.

1984, Feb. 15 **Litho.**

471 A65	50c multicolored	.25	.20
472 A65	2e multicolored	.30	.25
473 A65	10e multicolored	1.10	.50
474 A65	13e multicolored	1.25	.85
475 A65	20e multicolored	1.90	1.25
476 A65	50e multicolored	4.50	2.50
	Nos. 471-476 (6)	9.30	5.55

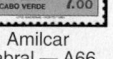

Amilcar Cabral — A66

A67

1983, Jan. 17 **Litho.** ***Perf. 14½***

477 A66	7e multi	1.00	.50
478 A66	10.50e multi	1.50	.90
a.	Souvenir sheet of 2, #477-478	30.00	30.00

Amilcar Cabral Symposium, Jan. 17-20. No. 478a sold for 30e.

1983, Dec. 10 **Photo.** ***Perf. 14½***

479 A67 7e Cross overshadowing islands 1.10 .50

Christianity in Cape Verde, 450th anniv.

Natl. Solidarity Campaign A68

1984, Sept. 12 ***Perf. 13½***

480 A68	6.50e multi	1.10	.25
481 A68	13.50e multi	2.10	.85

2nd Conference of Natl. Women's Orgs., Mar. 23-27 — A69

1985, Mar. 27 **Litho.** ***Perf. 13½***

482 A69 8e multicolored *1.10* .55

Miniature Sheet

483 A69 30e multicolored *100.00 100.00*

Natl. Independence, 10th Anniv. — A70

1985, July 5 **Litho.** ***Perf. 14***

484 A70	8c multicolored	1.25	.55
485 A70	12e multicolored	1.90	.80

Intl. Youth Year — A71

1985, Sept. 12 **Litho.** ***Perf. 14***

486 A71 12e multicolored 2.50 .90

Vapor, by Hundertwasser A72

Photogravure and Engraved

1986, Apr. 25 ***Perf. 14***

Black Surcharge

487 A72 30e on 10e multi 20.00 4.00

Souvenir Sheets

Background Color

488	Sheet of 4	140.00	
a.	A72 50e yellow & multi	15.00	15.00
489	Sheet of 4	140.00	
a.	A72 50e red & multi	15.00	15.00
490	Sheet of 4	140.00	
a.	A72 50e green & multi	15.00	15.00

No. 487 exists without surcharge. Value $27.50.

World Wildlife Fund — A73

Perf. 13½x14½

1986, June 15 **Litho.**

491 A73	8e Mabuya vaillanti	5.00	2.00
492 A73	10e Tarentola gigas brancoensis	6.50	2.75
493 A73	15e Tarentola gigas gigas	9.50	3.50
494 A73	30e Hemidactylus bouvieri	18.00	4.50
	Nos. 491-494 (4)	39.00	12.75

Souvenir Sheet

495	Sheet of 2	25.00	20.00
a.	A73 50e Mabuya vaillanti	12.00	9.00
b.	A73 50e Hemidactylus bouvieri	12.00	9.00

No. 495 printed with center label picturing progress union emblem. Nos. 495a-495b printed without WWF emblem.

World Food Day — A74

Intl. Peace Year — A75

1986, June 20 ***Perf. 14***

496 A74	8e Cauldron	.50	.25
497 A74	12e Mortar & pestle	.80	.35
498 A74	15e Quern stone	1.40	.50
	Nos. 496-498 (3)	2.70	1.10

1986, Dec. 24 **Litho.** ***Perf. 14***

499 A75	12e multicolored	.60	.25
500 A75	30e multicolored	2.10	1.40

Natl. Child Survival Campaign A76

1987, Mar. 27 **Litho.** ***Perf. 14***

501 A76	8e multicolored	.45	.20
502 A76	10e multicolored	.55	.25
503 A76	12e multicolored	.65	.35
504 A76	16e multicolored	.95	.50
505 A76	100e multicolored	4.50	2.75
	Nos. 501-505 (5)	7.10	4.05

Tourism A77

1987, May 17

506 A77	1e Bay, Mindelo	.20	.20
507 A77	2.50e Hill country	.20	.20
508 A77	5e Mountain peak	.25	.25
509 A77	8e Monument	.45	.25
510 A77	10e Mountain peaks	.65	.30
511 A77	12e Beached boats	.85	.40
512 A77	100e Harbor	5.25	3.00
	Nos. 506-512 (7)	7.85	4.60

For surcharge see No. 710.

Ships — A78

1987, Aug. 3 ***Perf. 13½x14½***

513 A78	12e Carvalho, 1937	.75	.25
514 A78	16e Nauta, 1943	1.25	.25
515 A78	50e Maria Sony, 1911	3.75	1.25
	Nos. 513-515 (3)	5.75	1.75

Souvenir Sheet

516	Sheet of 2	9.00	9.00
a.	A78 60e Madalan, 1928	4.00	4.00

Crop Protection A80

1988, May 9 **Litho.** ***Perf. 13½***

518 A80	50c Identification of insect plague	.20	.20
519 A80	2e Use of insecticides	.20	.20
520 A80	9e Import of parasites	.50	.25
521 A80	13e Import of predators	.60	.25
522 A80	16e Locust	1.00	.40
523 A80	19e Estimation of crop loss	1.25	.60
	Nos. 518-523 (6)	3.75	1.90

Souvenir Sheet

524 A80 50e Agricultural Research Institute 5.00 5.00

Maps — A81

1988, July 5 **Litho.** ***Perf. 14***

525 A81	1e	Dutch, 17th cent.	.20	.20
526 A81	2.50e	Belgian, 18th cent.	.20	.20
527 A81	4.50e	French, 18th cent.	.30	.20
528 A81	9.50e	English, 18th cent.	.60	.25
529 A81	19.50e	English, 19th cent.	1.25	.55
530 A81	20e	French, 18th cent., vert.	1.40	.65
		Nos. 525-530 (6)	3.95	2.05

Churches A82

5e, St. Amaro Abade, Tarrafal, Santiago Is. 8e, Our Lady of the Light, Maio Is. 10e, Nazarene, Praia, Santiago Is. 12e, Our Lady of Rosa'rio, Sao Nicolau Is. 15e, Nazarene, Mindelo, Sao Vicente Is. 20e, Our Lady of Grace, Praia, Santiago Is.

1988, Aug. 15 ***Perf. 13½x14½***

531 A82	5e multicolored	.20	.20
532 A82	8e multicolored	.45	.20
533 A82	10e multicolored	.55	.25
534 A82	12e multicolored	.60	.25
535 A82	15e multicolored	.85	.35
536 A82	20e multicolored	1.25	.45
	Nos. 531-536 (6)	3.90	1.70

Water Conservation — A83

1988, Sept. 26 **Litho.** ***Perf. 14***

537 A83 12e multicolored .75 .35

Intl. Red Cross, 125th Anniv. — A84

1988, Oct. 20

538 A84 7e multi .45 .25

3rd Communist Party (PAICV) Congress — A85

Portrait of Pres. Pereira, PAICV secretary-general, and: 7e, S. Jorginho Vocational Training Center. 10.50e, UN Secretary-General Perez de Cuellar. 30e, 100e, Star and text.

Perf. 14½x13½

1988, Nov. 25 **Litho.**

539	A85	7e multi	.40	.25
540	A85	10.50e multi	.60	.25
541	A85	30e multi	1.75	.75
		Nos. 539-541 (3)	2.75	1.25

Souvenir Sheet

542	A85	100e multi	6.25	6.25

1988 Summer Olympics, Seoul — A86

1988, Dec. 26

543	A86	12e shown	.60	.25
544	A86	15e Tennis	.90	.35
545	A86	20e Soccer	1.25	.50
546	A86	30e Boxing	1.75	.90
		Nos. 543-546 (4)	4.50	2.00

Souvenir Sheet

547	A86	50e Long jump	4.00	4.00

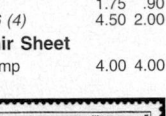

Roberto Duarte Silva (1837-89), Chemist A86a

1989, May 2 **Litho.** *Perf. 14¼x14*

547A	A86a	12.50e multi	.45	.25

2nd JAAC-CV Congress, Sept. 7-12 — A87

1989, Apr. 7 **Litho.** *Perf. 14*

548	A87	30e Hot air balloon	1.10	.75

Liberty Guiding the People — A88

Relief, Arc de Triomphe — A89

1989, July 7 **Litho.** *Perf. 14*

549	A88	20e multicolored	.85	.45
550	A88	24e multicolored	1.10	.55
551	A88	25e multicolored	1.25	.65
		Nos. 549-551 (3)	3.20	1.65

Souvenir Sheet

Perf. 14½x13½

552	A89	100e multicolored	5.50	5.50

French revolution, bicent.

Interparliamentary Union, Cent. — A90

1989, Sept. 18 **Litho.** *Perf. 14*

553	A90	2e shown	.20	.20
554	A90	4e Dove	.25	.20
555	A90	13e Natl. Assembly Bldg.	.45	.20
		Nos. 553-555 (3)	.90	.60

Traditional Ceramics A91

1989, Nov. 13 **Litho.** *Perf. 13½*

Panel Colors

556	A91	13e lilac	.50	.25
557	A91	20e red, vert.	.70	.40
558	A91	24e brown	.90	.50
559	A91	25e orange, vert.	1.00	.55
		Nos. 556-559 (4)	3.10	1.70

Outdoor Toys — A92

1989, Dec. 23

560	A92	1e Yellow truck	.20	.20
561	A92	6e Car	.20	.20
562	A92	8e White truck	.35	.20
563	A92	11.50e Trucks	.45	.25
564	A92	18e Scooter	.75	.45
565	A92	100e Boat	4.00	2.25
		Nos. 560-565 (6)	5.95	3.55

Visit of Pope John Paul II — A93

1990, Jan. 25

566	A93	13e blue & multi	.40	.25
567	A93	20e purple & multi	.75	.40

Souvenir Sheet

568	A93	200e multi, diff.	8.00	8.00

Turtles A94

1990, May 17 **Litho.** *Perf. 13½*

569	A94	50c Chelonia mydas	.20	.20
570	A94	1e Dermochelys coriacea	.20	.20
571	A94	5e Lepidochelys olivacea	.35	.20
572	A94	10e Caretta caretta	.60	.25
573	A94	42e Eretmochelys imbricata	2.75	.90
		Nos. 569-573 (5)	4.10	1.75

Women's Congress A95

1990, Aug. 13

574	A95	9e multicolored	.35	.20

A96

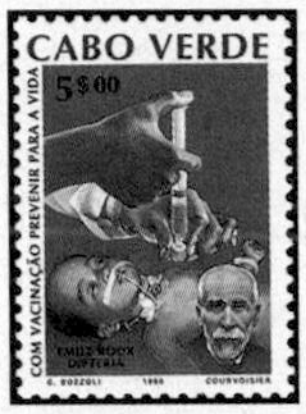

A97

Various drawings of soccer players in action.

1990, Aug. 7

575	A96	4e multicolored	.20	.20
576	A96	7.50e multicolored	.25	.20
577	A96	8e multicolored	.25	.20
578	A96	100e multicolored	3.50	2.10
		Nos. 575-578 (4)	4.20	2.70

Souvenir Sheet

579	A96	100e multi, diff.	4.50	4.50

World Cup Soccer Championships, Italy.
For surcharges see Nos. 711-712.

1990, Oct. 15 *Perf. 11½*

Vaccinations: 5e, Emile Roux (1853-1933), diphtheria. 13e, Robert Koch (1843-1910), tuberculosis. 20e, Gaston Ramon (1886-1963), tetanus. 24e, Jonas Salk (1914-95), polio.

Granite Paper

580	A97	5e multicolored	.35	.20
581	A97	13e multicolored	1.00	.25
582	A97	20e multicolored	1.40	.40
583	A97	24e multicolored	1.75	.50
		Nos. 580-583 (4)	4.50	1.35

Intl. Literacy Year — A98

Designs: 3e, Adult literacy class. 15e, Teacher holding flash card, children. 19e, Teacher, student at blackboard.

1990, Sept. 28

Granite Paper

584	A98	2e shown	.20	.20
585	A98	3e multicolored	.20	.20
586	A98	15e multicolored	.50	.25
587	A98	19e multicolored	.75	.30
		Nos. 584-587 (4)	1.65	.95

Traditional Fairy Tales A99

1990, Dec. 20 **Litho.** *Perf. 12½*

588	A99	50c shown	.20	.20
589	A99	2.50e Man catching mermaid	.25	.25
590	A99	12e Woman, snake	.50	.45
591	A99	25e Man, eggs, woman	1.00	.40
		Nos. 588-591 (4)	1.95	1.30

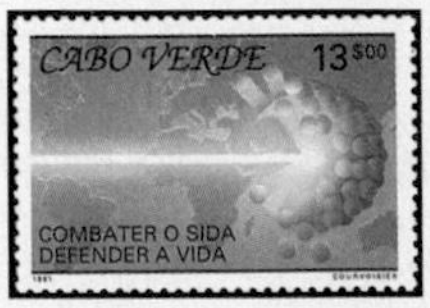

Fight Against AIDS A100

1991, Feb. 20 **Litho.** *Perf. 14*

Granite Paper

592	A100	13e multicolored	.55	.25
593	A100	24e multi, diff.	1.00	.65

Fishing — A101

24e, Man removing hook from fish. 25e, Fishing boats. 50e, Two men long-line fishing.

1991, Apr. 23 **Litho.** *Perf. 11½*

594	A101	10e multicolored	.35	.25
595	A101	24e multicolored	1.10	.60
596	A101	25e multicolored	1.25	.65
597	A101	50e multicolored	2.40	1.50
		Nos. 594-597 (4)	5.10	3.00

Medicinal Plants — A102

10e, Lavandula rotundifolia. 15e, Micromeria forbesii. 21e, Sarcostemma daltonii. 24e, Periploca chevalieri. 30e, Echium hypertropicum. 35e, Erysimum caboverdeanum.

1991, July 5 **Litho.** *Perf. 11½*

598	A102	10e multicolored	.30	.20
599	A102	15e multicolored	.55	.25
600	A102	21e multicolored	.70	.30
601	A102	24e multicolored	.90	.35
602	A102	30e multicolored	1.10	.45
603	A102	35e multicolored	1.40	.55
		Nos. 598-603 (6)	4.95	2.10

Landmarks in Old Ribeira Grande on Santiago Island A103

12.50e, Church of Our Lady of the Rosary, 1495. 15e, Ruins of the Cathedral, 1556. 20e, Fortress of San Felipe, 1587. 30e, Ruins of the Convent of St. Francis, 1642. 100e, Pillory, 1520, vert.

1991, June 25 **Litho.** *Perf. 11½*

604	A103	12.50e multicolored	.45	.25
605	A103	15e multicolored	.55	.25
606	A103	20e multicolored	.75	.45
607	A103	30e multicolored	1.10	.75
		Nos. 604-607 (4)	2.85	1.70

Souvenir Sheet

608	A103	100e multicolored	4.00	4.00

Musical Instruments — A104

1991, Oct. 9 Litho. *Perf. 11½*

609 A104 10e 6-string guitar .35 .20
610 A104 20e Violin .85 .55
611 A104 29e 5-string guitar 1.40 .65
612 A104 47e Cimba 2.00 1.25
Nos. 609-612 (4) 4.60 2.65

Souvenir Sheet

613 A104 60e Accordion, horiz. 3.00 3.00

Christmas A105

1991, Dec. 20 Litho. *Perf. 11½*

614 A105 31e Nativity scene 1.10 .50
615 A105 50e Nativity scene, diff. 1.75 .90

Discovery of America, 500th Anniv. A106

1992, Mar. 31 Litho. *Perf. 11½*

616 A106 40e shown 2.00 1.10
617 A106 40e Columbus on ship 2.00 1.10
a. Pair, #616-617 4.50 4.50

Souvenir Sheet

618 A106 Sheet of 2 8.00 8.00

Stamps in No. 618 are smaller, without white border and "Luis Duran" and "Courvoisier" inscriptions. No. 618 was printed in continuous design and sold for 150e.

Souvenir Sheet

Granada '92 — A107

Illustration reduced.

1992, Apr.24 *Perf. 11½*

619 A107 50e multicolored 8.00 8.00

No. 619 sold for 150e.

Tropical Fruits A108

1992, Feb. 29 *Perf. 12x11½*

620 A108 16e Syzygium jambos .65 .30
621 A108 25e Mangifera indica 1.10 .50
622 A108 31e Anacardium occidentale 1.40 .65
623 A108 32e Persea americana 1.60 .75
Nos. 620-623 (4) 4.75 2.20

1992 Summer Olympics, Barcelona A109

1992, June 30 Litho. *Perf. 13½*

624 A109 16e Women's javelin .60 .25
625 A109 20e Weight lifting .75 .30
626 A109 32e Women's pole vault 1.40 .65
627 A109 40e Women's shot put 1.60 .85
Nos. 624-627 (4) 4.35 2.05

Souvenir Sheet

628 A109 100e Women's gymnastics 4.25 4.25

Sugar Cane Production — A110

Designs: 19e, Oxen, sugar cane. 20e, Oxen yoked to press. 37e, Man placing cane inside press. 38e, Refining process.

1992, Nov. Litho. *Perf. 11*

629 A110 19e multicolored .65 .30
630 A110 20e multicolored .65 .30
631 A110 37e multicolored 1.25 .60
632 A110 38e multicolored 1.40 .60
Nos. 629-632 (4) 3.95 1.80

Domestic Animals A111

1992, Nov. *Perf. 13½*

633 A111 16e Cat .65 .40
634 A111 31e Chickens 1.10 .80
635 A111 32e Dog, vert. 1.25 .90
636 A111 50e Horse 2.00 1.25
Nos. 633-636 (4) 5.00 3.35

Corals A112

1993, Apr. 29 Litho. *Perf. 11½*

637 A112 5e Tubastrea aurea .20 .20
638 A112 31e Corallium rubrum 1.25 .80
639 A112 37e Porites porites 1.50 1.00
640 A112 50e Millepora alcicornis 2.00 1.25
Nos. 637-640 (4) 4.95 3.25

Treaty of Tordesillas, 500th Anniv. (in 1994) A113

Designs: No. 641, King Ferdinand, Queen Isabella of Spain, Pope Alexander VI. No. 642, Pope Julius II, King John II of Portugal. No. 643, Astrolabe, treaty signing. No. 644, Compass rose, map.

1993, Aug. 1 Litho. *Perf. 12x11½*

641 A113 37e multicolored 1.40 .65
642 A113 37e multicolored 1.40 .65
a. Pair, #641-642 3.25 3.25
643 A113 38e multicolored 1.40 .65
644 A113 38e multicolored 1.40 .65
a. Pair, #643-644 3.25 3.25
Nos. 641-644 (4) 5.60 2.60

Souvenir Sheet

Santiago Island, 1806 — A114

1993, July 30 *Perf. 13½*

645 A114 100e multicolored 4.25 4.25

Brasiliana '93.

Lobsters — A115

1993, Sept. 29 Litho. *Perf. 11½*

646 A115 2e Palinurus charlestoni .30 .20
647 A115 10e Panulirus echinatus .60 .25
648 A115 17e Panulirus regius 1.10 .50
649 A115 38e Scyllarides latus 2.50 1.00
Nos. 646-649 (4) 4.50 1.95

Souvenir Sheet

650 A115 100e Panulirus regius, diff. 6.00 6.00

No. 650 contains one 51x36mm stamp.

Birds A116

1993, Oct. 29 Litho. *Perf. 12x11½*

651 A116 10e Calonectris edwardsii .75 .25
652 A116 30e Sula leucogaster 2.25 .85
653 A116 40e Fregata magnificens 3.00 1.10
a. Souvenir sheet of 1 10.00 10.00
654 A116 41e Phaeton aethereus 3.25 1.10
Nos. 651-654 (4) 9.25 3.30

Hong Kong '94 (#653a). No. 653a sold for 150e.

Flowers A117

1993, Dec. 16 Litho. *Perf. 12x11½*

655 A117 5e Rosa alexandra .20
656 A117 30e Strelitzia reginae 1.10 .80
657 A117 37e Dianthus barbatus 1.50 1.00
a. Souvenir sheet of 1 6.50 6.50
658 A117 50e Dahlia 1.90 1.25
Nos. 655-658 (4) 4.70 3.05

Singapore '95 (#657a). Issued 9/1/95. No. 657a sold for 150e.

1994 World Cup Soccer Championships, US — A118

Players, US flag, and: 1e, Giant's Stadium, New Jersey. 20e, Rose Bowl Stadium, Pasadena. 37e, Foxboro Stadium, Boston. 38e, Silverdome, Pontiac. 100e, RFK Stadium, Washington DC.

1994, May 31 Litho. *Perf. 11½*

659 A118 1e multicolored .20 .20
660 A118 20e multicolored .85 .50
661 A118 37e multicolored 1.50 1.00
662 A118 38e multicolored 1.60 1.10
Nos. 659-662 (4) 4.15 2.80

Souvenir Sheet

663 A118 100e multicolored 4.25 4.25

Prince Henry the Navigator (1394-1460) — A119

Illustration reduced.

1994, Mar. 4 Litho. *Perf. 12*

664 A119 37e multicolored 2.00 1.00

See Brazil #2463, Macao #719, Portugal #1987.

Sharks A120

1994, June 27 Litho. *Perf. 12x11½*

665 A120 21e Eugomphodus taurus .85 .50
666 A120 27e Carcharhinus limbatus 1.10 .70
667 A120 37e Rhiniodon typus 1.50 1.00
668 A120 38e Etmopterus spinax 1.75 1.10
Nos. 665-668 (4) 5.20 3.30

Bananas A121

1994, Aug. 16 Litho. *Perf. 11½*

669 A121 12e Prata, vert. .40 .25
670 A121 16e Pao .65 .40
671 A121 30e Ana roberta, vert. 1.25 .85
672 A121 40e Roxa, vert. 1.50 1.10
Nos. 669-672 (4) 3.80 2.60

Souvenir Sheet

673 A121 100e Prata, diff., vert. 7.75 7.75

PHILAKOREA '94, SINGPEX '94 (#673). No. 673 sold for 150e.

Lighthouses — A122

1994, Oct. 17 *Perf. 12*

674 A122 2e Fontes Pereira de Melo .20 .20
675 A122 37e Morro Negro 1.50 1.00
676 A122 38e Amelia, vert. 1.50 1.10
677 A122 50e Maria Pia, vert. 2.00 1.40
Nos. 674-677 (4) 5.20 3.70

Wilhelm Roentgen (1845-1923), Discovery of the X-Ray, Cent. — A123

1995, Mar. 31 Litho. *Perf. 12*

678 A123 20e yellow & multi .80 .50
679 A123 37e blue & multi 1.50 1.00
a. Souvenir sheet of 2, #678-679 4.50 4.50

No. 679a sold for 100e.

A124

FAO, 50th Anniv. — A125

1995, May 17 Litho. Perf. 12
680 A124 37e multicolored 1.50 .90
681 A125 38e multicolored 1.50 .90

Dogs A126

Dog, scene depicting story of dogs: 1e, Fox terrier, Two foxhounds and fox terrier, by John Emms. 10e, Cavalier King Charles, Shooting over Dogs, by Richard Ansdell. 40e, Rough collie, German shepherd. 50e, Braco, Hounds at Full Cry, by Thomas Blinks.

1995, June 16 Litho. Perf. 12x11½
682 A126 1e multicolored .25 .20
683 A126 10e multicolored .55 .25
684 A126 40e multicolored 2.25 1.25
685 A126 50e multicolored 2.75 1.10
Nos. 682-685 (4) 5.80 2.80

Independence, 20th Anniv. — A127

1995, July 20 Litho. Perf. 12
686 A127 37e multicolored 1.90 1.25

Traditional Festival A128

Designs: 2e, Horse race. 10e, Horseman leading parade. 37e, People singing, playing drums. 40e, Playing game on horseback.

1995, Oct. 9 Perf. 12x11½
687 A128 2e multicolored .20 .20
688 A128 10e multicolored .45 .25
689 A128 37e multicolored 1.50 .85
690 A128 40e multicolored 1.75 1.00
Nos. 687-690 (4) 3.90 2.30

Children's Stories A130

Designs: 10e, The cicadas making music, ants. 25e, Cicada being exposed to light. 38e, Cicada with guitar, ants working. 45e, Ants at table making fun of cicada.

1995, Dec. 15 Litho. Perf. 11½
692 A130 10e multicolored .40 .55
693 A130 25e multicolored .85 .85
694 A130 38e multicolored 1.40 1.10
695 A130 45e multicolored 1.60 1.00
Nos. 692-695 (4) 4.25 3.50

Endangered Plants — A131

20e, Sonchus daltonii. 37e, Echium vulcanorum. 38e, Nauplius smithii. 50e, Campanula jacobaea.

1996, Apr. 24 Litho. Perf. 11½
696 A131 20e multicolored .65 .40
697 A131 37e multicolored 1.20 .75
698 A131 38e multicolored 1.20 .75
699 A131 50e multicolored 1.60 1.10
Nos. 696-699 (4) 4.65 3.00

1996 Summer Olympic Games, Atlanta A132

1996, June 30 Litho. Perf. 11½
700 A132 1e Tennis .20 .20
701 A132 37e Gymnastics 1.10 .75
702 A132 100e Athletics 3.25 2.10
Nos. 700-702 (3) 4.55 3.05

UNICEF, 50th Anniv. — A133

Water Sports — A134

1996, Aug. 1 Litho. Perf. 12
703 A133 20e Young girl .90 .40
704 A133 40e Mother, child 1.75 .85

1996, Oct. 9 Litho. Perf. 12

Designs: 2.50e, Fishing. 10e, Windsurfing. 22e, Jet skiing. No. 708, Surfing, horiz. No. 709, Diver's hand, pufferfish, horiz.

705 A134 2.50e multicolored .20 .20
706 A134 10e multicolored .35 .20
707 A134 22e multicolored .70 .45
708 A134 100e multicolored 3.25 2.10
Nos. 705-708 (4) 4.50 2.95

Souvenir Sheet

709 A134 100e multicolored 4.50 4.50

No. 709 contains one 80x61mm stamp.

Nos. 507, 575-576 Surcharged

a

b

1997 Litho. Perf. 14
710 A77(a) 3e on 2.50e #507 .20 .20

Perf. 13½
711 A96(b) 37e on 4e #575 1.25 .75
712 A96(a) 38e on 7.50e #576 1.25 .75
Nos. 710-712 (3) 2.70 1.70

Natl. Symbols A135

1997 Perf. 12
713 A135 25e Arms .80 .50
714 A135 37e Anthem 1.10 .75
715 A135 50e Flag 1.60 1.00
Nos. 713-715 (3) 3.50 2.25

World Wildlife Fund A136

Pristis pectinata: a, On seabed. b, Swimming, school of small fish. c, Swimming along seabed, small fish. d, Two near seabed.

1997 Litho. Perf. 11½
716 A136 15e Strip of 4, #a.-d. 9.00 9.00

Legends of the Sea — A137

a, Fish, dolphins. b, Merman, mermaid. c, Fish swimming through portal, moray eel.

1997 Litho. Perf. 11½
717 A137 45e Strip of 3, #a.-c. 4.00 4.00

Fish A138

Designs: 13e, Thunnus albacares. 21e, Thunnus obesus. 41e, Euthynnus alletteratus. 45e, Katsuwonus pelamis.

1997 Litho. Perf. 12
718 A138 13e multicolored .35 .30
719 A138 21e multicolored .65 .60
720 A138 41e multicolored 1.40 1.25
721 A138 45e multicolored 1.60 1.50
Nos. 718-721 (4) 4.00 3.65

1998 World Cup Soccer Championships, France — A139

Designs: 30e, Soccer ball in net, vert. 45e, Soccer player, ball, vert. 50e, Globe, ball, World Cup trophy, fans in stadium.

1998 Litho. Perf. 12x11½, 11½x12
722 A139 10e shown .30 .25
723 A139 30e multicolored .80 .80
724 A139 45e multicolored 1.25 1.25
725 A139 50e multicolored 1.50 1.40
Nos. 722-725 (4) 3.85 3.70

Traditional Cuisine A140

5e, Boiled fish. 25e, Xerém com friginato. 35e, Cachupa. 40e, Molho de Saint-Nicholas.

1998 Litho. Perf. 12x11½
726 A140 5e multicolored .20 .20
727 A140 25e multicolored .65 .65
728 A140 35e multicolored 1.00 1.00
729 A140 40e multicolored 1.10 1.10
Nos. 726-729 (4) 2.95 2.95

Early Exploration A141

a, Quotation from Lusiadas, two men looking at maps. b, Man with sword, man & woman. c, Compass, map, sailing ship, buildings on cliff.

1998 Perf. 11½
730 A141 50e Strip of 3, #a.-c. 4.00 4.00

Women's Traditional Costumes — A142

1998 Litho. Perf. 12
731 A142 10e Brava .25 .25
732 A142 18e Fogo .50 .50
733 A142 30e Boa Vista .80 .80
734 A142 50e Santiago 1.40 1.40
Nos. 731-734 (4) 2.95 2.95

Butterflies and Moths A143

Designs: 5e, Byblia ilithyia. 10e, Aganais speciosa. 20e, Utetheisia pulchella. 30e, Vanessa cardui. 50e, Trichoplusia ni. 100e, Grammodes congenita.

1999, Mar. 16 Litho. Perf. 11¾
735 A143 5e multi .20 .20
736 A143 10e multi .25 .25
737 A143 20e multi .50 .50
738 A143 30e multi .80 .80
a. Souvenir sheet, #737-738 4.00 4.00
739 A143 50e multi 1.25 1.25
740 A143 100e multi 2.60 2.60
Nos. 735-740 (6) 5.60 5.60

No. 738a sold for 100e.

First Concorde Flight, 30th Anniv. A144

Concorde: 30e, In flight. 50e, On ground.

1999, June 14 Litho. Perf. 12
741-742 A144 Set of 2 2.75 2.75

Famous People — A145

Design: 30e, Alain Gerbault (1893-1941), sailor, boats at dock. 50e, Roberto Duarte Silva (1837-89), chemist, Eiffel Tower.

1999, July 2 Litho. *Perf. 14½*

743	A145 30e multi	2.00	2.00
744	A145 50e multi	3.25	3.25
744a	Souvenir sheet, #743-744	6.50	6.50

Philex France 99 (#744a).

A146

UPU, 125th Anniv. A147

1999, Sept. 15 *Perf. 12x11¾*

745	A146 30e shown	20.00	20.00
746	A147 50e shown	20.00	20.00

With Country Name Added

747	A146 30e multi	.65	.65
748	A147 50e multi	1.10	1.10
	Nos. 745-748 (4)	41.75	41.75

Dance A148

Designs: 10e, Colá Sanjon, vert. 30e, Contradança, vert. 50e, Desfile de tabanca. 100e, Batuque.

Perf. 11¾x12, 12x11¾

1999, Nov. 5 Litho.

749-752 A148 Set of 4 5.00 5.00

Millennium — A149

Designs: 40e, Globe, hourglass and open antique book inscribed "2000," vert. 50e, "2000 Milenio."

2000, Jan. 31 Litho. *Perf. 11¾x11½*

753-754 A149 Set of 2 2.50 2.50

SOS Children's Villages A150

Emblem and child: 50e, Seated, vert. 100e, With arms outstretched.

smile ***Perf. 11¾x12, 12x11¾***

2000, Apr. 28 Litho.

755-756 A150 Set of 2 4.00 4.00

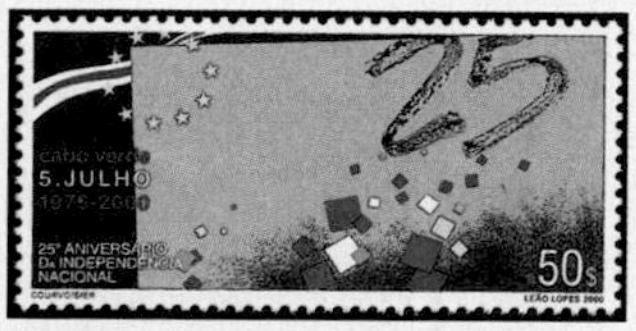

Independence, 25th Anniv. — A151

2000, July 5 *Perf. 11¾*

757 A151 50e multi 1.25 1.25

2000 Summer Olympics, Sydney A152

Designs: 10e, Women's gymnastics. 40e, Taekwondo. 50e, Women's hurdles.

2000, Sept. 15 Litho. *Perf. 11¾*

758-760	A152 Set of 3	2.60	2.60
760a	Souvenir sheet of 3, #758-760	2.75	2.75

Dragoeiro Tree — A153

2000, Oct. 9 Litho. *Perf. 11¾x11½*

761	A153 5e green	.20	.20
762	A153 40e red	1.00	1.00
763	A153 60e brown	1.60	1.60

Sao Nicolau Seminary and School — A154

No. 764: a, Seminarians and students (denomination at LR, 27x26mm). b, Seminarians and students (denomination at LL, 29x26mm). c, José Alves Feijo, Dr. Julio Dias and Canon António Bouças (56x26mm).

Illustration reduced.

2000, Dec. 15 Litho. *Perf. 14½*

764 A154 60e Horiz. strip of 3, #a-c 5.00 5.00

Fish A155

Designs: 10e, Diplodus sargus lineatus. 22e, Diplodus prayensis. 28e, Lithognathus mormyrus. 48e, Diplodus fasciatus. 60e, Diplodus puntazzo.

2001, Apr. 24 *Perf. 12x11¾*

765-769 A155 Set of 5 5.00 5.00

Spiders A156

Designs: 13e, Thomisus onustus. 16e, Scytodes velutina. 40e, Hersiliola simoni. 100e, Loxosceles rufescens.

2001, May 28

770-773 A156 Set of 4 5.00 5.00

Trees — A156a

Designs: 50e, Acacia albida. 60e, Ficus sycomorus.

2001, June 9 Litho. *Perf. 11¾x11½*

773A-773B A156a Set of 2 2.75 2.75

Souvenir Sheet

Belgica 2001 Intl. Stamp Exhibition, Brussels — A157

Perf. 11¾x11½

2001, June 9 Photo.

774 A157 100e multi 2.75 2.75

Medicinal Plants — A157a

Designs: 20e, Artimisia gorgonum. 27e, Globularia amygdalifolia. 47.50e, Sidereoxylon marginata, horiz. 50e, Umbilicus schmidtii, horiz. 60e, Verbascum cystolithicum. 100e, Limonium lobinii.

Perf. 11¾x12, 12x11¾

2001, Sept. 27 Litho.

774A-774F A157a Set of 6 8.00 8.00

Year of Dialogue Among Civilizations — A158

2001, Oct. 9 Litho. *Perf. 11¾x12*

775 A158 60e multi 1.60 1.60

António Aurélio Gonçalves (1901-84), Writer — A159

2001, Dec. 20 *Perf. 12¼*

776 A159 100e multi 2.75 2.75

Medicinal Plants A160

Designs: 10e, Euphorbia tuckeyna. 50e, Limonium sunding, vert. 60e, Aeonium gorgoneum, vert. 100e, Polycarpaea gayi, vert.

Perf. 12x11¾, 11¾x12

2002, Apr. 26 Litho.

777-780 A160 Set of 4 5.75 5.75

2002 World Cup Soccer Championships, Japan and Korea — A161

Designs: 60e, Player heading ball towards goal. 100e, Player kicking ball towards goal.

2002, July 22 *Perf. 12x11¾*

781-782 A161 Set of 2 4.00 4.00

Caretta Caretta A162

Designs: 10e, Pair mating. 20e, Female laying eggs, vert. 30e, Eggs hatching. 60e, Hatchlings heading for sea, vert. No. 787, 100e, Turtle swimming underwater.

No. 788, 100e, Turtle on beach.

2002, Sept. 9 *Perf. 12x11¾, 11¾x12*

783-787 A162 Set of 5 6.50 6.50

Souvenir Sheet

788 A162 100e multi 3.00 3.00

No. 788 contains one 80x60mm stamp.

Basketry A163

Baskets and basket weavers from: 20e, Sao Nicolau Island. 33e, Santo Antao Island. 60e, Santiago Island, 100e, Boa Vista Island.

2002, Oct. 29 *Perf. 12x11¾*

789-792 A163 Set of 4 6.50 6.50

Composers and Poets A164

Designs: 12e, Katcháss (1951-88), composer. 20e, Jorge Monteiro (1913-98), composer. 32e, Luis Rendall (1898-1986), composer. 47.50e, Jorge Barbosa (1902-71), poet. 60e, Januário Leite (1865-1930), poet. 100e, José Lopes (1872-1962), poet.

2003, Feb. 24

793-798 A164 Set of 6 7.50 7.50

Birds — A165

Designs: 10e, Ardea bournei. 27e, Ardea cinerea. 42e, Bubulcus ibis. 60e, Egretta garzeta.

2003, July 9 *Perf. 14x13¾*

799-802 A165 Set of 4 4.00 4.00

Cesaria Evora, Singer A166

Designs: 60e, Evora at left. 100e, Evora at right.
200e, Feet of Evora.

2003, May 26 *Perf. 13¾x14*
803-804 A166 Set of 2 4.50 4.50

Souvenir Sheet
Perf. 12¼x12
805 A166 200e multi + label 6.00 6.00

No. 805 contains one 50x38mm stamp.

Scouting in Cape Verde A167

Emblem and scout of: 60e, Scouts Association of Cape Verde. 100e, Cape Verde Scouts Corps.

2003, Oct. 24 Litho. *Perf. 13¾x14*
806-807 A167 Set of 2 4.50 4.50

Whales A168

Designs: 10e, Balaenoptera musculus. 20e, Physeter macrocephalus. 50e, Megaptera novaeangliae. 60e, Globicephala macrorhynchus.

2003, Nov. 25 *Perf. 12*
808-811 A168 Set of 4 6.00 6.00

First Dakar — Praia Seaplane Flight of Europe — Africa — South America Airmail Service, 75th Anniv. — A169

Seaplane and: 10e, Crew. 42e, Pilot Paulin Paris, map of South America — Africa route. 60e, Map of entire route.
100e, Like 10e.

2003, Dec. 11 *Perf. 14*
812-814 A169 Set of 3 3.25 3.25

Souvenir Sheet
815 A169 100e multi 3.00 3.00

Election of Pope John Paul II, 25th Anniv. — A170

Pope John Paul II and: 30e, Girl. 60e, Boats, horiz.
100e, Censer and crucifix.

2003, Dec. 29 *Perf. 14x13¾, 13¾x14*
816-817 A170 Set of 2 2.40 2.40

Souvenir Sheet
818 A170 100e multi 3.00 3.00

Trees A171

Windmill A172

Designs: 20e, Khaya senegalensis. 27e, Acacia nilotica. 60e, Ceiba pentandra. 100e, Phoenix atlantica.

2004, Jan. 25 *Perf. 14x13¾*
819-822 A171 Set of 4 5.50 5.50

2004, June 3 *Perf. 13¼x13*

Colors: 20e, Blue. 60e, Red. 100e, Green.

823-825 A172 Set of 3 4.75 4.75

2004 Summer Olympics, Athens — A173

Designs: 10e, Taekwondo. 60e, Rhythmic gymnastics. 100e, Boxing, horiz.

Perf. 13¼x13, 13x13¼
2004, Aug. 13 **Litho.**
826-828 A173 Set of 3 4.75 4.75

Lighthouses A174

Designs: 10e, Ponta do Barril Lighthouse, Sao Nicolau Island. 30e, Ponta Jalunga Lighthouse, Brava Island. 40e, D. Luis Lighthouse, Passaros Islands, horiz. 50e, Ponta Preta Lighthouse, Santiago Island, horiz.

2004, Sept. 7
829-832 A174 Set of 4 4.00 4.00

Houses on Fogo Island A175

Various houses: 20e, 40e, 50e, 60e.

2004, Oct. 9 *Perf. 13x13¼*
833-836 A175 Set of 4 4.75 4.75

Telephones — A176

Old telephones and: 10e, Switchboard. 40e, Operator. 60e, Telephone directory. 100e, Truck and telephone poles.

2004, Nov. 12
837-840 A176 Set of 4 5.50 5.50

Oral Stories and Legends A177

Designs: 10e, Stória Stória. 20e, Era um Vez! 30e, Sapatinha Ribera Baxu. 60e, Quem ki Sabi Mas, Conta Midjor!, vert.

Perf. 13x13¼, 13¼x13
2005, Feb. 21 **Litho.**
841-844 A177 Set of 4 3.50 3.50

Amilcar Cabral (1924-73), Revolutionary Leader — A178

2005, June 30 Litho. *Perf. 13¼x13*
845 A178 60e multi 1.60 1.60

Independence, 30th anniv.

Shells A179

Designs: 30e, Conus evorai. 40e, Harpa doris. 50e, Strombus lotus. 60e, Phyllonotus duplex.

2005, July 18 *Perf. 13x13¼*
846-849 A179 Set of 4 5.00 5.00

Birds — A180

Designs: 19e, Passer iagoensis. 42e, Estrilda astrild. 44e, Passer domesticus. 55e, Acrocephalus brevipennis.

2005, Aug. 8 *Perf. 13¼x13*
850-853 A180 Set of 4 4.25 4.25

World Summit on the Information Society, Tunis A181

2005, Nov. 16 Litho. *Perf. 13x13¼*
854 A181 60e multi 1.60 1.60

Artifacts of the Slave Trade A182

Designs: 5e, Pipe. 10e, Telescope. 30e, Cannon. 60e, Nautical instrument.
100e, Shackles.

2006, Jan. 31
855-858 A182 Set of 4 3.00 3.00

Souvenir Sheet
859 A182 100e multi 3.00 3.00

No. 859 contains one 80x60mm stamp.

AIR POST STAMPS

Common Design Type
Name and Value in Black
Perf. 13½x13

1938, July 26 **Unwmk.**

C1	CD39	10c	red orange	.60	.50
C2	CD39	20c	purple	.60	.50
C3	CD39	50c	orange	.60	.50
C4	CD39	1e	ultra	.60	.50
C5	CD39	2e	lilac brown	1.40	.80
C6	CD39	3e	dk green	1.75	1.40
C7	CD39	5e	red brown	5.50	2.10
C8	CD39	9e	rose carmine	9.00	3.75
C9	CD39	10e	magenta	9.75	5.00
			Nos. C1-C9 (9)	29.80	15.05
			Set, never hinged	50.00	

No. C7 exists with overprint "Exposicao Internacional de Nova York, 1939-1940" and Trylon and Perisphere.

POSTAGE DUE STAMPS

D1

D2

1904 **Unwmk.** **Typo.** *Perf. 12*

J1	D1	5r	yellow grn	.40	*.25*
J2	D1	10r	slate	.40	*.25*
J3	D1	20r	yellow brn	.50	*.40*
J4	D1	30r	red orange	1.25	*.40*
J5	D1	50r	gray brown	.50	*.35*
J6	D1	60r	red brown	9.25	4.25
J7	D1	100r	lilac	1.75	1.25
J8	D1	130r	dull blue	1.90	1.25
J9	D1	200r	carmine	1.60	1.60
J10	D1	500r	dull violet	5.00	*3.00*
			Nos. J1-J10 (10)	22.55	*13.00*

Overprinted in Carmine or Green

1911

J11	D1	5r	yellow grn	.30	.20
J12	D1	10r	slate	.30	.20
J13	D1	20r	yellow brn	.35	.20
J14	D1	30r	orange	.35	.20
J15	D1	50r	gray brown	.65	.40
J16	D1	60r	red brown	.65	.40
J17	D1	100r	lilac	.65	.40
J18	D1	130r	dull blue	.75	.65
J19	D1	200r	carmine (G)	2.00	1.50
J20	D1	500r	dull violet	2.50	1.75
			Nos. J11-J20 (10)	8.50	5.90

1921 *Perf. 11½*

J21	D2	½c	yellow grn	.30	.20
J22	D2	1c	slate	.30	.20
J23	D2	2c	red brown	.30	.20
J24	D2	3c	orange	.30	.20
J25	D2	5c	gray brown	.30	.20
J26	D2	6c	lt brown	.30	.20
J27	D2	10c	red violet	.30	.20
J28	D2	13c	dull blue	.55	*.40*
J29	D2	20c	carmine	.60	*.50*
J30	D2	50c	gray	1.75	*1.10*
			Nos. J21-J30 (10)	5.00	*3.40*

Catalogue values for unused stamps in this section, from this point to the end of the section, are for Never Hinged items.

Common Design Type
Photogravure and Typographed
1952 Unwmk. *Perf. 14*
Numeral in Red, Frame Multicolored

J31 CD45 10c chocolate .30 .25
J32 CD45 30c black brown .30 .25
J33 CD45 50c dark blue .30 .25
J34 CD45 1e dark blue .40 .25
J35 CD45 2e red brown .40 .30
J36 CD45 5e olive green 1.10 1.00
Nos. J31-J36 (6) 2.80 2.30

NEWSPAPER STAMP

N1

1893 Typo. Unwmk. *Perf. 11½*
P1 N1 2½r brown 1.50 .60
a. Perf. 12½ 3.00 1.50
b. Perf. 13½ 6.50 3.00

For surcharges see Nos. 79, 206.

POSTAL TAX STAMPS

Pombal Issue
Common Design Types
1925 Unwmk. Engr. *Perf. 12½*
RA1 CD28 15c dull vio & blk 1.25 1.10
RA2 CD29 15c dull vio & blk 1.25 1.10
RA3 CD30 15c dull vio & blk 1.25 1.10
Nos. RA1-RA3 (3) 3.75 3.30

St. Isabel — PT1

PT2

1948 Litho. *Perf. 11*
RA4 PT1 50c dark green 3.75 2.40
RA5 PT1 1e henna brown 7.50 3.00

Catalogue values for unused stamps in this section, from this point to the end of the section, are for Never Hinged items.

No. RA5 Surcharged with New Value and Bars
1959
RA6 PT1 50c on 1e henna brown 1.40 1.10

Perf. 14
RA7 PT1 50c carmine rose 2.10 1.00
RA8 PT1 1e blue 2.10 1.00

St. Isabel Type Redrawn
1967-73 Litho. *Perf. 14*
RA9 PT1 30c (blue panel) .40 .40
RA9A PT1 30c (orange panel) .40 .40
RA10 PT1 50c (lilac rose panel) .85 .85
RA11 PT1 50c (red panel) ('72) *.45 .45*
RA12 PT1 1e (brn panel) .90 .90
RA13 PT1 1e (red lilac panel) ('72) *.90 .90*
Nos. RA9-RA13 (6) *3.90 3.90*

Nos. RA9-RA13 are inscribed "ASSISTENCIA" in large letters in bottom panel and "PORTUGAL" and "CABO VERDE" in small letters in upper left corner.

Revenue Stamps Surcharged in Green, Blue or Black
1967-72 Typo. *Perf. 12*
Black "CABO VERDE" & Value
Pale Green Burelage
RA14 PT2 50c on 1c org (Bl) ('71) 1.40 .90
a. Black surcharge ('68?) *15.00 14.50*
RA15 PT2 50c on 2c org (Bk) ('69) *15.00 14.50*
c. Inverted surcharge *50.00 35.00*
RA16 PT2 50c on 3c org (G) ('72) 1.10 .60
RA17 PT2 50c on 5c org (G) ('72) 1.10 .60
RA18 PT2 50c on 10c org (G) ('71) 1.25 1.00
RA19 PT2 1e on 1c org (Bk) 2.75 2.10
RA20 PT2 1e on 2c org (G) ('71) 1.90 1.75
a. Blue surcharge ('71) 2.00 1.10
b. Black surcharge 2.10 2.10
Nos. RA14-RA20 (7) *24.50 21.45*

POSTAL TAX DUE STAMPS

Pombal Issue
Common Design Types
1925 Unwmk. *Perf. 12½*
RAJ1 CD28 30c dull vio & blk .75 .70
RAJ2 CD29 30c dull vio & blk .75 .70
RAJ3 CD30 30c dull vio & blk .75 .70
Nos. RAJ1-RAJ3 (3) 2.25 2.10

CAROLINE ISLANDS

ˈkar-ə-ˌlīn ˈī-lənds

LOCATION — A group of about 549 small islands in the West Pacific Ocean, north of the Equator.
GOVT. — German colony
AREA — 550 sq. mi.
POP. — 40,000 (approx. 1915)

100 Pfennig = 1 Mark

Watermark

Wmk. 125 — Lozenges

#2

#2a

Stamps of Germany 1889-90 Overprinted in Black
Overprinted at 56 degree Angle
1900 Unwmk. *Perf. 13½x14½*
1 A9 3pf dk brown 13.00 *14.00*
2 A9 5pf green 18.00 *18.00*
3 A10 10pf carmine 19.00 *19.00*
4 A10 20pf ultra 24.00 *30.00*
5 A10 25pf orange 55.00 *65.00*
6 A10 50pf red brown 55.00 *65.00*
Nos. 1-6 (6) 184.00 *211.00*

1899
Overprinted at 48 degree Angle
1a A9 3pf light brown 625.00 *750.00*
2a A9 5pf green 650.00 575.00
3a A10 10pf carmine 62.50 *150.00*
4a A10 20pf ultra 62.50 *150.00*
5a A10 25pf orange *1,650.* *3,100.*
6a A10 50pf red brown *900.00* *1,600.*

A3

Kaiser's Yacht "Hohenzollern" — A4

1901, Jan. Typo. *Perf. 14*
7 A3 3pf brown 1.10 *1.75*
8 A3 5pf green 1.10 *2.10*
9 A3 10pf carmine 1.10 *5.00*
a. Half used as 5pf on cover, back-stamped in Jaluit ('05) *110.00*
10 A3 20pf ultra 1.25 *9.00*
a. Half used as 10pf on cover ('10) *8,500.*
11 A3 25pf org & blk, *yel* 1.60 *14.50*
12 A3 30pf org & blk, *sal* 1.60 *14.50*
13 A3 40pf lake & blk 1.60 *16.50*
14 A3 50pf pur & blk, *sal* 2.00 *22.50*
15 A3 80pf lake & blk, *rose* 3.00 *25.00*

Perf. 14½x14
Engr.
16 A4 1m carmine 4.50 *62.50*
17 A4 2m blue 7.25 *87.50*
18 A4 3m black violet 10.00 *150.00*
19 A4 5m slate & carmine 160.00 *550.00*
Nos. 7-19 (13) 196.10 *960.85*

No. 9a is known as the "typhoon provisional" the stock of 5pf stamps having been destroyed during a typhoon. Covers (cards) without backstamp, value about $90.

Forged cancellations are found on #7-19.

No. 7 Handstamp Surcharged

1910, July 12
20 A3 5pf on 3pf brown *5,500.*
a. Inverted surcharge *7,750.*
b. Double surcharge *11,000.*

Values are for stamps tied to cover. Stamps on piece sell for about 40% less.

1915-19 Wmk. 125 Typo.
21 A3 3pf brown ('19) .90
22 A3 5pf green 12.50

Engr.
23 A4 5m slate & carmine 35.00
Nos. 21-23 (3) 48.40

Nos. 21-23 were not placed in use.

CASTELLORIZO

ˌkäs-tə-ˈlor-ə-ˌzō

(Castelrosso)

LOCATION — A Mediterranean island in the Dodecanese group lying close to the coast of Asia Minor and about 60 miles east of Rhodes.
GOVT. — Former Italian Colony
AREA — 4 sq. mi.
POP. — 2,238 (1936)

Formerly a Turkish possession, Castellorizo was occupied by the French in 1915 and ceded to Italy after World War I. In 1945 it became part of Greece.

25 Centimes = 1 Piaster
100 Centimes = 1 Franc

Used values in italics are for postally used copies. Stamps with CTO cancels sell for about the same as hinged, unused stamps.

Issued under French Occupation

Stamps of French Offices in Turkey Overprinted

1920 Unwmk. *Perf. 14x13½*
1 A2 1c gray 52.50 *60.00*
a. Inverted overprint 225.00 225.00
b. Double overprint 340.00 *440.00*
2 A2 2c vio brn 55.00 *65.00*
a. Double overprint 325.00 *400.00*
3 A2 3c red org 52.50 *60.00*
a. Inverted overprint 225.00 225.00
4 A2 5c green 80.00 80.00
a. Inverted overprint 260.00 260.00
5 A3 10c rose 92.50 92.50
6 A3 15c pale red 125.00 125.00
a. Inverted overprint 450.00 450.00
7 A3 20c brn vio 125.00 125.00
8 A5 1pi on 25c blue 120.00 120.00
a. Pair, one without overprint 800.00
9 A3 30c lilac 140.00 140.00

Overprint Reading Down
10 A4 40c red & pale bl 190.00 190.00
a. Inverted ovpt (reading up) 825.00 825.00
11 A6 2pi on 50c bis brn & lav 210.00 *225.00*
a. Inverted ovpt (reading up) 825.00 825.00
b. Double overprint 1,100. *1,100.*
12 A6 4pi on 1fr cl & ol grn 260.00 *300.00*
a. Double overprint 1,100. 1,100.
b. Inverted ovpt (reading up) 950.00 900.00
13 A6 20pi on 5fr dk bl & buff 600.00 *650.00*
a. Double overprint 1,600. *1,600.*
Nos. 1-13 (13) 2,102. 2,232.

No. 1-9 were overprinted in blocks of 25. Position 4 had "CASTELLORIZO" inverted and Positions 8 and 18 had "CASTELLORISO." The later variety also occurred in the setting of the form for Nos. 10-13.

"B. N. F." are the initials of "Base Navale Francaise".

Overprinted in Black or Red

1920
On Stamps of French Offices in Turkey
14 A2 1c gray 32.50 *36.00*
15 A2 2c vio brn 36.00 *40.00*
16 A2 3c red org 60.00 *65.00*
17 A2 5c green (R) 32.50 32.50
19 A3 10c rose 40.00 40.00
20 A3 15c pale red 65.00 65.00
21 A3 20c brn vio 92.50 92.50
22 A5 1pi on 25c bl (R) 60.00 60.00
23 A3 30c lilac (R) 67.50 67.50
24 A4 40c red & pale bl 65.00 65.00
25 A6 2pi on 50c bis brn & lav 60.00 60.00
26 A6 4pi on 1fr claret & ol grn 92.50 *100.00*
28 A6 20pi on 5fr dk bl & buff 360.00 360.00
Nos. 14-28 (13) 1,063. 1,083.

On Nos. 25, 26 and 28 the two lines of the overprint are set wider apart than on the lower values.

"O.N.F." are the initials of "Occupation Navale Francaise."

"Casetllorizo" and "astellorizo" varieties are known on Nos. 14-23.

Overprint on 8pi on 2fr (#37), value $900 unused, $1,000 used.

On Stamps of France
30 A22 10c red 45.00 45.00
a. Inverted overprint 200.00 200.00
31 A22 25c blue (R) 45.00 45.00
a. Inverted overprint 200.00 200.00

This overprint exists on 8 other 1900-1907 denominations of France (5c, 15c, 20c, 30c, 40c, 50c, 1fr, 5fr). These are believed not to have been issued or postally used. Values: 5c, $650; 15c, $650; 20c, $675; 30c, $1,000; 40c, $1,000; 50c, $1,000; 1fr, $1,100; 5fr, $10,000.

Stamps of France, 1900-1907, Handstamped in Black or Violet

O F CASTELLORISO

1920

33	A22	5c green	160.00	160.00
34	A22	10c red	160.00	160.00
35	A22	20c vio brn	160.00	160.00
a.		Overprint inverted (reading up)	1,400.	
b.		Double overprint		650.00
36	A22	25c blue	160.00	160.00
37	A18	50c bis brn & lav	950.00	1,050.
a.		Double overprint	1,400.	
38	A18	1fr cl & ol grn (V)	950.00	1,050.
		Nos. 33-38 (6)	2,540.	2,740.

Nos. 1-38 are considered speculative.

Forgeries of overprints on Nos. 1-38 exist. They abound of Nos. 33-38.

French Offices in Turkey Nos. 25//38 were hand-stamped "Occupation Francaise Castellorizo" locally by the officers in charge of the French Navy postal facilities but were not issued. Values: 5c, 10c, 15c, 20c, 1pi on 25c, each $875; 40c, 2pi on 50c, each $1,750; 4pi on 1fr, $2,000; 20pi on 5fr, $6.750.

Issued under Italian Dominion

100 Centesimi = 1 Lira

Italian Stamps of 1906-20 Overprinted

1922 Wmk. 140 *Perf. 14*

51	A48	5c green	4.25	24.00
52	A48	10c claret	2.50	24.00
53	A48	15c slate	3.50	24.00
54	A50	20c brn org	2.50	24.00
a.		Double overprint	340.00	
b.		Vertical pair, one without overprint	1,750.	
55	A49	25c blue	2.50	24.00
56	A49	40c brown	50.00	30.00
57	A49	50c violet	50.00	30.00
58	A49	60c carmine	50.00	42.50
a.		Diagonal overprint		650.00
59	A49	85c chocolate	5.00	50.00
		Nos. 51-59 (9)	170.25	272.50
		Set, never hinged	425.00	

Map of Castellorizo; Flag of Italy — A1

1923

60	A1	5c gray green	4.25	27.50
61	A1	10c dull rose	4.25	27.50
62	A1	25c dull blue	4.25	27.50
63	A1	50c gray lilac	4.25	27.50
64	A1	1 l brown	4.25	27.50
		Nos. 60-64 (5)	21.25	137.50
		Set, never hinged	52.50	

Italian Stamps of 1901-20 Overprinted

1924

65	A48	5c green	2.10	30.00
66	A48	10c claret	2.10	30.00
67	A48	15c slate	2.10	37.50
68	A50	20c brn orange	2.10	37.50
a.		Double overprint	120.00	
69	A49	25c blue	2.10	30.00
70	A49	40c brown	2.10	30.00
71	A49	50c violet	2.10	37.50
72	A49	60c carmine	2.10	47.50
a.		Double overprint	375.00	
73	A49	85c red brown	2.10	55.00
74	A46	1 l brn & green	2.10	55.00
		Nos. 65-74 (10)	21.00	390.00
		Set, never hinged	52.50	

Ferrucci Issue

Types of Italian Stamps of 1930, Overprinted in Red or Blue

1930 Wmk. Crowns (140)

75	A102	20c violet	8.50	8.50
76	A103	25c dark green	8.50	20.00
77	A103	50c black	8.50	8.50
78	A103	1.25 l deep blue	8.50	20.00
79	A104	5 l + 2 l dp car (Bl)	30.00	67.50
		Nos. 75-79 (5)	64.00	124.50
		Set, never hinged	160.00	

Garibaldi Issue

Types of Italian Stamps of 1932, Overprinted like Nos. 75-79 in Red or Blue

1932

80	A138	10c brown	25.00	50.00
81	A138	20c red brn (Bl)	25.00	50.00
82	A138	25c dp grn	25.00	50.00
83	A138	30c bluish slate	25.00	50.00
84	A138	50c red vio (Bl)	25.00	50.00
85	A141	75c cop red (Bl)	25.00	50.00
86	A141	1.25 l dull blue	25.00	50.00
87	A141	1.75 l + 25c brn	25.00	50.00
88	A144	2.55 l + 50c org (Bl)	25.00	50.00
89	A145	5 l + 1 l dl vio	25.00	50.00
		Nos. 80-89 (10)	250.00	500.00
		Set, never hinged	750.00	

CAYMAN ISLANDS

ˌkā-ˈman ˈī-lənds

LOCATION — Three islands in the Caribbean Sea, about 200 miles northwest of Jamaica

GOVT. — British Crown Colony, formerly a dependency of Jamaica

AREA — 100 sq. mi.

POP. — 39,335 (1999 est.)

CAPITAL — George Town, located on Grand Cayman

12 Pence = 1 Shilling

20 Shilling = 1 Pound

100 Cents = 1 Dollar (1969)

Watermark

Wmk. 362 — Basotho Hat Multiple

Catalogue values for unused stamps in this country are for Never Hinged items, beginning with Scott 112.

Victoria A1

Edward VII A2

1900 Typo. Wmk. 2 *Perf. 14*

1	A1	½p pale green	7.00	22.50
2	A1	1p carmine rose	7.00	3.75

1901-03

3	A2	½p green ('02)	6.00	32.50
4	A2	1p car rose ('03)	13.00	11.50
5	A2	2½p ultramarine	13.00	16.00
6	A2	6p chocolate	40.00	77.50
7	A2	1sh brown orange	80.00	140.00
		Nos. 3-7 (5)	152.00	277.50

1905 Wmk. 3

8	A2	½p green	8.50	11.50
9	A2	1p carmine rose	17.00	22.50
10	A2	2½p ultramarine	8.50	4.25
11	A2	6p chocolate	20.00	50.00
12	A2	1sh brown orange	40.00	62.50
		Nos. 8-12 (5)	94.00	150.75

For surcharge see No. 17.

1907, Mar. 13

13	A2	4p brown & blue	40.00	75.00
14	A2	6p ol green & rose	40.00	87.50
15	A2	1sh violet & green	70.00	110.00
16	A2	5sh ver & green	240.00	375.00
		Nos. 13-16 (4)	390.00	647.50

Numerals of 4p, 1sh and 5sh of type A2 are in color on colorless tablet.

For surcharges see Nos. 18-20.

Nos. 9, 16, 13 Handstamped

#17

#18

#19

#20

1907-08

17	A2	½p on 1p	60.00	100.00
18	A2	½p on 5sh	350.00	575.00
a.		Inverted surcharge	57,500.	
b.		Double surcharge	12,750.	12,750.
c.		Dbl. surch., one inverted		
d.		Pair, one without surcharge	75,000.	
19	A2	1p on 5sh	375.00	575.00
a.		Double surcharge	22,500.	20,000.
b.		Inverted surcharge	150,000.	
20	A2	2½p on 4p ('08)	2,000.	3,750.
a.		Double surcharge	45,000.	24,000.

No. 19b is unique. It exists on the upper left stamp in an upper left corner margin plate no. 1 block of four that is lightly hinged in the top margin only.

The 1p on 4p is a revenue stamp not authorized for postal use. Value about $300. Varieties exist.

A3

A4

1907-09 *Perf. 14*

21	A3	½p green	3.50	5.50
22	A3	1p carmine rose	2.10	1.10
23	A3	2½p ultramarine	4.75	5.25

Chalky Paper

24	A3	3p violet, *yellow*	4.50	9.75
25	A3	4p blk & red, *yel*	67.50	100.00
26	A3	6p violet	13.50	52.50
27	A3	1sh black, *grn*	11.00	32.50
28	A3	5sh grn & red, *yel*	52.50	90.00
		Nos. 21-28 (8)	159.35	296.60

Issued: ½p, 1p, 12/27; 2½p, 3p, 4p, 5sh, 3/30/08; 6d, 10/2/08; 1sh, 4/5/09.

Forged cancellations are found on No. 28.

1908, Mar. 30 Wmk. 2

29	A3	1sh black, *green*	85.00	125.00
30	A3	10sh grn & red, *grn*	225.00	400.00

Numerals of 3p, 4p, 1sh and 5sh of type A3 are in color on plain tablet.

Forged cancellations are found on No. 30.

1908 Wmk. 3

Ordinary Paper

31	A4	¼p brown	6.00	1.00

King George V

A5 A6

1912-20

32	A5	¼p brown ('13)	1.25	.50
33	A5	½p green	3.25	6.00
34	A5	1p carmine ('13)	4.00	3.00
35	A5	2p gray	1.25	12.50
36	A5	2½p ultra ('14)	8.50	13.50

Chalky Paper

37	A5	3p vio, *yel* ('13)	3.00	22.50
38	A5	4p blk & red, *yel* ('13)	1.25	12.50
39	A5	6p vio & red vio ('13)	4.50	9.00
40	A5	1sh blk, *grn* ('13)	4.25	32.50
41	A5	2sh vio & ultra, *bl*	14.50	57.50
42	A5	3sh green & vio	22.50	77.50
43	A5	5sh grn & red, *yel* ('14)	90.00	190.00
44	A5	10sh grn & red, *bl grn*, olive back ('18)	225.00	260.00
a.		10sh green & red, *grn* ('13)	150.00	240.00
		Nos. 32-44 (13)	383.25	697.00

The first printings of the 3p, 1sh and 10sh have a white back.

For surcharges see Nos. MR1-MR7.

1913, Nov. 19

Surface-colored Paper

45	A5	3p violet, *yel*	4.25	9.50
46	A5	1sh black, *green*	4.25	4.25
47	A5	10sh grn & red, *grn*	100.00	175.00
		Nos. 45-47 (3)	108.50	188.75

Numeral of ¼p, 2p, 3p, 4p, 1sh, 2sh, 3sh and 5sh of type A5 are in color on plain tablet.

1921-26 Wmk. 4 *Perf. 14*

50	A6	¼p yel brown	.60	1.75
51	A6	½p gray green	.60	.35
52	A6	1p rose red	1.75	1.00
53	A6	1½p orange brn	2.10	.35
54	A6	2p gray	2.10	4.75
55	A6	2½p ultramarine	.60	.60
56	A6	3p violet, *yel*	1.25	4.75
57	A6	4½p olive grn	2.75	3.75
58	A6	6p claret	6.50	37.50
59	A6	1sh black, *grn*	11.50	37.50
60	A6	2sh violet, *blue*	17.00	29.00
61	A6	3sh violet	27.50	19.00
62	A6	5sh green, *yel*	29.00	55.00
63	A6	10sh car, *green*	72.50	100.00
		Nos. 50-63 (14)	175.75	295.30

Issued: 1½p, 4/4/21; ¼p, ½p, 1p, 2p, 2½p, 6p, 2sh, 3sh, 4/1/22; 3p, 4½p, 6/29/23; 5sh, 2/15/25; 1sh, 5/15/25; 10sh, 9/5/26.

1921-22 Wmk. 3

64	A6	3p violet, *org*	1.75	9.50
65	A6	4p red, *yel*	1.25	4.75
66	A6	1sh black, *green*	1.50	11.50
67	A6	5sh green, *yel*	19.00	85.00
68	A6	10sh car, *green*	72.50	125.00
		Nos. 64-68 (5)	96.00	235.75

Issued: 4p, 4/1/22; others, 4/4/21.

King William IV, King George V A7

Perf. 12½

1932, Dec. 5 Wmk. 4 Engr.

69	A7	¼p brown	1.90	1.40
70	A7	½p green	3.25	10.50
71	A7	1p carmine	3.25	10.50
72	A7	1½p orange	3.25	3.75
73	A7	2p gray	3.25	4.75
74	A7	2½p ultramarine	3.25	2.00
75	A7	3p olive green	4.00	6.75
76	A7	6p red violet	11.50	30.00
77	A7	1sh brn & black	20.00	42.50
78	A7	2sh ultra & blk	55.00	100.00
79	A7	5sh green & blk	100.00	160.00
80	A7	10sh car & black	350.00	475.00
		Nos. 69-80 (12)	558.65	847.15
		Set, never hinged	1,225.	

Centenary of the formation of the Cayman Islands Assembly.

Common Design Types pictured following the introduction.

Silver Jubilee Issue
Common Design Type

1935, May 6 *Perf. 13½x14*

81	CD301	½p green & black	.30	*1.50*
82	CD301	2½p blue & brown	1.50	1.50
83	CD301	6p ol grn & lt bl	1.50	*4.75*
84	CD301	1sh brt vio & ind	10.50	10.00
		Nos. 81-84 (4)	13.80	17.75
		Set, never hinged	20.00	

King George V A8

Catboat A9

Red-footed Boobies A10

Conches and Coconut Palms — A11

Hawksbill Turtles A12

1935-36 *Perf. 12½*

85	A8	¼p brown & blk	.60	*1.25*
86	A9	½p yel grn & ultra	1.25	1.25
87	A10	1p car & ultra	5.00	3.00
88	A11	1½p org & black	1.75	*2.40*
89	A9	2p brown vio & ultra	4.50	1.50
90	A12	2½p dp blue & blk	4.00	1.60
91	A8	3p ol grn & blk	3.00	*3.75*
92	A12	6p red vio & blk	10.50	6.00
93	A9	1sh org & ultra	7.25	*9.25*
94	A10	2sh black & ultra	55.00	50.00
95	A12	5sh green & blk	60.00	70.00
96	A11	10sh car & black	125.00	*140.00*
		Nos. 85-96 (12)	277.85	290.00
		Set, never hinged	525.00	

Issued: #86, 2½p, 6p, 1sh, 1/1/36; others, 5/1/35.

Coronation Issue
Common Design Type

1937, May 13 *Perf. 11x11½*

97	CD302	½p deep green	.20	*1.50*
98	CD302	1p dark carmine	.25	.25
99	CD302	2½p deep ultra	.55	.55
		Nos. 97-99 (3)	1.00	2.30
		Set, never hinged	2.25	

Beach View, Grand Cayman A13

Dolphin — A14

Hawksbill Turtles — A16

Map of the Islands A15

Cayman Schooner A17

Perf. 12½; 11½x13 or 13x11½ (A14, #111); 14 (#104, 107)

1938-43 **Engr.**

100	A13	¼p red orange	.55	*.75*
a.		Perf. 13½x12½ ('43)	.20	*.85*
101	A14	½p yel green	.85	*.75*
a.		Perf. 14 ('43)	1.10	*1.75*
102	A15	1p carmine	.20	*1.00*
103	A13	1½p black	.20	.20
104	A16	2p dp violet ('43)	.50	.35
a.		Perf. 11½x13	2.50	.30
105	A17	2½p ultra	.30	.20
106	A15	3p orange	.30	.20
107	A16	6p dk ol grn ('43)	2.50	2.50
a.		Perf. 11½x13	7.25	5.25
108	A14	1sh reddish brown	5.75	2.00
a.		Perf. 14 ('43)	3.75	2.50
109	A13	2sh green	24.00	18.00
110	A17	5sh deep rose	27.50	19.00
111	A16	10sh dark brown	19.00	12.00
a.		Perf. 14 ('43)	19.00	12.00
		Nos. 100-111 (12)	81.65	56.95
		Never hinged	135.00	

See Nos. 114-115.

Catalogue values for unused stamps in this section, from this point to the end of the section, are for Never Hinged items.

Peace Issue
Common Design Type

1946, Aug. 26 **Wmk. 4** *Perf. 13½*

112	CD303	1½p black	.25	.20
113	CD303	3p orange	.25	.20

Types of 1938

1947, Aug. 25 *Perf. 12½*

114	A17	2½p orange	3.50	.65
115	A15	3p ultramarine	3.50	.45

Silver Wedding Issue
Common Design Types

1948, Nov. 29 **Photo.** *Perf. 14x14½*

116	CD304	½p dark green	.20	.65

Perf. 11½x11

Engr.; Name Typo.

117	CD305	10sh blue violet	18.00	18.00

UPU Issue
Common Design Types

Engr.; Name Typo. on #119, 120

1949, Oct. 10 *Perf. 13½, 11x11½*

118	CD306	2½p orange	.30	*1.00*
119	CD307	3p indigo	1.75	*2.50*
120	CD308	6p olive	.70	*2.50*
121	CD309	1sh red brown	.70	.40
		Nos. 118-121 (4)	3.45	6.40

Catboat A18

Designs: ½p, Coconut grove. 1p, Green turtle. 1½p, Thatch rope industry. 2p, Caymanian seamen. 2½p, Map. 3p, Parrot fish. 6p, Bluff, Cayman Brac. 9p, George Town harbor. 1sh, Turtle "crawl". 2sh, Cayman schooner. 5sh, Boat-building. 10sh, Government offices.

Perf. 11½x11

1950, Oct. 2 **Wmk. 4** **Engr.**

122	A18	¼p rose red & blue	.20	*.80*
123	A18	½p bl grn & red vio	.20	*1.75*
124	A18	1p dp blue & olive	.75	*1.00*
125	A18	1½p choc & bl grn	.45	*1.00*
126	A18	2p rose car & vio	1.75	*2.00*
127	A18	2½p sepia & aqua	1.75	.85
128	A18	3p bl & blue grn	2.10	2.00
129	A18	6p dp bl & org brn	2.50	1.75
130	A18	9p dk grn & rose red	10.50	2.50
131	A18	1sh red org & brn	4.50	3.75
132	A18	2sh red vio & vio	11.50	*14.50*
133	A18	5sh vio & olive	17.00	9.50
134	A18	10sh rose red & blk	22.50	19.00
		Nos. 122-134 (13)	75.70	60.40

Types of 1950 with Portrait of Queen Elizabeth II and

Lighthouse, South Sound — A20

Elizabeth II and Turtles — A21

Perf. 11½x11, 11x11½

1953-59 **Engr.**

135	A18	¼p rose red & bl	1.40	.80
136	A18	½p bl grn & red vio	1.10	.75
137	A18	1p dp bl & olive	1.00	.70
138	A18	1½p choc & bl grn	.75	.35
139	A18	2p rose car & vio	3.50	1.40
140	A18	2½p black & aqua	4.25	1.25
141	A18	3p blue & bl grn	5.25	1.00
142	A20	4p dp blue & black	2.50	.70
143	A18	6p dp bl & red brn	2.10	.30
144	A18	9p dk green & rose red	8.50	.40
145	A18	1sh red org & brn	4.75	.40
146	A18	2sh red vio & vio	16.00	11.50
147	A18	5sh violet & olive	17.50	10.00
148	A18	10sh rose red & blk	19.00	11.50
149	A21	£1 bright blue	37.50	16.00
		Nos. 135-149 (15)	125.10	57.05

Issued: 4p, 3/2; 2p, 2½p, 9p, 6/2/54; ½p, 1p, 1½p, 6p, 7/7/54; ¼p, 3p, 1sh-10sh, 2/21/55; £1, 1/6/59.

Coronation Issue
Common Design Type

1953, June 2 *Perf. 13½x13*

150	CD312	1p brt green & black	.40	*1.00*

Arms of Cayman Islands A22

Perf. 12

1959, July 4 **Wmk. 4** **Photo.**

151	A22	2½p dull blue & blk	.65	1.25
152	A22	1sh red orange & blk	.75	.50

Granting of a new constitution.

Cayman Parrot — A23

Catboat A24

1½p, Orchid. 2p, Map of Islands. 2½p, Fisherman casting net. 3p, West Bay Beach. 4p, Green turtle. 6p, Cayman schooner. 9p, Angler with kingfish. 1sh, Iguana. 1sh3p, Swimming pool, Cayman Brac. 1sh9p, Girl and sailboat. 5sh, Fort George. 10sh, Coat of Arms. £1, Queen Elizabeth II.

Perf. 11x11½, 11½x11

1962, Nov. 28 **Wmk. 314** **Engr.**

153	A23	¼p rose red & emer	1.00	*1.50*
154	A24	1p olive & black	.85	.40
155	A24	1½p purple & yel	4.25	1.25
156	A24	2p sepia & blue	1.10	.50
157	A24	2½p green & vio	.85	*1.50*
158	A24	3p car & blue	.40	.40
159	A24	4p pur & green	1.40	.95
160	A24	6p sepia & green	3.25	.55
161	A23	9p pur & vio bl	2.25	.85
162	A24	1sh rose & sepia	.85	.20
163	A24	1sh3p brn org & lt grn	3.75	3.50
164	A24	1sh9p vio & bl grn	15.00	2.25
165	A24	5sh grn & dl pur	11.50	9.50
166	A23	10sh blue & olive	21.00	13.00
167	A23	£1 blk & car rose	21.00	*24.00*
		Revenue cancel		.80
		Nos. 153-167 (15)	88.45	60.35

Freedom from Hunger Issue
Common Design Type

1963, June 4 **Photo.** *Perf. 14x14½*

168	CD314	1sh9p car rose	.60	.30

Red Cross Centenary Issue
Common Design Type

Wmk. 314

1963, Sept. 2 **Litho.** *Perf. 13*

169	CD315	1p black & red	.20	.20
170	CD315	1sh9p ultra & red	1.25	1.90

Shakespeare Issue
Common Design Type

1964, Apr. 23 **Photo.** *Perf. 14x14½*

171	CD316	6p deep lilac rose	.40	.30

ITU Issue
Common Design Type

1965, May 17 **Litho.** **Wmk. 314**

172	CD317	1p ultra & red lil	.20	.20
173	CD317	1sh3p rose lil & grn	.90	.75

Intl. Cooperation Year Issue
Common Design Type

1965, Oct. 25 **Wmk. 314** *Perf. 14½*

174	CD318	1p blue grn & claret	.20	.20
175	CD318	1sh lt vio & green	.65	.65

Churchill Memorial Issue
Common Design Type

1966, Jan. 24 **Photo.** *Perf. 14*

Design in Black, Gold and Carmine Rose

176	CD319	¼p bright blue	.25	1.25
177	CD319	1p green	.50	.50
178	CD319	1sh brown	.95	.65
179	CD319	1sh9p violet	1.60	.90
		Nos. 176-179 (4)	3.30	3.30

Royal Visit Issue
Common Design Type

1966, Feb. 4 **Litho.** *Perf. 11x12*

180	CD320	1p violet blue	.85	.30
181	CD320	1sh9p dk car rose	3.50	1.50

World Cup Soccer Issue
Common Design Type

1966, July 1 **Litho.** *Perf. 14*

182	CD321	1½p multicolored	.20	.20
183	CD321	1sh9p multicolored	.65	.65

WHO Headquarters Issue
Common Design Type

1966, Sept. 20 **Litho.** *Perf. 14*

184	CD322	2p multicolored	.75	.30
185	CD322	1sh3p multicolored	1.75	1.10

UNESCO Anniversary Issue
Common Design Type

1966, Dec. 1 **Litho.** *Perf. 14*

186	CD323	1p "Education"	.20	.20
187	CD323	1sh9p "Science"	1.10	.35
188	CD323	5sh "Culture"	2.25	1.10
		Nos. 186-188 (3)	3.55	1.65

Telephone and Map of Caymans — A25

Perf. 14½x14

1966, Dec. 5 Litho. Wmk. 314

189	A25	4p	multicolored	.20	.20
190	A25	9p	multicolored	.30	.30

Linking of the Cayman telephone system with the intl. system.

BAC 1-11 Jet Liner over Schooner — A26

1966, Dec. 17

191	A26	1sh	blue, ol & black	.35	.35
192	A26	1sh9p	ultra, grn & sepia	.75	.75

Opening of the Grand Cayman Airport jet service.

Water Skiing and ITY Emblem A27

ITY Emblem and: 6p, Skin diving. 1sh, Sport fishing. 1sh9p, Sailing.

Perf. 14½x14

1967, Dec. 1 Photo. Wmk. 314

193	A27	4p	multi & gold	.45	.20
a.			Gold omitted	110.00	
194	A27	6p	multi & gold	.45	.25
195	A27	1sh	multi & gold	.45	.40
196	A27	1sh9p	multi & gold	.65	.75
			Nos. 193-196 (4)	2.00	1.60

International Tourist Year.

Human Rights Flame and Freed Slaves A28

1968, June 3 Photo. Wmk. 314

197	A28	3p	slate bl, grn & gold	.20	.20
198	A28	9p	lt brn, grn & gold	.20	.20
199	A28	5sh	ultra, grn & gold	.70	.70
			Nos. 197-199 (3)	1.10	1.10

International Human Rights Year.

Long Jump A29

1sh3p, High jump. 2sh, Pole vault, vert.

1968, Oct. 1 Litho. *Perf. 13½*

200	A29	1sh	multicolored	.20	.20
201	A29	1sh3p	multicolored	.25	.25
202	A29	2sh	yellow & multi	.40	.40
			Nos. 200-202 (3)	.85	.85

19th Olympic Games, Mexico City, 10/12-27.

Adoration of Shepherds, by Carel Fabritius — A30

Christmas: 1p, 8p, 2sh, Adoration of the Shepherds, by Rembrandt.

Perf. 14x14½

1968, Nov. 18 Photo. Wmk. 314

203	A30	¼p	brown & multi	.20	.20
a.			Gold omitted	200.00	
204	A30	1p	violet & multi	.20	.20
205	A30	6p	multicolored	.20	.20
206	A30	8p	car & multi	.20	.20
207	A30	1sh3p	multicolored	.30	.30
208	A30	2sh	gray & multi	.45	.45
			Nos. 203-208 (6)	1.55	1.55

1969, Jan. 8 Unwmk.

209	A30	¼p	red lilac & multi	.20	.20

Grand Cayman Thrush A31

1p, Brahman cattle. 2p, Blowholes on coast. 2½p, Map of Grand Cayman. 3p, Town scene in George Town. 4p, Royal poinciana. 6p, Map of Cayman Brac and Little Cayman. 8p, Motor vessels at berth. 1sh, Basket making. 1sh3p, Beach scene. 1sh6p, Rope making. 2sh, Barracudas. 4sh, Government House. 10sh, Coat of arms. £1, Queen Elizabeth II.

Unwmk.

1969, June 5 Litho. *Perf. 14*

210	A31	¼p	multi	.20	*.90*
211	A31	1p	multi	.20	.20
212	A31	2p	multi	.20	.20
213	A31	2½p	multi	.20	.20
214	A31	3p	multi	.20	.20
215	A31	4p	multi	.20	.20
216	A31	6p	multi	.20	.20
217	A31	8p	multi	.20	.20
218	A31	1sh	multi	.25	.20
219	A31	1sh3p	multi	.30	*1.90*
220	A31	1sh6p	multi	.40	*1.90*
221	A31	2sh	multi	1.50	*1.40*
222	A31	4sh	multi	.70	*1.40*
223	A31	10sh	multi, vert.	1.50	*2.50*
224	A31	£1	multi, vert.	3.50	3.50
			Nos. 210-224 (15)	9.75	*15.10*

See #262-276. For surcharges see #227-241.

1969, Aug. 11 Wmk. 314 Sideways

225	A31	¼p	multicolored	.40	.40

Type of 1969 Surcharged

1969, Sept. 8 Wmk. 314 *Perf. 14*

227	A31	¼c	on ¼p multi	.20	*.85*
228	A31	1c	on 1p multi	.20	.25
229	A31	2c	on 2p multi	.20	.25
230	A31	3c	on 4p multi	.20	.25
231	A31	4c	on 2½p multi	.20	.25
232	A31	5c	on 6p multi	.20	.25
233	A31	7c	on 8p multi	.20	.25
234	A31	8c	on 3p multi	.20	.25
235	A31	10c	on 1s multi	.35	.25
236	A31	12c	on 1sh3p multi	.50	*1.90*
237	A31	15c	on 1sh6p multi	.65	*1.25*
238	A31	20c	on 2sh multi	2.25	2.10
239	A31	40c	on 4sh multi	.65	*1.25*
240	A31	$1	on 10sh multi	1.60	*3.75*
241	A31	$2	on £1 multi	2.50	*4.50*
			Nos. 227-241 (15)	10.10	17.60

The surcharge is arranged differently on various denominations.

Madonna and Child, by Alvise Vivarini — A32

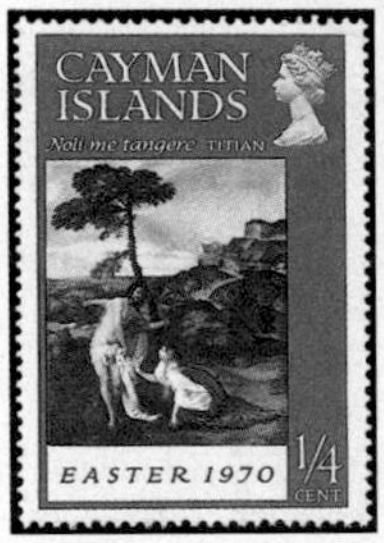

"Noli me Tangere," by Titian — A33

Christmas: 1c, 7c, 20c, The Adoration of the Kings, by Jan Gossaert.

1969, Nov. 4 Photo. *Perf. 14*

242	A32	¼c	blue & multi	.20	.20
243	A32	¼c	emer & multi	.20	.20
244	A32	¼c	red org & multi	.20	.20
245	A32	¼c	brt pink & multi	.20	.20
246	A32	1c	vio blue & multi	.20	.20
247	A32	5c	red org & multi	.20	.20
248	A32	7c	dk green & multi	.20	.20
249	A32	12c	emer & multi	.20	.20
250	A32	20c	multicolored	.20	.20
			Nos. 242-250 (9)	1.80	1.80

1970, Mar. 23 Litho. Unwmk.

251	A33	¼c	dull grn & multi	.20	.20
252	A33	¼c	dk car & multi	.20	.20
253	A33	¼c	violet & multi	.20	.20
254	A33	¼c	bister & multi	.20	.20
255	A33	10c	vio blue & multi	.20	.20
256	A33	12c	red brn & multi	.25	.25
257	A33	40c	brn vio & multi	.60	.60
			Nos. 251-257 (7)	1.85	1.85

Easter.

Barnaby from "Barnaby Rudge" by Dickens (1812-70), English Novelist — A34

Characters from Charles Dickens: 12c, Sairey Gamp, from "Martin Chuzzlewit." 20c, Mr. Micawber and David, from "David Copperfield." 40c, The Marchioness from "The Old Curiosity Shop."

1970, June 17 Photo. *Perf. 14½x14*

258	A34	1c	ol green, yel & blk	.20	.20
259	A34	12c	red brn, brick red & black	.20	.20
260	A34	20c	dk ol bister, gold & black	.35	.35
261	A34	40c	dp ultra, lt bl & blk	.75	.75
			Nos. 258-261 (4)	1.50	1.50

Type of Regular Issue 1969 Values in Cents and Dollars

Designs: ¼c, Grand Cayman thrush. 1c, Brahman cattle. 2c, Blowholes on coast. 3c, Royal poinciana. 4c, Map of Grand Cayman. 5c, Map of Cayman Brac and Little Cayman. 7c, Motor vessels at berth. 8c, Town scene in George Town. 10c, Basket making. 12c, Beach scene. 15c, Rope making. 20c, Barracudas. 40c, Government House. $1, Coat of arms, vert. $2, Queen Elizabeth II, vert.

Wmk. 314

1970, Sept. 8 Litho. *Perf. 14*

262	A31	¼c	multicolored	.60	.30
263	A31	1c	multicolored	.20	.20
264	A31	2c	multicolored	.20	.20
265	A31	3c	multicolored	.25	.20
266	A31	4c	multicolored	.25	.20
267	A31	5c	multicolored	.45	.20
268	A31	7c	multicolored	.40	.20
269	A31	8c	multicolored	.40	.20
270	A31	10c	multicolored	.40	.20
271	A31	12c	multicolored	1.40	1.10
272	A31	15c	multicolored	1.60	*3.50*
273	A31	20c	multicolored	3.75	1.75
274	A31	40c	multicolored	1.25	1.25
275	A31	$1	multicolored	1.60	*5.75*
276	A31	$2	multicolored	2.40	*5.75*
			Nos. 262-276 (15)	15.15	21.00

The Three Wise Men A35

Christmas: 1c, 10c, 20c, Nativity and globe.

1970, Oct. 8 Litho. *Perf. 14*

277	A35	¼c	brt grn & yel grn	.20	.20
278	A35	1c	bl grn, yel grn & blk	.20	.20
279	A35	5c	dp claret & org	.20	.20
280	A35	10c	red org, yel & blk	.20	.20
281	A35	12c	ultra & lt grnsh bl	.20	.20
282	A35	20c	grn, yel grn & blk	.25	.25
			Nos. 277-282 (6)	1.25	1.25

Grand Cayman Terrapin A36

Cayman Islands Turtles: 7c, Green turtle. 12c, Hawksbill turtle. 20c, Turtle farm.

1971, Jan. 28 *Perf. 14x14½*

283	A36	5c	multicolored	.70	.50
284	A36	7c	multicolored	.90	.50
285	A36	12c	multicolored	2.00	.60
286	A36	20c	multicolored	3.25	3.25
			Nos. 283-286 (4)	6.85	4.85

Dendrophylax Fawcetii — A37

Adoration of the Kings, 15th Century — A38

Wild Orchids of West Indies: 2c, Schomburgkia thomsoniana. 10c, Vanilla claviculata. 40c, Oncidium variegatum.

1971, Apr. 7 Wmk. 314 *Perf. 14*

287	A37	¼c	brown & multi	.25	*1.60*
288	A37	2c	ol green & multi	.85	*1.25*
289	A37	10c	gray bl & multi	3.25	1.00
290	A37	40c	lt violet & multi	6.25	5.00
			Nos. 287-290 (4)	10.60	*8.85*

1971, Sept. 27 *Perf. 14*

Christmas: 1c, 15c, Nativity (detail), Paris, 14th cent. 5c, 20c, Adoration of the Kings (detail), Burgundian, 15th cent.

291	A38	¼c	gold & multi	.20	.20
292	A38	1c	gold & multi	.20	.20
293	A38	5c	gold & multi	.20	.20
294	A38	12c	gold & multi	.20	.20
295	A38	15c	gold & multi	.30	.30
296	A38	20c	gold & multi	.40	.40
a.			Souvenir sheet of 6, #291-296	4.75	4.75
			Nos. 291-296 (6)	1.50	1.50

Underwater Cable, Turtle and Telephone — A39

1972, Jan. 10

297 A39 2c multicolored .20 .20
298 A39 10c multicolored .20 .20
299 A39 40c multicolored 1.00 1.00
Nos. 297-299 (3) 1.40 1.40

Coaxial cable for world communications.

Courthouse — A40

Designs: 15c, 40c, Legislative Assembly Building, George Town.

1972, Aug. 15 ***Perf. 13½x14***

300 A40 5c dp car & multi .20 .20
301 A40 15c lilac rose & multi .20 .20
302 A40 25c dull grn & multi .30 .30
303 A40 40c dk blue & multi .50 .50
a. Souvenir sheet of 4, #300-303 1.25 1.25
Nos. 300-303 (4) 1.20 1.20

New Cayman Islands government buildings.

Silver Wedding Issue, 1972
Common Design Type

Design: Queen Elizabeth II, Prince Philip, hawksbill turtle and conch.

1972, Nov. 20 Photo. ***Perf. 14x14½***

304 CD324 12c vio black & multi .25 .25
305 CD324 30c olive & multi .50 .50

$1 Note and 1c Coin A41

6c, $5 note and 5c coin. 15c, $10 note and 10c coin. 25c, $25 note and 25c coin.

1973, Jan. 15

306 A41 3c emerald & multi .20 .20
307 A41 6c yellow & multi .30 .60
308 A41 15c lilac & multi .75 .50
309 A41 25c orange & multi 1.50 .90
a. Souvenir sheet of 4, #306-309 5.25 5.25
Nos. 306-309 (4) 2.75 2.20

First Cayman Islands coinage and bank notes, May 1, 1972.

Last Supper A42

Stained Glass Windows: 10c, Christ Carrying Cross, vert. 12c, Resurrection, vert. 30c, Crucifixion.

Perf. 14½x14, 14x14½

1973, Apr. 11 Litho.

310 A42 10c pink & multi .20 .20
311 A42 12c yel green & multi .20 .20
312 A42 20c lt blue & multi .30 .30
313 A42 30c yellow & multi .40 .40
a. Souvenir sheet of 4 1.60 1.60
Nos. 310-313 (4) 1.10 1.10

Easter. No. 313a contains 4 stamps similar to Nos. 310-313 with simulated perforations.

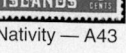

Nativity — A43

White-winged Dove — A44

Christmas: 5c, 12c, 25c, Adoration of the Magi, from Breviary of Queen Isabella. 9c, 15c, Like 3c, Nativity from Sforza Book of Hours.

1973, Oct. 2 ***Perf. 14½***

314 A43 3c dull green & multi .20 .20
315 A43 5c dull pur & multi .20 .20
316 A43 9c sepia & multi .20 .20
317 A43 12c dk blue & multi .20 .20
318 A43 15c dp rose & multi .20 .20
319 A43 25c black & multi .40 .40
Nos. 314-319 (6) 1.40 1.40

Princess Anne's Wedding Issue
Common Design Type

1973, Nov. 14 Wmk. 314 ***Perf. 14***

320 CD325 10c brt green & multi .20 .20
321 CD325 30c lilac & multi .30 .30

1974, Jan. 2 Litho. ***Perf. 14x14½***

322 A44 3c shown 2.75 .40
323 A44 10c Vitelline warblers 3.50 .40
324 A44 12c Greater Antillean grackles 3.50 .40
325 A44 20c West Indian red-bellied woodpecker 5.75 1.00
326 A44 30c Stripe-headed tanagers 7.25 2.25
327 A44 50c Yucatan vireos 9.75 6.25
Nos. 322-327 (6) 32.50 10.70

See Nos. 354-359.

One-room Schoolhouse — A45

Designs: 20c, New comprehensive school. 30c, Creative Arts Center, Mona, Jamaica.

1974, May 1 ***Perf. 14***

328 A45 12c multicolored .20 .20
329 A45 20c multicolored .20 .20
330 A45 30c multicolored .30 .30
Nos. 328-330 (3) .70 .70

25th anniv. of the University College of the West Indies.

Hermit Crab and Pirate Gold A46

Coat of Arms — A47

Elizabeth II — A48

Designs: 3c, Pirate, treasure chest and lion's paw. 4c, Spotted scorpionfish and crown. 5c, Flint-lock pistol and brain coral. 6c, Blackbeard on Grand Cayman and green turtle. 8c, 9c, Jeweled pomander and porkfish. 10c, Spiny lobster and gold coins. 12c, Jeweled sword, dagger and sea fan. 15c, Cabrit's murex and jeweled necklace. 20c, Queen conch, pistol and gold cup. 25c, Hogfish and pirate chest. 40c, Gold chalice and sea whip.

Wmk. 314 Upright, Sideways (#331-332, 336, 344-345)

1974-75 Litho. ***Perf. 14***

331 A46 1c multi ('75) 5.00 1.75
a. Wmk. upright 4.25 1.75
332 A46 3c multicolored 5.00 1.00
a. Wmk. upright 5.50 1.00
333 A46 4c multicolored .70 *.95*
334 A46 5c multicolored 4.25 1.00
335 A46 6c multicolored .50 *3.25*
336 A46 8c multicolored 3.50 *11.50*
337 A46 9c multicolored 5.25 *12.50*
338 A46 10c multicolored 6.25 1.10
339 A46 12c multicolored .50 *2.25*
340 A46 15c multicolored .65 *1.75*
341 A46 20c multicolored 5.00 4.00
342 A46 25c multicolored .65 *.95*
343 A46 40c multicolored 5.75 1.75
344 A47 $1 multicolored 4.00 *4.50*
345 A48 $2 multicolored 10.50 *9.00*
Nos. 331-345 (15) 57.50 *57.25*

Issued: #332, 11/12; 8c, 12/16; #331, 9/29; others, 8/1.

1976-77 Wmk. 373

332b A46 3c multicolored 1.40 *5.50*
333a A46 4c multi ('77) 1.75 *6.50*
334a A46 5c multi ('77) 9.00 8.25
336b A46 8c multicolored 10.50 7.25
338b A46 10c multicolored 4.00 *5.50*
341b A46 20c multicolored 4.50 4.25
344a A47 $1 multi ('77) 9.00 *13.50*
345b A48 $2 multicolored 10.00 9.25
Nos. 332b-345b (8) 50.15 *60.00*

Issued: 3c, 8c, 10c, 20c, $2, 9/3; 4c, 5c, $1, 10/19.

Design Smaller
Size: 40x25mm

Wmk. 373 (Sideways on 1c-40c)

1978-80

346 A46 1c multicolored 1.50 *2.25*
346A A46 3c multicolored 1.25 .85
346B A46 5c multi ('79) 3.25 *4.75*
347 A46 10c multicolored 2.50 1.25
347A A46 20c multicolored 5.25 2.25
347B A46 40c multi ('79) 21.00 30.00
347C A47 $1 multi ('80) 26.00 11.00
348 A48 $2 multi ('80) 9.50 *29.00*
Nos. 346-348 (8) 70.25 *81.35*

Issued: 1c, 3c, 3/16; 10c, 20c, 5/25; 5c, 12/11; $2, 4/3; $1, 7/30.

Sea Captain and Ship — A49

1974, Oct. 7 Wmk. 314 ***Perf. 14***

349 A49 8c shown .20 .20
350 A49 12c Thatch weaver .25 .20
351 A49 20c Farmer .55 .50
a. Miniature sheet of 3, #349-351 1.90 *2.50*
Nos. 349-351 (3) 1.00 .90

Arms of Cinque Ports and Lord Warden's Flag — A50

Churchill Coat of Arms — A51

1974, Nov. 30

352 A50 12c multicolored .20 .20
353 A51 50c multicolored .70 .70
a. Souvenir sheet of 2, #352-353 1.10 *1.25*

Sir Winston Churchill (1874-1965).

Bird Type of 1974

Wmk. 314

1975, Jan. 1 Litho. ***Perf. 14***

354 A44 3c Yellow-shafted flicker .75 .45
355 A44 10c West Indian tree duck 1.40 .45
356 A44 12c Yellow warblers 1.75 .70
357 A44 20c White-bellied dove 3.00 3.00
358 A44 30c Magnificent frigate bird 5.00 *5.00*
359 A44 50c Cayman amazon 6.00 *11.50*
a. Wmk. 362 (Lesotho) 600.00
Nos. 354-359 (6) 17.90 *21.10*

Ivory Crosier with Crucifixion — A52

Design: 35c, Crucifixion, ivory and gilt. Designs show heads of 14th century French pastoral staffs.

Wmk. 314

1975, Mar. 24 Litho. ***Perf. 14***

360 A52 15c plum & multi .20 .20
361 A52 35c gray & multi .65 .65
a. Souvenir sheet of 2, #360-361 1.10 1.10

Easter. No. 361a exists imperf.

See Nos. 366-367.

Israel Hands A53

Designs: Pirates and various scenes.

1975, July 25 Wmk. 314

362 A53 10c shown .60 .20
363 A53 12c John Fenn .60 .20
364 A53 20c Thomas Anstis .95 .45
365 A53 30c Edward Low 1.10 *1.75*
Nos. 362-365 (4) 3.25 2.60

Easter Type of 1975

Designs after ivory carved pastoral staffs showing Virgin and Child with angels, French, 14th century.

Wmk. 373

1975, Oct. 31 Litho. ***Perf. 14***

366 A52 12c dk green & multi .20 .20
367 A52 50c multicolored .70 .70
a. Souvenir sheet of 2, #366-367 1.40 *1.75*

Christmas.

Registered Letter with Nos. 1-2; Cayman Brac Government House and Sub Post Office — A54

Cayman Islands 1st postage stamps, 75th anniv.: 20c, Cayman Islands #1 and cancelation used 1890-94; 30c, #2, 20; 50c, #1-2.

1976, Mar. 12 Litho. ***Perf. 13½x14***

368 A54 10c lt blue & multi .20 .20
369 A54 20c pink & multi .25 .25
370 A54 30c multicolored .40 .40
371 A54 50c yellow & multi .60 .60
a. Souvenir sheet of 4, #368-371 4.25 4.25
Nos. 368-371 (4) 1.45 1.45

Seals of Georgia, Delaware and New Hampshire — A55

15c, Seals of SC, NJ, MD. 20c, Seals of VA, RI, MA. 25c, Seals of NY, CT, NC. 30c, Seal of PA, Liberty Bell and Great Seal of the US.

Wmk. 373

1976, May 29 Litho. ***Perf. 14***

372 A55 10c olive & multi .40 .20
373 A55 15c blue & multi .50 .20
374 A55 20c multicolored .70 .30
375 A55 25c blue grn & multi 1.00 .60

376 A55 30c red brn & multi 1.25 .85
a. Souvenir sheet of 5 + label *7.25 7.25*
Nos. 372-376 (5) 3.85 2.15

American Bicentennial. Nos. 372-376 printed in sheets of 5. No. 376a contains one each of Nos. 372-376 and corner label inscribed "USA 200."

French Class 470 Racing Dinghies — A56

Queen Elizabeth II — A57

Design: 50c, One racing dinghy.

1976, Aug. 16 Litho. *Perf. 14*
377 A56 20c multicolored .70 .45
378 A56 50c multicolored 1.25 1.25

21st Olympic Games, Montreal, Canada, July 17-Aug. 1.

Perf. 14x13½, 13½x14
1977, Feb. 7 Litho. Wmk. 373

8c, Prince Charles, 1973 visit. 50c, Preparation for anointing ceremony, horiz.

379 A57 8c multicolored .20 .20
380 A57 30c multicolored .35 .30
381 A57 50c multicolored .55 .50
Nos. 379-381 (3) 1.10 1.00

25th anniv. of the reign of Elizabeth II.

Scuba Diving A58

10c, Divers examining underwater wreck. 20c, Fairy basslets (fish). 25c, Sergeant majors (fish).

1977, July 25 *Perf. 13½*
382 A58 5c multicolored .20 .20
383 A58 10c multicolored .25 .25
384 A58 20c multicolored .50 .50
385 A58 25c multicolored .70 .65
a. Souvenir sheet of 4 3.00 3.00
Nos. 382-385 (4) 1.65 1.60

Tourist publicity. No. 385a contains one each of Nos. 382-385, perf. 14½.

Composia Fidelissima — A59

Butterflies: 8c, Heliconius charitonius. 10c, Danaus gilippus. 15c, Agraulis vanillae. 20c, Junonia evarete. 30c, Anartia jatrophae.

1977, Dec. 2 Wmk. 373 *Perf. 14x13*
386 A59 5c multicolored 1.25 .20
387 A59 8c multicolored 1.40 .30
388 A59 10c multicolored 1.50 .35
389 A59 15c multicolored 1.90 .55
390 A59 20c multicolored 2.10 .60
391 A59 30c multicolored 2.50 1.10
Nos. 386-391 (6) 10.65 3.10

Cruise Ship "Southward" A60

Designs: 5c, "Renaissance." 30c, New harbor, vert. 50c, "Daphne," vert.

1978, Jan. 23 Litho. *Perf. 14*
392 A60 3c multicolored .45 .20
393 A60 5c multicolored .45 .20
394 A60 30c multicolored 1.40 .65
395 A60 50c multicolored 1.90 .95
Nos. 392-395 (4) 4.20 2.00

New harbor and cruise ships.

Crucifixion, by Dürer — A61

Explorers, Singing Game — A62

Etchings by Dürer: 15c, Christ at Emmaus. 20c, Entry into Jerusalem. 30c, Christ washing Peter's feet.

1978, Mar. 20 Litho. *Perf. 12*
396 A61 10c multicolored .35 .20
397 A61 15c multicolored .50 .30
398 A61 20c multicolored .65 .40
399 A61 30c multicolored .75 .55
a. Souvenir sheet of 4, #396-399 6.50 *6.50*
Nos. 396-399 (4) 2.25 1.45

Easter; Albrecht Dürer (1471-1528). Nos. 396-399 issued in sheets of 6.

1978, Apr. 25 Litho. *Perf. 14*

10c, Girls' Brigade presenting flag. 20c, Guides studying Bible, playing guitar, tennis and volleyball. 50c, Guides setting table.

400 A62 3c multicolored .20 .20
401 A62 10c multicolored .45 .40
402 A62 20c multicolored .75 .70
403 A62 50c multicolored 1.60 1.60
Nos. 400-403 (4) 3.00 2.90

3rd Intl. Council Meeting of Girls' Brigade.

Elizabeth II Coronation Anniversary Issue
Common Design Types
Souvenir Sheet

1978, June 2 Unwmk. *Perf. 15*
404 Sheet of 6 2.50 *3.00*
a. CD326 30c Yale of Beaufort .40 .40
b. CD327 30c Elizabeth II .40 .40
c. CD328 30c Screech owl .40 .40

No. 404 contains 2 se-tenant strips of Nos. 404a-404c, separated by horizontal gutter with commemorative and descriptive inscriptions.

A63

A63a

A63: 1c, Trumpetfish. 3c, Nassau grouper. 5c, French angelfish. 10c, Schoolmaster snappers. 20c, Banded butterflyfish. 50c, Black-bar soldierfish.
A63a: 3c, Four-eyed butterflyfish. 5c, Grey angel fish. 10c, Squirrelfish. 15c, Parrotfish. 20c, Spanish hogfish. 30c, Queen angelfish.

1978-79 Wmk. 373 Litho. *Perf. 14*
405 A63 1c multicolored .20 .20
406 A63 3c multicolored .40 .20
407 A63a 3c multicolored .35 .20
408 A63a 5c multicolored .40 .20
409 A63 5c multicolored .35 .20
412 A63a 10c multicolored .65 .20
413 A63 10c multicolored .65 .20
414 A63a 15c multicolored .75 .35
415 A63a 20c multicolored 1.00 .45
416 A63 20c multicolored 1.25 .45
417 A63a 30c multicolored 2.00 .70
418 A63 50c multicolored 3.00 1.10
Nos. 405-418 (12) 11.00 4.45

Issued: design A63, 4/20/79; design A63a, 8/28/78.

Lockheed Lodestar — A64

Aircraft: 5c, Consolidated PBY. 10c, Vickers Viking. 15c, BAC1-11. 20c, Piper Cheyenne, HS 125 and Bell 47. 30c, BAC1-11.

1979, Feb. 5 *Perf. 14½*
420 A64 3c multicolored .40 .20
421 A64 5c multicolored .40 .20
422 A64 10c multicolored .55 .20
423 A64 15c multicolored 1.00 .40
424 A64 20c multicolored 1.25 .45
425 A64 30c multicolored 1.75 .55
Nos. 420-425 (6) 5.35 2.00

Opening of Owen Roberts Airport, 25th anniv.

Rowland Hill and No. 2 — A65

Sir Rowland Hill (1795-1879), originator of penny postage, and: 10c, Great Britain #132. 20c, Cayman Islands #149. 50c,Cayman Islands #20.

Perf. 13½x14½
1979, Aug. 15 Litho.
426 A65 5c multicolored .20 .20
427 A65 10c multicolored .20 .20
428 A65 20c multicolored .60 .60
Nos. 426-428 (3) 1.00 1.00

Souvenir Sheet

429 A65 50c multicolored 1.50 1.50

Flight into Egypt A66

Christmas: 20c, Shepherds, Star of Bethlehem. 30c, Nativity. 40c, Three Kings, Star of Bethlehem.

1979, Nov. 20 Litho. *Perf. 13½*
430 A66 10c multicolored .20 .20
431 A66 20c multicolored .25 .20
432 A66 30c multicolored .40 .25
433 A66 40c multicolored .70 .30
Nos. 430-433 (4) 1.55 .95

Bonaventure House, Rotary Emblem — A67

Perf. 14x13½, 13½x14
1980, Feb. 14 Litho. Wmk. 373
434 A67 20c shown .30 .20
435 A67 30c Paul P. Harris, vert. .50 .25
436 A67 50c Anniversary emblem, vert. .80 .50
Nos. 434-436 (3) 1.60 .95

Rotary International, 75th anniversary.

Mailman, London 1980 Emblem A68

1980, May 6 Litho. *Perf. 14*
437 A68 5c shown .20 .20
438 A68 10c Cat boat .20 .20
439 A68 15c Mounted mailman .25 .25
440 A68 30c Mail wagon .50 .35
441 A68 40c Mailman on bicycle .60 .45
442 A68 $1 Mail truck 1.25 .90
Nos. 437-442 (6) 3.00 2.35

London '80 Intl. Stamp Exhib., May 6-14.

Queen Mother Elizabeth Birthday Issue
Common Design Type

1980, Aug. 4 Litho. *Perf. 14*
443 CD330 20c multicolored .40 .40

Spondylus Americanus A69

1980, Aug. 12 *Perf. 14½x14*
444 A69 5c shown .90 .20
445 A69 10c Murex brevifrons .90 .30
446 A69 30c Cymatium femorale 1.75 .65
447 A69 50c Vasum muricatum 2.00 1.25
Nos. 444-447 (4) 5.55 2.40

See Nos. 502-505, 518-521.

Lantana — A70

1980, Oct. 21 Litho. *Perf. 14*
448 A70 5c shown .20 .20
449 A70 15c Bauhinia .35 .20
450 A70 30c Hibiscus .70 .30
451 A70 $1 Milk and wine lily 1.75 1.40
Nos. 448-451 (4) 3.00 2.10

See Nos. 478-481.

Juvenile Tarpon and Fire Sponges — A71

1980, Dec. 9 Litho. *Perf. 13½x13*

452	A71	3c shown	1.40	*2.25*
453	A71	5c Mangrove root oysters	1.60	*1.10*
a.		Wmk. 384	8.00	8.00
b.		Wmk. 384, perf. 14	6.75	7.00
454	A71	10c Mangrove crab	.65	*1.10*
a.		Wmk. 384, perf. 14	10.00	9.75
455	A71	15c Lizard, crescent spot butterfly	1.40	*2.25*
456	A71	20c Tricolored heron	1.90	*2.75*
457	A71	30c Red mangrove flower	.90	*1.40*
458	A71	40c Red mangrove seeds	.95	*1.60*
459	A71	50c Waterhouse's leaf-nosed bat	1.60	*2.25*
460	A71	$1 Black-crowned night heron	7.00	*7.50*
461	A71	$2 Cayman Isls. arms	2.75	*5.50*
462	A71	$4 Queen Elizabeth II	5.25	7.25
		Nos. 452-462 (11)	25.40	*34.95*

Nos. 452-462 also issued inscribed 1982 (Value, $45); 5c, 1984; 3c-$2, 1985. Other dates probably exist. No. 453a has large imprint date.

Issued: #453a, 4/86; #453b, 454a, 6/86.

Bread and Wine — A72

1981, Mar. 17 Wmk. 373 *Perf. 14*

463	A72	3c shown	.20	.20
464	A72	10c Crown of thorns	.20	.20
465	A72	20c Crucifix	.35	.35
466	A72	$1 Christ	1.00	*1.10*
		Nos. 463-466 (4)	1.75	1.85

Easter.

Wood Slave A73

1981, June 16 Litho. *Perf. 13½*

467	A73	20c shown	.45	.45
468	A73	30c Cayman iguana	.70	.70
469	A73	40c Lion lizard	.95	.95
470	A73	50c Freshwater turtle	1.10	1.10
		Nos. 467-470 (4)	3.20	3.20

Royal Wedding Issue

Common Design Type

1981, July 22 Litho. *Perf. 14*

471	CD331	20c Bouquet	.25	.25
472	CD331	30c Charles	.40	.40
473	CD331	$1 Couple	1.00	1.00
		Nos. 471-473 (3)	1.65	1.65

Intl. Year of the Disabled A74

1981, Sept. 29 Litho. *Perf. 14*

474	A74	5c Scuba divers	.20	.20
475	A74	15c Old School for Handicapped	.25	.25
476	A74	20c New School for Handicapped	.35	.35
477	A74	$1 Beach scene	1.75	1.75
		Nos. 474-477 (4)	2.55	2.55

Flower Type of 1980

1981, Oct. 20 Litho. *Perf. 14*

478	A70	3c Bougainvillea	.25	.20
479	A70	10c Morning glory	.25	.20
480	A70	20c Wild amaryllis	.55	.55
481	A70	$1 Cordia	3.00	3.00
		Nos. 478-481 (4)	4.05	3.95

TB Bacillus Centenary — A75

1982, Mar. 24 Litho. *Perf. 14½*

482	A75	15c Koch, horizontal microscope	.35	.35
483	A75	30c Koch, vert.	.75	.75
484	A75	40c Microscope, vert.	.90	.90
485	A75	50c Koch, diff., vert.	1.25	1.25
		Nos. 482-485 (4)	3.25	3.25

Princess Diana Issue

Common Design Type

1982, July 1 Litho. *Perf. 13*

486	CD333	20c Arms	*.65*	.40
487	CD333	30c Diana	*1.10*	.75
488	CD333	40c Wedding	*1.25*	.75
489	CD333	50c Portrait	*4.00*	*1.50*
		Nos. 486-489 (4)	*7.00*	*3.40*

Scouting Year A76

1982, Aug. 24 Wmk. 373 *Perf. 14*

490	A76	3c Pitching tent	.30	.20
491	A76	20c Cooking	.75	.75
492	A76	30c Troop	1.25	1.25
493	A76	50c Boating skills	1.75	1.75
		Nos. 490-493 (4)	4.05	3.95

Christmas 1982 — A77

Virgin and Child Paintings by Raphael.

1982, Oct. 26 *Perf. 14½*

494	A77	3c multicolored	.20	.20
495	A77	10c multicolored	.35	.35
496	A77	20c multicolored	.70	.70
497	A77	30c multicolored	1.00	1.00
		Nos. 494-497 (4)	2.25	2.25

Representative Govt. Sesquicentennial — A78

1982, Nov. 9 Litho. Wmk. 373

498	A78	3c Mace	.20	.20
499	A78	10c Old Courthouse	.20	.20
500	A78	20c Commonwealth Parliamentary Assoc. arms	.45	.45
501	A78	30c Legislative Assembley building	.75	.75
		Nos. 498-501 (4)	1.60	1.60

Shell Type of 1980

1983, Jan. 11 Litho. *Perf. 13½*

502	A69	5c Natica canrena	.20	.20
503	A69	10c Cassis tuberosa	.40	.40
504	A69	20c Strombus gallus	.90	.90
505	A69	$1 Cypraecassis testiculus	4.00	4.00
		Nos. 502-505 (4)	5.50	5.50

Visit of Queen Elizabeth II and Prince Philip A79

1983, Feb. 15 Litho. *Perf. 14*

506	A79	20c Legislative Building, Cayman Brac	.60	.60
507	A79	30c Leg. Bldg., Grand Cayman	1.00	.90
508	A79	50c Prince Philip	1.75	1.50
509	A79	$1 Queen Elizabeth II	3.00	3.00
a.		Souvenir sheet of 4, #506-509	7.25	7.25
		Nos. 506-509 (4)	6.35	6.00

A80

1983, Mar. 14

510	A80	3c Globe	.30	.20
511	A80	15c Flags	.70	.60
512	A80	20c Fisherman	.80	.70
513	A80	40c Elizabeth II	1.25	.95
		Nos. 510-513 (4)	3.05	2.45

Commonwealth Day.

Manned Flight Bicentenary and Mosquito Research and Control Unit — A81

Airplanes.

1983, Oct. 10 Litho. *Perf. 14½*

514	A81	3c MRCU Cessna	1.10	.70
515	A81	10c Consolidated Catalina PBY	1.25	.70
516	A81	20c Boeing 727	2.10	2.10
517	A81	40c Hawker Siddeley HS-748	3.00	*3.75*
		Nos. 514-517 (4)	7.45	7.25

Shell Type of 1980

1984, Jan. 18 *Perf. 14x14½*

518	A69	3c Natica floridana	1.50	.40
519	A69	10c Conus austini	1.75	.40
520	A69	30c Colubrania obscura	5.00	*5.00*
521	A69	50c Turbo cailletii	5.25	*5.25*
		Nos. 518-521 (4)	13.50	*11.05*

Lloyd's List Issue

Common Design Type

1984, May 16 Litho. *Perf. 14*

522	CD335	5c Cruise ship	.75	.20
523	CD335	10c The Old Harbor	.85	.30
524	CD335	25c Ridgefield	1.60	1.60
525	CD335	50c Goldfield	3.25	*3.25*
		Nos. 522-525 (4)	6.45	*5.35*

Souvenir Sheet

526	CD335	$1 Goldfield, diff.	3.75	3.75

No. 525 Overprinted: "U.P.U. CONGRESS HAMBURG 1984"

1984, June 18

527	CD335	50c multicolored	1.50	1.60

Local Birds — A82

Perf. 14x14½

1984, Aug. 15 Litho. Wmk. 373

528	A82	5c Snowy egret	1.40	.65
529	A82	10c Bananaquit	1.40	.65
530	A82	35c Kingfisher	4.75	3.25
531	A82	$1 Brown booby	8.50	*9.50*
		Nos. 528-531 (4)	16.05	*14.05*

Christmas — A83

Orchids — A84

#532a-532d, evening beach scenes. #533a-533d, daytime boating and beach scenes.

1984, Oct. 17 Litho. *Perf. 14*

532		Strip of 4	5.00	*5.00*
a.-d.		A83 5c Any single	1.25	*1.25*
533		Strip of 4	6.00	*5.00*
a.-d.		A83 25c Any single	1.50	*1.25*

Souvenir Sheet

534	A83	$1 Bonfire, diff.	6.50	6.50

No. 534 contains one stamp 29x48mm.

1985, Mar. 13 Litho. *Perf. 14x13½*

535	A84	5c Schomburgkia thomsoniana var.	1.75	.55
536	A84	10c Schomburgkia thomsoniana	1.75	.55
537	A84	25c Encyclia plicata	4.25	1.60
538	A84	50c Dendrophylax fawcetti	6.25	4.25
		Nos. 535-538 (4)	14.00	6.95

Shipwrecks A85

Unspecified shipwrecks found in Cayman waters.

1985, May 22 *Perf. 14*

539	A85	5c multicolored	1.50	.55
540	A85	25c multicolored	4.75	2.10
541	A85	35c multicolored	5.50	4.25
542	A85	40c multicolored	5.75	5.75
		Nos. 539-542 (4)	17.50	12.65

Intl. Youth Year — A86

5c, Natl. Athletic Assoc. track competition. 15c, High school students studying in Grand Cayman Campus Library. 25c, Amateur League Competition Football. 50c, Natl. Netball Assoc. competition.

1985, Aug. 14 *Perf. 14½*

543	A86	5c multicolored	.30	.25
544	A86	15c multicolored	.50	.40
545	A86	25c multicolored	1.10	.85
546	A86	50c multicolored	2.10	2.10
		Nos. 543-546 (4)	4.00	3.60

Telecommunications, 50th Anniv. — A87

Designs: 5c, Morse Code transmitter, 1935. 10c, Hand-cranked telephone, 1935. 25c, Tropospheric scatter dish, 1966. 50c, Earth dish receiver, 1979.

1985, Oct. 25 *Perf. 14*

547	A87	5c multicolored	.65	.65
548	A87	10c multicolored	.70	.70
549	A87	25c multicolored	1.90	1.10
550	A87	50c multicolored	3.25	*4.00*
		Nos. 547-550 (4)	6.50	6.45

Birds A88

1986, Mar. 20 Litho. Wmk. 384

551	A88	10c Magnificent frigatebird	2.50	1.10
552	A88	25c West Indian whistling duck	3.25	1.75
553	A88	35c La Sagra's flycatcher	3.75	3.75
554	A88	40c Yellow-faced grassquit	4.50	4.50
		Nos. 551-554 (4)	14.00	11.10

Nos. 552-553 vert.

Queen Elizabeth II 60th Birthday

Common Design Type

Designs: 5c, As bridesmaid at wedding of Lady Mary Cambridge, 1931. 10c, Royal visit to Norway, 1955. 25c, Inspecting West Indian troop, royal tour, 1985. 50c, Gulf tour, 1979. $1, Visiting Crown Agents' offices, 1983.

1986, Apr. 21 *Perf. 14x14½*

555	CD337	5c scar, blk & sil	.20	.20
556	CD337	10c ultra, blk & sil	.25	.25
557	CD337	25c grn & multi	2.00	.95
558	CD337	50c vio & multi	1.00	1.10
559	CD337	$1 rose vio & multi	1.60	*1.90*
		Nos. 555-559 (5)	5.05	4.40

Royal Wedding Issue, 1986

Common Design Type

Designs: 5c, Informal portrait. 50c, Andrew in uniform, helicopter.

Perf. 14½x14

1986, July 23 Litho. Wmk. 384

560	CD338	5c multicolored	.35	.25
561	CD338	50c multicolored	1.50	*1.90*

Marine Life — A89

Perf. 13½x13

1986, Sept. 15 Wmk. 373

562	A89	5c Rhynchocinetes rigeus	.80	*.65*
563	A89	10c Nemaster rubiginosa	.80	*.65*
a.		Wmk. 384, inscribed "1990"	2.75	3.00
564	A89	15c Calcinus tibicen	.70	*.75*
565	A89	20c Rhodactis sanctithomae	.70	*.95*
566	A89	25c Spirobranchus gigantea	.45	*3.00*
567	A89	35c Diodon holacanthus	.70	*3.25*
568	A89	50c Pseudocorynactis caribbeorum	.80	*5.00*
569	A89	60c Astrophyton muricatum	3.50	*9.50*
570	A89	75c Cyphoma gibbosum	9.50	*12.00*
571	A89	$1 Conolylactis gigantea	2.25	*3.25*
572	A89	$2 Malacoctenus boehlkei	5.00	*5.25*
573	A89	$4 Lima scabra	10.00	*8.25*
		Nos. 562-573 (12)	35.20	*52.50*

Nos. 562-565, 571-573 exist inscribed "1987." Value $22. Nos. 562-566, 571-572 exist inscribed "1990." Value $38.

Tourism A90

Perf. 13x13½

1987, Jan. 26 Wmk. 384

574	A90	10c Golfing	3.00	1.00
575	A90	15c Sailing	3.25	1.00
576	A90	25c Snorkeling	3.25	1.50
577	A90	35c Parasailing	3.25	2.00
578	A90	$1 Fishing	7.25	*9.75*
		Nos. 574-578 (5)	20.00	*15.25*

Fruit — A91

1987, May 20 *Perf. 14½*

579	A91	5c Akee	.95	.95
580	A91	25c Breadfruit	2.10	.70
581	A91	35c Papaya	2.10	1.00
582	A91	$1 Soursop	5.75	*6.75*
		Nos. 579-582 (4)	10.90	*9.40*

Lizards — A92

1987, Aug. 26 Litho. *Perf. 14*

583	A92	10c Lion lizard	2.40	.95
584	A92	50c Iguana	5.75	4.50
585	A92	$1 Anole	7.00	*8.25*
		Nos. 583-585 (3)	15.15	13.70

Flowers — A93

Herons — A95

Butterflies A94

1987, Nov. 18 *Perf. 14½x14*

586	A93	5c Poinsettia	1.25	.55
587	A93	25c Periwinkle	3.00	.90
588	A93	35c Yellow allamanda	3.00	1.25
589	A93	75c Blood lily	5.25	6.00
		Nos. 586-589 (4)	12.50	8.70

1988, Mar. 29 Wmk. 384 *Perf. 14*

Designs: 5c, Hemiargus ammon erembis and Strymon martialis. 25c, Phocides pigmalion batabano. 50c, Anaea troglodyta cubana. $1, Papilio andraemon andraemon.

590	A94	5c multicolored	2.00	.65
591	A94	25c multicolored	4.25	1.40
592	A94	50c multicolored	6.50	5.25
593	A94	$1 multicolored	8.25	8.25
		Nos. 590-593 (4)	21.00	15.55

1988, Jan. 26 Litho. *Perf. 14*

594	A95	5c Butorides striatus	2.50	.65
595	A95	25c Egretta tricolor	4.75	.90
596	A95	50c Nycticorax violaceus	6.00	6.00
597	A95	$1 Egretta caerulea	6.50	6.50
		Nos. 594-597 (4)	19.75	14.05

1988 Summer Olympics, Seoul — A96

1988, Sept. 21 *Perf. 14½*

598	A96	10c Cycling	2.25	.65
599	A96	50c Natl. team, passenger jet	3.75	2.75
600	A96	$1 Yachting	4.00	4.00
		Nos. 598-600 (3)	10.00	7.40

Souvenir Sheet

Wmk. 373

601	A96	$1 Tennis	7.00	7.00

No. 601 commemorates the 75th anniv. of the Intl. Tennis Federation.

Visit of Princess Alexandra A97

1988, Nov. 1 Wmk. 373 *Perf. 15*

602	A97	5c Portrait	2.75	1.25
603	A97	$1 Seated in garden	9.75	7.50

Cayman Islands P.O., Cent. — A98

Designs: 5c, P.O., Georgetown, 1889, and Jamaica #24, canceled. 25c, S.S. Orinoco and Cayman Isls. #1. 35c, Grand Cayman G.P.O. and #442. $1, Cayman Airways mail plane and #191.

1989, Apr. 12 Wmk. 384 *Perf. 14½*

604	A98	5c multicolored	1.25	1.25
605	A98	25c multicolored	2.75	1.50
606	A98	35c multicolored	3.00	1.75
607	A98	$1 multicolored	11.00	11.00
		Nos. 604-607 (4)	18.00	15.50

A99

A100

Mutiny on the Bounty: a, Capt. Bligh. b, HMS Providence, two crewmen. c, HMS Assistant, transplanted breadfruit. d, Moving breadfruit on land, in longboat. e, Midshipman among casks and crates.

1989, May 24 *Perf. 14*

608		Strip of 5	32.50	32.50
a.-e.		A99 50c any single	6.50	6.50

Perf. 14½x14

1989, Oct. 18 Litho. Wmk. 373

609	A100	5c Panton House	.90	.90
610	A100	10c Town Hall	.90	.90
611	A100	25c Old Courts House	2.00	.80
612	A100	35c Elmslie Memorial Church	2.10	1.10
613	A100	$1 Post office	5.00	5.25
		Nos. 609-613 (5)	10.90	8.95

Natl. Trust emblem & architecture, George Town.

Island Surveys A101

Maps or survey ships: 5c, Navigational instruments and George Gauld's map of 1773. 25c, Instruments and map created by surveyors aboard HMS *Vidal*, 1956. 50c, *Mutine*, 1914. $1, HMS *Vidal*.

1989, Nov. 15

614	A101	5c multicolored	1.75	1.40
615	A101	25c multicolored	4.50	1.75
616	A101	50c multicolored	7.00	*5.25*
617	A101	$1 multicolored	11.00	*11.00*
		Nos. 614-617 (4)	24.25	*19.40*

Angelfish A102

1990, Apr. 25 Wmk. 384 *Perf. 14*

618	A102	10c French	2.10	.65
619	A102	25c Gray	3.75	1.40
620	A102	50c Queen	5.50	5.50
621	A102	$1 Rock beauty	9.00	9.00
		Nos. 618-621 (4)	20.35	16.55

Queen Mother, 90th Birthday

Common Design Types

1990, Aug. 4 Wmk. 384 *Perf. 14x15*

622	CD343	50c King, Queen Elizabeth, 1948	1.75	*2.50*

Perf. 14½

623	CD344	$1 King, Queen with Churchill, 1940	3.75	*4.25*

Butterflies A103

1990, Oct. 24 *Perf. 14½x14*

624	A103	5c Soldier	1.60	1.25
625	A103	25c Pygmy blue	3.50	2.40
626	A103	35c Cayman crescent spot	4.50	2.75
627	A103	$1 Gulf fritillary	10.50	10.50
		Nos. 624-627 (4)	20.10	16.90

Expo '90, International Garden and Greenery Exposition, Osaka, Japan.

Hurricane Awareness — A104

Designs: 5c, Goes weather satellite. 30c, Meteorologist tracks storm. 40c, Hurricane damage. $1, Lockheed WP-3D Orion flying in hurricane's eye.

1991, Aug. 8 *Perf. 14*

628	A104	5c multicolored	1.60	1.50
629	A104	30c multicolored	3.75	1.75
630	A104	40c multicolored	4.00	2.10
631	A104	$1 multicolored	9.50	9.50
		Nos. 628-631 (4)	18.85	14.85

Christmas A105

Local flowers and Christmas scenes: 5c, Angel's trumpet, angels with trumpets. 30c,

Golden trumpet, Mary on donkey led by Joseph. 40c, Christmas flower, Adoration of the Magi. 60c, Tree of life, nativity scene.

1991, Nov. 6 **Wmk. 373**

632	A105	5c multicolored	1.00	1.00
633	A105	30c multicolored	3.00	.85
634	A105	40c multicolored	3.25	1.40
635	A105	60c multicolored	3.75	*5.00*
		Nos. 632-635 (4)	11.00	*8.25*

Island Scenes A106

Perf. 12½x13, 13x12½

1991, Dec. 11 **Litho.** **Wmk. 373**

636	A106	5c Coconut tree, vert.	.75	.55
637	A106	15c Beach scene	1.60	.55
638	A106	20c Poincianas in bloom	.85	.70
639	A106	30c Blowholes	2.25	.90
640	A106	40c Police band	3.75	2.25
641	A106	50c Downtown scene, vert.	3.00	2.25
642	A106	60c The Bluff, Cayman Brac	2.50	3.50
643	A106	80c Coat of arms, vert.	2.25	3.75
644	A106	90c View of Hell	2.25	3.75
645	A106	$1 Sportfishing	4.50	3.75
646	A106	$2 Harbor scene, vert.	9.50	9.00
647	A106	$8 Queen Elizabeth II, vert.	22.50	25.00
		Nos. 636-647 (12)	55.70	55.95

No. 636 exists inscribed "1994." Value $1.

Queen Elizabeth II's Accession to the Throne, 40th Anniv.

Common Design Type

Wmk. 373, 384 (40c)

1992, Feb. 6 **Litho.** ***Perf. 14***

648	CD349	5c multicolored	.45	.45
649	CD349	20c multicolored	1.60	.50
650	CD349	30c multicolored	1.75	.75
651	CD349	40c multicolored	1.75	1.40
652	CD349	$1 multicolored	3.25	*4.00*
		Nos. 648-652 (5)	8.80	7.10

1992 Summer Olympics, Barcelona A107

1992, Aug. 5 **Wmk. 373**

653	A107	15c Cyclist	2.25	.55
654	A107	40c Two cyclists	3.75	1.50
655	A107	60c Feet, pedals	4.50	4.50
656	A107	$1 Two cyclists, diff.	5.50	5.50
		Nos. 653-656 (4)	16.00	12.05

Island Heritage — A108

1992, Oct. 21

657	A108	5c Lady with donkey	.70	.70
658	A108	30c Making fish nets	1.75	1.00
659	A108	40c Maypole dancing	3.00	1.60
660	A108	60c Basket making	3.50	*3.50*
661	A108	$1 Cooking on caboose	4.25	*4.25*
		Nos. 657-661 (5)	13.20	*11.05*

Rays A109

Perf. 13½x14

1993, June 16 **Litho.** **Wmk. 373**

662	A109	5c Yellow stingray	1.10	.85
663	A109	30c Southern stingray	2.75	1.60
664	A109	40c Spotted eagle ray	3.25	1.90
665	A109	$1 Manta ray	7.00	7.00
		Nos. 662-665 (4)	14.10	11.35

A110

A111

Tourism: No. 666a, Turtle, sailboats. b, Diver, coral, boats. c, Golf. d, Beach, tennis. e, Pirates, sailing ship.

No. 667: a, Cruise ship, boat, sailboat. b, City street scene. c, Submarines. d, Cyclist, scooters. e, Jet planes.

Perf. 14x13½

1993, Sept. 30 **Litho.** **Wmk. 373**

666	A110	15c Strip of 5, #a.-e.	11.50	11.50
667	A110	30c Strip of 5, #a.-e.	12.50	12.50
f.		Booklet pane of 10, #666-667	30.00	

1993, Oct. 29 ***Perf. 14***

Various views of Grand Cayman Parrot.

668	A111	5c green & multi	1.40	1.40
669	A111	5c red & multi	1.40	1.40
670	A111	30c yellow & multi	3.50	3.50
671	A111	30c blue & multi	3.50	3.50
		Nos. 668-671 (4)	9.80	9.80

Christmas A112

Christmas scenes, orchids: 5c, Manger, Ionopsis utricularioides. 40c, Shepherd, lamb, Encyclia cochleata. 60c, Magi, Vanilla pompona. $1, Virgin in prayer, Oncidium caymanense.

Perf. 13½x14

1993, Dec. 6 **Litho.** **Wmk. 384**

672	A112	5c multicolored	1.40	.75
673	A112	40c multicolored	3.75	1.00
674	A112	60c multicolored	4.75	*4.75*
675	A112	$1 multicolored	6.25	*6.25*
		Nos. 672-675 (4)	16.15	*12.75*

Souvenir Sheet

Reef Life — A113

Designs: a, Holocanthus ciliaris. b, Bodianus pulchellus, anisotremus virginicus. c, Holocanthus tricolor, gramma loreto. d, Pomacanthus paru, chaeton striatus.

Perf. 14½x13

1994, Feb. 18 **Litho.** **Wmk. 373**

676	A113	60c Sheet of 4, #a.-d.	15.00	15.00

Hong Kong '94.

Royal Visit — A114

Designs: 5c, Cayman Islands, United Kingdom flags. 15c, Royal yacht Britannia. 30c, Queen Elizabeth II. $2, Queen, Prince Philip.

1994, Feb. 22 ***Perf. 14½***

677	A114	5c multicolored	2.00	.95
678	A114	15c multicolored	3.75	1.60
679	A114	30c multicolored	3.75	1.75
680	A114	$2 multicolored	10.50	10.50
		Nos. 677-680 (4)	20.00	14.80

West Indian Whistling Duck A115

5c, One standing. 15c, Landing in water. 20c, Four ducks, various activities. 80c, One raising wings. $1, Adult, chick.

Wmk. 373

1994, Apr. 21 **Litho.** ***Perf. 14***

681	A115	5c multi, vert.	1.50	.80
682	A115	15c multi	2.25	.85
683	A115	20c multi	2.25	.90
684	A115	80c multi, vert.	5.00	*5.50*
685	A115	$1 multi, vert.	5.75	*6.00*
a.		Souvenir sheet of 1	13.00	*13.00*
		Nos. 681-685 (5)	16.75	*14.05*

No. 685a has a continuous design and contains Cayman Islands Natl. Trust emblem.

Butterflies A116

No. 686: a, Fulvous hairstreak. b, Atala butterfly.

No. 687: a, Barred sulphur. b, Dorantes skipper.

Wmk. 373

1994, Aug. 16 **Litho.** ***Perf. 13½***

686	A116	10c Pair, #a.-b.	3.00	*3.25*
687	A116	$1 Pair, #a.-b.	14.50	*14.50*

Wreck of the Ten Sail, Bicent. — A117

Perf. 13½x14

1994, Oct. 12 **Litho.** **Wmk. 373**

688	A117	10c shown	.75	.75
689	A117	10c multicolored	.75	.75
690	A117	15c multicolored	1.25	.60
691	A117	20c multicolored	1.50	.70
692	A117	$2 multicolored	7.75	7.75
		Nos. 688-692 (5)	12.00	10.55

Sea Turtles A118

Wmk. 384

1995, Feb. 28 **Litho.** ***Perf. 14***

693	A118	10c Green	.85	.45
694	A118	20c Kemp's ridley	1.25	.55
695	A118	25c Hawksbill	1.40	.65
696	A118	30c Leatherback	1.60	.75
697	A118	$1.30 Loggerhead	5.75	5.75
698	A118	$2 Pacific ridley	7.25	7.25
a.		Souvenir sheet, #693-698	18.00	18.00
		Nos. 693-698 (6)	18.10	15.40

1995 CARIFTA & IAAF Games A119

1995, Apr. 15 **Litho.** ***Perf. 14***

699	A119	10c Running	1.00	.55
700	A119	20c Pole vault	1.50	1.10
701	A119	30c Javelin	2.10	1.25
702	A119	$1.30 Sailing	7.25	7.25
		Nos. 699-702 (4)	11.85	10.15

Souvenir Sheet

703	A119	$2 Medal winners	10.00	*10.00*

End of World War II, 50th Anniv.

Common Design Type

10c, Two soldiers, Cayman Home Guard. 25c, Freighter Comayagua torpedoed off Caymans, 5/14/42. 40c, Type IXc U-Boat U-125. $1, Navy airship L-3 used for U-boat patrol. $1.30, Reverse of War Medal 1939-45.

Wmk. 373

1995, May 8 **Litho.** ***Perf. 13½***

704	CD351	10c multicolored	1.50	.55
705	CD351	25c multicolored	3.00	.90
706	CD351	40c multicolored	3.50	2.25
707	CD351	$1 multicolored	6.50	*6.50*
		Nos. 704-707 (4)	14.50	*10.20*

Souvenir Sheet

Perf. 14

708	CD352	$1.30 multicolored	5.50	5.50

Souvenir Sheet

Queen Mother, 95th Birthday — A120

1995, Aug. 25 ***Perf. 14½***

709	A120	$4 multicolored	13.50	13.50

Singapore '95.

A121

A122

Animals of the Nativity.

1995, Nov. 1 *Perf. 14*

710 A121 10c Ox 1.00 .30
711 A121 20c Sheep, lamb 1.50 .50
712 A121 30c Donkey 2.50 .60
713 A121 $2 Camels 9.00 *10.50*
a. Souvenir sheet of 4, #710-713 14.00 *14.00*
Nos. 710-713 (4) 14.00 *11.90*

Wmk. 384

1996, Mar. 21 Litho. *Perf. 14*

Wild fruit.

714 A122 10c Sea grape .70 .50
715 A122 25c Guava 1.50 .70
716 A122 40c West Indian cherry 2.25 1.25
717 A122 $1 Tamarind 4.50 5.75
Nos. 714-717 (4) 8.95 8.20

Modern Olympic Games, Cent. — A123

Perf. 14x13½

1996, June 19 Litho. Wmk. 384

718 A123 10c Sailing .65 .45
719 A123 20c Sailboarding 1.25 .55
720 A123 30c Sailing, diff. 1.60 .80
721 A123 $2 Running 6.50 6.50
Nos. 718-721 (4) 10.00 8.30

Symbols of National Identity — A124

Designs: 10c, Guitar, music, natl. song. 20c, Boeing 737. 25c, Queen Elizabeth II opening Legislative Assembly. 30c, Seven Mile Beach. 40c, Scuba diver, stingrays. 60c, School children, Cayman Turtle Farm. 80c, Cayman parrot, natl. bird. 90c, Silver thatch palm, natl. tree. $1, Natl. flag. $2, Wild banana orchid, natl. flower. $4, Natl. arms. $6, Natl. currency.

Wmk. 373

1996, Sept. 26 Litho. *Perf. 14*

722 A124 10c multicolored .50 .45
Complete booklet, 10 #722 5.25
723 A124 20c multicolored 1.10 .85
724 A124 25c multicolored 1.25 .80
725 A124 30c multicolored 1.25 .80
Complete booklet, 10 #725 13.00
726 A124 40c multicolored 1.60 1.25
Complete booklet, 10 #726 17.00
727 A124 60c multicolored 2.25 1.60
728 A124 80c multicolored 3.75 3.00
a. Souvenir sheet of 1 3.75 3.75
729 A124 90c multicolored 2.50 3.00
730 A124 $1 multicolored 4.00 3.25
731 A124 $2 multicolored 7.25 7.00
732 A124 $4 multicolored 13.00 16.00
733 A124 $6 multicolored 17.00 20.00
Nos. 722-733 (12) 55.45 58.00

No. 728a for Hong Kong '97. Issued 2/3/97.
Nos. 723, 725, 727 exist dated "1999." Value, set $6.

Christmas A125

Designs: 10c, Christmas time on North Church Street. 25c, Santa "Gone Fishing." 30c, "Claus Encounters." $2, "Caymanian Christmas."

Wmk. 373

1996, Nov. 12 Litho. *Perf. 14*

734 A125 10c multicolored .65 .35
735 A125 25c multicolored 1.60 .90
736 A125 30c multicolored 2.00 1.25
737 A125 $2 multicolored 4.50 4.50
Nos. 734-737 (4) 8.75 7.00

Queen Elizabeth II and Prince Philip, 50th Wedding Anniv. — A126

#738, Queen. #739, Royal Guard. #740, Young Prince riding horse. #741, Queen in blue, Prince in military attire in open carriage. #742 Prince holding horse's reins. #743, Queen looking at horses.
$1, Queen, Prince in open carriage.

Perf. 14x13½

1997, July 10 Litho. Wmk. 373

738 A126 10c multicolored 1.25 1.25
739 A126 10c multicolored 1.25 1.25
a. Pair, #738-739 2.50 2.50
740 A126 30c multicolored 2.00 2.00
741 A126 30c multicolored 2.00 2.00
a. Pair, #740-741 4.00 4.00
742 A126 40c multicolored 2.40 2.40
743 A126 40c multicolored 2.40 2.40
a. Pair, #742-743 5.00 5.00
Nos. 738-743 (6) 11.30 11.30

Souvenir Sheet

744 A126 $1 multicolored 7.25 7.25

Telecommunications — A127

Designs: 10c, Children using the Internet. 25c, Cable and wireless ship. 30c, Children wearing numbers of new area code, "345." 60c, Cable and wireless satellite communications.

Perf. 14x14½

1997, Oct. 10 Litho. Wmk. 384

745 A127 10c multicolored .45 .30
746 A127 25c multicolored 1.25 .80
747 A127 30c multicolored 1.40 .95
748 A127 60c multicolored 2.25 2.25
Nos. 745-748 (4) 5.35 4.30

Christmas A128

Santa Claus: 10c, Relaxing in hammock, Little Cayman. 30c, With children on bluff, Cayman Brac. 40c, Playing golf. $1, Diving with stingrays.

Wmk. 373

1997, Dec. 3 Litho. *Perf. 13*

749 A128 10c multicolored .40 .25
750 A128 30c multicolored .85 .45
751 A128 40c multicolored 2.00 .80
752 A128 $1 multicolored 3.25 3.50
Nos. 749-752 (4) 6.50 5.00

Diana, Princess of Wales (1961-97)

Common Design Type

Portraits: a, 10c. b, 20c. c, 40c. d, $1.

Perf. 14½x14

1998 Litho. Wmk. 373

752A CD355 10c Like #753a 1.00 1.00
752B CD355 20c Like #753b 2.00 2.00

Sheet of 4

753 CD355 #a.-d. 6.00 6.00

No. 753 sold for $1.70 + 30c, with surtax from international sales being donated to the Princess Diana Memorial Fund and surtax from national sales being donated to designated local charity.

Royal Air Force, 80th Anniv.

Common Design Type of 1993 Re-Inscribed

Designs: 10c, Hawker Horsley. 20c, Fairey Hendon. 25c, Hawker Siddeley Gnat. 30c, Hawker Siddeley Dominie.
No. 758: a, 40c, Airco DH-9. b, 60c, Spad 13 Scout. c, 80c, Airspeed Oxford. d, $1, Martin Baltimore.

Wmk. 373

1998, Apr. 1 Litho. *Perf. 14*

754 CD350 10c multicolored 1.00 1.00
755 CD350 20c multicolored 1.40 1.40
756 CD350 25c multicolored 1.60 1.60
757 CD350 30c multicolored 2.00 2.00
Nos. 754-757 (4) 6.00 6.00

Souvenir Sheet

758 CD350 Sheet of 4, #a.-d. 10.00 10.00

Birds — A129

Designs: 10c, West Indian whistling duck. 20c, Magnificent frigatebird. 60c, Red footed booby. $1, Grand Cayman parrot.

1998 Litho. Wmk. 373 *Perf. 13½*

759 A129 10c multicolored 1.10 .60
760 A129 20c multicolored 2.00 .60
761 A129 60c multicolored 3.50 3.50
762 A129 $1 multicolored 4.25 4.25
Nos. 759-762 (4) 10.85 8.95

Christmas A130

Santa at various island locations: 10c, At Blowholes. 30c, Diving on wreck of MV Capt. Keith Tibbetts. 40c, Visiting Pedro Castle. 60c, Arriving at Little Cayman.

1998 *Perf. 14x14½*

763 A130 10c multicolored .40 .40
764 A130 30c multicolored 1.10 .85
765 A130 40c multicolored 1.50 1.10
766 A130 60c multicolored 3.00 3.00
Nos. 763-766 (4) 6.00 5.35

Easter A131

Artworks by Miss Lassie (Gladwyn Bush): 10c, "They Rolled the Stone Away." 20c, "Ascension," vert. 30c, "The World Praying for Peace." 40c, "Calvary," vert.

Wmk. 373

1999, Mar. 26 Litho. *Perf. 13*

767 A131 10c multicolored .50 .50
768 A131 20c multicolored .90 .90
769 A131 30c multicolored 1.40 1.40
770 A131 40c multicolored 1.50 1.50
Nos. 767-770 (4) 4.30 4.30

Vision 2008 A132

Children's drawings: 10c, "Cayman House." 30c, "Coral Reef." 40c, "Fisherman on North Sound." $2, "Three Fish and A Turtle."

1999, June *Perf. 13½*

771 A132 10c multicolored .35 .35
772 A132 30c multicolored 1.25 1.25
773 A132 40c multicolored 1.40 1.40
774 A132 $2 multicolored 7.00 7.00
Nos. 771-774 (4) 10.00 10.00

Wedding of Prince Edward and Sophie Rhys-Jones

Common Design Type

Perf. 13¾x14

1999, June 16 Litho. Wmk. 384

775 CD356 10c Separate portraits .50 .50
776 CD356 $2 Couple 5.50 5.50

1st Manned Moon Landing, 30th Anniv.

Common Design Type

Designs: 10c, Coast Guard during launch. 25c, 3rd stage fires and puts rocket in orbit. 30c, Aldrin descends to lunar surface. 60c, Lander module sent back to moon.
$1.50, Looking at earth from moon.

1999, July 20 *Perf. 14x13¾*

777 CD357 10c multicolored .45 .45
778 CD357 25c multicolored 1.10 1.10
779 CD357 30c multicolored 1.25 1.25
780 CD357 60c multicolored 2.50 2.50
Nos. 777-780 (4) 5.30 5.30

Souvenir Sheet

Perf. 14

781 CD357 $1.50 multicolored 5.50 5.50

No. 781 contains one circular stamp 40mm in diameter.

Queen Mother's Century

Common Design Type

Queen Mother: 10c, Looking at London's defenses, 1940. 20c, At Clarence House, 94th birthday. 30c, With Princes Charles and William. 40c, Reviewing the Chelsea Pensioners, 1986.
$1.50, At her wedding.

Wmk. 384

1999, Aug. 18 Litho. *Perf. 13¼*

782 CD358 10c multicolored .45 .45
783 CD358 20c multicolored .80 .80
784 CD358 30c multicolored 1.40 1.40
785 CD358 40c multicolored 1.75 1.75
Nos. 782-785 (4) 4.40 4.40

Souvenir Sheet

786 CD358 $1.50 multicolored 4.75 4.75

Christmas — A133

Wmk. 373

1999, Nov. 17 Litho. *Perf. 13¼*

787 A133 10c #242, vert. .40 .35
788 A133 30c #532d, vert. 1.10 .90
789 A133 40c #749, vert. 1.50 1.25
790 A133 $1 #431 3.00 3.00
a. Souv. sheet, #787-790, perf. 12 5.25 5.25
Nos. 787-790 (4) 6.00 5.50

British Monarchs — A134

No. 792: a, Henry VIII. b, Mary I. c, Charles II. d, Anne. e, George IV. f, George V.

Wmk. 373

2000, Feb. 29 Litho. *Perf. 14*

791	A134	10c Henry VII	.40	.40

Sheet of 6

792	A134	40c #a.-f.	8.00	8.00

The Stamp Show 2000, London.

Sesame Street — A135

Designs: 10c, Ernie. 30c, Big Bird.

No. 795: a, Grover. b, Zoe. c, Oscar the Grouch. d, The Count. e, Like 30c. f, Cookie Monster. g, Like 10c. h, Bert. i, Elmo in pond.

No. 796, Elmo collecting stamps.

Perf. 14½x14¾

2000, Mar. 15 Litho. Wmk. 373

793	A135	10c multi	.40	.40
794	A135	30c multi	1.10	1.10
795	A135	20c Sheet of 9, #a-i	6.25	6.25

Souvenir Sheet

796	A135	20c multi	1.90	1.90

Prince William, 18th Birthday

Common Design Type

10c, In checked shirt and in sweater and checked shirt. 20c, In white shirt and black bow tie. 30c, In blue casual shirt, vert. 40c, As child, with beret, vert. $1, As infant.

Perf. 14¼x13¾, 13¾x14¼

2000, June 21 Litho. Wmk. 373

Stamps With White Border

797	CD359	10c multi	.50	.40
798	CD359	20c multi	1.00	.95
799	CD359	30c multi	1.40	1.25
800	CD359	40c multi	1.90	1.90
		Nos. 797-800 (4)	4.80	4.50

Souvenir Sheet

Stamps Without White Border

Perf. 14¼

801	Sheet of 5	8.00	8.00
a.	CD359 10c multi	.35	.35
b.	CD359 20c multi	.75	.75
c.	CD359 30c multi	1.00	1.00
d.	CD359 40c multi	1.40	1.40
e.	CD359 $1 multi	4.00	4.00

Marine Life A136

10c, Green turtle. 20c, Queen angelfish. 30c, Parrotfish. $1, Green moray eel.

Wmk. 384

2000, Aug. 25 Litho. *Perf. 14*

802-805	A136	Set of 4	8.25	8.25

National Drug Council A137

Various children's drawings. Denominations, 10c, 15c, 30c, $2.

2000, Aug. 25

806-809	A137	Set of 4	12.00	12.00

Christmas A138

10c, Backing sand. 30c, Christmas dinner. 40c, Yard dance. 60c, Conch shell border.

Perf. 14½x14¼

2000, Nov. 14 Wmk. 373

810-813	A138	Set of 4	9.00	9.00

UN Women's Human Rights Campaign — A139

Wmk. 373

2001, Mar. 8 Litho. *Perf. 14*

814	A139	10c multi	.80	.80

Cayman Brac A140

Designs: 15c, Red mangrove. 20c, Peter's Cave, vert. 25c, Bight Road stairway, vert. 30c, Westerly Pond. 40c, Aerial view. 60c, Marshes.

2001, Apr. 21

815-820	A140	Set of 6	10.50	10.50

Non-profit Organizations — A141

Designs: Nos. 821, 826a, 15c, National Council of Voluntary Organizations. Nos. 822, 826b, 20c, Cayman Humane Society. Nos. 823, 826c, 25c, Red Cross/Red Crescent. Nos. 824, 826d, 30c, Cayman Islands Cancer Society, vert. Nos. 825, 826e, 40c, Lions Club of Tropical Gardens, vert.

Wmk. 373

2001, Aug. 15 Litho. *Perf. 14*

Stamps With White Margins

821-825	A141	Set of 5	8.00	8.00

Souvenir Sheet

Stamps With Pink Margins

826	A141	Sheet of 5, #a-e	8.00	8.00

No. 826 sold for $1.80, 50c of which went to the various organizations honored.

Transportation — A142

Designs: No. 827, Walking home. No. 828, Boy on donkey. 20c, Bananas by canoe. 25c, Horse and buggy. 30c, Catboats. 40c, Schooner. 60c, Police bicycle, vert. 80c, Lady drivers. 90c, Launcing Cimboco, vert. $1, Seaplane. $4, Freighter. $10, Boeing 767.

Perf. 14¼x14½, 14½x14¼

2001, Sept. 29 Litho. Wmk. 373

827	A142	15c multi	.40	.40
828	A142	15c multi	.40	.40
829	A142	20c multi	.55	.55
830	A142	25c multi	.70	.70
831	A142	30c multi	.80	.80
832	A142	40c multi	1.10	1.10
833	A142	60c multi	1.60	1.60
834	A142	80c multi	2.25	2.25
835	A142	90c multi	2.50	2.50
836	A142	$1 multi	2.75	2.75
837	A142	$4 multi	11.00	11.00
838	A142	$10 multi	26.00	26.00
		Nos. 827-838 (12)	50.05	50.05

Christmas A143

Santa Claus: 15c, With children on dock. 30c, On eagle ray. 40c, In catboat. 60c, Parasailing.

Perf. 14¼x14½

2001, Nov. 21 Litho. Wmk. 373

839-842	A143	Set of 4	6.50	6.50

In Remembrance of Sept. 11, 2001 Terrorist Attacks — A144

Perf. 14x14¾

2002, Jan. 22 Litho. Wmk. 373

843	A144	$1 multi	4.75	4.75

Reign Of Queen Elizabeth II, 50th Anniv. Issue

Common Design Type

Designs: Nos. 844, 848a, 15c, Princess Elizabeth as child. Nos. 845, 848b, 20c, In 1976. Nos. 846, 848c, 30c, With Princess Margaret, 1942. Nos. 847, 848d, 80c, In 1996. No. 848e, $1, 1955 portrait by Annigoni (38x50mm).

Perf. 14¼x14½, 13¾ (#848e)

2002, Feb. 6 Litho. Wmk. 373

With Gold Frames

844-847	CD360	Set of 4	4.25	4.25

Souvenir Sheet

Without Gold Frames

848	CD360	Sheet of 5, #a-e	10.50	10.50

Peanuts Comic Strip Characters A145

Designs: 15c, Snoopy painting Woodstock at Cayman Brac Bluff. 20c, Charlie Brown and Sally at Hell Post Office. 25c, Peppermint Patty and Marcie at Little Cayman beach. 30c, Snoopy and Boeing 737-200. 40c, Linus and Snoopy at Point of Sand. 60c, Charlie Brown at Links Golf Course.

Wmk. 373

2002, Mar. 9 Litho. *Perf. 14*

849-854	A145	Set of 6	9.50	9.50
854a		Souvenir sheet, #849-854	9.50	9.50

2002 World Cup Soccer Championships, Japan and Korea — A146

Denominations: 30c, 40c.

2002, Apr. 30 *Perf. 13¾*

855-856	A146	Set of 2	4.75	4.75

Queen Mother Elizabeth (1900-2002)

Common Design Type

Designs: 15c, Wearing hat (sepia photograph). 30c, Wearing dark blue hat. Nos. 859, 861a, 40c, Wearing hat (black and white photograph). Nos. 860, 861b, $1, Wearing tiara.

Perf. 13¾x14¼, 14¼ (#859-860)

2002, Aug. 5 Litho. Wmk. 373

With Purple Frames

857-860	CD361	Set of 4	8.75	8.75

Souvenir Sheet

Without Purple Frames

Perf. 14½x14¼

861	CD361	Sheet of 2, #a-b	8.75	8.75

Christmas A147

Designs: 15c, Hail Mary. 20c, Journey to Bethlehem. 30c, Her firstborn Son. 40c, I bring good tidings. 60c Star in the east.

Wmk. 373

2002, Oct. 18 Litho. *Perf. 14*

Stamps + labels

862-866	A147	Set of 5	6.25	6.25
866a		Souvenir sheet of 5, #862-866 + 5 labels	6.75	6.75

Aviation in the Cayman Islands, 50th Anniv. A148

Designs: 15c, PBY Catalina Flying Boat. 20c, First landing at Grand Cayman Airport, 1952. 25c, Cayman Brac Airways AC 50. 30c, Cayman Airways B-737. 40c, Concorde at original airport, 1984. $1.30, Island Air DHC6.

2002, Nov. 8

867-872	A148	Set of 6	11.50	11.50

Children's Games A149

Designs: 15c, Rope skipping. 20c, Maypole dancing. 25c, Gig. 30c, Hopscotch. $1, Marbles.

Wmk. 373

2003, May 27 Litho. *Perf. 13¾*

873-877	A149	Set of 5	9.00	9.00

Head of Queen Elizabeth II
Common Design Type
Wmk. 373
2003, June 2 Litho. *Perf. 13¾*
878 CD362 $4 multi 20.00 20.00

Coronation of Queen Elizabeth II, 50th Anniv.
Common Design Type

Designs: Nos. 879, 15c, 881a, 20c, Queen wearing crown. Nos. 880, $2, 881b, $4, Queen holding symbols of office.

Perf. 14¼x14½
2003, June 2 Litho. Wmk. 373
Vignettes Framed, Red Background
879-880 CD363 Set of 2 8.75 8.75
Souvenir Sheet
Vignettes Without Frame, Purple Panel
881 CD363 Sheet of 2, #a-b 14.50 14.50

Prince William, 21st Birthday
Common Design Type

Color photographs: 15c, William with backpack at right. 40c, William in suit and tie at left

No. 884: a, William with hand on chin at right. b, William with white bow tie at left.

Wmk. 373
2003, June 21 Litho. *Perf. 14¼*

882 CD364 15c multi		.50	.50
883 CD364 40c multi		1.40	1.40
884 Horiz. pair		5.75	5.75
a. CD364 80c multi		2.50	2.50
b. CD364 $1 multi		3.25	3.25
Nos. 882-884 (3)		7.65	7.65

Discovery of the Cayman Islands, 500th Anniv. A150

Designs: 15c, Turtle hatchlings. No. 886, 20c, Old waterfront. No. 887, 20c, Turtle and ship of Christopher Columbus. 25c, Nassau grouper. 30c, Cayman Brac schooner "Kirk-B." 40c, George Town harbor. 60c, Musical instruments. 80c, Smokewood tree. 90c, Little Cayman Baptist Church. $1, Thatch rope. $1.30, Children's dance troupe. $2, Parliament in session.

Wmk. 373
2003, July 24 Litho. *Perf. 13¾*
885-896 A150 Set of 12 29.00 29.00
896a Souvenir sheet, #885-896 29.00 29.00

Holiday Greetings A151

Various Christmas decorations and inscriptions of: 15c, Merry Christmas. 20c, Celebrate With Family. 30c, Happy New Year. 40c, Happy Holidays. 60c, Seasons Greetings.

Wmk. 373
2003, Nov. 4 Litho. *Perf. 13¼*
897-901 A151 Set of 5 8.50 8.50

Worldwide Fund for Nature (WWF) A152

Short-finned pilot whale: 15c, Adult and calf. 20c, Pod of four whales. 30c, Two whales at surface. 40c, One adult.

2003, Nov. 26 *Perf. 14*
902-905 A152 Set of 4 7.00 7.00
905a Sheet, 4 each #902-905 30.00 30.00

Shipping Registry, Cent. — A153

Ships: 15c, Lady Slater. 20c, Seanostrum. 30c, Kirk Pride. $1, Boadicea.

Perf. 14x14¾
2004, Jan. 29 Litho. Wmk. 373
906-909 A153 Set of 4 9.75 9.75

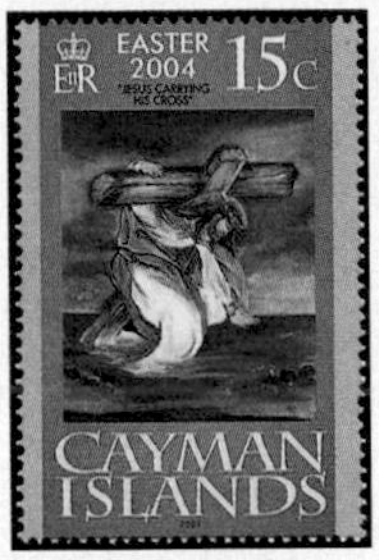

Easter — A154

Designs: 15c, Jesus Carrying His Cross. 30c, The Ascension.

2004, Mar. 16 *Perf. 14¾x14*
910-911 A154 Set of 2 3.00 3.00

2004 Summer Olympics, Athens — A155

Designs: 15c, Swimmer. 40c, Runner. 60c, Long jumper. 80c, Swimmers.

Perf. 13½x13¼
2004, Aug. 23 Litho. Wmk. 373
912-915 A155 Set of 4 7.25 7.25

Blue Iguana A156

Designs: 15c, Adult on rocks. 20c, Eggs. 25c, Four juveniles. 30c, Juvenile on finger. 40c, Adult with open mouth. 90c, Eye.

No. 922: a, 60c, On rock facing right. b, 80c, On rock facing left.

2004, Oct. 26 Litho. *Perf. 13¾*
916-921 A156 Set of 6 8.25 8.25
Souvenir Sheet
922 A156 Sheet of 2, #a-b 6.75 6.75

No. 922 sold for $1.90.

Battle of Trafalgar, Bicent. — A157

Designs: 15c, HMS Victory. 20c, HMS Tonnant tangles into the bow of the Algesiras. 25c, Flint cannon lock and linstock. No. 926, 60c, Royal Navy boatswain's mate. $1, Adm. Horatio Nelson, vert. No. 928, $2, HMS Orion in action against the Intrepide.

No. 929, vert.: a, 60c, French gunship Pluton. b, $2, HMS Tonnant.

Wmk. 373, Unwmkd. (15c)
2005, June 8 Litho. *Perf. 13¼*
923-928 A157 Set of 6 14.50 14.50
Souvenir Sheet
929 A157 Sheet of 2, #a-b 8.25 8.25

No. 923 has particles of wood from the HMS Victory embedded in the areas covered by a thermographic process that produces a raised, shiny effect.

Rotary International, Cent. — A158

Designs: 15c, Centennial emblem. 30c, PolioPlus emblem.

2005, June 30 Wmk. 373 *Perf. 13¾*
930-931 A158 Set of 2 2.00 2.00

Orchids A159

Designs: 15c, Myrmecophila albopurpurea. 20c, Prosthechea boothiana. 30c, Tolumnia calochila, vert. 40c, Encyclia phoenicia. 80c, Prosthechea cochleata, vert. $1.50, Encyclia kingsii.

2005, July 28 *Perf. 14*
932-936 A159 Set of 5 8.00 8.00
Souvenir Sheet
937 A159 $1.50 multi 6.50 6.50

Pope John Paul II (1920-2005) A160

2005, Aug. 18
938 A160 30c multi 1.50 1.50

A161

Butterflies A162

Designs: 15c, Queen. 20c, Mexican fritillary. 25c, Malachite. 30c, Cayman crescent spot. 40c, Cloudless sulphur. 90c, Swallowtail.

Wmk. 373
2005, Sept. 21 Litho. *Perf. 14*

939 A161 15c multi	.55	.55
940 A161 20c multi	.70	.70
941 A161 25c multi	.80	.80
942 A161 30c multi	1.00	1.00
943 A161 40c multi	1.40	1.40
944 A161 90c multi	3.00	3.00
Nos. 939-944 (6)	7.45	7.45

Booklet Stamps
Self-Adhesive
Unwmk.
Serpentine Die Cut 9½x9

945 A162 15c multi	.60	.60
a. Booklet pane of 10	6.00	
946 A162 20c multi	.70	.70
a. Booklet pane of 6	4.20	
947 A162 30c multi	1.00	1.00
a. Booklet pane of 10	10.00	
Nos. 945-947 (3)	2.30	2.30

Christmas A163

Designs: 15c, Angels. 30c, Magi, horiz. 40c, Holy Family. 60c, Shepherds, horiz.

Perf. 14x14¾, 14¾x14
2005, Oct. 26 Wmk. 373
948-951 A163 Set of 4 4.00 4.00
951a Souvenir sheet, #948-951, perf. 14¾ 4.00 4.00

Trees and Blossoms — A164

Designs: 15c, Wash wood. 20c, Red mangrove. 30c, Ironwood. 60c, West Indian cedar. $2, Spanish elm.

Wmk. 373
2006, Feb. 23 Litho. *Perf. 13¼*
Stamp + Label
952-956 A164 Set of 5 8.00 8.00

Queen Elizabeth II, 80th Birthday A165

Designs: 15c, As child. 40c, Wearing uniform and cap. $1, Wearing tiara. $2, Wearing sunglasses.

No. 961: a, 40c, Like #958. b, $1, Like #959.

2006, Apr. 21 *Perf. 14*
With White Frames
957-960 A165 Set of 4 8.75 8.75
Souvenir Sheet
Without White Frames
961 A165 Sheet of 2, #a-b 3.50 3.50

A166

Marine Life — A167

Designs: Nos. 962, 967a, 968, Hawksbill turtle. Nos. 963, 967b, 969, Gray angelfish. Nos. 964, 967c, 970, Queen angelfish. Nos. 965, 967c, 971, Diamond blenny. Nos. 966, 967e, Juvenile spotted drum,vert. Nos. 964 and 967c are vert.

Wmk. 373

2006, July 18 Litho. *Perf. 14*

With White Margins

962	A166	25c multi	.60	.60
963	A166	25c multi	.60	.60
964	A166	60c multi	1.50	1.50
965	A166	75c multi	1.90	1.90
966	A166	$1 multi	2.50	2.50
		Nos. 962-966 (5)	7.10	7.10

Souvenir Sheet

Without White Margin

967 A166 Sheet of 5, #a-e 7.25 7.25

Booklet Stamps

Self-Adhesive

Serpentine Die Cut 9½x9

Unwmk.

968	A167	25c multi	.60	.60
a.		Booklet pane of 10	6.00	
969	A167	25c multi	.60	.60
a.		Booklet pane of 10	6.00	
970	A167	60c multi	1.50	1.50
a.		Booklet pane of 10	15.00	
971	A167	75c multi	1.90	1.90
a.		Booklet pane of 10	19.00	
		Nos. 968-971 (4)	4.60	4.60

Birds A168

Designs: 25c, Bananaquit. 50c, Vitelline warbler. 75c, Grand Cayman parrot. 80c, Caribbean dove. $1, Caribbean elaenia. $1.50, West Indian woodpecker. $1.60, Thick-billed vireo. $2, Northern flicker. $4, Cuban bullfinch. $5, Western spindalis. $10, Loggerhead kingbird. $20, Red-legged thrush.

Perf. 13½x13¾

2006, Oct. 9 Litho. Wmk. 373

972	A168	25c multi	.60	.60
973	A168	50c multi	1.25	1.25
974	A168	75c multi	1.90	1.90
975	A168	80c multi	2.00	2.00
976	A168	$1 multi	2.50	2.50
977	A168	$1.50 multi	3.75	3.75
978	A168	$1.60 multi	4.00	4.00
979	A168	$2 multi	5.00	5.00
980	A168	$4 multi	9.75	9.75
981	A168	$5 multi	12.00	12.00
982	A168	$10 multi	24.00	24.00
983	A168	$20 multi	50.00	50.00
		Nos. 972-983 (12)	116.75	116.75

Booklet Stamps

Self-Adhesive

Unwmk.

983A	A168	25c multi	.60	.60
d.		Booklet pane of 10	6.00	
983B	A168	75c multi	1.90	1.90
e.		Booklet pane of 10	19.00	
983C	A168	80c multi	2.00	2.00
f.		Booklet pane of 10	20.00	
		Nos. 983A-983C (3)	4.50	4.50

Christmas A169

Designs: 25c, "Faith," Magi. 75c, "Hope," Prophet with scroll. 80c, "Joy," angel. $1, "Love," Madonna and Child.

Perf. 12½x13¼

2006, Oct. 26 Litho. Wmk. 373

984-987 A169 Set of 4 7.00 7.00

Island Scenes A170

Designs: 20c, Brac Reed dock. 25c, Waterfront buildings, Hog Sty Bay. 30c, East End blowholes, vert. 40c, Man in hammock, vert. 75c, Poinciana blooms. $1, Driftwood on Little Cayman.

Wmk. 373

2007, June 26 Litho. *Perf. 13¾*

988-993 A170 Set of 6 7.25 7.25

Scouting, Cent. A171

Designs: 25c, Wolf Cubs and leaders, hands lashing rope. 75c, Cub Scouts and leaders, hands with trumpet. 80c, Scouts camping, hand with compass. $1, Scout Drill Team, poppies.

No. 998, vert.: a, 50c, Scouts marching. b, $1.50, Lord Robert Baden-Powell and dog.

2007, July 9

994-997 A171 Set of 4 7.00 7.00

Souvenir Sheet

998 A171 Sheet of 2, #a-b 5.00 5.00

Wedding of Queen Elizabeth II and Prince Philip, 60th Anniv. — A172

Designs: 50c, Couple and wedding coach. 75c, Elizabeth wearing bridal veil. 80c, Princess Elizabeth, Philip, Queen Mother Elizabeth, King George VI, Princess Margaret. $1, Wedding procession, Westminster Abbey. $2, Couple.

Wmk. 373

2007, Sept. 12 Litho. *Perf. 13¾*

999-1002 A172 Set of 4 7.50 7.50

Souvenir Sheet

Perf. 14

1003 A172 $2 multi 5.00 5.00

No. 1003 contains one 42x57mm stamp.

Christmas A173

Stained-glass windows from local churches: 25c, Nativity, Wesleyan Holiness Church. 50c, Jesus Praying, Elmslie Memorial Church. 75c, Jesus Calling First Disciples, St. George's Anglican Church. 80c, Dove, East End Adventist Church. $1, Orb, First Baptist Church of Grand Cayman. $1.50, Shepherd, Frank Sound Church of God.

2007, Oct. 22 *Perf. 15x14*

1004-1009 A173 Set of 6 12.00 12.00

A174

Greetings A175

Nos. 1010-1015: a, Hello. b, Good Luck. c, Congratulations. d, You're Invited. e, Best Wishes. f, Love.

No. 1016, Hello. No. 1017, Congratulations. No. 1018, You're Invited. No. 1019, Love.

Wmk. 373

2008, Feb. 5 Litho. *Perf. 14¼*

1010	A174	20c Sheet of 6, #a-f	3.00	3.00
1011	A174	25c Sheet of 6, #a-f	3.75	3.75
1012	A174	50c Sheet of 6, #a-f	7.50	7.50
1013	A174	75c Sheet of 6, #a-f	11.00	11.00
1014	A174	80c Sheet of 6, #a-f	12.00	12.00
1015	A174	$1 Sheet of 6, #a-f	15.00	15.00
		Nos. 1010-1015 (6)	52.25	52.25

Booklet Stamps

Self-Adhesive

Serpentine Die Cut 9½x9

Unwmk.

1016	A175	20c multi	.50	.50
a.		Booklet pane of 10	5.00	
1017	A175	25c multi	.60	.60
a.		Booklet pane of 10	6.00	
1018	A175	25c multi	.60	.60
a.		Booklet pane of 10	6.00	
1019	A175	25c multi	.60	.60
a.		Booklet pane of 10	6.00	
		Nos. 1016-1019 (4)	2.30	2.30

Darwin Initiative A176

Fauna: 20c, Land crab. 25c, Needlecase. 75c, Little Cayman green anole, vert. 80c, Cayman Brac ground boa. $1, White-shouldered bat.

$2, Caribbean reef squid, vert.

Wmk. 373

2008, July 9 Litho. *Perf. 14*

1020-1024 A176 Set of 5 7.50 7.50

Souvenir Sheet

1025 A176 $2 multi 5.00 5.00

2008 Olympic Games, Beijing A177

Designs: 20c, Lanterns, swimming. 25c, Fish, swimming. 50c, Bamboo, running. 75c, Dragon, hurdles.

Wmk. 373

2008. Aug. 8 Litho. *Perf. 13¼*

1026-1029 A177 Set of 4 4.25 4.25

Water Authority, 25th Anniv. A178

Children's art: 25c, Stop Water Pollution. 75c, Water droplets. $2, Splash of Life.

Wmk. 373

2008, Oct. 16 Litho. *Perf. 13¼*

1030-1032 A178 Set of 3 7.50 7.50

Christmas A179

Santa Claus and: 25c, Ship. 75c, Horse-drawn carriage. 80c, Helicopter. $1, Race car.

2008, Nov. 12 *Perf. 13¾*

1033-1036 A179 Set of 4 7.00 7.00

WAR TAX STAMPS

No. 36 Surcharged:

a

b

1917, Feb. 26 Wmk. 3 *Perf. 14*

MR1	A5(a) 1½p on 2½p	11.00	*13.50*
a.	Fraction bar omitted	150.00	*210.00*
MR2	A5(b) 1½p on 2½p	2.10	*7.25*
a.	Fraction bar omitted	85.00	*150.00*

No. 1 exists with missing period. On No. 1 the distance between "WAR STAMP" and "1½" varies.

Surcharged

1917, Sept. 4

MR3 A5 1½p on 2½p ultra 1,000. *2,500.*

Surcharged

1917, Sept. 4

MR4 A5 1½p on 2½p ultra .30 *.65*

No. 33 Overprinted

1919, Feb. 4

MR5 A5 ½p green .70 *3.00*

The "brownish paper" variety comes from the interleaving used for shipment from England.

Type of 1912-16 Surcharged

1919, Feb. 4

MR6 A5 1½p on 2½p orange .95 *1.50*

Queen Victoria
A1 A2

1857 Engr. Wmk. 6 *Imperf.*

Blued Paper

1	A1	1p blue	—	260.00
2	A1	6p plum	*10,000.*	525.00

1857-59

White Paper

3	A1	1p deep turq	825.00	42.50
4	A1	2p deep green	190.00	72.50
a.		2p yellow green	600.00	105.00
5	A2	4p dl rose ('59)	*75,000.*	5,400.
6	A1	5p org brown	1,750.	175.00
6A	A1	6p plum	*2,400.*	160.00
7	A1	6p brown	*7,750.*	550.00
8	A2	8p brown ('59)	*30,000.*	*1,750.*
9	A2	9p lil brn ('59)	*50,000.*	1,050.
10	A1	10p vermilion	950.00	350.00
11	A1	1sh violet	5,500.	240.00
12	A2	1sh9p green ('59)	*950.00*	*950.00*
a.		1sh9p yellow green	*5,000.*	*3,600.*
13	A2	2sh blue ('59)	6,500.	1,400.

Stamps of type A2 frequently have repaired corners.

Nos. 3-4 exist unofficially rouletted. See the *Scott Classic Specialized Catalogue* for listings.

Beware of Nos. 17-57 trimmed to resemble Nos. 3-13. Values are for stamps with clear margins on all sides.

No. 5 was reproduced by the collotype process in a souvenir sheet distributed at the London International Stamp Exhibition 1950. The paper is unwatermarked.

A3

1857-58 Typo. Unwmk.

14	A3	½p lilac ('58)	210.00	*260.00*
15	A3	½p lilac, *bluish*	4,200.	600.00

No. 14 exists unofficially rouletted.

Nos. 14-15, 38 are printed on surface-glazed paper. Values are for stamps without cracking of the surface, and examples showing cracking should be discounted.

Clean-Cut Perf. 14 to 15½

1861 Wmk. 6 Engr.

17	A1	1p blue	190.00	18.00
18	A1	2p yel green	240.00	29.00
b.		Vert. pair, imperf between		—
19	A2	4p dull rose	2,400.	350.00
20	A1	5p org brown	110.00	10.00
20A	A1	6p brown	2,700.	140.00
b.		6p bister brown		215.00
21	A2	8p brown	2,400.	600.00
22	A2	9p lilac brown	8,400.	275.00
23	A1	1sh violet	120.00	17.50
24	A2	2sh blue	3,600.	775.00

Rough Perf. 14 to 15½

25	A1	1p blue	150.00	10.00
b.		Blued paper	700.00	25.00
26	A1	2p yel green	500.00	95.00
27	A2	4p rose red	540.00	110.00
28	A1	6p olive brown	1,000.	120.00
a.		6p deep brown	1,100.	115.00
b.		6p bister brown	1,775.	160.00
29	A2	8p brown	1,775.	650.00
30	A2	8p yel brown	1,800.	400.00
31	A2	9p olive brown	700.00	80.00
32	A2	9p deep brown	110.00	90.00
33	A1	10p vermilion	300.00	25.00
a.		Imperf. vert., pair		—
34	A1	1sh violet	300.00	17.50
35	A2	1sh9p green	825.00	
36	A2	2sh blue	800.00	160.00

The 1sh9p green was never placed in use.

1863 *Perf. 12½*

37	A1	10p vermilion	260.00	18.00

1864 Typo. Unwmk.

38	A3	½p lilac	260.00	210.00

See note following No. 15.

1863 Engr. *Perf. 13*

39	A1	1p blue	160.00	7.00
40	A1	5p car brown	1,900.	175.00
41	A1	6p deep brown	210.00	32.50
42	A2	9p brown	1,400.	110.00
43	A1	1sh grayish violet	2,100.	95.00

Parts of the papermaker's sheet watermark, "T. H. SAUNDERS 1862," may be found on some examples of Nos. 39-43.

Perf. 12

44	A1	1p blue	1,625.	150.00
a.		Horiz. pair, imperf. btwn.		*15,500.*

Two Types of Watermark Crown and CC (1)

1863-67 Typo. Wmk. 1a *Perf. 12½*

45	A3	½p lilac	60.00	45.00
a.		½p reddish lilac	77.50	52.50

Engr.

46	A1	1p blue	150.00	7.50
a.		1p dark blue	150.00	7.50
c.		Perf. 11½	3,000.	375.00
47	A1	2p gray green	90.00	14.00
48	A1	2p emerald	175.00	115.00
48A	A1	2p yel green	10,000.	475.00
48B	A1	2p bottle green		4,000.
49	A1	2p olive	300.00	260.00
50	A2	4p rose	525.00	110.00
a.		4p carmine rose	825.00	200.00
51	A1	5p car brown	240.00	90.00
52	A1	5p olive green	875.00	275.00
e.		5p deep sage green	2,100.	450.00
53	A1	6p choc brown	190.00	7.50
a.		Perf. 13	1,900.	225.00
b.		6p black brown	200.00	12.00
c.		As "b," double impression		3,750.
d.		6p reddish brown	240.00	14.00
54	A2	8p red brown	125.00	60.00
55	A2	9p brown	350.00	52.50
c.		Perf. 13	5,000.	950.00
56	A1	10p vermilion	2,400.	70.00
a.		10p orange	5,000.	500.00
58	A2	2sh blue	325.00	45.00

The ½p, 1p blue, 2p olive, 4p and 5p green exist imperf.

Wmk. 1b

46d	A1	1p blue	210.00	15.00
e.		1p dark blue	200.00	12.00
49d	A1	2p orange yellow	110.00	7.00
e.		2p olive yellow	175.00	24.00
f.		2p olive green	175.00	30.00
50b	A2	4p rose	275.00	65.00
c.		4p carmine rose	125.00	40.00
52b	A1	5p myrtle green	120.00	19.00
c.		5p olive green	125.00	19.00
d.		5p bronze green>	47.50	*60.00*
53d	A1	6p chocolate brown	47.50	42.50
e.		6p brown	105.00	12.00
54a	A2	8p red brown	95.00	72.50
55a	A2	9p dark brown	65.00	7.00
b.		9p bister brown	550.00	37.50
56b	A1	10p orange	110.00	14.00
c.		10p orange red	65.00	18.00
d.		10p vermilion	3,900.	160.00
57	A1	1sh purple	110.00	10.00
a.		1sh reddish lilac	325.00	32.50
58a	A2	2sh deep blue	160.00	15.00
b.		2sh indigo	300.00	22.50

The 1p blue and 6p brown exist imperf.
For overprints see Nos. O2, O4-O7.

A4

A5

1866 Typo. Wmk. 1 *Perf. 12½*

59	A5	3p rose	240.00	100.00
a.		Imperf., pair	900.00	

For overprint see No. O3.

1868 *Perf. 14*

61	A4	1p blue	30.00	11.00
62	A5	3p rose	95.00	55.00

For overprint see No. O1.

A6

A7

A8

A9

A10

A11

A12

A13

A14

A15

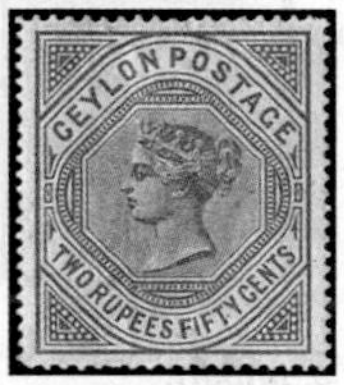
A16

1872-80 *Perf. 14*

63	A6	2c brown	26.00	3.75
64	A7	4c gray	47.50	1.75
65	A7	4c lil rose ('80)	72.50	1.75
66	A8	8c orange	47.50	6.50
a.		8c orange yellow	35.00	7.00
67	A9	16c violet	110.00	3.25
68	A10	24c green	72.50	2.40
69	A11	32c slate bl ('77)	175.00	17.50
70	A12	36c blue	190.00	26.00
71	A13	48c rose	95.00	8.50
72	A14	64c red brn ('77)	350.00	85.00
73	A15	96c olive gray	260.00	30.00
		Nos. 63-73 (11)	1,446.	186.40

For surcharges see #83-84, 94A-110, 112-114. For types surcharged see #124-129.

1872 *Perf. 12½*

74	A6	2c brown	3,500.	225.00
75	A7	4c gray	2,000.	325.00

1879 *Perf. 14x12½*

77	A6	2c brown	425.00	77.50
78	A7	4c gray	1,900.	35.00
79	A8	8c orange	450.00	57.50

Perf. 12½x14

82	A16	2r50c claret	650.00	350.00

The 32c and 64c are known perf. 14x12½, but were not regularly issued.

No. 82, perf. 12½, was not regularly issued.

See Nos. 142, 158. For surcharges see Nos. 111, 115, 130. For types surcharged see Nos. 160-161.

Nos. 68, 72 Surcharged

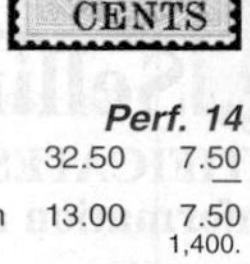

1882 *Perf. 14*

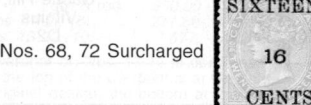

83	A10	16c on 24c green	32.50	7.50
a.		Inverted surcharge		
84	A14	20c on 64c red brn	13.00	7.50
a.		Double surcharge		1,400.

1883-99 Wmk. 2

85	A6	2c pale brown	72.50	2.50
86	A6	2c green ('84)	3.00	.20
a.		Perf. 12	5,000.	
87	A6	2c org brn ('99)	3.75	.40
88	A7	4c lilac rose	4.25	.35
89	A7	4c rose ('84)	7.50	*14.00*
a.		Perf. 12	5,000.	
90	A7	4c brt rose ('98)	10.00	10.50
91	A7	4c yellow ('99)	3.50	3.25
92	A8	8c orange	6.00	*11.00*
93	A9	16c violet	2,000.	190.00
94	A10	24c purple brown	1,650.	
b.		Perf. 12	5,400.	

Nos. 86a, 89a, 94 and 94b were never placed in use. A 48c brown, perf. 12, was prepared but not issued.

For surcharges and overprints see Nos.116-123, 143-151D, 155-156. O8-O9.

Issues of 1872-82 Surcharged:

a

b

c

d

1885 Wmk. 1 *Perf. 14*

94A	A9 (a)	5c on 16c		3,500.
95	A10 (a)	5c on 24c	3,900.	130.00
96	A11 (a)	5c on 32c	77.50	20.00
a.		Inverted surcharge		2,250.
97	A12 (a)	5c on 36c	350.00	14.00
a.		Inverted surcharge		3,000.
98	A13 (a)	5c on 48c	1,900.	72.50
99	A14 (a)	5c on 64c	130.00	9.50
a.		Double surcharge		1,900.
100	A15 (a)	5c on 96c	600.00	85.00
101	A9 (b)	10c on 16c	7,750.	3,000.
102	A10 (b)	10c on 24c	540.00	140.00
103	A12 (b)	10c on 36c	450.00	225.00
104	A14 (b)	10c on 64c	500.00	210.00
105	A10 (b)	20c on 24c	72.50	21.00
106	A11 (c)	20c on 32c	90.00	72.50
107	A11 (c)	25c on 32c	21.00	5.25
108	A13 (c)	28c on 48c	47.50	9.00
a.		Double surcharge		2,250.
109	A12 (b)	30c on 36c	19.00	13.00
a.		Inverted surcharge	300.00	130.00
110	A15 (b)	56c on 96c	30.00	25.00

Perf. 12½

111	A16 (d)	1r12c on 2r50c	650.00	120.00

Perf. 14x12½

112	A11 (a)	5c on 32c	900.00	60.00
113	A14 (a)	5c on 64c	950.00	52.50
114	A14 (b)	10c on 64c	82.50	*150.00*
a.		Vert. pair, imperf. btwn.	4,200.	

Perf. 12½x14

115	A16 (d)	1r12c on 2r50c	130.00	52.50

Perf. 14

Wmk. 2

117	A7 (a)	5c on 4c rose	27.50	5.00
a.		Inverted surcharge		350.00
118	A8 (a)	5c on 8c org	95.00	10.00
a.		Inverted surcharge		3,000.
b.		Double surcharge		2,500.
119	A9 (a)	5c on 16c vio	140.00	15.00
a.		Inverted surcharge		260.00
120	A10 (a)	5c on 24c pur brn	—	600.00
121	A9 (b)	10c on 16c vio	7,750.	1,750.

122 A10 (b) 10c on 24c pur brn 17.50 9.00
123 A9 (b) 15c on 16c vio 14.00 10.00

A 5c on 4c lilac rose and a 5c on 24c green are known to exist and are considered to be a forgeries.

Types of 1872-80 Surcharged

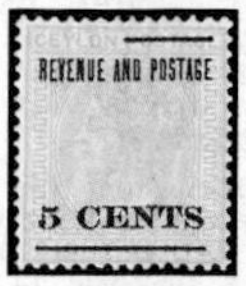

e

f

g

1885-87
124 A 8 (e) 5c on 8c lilac 25.00 1.75
125 A10 (f) 10c on 24c pur brn 13.00 9.50
126 A 9 (f) 15c on 16c org 72.50 14.00
127 A11 (f) 28c on 32c sl bl 30.00 3.00
128 A12 (f) 30c on 36c ol grn 32.50 16.00
129 A15 (f) 56c on 96c ol gray 60.00 17.50

Wmk. 1 Sideways
130 A16 (g) 1r12c on 2r50c cl 52.50 *120.00*
Nos. 124-130 (7) 285.50 *181.75*

A23

A24

FIVE CENTS
Type I — Thin lines in background. Hair and curl clear.
Type II — Thicker lines in background. Heavier shading under chin.

1886 **Wmk. 2**
131 A23 5c lilac, type I 3.25 .20
a. Type II 8.00 .20

For overprint see No. O12.

1886-1900
132 A24 3c org brn & green ('93) 4.25 .50
133 A24 3c green ('00) 3.75 .65
134 A24 6c rose & blk ('99) 1.75 .55
135 A24 12c ol grn & car ('00) 4.75 *8.50*
136 A24 15c olive green 7.50 1.75
137 A24 15c ultra ('00) 6.50 1.50
138 A24 25c brown 5.25 1.20
a. 25c brown, value in ol yel 140.00 90.00
139 A24 28c slate 26.00 1.60
140 A24 30c vio & org brown ('93) 5.00 2.60
141 A24 75c blk & org brown ('00) 7.25 *8.50*
Nos. 132-141 (10) 72.00 *27.35*

Numeral tablet of 3c, 12c and 75c has lined background with colorless value and "c."
For surcharges & overprints see #152-154, 157, 159, O10-O11, O13-O17.

1887 **Wmk. 1**
142 A16 1r12c claret 32.50 27.50

For overprint see No. O18.

Issue of 1883-84 Surcharged

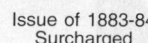

1888-90 **Wmk. 2**
143 A7 2c on 4c lilac rose 1.60 .95
a. Inverted surcharge 25.00 24.00
b. Double surcharge, one invtd. 325.00
144 A7 2c on 4c rose 2.50 .35
a. Inverted surcharge 18.00 *19.00*
b. Double surcharge 350.00

Surcharged

145 A7 2c on 4c lilac rose .90 .35
a. Inverted surcharge 37.50 37.50
b. Double surcharge 95.00 95.00
c. Double surcharge, one invtd. 77.50 77.50
146 A7 2c on 4c rose 7.50 .20
a. Double surcharge, one invtd. 105.00 *110.00*
b. Double surcharge 100.00 *105.00*
c. Inverted surcharge 350.00

Surcharged

147 A7 2c on 4c lilac rose 82.50 35.00
a. Inverted surcharge 150.00 47.50
b. Double surcharge, one inverted 190.00
148 A7 2c on 4c rose 3.00 .90
a. Inverted surcharge 17.50 10.00
b. Double surcharge, one inverted 9.50 *14.00*
c. Double surcharge 190.00 160.00

Surcharged

149 A7 2c on 4c lilac rose 65.00 27.50
a. Inverted surcharge 190.00 35.00
150 A7 2c on 4c rose 3.00 1.25
a. Inverted surcharge 17.50 7.00
b. Double surcharge 140.00 130.00
c. Double surcharge, one inverted 17.50 9.50

Surcharged

151 A7 2c on 4c rose 13.00 1.20
a. Inverted surcharge 24.00 6.50
b. Double surcharge 120.00 120.00
c. Double surch., one invtd. 26.00 12.00
i. "S" of "Cents" inverted 425.00 240.00
151D A7 2c on 4c lilac rose 65.00 35.00
e. Inverted surcharge 95.00 47.50
f. Double surcharge 350.00
g. Double surch., one invtd. 110.00 110.00
h. "S" of "Cents" inverted 550.00

Counterfeit errors of surcharges of Nos. 143 to 151D are prevalent.

No. 136 Surcharged

1890
152 A24 5c on 15c ol green 3.75 2.40
a. "Five" instead of "Five" 140.00 100.00
b. "REVENUE" omitted 200.00 190.00
c. Inverted surcharge 60.00 *65.00*
d. Double surcharge 120.00 *140.00*
e. As "a," inverted surcharge — 1,600.
f. Inverted "s" in "Cents" 95.00 *100.00*
g. As "f," inverted surcharge 2,000.
h. As "b," invtd. "s" in "Cents" 1,400.

Nos. 138-139 Surcharged

1891
153 A24 15c on 25c brown 16.00 15.00
154 A24 15c on 28c slate 19.00 10.00

Nos. 88, 89 and 139 Surcharged

1892
155 A7 3c on 4c lilac rose 1.20 *3.75*
156 A7 3c on 4c rose 6.00 *10.00*
a. Double surcharge, one invtd.
157 A24 3c on 28c slate 5.25 5.00
a. Double surcharge 175.00
Nos. 155-157 (3) 12.45 *18.75*

Type of 1879

1898
158 A16 2r50c violet, *red* 35.00 *62.50*

No. 136 Surcharged in Black

1899
159 A24 6c on 15c olive green 1.20 .85

Surcharged Type "g" in Black

1899 **Wmk. 1**
160 A16 1r50c on 2r50c gray 24.00 *52.50*
161 A16 2r25c on 2r50c yel 42.50 *95.00*

A35

1900 **Wmk. 1**
162 A35 1r50c car rose 29.00 *47.50*
163 A35 2r25c dull blue 42.50 *47.50*

King Edward VII
A36 A37

A38

A39

A40

1903-05 **Wmk. 2**
166 A36 2c org brown 2.40 .20
167 A37 3c green 2.40 1.20
168 A37 4c yel & blue 2.40 *4.50*
169 A38 5c dull lilac 1.75 .70
170 A39 6c car rose 11.00 1.75
171 A37 12c ol grn & car 6.00 *13.00*
172 A40 15c ultra 7.75 3.50
173 A40 25c bister 4.75 *9.50*
174 A40 30c vio & green 3.75 *4.75*
175 A37 75c bl & org ('05) 3.50 *24.00*
176 A40 1r50c gray ('04) 75.00 62.50
177 A40 2r25c brn & grn ('04) 82.50 60.00
Nos. 166-177 (12) 203.20 185.60

For overprints see Nos. O19-O24.

1904-10 **Wmk. 3**
178 A36 2c orange brown 1.75 .20
a. 2c orange 1.75 .60
179 A37 3c green 1.75 .20
180 A37 4c yel & blue 2.75 1.75
181 A38 5c dull lilac 3.00 1.50
a. Booklet pane of 12
182 A39 6c car rose 3.25 .20
183 A40 10c ol grn & vio ('10) 3.00 2.75
184 A37 12c ol grn & car 1.75 *2.00*
185 A40 15c ultra 3.25 .70
186 A40 25c bister ('05) 7.25 4.50
187 A40 25c slate ('10) 3.00 2.10
188 A40 30c vio & grn ('05) 3.00 *3.50*
189 A40 50c brown ('10) 4.75 *9.00*
190 A37 75c bl & org ('05) 6.25 *9.50*
191 A40 1r vio, *yel* ('10) 9.00 *12.00*
192 A40 1r50c gray ('05) 32.50 12.00
193 A40 2r scar, *yel* ('10) 17.50 *32.50*
194 A40 2r25c brn & grn 26.00 *35.00*
195 A40 5r blk, *grn* ('10) 45.00 *85.00*
196 A40 10r blk, *red* ('10) 105.00 *210.00*
Nos. 178-196 (19) 279.75 *424.40*

No. 181 exists on ordinary and chalky paper.

A41

A42

1908
197 A41 5c deep red violet 3.75 .20
a. Booklet pane of 12
198 A42 6c carmine rose 1.75 .20

1911, July 5
199 A40 3c green 1.10 .85

King George V — A44

King George V — A45

3 AND 6 CENTS
Type I — Small "c" after value, 2¼mm wide and 2mm high.
Type II — Large "c" after value, 2½mm wide and 2¼mm high.
1, 5 AND 9 CENTS are Type II, other denominations Type I.

Die I

For description of the dies, see back of this section of the Catalogue.

1912-25 **Wmk. 3**
200 A44 1c dp brn (Die Ib) ('20) 1.20 .20
201 A44 2c brown org .35 .20
202 A44 3c dp grn (Die Ia, type II) 4.25 .50
a. 3c deep green, die I, type I 5.25 1.25
203 A44 5c red violet 1.20 .70
204 A44 6c car (Die Ib, type II) 1.50 1.00
a. 6c carmine, die I, type I 13.00 1.00
b. As "a," bklt. pane of 6
205 A44 10c olive green 3.50 2.00
206 A44 15c ultra 2.10 1.50

Chalky Paper
207 A44 25c yel & ultra 2.10 2.10
208 A44 30c green & vio 4.75 3.75
209 A44 50c black & scar 1.75 *2.10*
210 A44 1r violet, *yel* 5.00 4.25
211 A44 2r blk & red, *yel* 3.75 *15.00*
212 A44 5r blk, *green* 20.00 *35.00*
a. 5r black, *bl grn, olive back* 21.00 *45.00*
b. 5r blk, *emer* (Die II) ('20) 52.50 *120.00*

Hands Reaching for UN Symbol
A98

Perf. 13x12½

1958, Dec. 10 Photo. Unwmk.

357 A98 10c red brown & red .20 .20
358 A98 85c Prus green & red .55 .55

10th anniv. of the signing of the Universal Declaration of Human Rights.

Pirivena Universities and Founders
A99

1959, Dec. 31

359 A99 10c brt ultra & dp org .40 .40

Institution of Pirivena Universities; founders Hikkaduwe Sri Sumangala Nayaka Thero and Ratmalane Sri Dharmaloka Nayake Thero.

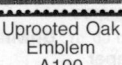

Uprooted Oak Emblem
A100

Prime Minister Bandaranaike
A101

1960, Apr. 7 Photo. *Perf. 11½*
Granite Paper

360 A100 4c chocolate & gold .20 *.50*
361 A100 25c vio blue & gold .20 .20

World Refugee Year, 7/1/59-6/30/60.

1961, Jan. 8 Granite Paper

Two types:
I — Gray hair at temple.
II — Dark hair at temple (redrawn).

362 A101 10c vio bl & gray bl (I) .40 .60
a. Type II .90 .20

Solomon West Ridgeway Dias Bandaranaike, assassinated Sept. 26, 1959.

Badge of Singhalese Scouts — A102

Malaria Eradication Emblem — A103

1962, Feb. 26 Unwmk. *Perf. 11½*
Granite Paper

363 A102 35c dark blue & ocher .35 .20

Boy Scouts of Ceylon, 50th anniv.

Perf. 14½x14

1962, Apr. 7 Photo. Wmk. 290

364 A103 25c lt sep, red org & brn .40 .40

WHO drive to eradicate malaria.

Monoplane 1938, and De Havilland Comet
IV — A104

1963, Feb. 28 Unwmk. *Perf. 11½*
Granite Paper

365 A104 50c lt grnsh blue & blk .60 .60

25th anniv. of Ceylonese airmail service.

Stylized Vase and Wheat Emblem
A105

1963, Mar. 21
Granite Paper

366 A105 5c blue & orange ver .75 *2.50*
367 A105 25c olive & brown 2.75 .75

FAO "Freedom from Hunger" campaign.

No. 340 Surcharged

Perf. 12x12½

1963, June 1 Engr. Wmk. 290

368 A79 2c on 4c brt red & choc .40 .40
a. Inverted surcharge 20.00
b. Double surcharge 40.00

Rural Life — A106

1963, July 5 Photo. *Perf. 14x14½*

369 A106 60c dull red & black 1.25 .75

50th anniv. of the Cooperative Movement.

Landscape and Elephant
A107

1963, Dec. 2 Wmk. 290

370 A107 5c blue & black .80 .45

National Conservation Week.

S.W.R.D. Bandaranaike
A108

Anagarika Dharmapala
A109

Perf. 11½

1963, Sept. 26 Unwmk. Engr.
Granite Paper

371 A108 10c blue .40 .40

Redrawn

1964, July 1 Photo.
Granite Paper

372 A108 10c grnsh gray & bl vio .40 .40

Frame redrawn on No. 372; inscription in bottom panel replaced by ornament.
For surcharge see No. 389.

1964, Sept. 16 Unwmk. *Perf. 11½*
Granite Paper

373 A109 25c gray brn & dull yel .40 .40

Anagarika Dharmapala, Buddhist missionary, birth cent.

Ceylon Jungle Fowl — A110

Vatadage Ruins at Madirigiriya
A111

Tea Picker — A112

Designs: 5c, Hill myna. 15c, Blue peafowl. 75c, Asiatic black-headed oriole. 5r, Girls, working in rice field. 10r, Map of Ceylon on scroll, showing agricultural development stations.

Wmk. 290, Unwmkd. (20c)

1964-69 Photo. *Perf. 14, 11½ (20c)*

374 A110 5c brt bl, blk, yel & grn 2.00 1.40
375 A110 15c yel, grn, blk, brt bl & rose 3.00 .25
376 A111 20c dk red brn, *buff* .20 .25
377 A110 60c yel & multi 4.25 1.10
a. Blue omitted 50.00
b. Red omitted 50.00
378 A110 75c ol, blk, org & brn 3.00 .75
a. Souvenir sheet of 4 10.00
b. As "a," overprinted 10.00
379 A112 1r brown & grn 1.00 .25
c. Brown omitted 125.00
379A A111 5r multicolored 6.00 4.00
379B A112 10r brown & multi 22.50 3.50
Nos. 374-379B (8) 41.95 11.50

No. 378a contains four imperf. stamps with simulated perforations similar to Nos. 374-375 and 377-378.

No. 378b is overprinted "First National Stamp Exhibition 1967" in two lines of black capitals.

No. 376 is on granite paper.

Issued: 20c, 1r, 10/1; 5c, 15c, 60c, 75c, 2/5/66; 5r, 8/15/69; 10r, 10/1/69.

See No. 325.

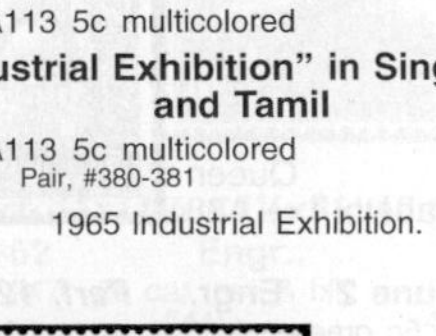
Exhibition Buildings, Cogwheels — A113

1964, Dec. 1 Unwmk. *Perf. 11*
"Industrial Exhibition" in Singhalese and English

380 A113 5c multicolored .20 *.50*

"Industrial Exhibition" in Singhalese and Tamil

381 A113 5c multicolored .20 *.50*
a. Pair, #380-381 .25 *1.00*

1965 Industrial Exhibition.

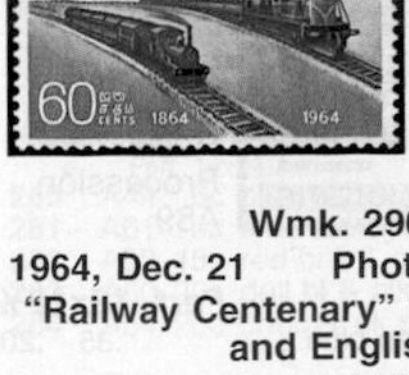
Railroad Trains, 1864-1964
A114

Wmk. 290

1964, Dec. 21 Photo. *Perf. 14*
"Railway Centenary" in Singhalese and English

382 A114 60c lil rose, bl & yel grn 3.25 .55

"Railway Centenary" in Singhalese and Tamil

383 A114 60c lil rose, bl & yel grn 3.25 .55
a. Vertical pair, #382-383 7.75 7.75

Centenary of Ceylonese railroads.

ITU Emblem, Old and New Communication Equipment — A115

1965, May 17 *Perf. 14*

384 A115 2c ultra & red 1.75 1.40
385 A115 30c brown & red 4.25 .55

ITU, centenary.

ICY Emblem
A116

1965, June 26 Unwmk. *Perf. 11½*
Granite Paper

386 A116 3c rose car & dk bl 1.75 1.40
387 A116 50c gold, rose car & blk 4.25 .60

International Cooperation Year.

Municipal Council Building
A117

1965, Oct. 29 Photo. *Perf. 11½*
Granite Paper

388 A117 25c gray & green .40 .40

Centenary of Colombo Municipal Council.

No. 372 Surcharged

1965, Dec. 18 Photo. *Perf. 11½*

389 A108 5c on 10c .40 .50

D. S. Senanayake — A118

View and Arms of Kandy — A119

1966, Mar. 22 Unwmk. *Perf. 11½*
Granite Paper

390 A118 10c bright green .85 .20

D. S. Senanayake, first prime minister of Ceylon, 14th death anniv. See No. 418.

Perf. 14x13½

1966, June 15 Photo. Wmk. 290

391 A119 25c multicolored .40 .40

Centenary of Kandy Municipal Council.

Opening of WHO Headquarters, Geneva A120

Unwmk.

1966, Oct. 8 Litho. *Perf. 14*

392 A120 4c multicolored 2.50 2.50
393 A120 1r multicolored 10.00 1.60

Rice, Map of Ceylon, FAO Emblem — A121

UNESCO Emblem A122

Design: 30c, Rice and globe.

1966, Oct. 25 Photo. *Perf. 11½*
Granite Paper

394 A121 6c dk green, org & brn .20 *.60*
395 A121 30c brt blue, org & brn .60 .20

Intl. Rice Year under sponsorship of the FAO.

1966, Nov. 3 Litho. *Perf. 12*

396 A122 3c tan & multi 4.00 4.00
397 A122 50c brt green & multi 7.75 1.60

20th anniv. of UNESCO.
For surcharge, see Sri Lanka No. 1578.

Map of Ceylon and UNESCO Emblem — A123

Worshippers at Buddhist Shrine A124

1966, Dec. 1 Unwmk. *Perf. 14*

398 A123 2c yel brn, yel & blue .45 *1.00*
399 A123 2r multicolored 1.75 *2.25*

Intl. Hydrological Decade (UNESCO), 1965-74.

1967, Jan. 2 Photo. *Perf. 12*

Designs: 20c, Muhintale Rock. 35c, Sacred Bo Tree. 60c, Adam's Peak.

400 A124 5c multicolored .20 *.40*
401 A124 20c multicolored .20 .20
402 A124 35c multicolored .20 .20
403 A124 60c multicolored .20 .20
Nos. 400-403 (4) .80 1.00

1st anniv. of the Poya Holiday System, Buddhist holiday replacing Sunday.
For surcharge, see Sri Lanka No. 1573.

Dutch Ramparts, Clock Tower and Arms of Galle A125

1967, Jan. 5 Litho. *Perf. 14x13½*

404 A125 25c dk green & multi .80 .20

Centenary of Galle Municipal Council.

Tea Research A126

40c, Tea tasting (cup & loose tea). 50c, Tea picking. 1r, Tea export (crate & freighter).

1967, Aug. 1 Unwmk. *Perf. 13½*

405 A126 4c multicolored .70 .70
406 A126 40c multicolored 2.10 1.60
407 A126 50c multicolored 2.10 .40
408 A126 1r multicolored 2.10 .20
Nos. 405-408 (4) 7.00 2.90

Centenary of the Ceylonese tea industry.

Elephant and ITY Emblem A127

1967, Aug. 15 Litho.

409 A127 45c multicolored 3.25 .85

Intl. Tourist Year.

Girl Guide, Jubilee Emblem and Flag — A128

1967, Sept. 19 *Perf. 12x12½*

410 A128 3c green & multi .60 .20
411 A128 25c org yel & multi .90 .20

Ceylon Girl Guide Assoc., 50th anniv.

Henry S. Olcott and Buddhist Flag A129

Perf. 13½

1967, Dec. 12 Unwmk. Litho.

412 A129 15c multicolored .40 .20

Colonel Henry S. Olcott (1832-1907), an American who reorganized the Buddhist hierarchy and school system in Ceylon and was the first president of the Theosophical Society.

Independence Memorial, Colombo A130

Design: 1r, Flag of Ceylon and mace.

1968, Feb. 4 Wmk. 290 *Perf. 14*

413 A130 5c multicolored .20 .50
414 A130 1r multicolored .60 .20

20th anniversary of independence.

D. B. Jayatilaka — A131

1968, Feb. 14 Photo.

415 A131 25c brown .40 .40

Sir Don Baron Jayatilaka (1868-1944), Buddhist leader and scholar.

Hygiene Institute, Kalutara A132

Perf. 11½x12

1968, Apr. 4 Litho. Wmk. 290

416 A132 50c multicolored .40 .40

WHO, 20th anniversary.

Jet over Colombo Terminal A133

1968, Aug. 5 *Perf. 13½*

417 A133 60c org brn, dk bl & org .55 .20

Opening of Colombo Airport.

D. S. Senanayake — A134

1968, Sept. 23 Photo. *Perf. 14*

418 A134 10c deep green .20 .20

See No. 390.

Open Koran A135

1968, Oct. 14 Photo. *Perf. 14*

419 A135 25c org brn, blk, blue & emerald .40 .40

1,400th anniversary of the Koran.

Human Rights Flame A136

Perf. 12½x13½

1968, Dec. 10 Unwmk.

420 A136 2c multicolored .20 .20
421 A136 20c multicolored .20 .20
422 A136 40c multicolored .20 .20
423 A136 2r multicolored .90 *1.90*
Nos. 420-423 (4) 1.50 2.50

International Human Rights Year.

Ceylon Buddhist Headquarters, Colombo — A137

1968, Dec. 19 Litho. *Perf. 13½*

424 A137 5c multicolored .40 *.60*

All-Ceylon Buddhist Cong., 50th anniv.
A multicolored 50c showing the Sri Padmaya (Sacred Footprint) on Adam's Peak was prepared but the issuance order was countermanded on Dec. 18. Some were sold in ignorance of the withdrawal order. Value $65.

E. W. Perera — A138

"Strength in Saving" — A139

Wmk. 290

1969, Feb. 17 Photo. *Perf. 14*

425 A138 60c brown .40 .50

E. W. Perera, member of Legislative Council.

1969, Mar. 20

426 A139 3c blue, yel & black .40 .40

National Savings Movement, 25th anniv.

A140

A141

4c, Seat of Enlightenment under Bodhi Tree. 6c, Buduresmala (disk symbolic of six-fold Buddha rays).

Wmk. 290

1969, Apr. 10 Litho. *Perf. 15*

427 A140 4c orange & multi .20 .25
428 A140 6c gold & multi .20 .25
429 A140 35c scarlet & multi .20 .20
Nos. 427-429 (3) .60 .70

Vesak Day, which commemorates the birth, enlightenment and death of Buddha.
For surcharges see Nos. 463, 466.

1969, Apr. 29 Photo. *Perf. 14x14½*

430 A141 15c org yel & multi .40 .40

Alexander Ekanayake Goonesingha (1891-1967), trade unionist, political leader and diplomat.

ILO, 50th Anniv. A142

1969, May 4 *Perf. 14½x14*

431 A142 5c grnsh bl & black .20 .20
432 A142 25c car rose & black .20 .20

Convocation Hall, University of Ceylon
A143

Elephant Lamp (Ath Pana) — A144

35c, "Lamp of Education," globe & flags. 50c, Uranium atom diagram. 60c, Symbols of science education. 1r, Aerial view of Sigiriya rock fortress.

Unwmk.

1969, Aug. 1 Litho. *Perf. 14*

Inscribed: "SIYAWASA"

433	A143	4c yellow & multi	.20	*.65*
434	A144	6c multicolored	.40	*1.25*
435	A143	35c multicolored	.20	.20
436	A144	50c red & multi	.20	.20
437	A143	60c blue & multi	.20	.20
438	A144	1r yel & multi	.50	.20
		Nos. 433-438 (6)	1.70	2.70

Centenary of public education and archaeological research.
For surcharges see Nos. 464-467.

Wild Water Buffalo
A145

15c, Slender loris. 50c, Axis deer. 1r, Leopard.

Perf. 14x13½

1970, May 11 Litho. Unwmk.

439	A145	5c lt blue & multi	.95	*1.40*
440	A145	15c buff & multi	1.50	.35
441	A145	50c salmon & multi	1.50	1.40
442	A145	1r gray & multi	1.50	*1.90*
		Nos. 439-442 (4)	5.45	5.05

Symbols of Agriculture and Industry
A146

1970, June 17

443 A146 60c multicolored .40 .40

Asian Productivity Year.

Inauguration of UPU Headquarters, Bern — A147

1970, Aug. 14 Litho. Unwmk.

444	A147	50c org, black & blue	.75	.20
445	A147	1.10r red, black & blue	4.75	.60

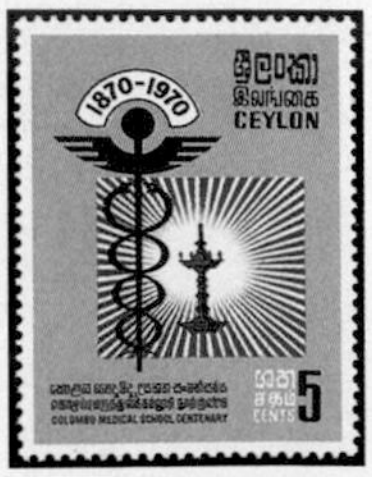

Caduceus and Oil Lamp — A148

1970, Sept. 1 *Perf. 13½x14*

446	A148	5c multicolored	1.00	*1.40*
447	A148	45c gray & multi	1.00	*1.10*

Centenary of the Ceylon Medical School.

Victory March and S.W.R.D. Bandaranaike
A149

1970, Sept. 25 *Perf. 14*

448 A149 10c red & multi .20 .20

For surcharge see No. 465.

UN Emblem and Dove — A150

Keppetipola Dissawe — A151

1970, Oct. 24 Photo. *Perf. 12½x14*

449 A150 2r dp orange & multi 3.00 *3.00*

25th anniversary of the United Nations.

1970, Nov. 26 Litho. *Perf. 14x14½*

450 A151 25c multicolored .40 .20

The 152nd anniversary of the execution of Keppetipola Dissawe, leader of the Great Rebellion of 1817-18.

Ola Leaf Manuscript and Education Year Emblem — A152

1970, Dec. 21 Photo. *Perf. 13*

451 A152 15c brown & multi 3.50 1.90

International Education Year.

Charles Henry de Soysa — A153

Edward Henry Pedris — A154

1971, Mar. 3 Litho. *Perf. 14x13½*

452 A153 20c orange & multi .40 .50

de Soysa (1836-90), philanthropist who founded hospitals and schools.

1971, July 8 Litho. *Perf. 14x14½*

453 A154 25c blue & multi .40 .40

Edward Henry Pedris (1888-1925), patriot.

A 5c stamp for the 10th Conf. of World Fellowship of Buddhists, Ceylon, May 9-13, was supposedly not issued without "1972" overprint. See Sri Lanka No. 471.

Lenin (1870-1924)
A156

Cumaratunga Munidasa
A157

1971, Aug. 31 *Perf. 14½*

455 A156 40c dp car & multi .70 .70

1971, Oct. 29 *Perf. 14*

Poets and Philosophers: #457, Ananda Coomaraswamy (1887-1947). #458, Rev. S. Mahinda Thero (1905-51). #459, Ananda Rajakaruna (1885-1957). #460, Arumuga Navalar (1822-78).

456	A157	5c brown	.20	.20
457	A157	5c slate	.20	.20
458	A157	5c deep orange	.20	.20
459	A157	5c dp vio blue	.20	.20
460	A157	5c brown red	.20	.20
		Nos. 456-460 (5)	1.00	1.00

CARE Package
A158

1971, Dec. 28 *Perf. 14x13*

461 A158 50c purple, blue & pink .55 .35

25th anniv. of CARE, a US-Canadian Cooperative for American Relief Everywhere.

Map of Ceylon, Colombo Plan Emblem
A159

1971, Dec. 28 Litho. *Perf. 14x14½*

462 A159 20c multicolored .40 .40

20th anniversary of the Colombo Plan.

Issues of 1969-70 Surcharged

a

b

c

d

e

Wmk. 290, Unwmkd.

1971, Dec. 5 *Perf. 15, 14*

463	A140 (a)	5c on 4c (#427)	7.50	2.50
464	A143 (b)	5c on 4c (#433)	.20	1.90
465	A149 (c)	15c on 10c (#448)	.20	.50
466	A140 (d)	25c on 6c (#428)	.80	.95
467	A144 (e)	25c on 6c (#434)	.80	*3.25*
		Nos. 463-467 (5)	9.50	9.10

Nos. 463-466 exist with surcharge inverted.

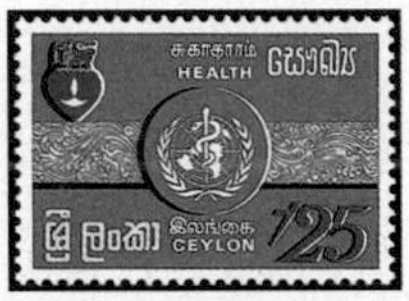

WHO Emblem and Heart — A160

1972, May 2 Unwmk. *Perf. 13x13½*

468 A160 25c multicolored 3.25 .90

"Your heart is your health," World Health Day.

UN Emblem, Map Showing Asian Highway
A161

1972, May 2 *Perf. 13x12½*

469 A161 85c lt blue & multi 6.50 3.25

Economic Commission for Asia and the Far East (ECAFE), 25th anniversary.

SEMI-POSTAL STAMPS

Catalogue values for unused stamps in this section are for Never Hinged items.

Lamp and Dharmachakra
SP1

Design: 10c+5c, Hand of Peace.

Perf. 11½

1956, May 10 Unwmk. Photo.

Granite Paper

B1	SP1	4c + 2c dp bl & lt yel	.35	.30
B2	SP1	10c + 5c dk gray, yel & brt pink	.50	.40

2500th anniv. of the birth of Buddha. The surtax went to the Buddha Jayanti Fund. For overprints, see Nos. 338-339.

WAR TAX STAMPS

Nos. 201, 202, 202a and 203 Overprinted

Die I

1918 **Wmk. 3** ***Perf. 14***

MR1 A44 2c brown orange .25 *.45*
a. Double overprint 35.00 47.50
b. Inverted overprint 60.00 *72.50*
MR2 A44 3c dp grn (Die Ia, type II) 2.60 .45
a. 3c dp green (Die I, type I) .25 *.60*
b. Double overprint (Die I) 95.00 *105.00*
MR3 A44 5c red violet .60 .35
a. Double overprint 52.50 *65.00*
b. Inverted overprint 120.00

Same Overprint on No. 223

MR4 A44 1c on 5c red violet .20 .30
a. Double overprint 210.00
Nos. MR1-MR4 (4) 3.65 1.55

OFFICIAL STAMPS

Regular Issues Overprinted

1869 **Wmk. 1** ***Perf. 12½, 14***

Black Overprint

O1 A4 1p blue 85.00
O2 A1 2p yellow 85.00
O3 A5 3p rose 150.00
O4 A2 8p red brown 85.00
O5 A1 1sh gray lilac 190.00

Red Overprint

O6 A1 6p brown 85.00
O7 A2 2sh blue 140.00
a. Imperf. *1,000.*
Nos. O1-O7 (7) 820.00

Nos. O1-O7 were never placed in use. The overprint measures 15mm on #O1, O3.

Regular Issues Overprinted in Black or Red

1895-1900 **Wmk. 2** ***Perf. 14***

O8 A6 2c green 13.00 .70
O9 A6 2c org brn ('00) 10.00 .70
O10 A24 3c org brn & grn 12.00 1.50
O11 A24 3c green ('00) 11.00 3.75
O12 A23 5c lilac 4.75 .40
O13 A24 15c olive green 17.50 .60
O14 A24 15c ultra ('00) 24.00 .70
O15 A24 25c brown 13.00 2.00
O16 A24 30c vio & org brn 15.00 .70
O17 A24 75c blk & org brn (R) ('99) 6.50 *7.50*

Wmk. 1

O18 A16 1r12c claret 100.00 65.00
Nos. O8-O18 (11) 226.75 83.55

1903-04 **Wmk. 2**

O19 A36 2c orange brown 17.50 1.20
O20 A37 3c green 12.00 2.40
O21 A38 5c dull lilac 26.00 1.75
O22 A40 15c ultramarine 37.50 3.25
O23 A40 25c bister 30.00 21.00
O24 A40 30c violet & green 17.50 1.75
Nos. O19-O24 (6) 140.50 31.35

CHAD

'chad

(Tchad)

LOCATION — Central Africa, south of Libya
GOVT. — Republic
AREA — 495,572 sq. mi.
POP. — 7,557,436 (1999 est.)
CAPITAL — N'Djamena

A former dependency of Ubangi-Shari, Chad became a separate French colony in 1920. In 1934, the colonies of Chad, Gabon, Middle Congo and Ubangi-Shari were grouped in a single administrative unit known as French Equatorial Africa, with the capital at Brazzaville. The Republic of Chad was proclaimed November 28, 1958.

100 Centimes = 1 Franc

Catalogue values for unused stamps in this country are for Never Hinged items, beginning with Scott 64 in the regular postage section, Scott B1 in the semi-postal section, Scott C1 in the air post section, Scott CB1 in the air post semi-postal section, Scott J23 in the postage due section, Scott M1 in the military stamp section, and Scott O1 in the officials section.

See French Equatorial Africa No. 190 for stamp inscribed "Tchad."

Types of Middle Congo, 1907-17, Overprinted

Perf. 14x13½, 13½x14

1922 **Unwmk.**

1 A1 1c red & violet .40 .50
a. Overprint omitted 225.00
2 A1 2c ol brn & salmon .50 .55
a. Overprint omitted 250.00
3 A1 4c ind & vio 1.10 1.20
4 A1 5c choc & grn 1.25 1.25
5 A1 10c dp grn & gray grn 2.25 2.25
6 A1 15c vio & red 2.50 2.50
7 A1 20c grn & vio 4.00 4.00
8 A2 25c ol brn & brn 9.00 9.00
9 A2 30c rose & pale rose 1.60 1.60
10 A2 35c dl bl & dl rose 2.75 2.75
11 A2 40c choc & grn 3.00 3.00
12 A2 45c vio & grn 2.25 2.25
13 A2 50c dk bl & pale bl 2.75 2.75
14 A2 60c on 75c vio, *pnksh* 3.75 3.75
a. "TCHAD" omitted 275.00
b. "60" omitted 300.00
15 A1 75c red & violet 3.00 3.00
16 A3 1fr indigo & salmon 11.00 11.00
17 A3 2fr indigo & violet 19.00 19.00
18 A3 5fr ind & olive brn 19.00 19.00
Nos. 1-18 (18) 89.10 89.35

See Nos. 26a, 32a, 38a, 55a.

Stamps of 1922 Overprinted in Various Colors:

Nos. 19-28

Nos. 29-50

1924-33

19 A1 1c red & vio .30 .30
a. "TCHAD" omitted 210.00 240.00
b. Double overprint 300.00
c. Violet omitted 275.00
20 A1 2c ol brn & sal .30 .40
a. "TCHAD" omitted 210.00
b. Double overprint 225.00
21 A1 4c ind & vio .30 .40
a. "TCHAD" omitted 875.00
22 A1 5c choc & grn (Bl) 1.00 1.00
a. "TCHAD" omitted 190.00
23 A1 5c choc & grn .50 .55
a. "TCHAD" omitted 210.00
24 A1 10c dp grn & gray grn (Bl) 1.10 .95
25 A1 10c dp grn & gray grn 1.10 .95
26 A1 10c red org & blk ('25) .50 .55
a. "Afrique Equatoriale Française" omitted 210.00 240.00
b. "TCHAD" omitted 225.00 240.00
27 A1 15c vio & red .55 .55
28 A1 20c grn & vio .80 .80
a. "TCHAD" omitted 210.00
b. "Afrique Equatoriale Française" doubled 325.00
29 A2 25c ol brn & brn .55 .55
a. "Afrique Equatoriale Française" doubled 150.00
30 A2 30c rose & pale rose .75 .80
31 A2 30c gray & bl (R) ('25) .50 .50
32 A2 30c dk grn & grn ('27) 1.10 1.20
a. "Afrique Equatoriale Française" omitted 325.00
33 A2 35c ind & dl rose .55 .65
34 A2 40c choc & grn 1.25 1.25
a. Dbl. overprint (R + Bk) 275.00
35 A2 45c vio & grn .90 .95
a. Dbl. overprint (R + Bk) 275.00
36 A2 50c dk bl & pale bl 1.40 1.50
a. Inverted overprint 150.00
37 A2 50c grn & vio ('25) 1.10 1.20
38 A2 65c org brn & bl ('28) 1.90 2.00
a. "Afrique Equatoriale Française" omitted 250.00
39 A2 75c red & vio 1.40 1.40
40 A2 75c dp bl & lt bl (R) ('25) .75 .95
a. "TCHAD" omitted 250.00
41 A2 75c rose & dk brn ('28) 2.60 2.40
42 A2 90c brn red & pink ('30) 7.25 7.50
43 A3 1fr ind & salmon 1.90 2.10
44 A3 1.10fr dl grn & bl ('28) 2.75 3.25
45 A3 1.25fr org brn & lt bl ('33) 8.00 8.00
46 A3 1.50fr ultra & bl ('30) 7.25 7.50
47 A3 1.75fr ol brn & vio ('33) 40.00 40.00
48 A3 2fr ind & vio 2.75 2.75
a. Double impression of frame 550.00
49 A3 3fr red vio ('30) 10.50 11.00
50 A3 5fr ind & ol brn 3.25 4.00
Nos. 19-50 (32) 104.85 107.90

See No. 58a.

Types of 1922 Overprinted like Nos. 29-50 and Surcharged with New Values

1924-27

51 A2 60c on 75c dk vio, *pnksh* .95 .95
a. "60" omitted 200.00
52 A3 65c on 1fr brn & ol grn ('25) 1.60 1.60
53 A3 85c on 1fr brn & ol grn ('25) 1.60 1.60
54 A2 90c on 75c brn red & rose red ('27) 1.40 1.40
55 A3 1.25fr on 1fr dk bl & ultra (R) ('26) .70 .70
a. "Afrique Equatoriale Française" omitted 175.00
56 A3 1.50fr on 1fr ultra & bl ('27) 1.50 1.50
57 A3 3fr on 5fr org brn & dl red ('27) 5.00 5.00
58 A3 10fr on 5fr ol grn & cer ('27) 12.00 13.00
a. "10fr" omitted 400.00
59 A3 20fr on 5fr vio & ver ('27) 18.00 18.00
Nos. 51-59 (9) 42.75 43.75

Common Design Types pictured following the introduction.

Colonial Exposition Issue

Common Design Types

1931 **Engr.** ***Perf. 12½***

Name of Country in Black

60 CD70 40c deep green 5.00 *5.00*
61 CD71 50c violet 5.00 *5.00*
62 CD72 90c red orange 5.00 *5.00*
63 CD73 1.50fr dull blue 5.00 *5.00*
Nos. 60-63 (4) 20.00 *20.00*

Catalogue values for unused stamps in this section, from this point to the end of the section, are for Never Hinged items.

Republic

"Birth of the Republic" A1

"Solidarity of the Community" A2

1959 **Unwmk.** **Engr.** ***Perf. 13***

64 A1 15fr ultra, grn & maroon .80 .20
65 A2 25fr dk grn & dp claret 1.00 .20

1st anniv. of the proclamation of the Republic.

Imperforates

Most Chad stamps from 1959 onward exist imperforate in issued and trial colors, and also in small presentation sheets in issued colors.

C.C.T.A. Issue

Common Design Type

1960

66 CD106 50fr rose lil & dk pur 1.75 .35

Flag and Map of Chad and UN Emblem — A3

Unwmk.

1961, Jan. 11 **Engr.** ***Perf. 13***

Flag in blue, yellow and carmine

67 A3 15fr brn & dk bl .60 .20
68 A3 25fr org brn & dk bl .90 .20
69 A3 85fr slate grn & dk bl 2.50 .40
Nos. 67-69 (3) 4.00 .80

Admission of Chad to United Nations.

Chari Bridge and Hippopotamus — A4

Abtouyoua Mountain and Ox — A5

Designs: 50c, Biltine and dorcas gazelle. 1fr, Logone and elephant. 2fr, Batha and lion. 3fr, Salamat and buffalo. 4fr, Ouaddai and Kudu. 15fr, Bessada and giant eland. 20fr, Tibesti mountains and mouflon. 25fr, Rocherg and antelope. 30fr, Kanem and cheetah. 60fr, Borkou and oryx. 85fr, Gorge of Archet and addax.

Perf. 13½x14, 14x13½

1961-62 **Typo.**

70 A5 50c yel grn & dk grn ('62) .20 .20
71 A5 1fr bl grn & dk bl grn ('62) .20 .20
72 A5 2fr dk red brn & blk ('62) .20 .20
73 A5 3fr ocher & dl grn ('62) .20 .20
74 A5 4fr dk crim & blk ('62) .20 .20
75 A4 5fr yellow & blk .20 .20
76 A5 10fr pink & blk .35 .20
77 A5 15fr lilac & blk ('62) .70 .20
78 A5 20fr red & blk .85 .20

79 A5 25fr blue & blk ('62) .90 .20
80 A5 30fr ultra & blk ('62) 1.00 .20
81 A5 60fr yel & ol grn ('62) 2.25 .20
82 A5 85fr org & blk 2.75 .25
Nos. 70-82 (13) 10.00 2.65

First anniversary of Independence.
For overprint see No. M1.

Abidjan Games Issue
Common Design Type

1962, July 21 Photo. *Perf. 12½x12*
83 CD109 20fr Relay race .80 .20
84 CD109 50fr High jump 2.00 .30
Nos. 83-84,C8 (3) 6.30 1.25

African-Malgache Union Issue
Common Design Type

1962, Sept. 8 Unwmk.
85 CD110 30fr dk bl, bluish grn, red & gold 1.25 .20

Pres. Ngarta Tombalbaye — A7

1963, Apr. 22 *Perf. 12x12½*
86 A7 20fr multi .65 .20
87 A7 85fr multi 1.75 .30

For surcharge, see No. 125.

Space Communciations Issue

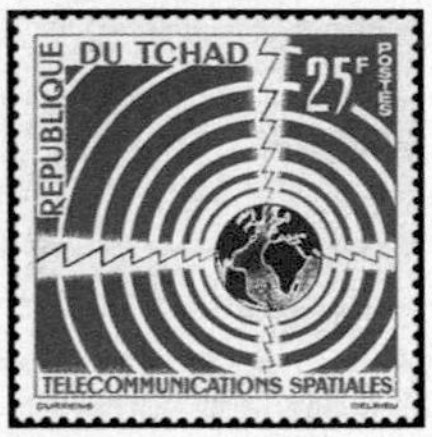

Waves Around Globe — A8

Design: 100fr, Orbit patterns around globe.

Perf. 12½
1963, Sept. 19 Unwmk. Photo.
88 A8 25fr grn & pur 1.00 .20
89 A8 100fr pink & ultra 3.00 .60

Ancestral Mask — A9

Excavated Sao Art: 5fr, Clay weight. 25fr, Ancestral clay statuette. 60fr, Gazelle, bronze. 80fr, Bronze pectoral.

1963, Dec. 2 Engr. *Perf. 13*
90 A9 5fr brt grn & red brn .20 .20
91 A9 15fr gray, dl cl & red .45 .20
92 A9 25fr dk bl & org brn 1.10 .25
93 A9 60fr org brn & slate grn 2.75 .35
94 A9 80fr org red & olive 3.00 .40
Nos. 90-94 (5) 7.50 1.40

UNESCO Emblem, Scales and Tree — A10

1963, Dec. 10
95 A1025fr green & maroon 1.00 .20

15th anniv. of the Universal Declaration of Human Rights.

Potter A11

Perf. 12½
1964, Feb. 5 Unwmk. Engr.
96 A11 10fr shown .35 .20
97 A11 30fr Boatmaker .90 .20
98 A11 50fr Weaver 1.50 .25
99 A11 85fr Smiths 2.25 .35
Nos. 96-99 (4) 5.00 1.00

Barograph and WMO Emblem A12

1964, Mar. 23 *Perf. 13*
100 A12 50fr red lil, pur & ultra 1.40 .25

Fourth World Meteorological Day.

Cotton A13

1964, Apr. 6 Photo. *Perf. 12½x13*
101 A13 20fr shown 1.75 .35
102 A13 25fr Royal poinciana 2.00 .40

Co-operation Issue
Common Design Type

1964, Nov. 7 Engr. *Perf. 13*
103 CD119 25fr ver, dk bl & dk brn 1.00 .25

National Guard and Map of Chad A14

Design: 25fr, Infantry, flag and map, vert.

Perf. 12½x13, 13x12½
1964, Dec. 11 Photo.
104 A14 20fr multi .85 .20
105 A14 25fr lt bl & multi .95 .20

Issued to honor the army of Chad.

Aoudad or Barbary Sheep A15

10fr, Addax. 20fr, Oryx. 25fr, Derby's eland, vert. 30fr, Giraffe, buffalo & lion, Zakouma Park, vert. 85fr, Great kudu at water hole, vert.

Perf. 12½x12, 12x12½
1965, Jan. 11 Unwmk.
106 A15 5fr dk brn, ultra & yel .50 .20
107 A15 10fr ultra, org & blk .75 .20
108 A15 20fr multi 1.50 .20
109 A15 25fr multi 1.75 .25
110 A15 30fr multi 2.50 .40
111 A15 85fr multi 5.00 .75
Nos. 106-111 (6) 12.00 2.00

Olsen Perforator A16

Designs: 60fr, Mildé telephone, vert. 100fr, Distributor of Baudot telegraph.

1965, May 17 Engr. *Perf. 13*
112 A16 30fr multi .75 .20
113 A16 60fr multi 1.25 .45
114 A16 100fr multi 2.00 .60
Nos. 112-114 (3) 4.00 1.25

Cent. of the ITU.

Motorized Police A17

Perf. 12½x12
1965, June 22 Photo. Unwmk.
115 A17 25fr ol, dk grn, gold & brn .75 .25

Issued to honor the national police.

Guitar A18

Musical Instruments from National Museum: 1fr, Drum and stool, vert. 3fr, Shoulder drums, vert. 15fr, Viol. 60fr, Harp, vert.

1965, Oct. 26 Engr. *Perf. 13*
Size: 22x36mm, 36x22mm
116 A18 1fr car, emer & brn .20 .20
117 A18 2fr red, brt lil & brn .20 .20
118 A18 3fr red & sepia .20 .20
119 A18 15fr red, ocher & sl grn .75 .20
120 A18 60fr maroon & slate grn 1.75 .60
Nos. 116-120,C23 (6) 5.85 2.25

Head and Bowl — A19

WHO Headquarters, Geneva — A20

Sao Art: 20fr, Head. 60fr, Head with crown. 80fr, Circlet with human head. From excavations at Bouta Kebira and Gawi.

1966, Apr. 1 Engr. *Perf. 13*
121 A19 15fr ol, choc & ultra .40 .20
122 A19 20fr dk red, brn & bl grn .75 .20
123 A19 60fr brt bl, choc & ver 1.75 .50
124 A19 80fr brn org, grn & pur 2.50 .60
Nos. 121-124 (4) 5.40 1.50

Issued to publicize the International Negro Arts Festival, Dakar, Senegal, Apr. 1-24.

No. 86 Surcharged with New Value and Two Bars in Orange

1966, Apr. 15 Photo. *Perf. 12x12½*
125 A7 25fr on 20fr multi .75 .30

1966, May 3
126 A20 25fr car, lt ultra & yel .60 .20
127 A20 32fr emer, ultra & yel .75 .20

New WHO Headquarters, Geneva.

Staff of Mercury and Map of Africa A21

1966, May 24 *Perf. 12½x12*
128 A21 30fr multi .75 .25

Central African Customs and Economic Union (Union Douaniere et Economique de l'Afrique Centrale, UDEAC).

Soccer Player — A22

Design: 60fr, Soccer player facing left.

1966, July 12 Engr. *Perf. 13*
129 A22 30fr grn, bl grn & mar .75 .25
130 A22 60fr dk bl, gray & car 1.40 .30

8th World Cup Soccer Championship, Wembley, England, July 11-30.

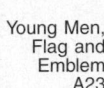

Young Men, Flag and Emblem A23

1966, Aug. 11 Photo. *Perf. 12½x13*
131 A23 25fr dk bl & multi .75 .20

Chad Youth Movement.

Greek Columns and UNESCO Emblem — A24

1966, Aug. 23 Engr. *Perf. 13*
132 A24 32fr sl bl, vio & car rose .75 .20

20th anniv. of UNESCO.

Reconstructed Skull of Chadanthropus — A25

1966, Sept. 20 Engr. *Perf. 13*
133 A25 30fr gray, red & ocher 1.90 .50

Yves Coppens' discovery of Lake Chad man.

Stone Axe — A26

Prehistoric Tools: 30fr, Flint arrow head. 85fr, Bone harpoon. 100fr, Sandstone millstone with grinder.

1966, Dec. 11 Engr. *Perf. 13*
134 A26 25fr dp bl, red & dk brn .55 .20
135 A26 30fr brn, dp bl & blk .80 .20
136 A26 85fr dk red, brt bl & brn 2.40 .50
137 A26 100fr Prus grn, dk brn & bis brn 2.75 .65
a. Miniature sheet of 4, #134-137 15.00 5.00
Nos. 134-137 (4) 6.50 1.55

Map of Chad and Various Sports — A27

1967, Apr. 10 Photo. *Perf. 12x12½*
138 A27 25fr multi .75 .30

Issued for Sports Day, Apr. 10, 1967.

Colotis Protomedia A28

Various Butterflies.

1967, May 23 Photo. *Perf. 12½x12*
139 A28 5fr blue & multi 1.75 .30
140 A28 10fr emerald & multi 4.25 .75
141 A28 20fr orange & multi 8.50 1.50
142 A28 130fr red & multi 17.50 2.50
Nos. 139-142 (4) 32.00 5.05

WHO Headquarters, Brazzaville — A29

1967, Sept. 23 Photo. *Perf. 12½x13*
143 A29 30fr vio bl & multi .75 .25

Opening of the Regional Office of the WHO, Brazzaville.

Jamboree Emblem and Boy Scouts A30

32fr, Jamboree emblem and Boy Scout.

1967, Oct. 17 Photo. *Perf. 12½x13*
144 A30 25fr multi .80 .20
145 A30 32fr multi .90 .20

12th Boy Scout World Jamboree, Farragut State Park, Idaho, Aug. 1-9.

Great Mills of Chad A31

30fr, Lake reclamation project, grain fields.

1967, Nov. 14 Engr. *Perf. 13*
146 A31 25fr brt bl, ind & sep .70 .20
147 A31 30fr ultra, emer & ol brn .90 .20

Economic development of Chad.

Woman and Harp Player A32

Rock Paintings: 30fr, Giraffes. 50fr, Camel rider hunting ostrich.

1967, Dec. 19 Engr. *Perf. 13*
Size: 36x22mm
148 A32 15fr bl, sal & mar 2.00 .20
149 A32 30fr grnsh bl, sal & mar 4.00 .40
150 A32 50fr emer, sal & mar 5.50 .55
Nos. 148-150,C38-C39 (5) 28.50 3.60

Balloud expedition in the Ennedi Mountains. See Nos. 163-166.

Rotary Emblem — A33

Map of Chad, WHO Emblem, Well, Physicians, Mother and Child — A34

1968, Jan. 9 Photo. *Perf. 13x12½*
151 A33 50fr multi 1.40 .40

Rotary Club of Chad, 10th anniversary.

1968, Apr. 6 *Perf. 13x12½*
152 A34 25fr multi .70 .20
153 A34 32fr multi .90 .20

20th anniv. of WHO.

"Water" Aiding Agriculture and Industry A35

1968, Apr. 23 Engr. *Perf. 13*
154 A35 50fr grnsh bl, brn & brt grn 1.10 .25

Hydrological Decade (UNESCO), 1965-74.

National Administration School — A36

1968, Aug. 20 Engr. *Perf. 13*
155 A36 25fr slate, brn red & rose vio .70 .20

Boy Learning to Write A37

1968, Sept. 10
156 A37 60fr dk bl, dk brn & blk 1.10 .30

Issued for National Literacy Day.

Cotton Harvest A38

Loom, Fort Archambault Factory — A39

Tiger Moth — A40

1968, Sept. 24 Engr. *Perf. 13*
157 A38 25fr Prus bl, choc & dk grn .80 .20
158 A39 30fr brt grn, ol & ultra .90 .20

Issued to publicize the cotton industry.

1968, Oct. 1 Photo.

Moths: 30fr, Owlet. 50fr, Saturnid (Gynanisa maja). 100fr, Saturnid (Epiphora bauhiniae).

159 A40 25fr multi 5.25 .60
160 A40 30fr multi 6.25 .75
161 A40 50fr multi 9.50 .85
162 A40 100fr multi 11.00 1.50
Nos. 159-162 (4) 32.00 3.70

Rock Paintings Type of 1967

Rock Paintings: 2fr, Archers. 10fr, Costumes (4 women, 1 man). 20fr, Funeral vigil. 25fr, Dispute.

1968, Nov. 19 Engr. *Perf. 13*
Size: 36x22mm
163 A32 2fr scar, salmon & brn .65 .20
164 A32 10fr pur, salmon & dk red 1.60 .20
165 A32 20fr grn, salmon & mar 3.25 .50
166 A32 25fr bl, salmon & maroon 3.50 .60
Nos. 163-166 (4) 9.00 1.50

Man and Human Rights Flame — A41

St. Paul — A42

1968, Dec. 10 Engr. *Perf. 13*
167 A41 32fr grn, brt bl & red .75 .20

International Human Rights Year.

1969, May 6 Litho. *Perf. 12½x13*

Apostles: 1fr, St. Peter. 2fr, St. Thomas. 5fr, St. John the Evangelist. 10fr, St. Bartholomew. 20fr, St. Matthew. 25fr, St. James the Less. 30fr, St. Andrew. 40fr, St. Jude. 50fr, St. James the Greater. 85fr, St. Philip. 100fr, St. Simon.

168 A42 50c multi .20 .20
169 A42 1fr multi .20 .20
170 A42 2fr multi .20 .20
171 A42 5fr multi .20 .20
172 A42 10fr multi .20 .20
173 A42 20fr multi .30 .20
174 A42 25fr multi .40 .20
175 A42 30fr multi .50 .20
176 A42 40fr multi .60 .20
177 A42 50fr multi .70 .20
178 A42 85fr multi 1.10 .40
179 A42 100fr multi 1.25 .40
a. Sheet of 12, #168-179 6.00 1.75

Jubilee Year of the Catholic Church in Chad.

Tractors and Trucks — A43

1969, June 19 Engr. *Perf. 13*
180 A43 32fr grn, red brn & ind .75 .20

50th anniv. of the ILO.

Deborah Meyer, US, 200 Meter Freestyle A44

Woman with Flowers, by Veneto — A45

Winners of 1968 Olympic Games: #182, Roland Matthes, East Germany, 100m backstroke. #183, Klaus DiBiasi, Italy, springboard diving. #184, Bruno Cipolla, Primo Baran and Renzo Sambo, Italy, pair with coxswain. #185, Annemarie Zimmermann and Rosewitha Esser, West Germany, women's kayak tandem. #186, Sailing, G.B. #187, Pierre Trentin, France, 1000 meter bicycling. #188, Pier Franco Vianelli, Italy, 196k bicycle road race. #189, Daniel Morelon and Pierre Trentin, France, tandem.

#190, Daniel R. Rebillard, France, 4000m pursuit (bicycle). #191, Ingrid Becker, West Germany, pentathlon. #192, Jean J. Guyon, France, equestrian. #193, Olympic dressage team, West Germany. #194, Bernd Klinger, West Germany, small bore rifle. #195, Manfred Wolke, East Germany, welterweight. #196, Randy Matson, US, shot put. #197, Colette Besson, France, 400m run. #198, Mohammed Gammoudi, Tunisia, 5,000m run. #199, Tommie Smith, US, 200m run.

#200, David Hemery, G.B., 200m hurdles. #201, Willie Davenport, US, 110m hurdles. #202, Bob Beamon, US, long jump. #203, Sawao Kato, Japan, all around gymnastics. #204, Dick Fosbury, US, high jump.

Paintings: #206, Holy Family, by Murillo, horiz. #207, Adoration of the Magi, by Rubens. #208, Portrait of an African Woman, by Bezombes. #209, Three Black Men, by Rubens. #210, Mother and Child, by Gauguin.

1969, June 30 Litho. *Perf. 12½x13*
181-204 A44 1fr set of 24 8.00 8.00

Perf. 12½x13, 13x12½
205-210 A45 1fr set of 6 1.90 1.90

Issued to stress the brotherhood of mankind.

For overprints see Nos. 244A-244F, 245A-245X.

Cochlospermum Tinctorium — A46

Flowers: 4fr, Parkia biglobosa. 10fr, Pancratium trianthum. 15fr, Morning glory.

1969, July 8 Photo. *Perf. 12½x13*
211 A46 1fr pink, yel & blk .60 .20
212 A46 4fr dk grn, yel & red .90 .20
213 A46 10fr dk grn, yel & gray 1.10 .20
214 A46 15fr vio bl & multi 1.90 .20
Nos. 211-214 (4) 4.50 .80

Meat Freezer, Farcha A47

30fr, Cattle at Farcha slaughterhouse.

1969, Aug. 19 Engr. *Perf. 13*

215 A47 25fr sl grn, ocher & red brn .60 .20
216 A47 30fr red brn, sl grn & gray .75 .20

Economic development in Chad.

Development Bank Issue

Common Design Type

1969, Sept. 10

217 CD130 30fr dl red, grn & ocher .70 .20

Tilapia Nilotica A48

Fish: 3fr, Citharinus latus. 5fr, Tetraodon fahaka strigosus. 20fr, Hydrocyon forskali.

1969, Nov. 25 Engr. *Perf. 13*

218 A48 2fr choc, grn & gray .55 .20
219 A48 3fr gray, red & bl 1.10 .20
220 A48 5fr ocher, blk & yel 1.75 .25
221 A48 20fr blk, red & grn 4.75 .60
Nos. 218-221 (4) 8.15 1.25

ASECNA Issue

Common Design Type

1969, Dec. 12 Engr. *Perf. 13*

222 CD132 30fr orange .75 .25

Pres. François Tombalbaye A49

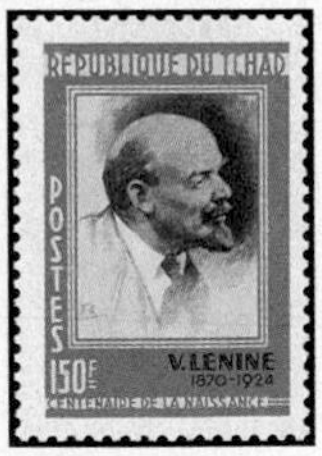

Lenin — A50

1970, Jan. 11 Litho. *Perf. 14*

223 A49 25fr multi .70 .20

1970, Apr. 22 Photo. *Perf. 11½*

224 A50 150fr gold, blk & buff 3.25 1.10

Lenin (1870-1924), Russian communist leader.

UPU Headquarters Issue

Common Design Type

1970, May 20 Engr. *Perf. 13*

225 CD133 30fr dk red, pur & brn .75 .25

During the 1970-73 period three different agents had entered into contracts to produce stamps with various officials of the Chad government, apparently including Pres. Tombalbaye.

In June 1973, Tombalbaye declared that some of the stamps produced by these agents were not recognized by the Chad government but might be put on sale at a later date, and that other stamps produced and shipped to Chad were refused by the government.

In July 1973, the Chad government announced that the stamps that were not recognized would be put on sale by the end of the year. We have no evidence that this actually happened.

Apollo Program A50a

Designs: 15fr, Apollo 11 in Lunar orbit. 25fr, Apollo 12 astronaut deploying lunar research equipment. 40fr, Astronaut, lunar module on moon. 50fr, Astronauts Conrad and Bean in life raft after splashdown, horiz.

1970, June 12 Litho. *Perf. 12x12½*

225A A50a Strip of 3, #b-d 6.00 —

Souvenir Sheet

Perf. 13½x13

225E A50a 50fr multicolored 10.00 —

No. 225E contains one 66x44mm stamp. 15fr, 25fr are airmail.

Expo '70, Japan — A50b

Japanese prints of women: 50c, by Kiyonaga. 1fr, by Utamaro. 2fr, from Heian period.

1970, June 12 Litho. *Perf. 12x12½*

225F A50b Strip of 3, #a-c 13.50 —

For overprint see No. 239C.

Adult Education Class and UN Emblem — A52

1970, June 16 Litho. *Perf. 14*

226 A52 100fr blue & multi 1.75 .50

International Education Year.

Bull's Head, Symbols of Weather and Agriculture — A53

1970, July 22 Engr. *Perf. 13*

227 A53 50fr org, gray & grn 1.00 .20

Issued for World Meteorological Day.

1970 World Cup Soccer Championships, Mexico City — A53a

Designs: 1fr, Three players, Italian flag. 4fr, Franz Beckenbauer, German flag. Nos. 227C, 227E, English players receiving World Cup trophy, 1966. No. 227D, Three players, Brazilian flag. No. 227F, Four players, "1970."

1970-71 Litho. *Perf. 12*

227A A53a 1fr multicolored
227B A53a 4fr multicolored
227C A53a 5fr multicolored
227D A53a 5fr multicolored
Nos. 227A-227D(3) 3.75 —

Embossed

Die Cut Perf 13

227E A53a 5fr gold 17.50 —

Souvenir Sheet

Litho.

Perf. 13½x13

227F A53a 15fr multicolored 6.25 —

No. 227F contains one 66x44mm stamp. Nos. 227D, 227F are airmail.

Issued: #227A-227D, 227F, 7/2; #227E, 11/1/71.

For overprints see Nos. 267A-267E.

Christmas A53b

Virgin and Child by: 3fr, Solario. 25fr, Durer. 32fr, Fouquet.

1970, Aug. 19 Litho. *Perf. 12x12½*

227G A53b 3fr multicolored
227H A53b 25fr multicolored
227I A53b 32fr multicolored
Nos. 227G-227I (3) 13.50 —

No. 227I is airmail.

Ahmed Mangue, Minister of Education — A54

1970, Sept. 15 Litho. & Engr.

228 A54 100fr gold, car & blk 1.50 .40

1972 Summer Olympics, Munich — A54a

Designs: No. 228A, 3fr, Horses pulling chariot. 8fr, Men running. 10fr, No. 228C, Woman hurdling. No. 228B, 20fr, Equestrian. 35fr, Woman diving. No. 228D, Woman diver in tuck position.

1970 Litho. *Perf. 12½x12*

228A A54a Strip of 3, #a-c 4.00 —

Perf. 12x12½

228B A54a Pair, #a-b + label 4.00 —

Embossed

Die Cut Perf 13

228C A54a 10fr gold 17.50 —

Souvenir Sheet

Litho.

Perf. 13½x13

228D A54a 40fr multicolored 10.00 —

10fr, 35fr, Nos. 228C-228D are airmail. No. 228D contains one 66x43mm stamp.

Issued: #228A-228B, 228D, Sept; #228C, 10/14.

For overprints see Nos. 239D-239F.

Tanner A55

Designs: 2fr, Cloth dyer, vert. 3fr, Camel turning oil press. 4fr, Water carrier. 5fr, Copper worker.

1970, Oct. 10 Engr. *Perf. 13*

229 A55 1fr ol brn, bl & brn .20 .20
229A A55 2fr dk brn, ol & ind .20 .20
229B A55 3fr pur, ol brn & rose car .30 .20
229C A55 4fr choc, lem & bl grn .40 .20
229D A55 5fr red, choc & sl grn .50 .20
Nos. 229-229D (5) 1.60 1.00

UN Emblem, Grain and Dove — A56

1970, Oct. 24 Photo. *Perf. 12x12½*

230 A56 32fr dk bl & multi .75 .25

25th anniversary of United Nations.

OCAM Headquarters, Map of Africa, Stars — A57

1971, Jan. 23 Photo. *Perf. 12½x12*

231 A57 30fr dk grn & multi .75 .20

OCAM (Organisation Commune Africaine, Malgache et Mauricienne) Summit Conference, N'djamena, Jan. 22-30.

Space Exploration — A57a

Illustration reduced.

1971, Feb. 16 Litho. *Perf. 13x13½*

231A A57a 8fr shown .60 —
231B A57a 10fr Apollo 11 .90 —
231C A57a 35fr Soviet space station 6.25 —
Nos. 231A-231C (3) 7.75

Embossed

Die Cut Perf 13

231D A57a 8fr gold, like #231A 8.25 —
f. Sheet of 1, Imperf.

Souvenir Sheet

Perf. 13½x13

231E A57a 40fr John F. Kennedy, Apollo spacecraft, vert. 10.00 —

Nos. 231C, 231E are airmail. No. 231Df contains one 73x45mm stamp with same size design as No. 231D. No. 231E contains one 33x50mm stamp.

Nos. 231D, 231Df probably were not available in Chad.

1972 Winter Olympics, Sapporo A57b

Paintings by Kiyonaga: 50c, Cherry Trees in Bloom, Tokyo. 1fr, Snowy Morning. 2fr, Sake Party.

1971 Litho. *Perf. 12x12½*

231G A57b 50c multicolored .80
231H A57b 1fr multicolored 1.40
231I A57b 2fr multicolored 2.25
Nos. 231G-231I (3) 4.45

Embossed

Die Cut Perf 13

231J A57b 2fr gold, like #231I 17.50
k. Sheet of 1, Imperf. 35.00

Issued: #231G-231I, 2/16; #231J-231Jk, 11/1. #231Jk contains one 43x54mm stamp with same size design as #231I.

For overprints see Nos. 246A-246C.

Nos. 231J-231Jk probably were not available in Chad.

Portraits of French Royalty — A57c

Designs: No. 232A, 25fr, The Dauphin (Louis XVII), by J.M. Vien the Younger. 32fr, Marie Antoinette, by E. Vigee-Lebrun. 60fr, Louis XVI, by J.S. Duplessis.

No. 232B, 25fr, Comtesse du Barry, by E. Vigee-Lebrun. 40fr, Louis XV, by M.Q. Delatour.

No. 232C, 40fr, Marie Antoinette, by Charpentier. 50fr, Louis XVI (Dauphin), by Michel Van Loo.

No. 232D, 35fr, Madame de Pompadour (detail), by Delatour. 70fr, Louis XV by Delatour.

No. 232E, 30fr, Madame de Pompadour (entire), by Delatour. 60fr, Marie Leszczynska, by Jean Marc Nattier. 80fr, Louis XV, by Van Loo.

No. 232F, 40fr, Duc D'Orleans as Regent, by 19th cent. French school. 200fr, Louis XIV, by H. Rigaud.

No. 232G, 100fr, Madame de Montespan, by Henry Gascard. 100fr, Madame de Maintenon, by Pierre Mignard.

No. 232H, 50fr, Colbert, by Claude Lefebvre. 200fr, Louis XIV, by J. Garnier.

No. 232J, 50fr, Marie Therese, by Mignard. 200fr, Louis XIV, by Marot.

No. 232K, 50fr, Marie de la Valliere, by English school. 200fr, Louis XIV, by French school.

No. 232L, 100fr, Giulio Cardinal Mazarin, by Mignard. 100fr, Anne of Austria, by Rubens.

No. 232M, 50fr, Vicomte de Turenne, by Champaigne. 200fr, Louis XIV as a Boy, by Mignard.

No. 232N, 100fr, Marquis de Cinq-Mars, by M. le Nain. 150fr, Cardinal Richelieu, by Champaigne.

No. 232P, 150fr, Anne of Austria, by Rubens. 250fr, Louis XIII (detail), by Simon Vouet.

No. 232Q, 150fr, Marriage of Marie de Medicis (looking right), by Rubens. 150fr, Mirror image.

No. 232R, 150fr, Duke of Sully, by Quesnel. 150fr, Mirror image.

No. 232S, 150fr, Henry IV, by Rubens. 150fr, Marie de Medicis, by Rubens.

No. 232T, 200fr, Gabrielle d'Estrees, by unknown artist. 250fr, Henry IV, by French school, c. 1595.

No. 232U, 150fr, Jeanne d'Albret, by Francois Clouet. 200fr, Marie de Medicis as a Girl, by Angelo Bronzino.

No. 232V, 200fr, Henry III, by Clouet. 250fr, Ambroise Pare, by 16th century French school.

No. 232W, 150fr, Catherine de Medicis, by Clouet. 250fr, Henry II, by Clouet.

No. 233A, 200fr, Elizabeth of Austria, by Clouet. 250fr, Charles IX, by Clouet.

No. 233B, 200fr, Mary Stuart, by 16th cent. Scottish school. 300fr, Diane of Poitiers, by Fontainbleau school.

No. 233C, 200fr, Elizabeth of Valois, by Alonso S. Coello. 250fr, Francis, Duke of Alencon, by Clouet.

No. 233D, 150fr, Marguerite d'Angouleme, by Clouet. 300fr, Francis I, by Clouet.

No. 233E, 200fr, Francis I, by Titian. 300fr, Francis I as Dauphin, by Corneille of Lyon.

No. 233F, 100fr, Anne of Austria, by Coello. 250fr, Louis XIII, by Champaigne.

No. 233G, 200fr, Marie de Medicis, by Rubens. 200fr, Marie de Medicis, Louis XIII, by Rubens.

No. 233H, 150fr, The Exchange of Princess Elizabeth of France and Princess Anne of Austria on the Andaye River, by Rubens. 250fr, Louis XIII of France and Navarre, by Vouet.

No. 233J, 250fr, Marie de Medicis, by Rubens. 250fr, Henry IV, by Rubens.

No. 233K, Louis XV and the Dauphin at Battle of Fontenoy. No. 233L, The Grand Dauphin and his Family, by Mignard. No. 233M, Madame de Montespan, horiz. No. 233N, Madame de la Valliere and her Children. No. 233P, The Birth of Louis XIII at Fontainebleau, by Rubens. No. 233Q, Reconciliation of the Queen and Louis XIII, by Rubens. No. 233R, Henry IV Entrusting Regency to Marie de Medici, by Rubens. No. 233S, The Majority of Louis XIII, by Rubens. No. 233T, The Apotheosis of Henry IV and the Proclamation of Regency, by Rubens. No. 233U, Felicity of the Regency, by Rubens.

Small numbers appear at the lower right on Nos. 232A-233J. To ease identication, these numbers are shown in parentheses after each listing.

1971-73 Litho. *Perf. 12½x13*

232A A57c Strip of 3, #aa-ac (58-60) 2.50
232B A57c Pair, #aa-ab (53-54) 1.50
232C A57c Pair, #aa-ab (56-57) 1.50
232D A57c Pair, #aa-ab (51-52) 1.90
232E A57c Strip of 3, #aa-ac (48-50) 3.75
232F A57c Pair, #aa-ab (45, 47) 3.75
232G A57c Pair, #aa-ab (44, 45B) 2.50
232H A57c Pair, #aa-ab (42-43) 3.75
232J A57c Pair, #aa-ab (40-41) 3.75
232K A57c Pair, #aa-ab (38-39) 3.75
232L A57c Pair, #aa-ab (36-37) 2.50
232M A57c Pair, #aa-ab (34-35) 3.75
232N A57c Pair, #aa-ab (32-33) 3.75
232P A57c Pair, #aa-ab (30-31) 6.00
232Q A57c Pair, #aa-ab (22-23) 4.00
232R A57c Pair, #aa-ab (22A-22B) 4.50
232S A57c Pair, #aa-ab (26, 27A) 4.50
232T A57c Pair, #aa-ab (18-19) 7.50
232U A57c Pair, #aa-ab (16-17) 5.50
232V A57c Pair, #aa-ab (16-16A) 7.50
232W A57c Pair, #aa-ab (14-15) 7.50
233A A57c Pair, #aa-ab (13-13A) 7.50
233B A57c Pair, #aa-ab (11-12) 8.00
233C A57c Pair, #aa-ab (10, 11A) 6.50
233D A57c Pair, #aa-ab (8-9) 7.50
233E A57c Pair, #aa-ab (7, 8A) 8.00
233F A57c Pair, #aa-ab (29, 32B) 6.00
233G A57c Pair, #aa-ab (24-25) 6.00
233H A57c Pair, #aa-ab (27-28) 6.00
233J A57c Pair, #aa-ab (20-21) 7.50
Nos. 232A-233J (30) 148.65

Souvenir Sheets

Perf. 13x13½, 13½x13, 13½

233K A57c 75fr multi 6.25
233L A57c 100fr multi 5.50
233M A57c 200fr multi 5.00
233N A57c 300fr multi 5.00
233P A57c 350fr multi 12.00
233Q A57c 400fr multi 16.00
233R A57c 400fr multi 10.00
233S A57c 400fr multi 10.00
233T A57c 400fr multi 6.00
233U A57c 500fr multi 13.50
Nos. 233K-233U (10) 89.25

Nos. 232A 60fr, 232B 40fr, 232C 50fr, 232D 70fr, 232E 80fr, 232F 200fr, 232G, 232H 200fr, 232J 200fr, 232K, 232L, 232M 200fr, 232N-233U are airmail.

Issued: 1971 — #232A, 2/24; #232B, 3/30; #232C, 3/4; #232D, 233K, 3/15; #232E, 4/12; #232F, 233L, 4/26; #232G, 8/10; #232H, 9/6; #232J, 9/23; #232K, 10/6; #232L, 10/26; #232M, 11/16; #232N, 11/20.

1972 — #232P, 233P, Jan.; #232Q, 233M-233N, Feb.; #233Q-233R, May; #232R, 233S, 6/15; #232S, 233T, 6/26; #232T, 8/8; #232U, 8/17; #232V, 8/30; #232W, 233U, 12/11; #233A, 12/18; #233B, 12/28.

1973 — #233C-233J.

Nos. 233K-233L, 233T-233U each contain one 37x62mm stamp. Nos. 233N, 233P each contain one 32x50mm stamp. No. 233M contains one 45x65mm stamp. Nos. 233Q-233R, 233U each contain one 65x45mm stamp.

Nos. 232Q-232V, 233G, 233J, 233R-233U and possibly 232P, 232W-233F, 233H probably were not available in Chad.

Symbolic Tree — A58

1971, Mar. 21 Engr. *Perf. 13*

236 A58 40fr bl grn, dk red & grn 1.00 .20

Intl. year against racial discrimination.

Paintings of Flowers A58a

Designs: 1fr, The Three Graces (detail), by Rubens. 4fr, Imperial Bouquet, by Van Os. 5fr, Bouquet, by Jan Brueghel.

1971, Apr. 28 Litho. *Perf. 12x12½*

236A A58a Strip of 3, #a-c 5.50

For overprint see No. 278A.

Summer Olympic Games — A58b

15fr, Swimming. 20fr, Women's relay races. 25fr, Swimming, medals. 50fr, Running.

Perf. 12x12½, 12½x12

1971, Apr. 28 Litho.

236B A58b 15fr multi, vert. 1.75
236C A58b 20fr multi, vert. 2.75
236D A58b 25fr multi 3.50
Nos. 236B-236D (3) 8.00

Embossed

Perf. 13

236E A58b 25fr gold, like No. 236D 17.50

Souvenir Sheet

Litho.

Die Cut Perf 13

236F A58b 50fr multicolored 10.00

Nos. 236D-236F are airmail. No. 236F contains one 62x36mm stamp.

Issued: #236B-236D, 236F, 4/28; #236E, 11/1.

For overprints see Nos. 251A-251D.

No. 236E probably was not available in Chad.

Map of Africa, Radar Antenna A59

Map of Africa and: 40fr, Communications tower. 50fr, Communications satellite.

1971, May 17 Engr. *Perf. 13*

237 A59 5fr ultra, org & dk red .20 .20
238 A59 40fr pur, emer & brn .75 .20
239 A59 50fr dk red, blk & brn 1.00 .20
Nos. 237-239 (3) 1.95 .60

3rd World Telecommunications Day.

Animals A79c

1973 Litho. *Perf. 13½*

294G A79c 20fr Sheep
294H A79c 30fr Camels
294J A79c 100fr Cats
294K A79c 130fr Dogs
294L A79c 150fr Horses
Nos. 294G-294L (5) 13.50

Nos. 294J-294L are airmail.
See note before No. 225A.

Christmas — A79d

30fr, The Virgin & Infant Surrounded by Saints, by Lorenzo Lotto. 40fr, Madonna and Child with St. Peter and a Martyred Saint, by Paolo Veronese (not Tintoretto), vert. 55fr, Nativity Scene, by Martin Schongauer, vert. 60fr, Nativity Scene, by Federico Barocci, vert. 250fr, Adoration of the Magi, by Stephan Lochner, vert. 400fr, Epiphany, by Hans Memling.

1973 Litho. *Perf. 11½*

294M A79d 30fr multicolored
294N A79d 40fr multicolored
294P A79d 55fr multicolored
294Q A79d 60fr multicolored
294R A79d 250fr multicolored
Nos. 294M-294R (5) 13.50

Souvenir Sheet

Perf. 15

294S A79d 400fr multicolored 13.50

Nos. 294Q-294S are airmail.
See note before No. 225A.

Dinothrombium Tinctorium A80

Rotary Emblem A81

1974, Sept. 3 Photo. *Perf. 13*

295 A80 25fr *shown* 1.50 .20
296 A80 30fr *Bupreste sternocera* 2.25 .20
297 A80 40fr *Diptere hyper-echia* 2.75 .25
298 A80 50fr *Chrysis* 3.25 .35
299 A80 100fr *Longicorn beetle* 4.75 .65
300 A80 130fr *Spider* 7.50 .95
Nos. 295-300 (6) 22.00 2.60

1975, Apr. 11 Typo. *Perf. 13*

301 A81 50fr multi 1.00 .20

Rotary International, 70th anniversary.

Craterostigma Plantagineum — A82

Flowers: 10fr, Tapinanthus globiferus. 15fr, Commelina forskalaei, vert. 20fr, Adenium obesum. 25fr, Yellow hibiscus. 30fr, Red hibiscus. 40fr, Kigelia africana.

1975, Sept. 25 Photo. *Perf. 13*

302 A82 5fr org & multi .40 .20
303 A82 10fr gray bl & multi .60 .20
304 A82 15fr yel grn & multi .75 .20
305 A82 20fr lt brn & multi 1.00 .20
306 A82 25fr lil & multi 1.75 .25
307 A82 30fr bis & multi 1.90 .35
308 A82 40fr ultra & multi 3.00 .50
Nos. 302-308 (7) 9.40 1.90

A. G. Bell, Satellite and Waves — A83

1976, June 10 Litho. *Perf. 12½*

309 A83 100fr bl, brn & ocher 1.40 .40
310 A83 125fr lt grn, brn & ocher 1.90 .60

Centenary of first telephone call by Alexander Graham Bell, Mar. 10, 1876.

Ice Hockey, USSR — A84

90fr, Ski jump, Karl Schnabl, Austria.

1976, June 21 *Perf. 14*

311 A84 60fr multi .75 .20
312 A84 90fr multi 1.25 .25
Nos. 311-312,C178-C179 (4) 8.25 2.05

12th Winter Olympic Games, winners. See No. C180.

High Hurdles A85

1976, July 12 Litho. *Perf. 13½*

313 A85 45fr multi .70 .20
Nos. 313,C187-C189 (4) 8.70 1.65

21st Summer Olympic Games, Montreal, Canada.
See No. C190.

Mars Landing and Viking Rocket A86

Mars Landing and: 90fr, Viking trajectory, Earth to Mars.

1976, July 23 *Perf. 14*

314 A86 45fr multi .50 .20
315 A86 90fr multi 1.00 .25
Nos. 314-315,C191-C193 (5) 7.35 2.05

Viking Mars project.
For overprints see Nos. 379-380.

Robert Koch, Medicine — A87

Design: 90fr, Anatole France, literature.

1976, Dec. 15

316 A87 45fr multi .75 .20
317 A87 90fr multi 1.50 .25
Nos. 316-317,C196-C198 (5) 9.75 2.00

Nobel Prize winners.

Map and Flag of Chad, Clasped Hands A88

120fr, Map of Chad, people & occupations.

1976, Sept. 15 Litho. *Perf. 12½x13*

318 A88 30fr multi .60 .20
319 A88 60fr orange & multi 1.10 .30
320 A88 120fr brown & multi 2.25 .50
Nos. 318-320 (3) 3.95 1.00

National reconciliation.

Freed Political Prisoners — A89

Designs: 60fr, Parade of cadets.

1976, Sept. 25 Litho. *Perf. 12½*

321 A89 30fr blue & multi .30 .20
322 A89 60fr black & multi .75 .20
323 A89 120fr red & multi 1.40 .25
Nos. 321-323 (3) 2.45 .65

Revolution of Apr. 13, 1975, 1st anniv.

Decorated Calabashes — A90

Designs: Various pyrographed calabashes.

1976, Nov. Litho. *Perf. 12½x13*

324 A90 30fr multi .40 .20
325 A90 60fr multi .90 .20
326 A90 120fr multi 1.75 .25
Nos. 324-326 (3) 3.05 .65

Germany No. C57 and Friedrichshafen, Germany — A91

1977, Mar. 30 *Perf. 14*

327 A91 100fr multi 1.40 .25
Nos. 327,C206-C209 (5) 11.55 2.10

75th anniversary of the Zeppelin.

Elizabeth II in Coronation Regalia and Clergy — A92

Design: 450fr, Elizabeth II and Prince Philip.

1977, June 15 Litho. *Perf. 14x13½*

328 A92 250fr multi 3.25 .75

Souvenir Sheet

329 A92 450fr multi 5.75 2.50

25th anniv. of the reign of Elizabeth II.
For overprints see Nos. 347-348.

Simon Bolivar A93

Famous Personalities: 175fr, Joseph J. Roberts. No. 332, Queen Wihelmina of Netherlands. No. 333, Charles de Gaulle. 325fr, King Baudouin and Queen Fabiola of Belgium.

1977, June 15 *Perf. 13½x14*

330 A93 150fr multi 1.50 .30
331 A93 175fr multi 2.25 .45
332 A93 200fr multi 3.00 .65
333 A93 200fr multi 3.00 .75
334 A93 325fr multi 4.00 1.00
Nos. 330-334 (5) 13.75 3.15

Post and Telecommunications Emblem — A94

Map of Chad and Waves — A95

Society Emblem — A96

1977, Aug. 15 Litho. *Perf. 13*

335 A94 30fr yel & blk .50 .20

Perf. 12½

336 A95 60fr multi .75 .20

Perf. 13½x13

337 A96 120fr multi 1.60 .50
Nos. 335-337 (3) 2.85 .90

Telecommunications (30fr); Natl. Telecommunications School, 10th anniv. (60fr); Intl. Telecommunication Soc. of Chad (120fr).

WHO Emblem and Man (Back Pain) — A97

World Rheumatism Year (WHO Emblem and): 60fr, Woman's head (neck pain), horiz. 120fr, Leg (knee pain).

Perf. 12½x13, 13x12½

1977, Nov. 10 Engr.

338 A97 30fr multi .50 .20
339 A97 60fr multi 1.00 .20
340 A97 120fr multi 1.40 .40
Nos. 338-340 (3) 2.90 .80

World Cup Emblems and Saving a Goal — A98

Designs (Argentina '78, World Cup Emblems and): 60fr, Heading the ball. 100fr, Referee whistling a goal. 200fr, World Cup poster. 300fr, Pelé. 500fr, Helmut Schoen and Munich stadium.

1977, Nov. 25 Litho. *Perf. 13½*

341 A98 40fr multi .50 .20
342 A98 60fr multi .75 .20
343 A98 100fr multi 1.10 .25
344 A98 200fr multi 2.50 .50
345 A98 300fr multi 3.75 .75
Nos. 341-345 (5) 8.60 1.90

Souvenir Sheet

346 A98 500fr multi 5.75 3.00

World Cup Soccer Championship, Argentina '78.

For overprints see Nos. 359-364.

Nos. 328-329 Overprinted in Silver: "ANNIVERSAIRE DU COURONNEMENT 1953-1978"

1978, Sept. 13 *Perf. 14x13½*

347 A92 250fr multi 3.00 1.00

Souvenir Sheet

348 A92 450fr multi 5.50 4.50

25th anniv. of coronation of Elizabeth II.

Abraham and Melchisedek, by Rubens — A99

Rubens Paintings: 120fr, Helene Fourment, vert. 200fr, David and the Elders of Israel. 300fr, Anne of Austria, vert. 500fr, Marie de Medicis, vert.

1978, Nov. 23 Litho. *Perf. 13½*

349 A99 60fr multi .75 .20
350 A99 120fr multi 1.75 .35
351 A99 200fr multi 3.00 .75
352 A99 300fr multi 4.50 1.25
Nos. 349-352 (4) 10.00 2.55

Souvenir Sheet

353 A99 500fr multi 6.75 3.00

Peter Paul Rubens (1577-1640).

Dürer Portrait A100

Dürer Paintings: 150fr, Jacob Muffel. 250fr, Young Woman. 350fr, Oswolt Krel.

1978, Nov. 23

354 A100 60fr multi .60 .20
355 A100 150fr multi 1.75 .50
356 A100 250fr multi 3.00 .80
357 A100 350fr multi 4.50 1.25
Nos. 354-357 (4) 9.85 2.75

Head, Village and Fly — A101

1978, Nov. 28 *Perf. 13*

358 A101 60f multi .75 .20

National Health Day.

Nos. 341-346 Overprinted in Silver:
a. 1962 BRESIL-TCHECOSLOVAQUIE / 3-1
b. 1966 / GRANDE BRETAGNE / -ALLEMAGNE (RFA) / 4-2
c. 1970 BRESIL-ITALIE 4-1
d. 1974 ALLEMAGNE (RFA)- / PAYS BAS 2-1
e. 1978 / ARGENTINE -/ PAYS BAS / 3-1
f. ARGENTINE -PAYS BAS / 3-1

1978, Dec. 30 Litho. *Perf. 13½*

359 A98(a) 40fr multi .50 .20
360 A98(b) 60fr multi .75 .20
361 A98(c) 100fr multi 1.40 .40
362 A98(d) 200fr multi 2.50 .75
363 A98(e) 300fr multi 3.50 1.25
Nos. 359-363 (5) 8.65 2.80

Souvenir Sheet

364 A98(f) 500fr multi 5.75 5.00

World Soccer Championship winners.

UPU Emblems, Camel Caravan, Satellites — A102

Design: 150fr, Obus woman and houses, Massa Territory, hibiscus.

1979, June 8 Litho. *Perf. 12x12½*

365 A102 60fr multi 3.00 .20
366 A102 150fr multi 5.00 .40

Philexafrique II, Libreville, Gabon, June 8-17. Nos. 365, 366 each printed in sheets of 10 with 5 labels showing exhibition emblem.

Wildlife Fund Emblem and Gazelle — A103

Protected Animals.

1979, Sept. 15 Litho. *Perf. 14½*

367 A103 40fr shown 1.90 .30
368 A103 50fr Addax 2.10 .50
369 A103 60fr Oryx antelope 2.50 .75
370 A103 100fr Cheetah 4.00 1.40
371 A103 150fr Zebra 5.50 1.90
372 A103 300fr Rhinoceros 11.00 3.00
Nos. 367-372 (6) 27.00 7.85

Souvenir Sheet

Holy Family, by Dürer — A104

1979, Sept. 1 *Perf. 13½*

373 A104 500fr brown & dull red 6.75 2.50

Boy and Handpainted Doors — A105

IYC Emblem and: 75fr, Oriental girl. 100fr, Caucasian girl, doves. 150fr, African boys. 250fr, Pencil and outlines of child's hands.

1979, Sept. 19 Litho. *Perf. 13½*

374 A105 65fr multi .60 .20
375 A105 75fr multi .75 .20
376 A105 100fr multi 1.00 .25
377 A105 150fr multi 1.50 .40
Nos. 374-377 (4) 3.85 1.05

Souvenir Sheet

378 A105 250fr multi 3.00 1.50

Nos. 314-315 Overprinted "ALUNISSAGE/APOLLO XI/JUILLET 1969" and Emblem

1979, Nov. 26 Litho. *Perf. 13½x14*

379 A86 45fr multi .60 .20
380 A86 90fr multi 1.00 .30
Nos. 379-380,C240-C242 (5) 7.45 2.50

Apollo 11 moon landing, 10th anniversary.

Ski Jump, Lake Placid '80 Emblem — A106

Lake Placid '80 Emblem and: 20fr, Slalom, vert. 40fr, Biathlon, vert. 150fr, Women's slalom, vert. 350fr, Cross-country skiing. 500fr, Downhill skiing.

1979, Dec. 18 *Perf. 14½*

381 A106 20fr multi .30 .20
382 A106 40fr multi .65 .20
383 A106 60fr multi .80 .20
384 A106 150fr multi 1.75 .50
385 A106 350fr multi 3.00 1.40
386 A106 500fr multi 4.50 1.90
Nos. 381-386 (6) 11.00 4.40

13th Winter Olympic Games, Lake Placid, NY, Feb. 12-24, 1980.

Jet over Map of Africa A107

1980, Feb. 20 Litho. *Perf. 12½*

387 A107 15fr yellow & multi .20 .20
388 A107 30fr blue & multi .40 .20
389 A107 60fr red & multi .60 .20
Nos. 387-389 (3) 1.20 .60

ASECNA (Air Safety Board), 20th anniv.

1982 World Cup Soccer Championships, Spain — A108

1996 Litho. *Perf. 13½*

721 A174 100fr Sheet of 9, #a-f 3.25 3.25
722 A174 170fr Sheet of 9, #a.-i. 5.50 2.75
723 A174 200fr Sheet of 9, #a.-i. 6.75 3.50
724 A174 300fr Sheet of 9, #a.-i. 10.50 5.25

Souvenir Sheets

724J A174 1500fr multi 5.50 5.50
724K A174 1500fr multi 5.50 5.50

Rotary Intl. — A175

Antelopes: a, 170fr, Damaliscus dorcas. b, 350fr, Oryx gazella. c, 500fr, Addax nasomaculatus. d, 600fr, Aepyceros melampus.

1996, Dec. 17

725 A175 Block of 4, #a.-d. 7.00 3.50

#725a-725d exist in souvenir sheets of 1.

No. 725 Overprinted in Gold

1996

726 A175 Block of 4, #a.-d. 7.00 3.50

#726a-726d exist in souvenir sheets of 1.

Marilyn Monroe (1926-1962) — A176

Various portraits.

1996

727 A176 250fr Sheet of 9, #a.-i. 10.50 6.50

Souvenir Sheet

728 A176 1500fr multicolored 5.75 2.75

No. 728 contains one 51x90mm stamp.

Famous People Type of 1997

Nobel Prize winners: 100fr, Mother Teresa (1910-97), humanitarian. 150fr, Martin Luther King, Jr. (1929-68), civil rights leader. 475fr, Otto Hahn (1879-1968), chemist, nuclear powered ship. 500fr, Ivan Pavlov (1849-1936), physiologist, Russian space dog, Laika. 600fr, Johannes van der Waals (1837-1923), physicist. 1000fr, Sir Edward Appleton (1892-1965), physicist, Concorde jet.

1998, Feb. 5

729-734 A173 Set of 6 14.50 7.00

Nos. 729-734 exist in souvenir sheets of 1.

Scouting A177

Wild animals: No. 735: a, Hyena. b, Mongoose.

No. 736: a, Wildcat. b, Addax nasomaculatus.

No. 737: a, Fennec. b, Hyena, diff.

1998, Feb. 6

735 A177 150fr Pair, #a.-b. 1.40 .65
736 A177 550fr Pair, #a.-b. 4.50 2.50
737 A177 600fr Pair, #a.-b. 5.25 2.75

Cats and Dogs — A178

No. 738: a, Maine coon. b. Singapore.

No. 739: a, Siberian husky. b, Malamute.

No. 740: a, Spitz. b, Eskimo.

No. 741: a, Siamese. b, Common cat.

No. 742, 1500fr, Abyssinian. No. 743, 1500fr, Samoyed.

1998, Feb. 6

738 A178 300fr Pair, #a.-b. 2.50 1.25
739 A178 450fr Pair, #a.-b. 3.75 1.90
740 A178 475fr Pair, #a.-b. 3.75 1.90
741 A178 500fr Pair, #a.-b. 4.00 2.00

Souvenir Sheets

742-743 A178 Set of 2 12.50 6.50

Nos. 742-743 each contain one 42x60mm stamp.

Airplanes, Ships, & Trains A179

No. 743A — Early aircraft: b, Latecoere 28, France. c, D'Equeuilly, France. d, Liore et Olivier Leo-213, France. e, Louis Bleriot monoplane. f, Graf Zeppelin LZ 127. g, Caproni CA 133, Italy.

No. 744 — Airplanes: a, Sikorsky VS-44A. b, Short S25/V Sandringham 4. c, Bristol 167 Brabazon 1. d, Savoia S13 Bis. e, Curtiss CR-3. f, Curtiss R3C-2.

No. 745 — Ships: a, Normandy, 1935. b, Persia, 1856. c, Queen Elizabeth II, 1968. d, Christian Radich, 1937. e, Amerigo Vespucci, 1933. f, Tovarich, 1933.

No. 745G — Classic sports cars: h, 1963-65 Porsche 356 SC. i, 1961-66 AC Cobra. j, 1960-61 Maserati Tipo 63 Birdcage. k, 1962-63 Austin Healey 3000 MK11. l, 1959-62 Ferrari 250 GT Berlinetta SWB. m, 1958 Aston Martin DB4.

No. 746 — Trains: a, BRB cog steam train. b, AE 4/7 10969. c, Crocodile of Saint-Gothard BE 6/8 111. d, RAE 2/4 1001. e, Steam train, Spain. f, RE 6/6 11612 express.

No. 746G — High speed trains: h, ETR 470, Italy. i, TGV Metro, France. j, Hikari, Japan. k, TGV 001 turbotrain, France. l, Eurostar 3203/3204 Metro train, France, Germany, Great Britain. m, 990 ICE train, Germany.

1500fr, Steam locomotive, C5/6 2978. 2000fr, TGV, France.

1998, Feb. 4

743A A179 150fr Sheet of 6, #b.-g. 3.75 1.90
744 A179 200fr Sheet of 6, #a.-f. 5.00 2.50
745 A179 250fr Sheet of 6, #a.-f. 6.25 3.25
745G A179 300fr Sheet of 6, #h.-m. 7.50 3.75
746 A179 350fr Sheet of 6, #a.-f. 9.00 4.50
746G A179 400fr Sheet of 6, #h.-m. 10.00 5.00

Souvenir Sheets

747 A179 1500fr multicolored 6.25 3.25
748 A179 2000fr multicolored 8.25 4.00

Nos. 747-748 contain one 36x42mm stamp.

Swiss rail service, 150th anniv. (#746-747).

Issued: #745G, 2/6.

See No. 758.

Diana, Princess of Wales (1961-97) A180

Various portraits.

2000fr, Portrait wearing high lace collar.

1997 Litho. *Perf. 13½*

749 A180 250fr Sheet of 9, #a.-i. 9.00 4.50

Souvenir Sheet

749J A180 2000fr multicolored 8.50 4.50

Literacy Campaign A181

Kellou Dahalob — A182

1997, June 16

750 A181 150fr olive & multi .55 .25
751 A181 300fr buff & multi 1.10 .50
752 A181 475fr salmon & multi 1.75 .80
Nos. 750-752 (3) 3.40 1.55

1998, Apr. 8

753 A182 50fr pink & multi .20 .20
754 A182 100fr blue & multi .40 .20
755 A182 150fr green & multi .65 .30
756 A182 300fr lilac & multi 1.10 .50
757 A182 400fr yellow & multi 1.50 .70
Nos. 753-757 (5) 3.85 1.90

Transportation Type of 1997

No. 758 — Modern aircraft: a, SAT, France, Germany. b, BAC/Aerospatiale Concorde. c, X001, Japan. d, Bell X-2, US. e, Douglas X-3, US. f, Aerospatiale STS 2000, France.

1998, Feb. 4 Litho. *Perf. 13½*

758 A179 475fr Sheet of 6, #a.-f. 12.00 6.25

Women — A183

Women: 50fr, 100fr, 150fr, Using grindstone. 300fr, 450fr, 500fr, Kneeling.

1997, June 16

759 A183 50fr vio & multi, vert. .20 .20
760 A183 100fr grn & multi, vert. .40 .20
761 A183 150fr yel & multi, vert. .55 .25
762 A183 300fr vio & multi 1.10 .50
763 A183 450fr grn & multi 1.75 .80
764 A183 500fr yel & multi 1.90 .85
Nos. 759-764 (6) 5.90 2.80

Protect the Ozone Layer — A184

1998, June 20 Litho. *Perf. 13½*

765 A184 150fr blue & multi .60 .25
766 A184 300fr green & multi 1.25 .55
767 A184 475fr pink & multi 1.90 .85
768 A184 500fr blue green & multi 1.90 .85
Nos. 765-768 (4) 5.65 2.50

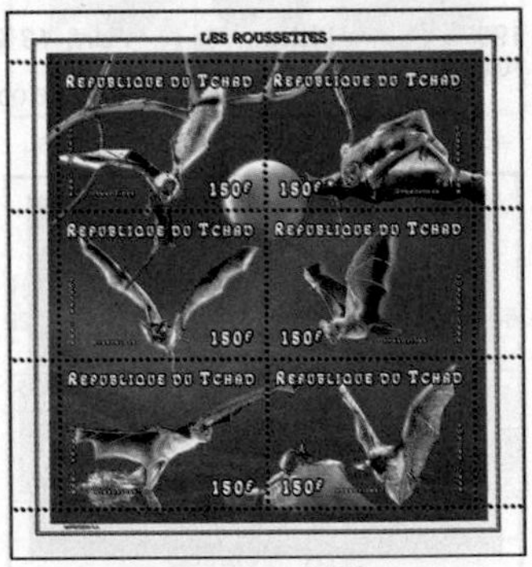

Fauna — A185

No. 769 — Bats: a, Holding mouse, tree branch. b, Drinking. c, One in flight, bottom of mouse. d, One flying left. e, One flying right. f, Mouse on rock, bat landing.

No. 769G — Horses: h, Gray Arabian. i, Brown Arabian. j, Przewalski's. k, Australian brumbies. l, Camargue. m, Zebras.

No. 769N — Sea mammals: o-t, Various portraits of Trichechus senegalensis.

No. 770 — Gorillas & chimpanzees: a, Chimpanzee scratching head. b, Gorilla walking on all fours. c, Gorilla seated. d, Chimpanzee swinging from branch. e, Chimpanzee using stick. f, Two gorillas.

No. 771 — Raptors: a, Terathopius ecaudatus. b, Buteo buteo. c, Sagittarius serpentarius. d, Polemaetus belligosus. e, Circaetus allicus. f, Aquila chrysaetos.

No. 771G — Reptiles: h, Crocodylus niloticus. i, Drendroaspis angusticeps. j, Bitis nasicornis. k, Chamaeleo johnstoni. l, Naja nigricolis. m, Meroles cuneirostris.

No. 771N — Mushrooms: o, Coprinus atramentarius. p, Romaria botrytis. q, Aleuria aurantia. r, Amanita muscaria. s, Macrolepiota rhacodes. t, Helvella crispa.

No. 771U — Mushrooms: v, Morchella vulgaris. w, Tuber aestiuum. x, Tuber melanosporum. y, Mitrophora hybrida. z, Morchella conica. aa, Choeromyces meandriformis.

No. 772 — Butterflies: a, Charaxes jasius. b, Hamanumidia daedalus. c, Charaxes bohemani. d, Hallimoides rumia, denomination LL. e, Hallimoides rumia, denomination LR. f, Pseudacraea boisduuali.

1500fr, Coelogyne ovalis, palla ussheri. 2000fr, Baleniceps, Neurophyllum clauatum.

1998, June 20

769	A185	150fr Sheet of 6, #a.-f.		4.00	2.10
769G	A185	250fr Sheet of 6, #h.-m.		5.50	2.75
769N	A185	300fr Sheet of 6, #o.-t.		6.50	6.50
770	A185	300fr Sheet of 6, #a.-f.		8.00	4.00
771	A185	350fr Sheet of 6, #a.-f.		9.25	4.50
771G	A185	450fr Sheet of 6, #h.-m.		10.00	10.00
771N	A185	475fr Sheet of 6, #o.-t.		10.50	10.50
771U	A185	500fr Sheet of 6, #v.-aa.		11.00	11.00
772	A185	600fr Sheet of 6, #a.-f.		16.00	8.00

Souvenir Sheets

773 A185 1500fr multicolored 6.50 3.25
773A A185 2000fr multicolored 7.50 3.75

Nos. 773-773A contain one 51x42mm stamp.

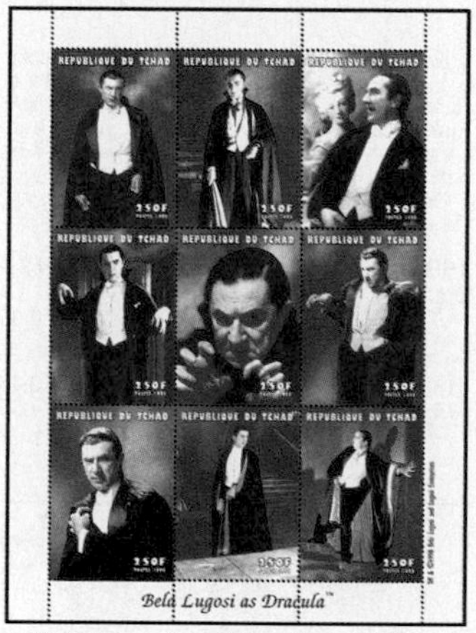

Bela Lugosi as Dracula — A185a

Lugosi in various poses.

1998, Dec. 11 Litho. *Perf. 13½*

773B A185a 250fr Sheet of 9, #d.-l. 8.50 8.50

Souvenir Sheet

773C A185a 1500fr multi, horiz. 5.75 5.75

Diana, Princess of Wales — A186

No. 774 — Various portraits: a, 200fr. b, 250fr. c, 300fr. d, 400fr. e, 475fr. f, 500fr. g, 800fr. h, 900fr. i, 1000fr.

1999, Jan. 10 Litho. *Perf. 12½*

774 A186 Sheet of 9, #a.-i. 17.50 9.00

Birds — A187

Designs: 75fr, Ibis ibis. 150fr, Ephippiorhynchus senegalensis. 200fr, Phoenicopterus ruber. 300fr, Leptoptilus crumeniferus. 400fr, Scopus umbretta. 475fr, Platalea alba.
1000fr, Balaeniceps rex.

1999, Jan. 15 Litho. *Perf. 12¾*

775-780 A187 Set of 6 5.75 2.75

Souvenir Sheet

781 A187 1000fr multicolored 3.50 1.75

No. 781 contains one 32x40mm stamp.

Fire Trucks A188

Designs: 50fr, 1840 model. 150fr, 1920 Fiat. 200fr, 1915 Mack. 300fr, 1930 Renault. 400fr, Pegaso M 1090. 500fr, 1960 Jet Fire Power.
700fr, 1720 King George III Fire Company.

1998, Dec. 30

782-787 A188 Set of 6 5.75 2.75

Souvenir Sheet

788 A188 700fr multicolored 2.50 1.25

No. 788 contains one 35x28mm stamp.

Minerals — A188a

No. 788A: a, Opal. b, Cyanite. c, Chalcopyrite. d, Apatite. e, Celestite. f, Scorodite.
No. 788B: a, Agate. b, Wulfenite. c, Barytine. d, Tanzanite. e, Amazonite. f, Malachite.

1998, Nov. 12 Litho. *Perf. 13½*

788A A188a 475fr Sheet of 6, #a.-f. 11.00 5.50
788B A188a 500f Sheet of 6, #a.-f. 11.50 5.75

Dinosaurs — A188b

No. 788C: a, Dilophosaurus. b, Argentinosaurus. c, Kritosaurus. d, Scutellosaurus. e, Ornithomimosaurus. f, Bactrosaurus.
No. 788D: a, Coelophysis. b, Kannemeyeria. c, Apatosaurus. d, Scipionyx. e, Lystrosaurus. f, Kentrosaurus.
No. 788E, Giganotosaurus, vert.

1998, Nov. 12 Litho. *Perf. 13¼*

Sheets of 6

788C A188b 400fr #a.-f. 9.25 4.75
788D A188b 450fr #a.-f. 10.50 5.25

Souvenir Sheet

788E A188b 2000fr multi 7.50 3.75

US Pres. Ronald Reagan — A189

No. 789: a, Family portrait as young boy. b, In front of family home. c, In football uniform, as radio announcer. d, Riding horse. e, Up close portrait. f, With Nancy, greeting Pope John Paul II. g, Making speech at podium. h, Being sworn in as president. i, At desk in Oval Office.
2000fr, At desk, White House.

1999, Feb. 2 Litho. *Perf. 13½*

789 A189 450fr Sheet of 9, #a.-i. 16.00 8.00

Souvenir Sheet

790 A189 2000fr multicolored 8.00 3.75

American Railroads — A190

No. 791 — Train, railroad pioneer: a, "Alco" Santa Fe, 1945, Cyrus Holliday. b, Rio Grande, 1961, J.F. Stevens. c, Amtrak, 1976, Thomas Dehone Judah. d, 250 Gobernador, 1884, Mark Hopkins. e, Meeting of Central Pacific and Union Pacific at Promontory Point, 1869, Leland Stanford, Thomas Durant. f, Great Northern W1, 1947, Jim Hill. g, Union Pacific Railroad, 1951, G.M. Dodge. h, Pennsylvania GG1, 1934, S.M. Vauclain. i, 151 Santa Fe U.P, 1917, S. Barstow Strong.

1999, Feb. 2

791 A190 200fr Sheet of 9, #a.-i. 7.00 3.50

Fossils and Cave Paintings — A191

No. 792: a, Harlania enigmatica. b, Spirophyton. c, Fossils, dunes of Djourab. d, Chain of people, oxen, Bardai. e, Man of Gonoa. f, Oxen, Kozen, Borkou.

1998, Dec. 11

792 A191 150fr Sheet of 6, #a.-f. 3.50 1.75

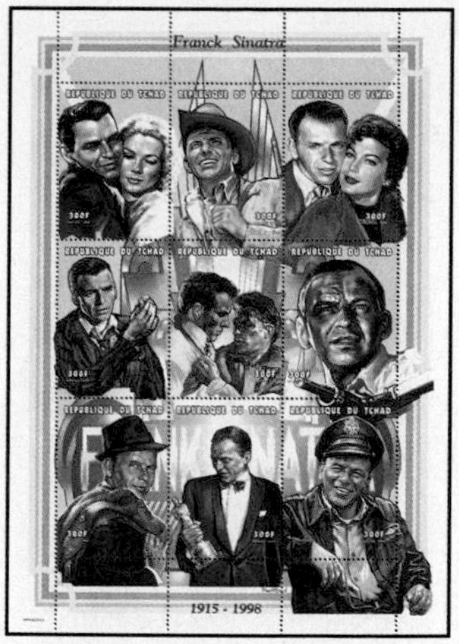

Frank Sinatra — A191a

No. 792G — Sinatra with: h, Blonde actress. i, Green jacket. j, Ava Gardner. k, Striped suit. l, Actor. m, Gun. n, Dark green hat. o, Oscar statuette. p, Military cap.

1998, Dec. 30 Litho. *Perf. 13½*

792G A191a 300fr Sheet of 9, #h.-p. 11.00 5.50

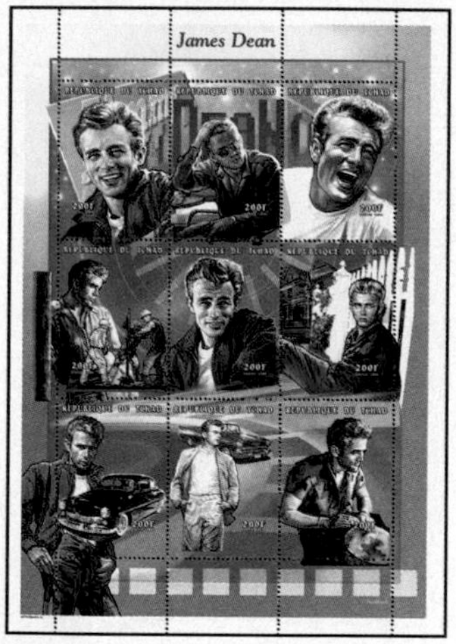

James Dean (1931-55), Actor — A192

Various portraits.

1999, Feb. 2

793 A192 200fr Sheet of 9, #a.-i. 7.00 3.50

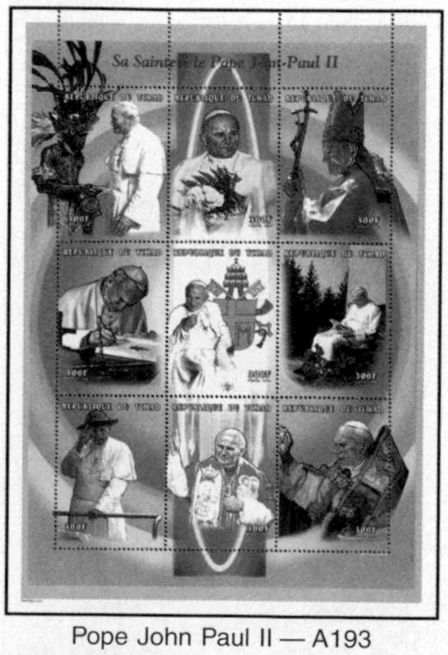

Pope John Paul II — A193

Various portraits.

1999, Feb. 2

794 A193 300fr Sheet of 9, #a.-i. 10.50 5.25

Souvenir Sheet

795 A193 1500fr multicolored 6.00 3.00

No. 795 contains one 58x51mm stamp.

John Glenn's Return to Space — A194

Various portraits.

1999, Feb. 11 Litho. *Perf. 13½*

796 A194 500fr Sheet of 9, #a.-i. 17.50 9.00

Souvenir Sheet

797 A194 2000fr multicolored 8.00 3.75

No. 797 contains one 57x51mm stamp.

Kofi Annan, UN Secretary-General — A195

Various portraits.

1999, Feb. 11

798 A195 150fr Sheet of 9, #a.-i. 5.25 2.75

Chess — A196

No. 798J: k, Paul Morphy. l, Chess board, Morphy-Anderssen, 1858. m, Adolf Anderssen. n, Emanuel Lasker. o, Chess board, Lasker-Capablanca, 1914. p, José Raul Capablanca. q, David Bronstein. r, Chess board, Bronstein-Botvinnik, 1951. s, Mikhail Botvinnik.

a, Bobby Fischer. b, Chess board, Fischer-Tal, 1961. c, Mikhail Tal. d, Boris Spassky. e, Chess board, Spassky-Petrosian, 1969. f, Tigran Petrosian. g, Garry Kasparov. h, Chess board, Kasparov-Karpov, 1960. i, Anatoly Karpov.

No. 800, Margrave Othon IV of Brandenburg.

No. 800A, King Louis XVI playing chess, horiz.

1999, Feb. 20

798J A196 375fr Sheet of 9, #k.-s. 13.00 6.50

799 A196 500fr Sheet of 9, #a.-i. 17.50 9.00

Souvenir Sheets

800 A196 2000fr multi 7.75 3.75

800A A196 2000fr multi — —

Dated 1998. No. 800 contains one 58x51mm stamp. No. 800A contains one 58x51mm stamp. Sheets of 3 stamps, containing Nos. 798Jk-798Jm, 798Jn-798Jp, 798Jq-798Js, 799a-799c, 799d-799f, or 799g-799i exist.

Souvenir Sheets

France, 1998 World Cup Champions — A197

No. 801: a, Bikente Lizarazu. b, Christian Karembeu. c, Frank Leboeuf. d, Emmanuel Petit.

No. 802: a, Fabien Barthez. b, Marcel Desailly. c, Didier Deschamps. d, Christophe Dugarry.

No. 803: Youri Djorkaeff. b, Aime Jacquet. c, Lilian Thuram. d, Zinedine Zidane.

2000fr, Deschamps holding World Cup.

1999, Feb. 20 Litho. *Perf. 13½*

801 A197 300fr Sheet of 4, #a.-d. 4.50 2.25

802 A197 400fr Sheet of 4, #a.-d. 6.25 3.00

803 A197 500fr Sheet of 4, #a.-d. 8.00 3.75

Perf. 13¼

804 A197 2000fr multicolored 8.00 3.75

No. 804 contains one 57x51mm stamp.

Hokusai Paintings A198

Designs: a, Voyagers Crossing the Oi River. b, Bird. c, On Totomi Mountain. d, Evening at Ueno. e, Higashimachi-matsuri-yatai-tenjou. f, Evening shower at Yoshiwara. g. Woman with Umbrella. h, Cascade. i, Courtesan.

1999, Sept. 10 Litho. *Perf. 13½*

805 A198 475fr Sheet of 9, #a.-i. 17.50 9.00

Japex '99.

Millennium — A199

No. 806 — Highlights of 1000-1899: a, Commercial routes in West Africa. b, Crusades. c, Notre Dame Cathedral. d, Ming dynasty tombs. e, Discovery of America. f, Albrecht Dürer. g, Sir Isaac Newton. h, American Independence. i, Napoleon.

No. 807 — 1900-24: a, Return of Halley's Comet. b, Lord Baden-Powell founds Scouting movement. c, Sinking of the Titanic. d, 1st film in Technicolor. e, Marconi sends 1st message across Atlantic, birth of radio. f, Harry Houdini. g, Capablanca-Lasker chess matches. h, Pierre & Marie Curie win Nobel Prize. i, Theft of the Mona Lisa.

No. 808 — 1925-49: a, Birth of Marilyn Monroe. b, Discovery of Pluto. c, Laurel and Hardy. d, Independence of India. e, Alexander Fleming discovers penicillin. f, Introduction of Volkswagen Beetle & Vespa motor scooter. g, Opening of film "Dracula." h, World War II. i, Discovery of Lascaux cave drawings.

No. 809 — 1950-74: a, 1st flight of the Concorde, 7 original astronauts. b, Death of Buddy Holly. c, 1st Super Bowl. d, Death of Eva Peron. e, Art by Andy Warhol. f, The Beatles. g, Cultural Revolution in China. h, Assassination of Pres. John F. Kennedy. i, Cuban Revolution.

No. 810 — 1975-99: a, Death of Princess Diana. b, Death of Enzo Ferrari. c, Akira. d, Argentina, 1986 World Cup Soccer champions. e, B. Lara breaks cricket records. f, France, 1998 World Cup Soccer champions. g, Explosion of the Space Shuttle Challenger. h, Pope John Paul II meets Lech Walesa. i, Deaths of Frank Sinatra, Freddie Mercury.

1999, Sept. 10

806 A199 150fr Sheet of 9, #a.-i. 5.25 2.50

807 A199 300fr Sheet of 9, #a.-i. 10.00 5.25

808 A199 450fr Sheet of 9, #a.-i. 15.00 7.75

809 A199 475fr Sheet of 9, #a.-i. 16.00 8.00

810 A199 500fr Sheet of 9, #a.-i. 16.00 8.25

Nos. 806-810 (5) 62.25 31.75

Souvenir Sheet

PhilexFrance '99 — A200

Illustration reduced.

1999, Sept. 10

811 A200 1500fr multi 6.00 3.00

I Love Lucy — A201

No. 812: a, Lucy leaning against tree, Ricky. b, Lucy, Ricky kissing. c, Lucy pointing gun. d, Ricky falling to ground. e, Lucy in apartment. f, Ricky holding animal. g, Ricky drinking from canteen. h, Lucy, Ricky talking. i, Lucy behind bush.

No. 813, Lucy in grape vat. No. 814, Lucy, Ricky in bed.

1999, Feb. 20 Litho. *Perf. 13¼*

812 A201 450fr Sheet of 9, #a.-i. 18.00 9.00

Souvenir Sheets

813 A201 1500fr multi 6.75 3.25

814 A201 2000fr multi 9.00 4.50

Dated 1998.

Betty Boop — A202

No. 815: a, With cat and dog. b, In flowered dress. c, Looking back over shoulder. d, With hammer, dresser. e, As majorette. f, In red dress with fur collar. g, Holding paper. h, Holding blue dress. i, Holding telephone.

No. 816, With feathered hat. No. 817, In leopard-spotted blouse.

1999, Feb. 20 Litho. *Perf. 13¼*

815 A202 450fr Sheet of 9, #a.-i. 18.00 9.00

Souvenir Sheets

816 A202 1500fr multi 6.75 3.25

817 A202 2000fr multi 9.00 4.50

Dated 1998.

Antique Automobiles — A203

150fr, 1900 F.N. 300fr, 1906 Bianchi. 400fr, 1906 Renault. 500fr, 1919 Pierce-Arrow. 700fr, 1919 Citroen 5CV. 900fr, 1928 Ford. 1000fr, 1898 Renault.

1999 Litho. *Perf. 13x12¾*
818-823 A203 Set of 6 14.00 6.75

Souvenir Sheet
Perf. 13x13¼
824 A203 1000fr multi 5.00 2.50

No. 824 contains one 40x31mm stamp.

Locomotives — A204

Designs: 150fr, 0-4-4-0. 300fr, Red 0-4-0. 400fr, Green 0-6-0. 500fr, Brown 0-4-0. 700fr, Blue 0-4-0. 900fr, Blue 0-6-0.
1000fr, Electric locomotive.

1999 *Perf. 12¾*
825-830 A204 Set of 6 14.00 6.50

Souvenir Sheet
Perf. 13x13¼
831 A204 1000fr multi 5.00 2.50

No. 831 contains one 36x28mm stamp.

Wonders of Forgotten Cultures — A205

Designs: 50fr, Easter Island. 150fr, Stonehenge. 300fr, Jericho. 400fr, Machu Picchu. 500fr, Valley of Statues. 700fr, Chichén Itzá. 900fr, Persepolis.

1999 *Perf. 12¾*
832-838 A205 Set of 7 15.00 7.00

Chad postal officials have declared the following items to be "not authorized:"
Set of six stamps of various denominations: New Year 2000 (Year of the Dragon)
Sheet of nine stamps of various denominations: Orchids
Sheet of nine 150fr stamps: Spanish Impressionist paintings
Sheet of nine 300fr stamps: Millennium (Composers), Van Gogh paintings
Sheet of nine 450fr stamps: Millennium (Marilyn Monroe), French Impressionist paintings
Sheet of nine 475fr stamps: Impressionist paintings
Sheet of nine 500fr stamps: Renoir nudes, Elvis Presley, Olympics
Souvenir sheets of one: Millennium (three 300fr, two 450fr, one 475fr, three 500fr, one 1500fr), New Year 2000 (1000fr), Palace of Versailles (1500fr, 2000fr), Hiroshige paintings (1500fr, 2000fr).

Minerals A206

Designs: 150fr, Wulfenite. 200fr, Argentite. 400fr, Siderite. 500fr, Dolomite and quartz. 700fr, Azurite. 900fr, Spinel and calcite.
1000fr, Cassiterite.

2000, Jan. 15 Litho. *Perf. 12¾*
839-844 A206 Set of 6 14.00 14.00

Souvenir Sheet
845 A206 1000fr multi 5.00 5.00

Dated 1999.

Elvis Presley — A207

No. 846: a, Playing guitar, wearing red jacket. b, Holding microphone and guitar, wearing red jacket. c, Holding guitar, wearing gold jacket. d, Playing guitar wearing black leather jacket. e, Playing guitar, wearing black jacket. f, Playing guitar, wearing blue jacket. g, Holding microphone, wearing blue shirt. h, Singing, wearing brown jacket. i, Holding microphone, wearing striped yellow jacket.

2000, Mar. 10 *Perf. 13¼*
846 A207 300fr Sheet of 9, #a-i 12.00 12.00

Dated 1999.

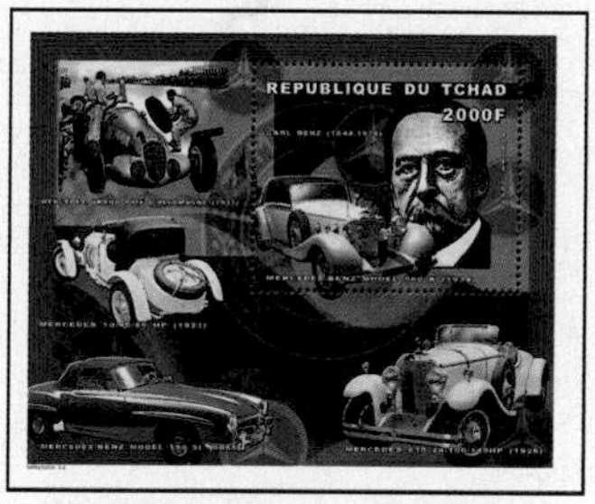

Carl Benz and Mercedes-Benz Automobiles — A208

No. 847: a, 1934 W-25. b, 1934 500 K. c, 1964 230 SL. d, 1935 150. e, 1954 300 SL. f, 1971 280 SE.
2000fr, 1934 500 K, diff.

2000, Mar. 10
847 A208 250fr Sheet of 6, #a-f 7.00 7.00

Souvenir Sheet
848 A208 2000fr multi 9.00 9.00

No. 847 contains six 30x30mm stamps. Dated 1999.

Trains — A209

No. 849: a, FES 3228, European Union flag. b, TGV Duplex, French flag. c, 500 Series Unit W1, Japanese flag. d, AVE Class 100, Spanish flag. e, ICE3, German flag. f, ETR 500, Italian flag.
2000fr, TGC 001 V56, TGV Duplex, Etienne Chambron.

2000, Mar. 10
849 A209 600fr Sheet of 6, #a-f 11.50 11.50

Souvenir Sheet
850 A209 2000fr multi 6.50 6.50

No. 849 contains six 30x30mm stamps. Dated 1999.

French Rulers — A210

No. 851, 150fr: a, Charlemagne. b, King Charles VIII. c, King Francis I. d, King Henry II. e, Catherine de Medici. f, King Henry III.
No. 852, 200fr: a, King Louis XII. b, King Louis XIII. c, King Louis XIV. d, King Louis XV. e, King Louis XVI. f, King Louis XVIII.
No. 853, 300fr — Napoleon Bonaparte: a, Standing, wearing red cape. b, On horseback, wearing red cape. c, On horseback, with soldier at right. d, On horseback, with crowd at right. e, Standing with opter people. f, On white horse, leading battle.

2000, Mar. 10
Sheets of 6, #a-f
851-853 A210 Set of 3 17.50 17.50

Dated 1999.

Pope John Paul II — A211

No. 854 — Pope John Paul II and: a, Dalai Lama. b, Fidel Castro. c, King Hassan II of Morocco. d, Grand Rabbi Elio Toaff. e, Patriarch Bartholomew I. f, Mother Teresa.

2000, Mar. 10
854 A211 475fr Sheet of 6, #a-f 13.00 13.00

Dated 1999.

Space — A212

No. 855: a, Sputnik, dog Laika. b, Yuri Gagarin, Vostok 1. c, Konstantin Feoktistov, Vladimir Komarov, Boris Yegorov, Voskhod 1. d, Luna 1, chimpanzee Ham. e, Neil Armstrong, Michael Collis, Edwin Aldrin, Apollo 11. f, Aldrin, splashdown of capsule.

2000, Mar. 10
855 A212 500fr Sheet of 6, #a-f 13.00 13.00

Dated 1999.

Betty Boop Type of 1999

No. 856: a, Wearing red and violet striped leotard, kicking leg up. b, As cheerleader. c, At football field, holding pennant. d, At ice cream shop. e, Wearing yellow and green striped leotard. f, Wearing baseball cap and orange shorts. g, Wearing baseball cap and checked shirt. h, Seated, drinking beverage. i, Wearing cut-off shorts.
No. 857, 1500fr, Riding bicycle. No. 858, 2000fr, Wearing glasses, elbow and knee pads.

2000, Mar. 30
856 A202 250fr Sheet of 9, #a-i 10.00 10.00

Souvenir Sheets
857-858 A202 Set of 2 16.00 16.00

The Three Stooges — A213

No. 859, 250fr, horiz.: a, Larry, in surgeon's gown, and Curly. b, Curly, Moe, Larry around barrel. c, Moe, Larry and Curly on horse. d, Larry attacking man. e, Moe getting hair pulled. f, Moe with mallet. g, Curly, Moe and Larry in western outfits, outdoors. h, Larry, Curly and Moe in white doctor's jackets. i, Man looking at Moe.
No. 860, 300fr, horiz.: a, Larry grabbing Moe's chin. b, Moe and Larry holding scrolls. c, Moe, yellow background. d, Larry, blue background. e, Moe, Shemp and Larry. f, Shemp, blue background. g, Shemp, yellow background. h, Shemp pointing bellows at Larry. i, Moe and Larry in white.
No. 861, 1500fr, Moe in surgeon's gown. No. 862, 1500fr, Moe wearing hat. No. 863, 2000fr, Curly, Moe and Larry in western outfits, outdoors. No. 864, 2000fr, Larry with violin.

2000
Sheets of 9, #a-i
859-860 A213 Set of 2 22.50 22.50

Souvenir Sheets
861-864 A213 Set of 4 32.50 32.50

Issued: Nos. 859, 861, 863, 3/30; Nos. 860, 862, 864, 5/29.

I Love Lucy Type of 1999

No. 865: a, Lucy dancing, man in background. b, Lucy dancing, with knees bent and arms extended. c, Lucy in doorway. d, Lucy dancing behind sofa. e, Lucy kicking out leg. f, Lucy being caught by two men. g, Lucy with one arm extended. h, Lugy being sprayed with seltzer water. i, Lucy with leg on dance rail.
No. 866, 1500fr, Lucy looking at clown, horiz. No. 867, 2000fr, Lucy with clown costume and arms extended.

2000, May 29
865 A201 225fr Sheet of 9, #a-i 9.00 9.00

Souvenir Sheets
866-867 A201 Set of 2 16.00 16.00

N'Djamena, Cent. A213a

Background colors: 150fr, Blue. 300fr, Red. 475fr, Green.

2000, May 29 Litho. *Perf. 13¼*
867A-867C A213a Set of 3 — —

Chadian Political History — A214

No. 868, 150fr: a, Louis Léon César Faidherbe. b, François Joseph Lamy. c, Henri Eugène Gouraud. d, Gustav Nachtigal. e, Head of Rabah on spike. f, Fernand Foureau.
No. 869, 300fr: a, Pierre Savorgnan de Brazza. b, Philippe Marie de Hautecloque Leclerc. c, Emile Gentil. d, Gabriel Lisette. e, Charles de Gaulle. f, Felix Eboué.

2000, May 29 *Perf. 13½*
Sheets of 6, #a-f

868-869 A214 Set of 2 18.00 18.00

Wildlife, Map of Chad, Scouting Emblem — A215

No. 870, 150fr — Giraffa camelopardalis: a, Pair, one with head lowered. b, Pair, both with heads extended. c, Pair near forest. d, Trio.
No. 871, 200fr: a, Pair of Gazella granti in field. b, Gazella cuiveri. c, Gazella dorcas. d, Pair of Gazella granti at waterhole.
No. 872, 250fr — Addax nasomaculatus: a, View of head. b, Lying in grass. c, Standing. d, Grazing.
No. 873, 300fr — Ammotragus lervia: a, Pair. b, View of head. c, Standing on mountain ledge. d, Standing, with purple mountain in background
No. 874, 375fr — Diceros bicornis: a, View of head. b, Facing right, line of dark green foliage in background. c, Facing left. d, Facing right, with trees in background.
No. 875, 400fr — Panthera pardus: a, On tree branch. b, Lying in grass. c, Standing. d, View of head.
No. 876, 450fr: a, Head of Theropithecus gelada. b, Cercopithecus aethiops. c, Papio anubis. d, Adult and juvenile Thereopithecus gelada.
No. 877, 450fr — Hippopotamus amphibius: a, Pair laying in mud. b, With open mouth. c, Standing. d, Herd.
No. 878, 475fr — Oryx dammah: a, Facing right, green foliage in background. b, View of head. c, Pair. d, Grazing, mountain in background.
No. 879, 500fr — Panthera leo: a, Male on female. b, Females at waterhole. c, Female and cub. d, Female and male.
No. 880, 600fr — Loxodonta africana: a, With tree at right. b, Facing right. c, View of head. With tree and mountain in background.
No. 881, 750fr — Syncerus caffer: a, Juvenile, adult grazing. b, Adult in field. c, Pair lying on ground. d, With grass in mouth.
No. 882, 1000fr, Pair of Diceros bicornis. No. 883, 1000fr, Pair of Hippopotamus amphibius fighting. No. 884, 1500fr, Panthera leo with kill.
Illustration reduced.

2000, Aug. 1 *Perf. 13¼*
Horiz. Strips of 4, #a-d

870-881 A215 Set of 12 90.00 90.00

Souvenir Sheets

882-884 A215 Set of 3 16.00 16.00

Nos. 882-884 each contain one 36x51mm stamp.

Miniature Sheet

Baseball Player — A216

2000, Oct. 11 **Litho. & Embossed**

885 A216 3000fr gold & multi 10.00 10.00

Exists with silver background.

High-five of Teenagers — A217

No. 886: a, Moon Hee-jun and Lee Jae-won. b, Jang Woo-hyuk and ear of Tony An. c, Tony an and Kang Ta. d, Jang Woo-hyuk. e, Entire group. f, Kang Ta. g, Moon Hee-jun. h, Lee Jae-won. i, Tony An.

2000 **Litho.**

886 A217 150fr Sheet of 9, #a-i 4.50 4.50

Sports and Chess — A218

No. 887, 30fr — Dogs involved in sport activities: a, Sled dogs. b, Dog racing. c, Hunting dogs. d, Dogs and skier.
No. 888, 70fr — Various sports: a, Petanque. b, Rugby. c, Archery. d, Jai alai.
No. 889, 250fr — 2000 Summer Olympics, Sydney: a, Fencing. b, Judo. c, Tennis. d, Boxing.
No. 890, 300fr — 2000 Summer Olympics, Sydney: a, Cycling. b, Basketball. c, Beach volleyball. d, Baseball.
No. 891, 400fr — Soccer players: a, Zinedine Zidane. b, Lilian Thuram. c, Yuri Djorkaeff. d, Nicolas Anelka
No. 892, 475fr — 2000 Summer Olympics, Sydney: a, Table tennis. b, Equestrian. c, Swimming. d, Kayaking.
No. 893, 500fr — Golf: a, Man with white pants swinging club. b, Golfer analyzing putt. c, Man with black pants swinging club. d, Woman golfer.
No. 894, 750fr — Formula I race drivers: a, Michael Schumacher. b, Mikka Hakkinen. c, Ralf Schumacher. d, David Coulthard.
No. 895, 1000fr — Chess: a, Knight with shield. b, Knight on donkey. c, Knight with attendant. d, Horses and wheeled castle.
2000fr, Venus Williams.

2001, Jan. 31 *Perf. 13¼*
Sheets of 4, #a-d

887-895 A218 Set of 9 67.50 67.50

Souvenir Sheet

896 A218 2000fr multi 9.00 9.00

2000 Summer Olympics, Sydney (No. 896).
No. 896 contains one 36x51mm stamp.

Trains — A219

No. 897, 200fr: a, Mallard, 1935. b, P8 Prussian, 1908. c, F2A, 1936. b, 240 P, 1940.
No. 898, 300fr: a, NSB No. 3641. b, New Zealand Railways Sereis EW. c, Series 277, Renfe. d, Series DF4 Vent d'Est IV Co-Co.
No. 899, 400fr: a, SNCF Series 9100 2-D-2, 1950. b, SNCF Series 72000 C-C, 1967. c, CC 21000, 1969. d, VL-80, 1963.
No. 900, 475fr: a, GNER Eurostar. b, Electric EMU ETR 500. c, DER OBB 1016 001. d, GNER train.
No. 901, 500fr: a, OL-49, 1951. b, Pacific Series 16E, 1935. c, Andaluces 030, 1877. d, Franco-Crosti Gr. 743, 1937.
No. 902, 500fr: a, JR West 8-car unit E4. b, TGV KTX. c, 300 Series unit J3. d, E3 Series unit R6.
No. 903, 600fr: a, 2D2 PO, 1926. b, Metropolitan BB Vickers, 1920. c, DB ET 491, 1935. d, Series D, 1925.
No. 904, 600fr: a, Electric EMU 490. b, Acela, 2001. c, CFF-FFS Electric EMU RABe 500. d, ICE-T Bavereihe 41.
No. 905, 750fr: a, Single Driver, 1870. b, Great Western Railway Castle, 1923. c, Schools Class, 1930. d, 230 Besa, 1905.
No. 906, 750fr: a, TGV Thalys. b, TGV Duplex. c, TGV La Poste. d, TGV Atlantique.
1500fr, SAR Series 26 2-D-2. 2000fr, TGV Sud-est.

2001, June 22 **Litho.**
Sheets of 4, #a-d

897-906 A219 Set of 10 90.00 90.00

Souvenir Sheets

907-908 A219 Set of 2 16.00 16.00

Nos. 907-908 each contain one 51x36mm stamp.

British Royalty — A220

No. 909, 300fr — Queen Mother: a, With King George VI. b, With young daughter. c, With Prince Charles. d, Waving. e, Wearing tiara and yellow dress. f, Wearing pink dress and hat. g, Wearing green dress and hat. h, Holding flowers. i, With dogs.
No. 910, 300fr — Prince William wearing: a, Black suit with lapel handkerchief. b, Suit with red and blue vest. c, Suit with gold vest. d, Sweater, looking right. e, Black suit and dark blue tie. f, Sweater, facing forward. g, Blue shirt with button. h, Dark blue shirt without button. i, Light blue suit.

2001, July 22 *Perf. 13¼*
Sheets of 9, #a-i

909-910 A220 Set of 2 24.00 24.00

No. 910 contains nine 36x51mm stamps.

French Rulers — A221

No. 911, 300fr: a, King Francis I. b, King Louis XIII. c, Elizabeth of Austria, consort of King Charles IX. d, King John II the Good.
No. 912, 375fr: a, King Louis XIV. b, King Francis I, diff. c, King Louis XVI. d, King Louis XVIII.
No. 913, 475fr: a, King Louis XV as child. b, King Louis XV as adult. c, Queen Marie Antoinette. d, King Charles VII.
No. 914, 500fr — Napoleon Bonaparte wearing: a, White tunic. b, Black jacket. c, Emperor's robes. d, Red tunic.

2001, July 22
Sheets of 4, #a-d

911-914 A221 Set of 4 30.00 30.00

Stamps of Nos. 911-913 exist in souvenir sheets of 1. Value, set $70.

Pope John Paul II — A222

No. 915, 800fr: a, Standing in room, looking left. b, Waving, c, Holding flowers. d, With blue sky background.
No. 916, 1000fr: a, Wearing red hat. b, Wearing miter, waving. c, Bending to kiss ground. d, Wearing miter, holding crucifix.
4000fr, Wearing zucchetto.

2001 **Litho.** *Perf. 13¼*
Sheets of 4, #a-d

915-916 A222 Set of 2 32.50 32.50

Miniature Sheet
Litho. & Embossed

917 A222 4000fr gold & multi 22.50 22.50

Issued: Nos. 915-916, 7/22; No. 917, 7/23.
No. 917 contains one 60x90mm stamp and exists with a silver background. Stamps of Nos. 915-916 exist in souvenir sheets of 1. Value, set $60.

Famous Men — A223

Designs: 200fr, Charles Darwin (1809-82), naturalist. 250fr, Christopher Columbus (1451-1506), explorer. 300fr, Jacques-Yves Cousteau (1910-97), marine scientist. 350fr, Albert Schweitzer (1875-1965), missionary. 400fr, Juan Manuel Fangio (1911-95), race car driver. 450fr, Nicolaus Copernicus (1473-1543), astronomer. 500fr, Robert Stephenson

(1803-59), engineer. 550fr, Etienne Chambron, high speed rail pioneer. 600fr, Garry Kasparov, chess player. 750fr, Lord Robert Baden-Powell (1857-1941), founder of scouting. 800fr, Neil Armstrong, astronaut. 1000fr, Sir Alexander Fleming (1881-1955), bacteriologist.

2001, Oct. 30 **Litho.**
918-929 A223 Set of 12 29.00 29.00

Nos. 918-929 exist in souvenir sheets of 1. Value, set $115.

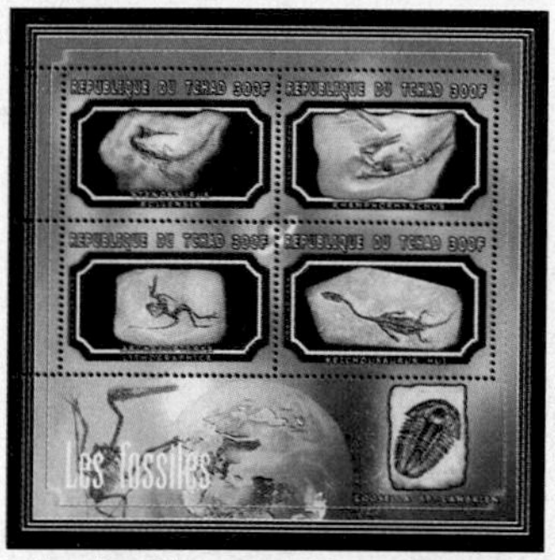

Fossils, Dinosaurs, Meteorites and Minerals — A224

No. 930, 300fr — Fossils: a, Stenosaurus bollensis. b, Rhamphorhynchus. c, Archaeopteryx lithographica. d, Keichousaurus hui.
No. 931, 375fr — Dinosaurs: a, Mesadactylus. b, Pteranodon. c, Tropeognathus. d, Quetzalcoatlus.
No. 932, 400fr — Meteorites found in: a, India. b, Nigeria. c, US. d, Australia.
No. 933, 500fr — Dinosaurs: a, Deinonychus. b, Seismosaurus. c, Pleurocoelus, Acrocanthosaur. d, Styracosaurus.
No. 934, 500fr — Minerals: a, Fluorite. b, Pyrite. c, Wulfenite. d, Merovingian scoria.
No. 935, 550fr — Meteorites found in: a, Antarctica. b, Libya. c, USSR. d, China.
No. 936, 600fr — Minerals: a, Magnetite. b, Kunzite. c, Apophyllite, Stilbite. d, Fluorite, diff.
No. 937, 750fr — Minerals: a, Quartz. b, Merovingian scoria, diff. c, Epidote. d, Amethyst, agate.
3000fr, Tyrannosaurus rex, vert.

2001, Dec. 27 **Litho.**
Sheets of 4, #a-d
930-937 A224 Set of 8 72.50 72.50

Miniature Sheet
Litho. & Embossed

938 A224 3000fr gold & multi 17.00 17.00

No. 938 contains one 60x90mm stamp and exists with silver background.

French Kings — A225

Designs: No. 939, 3000fr, Louis IX. No. 940, 3000fr, Francis I. No. 941, 3000fr, Henry IV. No. 942, 3000fr, Louis XIII. No. 943, 3000fr, Louis XV.

2002, Apr. 10 **Litho. & Embossed**
Gold & Multicolored
939-943 A225 Set of 5 50.00 50.00

Nos. 939-943 exist with silver background.

Egyptian Treasures A225a

Designs: No. 943A, 3000fr, Painted wooden box. No. 943B, 3000fr, Nekhbet vulture. No. 943C, 3000fr, Oushebti of Tutankhamen, vert. No. 943D, 3000fr, Pair of royal scepters, vert. No. 943E, 3000fr, Diadem, vert. No. 943F, 3000fr, Gold-plated throne, vert. No. 943G, 3000fr, Cynocephalic pectoral, vert. No. 943H, 3000fr, Coffin of Tutankhamen, vert. No. 943I, 3000fr, Statue of Ka, vert. No. 943J, 3000fr, Duck earring, vert. No. 943K, 3000fr, Lion-shaped vase, vert. No. 943L, 3000fr, Canopic dais and chapel, vert.

Embossed on Gold Paper
2002, Apr. 10 ***Perf. 13¼***
943A-943L A225a Set of 12 140.00 140.00

Artists and Their Paintings — A226

On Nos. 944-957, painting titles (in French) and artist's birth and death dates are in margins adjacent to each stamp. On Nos. 958-962 painting titles are not shown, but artist's name is in sheet margin
No. 944, 150fr: a, Berthe Morisot (1841-95). b, Cache-cache. c, Le Berceau. d, Au bal. e, Jeune femme se poudrant. f, Paule Gobillard peignant.
No. 945, 200fr: a, Marc Chagall (1887-1985). b, Nature morte. c, Le violoniste vert. d, La maison bleue. e, Mariage. f, Le soldat ivre.
No. 946, 250fr: a, Camille Pissarro (1830-1903). b, Les chataigniers a Osny. c, Le verger. d, Le repos des glaneuses. e, Jeune paysanne prenant son cafe. f, Le bergére.
No. 947, 300fr: a, Alfred Sisley (1839-99). b, Le pont de Villeneuve la Garenne. c, Allee de jardin a Louveciennes. d, Meule de foin bord du Loing. e, Moret sur Loing. f, Moulin a Moret.
No. 948, 325fr: a, Paul Delvaux (1897-1994). b, La voix publique. c, Nocturnes. d, Balgnade des Nymphes. e, Pygmalion. f, Jeunes femmes revant.
No. 949, 350fr: a, Edouard Manet (1832-83). b, Le Déjeuner sur l'herbe. c, Olympia. d, Le fifre. e, La serveuse de bocks. f, Le balcon.
No. 950, 375fr: a, Vincent van Gogh (1853-90). b, Champ de blé avec cypres. c, Rue a Auvers. d, La sieste. e, Chambre jaune a Arles. f, Rue de village.
No. 951, 400fr: a, Salvador Dali (1904-89). b, Cannibalisme en automne. c, Corpus Hypercubicus. d, Le sommeil. e, Le tentation de St. Antoine. f, Meditation sur harpe.
No. 952, 425fr: a, Paul Cézanne (1839-1906). b, Les baigneurs. c, Les grandes baigneuses (light blue background). d, Les grandes baigneuses, diff. (dark blue background). e, Les baigneueses. f, Les baigneurs au repos.
No. 953, 450fr: a, Pablo Picasso (1881-1973). b, Les demoiselles d'Avignon. c, Femme a l'eventail. d, La danse. e, La vie. f, La mere et son fils.
No. 954, 475fr: a, Amadeo Modigliani (1884-1920). b, Nu souche sur un divan. c, Nu debout. d, Cariatide debout. e, Nu allongé. f, Nu assis de dos.
No. 955, 500fr: a, Auguste Renoir (1841-1919). b, Diane chasseresse. c, Nu allongé. d, Baigneuses. e, Baigneuse assise. f, Nymphe au printemps.
No. 956, 550fr: a, Edgar Degas (1834-1917). b, Femme se coiffant. c, Aprés le bain (view of front of seated woman). d, Femme se peignant. e, Aprés le bain (view of back of woman). f, Aprés le bain (woman dressing).
No. 957, 600fr: a, Henri Matisse (1869-1954). b, Le nu bleu. c, Le genou levé. d, Nu assis sur un fauteuil. e, Odalisques. f, Nu allongé.
No. 958, 1500fr, Gustave Caillebotte. No. 959, 1500fr, Picasso, diff. No. 960, 1500fr, Auguste Renoir, diff. No. 961, 2000fr, Pablo Picasso, diff. No. 962, 2000fr, Van Gogh, diff.

2002, Apr. 10 ***Perf. 12¾x13¼***
Sheets of 6, #a-f
944-957 A226 Set of 14 140.00 140.00

Souvenir Sheets
Perf. 13¼x12¾
958-962 A226 Set of 5 27.50 27.50

Nos. 944a-955a and 957a exist in souvenir sheets of 1 that are perf. 13¼x12¾. Value, set $92.50.

Miniature Sheet

Zeppelin NT — A227

No. 963: a, 475fr, Over Lake Constance. b, 500fr, Over Frankfurt. c, 600fr, Over Nürburgring, Germany. d, 750fr, At 2001 Salon du Bourget.

2002, Oct. 30 ***Perf. 13¼***
963 A227 Sheet of 4, #a-d 11.00 11.00

Nos. 963a-963d exist in souvenir sheets of 1. Value, set $45.

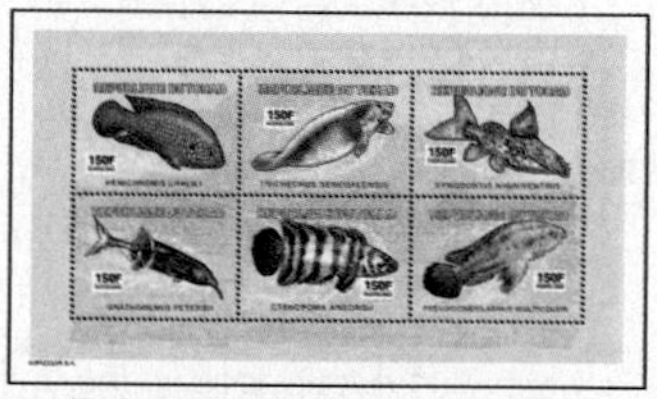

Fauna and Mushrooms — A228

No. 964, 150fr: a, Hemichromis lifalili. b, Trichechus senegalensis. c, Synodontis nigriventris. d, Gnathonemus petersii. e, Ctenopoma ansorgii. f, Pseudocrenilabrus multicolor.
No. 965, 300fr, vert.: a, Nectarina venusta. b, Lamprotornis splendidus. c, Poicephalus meyeri. d, Halcyon leucocephala. e, Quelea quelea. f, Merops pusillus.
No. 966, 350fr, vert.: a, Terathopius ecaudatus. b, Gymnogyps californianus. c, Buteo jamaicensis. d, Lophaetus occipitalis. e, Aquila rapax. f, Melierax metabates.
No. 967, 375fr, vert.: a, Elanus caeruleus. b, Harpia harpyja. c, Gyps rueppellii. d, Milvus migrans. e, Torgos tracheliotus. f, Aquila chrysaetos.
No. 968, 550fr: a, Kallimoides rumia. b, Zophopetes dysmephila. c, Megalopalpus zymna. d, Coeliades forestan. e, Catopsilia florella. f, Anaphaesis aurota.
No. 969, 600fr: a, Amanita muscaria. b, Amanita rubescens. c, Cortinarius orellanus. d, Hygrophorus hypothejus. e, Leccinum piceinum. f, Strobilomyces strobilaceus.

2003, June 2 **Litho.**
Sheets of 6, #a-f
964-969 A228 Set of 6 55.00 55.00

Stamps of Nos. 965-969 exist in a set of twelve souvenir sheets of two, with each souvenir sheet of two containing adjacent stamps found in the sheet of six. Value, set $160.

Chad - Taiwan Cooperation — A229

Flags and: 50fr, Grain. 100fr, Surgeon's hands, Red Cross. 150fr, Bridge. 300fr, Handshake, maps.

2003, Dec. 1
970-973 A229 Set of 4 2.50 2.50
973a Booklet pane, 2 each #970-973 5.00 —
Complete booklet, #973a 5.00
973b Souvenir sheet, #970-973 2.50 2.50

AIDS Prevention A230

Red ribbon and: 50fr, People under umbrella. 100fr, Man and woman. 150fr, Doctor. 300fr, "Prudence, Abstinence, Fidelité."

2004, July 7 **Litho.** ***Perf. 13x12¾***
974-977 A230 Set of 4 2.50 2.50

Opening of Petroleum Refinery, 1st Anniv. A231

Pres. Idriss Deby opening pipeline and: 150fr, Storage tank. 350fr, Storage tanks. 400fr, Refinery. 500fr, Tower, vert.

2004, Oct. 10 ***Perf. 12¾x13, 13x12¾***
978-981 A231 Set of 4 6.50 6.50

Women's Hairstyles A232

Designs: 150fr, Figuerier. 350fr, Sakkindjala. 550fr, Kileskou. 575fr, Dabbou.

2005, Mar. 8 ***Perf. 13***
982-985 A232 Set of 4 8.00 8.00

Toumai Skull A233

Color of skull: 25fr, Purple. 50fr, Green. 100fr, Gray. 150fr, Red. 1500fr, Gray.

2005, July 19 **Litho.** ***Perf. 12¾x13***
986-989 A233 Set of 4 1.40 1.40

Souvenir Sheet

990 A233 1500fr multi 5.75 5.75

SEMI-POSTAL STAMPS

Catalogue values for unused stamps in this section are for Never Hinged items.

Anti-Malaria Issue
Common Design Type
Perf. 12½x12

1962, Apr. 7 Engr. Unwmk.
B1 CD108 25fr + 5fr orange 1.00 .45

Freedom from Hunger Issue
Common Design Type

1963, Mar. 21 ***Perf. 13***
B2 CD112 25fr + 5fr dk grn, dk bl & brn 1.00 .45

Red Cross, Mother and Children — SP1

1974, Oct. 2 Photo. ***Perf. 12½x13***
B3 SP1 30fr + 10fr multi 1.00 .20

Red Cross of Chad, first anniversary.

AIR POST STAMPS

Catalogue values for unused stamps in this section are for Never Hinged items.

Olympic Games Issue
French Equatorial Africa No. C37 Surcharged in Red

Unwmk.

1960, Dec. 15 Engr. ***Perf. 13***
C1 AP8 250fr on 500fr grnsh blk, blk & slate 12.00 5.00

17th Olympic Games, Rome, Aug. 25-Sept. 11. Surcharge 46mm wide; illustration reduced.

Red Bishops — AP1

Discus Thrower — AP2

Birds in pairs: 100fr, Scarlet-chested sunbird. 200fr, African paradise flycatcher. 250fr, Malachite kingfisher. 500fr, Nubian carmine bee-eater.

1961-63 Unwmk. Engr. ***Perf. 13***
C2 AP1 50fr dk grn, mag & blk 1.25 .35
C3 AP1 100fr multi 3.75 1.25
C4 AP1 200fr multi 6.50 1.90
C5 AP1 250fr dk bl, grn & dp org ('63) 10.00 3.00
C6 AP1 500fr multi 22.50 9.50
Nos. C2-C6 (5) 44.00 16.00

Air Afrique Issue
Common Design Type

1962, Feb. 17 Unwmk. ***Perf. 13***
C7 CD107 25fr lt bl, org brn & blk 1.00 .20

Abidjan Games Issue

1962, July 21 Photo. ***Perf. 12x12½***
C8 AP2 100fr brn, lt grn & blk 3.50 .75

African Postal Union Issue
Common Design Type

1963, Sept. 8 Unwmk. ***Perf. 12½***
C9 CD114 85fr dk bl, ocher & red 2.40 .40

Air Afrique Issue, 1963
Common Design Type

1963, Nov. 19 ***Perf. 13x12***
C10 CD115 50fr multi 2.40 .40

Europafrica Issue
Common Design Type

1963, Nov. 30 Photo. ***Perf. 12x13***
C11 CD116 50fr dp grn, yel & dk brn 1.75 .40

Mail Truck and Broussard Plane — AP4

Unwmk.

1963, Dec. 16 Engr. ***Perf. 13***
C12 AP4 100fr sl grn, ultra & red brn 4.00 .20

Chiefs of State Issue

Map and Presidents of Chad, Congo, Gabon and Central African Republic AP4a

1964, June 23 Photo. ***Perf. 12½***
C13 AP4a 100fr multi 2.40 .20

See note after Central African Republic No. C19.

Europafrica Issue, 1964

Globe and Emblems of Industry and Agriculture — AP5

1964, July 20 ***Perf. 13x12***
C14 AP5 50fr brn, pur & dp org 1.75 .30

See note after Cameroun No. 402.

Soccer — AP6

Designs: 50fr, Javelin throw, vert. 100fr, High jump, vert. 200fr, Runners.

1964, Aug. 12 Engr. ***Perf. 13***
C15 AP6 25fr yel grn, sl grn & org brn .75 .20
C16 AP6 50fr org brn, ind & brt bl 1.75 .30
C17 AP6 100fr blk, red & brt grn 3.50 .50
C18 AP6 200fr bis, blk & car 6.00 1.10
a. Min. sheet of 4, #C15-C18 18.00 6.50
Nos. C15-C18 (4) 12.00 2.10

18th Olympic Games, Tokyo, 10/10-25/64.

Communications Symbols — AP7

1964, Nov. 2 Litho. ***Perf. 12½x13***
C19 AP7 25fr lil, dk brn & lt red brn 1.00 .20

Pan-African and Malagasy Posts and Telecommunications Cong., Cairo, Oct. 24-Nov. 6.

President John F. Kennedy (1917-63) — AP8

1964, Nov. 3 Photo. ***Perf. 12½***
C20 AP8 100fr multi 2.40 .70
a. Souvenir sheet of 4 12.00 6.00

ICY Emblem — AP9

1965, July 5 Photo. ***Perf. 13***
C21 AP9 100fr multi 1.50 .25

International Cooperation Year, 1965.

Abraham Lincoln — AP10

1965, Sept. 7 Unwmk. ***Perf. 13***
C22 AP10 100fr multi 2.25 .35

Centenary of death of Abraham Lincoln.

Musical Instrument Type
Design: 100fr, Xylophone (marimba).

1965, Oct. 26 Engr. ***Perf. 13***
Size: 48x27mm
C23 A18 100fr ocher, brt bl & vio bl 2.75 .85

Sir Winston Spencer Churchill (1874-1965) AP11

1965, Nov. 23 Engr. ***Perf. 13***
C24 AP11 50fr dk grn & blk 1.40 .20

Dr. Albert Schweitzer and Outstretched Hands — AP12

1966, Feb. 15 Photo. ***Perf. 12½***
C25 AP12 100fr multi 2.75 .50

Dr. Albert Schweitzer (1875-1965), medical missionary, theologian and musician.

Air Afrique Issue, 1966
Common Design Type

1966, Aug. 31 Photo. ***Perf. 13***
C26 CD123 30fr yel grn, blk & gray .75 .20

White-throated Bee-eater — AP13

Birds: 50fr, Blue-eared glossy starling. 200fr, African pygmy kingfisher. 250fr, Red-throated bee-eater. 500fr, Little green bee-eater.

1966-67 Photo. ***Perf. 13x12½***
C27 AP13 50fr gold & multi 1.25 .40
C28 AP13 100fr bluish gray & multi 3.50 1.00
C29 AP13 200fr grnsh gray & multi 6.75 1.75
C30 AP13 250fr pale bl & multi 7.50 1.75
C31 AP13 500fr pale sal & multi 14.00 3.25
Nos. C27-C31 (5) 33.00 8.15

Issued: 100fr, 200fr, 500fr, 8/18/66; others, 3/21/67.

For surcharges see Nos. C67-C69.

Congress Hall — AP14

1967, Jan. 5 Photo. ***Perf. 12½***
C32 AP14 25fr multi .75 .20

Opening of the new Congress Hall.

Breguet 19 Biplane — AP15

Planes: 30fr, Latécoère 631 hydroplane. 50fr, Douglas DC-3. 100fr, Piper Cherokee 6.

1967, Aug. 1 Engr. *Perf. 13*

C33	AP15	25fr sky bl, sl grn & lt brn	.75	.25
C34	AP15	30fr sky bl, indigo & grn	1.00	.30
C35	AP15	50fr sky bl, ol bis & sl grn	1.75	.50
C36	AP15	100fr dk bl, sl grn & dk red	3.50	.75
		Nos. C33-C36 (4)	7.00	1.80

First anniversary of Air Chad.

African Postal Union Issue, 1967
Common Design Type

1967, Sept. 9 Engr. *Perf. 13*

C37	CD124	100fr ol, brt pink & red brn	1.90	.40

Rock Painting Type of Regular Issue

1967, Dec. 19 Engr. *Perf. 13*
Size: 48x27mm

C38	A32	100fr Masked dancers	8.00	.95
C39	A32	125fr Rabbit hunt	9.00	1.50

Downhill Skiing — AP16

1968, Feb. 5 Engr. *Perf. 13*

C40	AP16	30fr shown	1.25	.20
C41	AP16	100fr Ski jump, vert.	3.25	.50

10th Winter Olympic Games, Grenoble, France, Feb. 6-18.

Konrad Adenauer (1876-1967), Chancellor of West Germany (1949-63) AP17

1968, Mar. 19 Photo. *Perf. 12½*

C42	AP17	52fr grn, dk brn & lt lil	1.40	.30
a.		Souvenir sheet of 4	6.00	2.40

The Snake Charmer, by Henri Rousseau — AP18

Design: 130fr, "War" by Henri Rousseau.

1968, May 14 Photo. *Perf. 13½*
Size: 41x41mm

C43	AP18	100fr ultra & multi	3.50	.30

Size: 48x35mm
Perf. 12½

C44	AP18	130fr brn & multi	5.50	.40

Hurdlers — AP19

1968, Oct. 16 Engr. *Perf. 13*

C45	AP19	32fr shown	1.00	.20
C46	AP19	80fr Relay race	2.75	.20

19th Olympic Games, Mexico City, 10/12-27.

PHILEXAFRIQUE Issue

The Actor Wolf (Bernard), by Jacques L. David AP20

1969, Jan. 15 Photo. *Perf. 12½*

C47	AP20	100fr multi	3.75	1.75

PHILEXAFRIQUE, Philatelic Exhib. in Abidjan, Feb. 14-23. Printed with alternating label.

2nd PHILEXAFRIQUE Issue
Common Design Type

50fr, Chad #J12 and Moundang Dancers.

1969, Feb. 14 Engr. *Perf. 13*

C48	CD128	50fr red, brt bl, brn & grn	2.25	1.25

Gustav Nachtigal and Tibesti Gorge, 1869 — AP21

#C50, Heinrich Barth & Lake Chad, 1851.

1969, Feb. 17

C49	AP21	100fr vio bl, dk brn & brn	2.40	.50
C50	AP21	100fr grn, pur & bl	2.40	.50

German explorers Gustav Nachtigal (1834-85) and Heinrich Barth (1821-65), and state visit of the Pres. of West Germany Heinrich Lubke.

Apollo 8, Earth and Moon — AP22

1969, Apr. 10 Photo. *Perf. 13*

C51	AP22	100fr multi	2.10	.60

US Apollo 8 mission, the 1st men in orbit around the moon, Dec. 21-27, 1968.

Mahatma Gandhi — AP23

#C53, John F. Kennedy. #C54, Dr. Martin Luther King, Jr. #C55, Robert F. Kennedy.

1969, May 20 Photo. *Perf. 12½*

C52	AP23	50fr blk & lt grn	1.25	.40
C53	AP23	50fr blk & tan	1.25	.40
C54	AP23	50fr blk & pink	1.25	.40
C55	AP23	50fr blk & lt vio bl	1.25	.40
a.		Souvenir sheet of 4, #C52-C55	6.00	6.00
		Nos. C52-C55 (4)	5.00	1.60

Issued to honor exponents of non-violence.

Presidents Tombalbaye and Mobutu, Map and Flags of Chad and Congo — AP24

Embossed on Gold Foil
1969 *Die-cut; Perf. 13½*

C56	AP24	1000fr gold, dk bl & red	27.50	27.50

1st anniv. of the establishment of the Union of Central African States, comprising Chad, Congo Democratic Republic and Central African Republic.

Napoleon Visiting Hospital, by Alexandre Veron-Bellecourt — AP25

Paintings: 85fr, Battle of Wagram, by Horace Vernet. 130fr, Battle of Austerlitz, by Francois Pascal Gerard.

1969, July 23 Photo. *Perf. 12x12½*

C57	AP25	30fr multi	1.10	.25
C58	AP25	85fr multi	2.40	.65
C59	AP25	130fr multi	4.25	1.25
		Nos. C57-C59 (3)	7.75	2.15

Bicentenary of birth of Napoleon I.

Apollo 11 Issue

Astronaut on Moon — AP26

Embossed on Gold Foil
1969, Oct. 17 *Die-cut; Perf. 13½*

C60	AP26	1000fr gold	27.50	19.00

See note after Algeria No. 427.

Village Life, by Goto Narcisse — AP27

No. 62, Women at the Market, by Iba N'Diaye. No. 63, Woman with Flowers, by Iba N'Diaye, vert.

1970 Photo. *Perf. 12x12½, 12½x12*

C61	AP27	100fr multi	3.25	.20
C62	AP27	250fr grn & multi	5.00	.35
C63	AP27	250fr brn & multi	5.00	.35
		Nos. C61-C63 (3)	13.25	.90

Issued: 100fr, Mar. 17; #C62-C63, Aug. 28.

Napoleon — AP27a

Designs: Nos. C63A, C63E, Napoleon II, Duke of Reichstadt, vert.
No. C63B: g, 10fr, Crossing the Grand St. Bernard, by David. h, 25fr, Emperor Napoleon, by Gerard. i, 32fr, Marriage of Napoleon and Marie Louise, by Rouget.
40fr, Napoleon after return from Elba, vert.

Perf. 12x12½, 12½x12
1970-71 Litho.

C63A	AP27a	10fr multicolored	4.00	—
C63B	AP27a	Strip of 3, #g.-i.	13.50	—

Embossed
Perf. 13

C63C	AP27a	10fr gold	20.00	—
f.		Sheet of 1, Imperf.	37.50	—

Souvenir Sheets
Litho.
Perf. 13x13½

C63D	AP27a	40fr multicolored	10.00	—

Embossed
Imperf

C63E	AP27a	10fr gold, like #C63A	37.50	—

#C63A is printed se-tenant with label. #C63D contains one 43x67mm stamp. #C63Cf contains one 53x42mm stamp with same size design as #C63Bg. #C63E contains one 43x104mm stamp with same size design as #C63A.
No. C63E probably was not available in Chad.
Issued: #C63B, 6/12; #C63A, C63D-C63E, 4/1971; #C63C, 11/1/71.

EXPO Emblem and Osaka Print — AP28

EXPO Emblem and: 100fr, Tower of the Sun. 125fr, Osaka print, diff.

1970, June 30 Engr. *Perf. 13*

C64 AP28 50fr bl, red brn & sl grn .70 .20
C65 AP28 100fr red, yel grn & Prus bl 1.40 .20
C66 AP28 125fr blk, dk red & bis 1.90 .25
Nos. C64-C66 (3) 4.00 .65

Issued to publicize EXPO '70 International Exhibition, Osaka, Japan, Mar. 15-Sept. 13.

1968 Summer Olympics, 1970 World Cup Soccer Championships, Mexico AP28a

1970, July 1 Litho. *Perf. 12½x12*

C66A AP28a 5fr Flags, soccer players 1.40

Souvenir Sheet

Perf. 13½x13

C66C AP28a 15fr Olympic torch, soccer player 6.25

No. C66A printed in sheets of 2 + 2 labels.
No. C66C contains one 66x43mm stamp.
For overprints see Nos. C88A-C88B.

Nos. C28-C30 Surcharged in Carmine with New Value and Bars and Overprinted:

a. "APOLLO XI / 1er débarquement sur la lune/20 juillet 1969"
b. "APOLLO XII / Exploration de la lune / 19 Novembre 1969"
c. "APOLLO XIII / Exploit spatial / 11-17 avril 1970"

1970, July 9 Photo. *Perf. 13x12½*

C67 AP13 (a) 50fr on 100fr 1.90 .25
C68 AP13 (b) 100fr on 200fr 3.25 .45
C69 AP13 (c) 125fr on 250fr 4.75 .55
Nos. C67-C69 (3) 9.90 1.25

Space missions of Apollo 11, 12 and 13.

DC-8 "Fort Lamy" over Airport — AP29

1970, Aug. 5 *Perf. 12½*

C70 AP29 30fr dk sl grn & multi 1.10 .20

Souvenir Sheet

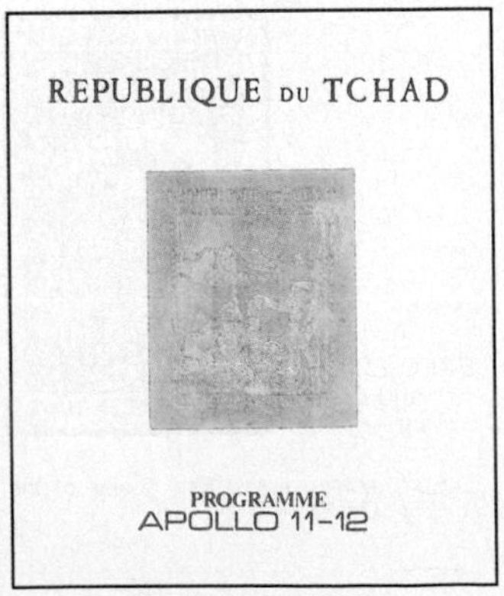

Apollo 12 — AP29a

1970, Sept. Embossed *Imperf.*

C70A AP29a 25fr gold 35.00

No. C70A probably was not available in Chad.

The Visitation, Venetian School, 15th Century AP30

Paintings, Venetian School: 25fr, Nativity, 15th century. 30fr, Virgin and Child, c. 1350.

1970, Dec. 15 Photo. *Perf. 12½x12*

C71 AP30 20fr gold & multi .75 .20
C72 AP30 25fr gold & multi 1.10 .20
C73 AP30 30fr gold & multi 1.25 .20
Nos. C71-C73 (3) 3.10 .60

Christmas 1970. See Nos. C144-C147.

Post Office Mauritius and Emblem AP31

1971, Jan. 23 Engr. *Perf. 13*

C74 AP31 10fr shown .20 .20
C75 AP31 20fr Tuscany #23 .40 .20
C76 AP31 30fr France #8 .60 .20
C77 AP31 60fr US #2 1.10 .25
C78 AP31 80fr Japan #8 1.50 .30
C79 AP31 100fr Saxony #1 1.90 .40
a. Souvenir sheet of 6, #C74-C79 8.00 5.00
Nos. C74-C79 (6) 5.70 1.55

Publicity for PHILEXOCAM, philatelic exhibition, Fort Lamy, Jan. 23-30.

Gamal Abdel Nasser — AP32

1971, Feb. 16 Photo. *Perf. 12½*

C80 AP32 75fr multi 1.10 .20

In memory of Gamal Abdel Nasser (1918-1970), President of Egypt.

Presidents Mobutu, Bokassa and Tombalbaye — AP33

1971, Apr. 28 Photo. *Perf. 13*

C81 AP33 100fr multi 1.75 .20

Return of Central African Republic to the United States of Central Africa which also includes Congo Democratic Republic and Chad.

Map of Africa, Communications Network and Symbols — AP34

1971, May 17 Engr. *Perf. 13*

C82 AP34 125fr ultra, sl grn & brn red 2.25 .20

Pan-African telecommunications system.

Boys Around Campfire, Torii AP35

1971, Aug. 24 Photo. *Perf. 12½*

C83 AP35 250fr multi 5.50 .40

13th Boy Scout World Jamboree, Asagiri Plain, Japan, Aug. 2-10.

White Egret — AP36

1971, Sept. 28 Photo. *Perf. 13x12½*

C84 AP36 1000fr blk, dk bl & ocher 75.00 6.75

Greek Marathon Runners — AP37

45fr, Ancient Olympic Stadium. 75fr, Greek wrestlers. 130fr, Olympic Stadium, Athens, 1896.

1971, Oct. 5 *Perf. 12½*

C85 AP37 40fr multi .75 .20
C86 AP37 45fr multi 1.00 .20
C87 AP37 75fr multi 1.75 .25
C88 AP37 130fr multi 1.90 .35
Nos. C85-C88 (4) 5.40 1.00

75th anniv. of modern Olympic Games.

Nos. C66A, C66C Ovptd. in Gold

1971 Litho. *Perf. 12½x12*

C88A AP28a 5fr on #C66A 2.50

Souvenir Sheet

Perf. 13½x13

C88B AP28a 15fr on #C66C 5.50

Overprint on No. C88B is 36mm long.

Duke Ellington — AP38

Charles de Gaulle — AP39

50fr, Sidney Bechet. 100fr, Louis Armstrong.

1971, Oct. 20 Litho. *Perf. 13*

C89 AP38 50fr multi 2.00 .50
C90 AP38 75fr lt bl & multi 3.00 .70
C91 AP38 100fr multi 5.00 .85
Nos. C89-C91 (3) 10.00 2.05

Famous American jazz musicians.

Lithographed and Embossed

1971, Nov. 9 *Perf. 12½*

Design: No. C93, Félix Eboué.

C92 AP39 200fr grn, yel grn & gold 8.00 4.00
C93 AP39 200fr bl, lt bl & gold 8.00 4.00
a. Souv. sheet, #C92-C93 + label 20.00 20.00

Charles de Gaulle (1890-1970), pres. of France.

African Postal Union Issue, 1971

Common Design Type

Design: 100fr, Sao antelope head and UAMPT building, Brazzaville, Congo.

1971, Nov. 13 Photo. *Perf. 13x13½*

C94 CD135 100fr bl & multi 1.50 .20

Apollo 15 Rocket AP40

80fr, Apollo 15 capsule, horiz. 150fr, Lunar module on Moon, horiz. 250fr, Astronaut making tests. 300fr, Moon-buggy. #C100, Successful splashdown, horiz. #C101, Apollo 15 insignia.

1972, Jan. 5 Litho. *Perf. 13½*

C95 AP40 40fr multi .50 .20
C96 AP40 80fr multi .90 .20
C97 AP40 150fr multi 1.50 .30
C98 AP40 250fr multi 2.50 .45
C99 AP40 300fr multi 3.00 .60
C100 AP40 500fr multi 5.50 1.40
Nos. C95-C100 (6) 13.90 3.15

Souvenir Sheet

C101 AP40 500fr multi 8.00 1.25

Apollo 15 moon landing.

Soyuz 11 Link-up — AP41

Designs: 30fr, Soyuz 11 on launching pad, vert. 50fr, No. C108, Cosmonauts in uniform. 200fr, V. I. Patsayev. No. C106, V. N. Volkov. 400fr, G. L. Dobrovolsky. No. C109, Three cosmonauts.

1972, Jan. 5 *Perf. 13½x13*

C102 AP41 30fr multi .25 .20
C103 AP41 50fr multi .45 .20
C104 AP41 100fr multi .80 .25
C105 AP41 200fr multi 2.00 .50
C106 AP41 300fr multi 3.25 .75
C107 AP41 400fr multi 4.25 1.10
Nos. C102-C107 (6) 11.00 3.00

Souvenir Sheets

C108 AP41 300fr multi 3.50 1.00
C109 AP41 400fr multi 4.00 1.40

Soyuz 11 link-up project.

Bobsledding — AP42

Design: 100fr, Slalom.

1972, Feb. 24 **Engr.** *Perf. 13*

C110 AP42 50fr Prus bl & rose red 1.00 .20
C111 AP42 100fr red lil & slate grn 1.90 .20

11th Winter Olympic Games, Sapporo, Japan, Feb. 3-13.

Pres. Tombalbaye Type, 1972

1972, Apr. 13 **Litho.** *Perf. 13*

C112 A63 70fr multi .90 .20
C113 A63 80fr multi 1.10 .20

11th Winter Olympic Type, 1972

130fr, Speed skating. #C115, Ice hockey. #C116, Ski jumping. 250fr, 4-man bobsled.

1972, Apr. 13 *Perf. 13½*

C114 A64 130fr multi 1.40 .45
C115 A64 200fr multi 2.50 .60

Souvenir Sheets

C116 A64 200fr multi 3.25 .75
C117 A64 250fr multi 4.25 1.10

Scout Jamboree Type, 1972

Designs: 100fr, Cooking preparation. 120fr, Lord Baden Powell. 250fr, Hiking.

1972, May 15

C118 A67 100fr multi 2.10 .30
C119 A67 120fr multi 2.40 .40

Souvenir Sheet

C120 A67 250fr multi 8.50 .75

Zebras — AP43

African wild animals: 30fr, Mandrills. 100fr, African elephants. 130fr, Gazelles. 150fr, Hippopotamuses. 200fr, Lion cub.

1972, May 15 **Litho.** *Perf. 13*

C121 AP43 20fr multi .35 .20
C122 AP43 30fr multi .50 .20
C123 AP43 100fr multi 1.40 .35
C124 AP43 130fr multi 2.25 .50
C125 AP43 150fr multi 3.50 .75
Nos. C121-C125 (5) 8.00 2.00

Souvenir Sheet

C126 AP43 200fr multi 35.00 25.00

View of Venice, by Caffi — AP44

Paintings by Ippolito Caffi: 40fr, Sailing ship and Doge's Palace, vert. 140fr, Grand Canal, vert.

1972, May 23 **Photo.**

C127 AP44 40fr gold & multi 1.10 .20
C128 AP44 45fr gold & multi 1.90 .20
C129 AP44 140fr gold & multi 3.50 .60
Nos. C127-C129 (3) 6.50 1.00

UNESCO campaign to save Venice.

11th Winter Olympic Winners Type, 1972

Designs: 150fr, Slalom, B. Cochran, US. 200fr, Women's figure skating, B. Schuba, Austria. 250fr, Ice hockey, USSR. 300fr, 2-man bobsled. W. Zimmerer and P. Utzschneider, West Germany.

1972, June 15 *Perf. 14½*

C130 A69 150fr gold & multi 3.00 .75
C131 A69 200fr gold & multi 3.75 1.00

Souvenir Sheets

C132 A69 250fr gold & multi 3.25 2.75
C133 A69 300fr gold & multi 3.75 3.00

Nos. C130-C131 exist se-tenant with label showing earth satellite.

Daudet, "Tartarin de Tarascon," Book Year Emblem — AP45

1972, July 22 **Engr.** *Perf. 13*

C134 AP45 100fr dk red, lil & dk brn 1.90 .20

Intl. Book Year, 1972, and to honor Alphonse Daudet (1840-1897), French writer.

20th Summer Olympics Type, 1972

Designs (TV Tower, Munich and): 100fr, Gymnast. 120fr, Pole vault. 150fr, Fencing. 250fr, Hammer throw. 300fr, Boxing.

1972, Aug. 15

C135 A70 100fr gold & multi 2.10 .50
C136 A70 120fr gold & multi 2.50 .60
C137 A70 150fr gold & multi 3.25 .80
Nos. C135-C137 (3) 7.85 1.90

Souvenir Sheets

C138 A70 250fr gold & multi 3.50 2.75
C139 A70 300fr gold & multi 4.00 3.00

Nos. C135-C137 exist se-tenant with label showing arms of Munich.

Lunokhod on Moon — AP46

Russian moon missions: 100fr, Luna 16 on moon and rocket in flight, vert.

1972, Sept. 19

C140 AP46 100fr dk bl, pur & bis 1.90 .50
C141 AP46 150fr slate, brn & lil 2.50 .75

Farcha Laboratory, Cattle, Scientist — AP47

1972, Nov. 11 **Photo.** *Perf. 13*

C142 AP47 75fr yellow & multi 1.40 .30

20th anniversary of the Farcha Laboratory for veterinary research.

King Faisal and Holy Kaaba, Mecca — AP48

1972, Nov. 17

C143 AP48 75fr multi 1.40 .25

Visit of King Faisal of Saudi Arabia.

Christmas Type of 1970

Christmas: 40fr, Virgin and Child, by Giovanni Bellini. 75fr, Virgin and Child, by Dall'Occhio. 80fr, Nativity, by Fra Angelico, horiz. 95fr, Adoration of the Kings, by Il Perugino.

1972, Dec. 15 **Photo.** *Perf. 13*

C144 AP30 40fr gold & multi .20 .20
C145 AP30 75fr gold & multi 1.75 .30
C146 AP30 80fr gold & multi 2.00 .40
C147 AP30 95fr gold & multi 2.00 .50
Nos. C144-C147 (4) 5.95 1.40

Summer Olympic Winners Type, 1972

Olympic Emblems and: 150fr, Pole vault, Nordwig, East Germany. 250fr, Hurdles, Milburn, US. 300fr, Javelin, Wolfermann, West Germany.

1972, Dec. 22

C148 A76 150fr multi 3.00 .60
C149 A76 250fr multi 4.25 .75

Souvenir Sheet

C150 A76 300fr multi 15.00 3.00

Summer Olympic Winners Type, 1972

Olympic Emblem and: 150fr, Dressage, Mancinelli, Italy. #C152, Finn class sailing, Serge Maury, France. #C153, Swimming, Mark Spitz.

1972, Dec. 22 **Litho.** *Perf. 11*

C151 A77 150fr gold & multi 3.25 .75
C152 A77 250fr gold & multi 5.00 1.00

Souvenir Sheet

C153 A77 250fr multi 15.00 3.00

Copernicus and Solar System — AP49

1973, Mar. 31 **Engr.** *Perf. 13*

C154 AP49 250fr gray, mag & brn 5.25 1.25

500th anniversary of the birth of Nicolaus Copernicus (1473-1543), Polish astronomer.

Horses — AP49a

Details from paintings: 20fr, A Horse Frightened by Lightning, by Theordore Gericault. 60fr, The White Horse, by Paul Potter. 100fr, Mares and Foals, by George Stubbs. 150fr, Horse Head, by Theordore Gericault, vert. 500fr, The Carriage, by Vernet.

1973 **Litho.** *Perf. 11½*

C154A AP49a 20fr multi
C154B AP49a 60fr multi
C154C AP49a 100fr multi
C154D AP49a 150fr multi
Nos. C154A-C154D (4) 14.00

Souvenir Sheet

Perf. 15

C154E AP49a 500fr multicolored 15.00

See note before No. 225A.

Airplanes — AP49b

1973 **Litho.** *Perf. 12*

C154F AP49b 5fr Fokker F VII/3M
C154G AP49b 25fr DH 89A Rapide
C154H AP49b 70fr Viscount
C154J AP49b 150fr Boeing 747
C154K AP49b 200fr Concorde
Nos. C154F-C154K (5) 14.00

Souvenir Sheet

Perf. 12

C154L AP49b 350fr Concorde, diff. 14.00

Nos. C154L contains one 60x40mm stamp. See note before No. 225A.

Skylab over Africa — AP50

1974, Aug. 6 **Engr.** *Perf. 13*

C155 AP50 100fr shown 1.50 .25
C156 AP50 150fr Skylab 2.50 .35

Exploits of Skylab, US manned space station.

Soccer — AP51

125fr, 150fr, Soccer players; 125fr, vert.

1974, Oct. 22 Engr. *Perf. 13*

C157 AP51	50fr dl red & choc	.75	.25
C158 AP51	125fr red & dp grn	1.75	.50
C159 AP51	150fr grn & rose red	2.50	.75
	Nos. C157-C159 (3)	5.00	1.50

World Cup Soccer Championship, Munich, June 13-July 7.

Family and WPY Emblem — AP52

1974, Nov. 11

C160 AP52 250fr multi 3.75 1.25

World Population Year.

Mail Delivery by Canoe — AP53

UPU Cent.: 40fr, Diesel train. 100fr, Jet. 150fr, Spacecraft.

1974, Dec. 20 Engr. *Perf. 13*

C161 AP53	30fr car & multi	.60	.20
C162 AP53	40fr ultra & blk	1.00	.20
C163 AP53	100fr brn, ultra & blk	1.90	.40
C164 AP53	150fr grn, lil & ol	2.40	.55
	Nos. C161-C164 (4)	5.90	1.35

Women of Different Races, IWY Emblem — AP54

1975, June 25 Photo. *Perf. 13*

C165 AP54 250fr bl & multi 4.50 1.25

International Women's Year 1975.

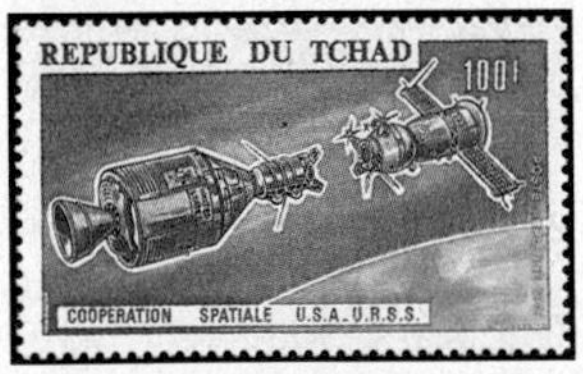

Apollo and Soyuz Before Link-up — AP55

130fr, Apollo and Soyuz after link-up.

1975, July 15 Engr. *Perf. 13*

C166 AP55	100fr ultra, choc & grn	1.50	.40
C167 AP55	130fr vio bl, brn & grn	2.00	.50

Apollo Soyuz space test project (Russo-American space cooperation), launching 7/15; link-up 7/17.

For overprints see Nos. C171-C172.

Soccer Player, View of Montreal — AP56

Olympic Rings, Montreal Skyline: 100fr, Discus thrower. 125fr, Runner.

1975, Oct. 14 Engr. *Perf. 13*

C168 AP56	75fr car & slate grn	1.00	.25
C169 AP56	100fr car, choc & bl grn	1.40	.40
C170 AP56	125fr brn, bl & car	1.90	.75
	Nos. C168-C170 (3)	4.30	1.40

Pre-Olympic Year 1975.

Nos. C166-C167 Overprinted: "JONCTION / 17 JUILLET 1975"

1975, Nov. 4 Engr. *Perf. 13*

C171 AP55	100fr multi	1.75	.25
C172 AP55	130fr multi	2.10	.35

Apollo-Soyuz link-up in space, July 17.

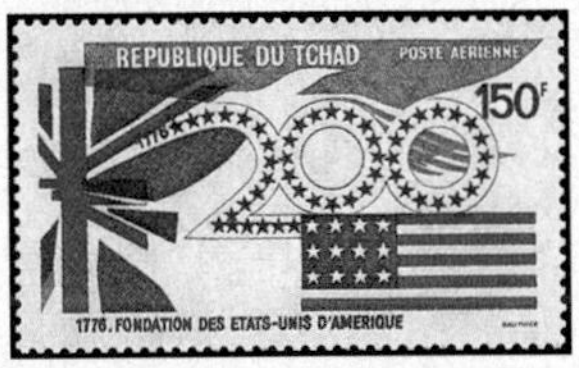

Stylized British and American Flags, "200" — AP57

1975, Dec. 5 Engr. *Perf. 13*

C173 AP57 150fr vio bl, car & ol bis 2.25 .75

American Bicentennial.

Adoration of the Shepherds, by Murillo — AP58

Christmas (Paintings): 75fr, Adoration of the Shepherds, by Georges de La Tour. 80fr, Virgin and Child with Bible, by Rogier van der Weyden, vert. 100fr, Holy Family, by Raphael, vert.

1975, Dec. 15 Litho. *Perf. 13x12½*

C174 AP58	40fr yel & multi	.75	.25
C175 AP58	75fr yel & multi	1.25	.35
C176 AP58	80fr yel & multi	1.75	.40
C177 AP58	100fr yel & multi	2.75	.75
	Nos. C174-C177 (4)	6.50	1.75

12th Winter Olympic Winners Type, 1976

250fr, 4-man bobsled, West Germany. 300fr, Speed skating, J. E. Storholt, Norway. 500fr, Downhill skiing, F. Klammer, Austria.

1976, June 21 *Perf. 14*

C178 A84	250fr multi	2.75	.60
C179 A84	300fr multi	3.50	1.00

Souvenir Sheet

C180 A84 500fr multi 6.00 3.00

Paul Revere's Ride and Portrait by Copley — AP59

American Bicentennial: 125fr, Washington crossing Delaware. 150fr, Lafayette offering his services to America. 200fr, Rochambeau at Yorktown with Washington. 250fr, Franklin presenting Declaration of Independence. 400fr, Count de Grasse's victory at Cape Charles.

1976, July 4 Litho. *Perf. 14*

C181 AP59	100fr multi	1.10	.30
C182 AP59	125fr multi	1.25	.35
C183 AP59	150fr multi	1.90	.40
C184 AP59	200fr multi	2.25	.50
C185 AP59	250fr multi	3.00	.55
	Nos. C181-C185 (5)	9.50	2.10

Souvenir Sheet

C186 AP59 400fr multi 6.00 3.00

Summer Olympics Type, 1976

1976, July 12

C187 A85	100fr Boxing	1.50	.30
C188 A85	200fr Pole vault	2.50	.50
C189 A85	300fr muShot put	4.00	.65
	Nos. C187-C189 (3)	8.00	1.45

Souvenir Sheet

C190 A85 500fr Sprint 6.00 3.00

Viking Mars Project Type, 1976

Mars Lander and: 100fr, Viking landing on Mars. 200fr, Capsule over Mars. 250fr, Lander over Mars. 450fr, Lander and probe.

1976, July 23 Litho. *Perf. 14*

C191 A86	100fr multi	1.10	.30
C192 A86	200fr multi	2.25	.55
C193 A86	250fr multi	2.50	.75
	Nos. C191-C193 (3)	5.85	1.60

Souvenir Sheet

C194 A86 450fr multi 7.50 3.00

For overprints see Nos. C240-C243.

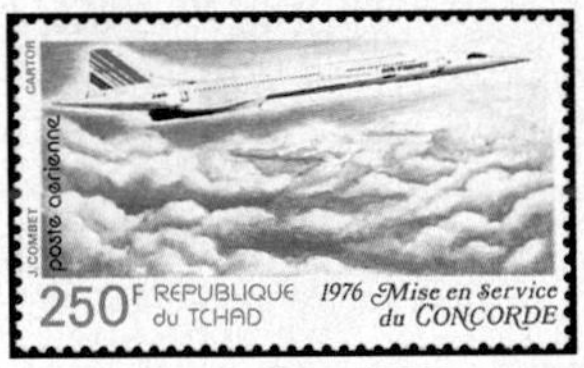

Concorde — AP60

1976, Oct. 15 Litho. *Perf. 12½*

C195 AP60 250fr bl, blk & ver 6.00 1.75

First commercial flight of supersonic jet Concorde, Jan. 21.

Nobel Prize Type, 1976

100fr, Albert Einstein, physics. 200fr, Dag Hammarskjold, peace. 300fr, Shinichiro Tomanaga, physics. 500fr, Alexander Fleming, medicine.

1976, Dec. 15

C196 A87	100fr multi	1.50	.30
C197 A87	200fr multi	2.50	.55
C198 A87	300fr multi	3.50	.70
	Nos. C196-C198 (3)	7.50	1.55

Souvenir Sheet

C199 A87 500fr multi 8.00 3.50

Adoration of the Shepherds, by Gerard van Honthorst — AP61

Christmas (Paintings): 30fr, Nativity, by Albrecht Altdorfer, vert. 60fr, Nativity, by Hans Holbein, vert. 150fr, Adoration of the Kings, by Gerard David.

1976, Dec. 22 Litho. *Perf. 12½*

C200 AP61	30fr gold & multi	.50	.20
C201 AP61	60fr gold & multi	.75	.20
C202 AP61	120fr gold & blk	1.50	.50
C203 AP61	150fr gold & blk	2.25	.75
	Nos. C200-C203 (4)	5.00	1.65

Lesdiguières Bridge, by Jongkind — AP62

Design: 120fr, Sailing Ship and Boats, by Johan Barthold Jongkind (1819-1891).

1976, Dec. 27 Photo. *Perf. 13*

C204 AP62	100fr multi	1.75	.55
C205 AP62	120fr multi	2.25	.60

Centenary of impressionism.

Zeppelin Type of 1977

125fr, Germany #C40, North Pole. 150fr, Germany #C45, Chicago department store. 175fr, Germany #C38 and scenes of NYC and London. 200fr, 500fr, US #C15, NYC.

1977, Mar. 30 *Perf. 11*

C206 A91	125fr multi	1.90	.35
C207 A91	150fr multi	2.25	.40
C208 A91	175fr multi	2.75	.50
C209 A91	200fr multi	3.25	.60
	Nos. C206-C209 (4)	10.15	1.85

Souvenir Sheet

C210 A91 500fr multi 8.00 3.00

Sassenage Castle, Grenoble — AP63

1977, May 21 Litho. *Perf. 12½*

C211 AP63 100fr multi 1.00 .30

Intl. French Language Council, 10th Anniv.

Lafayette and Ships — AP64

American Bicentennial: 120fr, Abraham Lincoln, eagle and flags, vert. 150fr, James Madison and family.

1977, July 30 Engr. *Perf. 13*

C212 AP64	100fr multi	1.40	.35
C213 AP64	120fr multi	1.75	.40
C214 AP64	150fr multi	2.25	.50
	Nos. C212-C214 (3)	5.40	1.25

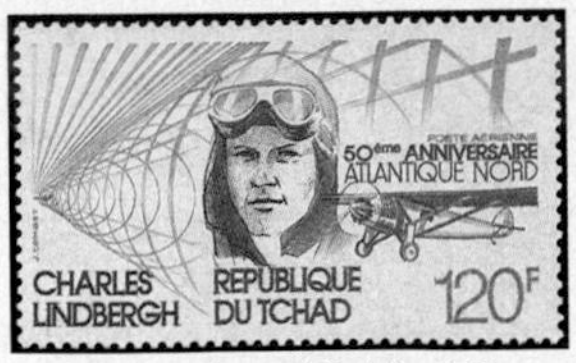

Lindbergh and Spirit of St. Louis — AP65

100fr, Concorde. 150fr, 200fr, 300fr, Various Lindbergh portraits & Spirit of St. Louis.

1977, Sept. 27

C215 AP65 100fr multi 1.25 .30
C216 AP65 120fr multi 1.25 .40
C217 AP65 150fr multi 1.40 .55
C218 AP65 200fr multi 2.25 .65
C219 AP65 300fr multi 3.00 .90
Nos. C215-C219 (5) 9.15 2.80

Charles A. Lindbergh's solo transatlantic flight from NY to Paris, 50th anniv., and 1st supersonic transatlantic flight of Concorde.
For overprint see No. C227.

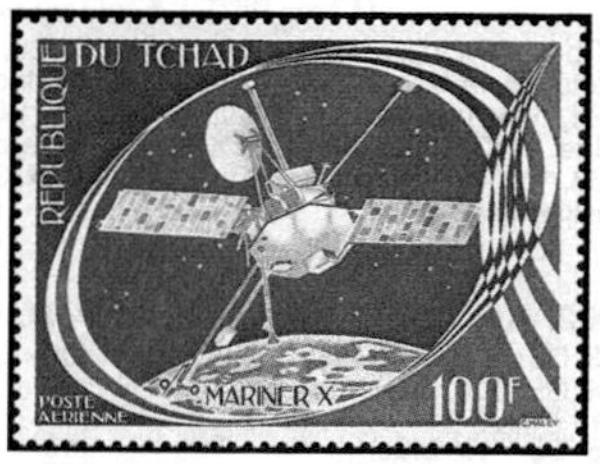

Mariner 10 — AP66

Spacecraft: 200fr, Lunokhod on moon, Luna 21. 300fr, Viking on Mars.

1977, Oct. 10 Engr. *Perf. 13*

C220 AP66 100fr multi 1.25 .40
C221 AP66 200fr multi 2.00 .70
C222 AP66 300fr multi 2.75 .90
Nos. C220-C222 (3) 6.00 2.00

Running — AP67

1977, Oct. 24 Engr. *Perf. 13*

C223 AP67 30fr shown .40 .20
C224 AP67 60fr Volleyball .85 .20
C225 AP67 120fr Soccer 1.50 .45
C226 AP67 125fr Basketball 1.25 .50
Nos. C223-C226 (4) 4.00 1.35

No. C215 Overprinted: "PARIS NEW-YORK / 22.11.77"

1977, Nov. 22

C227 AP65 100fr multi 3.25 .20

Concorde, 1st commercial flight Paris-NYC.

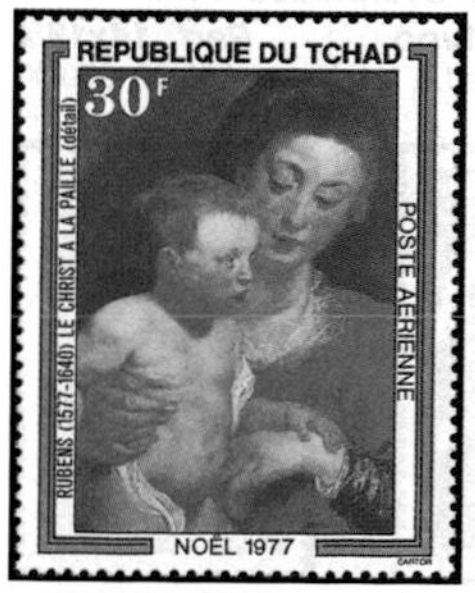

Virgin and Child, by Rubens AP68

Rubens Paintings: 60fr, Virgin and Child and Two Donors. 100fr, Adoration of the Shepherds. 125fr, Adoration of the Kings.

1977, Dec. 20 Litho. *Perf. 12½x12*

C228 AP68 30fr multi .75 .20
C229 AP68 60fr multi 1.10 .30
C230 AP68 100fr multi 1.50 .40
C231 AP68 125fr multi 1.90 .60
Nos. C228-C231 (4) 5.25 1.50

Christmas 1977.

Antoine de Saint-Exupéry — AP69

50fr, Wilbur & Orville Wright & Flyer. 80fr, Hugo Junkers & his plane. 100fr, Gen. Italo Balbo & his plane. 120fr, Concorde. 500fr, Wilbur & Orville Wright & Flyer.

1978, Oct. 25 Litho. *Perf. 13½*

C232 AP69 40fr multi .60 .20
C233 AP69 50fr multi .75 .20
C234 AP69 80fr multi 1.10 .30
C235 AP69 100fr multi 1.50 .40
C236 AP69 120fr multi 1.75 .50
Nos. C232-C236 (5) 5.70 1.60

Souvenir Sheet

C237 AP69 500fr multi 6.75 2.00

History of aviation and 75th anniversary of 1st powered flight.

Philexafrique II-Essen Issue
Common Design Types

#C238, Rhinoceros & Chad #C6. #C239, Kingfisher & Mecklenburg-Strelitz #1.

1978, Nov. 1 *Perf. 12½*

C238 CD138 100fr multi 3.00 1.00
C239 CD139 100fr multi 3.00 1.00
a. Pair, #C238-C239 + label 8.00 4.00

Nos. C191-C194 Overprinted "ALUNISSAGE/APOLLO XI/ JUILLET 1969"

1979, Nov. 26 Litho. *Perf. 13½x14*

C240 A86 100fr multi 1.10 .35
C241 A86 200fr multi 2.25 .65
C242 A86 250fr multi 2.50 1.00
Nos. C240-C242 (3) 5.85 2.00

Souvenir Sheet

C243 A86 450fr multi 5.50 4.50

Apollo 11 moon landing, 10th anniversary.

Hurdles, Moscow '80 Emblem — AP70

Emblem and: 30fr, Field hockey. 250fr, Swimming. 350fr, Running. 500fr, Yachting.

1979, Nov. 30 *Perf. 13½*

C244 AP70 15fr multi .20 .20
C245 AP70 30fr multi .30 .20
C246 AP70 250fr multi 1.90 .60
C247 AP70 350fr multi 3.00 1.10
Nos. C244-C247 (4) 5.40 2.10

Souvenir Sheet

C248 AP70 500fr multi 5.75 3.00

Pre-Olympic Year.
For overprints see Nos. C254-C255.

Austria Jubilee Issue of 1910, Canoe, Hill — AP71

Hill, Stamps & Vessels: 100fr, US design A97, dhow. 200fr, France #21, Sidewheeler. 300fr, Holstein #16, ocean liner. 500fr, Chad #J13, ocean liner.

1979, Dec. 3 *Perf. 14x13½*

C249 AP71 65fr multi .60 .20
C250 AP71 100fr multi 1.40 .25
C251 AP71 200fr multi 2.25 .45
C252 AP71 300fr multi 2.75 .70
Nos. C249-C252 (4) 7.00 1.60

Souvenir Sheet

C253 AP71 500fr multi 5.75 3.00

Sir Rowland Hill (1795-1879), originator of penny postage.
For overprints see Nos. C256-C257.

Nos. C244-C245, C249-C250 Overprinted: "POSTES 1981" in Red or Overprinted and Surcharged Silver on Red

Perf. 13½, 14x13½

1981, Nov. 15 Litho.

C254 AP70 30fr on 15fr multi 1.25 .40
C255 AP70 30fr multi 1.25 .40
C256 AP71 60fr on 65fr multi 2.25 .70
C257 AP71 60fr on 100fr multi 2.25 .70
Nos. C254-C257 (4) 7.00 2.20

Soccer Type of 1982 and

1982 World Cup Soccer Championships, Spain — AP71a

#C259C, Soccer players, ball, & trophy, vert.

1982 Litho. *Perf. 13½*

C258 A108 80fr Brazil 1.00 .20
C259 A108 300fr W. Germany 3.00 .50

Souvenir Sheet

C259A A108 500fr like 300fr 6.00 2.00

Litho. & Embossed

C259B AP71a 1500fr gold & multi 16.00

Souvenir Sheet

C259C AP71a 1500fr gold & multi 14.00

No. C259A contains one 42x51mm stamp.
No. C259B exists in a souvenir sheet of 1. Value $42.50.
For surcharge see No. C305.

Diana Type of 1982 and

Princess Diana, 21st Birthday — AP71b

Design: No. C262A, Portrait, horiz.

1982, July 2 Litho. *Perf. 13½*

C260 A109 80fr 1977 1.00 .25
C261 A109 300fr 1980 3.00 .95

Souvenir Sheet

C262 A109 500fr 1981 5.50 2.00

Litho. & Embossed

C262A AP71b 1500fr gold & multi 16.00

Souvenir Sheet

C262B AP71b 1500fr gold & multi 16.00

No. C262A exists in a souvenir sheet of 1. Value $42.50.
For overprints see Nos. 419A-419B.

Manned Flight Bicentenary AP72

Balloons: 100fr, Charles' & Roberts', 1783. 200fr, J.P. Blanchard, Berlin, 1788. 300fr, Charles Green, London, 1837. 400fr, Modern blimp. 500fr, Montgolfiere, 1783.

1983, Apr. Litho. *Perf. 13*

C263 AP72 100fr multi, vert. 1.25 .25
C264 AP72 200fr multi, vert. 2.50 .40
C265 AP72 300fr multi 3.50 .60
C266 AP72 400fr multi 4.75 .75
Nos. C263-C266 (4) 12.00 2.00

Souvenir Sheet

C267 AP72 500fr multi, vert. 5.75 2.50

Balloon Type and

First Balloon Ascension, Bicent. — AP72a

80fr, Steam Powered Airship, H. Giffard. 250fr, Graf Zeppelin; Airship L-1, 1st flight. 300fr, 1st Balloon Flight, Montgolfier & Rozier. #C270A, Airship Hindenburg, Count Ferdinand von Zeppelin. #C270B, Jean-Francois Pilatre de Rozier & Marquis d'Arlandes, 1st balloon ascension.

1983, May 30 Litho. *Perf. 13*

C268 A116 80fr multi 1.00 .25
C269 A116 250fr multi 3.00 .40

Souvenir Sheet

C270 A116 300fr multi 3.75 2.50

Litho. & Embossed

Perf. 13½

C270A AP72a 1500fr gold & multi 16.00

Souvenir Sheet

C270B AP72a 1500fr gold & multi 12.00

No. C270A exists in a souvenir sheet of 1. Value $25.
For surcharge see No. C299.

1984 Summer Olympics — AP73

Various kayak scenes.

Protected Whales — A719

Designs: 250p, Eubalaena australis. 500p, Balaenoptera acutorostrata.
2000p, Physeter macrocephalus.

2002, Nov. 2
1413-1414 A719 Set of 2 3.50 1.50

Souvenir Sheet

1415 A719 2000p multi 10.00 10.00

Violence Against Women Prevention Day — A720

2002, Nov. 22
1416 A720 230p multi 1.00 .50

Town of Puerto Varas, 150th Anniv. A721

2002, Nov. 29
1417 A721 190p multi .80 .40

Bird Type of 1998

Designs: 500p, Campephilus magellanicus, vert. 1000p, Falco peregrinus cassini, vert.

2003, Jan. 15 Litho. *Perf. 13¼*
1418 A640 500p multi 2.10 .75
1419 A640 1000p multi 4.00 1.75

Puerto Montt, 150th Anniv. A722

2003, Feb. 13
1420 A722 240p multi 1.00 .45

Claudio Arrau (1903-91), Pianist — A723

2003, June 9 Litho. *Perf. 13¼*
1421 A723 200p multi .85 .30

First Chilean Postage Stamps, 150th Anniv. — A724

No. 1422 — Mailbox, building and: a, #1. b, #2.
2000p, Building, #1 and various other stamps.
Illustration reduced.

2003, July 1
1422 A724 300p Horiz. pair, #a-b 1.75 .85

Souvenir Sheet

1423 A724 2000p multi 8.00 3.00

America Issue — Flora and Fauna — A725

Designs: 240p, Trees, flowers, cactus. 300p, Frog, fox, butterfly, pudu, parrot.

2003, Oct. 12 Litho. *Perf. 13¼*
1424-1425 A725 Set of 2 2.00 1.00

Supreme Court, 180th Anniv. — A726

2003, Nov. 5
1426 A726 200p multi .85 .35

Chilean Red Cross, Cent. A727

2003, Nov. 18
1427 A727 200p black & red .85 .35

Christmas — A728

2003, Nov. 28
1428 A728 190p multi .80 .30

Inscribed "DS-20"

1429 A728 190p multi .80 .30

Powered Flight, Cent. — A729

2003, Dec. 11
1430 A729 200p multi .85 .35

Cristo Redentor Statue, Cent. A730

2004, Apr. 22 Litho.
1431 A730 200p multi .85 .30

Seventh World Conference of Grand Masonic Lodges — A731

2004, May 5 *Perf. 13¼*
1432 A731 190p multi .80 .30

Pablo Neruda (1904-73), Poet — A732

2004, June 11
1433 A732 300p multi 1.25 .45

Social Security, 80th Anniv. — A733

2004, Aug. 18
1434 A733 190p multi .80 .30

America Issue — Environmental Protection — A734

Designs: 100p, Burnt forest, logs, field of flowers, puma, flower. 600p, Flower, wildlife, tanker truck, smokestacks.

2004, Sept. 27
1435-1436 A734 Set of 2 2.60 1.50

German Institute, Osorno, 150th Anniv. — A735

2004, Oct. 6
1437 A735 250p multi 1.10 .40

Tematica 2004 National Philatelic Exhibition A736

2004, Oct. 19
1438 A736 310p multi 1.25 .55

Naval Telecommunications, Cent. — A737

2004, Nov. 5
1439 A737 400p multi 1.75 .80

Electricity and Fuel Superintendency, Cent. — A738

2004, Dec. 7
1440 A738 240p multi 1.00 .40

Chilean Air Force, 75th Anniv. — A739

Illustration reduced.

2005, Mar. 15 Litho. *Perf. 13¼*
1441 A739 230p multi 1.00 .40

Law No. 20,000 — A740

2005, May 4
1442 A740 220p multi .95 .40

Pope John Paul II (1920-2005) — A741

Pope John Paul II and: a, Child, condor, mountain. b, Crucifix, Chilean flag, mountain. c, Church, Chilean flag.

2005, May 13
1443 Horiz. strip of 3 3.25 1.75
a.-c. A741 230p Any single 1.00 .50

Rotary International, Cent. — A742

2005, June 30 Litho. *Perf. 13¼*
1444 A742 230p multi 1.00 .40

Treasury Building, Bicent. — A743

2005, June 30
1445 A743 230p multi 1.00 .40

Publication of Don Quixote, 400th Anniv. A744

No. 1446: a, Don Quixote on horseback. b, Windmill. c, Windmills. d, Miguel de Cervantes, author.

2005, July 14
1446 Horiz. strip of 4 .25 .20
a.-b. A744 10p Either single .20 .20
c.-d. A744 20p Either single .20 .20

El Teniente Copper Mine, Cent. — A745

2005, Aug. 3
1447 A745 390p multi 1.75 .75

Undersecretariat of Aviation, 75th Anniv. — A746

Illustration reduced.

2005, Aug. 19
1448 A746 400p multi 1.75 1.00

Valparaiso Customs House, 150th Anniv. — A747

2005, Sept. 1
1449 A747 390p multi 1.75 .75

Bicentennial Fountain, Santiago — A748

2005, Sept. 5
1450 A748 230p multi 1.00 .45

America Issue — Fight Against Poverty — A749

No. 1451: a, Denomination at right. b, Denomination at left.
Illustration reduced.

2005, Oct. 3 Litho. *Perf. 13¼*
1451 A749 250p Horiz. pair, #a-b 2.25 .95

Canonization of Father Alberto Hurtado (1901-52) — A750

2005, Oct. 13 Litho. *Perf. 13¼*
1452 A750 390p multi 1.75 .75

Expo Austral 2005 Philatelic Exhibition, Punta Arenas — A751

2005, Oct. 22
1453 A751 390p multi 1.75 .75

New Civil Matrimony Law — A752

2005, Nov. 18 Litho. *Perf. 13¼*
1454 A752 260p multi 1.10 .50

German Clinic, Cent. — A753

2005, Nov. 23
1455 A753 230p multi 1.00 .45

Restoration of Central Post Office, Santiago A754

2005, Nov. 30
1456 A754 230p multi 1.00 .45

Political Constitution A755

2005, Dec. 1
1457 A755 230p multi 1.00 .45

Department of Physical Education, Sports and Recreation, Cent. — A756

2006, Mar. 6 Litho. *Perf. 13¼*
1458 A756 230p multi 1.00 .45

Intl. Women's Day — A757

2006, Mar. 7
1459 A757 390p multi 1.75 .75

Wulff Castle, Cent. — A758

No. 1460 — Castle, arms of Vina del Mar and: a, Birds. b, Windmill.

2006, Mar. 21
1460 Horiz. pair 3.00 1.50
a. A758 230p multi 1.00 .55
b. A758 390p multi 1.75 .85

Tourism — A759

No. 1461: a, Morro de Arica. b, Moais, Easter Island. c, Palafittes, Castro. d, Torres del Paine. e, Penguins, Chilean Antarctic Territory.

2006, May 19
1461 Horiz. strip of 5 4.50 2.25
a.-e. A759 230p Any single .90 .45

Don Quixote Type of 2005

No. 1462: a, Building. b, Windmills. c, Windmill, country name at LR. d, Don Quixote and Sancho Panza.

2006, May 31
1462 Horiz. strip of 4 .20 .20
a.-d. A744 10p Any single .20 .20

1949, May *Perf. 12½, 13, 14*
Without Gum
960 A95 $30 dark violet 75.00 55.00
Engr.
961 A95 $200 violet brown 10.00 6.00
962 A95 $500 dark green 14.00 10.00
Nos. 960-962 (3) 99.00 71.00

A similar overprint appears on #C63, E13, F3, differing in 2nd and 3rd characters of bottom row.

Silver Yuan Surcharge in Black or Other Colors

1949 **Litho.**
963 A95 1c on $5000 brn (G) 5.00 6.00
964 A95 4c on $100 ol grn (Bl) 2.25 2.00
965 A95 4c on $3000 org) 2.25 2.00
966 A95 10c on $50 dk bl (RV) 3.50 2.00
967 A95 10c on $1000 car 4.50 2.00
a. Inverted surcharge 60.00
968 A95 20c on $1000 red (V) 5.00 3.00
b. Inverted surcharge
968A A95 50c on $30 dk vio (C) 30.00 6.00
969 A95 50c on $50 dk bl (C) 6.00 2.00
970 A95 $1 on $50 dk bl 15.00 *20.00*
Nos. 963-970 (9) 73.50 45.00

Nos. 963-965 and 967 are engraved.

Sun Type of 1949 Redrawn
Coarse Impression

1949 ***Perf. 12½, 13 or Compound***
973 A94 1c apple green 16.00 *6.00*
974 A94 2c orange 3.50 *4.00*
975 A94 4c blue green .20 *2.00*
976 A94 10c deep lilac .20 *2.00*
977 A94 16c orange red .45 *3.00*
978 A94 20c blue .25 *2.00*
979 A94 50c dk brown 1.40 *48.00*
980 A94 100c deep blue 325.00 275.00
981 A94 500c scarlet 450.00 325.00
Nos. 973-981 (9) 797.00 667.00

For surcharges see Nos. 1057-1060.

Flying Geese Over Globe — A97

Pigeons, Globe and Wreath — A98

1949, May **Litho.** *Perf. 12½*
Without Gum
984 A97 $1 brown org 5.00 *10.00*
985 A97 $2 blue 40.00 16.00
986 A97 $5 car rose 40.00 20.00
987 A97 $10 blue grn 40.00 35.00
Nos. 984-987 (4) 125.00 81.00

Five other denominations — 10c, 16c, 50c, $20 and $50 — were also printed at Shanghai, but were not issued.

For surcharges see Nos. 1007-1011, 1042-1045, 1061-1063, People's Republic of China 49-56, 5LQ17-5LQ26, 7L17-7L18, 8L14-8L16.

Engraved and Typographed
1949, Aug. 1 **Without Gum** ***Imperf.***
988 A98 $1 org red & blk 7.00 *10.00*

75th anniv. of the UPU.
Exists with black denomination omitted.

Summer Palace, Peiping — A99

Bronze Bull and Kunming Lake — A100

Engraved and Typographed
1949, Aug. *Rouletted*
Without Gum
989 A99 15c org brn & grn 3.00 *3.00*
990 A100 40c dl grn & car 3.00 *3.00*
a. 2nd and 3rd characters at top transposed 160.00 200.00

Silver Yuan Surcharge in Black on 1949 Sun Yat-sen Issues

1949 ***Perf. 12½, 14***
991 A94 1c on $100 org brn (890) 9.25 10.00
992 A94 1c on $100 dk org brn (898) 9.25 10.00
993 A94 2½c on $500 rose lil (892) 11.00 11.00
a. Inverted surcharge 35.00
994 A94 2½c on $500 rose lil (900) 12.50 12.00
995 A94 15c on $10 grn (887) 17.50 25.00
a. Inverted surcharge 40.00
996 A94 15c on $20 vio brn (896) 27.50 *35.00*
Nos. 991-996 (6) 87.00 103.00

Silver Yuan Surcharge in Black or Carmine

997 A94 2½c on $50 grn (951) 1.60 3.50
998 A94 2½c on $50,000 bl (956) 4.50 3.50
999 A94 5c on $1000 dp bl (952) (C) 3.50 3.50
1000 A94 5c on $20,000 org (955) 2.25 3.00
1001 A94 5c on $200,000 vio (957) (C) 3.50 3.00
1002 A94 5c on $500,000 vio brn (958) 2.25 3.00
1003 A94 10c on $5000 car (953) 6.50 4.25
1004 A94 10c on $10,000 brn (954) 6.50 4.25
1005 A94 15c on $200 red org (891) 8.75 8.00
1006 A94 25c on $100 dk org brn (896) 17.50 17.50
Nos. 997-1006 (10) 56.85 53.50

REPUBLIC OF CHINA

ri-'pə-blik of 'chī-nə

(Taiwan)

LOCATION — Taiwan (since 1949) (Formosa)
GOVT. — Republic
AREA — 13,970 sq. mi.
POP. — 22,113,250 (1999 est.)
CAPITAL — Taipei

Stamps issued and used in Taiwan after Communist forces occupied the Chinese mainland include Taiwan Nos. 91-96, 101-103, J10-J17.

Catalogue values for unused stamps in this country are for Never Hinged items, beginning with Scott 1124 in the regular postage section, Scott B17 in the semi-postal section, Scott C69 in the airpost section, and Scott J142 in the postage due section.

Watermarks

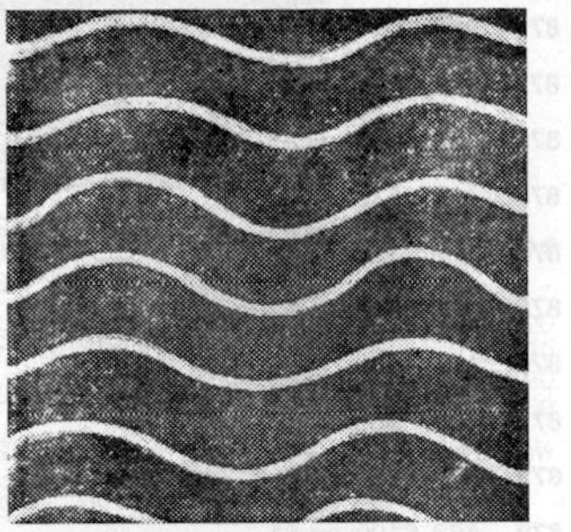

Wmk. 281 — Wavy Lines

Wmk. 323 — Seal Character (found with "Yu" in various arrangements)

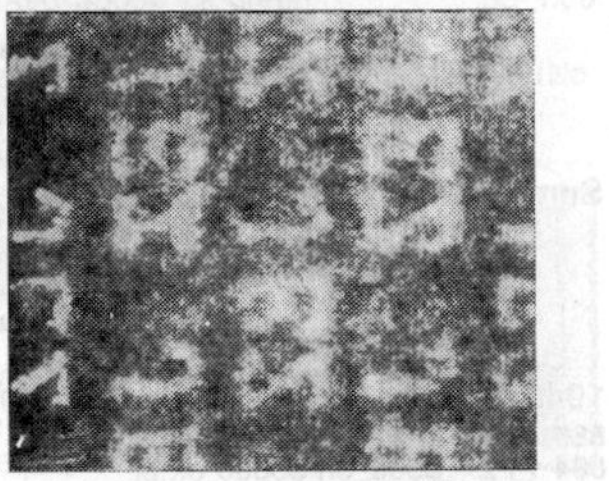

Wmk. 368 — JEZ Multiple

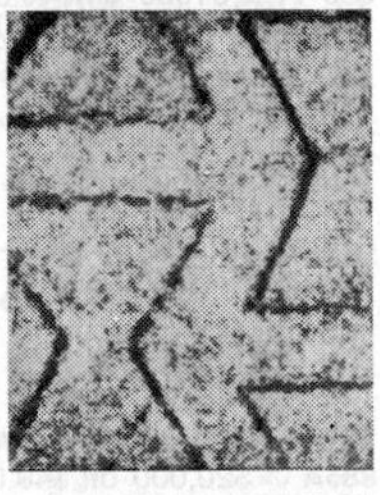

Wmk. 370 — Geometrical Design

Type of 1949 with Value Omitted Surcharged in Various Colors

1950, Jan. 1 **Unwmk.** ***Perf. 12½***
1007 A97 $1 green (Bk) 150.00 7.00
1008 A97 $2 green (C) 175.00 14.00
1009 A97 $5 green (V) 1,600. 65.00
1010 A97 $10 green (Br) 1,500. 130.00
1011 A97 $20 green (Dk Bl) 3,500. 550.00
Nos. 1007-1011 (5) 6,925. 766.00

Two printings of the $1 and $2 show minor differences.

Cheng Ch'eng-kung (Koxinga) — A101

1950, June 26 **Typo.** ***Rouletted***
Without Gum
1012 A101 3c dk gray grn 3.50 .85
1013 A101 10c orange brn 2.50 .25
1014 A101 15c orange yel 12.00 2.00
1015 A101 20c emerald 3.50 .20
1016 A101 30c claret 45.00 11.00
1017 A101 40c red orange 3.50 .25
1018 A101 50c chocolate 8.00 1.00
1019 A101 80c carmine 8.00 2.00
1020 A101 $1 ultra 4.00 1.00
1021 A101 $1.50 green 35.00 2.00
1022 A101 $1.60 blue 17.50 1.00
1023 A101 $2 red violet 20.00 .75
1024 A101 $5 aqua 125.00 22.50
Nos. 1012-1024 (13) 287.50 44.80

Part perf pairs exist of the 10c, 20c, 80c.
The 10c and 20c were reprinted from new plates. There are slight differences.
For surcharges see Nos. 1070-1072, 1105-1108, 1118-1119.

Nos. 751, 753, 788-791, 793, 795-799 Surcharged in Carmine or Black

1950 **Engr.** ***Perf. 14***
1025 A82 3c on $30,000 3.75 2.25
1026 A82 3c on $40,000 (C) 3.25 2.25
1027 A82 3c on $50,000 (C) 3.25 3.00
1028 A82 5c on $200,000 3.75 2.50
1029 A82 10c on $4000 32.50 4.00
1030 A82 10c on $6000 24.00 4.00
1031 A82 10c on $20,000 24.00 4.00
1032 A82 10c on $2,000,000 24.00 4.00
1033 A82 20c on $500,000 35.00 4.00
1034 A82 20c on $1,000,000 60.00 8.00
1035 A82 30c on $3,000,000 90.00 10.00
1036 A82 50c on $5,000,000 (C) 150.00 10.00
Nos. 1025-1036 (12) 453.50 58.00

Issued: #1025-1027, 3/6; #1028, 3/25; #1031, 6/10:#1029-1030, 1032, 1035-1036, 8/1; #1033-1034, 8/25.
Forgeries exist.

Inverted Surcharge
1029a A82 10c on $4000 160.00
1030a A82 10c on $6000 350.00
1031a A82 10c on $20,000 200.00
1032a A82 10c on $2,000,000 210.00
1033a A82 20c on $500,000 275.00
1034a A82 20c on $1,000,000 275.00

Allegory of Election A102

Perf. 12x12½, Imperf.
1951, Mar. 20 **Engr.** **Unwmk.**
Without Gum
1037 A102 40c carmine 14.00 1.00
a. Horiz. pair, imperf. btwn. 85.00
1038 A102 $1 dp blue 30.00 2.75
1039 A102 $1.60 purple 55.00 4.00
1040 A102 $2 brown 80.00 4.00
Nos. 1037-1040 (4) 179.00 11.75

Souvenir Sheet
Imperf
1041 A102 $2 dp blue grn *425.00 350.00*

Adoption of local self-government in Taiwan.

Design A97 Surcharged A103

Farmer and Scroll Announcing Tax Reduction A104

Surcharge in Various Colors

1951, July 19 *Perf. 12½*

Without Gum

1042	A103	$5 green (R Br)	57.50	11.00
1043	A103	$10 green (Bk)	130.00	12.00
1044	A103	$20 green (R)	500.00	30.00
1045	A103	$50 green (P)	900.00	95.00
		Nos. 1042-1045 (4)	1,587.	148.00

1952, Jan. 1 *Perf. 14*

Without Gum

1046	A104	20c red orange	9.00	1.50
1047	A104	40c dk green	12.50	2.75
1048	A104	$1 brown	20.00	6.50
1049	A104	$1.40 dp blue	30.00	4.50
1050	A104	$2 dk gray	90.00	40.00
1051	A104	$5 brown car	125.00	16.00
		Nos. 1046-1051 (6)	286.50	71.25

Land tax reduction of 37.5% in Taiwan.
Value, imperf. set, $575.

Pres. Chiang Kai-shek, Flag and Followers A105

1952, Mar. 1 **Unwmk.** *Perf. 14*

Without Gum

Flag in Violet Blue and Carmine

1052	A105	40c rose car	8.00	.50
a.		Vert. pair, imperf. btwn.	75.00	
1053	A105	$1 dp green	15.00	2.25
1054	A105	$1.60 brown org	30.00	1.10
a.		Horiz. pair, imperf. btwn.	160.00	
1055	A105	$2 brt blue	60.00	19.00
1056	A105	$5 violet brn	67.50	5.00
		Nos. 1052-1056 (5)	180.50	27.85

2nd anniv. of Chiang Kai-shek's return to the presidency.
Value, imperf. set, $460.
See Nos. 1064-1069.

Nos. 975-976, 978-979 Surcharged in Black

1952, Aug. 1 *Perf. 12½*

1057	A94	3c on 4c bl grn	4.50	3.00
1058	A94	3c on 10c dp lil	4.50	3.00
a.		Inverted surcharge		
1059	A94	3c on 20c blue	6.25	4.25
1060	A94	3c on 50c dk brn	7.25	5.00
		Nos. 1057-1060 (4)	22.50	15.25

Forgeries exist.

Geese Type of 1949 with Value Omitted Surcharged

1952, Dec. 8

1061	A97	$10 green (P)	95.00	16.00
1062	A97	$20 green (R)	275.00	27.50
1063	A97	$50 green (Bk)	2,000.	750.00
		Nos. 1061-1063 (3)	2,370.	793.50

Chiang Type of 1952 Redrawn

Perf. 12½

1953, Mar. 1 **Engr.** **Unwmk.**

Without Gum

Flag in Dark Blue & Carmine

1064	A105	10c red orange	4.00	1.50
1065	A105	20c green	8.50	1.50
1066	A105	40c rose pink	12.00	2.00
1067	A105	$1.40 blue	35.00	3.25
1068	A105	$2 brown	90.00	6.00
1069	A105	$5 rose violet	140.00	16.00
		Nos. 1064-1069 (6)	289.50	30.25

Chiang Kai-shek's return to presidency, 3rd anniv.
Many differences in redrawn design. Value, imperf. set, $460.

Nos. 1020, 1014, 1016 and 1022 Surcharged in Various Colors

1953 *Rouletted*

1070	A101	3c on $1 ultra (C)	1.60	.35
1070A	A101	10c on 15c org yel (G) ('54)	5.75	.75
1071	A101	10c on 30c cl (Bl)	3.00	1.00
1072	A101	20c on $1.60 bl (Bk)	3.50	1.10
		Nos. 1070-1072 (4)	13.85	3.20

Chinese characters and ornamental device at bottom differ on each value.
Issued: #1071, 2/1; #1070, 5/25; #1072, 6/13; #1070A, 7/16.

Nurse & Patients — A106

Chiang Kai-shek — A107

1953, July 1 **Litho.** *Perf. 12½*

Without Gum

Cross in Red, Burelage Color in Italics

1073	A106	40c brown, *buff*	12.50	1.50
1074	A106	$1.60 blue, *bl*	30.00	1.40
1075	A106	$2 green, *yel*	47.50	2.25
1076	A106	$5 red org, *org*	80.00	10.00
		Nos. 1073-1076 (4)	170.00	15.15

Chinese Anti-Tuberculosis Association.

1953, Oct. 31 **Engr.**

Without Gum

1077	A107	10c dk brown	4.75	.25
1078	A107	20c lilac	4.75	.25
1079	A107	40c dp green	4.75	.25
1080	A107	50c dp pink	6.50	.45
1081	A107	80c brown bis	17.50	2.00
1082	A107	$1 dp olive grn	8.25	.25
1083	A107	$1.40 dp blue	8.25	.25
1084	A107	$1.60 dp carmine	8.25	.25
1085	A107	$1.70 apple grn	8.25	1.10
1086	A107	$2 brown	9.75	.25
1087	A107	$3 dark blue	150.00	5.00
1088	A107	$4 aqua	9.75	.70
1089	A107	$5 red orange	15.00	.70
1090	A107	$10 dk green	65.00	3.25
1091	A107	$20 dk brn lake	85.00	10.00
a.		Souvenir folder	450.00	
		Nos. 1077-1091 (15)	405.75	24.95

67th birthday of Pres. Chiang Kai-shek.
#1091a contains #1077-1091 imperf, arranged in 3 sheets of 5 stamps each.

Silo Highway Bridge — A108

Forest of Evergreens — A109

$1.60 and $5, Silo bridge, side view.

1954, Jan. 28 **Unwmk.** *Perf. 12½*

Without Gum

Various Frames

1092	A108	40c vermilion	17.50	1.00
1093	A108	$1.60 blue violet	80.00	1.75
1094	A108	$3.60 sepia	50.00	5.00
1095	A108	$5 magenta	125.00	9.00
a.		Souvenir folder	1,375.	
		Nos. 1092-1095 (4)	272.50	16.75

Opening of Silo bridge, 1st anniversary.
No. 1095a contains one sheet of 4 containing Nos. 1092-1095 imperforate.

1954, Mar. 12 *Perf. 12x12½*

Without Gum

1096	A109	40c shown	15.00	1.50
1097	A109	$10 Nursery	110.00	10.00

Issued to publicize forest conservation.

Runner — A110

Globe, Bridge and Ship — A111

1954, Mar. 29

Without Gum

1098	A110	40c dp ultra	10.00	1.75
1099	A110	$5 carmine	75.00	9.50

11th Youth Day, Mar. 29, 1954.

1954, Oct. 21 *Perf. 12*

Without Gum

1100	A111	40c red orange	15.00	1.00
1101	A111	$5 deep blue	17.50	4.50

2nd Overseas Chinese Day, Oct. 21, 1954.

Ex-Prisoner with Broken Chains — A112

Designs: $1, Ex-prisoner with torch and flag, UN emblem. $1.60, Torch and date.

1955, Jan. 23

1102	A112	40c blue green	2.00	.65
a.		Vert. pair, imperf. btwn.	140.00	
1103	A112	$1 sepia	14.50	5.00
1104	A112	$1.60 lake	14.50	4.25
		Nos. 1102-1104 (3)	31.00	9.90

Honoring Chinese who fought on the side of the North Korean army, who, when released January 23, 1954, chose to return to the Republic of China.

Nos. 1019-1021, 1017 Surcharged in Brown, Blue or Green:

a

b

c

1955 *Rouletted*

1105	A101(a)	3c on $1 (Br)	2.00	.50
1106	A101(b)	10c on 80c (Bl)	2.75	.50
1107	A101(b)	10c on $1.50 (Bl)	2.75	.50
1108	A101(c)	20c on 40c (G)	3.25	.85
		Nos. 1105-1108 (4)	10.75	2.35

Issued: #1105, 1108, 2/18; #1106-1107, 8/1.

Hand Planting Evergreen Tree — A113

Chiang Kai-shek, Flags, Building A114

Design: $50, Seedling and map of Taiwan.

1955, Apr. 1 *Perf. 12*

Without Gum

1109	A113	$20 dp carmine	32.50	1.25
1110	A113	$50 blue	80.00	5.75

Issued to publicize forest conservation.

1955, May 20 **Engr.** *Perf. 12*

Without Gum

1111	A114	20c olive	3.25	.30
1112	A114	40c blue green	3.00	.30
1113	A114	$2 car rose	8.00	.90
1114	A114	$7 dp ultra	12.50	1.50
a.		Souv. sheet of 4, #1111-1114, imperf.	*175.00*	*150.00*
		Nos. 1111-1114 (4)	26.75	3.00

First anniversary of Pres. Chiang Kai-shek's re-election.
No. 1114a is perf. 12 at right edge of sheet. Value is for sheet with right selvage.

Armed Forces Emblem — A115

1955, Sept. 3

Without Gum

1115	A115	40c dk blue	3.50	.50
1116	A115	$2 org ver	12.50	1.50
1117	A115	$7 bl grn	20.00	1.75
a.		Sheet of 3, #1115-1117, imperf.	*450.00*	*325.00*
		Nos. 1115-1117 (3)	36.00	3.75

Armed Forces Day, Sept. 3.
No. 1117a is perf. 12 at right edge of sheet. Value is for sheet with right selvage.

Nos. 1017, 1018 and C64 Surcharged in Magenta

1955, Sept. 16 **Typo.** *Rouletted*

1118	A101	20c on 40c red org	4.00	.40
1119	A101	20c on 50c choc	4.00	.40
1120	AP6	20c on 60c dp blue	5.00	.50
		Nos. 1118-1120 (3)	13.00	1.30

Flags of UN and China A116

1955, Oct. 24 **Engr.** *Perf. 11½*

Without Gum

1121	A116	40c dk blue	2.25	.50
1122	A116	$2 dk car rose	4.50	1.00
1123	A116	$7 slate green	7.75	1.75
		Nos. 1121-1123 (3)	14.50	3.25

10th anniv. of the UN, Oct. 24, 1955.

Catalogue values for unused stamps in this section, from this point to the end of the section, are for Never Hinged items.

Pres. Chiang Kai-shek A117

Birthplace of Sun Yat-sen A118

1955, Oct. 31 Photo. *Perf. 13½*

1124	A117	40c dk bl, red & brn	4.25	.50
1125	A117	$2 grn, red & dk bl	10.50	1.10
1126	A117	$7 brn, red & grn	14.00	2.25
a.		Souv. sheet of 3, #1124-1126, imperf.	*140.00*	*140.00*
		Nos. 1124-1126 (3)	28.75	3.85

69th birthday of Pres. Chiang Kai-shek.
No. 1126a is perf. 12 at right edge of sheet. Value is for sheet with right selvage.

1955, Nov. 12 Engr. *Perf. 12*
Without Gum

1127	A118	40c blue	1.75	.45
1128	A118	$2 red brown	6.00	1.00
1129	A118	$7 rose lake	10.00	2.00
		Nos. 1127-1129 (3)	17.75	3.45

90th anniversary, birth of Sun Yat-sen.

No. 959a Surcharged in Bright Green

1956, Feb. 10 Litho. *Rouletted*

1130	A96	20c on orange	.45	.20

See No. 1213.

China Map and Transportation Methods — A119

Wmk. 281
1956, Mar. 20 Engr. *Perf. 12*
Without Gum

1131	A119	40c dk carmine	1.75	.25
1132	A119	$1 intense blk	3.50	.50
1133	A119	$1.60 chocolate	4.50	.35
1134	A119	$2 dk green	5.50	1.00
		Nos. 1131-1134 (4)	15.25	2.10

60th anniv. of the founding of the modern Chinese postal system.

Souvenir Sheets
Imperf

1135	A119	$2 magenta	*45.00*	*25.00*
1136	A119	$2 red	*45.00*	*25.00*

Exhib. for the 60th anniv. of the modern Chinese postal system, Mar. 20, 1956.

Children at Play — A120

Early and Modern Locomotives A121

1956, Apr. 4 Unwmk. *Perf. 12*
Without Gum

1137	A120	40c emerald	1.50	.25
1138	A120	$1.60 dk blue	3.00	.50
1139	A120	$2 dk carmine	3.50	.90
		Nos. 1137-1139 (3)	8.00	1.65

Children's Day, Apr. 4, 1956.

1956, June 9 Wmk. 281 Vert.
Without Gum

1140	A121	40c rose car	3.25	.40
1141	A121	$2 blue	6.50	.65
1142	A121	$8 green	8.00	1.40
		Nos. 1140-1142 (3)	17.75	2.45

75th anniversary of Chinese Railroads.

Pres. Chiang Kai-shek
A122 A123

A124

Various Portraits of Chiang
Perf. 14½x13½, 14½ (A123), 13½x14½

1956, Oct. 31 Photo. Unwmk.

1143	A122	20c red orange	4.00	.20
1144	A122	40c carmine rose	6.25	.20
1145	A123	$1 brt ultra	8.25	.25
1146	A123	$1.60 red lilac	10.50	.20
1147	A124	$2 red brown	12.50	.30
1148	A124	$8 brt grnsh blue	21.00	.60
		Nos. 1143-1148 (6)	62.50	1.75

70th birthday of Pres. Chiang Kai-shek.

Types of Special Delivery, Air Post and Registration Stamps of 1949 Surcharged in Black or Maroon

a

b

c

1956 Unwmk. Litho. *Rouletted*
Without Gum

1150	SD2(a)	3c red violet	1.25	.20
a.		Perf. 12½	2.75	.30
1151	AP5(b)	3c blue green (M)	1.25	.20
1152	R2(c)	10c bright red	1.25	.20
		Nos. 1150-1152 (3)	3.75	.60

Issued: #1150, 4/25; #1151, 11/11; #1152, 12/25.

Telecommunications Emblem and Radio Tower — A125

Wmk. 281
1956, Dec. 28 Engr. *Perf. 12*
Without Gum

1153	A125	40c deep ultra	1.60	.20
1154	A125	$1.40 carmine	2.25	.20
1155	A125	$1.60 dark green	3.25	.20
1156	A125	$2 chocolate	4.25	.40
		Nos. 1153-1156 (4)	11.35	1.00

Chinese telegraph service, 75th anniv.

Map of China A126

Mother Instructing Mencius A127

Pin Perf., Perf. 12x12½
1957 Litho. Wmk. 281
Without Gum

1157	A126	3c brt blue	.90	.20
1158	A126	10c violet	1.40	.20
1159	A126	20c red orange	.90	.20
1160	A126	40c rose red	1.75	.20

Unwmk.

1161	A126	$1 orange brown	2.50	.20
1162	A126	$1.60 green	3.75	.25
		Nos. 1157-1162 (6)	11.20	1.25

Map inscription reads: "Recovery of Mainland."
See Nos. 1177-1182.

Unwmk.
1957, May 12 Engr. *Perf. 12*

Design: $3, Mother tattooing Yueh Fei.

Without Gum

1163	A127	40c green	1.50	.20
1164	A127	$3 redsh brown	2.75	.40

Issued to honor Mother's Day, 1957.

Badge of Chinese Boy Scouts — A128

1957, Aug. 11
Without Gum

1165	A128	40c lilac	.75	.20
1166	A128	$1 green	1.50	.35
1167	A128	$1.60 dk blue	2.25	.25
		Nos. 1165-1167 (3)	4.50	.80

Cent. of the birth of Lord Baden-Powell and to publicize the World Scout Jubilee Jamboree, England, Aug. 1-12.

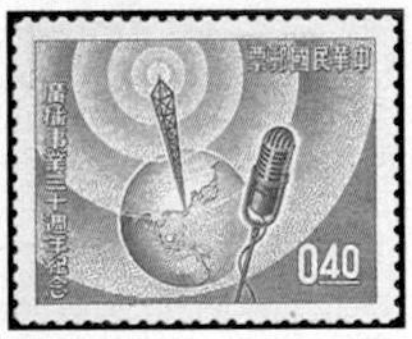

Globe, Radio Tower and Microphone A129

1957, Sept. 16
Without Gum

1168	A129	40c vermilion	.60	.20
1169	A129	50c brt rose lilac	1.00	.20
1170	A129	$3.50 dark blue	1.50	.50
		Nos. 1168-1170 (3)	3.10	.90

30th anniv. of Chinese broadcasting.

Map of Taiwan — A130

1957, Oct. 26
Without Gum

1171	A130	40c blue green	2.75	.35
1172	A130	$1.40 lt ultra	4.50	1.00
1173	A130	$2 gray	6.25	1.50
		Nos. 1171-1173 (3)	13.50	2.85

Start of construction on the Cross Island Highway, Taiwan.

Freighter "Hai Min" and River Boat "Kiang Foo" — A131

1957, Dec. 16 Engr. *Perf. 12*
Without Gum

1174	A131	40c deep ultra	.75	.25
1175	A131	80c rose lake	1.50	.95
1176	A131	$2.80 vermilion	2.25	1.40
		Nos. 1174-1176 (3)	4.50	2.60

85th anniv. of the establishment of the China Merchants Steam Navigation Co.

Type of 1957
Pin Perf., Perf. 12x12½
1957, Dec. 25 Typo. Unwmk.
Without Gum
Dark Blue Frames

1177	A126	3c brt blue	.30	.20
1178	A126	10c violet	.55	.20
1179	A126	20c brick red	.85	.20
1180	A126	40c rose red	1.00	.20
1181	A126	$1 dp org brn	3.25	.25
1182	A126	$1.60 dp green	4.00	.30
		Nos. 1177-1182 (6)	9.95	1.35

Stamps with bars obliterating the face value are specimens.

Butterfly A132

Mme. Chiang Kai-shek Orchid A133

Perf. 13½
1958, Mar. 20 Unwmk. Photo.
Various Insects in Natural Colors

1183	A132	10c pale grn, grn & blk	1.25	.50
1184	A132	40c lem, pink, grn & blk	1.25	.50
1185	A132	$1 yel grn & mar	2.25	.60
1186	A132	$1.40 yel, org & blk	2.75	.75
1187	A132	$1.60 pale brn & dk pur	4.00	.90
1188	A132	$2 brt yel, org & blk	4.75	1.25
		Nos. 1183-1188 (6)	16.25	4.50

1958, Mar. 20

Orchids: 20c, Formosan Wilson, horiz. $1.40, Klotzsch. $3, Fitzgerald, horiz.

Orchids in Natural Colors

1189	A133	20c chocolate	2.00	.40
1190	A133	40c purple	2.25	.40
1191	A133	$1.40 dk vio brn	3.00	.60
1192	A133	$3 dark blue	4.25	1.10
		Nos. 1189-1192 (4)	11.50	2.50

World Health Organization Emblem — A134

1958, May 28 Engr. *Perf. 12*
Without Gum

1193	A134	40c dark blue	.50	.20
1194	A134	$1.60 brick red	.65	.20
1195	A134	$2 deep red lilac	.85	.40
		Nos. 1193-1195 (3)	2.00	.80

10th anniv. of the WHO.

President's Mansion, Taipei — A135

Wmk. 323
1958, Sept. 20 Engr. *Perf. 12*
Without Gum

1196	A135	$10 blue green	8.00	.30
a.		Granite paper	10.00	.30
1197	A135	$20 car rose	18.00	.50
a.		Granite paper	18.00	.50
1198	A135	$50 red brown	55.00	2.00
1199	A135	$100 dk blue	85.00	4.75
		Nos. 1196-1199 (4)	166.00	7.55

Issued: #1196a, 1197a, 5/24/63.
See #1349-1351. For surcharge see #J131.

Taiwan Farm Scene A136

1958, Oct. 1 Unwmk.
Without Gum

1200	A136	20c emerald	1.25	.20
1201	A136	40c black	1.50	.20
1202	A136	$1.40 brt magenta	2.00	.25
1203	A136	$3 ultra	3.75	.75
		Nos. 1200-1203 (4)	8.50	1.40

10th anniversary of the Joint Commission on Rural Reconstruction.

Pres. Chiang Kai-shek A137

1958, Oct. 31 Photo. *Perf. 13½*

1204	A137	40c multicolored	1.25	.45

Pres. Chiang Kai-shek on his 72nd birthday.

UNESCO Building, Paris A138

1958, Nov. 3 Engr. *Perf. 12*
Without Gum

1205	A138	20c dark blue	.30	.20
1206	A138	40c green	.40	.20
1207	A138	$1.40 orange ver	.60	.35
1208	A138	$3 red lilac	1.00	.50
		Nos. 1205-1208 (4)	2.30	1.25

UNESCO Headquarters in Paris opening, Nov. 3.

Flame from Liberty Torch Encircling Globe — A139

1958, Dec. 10 Unwmk.
Without Gum

1209	A139	40c green	.20	.20
1210	A139	60c gray brown	.30	.20
1211	A139	$1 carmine	.50	.20
1212	A139	$3 ultra	.75	.40
		Nos. 1209-1212 (4)	1.75	1.00

10th anniversary of the signing of the Universal Declaration of Human Rights.

No. 959a Surcharged in Bright Green

Rouletted
1958, Dec. 11 Litho. Unwmk.
Without Gum

1213	A96	20c on orange	.55	.20

Ballot Box, Scales and Constitution — A140

1958, Dec. 25 Engr. *Perf. 12*
Without Gum

1214	A140	40c green	.90	.20
1215	A140	50c dull purple	1.25	.20
1216	A140	$1.40 car rose	1.50	.25
1217	A140	$3.50 dk blue	2.50	.75
		Nos. 1214-1217 (4)	6.15	1.40

Adoption of the constitution, 10th anniv.

Chu Kwang Tower, Quemoy — A141

1959-60 Wmk. 323 Litho. *Perf. 12*
Without Gum

1218	A141	3c orange	.35	.20
1218A	A141	5c lt yel grn ('60)	.40	.20
1219	A141	10c lilac	.50	.20
1220	A141	20c ultra	.65	.20
1221	A141	40c brown	.80	.20
1222	A141	50c bluish grn	1.00	.20
1223	A141	$1 rose red	1.10	.20
1224	A141	$1.40 yel grn	1.50	.20
1225	A141	$2 gray grn	2.00	.20
1226	A141	$2.80 rose pink	2.75	.25
1227	A141	$3 slate blue	3.00	.25
		Nos. 1218-1227 (11)	14.05	2.30

See Nos. 1270-1283.

ILO Emblem and Headquarters, Geneva — A142

1959, June 15 Engr. *Perf. 12*
Without Gum

1228	A142	40c blue	.30	.20
1229	A142	$1.60 dk brown	.40	.20
1230	A142	$3 brt blue grn	.50	.20
1231	A142	$5 orange ver	1.00	.50
		Nos. 1228-1231 (4)	2.20	1.10

40th anniversary of the ILO.

Bugler and Tents A143

1959, July 8 Unwmk.
Without Gum

1232	A143	40c carmine	.95	.20
1233	A143	50c dark blue	1.10	.25
1234	A143	$5 green	1.90	.55
		Nos. 1232-1234 (3)	3.95	1.00

10th World Boy Scout Jamboree, Makiling National Park, Philippines, July 17-26.

Inscribed Stone, Mt. Tai-wu, Quemoy — A144

Map of Taiwan Straits A145

1959, Sept. 3 Engr. *Perf. 12*
Without Gum

1235	A144	40c brown	.75	.20
1236	A145	$1.40 ultra	.85	.20
1237	A145	$2 green	1.50	.20
1238	A144	$3 dark blue	1.75	.30
		Nos. 1235-1238 (4)	4.85	.90

Defense of Quemoy and Matsu islands.
For overprints see Nos. 1258-1259.

Pigeons Circling Globe A146

1959, Oct. 4
Without Gum

1239	A146	40c blue	.35	.20
1240	A146	$1 rose carmine	.60	.20
1241	A146	$2 gray brown	.85	.20
1242	A146	$3.50 red orange	1.00	.50
		Nos. 1239-1242 (4)	2.80	1.10

Intl. Letter Writing Week, Oct. 4-10.

National Taiwan Science Hall, Taipei — A147

1959, Nov. 12 Photo. *Perf. 13x13½*

1243	A147	40c shown	1.10	.20
1244	A147	$3 Front view	2.40	.70

Emblem A148

1959, Dec. 7 Engr. *Perf. 12*
Without Gum

1245	A148	40c blue green	.40	.25
1246	A148	$1.60 red lilac	.50	.25
1247	A148	$3 orange	.95	.60
		Nos. 1245-1247 (3)	1.85	1.10

Intl. Confederation of Free Trade Unions, 10th anniv.

Sun Yat-sen, Lincoln and Flags A149

Perf. 13½, 12
1959, Dec. 25 Photo. Unwmk.

1248	A149	40c multicolored	.25	.25
1249	A149	$3 multicolored	1.00	.60

Issued to honor Sun Yat-sen and Abraham Lincoln as "Leaders of Democracy."

Mailman on Motorcycle Delivering Night Mail — A150

Postal Launch A151

1960, Mar. 20 Engr. *Perf. 11½*
Without Gum

1250	A150	$1.40 dk violet brn	1.10	.25
1251	A151	$1.60 ultra	1.10	.25

Issued to publicize the Prompt Delivery Service.

WRY Uprooted Oak Emblem — A152

1960, Apr. 7 Photo. *Perf. 13*

1252	A152	40c blk, red brn & emer	.50	.20
1253	A152	$3 blk, red org & grn	.90	.35

World Refugee Year, 7/1/59-6/30/60.

Cross Island Highway, Taiwan — A153

Design: $1, $2, Road through tunnel, vert.

Perf. 11½

1960, May 9 Engr. Unwmk.

Without Gum

1254	A153	40c	green	1.00	.20
1255	A153	$1	dk blue	1.75	.25
1256	A153	$2	brown vio	2.00	.30
1257	A153	$3	brown	3.00	.35
a.			Souv. sheet of 2, #1255, 1257, wmk. 323, imperf.	*190.00*	*75.00*
			Nos. 1254-1257 (4)	7.75	1.10

Opening of the Cross Island Highway, Taiwan.

Red Overprint on Nos. 1237-1238 Chinese and English: "Welcome U.S. President Dwight D. Eisenhower 1960"

1960, June 18 Unwmk. *Perf. 12*

1258	A145	$2	green	.90	.30
a.			Inverted overprint	2,250.	2,250.
1259	A144	$3	dk blue	1.40	.45

Eisenhower's visit to China, June 18, 1960.

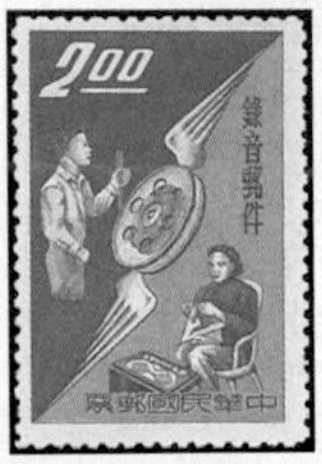

Phonopost — A154

1960, June 27

Without Gum

1260	A154	$2	red orange	1.60	.40

Phonopost Service of the Chinese armed forces.

Two Horses and Groom, by Han Kan — A155

Paintings from Palace Museum, Taichung: $1, Two Riders, by Wei Yen. $1.60, Flowers and Birds by Hsiao Yung, vert. $2, Pair of Mandarin Ducks by Monk Hui Ch'ung.

1960, Aug. 4 Photo. *Perf. 13*

1261	A155	$1	ol gray, blk & brn	3.25	.55
1262	A155	$1.40	bis brn, blk & fawn	6.00	1.00
1263	A155	$1.60	multicolored	8.00	1.50
1264	A155	$2	beige, blk & gray grn	14.00	2.75
			Nos. 1261-1264 (4)	31.25	5.80

Chinese paintings, 7th-11th centuries.

For other painting types with large straight numerals in the upper corners and large Chinese characters on the side see A186, A241 and A285.

Youth Corps Flag and Summer Activities A156

Reforestation A157

Design: $3, similar to 50c, horiz.

1960, Aug. 20 Engr. *Perf. 12*

Without Gum

1265	A156	50c	slate green	.50	.20
1266	A156	$3	copper brown	1.10	.45

Summer activities of China Youth Corps.

1960, Aug. 29 Photo. *Perf. 13½x13*

$2, Protection of forest. $3, Timber industry.

1267	A157	$1	multicolored	1.25	.20
1268	A157	$2	multicolored	1.75	.25
1269	A157	$3	multicolored	2.50	.60
a.			Souvenir sheet of 3	25.00	17.50
			Nos. 1267-1269 (3)	5.50	1.05

Fifth World Forestry Congress, Seattle, Washington, Aug. 29-Sept. 10.

No. 1269a contains Nos. 1267-1269 assembled as a triptych, 65½x40mm and imperf., but with simulated black perforations.

Chu Kwang Tower, Quemoy — A158

Sports — A159

1960-61 Wmk. 323 Litho. *Perf. 12*

Without Gum

1270	A158	3c	lt red brown	.50	.20
1271	A158	40c	pale violet	.50	.20
1272	A158	50c	orange ('61)	.80	.20
1273	A158	60c	rose lilac	1.00	.20
1274	A158	80c	pale green	1.10	.20
1275	A158	$1	gray grn ('61)	1.25	.20
1276	A158	$1.20	gray olive	1.25	.20
1277	A158	$1.50	ultra	1.50	.25
1278	A158	$2	car rose ('61)	1.75	.20
1279	A158	$2.50	pale blue	1.90	.25
1280	A158	$3	bluish green	2.00	.25
1281	A158	$3.20	lt red brown	1.75	.20
1282	A158	$3.60	vio blue ('61)	3.75	.30
1283	A158	$4.50	vermilion	7.00	.35
			Nos. 1270-1283 (14)	26.05	3.20

For surcharges see Nos. J132-J134.

1962-64

Granite Paper

Without Gum

1270a	A158	3c	light red brown	.50	.20
1270B	A158	10c	emerald ('63)	1.50	.20
1271a	A158	40c	pale violet	.50	.20
1274a	A158	80c	pale green	.50	.20
1275a	A158	$1	gray grn ('63)	8.00	.20
1278a	A158	$2	carmine rose	4.00	.20
1281a	A158	$3.20	red brn ('64)	10.00	.20
1282A	A158	$4	brt blue grn	10.00	.20
1283a	A158	$4.50	vermilion	15.00	.50
			Nos. 1270a-1283a (9)	50.00	2.10

Two types of No. 1271a: I. Seven lines in "0" of "40." II. Eight lines in "0."

Perf. 12½

1960, Oct. 25 Photo. Unwmk.

1284	A159	50c	Diving	1.25	.20
1285	A159	80c	Discus thrower	1.00	.20
1286	A159	$2	Basketball	2.50	.20
1287	A159	$2.50	Soccer	2.50	.40
1288	A159	$3	Hurdling	3.00	.40
1289	A159	$3.20	Runner	3.25	.60
			Nos. 1284-1289 (6)	13.50	2.00

Bronze Wine Container, 1751-1111 B.C. — A160

Flat Bowl, 1111-771 B.C. — A161

Ancient Chinese Art Treasures: $1, Cauldron, 1111-771 B.C. $1.20, Porcelain vase, 960-1126 A.D. $1.50, Perforated tube, 1111-771 B.C. $2, Jug in shape of monk's cap, 1368-1661 A.D. $2.50, Jade flower vase, 1368-1661, A.D.

1961 Photo. *Perf. 13*

1290	A160	80c	lt ol, blk & dk vio	1.50	.20
1291	A160	$1	sal, bl & blk	1.90	.25
1292	A160	$1.20	yel, brn & ultra	2.75	.35
1293	A160	$1.50	lil, bl & sep	3.75	.60
1294	A160	$2	pale grn, dk grn & red brn	5.50	.70
1295	A160	$2.50	grnsh bl & dk vio	9.25	1.00
			Nos. 1290-1295 (6)	24.65	3.10

Issue dates: Nos. 1290, 1292, 1295, Feb. 1. Nos. 1291, 1293-1294, May 1.

1961

80c, Palace perfumer, 1662-1911. $1, Corn vase, 770-221 B.C. $2, Jade tankard, 960-1126 A.D. $4, Glazed washer, 1127-1279 A.D. $4.50, Jade chimera, 8 B.C.-206 A.D.

1296	A160	80c	pink, brn, bl & yel	1.50	.30
1297	A160	$1	cit, blk & brn	2.00	.60
1298	A161	$1.50	sal & ind	4.00	.70
1299	A160	$2	bl, blk & rose	4.00	.60
1300	A161	$4	red, blk & bluish gray	6.00	1.25
1301	A161	$4.50	grnsh bl, blk & brn	24.00	3.00
			Nos. 1296-1301 (6)	41.50	6.45

Issued: #1296-1298, 8/15; #1299-1301, 9/15.

1962

Designs: 80c, Topaz twin wine vessels, 1662-1911 A.D. $1, Squat pouring vase, 1751-1111 B.C. $2.40, Vase, 1368-1661 A.D. $3, Wine vase, 1751-1111 B.C. $3.20, Covered porcelain jar, 1662-1911 A.D. $3.60, Perforated disc, 206 B.C.-8 A.D.

1302	A160	80c	crim, blk & ocher	1.00	.20
1303	A160	$1	blue & vio blk	1.25	.25
1304	A160	$2.40	hn brn, blk & bl	13.50	1.00
1305	A160	$3	blue, blk & pink	15.00	.90
1306	A160	$3.20	ultra, lt grn & red	13.00	.90
1307	A160	$3.60	yel, blk & brn	21.00	1.25
			Nos. 1302-1307 (6)	64.75	4.50

Issue dates: Nos. 1303-1304, 1307, Jan. 15. Nos. 1302, 1305-1306, Feb. 15.

Farmer with Mechanized Plow — A162

Madame Chiang Kai-shek and League Emblem — A163

1961, Feb. 4 Engr. *Perf. 12*

Without Gum

1308	A162	80c	rose violet	1.40	.20
1309	A162	$2	green	2.50	.30
1310	A162	$3.20	vermilion	4.00	.30
			Nos. 1308-1310 (3)	7.90	.80

1961 agricultural census.

Unwmk.

1961, Mar. 8 Photo. *Perf. 13*

Portrait in Black

1311	A163	80c	lt grn & car rose	2.10	.20
1312	A163	$1	yel grn & car rose	2.75	.60
1313	A163	$2	org brn & car rose	3.50	.70
1314	A163	$3.20	lil & car rose	4.25	1.00
			Nos. 1311-1314 (4)	12.60	2.50

10th anniversary of the Chinese Women's Anti-Aggression League.

Spiny Lobster and Mail Order Service Emblem — A164

Jeme Tien-yow and Pataling Tunnel — A165

1961, Mar. 20 Engr. *Perf. 11½*

Without Gum

1315	A164	$3	slate green	3.50	.35

Issued to publicize the mail order service for consumer goods.

1961, Apr. 26 *Perf. 11½*

Without Gum

$2, Jeme Tien-yow & 1909 locomotive.

1316	A165	80c	lilac	1.40	.20
1317	A165	$2	black, horiz.	2.10	.50

Centenary of the birth of Jeme Tien-yow, builder of the Peking-Kalgan railroad.

Map of China inscribed: "Recovery of the Mainland" — A166

Pres. Chiang Kai-shek — A167

1961, May 20 Photo. *Perf. 13½*

1318	A166	80c	multicolored	2.50	.25
1319	A167	$2	multicolored	4.00	1.10
a.			Souvenir sheet of 2	14.00	*12.50*

1st anniversary of Pres. Chiang Kai-shek's 3rd term inauguration.

No. 1319a contains one each of Nos. 1318-1319, imperf. with simulated perforations. Without gum.

Convair 880-M, Biplane of 1921 and Flag — A168

1961, July 1 *Perf. 13x12½*

1320	A168	$10	multicolored	3.00	1.10

40th anniversary of civil air service.

Sun Yat-sen and Chiang Kai-shek — A169

Flag and Map of China — A170

Perf. 13½

1961, Oct. 10 Unwmk. Photo.

1321 A169 80c gray, lt brn & sl 1.60 .20
1322 A170 $5 gray, ultra, red & beige 3.25 1.40
a. Souvenir sheet of 2 12.00 10.00

50th anniv. of the Republic of China. No. 1322a contains one each of Nos. 1321-1322, imperf. with simulated perforations. No gum.

Green Lake A171

Oil Refinery A173

Lotus Pond A172

Taiwan Scenery: $2, Sun-Moon Lake. $3.20, Wulai waterfalls.

Perf. 13½x14, 14x13½

1961, Oct. 31 Unwmk.

1323 A171 80c multicolored 4.00 .20
1324 A172 $1 multicolored 9.00 .50
1325 A172 $2 multicolored 9.00 .70
1326 A171 $3.20 multicolored 12.00 .90
Nos. 1323-1326 (4) 34.00 2.30

1961, Nov. 14 ***Perf. 11½***

Designs: $1.50, Steel works. $2.50, Aluminum plant. $3.20, Fertilizer plant, horiz.

1327 A173 80c multicolored 1.60 .20
1328 A173 $1.50 multicolored 3.25 .50
1329 A173 $2.50 multicolored 4.25 .55
1330 A173 $3.20 multicolored 5.00 .65
Nos. 1327-1330 (4) 14.10 1.90

Chinese industrial development and the Golden Jubilee Convention of the Chinese Institute of Engineers, Nov. 13-16.

Atomic Reactor, Tsing-Hwa University A174

Atomic Reactor in Operation A175

Design: $3.20, Atomic symbol and laboratory, Tsing-Hwa, horiz.

1961-62 Photo. ***Perf. 12½***

1331 A174 80c multicolored 2.25 .20
1332 A175 $2 multicolored 4.50 1.40
1333 A175 $3.20 multicolored 4.25 .85
Nos. 1331-1333 (3) 11.00 2.45

Inauguration on Apr. 13, 1961, of the 1st Chinese atomic reactor at the National Tsing-Hwa University Institute of Nuclear Science.
Issued: 80c, 12/2; $2, $3.20, 3/20/62.

Microwave Reflector and Telegraph Wires — A176

Design: $3.20, Microwave parabolic antenna and mountains, horiz.

1961, Dec. 28 ***Perf. 12½***

1334 A176 80c multicolored 1.25 .20
1335 A176 $3.20 multicolored 2.00 .80

80th anniv. of Chinese telecommunications.

Mechanical Postal Equipment and Twine Tying Machine — A176a

Wmk. 323

1962, Mar. 20 Engr. ***Perf. 11½***

Without Gum

1336 A176a 80c chocolate 1.10 .30

Yu Shan Observatory A177

Observation Balloon, Earth and Cumulus Clouds A178

Design: $1, Map showing route of typhoon Pamela, Sept. 1961, horiz.

1962

Without Gum

1337 A177 80c brown .70 .20
1338 A178 $1 bluish black 1.40 .30
1339 A178 $2 green 1.90 .65
Nos. 1337-1339 (3) 4.00 1.15

Issue dates: 80c, $2, Mar. 23; $1, May 7.
World Meteorological Day, Mar. 23.

Child Receiving Milk, UN Emblem A179

1962, Apr. 4

Without Gum

1340 A179 80c rose red .85 .20
1341 A179 $3.20 green 1.75 .50
a. Souvenir sheet of 2 11.50 3.50

15th anniv. of UNICEF. No. 1341a contains one each of Nos. 1340-1341 imperf. with simulated perforations.

Malaria Eradication Emblem — A180

Unwmk.

1962, Apr. 7 Photo. ***Perf. 13***

1342 A180 80c dk bl, red & lt grn .60 .20
1343 A180 $3.60 brn, pink & grn 1.10 1.00

WHO drive to eradicate malaria.

Yu Yu-jen — A181

Cheng Ch'eng-kung (Koxinga) — A182

1962, Apr. 24 ***Perf. 13***

1344 A181 80c gray, blk & pink 1.60 .25

Issued to honor Yu Yu-jen, newspaper reporter, revolutionary leader and co-worker of Sun Yat-sen, on his 84th birthday.

1962, Apr. 29

1345 A182 80c deep claret 1.50 .20
1346 A182 $2 dark green 2.50 .55

300th anniversary (in 1961) of the recovery of Taiwan from the Dutch by Koxinga.

Emblem of Intl. Cooperative Alliance — A183

Clasped Hands Across Globe — A184

Wmk. 323

1962, July 7 Engr. ***Perf. 12***

Without Gum

1347 A183 80c brown .70 .20
1348 A184 $2 violet 1.10 .45

Intl. Cooperative Movement and 40th Intl. Cooperative Day, July 7, 1962.

Mansion Type of 1958

1962, July 20

Without Gum

1349 A135 $5 gray green 2.00 .20
1350 A135 $5.60 violet 2.75 .20
1351 A135 $6 orange 2.40 .20
Nos. 1349-1351 (3) 7.15 .60

1963

Granite Paper

1349a A135 $5 gray green 2.50 .20
1350a A135 $5.60 violet 3.00 .20
1351a A135 $6 orange 4.00 .20
Nos. 1349a-1351a (3) 9.50 .60

"Art and Science" — A185

$2, "Education," book and UNESCO emblem, horiz. $3.20, "Communications," globes, horiz.

1962, Aug. 28 Wmk. 323 ***Perf. 12***

Without Gum

1352 A185 80c lilac rose .60 .20
1353 A185 $2 rose claret .95 .40
1354 A185 $3.20 yellow green 1.10 .30
Nos. 1352-1354 (3) 2.65 .90

UNESCO activities in China.

Emperor T'ai Tsung, T'ang Dynasty, 627-649 A186

Emperors: $2, T'ai Tsu, Sung dynasty, 960-975. $3.20, T'ai Tsu, Yuan dynasty (Genghis Khan), 1206-27. $4, T'ai Tsu, Ming dynasty, 1368-98.

1962, Sept. 20 Photo. Unwmk.

1355 A186 80c multicolored 10.00 2.25
1356 A186 $2 multicolored 27.50 7.00
1357 A186 $3.20 multicolored 47.50 7.50
1358 A186 $4 multicolored 60.00 19.50
Nos. 1355-1358 (4) 145.00 36.25

Lions International Emblem A187

1962, Oct. 8 ***Perf. 13½***

1359 A187 80c multicolored 1.10 .20
1360 A187 $3.60 multicolored 2.10 .80
a. Souvenir sheet of 2 14.00 7.00

45th anniv. of Lions Intl. No. 1360a contains one each of Nos. 1359-1360, imperf. with simulated perforations.

Pole Vaulting — A188

Shooting A189

1962, Oct. 25 Unwmk. ***Perf. 13***

1361 A188 80c multicolored .90 .20
1362 A189 $3.20 multicolored 2.10 .40

Sports meet.

Young Farmers and 4-H Emblem — A190

Flag, Liner of China Merchants' Steam Navigation Co. — A191

Design: $3.20, 4-H emblem and rice.

Wmk. 323

1962, Dec. 7 Engr. ***Perf. 12***

Without Gum

1363 A190 80c carmine .60 .20
1364 A190 $3.20 green 1.90 .55
a. Souvenir sheet of 2 13.00 9.00

10th anniv. of the 4-H Club in China. No. 1364a contains one each of Nos. 1363-1364, imperf. with simulated perforations.

Perf. 13½

1962, Dec. 16 Unwmk. Photo.

Design: $3.60, Company's Pacific navigation chart and freighter, horiz.

1365	A191	80c	multicolored	1.60	.20
1366	A191	$3.60	multicolored	2.50	.80

90th anniversary of the China Merchants' Steam Navigation Co., Ltd.

Farm Woman, Tractor and Plane Dropping Food over Mainland — A192

Perf. 12½

1963, Mar. 21 Unwmk. Photo.

1367	A192	$10	multicolored	4.00	.70

FAO "Freedom from Hunger" campaign.

Torch, Young Couple and Martyrs' Monument, Canton A193

Wmk. 323

1963, Mar. 29 Engr. *Perf. 11½*

Without Gum

1368	A193	80c	purple	.75	.20
1369	A193	$3.20	green	1.50	.40

Issued for the 20th Youth Day.

Swallows, Pagoda and AOPU Emblem — A194

Designs: $2, Northern gannet, horiz. $6, Japanese crane and pine.

Unwmk.

1963, Apr. 1 Photo. *Perf. 13*

1370	A194	80c	multicolored	4.00	.55
1371	A194	$2	multicolored	5.50	.65
1372	A194	$6	multicolored	8.25	2.10
			Nos. 1370-1372 (3)	17.75	3.30

1st anniversary of the formation of the Asian-Oceanic Postal Union, AOPU.

Refugee Girl (Li Ying) and Map of China — A195

Refugees Fleeing Mainland A196

Wmk. 323

1963, June 27 Engr. *Perf. 11½*

Without Gum

1373	A195	80c	bluish black	1.00	.20
1374	A196	$3.20	dp claret	2.25	.30

1st anniv. of the evacuation of Chinese mainland refugees from Hong Kong to Taiwan. Designs from photographs of refugees.

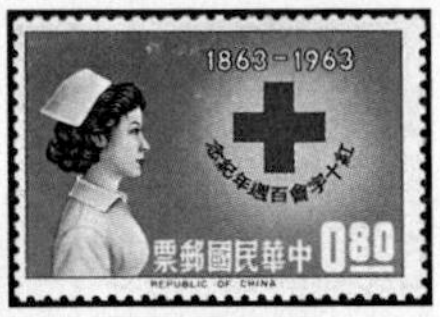

Nurse and Red Cross A197

Design: $10, Globe and Red Cross.

Perf. 12½

1963, Sept. 1 Unwmk. Photo.

1375	A197	80c	black & carmine	5.25	.25
1376	A197	$10	slate, gray & car	6.25	2.25

Centenary of International Red Cross.

Basketball Player, Stadium and Asian Cup — A198

$2, Hands reaching for ball and Asian cup.

Wmk. 323

1963, Nov. 20 Engr. *Perf. 12*

Without Gum

1377	A198	80c	lilac rose	.90	.20
1378	A198	$2	violet	1.75	.60

The 2nd Asian Basketball Championship, Taipei, Nov. 20.

UN Emblem, Torch and Men — A199

Scales and Men of Various Races A200

1963, Dec. 10 Wmk. 323 *Perf. 11½*

Without Gum

1379	A199	80c	brt green	.70	.30
1380	A200	$3.20	maroon	1.40	.65

Universal Declaration of Human Rights, 15th anniversary.

Village and Orchids A201

"Kindle the Fire of Conscience" A202

Perf. 13½x13

1963, Dec. 17 Photo. Unwmk.

1381	A201	40c	multicolored	2.50	.35
1382	A202	$4.50	multicolored	4.00	1.60

Contribution of the Good-People-Good-Deeds campaign to improve ethical standards.

Sun Yat-sen and Book, "Three Principles of the People" A203

1963, Dec. 25 *Perf. 13*

1383	A203	$5	blue & multi	6.75	1.00

"Land-to-the-Tillers" program, 10th anniv. An 80c was prepared but not issued.

Torch — A204

Hands Unchained — A205

Wmk. 323

1964, Jan. 23 Engr. *Perf. 11½*

Without Gum

1384	A204	80c	red orange	.60	.20
1385	A205	$3.20	indigo	1.90	.35

Liberty Day, 10th anniversary.

Broadleaf Cactus A206

Wu Chih-hwei A207

Designs: $1, Crab cactus. $3.20, Nopalxochia. $5, Grizzly bear cactus.

Perf. 12½

1964, Feb. 27 Unwmk. Photo.

Plants in Original Colors

1386	A206	80c	dp plum & fawn	2.50	.20
1387	A206	$1	dk blue & car	4.25	.90
1388	A206	$3.20	green	6.25	.20
1389	A206	$5	lilac & yellow	6.75	1.10
			Nos. 1386-1389 (4)	19.75	2.40

Wmk. 323

1964, Mar. 25 Engr. *Perf. 11½*

Without Gum

1390	A207	80c	black brown	1.40	.20

Centenary of the birth of Wu Chih-hwei (1865-1953), politician and leader of the Kuomintang.

Chu Kwang Tower, Quemoy — A208

Perf. 13x12½

1964-66 Wmk. 323 Litho.

Granite Paper; Without Gum

1391	A208	3c	sepia	.25	.20
1392	A208	5c	brt yel grn ('65)	.25	.20
1393	A208	10c	yellow grn	.25	.20
1394	A208	20c	slate grn ('65)	.25	.20
1395	A208	40c	rose red	.25	.20
1396	A208	50c	brown	.25	.20
1397	A208	80c	orange ('65)	.25	.20
1398	A208	$1	violet ('65)	.25	.20
1399	A208	$1.50	brt lilac ('66)	2.25	.25
1400	A208	$2	lilac rose	.25	.20
1401	A208	$2.50	ultra ('65)	2.25	.25
1402	A208	$3	slate	2.25	.30
1403	A208	$3.20	brt blue	4.00	.20
1404	A208	$4	brt green	4.50	.25
			Nos. 1391-1404 (14)	17.50	3.05

Nurses Holding Candles A209

Florence Nightingale and Student Nurse — A210

1964, May 12 Engr. *Perf. 11½*

Without Gum

1406	A209	80c	violet blue	1.40	.25
1407	A210	$4	red	2.25	.50

Issued for Nurses Day.

Shihmen Reservoir A211

Designs: $1, Irrigation system. $3.20, Main dam and power plant. $5, Spillway.

Perf. 12½

1964, June 14 Unwmk. Photo.

1408	A211	80c	multicolored	1.75	.25
1409	A211	$1	multicolored	2.25	.45
1410	A211	$3.20	multicolored	6.25	.55
1411	A211	$5	multicolored	7.00	1.40
			Nos. 1408-1411 (4)	17.25	2.65

Completion of Shihmen Reservoir.

15th Century Ship, Modern Liner — A212

Wmk. 323

1964, July 11 Engr. *Perf. 11½*

Without Gum

1412	A212	$2	orange	.80	.20
1413	A212	$3.60	brt green	1.25	.35

China's 10th Navigation Day.

Bananas A213

Unwmk.

1964, July 25 Photo. *Perf. 14*

1414	A213	80c	shown	*8.50*	.40
1415	A213	$1	Oranges	*15.00*	1.00
1416	A213	$3.20	Pineapple	*18.00*	1.00
1417	A213	$4	Watermelon	*27.50*	3.25
			Nos. 1414-1417 (4)	*69.00*	5.65

Artillery, Warships, Jet Fighters A214

Wmk. 323
1964, Sept. 3 Engr. *Perf. 11½*
Without Gum

1418 A214 80c dk blue 1.10 .20
1419 A214 $6 violet brown 2.75 .50

Issued for the 10th Armed Forces Day.

Unisphere, Flags of China and U.S. — A215

Chinese Pavilion, NY World's Fair — A216

1964, Sept. 10 Photo. Unwmk.

1420 A215 80c violet & multi 1.25 .25
1421 A216 $5 blue & multi 2.75 .90

NY World's Fair, 1964-65. See #1450-1451.

Cowboy Carrying Calf, and Ranch — A217

Bicycling — A218

Wmk. 323
1964, Sept. 24 Engr. *Perf. 11½*
Without Gum

1422 A217 $2 brown lake 1.10 .20
1423 A217 $4 dark violet blue 2.25 .80

Animal Protection Week, Sept. 24-30.

1964, Oct. 10 Without Gum

Sports: $1, Runner. $3.20, Gymnast on rings. $10, High jump.

1424 A218 80c violet blue .80 .20
1425 A218 $1 rose red 1.40 .20
1426 A218 $3.20 dull blue grn 1.75 .25
1427 A218 $10 lilac 3.00 1.50
Nos. 1424-1427 (4) 6.95 2.15

18th Olympic Games, Tokyo, Oct. 10-25.

Hsü Kuang-chi A219

Pharmaceutical Industry A220

Textile Industry A221

1964, Nov. 8 Engr. *Perf. 11½*
Without Gum

1428 A219 80c indigo 2.00 .20

Issued to honor Hsü Kuang-chi (1562-1633), scholar and statesman.

1964, Nov. 11 Photo. Unwmk.

$2, Chemical industry. $3.60, Cement industry.

1429 A220 40c multi 2.25 .20
1430 A221 $1.50 multi 3.00 .70
1431 A220 $2 multi 4.50 .50
1432 A221 $3.60 multi 5.25 1.10
Nos. 1429-1432 (4) 15.00 2.50

Dr. Sun Yat-sen — A222

Eleanor Roosevelt and Scales of Justice — A223

1964, Nov. 24 Engr. Wmk. 323
Without Gum

1433 A222 80c green 1.40 .30
1434 A222 $3.60 purple 3.75 .65

Founding of the Kuomintang by Sun Yat-sen, 70th anniversary.

Unwmk.
1964, Dec. 10 Photo. *Perf. 13*

1435 A223 $10 violet & brown 1.60 .40

Issued to honor Eleanor Roosevelt (1884-1962) on the 16th anniversary of the Universal Declaration of Human Rights.

Scales, Code Book and Plum Blossom A224

Rotary Emblem and Mainspring A225

Wmk. 323
1965, Jan. 11 Engr. *Perf. 11½*
Without Gum

1436 A224 80c carmine rose .45 .20
1437 A224 $3.20 dull slate grn .70 .40

The 20th Judicial Day.

1965, Feb. 23 Wmk. 323 *Perf. 11½*
Without Gum

1438 A225 $1.50 vermilion .60 .20
1439 A225 $2 emerald .70 .20
1440 A225 $2.50 blue .90 .30
Nos. 1438-1440 (3) 2.20 .70

Rotary International, 60th anniversary.

Double Carp Design A226

Madame Chiang Kai-shek A227

Wmk. 323
1965, Mar. 29 Engr. *Perf. 11½*
Granite Paper; Without Gum

1441 A226 $5 purple 9.00 .95
1442 A226 $5.60 dp blue 15.00 1.10
1443 A226 $6 brown 13.50 .95
1444 A226 $10 lilac rose 22.50 .95
1445 A226 $20 rose car 26.00 1.60
1446 A226 $50 green 30.00 3.50
1447 A226 $100 crim rose 37.50 5.75
Nos. 1441-1447 (7) 153.50 15.30

New dies used to reprint #1444-1447, 8/20/67. Remainders of #1441-1447 issued with gum, 11/1/71.

1965, Apr. 17 Photo. Unwmk.

1448 A227 $2 multicolored 12.50 .50
1449 A227 $6 salmon & multi 22.50 3.00

Chinese Women's Anti-Aggression League, 15th anniversary.

Unisphere and Chinese Pavilion — A228

"100 Birds Paying Homage to Queen Phoenix" and Unisphere — A229

1965, May 8

1450 A228 $2 blue & multi 12.00 1.25
1451 A229 $10 red, ocher & bis 14.00 2.00

New York World's Fair, 1964-65.

ITU Emblem, Old and New Communication Equipment A230

Design: $5, similar to 80c, vert.

Perf. 13½x13, 13x13½
1965, May 17 Photo. Unwmk.

1452 A230 80c multicolored .60 .20
1453 A230 $5 multicolored 1.75 .55

Centenary of the ITU.

Red Sea Bream A231

Fish: 80c, White pomfret. $2, Skipjack, vert. $4, Moonfish.

1965, July 1 *Perf. 13*

1454 A231 40c multicolored 1.60 .20
1455 A231 80c multicolored 2.50 .30
1456 A231 $2 multicolored 5.75 1.00
1457 A231 $4 multicolored 10.00 1.50
Nos. 1454-1457 (4) 19.85 3.00

Issued for Fishermen's Day.

Confucius A232

ICY Emblem A233

Portraits: $2.50, Yueh Fei. $3.50, Wen Tien-hsiang. $3.60, Mencius.

Wmk. 323
1965-66 Engr. *Perf. 11½*
Without Gum

1458 A232 $1 deep carmine 3.00 .35
1459 A232 $2.50 black brown 2.00 .35
1460 A232 $3.50 dark red 4.50 .50
1461 A232 $3.60 dark blue 5.25 .60
Nos. 1458-1461 (4) 14.75 1.80

The $2.50 and $3.50 have colored background.

Forgeries of #1461 exist.

Issued: #1458, 1461, 9/28/65; #1459-1460, 9/3/66.

See Nos. 1507-1508, design A251.

Unwmk.
1965, Oct. 24 Photo. *Perf. 13*

Design: $6, ICY emblem, horiz.

1462 A233 $2 brn, blk & gold 1.25 .20
1463 A233 $6 brt grn, red & gold 2.75 1.00

International Cooperation Year, 1965.

Street Crossing, Traffic Light A234

Sun Yat-sen A235

Wmk. 323
1965, Nov. 1 Engr. *Perf. 11½*
Without Gum

1464 A234 $1 brown violet 1.25 .25
1465 A234 $4 crimson rose 2.40 .80

Issued to publicize traffic safety.

Perf. 13½
1965, Nov. 12 Unwmk. Photo.

Designs: $4, Dr. Sun Yat-sen, portrait at right. $5, Sun Yat-sen and flags, horiz.

1466 A235 $1 multicolored 2.50 .20
1467 A235 $4 multicolored 7.75 .60
1468 A235 $5 multicolored 9.25 1.75
Nos. 1466-1468 (3) 19.50 2.55

Children with New Year's Firecrackers A236

Dragon Dance, "Dragon Playing Ball" A237

1965, Dec. 1 Photo. *Perf. 13*

1469 A236 $1 multi 3.50 .30
1470 A237 $4.50 multi 8.00 1.10

Lien Po from "Marshal and Prime Minister Reconciled" — A238

Facial Paintings for Chinese Operas: $3, Kuan Yü from "Reunion at Ku City." $4, Gen. Chang Fei from "The Battle of Chang Pan Hill." $6, Buddha from "The Flower-Scattering Angel."

1966, Feb. 15 Unwmk. *Perf. 11½*

1471 A238 $1 olive & multi 8.00 .50
1472 A238 $3 multicolored 13.50 1.00
1473 A238 $4 multicolored 24.00 1.50
1474 A238 $6 ver & multi 29.00 2.75
Nos. 1471-1474 (4) 74.50 5.75

Labels with a similar appearance to these stamps exist. These labels have the numbers 1 to 20 in the upper right corner, but lack the "00."

Red Cross Society, Cent. — A878

No. 3539: a, Heart, stylized people with arms raised. b, Heart, stylized people doing Red Cross activities.

Illustration reduced.

2004, Mar. 9 ***Perf. 11¼x11½***

3539 A878 $5 Horiz. pair, #a-b .75 .30

A Young Girl From Lu Kai, by Yan Shui-long A879

Old Street in Taipei, by Yang San-lang A880

Happy Farmers, by Lee Shih-chiao A881

Fish Shop, by Liu Chi-hsiang A882

Perf. 11¼x11½, 11½x11¼

2004, Mar. 25

3540	A879	$5 multi		.40	.20
3541	A880	$5 multi		.40	.20
3542	A881	$10 multi		.80	.30
3543	A882	$20 multi		1.40	.60
	Nos. 3540-3543 (4)			3.00	1.30

Butterflies A883

Designs: No. 3544, $5, Parantica sita niphonica. No. 3545, $5, Choaspes benjaminii formosanus. $17, Junonia almana. $20, Artipe eryx horiella.

2004, Apr. 21 ***Perf. 11½x11¼***

3544-3547 A883 Set of 4 3.50 1.50

Yijhen Folk Art Performers A884

Designs: No. 3548, $5, Eight Generals (buff background). No. 3549, $5, Song Jiang Battle Array (grayish blue background). $11, Drum Dance. $25, Stilt walkers.

2004, May 11

3548-3551 A884 Set of 4 3.25 1.40

Inauguration of Pres. Chen Shiu-bian and Vice-President Hsiu-lien Annette Lu — A885

No. 3552 — President, Vice-President and: a, Map of Taiwan, flag, crowd. b, Map of People's Republic of China and Taiwan, handshake, flowers. c, Buildings, crowd. d, Train, highway, buildings.

$12, President, Vice-President, buildings, train, highway.

2004, May 20 ***Perf. 12½***

3552 Horiz. strip of 4 1.50 .60

a.-d. A885 $5 Any single .35 .20

Souvenir Sheet

Perf. 12

3553 A885 $12 multi 1.00 .75

No. 3553 contains one 80x30mm stamp.

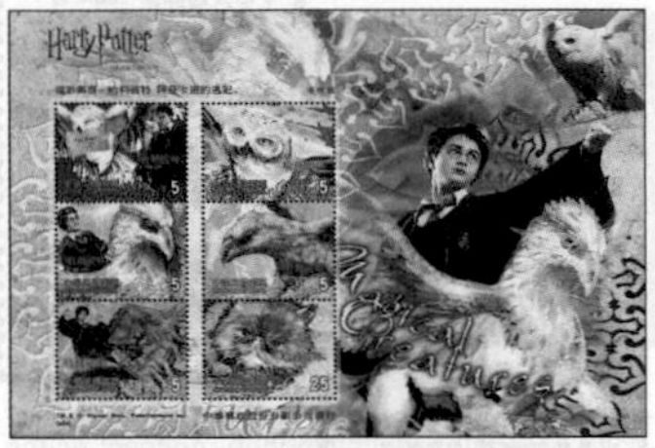

Opening of Movie, *Harry Potter and the Prisoner of Azkaban* — A886

No. 3554: a, $5, Harry, messenger owl, Hedwig, with letter. b, $5, Hedwig, rose background. c, $5, Harry riding Hippogriff. d, $5, Hippogriff, green background. e, $5, Harry, Monster Book of Monsters. f, $25, Crookshanks the Cat.

No. 3555: a, $5, Harry playing quidditch. b, $5, Harry playing quidditch, Dementors. c, $5, Harry and Hermoine riding Hippogriff. d, $5, Harry holding wand, Hogwarts. e, $5, Harry practicing Patronus Charm to repel Dementors. f, $25, Harry thrusting wand.

2004, June 4 ***Perf. 12***

Sheets of 6, #a-f

3554-3555 A886 Set of 2 8.00 5.00

Nos. 3554-3555 were not sold directly to customers at foreign addresses but were made available abroad through Canada Post's philatelic agency.

Old Train Stations A887

Designs: No. 3556, $5, Keelung Station, rickshaws. No. 3557, $5, Taipei Station, automobile. $15, Hsinchu Station, ox and cart. $25, Taichung Station, wagons.

2004, June 9 ***Perf. 13½x13¾***

3556-3559 A887 Set of 4 3.50 1.50

Compare Type A887 with Types A926-A929.

Iron Fort, Nangan Island A888

Cinbi, Beigan Island A889

Fujheng, Tungchu Island A890

Lienyuyikeng, Tungyin Island — A891

2004, July 1 **Litho.** ***Perf. 11½x11¼***

3560	A888	$5	multi	.40	.20
3561	A889	$5	multi	.40	.20
3562	A890	$9	multi	.65	.25
3563	A891	$25	multi	1.75	.75
	Nos. 3560-3563 (4)			3.20	1.40

Matsu National Scenic Area.

Crabs A892

Designs: No. 3564, $3.50, Uca formosensis. No. 3565, $3.50, Uca borealis. $5, Uca arcuata. $25, Uca lactea.

2004, July 21

3564-3567 A892 Set of 4 2.50 1.10

Souvenir Sheet

Listening to the Lute, Attributed to Li Sung — A893

No. 3568: a, $5, Lute player. b, $25, Scholar and woman.

2004, Aug. 6 ***Perf. 12***

3568 A893 Sheet of 2, #a-b 2.00 1.40

Souvenir Sheet

Taipei 2005 Intl. Stamp Exhibition — A894

No. 3569: a, $5, Sun Moon Lake. b, $25, Mt. Ali.

2004, Aug. 27 ***Perf. 11½x11¼***

3569 A894 Sheet of 2, #a-b 2.00 1.40

Intl. Day of Peace A895

2004, Sept. 21 ***Perf. 12¼x11¾***

3570 A895 $15 multi 1.00 .45

Souvenir Sheets

Hello Kitty — A896

No. 3571, oval stamps: a, $5, Dear Daniel, donuts. b, $15, Hello Kitty, Taipei 101 Building.

No. 3572, rectangular stamps: a, $5, Hello Kitty, bird, horiz. b, $15, Dear Daniel, Fisherman's Wharf, Danshuei.

2004, Sept. 24 ***Perf.***

3571 A896 Sheet of 2, #a-b 1.50 1.00

Perf. 12

3572 A896 Sheet of 2, #a-b 1.50 1.00

Sayings With Numbers Greeting Stamps

One Sea of Smooth Sailing A897

Two Lions Bring Good Fortune
A898

Three Goats of Auspiciousness — A899

Safety in All Four Seasons
A900

Five Blessings at the Door
A901

Six is Silky Smooth
A902

Married for Seven Lives
A903

Eight Immortals Wish for Your Perfection
A904

Nine Means Success
A905

Ten is All Around Perfection
A906

2004, Oct. 10 *Perf. 12½*

3573	Block of 10	2.10	1.10
a.	A897 $3.50 multi	.20	.20
b.	A898 $3.50 multi	.20	.20
c.	A899 $3.50 multi	.20	.20
d.	A900 $3.50 multi	.20	.20
e.	A901 $3.50 multi	.20	.20
f.	A902 $3.50 multi	.20	.20
g.	A903 $3.50 multi	.20	.20
h.	A904 $3.50 multi	.20	.20
i.	A905 $3.50 multi	.20	.20
j.	A906 $3.50 multi	.20	.20

Changed Colors

3574	Block of 10	3.00	1.50
a.	A897 $5 multi	.30	.20
b.	A898 $5 multi	.30	.20
c.	A899 $5 multi	.30	.20
d.	A900 $5 multi	.30	.20
e.	A901 $5 multi	.30	.20
f.	A902 $5 multi	.30	.20
g.	A903 $5 multi	.30	.20
h.	A904 $5 multi	.30	.20
i.	A905 $5 multi	.30	.20
j.	A906 $5 multi	.30	.20
k.	Sheet, #3574a-3574j + 10 attached labels ('04)	10.00	10.00

No. 3574k sold for $170 and has labels, which could be personalized, that are separated from the stamps by simulated perforations. Issued 10/10/04.

Kaohsiung Medical University. 50th Anniv.
A907

Designs: No. 3575, $5, University gate and buildings. No. 3576, $5, Building, researcher, beaker, mosquito and snake.

2004, Oct. 16 *Perf. 12½*

3575-3576	A907	Set of 2	.75	.30

Main Peak, Mt. Cilai
A908

North Peak, Mt. Cilai
A909

South Peak, Mt. Cilai
A910

Grasslands, Mt. Cilai — A911

2004, Oct. 16 *Perf. 11½x11¼*

3577	A908	$5 multi	.30	.20
3578	A909	$5 multi	.30	.20
3579	A910	$12 multi	.75	.35
3580	A911	$25 multi	1.50	.75
		Nos. 3577-3580 (4)	2.85	1.50

Sports In Which Taiwanese Athletes Won Medals At 2004 Summer Olympics
A912

Designs: No. 3581, $5, Women's Taekwondo. No. 3582, $5, Men's Taekwondo, vert. $9, Archery. $12, Athletes on winner's platform, vert.

Perf. 11¼x11½, 11½x11¼

2004, Oct. 22

3581-3584	A912	Set of 4	2.00	.95

Platalea Minor
A913

Designs: No. 3585, $2.50, Pair in flight. No. 3586, $2.50, Pair standing on one leg. $15, With wings spread. $25, Foraging for food. $20, Birds in water.

2004, Oct. 30 *Perf. 13½x13¼*

3585-3588	A913	Set of 4	3.00	1.40

Souvenir Sheet

3589	A913	$20 multi	1.50	1.00

No. 3589 contains one 80x30mm stamp.

Pres. Yen Chia-kan (1905-93)
A914

2004, Nov. 5 *Perf. 13¼x13½*

3590	A914	$12 multi	.80	.35

New Year 2005 (Year of the Cock) — A915

Designs: $3.50, Cock on lantern. $13, Lanterns, cock
$5, Cock, hen and chick, horiz.

2004, Nov. 10 *Perf. 12¼x11¾*

3591-3592	A915	Set of 2	1.00	.50

Souvenir Sheet

Perf. 11¾x11¼

3593	A915	$5 multi	.50	.35

No. 3593 contains one 46x26mm stamp.

Prefectural Hall, Chiayi
A916

East Gate, Chiayi
A917

2004, Nov. 20 *Perf. 13½x13¼*

3594	A916	$5 multi	.30	.20
3595	A917	$5 multi	.30	.20

Chiayi, 300th anniv.

Embroidered Squares for Ching Dynasty Civil Official Court Dresses — A918

Designs: No. 3596, $3.50, Manchurian crane (orange background). No. 3597, $3.50, Golden pheasant (green background). $5, Peacock. $25, Goose.

2005, Jan. 20 Litho. *Perf. 11½x11¼*

3596-3599	A918	Set of 4	2.40	1.25

See Nos. 3727-3730.

Greetings
A919

No. 3600 — Cartoon balloon with various keyboard characters creating faces and backgrounds with: a, Hands. b, Envelopes. c, Hearts. d, Flowers.

2005, Jan. 31 *Perf. 12½*

3600	Horiz. strip of 4	1.25	.65
a.-d.	A919 $5 Any single	.30	.20
e.	Sheet, #3600a-3600d + 4 attached labels	9.00	9.00

No. 3600e sold for $140 and has labels, which could be personalized, that are separated from the stamps by simulated perforations. Sheets exist with various arrangements of stamps and positions of labels respective to the stamps (at left, above or below).

Rotary International, Cent. — A920

Rotary emblem and: $5, Map of Taiwan. $12, Dove.

2005, Feb. 23 *Perf. 13½x13¼*

3601-3602	A920	Set of 2	1.10	.55

Mangroves
A921

Designs: No. 3603, $3.50, Kandelia obovata. No. 3604, $3.50, Rhizophora stylosa. No. 3605, $5, Avicennia marina. No. 3606, $5, Lumnitzera racemosa.

2005, Mar. 10 *Perf. 11½x11¼*

3603-3606	A921	Set of 4	1.10	.55

Longshan Temple, Mengjia
A922

Lin Ben Yuan Garden, Banciao
A923

Designs: $13, Chaotain Temple, Beigang. $15, Fort Anping, Tainan.

2005, Mar. 18

3607	A922	$5 multi	.35	.20
3608	A923	$5 multi	.35	.20
3609	A923	$13 multi	.85	.40
3610	A923	$15 multi	.95	.45
		Nos. 3607-3610 (4)	2.50	1.25

Souvenir Sheet

Taipei 2005 Intl. Stamp Exhibition — A924

No. 3611: a, $5, Wood carving, Mandarin Ducks Playing in a Lotus Pond. b, $25, Hand puppets, horiz.

2005, Apr. 19 ***Perf. 12***

3611	A924	Sheet of 2, #a-b	2.00	1.00

Coral Reef Fish
A925

Designs: No. 3612, $5, Rhinomuraena quaesita. No. 3613, $5, Pomacanthus semicirculatus. $12, Forcipiger flavissimus. $25, Pterois volitans.

2005, May 16 ***Perf. 11½x12***

3612-3615	A925	Set of 4	3.00	1.50
a.		Sheet, 2 each #3612-3615	6.00	6.00

Changhua Train Station, 1918
A926

Chiayi Train Station, 1933
A927

Tainan Train Station, 1936
A928

Kaohsiung Train Station, 1941
A929

2005, June 9 ***Perf. 13½x13¾***

3616	A926	$5 multi	.35	.20
3617	A927	$5 multi	.35	.20
3618	A928	$15 multi	.95	.50
3619	A929	$25 multi	1.60	.80
		Nos. 3616-3619 (4)	3.25	1.70

Compare with type A887.

Novel "The Romance of the Three Kingdoms"
A930

Designs: No. 3620, $3.50, Mayhem in the Fengyi Pavilion (man and woman near pavilion railing). No. 3621, $3.50, Deterring the Enemy in Changban (horse and rider on bridge). $5, Releasing Tsao Tsao (rider on horse near flag). $20, A Trick in the Bag (man in bed holding bag).

Perf. 11½x11¼

2005, June 23 **Litho.**

3620-3623	A930	Set of 4	2.10	1.10
3623a		Souvenir sheet, #3620-3623	2.10	1.10

Lifeline Suicide Prevention Hotline — A931

2005, July 1 ***Perf. 12x11½***

3624	A931	$12 multi	.75	.40

Albert Einstein's Theory of Relativity, Cent. — A932

2005, July 1

3625	A932	$15 multi	.95	.45

Souvenir Sheets

Mickey Mouse — A933

No. 3626: a, $5, At ship's wheel, in *Steamboat Willie.* b, $25. As wizard, in *Fantasia.*

No. 3627: a, $5, Holding sword, in *The Prince and the Pauper.* b, $25. With Pluto, in *Mickey's Twice Upon a Christmas.*

2005, Aug. 3 ***Perf. 12***

Sheets of 2, #a-b

3626-3627	A933	Set of 2	3.75	1.90

Rooster-shaped Wine Vessel — A934

2005, Aug. 19 ***Perf. 11¼x11½***

3628	A934	$15 multi	.95	.45
a.		Sheet of 6, perf. 12	5.75	3.00

Taipei 2005 Intl. Stamp Exhibition.

Souvenir Sheets

A935

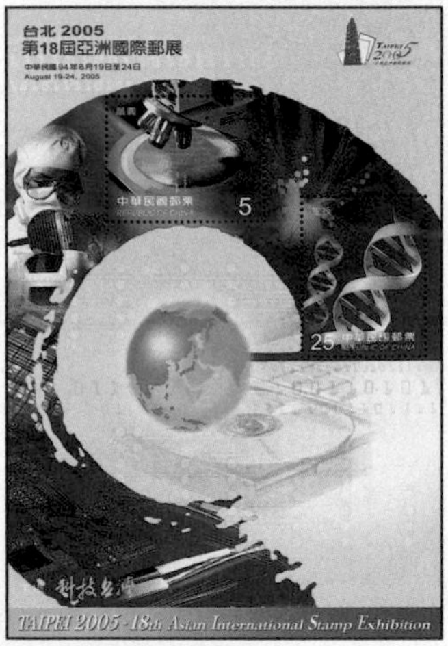

A936

A937

A938

A939

Taipei 2005 Intl. Stamp Exhibition — A940

No. 3629: a, $5, Green Island and shoreline. b, $25, Formosan rock monkey.
No. 3630: a, $5, Microscope. b, $25, DNA double helices, vert.
No. 3631: a, $5, Flowers. $25, Fruit.
No. 3632: a, $5, Ear Shooting Ceremony, vert. b, $25, Dragon boat in race.
No. 3633: a, $5, Bowl of food and ladle. b, $25, Rice cakes.
No. 3634: a, $5, Royal empress angelfish. b, $25, Red horny coral.

2005 ***Perf.***
3629 A935 Sheet of 2, #a-b 1.90 .95

Perf. 13½x13, 13x13½
3630 A936 Sheet of 2, #a-b 1.90 .95

Perf. 13½
3631 A937 Sheet of 2, #a-b 1.90 .95

Perf. 13¼x13½, 13½x13¼
3632 A938 Sheet of 2, #a-b 1.90 .95

Perf. 12
3633 A939 Sheet of 2, #a-b 1.90 .95

Perf.
3634 A940 Sheet of 2, #a-b 1.90 .95
Nos. 3629-3634 (6) 11.40 5.70

Issued: No. 3629, 8/19; No. 3630, 8/20; No. 3631, 8/21; No. 3632, 8/22; No. 3633, 8/23; No. 3634, 8/24. No. 3629 contains two 38mm diameter stamps. No. 3634 contains two 43x33mm oval stamps.

Novel, "Journey to the West" — A941

Designs: No. 3635, $3.50, Stone Monkey (monkeys at waterfall). No. 3636, $3.50, Buddhist Baby in the River. $5, Making a Pass at Chang E. $20, Taming the Monster of the River of Flowing Sands.

2005, Sept. 15 ***Perf. 11¼x11½***
3635-3638 A941 Set of 4 2.00 1.00

Souvenir Sheet

Kaohsiung 2005 Intl. Stamp Exhibition — A942

No. 3639: a, $5, Loyalty and Filial Piety, by Cian Syuan, vert. b, Gilt scepter.

Perf. 13¼x13½, 13½x13¼
2005, Oct. 7
3639 A942 Sheet of 2, #a-b 1.90 .95

Souvenir Sheets

A943

Opening of Movie, *Harry Potter and the Goblet of Fire* — A944

No. 3640: a, $5, Triwizard Cup. b, $5, Harry and Hungarian Horntail. c, $5, Golden Egg. d, $5, Harry swimming. e, $5, Harry summoning Firebolt with wand. f, $25, Harry and Triwizard Cup.
No. 3641: a, $5, Hungarian Horntail. b, $5, Harry on Firebolt. c, $5, Voldemort's snake, Nagini. d, $5, Grindylows. e, $5, Dumbledore's phoenix, Fawkes. f, $25, Merchieftainess.

2005, Nov. 18 ***Perf. 12***
3640 A943 Sheet of 6, #a-f 3.00 1.50
3641 A944 Sheet of 6, #a-f 3.00 1.50

New Year 2006 (Year of the Dog) — A945

Designs: $3.50, Dog at left. $13, Dog at lower right.
$12, Three dogs, horiz.

2005, Dec. 1 ***Perf. 12¼x11¾***
3642-3643 A945 Set of 2 1.00 .50

Souvenir Sheet

Perf. 11¾x11¼
3644 A945 $12 multi .80 .40

No. 3644 contains one 46x26mm stamp.

Pets — A946

Designs: $3.50, Siberian husky. $5, Golden retriever. $12, Himalayan cat. $25, Scottish fold cat.

Perf. 13½x12½
2005, Dec. 22 **Litho.**

Country Name in Green

3645 A946 $3.50 multi .25 .20
3646 A946 $5 multi .30 .20
3647 A946 $12 multi .75 .35
3648 A946 $25 multi 1.50 .75
Nos. 3645-3648 (4) 2.80 1.50

See Nos. 3652-3655, 3685-3688.

Tea Ceremony A947

No. 3649: a, Preparation of tea set (dull orange panel). b, Placing of tea leaves in pot (lemon panel). c, Pouring hot water over pots and cups (light green panel). d, Drying of pot and pouring of tea (blue geen panel). e, Smelling and drinking of tea (gray blue panel).

2006, Jan. 26 ***Perf. 13½***
3649 Horiz. strip of 5 1.60 .80
a.-e. A947 $5 Any single .30 .20

Taipei 101 Building — A948

Designs: $5, In day. $12, At night.

2006, Mar. 23 ***Perf. 12***
3650-3651 A948 Set of 2 1.10 .55

Pets Type of 2005

Designs: $2.50, Labrador retriever. $7, St. Bernard. $10, Siamese cat. $32, Persian cat.

2006, Mar. 8 ***Perf. 13½x12½***

Country Name in Blue

3652 A946 $2.50 multi .20 .20
3653 A946 $7 multi .45 .20
3654 A946 $10 multi .60 .30
3655 A946 $32 multi 2.00 1.00
Nos. 3652-3655 (4) 3.25 1.70

See Nos. 3712-3715.

King Penguins A949

Aptenodytes patagonicus: No. 3656, $5, Adult and juvenile. No. 3657, $5, Courtship. $9, Swimming and diving, horiz. $12, Gliding and preening, horiz.
$15, Colony, horiz.

Perf. 11¼x11½, 11½x11¼
2006, Mar. 26
3656-3659 A949 Set of 4 1.90 .95

Souvenir Sheet

Perf. 12
3660 A949 $15 multi .95 .45

No. 3660 contains one 80x30mm stamp.

Miniature Sheet

Children's Art — A950

No. 3661 — Winning drawings in children's stamp design competition: a, Birds with black bills. b, People with red faces. c, Pheasants. d, Chinese celebration. e, Fishing boats and catch. f, People with large flowers and fruit. g, Man painting Chinese lantern. h, Bridge and ducks. i, Train. j, Bees and flowers. k, People with black faces. l, Boy on ladder. m, People and chickens. n, Ring of people around dancers and musicians. o, People and large lions. p, Two cats. q, People and cow. r, Whale and fish. s, People with white faces bending backwards. t, Bus.

2006, Apr. 4 ***Perf. 11½***
3661 A950 $5 Sheet of 20, #a-t 6.25 3.25

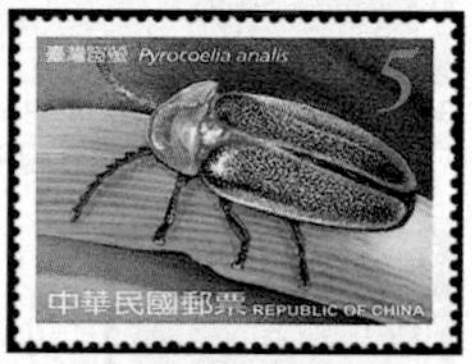

Fireflies A951

Designs: No. 3662, $5, Pyrocoelia analis. No. 3663, $5, Diaphanes citrinus. No. 3664, $5, Diaphanes niveus. No. 3665, $5, Diaphanes formosus.

2006, May 25 ***Perf. 13½x13¼***
3662-3665 A951 Set of 4 1.25 .60

Souvenir Sheet

Completion of Nangang to Suao Section of National Expressway 5 — A952

2006, June 16 **Litho.** ***Perf. 11½***
3666 A952 $12 multi .75 .35

Souvenir Sheets

Winnie the Pooh — A953

No. 3667: a, $5, Winnie the Pooh pushing Piglet in wheelbarrow. b, $25, Winnie the Pooh, Piglet and Tigger floating in inner tube.
No. 3668: a, $5, Winnie the Pooh and Piglet running in autumn. b, $25, Winnie the Pooh and Tigger ice fishing.

2006, June 21 ***Perf. 12***

Sheets of 2, #a-b

3667-3668 A953 Set of 2 3.75 1.90

London Print Issue of China, 1931-37, Overprinted

1932-34 Unwmk. Perf. 12½

Type I (double circle)

29	A37	1c orange	2.50	1.75
30	A37	2c olive grn	3.00	3.50
31	A37	4c green	2.00	3.50
32	A37	20c ultra	2.00	2.00
33	A37	$1 org brn & dk brn	30.00	35.00
34	A37	$2 bl & org brn	50.00	55.00
35	A37	$5 dl red & blk	150.00	190.00
		Nos. 29-35 (7)	239.50	290.75

Type II (single circle)

36	A37	2c olive grn	17.00	17.00
37	A37	4c green	11.00	7.00
38	A37	5c green	10.00	6.75
39	A37	15c dk green	5.25	5.75
40	A37	15c scar ('34)	5.25	6.50
41	A37	25c ultra	7.00	7.50
42	A37	$1 org brn & dk brn	45.00	45.00
43	A37	$2 bl & org brn	77.50	77.50
44	A37	$5 dl red & blk	175.00	175.00
		Nos. 36-44 (9)	353.00	348.00

Nos. 36-39, 41-44 were overprinted in London as well as in Peking. The London overprints are 11mm in length; the Peking overprints are 12mm in length. There are other minor differences. Value of London overprints is significantly more than the Peking overprints, which are valued above.

Tan Yuan-chang Issue of China, 1933, Overprinted

1933 Perf. 14

45	A49	2c olive green	1.10	1.10
46	A49	5c green	1.90	1.50
47	A49	25c ultra	3.25	3.50
48	A49	$1 red	50.00	40.00
		Nos. 45-48 (4)	56.25	46.10

Martyrs Issue of China, 1932-34, Overprinted

1933

49	A39	½c blk brown	1.00	.90
50	A40	1c orange	2.00	1.50
51	A39	2½c rose lilac	2.25	2.50
52	A48	3c deep brown	3.50	1.25
53	A45	8c brown org	1.50	1.50
54	A46	10c dull vio	2.25	2.50
55	A45	13c blue grn	1.40	.60
56	A46	17c brn olive	7.00	7.00
57	A47	20c brown red	1.75	1.75
58	A48	30c brown vio	5.50	5.50
59	A47	40c orange	26.00	26.00
60	A40	50c green	26.00	26.00
		Nos. 49-60 (12)	80.15	77.00

China No. 324 was overprinted with characters arranged vertically, like Sinkiang No. 114, but was not issued.

China Stamps of 1945-49 Surcharged in Black or Blue

Engraved; Lithographed; Typographed

1949 Perf. 12, 12½, 14

61	A82	1c on $200,000 brn vio	12.50	12.50
62	A82	1.2c on $40,000 grn	12.50	14.00
63	A94	6c on $200 red org	12.50	12.50
64	A94	10c on $20,000 org	12.50	14.00
65	A94	12c on $50 dk Prus grn (Bl)	12.50	12.50
66	A72	12c on $50 grnsh gray (Bl)	12.50	12.50
67	A72	12c on $200 brn vio (Bl)	12.50	14.00
68	A94	30c on $20 vio brn	12.50	12.50
69	A82	$1.20 on $100,000 dl grn	20.00	22.50
		Nos. 61-69 (9)	120.00	127.00

China No. 888 and 630 Surcharged

1949 Engr. Perf. 14

70	A94	4c on $20 vio brn	225.00

Typo. Perf. 12

71	A72	12c on $200 brn vio	225.00

Manchuria

Kirin and Heilungkiang Issue

Stamps of China, 1923-26, Overprinted

The overprint reads: "For use in Ki-Hei District" the two names being abbreviated.

The intention of the overprint was to prevent the purchase of stamps in Manchuria, where the currency was depreciated, and their resale elsewhere.

1927 Unwmk. Perf. 14

1	A29	½c black brn	1.10	.20
2	A29	1c orange	1.10	.20
3	A29	1½c violet	1.50	1.10
4	A29	2c yellow grn	1.50	.20
5	A29	3c blue grn	1.00	.45
6	A29	4c olive grn	.50	.20
7	A29	5c claret	1.00	.20
8	A29	6c red	1.50	1.10
9	A29	7c violet	3.00	1.10
10	A29	8c brown org	2.00	1.10
11	A29	10c dk blue	1.10	.30
12	A30	13c brown	2.25	1.75
13	A30	15c dk blue	2.25	1.75
14	A30	16c olive grn	2.25	1.60
15	A30	20c brown red	3.50	1.90
16	A30	30c brown vio	5.00	2.00
17	A30	50c dp green	7.00	2.40
18	A31	$1 org brn & sep	15.00	5.00
19	A31	$2 bl & red brn	40.00	11.00
20	A31	$5 red & slate	190.00	190.00
		Nos. 1-20 (20)	282.55	223.55

Several values of this issue exist with inverted overprint, double overprint and in pairs with one overprint omitted. These "errors" were not regularly issued. Forgeries also exist.

Chang Tso-lin Stamps of 1928 Overprinted in Red or Blue

1928 Perf. 14

21	A34	1c brown org (R)	1.75	1.10
22	A34	4c olive grn (R)	1.10	1.10
23	A34	10c dull blue (R)	3.00	2.25
24	A34	$1 red (Bl)	30.00	27.50
		Nos. 21-24 (4)	35.85	31.95

Unification Issue of China, 1929, Overprinted in Red as in 1928

1929

25	A35	1c brown orange	1.25	1.25
26	A35	4c olive green	2.25	2.00
27	A35	10c dark blue	8.00	7.50
28	A35	$1 dark red	65.00	60.00
		Nos. 25-28 (4)	76.50	70.75

Similar Overprint in Black on Sun Yat-sen Mausoleum Issue of China Characters 15-16mm apart

1929 Perf. 14

29	A36	1c brown orange	1.40	1.60
30	A36	4c olive green	1.75	1.90
31	A36	10c dark blue	5.25	3.25
32	A36	$1 dark red	52.50	40.00
		Nos. 29-32 (4)	60.90	46.75

Sinkiang

Stamps of China, 1913-19, Overprinted in Black or Red

The first character of overprint is ½mm out of alignment, to the left, and the overprint measures 16mm.

1915 Unwmk. Perf. 14

1	A24	½c black brn	1.10	.60
2	A24	1c orange	1.10	.45
3	A24	2c yellow grn	1.50	.80
4	A24	3c slate grn	1.50	.40
5	A24	4c scarlet	3.00	.70
6	A24	5c rose lilac	2.25	.60
7	A24	6c gray	4.00	1.75
8	A24	7c violet	4.00	5.25
9	A24	8c brown orange	3.50	3.50
10	A24	10c dark blue	3.50	1.75
11	A25	15c brown	4.00	2.25
12	A25	16c olive grn	8.00	5.75
13	A25	20c brown red	8.00	4.50
14	A25	30c brown violet	9.00	7.00
15	A25	50c deep green	25.00	11.50
16	A26	$1 ocher & blk (R)	90.00	40.00
a.		Second & third characters of overprint transposed	16,000.	
		Nos. 1-16 (16)	169.45	86.80

Stamps of China, 1913-19, Overprinted in Black or Red

The five characters of overprint are correctly aligned and measure 15½mm.

1916-19

17	A24	½c black brn	1.25	1.50
18	A24	1c orange	2.00	1.10
19	A24	1½c violet	2.75	2.50
20	A24	2c yellow grn	2.00	1.10
21	A24	3c slate grn	3.50	.45
22	A24	4c scarlet	3.50	.75
23	A24	5c rose lilac	3.50	.55
24	A24	6c gray	5.00	.75
25	A24	7c violet	5.00	7.00
26	A24	8c brown org	5.50	5.25
27	A24	10c dark blue	5.50	.75
28	A25	13c brown	3.00	5.00
29	A25	15c brown	3.75	5.25
30	A25	16c olive grn	3.50	2.50
31	A25	20c brown red	2.75	1.90
32	A25	30c brown vio	4.25	3.75
33	A25	50c deep green	5.75	3.50
34	A26	$1 ocher & blk (R)	18.00	6.75
35	A26	$2 dk bl & blk (R)	17.50	7.50
36	A26	$5 scar & blk (R)	67.50	24.00
37	A26	$10 yel grn & blk (R)	175.00	110.00
38	A26	$20 yel & blk (R)	900.00	550.00
		Nos. 17-38 (22)	1,240.	741.85

For overprint see No. C4.

China Nos. 243-246 Overprinted

1921 Perf. 14

39	A27	1c orange	1.10	1.10
40	A27	3c blue green	2.25	2.25
41	A27	6c gray	8.50	6.00
42	A27	10c blue	50.00	50.00
		Nos. 39-42 (4)	61.85	59.35

Constitution Issue of China, 1923, Overprinted

1923

43	A32	1c orange	3.75	3.75
44	A32	3c blue green	4.25	4.25
45	A32	4c red	6.25	6.25
46	A32	10c blue	17.50	17.50
		Nos. 43-46 (4)	31.75	31.75

Stamps of China, 1923-26, Overprinted as in 1916-19, in Black or Red

1924 Re-engraved

47	A29	½c black brn	.90	1.75
48	A29	1c orange	.90	.70
49	A29	1½c violet	1.60	3.00
50	A29	2c yellow grn	2.50	.85
51	A29	3c blue grn	2.50	.75
52	A29	4c gray	2.50	4.00
53	A29	5c claret	.85	.60
54	A29	6c red	4.50	1.60
55	A29	7c violet	5.00	4.50
56	A29	8c org brn	10.00	9.00
57	A29	10c dark blue	4.00	1.10
58	A30	13c red brown	3.50	5.00
59	A30	15c deep blue	5.25	4.00
60	A30	16c olive grn	6.00	5.75
61	A30	20c brown red	5.00	3.75
62	A30	30c brown vio	5.75	4.00
63	A30	50c deep green	6.00	4.00
64	A31	$1 org brn & sep (R)	10.50	5.00
65	A31	$2 bl & red brn (R)	22.50	7.25
66	A31	$5 red & slate (R)	57.50	19.00
67	A31	$10 grn & claret (R)	175.00	100.00
68	A31	$20 plum & bl (R)	250.00	190.00
		Nos. 47-68 (22)	582.25	375.60

See #69, 114. For overprints see #C1-C3.

Same Overprint on China No. 275

1926

69	A29	4c olive green	2.50	2.50

Chang Tso-lin Stamps of China, 1928, Overprinted in Red or Blue

1928 Perf. 14

70	A34	1c brn org (R)	1.10	1.10
71	A34	4c ol grn (R)	1.75	1.75
72	A34	10c dull bl (R)	4.00	4.00
73	A34	$1 red (Bl)	35.00	30.00
		Nos. 70-73 (4)	41.85	36.85

Unification Issue of China, 1929, Overprinted in Red as in 1928

1929

74	A35	1c brown org	1.75	1.75
75	A35	4c olive grn	3.00	3.00
76	A35	10c dk blue	7.00	7.00
77	A35	$1 dk red	55.00	45.00
		Nos. 74-77 (4)	66.75	56.75

Similar Overprint in Black on Sun Yat-sen Mausoleum Issue of China Characters 15mm apart

1929 Perf. 14

78	A36	1c brown org	1.10	1.10
79	A36	4c olive grn	1.65	1.75
80	A36	10c dark blue	3.75	4.00
81	A36	$1 dark red	47.50	37.50
		Nos. 78-81 (4)	54.00	44.35

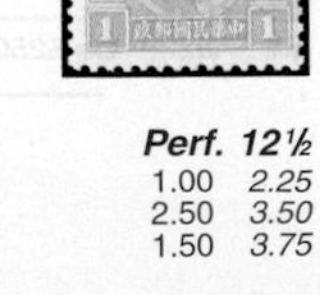

Stamps of Sun Yat-sen Issue of 1931-37 Overprinted

1932 Type I Perf. 12½

82	A37	1c orange	1.00	2.25
83	A37	2c olive grn	2.50	3.50
84	A37	4c green	1.50	3.75

85	A37	20c ultra	2.25	*4.75*
86	A37	$1 org brn & dk brn	7.00	*11.50*
87	A37	$2 bl & org brn	20.00	*24.00*
88	A37	$5 dl red & blk	22.50	*35.00*
		Nos. 82-88 (7)	56.75	*84.75*

No. 83 was overprinted in Shanghai in 1938. The overprint differs in minor details.

1932-38

Type II

89	A37	2c olive grn	.25	*1.10*
90	A37	4c green	.70	*2.25*
91	A37	5c green	.45	*2.25*
92	A37	15c dk green	.60	*2.25*
93	A37	15c scar ('34)	.60	*2.25*
93A	A37	20c ultra ('38)	.45	*1.50*
94	A37	25c ultra	.70	*2.25*
95	A37	$1 org brn & dk brn	5.25	*6.00*
96	A37	$2 bl & org brn	11.00	*17.50*
97	A37	$5 dl red & blk	22.50	*35.00*
		Nos. 89-97 (10)	42.50	*72.35*

Nos. 89, 90 and 94 were overprinted in London, Peking and Shanghai. Nos. 92, 95-97 exist with London and Peking overprints. Nos. 91 and 93 exist with Peking and Shanghai overprints. No. 93A is a Shanghai overprint. The overprints differ in minor details.

Tan Yuan-chang Issue of China, 1933, Overprinted as in 1928

1933 ***Perf. 14***

98	A49	2c olive grn	2.40	2.40
99	A49	5c green	3.00	3.00
100	A49	25c ultra	9.50	9.50
101	A49	$1 red	47.50	40.00
		Nos. 98-101 (4)	62.40	54.90

Stamps of China Martyrs Issue of 1932-34 Overprinted

1933-34

102	A39	½c black brown	.20	*1.25*
103	A40	1c orange	1.10	*1.50*
104	A39	2½c rose lilac	.25	*1.10*
105	A48	3c deep brown	.25	*1.10*
106	A45	8c brown orange	.75	*1.25*
107	A46	10c dull violet	.25	*1.10*
108	A45	13c blue green	.25	*1.60*
109	A46	17c brown olive	.25	*.90*
110	A47	20c brown red	1.10	*2.25*
111	A48	30c brown violet	.40	*1.60*
112	A47	40c orange	.60	*1.10*
113	A40	50c green	.70	*2.25*
		Nos. 102-113 (12)	6.10	*17.00*

Nos. 102-113 were originally overprinted in Peking. In 1938, Nos. 103-105, 108-112 were overprinted in Shanghai. The two overprints differ in minor details. No. 105, Shanghai overprint, is scarce. Value $35.

China No. 324 Overprinted as in 1916-19

1936 ***Perf. 14***

114	A29	6c brown	11.50	*12.00*

Stamps of China, 1939-40 Overprinted in Black

1940-45 **Unwmk.** ***Perf. 12½***

Type III

115	A57	2c olive green	.85	*1.00*
116	A57	3c dull claret ('41)	.20	*1.50*
117	A57	5c green	.20	*1.50*
118	A57	5c olive green	.20	*1.50*
119	A57	8c olive green ('41)	.20	*.75*
120	A57	10c green ('41)	.20	*1.10*
121	A57	15c scarlet	.55	*2.50*
122	A57	16c olive gray ('41)	.40	*1.00*
123	A57	25c dark blue	.55	*2.75*
124	A57	$1 hn & dk brn (type II)	6.25	*11.00*
125	A57	$2 dp bl & org brn (type I)	4.50	*11.00*
126	A57	$5 red & grnsh blk	26.00	*32.50*
		Nos. 115-126 (12)	40.10	*68.10*

Perf. 14

With Secret Marks

127	A57	8c ol grn (#383a)	1.10	*1.65*
a.		On #383	19.00	*22.50*
128	A57	10c green ('41)	10.00	*13.00*
129	A57	30c scarlet ('45)	.30	*1.10*
130	A57	50c dk blue ('45)	.55	*1.75*
131	A57	$1 org brn & sep	.55	*2.25*
132	A57	$2 dp bl & org brn	.55	*2.25*
133	A57	$5 red & sl grn	.65	*3.75*
134	A57	$10 dk grn & dl pur	1.90	*2.75*
135	A57	$20 rose lake & dk bl	3.50	*5.50*
		Nos. 127-135 (9)	19.10	*34.00*

Wmk. Character Yu (Post) (261)

Perf. 14

136	A57	5c olive green	.20	*1.10*
137	A57	10c green	.25	*1.75*
138	A57	30c scarlet	.25	*2.25*
139	A57	50c dark blue	.30	*1.10*
		Nos. 136-139 (4)	1.00	*6.20*

Martyrs Issue, 1940-41, Overprinted in Black

Perf. 12, 12½, 13, 13x12, 13½x13

1941-45 **Wmk. 261**

140	A40	1c orange	.20	*.65*
141	A39	2½c rose lilac	.20	*1.25*
142	A45	8c dp org ('45)	3.25	3.25
143	A46	10c dull vio	.25	*.85*
144	A45	13c dp yel grn	.55	*1.50*
145	A46	17c brown olive	.55	*1.40*
146	A40	25c red vio ('45)	1.10	*2.00*
147	A47	40c orange ('45)	1.90	*2.50*
		Nos. 140-147 (8)	8.00	*13.40*

Unwmk.

148	A39	½c olive blk	.20	*.85*
149	A40	1c orange ('45)	.20	*.65*
150	A46	2c dp blue ('45)	1.75	1.00
151	A48	3c dp yel brn	.20	*1.25*
152	A39	4c pale vio ('45)	.20	*1.25*
153	A45	8c dp orange	.20	*1.50*
154	A45	13c dp yel grn ('45)	.35	*1.10*
155	A48	15c brn car ('45)	.20	*1.10*
156	A46	17c brn ol ('45)	.55	*1.25*
157	A47	20c lt blue ('45)	.20	*.90*
158	A45	21c ol brn ('45)	.65	*1.25*
159	A46	28c olive ('45)	.80	*1.50*
160	A47	40c orange ('45)	1.65	*3.75*
161	A40	50c green ('45)	1.10	*1.90*
		Nos. 148-161 (14)	8.25	*19.25*

Stamps of China, 1942-43 Overprinted in Carmine, Black or Red

1944 ***Perf. 12½, 13***

Without Gum

162	A62	10c dp grn (C)	1.10	*2.75*
163	A62	20c dk ol grn (C)	1.25	*2.75*
164	A62	25c violet brn	.20	*3.00*
165	A62	30c dk orange	.60	*3.25*
166	A62	40c red brown	.20	*3.00*
167	A62	50c sage green	.20	*1.75*
a.		Perf. 11	10.00	8.50
168	A62	$1 rose lake	2.25	1.75
169	A62	$1 dull green	.20	*3.00*
170	A62	$1.50 dp bl (C)	.20	*3.25*
171	A62	$2 dk bl grn (R)	1.50	*2.50*
172	A62	$3 yellow	.20	*4.25*
173	A62	$5 cerise	1.50	*4.00*
		Nos. 162-173 (12)	9.40	*35.25*

For surcharges see Nos. 194-195.

Same Overprint on Stamps of China, 1942-43, in Black

1944-46 ***Imperf.***

174	A57	$10 red brown	50.00	*67.50*
175	A57	$20 rose red	1.90	*7.25*
176	A57	$30 dull vio	1.25	*7.25*
177	A57	$40 rose red	1.90	*8.00*
178	A57	$50 blue ('46)	625.00	*675.00*
179	A57	$100 orange brn	2.50	*8.00*

Perf. 13½

180	A57	$4 dp blue	.20	*4.00*
181	A57	$5 lilac gray	.30	*4.50*
182	A57	$10 red brn	.30	*4.50*
183	A57	$20 blue grn	.90	*5.00*
184	A57	$20 rose red	85.00	80.00
185	A57	$30 dull vio	1.25	*5.50*
186	A57	$40 rose	1.25	*6.00*
187	A57	$50 blue	1.60	*5.00*
188	A57	$100 orange brn	67.50	67.50
		Nos. 174-177,179-188 (14)	215.85	*280.00*

Beware of trimmed copies of Nos. 182 and 187 offered as Nos, 174 and 178.

Nos. 162 and 164 Surcharged in Black

1944, Aug. 1

194	A62	12c on 10c dp grn	1.40	*3.50*
195	A62	24c on 25c brn vio	2.00	*3.25*

Stamps of China, 1940-41, Overprinted in Black at Chengtu, Szechwan

1943

196	A57	10c green (#354)	15.00	*30.00*
197	A47	20c lt blue (#433)	15.00	*30.00*

Wmk. 261 ***Perf. 14***

198	A57	50c dk blue (#396)	15.00	*30.00*

China Nos. 565 and 567 Overprinted in Black

1945 **Unwmk.** ***Perf. 12½***

200	A63	40c brown red	.30	.65
201	A63	$3 red	.30	.65

China Nos. 640-642, 788, 751, 753 Surcharged in Black or Red

1949 **Engr.** ***Perf. 14***

202	A73	1c on $100 dk car	19.00	*22.50*
203	A73	3c on $200 ol grn (R)	19.00	*22.50*
204	A73	5c on $500 brt bl grn (R)	19.00	*22.50*
205	A82	10c on $20,000 rose pink	16.00	*20.00*
206	A82	50c on $4000 gray (R)	62.50	62.50
207	A82	$1 on $6000 rose lil	72.50	72.50
		Nos. 202-207 (6)	208.00	*222.50*

AIR POST STAMPS

Sinkiang Nos. 53, 57, 59, 32 Overprinted in Red

1932-33 **Unwmk.** ***Perf. 14***

C1	A29	5c claret ('33)	165.00	90.00
C2	A29	10c dark blue ('33)	165.00	85.00
C3	A30	15c deep blue	1,000.	275.00
C4	A25	30c brown violet	400.00	325.00

Counterfeits exist of Nos. C1-C19.

Air Post Stamps of China, 1932-37 Handstamped in Dull Red

1942

C5	AP3	15c gray green	4.25	*5.50*
C6	AP3	25c orange	250.00	250.00
C7	AP3	30c red	10.00	*16.00*
C8	AP3	45c brown vio	6.25	*10.50*
C9	AP3	50c dk brown	26.00	*32.50*
C10	AP3	60c dk blue	6.25	*13.00*
C11	AP3	90c olive grn	35.00	*47.50*
C12	AP3	$1 yellow grn	7.25	*11.50*
		Nos. C5-C12 (8)	345.00	*386.50*

Same Handstamped Overprint on Air Post Stamps of China, 1940-41 in Dull Red

1942 **Wmk. 261** ***Perf. 12½, 13, 13½***

C13	AP3	15c gray green	3.25	*4.00*
C14	AP3	25c yellow orange	3.25	*4.00*

1942 **Unwmk.**

C15	AP3	25c light orange	2.75	2.75
C16	AP3	30c light red	4.00	4.00
C17	AP3	50c brown	5.50	5.50
C18	AP3	$2 light brown	26.00	26.00
C19	AP3	$5 lake	26.00	26.00
		Nos. C15-C19 (5)	64.25	64.25

Twelve values exist with this overprint in black. Their status has not been determined. Inverted overprints exist in both red and black.

Official Perforated Characters

For use on official mail, various Sinkiang stamps were perforated with an arrangement of four Chinese characters ("For Official Business Only"). These include Nos. 1-38, 47-69, 114.

OFFICES IN TIBET

12 Pies = 1 Anna
16 Annas = 1 Rupee

Stamps of China, Issues of 1902-10, Surcharged

1911 **Unwmk.** ***Perf. 12 to 16***

1	A17	3p on 1c ocher	15.00	*27.50*
a.		Inverted surcharge	3,500.	
2	A17	½a on 2c grn	15.00	*27.50*
3	A17	1a on 4c ver	15.00	*27.50*
4	A17	2a on 7c mar	15.00	*27.50*
5	A17	2½a on 10c ultra	20.00	*32.50*
6	A18	3a on 16c ol grn	40.00	*50.00*
a.		Large "S" in "Annas"	1,250.	
7	A18	4a on 20c red brn	40.00	*50.00*
8	A18	6a on 30c rose red	60.00	*72.50*
9	A18	12a on 50c yel grn	175.00	*250.00*
10	A19	1r on $1 red & pale rose	475.00	*600.00*
11	A19	2r on $2 red & yel	900.00	*1,200.*
		Nos. 1-11 (11)	1,770.	2,365.

CHINA, PEOPLE'S REPUBLIC OF

'pē-pəls ri-'pə-blik of 'chī-nə

LOCATION — Eastern Asia
GOVT. — Communist Republic
POP. — 1,246,871,951 (1999 est.)
CAPITAL — Beijing (Peking)

The communists completed their conquest of all mainland China in 1949. They established the Central Government and General Postal Administration in Peking. They ordered all but two regions to stop selling regional issues by June 30, 1950, extending validity one year from that date. The Northeast and Port Arthur-Dairen regions were exempted because their currency had a different value. These two regions stopped using separate issues at the end of 1950. Thereafter unified issues were used throughout mainland China.

On July 1, 1997 Hong Kong returned to Chinese control as an administrative district. Hong Kong stamps issued under Chinese rule will continue to be listed under "Hong Kong."

Reprints

After currency revaluation Mar. 1, 1955, reprints were prepared and put on sale by the Philatelic Agency in order to supply stocks of exhausted issues for collectors. Minor differences in design or paper distinguish the reprints. They are of commemorative and special issues up to the gymnastics set of 1952. Reprints are less expensive. Values are for original issues. Reprint distinctions are footnoted.

Used Stamps

Most used stamps before 1970 exist primarily canceled to order. Postally used copies generally sell for ½ the unused value.

Beginning in 1987 the PRC stopped furnishing quantities of used stamps to the philatelic market. When available, used stamps of these issues sell for the same or more than unused copies.

PRC Issue Numbers

Commemorative issues, beginning in 1949, and special issues, beginning in 1951, bear 4 numbers in lower margin: 1. Issue number. 2. Total of stamps in set. 3. Position of stamp in set. 4. Cumulative number of stamp (usually in parenthesis). A fifth number, the year of issue, was added in 1952.

The numbering system varies at times, with all numbers omitted on Scott 938-1046.

In certain sets listings include parenthetically the position-in-set number. During some periods these parentheses in listings hold the stamp's cumulative number. Issue numbers are noted when one or more designs are not illustrated.

Gum

All stamps to the beginning of 1960 were issued without gum, except as noted. After that date, most stamps have gum, which is translucent and almost invisible. All issues are unwatermarked, unless otherwise noted.

100 fen = 1 yuan ($)

Catalogue values for unused stamps in this country are for Never Hinged items, beginning with Scott 487 in the regular postage section, Scott B1 in the semi-postal section.

Syncopated Perforations

Type A (1st stamp #2880): On the two shorter sides, an oval hole equal in width to three holes is centered.

Lantern and Gate of Heavenly Peace — A1

Globe and Hand Holding Hammer — A2

1949, Oct. 8 Litho. *Perf. 12½*

1	A1	$30 blue		2.50	1.75
2	A1	$50 rose red		2.50	1.75
3	A1	$100 green		2.50	1.75
4	A1	$200 maroon		2.50	1.75
		Nos. 1-4 (4)		10.00	7.00

1st session of Chinese People's Consultative Political Conference. See #1L121-1L124.

Original

Reprint

Reprints have altered ornament on lantern base. On originals, it is a full oval; in reprints, only a partial circle. Value, set: unused $3; used $1.25.

1949, Nov. 16

5	A2	$100 carmine	7.00	2.50
6	A2	$300 slate green	7.00	2.50
7	A2	$500 dark blue	7.00	2.50
		Nos. 5-7 (3)	21.00	7.50

Asiatic and Australasian Congress of the World Federation of Trade Unions, Peking.
The $100, imperf., is of dubious status.
See Nos. 1L133-1L135.

Original

Reprint

Reprints show heavier shading on index finger and thumb. Value, set $5.00 unused or $2.40 used.

Conference Hall, Peking — A3

Mao Tse-tung on Rostrum A4

1950, Feb. 1 Engr. *Perf. 14*

8	A3	$50 red	3.50	3.25
9	A3	$100 blue	3.50	3.25
10	A4	$300 red brown	3.50	3.00
11	A4	$500 green	3.50	3.50
		Nos. 8-11 (4)	14.00	13.00

Chinese People's Consultative Political Conference. See Nos. 1L136-1L139.

Original

Reprint

Nos. 8-9: First character in top inscription shows a square, reprints an oblong.

Nos. 10-11: Originals have heavy cross-hatching and lines which touch back of head and top of rostrum. Reprints have lighter lines which do not touch head or top of rostrum. Reprints, value set $4.75.

Gate of Heavenly Peace (actual size) — A5

First Issue: Top line of shading broken at right.

1950, Feb. 10 Litho. *Perf. 12½*

12	A5	$200 green	6.00	2.00
13	A5	$300 brown red	.20	*2.00*
14	A5	$500 red	.20	*2.00*
15	A5	$800 orange	70.00	2.00
16	A5	$1000 dull violet	1.25	*2.00*
17	A5	$2000 olive	8.00	2.00
18	A5	$5000 brt pink	.20	*2.00*
19	A5	$8000 blue	.20	*20.00*
20	A5	$10,000 brown	.60	*2.00*
		Nos. 12-20 (9)	86.65	*36.00*

1950, June 9 Typo.

Second Issue: Top line of shading extends to frame line at right.

21	A5	$1000 dull violet	1.10	*1.50*
22	A5	$3000 red brown	1.10	*1.50*
23	A5	$10,000 brown	1.10	*1.50*
		Nos. 21-23 (3)	3.30	*4.50*

Other Gate of Heavenly Peace issues are illustrated where they are listed. See A10, A13, A14 and A42 for similar designs.

For similar types with Chinese characters in upper right corner see Northeast China A28, A29, Port Arthur & Darien A11, North China A8.

China Nos. 959, C62, E12, F2 Surcharged in Blue, Black, Green or Red

Rouletted, Perf. 12½ (#27, 29)

1950, Mar. Litho.

24	SD2	$100 on red vio (Bl)	.25	.85
a.		Perf. 12½	7.50	3.00
25	R2	$200 on red (Bk)	2.50	.60
a.		Perf. 12½	55.00	3.50
26	AP5	$300 on bl grn (Bk)	.25	.85
a.		Perf. 12½	1.00	1.00
27	A96	$500 on org (Bk)	.20	.30
a.		Perf. 14	67.50	60.00
28	A96	$800 on org (R)	2.50	.20
a.		Perf. 12½	22.50	2.50
b.		Perf. 14	*900.00*	70.00
29	A96	$1000 on org (Bk)	.20	.20
a.		Perf. 14	.20	.20
		Nos. 24-29 (6)	5.90	3.00

No. 27 exists with green surcharge.

Harvesters with Ox — A6

1950, May

30	A6	$20,000 on $10,000 red	475.00	95.00

No. 30 is surcharged on an unissued stamp of East China.

Flag, Mao Tse-tung, Gate of Heavenly Peace — A7

1950, July 1 *Perf. 14*

Yellow Stars

31	A7	$800 green & red	35.00	8.00
32	A7	$1000 brn & red	42.50	8.00
33	A7	$2000 dk brn & red	55.00	8.00
34	A7	$3000 dk blue & red	75.00	11.00
		Nos. 31-34 (4)	207.50	35.00

Inauguration of the People's Republic, Oct. 1, 1949. See Nos. 1L150-1L153.

Original

Reprint

Originals have a single curved line in jacket button, reprints have an extra dot in button. Value, set $14.

Sun Yat-sen Stamps of Northeastern Provinces Surcharged in Red, Black or Blue

1950, July 1 Engr.

35	A2	$50 on 20c yel grn	3.50	*8.00*
36	A2	$50 on 25c blk brn	6.50	4.00
37	A2	$50 on 50c red org (Bk)	2.00	3.00
38	A2	$100 on $2.50 ind	1.90	3.00
39	A2	$100 on $3 brn (Bk)	2.10	2.00
40	A2	$100 on $4 org brn, Type II (Bl)	5.00	*8.00*
a.		Type I	*800.00*	125.00
41	A2	$100 on $5 dk grn (Bk)	2.10	2.00
42	A2	$100 on $10 crim, Type II (Bl)	20.00	12.00
a.		Type I	*7,500.*	
43	A2	$400 on $20 ol, Type II (Bl)	50.00	50.00
a.		Type I	*900.00*	100.00
44	A2	$400 on $44 dk car rose (Bl)	1.10	8.00
45	A2	$400 on $65 dl grn	120.00	75.00
46	A2	$400 on $100 dp grn	30.00	10.00
47	A2	$400 on $200 rose brn (Bk)	80.00	20.00
48	A2	$400 on $300 bluish grn	80.00	25.00
		Nos. 35-48 (14)	404.20	230.00

Flying Geese Type of China Surcharged in Red, Blue, Green, Brown or Black

1950, Aug. 1 *Perf. 12½, Imperf.*

49	A97	$50 on 10c dk bl (R)	.20	.35
50	A97	$100 on 16c ol, imperf. (Bl)	.20	.35
51	A97	$100 on 50c dl grn, imperf. (Bl)	.20	.20
52	A97	$200 on $1 org (G)	.20	.20
53	A97	$200 on $2 bl (Br)	6.00	.80
54	A97	$400 on $5 car rose (Bk)	.20	.35
55	A97	$400 on $10 bl grn (Bk)	.20	1.00
56	A97	$400 on $20 pur (Bk)	.20	*2.75*
		Nos. 49-56 (8)	7.40	6.00

Dove of Peace, by Picasso — A8

Chinese Flag and "1" — A9

1950, Aug. 1 Engr. *Perf. 14*

57	A8	$400 brown	13.00	4.00
58	A8	$800 green	13.00	4.00
59	A8	$2000 blue	17.50	4.00
		Nos. 57-59 (3)	43.50	12.00

World Peace Campaign. See #1L154-1L156.

Paper of originals appears bright under ultraviolet lamp. That of reprints looks dull. Value, set $3.

1950 Engr. & Litho.

Flag in Red & Yellow

60	A9	$100 purple	18.00	4.00
61	A9	$400 red brown	22.00	4.00
62	A9	$800 green	22.00	4.00
63	A9	$1000 lt olive	35.00	8.00
64	A9	$2000 blue	50.00	10.00
		Nos. 60-64 (5)	147.00	30.00

1st anniv. of the Chinese People's Republic. Size of $800: 38x46mm; others 26x32mm.

Issue dates: No. 62, Oct. 1; others Oct. 31. See Nos. 1L157-1L161.

$800

Original

Reprint

Reprints are a brighter red, leaves beside "1" are gray brown instead of reddish brown. On the $800 the arrangement of dots in background differs in relationship to large star. Value, set $4.

Gate of Heavenly Peace (actual size) — A10

Third Issue: Cloud almost touches character at upper left. Cloud breaks inner frame line at top.

1950 Litho.

65	A10	$100 lt grnsh bl	40.00	8.00
66	A10	$200 green	250.00	15.00
67	A10	$300 dk carmine	2.75	*5.00*
68	A10	$400 grnsh gray	1.00	*3.00*
69	A10	$500 carmine	.75	*2.00*
70	A10	$800 orange	7.00	1.00
71	A10	$2000 gray olive	1.50	1.00
		Nos. 65-71 (7)	303.00	*35.00*

Issued: $800, 10/8; $500, $2000, 12/1; others, 10/6.

"Communication" and Map of China — A11

1950, Nov. 1 Litho.

72	A11	$400 green & brn	16.00	4.00
73	A11	$800 carmine & grn	16.00	4.00

First All-China Postal Conference, Peking. See Nos. 1L162-1L163.

Original

Reprint

Originals have 3 lines below horizontal bar (2nd character); reprints have four. Value, set $1.75.

Stalin and Mao Tse-tung — A12

1950, Dec. 1 Engr. *Perf. 14*

74	A12	$400 red	11.00	4.25
75	A12	$800 dp green	11.00	3.25
76	A12	$2000 dk blue	15.00	4.25
		Nos. 74-76 (3)	37.00	11.75

Signing of Sino-Soviet Treaty of Friendship, Alliance and Mutual Assistance. See Nos. 1L176-1L178.

Paper of originals appears bright under ultraviolet lamp. That of reprints looks dull. Value, set $3.75.

East China Issue of 1949 Surcharged in Red, Black, Brown or Blue

Train and Postal Runner — A12a

1950, Dec. Litho. *Perf. 12½*

77	A12a	$50 on $10 dp ultra (R)	.20	.20
78	A12a	$100 on $15 org ver (Bk)	.20	.20
a.		$100 on $15 red (Bk), perf. 14	.20	.20
79	A12a	$300 on $50 car (Bk)	.20	.20
80	A12a	$400 on $1600 vio bl (Br)	2.00	.20
81	A12a	$400 on $2000 brn vio (Bl)	.85	.20
		Nos. 77-81 (5)	3.45	1.00

East China Issue of 1949 Surcharged in Red or Black

Chairman Mao — A12b

1950, Dec.

82	A12b	$50 on $10 ultra (R)	.25	.20
83	A12b	$400 on $15 ver (Bk)	.25	.20
84	A12b	$400 on $2000 grn (Bk)	1.75	.20
		Nos. 82-84 (3)	2.25	.60

(actual size) — A13

(actual size) — A14

Fourth Issue: Similar to 3rd issue, but large cloud does not break inner frame line at top.

1950-51 Litho.

85	A13	$100 lt blue	1.60	1.00
86	A13	$200 dull green	1.75	2.00
87	A13	$300 dull lilac	.40	*5.25*
88	A13	$400 gray grn	.40	*1.00*
89	A13	$500 carmine	.20	*1.10*
90	A13	$800 orange	85.00	4.00
a.		Imperf., pair	—	
91	A13	$1000 violet	.50	*1.00*
92	A13	$2000 olive	240.00	6.00
93	A13	$3000 brown	.20	*6.00*
94	A13	$5000 pink	.20	*6.00*
		Nos. 85-94 (10)	330.25	*33.35*

Issued: $200, $300, $500, $800, $2000, $5000, 12/22/50; others 6/8/51.

1951, Jan. 18 Engr. *Perf. 14*

Fifth Issue: Colored network on surface in salmon.

95	A14	$10,000 brown	1.40	*10.00*
96	A14	$20,000 olive	1.40	*8.25*
97	A14	$30,000 green	40.00	*60.00*
98	A14	$50,000 violet	90.00	17.00
99	A14	$100,000 scarlet	2,250.	250.00
100	A14	$200,000 blue	2,250.	250.00
		Nos. 95-100 (6)	4,632.	595.25

Unit Issue of China Surcharged

1951, May 2 Litho. *Perf. 12½*

101	SD2	$5 on rose lilac	3.50	.50
102	AP5	$10 on brt grn	.25	.25
103	R2	$15 on red	.20	.25
104	A96	$25 on orange	.70	.25
		Nos. 101-104 (4)	4.65	1.25

Issued for use in Northeast China, but available for use throughout China. Nos. 101-104 rouletted were sold for philatelic purposes only. Value, set $4.00.

Chairman Mao Tse-tung — A15

1951, July 1 Engr. *Perf. 14*

105	A15	$400 chestnut	4.50	1.25
106	A15	$500 deep green	4.50	1.25
107	A15	$800 crimson	4.50	1.25
		Nos. 105-107 (3)	13.50	3.75

Chinese Communist Party, 30th anniv.

Reprints are on whiter, thinner and harder paper. Value, set $3.50.

Picasso Dove — A16

1951, Aug. 15 *Perf. 12½*

108	A16	$400 orange brn	13.00	4.50
109	A16	$800 blue grn	13.00	4.00
110	A16	$1000 dull vio	13.00	4.50
		Nos. 108-110 (3)	39.00	13.00

Reprints are perf 14. Value, set $12.

Remittance Stamp of China Surcharged in Carmine or Black

(same size) — A17

Engraved, Commercial Press

1951, Sept. *Perf. 12½*

111	A17	$50 on $2 bl grn (C)	.30	*1.00*

Typo., Kang Hwa Printing Co.

Rouletted 9½

112	A17	$50 on $2 gray bl (C)	.85	*7.00*
113	A17	$50 on $5 red org (Bk)	.20	*1.00*
114	A17	$50 on $50 gray (C)	8.00	*4.00*

Lithographed, Central Trust Co.

Perf. 13

115	A17	$50 on $50 gray blk (C)	.20	*.40*

Lithographed, Chung Hwa Book Co.

Perf. 11½x10

116	A17	$50 on $50 gray (C)	2.00	.75
a.		Perf. 11½	1.00	1.00
		Nos. 111-116 (6)	11.55	*14.15*

National Emblem — A18

Engraved; Background Network Lithographed in Yellow

1951, Oct. 1 *Perf. 14*

117	A18	$100 Prus blue	6.00	3.00
118	A18	$200 brown	6.00	3.00
119	A18	$400 orange	6.00	4.00
120	A18	$500 green	6.00	1.50
121	A18	$800 carmine	6.00	1.50
		Nos. 117-121 (5)	30.00	13.00

Reprints exist but are difficult to distinguish; paper whiter, and colors slightly brighter. Value, set $6.

Rough Perfs

Rough perforations are normal on many early issues. These include Nos. 122-123, 136-140, 155-176, 239-240, 299-300, 453-456, 467-482, 629-634, 684-707, 737-745 and probably others.

Lu Hsun and Quotation A19

1951, Oct. 19 Litho. *Perf. 12½*

122 A19 $400 lilac 4.75 3.00
123 A19 $800 green 7.25 1.50

15th anniversary of the death of Lu Hsun (1881-1936), writer.

Original

Reprint

Reprints have dot in triangle at lower right; no dot in original. Value, set $2.25.

Peasant Uprising, Chintien — A20

Design: Nos. 126-127, Coin of Taiping Regime and decrees of peasant government.

1951, Dec. 15 Engr. *Perf. 14*

124 A20 $400 green 7.50 5.00
125 A20 $800 scarlet 7.50 3.00
126 A20 $800 orange 7.50 4.00
127 A20 $1000 deep blue 7.50 3.00
Nos. 124-127 (4) 30.00 15.00

Centenary of Taiping Peasant Rebellion.

Original

Reprint

Reprints of Nos. 124-125 have additional short stroke at upper left.

Original

Reprint

Reprints of Nos. 126-127 have two short strokes on scale near tail of right dragon on coin. Value, Nos. 124-127, $4.25.

Old and New Methods of Agriculture — A21

1952, Jan. 1

128 A21 $100 scarlet 7.50 2.50
129 A21 $200 bright blue 7.50 2.50
130 A21 $400 deep brown 7.50 1.65
131 A21 $800 green 7.50 1.65
Nos. 128-131 (4) 30.00 8.30

Agrarian reform.

Original

Reprint

One short horizontal line between legs of plower; 2 lines in reprints. Value, set $3.50.

Potala Monastery, Lhasa — A22

Nos. 134-135, Farmer plowing with yaks.

1952, Mar. 15 *Perf. 12½*

132 A22 $400 vermilion 7.50 2.50
133 A22 $800 claret 7.50 2.50
134 A22 $800 blue grn 7.50 1.60
135 A22 $1000 dull vio 7.50 1.60
Nos. 132-135 (4) 30.00 8.20

Liberation of Tibet.

Reprints, perf 14, have a small Chinese character at lower left of the vignette which is missing in the original. Value, set $4.25.

Children of Four Races A23

Hammer and Sickle on Numeral 1 A24

1952, Apr. 12 Litho.

136 A23 $400 dull grn .50 .30
137 A23 $800 vio blue .50 .30

Intl. Child Protection Conf., Vienna.

1952, May 1

Labor Day: #139, Dove rising from worker's hand. #140, Dove, hammer, wheat & chimneys.

138 A24 $800 scarlet .20 .20
139 A24 $800 blue grn .20 .20
140 A24 $800 orange brn .60 .20
Nos. 138-140 (3) 1.00 .60

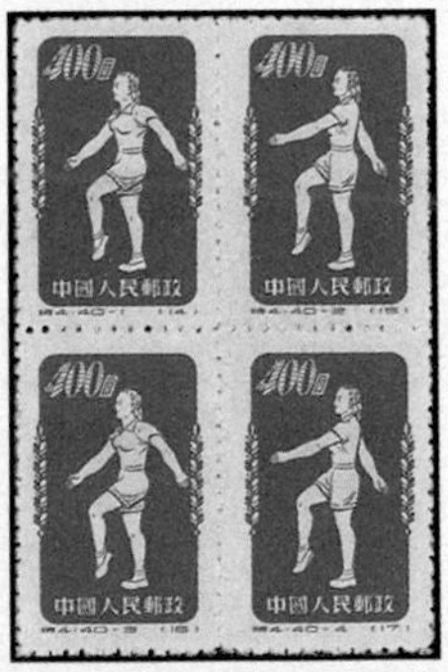

Physical Exercises — A25

Stamps printed in blocks of four for each color, each block representing a specific setting-up exercise; exercises coincided with a national radio program. Where exercise positions are identical within the block, the serial number (in parenthesis) is the only means of differentiation.

1952, June 20

141 A25 Block of 4 40.00 30.00
a. $400 vermilion (1) 6.00 1.75
b. $400 vermilion (2) 6.00 1.75
c. $400 vermilion (3) 6.00 1.75
d. $400 vermilion (4) 6.00 1.75
142 A25 Block of 4 40.00 30.00
a. $400 blue (5) 6.00 1.75
b. $400 blue (6) 6.00 1.75
c. $400 blue (7) 6.00 1.75
d. $400 blue (8) 6.00 1.75
143 A25 Block of 4 40.00 30.00
a. $400 brown red (9) 6.00 1.75
b. $400 brown red (10) 6.00 1.75
c. $400 brown red (11) 6.00 1.75
d. $400 brown red (12) 6.00 1.75
144 A25 Block of 4 40.00 30.00
a. $400 yellow green (13) 6.00 1.75
b. $400 yellow green (14) 6.00 1.75
c. $400 yellow green (15) 6.00 1.75
d. $400 yellow green (16) 6.00 1.75
145 A25 Block of 4 40.00 30.00
a. $400 red orange (17) 6.00 1.75
b. $400 red orange (18) 6.00 1.75
c. $400 red orange (19) 6.00 1.75
d. $400 red orange (20) 6.00 1.75
146 A25 Block of 4 40.00 30.00
a. $400 dull blue (21) 6.00 1.75
b. $400 dull blue (22) 6.00 1.75
c. $400 dull blue (23) 6.00 1.75
d. $400 dull blue (24) 6.00 1.75
147 A25 Block of 4 40.00 30.00
a. $400 orange (25) 6.00 1.75
b. $400 orange (26) 6.00 1.75
c. $400 orange (27) 6.00 1.75
d. $400 orange (28) 6.00 1.75
148 A25 Block of 4 40.00 30.00
a. $400 dull purple (29) 6.00 1.75
b. $400 dull purple (30) 6.00 1.75
c. $400 dull purple (31) 6.00 1.75
d. $400 dull purple (32) 6.00 1.75
149 A25 Block of 4 40.00 30.00
a. $400 yellow bister (33) 6.00 1.75
b. $400 yellow bister (34) 6.00 1.75
c. $400 yellow bister (35) 6.00 1.75
d. $400 yellow bister (36) 6.00 1.75
150 A25 Block of 4 40.00 30.00
a. $400 sky blue (37) 6.00 1.75
b. $400 sky blue (38) 6.00 1.75
c. $400 sky blue (39) 6.00 1.75
d. $400 sky blue (40) 6.00 1.75
Nos. 141-150 (10) 400.00 300.00

Originals are on thin gray paper, colors darker. Reprints on thicker white paper, colors brighter. Value, set $16.50.

Hunting, Wei Dynasty, A.D. 386-580 A26

Designs from Murals in Cave Temples at Tunhuang, Kansu Province: No. 152, Lady attendants, Sui Dynasty, 581-617 A.D. No. 153, Gandharvas (mythology), Tang Dynasty, 618-906. No. 154, Dragon, Tang Dynasty.

1952, July 1 Engr.

151 A26 $800 slate green (1) .50 .25
152 A26 $800 chocolate (2) .50 .25
153 A26 $800 indigo (3) .50 .25
154 A26 $800 dk vio (4) .50 .25
Nos. 151-154 (4) 2.00 1.00

"Glorious Mother Country," 1st series.

Marco Polo Bridge, near Peking A27

Designs: No. 156, Cavalry passing through Great Wall. No. 157, Departure of New Fourth Army. No. 158, Mao Tse-tung and Gen. Chu Teh planning counter-attack.

1952, July 7 Litho. *Perf. 14*

155 A27 $800 brt blue .60 .30
156 A27 $800 blue grn 1.25 .70
157 A27 $800 plum .60 .30
158 A27 $800 scarlet .30 .20
Nos. 155-158 (4) 2.75 1.50

15th anniversary of war against Japan.

Soldier and Tanks — A28

#159, Soldier, sailor & airman, vert. #161, Sailor & warships. #162, Airman & planes.

1952, Aug. 1 Engr. *Perf. 12½*

159 A28 $800 carmine .50 .20
160 A28 $800 deep green 1.25 .40
161 A28 $800 purple .50 .20
162 A28 $800 orange brown .50 .20
Nos. 159-162 (4) 2.75 1.00

25th anniv. of People's Liberation Army.

Huai River Sluice Dam A29

#164, Train on the Chengtu-Chungking Railway. #165, Oil refinery and derricks in the Northwest. #166, Mechanized state farm.

1952, Oct. 1 *Perf. 14*

163 A29 $800 dk violet .40 .25
164 A29 $800 red .40 .25
165 A29 $800 dk vio brn .60 .25
166 A29 $800 dp green .60 .25
Nos. 163-166 (4) 2.00 1.00

"Glorious Mother Country," 2nd series.

Doves and Globe A30

Designs: Nos. 167-168, Picasso dove over Pacific, vert. $2500, as No. 169.

1952, Oct. 2 *Perf. 14*

167 A30 $400 maroon .30 .25
168 A30 $800 red .30 .25
169 A30 $800 brown orange .30 .25
170 A30 $2500 deep green .60 .50
Nos. 167-170 (4) 1.50 1.25

Peace Conf. of the Asian and Pacific Regions.

Volunteers on the March — A31

#172, Chinese peasants loading supplies. #173, Volunteers attacking across river. #174, Meeting of Chinese & Korean troops.

1952, Oct. 25

171 A31 $800 blue green (1) .60 .25
172 A31 $800 vermilion (2) .60 .25
173 A31 $800 violet (3) .75 .25
174 A31 $800 lake brown (4) 1.10 .30
Nos. 171-174 (4) 3.05 1.05

2nd anniv. of Chinese Volunteers in Korea.

Woman Textile Worker A32

Design: No. 176, Farm woman with sickle.

1953, Mar. 10

175 A32 $800 carmine .50 .30
176 A32 $800 emerald .50 .30

International Women's Day.

Textile Worker — A33

Karl Marx — A34

$200, Shepherdess. $250, Stone lion. $800, Lathe operator. $1600, Coal miners. $2000, Corner tower of Forbidden City, Peking.

1953 Litho. *Perf. 14, 12½ ($250)*

177 A33 $50 magenta .80 .20
178 A33 $200 emerald 1.50 .40
179 A33 $250 ultra 4.00 2.25
180 A33 $800 blue grn .70 .20
181 A33 $1600 gray .80 .40
182 A33 $2000 red org 2.50 .20
Nos. 177-182 (6) 10.30 3.65

Issued: #177-181, Mar. 25; #182, May 23.

1953, May 20 **Engr.** ***Perf. 14***

183	A34	$400 dk brown	.50	.25
184	A34	$800 slate grn	1.00	.35

135th anniv. of the birth of Karl Marx.

Workers and Banners — A35

1953, June 25

185	A35	$400 Prus blue	.80	.30
186	A35	$800 carmine	.65	.30

7th All-China Trade Union Congress.

Picasso Dove — A36

1953, July 25

187	A36	$250 blue grn	.90	.30
188	A36	$400 orange brn	.50	.30
189	A36	$800 purple	.70	.30
		Nos. 187-189 (3)	2.10	.90

World Peace.

Groom, Wei Dynasty, 386-580 — A37

Scenes from Tunhuang Murals: No. 191, Court Players, Wei Dynasty. No. 192, Battle Scene, Sui Dynasty, 581-617. No. 193, Ox-drawn palanquin, Tang Dynasty, 618-906.

1953, Sept. 1

190	A37	$800 dp green (1)	2.00	.25
191	A37	$800 red org (2)	.50	.25
192	A37	$800 Prus blue (3)	1.00	.25
193	A37	$800 carmine (4)	.50	.25
		Nos. 190-193 (4)	4.00	1.00

"Glorious Mother Country," 3rd series.

Stalin and Mao on Kremlin Terrace — A38

Statue of Stalin at Volga-Don Canal — A39

Designs: No. 195, Lenin proclaiming Soviet power. No. 197, Stalin as orator.

1953, Oct. 5

194	A38	$800 green (1)	.50	.25
195	A38	$800 carmine (2)	.50	.25
196	A39	$800 brt blue (3)	.75	.30
197	A39	$800 org brn (4)	.75	.30
		Nos. 194-197 (4)	2.50	1.10

Russian October Revolution, 35th anniv.

Stamps in same designs with two additional characters meaning "Soviet" in the single-line Chinese inscription, and in different colors, were unofficially released at several small post offices in Hunan, Fukien and Canton areas in February, 1953, but were withdrawn after only a small number had been sold. Value, set $7,250 unused, $2,000 canceled.

Compass, 3rd Century B.C. — A40

#199, Seismoscope, later Han Dynasty. #200, Drum cart to measure distance, Chin Dynasty. #201, Armillary sphere, Ming Dynasty.

1953, Dec. 1

198	A40	$800 indigo (1)	.60	.25
199	A40	$800 dk green (2)	.60	.25
200	A40	$800 dk blue (3)	.60	.25
201	A40	$800 choc (4)	.60	.25
		Nos. 198-201 (4)	2.40	1.00

Major inventions by ancient and medieval Chinese scientists.

"Glorious Mother Country," 4th series.

Francois Rabelais — A41

(same size) Gate of Heavenly Peace — A42

Designs: $400, Jose Marti, Cuban revolutionary. $800, Chu Yuan (350-275 B.C.), philosopher. $2200, Nicolaus Copernicus, astronomer.

1953, Dec. 30

202	A41	$250 slate grn (3)	.60	.25
203	A41	$400 brown blk (4)	.60	.25
204	A41	$800 indigo (1)	.60	.25
205	A41	$2200 choc (2)	.60	.25
		Nos. 202-205 (4)	2.40	1.00

1954, Apr. 16 **Litho.**

Sixth Issue: Inscription at upper right.

206	A42	$50 carmine	.20	.20
207	A42	$100 lt blue	.20	.20
208	A42	$200 green	.20	.20
209	A42	$250 ultra	3.00	.30
210	A42	$400 gray grn	.20	.20
211	A42	$800 orange	.20	.20
212	A42	$1600 gray	.20	*.65*
213	A42	$2000 olive	.20	*.30*
		Nos. 206-213 (8)	4.40	2.25

Textile Plant, Harbin — A43

Lenin — A44

Designs: $200, Tangku Harbor. $250, Tienshui-Lanchow railroad bridge, Kansu Province. $400, Heavy machine-building plant, Taiyuan, Shansi. No. 218, Automatic blast, furnace, Anshan, Manchuria. No. 219, Fushun open-cut coal mine. $2000, Automatic power plant, Northeast. $3200, Prospecting in Tayeh district, Hupeh.

1954, May 1 **Engr.**

214	A43	$100 brown olive	.35	.20
215	A43	$200 blue green	.50	.20
216	A43	$250 violet	.35	.20
217	A43	$400 black	.35	.20
218	A43	$800 claret	.35	.20
219	A43	$800 indigo	.35	.20
220	A43	$2000 red	.45	.20
221	A43	$3200 dark brown	.45	.30
		Nos. 214-221 (8)	3.15	1.70

Economic progress.

1954, June 30 **Engr.**

$400, Lenin and Stalin Monument, Gorki, horiz. $2000, Lenin proclaiming Soviet power.

222	A44	$400 deep green	.55	.25
223	A44	$800 dark brown	.30	.25
224	A44	$2000 deep carmine	2.25	.45
		Nos. 222-224 (3)	3.10	.95

30th anniversary of the death of Lenin.

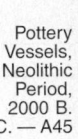

Pottery Vessels, Neolithic Period, 2000 B.C. — A45

Archeological Treasures: No. 226, Stone clime, Shang Dynasty, c. 1200 B.C. No. 227, Kuo Chi Tsu-pai bronze basin, Middle Chou Dynasty, 816 B.C. No. 228, Lacquered box and wine cup, Warring States Period, 403-221 B.C.

1954, Aug. 25

225	A45	$800 brown	.50	.25
226	A45	$800 indigo	.50	.25
227	A45	$800 Prus bl	.50	.25
228	A45	$800 dk car	.50	.25
		Nos. 225-228 (4)	2.00	1.00

"Glorious Mother Country," 5th series.

Pipe Production, Anshan Steel Mill — A46

Stalin Statue, by Tomsky — A47

Design: $800, Rolling mill, Anshan.

1954, Oct. 1

229	A46	$400 Prus green	1.00	.50
230	A46	$800 vio brown	1.00	.50

1954, Oct. 15

Designs: $800, Stalin portrait. $2000, Stalin viewing hydroelectric plant.

Size: 21x45mm

231 A47 $400 black 1.25 .50

Size: 26x37mm

232 A47 $800 black brown .70 .20

Size: 42x26mm

233 A47 $2000 deep red .70 .30
Nos. 231-233 (3) 2.65 1.00

First anniversary of the death of Stalin.

Exhibition Building, Peking — A48

1954, Nov. 7

234 A48 $800 brown, *cream* 13.00 3.75
a. Size: 53½x24mm 14.00 3.75

Russian Economic and Cultural Exhibition, Peking. No. 234 measures 52½x24½mm.

Apprentices and Lathe — A49

Progress in Technology: $800, Heavy machinery and workers.

1954, Dec. 15

235	A49	$400 dk olive grn	.85	.40
236	A49	$800 bright red	.65	.40

Woman Worker Voting — A50

People Celebrating Opening of Congress — A51

1954, Dec. 30

237	A50	$400 deep claret	.45	.30
238	A51	$800 bright red	1.00	.30

First National Congress.

Flags, Worker and Woman Holding Constitution — A52

1954, Dec. 30

239	A52	$400 brown, *buff*	.70	.20
240	A52	$800 brt red, *yel*	1.00	.40

Adoption of Constitution.

High-tension Pylon — A53

1955, Feb. 25

241 A53 $800 dk Prus bl 2.40 .30

Development of electric power.

Factory Health Workers and Red Cross — A54

1955, June 25 **Engr.; Cross Typo.**

242 A54 8f dp grn & red 8.00 2.00

50th anniversary of Chinese Red Cross.

Stalin and Mao in Kremlin — A55

Soviet Specialist and Chinese Worker — A56

1955, July 25 **Engr.**

243	A55	8f brown red	7.25	.50
244	A56	20f olive blk	11.00	1.50

5th anniv. of Sino-Soviet Friendship Treaty.

Chang Heng (78-139), Astronomer — A57

Portraits of Scientists: No. 246, Tsu Chung-chih (429-500), mathematician. No. 247, Chang Sui (683-727), astronomer. No. 248, Li Shih-chen (1518-1593), physician and pharmacologist.

1955, Aug. 25 ***Perf. 14***

245	A57	8f sepia, *buff*	2.50	.30
a.		Min. sheet, sepia, *white*	30.00	6.75
246	A57	8f dp grn, *buff*	2.50	.30
a.		Min. sheet, deep green, *white*	30.00	6.75
247	A57	8f black, *buff*	2.50	.30
a.		Min. sheet, blk, *white*	30.00	6.75
248	A57	8f claret, *buff*	2.50	.30
a.		Min. sheet, claret, *white*	30.00	6.75
		Nos. 245-248 (4)	10.00	1.20

Miniature sheets contain one imperf. stamp.

Steel Pouring Ladle A58

1955-56 **Litho.**

Position-in-set number in ( )

249	A58	8f shown (1)	1.10	.20
250	A58	8f High tension line (2)	1.10	.20
251	A58	8f Mechanized coal mining (3)	1.10	.20
252	A58	8f Tank cars and derricks (4)	1.10	.20
253	A58	8f Heavy machine shop (5)	1.10	.20
254	A58	8f Soldier on guard (6)	1.10	.20
255	A58	8f Spinning machine (7)	1.10	.20
256	A58	8f Workers discussing 5-year plan (8)	1.10	.20
257	A58	8f Combine harvester (9)	1.10	.20
258	A58	8f Milk production (10)	1.10	.20
259	A58	8f Dam (11)	1.10	.20
260	A58	8f Pottery industry (12) ('56)	1.10	.20
261	A58	8f Truck (13)	1.10	.20
262	A58	8f Ship at dock (14)	1.10	.20
263	A58	8f Geological survey (15)	1.10	.20
264	A58	8f Higher education (16)	1.10	.20
265	A58	8f Family (17)	1.10	.20
266	A58	8f Workers' rest home (18) ('56)	1.10	.20
		Nos. 249-266 (18)	19.80	3.60

1st 5 Year Plan. Issued: #249-257, 10/1; #258-259, 261-265, 12/15; #260, 266, 2/24/56.

Lenin — A59

Engels — A60

1955, Dec. 15 **Engr.** ***Perf. 14***

267	A59	8f dk blue grn	10.00	.25
268	A59	20f dk rose car	10.00	1.75

85th anniversary of the birth of Lenin.

1955, Dec. 15

269	A60	8f deep orange	10.00	.25
270	A60	20f brown	10.00	1.75

135th anniversary of the birth of Friedrich Engels (1820-1895), German socialist.

Storming Lu Ting Bridge — A61

Crossing Great Snow Mountains A62

1955, Dec. 30

271	A61	8f dark red	7.00	.35
272	A62	8f dark blue	13.00	1.60

Long March of Chinese Communist army, 20th anniversary.

Miner — A63

Gate of Heavenly Peace — A64

Designs: 1f, Machinist. 2f, Airman. 2½f, Nurse. 4f, Soldier. 8f, Steel worker. 10f, Scientist. 20f, Farm woman. 50f, Sailor.

1955-56 Litho. *Perf. 14*

273	A63	½f orange brn	1.90	.20
274	A63	1f purple	1.90	.20
275	A63	2f green	1.90	.20
276	A63	2½f blue ('56)	1.90	.20
277	A63	4f gray olive	1.90	.45
278	A63	8f red org (Peking printing)	1.90	.65
a.		Perf. 12½ (Shanghai printing)	400.00	15.00
279	A63	10f claret ('56)	26.00	.20
280	A63	20f dp blue	6.75	.20
281	A63	50f gray	6.75	.20
		Nos. 273-281 (9)	50.90	2.50

Engr.

282	A64	$1 claret ('56)	.65	.25
283	A64	$2 sepia ('55)	1.10	.25
284	A64	$5 indigo ('56)	1.75	.40
285	A64	$10 dp org ('56)	5.50	4.25
286	A64	$20 gray vio ('56)	9.00	*17.00*
		Nos. 282-286 (5)	18.00	22.15

Nos. 282-286 are the 7th Gate Issue.

Trucks, Mountains, Highway Map — A65

Suspension Bridge over Tatu River — A66

#289, 1st truck arriving in Lhasa, & the Potala.

1956, Mar. 10 Engr.

287	A65	4f dp blue	.85	.20
288	A66	8f dk brown	.85	.20
289	A65	8f carmine	.85	.20
		Nos. 287-289 (3)	2.55	.60

Completion of Sikang-Tibet and Chinghai-Tibet Highways.

Summer Palace and Marble Boat A67

Famous Views of Imperial Peking: No. 291, Peihai Park with Jade Belt Marble Bridge. No. 292, Gate of Heavenly Peace. No. 293, Temple of Heaven. No. 294, Great Throne Hall, Forbidden City.

1956-57

290	A67	4f car rose (1)	3.00	.25
291	A67	4f blue grn (2)	3.00	.25
292	A67	8f red org (3) ('57)	8.00	.25
293	A67	8f Prus blue (4)	3.00	.25
294	A67	8f yellow brn (5)	3.00	.25
		Nos. 290-294 (5)	20.00	1.25

Issued: #292, 2/20/57; others, 6/15/56.
No. 292 exists with sun rays in background.

Salt Making A68

Designs: No. 296, Dwelling of the Eastern Han period. No. 297, Duck hunting and harvesting. No. 298, Carriage crossing bridge.

1956, Oct. 1

295	A68	4f gray olive	.40	.20
296	A68	4f slate blue	.40	.20
297	A68	8f gray brown	.40	.20
298	A68	8f sepia	.40	.20
		Nos. 295-298 (4)	1.60	.80

Murals, Tung Han Dynasty, 250 B.C.-220 A.D., found near Chengtu.

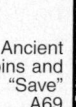

Ancient Coins and "Save" A69

1956, Oct. 1

299	A69	4f yellow brown	7.50	.60
300	A69	8f rose red	7.50	.60

Promotion of saving.

Gate of Heavenly Peace — A70

Sun Yat-sen — A71

1956, Nov. 10

301	A70	4f dk green	7.00	.40
302	A70	8f brt red	9.00	.40
303	A70	16f dk carmine	9.00	.80
		Nos. 301-303 (3)	25.00	1.60

8th National Congress of the Communist Party of China.

1956, Nov. 12

304	A71	4f brown, *cream*	17.50	.20
305	A71	8f dp blue, *cream*	7.50	1.25

90th anniversary of birth of Sun Yat-sen.

Weight Lifting — A72

1957, Mar. 20 Litho. *Perf. 12½*
Hibiscus red and green; inscription brown

306	A72	4f Shot put (2)	1.25	.20
307	A72	4f shown (5)	1.25	.20
308	A72	8f Track (1)	1.25	.20
309	A72	8f Soccer (3)	1.25	.20
310	A72	8f Bicycling (4)	1.25	.20
		Nos. 306-310 (5)	6.25	1.00

First National Workers' Sports Meeting.

Truck Factory No. 1, Changchun — A73

China's truck industry: 8f, Trucks rolling off assembly line.

1957, May 1 Engr. *Perf. 14*

311	A73	4f light brown	.50	.25
312	A73	8f slate green	1.00	.40

Nanchang Uprising — A74

#314, Mao and Chu Teh at Chingkanshan. #315, Crossing Yellow River. #316, Liberation of Nanking, 4/23/49.

1957

313	A74	4f blk vio (1)	10.00	.90
314	A74	4f slate grn (2)	10.00	.90
315	A74	8f red brn (3)	10.00	.45
316	A74	8f dp blue (4)	10.00	.45
		Nos. 313-316 (4)	40.00	2.70

People's Liberation Army, 30th anniv. Issued: #313, 315, 8/10; #314, 8/30; #316, 12/30.

Congress Emblem — A75

1957, Sept. 30

317	A75	8f chocolate	4.00	.40
318	A75	22f indigo	7.00	.60

4th Intl. Trade Union Cong., Leipzig, 10/4-15.

Yangtze River Bridge A76

20f, Road leading to and over bridge.

1957, Oct. 1

319	A76	8f scarlet	.60	.25
320	A76	20f slate blue	1.40	.40

Completion of Yangtze River Bridge at Wuhan.

Fireworks over Kremlin — A77

Designs: 8f, Hammer and sickle over globe and broken chain. 20f, Stylized dove and olive branch. 22f, Hands of three races holding book with Marx and Lenin. 32f, Star and pylon.

1957, Nov. 7

321	A77	4f brt red	6.50	.35
322	A77	8f chocolate	6.50	.35
323	A77	20f dp green	6.50	.35
324	A77	22f red brown	6.50	.35
325	A77	32f dp blue	6.50	2.00
		Nos. 321-325 (5)	32.50	3.40

40th anniv. of Russian October Revolution.

Map of Yellow River Basin A78

#327, Sanmen Gorge dam & powerhouse. #328, ocean liner on Yellow River. #329, Dam, irrigation canals & tree-bordered fields.

1957, Dec. 30

326	A78	4f deep orange (1)	12.00	1.25
327	A78	4f deep blue (2)	12.00	1.25
328	A78	8f deep lake (3)	12.00	.60
329	A78	8f blue green (4)	12.00	1.00
		Nos. 326-329 (4)	48.00	4.10

Yellow River control plan.

Old Man and Young Drummer A79

Crane, Dove and Flowers A80

1957, Dec. 30 **Litho.**

330 A79 8f shown (1) .55 .20
331 A79 8f Plowman (2) .55 .20
332 A79 8f Woman planting tree (3) .55 .20
333 A79 8f Harvest (4) .55 .20
Nos. 330-333 (4) 2.20 .80

Agricultural cooperation.

1958, Jan. 30 **Engr.**

Designs (Congratulatory Banner and): 8f, Crane with hot ingots, cotton bolls and wheat. 16f, Train on bridge, ship and plane.

334 A80 4f emer, *cream* .45 .20
335 A80 8f red, *cream* .45 .25
336 A80 16f ultra, *cream* .60 .20
Nos. 334-336 (3) 1.50 .65

Fulfillment of First Five-Year Plan.

Sungyu Pagoda, Honan — A81

Trilobite, Kaoli — A82

Ancient Pagodas: No. 338, Chienhsun Pagoda, Yunnan. No. 339, Sakyamuni Pagoda, Shansi. No. 340, Flying Rainbow Pagoda, Shansi.

1958, Mar. 15 **Engr.**

337 A81 8f sepia (1) 1.40 .20
338 A81 8f Prus blue (2) 1.40 .20
339 A81 8f maroon (3) 1.40 .20
340 A81 8f dp green (4) 1.40 .25
Nos. 337-340 (4) 5.60 .85

1958, Apr. 15

Designs: 8f, Lufeng dinosaur. 16f, Choukoutien sino-megaceros.

341 A82 4f black .80 .20
342 A82 8f sepia .80 .25
343 A82 16f slate green 1.25 .30
Nos. 341-343 (3) 2.85 .75

Prehistoric animals of China.

Heroes Monument A83

1958, May 1

344 A83 8f scarlet 14.50 1.25
a. Souvenir sheet, imperf. 125.00 50.00

Unveiling of People's Heroes Monument, Peking. No. 344a issued May 30.

Karl Marx — A84

Cogwheels and Factories — A85

Design: 22f, Marx Speaking to German Workers' Educational Association, London, painting by Zhukow.

1958, May 5

345 A84 8f chocolate 12.50 1.00
346 A84 22f dk green 12.50 2.00

Karl Marx (1818-83), 140th birth anniv.

1958, May 25

347 A85 4f brt grnsh bl 7.00 2.50
348 A85 8f red lilac 12.00 .60

8th All-China Trade Union Cong., Peking.

Dove over Globe — A86

Mother and Child — A87

1958, June 1

349 A86 8f violet blue 6.25 .25
350 A86 20f blue green 8.25 3.25

4th Congress of the Intl. Democratic Women's Federation, Vienna, June 1958.

1958, June 1 **Litho.**

Children's Day: No. 352, Watering sunflowers. No. 353, Playing hide-and-seek. No. 354, Sailing toy boat.

351 A87 8f green & multi (1) 12.50 1.60
352 A87 8f green & multi (2) 12.50 1.60
353 A87 8f green & multi (3) 12.50 1.60
354 A87 8f green & multi (4) 12.50 1.60
Nos. 351-354 (4) 50.00 6.40

Kuan Han-ching A88

Designs (Operas): 4f, "Dream of Butterflies." 20f, "The Riverside Pavilion."

1958, June 20 **Engr.**

355 A88 4f indigo, *cr* 10.00 3.50
356 A88 8f brown, *cr* 10.00 .60
357 A88 20f black, *cr* 17.50 .90
a. Souvenir sheet of 3, *ivory* 260.00 75.00
Nos. 355-357 (3) 37.50 *5.00*

700th anniversary of publication of works of Kuan Han-ching (1210-1280), dramatist. No. 357a contains 3 imperf. stamps similar to Nos. 355-357. Size: 130x100mm. Issued June 28.

Planetarium A89

20f, Telescope and stars over Peking.

1958, June 25

358 A89 8f dk green 5.00 .80
359 A89 20fr indigo 7.00 1.60

First Chinese planetarium, Peking.

Marx and Engels — A90

Wild Goose and Broadcasting Tower — A91

8f, Cover of 1st edition of the Communist Manifesto.

1958, July 1

360 A90 4f dk red vio 8.50 2.25
361 A90 8f Prus blue 16.50 1.25

110th anniversary of publication of the Communist Manifesto.

1958, July 10

362 A91 4f ultra 7.00 2.00
363 A91 8f deep green 13.00 1.00

1st Conference of the Ministers of Posts and Telecommunications of Socialist Countries, Moscow, Dec. 3-17, 1957.

Peony and Doves — A92

Bronze Weather Vane — A93

8f, Olive branch with ribbon & clouds. 22f, Atomic energy symbol over factories.

1958, July 20

364 A92 4f red 10.00 1.50
365 A92 8f green 10.00 3.50
366 A92 22f red brown 8.50 3.75
Nos. 364-366 (3) 28.50 8.75

Congress for Disarmament and International Cooperation, Stockholm, July 17-22.

1958, Aug. 25

Designs: No. 368, Weather balloon. No. 369, Typhoon tower and weather map of Asia.

367 A93 8f yel bis & blk (1) .85 .25
368 A93 8f blue & blk (2) .85 .25
369 A93 8f brt grn & blk (3) .85 .25
Nos. 367-369 (3) 2.55 .75

Meteorological services in ancient and modern China.

"5" Encircling IUS Emblem — A94

1958, Sept. 4

370 A94 8f rose lilac 6.00 .30
371 A94 22f dp blue grn 8.00 .90

Intl. Union of Students, 5th Cong., Peking, 9/4-13.
Copies exist with incorrect inscription.

Telegraph Building, Peking A95

1958, Sept. 29

372 A95 4f greenish black 2.50 .60
373 A95 8f rose red 3.50 .60

Opening of Telegraph Building, Peking.

Exhibition Emblem and Exhortation A96

Designs: No. 375, Dragon over clouds signifying "aiming high." No. 376, Flying horses, signifying "great leap forward" in production.

1958, Oct. 1

374 A96 8f slate grn (1) 5.00 1.00
375 A96 8f rose car (2) 7.00 1.00
376 A96 8f red brown (3) 7.00 2.00
Nos. 374-376 (3) 19.00 4.00

National Exhibition of Industry and Communications, Peking.

Worker and Excavator A97

Design: 8f, Completed dam and pylon.

1958, Oct. 25

377 A97 4f dark brown .75 .40
378 A97 8f deep Prussian blue 1.75 .40

13 Ming Tombs Reservoir completion.

Sputnik over Armillary Sphere — A98

Designs: 8f, Sputnik 3 in orbit. 10f, Trajectories of 3 Sputniks over earth.

1958, Oct. 30

379 A98 4f scarlet 2.00 .25
380 A98 8f dp violet bl 2.50 .75
381 A98 10f dp green 3.00 1.60
Nos. 379-381 (3) 7.50 2.60

Anniversary of first earth satellite launched by the USSR.

Chinese and North Korean Soldiers A99

Designs: No. 383, Chinese soldier embracing Korean woman. No. 384, Chinese girl presenting flowers to returning soldier.

1958, Nov. 20

382	A99 8f brt purple (1)	1.75	.35
383	A99 8f chestnut (2)	1.75	.35
384	A99 8f rose car (3)	1.75	.35
	Nos. 382-384 (3)	5.25	1.05

Return of the Chinese Volunteers from Korea.

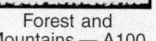

Forest and Mountains — A100

Peony — A101

Afforestation: No. 386, Mounted forest patrol. No. 387, Mechanized lumbering, horiz. No. 388, Tree-planting: "Turning the Country Green," horiz.

1958, Dec. 15

385	A100 8f dp blue grn (1)	2.50	1.00
386	A100 8f slate grn (2)	2.50	.60
387	A100 8f dk purple (3)	2.50	.60
388	A100 8f indigo (4)	2.50	.70
	Nos. 385-388 (4)	10.00	2.90

1958, Sept. 25 **Litho.**

Designs: 3f, Lotus. 5f, Chrysanthemums.

389	A101 1½f lilac rose	3.50	.50
390	A101 3f blue grn	8.00	1.60
391	A101 5f dp orange	3.00	.35
	Nos. 389-391 (3)	14.50	2.45

Atomic Reactor A102

1958, Dec. 30 **Engr.**

392	A102 8f shown	6.50	1.50
393	A102 20f Cyclotron	8.50	2.00

Inauguration of China's first atomic reactor and cyclotron, Peking.

Children Launching Model Planes — A103

Camel Carrying Load — A104

8f, Gliders over trees. 10f, Parachutists descending. 20f, Small monoplanes in mid-air.

1958, Dec. 30

394	A103 4f carmine	.90	.30
395	A103 8f dp slate grn	1.00	.25
396	A103 10f dk brown	1.00	.25
397	A103 20f Prus blue	1.10	.30
	Nos. 394-397 (4)	4.00	1.10

Sports-aviation publicity.

1959, Jan. 1

Designs: No. 399, Pomegranates. No. 400, Rooster. No. 401, Theatrical figure.

398	A104 8f vio & blk (1)	6.50	.65
399	A104 8f dp bl grn & blk (2)	6.50	.65
400	A104 8f red & blk (3)	6.50	.65
401	A104 8f dp bl & blk (4)	6.50	.65
	Nos. 398-401 (4)	26.00	2.60

Paper cut-outs (folk art).

Red Flag, Mao and Workers — A105

Women Workers and Atomic Model — A106

Designs: 8f, Traditional and modern blast furnaces. 10f, Steel works and workers.

1959

402	A105 4f brt red	7.00	1.40
403	A105 8f lake	7.50	1.40
404	A105 10f deep red	8.00	1.40
	Nos. 402-404 (3)	22.50	4.20

"Great Leap Forward" in steel production.
Issue dates: 4f, 8f, Feb. 19; 10f, May 25.

1959, Mar. 8

Design: 22f, Chinese and Soviet women holding banners dated "3.8."

405	A106 8f emerald, *cr*	.90	.40
406	A106 22f magenta, *cr*	.90	.20

International Women's Day.

Natural History Museum A107

1959, Apr. 1

407	A107 4f greenish blue	.90	.40
408	A107 8f olive brown	.90	.40

Opening of Museum of Natural History, Peking.

Wheat — A108

Designs on Chinese Flag: No. 410, Rice. No. 411, Cotton bolls. No. 412, Soybeans, rapeseed and peanuts.

1959, Apr. 25

409	A108 8f red (1)	2.00	.40
410	A108 8f red (2)	2.00	.40
411	A108 8f red (3)	2.00	.40
412	A108 8f red (4)	2.00	.40
a.	Block of 4, #409-412	14.00	4.00

Successful harvest, 1958.

A109

A110

Designs: 4f, Marx, Lenin and workers. 8f, Black, yellow and white fists holding banner. 22f, Steel workers parading with banners dated "5.1."

1959, May 1

413	A109 4f ultra	5.00	2.00
414	A109 8f red	6.00	1.25
415	A109 22f emerald	4.50	1.00
	Nos. 413-415 (3)	15.50	4.25

International Labor Day.

1959, June 20

8f, Peking airport. 10f, Plane loading on runway.

416	A110 8f lilac & blk	12.00	.40
417	A110 10f ol gray & blk	12.00	1.00

Opening of new Peking Airport.

Students with Marx-Lenin Banners A111

Design: 8f, Workers with banners of Mao.

1959, July 1 **Photo.** ***Perf. 11x11½***

418	A111 4f gray, red & dk brn	17.50	6.00
419	A111 8f bis, red & dk brn	22.50	4.00

40th anniv. of the May 4th students' uprising.

Frederick Joliot-Curie — A112

22f, Three races, dove and olive branch.

1959, July 25 **Engr.** ***Perf. 11½***

420	A112 8f violet brn	6.50	1.75
421	A112 22f dk violet	8.50	1.50

10th anniv. of the World Peace Movement.

Stamp Printing Plant, Peking A113

1959, Aug. 15 ***Perf. 11x11½***

422	A113 8f dp blue grn	7.25	2.00

Sino-Czechoslovak cooperation in stamp production.

Table Tennis — A114

1959, Aug. 30 **Litho.** ***Perf. 14***

423	A114 4f black & blue	2.25	.45
424	A114 8f black & red	2.75	.65

25th World Table Tennis Championships, Dortmund, German Democratic Republic.

Soviet Space Rocket A115

Backyard Steel Production A116

1959, Sept. 10 **Photo.** ***Perf. 11½***

425	A115 8f Prus bl, red & blk	10.00	2.40

Launching of first Russian space rocket, Jan. 2, 1959.

1959, Sept. 25 **Engr.**

Designs: #426, Sun rising over "industry and agriculture." #428, Farming. #429, Trade. #430, Education. #431, Militia. #432, Communal dining. #433, Nursery. #434, Care for the aged. #435, Health services. #436, Flutist; culture and sports. #437, Flower symbolizing unity of industry, agriculture, trade, education and armed forces.
Position-in-set number in ( ).

426	A116 8f rose (1)	.85	.20
427	A116 8f violet brn (2)	.85	.20
428	A116 8f dp orange (3)	.85	.20
429	A116 8f slate grn (4)	.85	.20
430	A116 8f dp blue (5)	.85	.20
431	A116 8f olive (6)	.85	.20
432	A116 8f indigo (7)	.85	.20
433	A116 8f lilac rose (8)	.85	.20
434	A116 8f gray blk (9)	.85	.20
435	A116 8f emerald (10)	.85	.20
436	A116 8f dk violet (11)	.85	.20
437	A116 8f red (12)	.85	.20
	Nos. 426-437 (12)	10.20	2.40

First anniversary of Peoples' Communes.

Mao and Gate of Heavenly Peace — A117

National Emblem A118

Blast Furnaces — A119

Celebration at Gate of Heavenly Peace — A120

Mao Proclaiming Republic — A121

Designs: #439, Marx, Lenin and Kremlin. 22f, Dove over globe.

Perf. 11½ x 11

1959, Sept. 28 **Photo.**

With Gum

438 A117 8f lt brown & red 14.00 5.50
439 A117 8f dull blue & red 14.00 1.75
440 A117 22f blue grn & red 12.00 1.00
Nos. 438-440 (3) 40.00 8.25

1959, Oct. 1 **Litho.** ***Perf. 14***

441 A118 4f pale grn, red & gold 9.00 4.25
442 A118 8f gray, red & gold 9.00 1.00
443 A118 10f lt blue, red & gold 9.00 1.00
444 A118 20f pale brn, red & gold 13.00 1.50
Nos. 441-444 (4) 40.00 7.75

Engraved and Photogravure

1959, Oct. 1 ***Perf. 11½ x 11***

#446, Large coal mine. #447, Planer, Wuhan heavy machinery plant. #448, Wuhan Yangtze River Bridge. #449, Combine harvester. #450, Hsinankiang hydroelectric station. #451, Spinning machine. #452, Kirin chemical fertilizer plant.

With Gum

445 A119 8f brown & rose red (1) 1.00 .50
446 A119 8f brown & gray (2) 1.00 .50
447 A119 8f brown & yel brn (3) 1.00 .50
448 A119 8f brown & stl bl (4) 1.00 .50
449 A119 8f brown & org (5) 1.00 .50
450 A119 8f brown & ol (6) 1.00 .50
451 A119 8f brown & bl grn (7) 1.00 .50
452 A119 8f brown & vio (8) 1.00 .50
Nos. 445-452 (8) 8.00 4.00

1959, Oct. 1 **Litho.** ***Perf. 14***

Designs: 10f, Workers and factory, vert. 20f, People rejoicing, vert.

453 A120 8f cream & multi 5.00 1.60
454 A120 10f cream & multi 5.00 1.60
455 A120 20f cream & multi 5.00 1.60
Nos. 453-455 (3) 15.00 4.80

1959, Oct. 1 **Engr.**

456 A121 20f deep carmine 50.00 11.00

Nos. 438-456 commemorate 10th anniversary of the Proclamation of the People's Republic of China.

A122

A123

Designs: No. 457, Pioneers' emblem. No. 458, Pioneer Bugler. No. 459, Schoolgirl. No. 460, Girl using rain gauge. No. 461, Boy planting tree. No. 462, Girl figure skater.

1959, Nov. 10 **Photo.** ***Perf. 11½***

457 A122 4f red yel & blk (1) 3.50 .50
458 A122 4f Prus bl & red (2) 3.50 .50
459 A122 8f brn & red (3) 3.50 .50
460 A122 8f dk bl & red (4) 3.50 .50
461 A122 8f red & grn (5) 3.50 .50
462 A122 8f mag & red (6) 3.50 .50
Nos. 457-462 (6) 21.00 3.00

10th anniversary of the Young Pioneers. Black inscription on No. 457 engraved.

1959, Dec. 1 **Engr.**

4f, Exhibition emblem, communications symbols. 8f, Exhibition emblem & chimneys.

463 A123 4f dark blue .45 .40
464 A123 8f red .75 .40

Exhibition of Industry and Communications, Peking.

Palace of Nationalities A124

Engraved, Frame Lithographed

1959, Dec. 10 ***Perf. 14***

465 A124 4f red & blk 4.00 .50
466 A124 8f brt grn & blk 4.00 .80

Inauguration of the Cultural Palace of Nationalities, Peking.

Athletes' Monument and Track — A125

#468, Parachuting. #469, Marksmanship. #470, Diving. #471, Table tennis. #472, Weight lifting. #473, High jump. #474, Rowing. #475, Track. #476, Basketball. #477, Traditional Chinese fencing. #478, Motorcycling. #479, Gymnastics. #480, Bicycling. #481, Horsemanship. #482, Soccer.

1959, Dec. 28 **Litho.**

467 A125 8f bis, blk & gray (1) 3.25 .40
468 A125 8f dl bl, blk & gray (2) 3.25 .40
469 A125 8f red brn & blk (3) 3.25 .40
470 A125 8f grn, blk & brn (4) 3.25 .40
471 A125 8f brt grn, blk, brn & gray (5) 3.25 .40
472 A125 8f gray, blk & brn (6) 3.25 .40
473 A125 8f dl bl, blk & brn (7) 3.25 .40
474 A125 8f Prus grn, blk & brn (8) 3.25 .40
475 A125 8f org, blk & brn (9) 3.25 .40
476 A125 8f dl vio, blk & brn (10) 3.25 .40
477 A125 8f lt ol, blk & brn (11) 3.25 .40
478 A125 8f bl, blk & gray (12) 3.25 .40
479 A125 8f gray bl, blk, grn, & bl (13) 3.25 .40
480 A125 8f gray, blk, brn, & vio (14) 3.25 .40
481 A125 8f red org, blk, brn, & gray (15) 3.25 .40
482 A125 8f lt gray, blk, brn, & red (16) 3.25 .40
Nos. 467-482 (16) 52.00 6.40

First National Sports Meeting, Peking.

Wheat and Main Pavilion A126

Designs (Pavilion and): 8f, Meteorological symbols. 10f, Domestic animals. 20f, Fish.

1960, Jan. 20 **Engr. & Litho.**

Cream Background

483 A126 4f black & org .75 .25
484 A126 8f black & dull bl .75 .25
485 A126 10f black & org brn .75 .25
486 A126 20f black & grnsh bl .75 .30
Nos. 483-486 (4) 3.00 1.05

Opening of the National Agricultural Exhibition Halls, Peking.

With Gum
From No. 487 onward all stamps were issued with gum except as noted.

Catalogue values for unused stamps in this section, from this point to the end of the section, are for Never Hinged items.

Conference Hall, Tsunyi A127

Designs: 8f, Mao addressing conference. 10f, Crossing Chinsha River.

Engraved (4f, 10f); Photogravure (8f)

1960, Jan. 25 ***Perf. 11x11½***

487 A127 4f violet & blue 13.00 2.75
488 A127 8f red & multi 14.00 4.50
489 A127 10f slate green 19.50 2.75
Nos. 487-489 (3) 46.50 10.00

25th anniversary of the Communist Party Conference at Tsunyl.

Clara Zetkin (1857-1933) A128

Chinese and Russian Workers — A129

8f, Mother, child and dove. 10f, Woman tractor driver. 22f, Women of three races.

1960, Mar. 8 **Photo.** ***Perf. 11½x11***

490 A128 4f black & multi 3.00 .35
491 A128 8f black & multi 3.00 .35
492 A128 10f black & multi 3.00 .35
493 A128 22f black & multi 3.00 .60
Nos. 490-493 (4) 12.00 1.65

50th anniv. of International Women's Day.

1960, Mar. 10

Designs: 8f, Chinese and Russian flags. 10f, Chinese and Russian soldiers.

494 A129 4f dk brown 6.00 2.25
495 A129 8f red, yel & blk 7.00 2.25
496 A129 10f dp blue 10.00 2.25
Nos. 494-496 (3) 23.00 6.75

10th anniv. of Sino-Soviet Treaty of Friendship. Black inscription engraved on No. 495.

Flags of Hungary and China A130

Design: 8f, Parliament Building, Budapest.

1960, Apr. 4 ***Perf. 11 x 11½***

497 A130 8f yel, blk, red & grn 10.00 2.10
498 A130 8f blue, red & blk 10.00 4.25

15th anniv. of the liberation of Hungary.

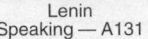

Lenin Speaking — A131

Lunik 2, Earth and Russian Arms — A132

Designs: 8f, Portrait of Lenin. 20f, Lenin talking with Smolny Palace guard.

Engraved (4f, 20f); Engraved and Photogravure (8f)

1960, Apr. 22 ***Perf. 11½ x 11***

499 A131 4f violet brn 8.00 1.00
500 A131 8f org red & blk 12.00 4.00
501 A131 20f dk brown 20.00 2.00
Nos. 499-501 (3) 40.00 7.00

90th anniversary of the birth of Lenin.

1960, Apr. 30 **Engr.** ***Perf. 11½***

Design: 10f, Lunik 3 over earth.

502 A132 8f red 4.00 .90
503 A132 10f green 6.00 .90

Russian space flights.

Pioneers and Flags of Czechoslovakia and China — A133

View of Prague with Charles Bridge A134

Perf. 11½x11; 11x11½

1960, May 9 **Photo.**

504 A133 8f yellow & multi 10.00 1.40
505 A134 8f deep green 10.00 2.75

Liberation of Czechoslovakia, 15th anniv.

Nostril Bouquet A135

Designs: Various goldfish.

1960, June 1 ***Perf. 11x11½***

506 A135 4f shown (1) 30.00 4.00
507 A135 4f Black-back dragon eye (2) 32.50 4.00
508 A135 4f Bubble eye (3) 32.50 4.50
509 A135 4f Red tiger head (4) 10.00 3.25
510 A135 8f Pearl scale (5) 50.00 6.00
511 A135 8f Blue dragon eye (6) 50.00 6.00
512 A135 8f Skyward eye (7) 10.00 3.00
513 A135 8f Red cap (8) 10.00 3.00
514 A135 8f Purple cap (9) 10.00 3.00
515 A135 8f Red head (10) 10.00 3.00
516 A135 8f Red and white dragon eye (11) 32.50 5.25
517 A135 8f Red dragon eye (12) 32.50 5.25
Nos. 506-517 (12) 310.00 50.25

Sow with Litter A136

#519, Pig being inoculated. #520, Pigs. #521, Pig and mechanized feeding. #522, Pig and bales.

1960, June 15

518 A136 8f red & blk (1) 22.50 1.75
519 A136 8f dp grn & blk (2) 22.50 1.75
520 A136 8f lil rose & blk (3) 22.50 1.75
521 A136 8f lt yel grn & blk (4) 22.50 1.75
522 A136 8f org & blk (5) 30.00 4.75
Nos. 518-522 (5) 120.00 11.75

Flag Inscribed "Serving the Workers" — A137

Flowers, Flags of North Korea and China — A138

Design: 8f, Inscribed stone seal.

1960, July 30 Photo. *Perf. 11½x11*

523 A137 4f lt grn, red, pink & brn 12.00 1.50

Photogravure & Engraved

524 A137 8f pale bl, red & bis 18.00 3.00

3rd Natl. Cong. for Literature and Arts, Peking.

1960, Aug. 15 Photo.

Design: 8f, Flying horse of Korea.

525 A138 8f red & multi 14.00 2.50
526 A138 8f ultra, red & indigo 15.00 6.00

15th anniversary of the liberation of Korea.

Railroad Station, Peking — A139

Design: 10f, Train arriving at station.

1960, Aug. 30 *Perf. 11½*

527 A139 8f blue, cream & brn 15.00 4.50
528 A139 10f bluish grn, cr & ind 20.00 4.50

Opening of new Peking Railroad Station.

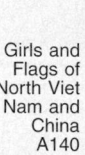

Girls and Flags of North Viet Nam and China A140

Lake of the Returning Sword, Hanoi A141

Worker and Fresh-air Installation A142

1960, Sept. 2 *Perf. 11x11½, 11½x11*

529 A140 8f red & multi 6.00 1.00
530 A141 8f red, gray grn & gray 6.00 3.00

15th anniversary of the Democratic Republic of North Viet Nam.

1960, Sept. 10 *Perf. 11½*

Designs: No. 532, Exterminator. No. 533, Window cleaning. No. 534, Medical examination of child. No. 535, Physical exercise.

531 A142 8f black & orange (1) 2.25 .25
532 A142 8f indigo & slate (2) 2.25 .25
533 A142 8f brown & blue (3) 2.25 .25
534 A142 8f maroon & ocher (4) 2.25 .25
535 A142 8f indigo & brt grn (5) 2.25 .45
Nos. 531-535 (5) 11.25 1.45

National health campaign.

Great Hall of the People — A143

Design: 10f, Inside view.

1960, Oct. 1

536 A143 8f yellow & multi 14.00 2.50
537 A143 10f brown & multi 20.00 3.00

Completion of the Great Hall of the People, Peking.

Dr. Norman Bethune — A144

Engels Addressing Congress at The Hague — A145

No. 539, Dr. Bethune operating on a soldier.

Photo. (No. 538); Engr. (No. 539)

1960, Nov. 20 *Perf. 11½x11*

538 A144 8f red & multi 6.50 1.00
539 A144 8f sepia 6.50 .80

Dr. Norman Bethune (1890-1939), Canadian surgeon with 8th Army.

1960, Nov. 28 Engr.

540 A145 8f shown 8.50 1.25

Photo.

541 A145 10f Portrait of Engels 10.00 3.00

140th anniversary of the birth of Friedrich Engels (1820-1895), German Socialist.

"Hwang Shi Ba" A146

Freighter A147

1960-61 Photo.

Various Chrysanthemums in Natural Colors

542 A146 4f bl gray (1) 14.00 1.10
543 A146 4f pink (2) 27.50 1.10
544 A146 8f dk gray (3) 13.00 1.10
545 A146 8f dp blue (4) 13.00 1.10
546 A146 8f green (5) 13.00 1.10
547 A146 8f magenta (6) 13.00 1.10
548 A146 8f olive (7) 13.00 1.10
549 A146 8f grnsh bl (8) 47.50 1.10
550 A146 10f gray (9) 13.00 1.10
551 A146 10f choc (10) 13.00 1.10
552 A146 20f dp blue (11) 13.00 1.10
553 A146 20f brt red (12) 37.50 3.25
554 A146 22f olive bis (13) 25.00 7.00
555 A146 22f carmine (14) 47.50 11.00
556 A146 30f grnsh gray (15) 16.00 4.50
557 A146 30f brt pink (16) 16.00 4.50
558 A146 35f dp green (17) 20.00 4.50
559 A146 52f brt lilac rose (18) 21.00 8.75
Nos. 542-559 (18) 376.00 55.60

Issued: #548-550, 557-559, 12/10/60; #545-547, 554-556, 1/18/61; #542-544, 2/24/61.

1960, Dec. 15 *Perf. 11½*

Without Gum

560 A147 8f deep blue 3.50 1.40

1st 10,000-ton Chinese-built freighter, launching.

Pantheon, Paris — A148

Design: 8f, Proclamation of the Commune.

Engraved and Photogravure

1961, Mar. 18 *Perf. 11½x11*

561 A148 8f gray blk & red 11.00 3.00
562 A148 8f brown & red 11.00 3.00

90th anniversary of the Paris Commune.

Championship Symbol and Jasmine — A149

Designs: 10f, Table tennis racket and ball; Temple of Heaven. 20f, Table tennis match. 22f, Peking workers' gymnasium.

1961, Apr. 5 Photo. *Perf. 11*

563 A149 8f multicolored .80 .50
564 A149 10f multicolored 1.10 1.25
565 A149 20f multicolored 1.60 1.25
566 A149 22f multicolored 2.75 .50
a. Souv. sheet, #563-566 *700.00 325.00*
Nos. 563-566 (4) 6.25 3.50

26th World Table Tennis Championships, Peking.

Jeme Tien-yow — A150

Design: 10f, Train and tunnel, Peking-Changchow Railroad.

1961, June 20 *Perf. 11½x11*

567 A150 8f ol grn & blk 2.50 .65
568 A150 10f org brn & brn 5.00 2.00

Centenary of the birth of Jeme Tien-yow, railroad construction engineer.

Congress Building, Shanghai — A151

Designs: 8f, August 1st Building, Nanchang. 10f, Provisional Central Government Office, Juikin. 20f, Pagoda Hill, Yenan. 30f, Gate of Heavenly Peace, Peking.

1961, July 1 *Perf. 11½*

569 A151 4f gold, red & cl 12.00 1.00
570 A151 8f gold, red & bl grn 32.50 1.50
571 A151 10f gold, red & yel brn 14.00 4.50
572 A151 20f gold, red & ultra 20.00 1.00
573 A151 30f gold, red & org red 27.50 2.00
Nos. 569-573 (5) 106.00 10.00

40th anniv. of the Chinese Communist Party.

August 1 Building, Nanchang — A152

3f, 4f, 5f, Trees & Sha Cho Pa Building, Juikin. 8f, 10f, 20f, Pagoda Hill, Yenan. 22f, 30f, 50f, Gate of Heavenly Peace, Peking.

1961-62 Engr. *Perf. 11*

Without Gum

Size: 24x16mm

574 A152 1f vio blue 7.00 .25
575 A152 1½f maroon 13.00 .25
576 A152 2f indigo 7.00 .95
577 A152 3f dull vio 27.50 1.40
578 A152 4f green 2.40 .20
579 A152 5f gray 1.60 .25
580 A152 8f sepia 1.60 .20
581 A152 10f brt lil rose 4.50 .20
582 A152 20f grnsh bl 1.60 .20
583 A152 22f brown .80 .20
584 A152 30f blue 1.60 .20
585 A152 50f vermilion 1.60 .20
Nos. 574-585 (12) 70.20 4.50

Issued: 1f, 1½f, 5f, 7/20/62; others 7/20/61.
See Nos. 647-654, 1059-1064.

Flowers, Flags of Mongolia and China A153

Design: 10f, Parliament, Ulan Bator, and statue of Sukhe Bator.

1961, July 11 Photo. *Perf. 11x11½*

586 A153 8f crim, ultra & yel 17.50 2.00
587 A153 10f orange, blk & yel 27.50 9.50

40th anniv. of the Mongolian People's Republic.

Military Museum — A154

Photo. & Engr.

1961, Aug. 1 *Perf. 11½*

588 A154 8f gray bl, brn & grn 25.00 .85
589 A154 10f gray, blk & grn 37.50 1.40

Opening of the People's Revolutionary Military Museum.

Uprising at Wuchang A155

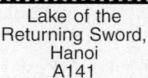

Sun Yat-sen — A156

Perf. 11x11½, 11½x11

1961, Oct. 10 **Photo.**

590	A155	8f gray & blk	15.00	1.75
591	A156	10f tan & black	30.00	.90

50th anniversary of the 1911 Revolution.

Donkey — A157

Rejoicing Tibetans — A158

Designs: 8f, 10f, 20f, 22f, Horses; 30f, 50f, Camels. Ceramic statuettes from Tang Dynasty (618-906) graves.

1961, Nov. 10 ***Perf. 11½x11***

Statuettes in Original Colors

592	A157	4f dull blue	6.00	1.00
593	A157	8f gray green	7.00	1.00
594	A157	8f dp purple	7.00	1.00
595	A157	10f dp blue	7.00	1.00
596	A157	20f olive	9.00	2.00
597	A157	22f blue grn	14.00	2.75
598	A157	30f red brown	18.00	8.00
599	A157	50f slate	18.00	4.50
		Nos. 592-599 (8)	86.00	21.25

1961, Nov. 25

Designs: 8f, Woman sower. 10f, Celebration of bumper crop. 20f, People's representatives. 30f, Tibetan children.

600	A158	4f brn & ocher	6.00	1.00
601	A158	8f brn & lt bl grn	6.00	1.00
602	A158	10f brn & yel	20.00	1.75
603	A158	20f brn & rose	27.50	2.50
604	A158	30f brn & bluish gray	47.50	3.25
		Nos. 600-604 (5)	107.00	9.50

Rebirth of the Tibetan people.

Lu Hsun — A159

1962, Feb. 26

605	A159	8f red brown & blk	3.00	1.00

80th anniv. of the birth of Lu Hsun, writer.

An Chi Bridge, Chao Hsien — A160

Bridges of Ancient China: 8f, Pao Tai, Soochow. 10f, Chu Pu, Kwan Hsien. 20f, Chen Yang, San Kiang.

1962, May 15 ***Perf. 11***

606	A160	4f dk gray blue	2.00	.20
607	A160	8f dp green	2.00	.20
608	A160	10f brown	2.00	.90
609	A160	20f grnsh blue	3.50	1.25
		Nos. 606-609 (4)	9.50	2.55

Tu Fu — A161

Cranes and Bamboo — A162

4f, Tu Fu memorial pavilion, Chengtu.

1962, May 25 ***Perf. 11½x11***

610	A161	4f ol bis & blk	15.00	1.00
611	A161	8f grnsh bl & blk	15.00	2.00

Poet Tu Fu, 1,250th anniversary of birth.

1962, June 10

10f, Two cranes in flight. 20f, Crane on rock.

612	A162	8f tan & multi	10.00	2.00
613	A162	10f blue & multi	15.00	3.00
614	A162	20f bister & multi	29.00	4.00
		Nos. 612-614 (3)	54.00	9.00

"The Sacred Crane," from paintings by Chen Chi-fo.

Cuban Soldier and Flag A163

Designs: 10f, Sugar cane worker. 22f, Militiaman and woman.

1962, July 10 ***Perf. 11x11½***

615	A163	8f car, rose & blk	32.50	9.00
616	A163	10f green & blk	32.50	2.75
617	A163	22f ultra & blk	70.00	16.00
		Nos. 615-617 (3)	135.00	27.75

Support of Cuba.

Torch and Map of Algeria — A164

Mei Lan-fang — A165

Design: 22f, Algerian soldiers and flag.

1962, July 10 ***Perf. 11½x11***

618	A164	8f dp brown & red org	1.00	.25
619	A164	22f ocher & dp brn	2.00	.75

Support of Algeria.

1962 ***Perf. 11½x11, 11x11½***

Designs (Mei Lan-fang in Women's Roles): No. 621, Beating drum. No. 622, With fan. 10f, Lady Yu with swords. 20f, With bag. 22f, Heavenly Maiden, horiz. 30f, With spinning wheel, horiz. 50f, Kneeling, horiz. $3, Scene from opera "Drunken Beauty."

620	A165	4f tan & multi	275.00	25.00
621	A165	8f tan & multi	50.00	7.00
622	A165	8f gray & multi	50.00	7.00
623	A165	10f gray & multi	60.00	8.00
624	A165	20f lt grn & multi	60.00	17.50
625	A165	22f cream & multi	70.00	19.00
626	A165	30f lt blue & multi	100.00	47.50
627	A165	50f buff & multi	100.00	30.00
		Nos. 620-627 (8)	765.00	161.00

Souvenir Sheet

Perf. 11

628	A165	$3 brown & multi	*6,500.*	*1,200.*

Stage art of Mei Lan-fang, actor.

Issued: 4f, 8f, 10f, 8/8; $3, 9/15; others 9/1.

Nos. 620-627 exist imperf. Value, set $3,500.

No. 628 contains one 48x58mm stamp and almost always has some faults. Value above is for fault-free examples. Value for No. 628 with small faults, unused $2,500. Excellent forgeries exist.

Flower Drum Dance, Han — A166

Folk Dances: 8f, Ordos, Mongolia. 10f, Catching shrimp, Chuang. 20f, Friend, Yi. 30f, Fiddle dance, Tibet. 50f, Tambourine dance, Uighur.

Cumulative numbers 246-251 at lower right.

1962, Oct. 15 **Litho.** ***Perf. 12½***

Without Gum

629	A166	4f cream & multi	.60	.35
630	A166	8f cream & multi	.60	.35
631	A166	10f cream & multi	.85	.35
632	A166	20f cream & multi	.85	.35
633	A166	30f cream & multi	1.75	.70
634	A166	50f cream & multi	3.50	1.40
		Nos. 629-634 (6)	8.15	3.50

See Nos. 696-707.

Soldiers Storming Winter Palace — A167

Design: 8f, Lenin leading soldiers, vert.

1962, Nov. 7 **Photo.** ***Perf. 11½***

635	A167	8f black & red	20.00	1.00
636	A167	20f slate grn & red	40.00	3.00

45th anniversary of the Russian Revolution.

Monument and Map of Albania — A168

Tsai Lun, Inventor of Papermaking A169

Design: 10f, Albanian flag and Girl Pioneer.

1962, Nov. 28 ***Perf. 11½x11***

637	A168	8f Prus blue & sepia	2.25	.35
638	A168	10f red, yel, & blk	2.50	1.00

50th anniversary of Albanian independence.

1962, Dec. 1 ***Perf. 11½x11***

Designs: No. 640, Paper making. No. 641, Sun Szu-miao, physician. No. 642, Writing medical treatise. No. 643, Shen Ko, geologist. No. 644, Making field notes. No. 645, Kuo Shou-chin, astronomer. No. 646, Astronomical instrument.

Cumulative numbers 297-304 at lower right.

639	A169	4f multicolored	8.00	.75
640	A169	4f multicolored	4.00	.75
641	A169	8f multicolored	4.00	.75
642	A169	8f multicolored	4.00	.75
643	A169	10f multicolored	4.00	.75
644	A169	10f multicolored	4.00	.75
645	A169	20f multicolored	8.00	.90
646	A169	20f multicolored	8.00	.90
		Nos. 639-646 (8)	44.00	6.30

Scientists of ancient China.

No. 639 exists with an extra character in the inscription.

Building Type of 1961

Designs: 1f, 2f, Building, Nanchang. 3f, 4f, Trees and Sha Cho Pa Building. 8f, 10f, 20f, Pagoda Hill, Yenan. 30f, Gate of Heavenly Peace, Peking.

1962, Jan. **Litho.** ***Rough Perf. 12½***

Size: 21x16mm

Without Gum

647	A152	1f ultra	.75	.20
648	A152	2f greenish gray	.75	.20
649	A152	3f violet gray	.75	.20
650	A152	4f green	.75	.20
651	A152	8f dk olive, perf. 14	1.50	.20
b.		Perf. 11x11½	5.00	
652	A152	10f brt rose lilac	2.50	.20
653	A152	20f slate blue	2.50	.20
654	A152	30f dull blue	3.50	.25
		Nos. 647-654 (8)	13.00	1.65

Tank Monument, Havana A170

Crowd in Peking — A171

Designs: No. 656, Cuban revolutionaries. No. 657, Crowd in Havana. No. 659, Cuban soldier. No. 660, Castro and Cuban flag.

Perf. 11½, 11x11½

1963, Jan. 1 **Photo.**

655	A170	4f red & blk brn	35.00	1.90
656	A170	4f green & blk	35.00	1.90
657	A171	8f dull red & brn	40.00	1.90
658	A171	8f dull red & brn	75.00	12.00
659	A170	10f ocher & blk	65.00	5.50
660	A170	10f red, blue & blk	75.00	*16.00*
		Nos. 655-660 (6)	325.00	*39.20*

4th anniversary of the Cuban revolution.

Green Dragontail — A172

Karl Marx — A173

1963 Without Gum *Perf. 11*

661	A172	4f Tibetan clouded yellow (1)	12.50	5.00
662	A172	4f Tritailed glory (2)	12.50	1.00
663	A172	4f Neumogeni jungle queen (3)	12.50	1.00
664	A172	4f Washan swordtail (4)	12.50	1.00
665	A172	4f Striped ringlet (5)	12.50	1.00
666	A172	8f shown (6)	15.00	1.00
667	A172	8f Dilunulated peacock (7)	15.00	1.00
668	A172	8f Yamfly (8)	15.00	1.00
669	A172	8f Golden kaiser-i-hind (9)	15.00	1.00
670	A172	8f Mushaell hairstreak (10)	15.00	1.00
671	A172	10f Yellow orange-tip (11)	15.00	2.00
672	A172	10f Great jay (12)	15.00	2.00
673	A172	10f Striped punch (13)	15.00	2.00
674	A172	10f Hainan violet-beak (14)	15.00	2.00
675	A172	10f Omeiskipper (15)	15.00	3.50
676	A172	20f Philippines birdwing (16)	12.50	3.50
677	A172	20f Richtofenis red apollo (17)	12.50	4.25
678	A172	22f Blue-banded king crow (18)	12.50	4.25
679	A172	30f Solskyi copper (19)	12.50	4.25
680	A172	50f Yunnan clipper (20)	12.50	5.50
		Nos. 661-680 (20)	275.00	47.25

Issued: #666-675, July 15; others Apr. 5.

1963, May 5 *Perf. 11½*

Designs: No. 682, "Workers of the World, Unite" on cover of first edition of Communist Manifesto. No. 683, Marx and Engels.

Without Gum

681	A173	8f black, gold & sal (1)	6.75	2.00
682	A173	8f gold & red (2)	6.75	2.00
683	A173	8f gold & choc (3)	6.75	2.00
		Nos. 681-683 (3)	20.25	6.00

145th anniversary of birth of Karl Marx (1818-1883), German political philosopher.

Child with Top — A174

Child: #685, eating berries. #686, as traffic policeman. #687, with windmill. #688, listening to caged cricket. #689, with sword. #690, embroidering. #691, with umbrella. #692, playing with sand. #693, playing table tennis. #694, learning to add. #695, with kite.

1963, June 1 Litho. *Perf. 12½*
Without Gum
Multicolored Designs

684	A174	4f grnsh gray (1)	1.25	.20
685	A174	4f tan (2)	1.25	.20
686	A174	8f gray (3)	1.25	.20
687	A174	8f blue (4)	1.25	.20
688	A174	8f tan (5)	1.25	.20
689	A174	8f dp gray (6)	1.25	.20
690	A174	8f citron (7)	1.25	.20
691	A174	8f gray (8)	1.25	.20
692	A174	10f green (9)	1.50	.45
693	A174	10f violet (10)	1.50	.45
694	A174	20f bister (11)	4.00	1.00
695	A174	20f green (12)	4.00	1.00
		Nos. 684-695 (12)	21.00	4.50

Children's Day. Value, imperf set $175.

Dance Type of 1962

Folk Dances: 4f, Weavers' dance, Puyi. 8f, Kazakh. 10f, Olunchun. 20f, Labor dance, Kaochan. 30f, Reed pipe dance, Miao. 50f, Fan dance, Korea.
Cumulative numbers 261-266 at lower right.

1963, June 15 *Perf. 12½*
Without Gum

696	A166	4f cream & multi	.75	.35
697	A166	8f cream & multi	.75	.35
698	A166	10f cream & multi	1.25	.35
699	A166	20f cream & multi	1.25	.35
700	A166	30f cream & multi	2.75	.70
701	A166	50f cream & multi	2.75	.70
		Nos. 696-701 (6)	9.50	2.80

1963, June 30 Without Gum

Folk Dances: 4f, "Wedding Ceremony," Yu. 8f, "Encircling Mountain Forest," Pai. 10f, Long drum dance, Yao. 20f, Third day of the third month dance, Li. 30f, Knife dance, Kawa. 50f, Peacock dance, Thai.
Cumulative numbers 279-284 at lower right.

702	A166	4f cream & multi	.75	.35
703	A166	8f cream & multi	.75	.35
704	A166	10f cream & multi	1.10	.35
705	A166	20f cream & multi	1.10	.35
706	A166	30f cream & multi	2.75	.60
707	A166	50f cream & multi	4.00	1.00
		Nos. 702-707 (6)	10.45	3.00

Giant Panda Eating Apples — A175

Table Tennis Player — A176

Designs: No. 709, Giant panda eating bamboo shoots. 10f, Two pandas, horiz.

1963, Aug. 5 Photo. *Perf. 11½x11*
Size: 28x38mm

708	A175	8f pale blue & blk	27.50	2.00
709	A175	8f pale blue & blk	27.50	6.25

Size: 50x29mm
Perf. 11½

710	A175	10f olive & blk	27.50	3.75
		Nos. 708-710 (3)	82.50	12.00

Value, imperf set $240.

1963, Sept. 10 Engr. *Perf. 11½*

No. 712, Trophies won by Chinese team.

711	A176	8f dk olive grn	13.00	.80
712	A176	8f brown	13.00	1.75

27th World Table Tennis Championships.

Snub-nosed Langur — A177

Jade-green Screen Mountain — A178

Designs: 10f, Two monkeys playing. 22f, Two monkeys grooming.

1963, Sept. 23 Photo. *Perf. 11½x11*

713	A177	8f gray & multi	8.00	1.10
714	A177	10f gray & multi	8.00	1.10
715	A177	22f gray & multi	13.00	4.50
		Nos. 713-715 (3)	29.00	6.70

Value, imperf set $225.

Engraved and Photogravure
1963, Oct. 15 *Perf. 11½*

Hwang Shan Landscapes (Yellow Mountains), Anhwei Province. #724-731 horiz.

Design A178

716	4f shown (1)	15.00	1.25
717	4f "Guests Welcoming Pines" (2)	15.00	1.25
718	4f Pines and Rock Behind the Sea (3)	15.00	1.75
719	4f Terrace of Keeping Cool (4)	15.00	1.75
720	8f Mount of Heavenly Capital (5)	18.50	1.75
721	8f Mount of Scissors (6)	18.50	1.75
722	8f Forest of Ten Thousand Pines (7)	18.50	1.75
723	8f "Brush Blooming in Dream" (8)	20.00	1.75
724	10f Mount of Lotus Flower (9)	27.50	1.75
725	10f Cumulus Cloud over West Sea (10)	27.50	1.75
726	10f Old Pines of Hwang Shan (11)	32.50	1.75
727	10f "Watching the Clouds over West Sea" (12)	50.00	1.75
728	20f Mount of Stalagmites (13)	60.00	6.00
729	22f "Stone Monkey Watching the Sea" (14)	60.00	9.50
730	30f Forest of Lions (15)	75.00	45.00
731	50f Three Fairy Tales of Pen Lai (16)	75.00	30.00
	Nos. 716-731 (16)	543.00	110.50

Soccer Player — A179

Athletes and Banners — A180

#733, Discus, women's. #734, Diving, men's. #735, Gymnastics, women's.

Engraved and Photogravure
1963, Nov. 17 *Perf. 11*

732	A179	8f gray, red & blk (1)	11.00	.80
733	A179	8f gray, ultra & blk (2)	11.00	.80
734	A179	8f lt grn, brn & blk (3)	11.00	.80
735	A179	8f gray, lil rose & blk (4)	11.00	.80

Photo. *Perf. 11½*

736	A180	10f red & multi (5)	11.00	3.25
		Nos. 732-736 (5)	55.00	6.45

Games of the Newly Emerging Forces, Djakarta.

Clay Rooster and Goat — A181

Chinese Folk Toys: No. 738, Cloth camel. No. 739, Cloth tigers. No. 740, Clay ox and rider. No. 741, Cloth rabbit, wooden doll, clay roosters. No. 742, Straw rooster. No. 743, Cloth donkey and bird. No. 744, Clay lion. No. 745, Cloth tiger and tumbler doll.

1963, Dec. 10 Litho. *Perf. 11½*
Toys Multicolored; Without Gum

737	A181	4f bister (1)	.70	.20
738	A181	4f gray (4)	.70	.20
739	A181	4f lt blue (7)	.70	.20
740	A181	8f bister (2)	.70	.20
741	A181	8f gray (5)	.70	.20
742	A181	8f lt blue (8)	.70	.25
743	A181	10f bister (3)	.70	.25
744	A181	10f gray (6)	.70	.25
745	A181	10f lt blue (9)	.70	.25
		Nos. 737-745 (9)	6.30	2.00

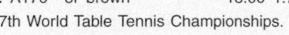

Armed Vietnamese Family — A182

Flags of Cuba and China — A183

Liberation of South Viet Nam: No. 747, Militia with Vietnamese flag.

1963, Dec. 20 Photo. *Perf. 11½x11*

746	A182	8f tan, blk & red	6.00	.80
747	A182	8f red & multi	6.00	1.60

1964, Jan. 1

Design: No. 749, Boy waving Cuban flag.

748	A183	8f red, yel, bl & ind	15.00	1.00
749	A183	8f multicolored	30.00	6.00

5th anniversary of the liberation of Cuba.

Woman Driving Tractor — A184

Woman of the People's Commune: No. 751, harvesting. No. 752, picking cotton. No. 753, picking fruit. No. 754, reading book. No. 755, on guard duty.

1964, Mar. 8

750	A184	8f ol, pink & brn (1)	1.00	.20
751	A184	8f brn yel & org (2)	1.00	.20
752	A184	8f gray & multi (3)	1.00	.20
753	A184	8f black, org & bl (4)	1.25	.20
754	A184	8f green & multi (5)	1.25	.20
755	A184	8f lilac & multi (6)	1.25	.30
		Nos. 750-755 (6)	6.75	1.30

Chinese and African Men A185

Design: No. 757, African drummer.

1964, Apr. 12 Photo. *Perf. 11*

756	A185	8f red & multi	.90	.25
757	A185	8f black & dk brn	.90	.25

African Freedom Day.

Marx, Engels, Lenin and Stalin — A186

Design: No. 759, Banners and workers.

1964, May 1 *Perf. 11½*

758	A186	8f gold, red & blk	22.50	*6.00*
759	A186	8f gold, red & blk	8.00	*2.00*

Labor Day.

Orchard, Yenan A187

Yenan, Shrine of the Chinese Revolution: No. 761, Central Auditorium, Yang Chia Ling. No. 762, Mao's office and residence. No. 763, Auditorium, Wang Chia Ping. No. 764, Border Region Assembly Hall. No. 765, Pagoda Hill and Bridge.

1964, July 1 Photo. *Perf. 11x11½*

760	A187	8f multicolored (1)	22.50	1.50
761	A187	8f multicolored (2)	3.75	.60
762	A187	8f multicolored (3)	3.75	.60
763	A187	8f multicolored (4)	3.75	.60
764	A187	8f multicolored (5)	18.00	2.00
765	A187	52f multicolored (6)	12.50	4.00
		Nos. 760-765 (6)	64.25	9.30

Map and Flag of Viet Nam — A188

Alchemist's Glowing Crucible — A189

1964, July 20 *Perf. 11½*

766	A188	8f multicolored	16.00	5.00

Victory in South Viet Nam.

1964, Aug. 5 *Perf. 11½x11*

767	A189	4f shown (1)	6.00	1.00
768	A189	4f Night-shining jade (2)	6.00	1.00
769	A189	8f Purple Kuo's cap (3)	9.50	1.00
770	A189	8f Chao pink (4)	9.50	1.00
771	A189	8f Yao yellow (5)	9.50	1.00
772	A189	8f Twin beauty (6)	9.50	1.00
773	A189	8f Ice-veiled ruby (7)	9.50	1.40
774	A189	10f Gold-sprinkled Chinese ink (8)	11.50	1.40
775	A189	10f Cinnabar jar (9)	11.50	1.40
776	A189	10f Lan Tien jade (10)	13.50	2.10
777	A189	10f Imperial robe yellow (11)	14.00	2.10
778	A189	10f Hu red (12)	14.00	2.10
779	A189	20f Pea green (13)	29.00	*5.00*
780	A189	43f Wei purple (14)	40.00	*17.50*
781	A189	52f Intoxicated celestial peach (15)	57.50	*20.00*
		Nos. 767-781 (15)	250.50	*59.00*

Souvenir Sheet

Perf. 11½

Without Gum

782	A189	$2 Glorious crimson & great gold pink	*1,200.*	*500.00*

No. 782 contains one 48x59mm stamp.

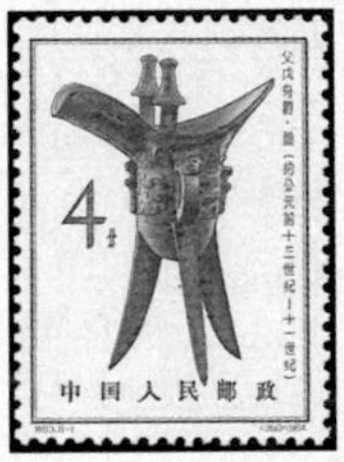

Wine Cup — A190

Grain Harvest — A191

Designs: Sacrificial bronze vessels of Yin dynasty, prior to 1050 B.C.

Engraved and Photogravure

1964, Aug. 25 *Perf. 11½x11*

783	A190	4f shown (1)	8.75	.90
784	A190	4f Ku beaker (2)	8.75	.90
785	A190	8f Kuang wine urn (3)	8.75	.90
786	A190	8f Chia wine cup (4)	9.50	.90
787	A190	10f Tsun wine vessel (5)	9.50	.90
788	A190	10f Yu wine urn (6)	9.50	.90
789	A190	20f Tsun wine vessel (7)	14.50	3.50
790	A190	20f Ceremonial cauldron (8)	14.50	3.50
		Nos. 783-790 (8)	83.75	12.40

1964, Sept. 26 Photo.

Designs: #792, Students planting trees. #793, Study period. #794, Scientific experimentation.

791	A191	8f multicolored (1)	1.75	.25
792	A191	8f multicolored (2)	1.75	.25
793	A191	8f multicolored (3)	1.75	.25
794	A191	8f multicolored (4)	1.75	.25
		Nos. 791-794 (4)	7.00	1.00

Youth helping in agriculture.

Marx, Engels, Trafalgar Square, London — A192

People with Banners — A193

1964, Sept. 28 *Perf. 11½*

795	A192	8f red, gold & red brn	42.50	16.00

Centenary of the First International.

Gold Ink

Stamps with gold ink often show some tarnishing. Values are for untarnished gold color. Tarnished stamps will sell for less.

1964, Oct. 1

No. 797, Gate of Heavenly Peace and Chinese flag. No. 798, People with banners, facing left.

796	A193	8f cream & multi (1)	27.50	2.75
797	A193	8f cream & multi (2)	27.50	2.75
798	A193	8f cream & multi (3)	27.50	2.75
a.		Souvenir sheet of 3	*2,100.*	*650.00*
b.		Strip of 3, #796-798	140.00	15.00
		Nos. 796-798 (3)	82.50	8.25

15th anniv. of the People's Republic.

No. 798a contains No. 798b in continuous design without separating perfs. No. 798a almost always has disturbed gum, with interleaving paper sticking to it, or tarnished gilt. Such copies sell for considerably less than the very fine example valued above.

Values for No. 798b are for an unfolded strip.

Oil Derricks — A194

Oil industry: 4f, Geological surveyors and truck, horiz. 8f, "Christmas tree" and extraction accessories. 10f, Oil refinery. 20f, Tank cars, horiz.

1964, Oct. 1

799	A194	4f lt blue & multi	50.00	4.00
800	A194	8f lt blue & multi	22.50	1.75
801	A194	8f lilac & multi	22.50	1.75
802	A194	10f slate & multi	50.00	1.75
803	A194	20f brown & multi	100.00	*23.50*
		Nos. 799-803 (5)	245.00	*32.75*

Albanian and Chinese Flags A195

10f, Enver Hoxha and Albanian coat of arms.

1964, Nov. 29 *Perf. 11x11½*

804	A195	8f red & multi	10.00	2.00
805	A195	10f red, yel & blk	15.00	8.00

20th anniv. of the liberation of Albania.

Power Dam Construction A196

No. 807, Installation of turbogenerator rotor. No. 808, Main dam. 20f, Pylon.

1964, Dec. 15 *Perf. 11½*

806	A196	4f multicolored	65.00	2.25
807	A196	8f multicolored	25.00	.85
808	A196	8f multicolored	50.00	1.40
809	A196	20f multicolored	100.00	20.00
		Nos. 806-809 (4)	240.00	24.50

Hsin An Kiang Dam and hydroelectric power station.

Fertilizer Industry — A197

Chemical Industry: #811, Plastics. #812, Medicines. #813, Rubber. #814, Insecticides. #815, Industrial acids. #816, Industrial alkaloids. #817, Synthetic fibers.

1964, Dec. 30 Photo. & Engr.

810	A197	8f red & blk (1)	2.25	.25
811	A197	8f yel grn & blk (2)	2.25	.25
812	A197	8f brown & blk (3)	2.25	.25
813	A197	8f lilac rose & blk (4)	2.25	.25
814	A197	8f blue & blk (5)	2.25	.25
815	A197	8f orange & blk (6)	2.25	.25
816	A197	8f violet & blk (7)	2.25	.25
817	A197	8f brt green & blk (8)	2.25	.25
		Nos. 810-817 (8)	18.00	2.00

Mao Studying Map — A198

Mao Tse-tung — A199

Design: No. 819, Victory at Lushan Pass.

1965, Jan. 31 Photo. ***Perf. 11***

818 A198 8f red & multi 40.00 10.00
819 A198 8f red & multi 30.00 10.00

Perf. 11½x11

820 A199 8f gold & multi 35.00 10.00
Nos. 818-820 (3) 105.00 30.00

Tsunyi Conference, 30th anniversary.

Conference Hall, Bandung — A200

Lenin — A201

#822, Asians and Africans applauding.

1965, Apr. 18 ***Perf. 11½x11***

821 A200 8f cream & multi .90 .20
822 A200 8f cream & multi .90 .20

10th anniversary of the Bandung, Indonesia, Conference, Apr. 1955.

1965, Apr. 25 ***Perf. 11½***

823 A201 8f red, choc & salmon 20.00 5.00

95th anniversary of the birth of Lenin.

Chinese Player — A202

1965, Apr. 25 ***Perf. 11½***

824 A202 8f shown (1) .50 .20
825 A202 8f European woman (2) .50 .20
826 A202 8f Chinese woman (3) .50 .20
827 A202 8f European man (4) .50 .20
a. Block of 4, #824-827 2.75 .80

28th World Table Tennis Championships, Ljubljana, Yugoslavia, Apr. 15-25.

Climbers on Mt. Minya Konka — A203

Marx and Lenin — A204

Mountain Climbers: No. 829, on Muztagh Ata. No. 830, on Mt. Jolmo Lungma (Mt. Everest). No. 831, Women camping on Kongur Tiubie Tagh. No. 832, on Shisha Pangma.

1965, May 25 Photo. & Engr.

828 A203 8f blue, blk & ol (1) 5.25 .75
829 A203 8f blue, blk & ol (2) 5.25 .75
830 A203 8f ultra, blk & gray (3) 5.25 .75
831 A203 8f lt bl, blk & yel gray (4) 5.25 .75
832 A203 8f ultra, blk & gray (5) 5.50 3.25
Nos. 828-832 (5) 26.50 6.25

Chinese mountaineering achievements, 1957-64.

1965, June 21 Photo. ***Perf. 11½x11***

833 A204 8f red, yel & blk 15.00 5.00

Postal Ministers' Congress, Peking.

Tseping Valley A205

Chingkang Mountains, Cradle of the Chinese Revolution.

1965, July 1 ***Perf. 11x11½***

834 A205 4f shown (1) 8.00 1.00
835 A205 8f San Wan Tsun (2) 10.00 1.00
836 A205 8f Octagon Bldg., Mao Ping (3) 32.50 1.00
837 A205 8f River and Bridge at Lung Shih (4) 37.50 1.75
838 A205 8f Ta Ching Tsun (5) 16.00 2.75
839 A205 10f Bridge across the Lung Yuan (6) 16.00 2.00
840 A205 10f Hwang Yang Mountain (7) 13.50 5.00
841 A205 52f Chingkang peaks (8) 12.00 7.00
Nos. 834-841 (8) 145.50 21.50

Soldiers with Books — A206

1965, Aug. 1 ***Perf. 11½***

Without Gum

842 A206 8f shown (1) 20.00 2.50
843 A206 8f Soldiers reading Little Red Books (2) 20.00 2.50
844 A206 8f With shell and artillery (3) 20.00 2.50
845 A206 8f Rifle instruction (4) 20.00 2.50
846 A206 8f Sewing jacket (5) 20.00 2.50
847 A206 8f Bayonet charge (6) 20.00 6.00
848 A206 8f With Banner (7) 22.50 6.00
849 A206 8f Military band (8) 22.50 6.00
Nos. 842-849 (8) 165.00 30.50

People's Liberation Army. Nos. 846-849 vertical.

"Welcome to Peking" — A207

#851, Chinese and Japanese young men. #852, Chinese and Japanese girls. #853, Musical entertainment. #854, Emblem of meeting.

1965, Aug. 25 ***Perf. 11½x11***

850 A207 4f yellow & multi 1.25 .25
851 A207 8f pink & multi 1.25 .25
852 A207 8f multicolored 1.25 .25
853 A207 10f multicolored 1.75 .25
854 A207 22f lt blue & multi 3.00 .50
Nos. 850-854 (5) 8.50 1.50

Chinese-Japanese Youth Meeting, Peking.

North Vietnamese Soldier — A208

Peoples of the World — A209

Designs: No. 856, Soldier with guns. No. 857, Soldier giving victory salute.

1965, Sept. 2 ***Perf. 11½x11***

855 A208 8f red & red brn (1) 1.50 .35
856 A208 8f red & blk (2) 1.50 .35
857 A208 8f red & vio brn (3) 1.50 .35

Perf. 11½

858 A209 8f black & red (4) 1.50 .35
Nos. 855-858 (4) 6.00 1.40

Struggle of the people of Viet Nam.

Mao Tse-tung at His Desk — A210

Crossing Yellow River A211

Victory Monument A212

Design: No. 862, Recruits in cart.

1965, Sept. 3 ***Perf. 11***

859 A210 8f red & multi (1) 30.00 6.50

Perf. 11x11½, 11½x11

860 A211 8f red & dk grn (2) 10.00 .90
861 A212 8f red & dk brn (3) 10.00 .90
862 A211 8f red & dk grn (4) 10.00 .90
Nos. 859-862 (4) 60.00 9.20

20th anniversary of victory over Japan.

2nd National Games — A213

National Games Opening Ceremonies — A214

Perf. 11½x11, 11 (A214)

1965, Sept. 28

863 A213 4f Soccer (1) 10.00 .85
864 A213 4f Archery (2) 10.00 .85
865 A213 8f Javelin (3) 10.00 .85
866 A213 8f Gymnastics (4) 10.00 .85
867 A213 8f Volleyball (5) 10.00 .85
868 A214 10f shown (6) 42.50 .85
869 A213 10f Bicyling (7) 60.00 .85
870 A213 20f Diving (8) 55.00 2.50
871 A213 22f Hurdles (9) 10.00 2.50
872 A213 30f Weight lifting (10) 10.00 5.50
873 A213 43f Basketball (11) 14.50 9.00
Nos. 863-873 (11) 242.00 25.45

Government Building A215

Textile Workers A216

1½f, 5f, 22f, Gate of Heavenly Peace. 2f, 8f, 30f, People's Hall. 3f, 10f, 50f, Military Museum.

1965-66 ***Perf. 11½x11***

Without Gum

874 A215 1f brown .20 .20
875 A215 1½f red lilac .20 *.50*
876 A215 2f green .20 .20
877 A215 3f blue grn .20 .20
878 A215 4f brt blue .20 .20
879 A215 5f vio brn ('66) .40 .20
880 A215 8f rose red .40 .20
881 A215 10f gray olive .80 .20
882 A215 20f violet .80 .20
883 A215 22f orange 1.60 .25
884 A215 30f yellow grn 2.50 .30
885 A215 50f dp blue ('66) 7.50 *3.25*
Nos. 874-885 (12) 15.00 *5.90*

1965, Nov. 30

886 A216 8f shown (1) 14.00 1.25
887 A216 8f Machine shop (2) 14.00 1.25
888 A216 8f Welder (3) 14.00 1.25
889 A216 8f Students (4) 14.00 1.25
890 A216 8f Militia (5) 14.00 1.50
Nos. 886-890 (5) 70.00 6.50

Women workers.

Soccer — A217

Children's Sports: No. 892, Racing. No. 893, Tobogganing and skating. No. 894, Gymnastics. No. 895, Swimming. No. 896, Rifle practice. No. 897, Jumping rope. No. 898, Table tennis.

1966, Feb. 25 ***Perf. 11***

891 A217 4f emerald & multi (1) .50 .20
892 A217 4f yel brown & multi (2) .50 .20
893 A217 8f blue & multi (3) .50 .20
894 A217 8f yellow & multi (4) .50 .20
895 A217 8f grnsh bl & multi (5) .75 .20
896 A217 8f green & multi (6) .75 .20
897 A217 10f orange & multi (7) 1.75 .40
898 A217 52f grnsh gray & multi (8) 3.00 1.25
Nos. 891-898 (8) 8.25 2.85

Mobile Transformer A218

New Industrial Machinery: No. 900, Electron microscope, vert. No. 901, Lathe. No. 902, Vertical boring and turning machine, vert. No. 903, Gear-grinding machine. No. 904, Hydraulic press. No. 905, Milling machine. No. 906, Electron accelerator, vert.

Perf. 11x11½, 11½x11

1966, Mar. 30 **Photo. & Engr.**

899 A218 4f yellow & blk (1) 13.00 .90
900 A218 8f blk & lt ultra (2) 15.00 .90
901 A218 8f sal pink & blk (3) 15.00 .90
902 A218 8f olive & blk (4) 15.00 .90
903 A218 8f rose lil & blk (5) 15.00 .90
904 A218 10f gray & blk (6) 20.00 .90
905 A218 10f bl grn & blk (7) 20.00 3.50
906 A218 22f lilac & blk (8) 37.50 5.50
Nos. 899-906 (8) 150.50 14.40

Military and Civilian Workers A219

Women in Various Occupations: No. 908, Train conductor. No. 909, Red Cross worker. No. 910, Kindergarten teacher. No. 911, Road sweeper. No. 912, Hairdresser. No. 913, Bus conductor. No. 914, Traveling saleswoman. No. 915, Canteen worker. No. 916, Rural mail carrier.

1966, May 10 ***Perf. 11x11½***

907 A219 8f red & multi (1) .60 .25
908 A219 8f pale grn & multi (2) .60 .25
909 A219 8f yellow & multi (3) .60 .25
910 A219 8f green & multi (4) .60 .25
911 A219 8f salmon & multi (5) .60 .25
912 A219 8f pale bl & bl (6) .60 .25
913 A219 8f yellow & multi (7) .60 .25
914 A219 8f tan & multi (8) .60 .25
915 A219 8f yel grn & multi (9) .60 .25
916 A219 8f green & multi (10) .60 .25
Nos. 907-916 (10) 6.00 2.50

Statue "Thunderstorm" — A220

22f, Open book and association emblem.

1966, June 27 ***Perf. 11***

917 A220 8f red & black 2.00 .35
918 A220 22f red, gold & yel 6.00 .75

Afro-Asian Writers' Assoc. Conf., Peking.

Sun Yat-sen — A221

1966, Nov. 12 ***Perf. 11½x11***

919 A221 8f sepia & lt buff 70.00 9.00

Birth centenary of Sun Yat-sen.

Athletes Holding Portrait of Mao — A222

Two Women Athletes with Little Red Book A223

#921, Athletes holding Little Red Books. #923, Athletes reading Mao texts.

1966, Dec. 31 ***Perf. 11***

920 A222 8f red & multi (1) 30.00 7.00
921 A222 8f red & multi (2) 30.00 7.00

Perf. 11x11½

922 A223 8f blue & multi (3) 30.00 7.00
923 A223 8f blue & multi (4) 30.00 7.00
Nos. 920-923 (4) 120.00 28.00

1st Athletic Games of the New Emerging Nations.

Appreciation of Lu Hsun by Mao — A224

"Be Resolute ...," by Mao Tse-tung — A225

Designs: No. 925, Portrait of Lu Hsun. No. 926, Lu Hsun's handwriting (3 vert. rows).

Engr. & Photo.; Photo. (#925)

1966, Dec. 31 ***Perf. 11½***

924 A224 8f red & black (1) 62.50 13.00
925 A224 8f red & multi (2) 22.50 12.00
926 A224 8f red & black (3) 42.50 13.00
Nos. 924-926 (3) 127.50 38.00

Lu Hsun, Revolutionary writer (1881-1936).

Perf. 11½x11, 11½ (No. 928)

1967, Mar. 10 **Photo.**

Designs: No. 928, Drilling crew fighting natural gas fire, horiz. No. 929, Attempt to close fire-engulfed valve.

Sizes: Nos. 927, 929, 26x38mm; No. 928, 49x29mm

927 A225 8f red, gold & blk 30.00 12.50
928 A225 8f brick red & blk 30.00 6.00
929 A225 8f brick red & blk 30.00 6.00
Nos. 927-929 (3) 90.00 24.50

Heroic oil well firefighters.

Liu Ying-chun A226

1967, Mar. 25 ***Perf. 11½x11***

930 A226 8f shown (1) 25.00 7.75
931 A226 8f With book by Mao (2) 25.00 6.00
932 A226 8f Holding bridle of horse (3) 27.50 10.00
933 A226 8f With film slide (4) 27.50 6.00
934 A226 8f Lecturing (5) 27.50 5.25
935 A226 8f Fatal attempt to stop runaway horse (6) 27.50 5.25
Nos. 930-935 (6) 160.00 40.25

In memory of soldier Liu Ying-chun, hero.

Third 5-Year Plan — A227

Design: No. 936, Banners, 3 workers and male soldier facing right (industrial growth). No. 937, Banners, 3 workers and female militia member facing left (agricultural growth).

1967, Apr. 15 ***Perf. 11***

936 A227 8f red & multi 40.00 8.00
937 A227 8f red & multi 40.00 8.00

Third Five-Year Plan.

Mao Tse-tung — A228

Thoughts of Mao — A229

1967, Apr. 20 ***Perf. 11½***

938 A228 8f red & multi 35.00 17.50

Red & Gold

939 A229 8f 39 characters 75.00 17.50
940 A229 8f 50 characters 75.00 17.50
941 A229 8f 39 characters in 6 lines 75.00 17.50
942 A229 8f 53 characters 75.00 17.50
943 A229 8f 46 characters 75.00 17.50
a. Strip of 5, #939-943 1,100. 250.00

Gold & Red

944 A229 8f 41 characters 90.00 20.00
945 A229 8f 49 characters 90.00 20.00
946 A229 8f 35 characters 90.00 20.00
947 A229 8f 22 characters 90.00 20.00
948 A229 8f 29 characters 90.00 20.00
a. Strip of 5, #944-948 1,100. 250.00
Nos. 938-948 (11) 860.00 205.00

Thoughts of Mao Tse-tung.

Values for Nos. 943a and 948a are for unfolded strips without tarnishing.

No numbers appear below design on Nos. 938-1046.

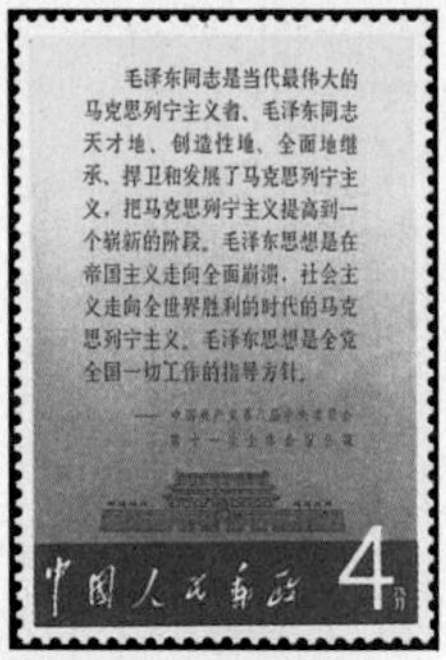

Gate of Heavenly Peace and Text from C. C. P. Communique Praising Mao — A230

Mao and Lin Piao A231

#950, Mao and poem. #951, Mao among people of various races. #952, Mao facing left and Red Guards with books. #953, Mao with upraised right hand. #954, Mao leaning on rail, horiz. 10f, Mao and Lin Piao in discussion, horiz.

Engraved and Photogravure

1967 ***Perf. 11x11½***

Size: 36x56mm

949 A230 4f yel, red & mar 40.00 14.00

Photo.

950 A230 8f yel, brn, & red 50.00 14.00
951 A230 8f yel, red & multi 47.50 14.00
952 A230 8f yel, red & multi 65.00 14.00

Size: 36x50mm, 50x36mm

Perf. 11

953 A231 8f black & multi 40.00 14.00
954 A231 8f black & multi 190.00 30.00
955 A231 8f lt blue & multi 30.00 14.00
956 A231 10f black & multi 190.00 30.00
Nos. 949-956 (8) 652.50 144.00

"Mao Tse-tung Our Great Teacher."
Issued: #949-953, 5/1; #954-956, 9/20.

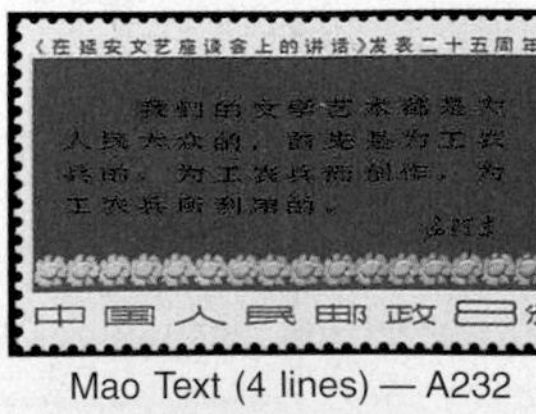

Mao Text (4 lines) — A232

Parade of Supporters — A233

Design: No. 958, Mao text (5 lines).

Engraved and Photogravure

1967, May 23 *Perf. 11½*

957	A232	8f black, red & yel	175.00	35.00
958	A232	8f black, red & yel	225.00	45.00

Photo. *Perf. 11*

959	A233	8f multicolored	225.00	45.00
		Nos. 957-959 (3)	625.00	125.00

25th anniversary of Mao Tse-tung's "Talks on Literature and Art" in Yenan.

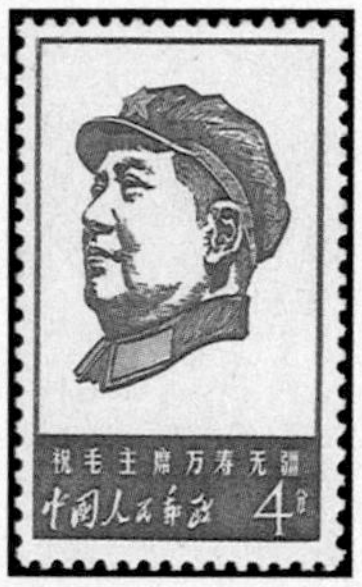

Mao Tse-tung — A234

1967 **Engr.** *Perf. 11*

960	A234	4f brown	15.00	*12.00*
961	A234	8f carmine	200.00	*25.00*
962	A234	35f dk brown	7.50	*12.00*
963	A234	43f vermilion	7.50	*12.00*
964	A234	52f carmine	7.50	*12.00*
		Nos. 960-964 (5)	237.50	*73.00*

46th anniv. of Chinese Communist Party. Issue dates: 8f, July 1; others Sept.

Mao, "Sun of the Revolution" — A235

No. 966, Mao and people of various races.

1967, Oct. 1 *Perf. 11½x11*

965	A235	8f multicolored	15.00	*11.00*
966	A235	8f multicolored	90.00	13.00

People's Republic of China, 18th anniv.

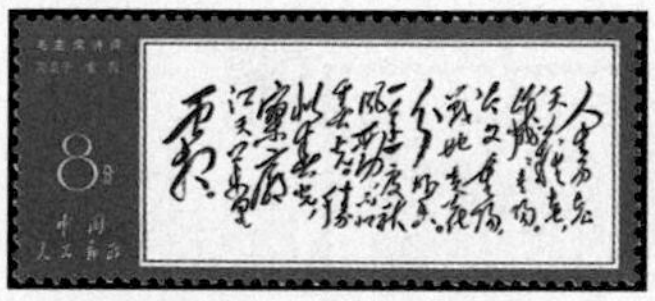
"September 9" — A236

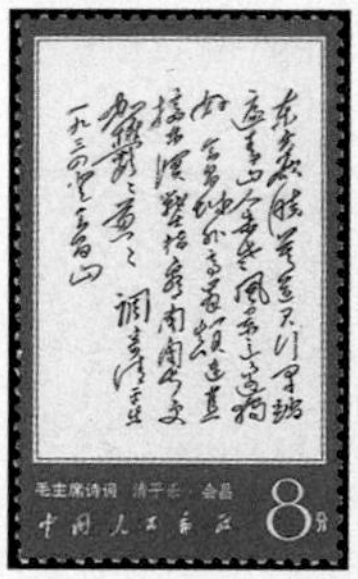
"Huichang" A237

"Peitaiho" A238

Reply to Comrade Kuo Mo-jo — A239

Mao Tse-tung Writing Poems — A240

Poems by Mao: #967, "The Long March." #968, "Liupanshan." #969, shown. #970, "The Cave of the Fairies." #971, "Snow." #972, "Lushan Pass." #975, "Conquest of Nanking." #976, "The Yellow Crane Pavilion." #977, "Swimming." #979, "Changsha."

1967-68 **Photo.** *Perf. 11*

Size: 79x18½mm

967	A236	4f 9 characters, UL panel	20.00	*17.50*
968	A236	4f 11 characters, UL panel	10.00	*17.50*

Size: 60x24mm

Perf. 11½

969	A236	8f shown, 10 characters in UL panel	90.00	20.00
970	A236	8f 21 characters in UL panel	80.00	20.00
971	A236	8f 11 characters in UL panel	90.00	22.00
972	A236	8f 9 characters in UL panel	90.00	22.00

Size: 29x50mm

973	A237	8f shown	200.00	45.00
974	A238	8f shown	450.00	50.00
975	A238	8f 3 rows in bottom panel	175.00	40.00
976	A238	8f 2 rows in bottom panel	260.00	35.00

Size: 52x38mm

Perf. 11

977	A239	8f 3 short vert. rows, at left of poem	260.00	30.00
978	A239	10f shown	10.00	*17.50*
979	A239	10f undivided text	11.00	*17.50*
980	A240	10f red, yel & multi	12.00	*17.50*
		Nos. 967-980 (14)	1,758.	371.50

Issued: #969-970, 980, 10/1; #973-974, 977, 5/20/68; others 7/20/68.

Lin Piao's Epigram on Mao Tse-tung A241

1967, Dec. 26 **Photo.** *Perf. 11x11½*

981	A241	8f red & gold	22.00	14.00

Mao and Parade of Artists — A242

"Raid on White Tiger Regiment" — A243

"Red Detachment of Women" — A244

1968 *Perf. 11½x11; 11 (983, 990)*

982	A242	8f shown (56x36mm)	55.00	12.00
983	A242	8f "The Red Lantern," vert.	55.00	12.00
984	A243	8f shown	55.00	14.00
985	A243	8f "Shachiapang" (women & soldier)	55.00	14.00
986	A243	8f "On the Dock"	55.00	14.00
987	A243	8f "Taking Bandits' Fort"	55.00	14.00
988	A244	8f shown	55.00	14.00
989	A244	8f "The White-haired Girl"	55.00	14.00
990	A242	8f Mao with Orchestra & Chorus (50x36mm)	75.00	17.50
		Nos. 982-990 (9)	515.00	125.50

Mao's direction for revolutionary literature and art. Issued: #982-987, Jan. 30; #988-990, May 1.

"Unite still more closely . . ." — A245

1968, May 31 **Photo.** *Perf. 11*

991	A245	8f red, gold & red brn	95.00	20.00

Mao Tse-tung's statement of support of Afro-Americans.

Statement about Cultural Revolution A246

Directives of Chairman Mao: No. 993, Experiences of Revolutionary Committee. No. 994, Leadership role of Revolutionary Committee. No. 995, Basic principle of reform. No. 996, Purpose of Cultural Revolution.

1968, July 20 **Photo.** *Perf. 11½*

No. of Lines Over Signature

992	A246	8f shown	100.00	37.50
993	A246	8f 5	100.00	37.50
994	A246	8f 4½	100.00	37.50
995	A246	8f 4	100.00	37.50
996	A246	8f 8	100.00	37.50
a.		Strip of 5, #992-996	*3,000.*	600.00
		Nos. 992-996 (5)	500.00	187.50

Value for No. 996a is for an unfolded strip.

Lin Piao's Statement, July 26, 1965 — A247

1968, Aug. 1 **Engr. & Photo.**

997	A247	8f red, gold & blk	10.50	5.50

Chinese People's Liberation Army, 41st anniv.

Mao Tse-tung Going to An Yuan, 1921 A248

1968, Aug. 1 *Perf. 11x11½*

998	A248	8f multicolored	75.00	8.00

Shade varieties include varying amount of red in clouds.

Directive of Chairman Mao — A249

1968, Nov. 30 *Perf. 11½*

999	A249	8f red & blk brn	90.00	25.00

China Map, Worker, Farmer and Soldier A249a

1968, Nov. **Photo.** *Perf. 11½x11*

999A	A249a	8f red, bl & bis	*20,000.*	*15,000.*

Map inscribed: "The entire nation is red." Issued in Canton and quickly withdrawn because Taiwan appears white instead of red.

No. 999A most often is found repaired. Values are for sound, unrepaired examples.

Counterfeits exist.

Woman, Miner and Soldier Holding Little Red Book A250

1968, Dec. 26 ***Perf. 11x11½***

1000 A250 8f multicolored 25.00 3.75

Canceled-to-order

From about this point on stamps are valued postally used.

Yangtze Bridge, Nanking A251

Road across Bridge — A252

No. 1003, Side view. 10f, Aerial view.

Lithographed, *Perf. 11½x11 (A251);*
Photogravure, *Perf. 11½ (A252)*

1969

Without Gum

1001 A251 4f multicolored 4.50 2.25
1002 A252 8f multicolored 18.00 6.75
1003 A252 8f multicolored 12.50 6.75
1004 A251 10f multicolored 4.50 2.25
Nos. 1001-1004 (4) 39.50 18.00

Inauguration of Yangtze Bridge at Nanking on Dec. 29, 1968.

Singer and Pianist A253

(Piano Music from the Opera, "The Red Lantern"): #1006, Woman singer and pianist.

1969, Aug. **Photo.** ***Perf. 11x11½***

Without Gum

1005 A253 8f multicolored 10.00 7.50
1006 A253 8f multicolored 52.50 11.00

Harvest A254

1969, Oct.

Without Gum

1007 A254 4f shown 5.00 2.25
a. Brown omitted 20.00 20.00
1008 A254 8f Two harvesters 10.00 1.50
1009 A254 8f Harvesters with Little Red Books 60.00 9.00
1010 A254 10f Red Cross Worker examining baby 5.25 2.50
Nos. 1007-1010 (4) 80.25 15.25

Agriculture students.

Armed Forces and Slogan — A255

Guarding the Coast — A256

Designs: No. 1013, 43f, Snow patrol, vert.

1969, Oct. ***Perf. 11½***

Without Gum

1011 A255 8f red & multi 27.50 *10.00*
a. Bayonets omitted 80.00 40.00
1012 A256 8f blue & multi 4.50 *3.50*
1013 A256 8f blue & multi 4.50 *3.50*
1014 A256 35f black & multi 4.50 *3.50*
1015 A256 43f black & multi 4.50 *3.50*
Nos. 1011-1015 (5) 45.50 *24.00*

Defense of Chen Pao-tao (Damansky Islands) in Ussuri River.

Farm Woman A257

Designs: 8f, Foundry worker. 10f, Soldier.

1969, Dec. ***Perf. 10; 11½***

Without Gum

1016 A257 4f ver & dk pur .50 *.40*
a. Perf 11½ 1.75 1.10
1017 A257 8f ver & dk brn 1.00 *.60*
a. Perf 11½ 1.75 1.10
1018 A257 10f ver & blk 2.00 *1.10*
a. Perf 11½ —
Nos. 1016-1018 (3) 3.50 *2.10*

Perforation

Nos. 1016-1018 and some succeeding issues bear two kinds of perforation: clean (Peking) and rough (Shanghai).

Building — A258

Communist Party Building, Shanghai A259

Agriculture Building, Canton — A260

Foundry Worker — A261

Two types of 8f Gate of Heavenly Peace:

I — Strong, definite halo around sun.
II — Halo missing, white shades gradually into red.

1969-72 **Photo.** ***Perf. 10, 11½***

Without Gum

1019 A258 1f shown .20 *.20*
1020 A259 1½f shown .65 .70
a. Perf. 11½ 5.50 4.00
1021 A260 2f shown .20 *.20*
1022 A260 3f 1929 Party Day House, Pu Tien .20 .20
1023 A260 4f Mao's Home and Office, Yunnan .20 *.20*
1024 A261 5f Woman Tractor Driver 1.75 .75
1025 A260 8f Gate of Heavenly Peace, type II .65 .35
a. Type I 2.50 1.25
1026 A259 8f Heroes Monument 1.25 .70
a. Perf. 11½ 4.50 3.00
1027 A260 8f Pagoda Hill, Yenan 1.25 *3.50*
1028 A260 8f Gate of Heavenly Peace (no sun) .20 .20
1029 A260 10f Monument, Tsu Ping .30 .20
1030 A259 20f Conference Hall, Tsunyi 1.90 1.40
a. Perf. 11½ 6.00 4.50
1031 A260 20f Highway ('72) .40 .20
1032 A260 22f Shao Shan Village, Birthplace of Mao .75 .35
1033 A260 35f Conference Hall 1.00 .35
1034 A260 43f Chingkang Peaks 1.50 .35
1035 A259 50f as 4f, different view 1.50 1.40
1036 A260 52f People's Hall, Peking 2.25 .35
1037 A261 $1 shown ('70) 5.00 2.75
Nos. 1019-1037 (19) 21.15 14.35

Kin Hsün-hua A262

Mounted Patrol — A263

1970, Jan. **Without Gum** ***Perf. 11½***

1045 A262 8f red & black 21.00 *16.00*
a. 8f red & gray brown 23.00 12.00

Death of Kin Hsün-hua in Kirin border flood.

1970, Aug. 1

Without Gum

1046 A263 8f yel grn & multi 7.00 6.00

People's Liberation Army, 43rd anniv.

Commemorative stamps from Nos. 1047 to 1142 and 1211-1214, carry a cumulative number in parenthesis at lower left and the year at lower right. Where such numbers help to identify, they are quoted in parenthesis.

Cpl. Yang Tse-jung — A264

Ensemble A265

1970, Aug. 1 ***Perf. 11½x11, 11x11½***

Without Gum

1047 A264 8f shown (1) 32.50 8.00
1048 A264 8f Armed guards (2) 3.50 2.50
1049 A264 8f Yang leaping through forest (3) 3.50 2.50
1050 A265 8f shown (4) 27.50 8.00
1051 A265 8f Yang in folk costume (5) 3.50 2.50
1052 A265 8f Four actors (6) 21.00 8.00
Nos. 1047-1052 (6) 91.50 31.50

Scenes from opera "Taking Tiger Mountain by Strategy." Nos. 1048, 1052, horizontal.

Frontier Guard A266

1971, Jan. **Litho.** ***Perf. 10***

Without Gum

1053 A266 4f multicolored 2.00 1.50
a. Perf. 11½ 2.10 1.10
b. Perf. 11½x10 3.00
c. Perf. 10x11½ 4.00

Banner of the Commune A267

Street Battle, Paris, 1871 A268

10f, Proclamation of the Commune. 22f, Rally.

Perf. 11½x11, 11x11½

1971, Mar. 18 **Litho. & Engr.**

Without Gum

1054 A267 4f sal & multi 25.00 8.00
1055 A268 8f ver, pink & brn 200.00 25.00
1056 A267 10f ver, pink & dk brn 9.00 8.00
1057 A268 22f ver, pink & dk brn 3.50 *8.00*
Nos. 1054-1057 (4) 237.50 49.00

Centenary of the Paris Commune.

Redrawn Building Type of 1961

Designs: 2f, 3f, August 1 building, Nanchang. 4f, 52f, Gate of Heavenly Peace, Peking. 10f, 20f, Pagoda Hill, Yenan.

1971, July 1 Litho. *Perf. 11x11½*
Size: 21x16mm
Without Gum

1059	A152	2f	slate green	1.50	.75
1060	A152	3f	sepia	2.00	1.25
1061	A152	4f	brt pink	2.00	1.25
1062	A152	10f	brt rose lil	4.75	1.25
1063	A152	20f	dk blue grn	2.75	1.25
1064	A152	52f	orange	1.50	1.25
			Nos. 1059-1064 (6)	14.50	7.00

Paper of Nos. 1059-1064 is white. That of Nos. 647-654 is toned.

Communist Party Building, Shanghai — A269

People and Factories — A270

Designs: No. 1068, Peasant Movement Training Institute. No. 1069, Ching Kang Peaks. No. 1070, Conference Building, Tsunyi. No. 1071, Pagoda Hill, Yenan. No. 1073, People and People's Hall, Peking. No. 1074, People and Pagoda Hill, Yenan. 22f, Gate of Heavenly Peace, Peking.

1971, July 1 Photo. *Perf. 11½*
Red and Gold Frame
Without Gum

1067	A269	4f	vermilion (12)	5.00	1.25
1068	A269	4f	brt grn (13)	5.00	1.25
1069	A269	8f	grnsh bl & red (14)	4.00	1.25
1070	A269	8f	ol blk (15)	4.00	1.25
1071	A269	8f	bis, grn & red (16)	15.00	2.75
1072	A270	8f	yel, red & multi (18)	15.00	2.75
1073	A270	8f	yel, red & multi (19)	15.00	2.75
1074	A270	8f	yel, red & multi (20)	15.00	2.75
a.			Strip of 3, #1072-1074	95.00	40.00
1075	A269	22f	red, gold & brn (17)	35.00	3.00
			Nos. 1067-1075 (9)	113.00	19.00

50th anniv. of the Chinese Communist Party. No. 1074a has a continuous design and is valued as an unfolded strip.

Chinese Welcome A271

Enver Hoxha — A272

#1077, Chinese & African players. #1078, Chinese & African girl players. 43f, Games' emblem.

1971, Nov. 3 Litho. *Perf. 11½*
Without Gum

1076	A271	8f	lil rose & multi	7.00	1.75
1077	A271	8f	lt yellow & multi	7.00	1.75
1078	A271	8f	dk grn & multi	7.00	1.75
1079	A271	43f	grn, gold & org	4.00	1.75
			Nos. 1076-1079 (4)	25.00	7.00

Afro-Asian Table Tennis Games, Peking.

1971, Nov. 3 Photo. *Perf. 11*

#1081, Party's birthplace. #1082, Albanian flag. 52f, Albanian partisans, horiz.

Without Gum

1080	A272	8f	Prus blue & multi	8.50	5.00
1081	A272	8f	buff & multi	6.75	3.00
1082	A272	8f	red, yel & multi	6.75	3.00
1083	A272	52f	lt blue & multi	7.75	5.00
			Nos. 1080-1083 (4)	29.75	16.00

30th anniversary of the founding of Albanian Communist Party.

Yenan Pagoda and 1942 Meeting House A273

1972, May 23 Photo. *Perf. 11*
Without Gum

1084	A273	8f	shown (33)	6.00	2.00
1085	A273	8f	Uniformed choir (34)	6.00	2.00
1086	A273	8f	"Brother & Sister" (35)	7.00	2.00
1087	A273	8f	Outdoor performance (36)	7.00	2.00
1088	A273	8f	"The Red Signal Lantern" (37)	7.00	2.00
1089	A273	8f	Dancer from "The Red Company of Women" (38)	7.00	2.00
			Nos. 1084-1089 (6)	40.00	12.00

30th anniversary of the publication of the Discussions on Literature and Art at the Yenan Forum.

Various Ball Games — A274

Workers' Gymnastics A275

1972, June 10

1090	A274	8f	shown (39)	7.50	1.25
1091	A275	8f	shown (40)	7.50	1.25
1092	A275	8f	Tug of war (41)	7.50	1.25
1093	A275	8f	Mountain climbers and tents (42)	7.50	1.25
1094	A275	8f	Children diving & swimming (43)	7.50	1.25
			Nos. 1090-1094 (5)	37.50	6.25

10th anniversary of Mao Tse-tung's edict on physical culture.

Ocean Freighter Fenglei — A276

1972, July 10 Photo. *Perf. 11½*
Without Gum

1095	A276	8f	shown (29)	16.00	2.50
1096	A276	8f	Tanker Taching No. 30 (30)	16.00	2.50
1097	A276	8f	Cargo-passenger ship Changzeng (31)	16.00	2.50
1098	A276	8f	Dredger Xienfeng (32)	16.00	2.50
			Nos. 1095-1098 (4)	64.00	10.00

Table Tennis Players' Welcome A277

1972, Sept. 2 *Perf. 11½x11, 11x11½*
Without Gum

1099	A277	8f	Championship emblem, vert. (45)	3.00	1.00
1100	A277	8f	shown (46)	3.00	1.00
1101	A277	8f	Table tennis (47)	3.00	1.00
1102	A277	22f	Women from different countries, vert. (48)	7.00	3.00
			Nos. 1099-1102 (4)	16.00	6.00

First Asian table tennis championships.

Wang Chin-hsi — A278

Workers on Cliffs along Canal — A279

Engraved and Photogravure
1972, Dec. 25 *Perf. 11½x11*

1103	A278	8f	multicolored (44)	10.00	2.00

Wang Chin-hsi, the Iron Man, fighter for the working class.

1972, Dec. 30

#1105, Canal flowing through tunnel. #1106, Bridge. #1107, Canal along cliffs.

1104	A279	8f	multicolored (49)	2.25	1.00
1105	A279	8f	multicolored (50)	2.25	1.00
1106	A279	8f	multicolored (51)	2.25	1.00
1107	A279	8f	multicolored (52)	2.25	1.00
			Nos. 1104-1107 (4)	9.00	4.00

Construction of Red Flag Canal, Linhsien county, Honan.

Giant Panda — A280

Woman Coal Miner — A281

Designs: Pandas in various positions. The 8f stamps are horizontal.

Perf. 11½x11, 11x11½
1973, Jan. 15 Photo.
Designs in Black and Red

1108	A280	4f	lt yel grn (61)	2.00	*2.50*
1109	A280	8f	buff (59)	2.00	*2.50*
1110	A280	8f	lt tan (60)	2.00	*2.50*
1111	A280	10f	pale green (58)	80.00	20.00
1112	A280	20f	pale bl gray (57)	55.00	20.00
1113	A280	43f	pale lilac (62)	8.50	*9.50*
			Nos. 1108-1113 (6)	149.50	57.00

1973, Mar. 8 Photo. *Perf. 11½x11*

1114	A281	8f	shown (63)	2.25	1.50
1115	A281	8f	Committee member (64)	2.25	1.50
1116	A281	8f	Telephone line worker (65)	2.25	1.50
			Nos. 1114-1116 (3)	6.75	4.50

Intl. Working Women's Day. Designs are after paintings from an exhib. for 30th anniv. of the Yenan Forum on Literature and Art.

Dancing Girl — A282

1973, June 1 Photo. *Perf. 11*

1117	A282	8f	shown (86)	1.50	1.25
1118	A282	8f	Musician, boy (87)	1.50	1.25
1119	A282	8f	Girl with scarf (88)	1.50	1.25
1120	A282	8f	Boy with tambourine (89)	1.50	1.25
1121	A282	8f	Girl with drum (90)	1.50	1.25
a.			Strip of 5, #1117-1121	9.50	7.50
			Nos. 1117-1121 (5)	7.50	6.25

Values for No. 1121a are for an unfolded strip.

Tournament Emblem — A283

1973, Aug. 25 Photo. *Perf. 11½*

#1123, Visitors from Asia, Africa and Latin America arriving by plane. #1124, Woman player. 22f, African, Asian & Latin American women.

1122	A283	8f	multicolored (91)	2.25	.90
1123	A283	8f	multicolored (92)	2.25	.90
1124	A283	8f	multicolored (93)	2.25	.90
1125	A283	22f	multicolored (94)	1.10	.90
			Nos. 1122-1125 (4)	7.85	3.60

Asian, African and Latin American Table Tennis Friendship Invitational Tournament.

The White-haired Girl — A284

Designs: Scenes from the ballet "The White-haired Girl." Nos. 1126, 1129 vert.

1973, Sept. 25 Photo. *Perf. 11½*

1126 A284 8f multicolored (53) 5.00 1.10
1127 A284 8f multicolored (54) 5.00 1.10
1128 A284 8f multicolored (55) 5.00 1.10
1129 A284 8f multicolored (56) 5.00 1.10
Nos. 1126-1129 (4) 20.00 4.40

Fair Building, Canton — A285

1973, Oct. 15 Photo. *Perf. 11*

1130 A285 8f multicolored (95) 4.25 2.25

Export Commodities Fall Fair, Canton.

Teapot with Blue Phoenix Design — A286

Excavated Works of Art: No. 1132, Silver pot with horse design. No. 1133, Black pottery horse. No. 1134, Woman, clay figurine. No. 1135, Carved stone pillar base. No. 1136, Galloping bronze horse. No. 1137, Bronze inkwell (toad). No. 1138, Bronze lamp, Chang Hsin Palace. No. 1139, Bronze tripod. No. 1140, Square bronze pot. 20f, Bronze wine vessel. 52f, Painted red clay tripod.

1973, Nov. 20 *Perf. 11½*

1131 A286 4f ol bis & multi (66) 1.50 1.00
1132 A286 4f ver & multi (67) 1.50 1.00
1133 A286 8f yel grn & multi (68) 1.10 .50
1134 A286 8f brt rose & multi (69) 1.10 .50
1135 A286 8f lt vio & multi (70) .80 .50
1136 A286 8f yel bis & multi (71) .80 .50
1137 A286 8f lt bl & multi (72) .80 .50
1138 A286 8f gray & multi (73) .80 .50
1139 A286 10f yel bis & multi (74) .35 *.50*
1140 A286 10f dp org & multi (75) .35 *.50*
1141 A286 20f lil & multi (76) 1.50 1.25
1142 A286 52f grn & multi (77) 1.50 *2.00*
Nos. 1131-1142 (12) 12.10 9.25

Marginal Markings

Marginal inscriptions on stamps of 1974-91 start at lower left with "J" for commemoratives and "T" for "special issues," followed by three numbers indicating (a) set sequence for the year, (b) total of stamps in set, and (c) number of stamp within set. At right appears the year date. Listings include the "c" number parenthetically. The "a" number is included only when it will help identify stamps not illustrated.

Example: T26 (6-3), the 3rd stamp of 6 from the 26th special set. Set numbers and or positions will be shown only when they help identify a stamp. An illustrated single stamp set will not have these numbers in the listings.

Woman Gymnast — A287

Designs: No. 1144, Gymnast on rings. No. 1145, Aerial split over balance beam, woman. No. 1146, Gymnast on parallel bars. No. 1147, Uneven bars, woman. No. 1148, Gymnast on horse. T.1.

1974, Jan. 1 Photo. *Perf. 11½x11*

1143 A287 8f lt grn & multi (1) 8.00 3.00
1144 A287 8f lt vio & multi (2) 8.00 3.00
1145 A287 8f lt blue & multi (3) 8.00 3.00
1146 A287 8f sal & multi (4) 8.00 3.00
1147 A287 8f yel & multi (5) 9.00 4.00
1148 A287 8f lil rose & multi (6) 9.00 4.00
Nos. 1143-1148 (6) 50.00 20.00

Girls Twirling Bamboo Diabolos — A288

Designs: No. 1149, Lion Dance, vert. No. 1150, Handstand on chairs, vert. No. 1152, Men balancing jar. No. 1153, Plate spinning, vert. No. 1154, Twirling umbrella, vert. T.2.

1974, Jan. 21 *Perf. 11*

1149 A288 8f brn & multi (1) 5.75 2.75
1150 A288 8f Prus bl & multi (2) 5.75 2.75
1151 A288 8f lilac & multi (3) 5.75 2.75
1152 A288 8f dull bl & multi (4) 7.00 2.75
1153 A288 8f ol grn & multi (5) 7.00 2.75
1154 A288 8f gray & multi (6) 7.00 2.75
Nos. 1149-1154 (6) 38.25 16.50

Traditional acrobatics.

Shao Shan — A289

Transportation by Railroad — A290

1½f, Site of 1st National Communist Party Congress. 2f, Peasant Movement Institute, Kwangchow. 3f, Headquarters of Nanchang Uprising. 4f, Great Hall of the People, Peking. 5f, View of Wen Chia Shih. 8f, Tien An Men. 10f, Tzeping in Chingkang Mountains. 20f, Site of Kutien Meeting. 22f, Tsunyi Conference site. 35f, Yenan (bridge). 43f, Hsi Pai Ho, Communist Party meeting site. 50f, Fairy Cave, Lushan. 52f, Monument to People's Heroes. $2, Trucks on mountain road.

1974 Litho. *Perf. 11*
Without Gum

1163 A289 1f sl grn & pale grn .50 .20
1164 A289 1½f car & buff .50 .20
1165 A289 2f dk blue & pale grn .50 .20
1166 A289 3f dk ol & yel .50 .20
1167 A289 4f red & yel .50 .20
1168 A289 5f brn & lt yel .50 .20
1169 A289 8f dull mag & buff .50 .20
a. Perf. 11½x12 8.00
1170 A289 10f blue & pink .50 .20
1171 A289 20f dk red & buff 1.25 .20
1172 A289 22f vio & lt yel 1.90 .25
1173 A289 35f mar & lt yel 2.50 .75
1174 A289 43f red brn & buff 3.25 *1.25*
1175 A289 50f dk blue & pink *3.75* *2.00*
1176 A289 52f sepia & buff 5.00 2.50

Photogravure & Engraved

1177 A290 $1 multicolored 1.25 .20
1178 A290 $2 multicolored 2.50 .40
Nos. 1163-1178 (16) 25.40 9.15

Capital Stadium — A290a

Design: 8f, Hotel Peking.

1974, Dec. 1 Photo. *Perf. 11*
Without Gum

1179 A290a 4f black & yel grn .20 .20
1180 A290a 8f black & ultra .30 .20

"Veteran Secretary" — A291

Well Diggers — A292

Designs: Nos. 1183-1186 horizontal. T.3.

1974, Apr. 20 Photo. *Perf. 11*

1181 A291 8f shown (1) 1.60 1.10
1182 A292 8f shown (2) 1.60 1.10
1183 A291 8f Spring hoeing (3) 1.60 1.10
1184 A291 8f Farmers (4) 1.60 1.10
1185 A292 8f Farm (5) 2.40 1.10
1186 A291 8f Bumper crops (6) 2.40 1.10
Nos. 1181-1186 (6) 11.20 6.60

Paintings by farmers of Huhsien County, shown at exhibition in Peking.

Mailman on Motorcycle — A293

1974, May 15 Photo. *Perf. 11*

1187 A293 8f shown (1) 6.25 3.50
1188 A293 8f People of the world (2) 6.25 3.50
1189 A293 8f Great Wall (3) 6.25 3.50
Nos. 1187-1189 (3) 18.75 10.50

Centenary of the UPU. J.1.

Barefoot Doctor Inoculating Children A294

Designs (Barefoot Doctors): No. 1191, Crossing stream at night to reach patient, vert. No. 1192, Gathering herbs, vert. No. 1193, Acupuncture treatment for farmer in the field.

Perf. 11x11½, 11½x11
1974, June 26 Photo.

1190 A294 8f multicolored (82) 1.40 1.00
1191 A294 8f multicolored (83) 1.40 1.00
1192 A294 8f multicolored (84) 1.40 1.00
1193 A294 8f multicolored (85) 1.40 1.00
Nos. 1190-1193 (4) 5.60 4.00

Steel Worker Wang Chin-hsi — A295

#1195, Workers studying Mao's writings around campfire. #1196, Drilling for oil in winter. #1197, Scientific industrial management. #1198, Oil derricks and farms. T.4.

1974, Sept. 30 Photo. *Perf. 11*

1194 A295 8f multicolored (5-1) 1.25 .90
1195 A295 8f multicolored (5-2) 1.25 .90
1196 A295 8f multicolored (5-3) 1.25 .90
1197 A295 8f multicolored (5-4) 1.25 .90
1198 A295 8f multicolored (5-5) 1.25 .90
Nos. 1194-1198 (5) 6.25 4.50

Workers of Taching as examples of achievement.

Members of Tachai Commune — A296

#1200, Farmers leveling mountains and fields in winter. #1201, Scientific farming. #1202, Trucks carrying surplus harvest. #1203, Young workers with banner. T.5.

1974, Sept. 30

1199 A296 8f multi (5-1) 1.75 .80
1200 A296 8f multi (5-2) .90 .80
1201 A296 8f multi (5-3) 1.75 .80
1202 A296 8f multi (5-4) .90 .80
1203 A296 8f multi (5-5) .90 .80
Nos. 1199-1203 (5) 6.20 4.00

Farmers of Tachai as examples of achievement.

Arms of Republic and Members of Ethnic Groups — A297

1974, Oct. 1

1204 A297 8f multi (1-1) 6.00 3.50

Taching Steel Worker — A298

Designs: No. 1206, Tachai farm woman. No. 1207, Soldier, planes and ships. J.3.

1974, Oct. 1

1205 A298 8f multi (3-1) 1.75 1.50
1206 A298 8f multi (3-2) 1.75 1.50
1207 A298 8f multi (3-3) 1.75 1.50
a. Strip of 3, #1205-1207 6.00 5.25

People's Republic of China, 25th anniv. Values for No. 1207a are for an unfolded strip.

Export Commodities Fair Building, Canton — A299

1974, Oct. 15

1208 A299 8f multicolored 3.50 1.50

Chinese Export Commodities Fair, Canton.

Guerrillas' Monument, Permet, Albania — A300

Albanian Patriots and Coat of Arms — A301

1974, Nov. 29 Photo. *Perf. 11½x11*

1209	A300	8f	multicolored	3.75	1.50
1210	A301	8f	multicolored	3.75	1.50

Albania's liberation, 30th anniversary.

Water-cooled Generator — A302

Industrial Products: No. 1212, Motorized rice sprouts transplanter. No. 1213, Universal cylindrical grinding machine. No. 1214, Open-air rock drill, vert. All dated 1973.

Photogravure and Engraved

1974, Dec. 23 *Perf. 11*

1211	A302	8f	vio & multi (78)	37.50	6.00
1212	A302	8f	yel grn & multi (79)	37.50	6.00
1213	A302	8f	ver & multi (80)	37.50	6.00
1214	A302	8f	blue & multi (81)	37.50	6.00
			Nos. 1211-1214 (4)	150.00	24.00

Congress Delegates — A303

Designs: No. 1216, Red flags, constitution and flowers. No. 1217, Worker, farmer and soldier, agriculture and industry.

1975, Jan. 25 Photo. *Perf. 11½*

1215	A303	8f	gold & multi (3-1)	5.00	1.75
1216	A303	8f	gold & multi (3-2)	5.00	1.75
1217	A303	8f	gold & multi (3-3)	5.00	1.75
			Nos. 1215-1217 (3)	15.00	5.25

Fourth National People's Congress, Peking.

Teacher Studying Revolutionary Works — A304

#1219, Teacher, children and horse. #1220, Outdoors class. #1221, Class held in boat. T.9.

1975, Mar. 8 Photo. *Perf. 11*

1218	A304	8f	multi (4-1)	9.00	3.00
1219	A304	8f	multi (4-2)	9.00	3.00
1220	A304	8f	multi (4-3)	9.00	3.00
1221	A304	8f	multi (4-4)	9.00	3.00
			Nos. 1218-1221 (4)	36.00	12.00

Rural women teachers and for International Working Women's Day.

"Broadsword," Encounter Position — A305

#1223, Exercise with 2 swords (woman). #1224, Graceful boxing (woman). #1225, Man leaping with spear. #1226, Woman holding fighting staff. 43f, 2 women with spears against man with 3-section staff.

1975, June 10 Photo. *Perf. 11x11½*

Size: 39x29mm

1222	A305	8f	(6-1)	4.50	3.00
1223	A305	8f	(6-2)	4.50	3.00
1224	A305	8f	(6-3)	4.50	3.00
1225	A305	8f	(6-4)	4.50	3.00
1226	A305	8f	(6-5)	4.50	3.00

Size: 59x29mm

1227	A305	43f	red & multi (6-6)	4.50	6.00
			Nos. 1222-1227 (6)	27.00	21.00

Wushu ("Kung Fu"), self-defense exercises. Tête bêche in sheets of 50 (5x10).

Mass Judgment and Criticisms — A306

No. 1229, Brigade leader writing wall newspaper. No. 1230, Study and criticism on battlefield, horiz. No. 1231, Former "slave" led into battle by criticism of Lin Piao and Confucius, horiz. T.8.

Perf. 11½x11, 11x11½

1975, Aug. 20 Photo.

1228	A306	8f	red & multi (4-1)	6.50	2.50
1229	A306	8f	red & multi (4-2)	6.50	2.50
1230	A306	8f	red & multi (4-3)	6.50	2.50
1231	A306	8f	red & multi (4-4)	6.50	2.50
			Nos. 1228-1231 (4)	26.00	10.00

Campaign to encourage criticism of Lin Piao and Confucius.

Athletes Studying Theory of Dictatorship of Proletariat — A307

3rd National Sports Meet: No. 1232, Women athletes leading parade, vert. No. 1234, Women volleyball players. No. 1235, Runner, soldier, farmer and worker, vert. No. 1236, Young athlete and various sports. No. 1237, Athletes of various races and horse race. 35f, Children and diving tower, vert. J.6.

1975, Sept. 12 Photo. *Perf. 11½*

1232	A307	8f	multi (7-1)	1.25	.85
1233	A307	8f	multi (7-2)	1.25	.85
1234	A307	8f	multi (7-3)	1.25	.85
1235	A307	8f	multi (7-4)	1.25	.85
1236	A307	8f	multi (7-5)	1.25	.85
1237	A307	8f	multi (7-6)	1.25	.85
1238	A307	35f	multi (7-7)	4.25	4.25
			Nos. 1232-1238 (7)	11.75	9.35

Mountaineers A308

Mt. Everest A309

Design: No. 1240, Mountaineers raising Chinese flag on summit, horiz. T.15.

1975 Photo. *Perf. 11½x11, 11x11½*

1239	A308	8f	multi (3-2)	.65	.35
1240	A308	8f	multi (3-3)	.65	.35
1241	A309	43f	multi (3-1)	.95	.75
			Nos. 1239-1241 (3)	2.25	1.45

Chinese Mt. Everest expedition.

Agricultural Workers with Book — A310

#1243, Workers carrying load. #1244, Woman driving harvester combine. J.7.

1975, Oct. 1 *Perf. 11½*

1242	A310	8f	multi (3-1)	3.75	1.25
1243	A310	8f	multi (3-2)	3.75	1.25
1244	A310	8f	multi (3-3)	3.75	1.25
			Nos. 1242-1244 (3)	11.25	3.75

National Conference to promote learning from Tachai's achievements in agriculture.

Girl Giving Boy Red Scarf — A311

Designs (Children): No. 1246, Putting up wall posters criticizing Lin Piao and Confucius. No. 1247, Studying. No. 1248, Harvesting. 52f, Physical training. T.14.

1975, Dec. 1 Photo. *Perf. 11½*

1245	A311	8f	multi (5-1)	1.25	1.00
1246	A311	8f	multi (5-2)	1.25	1.00
1247	A311	8f	multi (5-3)	1.25	1.00
1248	A311	8f	multi (5-4)	1.25	1.00
1249	A311	52f	multi (5-5)	5.75	3.50
			Nos. 1245-1249 (5)	10.75	7.50

Moral, intellectual and physical progress of Chinese children.

Woman Plowing Rice Field A312

#1251, Mechanized rice planting. #1252, Drainage and irrigation. #1253, Woman spraying insecticide over cotton field. #1254, Combine. T.13.

1975, Dec. 15 *Perf. 11*

1250	A312	8f	multi (5-1)	2.10	1.25
1251	A312	8f	multi (5-2)	2.10	1.25
1252	A312	8f	multi (5-3)	2.10	1.25
1253	A312	8f	multi (5-4)	2.10	1.25
1254	A312	8f	multi (5-5)	2.10	1.25
			Nos. 1250-1254 (5)	10.50	6.25

Priority program of farm mechanization.

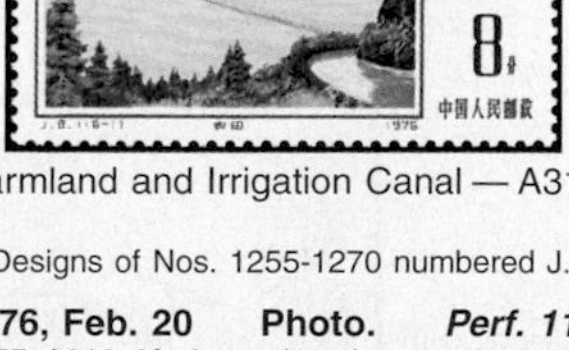

Farmland and Irrigation Canal — A313

Designs of Nos. 1255-1270 numbered J.8.

1976, Feb. 20 Photo. *Perf. 11½*

1255	A313	8f	shown (16-1)	3.50	2.00
1256	A313	8f	Irrigation canal (16-2)	3.50	2.00
1257	A313	8f	Fertilizer plant (16-3)	3.50	2.00
1258	A313	8f	Textile plant (16-4)	3.50	2.00
1259	A313	8f	Anshan Iron and Steel Co. (16-5)	3.50	2.00

Nos. 1255-1270 commemorate fulfillment of 4th Five-year Plan.

1976, Apr. 9

1260	A313	8f	Coal freight trains (16-6)	3.75	2.00
1261	A313	8f	Hydroelectric station (16-7)	3.75	2.00
1262	A313	8f	Ship building (16-8)	3.75	2.00
1263	A313	8f	Oil industry (16-9)	3.75	2.00
1264	A313	8f	Pipe line and port (16-10)	3.75	2.00

1976, June 12

1265	A313	8f	Train on viaduct (16-11)	5.00	2.00
1266	A313	8f	Scientific research (16-12)	5.00	2.00
1267	A313	8f	Classroom (16-13)	5.00	2.00
1268	A313	8f	Health Center (16-14)	5.00	2.00
1269	A313	8f	Apartment houses (16-15)	5.00	2.00
1270	A313	8f	Department store (16-16)	5.00	2.00
			Nos. 1255-1270 (16)	66.25	32.00

Heart Surgery with Acupuncture Anesthesia — A314

Operating Room and: #1272, Man driving tractor with severed arm restored. #1273, Man exercising broken arm in cast. #1274, Patient threading needle after cataract operation. T.12.

1976, Apr. 9 Photo. *Perf. 11½*

1271	A314	8f	brn & multi (4-1)	3.00	1.00
1272	A314	8f	yel grn & multi (4-2)	3.00	1.00
1273	A314	8f	bl grn & multi (4-3)	3.00	1.00
1274	A314	8f	vio bl & multi (4-4)	3.00	1.00
			Nos. 1271-1274 (4)	12.00	4.00

Achievements in medical and health services.

Students in May 7 School — A315

Designs: No. 1276, Students as farm workers. No. 1277, Production brigade. J.9.

1976, May 7 Photo. *Perf. 11½*

1275	A315	8f	multi (3-1)	1.75	1.40
1276	A315	8f	multi (3-2)	1.75	1.40
1277	A315	8f	multi (3-3)	1.75	1.40
			Nos. 1275-1277 (3)	5.25	4.20

Chairman Mao's May 7 Directive, 10th anniv.

Mass Training in Swimming — A316

No. 1279, Swimmers crossing Yangtze River. No. 1280, Swimmers walking into the surf. J.10.

1976, July 16 Photo. *Perf. 11½*

Size: 47x27mm

1278	A316	8f	multi (3-1)	1.75	1.10

Size: 35x27mm

1279	A316 8f multi (3-2)		1.75	1.10
1280	A316 8f multi (3-3)		1.75	1.10
	Nos. 1278-1280 (3)		5.25	3.30

Chairman Mao's swim in Yangtze River, 10th anniversary.

Workers, Peasants and Soldiers Going to College — A317

#1282, Classroom. #1283, Instruction on construction site. #1284, Computer room. #1285, Graduates returning home. T.18.

1976, Sept. 6 Photo. *Perf. 11½*

1281	A317 8f multi (5-1)	2.50	1.10
1282	A317 8f multi (5-2)	2.50	1.10
1283	A317 8f multi (5-3)	2.50	1.10
1284	A317 8f multi (5-4)	2.50	1.10
1285	A317 8f multi (5-5)	2.50	1.10
	Nos. 1281-1285 (5)	12.50	5.50

Success of proletarian education system.

Power Line Repair by Woman — A318

#1287, Insulator repair. #1288, Cherry picker. #1289, Transformer repair. T.16.

1976, Sept. 15

1286	A318 8f multi (4-1)	1.50	1.40
1287	A318 8f multi (4-2)	1.50	1.40
1288	A318 8f multi (4-3)	3.00	1.40
1289	A318 8f multi (4-4)	3.00	1.40
	Nos. 1286-1289 (4)	9.00	5.60

Maintenance of high power lines.

Lu Hsun A319

#1291, Lu Hsun sick, writing in bed. #1292, Lu Hsun with worker, soldier and peasant. J.11.

Photo. & Engr.

1976, Oct. 19 *Perf. 11x11½*

1290	A319 8f multi (3-1)	4.50	1.75

Photo.

1291	A319 8f multi (3-2)	4.50	1.75
1292	A319 8f multi (3-3)	4.50	1.75
	Nos. 1290-1292 (3)	13.50	5.25

Lu Hsun (1881-1936), writer and revolutionary leader.

Old Farmer Tying Towel on Student's Head — A320

Designs: No. 1294, Student teaching farm woman, horiz. No. 1295, Students climbing mountain for new water resources. No. 1296, Student testing wheat, horiz. 10f, Student feeding lamb. 20f, Frontier guards, horiz. T.17.

1976, Dec. 22 Photo. *Perf. 11½*

1293	A320 4f multi (6-1)	.75	.45
1294	A320 8f multi (6-2)	.75	.45
1295	A320 8f multi (6-3)	.75	.45
1296	A320 8f multi (6-4)	.75	.45
1297	A320 10f multi (6-5)	2.25	1.00
1298	A320 20f multi (6-6)	4.50	2.00
	Nos. 1293-1298 (6)	9.75	4.80

Students' efforts to help poor country people.

Mao's Home, Shaoshan — A321

Shaoshan, Mao's birthplace: No. 1300, School building. No. 1301, Farmers' Association building. 10f, Railroad station. T.11.

1976, Dec. 26 *Perf. 11*

1299	A321 4f multi (4-1)	.80	.75
1300	A321 8f multi (4-2)	1.25	.75
1301	A321 8f multi (4-3)	1.25	.75
1302	A321 10f multi (4-4)	2.00	1.75
	Nos. 1299-1302 (4)	5.30	4.00

Chou En-lai — A322

#1304, Chou giving report at 10th Party Congress. #1305, Chou with Wang Chin-hsi, famous oil worker, horiz. #1306, Chou with people of Tachai, 1973, horiz. J.13.

1977, Jan. 8 Photo. *Perf. 11½*

1303	A322 8f multi (4-1)	.70	.70
1304	A322 8f multi (4-2)	.70	.70
1305	A322 8f multi (4-3)	.70	.70
1306	A322 8f multi (4-4)	5.00	.70
	Nos. 1303-1306 (4)	7.10	2.80

Premier Chou En-lai (1898-1976), a founder of Chinese Communist Party, 1st death anniversary.

Liu Hu-lan, an Inspiration A323

Liu Hu-lan, Chinese heroine: No. 1307, Liu Hu-lan monument. No. 1308, Mao Tse-tung quotation: "A great life-a glorious death." J.12.

1977, Jan. 31

1307	A323 8f multi (3-1)	6.00	2.50
1308	A323 8f multi (3-2)	2.25	1.75
1309	A323 8f multi (3-3)	2.25	1.75
	Nos. 1307-1309 (3)	10.50	6.00

Uprising in Taiwan A324

Design: 10f, Gate of Heavenly Peace, Peking; Sun Moon Lake, Taiwan, Taiwanese people holding PRC flag. J.14.

1977, Feb. 28 Photo. *Perf. 11*

1310	A324 8f multi (2-1)	.90	.70
1311	A324 10f multi (2-2)	2.25	1.40

Uprising of the people of Taiwan, 2/28/47.

Sharpshooters — A325

Militia Women: No. 1313, Women horseback riders. No. 1314, Underground defense tunnel. T.10.

1977, Mar. 8 *Perf. 11½*

1312	A325 8f multi (3-1)	4.25	2.75
1313	A325 8f multi (3-2)	4.25	2.75
1314	A325 8f multi (3-3)	4.25	2.75
	Nos. 1312-1314 (3)	12.75	8.25

Forestry — A326

Designs: 1f, Coal mining. 1½f, Sheepherding. 2f, Export (loading railroad car onto ship). 4f, Hydroelectric station. 5f, Fishery. 8f, Combine in field. 10f, Radio tower and mail truck. 20f, Steel production. 30f, Trucks on mountain road. 40f, Textiles. 50f, Tractor assembly line. 60f, Offshore oil rigs and birds, setting sun. 70f, Railroad bridge, Yangtze Gorge. No numbers.

1977 Photo. *Perf. 11½*

1315	A326	1f yel grn, red & blk	.20	.20
1316	A326	1½f bl grn, yel grn & brn	.20	*.20*
1317	A326	2f org, bl & blk	.20	.20
1318	A326	3f ol & dk grn	.20	.20
1319	A326	4f lil, org & blk	.20	.20
1320	A326	5f lt ol & ultra	.20	.20
1321	A326	8f red & yel	.20	.20
1322	A326	10f lt grn, org & bl	.25	.20
1323	A326	20f org, yel & brn	.30	.20
1324	A326	30f bl, lt grn & blk	.30	.20
1325	A326	40f multicolored	.40	.20
1326	A326	50f cit, red & blk	.50	.20
1327	A326	60f pur, yel & org	.60	.25
1328	A326	70f blue & multi	.90	.30
		Nos. 1315-1328 (14)	4.65	2.95

Address by Party Committee A327

Designs: No. 1330, Planting new rice fields. No. 1331, Farmers reading wall newspaper. No. 1332, Land reclamation. T.22.

1977, Apr. 9 *Perf. 11x11½*

1329	A327 8f multi (4-1)	.90	.75
1330	A327 8f multi (4-2)	.90	.75
1331	A327 8f multi (4-3)	.90	.75
1332	A327 8f multi (4-4)	.90	.75
	Nos. 1329-1332 (4)	3.60	3.00

Building Tachai-type communities throughout China.

Worker at Microphone — A328

Designs: No. 1334, Drilling for oil during snowstorm. No. 1335, Crowd advancing under Red banner. No. 1336, Workers, industrial complex, rocket blast-off. J.15.

1977, Apr. 25 *Perf. 11*

1333	A328 8f multi (4-1)	1.50	1.10
1334	A328 8f multi (4-2)	1.50	1.10
1335	A328 8f multi (4-3)	1.50	1.10
1336	A328 8f multi (4-4)	1.50	1.10
	Nos. 1333-1336 (4)	6.00	4.40

Conference on learning from Taching workers in industry.

Mongolians Hailing Anniversary A329

10f, Iron and steel complex, iron ore train. 20f, Cattle grazing in improved pasture. J.16.

1977, May 1 *Perf. 11x11½*

1337	A329 8f multi (3-1)	.40	.20
1338	A329 10f multi (3-2)	.40	.30
1339	A329 20f multi (3-3)	1.50	.95
	Nos. 1337-1339 (3)	2.30	1.45

30th anniversary of Inner Mongolian Autonomous Region.

1877 Flag of Romania and Oak Leaves — A330

Mihai Viteazu Memorial (16th Century Hero) — A331

10f, Battle of Smirdan, by N. Grigorescu. J.17.

1977, May 9 Photo. *Perf. 11*

1340	A330 8f multi (3-1)	.75	.60
1341	A331 10f multi (3-2)	.75	.60
1342	A331 20f multi (3-3)	2.10	1.75
	Nos. 1340-1342 (3)	3.60	2.95

Centenary of Romanian independence.

Yenan "Let 100 Flowers Bloom" A332

#1344, Hammer, sickle, gun & flowers; "Proletarian revolutionary literature will prosper." J.18.

1977, May, 23

1343	A332 8f grn, red & gold	.90	.55
1344	A332 8f lt brn, red & gold	.90	.55

Yenan Forum on Literature & Art, 35th anniv.

Zhu De — A333

Designs: No. 1346, Zhu De, last address to Congress. No. 1347, Zhu De at his desk, horiz. No. 1348, Zhu De on horseback as commander of Red Army. J.19.

1977, July 6 Photo. ***Perf. 11½***

1345	A333 8f multi (4-1)	.65	.35
1346	A333 8f multi (4-2)	.65	.35
1347	A333 8f multi (4-3)	.65	.35
1348	A333 8f multi (4-4)	.65	.35
	Nos. 1345-1348 (4)	2.60	1.40

Zhu De (1886-1976), Commander of Red Army, Chairman of National People's Congress.

Military under Mao's Banner — A334

#1350, Red Flag, Soldiers, Chingkang Mountains. #1351, Guerrilla fighters returning to base. #1352, Guerrillas crossing Yangtze. #1353, National defense. J.20.

1977, Aug. 1

1349	A334 8f multi (5-1)	1.75	1.10
1350	A334 8f multi (5-2)	1.75	1.10
1351	A334 8f multi (5-3)	1.75	1.10
1352	A334 8f multi (5-4)	1.75	1.10
1353	A334 8f multi (5-5)	1.75	1.10
	Nos. 1349-1353 (5)	8.75	5.50

Liberation Army Day, 50th anniversary of People's Army.

Gate of Heavenly Peace, People and Red Flags — A335

Designs: No. 1355, People marching under Red Flag with Mao's portrait. No. 1356, People marching under Red Flag with hammer and sickle. J.23.

1977, Aug. 22 Photo. ***Perf. 11½x11***

1354	A335 8f multi (3-1)	4.25	2.75
1355	A335 8f multi (3-2)	4.25	2.75
1356	A335 8f multi (3-3)	4.25	2.75
	Nos. 1354-1356 (3)	12.75	8.25

11th National Congress of the Communist Party of China.

Chairman Mao — A336

Designs (Mao Portraits): No. 1358, as young man in Shansi. No. 1359, addressing Communist Party in Plenary Session. No. 1360, Proclaiming People's Republic at Gate of Heavenly Peace. No. 1361, at airport with Chou En-lai and Zhu De, horiz. No. 1362, Reviewing Army as old man. J.21.

1977, Sept. 9 Photo. ***Perf. 11½***

1357	A336 8f multi (6-1)	1.10	.90
1358	A336 8f multi (6-2)	1.10	.90
1359	A336 8f multi (6-3)	1.10	.90
1360	A336 8f multi (6-4)	1.10	.90
1361	A336 8f multi (6-5)	1.10	.90
1362	A336 8f multi (6-6)	1.10	.90
	Nos. 1357-1362 (6)	6.60	5.40

Mao-Tse-tung (1893-1976), first death anniversary.

Mao Memorial Hall — A337

Completion of Mao Memorial Hall: No. 1364, Chairman Hua's inscription. J.22.

1977, Sept. 9

1363	A337 8f lt ultra & multi	2.25	1.50
1364	A337 8f lt grn, tan & gold	2.25	1.50

Tractors Moving Drilling Tower — A338

#1366, Shui Pow Tsi oil well and women workers. #1367, Construction of oil pipe line, Taching, and silos. #1368, Tung Fang Hung oil refinery, Peking. #1369, Taching oil loaded into tanker in harbor. 20f, Off-shore drilling platform "Pohai No. 1." T.19.

1978, Jan. 31 Photo. ***Perf. 11***

1365	A338 8f multi (6-1)	.35	.40
1366	A338 8f multi (6-2)	.35	.40
1367	A338 8f multi (6-3)	.35	.40
1368	A338 8f multi (6-4)	.35	.40
1369	A338 8f multi (6-5)	.35	.40
1370	A338 20f multi (6-6)	1.90	.90
	Nos. 1365-1370 (6)	3.65	2.90

Development of Chinese oil industry.

"Army Teaching Militia" — A339

#1372, "Army helping with rice planting." T.23.

1978, Feb. 5 Photo. ***Perf. 11***

1371	A339 8f multi (2-1)	1.40	1.10
1372	A339 8f multi (2-2)	1.40	1.10

Army and people working as a family.

Red Flags, Mao Tse-tung — A340

Constitution and Red Flags — A341

#1375, Atom symbol over symbols of agriculture & industry. All designs include Great Hall of the People, Peking, & flowers. J.24.

1978, Feb. 26

1373	A340 8f multi (3-1)	.90	.75
1374	A341 8f multi (3-2)	.90	.75
1375	A340 8f multi (3-3)	.90	.75
	Nos. 1373-1375 (3)	2.70	2.25

5th National People's Congress.

Mao's Eulogy for Lei Feng — A342

Lei Feng, Studying Mao's Works — A343

#1377, Chairman Hua's thoughts (5 lines). J.26.

1978, Mar. 5

1376	A342 8f gold & red (3-1)	1.40	1.10
1377	A342 8f gold & red (3-2)	1.40	1.10
1378	A343 8f multicolored (3-3)	1.40	1.10
	Nos. 1376-1378 (3)	4.20	3.30

Lei Feng (1940-1962), communist fighter; 15th anniversary of Chairman Mao's eulogy "Learn from Comrade Lei Feng."

Hsiang Ching-yu — A344

Yang Kai-hui — A345

1978, Mar. 8

1379	A344 8f multi (2-1)	.95	.75
1380	A345 8f multi (2-2)	.95	.75

Hsiang Ching-yu, pioneer of Women's Movement, executed 1928; Yang Kai-hui, communist fighter, executed 1930. J.27.

A346

A346a

A346b

#1381, Conference emblem. #1382, Banners symbolizing industry, agriculture, defense & science. #1383, Red flag, atom symbol & globe. J.25.

1978, Mar. 18 Litho. ***Perf. 11½x11***

1381	A346 8f gold & red (3-1)	.90	.70
1382	A346a 8f multi (3-2)	.90	.70
1383	A346b 8f multi (3-3)	.90	.70
a.	Souvenir sheet of 3	*325.00*	250.00
	Nos. 1381-1383 (3)	2.70	2.10

Natl. Science Conf. #1383a contains #1381-1383 with simulated perforations. Sold for 50f.

Release of Weather Balloon A347

Weather Observations: No. 1385, Radar station, typhoon watch. No. 1386, Computer, weather maps. No. 1387, Local weather observers. No. 1388, Rockets intercepting hail clouds. T.24.

1978, Apr. 25 Photo. ***Perf. 11x11½***

1384	A347 8f multi (5-1)	.60	.50
1385	A347 8f multi (5-2)	.60	.50
1386	A347 8f multi (5-3)	.60	.50
1387	A347 8f multi (5-4)	.60	.50
1388	A347 8f multi (5-5)	.60	.50
	Nos. 1384-1388 (5)	3.00	2.50

Galloping Horse — A348

Children Playing Soccer — A349

Designs: Galloping Horses, by Hsu Peihung (1895-1953). 40f, 50f, 60f, 70f, $5, horiz. T.28.

1978, May 5 ***Perf. 11½x11, 11x11½***

1389	A348 4f multi (10-1)	.85	.75
1390	A348 8f multi (10-2)	.85	.75
1391	A348 8f multi (10-3)	.85	.75
1392	A348 10f multi (10-4)	.85	.75
1393	A348 20f multi (10-5)	3.50	.75
1394	A348 30f multi (10-6)	2.50	.75
1395	A348 40f multi (10-7)	2.50	1.50
1396	A348 50f multi (10-8)	3.50	1.50
1397	A348 60f multi (10-9)	2.50	3.00
1398	A348 70f multi (10-10)	3.50	4.25
	Nos. 1389-1398 (10)	21.40	14.75

Souvenir Sheet

1399	A348 $5 multicolored	*275.00*	150.00

No. 1399 contains one stamp showing 4 horses, size: 89x39mm.

1978, June 1 ***Perf. 11½***

Designs: No. 1401, Children on the beach. No. 1402, Little girls dancing. No. 1403, Children taking long walks. 20f, Children exercising for good health. T.21.

Size: 22x27mm

1400	A349 8f multi (5-2)	.45	.40
1401	A349 8f multi (5-3)	.45	.40
1402	A349 8f multi (5-4)	.45	.40
1403	A349 8f multi (5-5)	.45	.40

Size: 48x28mm

1404	A349 20f multi (5-1)	.90	.70
	Nos. 1400-1404 (5)	2.70	2.30

Build up your health while young.

Synthetic Fiber Feeder
A350

Designs: No. 1406, Drawing out threads. No. 1407, Weaving. No. 1408, Dyeing and printing. No. 1409, Finished products. T.25.

1978, June 15 Photo. *Perf. 11½*

1405	A350 8f multi (5-1)	.60	.50
1406	A350 8f multi (5-2)	.60	.50
1407	A350 8f multi (5-3)	.60	.50
1408	A350 8f multi (5-4)	.60	.50
1409	A350 8f multi (5-5)	.60	.50
a.	Strip of 5, #1405-1409	3.50	3.00
	Nos. 1405-1409 (5)	3.00	2.50

Chemical fiber industry. No. 1409a has continuous design.

Conference Emblem
A351

"Develop Economy and Ensure Supplies"
A352

1978, June 20 *Perf. 13*

1410	A351 8f multi (2-1)	.40	.30
1411	A352 8f multi (2-2)	.40	.30

Natl. Conf. on Learning from Taching and Tachai in Finance and Trade. J.28.

New Pastures, Mongolia — A353

Designs: No. 1413, Kazakh shepherds selecting sheep for breeding. No. 1414, Mechanized shearing of sheep, Tibet, T.27.

1978, June 30 Photo. *Perf. 11½*

1412	A353 8f multi (3-1)	1.10	.55
1413	A353 8f multi (3-2)	1.10	.55
1414	A353 8f multi (3-3)	1.10	.55
	Nos. 1412-1414 (3)	3.30	1.65

Learning from Tachai in developing animal husbandry and new pastoral areas.

Coke Oven — A354

Iron and Steel Industry: No. 1416, Iron furnace. No. 1417, Pouring steel. No. 1418, Steel rolling. No. 1419, Finished iron and steel products. T.26.

1978, July 22

1415	A354 8f multi (5-1)	.70	.45
1416	A354 8f multi (5-2)	.70	.45
1417	A354 8f multi (5-3)	.70	.45
1418	A354 8f multi (5-4)	.70	.45
1419	A354 8f multi (5-5)	.70	.45
	Nos. 1415-1419 (5)	3.50	2.25

Iron Fist to Prevent Revisionism
A355

Jug in Shape of Sheep — A356

#1421, "Carrying forward revolutionary tradition." #1422, "Strenuous training in military skills to wipe out enemy." T.32.

1978, Aug. 1 Photo. *Perf. 11½*

1420	A355 8f multi (3-1)	.90	.45
1421	A355 8f multi (3-2)	.90	.45
1422	A355 8f multi (3-3)	.90	.45
	Nos. 1420-1422 (3)	2.70	1.35

"Learn from Hard-boned 6th Company." (A military unit since 1939).

1978, Aug. 26

Arts and Crafts: 4f, Giant lion (toy; horiz.). No. 1425, Rhinoceros (lacquer ware; horiz). 10f, Cat (embroidery). 20f, Bag (weaving; horiz.). 30f, Teapot in shape of peacock (cloisonné). 40f, Plate with lotus, and swan-shaped box (lacquer ware; horiz.). 50f, Dragon flying in sky (ivory). 60f, Sun rising (jade; horiz.). 70f, Flight to human world (ivory). $3, Flying fairies (arts and crafts; horiz.). T.29.

1423	A356 4f multi (10-1)	.45	.25
1424	A356 8f multi (10-2)	.45	.25
1425	A356 8f multi (10-3)	.45	.25
1426	A356 10f multi (10-4)	.45	.40
1427	A356 20f multi (10-5)	.45	.40
1428	A356 30f multi (10-6)	.45	.40
1429	A356 40f multi (10-7)	.90	.75
1430	A356 50f multi (10-8)	1.75	1.00
1431	A356 60f multi (10-9)	1.75	1.00
1432	A356 70f multi (10-10)	1.75	1.25
	Nos. 1423-1432 (10)	8.85	5.95

Souvenir Sheet

1433	A356 $3 multi	*250.00*	160.00

No. 1433 contains one 85x36mm stamp.

Women, Atom Symbol, Rocket and Wheat
A357

1978, Sept. 8 Photo. *Perf. 11*

1434	A357 8f multicolored	1.40	.90

4th National Women's Congress.

Ginseng — A358

Flag, Wheat, Cogwheel, Plane, Atom Symbols — A359

Medicinal Plants: No. 1436, Horn of plenty. No. 1437, Blackberry lily. No. 1438, Balloon-flower. 55f, Rhododendron dauricum. T.30.

1978, Sept. 15

1435	A358 8f multi (5-1)	.45	.25
1436	A358 8f multi (5-2)	.45	.25
1437	A358 8f multi (5-3)	.45	.25
1438	A358 8f multi (5-4)	.45	.25
1439	A358 55f multi (5-5)	1.75	.80
	Nos. 1435-1439 (5)	3.55	1.80

1978, Oct. 11 Photo. *Perf. 11*

1440	A359 8f multicolored	2.25	1.75

9th National Trade Union Congress.

Youth League Emblem
A360

1978, Oct. 16

1441	A360 8f multicolored	1.75	1.10

10th Natl. Communist Youth League Cong.

Chinese and Japanese Girls Exchanging Gifts
A361

Great Wall and Mt. Fuji
A362

1978, Oct. 22

1442	A361 8f multicolored	.65	.40
1443	A362 55f multicolored	1.75	1.50

Signing of Sino-Japanese Peace and Friendship Treaty.

Moslem, Chinese and Mongolian People — A363

Chinsha River Bridge, West Szechuan
A364

#1445, Loading coal at Holan Mountain. 10f, Irrigated rice fields & boxthorn. J.29.

1978, Oct. 25

1444	A363 8f multi (3-1)	.90	.75
1445	A363 8f multi (3-2)	.90	.75
1446	A363 10f multi (3-3)	.90	.75
	Nos. 1444-1446 (3)	2.70	2.25

20th anniversary of founding of Ningsia Moslem Autonomous Region.

1978, Nov. 1 Photo. *Perf. 11½x11*

Highway Bridges: No. 1448, Hsinhong bridge, Wuhsi. No. 1449, Chiuhsikou bridge, Fengdu. No. 1450, Chinsha River bridge, West Szechuan. 60f, Shangyeh bridge, Sanmen. $2, Hsiang-kiang River bridge. T.31.

1447	A364 8f multi (5-1)	.45	.30
1448	A364 8f multi (5-2)	.45	.30
1449	A364 8f multi (5-3)	.45	.30
1450	A364 8f multi (5-4)	.45	.30
1451	A364 60f multi (5-5)	2.50	1.25
	Nos. 1447-1451 (5)	4.30	2.45

Souvenir Sheet

1452	A364 $2 multi	*250.00*	140.00

No. 1452 contains one 86x37mm stamp.

Mechanical Transplanting of Rice Seedlings
A365

Paintings: No. 1454, Spraying fields. No. 1455, Seed selection. No. 1456, Trade. No. 1457, Delivery of public grain in city. T.34.

1978, Nov. 30 *Perf. 11½*

1453	A365 8f multi (5-1)	5.00	2.50
1454	A365 8f multi (5-2)	5.00	2.50
1455	A365 8f multi (5-3)	5.00	2.50
1456	A365 8f multi (5-4)	5.00	2.50
1457	A365 8f multi (5-5)	5.00	2.50
a.	Strip of 5, #1453-1457	29.00	15.00

Agricultural progress. No. 1457a has a continuous design.

Dancers and Fireworks — A366

Designs: No. 1459, Industry, vert. 10f, Agriculture, vert. J.33.

1978, Dec. 11 Photo. *Perf. 11*

1458	A366 8f multi (3-1)	2.00	.60
1459	A366 8f multi (3-2)	2.00	.60
1460	A366 10f multi (3-3)	1.00	1.00
	Nos. 1458-1460 (3)	5.00	2.20

20th anniversary of Kwangsi Chuang Autonomous Region.

Miners with Pneumatic Drill
A367

Mine Development: 4f, Old Tibetan peasant reporting to surveyor. 10f, Open-cut mining with power shovel. 20f, Loaded electric train in pit. T.20.

1978, Dec. 29 Photo. & Engr.

1461	A367 4f multi (4-1)	.55	.30
1462	A367 8f multi (4-2)	.55	.30
1463	A367 10f multi (4-3)	1.25	1.00
1464	A367 20f multi (4-4)	1.25	1.10
	Nos. 1461-1464 (4)	3.60	2.70

A368

A369

Golden Pheasants: 4f, Roosting on rock. 8f, In flight. 45f, Seeking food. T.35.

1979, Jan. 25 Photo. *Perf. 11½*

1465	A368	4f multi (3-1)	1.10	1.00
1466	A368	8f multi (3-2)	3.25	1.00
1467	A368	45f multi (3-3)	2.25	2.00
		Nos. 1465-1467 (3)	6.60	4.00

1979, Mar. 14 Photo. *Perf. 11½x11*

1468	A369	8f Albert Einstein, equation	2.25	1.75

Phoenix Battling Monster, Praying Woman A370

60f, Man riding dragon to heaven. Designs from silk paintings found in Changsha tomb, Warring States Period (475-221 B.C.). T.33.

1979, Mar. 29 *Perf. 11*

1469	A370	8f multi (2-1)	2.40	.75
1470	A370	60f multi (2-2)	1.60	1.50

Summer Palace — A371

Photo., Photo. & Engr. ($5)

1979-80 *Perf. 13*

1471	A371	$1 Pagoda ('80)	.60	.20
1472	A371	$2 Shown	1.25	.50
1473	A371	$5 Temple, Beihai Park	4.00	1.10
		Nos. 1471-1473 (3)	5.85	1.80

Issued: $2, June 16, 1979.

Hammer and Sickle "51" and Bars from "International" — A372

1979, May 1 Photo. *Perf. 11*

1474	A372	8f multicolored	.90	.75

International Labor Day, 90th anniv.

"Tradition of May 4th Movement" A373

Young Woman, Rocket, Antenna, Nuclear Reactor A374

1979, May 4

1475	A373	8f multicolored	.65	.50
1476	A374	8f multicolored	.65	.50

60th anniversary of May 4th Movement.

IYC Emblem, Children Holding Balloons — A375

Children of Three Races, IYC Emblem — A376

1979, May 25 *Perf. 11½*

1477	A375	8f multicolored	1.00	.65
1478	A376	60f multicolored	7.00	5.25

International Year of the Child.

Great Wall in Spring A377

Designs (The Great Wall): No. 1480, in summer. No. 1481, in autumn. 60f, in winter. $2, Guard tower. T.38.

1979, June 25 Photo. *Perf. 11*

1479	A377	8f multi (4-1)	1.00	.80
1480	A377	8f multi (4-2)	1.00	.80
1481	A377	8f multi (4-3)	1.00	.80
1482	A377	60f multi (4-4)	5.75	4.75
		Nos. 1479-1482 (4)	8.75	7.15

Souvenir Sheet

1483	A377	$2 multi	*125.00*	75.00

For overprint see No. 1492.

Roaring Tiger — A379

Manchurian Tiger: 8f, Two young tigers. 60f, Tiger at rest. T.40.

1979, July 20 *Perf. 11½x11*

1484	A379	4f multi (3-1)	1.50	1.00
1485	A379	8f multi (3-2)	1.50	1.00
1486	A379	60f multi (3-3)	4.00	2.00
		Nos. 1484-1486 (3)	7.00	4.00

Mechanical Harvesting — A380

Work of the Communes: No. 1488, Forestry. No. 1489, Raising ducks. No. 1490, Women weaving baskets. 10f, Fishing. T.39.

1979, Aug. 10 *Perf. 11½*

1487	A380	4f multi (5-1)	.50	.40
1488	A380	8f multi (5-2)	1.00	.90
1489	A380	8f multi (5-3)	1.00	.90
1490	A380	8f multi (5-4)	1.00	.90
1491	A380	10f multi (5-5)	2.00	1.25
		Nos. 1487-1491 (5)	5.50	4.35

No. 1483 Overprinted with Gold Inscription and "1979"

Souvenir Sheet

1979, Aug. 25 Photo. *Perf. 11*

1492	A377	$2 multicolored	*400.00*	

31st International Stamp Exhibition, Riccione, Italy. J41 (1-1).

Forged overprints exist.

Games Emblem, Sports — A381

#1494, Soccer, badminton, high jump, speed skating. #1495, Fencing, skiing, gymnastics, diving. #1496, Motorcycling, table tennis, basketball, archery. #1497, Emblem only. J.43.

1979, Sept. 15 *Perf. 11½x11*

1493	A381	8f multi (4-1)	.50	.40
1494	A381	8f multi (4-2)	.50	.40
1495	A381	8f multi (4-3)	.50	.40
1496	A381	8f multi (4-4)	.50	.40
	a.	Block of 4, #1493-1496	2.75	2.50

Souvenir Sheet

Perf. 11½

1497	A381	$2 multi, vert.	*40.00*	25.00

4th National Games. Size of stamp in No. 1497: 22x26mm.

Flag and Rainbow — A382

Design: No. 1499, Flag and mountains.

1979, Oct. 1 Photo. *Perf. 11½*

1498	A382	8f multicolored	1.60	1.25
1499	A382	8f multicolored	1.60	1.25

National Emblem — A383

Dancers — A384

1979, Oct. 1 Photo. *Perf. 11½*

1500	A383	8f multicolored	2.00	1.00

Souvenir Sheet

1501	A383	$1 multicolored	*40.00*	25.00

1979, Oct. 1 Photo. *Perf. 11½*

Designs: #1503-1505, various dances. J.47.

1502	A384	8f multi (4-1)	.60	.30
1503	A384	8f multi (4-2)	.60	.30
1504	A384	8f multi (4-3)	.60	.30
1505	A384	8f multi (4-4)	.60	.30
	a.	Block of 4, #1502-1505	2.75	2.25

Tractor, Aerial Crop Spraying, Irrigation — A385

#1507, Gear, computers. #1508, Rocket, submarine, jets. #1509, Atom symbol. J.48.

1979, Oct. 1 Photo. *Perf. 11½*

1506	A385	8f multi (4-1)	.65	.55
1507	A385	8f multi (4-2)	.65	.55
1508	A385	8f multi (4-3)	.65	.55
1509	A385	8f multi (4-4)	.65	.55
		Nos. 1506-1509 (4)	2.60	2.20

National Anthem A386

1979, Oct. 1 Engr. *Perf. 11*

1510	A386	8f multicolored	2.75	2.75

Exhibition Emblem — A387

Children Flying Model Planes — A388

1979, Oct. 3

1511	A387	8f multicolored	.90	.55

Junior National Scientific and Technological Exhibition.

1979, Oct. 3

#1513, Girls and microscope. #1514, Children and telescope. #1515, Boy catching butterflies. #1516, Girl taking meteorological readings. #1517, Boys sailing model boat. #1518, Girl with book. T.41.

1512	A388	8f multi (6-1)	.50	.40
1513	A388	8f multi (6-2)	.50	.40
1514	A388	8f multi (6-3)	.50	.40
1515	A388	8f multi (6-4)	.50	.40
1516	A388	8f multi (6-5)	.50	.40
1517	A388	60f multi (6-6)	2.75	1.75
		Nos. 1512-1517 (6)	5.25	3.75

Souvenir Sheet

Perf. 11

1518	A388	$2 multi	*875.00*	425.00

Study Science from Childhood. No. 1518 contains one stamp, size: 90x40mm.

Yu Shan Mountain A389

Taiwan Landscapes: No. 1520, Sun and Moon Lake. No. 1521, Chihkan Tower. No. 1522, Suao-Hualien Highway. 55f, Tian Xiang Falls. 60f, Banping Mountain. T.42.

1979, Oct. 20 Photo. *Perf. 11x11½*

1519	A389	8f multi (6-1)	.80	.65
1520	A389	8f multi (6-2)	.80	.65
1521	A389	8f multi (6-3)	.80	.65
1522	A389	8f multi (6-4)	.80	.65
1523	A389	55f multi (6-5)	2.40	1.40
1524	A389	60f multi (6-6)	3.25	2.75
		Nos. 1519-1524 (6)	8.85	6.75

Arts Symbols A390

8f, Seals and modernization symbols. J.39.

1979, Oct. 30

1525	A390	4f multicolored	.55	.45
1526	A390	8f multicolored	1.25	.70

4th Natl. Cong. of Literary and Art Workers.

Train in Tunnel A391

Railroads: No. 1528, Mountain bridge. No. 1529, Freight train. T.36.

1979, Oct. 30 Photo. & Engr.

1527	A391	8f multi (3-1)	.90	.75
1528	A391	8f multi (3-2)	.90	.75
1529	A391	8f multi (3-3)	.90	.75
		Nos. 1527-1529 (3)	2.70	2.25

Chrysanthemum Petal — A392

Camellias: No. 1531, Lion head. No. 1532, Camellia chryantha. 10f, Small osmanthus leaf. 20f, Baby face. 30f, Cornelian. 40f, Peony camellia. 50f, Purple gown. 60f, Dwarf rose. 70f, Willow leaf spinel pink. $2, Red jewelry. T.37.

1979, Nov. 10 Photo. *Perf. 11x11½*

1530	A392	4f multi (10-1)	.80	.50
1531	A392	8f multi (10-2)	.80	.50
1532	A392	8f multi (10-3)	.80	.50
1533	A392	10f multi (10-4)	.80	.50
1534	A392	20f multi (10-5)	1.60	1.00
1535	A392	30f multi (10-6)	3.25	1.00
1536	A392	40f multi (10-7)	2.40	1.00
1537	A392	50f multi (10-8)	2.40	1.00
1538	A392	60f multi (10-9)	1.60	1.00
1539	A392	70f multi (10-10)	1.60	1.00
		Nos. 1530-1539 (10)	16.05	8.00

Souvenir Sheet

Perf. 11½x11

1540	A392	$2 multi	*125.00*	80.00

No. 1540 contains one 86x36mm stamp.

No. 1540 Overprinted and Numbered in Gold in Margin

Souvenir Sheet

1979, Nov. 10

1541	A392	$2 multicolored	*250.00*

People's Republic of China Phil. Exhib., Hong Kong, 1979. J.42 (1-1).

Forged overprints exist.

Norman Bethune Treating Soldier — A393

Design: 70f, Bethune statue.

1979, Nov. 12

1542	A393	8f multi (2-2)	2.25	1.50
1543	A393	70f multi (2-1)	.45	.30

Dr. Norman Bethune, 40th death anniv. J.50.

Central Archives Hall A394

Intl. Archives Weeks: No. 1545, Gold archive cabinet, vert. 60f, Pavilion. J.51.

Perf. 11x11½, 11½x11

1979, Nov. 26 Photo.

1544	A394	8f multi (3-1)	.40	.35
1545	A394	8f multi (3-2)	.40	.35
1546	A394	60f multi (3-3)	5.25	2.00
		Nos. 1544-1546 (3)	6.05	2.70

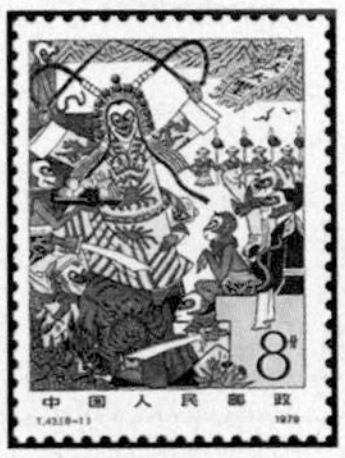

Monkey King in Waterfall Cave — A395

Monkey King, Scenes from Pilgrimage to the West (Novel): No. 1548, Fighting Necha, son of Prince Li. No. 1549, In Mother Queen's peach orchard. No. 1550, In the alchemy furnace. 10f, Subduing the white bone demon. 20f, With palm leaf fan. 60f, In cobweb cave. 70f, Walking on scripture-seeking route. T.43.

1979, Dec. 1 *Perf. 11½x11*

1547	A395	8f multi (8-1)	1.60	1.40
1548	A395	8f multi (8-2)	1.60	1.40
1549	A395	8f multi (8-3)	1.60	1.40
1550	A395	8f multi (8-4)	1.60	1.40
1551	A395	10f multi (8-5)	4.75	1.40
1552	A395	20f multi (8-6)	4.75	1.40
1553	A395	60f multi (8-7)	7.75	4.00
1554	A395	70f multi (8-8)	7.75	4.00
		Nos. 1547-1554 (8)	31.40	16.40

Stalin Delivering Speech A396

Joseph Stalin (1879-1953): No. 1555, Portrait of Stalin, vert. J.49.

Perf. 11x11½, 11½x11

1979, Dec. 21 Engr.

1555	A396	8f brown (2-1)	1.10	.90
1556	A396	8f black (2-2)	1.10	.90

A397

A398

1980 Photo. *Perf. 11½*

1557	A397	4f Peony (16-1)	.75	.65
1558	A397	4f Squirrels and grapes (16-2)	.75	.65
1559	A397	8f Crabs candle and wine (16-3)	.75	.65
1560	A397	8f Tadpoles in mountain spring (16-4)	.75	.65
1561	A397	8f Chicks (16-5)	.75	.65
1562	A397	8f Lotus (16-6)	.75	.65
1563	A397	8f Red plum (16-7)	.75	.65
1564	A397	8f Kingfisher (16-8)	.75	.65
1565	A397	10f Bottle gourd (16-9)	1.50	.65
1566	A397	20f Voice of autumn (16-10)	1.50	.65
1567	A397	30f Wisteria (16-11)	1.50	1.10
1568	A397	40f Chrysanthemums (16-12)	1.50	1.10
1569	A397	50f Shrimp (16-13)	3.00	1.50
1570	A397	55f Litchi (16-14)	3.75	1.90
1571	A397	60f Cabbages, mushrooms (16-15)	5.25	3.75
1572	A397	70f Peaches (16-16)	6.00	5.50
		Nos. 1557-1572 (16)	30.00	21.35

Souvenir Sheet

1573	A397	$2 Hyacynth	*135.00*	55.00

Qi Baishi paintings. Issued: #1557-1560, 1569-1572, 1/15; others, 5/20. #1573 contains one 37½x61mm stamp. T. 44.

1980, Jan. 25 *Perf. 11½x11*

Opera Masks: No. 1574, Meng Liang Mask from Hongyang Cave Opera. No. 1575, Li Kui, from Black Whirlwind. No. 1576, Huang Gai, from Meeting of Heroes. No. 1577, 10f, Lu Zhishen, from Wild Boar Forest. 20f, Lian Po, from Reconciliation between the General and Minister. 60f, Zhang Fei, from Reed Marsh. 70f, Dou Erdun, from Stealing the Emperor's Horse, T. 45.

1574	A398	4f multi (8-1)	.90	.75
1575	A398	4f multi (8-2)	3.50	.75
1576	A398	8f multi (8-3)	1.75	.75
1577	A398	8f multi (8-4)	1.75	.75
1578	A398	10f multi (8-5)	3.50	1.75
1579	A398	20f multi (8-6)	3.50	1.75
1580	A398	60f multi (8-7)	7.25	3.50
1581	A398	70f multi (8-8)	9.00	5.25
		Nos. 1574-1581 (8)	31.15	15.25

Speed Skating, Olympic Rings — A399

Monkey, New Year — A400

Olympic Rings and: No. 1582, Chinese flag. No. 1584, Figure skating. 60f, Downhill skiing. J.54.

1980, Feb. 13

1582	A399	8f multi (4-1)	.45	.30
1583	A399	8f multi (4-2)	.45	.30
1584	A399	8f multi (4-3)	.45	.30
1585	A399	60f multi (4-4)	4.75	1.75
		Nos. 1582-1585 (4)	6.10	2.65

13th Winter Olympic Games, Lake Placid, NY, Feb. 12-24.

Engraved and Photogravure

1980, Feb. 15 *Perf. 11½*

1586	A400	8f multicolored	*575.00*	*95.00*

Clara Zetkin — A401

Photogravure & Engraved

1980, Mar. 8 *Perf. 11½x11*

1587	A401	8f black & yellow	1.10	.90

International Working Women's Day, 70th anniv., founded by Clara Zetkin (1857-1933).

Orchard A402

Afforestation: 8f, Trees lining highway. 10f, Aerial seeding. 20f, Trees surrounding factory. T.48.

1980, Mar. 12 *Perf. 11x11½*

1588	A402	4f multi (4-1)	.45	.25
1589	A402	8f multi (4-2)	.45	.25
1590	A402	10f multi (4-3)	.90	.50
1591	A402	20f multi (4-4)	.90	.50
		Nos. 1588-1591 (4)	2.70	1.50

Apsaras, Symbols of Modernization — A403

1980, Mar. 15 Photo. *Perf. 11½*

1592	A403	8f multicolored	1.75	1.25

2nd National Conference of the Scientific and Technical Association of China.

Mail Transport (T.49) — A404

1980, Mar. 20 *Perf. 11x11½*

1593	A404	2f Ship (4-1)	1.00	1.00
1594	A404	4f Bus (4-2)	1.00	1.00
1595	A404	8f Train (4-3)	2.00	1.00
1596	A404	10f Jet (4-4)	3.00	2.00
		Nos. 1593-1596 (4)	7.00	5.00

Forgeries exist.

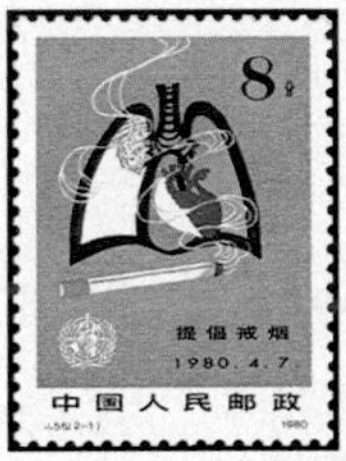

Lungs, Heart, Cigarette, WHO Emblem — A405

Statue of Chien Chen (688-763) — A406

1980, Apr. 7 *Perf. 11½x11*

1597	A405	8f shown (2-1)	.80	.45
1598	A405	60f Faces (2-2)	5.00	2.75

Fight against cigarette smoking. J.56.

1980, Apr. 13 *Perf. 11x11½, 11½x11*

Loan to China by Japan of statue of Chien Chen (Jian Zhen), Buddhist missionary to Japan (754-763): No. 1600, Chien Chen Memorial Hall, Yangchou, horiz. 60f, Chien Chen's ship, horiz. His name in Japan is Ganjin. J.55.

1599	A406	8f multi (3-1)	2.40	.85
1600	A406	8f multi (3-2)	2.40	.85
1601	A406	60f multi (3-3)	15.00	6.75
		Nos. 1599-1601 (3)	19.80	8.45

Lenin's 110th Birthday — A407

Swallow Chick Kite — A408

Photogravure and Engraved

1980, Apr. 22 ***Perf. 11½x11***

1602 A407 8f multicolored 1.40 .90

1980, May 10 **Photo.** ***Perf. 11½***

Designs: Kites. T.50.

1603 A408 8f shown (4-1) 2.50 1.10
1604 A408 8f Slender-swallow (4-2) 2.50 1.10
1605 A408 8f Semi-slender swallow (4-3) 2.50 1.10
1606 A408 70f Dual swallows (4-4) 10.00 4.50
Nos. 1603-1606 (4) 17.50 7.80

Hare Running from Fallen Papaya A409

1980, June 1 **Photo.** ***Perf. 11x11½***

1607 Strip of 4 + label 7.25 6.00
a. A409 8f shown (4-1) 1.40 1.25
b. A409 8f Hare fox, monkey running away (4-2) 1.40 1.25
c. A409 8f Lion instructing animals (4-3) 1.40 1.25
d. A409 8f Discovery of fallen papaya (4-4) 1.40 1.25

Gu Dong fairy tale. T.51.

Terminal Building, Jets — A410

1980, June 20 ***Perf. 11½***

1608 A410 8f Shown (2-1) 1.10 1.00
1609 A410 10f Runways, jets (2-2) 1.60 1.00

Peking Intl. Airport opening. T.47.

Sika Stag — A411

White Lotus — A412

1980, July 18 **Photo.** ***Perf. 11½***

1610 A411 4f Shown (3-1) 1.25 1.25
1611 A411 8f Doe and fawn (3-2) 1.25 1.25
1612 A411 60f Herd (3-3) 6.00 5.00
Nos. 1610-1612 (3) 8.50 7.50

T.52.

1980, Aug. 4

1613 A412 8f Shown (4-1) 3.25 1.25
1614 A412 8f Rose-tipped snow (4-2) 2.25 1.25
1615 A412 8f Buddha's seat (4-3) 2.25 1.25
1616 A412 70f Variable charming face (4-4) 17.00 7.50
Nos. 1613-1616 (4) 24.75 11.25

Souvenir Sheet

1617 A412 $1 Fresh lotus on rippling water 150.00

#1617 contains one 48x88mm stamp. T.54.

Pearl Cave, Sword-cut Stone Sculptures — A413

Guilin Landscapes: No. 1619, Three mountains, distant views. No. 1620, Nine-horse fresco hill. No. 1621, Egrets around aged banyan. No. 1622, Western hills at sunset, vert. No. 1623, Moonlight on Lijiang River, vert. 60f, Springhead, ancient ferry, vert. 70f, Scenic path, Yangshue, vert. T.53.

1980, Aug. 30 **Photo.** ***Perf. 11½***

1618 A413 8f multi (8-1) 1.25 .60
1619 A413 8f multi (8-2) 1.25 .60
1620 A413 8f multi (8-3) 1.25 .60
1621 A413 8f multi (8-4) 1.25 .60
1622 A413 8f multi (8-5) 1.25 .60
1623 A413 8f multi (8-6) 1.25 .60
1624 A413 60f multi (8-7) 9.00 3.50
1625 A413 70f multi (8-8) 10.00 4.75
Nos. 1618-1625 (8) 26.50 11.85

Entrance Gate and Good Fairies A414

Great Wall, Symbols of Chicago, San Francisco and New York A415

1980, Sept. 13 **Photo.** ***Perf. 11x11½***

1626 A414 8f multicolored .80 .70
1627 A415 70f multicolored 5.50 2.75

Exhibitions of the People's Republic of China in San Francisco, Chicago and New York, Sept.-Dec. Sheets of 12 were sold only at the US exhibitions at increasing prices. Retail value of set of two sheets of 12, approximately $500.

Romanian Flag, Warrior and Scroll — A416

1980, Sept. 20 **Photo.** ***Perf. 11½x11***

1628 A416 8f multicolored 1.75 1.25

2050th anniv. of Dacia, 1st independent Romanian state.

UNESCO Exhibition of Drawings and Paintings (J.60) — A417

1980, Oct. 8 ***Perf. 11½***

1629 A417 8f Sea of Clouds, by Liu Haisu (3-1) 1.25 .55
1630 A417 8f Oriole and Magnolia, by Yu Feian, vert., (3-2) 1.25 .55
1631 A417 8f Camels, by Wu Zuoren (3-3) 1.25 .55
Nos. 1629-1631 (3) 3.75 1.65

Scenes from Tarrying Garden (T.56) — A418

1980, Oct. 25 **Photo.** ***Perf. 11½***

1632 A418 8f Quxi Tower (4-1) *5.00* 3.00
1633 A418 8f Yuancui Pavilion (4-2) *5.00* 3.00
1634 A418 10f Hanbi Shanfang (4-3) *5.00* 3.00
1635 A418 60f Guanyun Peak (4-4) *45.00* 15.00
Nos. 1632-1635 (4) *60.00* 24.00

Xu Guangpi (1562-1633), Agronomist A419

Shooting, Olympic Rings — A420

Scientists of Ancient China: No. 1637, Li Bing, hydraulic engineer, 3rd century B.C. No. 1638, Jia Sixie, agronomist, 5th century. 60f, Huang Daopo, textile expert, 13th century. J.58.

Photogravure and Engraved

1980, Nov. 20 ***Perf. 11½x11***

1636 A419 8f multi (4-1) 1.75 .85
1637 A419 8f multi (4-2) 1.75 .85
1638 A419 8f multi (4-3) 1.75 .85
1639 A419 60f multi (4-4) 11.00 5.00
Nos. 1636-1639 (4) 16.25 7.55

1980, Nov. 26 **Photo.**

1640 A420 4f shown (5-1) .45 .20
1641 A420 8f Gymnastics (5-2) .90 .25
1642 A420 8f Diving (5-3) .90 .25
1643 A420 10f Volleyball (5-4) 1.40 .60
1644 A420 60f Archery (5-5) 3.50 1.75
Nos. 1640-1644 (5) 7.15 3.05

Return to International Olympic Committee, 1st anniversary. J.62.

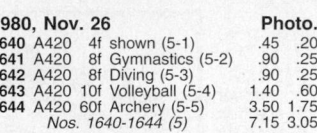

Chinese River Dolphin A421

Photogravure & Engraved

1980, Dec. 25 ***Perf. 11x11½***

1645 A421 8f shown (2-1) 1.25 .50
a. Booklet pane of 6 16.00
1646 A421 60f Dolphins (2-2) 5.00 1.50
a. Booklet pane of 1 16.00

Stamps from No. 1645a have straight edges on top or bottom.

Cock — A422

Photogravure & Engraved

1981, Jan. 5 ***Perf. 11½***

1647 A422 8f multicolored 5.50 2.75
a. Booklet pane of 12 35.00

New Year 1981.
Stamps from booklet pane have straight edges on top or bottom.

Early Morning in Xishuang Bana (T.55) A423

Perf. 11x11½, 11½x11

1981, Jan. 20 **Photo.**

1648 A423 4f shown (6-1) .90 .60
1649 A423 4f Dai mountain village (6-2) .90 .60
1650 A423 8f Rainbow over Lanchang River (6-3) 1.60 .60
1651 A423 8f Ancient temple vert. (6-4) 1.60 .60
1652 A423 8f Moonlit night, vert. (6-5) 1.60 .60
1653 A423 60f Phoenix tree, vert. (6-6) 7.00 4.00
Nos. 1648-1653 (6) 13.60 7.00

Flower Basket Palace Lantern — A424

Designs: Palace lanterns. T.60.

1981, Feb. 19 **Photo.** ***Perf. 11½***

1654 A424 4f multi (6-1) 1.60 .90
1655 A424 8f multi (6-2) 1.60 .90
1656 A424 8f multi (6-3) 1.60 .90
1657 A424 8f multi (6-4) 1.60 .90
1658 A424 20f multi (6-5) 4.00 3.50
1659 A424 60f multi (6-6) 9.50 7.00
Nos. 1654-1659 (6) 19.90 14.10

Crossing River, Scene from Marking the Gunwale A425

Scenes from Marking the Gunwale fable. T.59.

1981, Mar. 10 Photo. ***Perf. 11x11½***

1660 A425 8f Text (5-1) 1.25 1.00
1661 A425 8f shown (5-2) 1.25 1.00
1662 A425 8f Dropping sword in water (5-3) 1.25 1.00
1663 A425 8f Marking gunwale (5-4) 1.25 1.00
1664 A425 8f Searching for sword (5-5) 1.25 1.00
a. Bklt. pane, 2 each #1660-1664 21.00
b. Strip of 5, #1660-1664 8.00 6.50

Chinese Juniper A426

Designs: Miniature landscapes. T.61.

1981, Mar. 31 ***Perf. 11½***

1665 A426 4f Chinese elm, vert. (6-1) .75 .65
1666 A426 8f Juniper, vert. (6-2) .75 .65
1667 A426 8f Maidenhair tree, vert. (6-3) .75 .65
1668 A426 10f shown (6-4) .75 .65
1669 A426 20f Persimmon (6-5) 1.50 1.25
1670 A426 60f Juniper (6-6) 4.50 3.00
Nos. 1665-1670 (6) 9.00 6.85

Vase with Tiger-shaped Handles — A427

Cizhou Kiln Ceramic Pottery: 4f, Vase with 2 tigers, Song Dynasty. #1672, Black glazed jar, Jin Dynasty. #1673, Amphora. #1674, Jar with 2 phoenixes (Yuan Dynasty). 10f, Flat flask, Yuan Dynasty. T.62.

1981, Apr. 15 Photo. ***Perf. 11½x11***

1671 A427 4f multi, vert. (6-1) .35 .30
1672 A427 8f multi (6-2) .75 .70
1673 A427 8f multi, vert. (6-3) .75 .70
1674 A427 8f multi (6-4) .75 .70
1675 A427 10f multi (6-5) 1.50 1.40
1676 A427 60f multi (6-6) 3.25 2.75
Nos. 1671-1676 (6) 7.35 5.85

Panda and Colored Stamps — A428

1981, Apr. 29 Photo. ***Perf. 11½x11***

1677 A428 8f shown (2-1) .25 .25
1678 A428 60f Boat, bird (2-2) 2.50 1.40
a. Booklet pane (8 #1677, souv. sheet with 1677-1678) 9.00

Qinchuan Steer A429

Cattle Breeds: #1680, Binhu buffalo. #1681, Yak. #1682, Black and white dairy cows. 10f, Pasture red cow. 55f, Simmental cross-breed. T.63.

1981, May 5 ***Perf. 11x11½***

1679 A429 4f multi (6-1) .35 .30
1680 A429 8f multi (6-2) .35 .55
1681 A429 8f multi (6-3) .35 .55
1682 A429 8f multi (6-4) .35 .55
1683 A429 10f multi (6-5) .75 .55
1684 A429 55f multi (6-6) 4.50 2.10
Nos. 1679-1684 (6) 6.65 4.60

Mail Delivery Slogan — A430

13th World Telecommunications Day — A431

1981, May 9 ***Perf. 11***

1685 A430 8f multicolored .70 .20

1981, May 17 ***Perf. 11½x11***

1686 A431 8f multicolored .70 .20

Construction Worker — A432

Telephone Building, Peking — A433

1981, May 20 ***Perf. 11½***

1687 A432 8f shown (4-1) .55 .45
1688 A432 8f Miner (4-2) .55 .45
1689 A432 8f Children crossing street (4-3) .55 .45
1690 A432 8f Farm worker (4-4) .55 .45
Nos. 1687-1690 (4) 2.20 1.80

National Safety Month. J.65.

1981, June 5 Engr. ***Perf. 11½x11***

1691 A433 8f violet brown .90 .55

Swaythling Cup, Men's Team Table Tennis — A434

36th World Table Tennis Championships Victory — #1692: a, St. Bride Vase, men's singles (7-3). b, Iran Cup, men's doubles (7-4). c, G. Geist Prize, women's singles (7-5). d, W.J. Pope Trophy, women's doubles (7-6). e, Heydusek Prize, mixed doubles (7-7). #1694, Marcel Corbillon Cup, women's team. #1693-1694 printed in sheets of 16 (8 each) + 2 labels. J.71.

1981, June 30 Photo. ***Perf. 11½x11***

1692 Strip of 5 1.60 1.50
a.-e. A434 8f multi .20 .20
1693 A434 20f multi (7-1) .80 .75
1694 A434 20f multi (7-2) .80 .75

Chinese Communist Party, 60th Anniv. A435

1981, July 1 Photo. ***Perf. 11x11½***

1695 A435 8f multicolored .55 .30

Hanpo Pass, Lushan Mountains (T.67) A436

Photogravure & Engraved

1981, July 20 ***Perf. 12½x12***

1696 8f Five-veteran Peak, vert. (7-1) .85 .60
1697 8f shown (7-2) .85 .60
1698 8f Yellow Dragon Pool, vert. (7-3) .85 .60
1699 8f Sunlit Peak (7-4) .85 .60
1700 8f Three-layer Spring, vert. (7-5) .85 .60
1701 8f Stone and pines (7-6) .85 .60
1702 60f Dragon-head Cliff, vert. (7-7) 7.25 4.00
Nos. 1696-1702 (7) 12.35 7.60

Tremella Fuciformis A437

Designs: Edible mushrooms. T.66.

1981, Aug. 6 Photo. ***Perf. 11½***

1703 A437 4f shown (6-1) .30 .25
1704 A437 8f Dictyophora indusiata (6-2) .60 .40
1705 A437 8f Hericium erinaceus (6-3) .60 .40
1706 A437 8f Russula rubra (6-4) .60 .40
1707 A437 10f Lentinus edodes (6-5) .90 .40
1708 A437 70f Agaricus bisporus (6-6) 2.50 1.60
Nos. 1703-1708 (6) 5.50 3.45

Quality Month (J.66) — A438

Lunan Stone Forest, Yunn — A439

1981, Sept. 1 Photo. ***Perf. 11½x11***

1709 A438 8f Silver medal (2-1) .45 .40
1710 A438 8f Gold medal (2-2) .45 .40

1981, Sept. 18 ***Perf. 11½***

Designs: Views of limestone formations, Lunan Stone Forest. #1711-1713 horiz. T.64.

1711 A439 8f multi (5-1) .75 .50
1712 A439 8f multi (5-2) .75 .50
1713 A439 8f multi (5-3) .75 .50
1714 A439 10f multi (5-4) .75 .50
1715 A439 70f multi (5-5) 3.75 4.00
Nos. 1711-1715 (5) 6.75 6.00

Lu Xun, Writer, Birth Centenary (J.67) A440

1981, Sept. 25

1716 A440 8f shown (2-1) .70 .40
1717 A440 20f Portrait (diff.) (2-2) 1.10 1.00

Sun Yat-sen and Text A441

70th Anniv. of 1911 Revolution: No. 1719, 72 Martyrs Grave, Huang Hua Gang. No. 1720, Hubei Provincial Government Headquarters, 1911. J.68.

1981, Oct. 10 Photo. ***Perf. 11x11½***

1718 A441 8f multi (3-1) .55 .35
1719 A441 8f multi (3-2) .55 .35
1720 A441 8f multi (3-3) .55 .35
Nos. 1718-1720 (3) 1.65 1.05

Asian Conference of Parliamentarians on Population and Development, Peking, Oct. 27 (J.73) — A442

1981, Oct. 27 ***Perf. 11½x11, 11x11½***

1721 A442 8f Tree, vert. (2-1) .20 .20
1722 A442 70f shown (2-2) .70 .60

Huang Guo Shu Falls — A443

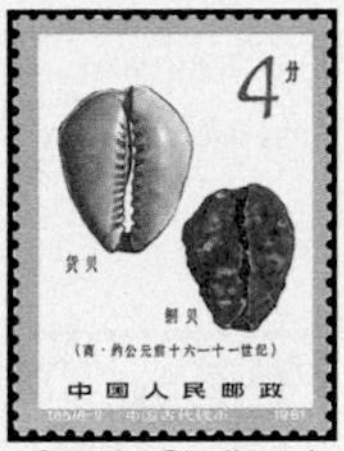

Cowrie Shell and Shell-shaped Coin — A444

Nos. 1731-1739 are horizontal.

Perf. 11¼, 13x13¼ (#1726, 1729), 13¼x13 (#1731)

1981-83 **Engr.**

1723	A443	1f	Xishuang Banna	.20	.20
1724	A443	1½f	Mt. Hua	.20	.20
1725	A443	2f	Mt. Tai	.20	.20
1726	A443	3f	shown	.20	.20
1727	A443	4f	Hainan Isld.	.20	.20
b.			Perf. 11½x11	10.00	10.00
1728	A443	5f	Tiger Hill, Suzhou	.20	.20
1729	A443	8f	Great Wall	.20	.20
1730	A443	10f	Immense Forest	.20	.20
1731	A443	20f	Mt. Tian	.25	.20
1732	A443	30f	Grassland, Inner Mongolia	.25	.20
1733	A443	40f	Stone Forest	.35	.20
1734	A443	50f	Banping Mountain	.45	.25
1735	A443	70f	Mt. Qomolangma	.55	.40
1736	A443	80f	Seven-Star Crag	.55	.50
1737	A443	$1	Three Gorges, Changjiang River	.75	.55
1738	A443	$2	Guilin landscape	.90	1.10
1739	A443	$5	Mt. Huangshan	2.40	2.00
			Nos. 1723-1739 (17)	8.05	7.00

Issued: #1737-1739, 10/9/82; #1732, 1734-1736 4/1/83.

Photo.

Perf. 11½

1726a	A443	3f	.20	.20
1727a	A443	4f	.20	.20
1729a	A443	8f	.30	.25
1730a	A443	10f	.40	.35
1731a	A443	20f	.80	.70
		Nos. 1726a-1731a (5)	1.90	1.70

Nos. 1727a, 1729a, 1730a exist tagged. Values 10-15% higher.

Photogravure and Engraved

1981, Oct. 29 ***Perf. 11½x11***

Ancient Coins. T.65.

1740	A444	4f	shown (8-1)	.30	.25
1741	A444	4f	Shovel (8-2)	.30	.25
1742	A444	8f	Shovel, diff. (8-3)	.60	.25
1743	A444	8f	Shovel, diff. (8-4)	.60	.25
1744	A444	8f	Knife (8-5)	.60	.25
1745	A444	8f	Knife (8-6)	.60	.25
1746	A444	60f	Knife, diff. (8-7)	1.90	1.10
1747	A444	70f	Gong (8-8)	3.00	1.90
			Nos. 1740-1747 (8)	7.90	4.50

See Nos. 1765-1772.

A445

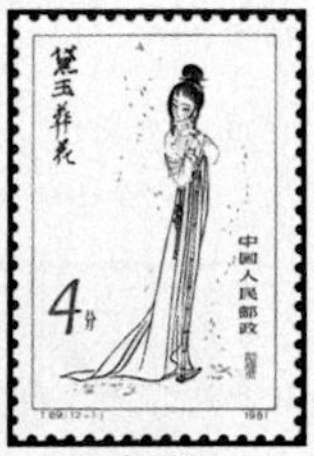

A446

1981, Nov. 10 **Photo.** ***Perf. 11½x11***

1748 A445 8f multicolored .35 .20

Intl. Year of the Disabled.

1981-82 **Photo.** ***Perf. 11***

Twelve Beauties, from The Dream of Red Mansions, by Cao Xueqin.

1749	A446	4f	Daiyu (12-1)	1.00	.70
1750	A446	4f	Baochai (12-2)	1.00	.70
1751	A446	8f	Yuanchun (12-3)	1.00	.75
1752	A446	8f	Yingchun (12-4)	1.00	.75
1753	A446	8f	Tanchun (12-5)	1.00	.75
1754	A446	8f	Xichun (12-6)	1.00	.75
1755	A446	8f	Xiangyuh (12-7)	1.00	.75
1756	A446	10f	Liwan (12-8)	1.75	.75
1757	A446	20f	Xifeng (12-9)	2.00	.80
1758	A446	30f	Sister Qiao (12-10)	3.00	.90
1759	A446	40f	Keqing (12-11)	4.00	2.75
1760	A446	80f	Miaoyu (12-12)	7.25	4.00
			Nos. 1749-1760 (12)	25.00	14.35

Souvenir Sheet

1761 A446 $2 Baoyu, Daiyu 110.00 50.00

No. 1761 contains one 59x39mm stamp. Issued: #1749, 1751, 1753, 1755, 1757, 1759, 1761, 11/20/81; others, 4/24/82. T.69.

A447

A448

1981, Dec. 21 **Photo.**

1762	A447	8f	Girl playing (2-1)	.20	.20
1763	A447	20f	Girl holding trophy (2-2)	.60	.45

Women's team victory in 3rd World Cup Volleyball Championship (J.76).

Photogravure & Engraved

1982, Jan. 5 ***Perf. 11½***

1764	A448	8f multicolored	3.50	2.10
a.		Booklet pane of 10 + label	13.50	

New Year 1982 (Year of the Dog). Stamps from No. 1764a have straight edges at top or bottom.

Coin Type of 1981

1982, Feb. 12

1765	A444	4f	Guilian mask (8-1)	.60	.45
1766	A444	4f	Shu shovel (8-2)	.60	.45
1767	A444	8f	Xia zhuan shovel (8-3)	.60	.45
1768	A444	8f	Han Dan shovel (8-4)	.60	.45
1769	A444	8f	Knife (8-5)	.60	.45
1770	A444	8f	Ming knife (8-6)	.60	.60
1771	A444	70f	Jin hua knife (8-7)	1.10	.90
1772	A444	80f	Yi Liu Hua coin (8-8)	2.25	2.00
			Nos. 1765-1772 (8)	6.95	5.75

T.71.

Nie Er (1912-1935), Natl. Anthem Composer — A449

1982, Feb. 15 ***Perf. 11x11½***

1773 A449 8f multicolored .30 .20

Intl. Drinking Water and Sanitation Decade, 1981-1990 A450

1982, Mar. 1 ***Perf. 11½x11***

1774 A450 8f multicolored .30 .20

TB Bacillus Centenary A451

1982, Mar. 24 ***Perf. 11x11½***

1775 A451 8f multicolored .30 .20

Fire Control (T.76) — A452

1982, May 8 **Photo.** ***Perf. 11½x11***

1776	A452	8f	Water hoses (2-1)	.45	.20
1777	A452	8f	Chemical extinguisher (2-2)	.45	.20

Syzygy of the Nine Planets, Mar. 10 and May 16 — A453

1982, May 16 ***Perf. 11½***

1778 A453 8f multicolored .60 .25

Medicinal Herbs — A454

Soong Ching Ling (1893-1981), Sun Yat-sen's Widow — A455

1982, May 20 ***Perf. 11½x11***

1779	A454	4f	Hemerocallis flava (6-1)	.40	.35
1780	A454	8f	Fritillaria unibracteata (6-2)	.40	.35
1781	A454	8f	Aconitum carmichaeli (6-3)	.40	.35
1782	A454	10f	Lilium brownii (6-4)	.40	.35
1783	A454	20f	Arisaema (6-5)	.75	.50
1784	A454	70f	Paeonia lactiflora (6-6)	2.25	1.00
			Nos. 1779-1784 (6)	4.60	2.90

Souvenir Sheet

1785 A454 $2 Iris tectorum maxim 11.00 8.50

No. 1785 contains one 89x39mm stamp. Nos. 1779-1784 numbered T.72.

1982, May 29 ***Perf. 11½***

1786	A455	8f	Addressing Consultative Conf. (2-1)	.40	.35
1787	A455	20f	Portrait (2-2)	1.25	1.10

J.82.

Sable (T.68) A456

1982, June 20 **Photo.** ***Perf. 11½***

1788	A456	8f	shown (2-1)	.65	.45
1789	A456	80f	Sable, diff. (2-2)	3.75	3.00
a.			Bklt. pane of 8, 6 8f plus sheetlet of 2 (8f, 80f)	10.50	

A457

A458

1982, June 30 ***Perf. 11½x11***

1790 A457 8f multicolored .20 .20

Natl. census, July 1.

1982, July 25 **Photo.** ***Perf. 11½x11***

1791 A458 8f multicolored .20 .20

2nd UN Conference on Peaceful Uses of Outer Space, Vienna, Aug. 9-21.

Strolling in Autumn Woods, by Shen Zhou, Ming Dynasty — A459

Fan Paintings (Ming or Qing Dynasty): No. 1793, Jackdaw on Withered Tree, by Tang Yin. No. 1794 Bamboo and Sparrows, by Zhou Zhimian. 10f, Writing Poem under Pine, by Chen Hongshou and Bai Han. 20f, Chrysanthemums, by Yun Shouping, Qing. 70f, Birds, Crape Myrtle and Chinese Parasol, by Wang Wu, Qing. T.77.

1982, July 31 ***Perf. 11½***

1792	A459	4f	multi (6-1)	.40	.30
1793	A459	8f	multi (6-2)	.80	.60
1794	A459	8f	multi (6-3)	.80	.60
1795	A459	10f	multi (6-4)	.80	.60
1796	A459	20f	multi (6-5)	1.10	.60
1797	A459	70f	multi (6-6)	2.25	1.75
			Nos. 1792-1797 (6)	6.15	4.45

A460

A461

1982, Aug. 25 *Perf. 11½x11*
1798 A460 8f multicolored .20 .20

60th anniv. of Chinese Geological Society.

1982, Aug. 25 Photo. *Perf. 11½x11*
1799 A461 4f Orpiment (4-1) .20 .20
1800 A461 8f Stibnite (4-2) .20 .20
1801 A461 10f Cinnabar (4-3) .40 .20
1802 A461 20f Wolframite (4-4) .65 .45
Nos. 1799-1802 (4) 1.45 1.05

T.73.

Souvenir Sheet

Messenger, Tomb Mural, Jiayu Pass, Wei-Jin Period — A462

1982, Aug. 25
1803 A462 $1 multicolored 10.00 7.50

All-China Philatelic Federation, 1st Cong.

12th Natl. Communist Party Congress A463

Hoopoe — A464

1982, Sept. 1 *Perf. 11½*
1804 A463 8f multicolored .20 .20

1982, Sept. 10 *Perf. 11½x11*
1805 A464 8f shown (5-1) .65 .30
1806 A464 8f Swallows (5-2) .65 .30
1807 A464 8f Oriole (5-3) .65 .30
1808 A464 20f Chickadees (5-4) 1.00 .50
1809 A464 70f Woodpecker (5-5) 2.75 2.50
Nos. 1805-1809 (5) 5.70 3.90

Souvenir Sheet

1810 A464 $2 Cuckoos 22.50

#1810 contains one 56x36mm stamp. T.79.

Japan-China Relations Normalization, 10th Anniv. — A465

World Food Day — A466

Flower Paintings: 8f, Plum blossoms, by Guan Shanyue. 70f, Hibiscus, by Xiao Shufang. J.84.

1982, Sept. 29 *Perf. 11*
1811 A465 8f multi (2-1) .35 .20
1812 A465 70f multi (2-2) .65 .55

1982, Oct. 16 *Perf. 11½*
1813 A466 8f multicolored .20 .20

Guo Morou (1892-1978), Acad. of Sciences Pres. A467

Bodhisattva, 11th Cent. Sculpture A468

Designs: Portraits. J.87.

1982, Nov. 16 Photo. *Perf. 11½x11*
1814 A467 8f multi (2-1) .20 .20
1815 A467 20f multi (2-2) .30 .25

1982, Nov. 19 *Perf. 11*

Liao Dynasty Buddha Sculptures, Lower Huayan Monastery. T.74.

1816 A468 8f multi (4-1) .40 .30
1817 A468 8f multi (4-2) .40 .30
1818 A468 8f multi (4-3) .40 .30
1819 A468 70f multi (4-4) 3.25 2.25
Nos. 1816-1819 (4) 4.45 3.15

Souvenir Sheet

Perf. 11x11½

1820 A468 $2 multicolored 20.00 9.00

No. 1820 contains one 36x55mm stamp.

Dr. D.S. Kotnis, Indian Physician in 8th Army (J.83) A469

Perf. 11½x11, 11x11½
1982, Dec. 9 **Photo.**
1821 A469 8f Portrait, vert. (2-1) .45 .20
1822 A469 70f Riding horse (2-2) 1.75 1.25

11th Communist Youth League Natl. Congress A470

1982, Dec. 20 *Perf. 11x11½*
1823 A470 8f multicolored .20 .20

Bronze Wine Container — A471

Western Zhou Dynasty Bronze (1200-771 B.C.): No. 1825, Three-legged cooking pot. No. 1826, Food bowl. No. 1827, Three-legged cooking pot (diff.). No. 1828, Animal-shaped wine container. 10f, Wine container with lid. 20f, Round food bowl. 70f, Square wine container. T.75.

Photogravure & Engraved

1982, Dec. 25 *Perf. 11*
1824 A471 4f multi (8-1) .85 .55
1825 A471 4f multi (8-2) .85 .55
1826 A471 8f multi (8-3) .85 .55
1827 A471 8f multi (8-4) .85 .55
1828 A471 8f multi (8-5) .85 .55
1829 A471 10f multi (8-6) 1.75 .55
1830 A471 20f multi (8-7) 1.75 1.10
1831 A471 70f multi (8-8) 6.00 2.10
Nos. 1824-1831 (8) 13.75 6.50

A472

1983, Jan. 5 *Perf. 11½*
1832 A472 8f multicolored 4.00 3.50
a. Booklet pane of 12 18.00

New Year 1983 (Year of the Pig).
Stamps from No. 1832a have straight edges at top or bottom.

A473

A474

Stringed Instruments (T.81).

1983, Jan. 20 *Perf. 11½x11, 11x11½*
1833 A473 4f Konghou (5-1) *1.40* .70
1834 A473 8f Ruan (5-2) *1.40* .70
1835 A473 8f Qin, horiz. (5-3) *1.40* .70
1836 A473 10f Piba (5-4) *1.40* .70
1837 A473 70f Sanxian (5-5) *12.00* 3.50
Nos. 1833-1837 (5) *17.60* 6.30

1983, Feb. 7 Photo. *Perf. 11½x11*
1838 A474 8f Memorial Tower, Zhengzhou (2-1) .40 .30
1839 A474 8f Monument, Jiangan (2-2) .40 .30

60th Anniv. of Peking-Hankow Railroad Workers' Strike (J.89).

The Western Chamber, Traditional Opera, by Wang Shifu (1271-1368) A475

Scenes from the opera.

1983, Feb. 21 Photo. *Perf. 11x11½*
1840 A475 8f multi (4-1) 1.50 .80
1841 A475 8f multi (4-2) 1.50 .80
1842 A475 10f multi (4-3) 3.00 1.60
1843 A475 80f multi (4-4) 12.00 4.50
Nos. 1840-1843 (4) 18.00 7.70

Souvenir Sheet

Photogravure and Engraved

Perf. 12

1844 A475 $2 multicolored 70.00 30.00

#1844 contains one 27x48mm stamp. T.82.

Karl Marx (1818-1883) (J.90) — A476

Photogravure & Engraved

1983, Mar. 14 *Perf. 11½x11*
1845 A476 8f Portrait (2-1) .20 .20
1846 A476 20f Making speech (2-2) .50 .25

Tomb of the Yellow Emperor (T.84) A477

Photogravure & Engraved

1983, Apr. 5 *Perf. 11½*
1847 A477 8f Tomb, vert. (3-1) .90 .40
1848 A477 10f Hall of Founder of Chinese Culture (3-2) 1.40 .40
1849 A477 20f Cypress tree, vert. (3-3) 2.25 .80
Nos. 1847-1849 (3) 4.55 1.60

World Communications Year — A478

1983, Apr. 28 Photo. *Perf. 11½*
1850 A478 8f multicolored .45 .20

Male Chinese Alligator (T.85) — A479

Photogravure & Engraved

1983, May 24 *Perf. 11*

1851 A479 8f shown (2-1) .80 .40
1852 A479 20f Female, hatching eggs (2-2) 1.60 .70

Kitten, by Tan Arxi — A480

Various children's drawings. T.86.

1983, June 1 *Perf. 11½x11*

1853 A480 8f multi (4-1) .25 .20
1854 A480 8f multi (4-2) .25 .20
1855 A480 8f multi (4-3) .25 .20
1856 A480 8f multi (4-4) .25 .20
Nos. 1853-1856 (4) 1.00 .80

6th Natl. People's Congress (J.94) A481

1983, June 6 *Perf. 11x11½*

1857 A481 8f Hall (2-1) .20 .20
1858 A481 20f Natl. anthem score (2-2) .75 .35

Terra Cotta Figures, Qin Dynasty (221-207 BC) A482

1983, June 30

1859 A482 8f Soldiers (4-1) .80 .60
1860 A482 8f Heads (4-2) .80 .60
1861 A482 10f Soldiers, horses (4-3) .80 .60
1862 A482 70f Excavation site (4-4) 4.75 2.75
a. Bklt. pane of 8 (#1859, 3 #1860, 3 #1861, #1862) 57.50 27.50
Nos. 1859-1862 (4) 7.15 4.55

Souvenir Sheet

1863 A482 $2 Soldier leading horse 55.00 21.00
a. Booklet pane 55.00

#1863 contains one 59x39mm stamp. T.88.

A483

A484

Female roles in Peking opera (T.87).

1983, July 20 **Photo.** *Perf. 11*

Design A483

1864 4f Sun Yujiao (8-1) .75 .35
1865 8f Chen Miaochang (8-2) .75 .35
1866 8f Bai Suzhen (8-3) .75 .35
1867 8f Sister Thirteen (8-4) .75 .35
1868 10f Qin Xianglian (8-5) .75 .35
1869 20f Yang Yuhuan (8-6) 2.25 .75
1870 50f Cui Yingying (8-7) 4.50 1.60
1871 80f Mu Guiying (8-8) 5.75 2.00
Nos. 1864-1871 (8) 16.25 6.10

1983, Aug. 10 **Photo.** *Perf. 11½*

Paintings by Liu Lingcang.

1872 A484 8f Li Bai (4-1) .55 .25
1873 A484 8f Du Fu (4-2) .55 .25
1874 A484 8f Han Yu (4-3) .55 .25
1875 A484 70f Liu Zongyuan (4-4) 3.25 2.25
Nos. 1872-1875 (4) 4.90 3.00

Poets and philosophers of ancient China (J.92).

5th Natl. Women's Congress — A485

1983, Sept. 1 **Photo.** *Perf. 11½*

1876 A485 8f multicolored .20 .20

5th National Games (J.93) — A486

1983, Sept. 16 **Photo.** *Perf. 11½*

1877 A486 4f Emblem (6-1) .45 .25
1878 A486 8f Gymnast (6-2) .45 .25
1879 A486 8f Badminton (6-3) .45 .25
1880 A486 8f Diving (6-4) .45 .25
1881 A486 20f High jump (6-5) .80 .70
1882 A486 70f Wind surfing (6-6) 2.00 1.75
Nos. 1877-1882 (6) 4.60 3.45

Family Planning (T.91) A487

1983, Sept. 19 *Perf. 11x11½*

1883 A487 8f One child (2-1) .20 .20
1884 A487 8f Cultivated land (2-2) .20 .20

10th Intl. Trade Union Congress — A488

1983, Oct. 18 **Litho.** *Perf. 11½*

1885 A488 8f multicolored .20 .20

Swans (T.83) A489

Perf. 11x11½ on 3 sides

1983, Nov. 18 **Photo.**

1886 A489 8f (4-1) .30 .30
1887 A489 8f (4-2) .30 .30
1888 A489 10f (4-3) .55 .30
1889 A489 80f (4-4) 2.00 1.50
a. Booklet pane, 7 #1886, 1 each #1887-1889 10.00
Nos. 1886-1889 (4) 3.15 2.40

A490

A491

Various photos. J.96.

1983, Nov. 24 **Photo.** *Perf. 11½*

1890 A490 8f multi (4-1) .40 .35
1891 A490 8f multi (4-2) .40 .35
1892 A490 8f multi (4-3) .40 .35
1893 A490 8f multi (4-4) .40 .35
Nos. 1890-1893 (4) 1.60 1.40

85th birth anniv. of Liu Shaoqi, political leader.

1983, Nov. 29 **Photo.** *Perf. 11½*

1894 A491 8f No. 117 (2-1) .20 .20
1895 A491 20f No. 4L1 (2-2) .50 .25

CHINAPEX '83 Natl. Philatelic Exhibition (J.99).

A492

A493

Various portraits. J.97.

1983, Dec. 26 **Photo.** *Perf. 11½*

1896 A492 8f 1925 (4-1) .20 .20
1897 A492 8f 1945 (4-2) .20 .20
1898 A492 10f 1952 (4-3) .45 .25
1899 A492 20f 1961 (4-4) 1.00 .90
Nos. 1896-1899 (4) 1.85 1.55

90th birth anniv. of Mao Tse-tung.

Photogravure and Engraved

1984, Jan. 5 *Perf. 11½*

1900 A493 8f multicolored 2.50 1.10
a. Booklet pane of 12 16.00

New Year 1984 (Year of the Rat).

Stamps from No. 1900a have straight edge at top or bottom.

Beauties Wearing Flowers — A494

Portions of painting by Zhou Fang (Tang Dynasty). T.89.

1984, Mar. 24 **Photo.** *Perf. 11*

1901 A494 8f multi (3-1) .80 .30
1902 A494 10f multi (3-2) .80 .30
1903 A494 70f multi (3-3) 4.00 2.25
Nos. 1901-1903 (3) 5.60 2.85

Souvenir Sheet

1904 A494 $2 Entire painting 110.00 50.00

No. 1904 contains one 162x40mm stamp.

Chinese Roses (T.93) — A495

Ren Bishi (1904-50), Statesman A496

1984, Apr. 20 **Photo.** *Perf. 11½*

1905 A495 4f Spring of Shanghai (6-1) .35 .20
1906 A495 8f Rosy Dawn of Pujiang River (6-2) .35 .20
1907 A495 8f Pearl (6-3) .35 .20
1908 A495 10f Black whirlwind (6-4) .35 .25
1909 A495 20f Yellow flower in battlefield (6-5) .65 .35
1910 A495 70f Blue Phoenix (6-6) 1.75 1.10
Nos. 1905-1910 (6) 3.80 2.30

1984, Apr. 30 *Perf. 11½x11*

1911 A496 8f multicolored .20 .20

Crested Ibis (T.94) A497

1984, May 15 **Photo.** *Perf. 11x11½*

1912 A497 8f Flying (3-1) .50 .20
1913 A497 8f Wading (3-2) .50 .20
1914 A497 80f Perching (3-3) 1.50 1.25
Nos. 1912-1914 (3) 2.50 1.65

Chinese Red Cross Society, 80th Anniv. — A498

1984, May 29 ***Perf. 11½***

1915 A498 8f multicolored .20 .20

Gezhou Dam, Yangtze River (T.95) — A499

1984, June 15 **Photo.**

1916 A499 8f Dam (3-1) .25 .25
1917 A499 10f Bridge, vert. (3-2) .30 .25
1918 A499 20f Lock Gate #2 (3-3) .60 .50
Nos. 1916-1918 (3) 1.15 1.00

Zhuo Zheng Garden, Suzhou (T.96) — A500

Photogravure & Engraved

1984, June 30 ***Perf. 11½x11***

1919 A500 8f Inverted Image Tower (4-1) .60 .35
1920 A500 8f Loquat Garden (4-2) .60 .35
1921 A500 10f Water Court, Xiao Cang Lang (4-3) .60 .35
1922 A500 70f Yuanxiang Hall, Yiyu Study (4-4) 1.75 1.40
Nos. 1919-1922 (4) 3.55 2.45

1984 Summer Olympics A501

1984, July 28 **Photo.** ***Perf. 11½***

1923 A501 4f Shooting (6-1) .20 .20
1924 A501 8f High jump (6-2) .20 .20
1925 A501 8f Weight lifting (6-3) .20 .20
1926 A501 10f Gymnastics (6-4) .25 .20
1927 A501 20f Volleyball (6-5) .25 .25
1928 A501 80f Diving (6-6) 1.00 .35
Nos. 1923-1928 (6) 2.10 1.40

Souvenir Sheet

1929 A501 $2 Athletes, rings 4.50

#1929 contains one 61x38mm stamp. J.103.

Calligraphy A502

Luanhe River Water Diversion Project (T.97) A503

Artworks by Wu Changshuo. T.98.

1984, Aug. 27 **Photo.** ***Perf. 11½***

1930 A502 4f shown (8-1) .40 .25
1931 A502 4f A Pair of Peaches (8-2) .40 .25
1932 A502 8f Lotus (8-3) .40 .25
1933 A502 8f Wisteria (8-4) .40 .25
1934 A502 8f Peony (8-5) .40 .25
1935 A502 10f Chrysanthemum (8-6) .80 .45
1936 A502 20f Plum Blossom (8-7) .80 .45
1937 A502 70f Seal Cutting (8-8) 2.00 1.60
Nos. 1930-1937 (8) 5.60 3.75

Perf. 11½x11, 11 (#1939)

1984, Sept. 11 **Photo.**

1938 A503 8f multi (3-1) .20 .20
1939 A503 10f multi, horiz. (3-2) .20 .20
1940 A503 20f multi (3-3) .30 .25
Nos. 1938-1940 (3) .70 .65

Chinese-Japanese Youth (J.104) — A504

1984, Sept. 24 **Photo.** ***Perf. 11½***

1941 A504 8f Neighbors (3-1) .20 .20
1942 A504 20f Planting tree (3-2) .20 .20
1943 A504 80f Dancing (3-3) .60 .50
Nos. 1941-1943 (3) 1.00 .90

People's Republic, 35th Anniv. (J.105) — A505

1984, Oct. 1 **Photo.** ***Perf. 11½x11***

Size: 26x35mm

1944 A505 8f Engineer (5-1) .20 .20
1945 A505 8f Farm woman (5-2) .20 .20
1946 A505 8f Scientist (5-4) .20 .20
1947 A505 8f Soldier (5-5) .20 .20

Size: 36x48mm

Perf. 11

1948 A505 20f Cranes (5-3) .30 .25
Nos. 1944-1948 (5) 1.10 1.05

110th Birth Anniv. of Chen Jiageng (J.106) A506

1984, Oct. 21 **Photo.** ***Perf. 12½x12***

1949 A506 8f Chen Jiageng (2-1) .20 .20
1950 A506 80f Jimei School (2-2) .45 .30

The Maiden's Study A507

Scenes from The Peony Pavilion, by Tang Xianzu. T.99.

Photogravure & Engraved

1984, Oct. 30 ***Perf. 11***

1951 A507 8f shown (4-1) .45 .35
1952 A507 8f In the dreamland (4-2) .45 .35
1953 A507 20f Du Liniang drawing self-portrait (4-3) .80 .65
1954 A507 70f Married to Liu Mengmai (4-4) 2.50 2.50
Nos. 1951-1954 (4) 4.20 3.85

Souvenir Sheet

Perf. 11½

1955 A507 $2 Playing in the garden 24.00 12.00

No. 1955 contains one 90x60mm stamp.

Emei Shan Mountain Scenery (T.100) — A508

1984, Nov. 16 ***Perf. 11***

1956 A508 4f Baoguo Temple (6-1) .45 .25
1957 A508 8f Leiyin Temple (6-2) .45 .30
1958 A508 8f Hongchun Lawn (6-3) .45 .30
1959 A508 10f Elephant bath (6-4) .45 .40
1960 A508 20f Woyun Temple (6-5) 1.00 .90
1961 A508 80f Shining Cloud Sea at Jinding (6-6) 3.75 2.40
Nos. 1956-1961 (6) 6.55 4.55

A509

A510

Portraits.

1984, Dec. 15 **Photo.** ***Perf. 11½x11***

1962 A509 8f During the Long March (3-1) .20 .20
1963 A509 10f At 7th Natl. Party Congress (3-2) .20 .20
1964 A509 20f In motorcade (3-3) .25 .20
Nos. 1962-1964 (3) .65 .60

Former party secretary Ren Bishi (1904-50).

1984, Dec. 25 ***Perf. 11***

1965 A510 8f Flower arrangement .20 .20

Chinese insurance industry.

New Year 1985 (Year of the Ox) — A511

Photogravure & Engraved

1985, Jan. 5 ***Perf. 11½***

1966 A511 8f T.102 .40 .30
a. Bklt. pane of 4 + 8 plus label 13.50

Stamps from No. 1966a have straight edge at top or bottom.

Zunyi Meeting, 50th Anniv. — A512

Paintings: 8f, The Zunyi Meeting, by Liu Xiangping. 20f, The Red Army Successfully Arrived in Northern Shaanxi, by Zhao Yu. J.107.

1985, Jan. 15 **Photo.** ***Perf. 11x11½***

1967 A512 8f multi (2-1) .25 .25
1968 A512 20f multi (2-2) .60 .50

A513

A514

Lantern Folk Festival: No. 1969, Lotus of Good Luck. No. 1970, Auspicious dragon and phoenix. No. 1971, A hundred flowers blossoming. 70f, Prosperity and affluence. T.104.

1985, Feb. 28 ***Perf. 11½***

1969 A513 8f multi (4-1) .40 .20
1970 A513 8f multi (4-2) .40 .20
1971 A513 8f multi (4-3) .40 .20
1972 A513 70f multi (4-4) 2.10 1.10
Nos. 1969-1972 (4) 3.30 1.70

1985, Mar. 8

1973 A514 20f multicolored .20 .20

UN Decade for Women (1976-85).

Mei (Prunus mume) (T.103) — A515

1985, Apr. 5 *Perf. 11*

1974 A515 8f Green calyx (6-1) .20 .20
1975 A515 8f Pendant mei (6-2) .20 .20
1976 A515 8f Contorted dragon (6-3) .20 .20
1977 A515 10f Cinnabar (6-4) .30 .20
1978 A515 20f Versicolor mei (6-5) .45 .25
1979 A515 80f Apricot mei (6-6) 2.00 .90
Nos. 1974-1979 (6) 3.35 1.95

Souvenir Sheet

Perf. 11½

1980 A515 $2 Duplicate and condensed fragrance mei 16.00

No. 1980 contains one 93x52mm stamp.

A516

A518

A517

1985, May 1 **Photo.** *Perf. 11*

1981 A516 8f Huizo Guild Hall, Guangzhou .20 .20

All-China Fed. of Trade Unions.

1985, May 4 **Photo.**

1982 A517 20f multicolored .20 .20

Intl. Youth Year.

1985, May 24 *Perf. 11½*

Paintings of giant pandas: 8f, 20f, 50f, 80f, by Han Meilin; $3, by Wu Zuoren. T.106.

1983 A518 8f multi (4-1), vert. .25 .20
1984 A518 20f multi (4-2) .25 .25
1985 A518 50f multi (4-3), vert. .35 .30
1986 A518 80f multi (4-4) .50 .45
Nos. 1983-1986 (4) 1.35 1.20

Souvenir Sheet

Perf. 11x11½

1987 A518 $3 multi, vert. 3.25
a. Ovptd. in sheet margin 6.00

No. 1987 contains one 39x59mm stamp.

No. 1987a ovptd. in sheet margin with panda hologram, PJZ-4 and horizontal Chinese inscription in gold. Issued 10/9/96.

No. 1987a was sold in a mount affixed to a small card.

Xian Xinghai (1905-1945), Composer A519

Agnes Smedley, 1892-1950 (3-1) — A520

Design: Bust, by Cao Chongen and music from The Yellow River Cantata.

1985, June 13 **Photo.** *Perf. 11½x11*

1988 A519 8f multicolored .20 .20

1985, June 25

American journalists: 20f, Anna Louise Strong, 1885-1970 (3-2). 80f, Edgar Snow, 1905-1972 (3-3). J.112.

1989 A520 8f multicolored .20 .20
1990 A520 20f multicolored .20 .20
1991 A520 80f multicolored .55 .35
Nos. 1989-1991 (3) .95 .75

Zheng He's West Seas Expedition, 580th Anniv. — A521

#1992, Portrait of the navigator. #1993, Peace envoy. 20f, Trade, cultural exchange. 80f, Honored for navigational feats. J.113.

1985, July 11 *Perf. 11½*

1992 A521 8f multi (4-1) .20 .20
1993 A521 8f multi (4-2) .20 .20
1994 A521 20f multi (4-3) .35 .30
1995 A521 80f multi (4-4) 1.10 .60
Nos. 1992-1995 (4) 1.85 1.30

Xu Beihong, 1895-1953, Painter (J.114) A522

1985, July 19 *Perf. 11½x11, 11x11½*

1996 A522 8f Self-portrait (2-1), vert. .20 .20
1997 A522 20f shown (2-2) .55 .20

A523

A524

Designs: 8f, Lin Zexu, 1785-1850, statesman, patriot. 80f, Burning opium at Humen, bas-relief.

1985, Aug. 30 *Perf. 11*

1998 A523 8f multi (2-1) .20 .20

Size: 51x22mm

1999 A523 80f multi (2-2) .35 .25

Lin Zexu's ban of the opium trade catalyzed the Anglo-Chinese Opium Wars. J.115.

1985, Sept. 1 *Perf. 11½x11*

2000 A524 8f Prosperity (3-1) .20 .20
2001 A524 10f Celebration (3-2) .20 .20
2002 A524 20f Abundant Harvest (3-3) .45 .45
Nos. 2000-2002 (3) .85 .85

Tibet Autonomous Region, 20th anniv. (J.116).

End of World War II, 40th Anniv. A525

Woodcuts by Wu Biduan: 8f, The Chinese Army Rose Against the Japanese Agressors at Logouqiao (2-1). 80f, The Eighth Route Army and Militia Fought Around the Great Wall (2-2). J.117.

1985, Sept. 3 *Perf. 11*

2003 A525 8f multi .20 .20
2004 A525 80f multi .25 .20

2nd Natl. Worker's Games, Sept. 8-15, Beijing A526

Competitors from various events and: 8f, Men's bicycling (2-1). 20f, Women hurdlers (2-2). J.118.

1985, Sept. 8 *Perf. 11x11½*

2005 A526 8f multi .60 .50
2006 A526 20f multi .80 .75

Xinjiang Uygur Autonomous Region, 30th Anniv. (J.119) A527

1985, Oct. 1 **Photo.** *Perf. 11½*

2007 A527 8f Oasis in the Gobi, woman (3-1) .20 .20
2008 A527 10f Oil field, Lake Tianchi (3-2) .20 .20
2009 A527 20f Tianshan pasture, woman (3-3) .20 .20
Nos. 2007-2009 (3) .60 .60

Size of No. 2008, 60x30mm.

1st Natl. Youth Games, Oct. 6-15, Zhengzhou (J.121) — A528

1985, Oct. 6 *Perf. 11½x11*

2010 A528 8f Girls' track & field (2-1) .20 .20
2011 A528 20f Boys' basketball (2-2) .30 .30

Forbidden City Main Buildings — A529

1985, Oct. 10 *Perf. 11½*

2012 A529 8f multi (4-1) .20 .20
2013 A529 8f multi (4-2) .20 .20
2014 A529 20f multi (4-3) .20 .20
2015 A529 80f multi (4-4) .45 .45
a. Vert. strip of 4, #2012-2015 .90 .90

Palace Museum, 60th anniv. J.120.

Zou Taofen (1895-1935), Journalist (J.122) — A530

1985, Nov. 5 *Perf. 11½x11*

2016 A530 8f Portrait (2-1) .20 .20
2017 A530 20f Epitaph by Zhou Enlai (2-2) .20 .20
a. Pair, #2016-2017 .30 .30

December 9th Revolution, 50th Anniv. — A531

1985, Dec. 9 *Perf. 11½*

2018 A531 8f Memorial Pavilion .20 .20

New Year 1986 — A532

Natl. Space Industry — A533

Photogravure & Engraved

1986, Jan. 5 *Perf. 11½*

2019 A532 8f multicolored .40 .40
a. Bklt. pane of 4 + 8 with label btwn 5.50

1986, Feb. 1 **Photo.**

4f, 1st experimental satellite. #2021, Recoverable satellite. #2022, Underwater rocket launch. 10f, Rocket launch. 20f,Earth satellite receiver. 70f, Satellite trajectory diagram. T.108.

2020 A533 4f multi (6-1) .20 .20
2021 A533 8f multi (6-2) .20 .20
2022 A533 8f multi (6-3) .20 .20
2023 A533 10f multi (6-4) .20 .20
2024 A533 20f multi (6-5) .20 .20
2025 A533 70f multi (6-6) .60 .30
Nos. 2020-2025 (6) 1.60 1.30

Dong Biwu (1886-1975), Party Founder (J.123) — A534

Lin Boqu (1886-1960), Party Leader (J.124) — A535

Photogravure and Engraved

1986, Mar. 5 *Perf. 11½x11*

2026 A534 8f 1975 (2-1) .20 .20
2027 A534 20f 1945 (2-2) .20 .20

1986, Mar. 20

2028 A535 8f shown (2-1) .20 .20
2029 A535 20f Lin standing (2-2) .20 .20

Marshal He Long (1896-1969), Revolution Leader (J.126) — A536

1986, Mar. 22 *Perf. 11x11½*

2030 A536 8f shown (2-1) .20 .20
2031 A536 20f On horseback (2-2) .20 .20

Halley's Comet — A537

1986, Apr. 11 Photo. *Perf. 11½*
2032 A537 20f dk bl & gray .20 .20

White Crane (T.110) A538

1986, May 22 *Perf. 11x11½, 11½x11*
2033 A538 8f Two cranes (3-1) .20 .20
2034 A538 10f One flying (3-2), vert. .20 .20
2035 A538 70f Four cranes (3-3), vert. .45 .20
Nos. 2033-2035 (3) .85 .60

Souvenir Sheet

2036 A538 $2 Flock *5.50*

No. 2036 contains one 116x25mm stamp.

Li Weihan (1896-1984), Party Leader (J.127) — A539

1986, June 2 *Perf. 11x11½*
2037 A539 8f Portrait (2-1) .20 .20
2038 A539 20f Writing (2-2) .20 .20

Intl. Peace Year A540

1986, June 16 *Perf. 11*
2039 A540 8f multi .20 .20

Mao Dun (1896-1981), Writer (J.129) — A541

1986, July 4 *Perf. 11x11½*
2040 A541 8f Portrait (2-1) .20 .20
2041 A541 20f Portrait, diff. (2-2) .20 .20

Wang Jiaxiang (1906-1974), Party Leader (J.130) — A542

1986, Aug. 15
2042 A542 8f Portrait (2-1) .20 .20
2043 A542 20f Portrait, diff. (2-2) .20 .20

Teacher's Day A543

1986, Sept. 10 *Perf. 11*
2044 A543 8f multi .20 .20

Magnolia Liliflora (T.111) A544

1986, Sept. 23 *Perf. 11x11½*
2045 A544 8f Blossom (3-1) .30 .30
2046 A544 8f Two blossoms (3-2) .30 .30
2047 A544 70f Blossom, diff. (3-3) 2.10 2.10
Nos. 2045-2047 (3) 2.70 2.70

Souvenir Sheet

2048 A544 $2 Three blossoms *9.00*

No. 2048 contains one 132x70mm stamp.

Folk Houses — A545

Perf. 13x13½, 11x11½, (1½f, 3f, #2057-2062)

1986, Apr. 1 Photo.
2049 A545 1f Inner Mongolia .20 .20
2050 A545 1½f Tibet .20 .20
2051 A545 2f Northeastern China .20 .20
2052 A545 3f Hunan .20 .20
2053 A545 4f So. Yangtze River .20 .20
2054 A545 8f Beijing .20 .20
2055 A545 10f Yunnan .20 .20
2056 A545 20f Shanghai .20 .20
2057 A545 30f Anhui .25 .20
2058 A545 40f No. Shaanxi .35 .25
2059 A545 50f Sichuan .40 .35
2060 A545 90f Taiwan .70 .50
2061 A545 $1 Fujian .75 .60
2062 A545 $1.10 Zhejiang .80 .70
Nos. 2049-2062 (14) 4.85 4.20

Issue dates: 3f, Dec. 25; 4f, $1, Oct. 15; 20f, 50f, Sept. 10; 40f, Nov. 15; others, Apr. 1.
Postal forgeries of No. 2056 exist.
See Nos. 2198-2207.

1989-90 Photo.
2055a Perf. 11x11½ ('89) .25 .20
2056a Perf. 11x11½ ('89) .35 .25
2057a Perf. 13x13½ ('90) .65 .35
2058a Perf. 13x13½ .85 .45
2059a Perf. 13x13½ ('89) 1.10 .60
2061a Perf. 13x13½ ('90) 2.25 1.25
Nos. 2055a-2061a (6) 5.45 3.10

Souvenir Sheet

All-China Philatelic Federation, 2nd Congress — A546

1986, Oct. 17 Litho. *Perf. 11½*
2063 A546 $2 Jade lion *3.25*

Leaders of the 1911 Revolution (J.132) A547

1986, Oct. 10 Photo. *Perf. 11x11½*
2064 A547 8f Sun Yat-sen (3-1) .20 .20
2065 A547 10f Huang Xing (3-2) .20 .20
2066 A547 40f Zhang Taiyan (3-3) .90 .90
Nos. 2064-2066 (3) 1.30 1.30

Souvenir Sheet

Sun Yat-sen (1866-1925) — A548

1986, Nov. 12 *Perf. 11½*
2067 A548 $2 multicolored *6.25*

Marshal Zhu De (1886-1976) (J.134) — A549

Designs: 20f, Orating.

1986, Dec. 1 Engr. *Perf. 11½x11*
2068 A549 8f sepia (2-1) .20 .20
2069 A549 20f myrtle grn (2-2) .30 .20

Sports of Ancient China A550

Stone carvings. T.113.

Perf. 11½x11, 11x11½

1986, Dec. 20 Photo.
2070 A550 8f Archery (4-1), vert. .25 .20
2071 A550 8f Weiqi (4-2) .25 .20
2072 A550 10f Golf (4-3) .35 .25
2073 A550 50f Soccer (4-4), vert. 2.75 1.75
Nos. 2070-2073 (4) 3.60 2.40

A551

A552

Photogravure & Engraved

1987, Jan. 5 *Perf. 11½*
2074 A551 8f blk, dk pink & yel grn .20 .20
a. Bklt. pane of 4 + 8 + label *4.50*

New Year 1987 (Year of the Hare).

1987, Feb. 20 Photo. *Perf. 11½*
2075 A552 8f Traveling (3-1) .35
2076 A552 20f Cave writing (3-2) 1.60
2077 A552 40f Mountain climbing (3-3) 3.25
Nos. 2075-2077 (3) 5.20

Xu Xiake (1587-1621), Ming Dynasty geographer (J.136).

Birds of Prey (T.114) — A553

1987, Mar. 20
2078 A553 8f Kite (4-1) .25 .20
2079 A553 8f Sea eagle (4-2), vert. .25 .20
2080 A553 10f Vulture (4-3), vert. .35 .20
2081 A553 90f Buzzard (4-4) 4.50 1.00
Nos. 2078-2081 (4) 5.35 1.60

Liao Zhongkai (1877-1925), National Party Leader (J.137) — A554

1987, Apr. 23 *Perf. 11½x11*
2082 A554 8f shown (2-1) .20
2083 A554 20f Liao, He Xiangning (2-2) .25

Kites (T.115) — A555

A556

1987, Apr. 1

2084 A555 8f Hawk (4-1) .40
2085 A555 8f Dragon (4-2) .40
a. Pair, #2084-2085 .80
2086 A555 30f Symbolic octagon (4-3) 1.50
2087 A555 30f Phoenix (4-4) 1.50
a. Pair, #2086-2087 3.00
Nos. 2084-2087 (4) 3.80

Nos. 2085a, 2087a have continuous designs.

1987, Apr. 28

Portraits of Ye Jianying (1897-1986), central committee vice chairman (J.138).

2088 A556 8f multi (3-3) .25 .25
2089 A556 10f multi (3-2) .35 .35
2090 A556 30f multi (3-1) 1.60 1.60
Nos. 2088-2090 (3) 2.20 2.20

Caves of the Thousand Buddhas, Dunhuang, Gansu Province — A557

Wall Paintings: 8f, Worshipping Bodhisattvas, Northern Liang Dynasty. 10f, Deer King Jatka, Northern Wei Dynasty. 20f, Heavenly Musicians, Northern Wei Dynasty. 40f, Flying Devata, Northern Wei Dynasty. $2, Mahasattva Jataka. T.116.

1987, May 20 ***Perf. 11½***

2091 A557 8f multi (4-1) .35 .20
2092 A557 10f multi (4-2) .40 .25
2093 A557 20f multi (4-3) 1.10 .60
2094 A557 40f multi (4-4) 2.25 1.10
Nos. 2091-2094 (4) 4.10 2.15

Souvenir Sheet

2095 A557 $2 multi *20.00*

No. 2095 contains one 92x73mm stamp.
See Nos. 2149-2152, 2283-2286, 2407-2411, 2505-2508, 2704-2707.

Children's Day Festival A558

Children's drawings: No. 2096, Happy Holiday, by Yan Qinghui, age 7. No. 2097, Peace and Happiness, by Liu Yuan, age 7. T.117.

1987, June 1 ***Perf. 12½x12***

2096 A558 8f shown (2-1) .20 .20
2097 A558 8f multi, vert. (2-2) .20 .20

Rural Development A559

Postal Savings Bank Inauguration A560

1987, June 25 ***Perf. 11½***

2098 A559 8f Village, southeast China (4-1) .35 .35
2099 A559 8f Market (4-2) .35 .35
2100 A559 10f Dairy industry (4-3) .50 .50
2101 A559 20f Theater (4-4) 1.00 1.00
Nos. 2098-2101 (4) 2.20 2.20

Nos. 2099-2100 horiz. T.118.

1987, July 1

2102 A560 8f multicolored .20 .20

Esperanto Language Movement, Cent. — A561

1987, July 26

2103 A561 8f lt olive grn, blk & brt blue .20

People's Liberation Army, 60th Anniv. (J.140) A562

1987, Aug. 1 ***Perf. 11***

2104 A562 8f Flag, Great Wall (4-1) .30
2105 A562 8f Rocket launch, soldier, village (4-2) .30
2106 A562 10f Submarine, sailor (4-3) .40
2107 A562 30f Aircraft, pilot (4-4) 1.10
Nos. 2104-2107 (4) 2.10

Intl. Year of Shelter for the Homeless A563

1987, Aug. 20 ***Perf. 11***

2108 A563 8f gray, dk car rose & blk .20

Chinese Art Festival, Sept. 5-25, Beijing — A564

Fairy Tales — A565

1987, Sept. 5 ***Perf. 11***

2109 A564 8f brt red, gold & blk .20

1987, Sept. 25 ***Perf. 11½***

4f, Pan Gu inventing the universe. #2111, Nu Wa creating man. #2112, Yi shooting nine suns. 10f, Chang'e flying to the moon. 20f, Kua Fu pursuing the sun. 90f, Jing Wei filling the sea. T.120.

2110 A565 4f multi (6-1) .20 .20
2111 A565 8f multi (6-2) .25 .20
2112 A565 8f multi (6-3) .25 .20
2113 A565 10f multi (6-4) .35 .20
2114 A565 20f multi (6-5) .60 .30
2115 A565 90f multi (6-6) 2.50 1.10
Nos. 2110-2115 (6) 4.15 2.20

Communist Party of China, 13th Natl. Congress A566

1987, Oct. 25 ***Perf. 11***

2116 A566 8f multicolored .20

Yellow Crane Tower (T.121) A567

1987, Oct. 30

2117 A567 8f shown (4-1) .30 .20
2118 A567 8f Yue Yang Tower (4-2) .30 .30
2119 A567 10f Teng Wang Pavilion (4-3) .35 .35
2120 A567 90f Peng Lai Pavilion (4-4) 3.25 3.25
a. Min. sheet of 4, #2117-2120 *12.00*
Nos. 2117-2120 (4) 4.20 4.10

No. 2120a sold for $1.50.

6th Natl. Games (J.144) — A568

1987, Nov. 20 ***Perf. 11½x11***

2121 A568 8f Pole vault (4-1) .20
2122 A568 8f Softball (4-2) .20
2123 A568 30f Weight lifting (4-3) .50
2124 A568 50f Diving (4-4) .90
Nos. 2121-2124 (4) 1.80

Souvenir Sheet

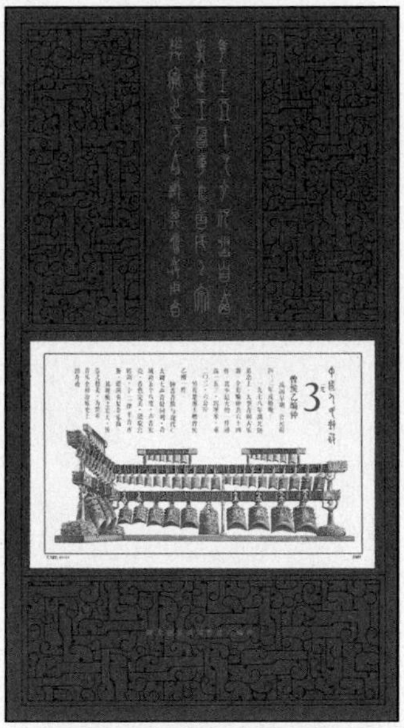

Bronze Bells from the Tomb of Marquis Yi of the Zeng State (c. 433 B.C.), Hubei Province — A569

1987, Dec. 10 **Litho.** ***Imperf.***

2125 A569 $3 multicolored *6.25*

Classic Literature — A570

Outlaws of the Marsh: 8f, Shi Jin practicing martial arts. 10f, Sagacious Lu, the "Tattooed Monk," uprooting a willow tree. 30f, Lin Chong seeking shelter from snow storm at the Mountain Spirit Temple. 50f, Song Jiang helps Ward Chief Chao Gai flee. $2, Outlaws of the Marsh capture treasures. T.123.

1987, Dec. 20 **Photo.** ***Perf. 11***

2126 A570 8f multi (4-1) .35
2127 A570 10f multi (4-2) .45
2128 A570 30f multi (4-3) 1.50
2129 A570 50f multi (4-4) 2.00
Nos. 2126-2129 (4) 4.30

Souvenir Sheet

Perf. 11½x11

2130 A570 $2 multi *16.00*

No. 2130 contains one 90x60mm stamp.
See Nos. 2216-2219, 2373-2377, 2449-2452, 2822-2826, 2889-2893.

New Year 1988 (Year of the Dragon) — A571

Cai Yuanpei (1868-1940), Education Reformer ((J.145) — A572

Photo. & Engr.

1988, Jan. 5 ***Perf. 11½***

2131 A571 8f multicolored *.20*
a. Bklt. pane of 4 + 8 with label between *5.50*

1988, Jan. 11 **Photo.** ***Perf. 11½x11***

2132 A572 8f shown (2-1) .20
2133 A572 20f Seated (2-2) .20

Tao Zhu (1908-1969), Party Leader (J.146) — A573

1988, Jan. 16 ***Perf. 11x11½***

2134 A573 8f shown (2-1) .20
2135 A573 20f Tao, diff. (2-2) .20

Folklore (T.125) A574

1988, Feb. 10

2136 A574 8f shown (4-1) .20
2137 A574 10f multi, diff. (4-2) .20
2138 A574 20f multi, diff. (4-3) .40
2139 A574 30f multi, diff. (4-4) .65
Nos. 2136-2139 (4) 1.45

A575

A576

1988, Mar. 25 **Photo.** ***Perf. 11½***

2140 A575 8f multicolored .20

7th Natl. People's Congress.

1988, Apr. 20 Photo. *Perf. 11½*

2141 A576 8f Wuzhi Mountain (4-1) .20
2142 A576 10f Wanquan River (4-2) .20
2143 A576 30f "End of the Earth" (4-3) .20
2144 A576 $1.10 "Deer Turning Its Head" (4-4) .50
Nos. 2141-2144 (4) 1.10

Establishment of Hainan Province (J.148).

Modern Scientists A577

Designs: 8f, Li Siguang, geologist. 10f, Zhu Kezhen, meteorologist and geographer. 20f, Wu Youxun, physicist. 30f, Hua Luogeng, mathematician. J.149.

1988, Apr. 28 *Perf. 11x11½*

2145 A577 8f multi (4-1) .20
2146 A577 10f multi (4-2) .20
2147 A577 20f multi (4-3) .20
2148 A577 30f multi (4-4) .25
Nos. 2145-2148 (4) .85

Wall Paintings Type of 1987

Caves of the Thousand Buddhas, Dunhuang, Gansu Province: No. 2149, Hunting, Western Wei Dynasty. No. 2150, Fishing, Western Wei Dynasty. 10f, Farming, Northern Zhou Dynasty. 90f, Building a Pagoda, Northern Zhou Dynasty. T.126.

1988, May 25 *Perf. 11½x11*

2149 A557 8f multi (4-1) *.20*
2150 A557 8f multi (4-2) *.20*
2151 A557 10f multi (4-3) *.25*
2152 A557 90f multi (4-4) *2.00*
Nos. 2149-2152 (4) *2.65*

Environmental Protection — A578

1988, June 5 Photo. *Perf. 11*

2153 A578 8f Soil (4-1) .20
2154 A578 8f Air (4-2) .20
2155 A578 8f Water (4-3) .20
2156 A578 8f Prevent noise pollution (4-4) .20
a. Block of 4, #2153-2156 .55

Souvenir Sheet

China Nos. 1-3 — A579

Photo. & Engr.

1988, July 2 *Perf. 13*

2157 A579 $3 multicolored *4.25*

Postage stamps of China, 110th anniv.

11th Asian Games (in 1990), Beijing (J.151) A580

1988, July 20 Photo. *Perf. 11x11½*

2158 A580 8f Emblem (2-1) .20 .20
2159 A580 30f Character trademark (2-2) .20 .20

See No. 2300a.

Signing of the Sino-Japanese Peace Treaty, 10th Anniv. (J.152) — A581

1988, Aug. 12 Photo. *Perf. 11*

2160 A581 8f Peony (2-1) .20
2161 A581 $1.60 Sakura (2-2) .80
a. Pair, #2160-2161 .90

Achievements in Construction — A582

Designs: 8f, Coal-loading wharf, Ch'in-huang-tao Port. 10f, Ethylene refinery, Qilu. 20f, Pao-shan steel plant, Shanghai. 30f, Central Television Broadcasting Station. T.128.

1988, Sept. 2 Photo. *Perf. 11*

2162 A582 8f multi (4-1) .20
2163 A582 10f multi (4-2) .20
2164 A582 20f multi (4-3) .20
2165 A582 30f multi (4-4) .20
Nos. 2162-2165 (4) .80

See #2221-2224, 2279-2282, 2354-2357.

Mt. T'ai Shan, Shantung Province (T.130) — A583

1988, Sept. 14 Photo. & Engr.

2166 A583 8f T'ai Shan Temple (4-1) .25
2167 A583 10f Ladder to Heaven (4-2) .35
2168 A583 20f Daguang peak (4-3) .65
2169 A583 90f Sun-watching peak (4-4) 2.75
Nos. 2166-2169 (4) 4.00

Liao Chengzhi (1908-1983), Party Leader (J.153) — A584

1988, Sept. 25 Photo. *Perf. 11½x11*

2170 A584 8f shown (2-1) .20
2171 A584 20f Writing (2-2) .20

Marshal Peng Dehuai (1898-1974), Party Leader (J.155) — A585

1988, Oct. 24 Photo. *Perf. 11x11½*

2172 A585 8f shown (2-1) .20
2173 A585 20f Peng in uniform (2-2) .20

1st Natl. Farmers' Games (J.154) A586

1988, Oct. 9 Photo. *Perf. 11½*

2174 A586 8f Cycling (2-1) .20
2175 A586 20f Javelin (2-2) .20

Literary Masterpieces — A587

The Romance of the Three Kingdoms, by Luo Guanzhong, 14th cent.: No. 2176, Three heroes' sworn brotherhood (4-1). No. 2177, Battle between Lu Bu and the heroes, vert. (4-2). No. 2178, Struggle between man and woman at Fengyi Pavilion (4-3). No. 2179, Two noblemen, vert. (4-4). No. 2180, Guan Yu's battle through five passes. T.131.

Perf. 11½x11, 11x11½

1988, Nov. 25 Photo.

2176 A587 8f multicolored .30
2177 A587 8f multicolored .30
2178 A587 30f multicolored .80
2179 A587 50f multicolored 1.40
Nos. 2176-2179 (4) 2.80

Souvenir Sheet

Perf. 11

2180 A587 $3 multicolored *16.00*

See #2310-2313, 2403-2406, 2539-2543.

A588

A589

1988, Dec. 5 Photo. *Perf. 11*

2181 A588 20f multicolored .20

Intl Volunteers' Day.

1988, Dec. 20 Photo. *Perf. 11½x11*

Milu, *Elaphurus davidianus* (T.132).

2182 A589 8f Buck (2-1) .25
2183 A589 40f Herd (2-2) 1.10

Exist imperf. Value, pairs each $5.50.

Orchids (T.129) — A590

1988, Dec. 25 *Perf. 12*

2184 A590 8f Da yi pin (4-1) .20
2185 A590 10f Dragon (4-2) .25
2186 A590 20f Large phoenix tail (4-3) .40
2187 A590 50f Silver-edged black (4-4) 1.00
a. Strip of 4, #2184-2187 1.90
Nos. 2184-2187 (4) 1.85

Souvenir Sheet

Perf. 11½x11

2188 A590 $2 Red lotus petal *13.00*

No. 2188 contains one 55x37mm stamp.

A591

A592

Grotto Statuary: $2, Buddha. $5, Warrior, Longmen Grotto, Henan. $10, Goddess. $20, Woman and birds.

Photo & Engr.

1988-89 *Perf. 11½x11*

2189 A591 $2 buff & reddish blk .45 .25
2190 A591 $5 buff & grnh blk 1.10 .55
2191 A591 $10 buff & brn blk 2.40 1.10
a. Souv. sheet of 1, buff & sep *17.00*
2192 A591 $20 buff & indigo 5.00 2.25
Nos. 2189-2192 (4) 8.95 4.15

Issued: $2, 11/30; $5, 8/10; $10, 10/15; $20, 10/20.

No. 2191a released on Oct. 12, 1989, for the China Natl. Philatelic Exhibition and the 40th anniv. of the People's Republic.

Nos. 2189-2192, 2191a are almost always found with small ink spots on the stamps. Values are for stamps in this condition.

Photo. & Engr.

1989, Jan. 5 *Perf. 11½*

2193 A592 8f multicolored .25
a. Bklt. pane of 4+8 with label between *4.50*

New Year 1989 (Year of the Snake).

Qu Qiubai (1899-1935), Party Leader (J.157) — A593

1989, Jan. 29 Photo. *Perf. 11x11½*

2194 A593 8f multi (2-1) .20
2195 A593 20f multi, diff. (2-2) .20

Brown-eared Pheasant, *Crossoptilon mantchuricum* (T.134) — A594

1989, Feb. 21 *Perf. 11½*

2196 A594 8f multi (2-1) .20
2197 A594 50f multi, diff. (2-2) .30

Folk Houses Type of 1986

1989-91 Photo. *Perf. 13x13½*

2198 A545 5f Shandong .20 .20
2199 A545 15f Guangxi .20 .20
2200 A545 25f Ningxia .20 .20
2201 A545 80f Shanxi .40 .25
2202 A545 $1.30 Qinghai .50 .30
2203 A545 $1.60 Guizhou .65 .35
2204 A545 $2 Jiangxi .65 .35
Nos. 2198-2204 (7) 2.80 1.85

Issued: 5f, 6/10/91; 15f, 11/25/90; 25f, 11/10/90; 80f, 9/20/90; $1.30, $1.60, 3/10/89; $2, 4/25/91.

Silk Painting Excavated from Han Tomb No. 1 at Mawangdui, Changsha (T.135)
A595

1989, Mar. 25 Photo. *Perf. 11½*

2208 A595 8f In the Heavens (3-1) .20
2209 A595 20f On the Earth, vert. (3-2) .20
2210 A595 30f In the Netherworld, vert. (3-3) .20
Nos. 2208-2210 (3) .60

Textured Paper, Without Gum

Size: 90x165mm

Imperf

2211 A595 $5 Entire painting *4.00*

Prevention and Resistance of Cancer (T.136) — A596

1989, Apr. 7 Litho. *Perf. 12*

2212 A596 8f shown (2-1) .20
2213 A596 20f Woman's thermogram (2-2) .20

May Fourth Movement, 70th Anniv. (J.158)
A597

1989, May 4 Photo. *Perf. 11*

2214 A597 8f Bas-relief .20

Interparliamentary Union, Cent. — A598

1989, June 29 Photo. *Perf. 11x11½*

2215 A598 20f multi .20

Literature Type of 1987

Outlaws of the Marsh: 8f, Wu Song slaying a tiger on Jingyang Ridge. 10f, Qin Ming dodging arrows. 20f, Hua Rong shooting a wild goose on Mt. Liangshan. $1.30, Li Kui fighting Zhang Shun from a junk. T.138.

1989, July 25 Photo. *Perf. 11*

2216 A570 8f multi (4-1) .20
2217 A570 10f multi (4-2) .20
2218 A570 20f multi (4-3) .25
2219 A570 $1.30 multi (4-4) 1.50
Nos. 2216-2219 (4) 2.15

Asia-Pacific Telecommunity, 10th Anniv. — A599

1989, Aug. 4 Litho. *Perf. 12*

2220 A599 8f multi .20

Type of 1988

Achievements in Engineering and Construction: 8f, Beijing Intl. Telecommunications Building, vert. 10f, Xi Qu Coal Mine, Gu Jiao, Shanxi Province. 20f, Long Yang Gorge Hydroelectric Power Station, Qinghai Province. 30f, Da Yao Shan Tunnel of the Guangzhou-Heng Yang Railway. T.139.

1989, Aug. 10 Photo. *Perf. 11*

2221 A582 8f multi (4-1) .20
2222 A582 10f multi (4-2) .20
2223 A582 20f multi (4-3) .20
2224 A582 30f multi (4-4) .20
Nos. 2221-2224 (4) .80

Mt. Huashan — A601

Designs: 8f, Five prominent peaks. 10f, View from atop Huashan. 20f, 1000-foot precipice. 90f, Blue Dragon Ridge. T.140.

1989, Aug. 25 Photo. & Engr.

2225 A601 8f multi (4-1) .20
2226 A601 10f multi (4-2) .20
2227 A601 20f multi (4-3) .30
2228 A601 90f multi (4-4) .90
Nos. 2225-2228 (4) 1.60

Modern Art — A602

Paintings: 8f, *The Fable of the White Snake*, by Ye Qianyu. 20f, *Li River in Fine Rain*, by Li Keran. 50f, *Marching Together*, by Wu Zuoren. T.141

1989, Sept. 1 Photo.

2229 A602 8f multi (3-1) .20
2230 A602 20f multi (3-2) .25
2231 A602 50f multi (3-3) .55
Nos. 2229-2231 (3) 1.00

People's Political Conference
A603

1989, Sept. 21 *Perf. 12*

2232 A603 8f No. 2 .20

A604

Confucius (551-479 B.C.) — A605

Designs: 8f, The lecture in the Apricot Temple, Qufu. $1.60, Confucius riding in an ox cart. J.162.

1989, Sept. 28 Photo. *Perf. 11*

2233 A604 8f shown (2-1) .20
2234 A604 $1.60 multi (2-2) .70

Souvenir Sheet

Litho. *Imperf.*

Without Gum

2235 A605 $3 multicolored *3.25*

A606

Gate of Heavenly Peace — A607

1989, Oct. 1 Photo. *Perf. 11x11½*

2236 A606 8f shown (4-1) .20
2237 A606 10f Flowers (4-2) .20
2238 A606 20f Five stars (4-3) .20
2239 A606 40f Construction (4-4) .25
Nos. 2236-2239 (4) .85

Souvenir Sheet

Litho. *Imperf.*

Without Gum

2240 A607 $3 shown *1.75*

PRC, 40th anniv. J.163.

Photography, Sesquicentennial — A608

1989, Oct. 15 Photo. *Perf. 11*

2241 A608 8f multicolored .20

Li Dazhao (1889-1927), Party Leader (J.164) — A609

1989, Oct. 29 Photo. *Perf. 11½*

2242 A609 8f Li, soldiers (2-1) .20
2243 A609 20f Li, text (2-2) .20

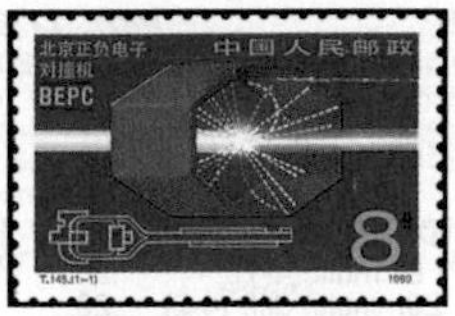

Positron Collider Produced in Beijing
A610

1989, Nov. 1 *Perf. 11*

2244 A610 8f multicolored .20

Rocket Defense
A611

Designs: 4f, Transporting 3 rockets. 8f, Disassembled rocket on transport. 10f, Launch, vert. 20f, Stage separation in space. T.143.

1989, Nov. 15 Litho. *Perf. 12*

2245 A611 4f multicolored (4-1) .20
2246 A611 8f multicolored (4-2) .20
2247 A611 10f multicolored (4-3) .20
2248 A611 20f multicolored (4-4) .20
Nos. 2245-2248 (4) .80

A612

Views of West Lake (T.144) — A613

1989, Nov. 25 Photo. *Perf. 11x11½*

2249 A612 8f multi (4-1) .20
2250 A612 10f multi, diff. (4-2) .20
2251 A612 30f multi, diff. (4-3) .25
2252 A612 40f multi, diff. (4-4) .35
Nos. 2249-2252 (4) 1.00

Souvenir Sheet

Perf. 11½x11

2253 A613 $5 multicolored *3.50*

11th Asian Games
A614

Various stadiums. J.165.

1989, Dec. 15 *Perf. 11x11½*

2254 A614 8f multi (4-1) .20
2255 A614 10f multi (4-2) .20
2256 A614 30f multi (4-3) .20
2257 A614 $1.60 multi (4-4) .30
Nos. 2254-2257 (4) .90

See Nos. 2295-2300.

The Great Wall — A730

Jiuhua Mountains — A731

1995, Oct. 5 Photo. *Perf. 12½*

2611	A730	60f shown	.20
2612	A730	230f Shanhaiguan Pass	.60
2613	A730	290f Jinshanling	.80
		Nos. 2611-2613 (3)	1.60

See Nos. 2755, 2792-2795, 2907-2910, 2934-2941, 2952-2955.

1995, Oct. 9 *Perf. 12*

10f, Sunrise at Peak Terrace, horiz. #2615, Hall of Meditation. #2616, Temple of Bodhisattva, horiz. #2617, Sunset at Zhiyuan, horiz. #2618, Great Rock. #2619, Phoenix Pine, horiz.

2614	A731	10f multi (6-1)	.20
2615	A731	20f multi (6-2)	.20
2616	A731	20f multi (6-3)	.20
2617	A731	50f multi (6-4)	.20
2618	A731	50f multi (6-5)	.20
2619	A731	290f multi (6-6)	.50
		Nos. 2614-2619 (6)	1.50

Motion Pictures, Cent. A732

Projector and: 20f, Black and white film. 50f, Color film.

1995, Oct. 13

2620	A732	20f blue & black	.20
2621	A732	50f multicolored	.20

UN, 50th Anniv. A733

Designs: 20f, UN flag, Headquarters. 50f, Stylized flags, UN emblem, "50."

1995, Oct. 24 Litho.

2622	A733	20f multi	.20
2623	A733	50f multi	.20

Sanqing Mountains — A734

#2624, Good Fortune Land. #2625, Sichun Goddess. 50f, Bodhisattva Enjoys Music. 100f, Huge Boa out of Mountain.

1995, Nov. 1 Photo. *Perf. 12*

2624	A734	20f multi (4-1)	.20
2625	A734	20f multi (4-2)	.20
2626	A734	50f multi, vert. (4-3)	.20
2627	A734	100f multi, vert. (4-4)	.20
		Nos. 2624-2627 (4)	.80

Mt. Hengshan Type of 1990

Songshan Mountains: 20f, Ancient Temple of Mount Song. 50f, Moon waiting at Songmen Gate. 60f, Shaolin Temple. $1, Panorama view of Mt. Song.

Photo. & Engr.

1995, Nov. 10 *Perf. 11*

2628	A631	20f multi	.20
2629	A631	50f multi	.20
2630	A631	60f multi	.20
2631	A631	$1 multi	.20
		Nos. 2628-2631 (4)	.80

Scenic Views of Hong Kong — A735

Designs: 20f, Victoria Harbor. 50f, Central Plaza at night. 60f, Hong Kong Cultural Center. 290f, Repulse Bay.

1995, Nov. 28 Photo. *Perf. 12*

2632	A735	20f multi	.20
2633	A735	50f multi	.20
2634	A735	60f multi	.20
2635	A735	290f multi	.50
		Nos. 2632-2635 (4)	1.10

Sun Zi's Art of War — A736

Drawings depicting: No. 2637, Discussing strategy. 30f, Capturing Ying. 50f, Battle at Ailing. 100f, Meeting of sovereigns, Huangchi.

1995, Dec. 4 *Perf. 11x11½*

2636	A736	20f multi (5-1)	.20
2637	A736	20f multi (5-2)	.20
2638	A736	30f multi (5-3)	.20
2639	A736	50f multi (5-4)	.20
2640	A736	100f multi (5-5)	.20
		Nos. 2636-2640 (5)	1.00

New Year 1996 (Year of the Rat) A737 A738

Photo. & Engr.

1996, Jan. 5 *Perf. 11½*

2641	A737	20f multi	.20
2642	A738	50f multi	.20

3rd Asian Winter Games A739

#2643, Speed skating. #2644, Ice hockey. #2645, Figure skating. #2646, Skiing.

1996, Feb. 4 Litho. *Perf. 12*

2643	A739	50f multi (4-1)	.20
2644	A739	50f multi (4-2)	.20
2645	A739	50f multi (4-3)	.20
2646	A739	50f multi (4-4)	.20
a.		Block of 4, #2643-2646	.50

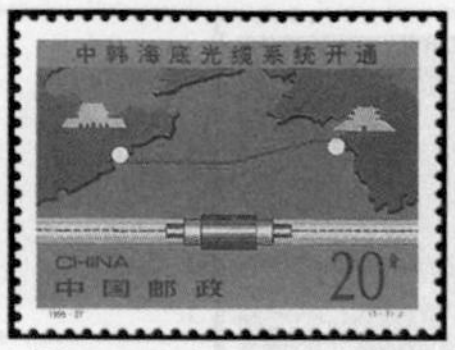

China/Korea Submarine Fiber Optic Cable System — A740

1996, Feb. 8 Litho. *Perf. 12*

2647	A740	20f multicolored	.20

First day covers are dated 12/15/95.
See Korea No. 1863.

Shenyang Imperial Palace — A741

Designs: No. 2648, Buildings, denomination UL. No. 2649, Buildings, denomination LR.

1996, Mar. 18 Photo. *Perf. 12*

2648	A741	50f multi (2-1)	.20
2649	A741	50f multi (2-2)	.20
a.		Pair, Nos. 2648-2649	.30

China Post, Cent. A742

Post Office buildings: 10f, Tianjin Posts Bureau. 20f, Beijing Postal Administration. 50f, Directorate of Posts of China. 100f, Beijing postal hub.

500f, China #78-85.

1996, Mar. 20 *Perf. 11½*

2650	A742	10f multi	.20
2651	A742	20f multi	.20
2652	A742	50f multi	.20
2653	A742	100f multi	.20
		Nos. 2650-2653 (4)	.80

Souvenir Sheet

Perf. 11

2654	A742	500f multicolored	*5.00*

No. 2654 contains one 89x59mm stamp.

Huang Binhong, Artist — A743

#2655, Calligraphy. #2656, Landscape. 40f, Qingcheng Mts. #2658, View from Xiing. #2659, Colored landscape. 230f, Flowers.

1996, Apr. 5 *Perf. 11½*

2655	A743	20f multi (6-1)	*.20*
2656	A743	20f multi (6-2)	*.20*
2657	A743	40f multi (6-3)	*.40*
2658	A743	50f multi (6-4)	*.50*
2659	A743	50f multi (6-5)	*.50*
2660	A743	230f multi (6-6)	*2.25*
		Nos. 2655-2660 (6)	*4.05*

Aircraft — A744

1996, Apr. 17 *Perf. 12*

2661	A744	20f F-8 (4-1)	.20
2662	A744	50f A-5 (4-2)	.20
2663	A744	50f Yun-7 (4-3)	.20
2664	A744	100f Yun-12 (4-4)	.20
		Nos. 2661-2664 (4)	.80

Potted Landscapes — A745

#2665-2666, Lijing & Divine Peak. #2667-2668, Melting Snow & Eagle Rock. #2668-2669, Manch & Rosy Clouds.

1996, Apr. 18

2665	A745	20f multi (6-1)	.20
2666	A745	20f multi (6-2)	.20
a.		Pair, #2665-2666	.40
2667	A745	50f multi (6-3)	.20
2668	A745	50f multi (6-4)	.20
a.		Pair, #2667-2668	.60
2669	A745	100f multi (6-5)	.20
2670	A745	100f multi (6-6)	.20
a.		Pair, #2669-2670	1.25
		Nos. 2665-2670 (6)	1.20

Iron Trees — A746

#2671, Cycas revoluta. #2672, Cycas panzhihuaensis. 50f, Cycas pectinata. 230f, Cycas multipinnata.

1996, May 2 Litho. *Perf. 12*

2671	A746	20f multi (4-1)	.20
2672	A746	20f multi (4-2)	.20
2673	A746	50f multi (4-3)	.20
2674	A746	230f multi (4-4)	.35
		Nos. 2671-2674 (4)	.95

China-San Marino Relations, 25th Anniv. A747

1996, May 6 Photo. *Perf. 12*

2675	A747	100f Great Wall of China (2-1)	.30
2676	A747	100f Mt. Titano (2-2)	.30
a.		Pair, #2675-2676	.60

See San Marino Nos. 1356-1357.

Artifacts from Hemudu Ruins — A748

Designs: 20f, Agricultural tool. 50f, Pile to support building. 100f, Paddles for boats. 230f, Bird and sun carved in wood.

1996, May 12 Litho. *Perf. 12*

2677	A748	20f multi	.20
2678	A748	50f multi	.20
2679	A748	100f multi	.20
2680	A748	230f multi	.50
		Nos. 2677-2680 (4)	1.10

Souvenir Sheet

CHINA '96, 9th Asian Intl. Philatelic Exhibition — A749

1996, May 18 *Perf. 11½x12*

2681	A749	500f multicolored	*6.00*
a.		Overprinted in gold	*7.75*

No. 2681 exists imperf. Value, $16.

Overprint in margin of No. 2681a includes Chinese characters, Shanghai '97 exhibition emblem, and "PJZ-6." Issued in 1998.

Children's Activities A750

Designs: 20f, Singing, playing musical instruments. 30f, Pushing child in wheelchair, holding umbrella. 50f, Placing flag on South Pole, penguins. 100f, Planting tree.

1996, June 1 *Perf. 12*

2682	A750	20f multi	.20
2683	A750	30f multi	.20
2684	A750	50f multi	.20
2685	A750	100f multi	.20
		Nos. 2682-2685 (4)	.80

Modern Olympic Games, Cent. — A751

1996, June 23 Photo. *Perf. 12*

2686	A751	20f multicolored	.20

Protection of Land A752

Stylized designs representing: 20f, Making use of land. 50f, Protection of farmland.

1996, June 25 *Perf. 11x11½*

2687	A752	20f multi	.20
2688	A752	50f multi	.20

A753

Military Terraces — A754

1996, July 9 Litho. *Perf. 12*

2689	A753	20f multi	.20
2690	A754	50f multi	.20

Vehicles — A755

#2691, Red Flag, 4-door limousine. #2692, Dongfeng, stake truck. 50f, Jiefang, 4-door truck. 100f, Beijing, canvas-topped jeep.

1996, July 15 Photo. *Perf. 12*

2691	A755	20f multi (4-1)	.20
2692	A755	20f multi (4-2)	.20
2693	A755	50f multi (4-3)	.25
2694	A755	100f multi (4-4)	.40
		Nos. 2691-2694 (4)	1.05

New Tangshan Built Following 1976 Earthquake — A756

1996, July 28 *Perf. 11½*

2695	A756	20f Farm cottages (4-1)	.20
2696	A756	50f Factory (4-2)	.20
2697	A756	50f Street (4-3)	.20
2698	A756	100f Port (4-4)	.20
		Nos. 2695-2698 (4)	.80

30th Intl. Geological Conference — A757

1996, Aug. 4 Litho. *Perf. 12*

2699	A757	20f multicolored	.20

Tianchi Lake, Tianshan Mountains — A758

20f, High mountain lake. #2701, Splendid Waterfalls. #2702, Snow-capped peaks. 100f, Lakeside scenery.

1996, Aug. 8

2700	A758	20f multi (4-1)	.20
2701	A758	50f multi, vert. (4-2)	.20
2702	A758	50f multi, vert. (4-3)	.20
2703	A758	100f multi (4-4)	.40
		Nos. 2700-2703 (4)	1.00

Wall Paintings Type of 1987

10f, Illustration of Mount Wutai. 20f, King of Khotan, vert. 50f, Savior Avalokitesvara. 100f, Worshipping Bodhisattvas.

$5, Thousand Arm Avalokitesvara.

1996, Aug. 15 Photo. *Perf. 11*

2704	A557	10f multi, vert.	.20
2705	A557	20f multi	.20
2706	A557	50f multi	.20
2707	A557	100f multi	.20
		Nos. 2704-2707 (4)	.80

Souvenir Sheet

2708	A557	500f multicolored	*6.00*

No. 2708 contains one 46x102mm stamp.

Mausoleums of Western Xia — A759

Designs: No. 2709: Mausoleum terrace. No. 2710, Ornament on Divine Gate. 50f, Stele. 100f, Stele remnant, Shouling.

1996, Aug. 22 Photo. *Perf. 11½*

2709	A759	20f multi (4-1)	.20
2710	A759	20f multi (4-2)	.20
2711	A759	50f multi (4-3)	.20
2712	A759	100f multi (4-4)	.40
		Nos. 2709-2712 (4)	1.00

Railways in China — A760

Designs: 15f, Datong-Quinhuangdao Railway. 20f, Lanzhou-Xinjiang Two-Track Railway. 50f, Beijing-Kowloon Railway. 100f, Beijing Western Railway Station

1996, Sept. 1

2713	A760	15f multi	.20
2714	A760	20f multi	.20
2715	A760	50f multi	.20
2716	A760	100f multi	.20
		Nos. 2713-2716 (4)	.80

A761

A762

Chinese Archives: No. 2717, Archives on tortoise shells, Shang Dynasty. No. 2718, Archives on wood slips, Han Dynasty. 50f, Iron scrolls, Ming Dynasty. 100f, Books of Ch'ing Dynasty.

1996, Sept. 2 Litho. *Perf. 12*

2717	A761	20f multi (4-1)	.20
2718	A761	20f multi (4-2)	.20
2719	A761	50f multi (4-3)	.20
2720	A761	100f multi (4-4)	.20
		Nos. 2717-2720 (4)	.80

1996, Sept. 10 *Perf. 12*

2721	A762	20f Portrait	.20
2722	A762	50f In uniform	.20

Ye Ting (1896-1946), co-founder of Chinese People's Liberation Army.

96th Conference of Inter-Parliamentary Union — A763

1996, Sept. 16 *Perf. 11½*

2723	A763	20f multi	.30

Shanghai — A764

Photo. & Engr.

1996, Sept. 21 *Perf. 11½*

2724	A764	10f Communication (6-1)	.20
2725	A764	20f Lujiazui (6-2)	.20
2726	A764	20f Jinqiao (6-3)	.20
2727	A764	50f Zhanghiang (6-4)	.20
2728	A764	60f Waigaoqiao (6-5)	.20
2729	A764	100f Residential (6-6)	.20
		Nos. 2724-2729 (6)	1.20

Souvenir Sheet

Perf. 11

2730	A764	500f Panoramic view	*6.00*	
a.		Margin ovptd.	14.00	—

No. 2730 contains one 90x45mm stamp.

No. 2730a issued 10/20/01. It is inscribed in margin with multicolored emblems and gold "PJZ-14," "APEC CHINA 2001," and Chinese characters.

Space Navigation — A765

1996, Oct. 7 Litho. *Perf. 12*

2731	A765	20f Rocket lift-off	.25
2732	A765	100f Satellite in orbit	.40

Singapore Waterfront — A766

Design: 290f, Panmen, Suzhou, China.

1996, Oct. 9 Photo. *Perf. 11½*

2733	A766	20f multi	.20
2734	A766	290f multi	.75

See Singapore Nos. 768-769.

Victory of Long March, 60th Anniv. — A767

Designs: 20f, Red Army through Marshland. 50f, Reunion of Three Armies.

1996, Oct. 22 Litho. *Perf. 12*

2735 A767 20f multi .30 .20
2736 A767 50f multi .70 .20

Colored Sculpture of Tianjin A768

Designs: 20f, The Two Immortals. No. 2738, Making Candy. No. 2739, Returning from Fishing. 100f, Xi Chun in Painting.

1996, Nov. 5 Photo. *Perf. 11½*

2737 A768 20f multi (4-1) .20
2738 A768 50f multi (4-2) .20
2739 A768 50f multi (4-3) .20
2740 A768 100f multi (4-4) .20
Nos. 2737-2740 (4) .80

Hong Kong A769

20f, Bank of China. 40f, Container Terminal. 60f, Kai Tak Airport. 290f, Stock Exchange.

1996, Dec. 19 Litho. *Perf. 12*

2741 A769 20f multi (4-1) .20
2742 A769 40f multi (4-2) .20
2743 A769 60f multi (4-3) .20
2744 A769 290f multi (4-4) .45
Nos. 2741-2744 (4) 1.05

A770 A771

1997, Jan. 1

2745 A770 50f Visit China .20

1997, Jan. 1

2746 A771 50f multicolored .20

First natl. agricultural census.

New Year 1997 (Year of the Ox)
A772 A773

Photo. & Engr.

1997, Jan. 5 *Perf. 11½*

2747 A772 50f multi (2-2) .20
2748 A773 150f multi (2-1) .40

Paintings by Pan Tianshou (1897-1971) A774

#2749, Pines on the Yellow Mountain. #2750, Rosy Clouds of Dawn. #2751, Clearing Up after Mould Rains. #2752, Chrysanthemum and Bamboo. #2753, Sleeping Cat. #2754, A Corner of Lingyan Brook.

1997, Mar. 14 Photo. *Perf. 11½*

2749 A774 50f multi (6-1) .30
2750 A774 50f multi (6-2) .30
2751 A774 100f multi (6-3) .65
2752 A774 100f multi (6-4) .65
2753 A774 150f multi (6-5) 1.00
2754 A774 150f multi (6-6) 1.00
Nos. 2749-2754 (6) 3.90

Great Wall Type of 1995

1997, Apr. 1 Photo. *Perf. 13x12*

2755 A730 50f multicolored .20

A776

A777

Tea: No. 2756, People forming circle beside tea tree. No. 2757, Statue of tea sage. No. 2758, Tea utensils, horiz. No. 2759, Painting of tea party, horiz.

1997, Apr. 8 Litho. *Perf. 12*

2756 A776 50f multi (4-1) .20
2757 A776 50f multi (4-2) .20
2758 A776 150f multi (4-3) .45
2759 A776 150f multi (4-4) .45
Nos. 2756-2759 (4) 1.30

1997, May 1 Photo. *Perf. 11½*

Stylized designs depicting: No. 2760, Celebration. No. 2761, Unity (group of people), horiz. 200f, Advance (horses running), horiz.

2760 A777 50f multi (3-1) .20
2761 A777 50f multi (3-2) .20
2762 A777 200f multi (3-3) .80
Nos. 2760-2762 (3) 1.20

Inner Mongolia Autonomous Region, 50th anniv.

Pheasants A778

Designs: 50f, Chinese copper pheasant. 540f, Common pheasant.

Litho. & Engr.

1997, May 9 *Perf. 11½x11*

2763 A778 50f multi (2-1) .20
2764 A778 540f multi (2-2) 1.10

See Sweden Nos. 2225-2226.

Dong Architecture A779

Maiji Grottoes — A780

#2765, Zengchong Drum Tower. #2766, Bai'er Drum Tower. #2767, Wind and Rain Bridge over the River, horiz. #2768, Wind and Rain Bridge in the Field, horiz.

1997, June 2 Litho. *Perf. 12*

2765 A779 50f multi (4-1) .20
2766 A779 50f multi (4-2) .20
a. Pair, #2765-2766 .30
2767 A779 150f multi (4-3) .45
2768 A779 150f multi (4-4) .45
a. Pair, #2767-2768 .90
Nos. 2765-2768 (4) 1.30

1997, June 13

Statues: No. 2769, Buddha and Xieshi Bodhisattva. No. 2770, Xieshi Bodhisattva and his disciple. 100f, Maid. No. 2772, Buddha. No. 2773, Xieshi Bodhisattva. 200f, Provider.

2769 A780 50f multi (6-1) .20
2770 A780 50f multi (6-2) .20
2771 A780 100f multi (6-3) .25
2772 A780 150f multi (6-4) .35
2773 A780 150f multi (6-5) .35
2774 A780 200f multi (6-6) .45
Nos. 2769-2774 (6) 1.80

A780a

A781

Texts surrounded by flowers: 50f, Sino-British Joint Declaration. 150f, Basic Law of the Hong Kong Special Adminstrative Region. 800f, Deng Xiaoping.

1997, July 1 Litho. *Perf. 12*

2774A A780a 50f multi (2-1) .30
2774B A780a 150f multi (2-2) .80

Souvenir Sheets

2774C A781 800f multi *2.75*
d. Overprinted in sheet margin *3.25*

Litho. (stamp) & Embossed (margin)

Perf. 13½

2775 A781 $50 gold & multi *32.50*
a. Overprinted in margin *45.00 45.00*

Deng Xiaoping (1904-97), return of Hong Kong to China.

No. 2775 was released in special souvenir folder.

No. 2774d contains gold Chinese inscription for Hong Kong's Return Exhibition Tour, emblem, and "PJZ-8" in sheet margin. Issued: 6/19/98.

Overprint in margin on No. 2775a is Chinese inscription, "2000-1" and "(2-1)J." Issued: 1/1/00.

Ancient Temples of Wutai Mountain — A782

Designs: 40f, Taihuai Township. No. 2777, Nanchan Temple. No. 2778, Foguang Temple. No. 2779, Xiantong Temple. No. 2780, Bodhisattva Summit. 200f, Zhenhai Temple.

1997, July 26 Litho. *Perf. 12*

2776 A782 40f multi (6-1) .20
2777 A782 50f multi (6-2) .20
2778 A782 50f multi (6-3) .20
2779 A782 150f multi (6-4) .35
2780 A782 150f multi (6-5) .35
2781 A782 200f multi (6-6) .45
Nos. 2776-2781 (6) 1.75

Chinese People's Liberation Army, 70th Anniv. — A783

#2782, Land Force. #2783, Naval Force. #2784, Air Force. #2785, Strategic Missile Troops. 200f, Joint military maneuvers.

1997, Aug. 1

2782 A783 50f multi (5-1) .20
2783 A783 50f multi (5-2) .20
2784 A783 50f multi (5-3) .20
2785 A783 50f multi (5-4) .20
2786 A783 200f multi (5-5) .50
Nos. 2782-2786 (5) 1.30

Shoushan Stone Carvings A784

Designs: No. 2787, "Rhythm of Autumn," vert. No. 2788, "Rhinoceros under Sunshine,", vert. No. 2789, "Jade's Fragrance," (basket of fruit). No. 2790, "Drunken Joy."

800f, Qianlong's Chain Seals.

1997, Aug. 17 Litho. *Perf. 12*

2787 A784 50f multi (4-1) .20
2788 A784 50f multi (4-2) .20
2789 A784 150f multi (4-3) .45
2790 A784 150f multi (4-4) .45
Nos. 2787-2790 (4) 1.30

Souvenir Sheet

2791 A784 800f multi 5.00

No. 2791 contains one 60x60mm stamp.

Great Wall Type of 1995

Gates: 30f, Huangyaguan. 100f, Badaling. 150f, Joyongguan. 200f, Zijingguan.

1997, Sept. 1 Photo. *Perf. 13x12*

2792 A730 30f yellow & black .20
2793 A730 100f vermilion & black .25
2794 A730 150f green & black .40
2795 A730 200f red & black .50
Nos. 2792-2795 (4) 1.35

Communist Party of China, 15th Natl. Congress A785

1997, Sept. 12 Litho. *Perf. 12*

2796	A785	50f multicolored	.50

A786

#2797, China Rose. #2798, New Zealand Monthly Rose.

1997, Oct. 9 Photo. *Perf. 11½*

2797		150f multi (2-1)	.50	
2798		150f multi (2-2)	.50	
a.	A786	Pair, #2797-2798	1.00	

See New Zealand Nos. 1469-1470.

Eighth Natl. Games A788

1997, Oct. 12 Litho. *Perf. 12*

2799	A788	50f Athletes (2-1)	.20
2800	A788	150f Stadium)2-2)	.45
a.		Souv. sheet, #2799-2800	*5.00*

No. 2800a sold for 300f.

Temple of Heaven, Beijing — A789

#2801, Hall of Prayers for Bumper Harvests. #2802, Imperial Vault of Heaven. #2803, Circular Mound Altar. #2804, Fasting Palace.

1997, Oct. 16 Litho. *Perf. 12*

2801	A789	50f multi (4-1)	.20
2802	A789	50f multi (4-2)	.20
a.		Pair, #2801-2802	.25
2803	A789	150f multi (4-3)	.40
2804	A789	150f multi (4-4)	.40
a.		Pair, #2803-2804	.80
		Nos. 2801-2804 (4)	1.20

Mt. Huangshan — A790

a, Mt. Huangshan at sunrise (8-1). b, Xihai Peaks (8-2). c, Flying Rock in surging clouds (8-3). d, Beihai in drifting clouds (8-4). e, Yuping Peak (8-5). f, Mystical stone (8-6). g, Tiandu Peak over clouds (8-7). h, Fabled Abode of Immortals (8-8).

1997, Oct. 20 Photo. *Perf. 11½*
Sheet of 8 + Label

2805	A790	200f #a.-h.	*10.00*

Nos. 2805d, 2805e are each 36x46mm.
22nd UPU Congress, Beijing, 1999.

City Wall of Xi'an A791

Designs: No. 2806, Surrounding tower. No. 2807, Arrow Tower. No. 2808, Watch Tower. No. 2809, Corner Tower.

1997, Oct. 24 Litho. *Perf. 12*

2806	A791	50f multi (4-1)	.20
2807	A791	50f multi (4-2)	.20
2808	A791	150f multi (4-3)	.40
2809	A791	150f multi (4-4)	.40
		Nos. 2806-2809 (4)	1.20

Three Gorges Dam Project on Yangtze River — A792

#2810, New channel being opened to navigation. #2811, Damming Yangtze River.

1997, Nov. 8 Photo. *Perf. 11½*

2810	A792	50f multi (2-1)	.20
2811	A792	50f multi (2-2)	.20
a.		Pair, #2810-2811	.25

Macao Landmarks — A793

50f, Ma Kok Temple. 100f, Lin Fong Temple. 150f, St. Paul's Ruins. 200f, Guia Lighthouse.

1997, Nov. 11 Litho. *Perf. 12*

2812	A793	50f multi (4-1)	.20
2813	A793	100f multi (4-2)	.25
2814	A793	150f multi (4-3)	.35
2815	A793	200f multi (4-4)	.50
		Nos. 2812-2815 (4)	1.30

Steel Production Exceeds 100 Million Tons in 1996 A794

50f, Ancient method of producing steel. 150f, Modern mill, pouring steel from smelter.

1997, Nov. 25

2816	A794	50f multi (2-1)	.20
2817	A794	150f multi (2-2)	.45

Telecommunications — A795

Stylized designs: #2818, Digital transmissions. #2819, Computer, "X-changing" data. #2820, Computer receiving signals, Chinese landmarks. #2821, Cellular phone transmission, man's head.

1997, Dec. 10

2818	A795	50f multi (4-1)	.20
2819	A795	50f multi (4-2)	.20
2820	A795	150f multi (4-3)	.35
2821	A795	150f multi (4-4)	.35
		Nos. 2818-2821 (4)	1.10

Literature Type of 1987

Outlaws of the Marsh: 40f, Huyan Zhuo coaxes Guan Sheng in a moonlit night. No. 2823, Lu Junyi captures Shi Wengong. No. 2824, Yan Qing defeats sky supporting pillar. 150f, Thunderbolt defeats Imperial Army.

800f, Heroes of Mount Liangshan take seats in order of rank.

1997, Dec. 22 Photo. *Perf. 11*

2822	A570	40f multi (4-1)	.20
2823	A570	50f multi (4-2)	.20
2824	A570	50f multi (4-3)	.20
2825	A570	150f multi (4-4)	.60
		Nos. 2822-2825 (4)	1.20

Souvenir Sheet

2826	A570	800f multicolored	3.25

No. 2826 contains one 60x90mm stamp.

New Year 1998 (Year of the Tiger)
A796 A797

Photo. & Engr.

1998, Jan. 5 *Perf. 11½*

2827	A796	50f multi (2-1)	.20
2828	A797	150f multi (2-2)	.35

Gardens of Lingnan — A798

1998, Jan. 18 Litho. *Perf. 12*

2829	A798	50f Keyaun (4-1)	.20
2830	A798	50f Liangyuan (4-2)	.20
2831	A798	100f Qinghui (4-3)	.25
2832	A798	200f Yuyin Villa (4-4)	.50
		Nos. 2829-2832 (4)	1.15

Deng Xiaoping (1904-97) — A799

#2833, At middle age. #2834, During Liberation War. #2835, With Mao Tse-tung. 100f, As Chairman of Central Military Commission. 150f, Making speech on 35th anniversary of People's Republic. 200f, Making speech, hand raised, 1992.

1998, Feb. 19 Photo. *Perf. 11½*

2833	A799	50f multi (6-1)	.20
2834	A799	50f multi (6-2)	.20
2835	A799	50f multi (6-3)	.20
2836	A799	100f multi (6-4)	.25
2837	A799	150f multi (6-5)	.35
2838	A799	200f multi (6-6)	.50
		Nos. 2833-2838 (6)	1.70

Chinese People's Police — A800

Designs: 40f, Golden shield. No. 2840, Blitz operation. No. 2841, Cooperation between police and people. 100f, Traffic control. 150f, Fire police. 200f, Border guards.

1998, Feb. 28 Litho. *Perf. 12*

2839	A800	40f multi (6-1)	.20
2840	A800	50f multi (6-2)	.20
2841	A800	50f multi (6-3)	.20
2842	A800	100f multi (6-4)	.25
2843	A800	150f multi (6-5)	.35
2844	A800	200f multi (6-6)	.50
		Nos. 2839-2844 (6)	1.70

A801

A802

1998, Mar. 5

2845	A801	50f multi (1-1)	.20	.20

Ninth Natl. People's Congress, Beijing.

1998, Mar. 5 Photo. *Perf. 11½*

Chou En-lai (1898-1976), Communist Party leader: No. 2846, In military uniform on horse. No. 2847, As First Premier, walking. No. 2848, As diplomat wearing lei. No. 2849, Standing and applauding.

2846	A802	50f multi (4-1)	.20
2847	A802	50f multi (4-2)	.20
2848	A802	150f multi (4-3)	.30
2849	A802	150f multi (4-4)	.30
		Nos. 2846-2849 (4)	1.00

Nine-Village Valley — A803

Designs: No. 2850, Fangcao Lake. No. 2851, Wuhua Lake. No. 2852, Shuzheng Waterfalls. No. 2853, Nuorilang Waterfalls.

1998, Mar. 26 Litho. *Perf. 12*

2850	A803	50f multi (4-1)	.20
2851	A803	50f multi (4-2)	.20
2852	A803	150f multi (4-3)	.30
2853	A803	150f multi (4-4)	.30
		Nos. 2850-2853 (4)	1.00

Souvenir Sheet

2854	A803	800f Long Lake	3.00

No. 2854 contains one 93x52mm stamp.

Dai Architecture — A804

#2855, Building on stilts. #2856, Well. #2857, Pavilion. #2858, Pagoda.

1998, Apr. 12 Photo. *Perf. 11½*

2855	A804	50f multi (4-1)	.20
2856	A804	50f multi (4-2)	.20
2857	A804	150f multi (4-3)	.30
2858	A804	150f multi (4-4)	.30
		Nos. 2855-2858 (4)	1.00

Construction, Hainan Special Economic Zone — A805

#2859, Urban construction, Haikou. #2860, Economic development zone, Yangpu. #2861, Phoenix Intl. Airport, Sanya. #2862, Natl. tourism and resort zone, Yalongwan.

1998, Apr. 13 Litho. *Perf. 12*

2859 A805 50f multi (4-1) .20
2860 A805 50f multi (4-2) .20
a. Pair, #2859-2860 .40
2861 A805 150f multi (4-3) .30
2862 A805 150f multi (4-4) .30
a. Pair, #2861-2862 .60
Nos. 2859-2862 (4) 1.00

Ancient Academies — A806

Designs: No. 2863, Yingtian. No. 2864, Songyang. No. 2865, Yuelu. No. 2866, Bailu.

1998, Apr. 29

2863 A806 50f multi (4-1) .20
2864 A806 50f multi (4-2) .20
2865 A806 150f multi (4-3) .30
2866 A806 150f multi (4-4) .30
Nos. 2863-2866 (4) 1.00

Beijing University, Cent. A807

1998, May 4 Litho. *Perf. 12*

2867 A807 50f multicolored .20

22nd UPU Congress, Beijing A808

1998, May 15 Litho. *Perf. 12*

2868 A808 50f Emblem (2-1) .20
2869 A808 540f Emblem, vert. (2-2) 1.50

Shennongjia Nature Reserve — A809

#2870, Mountain peaks. #2871, River, gorge. #2872, Primitive forest. #2873, Grasslands.

1998, June 6

2870 A809 50f multi (4-1) .20
2871 A809 50f multi (4-2) .20
2872 A809 150f multi (4-3) .40
2873 A809 150f multi (4-4) .40
Nos. 2870-2873 (4) 1.20

Chongqing — A810

1998, June 18 Litho. *Perf. 12*

2874 A810 50f Great Hall (2-1) .20
2875 A810 150f Port (2-2) .40

Xilinguole Grassland — A811

Designs: No. 2876, Sheep grazing, sheep herders. No. 2877, Cattle grazing, flowers. 150f, Poplar and birch forest, deer.
800f, Xilinguole River Bend.

1998, June 24

2876 A811 50f multi (3-1) .20
2877 A811 50f multi (3-2) .20
2878 A811 150f multi (3-3) .40
Nos. 2876-2878 (3) .80

Souvenir Sheet

2879 A811 800f multicolored 2.75

No. 2879 contains one 56x36mm stamp.

Paintings, by He Xiangning (1878-1972) — A812

Perf. 12½ Syncopated Type A (2 Sides)

1998, June 27 Photo.

2880 A812 50f Tiger (3-1) .25
2881 A812 100f Lion, vert. (3-2) .30
2882 A812 150f Plum blossom, vert. (3-3) .45
Nos. 2880-2882 (3) 1.00

Jingpo Lake — A813

Views of lake: No. 2883, Bridge, houses on cliff, boat. No. 2884, Islands, boats at shore. No. 2885, Boat, island. No. 2886, Waterfalls.

1998, Aug. 15 Litho. *Perf. 12*

2883 A813 50f multi (4-1) .20
2884 A813 50f multi (4-2) .20
2885 A813 50f multi (4-3) .20
2886 A813 50f multi (4-4) .20
a. Strip of 4, #2883-2886 .55

Würzburg Palace — A814

Puning Temple, Chengde — A815

1998, Aug. 20 Litho. *Perf. 12*

2887 A814 50f multi (2-1) .20 .20
2888 A815 540f multi (2-2) 1.25 1.25

See Germany Nos. 2012-2013.

Literature Type of 1987

Romance of the Three Kingdoms: No. 2889, Liu Bei finds a guardian for his heir at Baidi City. No. 2890, Zhuge Liang leads his army home, vert. 100f, Death of Zhuge Liang. 150f, Three Kingdoms united under the reign of Jin, vert.
800f, The Stratagem of Empty City.

1998, Aug. 26 Photo. *Perf. 11½*

2889 A570 50f multi (4-1) .20 .20
2890 A570 50f multi (4-2) .20 .20
2891 A570 100f multi (4-3) .25 .25
2892 A570 150f multi (4-4) .45 .45
Nos. 2889-2892 (4) 1.10 1.10

Souvenir Sheet

2893 A570 800f multicolored 4.00 3.50

No. 2893 contains one 158x37mm stamp.

Flood Victims Relief — A816

1998, Sept. 10 Photo. *Perf. 13x13½*

2894 A816 50f + 50f label .30 .30

The Louvre, France A817

Design: 200f, Hall of Heavenly Peace, Imperial Palace, China.

1998, Sept. 12 Photo. *Perf. 13x13½*

2895 A817 50f multi (2-1) .20 .20
2896 A817 200f multi (2-2) .50 .50

See France Nos. 2669-2670.

Cliff Paintings of Helan Mountains — A818

1998, Sept. 23 Litho. *Perf. 12*

2897 A818 50f Human face (3-1) .20 .20
2898 A818 100f Hunting (3-2) .25 .25
2899 A818 150f Ox (3-3) .35 .35
Nos. 2897-2899 (3) .80 .80

Longquan Pottery and Porcelain — A819

Designs: No. 2900, Vase with five spouts. No. 2901, Vase with phoenix ears. No. 2902, Double gourd vase. 150f, Ewer.

1998, Oct. 13

2900 A819 50f multi (4-1) .20 .20
2901 A819 50f multi (4-2) .20 .20
2902 A819 50f multi (4-3) .20 .20
2903 A819 150f multi (4-4) .40 .40
Nos. 2900-2903 (4) 1.00 1.00

Mausoleum of Yandi A820

Designs: 50f, Meridian Gate. 100f, Saluting Pavilion. 150f, Tomb.

1998, Oct. 28 Litho. *Perf. 12*

2904 A820 50f multi (3-1) .20 .20
2905 A820 100f multi (3-2) .25 .25
2906 A820 150f multi (3-3) .35 .35
a. Souvenir sheet, #2904-2906 1.75 1.50
Nos. 2904-2906 (3) .80 .80

Great Wall Type of 1995

10f, Jiumenko Pass. 300f, Niagziguan Pass. 420f, Pianguan Pass. 500f, Bianjing Tower.

1998, Nov. 1 Photo. *Perf. 13x12*

2907 A730 10f apple green & black .20 .20
2908 A730 300f olive & black .75 .75
2909 A730 420f brn org & blk 1.00 1.00
2910 A730 500f blue, black & brown 1.25 1.25
Nos. 2907-2910 (4) 3.20 3.20

Major Campaigns in Liberation War — A821

#2911, Making plans. #2912, Conquering Jinzhou. #2913, Battle in Huaihai. #2914, Liberating Beijing. 150f, People moving supplies.

1998, Nov. 14 Litho. *Perf. 12*

2911 A821 50f red & multi (5-1) .20 .20
2912 A821 50f gray & multi (5-2) .20 .20
2913 A821 50f org yel & multi (5-3) .20 .20
2914 A821 50f orange & multi (5-4) .20 .20
2915 A821 150f brn org & multi (5-5) .35 .35
Nos. 2911-2915 (5) 1.15 1.15

Liu Shaoqi (1898-1969), Communist Party Leader — A822

Various portraits.

1998, Nov. 24 Photo. *Perf. 11½*

2916 A822 50f multi (4-1), vert. .20 .20
2917 A822 50f multi (4-2), vert. .20 .20
2918 A822 50f shown (4-3) .20 .20
2919 A822 150f multi (4-4) .35 .35
Nos. 2916-2919 (4) .95 .95

Chillon Castle, Lake Geneva
A823

Bridge 24, Slender West Lake, Yangzhou
A824

1998, Nov. 25 ***Perf. 11x11½***
2920 A823 50f multi (2-1) .20 .20
2921 A824 540f multi (2-2) 1.30 1.30

See Switzerland Nos. 1037-1039.

Lingqu Canal — A825

#2922, Dam. #2923, Bridge over canal, vert. 150f, Boat approaching lock, vert.

1998, Dec. 1 **Litho.** ***Perf. 12***
2922 A825 50f multi (3-1) .20 .20
2923 A825 50f multi (3-2) .20 .20
2924 A825 150f multi (3-3) .35 .35
Nos. 2922-2924 (3) .75 .75

Buildings in Macao — A826

Designs: 50f, Building complex, Nanwan. 100f, Friendship Bridge. 150f, Macao Stadium. 200f, Macao Intl. Airport.

1998, Dec. 12 **Litho.** ***Perf. 12***
2925 A826 50f multi (4-1) .20 .20
2926 A826 100f multi (4-2) .25 .25
2927 A826 150f multi (4-3) .35 .35
2928 A826 200f multi (4-4) .55 .55
Nos. 2925-2928 (4) 1.35 1.35

11th Communist Party Congress, 20th Anniv. — A827

1998, Dec. 18
2929 A827 50f Deng Xiaoping (2-1) .20 .20
2930 A827 150f Handbill, buildings (2-2) .35 .35

Fish of the Coral Reef
A828

a, Pomacanthus imperator (8-1). b, Plectropomus maculatus (8-2). c, Chaetodon plebeius (8-3). d, Chaetodon chrysurus (8-4), vert. e, Heniochus acuminatus (8-5), vert. f, Lutjanus sebae (8-6). g, Balistoides conspicillum (8-7). h, Pygoplites diancanthus (8-8).

1998, Dec. 22 **Photo.** ***Perf. 11½***
Sheet of 8
2931 A828 200f #a.-h. + label 5.00 5.00
i. As No. 2931, with margin ovptd. in gold *6.00 6.00*

UPU, 22nd Congress, Beijing '99 World Philatelic Exhibition.

Nos. 2931d-2931e are each 40x49mm.

No.2931i issued 7/15/00. No. 2931i inscribed in margin in gold "PJZ-12", "1997-1999" and Chinese characters. Inscription for best philatelic item from 1997-99.

New Year 1999 (Year of the Rabbit)
A829 A830

Photo. & Engr.

1999, Jan. 5 ***Perf. 11½***
2932 A829 50f Stylized rabbit (2-1) .20 .20
2933 A830 150f Symbol for rabbit (2-2) .35 .35

Great Wall Type of 1995

5f, Hushan Section. 20f, Shanhaiguan Pass. 40f, Jinshanling Section. 80f, Mutianyu Section. 270f, Pingxingguan Pass. 320f, Desheng Pass. 440f, Yanmen Pass. 540f, Zhenbei Tower.

1999, Mar. 1 **Photo.** ***Perf. 13x12***
2934 A730 5f bl, blk & bl grn .20 .20
2935 A730 20f vio & blk .20 .20
2936 A730 40f pink & blk .20 .20
2937 A730 80f grn, blk & ol .20 .20
2938 A730 270f grn, blk & brn .65 .65
2939 A730 320f vio, blk & bwn .75 .75
2940 A730 440f red brn, blk & bwn 1.10 1.10
2941 A730 540f blue & black 1.25 1.25
Nos. 2934-2941 (8) 4.55 4.55

Stone Carvings of the Han Dynasty
A831

#2942, Plowing fields with oxen. #2943, Group weaving. #2944, Three figures dancing in front of fire. #2945, Horses, carriage. #2946, Group in assassination attempt. #2947, Goddess Chang'e.

1999, Mar. 16 ***Perf. 12***
2942 A831 50f dark green & blk .20 .20
2943 A831 50f brown & blk .20 .20
2944 A831 50f dark blue & blk .20 .20
2945 A831 150f dark brown & blk .35 .35
2946 A831 150f brown olive & blk .35 .35
2947 A831 150f dark purple & blk .35 .35
Nos. 2942-2947 (6) 1.65 1.65

A832

A833

Chinese Ceramics (Porcelain from the Jun Kiln): 80f, Halberd-shaped cup. 100f, Cup. 150f, Dual-handled stove. 200f, Dual-handled vase with base.

1999, Apr. 8 **Photo.** ***Perf. 11½***
2948 A832 80f multi (4-1) .20 .20
2949 A832 100f multi (4-2) .25 .25
2950 A832 150f multi (4-3) .35 .35
2951 A832 200f multi (4-4) .50 .50
Nos. 2948-2951 (4) 1.30 1.30

Great Wall Type of 1995

Designs: 60f, Huanghua Tower. $10, Huama section. $20, Sanguankou Pass. $50 Jiayuguan Pass.

1999, May 1 **Photo.** ***Perf. 13x12***
2952 A730 60f multicolored .30 .30

Size: 28x22mm
Perf. 11½
Photo. & Engr.

2953 A730 $10 multicolored 3.00 3.00
2954 A730 $20 multicolored 5.75 5.75
2955 A730 $50 multicolored 14.50 14.50
Nos. 2952-2955 (4) 23.55 23.55

1999, May 1 **Litho.** ***Perf. 12***
2956 A833 80f shown (2-1) .20 .20
2957 A833 200f Tree (2-2) .50 .50

Kunming World Horticultural Fair.

Red Deer
A834

1999, May 18 **Litho.** ***Perf. 11x11½***
2958 A834 80f Bucks .20 .20
2959 A834 80f Does .20 .20
a. Pair, #2958-2959 .45 .45

See Russia No. 6514.

Beauty of Putuo Mountain — A835

1999, June 3 **Litho.** ***Perf. 12***
2960 A835 30f Puji Temple (6-1) .20 .20
2961 A835 60f Nantian Gate, vert. (6-2) .20 .20
2962 A835 60f 100-step Sand (6-3) .20 .20
2963 A835 80f Pantuo Rock (6-4) .20 .20
2964 A835 80f Fanyin Cave, vert. (6-5) .20 .20
2965 A835 280f Fayu Temple (6-6) .65 .65
Nos. 2960-2965 (6) 1.65 1.65

Fang Zhimin (1899-1935), Revolutionary
A836

1999, Aug. 21 **Photo.** ***Perf. 11¼***
2966 A836 80f Close-up (2-1) .30 .30
2967 A836 80f Standing (2-2) .30 .30

Souvenir Sheet

China 1999 World Philatelic Exhibition — A837

Illustration reduced.

1999, Aug. 21 ***Perf. 11½x11¼***
2968 A837 800f multicolored 3.25 3.25

Exists overprinted in upper corners in gold. Value, $10.

A838

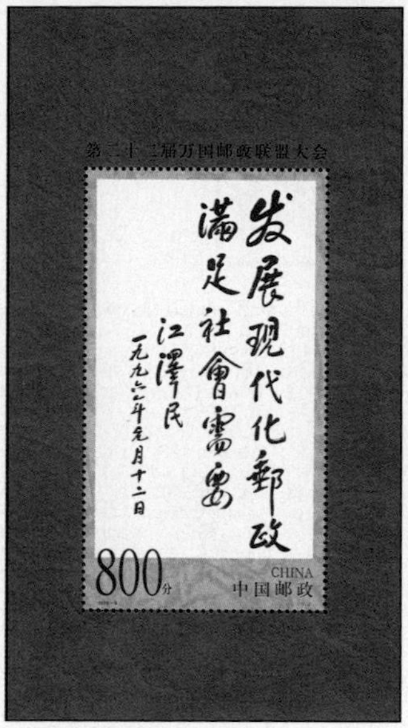
22nd UPU Congress — A839

Congress sites: 80f, 1st, Bern. 540f, 22nd, Beijing.
800f, Inscription by Pres. Jiang Zemin.
A839 illustration reduced.

1999, Aug. 23 **Litho.** ***Perf. 12***
2969 A838 80f multi (2-1) .20 .20
2970 A838 540f multi (2-2) 1.25 1.25

Souvenir Sheet
Perf. 12¼

2971 A839 800f multicolored 2.75 2.75

UPU, 125th Anniv. — A840

Intl. Year of the Elderly — A841

1999, Sept. 7 **Litho.** ***Perf. 12***
2972 A840 80f multicolored .30 .30

1999, Sept. 9
2973 A841 80f multicolored .20 .20

Chinese People's Political Consultative Conference, 50th Anniv. — A842

1999, Sept. 21

2974 A842 60f Building (2-1) .20 .20
2975 A842 80f Mao Zedong, vert. (2-2) .20 .20

Ethnic Groups in China — A843

Designs (stamp number following "56-" at LR): a, Han (1). b, Mongols (2). c, Hui (3). d, Tibetans (4). e, Uygurs (5) f, Miao (6). g, Yi (7). h, Zhuang (8). i, Bouyei (9). j, Koreans (10). k, Manchu (11). l, Dongs (12). m, Yao (13). n, Bai (14). o, Tujia (15). p, Hani (16). q, Kazak (17). r, Dai (18). s, Li (19). t, Lisu (20). u, Va (21). v, She (22). w, Gaoshan (23). x, Lahu (24). y, Shui (25). z, Dongxiang (26). aa, Naxi (27). ab, Jingpo (28). ac, Kirgiz (29). ad, Tu (30). ae, Daur (31). af, Mulam (32). ag, Qiang (33). ah, Blang (34). ai, Salas (35). aj, Maonan (36). ak, Gelao (37). al, Xibe (38). am, Achang (39). an, Pumi (40). ao, Tajiks (41). ap, Nu (42). aq, Uzbeks (43). ar, Russians (44). as, Ewenki (45). at, De'ang (46). au, Bonan (47). av, Yugur (48). aw, Jing (49). ax, Tartars (50). ay, Drung (51). az, Oroqen (52). ba, Hezhe (53). bb, Moiba (54). bc, Lhoba (55). bd, Jino (56).

1999, Oct. 7 Photo. Perf. 13¼

2976 A843 80f Sheet of 56, #a.-bd. 15.00 15.00

Mountains — A844

1999, Oct. 5 Perf. 11½x11¼

2977 A844 80f Lushan (2-1) .20 .20
2978 A844 80f Kuryongyon (2-2) .20 .20

Project Hope, 10th Anniv. — A845

Li Lisan (1899-1967), Minister of Labor — A847

Scientific and Technological Achievements — A846

1999, Oct. 30 Photo. Perf. 11½

2979 A845 80f multi .20 .20

1999, Nov. 1 Litho. Perf. 12

Designs: No. 2980, Cambrian era fossil. No. 2981, Underwater robot. No. 2982, Best result of Goldbach conjecture, vert. No. 2983, 2.16m telescope, vert.

2980 A846 80f multi (4-1) .20 .20
2981 A846 80f multi (4-2) .20 .20
a. Pair, #2980-2981 .45 .45
2982 A846 80f multi (4-3) .20 .20
2983 A846 80f multi (4-4) .20 .20
a. Pair, #2982-2983 .45 .45
Nos. 2980-2983 (4) .80 .80

1999, Nov. 19 Photo. Perf. 11½

2984 A847 80f As young man (2-1) .20 .20
2985 A847 80f Wearing glasses (2-2) .20 .20

Return of Macao to China — A848

Designs: 80f, Sino-Portuguese declaration, flower. 150f, Basic Law of Macao Special Administrative Region, Great Wall.
800f, $50, Deng Xiaoping.

1999-2000 Photo. Perf. 11¾x11½

2986 A848 80f multi (2-1) .20 .20
2987 A848 150f multi (2-2) .35 .35

Souvenir Sheets

Perf. 13

2988 A848 800f multi 3.50 3.50

Litho. (stamp) & Embossed (margin)

Perf. 12

2989 A848 $50 multi *24.00 24.00*
a. Overprinted in margin *37.50 37.50*

No. 2988 contains one 60x50mm stamp with star-shaped perforations in the corners.

Overprint in margin on No. 2989a is Chinese inscription, "2000-1" and "(2-2)J."

Issued: No. 2989a, 1/1/00; others, 12/20/99.

Nie Rongzhen (1899-1992), Military Leader — A849

New Year 2000 (Year of the Dragon) — A851

Millennium — A850

1999, Dec. 29 Litho. Perf. 12

2990 A849 80f In uniform (2-1) .20 .20
2991 A849 80f Seated (2-2) .20 .20

1999, Dec. 31 Litho. Perf. 12

No. 2992, Sun Yat-sen, #590. No. 2993, #2214. No. 2994, #2339. No. 2995, #2601. No. 2996, Mao Zedong, #456. 200f, #2248. 260f, #2730. 280f, Deng Xiaoping, #2774C.

2992 A850 60f multi (8-1) .20 .20
2993 A850 60f multi (8-2) .20 .20
2994 A850 80f multi (8-3) .20 .20
2995 A850 80f multi (8-4) .20 .20
2996 A850 80f multi (8-5) .20 .20
2997 A850 200f multi (8-6) .45 .45
2998 A850 260f multi (8-7) .60 .60
2999 A850 280f multi (8-8) .65 .65
Nos. 2992-2999 (8) 2.70 2.70

Photo. & Engr.

2000, Jan. 5 Perf. 11½x11¾

3000 A851 80f Dragon (2-1) .20 .20
3001 A851 $2.80 Rising sun (2-2) .60 .60

A852

Spring Festival: No. 3002, Welcoming the Spring Festival. No. 3003, Bidding farewell to outgoing year. $2.80, Offering sacrifices to god of land.

$8, Family reunion, horiz.

2000, Jan. 29 Photo. Perf. 11¼

3002 A852 80f multi (3-1) .20 .20
3003 A852 80f multi (3-2) .20 .20
3004 A852 $2.80 multi (3-3) .65 .65
Nos. 3002-3004 (3) 1.05 1.05

Souvenir Sheet

Perf. 11¼x11

3005 A852 $8 multi *5.00 5.00*
a. Ovptd. in sheet margin *7.50 7.50*

No. 3005 contains one 90x60mm stamp.

No. 3005a contains gold Chinese inscription for New Century Philatelic Exhibition, "2000," and "PJZ-11" in sheet margin. Issued: 4/28.

A853

2000, Feb. 25 Photo. Perf. 13¼x13

Wildlife.

3006 Sheet of 10 + 2 labels 6.00 6.00
a. A853 30f Nipponia nippon .20 .20
b. A853 60f Teinopalpus aureus .20 .20
c. A853 80f Ailuropoda melanoleuca .20 .20
d. A853 $1 Crossoptilon manchuricum .20 .20
e. A853 $1.50 Acipenser sinensis .30 .30
f. A853 $2 Rhinopithecus roxellanae .40 .40
g. A853 $2.60 Lipotes vexillifer .55 .55
h. A853 $2.80 Grus japonensis .60 .60
i. A853 $3.70 Panthera tigris .80 .80
j. A853 $5.40 Alligator sinensis 1.25 1.25

Cultural Relics — A854

Designs; 60f, Neolithic Age jade dragon. No. 3008, Dragon-shaped ornament. No. 3009, Carved tile with dragon. No. 3010, Copper mirror with dragon. No. 3011, Bronze dragon. $2.80, Dragon on sandalwood throne.

2000, Mar. 7 Litho. Perf. 12

3007 A854 60f multi (6-1) .20 .20
3008 A854 80f multi (6-2) .20 .20
3009 A854 80f multi (6-3) .20 .20
3010 A854 80f multi (6-4) .20 .20
3011 A854 80f multi (6-5) .20 .20
3012 A854 $2.80 multi (6-6) .60 .60
Nos. 3007-3012 (6) 1.60 1.60

Yangtze River Highway Bridges — A855

2000, Mar. 26 Litho. Perf. 12

3013 A855 80f Wanxian (4-1) .20 .20
3014 A855 80f Huangshi (4-2) .20 .20
3015 A855 80f Tongling (4-3) .20 .20
3016 A855 $2.80 Jiangyin (4-4) .60 .60
Nos. 3013-3016 (4) 1.20 1.20

Landscapes in Dali — A856

Designs: No. 3017, Cangshan Mountain and Erhai Lake. No. 3018, Pagodas at Chongsheng Temple. No. 3019, Jizu Mountain. $2.80, Shibao Mountain.

Perf. 11¾x11½

2000, Apr. 19 Photo.

3017 A856 80f multi (4-1) .20 .20
3018 A856 80f multi (4-2) .20 .20
3019 A856 80f multi (4-3) .20 .20
3020 A856 $2.80 multi (4-4) .65 .65
Nos. 3017-3020 (4) 1.25 1.25

Legend of Mulan — A857

Mulan: No. 3021, Weaving cloth. No. 3022, Joining army. No. 3023, On expedition. No. 3024, Returning home.

2000, Apr. 30 Litho. Perf. 12

3021 A857 80f multi (4-1) .20 .20
3022 A857 80f multi (4-2) .20 .20
3023 A857 80f multi (4-3) .20 .20
3024 A857 80f multi (4-4) .20 .20
a. Strip, #3021-3024 *2.00 2.00*

Taer Lamasery — A858

#3025, Good Luck Treasure Pagoda. #3026, Big Golden Tile Palace. #3027, Big Scripture Hall. $2.80, Banqen residence.

2000, May 5

3025 A858 80f multi (4-1) .20 .20
3026 A858 80f multi (4-2) .20 .20
3027 A858 80f multi (4-3) .20 .20
3028 A858 $2.80 multi (4-4) .65 .65
Nos. 3025-3028 (4) 1.25 1.25

Designs: No. 3141, 80f, Mask of San Xing Dui (2-1). No. 3142, 80f, Funerary mask of King Tutankhamun, Egypt (2-2).

2001, Oct. 12 *Perf. 11¾x11½*
3141-3142 A895 Set of 2 .60 .60

See Egypt Nos. 1807-1808.

People's Republic of China as 2001 Asia-Pacific Economic Cooperation Head
A896

2001, Oct. 20 **Litho.** *Perf. 12*
3143 A896 80f multi .25 .25

Souvenir Sheet

Ertan Hydroelectric Plant — A897

2001, Oct. 20 **Litho.** *Perf. 12¼*
3144 A897 $8 multi 3.00 3.00

Horses, Zhaoling Mausoleum
A898

Horse: a, Facing right, galloping (6-1). b, Facing right, galloping, diff. (6-2). c, Facing right, walking (6-3). d, With attendant (6-4). e, Facing left, walking (6-5). f, Facing left, galloping (6-6).

2001, Oct. 28 **Photo.** *Perf. 12*
Fawn Background

3145	Horiz. strip of 6	1.75	1.75
a.	A898 60f multi	.20	.20
b.-e.	A898 80f multi	.20	.20
f.	A898 $2.80 multi	.75	.75
g.	Sheet, 2 each #3145a-3145c, white background, photo. & embossed	16.00	—
h.	Sheet, 2 each #3145d-3145f, white background, photo. & embossed	16.00	—

Sailing Ships — A899

No. 3146: a, Chinese junk, 13th cent. (2-1). b, Portuguese caravel, 15th cent. (2-2).
Illustration reduced.

2001, Nov. 8 *Perf. 13x13¼*
3146 A899 80f Horiz. pair, #a-b .45 .45

See Portugal No. 2454.

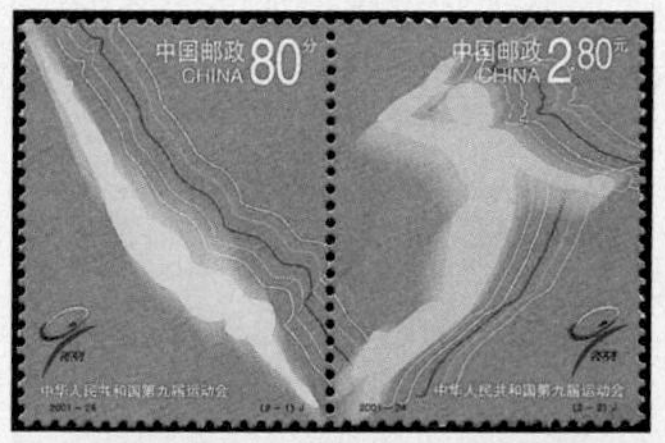

9th Natl. Games — A900

No. 3147: a, 80f, Diving (2-1). b, $2.80, Volleyball (2-2).

2001, Nov. 11 **Litho.** *Perf. 12*
3147 A900 Horiz. pair, #a-b 1.00 1.00
c. Souvenir sheet, #3147 3.75 3.75

Liupan Shan Mountains — A901

Various landscapes: No. 3148, 80f (4-1). No. 3149, 80f (4-2). No. 3150, 80f (4-3). $2.80, (4-4).

Photo. & Engr.

2001, Nov. 24 *Perf. 11¼x11½*
3148-3151 A901 Set of 4 1.60 1.60

Xiu Xian and the White Snake — A902

Designs: No. 3152, Women, umbrella (4-1). No. 3153, Three men (4-2). No. 3154, Man with sword, man with bowl (4-3). $2.80, Women on bridge (4-4).

Perf. 11½, 11½x11 (#3153-3154)

2001, Dec. 5 **Photo.**

3152	A902 80f multi	.20	.20
a.	Booklet pane of 1	1.00	—
3153	A902 80f multi	.20	.20
a.	Booklet pane of 1	1.00	—
3154	A902 80f multi	.20	.20
a.	Booklet pane of 1	1.00	—
3155	A902 $2.80 multi	.75	.75
a.	Booklet pane of 1	3.75	—
	Booklet, #3152a-3155a	6.75	
	Nos. 3152-3155 (4)	1.35	1.35

Admission to World Trade Organization
A903

2001, Dec. 11 **Photo.** *Perf. 13¼x13*
3156 A903 80f multi 1.25 1.25

Koxinga's Recovery of Taiwan from the Dutch, 340th Anniv. — A904

Koxinga and: No. 3157, 80f, Warriors, ships (3-1). No. 3158, 80f, Warriors, horse (3-2). $2.80, People, trees (3-3).

Perf. 11½x11¼

2001, Dec. 13 **Photo.**
3157-3159 A904 Set of 3 1.50 1.50

Souve

Qinhai - Tibet I

2001, Dec. 29
3160 A905 $8 multi

Ne
of
Ho

Designs: 80f, Ceram
Flowers, Chinese symb

Photo. &

2002, Jan. 5
3161-3162 A906 Set

Nos. 3161-3162 each
sheet of six. Value, eac

Art of Badashanren (1626-1705)
A907

Designs: 60f, Two Ea
80f, Pine Tree (6-2). N
Flowers (6-3). No. 3166,
in Vase (6-4). $2.60, Two
(6-5). $2.80, Landscape
6).

Perf. 11¼

2002, Jan. 20
3163-3168 A907 Set o

Envir
Prote

Designs: 5f, Keeping bir
est conservation. 30f, Con
resources. 60f, Preventin
Conservation of water. $1.
ocean resources.

Perf. 12¾x13¼ S

2002

3169	A908	5f multi
3170	A908	10f multi
3171	A908	30f multi
3172	A908	60f multi
3173	A908	80f multi
3174	A908	$1.50 multi

Nos. 3169-3174 (6

Issued: 10f, 60f, 2/1;

Cai Chang and Li Fuchun
A859

2000, May 22
3029 A859 80f multi .20 .20

Stampin' the Future Children's Stamp Design Contest Winners — A860

Various children's drawings: #3030, 30f, (8-1). #3031, 60f, (8-2). #3032, 60f, (8-3). #3033, 80f, (8-4). #3034, 80f, (8-5). #3035, 80f, (8-6). $2.60, (8-7). $2.80, (8-8).

Perf. 11½x11¼

2000, June 1 **Photo.**
3030-3037 A860 Set of 8 2.25 2.25

Chen Yun (1905-95), Statesman
A861

#3038, 80f, As a young man (4-1). #3039, 80f, In uniform, vert. (4-2). #3040, 80f, In black jacket, vert. (4-3). $2.80, As old man (4-4).

Perf. 13x13¼, 13¼x13

2000, June 13
3038-3041 A861 Set of 4 1.25 1.25

Pots
A862

Designs: No. 3042, 80f, Wine vessel (2-1). No. 3042, 80f, Horse milk pot (2-2).

2000, June 28 **Litho.** *Perf. 12*
3042-3043 A862 Set of 2 .40 .40

See Kazakhstan No. 305.

Laoshan Mountain — A863

#3044, 80f, Huge Peak (4-1). #3045, 80f, Yangkou Bay (4-2). #3046, 80f, Beijiu Lake (4-3). $2.80, Taiqing Palace (4-4).

Perf. 11½x11¼

2000, July 15 **Photo.**
3044-3047 A863 Set of 4 1.50 1.50
3047a Souvenir sheet, #3044-3047 6.00 6.00

Souvenir Sheet

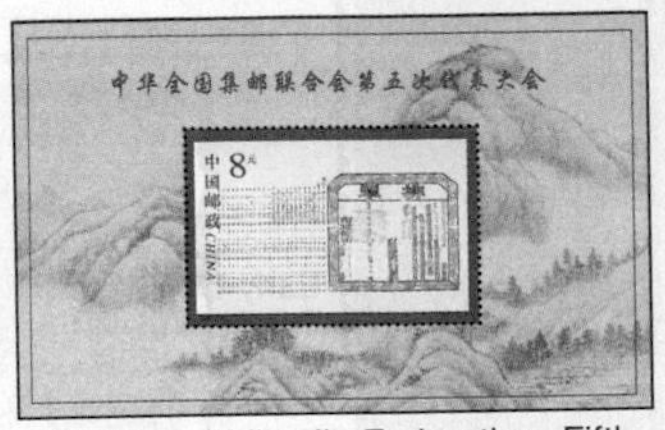

All-China Philatelic Federation, Fifth Congress — A864

Illustration reduced.

2000, July 18 **Litho.** *Perf. 12*
3048 A864 $8 multi 4.75 4.75
a. Margin ovptd. in gold 5.25 —

No. 3048a issued 9/21/01. It is inscribed in margin in gold "PJZ-13," "2001," with Chinese characters and Nanjing 2001 Philatelic Exhibition mascot.

Small Carp Leap Through Dragon Gate Legend — A865

No. 3049: a, Grandma Carp tells a story (5-1). b, Small Carp look for Dragon Gate (5-2). c, Help from Uncle Crab (5-3). d, Small Carp leap through Dragon Gate (5-4). e, Aunt Swallow passes on a letter (5-5).

2000, Aug. 8 **Photo.** *Perf. 11½*

3049	A865 80f Horiz. strip of 5, #a-e	2.00	2.00
f.	Booklet pane, #3049 + 2 labels, perf. 12	10.00	
	Booklet, #3049f	1.00	

Shenzhen Special Eonomic Zone — A866

No. 3050: a, 80f, Financial Center district (5-1). b, 80f, China Intl. Exhibition Center (5-2). c, 80f, Yantian Harbor area (5-3). d, 80f, Shenzhen Bay tourist area (5-4). e, $2.80, Shekou industrial district (5-5).

2000, Aug. 26 **Litho.** *Perf. 12*
3050 A866 Horiz. strip of 5, #a-e 1.50 1.50

2000 Summer Olympics, Sydney — A867

Illustration reduced.

2000, Sept. 15 **Photo.** *Perf. 13¼x13*
3051 A867 $8 multi 3.75 3.75
a. Sheet of 2 40.00 40.00

No. 3051a issued 10/31/00.

Beaches — A868

a, Coconuts Bay, PRC (2-1). b, Varadero Beach, Cuba (2-2).

2000, Sept. 26 **Litho.** *Perf. 12*
3052 A868 Pair .40 .40
a.-b. 80f Any single .20 .20

See Cuba Nos. 4108-4109.

Masks and Puppets
A869

No. 3053, Tan background (2-1). No. 3054, Violet blue background (2-2).

2000, Oct. 9 **Photo.** *Perf. 13x13½*
3053-3054 A869 80f Set of 2 .40 .40

See Brazil Nos. 2767-2768.

Relics from the Tomb of Prince Jing of Zhongshan — A870

#3055, 80f, Eternal Fidelity palace lamp (4-1). #3056, 80f, Bronze pot (4-2). #3057, 80f, Boshan incense burner (4-3). $2.80, Cup (4-4).

2000, Oct. 20 *Perf. 13½x13¼*
3055-3058 A870 Set of 4 1.25 1.25

Ancient Thinkers — A871

#3059, 60f, Confucius (6-1). #3060, 80f, Mencius (6-2). #3061, 80f, Lao Zi (6-3). #3062, 80f, Zhuang Zi (6-4). #3063, 80f, Mo Zi (6-5). $2.80, Xun Zi (6-6).

Photo. & Engr.

2000, Nov. 11 *Perf. 11¼x11*
3059-3064 A871 Set of 6 1.60 1.60

Test of Shenzhou Spacecraft, 1st Anniv. — A872

No. 3065: a, Launch (2-1). b, In orbit (2-2).
Illustration reduced.

2000, Nov. 20 **Photo.** *Perf. 11½*
3065 A872 Pair 1.75 1.75
a.-b. 80f Any single .20 .20
c. Sheet, 6 #3065 35.00 35.00

World Meteorological Organization, 50th Anniv. — A873

Designs: No. 3066, 80f, Weather satellite (4-1). No. 3067, 80f, Weather measuring equipment on Qinghai-Tibetan Plateau (4-2). No. 3068, 80f, Weather-predicting computer (4-3). $2.80, Airplane for cloud seeding (4-4).

2000, Nov. 22 **Litho.** *Perf. 12*
3066-3069 A873 Set of 4 1.25 1.25

Flowers — A874

#3070, 80f, Scarlet kaffir lily (4-1). #3071, 80f, Noble clivia (4-2). #3072, 80f, Golden striated lily (4-3). $2.80, White kaffir lily (4-4).

Perf. 11¼x11½

2000, Dec. 12 **Photo.**
3070-3073 A874 Set of 4 1.25 1.25
3073a Souv. sheet, #3070-3073 6.00 6.00

Ancient Bells — A875

#3074, 80f, Jingshu bell (4-1). #3075, 80f, Su chime bell (4-2). #3076, 80f, Jingyun bell (4-3). $2.80, Qianlong bell (4-4).

2000, Dec. 31 *Perf. 11¼x11½*
3074-3077 A875 Set of 4 1.25 1.25

Advent of New Millennium
A876

Designs: 60f, Sun, moon, date, time, building (5-1). No. 3079, 80f, Dove, Earth (5-2). No. 3080, 80f, Map, leaf, infant's hands (5-3). No. 3081, 80f, Circuitboard, head, Earth, horiz. (5-4). $2.80, Moon, stars, sundial (5-5).

2001, Jan. 1 **Litho.** *Perf. 12*
3078-3082 A876 Set of 5 1.40 1.40

New Year 2001 (Year of the Snake) — A877

Snake and: 80f, Flower (2-1). $2.80, Chinese character for snake (2-2).

Photo. & Engr.

2001, Jan. 5 *Perf. 11½x11¾*

3083	A877 80f multi	.20	.20
a.	Sheet of 6	6.00	6.00
3084	A877 $2.80 multi	.70	.70
a.	Sheet of 6	20.00	20.00

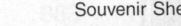

Clown Roles in Peking Opera — A878

Designs: No. 3085, 80f, Tang Qin (6-1). No. 3086, 80f, Lin Lihua (6-2). No. 3087, 80f, Gao Lishi (6-3). No. 3088, 80f, Jiang Gan (6-4). No. 3089, 80f, Yang Xiangwu (6-5). $2.80, Shi Qian (6-6).

2001, Feb. 15 Photo. ***Perf. 11½x11***
3085-3090 A878 Set of 6 1.60 1.60

Wildlife — A879

2001, Mar. 16 ***Perf. 13¼x13***

3091	Sheet of 10 + 2 labels	*9.00*	*9.00*
a.	A879 30f Budorcas taxicolor	*.20*	*.20*
b.	A879 60f Psephurus gladius	*.40*	*.40*
c.	A879 60f Elaphurus davidianus	*.40*	*.40*
d.	A879 80f Acipenser dabryanus	*.50*	*.50*
e.	A879 80f Capra ibex	*.50*	*.50*
f.	A879 80f Haliaeetus pelagicus	*.50*	*.50*
g.	A879 80f Camelus bactrianus	*.50*	*.50*
h.	A879 $1 Uncia uncia	*.65*	*.65*
i.	A879 $2.60 Martes zibellina	*1.75*	*1.75*
j.	A879 $5.40 Saiga tatarica	*3.50*	*3.50*

Ancient Towns — A880

Designs: No. 3092, 80f, Zhouzhuang, Kunshan (6-1). No. 3093, 80f, Tongli, Wujiang (6-2). No. 3094, 80f, Wuzhen, Tongxiang (6-3). No. 3095, 80f, Nanxun, Huzhou (6-4). No. 3096, 80f, Luzhi, Wuxian (6-5). $2.80, Xitang, Jiashan (6-6).

2001, Apr. 7 Photo. ***Perf. 11½x11¼***
3092-3097 A880 Set of 6 2.10 2.10
3097a Booklet pane, #3092-3097 + 6 labels *8.75*
Booklet, #3097a *8.75*

Strange Stories From a Chinese Studio, by Pu Songling A881

Designs: 60f, Ying Ning (4-1). No. 3099, 80f, A Bao (4-2). No. 3100, 80f, Mask of Evildoer (4-3). $2.80, Stealing Peach (4-4).
$8, Taoist Priest from Laoshan.

2001, Apr. 21 ***Perf. 11½***
3098-3101 A881 Set of 4 1.60 1.60

Souvenir Sheet
Perf. 13½x13

3102 A881 $8 multi *10.00 10.00*

No. 3102 contains one 90x60mm stamp.

Yongle Temple Murals A882

No. 3103: a, Lady Queen Mother (4-1). b, Jade Lady Presenting Treasure (4-2). c, Celestial Worthy of the East (4-3). d, Venus and Mercury (4-4).

2001, May 5 Litho. ***Perf. 12***

3103	Horiz. strip of 4	1.60	1.60
a.	A882 60f multi	.20	.20
b.-c.	A882 80f Any single	.25	.25
d.	A882 $2.80 multi	.90	.90

Mount Wudang — A883

Designs: 60f, Nanyan Hall (3-1). No. 3105, 80f, Zixiao Temple (3-2). No. 3106, 80f, Taizi Slope (3-3).
$8, Golden Crown in spring.

Perf. 11¼x11½
2001, May 26 Photo.
3104-3106 A883 Set of 3 .65 .65

Souvenir Sheet
Perf. 12¼x12½

3107 A883 $8 multi + label *7.00 7.00*

No. 3107 contains one 47x71mm stamp.

Ancient Chinese Receptacles A884

Designs: No. 3108, 80f, Earthenware vase. No. 3109, 80f, Porcelain coffee pot.

2001, June 12 ***Perf. 11¼x11½***
3108-3109 A884 Set of 2 .40 .40

See Belgium Nos. 1858-1859.

Dragon Boat Festival A885

Designs: No. 3110, Dragon boat race (3-1). No. 3111, Making Zongzi (3-2). $2.80, Expelling five poisons (3-3).

2001, June 25 Photo. ***Perf. 13x13½***

3110 A885	80f multi	.20	.20
a.	Sheet of 9	*8.00*	
3111 A885	80f multi	.20	.20
a.	Sheet of 9	*8.00*	
3112 A885	$2.80 multi	.70	.70
a.	Sheet of 9	*30.00*	
	Nos. 3110-3112 (3)	1.10	1.10

Nos. 3110-3112 each issued in sheets of 40.

Designs: No. 3113,
No. 3114, 80f, Zhao
80f, Deng Enming (5
Hesen (5-4). No. 3117

2001, June 28
3113-3117 A886 S

Communist Party, 80th Anniv. A887

2001, July 1 Ph
3118 A887 80f multi
a. Sheet of 8

No. 3118 issued

Emblem of 2008 S
Beijing

2001, July 14
3119 A888 80f multi
a. Sheet of 36 + 39

No. 3119 printed in
label pairs with one la
Hong Kong No. 940, M
No. 3119a contains
Hong Kong No. 940 (
label), and Macao Nc
adjacent label).

Designs: No. 3120, 80
No. 3121, 80f, Doupota
3122, 80f, Dishuitan (3-
$8, Huangguoshu.

Perf. 12¼x1
2001, July 22
3120-3122 A889 Set

Souvenir
Perf.

3123 A889 $8 multi

No. 3123 contains one

Beidaihe Bea

Strange Stories from a Chinese Studio, by Pu Songling A914

No. 3191: a, 60f, Xi Fangping (4-1). b, 80f, Pianpian (4-2).
No. 3192: a, 80f, Tian Qilang (4-3). b, $2.80, Bai Qiulian (4-4).

2002, Apr. 21 Photo. ***Perf. 11½***
3191 A914 Vert. pair, #a-b .40 .40
3192 A914 Horiz. pair, #a-b .95 .95

Qianshan Mountain — A915

No. 3193: a, Wuliang Taoist Temple (4-1). b, Maitreya Peak (4-2). c, Longquan Temple (4-3). d, Terrace of Immortals (4-4).

2002, Apr. 26 ***Perf. 12***

3193	Horiz. strip of 4	1.25	1.25
a.-c.	A915 80f Any single	.20	.20
d.	A915 $2.80 multi	.65	.65

Ancient City of Lijiang — A916

Designs: No. 3194, 80f, Sifang Street (3-1). No. 3195, 80f, Stream, vert. (3-2). $2.80, House of Naxi people (3-3).

2002, May 1 ***Perf. 11½***
3194-3196 A916 Set of 3 1.10 1.10
a. Souvenir sheet, #3194-3196 1.60 1.60

No. 3196a sold for $6.60.

Ruyi (Good Luck Symbol) — A917

2002, May 10 Litho. ***Perf. 12***
3197 A917 80f multi + label .20 .20

Exists in miniature sheet of 4 + 4 vert. labels and in sheet of 16 + 16 horiz. labels.

Stamps with Attached Labels

Starting with No. 3197, stamps listed as having attached labels are known to have been issued in dozens of different sheets having various margin and label designs, various numbers of stamps and labels in the sheets, and different stamp and label combinations. Little information has been made available about these sheets, and all seem to have been sold for prices significantly above face value. Labels on these sheets do not seem to have been personalizable with personal photos but have illustrations with approved designs.

2002 World Cup Soccer Championships, Japan and Korea — A918

No. 3198: a, 80f, Player (2-1). b, $2.80, Players (2-2).
Illustration reduced.

2002, May 16 Photo. ***Perf. 12¼***
3198 A918 Horiz. pair, #a-b .65 .65

A souvenir sheet containing People's Republic of China No. 3198, Hong Kong Nos. 978a-978b and Macao 1091a-1091b exists, and sold for premium over face value.

Lighthouses A919

Nautical charts and: No. 3199, 80f, Maota Pagoda Lighthouse (5-1). No. 3200, 80f, Jiangxin Pagoda Lighthouses (5-2). No. 3201, 80f, Huaniaoshan Lighthouse (5-3). No. 3202, 80f, Laotieshan Lighthouse (5-4). No. 3203, 80f, Lin'gao Lighthouse (5-5).

Photo. & Engr.
2002, May 18 ***Perf. 11½x11***
3199-3203 A919 Set of 5 1.00 1.00

Yellow River Dams A920

Designs: No. 3204, 80f, Lijia Gorge (4-1). No. 3205, 80f, Liujia Gorge (4-2). No. 3206, 80f, Qingtong Gorge (4-3). No. 3207, 80f, Sanmen Gorge (4-4).
$8, Xiaolangdi, vert.

2002, June 8 Photo. ***Perf. 12***
3204-3207 A920 Set of 4 1.00 1.00

Souvenir Sheet
Perf. 13x13¼

3208 A920 $8 multi 1.90 1.90

No. 3208 contains one 40x60mm stamp.

Dazu Stone Carvings — A921

Designs: No. 3209, 80f, Avalokitesvara of the Sun and Moon, North Mountain (4-1). No. 3210, 80f, Samantabhadra, North Mountain (4-2). No. 3211, 80f, Three Avatamasaka Sages, Holy Summit Mountain (4-3). No. 3212, 80f, Statue in Cave of the Three Emperors, Stone Gate Mountain (4-4).
$8, Avalokitesvara of a Thousand Hands, Holy Summit Mountain.

2002, June 18 Litho. ***Perf. 12***
3209-3212 A921 Set of 4 .80 .80

Souvenir Sheet
Photo.
Perf. 13x13¼

3213 A921 $8 multi 1.90 1.90

No. 3213 contains one 40x60mm stamp.

Desert Flowers A922

No. 3214: a, Ammopiptanthus mongolicus (4-1). b, Calligonum rubicandum (4-2). c, Hedysarum scoparium (4-3). d, Tamarix leptostachys (4-4).

2002, June 29 Photo. ***Perf. 13x13¼***

3214	Vert. strip of 4	1.25	1.25
a.-c.	A922 80f Any single	.20	.20
d.	A922 $2 multi	.50	.50

Antarctic Scenes A923

Designs: No. 3215, 80f, Penguins (3-1). No. 3216, 80f, Aurora Australis (3-2). $2, Bird, Grove Mountains (3-3).

2002, July 15 Litho. ***Perf. 12***
3215-3217 A923 Set of 3 .90 .90

Qinghai Lake — A924

Designs: No. 3218, 80f, Lake shore (3-1). No. 3219, 80f, Birds on rock (3-2). $2.80, View of lake and birds (3-3).

2002, July 20
3218-3220 A924 Set of 3 1.10 1.10

Early Communist Party Leaders — A925

Designs: No. 3221, 80f, Huang Gonglue (1898-1931) (5-1). No. 3222, 80f, Xu Jishen (1901-31) (5-2). No. 3223, 80f, Cai Shengxi (1906-32) (5-3). No. 3224, 80f, Wei Baqun (1894-1932) (5-4). No. 3225, 80f, Liu Zhidan (1903-36) (5-5).

2002, Aug. 1 Photo.
3221-3225 A925 Set of 5 1.00 1.00

Scientists of Ancient China — A926

Designs: No. 3226, 80f, Bian Que (4-1). No. 3227, 80f, Liu Hui (4-2). No. 3228, 80f, Su Song (4-3). No. 3229, 80f, Song Yingxing (4-4).

Photo. & Engr.
2002, Aug. 20 ***Perf. 11¼x11***
3226-3229 A926 Set of 4 .80 .80

Yandangshan Mountain — A927

Designs: No. 3230, 80f, Xianshengmen Gate (4-1). No. 3231, 80f, Dalongqui Pond (4-2). No. 3232, 80f, Beidou Cave, horiz. (4-3). No. 3233, 80f, Guanyin Peak, horiz. (4-4).

2002, Sept. 7 Litho. ***Perf. 12¾***
3230-3233 A927 Set of 4 1.00 1.00

Mid-Autumn Festival — A928

Designs: No. 3234, 80f, Family reunion (3-1). No. 3235, 80f, People looking at Moon (3-2). $2, The Moon as a matchmaker (3-3).

2002, Sept. 21 ***Perf. 12***
3234-3236 A928 Set of 3 .90 .90

Each printed in sheets of 20. Sheets of nine containing three of each stamp exist with a decorative border and a border with Chinese text for the Beijing 2002 Stamp Exhibition.

Peng Zhen (1902-97) — A929

Designs: No. 3237, 80f, Head of Peng Zhen (2-1). No. 3238, 80f, Peng Zhen standing (2-2).

2002, Oct. 12 ***Perf. 11¾x12***
3237-3238 A929 Set of 2 .40 .40

Architecture in Slovakia and China — A930

No. 3239: a, Bojnice Castle, Slovakia (2-1). b, Handan Congtai Pavilion, China (2-2).

Photo. & Engr.

2002, Oct. 12 ***Perf. 11¼x11***
3239 A930 80f Horiz. pair, #a-b .40 .40

See Slovakia No. 410.

Dong Yong and Lady — A931

No. 3240: a, Dong Yong's filial love moves immortals (5-1). b, Dong Yong marries seventh immortal maiden (5-2). c, Immortal maiden weaving brocade (5-3). d, Dong Yong returns home (5-4). e, Everlasting love (5-5).

2002, Oct. 26 Litho. ***Perf. 13¼x13***
3240 Horiz. strip of 5 1.25 1.25
a.-d. A931 80f Any single .20 .20
e. A931 $2 multi .45 .45

Nos. 3240a-3240e exist in booklet panes of one that made up a booklet that had limited distribution to people with standing order accounts.

Flower — A932

2002, Nov. 8 Litho. ***Perf. 12***
3241 A932 80f multi + label .25 .25

Exists in a miniature sheet of 4 + 4 labels.

Souvenir Sheet

Hukou Waterfall — A933

Photo. (Margin Photo. & Embossed)

2002, Nov. 8 ***Perf. 13¼x13***
3242 A933 $8 multi 1.90 1.90

Museums — A934

Designs: No. 3243, 80f, Shanxi History Museum (5-1). No. 3244, 80f, Shanghai Museum (5-2). No. 3245, 80f, Henan Museum (5-3). No. 3246, 80f, Tibet Museum (5-4). No. 3247, 80f, Tianjin Natural Museum.

2002, Nov. 9 Photo. ***Perf. 12¾***
3243-3247 A934 Set of 5 1.00 1.00

Martial Arts A935

No. 3248: a, Kung Fu (2-1). b, Taekwondo (2-2)

2002, Nov. 20 Photo. ***Perf. 12***
3248 A935 80f Vert. pair, #a-b .40 .40

No. 3248 is a joint issue with South Korea No. 2109.

Gibbons — A936

Designs: No. 3249, 80f, Hylobates lar (4-1). No. 3250, 80f, Hylobates leucogenys (4-2). No. 3251, 80f, Hylobates concolor (4-3). $2, Hylobates hoolock (4-4).

Photo. & Engr.

2002, Dec. 7 ***Perf. 11¼x11***
3249-3252 A936 Set of 4 1.10 1.10

New Year 2003 (Year of the Ram) — A937

Designs: 80f, Ram (2-1). $2, Chinese symbol (2-2).

Photo. & Engr.

2003, Jan. 5 ***Perf. 11½***
3253-3254 A937 Set of 2 .70 .70

Sheets of 8 + central label of Nos. 3253-3254 exist. Value, each $8.

Yangliuqing New Year Woodprints A938

Designs: No. 3255, 80f, Five boys wrestling for a lotus (4-1). No. 3256, 80f, Zhong Kui, vert. (4-2). No. 3257, 80f, Steaing the herb of immortality (4-3). $2, Wealth in a jade hall (4-4).

2003, Jan. 25 Photo. ***Perf. 12***
3255-3258 A938 Set of 4 1.10 1.10

A sheetlet containing two each #3255-3258 exists. Value $11.

Seal Characters A939

Designs: No. 3259, 80f, 24 characters (2-1). No. 3260, 80f, 12 characters (2-2).

2003, Feb. 22 Litho.
3259-3260 A939 Set of 2 .40 .40

A sheetlet exists containg four each Nos. 3259-3260. Value $11.

Knot A940

2003, Feb. 3
3261 A940 80f multi + label .30 .30

Exists in sheets of 4 stamps + 4 labels. Value $20.

Perf 12¾ examples come from a sheetlet containing four examples with labels below the stamps that also contain four #3375. The sheetlet sold for $15.

Lilies A941

Designs: 60f, Lilium taliense (4-1). No. 3263, 80f, Lilium lankongense (4-2). No. 3264, 80f, Lilium distichum (4-3). $2, Lilium lophophorum (4-4).
$8, Lilium leucanthum.

2003, Mar. 5 Photo. ***Perf. 13x13¼***
3262-3265 A941 Set of 4 1.25 1.25

Souvenir Sheet

Perf. 13¼

3266 A941 $8 multi 2.50 2.50

Nos. 3262-3265 each exist in sheetlets of 10. Value, set of 4, $22.
No. 3266 contains one 75x53mm stamp.

Arch Bridges — A942

Designs: No. 3267, 80f, Maple Bridge (4-1). No. 3268, 80f, Xiaoshang Bridge (4-2). No. 3269, 80f, Lugouqiao Bridge (4-3). No. 3270, 80f, Double Dragon Bridge (4-4).

Photo. & Engr.

2003, Mar. 29 ***Perf. 11½***
3267-3270 A942 Set of 4 1.00 1.00

A sheetlet of 8 exists for each of Nos. 3267-3270. Value, set of 2, $22.

Chinese and Iranian Buildings A943

Designs: No. 3271, 80f, Bell Tower, Xian, China (2-1). No. 3272, 80f, Mosque, Isfahan, Iran (2-2).

2003, Apr. 15 Photo. ***Perf. 13x13¼***
3271-3272 A943 Set of 2 .50 .50

See Iran No. 2856.
A sheetlet exists containing 4 each Nos. 3271-3272. Value $13.

Souvenir Sheet

Leshan Giant Buddha — A944

Photo. & Engr.

2003, Apr. 28 ***Perf. 12***
3273 A944 $8 multi 2.50 2.50

Gulangyu Island — A945

No. 3274: a, Eight Diagram Building (3-1). b, Sunlight Rock (3-2). c, Shuzhuang Park (3-3)

2003, May 2 Photo. ***Perf. 12***
3274 Horiz. strip of 3 1.00 1.00
a.-b. A945 80f Either single .20 .20
c. A945 $2 multi .50 .50
d. Souvenir sheet, #3274 1.40 1.40

A souvenir sheet exists containing three No. 3274. Value $13.

Campaign to Combat Epidemic of Severe Acute Respiratory Syndrome — A946

2003, May 19 ***Perf. 13¼x13***
3275 A946 80f multi 3.00 3.00

Strange Stories from a Chinese Studio, by Pu Songling A947

Designs: 10f, Xiang Yu (6-1). 30f, Tiger of Zhaocheng (6-2). 60f, Huanniang (6-3). 80f, Ah Xiu (6-4). $1.50, Wang Gui'an (6-5). $2, Goddess (6-6).
$8, Princess of Dongting Lake, horiz.

2003, May 16 ***Perf. 12***
3276-3281 A947 Set of 6 3.00 3.00

Souvenir Sheet

Perf. 13¼x13

3282 A947 $8 multi 4.50 4.50

No. 3282 contains one 90x60mm stamp.
Sheetlets exist containing 4 each of Nos. 3276-3277, 3278-3279 and 3280-3281. Value, set $16.

1976 Meteorite Shower Over Jilin — A948

Designs: No. 3283, 80f, Meteorites falling (3-1). No. 3284, 80f, Dispersal of meteorites (3-2). $2, Meteorite (3-3).

2003, June 21 **Litho.**
3283-3285 A948 Set of 3 1.00 1.00

A sheetlet exists containing 3 each of Nos. 3283-3285. Value $13.

Master-of-Nets Garden, Suzhou — A949

No. 3286: a, 80f, Late Spring Cottage (4-1). b, 80f, Pavilion Greeting the Moon and Breeze (4-2). c, 80f, Veranda of Bamboo (4-3). d, $2, Hall of Ten Thousand Volumes (4-4).
Illustration reduced.

2003, June 29 **Photo.** ***Perf. 12¾***
3286 A949 Horiz. strip of 4, #a-d 1.25 1.25

Tibetan Antelopes A950

Designs: 80f, Antelopes and mountain (2-1). $2, Antelope's head, adult with young (2-2).

Photo. & Engr.

2003, July 20 ***Perf. 11x11¼***
3287-3288 A950 Set of 2 .90 .90

Kongtong Mountain — A951

No. 3289: a, 80f, Town of Huangcheng (4-1). b, 80f, Gorge of Playing the Zither (4-2). c, 80f, Pagoda Courtyard (4-3). d, $2, Peak of Thunder (4-4).
Illustration reduced.

2003, July 26 **Litho.** ***Perf. 12***
3289 A951 Block of 4, #a-d 1.25 1.25

Sailing Ship — A952

2003, Aug. 5
3290 A952 80f multi + label 1.00 1.00

Exists in sheets of 4 stamps + 4 labels. Value $6.

Powered Flight, Cent. — A953

Designs: 80f, Foreign airplanes (2-1). $2, Chinese airplanes (2-2).

2003, Aug. 9 **Photo.** ***Perf. 12¾***
3291-3292 A953 Set of 2 .90 .90

Jinci Temple Painted Statues — A954

Designs: No. 3293, 80f, Ruyi maid (4-1). No. 3294, 80f, Maid holding a towel (4-2). No. 3295, 80f, Maid carrying a royal seal (4-3). $2, Maid singing and dancing (4-4).

2003, Aug. 16 ***Perf. 11¾x12***
3293-3296 A954 Set of 4 1.25 1.25

Sheetlets exist containing four each of Nos. 3293-3294 and 3295-3296. Value $16.

Three Gorges Project — A955

Designs: No. 3297, 80f, Dam and reservoir (3-1). No. 3298, 80f, Ship locks (3-2). $2, Power plant and high tension wire towers (3-3).

2003, Aug. 20 **Litho.** ***Perf. 12***
3297-3299 A955 Set of 3 1.00 1.00

Traditional Sports of Ethnic Minorities A956

Designs: No. 3300, 80f, Wrestling (4-1). b, No. 3301, 80f, Archery (4-2). No. 3302, 80f, Horse racing (4-3). No. 3303, 80f, Swinging (4-4).

2003, Sept. 5 **Photo.** ***Perf. 13x13½***
3300-3303 A956 Set of 4 .90 .90
3303a Souvenir sheet, #3300-3303 1.40 1.40

No. 3303a sold for $5. Sheets exist containing four each of No. 3300-3301 and 3302-3303. Value set, $16.

Tienanmen Gate, Beijing — A957

2003, Sept. 10 **Litho.** ***Perf. 12***
3304 A957 80f multi + label .30 .30

Two different sheets each containing four examples of No. 3304 were included in a souvenir folder sold only at the International Stamp and Coin Expo in Beijing in 2004.

General Yue Fei (1103-42) — A958

Designs: No. 3305, 80f, Mother tattooing "Loyalty to the Country" on Yue Fei's back (3-1). No. 3306, 80f, Yue Fei standing with sword (3-2). $2, Yue Fei seated (3-3).

2003, Sept. 25
3305-3307 A958 Set of 3 1.00 1.00

Souvenir Sheet

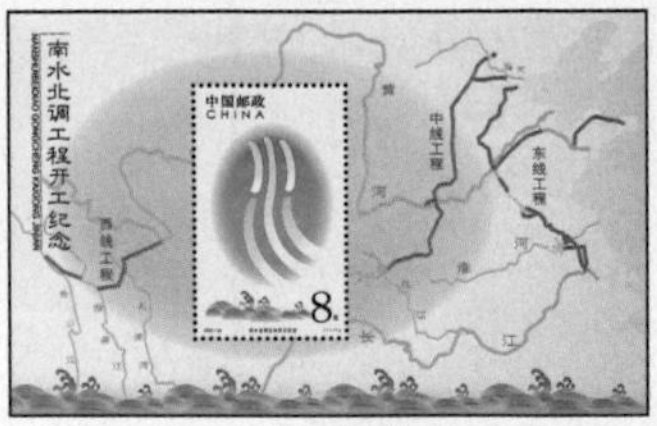

Water Diversion Projects — A959

2003, Sept. 26 **Photo.** ***Perf. 12¾***
3308 A959 $8 multi 2.25 2.25

Book Printing — A960

Designs: No. 3309, 80f, Ritual of Zhou, China (2-1). No. 3310, 80f, Hungarian Illuminated Chronicle, 1473 (2-2).

2003, Sept. 30 **Litho.** ***Perf. 12***
3309-3310 A960 Set of 2 .50 .50

Nos. 3309-3310 have large perforation holes at the stamp corners. See Hungary Nos. 3863-3864.

Double Ninth Festival — A961

Designs: No. 3311, 80f, Climbing mountain (3-1). No. 3312, 80f, Enjoying the beauty of chrysanthemums (3-2). $2, Playing chess and drinking wine (3-3).

2003, Oct. 4 **Photo.** ***Perf. 11½***
3311-3313 A961 Set of 3 1.00 1.00

Launch of First Manned Chinese Spacecraft A962

No. 3314: a, 80f, Astronaut, Shenzhou spacecraft (2-1). b, $2, Yang Liwei, flag (2-2).

2003, Oct. 16 ***Perf. 13x13¼***
3314 A962 Pair, #a-b .90 .90

A booklet containing No. 3314, Hong Kong No. 1062 and Macao No. 1128 exists. The booklet sold for a premium over face value.

Folktale of Liang Shanbo and Zhu Yingtai — A963

Designs: No. 3315, 80f, Zhu Yingtai, disguised as a man, and Liang Shanbo become sworn brothers at Caoqiao (5-1). No. 3316, 80f, Classmates for three years (5-2). No. 3317, 80f, Bidding farewell (5-3). No. 3318, 80f, Sad parting on the terrace (5-4). $2, Turning into butterflies (5-5).

2003, Oct. 18 ***Perf. 12***
3315-3319 A963 Set of 5 1.40 1.40

A booklet containing booklet panes of one of each of Nos. 3315-3319 exists.

China 2003 Intl. Stamp Exhibition, Mianyang A964

2003, Nov. 20 **Photo.** ***Perf. 13¼***
3320 A964 80f multi .30 .30

World AIDS Day — A965

2003, Dec. 1 ***Perf. 11¼x11***
3321 A965 80f multi .30 .30

Mao Zedong (1893-1976) — A966

Mao: No. 3322, 80f, Seated in folding chair (4-1). No. 3323, 80f, Standing (4-2). No. 3324, 80f, Seated on bench (4-3). No. 3325, 80f, Seated at desk (4-4).

Litho. & Engr.

2003, Dec. 6 ***Perf. 12***
3322-3325 A966 Set of 4 1.00 1.00

Bronze Objects of Eastern Zhou Dyansty — A967

Designs: No. 3326, 60f, Square plate with turtle and fish patterns (8-1). No. 3327, 60f, Gui of the Duke of Qin (handled bowl with lid) (8-2). No. 3328, 80f, Iron-footed tripod of the King of Zhongshan (8-3). No. 3329, 80f, Gourd-shaped ladle of Yi, the Marquis of Zeng (8-4). No. 3330, 80f, Divine animal wine vessel, vert. (8-5). No. 3331, 80f, Wine vessel with phoenix pattern, vert. (8-6). $1, Square pot with lotus and cranes design, vert. (8-7). $2, Tripod with a dragon-shaped handle, vert. (8-8).

Perf. 11½x11¼, 11¼x11½

2003, Dec. 13 **Photo. & Engr.**
3326-3333 A967 Set of 8 2.40 2.40

Environmental Protection Type of 2002

Designs: 50f, Prevention and control of desertification. $4.50, Protection of biodiversity.

Perf. 12¾x13¼ Syncopated

2004, Jan. 1 **Photo.**

3334 A908 50f multi .30 .30
3335 A908 $4.50 multi 1.25 1.25

Bird Type of 2002

Designs: $5, Yellow-bellied tit. $6, Yunnan nuthatch.

2004, Jan. 1 ***Perf. 13¼***

3336 A909 $5 multi 1.50 1.50
3337 A909 $6 multi 1.75 1.75

New Year 2004 (Year of the Monkey) A968

2004, Jan. 5 ***Perf. 13 Syncopated***

3338 A968 80f multi 1.00 1.00
a. Booklet pane of 10 4.75 —
Complete booklet, #3338a 6.00

Sheets of 4 and sheets of 6 exist.

Taohuawu New Year Pictures — A969

Designs: No. 3339, 80f, Feelings of Pipa (4-1). No. 3340, 80f, Kylin Bringing a Son (4-2). No. 3341, 80f, Liu Hai Playing with the Golden Toad (4-3). $2, Ten Beauties Playing Football (4-4).

2004, Jan. 14 **Litho.** ***Perf. 12***

3339-3342 A969 Set of 4 1.25 1.25
3342a Souvenir sheet, #3339-3342 3.00 3.00

Deng Yingchao (1904-92), Communist Party Leader — A970

No. 3343: a, Holding book. b, Portrait.

2004, Feb. 4 **Litho. & Engr.**

3343 A970 80f Vert. pair, #a-b 1.00 1.00

Suzhou Industrial Park, 10th Anniv. A971

2004, Mar. 1 **Photo.** ***Perf. 13x13¼***

3344 A971 80f multi .30 .30

See Singapore No. 1084.

Red Cross Society, Cent. — A972

2004, Mar. 10 ***Perf. 11¼x11***

3345 A972 80f multi .30 .30

Stories Explaining Chinese Idioms A973

Idioms: No. 3346, 80f, Trying to learn the Handan walk (4-1). No. 3347, 80f, Lord Ye's love for dragon (4-2). No. 3348, 80f, Filling a position in a Yu band (4-3). No. 3349, 80f, When the snipe and the clam grapple (4-4).

Perf. 12½x13¼ Syncopated

2004, Apr. 2

3346-3349 A973 Set of 4 1.10 1.10

Peacocks — A974

Designs: No. 3350, 80f, Blue peacock (2-1). No. 3351, 80f, Albino peacock, vert. (2-2). $6, Green peacocks.

2004, Apr. 13 ***Perf. 12¾***

3350-3351 A974 Set of 2 .50 .50

Souvenir Sheet

Perf. 13¼x13

3352 A974 $6 multi 2.00 2.00

No. 3352 contains one 60x40mm stamp

Nanxi River — A975

No. 3353: a, River and mountain (4-1). b, Tree and boat in foreground, mountains in background (4-2). c, Rocks, boat in river (4-3). d, Boat, spit of land with trees (4-4).

2004, Apr. 24 **Photo.** ***Perf. 12¾***

3353 Horiz. strip of 4 1.25 1.25
a. A975 60f multi .25 .25
b.-c. A975 80f Either single .25 .25
d. A975 $2 multi .50 .50

Danxia Mountain — A976

Designs: 60f, Sengmao Peak (4-1). No. 3355, 80f, Xianlong Lake (4-2). No. 3356, 80f, Chahu Peak (4-3). $2, Jinjiang River (4-4).

2004, May 1 **Litho. & Engr.** ***Perf. 12***

3354-3357 A976 Set of 4 1.25 1.25

Economic and Technological Development Zones, 20th Anniv. — A977

2004, May 4 **Litho.**

3358 A977 80f multi .30 .30

Exists in a sheet of 8 stamps + 8 labels.

Hometowns of Returned Chinese — A978

Designs: No. 3359, 80f, Xinglong Overseas Chinese Farm (4-1). No. 3360, 80f, Jinan University (4-2). No. 3361, 80f, Fuqing Rongqiao Development Zone (4-3). No. 3362, 80f, Kaiping (4-4).

2004, May 15 **Photo.** ***Perf. 11x11¼***

3359-3362 A978 Set of 4 1.00 1.00

Sima Guang Breaking the Vat — A979

Designs: No. 3363, 80f, Sima Guang falling into water (3-1). No. 3362, 80f, Breaking vat (3-2). No. 3363, $2, Rescued (3-3).

2004, June 1 ***Perf. 12***

3363-3365 A979 Set of 3 1.10 1.10

Scenes of Villages of Southern Anhui Province A980

Designs: No. 3366, 80f, Archway (4-1). No. 3367, 80f, Old buildings (4-2). No. 3368, 80f, Buildings on South Lake (4-3). No. 3369, 80f, Moon Pond (4-4).

Photo. & Engr.

2004, June 25 ***Perf. 11x11¼***

3366-3369 A980 Set of 4 1.00 1.00

Liu Yi Delivering a Letter — A981

Designs: No. 3370, 80f, Dragon Princess asking Liu Yi to deliver a letter (4-1). No. 3371, 80f, Delivering letter to Dongting Lake (4-2). No. 3372, 80f, Family reunion (4-3). $2, Couple embracing (4-4).

2004, July 17 **Photo.** ***Perf. 13¼x13***

3370 A981 80f multi .25 .25
a. Booklet pane of 1 .30 —
3371 A981 80f multi .25 .25
a. Booklet pane of 1 .30 —
3372 A981 80f multi .25 .25
a. Booklet pane of 1 .30 —
3373 A981 $2 multi .55 .55
a. Booklet pane of 1 .75 —
Complete booklet, #3370a-3373a 1.90
Nos. 3370-3373 (4) 1.30 1.30

Complete booklet sold for $6.

Souvenir Sheet

Eight Immortals Crossing the Sea — A982

2004, July 30 ***Perf. 12 Syncopated***

3374 A982 $6 multi 2.25 2.25

Peony — A983

2004, July 31 **Litho.** ***Perf. 12¾***

3375 A983 80f multi + label .30 .30

Perf 12¾ examples come from a sheetlet containing four examples with labels below the stamps that also contain four #3261. The sheetlet sold for $15.

2004 Summer Olympics, Athens — A984

Olympic rings and: No. 3376, 80f, Parthenon, Athens (2-1). No. 3377, 80f, Hall of Good Harvest, Temple of Heaven, Beijing.

2004, Aug. 13 **Photo.** ***Perf. 12¾***

3376-3377 A984 Set of 2 .50 .50

Perf 12¾ examples come from a sheetlet containing four examples with labels below the stamps that also contain four #3261. The sheetlet sold for $15. See Greece Nos. 2124-2125.

Deng Xiaoping (1904-97), Chinese Leader — A985

Designs: No. 3378, 80f, Walking (2-1). No. 3379, 80f, Saluting, horiz. (2-2). $6, Seated.

2004, Aug. 22 ***Perf. 12 Syncopated***

3378-3379 A985 Set of 2 .50 .50

Souvenir Sheet

Perf. 13 Syncopated

3380 A985 $6 multi 2.25 2.25

No. 3380 contains one 47x57mm stamp.

South China Tiger A986

Designs: 80f, Head (2-1). $2, Adult and young (2-2).

2004, Aug. 23 Litho. *Perf. 12*
3381-3382 A986 Set of 2 .85 .85

People's Congress, 50th Anniv. — A987

Designs: No. 3383, 80f, Congress members arriving at Huairentang Hall of Zhongnanhai (2-1). No. 3384, 80f, Interior of Great Hall of the People (2-2).

2004, Sept. 15 *Perf. 13¼*
3383-3384 A987 Set of 2 .50 .50

A sheet containing 3 pairs of Nos. 3383-3384 exists.

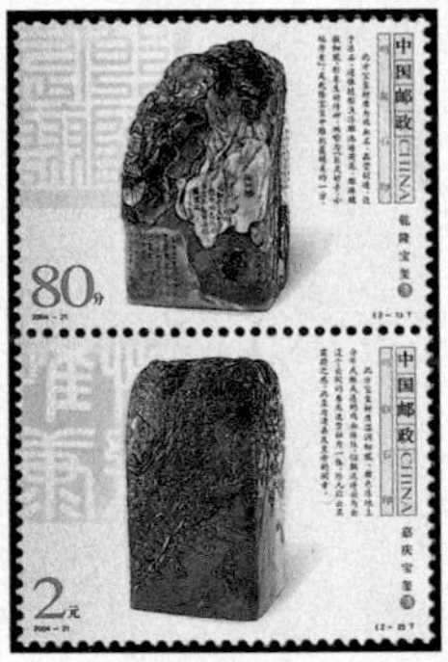

Bloodstone Seals A988

No. 3385: a, 80f, Seal of Emperor Qianlong (2-1). b, $2, Seal of Emperor Jiaqing (2-2).

Litho. & Embossed

2004, Sept. 17 *Perf. 13x13¼*
3385 A988 Pair, #a-b .90 .90

Celery Wormwood A989

Designs: No. 3386, 80f, Purple flowers (4-1). No. 3387, 80f, Blue flowers (4-2). No. 3388, 80f, Red flowers (4-3). $2, Yellow flowers (4-4).

2004, Sept. 19 Photo. *Perf. 13¼x13*
3386-3389 A989 Set of 4 1.40 1.40

A sheet containing 2 strips of 3386-3389 exists.

Chinese and Romanian Handicrafts A990

Designs: No. 3390, 80f, Drum with tigers and birds, China (2-1). No. 3391, 80f, Cucuteni pottery jar, Romania (2-2).

2004, Sept. 22 *Perf. 13 Syncopated*
3390-3391 A990 Set of 2 .50 .50

A sheet containing 4 pairs of Nos. 3390-3391 exists.

See Romania No. 4668.

National Symbols A991

Designs: No. 3392, 80f, Flag (2-1). No. 3393, 80f, Arms, vert. (2-2).

Perf. 13¼x13 Syncopated, 13x13¼ Syncopated

2004, Sept. 30
3392-3393 A991 Set of 2 .50 .50

A sheet of 4 self-adhesive examples of both Nos. 3392 and 3393 was included in a souvenir folder sold only at the International Stamp and Coin Expo in Beijing in 2004.

Landscapes of Chinese Borderlands — A992

Designs: No. 3394, 80f, Forest, Xing'an Mountains (12-1). No. 3395, 80f, Lake in Yalu River Basin (12-2). No. 3396, 80f, Reefs in Yellow Sea (12-3). No. 3397, 80f, Zhoushan Archipelago (12-4). No. 3398, 80f, Coast of Taiwan (12-5). No. 3399, 80f, Xisha Islands (12-6). No. 3400, 80f, Karst landscape, Southern Guangxi (12-7). No. 3401, 80f, Rain forest, Southern Yunnan (12-8). No. 3402, 80f, Mt. Qomolangma (12-9). No. 3403, 80f, Pamirs (12-10). No. 3404, 80f, Badain Jaran Desert (12-11). No. 3405, 80f, Hulun Buir Steppe (12-12).

2004, Oct. 1 *Perf. 12¾*
3394-3405 A992 Set of 12 2.75 2.75
3405a Sheet of 12, #3394-3405 + central label 3.00 3.00

Buildings in China and Spain — A993

Designs: No. 3406, 80f, Jinmao Tower, China (2-1). No. 3407, 80f, Park Guell, Spain.

2004, Oct. 8 *Perf. 13¼x13*
3406-3407 A993 Set of 2 .50 .50

See Spain Nos. 3319-3320.

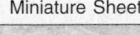

Miniature Sheet

The Festival of Pure Brightness on the River, by Zhang Zeduan — A994

No. 3408 — Various details from painting: a, 60f, Trees (9-1). b, 80f, Trees, people on horseback (9-2). c, 80f, Buildings, boats on river (9-3). d, 80f, Buildings, boats on river, diff. (9-4). e, 80f, Bridge (9-5). f, 80f, Buildings, boats on river (9-6). g, 80f, Buildings (9-7). h, $1, Tower (9-8). i, $2, Intersection (9-9).

Litho. & Engr.

2004, Oct. 18 *Perf. 12*
3408 A994 Sheet of 9, #a-i 2.10 2.10

Phoenix — A995

2004, Nov. 1 Litho. *Perf. 12¾*
3409 A995 80f multi + label .20 .20

A sheet of 10 serpentine die cut 12¼ self-adhesive stamps like No. 3409 + 10 labels depicting Snoopy for 25 yuan.

Pavilions — A996

Designs: No. 3410, 80f, Aiwan (4-1). No. 3411, 80f, Pipa (4-2). No. 3412, 80f, Lan (4-3). No. 3413, 80f, Zuiweng (4-4).

2004, Nov. 6 Photo. *Perf. 13¼x13*
3410-3413 A996 Set of 4 .80 .80

Ancient Calligraphy A997

Designs: No. 3414, 80f, Yiying stele (4-1). No. 3415, 80f, Zhangqian stele (4-2). No. 3416, 80f, Caoquan stele (4-3). No. 3417, 80f, Shimen song (4-4).

Photo. & Engr.

2004, Dec. 5 *Perf. 11¼x11*
3414-3417 A997 Set of 4 .80 .80

New Year 2005 (Year of the Rooster) A998

Perf. 13 Syncopated

2005, Jan. 5 Photo.
3418 A998 80f multi .20 .20
a. Booklet pane of 10 2.00 —
Complete booklet, #3418a 2.00

No. 3418 exists in a sheet of 4.

Tarim-Baihe Gas Pipeline — A999

No. 3419: a, 80f, Derrick (2-1). b, $3, Pipes (2-2).

Illustration reduced.

2005, Jan. 8 Litho. *Perf. 12*
3419 A999 Horiz. pair, #a-b .95 .95

Historic Structures in Taiwan A1000

No. 3420: a, North Gate, Taipei City Wall (5-1). b, Confucian Temple (5-2). c, Longshan Temple, Lugang (5-3). d, Erkunshen Cannon Fort, Tainan (5-4). e, Matsu Temple, Penghu (5-5).

Perf. 13 Syncopated

2005, Jan. 30 Litho. & Engr.
3420 Vert. strip of 5 1.25 1.25
a.-d. A1000 80f Any single .20 .20
e. A1000 $1.50 multi .40 .40

Yangjiabu New Year Woodprints A1001

Designs: No. 3421, 80f, Door God (4-1). No. 3422, 80f, Abundance for year (4-2). No. 3423, 80f, Good news on New Year's Day (4-3). No. 3424, 80f, Goddess strewing flowers from heaven (4-4).

2005, Feb. 1 Litho. *Perf. 13¼x13*
3421-3424 A1001 Set of 4 .80 .80
3424a Souvenir sheet, #3421-3424 1.25 1.25

No. 3424a sold for $4.80. A miniature sheet containing 2 of each stamp exists.

Magnolias A1002

Designs: No. 3425, 80f, Magnolia dennudata (4-1). No. 3426, 80f, Magnolia delavayi (4-2). No. 3427, 80f, Magnolia grandiflora (4-3). No. 3428, 80f, Magnolia liliflora (4-4).

2005, Mar. 5 Photo. *Perf. 13x13¼*
3425-3428 A1002 Set of 4 .80 .80

Great Wall of China — A1003

2005, Apr. 1 Litho. *Perf. 12¾*
3429 A1003 80f multi + label .20 .20

Earth Day — A1004

2005, Apr. 22 Photo. *Perf. 13¼*
3430 A1004 80f multi .20 .20

A ring of syncopated perforations surrounds the vignette.

Jigong Mountains
A1005

No. 3431: a, Mountain at daybreak (4-1). b, Garden in clouds (4-2). c, Moon Pond (4-3). d, Black Dragon Waterfall (4-4).

Perf. 12½ Syncopated

2005, Apr. 28 **Litho.**

3431 Horiz. strip of 4 .80 .80
a.-d. A1005 80f Any single .20 .20

All-China Federation of Trade Unions, 80th Anniv. — A1006

2005, May 1 ***Perf. 12***
3432 A1006 80f multi .20 .20

Paintings of Flower Arrangements
A1007

Designs: No. 3433, 80f, Magnolia Flowers, by Chen Hongshou (2-1). No. 3434, 80f, Flower Vase in a Window Niche, by Ambrosius Bosschaert the Elder (2-2).

Perf. 12½ Syncopated

2005, May 18 **Photo.**
3433-3434 A1007 Set of 2 .40 .40

See Liechtenstein Nos. 1315-1316.

Dalian Bay Area Views — A1008

No. 3435: a, Tiger Beach (4-1). b, Bangchui Island (4-2). c, Golden Pebble Beach (4-3). d, Lushunkou (4-4).

2005, May 21 ***Perf. 12¾ Syncopated***
3435 Horiz. strip of 4 .80 .80
a.-d. A1008 80f Any single .20 .20

Fudan University, Cent.
A1009

Litho., Engr. & Embossed

2005, May 27 ***Perf. 12***
3436 A1009 80f multi .20 .20

Hans Christian Andersen (1805-75), Author
A1010

No. 3437 — Fairy tales by Andersen: a, The Emperor's New Clothes (5-1). b, The Little Mermaid (5-2). c, Thumbelina (5-3). d, The Little Match Girl (5-4). e, The Ugly Duckling (5-5).

Perf. 13¼ Syncopated

2005, June 1 **Photo.**

3437 Horiz. strip of 5 1.00 1.00
a.-e. A1010 80f Any single .20 .20
f. Booklet pane of 1, #3437a .30 —
g. Booklet pane of 1, #3437b .30 —
h. Booklet pane of 1, #3437c .30 —
i. Booklet pane of 1, #3437d .30 —
j. Booklet pane of 1, #3437e .30 —
Complete booklet, #3437f-3437j 1.50

The complete booklet sold for $6.

A sheet of ten serpentine die cut 10 self-adhesive stamps containing two of each of the designs of Nos. 3437a-3437e and ten labels exists.

Voyages of Admiral Zheng He, 600th Anniv. — A1011

No. 3438: a, Admiral Zheng He (3-1). b, Building, map of voyages (3-2). c, Compass, drawing of ship (3-3)
$6, Ship, horiz.

2005, June 28 **Litho.**
3438 Horiz. strip of 3 .60 .60
a.-c. A1011 80f Any single .20 .20

Souvenir Sheet

3439 A1011 $6 multi 1.50 1.50

No. 3439 contains one 70x50mm stamp.

Nantong Museum — A1012

No. 3440: a, Southern Hall (2-1). b, Central Hall (2-2).
Illustration reduced.

Photo. & Engr.

2005, June 16 ***Perf. 12½x12¾***
3440 A1012 80f Horiz. pair, #a-b .40 .40

Xianghai National Nature Reserve — A1013

Designs: No. 3441, 80f, Red-crowned cranes in nest (4-1). No. 3442, 80f, Three birds in flight, trees (4-2). No. 3443, 80f, Birds at lake (4-3). No. 3444, 80f, Eagles flying above steppe (4-4).

2005, July 30 **Photo.** ***Perf. 12¾***
3441-3444 A1013 Set of 4 .80 .80

Miniature Sheet

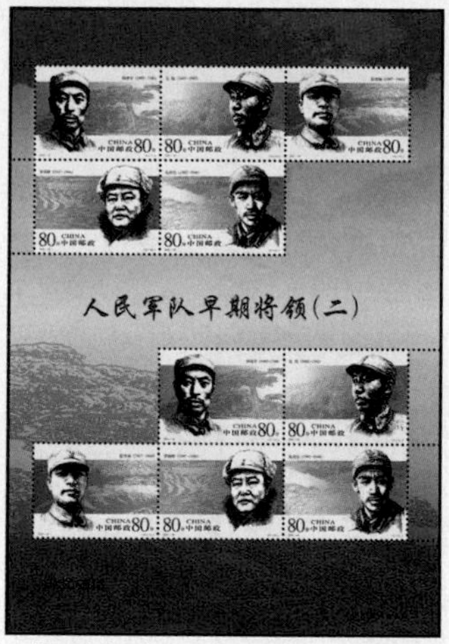

People's Army Generals — A1014

No. 3445: a, Yang Jingyu (5-1). b, Zuo Quan (5-2). c, Peng Xuefeng (5-3). d, Luo Binghui (5-4). e, Guan Xiangying (5-5).

2005, Aug. 1 ***Perf. 12***
3445 A1014 80f Sheet of 10, 2 each #a-e 2.00 2.00

End of World War II, 60th Anniv. — A1015

No. 3446: a, Soldiers with machine guns (4-1). b, Bugler (4-2). c, Soldier holding gun, troops landing in Normandy (4-3). d, Conquering Berlin (4-4).
$6, Dove, vert.
Illustration reduced.

Perf. 12¾ Syncopated

2005, Aug. 15 **Litho.**
3446 A1015 80f Block of 4, #a-d .80 .80

Souvenir Sheet

Photo.

Perf. 12¾

3447 A1015 $6 multi 1.50 1.50

Tibet Autonomous Region, 40th Anniv. — A1016

2005, Aug. 26 **Photo.** ***Perf. 13¼***
3448 A1016 80f multi .20 .20

Chinese Motion Pictures, Cent. — A1017

2005, Aug. 28 **Litho.** ***Perf. 12¾x13***
3449 A1017 80f multi .20 .20

Exists in a sheet of 8 stamps + 8 labels.

"Five Happinesses Arrive" — A1018

2005, Sept. 16 ***Perf. 12¾***
3450 A1018 80f multi + label .20 .20

Fanjing Mountain Nature Reserve
A1019

No. 3451: a, Golden Summit (4-1). b, Mushroom Rock (4-2). c, Forest (4-3). d, Heiwan River (4-4).

2005, Sept. 18 **Photo.** ***Perf. 13x13¼***
3451 Horiz. strip of 4 .80 .80
a.-d. A1019 80f Any single .20 .20

Farm Technology
A1020

Sheep and: No. 3452, 80f, Chinese water wheel (2-1). No. 3453, 80f, Dutch windmill (2-2).

2005, Sept. 22 ***Perf. 12***
3452-3453 A1020 Set of 2 .40 .40

See Netherlands Nos. 1203-1204.

Miniature Sheet

People's Liberation Army Generals — A1021

No. 1021: a, Su Yu (10-1). b, Xu Haidong (10-2). c, Huang Kecheng (10-3). d, Chen Geng (10-4). e, Tan Zheng (10-5). f, Xiao Jinguang (10-6). g, Zhang Yunyi (10-7). h, Luo Ruiqing (10-8). i, Wang Shusheng (10-9). j, Xu Guangda (10-10).

Litho. & Engr.

2005, Sept. 27 ***Perf. 13¼x13***
3454 A1021 80f Sheet of 10, #a-j 2.00 2.00

Miniature Sheet

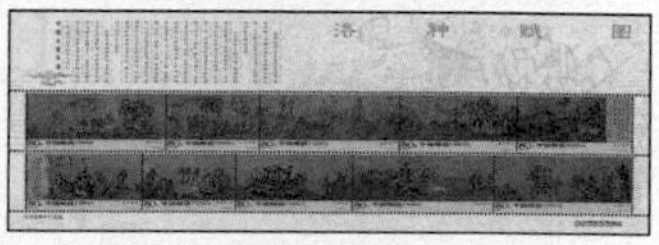

Goddess of the River Luo, by Gu Kaizhi — A1022

Various painting details with width of: a, 50mm (10-1). b, 50mm (10-2). c, 60mm (10-3). d, 40mm (10-4). e, 60mm (10-5). f, 60mm (10-6). g, 60mm (10-7). h, 50mm (10-8). i, 40mm (10-9). j, 50mm (10-10).

2005, Sept. 28 ***Perf. 12***
3455 A1022 80f Sheet of 10, #a-j 2.00 2.00

Xinjiang Uygur Autonomous Region, 50th Anniv. — A1023

No. 3456: a, Male dancers and musicians (3-1). b, Male and female dancers (3-2). c, Women carrying plates of food (3-3).

Perf. 12x12½ Syncopated

2005, Oct. 1 **Litho.**

3456 Horiz. strip of 3 .60 .60
a.-c. A1023 80f Any single .20 .20

Souvenir Sheet

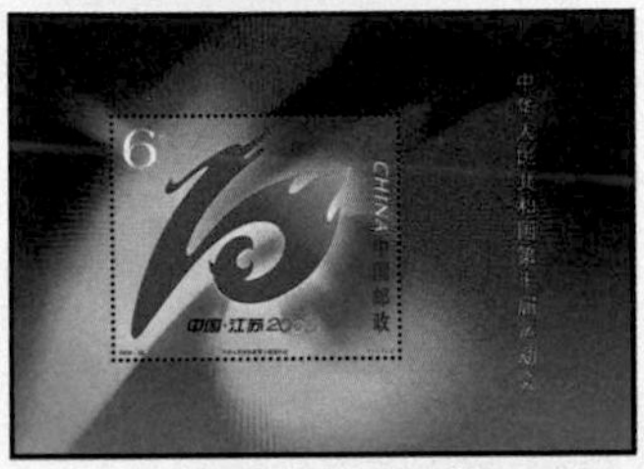

10th National Games, Jiangsu Province — A1024

2005, Oct. 12 **Photo.** ***Perf. 12¾***

3457 A1024 $6 multi 1.50 1.50

Wild Cats A1025

Designs: No. 3458, 80f, Panthera pardus orientalis (2-1). No. 3459, 80f, Puma concolor (2-2).

2005, Oct. 13 **Photo.** ***Perf. 13x13¼***

3458-3459 A1025 Set of 2 .40 .40

See Canada Nos. 2122-2123.

"Be Safe Every Year" — A1026

Illustration reduced.

2005, Nov. 6 **Litho.** ***Perf. 13¼***

3460 A1026 80f red & blk + label .20 .20

Relics From Chengtoushan Archaeological Site — A1027

2005, Nov. 6 **Photo.** ***Perf. 12½***

3461 A1027 80f multi .20 .20

"Beam With Delight" — A1028

2005, Nov. 11 **Litho.** ***Perf. 12¾***

3462 A1028 80f multi + label .20 .20

2008 Summer Olympics, Beijing — A1029

Designs: No. 3463, Beijing Olympics emblem, Olympic rings (6-1).

No. 3464 — Beijing Olympic mascots with emblem on chest: a, Beibei (6-2). b, Jingjing (6-3). c, Huanhuan (6-4). d, Yingying (6-5). e, Nini (6-6).

2005, Nov. 12 **Photo.** ***Perf. 13¼x13***

3463 A1029 80f multi .20 .20
3464 A1029 80f Horiz. strip of 5, #a-e 1.00 1.00

Beijing Olympics Type of 2005

No. 3465: a, Like #3463. b, Like #3464a. c, Like #3464b. d, Like #3464c. e, Like #3464d. f, Like #3464e.

Serpentine Die Cut 11¾

2005, Nov. 12 **Photo.**

Self-Adhesive

3465 A1029 80f Sheet, 2 each #a-f 2.40 2.40

New Year 2006 (Year of the Dog) A1030

Perf. 13 Syncopated

2006, Jan. 5 **Photo.**

3466 A1030 80f multi .20 .20
a. Sheet of 6 *3.75 3.75*
b. Booklet pane of 10 2.00 —
Complete booklet, #3466b 2.00

A sheet of 4 exists that was a giveaway for standing order customers.

Wuqiang New Year Woodprints A1031

Designs: No. 3467, 80f, Being Safe All Year Round (4-1). No. 3468, 80f, Five Blessings Approach Your Door (4-2). No. 3469, 80f, Flower of Prosperity Blossoms (4-3). No. 3470, 80f, Lion Rolling the Embroidered Ball (4-4).

Litho. & Engr.

2006, Jan. 22 ***Perf. 12***

3467-3470 A1031 Set of 4 .80 .80
3470a Souvenir sheet, #3467-3470 .80 .80
3470b Souvenir sheet, 2 each #3467-3470 1.60 1.60

Lanterns A1032

Designs: No. 3471, 80f, Fish lantern (5-1). No. 3472, 80f, Chinese white cabbage lantern (5-2). No. 3473, 80f, Lotus lantern (5-3). No. 3474, 80f, Dragon and phoenix lantern (5-4). $1.50, Butterfly lantern (5-5).

2006, Feb. 12 **Photo.** ***Perf. 13¼x13***

3471-3475 A1032 Set of 5 1.25 1.25
3475a Sheet, 2 each #3471-3475 2.50 2.50

Abolition of Agricultural Tax — A1033

Perf. 13½ Syncopated

2006, Feb. 22

3476 A1033 80f multi .20 .20

Lijiang River — A1034

No. 3477: a, Yangdi (4-1). b, Langshi (4-2). c, Huangbu (4-3). d, Xingping (4-4).

2006, Feb. 25 ***Perf. 12¾***

3477 Horiz. strip of 4 .80 .80
a.-d. A1034 80f Any single .20 .20

Relic Plants — A1035

Designs: No. 3478, 80f, Ginkgo biloba (4-1). No. 3479, 80f, Glyptostrobus pensilis (4-2). No. 3480, 80f, Davidia involucrata (4-3). No. 3481, 80f, Liriodendron chinense (4-4).

Perf. 12x12¼ Syncopated

2006, Mar. 12 **Litho.**

3478-3481 A1035 Set of 4 .80 .80

Dogs A1036

Designs: Nos. 3482, 3486a, 80f, Pekingese (4-1). Nos. 3483, 3486b, 80f, Pug, vert. (4-2). Nos. 3484, 3486c, 80f, Chow chow (4-3). Nos. 3485, 3486d, 80f, Tibetan mastiff, vert. (4-4).

Perf. 13¼ Syncopated

2006, Mar. 19 **Litho. & Engr.**

3482-3485 A1036 Set of 4 .80 .80

Self-Adhesive

Serpentine Die Cut 11¾ on 2 Sides

3486 A1036 80f Sheet, 2 each #3486a-3486d 1.60 1.60

Qingcheng Mountain A1037

Designs: 60f, Remote mountain gate (4-1). No. 3488, 80f, Winding path (4-2). No. 3489, 80f, Ancient temple (4-3). No. 3490, 80f, Spring (4-4).

2006, Apr. 12 ***Perf. 13¼ Syncopated***

3487-3490 A1037 Set of 4 .75 .75

Statues in Yungang Grottoes — A1038

Designs: No. 3491, 80f, Sakyamuni (4-1). No. 3492, 80f, Bodhisattva (4-2). No. 3493, 80f, Head of Bodhisattva (4-3). No. 3494, 80f, Xieshi Bodhisattva (4-4).

$6, Sakyamuni, diff.

Perf. 13¼x13½ Syncopated

2006, Apr. 13 **Photo.**

3491-3494 A1038 Set of 4 .80 .80

Souvenir Sheet

Perf. 13 Syncopated

3495 A1038 $6 multi 1.50 1.50

No. 3495 contains one 40x60mm stamp.

Tianzhu Mountain — A1039

Designs: 60f, Green Dragon Mountain Stream (4-1). No. 3497, 80f, Taoist Practice Terrace (4-2). No. 3498, 80f, Sanzu Temple (4-3). No. 3499, 80f, Qingtian Peak (4-4).

2006, Apr. 22 ***Perf. 11½x11¼***

3496-3499 A1039 Set of 4 .75 .75

Scientists A1040

Designs: No. 3500, 80f, Liang Xi (1883-1958), forester (4-1). No. 3501, 80f, Mao Yisheng (1896-1989), civil engineer (4-2). No. 3502, 80f, Yan Jici (1900-96), physicist (4-3). No. 3503, 80f, Zhou Peiyuan (1902-93), physicist (4-4).

Litho. & Engr.

2006, May 13 ***Perf. 12***

3500-3503 A1040 Set of 4 .80 .80

Lighthouses A1041

No. 3504: a, Dagu Lighthouse (4-1). b, Guishan Island Lighthouse (4-2). c, Wusongkou Lighthouse (4-3). d, Mulantou Lighthouse (4-4).

2006, May 22 Photo. *Perf. 12¾*

3504	Horiz. strip of 4	.80	.80
a.-d.	A1041 80f Any single	.20	.20

Chinese Space Program, 50th Anniv. — A1042

No. 3505: a, Geospace Double Star Exploration (2-1). b, Shenzhou 6 (2-2).
Illustration reduced.

Perf. 12x11¼ Syncopated

2006, June 8 Litho.

3505	A1042 80f Horiz. pair, #a-b	.40	.40

Silver and Gold Objects — A1043

Designs: No. 3506, 80f, Jeeweled Qing Dynasty cup, China (2-1). No. 3507, 80f, Tankard with Biblical designs, by Peter Rohde, Poland.

2006, June 20 Photo. *Perf. 13¼x13*

3506-3507	A1043 Set of 2	.40	.40

See Poland No. 3829.

Olympic Rings and Emblem of 2008 Summer Olympics, Beijing — A1043a

2006, June 23 Litho. *Perf. 12*

3507A	A1043a 80f multi + label	.20	.20

Printed in sheets of 15 stamps + 15 labels, sheets of 5 stamps + 5 labels, sheets of 4 stamps + 4 labels to right of stamps, sheets of 4 stamps + 4 labels below stamps, and sheets of 8 stamps + 8 labels.

Early Communist Leaders A1044

Designs: No. 3508, 80f, Gao Junyu (1896-1925) (5-1). No. 3509, 80f, Wang Hebo (1882-1927) (5-2). No. 3510, 80f, Su Zhaozheng (1885-1929) (5-3). No. 3511, 80f, Peng Pai (1896-1929) (5-4). No. 3512, 80f, Deng Xhongxia (1894-1933) (5-5).

2006, June 30 Litho. & Engr.

3508-3512	A1044 Set of 5	1.00	1.00

Opening of Qinghai-Tibet Railway — A1045

Designs: No. 3513, 80f, Bridge across Kekexili, antelopes (3-1). No. 3514, 80f, Train crossing Danggula Mountains, cattle (3-2). No. 3515, 80f, Lhasa Railway Station, birds (3-3).

Perf. 12½x12 Syncopated

2006, July 1 Litho.

3513-3515	A1045 Set of 3	.60	.60

Kanasi Nature Reserve — A1046

Designs: No. 3516, 80f, Kanasi Lake (4-1). No. 3517, 80f, Crouching Dragon Bend (4-2). No. 3518, 80f, Celestial Bend (4-3). No. 3519, 80f, Moon Bend (4-4).

2006, July 8 Photo. *Perf. 12¾*

3516-3519	A1046 Set of 4	.80	.80

Earthquake Protection and Damage Mitigation A1047

2006, July 26 *Perf. 13½x13*

3520	A1047 80f multi	.20	.20

2008 Summer Olympics, Beijing — A1048

Designs: Nos. 3521, 3525a, 60f, Basketball (4-1). Nos. 3522, 3525b, 80f, Fencing (4-2). Nos. 3523, 3525c, Sailing (4-3). Nos. 3524, 3525d, $3, Gymnastics (4-4).

2006, Aug. 8 Photo. *Perf. 13¼x13*

3521-3524	A1048 Set of 4	1.40	1.40

Self-Adhesive

Serpentine Die Cut 11¾

3525	A1048 Sheet of 8, 2 each #a-d	3.00	3.00

Portions of the designs of Nos. 3525a-3525d were applied by a thermographic process, producing a shiny, raised effect.

Treasures of the Study — A1049

Designs: No. 3526, 80f, Brushes (4-1). No. 3527, 80f, Ink (4-2). No. 3528, 80f, Paper (4-3). No. 3529, 80f, Ink stone (4-4).

Perf. 12x12½ Syncopated

2006, Sept. 10 Litho.

3526-3529	A1049 Set of 4	.80	.80

All-China Federation of Returned Overseas Chinese, 50th Anniv. A1050

Perf. 12½x12 Syncopated

2006, Sept. 25

3530	A1050 80f multi	.20	.20

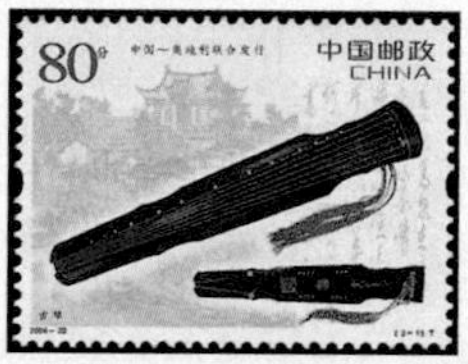

Musical Instruments — A1051

Designs: No. 3531, 80f, Seven-stringed qin, China (2-1). No. 3532, 80f, Bösendorfer piano, Austria (2-2).

Perf. 13x12½ Syncopated

2006, Sept. 26 Litho.

3531-3532	A1051 Set of 2	.40	.40

See Austria Nos. 2066-2067.

Chinese Export Commodities Fair — A1052

Perf. 13½x13¼ Syncopated

2006, Oct. 15 Photo.

3533	A1052 80f multi	.20	.20

Long March, 70th Anniv. — A1053

Designs: No. 3534, 80f, Setting Out (4-1). No. 3535, 80f, Zunyi Conference (4-2). No. 3536, 80f, Speedily Occupy the Luding Bridge (4-3). No. 3537, 80f, The Red Army Through the Marshland (4-4).
$6, Reunion.

2006, Oct. 22 *Perf. 13x13¼*

3534-3537	A1053 Set of 4	.80	.80

Souvenir Sheet

3538	A1053 $6 multi	1.60	1.60

No. 3538 contains one 80x50mm stamp.

Dialogue With ASEAN, 15th Anniv. A1054

Perf. 12½x12 Syncopated

2006, Oct. 30 Litho.

3539	A1054 80f multi	.20	.20

"Enjoying Prosperity Year After Year" A1055

"Happy New Year" — A1055a

Perf. 12¾ Syncopated

2006, Nov. 1 Photo.

3540	A1055 80f multi	.20	.20
3541	A1055a $3 multi	.80	.80

Beijing Summit of Forum on China-Africa Cooperation — A1056

2006, Nov. 3 Litho. *Perf. 13¼*

3542	A1056 80f multi	.20	.20

Buildings Associated With Dr. Sun Yat-sen (1826-1925) A1057

Designs: No. 3543, 80f, Sun Yat-sen Villa (4-1). No. 3544, 80f, Mausoleum (4-2). No. 3545, 80f, Sun Yat-sen Memorial Hall (4-3). No. 3546, 80f, Sun Yat-sen University (4-4).

Perf. 13¼ Syncopated

2006, Nov. 12 Litho. & Engr.

3543-3546	A1057 Set of 4	.85	.85

Birds Type of 2002

Designs: 40f, Chinese monal pheasant. $1.20, Taiwan yuhinas.

Perf. 13½ Syncopated

2006, Nov. 15 Photo.

3547	A909 40f multi	.20	.20
3548	A909 $1.20 multi	.30	.30

Heavenly Steed, Silk Roll Painting — A1058

No. 3549: a, Horse and rider. b, People looking at horse.
Illustration reduced.

2006, Dec. 3 Photo. ***Perf. 12¾***
3549 A1058 $1.20 Horiz. pair, #a-b .60 .60

Wu Lanfu (1906-88), Politician A1059

2006, Dec. 23 ***Perf. 13¼x13***
3550 A1059 $1.20 multi .30 .30

Trains — A1060

Designs: No. 3551, $1.20, Locomotive, blue background (4-1). No. 3552, $1.20, Locomotive, red brown background (4-2). No. 3553, $1.20, Box car (4-3). No. 3554, $1.20, Log cars and gateway (4-4).
$6, Locomotive and city skyline.

2006, Dec. 28 ***Perf. 13x13¼***
3551-3554 A1060 Set of 4 1.25 1.25

Souvenir Sheet

Perf. 13¼x13

3555 A1060 $6 multi 1.50 1.50

No. 3555 contains one 90x40mm stamp.

China Post, 110th Anniv. — A1061

Perf. 12x11½ Syncopated

2006, Dec. 30 Litho.
3556 A1061 $1.20 multi .30 .30

New Year 2007 (Year of the Pig) — A1062

Perf. 13 Syncopated

2007, Jan. 5 Photo.
3557 A1062 $1.20 multi .30 .30
a. Souvenir sheet of 6 1.80 1.80
b. Booklet pane of 10 3.00 —
Complete booklet, #3557b 3.00

6th Asian Winter Games — A1063

Perf. 12x12½ Syncopated

2007, Jan. 28 Litho.
3558 A1063 $1.20 multi .30 .30

Shiwan Pottery Figurines A1064

Designs: No. 3559, $1.20, Ta Xue Xun Mei (2-1). No. 3560, $1.20, Wang Zhaojun Chu Sai (2-2).

2007, Feb. 3 Photo. ***Perf. 13¼x13***
3559-3560 A1064 Set of 2 .60 .60
3560a Miniature sheet, 4 each #3559-3560 2.40 2.40

"Divine Birds of the Sun" — A1065

2007, Feb. 9 Litho. ***Perf. 12***
3561 A1065 $1.20 multi + label .30 .30

Printed in sheets of 8 + 8 labels and 15 + 15 labels.

Mianzhu New Year Woodcuts A1066

Designs: No. 3562, $1.20, Zuo Zuo Ti Dao (4-1). No. 3563, $1.20, Mu Guiying (4-2). No. 3564, $1.20, Shuang Xi Tong Zi (4-3). No. 3565, $1.20, Zhang Xian She Gou (4-4).

Perf. 12x11½ Syncopated

2007, Feb. 10 Litho. & Engr.
3562-3565 A1066 Set of 4 1.25 1.25
3565a Souvenir sheet of 4, #3562-3565 1.25 1.25
3565b Miniature sheet of 8, 2 each #3562-3565 2.50 2.50

A lithographed sheet similar to No. 3565b on a textured silk-faced paper exists.

Beijing Opera — A1067

Designs: 80f, Lin Xiangru (6-1). No. 3567, $1.20, Song Shijie (6-2). No. 3568, $1.20, Zhou Yu (6-3). No. 3569, $1.20, Xu Xian (6-4). No. 3570, $1.20, Gao Chong (6-5). No. 3571, $1.20, Ren Tanghui (6-6).

2007, Mar. 10 Photo. ***Perf. 13¼x13***
3566-3571 A1067 Set of 6 1.75 1.75

Postal Savings Bank — A1068

2007, Mar. 20 ***Perf. 12¾***
3572 A1068 $1.20 multi .30 .30
a. Miniature sheet of 8 2.40 2.40

Writings of Li Keran A1069

Designs: No. 3573, $1.20, Man viewing waterfall (6-1). No. 3574, $1.20, Mountains with red-leaved trees (6-2). No. 3575, $1.20, People looking at scroll (6-3). No. 3576, $1.20, Crane flying above man under tent (6-4). No. 3577, $1.20, Cattle and driver in pond (6-5). No. 3578, $1.20, Raining in Jiangnan (6-6).

Perf. 13x13¼ Syncopated

2007, Mar. 26
3573-3578 A1069 Set of 6 1.90 1.90

Modern Chinese Drama, Cent. A1070

Perf. 13 Syncopated

2007, Apr. 6 Litho.
3579 A1070 $1.20 multi .30 .30

Yangzhou Garden — A1071

No. 3580: a, He Garden (3-1). b, Ge Garden (3-2). c, Xu Garden (3-3).

Perf. 12x11½ Syncopated

2007, Apr. 8
3580 Horiz. strip of 3 .90 .90
a.-c. A1071 $1.20 Any single .30 .30

Dances — A1072

Designs: No. 3581, $1.20, Dragon dance (2-1). No. 3582, $1.20, Lion dance (2-2).

2007, Apr. 13 Litho. ***Perf. 12¾x13***
3581-3582 A1072 Set of 2 .65 .65

See Indonesia No. 2100.

Torch Relay for 2008 Summer Olympics, Beijing — A1073

2007, Apr. 27 ***Perf. 12***
3583 A1073 $1.20 multi + label .35 .35

Inner Mongolia Autonomous Region, 60th Anniv. — A1074

Designs: No. 3584, $1.20, Horsemen, wrestlers, archer (2-1). No. 3585, $1.20, Seven women (2-2).

Perf. 12½x12 Syncopated

2007, May 1
3584-3585 A1074 Set of 2 .65 .65
3585a Souvenir sheet, #3584-3585 .65 .65

Mausoleums of Qing Emperors A1075

Designs: No. 3586, $1.20, Zhaoling Mausoleum (3-1). No. 3587, $1.20, Xiaoling Mausoleum (3-2). No. 3588, Tailing Mausoleum (3-3).

2007, May 12 Photo. ***Perf. 12¾***
3586-3588 A1075 Set of 3 .95 .95

Tongji University, Cent. A1076

2007, May 20 ***Perf. 12½ Syncopated***
3589 A1076 $1.20 multi .35 .35

Kong Rong and Pears — A1077

Nos. 3590 and 3591: a, Denomination at LL (2-1). b, Denomination at LR (2-2).

2007, June 1 ***Perf. 13¼x13***
3590 A1077 $1.20 Horiz. pair, #a-b .65 .65

Self-Adhesive

Booklet Stamps

Serpentine Die Cut 11¾

3591 A1077 $1.20 Horiz. pair, #a-b .65 .65
c. Booklet pane, 4 #3591 2.60

Chongqing — A1078

No. 3592: a, City skyline (2-1). b, City and highway interchange (2-2).
Illustration reduced.

Perf. 12x11½ Syncopated

2007, June 8 Litho.

3592 A1078 $1.20 Horiz. pair, #a-b .65 .65

Wudalianchi Natl. Park — A1079

No. 3593: a, Heilong Mountain (3-1). b, Sanchi Pool (3-2). c, Sea of Rock (3-3).

2007, June 19 Photo. *Perf. 12¾*

3593 Horiz. strip of 3 .95 .95
a.-c. A1079 $1.20 Any single .30 .30

Return of Hong Kong, 10th Anniv. A1080

Designs: No. 3594, $1.20, Flags of People's Republic of China and Hong Kong, doves, monument (3-1). No. 3595, $1.20, "CEPA" and stylized buildings (3-2). No. 3596, $1.20, Hong Kong buildings, bridge (3-3).

Perf. 13¼x12¾ Syncopated

2007, July 1

3594-3596 A1080 Set of 3 .95 .95

A souvenir sheet containing Nos. 3594-3596 and Hong Kong No. 1275 sold for $12.95 in Hong Kong currency.

Pres. Yang Shangkun (1907-98) A1081

Designs: No. 3597, $1.20, Standing in uniform (2-1). No. 3598, $1.20, Seated at desk, horiz. (2-2).

Perf. 11½x11, 11x11½

2007, July 5 Photo. & Engr.

3597-3598 A1081 Set of 2 .65 .65

Nanji Islands Marine Reserve — A1082

Shells and: No. 3599, $1.20, Sanpanwei (3-1). No. 3600, $1.20, Longchuanjiao (3-2). No. 3601, $1.20, Dashaao (3-3).

Perf. 12¾x12½ Syncopated

2007, July 10 Photo.

3599-3601 A1082 Set of 3 .95 .95

Emblem of People's Liberation Army — A1083

2007, July 15 Litho. *Perf. 12*

3602 A1083 $1.20 multi + label .35 .35

Souvenir Sheet

All-China Philatelic Federation, 6th Congress — A1084

Perf. 12½ Syncopated

2007, July 28 Litho. & Engr.

3603 A1084 $6 multi 1.60 1.60

People's Liberation Army, 80th Anniv. — A1085

Designs: No. 3604, $1.20, Soldiers saluting (4-1). No. 3605, $1.20, Soldier carrying sack (4-2). No. 3606, $1.20, Soldier with rifle (4-3). No. 3607, $1.20, Soldiers wearing UN Peacekeeper berets (4-4).

Perf. 13¼x12½ Syncopated

2007, Aug. 1 Photo.

3604-3607 A1085 Set of 4 1.25 1.25

Olympic Sports — A1086

Designs: Nos. 3608, 3614a, $1.20, Diving (6-1). Nos. 3609, 3614b, $1.20, Shooting (6-2). Nos. 3610, 3614c, $1.20, Athletics (6-3). Nos. 3611, 3614d, $1.20, Volleyball (6-4). Nos. 3612, 3614e, $1.20, BMX bicycling (6-5). Nos. 3613, 3614f, $1.20, Weight lifting (6-6).

2007, Aug. 8 Photo. *Perf. 13¼x13*

3608-3613 A1086 Set of 6 1.90 1.90
3613a Sheet of 10, #3521-3524, 3608-3613, + label 5.50 5.50

Self-Adhesive

Serpentine Die Cut 11¾

3614 Miniature sheet of 12, 2 each #a-f 4.00
a.-f. A1086 $1.20 Any single .30 .30

No. 3613a sold for $18.60.

Tengchong Volcano Area — A1087

Designs: No. 3615, $1.20, Rehai (3-1). No. 3616, $1.20, Volcanoes, vert. (3-2). No. 3617, $1.20, Shenzhu Valley, vert. (3-3).

Perf. 12x12½ Syncopated, 12½x12 Syncopated

2007, Aug. 18

3615-3617 A1087 Set of 3 .95 .95

Nos. 3615-3617 were printed together in a sheet of 15 stamps + a horizontal label. The first row consists of the label and 2 #3615; the second row, 3 #3615; the third row, 5 #3616; and the fourth row, 5 #3617.

Jin Hu — A1088

No. 3618: a, Da Chibi (2-1). b, Maoer Mountain (2-2).
Illustration reduced.

Perf. 12¾ Syncopated

2007, Sept. 2 Litho.

3618 A1088 $1.20 Horiz. pair, #a-b .65 .65

2007 Women's Soccer World Cup, People's Republic of China A1089

2007, Sept. 10 Photo. *Perf. 13¼*

3619 A1089 $1.20 multi .35 .35

Values are for stamps with surrounding selvage.

2007 World Summer Special Olympics, Shanghai — A1090

2007, Oct. 2 *Perf. 13¼*

3620 A1090 $1.20 multi .35 .35

Historic Sites in Three Gorges Reservoir Area — A1091

Designs: No. 3621, $1.20, Zhang Fei Temple (4-1). No. 3622, $1.20, Shibaozhai Village, vert. (4-2). No. 3623, $1.20, Ancient Dachang, vert. (4-3). No. 3624, $1.20, Quyuan's Grave (4-4).

Perf. 13¼ Syncopated

2007, Oct. 13 Litho. & Engr.

3621-3624 A1091 Set of 4 1.40 1.40

17th Natl. Communist Party Congress — A1092

Designs: No. 3625, $1.20, Memorial for First Natl. Communist Party Congress (2-1). No. 3626, $1.20, Site of Second Plenary Session of the Seventh Central Committee.
$6, Dove and monument.

Perf. 13¼x13 Syncopated

2007, Oct. 15 Photo.

3625-3626 A1092 Set of 2 .65 .65

Souvenir Sheet

Perf. 13¼x13

3627 A1092 $6 multi 1.60 1.60

No. 3627 contains one 60x40mm stamp.

"Happiness" A1093

Perf. 12¾ Syncopated

2007, Nov. 1 Photo.

3628 A1093 $1.20 multi .35 .35

A sheet containing Nos. 3628, 3541 and four labels exists.

Ancient Calligraphy A1094

Designs: No. 3629, $1.20, Proclamation (6-1). No. 3630, $1.20, Zhang Menglong Stele (6-2). No. 3631, $1.20, Inscription for Sweet Spring at Jiucheng Palace (6-3). No. 3632, $1.20, Preface for Sacred Religion at Wild Goose Pagoda (6-4). No. 3633, $1.20, Yan Qinli Stele (6-5). No. 3634, $1.20, Mysterious Pagoda Stele (6-6).

Perf. 12x11½ Syncopated

2007, Nov. 5 Litho.

3629-3634 A1094 Set of 6 2.00 2.00

A sheet containing 2 each of lithographed and embossed examples of Nos. 3629-3634 exists.

Mountains — A1095

Designs: No. 3635, $1.20, Mount Gongga, People's Republic of China (2-1). No. 3636, $1.20, Popocatepetl, Mexico (2-2).

Perf. 12¾ Syncopated

2007, Nov. 22

3635-3636 A1095 Set of 2 .65 .65

See Mexico Nos. 2561-2562.

Launch of China's First Lunar Probe A1096

2007, Nov. 26 Litho. & Embossed

3637 A1096 $1.20 multi .35 .35

Emblem of Expo 2010, Shanghai A1097

Mascot of Expo 2010 — A1098

Perf. 11½ Syncopated

2008, Dec. 19 Litho.

3638 A1097 $1.20 multi .35 .35
- *a.* Booklet pane of 1 .35 —

3639 A1098 $1.20 multi .35 .35
- *a.* Booklet pane of 1 .35 —
- *b.* Booklet pane of 10, 5 each #3638-3639 3.50 —
- Complete booklet, #3638a, 3639a, 3639b 4.25

Venues at 2008 Summer Olympics, Beijing — A1099

Designs: 80f, China Agricultural University Gymnasium (6-1). No. 3641, $1.20, Laoshan Mountain Bike Course (6-2). No. 3642, $1.20, National Indoor Stadium (6-3). No. 3643, $1.20, Beijing University Gymnasium (6-4). No. 3644, $1.20, National Aquatics Center (6-5). No. 3645, $3, Qingdao Olympic Sailing Center (6-6).
$6, National Stadium.

2007, Dec. 20 Photo. *Perf. 13x13¼*

3640-3645 A1099 Set of 6 2.40 2.40

Souvenir Sheet

Perf. 13

3646 A1099 $6 multi 1.75 1.75

No. 3646 contains one pentagonal 65x62mm stamp.

New Year 2008 (Year of the Rat) A1100

Perf. 12¾ Syncopated

2008, Jan. 5 Photo.

3647 A1100 $1.20 multi .35 .35
- *a.* Booklet pane of 10 3.50 —
- Complete booklet, #3647a 3.50

Miniature sheets containing 4 and 6 stamps exist.

Zhuxian New Year Woodprints A1101

Designs: No. 3648, $1.20, Gate guardian (4-1). No. 3649, $1.20, Woman lecturing son (4-2). No. 3650, $1.20, Come back with fruitful result (4-3). No. 3651, $1.20, Chivalrous women (4-4).

2008, Jan. 15 Photo. *Perf. 13¼x13*

3648-3651 A1101 Set of 4 1.40 1.40
- *3651a* Souvenir sheet of 4, #3648-3651 2.00 2.00

No. 3651a sold for $7.20. A miniature sheet containing two each of #3648-3651 exists.

Beijing Opera Characters A1102

Designs: 80f, Zhang Fei (6-1). No. 3653, $1.20, Cao Cao (6-2). No. 3654, $1.20, Bao Zheng (6-3). No. 3655, $1.20, Lian Po (6-4). No. 3656, $1.20, Xu Yanzhao (6-5). No. 3657, $1.20, Yang Yansi (6-6).

Perf. 12x11½ Syncopated

2008, Feb. 23 Litho.

3652-3657 A1102 Set of 6 1.90 1.90

Miniature Sheet

Birds — A1103

No. 3658: a, Urocissa caerulea (6-1). b, Emberiza koslowi (6-2). c, Tragopan caboti (6-3). d, Garrulax sukatschewi (6-4). e, Chrysolophus pictus (6-5). f, Podoces biddulphi (6-6).

2008, Feb. 28 Photo. *Perf. 13¼x13*

3658 A1103 $1.20 Sheet of 6, #a-f 2.10 2.10

11th National People's Congress — A1104

2008, Mar. 5

3659 A1104 $1.20 multi .35 .35

Olympic Torch Relay — A1105

Designs: $1.20, Lighting of torch in Greece, mascot holding torch (2-1). $3, Torch, torch bearer, vert. (2-2).

2008, Mar. 5 Photo. *Perf. 13¼*

3660-3661 A1105 Set of 2 1.25 1.25
- *3661a* Souvenir sheet, #3660-3661 1.90 1.90

No. 3661a sold for $6.30. A sheet containing 4 self-adhesive examples each of Nos. 3660-3661 exists.

Suzhou-Nantong Yangtze River Bridge — A1106

No. 3662 — Denomination at: a, Left (2-1). b, Right (2-2).
Illustration reduced.

2008, Apr. 12 *Perf. 13¼*

3662 A1106 $1.20 Horiz. pair, #a-b .70 .70

Boao Forum For Asia — A1107

No. 3663: a, Dongyu Island (2-1). b, Forum venue (2-2).
Illustration reduced.

Perf. 12x11½ Syncopated

2008, Apr. 13 Litho.

3663 A1107 $1.20 Horiz. pair, #a-b .70 .70

Qiandao Lake — A1108

No. 3664 — Islands with denomination at: a, Left (2-1). b, Right (2-2).
Illustration reduced.

2008, Apr. 16 *Perf. 12¾ Syncopated*

3664 A1108 $1.20 Horiz. pair, #a-b .70 .70
- *c.* Souvenir sheet, #3664 1.10 1.10

No. 3664c sold for $3.60.

A1109

Olympic Expo, Beijing — A1110

2008, Apr. 30 Photo. *Perf. 11¼x11*

3665 A1109 $1.20 multi .35 .35

Litho.

Perf. 12½

3666 A1110 $1.20 multi .35 .35

A circle of perforations surrounds the circular design on No. 3665.

Summer Palace — A1111

Designs: No. 3667, $1.20, Shiqikong Bridge (6-1). No. 3668, $1.20, Corridor (6-2). No. 3669, $1.20, Boat (6-3). No. 3670, $1.20, Garden of Harmonious Pleasures (6-4). No. 3671, $1.20, Yudai Bridge (6-5). No. 3672, $1.20, Houhu Lake (6-6).
$6, Tower of the Fragrance of Buddha, vert.

Litho. & Engr.

2008, May 10 *Perf. 12*

3667-3672 A1111 Set of 6 2.10 2.10

Souvenir Sheet

Perf. 12x11¾

3673 A1111 $6 multi 1.75 1.75

No. 3673 contains one 50x62mm stamp.

Cao Chong Weighs the Elephant A1112

Cao Chong: Nos. 3674, 3676, $1.20, Marking water level on boat carrying elephant (2-1). Nos. 3675, 3677, $1.20, Replacing elephant with weighable objects (2-2).

2008, June 1 Photo. ***Perf. 13x13¼***
3674-3675 A1112 Set of 2 .70 .70

Booklet Stamps
Self-Adhesive
Serpentine Die Cut 11¾

3676-3677 A1112 Set of 2 .70 .70
3677a Booklet pane of 8, 4 each #3676-3677 2.80

Temples A1113

Designs: No. 3678, $1.20, White Horse Temple, China (2-1). No. 3679, $1.20, Maha Bodhi Temple, India (2-2).

2008, June 6 ***Perf. 13¼x13***
3678-3679 A1113 Set of 2 .70 .70

See India No. 2246.

Development on the Taiwan Strait — A1114

Designs: No. 3680, $1.20, Minjiang River development (4-1). No. 3681, $1.20, Port of Xiamen (4-2). No. 3682, $1.20, Exhibition Hall (4-3). No. 3683, $1.20, Fujian-Taiwan Kinship Museum (4-4).

2008, June 18 ***Perf. 12¾***
3680-3683 A1114 Set of 4 1.40 1.40

A sheet containing 2 each of Nos. 3680-3683 + 1 label exists.

Second Land Survey — A1115

Designs: No. 3684, $1.20, Satellite, rural land survey (2-1). No. 3685, $1.20, Theodolite, urban land survey (2-2).

Perf. 12¾x12½
2008, June 25 Litho.
3684-3685 A1115 Set of 2 .70 .70

Qiuci Grotto Murals A1116

Designs: No. 3686, $1.20 Heavenly Kings (4-1). No. 3687, $1.20, Bodhisattva (4-2). No. 3688, $1.20, Flying Apsaras, horiz. (4-3). No. 3689, $1.20, Maitreya Preaching, horiz. (4-4).

2008, July 6 Photo. ***Perf. 13¼***
3686-3689 A1116 Set of 4 1.40 1.40

General Qi Jiguang (1528-88) A1117

Qi Jiguang: No. 3690, $1.20, Standing (2-1). No. 3691, $1.20, On horse (2-2).

Perf. 12x12½ Syncopated
2008, July 19 Litho.
3690-3691 A1117 Set of 2 .70 .70

Opening of 2008 Summer Olympics, Beijing — A1118

2008, Aug. 8 Photo. ***Perf. 13¼***
3692 A1118 $1.20 multi .35 .35

A sheet of eight self-adhesive stamps similar to No. 3692 exists.

Olympex 2008 Philatelic Exhibition, Beijing — A1119

Designs: No. 3693, $1.20, Greece #127 (2-1). No. 3694, $1.20, Portugal #RA14 (2-2). $6, Greece #127, gold medal and mascots of 2004 Summer Olympics.

2008, Aug. 8 Photo. ***Perf. 13¼x13***
3693-3694 A1119 Set of 2 .70 .70

Souvenir Sheet
Litho.
Perf.

3695 A1119 $6 multi 1.75 1.75

No. 3695 contains one 56mm diameter stamp.

Closing of 2008 Summer Olympics A1120

Designs: No. 3696, $1.20, National Stadium, Beijing (4-1). No. 3697, $1.20, Tower, Forbidden City, Beijing (4-2). No. 3698, $1.20, Millennium Wheel, London (4-3). No. 3699, $1.20, Tower of London (4-4).

2008, Aug. 24 Photo. ***Perf. 13¼***
3696-3699 A1120 Set of 4 1.40 1.40

A sheet containing three self-adhesive examples each of Nos. 3696-3699 exists.

China Central Television, 50th Anniv. A1121

Perf. 13½x13 Syncopated
2008, Sept. 2
3700 A1121 $1.20 multi .35 .35

Emblem of 2008 Paralympic Games, Beijing — A1122

Paralympic Games Mascot — A1123

2008, Sept. 6 ***Perf. 13¼x13***
3701 A1122 $1.20 multi .35 .35
3702 A1123 $1.20 multi .35 .35

University of Science and Technology, 50th Anniv. — A1124

Perf. 12x11¼ Syncopated
2008, Sept. 20 Litho.
3703 A1124 $1.20 multi .35 .35

Ningxia Hui Autonomous Region, 50th Anniv. — A1125

No. 3704: a, Windmills (3-1). b, Trees and wildlife in desert (3-2). c, People holding flower bouquets (3-3).

Perf. 13¼x12¾ Syncopated
2008, Sept. 23 Photo.
3704 Horiz. strip of 3 .95 .95
a. A1125 80f multi .25 .25
b.-c. A1125 $1.20 Either single .35 .35

Airports — A1126

No. 3705: a, Beijing Capital International Airport (3-1). b, Shanghai Pudong International Airport (3-2). c, Guangzhou Baiyun International Airport (3-3).

2008, Sept. 28 ***Perf. 12¾***
3705 Vert. strip of 3 1.10 1.10
a.-c. A1126 $1.20 Any single .35 .35

Guangxi Zhuang Autonomous Region, 50th Anniv. — A1127

No. 3706: a, Dancers (3-1). b, Building (3-2). c, Port (3-3).

Perf. 12¾ Syncopated
2008, Oct. 18 Litho.
3706 Horiz. strip of 3 .95 .95
a. A1127 80f multi .25 .25
b.-c. A1127 $1.20 Either single .35 .35

SEMI-POSTAL STAMPS

Catalogue values for unused stamps in this section are for Never Hinged items.

Girl Holding Ball — SP1

Hands Reading Braille — SP2

1984, Feb. 16 Photo. ***Perf. 11½***
B1 SP1 8f + 2f shown (2-1) .25 .20
B2 SP1 8f + 2f Boy, panda (2-2) .25 .20

Surtax for China Children's Fund. T.92.

1985, Mar. 15 Photo. ***Perf. 11½***
B3 SP2 8f + 2f shown (4-1) 1.00 .60
B4 SP2 8f + 2f Sign language, lip reading (4-2) 1.00 .60
B5 SP2 8f + 2f Artificial limb (4-3) 1.00 .60
B6 SP2 8f + 2f Handicapped person in wheelchair (4-4) 1.00 .60
Nos. B3-B6 (4) 4.00 2.40

Surtax for China Welfare Fund. T.105.

Children (T.137) SP3

1989, June 1 Litho. ***Perf. 12***
B7 SP3 8f +4f Friends (4-1) .20 .20
B8 SP3 8f +4f Penguins (4-2) .20 .20
B9 SP3 8f +4f Bird, Moon, Sun (4-3) .20 .20
B10 SP3 8f +4f Girl, boy playing ball (4-4) .20 .20
a. Strip of 4, #B7-B10 .50 .50

Intl Children's Day, 40th anniv., and 10th Intl. Year of the Child. Surtax for China Children's Fund.

Sichuan Earthquake Relief — SP4

2008, May 20 Photo. *Perf. 13x13¼*

B11 SP4 $1.20 + $1 multi + label	.65	.65

AIR POST STAMPS

Mail Plane and Temple of Heaven — AP1

1951, May 1 Engr. *Perf. 12½*
Without Gum

C1	AP1 $1000 carmine	.20	.20
C2	AP1 $3000 green	.30	.20
C3	AP1 $5000 orange	.20	.20
C4	AP1 $10,000 vio brn & grn	.25	.25
C5	AP1 $30,000 dk bl & brn	8.50	1.25
	Nos. C1-C5 (5)	9.45	2.10

Planes at Airport — AP2

Designs: 28f, Plane over winding mountain highway. 35f, Plane over railroad yard. 52f, Plane over ship.

1957-58 *Perf. 14*
Without Gum

C6	AP2 16f indigo	10.00	.25
C7	AP2 28f olive black	10.00	.25
C8	AP2 35f slate	10.00	5.00
C9	AP2 52f Prus blue ('58)	10.00	.75
	Nos. C6-C9 (4)	40.00	6.25

POSTAGE DUE STAMPS

Grain and Cogwheel — D1

D2

1950, Sept. 1 Typo. *Perf. 12½*
Without Gum

J1	D1 $100 steel blue	.20	.20
J2	D1 $200 steel blue	.20	.20
J3	D1 $500 steel blue	.20	.20
J4	D1 $800 steel blue	27.50	.20
J5	D1 $1000 steel blue	.45	.40
J6	D1 $2000 steel blue	.45	.40
J7	D1 $5000 steel blue	.30	.60
J8	D1 $8000 steel blue	.30	1.00
J9	D1 $10,000 steel blue	.60	2.00
	Nos. J1-J9 (9)	30.20	5.20

1954, Aug. 18 Litho. *Perf. 14*
Without Gum

J10	D2 $100 red	2.00	.20
J11	D2 $200 red	.60	.20
J12	D2 $500 red	2.00	.20
J13	D2 $800 red	.20	.20
J14	D2 $1600 red	.20	.20
	Nos. J10-J14 (5)	5.00	1.00

MILITARY STAMP

Red Star, 8-1 in Center — M1

1953, Aug. Litho. *Perf. 14*
Without Gum

M1	M1 $800 yel, org & red	85.00	27.50

This stamp also was printed in deep purple, orange & red, and blue, orange & red. These were not issued.

While it has been assumed for many years that each color was for a separate branch of the armed forces (army, air force and navy), there is no documentation to support that theory. Quantities printed also do not correspond to the number of servicemen in each branch.

M2

1995 Litho. *Perf. 12*

M4	M2 20f multicolored	8.00

NORTHEAST CHINA

The Northeast Liberation Area included the provinces of Liaoning, Kirin, Jehol and Heilungkiang, the area generally known as Manchuria under the Japanese. The first post war issues were local overprints on stamps of Manchukuo. In early 1946, a Ministry of Posts and Telegraphs served the areas already liberated, and in August, 1946, a Communications Committee of the Political Council was established. In June, 1947, these postal services were subordinated to the Harbin General Post Office, and this was extended to Changchun on Oct. 22, 1948, and to Mukden on Nov. 4, 1948. It was rapidly extended to cover all Manchuria.

Rough Perfs

Rough perforations are normal on most regional issues.

All Stamps Issued without Gum

Mao Tse-tung
A1 A2

1946, Feb. Unwmk. Litho. *Perf. 11*

1L1	A1 $1 violet	20.00	10.00
1L2	A2 $2 vermilion	1.50	1.00
1L3	A2 $5 orange	1.75	1.00
a.	Booklet pane of 6	250.00	
1L4	A2 $10 blue	2.00	1.25
a.	Booklet pane of 6	250.00	
	Nos. 1L1-1L4 (4)	25.25	13.25

Value, imperf set $125.

For surcharges see Nos. 1L20-1L23, 1L49-1L50, 1L89, 1L91, 1L93.

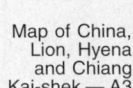

Map of China, Lion, Hyena and Chiang Kai-shek — A3

1946, Dec. 12 *Perf. 10½*

1L5	A3 $1 violet	2.00	1.50
1L6	A3 $2 orange	2.00	1.50
1L7	A3 $5 org brn	7.00	7.00
1L8	A3 $10 lt grn	10.00	10.00
a.	Imperf., pair	60.00	
	Nos. 1L5-1L8 (4)	21.00	20.00

10th anniversary of the capture of Chiang Kai-shek at Sian.

Railroad Workers, Chengchow A4

1947, Feb. 7 *Perf. 10½*

1L9	A4 $1 pink	1.00	*1.10*
1L10	A4 $2 dull grn	1.00	*1.10*
1L11	A4 $5 pink	1.75	1.60
1L12	A4 $10 dull grn	3.75	3.75
	Nos. 1L9-1L12 (4)	7.50	7.55

24th anniversary of the Chengchow railroad workers' strike and massacre.

Women (Worker, Soldier and Farmer) — A5

Wmk. Chinese Characters in Sheet
1947, Mar. 8 *Perf. 10½x11*

1L13	A5 $5 brick red	1.00	1.00
1L14	A5 $10 brown	1.00	1.00

International Women's Day, March 8. Exists imperf.

Same Overprinted in Green ("Northeast Postal Service")

1947, Mar. 18

1L15	A5 $5 brick red	3.00	4.50
1L16	A5 $10 brown	3.00	4.50

Exists imperf.

Children Carrying Banner — A6

1947, Apr. 4 *Perf. 11x10½*
Granite Paper

1L17	A6 $5 rose red	1.50	2.25
1L18	A6 $10 lt green	3.25	3.00
1L19	A6 $30 orange	5.00	4.00
	Nos. 1L17-1L19 (3)	9.75	9.25

Children's Day.

Nos. 1L1-1L2 Surcharged in Red, Brown, Black, Blue or Green

1947, Apr. Unwmk. *Perf. 11*

1L20	A1 $50 on $1 vio (R)	24.00	25.00
a.	Brown surcharge	24.00	25.00
1L21	A2 $50 on $2 ver	24.00	25.00
a.	Brown surcharge	24.00	25.00
1L22	A1 $100 on $1 vio	24.00	25.00
a.	Green surcharge	24.00	25.00
1L23	A2 $100 on $2 ver (Bl)	24.00	25.00
a.	Green surcharge	24.00	25.00
	Nos. 1L20-1L23 (4)	96.00	100.00

Farmer and Worker — A7

Ax Severing Chain — A8

Wmk. Chinese Characters in Sheet
1947, May 1 *Perf. 10½x11*
Granite Paper

1L24	A7 $10 orange red	2.25	2.25
1L25	A7 $30 ultra	2.75	2.75
1L26	A7 $50 gray green	4.25	4.25
	Nos. 1L24-1L26 (3)	9.25	9.25

Labor Day. Value, imperf. pairs, set $425.

1947, May 4 *Perf. 11*

1L27	A8 $10 brt green	2.50	2.50
1L28	A8 $30 brown	2.50	2.50
1L29	A8 $50 violet	3.00	3.00
	Nos. 1L27-1L29 (3)	8.00	8.00

28th anniversary of the students' revolt at Peking University against the 1918 peace treaty. Value, imperf. pairs, set $525.

Workers with Banner: "Oppose Imperialist Aggression" — A9

1947, May 30 *Perf. 10½x11*
Banner in Red

1L30	A9 $2 brt lilac	2.25	*3.00*
1L31	A9 $5 brt green	2.25	*3.00*
1L32	A9 $10 yellow	2.75	*3.00*
1L33	A9 $20 violet	2.75	*3.00*
1L34	A9 $30 red brown	2.75	*3.00*
1L35	A9 $50 dk blue	4.75	3.00
1L36	A9 $100 brown	6.75	3.00
a.	Souvenir sheet of 7	150.00	
	Nos. 1L30-1L36 (7)	24.25	21.00

22nd anniversary of the Shanghai-Nanking Road incident. No. 1L36a is on granite paper and contains 7 imperf. stamps similar to Nos. 1L30-1L36. Size: 215x158mm. Value, imperf. pairs, ordinary paper, set $1,300.

Mao and Communist Flag — A10

1947, July 1 *Perf. 10½x11*

1L37	A10 $10 red	9.50	*11.00*
1L38	A10 $30 brt lilac	9.50	*11.00*
1L39	A10 $50 rose brn	20.00	*26.00*
1L40	A10 $100 vermilion	25.00	*29.00*
	Nos. 1L37-1L40 (4)	64.00	*77.00*

26th anniversary of the founding of the Chinese Communist Party.

Hand Holding Rifle — A11

1947, July 7 ***Perf. 10½***

1L41 A11 $10 orange 3.75 *4.75*
1L42 A11 $30 green 3.75 *4.75*
1L43 A11 $50 dull blue 5.75 5.75
1L44 A11 $100 brown 8.00 8.00
a. Souvenir sheet of 4 160.00 *175.00*
Nos. 1L41-1L44 (4) 21.25 23.25

10th anniversary of the start of Sino-Japanese War. No. 1L44a contains 4 imperf. stamps similar to Nos. 1L41-1L44. Size: 149x107mm.
Exist imperf. Value, set of pairs $1,100.

White Mountain and Black Water, Northeast China — A12

Wmk. Zigzag Lines (141)

1947, Aug. 15 ***Perf. 10½***

1L45 A12 $10 brown org 3.00 *7.50*
1L46 A12 $30 lt ol grn 3.00 *7.50*
1L47 A12 $50 blue grn 12.00 *13.00*
1L48 A12 $100 sepia 21.00 *18.00*
Nos. 1L45-1L48 (4) 39.00 *46.00*

2nd anniversary of the reoccupation of Northeast China and the surrender of Japan.
Exist imperf. Value, set of pairs $700.

Nos. 1L1-1L2 Surcharged in Black, Red, Green or Blue

1947, Aug. 29 **Unwmk.** ***Perf. 11***

1L49 A1 $5 on $1 vio 22.50 22.50
a. Red surcharge 22.50 22.50
b. Green surcharge 22.50 22.50
1L50 A2 $10 on $2 ver 22.50 22.50
a. Blue surcharge 22.50 22.50
b. Green surcharge 22.50 22.50

Map of Manchuria — A13

1947, Sept. 18 **Unwmk.**

White Paper

1L51 A13 $10 gray green 4.50 8.75
1L52 A13 $20 rose lilac 4.50 8.75
1L53 A13 $30 black brown 8.75 8.75
1L54 A13 $50 carmine 8.75 8.75
Nos. 1L51-1L54 (4) 26.50 35.00

16th anniversary of Japanese attack on Mukden, Sept. 18, 1931.

Northeast Political Council Offices — A14

Mao Tse-tung (Value figures repeated) — A15

1947, Oct. 10 ***Perf. 10½***

1L55 A14 $10 yel orange 30.00 30.00
1L56 A14 $20 rose red 30.00 30.00
1L57 A14 $100 brown 77.50 77.50
Nos. 1L55-1L57 (3) 137.50 137.50

35th anniversary of the founding of the Chinese Republic.

1947, Oct. 10 White Paper ***Perf. 11***

1L58 A15 $1 brown .35 1.50
1L59 A15 $5 gray green 2.00 1.50
1L60 A15 $10 brt green 8.00 8.00
1L61 A15 $15 bluish lilac 8.00 8.00
1L62 A15 $20 brt rose .80 1.50
1L63 A15 $30 green .80 2.00
1L64 A15 $50 black brown 15.00 12.00
1L65 A15 $90 blue 4.50 4.00
Nos. 1L58-1L65 (8) 39.45 38.50

Newsprint

1L66 A15 $100 red .70
a. White paper 7.00 4.00
1L67 A15 $500 red orange 27.50 16.00
a. White paper 27.50 25.00

Type A22 resembles A15, but has "YUAN" at upper right.
The $1, $90 were also printed on newsprint.
See footnote following No. 1L72.
See Nos. 1L68-1L72. For surcharges see Nos. 1L84-1L88, 1L90, 1L92, 1L94.

1947, Nov. **Redrawn**

White Paper

1L68 A15 $50 lt grn 1.00 *1.50*
1L69 A15 $150 red org, wmkd. Chinese characters 2.25 1.50
a. Unwatermarked 2.75
1L70 A15 $250 bluish lil .90 *1.50*
a. Wmkd. Chinese characters 1.25 *1.50*

Nos. 1L69 and 1L69a exist in same sheet.

1947, Dec. **Unwmk.**

Newsprint

1L71 A15 $300 green 52.50 27.50
1L72 A15 $1000 yellow 1.50 1.50
a. White paper 1.50 1.50
Nos. 1L68-1L72 (5) 58.15 33.50

Panel below portrait 8½x3mm on Nos. 1L68-1L70; 7x3mm on No. 1L58-1L67. Nos. 1L68-1L70 have different ornamental border. Nos. 1L71-1L72 without zeros for cents.
For surcharges see Nos. 1L90, 1L92, 1L94.

Hand Holding Torch — A16

1947, Dec. 12 **Unwmk.** ***Perf. 11***

White Paper

1L73 A16 $30 rose red 6.00 *8.50*
1L74 A16 $90 dk bl 8.00 *8.50*
1L75 A16 $150 green 12.00 8.50
Nos. 1L73-1L75 (3) 26.00 25.50

11th anniversary of the capture of Chiang Kai-shek at Sian.

Tomb of Gen. Li Chao-lin — A17

Globe and Banner — A18

1948, Mar. 9 **Unwmk.** ***Perf. 10½x11***

1L76 A17 $30 green 12.00 12.00
a. Granite paper, wmkd. 12.00 12.00
1L77 A17 $150 vio gray 12.00 12.00
a. Granite paper, wmkd. 12.00 12.00

2nd anniversary of the assassination of Gen. Li Chao-lin, Commander of 3rd Army.

Wmk. Chinese Characters in Sheet

1948, May 1 ***Perf. 11x10½***

1L78 A18 $50 red 8.00 *12.00*
1L79 A18 $150 green 3.00 *18.00*
1L80 A18 $250 lilac 3.00 *35.00*
Nos. 1L78-1L80 (3) 14.00 *65.00*

Labor Day.

Student, Torch and Banner — A19

1948, May 4 **Unwmk.** ***Perf. 10½x11***

Granite paper

1L81 A19 $50 green 8.00 7.00
1L82 A19 $150 brown 8.00 11.00
1L83 A19 $250 red 15.00 17.00
Nos. 1L81-1L83 (3) 31.00 35.00

Youth Day, May 4.

Nos. 1L58, 1L61, 1L59, 1L63, 1L65, 1L2-1L4, 1L68-1L69, 1L71 Surcharged in Black, Blue, Red or Green

1948-49 ***Perf. 11***

1L84 A15 $100 on $1 75.00 90.00
a. Blue surcharge 50.00 50.00
1L85 A15 $100 on $15 18.00 17.50
a. Blue surcharge 50.00 50.00
1L86 A15 $300 on $5 (R) 55.00 25.00
1L87 A15 $300 on $30 (R) 6.00 10.00
1L88 A15 $300 on $90 (R) 6.00 10.00
1L89 A2 $500 on $2 6.00 6.00
1L90 A15 $500 on $50 (R, '49) 27.50 20.00
1L91 A2 $1500 on $5 (Bl) 6.00 7.50
1L92 A15 $1500 on $150 (G; '49) 22.50 15.00
a. Blue surcharge 50.00 50.00
1L93 A2 $2500 on $10 (R) 7.50 9.00
1L94 A15 $2500 on $300 ('49) 9.00 12.00
Nos. 1L84-1L94 (11) 238.50 222.00

Crane Operator — A20

Wmk. Chinese Characters in Sheet

1948, May ***Perf. 11***

1L95 A20 $100 red & pink 1.25 1.00
1L96 A20 $300 vio brn & yel 1.50 1.50
1L97 A20 $500 bl & grn 2.00 2.00
Nos. 1L95-1L97 (3) 4.75 4.50

6th All-China Labor Conference, Harbin.

Farmer, Worker and Soldier Saluting — A21

Mao Tse-tung ("YUAN" at upper right) — A22

1948, Dec. 3 **Unwmk.** ***Perf. 11x10½***

White paper

1L98 A21 $500 vermilion 8.00 8.00
1L99 A21 $1500 brt grn 12.00 12.00
1L100 A21 $2500 brown 21.00 21.00
Nos. 1L98-1L100 (3) 41.00 41.00

Liberation of Northeast China.
Values for Nos. 1L98-1L100 are for fine stamps.

1949, Feb. ***Perf. 11***

1L101 A22 $300 olive .50 *1.00*
1L102 A22 $500 orange 1.50 *1.75*
1L103 A22 $1500 bl grn .50 *1.00*
1L104 A22 $4500 brown .50 *1.00*
1L105 A22 $6500 dk bl .50 *1.00*
Nos. 1L101-1L105 (5) 3.50 *5.75*

See type A15. For surcharges see Nos. 1L126-1L129, 1L131-1L132.

Workers, Globe and Flag — A23

Fields and Factories — A24

1949, May 1 ***Perf. 11½***

1L106 A23 $1000 red & dl bl .35 *.65*
1L107 A23 $1500 red & pale bl .35 *.65*
1L108 A23 $4500 rose & ol brn .50 *1.00*
1L109 A23 $6500 dl org & grn .50 *1.00*
1L110 A23 $10,000 mar & ultra .60 *1.40*
Nos. 1L106-1L110 (5) 2.30 *4.70*

Labor Day.

1949 ***Perf. 10, 11***

1L111 A24 $5000 Prus bl 4.50 3.25
1L112 A24 $10,000 org brn .35 *1.60*
1L113 A24 $50,000 green .45 *2.40*
1L114 A24 $100,000 violet .90 *12.00*
Nos. 1L111-1L114 (4) 6.20 *19.25*

Production in agriculture and industry.

Workers with Flags — A25

Heroes' Monument, Harbin — A26

1949, July 1 ***Perf. 11***

1L115 A25 $1500 vio, lt bl & red .50 *.65*
1L116 A25 $4500 dk brn, lt bl & ver .50 *.65*
1L117 A25 $6500 gray, lt bl & rose red .90 *1.25*
Nos. 1L115-1L117 (3) 1.90 *2.55*

28th anniversary of the founding of the Chinese Communist Party.

1949, Aug. 15 ***Perf. 11½x11***

1L118 A26 $1500 brick red .90 *1.20*
1L119 A26 $4500 yel grn .90 *1.20*
1L120 A26 $6500 lt blue 1.00 *1.20*
Nos. 1L118-1L120 (3) 2.80 *3.60*

4th anniversary of the Reoccupation, and the surrender of Japan.

東北貼用

"Northeast Postal Service"

The following commemorative issues are similar to those of the People's Republic of China, with the 4 characters shown added in different sizes and various arrangements. Reprints were also issued similar to those of the PRC.

Chinese Lantern Type of PRC, 1949

1949, Sept. 12 **Litho.** ***Perf. 12½***

1L121 A1 $1000 dp blue 3.00 5.00
1L122 A1 $1500 scarlet 4.00 5.00
1L123 A1 $3000 green 6.00 *6.50*
1L124 A1 $4500 maroon 7.00 *7.50*
Nos. 1L121-1L124 (4) 20.00 *24.00*

Reprints exist. Value, set $1.10.

Factory — A27

1949, Oct. *Perf. 11x10½*

1L125 A27 $1500 orange .90 *1.25*

For surcharge see No. 1L130.

Nos. 1L101, 1L103-1L105, 1L125 Surcharged in Black or Green

1949, Nov. 20

1L126 A22 $2000 on $300 22.50 4.25
1L127 A22 $2000 on $4500 (G) 47.50 *32.50*
1L128 A22 $2500 on $1500 .70 *5.00*
1L129 A22 $2500 on $6500 24.00 *32.50*
1L130 A27 $5000 on $1500 .60 *1.75*
1L131 A22 $20,000 on $4500 .40 *5.00*
1L132 A22 $35,000 on $300 .50 *6.75*
Nos. 1L126-1L132 (7) 96.20 *87.75*

Globe and Hammer Type of PRC

1949, Nov. 15 *Perf. 12½*

1L133 A2 $5000 crimson 150.00 60.00
1L134 A2 $20,000 dp green 250.00 70.00
1L135 A2 $35,000 vio blue 350.00 90.00
Nos. 1L133-1L135 (3) 750.00 220.00

Reprints, value; #1L133-1L134, each $1.50; #1L135, $1.75.

Mao and Conference Hall Types of PRC

1950, Feb. 1 *Perf. 14*

1L136 A3 $1000 vermilion 10.00 13.00
1L137 A3 $1500 dp blue 10.00 13.00
1L138 A4 $5000 dk vio brn 20.00 14.00
1L139 A4 $20,000 green 20.00 *20.00*
Nos. 1L136-1L139 (4) 60.00 60.00

Reprints exist. Value, set $4.

Gate of Heavenly Peace — A28

1950 *Perf. 10½*

Narrow horizontal shading

1L140 A28 $500 olive 1.50 .55
1L141 A28 $1000 orange 1.75 .55
1L142 A28 $1000 lil rose 4.00 .55
1L143 A28 $2000 gray grn 1.25 .30
1L144 A28 $2500 yellow 4.50 .30
1L145 A28 $5000 dp org 20.00 .30
1L146 A28 $10,000 brn org 2.25 .55
1L147 A28 $20,000 vio brn 1.25 .30
1L148 A28 $35,000 dp blue 1.25 .40
1L149 A28 $50,000 brt grn 20.00 .80
Nos. 1L140-1L149 (10) 57.75 4.60

See A29.

Flag and Mao Type of PRC

1950, July 1 *Perf. 14*

Yellow Stars

1L150 A7 $5000 grn & red 57.50 52.50
1L151 A7 $10,000 brn & red 72.50 52.50
1L152 A7 $20,000 dk brn & red 80.00 52.50
1L153 A7 $30,000 dk vio bl & red 110.00 72.50
Nos. 1L150-1L153 (4) 320.00 230.00

Reprints exist. Value, set $7.

Picasso Dove Type of PRC

1950, Aug. 1 **Engr.** *Perf. 14*

1L154 A8 $2500 brown 10.00 18.00
1L155 A8 $5000 green 15.00 18.00
1L156 A8 $20,000 blue 20.00 18.00
Nos. 1L154-1L156 (3) 45.00 54.00

Reprints exist. Value, set $4.75.

Flag Type of PRC

1950, Oct. 1 **Engr. & Litho.**

Flag in Red & Yellow

1L157 A9 $1000 purple 35.00 27.50
1L158 A9 $2500 org brn 52.50 35.00
1L159 A9 $5000 dp grn 60.00 45.00
1L160 A9 $10,000 olive 80.00 45.00
1L161 A9 $20,000 blue 125.00 72.50
Nos. 1L157-1L161 (5) 352.50 225.00

Size of #1L159: 38x47mm, others 26x33mm.
Reprints exist. Value, set $7.

Postal Conference Type of PRC

1950, Nov. 1 **Litho.**

1L162 A11 $2500 grn & dp org 12.00 9.50
1L163 A11 $5000 car & grn 12.00 9.50

Reprints exist. Value, set, $5.

Gate of Heavenly Peace — A29

1950-51 *Perf. 10½*

Wide horizontal shading

1L164 A29 $5000 orange 6.00 *6.25*
1L165 A29 $30,000 scarlet 2.25 *15.00*
1L166 A29 $100,000 violet 10.00 *16.00*

Wmk. Zigzag Lines (141)

1L167 A29 $250 brown .90 *1.50*
1L168 A29 $500 olive .90 *1.50*
1L169 A29 $1000 lil rose 1.25 *2.50*
1L170 A29 $2000 dl grn ('51) 2.00 *2.50*
1L171 A29 $2500 yellow .90 *2.50*
1L172 A29 $5000 orange 2.25 *2.50*
1L173 A29 $10,000 brn org ('51) 1.60 *2.50*
1L174 A29 $12,500 maroon .90 *2.50*
1L175 A29 $20,000 dp brn ('51) 1.75 *5.00*
Nos. 1L164-1L175 (12) 30.70 *60.25*

A $50,000 green was prepared, but not issued. Value $150.

Stalin and Mao Tse-tung Type of PRC

Unwmk.

1950, Dec. 1 **Engr.** *Perf. 14*

1L176 A12 $2500 red 20.00 10.00
1L177 A12 $5000 dp green 25.00 10.00
1L178 A12 $20,000 dk blue 25.00 10.00
Nos. 1L176-1L178 (3) 70.00 30.00

Reprints exist. Value, set $2.75.

NORTHEAST CHINA PARCEL POST STAMPS

Locomotive — PP1

1951 **Litho.** *Perf. 10½*

1LQ1 $100,000 purple 200.00

Imperf

1LQ2 $300,000 brown 400.00
1LQ3 $500,000 grnsh bl 700.00
1LQ4 $1,000,000 ver 1,100.

Value, Nos. 1LQ2-1LQ4 perf. 10½, $2,650.
For similar type see North China PP1.

PORT ARTHUR AND DAIREN

The Liaoning Postal Administration was established on April 1, 1946, in accordance with the Sino-Soviet Treaty, but was renamed one week later the Port Arthur and Dairen Postal Administration. On Apr. 3, 1947, it was combined with telecommunications and renamed the Kwantung Post and Telegraph General Administration.

On May 1, 1949, the name was again changed to Port Arthur and Dairen Post and Telegraph Administration. Postal tariffs were based on local currency and both Manchukuo and Japanese stamps were overprinted for use.

Gum

#2L1-2L55 were issued with gum.

Manchukuo Nos. 162 and 94 Handstamp Surcharged in Violet ("Liaoning Post")

1946, Mar. 15

2L1 A19 20f on 30f buff 72.50 72.50
2L2 A18 1y on 12f org 37.50 37.50

Same Surcharge on Japan Nos. 260, 337, 195, 244, 263, 342 in Violet, Red or Black

1946, Apr. 1

2L3 A85 20f on 3s grn (V) 19.50 *21.00*
2L4 A151 1y on 17s gray vio (R) 16.00 *18.00*
2L5 A57 5y on 6s car 29.00 27.50
2L6 A57 5y on 6s crim 29.00 27.50
2L7 A88 5y on 6s org 22.00 20.00
2L8 A154 15y on 40s dk vio 110.00 *125.00*
Nos. 2L1-2L8 (8) 335.50 349.00

Surcharge sideways on Nos. 2L5-2L6.

Japan Nos. 260 and 263 Surcharged

1946, Apr.

2L9 A85 1y on 3s grn —
2L10 A88 5y on 6s org —

Sha Ho Kow (suburb of Dairen) issue. The status of this issue is in question.

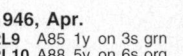

Manchukuo Nos. 84, 88 and 98 Handstamp Surcharged in Green, Red or Black

1946, May 1

2L11 A16 1y on 1f red brn (G) 18.00 *24.00*
2L12 A18 5y on 4f lt ol grn (R) 24.00 *32.50*
2L13 A19 15y on 30f chnt brn 52.50 *62.50*
Nos. 2L11-2L13 (3) 94.50 *119.00*

Transfer of postal administration and Labor Day.

Manchukuo Nos. 159, 86 and 94 Surcharged in Green, Red or Black

1946, July 7

2L14 A17 1y on 6f crim rose (G) 11.50 *20.00*
2L15 A17 5y on 2f lt grn (R) 52.50 *85.00*
2L16 A18 15y on 12f dp org 110.00 110.00
Nos. 2L14-2L16 (3) 174.00 215.00

Outbreak of war with Japan, 9th anniv.

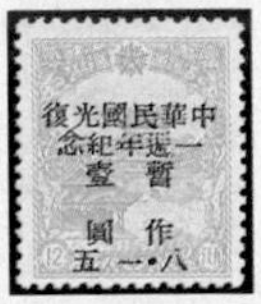

Manchukuo Nos. 94, 84 and 158 Surcharged in Black, Green or Red

1946, Aug. 15

2L17 A18 1y on 12f dp org 22.50 *27.50*
2L18 A16 5y on 1f red brn (G) 52.50 50.00
2L19 A10 15y on 5f gray blk (R) 110.00 100.00
Nos. 2L17-2L19 (3) 185.00 177.50

Surrender of Japan, first anniversary.

Manchukuo Nos. 159, 94 and 86 Surcharged in Green, Black or Red

1946, Oct. 10

2L20 A17 1y on 6f crim rose (G) 32.50 30.00
2L21 A18 5y on 12f dp org 57.50 55.00
2L22 A17 15y on 2f lt grn (R) 110.00 100.00
Nos. 2L20-2L22 (3) 200.00 185.00

35th anniversary of Chinese revolution.

Manchukuo Nos. 84, 159 and 94 Surcharged in Black, Green or Blue

1946, Oct. 19

2L23 A16 1y on 1f red brn 47.50 45.00
2L24 A17 5y on 6f crim rose (G) 87.50 85.00
2L25 A18 15y on 12f dp org (Bl) 125.00 125.00
Nos. 2L23-2L25 (3) 260.00 255.00

10th anniversary of the death of Lu Hsun (1881-1936), writer.

Manchukuo Nos. 86, 159 and 95 Surcharged in Red, Green or Black

1947, Feb. 20

2L26 A17 1y on 2f lt grn (R) 80.00 77.50
2L27 A17 5y on 6f crim rose (G) 160.00 150.00
2L28 A18 15y on 13f dk red brn 325.00 300.00
Nos. 2L26-2L28 (3) 565.00 527.50

29th anniversary of the Red (USSR) Army.

Manchukuo Nos. 86, 159 and 162 Surcharged in Red, Green or Black

1947, May 1

2L29 A17 1y on 2f lt grn (R) 24.00 24.00
2L30 A17 5y on 6f crim rose (G) 67.50 65.00
2L31 A19 15y on 30f buff 110.00 100.00
Nos. 2L29-2L31 (3) 201.50 189.00

Labor Day.

Manchukuo Nos. 86, 88, 98 and 162 Surcharged ("Kwantung Postal Service, China")

1947, Sept. 15

2L32 A17 5y on 2f lt grn 40.00 40.00
2L33 A18 15y on 4f lt ol grn 65.00 62.50
2L34 A19 20y on 30f red brn 100.00 95.00
2L35 A19 20y on 30f buff 110.00 100.00
Nos. 2L32-2L35 (4) 315.00 297.50

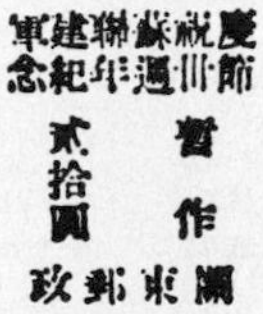

Manchukuo Nos. 86 and 159 Surcharged in Red and Green

Sacred Golden Kite (same size) — A1

1948, Feb. 20

2L36 A17 10y on 2f lt grn (R) 140.00 140.00
2L37 A17 20y on 6f crim rose (G) 175.00 175.00
2L38 A1 100y on bl & red brn 725.00 725.00

30th anniversary of the Red (USSR) Army. No. 2L38 is on an ungummed label for the 2600th anniv. of the Japanese Empire.

Japan No. 260 and Manchukuo Nos. 84, 86 and 88 Surcharged in Red, Blue or Black

1948, July

2L39 A85 5y on 3s grn (R) 125.00 125.00
2L40 A16 10y on 1f red brn (Bl) 225.00 250.00
2L41 A17 50y on 2f lt grn 500.00 475.00
2L42 A18 100y on 4f lt ol grn (R) 875.00 900.00

Smaller Characters on Bottom Line

2L43 A17 10y on 2f lt grn (R) 300.00 225.00
2L44 A16 50y on 1f red brn 350.00 300.00

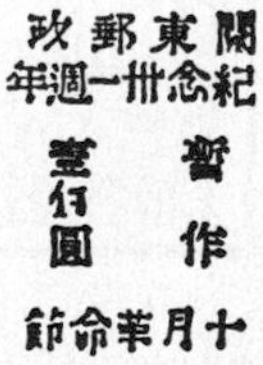

Stamps of Manchukuo Nos. 84, 86 and 88 Surcharged in Blue, Red or Black

1948, Nov. 1

2L45 A16 10y on 1f red brn (Bl) 275.00 600.00
2L46 A17 50y on 2f lt grn (R) 450.00 600.00
2L47 A18 100y on 4f lt ol grn 1,100. 600.00

31st anniversary of the Russian Revolution.

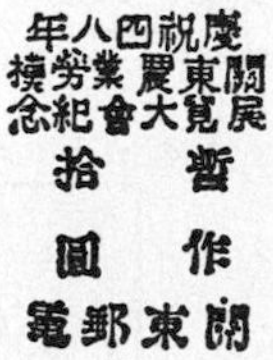

Manchukuo Nos. 86 and 161 Surcharged in Red or Green

1948, Nov. 15

2L48 A17 10y on 2f lt grn 1,050. 1,050.
2L49 A17 50y on 20f brn (G) 1,200. 1,200.

Kwantung Agricultural and Industrial Exhibition.

Manchukuo Nos. 86, 88 and 161 Surcharged in Red, Black or Green

1949, Jan.

2L50 A17 20y on 2f lt grn (R) 500.00
2L51 A18 50y on 4f lt ol grn 700.00
2L52 A17 100y on 20f brn (G) 700.00

Without Gum

From No. 2L56 onward all stamps were issued without gum except as noted.

Farmer and Worker — A2

Train and Ship — A3

Ship at Dock (No. 2L55) — A4

(No. 2L56)

1949 Litho. *Perf. 11, 11½*

2L53 A2 5y pale grn 2.25 *4.00*
2L54 A3 10y orange 12.00 11.00
2L55 A4 50y vermilion 17.50 16.00
2L56 A4 50y red (redrawn) 24.00 24.00
Nos. 2L53-2L56 (4) 55.75 55.00

Issue dates: #2L56, July 7; others Apr. 1.
For surcharges see Nos. 2L62-2L66.

Worker, Flag and Means of Transport A5

1949, May 1 *Perf. 11*

2L57 A5 10y rose pink 17.50 *18.00*
a. 10y vermilion 75.00 75.00

Labor Day. #2L57a is from a worn plate.

Mao Tse-tung and Red Flag — A6

Heroes Monument, Dairen — A7

1949, July 1

2L59 A6 50y red 32.50 35.00

28th anniversary of the founding of the Chinese Communist Party.

1949, Sept.

2L60 A7 10y red, bl & olive 16.00 13.00
a. 10y red, blue & pale blue 100.00 85.00

4th anniversary of victory over Japan and opening of the Dairen Industrial Fair.

Nos. 2L53-2L54 Surcharged in Red or Black

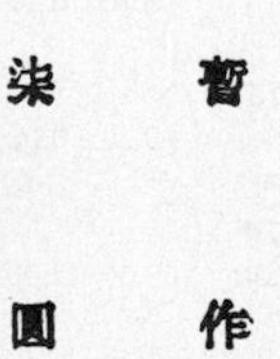

a

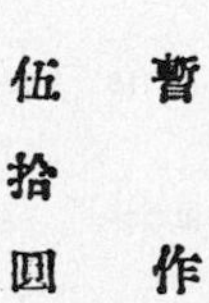

b

c

1949, Sept. With Gum

2L62 A2(a) 7y on 5y (R) 37.50 32.50
2L63 A2(a) 7y on 5y 35.00 32.50
2L64 A2(b) 50y on 5y (R) 90.00 80.00
2L65 A3(b) 100y on 10y 450.00 350.00
2L66 A3(c) 500y on 10y (R) 600.00 400.00
Nos. 2L62-2L66 (5) 1,212. 895.00

Size of surcharge on No. 2L63: 16x19mm.
A 500y on 5y, red surcharge "c," and a 500y on 10y orange, surcharge "b" were prepared but not issued.

Stalin and Lenin — A8

1949, Nov. 7 *Perf. 11x11½*

2L68 A8 10y dl bl grn (shades) 15.00 *16.00*

32nd anniversary of the Russian Revolution.

Workers Saluting Mao, Star and Flag — A9

1949, Nov. 16 *Perf. 11*

2L69 A9 35y dk bl, red, & yel 20.00 20.00

Founding of the People's Republic of China.

Stalin — A10

(same size) Gate of Heavenly Peace — A11

1949, Dec. 20 *Perf. 11½*

2L70 A10 20y dull magenta 37.50 *40.00*
2L71 A10 35y rose red 37.50 *40.00*

70th birthday of Stalin.

1950, Mar. 10 Typo. *Perf. 10½*

2L72 A11 10y Prus blue *210.00* *85.00*
2L73 A11 20y dull grn *110.00* *110.00*
2L74 A11 35y red *22.50* *22.50*
2L75 A11 50y deep pur *16.00* *16.00*
2L76 A11 100y lilac rose *22.50* *22.50*
Nos. 2L72-2L76 (5) *381.00* *256.00*

NORTH CHINA

The North China Liberation Area included the provinces of Hopeh, Chahar, Shansi and Suiyuan. The original postal service, begun in the Shansi-Hopeh-Chahar Border Area in December, 1937, became the North China Postal and Telegraph Administration in May, 1949.

All Stamps Issued without Gum Except as Noted

Large Victory Issue

Cavalry Man Holding Nationalist Flag — A1

Wmk. Wavy Lines

1946, Mar. *Perf. 10½*

Granite Paper

Size: 34½x42mm

3L1 A1 $1 red brown 1.25 1.40
a. Newsprint 10.00 12.00
3L2 A1 $2 gray grn 1.25 1.25
3L3 A1 $4 vermilion 1.40 1.25
3L4 A1 $5 vio brn 4.25 1.25
3L5 A1 $8 vio bl 4.25 1.25
3L6 A1 $10 dp car 1.40 1.25
3L7 A1 $12 yellow 4.00 4.50
3L8 A1 $20 lt green 8.50 8.00
Nos. 3L1-3L8 (8) 26.30 20.15

Defeat of Japan.

Small Victory Issue

Perf. 10½x10, 9½ rough

1946, May Unwmk.

Granite paper

Size: 20x21mm

3L9 A1 $1 red org 1.50 *2.00*
3L10 A1 $2 green 2.40 2.00
3L11 A1 $3 lt lilac 4.50 *8.00*
3L12 A1 $5 dull pur 6.00 .35
3L13 A1 $8 dk blue 12.50 *16.00*
3L14 A1 $10 rose red 2.40 *4.00*
3L15 A1 $15 purple *50.00* *40.00*
3L16 A1 $20 green 4.50 *6.00*
3L17 A1 $30 brt grnsh bl 3.75 *7.00*
3L18 A1 $40 brt rose lilac 4.50 3.00
3L19 A1 $50 brown *26.00* .70
3L20 A1 $60 myrtle green *50.00* 1.50

Wmk. Wavy Lines

3L21 A1 $100 orange 1.60 *4.00*
3L22 A1 $200 dull blue 1.60 *4.00*
3L23 A1 $500 rose 47.50 *50.00*
Nos. 3L9-3L23 (15) *218.75* *148.55*

North China Postal and Telegraph Administration

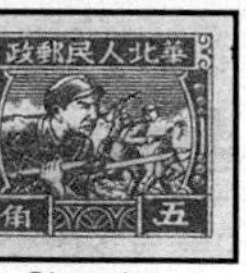

Charging Infantrymen A2

Agriculture and Industry A3

1949, Jan. Unwmk. *Imperf.*

White Paper

3L24 A2 50c brown lake 1.10 1.10
3L25 A2 $1 Prussian blue 1.10 1.10

Newsprint

3L26 A2 $2 apple green 1.10 1.10
3L27 A2 $3 dull violet 1.10 1.10
3L28 A2 $5 brown 1.10 1.10
3L29 A3 $6 deep rose 1.10 1.10
a. White paper 1.10 1.10
3L30 A2 $10 blue grn .40 *.50*
3L31 A2 $12 dp car 1.25 1.25
Nos. 3L24-3L31 (8) 8.25 8.35

No. 3L29 issued in Peking, others in Tientsin.

Remittance Stamps of China Surcharged

A4

壹
$1

叁
$3

1949, Jan. **Engr.** ***Perf. 13***

Small Central Characters

3L32 A4 50c on $50 brn blk 3.25 *3.50*
3L33 A4 $1 on $50 gray blk 2.25 *2.75*
3L34 A4 $3 on $50 gray 2.50 2.50

Large Central Characters

3L35 A4 50c on $50 blk 1.60 1.60
3L36 A4 $6 on $20 dk vio brn 1.60 1.60
Nos. 3L32-3L36 (5) 11.20 11.95

Issued in Tientsin.
For surcharges see Nos. 3LQ10-3LQ21.

Sun Yat-sen Type A2 of Northeastern Provinces and China No. 640 Surcharged in Black, Red, Green or Blue

#3L37-3L45, 3L47-3L50, 3L52

#3L46, 3L51, 3L53

c

Type "b," bottom character of left vertical row (yuan) differs. Type "c," top character of right vertical row differs.

1949, Mar. 7 ***Perf. 14***

3L37 A2 50c on 5c lake .45 *2.40*
3L38 A2 $1 on 10c org .45 *1.90*
3L39 A2 $2 on 20c yel grn 42.50 22.50
3L40 A2 $3 on 50c red org .45 *1.50*
3L41 A2 $4 on $5 dk grn 4.75 1.90
3L42 A2 $6 on $10 crim 1.50 *1.90*
3L43 A2 $10 on $300 bluish grn 3.00 *3.75*
3L44 A2 $12 on $1 bl 1.25 *2.75*
3L45 A2 $18 on $3 brn 1.25 *1.40*
3L46 A2 $20 on 50c red org (Bl) 1.50 1.25
3L47 A2 $20 on $20 ol, II 3.00 *4.00*
a. Type I 12.00 *13.50*
3L48 A2 $30 on $2.50 ind (R) 3.00 *3.75*
3L49 A2 $40 on 25c blk brn (R) 4.50 *5.75*
3L50 A2 $50 on $109 dk grn (R) 9.50 7.75
3L51 A2 $80 on $1 bl (R) 12.50 4.00
3L52 A2 $100 on $65 dl grn (R) 16.00 7.75
3L53 A73 $100 on $100 dk car, surch. 16mm wide (Bl) 20.00 2.75
a. Surcharge 14mm wide 20.00 10.00

1949, Apr.

3L55 A2 (c) $2 on 20c yel grn 1.50 *2.75*
3L56 A2 (c) $3 on 50c red org .75 *1.90*
3L57 A2 (c) $4 on $5 dk grn 6.00 3.75
3L58 A2 (c) $6 on $10 crim, I 4.25 3.75
a. Type II 15.00 10.00
3L59 A2 (c) $12 on $1 blue 1.50 *1.50*

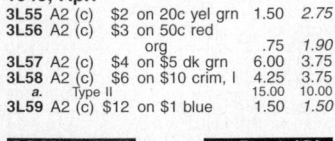

d

e

1949, Apr.

Type "d"

3L60 A2 $1 on 25c blk grn (G) .45 *1.10*
3L61 A2 $10 on $300 bluish grn (R) 9.50 5.25
3L62 A2 $20 on 50c red org (G) 18.00 *22.50*
3L63 A2 $20 on $20 ol (R) 6.50 3.75
3L64 A2 $40 on 25c blk brn (R) 6.50 4.50
3L65 A2 $50 on $109 dk grn, surch. 15mm wide (R) 9.50 *11.50*
a. Surcharge 13mm wide 30.00 *30.00*
3L66 A2 $80 on $1 bl (R) 6.50 5.75

Type "d" On Stamps on China

3L67 A73 $100 on $100 dk car (G) 52.50 30.00
3L68 A73 $300 on $700 red brn (Bl) 11.00 11.00
3L69 A82 $500 on $500 bl grn (R) 8.00 3.75
3L70 A82 $3000 on $3000 bl (R) 12.00 7.50

Type "e" On Stamps of Northeastern Provinces

1949, Aug.

3L71 A2 $10 on $10 crim, II (Bl) 6.50 3.00
a. Type I 12.50 12.00
3L72 A2 $30 on 20c yel grn (R) 6.50 1.90
3L73 A2 $50 on $44 dk car rose (Bl) 6.50 1.00
3L74 A2 $100 on $3 brn (Bl) 12.00 5.75
3L75 A2 $200 on $4 org brn, II (Bl) 30.00 19.00
a. Type I 1,100. 450.00

On China No. 754 in Blue

3L76 A82 $10 on $7000 lt red brn 11.00 7.75
Nos. 3L37-3L76 (39) 352.55 235.65

Overprints on Nos. 3L71 and 3L76 have 2 characters in center row.

Farmer and Worker on Globe — A5

1949, May 1 **Engr.** ***Perf. 14***

3L77 A5 $20 crimson 1.75 .65
3L78 A5 $40 dark blue 1.75 .80
3L79 A5 $60 brown org 1.75 .65
3L80 A5 $80 dk green 1.75 1.00
3L81 A5 $100 purple 1.75 1.00
Nos. 3L77-3L81 (5) 8.75 4.10

Labor day. Exists imperf. Value, set $12.50. Also issued in blocks of 4, imperf between. Value, unused or used, $13.50.

Mao Tse-tung (Chinese Numeral) — A6

Mao Tse-tung (Arabic Numeral) — A7

1949, July 1 ***Perf. 14***

3L82 A6 $10 red .80 *.60*
3L83 A7 $20 dk blue .80 *.60*
3L84 A6 $50 orange 5.00 .60
3L85 A7 $80 dk green 1.00 *1.00*
3L86 A6 $100 purple 5.00 1.00
3L87 A7 $120 olive .70 *1.00*
3L88 A6 $140 vio brn 5.00 1.00
Nos. 3L82-3L88 (7) 18.30 5.80

28th anniv. of the founding of the Chinese Communist Party. Value, imperf, set $40.

Gate of Heavenly Peace — A8

Farmers and Factory — A9

1949, Nov. 26 **Litho.** ***Perf. 12½***

3L89 A8 $50 orange .30 *3.50*
3L90 A8 $100 crimson .30 *1.00*
3L91 A8 $200 green .70 *1.00*
3L92 A8 $300 rose brn 9.00 2.25
3L93 A8 $400 blue 9.00 2.25
3L94 A8 $500 brown 9.00 1.25
3L95 A8 $700 violet 3.25 3.50
Nos. 3L89-3L95 (7) 31.55 14.75

1949, Dec. **Engr.** ***Perf. 14***

3L96 A9 $1000 orange 2.75 1.50
3L97 A9 $3000 dark blue .30 *1.25*
3L98 A9 $5000 crimson .30 *2.40*
3L99 A9 $10,000 red brown .30 *4.75*
Nos. 3L96-3L99 (4) 3.65 *9.90*

NORTH CHINA PARCEL POST STAMPS

Parcel Post Stamps of China Nos. Q23-Q27 (Type PP3) Surcharged in Red, Black (#3LQ6-3LQ9) or Blue (#3LQ2)

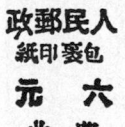

政郵民人
元百捌
北 華
a

作圓佰伍暫
電郵北華
作 暫
500
b

1949, June

Surcharged Type "a"

3LQ1 $300 on $6,000,000 55.00
3LQ2 $400 on $8,000,000 55.00
3LQ3 $500 on $10,000,000 55.00
3LQ4 $800 on $5,000,000 55.00
3LQ5 $1000 on $3,000,000 75.00

Surcharged Type "b"

3LQ6 $500 on $3,000,000 75.00
3LQ7 $1000 on $5,000,000 90.00
3LQ8 $3000 on $8,000,000 225.00
3LQ9 $5000 on $10,000,000 300.00
Nos. 3LQ1-3LQ9 (9) 985.00

Nos. 3LQ8-3LQ9 have large numerals unboxed.

Remittance Stamps of China (like North China Type A4) Surcharged in Black or Red

政郵民人
紙印褒包
元 六
北 華
a

b

Peking Surcharge "a"

1949, June **Litho.** ***Perf. 13***

3LQ10 $6 on $5 ver 11.00 3.50
3LQ11 $20 on $50 gray 11.00 3.50
3LQ12 $50 on $20 dk vio brn 11.00 3.50
3LQ13 $100 on $10 ol grn 11.00 7.00

Tientsin Surcharge "b"

Engr. ***Perf. 14***

3LQ14 $20 on $1 brn org 13.00 6.00
a. Perf. 12½ 22.50 7.50
3LQ15 $30 on $2 dk grn 13.00 5.00
a. Red surcharge 22.50 11.00
3LQ16 $30 on $10 ol grn *100.00* *42.50*
3LQ17 $100 on $10 gray grn (R) 13.00 6.00

Litho.
Perf. 13

3LQ18 $50 on $5 red 13.00 6.00

Engr.
Perf. 14

3LQ19 $20 on $1 org brn 37.50 17.00

Perf. 12½

3LQ20 $100 on $10 yel grn (R) 62.50 30.00

Typo.
Roulette 9½

3LQ21 $30 on $2 bl grn (R) 47.50 20.00

The surcharge on No. 3LQ19 is without first and last lines.

Nos. 3LQ14, 3LQ14a, 3LQ15, 3LQ15a, 3LQ16-3LQ17, 3LQ19-3LQ20 issued with gum.

Locomotive — PP1

1949, Nov. **Engr.** ***Perf. 14***

3LQ22 PP1 $500 crimn 9.00 13.00
3LQ23 PP1 $1000 dp bl *65.00* 22.50
3LQ24 PP1 $2000 green *65.00* 32.50
3LQ25 PP1 $5000 dp ol *100.00* 70.00
3LQ26 PP1 $10,000 orange *175.00* 130.00
3LQ27 PP1 $20,000 red brn *350.00* 325.00
3LQ28 PP1 $50,000 brn pur *750.00* 625.00
Nos. 3LQ22-3LQ28 (7) *1,493.* 1,206.

NORTHWEST CHINA

The Northwest China Liberation Area consisted of the provinces of Sinkiang, Tsinghai, Ningsia and the western part of Shensi. The area was first established as the Shensi-Kansu-Ningsia Border Area in October, 1936, after the Long March to Yenan. Remote Sinkiang was not included until late 1949.

All Stamps Issued without Gum

Pagoda on Yenan Hill — A1

1945, Mar. **Litho.** ***Imperf.***

4L1 A1 $1 green 23.00
4L2 A1 $5 dk blue 125.00
4L3 A1 $10 rose red 19.00
4L4 A1 $50 dull pur 24.00
4L5 A1 $100 yel org 45.00
Nos. 4L1-4L5 (5) 236.00

Rouletted 9

4L1a A1 $1 82.50
4L2a A1 $5 125.00
4L3a A1 $10 82.50

First issue; denomination in Chinese and Arabic. Heavy shading at top of vignette. Columns at sides.

See types A2, A3 and A4. For surcharges see Nos. 4L6-4L10, 4L23.

Nos. 4L1-4L2 Surcharged in Red:

a

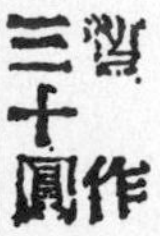
b

c

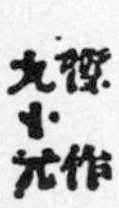
d

1946, Nov.

4L6 A1 (a) $30 on $1 grn 25.00
4L7 A1 (b) $30 on $1 grn *125.00*
a. Rectangular lower left character *1,000.*
4L8 A1 (c) $30 on $1 grn 15.00
4L9 A1 (b) $60 on $1 grn 2,500.
4L10 A1 (d) $90 on $5 dk bl 24.00

Surcharge on Nos. 4L7a is type "b" as illustrated. Surcharge on No. 4L7 differs from "b," having lower left character as in type "a."

Surcharge on No. 4L9 the upper left surcharge character differs from that shown in "b."

A2

Pagoda on Yenan Hill (same size) — A3

1948, June

4L11 A2 $100 buff 160.00
4L12 A2 $300 rose pink 6.00
4L13 A2 $500 red 6.00
4L14 A2 $1000 blue 6.00
4L15 A2 $2000 yel grn 20.00
4L16 A2 $5000 dull pur 18.00
Nos. 4L11-4L16 (6) 216.00

Second issue; denominations in Chinese only. Many shades and proofs exist.

For surcharge see No. 4L24.

1948, Dec.

4L17 A3 10c yel org 1.75
4L18 A3 20c lemon 1.75
4L19 A3 $1 dk blue 1.75
4L20 A3 $2 vermilion 1.75
4L21 A3 $5 pale bl grn 9.50
4L22 A3 $10 violet 14.50
Nos. 4L17-4L22 (6) 31.00

Third issue; ornamental border at sides. Many shades exist.

Nos. 4L2 and 4L13 Surcharged in Red or Black

1949, Jan.

4L23 A1 $1 on $5 dk bl 40.00
4L24 A2 $2 on $500 red 25.00

Pagoda on Yenan Hill — A4

1949, May 1

4L25 A4 50c yel to olive .50 .45
4L26 A4 $1 dl bl to indigo .50 .45
4L27 A4 $3 ol yel to org yel .50 .45
4L28 A4 $5 blue green 1.75 .50
a. Upper left character as on #4L25
4L29 A4 $10 vio to dp vio 4.50 *5.50*
4L30 A4 $20 pink to rose red 9.00 *12.00*
Nos. 4L25-4L30 (6) 16.75 19.35

Fourth issue; light shading at top of vignette, columns without ornaments at sides. Many shades exist.

人民郵政(陝)

China Nos. 959, F2 and E12 Overprinted ("People's Post, Shensi")

1949, June 13 Engr. *Perf. 12½*

4L31 A96 orange 16.00 16.00
4L32 R2 carmine 29.00 29.00
4L33 SD2 red vio 29.00 29.00
Nos. 4L31-4L33 (3) 74.00 74.00

Stamps of China, Sun Yat-sen Type A94 of 1949, Overprinted in Black or Red ("People's Post, Shensi")

Lithographed; Engraved

1949, July 1 *Perf. 14, 12½*

4L34 $10 green (887) 1.25 1.25
4L35 $20 vio brn (888) 1.25 *2.25*
4L36 $20 vio brn (896) 1.25 1.25
4L37 $50 dk Prus grn (889; R) 6.00 5.25
4L38 $50 grn (951) 6.00 5.25
4L39 $100 org brn (890) 14.50 6.25
4L40 $500 ros lil (892) 20.00 6.25
4L41 $1000 dp bl (952; R) 27.50 15.00
4L42 $2000 vio (902;R) 27.50 18.00
4L43 $5000 car (953) 40.00 37.50
4L44 $10,000 brn (954) 75.00 75.00
Nos. 4L34-4L44 (11) 220.25 173.25

Kansu-Ningsia-Tsinghai Area, Lanchow Overprints

China Nos. 959a, F2 and E12 Overprinted ("People's Post, Kansu")

1949, Oct. Engr. *Rouletted*

4L45 A96 orange 16.00 10.00

Perf. 12½

4L46 R2 carmine 20.00 17.00
4L47 SD2 red vio 20.00 20.00
Nos. 4L45-4L47 (3) 56.00 47.00

Stamps of China, Sun Yat-sen Type A94 of 1949, Overprinted ("People's Post, Kansu")

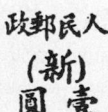

Engraved; Lithographed

1949, Oct. *Perf. 14, 12½*

4L48 $10 grn (887) 2.25 2.25
4L49 $20 vio brn (888) 2.25 3.25
4L50 $50 dk Prus grn (889) 5.25 *8.25*
4L51 $100 org brn (890) 3.50 3.25
4L52 $100 dk org brn (898) 5.25 *6.00*
4L53 $200 red org (891) 6.50 5.25
4L54 $500 rose lil (892) 6.50 5.25
4L55 $1000 blue (894) 3.50 3.25
4L56 $1000 dp bl (901) 6.50 *7.50*
4L57 $2000 vio (902) 11.00 *15.00*
4L58 $5000 lt bl (903) 22.00 *27.50*
4L59 $10,000 sepia (904) 30.00 *37.50*
4L60 $20,000 ap grn (905) 60.00 *72.50*
Nos. 4L48-4L60 (13) 164.50 196.75

No. 4L54-4L60 exist with wider spaced overprints.

China Nos. 959, F2 and 791-792 Surcharged in Black or Red ("People's Post, Sinkiang")

政郵民人 (新) 圓壹

1949, Oct.

4L61 A96 $1 on org 10.00 11.00
4L62 R2 $3 on car 16.00 19.00
4L63 A82 10c on $50,000 dp bl (R) 30.00 30.00
4L64 A82 $1.50 on $100,000 dl grn (R) 60.00 60.00
Nos. 4L61-4L64 (4) 116.00 120.00

Northwest People's Post

Mao Tse-tung — A5

Great Wall — A6

1949, Oct. 15 Litho. *Imperf.*

4L65 A5 $50 rose 1.75 *2.50*
a. $200 cliche in $50 plate 200.00
4L66 A6 $100 dark blue 1.00 *1.10*
4L67 A5 $200 orange 1.00 *4.00*
4L68 A6 $400 sepia 3.50 4.00
Nos. 4L65-4L68 (4) 7.25 *11.60*

EAST CHINA

The East China Liberation Area included the provinces of Shantung, Kiangsu, Chekiang, Anhwei and Fukien. The original postal service established in Shantung in 1941, became the East China Posts and Telegraph General Office in July, 1948.

All Stamps Issued without Gum

Mao Tse-tung — A1

Transportation and Tower — A2

1948, Mar. Litho. *Perf. 10½*

5L1 A1 $50 yel org 1.60 1.50
5L2 A1 $100 dp rose 4.25 2.50
5L3 A1 $200 dk vio bl 4.25 2.50
5L4 A1 $300 brt grn 5.25 2.50
5L5 A1 $500 dp blue 2.00 2.50
5L6 A1 $800 vermilion 5.25 1.75
5L7 A1 $1000 dk blue 8.00 8.00
5L8 A1 $5000 rose 18.00 18.00
5L9 A1 $10,000 dp car 45.00 45.00
Nos. 5L1-5L9 (9) 93.60 84.25

Many varieties, including unissued imperforates exist.

Perf. 9 to 11 and compound

1949, Apr. Litho.

5L10 A2 $1 yel grn .25 .20
5L11 A2 $2 blue grn .25 .20
5L12 A2 $3 dull red .25 .20
5L13 A2 $5 pale brn (ovpt. 4x4mm) .25 .20
a. Without overprint 65.00 65.00
b. Overprint 3x3mm 1.25 1.00
c. As "b," purple overprint 65.00
5L14 A2 $10 ultra .25 .20
5L15 A2 $13 brt vio .25 .20
5L16 A2 $18 brt blue .25 .20
5L17 A2 $21 vermilion .25 .20
5L18 A2 $30 gray .25 .30
5L19 A2 $50 crimson .40 *.55*
5L20 A2 $100 olive 16.00 9.50
Nos. 5L10-5L20 (11) 18.65 11.95

Seventh anniv. of Shantung Communist Postal Administration. The overprint on the $5, character "yu" meaning "Posts," obliterates Japanese flag on tower, erroneously included in design. Value, imperfs. of Nos. 5L10-5L12, 5L13c, 5L14-5L20 on different paper, set $125.

Train and Postal Runner (1949.2.7) — A3

Mao, Soldiers, Map — A4

1949, Apr. Litho. *Perf. 8 to 11*

5L21 A3 $1 brt emer .20 .20
5L22 A3 $2 blue grn .20 .20
5L23 A3 $3 dk red .20 .20
5L24 A3 $5 brown .25 .25
5L25 A3 $10 ultra .45 .25
5L26 A3 $13 brt vio .25 .25
5L27 A3 $18 brt blue .25 .25
5L28 A3 $21 vermilion .25 .25
5L29 A3 $30 slate .25 *.35*
5L30 A3 $50 crimson .35 .35
5L31 A3 $100 olive .75 .70
Nos. 5L21-5L31 (11) 3.40 3.25

7th anniv. of Shantung P. O., Feb. 7. Imperf. sets were sold by the Philatelic Dept., Tientsin P.O. Value $40. See Nos. 5L69-5L76. For surcharges see People's Republic of China Nos. 77-81.

Perf. 9½ to 11 and comp.

1949, Apr.

5L32 A4 $1 brt emer .20 .20
5L33 A4 $2 blue grn .20 .20
5L34 A4 $3 dull red .20 .20
5L35 A4 $5 brown .20 .20
5L36 A4 $10 ultra .25 .20
5L37 A4 $13 brt vio .25 .25
5L38 A4 $18 brt blue .25 .25
5L39 A4 $21 vermilion .25 .25
5L40 A4 $30 gray .25 .25
5L41 A4 $50 crimson .25 .25
5L42 A4 $100 olive 2.25 2.25
Nos. 5L32-5L42 (11) 4.55 4.50

Victory of Hwai-Hai (Hwaiying and Haichow). Imperf. sets were sold by the Philatelic Dept., Tientsin P.O. Value, set $100.

Stamps of China, Sun Yat-sen Type of 1949, Surcharged in Red or Black

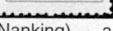

(Nanking) — a

(Wuhu) — b

1949, May 4 Engr. *Perf. 12½*

5L43 A94 (a) $1 on $10 grn (895, R) .55 .50
a. Perf. 13 3.25 3.00
5L44 A94 (a) $3 on $20 vio brn (896) .55 .55
a. Perf. 13 .75 2.25
b. Perf. 14 5.75 5.50
c. Surcharge inverted 200.00

Sun Yat-sen Type A94 Surcharged Type "b"

Lithographed, Engraved

1949, May *Perf. 12½, 14*

5L45 $30 on $1000 dp bl (901 8.00 6.00
5L46 $30 on $1000 bl (894) 8.00 6.00
5L47 $50 on $200 org red (899) 8.00 6.00
5L48 $100 on $5000 lt bl (903, R) 16.00 16.00
5L49 $300 on $10,000 sep (904, R) 50.00 50.00
5L50 $500 on $200 org red (899) 75.00 75.00
Nos. 5L45-5L50 (6) 165.00 159.00

Many varieties exist.

China Nos. 913a and 913 Surcharged in Blue, Green, Black or Red

(East China)

1949, May Litho. *Perf. 12½*

5L51 A95	$5 on 50c on $20 brn, II (B)	14.00	13.00
a.	Green surcharge	100.00	100.00
5L52 A95	$10 on 50c on $20 brn, II	14.00	14.00
5L53 A95	$20 on 50c on $20 red brn, II (R)	14.00	14.00
a.	Type I (R)	21.00	21.00
	Nos. 5L51-5L53 (3)	42.00	41.00

Stamps of China, Sun Yat-sen Type of 1949, Surcharged in Black or Red

(Hangchow)

Engr., Litho. (No. 5L57)

1949, June 25 *Perf. 14, 12½*

5L54 A94	$1 on $1 org (886)	1.50	1.60
5L55 A94	$3 on $20 vio brn (896, R)	.80	.80
5L56 A94	$5 on $100 org brn (890)	4.00	4.00
5L57 A94	$5 on $100 dk org brn (898)	1.90	1.50
5L58 A94	$10 on $50 dk Prus grn (889, R)	13.00	13.00
5L59 A94	$13 on $10 grn (895)	1.00	*1.00*
	Nos. 5L54-5L59 (6)	22.20	21.90

East China Liberation Area

Maps of Shanghai and Nanking — A5

1949, May 30 Litho. *Perf. 8½ to 11*

5L60 A5	$1 orange ver	.20	*.30*
5L61 A5	$2 blue green	.20	*.30*
5L62 A5	$3 brt violet	.25	*.25*
5L63 A5	$5 violet brn	.25	*.25*
5L64 A5	$10 ultra	.25	*.25*
5L65 A5	$30 slate	.25	*.30*
5L66 A5	$50 carmine	.25	*.60*
5L67 A5	$100 olive	.25	*.45*
5L68 A5	$500 orange	4.00	2.25
	Nos. 5L60-5L68 (9)	5.90	*4.95*

Liberation of Shanghai and Nanking. Many shades, paper and perforation varieties and imperfs. exist.

Train and Postal Runner Type Dated "1949"

1949, July-1950, Feb. *Perf. 12½, 14*

5L69 A3	$10 dp ultra	.25	*.25*
5L70 A3	$15 orange ver	.25	*.45*
a.	$15 red, perf. 14	.50	.30
5L71 A3	$30 slate green	.25	.25
a.	Perf. 12½	.50	.30
5L72 A3	$50 carmine	.25	*.50*
5L73 A3	$60 bl grn, perf. 14	.25	*1.00*
5L74 A3	$100 ol, perf. 14	2.50	.50
5L75 A3	$1600 vio bl ('50)	.60	*3.00*
5L76 A3	$2000 brn vio ('50)	.75	*3.00*
	Nos. 5L69-5L76 (8)	5.10	*8.95*

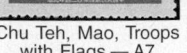

Chu Teh, Mao, Troops with Flags — A7

Mao Tse-tung — A8

1949, Aug. 17 *Perf. 12½*

5L77 A7	$70 orange	.20	*.25*
5L78 A7	$270 crimson	.20	*.25*
5L79 A7	$370 emerald	.35	.35
5L80 A7	$470 vio brn	.55	.45
5L81 A7	$570 blue	.25	*.40*
	Nos. 5L77-5L81 (5)	1.55	1.70

22nd anniv. of the People's Liberation Army. For similar type see Southwest China A1.

1949, Oct.

5L82 A8	$10 dk blue	2.25	*3.00*
5L83 A8	$15 vermilion	2.75	*3.75*
5L84 A8	$70 brown	.25	.20
5L85 A8	$100 vio brn	.25	.20
5L86 A8	$150 orange	.25	.25
5L87 A8	$200 grnsh gray	.25	.25
5L88 A8	$500 gray bl	.25	.25
5L89 A8	$1000 rose	.25	.25
5L90 A8	$2000 emerald	.25	.25
	Nos. 5L82-5L90 (9)	6.75	*8.40*

For surcharges see People's Republic of China Nos. 82-84.

Stamps of China, Sun Yat-sen Type of 1949 Surcharged in Black or Red

1949, Nov. Litho. *Perf. 12½*

5L91 A94	$400 on $200 org red (899)	22.50	1.50
5L92 A94	$1000 on $50 grnsh gray (897, R)	2.25	.70
5L93 A94	$1200 on $100 dk org brn (898)	.30	*1.50*
5L94 A94	$1600 on $20,000 ap grn (905)	.30	*3.00*
5L95 A94	$2000 on $1000 dp bl (952,R)	.30	*.75*
a.	Perf. 14	45.00	25.00
	Nos. 5L91-5L95 (5)	25.65	*7.45*

EAST CHINA PARCEL POST STAMPS

Parcel Post Stamps of China 1945-48 Surcharged

(Shantung)

1949, Aug. 1 Engr. *Perf. 13*

5LQ1 PP1	$200 on $500 grn	8.00	8.00
5LQ2 PP1	$500 on $1000 bl	18.00	18.00

Type PP3 *Perf. 13½*

5LQ3	$200 on $200,000 dk grn	16.00	16.00
5LQ4	$200 on $10,000,000 sage grn	14.00	14.00
5LQ5	$500 on $7000 dl bl	40.00	40.00
5LQ6	$500 on $50,000 indigo	10.00	10.00
5LQ7	$1000 on $10,000 car rose	10.00	10.00
5LQ8	$1000 on $100,000 dk rose brn	18.00	18.00
5LQ9	$1000 on $300,000 pink	10.00	10.00
5LQ10	$1000 on $500,000 vio brn	52.50	45.00
5LQ11	$1000 on $8,000,000 org ver	12.00	12.00
5LQ12	$2000 on $5,000,000 dl vio	30.00	30.00
5LQ13	$2000 on $6,000,000 brn blk	35.00	35.00
5LQ14	$3000 on $30,000 ol	35.00	35.00
5LQ15	$3000 on $70,000 org brn	24.00	24.00
5LQ16	$5000 on $3,000,000 dl bl	52.50	52.50
	Nos. 5LQ1-5LQ16 (16)	385.00	377.50

China Type A97, No. 987 Surcharged

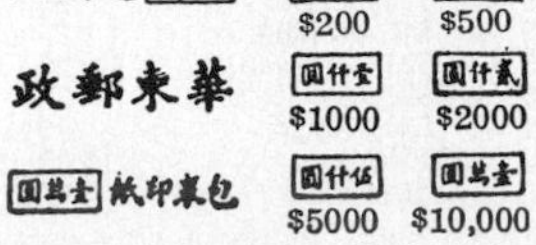

1949, Sept. 7 Litho. *Perf. 12½*

5LQ17	$200 on $10	35.00	15.00
5LQ18	$500 on $10	35.00	15.00
5LQ19	$1000 on $10	35.00	15.00
5LQ20	$2000 on $10	50.00	30.00
5LQ21	$5000 on $10	75.00	45.00
5LQ22	$10,000 on $10	150.00	60.00
	Nos. 5LQ17-5LQ22 (6)	380.00	180.00

Flying Geese Type of China, 1949, and China Nos. 984-986 Surcharged in Red or Black

1950, Jan. 28

5LQ23 A97	$5000 on 10c bl vio (R)	30.00	25.00
5LQ24 A97	$10,000 on $1 brn org	45.00	40.00
5LQ25 A97	$20,000 on $2 bl	75.00	70.00
5LQ26 A97	$50,000 on $5 car rose	130.00	130.00
	Nos. 5L23-5L26 (4)	280.00	265.00

Parcel Post Stamps of China Type PP3, Nos. Q1-Q2, Q12-Q13 Surcharged in Red or Black

1950, Jan. 28 Engr. *Perf. 13, 13½*

5LQ27	$5000 on $500 grn (R)	.60	*15.00*
5LQ28	$10,000 on $1000 bl (R)	75.00	60.00
5LQ29	$20,000 on $3000 bl grn	125.00	100.00
5LQ30	$50,000 on $5000 org red	7.50	*75.00*
	Nos. 5L27-5L30 (4)	208.10	250.00

CENTRAL CHINA

The Central Chinese Liberation Area included the provinces of Honan, Hupeh, Hunan and Kiangsi. The area was established between August and September, 1949, following the occupation of Hankow by Red Army forces.

All Stamps Issued without Gum

Hupeh Postal and Telegraph Administration

Stamps of China, Sun Yat-sen Type A94 of 1949, Surcharged ("Chinese P.O., Temporary Use")

Engraved; Lithographed

1949, June 4 *Perf. 14, 12½*

Thin parallel lines

6L1	$1 on $200 red org (891)	.85	*1.25*
6L2	$6 on $10,000 sep (904)	.85	*1.25*
6L3	$15 on $1 org (886)	.85	*1.25*
6L4	$30 on $100 org brn (890)	4.00	2.50
6L5	$30 on $100 dk org brn (898)	.85	*1.25*
6L6	$50 on $20 vio brn (896)	18.00	11.00
6L7	$80 on $1000 dp bl (901)	2.40	1.25

Thick parallel lines

6L8	$1 on $200 red org (891)	3.75	3.50
6L9	$3 on $5000 lt bl (903)	.65	*1.50*
6L10	$10 on $500 rose lil (892)	.65	*1.50*
6L11	$10 on $500 rose lil (900)	3.75	3.50
6L12	$50 on $20 vio brn (888)	3.75	3.50
6L13	$50 on $20 vio brn (896)	1.25	*3.00*
6L14	$80 on $1000 bl (894)	4.00	3.75
6L15	$80 on $1000 dp bl (901)	20.00	12.00
6L16	$100 on $50 dk Prus grn (903)	1.75	*3.75*
	Nos. 6L1-6L16 (16)	67.35	55.75

Kiangsi Postal and Telegraph Administration.

Central Trust Revenue Stamps of China Surcharged ("People's Post, Kiangsi")

(same size) — A1

$30

$60

1949, June 20 Engr. *Perf. 12½*

6L17 A1	$3 on $30 pur	1.25	1.25
6L18 A1	$15 on $15 red org	1.25	1.25
6L19 A1	$30 on $50 dk bl	1.25	1.25
6L20 A1	$60 on $50 dk bl	1.25	1.25
6L21 A1	$130 on $15 red org	1.25	1.25

The $15 surcharge has 3 characters in left vertical row, the $130 surcharge has 5.

Same Surcharge on Sun Yat-sen Issues of China, 1945-49

Engraved, Lithographed

Perf. 14, 12½

6L22 A82	$1 on $250 dp lil (746)	3.25	3.25
6L23 A94	$5 on $1000 dp bl (901)	3.25	3.25
6L24 A94	$5 on $2000 vio (902)	3.25	3.25
6L25 A94	$5 on $5000 lt bl (903)	1.25	1.25
6L26 A94	$10 on $1000 bl (894)	3.25	3.25
6L27 A82	$20 on $4000 gray	1.25	1.25
6L28 A73	$30 on $100 dk car	3.25	3.25
6L29 A82	$30 on $20,000 rose pink	1.25	1.25
6L30 A94	$80 on $500 rose lil (900)	1.25	1.25
6L31 A94	$100 on $1000 dp bl (901)	1.25	1.25
6L32 A82	$200 on $250 dp lil	2.25	2.25
	Nos. 6L17-6L32 (16)	31.00	31.00

Central China Posts and Telegraph Administration

Farmer, Soldier and Worker
A2 A3

I — Top white line of square character (yuan) at upper left does not touch left vertical stroke. No gap in shading between soldier's feet.

II — Top line connects with left vertical stroke. Gap in shading between feet.

Perf. 10 to 11½ & Comp.

1949 Litho.

6L33 A2	$1 orange	7.50	2.25
6L34 A2	$3 brn org	2.75	2.25
6L35 A2	$6 emerald	3.00	2.25
6L36 A3	$7 yel brn	.50	*2.25*
6L37 A2	$10 bl grn	.25	*.35*
6L38 A3	$14 org brn	15.00	14.00
6L39 A2	$15 ultra	.40	*.50*
6L40 A2	$30 grn, type I	.25	*.40*
a.	Type II	.30	.30
6L41 A3	$35 gray bl	10.00	*16.00*
6L42 A2	$50 rose vio	8.50	12.00
6L43 A3	$70 dp grn	.25	.25
6L44 A2	$80 pink	.55	*.90*
6L45 A3	$100 bl grn	.40	*.95*
6L46 A3	$220 rose red	3.50	*.75*
	Nos. 6L33-6L46 (14)	52.85	55.10

For surcharges & overprints see #6L63-6L65, 6L66-6L73, 6L75, 6L90-6L98, 6L100-6L108.

Star Enclosing Map of Hankow Area — A4

Two types of $500:
I — Thick numerals of "500." No period after "500."
II — Thin numerals and period.

Two types of $1000:
I — No period after "1000."
II — Period after "1000."

1949, July

6L48	A4	$110	org brn	.30	*1.25*
6L49	A4	$130	violet	4.00	2.00
6L50	A4	$200	dp org	.25	*.50*
6L51	A4	$290	brown	1.60	.50
6L52	A4	$370	dk bl	1.60	1.25
6L53	A4	$500	lt bl, I	4.00	.60
a.		$500 blue, II		18.00	7.00
6L54	A4	$1000	dull red, II	18.00	1.50
a.		$1000 dark red, I		25.00	8.00
6L55	A4	$5000	brown	.85	3.00
6L56	A4	$10,000	brt pink	1.75	6.00
		Nos. 6L48-6L56 (9)		32.35	16.60

For surcharges and overprints see Nos. 6L74, 6L76-6L81, 6L99, 6L109.

Hankow River Customs Building A5

River Wall, Wuchang — A6

Design: $290, $370, River scene, Hanyang.

1949, Aug. 16 ***Perf. 11***

6L57	A5	$70	green	1.40	.90
6L58	A5	$220	crimson	1.40	1.25
6L59	A5	$290	brown	1.40	1.25
6L60	A5	$370	brt blue	1.40	1.25
6L61	A6	$500	purple	1.40	*1.75*
6L62	A6	$1000	vermilion	1.25	*1.75*
		Nos. 6L57-6L62 (6)		8.25	*8.15*

Liberation of Hankow, Wuchang and Hanyang.
Exist imperf. About the same value.
For overprints see Nos. 6L82-6L87.

Nos. 6L35, 6L39 and 6L40 Surcharged in Red ("Honan Renminbi Currency")

1949, July

6L63	A2	$7 on $6	emer	3.00	4.00
6L64	A2	$14 on $15	ultra	4.50	*6.00*
6L65	A2	$70 on $30	grn	7.50	*10.00*
		Nos. 6L63-6L65 (3)		15.00	20.00

Surcharge shown is for $70. The $7 has 5 characters in left column and no bottom line.

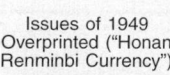

Issues of 1949 Overprinted ("Honan Renminbi Currency")

1949, Aug.

6L66	A2	$3	brn org	.95	.90
6L67	A3	$7	yel brn	.95	.90
6L68	A2	$10	bl grn	1.90	1.90
6L69	A3	$14	org brn	1.90	*3.00*
6L70	A2	$30	yel grn (6L40a)	2.00	*3.00*
6L71	A3	$35	gray bl	.95	*5.00*
6L72	A2	$50	rose vio	7.00	5.00
6L73	A3	$70	dp grn	2.00	*3.75*
6L74	A4	$110	org brn	7.00	7.00
6L75	A3	$220	rose red	6.00	6.00
6L76	A4	$290	brown	6.00	6.00
6L77	A4	$370	blue	10.00	10.00
6L78	A4	$500	bl, II	12.00	*14.00*
6L79	A4	$1000	dk red, I	25.00	*30.00*
6L80	A4	$5000	brown	100.00	*110.00*
6L81	A4	$10,000	brt pink	200.00	*225.00*
		Nos. 6L66-6L81 (16)		383.65	431.45

Width of the overprint varies slightly.

Nos. 6L57-6L62 Overprinted ("Honan Renminbi Currency")

1949, Aug. ***Perf. 11***

6L82	A5	$70	green	2.00	*2.50*
6L83	A5	$220	crimson	3.50	*3.75*
6L84	A5	$290	brown	3.50	*3.75*
6L85	A5	$370	brt bl	5.50	*6.00*
6L86	A6	$500	purple	5.50	*6.00*
6L87	A6	$1000	vermilion	7.50	*8.00*
		Nos. 6L82-6L87 (6)		27.50	30.00

Width of overprint on Nos. 6L82-6L85, 7mm; on Nos. 6L86-6L87, 12mm.
Exist imperf. About the same value.

Changchow Issue Surcharged in Red ("Honan Renminbi Currency")

(same size) Mao Tse-tung — A7

1949, Sept. ***Perf. 10***

6L88	A7	$290 on $30 yel grn	35.00	*40.00*
6L89	A7	$370 on $30 yel grn	52.50	*57.50*

Issues of 1949 Surcharged

1950, Jan.

6L90	A2	$200 on $1	.55	*1.75*
6L91	A2	$200 on $3	3.00	1.60
6L92	A2	$200 on $6	.55	*1.75*
6L93	A3	$200 on $7	3.00	1.60
6L94	A3	$200 on $14	3.00	1.60
6L95	A3	$200 on $35	3.25	2.40
6L96	A3	$200 on $70	3.00	1.60
6L97	A2	$200 on $80	3.00	1.60
6L98	A3	$200 on $220	3.00	1.60
6L99	A4	$200 on $370	.50	*1.75*
6L100	A3	$300 on $70	.50	*2.50*
6L101	A2	$300 on $80	.50	*1.75*
6L102	A3	$300 on $220	.25	*1.75*
6L103	A2	$1200 on $3	27.50	22.50
6L104	A3	$1200 on $7	5.75	5.00
6L105	A3	$1500 on $14	8.25	6.75
6L106	A2	$2100 on $1	37.50	22.50
6L107	A2	$2100 on $6	37.50	22.50
6L108	A3	$2100 on $35	12.00	9.75
6L109	A4	$5000 on $370	5.00	5.00
		Nos. 6L90-6L109 (20)	157.60	117.25

Two types of surcharge exist, differing in spacing of characters in top row.

CENTRAL CHINA PARCEL POST STAMPS

Star and Map of Hankow — PP1

1949, Nov. **Litho.** ***Perf. 11, 11½***

6LQ1	PP1	$5000	brown	2.00	*3.75*
6LQ2	PP1	$10,000	scarlet	9.50	9.00
6LQ3	PP1	$20,000	dk sl grn	4.50	*11.00*
6LQ4	PP1	$50,000	vermilion	2.00	*32.50*
		Nos. 6LQ1-6LQ4 (4)		18.00	*56.25*

SOUTH CHINA

The South China Liberation Area included the provinces of Kwangtung and Kwangsi and Hainan Island. The South China Postal and Telegraph Administration was organized on or about Nov. 4, 1949.

All Stamps Issued without Gum

Pearl River Bridge, Canton — A1

1949, Nov. 4 **Litho.** ***Imperf.***

7L1	A1	$10	green	.30	.25
7L2	A1	$20	sepia	.30	.25
7L3	A1	$30	violet	.30	.25
7L4	A1	$50	carmine	.30	.25
7L5	A1	$100	ultramarine	.50	.25
		Nos. 7L1-7L5 (5)		1.70	1.25

For surcharges see Nos. 7L19-7L23.

China Nos. 993-995 With Additional Overprint in Red ("Liberation of Swatow")

1949, Nov. 9

7L6	A94	2½c on $500 rose lil (993)	16.00	16.00
a.		Handstamped	40.00	40.00
7L7	A94	2½c on $500 rose lil (994)	20.00	20.00
a.		Handstamped	47.50	47.50
7L8	A94	15c on $10 grn (995)	24.00	24.00
a.		Handstamped	90.00	90.00

On Unit Issues of China, 1949

7L9	A96	org (959)	19.00	12.50
7L10	AP5	bl grn (C62)	24.00	*27.50*
7L11	SD2	red vio (E12)	24.00	*27.50*
7L12	R2	car (F2)	20.00	*27.50*

On Sun Yat-sen and Flying Geese Issues of China

7L13	A94	2c	org (974)	150.00	*175.00*
7L14	A94	4c	bl grn (975)	300.00	*375.00*
7L15	A94	10c	dp lil (976)	13.50	*20.00*
7L16	A94	20c	bl (978)	22.50	*32.50*
7L17	A97	$1	brn org (984)	37.50	25.00
7L18	A97	$10	bl grn (987)	450.00	375.00
		Nos. 7L6-7L18 (13)		1,120.	1,157.

Forgeries exist of #7L13-7L14, 7L18.

Nos. 7L1-7L3 Surcharged in Red or Green

1950, Jan.

7L19	A1	$300 on $30 vio (R)	3.25	1.00
7L20	A1	$500 on $20 brn (R)	3.25	1.25
7L21	A1	$800 on $30 vio (G)	3.50	2.00
7L22	A1	$1000 on $10 gray grn (R)	4.25	3.00
7L23	A1	$1000 on $20 brn (R)	4.25	2.25
		Nos. 7L19-7L23 (5)	18.50	9.50

SOUTHWEST CHINA

The Southwest China Liberation Area included the provinces of Kweichow, Szechwan, Yunnan, Sikang and Tibet. The Southwest Postal and Telegraph Administration was organized on or about Nov. 15, 1949 after the liberation of Kweiyang, capital of Kweichow Province.

All Stamps Issued without Gum

Chu Teh, Mao and Troops — A1

1949, Dec. **Litho.** ***Perf. 12½***

8L1	A1	$10	deep blue	2.50	*3.75*
8L2	A1	$20	rose claret	.40	*1.25*
8L3	A1	$30	dp org	.55	*1.25*
8L4	A1	$50	gray grn	.55	*1.25*
8L5	A1	$100	carmine	.90	.75
8L6	A1	$200	blue	1.25	1.00
8L7	A1	$300	bl vio	1.50	1.50
8L8	A1	$500	dk gray	2.75	2.25
8L9	A1	$1000	pale pur	7.50	6.00
8L10	A1	$2000	green	17.50	*20.00*
8L11	A1	$5000	orange	55.00	*60.00*
		Nos. 8L1-8L11 (11)		90.40	99.00

For surcharges and overprints see Nos. 8L21-8L29, 8L40-8L47, 8L55.

China Nos. 974-975, 984, 986-987 Surcharged ("Kweichow People's Post")

1949, Dec. 1 ***Perf. 12½***

8L12	A94	$20 on 2c org	3.50	*4.50*
8L13	A94	$50 on 4c bl grn	5.00	5.00
8L14	A97	$100 on $1 brn org	10.00	7.25
8L15	A97	$400 on $5 car rose	16.00	*22.50*
8L16	A97	$2000 on $10 bl grn	62.50	57.50
		Nos. 8L12-8L16 (5)	97.00	96.75

Map of China, Flag Planted in Southwest A2

1950, Jan. **Litho.** ***Perf. 9 to 11½***

8L17	A2	$20	dark blue	.40	*.65*
8L18	A2	$30	green	.40	*.65*
8L19	A2	$50	red	.40	*.95*
8L20	A2	$100	brown	.40	*.95*
		Nos. 8L17-8L20 (4)		1.60	*3.20*

Liberation of the Southwest.
For surcharges see #8L30-8L39, 8L56-8L59.

Nos. 8L5-8L6 Surcharged

Perf. 12½

8L21	A1	$300 on $100 car	3.50	4.00
8L22	A1	$500 on $100 car	3.50	4.00
8L23	A1	$1200 on $100 car	7.00	7.00
8L24	A1	$1500 on $200 bl	7.00	7.00
8L25	A1	$2000 on $200 bl	11.00	10.00
		Nos. 8L21-8L25 (5)	32.00	32.00

Nos. 8L5-8L6 Overprinted ("East Szechwan")

1950, Jan.

8L26	A1	$100	carmine	6.00	7.50
8L27	A1	$200	blue	6.00	7.50

Nos. 8L5-8L6 Handstamp Surcharged

1950, Jan.

8L28	A1	$1200 on $100 car	15.00	*27.50*
8L29	A1	$1500 on $200 bl	40.00	*27.50*

Many varieties, including wide and narrow settings, exist.

Nos. 8L17-8L20 Surcharged in Black or Red

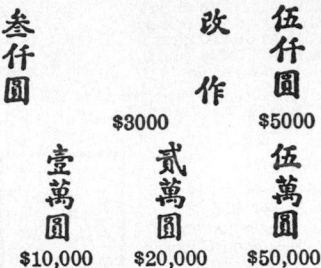

叁仟圓 改作 伍仟圓

$3000 $5000

壹萬圓 貳萬圓 伍萬圓

$10,000 $20,000 $50,000

$60

$300

1950 ***Perf. 9 to 11½***

8L30	A2	$60 on $30	20.00	9.00
8L31	A2	$150 on $30	20.00	9.00
8L32	A2	$300 on $20 (R)	2.00	*4.00*
8L33	A2	$300 on $100	20.00	9.00
8L34	A2	$1500 on $100	32.50	22.50
8L35	A2	$3000 on $50	7.75	*22.50*
8L36	A2	$5000 on $50	3.50	*22.50*
8L37	A2	$10,000 on $50	60.00	42.50
8L38	A2	$20,000 on $50	4.00	*42.50*
8L39	A2	$50,000 on $50	5.75	*60.00*
		Nos. 8L30-8L39 (10)	175.50	243.50

Nos. 8L5-8L7 Overprinted ("West Szechwan")

1950, Jan. ***Perf. 12½***

8L40	A1	$100 carmine	10.50	*11.00*
8L41	A1	$200 pale blue	17.00	*18.50*
8L42	A1	$300 blue violet	26.00	*28.00*
		Nos. 8L40-8L42 (3)	53.50	57.50

Nos. 8L4-8L7 Surcharged

1950, Jan.

8L43	A1	$500 on $100	8.75	8.75
a.		Narrow spacing	70.00	60.00
8L44	A1	$800 on $100	8.75	8.75
8L45	A1	$1000 on $50	11.00	11.00
8L46	A1	$2000 on $200	22.50	27.50
8L47	A1	$3000 on $300	35.00	45.00
		Nos. 8L43-8L47 (5)	86.00	101.00

Two lines of surcharge 7mm apart on No. 8L43, 4mm on No. 8L43a.

China Nos. 975 and 977 Surcharged

Perf. 12½, 13 or Compound

1950, Jan.

8L48	A94	$100 on 4c	13.50	13.50
8L49	A94	$200 on 4c	24.00	22.50
8L50	A94	$800 on 16c	67.50	67.50
8L51	A94	$1000 on 16c	300.00	*375.00*
		Nos. 8L48-8L51 (4)	405.00	478.50

Unit Issue of China Overprinted ("Southwest People's Post")

1950, Jan. **Engr.** ***Rouletted***

8L52	A96	orange	150.00	175.00
a.		Perf. 12½	225.00	250.00

Perf. 12½

8L53	SD2	red violet	225.00	250.00
8L54	R2	carmine	225.00	250.00
		Nos. 8L52-8L54 (3)	600.00	675.00

On No. 8L54, space between overprint columns is 3mm and right column is raised to height of left.

Nos. 8L3, 8L17-8L20 Surcharged in Black or Red

1950, Mar. ***Perf. 12½, 9 to 11½***

8L55	A1	$800 on $30	42.50	40.00
8L56	A2	$1000 on $50	9.00	*12.00*
8L57	A2	$2000 on $100	12.50	*18.00*
8L58	A2	$4000 on $20 (R)	35.00	*37.50*
8L59	A2	$5000 on $30	55.00	55.00
		Nos. 8L55-8L59 (5)	154.00	162.50

CHRISTMAS ISLAND

'kris-məs 'ī-lənd

LOCATION — In the Indian Ocean, 230 miles south of Java

GOVT. — A territory of Australia

AREA — 52 sq. mi.

POP. — 2,373 (1999 est.)

Australia took over Christmas Island from Singapore in 1958.

Catalogue values for all unused stamps in this country are for Never Hinged items.

Queen Elizabeth II — A1

Engr.; Name and Value Typo. in Black

1958, Oct. 15 **Unwmk.** ***Perf. 14½***

1	A1	2c yellow orange	.90	1.90
2	A1	4c brown	.95	.75
3	A1	5c lilac	.95	.75
4	A1	6c dull blue	2.50	.75
5	A1	8c gray brown	5.00	1.25
6	A1	10c violet	3.50	.75
7	A1	12c carmine rose	5.25	4.25
8	A1	20c ultramarine	3.50	4.25
9	A1	50c yellow green	6.00	4.25
10	A1	$1 greenish blue	6.25	4.25
		Nos. 1-10 (10)	34.80	23.15
		Set, hinged	13.00	

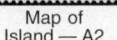

Map of Island — A2

Island Scene — A3

4c, Moonflower. 5c, Robber crab. 8c, Phosphate train. 10c, Crane loading phosphate. 12c, Flying fish cove. 20c, Loading ship. 50c, Frigate bird. $1, Yellow-billed tropic bird.

Perf. 14x14½, 14½x14

1963, Aug. 28 **Engr.**

11	A2	2c orange	.80	.70
12	A2	4c red brown	.45	.30
13	A2	5c rose lilac	.45	.40
14	A3	6c slate	.40	*.70*
15	A2	8c black	2.50	.70
16	A2	10c violet	.40	.30
17	A3	12c dull red	.40	.50
18	A3	20c dark blue	.95	.40
19	A3	50c green	1.25	.40

Size: 35x21mm

20	A3	$1 orange yellow	2.40	.70
		Nos. 11-20 (10)	10.00	5.10

"Simpson and His Donkey" by Wallace Anderson — A3a

1965, Apr. 14 **Photo.** ***Perf. 13½x13***

21	A3a	10c brt grn, sepia & blk	.75	*1.00*

ANZAC issue. See note after Australia No. 387.

Moorish Goddess A4

Fish: 1c, Golden striped grouper. 3c, Forceps fish. 4c, Queen triggerfish. 5c, Regal angelfish. 9c, Surgeonfish. 10c, Turkeyfish. 15c, Saddleback butterflyfish. 20c, Clown butterflyfish. 30c, Ghost pipefish. 50c, Lined surgeonfish. $1, Meyer's butterflyfish.

1968-70 **Photo.** ***Perf. 13½***

22	A4	1c multicolored	.75	1.25
23	A4	2c multicolored	1.00	.55
24	A4	3c multicolored	1.00	.85
25	A4	4c multicolored	1.00	.55
26	A4	5c multicolored	1.00	.55
27	A4	9c multicolored	1.00	1.10
28	A4	10c multicolored	1.00	.55
29	A4	15c multicolored	14.50	7.00
30	A4	20c multicolored	2.75	1.50
31	A4	30c multicolored	14.50	7.00
32	A4	50c multicolored	3.50	*4.25*
33	A4	$1 multicolored	3.50	*5.50*
		Nos. 22-33 (12)	45.50	30.65

Issued: 15c, 30c, 12/14/70; others, 5/6/68.

Christmas Issues

"Hark the Herald Angels Sing" — A5

1969, Nov. 10 **Photo.** ***Perf. 13½***

34	A5	5c dk blue, gold, buff & red	.40	.40

A6

A7

3c, The Ansidei Madonna, by Raphael. 5c, Virgin and Child, by Morando.

1970, Oct. 26 **Photo.** ***Perf. 14x14½***

35	A6	3c gold & multi	.20	.20
36	A6	5c silver & multi	.25	.25

1971, Oct. 4

5c, Adoration of the Shepherds, Seville School. 20c, Adoration of the Shepherds, by Guido Reni.

37	A7	6c black & multi	.75	.50
38	A7	20c dark blue & multi	1.60	1.25

"Flying Fish," 1887 — A8

Ships and Map of Christmas Island: 1c, "Eagle," 1714. 2c, "Redpole," 1890. 3c, "Hoi Houw," 1959. 4c, "Pigot," 1771. 5c, "Valetta," 1968. 7c, "Asia," 1805. 8c, "Islander," 1929-60. 9c, "Imperieuse," 1888 (incorrectly inscribed "Imperious"). 10c, "Egeria," 1887. 20c, "Thomas," 1615. 25c, "Gordon," 1864. 30c, "Cygnet," 1688. 35c, "Triadic," 1958. 50c, "Amethyst," 1857. $1, "Royal Mary," 1643.

1972-73 **Photo.** ***Perf. 14½x13½***

39	A8	1c yel green & multi	.30	.60
40	A8	2c lt red brn & multi	.35	.70
41	A8	3c dp rose & multi	.35	.70
42	A8	4c multicolored	.50	.75
43	A8	5c multicolored	.50	.75
44	A8	6c lilac & multi	.50	.75
45	A8	7c lt green & multi	.50	.75
46	A8	8c blue & multi	.55	.75
47	A8	9c org & multi	.80	.60
48	A8	10c lem & multi	.65	.70
49	A8	20c tan & multi	.85	.90
50	A8	25c multicolored	.90	1.50
51	A8	30c multicolored	.90	.90
52	A8	35c tan & multi	.90	.90
53	A8	50c ultra & multi	.90	1.50
54	A8	$1 yellow & multi	1.25	1.75
		Nos. 39-54 (16)	10.70	14.50

Issued: 6c, 7c, 8c, 20c, 2/5/72; 1c, 2c, 3c, $1, 6/5/72; 4c, 5c, 9c, 50c, 2/6/73; 10c, 25c, 30c, 35c, 6/4/73.

A9 "Peace"

A9a "Joy"

1972, Oct. 2 **Litho.** ***Perf. 14½***

55	A9	3c black & multi	.65	.40
56	A9a	3c black & multi	.65	.40
a.		Pair, #55-56	1.40	1.40
57	A9	7c black & multi	.85	.75
58	A9a	7c black & multi	.85	.75
a.		Pair, #57-58	1.75	1.75
		Nos. 55-58 (4)	3.00	2.30

Mother and Child, Christmas Island Map — A10

1973, Oct. 2 Photo. *Perf. 14½x13½*

59 A10 7c blue & multi 1.00 .60
60 A10 25c brt green & multi 3.00 2.25

Christmas.

Mother and Child with Star and Cross — A11

1974, Oct. 2 Photo. *Perf. 13½x14½*

61 A11 7c black & lilac rose .75 .60
62 A11 30c black & yellow 2.25 2.25

Christmas.

Flight into Egypt — A12

1975, Oct. 2 Photo. *Perf. 14½x13½*

63 A12 10c gold, black & yel .70 .40
64 A12 35c gold, vio blk & rose 1.40 1.60

Christmas.

Star of Bethlehem and Dove
A13 A14

1976, Oct. 2 Photo. *Perf. 13½*

65 A13 10c red & multi .65 .40
66 A14 10c red & multi .65 .40
a. Pair, #65-66 1.40 1.40
67 A13 35c blue & multi .85 .75
68 A14 35c blue & multi .85 .75
a. Pair, #67-68 1.75 1.75
Nos. 65-68 (4) 3.00 2.30

Christmas.

Andrew Clunies-Ross (first settler) A15

Famous Visitors: 1c, William Dampier, explorer, buccaneer. 2c, Capt. Willem de Vlamingh, Dutch explorer. 3c, Vice Adm. John F. L. P. Maclear, Royal Navy. 4c, John Murray, oceanographer, scientist. 5c, Adm. Pelham Aldrich and crew collecting specimen. 7c, Joseph Jackson Lister, naturalist, and arenga listeri plant. 8c, Adm. William Henry May. 9c, Henry Nicholas Ridley, botanist. 10c, George Clunies-Ross, pioneer phosphate miner. 20c, Capt. Joshua Slocum. 45c, Charles William Andrews, zoologist, and frigate birds. 50c, Karl Richard Hanitsch, zoologist, and fruit pigeon. 75c, Victor W. W. Saunders Purcell, Sinologist. $1, Fam Choo Beng, educator. $2, Harold Spencer-Jones, astronomer.

1977-78 Photo. *Perf. 14x13½*

69 A15 1c multicolored .20 .80
70 A15 2c multicolored .20 .80
71 A15 3c multicolored .25 .80
72 A15 4c multicolored .30 .90
73 A15 5c multicolored .30 .35
74 A15 6c multicolored .30 .65
75 A15 7c multicolored .30 .40
76 A15 8c multicolored .35 .70
77 A15 9c multicolored .40 2.00
78 A15 10c multicolored .35 .60
79 A15 20c multicolored .45 .75
80 A15 45c multicolored .85 .45
81 A15 50c multicolored 1.00 2.00
82 A15 75c multicolored .90 1.60
83 A15 $1 multicolored .90 1.60
84 A15 $2 multicolored 1.50 2.50
Nos. 69-84 (16) 8.55 16.90

Issued: 1c, 6c, 9c, $1, 4/30/77; 2c, 3c, 4c, $2, 2/22/78; 5c, 7c, 45c, 50c, 5/31/78; 8c, 10c, 20c, 75c, 9/1/78.

Australian Arms, Map of Christmas Island — A16

1977, June 2 Litho. *Perf. 14½x13½*

85 A16 45c multicolored .80 .80

25th anniv. of reign of Elizabeth II.

Souvenir Sheet

Partridge in a Pear Tree — A17

Twelve Days of Christmas: a, Partridge in a pear tree. b, 2 turtle doves. c, 3 French hens. d, 4 calling birds. e, 5 gold rings. f, 6 geese. g, 7 swans. h, 8 maids a-milking. i, 9 ladies dancing. j, 10 lords a-leaping. k, 11 pipers piping. l, 12 drummers drumming.

Unwmk.

1977, Oct. 20 Litho. *Perf. 14*

86 Sheet of 12 1.90 2.25
a.-l. A17 10c, single stamp .20 .20
m. Wmk. 373 ('78) 2.50 3.50

Christmas.

Common Design Types pictured following the introduction.

Elizabeth II Coronation Anniversary

Common Design Types

Souvenir Sheet

1978, Apr. 21 Litho. *Perf. 15*

87 Sheet of 6 4.25 4.25
a. CD326 45c White swan of Bohun .70 *.90*
b. CD327 45c Elizabeth II .70 *.90*
c. CD328 45c Abbott's booby .70 *.90*

No. 87 contains 2 se-tenant strips of Nos. 87a-87c, separated by horizontal gutter with commemorative and descriptive inscriptions.

Souvenir Sheet

Christ Child — A18

Song of Christmas: a, Christ Child. b, Herald angels. c, Redeemer. d, Israel. e, Star. f, Three Wise Men. g, Manger. h. "All He stands for." i, "Shepherds came."

1978, Oct. 2 Litho. *Perf. 14*

88 A18 Sheet of 9 1.75 2.00
a.-i. 10c single stamp .20 .20

Christmas. Each stamp design incorporates one letter of "Christmas."

IYC Emblem, Oriental Children — A19

Design: IYC emblem and children of different races holding hands, continuous design.

1979, Apr. 20 Litho. *Perf. 14*

89 Strip of 5 1.90 2.00
a. A19 20c single stamp .35 .50

International Year of the Child.

Rowland Hill and No. 25 A20

Sir Rowland Hill (1795-1879), originator of penny postage, and Christmas Island stamps: a, #1. b, #11. c, #21. d, #25. e, #34.

1979, Aug. 27 Litho. *Perf. 13x13½*

90 Strip of 5 1.40 1.50
a.-e. A20 20c any single .20 .30

Three Kings Bearing Gifts — A21

Christmas: 55c, Virgin and Child, globe.

1979, Oct. 22 Litho. *Perf. 14x14½*

91 A21 20c multicolored .25 .25
92 A21 55c multicolored .60 .50

25 Years of Golf — A22

1980, Feb. 12 Litho. *Perf. 14½x14*

93 A22 20c shown .40 .45
94 A22 55c Clubhouse 1.00 1.25

Surveyor, Phosphate Industry A23

1980, May 5 Litho. *Perf. 14x14½*

95 A23 15c shown .30 .40
96 A23 22c Drilling for samples .30 .40
97 A23 40c Sample analysis .35 .45
98 A23 55c Mine planning .55 .65

1980, July 14

99 A23 15c Jungle clearing .30 .30
100 A23 22c Overburden removal .30 .30
101 A23 40c Open cut mining .35 .35
102 A23 55c Restoration .55 .55

1981, Feb. 9

103 A23 22c Screening and stockpiling .30 .30
104 A23 28c Loading train .40 .40
105 A23 40c Rail transport .50 .50
106 A23 60c Drying .60 .60

1981, May 4

107 A23 22c Crushing .30 .35
108 A23 28c Pipeline .40 .45
109 A23 40c Bulk storage .50 .55
110 A23 60c Loading ship .60 .65
Nos. 95-110 (16) 6.60 7.20

Souvenir Sheet

Virgin and Child — A24

1980, Oct. 6 Litho. *Perf. 13½x13*

111 Sheet of 6 2.25 2.40
a. A24 15c Angel .20 .20
b. A24 22c shown .25 .30
c. A24 60c Angel .35 .35
d. A24 15c Angel holding soldier .20 .20
e. A24 22c Kneeling woman and man .25 .30
f. A24 60c Chinese, Indian, European children .35 .35

Christmas. No. 111 contains 2 strips of 3 (Nos. 111a-111c and 111d-111f) with gutter between.

Cryptoblepharus Egeriae — A25

Designs: Reptiles.

1981, Aug. 10 Litho. *Perf. 13x13½*

112 A25 24c shown .30 .30
113 A25 30c Emoia nativitata .50 .50
114 A25 40c Lepidodactylus listeri .60 .60
115 A25 60c Cyrtodactylus nov. .75 .75
Nos. 112-115 (4) 2.15 2.15

Souvenir Sheet

Nativity A26

1981, Oct. 19 Litho. *Perf. 14½x14*

116 Sheet of 4 1.60 1.75
a. A26 18c Angels, star .20 *.25*
b. A26 24c shown .25 *.30*
c. A26 40c Children praying to Jesus .50 *.55*
d. A26 60c Children praying .60 *.70*

Christmas.

Reef Heron A27

1982-83 Litho. *Perf. 14*

117 A27 1c shown .70 .20
118 A27 2c Noddies .70 .20
119 A27 3c Glossy swiftlet .70 .70
120 A27 4c Imperial pigeon .70 .70
121 A27 5c Christmas Isld. silvereyes .85 .85
122 A27 10c Thrush .70 .70
123 A27 25c Silver bosunbird 1.25 .70
124 A27 30c Christmas Isld. emerald doves .75 .75
125 A27 40c Brown boobies .75 .60
126 A27 50c Red-footed boobies .75 .60
127 A27 65c Christmas Isld. frigatebird .75 .60
128 A27 75c Golden bosunbirds .90 .80
129 A27 80c Nankeen kestrel, vert. 1.25 *1.75*
130 A27 $1 Christmas Isld. hawk owl, vert. 2.75 1.75
131 A27 $2 Goshawk, vert. 2.00 *4.25*
132 A27 $4 Abbott's boobies, vert. 3.25 3.25
Nos. 117-132 (16) 18.75 18.40

Issued: 1c, 2c, 25c $4, 3/8; 3c, 4c, 10c, $2, 6/14; 40c, 50c, 65c, 75c, 8/23; 5c, 30c, 80c, $1, 2/21/83.

Christmas — A28

25th Anniv. of Boat Club — A29

Paper sculptures.

1982, Oct. 18 Litho. & Embossed
135 A28 27c Joseph .40 .40
136 A28 50c Angel .55 .55
137 A28 75c Mary, Baby Jesus .80 .80
a. Strip of 3, #135-137 1.75 1.75

Perf. 14x14½, 14½x14
1983, May 2 Litho.

Designs: Various boating activities.

138 A29 27c multicolored .50 .50
139 A29 35c multicolored .50 .50
140 A29 50c multi, horiz. .60 .75
141 A29 75c multi, horiz. .65 .75
Nos. 138-141 (4) 2.25 2.50

25th Anniv. of Australian Territory A30

1983, Oct. 1 Litho. *Perf. 14*
142 A30 24c Maps. golden bosun bird, kangaroo .65 .40
143 A30 30c Map, flag .75 .75
144 A30 85c Boeing 727, maps 1.50 1.50
Nos. 142-144 (3) 2.90 2.65

Christmas — A31

Designs: Christmas candles.

1983, Oct. 31 Litho. *Perf. 13½x13*
145 A31 24c multicolored .30 .30
146 A31 30c multicolored .45 .50
147 A31 85c multicolored 1.10 1.40
Nos. 145-147 (3) 1.85 *2.20*

Red Land Crab — A32

1984, Feb. 20 Litho. *Perf. 14x14½*
148 A32 30c Feeding .65 .65
149 A32 40c Migration .75 .75
150 A32 55c Developmental stages .75 .75
151 A32 85c Adult female, young 1.10 1.10
Nos. 148-151 (4) 3.25 3.25

Local Fungi — A33

1984, Apr. 30 *Perf. 13½x14½*
152 A33 30c Leucocoprinus fragilissimus .60 .60
153 A33 40c Microporus xanthopus .75 .75
154 A33 45c Trogia anthidepas .90 .90
155 A33 55c Haddowia longipes 1.00 1.00
156 A33 85c Phillipsia domingensis 1.25 1.25
Nos. 152-156 (5) 4.50 4.50

Cricket on Christmas Isld., 25th Anniv. A34

1984, July 23 Litho. *Perf. 14*
157 A34 30c Runout .70 *.85*
158 A34 40c Catch at point .75 *1.10*
159 A34 55c Batsman .80 *1.50*
160 A34 85c Batsman hitting 1.00 *1.75*
Nos. 157-160 (4) 3.25 *5.20*

Souvenir Sheet

Christmas; Ausipex '84 A35

1984, Sept. 21 Litho. *Perf. 13½*
161 Sheet of 3 + 3 labels 3.00 3.00
a. A35 30c Father Christmas arriving .50 .50
b. A35 55c Distributing gifts 1.00 1.00
c. A35 85c Waving good-bye 1.40 1.40

Crabs A36

1985 Litho. *Perf. 13x13½*
162 A36 30c Birgus latro 1.00 .80
163 A36 33c Cardiosoma hirtipes 1.00 .80
164 A36 33c Gecarcoidea natalis 1.10 .90
165 A36 40c Ocypode ceratophthalma 1.10 .90
166 A36 45c Ceonobita rugosa 1.10 1.10
167 A36 45c Metasesarma rousseauxi 1.40 1.40
168 A36 55c Coenobita brevimana 1.40 1.40
169 A36 60c Geograpsus stormi 1.75 1.75
170 A36 60c Grapsus tenuicrustatus 2.25 2.25
171 A36 85c Geograpsus grayi 2.50 2.50
172 A36 90c Ocypode cordimana 2.50 *3.50*
173 A36 90c Geograpsus crinipes 3.00 *4.00*
Nos. 162-173 (12) 20.10 21.30

Issued: 30c, 40c, 55c, 85c, 1/30; #163, 166, 169, 172, 4/29; #164, 167, 170, 173, 7/22.

Once in Royal David's City — A37

Songs: 33c, While Shepherds Watched Their Flocks by Night. 45c, Away in a Manger. 60c, We Three Kings of Orient Are. 90c, Hark! The Herald Angels Sing.

1985, Oct. 28 Litho. *Perf. 14x14½*
174 A37 27c multicolored .90 *1.10*
175 A37 33c multicolored 1.00 *1.25*
176 A37 45c multicolored 1.25 *1.40*
177 A37 60c multicolored 1.40 *1.50*
178 A37 90c multicolored 1.50 *1.60*
a. Strip of 5, #174-178 7.50 *8.00*

Christmas.

Halley's Comet A38

1986, Apr. 30 Litho. *Perf. 14*
179 A38 33c Over island .60 *.65*
180 A38 45c Edmond Halley .80 *1.00*
181 A38 60c Over phosphate shipping 1.10 *1.90*
182 A38 90c Over Flying Fish Cove 1.75 *2.25*
Nos. 179-182 (4) 4.25 *5.80*

Indigenous Flowers — A39

1986, June 30 Litho. *Perf. 14*
183 A39 33c Ridley's orchid 1.50 .55
184 A39 45c Hanging flower .95 *.90*
185 A39 60c Hoya .95 *1.60*
186 A39 90c Sea hibiscus 1.25 *2.25*
Nos. 183-186 (4) 4.65 *5.30*

Royal Wedding Issue, 1986
Common Design Type

Designs: 33c, Couple in Buckingham Palace garden. 90c, Andrew operating helicopter.

1986, July 23 Litho. *Perf. 14½x14*
187 CD338 33c multicolored .60 *.50*
188 CD338 90c multicolored 1.40 *1.60*

Christmas A40

Santa Claus at Christmas Island.

1986, Sept. 30 Litho. *Perf. 13x13½*
189 A40 30c Speedboating .90 .70
190 A40 36c At the beach 1.00 .70
191 A40 55c Fishing 1.50 1.50
192 A40 70c Golfing 2.50 *3.75*
193 A40 $1 Sleeping in hammock 2.50 *4.25*
Nos. 189-193 (5) 8.40 10.90

Visiting Ships, Cent. A41

1987, Jan. 21 *Perf. 14½*
194 A41 36c Flying Fish 1.25 .75
195 A41 90c Egeria 2.25 2.25

Wildlife A42

1987-89 Litho. *Perf. 14*
196 A42 1c Blind snake .55 .90
197 A42 2c Blue-tailed skink .55 .90
198 A42 3c Insectivorous bat 1.00 .90
199 A42 5c Green cricket 1.00 .90
200 A42 10c Christmas Is. fruit bat 1.00 .90
201 A42 25c Gecko 1.25 1.00
202 A42 30c Praying mantis 1.50 1.25
203 A42 36c Hawk owl 3.25 2.00
204 A42 40c Bull-mouth helmet shell 2.00 1.75
204A A42 41c Nudibranch ('89) 1.50 .80
205 A42 50c Textile cone shell 2.25 2.00
206 A42 65c Brittle-stars 1.50 1.25
207 A42 75c Royal angelfish 1.50 *1.75*
208 A42 90c Christmas Is. white butterfly 4.50 4.00
209 A42 $1 Mimic butterfly 4.50 4.00
210 A42 $2 Shrew 4.50 *7.50*
211 A42 $5 Green turtle 5.50 *8.00*
a. Sheet of 16, #196-204, 205-211 52.50 52.50
Nos. 196-211 (17) 37.85 39.80

Issued: 1c, 2c, 25c, $5, 3/25; 3c, 10c, 36c, $2, 6/24; 40c, 50c, 65c, 75c, 8/26; 5c, 30c, 90c, $1, 3/1/88; 41c, 9/1/89.

Stamps contained in No. 211a inscribed "1988" at bottom.

For overprint see Nos. 246-247.

Souvenir Sheet

Santa Claus Delivering Presents — A43

Illustration reduced.

1987, Oct. 7 Litho. *Perf. 13½*
212 A43 Sheet of 4 5.75 5.75
a. 30c multicolored .60 .60
b. 37c multicolored .65 .65
c. 90c multicolored 1.75 1.75
d. $1 multicolored 1.90 1.90

Christmas. Nos. 212a-212d printed in a continuous design.

Australia Bicentennial A44

Designs: a, First Fleet sighted by 5 Aborginals on land. b, Four Aboriginals on land, one in canoe. c, Ships entering bay, kangaroos. d, Europeans land. e, Flag raising.

1988, Jan. 26 Litho. *Perf. 13*
213 Strip of 5 8.00 8.00
a.-e. A44 37c any single 1.50 1.50

Nos. 213a-213e printed in a continuous design. See Cocos Islands No. 172.

Annexation of the Island, Cent. — A45

1988, June 8 Litho. *Perf. 14½*
214 A45 37c Capt William Henry May .75 .75
215 A45 53c Annexation ceremony 1.00 1.00
216 A45 95c HMS Imperieuse 1.75 1.75
217 A45 $1.50 Building cairn of stones 2.25 2.25
Nos. 214-217 (4) 5.75 5.75

Settlement of Christmas Is., Cent. — A46

Transportation: 37c, Horse and cart, 1910. 55c, Phosphate mining, 1910. 70c, Steam locomotive, 1914. $1, Arrival of first aircraft, 1957.

1988, Aug. 24 Litho. *Perf. 14½*
218 A46 37c multicolored .85 .50
219 A46 55c multicolored 1.25 .65
220 A46 70c multicolored 1.75 .95
221 A46 $1 multicolored 2.00 1.50
Nos. 218-221 (4) 5.85 3.60

Christmas Presents — A47

1988, Nov. 15 *Perf. 14x14½*
222 A47 32c Bucket, shovel, boat .65 .65
223 A47 39c Snorkeling equipment .80 .80
224 A47 90c Toy soldier, doll, stuffed animals 1.75 1.75
225 A47 $1 Race car, truck, plane 2.00 2.00
Nos. 222-225 (4) 5.20 5.20

Chinese New Year — A48

1989, Jan. 31 *Perf. 14½*
226 A48 39c Good harvest .75 .65
227 A48 70c Prosperity 1.40 1.25
228 A48 90c Good fortune 1.90 1.50
229 A48 $1 Progress 2.10 1.75
Nos. 226-229 (4) 6.15 5.15

Sir John Murray (1841-1914), Oceanographer — A49

1989, Mar. 16 *Perf. 14½x14*
230 A49 39c Portrait .75 .75
231 A49 80c Murray Hill (map) 1.40 1.40
232 A49 $1 Murray's equipment 1.75 1.75
233 A49 $1.10 HMS Challenger 2.10 2.10
Nos. 230-233 (4) 6.00 6.00

Malay-Hari Raya Folk Celebration — A50

1989, May 31 *Perf. 14*
234 A50 39c Children .65 .60
235 A50 55c Tambourine player 1.00 .85
236 A50 80c Girl 1.50 1.25
237 A50 $1.10 Minaret 2.10 1.90
Nos. 234-237 (4) 5.25 4.60

Ferns A51

Christmas A52

1989, Aug. 16
238 A51 41c *Huperzia phlegmaria* .90 .90
239 A51 65c *Asplenium polydon* 1.25 1.25
240 A51 80c *Davallia denticulata* 1.50 1.25
241 A51 $1.10 *Asplenium nidus* 2.10 2.10
Nos. 238-241 (4) 5.75 5.50

1989, Oct. 4 **Litho.** *Perf. 14½x15*

Biblical scenes: 36c, Joseph. 41c, Manger. 80c, Shepherds see star. $1.10, Magi riding camels.

242 A52 36c multi .70 .50
243 A52 41c multi .75 .55
244 A52 80c multi 1.90 .80
245 A52 $1.10 multi 2.00 1.10
Nos. 242-245 (4) 5.35 2.95

Nos. 204A and 209 Overprinted

1989, Oct. 18 **Litho.** *Perf. 14*
246 A42 41c multicolored 1.25 .55
247 A42 $1 multicolored 4.25 1.25

STAMPSHOW '89, Melbourne. No. 247 is dated "1989."

1st Sighting of Christmas Is., 375th Anniv. — A53

Sightings of the island: 41c, John Milward, master of the British East India ship *Thomas,* 1615. $1.10, William Mynors, captain of *Royal Mary,* 1643.

1990, Jan. 31 **Litho.** *Perf. 14x15*
248 A53 41c multicolored 2.00 .60
249 A53 $1.10 multicolored 2.50 1.60

Transport Through the Ages — A55

Perf. 14x13½, 13½x14

1990 **Litho.** **Unwmk.**
254 A55 1c Phosphate transport .25 .25
255 A55 2c Phosphate train .50 .50
256 A55 3c Rail car, vert. .35 .35
257 A55 5c Road train .55 .55
258 A55 10c Trishaw, vert. .45 .45
259 A55 15c Terex 1.10 .95
260 A55 25c Long bus .45 .45
261 A55 30c Passenger rake, vert. .45 .45
262 A55 40c Passenger barge, vert. .55 .45
263 A55 50c Kolek canoe .75 .55
264 A55 65c Flying doctor, ambulance 5.00 2.10
265 A55 75c Tradestore van 2.40 2.40
266 A55 90c Vintage truck 2.40 2.40
267 A55 $1 Water tanker 2.75 2.40
268 A55 $2 Traction engine 3.50 3.50
269 A55 $5 Steam locomotive, flat car 4.75 *6.25*
Nos. 254-269 (16) 26.20 24.00

Issued: 1c, 3c, 10c, 25c, 30c, 40c, 50c, $5, Apr. 18; others, Aug. 22.

World Wildlife Fund — A56

Abbott's boobies *(Sula abbotti):* 20c, Adult (facing left). 29c, Adult (facing right). No. 273, Adults, nest, hatchling. No. 274a, Adult landing on tree branch. No. 274b, Adult resting on branch. No. 274c, Adult, young in nest.

Perf. 14x14½

1990, June 6 **Litho.** **Unwmk.**
270 A56 10c shown 1.75 1.75
271 A56 20c multicolored 2.25 2.25
272 A56 29c multicolored 2.50 2.50
273 A56 41c multicolored 3.25 3.25
Nos. 270-273 (4) 9.75 9.75

Souvenir Sheet

Perf. 14½

274 Sheet of 3 10.00 10.00
a.-c. A56 41c any single 3.25 3.25
d. Overprinted in purple *14.00 14.00*
e. Overprinted in green *20.00 20.00*

No. 274d overprint reads "WORLD STAMP EXHIBITION / AUCKLAND, NEW ZEALAND, 24 AUGUST-2 SEPTEMBER 1990."

No. 274e overprint reads "BIRDPEX '90 National Philatelic Exhibition / University of Canterbury Christchurch NZ 6-9 Dec 1990 / In Conjunction / With The 20th International Ornithological Congress" and Bird's head.

Issued: #274d, Aug. 24; #274e, Dec. 6.

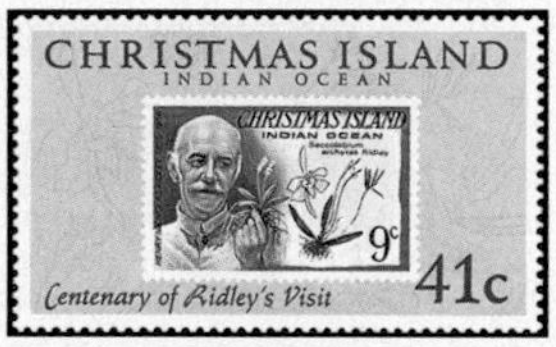

Centenary of Visit by Botanist Henry Ridley — A57

1990, July 11 **Litho.** *Perf. 14½*
275 A57 41c No. 77 1.50 *.80*
276 A57 75c Ridley, vert. 2.25 *2.00*

Christmas A58

Flowers.

1990, Oct. 3 **Litho.** *Perf. 14½*
294 A58 38c Corymborkus veratrifolia 1.00 .90
295 A58 43c Hoya aldrichii 1.25 1.00
296 A58 80c Quisqualis indica 2.00 2.00
297 A58 $1.20 Barringtonia racemosa 3.00 *3.50*
Nos. 294-297 (4) 7.25 7.40

1st Phosphate Mining Lease, Cent. — A59

1991, Feb. 13 **Litho.** *Perf. 14½*
298 A59 43c Freighter 1.25 1.25
299 A59 43c Loading rail cars 1.25 1.25
300 A59 85c Shay locomotive 1.50 1.50
301 A59 $1.20 Bucket shovel 2.00 2.00
302 A59 $1.70 Reforestation 2.50 2.50
a. Strip of 5, #298-302 9.00 9.00

Island Police Force — A60

1991, Apr. 17 **Litho.** *Perf. 14½*
303 A60 43c Community relations 1.75 1.75
304 A60 43c Traffic control 1.75 1.75
305 A60 90c Customs and quarantine 2.50 2.50
306 A60 $1.20 Search and rescue 3.25 3.25
a. Souvenir sheet of 4, #303-306 9.50 8.00
Nos. 303-306 (4) 9.25 9.25

Maps — A61

1991, June 19 **Litho.** *Perf. 14*
307 A61 43c 1991 1.25 1.25
308 A61 75c Goos Atlas, 1666 2.25 2.00
309 A61 $1.10 Apres De Manevillette, 1745 2.75 2.75
310 A61 $1.20 Comberford, 1667 3.00 3.00
Nos. 307-310 (4) 9.25 9.00

Trees A62

1991, Aug. 21 **Litho.** *Perf. 14*
311 A62 43c Bruguiera gymnorrhiza 1.50 1.50
312 A62 70c Syzygium operculatum 2.00 2.00
313 A62 85c Ficus microcarpa 2.25 2.25
314 A62 $1.20 Arenga listeri 2.50 2.50
Nos. 311-314 (4) 8.25 8.25

Christmas A63

Drawings of "What Christmas Means to Me" by: No. 315a, S'ng Yen Luiw. b, Liew Ann Nee. c, Foo Pang Chuan. d, Too Lai Peng. e, Jesamine Wheeler. 43c, Ho Puay Ha. $1, Ng Hooi Hua. $1.20, Yani Kawi.

1991, Oct. 2 **Litho.** *Perf. 14½*
315 Strip of 5 5.00 5.00
a.-e. A63 38c any single .90 .90
316 A63 43c multicolored 1.00 .85
317 A63 $1 multicolored 2.25 2.25
318 A63 $1.20 multicolored 2.50 2.50
Nos. 315-318 (4) 10.75 10.60

A64

Shells — A65

War Time Evacuation, 50th Anniv.: No. 319, Conference to decide upon evacuation. No. 320, Europeans awaiting barge. $1.05, Barge approaching waiting ship. $1.20, Remaining population waving to TSS Islander.

1992, Feb. 19 **Litho.** *Perf. 14½*
319 A64 45c multicolored 1.25 1.25
320 A64 45c multicolored 1.25 1.25
321 A64 $1.05 multicolored 2.75 2.75
322 A64 $1.20 multicolored 3.00 3.00
Nos. 319-322 (4) 8.25 8.25

1992 **Litho.** *Perf. 15x14½*
326 A65 5c Cypraea tigris .65 *.90*
327 A65 10c Cypraea caputserpentis .95 .90
328 A65 15c Lambis scorpius 1.25 .90
329 A65 20c Chlamys pallium 1.25 .90
330 A65 25c Engina mendicaria 1.25 .90
331 A65 30c Drupa ricinus 1.25 .90
332 A65 40c Distorsio reticulata 1.25 1.00
333 A65 45c Turbo petholatus 1.60 1.00
334 A65 50c Cantharus pulcher 1.60 1.00

335 A65 60c Conus capitaneus 2.00 1.10
336 A65 70c Turbo lajonkairii 2.00 1.25
337 A65 80c Lambis chiragra 2.50 1.40
338 A65 90c Angaria delphinus 2.50 1.60
339 A65 $1 Vasum ceramicum 2.50 1.90
340 A65 $2 Tonna perdix 1.90 *2.75*
341 A65 $5 Drupa rubusidaea 4.75 4.50
Nos. 326-341 (16) 29.20 22.90

Issued: 10c, 20c, 30c, 45c, 60c, 80c, $1, $2, 4/15; 5c, 15c, 25c, 40c, 50c, 70c, 90c, $5, 8/19.

For overprint see No. 348.

Sinking of Eidsvold and Nissa Maru, 50th Anniv. A66

Designs: 45c, Eidsvold hit by torpedo. 80c, Eidsvold sinking. $1.05, Nissa Maru hit by torpedo. $1.20, Nissa Maru sinking.

1992, June 17 Litho. ***Perf. 14x13½***
343 A66 45c multicolored 1.75 1.25
344 A66 80c multicolored 2.50 2.50
345 A66 $1.05 multicolored 3.00 3.00
346 A66 $1.20 multicolored 3.00 3.00
Nos. 343-346 (4) 10.25 9.75

Christmas — A67

Coastline, booby birds: a, 40c, Plants on shore, birds. b, 40c, Birds, rocks offshore. c, 45c, Birds on shore. d, $1.05, Birds in flight, coastline. e, $1.20, Forest, rocky coastline.

1992, Oct. 7 Litho. ***Perf. 14½***
347 A67 Strip of 5, #a.-e. 7.75 *8.50*

No. 341 Ovptd. in Red Violet

1992, Sept. 1 Litho. ***Perf. 15x14½***
348 A65 $5 on #342 12.00 8.00

Kuala Lumpur Philatelic Exhibition.

Starting with No. 349, Christmas Island stamps are valid for postage on items mailed in Australia and Australian stamps are valid on items posted on Christmas Island.

Seabirds — A68

Designs: a, Abbott's booby. b, Christmas Island frigatebird. c, Common noddy. d, Golden bosunbird. e, Brown booby.

1993, Mar. 4 Litho. ***Perf. 14½x14***
349 A68 45c Strip of 5, #a.-e. 4.25 *4.50*
f. Souvenir sheet of 5, #a.-e. 5.00 5.00
g. As "f," overprinted *10.00 10.00*
h. As "f," overprinted *8.00 8.00*

No. 349g Ovptd. in Gold in sheet margin with Taipei '93 emblem and: "ASIAN INTERNATIONAL INVITATION STAMP EXHIBITION / TAIPEI '93" in Chinese and English.

No. 349h Ovptd. in Gold in Sheet Margin with "INDOPEX '93 / 6TH ASIAN INTERNATIONAL PHILATELIC EXHIBITION 1993 / PAMERAN INTERNASIONAL PENGUMPULAN / KEENAM DI ASIA TAHUN 1993" and show emblem.

Issued: #349g, 4/93; #349h, 5/29/93.

Scenic Views — A69

1993, June 1 ***Perf. 14x14½***
350 A69 85c Dolly Beach 1.75 1.75
351 A69 95c Blow holes 2.00 2.00
352 A69 $1.05 Merrial Beach 2.25 2.25
353 A69 $1.20 Rain forest 2.50 2.50
Nos. 350-353 (4) 8.50 8.50

Christmas — A70

1993, Sept. 2 Litho. ***Perf. 14½x14***
354 A70 40c Turtle on beach 1.25 1.25
355 A70 45c Crabs, wave 1.25 1.25
356 A70 $1 Frigatebird, rainforest 2.75 2.75
Nos. 354-356 (3) 5.25 5.25

Naming of Christmas Island, 350th Anniv. — A71

1993, Dec. 1 Litho. ***Perf. 14x14½***
357 A71 $2 multicolored 4.00 4.00

New Year 1994 (Year of the Dog) — A72

1994, Jan. 20 Litho. ***Perf. 14x14½***
358 A72 45c shown 1.40 *1.50*
359 A72 45c Pekingese 1.40 *1.50*
a. Pair, #358-359 3.00 *3.75*
b. Souvenir sheet of 1, #359a 4.25 *4.25*
c. As "b," overprinted *4.50 4.50*
d. As "b," overprinted *7.50 7.50*
e. As "b," overprinted *4.50 4.50*
f. As "b," overprinted *12.50 12.50*

No. 359c Ovptd. in gold in sheet margin with dog and "Melbourne / STAMP & COIN SHOW / 11-13 February 1994;" No. 359d with "HONG KONG '94 STAMP EXHIBITION" and show emblem; No. 359e with "Canberra /Stamp Show '94 / 19-21 March / 1994" and show emblem; No. 359f with "QUEENSLAND STAMP & COIN SHOW 1994 / JUNE 11, 12, 13."

Issued: #359c, 2/11/94; #359d, 2/18/94; #359e, 3/19/94; #359f, 1995.

Christmas Island Railway Steam Locomotives A73

1994, May 19 Litho. ***Perf. 14x14½***
360 A73 85c Locomotive No. 4 2.00 1.75
361 A73 95c Locomotive No. 9 2.25 1.75
362 A73 $1.20 Locomotive No. 1 2.75 2.00
Nos. 360-362 (3) 7.00 5.50

Orchids — A74

a, Brachypeza archytas. b, Thelasis capitata. c, Corymborkis veratrifolia. d, Flickingeria nativitatis. e, Dendrobium crumenatum.

1994, Aug. 16 Litho. ***Perf. 14½x14***
363 A74 45c Strip of 5, #a.-e. 7.00 7.00

Christmas A75

1994, Sept. 8 Litho. ***Perf. 14x14½***
364 A75 40c Angel 1.10 .80
365 A75 45c Wise man 1.25 .80
366 A75 80c Bethlehem 1.75 1.50
Nos. 364-366 (3) 4.10 3.10

New Year 1995 (Year of the Boar) — A76

Design: 85c, Stylized boar, diff.

1995, Jan. 12 Litho. ***Perf. 14x14½***
367 A76 45c shown .90 .85
368 A76 85c multicolored 1.60 1.40
a. Souvenir sheet, #367-368 3.25 3.25
b. As "a," overprinted *6.00 6.00*

No. 368b ovptd. in gold in sheet margin with outline of boar and: "STAMP & COIN FAIR / ROYAL EXHIBITION BUILDING / MELBOURNE VIC. 3000 . 10-12 FEB 1995."

Christmas Island Golf Course, 40th Anniv. — A77

1995, May 11 Litho. ***Perf. 14***
369 A77 $2.50 multicolored 7.50 7.50

Christmas A78

Santa Claus riding great frigatebird: 40c, Reading map. 45c, Dropping presents. 80c, Waving.

1995, Sept. 14 Litho. ***Perf. 14x14½***
370 A78 40c multicolored 1.00 .85
371 A78 45c multicolored 1.10 .85
372 A78 80c multicolored 1.75 1.40
Nos. 370-372 (3) 3.85 3.10

End of World War II, 50th Anniv. — A79

#373a, RAAF reconnaissance flight, 1945. #373b, Arrival of HMS Rother, 1945.

Litho. & Engr.

1995, Oct. 12 ***Perf. 14x14½***
373 Pair 3.00 3.00
a.-b. A79 45c any single 1.40 1.40

Angelfish A80

1995, Oct. 12 **Litho.**
374 A80 75c Lemonpeel 1.60 1.60
375 A80 $1 Emperor 2.00 2.00

New Year 1996 (Year of the Rat) A81

1996, Jan. 9 Litho. ***Perf. 14x14½***
376 A81 45c Facing right 1.10 1.10
377 A81 45c Facing left 1.10 1.10
a. Pair, #376-377 2.25 2.25
b. Souvenir sheet, #377a 2.50 2.50
c. As "b," overprinted 3.25 3.25

No. 377c overprinted in gold in sheet margin "STAMP AND COIN FAIR / MELBOURNE / 23-25 February 1996."

Fish — A82

1996-97 Litho. ***Perf. 14x14½***
381 A82 20c Pinktail triggerfish .55 .55
382 A82 30c Longnose filefish .70 .70
383 A82 45c Princess anthias .90 .90
384 A82 85c Green moon wrasse 1.50 1.50
385 A82 90c Spotted boxfish 1.75 1.75
386 A82 95c Moorish idol 1.75 1.75
387 A82 $1.20 Glass bigeye 2.25 1.90
Nos. 381-387 (7) 9.40 9.05

Issued: 20c, 30c, 45c, 90c, 4/18/96; 85c, 95c, $1.20, 7/17/97.

Birds — A83

1996, July 11 Litho. ***Perf. 14½x14***
399 A83 45c White-eye 1.25 1.25
400 A83 85c Hawk-owl 2.00 2.00

Christmas A84

Sailing ships, words from Christmas carol: 40c, "I Saw Three Ships." 45c, "Come sailing in." 80c, "On Christmas day in the morning."

1996, Sept. 12 Litho. *Perf. 14*

401 A84 40c multicolored	1.00	.70
402 A84 45c multicolored	1.10	.80
403 A84 80c multicolored	1.75	1.40
Nos. 401-403 (3)	3.85	2.90

Exploration of Australian Coast & Christmas Island by Willem de Vlamingh, 300th Anniv. — A85

"Portrait of a Dutch Navigator," by Jan Verkolje.

1996, Oct. 27 Litho. *Perf. 14*

404 A85 45c multicolored 1.50 1.50

No. 404 was issued se-tenant with Australia No. 1571 (No. 1571a).

New Year 1997 (Year of the Ox) — A86

Constellation and: No. 405, Ox facing right. No. 406, Ox facing left.

1997, Jan. 6 Litho. *Perf. 14x14½*

405 A86 45c multicolored	1.10	1.10
406 A86 45c multicolored	1.10	1.10
a. Pair, #405-406	2.40	2.40
b. Souvenir sheet, #405-406	2.75	*3.00*

Christmas A87

Santa on Christmas Island: 40c, Reading letters. 45c, Making toys. 80c, In sleigh.

1997, Sept. 11 Litho. *Perf. 14x14½*

407 A87 40c multicolored	.90	.85
408 A87 45c multicolored	.95	.90
409 A87 80c multicolored	2.10	1.75
Nos. 407-409 (3)	3.95	3.50

New Year 1998 (Year of the Tiger) — A88

1998, Jan. 5 Litho. *Perf. 14x14½*

410 A88 45c shown	1.25	1.25
411 A88 45c Looking backward	1.25	1.25
a. Pair, #410-411	2.75	2.75
b. Souvenir sheet of 2, #410-411	3.25	*3.50*

Marine Life — A89

Designs: a, 5c, Frigatebird. b, 5c, Ambon chromis, denomination LR. c, 5c, Ambon chromis, denomination LL. d, 5c, Pink anemonefish, denomination, UR. e, 5c, Pink anemonefish, denomination LL. f, 10c, Eastern reef egret. g, 10c, Whitelined cod. h, 10c, Pyramid butterfly fish. i, 10c, Dusky parrotfish. j, 10c, Spotted garden eel. k, 25c, Sooty tern. l, 25c, Scissortail sergeant. m, 25c, Thicklip wrasse. n, 25c, Blackaxil chromis. o, 25c, Orange anthias. p, 45c, Brown booby. q, 45c, Green turtle. r, 45c, Pink anemonefish. s, 45c, Blue sea star. t, 45c, Kunie's chromodoris.

1998, Mar. 12 Litho. *Perf. 14*

412 A89 Sheet of 20, #a.-t. 10.00 10.00

Tree Flowers of Christmas — A90

1998, Sept. 3 Litho. *Perf. 14½x14*

413 A90 40c Orchid tree	.80	.80
414 A90 80c Flame tree	1.75	1.75
415 A90 95c Sea hibiscus	1.90	1.90
Nos. 413-415 (3)	4.45	4.45

New Year 1999 (Year of the Rabbit) A91

1999, Jan. 14 Litho. *Perf. 14x14½*

416 A91 45c shown	1.25	1.25
417 A91 45c Rabbit looking left	1.25	1.25
a. Pair, #416-417	2.75	2.75
b. Souvenir sheet, #417a	3.00	3.00

Festivals on Christmas Island — A92

Children's drawings: No. 418, Carrying balloons in parade, by Fong Jason. No. 419, Giant crab, by Siti Zanariah Zainal. 85c, Children at night, by Tan Diana, vert. $1.20, Green mosque, tree, by Anwar Ramian, vert.

1999, July 15 Litho. *Perf. 14x14½*

418 A92 45c multicolored	.90	.80
419 A92 45c multicolored	.90	.80
a. Pair, #418-419	1.90	1.90

Perf. 14½x14

420 A92 85c multicolored	1.40	1.40
421 A92 $1.20 multicolored	2.00	2.00
Nos. 418-421 (4)	5.20	5.00

Christmas A93

Designs: 40c, Santa Claus in hammock. 45c, Santa, birds, crab, lizard, cake. 95c, Santa, booby-drawn sleigh.

1999, Sept. 9 Litho. *Perf. 14x14½*

422 A93 40c multicolored	.95	.80
423 A93 45c multicolored	1.10	.95
424 A93 95c multicolored	1.75	1.75
Nos. 422-424 (3)	3.80	3.50

New Year 2000 (Year of the Dragon) A94

2000, Jan. 13 Litho. *Perf. 14x14½*

425 A94 45c shown	1.25	1.25
426 A94 45c Dragon facing left	1.25	1.25
a. Pair, #425-426	2.75	2.75
b. Souvenir sheet, #426a	3.00	*3.25*

Faces of Christmas Island — A95

Ordinary people: a, Yeow Jian Min, without shirt. b, Ida Chin, with blue shirt. c, Ho Tak Wah, old man. d, Thomas Faul and James Neill. e, Siti Sanniah Kawi, with striped blouse.

2000, Apr. 13 Litho. *Perf. 14½x14*

427 A95 45c Strip of 5, #a.-e. 5.00 5.50

Christmas — A96

No. 428: a, We three kings of Orient are. b, Bearing gifts we traverse afar. 45c, Star of wonder, star of night.

2000, Sept. 5 Litho. *Perf. 14½x14*

428 Pair	1.60	1.60
a.-b. A96 40c Any single	.80	.70
429 A96 45c multi	.80	.70

New Year 2001 (Year of the Snake) A97

Snake color: 45c, Green. $1.35, Silver.

Litho. with Foil Application

2001, Jan. 8 *Perf. 14x14½*

430-431 A97 Set of 2	3.00	3.00
a. Souvenir sheet, #430-431	4.00	*4.50*

Fungi — A98

Designs: $1, Chaetocalathus semisupinus. $1.50, Pycnoporus sanguineus.

2001, Oct. 25 Litho. *Perf. 14x14½*

432-433 A98 Set of 2 4.00 *4.25*

New Year 2002 (Year of the Horse) — A99

Zodiac Animals and Their Chinese Characters A100

Designs: 45c, Purple horse. $1.35, Gold horse.

No. 436: a, Rat. b, Ox. c, Tiger. d, Rabbit. e, Dragon. f, Snake. g, Horse. h, Sheep. i, Monkey. j, Cock. k, Dog. l, Boar.

Litho. With Gold Foil Application

2002, Jan. 8 *Perf. 14x14½*

434-435 A99 Set of 2	3.25	3.25
a. Souvenir sheet, #434-435	4.00	4.00
436 Sheet of 14, #a-l, #435a	10.00	10.00
a.-d. A100 5c Any single	.45	.45
e.-h. A100 15c Any single, orange background	.50	.50
i.-l. A100 25c Any single, orange background	.55	.55

See No. 442.

Worldwide Fund for Nature (WWF) — A101

Christmas Island birds - No. 437: a, Imperial pigeon. b, Hawk owl.

$1, Goshawk. $1.50, Thrush.

2002, May 1 Litho. *Perf. 14½x14*

437 A101 45c Horiz. pair, #a-b	1.50	1.50
438 A101 $1 multi	1.50	1.50
439 A101 $1.50 multi	2.50	2.50
Nos. 437-439 (3)	5.50	5.50

Zodiac Animals Type of 2002 and

New Year 2003 (Year of the Ram) A102

Designs: 50c, Yellow and orange ram. $1.50, Blue ram.

No. 442: a, Rat. b, Ox. c, Tiger. d, Rabbit. e, Dragon. f, Snake. g, Horse. h, Sheep. i, Monkey. j, Cock. k, Dog. l, Boar.

Litho. With Gold Foil Application

2003, Jan. 7 *Perf. 14x14½*

440-441 A102 Set of 2	3.50	3.50
a. Souvenir sheet, #440-441	4.00	4.00
442 Sheet of 14, #a-l, #441a	10.00	10.00
a.-d. A100 10c Any single, red violet background	.40	.40
e.-h. A100 15c Any single, red violet background	.50	.50
i.-l. A100 25c Any single, red violet background	.60	.60

Christmas — A103

Designs: 45c, Arrival of Santa Claus on whale shark. 50c, Santa giving gifts to red crabs.

2003, Oct. 31 Litho. *Perf. 14½x14*

443-444 A103 Set of 2 2.25 2.25

Zodiac Animals Type of 2002 and

New Year 2004 (Year of the Monkey) A104

Designs: 50c, Yellow and orange monkey. $1.45, Red orange monkey, lotus flower.

No. 447: a, Rat. b, Ox. c, Tiger. d, Rabbit. e, Dragon. f, Snake. g, Horse. h, Sheep. i, Monkey. j, Cock. k, Dog. l, Boar.

Litho. With Gold Foil Application

2004, Jan. 6 *Perf. 14x14½*

445-446 A104 Set of 2	4.00	4.00
446a Souvenir sheet, #445-446	5.00	5.00
447 Sheet of 14, #a-l, #446a	10.00	10.00
a.-d. A100 10c Any single, light and dark blue background	.40	.40
e.-h. A100 15c Any single, light and dark blue background	.50	.50
i.-l. A100 25c Any single, light and dark blue background	.60	.60

No. 446a exists with a 2004 Hong Kong Stamp Expo overprint in sheet margin in red. This sheet was sold at the show, but not on Christmas Island.

Marine Life — A105

No. 448: a, Two butterflyfish, rear of whale shark. b, Three striped fish, front of whale shark. c, Four fish. d, Two fish. e, Two green turtles. f, Two triggerfish (polka dots), red coral at LL. g, Two fish with thin horizontal stripes with yellow tails. h, Two fish with thick vertical stripes. i, Black and white fish. j, Three fish. k, Yellow fish with black spot, blue fish, red coral, yellow coral. l, Striped fish, clam. m, Black fish, small red fish. n Red fish, divers. o, Two striped fish, red coral under denomination. p, Blue and yellow fish, red and white spotted fish, yellow coral. q, Blue and yellow fish, yellow coral, sea anemones. r, Three blue fish with orange spots. s, Sea anemone and two anemonefish. t, Nudibranch, red coral and starfish.

2004, July 13 Litho. *Perf. 14½x14*

448	A105	Sheet of 20	9.50	9.50
a.-e.		10c Any single	.20	.20
f.-o.		25c Any single	.40	.40
p.-t.		50c Any single	.85	.85

Zodiac Animals Type of 2002 and

New Year 2005 (Year of the Cock) A106

Designs: 50c, Cock, spirals at right. $1.45, Cock, spirals at right.

No. 451: a, Rat. b, Ox. c, Tiger. d, Rabbit. e, Dragon. f, Snake. g, Horse. h, Sheep. i, Monkey. j, Cock. k, Dog. l, Boar.

Litho. With Gold Foil Application

2005, Jan. 4 *Perf. 14x14½*

449-450	A106	Set of 2	4.00	4.00
450a		Souvenir sheet, #445-446	4.00	4.00
450b		As "a," with Taipei 2005 emblem overprinted in margin	3.00	3.00
451		Sheet of 14, #a-l, #450a	10.00	10.00
a.-d.		A100 10c Any single, red and yellow background	.35	.35
e.-h.		A100 15c Any single, red and yellow background	.35	.35
i.-l.		A100 25c Any single, red and yellow background	.55	.55

Christmas A107

Santa Claus, birds and: 45c, Palm tree, presents. 90c, Sleigh, crabs.

2005, Nov. 1 Litho. *Perf. 14¼x14*

452	A107	45c multi	.75	.75
a.		Booklet pane of 4	3.50	—
453	A107	90c multi	1.60	1.60

No. 452a exists with two different margins. These two panes were issued in a booklet that also contained three examples of Australia No. 2423a. The entire booklet sold for $9.95.

Zodiac Animals Type of 2002 and

New Year 2006 (Year of the Dog) A108

Designs: 50c, Purple dog. $1.45, Copper dog.

No. 456: a, Rat. b, Ox. c, Tiger. d, Rabbit. e, Dragon. f, Snake. g, Horse. h, Sheep. i, Monkey. j, Cock. k, Dog. l, Boar.

Litho. With Copper Foil Application

2006, Jan. 5 *Perf. 14x14½*

454-455	A106	Set of 2	3.00	3.00
455a		Souvenir sheet, #454-455	3.00	3.00
456		Sheet of 14, #a-l, #455a	6.00	6.00
a.-d.		A100 10c Any single, brown and yellow background	.20	.20
e.-h.		A100 15c Any single, brown and yellow background	.20	.20
i.-l.		A100 25c Any single, brown and yellow background	.35	.35

Buildings — A109

Designs: 50c, Mosque. $1.45, Tai Jin House.

No. 458: a, Tai Pak Kong Temple. b, Soon Tian Temple.

2006, June 13 Litho. *Perf. 14½x14*

457	A109	50c multi	.75	.75
458	A109	$1 Horiz. pair, #a-b	3.00	3.00
459	A109	$1.45 multi	2.25	2.25
		Nos. 457-459 (3)	6.00	6.00

Zodiac Animals Types of 1996-2006 and

New Year 2007 (Year of the Boar) A110

Zodiac Animals A111

Designs: Nos. 460, 463l, 50c, Boar facing right. $1.45, Boar facing left.

No. 462: a, Rat. b, Ox. c, Tiger. d, Rabbit. e, Dragon. f, Snake. g, Horse. h, Sheep. i, Monkey. j, Cock. k, Dog. l, Boar.

Litho. With Copper Foil Application

2007, Jan. 9 *Perf. 14x14½*

460-461	A110	Set of 2	3.25	3.25
461a		Souvenir sheet, #460-461	3.25	3.25
462		Sheet of 14, #a-l, #461a	6.50	6.50
a.-d.		A100 10c Any single, multicolored background	.20	.20
e.-h.		A100 15c Any single, multicolored background	.20	.20
i.-l.		A100 25c Any single, multicolored background	.40	.40

Self-Adhesive

Serpentine Die Cut 12¼ Syncopated (#463a-463l), Serpentine Die Cut (#463m)

463	Sheet of 13	11.50	
a.	A81 50c Like #376	.80	.80
b.	A86 50c Like #405	.80	.80
c.	A88 50c Like #410	.80	.80
d.	A91 50c Like #416	.80	.80
e.	A94 50c Like #425	.80	.80
f.	A97 50c Like #430	.80	.80
g.	A99 50c Like #434	.80	.80
h.	A102 50c Like #440	.80	.80
i.	A104 50c Like #445	.80	.80
j.	A106 50c Like #449	.80	.80
k.	A108 50c Like #454	.80	.80
l.	A110 50c Like #460	.80	.80
m.	A111 $1 multi	1.60	1.60
n.	Booklet pane, 2 each #463a-463b	3.50	
o.	Booklet pane, 2 each #463c-463d	3.50	
p.	Booklet pane, 2 each #463e-463f	3.50	
q.	Booklet pane, 2 each #463g-463h	3.50	
r.	Booklet pane, 2 each #463i-463j	3.50	
s.	Booklet pane, 2 each #463k-463l	3.50	
	Complete booklet, #463n-463s	21.00	

Complete booklet sold for $12.95.

Christmas A112

Santa Claus: 45c, In boat. 50c, Hoisted by crane. $1.10, On beach.

2007, Nov. 1 Litho. *Perf. 14x14½*

464-466	A112	Set of 3	3.75	3.75

New Year 2008 (Year of the Rat) — A113

Designs: 50c, Rat. $1.45, Chinese character for "rat."

No. 469: a, Rat, diff. b, Ox. c, Dragon. d, Snake. e, Tiger. f, Rabbit. g, Horse. h, Pig. i, Goat. j, Monkey. k, Rooster. l, Dog.

Litho. With Foil Application

2008, Jan. 8 *Perf. 14*

467	A113	50c multi	.90	.90
a.		Perf. 14¾x14	.90	.90

Perf. 14¾x14

468	A113	$1.45 multi	2.60	2.60
a.		Souvenir sheet, #467a, 468	3.50	3.50
469		Sheet of 14, #467a, 468, 469a-469l	7.00	7.00
a.-d.		A113 10c Any single	.20	.20
e.-h.		A113 15c Any single	.25	.25
i.-l.		A113 25c Any single	.40	.40
m.		Booklet pane of 4, #469a, 469b, 2 #468	6.25	—
n.		Booklet pane of 4, #469e, 469f, 2 #467a	2.60	—
o.		Booklet pane of 4, #469c, 469d, 2 #467a	2.40	—
p.		Booklet pane of 4, #469g, 469i, 2 #467a	2.75	—
q.		Booklet pane of 4, #469j, 469k, 2 #467a	3.00	—
r.		Booklet pane of 4, #469h, 469l, 2 #467a	2.75	—
		Complete booklet, #469m-469r	20.00	

Complete booklet sold for $10.95.

Territorial Status of Christmas Island, 50th Anniv. A114

No. 470: a, Gecarcoidea natalis. b, Papasula abbotti. c, Asplenium listeri.

$1.45, Seal of Union of Christmas Island Workers. $2.45, Christmas Island flag.

2008, June 10 Litho. *Perf. 14¼*

470		Horiz. strip of 3	3.00	3.00
a.-c.	A114	50c Any single	1.00	1.00
471	A114	$1.45 multi	3.00	3.00
472	A114	$2.45 multi	4.75	4.75
		Nos. 470-472 (3)	10.75	10.75

Christmas — A115

Designs: 50c, Christmas tree, bird, crabs and shells. $1.20, Crabs with gifts and Christmas lights.

2008, Oct. 31 Litho. *Perf. 14½x14*

473-474	A115	Set of 2	2.25	2.25

CILICIA

sə-'li-sh,ē-,ə

LOCATION — A territory of Turkey, in Southeastern Asia Minor
GOVT. — Former French occupation
AREA — 6,238 sq. mi.
POP. — 383,645
CAPITAL — Adana

British and French forces occupied Cilicia in 1918 and in 1919 its control was transferred to the French. Eventually part of Cilicia was assigned to the French Mandated Territory of Syria but by the Lausanne Treaty of 1923 which fixed the boundary between Syria and Turkey, Cilicia reverted to Turkey.

40 Paras = 1 Piaster

Issued under French Occupation

The overprint on Nos. 2-93 is often found inverted, double, etc.

Numbers in parentheses are those of basic Turkish stamps.

Turkish Stamps of 1913-19 Handstamped

Perf. 11½, 12, 12½, 13½

1919 Unwmk.

		On Pictorial Issue of 1913		
2	A24	2pa red lil (254)	6.50	6.50
3	A25	4pa dk brn (255)	6.00	6.00
4	A27	6pa dk bl (257)	20.00	14.00
5	A32	1¾pi sl & red brn (262)	7.25	6.75
		On Issue of 1915		
6	A17	1pi bl (300)	2.25	2.25
7	A21	20pa car rose (318)	11.00	8.75
9	A22	20pa car rose (330)	30.00	26.00
		On Commemorative Issue of 1916		
9A	A41	5pa green (345)	110.00	72.50
10	A41	20pa ultra (347)	5.25	5.25
11	A41	1pi vio & blk (348)	7.25	7.25
12	A41	5pi yel brn & blk (349)	3.50	2.25
		On Issue of 1916-18		
13	A44	10pa grn (424)	7.25	7.25
14	A47	50pa ultra (428)	37.50	30.00
15	A51	25pi car, *straw* (434)	7.25	7.25
16	A52	50pi car (437)	7.25	7.25
17	A52	50pi ind (438)	26.00	26.00
		On Issue of 1917		
18	A53	5pi on 2pa Prus bl (547)	11.00	4.50
		On Issue of 1919		
19	A47	50pa ultra (555)	32.50	3.75
20	A48	2pi org brn & ind (556)	32.50	4.00
21	A49	5pi pale bl & blk (557)	32.50	4.00
		On Newspaper Stamp of 1916		
22	A10	5pa on 10pa gray grn (P137)	3.75	3.75
		On Semi-Postal Stamps of 1915		
22A	A21	20pa car rose (B8)	90.00	62.50
22B	A21	1pi ultra (B9)	2,000.	1,100.
22C	A21	1pi ultra (B13)	1,750.	1,500.
		On Semi-Postal Stamps of 1916		
23	A17	1pi bl (B19)	7.25	7.25
24	A21	20pa car rose (B28)	2.25	2.25
25	A21	1pi ultra (B29)	8.75	8.75

Turkish Stamps of 1913-18 Handstamped

1919

On Pictorial Issue of 1913

31 A24 2pa red lil (254) 2.25 2.25
32 A25 4pa dk brn (255) 12.50 12.50

On Issue of 1915

33 A17 1pi blue (300) 11.00 11.00
34 A22 20pa car rose (330) 3.75 3.75

On Commemorative Issue of 1916

35 A41 20pa ultra (347) 12.50 12.50
36 A41 1pi vio & blk (348) 2.25 2.25

On Issue of 1917

40 A53 5pi on 2pa Prus bl (547) 11.00 11.00

On Newspaper Stamp of 1916

41 A10 5pa on 10pa gray grn (P137) 21.00 21.00

On Semi-Postal Stamp of 1915

41A A21 20pa car rose (B8) 160.00 125.00

On Semi-Postal Stamps of 1916

42 A17 1pi blue (B19) 4.00 2.50
43 A21 20pa car rose (B28) 5.25 5.50

Turkish Stamps of 1913-19 Handstamped

1919

On Pictorial Issue of 1913

51 A24 2pa red lil (254) 8.75 8.75
52 A25 4pa dk brn (255) 3.00 2.25

On Issue of 1915

53 A17 1pi blue (300) 4.50 4.50
55 A22 5pa ocher (328) 32.50 30.00
56 A22 20pa car rose (330) 3.00 3.00

On Commemorative Issue of 1916

57 A41 20pa ultra (347) 3.00 3.00
58 A41 1pi vio & blk (348) 2.25 2.25
59 A41 5pi yel brn & blk (349) 9.50 9.50

On Issue of 1916

59A A17 1pi blue (372) 80.00 55.00

On Issue of 1916-18

60 A43 5pa org (421) 32.50 30.00
61 A46 1pi dl vio (426) 11.00 11.00
63 A52 50pi grn, *straw* (439) 30.00 21.00

On Issue of 1917

64 A53 5pi on 2pa Prus bl (547) 26.00 21.00

On Newspaper Stamp of 1916

65 A10 5pa on 10pa gray grn (P137) 7.50 7.50

On Semi-Postal Stamp of 1915

65A A21 20pa car rose (B8) 1,100. 675.00

On Semi-Postal Stamps of 1916

66 A17 1pi blue (B19) 8.00 2.50
67 A19 20pa car (B26) 9.00 4.00
68 A21 20pa car rose (B28) 125.00 67.50
69 A21 20pa car rose (B31) 7.50 2.50

Turkey No. 424 Handstamped

1919

71 A44 10pa green 7.50 7.50

"T.E.O." stands for "Territoires Ennemis Occupés."

Turkish Stamps of 1913-19 Overprinted in Black, Red or Blue

In this setting there are various broken and wrong font letters and the letter "i" is sometimes replaced by a "t."

1919 On Pictorial Issue of 1913

75 A30 1pi blue (R) (260) 3.75 3.75

On Issue of 1915

76 A21 20pa car rose (318) 7.50 7.50

On Commemorative Issue of 1916

76A A41 5pa green (345) 150.00 75.00
77 A41 20pa ultra (347) 11.00 11.00
78 A41 1pi vio & blk (348) 18.00 18.00

On Issue of 1916-18

79 A43 5pa org (Bl) (421) 3.75 3.75
80 A44 10pa green (424) 7.25 7.50
81 A45 20pa dp rose (Bk) (425) 25.00 22.50
82 A45 20pa dp rose (Bl) (425) 2.00 .75
83 A48 2pi org brn & ind (429) 3.00 1.25
83C A49 5pi pale bl & blk (R) (430) 3.50 1.50
84 A51 25pi car, *straw* (434) 9.00 5.25
85 A52 50pi grn, *straw* (439) 105.00 72.50

On Issue of 1917

85A A53 5pi on 2pa Prus bl (547) —
86 A53 5pi on 2pa Prus bl (548) 11.00 11.00

On Newspaper Stamps of 1916-19

87 A10 5pa on 10p gray grn (P137) 3.00 2.00
88 A21 5pa on 2pa ol grn (P173) 1.75 .75

On Semi-Postal Stamps of 1915-17

90 A21 20pa car rose (B28) 7.25 7.25
91 A41 10pa car (B42) 2.25 2.25
92 A11 10pa on 20pa vio brn (B38) 2.50 2.25
93 SP1 10pa red vio (B46) 3.00 1.50

It is understood that the newspaper and semi-postal stamps overprinted "Cilicie" were used as ordinary postage stamps.

A1

1920 Blue Surcharge ***Perf. 11½***

98 A1 70pa on 5pa red 2.50 2.25
- *a.* Double surcharge 32.50 32.50
- *b.* Triple surcharge 200.00

99 A1 3½pi on 5pa red 3.50 2.25
- *a.* Se-tenant with No. 98, horiz. pair 100.00 100.00
- *b.* As "a," inverted surcharge 200.00 200.00
- *c.* Double surcharge 32.50 32.50
- *d.* Inverted surcharge 30.00 30.00
- *e.* Double surcharge, one inverted 37.50 37.50

Nos. 98-99 exist with surcharge misspelled "OCCUPTTION," "OCCCPATION," "OCCUPITION". Value $9 each.

French Offices in Turkey No. 26 Surcharged

1920 ***Perf. 14x13½***

100 A3 20pa on 10c rose red 2.50 1.25
- *a.* "PARAS" omitted 62.50 62.50
- *b.* Surcharged on back 22.50 22.50

Three types of "20" exist on No. 100.

Stamps of France, 1900-17, Surcharged

1920

101 A16 5pa on 2c vio brn 1.50 1.50
102 A22 10pa on 5c green 1.90 1.90
- *a.* Inverted surcharge 17.50 *22.50*

103 A22 20pa on 10c red 3.00 3.00
104 A22 1pi on 25c blue 2.75 2.25
105 A20 2pi on 15c gray grn 10.00 10.00
106 A18 5pi on 40c red & gray bl 21.00 22.50
107 A18 10pi on 50c bis brn & lav 25.00 26.00
108 A18 50pi on 1fr cl & ol grn 150.00 150.00
109 A18 100pi on 5fr dk bl & buff 725.00 725.00
Nos. 101-109 (9) 940.15 942.15

Nos. 106 to 109 surcharged in four lines.
"O.M.F." stands for "Occupation Militaire Francaise."

Stamps of France, 1917, Surcharged

1920

110 A16 5pa on 2c vio brn 10.00
111 A22 10pa on 5c green 10.00
112 A22 20pa on 10c red 7.25
113 A22 1pi on 25c blue 5.50
114 A20 2pi on 15c gray grn 21.00
115 A18 5pi on 40c red & gray bl 55.00
116 A18 20pi on 1fr cl & ol grn 150.00
- *a.* "O.M.F. Cilicie" omitted 525.00
- *b.* Double surcharge 525.00

Nos. 110-116 (7) 258.75

On Nos. 115 and 116 "SAND. EST" is placed vertically. "Sand. Est" is an abbreviation of Sandjak de l'Est (Eastern County).
Nos. 110-116 were prepared for use, but never issued.

Stamps of France, 1900-17, Surcharged

1920

117 A16 5pa on 2c vio brn 1.75 .75
- *a.* Inverted surcharge 26.00 22.50
- *b.* Double surcharge 30.00 *30.00*
- *c.* "Cililie" *30.00* *30.00*
- *d.* Surcharge 5pi (error) 47.50 *47.50*

119 A22 10pa on 5c green 1.75 .75
- *a.* Inverted surcharge 26.00 22.50
- *b.* Surch. 5pa (error), invtd. 65.00 60.00
- *c.* Surch. 5pa (error), upright 47.50 47.50

121 A22 20pa on 10c red 1.75 .75
- *a.* Inverted surcharge 26.00 22.50
- *b.* Surch. 10pa (error), invtd. 65.00 60.00
- *c.* Surch. 10pa (error), upright 47.50 47.50
- *d.* Double surcharge 30.00 30.00

122 A22 1pi on 25c blue 1.25 1.10
- *a.* Double surcharge 62.50 62.50
- *b.* Inverted surcharge 30.00 26.00

123 A20 2pi on 15c gray grn 1.75 1.75
- *a.* Double surcharge 37.50 37.50
- *b.* Inverted surcharge 30.00 26.00

124 A18 5pi on 40c red & gray bl 3.00 3.00
- *a.* Double surcharge 55.00 55.00
- *b.* Inverted surcharge 32.50 32.50
- *c.* "PIASRTES" 62.50 62.50

125 A18 10pi on 50c bis brn & lavender 10.00 10.00
- *a.* "PIASRTES" 62.50 62.50
- *b.* Double surcharge 55.00 55.00
- *c.* Inverted surcharge 47.50 40.00

126 A18 50pi on 1fr claret & ol grn 15.00 15.00
- *a.* "PIASRTES" 72.50 72.50
- *b.* Inverted surcharge 110.00 26.00

127 A18 100pi on 5fr dk bl & buff 37.50 37.50
- *a.* "PIASRTES" *750.00*
- *b.* Inverted surcharge 150.00 150.00

Nos. 117-127 (9) 73.75 70.60

This surcharge has "O.M.F." in thicker letters than the preceding issues.
There were two printings of this surcharge which may be distinguished by the space of 1 or 2mm between "Cilicie" and the numeral.
For overprints see Nos. C1-C2.

AIR POST STAMPS

Nos. 123 and 124 Handstamped

Perf. 14x13½

1920, July 15 Unwmk.

C1 A20 2pi on 15c gray grn *8,000.*
C2 A18 5pi on 40c red & gray bl *8,000.*
- *a.* "PIASRTES"

A very limited number of Nos. C1 and C2 were used on two air mail flights between Adana and Aleppo. At a later date impressions from a new handstamp were struck "to oblige" on stamps of the regular issue of 1920 (Nos. 123, 124, 125 and 126) that were in stock at the Adana Post Office.
Counterfeits exist.

POSTAGE DUE STAMPS

Turkish Postage Due Stamps of 1914 Handstamped

Handstamped

1919 Unwmk. ***Perf. 12***

J1 D1 5pa claret 18.00 18.00
J2 D2 20pa red 18.00 18.00
J3 D3 1pi dark blue 30.00 30.00
J4 D4 2pi slate 35.00 35.00
Nos. J1-J4 (4) 101.00 101.00

Handstamped

J5 D1 5pa claret 21.00 21.00
J6 D2 20pa red 25.00 25.00
J7 D3 1pi dark blue 30.00 30.00
J8 D4 2pi slate 30.00 30.00
Nos. J5-J8 (4) 106.00 106.00

Handstamped

J9 D1 5pa claret 21.00 21.00
J10 D2 20pa red 25.00 25.00
J11 D3 1pi dark blue 30.00 30.00
J12 D4 2pi slate 30.00 30.00
Nos. J9-J12 (4) 106.00 106.00

Postage Due Stamps of France Surcharged

1921

J13	D2	1pi on 10c choc	9.50	9.50
J14	D2	2pi on 20c olive grn	9.50	9.50
J15	D2	3pi on 30c red	8.75	8.75
J16	D2	4pi on 50c vio brn	8.75	8.75
		Nos. J13-J16 (4)	36.50	36.50

COCHIN CHINA

ˈkō-chən ˈchī-nə

LOCATION — The southernmost state of French Indo-China in the Cambodian Peninsula.
GOVT. — French Colony
AREA — 26,476 sq. mi.
POP. — 4,615,968
CAPITAL — Saigon

100 Centimes = 1 Franc

Values for unused stamps are for examples without gum, as most stamps were issued in that condition.

Surcharged in Black on Stamps of French Colonies:

a

b

c

1886-87 Unwmk. *Perf. 14x13½*

1	A9(a)	5c on 25c yel, *straw*	210.00	110.00
2	A9(b)	5c on 2c brn, *buff*	40.00	*30.00*
3	A9(b)	5c on 25c yel, *straw*	32.50	26.00
a.		Inverted surcharge	*200.00*	*200.00*
4	A9(c)	5c on 25c blk, *rose* ('87)	60.00	45.00
a.		Dbl. surch., one of type b	*3,100.*	*2,750.*
b.		Triple surch., two of type b	—	—
c.		Inverted surcharge	350.00	350.00
d.		Double surch., both type "a"	*2,250.*	*2,500.*
e.		Triple surch., types "a," "b" and "c"		*6,750.*
		Nos. 1-4 (4)	342.50	211.00

1888

5	A9	15c on half of 30c brn, *bis*	72.50	

No. 5 was prepared but not issued.

The so-called Postage Due stamps were never issued.

Stamps of Cochin China were superseded by those of Indo-China in 1892.

COCOS ISLANDS

ˈkō-kəs ˈī-ləndz

(Keeling Islands)

LOCATION — Indian Ocean, 1,330 miles northwest of Australia, 580 miles southwest of Java
GOVT. — A territory of Australia
AREA — 6 sq. mi.
POP. — 670 (1994)

Of 27 small coral islands making up two atolls, two islands are inhabited. Cocos Islands stamps are also valid within Australia.

12 Pence = 1 Shilling
100 Cents = 1 Dollar (1969)

Catalogue values for all unused stamps in this country are for Never Hinged items.

Copra Industry — A1

Super Constellation A2

Map of Islands — A3

Designs: 1sh, Coco palms. 2sh, Sailboat (dukong). 2sh3p, Fairy tern.

Perf. 14½

1963, June 11 Unwmk. Engr.

1	A1	3p	dk red brown	1.40	1.25
2	A2	5p	vio blue	1.75	1.00
3	A3	8p	red	3.75	1.75
4	A1	1sh	green	3.75	1.00
5	A3	2sh	dull purple	7.00	3.75
6	A2	2sh3p	green	25.00	5.25
			Nos. 1-6 (6)	42.65	14.00
			Set, hinged	18.00	

"Simpson and His Donkey" by Wallace Anderson — A3a

1965, Apr. 14 Photo. *Perf. 13½x13*

7	A3a	5p brt grn, sepia & blk	1.00	.85

ANZAC issue. See note after Australia No. 387.

Turbo Lajonkairii — A4

Blenny — A5

Designs: 2c, Tridacna crocea (shell). 3c, Tridacna derasa (shell). 5c, Porites cocosensis (coral). 6c, Flyingfish. 10c, Banded rail (bird). 15c, Java sparrow. 20c, Red-tailed tropic bird. 30c, Sooty tern. 50c, Eastern reef heron. $1, Great frigate bird.

Perf. 13½

1969, July 9 Unwmk. Photo.

Size: 21½x27mm, 26½x22mm

8	A4	1c multicolored	.25	*.50*
9	A4	2c multicolored	.90	.65
10	A5	3c multicolored	.35	.20
11	A5	4c multicolored	.25	*.40*
12	A5	5c multicolored	.30	.25
13	A5	6c multicolored	.75	.70
14	A5	10c multicolored	1.10	.75
15	A5	15c multicolored	1.10	.55
16	A5	20c multicolored	1.10	.40
17	A5	30c multicolored	1.10	.45
18	A5	50c multicolored	1.10	.45

Size: 21½x34mm

19	A4	$1 multicolored	3.00	1.40
		Nos. 8-19 (12)	11.30	6.70

"Dragon" — A6

"Juno" — A7

Perf. 13½x13, 13x13½

1976, Mar. 29 Photo.

20	A6	1c shown	.40	.40
21	A7	2c shown	.40	.40
22	A7	5c "Beagle"	.40	.40
23	A7	10c "Sydney"	.45	.45
24	A7	15c "Emden"	.85	.85
25	A7	20c "Ayesha"	.85	.85
26	A6	25c "Islander"	.85	.85
27	A6	30c "Cheshire"	.85	.85
28	A7	35c "Jukung"	.85	.85
29	A7	40c "Scotia"	.85	.85
30	A6	50c "Orontes"	.85	.85
31	A6	$1 Royal Yacht "Gothic"	1.50	1.50
		Nos. 20-31 (12)	9.10	9.10

Historic ships.

Flag, Southern Cross, Islands' Map — A8

Council Emblem, Sailboat A9

1979, Sept. 3 Litho. *Perf. 15½*

32	A8	20c multicolored	.35	*.30*
33	A9	50c multicolored	.55	*.70*

Inauguration of Cocos Islands' postal service (20c), and establishment of Cocos Islands Council (50c).

Forcipiger Flavissimus A10

Fish: 2c, Chaetodon ornatissimus. 5c, Anthias. 10c, Meyer's coralfish. 15c, Halichoeres. 20c, Amphiprion clarkii. 22c, Balistapus undulatus. 25c, Maori wrasse. 28c, Macropharyngodon meleagris. 30c, Chaetodon madagascariensis. 35c, Centropyge colini. 40c, Bodianus axillaris. 50c, Corisgaimardi. 55c, Spotted wrasse. 60c, Epinepnelus tauvina. $1, Paracanthurus hepatus. $2, Striped butterflyfish.

1979-80 Litho. *Perf. 15½*

34	A10	1c multicolored	.20	*.90*
35	A10	2c multicolored	.20	*.30*
36	A10	5c multicolored	.40	*.95*
37	A10	10c multi ('80)	.20	*.90*
38	A10	15c multicolored	.35	.30
39	A10	20c multicolored	.45	.30
40	A10	22c multi ('80)	.40	.30
41	A10	25c multi ('80)	.45	*.90*
42	A10	28c multi ('80)	.40	.30
43	A10	30c multicolored	.55	.40
44	A10	35c multicolored	.65	*1.40*
45	A10	40c multicolored	.70	.50
46	A10	50c multicolored	.95	.70
47	A10	55c multi ('80)	.85	*1.10*
48	A10	60c multi ('80)	.75	.70
49	A10	$1 multicolored	1.10	*2.75*
50	A10	$2 multi ('80)	2.25	*3.00*
		Nos. 34-50 (17)	10.85	*15.70*

Sailboats in Lagoon A11

Christmas: 25c, Yachts and seagulls, vert.

1979, Oct. 22 Litho. *Perf. 15½*

51	A11	25c multicolored	.35	.25
52	A11	55c multicolored	.55	*.65*

Star of Bethlehem, Map of Cocos Islands A12

Christmas (Map of Cocos Islands and): 28c, Three kings. 60c, Nativity.

1980, Oct. 22 Litho. *Perf. 13½x13*

53	A12	15c multicolored	.20	.20
54	A12	28c multicolored	.25	.25
55	A12	60c multicolored	.80	.80
		Nos. 53-55 (3)	1.25	1.25

Flag and Arms of Great Britain — A13

Australian Territory Status, 25th Anniv. (British Flag and Arms of Past Administrators): No. 57, Ceylon, 1878, 1942-1946. No. 58, Straits Settlements, 1886. No. 59, Singapore, 1946. No. 60, Australia (flag), 1955.

1980, Nov. 24 Litho. *Perf. 13½x13*

56	A13	22c multicolored	.30	.30
57	A13	22c multicolored	.30	.30
58	A13	22c multicolored	.30	.30
59	A13	22c multicolored	.30	.30
60	A13	22c multicolored	.30	.30
a.		Strip of 5, Nos. 56-60	1.75	1.75

Eye of the Wind, Map of Cocos Islands — A14

1980, Dec. 18 *Perf. 13x13½, 13½x13*

61	A14	22c shown	.45	.45
62	A14	28c Expedition routes, horiz.	.45	.45
63	A14	35c Francis Drake, Golden Hinde	.45	.45
64	A14	60c Prince Charles, Eye of the Wind	.75	.75
		Nos. 61-64 (4)	2.10	2.10

Operation Drake circumnavigation.

Livestock in Quarantine
A15

1981, May 12 Litho. *Perf. 13½x13*

65 A15 22c Aerial view of station .35 .35
66 A15 45c shown .50 .50
67 A15 60c Livestock, diff. .85 .85
Nos. 65-67 (3) 1.70 1.70

West Island Quarantine Station opening.

Catalina Guba II
A16

Inauguration of Air Service to Indian Ocean: No. 69, Avro Lancastrian. No. 70, Douglas DC4 Skymaster, Lockheed Constellation. No. 71, Lockheed Electra. No. 72, Boeing 727.

1981, June 23 Litho. *Perf. 13½x13*

68 A16 22c multicolored .40 .40
69 A16 22c multicolored .40 .40
70 A16 22c multicolored .40 .40
71 A16 22c multicolored .40 .40
72 A16 22c multicolored .40 .40
a. Strip of 5, #68-72 2.25 2.25

Prince Charles and Lady Diana — A17

1981, July 29 Litho. *Perf. 13½x13*

73 A17 24c multicolored .35 .35
74 A17 60c multicolored .90 .90

Royal Wedding.

Angels We Have Heard on High — A18

Christmas: Carols.

1981, Oct. 22 Photo. *Perf. 13½x13*

75 A18 18c shown .35 .35
76 A18 30c Shepherds Why this Jubilee .50 .50
77 A18 60c Come to Bethlehem and See Him .70 .70
Nos. 75-77 (3) 1.55 1.55

Sesquicentennial of Charles Darwin's Visit — A19

1981, Dec. 28 Litho. *Perf. 13½x13*

78 A19 24c Coral .35 .35
79 A19 45c Darwin, coral .50 .50
80 A19 60c Beagle, coral .75 .75
Nos. 78-80 (3) 1.60 1.60

Souvenir Sheet

81 Sheet of 2 1.25 1.25
a. A19 24c Atoll .60 .60
b. A19 24c Atoll, diff. .60 .60

125th Anniv. of Annexation to the British Dominions
A20

1982, Mar. 31 Litho. *Perf. 13½x14*

82 A20 24c Queen Victoria .40 .40
83 A20 45c British flag .75 .75
84 A20 60c Capt. Fremantle .85 .85
Nos. 82-84 (3) 2.00 2.00

Scouting Year — A21

Perf. 13½x14, 14x13½

1982, July 21 Litho.

85 A21 27c Baden-Powell .55 .55
86 A21 75c Emblem, map, vert. 1.10 1.10

Macroglossum Corythus — A22

1982, Sept. 6

87 A22 1c Presic villida, vert. 1.25 .70
88 A22 2c Cephonodes picus .45 .45
89 A22 5c shown 1.90 .80
90 A22 10c Chasmina candida, vert. .45 .45
91 A22 20c Nagia linteola .45 *.55*
92 A22 25c Eublemma rivula, vert. .45 *.65*
93 A22 30c Eurrhyparodes tricoloralis, vert. .45 *.55*
94 A22 35c Hippotion boerhaviae 2.00 .85
95 A22 40c Euploea core corinna, vert. .45 *.70*
96 A22 45c Psara hipponalis .60 *.70*
97 A22 50c Danaus chrysippus .70 *1.25*
98 A22 55c Hypolimas misippus, vert. .70 *.80*
99 A22 60c Spodoptera litura, vert. .75 *1.75*
100 A22 $1 Achaea janata, vert. 3.50 3.25
101 A22 $2 Hippotion velox 2.50 *3.25*
102 A22 $3 Utetheisa pulchelloides 3.50 3.25
Nos. 87-102 (16) 20.10 19.95

Christmas
A23

1982, Oct. 25 *Perf. 13x13½*

104 A23 21c Holy Family .30 .20
105 A23 35c Angel .45 .30
106 A23 75c Flight into Egypt 1.25 1.25
Nos. 104-106 (3) 2.00 1.75

Christmas
A24

Cocos-Malay Culture
A25

The Birth of Christ: a, God Will Look After Us; b, Our Baby King Jesus; c, Your Saviour is Born; d, Wise Men Followed the Star; e, And Worship the Lord.

1983, Oct. 31 Litho. *Perf. 14x13½*

107 Strip of 5 1.75 1.75
a.-e. A24 24c any single .30 .30

1984, Jan. 27 Litho. *Perf. 14x13½*

Festive Occasions.

108 A25 45c Hari Raya .65 .45
109 A25 75c Melenggok dance 1.00 .65
110 A25 85c Wedding 1.25 .75
Nos. 108-110 (3) 2.90 1.85

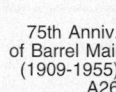

75th Anniv. of Barrel Mail (1909-1955)
A26

Designs: 35c, Mail distribution, Direction Isld. 55c, Jukongs retrieving barrels from ocean liner. 70c, Morea receiving outgoing barrel mail, 1909. $1, Barrel mail recovery.

1984, Apr. 20 Litho. *Perf. 13½x14*

111 A26 35c multicolored .60 .60
112 A26 55c multicolored 1.00 1.00
113 A26 70c multicolored 1.10 1.10
Nos. 111-113 (3) 2.70 2.70

Souvenir Sheet

114 A26 $1 multicolored 2.50 *2.50*

375th Anniv. of Islands' Discovery — A27

1984, July 10 Litho. *Perf. 14x13½*

115 A27 30c Capt. William Keeling .75 .50
116 A27 65c The Hector 1.50 1.10
117 A27 95c Astrolabe 1.90 1.50
118 A27 $1.10 Map, 1666 2.10 1.75
Nos. 115-118 (4) 6.25 4.85

AUSIPEX '84 — A28

45c, Malay Settlement, Home Island. 55c, West Island Air Strip, settlement. $2, Jukong ships racing, Melbourne Exhibition Center.

1984, Sept. 21 Litho. *Perf. 13½*

119 A28 45c multicolored .70 .50
120 A28 55c multicolored .80 .65

Souvenir Sheet

121 A28 $2 multicolored 3.25 3.25

Christmas
A29

1984, Oct. 31 Litho. *Perf. 13½*

122 A29 24c Fish .45 .45
123 A29 35c Butterfly .70 .70
124 A29 55c Bird 1.10 1.10
Nos. 122-124 (3) 2.25 2.25

Souvenir Sheet

Act of Self-Determination — A30

Integration with Australia: a, Australians welcoming Cocos islanders. b, Australian flag over the islands.

1984, Nov. 30 Litho. *Perf. 13½x14*

125 Sheet of 2 3.00 3.00
a.-b. A30 30c any single 1.25 1.25

Crafts — A31

1985, Jan. 30 *Perf. 14x13½*

126 A31 30c Boat building .60 .30
127 A31 45c Blacksmith .90 .45
128 A31 55c Woodcarving 1.25 .75
Nos. 126-128 (3) 2.75 1.50

Cable-laying Ships — A32

1985, Apr. 24 *Perf. 13½x14*

129 A32 33c Scotia 1.60 .90
130 A32 65c Anglia 2.50 1.50
131 A32 80c Patrol 2.50 2.50
Nos. 129-131 (3) 6.60 4.90

Birds
A33

1985, July 17 *Perf. 13½*

132 A33 33c Redfooted booby, vert. 2.75 2.75
133 A33 60c Nankeen night heron 3.25 3.25
134 A33 $1 Buff-banded rail 3.50 3.50
a. "Block" of 3, #132-134 11.00 11.00

Nos. 132-134 printed in a continuous design.

Seashells
A34

1985-86 Litho. *Perf. 13½x14*

135 A34 1c Trochus maculatus .70 *1.00*
136 A34 2c Smaragdia rangiana .70 *1.00*
137 A34 3c Chama .70 *1.00*
138 A34 4c Cypraea moneta 1.25 *1.00*
139 A34 5c Drupa morum .70 *1.00*
140 A34 10c Conus miles .80 *2.10*
141 A34 15c Terebra maculata 2.40 1.75
142 A34 20c Fragum fragum 2.40 2.00
143 A34 30c Turbo lajonkairii 2.40 2.00
144 A34 33c Mitra fissurata 2.50 2.00
145 A34 40c Lambis lambis 2.50 2.00
146 A34 50c Tridacna squamosa 2.50 *2.75*
147 A34 60c Cypraea histrio 2.50 *3.00*
148 A34 $1 Phillidia varicosa 3.75 *4.00*
149 A34 $2 Halgerda tessellata 4.00 *5.00*
150 A34 $3 Harminoea cymbalum 5.00 *6.00*
Nos. 135-150 (16) 34.80 37.60

Issue dates: 1c, 5c, 33c, $1, Sept. 18. 2c, 3c, 10c, $3, Jan. 29, 1986. 15c-30c, 40c, Apr. 30, 1986. 4c, 50c, 60c, $2, July 30, 1986.

For surcharges see #225, 228-229, 231-233.

Souvenir Sheet

Christmas
A35

a, Star LR. b, Star LL. c, Star UR. d, Star UL.

1985, Oct. 30 *Perf. 13½x14*

151 Sheet of 4 3.00 3.00
a.-d. A35 27c any single .70 .70

Darwin's Visit to the Islands — A36

1986, Apr. 1 Litho. *Perf. 14x13½*

152 A36 33c Charles Darwin 1.00 .70
153 A36 60c Map of voyage 1.75 *1.90*
154 A36 $1 HMS Beagle 2.50 *3.00*
Nos. 152-154 (3) 5.25 *5.60*

Christmas A37

1986, Oct. 20 Litho. *Perf. 13½x14*

155 A37 30c Coconut palm, holly .75 .75
156 A37 90c Shell, ornament 2.75 *2.75*
157 A37 $1 Tropical fish, bell 2.75 *2.75*
Nos. 155-157 (3) 6.25 *6.25*

Sailboats A38

a, Jukong. b, Ocean racers. c, Sarimanok. d, Ayesha. #158 has a continuous design.

1987, Jan. 28

158 Strip of 4 6.00 6.00
a.-d. A38 36c any single 1.10 1.10

Island Views — A39

1987, Apr. 8

159 A39 70c Direction Is. 1.50 1.40
160 A39 90c West Is. 1.75 *2.00*
161 A39 $1 Golf course, Cocos 2.50 *2.75*
Nos. 159-161 (3) 5.75 6.15

Communications — A40

1987, July 29 Litho. *Perf. 13½x14*

162 A40 70c Radio 1.40 1.40
163 A40 75c Air service 1.50 1.50
164 A40 90c Satellite 1.75 1.75
165 A40 $1 Airmail 2.00 2.00
Nos. 162-165 (4) 6.65 6.65

Industries A41

1987, Sept. 16

166 A41 45c Batik printing 1.40 1.40
167 A41 65c Boat building 1.90 1.90
168 A41 75c Copra production 2.25 2.25
Nos. 166-168 (3) 5.55 5.55

Industrial activities of the Cocos Malay people.

Christmas — A42

1987, Oct. 28 *Perf. 14x13½*

169 A42 30c Peace on Earth .55 .55
170 A42 90c Unity 1.50 1.50
171 A42 $1 Goodwill Towards All 2.00 2.00
Nos. 169-171 (3) 4.05 4.05

Australia Bicentennial A43

Arrival of the First Fleet, Sydney Cove, Jan. 1788: a, Five aboriginals on shore. b, Four aboriginals on shore, one in canoe. c, Ships entering bay, kangaroos. d, Europeans land, white cranes. e, Flag raising.

1988, Jan. 26 Litho. *Perf. 13*

172 Strip of 5 9.00 9.00
a.-e. A43 37c any single 1.10 1.10

No. 172 has a continuous design. See Christmas Is. No. 213.

Life Cycle of the Coconut — A44

1988, Apr. 13 Litho. *Perf. 14x13½*

173 A44 37c Flower .75 .70
174 A44 65c Small nut stage 1.40 1.40
175 A44 90c Mature nuts 1.60 *1.75*
176 A44 $1 Seedlings 2.00 *2.00*
a. Souvenir sheet of 4, #173-176 7.00 7.00
Nos. 173-176 (4) 5.75 5.85

For surcharge see No. O1.

Cocos Postage Stamps, 25th Anniv. A45

Litho. & Engr.

1988, June 15 *Perf. 15x14*

177 A45 37c No. 1 1.25 .90
178 A45 55c No. 4 1.60 1.25
179 A45 65c No. 2 1.75 1.75
180 A45 70c No. 3 1.90 1.75
181 A45 90c No. 5 2.25 *2.75*
182 A45 $1 No. 6 2.40 *2.75*
Nos. 177-182 (6) 11.15 11.15

For overprint and surcharge see #216, 236.

Flowering Plants — A46

1988-89 Litho. *Perf. 14x13½*

183 A46 1c Pisonia grandis .70 *.90*
184 A46 2c Cocos nucifera .70 *.90*
185 A46 5c Morinda citrifolia 1.40 1.00
186 A46 10c Cordia subcordata .95 *1.00*
189 A46 30c Argusia argentea 1.40 *1.50*
190 A46 37c Calophyllum inophyllum 2.00 1.25
191 A46 40c Barringtonia asiatica 1.40 *1.50*
192 A46 50c Caesalpinia bonduc 1.75 *3.25*
194 A46 90c Terminalia catappa 2.40 *4.75*
195 A46 $1 Pemphis acidula 2.40 *2.75*
197 A46 $2 Scaevola sericea 3.00 3.00
198 A46 $3 Hibiscus tiliaceus 4.75 4.25
Nos. 183-198 (12) 22.85 26.05

Issued: 1c, 5c, 37c, $3, 7/29; 2c, 10c, 30c, $2, 1/18/89; 40c, 50c, 90c, $1, 4/19/89.

For self-adhesive sheet of 3 see No. 217.

Souvenir Sheet

1988, July 30

199 A46 $3 like No. 198 *8.50 8.50*

SYDPEX '88.

Christmas A47

1988, Oct. 12 Litho. *Perf. 13½x14*

200 A47 32c multicolored 1.00 1.00
201 A47 90c multicolored 2.25 2.25
202 A47 $1 multicolored 2.75 2.75
Nos. 200-202 (3) 6.00 6.00

1st Aerial Survey of the Indian Ocean Air Route, 50th Anniv. — A48

40c, P.G. Taylor, pilot. 70c, *Guba II* seaplane and crew. $1, *Guba II* landing off Direction Island. $1.10, Unissued 5sh stamp of Australia, 1939.

1989, July 19 Litho. *Perf. 14x13½*

203 A48 40c multicolored 1.00 1.00
204 A48 70c multicolored 1.60 1.60
205 A48 $1 multicolored 2.25 2.25
206 A48 $1.10 multicolored 2.50 2.50
Nos. 203-206 (4) 7.35 7.35

Jukong, Traditional Sailing Vessel of the Cocos Malay People — A49

1989, Oct. 18 Litho. *Perf. 14x13½*

207 A49 35c multicolored .95 .90
208 A49 80c multicolored 2.25 2.25
209 A49 $1.10 multicolored 3.00 3.00
Nos. 207-209 (3) 6.20 6.15

Christmas.

Naval Engagement of the HMAS *Sydney* and the German Raider SMS *Emden,* 75th Anniv. — A50

Designs: 40c, HMAS *Sydney.* 70c, SMS *Emden.* $1, Steam launch belonging to the *Emden.* $1.10, HMAS *Sydney* and naval crest.

1989, Nov. 9 Litho. *Perf. 13½x14*

210 Strip of 4 + label 7.25 *7.50*
a. A50 40c multicolored .65 .65
b. A50 70c multicolored 1.25 1.25
c. A50 $1 multicolored 1.75 1.75
d. A50 $1.10 multicolored 1.90 1.90
e. Souvenir sheet of 4, #210a-210d 9.00 9.00

Crabs — A52

1990, May 31 Litho. *Perf. 14½*

212 A52 45c Xanthid 1.25 1.25
213 A52 75c Ghost 2.25 2.25
214 A52 $1 Red-backed mud crab 2.50 2.50
215 A52 $1.30 Coconut, vert. 3.00 3.00
Nos. 212-215 (4) 9.00 9.00

No. 180 Overprinted in Red

Litho. & Engr.

1990, Aug. 24 *Perf. 15x14*

216 A45 70c gray, black & red 7.50 7.50

Flowering Plants Type of 1988

1990, Aug. 24 Photo. *Rouletted 9½*

Self-Adhesive

217 Sheet of 3 10.50 10.50
a. A46 10c like No. 186 .40 .40
b. A46 90c like No. 194 2.75 2.75
c. A46 $2 like No. 197 6.25 6.25

World Stamp Exhibition, New Zealand 1990. Nos. 217a-217c inscribed 1990.

Explorers and Their Ships A54

45c, Capt. Keeling, Hector, 1609. 75c, Capt. Fitzroy, Beagle, 1836. $1, Capt. Belcher, Samarang, 1846. $1.30, Capt. Fremantle, Juno, 1857.

1990, Aug. 24 Litho. *Perf. 14½*

218 A54 45c violet brown 1.75 1.60
219 A54 75c pale bl & vio brn 3.00 *3.50*
220 A54 $1 pale yel & vio brn 3.50 *4.50*
221 A54 $1.30 buff & vio brn 5.50 *6.75*
a. Souv. sheet of 4, #218-221, imperf. 12.00 12.00
Nos. 218-221 (4) 13.75 *16.35*

Christmas — A55

1990, Dec. 12 Litho. *Rouletted 5*

222 A55 40c Star at left 1.00 1.00
a. Bklt. pane of 10 + 2 labels 15.00
223 A55 70c Star in center 2.00 2.00
a. Bklt. pane, 4 #222, 2 #223 + 6 labels 20.00
224 A55 $1.30 Star at right 3.50 3.50
Nos. 222-224 (3) 6.50 6.50

Nos. 140, 141, 143, 146-147, 179 Surcharged in Blue or Black

Litho., Litho. & Engr.

1990-91 *Perf. 13½x14, 15x14*

225	A34	(1c) on 30c #143	*14.00*	*5.00*
228	A34	(43c) on 10c #140	*24.00*	*27.50*
229	A34	(43c) on 10c #140	*17.50*	*9.75*
231	A34	70c on 60c #147 (bk)	*5.50*	*5.00*
232	A34	80c on 50c #146 (bk)	*5.50*	*5.00*
233	A34	$1.20 on 15c #141 (bk)	*5.50*	*5.00*
236	A45	$5 on 65c #179	*52.50*	*35.00*
		Nos. 225-236 (7)	*124.50*	*92.25*

Obliterator consists of diagonal lines on No. 228, crosshatched lines on No. 229.

Additional text in surcharges reads: "MAINLAND / POSTAGE PAID" (Nos. 228-229), "ZONE 1 / POSTAGE PAID" (No. 231), "ZONE 2 / POSTAGE PAID" (No. 232), "ZONE 5 / POSTAGE PAID" (No. 233).

Issued: #236, 11/11; #228, 12/18; #225, 229, 231-233, 1/1991.

Beaded Sea Star — A56

1991, Feb. 28 **Litho.** *Perf. 14½*

237	A56	45c shown	1.10	1.10
238	A56	75c Feather star	1.75	1.75
239	A56	$1 Slate pencil urchin	2.40	2.40
240	A56	$1.30 Globose sea urchin	3.25	3.25
		Nos. 237-240 (4)	8.50	8.50

Hari Raya — A57

1991, Mar. **Litho.** *Perf. 14½*

241	A57	45c multicolored	1.25	1.25
242	A57	75c multi, diff.	2.00	2.00
243	A57	$1.30 multi, diff.	3.50	3.50
		Nos. 241-243 (3)	6.75	6.75

Christmas — A58

1991, Nov. 6 **Litho.** *Perf. 15½*

244	A58	38c Child praying	.80	.80
245	A58	43c Child sleeping	1.00	1.00
246	A58	$1 Child singing	2.25	2.25
247	A58	$1.20 Child in wonder	2.75	2.75
		Nos. 244-247 (4)	6.80	6.80

Souvenir Sheet

248	Sheet of 4	8.00	8.00
a.	A58 38c Two children	.75	.75
b.	A58 43c Three girls	.95	.95
c.	A58 $1 Boy, two girls	2.25	2.25
d.	A58 $1.20 Boy, girl	2.75	2.75

Nos. 248a-248d are in a continuous design depicting a children's choir.

Crustaceans A59

Designs: 5c, Lybia tessellata. 10c, Pilodius areolatus. 20c, Trizopagurus strigatus. 30c, Lophozozymus pulchellus. 40c, Thalamitoides quadridens. 45c, Calcinus elegans, vert. 50c, Clibarius humilis. 60c, Trapezia rufopunctata, vert. 80c, Pylopaguropsis magnimanus, vert. $1, Trapezia ferruginea, vert. $2, Trapezia guttata, vert. $3, Trapezia cymodoce, vert.

1992 **Litho.** *Perf. 14½*

249	A59	5c multicolored	1.25	*1.60*
250	A59	10c multicolored	1.25	*1.60*
251	A59	20c multicolored	1.25	*1.60*
252	A59	30c multicolored	1.40	*2.75*
253	A59	40c multicolored	1.50	*2.75*
254	A59	45c multicolored	1.60	*2.75*
255	A59	50c multicolored	1.60	*3.75*
256	A59	60c multicolored	1.90	*3.75*
257	A59	80c multicolored	2.25	*3.75*
258	A59	$1 multicolored	3.00	*3.75*
259	A59	$2 multicolored	6.00	6.00
260	A59	$3 multicolored	9.25	9.25
		Nos. 249-260 (12)	32.25	*43.30*

Issued: 10c, 30c, 50c, 80c, $1, $2, 8/11; others, 2/28.

Discovery of America, 500th Anniv. — A60

1992, May 22 **Litho.** *Perf. 14½*

261	A60	$1.05 multicolored	3.50	3.50

Buff-banded Rail — A61

No. 262: a, 10c, Bird looking for food. b, 15c, Adult with chick. c, 30c, Two adults eating. d, 45c, Adult with eggs, hatchling.

No. 263: a, 45c, Two birds, one in water. b, 85c, Chick in nest. c, $1.20, Bird's head.

1992, June 18 **Litho.** *Perf. 14*

262	A61	Strip of 4, #a.-d.	6.00	6.00

Souvenir Sheet

263	A61	Sheet of 3, #a.-c.	7.50	7.50

World Wildlife Fund (#262).

World War II, 50th Anniv. — A62

45c, Royal Air Force Spitfire fighters. 85c, Japanese bombing of Kampong. $1.20, Sunderland reconnaissance flying boat.

1992, Oct. 13 **Litho.** *Perf. 14½*

264	A62	45c multicolored	1.50	1.50
265	A62	85c multicolored	2.75	2.75
266	A62	$1.20 multicolored	3.75	3.75
		Nos. 264-266 (3)	8.00	8.00

Festive Season — A63

Corals — A64

40c, Storm waves on reef edge. 80c, Direction Island. $1, Moorish idols among coral.

1992, Nov. 10 **Litho.** *Perf. 15x14½*

267	A63	40c multicolored	1.25	1.25
268	A63	80c multicolored	2.25	2.25
269	A63	$1 multicolored	3.00	3.00
		Nos. 267-269 (3)	6.50	6.50

1993, Jan. 28 **Litho.** *Perf. 14½*

270	A64	45c Lobophyllia hemprichii	.90	.90
271	A64	85c Pocillopora eydouxi	1.60	1.60
272	A64	$1.05 Fungia scutaria	2.25	2.25
273	A64	$1.20 Sarcophyton sp.	2.75	2.75
		Nos. 270-273 (4)	7.50	7.50

A65

A66

Island Currency Tokens: 45c, 5r token, 1968. 85c, Island scene token, 1968. $1.05, 150r token, 1977. $1.20, Token, 1910.

1993, Mar. 30 **Litho.** *Perf. 15x14½*

274	A65	45c multicolored	.90	.90
275	A65	85c multicolored	1.60	1.60
276	A65	$1.05 multicolored	2.25	2.25
277	A65	$1.20 multicolored	2.75	2.75
		Nos. 274-277 (4)	7.50	7.50

1993, June 1 **Litho.** *Perf. 14½*

Education: 5c, Primary classroom activities. 45c, Secondary studies. 85c, Crafts, traditional basket weaving. $1.05, Office staff, higher education. $1.20, Marine officers, coxswain's training.

278	A66	5c multicolored	.75	.75
279	A66	45c multicolored	1.25	1.25
280	A66	85c multicolored	2.10	2.10
281	A66	$1.05 multicolored	2.40	2.40
282	A66	$1.20 multicolored	2.75	2.75
		Nos. 278-282 (5)	9.25	9.25

Air-Sea Rescue Service A67

45c, Men in lifeboat. 85c, Westwind Seascan. $1.05, R.J. Hawke inter-island ferry.

1993, Aug. 17 **Litho.** *Perf. 14½*

283	A67	45c multicolored	1.25	1.25
284	A67	85c multicolored	2.00	2.00
285	A67	$1.05 multicolored	2.75	2.75
a.		Souvenir sheet of 3, #283-285	8.50	8.50
		Nos. 283-285 (3)	6.00	6.00

A limited printing exists of No. 285a with Taipei '95 overprint. Value, $60.

Festive Season — A68

1993, Oct. 24 **Litho.** *Perf. 14½*

286	A68	40c pink & multi	1.00	1.00
287	A68	80c blue & multi	2.00	2.00
288	A68	$1 yellow & multi	3.00	3.00
		Nos. 286-288 (3)	6.00	6.00

Map and Reef Life — A69

Puppets — A70

Reef triggerfish — No. 289: a, Two fish, purple coral (b). b, Three fish. c, Two fish. d, Two fish, red coral (e). e, One fish.

Green turtles — No. 290: a, Eggs, turtles. b, Two turtles (c). c, Group of baby turtles. d, Baby turtle. e, Fish, large turtle.

Pyramid butterflyfish — No. 291: a, Three fish. b, Two small, one large fish, coral (c). c, One small, one large fish, coral (d). d, Three fish, coral (e). e, Coral, one fish.

Junkongs sailing craft — No. 292: a, One boat, red sail. b, Two boats, one blue & white sail, one red sail. c, One boat, yellow sail. d, Two boats sailing away. e, Two boats, one red sail, one white & blue sail.

1994, Feb. 17 **Litho.** *Perf. 14½x14*

289	A69	5c Strip of 5, #a.-e.	1.25	*1.60*
290	A69	10c Strip of 5, #a.-e.	1.60	*2.00*
291	A69	20c Strip of 5, #a.-e.	2.00	*2.75*
292	A69	45c Strip of 5, #a.-e.	4.75	*5.25*
f.		Sheet of 20, #289-292	10.00	*13.00*

No. 292 also produced in sheets of 20.

1994, June 16 **Litho.** *Perf. 14½x14*

293	A70	45c Prabu Abjasa	.85	.85
294	A70	90c Prabu Pandu	1.60	1.60
295	A70	$1 Judistra	1.75	1.75
296	A70	$1.35 Abimanju	2.25	2.25
		Nos. 293-296 (4)	6.45	6.45

Christmas A71

1994, Oct. 31 **Litho.** *Perf. 14x14½*

297	A71	40c Angel	.75	.75
298	A71	45c Wise man	.95	.95
299	A71	80c Bethlehem	1.50	1.50
		Nos. 297-299 (3)	3.20	3.20

Seabirds A72

45c, White-tailed tropicbird, masked booby. 85c, Great frigatebird, white tern.

1995, Mar. 16 **Litho.** *Perf. 14x14½*

300	A72	45c multicolored	.75	.75
301	A72	85c multicolored	1.50	1.50
a.		Souvenir sheet of 2, #300-301	2.75	2.75
b.		As "a," overprinted	7.00	7.00

No. 301b ovptd. in gold in sheet margin with Jakarta '95 exhibition emblem and: "8th Asian International Philatelic Exhibition / PAMERAN FILATELI INTERNASIONAL ASIA VIII."

No. 301b issued 8/19/95.

Insects — A73

#302a, Yellow crazy ant. b, Aedes mosquito. c, Hawk moth. d, Scarab beetle. e, Lauxaniid fly.

$1.20, Common eggfly butterfly.

1995, July 13 Litho. *Perf. 14½x14*

302	A73	45c Strip of 5, #a.-e.	5.50	5.50
303	A73	$1.20 multicolored	2.50	2.50

Fish — A74

Designs: 5c, Redspot wrasse. 30c, Gilded triggerfish. 40c, Saddled butterflyfish. 45c, Ringeyed hawkfish. 75c, Orangespine unicornfish. 80c, Blue tang. 85c, Humpback wrasse. 90c, Threadfin butterflyfish. $1, Bluestripe snapper. $1.05, Longnosed butterflyfish. $1.20, Freckled hawkfish. $2, Powder blue surgeonfish.

1995-97 Litho. *Perf. 14x14½*

304	A74	5c multicolored	.35	.35
305	A74	30c multicolored	.55	.55
306	A74	40c multicolored	.85	.85
307	A74	45c multicolored	1.00	1.00
308	A74	75c multicolored	1.50	1.50
309	A74	80c multicolored	1.60	1.60
310	A74	85c multicolored	1.60	1.60
311	A74	90c multicolored	1.90	1.90
312	A74	$1 multicolored	2.10	2.10
313	A74	$1.05 multicolored	2.10	2.10
314	A74	$1.20 multicolored	2.75	2.75
315	A74	$2 multicolored	4.75	4.75
		Nos. 304-315 (12)	21.05	21.05

Issued: 40c, 80c, $1.05, 11/1/95; 30c, 45c, 85c, $2, 8/8/96; 5c, 75c, 90c, $1, $1.20, 8/14/97.

See Nos. 327-329.

Festive Season — A75

Designs: 45c, Greeting others, asking forgiveness. 75c, Drum beaters celebrate Hari Raya Puasa. 85c, Sharing food with friends.

1996, Feb. 19 Litho. *Perf. 14*

316	A75	45c multicolored	.75	.75
317	A75	75c multicolored	1.75	1.75
318	A75	85c multicolored	2.00	2.00
		Nos. 316-318 (3)	4.50	4.50

Animals Imported Into Australia Through Cocos Islands Quarantine Station — A76

1996, June 13 Litho. *Perf. 14½x14*

319	A76	45c Black rhinoceros	1.00	1.00
320	A76	50c Alpacas	1.25	1.25
321	A76	$1.05 Boran cattle	2.25	2.25
322	A76	$1.20 Ostrich	3.25	3.25
		Nos. 319-322 (4)	7.75	7.75

A77

A78

Festive Season: 45c, Tambourine, dancing on shore, bird. 75c, Woman clapping, sailboats racing. 85c, Fish, night scene on beach.

1997, Jan. 6 Litho. *Perf. 14x14½*

323	A77	45c multicolored	.85	.85
324	A77	75c multicolored	1.40	1.40
325	A77	85c multicolored	1.75	1.75
		Nos. 323-325 (3)	4.00	4.00

1998, Jan. 22 Litho. *Perf. 14*

Children's drawings: a, Gift package. b, Mosque. c, Cocos Malay woman. d, Island scene. e, Two dancers.

326	A78	45c Strip of 5, #a.-e.	4.75	4.75

Festive Season.

Marine Life Type of 1995

Designs: 70c, Crowned squirrelfish. 95c, Sixstripe wrasse. $5, Goldback anthias.

1998, Aug. 13 Litho. *Perf. 14x14½*

327	A74	70c multicolored	1.10	1.10
328	A74	95c multicolored	1.40	1.40
329	A74	$5 multicolored	7.50	7.50
		Nos. 327-329 (3)	10.00	10.00

Jukong Boats, Hari Raya Festival — A79

a, Women placing items in leaves, people along beach. b, Two women, boats along beach. c, Flowers, man in boat. d, Palm trees, two men, man in boat. e, Two people in boat.

1999, Feb. 11 Litho. *Perf. 14½x14*

330	A79	45c Strip of 5, #a.-e.	4.25	4.25

Flora and Fauna — A80

a, 45c, Two birds on tree branch. b, 25c, Bird in flight. c, 10c, Sailboat with sail down. d, 5c, Sailboat with red sails. e, 45c, Two birds in flight. f, 25c, Butterflies. g, 10c, School of fish. h, 5c, School of fish swimming left, coral. i, 45c, Red hibiscus flower. j, 25c, Three birds in flight. k, 10c, Two moorish idols. l, 5c, Turtles. m, 45c, Butterfly, flowers. n, 25c, Moth with wings folded, flowers. o, 10c, Two gold fish. p, 5c, Various fish swimming right. q, 45c, Yellow hibiscus. r, 25c, Butterfly on flowers. s, 10c, Two birds in flight. t, 5c, Large fish, coral.

1999, June 17 Litho. *Perf. 14x14½*

331	A80	Sheet of 20, #a.-t.	15.00	15.00

Faces of Cocos Islands A81

Ordinary people: a, Ratma Anthoney, with white shirt. b, Nakia Haji Dolman, with multicolored head covering. c, Muller Eymin, with white head covering. d, Courtney Press, with flowered outfit. e, Mhd Abu-Yazid, with blue shirt with stripes.

2000, Apr. 13 Litho. *Perf. 14x14½*

332	A81	45c Strip of 5, #a.-e.	4.50	4.50

Worldwide Fund for Nature — A82

#333: a, Purple crab. b, Little nipper crab.
#334: a, Horn-eyed ghost crab. b, Smooth-banded ghost crab.

Illustration reduced.

2000, June 20 Litho. *Perf. 14x14¾*

333	A82	5c Pair, #a-b	1.00	1.00
334	A82	45c Pair, #a-b	2.00	2.00

Fish Type of 1995

No. 335: a, Wideband fusilier. b, Striped surgeonfish. c, Orangeband surgeonfish. d, Indo-Pacific sergeant.

2001, Feb. 8 Litho. *Perf. 14x14½*

335		Block of 4	5.00	5.00
a.-d.		A74 45c Any single	.90	.85

Turtles — A83

No. 336: a, Loggerhead. b, Hawksbill. c, Leatherback. d, Green.

Illustration reduced.

2002, Oct. 1 Litho. *Perf. 14x14½*

336	A83	Block of 4	5.00	5.00
a.-d.		45c Any single	.90	.90

Shore Birds — A84

No. 337: a, Eastern reef egret. b, Sooty tern. c, Ruddy turnstone. d, Whimbrel.

2003, June 17 Litho. *Perf. 14x14½*

337		Horiz. strip of 4	6.00	6.00
a.-d.		A84 50c Any single	1.10	1.10

Royal Visit, 50th Anniv. — A85

Queen Elizabeth II and: No. 338a, Cocos Malay musicians. No. 338b, Royal Yacht Gothic. $1, Clunies Ross (Oceania) House. $1.45, Dignitary presenting model of Malay jukong.

2004, Mar. 16 Litho. *Perf. 14x14½*

338	A85	50c Horiz. pair, #a-b	2.25	2.25
339	A85	$1 multi	2.25	2.25
340	A85	$1.45 multi	3.50	3.50
a.		Souvenir sheet, #338a, 338b, 339, 340	8.25	8.25
b.		As "a," with 2004 World Stamp Championship emblem ovptd. in gold in margin	9.00	9.00
		Nos. 338-340 (3)	8.00	8.00

No. 340b issued 8/28.

Worldwide Fund for Nature (WWF) A86

Designs: No. 341a, Blacktip reef shark. No. 341b, Gray reef sharks. $1, Blacktip reef sharks. $1.45, Gray reef shark.

2005, June 21 Litho. *Perf. 14½x14*

341	A86	50c Horiz. pair, #a-b	2.00	2.00
342	A86	$1 multi	2.00	2.00
343	A86	$1.45 multi	3.00	3.00
		Nos. 341-343 (3)	7.00	7.00

Miniature Sheet

Wildlife — A87

No. 344: a-e, Various birds. f-t, Various fish and marine life.

2006, June 13 Litho. *Perf. 14¾x14*

344	A87	Sheet of 20	10.00	10.00
a.-e.		10c Any single	.25	.25
f.-o.		25c Any single	.40	.40
p.-t.		50c Any single	.90	.90

Mollusks A88

Designs: No. 345a, Oriental moonsnail. No. 345b, Pearly nautilus. $1, Partridge tun. $1.45, Giant clam.

2007, Mar. 20 Litho. *Perf. 14x14½*

345	A88	50c Horiz. pair, #a-b	1.60	1.60
346	A88	$1 multi	1.60	1.60
347	A88	$1.45 multi	2.40	2.40
		Nos. 345-347 (3)	5.60	5.60

Birds — A89

No. 348, vert.: a, Black-winged stilt. b, Chinese pond heron.

$1, White-breasted waterhen. $1.45, Saunders' tern.

2008, Feb. 26 Litho. *Perf. 14*

348	A89	50c Horiz. pair, #a-b	1.90	1.90
349	A89	$1 multi	1.90	1.90
350	A89	$1.45 multi	2.75	2.75
		Nos. 348-350 (3)	6.55	6.55

OFFICIAL STAMP

No. 175 Ovptd. and Surcharged in Dark Blue

1991, Jan. 25 Litho. *Perf. 14x13½*

O1	A44	(43c) on 90c multi		*120.00*

No. O1 was not sold to the public unused. Used value is for a canceled-to-order example. Mint examples exist in the marketplace. Value the same as used.

COLOMBIA

kə-'ləm-bē-ə

LOCATION — On the northwest coast of South America, bordering on the Caribbean Sea and the Pacific Ocean
GOVT. — Republic
AREA — 456,535 sq. mi.
POP. — 39,309,422 (1999 est.)
CAPITAL — Bogota

In 1810 the Spanish Viceroyalty of New Granada gained its independence and with Venezuela and Ecuador formed the State of Greater Colombia. In 1832 this state split into three independent units as Venezuela, Ecuador and the Republic of New Granada. The name of the country has been, successively, Granadine Confederation (1858-61), United States of New Granada (1861), United States of Colombia (1861-65), and the Republic of Colombia (1885 to date).

100 Centavos = 1 Peso

Catalogue values for unused stamps in this country are for Never Hinged items, beginning with Scott 594 in the regular postage section, Scott B1 in the semi-postal section, Scott C200 in the airpost section, Scott CE1 in the airpost special delivery section, Scott E2 in the special delivery section, and Scott RA33 in the postal tax section.

In the earlier days many towns did not have handstamps for canceling and stamps were canceled with pen and ink. Pen cancellations, therefore, do not indicate fiscal use. (Postage stamps were not used for revenue purposes.) Used values for Nos. 1-128 are for stamps with illegible manuscript cancels or handstamp cancels of Bogota or Medellin. Stamps with legible manuscript or other handstamped town-name cancels sell for more.

Fractions of many Colombian stamps of both early and late issues are found canceled, their use to pay postage having been tolerated even though forbidden by the postal laws and regulations. Many are known to have been made for philatelic purposes.

Watermarks

Wmk. 116 — Crosses and Circles

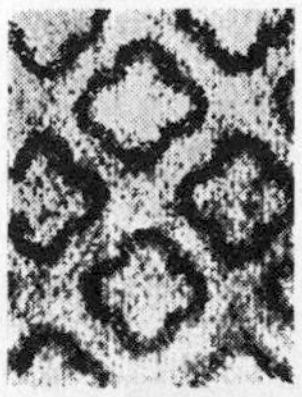

Wmk. 127 — Quatrefoils

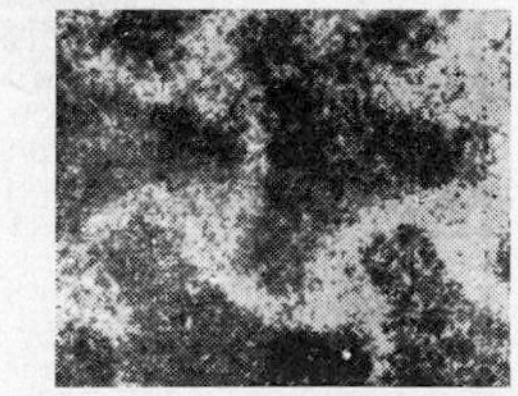

Wmk. 194 — Multiple Curvilinear Triangles

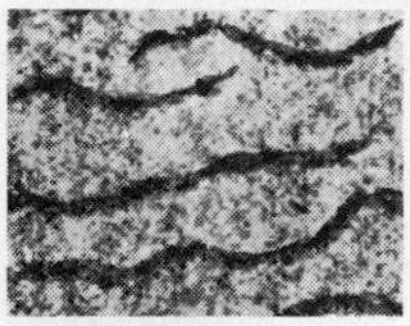

Wmk. 229 — Wavy Lines

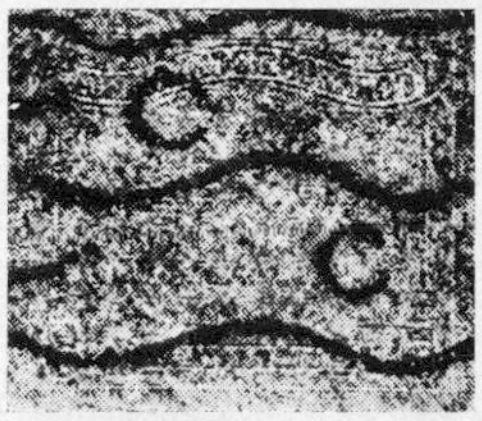

Wmk. 255 — Wavy Lines and C Multiple

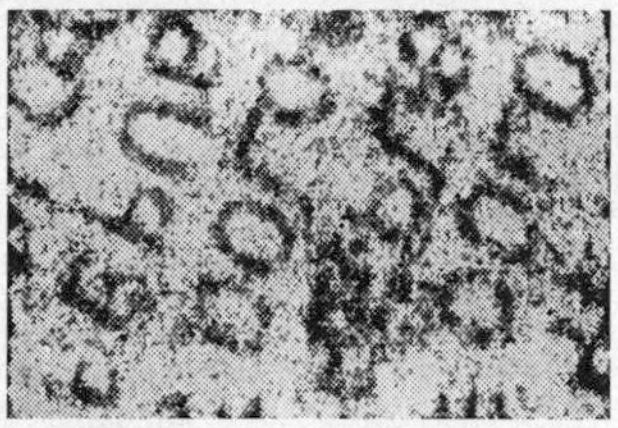

Wmk. 331 — REPUBLICA DE COLOMBIA

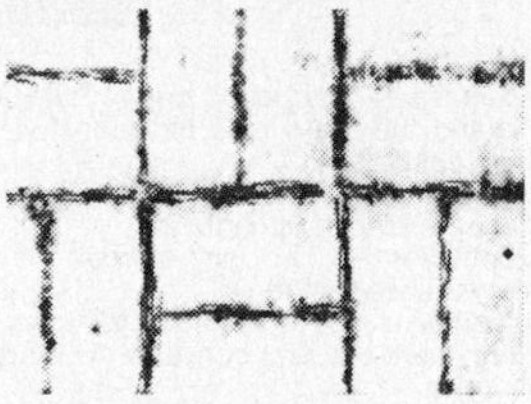

Wmk. 334 — Rectangles

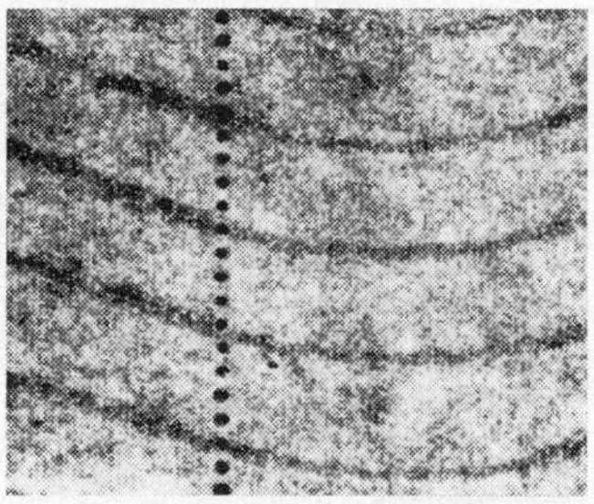

Wmk. 346 — Parallel Curved Lines

Stamps inscribed "Colombia" that show the Panama Canal area were used in Panama and can be found in Vol. 5.

Granadine Confederation

A1

A2 Coat of Arms

Type A1 — Asterisks in frame. Wavy lines in background.

Type A2 — Diamond-shaped ornaments in frame. Straight lines in background. Numerals larger.

1859 Unwmk. Litho. *Imperf.*
Wove Paper

1 A1 2½c green 95.00 95.00
a. 2½c yellow green 95.00 95.00
2 A1 5c blue 110.00 75.00
a. Tête bêche pair 3,500. 5,750.
b. "50" instead of "5" 7,500.
3 A1 5c violet 300.00 95.00
a. Tête bêche pair 6,000. 6,000.
b. "50" instead of "5" 15,000.
4 A1 10c red brown 110.00 65.00
a. 10c buff 110.00 65.00
6 A1 20c blue 95.00 55.00
a. 20c gray blue 95.00 55.00
b. Se-tenant with 5c — —
c. Tête bêche pair *40,000.* *25,000.*
7 A1 1p carmine 70.00 *100.00*
a. 1p rose 85.00 125.00
8 A1 1p rose, *bluish* 350.00

The 10c green is an essay.

Reprints of No. 7 are in brown rose or brown red. Wavy lines of background are much broken; no dividing lines between stamps.

1860

Laid Paper

9 A2 5c lilac 250.00 175.00

Wove Paper

10 A2 5c gray lilac 65.00 50.00
a. 5c lilac 65.00 50.00
11 A2 10c yellow buff 75.00 45.00
a. Tête bêche pair 7,000.
12 A2 20c blue 160.00 110.00

United States of New Granada

Arms of New Granada — A3

1861

13 A3 2½c black 1,100. 300.00
14 A3 5c yellow 325.00 140.00
a. 5c buff 325.00 140.00
16 A3 10c blue 950.00 140.00
17 A3 20c red 400.00 190.00
18 A3 1p pink 950.00 300.00

There are 54 varieties of the 5c, 20c, and 1 peso.

Forgeries exist of Nos. 13-18.

United States of Colombia

Coat of Arms
A4 A5 A6

1862

19 A4 10c blue 200.00 100.00
20 A4 20c red *3,600.* 600.00
21 A4 50c green 200.00 140.00
22 A4 1p red lilac 475.00 140.00
23 A4 1p red lil, *bluish* *4,250.* *1,450.*

No. 23 is on a thinner, coarser wove paper than Nos. 19-22.

1863

24 A5 5c orange 80.00 52.50
a. Star after "Cent" 90.00 60.00
25 A5 10c blue 160.00 19.00
a. Period after "10" 180.00 25.00
26 A5 20c red 175.00 62.50
a. Star after "Cent" 200.00 70.00
b. Transfer of 50c in stone of 20c *14,000.* *4,500.*

Bluish Paper

28 A5 10c blue 140.00 27.50
a. Period after "10" 150.00 30.00
29 A5 50c green 175.00 62.50
a. Star after "Cent" 175.00 70.00

Ten varieties of each.

1864

Wove Paper

30 A6 5c orange 57.50 30.00
a. Tête bêche pair 350.00 325.00
31 A6 10c blue 42.50 12.50
a. Period after 10 42.50 12.50
32 A6 20c scarlet 80.00 45.00
33 A6 50c green 65.00 45.00
34 A6 1p red violet 275.00 140.00

Two varieties of each.

Arms of Colombia
A7 A9

A8

1865

35 A7 1c rose 8.00 8.00
a. bluish pelure paper 22.50 17.50
36 A8 2½c black, *lilac* 16.00 11.00
37 A9 5c yellow 35.00 16.00
a. 5c orange 35.00 16.00
38 A9 10c violet 52.50 3.50
39 A9 20c blue 52.50 16.00
40 A9 50c green 92.50 42.50
41 A9 50c grn (small figures) 92.50 42.50
42 A9 1p vermilion 100.00 15.00
a. 1p rose red 100.00 15.00
b. Period after "PESO" 120.00 17.50

Ten varieties of each of the 5c, 10c, 20c, and 50c, and six varieties of the 1 peso. No. 36 was used as a carrier stamp.

A10 A11 A12

A13 A14

A15 A16

1866

White Wove Paper

45 A10 5c orange 55.00 22.50
46 A11 10c lilac 13.00 4.25
a. Pelure paper 17.50 10.00
47 A12 20c light blue 32.50 17.50
a. Pelure paper 50.00 42.50
48 A13 50c green 13.00 10.00
49 A14 1p rose red, *bluish* 72.50 26.00
a. 1p vermilion 72.50 26.00
51 A15 5p blk, *green* 400.00 175.00
52 A16 10p blk, *vermilion* 275.00 160.00

There are several varieties of the 1 peso having the letters "U," "N," "S" and "O" smaller.

A17 A18

A19 A20

A21

TEN CENTAVOS:

Type I — "B" of "COLOMBIA" over "V" of "CENTAVOS".

Type II — "B" of "COLOMBIA" over "VO" of "CENTAVOS."

ONE PESO:

Type I — Long thin spear heads. Diagonal lines in lower part of shield.

Type II — Short thick spear heads. Horizontal and a few diagonal lines in lower part of shield.

Type III — Short thick spear heads. Crossed lines in lower part of shield. Ornaments at each side of circle are broken. (See No. 97.)

1868

53 A17 5c orange 55.00 42.50
54 A18 10c lilac (I) 3.25 .90
a. 10c red violet (I) 3.25 .90
b. 10c lilac (II) 3.25 .90
c. 10c red violet (II) 3.25 .90
d. Printed on both sides 6.25 2.00
55 A19 20c blue 2.25 1.00
56 A20 50c yellow green 2.75 2.00
57 A21 1p ver (II) 3.25 1.75
a. Tête bêche pair 110.00 85.00
b. 1p rose red (I) 45.00 22.50
c. 1p rose red (II) 3.00 1.75
Nos. 53-57 (5) 66.50 48.15

See Nos. 83-84, 96-97.

Counterfeits or reprints.

10c — There is a large white dot at the upper left between the circle enclosing the "X" and the ornament below.

50c — There is a shading of dots instead of dashes below the ribbon with motto. There are crossed lines in the lowest section of the shield instead of diagonal or horizontal ones.

1p — The ornaments in the lettered circle are broken. There are crossed lines in the lowest section of the shield. These counterfeits, or reprints, are on white paper, wove and laid, on colored wove paper and in fancy colors.

A22

Two varieties

1869-70

Wove Paper

59 A22 2½c black, *violet* 3.50 2.10
a. Laid paper ('70) 250.00 210.00
b. Laid batonné paper ('70) 22.50 19.00

Nos. 59, 59a, 59b were used as carrier stamps.

Counterfeits, or reprints, are on magenta paper wove or ribbed.

A23

A24

1870

Wove Paper

62 A23 5c orange 1.60 1.10
a. 5c yellow 1.60 1.10
63 A24 25c black, *blue* 13.00 11.00

See No. 89.

In the counterfeits, or reprints, of No. 63, the top of the "2" of "25" does not touch the down stroke. The counterfeits are on paper of various colors.

A25

A26

5 pesos — The ornament at the left of the "C" of "Cinco" cuts into the "C," and the shading of the flag is formed of diagonal lines.

10 pesos — The stars have extra rays between the points, and the central part of the shield has some horizontal lines of shading at each end.

1870

Surface Colored, Chalky Paper

64 A25 5p blk, *green* 80.00 55.00
65 A26 10p blk, *vermilion* 92.50 55.00

See Nos. 77-79, 125-126.

A27

A28

A29

TEN CENTAVOS:

Type I — "S" of "CORREOS" 2½mm high. First "N" of "NACIONALES" small.

Type II — "S" of "CORREOS" 2mm high. First "N" of "NACIONALES" wide.

1871-74

Thin Porous Paper

66 A27 1c green ('72) 2.75 2.75
67 A27 1c rose ('73) 2.75 2.75
a. 1c carmine ('73) 2.75 2.75
68 A28 2c brown 1.25 1.25
a. 2c red brown 1.25 1.25
69 A29 10c vio (I) ('74) 2.00 1.60
a. 10c lilac (I) ('74) 2.00 1.60
b. 10c violet (II) ('74) 2.00 1.60
c. 10c lilac (II) ('74) 2.00 1.60
d. Laid paper ('72) 110.00 110.00
e. As "b," laid paper ('72) 110.00 110.00
Nos. 66-69 (4) 8.75 8.35

Counterfeits or reprints.

1c — The outer frame of the shield is broken near the upper left corner and the "A" of "Colombia" has no cross-bar.

2c — There are scratches across "DOS" and many white marks around the letters on the large "2." The counterfeits, or reprints, are on white wove and bluish white laid paper.

Condor — A30

Liberty Head
A31 A32

5 pesos, redrawn — The ornament at the left of the "C" only touches the "C," and the shading of the flag is formed of vertical and diagonal lines.

10 pesos, redrawn — The stars are distinctly five pointed, and there is no shading in the central part of the shield.

1877

Wove Paper

73 A30 5c purple 5.50 1.75
a. 5c lilac 5.50 1.75
74 A31 10c bister brown 2.75 .75
a. 10c red brown 2.75 .75
b. 10c violet brown 2.75 .75
75 A32 20c blue 3.25 1.10
a. 20c violet blue 6.50 2.75
77 A26 10p blk, *rose* 92.50 57.50
78 A25 5p blk, *lt grn,* redrawn 32.50 27.50
79 A26 10p blk, *rose,* redrawn 13.00 2.25
a. 10p blk, *dark rose,* redrawn 13.00 2.25
Nos. 73-79 (6) 149.50 90.85

Stamps of the issues of 1871-77 are known with private perforations of various gauges, also with sewing machine perforations.

In the counterfeits, or reprints, of the 5 pesos the ornament at the left of the "C" of "Cinco" is separated from the "C" by a black line.

In the counterfeits, or reprints, of the 10 pesos the outer line of the double circle containing "10" is broken at the top, below "OS" of "Unidos," and the vertical lines of shading contained in the double circle are very indistinct. There is a colorless dash below the loop of the "P" of "Pesos."

1876-79

Laid Paper

80 A30 5c lilac 65.00 52.50
81 A31 10c brown 35.00 2.25
82 A32 20c blue 80.00 55.00
83 A20 50c green ('79) 77.50 52.50
84 A21 1p pale red (II) ('79) 50.00 12.50
Nos. 80-84 (5) 307.50 174.75

1879

Wove Paper

89 A24 25c green 26.00 26.00

1881

Blue Wove Paper

93 A30 5c violet 16.00 10.50
a. 5c lilac 16.00 10.50
94 A31 10c brown 9.25 2.10
95 A32 20c blue 9.25 2.10
96 A20 50c yellow green 9.50 6.00
97 A21 1p ver (III) 13.00 6.00
Nos. 93-97 (5) 57.00 26.70

For types of 1p, see note over No. 53.

Reprints of the 10c and 20c are much worn. On the 10c the letters "TAVOS" of "CENTAVOS" often touch. On the 20c the letters "NT" of "VEINTE" touch and the left arm of the "T" is too long. Reprints of the 25c, 50c and 1p have the characteristics previously described. The reprints are on white wove or laid paper, on colored papers, and in fancy colors. Stamps on green paper exist only as reprints.

A34

A35

A36

1 centavo — The period before "UNION" is round and there are rays between the stars and the condors.

2 centavos — The "2's" and "C's" in the corners are placed upright.

5 centavos — The last star at the right almost touches the frame.

10 centavos — The letters of the inscription are thin; there are rays between the stars and the condor.

1881 ***Imperf.***

White Wove Paper

103 A34 1c green 3.75 3.25
104 A35 2c vermilion 1.60 1.25
a. 2c rose 1.90 1.25
106 A34 5c blue 4.50 1.40
a. Printed on both sides
107 A36 10c violet 3.25 1.00
108 A34 20c black 3.50 1.60
Nos. 103-108 (5) 16.60 8.50

The stamps of this issue are found with perforations of various gauges, also sewing machine perforations, all of which are unofficial.

See Nos. 112, 114-115.

Liberty Head — A37

A37a

1881 ***Imperf.***

109 A37 1c blk, *green* 2.50 *4.00*
110 A37 2c blk, *lilac rose* 2.50 *4.00*
111 A37 5c blk, *lilac* 6.50 1.50
Nos. 109-111 (3) 11.50 *9.50*

Nos. 109 to 111 are found with regular or sewing machine perforation, unofficial.

Reprints:

1c — The top line of the stamp and the top frame extend to the left. 2c — There is a curved line over the scroll below the "AV" of "CENTAVOS."

5c — There are scratches across the "5" in the upper left corner. All three values were reprinted on the three colors of paper of the originals.

Redrawn

1 centavo — The period before "UNION" is square and the rays between the stars and the condor have been wholly or partly erased.

2 centavos — The "2's" and "C's" in the corners are placed diagonally.

5 centavos — The last star at the right touches the wing of the condor.

10 centavos — The letters of the inscription are thick; there are no rays under the stars; the last star at the right touches the wing of the condor and this wing touches the frame.

1883 ***Imperf.***

112 A34 1c green 4.75 4.25
113 A37a 2c rose 1.60 1.40
114 A34 5c blue 4.00 1.00
a. 5c ultramarine 4.00 1.00
b. Printed on both sides, reverse ultra 25.00 20.00
115 A36 10c violet 5.00 1.40
Nos. 112-115 (4) 15.35 8.05

The stamps of this issue are found with regular or sewing machine perforations, privately applied.

A38

A39

1883 ***Perf. 10½, 12, 13½***

116 A38 1c gray grn, *grn* .80 .80
a. Imperf., pair 4.00 4.00
117 A39 2c red, *rose* .80 *1.10*
a. 2c org red, *rose* .80 *1.10*
b. 2c red, *buff* 10.00 10.00
c. Imperf., pair (No. 117 or 117a) 6.50 6.50
d. "DE LOS" in very small caps 12.50 12.50
118 A38 5c blue, *bluish* 2.00 1.25
a. 5c dk bl, *bluish* 2.00 .90
b. 5c blue 2.75 2.00
c. Imperf., pair (No. 118 or 118a) 6.50 6.50
d. As "b," imperf., pair 10.00 10.00
119 A39 10c org, *yel* 1.00 *1.10*
a. "DE LOS" in large caps 45.00 20.00
b. Imperf., pair 13.00 13.00
120 A39 20c vio, *lilac* 1.10 1.10
a. Imperf., pair 13.00 13.00
122 A38 50c brn, *buff* 2.25 2.50
a. Perf. 12 2.25 2.50
123 A38 1p claret, *bluish* 4.25 1.60
a. Imperf., pair 13.00 13.00
Nos. 116-123 (7) 12.20 9.45

Redrawn Types of 1877

1883 (?) ***Perf. 10½, 12***

125 A25 5p orange brown 6.00 6.00
126 A26 10p black, *gray* 6.50 *7.25*

1886 ***Perf. 10½, 11½, 12***

127 A38 5p brown, *straw* 8.00 4.75
a. Imperf., pair 26.00 26.00
128 A38 10p black, *rose* 8.00 4.75
a. Imperf., pair 26.00 26.00

Republic of Colombia

A40

Simón Bolívar — A41

Pres. Rafael Núñez — A42

1886 ***Perf. 10½ and 13½***

129 A40 1c grn, *grn* 1.25 .60
a. Imperf., pair 5.50 5.50
130 A41 5c blue, *bl* 1.25 .35
a. 5c ultra, *blue* 1.25 .35
b. Imperf., pair (#130) 5.50 5.50
131 A42 10c orange 2.75 .60
a. Imperf., pair 7.50 7.50
b. Pelure paper 3.50 .85
Nos. 129-131 (3) 5.25 1.55

Gen. Antonio Jose de Sucre y Alcala
A43

Gen. Antonio Nariño
A44

1887

133 A43 2c org red, *rose* 1.75 .85
a. 2c orange red, *yellowish* 4.50 4.50
b. 2c orange red 5.25 5.25
c. Imperf., pair (No. 133) 8.00 8.00

134 A44 20c pur, *grysh* 2.25 .85
a. Imperf., pair 6.50 6.50
b. Pelure paper 2.75 1.75

Impressions of No. 134 on white, blue or greenish blue paper were not regularly issued.

Arms — A45

Nariño — A46

1888

135 A45 50c brn, *buff* 1.40 *1.50*
a. Imperf., pair 4.75 4.75
136 A45 1p claret, *bluish* 6.00 1.75
137 A45 1p claret 2.50 1.25
138 A45 5p org brn 6.50 5.50
139 A45 5p black 11.00 8.00
140 A45 10p black, *rose* 16.00 5.50
Nos. 135-140 (6) 43.40 23.50

See Nos. 154, 156-157.

1889

141 A46 20c pur, *grayish* 1.50 1.00
a. Imperf., pair 7.50 7.50

Impressions on white, blue or greenish blue paper were not regularly issued.

A47

A48

A49

A50

A51

1890-91 ***Perf. 10½, 13½, 11***

142 A47 1c grn, *grn* 1.50 1.25
143 A48 2c org red, *rose* .75 *.75*
144 A49 5c bl, *grnsh bl* 1.10 .35
a. 5c deep blue, *blue* 1.10 .35
b. Imperf., pair 4.50 4.50
146 A50 10c brn, *yel* .80 .35
a. 10c brown, *buff* .80 .35
147 A51 20c vio, pelure paper 2.75 *3.50*
Nos. 142-147 (5) 6.90 *6.20*

A52

A52a

A53

A53a

A54

Perf. 10½, 12, 13½, 14 to 15½

1892-99

Ordinary Paper

148 A47 1c red, *yel* .65 .35
149 A52 2c red, *rose* 32.50 32.50
150 A52 2c green .40 .25
a. 2c yellow green .40 .25
151 A49 5c blk, *buff* 10.00 .30
152 A52a 5c org brn, *pale buff* .85 .25
a. 5c red brown, *salmon* ('97) .85 .25
153 A50 10c bis brn, *rose* .60 .35
a. 10c brown, *brownish* 1.60 1.25
154 A53 20c brn, *bl* .60 .35
a. 20c red brown, *blue* .60 .35
b. 20c yel brn, *grnsh bl* ('97) 4.50 *11.00*
c. 20c brown, *buff* ('97) 15.00 11.00
155 A45 50c vio, *vio* 1.00 .60
156 A53a 50c red vio, *vio* ('99) 1.25
157 A54 1p bl, *grnsh* 1.60 .75
a. 1p blue, *buff* 1.60 .75
158 A45 5p red, *pale rose* 6.00 2.75
159 A45 10p blue 12.50 2.75
a. Thin, pale rose paper 22.50 6.00
Nos. 148-159 (12) 67.95
Nos. 148-155,157-159 (11) 41.20

Type A53a is a redrawing of type A45. The letters of the inscriptions are slightly larger and the numerals "50" slightly smaller than in type A45.

The 20c brown on white paper is believed to be a chemical changeling.

Nos. 148, 150-152a, 153-155, 157, 159 exist imperf. Value per pair, $5-$7.50.

A56

1899

162 A56 1c red, *yellow* .55 .30
163 A56 5c red brn, *sal* .55 .30
164 A56 10c brn, *lil rose* 1.60 .80
165 A56 50c blue, *lilac* 1.10 1.00
Nos. 162-165 (4) 3.80 2.40

Cartagena Issues

A57

1899 **Blue Overprint** ***Imperf.***

167 A57 5c red, *buff* 24.00 24.00
a. Sewing machine perf. 24.00 24.00
168 A57 10c ultra, *buff* 24.00 24.00
a. Sewing machine perf. 24.00 24.00

Nos. 168 and 168a differ slightly from the illustration.

Bolivar No. 55 Overprinted with 7 Parallel Wavy Lines and:

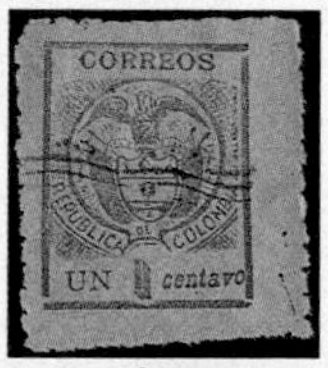
A58

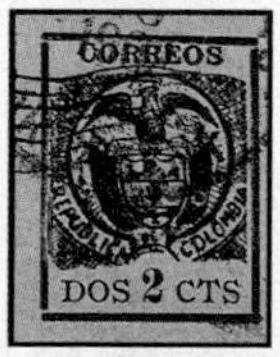
A59

A60

A61

Perf. 14 (No. 169), Sewing Machine Perf.

1899 **Purple Overprint**

169 A18 1c black 50.00 50.00
170 A58 1c brn, *buff* 17.00 17.00
a. Altered from 10c 25.00 25.00
171 A59 2c blk, *buff* 17.00 17.00
a. Altered from 10c 25.00 25.00
172 A60 5c mar, *grnsh bl* 15.00 15.00
a. Perf. 12 15.00 15.00
b. Without overprint 8.75 8.75
173 A61 10c red, *sal* 15.00 15.00
a. Perf. 12 15.00 15.00
Nos. 169-173 (5) 114.00 114.00

Types A58 and A59 illustrate Nos. 170a and 171a, which were made from altered plates of the 10c (No. 168). Nos. 170 and 171 were made from altered plate of the 5c denomination (No. 167), show part of the top flag of the "5" and differ slightly from the illustrations.

Nos. 170-173 exist imperf. Values about same as perf.

A62

1900 ***Imperf.***

Purple Overprint

174 A62 5c red 20.00 20.00
a. Perf. 12 27.50 27.50

A63

A64

"Gobierno Provisorio" at Top

1900 **Litho.** ***Perf. 12 Vertically***

175 A63 1c (ctvo) blk, *bl grn* 35.00 6.50
a. "cvo." 92.50 12.00
b. "cvos." 35.00 6.50
c. "centavo" 42.50 40.00
176 A63 2c black 25.00 4.00
177 A63 5c blk, *pink* 25.00 4.00
a. Name at side (V) 50.00 7.50
178 A63 10c blk, *pink* 25.00 4.00
a. Name at side (V) 50.00 7.50
179 A63 20c blk, *yellow* 35.00 6.50
a. Name at side (G) 75.00 10.00
Nos. 175-179 (5) 145.00 25.00

"Gobierno Provisional" at Top
Name at Side in Black or Green

180 A64 1c (ctvo.) blk, *bl grn* 35.00 5.00
a. "centavo" 100.00 40.00
181 A64 2c blk, *bl grn* 20.00 5.00
182 A64 5c blk (G) 20.00 5.00
a. "ctvos." smaller 40.00 7.50
183 A64 10c blk, *pink* 20.00 5.00
184 A64 20c blk, *yel* (G) 35.00 7.50
Nos. 180-184 (5) 130.00 27.50

Issues of the rebel provisional government in Cucuta.

A65

A66

1901 ***Sewing Machine Perf.***

Purple Overprint

185 A65 1c black .85 .85
a. Without overprint 1.90 1.90
b. Double overprint 2.00 2.00
c. Imperf., pair 2.00 2.00
d. Inverted overprint 1.00 1.00
186 A66 2c blk, *rose* .85 .85
a. Imperf., pair 2.00 2.00
b. Without overprint 1.90 1.90
c. Double overprint 2.00 2.00

A67

A68

1901

Rose Overprint

187 A67 1c blue .85 .85
a. Imperf., pair 3.00 3.00
188 A68 2c brown .85 .85
a. Imperf., pair 3.00 3.00
b. Without overprint .85 .85

A69

A70

Sewing Machine or Regular Perf. 12, 12½

1902

Magenta Overprint

189 A69 5c violet 1.75 1.75
a. Without overprint 1.75 1.75
b. Double overprint 1.75 1.75
c. Imperf., pair 3.75 3.75
190 A70 10c yel brn 1.75 1.75
a. Double overprint 1.75 1.75
b. Imperf., pair 3.75 3.75
c. Without overprint 1.75 1.75
d. Printed on both sides 2.50 2.50

A71

A72

1902

Magenta Overprint

191 A71 5c yel brn 1.75 1.75
a. Without overprint 1.60 1.60
b. Imperf., pair 5.00 5.00
192 A71 10c black 1.25 1.25
a. Without overprint 1.00 1.00
b. Imperf., pair 7.50 7.50
193 A72 20c maroon 4.00 2.50
b. Imperf., pair 12.50 12.50
Nos. 191-193 (3) 7.00 5.50

Nos. 191-193 exist tête bêche. Value of 10c and 20c, each $12.50.

Washed examples of Nos. 167-174, 185-193 are offered as "without overprint."

Barranquilla Issues

Magdalena River — A75

Iron Quay at Sabanilla — A76

La Popa Hill — A77

1902-03 ***Imperf.***

194 A75 2c green 1.25 1.25
195 A75 2c dk bl 1.25 1.25
196 A75 2c rose 18.00 18.00
197 A76 10c scarlet .85 .85
198 A76 10c orange 10.00 10.00
199 A76 10c rose 1.25 1.25
200 A76 10c maroon 1.40 1.40
201 A76 10c claret 1.40 1.40
202 A77 20c violet 2.75 2.75
a. Laid paper 7.50
203 A77 20c dl bl 7.50 7.50
204 A77 20c dl bl, *pink* *110.00* *110.00*
205 A77 20c car rose 16.00 16.00
Nos. 194-205 (12) *171.65* *171.65*

Sewing Machine Perf. and Perf. 12

194a A75 2c green 7.50 7.50
195a A75 2c dark blue 7.50 7.50
196a A75 2c carmine *35.00* *35.00*
197a A76 10c scarlet 3.50 3.50
198a A76 10c orange *27.50* *27.50*
199a A76 10c rose 5.50 5.50
200a A76 10c maroon 5.50 5.50
201a A76 10c claret 5.00 5.00
202b A77 20c purple .55 .55
c. 20c lilac .55 .55
203a A77 20c dull blue 7.50 7.50
204a A77 20c dull blue, *rose* *140.00* *140.00*
205b A77 20c carmine rose *55.00* *55.00*
Nos. 194a-205b (12) *300.05* *300.05*

See Nos. 240-245.

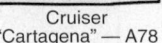

Cruiser "Cartagena" — A78

Bolívar — A79

General Próspero Pinzón — A80

A81

A82

1903-04 *Imperf.*

209	A78	5c blue	2.10	2.10
210	A78	5c bister	3.50	3.50
211	A79	50c yellow	3.00	3.00
212	A79	50c green	3.50	3.50
213	A79	50c scarlet	3.50	3.50
214	A79	50c carmine	3.50	3.50
a.		50c rose	3.50	3.50
215	A79	50c pale brown	3.50	3.50
216	A80	1p yellow brn	1.25	1.25
217	A80	1p rose	2.00	2.00
218	A80	1p blue	2.00	2.00
219	A80	1p violet	20.00	20.00
220	A81	5p claret	4.25	4.25
221	A81	5p pale brown	6.50	6.50
222	A81	5p blue green	6.00	6.00
223	A82	10p pale green	6.25	6.25
224	A82	10p claret	20.00	20.00
		Nos. 209-224 (16)	90.85	90.85

Nos. 216 and 217 measure 20½x26½mm and No. 218, 18x24mm. Stamps of this issue exist with forged perforations.

Perf. 12

209a	A78	5c blue	7.50	7.50
210a	A78	5c bister	7.50	7.50
211a	A79	50c yellow	12.50	12.50
b.		50c orange	20.00	20.00
212a	A79	50c green	20.00	20.00
213a	A79	50c scarlet	9.00	9.00
214b	A79	50c rose	9.00	9.00
215a	A79	50c pale brown	9.00	9.00
216a	A80	1p yellow brown	4.00	4.00
217a	A80	1p rose	6.00	6.00
218a	A80	1p blue	7.50	6.00
219a	A80	1p violet	50.00	50.00
220a	A81	5p claret	16.00	16.00
221a	A81	5p pale brown	18.00	18.00
222a	A81	5p blue green	18.00	18.00
223a	A82	10p pale green	25.00	25.00
224a	A82	10p claret	60.00	60.00
		Nos. 209a-224a (16)	279.00	277.50

Laid Paper *Imperf.*

240	A76	10c dk bl, *lil*	5.00	5.00
241	A76	10c dk bl, *bluish*	3.00	3.00
242	A76	10c dk bl, *brn*	3.00	3.00
243	A76	10c dk bl, *sal*	7.50	7.50
244	A76	10c dk bl, *grnsh bl*	4.00	4.00
245	A76	10c dk bl, *dp rose*	3.00	3.00
		Nos. 240-245 (6)	25.50	25.50

Perf. 12

240a	A76	10c dk bl, *lilac*	10.50	10.50
241a	A76	10c dk bl, *bluish*	7.50	7.50
242a	A76	10c dk bl, *brn*	7.50	7.50
243a	A76	10c dk bl, *salmon*	55.00	55.00
244a	A76	10c dk bl, *grnsh bl*	16.00	16.00
245a	A76	10c dk bl, *deep rose*	7.50	7.50
		Nos. 240a-245a (6)	104.00	104.00

A82a

Imperf., Sewing Machine Perf.

1902 **Typeset**

255	A82a	10c black, *rose*	3.50	3.50
256	A82a	20c blk, *orange*	2.50	2.50

This issue was printed in either Cali or Popayan.

Medellin Issue

A83

1902

257	A83	1c grn, *straw*	.25	*.40*
258	A83	2c salmon, *rose*	.25	*.40*
259	A83	5c dp bl, *grnsh*	.25	*.40*
260	A83	10c pale brn, *straw*	.25	*.40*
261	A83	20c pur, *rose*	.35	*.40*
262	A83	50c dl rose, *grnsh*	1.75	*2.50*
263	A83	1p blk, *yellow*	3.50	*5.25*
264	A83	5p slate, *blue*	27.50	27.50
265	A83	10p dk brn, *rose*	17.50	17.50
		Nos. 257-265 (9)	51.60	54.75

For overprint see No. L8.

Imperf., Pairs

257a	A83	1c	8.50	8.50
258a	A83	2c	8.50	8.50
259a	A83	5c	8.50	8.50
260a	A83	10c	8.50	8.50
261a	A83	20c	8.50	8.50
262a	A83	50c	8.50	8.50
263a	A83	1p	22.50	22.50
264a	A83	5p	62.50	62.50
265a	A83	10p	50.00	50.00

Regular Issue

A84

A85

A86

A87

A88

A89

A90

A91

A92

1902 *Imperf.*

266	A84	2c blk, *rose*	.20	.20
267	A85	4c red, *grn*	.20	.20
268	A86	5c grn, *bl*	.20	.20
269	A87	10c blk, *pink*	.20	.20
c.		10c blk, *rose*	.75	.75
270	A88	20c brn, *buff*	.20	.20
271	A89	50c dk grn, *rose*	1.10	1.10
272	A90	1p pur, *buff*	.45	.45
273	A91	5p grn, *bl*	3.25	3.25
274	A92	10p grn, *pale grn*	10.00	5.00
		Nos. 266-274 (9)	15.80	10.80

For overprint see No. H13.

Sewing Machine Perf.

266a	A84	2c blk, *rose*	1.50	1.50
267a	A85	4c red, *grn*	1.25	1.25
268a	A86	5c grn, *blue*	1.50	1.50
269a	A87	10c blk, *pink*	1.50	1.50
270a	A88	20c brn, *buff*	2.50	2.00
271a	A89	50c dk grn, *rose*	5.00	4.00
272a	A90	1p pur, *buff*	6.00	5.00
273a	A91	5p grn, *blue*	27.50	27.50
274a	A92	10p grn, *pale grn*	50.00	50.00
		Nos. 266a-274a (9)	96.75	94.25

1903 ***Perf. 12***

266b	A84	2c blk, *rose*	1.10	1.10
269b	A87	10c blk, *pink*	1.25	1.25
270b	A88	20c brn, *buff*	1.25	1.25
272b	A90	1p pur, *buff*	2.50	2.50
273b	A91	5p grn, *blue*	22.50	22.50
274b	A92	10p grn, *pale grn*	40.00	35.00
		Nos. 266b-274b (6)	68.60	63.60

1903 ***Imperf.***

284	A85	4c blue, *grn*	.25	.25
285	A86	5c blue, *blue*	.25	.25
286	A88	20c blue,*buff*	.25	.25
288	A89	50c blue, *rose*	1.40	1.40
		Nos. 284-288 (4)	2.15	2.15

Sewing Machine Perf.

284a	A85	4c blue, *grn*	1.75	1.40
285a	A86	5c blue, *blue*	1.75	1.40
286a	A88	20c blue, *buff*	2.50	2.00
288a	A89	50c blue, *rose*	5.00	4.50
		Nos. 284a-288a (4)	11.00	9.30

Perf. 12

284b	A85	4c blue, *grn*	2.00	2.00
285b	A86	5c blue, *blue*	2.00	2.00
286b	A88	20c blue, *buff*	2.75	2.75
288b	A89	50c blue, *rose*	7.50	7.50
		Nos. 284b-288b (4)	14.25	14.25

A93

1904 **Pelure Paper** ***Imperf.***

303	A93	½c yellow brn	1.00	1.00
304	A90	1c blue green	1.00	1.00
a.		1c yellow green	1.00	1.00
306	A84	2c blue	.90	.60
307	A86	5c carmine	1.00	1.00
308	A87	10c violet	1.00	.90
		Nos. 303-308 (5)	4.90	4.50

For overprint see No. H13.

1904 ***Perf. 13***

303a	A93	½c yellow brown	3.00	3.00
304b	A90	1c blue green	4.00	3.50
c.		1c yellow green	5.00	4.50
306a	A84	2c blue	2.50	2.50

Perf. 12

307a	A86	5c carmine	2.25	2.25
308a	A87	10c violet	2.25	2.25
		Nos. 303a-308a (5)	14.00	13.50

A94

A95

Pres. José Manuel Marroquín — A96

Imprint: "Lit. J.L.Arango Medellin. Col."

1904 **Wove Paper** ***Perf. 12***

314	A94	½c yellow	.65	.20
315	A94	1c green	.65	.20
316	A94	2c rose	.65	.20
317	A94	5c blue	1.00	.20
318	A94	10c violet	1.40	.20
319	A94	20c black	1.40	.25
320	A95	1p brown	15.00	2.50
321	A96	5p red & blk, *yel*	45.00	45.00
322	A96	10p bl & blk, *grnsh*	45.00	45.00
		Nos. 314-322 (9)	110.75	93.75

Redrawn

314a	A94	½c	.65	.20
315a	A94	1c	.65	.20
316a	A94	2c	.65	.20
317a	A94	5c	1.00	.20
319a	A94	20c	1.40	.20
		Nos. 314a-319a (5)	4.35	1.00

Imperf., Pairs

314b	A94	½c	2.50	2.50
315b	A94	1c	2.00	2.00
316b	A94	2c	2.50	2.50
317b	A94	5c	2.50	2.50
318a	A94	10c	3.25	3.25
319b	A94	20c	6.00	6.00
320a	A95	1p	50.00	50.00
		Nos. 314b-320a (7)	68.75	68.75

On the redrawn types, the imprint is close to the base of the design instead of being spaced from it. On the redrawn 2c and 5c, the lower end of the vertical white line below "OR" of "CORREOS" forms a hook which turns to the right instead of to the left as in the originals.

See Nos. 325-330. For surcharges see Nos. 351-354, L1-L7, L9-L13, L15-L25.

A97

100p has different frame.

1903 ***Imperf.***

323	A97	50p org yel, *pale pink*	75.00	75.00
324	A97	100p dk bl, *dk rose*	60.00	60.00

Imprint: "Lit. Nacional"

Perf. 10, 13, 13½ and Compound

1908

325	A94	½c orange	.60	.20
a.		½c yellow	.60	.20
b.		Imperf., pair	2.00	1.50
c.		Without imprint	4.00	4.00
326	A94	1c yel grn	.60	.20
a.		Without imprint	.60	.20
d.		Imperf., pair	3.00	2.50
327	A94	2c red	.60	.20
a.		2c carmine	.60	.20
b.		Imperf., pair	3.00	2.50
328	A94	5c blue	.50	.20
a.		Imperf., pair	5.00	4.00
329	A94	10c violet	*40.00*	.70
330	A94	20c gray blk	*40.00*	.50
		Nos. 325-330 (6)	*82.30*	2.00

The above stamps may be easily distinguished from those of 1904 by the perforation, by the height of the design, 24mm instead of 23mm, and by the "Lit. Nacional" imprint.

Camilo Torres A99

Policarpa Salavarrieta A100

Bolívar Demanding Liberation of Slaves — A105

Designs: 2c, Nariño. 5c, Bolívar. 10c, Francisco José de Caldas. 20c, Francisco de Paula Santander. 10p, Bolívar Resigning.

1910, Aug. **Engr.** ***Perf. 12***

331	A99	½c violet & blk	.50	.25
a.		Center inverted	425.00	425.00
332	A100	1c deep green	.40	.25
333	A100	2c scarlet	.40	.25
334	A100	5c deep blue	1.25	.45
335	A100	10c plum	10.00	5.00
336	A100	20c black brn	15.00	5.50
337	A105	1p dk violet	65.00	20.00
338	A105	10p claret	250.00	200.00
		Nos. 331-338 (8)	342.55	231.70

Colombian independence centenary.

Caldas
A107

Monument to Battle of Boyacá
A113

View of Cartagena
A114

Coat of Arms
A118

Designs: 1c, Torres. 2c, Narino. 4c, Santander. 5c, Bolivar. 10c, Jose Maria Cordoba. 1p, Sucre. 2p, Rufino Cuervo. 5p, Antonio Ricaurte y Lozano.

1917	Engr.		Perf. 14	
339	A107	½c bister	.35	.20
340	A107	1c green	.30	.20
341	A107	2c car rose	.30	.20
342	A107	4c violet	.90	.30
343	A107	5c dull blue	2.25	.20
344	A107	10c gray	2.25	.20
345	A113	20c red	1.25	.20
346	A114	50c carmine	1.50	.20
347	A107	1p brt blue	11.00	.40
348	A107	2p orange	12.00	.45
349	A107	5p gray	30.00	8.50
350	A118	10p dk brown	35.00	10.00
		Nos. 339-350 (12)	97.10	21.05

The 1c, 5c, 10c, 50c, 2p, 5p and 10p also exist perf. 11½ and 11½ compounded with 14.

Litho. varieties of Nos. 343, 345 and 346 are counterfeits made to defraud the government.

Imperforate examples of Nos. 339-350 are not known to have been regularly issued.

See Nos. 373-374, 400-405. For overprints and surcharges see Nos. 369-370, 377, 409-410, 440, C1, O3, O5-O9.

Nos. 318-319, 329-330 Surcharged in Red

1918

On Issue of 1904

351	A94	½c on 20c black	1.00	.25
352	A94	3c on 10c violet	2.50	.50

On Issue of 1908

353	A94	½c on 20c gray blk	8.00	5.00
354	A94	3c on 10c violet	12.00	4.25
		Nos. 351-354 (4)	23.50	10.00

Nos. 351-354 inclusive exist with surcharge reading up or down. On one stamp in each sheet the letter "S" in "Especie" is omitted. All denominations exist with a small zero before the decimal in the surcharge.

A119

A120

1918	Litho.		Perf. 13½	
358	A119	3c red	.50	.20
a.		Imperf., pair	4.00	4.00

1920	Engr.		Perf. 14	
359	A120	3c red, *org*	.30	.20
a.		Imperf., pair	3.00	3.00

See Nos. 371-372. For surcharge see No. 453.

A121

A122

A123

Perf. 10, 13½ and Compound

1920-21			Litho.	
360	A121	½c yellow	.50	.25
361	A121	1c green	.85	.20
362	A121	2c red	.65	.20
363	A122	3c green	.65	.20
a.		3c yellow green	.65	.20
364	A121	5c blue	.95	.25
365	A121	10c violet	3.00	1.50
366	A121	20c deep green	8.00	3.50
367	A123	50c dark red	8.00	3.50
		Nos. 360-367 (8)	22.60	9.60

The tablet with "PROVISIONAL" was added separately to each design on the various lithographic stones and its position varies slightly on different stamps in the sheet. For some values there were two or more stones, on which the tablet was placed at various angles.

Nos. 360-366 exist imperf.

See No. 375.

No. 342 Surcharged in Red

a

(15mm wide) — b

1921				
369	A107 (a)	3c on 4c violet	.80	.25
a.		Double surcharge	13.00	
370	A107 (b)	3c on 4c violet	3.50	2.00

See No. 377.

Types of 1917-21

1923-24	Engr.		Perf. 13½	
371	A120	1½c chocolate	1.00	.50
372	A120	3c blue	.50	.20
373	A107	5c claret ('24)	2.00	.20
374	A107	10c blue	7.50	.40
		Litho.		
375	A121	10c dark blue	10.00	6.00
		Nos. 371-375 (5)	21.00	7.30

No. 342 Surcharged in Red

(18mm wide)

1924				
377	A107	3c on 4c vio	3.00	1.25
a.		Double surcharge	12.00	
b.		Double surch., one invtd.	12.00	
c.		With added surch. "3cs." in red		

A124

1924-25	Litho.		Perf. 10, 10x13½	
379	A124	1c red	.70	.20
380	A124	3c dp blue ('25)	.70	.20

Nos. 379-380 exist imperf. Value, each pair $5.

A125

A126

Black, Red or Green Surch. & Ovpt.

Imprint of Waterlow & Sons

1925			Perf. 14, 14½	
382	A125	1c on 3c bis brn	.30	.20
383	A126	4c violet (R)	.40	.20
a.		Inverted surcharge	7.00	7.00

Imprint of American Bank Note Co.

Perf. 12

384	A125	1c on 3c bis brn	6.00	5.00
a.		Inverted surcharge	15.00	15.00
385	A126	4c violet (G)	.40	.30
a.		Inverted overprint	7.50	7.50
		Nos. 382-385 (4)	7.10	5.70

Correos

Provisional

Revenue stamps of basic types A125 and A126 were handstamped as above in violet or blue by the Cali post office in 1925, but were not authorized by the government. Denominations so overprinted are 1c, 2c, 3c, 4c and 5c.

A127

A128

Perf. 10, 13½x10

1926	Litho.		Wmk. 194	
395	A127	1c gray green	.40	.20
396	A128	4c deep blue	.45	.20

Nos. 395-396 exist imperf. Value, each pair $4.

Types of 1917 and

Sabana Station — A129

1926-29	Unwmk.	Engr.	Perf. 14	
400	A107	4c deep blue	.40	.20
401	A118	8c dark blue	.50	.20
402	A107	30c olive bister	4.75	.60
403	A129	40c brn & yel brn	7.50	1.00
404	A107	5p violet	7.50	.70
a.		Perf. 11 ('29)	12.00	1.00
405	A118	10p green	12.00	2.00
a.		Perf. 11 ('29)	25.00	4.00
		Nos. 400-405 (6)	32.65	4.70

For surcharges & overprint see Nos. 409-410, O4.

Death of Bolívar
A130

1930, Dec. 17			Perf. 12½	
408	A130	4c dk blue & blk	.60	.35

Cent. of the death of Simón Bolívar. See Nos. C80-C82.

Nos. 400 and 402 Surcharged in Red or Dark Blue

1932, Jan. 20			Perf. 14	
409	A107	1c on 4c dp bl (R)	.30	.20
a.		Inverted surcharge	5.25	5.25
410	A107	20c on 30c ol bis	8.00	.70
a.		Inverted surcharge	17.50	
b.		Double surcharge	17.50	

Emerald Mine — A131

Oil Wells — A132

Coffee Cultivation
A133

Platinum Mine — A134

Gold Mining — A135

Christopher Columbus — A136

Imprint: "Waterlow & Sons Ltd. Londres"

1932	Wmk. 229		Perf. 12½	
411	A131	1c green	.50	.20
412	A132	2c red	.50	.20
413	A133	5c brown	.60	.20
414	A134	8c blue blk	3.75	.50
415	A135	10c yellow	2.75	.20
416	A136	20c dk blue	8.00	.35
		Nos. 411-416 (6)	16.10	1.65

See Nos. 441-442, 464-466a, 517. For surcharges see Nos. 455, 527, O1, O10-O11, O13, RA30.

Pedro de Heredia — A137

Coffee Picking — A138

Perf. 11½

1934, Jan. 10 Unwmk. Litho.

417	A137	1c dark green	2.40	.70
418	A137	5c chocolate	3.25	.60
419	A137	8c dark blue	2.40	.70
		Nos. 417-419 (3)	8.05	2.00

Cartagena, 400th anniv. See Nos. C111-C114.

1934, Dec. Engr. *Perf. 12*

420	A138	5c brown	3.00	.20

Discus Thrower — A139

Post and Telegraph Building — A145

Allegory of Olympic Games at Barranquilla — A140

Foot Race A141

Tennis A142

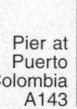

Pier at Puerto Colombia A143

View of the Bay A144

Designs: 2c, Soccer. 10c, Hurdling. 15c, Athlete in stadium. 18c, Baseball. 24c, Swimming. 50c, View of Barranquilla. 2p, Monument to Flag. 5p, Coat of Arms. 10p, Condor.

1935, Jan. 26 Litho. *Perf. 11½*

421	A139	2c bluish grn & buff	1.25	.40
422	A139	4c deep green	1.25	.40
423	A140	5c dk brn & yel	1.25	.40
a.		Horiz. pair, imperf. btwn.	200.00	
424	A141	7c dk carmine	2.50	1.50
425	A142	8c blk & pink	2.00	2.00
426	A141	10c brown & bl	2.75	1.50
427	A143	12c indigo	3.25	2.50
428	A141	15c bl & red brn	5.50	4.25
429	A141	18c dk vio & buff	8.00	6.50
430	A144	20c purple & grn	6.50	5.50
431	A144	24c bluish grn & ultra	6.50	5.25
432	A144	50c ultra & buff	10.00	8.50
433	A145	1p drab & blue	92.50	50.00
434	A145	2p dull grn & gray	110.00	90.00
435	A145	5p pur blk & bl	350.00	275.00
436	A145	10p black & gray	425.00	400.00
		Nos. 421-436 (16)	1,028.	853.70

3rd Natl. Olympic Games, Barranquilla. Counterfeits of 10p exist.

Oil Wells — A155

Gold Mining — A157

Imprint: "American Bank Note Co."

1935, Mar. Unwmk. Engr. *Perf. 12*

437	A155	2c carmine rose	.35	.20
439	A157	10c deep orange	20.00	.20

See Nos. 468, 470, 498, 516. For surcharge and overprints see Nos. 496, 596, O2.

No. 347 Surcharged in Black

1935, Aug. *Perf. 14*

440	A107	12c on 1p brt bl	3.50	1.50

Types of 1932

Imprint: "Lit. Nacional Bogotá"

1935-36 Litho. *Perf. 11, 11½, 12½*

441	A131	1c lt green	.20	.20
a.		Imperf., pair	3.50	
442	A133	5c brown ('36)	.55	.20
a.		Imperf., pair	4.00	4.00

For surcharge see No. 527.

Bolívar A159

Tequendama Falls A160

Wmk. Wavy Lines. (229)

1937 Engr. *Perf. 12½*

443	A159	1c deep green	.20	.20
a.		Perf. 14		
444	A160	12c deep blue	3.25	1.10

See No. 570. For surcharges and overprints see Nos. 454, 456, C231, C326, O12.

Soccer Player — A161

Runner — A163

Discus Thrower — A162

1937, Jan. 4 Photo. Unwmk.

445	A161	3c lt green	1.40	.85
446	A162	10c carmine rose	3.00	1.75
447	A163	1p black	27.50	24.00
		Nos. 445-447 (3)	31.90	26.60

National Olympic Games, Manizales. For surcharge see No. 452.

Exposition Palace — A164

Stadium at Barranquilla A165

Monument to the Colors A166

1937, Jan. 4

448	A164	5c violet brown	2.75	.40
449	A165	15c blue	6.75	4.50
450	A166	50c orange brn	19.00	9.75
		Nos. 448-450 (3)	28.50	14.65

Barranquilla National Exposition.

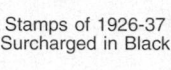

Stamps of 1926-37 Surcharged in Black

1937-38 Unwmk. *Perf. 12½*

452	A161	1c on 3c lt grn	.75	.75
a.		Inverted surcharge	1.75	1.75
453	A118	5c on 8c dk bl	.40	.35
a.		Inverted surcharge	1.75	1.75

Wmk. 229

454	A160	2c on 12c dp bl	.40	.35
455	A134	5c on 8c bl blk	.45	.55
a.		Invtd. surcharge	1.50	1.50
456	A160	10c on 12c dp bl ('38)	4.25	.85
a.		Dbl. surcharge	8.50	8.50
		Nos. 452-456 (5)	6.25	2.85

Calle del Arco — A168

Entrance to Church of the Rosary — A169

Arms of Bogotá A170

Gonzálo Jiménez de Quesada A171

Bochica A172

Santo Domingo Convent A173

Mass of the Conquistadors — A174

1938, July 27 Unwmk. *Perf. 12½*

457	A168	1c yellow green	.20	.20
458	A169	2c scarlet	.20	.20
459	A170	5c brown blk	.25	.20
460	A171	10c brown	.60	.30
461	A172	15c brt blue	3.00	1.25
462	A173	20c brt red vio	3.00	1.25
463	A174	1p red brown	40.00	22.50
		Nos. 457-463 (7)	47.25	25.90

Bogotá, 400th anniversary.

Types of 1932

Imprint: "Litografia Nacional Bogotá"

1938, Dec. 5 Litho. *Perf. 10½, 11*

464	A132	2c rose	.80	.30
465	A135	10c yellow	2.00	.30
466	A136	20c dull blue	8.00	1.00
a.		20c dark blue, perf. 12½ ('44)	50.00	5.00
		Nos. 464-466 (3)	10.80	1.60

Types of 1935 and

Bolívar A175

Coffee Picking A176

Arms of Colombia A177

Christopher Columbus A178

Caldas A179

Sabana Station A180

Imprint: "American Bank Note Co."

Wmk. 255

1939, Mar. 3 Engr. *Perf. 12*

467	A175	1c green	.20	.20
468	A155	2c car rose	.20	.20
469	A176	5c dull brown	.20	.20
470	A157	10c deep orange	.40	.20
471	A177	15c dull blue	1.25	.20
472	A178	20c violet blk	14.00	.20
473	A179	30c olive bister	4.25	.30
474	A180	40c bister brn	13.00	2.75
		Nos. 467-474 (8)	33.50	4.25

See Nos. 497-499, 515, 518, 574. For surcharges and overprints see Nos. 506-507, 520-522, 596, RA26, RA47.

Gen. Santander A181

Allegory A182

Gen. Santander A183

Statue at Cúcuta A184

Birthplace of Santander A185

Church at Rosario A186

Paya — A187

Bridge at Boyacá — A188

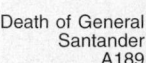

Death of General Santander A189

Invasion of the Liberators A190

Perf. 13x13½, 13½x13

1940, May 6 Engr. Wmk. 229

475	A181	1c olive green	.20	.20
476	A182	2c dk carmine	.40	.25
477	A183	5c sepia	.20	.20
478	A184	8c carmine	1.50	1.50
479	A185	10c orange yel	.65	.50
480	A186	15c dark blue	1.75	1.10
481	A187	20c green	2.25	1.75
482	A188	50c violet	5.25	5.00
483	A189	1p deep rose	17.00	17.00
484	A190	2p orange	55.00	55.00
		Nos. 475-484 (10)	84.20	82.50

Death of General Francisco Santander, cent.

Tobacco Plant — A194

Gen. Santander A195

Garcia Rovira A196

R. Galan — A197

Antonio Sucre — A198

1940-43 Engr. Wmk. 255 *Perf. 12*

488	A194	8c rose car & grn	1.00	.55
489	A195	15c dp blue ('43)	1.10	.25
490	A196	20c gray blk ('41)	3.50	.40
491	A197	40c brown bis ('41)	2.10	.40
492	A198	1p black	6.75	.50
		Nos. 488-492 (5)	14.45	2.10

See Nos. 500, 554. For overprint see No. RA28.

Arms of Palmira — A199

Unwmk.

1942, July 4 Litho. *Perf. 11*

493	A199	30c claret	4.25	.60

8th Natl. Agricultural Exposition, held at Palmira.

Paradise of Isaacs, Palmira — A200

Signing Treaty of the Wisconsin A201

1942, July 4

494	A200	50c lt blue grn	4.25	.85

Issued in honor of the writer, Jorge Isaacs.

1942, Nov. 21 *Perf. 10½*

495	A201	10c dull orange	3.00	.50
a.		"2. XI.1902" instead of "21. XI. 1902"	17.50	*20.00*
b.		Perf. 12	5.00	5.00

40th anniv. of the signing of the Treaty of the Wisconsin, Nov. 21, 1902.

No. 470 Surcharged in Black

1944 Wmk. 255 *Perf. 12*

496	A157	5c on 10c dp org	.20	.20

Counterfeits exist of No. 496 with inverted or double surcharge.

Types of 1935-41 and

National Shrine — A202

San Pedro Alejandrino A203

Imprint: "Columbian Bank Note Co."

1944-45 Unwmk. Engr. *Perf. 11*

497	A175	1c green	.20	.20
498	A155	2c rose	.20	.20
499	A176	5c dull brown	.20	.20
500	A196	20c gray black	3.00	.75
501	A202	30c dl ol grn ('45)	1.75	.95
502	A203	50c rose	1.75	.95
		Nos. 497-502 (6)	7.10	3.25

No. 499 Surcharged in Black

1944, Oct.

506	A176	1c on 5c dull brn	.20	.20
507	A176	2c on 5c dull brn	.20	.20

Nos. 506 and 507 exist with inverted or double surcharge, created by favor.

Flag — A204

Arms — A205

Murillo Toro — A206

Hospital of St. John of God A207

Virrey Solis A208

1944, Oct. 10 Litho.

508	A204	2c ultra & bis	.30	.30
a.		Sheet of 18	15.00	
b.		Imperf., pair	15.00	
509	A205	5c ultra & bis	.45	.45
a.		Sheet of 22	18.00	
b.		Imperf., pair	15.00	
510	A206	20c blk & bluish grn	1.50	1.50
a.		Sheet of 8	16.00	
b.		Imperf., pair	22.50	
511	A207	40c blk & red	6.25	6.25
a.		Sheet of 4	26.00	
512	A208	1p blk & red	14.00	14.00
a.		Sheet of 2	30.00	
		Nos. 508-512 (5)	22.50	22.50

Souvenir Sheet

Perf. 11x11½ All Around, Stamps Imperf.

513		Sheet of 5, #508-512	25.00	25.00

75th anniv. of Gen. Benevolent Assoc. of Cundinamarca.

Nos. 508-513 were printed in composite sheets containing one each of Nos. 508a, 509a, 510a, 511a and 512a, and two of 513. Fifty of these were presented to government officials.

Murillo Toro — A210

San Pedro Alejandrino — A211

1944, Nov. 10 *Perf. 11*

514	A210	5c lt brown	.30	.20

Types of 1932-39 and A211

Imprint: "Litografia Nacional Bogota"

1944 Litho. *Perf. 12½*

515	A175	1c dp green	.35	.20
a.		1c olive green	.35	.20
b.		Imperf., pair	1.75	1.75
516	A155	2c dk carmine	.40	.20
a.		Imperf., pair	1.75	1.75
517	A135	10c yellow org	2.75	.45
518	A179	30c gray olive	7.50	3.50
a.		Imperf., pair	27.50	
519	A211	50c rose	8.00	3.75
		Nos. 515-519 (5)	19.00	8.10

No. 469 Overprinted in Green, Blue or Red

Wmk. 255

1945, July 19 Engr. *Perf. 12*

520	A176	5c dull brn (G)	.40	.25
521	A176	5c dull brn (R)	.40	.25
522	A176	5c dull brn (Bl)	.40	.25
		Nos. 520-522 (3)	1.20	.75

Portraits are Joseph Stalin, Franklin D. Roosevelt and Winston Churchill.

Nos. 520-522 exist with overprint inverted. Value, $20 each.

Clock Tower, Cartagena — A212

1945, Nov. 15

523	A212	50c olive black	4.25	1.50

For overprints see Nos. 543-544.

Sierra Nevada of Santa Marta A213

Designs: 30c, Seaplane Tolima. 50c, San Sebastian Fort, Cartagena.

Unwmk.

1945, Dec. 14 Litho. *Perf. 11*

524	A213	20c light green	2.00	1.25
525	A213	30c pale blue	2.00	1.25
526	A213	50c salmon pink	2.00	1.25
		Nos. 524-526 (3)	6.00	3.75

25th anniv. of the 1st airmail service in America, according to the inscription, but earlier services are known to have existed.

No. 442 Surcharged in Black

1946, Mar. 8 *Perf. 11x11½, 12½*

527	A133	1c on 5c brown	.20	.20
a.		Inverted surcharge	.90	

Gen. Antonio Jose de Sucre — A216

Wmk. 255

1946, Apr. 16 Engr. *Perf. 12*

Size: 19x26½mm

528	A216	1c brn & turq grn	.20	.20
529	A216	2c vio & rose car	.20	.20

Size: 23x31mm

530	A216	5c sepia & blue	.20	.20
531	A216	9c dk grn & red	.85	.85
532	A216	10c ultra & org	.65	.65
533	A216	20c blk & dp org	.65	.65
534	A216	30c brn red & grn	.90	.35
535	A216	40c ol blk & red vio	.90	.40
536	A216	50c dp brn & vio	.90	.40
		Nos. 528-536 (9)	5.45	3.90

Map of South America A217

National Observatory A218

Unwmk.

1946, June 7 Litho. *Perf. 11*

537 A217 15c ultra .50 .30
a. Imperf., pair 4.00

1946, Aug.

538 A218 5c fawn .30 .20
a. Imperf., pair 6.00

See No. 565.

Andrés Bello — A219

Joaquín de Cayzedo y Cuero — A220

Wmk. 255

1946, Sept. 3 Engr. *Perf. 12*

539 A219 3c sepia .25 .20
540 A219 10c orange .60 .30
541 A219 15c slate black .75 .35
Nos. 539-541,C145 (4) 1.80 1.05

Bello (1781-1865), poet and educator.

1946, Sept. 20 Wmk. 229 *Perf. 12½*

542 A220 2p bluish green 4.50 1.25

See No. 568. For surcharge see No. 613.

Type of 1945, Overprinted in Black or Green

1946, Dec. 6 Wmk. 255 *Perf. 12*

543 A212 50c red (Bk) 4.00 2.25
a. Double overprint 25.00
544 A212 50c red (G) 4.00 2.25
a. Double overprint 25.00

5th Central American and Caribbean Championship Games.

Coffee — A221

Engraved and Lithographed

1947, Jan. 10 Wmk. 229 *Perf. 12½*

545 A221 5c multicolored .40 .20

Colombian Orchid: Masdevallia Nycterina A222

Designs (Orchids): 2c, Miltonia vexillaria. No. 548, Cattleya chocoensis. No. 549, Odontoglossum crispum. No. 550, Cattleya dowiana aurea. 10c, Cattleya labiata trianae.

1947, Feb. 7 Wmk. 255 *Perf. 12*

546 A222 1c multicolored .50 .20
547 A222 2c multicolored .50 .20
548 A222 5c multicolored 1.50 .20
549 A222 5c multicolored 1.50 .20
550 A222 5c multicolored 1.50 .20
551 A222 10c multicolored 2.25 .35
Nos. 546-551 (6) 7.75 1.35

Antonio Nariño — A228

Alberto Urdaneta y Urdaneta — A229

Perf. 12½

1947, May 9 Litho. Unwmk.

552 A228 5c blue, *grnsh* .25 .20
553 A229 10c red brn, *grnsh* .30 .20
Nos. 552-553,C146-C147 (4) 1.40 1.05

4th Pan-American Press Congress, 1946.

Sucre Type of 1940

1947 Wmk. 255 Engr. *Perf. 12*

554 A198 1p violet 2.50 1.00

José Celestino Mutis and José Jerónimo Triana A230

Miguel A. Caro and Rufino J. Cuervo — A231

1947 Wmk. 229 *Perf. 12½*

555 A230 25c olive green .75 .30
556 A231 3p dark purple 4.50 3.50

See Nos. 567, 569. For surcharge see No. 610.

Metropolitan Cathedral, Plaza Bolívar, Bogotá — A232

National Capitol A233

Ministry of Foreign Affairs A234

A235

1948, Apr. 2

557 A232 5c black brown .20 .20
558 A233 10c orange .55 .55
559 A234 15c dark blue .55 .55
Nos. 557-559,C148-C149 (5) 2.40 2.40

Miniature Sheet

Imperf

560 A235 50c slate 2.00 1.60

9th Pan-American Conf., Bogotá.

No. RA5A Overprinted in Black

1948 Unwmk. *Perf. 12½*

Without Gum

561 PT3 1c yellow orange .20 .20

The letter "C" is the initial of "CORREOS."

Nos. RA33, RA24 and RA25 Overprinted in Black

1948 Wmk. 255 *Perf. 12.*

562 PT6 1c olive .20 .20
563 PT6 2c green .20 .20
564 PT6 20c brown .20 .20
Nos. 562-564 (3) .60 .60

Nos. 561-564 exist with inverted and double overprints.

Observatory Type of 1946

Unwmk.

1948, June 30 Litho. *Perf. 11*

565 A218 5c blue .20 .20

Simón Bolívar — A236

Carlos Martinez Silva — A237

Wmk. 255

1948, May 29 Engr. *Perf. 12*

566 A236 15c green .40 .20

Types of 1946-47

1948 Unwmk. *Perf. 12½*

567 A230 25c green .30 .20
568 A220 2p dp green .55 .20
569 A231 3p dp red violet .70 .20
Nos. 567-569 (3) 1.55 .60

Falls Type of 1937

1948 Wmk. 229

570 A160 10c red .20 .20

For overprints see Nos. C231, C326.

Perf. 13½

1948, Dec. 21 Unwmk. Litho.

571 A237 40c carmine .40 .25

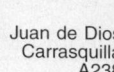

Juan de Dios Carrasquilla A238

1949, May 20 Wmk. 229 *Perf. 12½*

572 A238 5c bister .20 .20

75th anniv. of the foundation of the Colombian Soc. of Agriculture.

Julio Garavito Armero A239

Arms of Colombia A240

Wmk. 229

1949, Apr. 24 Engr. *Perf. 12*

573 A239 4c green .35 .20

Issued to honor Julio Garavito Armero (1865-1920), mathematician.

Coffee Type of 1939.
Imprint: "American Bank Note Co."

1949, Aug. 4 Wmk. 255

574 A176 5c blue .20 .20

1949, Oct. 7 Unwmk. *Perf. 13*

575 A240 15c blue .20 .20

Issued to honor the new Constitution. See Nos. C164-C165.

Shield and Tree — A241

Francisco Javier Cisneros — A242

1949, Oct. 13 Wmk. 229 *Perf. 12½*

576 A241 5c olive .20 .20

4th anniv. of Colombia's 1st Forestry Cong. and propaganda for the government's reforestation program.

1949, Dec. 15 Photo. Unwmk.

577 A242 50c red vio & yel 1.00 .60
578 A242 50c green & vio 1.00 .60
579 A242 50c brown & lt bl 1.00 .60
Nos. 577-579 (3) 3.00 1.80

50th anniv. (in 1948) of the death of Francisco Javier Cisneros.

Masdevallia Chimaera A243

Odontoglossum Crispum — A244

Eastern Hemisphere — A245

Designs: 3c, Cattleya labiata trianae. 4c, Masdevallia nycterina. 5c, Cattleya dowiana aurea. 11c, Miltonia vexillaria. 18c, Santo Domingo post office.

1950, Aug. 22 Photo. *Perf. 13*

580 A243 1c brown .20 .20
581 A244 2c violet .20 .20
582 A243 3c rose lilac .25 .20
583 A243 4c emerald .30 .20
584 A243 5c red orange .75 .20
585 A244 11c red 1.75 1.50
586 A244 18c ultra 2.75 .50
Nos. 580-586 (7) 6.20 3.00

Miniature Sheet

Imperf

587 A245 50c orange yel 1.50 1.50

75th anniv. (in 1949) of the UPU. See No. C199. For surcharge see No. C232.

Antonio Baraya — A246

Perf. 12½

1950, Nov. 27 Unwmk. Engr.

588 A246 2c red .20 .20

Colombian Farm A247

1950, Dec. 28 Photo. *Perf. 11½*

589 A247 5c dp car & buff .20 .20
590 A247 5c bl grn & gray .20 .20
591 A247 5c vio bl & gray .20 .20
Nos. 589-591 (3) .60 .60

Issued to publicize rural life.

Arms of Bogotá A248

Arms of Colombia A249

Perf. 12x12½

1950, Dec. 28 Engr. Wmk. 255

592 A248 5p deep green 2.50 1.25
593 A249 10p red orange 7.50 1.75

Catalogue values for unused stamps in this section, from this point to the end of the section, are for Never Hinged items.

Map and Badge A250

Guillermo Valencia A251

Perf. 12½x13

1951, Jan. 30 Photo. Unwmk.

594 A250 20c red, yel & bl .45 .25

60th anniversary (in 1947) of the formation of the Colombian Society of Engineers.

1951, Oct. 20 Engr. *Perf. 13x13½*

595 A251 25c black .90 .25

Issued to honor Guillermo Valencia (1873-1943), newspaper founder, governor of Cauca, presidential candidate, author.

No. 468 Overprinted in Black

1951, Dec. 11 Wmk. 255 *Perf. 12*

596 A155 2c carmine rose .30 .20

Issued to publicize the reversion of the Mares oil concession to Colombia.

Nicolas Osorio — A252

No. 598, Pompilio Martinez. No. 599, Ezequiel Uricoechea. No. 600, Jose M. Lombana.

Perf. 11½

1952, Aug. 6 Unwmk. Engr.

Various Frames

597 A252 1c deep blue .25 .20
598 A252 1c deep blue .25 .20
599 A252 1c deep blue .25 .20
600 A252 1c deep blue .25 .20
Nos. 597-600 (4) 1.00 .80

Nos. 597-600 were printed in a single sheet containing four panes of twenty-five each, separated by double rows of ornamental tabs. Although inscribed "sobretasa," the stamps were for ordinary postage.

Types of Postal Tax Stamps of 1945-50 and

Communications Building A253 A253a

1952 *Perf. 12*

601 A253 5c ultra .30 .25

Wmk. 255

602 PT10 20c brown 8.00 4.00
603 PT6 25c dk gray *32.50 32.50*
604 PT10 25c blue green .85 .25
605 A253a 50c orange yel 21.00 12.50
606 A253a 1p rose carmine 2.00 .30
607 A253a 2p lilac rose 21.00 8.50
608 A253a 2p violet 2.25 .60
Nos. 601-608 (8) 87.90 58.90

Although inscribed "sobretasa," Nos. 601-608 were issued for ordinary postage.

For surcharges see Nos. 612, RA48.

Cathedral of Manizales — A254

Perf. 11½

1952, Oct. 10 Photo. Unwmk.

609 A254 23c blue & gray blk .45 .25

Centenary of city of Manizales.

For surcharge see No. 619.

No. 555 Surcharged in Blue

1952, Oct. 30 Wmk. 229 *Perf. 12½*

610 A230 15c on 25c olive green .45 .25

Latin American Siderurgical Conf., 1952. See No. C226.

Queen Isabella I and Monument A255

Perf. 12½

1953, Mar. 10 Unwmk. Engr.

611 A255 23c blue & black .75 .55

5th cent. of the birth of Queen Isabella I of Spain.

For surcharge see No. 693.

Nos. 606 and 568 Surcharged with New Values in Dark Blue

1953, Oct. 19 Wmk. 255

612 A253a 40c on 1p rose car 1.40 .25
613 A220 50c on 2p dp green 1.40 .25

Manuel Ancizar A256

Portraits: 23c, José Jeronimo Triana. 30c, Manuel Ponce de Leon. 1p, Agustin Codazzi.

Perf. 12½x13

1953, Nov. Engr. Unwmk.

Frames in Black

614 A256 14c rose red .60 .55
615 A256 23c ultra .55 .25
616 A256 30c chocolate .40 .25
617 A256 1p emerald .40 .25
Nos. 614-617 (4) 1.95 1.30

Cent. (in 1950) of the establishment of the Chorographic Commission. For surcharges and overprint see Nos. 620, 687, 690, 692, C284.

Murillo Toro and Map — A257

Engraved and Lithographed

1953, Dec. 12 Wmk. 255 *Perf. 12*

Black Surcharge

618 A257 5c on 5p multi .35 .20

2nd Natl. Phil. Exhib., Bogotá, Dec. 1953. See No. C237.

Nos. 609 and 614 Surcharged with New Value or New Value and Ornaments

1953 Unwmk. *Perf. 11½, 12½x13*

619 A254 5c on 23c (C) .35 .20
620 A256 5c on 14c (Bk) .35 .25

No. 614 surcharged "CINCO" in blue is listed as No. 687.

Symbolical of St. Francis Receiving Christ's Wounds — A258

1954, Apr. 23 Photo. *Perf. 11½*

621 A258 5c sepia & green .35 .20

400th anniversary of the establishment of Colombia's first Franciscan community.

Soldier, Map and Arms A259

1954, June 13 Engr. *Perf. 13*

622 A259 5c dull blue .25 .20

1st anniv. of the assumption of the presidency by Gen. Gustavo Rojas Pinilla. See Nos. C255, 637a.

Sports Emblem — A260

Design: 10c, Stadium and athlete holding arms of Colombia.

1954, July 18 Unwmk.

623 A260 5c deep blue .40 .20
624 A260 10c red .75 .20
Nos. 623-624,C256-C257 (4) 3.05 .95

7th Natl. Athletic Games, Cali, July 1954.

History Academy Seal — A261

1954, July 24

625	A261	5c ultra & green	.25	.20

50th anniversary (in 1952) of the Colombian Academy of History.

Convent and Cell of St. Peter Claver — A262

1954, Sept. 9

627	A262	5c dark green	.25	.20
a.		Souvenir sheet	5.50	5.50

300th anniv. of the death of St. Peter Claver.

No. 627a contains one stamp similar to No. 627, but printed in greenish black. Sheet size: 121x129½mm. See Nos. C258-C258a.

Mercury — A263

1954, Oct. 29

628	A263	5c orange	.50	.25
		Nos. 628,C259-C260 (3)	1.20	.65

1st Intl. Fair and Exhibition, Bogota, 1954.

Tapestry Madonna A264

College Cloister A265

Designs: 10c, Brother Cristobal de Torres. 20c, College chapel and arms.

Perf. 12½x11½, 11½x12½

1954, Dec. 6

629	A264	5c orange & blk	.35	.20
630	A264	10c blue	.35	.20
631	A265	15c violet brn	.40	.20
632	A265	20c black & brn	1.00	.35
a.		Souvenir sheet	8.50	8.50
		Nos. 629-632,C263-C266 (8)	4.45	2.15

Founding of the Senior College of Our Lady of the Rosary, Bogota, 300th anniv. (in 1953).

No. 632a contains four stamps similar to Nos. 629-632, but printed in different colors: 5c yellow and black, 10c green, 15c dull violet, 20c black and light-blue.

Steel Mill — A266

José Marti — A267

1954, Dec. 12 ***Perf. 12½x13***

633	A266	5c ultra & blk	.25	.20

Issued to mark the opening of the Paz del Rio steel mill, October 1954. See No. C267.

1955, Jan. 28 ***Perf. 13½x13***

634	A267	5c deep carmine	.25	.20

Centenary of the birth of José Marti (1853-1895), Cuban patriot. See No. C268.

Arms, Flags and Soldiers Building Bridge A268

1955, Mar. 23 ***Perf. 12½***

635	A268	10c claret	.30	.20

Issued to honor Colombian soldiers who served in Korea, 1951-53. See Nos. 637a, C269.

Fleet Emblem — A269

M. S. City of Manizales and New York Skyline A270

1955, Apr. 12 **Unwmk.**

636	A269	15c deep green	.20	.20
637	A270	20c violet	.40	.20
a.		Souvenir sheet	7.50	7.50
		Nos. 636-637,C270-C271 (4)	1.45	.90

Grand-Colombian Merchant Fleet.

No. 637a contains four stamps similar to Nos. 622, 635-637, but printed in different colors: 5c blue, 10c dark carmine, 15c green, 20c purple.

Hotel Tequendama and Church of San Diego — A271

1955, May 16 **Photo.** ***Perf. 11½x12***

638	A271	5c blue	.25	.20

See No. C273.

Bolivar's Country Estate, Bogotá A272

1955, Sept. 28 **Engr.** ***Perf. 12½***

639	A272	5c deep ultra	.25	.20

50th anniv. of Rotary Intl. See No. C274.

Belalcazar, Jiménez de Quesada and Balboa A273

Caravels and Columbus A274

5c, San Martin, Bolivar and Washington.

Engraved and Photogravure

1955, Oct. 29 ***Perf. 13x12½***

640	A273	2c yel grn & brn	.40	.25
641	A273	5c brt bl & brn	.40	.25
642	A274	23c lt ultra & blk	.45	.25
a.		Souvenir sheet	17.50	17.50
		Nos. 640-642,C275-C280 (9)	18.50	12.30

7th Cong. of the Postal Union of the Americas and Spain, Bogota, Oct. 12-Nov. 9, 1955.

No. 642a contains one each of Nos. 640-642, printed in slightly different shades.

José Eusebio Caro — A275

1955, Nov. 29 **Engr.** ***Perf. 13½x13***

643	A275	5c brown	.25	.20

José Eusebio Caro (1817-53), poet. See No. C281.

Departmental Issue

Map — A276

View of San Andres Harbor — A277

Cattle at Waterhole A278

Designs: 2c, Docks, Atlantico. 3c, "Industry," Antioquia. 4c, Cartagena Harbor, Bolivar. #647, Steel Mill, Boyaca. #648, Cattle, Cordoba. #649, Map. #650, San Andres Harbor. #651, Cacao picker, Cauca. 10c, Coffee picker, Caldas. 15c, Salt Mine Chapel, Zipaquira, Cundinamarca. 20c, Tropical plants and map, Choco. 23c, Harvester, Huila. 25c, Banana Plantation, Magdalena. 30c, Gold mining, Narifio. 40c, Tobacco plantation, Santander. 50c, Oil wells, North Santander. 60c, Cotton plantation, Tolima. 1p, Sugar industry, Cauca. 3p, Amazon river at Leticia, Amazonas. 5p, Windmills and panoramic view, La Guajira. 10p, Rubber plantation, Vaupes.

Perf. 13½x13, 13x13½, 13

Engr.; Engr. & Litho.

1956 **Unwmk.**

Various Frames

644	A277	2c car & grn	.20	.20
645	A276	3c brn vio & blk	.20	.20
646	A277	4c grn & blk	.20	.20
647	A276	5c dk brn & bl	.20	.20
648	A277	5c ol & dk vio brn	.30	.20
649	A276	5c bl & blk	.25	.20
650	A277	5c car & grnsh bl	.20	.20
651	A277	5c ol grn & red brn	.20	.20
652	A276	10c org & blk	.40	.20
653	A276	15c ultra & blk	.25	.20
654	A276	20c dk brn & bl	.25	.20
655	A277	23c ultra & ver	.30	.20
656	A277	25c ol grn & blk	.30	.20
657	A277	30c ultra & brn	.25	.20
658	A277	40c dl pur & red brn	.25	.20
659	A277	50c dk grn & blk	.25	.20
660	A277	60c pale brn & grn	.25	.20
661	A278	1p mag & grnsh bl	1.60	.20
662	A278	2p grn & red brn	2.40	.25
663	A278	3p car & blk	2.75	.45
664	A278	5p brn & lt ultra	5.00	1.00
665	A276	10p red brn & grn	14.00	6.00
		Nos. 644-665 (22)	30.00	11.30

Nos. 645, 647, 649, 652-654 measure 27x32mm, No. 665 27x37mm. See Nos. 681-684, 685, 688-689. For surcharges and overprints see Nos. 685, 688-689, C289, C312.

Columbus and Proposed Lighthouse A279

1956, Oct. 12 **Photo.** ***Perf. 12***

666	A279	3c gray black	.50	.25

Issued in honor of Christopher Columbus. See Nos. C285, C306.

Altar of St. Elizabeth and Tomb of Jimenez de Quesada A280

1956, Nov. 19 **Unwmk.**

667	A280	5c red lilac	.25	.20

7th cent. of St. Elizabeth of Hungary, patron saint of Sante Fé de Bogotá. See No. C286.

St. Ignatius of Loyola — A281

Javier Pereira — A282

1956, Nov. 26 Engr. *Perf. 12½x13*
668 A281 5c blue .25 .20

400th anniv. of the death of St. Ignatius of Loyola. See No. C287. For overprint see No. C324.

1956, Dec. 28 Unwmk. *Perf. 12*
669 A282 5c blue .25 .20

Issued to honor 167-year-old Javier Pereira. See No. C288.

Emblem and Dairy Farm A283

Designs: 2c, Emblem and tractor. 5c, Emblem, coffee and corn.

1957, Mar. 5 Photo. *Perf. 14x13½*
670 A283 1c lt ol grn .25 .20
671 A283 2c lt brn .25 .20
672 A283 5c lt bl .25 .20
Nos. 670-672,C292-C296 (8) 2.85 1.80

Agrarian Savings Bank of Colombia, 25th anniv.
For overprint see No. C322.

Arms of Military Academy and Gen. Rafael Reyes A284

Design: 10c, Arms and Academy.

1957, July 20 Engr. *Perf. 12½*
673 A284 5c blue .20 .20
674 A284 10c orange .30 .20
a. Souv. sheet of 2 18.00 18.00
Nos. 673-674,C299-C300 (4) .95 .80

50th anniv. of the Colombian Military Academy.
No. 674a contains one each of Nos. 673-674 in slightly different shades.
For overprints see Nos. C328, C312.

Statue of José Matias Delgado — A285

1957, Sept. 16 Photo. *Perf. 12*
675 A285 2c rose brn .25 .20

Issued in honor of Jose Matias Delgado, liberator of El Salvador. See No. C301.

Santo Michelena, Marcos y Crespo, P. Alcantara Herran and UPU Monument A286

1957, Oct. 10 Unwmk.
676 A286 5c green .20 .20
677 A286 10c gray .30 .20
Nos. 676-677,C302-C303 (4) .90 .80

Intl. Letter Writing Week and 14th UPU Cong.

St. Vincent de Paul and Children — A287

1957, Oct. 18
678 A287 1c dark olive green .25 .20

Colombian Society of St. Vincent de Paul, cent. See No. C304. For overprint see No. C323.

Fencer A288

1957, Nov. 22 Photo. *Perf. 12*
679 A288 4c lilac .25 .20

3rd South American Fencing Championship. See No. C305. For overprint see No. C332.

Francisco José de Caldas and Hypsometer — A289

1958, May 12 Unwmk. *Perf. 12*
680 A289 10c black .25 .20
Nos. 680,C309-C310 (3) 1.05 .60

International Geophysical Year, 1957-58.

Departmental Issue
Type of 1956

Designs as before.

1958 Engr. *Perf. 13*
681 A276 3c ultra & brn .25 .20
682 A276 3c ol grn & pur .25 .20
683 A276 10c grn & brn .25 .20
684 A276 10c dk bl & brn .25 .20
Nos. 681-684 (4) 1.00 .80

Nos. 646, C291, 614, 653, 655, 616, C308, 615 and 611 Surcharged with New Value, and Old Value Obliterated, or Overprinted in Dark Blue or Green

Perf. 12½, 12½x13, 13

1958-59 Unwmk.
685 A277 2c on 4c grn & blk .25 .20
686 AP48 5c dp plum & multi ('59) .25 .20
687 A256 5c on 14c blk & rose red ("CINCO") ('59) .30 .30
688 A276 5c on 15c ultra & blk .25 .20
689 A277 5c on 23c ultra & ver (G) .25 .20
690 A256 5c on 30c blk & choc .25 .20
691 AP40 10c on 25c rose vio .25 .20
692 A256 20c on 23c blk & ultra (G) ('59) .30 .20
693 A255 20c on 23c bl & blk ('59) .30 .20
Nos. 685-693 (9) 2.40 1.90

On No. 686 the words "Correo Extra Rapido" are obliterated in dark blue.

Father Rafael Almanza and Church of San Diego, Bogota A290

1958, Oct. 23 Photo. *Perf. 14x13*
695 A290 10c purple .25 .20
Nos. 695,C313-C314 (3) .70 .60

For overprint see No. C336.

Msgr. R. M. Carrasquilla and Church A291

1959, Jan. 22 *Perf. 14x13*
696 A291 10c dk red brn .25 .20
Nos. 696,C315-C316 (3) 1.05 .60

Cent. of the birth of Msgr. R. M. Carrasquilla (1857-1930), rector of Our Lady of the Rosary Seminary, Bogotá. For overprints see Nos. C335, C341.

Miss Universe 1959 — A292

Jorge Eliecer Gaitan — A293

1959, June 26 Photo. *Perf. 11½*
697 A292 10c multi .70 .25
Nos. 697,C317-C318 (3) 42.10 38.85

Luz Marina Zuluaga, Miss Universe, 1959.
For overprint see No. C342.

1959, July 28 Engr. *Perf. 12x13½*
698 A293 10c on 3c gray bl (Bl) .25 .20
699 A293 30c rose vio .45 .25
Nos. 698-699,C319-C320 (4) 3.50 2.95

Issued in honor of Jorge Eliecer Gaitan (1898-1948), lawyer and politician.
No. 698 exists without blue surcharge.

Gen. Francisco de Paula Santander — A294

Designs: Nos. 701, 703, Simon Bolivar.

1959 Litho. Wmk. 331 *Perf. 12½*
700 A294 5c brown & yel .25 .20
701 A294 5c ultra & bl .25 .20
702 A294 10c gray & grn .25 .20
703 A294 10c gray & red .25 .20
Nos. 700-703,C389 (5) 4.00 1.20

Capitol, Bogota A295

1959
704 A295 2c dk bl & red brn .25 .20
705 A295 3c blk brn & lilac .25 .20

Stamp of 1859 and Mail Transport by Mule — A296

Two-Toed Sloth — A297

Designs (various stamps of 1859 and): 10c, Mail boat on the Magdalena river. 15c, as 5c. 25c, Train.

Unwmk.

1959, Dec. 1 Photo. *Perf. 12*
709 A296 5c org & grn .20 .20
710 A296 10c rose cl & bl .20 .20
711 A296 15c car rose & grn .40 .40
712 A296 25c bl & red brn .50 .50
Nos. 709-712,C351-C354 (8) 5.00 3.30

Centenary of Colombian postage stamps.

1960, Feb. 12 *Perf. 12*

Designs: 10c, Alexander von Humboldt. 20c, Spider monkey.

713 A297 5c grnsh bl & brn .30 .20
714 A297 10c blk & dp car .40 .20
715 A297 20c cit & gray brn .30 .20
Nos. 713-715,C357-C359 (6) 6.65 4.30

Cent. of the death of Alexander von Humboldt (1769-1859), German naturalist and geographer.
For overprint and surcharge see Nos. C411, C413.

Anthurium Andreanum A298

Lincoln Statue, Washington A299

Flower: 20c, Espeletia grandiflora.

1960, May 10
716 A298 5c multi .60 .25
717 A298 20c brn, yel & gray ol .60 .25
Nos. 716-717,C360-C370 (13) 13.95 15.20

See Nos. C420-C425. For overprint see No. C412.

Wmk. 331

1960, June 10 Litho. *Perf. 10½*
718 A299 20c rose lil & blk .30 .25
Nos. 718,C375-C376 (3) 1.40 1.05

Florero House, Cradle of the Republic A300

Arms of Santa Cruz de Mompox — A301

Design: 5c, First coins of Republic.

Unwmk.

1960, July 19 Photo. *Perf. 12*
719 A301 5c grn & ocher .25 .20
720 A300 20c ol bis & mar .25 .20
721 A301 20c multi .25 .20
Nos. 719-721,C377-C385 (12) 6.25 4.90

Colombia's independence, 150th anniv.

St. Isidore and Farm Animals — A302

Design: 20c, Nativity by Gregorio de Arce Vasquez y Ceballos.

1960, Sept. 26 *Perf. 12*
722 A302 10c multi .20 .20
723 A302 20c multi .25 .20
Nos. 722-723,C387 (3) .70 .60

St. Isidore the Farmer, patron saint of the rural people.
See Nos. 747, C388, C439-C440.

UN Headquarters and Emblem A303

Wmk. 331
1960, Oct. 24 Litho. *Perf. 11*
724 A303 20c blk & pink .25 .20

Souvenir Sheet
Imperf
725 A303 50c dk brn, brt grn & blk 4.00 4.00

15th anniversary of the United Nations.

Pan-American Highway through Colombia — A304

Alfonso Lopez — A305

1961, Mar. 7 Unwmk. *Perf. 10½x11*
726 A304 20c brn & grnsh bl .75 .70
Nos. 726,C390-C393 (5) 2.75 2.70

8th Pan-American Highway Congress, Bogota, May 20-29, 1960.

1961, Mar. 22 Photo. *Perf. 12½*
727 A305 10c brt rose & brn .25 .20
728 A305 20c vio & brn .25 .20
Nos. 727-728,C394-C395 (4) 1.20 .80

Alfonso Lopez (1886-1959), President of Colombia. See No. C396.

Cauca River Bridge, Cali A306

Page from Resolutions of Confederated Cities — A307

1961-62 *Perf. 12½x13, 13½x13*
729 A306 10c red brn, bl, grn & red ('62) .25 .20
730 A307 20c pale brn & blk .25 .20
Nos. 729-730,C397-C401 (7) 3.00 2.05

50th anniversary (in 1960) of the Department of Valle del Cauca.

View of Cucuta and Arms A308

No. 732, Arms of Ocana and Pamplona.

1961, Aug. 29 *Perf. 13x13½*
731 A308 20c bl, blk, yel & red .25 .20
732 A308 20c ocher, ultra & red .25 .20
Nos. 731-732,C402-C403 (4) 1.30 .80

50th anniv. (in 1960) of the Department of North Santander.

Arms of Popayan A309

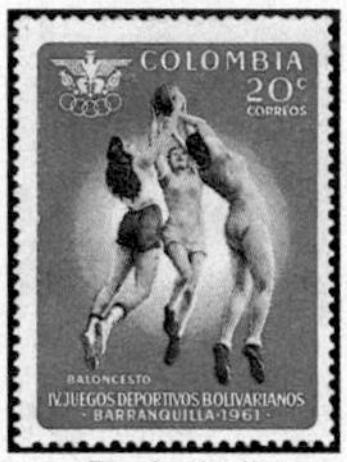
Basketball A310

Designs: No. 734, Arms of Barranquilla. No. 735, Arms of Bucaramanga.

Perf. 12½x13
1961, Oct. 10 Unwmk.
Arms in Multicolor
733 A309 10c blue & silver .25 .20
734 A309 20c blue & yellow .25 .20
735 A309 20c blue & gold .25 .20
Nos. 733-735,C404-C408 (8) 2.75 1.60

Issued to honor Atlantico Department.

1961, Dec. 16 Litho. *Perf. 13½x14*
736 A310 20c shown .25 .20
737 A310 20c Runners .25 .20
738 A310 20c Boxers .40 .25
739 A310 25c Soccer .25 .20
Nos. 736-739,C414-C418 (9) 3.75 2.20

4th Bolivarian Games, Barranquilla, 1961.

Colombian Anti-Malaria Emblem — A311

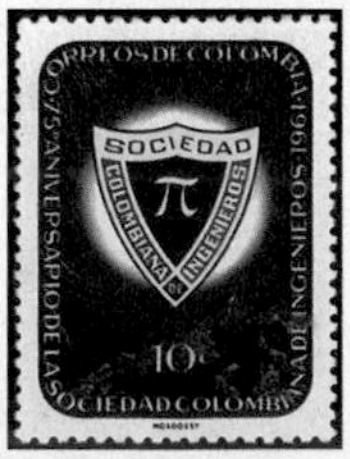
Engineers Society Emblem — A312

Design: 50c, Malaria eradication emblem and mosquito in swamp.

1962, Apr. 12 Unwmk. *Perf. 12*
740 A311 20c lt bis & red .25 .20
741 A311 50c bis & ultra .30 .20
Nos. 740-741,C426-C428 (5) 4.80 4.50

1962, June 12 Photo. *Perf. 11½x12*
742 A312 10c multi .25 .25
Nos. 742,C429-C432 (5) 2.40 2.35

Colombian Society of Engineers, 75th anniv.

Flags of American Nations A313

Woman Casting Ballot and Statue of Policarpa Salavarrieta A314

1962, June 28 *Perf. 13*
Flags in National Colors
743 A313 25c blk & org ver .25 .20

Souvenir Sheet
744 A313 2.50p blk & yel 5.75 5.75

70th anniv. of the founding of the Organization of American States.
See No. C433.

Perf. 12x12½
1962, July 20 Litho. Wmk. 229
745 A314 10c lt bl, gray & blk .25 .20

Issued to publicize women's political rights. See Nos. 752, C434, C448-C450.

Scouts at Campfire and Tents A315

Railroad Map of Colombia A316

Perf. 11½x12
1962, July 28 Photo. Unwmk.
746 A315 10c brt grnsh bl & brn .35 .30
Nos. 746,C435-C438 (5) 5.60 4.80

Colombian Boy Scouts, 30th anniv.

St. Isidore Type of 1960 Redrawn
1962, Aug. 28 *Perf. 12*
747 A302 10c pink & multi .25 .20
Nos. 747,C439-C440 (3) 4.20 3.90

The frame on No. 747 is solid color with white inscription similar to type AP82.

1962, Sept. 28 *Perf. 12½*
748 A316 10c blk, gray, grn & red .20 .20
Nos. 748,C441-C444 (5) 5.75 4.55

Progress of Colombian railroads and the completion of the Atlantic Line from Santa Marta to Bogota.

Post Horn — A317

Perf. 13½x14
1962, Oct. 18 Litho. Wmk. 346
749 A317 20c gold, dl gray vio & blk .25 .20
Nos. 749,C445-C446 (3) .80 .60

50th anniv. of the founding of the Postal Union of the Americas and Spain, UPAE.

"Virgin of the Rock" A318

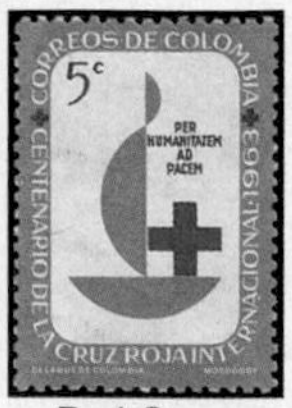
Red Cross Centenary Emblem A319

1963, Mar. 11 Wmk. 346
750 A318 60c multi .25 .20

Vatican II, the 21st Ecumenical Council of the Roman Catholic Church. See No. C447.

1963, May 1 *Perf. 12x12½*
751 A319 5c olive bister & red .25 .20

Centenary of International Red Cross.

Women's Rights Type of 1962
1963, July 11 Wmk. 346
752 A314 5c org, gray & blk .25 .20
Nos. 752,C448-C450 (4) 1.05 .80

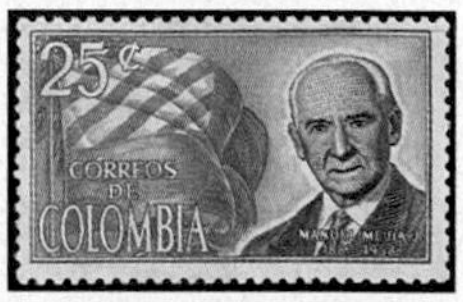
Manuel Mejia J. and Flag of National Coffee Growers Assn. A320

Perf. 12½x13
1965, Feb. 10 Engr. Unwmk.
753 A320 25c rose & blk .25 .20
Nos. 753,C464-C466 (4) 4.60 .95

Manuel Mejia J. (1887-1958), banker and manager of the National Coffee Growers Association.

Julio Arboleda (1817-62), Writer, Soldier and Statesman A321

1966, Mar. 9 Litho. *Perf. 14x13½*
754 A321 5c lt brn, lt yel grn & blk .30 .20

Spanish Galleon, 16th Century A322

History of Maritime Mail: 15c, Rio Hacha brigantine, 1850. 20c, Uraba canoe. 40c, Magdalena River steamship and barge, 1900. 50c, Modern motor ship and sea gull.

1966, June 16 Photo. Unwmk.
755 A322 5c org & multi .35 .20
756 A322 15c car rose, blk & brn .35 .20
757 A322 20c brt grn, org & blk .35 .20
758 A322 40c dp bl & multi .50 .20
759 A322 50c pale bl & multi 1.00 .40
Nos. 755-759 (5) 2.55 1.20

Plumed Hogfish A323

Design: 10p, Bat ray and brittle starfish.

1966, Aug. 25 Photo. *Perf. 12½x13*
760 A323 80c multi .25 .20
761 A323 10p multi 8.25 5.25
Nos. 760-761,C481-C483 (5) 26.75 18.55

Arms of Venezuela, Colombia and Chile
A324

1966, Oct. 11 Litho. *Perf. 14x13½*

762 A324 40c yel & multi .25 .20
Nos. 762,C484-C485 (3) .70 .60

Visits of Eduardo Frei and Raul Leoni, presidents of Chile and Venezuela.

Camilo Torres, 1766-1816, Lawyer — A325

Portraits: 60c, Jorge Tadeo Lozano (1771-1816), naturalist. 1p, Francisco Antonio Zea (1776-1822), naturalist and politician.

Perf. 13½x14

1967, Jan. 18 Litho. Unwmk.

763 A325 25c vio & bis .25 .20
764 A325 60c dk red brn & bis .25 .20
765 A325 1p grn & bis .35 .25
Nos. 763-765,C486-C487 (5) 1.30 1.05

Issued to honor famous men of Colombia.

Map of South America and Arms
A326

1967, Feb. 2 Litho. *Perf. 14x13½*

766 A326 40c multi .25 .20
767 A326 60c multi .25 .20
Nos. 766-767,C488 (3) .85 .60

Declaration of Bogota for cooperation and world peace, signed by Colombia, Chile, Ecuador, Peru and Venezuela.

Monochaetum Orchid and Bee — A327

Orchid: 2p, Passiflora vitifolia and butterfly.

1967, May 23 Litho. *Perf. 14*

768 A327 25c multi .25 .20
769 A327 2p multi 4.25 2.75
Nos. 768-769,C489-C491 (5) 14.70 4.40

1st Natl. Orchid Exhib. and the Topical Phil. Flora and Fauna Exhib., Medellin, Apr. 1967.

Lions Emblem — A328

SENA Emblem — A329

1967, July 12 Litho. *Perf. 13½x14*

770 A328 10p multi 3.50 2.00

50th anniv. of Lions Intl. See No. C492.

Lithographed and Embossed

1967, Sept. 20 Unwmk.

771 A329 5p gold, brt grn & blk 1.50 .25

10th anniv. of Natl. Apprenticeship Service, SENA. See No. C494.

Gold Diadem in Calima Style — A330

Radar Installation
A331

Pre-Columbian Art: 3p, Gold statuette, ornamental globe and bird, horiz.

Perf. 13½x14, 14x13½

1967, Oct. 13 Photo.

772 A330 1.60p brt rose lil, gold & brn .95 .25
773 A330 3p dk bl, gold & brn 1.40 .40
Nos. 772-773,C495-C497 (5) 20.45 11.35

Meeting of the UPU Committee of Postal Studies, Bogota, Oct., 1967.

1968, May 14 Litho. *Perf. 13½x14*

1p, Map of communications network.

774 A331 50c brt yel grn, blk & org brn .20 .20
775 A331 1p multi .30 .20
Nos. 774-775,C498-C499 (4) 1.00 .80

20th anniv. of the National Telecommunications Service (TELECOM).

The Eucharist — A332

St. Augustin, by Gregorio Vasquez — A333

1968, June 6 Litho. *Perf. 13½x14*

776 A332 60c multi .25 .20
Nos. 776,C500-C501 (3) .75

39th Eucharistic Cong., Bogotá, 8/18-25.

1968, Aug. 13 Photo. *Perf. 13*

Designs: 60c, The Gathering of Manna, by Gregorio Vasquez. 1p, The Marriage of the Virgin, by Baltazar de Figueroa. 5p, Jeweled monstrance, c. 1700. 10p, Pope Paul VI, painting by Roman Franciscan nuns.

777 A333 25c multicolored .20 .20
778 A333 60c multicolored .20 .20
779 A333 1p multicolored .20 .20
780 A333 5p multicolored .65 .20
781 A333 10p multicolored 1.25 .45
a. Souvenir sheet of 2 3.50 3.50
Nos. 777-781,C502-C506 (10) 7.95 4.05

39th Eucharistic Congress. Bogotá, Aug. 18-25. No. 781a contains two imperf. stamps similar to Nos. 780-781.

Pope Paul VI — A334

Arms of National University — A335

1968, Aug. 22 Litho. *Perf. 13½x14*

782 A334 25c multi .25 .20
Nos. 782,C507-C509 (4) .95 .80

Visit of Pope Paul VI to Colombia, 8/22-24.

1968, Oct. 29 Litho. *Perf. 13½x14*

783 A335 80c multi .35 .25

Centenary of the founding of the National University. See No. C510.

Stamp of Antioquia, 1868 — A336

Institute Emblem — A337

1968, Nov. 20 Litho. *Perf. 12x12½*

784 A336 30c emer & bl .30 .20

Souvenir Sheet

785 A336 5p lt olive & blue 5.50 5.50

Cent. of the 1st postage stamps of Antioquia and the 7th Natl. Phil. Exhib., Medellin, Nov. 20-29.

1969, Mar. 5 Litho. *Perf. 13½x14*

786 A337 20c multi .35 .25

25th anniv. (in 1967) of the Inter-American Agricultural Sciences Institute. See No. C511.

Battle of Boyaca (Detail), by José Maria Espinosa — A338

Design: 30c, Army of liberation crossing Pisba Pass, by Francisco Antonio Caro.

1969, July 24 Litho. *Perf. 13½x14*

787 A338 20c gold & multi .35 .25
788 A338 30c gold & multi .35 .25
Nos. 787-788,C517 (3) 1.70 .85

Fight for independence, sesquicentennial.

"Poverty"
A339

1970, Mar. 1 Litho. *Perf. 14*

789 A339 30c bl & multi .35 .25

Colombian Institute for Family Welfare and 10th anniv. of the Children's Rights Law.

Greek Mask and Pre-Columbian Symbol of Literary Contest — A340

1970, Sept. 12 Litho. *Perf. 14x13½*

790 A340 30c dk brn, red org & ocher .25 .20

3rd Latin American Theatrical Festival of the Universities, Manizales, Sept. 12-20.

Colombian Stamps, Envelope and Emblem
A341

1970, Sept. 24 Litho. *Perf. 14x13½*

791 A341 2p brt bl & multi .30 .25

Issued to publicize Philatelic Week.

Arms of Ibague and Discobolus
A342

1970, Oct. 13

792 A342 80c buff, emer & sepia .25 .20

9th National Games in Ibague.

St. Theresa, by Baltazar de Figueroa — A343

1970, Oct. 28 Litho. *Perf. 13½x14*

793 A343 2p multi .40 .25

Elevation of St. Theresa (1515-1582), to Doctor of the Church. See No. C568. For overprint see No. C568.

Casa Cural A344

1971, May 20 Litho. ***Perf. 14x13½***
794 A344 1.10p multi .30 .20

Fourth centenary (in 1970) of the founding of Guacari, Valle. See No. 809.

Dancers and Music, Currulao — A345

1p, Chicha Maya dancers and music.

1971 Litho. ***Perf. 13½x14***
795 A345 1p pink & multi .35 .25
796 A345 1.10p lt bl & multi .35 .25

Souvenir Sheets
Imperf

797 Sheet of 3 4.00 4.00
a. A345 2.50p Napanga .50 .50
b. A345 2.50p Joropo .50 .50
c. A345 5p Guabina 1.00 1.00
798 Sheet of 3 4.00 4.00
a. A345 4p Bambuco .75 .75
b. A345 4p Cumbia .75 .75
c. A345 4p Currulao .75 .75

Issued: No. 795, 12/20; No. 796, 8/5; Nos. 797-798, 8/10.

Constitutional Assembly, by Delgado A346

1971, Oct. 2 ***Perf. 14***
801 A346 80c multi .25 .20

Sequicentennial of Gran Colombian Constitutional Assembly in Rosario del Cucuta.
See No. C589. For overprint see No. C589.

Arrows Emblem — A347

1972, Feb. 24 ***Perf. 13½x14***
802 A347 60c blk & gray .30 .20

Inter-Governmental Committee on European Migration, 20th anniversary.

Student and World Map A348

1972, Mar. 15 ***Perf. 14x13½***
803 A348 1.10p lt grn & brn .25 .20

20th anniv. of ICETEX, an organization which furnishes financial help for educational purposes and for technical studies abroad.

UN Emblem, Soldier and Frigate A349

1972, Apr. 7
804 A349 1.20p lt bl & multi .25 .20

Colombian Battalion in Korea, 20th anniv.

Mother Francisca Josefa del Castillo — A350

Handicraft A351

1972, Apr. 6 ***Perf. 13½x14***
805 A350 1.20p brn & multi .25 .20

Tercentenary (in 1971) of the birth of Mother Francisca Josefa del Castillo, Poor Clare abbess and writer.

1972, Apr. 11
806 A351 1.10p multi .35 .20
Nos. 806,C569-C571 (4) 1.55 .85

Colombian artisans.

Maxillaria Triloris — A352

Emeralds — A353

1972, Apr. 20
807 A352 20p green & multi 7.25 .75

10th Natl. Phil. Exhib., Medellin.

1972, June 16 Litho. ***Perf. 13½x14***
808 A353 1.10p multi 1.00 .20

Type of 1971

Design: Antonio Nariño House.

1972, June 17 ***Perf. 14x13½***
809 A344 1.10p multi .50 .25

4th centenary, town of Leyva.

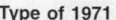

San Andres and Providencia Islands — A354

1972, June 24 ***Perf. 13½x14***
810 A354 60c bl & multi .25 .20

Sesquicentennial of annexation by Colombia of San Andres and Providencia Islands.

Postal Service Emblem A355

1972, Nov. 15 Litho. ***Perf. 12½x12***
811 A355 1.10p emerald .25 .20

Family A356

1972, Nov. 23
812 A356 60c orange .25 .20

Social progress.

Radio League Emblem A357

Human Figure, Tamalameque A358

1973, Apr. 6 Litho. ***Perf. 12x12½***
813 A357 60c lt bl, ultra & red .25 .20

40th anniversary of the Colombian Radio Amateurs' League.

1973, June 15 Litho. ***Perf. 13½x14***

Excavated Ceramic Artifacts: 1p, Winged urn, Tairona. 1.10p, Jug, Muisca.

814 A358 60c lt bl & multi .35 .25
815 A358 1p org & multi .70 .25
816 A358 1.10p vio bl & multi .40 .25
Nos. 814-816,C583-C586 (7) 4.60 2.50

Antonio Nariño, by José M. Espinosa — A359

Child — A360

1973, Dec. 13 Litho. ***Perf. 13½x14***
817 A359 60c multi .25 .20

Sesquicentennial of the death of General Antonio Nariño (1765-1823).

1973, Dec. 17
818 A360 1.10p multi .25 .20

National Campaign for Children's Welfare.

Symbols of Financial Controls A361

1973, Dec. 20 Litho. ***Perf. 14x13½***
819 A361 80c ultra, ocher & blk .25 .20

50th anniv. of Comptroller-general's Office.

Mother Laura Montoya — A362

1974, June 18 Litho. ***Perf. 13½x14***
820 A362 1p multi .25 .20

Mother Laura Montoya (1874-1949), founder and Mother Superior of the Missionaries of Mary Immaculata and St. Catherine of Siena.

Runner and Games' Emblem A363

1974, July 18 Litho. ***Perf. 14x13½***
821 A363 2p ver, yel & brn .35 .20

10th National Games, Pereira.

José Rivera A364

1974, Aug. 3 Litho. ***Perf. 14x13½***
822 A364 10p grn & multi 1.25 .20

50th anniv. of the publication of "La Voragine" (The Whirlpool) by José Eustasio Rivera.

Abstract Pattern — A365

Train Emerging from Tunnel — A366

1974, Oct. 24 Litho. ***Perf. 13½x14***
823 A365 1.10p multi .25 .20

Cent. of Natl. Insurance Co. See No. C610.

1974, Nov. 27 Litho. ***Perf. 13½x14***
824 A366 1.10p multi .25 .20

Centenary of the Antioquia railroad.

Boy, Puppy and Soccer Ball — A367

Christmas: 1p, Girl with racket and kitten.

1974, Dec. 9
825 A367 80c multi .25 .20
826 A367 1p multi .25 .20

A368

1975, Apr. 11 Litho. ***Perf. 14x13½***
827 A368 80c Gold Animal .40 .25
828 A368 1.10p Gold necklace .40 .25
Nos. 827-828,C621-C622 (4) 6.45 1.30

Pre-Columbian Sinu culture artifacts. For surcharge see No. 840.

Guglielmo Marconi — A369

Santa Marta Cathedral — A370

1975, June 2 Litho. ***Perf. 13½x14***
829 A369 3p multi .30 .20

Birth centenary of Guglielmo Marconi (1874-1937), Italian electrical engineer and inventor.

1975, July 26
830 A370 80c multi .30 .20

400th anniv. of Santa Marta City. See No. C623.

Rafael Nuñez — A371

Arms of Medellin — A372

1975, Sept. 28 Litho. ***Perf. 13½x14***
831 A371 1.10p multi .30 .20

Rafael Nunez (1825-1894), philosopher, poet, political leader, birth sesquicentenary. For surcharge see No. 848.

1975-79 ***Perf. 13½x14, 12 (1.20p)***

832	A372	1p	shown	.35	.20
833	A372	1.20p	Ibagué	.30	.20
834	A372	1.20p	Tunja	.20	.20
835	A372	1.50p	Cucuta	.50	.20
836	A372	1.50p	Cartagena	.20	.20
836A	A372	4p	Sogamoso	.90	.20
837	A372	5p	Popayan	.45	.20
838	A372	5p	Barranquilla	.45	.20
839	A372	10p	San Gil	.90	.20
839A	A372	10p	Socorro	.90	.20
			Nos. 832-839A (10)	5.15	2.00

1p for the tercentenary of Medellin; No. 835, the cent. of Cucuta's reconstruction.

Issued: 1p, 11/4; No. 835, 11/29; No. 836, 2/10/76; No. 833, 7/30/76; No. 834, 12/2076; No. 837, 8/30/77; No. 838, 9/20/77; 10p, 8/9/79; 4p, 9/14/79.

See Nos. 905-913, C818. For surcharge see No. 849.

No. 827 Surcharged

1975 ***Perf. 14x13½***
840 A368 1.20p on 80c multi .25 .20

Purace Indians, Cauca — A373

1976, Nov. 10 Litho. ***Perf. 13½x14***
841 A373 1.50p multi .25 .20

Callicore A374

5p, Morpho (butterfly). 20p, Anthurium.

1976, Nov. 17 ***Perf. 12***
842 A374 3p multicolored .90 .25
843 A374 5p multicolored 1.50 .25
844 A374 20p multicolored 4.25 1.00
Nos. 842-844 (3) 6.65 1.50

Rotary Emblem — A375

1976, Dec. 3 Litho. ***Perf. 12***
845 A375 1p multicolored .25 .20

Rotary Club of Colombia, 50th anniversary.

Declaration of Independence, by John Trumbull — A376

1976, Dec. 21 Litho. ***Perf. 12***
846 A376 Strip of 3 10.00 *11.50*
a.-c. 30p any single 2.75 2.00

American Bicentennial. No. 846 printed in sheets of 4 triptychs.

Policeman with Dog — A377

1976, Dec. 29 ***Perf. 13½x14***
847 A377 1.50p multicolored .25 .20

Honoring the National Police. For surcharge see No. 850.

Nos. 831, 834, 847 Surcharged in Light Brown

1977, June Litho. ***Perf. 13½x14, 12***
848 A371 2p on 1.10p multi .40 .20
849 A372 2p on 1.20p multi .20 .20
850 A377 2p on 1.50p multi .25 .20
Nos. 848-850 (3) .85 .60

Souvenir Sheet

Postal Museum, Bogota — A378

1977, July 27 Litho. ***Perf. 14***
855 A378 25p multi 2.50 2.50

Postal Museum, Bogota.

Mother and Child — A379

1977-78 Litho. ***Perf. 12***
856 A379 2p multi .20 .20
857 A379 2.50p multi ('78) 1.50 .20

National good nutrition plan.
Issue dates: 2p, Aug. 30; 2.50p, Jan. 26.

Jacana and Eichhornia A380

Fidel Cano, by Francisco Cano — A381

20p, Mayan cotinga and pyrostegia venusta.

1977, Sept. 6 Litho. ***Perf. 14***
858 A380 10p multicolored 2.50 .25
859 A380 20p multicolored 4.00 .50
Nos. 858-859,C644-C647 (6) 10.20 1.55

1977, Sept. 16 ***Perf. 14***
860 A381 4p multicolored .25 .20

90th anniversary of El Espectador, newspaper founded by Fidel Cano.

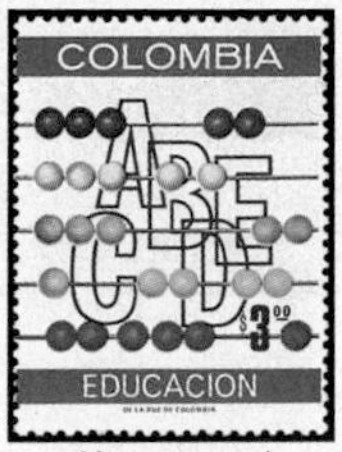

Abacus and Alphabet A382

Cattleya Triannae A383

1977, Sept. 16 ***Perf. 13½x14***
861 A382 3p multicolored .25 .20

Popular education.

1978-79 Litho. ***Perf. 12***
862 A383 2.50p multi .75 .20
863 A383 3p multi ('79) .75 .20

Issue dates: 2.50p, Apr. 18. 3p, May 10.

Sprinting and Games Emblem A384

Sports: a, sprinting. b, basketball. c, baseball. d, boxing. e. bicycling. f, fencing. g, soccer. h, gymnastics. i, judo. j, weight lifting. k, wrestling. l, swimming. m, tennis. n, target shooting. o, volleyball. p, water polo.

1978, June 27 Litho. *Perf. 14*

868	Sheet of 16	26.50	26.50
a.-p.	A384 10p, any single	1.10	.20

13th Central American and Caribbean Games, Medellin.

"Sigma 2" by Alvaro Herrán A385

1978, June 30

869 A385 8p multicolored .45 .20

Chamber of Commerce, Bogota, centenary.

Gen. Tomás Cipriano de Mosquera (1778-1878), Statesman A386

1978, Oct. 6 Litho. *Perf. 12*

870 A386 6p multicolored .45 .20

Anthurium Narinenses — A387

1979, July 23 *Perf. 12*

871	A387 3p red & multi	.25	.20
872	A387 3p purple & multi	.25	.20
873	A387 3p rose & purple	.25	.20
874	A387 3p white & multi	.25	.20
a.	Block of 4, #871-874	1.75	1.75

Gen. Rafael Uribe, by Acevedo Bernal — A388

1979, Oct. 31 Litho. *Perf. 12*

875 A388 8p multicolored .40 .20

Gen. Uribe, statesman, 60th death anniv.

Village, by Leonor Alarcon — A389

1979, Nov. 22 *Perf. 14*

876 A389 15p multicolored 1.00 .35

Community Work Boards, 20th anniversary.

Introduction of Color Television A390

1980, Mar. 4 Litho. *Perf. 14*

877 A390 5p multicolored .50 .20

Bullfight, Arms of Cali A391

1980, Mar. 25

878 A391 5p multicolored .70 .20

Cali Tourist Festival, 12/25/79-1/2/80.

"Learn to Write" — A392

a, shown. b, "a." c, "b." d, "c." e, "ch." f, "d." g, "e." h, "f." i, "g." j, "h." k, "i." l, "j." m, "k." n, "l." o, "ll." p, "m." q, "n." r, "ñ." s, "o." t, "p." u, "q." v, "r." w, "s." x, "t." y, "u." z, "v." aa, "w." ab, "x." ac, "y." ad, "z."

1980, Apr. 25 Litho. *Perf. 12½*

879	Block of 30	27.50	27.50
a.-ad.	A392 4p, any single	.75	.20

Each stamp shows letter of alphabet and corresponding animal or subject. Issued in sheets of 90 (10x9).

Villavicencio Festival — A393

Design: 9p, Vallenato festival.

1980 Litho. *Perf. 14*

880	A393 5p multicolored	.45	.20
881	A393 9p multicolored	.45	.20

Issue dates: 5p, July 15; 9p, June 17.

Gustavo Uribe Ramirez and Tree A394

1980, Aug. 5 Litho. *Perf. 12*

882 A394 10p multicolored .90 .20

Gustavo Uribe Ramirez (1893-1968), ecologist.

Narino Palace (Former Presidential Residence) — A395

1980, Sept. 19 Litho. *Perf. 14*

883 A395 5p multicolored .60 .20

Monument to First Pioneers of 1819, Armenia A396

1980, Oct. 14

884 A396 5p multicolored .50 .20

11th National Games, Neiva — A397

Fight against Cancer — A398

1980, Nov. 28 *Perf. 13½x14*

885 A397 5p multicolored .45 .20

1980, Dec. 9

886 A398 10p multicolored .40 .20

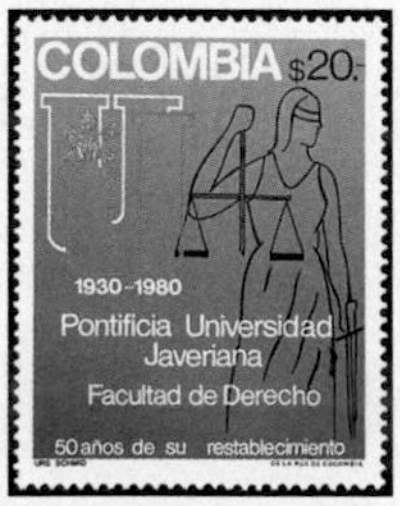

Xavier University Law Faculty, 50th Anniversary A399

1980, Dec. 16 Litho. *Perf. 14½*

887 A399 20p multicolored .60 .20

Death of Bolivar — A400

1980, Dec. 17 *Perf. 12*

888 A400 25p multicolored 1.00 .60

Simon Bolivar, death sesquicentennial. See No. C696.

José Maria Obando, President of Colombia A401

115th Anniv. of Constitution (Former Presidents): b, Jose Hilario Lopez. c, Manuel Murillo Toro. d, Santiago Perez. e, Rafael Reyes. f, Carlos E. Restrepo. g, Jose Vicente Concha. h, Miguel Abadia Mendez. i, Eduardo Santos. j, Mariano Ospina Perez.

1981, June 9 Litho. *Perf. 12*

889	Strip of 10	*6.00*	
a.-j.	A401 5p multicolored	.50	.20

1981, Sept. 23 Litho. *Perf. 12*

Designs: a, Rafael Nunez (1825-94). b, Marco Fidel Suarez (1855-1927). c, Pedro Nel Ospina (1858-1927). d, Enrique Olaya Herrera (1880-1937). e, Alfonso Lopez Pumarejo (1886-1959). f, Aquileo Parra (1825-1900). g, Santos Gutierrez (1820-72). h, Tomas Cipriano de Mosquera (1789-1878). i, Mariano Ospina Rodriguez. j, Pedro Alcantara Herran (1800-72).

890	Strip of 10	*50.00*	
a.-j.	A401 7p multicolored	3.50	.50

1981, Aug. 11 Litho. *Perf. 12*

Designs like No. 889.

891	Strip of 10	*50.00*	
a.-j.	A401 7p multicolored	4.00	1.00

1981, Nov. 11 Litho. *Perf. 12*

Designs: a, Manuel Maria Mallarino. b, Santos Acosta. c, Eustorgio Salgar. d, Julian Trujillo. e, Francisco Javier Zaldua. f, Guillermo Leon Valencia. g, Laureano Gomez. h, Manuel A. Sanclemente. i, Miguel Antonio Caro. j, Jose Eusebio Otalora.

892	Strip of 10	*30.00*	
a.-j.	A401 7p multicolored	2.50	.40

1981, Dec. 15 Litho. *Perf. 12*

Designs: a, Ruben Piedrahita Arango. b, Jorge Holguin. c, Ramon Gonzalez Valencia. d, Jose Manuel Marroquin. e, Carlos Holguin. f, Bartolome Calvo. g, Sergio Camargo. h, Jose Maria Rojas Garrido. i, J.M. Campo Serrano. j, Eliseo Payan.

893	Strip of 10	25.00	
a.-j.	A401 7p multicolored	1.75	.30

1982, May 3 *Perf. 12*

Designs: a, Simon Bolivar. b, Francisco de Paula Santander. c, Joaquin Mosquera. d, Domingo Caicedo. e, Jose Ignacio de Marquez. f, Roberto Urdaneta Arbelaez. g, Carlos Lozano y Lozano. h, Guillermo Quintero Calderon. i, Jose de Obaldia. j, Juan de Dios Aranzazu.

894	Strip of 10	13.50	
a.-j.	A401 7p multicolored	1.25	.20

See No. 1110.

Jose Maria Villa and West Bridge over Cauca River A404

1981, Nov. 25 Litho. *Perf. 14x13½*

895 A404 60p multicolored 1.40 .30

Agrarian, Mineral and Industrial Credit Bank, 50th Anniv. — A405

Los Nevados Park — A406

1981, Dec. 9 Litho. *Perf. 14*
896 A405 15p multicolored .35 .20

1981, Dec. 10 Litho. *Perf. 13½x14*
897 A406 20p multicolored .60 .20

Girl Sitting on Fence — A407

1982, Feb. 22 Litho. *Perf. 12½x12*
898 Strip of 3 4.50 4.50
a. A407 30p shown 1.00 .35
b. A407 30p Girl, basket 1.00 .35
c. A407 30p Boy, wheelbarrow 1.00 .35

Floral Bouquet — A408

Hipotecario Bank, 50th Anniv. — A409

Various floral arrangements (background): a, Flowers in vase (gray). b, Roses (red). c, Daisies (green). d, Roses (blue). e, Assorted (red). f, Yellow & orange flowers (green). g, Assorted (lilac). h, Roses (gray). i, Pink flowers (green). j, Flowers in basket (gray).

1982, July 28
900 Strip or block of 10 15.00 15.00
a.-j. A408 7p, any single 1.50 .30

1982, July 29 *Perf. 14*
901 A409 9p black & green .35 .20

St. Thomas Aquinas (1225-1274) A410

Paintings by Zurbaran.

1982 Litho. *Perf. 12*
902 A410 5p multicolored .25 .20
903 A410 5p St. Teresa of Avila .25 .20
904 A410 5p St. Francis of Assisi .25 .20
Nos. 902-904 (3) .75 .60

Issued: No. 902, 8/6; No. 903, 9/28; No. 904, 10/4.

Arms Type of 1975

1982-90 Litho. *Perf. 14, 12 (50p)*
905 A372 10p Buga .35 .20
906 A372 10p San Juan de Pasto 1.10 .20
907 A372 16p Rionegro .60 .20
908 A372 20p Santa Fe de Bogota .90 .20
909 A372 20p Santiago de Cali .25 .20
910 A372 23p Honda .65 .25
911 A372 50p Cartago .60 .20
912 A372 55p Antioquia ('86) .90 .25
Nos. 905-912 (8) 5.35 1.70

Issued: 16p, 23p, No. 905, 12/7; No. 908, 3/1/83; No. 906, 4/12/83; No. 909, 7/25/86; 55p, 8/5/86; 50p, 5/30/90.
See No. C818.

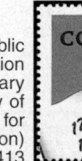

Gabriel Marquez, 1982 Nobel Prize, Literature — A412

1982, Dec. 10 *Perf. 13½x14*
917 A412 7p gray & green .25 .20
See Nos. C731-C732.

Public Education Bicentenary (Society of Mary for Education) A413

1983, May 6
918 A413 9p gold & blk .35 .20

José Maria Espinosa Prieto, Painter — A414

250th Anniv. of City of Cucuta — A415

1983, June 3 *Perf. 12*
919 A414 9p Self-portrait, 1860 .30 .20

1983, June 23 Litho. *Perf. 12*
920 A415 9p multicolored .25 .20

Porfirio Barba-Jacob (1883-1942), Poet — A416

1983, July 29 Litho. *Perf. 13½x14*
921 A416 9p Portrait .25 .20

Simon Bolivar, 200th Birth Anniv. A417

1983, July 24 *Perf. 12*
922 A417 9p multicolored .25 .20
See Nos. C736-C737.

Royal Spanish Botanical Expedition, 200th Anniv. — A418

1983, Aug. 18 *Perf. 14*
923 A418 9p Cinchona lancefolia .25 .20
924 A418 9p Passiflora laurifolia .25 .20
925 A418 60p Cinchona cordifolora 1.75 .50
Nos. 923-925,C738-C740 (6) 6.25 1.70

Dawn in the Andes, by Alejandro Obregon A420

1983, Oct. 5 Litho. *Perf. 12*
928 A420 20p multicolored .45 .20
See No. C741.

Francisco de Paula Santander (1792-1840), General — A421

1984, Mar. 6 Litho. *Perf. 14½x14*
929 A421 12p light olive green .25 .20
930 A421 12p pale carmine .25 .20
931 A421 12p light ultra .25 .20
Nos. 929-931 (3) .75 .60

Admiral Jose Prudencio Padilla (1784-1831) — A423

1984, May 17 Litho. *Perf. 12*
933 A423 10p multicolored .30 .20

Luis Antonio Calvo (1882-1945) Composer — A424

1984, July 26
934 A424 18p multicolored .30 .20

Diego Fallon (1834-1905), Educator, Musician, Poet — A425

1984, Aug. 31 *Perf. 12*
935 A425 20p multicolored .45 .20

Candelario Obeso (1849-1884), Writer — A426

1984, Sept. 4 *Perf. 14x13½*
936 A426 20p multicolored .45 .20

Site of Marandua, Future City A427

1984, Sept. 28 *Perf. 12*
937 A427 15p multicolored .30 .20
See No. C744.

Christmas 1984 A428

Nativity and Children Playing, by Jose Uriel Sierra, Age 7.

1984, Dec. 14
938 A428 12p multicolored .30 .20
See No. C746.

Dr. Luis Eduardo Lopez, Education Minister A429

1984, Dec. 21
939 A429 22p multicolored .35 .20

Maria Concepcion Loperena de Fernandez de Castro, Independence War Heroine — A430

1985, Jan. 6
940 A430 12p multicolored .25 .20

Gonzalo Mejia (1885-1956) — A431

1985, Feb. 25
941 A431 12p Portrait, biplane, camera .35 .20

Aviation, motion picture and meat exporting industrialist.

Self-portrait with Wife — A432

1985, Feb. 25
942 A432 37p multicolored .65 .30

Pedro Nel Gomez (1899-1984), painter. See No. C748.

Fauna A433

1985 ***Perf. 14***
943 A433 12p Hydrochaeris hydrochaeris .45 .30

Perf. 13
944 A433 15p Felis pardalis .45 .25
945 A433 15p Tremarctos ornatus, vert. .45 .25
946 A433 20p Tapirus pinchaque .75 .30
Nos. 943-946,C758 (5) 3.60 1.35

Carlos Gardel (1890-1935), Entertainer A434

Camina Literacy Program — A435

1985, June 23 ***Perf. 14***
947 A434 15p Portrait, Fokker F-31 Trimotor .25 .20

1985, Nov. 25 ***Perf. 13½x14***
948 A435 15p Tree, alphabet .30 .20

Christmas 1985 A436

1985, Dec. 4 **Litho.** ***Perf. 13***
949 A436 15p multicolored .35 .20

Rafael Pombo Children's Foundation. See No. C755.

Eduardo Carranza (b. 1913), Poet — A437

Colombian Free University, Cent. — A438

1986, Feb. 13
950 A437 18p multicolored .25 .20

1986, Feb. 14
951 A438 18p multicolored .30 .20

Gen. Antonio Ricaurte (b. 1786), Liberator A439

1986, May 7 **Litho.** ***Perf. 13***
952 A439 18p Leiva birthplace .25 .20

Jose Asuncion Silva (1865-1896), Poet, and Scene from Nocturno — A440

1986, May 30 **Litho.** ***Perf. 12***
953 A440 18p multicolored .25 .20

Fernando Gomez Martinez (1897-1985), Journalist — A441

1986, June 19
954 A441 24p multicolored .30 .20

Santiago de Cali, 450th Anniv. A442

1986, July 25 **Litho.** ***Perf. 13***
955 A442 25p La Merced .30 .20

A443

A444

Monsignor Jose Vicente Castro Silva (1885-1968), rector of the Mayor del Rosario School: portrait by Ricardo Gomez.

1986, Aug. 4 **Litho.** ***Perf. 12***
956 A443 20p multicolored .25 .20

1986, Oct. 14 **Litho.** ***Perf. 12***
957 A444 40p Natl. University .45 .20

Faculties: Fine Arts, cent., and Architecture, 50th anniv.

Rafael Maya (1897-1980), Poet, and Salamanca University Entrance — A445

1986, Oct. 15
958 A445 25p multicolored .30 .20

See No. C772.

Condor in Flight — A446

Inia goefrenis A446a

No. 962, Inia goeffrensis. No. 963, Procyon cancrivorus. No. 964, Monachus tropicalis. No. 965, Pteronura brasiliensis. No. 966, Trichechus manatus. No. 967, Odocoileus virginianus. No. 968, Trogon personatus personatus. Nos. 962-968 horiz.

1986-89 **Litho.** ***Perf. 12***
959 A446 20p ultra .25 .20
960 A446 25p ultra ('87) .30 .20

Perf. 14½x14, 14x14½
961 A446a 30p grn ('87) .45 .20
962 A446a 30p dull vio ('87) .45 .20

Engr.
Wmk. 334
963 A446a 35p chest brn ('88) .65 .20
964 A446a 35p dark grn ('88) .65 .20
965 A446a 40p deep org ('88) .65 .20
966 A446a 40p gray ('88) .75 .20
967 A446a 40p tan ('89) .75 .20
968 A446a 45p dark vio ('88) .75 .20
Nos. 959-968 (10) 5.65 2.00

Issued: 20p, 11/6; 25p, 5/25; No. 961, 6/8; No. 962, 12/24; No. 963, 8/6; No. 964, 9/20; No. 965, 9/20; No. 966, 11/29; No. 967, 4/29; No. 968, 12/16.

See Nos. 996, 1000, C778-C781.

A447

A448

1987, Jan. 29 **Unwmk.** ***Perf. 12***
969 A447 25p multicolored .45 .20

Pedro Uribe Mejia (1886-1972), pioneer of Colombian coffee industry.

1987, May 3 ***Perf. 13½x13***
970 A448 500p Santa Barbara Church 5.50 1.75

Mompox, 450th anniv.

Writers A449

Portraits and scenes from works: 70p, Jorge Isaacs (1837-1895), novelist, and scene from *Maria*. 90p, Aurelio Martinez Mutis (1884-1954), poet, and scene from *La Epopeya del Condor*.

1987 ***Perf. 12***
971 A449 70p multicolored .75 .25
972 A449 90p multicolored 1.10 .40

Issue dates: 70p, July 28. 90p, Sept. 2.

A450

A451

Social Security & Communications.

1987 **Litho.** ***Perf. 13½x13***
973 A450 35p multicolored .40 .20

1988, May 25 Litho. *Perf. 12*

Natl. Anthem, Cent.: Score, lyricist Rafael Nunez and composer Oreste Sindici. Dated 1987.

974 A451 70p multicolored .65 .25

Human Rights — A452

Perf. 14½x14, 14x14½

1988-89 Engr.

975 A452 30p Life .30 .20
976 A452 35p Suffrage .30 .20
977 A452 40p Association, horiz. .40 .20
978 A452 45p Culture, horiz. .30 .20
Nos. 975-978 (4) 1.30 .80

Issued: 30p, 35p, 5/12; 40p, 7/1; 45p, 10/27/89.

See Nos. C797, C807.

Pasto, 450th Anniv. A453

1988, May 20 Litho. *Perf. 12*

979 A453 60p Cathedral, Pasto .60 .20

Dated 1987.

Bogota Aqueduct and Sewage System, Cent. — A454

1988, May 20

980 A454 100p Waterfall 1.10 .30

Maria Currea de Aya (1888-1985), Women's Rights Activist — A455

1988, May 27

981 A455 80p multicolored .85 .25

A456

A457

Sailfish, *Istiaophorus Americanus.*

Perf. 14x13½

1988, July 19 Engr. Wmk. 334

982 A456 (A) dark blue 4.25 2.25
983 A456 (B) Prus blue 1.25 .40

At the time of issue, No. 982 was sold for 400p and No. 983 for 100p. See type A486.

Unwmk.

1988, Aug. 10 Litho. *Perf. 12*

984 A457 120p multicolored 1.10 .35

San Bartolome College, founded in 1604.

Jorge Alvarez Lleras (1885-1952), Engineer and Director of the Natl. Astronomical Observatory — A458

1988, Aug. 17

985 A458 90p multicolored .80 .35

Pres. Eduardo Santos (1888-1974) A459

1988, Aug. 30

986 A459 80p multicolored .70 .20

Andres Bello Seminary A460

Unwmk.

1988, Dec. 27 Litho. *Perf. 12*

987 A460 115p multicolored .95 .20

Adpostal, 25th Anniv. A461

1989, May 3

988 A461 45p multicolored .35 .20

Military Leaders — A462

Bolivar and Santander at the Los Llanos Campaign — A463

1989 Litho. *Perf. 12*

989 A462 40p Santander .50 .25
990 A462 40p Bolivar .50 .25
991 A463 45p multicolored .50 .25
Nos. 989-991 (3) 1.50 .75

Liberation campaign, 170th anniv.

Issued: No. 989, 8/25; No. 990, 7/25; 45p, 8/7.

From Boyaca to Santa Fe — A464

1989, Aug. 7 Litho. *Perf. 12*

992 45p multicolored 1.50 .45
993 45p multicolored 1.50 .45
a. A464 Pair, #992-993 4.00 2.00

Liberation campaign, 170th anniv.

Liberation Campaign Triptych — A466

Designs: a, Gen. Santander, liberation force. b, Simon Bolivar riding mount. c, Insurgent cavalry.

Unwmk.

1989, Aug. 7 Litho. *Perf. 13*

994 A466 Strip of 3 3.50 1.50
a.-c. 45p any single 1.00 .35

Liberation Campaign, 170th anniv.

Tunja, 450th Anniv. A467

1989, Aug. 8 *Perf. 12*

995 A467 45p multicolored .35 .20

Fauna Type of 1988

Designs: No. 996, Harpia harpyja, horiz. No. 997, Urocyon cinereoargenteus. No. 998, Dendrobates histrionicus. No. 1000, Phenacosaurus indenenae. No. 1001, Cebuella pygmaea. No. 1002, Eurypyga helias, horiz.

Perf. 14½x14, 14x14½

1989-90 Engr. Wmk. 334

996 A446a 45p black 1.00 .20
997 A446a 50p blue gray .50 .20
998 A446a 50p deep claret .30 .20
999 A446a 55p red brown .75 .20
1000 A446a 60p brown .50 .20
1001 A446a 60p org brown .50 .20
Nos. 996-1001 (6) 3.55 1.20

Issued: 45p, 9/7; Nos. 997, 1000, 3/1/90; No. 998, 4/25; 55p, 8/18; No. 1001, 8/6.

A468

A469

1989, Aug. 30 Unwmk. *Perf. 12*

1011 A468 135p multicolored 1.10 .75

City of Armenia, cent.

1990, Mar. 28 Litho. *Perf. 12*

1012 A469 60p Espeletia hartwegiana .35 .20

Gen. Francisco De Paula Santander (1792-1840) — A470

1990, May 6 *Perf. 14x13½*

1013 A470 50p multicolored .35 .20
Nos. 1013,C823-C827 (6) 3.75 2.50

See Nos. 1046-1047.

General Santander Police Academy, 50th Anniv. — A471

1990, May 16 *Perf. 12*

1014 A471 60p multicolored .35 .20

Department of La Guajira A473

1990, July 1 *Perf. 12*

1016 A473 60p multicolored .55 .20

Ceiba Pentandra A474

1990, July 15 Litho. *Perf. 12*

1017 A474 60p multicolored .35 .20

A475

A476

1990, Aug. 8 Litho. *Perf. 12*
1018 A475 70p Tibouchina lepidota .65 .25

Unwmk.
1990, Aug. 28 Litho. *Perf. 14*
1019 A476 70p Ceroxylon quindiuense .40 .20

A477

A478

1990, Sept. 28 *Perf. 12*
1020 A477 60p St. John Bosco .45 .20

Salesian Order in Colombia, cent.

1991, Mar. 28 Litho. *Perf. 12*
1021 A478 70p multicolored .40 .20

Miraculous Christ, Pilgrimage Church of Buga.

Moths and Butterflies A479

1991, Apr. 18 Litho. *Perf. 14*
1022 A479 70p Callithea philotima .65 .20
1023 A479 70p Anaea syene, vert. .65 .20
1024 A479 80p Thecla coronata, vert. .80 .20
1025 A479 80p Agrias amydon .85 .20
1026 A479 170p Morpho rhetenor 1.75 .30
1027 A479 190p Heliconius longarenus 2.00 .30
Nos. 1022-1027 (6) 6.70 1.40

Nos. 1025-1027 are airmail.

New Constitution A480

1991, July 4 Litho. *Perf. 14*
1028 A480 70p multicolored .35 .20

A481

A482

1991, July 19 *Perf. 12*
1029 A481 80p multicolored .40 .20

Pres. Dario Echandia Olaya (1897-1989). See No. 1042.

1991, Aug. 7
1030 A482 70p multicolored .35 .20

Col. Antanasio Girardot (1791-1813).

A483

A484

1991, Aug. 15 Litho. *Perf. 14*
1031 A483 80p multicolored .40 .20

Luis Carlos Galan Sarmiento (1943-1989), political reformer.

1991, Aug. 24 *Perf. 12*

Pre-Columbian Artifacts: 80p, Statue of cat god. No. 1033, Pitcher from tomb of high official. No. 1034, Statue with two heads. 210p, Flying fish, horiz.

1032 A484 80p multicolored .55 .20
1033 A484 90p multicolored .75 .20
1034 A484 90p multicolored .75 .20
1035 A484 210p multicolored 1.75 .30
Nos. 1032-1035 (4) 3.80 .90

Nos. 1034-1035 are airmail.

Colonial Architecture A485

80p, Cloister of St. Augustine, Tunja. No. 1037, Community Bridge, Chia. No. 1038, Roadside Chapel, Pamplona. 190p, Church of Immaculate Conception, Bogota.

1991 Litho. *Perf. 12*
1036 A485 80p multi .55 .20
1037 A485 90p multi .90 .20
1038 A485 90p multi, vert. .75 .20
1039 A485 190p multi, vert. 1.50 .25
Nos. 1036-1039 (4) 3.70 .85

Issue dates: No. 1037, Sept. 9; others, Sept. 27. Nos. 1038-1039 are airmail.

Istiaphorus Americanus A486

1991, Sept. 3 *Perf. 14*
1040 A486 830p multicolored 5.50 1.40

Colombian Police Force, Cent. A487

1991, Oct. 12 *Perf. 12*
1041 A487 80p multicolored .45 .20

President Type of 1991

Pres. Alberto Lleras Camargo (1906-1990)

1991, Nov. 5
1042 A481 80p multicolored .40 .20

A489

A490

1991, Dec. 17 Litho. *Perf. 12*
1043 A489 80p Sogamoso City Hall .45 .20

1992 Litho. *Perf. 14*

Designs: No. 1044, Diana Turbay Quintero (1950-91), journalist. No. 1045, Indalecio Lievano Aguirre (1917-82), diplomat.

1044 A490 80p multicolored .40 .20
1045 A490 80p multicolored .40 .20

Issued: No. 1044, Jan. 24; No. 1045, Apr. 21.

Santander Type of 1990 and

Battle of Boyaca — A491a

1992, Apr. 2 *Perf. 14*
Size: 26x37mm
1046 A470 80p Monument .40 .30
1047 A470 190p Portrait 1.00 .65

Souvenir Sheet
Perf. 13½x14
1047A A491a 950p multicolored 5.50 5.50

Nos. 1047-1047A are airmail. Gen. Francisco de Paula Santander, bicent. of birth.

A492

A493

Ministers of Justice: 100p, Enrique Low Murtra (1939-91). 110p, Rodrigo Lara Bonilla (1946-84).

1992, Apr. 30 Litho. *Perf. 12*
1048 A492 100p multicolored .40 .20
1049 A492 110p multicolored .50 .20

1992, May 18 *Perf. 14*
1050 A493 110p multicolored .60 .30

15th natl. games, Barranquilla.

Wildlife — A494

1992, Apr. 14 Litho. *Perf. 12*
1051 A494 (B) Oroaetus icidori 1.75 .75
1052 A494 (A) Tremarctos ornatus 8.25 2.75

Nos. 1051-1052 had face values of 200p and 950p respectively on date of issue.

Endangered Species A495

1992, Aug. 4
1053 A495 100p Crocodylus acatus 1.00 .35
1054 A495 100p Vultur gryphus, vert. 1.00 .35

A496

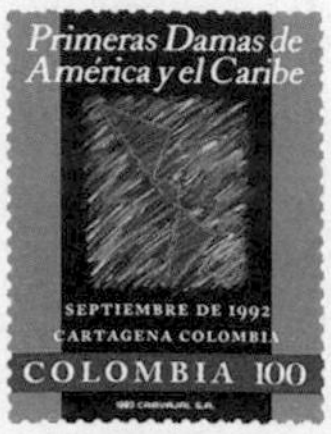

A497

1992, Aug. 24 Litho. *Perf. 14*

1055 A496 100p multicolored .45 .30
1056 A496 110p multicolored .45 .30

Maria Lopez de Escobar, founder of the House of the Mother and Child. No. 1056 is airmail.

1992, Sept. 23 Litho. *Perf. 12*

1057 A497 100p multicolored .45 .30

Conference of First Ladies of the Americas and Caribbean, Cartagena.

Recycling — A498

1992, Oct. 9 Litho. *Perf. 12*

1058 A498 100p multicolored .45 .30

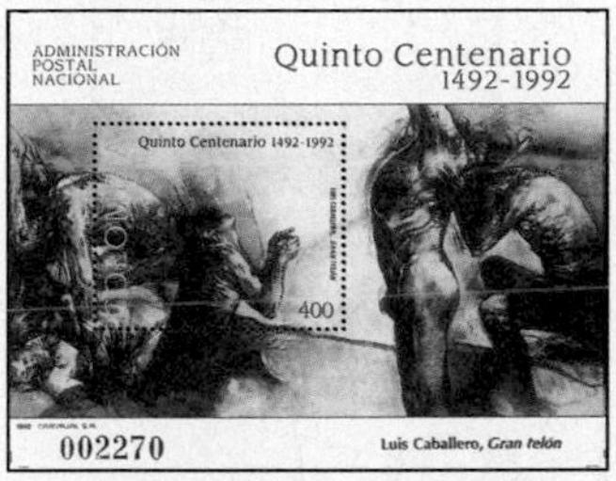

Discovery of America, 500th Anniv. — A499

Paintings: 100p, Zenaida, by Ana Mercedes Hoyos. No. 1060, Estudio Para 1/500, by Beatriz Gonzalez. No. 1061, Blue Eagle, by Alejandro Obregon. 230p, Cantileo, by Luis Luna. 260p, Corn, by Antonio Caro. 400p, Grand Curtain, by Luis Caballero. 440p, Homage to Guatavita, by Alejandro Obregon.

1992, Oct. 5 Litho. *Perf. 13½x14*

1059 A499 100p multicolored .40 .30
1060 A499 110p multicolored .45 .30
1061 A499 110p multicolored .45 .30
1062 A499 230p multicolored .95 .70
1063 A499 260p multicolored 1.10 .80
Nos. 1059-1063 (5) 3.35 2.40

Souvenir Sheets

Perf. 12

1064 A499 400p multicolored 2.00 2.00
1065 A499 440p multicolored 2.00 2.00

Nos. 1061-1063 are airmail.

World Post Day — A500

1992, Oct. 19 Litho. *Perf. 12*

1066 A500 (B) multicolored .95 .65

No. 1066 had face value of 200p on day of issue.

Christmas — A501

Children's paintings of: 100p, Nativity scene. 110p, Adoration of the Magi.

1992, Nov. 20 Litho. *Perf. 12*

1067 A501 100p multicolored .45 .30
1068 A501 110p multicolored .45 .30

No. 1068 is airmail.

Three Musicians, by Fernando Botero A502

1993, Feb. 5 Litho. *Perf. 12*

1069 A502 (B) multicolored .95 .65

No. 1069 had a face value of 250p on day of issue.

Lions Intl. Campaign Against Amblyopia A503

1993, Mar. 26 *Perf. 14*

1070 A503 100p multicolored .40 .30

Holy Week in Popayan A504

1993, Apr. 5 *Perf. 14x13½*

1071 A504 (B) multicolored .95 .65

No. 1071 had a face value of 250p on day of issue.

A505

A506

1993, Apr. 7 *Perf. 12*

1072 A505 (B) multicolored .95 .65

Pan American Health Org., 90th anniv.

No. 1072 had a face value of 250p on day of issue.

1993, Apr. 14

1073 A506 (B) multicolored .95 .65

Franciscans of Mary Immaculate, cent. No. 1073 had a face value of 250p on day of issue.

A507

A508

1993, Apr. 22 Litho. *Perf. 14*

1074 A507 (B) multicolored .90 .60

EXFILBO '93, 18th Natl. Philatelic Exhibition. No. 1074 had a face value of 250p on day of issue.

1993, July 2 Litho. *Perf. 12*

1075 A508 250p Guillermo Cano, writer 1.00 .65

Human Rights A509

Rights: a, 150p, Of prisoners. b, 150p, Of the elderly. c, 200p, Of the infirm. d, 200p, Of children. e, 220p, Of women. f, 220p, Of the poor. g, 460p, To clean environment. h, 520p, Of indigenous people.

Painting: 800p, Peace, Rights, and Freedom, by Alfredo Vivero, vert.

1993, June 10 *Perf. 14*

1076 A509 Block of 8, #a.-h. 10.00 7.00

Souvenir Sheet

1077 A509 800p multicolored 5.00 5.00

Nos. 1076e-1076h are airmail.

Amazon Region of Colombia — A510

No. 1078a, Parrot. No. 1078b, Anaconda. No. 1079a, Victoria regia. No. 1079b, Flor ipecacuana. 880p, Map, native, horiz.

1993 Litho. *Perf. 12*

1078 A510 150p Pair, #a.-b. 1.25 .75
1079 A510 220p Pair, #a.-b. 1.75 1.00

Souvenir Sheet

1080 A510 880p multicolored 4.00 4.00

Nos. 1079-1080 are airmail.

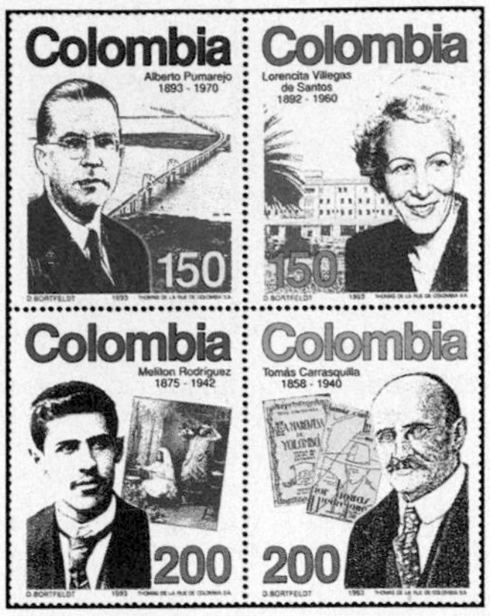

Famous People — A511

Designs: a, 150p, Alberto Pumarejo (1893-1970). b, 150p, Lorencita Villegas de Santos (1892-1960). c, 200p, Meliton Rodriguez (1875-1942). d, 200p, Tomas Carrasquilla (1858-1940).

1993 Litho. *Perf. 14x13½*

1081 A511 Block of 4, #a.-d. 2.50 1.60

Christmas — A512

1993, Nov. 30 *Perf. 12*

1082 A512 200p Holy Family .90 .50
1083 A512 220p Shepherd 1.50 1.00

No. 1083 is airmail.

Tourism A513

Designs: No. 1084a, San Andres Providence. b, Cocuy Natl. Park. c, Lake Cocha. d, Waterfalls, Serrania de la Macarena. 250p, Lake Otun. No. 1086a, Chicamocha River. b, Sierra Nevada de Santa Marta mountains. 520p, Penol Reservoir.

1993, Dec. 1 Litho. *Perf. 12*

1084 A513 220p Block of 4, #a.-d. 4.00 3.00
1085 A513 250p multicolored 1.10 .55
1086 A513 460p Pair, #a.-b. 4.00 3.00
1087 A513 520p multicolored 2.40 1.50
Nos. 1084-1087 (4) 11.50 8.05

Nos. 1084, 1086-87 are airmail.

A514

A515

1993, Dec. 21 Litho. *Perf. 14*

1088 A514 150p multicolored .50 .35

Natl. Museum, 170th anniv.

1994, Jan. 25 Litho. *Perf. 14*

1089 A515 300p Marie Poussepin 1.10 .70

A516

A517

Birds: 180p, Ognorhynchus icterotis. 240p, Rallus semiplumbeus. 270p, Semnornis ramphastinus. 560p, Anas cyanoptera.

1994, Mar. 4

1090 A516 180p multi 1.25 .40
1091 A516 240p multi 1.50 .55
1092 A516 270p multi, horiz. 1.75 .65
1093 A516 560p multi, horiz. 3.50 1.25
Nos. 1090-1093 (4) 8.00 2.85

Nos. 1092-1093 are airmail.

1994, Apr. 11 Litho. *Perf. 14*

1094 A517 300p multicolored 1.25 .80

Air Force, 75th anniv.

Latin American Presidential Summit, Cartagena A518

1994, June 14 Litho. *Perf. 14*

1095 A518 300p shown .95 .60
1096 A518 630p Flags 2.00 1.40

No. 1096 is airmail.

1994 World Cup Soccer Championships, US — A519

World Cup Trophy and: 180p, Soccer player, Colombian flag. 270p, Two players with ball. 560p, Soccer ball, Colombian flag, vert.
1110p, Soccer player offering hand to another.

1994, May 26 *Perf. 12*

1097 A519 180p multicolored .60 .40
1098 A519 270p multicolored .90 .55
1099 A519 560p multicolored 2.00 1.25
Nos. 1097-1099 (3) 3.50 2.20

Souvenir Sheet

1100 A519 1110p multicolored 5.00 5.00

Nos. 1098-1099 are airmail.

Ricardo Rendon (1894-1931), Artist — A520

1993 Census — A521

1994, June 30 Litho. *Perf. 12*

1101 A520 240p black .90 .45

1994, Aug. 12 *Perf. 14*

1102 A521 240p multicolored .80 .45

Ministry of Communications Inravision, 30th Anniv. — A522

1994, Aug. 3

1103 A522 180p multicolored .65 .30

Intl. Year of the Family A523

1994, Sept. 1 Litho. *Perf. 14*

1104 A523 300p multicolored 1.00 .65

America Issue — A524

Methods of mail delivery: 270p, Horse, bicycle. 300p, Men holding stamps showing truck, ship, plane.

1994, Oct. 18 Litho. *Perf. 13*

1105 A524 270p multicolored 1.00 .60
1106 A524 300p multicolored 1.50 .65

No. 1105 is airmail.

Colombian Society of Engineers, Cent. A525

1994, Oct. 20 Litho. *Perf. 12*

1107 A525 180p multicolored .60 .40

Christmas A526

1994, Nov. 22 Litho. *Perf. 13½x13*

1108 A526 270p Magi .90 .60
1109 A526 300p Holy family 1.00 .65

No. 1108 is airmail.

Former President Type of 1981
Miniature Sheet of 20

Designs: a, Jose Miguel Pey. b, Jorge Tadeo Lozano. c, Antonio Narino. d, Camilo Torres. e, Jose Fernandez Madrid. f, Jose Maria del Castillo y Rada. g, Custodio Garcia Rovira. h, Antonio Villavicencio. i, Liborio Mejia. j, Rafael Urdaneta. k, Juan Garcia del Rio. l, Jose Maria Melo. m, Tomas Herrera. n, Froilan Largacha. o, Salvador Camacho Roldan. p, Ezequiel Hurtado. q, Dario Echandia Olaya. r, Alberto Lleras Camargo. s, Gustavo Rojas Pinilla. t, Carlos Lleras Restrepo.

1995, Apr. 4 Litho. *Perf. 12*

1110 A401 270p #a.-t. 35.00 35.00

World Offroad Bicycle Championships, Melgar — A527

1995, Mar. 30 *Perf. 14*

1111 A527 400p multicolored 1.40 .90

A528

A529

1995, Oct. 12 Litho. *Perf. 12*

1112 A528 220p multicolored .65 .30

Gen. Jose Maria Obando (1795-1861), President.

1995, Nov. 28 *Perf. 14*

1113 A529 400p Clean air 1.10 .55
1114 A529 400p Clean water 1.10 .55

Preserve the environment. America issue.

Christmas A530

Stained glass windows: 220p, Flight into Egypt. 330p, Nativity.

1995, Dec. 18 *Perf. 12*

1115 A530 220p multicolored .75 .30
1116 A530 330p multicolored 1.10 .55

No. 1116 is airmail.

Bogotá to Boyacá World Cycling Championship — A531

1995, Oct. 4 Litho. *Perf. 12*

1117 A531 400p multicolored 1.25 .65

León De Greiff (1895-1976), Poet — A532

1996, May 2 Litho. *Perf. 12*

1118 A532 400p black 1.40 .40

Mosquera Courtyard, Natl. Capitol A533

1996, July 18 Litho. *Perf. 14*

1119 A533 400p multicolored 1.10 .40

Medellin Rapid Transit System A534

1996, July 2 *Perf. 12*

1120 A534 500p multicolored 1.75 .90

A535

A536

1996, June 20
1121 A535 500p multicolored 1.40 .50

Community of St. John of God in Colombia, 400th anniv.

1996, June 25

Arms: a, Santa Maria la Antigua del Darien. b, San Sebastian de Mariquita. c, Villa de la Marinilla. d, Villa of Santa Cruz of Mompox.

1122 A536 400p Block of 4, #a.-d. 4.25 3.00
e. As "d," inscribed AEREO 10.00
f. Block of 4, #1122a-1122c, 1122e 12.00

Issued in sheets of 16 stamps.

1996 Summer Olympic Games, Atlanta — A537

1996, July 16
1123 A537 500p multicolored 1.40 .50

SAYCO (Colombian Authors and Composers Society), 50th Anniv. — A538

1996, Aug. 17 **Litho.** ***Perf. 12***
1124 A538 400p multicolored 1.25 .50

Exfilbo '96, 20th Natl. Philatelic Exhibition A539

Jewelry from Gold Museum, Bogotá.

1996, Oct. 19 **Litho.** ***Perf. 12***
1125 A539 400p multicolored 1.25 .50

Souvenir Sheet

Founders Theater, Manizales, 30th Anniv. — A540

Drop curtain: a, Eagle, people watching man drawing on ground, vert. b, People, animals on hillside.

1996, Oct. 28 ***Perf. 14***
1126 A540 4000p #a.-b. 20.00 20.00

Christmas A541

Designs: No. 1127, Mailman handing woman letter. No. 1128, Woman reading letter, mailman holding bundle of mail.

1996, Nov. 22
1127 A541 400p multicolored 1.10 .40
1128 A541 400p multicolored 1.10 .40

No. 1128 is airmail.

America Issue — A542

1996, Nov. 29 ***Perf. 12***
1129 A542 500p Men's costume 1.40 .50
1130 A542 500p Women's costume 1.40 .50

Historical Landmarks — A543

a, Cemetery, Santa Cruz of Mompox. b, Carved face, San Agustin Archaelogical Park. c, Entrance, Palace of the Inquisition, Cartagena de Indias. d, Inside ruins, Tierradentro Archaelogical Park.

1996, Dec. 6 ***Perf. 14***
1131 A543 400p Block of 4, #a.-d. 10.00 10.00

Alvaro Gomez Hurtado (1919-95), Politician, Writer — A544

1997, Mar. 18 **Litho.** ***Perf. 12***
1132 A544 400p multicolored 1.00 .40

Bogotá Journalists Assoc., 50th Anniv. A545

1997, July 10 **Litho.** ***Perf. 12***
1133 A545 400p multicolored 1.00 .40

Natl. Festival of Porro — A546

1997, June 26 ***Perf. 13½x14***
1134 A546 400p multicolored 1.00 .40

Pres. Virgilio Barco (1921-97) — A547

1997, Nov. 27 **Litho.** ***Perf. 14***
1135 A547 500p multicolored 1.25 .40

Colombia in Peace A548

1997, Dec. 30 **Litho.** ***Perf. 12***
1136 A548 500p Children playing 1.10 .40
1137 A548 1100p Children dancing 2.50 .90

No. 1137 is airmail.

America Issue A549

1997, Dec. 30
1138 A549 500p Postman by day 1.25 .45
1139 A549 1100p Postman by night 2.75 1.00

No. 1139 is airmail.

Jorge Eliecer Gaitan (1903-48), Politician — A550

1998, Apr. 24 **Litho.** ***Perf. 14***
1140 A550 500p multicolored 1.10 .40

Free University, 75th Anniv. A551

1998, July 1 **Litho.** ***Perf. 14***
1141 A551 500p black & red 1.00 .35

Santander Industrial University, 50th Anniv. — A552

1998, May 14 ***Perf. 12***
1142 A552 500p multicolored 1.10 .35

City of Manizales, 150th Anniv. — A553

1998, July 24 **Litho.** ***Perf. 12***
1143 A553 500p multicolored 1.00 .40

A554

A555

Pre-Columbian art, agency: a, Tairona, Bank of the Republic. b, Malagana, Controller General. c, Quimbaya, Bank Superintendent.

1998, July 24
1144 A554 500p Strip of 3, #a.-c. 3.00 2.00

Natl. financial agencies, 70th anniv.

1998, Aug. 21 ***Perf. 14***
1145 A555 500p multicolored 1.00 .40

Pres. Misael Pastrana Borrero (1923-97).

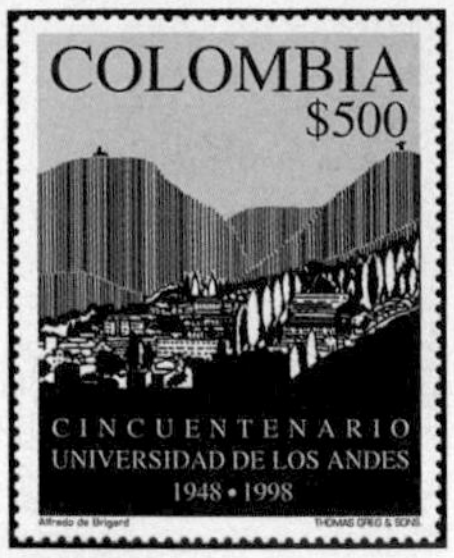

University of the Andes, 50th Anniv. A556

1998, Sept. 28
1146 A556 500p multicolored .80 .40

Christmas A557

Designs: 500p, Woman kneeling down to get water with bowl, cherubs in sky. No. 1148a, Magi. No. 1148b, Nativity scene.

1998, Nov. 19 Litho. ***Perf. 14***
1147 A557 500p multicolored 1.00 .50
1148 A557 1000p Pair, #a.-b. 4.00 3.00

No. 1148 is airmail.

A558

A559

Emblems of Colombian Academies: a, Language. b, Medicine. c, Law. d, History. e, Science. f, Ecomonics. g, Religion.

1998, Dec. 15 ***Perf. 12***
Sheet of 7 + Label
1149 A558 500p #a.-g. 14.00 14.00

1999, Apr. 16 ***Perf. 14***
1150 A559 1000p multicolored 1.25 .60

Gen. José Hilario López.

Famous Women — A559a

America Issue: 600p, Soledad Román de Nuñez. 1200p, Bertha Herández de Ospina.

1999, Mar. 25 Litho. ***Perf. 12***
1151 A559a 600p multicolored 1.50 .40
1152 A559a 1200p multicolored 2.75 .70

No. 1152 is airmail.

Turtles — A560

a, Chelonia mydas. b, Dermochelys coriacea. c, Eretmochelys imbricata.

1999, Apr. 16 ***Perf. 14***
1153 A560 1300p Strip of 3, #a.-c. 10.00 10.00

Dr. Eduardo Zuleta Angel, Diplomat (b. 1899) — A561

1999, Sept. 9 Litho. ***Perf. 12***
1154 A561 600p multicolored 1.25 .35

Pamplona, 450th Anniv. A562

1999 Litho. ***Perf. 12***
1155 A562 1000p multicolored 2.25 .60

Sovereign Military Order of Malta, 900th Anniv. — A563

1999, June 24 ***Perf. 14***
1156 A563 1200p multicolored 3.00 .85

Japanese Immigration to Colombia — A564

Designs: a, Red at right. b, Red at left.

1999, May 12 ***Perf. 13½x14***
1157 A564 1300p Pair, #a.-b. 5.00 5.00

Pan American Games, Winnipeg, Manitoba A565

Designs: a, Flag, Olympic rings. b, Runner facing right. c, Weight lifter facing left. d, Cyclist facing right. e, Shooter facing left. f, Roller skater facing right. g, Runner facing left. h, Weight lifter facing right. i, Cyclist facing left. j, Shooter facing right. k, Roller skater facing left. l, Like "a," with lilac line under "12."

1999, July 23 Litho. ***Perf. 14***
1158 A565 1200p Sheet of 12, #a.-l. 30.00 30.00

Luis A. Robles (b. 1849) — A566

1999, Oct. 27
1159 A566 600p multi .95 .40

Manufacture of Aspirin, Cent. A567

1999, Dec. 1 ***Perf. 12¾***
1160 A567 600p multi .95 .40

Value is for stamp with surrounding selvage.

UPU, 125th Anniv. A568

1999, Oct. 29 ***Perf. 14¼***
1161 A568 1000p "125" 1.50 .65
1162 A568 1300p "1874-1999" 2.50 .85

Inter-American Development Bank, 40th Anniv. — A569

Abstract art: a, "Colombia" in yellow. b, "Colombia" in red.

1999, Nov. 19 ***Perf. 14x14¼***
1163 A569 1000p Pair, #a.-b. 3.25 1.40

America Issue, A New Millennium Without Arms — A570

a, Stylized hands. b, Large flower at LR.

1999, Nov. 9 ***Perf. 14***
1164 A570 1200p Pair, #a.-b. 4.00 1.75

Christmas — A571

a, Holy Family, animals. b, Angel, Magi.

1999, Nov. 29 ***Perf. 13½x14***
1165 A571 600p Pair, #a.-b. 2.00 .80

Millennium — A572

Designs: a, Nude man, flag, dove. b, Globe, rainbow, "2000."

2000, Jan. 3 ***Perf. 14***
1166 A572 1000p Pair, #a.-b. 3.00 3.00

University of Medellin, 50th Anniv. A573

2000 Litho. ***Perf. 14***
1167 A573 1000p multi 1.25 .55

Father José Rafael Faría Bermúdez (1896-1979) A574

2000, Mar. 6 Litho. ***Perf. 14***
1168 A574 1300p multi 1.50 .75

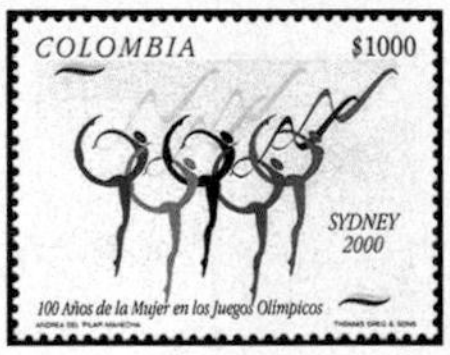

2000 Summer Olympics, Sydney A575

2000, Apr. 21
1169 A575 1000p multi 1.50 .65

Popayán Religious Music Festival A576

2000, July 7
1170 A576 1000p multi 1.90 .65

America Issue, Campaign Against AIDS A577

2000 Litho. ***Perf. 14x13½***
1171 A577 1000p multi 3.00 1.25

Radio Station HJCK, 50th Anniv. — A578

2000, Sept. 28 Litho. ***Perf. 14***
1172 A578 1000p multi 1.25 .55

Birth Registration A579

2000 Litho. ***Perf. 14¼***
1173 A579 1000p multi 1.10 .50

Paintings A580

No. 1174: a, Archangel, by Fernando Botero. b, Gypsy Woman With Tamourine, by Jean-Baptiste-Camille Corot. c, Vera Sergine Renoir, by Renoir. d, Man on Horse, by Botero. e, Mother Superior, by Botero. f, A Town, by Botero. g, Flowers, by Botero. h, Cézanne, by Botero. i, Patio, by Botero. j, Absinthe Drinker in Grenelle, by Toulouse-Lautrec. k, A Little Valley, by Corot. l, The Studio, by Botero.

2000 ***Perf. 12***
1174 Sheet of 12 12.00 12.00
a.-l. A580 650p Any single .75 .35

Children's Day — A581

2001, Mar. 15 Litho. ***Perf. 14***
1175 A581 1100p multi 2.75 1.00

Abolition of Slavery, 150th Anniv. — A582

2001, May 21 Litho. ***Perf. 14¼x14***
1176 A582 1100p multi 2.75 1.00

Discovery of Magdalena River, 500th Anniv. — A583

2001, June 13 Litho. ***Perf. 14***
1177 A583 1100p multi 2.75 1.00

Copa America Soccer Tournament A584

2001, July 18 Litho. ***Perf. 12¾***
1178 A584 1900p multi 3.00 1.25

Values are for examples with surrounding selvage.

America Issue — Los Katios Natl. Park, UNESCO World Heritage Site — A585

2001, Aug. 17 ***Perf. 13¾x14***
1179 A585 2100p multi 3.00 1.25

Year of Dialogue Among Civilizations A586

2001, Oct. 9 ***Perf. 14***
1180 A586 650p multi 1.75 .60

Reclining Woman, by Fernando Botero — A587

2001 ***Perf. 14¼***
1181 A587 1100p multi 2.75 1.00

Christmas A588

2001 ***Perf. 14***
1182 A588 1100p multi 2.75 1.00

National Beauty Pageant — A589

Flag, Miss Colombia Vanesa A. Mendoza Bustos and: a, Cartagena de Indias. b, St. Francis of Assisi Cathedral, Quibdo.
Illustration reduced.

2002, Jan. 22 ***Perf. 14x14¼***
1183 A589 800p Horiz. pair, #a-b 2.00 .80

Natural Riches of Colombia — A590

Parts of map of Colombia, various wildlife and/or natives and: a, Bird and clouds at left. b, Turtle at upper left. c, Fish and whales at left. d, Man on horse at center. e, Volcano at upper left. f, Red and blue parrots at right. g, Flamingos at left. h, Snake at upper left.

2002, Feb. 1 ***Perf. 14¼x14***
1184 A590 2300p Sheet of 8, #a-h 25.00 25.00

Children's Day — A591

2002, Feb. 18 ***Perf. 12***
1185 A591 1400p multi 1.75 .75

New Emblem of Adpostal — A592

2002, Mar. 7 ***Perf. 14***
1186 A592 800p multi 1.10 .40

7th South American Games A593

2002
1187 A593 2100p multi 2.50 1.10

Oxyura Jamaicensis A594

2002, Apr. 30 Litho. ***Perf. 12***
1188 A594 3900p multi 5.00 2.25

Souvenir Sheet

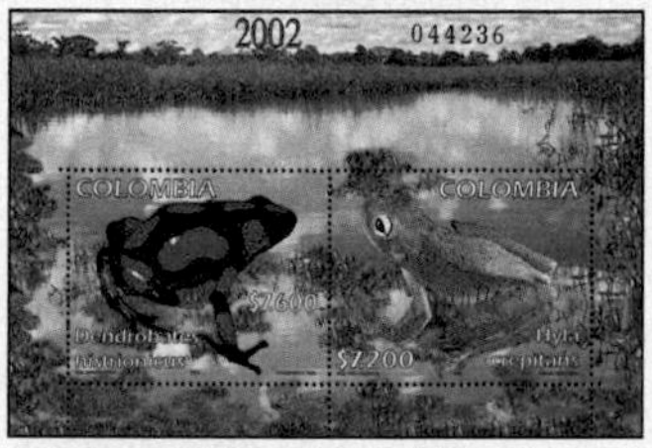

Frogs — A595

No. 1189: a, 7200p, Hyla crepitans. b, 7600p, Dendrobates histrionicus.

2002, Apr. 30 ***Perf. 13¾x14***
1189 A595 Sheet of 2, #a-b 20.00 20.00

Souvenir Sheet

Butterflies — A596

No. 1190: a, Dryas iulia. b, Dryadula phaetusa, vert.

2002, Apr. 30 ***Perf. 12***
1190 A596 13,700p Sheet of 2, #a-b 35.00 35.00

Foundation for Reconstructive Surgery, 25th Anniv. — A597

2002, May 24 ***Perf. 14***
1191 A597 1000p multi 1.25 .50

Pre-Columbian Art — A598

No. 1192, 800p: a, Nariño pectoral. b, Nariño disc.
No. 1193, 1400p: a, Calima diadem. b, Calima pectoral.
No. 1194, 2100p: a, Anthropomorphic Tairona pectoral. b, Round Tairona pectoral.
Illustration reduced.

2002, June 7 *Perf. 13½x14*

Horiz. Pairs, #a-b

1192-1194 A598 Set of 3 12.00 12.00

Surgical Society of Bogota San José Hospital, Cent. — A599

No. 1195: a, Early doctors and nurse. b, Hospital.

2002, July 22 *Perf. 14*

1195 A599 800p Horiz. pair, #a-b 2.00 2.00

Consuelo Araújo Noguera (1940-2001), Assassinated Former Minister of Culture — A600

2002, Aug. 1

1196 A600 1400p multi 2.00 .80

Union Network International A601

2002, Aug. 12

1197 A601 1000p multi 1.25 .50

America Issue — Youth, Education and Literacy — A602

No. 1198: a, Person reading book. b, Letters amd words.

2002, Oct. 9

1198 A602 2500p Horiz. pair, #a-b 5.50 4.50

Christmas A603

2002, Nov. 6 Litho. *Perf. 14x13¾*

1199 A603 800p multi 1.25 .50

Colombian History Academy, Cent. — A604

No. 1200: a, Mural scene with Simon Bolivar at UR. b, Mural scene with horsemen at top. c, Mural scene with man with outstretched arms at UL. d, Cafetal, 1956. e, Batalla de Palonegro, 1905. f, Tigre Cazando Sabanera, 1963. g, El Barqueo, 1936. h, Colombia Asesinada, 1902. i, Dos Mujeres, 1951. j, Bearded man at left, Plaza de Santander. k, Carriage, Plaza de Santander. l, Horse, man and woman, Plaza de Santander.

2002, Nov. 19 *Perf. 13¾x14*

1200 A604 800p Sheet of 12, #a-l 21.00 21.00

Peace Treaty Ending War of 1,000 Days, Cent. A605

2002, Nov. 21 *Perf. 14x13¾*

1201 A605 1600p multi 3.00 .90

Carnival A606

No. 1202: a, shown. b, Participants holding masks on sticks. c, Participants on float.

2003, Jan. 4 *Perf. 14*

1202 Horiz. strip of 3 5.50 5.50
a.-b. A606 1000p Either single 1.10 1.10
c. A606 1200p multi 1.40 1.40

Printed in sheets of 3 horizontal strips and 2 horiz. strips of 3 labels.

Articulated Bus, Bogota A607

2003, Mar. 13 *Perf. 12*

1203 A607 1000p multi 1.10 .45

Departments — A608

No. 1204 — Caldas Department: a, 1200p, Arms. b, 1200p, Government office building, Manizales, horiz. c, 1200p, Campesinos, 1957. d, 2400p, Church, Salamina. e, 2400p, Neira, 1997, horiz. f, 2400p, Enea Chapel, Manizales. g, 2800p, Laguna Verde, Villamaria. h, 2800p, Aguadas, horiz. i, 2800p, Devil's carnival, Riosucio. j, 4100p, Miner, Marmato. k, 4100p, Mariposas del Eje Cafetero, 2001, horiz. l, 4100p, Pacora.

No. 1205, 1000p — Huila Department: a, Arms. b, Government office building, Neiva, horiz. c, La Gaitana. d, Bordones Waterfall, Isnos. e, San Agustín World Heritage Archaeological Park, horiz. f, Lavapatas Spring, San Agustín. g, La Tatacoa Desert, Villavieja. h, Liberty tree, Gigante, horiz. i, Sombrero maker, Suaza. j, Nuestra Señora de los Dolores Church, Aipe. k, Paisaje, horiz. l, Dancers.

No. 1206 — 2400p: a, Historic center of Barichara. b, Ophthalmologic Foundation of Santander, Bucaramanga, horiz. c, Girón. d, Santander Industrial University Intl. Piano Festival, 20th anniv. emblem. e, Petroleum Christ Statue, refinery, Barrancabermeja, horiz. f, Church, San Andrés. g, Gustavo Cote Uribe (1918-94), writer. h, Chamber of Commerce, Bucaramanga, horiz. i, Carnival of Eastern Colombia, Bucaramanga. j, Historic center of Albania. k, Chicamocha River Canyon, Cepitá, horiz. l, Entreguerras.

2003 *Perf. 12*

Sheets of 12, #a-l, + 8 labels

1204	A608	Caldas	37.50	37.50
1205	A608	Huila	15.00	15.00
1206	A608	Santander	25.00	25.00

Issued: No. 1204, Apr. 11. No. 1205, June 29. No. 1206, June 22. Size of horiz. stamps: 46x37mm.

See Nos. 1224-1226, 1246, 1265-1267, 1273.

Fish and Coral of the Rosario Islands — A609

2003, Jan. 16 Litho. *Perf. 12*

1207 A609 1000p multi 2.25 .60

Hapalopsittaca Fuertesi — A610

2003, June 13

1208 A610 1000p multi 2.25 .60

Souvenir Sheets

Orchids — A611

No. 1209 — 2400p: a, Masdevallia ignea. b, Miltoniopsis vexillaria, horiz.

No. 1210 — 2800p: a, Odontoglossum crispum, horiz. b, Masdevallia macrura.

No. 1211 — 5000p: a, Cimbidium. b, Oncidium obryzatum.

No. 1212 — 7000p: a, Cattleya dowiana. b, Cattleya trianaei (49x49mm).

Perf. 14¼, 13¾x14 (#1212b)

2003, June 13

Sheets of 2, #a-b

1209-1212 A611 Set of 4 45.00 45.00

Tejo, National Sport A612

No. 1213: a, Players, tree in foreground (49x39mm). b, Players, light poles (49x39mm). c, Cacique Turmeque.

2003, July 25 *Perf. 12*

1213 Horiz. strip of 3 9.00 9.00
a.-c. A612 2400p Any single 2.10 1.25

America Issue — A613

Flora and fauna: a, Denomination at UR. b, Denomination at LR.

2003, Oct. 9 Litho. *Perf. 12*

1214 A613 1600p Vert. pair, #a-b 4.00 4.00

Printed in sheets of four pairs and four labels.

Souvenir Sheet

Colombia Libraries National Reading Plan — A614

No. 1215: a, 1200p, Building. b, 4100p, Building, diff.

2003, Oct. 30 **Litho.** ***Perf. 12***
1215 A614 Sheet of 2, #a-b 7.00 7.00

General Ramón Arturo Rincón Quiñones (1922-75) — A615

2003, Oct. 31
1216 A615 1000p multi 1.50 .40

Souvenir Sheet

Administrative Security Deparment, 50th Anniv. — A616

2003, Oct. 31
1217 A616 4100p multi 6.00 6.00

Armed Forces A617

No. 1218 — Arms and mottos (#a-d): a, General Command of Military Forces. b, National Army. c, National Navy. d, Air Force. e, Colombian Forces in Korea, 50th anniv.

2003, Nov. 7
1218 Vert. strip of 5 7.50 7.50
a.-e. A617 1200p Any single 1.00 .50

Christmas — A618

No. 1219: a, Good Shepherd, sheep. b, Tree, comet, airplane, rabbit. c, Rabbits, dog. d, Automobile, angel, reindeer, horse. e, Sheep, woman with basket, swan, house. f, Branch with leaves, horse and rider, duck, Indian with bow and arrow.

2003, Dec. 2 **Litho.** ***Perf. 12***
1219 Block of 6 8.00 8.00
a.-f. A618 1000p Any single .95 .55

Colombia and the Eldorado Legend — A619

No. 1220: a, Print of Eldorado ceremony, by Teodoro De Bry, 1595. b, Watercolor painting of Lake Guatavita, by M. María Paz, 1855. c, Watercolor painting of Lake Guatavita, by Gonzalo Ariza, 1984. d, Print of Lake Guatavita, by A. Humboldt Thibault and F. Schoell, 1813. e, Photo of Lake Guatavita, by Fernando Urbina Rangel, 1983. f, Print of Lake Guatavita, by Eustacio Barreto, 1883.

No. 1221 — Muisca raft: a, 1700p, Front. b, 2000p, Back, vert.

2004, Mar. 10
1220 A619 2800p Sheet of 6, #a-f, + 3 labels 13.00 13.00

Souvenir Sheet

1221 A619 Sheet of 2, #a-b 3.00 3.00

Locomotives — A620

No. 1222, 1100p: a, 2-8-2. b, 4-8-0.
No. 1223, 1300p: a, 2-6-2. b, 4-6-2.
Illustration reduced.

2004, Mar. 19

Horiz. Pairs, #a-b

1222-1223 A620 Set of 2 12.00 12.00

Nos. 1222-1223 each printed in sheets of four pairs and two pairs of labels.

Departments Type of 2003

No. 1224, 1100p — Nariño Department: a, Galeras Volcano, San Juan de Pasto, horiz. b, Statue of Gen. Antonio Nariño. c, Nariño Government Building, San Juan de Pasto, horiz. d, Farm, Catambuco, horiz. e, Nuestra Señora de las Lajas Sanctuary, Ipiales. f, Sandoná city center, horiz. g, Gallery of Mirrors, horiz. h, Barnizadores de Pasto Chorography Commission. i, Golden palms, horiz. j, El Morro, Tumaco, horiz. k, Virgen de la Playa Sanctuary, San Pablo. l, Festival of Whites and Blacks, horiz.

No. 1225, 2000p — Tolima Department: a, Nevado del Tolima, horiz. b, Tolima arms. c, Ambalema, horiz. d, Bowls, La Chamba, horiz. e, Natural Bridge, Icononzo. f, Hermitage, Mariquita, horiz. g, Matachos, horiz. h, Prison, Ibagué. i, Alberto Castilla Conservatory Room, horiz. j, Fishermen, Magdalena River, horiz. k, Cacique Calarcá. l, Tolima Art Museum, Ibagué.

No. 1226, 3000p — Chocó Department: a, Coat of Arms. b, Quibdó skyline, horiz. c, Indian girls. d, San Pacho Fiesta. e, Carrasquilla College, Quibdó, horiz. f, Houses, Nóvita. g, Canoe on San Juan River. h, Women grinding corn meal, horiz. i, Nuestra Senora del Rosario Church, Condoto. j, Utría Bay. k, Bellavista Church, Bojayá, horiz. l, Goldsmith, Acandí.

Horiz. stamps are 46x37mm.

2004 **Litho.** ***Perf. 13¾x14***

Sheets of 12, #a-l, +8 labels

1224 A608 Nariño 10.50 10.50
1225 A608 Tolima 18.00 18.00
1226 A608 Chocó 30.00 30.00
Nos. 1224-1226 (3) 58.50 58.50

Issued: No. 1224, 8/5; No. 1225, 4/16. No. 1226, 11/17

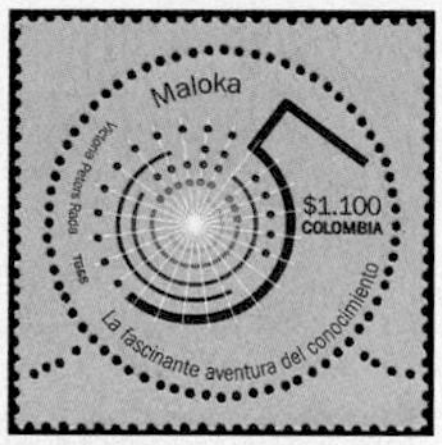

Maloka Science and Technology Center A621

2004, June 6 **Litho.** ***Perf. 12¾***
1227 A621 1100p multi .80 .80

Values are for stamps with surrounding selvage.

2004 Summer Olympics, Athens — A622

2004, Aug. 5 ***Perf. 13¾x14***
1228 A622 4400p multi 3.50 3.50

Natl. Association of Contractors, 60th Anniv. A623

No. 1229: a, Denomination in white. b, Denomination in black.

2004, Aug. 5 ***Perf. 14x13¾***
1229 Pair 4.50 4.50
a.-b. A623 2800p Either single 2.25 2.25

Printed in sheets containing 6 pairs and one large central label.

FIFA (Fédération Internationale de Football Association), Cent. — A624

2004, Aug. 25 ***Perf. 13¼x14***
1230 A624 3500p multi 2.75 2.75

Women's Citizenship, 50th Anniv. — A625

2004, Sept. 24 ***Perf. 14***
1231 A625 15,000p multi 12.00 12.00

Fair and Expositions Corporation, 50th Anniv. — A626

2004, Oct. 14 ***Perf. 13½x13***
1232 A626 1300p multi 1.10 1.10

Colombian Radio Announcers Association, 50th Anniv. — A627

2004, Oct. 21 ***Perf. 14***
1233 A627 1700p multi 1.50 1.50

17th National Games — A628

Illustration reduced.

2004, Dec. 10 **Litho.** ***Perf. 12¾***
1234 A628 7000p multi + label 5.75 5.75

Printed in sheets of 4 + 5 labels.

America Issue — Environmental Conservation — A629

Designs: No. 1235, 5000p, Whale, Gorgona National Nature Park. No. 1236, 5000p, Hammerhead sharks, Malpelo Flora and Fauna Sanctuary.

2004, Dec. 14 ***Perf. 14***
1235-1236 A629 Set of 2 8.50 8.50

Miniature Sheet

Christmas — A630

No. 1237 — Inscriptions: a, Jesús en la mansion de su padre. b, Eterna sumision a Dios. c, Jesús desciende al seno de su madre. d, Aceptacion de milagro divino. e, La ilusion de Maria. f, Voluntad divina en manos del emperador. g, Paciencia, expectativa y anhelo. h, Belén: Humilde hospedaje. i, Nacimiento, la faz de Dios encarnado.

2004, Dec. 15
1237 A630 2800p Sheet of 9, #a-i 22.00 22.00

Pre-Columbian Gold Artifacts From Gold Museum — A631

No. 1238, 1200p: a, Tumaco ear covering. b, Zenú nose ring.
No. 1239, 1800p: a, Cauma nose ring. b, Tierradentro bracelet.
Illustration reduced.

2005 ***Perf. 12x12½***
Pairs, #a-b
1238-1239 A631 Set of 2 5.25 5.25

Issued: No. 1238, 1/21; No. 1239, 3/28.

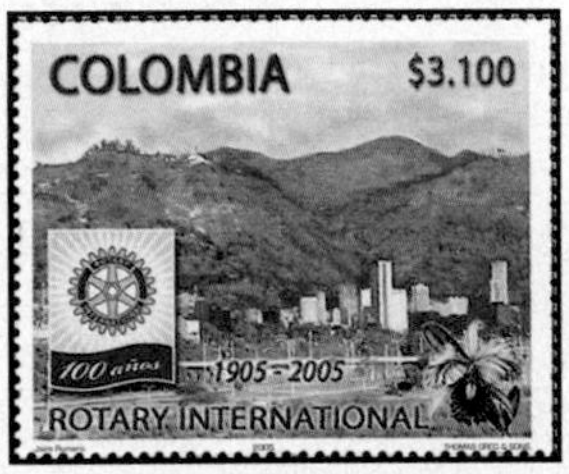

Rotary International, Cent. — A632

2005, Feb. 23 ***Perf. 13½x14***
1240 A632 3100p multi 2.75 2.75

Souvenir Sheet

Butterflies — A633

No. 1241: a, Protographium tyastes panamensis. b, Dismorphia zaela laura. c, Actinote ozomene.

2005 **Litho.** ***Perf. 14¼***
1241 A633 4600p Sheet of 3, #a-c 12.50 12.50

FENALCO (Natl. Federation of Retailers), 60th Anniv. A634

2005 ***Perf. 14***
1242 A634 1200p multi 1.10 1.10

Souvenir Sheets

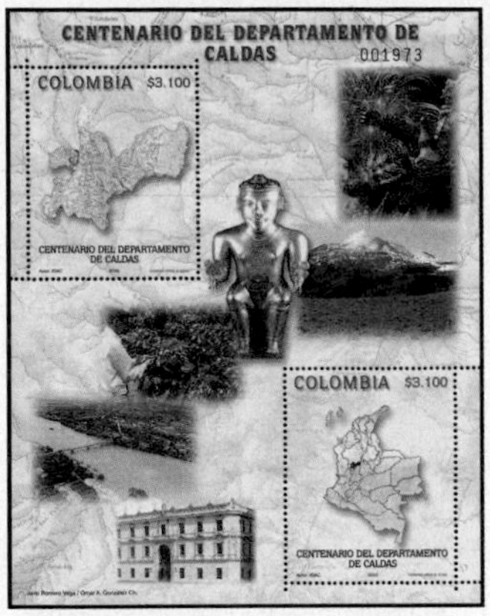

Department Centenaries — A635

No. 1243, 3100p: a, Map of Caldas Department. b, Map of Colombia highlighting Caldas.
No. 1244, 3700p: a, Map of Huila Department. b, Map of Colombia highlighting Huila.
No. 1245, 4200p: a, Map of Atlantico Department. b, Map of Colombia highlighting Atlantico.

2005 ***Perf. 14x13½***
Sheets of 2, #a-b
1243-1245 A635 Set of 3 19.50 19.50

Departments Type of 2003

No. 1246 — San Andrés y Providencia Department: a, Aerial view of San Andrés, horiz. b, Arms. c, Aerial view of Johnny Cay, horiz. d, Cayo Cangrejo, horiz. e, Artisan. f, Culture House, San Andrés, horiz. g, Morgan Head, Santa Catalina Island, horiz. h, Island view. i, Ensenada, San Andrés, horiz. j, Island architecture, horiz. k, Baptist Church, San Andrés. l, Aerial view of Providencia and Santa Catalina Islands.
Horiz. stamps are 46x37mm.

2005 ***Perf. 13¾x14***
1246 A608 1200p Sheet of 12, #a-l 13.00 13.00

Bogota Botanical Gardens — A636

2005 ***Perf. 14***
1247 A636 1400p multi 1.25 1.25

15th Bolivarian Games — A637

2005 ***Perf. 13¾x14***
1248 A637 3500p multi 3.25 3.25

Association of Graduates of the University of the Andes, 50th Anniv. A638

2005 ***Perf. 14***
1249 A638 2000p multi 1.75 1.75

Intl. Day of Ozone Layer Protection A639

2005
1250 A639 2000p multi 1.75 1.75

Souvenir Sheet

Publication of Don Quixote, 400th Anniv. — A640

No. 1251 — Paintings of Miguel de Cervantes by: a, Ricardo Rendón Bravo. b, Eduardo Ramírez Villamizar, vert. c, Santiago Martínez Delgado, vert.

Perf. 13½x14 (#1251a), 14x13½
2005
1251 A640 1300p Sheet of 3, #a-c 3.50 3.50

Colpatria Bank, 50th Anniv. A641

2005 ***Perf. 14x13½***
1252 A641 1200p multi 1.10 1.10

Arms of City of Facatativá A642

2005 **Litho.** ***Perf. 14***
1253 A642 1800p multi 1.75 1.75

Latin Union, 50th Anniv. — A643

2005 ***Perf. 13½x14***
1254 A643 5000p multi 4.75 4.75

Printed in sheets of 4.

Souvenir Sheet

America Issue, Fight Against Poverty — A644

2005 ***Perf. 14x13½***
1255 A644 Sheet of 2 #1255a 9.50 9.50
a. 5000p Single stamp 4.75 4.75

Souvenir Sheet

Escuela de Lanceros (Military School), 50th Anniv. — A645

2005 ***Perf. 14***
1256 A645 Sheet of 2 #1256a 19.00 19.00
a. 10,000p Single stamp 9.50 9.50

Christmas A646

2005 ***Perf. 14***
1257 A646 3100p multi 3.00 3.00

Printed in sheets of 7.

Colombian Journalism A647

2006 **Litho.**
1258 A647 2000p multi 1.90 1.90

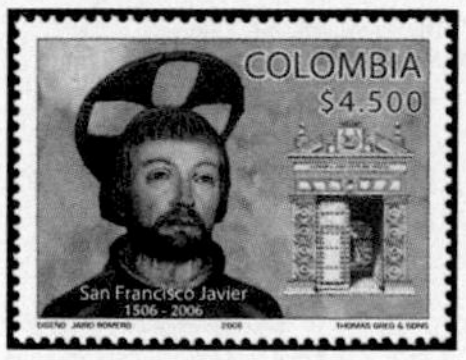

St. Francis Xavier (1506-52) A648

2006

1259 A648 4500p multi 3.75 3.75

Pope John Paul II (1920-2005) A649

2006

1260 A649 4800p multi 3.75 3.75

Souvenir Sheet

Frederic Chopin (1810-49), Composer A650

2006 ***Perf. 13½x13***

1261 A650 5300p multi 4.25 4.25

Printed in sheets of 4.

Gold Artifacts Type of 2005

No. 1262: a, Quimbaya striated lime receptacle with handles. b, Quimbaya thin lime receptacle.

2006 ***Perf. 12x12½***

1262 A631 1500p Horiz. pair, #a-b 2.50 2.50

Italian Cultural Institute of Bogota, 50th Anniv. — A651

No. 1263: a, Lute at lower left. b, Violin at lower right.

Illustration reduced.

2006 ***Perf. 14***

1263 A651 1300p Horiz. pair, #a-b 2.25 2.25

Souvenir Sheet

Rayo Museum, 25th Anniv. — A652

No. 1264: a, Artwork in blue, white, red, yellow and black. b, Artwork in white, blue, tan and black.

2006 ***Perf. 13½x13***

1264 A652 Sheet, 2 each #a-b 4.50 4.50

a.-b. 1300p Either single 1.10 1.10

Departments Type of 2003

No. 1265 — Valle del Cauca Department: a, Mapping Commission drawing of Cali, horiz. b, Arms of Valle del Cauca. c, Arms and panoramic view of Sevilla, horiz. d, Calima Lake, El Darién, horiz. e, La Ermita, Santiago de Cali. f, Port of Buenaventura, horiz. g, Railroad station, Palmira, horiz. h, Sugar cane. i, Salsa dancers, Cali, horiz. j, El Paraiso Museum, El Cerrito, horiz. k, Basilica, Buga. l, Aerial view of Valle del Cauca, horiz.

No. 1266 — Boyacá Department: a, Plaza de Bolivar, Tunja, horiz. b, Arms of Boyacá. c, Mapping Commission drawing of Campo de Boyacá, horiz. d, Bolivar Monument, Campo de Boyacá, horiz. e, Altar of the Virgin of Chiquinquirá. f, Panoramic view of Garagoa, horiz. g, Plaza de los Libertadores, Duitama, horiz. h, Emeralds. i, Plaza Mayor, Villa de Leyva, horiz. j, Sierra Nevada del Cocuy, horiz. k, Temple of the Sun, Sogamoso. l, El Salitre Farm, Paipa, horiz.

No. 1267 — Quindío Department: a, Quindío Pass, 1836, horiz. b, Quimbaya culture sculpture. c, Coffee plantation house, Quimbaya, horiz. d, Coffee bean picker, Pijao, horiz. e, Valle de Cocora, Salento. f, Botanical Gardens, Calarca, horiz. g, La Estación Metropolitan Cultural Center, Armenia, horiz. h, Monument and government building, Armenia. i, Free Cemetery, Circasia, horiz. j, Aerial view of Buenavista, horiz. k, San José Temple, Génova. l, Founding of Armenia, horiz.

Horizontal stamps are 46x37mm.

2006 ***Perf. 13½x14***

Sheets of 12, #a-l, + 8 labels

1265 A608 1300p Valle del Cauca 13.00 13.00

1266 A608 2000p Boyacá 20.00 20.00

1267 A608 3300p Quindío 32.50 32.50

Nos. 1265-1267 (3) 65.50 65.50

20th Central American and Caribbean Games A653

2006 **Litho.** ***Perf. 14***

1268 A653 2000p multi 1.75 1.75

Pres. Alberto Lleras Camargo (1906-90) — A654

Denominations: a, 1300p. b, 3300p.

Illustration reduced.

2006 **Litho.** ***Perf. 14x13¾***

1269 A654 Horiz. pair, #a-b + alternating labels 4.25 4.25

Souvenir Sheet

America Issue, Energy Conservation — A655

No. 1270: a, Left hand. b, Right hand.

2006 ***Perf. 12***

1270 A655 5000p Sheet of 2, #a-b 9.00 9.00

Christmas — A656

Denominations: a, 1300p. b, 3300p.

2006, Dec. 13 ***Perf. 13¾x14***

1271 A656 Vert. pair, #a-b 4.25 4.25

General José Maria Cordova Military School, Cent. — A657

2007, May 30 ***Perf. 14***

1272 A657 10,000p multi 11.00 11.00

Departments Type of 2003

No. 1273 — Sucre Department: a, Coat of arms. b, St. Francis of Assisi Cathedral, Sincelejo, horiz. c, Palm trees, Tolú. d, Cattle, Sucre. e, Bull ring, Sincelejo, horiz. f, Church, Corozal. g, Musical score of "Fiesta en Corraleja." h, Painting of fandango dancers, horiz. i, Fisherman, Caimito. j, Palm trees, Sincelejo. k, Cane weaver, Sampués, horiz. l, Hammocks, Morroa.

Horizontal stamps are 46x37mm.

2007, May 30 ***Perf. 12***

Sheet of 12, #a-l, + 8 Labels

1273 A608 3300p Sucre 42.50 42.50

Miniature Sheet

Scouting, Cent. — A658

No. 1274: a, International and Colombian Scouting emblems, Scouts with Lord Robert Baden-Powell. b, Emblem of 21st World Scout Jamboree, Colombian Scouting emblem, children's drawing of Colombian scout. c, Scouting emblem, Lord Robert Baden-Powell. d, International and Colombian Scouting emblems, animal track.

2007, June 26 ***Perf. 14***

1274 A658 1500p Sheet of 8, 2 each #a-d, + central label 12.50 12.50

Souvenir Sheet

El Espectador Newspaper, 120th Anniv. — A659

No. 1275: a, Newspaper from 1887. b, Paperboy, horiz.

2007, June 28 ***Perf. 12***

1275 A659 4500p Sheet of 2, #a-b 9.25 9.25

Pan American Games, Rio de Janeiro — A660

2007, July 9 ***Perf. 14***

1276 A660 3700p multi 3.75 3.75

Fourth Spanish Language Intl. Congress — A661

2007, June 25

1277 A661 5300p multi + label 5.25 5.25

Caja de Compensación Familiar, 50th Anniv. — A662

2007, Oct. 10 **Litho.** ***Perf. 14***

1278 A662 3500p multi 3.75 3.75

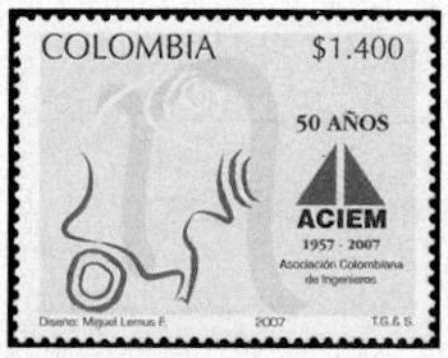

Colombian Association of Engineers, 50th Anniv. A663

2007, Oct. 17

1279 A663 1400p multi 1.40 1.40

Bogota Honors and Awards — A664

No. 1280: a, 2007 UNESCO World Book Capital. b, Venice Biennale Golden Lion Award

for Architecture. c, 2007 Latin American Cultural Capital.
Illustration reduced.

2007, Oct. 23
1280 A664 3700p Horiz. strip of 3, #a-c 11.00 11.00

Minuto de Dios, 50th Anniv. A665

2007, Nov. 22
1281 A665 1600p multi 1.60 1.60

Christmas A666

2007, Nov. 27
1282 A666 3300p multi 3.25 3.25

America Issue, Education For All — A667

2007, Dec. 13
1283 A667 3500p multi 3.50 3.50

SEMI-POSTAL STAMP

Catalogue values for unused stamps in this section are for Never Hinged items.

Girl Giving First Aid — SP1

Perf. 13½x14
1966, Apr. 26 Litho. Unwmk.
B1 SP1 5c + 5c multicolored .25 .20

Issued for the Red Cross.

AIR POST STAMPS

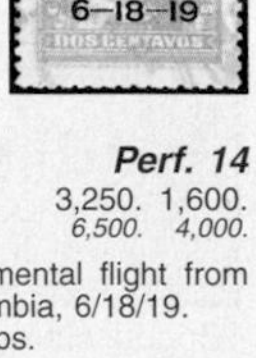

No. 341 Overprinted

1919 Unwmk. *Perf. 14*
C1 A107 2c car rose 3,250. 1,600.
a. Numerals "1" with serifs *6,500. 4,000.*

Used for the first experimental flight from Barranquilla to Puerto Colombia, 6/18/19.
Values are for faulty stamps.

Issued by Compania Colombiana de Navegacion Aerea

From 1920 to 1932 the internal airmail service of Colombia was handled by the Compania Colombiana de Navegacion Aerea (1920) and the Sociedad Colombo-Alemana de Transportes Aéreos, known familiarly as "SCADTA" (1920-1932).

These organizations, under government contracts, operated and maintained their own post offices and issued stamps which were the only legal franking for airmail service during this period, both in the internal and international mails. All letters had to bear government stamps as well.

Woman and Boy Watching Plane — AP1

Designs: No. C3, Clouds and small biplane at top. No. C4, Tilted plane viewed close-up from above. No. C5, Flier in plane watching biplane. No. C6, Lighthouse. No. C7, Fuselage and tail of biplane. No. C8, Condor on cliff. No. C9, Plane at rest; pilot foreground. No. C10, Ocean liner.

1920, Feb. Unwmk. Litho. *Imperf.*
Without Gum

C2	AP1	10c	multicolored	2,750.	1,750.
C3	AP1	10c	multicolored	3,500.	1,750.
C4	AP1	10c	multicolored	4,250.	1,750.
C5	AP1	10c	multicolored	3,250.	1,750.
C6	AP1	10c	multicolored	2,750.	1,750.
C7	AP1	10c	multicolored	10,000.	3,500.
C8	AP1	10c	multicolored	5,500.	2,750.
C9	AP1	10c	multicolored	3,250.	1,750.
C10	AP1	10c	multicolored	4,250.	2,500.

Nos. C2-C10 were overprinted on the nine lighter-colored varieties of a set of 18 publicity labels produced by the Curtis Co. for inclusion with packs of cigarettes. These labels were printed se-tenant, in panes of 18 (3x6). Value for the set of 18 values without overprint: $4,000.

Flier in Plane Watching Biplane — AP2

1920, Mar.
C11 AP2 10c green 50.00 *85.00*

Four other 10c stamps, similar to No. C11, have two designs showing plane, mountains and water. They are printed in deep green or light brown red. Some authorities state that these four were not used regularly.

Issued by Sociedad Colombo-Alemana de Transportes Aereos (SCADTA)

Seaplane over Magdalena River — AP3

1920-21 Litho. *Perf. 12*

C12	AP3	10c yellow ('21)	35.00	30.00
C13	AP3	15c blue ('21)	40.00	32.50
C14	AP3	30c blk, *rose*	22.50	13.00
C15	AP3	30c rose ('21)	35.00	27.50
C16	AP3	50c pale green	35.00	30.00
		Nos. C12-C16 (5)	167.50	133.00

For surcharges see Nos. C17-C24, C36-C37.

No. C16 Handstamp Surcharged in Violet or Black:

(Illustrations of types "a" to "e" are reduced in size.)

VALOR 10 CENTAVOS
a

VALOR 10 CENTAVOS
b

Valor 10 Céntavos
c

d

30¢ 30¢
e

f

$030¢
g

1921

C17	AP3 (a)	10c on 50c	900.	850.
C18	AP3 (b)	10c on 50c	900.	850.
C19	AP3 (c)	10c on 50c	900.	850.
C20	AP3 (b)	30c on 50c	700.	600.
C21	AP3 (d)	30c on 50c	700.	600.
C22	AP3 (e)	30c on 50c	1,100.	1,100.
C23	AP3 (f)	30c on 50c	1,300.	1,100.
C24	AP3 (g)	30c on 50c	1,300.	1,100.

Plane over Magdalena River — AP4

Plane over Bogota Cathedral AP5

1921 *Perf. 11½*

C25	AP4	5c orange yellow	3.00	3.00
C26	AP4	10c slate green	1.25	1.00
C27	AP4	15c orange brown	1.25	1.10
C28	AP4	20c red brown	3.00	1.40
a.		Horiz. pair, imperf. vert.	*140.00*	
C29	AP4	30c green	1.40	.70
C30	AP4	50c blue	2.40	.75
C31	AP4	60c vermilion	50.00	22.50
C32	AP5	1p gray black	14.00	3.75
C33	AP5	2p rose	26.00	14.00
C34	AP5	3p violet	80.00	52.50
C35	AP5	5p olive green	225.00	210.00
		Nos. C25-C35 (11)	407.30	310.70

Nos. C25-C35 exist imperf.
For surcharge see No. C52.

Nos. C16 and C12 Handstamp Surcharged

Illustration of type "h" is reduced in size.

VALOR 20 Ctvs.
h

30 cent.
i

1921-22 *Perf. 12*

C36	AP3 (h)	20c on 50c	2,250.	1,700.
C37	AP3 (i)	30c on 10c	575.	—

Seaplane over Magdalena River — AP6

Plane over Bogota Cathedral AP7

1923-28 Wmk. 116 *Perf. 14x14½*

C38	AP6	5c orange yellow	1.00	.20
C39	AP6	10c green	1.00	.20
C40	AP6	15c carmine	1.00	.20
C41	AP6	20c gray	1.00	.20
C42	AP6	30c blue	1.00	.20
C43	AP6	40c purple ('28)	8.00	5.50
C44	AP6	50c green	1.25	.20
C45	AP6	60c brown	2.10	.20
C46	AP6	80c olive grn ('28)	21.00	20.00
C47	AP7	1p black	9.00	2.00
C48	AP7	2p red orange	13.00	4.00
C49	AP7	3p violet	27.50	17.50
C50	AP7	5p olive green	45.00	24.00
		Nos. C38-C50 (13)	131.85	74.40

For surcharges and overprints see Nos. C51, C53-C54, CF1.

Nos. C41 and C31 Surcharged in Carmine and Dark Blue:

No. C51

No. C52

1923

C51	AP6	30c on 20c gray (C)	60.00	40.00
C52	AP4	30c on 60c ver	52.50	27.50

Nos. C41-C42 Overprinted in Black

1928 Wmk. 116 *Perf. 14x14½*

C53	AP6	20c gray	42.50	40.00
C54	AP6	30c blue	42.50	40.00

Goodwill flight of Lt. Benjamin Mendez from New York to Bogota.

Magdalena River and Tolima Volcano AP8

Columbus' Ship and Plane AP9

1929, June 1 Wmk. 127 *Perf. 14*

C55	AP8	5c yellow org	.65	.20
C56	AP8	10c red brown	.65	.20
C57	AP8	15c deep green	.65	.20
C58	AP8	20c carmine	.65	.20
C59	AP8	30c gray blue	.65	.20
C60	AP8	40c dull violet	.65	.25
C61	AP8	50c dk olive grn	1.25	.25

C62 AP8 60c orange brown 2.10 .25
C63 AP8 80c green 5.50 2.25
C64 AP9 1p blue 6.50 1.75
C65 AP9 2p brown orange 9.75 4.25
C66 AP9 3p pale rose vio 24.00 14.00
C67 AP9 5p olive green 60.00 26.00
Nos. C55-C67 (13) 113.00 50.00

For surcharges and overprints see Nos. C80-C95, CF2, CF4.

For International Airmail

AP10

AP11

1929, June 1 Wmk. 127 *Perf. 14*
C68 AP10 5c yellow org 3.50 *4.25*
C69 AP10 10c red brown .65 *1.75*
C70 AP10 15c deep green .65 *1.75*
C71 AP10 20c carmine .65 *2.10*
C72 AP10 25c violet blue .65 .35
C73 AP10 30c gray blue .65 .55
C74 AP10 50c dk olive grn .65 *1.00*
C75 AP10 60c brown 1.50 *1.75*
C76 AP11 1p blue 3.00 *4.25*
C77 AP11 2p red orange 4.50 *5.75*
C78 AP11 3p violet 60.00 60.00
C79 AP11 5p olive green 80.00 *90.00*
Nos. C68-79 (12) 156.40 *173.50*

This issue was sold abroad for use on correspondence to be flown from coastal to interior points of Colombia. Cancellations are those of the country of origin rather than Colombia.
For overprint see No. CF3.

Nos. C63, C66 and C64 Surcharged in Black:

m

n

1930, Dec. 15
C80 AP8(m) 10c on 80c 4.25 4.25
C81 AP9(n) 20c on 3p 8.25 *9.00*
C82 AP9(n) 30c on 1p 10.00 9.00
Nos. C80-C82 (3) 22.50 *22.25*

Simon Bolivar (1783-1830).

Colombian Government Issues
Nos. C55-C67 Overprinted in Black:

o

p

Wmk. 127
1932, Jan. 1 Typo. *Perf. 14*
C83 AP8(o) 5c yellow org 8.00 8.00
C84 AP8(o) 10c red brown 1.75 .50
C85 AP8(o) 15c deep green 3.00 3.00
C86 AP8(o) 20c carmine 1.50 .30
C87 AP8(o) 30c gray blue 1.50 .50
C88 AP8(o) 40c dull violet 2.00 1.00
C89 AP8(o) 50c dk ol grn 4.00 3.00
C90 AP8(o) 60c orange brn 3.25 3.00
C91 AP8(o) 80c green 14.00 14.00
C92 AP9(p) 1p blue 11.00 9.00
C93 AP9(p) 2p brown org 30.00 27.50
C94 AP9(p) 3p pale rose vio 60.00 52.50
C95 AP9(p) 5p olive green 100.00 *110.00*
Nos. C83-C95 (13) 240.00 232.30

Coffee
AP12

Gold
AP16

Designs: 10c, 50c, Cattle. 15c, 60c, Petroleum. 20c, 40c, Bananas. 3p, 5p, Emerald.

1932-39 Wmk. 127 Photo. *Perf. 14*
C96 AP12 5c org & blk brn .90 .25
C97 AP12 10c lake & blk 1.00 .20
C98 AP12 15c bl grn & vio blk .45 .20
C99 AP12 15c ver & vio blk ('39) 2.50 .20
C100 AP12 20c car & ol blk .70 .20
C101 AP12 20c turq grn & ol blk ('39) 3.50 .30
C102 AP12 30c dk bl & blk brn 1.60 .20
C103 AP12 40c dk vio & ol bis .85 .20
C104 AP12 50c dk grn & brnsh blk 3.50 1.25
C105 AP12 60c dk brn & blk vio 1.00 .25
C106 AP12 80c grn & blk brn 5.50 2.00
C107 AP16 1p dk bl & ol bis 9.00 1.25
C108 AP16 2p org brn & ol bis 10.00 2.25
C109 AP16 3p dk vio & emer 17.00 6.25
C110 AP16 5p gray blk & emer 47.50 20.00
Nos. C96-C110 (15) 105.00 35.00

For overprint see No. CF5.

Nos. C104, C106-C108 Surcharged:

a

b

1934, Jan. 5
C111 AP12(a) 10c on 50c 3.50 3.50
C112 AP12(a) 15c on 80c 4.75 4.75
C113 AP16(b) 20c on 1p 5.25 5.25
C114 AP16(b) 30c on 2p 5.75 5.75
Nos. C111-C114 (4) 19.25 19.25

400th anniversary of Cartagena.

Nos. C100 and C103 Surcharged in Black or Carmine:

1939, Jan. 15
C115 AP12 5c on 20c (Bk) .35 .35
C116 AP12 5c on 40c (C) .35 .25
C117 AP12 15c on 20c (Bk) 1.50 .50
a. Double surcharge 12.00
b. Pair, one with dbl. surch. 14.00
c. Inverted surcharge 12.00 12.00

No. CF5 Surcharged in Black
C118 AP12 5c on 20c .70 .70
Nos. C115-C118 (4) 2.90 1.80

Nos. C102-C103 Surcharged in Black or Red

1940, Oct. 20
C119 AP12 15c on 30c 1.25 .50
a. Inverted surcharge 12.00
C120 AP12 15c on 40c (R) 2.00 .75
a. Double surcharge 12.00

Pre-Columbian Monument — AP18

Proclamation of Independence — AP22

Designs: 10c, 40c, Symbol of Legend of El Dorado. 15c, 50c, Spanish Fortifications, Cartagena. 20c, 60c, Colonial Bogotá. 2p, 5p, National Library, Bogota.

Unwmk.
1941, Jan. 28 Engr. *Perf. 12*
C121 AP18 5c gray black .20 .20
C122 AP18 10c yellow org .20 .20
C123 AP18 15c carmine rose .20 .20
C124 AP18 20c yellow grn .35 .20
a. Horiz. pair, imperf. vert. 87.50
C125 AP18 30c deep blue .35 .20
C126 AP18 40c rose lake .70 .20
C127 AP18 50c turq green .70 .20
C128 AP18 60c sepia .70 .20
C129 AP18 80c olive blk 1.90 .40
C130 AP22 1p blue & blk 3.25 .50
C131 AP22 2p red org & blk 5.25 2.00
C132 AP22 3p violet & blk 14.00 5.00
C133 AP22 5p lt green & blk 27.50 17.50
Nos. C121-C133 (13) 55.30 27.00

See Nos. C151-C163, C217-C225. For overprints see Nos. C175-C198, C200-C216, C226, C290.

San Sebastian Fort, Cartagena — AP24

National Capitol, Bogotá
AP27

Designs: 5c, 20c, 50c, San Sebastian Fort, Cartagena. 10c, 30c, 60c, Tequendama Waterfall. 15c, 40c, 80c, Bay of Santa Maria.

Unwmk.
1945, Nov. 3 Litho. *Perf. 11*
C134 AP24 5c blue gray .20 .20
C135 AP24 10c yellow org .20 .20
C136 AP24 15c rose .20 .20
C137 AP24 20c lt yel grn .30 .20
C138 AP24 30c ultra .30 .20
C139 AP24 40c claret .50 .20
C140 AP24 50c bluish grn .55 .20
C141 AP24 60c lt vio brn 2.25 .80
C142 AP24 80c dk slate grn 3.50 .80
C143 AP27 1p dk blue 5.00 .75
C144 AP27 2p red orange 7.00 2.50
Nos. C134-C144 (11) 20.00 6.25

Part-perforate varieties exist for all denominations except 80c.

Imperf., Pairs
C134a AP24 5c 8.50
C135a AP24 10c 8.50
C136a AP24 15c 8.50
C137a AP24 20c 8.50
C138a AP24 30c 8.50
C139a AP24 40c 8.50
C140a AP24 50c 8.50
C141a AP24 60c 8.50
C142a AP24 80c 10.50
C143a AP27 1p 17.50
C144a AP27 2p 60.00

Bello Type of Regular Issue, 1946
Wmk. 255
1946, Sept. 3 Engr. *Perf. 12*
C145 A219 5c deep blue .20 .20

Francisco José de Caldas
AP29

Manuel del Socorro Rodriguez
AP30

Perf. 12½
1947, May 9 Litho. Unwmk.
C146 AP29 5c dp bl, *grnsh* .35 .20
C147 AP30 10c red org, *grnsh* .50 .45

4th Pan-American Press Congress (1946).

Chancellery Patio — AP31

Capitol, Patio Rafael Nunez
AP32

AP33

1948, Apr. 2 Engr. Wmk. 229
C148 AP31 5c dark brown .20 .20
C149 AP32 15c deep blue .90 .90

Miniature Sheet
Imperf
C150 AP33 50c brown 1.90 1.90

9th Pan-American Conference, Bogotá.

Types of 1941
1948, July 21 Unwmk. *Perf. 12*
C151 AP18 5c orange yel .20 .20
C152 AP18 10c scarlet .20 .20
C153 AP18 15c deep blue .20 .20
C154 AP18 20c violet .20 .20
C155 AP18 30c yellow grn .35 .20
C156 AP18 40c gray .40 .20
C157 AP18 50c rose lake .40 .20
C158 AP18 60c olive gray .70 .20
C159 AP18 80c red brn .85 .20
C160 AP22 1p ol grn & vio brn 1.50 .30
C161 AP22 2p dp grn & brt bl 2.50 .65
C162 AP22 3p rose car & blk 5.50 3.75
C163 AP22 5p lt brn & turq grn 14.00 7.00
Nos. C151-C163 (13) 27.00 13.50

"Air Week" 5c Blue

The War and Air Department issued a 5c blue stamp in May, 1949, to publicize Air Week (Semana de Aviacion). This stamp had no franking value and its use was optional during May 16-23.

Justice and Liberty AP34

Wing AP35

Design: 10c, Liberty holding tablet of laws.

1949, Oct. 7 Unwmk. *Perf. 13*

C164	AP34	5c blue green	.20	.20
C165	AP34	10c orange	.20	.20

Issued to honor the new Constitution.

For Domestic Postage

1950, June 22 Litho. *Perf. 12*

C166	AP35	5c orange yellow	.25	.25
C167	AP35	10c brown red	.35	.30
C168	AP35	15c lt blue	.40	.30
C169	AP35	20c lt green	.60	*.65*
C170	AP35	30c lilac gray	1.50	*2.00*
C171	AP35	60c chocolate	1.90	*2.50*

With Network as in Parenthesis

C172	AP35	1p gray (buff)	14.00	*16.00*
C173	AP35	2p bl (pale grn)	14.00	*16.00*
C174	AP35	5p red brn (red brn)	40.00	*45.00*
		Nos. C166-C174 (9)	73.00	*83.00*

No. C172 was issued both with and without network.

Nos. C151-C157 and C160-C163 Overprinted in Black

1950, July 18

C175	AP18	5c orange yel	.20	.20
C176	AP18	10c scarlet	.20	.20
C177	AP18	15c deep blue	.20	.20
C178	AP18	20c violet	.20	.20
C179	AP18	30c yellow green	.30	.20
C180	AP18	40c gray	.80	.25
C181	AP18	50c rose lake	.40	.25
C182	AP22	1p ol grn & vio brn	2.50	2.25
C183	AP22	2p dp grn & brt bl	3.75	3.25
C184	AP22	3p rose car & blk	11.00	11.00
C185	AP22	5p lt brn & turq grn	24.00	24.00
		Nos. C175-C185 (11)	43.55	42.00

Nos. C151-C163 Overprinted in Black

1950, July 12

C186	AP18	5c orange yel	.20	.20
C187	AP18	10c scarlet	.20	.20
C188	AP18	15c deep blue	.20	.20
C189	AP18	20c violet	.20	.20
C190	AP18	30c yellow green	.20	.20
C191	AP18	40c gray	.40	.20
C192	AP18	50c rose lake	.40	.20
C193	AP18	60c olive gray	.70	.20
C194	AP18	80c red brown	1.00	.40
C195	AP22	1p ol grn & vio brn	1.10	.50
C196	AP22	2p dp grn & brt bl	3.00	1.40
C197	AP22	3p rose car & blk	7.25	6.50
C198	AP22	5p lt brn & turq grn	16.00	14.00
		Nos. C186-C198 (13)	30.85	24.40

On Nos. C175-C198, "L" stands for LANSA, "A" for AVIANCA.

UPU Type
Miniature Sheet
Unwmk.

1950, Aug. 22 Photo. *Imperf.*

C199	A245	50c gray	1.00	1.00

75th anniv. (in 1949) of the UPU.

Catalogue values for unused stamps in this section, from this point to the end of the section, are for Never Hinged items.

Types of 1941 Overprinted at Lower Right in Black

Unwmk.

1951, Sept. 15 Engr. *Perf. 12*

C200	AP18	40c orange yel	1.50	1.25
C201	AP18	50c ultra	1.50	1.25
C202	AP18	60c gray	1.50	1.25
C203	AP18	80c car rose	1.10	.95
C204	AP22	1p red org & red brn	3.75	3.00
C205	AP22	2p rose car & bl	4.00	3.00
C206	AP22	3p choc & emer	10.00	8.00
C207	AP22	5p org & gray	30.00	30.00
		Nos. C200-C207 (8)	53.35	48.70

Types of 1941 Overprinted at Lower Right in Black

1951-54

C208	AP18	40c orange yel	3.25	.55
C209	AP18	50c ultra	4.00	.60
C210	AP18	60c gray	3.00	.45
a.		Overprint centered	2.00	.50
C211	AP18	80c car rose	.85	.30
C212	AP22	1p red org & red brn	3.25	.50
C213	AP22	1p ol grn & vio brn ('54)	4.00	.75
C214	AP22	2p rose car & bl	3.25	.55
C215	AP22	3p choc & emer	5.00	1.40
C216	AP22	5p org & gray	10.00	1.90
		Nos. C208-C216 (9)	36.60	7.00

All values except the 2p and 3p exist without overprint.

Types of 1941

1952, May 10 Engr.

C217	AP18	5c ultra	.45	.20
C218	AP18	10c ultra	.45	.20
C219	AP18	15c ultra	.45	.20
C220	AP18	20c ultra	.90	.25
C221	AP18	30c ultra	2.25	.55

Color Change

C222	AP18	5c car rose	.45	.20
C223	AP18	10c car rose	.45	.20
C224	AP18	20c car rose	.85	.20
C225	AP18	30c car rose	1.75	.30
		Nos. C217-C225 (9)	8.00	2.30

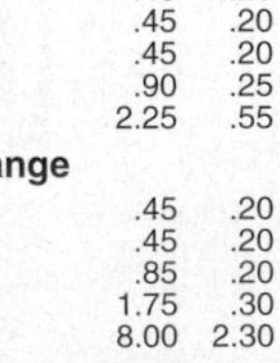

Type of 1941 Surcharged in Blue

1952, Oct. 30

C226	AP18	70c on 80c car rose	1.50	.70

Latin American Siderurgical Conf., 1952.

Type of Postal Tax Stamps, 1948-50, Nos. 602 and 604 Surcharged or Overprinted in Black

1953 Wmk. 255 *Perf. 12*

C227	PT10	5c on 8c blue	.20	.20
C228	PT10	15c on 20c brown	.25	.20
C229	PT10	15c on 25c bl grn	1.00	.20
C230	PT10	25c blue green	.55	.20
		Nos. C227-C230 (4)	2.00	.80

Many varieties of overprint or surcharge exist on Nos. C227-C231.

No. 570 Overprinted "AEREO" in Blue

1953, Aug. Wmk. 229 *Perf. 12½*

C231	A160	10c red	.25	.20

"Extra Rapido"

Stamps inscribed "Extra Rapido" are for use on domestic airmail carried by airlines other than AVIANCA.

No. 585 Surcharged and Overprinted "Extra Rapido" in Dark Blue

1953 Unwmk. *Perf. 13*

C232	A244	5c on 11c red	.50	.35

Capitol and Arms — AP37

Revenue Stamps Overprinted "Correo Extra-Rapido"
Gray Security Paper

1953 Wmk. 255 Engr. *Perf. 12*

C233	AP37	1c on 2c green	.25	.20
C234	AP37	50c red orange	.25	.20

AP38

Real Estate Tax Stamps Ovptd. "Correo Extra-Rapido" in Black or Carmine

1953

C235	AP38	5c red orange	.25	.20
C236	AP38	20c brown (C)	.30	.20

On 20c, overprint is at bottom of stamp and two lines of ornaments cover real estate tax inscription at top.

Castillo y Rada and Map — AP39

Real Estate Tax Stamp Surcharged "Correo Aereo, II Exposicion Filatelica Nacional, Bogota Dicbre 1953, 15 Centavos"

1953, Dec. 12 Engr. & Litho.

C237	AP39	15c on 10p multi	.40	.20

2nd Natl. Philatelic Exhib., Bogota, Dec. 1953.

No. RA45 Overprinted in Black

1953

C238	PT10	10c purple	.25	.20

Galeras Volcano — AP40

Retreat of San Diego — AP41

Designs: No. C241, Las Lajas Shrine, Narino. No. C242, 50c, Bolivar monument. 20c, 80c, Ruiz mountain, Manizales. 40c, George Isaacs monument, Cali. 60c, Monkey Fountain, Tunja. 1p, Stadium, Medellin. 2p, Pastelillo Fort, Cartagena. 3p, Santo Domingo University gate. 5p, Las Lajas Shrine. 10p, Map of Colombia.

Perf. 13½x13, 13

1954, Jan. 15 Engr. Unwmk.

C239	AP40	5c dp red vio	.20	.20
C240	AP41	10c black	.20	.20
C241	AP40	15c red orange	.20	.20
C242	AP40	15c car rose	.20	.20
C243	AP40	20c brown	.20	.20
C244	AP40	30c brown org	.25	.20
C245	AP40	40c blue	.25	.20
C246	AP40	50c dk violet brn	.30	.20
C247	AP40	60c dk brown	.40	.20
C248	AP40	80c red brown	.55	.20

Size: 37x27mm

Center in Black

C249	AP41	1p deep blue	2.75	.20
C250	AP41	2p dark green	4.25	.35
C251	AP41	3p carmine rose	9.50	1.25

Size: 38x32mm, 32x38mm

C252	AP41	5p dk grn & red brn	11.50	3.25
C253	AP40	10p gray grn & red org	16.00	6.50
		Nos. C239-C253 (15)	46.75	13.55

See Nos. C307-C308. For surcharges and overprints see Nos. 691, C321, C325, C330, C333-C334, C343-C346.

Condor Carrying Shield AP42

Inscribed: "Correo Extra-Rapido"

1954, Apr. 23 Litho. *Perf. 12½*

C254	AP42	5c lilac rose	.60	.30

For overprint see No. RA53.

Soldier-Map-Arms Type

1954, June 13 Engr. *Perf. 13*

C255	A259	15c carmine	.30	.20

See No. C271a.

Games Type

Design: 20c, Stadium and Athlete holding arms of Colombia.

1954, July 18

C256	A260	15c chocolate	.65	.20
C257	A260	20c deep blue green	1.25	.35

Church of St. Peter Claver, Cartagena AP45

1954, Sept. 9
C258 AP45 15c brown 1.25 .20
a. Souvenir sheet 3.50 3.00

St. Peter Claver, 300th death anniv.

No. C258a contains one stamp similar to No. C258, but printed in red brown.

Mercury Type

1954, Oct. 29
C259 A263 15c deep blue .35 .20

Inscribed "Extra Rapido"

C260 A263 50c scarlet .35 .20

Archbishop Manuel José Mosquera, Death Cent. — AP47

Inscribed: "Correo Extra Rapido"

1954, Nov. 17
C261 AP47 2c yellow green .25 .20

Virgin of Chiquinquira — AP48

Inscribed: "Correo Extra Rapido"

1954, Dec. 4 **Engr. & Litho.**
C262 AP48 5c org brn & multi .25 .20

See No. C291. For overprint see No. 686.

College Types

Designs: 20c, Brother Cristobal de Torres. 50c, College chapel and arms.

Perf. 12½x11½, 11½x12½

1954, Dec. 6 **Engr.** **Unwmk.**
C263 A264 15c orange & blk .25 .20
C264 A264 20c ultra .35 .20
C265 A265 25c dark brown .50 .20
C266 A265 50c black & car 1.25 .60
a. Souvenir sheet 4.75 4.75
Nos. C263-C266 (4) 2.35 1.20

No. C266a contains four stamps similar to Nos. C263-C266, but printed in different colors: 15c red and black, 20c pale purple, 25c brown, 50c black and olive green.

Steel Mill Type

1954, Dec. 12 ***Perf. 12½x13***
C267 A266 20c green & blk 1.00 .60

Marti Type

1955, Jan. 28 ***Perf. 13½x13***
C268 A267 15c deep green .30 .20

Korean Veterans Type

1955, Mar. 23 ***Perf. 12½***
C269 A268 20c dark green .50 .20

Merchant Fleet Types

1955, Apr. 12 ***Perf. 12½***
C270 A269 25c black .30 .20
C271 A270 50c dark green .55 .30
a. Souvenir sheet 6.00 5.25

No. C271a contains 4 stamps similar to Nos. C255, C269-C271, but printed in different colors; 15c lilac red, 20c olive, 25c bluish black, 50c bluish green.

Marco Fidel Suarez (1855-1927), Pres. 1918-21 — AP56

Inscribed: "Correo Extra Rapido"

1955, April 23 ***Perf. 13***
C272 AP56 10c deep blue .25 .20

Hotel-Church Type

1955, May 16 **Photo.** ***Perf. 11½x12***
C273 A271 15c rose brown .25 .20

Rotary Type

Unwmk.

1955, Oct. 17 **Engr.** ***Perf. 13***
C274 A272 15c dk carmine rose .25 .20

Atahualpa, Tisquesuza and Montezuma AP59

Ferdinand the Catholic and Queen Isabella I AP60

Designs: 15c, O'Higgins, Santander and Sucre. 20c, Marti, Hidalgo and Petion. 1p, Artigas, Solano Lopez and Murillo. 2p, Abdon Calderon, Baron de Rio Branco and José de La Mar.

1955, Oct. 12 **Engr. & Photo.**

Inscribed: "Extra Rapido"

C275 AP59 2c dull brn & blk .25 .20
C276 AP60 5c dk brn & yel .25 .20

Regular Air Post

C277 AP59 15c rose car & blk .30 .20
C278 AP59 20c pale brn & blk .45 .20
a. Souvenir sheet of 2 12.50 7.50

Inscribed: "Extra Rapido"

C279 AP60 1p ol gray & brn 10.00 6.00
C280 AP60 2p violet & blk 6.00 4.75
Nos. C275-C280 (6) 17.25 11.55

7th Cong. of the Postal Union of the Americas and Spain, Bogota, Oct. 12-Nov. 9, 1955.

No. C278a contains one each of Nos. C277-C278 printed in different shades.

Caro Type

1955, Nov. 29 **Engr.** ***Perf. 13½x13***
C281 A275 15c gray green .25 .20

University of Salamanca AP62

Inscribed: "Extra Rapido"

1955, Nov. 29 **Unwmk.** ***Perf. 13***
C282 AP62 20c dark brown .25 .20

University of Salamanca, 7th centenary.

Type of Postal Tax Stamp of 1948-50 Surcharged

1956 **Wmk. 255** **Engr.** ***Perf. 12***
C283 PT10 2c on 8c blue .25 .20

No. 617 Overprinted in Black

1956 **Unwmk.** ***Perf. 12½x13***
C284 A256 1p black & emerald .25 .20

Columbus Type

1956, Oct. 11 **Photo.** ***Perf. 12***
C285 A279 15c intense blue .55 .20

See No. C306.

St. Elizabeth Type

1956, Nov. 19
C286 A280 15c red brown .30 .20

St. Ignatius Type

1956, Nov. 26 **Engr.** ***Perf. 12½x13***
C287 A281 5c brown .25 .20

Javier Pereira — AP63

1956, Dec. 28 **Unwmk.** ***Perf. 12***
C288 AP63 20c rose carmine .25 .20

Issued to honor 167-year-old Javier Pereira.

No. 649 and Type of 1941 Overprinted in Red "EXTRA RAPIDO"

1957 ***Perf. 13½x13***
C289 A276 5c blue & black 6.00 2.50

Perf. 12

C290 AP22 5p orange & gray 6.50 5.00

The overprint measures 14mm.

Virgin Type of 1954

Engraved and Lithographed

1957, May 23 **Unwmk.** ***Perf. 13***
C291 AP48 5c dp plum & multi .25 .20

Bank Type

No. C292, 20c, Emblem, cow, horse & herd. 10c, Emblem & tractor. 15c, Emblem, coffee & corn. No. C293, Emblem & dairy farm.

1957 **Photo.** ***Perf. 14x13½***
C292 A283 5c chocolate .20 .20
C293 A283 5c orange .20 .20
C294 A283 10c green .55 .40
C295 A283 15c black .35 .20
C296 A283 20c dull red .80 .20
Nos. C292-C296 (5) 2.10 1.20

No. C292 is inscribed "Extra Rapido." Issued: No. C292, 3/5; others 5/23.

Cyclist AP64

1957, July 6 **Unwmk.** ***Perf. 12***
C297 AP64 2c brown .20 .20
C298 AP64 5c ultra .25 .20

Seventh Bicycle Tour of Colombia.

Academy Type

Designs: 15c, Coat of arms and Gen. Rafael Reyes. 20c, Coat of arms and Academy.

1957, July 20 **Engr.** ***Perf. 12½***
C299 A284 15c rose carmine .20 .20
C300 A284 20c brown .25 .20

Delgado Type

1957, Sept. 15 **Photo.** ***Perf. 12***
C301 A285 10c slate blue .25 .20

UPU Type

1957, Oct. 10
C302 A286 15c dark red brown .20 .20
C303 A286 25c dark blue .20 .20

St. Vincent de Paul Type

1957, Oct. 18
C304 A287 5c rose brown .25 .20

Fencing Type

1957, Nov. 23 ***Perf. 12***
C305 A288 20c dark red brown .25 .20

Columbus Type Inscribed "Extra Rapido"

1958, Jan. 8 **Unwmk.** ***Perf. 12***
C306 A279 3c dark green .25 .20

Scenic Type

Design: 25c, Las Lajas Shrine.

1958, June 20 **Engr.** ***Perf. 13***
C307 AP40 25c dark blue .30 .20
C308 AP40 25c rose violet .30 .20

IGY Type

1958, May 12 **Photo.** ***Perf. 12***
C309 A289 25c green .30 .20

Inscribed "Extra Rapido"

C310 A289 1p purple .50 .20

No. 659 Overprinted "AEREO" in Carmine

1958, Oct. 16 **Engr.** ***Perf. 13***
C312 A277 50c dk green & blk .40 .20

Almanza Type

1958, Oct. 23 **Photo.** ***Perf. 14x13***
C313 A290 25c dark gray .25 .20

Inscribed "Extra Rapido"

C314 A290 10c olive green .20 .20

Carrasquilla Type

1959, Jan. 22 **Photo.** ***Perf. 14x13***
C315 A291 25c carmine rose .20 .20
C316 A291 1p dark blue .60 .20

Miss Universe Type

1959, June 26 **Unwmk.** ***Perf. 11½***
C317 A292 1.20p multicolored 1.40 1.10
C318 A292 5p multicolored 40.00 37.50

Gaitan Type Inscribed "Extra Rapido" and Surcharged in Black or Blue

1959, July 28 **Engr.** ***Perf. 12x13½***
C319 A293 2p on 1p black 1.40 1.25
C320 A293 2p on 1p black (Bl) 1.40 1.25

The 1p black, type A293, exists without surcharge.

No. C247 Surcharged with New Value in Dark Blue; Old Value Obliterated

1959, Aug. 24 **Unwmk.** ***Perf. 13***
C321 AP40 50c on 60c dk brown 1.25 .40

Regular and Air Post Issues of 1948-59 Overprinted in Black or Red

1959-60
C322 A283 5c orange .35 .25
C323 A287 5c rose brn ('60) .50 .50
C324 A281 5c brown (R) .40 .30
C325 AP41 10c black .25 .20
a. Double overprint 2.50 2.50
C326 A160 10c red, #C231 .40 .20
a. Double overprint 1.40 1.40
C328 A284 15c rose car .25 .20
a. Inverted overprint 3.00 3.00
C330 AP40 20c brown .25 .20
a. Double overprint 1.40 1.40

C331	A284	20c brown	.25	.20
C332	A288	20c dk red brn ('60)	.25	.20
C333	AP40	25c rose vio ('60)	.25	.20
C334	AP40	25c dark blue	.25	.20
C335	A291	25c car rose	.25	.20
C336	A290	25c dark gray	.25	.20
C338	AP40	30c brown org	.25	.20
C340	AP40	50c on 60c dk brn	.40	.20
C341	A291	1p dark blue	.95	.20
a.		Double overprint	2.50	2.50
C342	A292	1.20p brn, ultra, car & ol	1.50	.80
C343	AP41	2p dk grn & blk	2.00	.20
C344	AP41	3p car rose & blk	6.00	.50
a.		Double overprint	10.00	10.00
C345	AP41	5p dk grn & red brn	8.00	1.10
a.		Double overprint	10.00	10.00
b.		Inverted overprint	10.00	10.00
C346	AP40	10p gray grn & red org	10.00	2.25
		Nos. C322-C346 (21)	33.00	8.50

Issued following agreement between the Colombian government and AVIANCA to unify the air postage used on all mail carried by AVIANCA.

Vertical overprint on Nos. C342 and C346.

Airmail Stamp of 1919 and Planes AP66

60c, Nos. C349a, C350a, Planes of 1919 and 1959. Nos. C349b, C350b, Stamp of 1919 and Planes.

Unwmk.

1959, Dec. 5 Photo. *Perf. 12*

C347	AP66	35c lt bl, blk & red	.40	.20
C348	AP66	60c yel grn & gray	.60	.35

Souvenir Sheets

C349		Sheet of 2	7.50	6.75
a.		AP66 1p orange & gray	1.50	1.00
b.		AP66 1p lilac, gray & red	1.50	1.00

Inscribed "Extra Rapido"

1960, May 17

C350		Sheet of 2	7.50	6.75
a.		AP66 1.50p red orange & gray	1.50	1.25
b.		AP66 1.50p olive, gray & rose	1.50	1.25

Nos. C347-C350 for the 40th anniv. of air post service and of the AVIANCA company.

Type of Regular Issue and

1859 Stamp and Seaplane AP67

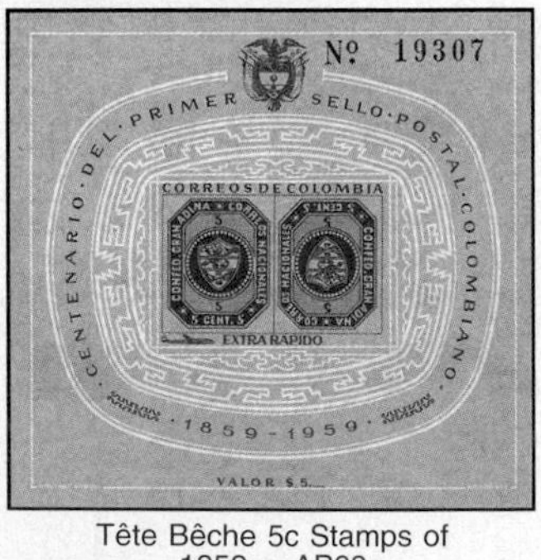

Tête Bêche 5c Stamps of 1859 — AP68

Designs (various stamps of 1859 and): 10c, Map of Colombia. 25c, Pres. Mariano Ospina. 1.20p, Plane over mountains.

1959, Dec. 1 Photo. *Perf. 12*

C351	A296	25c choc & red	.50	.20
C352	AP67	50c ver & ultra	1.00	.50
C353	AP67	1.20p yel grn & car	2.00	1.10

Inscribed "Extra Rapido"

C354	A296	10c lemon & vio	.20	.20
		Nos. C351-C354 (4)	3.70	2.00

Souvenir Sheet

Wmk. 331

1959, Dec. 23 Litho. *Imperf.*

C355	AP68	5p blue, *pink*	19.00	19.00

Cent. of Colombian postage stamps.

No. C355 exists with inscription "VALOR $5.10" instead of "VALOR $5."

Eldorado Airport, Bogota AP69

1960, Jan. 5 Wmk. 331 *Perf. 12½*

C356	AP69	35c black & ocher	.50	.20
C356A	AP69	60c ver & gray	.65	.35

Inscribed "Extra Rapido"

C356B	AP69	1p Prus bl & gray	.85	.50
		Nos. C356-C356B (3)	2.00	1.05

Ant Bear AP70

1.30p, Armadillo. 1.45p, Parrot fish.

Unwmk.

1960, Feb. 12 Photo. *Perf. 12*

C357	AP70	35c sepia	1.25	.20
C358	AP70	1.30p rose car & dk brn	2.40	2.25
C359	AP70	1.45p lt bl, bl & yel	2.00	1.25
		Nos. C357-C359 (3)	5.65	3.70

Alexander von Humboldt, German naturalist and geographer (1769-1859).

Flower Type

Nos. C360, C362, C366, Passiflora mollissima. Nos. C361, C364, C367, Odontoglossum luteo purpureum. Nos. C363, C369, Anthurium andreanum. Nos. C365, C370, Stanhopea tigrina. No. C368, Espeletia grandiflora.

1960, May 10 Photo. *Perf. 12*

Flowers in Natural Colors

C360	A298	5c dark blue	.20	.20
C361	A298	35c maroon	.40	.20
C362	A298	60c dark blue	.75	.55
C363	A298	1.45p dark brown	1.00	.85

Inscribed "Extra Rapido"

C364	A298	5c maroon	.20	.20
C365	A298	10c brown	.20	.20
C366	A298	1p dark blue	2.00	*2.50*
C367	A298	1p maroon	2.00	*2.50*
C368	A298	1p brown	2.00	*2.50*
C369	A298	1p brown	2.00	*2.50*
C370	A298	1p brown	2.00	*2.50*
		Nos. C360-C370 (11)	12.75	*14.70*

See Nos. C420-C425.

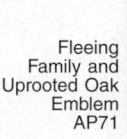

Fleeing Family and Uprooted Oak Emblem AP71

Perf. 10, 11

1960, May 24 Litho. Wmk. 331

C371	AP71	60c bl grn & gray	.30	.20

World Refugee Year, 7/1/59-6/30/60.

Souvenir Sheet

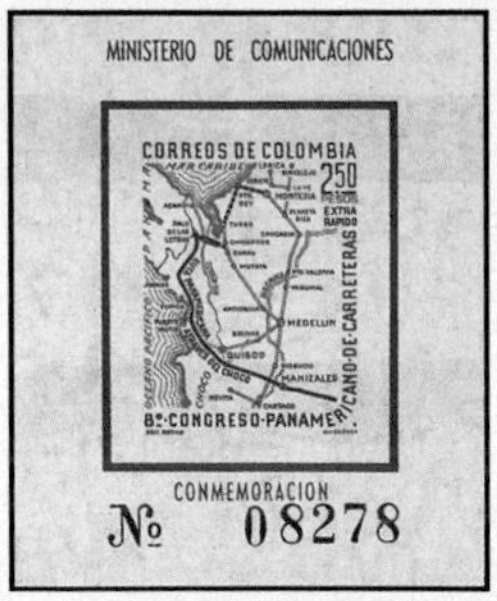

Pan-American Highway Through Colombia — AP72

1960, May 28 Litho. *Imperf.*

C372	AP72	2.50p brn & aqua	5.00	5.00

8th Pan-American Highway Congress, Bogota, May 20-29.

Lincoln Type

1960, June 6 *Perf. 10½*

C375	A299	40c dl red brn & blk	.85	.60
C376	A299	60c rose red & blk	.25	.20

Type of Regular Issue and

Joaquin Camacho, Jorge Tadeo Lozano and Jose Miguel Pey AP73

Flag, Coins and Arms of Mompox and Cartagena — AP74

No. C378, Arms of Cartagena. 35c, 1.45p, Colombian flag. 60c, Andres Rosillo, Antonio Villavicencio and Joaquin Caicedo. 1p, Manuel de Bernardo Alvarez and Joaquin Gutierrez. 1.20p, Jose Antonio Galan statue. 1.30p, Front page of newspaper La Bagatela, 1811. 1.65p, Antonia Santos, Jose Acevedo y Gomez and Liborio Mejia.

Unwmk.

1960, July 20 Photo. *Perf. 12*

C377	AP73	5c lilac & brn	.20	.20
C378	A301	5c dp bl grn & multi	.20	.20
C379	AP73	35c multicolored	.20	.20
C380	AP73	60c red brn & grn	.40	.20
C381	AP73	1p ver & sl grn	.85	.60
C382	A301	1.20p ultra & ind	.85	.60
C383	AP73	1.30p orange & blk	.85	.60
C384	AP73	1.45p multicolored	1.10	.85
C385	AP73	1.65p green & brn	.85	.85
		Nos. C377-C385 (9)	5.50	4.30

Souvenir Sheet

Stamps Inscribed "Extra Rapido"

C386	AP74	Sheet of 4	4.00	4.00
a.		50c deep claret & multi	.65	.65
b.		50c green & multi	.65	.65
c.		1p brown olive, yel, blue & car	.65	.65
d.		1p lilac & gray	.65	.65

150th anniv. of Colombia's independence.

St. Isidore Type

Designs: 35c, No. C388a, St. Isidore and farm animals. No. C388b, Nativity.

Unwmk.

1960, Sept. 26 Photo. *Perf. 12*

C387	A302	35c multicolored	.25	.20

Souvenir Sheet

Stamps Inscribed "Extra Rapido"

C388	A302	Sheet of 2	6.00	6.00
a.		1.50p multicolored	2.00	2.00
b.		1.50p multicolored	2.00	2.00

See Nos. C439-C440.

Type of Regular Issue, 1959

Wmk. 331

1960, Nov. 23 Litho. *Perf. 12½*

C389	A294	35c Bolivar	3.00	.40

Pan-American Highway Type

1961, Mar. 7 Unwmk. *Perf. 10½x11*

C390	A304	10c rose lil & emer	.50	*.50*
C391	A304	20c ver & lt bl	.50	*.50*
C392	A304	30c black & emer	.50	*.50*

Inscribed "Extra Rapido"

C393	A304	10c dk blue & emer	.50	*.50*
		Nos. C390-C393 (4)	2.00	*2.00*

8th Pan-American Highway Congress, Bogota, May 20-29, 1960.

Lopez Type

1961, Mar. 22 Photo. *Perf. 12½*

C394	A305	35c blue & brown	.50	.20

Inscribed "Extra Rapido"

C395	A305	10c emerald & brn	.20	.20

Souvenir Sheet

C396	A305	1p lilac & brn	4.00	3.50

Brother Damian and San Francisco Church, Cali AP75

Designs: 10c, View of Cali, vert. No. 398, Emblem of University del Valle, vert. 1.30p, Fine Arts School, Cali. 1.45p, Agricultural College, Palmira.

Perf. 13x13½, 13½x13

1961, Aug. 17 Photo. Unwmk.

C397	AP75	35c vio brn & ol	.30	.20
C398	AP75	35c olive & grn	.30	.20
C399	AP75	1.30p sepia & pink	.85	.45
C400	AP75	1.45p multicolored	.85	.60

Inscribed: "Extra Rapido"

C401	AP75	10c brn & yel grn	.20	.20
		Nos. C397-C401 (5)	2.50	1.65

50th anniv. (in 1960) of the department of Valle del Cauca.

View of Cucuta AP76

10c, Church of the Rosary, Cucuta, vert.

1961, Aug. 29

C402	AP76	35c brn ol & grn	.60	.20

Inscribed: "Extra Rapido"

C403	AP76	10c dk brn & gray grn	.20	.20

50th anniv. (in 1960) of the department of North Santander.

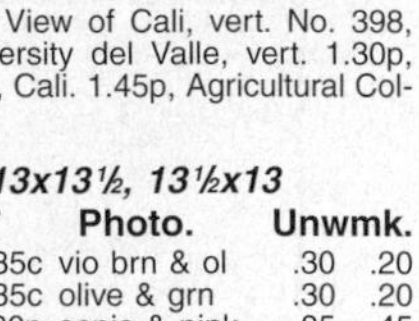

Old and New Ships of Barranquilla AP77

Arms and View of San Gil — AP78

Hotel, Popayan
AP79

Statue of Christ in Procession
AP80

Design: 1.45p, View of Velez.

Perf. 12½x13, 13x12½

1961, Oct. 10 Photo. Unwmk.

C404 AP77 35c gold & bl .45 .20
C405 AP78 35c bl grn, yel & red .45 .20
C406 AP79 35c car & brn .45 .20
C407 AP78 1.45p brown & grn .45 .20

Inscribed: "Extra Rapido"

C408 AP80 10c brown & yel .20 .20
Nos. C404-C408 (5) 2.00 1.00

Types of Regular and Air Post
Souvenir Sheets

Designs, No. C409: 35c, Barranquilla arms. 40c, Popayan arms. c, Arms and view of San Gil. d, Holy Week in Popayan.

No. C410: a, Old and new ships at Barranquilla. b, Hotel, Popayan. c, Bucaramanga arms. d, Holy Week in Popayan.

C409 Sheet of 4 6.00 6.00
a. A309 35c gold & multi .55 .55
b. A309 40c gold & multi .55 .55
c. AP78 1p blue, yellow & red 1.10 1.10
d. AP80 1p car rose & yellow 1.10 1.10

Stamps Inscribed: "Extra Rapido"

C410 Sheet of 4 6.00 6.00
a. AP77 50c gold & car rose .85 .85
b. AP79 50c gold & blue .85 .85
c. A309 50c pink & multi .85 .85
d. AP80 50c blue & yellow .85 .85

Nos. C404-C408 are in honor of the Atlantico Department. Nos. C409-C410 are in honor of the Departments of Atlantico, Cauca and Santander.

Nos. 713, 716 and 715 Overprinted and Surcharged

1961, Sept. *Perf. 12*

C411 A297 5c grnsh bl & brn .20 .20
C412 A298 5c multicolored .20 .20
C413 A297 10c on 20c cit & gray brn .20 .20
Nos. C411-C413 (3) .60 .60

"Aereo" in script on No. C412.
See Nos. C420-C425.

Sports Type

Designs: No. C414, Women divers. No. C415, Tennis, mixed doubles. 1.45p, No. C419b, Baseball. No. C417, Torch bearer. Nos. C418, C419a, Bolivar statue and flags of six participating nations. No. C419c, Soccer. No. C419d, Basketball.

1961, Dec. 16 Litho. *Perf. 13½x14*

C414 A310 35c ultra, yel & brn .60 .20
C415 A310 35c car, yel & brn .60 .20
C416 A310 1.45p Prus grn, yel & brn 1.00 .55

Inscribed: "Extra Rapido"

C417 A310 10c car lake, yel & brn .20 .20
C418 A310 10c ol, yel, bl & red .20 .20
Nos. C414-C418 (5) 2.60 1.35

Souvenir Sheet
Stamps Inscribed: "Extra Rapido"
Imperf

C419 Sheet of 4 6.00 6.00
a. A310 50c multi .40 .40
b. A310 50c multi .40 .40
c. A310 1p multi .85 .85
d. A310 1p multi .85 .85

Flower Type of 1960

5c, Passiflora mollissima. 10c, Espeletia grandiflora. 20c, 2p, Odontoglossum luteo purpureum. 25c, Stanhopea tigrina. 60c, Anthurium Andreanum.

Unwmk.

1962, Jan. 30 Photo. *Perf. 12*
Flowers in Natural Colors

C420 A298 5c gray .20 .20
C421 A298 10c gray blue .20 .20
C422 A298 20c rose lilac .20 .20
C423 A298 25c citron .30 .20
C424 A298 60c light brown .30 .20

Inscribed "Extra Rapido"

C425 A298 2p salmon pink 2.75 1.25
Nos. C420-C425 (6) 3.95 2.25

Anti-Malaria Type

Designs: 40c, Colombian anti-malaria emblem. 1p, 1.45p, Malaria eradication emblem and mosquito in swamp.

1962, Apr. 12 Litho. *Perf. 12*

C426 A311 40c yellow & red .25 .20
C427 A311 1.45p gray & ultra .50 .40

Inscribed "Extra Rapido"

C428 A311 1p yel grn & ultra 3.50 3.50
Nos. C426-C428 (3) 4.25 4.10

WHO drive to eradicate malaria.

Type of Regular Issue, 1962 and

Abelardo Ramos and Engineering School, Cauca — AP81

Designs: 10c, Miguel Triana, Andres A. Arroyo and Monserrate shrine with cable cars. 15c, Diodoro Sanchez and first meeting place of Engineers Society. 2p, Engineers Society emblem.

1962, June 12 Photo. *Perf. 11½x12*

C429 AP81 5c blue & dp rose .20 .20
C430 AP81 10c green & sepia .20 .20
C431 AP81 15c lilac & sepia .25 .20

Inscribed: "Extra Rapido"

C432 A312 2p blk, yel, red & bl 1.50 1.50
Nos. C429-C432 (4) 2.15 2.10

75th anniv. of the founding of the Colombian Soc. of Engineers and 6th Natl. Cong. of Engineers.

American States Type

1962, June 28 Photo. *Perf. 13*
Flags in National Colors

C433 A313 35c black & blue .35 .20

Women's Rights Type
Perf. 12x12½

1962, July 20 Litho. Wmk. 229

C434 A314 35c buff, gray & blk .25 .20

See Nos. C448-C450.

Scout Type

Designs: 15c, No. C438, Scouts at campfire and tents. 40c and No. C437, Girl Scouts.

Perf. 11½x12

1962, July 26 Photo. Unwmk.

C435 A315 15c brown & rose .20 .20
C436 A315 40c dp cl & pink .25 .20
C437 A315 1p blue & buff .80 .35

Inscribed "Extra Rapido"

C438 A315 1p purple & yel 4.00 3.75
Nos. C435-C438 (4) 5.25 4.50

Nos. C435 and C438 for 30th anniv. of the Colombian Boy Scouts. Nos. C436 and C437 for the 25th anniv. of the Girl Scouts.

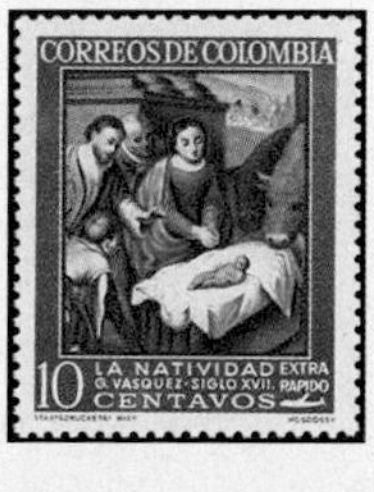

Nativity by Gregorio Vasquez
AP82

Design: 2p, St. Isidore, similar to type A302.

Inscribed "Extra Rapido"

Unwmk.

1962, Aug. 28 Photo. *Perf. 12*

C439 AP82 10c gray & multi .20 .20
C440 AP82 2p gray & multi 3.75 3.50

See Nos. C387-C388.

Type of Regular Issue, 1962 and

Pres. Aquileo Parra and Magdalena River Bridge
AP83

Design: 5c, Locomotives of 1854 and 1961. 10c, Railroad map of Colombia.

1962, Sept. 28 Photo. *Perf. 12½*

C441 AP83 5c sep & slate grn .20 .20
C442 A316 10c multicolored .20 .20

Engr.

C443 AP83 1p dull pur & brn 1.40 .20

Inscribed: "Extra Rapido."

C444 AP83 5p bl, brn & dl grn 3.75 3.75
Nos. C441-C444 (4) 5.55 4.35

Progress of Colombian railroads and completion of the Atlantic Line from Santa Maria to Bogota.

UPAE Type

Designs: 50c, Map of Americas and carrier pigeon. 60c, Post horn.

Perf. 13½x14

1962, Oct. 18 Litho. Wmk. 346

C445 A317 50c slate grn & gold .30 .20
C446 A317 60c gold & plum .25 .20

Pope John XXIII
AP84

1963, Mar. 11

C447 AP84 60c gold, red brn, buff & red .25 .20

Vatican II, the 21st Ecumenical Council of the Roman Catholic Church.

Women's Rights Type of 1962

1963-64 *Perf. 12x12½*

C448 A314 5c sal, gray & blk ('64) .20 .20
C449 A314 45c pale grn, gray & blk .30 .20
C450 A314 45c brt pink, gray & blk .30 .20
Nos. C448-C450 (3) .80 .60

Games Emblem — AP85

1963, Aug. 12 *Perf. 13x14*

C451 AP85 20c gray & multi .20 .20
C452 AP85 80c buff & multi .25 .20

South American Athletic Championships (22nd for men, 12th for women), Cali, June 30-July 7.

Bolivar Statue by Arenas-Betancourt — AP86

Perf. 14x13½

1963, Aug. 30 Unwmk.

C453 AP86 1.90p olive bis & blue .25 .20

Centenary of the city of Pereira.
For surcharge see No. C574.

Tennis Player — AP87

1963, Oct. 11 *Perf. 13½x14*

C454 AP87 55c multicolored .25 .20

30th South American Tennis Championships, Medellin, Oct. 3-13.

Pres. John F. Kennedy and Alliance for Progress Emblem
AP88

1963, Dec. 17 Litho. *Perf. 14x13½*

C455 AP88 10c multicolored .40 .20

President John F. Kennedy (1917-1963).

Church of the True Cross, National Pantheon, Bogota — AP89

2p, Christ of the Martyrs, bell and tomb.

Perf. 13½x14

1964, Mar. 10 Photo. Unwmk.

C459 AP89 1p multicolored .20 .20
C460 AP89 2p multicolored .35 .20

View of Cartagena
AP90

1964, Mar. 18 Litho. *Perf. 14x13½*

C461 AP90 3p vio, bl, ocher & brn 1.40 .60

Cartagena's independence in 1811, Simon Bolivar's visit in 1812 and the siege of 1815.

Eleanor Roosevelt
AP91

1964, Nov. 10 Photo. *Perf. 12*

C462 AP91 20c ol & dl red brn .25 .20

Eleanor Roosevelt (1884-1962).

Alberto Castilla and Score of "El Bunde" AP92

1964, Nov. 10 **Unwmk.**
C463 AP92 30c ol bis & Prus grn .25 .20

Department of Tolima and Maestro Alberto Castilla (1878-1937) who in 1906 founded the Tolima Conservatory of Music in Ibague.

Mejia Type

Mejia portrait and: 45c, Women picking coffee. 5p, Mules carrying coffee bags. 10p, Loading coffee on freighter "Manuel Mejia."

1965, Feb. 10 Engr. ***Perf. 12½x13***
C464 A320 45c brown & blk .20 .20
C465 A320 5p gray grn & blk 1.75 .25
C466 A320 10p ultra & blk 2.40 .30
Nos. C464-C466 (3) 4.35 .75

ITU Emblem AP93

1965, Oct. 25 Photo. ***Perf. 12***
C467 AP93 80c Prus bl, lt bl & red .25 .20

Cent. of the ITU.

Cattleya Trunae — AP94

Cent. of the Telegraph in Colombia — AP95

1965, Oct. 3 Litho. ***Perf. 13½x14***
C468 AP94 20c yellow & multi .25 .20

Fifth Philatelic Exhibition.

1965, Nov. 1 ***Perf. 13½x14, 14x13½***

No. C469, Pres. Manuel Murillo Toro statue, telegraph and orbits. No. C470, Telegraph and satellites over South America, horiz.

C469 AP95 60c multicolored .25 .20
C470 AP95 60c multicolored .25 .20

Junkers F-13 Seaplane, 1920 AP96

History of Colombian Aviation: 10c, Dornier Wal, 1924. 20c, Dornier Mercur, 1926. 50c, Trimotor Ford, 1932. 60c, De Havilland biplane, 1930. 1p, Douglas DC-4, 1947. 1.40p, Douglas DC-3, 1944. 2.80p, Superconstellation 1049, 1951. 3p, Boeing 720B jet, 1961.

Perf. 14x13½
1965-66 Photo. Unwmk.
C471 AP96 5c multicolored .20 .20
C472 AP96 10c multicolored .20 .20
C473 AP96 20c multicolored .20 .20
C474 AP96 50c multicolored .20 .20
C475 AP96 60c multicolored .40 .20
C476 AP96 1p multicolored .75 .20
C477 AP96 1.40p multicolored .90 .20
C478 AP96 2.80p multicolored 1.60 .60
C479 AP96 3p multicolored 2.40 .85
Nos. C471-C479 (9) 6.85 2.85
Nos. C471-C479,CE4 (10) 7.20 3.05

Issued: 5c, 60c, 3p, 12/13/65; 10c, 1p, 1.40p, 7/15/66; 20c, 50c, 2.80p, 12/14/66.

Automobile Club Emblem and Car on Road AP97

1966, Feb. 16 Litho. ***Perf. 14x13½***
C480 AP97 20c multicolored .25 .20

25th anniv. (in 1965) of the Automobile Club of Colombia.

Fish Type

Fish: 2p, Flying fish. 2.80p, Queen angelfish. 20p, King mackerel.

1966, Aug. 25 Photo. ***Perf. 12½x13***
C481 A323 2p multicolored .50 .20
C482 A323 2.80p multicolored 1.25 .90
C483 A323 20p multicolored 16.50 12.00
Nos. C481-C483 (3) 18.25 13.10

Coat of Arms Type

1966, Oct. 11 Litho. ***Perf. 14x13½***
C484 A324 1p ultra & multi .25 .20
C485 A324 1.40p red & multi .20 .20

Portrait Type

80c, Father Felix Restrepo Mejia, S.J. (1887-1965), theologian, scholar. 1.70p, José Joaquin Casas (1866-1951), educator, diplomat.

Perf. 13½x14
1967, Jan. 18 Litho. Unwmk.
C486 A325 80c dk bl & bis .20 .20
C487 A325 1.70p blk & bis .25 .20

Declaration of Bogota Type

1967, Feb. 2 Litho. ***Perf. 14x13½***
C488 A326 3p multicolored .35 .20

See note after No. 767.

Orchid Type

Orchids: 1p, Cattleya dowiana aurea, vert. 1.20p, Masdevallia coccinea, vert. 5p, Catasetum macrocarpum and bee.

1967, May 23 Litho. ***Perf. 14***
C489 A327 1p multicolored 1.60 .30
C490 A327 1.20p multicolored 1.10 .25
C491 A327 5p multicolored 7.50 .90
a. Souv. sheet of 3, #C489-C491 25.00 25.00
Nos. C489-C491 (3) 10.20 1.45

Lions Type

1967, July 12 Litho. ***Perf. 13½x14***
C492 A328 25c multicolored .25 .20

"First Caesarean Section" by Grau AP98

Perf. 14x13½
1967, Sept. 7 Litho. Unwmk.
C493 AP98 80c multicolored .25 .20

Issued to publicize the 6th Congress of Colombian Surgeons, Bogota, Sept. 25.

SENA Type
Lithographed and Embossed

1967, Sept. 20 ***Perf. 13½x14***
C494 A329 2p gold, ver & blk .50 .20

Pre-Columbian Art Type

Designs: 30c, Bird pectoral. 5p Ornamental pectoral. 20p, Pitcher.

1967, Oct. 13 Photo. ***Perf. 13½x14***
C495 A330 30c ver, gold & brn .35 .20
C496 A330 5p red, gold & brn 3.25 .50
a. Souvenir sheet of 2 10.00 10.00
C497 A330 20p vio, gold & brn 14.50 10.00
Nos. C495-C497 (3) 18.10 10.70

No. C496a also commemorates the 6th Natl. Phil. Exhib. No. C496a contains 2 imperf. stamps in changed colors similar to Nos. C495-C496 (30c has green background and 5p maroon background).

Telecommunications Type

Designs: 50c, Signal lights. 1p, Early Bird satellite, Southern Cross and radar.

Perf. 13½x14
1968, May 14 Litho. Unwmk.
C498 A331 50c blk, ver & emer .20 .20
C499 A331 1p ultra, yel & gray .30 .20

Eucharist Type

1968, June 6 Litho. ***Perf. 13½x14***
C500 A332 80c rose lil, red, yel & blk .20 .20
C501 A332 3p bl, red, yel & blk .30 .20

Eucharistic Congress Type

Designs: 80c, The Last Supper, by Gregorio Vasquez, horiz. 1p, St. Francis Xavier Preaching, by Gregorio Vasquez. 2p, The Dream of the Prophet Elias, by Gregorio Vasquez. 3p, Monstrance, c. 1700. 20p, Pope Paul VI, painting by Roman Franciscan nuns.

1968, Aug. 13 Photo. ***Perf. 13***
C502 A333 80c multicolored .20 .20
C503 A333 1p multicolored .25 .20
C504 A333 2p multicolored .35 .20
C505 A333 3p lil & multi .65 .20
C506 A333 20p gold & multi 4.00 2.00
Nos. C502-C506 (5) 5.45 2.80

Shrine of the Eucharist, Bogotá AP99

1.20p, Pope Paul VI giving blessing and Papal arms. 1.80p, Cathedral of Bogotá.

Perf. 14x13½, 13½x14
1968, Aug. 22 Litho.
C507 AP99 80c multi .20 .20
C508 AP99 1.20p multi, vert. .20 .20
C509 AP99 1.80p multi, vert. .30 .20
Nos. C507-C509 (3) .70 .60

Visit of Pope Paul VI to Colombia.

Computer Symbols — AP100

1968, Oct. 29 Litho. ***Perf. 13½x14***
C510 AP100 20c buff, car & grn .25 .20

Cent. of the Natl. University and the 1st Data Processing Cong. in 1967 at the University.

Agriculture Institute Type

1968, Mar. 5 Litho. ***Perf. 13½x14***
C511 A337 1p gray & multi .25 .20

Microscope and Pen — AP101

1969, Mar. 24 Litho. ***Perf. 14***
C512 AP101 5p blk, yel, ver & pur 2.40 .35

20th anniv. (in 1968) of the University of the Andes.

Alexander von Humboldt and Andes AP102

1969, May 3 Litho. ***Perf. 14x13½***
C513 AP102 1p grn & brn .65 .35

Alexander von Humboldt (1769-1859), German naturalist and traveler.

Map of Colombia, Amphibian Plane and Letter AP103

Design: 1.50p, No. C516b, Globe, letter, and jet of Avianca airlines.

1969, June 18 Litho. ***Perf. 14x13½***
C514 AP103 1p multi .45 .20
C515 AP103 1.50p multi .65 .25

Souvenir Sheet
Imperf

C516 Sheet of 2 7.50 7.50
a. AP103 5p green & multi 1.00 1.00
b. AP103 5p violet & multi 1.00 1.00

50th anniv. of the 1st air post flight in Colombia. No. C516 also for 8th Natl. Philatelic Exhibition, EXFILBA 69, Barranquilla, June 18-22. No. C516 contains 2 stamps in the designs of the 1p and 1.50p.

Independence Type

2.30p, Simon Bolivar, José Antonio Anzoategui, Francisco de Paula Santander and victorious army entering Bogotá, 9/18/1819; painting by Ignacio Castillo Cervantes.

1969, July 24 Litho. ***Perf. 13½x14***
C517 A338 2.30p gold & multi 1.00 .35

Social Security Emblem — AP104

Neurosurgeons' Congress Emblem — AP105

1969, Oct. 29 Litho. *Perf. 13½x14*
C518 AP104 20c emer & blk .25 .20

20th anniv. of the Colombian Institute of Social Security.

1969, Oct. 29
C519 AP105 70c vio, red & yel .50 .30

Issued to publicize the 13th Congress of Latin-American Neurosurgeons, Bogotá.

Junkers F-13 AP106

Nos. C521, C522b, Globe with airlines from Bogota & Boeing jet. No. C522a, like No. C520.

1969, Nov. 28 Litho. *Perf. 14x13½*
C520 AP106 2p grn & multi .75 .25
C521 AP106 3.50p ultra & multi 1.40 .50

Souvenir Sheet

Imperf

C522 Sheet of 2 7.50 7.50
a. AP106 3.50p lt grn & multi .75 .75
b. AP106 5p ultra & multi 1.00 1.00

50th anniv. of AVIANCA; No. C522 also publicizes the 1st Interamerican Phil. Exhib., Bogota, Nov. 28-Dec. 7.
No. C522 contains 2 imperf. stamps.

Child Mailing Letter — AP107

Christmas: 1.50p, Praying child and gifts.

1969, Dec. 16 Litho. *Perf. 13½x14*
C523 AP107 60c ocher & multi .80 .20
C524 AP107 1p multicolored .85 .25
C525 AP107 1.50p multicolored 1.10 .25
Nos. C523-C525 (3) 2.75 .70

Radar Station and Pre-Columbian Head — AP108

1970, Mar. 25 Litho. *Perf. 14x13½*
C526 AP108 1p dl grn, blk & brick red .30 .20

Issued to publicize the opening of the communications satellite earth station at Chocontá in Cundinamarca Province.

Emblem of Colombian Youth Sports Institute — AP109

Art Exhibition Emblem — AP110

2.30p, Games' emblem (dove and 3 rings).

1970, Apr. 6 Litho. *Perf. 13½x14*
C527 AP109 1.50p dk ol grn, yel & blk .30 .20
C528 AP109 2.30p red & multi .40 .20

9th Natl. Youth Games, Ibague, July 10-20.

1970, Apr. 30 Litho. *Perf. 13½x14*
C529 AP110 30c multicolored .25 .20

2nd Biennial Art Exhib., Medellin, 6/1-7/14.

Eduardo Santos, Rural and Urban Buildings AP111

1970, June 18 Litho. *Perf. 14x13½*
C530 AP111 1p grn, yel & blk .25 .20

Issued to commemorate the founding (in 1939) of the Territorial Credit Institute.

UN Emblem, Scales and Dove — AP112

EXFILCA Emblem — AP113

1970, June 26 *Perf. 13½x14*
C531 AP112 1.50p dk bl, lt bl & yel .25 .20

25th anniversary of United Nations.

1970, Nov. Litho. *Perf. 13½x14*
C532 AP113 10p bl, gold & blk 3.50 .25

EXFILCA 70, 2nd Interamerican Philatelic Exhib., Caracas, Venezuela, Nov. 27-Dec. 6.

Mother Juana Ruperta in Napanga Costume and Music by Efrain Orozco — AP114

Designs: 1p, Dancers from Eastern Plains and music by Alejandro Wills. No. C535, Guabina man, woman and folk song. No. C536, Bambuco man and woman, and music. No. C537, Man and woman dancing the Cumbia, and music.

1970-71 Litho. *Perf. 13½x14*
C533 AP114 60c dp lil rose & multi .50 .20
C534 AP114 1p ultra & multi .40 .20
C535 AP114 1.30p bl & multi .55 .20
C536 AP114 1.30p emer & multi ('71) .60 .20
C537 AP114 1.30p lil & multi ('71) .40 .20
Nos. C533-C537 (5) 2.45 1.00

Athlete and Games Emblem — AP115

Design: 2p, Games emblem.

1971, Mar. 11
C542 AP115 1.50p multicolored .90 .90
C543 AP115 2p blk, org & grn .80 .55

6th Pan-American Games, Cali, 7/30-8/13.

Gilberto Alzate Avendano AP116

1971, Apr. 29 Litho. *Perf. 14x13½*
C544 AP116 1p bl & multi .40 .25

Avendano (1910-60), journalist, popular leader.

Commemorative Medal — AP117

Lithographed and Embossed

1971, June 21 *Perf. 14x13½*
C545 AP117 1p slate grn & gold .55 .30

Centenary (in 1970) of the Bank of Bogota.

Olympic Center — AP118

Soccer — AP119

Designs (Games Emblem and): Nos. C546-C546C, Olympic Center. No. 547, Soccer. No. C548, Wrestling. No. C549, Bicycling. No. C550, Volleyball. No. C551, Diving (women). No. C552, Fencing. No. C553, Sailing. No. C554, Equestrian. No. C555, Jumping. No. C556, Rowing. No. C557, Cali emblem. No. C558, Basketball (women). No. C559, Stadium. No. C560, Baseball. No. C561, Hockey. No. C562, Weight lifting. No. C563, Medals. No. C564, Boxing. No. C565, Gymnastics (women). No. C566, Sharpshooting.

1971, July 16 Litho. *Perf. 13½x14*

Multicolored and Emblem Color:

C546	AP118	1.30p	yellow	1.25	.30
C546A	AP118	1.30p	green	1.25	.30
C546B	AP118	1.30p	blue	1.25	.30
C546C	AP118	1.30p	carmine	1.25	.30
C547	AP119	1.30p	emerald	1.25	.30
C548	AP119	1.30p	lilac	1.25	.30
C549	AP119	1.30p	blue	1.25	.30
C550	AP119	1.30p	carmine	1.25	.30
C551	AP119	1.30p	blue	1.25	.30
C552	AP119	1.30p	carmine	1.25	.30
C553	AP119	1.30p	blue	1.25	.30
C554	AP119	1.30p	gray	1.25	.30
C555	AP119	1.30p	green	1.25	.30
C556	AP119	1.30p	blue	1.25	.30
C557	AP118	1.30p	orange	1.25	.30
C558	AP119	1.30p	carmine	1.25	.30
C559	AP118	1.30p	light blue	1.25	.30
C560	AP119	1.30p	plum	1.25	.30
C561	AP119	1.30p	yel grn	1.25	.30
C562	AP119	1.30p	pink	1.25	.30
C563	AP118	1.30p	deep org	1.25	.30
C564	AP119	1.30p	plum	1.25	.30
C565	AP119	1.30p	lilac rose	1.25	.30
C566	AP119	1.30p	green	1.25	.30
a.	Sheet of 25, #C546-C566			35.00	35.00

6th Pan American Athletic Games, Cali. No. C546B appears twice in sheet.

Battle of Carabobo, by Martin Tovar y Tovar — AP120

1971, Nov. 25 Litho. *Perf. 13½x14*
C567 AP120 1.50p multicolored 1.00 .20

Sesquicentennial of the Battle of Carabobo.

St. Theresa Type Overprinted "AEREO"

1972 Litho. *Perf. 13½x14*
C568 A343 2p multicolored .30 .20

See note after No. 793.

Vendor — AP121

Designs: 50c, Woman wearing shawl, and woven shawl. 3p, Fruit vendor (puppet).

1972, Apr. 11 Litho. *Perf. 13½x14*
C569 AP121 50c multicolored .35 .20
C570 AP121 1p multicolored .35 .20
C571 AP121 3p multicolored .50 .25
Nos. C569-C571 (3) 1.20 .65

Colombian artisans.

Mormodes Rolfeanum AP122

1972, Apr. 20 ***Perf. 14x13½***
C572 AP122 1.30p multicolored .45 .20

7th World Orchidology Congress, Medellin.

Congo Grande Dancer — AP123

Laureano Gomez, by Ridriguez Cubillos — AP124

1972, June 21 **Litho.** ***Perf. 13½x14***
C573 AP123 1.30p multicolored .50 .20

International Carnival of Barranquilla.

No. C453 Surcharged in Brown

1972, Oct. 5 **Litho.** ***Perf. 14x13½***
C574 AP86 1.30p on 1.90p .55 .20

1972 ***Perf. 13½x14***

1.30p (#C576), Guillermo Leòn Valencia Muñoz.

C575 AP124 1.30p multicolored .25 .20
C576 AP124 1.30p multicolored .25 .20

Laureano Gomez (1898-1966), Guillermo Leon Valencia Munoz (1909-71), Presidents of Colombia.

Issued: No. C575, 10/17; No. C576, 11/28.

Benito Juarez — AP125

Rebecca Fountain AP126

1972, Dec. 12 ***Perf. 13½x14***
C577 AP125 1.50p multicolored .25 .20

Benito Juarez (1806-1872), revolutionary leader and president of Mexico.

1972, Dec. 19 **Litho.**
C578 AP126 80c multicolored .50 .45
C579 AP126 1p multicolored .45 .20

"Bucaramanga" — AP127

1972, Dec. 22 ***Perf. 14x13½***
C580 AP127 5p multicolored .85 .20

Founding of Bucaramanga, 350th anniv.

Xavier University AP128

1973, May 8 **Litho.** ***Perf. 14x13½***
C581 AP128 1.30p lt grn & sep .25 .20
C582 AP128 1.50p lt bl & sep .25 .20

350th anniversary of the founding of Xavier University in Bogotá.

Ceramic Type

Excavated Ceramic Artifacts: 1p, Winged urn, Tairona. 1.30p, Woman and child, Sinu. 1.70p, Two-headed figure, Quimbaya. 3.50p, Man, Tumaco.

1973 **Litho.** ***Perf. 13½x14***
C583 A358 1p multicolored 1.00 1.00
C584 A358 1.30p multicolored .50 .20
C585 A358 1.70p multicolored .55 .25
C586 A358 3.50p multicolored 1.10 .30
Nos. C583-C586 (4) 3.15 1.75

Issue dates: 1p, Oct. 11; others, June 15.

Battle of Maracaibo, by Manuel F. Rincon AP129

1973, July 24 **Litho.** ***Perf. 14x13½***
C587 AP129 10p bl & multi 2.00 .20

Battle of Maracaibo, sesquicentennial.

Bank Emblem AP130

1973, Oct. 1 **Litho.** ***Perf. 14x13½***
C588 AP130 2p multicolored .25 .20

50th anniv. of the Bank of the Republic.

No. 801 Overprinted "AEREO"

1973, Oct. 11 ***Perf. 14***
C589 A346 80c multicolored .30 .20

Pres. Pedro Nel Ospina, by Coroleano Leudo — AP131

Arms of Toro — AP132

1973, Nov. 9 ***Perf. 13½x14***
C590 AP131 1.50p multicolored .25 .20

50th anniversary of the Ministry of Communications founded under Pres. Ospina.

1973, Dec. 1
C591 AP132 1p multicolored .25 .20

Founding of Toro, Valle del Cauca, 4th cent.

Bolivar, Battle of Bombona AP133

1973, Dec. 7 **Litho.** ***Perf. 14x13½***
C592 AP133 1.30p multicolored .25 .20

Sesquicentennial (in 1972) of the Battle of Bombona.

Nicolaus Copernicus AP134

Andes, Map of South America AP135

1974, Feb. 19 **Litho.** ***Perf. 13½x14***
C593 AP134 2.50p multicolored .55 .20

500th anniversary of the birth of Nicolaus Copernicus (1473-1543), Polish astronomer.

1974, May 11 **Litho.** ***Perf. 14***
C594 AP135 2p multicolored .50 .20

Meeting of Communications Ministers of Members of the Andean Group, Cali, May 7-11, 1974.

Television Set AP136

1974, July 16 **Litho.** ***Perf. 14x13½***
C595 AP136 1.30p org, blk & brn .25 .20

20th anniversary of Colombian television and 10th anniversary of INRAVISION, the National Institute of Radio and Television.

Championship Emblem — AP137

1974, Aug. 5 **Litho.** ***Perf. 14x13½***
C596 AP137 4.50p multicolored .30 .20

2nd World Swimming Championships, Cali.

Condor — AP138

1974, Aug. 28 ***Perf. 14***
C597 AP138 1.50p multicolored .25 .20

Bank of Colombia centenary.

UPU Envelope AP139

1974, Sept. 9 **Litho.** ***Perf. 14***
C598 AP139 20p multicolored 2.50 .30

Centenary of Universal Postal Union.

Symbol of Flight — AP140

1974, Sept. ***Perf. 12x12½***
C599 AP140 20c olive .25 .20

Gen. José Maria Cordoba — AP141

White-tailed Trogon, Letter — AP142

1974, Oct. 14 **Litho.** ***Perf. 13½x14***
C609 AP141 1.30p multicolored .25 .20

Sesquicentennial of the Battles of Junin and Ayacucho.

Insurance Type

Design: 3p, Abstract pattern.

1974, Oct. 24 **Litho.** ***Perf. 13½x14***
C610 A365 3p multicolored .30 .20

Perf. 13½x14, 14x13½

1974, Nov. 14

Designs (UPU Letter and): 1.30p, Keelbilled Toucan, horiz. 2p, Peruvian cock-of-the-rock, horiz. 2.50p, Scarlet macaw.

C611 AP142 1p multicolored .75 .20
C612 AP142 1.30p multicolored .75 .20
C613 AP142 2p multicolored 1.00 .20
C614 AP142 2.50p multicolored 1.00 .20
Nos. C611-C614 (4) 3.50 .80

Centenary of Universal Postal Union.
For surcharge see No. C656.

Forest No. 1, by Roman Roncancio — AP143

Boy with Thorn in Finger, by Gregorio Vazquez AP144

Paintings: 3p, Women Fruit Vendors, by Miguel Diaz Vargas (1886-1956). 5p, Annunciation, Santafereña School, 17th-18th cent.

Perf. 13½x14, 14x13½

1975, Mar. 12 **Litho.**

C615 AP143 2p multicolored .75 .20
C616 AP144 3p multicolored .50 .20
C617 AP144 4p multicolored .65 .20
C618 AP144 5p multicolored 1.10 .25
Nos. C615-C618 (4) 3.00 .85

Modern and Colonial Colombian paintings.

Trees and Lake AP145

Design: 6p, Victoria regia, Amazon River.

1975, Mar. 12 ***Perf. 14x13½***

C619 AP145 1p yellow & multi .20 .20
C620 AP145 6p yellow & multi .60 .20

Nature conservation of trees and Amazon Region.

Gold Treasure Type

Designs: 2p, Nose pendant. 10p, Alligator-shaped staff ornament.

1975, Apr. 11 **Litho.** ***Perf. 14x13½***

C621 A368 2p grn, gold & brn .90 .20
C622 A368 10p multicolored 4.75 .60

El Rodadero, Santa Maria AP146

1975, July 26 **Litho.** ***Perf. 14x13½***

C623 AP146 2p multicolored .25 .20

400th anniversary of Santa Marta City.

AP147

AP148

1975, Aug. 31 **Litho.** ***Perf. 13½x14***

C624 AP147 4p multicolored .25 .20

Intl. Women's Year 1975. Maria de Jesus Paramo de Collazos founded 1st normal school for women in Bucaramanga in 1875.

1976, Mar. 12 **Litho.** ***Perf. 13½x14***

C625 AP148 5p "Sugar Cane" .85 .30

4th Congress of Latin-American and Caribbean sugar-exporting countries, Cali, 3/8-12.

View of Bogota — AP149

1976, July 2 **Litho.** ***Perf. 12***

C626 AP149 10p shown 1.25 .90
C627 AP149 10p Barranquilla 1.25 .90
C628 AP149 10p Cali 1.25 .90
C629 AP149 10p Medellin 1.25 .90
a. Block of 4, #C626-C629 6.00 6.00

Habitat, UN Conf. on Human Settlements, Vancouver, Canada, May 31-June 11.

University Emblem and "90" — AP150

1976, Aug. 6 **Litho.** ***Perf. 13½x14***

C630 AP150 5p lt blue & multi .50 .20

Univ. of Colombia day school, 90th anniv.

Miguel Samper — AP151

Telephone, 1895 — AP152

1976, Oct. 29 **Litho.** ***Perf. 13½x14***

C631 AP151 2p multicolored .25 .20

Samper (1825-99), economist and writer.

1976, Nov. 2

C632 AP152 3p multicolored .25 .20

Centenary of first telephone call by Alexander Graham Bell, Mar. 10, 1876.

747 Jumbo Jet AP153

1976, Dec. 3 **Litho.** ***Perf. 12***

C633 AP153 2p multicolored .25 .20

Inauguration of 747 jumbo jet service by Avianca.
For surcharge see No. C636.

Convent, Church and Plaza de San Francisco — AP154

1976, Dec. 29 **Litho.** ***Perf. 14***

C634 AP154 6p multicolored .50 .20

150th anniv. of the Congress of Panama.

Souvenir Sheet

Bank of the Republic Emblem — AP155

1977, June 6 **Litho.** ***Perf. 14***

C635 AP155 25p multicolored 11.00 11.00

Opening of Philatelic Museum of Medellin under auspices of Banco de la Republica.

No. C633 Surcharged in Light Brown

1977, June **Litho.** ***Perf. 12***

C636 AP153 3p on 2p multi .25 .20

Coffee AP156

Coffee Grower, Pack Mule AP157

1977-78 **Litho.** ***Perf. 12½***

C640 AP156 3p multi .50 .20
C641 AP156 3.50p multi ('78) .50 .20

Colombian coffee.

1977, Aug. 9 **Litho.** ***Perf. 13½x14***

C642 AP157 10p multicolored .50 .20

National Federation of Coffee Growers, 50th anniversary.

Beethoven and 9th Symphony AP158

Games' Emblem AP159

1977, Aug. 17

C643 AP158 8p multicolored .75 .20

Sesquicentennial of the death of Ludwig van Beethoven (1770-1827).

Bird Type

Tropical Birds and Plants: No. C644, Woodpecker and Meriania. C645, Purple gallinule and water lilies. No. C646, Xipholaena punicea and Cochlospermum orinocense. No. C647, Crowned flycatcher and Jacaranda copaia.

1977, Sept. 6 **Litho.** ***Perf. 14***

C644 A380 5p multicolored .75 .20
C645 A380 5p multicolored .75 .20
C646 A380 10p multicolored 1.10 .20
C647 A380 10p multicolored 1.10 .20
Nos. C644-C647 (4) 3.70 .80

1977, Sept. 9 ***Perf. 12x12½***

C648 AP159 6p multicolored .25 .20

13th Central American and Caribbean Games, Medellin, 1978.

La Cayetana, by Enrique Grau AP160

No. C650, Water Nymphs, by Beatriz Gonzalez.

1977, Sept. 13 ***Perf. 14x13½***

C649 AP160 8p multicolored .45 .20
C650 AP160 8p multicolored .45 .20

Women's suffrage, 20th anniversary.

Judge Francisco Antonio Moreno, by Joaquin Gutierrez AP161

Design: 25p, Viceroy Manuel de Guirior.

1977, Sept. 13 *Perf. 12*

C651	AP161	20p multicolored	1.25	.75
C652	AP161	25p multicolored	1.75	1.10

Bicentenary of National Library.

Federico Lleras Acosta — AP162

Cauca University Arms — AP163

1977, Sept. 27 **Litho.** *Perf. 14*

C653	AP162	5p multicolored	.30	.20

Dr. Federico Lleras Acosta, veterinarian and bacteriologist; birth centenary.

1977, Oct. 14

C654	AP163	5p multicolored	.30	.20

Sesquicentennial of the University of Cauca.

CUDECOM Building, Bogota AP164

1977, Oct. 14

C655	AP164	1.50p multicolored	.25	.20

Colombian Society of Engineers, 90th anniv.

No. C612 Surcharged with New Value and Bars in Brown

1977, Dec. 3 **Litho.** *Perf. 14x13½*

C656	AP142	2p on 1.30p multi	.30	.20

Lost City, Tayrona Culture AP165

Creator of Energy, by Arenas Betancourt AP166

1978, Apr. 18 **Litho.** *Perf. 12½*

C657	AP165	3.50p multicolored	.25	.20

1978, Apr. 25 *Perf. 12*

C658	AP166	4p blue & multi	.25	.20

Sesquicentennial of Antioquia University Law School.

Column of the Slaves — AP167

Statue of Catalina, Cartagena AP168

1978, May 9

C659	AP167	2.50p multicolored	.25	.20

Sesquicentennial of Ocana Convention (meeting of various political groups).

1978, May 30 **Litho.** *Perf. 12*

C660	AP168	4p blk & lt bl	.25	.20

Sesquicentennial of University of Cartagena.

Gold Pendant, Tolima — AP169

1978, July 11 **Litho.** *Perf. 12x12½*

C661	AP169	3.50p multicolored	.25	.20

Apotheosis of Spanish Language, by Luis Alberto Acuña — AP170

1978, Aug. 9 *Perf. 14*

C662	AP170	Strip of 3	4.75	4.75
a.-c.		11p, any single	1.10	1.10

Millennium of Spanish language.

Presidential Guard AP171

Figure, Muisca Culture AP172

1978, Aug. 16 *Perf. 13½x14*

C663	AP171	9p multicolored	.45	.45

Presidential Guard Battalion, 50th anniv.

1978, Sept. 12 **Litho.** *Perf. 12½*

C664	AP172	3.50p multicolored	.30	.20

Apse of Carmelite Church — AP173

1978, Oct. 12 *Perf. 13*

C665	AP173	30p multicolored	2.50	.40

Souvenir Sheet

Perf. 13½x14

C666	AP173	50p multicolored	3.50	3.50

ESPAMER '78 Philatelic Exhibition, Bogota, Oct. 12-21.

Owl, Gold Ornament, Calima AP174

Virgin and Child, by Gregorio Vasquez AP175

No. C669, Gold frog, Quimbaya culture. No. C670, Gold nose pendant, Tairona, horiz.

1978-80 **Litho.** *Perf. 12½*

C667	AP174	3.50p multi	.40	.20
C668	AP174	4p multi ('79)	.25	.20
C669	AP174	4p multi ('79)	.40	.20
C670	AP174	5p multi ('80)	.60	.20
		Nos. C667-C670 (4)	1.65	.80

1978, Nov. 28 *Perf. 13½x14*

C671	AP175	2.50p multicolored	.25	.20

Christmas 1978.

Bull Ring, Cathedral, Manizales AP176

1979, Jan. 6 **Litho.** *Perf. 14*

C672	AP176	7p multicolored	.60	.20

Manizales Fair.

Children Playing Hopscotch, and IYC Emblem — AP177

No. C674, Child at blackboard and UNESCO emblem. No. C675, The Paper Collector, by Omar Gordillo, and UN emblem.

1979, July 19 *Perf. 13½x14, 14x13½*

C673	AP177	8p multi	.40	.30
C674	AP177	12p multi, horiz.	.55	.45
C675	AP177	12p multi	.55	.45
		Nos. C673-C675 (3)	1.50	1.20

International Year of the Child.

Rio Prado Hydroelectric Station — AP178

1979, Aug. 24 *Perf. 13½x14*

C676	AP178	5p multicolored	.50	.20

Tomb, 6th Century — AP179

1979, Sept. 25 **Litho.** *Perf. 14*

C677	AP179	8p multicolored	.55	.35

San Augustin Archaeological Park.

Gonzalo Jimenez de Quesada, by C. Leudo AP180

1979, Oct. 11 *Perf. 12*

C678	AP180	20p multicolored	1.50	.50

Gonzalo Jimenez de Quesada (1500-1579), Spanish conquistador.

Hill, Penny Black, Colombia No. 1 — AP181

1979, Oct. 23 *Perf. 13½x14*

C679	AP181	15p multicolored	.60	.20

Sir Rowland Hill (1795-1879), originator of penny postage.

Amazon Region — AP182

Tourism: 14p, San Fernando Fortress.

1979	**Litho.**	***Perf. 13½x14***		
C680	AP182	7p multicolored	.40	.20
C681	AP182	14p multicolored	1.10	.60

Issue dates: 7p, Nov. 16; 14p, Nov. 9.
See Nos. C717-C719.

Nativity — AP183

Creche Sculptures: No. C682, Three Kings and soldiers. No. C684, Shepherds.

1979, Nov. 30		***Perf. 12***		
C682	AP183	3p multicolored	.35	.35
C683	AP183	3p multicolored	.35	.35
C684	AP183	3p multicolored	.35	.35
a.		Strip of 3, #C682-C684	1.40	1.40

Christmas 1979.

AP184

AP185

Magdalena Bridge, Avianca emblem.

1979, Dec. 5		***Perf. 14***		
C685	AP184	15p multicolored	.60	.20

Barranquilla, 350th anniversary; Avianca National Airline, 60th anniversary.

1980, Feb. 15 ***Perf. 13½x14***

Boy Playing Flute, by Judith Leyster.

C686	AP185	6p multicolored	.45	.20

2nd Intl. Music Competition, Ibague, Dec. 1979.

Gen. Antonio José de Sucre, 150th Death Anniversary AP186

1980, Feb. 15	**Litho.**	***Perf. 12½x12***		
C687	AP186	12p multicolored	.45	.20

The Watchman, by Edgar Negret AP187

1980, Feb. 26		***Perf. 12x12½***		
C688	AP187	25p multicolored	1.75	.80

Virgin Mary, by Real del Sarte, 1929 AP188

1980, May 23	**Litho.**	***Perf. 14x13½***		
C689	AP188	12p multicolored	.30	.20

Apparition of the Virgin Mary to Sister Catalina Labouri Gontard, 150th anniv.

San Gil Produce Market, by Luis Roncancio — AP189

1980, May 27		***Perf. 13½x14***		
C690	AP189	12p multicolored	.50	.25

Pres. Enrique Olaya Herrera, by Miguel Diaz Vargas — AP190

1980, Oct. 28	**Litho.**	***Perf. 12***		
C691	AP190	20p multicolored	1.00	.40

Enrique Olaya Herrera (1880-1936), president, 1930-1934.

The Boy Fishing in a Bucket AP191

Christmas (Christmas Stories by Rafael Pombo): No. C693, The Frog and the Mouse. No. C694, The Seven Lives of the Cat.

1980, Nov. 21	**Litho.**	***Perf. 14½***		
C692	AP191	4p multicolored	.20	.20
C693	AP191	4p multicolored	.20	.20
C694	AP191	4p multicolored	.20	.20
		Nos. C692-C694 (3)	.60	.60

28th World Golf Cup, Cajica — AP192

1980, Dec. 9	**Litho.**	***Perf. 13½x14***		
C695	AP192	30p multicolored	3.75	.50

Bolivar Type

Simon Bolivar Death Sesquicentennial: 6p, Portrait, last words to Colombia, vert.

1980, Dec. 17		***Perf. 12***		
C696	A400	6p multicolored	.60	.45

St. Peter Claver Holding Cross AP193

1981, Jan. 13		***Perf. 14½***		
C697	AP193	15p multicolored	.50	.20

St. Peter Claver (1580-1654), helped American Indians.

Sculptured Bird, San Augustin AP194

Archaeological Finds: No. C699, Funeral chamber, Tierradentro. No. C700, Chamber hallway, Tierradentro. No. C701, Statue of man, San Augustin.

1981, May 12	**Litho.**	***Perf. 14***		
C698	AP194	7p multicolored	1.00	.20
C699	AP194	7p multicolored	1.00	.20
C700	AP194	7p multicolored	1.00	.20
C701	AP194	7p multicolored	1.00	.20
a.		Block of 4, #C698-C701	5.00	5.00

See Nos. C707-C710D.

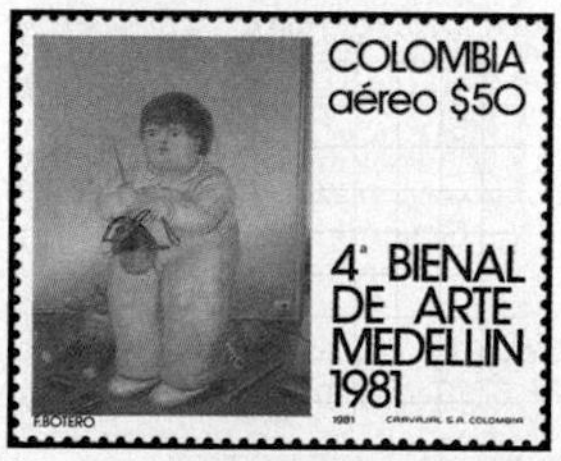

Child with Hobby Horse, by Fernando Botero — AP195

4th Biennial Arts show, Medellin: 20p, Square Abstract, by Omar Rayo. 25p, Flowers, by Alejandro Obregon.

1981, May 15		***Perf. 12***		
C702	AP195	20p multicolored	.85	.20
C703	AP195	25p multicolored	1.00	.30
C704	AP195	50p multicolored	1.75	.75
		Nos. C702-C704 (3)	3.60	1.25

8th South American Swimming Championships, Medellin — AP196

1981, June 5				
C705	AP196	15p multicolored	.50	.25

Santamaria Bull Ring, 50th Anniv. — AP197

1981, June 9	**Litho.**	***Perf. 12***		
C706	AP197	30p multicolored	2.00	1.25

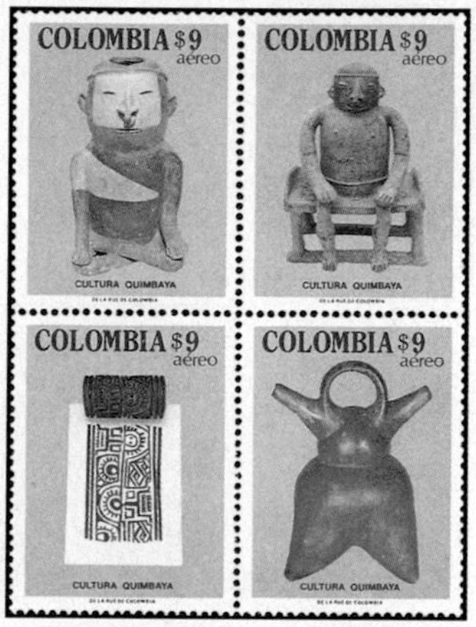

Quimbaya Culture — AP197a

1981, Sept. 23 **Litho.** ***Perf. 14***

Yellow Background

C707	9p	Man	1.00	.20
C708	9p	Seated man	1.00	.20
C709	9p	Seal, print	1.00	.20
C710	9p	Jug	1.00	.20
e.		AP197a Block of 4, #C707-C710	5.00	3.50

Calima Culture — AP197b

1981, Dec. 17

White Background

C710A	9p	Anthropomorphic container	1.25	.20
C710B	9p	Jar	1.25	.20
C710C	9p	Anthropomorphic jar	1.25	.20
C710D	9p	Urn	1.25	.20
f.		AP197b Block of 4, #C710A-C710D	6.00	4.50

Fruit
AP198

1981, Nov. 3 Litho. *Perf. 14*

C711	Block of 6	22.50	20.00
a.-f.	AP198 25p, any single	3.00	.80

Revolt of the Comuneros, 200th Anniv. — AP199

1981, Nov. 21 Litho. *Perf. 12*

C712	AP199 20p multicolored	.55	.30

Jose Manuel Restrepo, Historian, 1775?-1860?
AP200

Andres Bello, 1780?-1865
AP201

1981, Dec. 1 Litho. *Perf. 12*

C713	AP200 35p multicolored	1.00	.35

1981, Dec. 11 Litho. *Perf. 12*

C714	AP201 18p multicolored	.50	.20

Colombia's Admission to UPU, 100th Anniv.
AP202

30p, No. 103. 50p, Hemispheres, Nos. 104-108.

1981 Litho. *Perf. 12*

C715	AP202 30p multicolored	1.00	.35

Size: 100x70mm

Imperf

C716	AP202 50p multicolored	3.00	3.00

Issued: No. C715, Dec. 18. No. C716, Dec. 28.

Tourism Type of 1979

1982 Litho. *Perf. 12*

C717	AP182 20p Solano Bay	.50	.20
C718	AP182 20p Tota Lake, Boyaca	.50	.20
C719	AP182 20p Corrales, Boyaca	.50	.20
	Nos. C717-C719 (3)	1.50	.60

Issued: No. C717, 6/2; others, 6/16.

1982 World Cup — AP202a

Players and team emblems: a, "America." b, "A. B." c, "Cali." d, "C." e, "C/D." f, "Junior F.B.C." g, "D/M." h, Stadium. i, "M." j, "Club Atletico Nacional." k, "D/P." l, "Quindio." m, "Santa Fe." n, "T." o, "Santa Marta."

1982, June 21 *Perf. 14*

C720	Sheet of 15	10.00	6.75
a.-o.	AP202a 9p, any single	.70	.30

Bogota Gun Club Centenary
AP202b

1982, July 16 *Perf. 12*

C721	AP202b 20p multicolored	.50	.20

Gold Crocodile Figure, Tairona Culture
AP202c

Tairona Culture Exhibit, Gold Museum: Various figures. Nos. C723-C727 vert.

1982, July 28

Gold, Black and:

C722	AP202c 25p light brown	1.60	.45
C723	AP202c 25p bright pink	1.60	.45
C724	AP202c 25p green	1.60	.45
C725	AP202c 25p dark blue	1.60	.45
C726	AP202c 25p violet	1.60	.45
C727	AP202c 25p red	1.60	.45
	Nos. C722-C727 (6)	9.60	2.70

Government Buildings, Pereira — AP203

1982, Aug. 4 Litho. *Perf. 12*

C728	AP203 35p multicolored	1.00	.40

Biplane in Flight, by Edgar Antonio Bustos
AP204

1982, Aug. 5 *Perf. 14*

C729	AP204 18p multicolored	.50	.20

American Air Forces Cooperation System.

Magdalena River
AP205

1982, Oct. 21 Litho. *Perf. 12*

C730	AP205 30p multicolored	1.25	.35

Marquez Type

1982, Dec. 10 *Perf. 13½x14*

C731	A412 25p gray & blue	.60	.20
C732	A412 30p gray & brown	.85	.20

San Andres Archipelago — AP206

1983, Apr. 9 Litho. *Perf. 12*

C733	AP206 25p Liberty Fort	.50	.20

Opening of Las Gaviotas (The Seagulls) Ecological Center, Bogota — AP207

1983, June 1 Litho.

C734	AP207 12p multicolored	.30	.20

50th Anniv. of Radio Amateurs League
AP208

1983, June 11 *Perf. 14x13½*

C735	AP208 12p multicolored	.30	.20

Bolivar Type

1983, July 24 *Perf. 12*

C736	A417 30p multicolored	.60	.20
C737	A417 100p multicolored	2.00	1.50

Botanical Exhibition Type

1983, Aug. 18 *Perf. 14*

C738	A418 12p Begonia guaduensis	.55	.20
C739	A418 12p Chinchona ovaliflora	.55	.20
C740	A418 40p Begonia urticae	2.90	.40
	Nos. C738-C740 (3)	4.00	.80

Cartagena, 450th Anniv. — AP208a

1983, Sept. 9 Litho. *Perf. 12*

C740A	AP208a 12p Customs Square	.35	.20
C740B	AP208a 35p Historic sites, Cartagena	.90	.30

Painting Type

1983, Oct. 5 Litho. *Perf. 12*

C741	A420 30p multicolored	.50	.20

Scouting Year
AP209

Coffee Beans
AP210

1983, Oct. 24

C742	AP209 12p multicolored	.25	.20

1984, Mar. 28 Litho. *Perf. 14½x14*

C743	AP210 14p multicolored	.25	.20

Marandua City Type

1984, Sept. 28 *Perf. 12*

C744	A427 30p multicolored	.50	.20

AP211

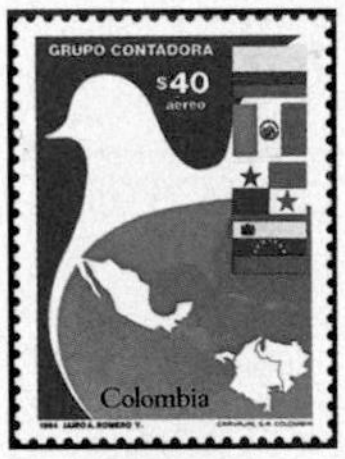

AP212

1984, Nov. 2

C745	AP211 45p multicolored	.70	.25

45th Cong. of Americanists, Bogota, 1985.

Christmas Type

1984, Dec. 14

C746	A428 14p multicolored	.30	.20

1985, Feb. 15

Design: Dove, map and flags of Colombia, Mexico, Costa Rica and Venezuela.

C747	AP212 40p multicolored	.70	.30

Contadora Group of Latin American countries.

Gomez Type

1985, Feb. 25

C748	A432 40p multicolored	.70	.30

Birds — AP213

AP214

1985

C749 AP213 14p Dryocopus lineatus nuperus .70 .25
C750 AP213 20p Xiphorhynchus picus 1.40 .25
C751 AP213 50p Eriocnemis cupreoventris 3.00 .30
C752 AP213 55p Momotus momota 3.75 .30
Nos. C749-C752 (4) 8.85 1.10

Issued: 14p, 4/12; 20p, 50p, 8/6; 55p, 8/29.

1985, July 15
C753 AP214 20p multicolored .30 .20

Admiral Padilla Naval School, 50th anniv.

1985 Census AP215

1985, Oct. 15 ***Perf. 12***
C754 AP215 20p multicolored .40 .20

Christmas Type

1985, Dec. 4 **Litho.** ***Perf. 13***
C755 A436 20p Girl, Christmas tree .30 .20

Alfonso Lopez Pumarejo (1886-1959), President, 1934-38, 1942-45 — AP216

1986, Jan. 31
C756 AP216 24p multicolored .30 .20

Coffee Berries, Natl. Cycling Team AP217

1986, Feb. 4
C757 AP217 60p multicolored 1.00 .60

Natl. Coffee Producers Assoc. sponsorship of natl. cycling team, 25th anniv.

Fauna Type of 1985

1986, Feb. 18
C758 A433 50p Pudu mephistophiles 1.50 .25

World Communications Day — AP218

Intl. Peace Year — AP219

1986, May 17 **Litho.** ***Perf. 13***
C759 AP218 50p multicolored .65 .25

1986, June 13 **Litho.** ***Perf. 13***
C760 AP219 55p multicolored .65 .25

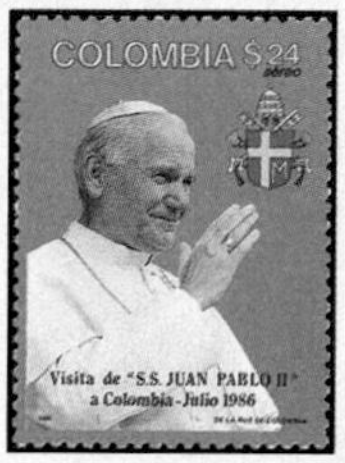

AP220

AP221

1986, July 1 **Litho.** ***Perf. 13***
C761 AP220 24p Portrait, papal arms 1.50 .20
C762 AP220 55p Portrait, Medellin cathedral, horiz. 1.50 .25
C763 AP220 60p Blessing crowd, horiz. 1.50 .25
Nos. C761-C763 (3) 4.50 .70

Souvenir Sheet

C764 AP220 200p Praying, Madonna of Bogota 3.00 3.00

Visit of Pope John Paul II.
Nos. C762-C763 each printed in sheets of 20 with se-tenant labels picturing religious symbols.

1986, July 15 ***Perf. 12***
C765 AP221 25p multicolored .30 .20

Enrique Santos Montejo (1886-1971), journalist.

Bach, Handel and Schutz, Composers AP222

1986, July 17 ***Perf. 13***
C766 AP222 70p Bach 1.50 .40
C767 AP222 100p Text, music 2.00 .55

Salesian Order Education in Colombia, Cent. AP223

1986, July 23 ***Perf. 12***
C768 AP223 25p De La Salle, founder .30 .20

Completion of Coal Mining Complex, El Cerrejon AP224

1986, July 29 **Litho.** ***Perf. 12***
C769 AP224 55p multi .80 .20

AP225

Natl. Constitution, Cent. — AP226

25p, The Five Signators, by R. Vasquez, detail, & Bogota Cathedral. 200p, Pres. Nunez & Miguel Antonio Caro, Natl. Council of Delegates chairman, & Presidential Palace, constitution.

1986, Aug. 5 **Litho.** ***Perf. 14***
C770 AP225 25p multi .30 .20

Souvenir Sheet

Perf. 12

C771 AP226 200p multi 2.25 2.25

Poet Type

Federico Garcia Lorca (1898-1936), poet, and birthplace, Fuentevaqueros, Granada, Spain.

1986, Sept. 26 **Litho.** ***Perf. 12***
C772 A445 60p multi .70 .25

Gratitude for Intl. Aid after the Armero Mudslide Disaster AP227

1986, Nov. 13
C773 AP227 50p multi .55 .20

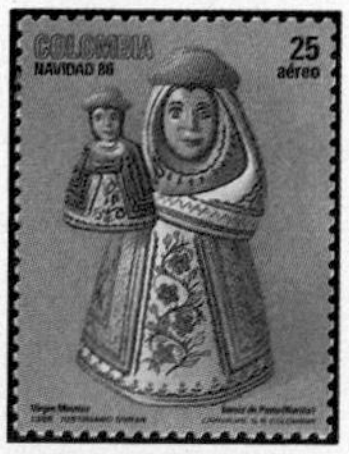

Christmas AP228

Wood sculpture: Virgin Mestiza, Nerina.

1986, Dec. 19 **Litho.** ***Perf. 12***
C774 AP228 25p multi .30 .20

The Apotheosis of Popayan, by Ephrain Martinez Zambrano (1898-1956) — AP229

1987, Jan. 13
C775 100p Popayan riding horse 1.50 .75
C776 100p Onlookers 1.50 .75
a. AP229 Pair, #C775-C776 3.50 3.50

AP230

AP231

1987, Mar. 16 **Litho.** ***Perf. 12***
C777 AP230 30p multi .40 .20

The Conversion of St. Augustine of Hippo, 1600th anniv.

Type of 1987

30p, Phoenicopterus ruber. 35p, Pseudemys scripta, horiz. No. C780, Crax alberti. No. C781, Symphysodon aequifasciatum, horiz.

Perf. 14½x14, 14x14½

1987-89 **Wmk. 334**
C778 A446a 30p lake .35 .20
C779 A446a 35p dark red brn .40 .20
C780 A446a 45p dark blue gray .30 .20
C781 A446a 45p blue .30 .20
Nos. C778-C781 (4) 1.35 .80

Issue dates: 30p, June 8. 35p, Dec. 24. No. C780, Dec. 6, 1988. No. C781, June 23, 1989.

Perf. 13½x13

1987, Apr. 10 **Unwmk.**
C783 AP231 25p multi .30 .20

Natl. University School of Mining, Medellin, cent.

Purebred Horses AP232

1987, June 17 ***Perf. 12***
C784 AP232 60p White horse 1.00 .25
C785 AP232 70p Black horse 1.00 .30

El Espectador Newspaper, Cent. AP233

Design: Frontispieces from 1887, 1915, 1948, 1974 and portraits of founder Don Fidel Cano, editors Don Luis Cano, Luis Gabriel Cano Isaza and Alfonso Cano Isaza.

1987, July 24 *Perf. 12½x12*
C786 AP233 60p multi .75 .25

Intl. Year of Shelter for the Homeless AP234

1987, Sept. 21 *Perf. 14*
C787 AP234 60p multi 1.10 .25

Flags AP235

1987, Nov. 27 **Litho.** *Perf. 13x13½*
C788 AP235 80p multi .80 .30

Ist Meeting of the eight Latin-American Presidents, Acapulco, Nov.

Christmas AP236

1987, Dec. 8 **Litho.** *Perf. 14*
C789 AP236 30p multi .45 .20

Rural Telephone System AP237

1988, Feb. 4 **Litho.** *Perf. 14*
C790 AP237 70p multi .80 .30

Founding of Bogota, 450th Anniv. — AP238

1988, Apr. 11 **Litho.** *Perf. 12*
C791 AP238 70p multi .75 .25

Bogota, 450th Anniv. AP238a

Unwmk.

1988, July 1 **Litho.** *Perf. 12*
C792 AP238a 80p Modern district, vert. .75 .25
C793 AP238a 90p Colonial district .85 .30

Gold Artifacts AP239

Artifacts in the Gold Museum: 70p, Mask. 80p, Two-headed human figure inside a circle, Muisca tribe. 90p, Ritual figure of the Quimbaya.

1988 *Perf. 12*
C794 AP239 70p multi .65 .30
C795 AP239 80p multi .75 .25
C796 AP239 90p multi 1.00 .35
Nos. C794-C796 (3) 2.40 .90

Issue dates: 70p, May 13; 80p, 90p, Oct. 7.

Human Rights Type

Perf. 14x14½

1988, July 1 **Engr.** **Wmk. 334**
C797 A452 40p Communication, horiz. .40 .20

AP240

AP241

1988, Sept. 28 **Litho.** *Perf. 12*
C798 AP240 80p multi .70 .20

Zipa Tisquesusa (d. 1538), Chibcha Indian leader during revolt against Spanish Conquistadors.

1988, Nov. 23 **Litho.** *Perf. 12*
C799 AP241 40p multi .50 .20

Christmas.

Agustin Nieto Caballero (1889-1975), Educator — AP242

Unwmk.

1989, Mar. 18 **Litho.** *Perf. 12*
C800 AP242 100p multi .75 .25

Pres. Laureano Gomez (1889-1965) AP243

1989, Mar. 29
C801 AP243 45p multi .30 .20

Intl. Coffee Organization — AP244

1989, Apr. 3
C802 AP244 110p multi .90 .30

12th Session of the UN Commission on Human Rights — AP245

1989, Apr. 28
C803 AP245 100p multi .90 .25

French Revolution, Bicent. AP246

1989, June 29 **Litho.** *Perf. 12*
C804 AP246 100p multi .75 .25

PHILEXFRANCE '89 — AP247

a, Bananas, tropical fruits. b, Fruits, flowers. c, Birds, animals. d, Precious gems, metals and mineral resources. e, View of fields, Colombian carrying produce basket. f, Waterfall. g, Fish, coast. Illustration reduced.

1989 **Litho.** *Perf. 14*
C805 AP247 Pane of 7 17.50 17.50
a.-g. 110p any single 1.75 .40

No. C805 printed in sheets containing panes of 7, rouletted between.

Souvenir Sheet

Los Lanceros, by R. Arenas Betancur — AP248

1989 **Litho.** *Perf. 12*
C806 AP248 250p multicolored 1.75 1.25

Human Rights Type

Perf. 14½x14

1989, Aug. 18 **Engr.** **Wmk. 334**
C807 A452 55p Family .40 .20

Natl. Anti-Drugs Campaign AP249

Unwmk.

1989, Aug. 23 **Litho.** *Perf. 12*
C808 AP249 115p multicolored .90 .25

America Issue AP250

UPAE emblem and artifacts or customs of pre-Columbian peoples: 115p, Quimbaya, Calima or Tolima gold smiths. 130p, Potter and Sinu ceramic figurine.

1989 *Perf. 12*
C809 AP250 115p multicolored 1.00 .25
C810 AP250 130p multicolored 1.10 .30

Issue dates: 115p, Oct. 12; 130p, Aug. 23.

Joaquin Quijano Mantilla (1878-1944), Journalist — AP251

1989, Sept. 29 *Perf. 12*
C811 AP251 170p multicolored 1.20 .40

Arts and Crafts in Barro-Raquira AP252

1989 **Litho.** *Perf. 12*
C812 AP252 55p multicolored .40 .20

Christmas.

Boeing 767
AP253

1989, Dec. 5 **Litho.** ***Perf. 12***
C813 AP253 130p multicolored .90 .30

Bolivar Installed at the Congress of Angostura, by Tito Salas — AP254

1989, Dec. 12
C814 AP254 130p multicolored .90 .30

Creation of the Republic, 1819.

Fathers of the Nation Leaving the Constitutional Convention
AP255

1989, Dec. 12
C815 AP255 130p shown .90 .30
C816 AP255 130p Arms .90 .30
C817 AP255 130p Temple of the Rosary .90 .30
Nos. C815-C817 (3) 2.70 .90

Constitution of the Republic, 1821.

Arms Type of Regular Issue, 1982

1990, Mar. 1 **Litho.** ***Perf. 12***
C818 A372 60p Velez .30 .20

Presidential Summit, Cartagena
AP256

1990, Feb. 15 **Litho.** ***Perf. 12***
C819 AP256 130p Plaza de la Aduana .55 .20

Colombian National Radio, 50th Anniv. — AP257

1990, Feb. 16 **Litho.** ***Perf. 12***
C820 AP257 150p multicolored 1.00 .20

Teresa Cuervo Borda (1889-1976), Art Historian — AP258

1990, Mar. 28 **Litho.** ***Perf. 12***
C821 AP258 60p multicolored .35 .20

Second Latin American Theater Festival, Bogota — AP259

1990, Apr. 10
C822 AP259 150p buff, tan & gold .80 .25

Santander Type

No. C823, Santander holding the Constitution. No. C824, Central Cemetery, Bogata and National Pantheon. No. C825, Santander, as organizer of public education. No. C826, "Postman of New Granada" (Man and burro) by Joseph Brown and Jose Maria del Castillo, horiz. 500p, Santander on death bed.

1990, May 6 ***Perf. 14x13½***
C823 A470 60p multicolored .30 .20
C824 A470 60p multicolored .30 .20
C825 A470 70p multicolored .40 .20
C826 A470 70p multicolored .40 .20
Nos. C823-C826 (4) 1.40 .80

Souvenir Sheet

Perf. 12

C827 A470 500p multi 2.00 1.50

No. C827 contains one 54x40mm stamp.

First Postage Stamp, 150th Anniv.
AP260

1990, May 6 ***Perf. 14***
C828 AP260 150p multicolored .80 .25

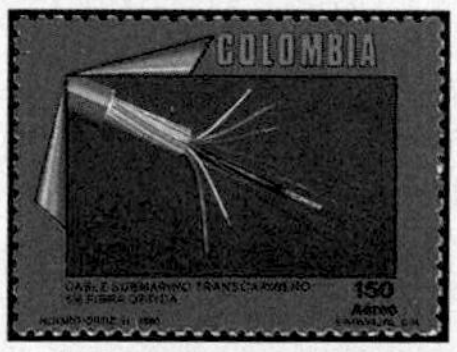

Trans-Caribbean Fiber Optic Cable — AP261

1990, May 19 ***Perf. 12***
C829 AP261 150p multicolored .80 .25

Institute of Industrial Development, 25th Anniv. — AP262

1990, May 22
C830 AP262 60p multicolored .40 .20

Souvenir Sheet

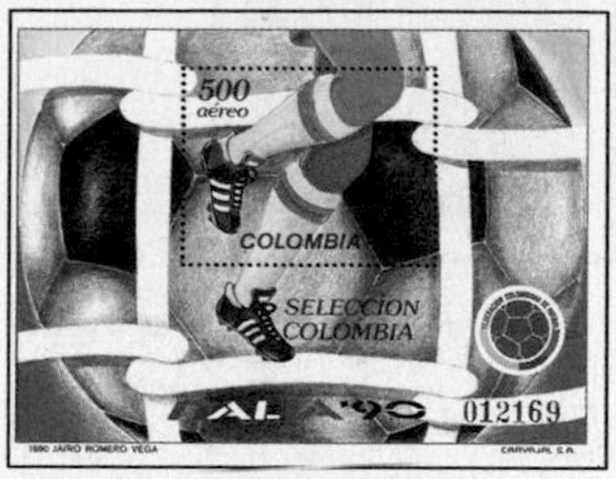

World Cup Soccer Championships, Italy — AP263

1990, June 8
C831 AP263 500p multicolored 3.00 2.25

AP264

AP265

1990, June 27
C832 AP264 130p multicolored .60 .20

Organization of American States, cent.

1990, July 26
C833 AP265 170p multicolored .80 .25

Museum of Gold, 50th Anniv.

Dolphins, Marine Birds
AP266

1990, Oct. 12 **Litho.** ***Perf. 12***
C834 AP266 150p shown 1.50 .20
C835 AP266 170p Jungle fauna, vert. 1.50 .25

AP267

AP268

1990, Nov. 16 **Litho.** ***Perf. 12***
C836 AP267 70p multicolored .40 .20

Monastery of Our Lady of Las Lajas.

1991, Feb. 8 **Litho.** ***Perf. 12***
C837 AP268 170p multicolored .80 .30

Newspaper Publishing, 200th Anniv.

AP269

AP270

1990, Nov. 1 **Litho.** ***Perf. 12***
C838 AP269 70p multicolored .40 .20

Christmas.

1991, May 31 **Litho.** ***Perf. 14***

Whales and Dolphins: 80p, Megaptera novaeangliae, breaching. 170p, Megaptera novaeangliae, diving. 190p, Inia geoffrensis, Sotalia fluviatilis, horiz.

C839 AP270 80p multicolored .90 .20
C840 AP270 170p multicolored 1.90 .30
C841 AP270 190p multicoloed 2.10 .30
Nos. C839-C841 (3) 4.90 .80

America Issue
AP271

1991, Oct. 11 **Litho.** ***Perf. 14***
C842 AP271 90p shown .45 .20
C843 AP271 190p Ship arriving in New World .85 .25

Adoration of the Magi — AP272

1991, Dec. 20 **Litho.** ***Perf. 14***
C844 AP272 90p multicolored .45 .20

Christmas.

AP273

AP274

1991, Dec. 2
C845 AP273 190p Country flags .85 .25

Fifth summit of Latin American presidents.

1992, Feb. 8 **Litho.** ***Perf. 12***
C846 AP274 210p multicolored 1.00 .30

8th UNCTAD Conference, Cartagena.

Proclamation of New Constitution, July 4, 1991 — AP275

1991, Nov. 27 **Litho.** ***Perf. 14***
C847 AP275 90p multicolored .40 .20

Export Products AP276

Copyright Protection AP277

1992, Mar. 11 ***Perf. 12***
C848 AP276 90p Flowers .40 .20
C849 AP276 210p Fruits, vegetables, horiz. 1.10 .30

1992, Apr. 13 **Litho.** ***Perf. 12***
C850 AP277 190p multicolored .85 .25

1992 Summer Olympics AP278

1992, June 4 **Litho.** ***Perf. 14***
C851 AP278 110p multicolored .75 .30

Earth Summit '92 AP279

a, Tree, mountain landscape. b, Birds in tree.

1992, June 2 **Litho.** ***Perf. 14***
C852 A279 230p Pair, #a.-b. 2.10 1.40

America Issue AP280

Paintings: 230p, Discovery of America by Christopher Columbus, by Salvador Dali. 260p, Magical America, Myth and Legend, by Alfredo Vivero.

1992, July 22 ***Perf. 14x13½***
C853 AP280 230p multicolored 1.00 .70
C854 AP280 260p multicolored 1.10 .75

McDonnell Douglas MD83 AP281

1992, Sept. 22 **Litho.** ***Perf. 12***
C855 AP281 110p multicolored .50 .30

Curtain of Colon Theatre AP282

1992, Oct. 12 **Litho.** ***Perf. 12***
C856 AP282 230p multicolored 1.00 .65

AP283

AP284

1992, Nov. 27 **Litho.** ***Perf. 12***
C857 AP283 230p Gloria Lara, 1938-82 1.00 .65

1993, June 7 **Litho.** ***Perf. 12***
C858 AP284 220p multicolored .95 .60

1993 American Soccer Cup, Ecuador.

Intl. Year of Indigenous People — AP285

1993, July 1 ***Perf. 14***
C859 AP285 460p multicolored 2.00 1.25

South American Eliminations for 1994 World Cup Soccer Championships, US — AP286

1993, July 31 **Litho.** ***Perf. 12***
C860 AP286 220p multicolored .95 .50

AP287

AP288

America Issue (Endangered species): a, 220p, Saguinus oedipus. b, 220p, Porphyrula martinica. c, 460p, Rupicola peruviana. d, 520p, Trichecus manatus.

1993, Oct. 19 **Litho.** ***Perf. 12***
C861 AP287 Block of 4, #a.-d. 7.50 7.50

1994, Mar. 21 **Litho.** ***Perf. 12***
C862 AP288 630p multicolored 2.25 1.40

Intl. Decade for Natural Disaster Reduction.

Beatification of Josemaria Escriva de Balaguer — AP289

1994, May 17 **Litho.** ***Perf. 13½x14***
C863 AP289 560p multicolored 1.90 1.25

First Airmail Delivery, 75th Anniv. AP290

Design: 270p, William Knox Martin, airplane over Port Colombia, 1919.

1994, July 29 **Litho.** ***Perf. 14***
C864 AP290 270p multicolored 1.00 .55

Natl. Institute of Medical Law & Forensic Sciences, 80th Anniv. AP291

1994, Oct. 27 **Litho.** ***Perf. 12***
C865 AP291 560p multicolored 1.90 1.25

Sociedad Colombo-Alemana de Transportes Aereos (SCADTA), 75th Anniv. — AP292

1995, Jan. 2 **Litho.** ***Perf. 12***
C866 AP292 330p No. C15 1.10 .50

Flora and Fauna — AP293

Iguana iguana: No. C867a, Facing right. b, Facing left.

Rain forest: No. C868a, Nuts on branch, flowers. b, Waterfall, hanging red flower.

1995, Jan. 17
C867 AP293 650p Pair, #a.-b. 4.50 3.00
C868 AP293 750p Pair, #a.-b. 5.50 4.00

Nos. C867-C868 are continuous designs.

SCADTA, 75th Anniv. AP294

1995, Mar. 30 **Litho.** ***Perf. 14***
C869 AP294 330p No. C9 1.50 .75

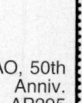

FAO, 50th Anniv. AP295

1995, Apr. 25 Litho. ***Perf. 13x13½***
C870 AP295 750p multicolored 2.25 1.25

Andres Bello Organization, 25th Anniv. — AP296

Colombian Firefighters, Cent. — AP297

1995, Apr. 27 ***Perf. 13½x13***
C871 AP296 650p multicolored 2.00 .85

1995, May 5 ***Perf. 12***
C872 AP297 330p multicolored 1.10 .45

Fenalco, 50th Anniv. — AP298

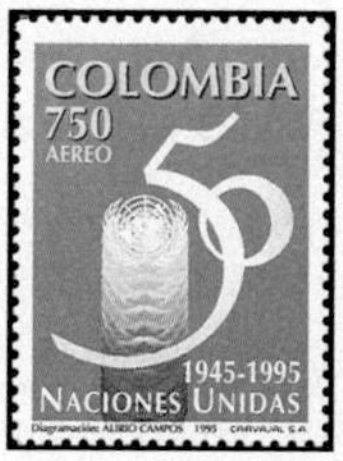

UN, 50th Anniv. — AP299

1995, May 25 ***Perf. 13½***
C873 AP298 330p multicolored 1.10 .45

1995, June 21 ***Perf. 12***
C874 AP299 750p multicolored 1.50 1.00

First Pacific Ocean Games — AP300

1995, June 23
C875 AP300 750p multicolored 2.25 1.25

11th Summit of Non-Aligned Countries, Cartagena — AP302

1995, Oct. 13 Litho. ***Perf. 12***
C877 AP302 650p multicolored 1.50 .90

Motion Pictures, Cent. AP303

Design: 330p, Charlie Chaplin and Jackie Coogan in "The Kid," Estela López Pomareda in "María," first Colombian feature length film.

1995, Oct. 19 ***Perf. 14***
C878 AP303 330p black & sepia .90 .45

AP304

AP305

1995, Nov. 23 ***Perf. 12***
C879 AP304 650p multicolored 1.90 .90

Andes Development Corporation (CAF), 25th Anniv.

1995, Nov. 21 ***Perf. 14***

Fight against illegal drug trafficking: No. C880, Locating illegally grown plants. No. C881, Hands in handcuffs, horiz.

C880 AP305 330p multicolored .70 .45
C881 AP305 330p multicolored .70 .45

Miniature Sheet of 16

Myths and Legends — AP306

Madre-Monte: a.-d.
La Llorna: e.-h.
El Mohán: i.-l.
Hombre Caimán: m.-p.

Background color changes from top to bottom rows. Top row is blue. Row 2 is blue green. Row 3 is green. Row 4 is lilac. Each design comes in all four colors.

1995, Dec. 6
C882 AP306 750p #a.-p. 27.50 27.50

See No. C886.

José Asunción Silva (1865-96), Poet AP307

1996, Apr. 23 Litho. ***Perf. 12***
C883 AP307 400p multicolored .90 .40

Isla de Providencia AP308

Policarpa Salavarrieta (1796-1817), Patriot — AP309

1996, Apr. 25 ***Perf. 14***
C884 AP308 800p multicolored 2.25 .80

1996, Apr. 26
C885 AP309 900p multicolored 2.50 .85

Myths and Legends Type

Designs: a, Kogui Creation. b, Yonna Wayu. c, Jaguar Man. d, Master of the Animals.

1996, Aug. 12 Litho. ***Perf. 13½x14***
C886 AP306 900p Block of 4, #a.-d. 13.00 13.00

Metropolitan Basilica, Medellin AP310

1996, July 12
C887 AP310 400p multicolored 1.10 .55

National Archives Building AP311

1996, July 30 Litho. ***Perf. 14***
C888 AP311 400p multicolored 1.10 .40

CERLALC, 25th Anniv. AP312

1996, Aug. 16 Litho. ***Perf. 12***
C889 AP312 800p multicolored 2.10 1.00

UNESCO.

Pioneers in Petroleum Industry — AP313

a, Jorge Isaacs, pumping oil. b, Francisco Burgos Rubio, refinery at night. c, Diego Martínez Camargo, derrick. d, Prisciliano Cabrales Lora, off-shore drilling. e, Manuel María Palacio, oil tanker loading offshore. f, Roberto De Mares, refinery, lake. g, General Virgilio Barco Maldonado, men positioning equipment. h, Roustabout, "ECOPETROL" emblem.

1996, Sept. 5 Litho. ***Perf. 13½x14***
C890 AP313 800p Block of 8, #a.-h. 20.00 20.00

Colombian Golf Federation, 50th Anniv. AP314

1996, Sept. 19 Litho. ***Perf. 12***
C891 AP314 400p multicolored 1.25 .50

Covenant for the Children AP315

1997, Feb. 28 Litho. ***Perf. 14***
C892 AP315 400p multicolored 1.40 .55

AP316

AP317

1997, Apr. 25 *Perf. 12*
C893 AP316 800p multicolored 1.75 1.40

Motion pictures in Colombia, cent.

1997, May 13 Litho. *Perf. 12*
C894 AP317 400p multicolored 1.50 .50

Social Security Institute, 50th anniv.

Ericsson in Colombia, Cent. — AP318

1997, May 22 *Perf. 13½x14*
C895 AP318 900p multicolored 2.50 1.40

Bogatá Colonial Bldg., Home of Natl. Mint and Numismatic Museum — AP319

1997, July 10 *Perf. 12*
C896 AP319 800p multicolored 2.50 1.40

Phytelephas Seemannii — AP320

1997, July 23 *Perf. 13½x14*
C897 AP320 900p multicolored 3.00 .90

Cordoba Cattle Fair AP321

1997, June 21 *Perf. 14*
C898 AP321 400p multicolored 1.25 .45

Personalities — AP322

No. C899: a, Cacique Gaitana, 16th cent., Indian resistance leader. b, Josefa Acevedo de Gómez (1803-61), writer. c, Domingo Bioho (d. 1621), black leader. d, Soledad Acosta de Samper (1831-1913), historian. e, Maria Cano Márquez (1897-1967), popular leader. f, Manuel Quintín Lame (1880-1967), native leader. g, Ezequiel Uricoechea (1834-80), linguist, naturalist. h, Juan Rodríguez Freyle (1566-1642), colonial reporter. i, Gerardo Reichel-Dolmatoff (1912-94), archaeologist. j, Ramón de Zubiría (1922-95), writer, educator. k, Esteban Jaramillo (1874-1947), economist. l, Pedro Fermín de Vargas (1762-c. 1810), economist.

No. 900: a, Luis Carlos "el turerto" López (1879-1950), poet. b, Aurelio Arturo (1906-74), poet. c, Enrique Pérez Arbeláez (1896-1972), botanist. d, José Maria González Benito (1843-1903), mathematician, astronomer. e, José Manuel Rivas Sacconi (1917-91), diplomat. f, Eduardo Lemaitre Román (1914-94), historian. g, Diójenes Arrieta (1848-93), politician. h, Gabriel Turbay Abunader (1901-47), politician, diplomat. i, Guillermo Echavarría Misas (1888-1985), aviation pioneer. j, Juan Friede Alter (1901-90), historian. k, Fabio Lozano Torrijos (1865-1947), diplomat. l, Lino de Pombo (1797-1862), engineer, diplomat.

1997, Dec. 19 Litho. *Perf. 13½x14*
Sheets of 12
C899 AP322 500p #a.-l. 22.50 22.50
C900 AP322 500p #a.-l. 22.50 22.50

Colombian Society of Orthopedic Surgery and Traumatology, 50th Anniv. — AP323

1997 *Perf. 12*
C901 AP323 1000p multicolored 3.00 1.00

AP324

AP325

1998, Apr. 30 Litho. *Perf. 14*
C902 AP324 1000p multicolored 3.00 .80

Organization of American States, 50th anniv.

1998, May 22
C903 AP325 1000p bl & org 3.00 .80

4th Bolivar Philatelic Exhibition, Santa Fe de Bogota.

World Health Organization, 50th Anniv. — AP326

1998, Apr. 7 *Perf. 12*
C904 AP326 1100p multicolored 3.00 1.00

1998 World Cup Soccer Championships, France — AP327

Stylized designs: a, Foot. b. Soccer ball. c, Hand.

1998, June 9 Litho. *Perf. 14*
C905 AP327 1100p Strip of 3, #a.-c. 9.00 9.00

Intl. Year of the Ocean — AP328

1998, May 22 *Perf. 12*
C906 AP328 1100p ARC Gloria 3.50 .95

Myths and Legends — AP329

Designs: a, Bochica. b, Chimingagua. c, Bachue and Huitica.

Perf. 13¼x12¾
1998, Nov. 27 Litho.
C907 AP329 1000p Strip of 3, #a.-c. 15.00 15.00

AIR POST SPECIAL DELIVERY STAMPS

Catalogue values for unused stamps in this section are for Never Hinged items.

Post Horn and Wings APSD1

Unwmk.
1958, May 19 Litho. *Perf. 12*
CE1 APSD1 25c dk bl & red .40 .20

Same Overprinted Vertically in Red

1959
CE2 APSD1 25c dk bl & red .50 .20

Jet Plane and Envelope — APSD2

1963, Oct. 4 *Perf. 14*
CE3 APSD2 50c red & blk .25 .20

Aviation Type

80c, Boeing 727 jet, 1966.

Perf. 14x13½
1966, Dec. 14 Photo. Unwmk.
CE4 AP96 80c crim & multi .35 .20

AIR POST REGISTRATION STAMPS

Issued by Sociedad Colombo-Alemana de Transportes Aereos (SCADTA)

No. C41 Overprinted in Red

1923 Wmk. 116 *Perf. 14x14½*
CF1 AP6 20c gray 2.50 1.10

No. C58 Overprinted in Black

1929 Wmk. 127 *Perf. 14*
CF2 AP8 20c carmine 4.50 1.10

Same Overprint on No. C71
CF3 AP10 20c carmine 6.50 6.00

Colombian Government Issues
Same Overprint on No. C86

1932
CF4 AP8 20c carmine 6.50 6.00

No. C100 Overprinted

CF5 AP12 20c car & ol blk 4.50 1.25

For surcharge see No. C118.

SPECIAL DELIVERY STAMPS

Special Delivery Messenger — SD1

1917 Unwmk. Engr. ***Perf. 14***
E1 SD1 5c gray green 25.00 *75.00*

Catalogue values for unused stamps in this section, from this point to the end of the section, are for Never Hinged items.

SD2

1987, July 31 Litho. ***Perf. 14***
E2 SD2 25p emerald & ver .30 .30
E3 SD2 30p emerald & ver .35 .35

REGISTRATION STAMPS

R1

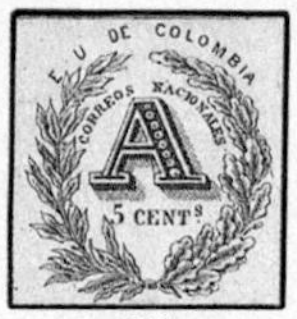

R2

1865 Unwmk. Litho. ***Imperf.***
F1 R1 5c black 80.00 40.00
F2 R2 5c black 75.00 40.00

R3

R4

1870

White Paper
Vertical Lines in Background
F3 R3 5c black 2.25 1.90
F4 R4 5c black 2.25 1.90

Horizontal Lines in Background
F5 R3 5c black 7.50 6.50
F6 R4 5c black 2.25 1.90
Nos. F3-F6 (4) 14.25 12.20

Reprints of Nos. F3 to F6 show either crossed lines or traces of lines in background.

R5

R6

1881 ***Imperf.***
F7 R5 10c violet 47.50 40.00
a. Sewing machine perf. 55.00 47.50
b. Perf. 11 60.00 50.00

1883 ***Perf. 12, 13½***
F8 R6 10c red, *orange* 1.50 *1.90*

R7

1889-95 ***Perf. 12, 13½***
F9 R7 10c red, *grysh* 5.25 2.50
F10 R7 10c red, *yelsh* 5.25 2.50
F11 R7 10c dp brn, *rose buff* ('95) 1.50 1.25
F12 R7 10c yel brn, *lt buff* ('92) 1.50 1.25
Nos. F9-F12 (4) 13.50 7.50

Nos. F9-F12 exist imperf. Values same as for perf.

R9

1902 ***Imperf.***
F13 R9 20c red brown, *blue* 1.40 1.40
a. Sewing machine perf. 3.75 3.75
b. Perf. 12 3.75 3.75

Medellin Issue

R10

1902 ***Perf. 12***

Laid Paper
F16 R10 10c blk vio 12.50 12.50
a. Wove paper 17.50 17.50

Regular Issue

1903 ***Imperf.***
F17 R9 20c blue, *blue* 1.40 1.40
a. Sewing machine perf. 4.00 4.00
b. Perf. 12 4.00 4.00

R11

1904 Pelure Paper ***Imperf.***
F19 R11 10c purple 3.00 3.00
a. Sewing machine perf. 4.00 3.00
b. Perf. 12 5.00 4.00

R12

Imprint: "J. L. Arango"

1904 ***Perf. 12***

Wove Paper
F20 R12 10c purple 2.00 .50
a. Imperf., pair 6.25 6.25

Imprint: "Lit. Nacional"

1909 ***Perf. 10, 14, 10x14, 14x10***
F21 R12 10c purple 2.25 .70
a. Imperf., pair 5.00 5.00

For overprints see Nos. LF1-LF4.

Execution at Cartagena in 1816 — R13

1910, July 20 Engr. ***Perf. 12***
F22 R13 10c red & black 17.50 *75.00*

Centenary of National Independence.

Pier at Puerto Colombia — R14

Tequendama Falls — R15

Perf. 11, 11½, 14, 11½x14
1917, Aug. 25
F23 R14 4c green & ultra .50 *2.50*
a. Center inverted 575.00 575.00
F24 R15 10c deep blue 1.90 .60

R16

1925 Litho. ***Perf. 10x13½***
F25 R16 (10c) blue 3.50 1.50
a. Imperf., pair 12.00 10.00
b. Perf. 13½x10 6.00 4.00

ACKNOWLEDGMENT OF RECEIPT STAMPS

AR1

AR2

1893 Unwmk. Litho. ***Perf. 13½***
H1 AR1 5c ver, *blue* 4.25 4.25

1894 ***Perf. 12***
H2 AR1 5c vermilion 3.50 *4.00*

1902-03 ***Imperf.***
H3 AR2 10c blue, *blue* 2.75 *4.00*
a. 10c, blue, *greenish blue* 2.75 *4.00*
b. Sewing machine perf. 2.75 *4.00*
c. Perf. 12 2.75 *4.00*

The handstamp "AR" in circle is believed to be a postmark.

AR2a

Purple Handstamp

1903 ***Imperf.***
H4 AR2a 10c black, *pink* 20.00 20.00

AR3

AR4

1904 Pelure Paper ***Imperf.***
H12 AR3 5c pale blue 10.50 10.50
a. Perf. 12 10.50 10.50

No. 307 Overprinted in Black, Green or Violet **A R**

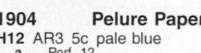

H13 A86 5c carmine 17.50 17.50

1904 ***Perf. 12***
H16 AR4 5c blue 3.25 2.75
a. Imperf., pair 8.75 8.75

For overprints see Nos. LH1-LH2.

General José Acevedo y Gómez — AR5

1910, July 20 **Engr.**
H17 AR5 5c orange & green 5.75 *16.00*

Centenary of National Independence.

Sabana Station AR6

Map of Colombia AR7

1917 ***Perf. 14***
H18 AR6 4c bister brown 1.75 *2.00*
H19 AR7 5c orange brown 1.50 *1.75*
a. Imperf., pair 11.00

LATE FEE STAMPS

LF1

LF2

1886 Unwmk. Litho. ***Perf. 10½***
I1 LF1 2½c blk, *lilac* 3.25 2.50
a. Imperf., pair 12.00 12.00

1892 ***Perf. 12, 13½***
I2 LF2 2½c dk bl, *rose* 2.75 2.00
a. Imperf., pair 12.00
I3 LF2 2½c ultra, *pink* 2.75 2.00

LF3

LF4

1902 ***Imperf.***
I4 LF3 5c purple, *rose* .85 .85
a. Perf. 12 1.75 1.75

1914 ***Perf. 10, 13½***
I6 LF4 2c vio brown 4.00 4.00
I7 LF4 5c blue green 4.00 3.25

Retardo

Refardo
1921

Overprints illustrated above are unauthorized and of private origin.

POSTAGE DUE STAMPS

These are not, strictly speaking, postage due stamps but were issued to cover an additional fee, "Sobreporte," charged on mail to foreign countries with which Colombia had no postal conventions.

D1

D2

D3

1866 Unwmk. Litho. *Imperf.*

J1	D1	25c black, *blue*	65.00	45.00
J2	D2	50c black, *yellow*	45.00	*65.00*
J3	D3	1p black, *rose*	140.00	*110.00*
		Nos. J1-J3 (3)	250.00	220.00

DEPARTMENT STAMPS

These stamps are said to be for interior postage, to supersede the separate issues for the various departments.

Regular Issues Handstamped in Black, Violet, Blue or Green — a

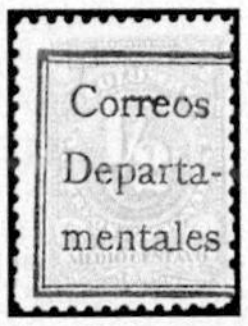

On Stamps of 1904

1909 Unwmk. *Perf. 12*

L1	A94	½c yellow	2.00	2.00
a.		Imperf., pair	6.00	6.00
L2	A94	1c yel grn	3.00	2.00
L3	A94	2c red	4.50	3.00
a.		Imperf., pair	12.50	12.50
L4	A94	5c blue	5.00	3.25
L5	A94	10c violet	7.00	7.00
L6	A94	20c black	11.00	10.00
L7	A95	1p brown	18.00	17.00

On Stamp of 1902

L8	A83	10p dk brn, *rose*	20.00	20.00
		Nos. L1-L8 (8)	70.50	64.25

On Stamps of 1908

Perf. 10, 13, 13½ and Compound

L9	A94	½c orange	2.00	2.00
a.		Imperf., pair	6.00	6.00
L10	A94	1c green	4.00	3.25
a.		Without imprint	5.00	5.00
L11	A94	2c red	4.50	3.25
a.		Imperf., pair		
L12	A94	5c blue	4.50	3.25
a.		Imperf., pair	12.50	12.50
L13	A94	10c violet	6.00	6.00

On Tolima Stamp of 1888

Perf. 10½

L14	A23	1p red brn	12.50	12.50
		Nos. L9-L14 (6)	33.50	30.25

Regular Issues Handstamped — b

On Stamps of 1904

Perf. 12

L15	A94	½c yellow	2.00	2.00
L16	A94	1c yellow grn	3.50	3.00
L17	A94	2c red	6.00	5.00
L18	A94	5c blue	6.00	5.00
L19	A94	10c violet	8.00	6.00
L20	A94	20c black	11.00	11.00
L21	A94	1p brown	20.00	20.00
		Nos. L15-L21 (7)	56.50	52.00

On Stamps of 1908

Perf. 10, 13, 13½

L22	A94	½c orange	2.25	2.25
L23	A94	1c yellow grn	6.25	6.25
L24	A94	2c red	5.00	5.00
a.		Imperf., pair	12.50	12.50
L25	A94	5c light blue	6.00	5.00
		Nos. L22-L25 (4)	19.50	18.50

The handstamps on Nos. L1-L25 are, as usual, found inverted and double.

DEPARTMENT OF REGISTRATION STAMPS

Registration Stamps Handstamped like Nos. L1-L25

On Registration Stamp of 1904

1909 Unwmk. *Perf. 12*

LF1	R12 (a)	10c purple	25.00	25.00
LF2	R12 (b)	10c purple	25.00	25.00

On Registration Stamp of 1909

Perf. 10, 13

LF3	R12 (a)	10c purple	25.00	25.00
LF4	R12 (b)	10c purple	25.00	25.00
		Nos. LF1-LF4 (4)	100.00	100.00

Nos. LF1-LF4 exist imperf. Value per pair, $100.

DEPARTMENT ACKNOWLEDGMENT OF RECEIPT STAMPS

Acknowledgment of Receipt Stamp of 1904 Handstamped like Nos. L1-L25

1909 Unwmk. *Perf. 12*

LH1	AR4 (a)	5c blue	25.00	25.00
a.		Imperf., pair	100.00	
LH2	AR4 (b)	5c blue	25.00	25.00
a.		Imperf., pair	100.00	

LOCAL STAMPS FOR THE CITY OF BOGOTA

A1

Pelure Paper

1889 Unwmk. Litho. *Perf. 12*

LX1	A1	½c black	.95	.95
a.		Imperf., pair	6.00	6.00

Impressions on bright blue and blue-gray paper were not regularly issued.

A2

A3

White Wove Paper

1896 *Perf. 12, 13½*

LX2	A2	½c black	.95	.95

1903 *Imperf.*

LX3	A3	10c black, *pink*	6.00	1.25
a.		Perf. 12	6.00	1.25

OFFICIAL STAMPS

Stamps of 1917-1937 Overprinted in Black or Red:

a

b

1937 Unwmk. *Perf. 11, 12, 13½*

O1	A131 (a)	1c green	.20	.20
O2	A157 (a)	10c dp org	.20	.20
O3	A107 (b)	30c olive bis	1.75	1.00
O4	A129 (b)	40c brn & yel brn	1.50	.80
O5	A114 (b)	50c car	1.00	.50
O6	A107 (b)	1p lt bl	5.00	4.00
O7	A107 (b)	2p org	10.00	6.50
O8	A107 (b)	5p gray	37.50	27.50
O9	A118 (b)	10p dk brn	110.00	100.00

Wmk. 229

Perf. 12½

O10	A132 (a)	2c red	.20	.20
O11	A133 (a)	5c brn	.20	.20
O12	A160 (a)	12c dp bl (R)	1.00	.50
O13	A136 (b)	20c dk bl (R)	1.60	.60
		Nos. O1-O13 (13)	170.15	142.20

Tall, wrong font "I's" in OFICIAL exist on all stamps with "a" overprint.

POSTAL TAX STAMPS

"Greatest Mother" PT1

Perf. 11½

1935, May 27 Unwmk. Litho.

RA1	PT1	5c olive blk & scar	2.50	.75

Required on all mail during Red Cross Week in 1935 (May 27-June 3) and in 1936.

Mother and Child — PT2

Perf. 10½, 10½x11

1937, May 24 Unwmk.

RA2	PT2	5c red	1.50	.60

Required on all mail during Red Cross Week. The tax was for the Red Cross.

PT3

Ministry of Posts and Telegraphs Building — PT4

1939-45 Litho. *Perf. 10½, 12½*

RA3	PT3	¼c dp bl	.20	.20
RA3A	PT3	¼c dk vio brn ('45)	.20	.20
RA4	PT3	½c pink	.20	.20
RA5	PT3	1c violet	.30	.20
RA5A	PT3	1c yel org ('45)	1.50	.60
RA6	PT3	2c pck grn	.40	.20
RA7	PT3	20c lt brn	3.50	1.25
		Nos. RA3-RA7 (7)	6.30	2.85

Obligatory on all mail. The tax was for the construction of the new Communications Building.

The 25c of type PT3 and PT4 were not usable on postal matter.

For overprint see No. 561.

Perf. 12½x13

1940, Jan. 20 Engr. Wmk. 229

RA8	PT4	¼c ultra	.20	.20
RA9	PT4	½c carmine	.20	.20
RA10	PT4	1c violet	.20	.20
RA11	PT4	2c bl grn	.25	.20
RA12	PT4	20c brown	1.00	.20
		Nos. RA8-RA12 (5)	1.85	1.00

See note after No. RA7. See No. RA18.

"Protection" — PT5

1940, Apr. 25 Wmk. 255 *Perf. 12*

RA13	PT5	5c rose carmine	.25	.20

See No. RA17.

Postal Tax Stamps of 1939 Surcharged in Black

1943 Unwmk. *Perf. 10½*

RA14	PT3	½c on 1c violet	.20	.20
a.		Inverted surcharge	1.50	
RA15	PT3	½c on 2c pck grn	.20	.20
RA16	PT3	½c on 20c lt brn	.20	.20
		Nos. RA14-RA16 (3)	.60	.60

Types of 1940

Imprint: "Litografia Colombia Bogota S.A."

1944 Litho. *Perf. 11*

RA17	PT5	5c dark rose	.35	.20

Imprint: "Lito-Colombia Bogota-Colombia"

RA18	PT4	¼c ultra	.20	.20

Ministry of Posts and Telegraphs Building — PT6

1945-48 Wmk. 255 Engr. *Perf. 12*

RA19	PT6	¼c ultra	.20	.20
RA20	PT6	¼c sepia ('46)	.20	.20
RA21	PT6	½c car rose	.20	.20
RA22	PT6	½c dp mag ('46)	.20	.20
RA23	PT6	1c vio ('46)	.20	.20
RA23A	PT6	1c red org ('46)	.20	.20
RA24	PT6	2c grn ('46)	.20	.20
RA25	PT6	20c brn ('46)	.90	.25
a.		20c red brown ('48)	.60	.20
		Nos. RA19-RA25 (8)	2.30	1.65

These stamps were obligatory on all mail. The surtax was for the construction of the new Communications Building. See Nos. 603, RA33. For overprints see Nos. 562-564.

No. 469 Overprinted in Carmine

1946, May 25

RA26	A176	5c dull brown	.35	.20

The surtax was for the Red Cross.

Ministry of Posts and Telegraphs Building — PT7

1946 Unwmk. Litho. *Perf. 11*

RA27 PT7 3c blue .20 .20

No. 490 Overprinted in Carmine

1947 Wmk. 255 *Perf. 12*

RA28 A196 20c gray black 3.75 1.25

Arms of Colombia and Red Cross — PT8

PT9

Perf. 12½

1947, Sept. Unwmk. Engr.

RA29 PT8 5c car lake .25 .20

The surtax of Nos. RA29 and RA40 was for the Red Cross. See No. RA40.

No. 466 Overprinted Like No. RA28 in Carmine

RA30 A136 20c dark blue 15.00 12.50

Catalogue values for unused stamps in this section, from this point to the end of the section, are for Never Hinged items.

Type of 1945

1947 Wmk. 255 Engr. *Perf. 12*

RA33 PT6 1c olive bister .30 .20

Black Surcharge

1948 Unwmk. Litho. *Perf. 11*

RA36 PT9 1c on 5c lt brn .30 .20
RA37 PT9 1c on 10c lt vio .30 .20
RA38 PT9 1c on 25c red .30 .20
RA39 PT9 1c on 50c ultra .30 .20
Nos. RA36-RA39 (4) 1.20 .80

Type of 1947

1948 *Perf. 10½*

RA40 PT8 5c vermilion .25 .20

Ministry of Posts and Telegraphs Building — PT10

Mother and Child — PT11

1948-50 Wmk. 255 Engr. *Perf. 12*

RA41 PT10 1c rose car ('49) .30 .20
RA42 PT10 2c green ('50) .30 .20
RA43 PT10 3c blue .30 .20
RA44 PT10 5c gray .30 .20
RA45 PT10 10c purple .30 .20
Nos. RA41-RA45 (5) 1.50 1.00

A 25c stamp of type PT10 was for use on telegrams, later for regular postage. See Nos. 602, 604. For overprints and surcharge see Nos. C227-C230, C238, C283, RA51.

Unwmk.

1950, May 25 Litho. *Perf. 11*

Dark Blue Surcharge

RA46 PT11 5c on 2c gray, red, blk & yel 1.00 .30
a. "195" instead of "1950" 2.00 2.00
b. Top bar and "19" of "1950" omitted 2.00 2.00

Marginal perforations omitted, creating 26 straight-edged stamps in each sheet of 44. Surtax for Red Cross.

No. 574 Overprinted in Black

1950, May 26 Wmk. 255 *Perf. 12*

RA47 A176 5c blue .25 .20
a. Inverted overprint 1.25

Telegraph Stamp Surcharged in Black

RA48 A253a 8c on 50c org yel .25 .20

Fiscal stamps of type A253a were available for postal use after May 9, 1952. See Nos. 605-608.

Arms and Cross — PT12

Bartolome de Las Casas Aiding Youth — PT13

Perf. 12½

1951, May Unwmk. Engr.

RA49 PT12 5c red .30 .20
RA50 PT13 5c carmine .30 .20

The surtax was for the Red Cross.

No. RA43 Surcharged with New Value in Black

1951 Wmk. 255 *Perf. 12*

RA51 PT10 1c on 3c blue .25 .20

Type of 1951

Engraved; Cross Lithographed

1953 Unwmk. *Perf. 12½*

RA52 PT13 5c grn & car .30 .20

Surtax of Nos. RA52-RA60 for the Red Cross.

No. C254 Overprinted with Cross and Bar in Carmine

1954

RA53 AP42 5c lilac rose .60 .50

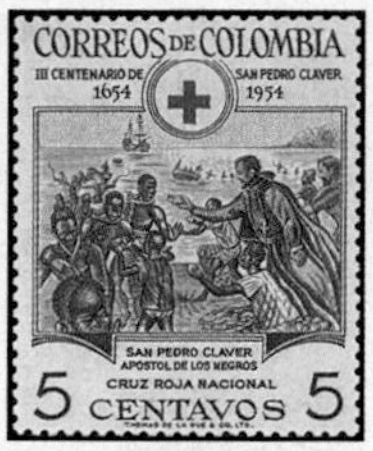

St. Peter Claver Offering Gifts to Slaves — PT14

Engraved; Cross Typographed

1955, May 2 Unwmk. *Perf. 13*

RA54 PT14 5c dp plum & red .30 .20

Death of St. Peter Claver, 300th anniv.

Jean Henri Dunant and Santiago Samper Brush PT15

Photo.; Red Cross & "Cruz Roja" Engr.

1956, June 1 Unwmk. *Perf. 13*

RA55 PT15 5c brown & red .30 .20

Nurses and Ambulances PT16

1958, June 2 Photo. *Perf. 12*

RA56 PT16 5c gray & red .30 .20

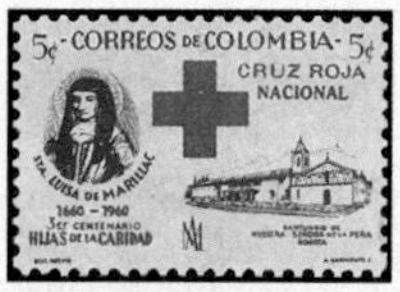

St. Louisa de Marillac and Church PT17

No. RA58, Henri Dunant and battle scene.

1960, Sept. 1 Litho. *Perf. 11*

RA57 PT17 5c brown & rose .25 .20
RA58 PT17 5c vio blue & rose .25 .20

No. RA57 for 3rd cent. of the Sisters of Charity. No. RA58 for cent. (in 1959) of the Red Cross idea.

Manuelita de la Cruz — PT18

Red Cross Worker, Patient — PT19

1961, Nov. 2 Engr. *Perf. 13*

RA59 PT18 5c dull pur & red .25 .20
RA60 PT18 5c brown & red .25 .20

Issued in memory of Red Cross Nurse Manuelita de la Cruz, who died in the line of duty during the floods of 1955. Obligatory on domestic mail for a month.

1965, Apr. 30 Photo. *Perf. 12*

RA61 PT19 5c blue gray & red .25 .20

Obligatory on domestic mail during May.

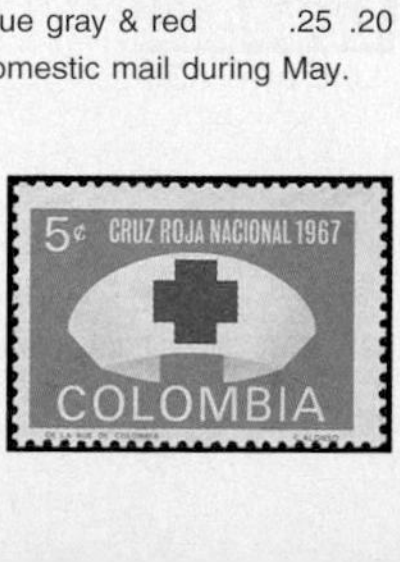

Nurse's Cap — PT20

Red Cross — PT21

1967, June 1 Litho. *Perf. 12*

RA62 PT20 5c brt bl & red .25 .20

1969, July 1 Litho. *Perf. 12x12½*

RA63 PT21 5c vio bl & red .25 .20

Child Care — PT22

1970, July 1 Litho. *Perf. 12½x12*

RA64 PT22 5c light bl & red .25 .20

ANTIOQUIA

ˌant-ē-ˈō-kē-ə

Originally a State, now a Department of the Republic of Colombia. Until the revolution of 1885, the separate states making up the United States of Colombia were sovereign governments in their own right. On August 4, 1886, the National Council of Bogotá, composed of two delegates from each state, adopted a new constitution which abolished the sovereign rights of states, which then became departments with governors appointed by the President of the Republic. The nine original states represented at the Bogotá Convention retained some of their previous rights, as management of their own finances, and all issued postage stamps until as late as 1904. For Panama's issues, see Panama Nos. 1-30.

Coat of Arms

A1 A2

A3

A4

Wove Paper

1868 Unwmk. Litho. *Imperf.*

1 A1 2½c blue *1,000. 750.*
2 A2 5c green *750. 575.*
3 A3 10c lilac *3,000. 1,000.*
4 A4 1p red *675. 750.*

Reprints of Nos. 1, 3 and 4 are on a bluish white paper and all but No. 3 have scratches across the design.

A5

A6

A7

A8

A9

A10

1869

5	A5	2½c blue	3.25	2.75
6	A6	5c green	5.00	4.50
7	A7	5c green	5.00	4.50
8	A8	10c lilac	6.25	3.25
9	A9	20c brown	6.25	3.25
10	A10	1p rose red	12.50	11.00
a.		1p vermilion	25.00	22.50
		Nos. 5-10 (6)	38.25	29.25

Reprints of Nos. 7, 8 and 10 are on a bluish white paper; reprints of Nos. 5 and 10a on white paper. The 10c blue is believed to be a reprint.

A11

A12

A13

A14

A15

A16

A17

A18

1873

12	A11	1c yellow grn	4.50	3.50
a.		1c green	4.50	3.50
13	A12	5c green	7.50	5.50
14	A13	10c lilac	22.50	19.00
15	A14	20c yellow brn	7.50	6.50
a.		20c dark brown	7.50	6.50
16	A15	50c blue	1.75	1.50
17	A16	1p vermilion	3.25	2.75
18	A17	2p black, *yellow*	7.75	7.00
19	A18	5p black, *rose*	55.00	47.50

A19

A20

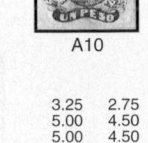

Liberty Head
A21 A22

Pedro Justo Berrio — A23

1875-85

20	A19	1c blk, *grn,* unglazed ('76)	1.60	1.40
a.		Glazed paper	2.25	1.90
b.		1c blk, *lt grn,* laid paper ('85)	3.75	3.50
21	A19	1c black ('76)	1.10	1.00
a.		Laid paper	140.00	100.00
22	A19	1c bl grn ('85)	2.25	1.90
23	A19	1c red lil, laid paper ('85)	2.25	1.90
24	A20	2½c blue	2.25	1.90
a.		Pelure paper ('78)	*1,500.*	*1,100.*
25	A21	5c green	15.00	12.50
a.		Laid paper	140.00	80.00
26	A22	5c green	15.00	12.50
a.		Laid paper	140.00	80.00
27	A23	10c lilac	22.50	19.00
a.		Laid paper	140.00	110.00
28	A20	10c vio, pelure paper ('78)	*900.00*	675.00

Arms — A24

Liberty — A25

A26

A27

1878-85

29	A24	2½c blue, pelure paper	2.50	2.25
30	A24	2½c green ('83)	2.25	1.90
a.		Laid paper ('83)	70.00	47.50
31	A24	2½c blk, *buff* ('85)	6.25	5.50
32	A25	5c green ('83)	3.75	3.25
a.		Pelure paper	30.00	25.00
b.		Laid paper ('82)	37.50	11.00
33	A25	5c violet ('83)	8.75	6.50
a.		5c blue violet ('83)	8.75	6.50
34	A26	10c vio, laid paper ('82)	160.00	55.00
35	A26	10c scar ('83)	2.25	1.90
a.		Tete beche pair	50.00	45.00
36	A27	20c brown ('83)	3.75	3.25
a.		Laid paper ('82)	5.00	4.50

A28

A29

Liberty — A30

Coat of Arms — A31

1883-85

37	A28	5c brown	4.50	3.00
a.		Laid paper	190.00	75.00
38	A28	5c green ('85)	125.00	40.00
a.		Laid paper ('85)	140.00	65.00
39	A28	5c yel, laid paper ('85)	5.00	4.00
40	A29	10c bl grn, laid paper	5.00	4.50
41	A29	10c bl, *bl* ('85)	5.00	4.00
42	A29	10c lil, laid paper ('85)	9.50	6.50
a.		Wove paper ('85)	100.00	40.00
43	A30	20c bl, laid paper ('85)	4.50	4.00

1886

Wove Paper

55	A31	1c grn, *pink*	.55	.50
56	A31	2½c blk, *orange*	.55	.50
57	A31	5c ultra, *buff*	1.75	1.60
a.		5c blue, *buff*	3.25	2.75
58	A31	10c rose, *buff*	1.60	1.40
a.		Transfer of 50c in stone of 10c	75.00	65.00
59	A31	20c dk vio, *buff*	1.60	1.40
61	A31	50c yel brn, *buff*	2.75	2.50
62	A31	1p yel, *grn*	4.50	4.00
63	A31	2p green, *vio*	4.50	4.00
		Nos. 55-63 (8)	17.80	15.90

1887-88

64	A31	1c red, *vio*	.45	.40
65	A31	2½c lil, *pale lil*	.45	*.55*
66	A31	5c car, *buff*	.60	.55
67	A31	5c red, *grn*	3.25	1.60
68	A31	10c brn, *grn*	.65	*.80*
		Nos. 64-68 (5)	5.40	3.90

Medellin Issue

A32

A33

A34

A35

1888 **Typeset**

69	A32	2½c blk, *yellow*	14.00	12.50
70	A33	5c blk, *yellow*	7.50	6.75
71	A34	5c red, *yellow*	4.50	4.00
		Nos. 69-71 (3)	26.00	23.25

Two varieties of No. 69, six of No. 70 and ten of No. 71.

1889

72	A35	2½c red	7.00	6.00

Ten varieties including "eentavos."

Regular Issue

Coat of Arms
A36 A37

A38

A39

A40

A41

1889 **Litho.** ***Perf. 13½***

73	A36	1c blk, *rose*	.25	.25
74	A36	2½c blk, *blue*	.25	.25
75	A36	5c blk, *yellow*	.30	.30
76	A36	10c blk, *green*	.30	.30
		Nos. 73-76 (4)	1.10	1.10

1890

78	A37	20c blue	1.25	1.25
79	A38	50c vio brn	2.50	2.50
a.		Transfer of 20c in stone of 50c	82.50	82.50
80	A38	50c green	2.00	2.00
81	A39	1p red	1.75	1.75
82	A40	2p blk, *mag*	12.50	12.50
83	A41	5p blk, *org red*	20.00	20.00
		Nos. 78-83 (6)	40.00	40.00

Nos. 73-76, 82-83 exist imperf.

The so-called "errors" of Nos. 73 to 76, printed on paper of wrong colors, are essays or, possibly, reprints. They exist perforated and imperforate.

See No. 96.

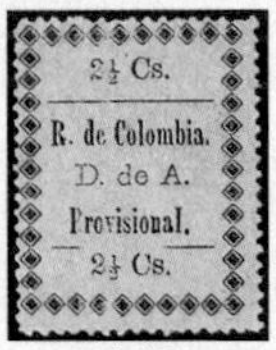

A42

A43

A44

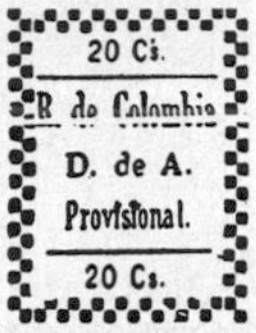

A45

1890 **Typeset** ***Perf. 14***

84	A42	2½c blk, *buff*	2.00	2.00
85	A43	5c blk, *orange*	2.00	2.00
86	A44	10c blk, *buff*	6.00	6.00
87	A44	10c blk, *rose*	7.50	7.50
88	A45	20c blk, *orange*	7.50	7.50
		Nos. 84-88 (5)	25.00	25.00

20 varieties of the 5c, 10 each of the other values.

A46

A47

1892 **Litho.** ***Perf. 13½***

89	A46	1c brn, *brnsh*	.35	.35
90	A46	2½c pur, *lil*	.35	.35
92	A46	5c blk, *gray*	1.00	.50
a.		Transfer of 2½c in stone of 5c	150.00	
		Nos. 89-92 (3)	1.70	1.20

1893

93	A46	1c blue	.25	.25
94	A46	2½c green	.35	.35
95	A46	5c vermilion	.25	.25
96	A36	10c pale brown	.25	.25
		Nos. 93-96 (4)	1.10	1.10

1896 ***Perf. 14***

97	A47	2c gray	.25	.25
98	A47	2c lilac rose	.25	.25
99	A47	2½c brown	.25	.25
100	A47	2½c steel blue	.25	.25
101	A47	3c orange	.25	.25
102	A47	3c olive grn	.25	.25
103	A47	5c green	.25	.25
104	A47	5c yellow buff	.30	.30
105	A47	10c brown vio	.55	.55
106	A47	10c violet	.55	.55
107	A47	20c brown org	1.25	1.25
108	A47	20c blue	1.25	1.25
109	A47	50c gray brn	1.25	1.25
110	A47	50c rose	1.10	1.10
111	A47	1p blue & blk	16.00	16.00
112	A47	1p rose red & blk	16.00	16.00
113	A47	2p orange & blk	47.50	47.50
114	A47	2p dk grn & blk	47.50	47.50
115	A47	5p red vio & blk	82.50	82.50
116	A47	5p purple & blk	82.50	82.50
		Nos. 97-116 (20)	300.00	300.00

Nos. 115-116 with centers omitted are proofs.

General José María Córdoba — A48

1899			Perf. 11	
117	A48	½c grnsh bl	.20	.20
118	A48	1c slate blue	.20	.20
119	A48	2c slate brown	.20	.20
120	A48	3c red	.20	.20
121	A48	4c bister brown	.20	.20
122	A48	5c green	.20	.20
123	A48	10c scarlet	.20	.20
124	A48	20c gray violet	.20	.20
125	A48	50c olive bister	.20	.20
126	A48	1p greenish blk	.20	.20
127	A48	2p olive gray	.20	.20
		Nos. 117-127 (11)	2.20	2.20

Numerous part-perf. and imperf. varieties of Nos. 117-127 exist.

A49

A50

A50a

1901		Typeset	Perf. 12	
128	A49	1c red	.20	.20
129	A50	1c ultra	.60	.60
130	A50	1c bister	.60	.60
130A	A50a	1c dull red	.60	.60
130B	A50a	1c ultra	4.00	4.00
		Nos. 128-130B (5)	6.00	6.00

Eight varieties of No. 128, four varieties of Nos. 129-130B.

A51

A52

Atanasio Girardot A53

Dr. José Félix Restrepo A54

1902		Litho.	Wove Paper	
131	A51	1c brt rose	.20	.20
a.		Laid paper	.60	.60
b.		Imperf., pair	2.50	
132	A51	2c blue	.20	.20
a.		Transfer of 3c in stone of 2c	5.00	5.00
133	A51	3c green	.20	.20
a.		Imperf., pair	4.00	
134	A51	4c dull violet	.20	.20
135	A52	5c rose red	.20	.20
136	A53	10c rose lilac	.20	.20
a.		Small head	5.00	5.00
b.		10c rose	.20	.20
137	A53	20c gray green	.20	.20
138	A53	30c brt rose	.20	.20
139	A53	40c blue	.20	.20
140	A53	50c brn, *yel*	.20	.20
		Laid Paper		
141	A54	1p purple & blk	.70	.70
142	A54	2p rose & blk	.70	.70
143	A54	5p sl bl & blk	1.25	1.25
		Nos. 131-143 (13)	4.65	4.65

1903				
		Wove Paper		
143A	A51	1c blue	.20	.20
144	A51	2c violet	.20	.20
a.		Imperf.	2.50	

A55

A56

A57

Designs: 1p, Francisco Antonio Zea. 2p, Custodio Garcia Rovira. 3p, La Pola (Policarpa Salavarrieta). 4p, J. M. Restrepo. 5p, José Fernández Madrid. 10p, Juan del Corral.

1903-04				
145	A55	4c yellow brn	.20	.20
146	A55	5c blue	.20	.20
147	A56	10c yellow	.20	.20
148	A56	20c purple	.20	.20
149	A56	30c brown	.60	.60
150	A56	40c green	.60	.60
151	A56	50c rose	.20	.20
152	A57	1p olive gray	.60	.60
153	A57	2p purple	.60	.60
154	A57	3p dark blue	.60	.60
155	A57	4p dull red	1.00	1.00
156	A57	5p red brown	3.00	1.50
157	A57	10p scarlet	6.50	3.50
		Nos. 145-157 (13)	14.50	10.00

Nos. 145-146, 151, 153-157 exist imperf. Value of pairs, $3 to $4.

Manizales Issue

Stamps of these designs are local private post issues.

OFFICIAL STAMPS Stamps of 1903-04 with overprint "OFICIAL" were never issued.

REGISTRATION STAMPS

R1

1896		Unwmk. Litho.	Perf. 14	
F1	R1	2½c rose	1.10	1.10
F2	R1	2½c dull blue	1.10	1.10

Córdoba R2

R3

R4

1899			Perf. 11	
F3	R2	2½c dull blue	.25	.25
F4	R3	10c red lilac	.25	.25

1902			Perf. 12	
F5	R4	10c purple, *blue*	.30	.30
a.		Imperf.		

ACKNOWLEDGMENT OF RECEIPT STAMPS

AR1

1902-03		Unwmk. Litho.	Perf. 12	
H1	AR1	5c black, *rose*	.90	.90
H2	AR1	5c slate ('03)	.30	.30

LATE FEE STAMPS

Córdoba — LF1

1899		Unwmk. Litho.	Perf. 11	
I1	LF1	2½c dark green	.25	.25
a.		Imperf., pair	2.75	

LF2

LF3

1901		Typeset	Perf. 12	
I2	LF2	2½c red violet	.50	.50
a.		2½c purple	.50	.50

1902			Litho.	
I3	LF3	2½c violet	.20	.20

City of Medellin

Stamps of the designs shown were not issued by any governmental agency but by the Sociedad de Mejoras Publicas.

BOLIVAR

bə-ˈlē-ˌvär

Originally a State, now a Department of the Republic of Colombia. (See Antioquia.)

A1

1863-66		Unwmk. Litho.	Imperf.	
1	A1	10c green	*1,100.*	*550.00*
a.		Five stars below shield	*2,400.*	*2,200.*
2	A1	10c red ('66)	25.00	*27.50*
a.		Diagonal half used as 5c on cover		55.00
b.		Five stars below shield	75.00	67.50
3	A1	1p red	6.25	*7.25*

Fourteen varieties of each. Counterfeits of Nos. 1 and 1a exist.

Coat of Arms

A2 A3

A4

A5

1873				
4	A2	5c blue	7.00	7.00
5	A3	10c violet	7.00	7.00
6	A4	20c yellow green	30.00	30.00
7	A5	80c vermilion	60.00	60.00
		Nos. 4-7 (4)	104.00	104.00

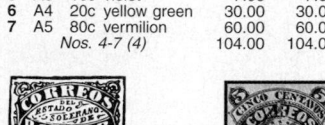

A6

A7

A8

Bolívar — A9

1874-78				
8	A6	5c blue	25.00	12.50
9	A7	5c blue ('78)	7.75	7.00
10	A8	10c violet ('77)	3.75	3.50
		Nos. 8-10 (3)	36.50	23.00

Dated "1879"

1879		White Wove Paper	Perf. 12½	
11	A9	5c blue	.25	.25
a.		Imperf., pair	.80	
12	A9	10c violet	.20	.20
13	A9	20c red	.25	.25
a.		20c green (error)	10.00	10.00
		Bluish Laid Paper		
15	A9	5c blue	.30	.30
a.		Imperf., pair	2.00	
16	A9	10c violet	1.60	1.60
a.		Imperf., pair	4.00	
17	A9	20c red	.40	.40
a.		Imperf., pair	1.75	
		Nos. 11-17 (6)	3.00	3.00

Stamps of 80c and 1p on white wove paper and 1p on bluish laid paper were prepared but not placed in use.

Dated "1880"

1880		White Wove Paper	Perf. 12½	
19	A9	5c blue	.25	.25
a.		Imperf., pair	1.60	
20	A9	10c violet	.35	.35
a.		Imperf., pair	1.60	
21	A9	20c red	.35	.35
a.		20c green (error)	13.00	13.00

23 A9 80c green 2.25 2.25
24 A9 1p orange 2.50 2.50
a. Imperf., pair 5.50
Nos. 19-24 (5) 5.70 5.70

Bluish Laid Paper

25 A9 5c blue .25 .25
a. Imperf., pair 1.25
26 A9 10c violet 2.25 2.25
27 A9 20c red .35 .35
a. Imperf., pair 2.75
28 A9 1p orange 400.00
a. Imperf. *450.00*

A11

A12

A13

A15

A16

Dated "1882"
White Wove Paper

1882 *Perf. 12, 16x12*
29 A11 5c blue .35 .35
30 A12 10c lilac .25 .25
31 A13 20c red .35 .35
33 A15 80c green .65 .65
34 A16 1p orange .65 .65
Nos. 29-34 (5) 2.25 2.25

Nos. 29, 30 and 34 are known imperforate. They are printer's waste and were not issued through post offices.

A17

A18

1882 **Engr.** *Perf. 12*
35 A17 5p blue & rose red .60 .60
a. Imperf., pair 4.75
b. Perf. 16 7.50 6.25
c. Perf. 14 6.25 6.25
36 A17 10p brown & blue 1.60 1.60
a. Imperf., pair 8.00
b. Perf. 16 7.00 5.50
c. Rouletted 8.00 8.00

Dated "1883"

1883 **Litho.** *Perf. 12, 16x12*
37 A11 5c blue .20 .20
a. Imperf., pair .80
b. Perf. 12 3.00 1.00
38 A12 10c lilac .25 .25
39 A13 20c red .25 .25
41 A15 80c green .30 .30
42 A16 1p orange .60 .60
a. Perf. 16x12 2.00 2.00
Nos. 37-42 (5) 1.60 1.60

Dated "1884"

1884
43 A11 5c blue .30 .30
a. Perf. 12 10.00 9.25
44 A12 10c lilac .20 .20
45 A13 20c red .20 .20
a. Perf. 12 4.25 4.25
47 A15 80c green .25 .25
a. Perf. 12 2.00 2.00
48 A16 1p orange .30 .30
Nos. 43-48 (5) 1.25 1.25

Dated "1885"

1885
49 A11 5c blue .20 .20
50 A12 10c lilac .20 .20
51 A13 20c red .20 .20
53 A15 80c green .25 .25
54 A16 1p orange .30 .30
Nos. 49-54 (5) 1.15 1.15

The note after No. 34 will also apply to imperforate stamps of the 1884-85 issues.

1891 *Perf. 14*
55 A18 1c black .30 .30
56 A18 5c orange .30 .30
a. Imperf., pair .80
57 A18 10c carmine .30 .30
58 A18 20c blue .60 .60
59 A18 50c green .90 .90
60 A18 1p purple .90 .90
Nos. 55-60 (6) 3.30 3.30

For overprint see Colombia No. 169.

Bolívar
A19

José Fernández Madrid
A20

Manuel Rodriguez Torices
A21

José María García de Toledo
A22

1903 **Laid Paper** *Imperf.*
62 A19 50c dk bl, *pink* .60 .60
a. Bluish paper .60 .60
63 A19 50c sl grn, *pink* .60 .60
a. Rose paper 2.00 2.00
b. Greenish blue paper 3.00 3.00
c. Yellow paper 4.00 4.00
d. Brown paper 4.00 4.00
e. Salmon paper 7.50 7.50
64 A19 50c pur, *pink* 2.00 2.00
a. White paper 4.00 4.00
b. Brown paper 4.00 4.00
c. Greenish blue paper 4.00 4.00
d. Lilac paper 4.00 4.00
e. Rose paper 3.50 3.50
f. Yellow paper 4.00 4.00
g. Salmon paper 6.00 6.00
h. As "a," wove paper 9.00 9.00
65 A20 1p org, *sal* .60 .60
a. Yellow paper 4.50 4.50
b. Greenish blue paper 15.00 15.00
66 A20 1p gray grn, *lil* 1.40 1.40
a. Yellow paper 6.50 6.50
b. Salmon paper 7.50 7.50
c. Green paper 7.50 7.50
d. White wove paper 10.00
67 A21 5p car rose, *lil* .60 .60
a. Brown paper 1.10 1.10
b. Yellow paper 1.10 1.10
c. Greenish blue paper 4.50 4.50
d. Bluish paper 6.00 6.00
e. Salmon paper 7.50 7.50
f. Rose paper 9.00 9.00
68 A22 10p dk bl, *bluish* 1.25 1.25
a. Greenish blue paper 1.25 1.25
b. Rose paper 7.50 7.50
c. Salmon paper 7.50 7.50
d. Yellow paper 7.50 7.50
e. Brown paper 8.50 8.50
f. Lilac paper 10.00 10.00
g. White paper 9.00 9.00
69 A22 10p pur, *grnsh bl* 3.50 3.50
a. Bluish paper 7.50 7.50
b. Rose paper 6.75 6.75
c. Yellow paper 7.50 7.50
d. Brown paper 7.50 7.50
Nos. 62-69 (8) 10.55 10.55

Sewing Machine Perf.
Laid Paper

70 A19 50c dk bl, *pink* 1.00 1.00
a. Bluish paper 1.00 1.00
71 A19 50c sl grn, *pink* 2.00 2.00
72 A19 50c pur, *grnsh bl* 4.00 4.00
a. White paper 4.00 4.00
b. White wove paper 7.50
73 A20 1p org, *sal* 2.00 2.00
74 A20 1p gray grn, *lil* 9.00 9.00
a. Yellow paper 9.00 9.00
75 A21 5p car rose, *yel* 1.60 1.60
a. Lilac paper 4.00 4.00
b. Brown paper 4.00 4.00
c. Bluish paper 5.50 5.50
d. White wove paper 9.00
76 A22 10p dk bl, *grnsh bl* 4.50 4.50
a. Bluish paper 7.00 7.00
b. Yellow paper 9.00 9.00
c. As "b," wove paper 10.00
77 A22 10p pur, *grnsh bl* 7.00 7.00
a. Bluish paper 11.00 11.00
b. Rose paper 8.00 8.00
c. Yellow paper 11.00 11.00
Nos. 70-77 (8) 31.10 31.10

José María del Castillo y Rada — A23

Manuel Anguiano — A24

Pantaleón C. Ribón — A25

1904 *Sewing Machine Perf.*
89 A23 5c black .25 .25
90 A24 10c brown .25 .25
91 A25 20c red .30 .30
92 A25 20c red brown .60 .60
Nos. 89-92 (4) 1.40 1.40

Imperf., pairs

89a A23 5c black 3.50 3.50
90a A24 10c brown 2.75 2.75
91a A25 20c red 6.50 6.50
92a A25 20c red brown 6.50 6.50

A26

A27

A28

1904 *Imperf.*
93 A26 ½c black .65 .65
a. Tête bêche pair 3.50 3.50
94 A27 1c blue 1.10 1.10
95 A28 2c purple 1.25 1.25
Nos. 93-95 (3) 3.00 3.00

REGISTRATION STAMPS

Simón Bolívar
R1 R2

White Wove Paper
Perf. 12½, 16x12

1879 **Unwmk.** **Litho.**
F1 R1 40c brown .70 .70

Bluish Laid Paper

F2 R1 40c brown .70 .70
a. Imperf., pair 3.25

Dated "1880"

1880

White Wove Paper

F3 R1 40c brown .30 .30

Bluish Laid Paper

F4 R1 40c brown .65 .65
a. Imperf., pair 3.50

Dated "1882" to "1885"
White Wove Paper

1882-85 *Perf. 16x12*
F5 R2 40c brown (1882) .30 .30
F6 R2 40c brown (1883) .25 .25
F7 R2 40c brown (1884) .25 .25
F8 R2 40c brown (1885) .30 .30
Nos. F5-F8 (4) 1.10 1.10

Perf. 12

F5a R2 40c 18.00
F6a R2 40c 9.25
F7a R2 40c 9.50
F8a R2 40c 2.50
Nos. F5a-F8a (4) 39.25

R3

Laid Paper

1903 *Imperf.*
F9 R3 20c orange, *rose* .60 .60
a. Salmon paper 1.10 1.10
b. Greenish blue paper 6.00 6.00

Sewing Machine Perf.

F10 R3 20c orange, *rose* 2.50 2.50
a. Salmon paper 2.50 2.50
b. Greenish blue paper 6.00 6.00

R4

1904

Wove Paper

F11 R4 5c black 3.25 3.25

ACKNOWLEDGMENT OF RECEIPT STAMPS

AR1 AR2

1903 **Unwmk.** **Litho.** *Imperf.*

Laid Paper

H1 AR1 20c org, *rose* 2.50 2.50
a. Yellow paper 1.25 1.25
b. Greenish blue paper 5.00 5.00
H2 AR1 20c dk bl, *yel* 2.00 2.00
a. Brown paper 3.50 3.50
b. Rose paper 2.50 2.50
c. Salmon paper 7.00 7.00
d. Greenish blue paper 7.00 7.00

Sewing Machine Perf.

H3 AR1 20c org, *grnsh bl* 6.25 6.25
a. Yellow paper 7.25 7.25
H4 AR1 20c dk bl, *yel* 7.25 7.25
a. Lilac paper 7.25 7.25
Nos. H1-H4 (4) 18.00 18.00

1904

Wove Paper

H5 AR2 2c red 1.10 1.10

LATE FEE STAMPS

LF1

1903 Unwmk. Litho. *Imperf.*
Laid Paper

I1 LF1 20c car rose, *bluish* .60 .60
I2 LF1 20c pur, *bluish* .55 .55
a. Rose paper 2.00 2.00
b. Brown paper 2.00 2.00
c. Lilac paper 2.00 2.00
d. Yellow paper 6.25 6.25

Sewing Machine Perf.

I3 LF1 20c car rose, *bluish* 3.50 3.50
I4 LF1 20c pur, *bluish* 3.50 3.50
a. Rose paper 6.00 6.00
b. Lilac paper 6.00 6.00
c. Yellow paper 10.00 10.00
Nos. I1-I4 (4) 8.15 8.15

BOYACA

Originally a State, now a Department of the Republic of Colombia. (See Antioquia.)

Diego Mendoza Pérez — A1

1902 Unwmk. Litho. *Perf. 13½*
Wove Paper

1 A1 5c blue green .70 .70
a. Bluish paper 90.00 90.00
b. Imperf., pair 12.50

Laid Paper
Perf. 12

2 A1 5c green 100.00 100.00

Coat of Arms
A2 A3

Gen. Próspero Pinzón — A4

A5

Monument of Battle of Boyacá — A6

President José Manuel Marroquin — A7

1903 Litho. *Imperf.*

4 A2 10c dark gray .25 .25
5 A3 20c red brown .30 .30
6 A5 1p red 3.00 3.00
a. 1p claret 3.50 3.50
8 A6 5p black, *rose* 1.10 1.10
a. 5p black, *buff* 11.00 11.00
9 A7 10p black, *buff* 1.10 1.10
a. 10p black, *rose* 11.00 11.00
b. Tête bêche pair 15.00
Nos. 4-9 (5) 5.75 5.75

Perf. 12

10 A2 10c dark gray .30 .30
11 A3 20c red brown .35 .35
12 A4 50c green .30 .30
13 A4 50c dull blue 2.00 2.00
14 A5 1p red .30 .30
a. 1p claret 3.00 3.00
16 A6 5p black, *rose* 11.00 11.00
a. 5p black, *buff* 9.50 9.50
17 A7 10p black, *buff* 1.10 1.10
a. 10p black, *rose* 11.00 11.00
b. Tête bêche pair 12.00 12.00
Nos. 10-17 (7) 15.35 15.35

Statue of Bolívar — A8

1904

18 A8 10c orange .25 .25
a. Imperf., pair 3.50 3.50

CAUCA

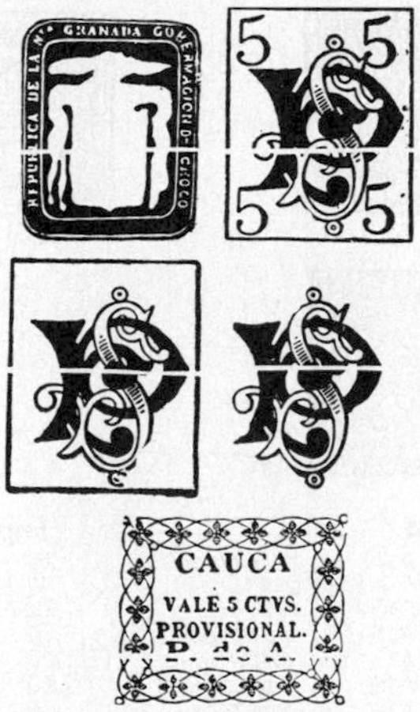

Stamps of these designs were issued by a provincial post between 1879(?) and 1890.

Stamps of this design are believed to be of private origin and without official sanction.

Items inscribed "No hay estampillas" (No stamps available) and others inscribed "Manuel E. Jiménez" are considered by specialists to be receipt labels, not postage stamps.

CUNDINAMARCA

ˌkün-di-nə-ˈmär-kə

Originally a State, now a Department of the Republic of Colombia. (See Antioquia.)

Coat of Arms
A1 A2

1870 Unwmk. Litho. *Imperf.*

1 A1 5c blue 4.75 4.75
2 A2 10c red 15.00 15.00

The counterfeits, or reprints, show traces of the cuts made to deface the dies.

A3

A4

A5

A6

1877-82

3 A3 10c red ('82) 3.25 3.25
a. Laid paper ('77) 4.25 4.25
4 A4 20c green ('82) 7.00 7.00
a. Laid paper ('77) 11.00 11.00
7 A5 50c purple ('82) 7.75 7.75
8 A6 1p brown ('82) 11.00 11.00
Nos. 3-8 (4) 29.00 29.00

A7

1884

10 A7 5c blue .75 .75
11 A7 5c blue (redrawn) .75 .75
a. Tête bêche pair 75.00 75.00

The redrawn stamp has no period after "COLOMBIA."

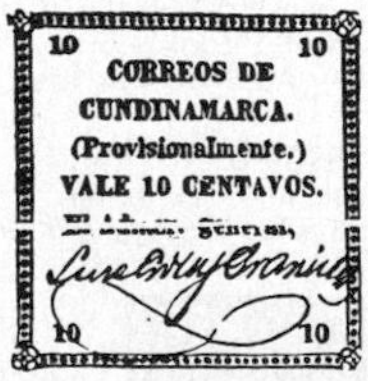

A8

A9

A10

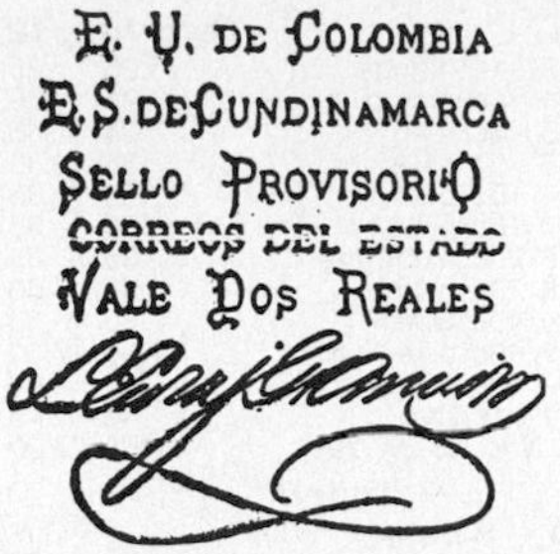

A11

1883 Typeset

13 A8 10c black, *yellow* 12.50 12.50
14 A9 50c black, *rose* 12.50 12.50
15 A10 1p black, *brown* 35.00 35.00
16 A11 2r black, *green* *2,000.*

Typeset varieties exist: 4 of the 10c, 2 each of 50c and 1p.

Some experts doubt that No. 16 was issued. The variety without signature and watermarked "flowers" is believed to be a proof. Forgeries exist.

A12

1886 Litho.

17 A12 5c blue .75 .75
18 A12 10c red 4.50 4.50
19 A12 10c red, *lilac* 2.50 2.50
20 A12 20c green 3.75 3.75
a. 20c yellow green 4.50 4.50
21 A12 50c purple 5.00 5.00
22 A12 1p orange brown 5.25 5.25
Nos. 17-22 (6) 21.75 21.75

Nos. 17 to 22 have been reprinted. The colors are aniline and differ from those of the original stamps. The impression is coarse and blurred.

A13

A14

A15

A16

A17

A18

A19

A20

A21

1904 *Perf. 10½, 12*

23 A13 1c orange .25 .25
24 A14 2c gray blue .25 .25
25 A15 3c rose .35 .35
26 A15 5c olive grn .35 .35
27 A16 10c pale brn .35 .35
28 A17 15c pink .35 .35
29 A18 20c blue, *grn* .35 .35
30 A18 20c blue .60 .60
31 A19 40c blue .60 .60
32 A19 40c blue, *buff* 17.50 17.50
33 A20 50c red vio .60 .60
34 A21 1p gray grn .45 .45
Nos. 23-34 (12) 22.00 22.00

Imperf

23a A13 1c orange .75 .75
24a A14 2c blue .75 .75
b. 2c slate 6.00 6.00
25a A15 3c rose .90 .90
26a A15 5c olive green 1.50 1.50
27a A16 10c pale brown 2.00 2.00
28a A17 15c pink .50 .50
29a A18 20c blue, *green* 2.00 2.00
30a A18 20c blue 2.00 2.00
31a A19 40c blue .70 .70
32a A19 40c blue, *buff* 17.50 17.50
33a A20 50c red violet .70 .70
34a A21 1p gray green .70 .70
Nos. 23a-34a (12) 30.00 30.00

REGISTRATION STAMPS

R1

1883 **Unwmk.** ***Imperf.***

F1 R1 black, *orange* 15.00 16.00

R2

1904 ***Perf. 12***

F2 R2 10c bister .80 .80
a. Imperf. 3.50 3.50

Magdalena

Items inscribed "No hay estampillas" (No stamps available) are considered by specialists to be not postage stamps but receipt labels.

Panama

Issues of Panama as a state and later Department of Colombia are listed with the Republic of Panama issues (Nos. 1-30).

SANTANDER

ˌsän-ˌtän-ˈdeˌər

Originally a State, now a Department of the Republic of Colombia.
(See Antioquia.)

Coat of Arms
A1 A2

1884 **Unwmk.** **Litho.** ***Imperf.***

1 A1 1c blue .30 .30
a. 1c gray blue .50 .50
2 A2 5c red .50 .50
3 A2 10c bluish purple 1.75 1.75
a. Tête bêche pair
Nos. 1-3 (3) 2.55 2.55

No. 2 exists unofficially perforated 14.

A3

A4

1886 ***Imperf.***

4 A3 1c blue .90 .90
5 A3 5c red .30 .30
6 A3 10c red violet .50 .50
a. 10c deep violet .50 .50
b. Inscribed "CINCO CENTAVOS" 25.00 25.00
Nos. 4-6 (3) 1.70 1.70

The numerals in the upper corners are omitted on No. 5, while on No. 6 there are no numerals in the side panels. No. 6 exists unofficially perforated 12.

1887

7 A4 1c blue .25 .25
a. 1c ultramarine 1.60 1.60
8 A4 5c red 1.60 1.60
9 A4 10c violet 5.00 5.00
Nos. 7-9 (3) 6.85 6.85

A5

A6

A7

1889 ***Perf. 11½ and 13½***

10 A5 1c blue .30 .30
11 A6 5c red 1.25 1.25
12 A7 10c purple .45 .45
a. Imperf., pair 16.00
Nos. 10-12 (3) 2.00 2.00

A8

A9

1892 ***Perf. 13½***

13 A8 5c red, *rose buff* 1.00 1.00

1895-96

14 A9 5c brown .70 .70
15 A9 5c yel grn ('96) .70 .70

A10

A11

A12

1899 ***Perf. 10***

16 A10 1c black, *green* .35 .35
17 A11 5c black, *pink* .35 .35

Perf. 13½

18 A12 10c blue .70 .70
a. Perf. 12 1.00 1.00
Nos. 16-18 (3) 1.40 1.40

A13

1903 ***Imperf.***

19 A13 50c red .55 .55
a. 50c rose .55 .55
b. "SANTENDER" 2.50 2.50
c. "Corrcos" 2.50 2.50
d. "Corceos" 2.50 2.50
e. Tête bêche pair 4.75 4.75
f. Pair, one without overprint 2.75 2.75

The overprint "Correos de Departmento Bucaramanga" on the 50c red revenue stamp has been proved to be a cancellation.

A14

A15

Arms
A16

Locomotive
A17

A18

A19

A20

1904 ***Imperf.***

22 A14 5c dark green .25 .25
a. 5c yellow green .40 .40
24 A15 10c rose .20 .20
25 A16 20c brown violet .20 .20
26 A17 50c yellow .20 .20
27 A18 1p black .20 .20
28 A19 5p dark blue .35 .35
29 A20 10p carmine .40 .40
Nos. 22-29 (7) 1.80 1.80

1905

30 A14 5c pale blue .40 .40
31 A15 10c red brown .40 .40
32 A16 20c yellow green .40 .40
33 A17 50c red violet .60 .60
34 A18 1p dark blue .60 .60
35 A19 5p pink .60 .60
36 A20 10p red 1.60 1.60
Nos. 30-36 (7) 4.60 4.60

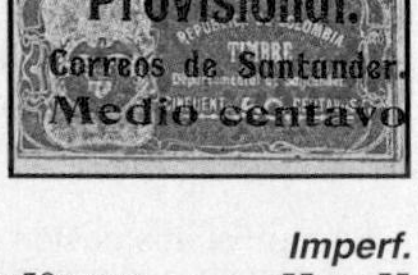
A21

1907 ***Imperf.***

37 A21 ½c on 50c rose .55 .55

City of Cucuta

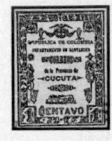

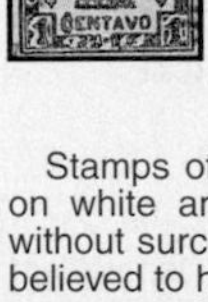

Stamps of these and similar designs on white and yellow paper, with and without surcharges of ½c, 1c or 2c, are believed to have been produced without government authorization.

TOLIMA

tə-lē-mə

Originally a State, now a Department of the Republic of Colombia.
(See Antioquia.)

A1

1870 **Unwmk.** **Typeset** ***Imperf.***

White Wove Paper

1 A1 5c black 50.00 50.00
2 A1 10c black 75.00 75.00
a. Vert. se-tenant pair 1,500. 1,500.

Printed from two settings. Setting I, ten types of 5c. Setting II, six types of 5c and four types of 10c.

Blue Laid Batonné Paper

3 A1 5c black *950.00*

Buff Laid Batonné Paper

4 A1 5c black 150.00 100.00

Blue Wove Paper

5 A1 5c black 70.00 45.00

Blue Vertically Laid Paper

6 A1 5c black 100.00 75.00
a. Paper with ruled blue vertical lines

Blue Horizontally Laid Paper

7 A1 5c black 200.00 150.00

Blue Quadrille Paper

8 A1 5c black 100.00 75.00

Ten varieties each of Nos. 3-5 and 7; 20 varieties each of Nos. 6 and 8.

Official imitations were made in 1886 from new settings of the type. There are only 2 varieties of each value. They are printed on blue and white paper, wove, batonné, laid, etc.

A2

A3

A4

A5

Yellowish White Wove Paper

1871 **Litho.** ***Imperf.***

9 A2 5c deep brown 2.25 2.25
a. 5c red brown 2.25 2.25
b. Value reads "CINGO" 37.50 37.50
10 A3 10c blue 6.00 6.00
11 A4 50c green 7.75 7.75
12 A5 1p carmine 12.00 12.00
Nos. 9-12 (4) 28.00 28.00

The 5p stamps, type A2, are bogus varieties made from an altered die of the 5c.

The 10c, 50c and 1 peso stamps have been reprinted on bluish white wove paper. They are from new plates and most examples show traces of fine lines with which the dies had been defaced. Reprints of the 5c have a large cross at the top. The 10c on laid batonné paper is known only as a reprint.

A6

A7

A8

A9

1879

Grayish or White Wove Paper

14	A6	5c yellow brown	.45	.45
a.		5c purple brown	.45	.45
15	A7	10c blue	.50	.50
16	A8	50c green, *bluish*	.50	.50
a.		White paper	1.60	1.60
17	A9	1p vermilion	2.25	2.25
a.		1p carmine rose	9.00	9.00
		Nos. 14-17 (4)	3.70	3.70

A10

Coat of Arms — A12

1883 ***Imperf.***

18	A6	5c orange	.45	.45
19	A7	10c vermilion	.90	.90
20	A10	20c violet	1.40	1.40
		Nos. 18-20 (3)	2.75	2.75

1884 ***Imperf.***

23	A12	1c gray	.20	.20
24	A12	2c rose lilac	.20	.20
a.		2c slate	.20	.20
25	A12	2½c dull orange	.20	.20
26	A12	5c brown	.20	.20
27	A12	10c blue	.35	.35
a.		10c slate	.25	.25
28	A12	20c lemon	.35	.35
a.		Laid paper	5.00	5.00
29	A12	25c black	.30	.30
30	A12	50c green	.30	.30
31	A12	1p vermilion	.40	.40
32	A12	2p violet	.60	.60
a.		Value omitted	27.50	27.50
33	A12	5p yellow	.40	.40
34	A12	10p lilac rose	1.10	1.10
a.		Laid paper	30.00	30.00
b.		10p gray	*160.00*	
		Nos. 23-34 (12)	4.60	4.60

A13

A14

Condor with Long Wings Touching Flagstaffs
A15 A16

1886 **Litho.** ***Perf. 10½, 11***

White Paper

36	A13	5c brown	1.25	1.25
a.		5c yellow brown	1.25	1.25
b.		Imperf., pair	16.00	
37	A14	10c blue	3.50	3.50
a.		Imperf., pair	16.00	
38	A15	50c green	3.00	3.00
a.		Imperf., pair	16.00	
39	A16	1p vermilion	2.50	2.50
a.		Imperf., pair	24.00	
		Nos. 36-39 (4)	10.25	10.25

No. 38 has been reprinted in pale gray green, perforated 10½, and No. 39 in bright vermilion, perforated 11½. The impressions show many signs of wear.

Lilac Tinted Paper

36c	A13	5c orange brown	12.00	12.00
37b	A14	10c blue	12.00	12.00
38b	A15	50c green	9.00	9.00
39b	A16	1p vermilion	8.00	8.00
		Nos. 36c-39b (4)	41.00	41.00

Items similar to A15 and A16 but with condor with long wings and upper flag-staffs omitted are forgeries.

A17

A18

Condor with Short Wings
A19 A20

1886 **White Paper** ***Perf. 12***

44	A19	1c gray	6.25	6.25
45	A17	2c rose lilac	6.50	6.50
46	A18	2½c dull org	19.00	19.00
47	A19	5c brown	8.50	8.00
48	A20	10c blue	8.00	8.00
49	A20	20c lemon	6.50	6.50
a.		Tête bêche pair	225.00	225.00
50	A20	25c black	6.25	6.25
51	A20	50c green	3.50	3.00
52	A20	1p vermilion	5.00	4.25
53	A20	2p violet	7.25	7.25
b.		Tête bêche pair	175.00	175.00
54	A20	5p orange	13.00	13.00
55	A20	10p lilac rose	7.25	7.25
		Nos. 44-55 (12)	97.00	95.25

Imperf., Pairs

44a	A19	1c	16.00
47a	A19	5c	27.50
48a	A20	10c	27.50
52a	A20	1p	20.00
53a	A20	2p	25.00
54a	A20	5p	32.50
55a	A20	10p	16.00

A23

1888 ***Perf. 10½***

62	A23	5c red	.20	.20
63	A23	10c green	.30	.30
64	A23	50c blue	.75	.75
65	A23	1p red brown	1.75	1.75
		Nos. 62-65 (4)	3.00	3.00

For overprint see Colombia No. L14.

1895 ***Perf. 12, 13½***

66	A23	1c blue, *rose*	.25	.25
67	A23	2c grn, *lt grn*	.25	.25
68	A23	5c red	.20	.20
69	A23	10c green	.50	.50
70	A23	20c blue, *yellow*	.30	.30
71	A23	1p brown	2.00	2.00
		Nos. 66-71 (6)	3.50	3.50

Imperf., Pairs

62a	A23	5c	2.75	
63a	A23	10c	3.25	
64a	A23	50c	4.75	4.75
65a	A23	1p	7.25	
66a	A23	1c	7.25	
67a	A23	2c	7.25	
70a	A23	20c	8.00	

"No Hay Estampillas"

Items inscribed "No hay estampillas" (No stamps available) are considered by specialists to be not postage stamps but receipt labels.

"Honda Issue"

This item seems to be of private origin.

A24

A25

A26

A27

A28

A29

A30

A31

Sewing Machine or Regular Perf. 12

1903-04 **Litho.**

79	A24	4c black, *green*	.25	.25
80	A25	10c dull blue	.25	.25
81	A26	20c orange	.50	.50
82	A27	50c black, *rose*	.25	.25
a.		50c black, *buff*	.20	.20
84	A28	1p brown	.20	.20
85	A29	2p gray	.20	.20
86	A30	5p red	.20	.20
a.		Tête bêche pair	5.00	5.00
87	A31	10p black, *blue*	.25	.25
a.		10p black, *light green*	.25	.25
b.		10p black, *grn*, glazed	3.50	3.50
		Nos. 79-87 (8)	2.10	2.10

Imperf

79a	A24	4c black, *green*	.25	.25
80a	A25	10c dull blue	.20	.20
81a	A26	20c orange	1.10	1.10
82b	A27	50c black, *rose*	1.50	1.50
c.		50c black, *buff*	1.50	1.50
84a	A28	1p brown	.20	.20
85a	A29	2p gray	.25	.25
86b	A30	5p red	.25	.25
c.		Tête bêche pair	5.00	5.00
87c	A31	10p black, *blue*	2.25	2.25
d.		Tête bêche pair		
e.		10p black, *light green*	3.50	3.50
f.		10p black, *green*, glazed	18.00	18.00
		Nos. 79a-87c (8)	6.00	6.00

COMORO ISLANDS

ˈkä-mə-ˌrō ˈī-ləndz

LOCATION — In Mozambique Channel between Madagascar and Mozambique
GOVT. — Republic
AREA — 838 sq. mi.
POP. — 562,723 (1999 est.)
CAPITAL — Moroni

The Comoro Archipelago consists of the islands of Mayotte, Anjouan, Grand Comoro (Grande Comore) and Moheli, which issued their own stamps as French protectorates or colonies from 1887-1914. The archipelago was attached to Madagascar from 1914 to 1946, when it became a separate French territory. In July 1975, Anjouan, Grand Comoro and Moheli united to declare independence as the State of Comoro. Mayotte remained French.

100 Centimes = 1 Franc

Catalogue values for all unused stamps in this country are for Never Hinged items.

Anjouan Bay — A2

Comoro Woman Grinding Grain — A3

Moroni Mosque on Grand Comoro A4

1950 **Unwmk.** **Engr.** ***Perf. 13***

30	A2	10c blue	.45	.30
31	A2	50c green	.45	.30
32	A2	1fr dk ol brn	.45	.30
33	A3	2fr brt grn	.80	.65
34	A3	5fr purple	1.40	1.00
35	A3	6fr vio brn	1.60	1.20
36	A4	7fr red	1.60	1.25
37	A4	10fr dk grn	1.60	1.25
38	A4	11fr dp ultra	2.00	1.50
		Nos. 30-38 (9)	10.35	7.75

Imperforates

Most Comoro Islands stamps exist imperforate in issued and trial colors, and also in small presentation sheets in issued colors.

Common Design Types pictured following the introduction.

Military Medal Issue

Common Design Type

1952 **Engraved and Typographed**

39	CD101 15fr multi	60.00	45.00

Mosque of Ouani, Anjouan — A5

Coelacanth A6

1952-54 **Engr.**

40	A5	15fr dark brown	4.00	3.00
41	A5	20fr red brown	5.50	4.25
42	A6	40fr aqua & indigo ('54)	35.00	18.00
		Nos. 40-42 (3)	44.50	25.25

FIDES Issue
Common Design Type

Design: 9fr, Women at water pump.

1956 **Unwmk.** ***Perf. 13x12½***

43	CD103	9fr dp vio	2.75	1.60

Human Rights Issue
Common Design Type

1958 **Engr.** ***Perf. 13***

44	CD105	20fr ol grn & dk bl	15.00	11.00

Flower Issue
Common Design Type

1959 **Photo.** ***Perf. 12½x12***

45	CD104	10fr Colvillea	6.50	4.50

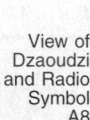

View of Dzaoudzi and Radio Symbol A8

Comoro radio station: 25fr, Radio tower and radio waves over Islands.

1960, Dec. 23 **Engr.** ***Perf. 13***

46	A8	20fr maroon, vio bl & grn	1.75	1.25
47	A8	25fr ultra, brn & grn	2.00	1.00

Harpa Conoidalis — A9

Sea Shells: 50c, Cypraecassis rufa. 2fr, Murex ramosus. 5fr, Turbo marmoratus. 20fr, Pterocera scorpio. 25fr, Charonia tritonis.

1962, Jan. 13 **Photo.**
Shells in Natural Colors

48	A9	50c lilac & brn	1.40	1.40
49	A9	1fr yel & red	1.40	1.40
50	A9	2fr pale grn & pink	2.75	2.75
51	A9	5fr yel & grn	4.25	4.25
52	A9	20fr salmon & brn	11.50	11.50
53	A9	25fr bister & pink	15.00	15.00
		Nos. 48-53,C5-C6 (8)	84.80	76.30

Wheat Emblem and Globe A10

1963, Mar. 21 **Engr.** ***Perf. 13***

54	A10	20fr choc & dk grn	5.50	4.50

FAO "Freedom from Hunger" campaign.

Red Cross Centenary Issue
Common Design Type

1963, Sept. 2 **Unwmk.** ***Perf. 13***

55	CD113	50fr emer, gray & car	9.50	8.00

Human Rights Issue
Common Design Type

1963, Dec. 10 **Engr.**

56	CD117	15fr dk red & yel grn	9.50	8.00

Tobacco Pouch — A13

Grand Comoro Canoe — A14

Designs: 4fr, Censer. 10fr, Carved lamp.

1963, Dec. 27 ***Perf. 13***
Size: 22x36mm

57	A13	3fr multi	.95	.95
58	A13	4fr org, dp cl & sl grn	1.00	1.00
59	A13	10fr org brn, dk red brn & grn	1.90	1.90
		Nos. 57-59,C8-C9 (5)	18.85	12.60

Philatec Issue
Common Design Type

1964, Mar. 31

60	CD118	50fr dk bl, red & grn	4.75	4.75

1964, Aug. 7 **Photo.** ***Perf. 13x12½***

Design: 30fr, Boutre felucca.

Size: 22x37mm

61	A14	15fr multi	3.50	3.50
62	A14	30fr lt grn & multi	5.50	5.50
		Nos. 61-62,C10-C11 (4)	20.50	13.25

Spiny Lobster — A15

Designs: 12fr, Hammerhead shark, horiz. 20fr, Turtle, horiz. 25fr, Merou fish.

1965, Dec. 20 **Engr.** ***Perf. 13***

63	A15	1fr grn, lil & ocher	1.00	.95
64	A15	12fr org red, slate & gray	2.10	1.60
65	A15	20fr org, red & bl grn	4.50	3.00
66	A15	25fr bl grn, dk brn & red	6.75	3.25
		Nos. 63-66 (4)	14.35	8.80

Hotel Itsandra, Moroni A16

Design: 15fr, Lake Salé, Grand Comoro.

1966, Dec. 19 **Photo.** ***Perf. 12½x13***

67	A16	15fr multi	1.25	.95
68	A16	25fr multi	1.50	1.00
		Nos. 67-68,C18-C19 (4)	16.75	10.20

Comoro Sunbird A17

Birds: 10fr, Malachite kingfisher. 15fr, Rothschild's fody. 30fr, Cuckoo-roller.

1967, June 20 **Photo.** ***Perf. 12½x13***
Size: 36x23mm

69	A17	2fr ocher & multi	2.75	2.75
70	A17	10fr lil & multi	6.00	5.25
71	A17	15fr yel grn & multi	7.25	6.50
72	A17	30fr pink & multi	13.00	13.00
		Nos. 69-72,C20-C21 (6)	52.50	42.00

For surcharge see No. 133.

WHO Anniversary Issue
Common Design Type

1968, May 4 **Engr.** ***Perf. 13***

73	CD126	40fr grn, vio & dp car	3.25	3.25

Surgeonfish A19

Design: 25fr, Imperial angelfish.

1968, Aug. 1 **Engr.** ***Perf. 13***
Size: 36x22mm

74	A19	20fr vio bl, yel & red brn	3.50	3.50
75	A19	25fr Prus bl, dk bl & org	4.25	4.25
		Nos. 74-75,C23-C24 (4)	25.75	17.00

For surcharge & overprint see #C52, C74.

Human Rights Year Issue
Common Design Type

1968, Aug. 10 **Engr.** ***Perf. 13***

76	CD127	60fr brn, grn & org	4.00	4.00

Msoila Prayer Rug and Praying Man — A20

Each stamp shows a different prayer position.

1969, Feb. 27 **Engr.** ***Perf. 13***

77	A20	20fr bl grn, rose red & pur	1.40	.95
78	A20	30fr pur, rose red & bl grn	1.60	1.40
79	A20	45fr rose red, pur & bl grn	3.00	1.75
		Nos. 77-79 (3)	6.00	4.10

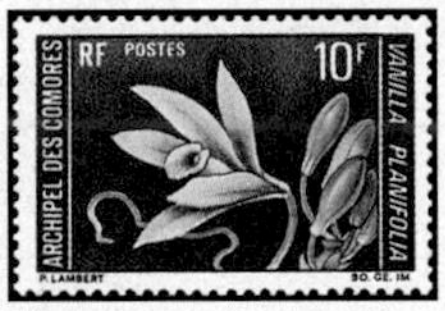

Vanilla Flower A21

Design: 15fr, Flower of ylang-ylang tree. 25fr, Poinsettia (country name at upper left).

1969-70 **Photo.** ***Perf. 12½x13***
Size: 36x23mm

80	A21	10fr multi	1.90	.85
81	A21	15fr multi	2.10	.95
82	A21	25fr multi ('70)	4.25	2.10
		Nos. 80-82,C26-C28 (6)	29.50	17.90

Issue dates: #80-81, Mar. 20. #82, Mar. 5.

ILO Issue
Common Design Type

1969, Nov. 24 **Engr.** ***Perf. 13***

83	CD131	5fr org, emerald & gray	1.60	1.20

UPU Headquarters Issue
Common Design Type

1970, May 20 **Engr.** ***Perf. 13***

84	CD133	65fr pur, bl grn & red brn	5.50	2.75

Chiromani Costume, Anjouan — A22

Friday Mosque — A23

25fr, Bouiboui costume, Grand Comoro.

1970, Oct. 30 **Photo.** ***Perf. 12½x13***

85	A22	20fr grn, yel & red	1.40	1.10
86	A22	25fr brn, yel & dk bl	2.10	1.25

1970, Dec. 18 **Engr.** ***Perf. 13***

87	A23	5fr rose car, grn & grnsh bl	.75	.75
88	A23	10fr dp lil, grn & vio	1.10	1.00
89	A23	40fr cop red, grn & dp brn	1.75	1.75
		Nos. 87-89 (3)	3.60	3.50

Great White Egret — A24

Pyrostegia Venusta — A25

Birds: 10fr, Comoro pigeon. 15fr, Green-backed heron. 25fr, Comoro blue pigeon. 35fr, Humbolt's flycatcher. 40fr, Allen's gallinule.

1971, Mar. 12 **Photo.** ***Perf. 12½x13***

90	A24	5fr multi	1.50	.80
91	A24	10fr yel & multi	2.00	.80
92	A24	15fr bl & multi	3.25	1.75
93	A24	25fr org & multi	4.75	2.00
94	A24	35fr yel grn & multi	6.50	2.50
95	A24	40fr gray & multi	8.00	3.25
		Nos. 90-95 (6)	26.00	11.10

For overprint see No. 145.

1971, July 19 **Photo.** ***Perf. 13***

Flowers: 3fr, Dogbane, horiz. 20fr, Frangipani.

Size: 22x36mm, 36x22mm

96	A25	1fr ver & grn	.95	.85
97	A25	3fr yel, grn & red	1.40	1.00
98	A25	20fr ver & grn	3.50	2.50
		Nos. 96-98,C37-C38 (5)	17.35	11.50

For surcharges see Nos. 131-132, C75, C83.

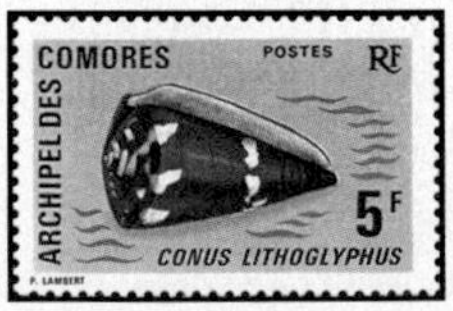

Lithograph Cone A26

Sea Shells: 10fr, Pacific lettered cone. 20fr, Aulicus cone. 35fr, Polita nerita. 60fr, Snake-head cowrie.

1971, Oct. 4

99	A26	5fr lt ultra & multi	1.25	1.00
100	A26	10fr multi	1.75	1.40
101	A26	20fr vio & multi	3.75	2.25
102	A26	35fr lt bl & multi	7.25	2.75
103	A26	60fr lt vio & multi	9.50	3.50
		Nos. 99-103 (5)	23.50	10.90

For surcharge see No. 150.

De Gaulle Issue
Common Design Type

Designs: 20fr, Gen. de Gaulle, 1940. 35fr, Pres. de Gaulle, 1970.

1971, Nov. 9 **Engr.** ***Perf. 13***

104	CD134	20fr dk car & blk	4.75	4.00
105	CD134	35fr dk car & blk	5.50	4.75

Louis Pasteur, Slides, Microscope A27

1972, Aug. 2

106	A27	65fr indigo, org, & ol brn	5.50	4.75

Sesquicentennial of the birth of Louis Pasteur (1822-1895), chemist.

Type of Air Post Issue 1971

Designs: 10fr, View of Goulaivoini. 20fr, Bay, Mitsamiouli. 35fr, Gate and fountain, Foumbouni. 50fr, View of Moroni.

1973, June 28 Photo. *Perf. 13*

107	AP10	10fr bl & multi	.85	.65
108	AP10	20fr grn & multi	1.50	1.10
109	AP10	35fr bl & multi	2.10	1.60
110	AP10	50fr bl & multi	2.60	2.25
		Nos. 107-110,C53 (5)	16.55	12.10

For overprint see No. 143.

Bank of Madagascar and Comoros — A28

Buildings in Moroni: 15fr, Post and Telecommunications Administration. 20fr, Prefecture.

1973, July 10 Photo. *Perf. 13x12½*

111	A28	5fr multi	.65	.55
112	A28	15fr multi	.90	.80
113	A28	20fr multi	1.25	1.00
		Nos. 111-113 (3)	2.80	2.35

For surcharge see No. 134.

Salimata Hamissi Mosque A29

20fr, Zaouiyat Chaduli Mosque, vert.

Perf. 12½x13, 13x12½

1973, Oct. 20 Photo.

114	A29	20fr multi	1.25	.95
115	A29	35fr multi	2.10	1.25

For surcharges see Nos. 135, 138.

Cheikh Mausoleum A30

Design: 50fr, Mausoleum of President Said Mohamed Cheikh (different view).

1974, Mar. 16 Engr. *Perf. 13*

116	A30	35fr grn, ol brn & blk	1.75	1.25
117	A30	50fr grn, ol brn & blk	2.50	1.75

For surcharge see No. 140.

Koran Stand, Anjouan A31

Designs: 15fr, Carved combs, vert. 20fr, 3-legged table, vert. 75fr, Sugar press.

1974, May 10 Photo. *Perf. 12½x13*

118	A31	15fr emer & multi	1.40	1.00
119	A31	20fr grn & multi	1.90	1.10
120	A31	35fr multi	2.90	1.90
121	A31	75fr multi	5.00	3.00
		Nos. 118-121 (4)	11.20	7.00

For overprints and surcharge see #137, 141, 149.

UPU Emblem, Symbolic Postmark A32

1974, Oct. 9 Engr. *Perf. 13x12½*

122	A32	30fr multi	2.00	1.75

Centenary of Universal Postal Union.
For surcharge see No. 155.

Bracelet A33

1975, Feb. 28 Engr. *Perf. 13*

123	A33	20fr shown	1.10	.95
124	A33	35fr Diadem	1.90	1.25
125	A33	120fr Saber	5.00	3.25
126	A33	135fr Dagger	7.00	4.00
		Nos. 123-126 (4)	15.00	9.45

For surcharges see Nos. 136, 142, 151, 154.

Mohani Village, Moheli — A34

50fr, Djoezi Village, Moheli. 55fr, Chirazi tombs.

1975, May 26 Photo. *Perf. 13*

127	A34	30fr vio bl & multi	2.00	1.40
128	A34	50fr Prus bl & multi	3.25	2.10
129	A34	55fr grn & multi	4.75	3.25
		Nos. 127-129 (3)	10.00	6.75

For overprints and surcharge see #139, 146, 148.

Scuba Diver Photographing Coelacanth — A35

1975, June 27 Engr. *Perf. 13*

130	A35	50fr multi	8.25	5.75

1975 coelacanth expedition.
For overprint see No. 147.

STATE OF COMORO

In 1978 the islands' name became the Federal and Islamic Republic of the Comoros.

Issues of 1971-75 Surcharged and Overprinted with Bars and: "ETAT COMORIEN" in Black, Silver or Red.

Tambourine Player — A36

#153, Women dancers & tambourine players.

Printing & Perforations as Before, Photogravure (A36)

1975 *Perf. 13 (A36)*

131	A25	5fr on 1fr	*1.00*	*.20*
132	A25	5fr on 3fr	*1.00*	*.20*
133	A17	10fr on 2fr	*1.00*	*.30*
134	A28	15fr on 20fr (R)	*.20*	*.20*
135	A29	15fr on 20fr (S)	*.20*	*.20*
136	A33	15fr on 20fr	*.20*	*.20*
137	A31	20fr	*.20*	*.20*
138	A29	25fr on 35fr	*.20*	*.20*
139	A34	30fr	*.40*	*.25*
140	A30	30fr on 35fr	*.80*	*.25*
141	A31	30fr on 35fr	*.80*	*.25*
142	A33	30fr on 35fr	*.40*	*.25*
143	AP10	35fr	*.40*	*.25*
144	SP2	35fr on 35fr + 10fr	*.40*	*.25*
145	A24	40fr	*2.50*	*.30*
146	A34	50fr	*.50*	*.50*
147	A35	50fr	*3.75*	*.40*
148	A34	50fr on 55fr (S)	*.90*	*.40*
149	A31	75fr	*2.10*	*.60*
150	A26	75fr on 60fr (S)	*3.75*	*.60*
151	A33	100fr on 120fr	*2.10*	*.80*
152	A36	100fr bl & multi	*6.75*	*.80*
153	A36	100fr on 150fr (S)	*6.75*	*.80*
154	A33	200fr on 135fr	*5.00*	*2.00*
155	A32	500fr on 30fr	*8.75*	*5.00*
		Nos. 131-155 (25)	*50.05*	*15.40*

Nos. 152-153 exist without overprint or surcharge. Value, each $75.
No. 155 exists with red surcharge.

Litho. & Embossed "Gold Foil" Stamps
These stamps generally are of a different design format than the rest of the issue. Since there is a commemorative inscription tieing them to the issue a separate illustration is not being shown.

Apollo-Soyuz — A37

Spacecraft and astronauts: 10fr, Soyuz lift-off, Alexei A. Leonov and Valeri N. Kubasov, vert. 30fr, Apollo lift-off, Thomas P. Stafford, Vance D. Brand, Donald K. Slayton, vert. 50fr, Meeting in space. 100fr, Chairman Brezhnev, President Ford talking with astronauts and cosmonauts. 200fr, Spacecraft preparing to dock. 400fr, Return to Earth. 500fr, Spacecraft, mission emblems. 1500fr, Apollo-Soyuz crew. No. 164, Preparing to dock, diff.

1975, Dec. 15 Litho. *Perf. 13½*

156	A37	10fr multicolored	.20	.20
157	A37	30fr multicolored	.50	.25
158	A37	50fr multicolored	.80	.55
159	A37	100fr multicolored	1.40	.60
160	A37	200fr multicolored	2.75	1.25
161	A37	400fr multicolored	5.00	2.50
		Nos. 156-161 (6)	10.65	5.35

Litho. & Embossed
Size: 45x45mm

162	A37	1500fr gold & multi	17.50	—

Souvenir Sheets
Litho.

163	A37	500fr multicolored	5.50	1.75

Litho. & Embossed

164	A37	1500fr gold & multi	17.50	—

Nos. 159-164 are airmail. No. 163 contains one 64x44mm stamp. No. 164 contains one 45x45mm stamp.
No. 162 exists in a souvenir sheet of 1. Value $50.
For overprints see Nos. 477-478.

A38

American Revolution, Bicent. — A39

Designs: 15fr, Lewis and Clark, Blackfoot Indian. 25fr, John C. Fremont, Kit Carson, Indian dancer. 35fr, Daniel Boone, Buffalo Bill Cody, wagon train. 40fr, Richard E. Egan, Johnny Frey, Pony Express. 75fr, Henry Wells, William G. Fargo, stagecoach. 400fr, Frontiersman, Indian. 500fr, Leland Stanford, Thomas C. Dunant, transcontinental railroad. 1000fr, George Washington, winter at Valley Forge. 1500fr, John Paul Jones, ship.

1976, Jan. 15 Litho.

165	A38	15fr multicolored	.20	.20
166	A38	25fr multicolored	.45	.25
167	A38	35fr multicolored	.75	.35
168	A38	40fr multicolored	.85	.45
169	A38	75fr multicolored	1.50	.60
170	A38	500fr multicolored	6.25	2.50
		Nos. 165-170 (6)	10.00	4.35

Litho. & Embossed

171	A39	1000fr gold & multi	13.50	—

Souvenir Sheets
Litho.

172	A38	400fr multicolored	5.50	1.75

Litho. & Embossed

173	A39	1500fr gold & multi	16.50	—

Nos. 170-173 are airmail. See Nos. 230, 232 and note after No. 479.
No. 171 exists in a souvenir sheet of 1. Value $55.

1976 Winter Olympics, Innsbruck — A40

1976, Mar. 30 Litho.

174	A40	5fr Women's figure skating	.20	.20
175	A40	30fr Slalom skiing	.25	.20
176	A40	35fr Speed skating	.35	.20
177	A40	50fr Downhill skiing	.60	.35
178	A40	200fr Ski jumping	2.10	1.00
179	A40	400fr Cross country skiing	4.50	1.25
		Nos. 174-179 (6)	8.00	3.20

Litho. & Embossed
Size: 56x35mm

180	A40	1000fr Downhill skier, hockey	*13.00*	—

Souvenir Sheets
Litho.

181	A40	500fr Hockey	5.50	1.75

Litho. & Embossed

182	A40	1000fr Olympic Rings	*11.00*	—

Nos. 178-182 are airmail. Nos. 181-182 contain one 58x35mm stamp. For overprint see No. 471.
No. 162 exists in a souvenir sheet of 1. Value $45.

1976 Summer Olympics, Montreal — A41

1976, Mar. 30 **Litho.**

183 A41 20fr Runner, Athens, 1896 .20 .20
184 A41 25fr Sprints .25 .20
185 A41 40fr High jump, Paris, 1900 .45 .20
186 A41 75fr High jump 1.00 .45
187 A41 100fr Women stretching, St. Louis, 1904 1.10 .50
188 A41 500fr Uneven parallel bars 6.00 1.75
Nos. 183-188 (6) 9.00 3.30

Souvenir Sheet

189 A41 400fr Olympic Stadium, Montreal 4.50 1.25

Nos. 187-189 are airmail.
For overprint see No. 476.

Fairy Tales — A42

1976, June 28

190 A42 15fr Hansel & Gretel .20 .20
191 A42 30fr Alice in Wonderland .50 .20
192 A42 35fr Pinocchio .65 .20
193 A42 40fr Good Little Henry .65 .25
194 A42 50fr Peter and the Wolf 1.00 .25
195 A42 400fr Thousand and One Nights 6.50 2.00
Nos. 190-195 (6) 9.50 3.10

#195 is airmail. #190-191, 193, 195 are vert.

Invention of Telephone, Cent. — A43

Designs: 10fr, A. G. Bell, 1st telephone. 25fr, Charles Bourseul, Paris-London phone service, 1891. 75fr, Philipp Reis, telephone operators. 100fr, Earth to Moon to Earth communications. 200fr, Satellite. 400fr, Ship-to-Satellite communications. No. 201, Satellite in orbit, antenna. No. 203, Global communications.

1976, July 1

196 A43 10fr multicolored .20 .20
197 A43 25fr multicolored .25 .20
198 A43 75fr multicolored .75 .30
199 A43 100fr multicolored 1.00 .50
200 A43 200fr multicolored 2.25 .90
201 A43 500fr multicolored 5.50 1.75
Nos. 196-201 (6) 9.95 3.85

Souvenir Sheets

202 A43 400fr multicolored 4.50 1.25
203 A43 500fr multicolored 5.50 1.75

Nos. 199-203 are airmail. Nos. 202-203 contain a 73x44mm stamp. For overprint see No. 472.

Comoro Flag, Map and Government Buildings — A44

1976, Nov. 18 **Litho.** ***Perf. 13½***

204 A44 30fr multi .75 .30
205 A44 50fr multi 1.25 .30

1st anniversary of independence.
For overprints and surcharges see Nos. 353-372.

Viking Probe to Mars — A45

Designs: 5fr, Nicolaus Copernicus, rocket launch. 10fr, Albert Einstein, Carl Sagan, Thomas Young, horiz. 25fr, Viking probe orbiting Mars. 35fr, Discovery of America by Vikings, horiz. 100fr, Flag, Viking landing on Mars. 500fr, Viking emblem, surface of Mars, horiz. 400fr, Viking probe. No. 212, Wagon train, frontiersman, rocket launch. No. 214, Viking on Martian surface, robotic shovel.

1976, Nov. 23

206 A45 5fr multicolored .20 .20
207 A45 10fr multicolored .20 .20
208 A45 25fr multicolored .25 .30
209 A45 35fr multicolored 1.10 .30
210 A45 100fr multicolored 1.75 .40
211 A45 500fr multicolored 10.50 1.50
Nos. 206-211 (6) 14.00 2.90

Litho. & Embossed

Size: 57x39mm

212 A45 1500fr gold & multi *14.00* —

Souvenir Sheets

Litho.

213 A45 400fr multicolored *5.00* 1.50

Litho. & Embossed

214 A45 1500fr gold & multi *15.00* —

American Revolution, bicentennial. Nos. 211-214 are airmail. No. 213 contains one 60x42mm stamp.
No. 212 exists in a souvenir sheet of 1. Value $50.

UN Postal Administration, 25th Anniv. — A46

Designs: 15fr, UN #24, irrigating field. 30fr, UN #43, doctor, nurse. 50fr, UN #162, mother holding child. 75fr, UN #42, communications satellite in orbit. 200fr, UN #32, Concorde, Zeppelin. 400fr, UN #18, cargo plane. 500fr, People passing letters around globe.

1976, Nov. 25 **Litho.**

215 A46 15fr multicolored .20 .20
216 A46 30fr multicolored .30 .20
217 A46 50fr multicolored .60 .30
218 A46 75fr multicolored .80 .30
219 A46 200fr multicolored 2.50 .50
220 A46 400fr multicolored 5.00 1.50
Nos. 215-220 (6) 9.40 3.00

Souvenir Sheet

221 A46 500fr multicolored *5.00* 2.00

Nos. 219-221 are airmail. No. 221 contains one 57x40mm stamp. For overprints see Nos. 282-284, 473.

Comoro Flag, UN Headquarters and Emblem — A47

1976, Nov. 25

222 A47 40fr multi 1.40 .30
223 A47 50fr multi 1.90 .40

1st anniv. of UN membership.

Type of 1976 and

US Bicentennial — A48

Civil War Battles: 10fr, Fort Sumter, Lincoln. 30fr, Bull Run, Gen. P.G.T. Beauregard, vert. 50fr, Antietam, Gen. Joseph E. Johnston. 100fr, Gettysburg, Gen. Meade. 200fr, Chattanooga, Gen. Sherman, vert. 400fr, Appomattox, Gen. Pickett. 500fr, Surrender at Appomattox, Generals Lee and Grant. 1000fr, Lincoln, battlefield. No. 230, Pres. Kennedy, lunar lander.

1976, Dec. 30 **Litho.**

224 A48 10fr multicolored .20 .20
225 A48 30fr multicolored .30 .20
226 A48 50fr multicolored .65 .25
227 A48 100fr multicolored 1.10 .45
228 A48 200fr multicolored 2.50 .80
229 A48 400fr multicolored 5.00 1.50
Nos. 224-229 (6) 9.75 3.40

Litho. & Embossed

Size: 61x51mm

230 A39 1500fr gold & multi *17.00* —

Souvenir Sheets

Litho.

231 A48 500fr multicolored *6.50* 1.75

Litho. & Embossed

232 A39 1000fr gold & multi *9.50* —

American Revolution bicentennial. Nos. 227-232 are airmail. No. 231 contains one 60x42mm stamp.
No. 230 exists in a souvenir sheet of 1. Value $50.

Endangered Species — A49

1976, Dec. 30 **Litho.**

233 A49 15fr Andean condor, vert. .30 .20
234 A49 20fr Australian tiger cat .45 .20
235 A49 35fr Leopard, vert. 1.00 .20
236 A49 40fr White rhinoceros 1.25 .45
237 A49 75fr Nyala, vert. 3.00 .55
238 A49 400fr Orangutan 8.00 1.50
Nos. 233-239 (7) 21.00 4.85

Souvenir Sheet

239 A49 500fr Lemur, vert. 7.00 1.75

Nos. 238-239 airmail. No. 239 contains one 40x58mm stamp.
See note after No. 479.

Endangered Species — A50

1977, Apr. 14

240 A50 10fr Wolf .20 .20
241 A50 30fr Aye-aye .45 .20
242 A50 40fr Cephalopus zebra .85 .25
243 A50 50fr Giant tortoise 1.00 .25
244 A50 200fr Ocelot 3.25 .75
245 A50 400fr Penguin 6.25 1.50
Nos. 240-245 (6) 12.00 3.15

Souvenir Sheet

246 A50 500fr Sumatran tiger 8.50 1.50

Nos. 244-246 airmail. No. 246 contains one 58x40mm stamp.

Giffard Airship, 1851 and Paris-St. Germain Train, 1837, France — A51

Airships & Locomotives: 25fr, Santos-Dumont's airship, 1906, Brazilian Tander 120FIN, Brazil. 50fr, Astra, 1914, Trans-Siberian Express, 1905, Russia. 75fr, R.34, 1919, Southern Belle, 1910, Great Britain. 200fr, Navy airship, Pacific Class locomotive, 1930, US. No. 252, Hindenburg, Rheingold Express, 1933, Germany. No. 253, Graf-Zeppelin, 1928, Nord-Express Type 231, 1925, Germany.

1977, Apr. 14

247 A51 20fr multicolored .30 .20
248 A51 25fr multicolored .30 .20
249 A51 50fr multicolored .75 .25
250 A51 75fr multicolored 1.10 .25
251 A51 200fr multicolored 2.75 .60
252 A51 500fr multicolored 6.25 1.60
Nos. 247-252 (6) 11.45 3.10

Souvenir Sheet

253 A51 500fr multi, horiz. 6.00 2.00

Nos. 251-253 are airmail. No. 253 contains one 58x39mm stamp.

Nobel Prize, 75th Anniv. — A52

Nobel Prize winners: 30fr, Medicine. 40fr, Physics. 50fr, Literature. 100fr, Physics. 200fr, Chemistry. 400fr, Peace.

1977, July 7

254 A52 30fr multicolored .75 .20
255 A52 40fr multicolored .75 .20
256 A52 50fr multicolored 1.25 .25
257 A52 100fr multicolored 3.25 .25
258 A52 200fr multicolored 5.50 .75
259 A52 400fr multicolored 12.50 1.25
Nos. 254-259 (6) 24.00 2.90

Souvenir Sheet

260 A52 500fr Nobel medal 5.50 1.75

Nos. 258-260 are airmail.
See note after No. 479.

Peter Paul Rubens, 400th Birth Anniv. — A53

Portraits: 20fr, Portrait of the Artist's Daughter, Clara. 25fr, Suzanne Fourment. 50fr, Toilet of Venus, (detail). 75fr, Ceres (detail). 200fr, Young Woman with Blonde Braided Hair. No. 266, Helene Fourment in her Wedding Dress. No. 267, Self-portrait.

1977, July 7

261 A53 20fr multicolored .20 .20
262 A53 25fr multicolored .30 .20
263 A53 50fr multicolored .65 .25
264 A53 75fr multicolored 1.10 .30
265 A53 200fr multicolored 2.50 .60
266 A53 500fr multicolored 6.25 1.50
Nos. 261-266 (6) 11.00 3.05

Souvenir Sheet

267 A53 500fr multicolored 5.50 1.75

Nos. 265-267 are airmail.
See note after No. 479.

Fish A54

1977, Nov. 21

268 A54 30fr Swordfish .50 .20
269 A54 40fr Gaterin 1.00 .20
270 A54 50fr Sea scorpion 1.75 .20
271 A54 100fr Chaetodon lunula 3.25 .45
272 A54 200fr Amphiprion 4.00 .75
273 A54 400fr Tetrodon 7.50 1.50
Nos. 268-273 (6) 18.00 3.30

Souvenir Sheet

274 A54 500fr Coelacanth 8.00 2.00

Nos. 272-274 airmail. No. 274 contains one 52x47mm stamp.

Space Exploration — A55

1977, Nov. 21

275 A55 30fr Jupiter lander .30 .20
276 A55 50fr Voyager probe, Uranus, vert. .60 .20
277 A55 75fr Pioneer probe, Venus 1.00 .25
278 A55 100fr Space shuttle, vert. 1.10 .40
279 A55 200fr Viking III, Mars 2.50 .60
280 A55 400fr Apollo-Soyuz, vert. 5.00 1.25
Nos. 275-280 (6) 10.50 2.90

Souvenir Sheet

281 A55 500fr Allegory of the Sun 5.00 1.75

Nos. 279-281 airmail. No. 281 contains one 52x42mm stamp.

No. 219 Overprinted in One Line in Gold, Silver or Red

"Paris-New-York - 22 Nov. 1977"

1977, Nov. 22

282 A46 200fr multicolored 5.00 2.75
283 A46 200fr multicolored (S) 30.00 —
284 A46 200fr multicolored (R) 10.00 —
Nos. 282-284 (3) 45.00 2.75

Birds — A56

1978, Feb. 6

285 A56 15fr Porphyrula alleni .35 .20
286 A56 20fr M. superciliosus .60 .20
287 A56 35fr Alcedo vintsioides johannae .95 .20
288 A56 40fr Terpsiphone 1.25 .25
289 A56 75fr Nectarinia comorensis 2.10 .30
290 A56 400fr Egretta alba 10.75 1.50
Nos. 285-290 (6) 16.00 2.65

Souvenir Sheet

291 A56 500fr Foudia eminentissima, horiz. 7.50 1.75

Nos. 290-291 are airmail. For overprint and surcharges see Nos. 444-448.

World Cup Soccer Championships, Argentina — A57

Designs: 30fr, Greece, 5th. cent. B.C. 50fr, Brittany, 19th cent. 75fr, London, 14th cent. 100fr, Italy, 18th cent. 200fr, England, 19th cent. 400fr, English Cup match, 1891. 500fr, English Cup final, 1962. No. 298, Player, satellite. No. 300, Players.

1978, Feb. 6

292 A57 30fr multicolored .30 .20
293 A57 50fr multicolored .60 .20
294 A57 75fr multicolored .75 .30
295 A57 100fr multicolored 1.10 .40
296 A57 200fr multicolored 2.50 .60
297 A57 400fr multicolored 5.00 1.25
Nos. 292-297 (6) 10.25 2.95

Litho. & Embossed

Size: 60x42mm

298 A57 1000fr gold & multi 11.00 —

Souvenir Sheets

Litho.

299 A57 500fr multicolored 6.00 1.75

Litho. & Embossed

300 A57 1000fr gold & multi 10.00 4.00

Nos. 296-300 are airmail. No. 300 contains one 60x42mm stamp.
No. 298 exists in a souvenir sheet of 1. Value $50.
For overprints and surcharges see Nos. 402-408, 449-453.

Composers — A58

1978, Apr. 5 **Litho.**

301 A58 30fr J.S. Bach .90 .20
302 A58 40fr W.A. Mozart 1.10 .20
303 A58 50fr Berlioz 1.50 .30
304 A58 100fr Verdi 3.00 .30
305 A58 200fr Tchaikovsky 4.50 .60
306 A58 400fr George Gershwin 9.00 1.25
Nos. 301-306 (6) 20.00 2.85

Souvenir Sheet

307 A58 500fr Beethoven 9.00 1.75

Nos. 305-307 are airmail. For overprints and surcharges see Nos. 454-458.

Albrecht Durer, 450th Death Anniv. — A59

Portraits: 20fr, Oswolt Krel. 25fr, Elspeth Tucher. 50fr, Hieronymus Holzschuher. 75fr, Young Woman. 200fr, Emperor Maximilian I. No. 313, Young Woman, (detail). No. 314, Self-portrait.

1978, Apr. 5

308 A59 20fr multicolored .20 .20
309 A59 25fr multicolored .30 .20
310 A59 50fr multicolored .65 .30
311 A59 75fr multicolored 1.00 .30
312 A59 200fr multicolored 2.50 .60
313 A59 500fr multicolored 6.00 1.60
Nos. 308-313 (6) 10.65 3.20

Souvenir Sheet

314 A59 500fr multicolored 5.50 1.75

Nos. 312-314 airmail. No. 314 contains one 42x52mm stamp. See note after No. 479.

Issues Not Valid for Postage

The government changed in May 1978. A number of sets that had not been issued seem to have been invalid for postage until they were overprinted with the new country name. These are a set of 9 for the 25th anniv. of Elizabeth's coronation, a set of 7 for butterflies, a set of 6 for the 10th Intl. Communications Year, a set of 7 for the history of aviation, a set of 9 for Rubens, and a set of 9 for Durer.

These sets, unoverprinted, exist both mint and cancelled to order. They are no scarcer than the previous listed issues.

See note after No. 479.

Islamic Republic

Nos. 204-205 Surcharged and Overprinted with 3 Lines and: "République / Fédérale / et Islamique / des Comores"

1978, July 24 **Litho.** ***Perf. 13½***

353 A44 30fr multi .30 —
354 A44 40fr on 30fr multi .30 —
355 A44 50fr multi .50 —
356 A44 100fr on 50fr multi .90 —
Nos. 353-356 (3) 1.50

Nos. 353 and 355 were also overprinted to commemorate World Cup Soccer winner; Albrecht Dürer; Railroad anniversary; Voyager I and II; 1980 Olympic Games; World Cup Soccer, Espana '82.

Nos. 353, 355 Overprinted

1978, July 25 **Litho.** ***Perf. 13½***

357 A44 30fr multi *6.00* —
358 A44 50fr multi *10.00* —

Coronation of Queen Elizabeth II, 25th anniv.

Nos. 353, 355 Overprinted

1978, July 26 **Litho.** ***Perf. 13½***

359 A44 30fr multi *6.00* —
360 A44 50fr multi *9.00* —

Birth of Capt. James Cook, 250th anniv.

Nos. 353, 355 Overprinted

1978, July 31 **Litho.** ***Perf. 13½***

365 A44 30fr multi *6.00* —
366 A44 50fr multi *10.00* —

Intl. Civil Aviation Organization.

Nos. 353, 355 Overprinted

1978, Aug. 3 **Litho.** ***Perf. 13½***

371 A44 30fr multi *11.00* —
372 A44 50fr multi *11.00* —

Intl. Year of the Child (in 1979).

Europe-Africa A66

Various satellites or spacecraft.

1978, Dec. 16

386 A66 10fr multicolored .20 .20
387 A66 25fr multicolored .20 .20
388 A66 35fr multicolored .40 .20
389 A66 50fr multicolored .65 .20
390 A66 100fr multicolored 1.10 .60
391 A66 500fr multicolored 5.50 1.25
Nos. 386-391 (6) 8.05 2.65

Souvenir Sheet

392 A66 500fr multicolored 5.50 1.75

Nos. 390-392 airmail. No. 392 contains one 61x40mm stamp.

Sir Rowland Hill — A67

1978, Dec. 16

393	A67	20fr Saxony #1	.20	.20
394	A67	30fr Netherlands #1	.30	.20
395	A67	40fr Great Britain #2	.60	.20
396	A67	75fr US #2	.75	.30
397	A67	200fr France #33	2.10	.60
398	A67	400fr Basel #3L1	4.50	1.25
		Nos. 393-398 (6)	8.45	2.75

Litho. & Embossed

Size: 39x58mm

399	A67	1500fr British Guiana #13	13.00	—

Souvenir Sheets

Litho.

400	A67	500fr Moheli, Mayotte, Anjouan, Grand Comoro #1	5.50	1.75

Litho. & Embossed

401	A67	1500fr Hill, Mauritius #3	13.00	—

Nos. 397-401 are airmail. No. 400 contains one 57x49mm stamp. No. 401 contains one 58x39mm stamp.

No. 399 exists in a souvenir sheet of 1. Value $40.

Nos. 292-297 Ovptd. with New Country Name in Black on Silver and
1 ARGENTINE
2 HOLLANDE
3 BRESIL

1978, Dec. 16

402	A57	30fr multicolored	.30	.20
403	A57	50fr multicolored	.60	.20
404	A57	75fr multicolored	.90	.20
405	A57	100fr multicolored	1.10	.45
406	A57	200fr multicolored	2.25	.60
407	A57	400fr multicolored	4.75	1.25
		Nos. 402-407 (6)	9.90	2.90

Souvenir Sheet

408	A57	500fr multicolored	5.50	1.25

Nos. 406-407 are airmail.

Exists with Country name in red on silver. Value approx. triple those of overprints in black.

Galileo and Voyager I — A68

Exploration of Solar System: 30fr, Kepler and Voyager II. 40fr, Copernicus and Voyager I, 100fr, Huygens and Voyager II. 200fr, William Herschel and Voyager II. 400fr, Urbain Leverrier and Voyager II. 500fr, Voyagers I and II, symbolic solar system.

1979, Feb. 19 Litho. *Perf. 13*

409	A68	20fr multi	.20	.20
410	A68	30fr multi	.30	.20
411	A68	40fr multi	.50	.20
412	A68	100fr multi	1.10	.25
413	A68	200fr multi	1.90	.50
414	A68	400fr multi	4.00	1.00
		Nos. 409-414 (6)	8.00	2.35

Souvenir Sheet

415	A68	500fr multi	5.00	1.50

Nos. 413-415 airmail.

Philidor, Anderssen, Steinitz and King — A69

100fr, Chess pieces and board, Venetian chess player. 500fr, Chess Grand Masters Alekhine, Spassky, Fischer, and bishop.

1979, Feb. 19

416	A69	40fr multi	.65	.20
417	A69	100fr multi	1.25	.20
418	A69	500fr multi	5.50	1.50
		Nos. 416-418 (3)	7.40	1.90

Chess Grand Masters. No. 418 airmail.

Nos. 419-425 are reserved for Summer Olympics set of 6 with one souvenir sheet, released Mar. 28, 1979.

Charaxes Defulvata — A71

Birds: 50fr, Leptosomus discolor. 75fr, Bee eater.

1979, Apr. 10 Litho. *Perf. 12½*

426	A71	30fr multi	1.50	.30
427	A71	50fr multi	3.75	.60
428	A71	75fr multi	6.25	1.00
		Nos. 426-428 (3)	11.50	1.90

Otto Lilienthal and Glider — A72

History of Aviation: No. 430, Wright brothers and Flyer A. No. 431, Louis Bleriot and Bleriot XI. 100fr, Claude Dornier and Dornier-Wal hydrofoil. 200fr, Charles Lindbergh and Spirit of St. Louis.

1979, May 2 *Perf. 13*

Black Overprint and Surcharge

429	A72	30fr multi	.50	.50
430	A72	50fr multi	.80	.80
431	A72	50fr on 75fr multi	.80	.80
432	A72	100fr multi	1.60	1.60
433	A72	200fr multi	2.50	2.50
		Nos. 429-433 (5)	6.20	6.20

No. 433 airmail.

For unoverprinted stamps see note after No. 314.

Papilio Dardanus Cenea A73

Butterflies: 15fr, Papilio dardanus. 30fr, Chrysiridia croesus. 50fr, Precis octavia. 75fr, Bunaea alcinoe.

1979, May 2

Black Overprint and Surcharge

434	A73	5fr on 20fr multi	.20	.20
435	A73	15fr multi	.35	.20
436	A73	30fr multi	.70	.45
437	A73	50fr multi	1.40	.95
438	A73	75fr multi	2.25	1.50
		Nos. 434-438 (5)	4.90	3.30

For unoverprinted stamps see note after No. 314.

Man Reading Proclamation — A74

1979, May 2 Litho. *Perf. 13½*

Black Surcharge and Overprint

439	A74	5fr on 25fr coronation coach	.20	.20
440	A74	10fr Drummer	.30	.30
441	A74	50fr on 40fr with crown, orb, scepter	.70	.70
442	A74	50fr on 200fr shown	1.10	1.10
443	A74	100fr St. Edward's Crown	1.40	1.40
		Nos. 439-443 (5)	3.70	3.70

No. 442 is airmail.

For unoverprinted stamps see note after No. 314.

Nos. 285-289 (Birds) Overprinted or Surcharged like A72-A74

1979, May 2 Litho. *Perf. 13*

444	A56	15fr multi	.30	.30
445	A56	30fr on 35fr multi	.70	.70
446	A56	50fr on 20fr multi	1.25	1.25
447	A56	50fr on 40fr multi	1.25	1.25
448	A56	200fr on 75fr multi	4.00	4.00
		Nos. 444-448 (5)	7.50	7.50

Nos. 292-296 (Soccer) Overprinted or Surcharged like A72-A74

1979, May 2 Litho. *Perf. 13*

449	A57	1fr on 100fr multi	.20	.20
450	A57	2fr on 75fr multi	.20	.20
451	A57	3fr on 30fr multi	.20	.20
452	A57	50fr multi	.90	.55
453	A57	200fr multi	2.25	2.25
		Nos. 449-453 (5)	3.75	3.40

No. 453 airmail.

Nos. 301-305 (Composers) Overprinted or Surcharged like A72-A74

1979, May 2 *Perf. 13½*

454	A58	5fr on 100fr multi	.20	.20
455	A58	30fr multi	1.25	1.25
456	A58	40fr multi	1.75	1.75
457	A58	50fr multi	2.25	2.25
458	A58	50fr on 200fr multi	3.50	3.50
		Nos. 454-458 (5)	8.95	8.95

No. 458 airmail.

Nos. 459-465 are reserved for Intl. Year of the Child set of 6 with one souvenir sheet, released May 30, 1979.

Litchi Nuts — A76

Basketball Players — A77

1979, June 15 Litho. *Perf. 12½*

466	A76	60fr shown	1.00	.30
467	A76	70fr Papayas	1.25	.45
468	A76	100fr Avocados	1.40	.55
469	A76	125fr Bananas	1.90	.90
		Nos. 466-469 (4)	5.55	2.20

For surcharges see Nos. 515, 533.

1979, Aug. 28 Litho. *Perf. 13*

470	A77	200fr multi	2.50	1.40

Indian Ocean Olympics.

Nos. 176, 198, 218, 187, 159-160 and Type A78 Overprinted in Black

Nimbus Weather Satellite — A78

No. 475, Apollo-Soyuz. No. 479, Molniya.

Printing & Perfs. as Before, Litho. (A78)

1979, Sept. 15 *Perf. 13 (A78)*

471	A40	35fr multi	.70	.70
472	A43	75fr multi	1.50	1.50
473	A46	75fr multi	1.50	1.50
474	A78	75fr multi	1.50	1.50
475	A78	100fr multi	2.10	2.10
476	A41	100fr multi	2.10	2.10
477	A37	100fr multi	2.10	2.10
478	A37	200fr multi	4.25	4.25
479	A78	200fr multi	4.25	4.25
		Nos. 471-479 (9)	20.00	20.00

Nos. 476-479 airmail.

For type A78 see note after No. 314.

Nos. 166-167, 169, 235-236, 257, 262, 309, 311, the unissued Rubens set (4 values) and Durer set (5 values) exist with this overprint, supposedly also issued Sept. 15.

Dugout on Beach A80

Anjouan Puppet — A81

1980, Jan. 4 Litho. *Perf. 13*

498	A80	60fr multi	1.00	.25
499	A81	100fr multi	1.50	.45

For surcharge see No. 534.

Sultan Said Ali — A82

1980, Feb. 20 *Perf. 12½x13*

500	A82	40fr shown	.60	.20
501	A82	60fr Sultan Ahmed	.75	.25

Sherlock Holmes, Doyle — A83

1980, Feb. 25 *Perf. 12½*
502 A83 200fr multi 4.75 1.75

Sir Arthur Conan Doyle (1859-1930), writer.
For surcharge see No. 513.

Grand Mosque, Holy Ka'aba, Mecca — A84

1980, Mar. 12 *Perf. 13x12½*
503 A84 75fr multi 1.00 .40

Hegira, 1500th anniv.
For surcharge see No. 514.

Year of the Holy City of Jerusalem A85

1980, Mar. 12 *Perf. 13x13½*
504 A85 60fr multi .75 .40

Kepler, Copernicus and Pluto — A86

1980, Apr. 30 **Litho.** *Perf. 12½*
505 A86 400fr multi 4.50 2.25

Discovery of Pluto, 50th anniversary.
For surcharge see No. 531.

Muscle System, Avicenna — A87

1980, Apr. 30 **Engr.** *Perf. 13*
506 A87 60fr multi .75 .40

Avicenna, Arab physician, birth millennium.

Soccer Players — A88

World Cup Soccer 1982; Various soccer scenes. 60fr, 150fr, 500fr, vert.

1981, Feb. 20 **Litho.** *Perf. 12½*
507 A88 60fr multi .65 .20
508 A88 75fr multi .75 .20
509 A88 90fr multi 1.25 .25
510 A88 100fr multi 1.10 .45
511 A88 150fr multi 1.90 .60
Nos. 507-511 (5) 5.65 1.70

Souvenir Sheet

512 A88 500fr multi 5.00 1.50

For overprints & surcharge see #532, 555-560.

Nos. 502-503, 469 Surcharged and

Merops Superciliosus A89

Perf. 12½, 13x12½ (No. 514)
1981, Feb. **Litho.**
Red, Black or Blue Surcharge
513 A83 15fr on 200fr multi .50 .50
514 A84 20fr on 75fr multi .50 .50
515 A76 40fr on 125fr multi (Bk) 1.50 1.50
516 A89 60fr on 75fr multi (Bl) 3.00 3.00
Nos. 513-516 (4) 5.50 5.50

A90

Space Exploration: 50fr, Apollo program, vert. 75fr, 100fr, 500fr, Columbia space shuttle.

1981, July 13 **Litho.** *Perf. 14*
517 A90 50fr multi .60 .20
518 A90 75fr multi .75 .20
519 A90 100fr multi 1.25 .30
520 A90 450fr multi 6.00 1.50
Nos. 517-520 (4) 8.60 2.20

Souvenir Sheet

521 A90 500fr multi 5.00 1.50

For overprints and surcharges see Nos. 599, 804F.

Prince Charles and Lady Diana, Buckingham Palace — A91

1981, Sept. 1 **Litho.** *Perf. 14½*
522 A91 125fr shown 1.10 .30
523 A91 200fr Highwood House 1.75 .60
524 A91 450fr Carnarvon Castle 3.75 1.25
a. Souvenir sheet of 3 6.75 2.00
Nos. 522-524 (3) 6.60 2.15

Royal wedding. No. 524a contains Nos. 522-524 in changed colors.
For overprints see Nos. 551-553.

Official Stamp Flag Type

1981, Oct. **Litho.** *Perf. 13*
526 O1 5fr multi .20 .20
527 O1 15fr multi .20 .20
528 O1 25fr multi .30 .20
529 O1 35fr multi .40 .20
530 O1 75fr multi .75 .35
Nos. 526-530 (5) 1.85 1.15

Nos. 505, 509, 468, 499 Surcharged

1981, Nov. **Litho.** *Perf. 12½*
531 A86 5fr on 400fr multi .40 .40
532 A88 20fr on 90fr multi .80 .80
533 A76 45fr on 100fr multi 2.00 .20
534 A81 45fr on 100fr multi 2.00 .20
Nos. 531-534 (4) 5.20 1.60

75th Anniv. of Grand Prix — A92

Designs: Winners and their Cars.

1981, Dec. 28 **Litho.** *Perf. 12½*
535 A92 20fr Mercedes, 1914 .30 .20
536 A92 50fr Delage, 1925 .65 .20
537 A92 75fr Rudi Caracciola, 1926 .90 .25
538 A92 90fr Stirling Moss, 1955 1.10 .35
539 A92 150fr Maserati, 1957 1.60 .45
Nos. 535-539 (5) 4.55 1.45

Souvenir Sheet

Perf. 13

540 A92 500fr Changing wheels, vert. 6.00 1.75

For overprint see No. 600.

Scouting Year — A93

1982, Jan. 5 *Perf. 12½*
541 A93 50fr Climbing rocks .60 .20
542 A93 75fr Boating .85 .25
543 A93 250fr Sailing 3.00 .90
544 A93 350fr Sailing, diff. 3.75 1.10
Nos. 541-544 (4) 8.20 2.45

Souvenir Sheet

Perf. 13

545 A93 500fr Baden-Powell 6.50 1.75

For overprint see No. 601.

21st Birthday of Princess of Wales — A94

Various portraits of Princess Diana.

1982, July 1 **Litho.** *Perf. 14*
546 A94 200fr multi 2.50 .60
547 A94 300fr multi 3.25 .90

Souvenir Sheet

548 A94 500fr multi 5.50 1.50

Johannes von Goethe (1749-1832) A95

1982, July
549 A95 75fr multi .75 .25
550 A95 350fr multi 3.75 .90

Nos. 522-524a Overprinted in Blue: "NAISSANCE ROYALE 1982"

1982, July 31 *Perf. 14½*
551 A91 125fr multi 1.50 .60
552 A91 200fr multi 2.50 .90
553 A91 450fr multi 4.50 2.00
a. Souvenir sheet of 3 8.75 8.75
Nos. 551-553 (3) 8.50 3.50

Birth of Prince William of Wales, June 21.

Nos. 507-512 Overprinted with Finalists and Score in Red

1982, Sept. 20 **Litho.** *Perf. 12½*
555 A88 60fr multi .65 .25
556 A88 75fr multi .75 .35
557 A88 90fr multi 1.00 .45
558 A88 100fr multi 1.10 .45
559 A88 150fr multi 1.40 .60
Nos. 555-559 (5) 4.90 2.10

Souvenir Sheet

560 A88 500fr multi 5.00 1.50

Italy's victory in 1982 World Cup.

Paintings by Norman Rockwell A96

1982, Oct. 11 **Litho.** *Perf. 14*
561 A96 60fr 1931 .65 .25
562 A96 75fr 1925 .70 .25
563 A96 100fr 1922 1.25 .25
564 A96 150fr 1919 1.40 .55
565 A96 200fr 1924 2.00 .60
566 A96 300fr 1918 3.50 1.00
Nos. 561-566 (6) 9.50 2.90

Sultans of Anjouan — A97

1982, Dec. *Perf. 12½x13, 13x12½*
567 A97 30fr Said Mohamed Sidi, vert. .40 .20
568 A97 60fr Ahmed Abdallah, vert. .75 .25
569 A97 75fr Salim 1.00 .25
570 A97 300fr Sidi, Abdallah 3.50 1.40
Nos. 567-570 (4) 5.65 2.10

Landscapes — A98

1983, Sept. 30 Litho. *Perf. 13*

571 A98 60fr D'Ziani Lake .75 .30
572 A98 100fr Sunset 1.25 .45
573 A98 175fr Anjouan, vert. 2.00 .75
574 A98 360fr Itsandra 4.00 1.25
575 A98 400fr Anjouan, diff. 5.00 1.60
Nos. 571-575 (5) 13.00 4.35

For surcharge see No. 815S.

Woman from Moheli
A99

1983, Oct. 17 Litho. *Perf. 12½x13*

576 A99 30fr shown .40 .20
577 A99 45fr Woman, diff. .55 .20
578 A99 50fr Man from Mayotte .55 .20
Nos. 576-578 (3) 1.50 .60

Horses — A100

1983, Nov. 30 Litho. *Perf. 13*

579 A100 75fr Arabian .70 .25
580 A100 100fr Anglo-Arabian 1.25 .30
581 A100 125fr Lippizaner 1.50 .40
582 A100 150fr Tennessee 1.75 .50
583 A100 200fr Appaloosa 2.00 .70
584 A100 300fr Pure English 3.50 1.00
585 A100 400fr Clydesdale 4.75 1.25
586 A100 500fr Andalusian 6.50 1.50
Nos. 579-586 (8) 21.95 5.90

Double Portrait, by Raphael
A101

1983, Dec. 30 Litho. *Perf. 13*

587 A101 100fr shown 1.25 .45
588 A101 200fr Girl, fresco detail 2.50 .80
589 A101 300fr St. George Killing Dragon 3.25 .90
590 A101 400fr Balthazar Castiglione 5.50 1.25
Nos. 587-590 (4) 12.50 3.40

For surcharges see Nos. 703, 800E, 815M.

Ships and Automobiles — A102

1984, Oct. 9 Litho. *Perf. 12½*

591 A102 100fr William Fawcett 1.25 .30
592 A102 100fr De Dion, 1885 1.50 .30
593 A102 150fr Lightning 1.90 .45
594 A102 150fr Benz Victoria, 1893 2.25 .60
595 A102 200fr Rapido 2.50 .75
596 A102 200fr Columbia Electric, 1901 3.00 .75
597 A102 350fr Sindia 4.50 1.00
598 A102 350fr Fiat, 1902 5.00 1.10
Nos. 591-598 (8) 21.90 5.25

For surcharge see No. 812Q.

Souvenir Sheets
Nos. 521, 540, 545, C126, C131 Ovptd. with Exhibition in Black, Blue, Red or Gold

1985, Mar. 11 *Perf. 14, 13*

599 A90 500fr '85 / HAMBOURG (Bk) 5.00 5.00
600 A92 500fr TSUKUBA EXPO '85 (Bl) 5.00 5.00
601 A93 500fr ARGENTINA '85/BUENOS AIRES (R) 5.00 5.00
602 AP31 500fr Rome, ITALIA '85 emblem (R) 5.00 5.00
603 AP32 500fr OLYMPHILEX/ '85 / LAUSANNE (G) 5.00 5.00
Nos. 599-603 (5) 25.00 25.00

Nos. 602-603 airmail.

Victor Hugo (1802-1885), Author, Pantheon, Paris — A103

Anniversaries and events: 200fr, IYY, Jules Verne (1828-1905), author. 300fr, IYY, Mark Twain (1835-1910), author. 450fr, Queen Mother, 85th birthday, vert. 500fr, Statue of Liberty, cent., vert.

1985, May 27 Litho. *Perf. 13*

604 A103 100fr multi 1.25 .30
605 A103 200fr multi 2.25 .60
606 A103 300fr multi 3.50 .90
607 A103 450fr multi 5.00 1.25
608 A103 500fr multi 6.00 1.50
Nos. 604-608 (5) 18.00 4.55

For surcharges see Nos. 704, 800A.

Sea Shells — A104

1985, Oct. 23 *Perf. 14*

609 A104 75fr Lambis chiragra 1.00 .20
610 A104 125fr Strombe lentifinosum 1.50 .35
611 A104 200fr Tonna gala 2.50 .60
612 A104 300fr Cymbium glans 4.00 .90
613 A104 450fr Lambis crocata 6.00 1.40
Nos. 609-613 (5) 15.00 3.45

Comoros Admission to UN, 10th Anniv. — A105

1985, Nov. 12 Litho. *Perf. 13x12½*

614 A105 5fr multi .20 .20
615 A105 30fr multi .30 .20
616 A105 75fr multi .90 .25
617 A105 125fr multi 1.40 .50
618 A105 400fr multi 4.50 1.50
Nos. 614-618 (5) 7.30 2.65

For surcharge see No. 800F.

Moroni Rotary Club, 20th Anniv. — A106

1985, Nov. 30 *Perf. 13*

619 A106 25fr multi .30 .20
620 A106 75fr multi .90 .40
621 A106 125fr multi 1.40 .45
622 A106 500fr multi 5.00 2.00
Nos. 619-622 (4) 7.60 3.05

Mushrooms — A107

1985, Dec. 24 *Perf. 13½*

623 A107 75fr Boletus edulis 1.00 .30
624 A107 125fr Sarcoscypha coccinea 1.50 .45
625 A107 200fr Hypholoma fasciculare 2.50 .60
626 A107 350fr Astraeus hygrometricus 4.00 .90
627 A107 500fr Armillariella mellea 7.00 1.50
Nos. 623-627 (5) 16.00 3.75

For surcharge see No. 815R.

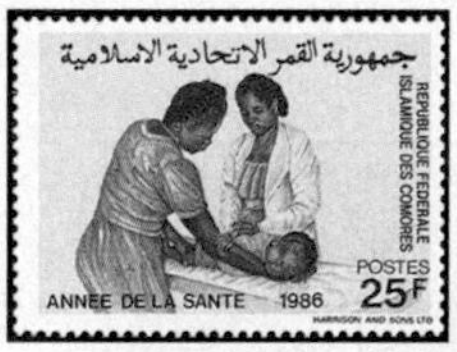

Health Year
A108

1986, Oct. 2 Litho. *Perf. 15x14½*

628 A108 25fr Pediatric examination .35 .20
629 A108 100fr Weighing child 1.50 .60
630 A108 200fr Immunization 2.75 1.25
Nos. 628-630 (3) 4.60 2.05

For surcharge see No. 705.

Musical Instruments
A109

1986, Dec. 24 Litho. *Perf. 13*

631 A109 75fr Ndzoumara .90 .40
632 A109 125fr Ndzedze 1.25 .60
633 A109 210fr Gaboussi 2.10 .90
634 A109 500fr Ngoma 6.00 1.75
Nos. 631-634 (4) 10.25 3.65

For surcharges see Nos. 796P, 796T, 800L, 815A.

Role of Women in National Development — A110

1987, Mar. 7 Litho. *Perf. 13*

635 A110 75fr Working fields .80 .30
636 A110 125fr Harvesting crops, vert. 1.40 .45
637 A110 1000fr Basketweaving 11.00 3.00
Nos. 635-637 (3) 13.20 3.75

Service Organizations — A111

Emblems and activities: 75fr, Nos. 642, Kiwanis or 643c, Rotary Intl. for child survival. 125fr, Nos. 641, Kiwanis or 643b, Lions Intl. for aid to the handicapped. 210fr, No. 643a, Kiwanis helping poor and homeless children.

1988 Litho. *Perf. 13½*

638 A111 75fr dk bl, lt bl & multi .75 .30
639 A111 125fr dk brn, lt brn & multi 1.40 .45
640 A111 210fr org, yel & multi 2.25 .75
641 A111 425fr red, pink & multi 4.50 1.75
642 A111 500fr bl, yel & multi 6.00 2.00
643 Strip of 3 13.00 6.00
 a. A111 210fr grn, lt grn & multi 2.10 .75
 b. A111 425fr pur, pink & multi 4.50 1.75
 c. A111 500fr red, orange & multi 6.00 2.00
Nos. 638-643 (6) 27.90 11.25

For surcharges see Nos. 654-656, 815B, 815W.

A112

1988 Olympics, Calgary and Seoul — A113

1988 Litho. *Perf. 13½*

644 A112 75fr Women's figure skating .65 .20
645 A112 100fr Running 1.00 .30
646 A112 125fr Women's speed skating 1.00 .40
647 A112 150fr Equestrian 1.50 .50
648 A112 350fr Two-man luge 3.25 .90
649 A112 400fr Biathlon 4.00 1.40
650 A112 500fr Pole vault 4.00 1.25
651 A112 600fr Soccer 6.00 1.50
Nos. 644-651 (8) 21.40 6.45

Souvenir Sheets

652 A113 750fr Women's downhill skiing, satellite 7.75 1.50
653 A113 750fr Track, satellite 7.75 1.50

Nos. 649 and 651-653 are airmail.

For surcharges see Nos. 800C, 800M, 815V.

No. 643 and Service Organization Types Surcharged

No. 655, like #643b. No. 656, like #643c.

1988, July 18 Litho. *Perf. 13½*

654 Strip of 3 5.50 5.00
 a. A111 75fr on 210fr #643a .65 .45
 b. A111 200fr on 425fr #643b 1.75 .90
 c. A111 300fr on 500fr #643c 2.75 1.25
655 A111 125fr on 425fr pur, lt pur & multi, blk letters 1.10 .60

656 A111 400fr on 500fr car, pink & multi 3.75 2.00
Nos. 654-656 (3) 10.35 7.60

Nos. 655-656 not issued without surcharge.

Discovery of America, 500th Anniv. (in 1992) — A114

Designs: 75fr, Christopher Columbus, *Santa Maria*. 125fr, Martin Alonzo Pinzon (c. 1441-1493), *Pinta*. 150fr, Vicente Yanez Pinzon (c. 1460-1523), *Nina*. 250fr, Search for Cipango, legendary rich islands off the coast of Asia. 375fr, *Santa Maria* shipwrecked. 450fr, Preparing for 4th voyage. 750fr, Samana Cay landing.

1988, Apr. 18 Litho. *Perf. 13½*

657 A114 75fr multi .65 .20
658 A114 125fr multi 1.10 .30
659 A114 150fr multi 1.50 .45
660 A114 250fr multi 2.10 .75
661 A114 375fr multi 3.75 1.00
662 A114 450fr multi 4.50 1.25
Nos. 657-662 (6) 13.60 3.95

Souvenir Sheet

663 A114 750fr multi, horiz. 7.75 1.50

Nos. 661-663 airmail. No. 663 contains one 42x30mm stamp.
For surcharges see Nos. 702, 815D.

1992 Summer Olympics, Barcelona A115

1988, Apr. 18

664 A115 75fr Discus, vert. .60 .20
665 A115 100fr shown .90 .30
666 A115 125fr Cycling 1.75 .45
667 A115 150fr Wrestling 2.25 .50
668 A115 375fr Basketball, vert. 5.25 1.00
669 A115 600fr Tennis, vert. 8.25 1.25
Nos. 664-669 (6) 19.00 3.70

Souvenir Sheet

670 A115 750fr Marathon, vert. 7.75 1.50

Nos. 668-670 are airmail.

Famous Men — A116

Rotary Intl. — A117

150fr, Yuri Gagarin (1934-68), USSR, cosmonaut. 300fr, Jean-Henri Dunant, Red Cross founder. 400fr, Roger Clemens, baseball player. 500fr, Gary Kasparov, USSR, 1985 world chess champion. 600fr, Paul Harris, US, Rotary founder. 750fr, Neil Armstrong walking on the Moon, John F. Kennedy. #678, The Thinker by Rodin, Rotary Intl. emblem.

1988, Dec. 6 Litho. *Perf. 13½*

671 A116 150fr multi 1.75 .50
672 A116 300fr multi 1.75 .50
673 A116 400fr multi 1.75 .50
674 A116 500fr multi 1.75 .50
675 A116 600fr multi 1.75 .50
a. Souv. sheet of 5, #671-675 + label 10.00 —
Nos. 665-669 (5) 18.40 3.50

Litho. & Embossed

676 A117 1500fr gold & multi 15.00 —

Souvenir Sheets

Litho.

677 A116 750fr multi 7.75 1.50

Litho. & Embossed

678 A117 1500fr gold & multi 15.00 —

Intl. Red Cross, 125th anniv. (300fr), Rotary Intl. (600fr, Nos. 676, 678). Nos. 674-678 are airmail.
#672-673 exist in souv. sheets of 1.
No. 676 exists in a souvenir sheet of 1. Value $42.50.

Inventors and Sportsmen A118

Portraits and modes of transportation: Designs: 75fr, Alain Prost, F-1 MacLaren-Honda. 125fr, George Stephenson and locomotive *Borsig of 1935*. 500fr, Ettore Bugatti (1881-1947), 1939 Bugatti Aravis Type 57. 600fr, Rudolf Diesel (1858-1913) and V200 BB diesel-electric locomotive. 750fr, Dennis Conner, captain of the *Stars and Stripes*, winner of the 1987 America's Cup. No. 684, Michael Fay, patron of the *New Zealand*, an entry in the America's Cup. No. 685, Enzo Ferrari and 1989 Ferrari Formula 1, horiz.

1988, Dec. 27 Litho. *Perf. 13½*

679 A118 75fr multi .75 .45
680 A118 125fr multi 1.25 .25
681 A118 500fr multi 5.00 1.25
682 A118 600fr multi 6.00 1.25
683 A118 750fr multi 7.00 1.25
684 A118 1000fr multi 10.00 1.25
Nos. 679-684 (6) 30.00 5.70

Souvenir Sheet

685 A118 1000fr multi 10.00 1.50

Nos. 683-685 are airmail.
#679-684 exist in souv. sheets of 1.

Scouts, Butterflies and Birds — A119

Scouts involved in various activities and species: 50fr, Gathering specimens, *Papilio nireus aristophontes oberthur* female. 75fr, Studying specimen and male. 150fr, Cooking out, *Charaxes fulvescens separanus poulton*. 375fr, Picking mushrooms, *Lonchura cucullatus*. 450fr, Examining specimen, *Charaxes castor comoranus rothschild*. 500fr, Identifying specimen, *Zosterops maderaspatana*. 750fr, Studying specimens, *Foudia omissa* and *Charaxes paradoxa lathy* female. No. 692, Photographing specimen, *Junonia rhadama*. No. 694, Examining specimen, *Agapornis cana cana*.

1989 Litho.

686 A119 50fr multi .50 .20
687 A119 75fr multi .60 .20
688 A119 150fr multi 1.40 .30
689 A119 375fr multi 4.00 .75
690 A119 450fr multi 4.75 1.00
691 A119 500fr multi 5.75 1.25
Nos. 686-691 (6) 17.00 3.70

Litho. & Embossed

692 A119 1500fr gold & multi 13.00 —

Souvenir Sheets

Litho.

693 A119 750fr multi 12.00 1.50

Litho. & Embossed

694 A119 1500fr gold & multi 13.00 —

Nos. 690-694 are airmail. Issue dates: Nos. 692, 694, May 15; others, Mar. 15.
No. 692 exists in a souvenir sheet of 1. Value $42.50.
For surcharges see Nos. 800D, 815T.

Gold Medalists of the 1988 Summer Olympics A120

Communication satellites, various equestrians and their mounts: 75fr, Nicole Uphoff, West Germany, individual dressage, and Aussat K3. 150fr, Pierre Durand, France, individual jumping, and Brazilsat. 375fr, Janos Martinek, Hungary, individual modern pentathlon, and ECS 4. 600fr, Mark Todd, New Zealand, individual three-day event, and Olympus. 750fr, Team jumping, West Germany, and satellite. No. 699, Pierre Durand, France, individual show jumping. No. 701, Nicole Uphoff, West Germany, individual dressage.

1989, Apr. 10 Litho. *Perf. 13½*

695 A120 75fr multi .65 .20
696 A120 150fr multi 1.25 .35
697 A120 375fr multi 3.00 .75
698 A120 600fr multi 5.00 1.25
Nos. 695-698 (4) 9.90 2.55

Litho. & Embossed

699 A120 1500fr gold & multi 13.00 —

Souvenir Sheets

Litho.

700 A120 750fr multi 6.75 1.50

Litho. & Embossed

701 A120 1500fr gold & multi 13.00 —

No. 701 contains one 39x38mm stamp. Nos. 698-701 are airmail.
No. 699 exists in a souvenir sheet of 1. Value $45.
For surcharges see Nos. 796Q, 804I.

Nos. 660, 588, 605 and 630 Surcharged

1989 Litho. *Perfs. as Before*

702 A114 25fr on 250fr #660 .20 .20
703 A101 150fr on 200fr #588 1.25 .50
704 A103 150fr on 200fr #605 1.25 .50
705 A108 150fr on 200fr #630 1.25 .50
Nos. 702-705 (4) 3.95 1.70

1992 Summer Olympics, Barcelona A121

1989, Apr. 26 Litho. *Perf. 13½*

706 A121 75fr Running .65 .20
707 A121 150fr Soccer 1.25 .40
708 A121 300fr Tennis 2.50 .60
709 A121 375fr Baseball 3.25 .80
710 A121 500fr Pommel horse 4.00 1.00
711 A121 600fr Table tennis 5.00 1.25
Nos. 706-711 (6) 16.65 4.25

Souvenir Sheet

712 A121 750fr Equestrian 6.75 1.50

Nos. 710-712 are airmail.
For surcharges see Nos. 796J, 796K, 800J, 812R.

Dr. Joseph-Ignace Guillotin (1738-1814) — A122

French Revolution, Bicent.: 150fr, French artillery, Gen. Francois-Christophe Kellermann (1735-1820). 375fr, Royalist insurgents & leader, Jean Cottereau (1757-94). 600fr, King Louis XVI (1774-92), troops. 1000fr, Storming of the Bastille & Jacques Necker, statesman (1732-1804). #717, Lafayette, Mounier, Sieyes & Declaration of the Rights of Man and Citizen. #719, Robespierre & St. Just before the Convention on 9 Thermidor.

1989, Oct. 25 Litho. *Perf. 13½*

713 A122 75fr multicolored .70 .20
714 A122 150fr multicolored 1.25 .35
715 A122 375fr multicolored 3.00 .60
716 A122 600fr multicolored 5.00 1.25
Nos. 713-716 (4) 9.95 2.40

Litho. & Embossed

717 A122 1500fr gold & multi 13.00 —

Souvenir Sheets

Litho.

718 A122 1000fr multicolored 8.50 1.75

Litho. & Embossed

719 A122 1500fr gold & multi 13.00

Philexfrance 1989. No. 716-719 are airmail.
No. 714 incorrectly inscribed "Francois-Etienne."
Nos. 713-716 exist in souvenir sheets of 1.
No. 717 exists in a souvenir sheet of 1. Value $22.
For surcharges see Nos. 796B, 800W, 804J.

Airport Pavilion A124

Designs: 10fr, 25fr, Airport pavilion. 50fr, 75fr, 150fr, Federal Assembly.

1990, Apr. 1 Litho. *Perf. 13*

722 A124 5fr brn, org & brt red .20 .20
723 A124 10fr brn, org & brt bl .20 .20
724 A124 25fr brn, org & brt grn .20 .20
725 A124 50fr blk & brt red .45 .20
726 A124 75fr blk & brt bl .75 .30
727 A124 150fr blk & grn 1.40 .60
Nos. 722-727 (6) 3.20 1.70

World Cup Soccer Championships, Italy — A125

Players from: 50fr, Brazil. 75fr, England. 100fr, Federal Republic of Germany. 150fr, Belgium. 375fr, Italy. 600fr, Argentina. 750fr, Argentina and Italy.

1990 Litho. *Perf. 13½*

728 A125 50fr multicolored .45 .20
729 A125 75fr multicolored .65 .30
730 A125 100fr multicolored .80 .35
731 A125 150fr multicolored 1.10 .45
732 A125 375fr multicolored 3.00 1.00
733 A125 600fr multicolored 5.00 1.25
Nos. 728-733 (6) 11.00 3.55

Litho. & Embossed

734 A125 1500fr gold & multi 13.00 5.00

Souvenir Sheets
Litho.

735 A125 750fr multicolored 6.75 1.50

Litho. & Embossed

736 A125 1500fr gold & multi 13.00 —

Nos. 732-736 are airmail.

No. 734 exists in a souvenir sheet of 1. Value $22.50.

For surcharges see Nos. 796L, 796O, 804K.

Telecom '91
A125a

1990, Oct. 29 Litho. *Perf. 13½*

736A A125a 75fr Emblem, vert. .75 .60
736B A125a 150fr shown 1.60 1.25

Nos. 736A-736B exist imperf.

A126

Designs: 75fr, Hubble Space Telescope placed in orbit. 150fr, Pope John Paul II, Pres. Gorbachev meet Dec. 3, 1989. 200fr, Kevin Mitchell, San Francisco Giants, Natl. League Most Valuable Player, 1989. 250fr, De Gaulle, France, and Adenauer, West Germany, meet in Sept. 1962. 300fr, Cassini probe to Titan, 2002. 375fr, Bullet train and Concorde, France. 450fr, Gary Kasparov, World Chess Champion. 500fr, Paul Harris (1868-1947), founder of Rotary Intl.

1990, Nov. 26 Litho. *Perf. 13½*

737 A126 75fr sil & multi .75 .25
738 A126 150fr sil & multi 1.50 .40
739 A126 200fr sil & multi 2.00 .40
740 A126 250fr sil & multi 2.50 .40
741 A126 300fr sil & multi 3.00 .50
742 A126 375fr sil & multi 3.75 .65
743 A126 450fr sil & multi 4.50 1.00
744 A126 500fr sil & multi 5.25 .75
Nos. 737-744 (8) 23.25 4.35

Nos. 743-744 are airmail.

#738, 744 exist in souv. sheets of 1.

For surcharges see Nos. 796A, 796R, 800I, 804A, 804L, 815E, 815U.

A127

A128

Winter Olympics participants: 75fr, Edi Reinalter, Switzerland, slalom, 1948. 100fr, Canadian hockey team, 1924. 375fr, Gratia Van der Oye, women's slalom, Holland, 1936. 600fr, Heikki Hasu, Finland, combined cross country and ski jumping, 1948. 750fr, Helene Engelman & Alfred Berger, Austria, pairs figure skating, 1924. No. 751, Speed skater, horiz. No. 751A, Luge, horiz.

1990, Dec. 10

746 A127 75fr multicolored .60 .20
747 A127 100fr multicolored .75 .30
748 A127 375fr multicolored 3.50 1.00
749 A127 600fr multicolored 6.00 1.25
Nos. 746-749 (4) 10.85 2.75

Souvenir Sheet

750 A127 750fr multicolored 8.25 1.50

Litho. & Embossed

751 A127 1500fr gold & multi 16.00 —

Souvenir Sheet

751A A127 1500fr gold & multi 15.00 —

1992 Winter Olympics, Albertville. Nos. 748-751A are airmail. No. 750 contains one 36x41mm stamp.

No. 751 exists in a souvenir sheet of 1. Value $22.

For surcharges see Nos. 796M, 800K, 804M, 812S.

1991, May 17 Litho. *Perf. 13½*

Ground station, Moroni Volo-Volo.

752 A128 75fr multicolored 1.00 .20
753 A128 150fr multicolored 1.60 .45
754 A128 225fr multicolored 2.40 .75
755 A128 300fr multicolored 3.50 1.00
756 A128 500fr multicolored 5.50 1.25
Nos. 752-756 (5) 14.00 3.65

For surcharge see 815N.

Indian Ocean Conference — A129

1991, June 17

757 A129 75fr multicolored .30 .20
758 A129 150fr multicolored .90 .75
759 A129 225fr multicolored 1.40 1.00
Nos. 757-759 (3) 2.60 1.95

World War II, 50th Anniv.
A130

Actors, Films: 150fr, Errol Flynn, Objective Burma. 300fr, Henry Fonda, The Longest Day. 450fr, Humphrey Bogart, Sahara.

1991, Aug. 5

760 A130 150fr sil & multi 1.75 .45
761 A130 300fr sil & multi 3.25 .75
762 A130 450fr sil & multi 5.00 .90
Nos. 760-762 (3) 10.00 2.10

No. 762 is airmail. Nos. 760-762 exist in souvenir sheets of 1.

For surcharges see Nos. 796D, 800H, 804B, 804G.

A131

Charles de Gaulle
A132

De Gaulle and: 125fr, Battle of Koufra. 375fr, Battle of Britain. 500fr, Battle of Monte Cassino. 1000fr, Airplanes. 1500fr, De Gaulle at podium.

1991, Aug. 5 Litho. *Perf. 13½*

763 A131 125fr multi 1.25 .30
764 A131 375fr multi 2.75 .75
765 A131 500fr multi 4.50 .90
Nos. 763-765 (3) 8.50 1.95

Souvenir Sheet

766 A131 1000fr multi 12.00 2.00

Litho. & Embossed

767 A132 1500fr gold & multi 16.00 —

Nos. 765-767 are airmail. No. 767 exists in souvenir sheet of 1. Value $20.

For surcharges see Nos. 796G, 804N, 816I.

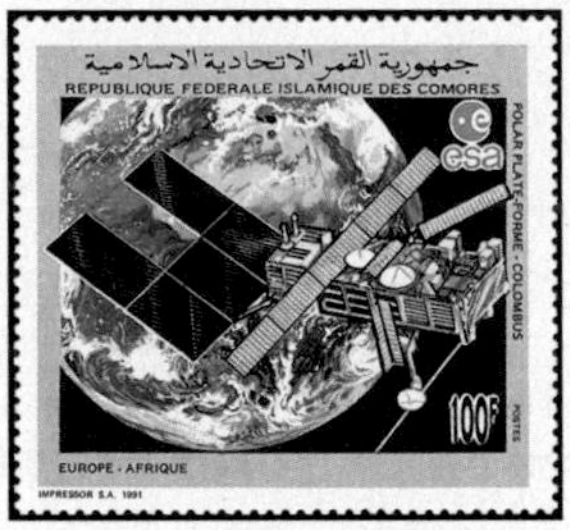

Anniversaries and Events — A133

Designs: 100fr, Satellite Columbus in polar orbit. 150fr, Gandhi. 250fr, Jean-Henri Dunant. 300fr, Wolfgang Amadeus Mozart. 375fr, Brandenburg Gate. 400fr, Konrad Adenauer. 450fr, Elvis Presley. 500fr, Ferdinand von Zeppelin.

1991, Nov. 18 Litho. *Perf. 13½*

768 A133 100fr multicolored 1.25 .30
769 A133 150fr multicolored 1.60 .35
770 A133 250fr multicolored 2.50 .60
771 A133 300fr multicolored 3.25 .60
772 A133 375fr multicolored 4.50 .90
773 A133 400fr multicolored 4.50 .90
774 A133 450fr multicolored 5.50 1.00
a. Souv. sheet, #771, 774 — —
775 A133 500fr multicolored 5.50 1.00
a. Souv. sheet, #772-773, 775 — —
Nos. 768-775 (8) 28.60 5.65

Nobel Peace Prize, 90th anniv. (#770). Mozart, bicent. of death (#771). Brandenburg Gate, bicent. (#772). Konrad Adenauer, 25th anniv. of death (#773). Elvis Presley, 15th anniv. of death (in 1992) (#774). Count Zeppelin, 75th anniv. of death (in 1992) (#775).

Nos. 774-775 are airmail. Nos. 768-775 exist in souvenir sheets of 1. Value, set $50.

For surcharges see Nos. 796F, 796H, 800G, 804C, 804O, 815F, 815O, 816J.

Mushrooms — A134

1992, Mar. 23 Litho. *Perf. 13½*

776 A134 75fr Cepe comestible .80 .40
777 A134 150fr Geastre en etoile 1.90 .60
778 A134 600fr Pezize ecarlate 8.25 1.50
Nos. 776-778 (3) 10.95 2.50

No. 778 is airmail. Nos. 776-778 exist imperf. and in souvenir sheets of one.

Shells
A135

1992, Mar. 23

779 A135 125fr Conus textile 1.60 .50
780 A135 150fr Cypraecassis rufa 2.10 .65
781 A135 500fr Leporicypraea mappa 6.50 1.90
Nos. 779-781 (3) 10.20 3.05

Souvenir Sheet

782 A135 750fr Nautilus pompilius 10.50 2.00

Nos. 781-782 are airmail. Nos. 779-781 exist imperf. and in souvenir sheets of one. No. 782 exists imperf.

For surcharges see Nos. 800N, 816K.

Space Programs
A136

Designs: 75fr, Mercury rocket, chimpanzee Ham, US. 125fr, Mars Observer, US. No. 785, Veronica rocket, cat Felix, France. No. 786, Mars rover, US, Mars car, USSR. 500fr, Phobos project, USSR. 600fr, Sputnik II, dog Laika, USSR. 1000fr, Viking, US, vert.

1992, Mar. 30 Litho. *Perf. 13½*

783 A136 75fr multicolored 1.25 .25
784 A136 125fr multicolored 1.75 .30
785 A136 150fr multicolored 2.25 .70
786 A136 150fr multicolored 2.10 .70
787 A136 500fr multicolored 6.50 1.25
a. Souv. sheet, #784, 786-787 — —
788 A136 600fr multicolored 7.75 1.40
a. Souv. sheet, #783, 785, 788 — —
Nos. 783-788 (6) 21.60 4.60

Souvenir Sheet

789 A136 1000fr multicolored 13.00 2.25

Nos. 787-789 are airmail. Nos. 783-788 exist imperf. and in souvenir sheets of one. No. 789 contains one 30x42mm stamp.

For surcharges see Nos. 800O, 804Q.

Voyages of Discovery
A137

Designs: 75fr, Space shuttle Endeavour, sailing ship Endeavour, Capt. Cook. 100fr, Satellite, sailing ship Golden Hinde, Sir Francis Drake. 150fr, ISO observation satellite, sailing ship Susan Constant, John Smith. 225fr, Probe B, sailing ship Discovery, Robert F. Scott. 375fr, Magellan probe over Venus, sailing ship, Ferdinand Magellan. 500fr, Newton probe, sailing ship Sao Gabriel, Vasco da Gama.

1000fr, Hermes-Columbus space shuttle, Columbus and his fleet.

1992, May 28 Litho. *Perf. 13½*

790 A137 75fr multicolored 1.25 .25
791 A137 100fr multicolored 1.40 .30
792 A137 150fr multicolored 2.25 .45
793 A137 225fr multicolored 2.75 .75
794 A137 375fr multicolored 5.25 1.00

795 A137 500fr multicolored 6.00 1.25
a. Souvenir sheet of 6, #790-795 15.00 7.00
Nos. 790-795 (6) 18.90 4.00

Souvenir Sheet

796 A137 1000fr multicolored 13.00 2.25

Nos. 794-796 are airmail. Nos. 790-795 exist imperf. in souvenir sheets of one.

For surcharges see Nos. 796E, 800P, 804P.

Various Stamps Surcharged

a — (Obliterator of dots)

Methods and Perfs as Before

1992-95

796A A126 10fr on 300fr #741 —
796B A122 15fr on 375fr #715 —
796C AP41 25fr on 210fr #C164 —
796D A130 25fr on 300fr #761 —
796E A137 25fr on 375fr #794 —
796F A133 35fr on 400fr #773 —
796G A131 50fr on 375fr #764 —
796H A133 50fr on 375fr #772 —
796I AP34 50fr on 475fr #C138 —
796J A121 75fr on 300fr #708 — —
796K A121 75fr on 375fr #709 —
796L A125 75fr on 375fr #732 —
796M A127 75fr on 375fr #748 —
796N AP42 75fr on 600fr #C170 —
796O A125 100fr on 375fr #732 —
796P A109 150fr on 210fr #633 —
796Q A120 150fr on 375fr #697 — —
796R A126 150fr on 375fr #742 —
796S AP40 150fr on 450fr #C162 —
796T A109 150fr on 500fr #634 —
796U AP42 150fr on 500fr #C169 —

No. 796J exists with quadruple surcharge.

No. 796Q exists with inverted surcharge and with double surcharge, one inverted.

Organization of African Unity, 30th Anniv. — A138

1993, Feb. 15 Litho. *Perf. 13½x13*

797 A138 25fr blue & multi .20 .20
798 A138 50fr pink & multi .50 .20

Perf. 12

799 A138 75fr green & multi 1.40 .45
800 A138 150fr vermilion & multi 2.25 1.00
Nos. 797-800 (4) 4.35 1.85

Various Stamps Surcharged

b — (Bar obliterator)

Methods and Perfs as Before

1992-95

800A A103 50fr on 450fr #607 —
x. Zero in surcharge thin at top and bottom —
800B AP47 75fr on 800fr #C192 —
800C A112 100fr on 350fr #648 —
800D A119 100fr on 375fr #689 —
g. Zero in surcharge thin at top and bottom —
y. 150fr on 375fr #689 (error) —
800E A101 100fr on 400fr #590 — —
800F A105 100fr on 400fr #618 —
h. Zero in surcharge thin at top and bottom —
800G A133 100fr on 400fr #773 —
i. Zero in surcharge thin at top and bottom —
800H A130 125fr on 450fr #762 —
800I A126 150fr on 250fr #740 — —
800J A121 150fr on 375fr #709 —
z. Zero in surcharge thin at top and bottom —
800K A127 150fr on 375fr #748 —
a. Zero in surcharge thin at top and bottom —
800L A109 150fr on 500fr #634 — —
k. Zero in surcharge thin at top and bottom —
800M A112 150fr on 500fr #650 —
b. Zero in surcharge thin at top and bottom —
800N A135 150fr on 500fr #781 — —
800O A136 150fr on 500fr #787 —
800P A137 150fr on 500fr #795 —
c. Zero in surcharge thin at top and bottom —
800Q AP41 150fr on 500fr #C165 —
d. Zero in surcharge thin at top and bottom —
800R AP44 150fr on 500fr #C177 —
l. Zero in surcharge thin at top and bottom —
m. Denomination above obliterator —
n. As "l," denomination above obliterator —
800S AP45 150fr on 500fr #C181 —
e. Zero in surcharge thin at top and bottom —
800T AP42 150fr on 500fr #C185 —
o. Zero in surcharge thin at top and bottom —
800U AP47 150fr on 500fr #C191 —
800V AP50 150fr on 500fr #C212 —
p. Zero in surcharge thin at top and bottom —
800W A122 150fr on 600fr #716 —

Surcharge on No. 800W is sideways reading top to bottom. Nos. 800B and 800F exist with inverted surcharge, Nos. 800F, 800R, 800W, and perhaps other values exist with misplaced surcharge.

No. 800F exists with zeros in surcharge in different sizes.

1994 World Cup Soccer Championships, U.S. — A139

Intl. Telecommunications Day — A140

1993, May 12 Litho. *Perf. 13x12½*

801 A139 25fr red & multi .20 .20
802 A139 75fr brown & multi .65 .30
803 A139 100fr blue & multi 1.40 .40
804 A139 150fr green & multi 1.60 .60
Nos. 801-804 (4) 3.85 1.50

Various Stamps Surcharged Type "b" in Black or Red

Methods and Perfs as Before

1992-95

804A A126 200fr on 300fr #741 —
s. Zero in surcharge thin at top and bottom —
804B A130 200fr on 300fr #761 —
804C A133 200fr on 300fr #771 —
w. Zero in surcharge thin at top and bottom — —
804D AP45 200fr on 300fr #C180 —
x. Zero in surcharge thin at top and bottom —
804E AP47 200fr on 300fr #C190 —
t. Zero in surcharge thin at top and bottom —
804F A90 200fr on 450fr #520 —
u. Overprint right side up —
y. Overprint right side up, zero in surcharge thin at top and bottom —
804G A130 200fr on 450fr #762 —
a. Zero in surcharge thin at top and bottom —
b. As "a," two obliterators —
804H AP40 200fr on 450fr #C162 —
c. Zero in surcharge thin at top and bottom —
804I A120 225fr on 375fr #697 —
804J A122 225fr on 375fr #715 —
804K A125 225fr on 375fr #732 —
804L A126 225fr on 375fr #742 —
804M A127 225fr on 375fr #748 —
v. "f" in surcharge omitted —
804N A127 225fr on 375fr #764 —
804O A133 225fr on 375fr #772 —
804P A137 225fr on 375fr #794 —
804Q A136 225fr on 500fr #787 —

Red Surcharge

804R AP40 200fr on 300fr #C161 —

Surcharge on No. 804F is inverted.

No. 804D exists with "020fr" surcharge and with zeroes in surcharge in different sizes. Nos. 804D and 804F exists with zeroes in surcharge in different sizes.

1993, May 17

805 A140 50fr red & multi .40 .20
806 A140 75fr blue & multi .65 .30
807 A140 100fr green & multi 1.10 .40
808 A140 150fr black & multi 1.60 .60
Nos. 805-808 (4) 3.75 1.50

Miniature Sheet

Prehistoric Animals A141

Designs: a, 75fr, Edaphosaurus. b, 75fr, Moschops. c, 75fr, Sauroctonus. d, 75fr, Ornitholestes. e, 75fr, Kentrosaurus. f, 75fr, Compsognathus. g, 75fr, Styracosaurus. h, 75fr, Acanthopholis. i, 150fr, Edmontonia. j, 150fr, Struthiomimus. k, 450fr, Dromiceiomimus. l, 450fr, Iguanodon. m, 150fr, Diatryma. n, 150fr, Uintatherium. o, 525fr, Synthetoceras. p, 525fr, Euryapteryx.

1200fr, Tyrannosaurus rex.

1994, Apr. 5 Litho. *Perf. 13½*

809 A141 Sheet of 16, #a.-p. 22.50 9.00

Souvenir Sheet

810 A141 1200fr multicolored 13.00 3.00

No. 810 is airmail and contains one 42x60mm stamp.

Miniature Sheets

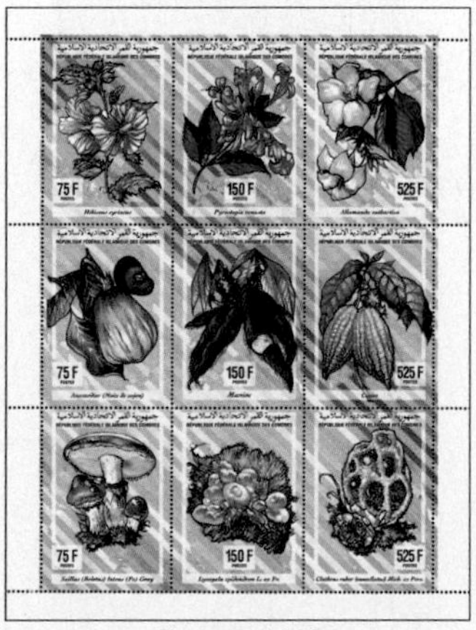

Flora — A142

Flowers: No. 811a, 75fr, Hibiscus syriacus. 150fr, Pyrostegia venusta. 525fr, Allamanda cathartica.

Vegetables: No. 811b, 75fr, Anacardier. 150fr, Manioc. 525fr, Cacao.

Mushrooms: No. 811c, 75fr, Suillus lutens. 150fr, Lycogala epidendron. 525fr, Clathrus ruber.

Butterflies, insects: No. 812a, 75fr, Colotis zoe. b, 150fr, Acherontia atropos. c, 450fr, Danaus chrysippus. d, 75fr, Charaxes comoranus. e, 150fr, Euchloron megaera. f, 450fr, Papilio phorbanta. g, 75fr, Hypurgus ova. h, 150fr, Onthophagus catta. i, 450fr, Echinosoma bolivari.

1994, May 24 Litho. *Perf. 13½*

811 A142 Sheet of 9 16.00 5.50
a. Strip of 3 4.25 1.50
b. Strip of 3 4.25 1.50
c. Strip of 3 4.25 1.50
d. Souvenir sheet of 3, #811a 16.00 5.00
e. Souvenir sheet of 3, #811b 16.00 5.00
f. Souvenir sheet of 3, #811c 16.00 5.00
812 A142 Sheet of 9, #a.-i. 15.00 5.00
j. Souv. sheet of 3, #812a-812c 16.00 5.00
k. Souv. sheet of 3, #812d-812f 16.00 5.00
l. Souv. sheet of 3, #812g-812i 16.00 5.00

For surcharges see No. 826F.

Independence, 20th Anniv. — A142a

Designs: 100fr, 200fr, 300fr, Maps of Grand Comoro, Moheli, Mayotte and Anjouan.

1995 (?) Litho. *Perf. 13x12¾*

812M A142a 100fr multi
812N A142a 200fr multi — —
812O A142a 300fr multi

For surcharge see No. 826M.

Various Stamps Surcharged in Gold

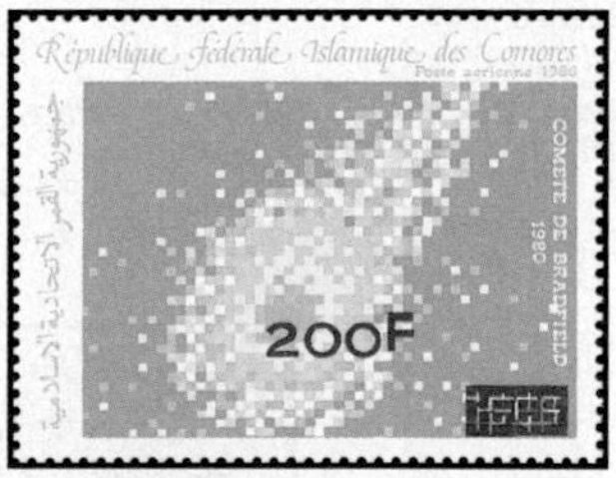

c — (Wide numerals, obliterator of small sqares in grid)

Methods and Perfs as Before

1996, Dec.

812P AP40 200fr on 300fr #C161 —
812Q A102 200fr on 350fr #598 —
812R A121 200fr on 375fr #709 —
v. "2" same size as "0" —
812S A127 200fr on 375fr #748 —
812T AP31 200fr on 400fr #C125 — —
812U AP44 200fr on 500fr #C177 —

Size of numerals and obliteration grids varies.

A143

A144

Diana, Princess of Wales (1961-97): Various portraits.

1997, Dec. 15 Litho. *Perf. 14*

813 A143 150fr Sheet of 12, #a.-l. 10.00 4.00
814 A143 375fr Sheet of 6, #a.-f. 12.00 5.00

Souvenir Sheet

815 A143 1000fr multicolored 5.50 2.25

Various Stamps Surcharged Type "c" in Black

Methods and Perfs as Before

1996, Dec.

815A A109 200fr on 210fr #633 —
815B A111 200fr on 210fr #640 —
815C AP41 200fr on 210fr #C164 — —
815D A114 200fr on 250fr #660 —
815E A126 200fr on 250fr #740 —
815F A133 200fr on 250fr #770 —
815G AP30 200fr on 250fr #C116 — —
815H AP38 200fr on 250fr #C151 —
815I AP38 200fr on 250fr #C152 —
x. Pair, #815H-815I + label —
815J AP42 200fr on 250fr #C168 —
815K AP42 200fr on 250fr #C184 —
815L AP28 200fr on 260fr #C110 — —
815M A101 200fr on 300fr #589 —
y. With gold obliterator over old value — —
815N A128 200fr on 300fr #755 —
815O A133 200fr on 300fr #771 —
815P AP31 200fr on 300fr #C124 —
815Q AP37 200fr on 300fr #C150 —
815R A107 200fr on 350fr #626 —
815S A98 200fr on 360fr #574 —
815T A119 200fr on 375fr #689 —
815U A126 200fr on 375fr #742 —
815V A112 200fr on 400fr #649 —
815W A111 200fr on 425fr #641 —

Size of surcharge numerals and obliteration grid varies. Black surcharge on No. 815My is misplaced. No. 815Q exists with misplaced surcharge that is faintly tripled, a surcharge with thinner zeroes, and a pair containing No. C150 next to No. 815Q with misplaced surcharge that is faintly tripled and has thinner zeroes. No. 815W exists with an inverted surcharge and with a double surcharge, one inverted.

1997, Dec. 15 Litho. *Perf. 14*

816 A144 200fr Mother Teresa (1910-97) 1.50 .45

No. 816 was issued in sheets of 9.

Aromatic Plants A144a

Designs: 25fr, 50fr, 1000fr, Piper nigrum. 100fr, 125fr, 200fr, Cinnamomum ceylanicum. 300fr, Syzigium aromaticum. 500fr, Myristica fragrans.

1997, Dec. 15 Litho. *Perf. 14*

816A A144a 25fr multi —
816B A144a 50fr multi —
816C A144a 100fr multi —
816D A144a 125fr multi —
816E A144a 200fr multi —
816F A144a 300fr multi —
816G A144a 500fr multi —
816H A144a 1000fr multi —

Various Stamps Surcharged Type "c" in Black

Methods and Perfs as Before

1996, Dec.

816I A131 200fr on 500fr #765 — —
816J A133 200fr on 500fr #775 — —
816K A135 200fr on 500fr #781 — —
816L AP42 200fr on 500fr #C169 — —
816M AP42 200fr on 500fr #C185 — —
816N AP42 200fr on 600fr #C170 — —
816O AP42 200fr on 600fr #C186 — —

Size of surcharge and obliteration grid varies.

Vertical Pairs from No. B4 Surcharged with Silver Bar to Obliterate Surtax

Methods and Perfs as before.

1996, Dec.

816P Surcharged pair of #B4a, B4e —
t. SP3 200fr on 200fr+10fr Galileo —
u. SP3 200fr on 200fr+10fr Planet A & 3 stars —
816Q Surcharged pair of #B4b, B4f —
v. SP3 200fr on 200fr+10fr Copernicus —
w. SP3 200fr on 200fr+10fr ICE —
816R Surcharged pair of #B4c, B4g —
x. SP3 200fr on 200fr+10fr Kepler —
y. SP3 200fr on 200fr+10fr Planet A & 5 stars —
816S Surcharged pair of #B4d, B4h —
z. SP3 200fr on 200fr+10fr Halley —
aa. SP3 200fr on 200fr+10fr Vega —

A full sheet of Nos. 816P-816S is not known to exist.

Cats A145

Designs, vert: 75fr, Silver banded. 150fr, Lac de Van. No. 819, 200fr, European short hair. No. 820, 200fr, Somali. No. 821, 375fr, Japanese bobtail. No. 822, 375fr, Egyptian mau.

No. 823, each 375fr: a, Poupée de chiffon. b, Maine coon. c, Norwegian forest cat. d, Persian. e, Droop-eared. f, Marbled American short hair.

No. 824, each 375fr: a, Manx. b, Cashmere. c, British shorthair. d, Cornish rex. e, American curl. f, Ocicat.

No. 825, 1500fr, Silver-chocolate Somali. No. 826, 1500fr, Chocolate Persian, vert.

1998, June 3 Litho. *Perf. 14*

817-822 A145 Set of 6 7.50 7.50

Sheets of 6

823-824 A145 Set of 2 24.00 24.00

Souvenir Sheets

825-826 A145 Set of 2 17.50 6.00

No. C215D Surcharged Type "c" in Red or Black

Methods and Perfs as Before

1997 (?)

826A AP52a 100fr on 225fr — —
826B AP52a 200fr on 225fr — —
826C AP52a 200fr on 225fr (Bk) —
826D AP52a 500fr on 225fr —
826E AP52a 600fr on 225fr —

Size of surcharge numerals varies. No. 826B exists with inverted surcharge, No. 826C exists with double surcharge.

No. 811 Surcharged on Six Stamps

d — (Obliterator of Triangles and Wavy Lines)

Methods and Perfs as Before

1998 (?)

826F Sheet of 9 —
g. A142 200fr on 150fr Pyrostegia venusta —
h. A142 200fr on 150fr Manioc —
i. A142 200fr on 150fr Lycogala epidendron —
j. A142 200fr on 525fr Allamanda cathartica —
k. A142 200fr on 525fr Cacao —
l. A142 200fr on 525fr Clathrus ruber —

The three 75fr stamps on the sheet received no surcharge.

No. 812O Surcharged

e — (Obliterator of Bars, Dots, and Semicircles)

Methods and Perfs as Before

1998 (?)

826M A142a 100fr on 300fr —

Size of surcharge numerals varies.

Marine Life A146

No. 827, each 150fr: a, Pomacanthus imperator. b, Cephalopholis miniatus. c, Diver. d, Nautilus pompilius. e, Sphyraena barracuda. f, Manta birostris. g, Lutjanus sebae. h, Chaetodonplus duboulayi. i, Amphiprion bicinctus.

No. 828, vert , each 150fr: a, Istiophorus platypterus. b, Sterna fuscata. c, Larus pipixcan. d, Hippocampus kuda. e, Amphiprion ocellaris (2 fish). f, Octopus vulgaris. g, Chaetodon striatus. h, Actini aquina. i, Acanthurus leucosternon.

No. 829: a, Diomedea exulans. b, Delphinus delphis. c, Sailboat. d, Sphyrna zygaena. e, Loligo forbesi. f, Galeocerdo cuvieri. g, Pomacanthus imperator, diff. h, Amphiprion ocellaris (1 fish). i, Forcipiger flavissimus. j, Electrophorus electricus. k, Dermochelys coriaoea. l, Asterias rubens.

No. 830, 1500fr, Mastigias papua, vert. No. 831, 1500fr, Sepia officinalis. No. 832, 1500fr, Zancius canescens.

1998, Aug. 10 Litho. *Perf. 14*

Sheets of 9 or 12

827-828 A146 Set of 2 13.00 13.00
829 A146 200fr #a.-l. 12.00 12.00

Souvenir Sheets

830-832 A146 Set of 3 22.50 22.50

Nos. 830-832 each contain one 51x38mm or 38x51mm stamp.

Betty Boop — A146a

No. 832A: b, Wearing hula skirt, dancing. c, With dog, wearing blue dress, in pink heart. d, Wearing polka dot dress. e, In bathtub. f, Face in red heart. g, Holding top hat. h, With flamingos. i, With dog, Wearing red dress, blue ribbon. j, Wearing hula skirt, on surf board.

1125fr, With fishing pole.

1998 Litho. *Perf. 13¼*

832A A146a 300fr Sheet of 9, #b-j — —

Souvenir Sheet

832K A146a 1125fr multi — —

No. 832A contains nine 35x41mm stamps.

Popeye — A146b

No. 832L: m, Wimpy. n, Popeye, Olive Oyl, ship's wheel. o, Swee'Pea. p, Head of Popeye. q, Popeye. r, Head of Olive Oyl. s, Jeep. t, Olive Oyl. u, Brutus.

No. 832V, 1125fr, Popeye with spinach can. No. 832W, 1125fr, Like #832Ln, horiz.

1998

832L A146b 450fr Sheet of 9, #m-u — —

Souvenir Sheets

832V-832W A146b Set of 2 — —

No. 832L contains nine 35x51mm stamps, No. 832W contains one 60x50mm stamp.

Coelacanth — A147

World Wildlife Fund: a, Swimming right, colored background. b, Swimming right, white background. c, In net. d, Swimming left.

No. 833E: f, Like #833a. g, Like #833d. h, Like #833c. i, Like #833b.

1998

833 A147 200fr Strip of 4, #a-d 6.00 6.00
833E A147 375fr Sheet of 4, #f-i 37.50

No. 833 was issued in sheets of 3 vertical strips.

No. 833E exists imperf. Value $45.

I Love Lucy — A147a

No. 833F, vert. — Lucy: g, With black ribbon in hair. h, Wearing burlap sack. i, With trapeze in mouth. j, With one arm raised. k, On telephone. l, Wearing red and white apron. m, Wearing bright green dress. n, Wearing blue dress. o, With fishing gear.

1125fr, With Ricky, with fishing gear.

1998 Litho. *Perf. 13¼*

833F A147a 250fr Sheet of 9, #g-o — —

Souvenir Sheet

833P A147a 1125fr multi — —

No. 833F contains nine 35x51mm stamps.

Diana, Princess of Wales (1961-97)
A148

Nos. 834-835, 835J, Various portraits.
No. 836, 1125fr, Wearing scarf, green dress. No. 837, 1125fr, Wearing black and white hat and outfit.

1998 Litho. *Perf. 13½*

Sheets of 9

834 A148 250fr #a.-i. 13.00 13.00
835 A148 350fr #a.-i. 18.00 18.00
835J A148 450fr #k.-s. 24.00 24.00

Souvenir Sheets

836-837 A148 Set of 2 13.00 13.00

Nos. 835, 835J contain 42x51mm stamps. Nos. 836-837 each contain one 42x60mm stamp.

Entertainers
A149

#838: Various portraits of Grace Kelly (Princess Grace of Monaco) (1929-92).
#839: Various portraits of Frank Sinatra (1915-98).

1998

Sheets of 9

838 A149 300fr #a.-i. 16.00 16.00
839 A149 500fr #a.-i. 26.50 26.50

Classic Automobiles — A150

No. 840, each 150fr: a, 1936 Jaguar SS. b, 1939 Lincoln Continental. c, 1903 Mercedes. d, 1936 MG-TA. e, 1946 Oldsmobile Custom Cruiser 98. f, 1933 Pontiac. g, 1940 Rolls-Royce Silver Ghost 40/50. h, 1950 Studebaker Starlight Coupe. i, 1932 Ford V8.
No. 841, each 150fr: a, 1927 Alfa Romeo RLSS. b, 1933 DuPont Model G. c, Bentley Speed Six. d, 1932 Cadillac 355. e, 1955 Corvette. f, 1934 Chrysler Airflow. g, Buick Coupe deVille. h, Model T Ford. i, 1920 Duesenberg Model A.
No. 842, 1500fr, Rolls-Royce Phantom II Continental. No. 843, 1500fr, 1927 Daimler Double Six.

1998, Oct. 29 Litho. *Perf. 14*

Sheets of 9

840-841 A150 Set of 2 13.00 13.00

Souvenir Sheets

842-843 A150 Set of 2 17.00 17.00

Birds — A151

No. 844, 75fr, Macareux moine. No. 845, 75fr, Calliste à tête verte. No. 846, 150fr, Soutmanga de la reine Christine. No. 847, 150fr, Rale d'eau. No. 848, 200fr, Lophophore replendissant. No. 849, 200fr, Francolin noir. No. 850, 375fr, Mesia â oreillonis argentes. No. 851, 375fr, Mérion splendide.
No. 852: a, Canard plongeur austral. b, Garrot a ceil d'or. c, Harle huppé. d, Canard colvert. e, Canard branchu. f, Sarcelle elegante.
No. 853: a, Emérillon. b, Nyctale de tengmalm. c, Aigle royal d, Kétoupa malais. e, Caracara. f, Chouette à lunettes
No. 854, Jacana du mexique. No. 855, Toucan de cuvier.

1999, Jan. 23 Litho. *Perf. 14*

844-851 A151 Set of 8 8.50 8.50

Sheets of 6, #a-f

852-853 A151 375fr Set of 2 22.50 22.50

Souvenir Sheets

854-855 A151 1500fr Set of 2 16.00 16.00

Fauna
A152

No. 856, vert, each 150fr: a, Giraffa camaloprdalis. b, Macaca fusata. c, Loxodonta africana. d, Ovis dalli. e, Phoenicopterus ruber. f, Orcinus orca. g, Ursus horribilis. h, Lemur catta.
No. 857, vert, each 150fr: a, Pongo pygmaeus. b, Ceratotherium simum. c, Ailuropoda melanoleuca. d, Tursiops truncartus. e, Felis caracel. g, Eudyptes chrysocome. h, Bison bison. i, Panthera uncia.
No. 858, vert, each 150fr: a, Phascolarctos cinereus. b, Ammotragus levia. c, Hippopatamus amphibius. d, Saimiri boliviensis. e, Acinonyx jubatus. f, Gorilla gorilla. g, Branta sandvicensis. h, Thalarctos maritimus.
No. 859, each 150fr: a, Panthera tigris. b, Phoca groenlandica. c, Acipenser sturio. d, Lepidochelys kempii. e, Ailuropoda melanoleuca. f, Isurus oxyrinchus. g, Chelydra serpentina. h, Eretmochelys imbricata.
Each 1500fr: No. 860: Pan troglodytes, vert. No. 861, Panthera tigris altaica, vert. No. 862, Oryx gazella, vert. No. 863, Hippotigris zebra. No. 864, Diceros bicornis. No. 865, Panthera leo. No. 866, Amazona viridgenalis. No. 867, Pygoscelis papua, vert.

1999, Jan. 25

Sheets of 8

856-859 A152 Set of 4 25.00 25.00

Souvenir Sheets

860-867 A152 Set of 8 65.00 65.00

Fish
A153

No. 868, 75fr, Pomacantus imperator. No. 869, 75fr, Heniochus intermedium. No. 870, 150fr, Mirolaprichthys. No. 871, 150fr, Pomacanthus paru. No. 872, 375fr, Ostzacion tuberculatus. No. 873, 375fr, Colisa calia.
No. 874, each 150fr: a, Coris aygula. b, Chromis caeruleys. c, Euxiphipops navarchus. d, Pseudobalistes fuscus. e, Zebrasoma flavescens. f, Mycteroperca urba. g, Epinephelus flavocaeruleus. h, Equetus lanceolatus. i, Acanthurus leucostemon.
No. 875, each 150fr: a, Chaetodon tinkeri. b, Ostzaciidae. c, Seatophagus argus. d, Adioryx coruscus. e, Pygoplites diacanthus. f, Paracanthurus hepatus. g, Chaetodon plebius. h, Lythrypnus dalli. i, Myrichthys oculatus.
Each 1500fr: No. 876, Amphipzion percula. No. 877, Cymnothorne undulatus.

1998, Oct.-Nov. Litho. *Perf. 14*

868-873 A153 Set of 6 7.00 7.00

Sheets of 9

874-875 A153 Set of 2 14.00 14.00

Souvenir Sheets

876-877 A153 Set of 2 16.00 16.00

Marine Life — A154

No. 878, 75fr, Tubastrea aurea. No. 879, 75fr, Condylachtis gigantea. No. 880, 150fr, Paracanthurus hepatus. No. 881, 150fr, Balistoides conspicillum. No. 882, 200fr, Diodon holocanthus. No. 883, 200fr, Sebastes rubrivintus. No. 884, 375fr, Trygonorhina fasciata. No. 885, 375fr, Phocoenoides dalli.
No. 886, each 150fr: a, Epinephelus guttatus. b, Diademichthys lineatus. c, Plotosus lineatus. d, Rhinomuraena quaesita. e, Zanclus cornutus. f, Persephona punctata. g, Murex pecten. h, Tetrosomus gibbosus.
No. 887, each 150fr: a, Lythrypnus dalli. b, Premnas biaculeatus. c, Pseudanthias tuka. d, Capros aper. e, Balistoides conspicillum. f, Oreaster reticulatus. g, Octopus joubini. h, Fasciolaris tulipa.
Each 1500fr: No. 888, S. picturatus. No. 889, Megaptera novaeangliae.

1999

878-885 A154 Set of 8 8.50 8.50

Sheets of 8

886-887 A154 Set of 2 17.00 17.00

Souvenir Sheets

888-889 A154 Set of 2 19.00 19.00

Prehistoric Animals — A155

No. 890, each 150fr: a, Meganeura. b, Archaeopteryx. c, Peteinosaurus. d, Eudimorphodon. e, Brachiosaurus. f, Gallimimus. g, Tarbosaurus. h, Parasaurolophus. i, Sauropelta. j, Herrarasaurus. k, Stegosaurus. l, Lambeosaurus.
No. 891, each 150fr: a, Ramphorhinchus. b, Quetzalcoatlus. c, Pterodactylus. d, Pteranodon. e, Dimorphodon. f. Camarasaurus. g, Tenontosaurus. h, Protoceratops. i, Coelurosaurus. j, Mixosaurus. k, Ceresiosaurus. l, Sharovipteryx.
Each 1500fr: No. 892, Ceratosaurus. No. 893, Mesosaurus. No. 894, Megazostrodon. No. 895, Diatryma.

1999

Sheets of 12

890-891 A155 Set of 2 19.00 19.00

Souvenir Sheets

892-895 A155 Set of 4 32.50 32.50

Prehistoric Animals, Lemurs and Butterflies — A156

Prehistoric animals — No. 895A — Prehistoric sea creatures: b, Eurhinodelphis. c, Stenopterygius. d, Ichthyosaurus. e, Pakicetus. f, Xenacanthus. g, Zygorhiza. h, Basilosaurus. i, Mesosaurus. j, Cetotherium.
No. 896: a, Elasmosaurus (b). b, Quetzalcoatl (c). c, Mesadactylus (b). d, Dimorphodon (e). e, Rhamphorhynchus (c, d, f, i). f, Pteranodon (c, i). g, Pterodactylus (h). h, Eudimorphodon (i). i, Ornithodesmus (g, h).
Lemurs — No. 897: a, Haplorhinien primitif. b, Aye aye (c, e, f). c, Lemur vari. d, Indri. e, Makis varis (f, i). f, Potto. g, Lemur catta. h, Lemur macaos. i, Microcebe souris.
Butterflies — No. 898: a, Charaxes nobilis. b, Charaxes eupale. c, Charaxes brutus. d, Lobobunea turlini. e, Papilio nobilis. f, Athletes gigas. g, Papilio antimachus. h, Epiphora albida. i, Papilio zalmoxis.

1998 *Perf. 13¼x13½*

Sheets of 9

895A A156 150fr Sheet of 9, #b-j 6.50 6.50
896 A156 200fr #a.-i. 9.75 9.75
897 A156 250fr #a.-i. 12.00 12.00
898 A156 300fr #a.-i. 14.50 14.50

See Nos. 928-933.

A157

Endangered Species — A157a

Designs: 75fr, Galago crassicaudatus. 150fr, Vulpes vulpes. 200fr, Anomalurus pusillus. 375fr, Loxodonta africana, vert.
Primates, vert: Nos. 903a-903c, Various views of Pan troglodytes. Nos. 903d-903f, Various views of gorilla gorilla. Nos. 903g-903i, Various views of pongo pygmaeus.
No. 904, each 375fr: a, Tragelaphus strepsiceros. b, Capra hircus. c, Egretta alba. d, Tockus flavirostris.
No. 905, each 375fr: a, Ursus maritimus. b, Megaptera novaeangliae. c, Phoca vitulina. d, Aptenodytes forsteri.
No. 906, each 375fr: a, Pelecanus occidentalis. b, Orcinus orca. c, Delphinus delphis. d, Iguana iguana.
No. 907: a, Panthera tigris altaica. b, Camelus bactrianus. c, Canus lupus. d, Cuon alpinus. e, Rangifer tarandus dawsoni. f, Gulo gulo.
Each 1500fr: No. 908, Loxodonta africana, vert. No. 909, Ursus thibetanus.

Perf. 14, 14½x14 (#904-906)

1999, Jan. 25 Litho.

899-902 A157 Set of 4 4.50 4.50
903 A157 150fr Sheet of 9, #a.-i. 8.00 8.00

Sheets of 4

904-906 A157a Set of 3 24.00 24.00

Sheet of and 6

907 A157 375fr #a.-f. 12.00 12.00

Souvenir Sheets

908-909 A157 Set of 2 16.00 16.00

Mushrooms
A158 A159

No. 910, 75fr, Russula xerampelina. No. 911, 75fr, Catathelasma imperiale. No. 912, 150fr, Cortinarius violaceus. No. 913, 150fr, Cortinarius camphoratus. No. 914, 200fr, Rozites caperata. No. 915, 200fr, Coprinus picaceus. No. 916, 375fr, Coprinus cromatus. No. 917, 375fr, Russula cavipes.
No. 918, each 150fr: a, Boletus edulis. b, Suillus grevillei. c, Boletinus cavipes. d,

Morchella esculenta. e, Morchella conica. f, Clitocybe dealbata. g, Hygrocybe nigrescens. h, Clitocybe geotropa. i, Lepiota cristata.

No. 919, each 150fr: a, Amanita citrina. b, Amanita phalloides. c, Cortinarius praestans. d, Phallus impudicus. e, Cortinarius bicolor. f, Cortinarius renidens. g, Lactarius torminosus. h, Boletus satanas. i, Cystolepiota bucknalii.

No. 920, each 375fr: a, Amanita muscaria. b, Coprinus comatus. c, Clitocybe odora. d, Cantharellus cibarius. e, Mycena epipterygia. f, Marasmius oreades.

No. 921, each 375fr: a, Boletus edulis. b, Laccaria laccata. c, Agaricus campestris. d, Hypholoma fasciculare. e, Lepiota procera. f, Russula aurata.

Each 1500fr: No. 922, Ramaria aurea, horiz. No. 923, Panellus serotinus. No. 924, Macrolepiota procera. No. 925, Amanita muscaria. No. 926, Hebeloma crustuliniforme. No. 927, Lepiota molybdites.

1999 Litho. *Perf. 14*

910-917	A158	Set of 8	8.50	8.50

Sheets of 9

918-919	A158	Set of 2	14.00	14.00

Sheets of 6

920-921	A159	Set of 2	24.00	24.00

Souvenir Sheets

922-925	A158	Set of 4	32.50	32.50
926-927	A159	Set of 2	16.00	16.00

Raptors — A160

No. 927A — Birds: b, Souimanga royal. c, Martin-pecheur huppe. d, Pie-grieche. e, Barbican a tete roughe. f, Beau-marquet. g, Rollier a poitrine lilas. h, Pintade vulturine. i, Grenadier. j, Outarde korhaon.

No. 928: a, Sparrow hawk. b, Red-tailed buzzard. c, Dark kite. d, African fish eagle. e, Bald eagle. f, Fawn-colored vulture. g, Peregrine falcon. h, Osprey. i, Harpie eagle.

Dinosaurs — No. 929: a, Dilophosaurus. b, Megalosaurus. c, Ceratosaurus. d, Coelophysis. e, Tyrannosaurus. f, Deinonychus. g, Allosaurus. h, Stegosaurus. i, Albertosaurus.

Gems — No. 930: a, Ruby. b, Liroconite. c, Emerald. d, Euclase. e, Diamond. f, Chrysoberyl. g, Plancheite. h, Kasolite. i, Indigolite.

Meteorites — No. 931: a, Martian. b, Antarctic. c, C2 Chondrite. d, Archondrite. e, Octaedrite moyenne. f, Iron. g, Tektite. h, Chondrite olivine. i, Iron, diff.

Mushrooms — No. 932: a, Paxillus atrotomentosus. b, Craterellus cornucopioides. c, Boletus satanas. d, Clavaria truncata. e, Phallus impudicus. f, Scleroderma aurantiacum. g, Amanita citrina. h, Catathe lasma. i, Inocybe fastigiata.

1125fr, Wulfenite.

1998 *Perf. 13¼x13½*

Sheets of 9

927A	A160	175fr Sheet of 9, #b-j	8.00	8.00
928	A160	200fr #a.-i.	9.75	9.75
929	A160	250fr #a.-i.	11.50	11.50
930	A160	375fr #a.-i.	17.50	17.50
931	A160	400fr #a.-i.	19.00	19.00
932	A160	400fr #a.-i.	19.00	19.00

Souvenir Sheet

933	A160	1125fr multicolored	5.75	5.75

No. 933 contains one 36x51mm stamp.

Captions on Nos. 928e and 928h are transposed.

See Nos. 896-898.

"Illegal" Stamps

Comoro Islands postal officials have declared as "illegal" the following items:

Muhammad Ali, sheet of nine 300fr stamps (previously No. 934);

Muhammad Ali, 1125fr souvenir sheet (previously No. 935);

Babe Ruth, sheet of nine 375fr stamps;

Babe Ruth, two 1125fr souvenir sheets;

Ocean Life, sheet of nine stamps with values of 100, 150, 250, 300, 350, 400, 450, and 500fr;

Horses, sheet of nine stamps with values of 100, 150, 250, 300, 350, 400, 450, and 500fr;

Pandas, sheet of nine stamps with values of 100, 150, 250, 300, 350, 400, 450, and 500fr;

Flora and Fauna: 25fr Harpe costata, 25fr Hibiscus, 50fr Volute lapponica, 50fr Tournesol de Comoros, 100fr Ghetonia mydas, 125fr Octopus vulgaris, 150fr Ylang ylang, 300fr Coelacanth, 300fr Tellina variegata.

Famous People: 250fr, Willy Messerschmitt, Messerschmitt BF-109G-6/R6. 300fr, Louis Pasteur, rabies vaccine administered to Joseph Meister. 350fr, Dr. Albert Schweitzer. 400fr, Ferdinand von Zeppelin, flying Zeppelin. 475fr, Henri Dunant, Nobel Prize. 500fr, Albert Einstein, Gravity Probe B. 550fr, Ayrton Senna, race car. 600fr, Pope John Paul II. 750fr, Iranian Pres. Mohammad Khatami, Pope John Paul II. 800fr, Crew of Apollo 11. 1125fr souvenir sheet, Lindbergh, Spirit of St. Louis.

Submarines — A161

No. 934: a, USS Salt Lake City, US. b, Le Terrible, France. c, Amethyste, France.

1999 Litho. *Perf. 13¼*

934	A161	150fr Sheet of 3, #a-c	3.00	3.00

Automobiles — A161a

No. 935: a, Cadillac Eldorado, Cadillac Series 62, US. b, Aston Martin DB2 IV Mark III, Austin Healey. c, Alfa Romeo Superlegera, Alfa Romeo Giuletta.

1125fr, Aston Martin DB5.

1999

935	A161a	200fr Sheet of 3, #a-c	3.50	3.50

Souvenir Sheet

935D	A161a	1125fr multi	7.00	7.00

No. 935D contains one 51x30mm stamp.

Motorcycles — A162

No. 935E: f, Honda NR. g, Christian Leliard and motorcycle. h, Joe S. Wright and motorcycle.

1999

935E	A162	250fr Sheet of 3, #f-h	4.50	4.50

Helicopters — A162a

No. 936: a, Westland Wessex. b, MIL MI-8. c, Sikorsky 5-76 Spirit.

1999

936	A162a	300fr Sheet of 3, #a-c	5.50	5.50

Dogs and Sleds A163

No. 937: a, Alaskan malamute, US. b, Greenlandic. c, Siberian husky.

1999

937	A163	400fr Sheet of 3, #a-c	7.00	7.00

Airplanes A164

No. 938: a, Tupolev Tu-160. b, Lockheed F-117A. c, Rafale C.01.

No. 939: a, Ilyshin Il-76. b, Boeing E-3. c, Concorde.

1125fr, Concorde, diff.

1999 Litho. *Perf. 13¼*

Sheets of 3

938	A164	375fr #a.-c.	6.50	6.50
939	A164	450fr #a.-c.	8.00	8.00

Souvenir Sheet

940	A164	1125fr mulicolored	7.00	7.00

No. 940 contains one 50x30mm stamp.

Trains A165

No. 941: a, Series E. b, Series 9100. c, Kitson-Still I-C-I.

No. 942: a, HST 125. b, TGV. c, RTG.

1125fr, Sereis DD40AX.

1999 Litho. *Perf. 13¼*

Sheets of 3

941	A165	400fr #a.-c.	7.25	7.25
942	A165	500fr #a.-c.	9.00	9.00

Souvenir Sheet

943	A165	1125fr mulicolored	7.00	7.00

No. 943 contains one 50x30mm stamp.

Space Achievements — A166

#944: a, Shuttles Discovery, Buran. b, Ariane V. c, John Glenn, Saturn V.

#945: a, Valentina Tereshkova, Soyuz 4. b, Dogs Laika, Bielka. c, Yuri Gagarin, Vostok 1.

1999 Litho. *Perf. 13¼*

Sheets of 3

944	A166	500fr #a.-c.	9.00	9.00
945	A166	600fr #a.-c.	11.00	11.00

Space Achievements Type of 1999

Souvenir Sheet

1125fr, Space Shuttle Discovery, John Glenn.

946	A166	1125fr multi	7.00	7.00

No. 946 contains one 51x30mm stamp.

Teams in 1998 World Cup Soccer Tournament — A167

Players in 1998 World Cup Soccer Tournament — A168

No. 947, 150fr: a, Italy. b, Chile, c, Cameroun. d, Austria. e, Netherlands. f, Belgium. g, South Korea. h, Mexico.

No. 948, 250fr: a, Brazil. b, Scotland. c, Morocco. d, Norway. e, Spain. f, Nigeria. g, Paraguay. h, Bulgaria.

No. 949, 300fr: a, France. b, South Africa. c, Saudi Arabia. d, Denmark. e, Germany. f, United States. g, Yugoslavia. h, Iran.

No. 950, 500fr: a, England. b, Colombia. c, Romania. d, Tunisia. e, Argentina. f, Croatia. g, Jamaica. h, Japan.

No. 951, 350fr: a, Desailly, French flag. b, Ronaldo, Brazilian flag. c, Suker, Croatian flag. d, Kluivert, Netherlands flag. e, French players, World Cup trophy. f, Brazilian player (yellow and green shirt). g, Croatian player (checked shirt). h, Netherlands player (orange shirt).

Illustrations reduced.

1998 Litho. *Perf. 13x13½*

Sheets of 8, #a-h

947-950	A167	Set of 4	50.00	50.00
951	A168	multi	14.50	14.50

Trucks — A169

No. 952: a, Truck with ornamentation over cab. b, Blue truck. c, Green truck. d, Yellow truck.

1999 Litho. *Perf. 13¼*

952	A169	350fr Sheet of 4, #a-d	—	—

Automobile Racing, Chess, Tennis and Table Tennis, Fishing and Diving — A170

No. 953, 250fr — Automobile racing: a, Giuseppe Farina and Alfa 1500. b, Juan Fangio and Mercedes 2.5L. c, Jack Brabham and Cooper Climax 2.5L. d, Jim Clark and Lotus Climax 1.5L.

No. 954, 300fr — Chess players: a, Garry Kasparov. b, Akiba Rubinstein. c, Max Euwe. d, Mikhail Botvinnik.

No. 955, 375fr — Fishing and diving: a, Shark fishing. b, Sport fishing. c, Diver, back half of shark. d, Diver, front half of shark.

No. 956, 500fr — Chess players: a, Bent Larsen. b, José Raúl Capablanca. c, Boris Spassky. d, Bobby Fischer.

No. 957, 600fr — Tennis and table tennis: a, Female tennis player. b, Male table tennis player. c, Female table tennis player. d, Male tennis player.

No. 958, 1125fr — Chess players: a, Samuel Reshevsky. b, Vassili Smyslov.

No. 959, 1125fr — Fishing and diving: a, Sport fishing, diff. b, Divers and marine life.

No. 960, 1125fr — Tennis and table tennis: a, Male table tennis player, diff. b, Women tennis players.

1999 *Perf. 13¼*

Sheets of 4, #a-d

953-957 A170 Set of 5 47.50 47.50

Souvenir Sheets of 2, #a-b

958-960 A170 Set of 3 21.00 21.00

Nos. 816E, 816G Surcharged

Methods and Perfs. As Before

2001, June 16

963 A144a 100fr on 500fr multi — —
964 A144a 125fr on 200fr multi — —

Traditional Costumes A171

Designs: 125fr, Woman. No. 966, 150fr, No. 969, 300fr, Woman, diff. No. 967, 150fr, No. 968, 300fr, Man.

2002, Apr. 8 **Litho.** *Perf. 13¼x13*
965-969 A171 Set of 5 *8.50 8.50*

Flowers — A172

Designs: 50fr, Cananga odorata. 600fr, Vanilla planifolia.

2003, Oct. 9
970-971 A172 Set of 2 *5.25 5.25*

Marine Mammals A173

Designs: 75fr, Peponocephala electra. 1000fr, Megaptera novaeangliae.

2003, Oct. 9 *Perf. 13x13¼*
972-973 A173 Set of 2 *9.00 9.00*

Wood Handicrafts A174

Designs: 100fr, Carved door. 300fr, Candleholder.

2003, Oct. 9 *Perf. 13¼x13*
974-975 A174 Set of 2 *3.25 3.25*

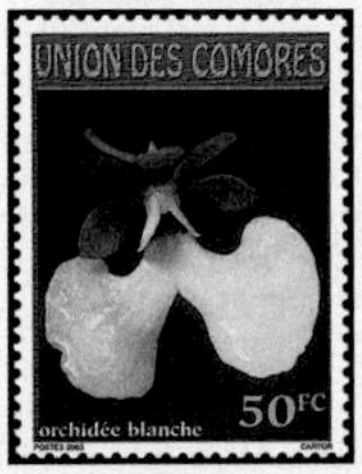

Orchids — A175

Orchid color: 50fr, White. 75fr, Yellow. 100fr, Mauve. 600fr, Red.

2003, Oct. 9
976-979 A175 Set of 4 *6.50 6.50*

Diplomatic Relations Between Comoro Islands and People's Republic of China, 30th Anniv. — A176

No. 980: a, 125fr, Chinese President Hu Jintao and Comoro Islands President Azali Assoumani, country flags. b, 125fr, Coelacanth, Worldwide Fund for Nature emblem, country arms. c, 300fr, Comoros Islands Broadcasting Center, country arms. d, 600fr, Comoros Islands People's Palace, country flags.

Illustration reduced.

2006, Jan. 1 **Litho.** *Perf. 12*
980 A176 Block of 4, #a-d 5.75 5.75

Comoro Islands postal officials have declared as "illegal" the following items:

Impressionist Paintings, sheet of five 500fr stamps.

Paintings in the Louvre, six different sheets of two 500fr stamps.

American Actors and Actresses, four different sheets of four 350fr stamps.

European Astronauts, three souvenir sheets of one 500fr stamp.

Disneyland, 50th anniv., souvenir sheet of one 500fr stamp.

Léopold Sédar Senghor (1906-2001), First President of Senegal — A177

Colors: No. 981, 125fr, Green and multicolored. No. 982, 125fr, Yellow and multicolored, vert. No. 983, 300fr, Green and black. No. 984, 300fr, Red violet and black, vert. 350fr, Purple and multicolored, vert. 500fr, Brown and black, vert.

Perf. 13x13¼, 13¼x13

2007, June 1 **Litho.**
981-986 A177 Set of 6 9.50 9.50

Medicinal Plants — A178

Designs: 75fr, Cymbopogon citratus. 125fr, Ocimum suave. 150fr, Aloe molucaca. 250fr, Like 75fr. 300fr, Like 150fr. 500fr, Like 125fr.

2007, June 1 *Perf. 13¼x13*
987-992 A178 Set of 6 7.75 7.75

SEMI-POSTAL STAMPS

Anti-Malaria Issue

Common Design Type

Perf. 12½x12

1962, Apr. 7 **Engr.** **Unwmk.**
B1 CD108 25fr + 5fr brt pink 4.00 4.00

WHO drive to eradicate malaria.

Nurse Feeding Infant — SP1

Mother and Child — SP2

1967, July 3 **Engr.** *Perf. 13*
B2 SP1 25fr + 5fr multi 3.25 3.25

For the Red Cross.

1974, Aug. 10 **Engr.** *Perf. 13*
B3 SP2 35fr + 10fr red & dk brn 2.75 2.75

For the Red Cross.
For surcharge see No. 144.

Miniature Sheet

Space Achievements SP3

World Philatelic Programs emblems (stamp collecting or Halley's Comet) and astronomer or satellite: a, Galileo. b, Copernicus. c, Kepler. d, Halley. e, *Planet A*, Japan, and 3 stars. f, *ICE*, US. g, *Planet A*, 5 stars. h, *Vega*, USSR.

1988 **Litho.** *Perf. 13½*
B4 Sheet of 8 15.00 15.00
a.-h. SP3 200fr +10fr multi 1.50 1.50

See No. C193.
For surcharges see Nos. 816P-816S.

AIR POST STAMPS

Comoro Village — AP1

Comoro Men and Moroni Mosque — AP2

Design: 200fr, Mosque of Ouani, Anjouan.

1950-54 **Unwmk.** **Engr.** *Perf. 13*
C1 AP1 50fr grn & red brn 4.50 1.40
C2 AP2 100fr dk brn & red 6.75 1.75
C3 AP1 200fr dk grn, rose brn & pur ('54) 25.00 9.50
Nos. C1-C3 (3) 36.25 12.65

Liberation Issue

Common Design Type

1954, June 6
C4 CD102 15fr sepia & red 47.50 24.00

Madrepora Fructicosa AP3

100fr, Coral, shells and sea anemones.

1962, Jan. 13 **Photo.** *Perf. 12½x13*
C5 AP3 100fr multi 16.00 16.00
C6 AP3 500fr multi 32.50 24.00

Telstar Issue

Common Design Type

1962, Dec. 5 **Engr.** *Perf. 13*
C7 CD111 25fr dp vio, dl pur & red lil 6.50 4.75

Type of Regular Issue

Unwmk.

1963, Dec. 27 **Engr.** *Perf. 13*

Size: 26½x48mm

C8 A13 65fr Baskets 5.00 3.50
C9 A13 200fr Pendant 10.00 5.25

Boat Type of Regular Issue

1964, Aug. 7 **Photo.** *Perf. 13*

Size: 27x48mm

C10 A14 50fr Mayotte pirogue 4.50 1.75
C11 A14 85fr Schooner 7.00 2.50

Olympic Torch and Boxers — AP4

Order of Star of Grand Comoro — AP5

1964, Oct. 10 Engr. *Perf. 13*
C12 AP4 100fr red brn, dk brn & gray grn 7.50 7.50

18th Olympic Games, Tokyo, Oct. 10-25.

1964, Dec. 10 Photo. *Perf. 13*
C13 AP5 500fr multi 20.00 20.00

ITU Issue
Common Design Type

1965, May 17 Engr. *Perf. 13*
C14 CD120 50fr gray, grnsh bl & ol 24.00 17.50

French Satellite A-1 Issue
Common Design Type

Designs: 25fr, Diamant rocket and launching installations. 30fr, A-1 satellite.

1966, Jan. 17 Engr. *Perf. 13*
C15 CD121 25fr dk pur & ultra 4.50 4.50
C16 CD121 30fr dk pur & ultra 6.00 6.00
a. Strip of 2, #C15-C16 + label 11.00 11.00

French Satellite D-1 Issue
Common Design Type

1966, May 16 Engr. *Perf. 13*
C17 CD122 30fr dk grn, org & brn 4.00 4.00

Old Gun Battery, Dzaoudzi — AP6

200fr, Ksar Castle, Mutsamudu, vert.

1966, Dec. 19 Photo. *Perf. 13*
C18 AP6 50fr multi 5.00 2.50
C19 AP6 200fr multi 9.00 5.75

Bird Type of Regular Issue

Birds: 75fr, Madagascar paradise flycatchers. 100fr, Blue-cheeked bee eaters.

1967, June 20 Photo. *Perf. 13*
Size: 27x48mm
C20 A17 75fr yel grn & multi 10.50 6.50
C21 A17 100fr lt bl & multi 13.00 8.00

Woman Skier — AP7

1968, Apr. 29 Engr. *Perf. 13*
C22 AP7 70fr brt grn, lt bl & choc 6.50 4.75

10th Winter Olympic Games, Grenoble, France, Feb. 6-18, 1968.

Fish Type of Regular Issue

50fr, Moorish idol. 90fr, Diagramma lineatus.

1968, Aug. 1 Engr. *Perf. 13*
Size: 47½x27mm
C23 A19 50fr plum blk & yel 8.00 4.00
C24 A19 90fr brt grn, yel & gray grn 10.00 5.25

For surcharge & overprint see #C52, C74.

Swimmer, Butterfly Stroke — AP8

1969, Jan. 27 Photo. *Perf. 12½*
C25 AP8 65fr ver, grnsh bl & blk 5.25 3.50

19th Olympic Games, Mexico City, 10/12-27.

Flower Type of Regular Issue

50fr, Heliconia sp. 85fr, Tuberose. 200fr, Orchid (angraecum eburneum).

1969, Mar. 20 Photo. *Perf. 13*
Size: 27x48mm
C26 A21 50fr multi, vert. 4.75 3.50
C27 A21 85fr multi, vert. 5.50 4.50
C28 A21 200fr multi, vert. 11.00 6.00
Nos. C26-C28 (3) 21.25 14.00

Concorde Issue
Common Design Type

1969, Apr. 17 Engr.
C29 CD129 100fr pur & brn org 24.00 16.00

View of EXPO, Globe and Moon — AP9

90fr, Geisha, map of Japan & EXPO emblem.

1970, Sept. 13 Photo. *Perf. 13*
C30 AP9 60fr slate & multi 4.50 2.40
C31 AP9 90fr multi 5.50 3.25

EXPO '70 International Exposition, Osaka, Japan, Mar. 15-Sept. 13.

Sunset over Mutsamudu — AP10

Map of Archipelago — AP11

Designs: 20fr, Sada Village, Mayotte. 65fr, Old Iconi Palace, Grand Comoro. 85fr, Nioumatchoua Island, Moheli.

1971, May 3 Photo. *Perf. 13*
C32 AP10 15fr dk bl & multi 1.20 .65
C33 AP10 20fr multi 1.75 .80
C34 AP10 65fr grn & multi 3.75 1.60
C35 AP10 85fr bl & multi 5.50 2.50

Engr.
C36 AP11 100fr brn red, grn & vio bl 7.50 5.50
Nos. C32-C36 (5) 19.70 11.05

See #107-110, C45-C49, C53, C62-C64. For overprints & surcharges see #143, C69, C71, C73, C76-C77, C79-C80, C82, C84.

Flower Type of Regular Issue

Flowers: 60fr, Hibiscus schizopetalus. 85fr, Acalypha sanderii.

1971, July 19 Photo. *Perf. 13*
Size: 27x48mm
C37 A25 60fr grn, ver & yel 5.00 2.40
C38 A25 85fr grn, red & yel 6.50 4.75

For surcharge see No. C75.

Mural, Moroni Airport — AP12

Designs: 85fr, Mural in Arrival Hall, Moroni Airport. 100fr, View of Moroni Airport.

1972, Mar. 30 Photo. *Perf. 13*
C39 AP12 65fr gray & multi 2.00 .85
C40 AP12 85fr gray & multi 2.25 1.20

Engr.
C41 AP12 100fr brn, bl & slate grn 3.75 2.10
Nos. C39-C41 (3) 8.00 4.15

New airport in Moroni.

Eiffel Tower and Moroni Telephone Exchange — AP13

75fr, Frenchman and Comoro Islander talking on telephone, radio tower and beacons.

1972, Apr. 24
C42 AP13 35fr dl red & gray 1.25 .85
C43 AP13 75fr dk car, vio & bl 2.25 .95

First radio-telephone connection between France and Comoro Islands.

Underwater Spear-fishing — AP14

1972, July 5 Engr. *Perf. 13*
C44 AP14 70fr vio bl, brt grn & mar 8.75 5.50

For surcharge see No. C78.

Types of 1971

1972, Nov. 15 Photo.

Designs: 20fr, Cape Sima. 35fr, Bambao Palace. 40fr, Domoni Palace. 60fr, Gomajou Peninsula. 100fr, Map of Anjouan Island.

C45 AP10 20fr brn & multi .85 .65
C46 AP10 35fr dk grn & multi 1.20 .80
C47 AP10 40fr bl & multi 1.75 .95
C48 AP10 60fr grnsh blk & multi 2.50 1.60

Engr.
C49 AP11 100fr mar, bl & sl grn 13.50 7.25
Nos. C45-C49 (5) 19.80 11.25

Pres. Said Mohamed Cheikh (1904-70) AP15

1973, Mar. 16 Photo. *Perf. 13*
C50 AP15 20fr multi 1.25 .80
C51 AP15 35fr multi 1.60 1.00

For overprints see Nos. C70, C72.

No. C24 Surcharged

1973, Apr. 30 Engr. *Perf. 13*
C52 A19 120fr on 90fr multi 12.50 7.25

Intl. Commission for Coelacanth Studies.

Map of Grand Comoro AP16

1973, June 28 Engr. *Perf. 13*
C53 AP16 135fr vio, bl & dk brn 9.50 6.50

See Nos. C65, C68. For surcharges see Nos. C90-C92.

Karthala Volcano AP17

1973, July 16 Photo. *Perf. 13x12½*
C54 AP17 120fr multi 7.50 5.50

Eruption of Karthala, Sept. 1972. For surcharge see No. C89.

Armauer G. Hansen — AP18

Design: 150fr, Nicolaus Copernicus (1473-1543), Polish astronomer.

1973, Sept. 5 **Engr.** ***Perf. 13***
C55 AP18 100fr brn, dk bl & sl grn 7.50 3.50
C56 AP18 150fr grnsh bl, vio bl & choc 7.00 5.25

Cent. of the discovery of the Hansen bacillus, the cause of leprosy.
For overprint & surcharge see #C81, C93.

Pablo Picasso (1881-1973) — AP19

1973, Sept. 30 **Photo.**
C57 AP19 200fr blk & multi 10.50 8.00

Souvenir Sheet

C58 AP19 100fr blk & multi 16.00 14.50

For overprint see No. C87.

Order of the Star of Anjouan — AP20

Said Omar ben Soumeth — AP21

1974, Jan. 7 **Photo.** ***Perf. 13***
C59 AP20 500fr brn, bl & gold 13.00 9.50

For overprint see No. C95.

1974, Jan. 31 ***Perf. 13x13½, 13½x13***

135fr, Grand Mufti Said Omar, horiz.

C60 AP21 135fr blk & multi 4.50 2.75
C61 AP21 200fr blk & multi 5.50 3.50

For overprint & surcharge see #C85, C88.

Types of 1971-73

Designs (Views on Mayotte): 20fr, Moya Beach. 35fr, Chiconi. 90fr, Port Mamutzu. 120fr, Map of Mayotte.

1974, Aug. 31 **Photo.** ***Perf. 13***
C62 AP10 20fr bl & multi 1.20 .95
C63 AP10 35fr grn & multi 3.50 2.00
C64 AP10 90fr multi 6.25 3.50

Engr.

C65 AP16 120fr ultra & grn 8.50 5.50
Nos. C62-C65 (4) 19.45 11.95

Jet Take-off — AP22

1975, Jan. 10 **Engr.** ***Perf. 13***
C66 AP22 135fr multi 7.25 4.75

First direct route Moroni-Hahaya-Paris.
For surcharge see No. C86.

Rotary Emblem, Meeting House, Map — AP23

1975, Feb. 23 **Photo.** ***Perf. 13***
C67 AP23 250fr multi 10.50 7.25

Rotary Intl., 70th anniv., Moroni Rotary Club, 10th anniv.
For surcharge see No. C94.

Map Type of 1973

Design: 230fr, Map of Moheli, horiz.

1975, May 26 **Engr.** ***Perf. 13***
C68 AP16 230fr ocher, ol grn & bl 11.00 8.00

STATE OF COMORO

Issues of 1968-75 Surcharged and Overprinted with Bars and: "ETAT COMORIEN" in Black, Silver, Red or Orange

1975 **Printing & Perfs. as Before**

C69	AP10	10fr on 20fr #C62	*.30*	*.20*
C70	AP15	20fr (S)	*.30*	*.20*
C71	AP10	30fr on 35fr (R) #C63	*.35*	*.20*
C72	AP15	35fr (S)	*.40*	*.25*
C73	AP10	40fr (O)	*.50*	*.25*
C74	A19	50fr	*.55*	*.30*
C75	A25	75fr on 60fr	*.80*	*.45*
C76	AP10	75fr on 60fr	*.80*	*.45*
C77	AP10	75fr on 65fr (O)	*.80*	*.45*
C78	AP14	75fr on 70fr	*.80*	*.45*
C79	AP11	100fr #C36	*1.00*	*.60*
C80	AP11	100fr #C49	*1.00*	*.60*
C81	AP18	100fr	*1.00*	*.60*
C82	AP10	100fr on 85fr (O)	*1.00*	*.60*
C83	A25	100fr on 85fr	*1.00*	*.60*
C84	AP10	100fr on 90fr	*1.00*	*.60*
C85	AP21	100fr on 135fr (S)	*1.00*	*.60*
C86	AP22	100fr on 135fr	*1.00*	*.60*
C87	AP19	200fr (S)	*2.10*	*1.25*
C88	AP21	200fr (S)	*2.10*	*1.25*
C89	AP17	200fr on 120fr	*2.10*	*1.25*
C90	AP16	200fr on 120fr	*2.10*	*1.25*
C91	AP16	200fr on 135fr	*2.10*	*1.25*
C92	AP16	200fr on 230fr	*2.10*	*1.25*
C93	AP18	400fr on 150fr	*4.75*	*2.50*
C94	AP23	400fr on 250fr	*4.75*	*2.50*
C95	AP20	500fr	*5.25*	*3.25*
		Nos. C69-C95 (27)	*40.95*	*23.75*

See postage section for airmail stamps that are part of joint postage/airmail sets.

Rotary Emblem, Landscape AP26

1979, July 31 **Litho.** ***Perf. 13x12½***
C107 AP26 400fr multi 7.00 3.00

Rotary International.

IYC Emblem, Mother and Child — AP27

1979, July 31 ***Perf. 13x13½***
C108 AP27 250fr multi 3.50 3.50

Intl. Year of the Child. See No. CB1. For surcharges see Nos. C121, C202.

Dimadjou Dispensary, Map of Southern Africa, Emblem AP28

1980, Feb. 23 **Litho.** ***Perf. 12½***
C109 AP28 100fr shown 1.25 .40
C110 AP28 260fr Globe, Concorde, emblem 3.00 1.00

Rotary International, 75th anniv. and Moroni Rotary Club, 15th anniv. (100fr).
For surcharges see Nos. 815L, C119-C120.

First Transatlantic Flight, 50th Anniversary — AP29

1980, May 30 **Litho.** ***Perf. 13***
C111 AP29 200fr multi 2.50 1.25

No. C111 Surcharged in Blue

1981, Feb. **Litho.** ***Perf. 13***
C112 AP29 30fr on 200fr multi 1.00 .35

The Dove and the Rainbow, by Picasso — AP30

Picasso Birth Centenary: 70fr, Still Life on a Sideboard. 150fr, Studio with Plaster Head. 250fr, Bowl and Pot, vert. 500fr, The Red Tablecloth.

1981, June 30 **Litho.** ***Perf. 12½***
C113 AP30 40fr multi .55 .20
C114 AP30 70fr multi .95 .20
C115 AP30 150fr multi 1.90 .50
C116 AP30 250fr multi 3.25 .70
C117 AP30 500fr multi 6.25 1.50
Nos. C113-C117 (5) 12.90 3.10

For surcharges see Nos. 815G, C118.

#C114, C109-C110, CB1 Surchd.

1981, Nov. **Litho.** ***Perf. 12½, 13***
C118 AP30 10fr on 70fr multi .40 .40
C119 AP28 10fr on 100fr multi .80 .80
C120 AP28 50fr on 260fr multi 2.00 .20
C121 AP27 50fr on 200fr+30fr multi 2.00 .20
Nos. C118-C121 (4) 5.20 1.60

Manned Flight Bicentenary — AP31

Balloons. 100fr, 200fr, 300fr, 500fr vert.

1983, Apr. 20 **Litho.** ***Perf. 13***
C122 AP31 100fr Montgolfiere, 1783 1.00 .30
C123 AP31 200fr Lunardi, 1784 1.90 .50
C124 AP31 300fr Blanchard and Jeffries, 1785 3.25 .90
C125 AP31 400fr Giffard, 1852 4.50 1.25
Nos. C122-C125 (4) 10.65 2.95

Souvenir Sheet

C126 AP31 500fr Paris Siege. 1870 5.50 1.50

For overprints and surcharges see Nos. 602, 812T, 815P.

Pre-Olympic Year Sailing — AP32

1983, June 30 **Litho.** ***Perf. 13***
C127 AP32 150fr Type 470 1.50 .40
C128 AP32 200fr Flying Dutchman 2.25 .50
C129 AP32 300fr Type 470, diff. 3.25 .90
C130 AP32 400fr Finn 4.75 1.00
Nos. C127-C130 (4) 11.75 2.80

Souvenir Sheet

C131 AP32 500fr Soling 5.50 1.50

For overprint and surcharge see Nos. 603, C206.

1984 Summer Olympics — AP33

1984, July 10 **Litho.** ***Perf. 13***
C132 AP33 60fr Basketball .50 .20
C133 AP33 100fr Basketball, diff. .90 .40
C134 AP33 165fr Basketball, diff. 1.50 .65
C135 AP33 175fr Baseball, horiz. 1.60 .65
C136 AP33 200fr Baseball, horiz. 1.90 .80
Nos. C132-C136 (5) 6.40 2.70

Souvenir Sheet

C137 AP33 500fr Basketball, diff. 8.00 1.50

Nos. C132-C134 vert.

Development Conference AP34

1984, July 2 Litho. *Perf. 13*
C138 AP34 475fr Tools for development 5.50 2.00

For surcharge see No. 796I.

Audubon Bicentenary — AP35

1985, Jan. 15 Litho. *Perf. 13*
C139 AP35 100fr Hirundo rustica, vert. 1.25 .40
C140 AP35 125fr Icterus galbula, vert. 1.50 .50
C141 AP35 150fr Buteo lineatus 2.00 .60
C142 AP35 500fr Sphyropicus varius 5.25 2.00
Nos. C139-C142 (4) 10.00 3.50

Moroni Port Missile Defense — AP36

No. C146, Ngome Ntsoudjini Scout troop.

1985, May 20 Litho. *Perf. 13x12½*
C145 AP36 200fr multi 3.25 1.25
C146 AP36 200fr multi 3.25 1.25
a. Pair, #C145-C146 + label 6.75 6.75

PHILEXAFRICA '85, Lome.
For surcharges see Nos. C207-C208.

Natl. Flag, Sun, Outline Map of Islands — AP37

1985, July 6
C147 AP37 10fr multi .30 .20
C148 AP37 15fr multi .30 .20
C149 AP37 125fr multi 2.25 .60
C150 AP37 300fr multi 5.50 1.50
Nos. C147-C150 (4) 8.35 2.50

Natl. independence, 10th anniv.
For surcharge see No. 815Q.

Runners — AP38

1985, Nov. 12
C151 AP38 250fr shown 2.75 1.75
C152 AP38 250fr Mining 2.75 1.75
a. Pair, #C151-C152 + label 6.00 6.00

PHILEXAFRICA '85, Lome, Togo, 11/16-24.
For surcharges see Nos. 815H-815I, C204-C205.

Air Transport Union, UTA, 50th Anniv. — AP39

1985, Dec. 30 Litho. *Perf. 13*
C153 AP39 25fr F-AOUL seaplane .20 .20
C154 AP39 75fr Camel driver, DC-8 .75 .30
C155 AP39 100fr Noratlas and Heron DC-4s 1.10 .40
a. Souv. sheet of 3, #C153-C155, perf. 12½ 3.50 2.25
C156 AP39 125fr UTA cargo plane 1.40 .60

Size: 40x52mm
Perf. 12½x13

C157 AP39 1000fr Aircraft, 1935-1985 12.00 6.00
a. Souv. sheet of 2, #C156-C157, perf. 12½ 13.00 8.00
Nos. C153-C157 (5) 15.45 7.50

Halley's Comet — AP40

Comets, astronomers and probes.

1986, Mar. 7 *Perf. 13*
C158 AP40 125fr Edmond Halley, Giotto probe 1.25 .45
C159 AP40 150fr Giacobini-Zinner, 1959 1.50 .50
C160 AP40 225fr Encke, 1961 2.50 .90
C161 AP40 300fr Bradfield, 1980 3.00 1.25
C162 AP40 450fr Planet A probe 5.00 1.75
Nos. C158-C162 (5) 13.25 4.85

For surcharges see Nos. 796S, 804H, 804R, 812P.

1986 World Cup Soccer Championships, Mexico — AP41

Various soccer plays.

1986, June 11 Litho. *Perf. 13*
C163 AP41 125fr multi 1.25 .45
C164 AP41 210fr multi 2.25 .80
C165 AP41 500fr multi 5.50 2.00
C166 AP41 600fr multi 6.00 2.25
Nos. C163-C166 (4) 15.00 5.50

For surcharges see Nos. 796C, 800Q, 815C.

Tennis at the 1988 Summer Olympics — AP42

Various players.

1987, Jan. 28 Litho. *Perf. 13½*
C167 AP42 150fr multi 1.75 .45
C168 AP42 250fr multi 3.00 .75
C169 AP42 500fr multi 5.50 1.50
C170 AP42 600fr multi 6.75 1.75
Nos. C167-C170 (4) 17.00 4.45

For overprints and surcharges see Nos. 796N, 796U, 815J, 816L, 816N, C183-C186, C203.

World Wildlife Fund — AP43

Various pictures of the mongoose lemur.

1987, Feb. 18 *Perf. 13*
C171 AP43 75fr multi, vert. 2.50 .50
C172 AP43 100fr multi 3.50 .75
C173 AP43 125fr multi 5.50 1.00
C174 AP43 150fr multi 6.50 1.25
Nos. C171-C174 (4) 18.00 3.50

1988 Winter Olympics, Calgary AP44

1987, Apr. 10 Litho. *Perf. 13½*
C175 AP44 150fr Slalom 1.25 .45
C176 AP44 225fr Ski jumping 2.25 .75
C177 AP44 500fr Women's giant slalom 5.50 1.60
C178 AP44 600fr Luge 6.00 2.25
Nos. C175-C178 (4) 15.00 5.05

For surcharges see Nos. 800R, 812U.

AP45

Aviation History AP46

Designs: 200fr, Inventors Didier Daurat and Raymond Vanier with 1935 Air Blue F-ANR1. 300fr, Farman biplane, 1st scheduled airmail delivery, Paris-LeMans-St. Nazaire, Aug. 17, 1918. 500fr, Bleriot aircraft, 1st scheduled airmail delivery, Villacoublay-Vendome-Poitiers-Pauillac, Oct. 15, 1913. 1000fr, Henri Pequet and his aircraft, Feb. 18, 1911.

1987, Dec. 29 Litho. *Perf. 13*
C179 AP45 200fr multi 2.25 .65
C180 AP45 300fr multi 3.25 1.00
C181 AP45 500fr multi 5.50 1.60

Perf. 12½x13

C182 AP46 1000fr multi 11.00 2.25
Nos. C179-C182 (4) 22.00 5.50

Airmail history exposition, Allahabad.
For surcharges see Nos. 800S, 804D.

Nos. C167-C170 Ovptd. in Red for 1988 Olympic Tennis Champions

Overprint includes name of athlete and "Medaille d'or / Seoul" or "Medaille / d'argent / Seoul."

1988, Nov. Litho. *Perf. 13½*
C183 AP42 150fr "Miloslav Mecir / (Tchec.)" 1.25 .75
C184 AP42 250fr "Tim Mayotte / (U.S.A.)" 1.90 1.40
C185 AP42 500fr "Steffi Graf / (R.F.A.)" 5.00 2.75
C186 AP42 600fr "Gabriela Sabatini / (Argentine)" 6.00 3.75
Nos. C183-C186 (4) 14.15 8.65

For surcharges see Nos. 800T, 815K, 816M, 816O.

Early Aviators and Aircraft — AP47

100fr, Alberto Santos-Dumont (1873-1932), & *Bagatelle,* 1st documented power flight in Europe, Oct. 23, 1906. 150fr, Wright Brothers & *Flyer A.* 200fr, Louis Bleriot (1872-1936) & *Bleriot XI,* 1st crossing of the English Channel in a heavier-than-air craft, July 25, 1909. 300fr, Henri Farman (1874-1958) & Voisin biplane, 1st fixed-route 1-kilometer circular flight, Jan. 13, 1908. 500fr, Gabriel (1880-1973) & Charles (1882-1912) Voisin, established 1st biplane factory (1908), & Voisin biplane. 800fr, Roland Garros (1888-1918), 1st trans-Mediterranean flight, Sept. 23, 1913.

1988, Dec. 7 Litho. *Perf. 13*
C187 AP47 100fr pur .90 .45
C188 AP47 150fr brt lil rose 1.60 .60
C189 AP47 200fr blk 2.00 .90
C190 AP47 300fr dark yel org 3.00 .90
C191 AP47 500fr dark blue 5.00 1.50
C192 AP47 800fr lt olive grn 7.50 3.00
Nos. C187-C192 (6) 20.00 7.35

For surcharges see Nos. 800B, 800U, 804E, C209.

Souvenir Sheet

Space Achievements — AP48

Design: World Philatelic Programs stamp collecting emblem, Soviet satellite and Edmond Halley.

1988 Litho. *Perf. 13½*
C193 AP48 750fr multi 8.00 1.50

Nos. C108, C168, C151-C152, C128, C145-C146 and C189 Surcharged

1989 Litho. *Perfs. as Before*
C202 AP27 5fr on 250fr #C108 .20 .20
C203 AP42 25fr on 250fr #C168 .20 .20
C204 AP38 50fr on 250fr #C151 .50 .20
C205 AP38 50fr on 250fr #C152 .50 .20
a. Pair, #C204-C205 + label 1.25 1.25
C206 AP32 150fr on 200fr #C128 1.40 .60
C207 AP36 150fr on 200fr #C145 1.40 .60
C208 AP36 150fr on 200fr #C146 1.40 .60
a. Pair, #C207-C208 + label 6.00 6.00
C209 AP47 150fr on 200fr #C189 1.40 .60
Nos. C202-C209 (8) 7.00 3.20

World Cup Soccer, Championships, Italy — AP50

Various soccer plays and map of Italy.

1990, June Litho. *Perf. 13*

C210 AP50	75fr	multicolored	.60	.30
C211 AP50	150fr	multicolored	1.40	.60
C212 AP50	500fr	multicolored	4.25	1.90
C213 AP50	1000fr	multicolored	8.75	4.00
	Nos. C210-C213 (4)		15.00	6.80

For surcharge see No. 800V.

Souvenir Sheet

Garry Kasparov, Anatoly Karpov, Russian Chess Champions — AP51

Litho. & Embossed

1991, Aug. 5 *Perf. 13½*

C214 AP51 1500fr gold & multi 12.00 —

World Chess Championships.

1992 Summer Olympics, Barcelona AP52

Litho. & Embossed

1992, July 28 *Perf. 13½*

C215 AP52 1500fr gold & multi 26.50 12.00

Sculpted Table — AP52a

1994 (?) Litho. *Perf. 13¼x13½*

Background Color

C215A AP52a	15fr	blue	—	—
C215B AP52a	75fr	green	—	—
C215C AP52a	100fr	pink	—	—
C215D AP52a	225fr	orange	—	—

For surcharges see Nos. 826A-826E.

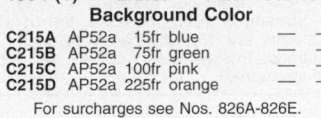

Sea Turtles AP53

1995 Litho. *Perf. 13½x13¼*

Frame Color

C216 AP53	10fr	blue	—	—
C217 AP53	25fr	pink	—	—
C218 AP53	30fr	green	—	—
C219 AP53	50fr	lilac	—	—

No. C215A Surcharged in Blue Violet

Perf. 13¼x13½

2001, June 16 Litho.

C220 AP52a 300fr on 15fr — —

AIR POST SEMI-POSTAL STAMP

Type of Air Post 1979

Design: IYC emblem, mother and son.

1979, July 31 Photo. *Perf. 13½x13*

CB1 AP27 200fr + 30fr multi 3.50 3.50

International Year of the Child.
For surcharge see No. C121.

POSTAGE DUE STAMPS

Anjouan Mosque D1

Coelacanth D2

1950 Unwmk. Engr. *Perf. 14x13*

J1 D1	50c	deep green	1.20	.95
J2 D1	1fr	black brown	1.20	1.00

1954

J3 D2	5fr	dk brown & green	1.10	1.00
J4 D2	10fr	gray & red brown	1.50	1.50
J5 D2	20fr	indigo & blue	2.75	2.50
	Nos. J3-J5 (3)		5.35	5.00

Hibiscus D3

2fr, 15fr, 40fr, 50fr, vertical.

1977, Nov. 19 Litho. *Perf. 13½*

J6 D3	1fr	shown	.35	.20
J7 D3	2fr	Pineapple	.35	.20
J8 D3	5fr	White butterfly	.35	.20
J9 D3	10fr	Chameleon	.35	.20
J10 D3	15fr	Blooming banana	.35	.20
J11 D3	20fr	Orchids	.35	.20
J12 D3	30fr	Allamanda cathartica	.50	.20
J13 D3	40fr	Cashews	.95	.20
J14 D3	50fr	Custard apple	1.10	.20
J15 D3	100fr	Breadfruit	2.10	.75
J16 D3	200fr	Vanilla	4.50	.95
J17 D3	500fr	Ylang ylang	10.75	1.50
	Nos. J6-J17 (12)		22.00	5.00

OFFICIAL STAMPS

Comoro Flag — O1

Perf. 13x12½

1979-85 Litho. Unwmk.

O1 O1	5fr	multi	.20	.20
O2 O1	10fr	multi	.20	.20
O3 O1	20fr	multi	.20	.20
O4 O1	30fr	multi	.50	.20
O5 O1	40fr	multi	.65	.25
O6 O1	60fr	multi ('80)	.60	.25
O7 O1	75fr	multi ('85)	.40	.25
O8 O1	100fr	multi	1.25	.60
	Nos. O1-O8 (8)		4.00	2.15

See Nos. 526-530.

Pres. Said Mohamed Cheikh (1904-1970) — O2

1980-85

O9 O2	100fr	multi	1.00	.40
O10 O2	125fr	multi ('85)	2.00	1.50
O11 O2	400fr	multi	3.00	1.25
	Nos. O9-O11 (3)		6.00	3.15

CONGO DEMOCRATIC REPUBLIC

ˌde-mə-ˈkra-tik ri-ˈpə-blik of ˈkäŋ-ˌgō

LOCATION — Central Africa
GOVT. — Republic
AREA — 895,348 sq. mi. (estimated)
POP. — 22,480,000 (est. 1971)
CAPITAL — Kinshasa (Leopoldville)

Congo was an independent state, founded by Leopold II of Belgium, until 1908 when it was annexed to Belgium as a colony. Congo became an independent republic in 1960. The name was changed to Republic of Zaire, Oct. 28, 1971. In 1998 some issues again used the name Congo Democratic Republic. See Zaire in Vol. 6 for later issues.

100 Centimes = 1 Franc
100 Sengi = 1 Li-Kuta,
100 Ma-Kuta = 1 Zaire (1967)

Catalogue values for all unused stamps in this country are for Never Hinged items.

Belgian Congo Flower Issue of 1952-53 Overprinted or Surcharged

Perf. 11½

1960, June 30 Photo. Unwmk.

Flowers in Natural Colors

Size: 21x25½mm

Granite Paper

323 A86	10c	dp plum & ocher	.20	.20
324 A86	10c	on 15c red & yel grn	.20	.20
325 A86	20c	grn & gray	.20	.20
326 A86	40c	grn & sal	.20	.20
327 A86	50c	on 60c bl grn & pink	.20	.20
328 A86	50c	on 75c dp plum & gray	.20	.20
329 A86	1fr	car & yel	.30	.20
330 A86	1.50fr	vio & ap grn	.30	.20
331 A86	2fr	ol grn & buff	.30	.20
332 A86	3fr	ol grn & pink	.45	.20
333 A86	4fr	choc & lil	1.40	1.00
334 A86	5fr	dp plum & lt bl grn	.55	.20
335 A86	6.50fr	dk car & lil	.70	.20
336 A86	8fr	grn & lt yel	.80	.30
337 A86	10fr	dp plum & pale ol	1.40	.30
338 A86	20fr	vio bl & dl sal	3.25	.80

Nos. 324, 327-328 exist without "CONGO" overprint but with surcharge, also without surcharge but with "CONGO." Inverted and double overprints exist. Values from $10 to $50 each.

Overprinted

Size: 22x32mm

339 A86	50fr	dp plum & gray bl	18.00	6.00
340 A86	100fr	grn & buff	42.50	10.00
	Nos. 323-340 (18)		71.15	20.80

Belgian Congo Animal Issue, Nos. 306-317, Overprinted or Surcharged in Red, Blue, Black or Brown

341 A92	10c	bl & brn (R)	.20	.20
342 A93	20c	red org & sl (Bl)	.20	.20
343 A92	40c	brn & bl (Bk)	.20	.20
344 A93	50c	brt ultra, red & sep (R)	.20	.20
345 A92	1fr	brn, grn & blk (Br)	.20	.20
346 A93	1.50fr	blk & org yel (R)	.20	.20
347 A92	2fr	crim, blk & brn (Bl)	.45	.20
348 A93	3.50fr	on 3fr blk, gray & lil rose (Bk)	.65	.20
349 A92	5fr	brn, dk brn & brt grn (Br)	.85	.20
350 A93	6.50fr	bl, brn & org yel (R)	1.00	.20
a.		Black overprint	1.75	.60
351 A92	8fr	org brn, ol bis & lil (Br)	1.25	.40
352 A93	10fr	multi (R)	1.60	.60
	Nos. 341-352 (12)		7.00	3.00

Inverted and double overprints exist. Values from $15 to $20 each.

Same Overprint on Belgian Congo No. 318

1960

353 A94 50c gldn brn, ocher & red brn 1.00 1.00

Same Overprint and Surcharge of New Value on Belgian Congo Nos. 321-322

Inscription in French

354 A95 3.50fr on 3fr gray & red 1.00 .70

Inscription in Flemish

355 A95	3.50fr	on 3fr gray & red	1.00	.70
	Nos. 353-355 (3)		3.00	2.40

Nos. 353-355 are known with inverted overprints. Value, each $10.

Map of Congo A93a

1960 **Photo.** ***Perf. 11½***

356	A93a	20c	brown	.20	.20
357	A93a	50c	rose red	.20	.20
358	A93a	1fr	green	.20	.20
359	A93a	1.50fr	red brn	.20	.20
360	A93a	2fr	rose car	.20	.20
361	A93a	3.50fr	lilac	.20	.20
362	A93a	5fr	brt bl	.20	.20
363	A93a	6.50fr	gray	.25	.20
364	A93a	10fr	orange	.40	.20
365	A93a	20fr	ultra	.75	.25
			Nos. 356-365 (10)	2.80	2.05

Congo's Independence.

Exists imperf.

For overprints see Nos. 371-380.

Flag, People and Broken Chain — A94

1961, Jan. 4 **Unwmk.** ***Perf. 11½***

Flag in Blue and Yellow

366	A94	2fr	rose vio	.25	.20
367	A94	3.50fr	vermilion	.25	.20
368	A94	6.50fr	yel brn	.25	.20
369	A94	10fr	brt grn	.30	.20
370	A94	20fr	car rose	.45	.30
			Nos. 366-370 (5)	1.50	1.10

Signing of the Independence Agreement by Belgium, Jan. 4, 1959.

Nos. 356-365 Overprinted in Blue, Black or Red: "Conference Coquilhatville Avril Mai 1961"

1961

371	A93a	20c	brn (Bl)	1.50	1.50
372	A93a	50c	rose red (Bk)	1.50	1.50
373	A93a	1fr	grn (R)	1.50	1.50
374	A93a	1.50fr	red brn (Bl)	1.50	1.50
375	A93a	2fr	rose car (Bk)	1.50	1.50
376	A93a	3.50fr	lil (Bl)	1.50	1.50
377	A93a	5fr	brt bl (R)	1.50	1.50
378	A93a	6.50fr	gray (R)	1.50	1.50
379	A93a	10fr	org (Bk)	1.50	1.50
380	A93a	20fr	ultra (R)	1.50	1.50
			Nos. 371-380 (10)	15.00	15.00

Coquilhatville Conf., Apr.-May, 1961.

Nos. 371-380 exist with inverted overprints. Value $15 each.

Pres. Joseph Kasavubu — A95

Kasavubu and Map of Congo — A96

10fr-100fr, Kasavubu in uniform and map.

Perf. 11½

1961, June 30 **Unwmk.** **Photo.**

Portrait and Inscription in Dark Brown

381	A95	10c	yellow	.20	.20
382	A95	20c	dp rose	.20	.20
383	A95	40c	bl grn	.20	.20
384	A95	50c	salmon	.20	.20
385	A95	1fr	lilac	.20	.20
386	A95	1.50fr	lt brn	.20	.20
387	A95	2fr	brt grn	.20	.20
388	A96	3.50fr	rose pink	.20	.20
389	A96	5fr	gray	*5.75*	.20
390	A96	6.50fr	ultra	.80	.20
391	A96	8fr	olive	.80	.20
392	A95	10fr	lt vio	2.10	.80
393	A95	20fr	orange	2.10	.20
394	A95	50fr	lt bl	3.50	.35
395	A95	100fr	apple green	5.75	.55
			Nos. 381-395 (15)	22.40	4.10

First anniversary of independence.

Exists imperf. Value, set $70.

Nos. 381-387, 389 and 392 Overprinted: "REOUVERTURE du PARLEMENT JUILLET 1961"

1961

Portrait and Inscription in Dark Brown

396	A95	10c	yellow	.20	.20
397	A95	20c	dp rose	.20	.20
398	A95	40c	bl grn	.20	.20
399	A95	50c	salmon	.50	.35
400	A95	1fr	lilac	.50	.35
401	A95	1.50fr	lt brn	1.25	1.00
402	A95	2fr	brt grn	1.25	1.00
403	A96	5fr	gray	1.25	1.00
404	A95	10fr	lt vio	1.25	1.00
			Nos. 396-404 (9)	6.60	5.30

Congolese parliament re-opening, 7/1961.

Nos. 396-404 exist with inverted overprints. Value $9 each.

Dag Hammarskjold and Map of Africa with Congo — A97

Malaria Eradication Emblem and Mosquito — A98

1962, Jan. 20 **Photo.** ***Perf. 11½***

Gray Background

405	A97	10c	dk brn	.20	.20
406	A97	20c	Prus bl	.20	.20
407	A97	30c	brown	.20	.20
408	A97	40c	dk bl	.20	.20
409	A97	50c	brn red	.20	.20
410	A97	3fr	ol grn	*4.25*	*1.25*
411	A97	6.50fr	dk vio	1.25	.35
412	A97	8fr	red brn	1.50	.50
			Nos. 405-412 (8)	8.00	3.10

Souvenir Sheets

Imperf

413	A97	25fr	blk brn	8.00	8.00
a.			Overprint in green	4.50	4.50

Dag Hammarskjold, Sec. Gen. of the UN, 1953-61.

No 413a is overprinted "30 Juin 1962" on stamp and "2eme Anniversaire de l'Independance" on sheet margin. Issued June 30, 1962.

For overprints see Nos. 417-424.

1962, June 15

Granite Paper

414	A98	1.50fr	yel, blk & dk red	.20	.20
415	A98	2fr	yel grn, brn & bl grn	.30	.20
416	A98	6.50fr	ultra, blk & mar	.40	.20
			Nos. 414-416 (3)	.90	.60

WHO drive to eradicate malaria.

Nos. 405-412 Overprinted in Blue, Purple, Black or Carmine

1962, Oct. 15

Gray Background

417	A97	10c	dk brn (Bl)	.20	.20
418	A97	20c	Prus bl (P)	.20	.20
419	A97	30c	brn (Bk)	.20	.20
420	A97	40c	dk bl (C)	.20	.20
421	A97	50c	brn red (Bl)	*2.00*	.75
422	A97	3fr	ol grn (P)	.20	.20
423	A97	6.50fr	dk vio (Bk)	.25	.20
424	A97	8fr	red brn (C)	.35	.20
			Nos. 417-424 (8)	3.60	2.15

Reorganization of Adoula administration.

Inverted overprints exist. Value, $8.00 each.

Canceled to Order

Starting in 1963, values in the used column are for "canceled to order" stamps. Postally used copies sell for much more.

A99

1963, Jan. 28 **Engr.** ***Perf. 10½x13***

425	A99	2fr	dull purple	*1.25*	*.90*
426	A99	4fr	red	.20	.20
427	A99	7fr	dark blue	.25	.20
428	A99	20fr	slate green	.50	.20
			Nos. 425-428 (4)	2.20	*1.50*

Congo's 1st participation at the UPU Cong., New Delhi, Mar. 1963.

An imperf sheet containing No. 428 in brown exists. Value $30.

For overprints see Nos. 468-471.

Shoebill — A100

Birds: 10c, Pelicans. 20c, Crested guinea fowl, horiz. 30c, Openbill. 40c, White-bellied storks, horiz. 2fr, Marabou. 3fr, Greater flamingos, horiz. 4fr, Congolese peacock. 5fr, Hartlaub ducks, horiz. 6fr, Secretary bird. 7fr, Black-casqued hornbill, horiz. 8fr, Sacred ibis and nest. 10fr, Crowned crane, horiz. 20fr, Saddle-bill stork, horiz.

1963 **Unwmk.** **Photo.** ***Perf. 11½***

429	A100	10c	pink, ultra & ocher	.20	.20
430	A100	20c	rose red, bl & blk	.20	.20
431	A100	30c	grn, ocher & blk	.20	.20
432	A100	40c	gray, org & blk	.20	.20
433	A100	1fr	brn, emer & gray	.20	.20
434	A100	2fr	gray, red & ind	*3.25*	.60
435	A100	3fr	ol grn, blk & rose	.20	.20
436	A100	4fr	car rose, vio bl & grn	.20	.20
437	A100	5fr	lake, lt bl & blk	.45	.20
438	A100	6fr	pur, yel & blk	*3.50*	.60
439	A100	7fr	bl grn, blk & ind	.55	.20
440	A100	8fr	yel, org & blk	.65	.20
441	A100	10fr	bl, blk & rose	.65	.20
442	A100	20fr	cit, red & blk	1.20	.20
			Nos. 429-442 (14)	11.65	3.60

Nos. 436 and 438 exist in imperf sheets of one. Value, each $35.

Cinchona Ledgeriana — A101

Red Cross Nurse — A102

10c, 30c, 5fr, Strophanthus sarmentosus.

Perf. 12½x13½, 13½x12½

1963, May 25 **Engr.** **Unwmk.**

Cross in Red

443	A101	10c	vio & dl grn	.20	.20
444	A101	20c	magenta & bl	.20	.20
445	A101	30c	grn & org	.20	.20
446	A101	40c	bl & vio	.20	.20
447	A101	5fr	ol & rose claret	.20	.20
448	A101	7fr	org & blk	.20	.20
449	A102	9fr	gray olive & red	.20	.20
450	A102	20fr	purple & red	*2.00*	.75
			Nos. 443-450 (8)	3.40	2.15

International Red Cross centenary.

A souvenir sheet of three contains imperf. 5fr, 7fr, and 20fr stamps similar to Nos. 447, 448 and 450, but in changed colors. Size: 109x75mm. Value $30.

Men Joining Hands and Map of Congo A103

1963, June 29 **Photo.** ***Perf. 11½***

451	A103	4fr	multi	1.25	.50
452	A103	5fr	multi	.20	.20
453	A103	9fr	multi	.20	.20
454	A103	12fr	multi	.35	.20
			Nos. 451-454 (4)	2.00	1.10

Issued to celebrate national reconciliation.

Bulldozer and Kabambare Sewer, Leopoldville — A104

Designs: 30c, 5fr, 12fr, Excavator and blueprint. 50c, 9fr, Building Ituri road.

1963, July 1 **Engr.** **Unwmk.**

455	A104	20c	multi	.20	.20
456	A104	30c	multi	.20	.20
457	A104	50c	multi	.20	.20
458	A104	3fr	multi	1.00	.40
459	A104	5fr	multi	.20	.20
460	A104	9fr	multi	.20	.20
461	A104	12fr	multi	.20	.20
			Nos. 455-461 (7)	2.20	1.60

Issued to publicize aid to Congo by the European Economic Community.

Leopoldville Airport N'Djili — A105

5fr, 7fr, 50fr, Tail assembly and airport.

1963, Nov. 30 **Photo.** ***Perf. 11½***

462	A105	2fr	gray, yel & red brn	.20	.20
463	A105	5fr	mag, vio & yel	.20	.20
464	A105	6fr	bl, yel & dk brn	1.40	.50
465	A105	7fr	multi	.20	.20
466	A105	30fr	lil, yel & ol	.40	.25
467	A105	50fr	multi	.60	.30
			Nos. 462-467 (6)	3.00	1.65

Issued to publicize Air Congo.

For surcharge see No. 606.

Nos. 425-428 Overprinted with Silver Frame on Three Sides and Black Inscription: "15e anniversaire / 10 DECEMBRE 1948 / DROITS DE L'HOMME / 10 DECEMBRE 1963"

Engraved and Typographed

1963, Dec. 10 ***Perf. 10½x13***

468	A99	2fr	dull purple	.20	.20
469	A99	4fr	red	.20	.20
470	A99	7fr	dark blue	.25	.20
471	A99	20fr	slate green	.30	.20
			Nos. 468-471 (4)	.95	.80

Universal Declaration of Human Rights, 15th anniv.

Nos. 468-471 exist with side date panels transposed ("1963" at left, "1948" at right). Value, each $15.

Laboratory Technician and Atomic Emblem A106

1.50fr, 60fr, University. 8fr, 75fr, First African nuclear reactor. 25fr, 100fr, University and crest.

1964, Feb. 1 Photo. *Perf. 14x12½*

472 A106 50c multi .20 .20
473 A106 1.50fr multi .20 .20
474 A106 8fr multi *2.50* *2.25*
475 A106 25fr multi .20 .20
476 A106 30fr multi .35 .20
477 A106 60fr multi .60 .35
478 A106 75fr multi .70 .60
479 A106 100fr multi 1.00 .80
a. Souv. sheet of 3 6.50 6.50
Nos. 472-479 (8) 5.75 4.80

Lovanium University, Leopoldville, 10th anniv.
No. 479a contains 3 imperf. multicolored stamps: 20fr, design as 50c; 30fr, as 8fr; 100fr.

Belgian Congo Issues of 1952-59 Overprinted "REPUBLIQUE DU CONGO" and Surcharged in Black on Overprinted Metallic Panels

1964 *Perf. 11½*

480 A93 1fr on 20c red org & sl (#307) .20 .20
481 A86 2fr on 1.50fr (#273) *10.00* *3.25*
482 A93 5fr on 6.50fr (#315) .80 .25
483 A86 8fr on 6.50fr (#278) 1.10 .35

Republic Issues of 1960-61 Surcharged in Black on Overprinted Metallic Rectangles or Ovals

484 A86 1fr on 6.50fr (#335) .20 .20
485 A93 1fr on 20c (#342) .20 .20
486 A86 2fr on 1.50fr (#330) .20 .20
487 A95 3fr on 20c (#382) .55 .25
488 A95 4fr on 40c (#383) .55 .25
489 A93 5fr on 6.50fr ("Congo" red) (#350) .80 .25
a. "Congo" black .80 .25
490 A93a 6fr on 6.50fr (#363) .80 .25
491 A93a 7fr on 20c (#356) .80 .25
Nos. 480-491 (12) 16.20 5.90

Pole Vault
A107

7fr, 20fr, Javelin, vert. 8fr, 100fr, Hurdling.

Perf. 11½
1964, July 13 Unwmk. Photo.
Granite Paper

492 A107 5fr gray, dk brn & car .20 .20
493 A107 7fr rose, vio & emer .95 .35
494 A107 8fr org, yel, red brn & vio bl .20 .20
495 A107 10fr bl, vio brn & mag .20 .20
496 A107 20fr gray grn, red brn & ver .25 .20
497 A107 100fr lil, dk brn & grn .95 .25
a. Souv. sheet of 3 10.00 10.00
Nos. 492-497 (6) 2.75 1.40

18th Olympic Games, Tokyo, Oct. 10-25.
No. 497a contains 3 imperf. stamps (20fr orange & dark brown, pole vault; 30fr citron and dark brown, hurdling; 100fr dull green and dark brown, javelin). Sheet issued Sept. 10.

National Palace, Leopoldville — A108

1964, Sept. 15
Granite Paper

498 A108 50c lil rose & bl .20 .20
499 A108 1fr bl & lil rose .20 .20
500 A108 2fr brn red & vio .20 .20
501 A108 3fr emer & red .20 .20
502 A108 4fr org & vio bl .20 .20
503 A108 5fr gray vio & emer .20 .20
504 A108 6fr sep & org .20 .20
505 A108 7fr gray ol & red brn .20 .20
506 A108 8fr rose red & vio bl *2.00* .30
507 A108 9fr vio bl & rose red .20 .20
508 A108 10fr brn ol & grn .20 .20
509 A108 20fr bl & brn org .20 .20
510 A108 30fr dk car rose & grn .25 .20
511 A108 40fr ultra & dk car rose .35 .20
512 A108 50fr brn org & grn .40 .20
513 A108 100fr slate & ver .85 .20
Nos. 498-513 (16) 6.05 3.30

For overprints and surcharges see Nos. 574-577, 593-598, 609-615, 670-671, 673-674, 676-677, 680, 684-687.

Pres. John F. Kennedy (1917-63)
A109

1964, Dec. 8 Photo. *Perf. 13½*

514 A109 5fr dk bl & blk .20 .20
515 A109 6fr rose claret & blk .20 .20
516 A109 9fr brn & blk .20 .20
517 A109 30fr pur & blk .55 .20
518 A109 40fr dl grn & blk *3.50* 1.00
519 A109 60fr red brn & blk 1.20 .35
Nos. 514-519 (6) 5.85 2.15

Souvenir Sheet

520 A109 150fr blk & mar 6.50 6.50

Rocket and Unisphere
A110

Basketball
A111

Engraved and Typographed
1965, Mar. 1 Unwmk. *Perf. 12*

521 A110 50c lil & blk .20 .20
522 A110 1.50fr bl & lil .20 .20
523 A110 2fr red brn & brt grn .20 .20
524 A110 10fr brt grn & dk red 1.00 .55
525 A110 18fr vio bl & brn .20 .20
526 A110 27fr rose red & grn .35 .20
527 A110 40fr gray & org .45 .20
Nos. 521-527 (7) 2.60 1.75

New York World's Fair, 1964-65.

1965, Apr. Photo. *Perf. 13½*

6fr, 40fr, Soccer, horiz. 15fr, 60fr, Volleyball.

528 A111 5fr blk, grnsh bl & ocher .20 .20
529 A111 6fr blk, bl gray & crim .20 .20
530 A111 15fr blk, org & yel grn .20 .20
531 A111 24fr blk, rose lil & brt grn .40 .20
532 A111 40fr blk, brt grn & ultra *2.00* .70
533 A111 60fr blk, bl & red lil .70 .20
Nos. 528-533 (6) 3.70 1.70

First African Games, Leopoldville, Mar. 31-Apr. 7, 1965.
For surcharges see Nos. 604-605.

Earth and Satellites
A112

Designs: 9fr, 15fr, 20fr, 40fr, Satellites at left, globe at right.

Perf. 14x14½
1965, June 28 Photo. Unwmk.

534 A112 6fr blk, sal & vio .20 .20
535 A112 9fr blk, lt grn & gray .20 .20
536 A112 12fr org, gray & blk .20 .20
537 A112 15fr grn, ultra & blk .20 .20
538 A112 18fr blk, lt grn & gray 1.10 .30
539 A112 20fr blk, sal & vio .20 .20
540 A112 30fr grn, ultra & blk .25 .20
541 A112 40fr org, gray & blk .30 .20
Nos. 534-541 (8) 2.65 1.70

Cent. of the ITU.

Congolese Paratrooper and Parachutes
A113

1965, July 5 *Perf. 13x14*

542 A113 5fr brt bl & brn .20 .20
543 A113 6fr org & brn .20 .20
544 A113 7fr br grn & brn .40 .25
545 A113 9fr brt pink & brn .20 .20
546 A113 18fr lem & brn .20 .20
Nos. 542-546 (5) 1.20 1.05

Fifth anniversary of independence.

Matadi Harbor and ICY Emblem — A114

ICY Emblem and: 8fr, 25fr, Katanga mines. 9fr, 60fr, Tshopo Dam, Stanleyville.

1965, Oct. 25 Photo. *Perf. 13x14*

547 A114 6fr ultra, blk & yel .20 .20
548 A114 8fr org red, blk & bl .20 .20
549 A114 9fr bl grn, blk & brn org .20 .20
550 A114 12fr car rose, blk & gray .75 .30
551 A114 25fr ol, blk & rose red .20 .20
552 A114 60fr gray, blk & org .55 .20
Nos. 547-552 (6) 2.10 1.30

International Cooperation Year, 1965.
For overprints and surcharges see Nos. 559-560, 607-608.

Soldiers Giving First Aid — A115

The Army Serving the Country: 7fr, Bridge building. 9fr, Feeding child. 19fr, Maintenance of telegraph lines. 20fr, House building. 30fr, Soldier and flag. (19fr, 20fr, 30fr, vert.)

Perf. 12½x13, 13x12½
1965, Nov. 17

553 A115 5fr sal, brn & red .20 .20
554 A115 7fr yel & grn .20 .20
555 A115 9fr ol & brn .20 .20
556 A115 19fr brt grn & brn 1.10 .60
557 A115 20fr lt bl & brn .30 .20
558 A115 30fr multi .50 .20
Nos. 553-558 (6) 2.50 1.60

See Nos. 582-586. For surcharges see Nos. 602, 678-679, 683.

Nos. 551-552 Overprinted with UN Emblem and "6e Journée Météorologique Mondiale / 23.3.66." on Metallic Strip

1966, Mar. 23 Photo. *Perf. 13x14*

559 A114 25fr ol & blk 1.40 .55
560 A114 60fr gray & blk 1.40 .65

6th World Meteorological Day.

Woman's Head and Goat — A116

10fr, Sculptured heads. 12fr, Sitting figure and two heads, vert. 53fr, Figure with earrings and kneeling woman with bowl, vert.

Perf. 11½x13, 13x11½
1966, Apr. 23 Litho. Unwmk.

561 A116 10fr red, blk & gray .20 .20
562 A116 12fr grn, blk & bl .25 .20
563 A116 15fr dp bl, blk & lil .30 .20
564 A116 53fr dp rose, blk & vio bl 1.50 1.10
Nos. 561-564 (4) 2.25 1.70

Intl. Negro Arts Festival, Dakar, Senegal, Apr. 1-24.

Pres. Joseph Desiré Mobutu and Fishing Industry
A117

Pres. Mobutu and: 4fr, Pyrethrum harvest. 6fr, Building industry. 8fr, Winnowing rice. 10fr, Cotton harvest. 12fr, Banana harvest. 15fr, Coffee harvest. 24fr, Pineapple harvest. No. 573a, Pres. Mobutu without cap, and men rolling up sleeves.

1966, May 1 Photo. *Perf. 11½*

565 A117 2fr dk brn & dk bl .20 .20
566 A117 4fr dk brn & org .20 .20
567 A117 6fr dk brn & ol .75 .60
568 A117 8fr dk brn & brt grnsh bl .20 .20
569 A117 10fr dk brn & brn red .20 .20
570 A117 12fr dk brn & vio .20 .20
571 A117 15fr dk brn & lt ol grn .20 .20
572 A117 24fr dk brn & lil rose .25 .20
Nos. 565-572 (8) 2.20 2.00

Souvenir Sheet
Perf. 11x11½

573 Sheet of 4 2.00 2.00
a. A117 15fr red, black & ultra .45 .45

Lt. Gen. Joseph Desiré Mobutu, Pres. of Congo, and publicizing the "Back to Work" campaign.
For surcharges see Nos. 601, 603, 616, 619-624, 672, 675, 681-682.

Nos. 510-513 Overprinted

1966, June 13 *Perf. 11½*

574 A108 30fr dk car rose & grn 1.10 1.10
575 A108 40fr ultra & dk car rose 1.20 1.20
576 A108 50fr brn org & grn 1.40 1.40
577 A108 100fr slate & ver 1.40 1.40
Nos. 574-577 (4) 5.10 5.10

Inauguration of WHO Headquarters, Geneva.

Soccer Player — A118

30fr, 2 soccer players. 50fr, 3 soccer players. 60fr, Jules Rimet Cup, soccer ball & globe.

1966, July 25 Photo. *Perf. 14*

578 A118 10fr ocher, vio & brt grn .20 .20
579 A118 30fr brt rose lil, vio & ap grn .45 .20
580 A118 50fr ap grn, Prus bl & tan 1.50 1.00
581 A118 60fr brt grn, dk brn & gold 1.50 .50
Nos. 578-581 (4) 3.65 1.90

World Cup Soccer Championship, Wembley, England, July 11-30.
For overprints see Nos. 587-590.

Army Type of 1965

The Army Serving the Country: 2fr, Soldiers giving first aid. 6fr, Feeding child. 10fr, House building, vert. 18fr, Bridge building. 24fr, Soldier and flag, vert.

1966, Aug. 8 *Perf. 12½x13, 13x12½*

582 A115 2fr ver, ind & red .20 .20
583 A115 6fr ultra red brn .20 .20
584 A115 10fr yel grn & red brn .75 .50
585 A115 18fr car rose & vio .20 .20
586 A115 24fr multi .25 .20
Nos. 582-586 (5) 1.60 1.30

#578-581 Overprinted in Black ("a"), Carmine or Green ("b"): "FINALE / ANGLETERRE-ALLEMAGNE / 4-2"

1966, Nov. 14 **Photo.** *Perf. 14*

587 A118 10fr pair, B and C .60 .60
588 A118 30fr pair, B and G 2.25 2.00
589 A118 50fr pair, B and C 3.50 2.50
590 A118 60fr pair, B and C 4.00 3.50
Nos. 587-590 (4) 10.35 8.60

England's victory in the World Soccer Cup Championship. The two colors of the overprint alternate in the sheets.

Souvenir Sheets

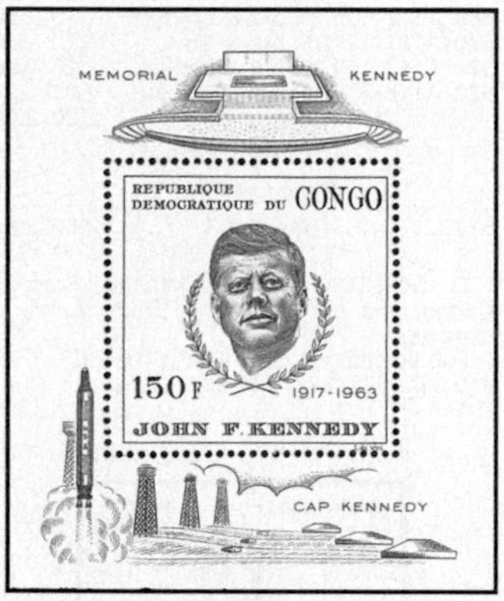

Pres. John F. Kennedy — A119

1966, Dec. 28 **Engr.** *Perf. 13*

591 A119 150fr brown 20.00 16.00
592 A119 150fr slate 20.00 16.00

Issued in memory of Pres. John F. Kennedy. No. 591 has slate green, No. 592 deep orange marginal design. Two imperf. sheets exist: 150fr brown with violet blue margin and 150fr slate with lilac margin. Size: 65x76mm. Values, $20 each.

Nos. 498-503 Surcharged in Black, Red or Maroon

1967, Sept. 11 **Photo.** *Perf. 11½*

593 A108 1k on 2fr .20 .20
a. Inverted overprint 5.00
594 A108 3k on 5fr .20 .20
595 A108 5k on 4fr .35 .20
596 A108 6.60k on 1fr (R) .50 .20
a. Inverted overprint 5.00
597 A108 9.60k on 50c .70 .30
a. Inverted overprint 5.00
598 A108 9.80k on 3fr (M) .75 .50
Nos. 593-598 (6) 2.70 1.60

Souvenir Sheet

Map of Africa, Torch — A120

599 A120 50k grnsh bl, blk & red 2.50 2.50

4th meeting of the Org. for African Unity, Kinshasa (Leopoldville), Sept. 9-11.

No. 599 in other colors was not a postal issue.

Souvenir Sheet

Horn Blower and EXPO Emblem — A121

1967, Sept. 28 **Engr.** *Perf. 11½*

600 A121 50k dk brn 3.25 3.25

EXPO '67, International Exhibition, Montreal, Apr. 28-Oct. 27, 1967.

Nos. 565-566 and 582 Overprinted: "NOUVELLE CONSTITUTION 1967" and Surcharged with New Value on Metallic Panel in Magenta or Brown

Perf. 11½, 12½x13

1967, Oct. 9 **Photo.**

601 A117 4k on 2fr (M) .25 .20
602 A115 5k on 2fr (B) .45 .20
603 A117 21k on 4fr (M) 1.50 .90
Nos. 601-603 (3) 2.20 1.30

Promulgation of the Constitution, June 4, 1967.

Nos. 528 and 530 Surcharged with New Value and Overprinted: "1ers Jeux Congolais / 25/6 au 2/7/1967 / Kinshasa"

1967, Oct. 16 **Photo.** *Perf. 13½*

604 A111 1k on 5fr multi .35 .20
605 A111 9.60k on 15fr multi .75 .65

First Congolese Games, Kinshasa, June 25-July 2, 1967.

No. 465 Surcharged with New Value and Overprinted: "1er VOL BAC / ONE ELEVEN / 14/5/67"

1967, Oct. 16 *Perf. 11½*

606 A105 9.60k on 7fr multi 1.20 .25

1st flight of the BAC 111 in the service of Air Congo, May 14, 1967.

Nos. 547 and 549 Surcharged in Red or Black: "JOURNEE MONDIALE / DE L'ENFANCE / 8-10-67"

1968, Feb. 10 **Photo.** *Perf. 13x14*

607 A114 1k on 6fr (R) .25 .20
608 A114 9k on 9fr (B) .95 .70

Intl. Children's Day. The surcharge is on a rectangle printed in metallic ink.

Nos. 498, 504 and 501 Surcharged in Blue or Red: "Année Internationale / du Tourisme 24-10-1967"

1968, Feb. 10 *Perf. 11½*

609 A108 5k on 50c lil rose & bl (Bl) .45 .25
610 A108 10k on 6fr sepia & org (R) .65 .55
611 A108 15k on 3fr emer & red (R) 1.00 1.00
Nos. 609-611 (3) 2.10 1.80

International Tourist Year. The surcharge is on a rectangle printed in metallic ink.

Nos. 500, 498 and 502 Surcharged in Black, Violet Blue or Gold

1968, July **Photo.** *Perf. 11½*

612 A108 1k on 2fr .30 .20
613 A108 2k on 50c (VBl) .45 .25
614 A108 2k on 50c (G) .45 .25
615 A108 9.60k on 4fr 2.00 1.10
Nos. 612-615 (4) 3.20 1.80

The surcharge on No. 612 consists of a black rectangle and new denomination in upper right corner; the surcharge on No. 613 has a violet blue rectangle with denomination printed in white on it; on No. 614 the rectangle is gold and the denomination black; on No. 615 the rectangle is black and the denomination white.

No. 565 Surcharged in White on Black Rectangle

1968, Oct. **Photo.** *Perf. 11½*

616 A117 10k on 2fr dk brn & dk bl .70 .20

Leopard A122

1968, Nov. 5 **Litho.** *Perf. 10½*

617 A122 2k brt grnsh bl & blk .30 .20
618 A122 9.60k red & blk 1.20 .20

Mobutu Type of 1966 Surcharged

1968, Dec. 20 **Photo.** *Perf. 11½*

619 A117 15s on 2fr sep & brt bl .20 .20
620 A117 1k on 6fr sep & brn .20 .20
621 A117 3k on 10fr sep & emer .20 .20
622 A117 5k on 12fr sep & org .30 .20
623 A117 20k on 15fr sep & brt grn 1.00 .50
624 A117 50k on 24fr sep & brt lil 2.75 1.40
Nos. 619-624 (6) 4.65 2.70

Human Rights Flame — A123

1968, Dec. 30 *Perf. 12½x13*

625 A123 2k lt ultra & brt grn .20 .20
626 A123 9.60k grn & dp car .65 .30
627 A123 10k brt lil & brn .65 .30
628 A123 40k org brn & pur 2.25 1.20
Nos. 625-628 (4) 3.75 2.00

International Human Rights Year.

Type of 1968 Overprinted in Gold

1969, Jan. 27 **Photo.** *Perf. 12½x13*

629 A123 2k ap grn & red brn .20 .20
630 A123 9.60k rose & emer .65 .30
631 A123 10k gray & ultra .65 .30
632 A123 40k grnsh bl & pur 2.25 1.20
Nos. 629-632 (4) 3.75 2.00

4th summit meeting of OCAM (Organisation Communitee Afrique et Malgache), Kinshasa, Jan. 27.

Kinshasa Fair Emblem and Cotton Boll — A124

Fair Emblem and: 6k, Copper. 9.60k, Coffee. 9.80k, Diamond. 11.60k, Oil palm fruits.

1969, May 2 **Photo.** *Perf. 12½x13*

633 A124 2k brt pur, gold & red lil .25 .20
634 A124 6k grn, gold & bl grn .95 .50
635 A124 9.60k brn, gold & lt brn 1.25 .40
636 A124 9.80k ultra & gold 1.40 .60
637 A124 11.60k hn brn, gold & brn 1.60 .90
Nos. 633-637 (5) 5.45 2.60

Kinshasa Fair, Limete, June 30-July 21.

Fair Entrance, Emblem — A125

Fair Emblem and: 3k, Gecomin Mining Co. Pavilion. 10k, Administration Building. 25k, Pavilion of the Organization for African Unity.

1969, June 30 **Photo.** *Perf. 11½*

Granite Paper

638 A125 2k brt rose lil & gold .20 .20
639 A125 3k blue & gold .20 .20
640 A125 10k lt ol grn & gold .80 .40
641 A125 25k copper red & gold 1.80 1.00
Nos. 638-641 (4) 3.00 1.80

Kinshasa Fair, Limete, June 30-July 21.

Congo Arms — A126

Pres. Mobutu — A127

1969, July-Sept. **Litho.** *Perf. 14*

642 A126 10s org & blk .20 .20
643 A126 15s ultra & blk .20 .20
644 A126 30s brt grn & blk .20 .20
645 A126 60s brt rose lil & blk .20 .20
646 A126 90s dp bister & blk .20 .20

Perf. 13

647 A127 1k sky bl & multi .20 .20
648 A127 2k org & multi .20 .20
649 A127 3k multi .30 .20
650 A127 5k brt rose & multi .40 .20
651 A127 6k ultra & multi .40 .25
652 A127 9.60k multi .70 .40
653 A127 10k lt lil & multi .90 .50
654 A127 20k yel & multi 1.75 1.00
655 A127 50k multi 4.75 2.50
656 A127 100k fawn & multi 9.50 6.00
Nos. 642-656 (15) 20.10 12.45

Well Driller, by Oscar Bonnevalle — A128

Paintings: 4k, Preparation of cocoa, by Jean Van Noten. 8k, Dock workers, by Constantin Meunier. 10k, Poultry shop, by Henri Evenepoel. 15k, Steel industry, by Constantin Meunier.

Perf. 13x14, 14x13 (8k)

1969, Dec. 15 **Litho.**

Size: 41x41mm

657	A128	3k multi	.20	.20
658	A128	4k multi	.20	.20

Size: 28x41mm

659	A128	8k multi	.45	.30

Size: 41x41mm

660	A128	10k multi	.70	.40
661	A128	15k multi	1.40	.70
		Nos. 657-661 (5)	2.95	1.80

50th anniv. of the ILO.

Souvenir Sheet

Adoration of the Kings, by Rubens — A129

1969, Dec. **Engr.** ***Perf. 13***

662	A129	50k red lilac	4.50	4.50

Issued for Christmas 1969.

Pres. Mobutu, Map and Flag of Congo A130

1970, June 30 **Litho.** ***Perf. 13½x13***

663	A130	10s multi	.20	.20
664	A130	90s pur & multi	.20	.20
665	A130	1k brn & multi	.20	.20
666	A130	2k multi	.20	.20
667	A130	7k multi	.35	.20
668	A130	10k multi	.55	.25
669	A130	20k multi	1.10	.60
		Nos. 663-669 (7)	2.80	1.85

10th anniversary of independence.

Issues of 1964-1966 Surcharged

Perf. 11½, 12½x13, 13x12½

1970, Sept. 24 **Photo.**

670	A108	10s on 1fr (#499)	.25	.20
671	A108	20s on 2fr (#500)	.25	.20
672	A117	20s on 2fr (#565)	1.00	.50
673	A108	30s on 3fr (#501)	.25	.20
674	A108	40s on 4fr (#502)	.25	.20
675	A117	40s on 4fr (#566)	1.00	.50
676	A108	60s on 7fr (#505)	3.00	1.75
677	A108	90s on 9fr (#507)	3.00	1.75
678	A115	90s on 9fr (#555)	.60	.40
679	A115	1k on 7fr (#554)	.60	.40
680	A108	1k on 6fr (#504)	.50	.20
681	A117	1k on 12fr (#570)	2.75	1.75
682	A117	2k on 24fr (#572)	1.25	.50
683	A115	2k on 24fr (#586)	1.25	.50
684	A108	3k on 30fr (#510)	2.25	1.25
685	A108	4k on 40fr (#511)	.50	.20
686	A108	5k on 50fr (#512)	9.00	5.00
687	A108	10k on 100fr (#513)	2.25	1.25
		Nos. 670-687 (18)	29.95	16.75

Telecommunications Building, Geneva — A131

Designs: 2k, 6.60k, UPU Headquarters, Bern. 9.80k, 10k, 11k, UN Headquarters, NY.

1970, Oct. 24 **Photo.** ***Perf. 11½***

688	A131	1k pink & grn	.20	.20
689	A131	2k org & grn	.20	.20
690	A131	6.60k grnsh bl & rose car	.40	.25
691	A131	9.60k yel & vio bl	.50	.35
692	A131	9.80k lt ultra & brn	.50	.35
693	A131	10k lt pur & brn	.50	.35
694	A131	11k rose & brn	.70	.45
		Nos. 688-694 (7)	3.00	2.15

ITU; new UPU Headquarters, Bern; 25th anniv. of the UN.

Pres. Mobutu, Congolese Flag and Arch — A132

1970, Nov. 24 **Litho.** ***Perf. 13***

695	A132	2k yel & multi	.20	.20
696	A132	10k bl & multi	.90	.50
697	A132	20k red & multi	2.10	1.50
		Nos. 695-697 (3)	3.20	2.20

Fifth anniversary of new government.

Apollo 11 in Flight A133

Designs: 2k, Astronaut and spacecraft on moon. 7k, Pres. Mobutu decorating astronauts' wives. 10k, Pres. Mobutu with Neil A. Armstrong, Col. Edwin E. Aldrin, Jr. and Lt. Col. Michael Collins. 30k, Armstrong, Aldrin and Collins in space suits.

1970, Dec. 24 ***Perf. 13x13½***

698	A133	1k bl & blk	.30	.20
699	A133	2k brt pur & blk	.50	.25
700	A133	7k dl org & blk	1.50	.85
701	A133	10k rose red & blk	1.75	1.25
702	A133	30k grn & blk	5.25	3.25
		Nos. 698-702 (5)	9.30	5.80

Visit of US Apollo 11 astronauts and their wives to Kinshasa.

Metopodontus Savagei — A134

Designs: Various insects of Congo.

1971, Jan. 25 **Photo.** ***Perf. 11½***

703	A134	10s dl rose & multi	.65	.25
704	A134	50s gray & multi	.65	.25
705	A134	90s multi	.65	.25
706	A134	1k citron & multi	.65	.25
707	A134	2k gray grn & multi	.65	.25
708	A134	3k lt vio & multi	1.40	.50
709	A134	5k bl & multi	4.50	1.75
710	A134	10k multi	6.25	2.25
711	A134	30k grn & multi	14.50	6.25
712	A134	40k ocher & multi	23.00	9.00
		Nos. 703-712 (10)	52.90	21.00

Colotis Protomedia — A135

Various butterflies and moths of Congo.

1971, Feb. 24

713	A135	10s lt ultra & multi	.65	.30
714	A135	20s choc & multi	.65	.30
715	A135	70s dp org & multi	.65	.30
716	A135	1k vio bl & multi	.65	.30
717	A135	3k multi	1.50	.50
718	A135	5k dk grn & multi	4.25	1.25
719	A135	10k multi	5.50	1.75
720	A135	15k emer & multi	10.00	3.00
721	A135	25k yel & multi	16.00	4.00
722	A135	40k multi	22.50	10.00
		Nos. 713-722 (10)	62.35	21.70

UN Emblem, Racial Unity — A136

1971, Mar. 21 **Photo.** ***Perf. 11½***

723	A136	1k lt grn & multi	.20	.20
724	A136	4k gray & multi	.20	.20
725	A136	5k lt lil & multi	.35	.25
726	A136	10k lt bl & multi	.75	.35
		Nos. 723-726 (4)	1.50	1.00

Intl. year against racial discrimination.

Hypericum Bequaertii A137

Flowers: 4k, Dissotis brazzae. 20k, Begonia wollastonii. 25k, Cassia alata.

1971, May 24 **Litho.** ***Perf. 14***

727	A137	1k multi	1.00	.25
728	A137	4k multi	1.75	.45
729	A137	20k multi	9.25	2.50
730	A137	25k multi	12.00	3.25
		Nos. 727-730 (4)	24.00	6.45

Obelisk at N'sele, Pres. Mobutu A138

1971, May 20 **Photo.** ***Perf. 11½***

731	A138	4k gold & multi	.45	.20

4th anniversary of the People's Revolutionary Movement.

Radar Station A139

Designs: 1k, Waves. 6k, Map of Africa with telecommunications network.

1971, June 25 **Photo.** ***Perf. 11½***

732	A139	1k rose & multi	.20	.20
733	A139	3k yel & multi	.50	.35
734	A139	6k lt bl & multi	1.25	.95
		Nos. 732-734 (3)	1.95	1.50

3rd World Telecommunications Day, May 17 (1k); opening of satellite telecommunications ground station, Kinshasa, June 30 (3k); Pan-African telecommunication system (6k).

Grass Monkeys A140

Designs: 20s, Moustached monkeys, vert. 70s, De Brazza's monkeys. 1k, Yellow baboons. 3k, Pygmy chimpanzee, vert. 5k, Mangabeys, vert. 10k, Owlfaced monkeys. 15k, Diana monkeys. 25k, Black-and-white colobus, vert. 40k, L'Hoest's monkeys, vert.

1971, Aug.

735	A140	10s vio & multi	.75	.35
736	A140	20s lt bl & multi	.75	.35
737	A140	70s ocher & multi	1.10	.45
738	A140	1k gray & multi	1.10	.45
739	A140	3k rose & multi	1.75	.90
740	A140	5k brn & multi	4.00	2.40
741	A140	10k multi	8.25	4.50
742	A140	15k multi	13.00	6.25
743	A140	25k brt bl & multi	22.50	10.50
744	A140	40k red & multi	30.00	15.00
		Nos. 735-744 (10)	83.20	41.15

Hotel Inter-Continental, Kinshasa — A141

1971, Oct. 2 **Photo.** ***Perf. 13***

745	A141	2k silver & multi	.25	.25
746	A141	12k gold & multi	.55	.25

Man Reading A142

Designs: 2.50k, Open book and abacus. 7k, Five letters surrounding symbolic head.

1971, Oct. 24

747	A142	50s multi	.20	.20
748	A142	2.50k multi	.20	.20
749	A142	7k multi	1.25	1.00
		Nos. 747-749 (3)	1.65	1.40

Fight against illiteracy.

Succeeding issues are listed in Vol. 6 under Zaire. Beginning in 1998, Zaire reverted to using the Congo name, at least temporarily. Until the situation is resolved, the current stamps inscribed "Congo" will be listed under Zaire.

SEMI-POSTAL STAMPS

Women Carrying Food, Wheat Emblem, and Tractor
SP22

1963, Mar. 21 Photo. *Perf. 14x13*

B48	SP22	5fr + 2fr multi	.25	.20
B49	SP22	9fr + 4fr multi	.40	.20
B50	SP22	12fr + 6fr multi	.45	.25
B51	SP22	20fr + 10fr multi	2.00	1.50
		Nos. B48-B51 (4)	3.10	2.15

FAO "Freedom from Hunger" campaign.

No. B51 exists in an imperf sheet of one, in light and dark violet. Value $30.

CONGO, PEOPLE'S REPUBLIC OF

'pē-pəls ri-'pə-blik of

'käŋ-,gō

(ex-French)

LOCATION — West Africa at equator
GOVT. — Republic
AREA — 132,046 sq. mi.
POP. — 2,716,814 (1999 est.)
CAPITAL — Brazzaville

The former French colony of Middle Congo became a member state of the French Community on November 28, 1958, and achieved independence on August 15, 1960. For some years before 1958, the colony was joined with three other French territories to form French Equatorial Africa. Issues of Middle Congo (1907-1933) are listed under that heading.

100 Centimes = 1 Franc

Catalogue values for all unused stamps in this country are for Never Hinged items.

Allegory of New Republic A7

1959 Unwmk. Engr. *Perf. 13*
89 A7 25fr brn, dp claret, org & ol .60 .25

1st anniv. of the proclamation of the Republic.

Imperforates
Most stamps of the Republic of the Congo exist imperforate in issued and trial colors, and also in small presentation sheets in issued colors.

Common Design Types pictured following the introduction.

C.C.T.A. Issue
Common Design Type

1960 Unwmk. *Perf. 13*
90 CD106 50fr dl grn & plum .80 .80

President Fulbert Youlou — A8

Flag, Map and UN Emblem — A9

1960
91 A8 15fr grn, blk & car .35 .35
92 A8 85fr indigo & car 2.00 .45

1961, Mar. 11 *Perf. 13*
Flag in Green, Yellow & Red
93 A9 5fr vio brn & dk bl .25 .20
94 A9 20fr org & dk bl .45 .25
95 A9 100fr grn & dk bl 2.00 .80
Nos. 93-95 (3) 2.70 1.25

Congo's admission to United Nations.

Rainbow Runner A10

Fish: 50c, 3fr, Rainbow runner. 1fr, 2fr, Sloan's viperfish. 5fr, Hatchet fish. 10fr, A deep-sea fish.

1961, Nov. 28 Engr.
96 A10 50c brn, ol grn & sal .25 .20
97 A10 1fr bl grn & sepia .25 .20
98 A10 2fr ultra, sep & dk grn .25 .20
99 A10 3fr dk bl, grn & salmon .35 .20
100 A10 5fr red brn, grn & blk .70 .25
101 A10 10fr blue & red brn 1.40 .30
Nos. 96-101 (6) 3.20 1.35

Brazzaville Market — A11

1962, Mar. 23 Unwmk. *Perf. 13*
102 A11 20fr blk, red & grn .60 .20

Abidjan Games Issue
Common Design Type

20fr, Boxing. 50fr, Running, finish line.

1962, July 21 Photo. *Perf. 12½x12*
103 CD109 20fr car, brt pink, brn & blk .45 .25
104 CD109 50fr car, brt pink, brn & blk .90 .30
Nos. 103-104,C7 (3) 3.85 1.80

African-Malgache Union Issue
Common Design Type

1962, Sept. 8
105 CD110 30fr multicolored 1.00 .40

Waves Around Globe A11a

Design: 100fr, Orbit patterns around globe.

1963, Sept. 19 *Perf. 12½*
106 A11a 25fr org, grn & ultra .50 .30
107 A11a 100fr lt red brn, bl & plum 1.60 .90

Issued to publicize space communications.

King Makoko's Collar — A12

Unwmk.
1963, Oct. 21 Engr. *Perf. 13*
108 A12 10fr shown .45 .25
109 A12 15fr Kebekebe mask .60 .25

UNESCO Emblem, Scales and Tree A12a

1963, Dec. 10 Unwmk. *Perf. 13*
110 A12a 25fr grn, dk bl & brn .70 .30

15th anniv. of the Universal Declaration of Human Rights.

Barograph and WMO Emblem A12b

1964, Mar. 23 Engr.
111 A12b 50fr grn, red brn & ultra 1.00 .60

Fourth World Meteorological Day.

Mechanic with Machine — A13

1964, Apr. 8
112 A13 20fr grnsh bl, mag & dk brn .60 .30

Training of technicians.

Corn and Tools A14

1964, Apr. 24 Unwmk. *Perf. 13*
113 A14 80fr brn, grn & brn car 1.10 .60

Importance of manual labor.

Diaboua Ballet A15

Kébékébé Dance — A16

Carved Figure — A17

1964, May 8 Engr.
114 A15 30fr multicolored 1.25 .30
115 A16 60fr multicolored 2.25 .65

1964, May 22
116 A17 50fr brn red & sepia 1.50 .55

Classroom A18

1964, May 26
117 A18 25fr dk brn, red & blue .60 .30

Issued to publicize education.

Type of Air Post Issue, 1963, Inscribed: "1er ANNIVERSAIRE DE LA REVOLUTION/FETE NATIONALE/15 AOUT 1964"

1964, Aug. 15 Photo. *Perf. 13x12*
118 AP5 20fr lt bl, red, ocher, dk brn & grn .50 .20

1st anniv. of the revolution and Natl. Feast Day, Aug. 15.

Fire Squid A19

15fr, Johnson's deep-sea angler (fish).

1964, Oct. 20 Engr. *Perf. 13*
119 A19 2fr ver, lt grn & brn .50 .20
120 A19 15fr vio, lt ol grn & dp cl 2.25 1.10

Cooperation Issue
Common Design Type

1964, Nov. 7 Unwmk. *Perf. 13*
121 CD119 25fr car, brt grn & dk brn .60 .35

Communications Emblems — A20

1965, Jan. 1 Litho. *Perf. 12½x13*
122 A20 25fr ol, red brn & blk .50 .25

Issued to commemorate the establishment of the national postal administration.

Sitatunga — A21

Dancer on Stilts — A22

Design: 20fr, Elephant, horiz.

1965, Mar. 15 Engr. *Perf. 13*
123 A21 15fr redsh brn, dl grn & bl .90 .40
124 A21 20fr blk, dp bl & sl grn .90 .40
125 A22 85fr lil & multi 3.50 1.50
Nos. 123-125 (3) 5.30 2.30

Pres. Alphonse Massamba-Debat A23

1965-66 Photo. *Perf. 12x12½*
126 A23 20fr dk brn, grn & yel .25 .20
127 A23 25fr brn, bl grn, emer & blk ('66) .30 .20

128 A23 30fr brn, bl grn, org & blk ('66) .45 .20
Nos. 126-128 (3) 1.00 .60

Soccer Player
A24

Designs: 25fr, Games' emblem (map of Africa and runners). 50fr, Field ball player. 85fr, Runner. 100fr, Bicyclist.

1965, July 17 Photo. *Perf. 12½*

Size: 28x28mm

129 A24 25fr blk, red, yel & grn .50 .30

Size: 34x34mm

130 A24 40fr yel grn & multi .70 .45
131 A24 50fr red & multi .70 .45
132 A24 85fr blk & multi 1.25 .65
133 A24 100fr yel & multi 1.75 .75
a. Min. sheet of 5, #129-133 7.50 7.50
Nos. 129-133 (5) 4.90 2.60

1st African Games, Brazzaville, July 18-25.

Arms of Congo — A25

1965, Nov. 15 Litho. *Perf. 12½x13*
134 A25 20fr multicolored .50 .20

Cooperative Village
A26

30fr, Gymnastic drill team with streamers.

1966, Feb. 18 *Perf. 12½x13*
135 A26 25fr multicolored .50 .25
136 A26 30fr multicolored .50 .30

Sculptured Mask — A27

Designs: 30fr, Weaver, painting. 85fr, String instrument, painting, horiz.

Perf. 13x12½, 12½x13

1966, Apr. 9 Photo.
137 A27 30fr multicolored .70 .30
138 A27 85fr multicolored 1.90 .70
139 A27 90fr multicolored 2.25 1.00
Nos. 137-139 (3) 4.85 2.00

Intl. Negro Arts Festival, Dakar, Senegal, 4/1-24.

Men and Clocks
A28

1966, Apr. 15 *Perf. 12½x12*
140 A28 70fr pale brn, ocher & dk brn 1.00 .30

Introduction of the shorter work day (less lunch time, earlier quitting time).

WHO Headquarters, Geneva — A29

1966, May 3 Photo. *Perf. 12½x13*
141 A29 50fr org yel, vio & bl .80 .40

Inauguration of the WHO Headquarters, Geneva.

Church of St. Peter Claver
A30

Women's Basketball
A31

1966, June 15 Photo. *Perf. 13x12½*
142 A30 70fr multicolored 1.00 .40

1966, July 15 Engr. *Perf. 13*

Sport: 1fr, Women's volleyball, horiz. 3fr, Women's field ball, horiz. 5fr, Athletes of various races. 10fr, Torch bearer. 15fr, Soccer and gold medal of First African Games.

143 A31 1fr ultra, choc & ol .20 .20
144 A31 2fr choc, grn & bl .25 .20
145 A31 3fr dk grn, dk car & choc .25 .20
146 A31 5fr slate, emer & choc .25 .20
147 A31 10fr dl bl, dk grn & vio .45 .20
148 A31 15fr vio, car & choc .50 .30
Nos. 143-148 (6) 1.90 1.30

Jules Rimet Cup and Globe
A32

1966, July 15 Photo. *Perf. 12½x12*
149 A32 30fr brt red, gold, blk & bl .90 .45

8th World Soccer Cup Championship, Wembley, England, July 11-30.

Savorgnan de Brazza School
A33

1966, Sept. 15 Photo. *Perf. 12½x12*
150 A33 30fr dk pur, grn, yel & blk .60 .25

Pointe-Noire Railroad Station — A34

1966, Oct. 15 Engr. *Perf. 13*
151 A34 60fr grn, red & brn 1.25 .60

Student with Microscope
A35

Balumbu Mask
A36

1966, Nov. 28 Engr. *Perf. 13*
152 A35 90fr brn, grn & ind 1.25 .70

20th anniv. of UNESCO.

1966, Dec. 12 Engr. *Perf. 13*

Masks: 10fr, Kuyu. 15fr, Bakwélé. 20fr, Batéké.

153 A36 5fr car rose & dk brn .45 .20
154 A36 10fr Prus bl & brn .50 .20
155 A36 15fr sep, dl org & dk bl .60 .20
156 A36 20fr dp bl & multi .80 .20
Nos. 153-156 (4) 2.35 .80

Order of the Revolution and Map — A37

Learning the Alphabet
A38

Design: 45fr, Harvesting and loading sugar cane, and sugar mill.

Perf. 12x12½, 12½x12

1967, Mar. 15 Photo.
157 A37 20fr org & multi .50 .30
158 A38 25fr blk, ocher & dk car .60 .35
159 A38 45fr blk, yel grn & lt bl 1.00 .30
Nos. 157-159 (3) 2.10 .95

Issued to honor the members of the Order of the Revolution (20fr); to publicize the literacy campaign (25fr); to publicize, sugar production (45fr).

Mahatma Gandhi — A39

Fruit Vendor — A40

1967, Apr. 21 Engr. *Perf. 13*
160 A39 90fr bl & blk 2.25 .75

Issued in memory of Mohandas K. Gandhi (1869-1948), Hindu nationalist leader.

1967, June Photo. *Perf. 13x12½*

Dolls: 5fr, "Elegant Lady." 25fr, Woman pounding saka-saka. 30fr, Mother and child.

161 A40 5fr gold & multi .25 .20
162 A40 10fr yel grn & multi .45 .20
163 A40 25fr lt ultra & multi .50 .20
164 A40 30fr multicolored .60 .20
Nos. 161-164 (4) 1.80 .80

ITY Emblem, Village and Waterfall
A41

1967, July 5 Engr. *Perf. 13*
165 A41 60fr rose cl, org & ol grn .70 .40

Issued for International Tourist Year, 1967.

Symbols of Cooperation
A42

Arms of Brazzaville
A43

Europafrica Issue, 1967

1967, July 20 Photo. *Perf. 12x12½*
166 A42 50fr multicolored .90 .30

1967, Aug. 15 Litho. *Perf. 12½x13*
167 A43 30fr yel & multi .60 .35

Fourth anniversary of the revolution.

UN Emblem, Dove and People — A44

Boy and UNICEF Emblem — A45

1967, Oct. 24 Photo. *Perf. 13x12½*
168 A44 90fr bl, dk brn, red brn & yel 1.60 .60

Issued for United Nations Day, Oct. 24.

1967, Dec. 11 Engr. *Perf. 13*
169 A45 90fr mar, blk & ultra 1.60 .60

21st anniv. of UNICEF.

Albert Luthuli, Dove and Globe
A46

1968, Jan. 29 Engr. *Perf. 13*
170 A46 30fr brt grn & ol bis .60 .35

Albert Luthuli (1899-1967) of South Africa, winner of 1960 Nobel Peace Prize.

Arms of Pointe Noire — A47

1968, Feb. 20 Litho. *Perf. 12½x13*
171 A47 10fr brt pink & multi .50 .30

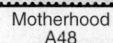

Motherhood
A48

Mayombe
Viaduct
A49

1968, May 25 **Engr.** ***Perf. 13***

172 A48 15fr dk car rose, sky bl & blk .50 .30

Issued for Mother's Day.

1968, June 24

173 A49 45fr maroon, slate grn & bl 1.75 .45

A50

1968, July 29 **Photo.** ***Perf. 13x12½***

174 A50 5fr Daimler, 1889 .45 .20
175 A50 20fr Berliet, 1897 .90 .30
176 A50 60fr Peugeot, 1898 1.75 .40
177 A50 80fr Renault, 1900 2.75 .70
178 A50 85fr Fiat, 1902 3.25 .90
Nos. 174-178,C67-C68 (7) 17.85 6.00

Tanker, Refinery and Map of Area Served — A50a

1968, July 30 ***Perf. 12½***

179 A50a 30fr multicolored .80 .30

Issued to commemorate the opening of the Port Gentil (Gabon) Refinery, June 12, 1968.

WHO Emblem and Tree of Life — A51

1968, Nov. 28 **Engr.** ***Perf. 13***

180 A51 25fr dk grn, red & dp lil .50 .30

20th anniv. of WHO.

Development Bank Issue

Common Design Type

1969, Sept. 10 **Engr.** ***Perf. 13***

181 CD130 25fr car rose, grn & ocher .35 .20
182 CD130 30fr bl, grn & ocher .35 .20

Bicycle
A52

Bicycles & Motorcycles: 75fr, Hirondelle. 80fr, Folding bicycle. 85fr, Peugeot. 100fr, Excelsior Manxman. 150fr, Norton. 200fr, Brough Superior "Old Bill." 300fr, Matchless and N.L.G.-J.A.P.S.

1969, Oct. 6 **Engr.** ***Perf. 13***

183 A52 50fr multicolored 1.25 .30
184 A52 75fr multicolored 1.50 .30
185 A52 80fr multicolored 1.75 .40
186 A52 85fr multicolored 2.00 .50
187 A52 100fr multicolored 3.00 .85
188 A52 150fr multicolored 4.00 1.00
189 A52 200fr multicolored 5.25 1.75
190 A52 300fr multicolored 9.50 2.75
Nos. 183-190 (8) 28.25 7.85

Mayombe Train and Tourist Year Emblem
A53

40fr, Train and Mbamba Tunnel, vert.

Perf. 13x12½, 12½x13

1969, Oct. 20 **Photo.**

191 A53 40fr multicolored 1.50 .40
192 A53 60fr multicolored 2.50 .65

Issued for African Tourist Year.

Loutete Cement Works
A54

Loutete Cement Works: 15fr, Mixing tower, vert. 25fr, Cable transport, vert. 30fr, General view of plant.

1969, Dec. 10 **Engr.** ***Perf. 13***

193 A54 10fr dk gray, rose cl & dk ol .25 .20
194 A54 15fr Prus bl, red brn & pur .50 .20
195 A54 25fr mar, brn & Prus bl .60 .20
196 A54 30fr vio brn, ultra & blk .70 .20
a. Min. sheet of 4, #193-196 2.75 2.75
Nos. 193-196 (4) 2.05 .80

ASECNA Issue

Common Design Type

1969, Dec. 12

197 CD132 100fr dull brown 1.60 .40

Pineapple Harvest and ILO Emblem
A55

30fr, Worker at lathe and ILO emblem.

1969, Dec. 20 **Engr.** ***Perf. 13***

198 A55 25fr bl, olive & brn .35 .25
199 A55 30fr rose red, choc & slate .50 .25

50th anniv. of the ILO.

SOTEXCO Textile Plant, Kinsoundi
A56

20fr, Women in spinnery. 25fr, Hand-printing textiles. 30fr, Checking woven cloth.

1970, Jan. 20

200 A56 15fr grn, blk & lil .45 .20
201 A56 20fr plum, car & sl grn .45 .20
202 A56 25fr bl, slate & brn .60 .20
203 A56 30fr gray, car rose & brn .60 .25
Nos. 200-203 (4) 2.10 .85

Hotel Cosmos, Brazzaville
A57

1970, Jan. 30

204 A57 90fr slate grn, bl & red brn 1.25 .30

The status of the three sets for Kennedy, etc., Summer Olympics, and Baroque paintings is not certain.

Linzolo Church — A58

Diosso Gorge
A59

Design: 90fr, Foulakari waterfall.

1970 **Engr.** ***Perf. 13***

205 A58 25fr multicolored .60 .20
206 A59 70fr multicolored 1.50 .30
207 A59 90fr multicolored 2.25 .40
Nos. 205-207 (3) 4.35 .90

Issue dates: 25fr, Feb. 10; others, Feb. 25.

Volvaria Esculenta — A60

Mushrooms: 10fr, Termitomyces entolomoides. 15fr, Termitomyces microcarpus. 25fr, Termitomyces aurantiacus. 30fr, Termitomyces mammiformis. 50fr, Tremella fuciformis.

1970, Mar. 31 **Photo.** ***Perf. 13***

208 A60 5fr multicolored 6.75 1.00
209 A60 10fr multicolored 9.00 1.40
210 A60 15fr multicolored 13.50 2.00
211 A60 25fr multicolored 22.50 4.00
212 A60 30fr multicolored 32.50 5.75
213 A60 50fr multicolored 70.00 10.00
Nos. 208-213 (6) 154.25 24.15

Laying Coaxial Cable
A61

Design: 30fr, Full view of rail car; 3 cable layers on railway roadbed.

1970, Apr. 30 **Engr.** ***Perf. 13***

214 A61 25fr dk brn & multi 1.00 .30
215 A61 30fr brn & multi 1.10 .60

Issued to publicize the laying of the coaxial cable linking Brazzaville and Pointe Noire.

For surcharges see Nos. 263-264.

UPU Headquarters Issue

Common Design Type

1970, May 20

216 CD133 30fr dk pur, gray & mag .70 .25

Mother Feeding Child — A62

Dag Hammarskjold, UN Emblem — A63

Design: 90fr, Mother nursing infant.

1970, May 30 **Photo.**

217 A62 85fr vio bl & multi 1.00 .30
218 A62 90fr lil & multi 1.10 .40

Issued for Mother's Day.

1970, June 20 **Engr.** ***Perf. 13***

UN Emblem and: No. 220, Trygve Lie, horiz. No. 221, U Thant, horiz.

219 A63 100fr scar, dk red & dk pur 1.40 .80
220 A63 100fr dk red, ultra & ind 1.40 .80
221 A63 100fr grn, emer & dk red 1.40 .80
a. Souv. sheet of 3, #219-221 5.50 5.50
Nos. 219-221 (3) 4.20 2.40

25th anniv. of the UN and to honor its Secretaries General.

Brillantaisia Vogeliana
A64

Sternotomis Variabilis — A65

Plants and Beetles: 2fr, Plectranthus decurrens. 3fr, Myrianthemum mirabile. 5fr, Connarus griffonianus. 15fr, Chelorrhina polyphemus. 20fr, Metopodontus savagei.

Perf. 12½x12, 12x12½

1970, June 30 **Photo.**

222 A64 1fr dk grn & multi .45 .25
223 A64 2fr multicolored .45 .25
224 A64 3fr indigo & multi .50 .25
225 A64 5fr lemon & multi 1.00 .25
226 A65 10fr lilac & multi 2.25 .40
227 A65 15fr orange & multi 3.00 .40
228 A65 20fr multicolored 3.25 .60
Nos. 222-228 (7) 10.90 2.40

For surcharge see No. 288.

Stegosaurus — A66

Prehistoric Fauna: 20fr, Dinotherium, vert. 60fr, Brachiosaurus, vert. 80fr, Arsinoitherium.

1970, July 20

229 A66 15fr dl grn, ocher & red brn .80 .30
230 A66 20fr lt bl & multi 2.75 .65
231 A66 60fr lt bl & multi 5.75 .95
232 A66 80fr lt bl & multi 7.50 1.75
Nos. 229-232 (4) 16.80 3.65

Mikado 141, 1932
A67

Locomotives: 60fr, Steam locomotive 130+032, 1947. 75fr, Alsthom BB 1100, 1962. 85fr, Diesel BB BB 302, 1969.

1970, Aug. 20 Engr. *Perf. 13*

233 A67 40fr mag, bl grn & blk	2.75	.80
234 A67 60fr blk, bl & grn	3.00	.90
235 A67 75fr red, bl & blk	4.50	1.25
236 A67 85fr car, sl grn & ocher	7.00	1.75
Nos. 233-236 (4)	17.25	4.70

Cogniauxia Padolaena A68

Green Night Adder A69

Tropical Flowers: 2fr, Celosia cristata. 5fr, Plumeria acutifolia. 10fr, Bauhinia variegata. 15fr, Poinsettia. 20fr, Thunbergia grandiflora.

1971, Feb. 10 Photo. *Perf. 12x12½*

237 A68 1fr lil & multi	.25	.20
238 A68 2fr yel & multi	.25	.20
239 A68 5fr ultra & multi	.25	.20
240 A68 10fr yel & multi	1.10	.20
241 A68 15fr multicolored	1.60	.30
242 A68 20fr dk red & multi	2.75	.40
Nos. 237-242 (6)	6.20	1.50

Perf. 12x12½, 12½x12

1971, June 26 Photo.

Reptiles: 10fr, African Egg-eating snake, horiz. 15fr, Flap-necked chameleon. 20fr, Nile crocodile, horiz. 25fr, Rock python, horiz. 30fr, Gaboon viper. 40fr, Brown house snake, horiz. 45fr, Jameson's mamba.

243 A69 5fr multicolored	.40	.20
244 A69 10fr multicolored	.40	.20
245 A69 15fr multicolored	1.40	.20
246 A69 20fr red & multi	2.25	.25
247 A69 25fr grn & multi	3.00	.35
248 A69 30fr multicolored	3.75	.75
249 A69 40fr bis & multi	4.25	.95
250 A69 45fr multicolored	5.75	1.00
Nos. 243-250 (8)	21.20	3.90

Pseudimbrasia Deyrollei — A70

Caterpillars: 15fr, Bunaea alcinoe, vert. 20fr, Epiphora vacuna ploetzi. 25fr, Imbrasia eblis. 30fr, Imbrasia dione, vert. 40fr, Holocera angulata.

1971, July 3 *Perf. 13*

251 A70 10fr ver, blk & grn	1.00	.20
252 A70 15fr multicolored	1.50	.30
253 A70 20fr yel grn, blk & ocher	2.25	.40
254 A70 25fr multicolored	3.50	.60
255 A70 30fr red, blk & yel	5.00	.90
256 A70 40fr bl, blk & org	6.75	1.25
Nos. 251-256 (6)	20.00	3.65

Boy Scout — A70a

Scouts, Lord Baden-Powell — A70b

Designs: c, Scout facing left. d, Scout facing forward. e, Lord Baden-Powell.

Embossed on Metallic Foil

1971, July 14 *Die Cut Perf. 10½*

256A A70a 90fr Block of 4, #b.-e, silver	*10.00*	*10.00*
256F A70b 1000fr gold	*30.00*	*30.00*

No. 256F is airmail.

Cymothoe Sangaris A71

Butterflies and Moths: 40fr, Papilio dardanus, vert. 75fr, Iolaus timon. 90fr, Papilio phorcas, vert. 100fr, Euchloron megaera.

1971, Oct. 15 *Perf. 12½x12, 12x12½*

257 A71 30fr yel & multi	1.75	.40
258 A71 40fr grn & multi	3.25	.65
259 A71 75fr multicolored	5.25	1.25
260 A71 90fr multicolored	7.00	1.90
261 A71 100fr ultra & multi	9.50	2.50
Nos. 257-261 (5)	26.75	6.70

Black and White Men Working Together — A72

1971, Oct. 30 *Perf. 13x12½*

262 A72 50fr org & multi	.65	.35

Intl. Year Against Racial Discrimination.

Nos. 214-215 Surcharged

1971, Nov. 18 Engr. *Perf. 13*

263 A61 30fr on 25fr multicolored	.50	.30
264 A61 40fr on 30fr multicolored	.75	.35

Inauguration of cable service between Brazzaville and Pointe Noire. Words of surcharge arranged differently on No. 264.

Map of Congo — A73

1971, Dec. 31 Photo. *Perf. 12½x13*

265 A73 30fr bl & multi	.35	.20
266 A73 40fr yel grn & multi	.45	.20
267 A73 100fr gray & multi	1.10	.40
Nos. 265-267 (3)	1.90	.80

"Labor, Democracy, Peace."

Lion — A74

2fr, African elephants. 3fr, Leopard. 4fr, Hippopotamus. 5fr, Gorilla, vert. 20fr, Potto. 30fr, De Brazza's monkey. 40fr, Pygmy chimpanzee, vert.

1972, Jan. 31 Engr. *Perf. 13*

268 A74 1fr grn & multi	.35	.20
269 A74 2fr dk red & multi	.50	.20
270 A74 3fr red brn & multi	.80	.20
271 A74 4fr vio & multi	1.00	.20
272 A74 5fr brn & multi	1.10	.25
273 A74 20fr org & multi	2.75	.35
274 A74 30fr ocher & multi	3.50	.45
275 A74 40fr Prus bl & multi	5.25	.75
Nos. 268-275 (8)	15.25	2.60

WHO, 25th Anniv. — A75

Perf. 12½x13, 13x12½

1973, June 30 Typo.

276 A75 40fr WHO Emblem	.60	.20
277 A75 50fr WHO emblem, horiz.	.70	.20

Kronenbourg Brewery — A76

Brewery Trademark and: 40fr, Laboratory. 75fr, Vats and controls. 85fr, Automatic control room. 100fr, Pressure room. 250fr, Bottling plant.

1973, July 15 Engr. *Perf. 13*

278 A76 30fr red & multi	.50	.20
279 A76 40fr red & multi	.60	.20
280 A76 75fr red & multi	1.00	.30
281 A76 85fr red & multi	1.50	.40
282 A76 100fr red & multi	1.60	.55
283 A76 250fr red & multi	3.25	1.00
Nos. 278-283 (6)	8.45	2.65

Kronenbourg Brewery, Brazzaville.

Golwe Locomotive, 1935 — A77

Locomotives: 40fr, Diesel, 1935. 75fr, Diesel Whithcomb, 1946. 85fr, Diesel CC200.

1973, Aug. 1 Engr. *Perf. 13*

284 A77 30fr indigo & multi	2.00	.50
285 A77 40fr vio bl & multi	3.00	.85
286 A77 75fr multicolored	4.25	1.50
287 A77 85fr multicolored	5.50	2.75
Nos. 284-287 (4)	14.75	5.60

No. 225 Surcharged with New Value, 2 Bars, and Overprinted in Ultramarine: "SECHERESSE SOLIDARITE AFRICAINE"

1973, Aug. 16 Photo. *Perf. 12½x12*

288 A64 100fr on 5fr multicolored	1.75	.60

African solidarity in drought emergency.

African Postal Union Issue

Common Design Type

1973, Sept. 12 Engr. *Perf. 13*

289 CD137 100fr bl grn, vio & brn	1.50	.45

Bees, Beehive, Honeycomb A78

1973, Dec. 10 Engr. *Perf. 13*

290 A78 30fr sl grn, dk red & bl	1.10	.20
291 A78 40fr sl bl, sl grn & lt grn	1.50	.20

"Work and economy."

Family, UN and FAO Emblems A79

40fr, Grain, emblems. 100fr, Grain, emblems, vert.

1973, Dec. 10

292 A79 30fr dk car & dk brn	.50	.20
293 A79 40fr dk grn, yel & ind	.60	.20
294 A79 100fr grn, brn & org	1.40	.40
Nos. 292-294 (3)	2.50	.80

World Food Program, 10th anniversary.

Amilcar Cabral, Cattle and Child — A80

1974, July 15 Engr. *Perf. 13*

295 A80 100fr multicolored	1.00	.60

First death anniversary of Amilcar Cabral (1924-1973), leader of anti-Portuguese guerrilla activity in Portuguese Guinea.

Félix Eboué, Cross of Lorraine
A81

1974, Aug. 31 **Litho.** ***Perf. 13***
296 A81 30fr bl & multi .60 .30
297 A81 40fr brt pink & multi 1.00 .60

Félix A. Eboué (1884-1944), Governor of Chad, first colonial governor to join Free French in WWII, 30th death anniversary.

Pineapples
A82

1974, Nov. 12
298 A82 30fr shown .60 .30
299 A82 30fr Bananas .70 .30
300 A82 30fr Safous .70 .30
301 A82 40fr Avocados 1.25 .30
302 A82 40fr Mangos 1.25 .30
303 A82 40fr Papaya 1.25 .30
304 A82 40fr Orange 1.25 .30
Nos. 298-304 (7) 7.00 2.10

Charles de Gaulle and Conference Building — A83

1974, Nov. 25 **Engr.** ***Perf. 13***
305 A83 100fr multicolored 3.25 1.90

Brazzaville Conference, 25th anniversary.

George Stephenson and Various Locomotives — A84

1974, Dec. 15
306 A84 75fr slate green & olive 4.00 1.00

George Stephenson (1781-1848), English inventor and railroad founder.

UDEAC Issue

Presidents and Flags of Cameroun, CAR, Congo, Gabon and Meeting Center — A84a

1974, Dec. 8 **Photo.** ***Perf. 13***
307 A84a 40fr gold & multi .60 .20

See note after Cameroun No. 595.
See No. C195.

Irish Setter
A85

1974, Dec. 15 **Photo.** ***Perf. 13x13½***
308 A85 30fr shown 1.25 .30
309 A85 40fr Borzoi 1.50 .30
310 A85 75fr Pointer 3.25 .75
311 A85 100fr Great Dane 4.50 .80
Nos. 308-311 (4) 10.50 2.15

1974, Dec. 15

Designs: Cats.

312 A85 30fr Havana chestnut 1.25 .30
313 A85 40fr Red Persian 1.50 .30
314 A85 75fr Blue British 3.25 .75
315 A85 100fr African serval 4.50 .80
Nos. 312-315 (4) 10.50 2.15

Labor Party Flags and People
A86

40fr, Hands holding flowers and tools.

1974, Dec. 31 **Engr.** ***Perf. 13x12½***
316 A86 30fr red & multi .50 .20
317 A86 40fr red & multi .60 .25

5th anniversary of Congolese Labor Party and of introduction of red flag.

Symbols of Development — A87

U Thant and UN Headquarters — A88

Paul G. Hoffman and UN Emblem
A89

Perf. 13x12½, 12½x13
1975, Feb. 28 **Litho.**
318 A87 40fr multicolored .60 .25
319 A88 50fr light blue & multi .60 .25
320 A89 50fr yellow & multi .60 .25
Nos. 318-320 (3) 1.80 .75

National economic development.

Map of China and Mao Tse-tung — A90

1975, Mar. 9 **Engr.** ***Perf. 13***
321 A90 75fr multicolored 4.50 1.50

25th anniv. of the PRC.

Woman Breaking Bonds, Women's Activities, Map of Congo
A91

1975, June 20 **Litho.** ***Perf. 12½***
322 A91 40fr gold & multi .60 .25

Revolutionary Union of Congolese Women, URFC, 10th anniversary.

CARA Soccer Team — A92

Design: 40fr, Team captain and manager receiving trophy, vert.

1975, July 15 **Litho.** ***Perf. 12½***
323 A92 30fr multicolored .50 .25
324 A92 40fr multicolored .60 .25

CARA team, winners of African Soccer Cup 1974.

Citroen, 1935 — A93

Designs: Early autombiles.

1975, July 17 ***Perf. 12***
325 A93 30fr shown .90 .40
326 A93 40fr Alfa Romeo, 1911 1.10 .40
327 A93 50fr Rolls Royce, 1926 1.40 .55
328 A93 75fr Duryea, 1893 2.75 .70
Nos. 325-328 (4) 6.15 2.05

Tipoyc Transport — A94

1975, Aug. 5
329 A94 30fr shown .90 .40
330 A94 40fr Dugout canoe 1.00 .65

Traditional means of transportation.

Raising Red Flag — A95

1975, Aug. 15
331 A95 30fr shown .50 .20
332 A95 40fr National Conference .60 .25

2nd anniv. of installation of popular power (30fr) and 3rd anniv. of Natl. Conf. (40fr).

Line Fishing — A96

Woman Pounding "Foufou" — A97

Traditional Fishing: 30fr, Trap fishing, horiz. 60fr, Spear fishing. 90fr, Net fishing, horiz.

1975, Aug. 31 **Litho.** ***Perf. 12***
333 A96 30fr multicolored .80 .25
334 A96 40fr multicolored .80 .30
335 A96 60fr multicolored 1.25 .50
336 A96 90fr multicolored 2.50 1.00
Nos. 333-336 (4) 5.35 2.05

1975, Sept. 5

Household Tasks: No. 338, Woman chopping wood. 40fr, Woman preparing manioc, horiz.

337 A97 30fr multicolored .60 .20
338 A97 30fr multicolored .60 .20
339 A97 40fr multicolored .90 .25
Nos. 337-339 (3) 2.10 .65

Musical Instruments
A98

1975, Sept. 20 ***Perf. 12½***
340 A98 30fr Esanga .75 .20
341 A98 40fr Kalakwa 1.25 .25
342 A98 60fr Likembe 1.50 .30
343 A98 75fr Ngongui 2.00 .40
Nos. 340-343 (4) 5.50 1.15

Dzeke (Congolese) Shell Money — A99

Ancient Money: No. 346, like No. 344. Nos. 345, 347, Okengo, Congolese, iron bar. 40fr, Gallic coin, c. 60 B.C. 50fr, Roman denarius, 37 B.C. 60fr, Danubian coin, 2nd cent. B.C. 85fr, Greek stater, 4th cent. B.C.

1975-76 Engr. *Perf. 13*

344 A99 30fr red & multi .60 .20
345 A99 30fr vio & multi .60 .20
346 A99 35fr ol & multi .90 .25
347 A99 35fr dk car rose & multi .90 .25
348 A99 40fr Prus bl & brn .90 .20
349 A99 50fr Prus bl & ol 1.00 .30
350 A99 60fr dk grn & brn 1.25 .35
351 A99 85fr mag & sl grn 2.10 .45
Nos. 344-351 (8) 8.25 2.20

Nos. 346-347 inscribed "1976" and issued Mar. 1976; others issued Oct. 5, 1975.

Moschops — A100

Pre-historic Animals: 70fr, Tyrannosaurus. 95fr, Cryptocleidus. 100fr, Stegosaurus.

1975, Oct. 15 Litho. *Perf. 13*

352 A100 55fr multicolored 2.25 .30
353 A100 75fr multicolored 3.25 .35
354 A100 95fr multicolored 5.75 .75
355 A100 100fr multicolored 8.00 1.25
Nos. 352-355 (4) 19.25 2.65

Albert Schweitzer (1875-1965), Medical Missionary — A101

1975, Oct. 15 Engr.

356 A101 75fr ol, brn & red 1.50 .40

Alexander Fleming A102

Designs: No. 358, André Marie Ampère. No. 359, Clement Ader.

1975, Nov. 15 Engr. *Perf. 13*

357 A102 60fr brn, grn & blk 1.00 .30
358 A102 95fr blk, red & grn 1.40 .40
359 A102 95fr red, blue & indigo 1.60 .40
Nos. 357-359 (3) 4.00 1.10

Fleming (1881-1955), developer of penicillin; Ampère (1775-1836), physicist; Ader (1841-1925), aviation pioneer.

UN Emblem "ONU" and "30" — A103

1975, Dec. 20 Engr. *Perf. 13*

360 A103 95fr car, ultra & grn 1.25 .45

United Nations, 30th anniversary.

Women's Broken Chain — A104

Design: 60fr, Equality between man and woman, globe, IWY emblem.

1975, Dec. 20 Litho. *Perf. 12½*

361 A104 35fr mag, ocher & gray .60 .20
362 A104 60fr ultra, brn & blk .70 .30

International Women's Year, 1975.

Pres. Marien Ngouabi, Flag and Workers — A105

Echo of the P.C.T. A106

1975, Dec. 31 *Perf. 12½x12, 13x12½*

363 A105 30fr multicolored .50 .20
364 A106 35fr multicolored .50 .20

6th anniversary of the Congolese Labor Party (P.C.T.). See No. C215.

A.G. Bell and 1876 Telephone A107

1976, Apr. 25 Litho. *Perf. 12½x13*

365 A107 35fr yel, brn & org brn .50 .20

Cent. of 1st telephone call by Alexander Graham Bell, Mar. 10, 1876. See No. C229.

Women Selling Fruit and Vegetables A108

1976, Sept. 19 Litho. *Perf. 12½x13*

366 A108 35fr shown .50 .20
367 A108 60fr Market scene 1.00 .30

Congolese Coiffure — A109

Designs: Various women's hair styles.

1976, Oct. 10 Litho. *Perf. 13*

368 A109 35fr multicolored .60 .20
369 A109 60fr multicolored 1.00 .25
370 A109 95fr multicolored 1.50 .35
371 A109 100fr multicolored 2.00 .40
Nos. 368-371 (4) 5.10 1.20

Pole Vault, Map of Central Africa A110

95fr, Long jump and map of Central Africa.

1976, Oct. 25 *Perf. 12½*

372 A110 60fr yel & multi .70 .25
373 A110 95fr yel & multi 1.25 .40
Nos. 372-373,C230-C231 (4) 6.45 2.50

Gold medalists, 1st Central African Games, Yaoundé, July 27-30, 1975.

Antelope A111

1976, Oct. 27 Litho. *Perf. 12½*

Size: 36x36mm

374 A111 5fr shown .55 .20
375 A111 10fr Buffalos .65 .20
376 A111 15fr Hippopotamus 1.00 .30
377 A111 20fr Wart hog 2.00 .35
378 A111 25fr Elephants 2.25 .40
Nos. 374-378 (5) 6.45 1.45

1976, Dec. 8

Designs: Birds.

Size: 26x36mm

379 A111 5fr Saddle-bill storks 1.00 .25

Size: 36x36mm

380 A111 10fr Malachite kingfisher 1.25 .25
381 A111 20fr Crowned cranes 3.00 .60
Nos. 379-381 (3) 5.25 1.10

Bicycling, Map of Participants A112

Heliotrope A113

1976, Dec. 21 Photo. *Perf. 12½x13*

382 A112 35fr shown .35 .20
383 A112 60fr Fieldball .60 .25
384 A112 80fr Running 1.00 .35
385 A112 95fr Soccer 1.25 .40
Nos. 382-385 (4) 3.20 1.20

First Central African Games, Libreville, Gabon, June-July 1976.

1976, Dec. 23 Photo. *Perf. 12½x13*

Flowers: 5fr, Water lilies. 15fr, Bird-of-paradise flower.

386 A113 5fr multicolored .25 .20
387 A113 10fr multicolored .35 .20
388 A113 15fr multicolored .60 .20
Nos. 386-388 (3) 1.20 .60

Torch and Olive Branches A114

1976, Dec. 25 Litho. *Perf. 12½x13*

389 A114 35fr multicolored .45 .20

National Pioneer Movement.

The Spirit of '76 — A115

125fr, Pulling down George III statue. 150fr, Battle of Princeton. 175fr, Generals of Revolutionary War. 200fr, Burgoyne's surrender at Saratoga. 500fr, Battle of Lexington.

1976, Dec. 29 Litho. *Perf. 14*

390 A115 100fr multicolored 1.00 .25
391 A115 125fr multicolored 1.10 .35
392 A115 150fr multicolored 1.60 .40
393 A115 175fr multicolored 2.00 .50
394 A115 200fr multicolored 2.25 .60
Nos. 390-394 (5) 7.95 2.10

Souvenir Sheet

395 A115 500fr multicolored 5.75 1.50

American Bicentennial.

Dugout Canoe Race A116

Design: 60fr, 2-man dugout canoes.

1977, Mar. 27 Litho. *Perf. 13x13½*

396 A116 35fr multicolored .60 .20
397 A116 60fr multicolored 1.00 .35

Dugout canoe races on Congo River.

Lilan Goua A117

Fresh-water Fish: 15fr, Liko ko. 25fr, Liyanga. 35fr, Mbessi. 60fr, Mongandza.

1977, June 15 Litho. *Perf. 12½*

398	A117	10fr multicolored	.75	.20
399	A117	15fr multicolored	.90	.20
400	A117	25fr multicolored	1.00	.20
401	A117	35fr multicolored	2.00	.30
402	A117	60fr multicolored	3.00	.45
		Nos. 398-402 (5)	7.65	1.35

Traditional Headdress — A118

1977, June 30 Litho. *Perf. 12½*

403	A118	35fr shown	.45	.30
404	A118	60fr Leopard cap	.90	.35

See Nos. C234-C235.

Bondjo Wrestling A119

40fr, 50fr, Bondjo wrestling, diff. 40fr, horiz.

1977, July 15

405	A119	25fr multicolored	.50	.20
406	A119	40fr multicolored	.55	.20
407	A119	50fr multicolored	.65	.30
		Nos. 405-407 (3)	1.70	.70

"Schwaben" LZ 10, 1911 — A120

Zeppelins: 60fr, "Viktoria Luise." LZ 11, 1913. 100fr, LZ 120. 200fr, LZ 127. 300fr, "Graf Zeppelin II" LZ 130.

1977, Aug. 5 Litho. *Perf. 11*

408	A120	40fr multicolored	.50	.20
409	A120	60fr multicolored	.75	.25
410	A120	100fr multicolored	1.25	.30
411	A120	200fr multicolored	2.50	.60
412	A120	300fr multicolored	4.00	.95
		Nos. 408-412 (5)	9.00	2.30

History of the Zeppelin. Exist imperf. See No. C236.

Coat of Arms and Rising Sun A121

1977, Aug. 15

413	A121	40fr multicolored	.50	.20

14th anniversary of the revolution.

Victor Hugo and The Hunchback of Notre Dame — A122

Designs (Hugo and): 60fr, Les Miserables. 100fr, Les Travailleurs de la Mer (octopus).

1977, Aug. 20 Engr. *Perf. 13*

414	A122	35fr multicolored	.75	.30
415	A122	60fr multicolored	1.00	.30
416	A122	100fr multicolored	1.50	.45
		Nos. 414-416 (3)	3.25	1.05

Victor Hugo (1802-1885), French novelist.

Mao Tse-tung A123

Lithographed; Gold Embossed

1977, Sept. 9 *Perf. 12x12½*

417	A123	400fr red & gold	7.50	5.50

Chairman Mao Tse-tung (1893-1976), Chinese Communist leader, 1st death anniv.

Peter Paul Rubens A124

1977, Sept. 20 Gold Embossed

418	A124	600fr gold & lt bl	10.00	5.00

Peter Paul Rubens (1577-1640), painter.

Child Leading Blind Woman Across Street A125

1977, Oct. 22 Litho. *Perf. 12½x13*

419	A125	35fr multicolored	.60	.25

World Health Day: To see is life.

Paul Kamba and Records A126

1977, Oct. 29

420	A126	100fr multicolored	1.00	.45

Paul Kamba (1912-1950), musician.

Trajan Vuia and Flying Machine — A127

Designs: 75fr, Louis Bleriot and plane. 100fr, Roland Garros and plane. 200fr, Charles Lindbergh and Spirit of St. Louis. 300fr, Tupolev Tu-144. 500fr, Lindbergh and Spirit of St. Louis over ship in Atlantic.

1977, Nov. 18 Litho. *Perf. 14*

421	A127	60fr multicolored	.60	.20
422	A127	75fr multicolored	.90	.25
423	A127	100fr multicolored	1.10	.30
424	A127	200fr multicolored	2.25	.50
425	A127	300fr multicolored	3.25	.70
		Nos. 421-425 (5)	8.10	1.95

Souvenir Sheet

426	A127	500fr multicolored	5.75	1.25

History of aviation.

Elizabeth II and Prince Philip A128

Design: 300fr, Elizabeth II wearing Crown.

1977, Dec. 21

427	A128	250fr multicolored	2.25	.65
428	A128	300fr multicolored	2.75	.70

Reign of Queen Elizabeth II, 25th anniv.
See #C239. For overprints see #468-469, C244.

King Baudouin A129

Design: No. 430, Charles de Gaulle.

1977, Dec. 21

429	A129	200fr multicolored	2.25	.65
430	A129	200fr multicolored	2.25	.65

King Baudouin of Belgium and Charles de Gaulle, president of France.

Ambete Sculpture A130

Congolese art: 85fr, Babembe sculpture.

1978, Feb. 18 Engr. *Perf. 13*

431	A130	35fr lt brn & multi	.65	.25
432	A130	85fr lt grn & multi	1.50	.45

St. Simon, by Rubens A131

Rubens Paintings: 140fr, Duke of Lerma. 200fr, Madonna and Saints. 300fr, Rubens and his Wife Helena Fourment. 500fr, Farm at Laeken.

1978, Mar. 7 Litho. *Perf. 13½x14*

433	A131	60fr gold & multi	.60	.20
434	A131	140fr gold & multi	1.50	.30
435	A131	200fr gold & multi	2.25	.45
436	A131	300fr gold & multi	3.50	.65
		Nos. 433-436 (4)	7.85	1.60

Souvenir Sheet

437	A131	500fr gold & multi	5.75	1.40

Peter Paul Rubens, 400th birth anniv.

Pres. Ngouabi and Microphones — A132

60fr, Ngouabi at his desk, horiz. 100fr, Portrait.

Perf. 12½x13, 13x12½

1978, Mar. 18 Litho.

438	A132	35fr multicolored	.45	.20
439	A132	60fr multicolored	.50	.25
440	A132	100fr multicolored	.90	.40
		Nos. 438-440 (3)	1.85	.85

Pres. Marien Ngouabi, 1st death anniv.

Ferenc Puskas and Argentina '78 Emblem — A133

Players and Emblem: 75fr, Giacinto Facchetti. 100fr, Bobby Moore. 200fr, Raymond Kopa. 300fr, Pele. 500fr, Franz Beckenbauer.

1978, Apr. 4 *Perf. 14x13½*

441	A133	60fr multicolored	.60	.20
442	A133	75fr multicolored	.70	.25
443	A133	100fr multicolored	1.10	.25
444	A133	200fr multicolored	2.25	.55
445	A133	300fr multicolored	3.25	.75
		Nos. 441-445 (5)	7.90	2.00

Souvenir Sheet

446	A133	500fr multicolored	6.25	1.25

11th World Cup Soccer Championship, Argentina, June 1-25.
For overprints see Nos. 481-486.

Pearl S. Buck and Chinese Women — A134

Nobel Prize winners: 75fr, Fridtjof Nansen, refugees and Nansen passport. 100fr, Henri Bergson, book and flame. 200fr, Alexander Fleming and Petri dish. 300fr, Gerhart Hauptmann and book. 500fr, Henri Dunant and Red Cross Station.

1978, Apr. 29

447 A134 60fr multicolored .60 .25
448 A134 75fr multicolored .70 .25
449 A134 100fr multicolored 1.10 .30
450 A134 200fr multicolored 2.00 .50
451 A134 300fr multicolored 2.75 .60
Nos. 447-451 (5) 7.15 1.90

Souvenir Sheet

452 A134 500fr multicolored 5.75 1.40

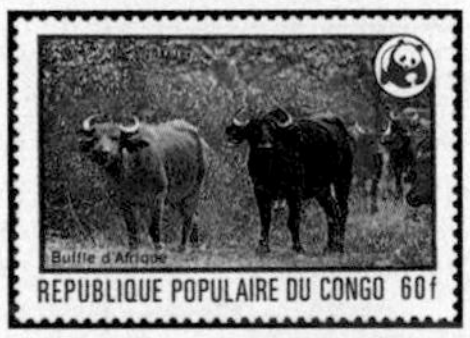

African Buffalos A135

Endangered animals and Wildlife Fund Emblem: 35fr, Okapi, vert. 85fr, Rhinoceros. 150fr, Chimpanzee, vert. 200fr, Hippopotamus. 300fr, Buffon's kob, vert.

1978 *Perf. 14½*

453 A135 35fr multicolored 1.00 .40
454 A135 60fr multicolored 1.50 .50
455 A135 85fr multicolored 3.75 .75
456 A135 150fr multicolored 5.50 1.00
457 A135 200fr multicolored 7.25 1.50
458 A135 300fr multicolored 13.50 2.25
Nos. 453-458 (6) 32.50 6.40

Issue dates: 35fr, Aug. 11; others, July 11.

Emblem, Young People, Gun and Fist — A136

1978, July 28 *Perf. 12½*

459 A136 35fr multicolored .50 .30

11th World Youth Festival, Havana, 7/28-8/5.

Pyramids and Camels — A137

Seven Wonders of the Ancient World: 50fr, Hanging Gardens of Babylon. 60fr, Statue of Zeus, Olympia. 95fr, Colossus of Rhodes. 125fr, Mausoleum of Halicarnassus. 150fr, Temple of Artemis, Ephesus. 200fr, Lighthouse, Alexandria. 300fr, Map of Eastern Mediterranean showing locations. 50fr, 60fr, 95fr, 125fr, 200fr, vertical.

1978, Aug. 12 **Litho.** *Perf. 14*

460 A137 35fr multicolored .50 .20
461 A137 50fr multicolored .60 .20
462 A137 60fr multicolored .75 .20
463 A137 95fr multicolored 1.00 .30
464 A137 125fr multicolored 1.25 .40
465 A137 150fr multicolored 1.50 .45
466 A137 200fr multicolored 2.00 .55
467 A137 300fr multicolored 2.75 .80
Nos. 460-467 (8) 10.35 3.10

Nos. 427-428 Overprinted in Silver: "ANNIVERSAIRE DU COURONNEMENT 1953-1978"

1978, Sept. **Litho.** *Perf. 14*

468 A128 250fr multicolored 2.25 .90
469 A128 300fr multicolored 2.75 1.25

25th anniversary of coronation of Queen Elizabeth II. See No. C244.

Kwame Nkrumah and Map of Africa — A138

1978, Sept. 23 **Litho.** *Perf. 13x12½*

470 A138 60fr multicolored .60 .40

Nkrumah (1909-72), Pres. of Ghana.

Wild Boar Hunt — A139

Local hunting and fishing: 50fr, Fish smoking. 60fr, Hunter with spears and dog, vert.

1978 **Litho.** *Perf. 12*

471 A139 35fr multicolored 2.00 .25
472 A139 50fr multicolored .60 .25
473 A139 60fr multicolored 3.00 .25
Nos. 471-473 (3) 5.60 .75

Issue dates: 35fr, 60fr, Oct. 5; 50fr, Oct. 10.

View of Kalchreut, by Dürer — A140

Paintings by Dürer: 150fr, Elspeth Tucher, vert. 250fr, "The Great Piece of Turf," vert. 350fr, Self-portrait, vert.

1978, Nov. 23 **Litho.** *Perf. 14*

474 A140 65fr multicolored .60 .20
475 A140 150fr multicolored 1.40 .35
476 A140 250fr multicolored 2.25 .65
477 A140 350fr multicolored 3.50 .90
Nos. 474-477 (4) 7.75 2.10

Albrecht Dürer (1471-1528), German painter.

Basketmaker A141

Productive Labor: 90fr, Woodcarver. 140fr, Women hoeing field.

1978, Nov. 18 **Litho.** *Perf. 12½*

Size: 25x36mm

478 A141 85fr multicolored .70 .40
479 A141 90fr multicolored 1.00 .40

Size: 27x48mm

Perf. 12

480 A141 140fr multicolored 1.50 .65
Nos. 478-480 (3) 3.20 1.45

Nos. 441-446 Overprinted in Silver:
a. "1962 VAINQUEUR: BRESIL"
b. "1966 VAINQUEUR: / GRANDE BRETAGNE"
c. "1970 VAINQUEUR: / BRESIL"
d. "1974 VAINQUEUR: / ALLEMAGNE (RFA)"
e. "1978 VAINQUEUR: / ARGENTINE"
f. "ARGENTINE-PAYS BAS 3-1/25 juin 1978"

1978, Nov. *Perf. 14x13½*

481 A133 (a) 60fr multicolored .60 .25
482 A133 (b) 75fr multicolored .70 .35
483 A133 (c) 100fr multicolored 1.00 .45
484 A133 (d) 200fr multicolored 2.00 .65
485 A133 (e) 300fr multicolored 2.75 1.00
Nos. 481-485 (5) 7.05 2.70

Souvenir Sheet

486 A133 (f) 500fr multicolored 5.75 2.40

Winners, World Soccer Cup Championships 1962-1978.

Heart and Charts A142

1978, Dec. 16 **Engr.** *Perf. 13*

487 A142 100fr multicolored 1.00 .45

Fight against hypertension.

Party Emblem and Road — A143

1978, Dec. 31 **Litho.** *Perf. 12½x12*

488 A143 60fr multicolored .60 .25

Congolese Labor Party, 9th anniversary.

Capt. Cook, Polynesians and House — A144

Capt. James Cook (1728-1779): 150fr, Island scene. 250fr, Polynesian longboats. 350fr, Capt. Cook's ships off Hawaii.

1979, Jan. 16 *Perf. 14½*

489 A144 65fr multicolored .60 .20
490 A144 150fr multicolored 1.40 .35
491 A144 250fr multicolored 2.25 .60
492 A144 350fr multicolored 3.50 1.00
Nos. 489-492 (4) 7.75 2.15

Pres. Marien Ngouabi — A145

1979, Mar. 18 **Litho.** *Perf. 12*

493 A145 35fr multicolored .35 .20
494 A145 60fr multicolored .50 .25

Assassination of President Ngouabi, 2nd anniv.

"1979," IYC Emblem, Child A146

A146a

1979, Apr. 30 **Litho.** *Perf. 12½x13*

495 A146 45fr multicolored .45 .20
496 A146 75fr multicolored .90 .35

Souvenir Sheet

Perf. 14½

496A A146a 250fr multicolored 2.75 1.00

International Year of the Child.
Issued: 45fr, 75fr, Apr. 30; 250fr, Sept. 5.

Pottery Vases and Solanum — A147

Design: 150fr, Mail runner, Concorde, train, UPU emblem, envelope.

1979, June 8 **Litho.** *Perf. 13*

497 A147 60fr multicolored 1.25 .60

Engr.

498 A147 150fr multicolored 2.75 1.25

Philexafrique II, Libreville, Gabon, June 8-17. Nos. 497, 498 each printed in sheets of 10 with 5 labels showing exhibition emblem.

Rowland Hill, Diesel Locomotive, Germany No. 78 — A148

Designs (Rowland Hill and): 100fr, Old steam locomotive and France No. B10. 200fr, Diesel locomotive and US No. 245. 300fr, Steam locomotive and England-Australia First Aerialpost vignette, 1919. 500fr, Electric train, Concorde and Middle Congo No. 75.

1979, June 30 *Perf. 14*

499 A148 65fr multicolored .60 .20
500 A148 100fr multicolored 1.00 .25
501 A148 200fr multicolored 2.25 .50
502 A148 300fr multicolored 2.75 .75
Nos. 499-502 (4) 6.60 1.70

Souvenir Sheet

503 A148 500fr multicolored 5.75 1.25

Sir Rowland Hill (1795-1879), originator of penny postage.

Salvador Allende, Flags, Demonstrators — A149

1979, July 21 Litho. ***Perf. 12½***
504 A149 100fr multicolored 1.00 .45

Salvador Allende, president of Chile.

Old Man Telling Stories — A150

1979, July 28
505 A150 45fr multicolored .60 .25

Story telling as education.

Handball Players A151

75fr, Players and ball. 250fr, Pres. Ngouabi, cup on map of Africa, player.

1979, July 31 Litho. ***Perf. 12½***
Size: 40x30mm, 30x40mm
506 A151 45fr multi .60 .20
507 A151 75fr multi, vert. 1.00 .25

Size: 22x40mm
Perf. 12x12½
508 A151 250fr multicolored 2.75 1.00

Marien Ngouabi Handball Cup.

Map and Flag of Congo — A152

1979, Aug. 15
509 A152 50fr multicolored .45 .25

16th anniversary of revolution.

Souvenir Sheet

Virgin and Child, by Dürer — A153

1979, Aug. 13 ***Perf. 13½***
510 A153 500fr red brn & lt grn 6.25 1.50

Albrecht Dürer (1471-1528), German engraver and painter.

Bach and Contemporary Instruments — A155

#512, Albert Einstein, astronauts on moon.

1979, Sept. 10 ***Perf. 13½***
511 A155 200fr multicolored 2.25 .75
512 A155 200fr multicolored 2.25 .75

Yoro Fishing Port A156

1979, Sept. 26 Litho. ***Perf. 12½***
513 A156 45fr shown .60 .20
514 A156 75fr Port at night .90 .35

Mukukulu Dam — A157

1979, Oct. 5 ***Perf. 12½x12***
515 A157 20fr multicolored .25 .20
516 A157 45fr multicolored .70 .25

Emblem, Control Tower, Jets A158

1979, Dec. 12 Litho. ***Perf. 12½***
517 A158 100fr multicolored 1.10 .50

ASECNA (Air Safety Board), 20th anniv.

Congolese Labor Party, 10th Anniversary A159

1979, Dec. 31
518 A159 45fr multicolored .45 .20

A160

A161

1980, Mar. 30 Litho. ***Perf. 12½***
519 A160 45fr multicolored .45 .20
520 A160 95fr multicolored .90 .30

Post Office, 15th Anniversary.

1980, May 5
521 A161 100fr multicolored 2.25 .50

Visit of Pope John Paul II.

Rotary International, 75th Anniversary — A162

1980, May 10 Litho. ***Perf. 12½***
522 A162 150fr multicolored 1.50 .50

Pointe Noire Foundry A163

1980, June 18 Litho. ***Perf. 12½***
523 A163 30fr shown .20 .20
524 A163 35fr Different view .50 .20

Claude Chappe, Tower — A164

1980, June 21 Litho. ***Perf. 12½***
525 A164 200fr multicolored 2.25 1.00

Claude Chappe (1763-1805), French engineer.

Mossaka Harbor — A165

1980, June 23
532 A165 45fr shown .50 .20
533 A165 90fr Different view 1.00 .25

Papilio Dardanus (Front and Back) — A167

Human Rights Emblem, People — A169

July 31st Hospital — A168

1980, July 12 Litho. ***Perf. 12½***
534 A167 5fr shown .80 .30
535 A167 15fr Kalima aethiops 1.50 .30
536 A167 20fr Papilio demodocus 1.50 .40
537 A167 60fr Euphaedra 4.00 .75
538 A167 90fr Hypolimnas misippus 7.25 1.00
Nos. 534-538 (5) 15.05 2.75

Souvenir Sheet

539 A167 300fr Charaxes smaragdalis 20.00 17.00

Nos. 534-536 also exist perf 12½x13. Values the same.

1980, July 31
540 A168 45fr multicolored .60 .25

1980, Aug. 2
541 A169 350fr shown 2.75 1.00
542 A169 500fr Man breaking chain 4.50 1.50

Human Rights Convention, 32nd anniv.

Citizens and Congolese Arms A170

1980, Aug. 15 ***Perf. 12½***
543 A170 75fr shown .70 .30
544 A170 95fr Dove on flag, fists, vert. .90 .30
545 A170 150fr Dove holding Congolese arms 1.40 .60
Nos. 543-545 (3) 3.00 1.20

August 13-15th Revolution, 17th anniv.

Coffee and Cocoa Trees on Map of Congo — A171

Coffee and Cocoa Day: 95fr, Branches, map of Congo.

1980, Aug. 18 *Perf. 13½x13*

546 A171 45fr multicolored .50 .20
547 A171 95fr multicolored 1.00 .40

Logging A172

1980, Aug. 28

548 A172 70fr shown .80 .30
549 A172 75fr Wood transport .80 .30

Pres. Neto of Angola, 1st Death Anniv. — A173

Lark — A174

1980, Sept. 11

550 A173 100fr multicolored .90 .30

1980, Sept. 17

Designs: Birds.

551 A174 45fr multi, horiz. 1.00 .30
552 A174 75fr multi, horiz. 1.25 .30
553 A174 90fr multi, horiz. 1.50 .35
554 A174 150fr multicolored 2.25 .50
555 A174 200fr multicolored 3.25 1.00
556 A174 250fr multicolored 3.75 1.25
a Souv. sheet of 6, #551-556 5.00 5.00
Nos. 551-556 (6) 13.00 3.70

World Tourism Conference, Manila, Sept. 27 — A175

1980, Sept. 27 **Litho.** *Perf. 13½x13*

557 A175 100fr multicolored .90 .35

First Day of School Term — A176

1980, Oct. 2 **Photo.** *Perf. 13*

558 A176 50fr multicolored .50 .20

First House in Brazzaville — A177

Brazzaville Centenary: 65fr, First native village. 75fr, Old Town Hall, 1912. 150fr, View from bank of Bacongo, 1912. 200fr, Meeting of explorer Savorgnan de Brazza and chief Makoko, 1880.

1980, Oct. 3 **Litho.** *Perf. 12½*

559 A177 45fr multicolored .50 .20
560 A177 65fr multicolored .70 .30
561 A177 75fr multicolored 1.00 .40
562 A177 150fr multicolored 1.75 .65
563 A177 200fr multicolored 2.25 1.00
Nos. 559-563 (5) 6.20 2.55

Boys on Bank of Congo River — A178

1980, Oct. 30

564 A178 80fr shown .70 .25
565 A178 150fr Djoue Bridge 1.60 .40

Revolutionary Stadium and Athletes — A179

1980, Nov. 20 *Perf. 13x12½*

566 A179 60fr multicolored .70 .25

Rebuilt Railroad Bridge over Congo River A180

1980, Nov. 29 *Perf. 13x13½*

567 A180 75fr multicolored .90 .30

Mangoes, Loudima Fruit Packing Station A181

1980, Dec. 2 *Perf. 13*

568 A181 10fr shown .25 .20
569 A181 25fr Oranges .50 .20
570 A181 40fr Citrons .60 .20
571 A181 85fr Mandarins 1.10 .30
Nos. 568-571 (4) 2.45 .90

African Postal Union, 5th Anniversary A182

1980, Dec. 24 *Perf. 13½*

572 A182 100fr multicolored .90 .30

Moungouni Earth Satellite Station A183

1980, Dec. 30 *Perf. 12½*

573 A183 75fr multicolored .60 .20

Hertzian Wave Communication, Brazzaville — A184

1980, Dec. 30 *Perf. 12½x12*

574 A184 150fr multicolored 1.25 .40

1980 African Handball Champion Team — A185

Perf. 12½x13, 13x12½

1981, Jan. 26 **Litho.**

575 A185 100fr Receiving cup, vert. 1.10 .35
576 A185 150fr shown 1.30 .60

Pres. Denis Sassou-Nguesso — A186

1981, Feb. 5 **Litho.** *Perf. 12½*

577 A186 45fr multicolored .45 .20
578 A186 75fr multicolored .60 .20
579 A186 100fr multicolored .90 .25
Nos. 577-579 (3) 1.95 .65

Columbia Space Shuttle Orbiting Earth — A187

Space Conquest: 100fr, Luna 17, 1970. 200fr, 300fr, 500fr, Columbia space shuttle, 1981.

1981, May 4 **Litho.** *Perf. 14x13½*

580 A187 100fr multicolored 1.00 .25
581 A187 150fr multicolored 1.40 .40
582 A187 200fr multicolored 2.00 .55
583 A187 300fr multicolored 2.75 .80
Nos. 580-583 (4) 7.15 2.00

Souvenir Sheet

584 A187 500fr multicolored 5.00 1.40

For overprint see No. 725.

Fight Against Apartheid — A188

Twin Palm Tree of Louingui — A189

1981, May 5 **Litho.** *Perf. 12½*

585 A188 100fr deep blue .90 .25

1981, May 22 *Perf. 12x12½*

586 A189 75fr multicolored 1.00 .25

13th World Telecommunications Day — A190

1981, June 6 *Perf. 12½*

587 A190 120fr multicolored 1.25 .30

Rubber Extraction — A191

1981, June 27 *Perf. 13*

588 A191 50fr shown .60 .20
589 A191 70fr Sap draining .90 .30

Intl. Year of the Disabled A192

1981, June 29 **Engr.**
590 A192 45fr multicolored .45 .20

See No. B7.

Bird Trap — A194

Designs: Animal traps. 10fr vert.

1981, July
596 A194 5fr multicolored 1.10 .20
597 A194 10fr multicolored 1.10 .20
598 A194 15fr multicolored 1.10 .20
599 A194 20fr multicolored 1.10 .20
600 A194 30fr multicolored 1.60 .25
601 A194 35fr multicolored 2.25 .30
Nos. 596-601 (6) 8.25 1.35

Mausoleum of King Maloango — A195

1981, July 4 **Litho.** ***Perf. 12½***
602 A195 75fr shown .70 .20
603 A195 150fr Mausoleum, portrait 1.25 .40

Prince Charles and Lady Diana, Coach A196

Royal wedding: Couple and coaches.

1981, Sept. 1 **Litho.** ***Perf. 14½***
604 A196 100fr multicolored 1.00 .25
605 A196 200fr multicolored 2.00 .55
606 A196 300fr multicolored 3.25 .80
Nos. 604-606 (3) 6.25 1.60

Souvenir Sheet

607 A196 400fr multicolored 4.00 1.10

World Food Day — A197

1981, Oct. 16 **Litho.** ***Perf. 13½x13***
608 A197 150fr multicolored 1.40 .55

12th World UPU Day A198

1981, Oct. 24 **Engr.** ***Perf. 13x12½***
609 A198 90fr multicolored .90 .25

Royal Guard A199

1981, Oct. 31 **Litho.** ***Perf. 12½x13***
610 A199 45fr multicolored .60 .20

Eradication of Manioc Beetle — A200

Natl. Red Cross — A201

1981, Nov. 18 **Litho.** ***Perf. 12½***
611 A200 75fr multicolored 1.00 .25

1981, Nov. 18 ***Perf. 13***
612 A201 10fr Bandaging patient .20 .20
613 A201 35fr Treating child .45 .20
614 A201 60fr Drawing well water .70 .25
Nos. 612-614 (3) 1.35 .65

Giant Baobab ("Tree of Savorgnan de Brazza") A202

1981, Dec. 19 **Litho.** ***Perf. 13***
615 A202 45fr multicolored .90 .20
616 A202 75fr multicolored 1.25 .30

Fetish Figure — A203

Designs: Various carved figures.

1981, Dec. 19 ***Perf. 13x12½***
617 A203 15fr multicolored .20 .20
618 A203 25fr multicolored .25 .20
619 A203 45fr multicolored .45 .20
620 A203 50fr multicolored .60 .20
621 A203 60fr multicolored .70 .20
Nos. 617-621 (5) 2.20 1.00

Nos. 617, 618 and 620 also exist perf 12½x13. Values the same.

Caves of Bangou A204

1981, Dec. 29 ***Perf. 13x13½***
622 A204 20fr multicolored .45 .20
623 A204 25fr multicolored .45 .20

King Makoko and His Queen, Ivory Sculptures by R. Engongodzo — A205

Perf. 13½x13, 13x13½
1982, Feb. 27 **Litho.**
624 A205 25fr Woman, vert. .35 .20
625 A205 35fr Woman, diff., vert. .45 .20
626 A205 100fr shown 1.00 .30
Nos. 624-626 (3) 1.80 .70

George Stephenson (1781-1848) and Inter City 125, Gt. Britain — A206

Locomotives: 150fr, Sinkansen Bullet Train, Japan. 200fr, Advanced Passenger Train, Gt. Britain. 300fr, TGV-001, France.

1982, Mar. 2 **Litho.** ***Perf. 12½***
627 A206 100fr multicolored 1.00 .25
628 A206 150fr multicolored 1.60 .40
629 A206 200fr multicolored 2.25 .55
630 A206 300fr multicolored 3.25 .80
Nos. 627-630 (4) 8.10 2.00

Scouting Year A207

1982, Apr. 13 **Litho.** ***Perf. 13***
631 A207 100fr Looking through binoculars 1.25 .25
632 A207 150fr Reading map 1.50 .40
633 A207 200fr Helping woman 2.25 .55
634 A207 300fr Crossing rope bridge 3.25 .80
Nos. 631-634 (4) 8.25 2.00

Souvenir Sheet

635 A207 500fr Hiking, horiz. 5.00 1.75

For overprint see No. 726.

Franklin Roosevelt A208

1982, June 12 **Litho.** ***Perf. 13***
636 A208 150fr shown 1.60 .40
637 A208 250fr Washington 2.75 .70
638 A208 350fr Goethe 3.25 .90
Nos. 636-638 (3) 7.60 2.00

21st Birthday of Princess Diana, July 1 — A209

1982, June 12 ***Perf. 14***
639 A209 200fr Candles 2.00 .55
640 A209 300fr "21" 2.75 .80

Souvenir Sheet

641 A209 500fr Diana 5.00 1.40

5-Year Plan, 1982-1986 A210

Perf. 13x12½, 12½x13
1982, June 19
642 A210 60fr Road construction .70 .20
643 A210 100fr Communications, vert. 1.10 .30
644 A210 125fr Operating room equipment, vert. 1.40 .35
645 A210 150fr Hydroelectric power, vert. 1.60 .40
Nos. 642-645 (4) 4.80 1.25

ITU Plenipotentiary Conference, Nairobi — A211

1982, June 26 ***Perf. 13***
646 A211 300fr multicolored 2.75 .90

Nos. 604-607 Overprinted in Blue: "NAISSANCE ROYALE 1982"

1982, July 30 ***Perf. 14½***
647 A196 100fr multicolored .90 .30
648 A196 200fr multicolored 1.75 .60
649 A196 300fr multicolored 2.75 1.00
Nos. 647-649 (3) 5.40 1.90

Souvenir Sheet

650 A196 400fr multicolored 3.50 2.50

Birth of Prince William of Wales, June 21.

Nutrition Campaign A212

1982, July 24 Litho. *Perf. 12½*

651	A212	100fr multicolored	1.00	.25

WHO African Headquarters, Brazzaville — A213

1982, July 24 Litho. *Perf. 12½*

652	A213	125fr multicolored	1.00	.45

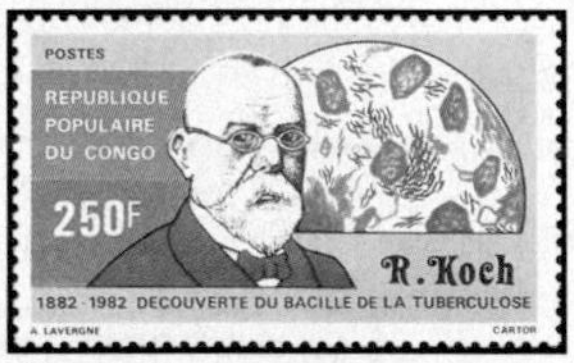

TB Bacillus Centenary — A214

1982, Aug. 7 *Perf. 12½x12*

653	A214	250fr Koch, bacillus	3.00	1.10

Pres. Sassou-Nguesso and 1980 Simba Prize — A215

1982, Oct. 20 Litho. *Perf. 13*

654	A215	100fr multicolored	.90	.30

Turtles — A216

Various turtles and tortoises.

1982, Dec. 1

655	A216	30fr multicolored	.75	.20
656	A216	45fr multicolored	1.00	.25
657	A216	55fr multicolored	1.50	.30
		Nos. 655-657 (3)	3.25	.75

Boy Gathering Coconuts — A217

Nest in Tree Trunk — A218

1982, Dec. 11

658	A217	100fr multicolored	.90	.30

1982, Dec. 29 *Perf. 12½*

659	A218	40fr shown	1.25	.20
660	A218	75fr Nests in palm tree	1.50	.20
661	A218	100fr Woven nest on thorn branch	1.60	.25
		Nos. 659-661 (3)	4.35	.65

Hertzian Wave Communication Network — A219

1982, Dec. 30 *Perf. 13x12½*

662	A219	45fr multicolored	.45	.20
663	A219	60fr multicolored	.50	.20
664	A219	95fr multicolored	.90	.30
		Nos. 662-664 (3)	1.85	.70

30th Anniv. of Customs Cooperation Council — A220

1983, Jan. 26 Litho. *Perf. 12½x13*

665	A220	100fr Headquarters	.90	.30

Mausoleum of Pres. Marien Ngouabi — A221

1983, Feb. 8 *Perf. 13*

666	A221	60fr multicolored	.50	.20
667	A221	80fr multicolored	.80	.20

Ironsmiths — A222

1983 *Perf. 12½*

668	A222	45fr shown	.50	.20
669	A222	150fr Weaver, vert.	1.25	.50

Issue dates: 45fr, Mar. 5; 150fr, Feb. 24.

Carved Chess Pieces, by R. Engongonzo — A223

Various pieces.

1983, Feb. 26 *Perf. 13*

670	A223	40fr multicolored	.40	.20
671	A223	60fr multicolored	1.00	.20
672	A223	95fr multicolored	2.00	.50
		Nos. 670-672 (3)	3.40	.90

Easter 1983 A224

Raphael drawings. 200fr, 400fr vert.

1983, Apr. 20 Litho. *Perf. 13*

673	A224	200fr Transfiguration study	2.00	.50
674	A224	300fr Deposition from Cross	3.25	.65
675	A224	400fr Christ in Glory	4.50	.85
		Nos. 673-675 (3)	9.75	2.00

Seashells A225

1983 Litho. *Perf. 15x14*

675A	A225	25fr multicolored	150.00	65.00
676	A225	35fr multicolored	1.25	.30
677	A225	65fr multicolored	1.60	.35

Dated 1982.

A226

A227

Various traditional combs.

1983, May *Perf. 14*

678	A226	30fr multicolored	.35	.20
679	A226	70fr multicolored	.90	.20
680	A226	85fr multicolored	1.00	.20
		Nos. 678-680 (3)	2.25	.60

Litho & Engr.

1983, Aug. 10 *Perf. 12½x13*

681	A227	60fr multicolored	.45	.20
682	A227	100fr multicolored	.90	.30

20th anniv. of revolution.

Centenary of the Arrival of Christian Missionaries — A228

Churches and Clergymen: 150fr, A. Carrie, Church of the Sacred Heart, Loango, vert. 250fr, Msgr. Augouard; St. Louis, Liranga; St. Joseph, Linzolo.

1983, Aug. 23 *Perf. 12½*

683	A228	150fr multicolored	1.60	.40
684	A228	250fr multicolored	2.75	.70

Local Flowers — A229

1984, Jan. 20 Litho. *Perf. 12½*

685	A229	5fr Liana thunderaie, vert.	.20	.20
686	A229	15fr Bougainvillea	.35	.20
687	A229	20fr Anthurium, vert.	.50	.20
688	A229	45fr Allamanda	1.00	.20
689	A229	75fr Hibiscus, vert.	1.40	.30
		Nos. 685-689 (5)	3.45	1.10

35th Anniv. of World Peace Council A230

1984, Mar. 31 Litho. *Perf. 13x12½*

690	A230	50fr multicolored	.45	.20
691	A230	100fr multicolored	.90	.30

Anti-Nuclear Arms Campaign A231

1984, May 31 Litho. *Perf. 12x12½*

692	A231	200fr Explosion, victims	1.75	.50

Agriculture Day A232

Perf. 13x13½, 13½x13

1984, June 30 **Litho.**
693 A232 10fr Rice .20 .20
694 A232 15fr Pineapples .20 .20
695 A232 60fr Manioc, vert. .60 .25
696 A232 100fr Palm tree, map, vert. 1.10 .35
Nos. 693-696 (4) 2.10 1.00

Congress Palace — A233

1984, July 27 *Perf. 13*
697 A233 60fr multicolored .50 .20
698 A233 100fr multicolored .90 .30

Chinese-Congolese cooperation.

CFCO-Congo Railways, 50th Anniv. — A234

1984, July 30 *Perf. 13½*
699 A234 10fr Loulombo Station .25 .20
700 A234 25fr Les Bandas Chinese Labor Camp .45 .20
701 A234 125fr "50" 2.00 .70
702 A234 200fr Admin. bldg. 4.50 1.00
Nos. 699-702 (4) 7.20 2.10

Locomotives — A235

Ships on the Congo River — A236

1984, Aug. 24 *Perf. 12½*
703 A235 100fr CC 203 1.10 .35
704 A236 100fr Tugboat 1.10 .35
705 A235 150fr BB 103 1.60 .50
706 A236 150fr Pusher tugboat 1.60 .50
707 A235 300fr BB-BB 301 3.25 1.10
708 A236 300fr Dredger 3.25 1.10
709 A235 500fr BB 420 L'Eclair 5.25 1.75
710 A236 500fr Cargo ship 5.25 1.75
Nos. 703-710 (8) 22.40 7.40

World Fisheries Year A237

1984, Oct. 16 *Perf. 13½*
711 A237 5fr Basket of fish .25 .20
712 A237 20fr Net fishermen in boat .45 .20
713 A237 25fr School of fish .60 .20
714 A237 40fr Net fisherman 1.00 .25
715 A237 55fr Trawler 1.60 .30
Nos. 711-715 (5) 3.90 1.15

Anti-polio Campaign A238

M'Bamou Palace Hotel, Brazzaville A239

1984, Oct. 30
716 A238 250fr Disabled men, hand 2.75 .90
717 A238 300fr Target, disabled women, horiz. 3.25 1.00

1984, Dec. 15 *Perf. 14½*
718 A239 60fr multicolored .45 .20
719 A239 100fr multicolored .90 .30

Fauna A240

1984, Dec. *Perf. 15x14½*
720 A240 30fr Pangolin 3.75 .75
721 A240 70fr Bat 8.00 1.50
722 A240 85fr Civet cat 9.75 2.00
Nos. 720-722 (3) 21.50 4.25

Congo River Logging A241

1984, Dec. *Perf. 13½x13*
723 A241 60fr Log raft, crew hut .60 .25
724 A241 100fr Tugboat pushing logs 1.25 .35

Souvenir Sheets

Nos. 584, 635 Ovptd. with Exhibition in Black or Green

1985, Mar. 8 *Perf. 14x13½, 13*
725 A187 500fr TSUKUBA EXPO '85 5.75 4.50
726 A207 500fr ITALIA '85 emblem, ROME (G) 5.75 4.50

See Nos. C336-C337.

Zonocerus Variegatus — A242

1985, Mar. 15 *Perf. 13*
727 A242 125fr multicolored 1.75 .35

Burial of a Teke Chief — A243

1985, Apr. 30 *Perf. 12½*
728 A243 225fr multicolored 2.25 .75

Edible Fruit A244

Perf. 13½, 13 (#732A), 13½x13¼ (#732B)

1985, June 15
729 A244 5fr Trichoscypha acuminata, vert. .20 .20
730 A244 10fr Aframomum africanum .20 .20
730A A244 90fr like #730
731 A244 125fr Gambeya lacuurtiana 1.40 .40
732 A244 150fr Landolphia jumelei 1.75 .55
732A A244 205fr like #731
732B A244 300fr Like #732 — —

Sizes: #729, 22x36mm, #731, 732A, 36x22mm.

Nos. 730A, 732A, 732B inscribed "Congo" only.

For overprints, see Nos. 1170, 1183-1185.
Compare type A244 with type A352.

Lions Club Intl., 30th Anniv. — A245

1985, June 25 *Perf. 12½*
733 A245 250fr Flag, District 403B 2.25 .70

Russian Soldier, Kremlin, Fall of Berlin A246

1985, July 27 *Perf. 12*
734 A246 60fr multicolored .50 .20

Defeat of Nazi Germany, end of World War II, 40th anniv.

Lady Olave Baden-Powell, Girl Guides Founder — A247

Anniversaries and events: 150fr, Girl Guides, 75th anniv. 250fr, Jacob Grimm, fabulist; Sleeping Beauty. 350fr, Johann Sebastian Bach, composer; European Music Year, St. Thomas Church organ, Leipzig. 450fr, Queen Mother, 85th birthday, vert. 500fr, Statue of Liberty, cent., vert.

1985, Aug. 26 *Perf. 13*
735 A247 150fr multicolored 1.60 .50
736 A247 250fr multicolored 2.25 .90
737 A247 350fr multicolored 2.75 1.25
738 A247 450fr multicolored 3.50 1.60
739 A247 500fr multicolored 5.00 2.00
Nos. 735-739 (5) 15.10 6.25

PHILEXAFRICA '85, Lome, Togo, Nov. 16-24 — A248

1985, Oct. 10 *Perf. 13x12½*
740 A248 250fr shown 2.25 1.00
741 A248 250fr Airport, postal van 2.25 1.00
a. Pair, #740-741 + label 5.25 5.25

Mushrooms — A249

1985, Dec. 14 **Litho.** *Perf. 13*
742 A249 100fr Coprinus, vert. 1.50 .35
743 A249 150fr Cortinarius 2.25 .50
744 A249 200fr Armillariella mellea 3.00 .85
745 A249 300fr Dictyophora 4.00 1.25
746 A249 400fr Crucibulum vulgare 6.00 1.50
Nos. 742-746 (5) 16.75 4.45

Arbor Day — A250

Children's Hoop Races — A251

1986, Mar. 6 *Perf. 13½*
747 A250 60fr Planting sapling .45 .20
748 A250 200fr Map, lifecycle diagram 1.90 .90

1986, Apr. 30 *Perf. 12½*
749 A251 5fr Two boys .20 .20
750 A251 10fr One boy .20 .20
751 A251 60fr Three boys, horiz. .50 .20
a. Souvenir sheet of 3, #749-751 1.25 1.00
Nos. 749-751 (3) .90 .60

A252

A253

1986, June 5 Litho. *Perf. 13½*

752 A252 60fr Garbage disposal .50 .20
753 A252 125fr Dumping garbage 1.00 .40

Intl. Environment Day.

1986, July 15 Litho. *Perf. 13x12½*

Traditional Modes of Transporting Goods: 5fr, Basket on head, child in sling carrier. 10fr, Child in carrier on hip, large basket strapped to forehead. 60fr, Man carrying load on shoulder.

754 A253 5fr multicolored .20 .20
755 A253 10fr multicolored .60 .25
756 A253 60fr multicolored .30 .20
Nos. 754-756 (3) 1.10 .65

Mission of the Sisters of St. Joseph of Cluny, Cent. A254

1986, Aug. 19 Litho. *Perf. 12½x13*

757 A254 230fr multicolored 2.40 1.25

A255

A256

1986, Aug. 30 Litho. *Perf. 13½*

758 A255 40fr multicolored .45 .20
759 A255 60fr multicolored .55 .20
760 A255 100fr multicolored 1.00 .35
Nos. 758-760 (3) 2.00 .75

UNESCO intl. communications development program.

1986, Sept. 15 Litho. *Perf. 13½*

761 A256 100fr multicolored .90 .30

Intl. Peace Year.

World Food Day A257

1986, Oct. 16

762 A257 75fr Food staples .80 .25
763 A257 120fr Mother feeding child 1.25 .40

UN Child Survival Campaign A258

Mothers, children and pinwheels in various designs.

1986, Oct. 27

764 A258 15fr multi, vert. .20 .20
765 A258 30fr multi .25 .20
766 A258 70fr multi, vert. .70 .30
Nos. 764-766 (3) 1.15 .70

A258a

A259

1986, Dec. 5 Litho. *Perf. 12x12½*

766A A258a 100fr multicolored 1.50 .35

27th Soviet Communist Party congress.

1987, Feb. 10 Litho. *Perf. 13½*

767 A259 30fr multicolored .25 .20
768 A259 45fr multicolored .45 .20
769 A259 75fr multicolored .70 .25
770 A259 120fr multicolored 1.10 .35
Nos. 767-770 (4) 2.50 1.00

Election of President Sassou-Nguesso, head of the Organization of African States.

Traditional Wedding A260

1987, Feb. 18 Litho. *Perf. 12½x13*

771 A260 5fr multicolored .20 .20
772 A260 15fr multicolored .25 .20
773 A260 20fr multicolored .25 .20
Nos. 771-773 (3) .70 .60

The Blue Lake — A261

1987, July 16 *Perf. 12½*

774 A261 5fr multicolored .20 .20
775 A261 15fr multicolored .20 .20
776 A261 75fr multicolored 1.00 .30
777 A261 120fr multicolored 1.25 .40
Nos. 774-777 (4) 2.65 1.10

Pres. Marien Ngouabi A262

Congress of African Scientists A263

1987, July 16 *Perf. 13*

778 A262 75fr multicolored .75 .30
779 A262 120fr multicolored 1.25 .40

Tenth death anniv.

1987, Sept. 10 *Perf. 13x12½*

780 A263 15fr multicolored .20 .20
781 A263 90fr multicolored .70 .30
782 A263 230fr multicolored 2.00 .80
Nos. 780-782 (3) 2.90 1.30

4th African Games, Nairobi — A264

1987, Oct. 30 *Perf. 12½*

783 A264 75fr multicolored .75 .40
784 A264 120fr multicolored 1.25 .60

Raoul Follereau (1903-1977), Philanthropist — A265

1987, Oct. 20 *Perf. 13½*

785 A265 120fr multicolored 1.50 .60

Cure leprosy.

FAO, 40th Anniv. — A266

1987, Nov. 17 *Perf. 12½*

786 A266 300fr multicolored 2.75 1.10

Anti-Apartheid Campaign A267

Nelson Mandela A268

Perf. 13½x15, 14½x15

1987, Sept. 21 Litho.

787 A267 60fr multicolored .60 .20
788 A268 240fr multicolored 2.25 .75

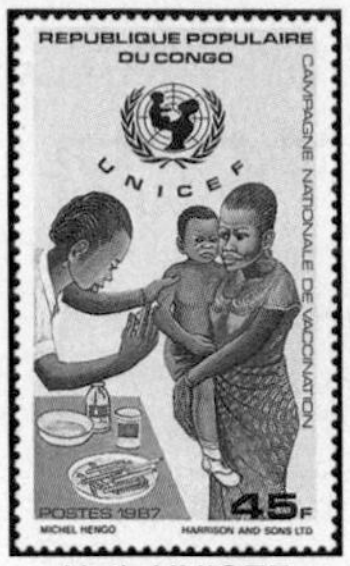

Natl. UNICEF Vaccination Campaign — A269

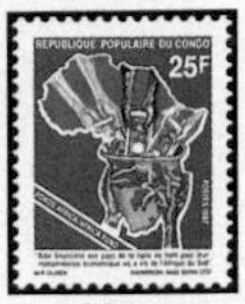

Africa Fund — A270

Perf. 13½x14½, 14½x13½

1987, Sept. 28

789 A269 30fr Inoculating adults, horiz. .25 .20
790 A269 45fr shown .50 .20
791 A269 500fr Inoculating children, horiz. 5.25 2.00
Nos. 789-791 (3) 6.00 2.40

No. 791 is airmail.

1987, Sept. 28 *Perf. 13½x15*

792 A270 25fr multicolored .25 .20
793 A270 50fr multicolored .40 .20
794 A270 70fr multicolored .75 .25
Nos. 792-794 (3) 1.40 .65

Self-sufficiency in Food Production by the Year 2000 — A271

1987, Nov. 20 Litho. *Perf. 13½*

795 A271 20fr multicolored .25 .20
796 A271 55fr multicolored .60 .20
797 A271 100fr multicolored 1.00 .35
Nos. 795-797 (3) 1.85 .75

Simon Kimbangu (b. 1887), Founder of the Church of Christ on Earth — A272

1987, Nov. 28 *Perf. 12½*

798 A272 75fr Kimbangu, vert. .70 .30
799 A272 120fr Kimbangu, parrot, vert. 1.10 .40
800 A272 240fr Kimbanguist Church, Nkamba 2.75 1.00
a. Souvenir sheet of 3, #798-800 5.75 5.00
Nos. 798-800 (3) 4.55 1.70

October Revolution, Russia, 70th Anniv. — A273

Lenin inspecting revolutionary troops, Red Square, from an unspecified painting.

1988, Feb. 19 Litho. *Perf. 12½x12*

801 A273 75fr multicolored 1.60 .60
802 A273 120fr multicolored 2.25 1.00

African Writers Opposing Apartheid — A274

Intl. Fund for Agricultural Development (IFAD), 10th Anniv. — A275

1988, Apr. 6 Litho. *Perf. 13½*

803 A274 15fr multicolored .20 .20
804 A274 60fr multicolored .50 .25
805 A274 75fr multicolored .80 .30
Nos. 803-805 (3) 1.50 .75

For overprint see #1157.

1988, Apr. 30

806 A275 240fr multicolored 2.00 .85

Invention of the Telegraph by Samuel Morse, 150th Anniv. (in 1987) — A276

1988, Apr. 28

807 A276 90fr Morse, vert. .90 .30
808 A276 120fr shown 1.10 .40

A277

A278

1988, Sept. 20 Litho. *Perf. 13½*

809 A277 5fr Eucalyptus trees, Brazzaville .30 .20
810 A277 10fr Stop cutting down trees .30 .20

Fight against desertification.

1988, Aug. 12 Litho. *Perf. 13½*

Campaigns: No. 812, Return to the Land Campaign (farming). 120fr, Self-sufficiency in food production.

811 A278 75fr shown .75 .30
812 A278 75fr multicolored .75 .30
813 A278 120fr multicolored .90 .40
Nos. 811-813 (3) 2.40 1.00

Congo Revolution, 25th anniv.

Yoro Fishing Village A279

1988, Sept. 1

814 A279 35fr shown .45 .20
815 A279 40fr Liberty Place .45 .20

Intl. Day for the Fight Against AIDS A280

1988, Dec. 1 Litho. *Perf. 13½*

816 A280 60fr shown .45 .20
817 A280 75fr Emblem .70 .20
818 A280 180fr Modified UN emblem, campaign emblem 1.75 .60
Nos. 816-818 (3) 2.90 1.00

Natl. Committee for the Fight Against AIDS and Evangelical Anglican Church of Congo anti-AIDS campaign.

February 5 Movement, 10th Anniv. A281

1989, Apr. 21 Litho. *Perf. 13½*

819 A281 75fr Rally .75 .30
820 A281 120fr Pres. Sassou-Nguesso, natl. achievements .90 .40

UN Declaration of Human Rights, 40th Anniv. (in 1988) A282

1989, May 19 *Perf. 13*

821 A282 120fr multicolored .90 .40
822 A282 350fr multicolored 2.50 1.20

Marien Nguabi, Founder of Congo Labor Party A282a

1989, July 31 Litho. *Perf. 12½x13*

822A A282a 240fr red & yellow 2.00 .75

Red Cross and Red Crescent Societies, 125th Annivs. A283

120fr, Dunant, emblem, Congo Red Cross.

1989, Sept. 19 Litho. *Perf. 13*

823 A283 75fr shown .90 .40
824 A283 120fr multicolored 1.00 .65

No. 824 is airmail.

Organization of African Unity, 25th Anniv. — A284

1989, Oct. 19 Litho. *Perf. 12½*

825 A284 120fr multicolored 1.10 .40

African Development Bank, 25th Anniv. — A285

1989, Dec. 22 Litho. *Perf. 12½x13*

826 A285 75fr multicolored .75 .35
827 A285 120fr multicolored 1.00 .40

WHO, 40th Anniv. (in 1988) A286

1989, Dec. 28 Litho. *Perf. 12½*

828 A286 60fr shown .75 .35
829 A286 75fr Blood donation, vert. .90 .50

See Nos. 846-847 for overprints.

Congo Labor Party (PCT), 20th Anniv. — A287

1989, Dec. 22 Litho. *Perf. 13x12½*

830 A287 75fr multicolored .75 .35
831 A287 120fr multicolored 1.10 .40

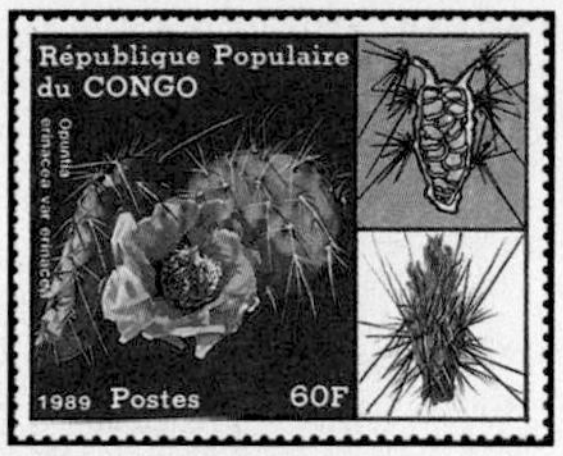

Cacti A288

Perf. 12½x13, 13x12½

1989, Nov. 22

832 A288 35fr *Opuntia phaeacantha discata* .35 .20
833 A288 40fr *Opuntia ficus indica* .50 .20
834 A288 60fr *Opuntia erinacea* .90 .25
835 A288 75fr *Opuntia rufida* 1.25 .30
836 A288 120fr *Opuntia leptocaulis* 1.75 .45
Nos. 832-836 (5) 4.75 1.40

Souvenir Sheet

Perf. 12½

837 A288 220fr *Opuntia compresa* 5.00 2.10

Nos. 832-833, 835 and 837 vert. No. 837 contains one 32x40mm stamp.

1992 Winter Olympics, Albertville A289

1989, Dec. 22 *Perf. 12½*

838 A289 75fr Ice dancing .60 .25
839 A289 80fr Nordic skiiing .60 .30
840 A289 100fr Speed skating .90 .35
841 A289 120fr Luge 1.10 .45
842 A289 200fr Alpine skiing 1.75 .70
843 A289 240fr Ice hockey 2.25 .85
844 A289 400fr Ski jumping 3.25 1.40
Nos. 838-844 (7) 10.45 4.30

Souvenir Sheet

Perf. 13

845 A289 500fr Bobsled 4.50 2.40

No. 845 contains one 32x40mm stamp.

Nos. 828-829 Ovptd. "NOTRE PLANETE, NOTRE SANTE PENSER GLOBALEMENT AGIR LOCALEMENT" in 3 or 5 Lines

1989, Dec. 28 *Perf. 12½*

846 A286 60fr multicolored .75 .45
847 A286 75fr multicolored .90 .60

Health care for everyone.

Intl. Literacy Year — A290

1990, June 26 Litho. *Perf. 13½*

848 A290 75fr bl, blk & yel .75 .35

Birds A291

Designs: 25fr, Tourterelle des bois. 50fr, Fauvette pitchou, vert. 70fr, Faucon crecerelle, vert. 150fr, Perroquet gris, vert.

1990, July 10

849 A291 25fr multicolored .35 .25
850 A291 50fr multicolored .70 .30
851 A291 70fr multicolored 1.10 .55
852 A291 150fr multicolored 2.10 1.25
Nos. 849-852 (4) 4.25 2.35

Dance Masks — A292

Flowering Plants — A293

1990, July 24 *Perf. 13*

853 A292 120fr Mondo 1.10 .40
854 A292 360fr Bapunu 3.50 1.25
855 A292 400fr Kwele 4.00 1.50
Nos. 853-855 (3) 8.60 3.15

For overprints see #1172, 1173.

1990, Sept. 15 Litho. *Perf. 12½*

856 A293 30fr Tournesol (sunflower) .25 .20
857 A293 45fr Cassia alata, horiz. .45 .20
858 A293 75fr Oeillette (opium poppy) .70 .25
859 A293 90fr Acalypha sanderil 1.00 .35
Nos. 856-859 (4) 2.40 1.00

1992 Summer Olympics, Barcelona — A294

1990, June 28 Litho. *Perf. 13½*

860 A294 100fr Street scene, vert. 1.00 .30
861 A294 150fr shown 1.40 .35
862 A294 200fr Sailing, diff. 1.75 .40
863 A294 240fr Marketplace 2.25 .55
864 A294 350fr Harbor 3.50 .75
865 A294 500fr Monument, vert. 4.75 .90
Nos. 860-865 (6) 14.65 3.25

Souvenir Sheet

866 A294 750fr Cathedral, vert. 5.50 3.50

Nos. 864-865 airmail. Nos. 860-865 exist in miniature sheets of 1.

Royal Necklaces A295

1990, Aug. 18 Litho. *Perf. 13½*

867 A295 75fr shown .75 .35
868 A295 100fr Necklace, diff. 1.00 .60

Boy Scouts Observing Nature A296

Scout: 35fr, Photographing butterfly, Euphaedra eusimoides. 40fr, Picking mushrooms, Armillaria mellea. 75fr, Drawing butterfly, Palla decius. 80fr, Using magnifying glass, Kallima ansorgei. 500fr, Using microscope, Cortinarius speciocissimus. 600fr, Feeding butterfly, Graphium illyris. 1500fr, Photographing butterfly, Berberia plistonax, horiz. 750fr, Photographing mushrooms, Volvariella bombycina.

1991, June 8 Litho. *Perf. 13½*

869 A296 35fr multicolored .20 .20
870 A296 40fr multicolored .45 .20
871 A296 75fr multicolored .60 .20
872 A296 80fr multicolored .70 .20
873 A296 500fr multicolored 4.00 1.25
874 A296 600fr multicolored 4.00 1.25
a. Min. sheet of 4, #869, 871-872, 874 7.50 3.75
Nos. 869-874 (6) 9.95 3.30

Litho. & Embossed

874B A296 1500fr gold & multi *32.50* —

Souvenir Sheet

875 A296 750fr multicolored 5.25 2.25

Nos. 869-874 exist in souvenir sheets of 1. Nos. 873-875 are airmail.

Medicinal Plants — A297

Designs: 15fr, Ocimum viride. 20fr, Kalanchoe pinnata, vert. 30fr, Euphorbia hirta. 60fr, Catharanthus roseus, vert. 75fr, Bidens pilosa, vert. 100fr, Brillantaisia patula, vert. 120fr, Cassia occidentalis, vert.

1991, Jan. 30 Litho. *Perf. 11½*

876 A297 15fr multicolored .20 .20
877 A297 20fr multicolored .25 .20
878 A297 30fr multicolored .25 .20
879 A297 60fr multicolored .50 .25
880 A297 75fr multicolored .70 .35
881 A297 100fr multicolored 1.00 .55
882 A297 120fr multicolored 1.10 .75
Nos. 876-882 (7) 4.00 2.50

Mushrooms A298

1991, Mar. 25 Litho. *Perf. 13*

883 A298 30fr Amanita rubescens .30 .20
883A A298 45fr Catathelasma imperiale .40 .20
883B A298 75fr Amanita caesarea .75 .25
883C A298 90fr Boletus regius .90 .25
883D A298 120fr Pluteus cervinus 1.10 .40
883E A298 150fr Boletus chrysenteron 1.50 .60
883F A298 200fr Agaricus arvensis 2.10 .75
Nos. 883-883F (7) 7.05 2.65

Souvenir Sheet

Perf. 12½

883G A298 350fr Boletus versipellis, horiz. 5.00 2.00

No. 883G contains one 40x32mm stamp.

Trains A298a

Designs: 75fr, TGV, France. 120fr, S350, Italy. 200fr, DE24000, Turkey. 250fr, DE1024, Germany.

1991, Apr. 10 Litho. *Perf. 12½x12¼*

883I A298a 75fr multi .65 .30
883J A298a 120fr multi 1.10 .45
883K A298a 200fr multi 2.00 .75
883L A298a 250fr multi 2.75 1.00

An additional stamp was issued in this set. The editors would like to examine it.

African Tourism Year — A299

1991, Apr. 15 Litho. *Perf. 13½*

884 A299 75fr shown .75 .35
885 A299 120fr Zebra, map 1.10 .60

Allegory of New Republic — A300

1991, May 13 Litho. *Perf. 13*

888 A300 15fr blue .20 .20
889 A300 30fr brt grn .25 .20
890 A300 60fr org yel .30 .20
891 A300 75fr brt pink .50 .30
892 A300 120fr dk brown .90 .45
Nos. 888-892 (5) 2.15 1.35

Trans-Siberian Railroad, Cent. — A301

1991, June 6 Litho. *Perf. 13*

899 A301 120fr Map 1.50 .50
900 A301 240fr Map, train 2.75 1.20

Telecom 91 — A302

1991, June 29 Litho. *Perf. 13*

901 A302 75fr multicolored .75 .30
902 A302 120fr multi, vert. 1.10 .60

6th World Forum and Exposition on Telecommunications, Geneva, Switzerland.

Insects — A303

A304

1991, July 2 *Perf. 12½*

903 A303 75fr Peanut beetle .90 .25
904 A303 120fr Centaur, horiz. 1.25 .45
905 A303 200fr Coffee beetle 2.00 .75
906 A303 300fr Goliath beetle 3.00 1.50
Nos. 903-906 (4) 7.15 2.95

1991, July 16 Litho. *Perf. 12½*

907 A304 75fr Water conservation .75 .35

Amnesty Intl., 30th Anniv. A305

Designs: 40fr, Candle, sun, vert. 75fr, "30," broken chains, vert.

1991, Aug. 13 *Perf. 13½*

908 A305 40fr multicolored .35 .20
909 A305 75fr multicolored .60 .25
910 A305 80fr multicolored .70 .35
Nos. 908-910 (3) 1.65 .80

Congo Postage Stamps, Cent. — A306

75fr, Similar to French Congo #1. 120fr, Similar to French Congo #35. 240fr, Similar to Congo Republic #89. 500fr, Similar to French Congo #1, 35 and Congo Republic #89.

Litho. & Engr.

1991, Aug. *Perf. 13x13½*

911 A306 75fr beige & dk grn .80 .30
912 A306 120fr beige, dk grn & brn 1.10 .45
913 A306 240fr multicolored 2.25 1.10
914 A306 500fr multicolored 4.50 2.00
a. Strip of 4, #911-914 10.00 9.00

Ducks A307

1991, Aug. 8 Litho. *Perf. 12½*

915 A307 75fr Anas acuta 1.25 .30
916 A307 120fr Somateria mollissima, vert. 1.50 .45
917 A307 200fr Anas clypeata, vert. 2.00 .75
918 A307 240fr Anas platyrhynchos 3.50 1.00
Nos. 915-918 (4) 8.25 2.50

Automobiles and Space — A308

Designs: 35fr, Ferrari 512S by Pininfarina. 40fr, Vincenzo Lancia, Lancia Stratos by

Bertone. 75fr, Maybach Zeppelin type 12, Wilhelm Maybach. 80fr, Mars Observer, 1992. 500fr, Magellan probe surveying Venus. 600fr, Magnification of Sun, Ulysses probe. 750fr, Crew of Apollo 11.

1991, Aug. 23 Litho. *Perf. 13½*

919 A308 35fr multicolored .30 .20
920 A308 40fr multicolored .30 .20
921 A308 75fr multicolored .60 .30
922 A308 80fr multicolored .65 .30
923 A308 500fr multicolored 4.25 2.25
924 A308 600fr multicolored 5.00 2.50
Nos. 919-924 (6) 11.10 5.75

Souvenir Sheet

925 A308 750fr multicolored 6.50 3.50

Nos. 923-925 are airmail. No. 925 contains one 60x42mm stamp.

Butterflies A309

1991, Aug. 31 *Perf. 11½*

926 A309 75fr Petit bleu 1.00 .30
927 A309 120fr Charaxe 1.25 .50
928 A309 240fr Papillon feuille, vert. 1.75 .80
929 A309 300fr Papillon de l'oranger, vert. 3.00 1.00
Nos. 926-929 (4) 7.00 2.60

For overprints see Nos. 1156, 1165.

Celebrities and Organizations — A310

Designs: 100fr, Bo Jackson, baseball and football player. 150fr, Nick Faldo, golfer. 200fr, Rickey Henderson, Barry Bonds, baseball players. 240fr, Garry Kasparov, World Chess Champion. 300fr, Starving child, Lions and Rotary Clubs emblems. 350fr, Wolfgang Amadeus Mozart. 400fr, De Gaulle, Churchill. 500fr, Jean-Henri Dunant, founder of Red Cross. 750fr, De Gaulle, vert.

1991, Sept. 2 *Perf. 13½*

930 A310 100fr multicolored .85 .40
931 A310 150fr multicolored 1.25 .60
932 A310 200fr multicolored 1.60 .80
933 A310 240fr multicolored 1.90 .95
934 A310 300fr multicolored 2.40 1.25
935 A310 350fr multicolored 2.75 1.40
936 A310 400fr multicolored 3.75 1.60
937 A310 500fr multicolored 4.50 2.00
Nos. 930-937 (8) 19.00 9.00

Souvenir Sheet

938 A310 750fr multicolored 6.50 3.50

Nos. 936-938 are airmail. No. 938 contains one 35x50mm stamp.
For overprint, see No. 1199.

Gen. Charles de Gaulle in Africa — A311

120fr, De Gaulle, Free French flag, vert. 240fr, De Gaulle, Appeal of Brazzaville, 1940.

1991, Sept. 2 *Perf. 13½x13, 13x13½*

939 A311 75fr multicolored .90 .40
940 A311 120fr multicolored 1.10 .60
941 A311 240fr multicolored 2.25 1.20
Nos. 939-941 (3) 4.25 2.20

A312

Paintings — A313

1991, Oct. 12 *Perf. 11½*

942 A312 75fr multicolored .75 .35
943 A313 120fr multicolored 1.10 .45

Discovery of America, 500th Anniv. (in 1992) — A314

20fr, Portrait of Christopher Columbus by Sebastian Del Pombo. 35fr, Portrait of Columbus. 40fr, Portrait of Columbus facing right. 55fr, Santa Maria. 75fr, Nina. 150fr, Pinta. 200fr, Arms & signature of Columbus.

1991, May 30 *Perf. 13*

944 A314 20fr multicolored .35 .20
945 A314 35fr multicolored .35 .20
946 A314 40fr multicolored .45 .35
947 A314 55fr multicolored .60 .35
948 A314 75fr multicolored .85 .35
949 A314 150fr multicolored 1.60 .85
950 A314 200fr multicolored 2.10 1.00
Nos. 944-950 (7) 6.30 3.30

Primates A315

1991, Dec. 13 Litho. *Perf. 13*

951 A315 30fr Cercopithecus diana .40 .20
952 A315 45fr Pan troglodytes .50 .20
953 A315 60fr Theropithecus gelada .85 .20
954 A315 75fr Papio hamadryas 1.25 .35
955 A315 90fr Macaca nemestrina 1.50 .50
956 A315 120fr Gorilla gorilla 1.75 .50
957 A315 240fr Mandrillus sphinx 3.75 .75
Nos. 951-957 (7) 10.00 2.70

Souvenir Sheet

958 A315 250fr Gorilla gorilla 4.25 1.50

Nos. 953-958 are vert.

Anniversaries and Events A316

Designs: 50fr, Launching of Sputnik II with dog, Laika, 1957. 75fr, Mahatma Gandhi and Martin Luther King, Jr. 1964. 120fr, Launching of Meteosat and ERS-1 over Europe and Africa. 240fr, Maybach Zeppelin automobile and Ferdinand von Zeppelin, 75th death anniversary. 300fr, Konrad Adenauer, 25th death anniversary and opening of the Brandenburg Gate, 1989. 500fr, Pope John Paul II's visit to Africa. 600fr, Elvis Presley, American entertainer.

1992, Feb. 4 Litho. *Perf. 13½*

959 A316 50fr multicolored .75 .25
960 A316 75fr multicolored .75 .25
961 A316 120fr multicolored 1.25 .45
962 A316 240fr multicolored 2.75 .85
963 A316 300fr multicolored 2.50 .80
964 A316 500fr multicolored 5.25 1.40
a. Souvenir sheet of 3, #960, 963-964 11.50 5.75
Nos. 959-964 (6) 13.25 4.00

Souvenir Sheet

965 A316 600fr multicolored 6.00 2.40

Nos. 959-964 exist in souvenir sheets of 1. Nos. 962, 964-965 are airmail.

Explorers A317

Birds — A318

Genoa '92: 75fr, Juan de la Cosa, nautical chart. 95fr, Martin Alonso Pinzon, astrolabe. 120fr, Alonso de Ojeda, hour glass. 200fr, Vicente Yanez Pinzon, sun dial. 250fr, Bartholomew Columbus, quadrant.
400fr, Columbus, flag, horiz.

1992, Oct. 21 Litho. *Perf. 13*

966 A317 75fr multicolored 1.00 .30
967 A317 95fr multicolored 1.10 .30
968 A317 120fr multicolored 1.75 .30
969 A317 200fr multicolored 2.25 .40
970 A317 250fr multicolored 2.75 .50
Nos. 966-970 (5) 8.85 1.80

Souvenir Sheet

971 A317 400fr multi 14.00 14.00

1992, Oct. 21

Designs: 60fr, Sagittarius serpentarius. 75fr, Ephippiorhynchus senegalensis. 120fr, Bugeranus carunculatus. 200fr, Ardea melanocephala. 250fr, Phoenicopterus ruber roseus.
400fr, Balearica regulorum.

972 A318 60fr multicolored .70 .20
973 A318 75fr multicolored .80 .20
974 A318 120fr multicolored 1.10 .30
975 A318 200fr multicolored 2.00 .40
976 A318 250fr multicolored 2.75 .50
Nos. 972-976 (5) 7.35 1.60

Souvenir Sheet

977 A318 400fr multi 4.00 1.00

For overprint, see No. 1191.

Wild Cats — A319

1992, Nov. 21 Litho. *Perf. 13*

978 A319 45fr Panthera leo .50 .50
979 A319 60fr Panthera tigris .60 .60
980 A319 75fr Lynx lynx .70 .70
981 A319 95fr Caracal caracal .80 .80
982 A319 250fr Leopardus pardalis 2.25 2.25
Nos. 978-982 (5) 4.85 4.85

Souvenir Sheet

983 A319 400fr Acinonyx jubatus 4.50 1.75

No. 983 contains one 32x40mm stamp.

1992 Winter Olympics, Albertville — A320

1992 Summer Olympics, Barcelona A321

Gold medalists: 150fr, N. Mishkutyonok, A. Dmitriev, pairs figure skating, Unified team. 200fr, I. Appelt, H. Winkler, G. Haldacher, T. Schroll, 4-man bobsled, Austria. 500fr, Gunda Niemann, speed skating, Germany. 600fr, Bjorn Daehlie, cross-country skiing, Norway. 750fr, Alberto Tomba, giant slalom, Italy.

1992, Dec. 21 Litho. *Perf. 13½*

984 A320 150fr multicolored 1.25 1.25
985 A320 200fr multicolored 1.60 1.60
986 A320 500fr multicolored 4.00 4.00
987 A320 600fr multicolored 4.75 4.75
Nos. 984-987 (4) 11.60 11.60

Souvenir Sheet

988 A320 750fr multicolored 6.00 6.00

Nos. 986-988 are airmail. No. 988 contains one 35x50mm stamp. Name on No. 987 spelled incorrectly.

1992, Dec. 21

Barcelona landmarks, Olympic event: 75fr, Steeple of La Sagrada Familia, baseball. 100fr, The Muse, Palace of Music, running. 150fr, Cupola interior, long jump. 200fr, St. Paul Hospital, pole vault. 400fr, Sculpture, by Miro, shot put. 500fr, Galley, Maritime Museum, table tennis. 750fr, La Sagrada Familia, tennis.

989 A321 75fr multicolored .60 .30
990 A321 100fr multicolored .80 .40
991 A321 150fr multicolored 1.25 .60
992 A321 200fr multicolored 1.60 .80
993 A321 400fr multicolored 3.25 3.25
994 A321 500fr multicolored 4.00 4.00
Nos. 989-994 (6) 11.50 9.35

Souvenir Sheet

995 A321 750fr multicolored 6.00 6.00

Nos. 993-995 are airmail.

Christmas A321a

Paintings: 95fr, The Madonna of the Grand Duke, by Raphael. 120fr, Virgin and Child, by Francesco Mazzo. 200fr, The Madonna with a Book, by Botticelli. 250fr, The Madonna Carondelet, by Fra Bartolommeo. 400fr, Madonna and Child, by Raphael.

1992, Dec. 20 Litho. *Perf. 12½*

995A	A321a	95fr multicolored	1.25	.30
995B	A321a	120fr multi	2.00	.65
995C	A321a	200fr multicolored	2.75	.75
995D	A321a	250fr multicolored	3.25	1.25
		Nos. 995A-995D (4)	9.25	2.95

Souvenir Sheet

995E	A321a	400fr multicolored	4.50	1.90

Nos. 995A-995E were not available until late 1993.

For overprint, see No. 1192.

Birds of Prey — A322

A323

1993, Jan. 15 Litho. *Perf. 12½x13*

996	A322	45fr Charognard	.50	.20
997	A322	75fr Vulture	1.50	.30
998	A322	120fr Eagle	2.00	.65
		Nos. 996-998 (3)	4.00	1.15

1993, Dec. 21 Litho. *Perf. 13½*

Traditional ceramics.

999	A323	45fr Liloko	.60	.30
1000	A323	75fr Mbeya	.95	.50
1001	A323	120fr Jug with ladles, Mbeya	1.40	.85
		Nos. 999-1001 (3)	2.95	1.65

1994 World Cup Soccer Championships, United States — A324

Design: 75fr, Player stretching to kick ball. 95fr, Goalie diving to stop ball. 120fr, Player stretching to kick ball. 200fr, Player kicking. 250fr, Goalie catching ball.

1993, Jan. 15 Litho. *Perf. 12¾*

1002	A324	75fr multi	1.20	.80
1003	A324	95fr multi	1.25	1.10
1004	A324	120fr multi	2.10	1.40
1005	A324	200fr multi	3.00	2.10
1006	A324	250fr multi	3.50	2.75

An additional stamps was issued in this set. The editors would like to examine any example.

Wild Animals A325

Designs: 60fr, Damaliscus lunatus. 75fr, Gazella granti. 95fr, Equus quagga. 120fr, Panthera pardus. 200fr, Syncerus caffer. 250fr, Hippopotamus ampibius. 350fr, Panthera leo.

1993, Feb. 20 Litho. *Perf. 13*

1008	A325	60fr Damaliscus lunatus	.75	.20
1009	A325	75fr Gazella granti	1.25	.20
1010	A325	95fr Equus quagga	1.40	.30
1011	A325	120fr Panthera pardus	1.90	.30
1012	A325	200fr Syncerus caffer	2.75	.40
1013	A325	250fr Hippopotamus amphibius	3.50	.40
1014	A325	300fr Necrosyrtes monachu	4.25	.40
1015	A325	350fr Panthera leo	4.75	.75
a.		Sheet of 8, #1008-1015	20.00	20.00
		Nos. 1008-1015 (8)	20.55	2.95

No. 1015a is a continuous design.

Wild Flowers — A326

Designs: 75fr, Hibiscus schizopetalus. 95fr, Pentas lanceolata. 120fr, Ricinus communis. 200fr, Delonix regia. 250fr, Stapelia gigantea.

1993, May 20 Litho. *Perf. 12½*

1016	A326	75fr multicolored	*1.25*	*.30*
1017	A326	95fr multicolored	*1.75*	*.40*
1018	A326	120fr multicolored	*3.00*	*.50*
1019	A326	200fr multicolored	*5.25*	*1.00*
1020	A326	250fr multicolored	*6.50*	*1.60*
		Nos. 1016-1020 (5)	*17.75*	*3.80*

Deep Sea Submersibles A327

1993, June 25

1021	A327	75fr Transport PC-1202	*1.60*	*.75*
1022	A327	95fr J. Sea Link 1	*2.00*	*1.00*
1023	A327	120fr Nemo	*2.50*	*1.25*
1024	A327	200fr Robot	*4.25*	*2.25*
1025	A327	250fr Alvin	*5.50*	*2.75*
		Nos. 1021-1025 (5)	*15.85*	*8.00*

Souvenir Sheet

1026	A327	400fr Star III	*9.00*	*6.75*

No. 1026 contains one 32x40mm stamp.

1996 Summer Olympic Games, Atlanta A329

Designs: 50fr, Equestrian. 75fr, Cycling. 120fr, Sailing. 240fr, shown. 300fr, Hurdles. 500fr, Women's basketball. 750fr, Running.

1993, Apr. 26 Litho. *Perf. 13½*

1030-1035	A329	Set of 6	10.00	4.00
1035a		Sheet of 6, #1030-1035	10.00	5.00

Souvenir Sheet

1036	A329	750fr multicolored	6.50	1.50

Nos. 1030-1036 exist imperf. Nos. 1030-1035 exist in souvenir sheets of 1.

Brasiliana '93 — A330

Birds: 75fr, Vidua whydah. 95fr, Vidua regia. 120fr, Steganura paradisea. 200fr, Vidua macroura. 250fr, Anthreptes platura.

400fr, Coliuspasser macrourus, horiz.

1993, July 15 Litho. *Perf. 12x12½*

1037-1041	A330	Set of 5	13.00	13.00

Souvenir Sheet

1042	A330	400fr multicolored	12.00	12.00

Prehistoric Animals — A331

1993, Aug. 20 Litho. *Perf. 13*

1043	A331	75fr Ichthyostega	*1.75*	*1.25*
1044	A331	95fr Archaeopteryx	*2.25*	*1.60*
1045	A331	120fr Brachiosaurus	*3.00*	*2.10*
1046	A331	200fr Tyrannosaurus	*4.75*	*3.50*
1047	A331	250fr Pteranodon, vert.	*6.50*	*4.25*
		Nos. 1043-1047 (5)	*18.25*	*12.70*

Souvenir Sheet

1048	A331	400fr Brontosaurus	*13.00*	*6.50*

No. 1048 contains one 32x40mm stamp.

Powered Flight, 90th Anniv. — A332

Designs: 75fr, Wilbur Wright, Model B airplane, vert. 95fr, Orville Wright and Model B biplane, vert. 120fr, First flight by Orville Wright. 200fr, Flight at Kitty Hawk. 250fr, Wright Brothers and airplane.

Perf. 12¼x12½, 12½x12¼

1993, Dec. 17 Litho.

1049	A332	75fr multi	.60	.60
1050	A332	95fr multi	.75	.75
1051	A332	120fr multi	.90	.90
1052	A332	200fr multi	1.60	1.60
1053	A332	250fr multi	2.10	2.10
		Nos. 1049-1053 (5)	5.95	5.95

Evolution of the Elephant A333

1994, June 20 Litho. *Perf. 12½*

1054	A333	25fr Palaeomastodon	*1.00*	*.50*
1055	A333	45fr Mammut	*1.75*	*.90*
1056	A333	50fr Amebelodon	*2.00*	*1.00*
1057	A333	75fr Platybelodon	*3.00*	*1.50*
1058	A333	120fr Mammuthus	*4.75*	*2.40*
		Nos. 1054-1058 (5)	*12.50*	*6.30*

Protection of Nature — A335

Designs: 50fr, Choeropsis liberiensis. 90fr, Hyemoschus aquaticus. 205fr, Taurotragus euryceros, vert. 300fr, Redunca redunca, vert.

1994, Aug. 27 Litho. *Perf. 12½*

1063	A335	50fr multicolored	*.65*	*.30*
1064	A335	90fr multicolored	*1.10*	*.30*
1065	A335	205fr multicolored	*2.50*	*1.10*
1066	A335	300fr multicolored	*3.25*	*1.60*
		Nos. 1063-1066 (4)	*7.50*	*3.30*

For overprint see #1167.

Seaplanes — A336

Designs: 30fr, Cant Z-505, Italy. 45fr, Martin Mariner PBM-3, US. No. 1069, E-59, Russia. No. 1070, Short Sunderland, Great Britain. No. 1071, Martin Mars XPB2M-1, US.

400fr, Boeing 314, US.

1994, Sept. 2 Litho. *Perf. 12½*

1067	A336	30fr multicolored	*.40*	*.40*
1068	A336	45fr multicolored	*.65*	*.65*
1069	A336	90fr multicolored	*1.50*	*1.50*
1070	A336	90fr multicolored	*1.50*	*1.50*
1071	A336	90fr multicolored	*1.50*	*1.50*
		Nos. 1067-1071 (5)	*5.55*	*5.55*

Souvenir Sheet

1071A	A336	400fr multicolored	*5.00*	*2.50*

No. 1071A contains one 40x32mm stamp.

Intl. Year of the Family — A337

1995, Jan. 28 Litho. *Perf. 12½*

1072	A337	90fr shown	*1.10*	*.40*
1073	A337	205fr African map, child	*2.25*	*1.00*
1074	A337	300fr Family, native huts	*3.50*	*1.50*
		Nos. 1072-1074 (3)	*6.85*	*2.90*

For overprint see No. 1168.

Insects — A338

1994, July 24 Litho. *Perf. 12½*

1075	A338	90fr Tarantula	*1.90*	*.40*
1076	A338	205fr Spider	*4.50*	*1.10*
1077	A338	240fr Ladybug	*5.00*	*1.25*
		Nos. 1075-1077 (3)	*11.40*	*2.75*

Souvenir Sheet

1078	A338	400fr Bee	*4.75*	*2.00*

Costumes — A338a

1995 Litho. *Perf. 12¾x12½*

1078A A338a 90fr M'Bochi 1.50 .75
1078B A338a 205fr Téké 2.00 1.00
1078C A338a 500fr Loango 5.00 1.75
Nos. 1078A-1078C (3) 8.50 3.50

Rotary Intl., 90th Anniv. A339

Designs: 90fr, Polio victim. No. 1080, Playing ball with children. No. 1081, Children with food. 300fr, Delivering polio vaccine.
1500fr, Paul Harris, Rotary emblem.

1996, Feb. 6 Litho. *Perf. 14*

1079 A339 90fr multicolored .60 .25
1080 A339 205fr multicolored 1.25 .50
1081 A339 205fr multicolored 1.25 .50
1082 A339 300fr multicolored 1.60 .60
Nos. 1079-1082 (4) 4.70 1.85

Souvenir Sheet

1083 A339 1500fr multicolored 7.50 3.25

For overprint, see Mo. 1201.

18th World Scout Jamboree, The Netherlands — A340

Designs: No. 1084, Handshake. No. 1085, Scout helping another with arm sling. 205fr, Saving life in water. 300fr, Lord Baden-Powell. 1000fr, Scout salute.

1996, Feb. 6 Litho. *Perf. 14*

1084 A340 90fr multicolored .45 .20
1085 A340 90fr multicolored .45 .20
1086 A340 205fr multicolored 1.10 .40
1087 A340 300fr multicolored 1.75 .50
Nos. 1084-1087 (4) 3.75 1.30

Souvenir Sheet

1088 A340 1000fr multicolored 4.25 2.10

1998 World Cup Soccer Tournament A340a

Various players. Denominations: 90fr, 150fr, 205fr, 300fr, 400fr, 500fr.

1996 Litho. *Perf. 12¾*

1088A-1088F A340a Set of 6 7.25 7.25

Souvenir Sheet

Perf. 13¼x13

1088G A340a 1000fr Player's legs 4.50 4.50

No. 1088G contains one 40x31mm stamp.

Antique Automobiles — A341

90fr, 1936 Armstrong Siddeley Twelve. 150fr, 1935 Aston Martin Mark II. 205fr, 1938 Morris 8. 300fr, 1955-62 MG Series MGA. 400fr, 1932 SS1. 500fr, 1938 Alvis 25 SB.

1996, Apr. 30 Litho. *Perf. 12½x12*

1089 A341 90fr multicolored .45 .20
1090 A341 150fr multicolored .75 .40
1091 A341 205fr multicolored 1.00 .50
1092 A341 300fr multicolored 1.50 .75
1093 A341 400fr multicolored 2.00 1.00
1094 A341 500fr multicolored 2.50 1.25
Nos. 1089-1094 (6) 8.20 4.10

Domestic Cats — A342

90fr, Persian. 150fr, Siamese. 205fr, Norwegian forest. 300fr, Exotic shorthair. 400fr, Maine coon. 500fr, Red abyssinian.
1000fr, Turkish Angora.

1996, Mar. 10 *Perf. 13x12½*

1095 A342 90fr multicolored .45 .20
1096 A342 150fr multicolored .75 .40
1097 A342 205fr multicolored 1.00 .50
1098 A342 300fr multicolored 1.50 .75
1099 A342 400fr multicolored 2.00 1.00
1100 A342 500fr multicolored 2.50 1.25
Nos. 1095-1100 (6) 8.20 4.10

Souvenir Sheet

1101 A342 1000fr multicolored 5.00 2.50

No. 1101 contains one 32x40mm stamp.

1996 Summer Olympic Games, Atlanta A343

1996 *Perf. 13x12½, 12½x13*

1102 A343 90fr Fencing, vert. .50 .25
1103 A343 150fr Archery, vert. .80 .40
1104 A343 205fr Basketball, vert. 1.10 .55
1105 A343 300fr Baseball, vert. 1.60 .80
1106 A343 400fr Volleyball 2.25 1.10
1107 A343 500fr 2-man kayak 2.50 1.25
Nos. 1102-1107 (6) 8.75 4.35

Souvenir Sheet

1108 A343 1000fr Judo, vert. 5.25 2.50

No. 1108 contains one 32x40mm stamp.

Flowers — A344

Designs: 90fr, Nerium oleander. 150fr, Eucaliptus globulus. 205fr, Centaurea cyanus. 300fr, Coffea arabica. 400fr, Hibiscus sabdariffa. 500fr, Cassia angustifolia.

1996, May 10 *Perf. 12½*

1109 A344 90fr multicolored .50 .25
1110 A344 150fr multicolored .80 .40
1111 A344 205fr multicolored 1.10 .55
1112 A344 300fr multicolored 1.60 .80
1113 A344 400fr multicolored 2.25 1.10
1114 A344 500fr multicolored 2.50 1.25
Nos. 1109-1114 (6) 8.75 4.35

Mother Carrying Baby — A345

1996 Litho. *Perf. 13*

1115 A345 40fr blue *4.00 2.00*
1116 A345 50fr violet brown *5.00 2.50*
1117 A345 90fr orange *9.00 4.50*
1118 A345 100fr green blue *10.00 5.00*
1119 A345 115fr gray *11.00 5.50*
1120 A345 205fr brown *20.00 10.00*
Nos. 1115-1120 (6) 59.00 29.50

It has been stated that this set was not issued.
See #1145-1150.
For overprint, see No. 1185A.

A346

Owls — A347

1996, Aug. 31 Litho. *Perf. 13½*

1121 A346 90fr orange & multi .45 .30
1122 A346 205fr green & multi 1.00 .60

Investiture of Pres. Pascal Lissouba, 4th anniv.

1996, Mar. 29 *Perf. 14½*

1123 A347 90fr Tyto alba .70 .25
1124 A347 205fr Bubo poensis 1.40 .50
1125 A347 300fr Scotopelia peli 2.00 .90
1126 A347 500fr Asio capensis 3.25 1.50
Nos. 1123-1126 (4) 7.35 3.15

Military Aircraft — A348

Designs: 90fr, Vought-Sikorsky Vindicator SB2U-1. 150fr, Grumman Wildcat F4F-3. 205fr, North American SNJ-2. 300fr, Brewster Bermuda. 400fr, Blackburn Skua 1. 500fr, Mitsubishi Type 98-1.
1000fr, P-40 Warhawk (Flying Tigers).

1996, June 24 Litho. *Perf. 12½x12*

1127 A348 90fr multicolored .45 .20
1128 A348 150fr multicolored .75 .30
1129 A348 205fr multicolored 1.00 .50
1130 A348 300fr multicolored 1.50 .75
1131 A348 400fr multicolored 2.00 1.00
1132 A348 500fr multicolored 2.50 1.25
Nos. 1127-1132 (6) 8.20 4.00

Souvenir Sheet

Perf. 13

1133 A348 1000fr multicolored 5.00 2.50

No. 1133 contains one 32x40mm stamp.

Aquatic Flowers — A348a

Design: 90fr, Cyrtosperma senegalense.

1996, July 3 Litho. *Perf. 14x14¼*

1133A A348a 90fr multi .50 .50

An additional stamp was issued in this set. The editors would like to examine it.

Crocodilians A348b

1996, July 16 Litho. *Perf. 14*

1133C A348b 205fr Nile crocodile — —
1133D A348b 255fr Gavial — —
1133E A348b 300fr Caiman — —

United Nations, 50th Anniv. — A348c

1996 Litho. *Perf. 12½*

1133F A348c 300fr multi — —

Arctocebus Calabarensis A349

a, 90fr, With young. b, 205fr, Touching leaf. c, 300fr, Climbing to left. d, 255fr, Walking on branch.

1998, June 3 Litho. *Perf. 14*

1134 A349 Strip of 4, #a.-d. 4.50 4.50

No. 1134 issued in sheets of 12 stamps. World Wildlife Fund.

Endangered Species — A350

#1135, Kabus defassa, vert. #1136, Caphalophus sylvicutor. 205fr, Potamochoerus porcus. 300fr, Tragelaplus spekei.

1996 Litho. *Perf. 14*

1135 A350 90fr multi .55 .25
1136 A350 90fr multi, vert. .55 .25
1137 A350 205fr multi, vert. 1.10 .45
1138 A350 300fr multi 1.60 .65
Nos. 1135-1138 (4) 3.80 1.60

Diana, Princess of Wales (1961-97) A351

#1139-1141: Various portraits with white rose.

Diana, rose, famous people in sheet margin: 750fr, Henry Kissinger, vert. No. 1143, Mother Teresa, vert. No. 1144, Hillary Clinton, vert.

1998, Aug. 31 Litho. *Perf. 14*

Sheets of 6

1139 A351 205fr #a.-f. 4.25 2.00
1140 A351 255fr #a.-f., vert. 5.25 2.75
1141 A351 300fr #a.-f., vert. 6.25 3.00

Souvenir Sheets

1142 A351 750fr multicolored 2.50 1.25
1143-1144 A351 1000fr each 3.50 1.75

Stamps of Type A345 inscribed only "Congo" ovptd.

1998 Litho. *Perf. 13*

1145 A345 40fr blue
1146 A345 50fr violet brown
1147 A345 90fr orange
1148 A345 100fr green blue — —
1149 A345 115fr gray
1150 A345 205fr brown

A352

Designs: 90fr, Aframomum africanum. 205fr, Gambeya lacuurtiana (37x24mm). 300fr, Landolphia jumeli.

Perf. 13½x13¼, 13 (#1152)

1998 Litho.

1151 A352 90fr multi
1152 A352 205fr multi — —
1153 A352 300fr multi

No. 1153 has denomination in yellow.

No. 732A Overprinted

No. 929 Overprinted

1998 Litho. *Perf. 13*

1155 A244 205fr multi — —
1156 A309 300fr multi — —

An additional stamp was issued in this set. The editors would like to examine them.

Nos. 732B, 804, 854, 855, 929, 1066, 1074, 1118, 1133D Ovptd. Like

and

A355

Perfs. as before, Perf. 14 (#1164), Perf. 13½x13¼ (#1170)

Methods as before, Litho. (#1164, 1170)

1998

1157 A274 60fr multi (#804)
1159 A345 100fr green blue (#1118)
1164 A348b 255fr multi (#1133D)
1165 A309 300fr multi (#929)
1167 A335 300fr multi (#1066)
a. Overprint reading horizontally
1168 A337 300fr multi (#1074)
1169 A355 300fr multi — —
1170 A244 300fr multi (#732B)
a. Overprint reading horizontally — —
1172 A292 360fr multi (#854)
a. Inverted overprint — —
1173 A292 400fr multi (#855) — —

Numbers have been reserved for additional overprinted stamps. Overprint reads horizontally on Nos. 1157, 1159, 1169, 1172 and 1173, vertically reading down on Nos. 1164, 1167, 1168 and 1170, and vertically reading up on No. 1165. No. 1170 has white denomination.

The editors would like to see examples of No. 1169 without the overprint.

1998 World Cup Soccer Championships, France — A358

Designs: 90fr, Netherlands, 4th place. 205fr, Croatia, bronze medal. 300fr, Brazil, silver medal. 500fr, France, gold medal.

1998, Nov. 16 Litho. *Perf. 13x13¼*

1175-1178 A358 Set of 4 — —

Masks — A359

Perf. 13¼x13½

1998, Nov. 20 Litho.

1179 A359 90fr Kwele wood mask
1180 A359 150fr Kwele wood mask
1181 A359 205fr Teke/Tsangui wood mask
1182 A359 205fr Kuyu wood mask

No. 732B Overprinted

Type I — Unserifed Upper and Lower Case Letters, 7x3mm

Type II — Serifed Upper and Lower Case Letters, 12x3mm

Type III — Upper Case Letters, 9x2mm

Methods and Perfs as Before

1999 ?

1183 A244 300fr multi (I) — —
1184 A244 300fr multi (II) — —
1185 A244 300fr multi (III) — —

No. 1119 Overprinted Like No. 1149 But With Wider "G" In Overprint

Method and Perf. As Before

1999 ?

1185A A345 115fr gray —

Nos. 934, 975, 995B, 1082, C342-C343 Overprinted Like No. 1157 and

A359a

Methods as Before, Litho. (#1204)

1999 ? *Perf. as Before, 12½ (#1204)*

1187 AP120 200fr multi (#C342) — —
1188 AP120 200fr multi (#C343) — —
a. Horiz. pair, #1187-1188, + central label — —
1191 A318 200fr multi (#975) — —
1192 A321a 200fr multi (#995B) — —
1199 A310 300fr multi (#934) — —
1201 A339 300fr multi (#1082) — —
1204 A359a 300fr multi — —

The editors would like to see examples of No. 1204 without the overprint. Overprint reads horizontally on No. 1204, horizontally and inverted on Nos. 1187-1188, vertically reading down on Nos. 1191 and 1199, and vertically reading up on Nos. 1192 and 1201.

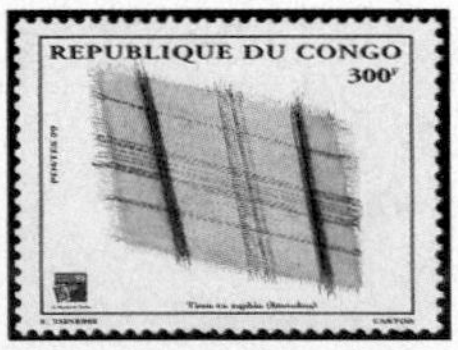

PhilexFrance 99 — A360

Design: 205fr, Raffia cloth with tassels. 300fr, Woven raffia cloth.

1999, July 2 Litho. *Perf. 13x13¼*

1211 A360 205fr multi —
1212 A360 300fr multi — —

First French Postage Stamp, 150th Anniv. A361

Litho. With Hologram

1999 *Perf. 13x13¼*

1213 A361 300fr multi — —

Central African Economic and Monetary Community Week — A363

Designs: 90fr, Map and flags. 205fr, Map and circle of flags.

1999 Litho. *Perf. 14½*

1227 A363 90fr multi — —
1228 A363 205fr multi — —

Additional stamps may exist in this set. The editors would like to examine any examples.

Third Pan-African Music Festival — A364

Designs: 120fr, Emblem. 270fr, Map of Africa with drummers.

2001, Aug. 4 Litho. *Perf. 13½x13*

1229-1230 A364 Set of 2 1.60 1.60

Independence, 40th Anniv. — A365

Designs: 90fr, Dove, vine, map, hands, people. 205fr, Tools, clasped and opened hands, map.

2001, Nov. 15 Litho. *Perf. 13¼x13*

1231-1232 A365 Set of 2 — —

Birds — A366

Designs: 90fr, Egretta garzetta. 120fr, Ardea cenerea. 270fr, Ciconia nigra.

2001 *Perf. 13¼*

1233 A366 90fr multi — —
1234 A366 120fr multi — —
1235 A366 270fr multi — —

Additional stamps may exist in this set. The editors would like to examine any examples.

Type of A345 Inscribed "REPUBLIQUE DU CONGO" Overprinted "LEGAL" Like No. 1145

2001 ? **Litho.** *Perf. 13*

1236 A345 90fr blue — —

Fruit — A367

Designs: 40fr, Mbila esobe. 50fr, Ikami. 70fr, Tsia, vert. 80fr, Bamou. 120fr, Malombo. 270fr, Ntondolo, vert.

2002, June 25 **Litho.** *Perf. 13½*

1237-1242 A367 Set of 6 — —

Birds — A368

Designs: 40fr, Calao (hornbill). 80fr, Cigogne blanche (white stork). 120fr, Grue cendrée (gray crane). 270fr, Marabout.

2002, July 23 *Perf. 13½x13*

1243-1246 A368 Set of 4 — —

Elephants A369

Designs; 120fr, Mammoth. 270fr, Elephant on savannah, horiz. 350fr, Elephant, horiz. 500fr, Forest elephant near lake.

Perf. 13¼x13, 13x13¼

2003, June 20

1247-1250 A369 Set of 4 5.75 5.75

Flowers — A370

Designs: 120fr, Muflier (antirrhinum). 270fr, Pivoine (peony). 400fr, Petunia. 600fr, Mauve (mallow), horiz.

2003, July 6

1251-1254 A370 Set of 4 6.50 6.50

Moringa Olifera — A371

Highlighted portion: 30fr, Bark. 70fr, Root. 90fr, Leaves. 115fr, Seeds and open pod. 120fr, Pod. 360fr, Pod.

2005, Feb. 3 **Litho.** *Perf. 13¼x13*

1255-1260 A371 Set of 6 3.25 3.25

Dated 2004.

Albert Einstein (1879-1955), Physicist — A373

2005, Aug. 17 **Litho.** *Perf. 13¼x13*

1265 A373 400fr multi 4.25 4.25

A374

Brazzaville, 125th Anniv. — A375

2005, Oct. 3 *Perf. 13¼x13*

1266 A374 120fr multi 1.10 1.10

Perf. 13½x13¼

1267 A375 360fr multi 3.25 3.25

Pope Benedict XVI A376

Pope Benedict XVI: 360fr, Waving. 500fr, Holding crucifix.

2005, Nov. 28 *Perf. 13¼x13½*

1268-1269 A376 Set of 2 3.75 3.75

Denis Sassou-Nguesso, President of African Union — A378

2006, Mar. 14 **Litho.** *Perf. 13x13¼*

1274 A378 500fr multi 2.40 2.40

Léopold Sédar Senghor (1906-2001), First President of Senegal — A379

2006, May 15

1275 A379 360fr multi 1.75 1.75

SEMI-POSTAL STAMPS

Anti-Malaria Issue
Common Design Type

1962, Apr. 7 **Engr.** *Perf. 12½x12*

B3 CD108 25fr + 5fr bister .90 .90

Freedom from Hunger Issue
Common Design Type

1963, Mar. 21 **Unwmk.** *Perf. 13*

B4 CD112 25fr + 5fr vio bl, bl grn & brn .90 .90

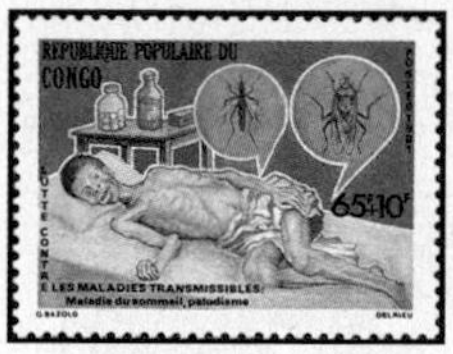

Boy Suffering from Sleeping Sickness SP1

Fight Against Communicable Diseases; 40fr+5fr, Examination, treatment, vert.

1981, June 6 **Litho.** *Perf. 13*

B5 SP1 40fr + 5fr multi .60 .25
B6 SP1 65fr + 10fr multi 1.00 .30

IYD Type of 1981

1981, June 29 *Perf. 12½*

B7 A192 75fr + 5fr multi .90 .35

AIR POST STAMPS

Olympic Games Issue
French Equatorial Africa No. C37 Surcharged in Red Like Chad No. C1

1960 **Unwmk.** **Engr.** *Perf. 13*

C1 AP8 250fr on 500fr grnsh blk, blk & sl 7.50 7.50

17th Olympic Games, Rome, 8/25-9/11.

Helicrysum Mechowiam — AP1

Flowers: 200fr, Cogniauxia podolaena. 500fr, Thesium tencio.

1961, Sept. 28 **Engr.** *Perf. 13*

C2 AP1 100fr grn, lil & yel 3.25 1.25
C3 AP1 200fr bl grn, yel & brn 5.25 1.75
C4 AP1 500fr brn red, yel & sl grn 16.00 5.00
Nos. C2-C4 (3) 24.50 8.00

Air Afrique Issue
Common Design Type

1961, Nov. 25 **Unwmk.** *Perf. 13*

C5 CD107 50fr lil rose, sl grn & grn 1.25 .50

Loading Timber, Pointe-Noire Harbor — AP2

1962, June 8 **Photo.** *Perf. 12½x12*

C6 AP2 50fr multicolored 1.50 .90

Opening of the Intl. Fair and Exhib., Pointe-Noire, June 8-11.

Abidjan Games — AP3

Costus Spectabilis AP4

1962, July 21 *Perf. 12x12½*

C7 AP3 100fr Basketball 2.50 1.25

1963 **Unwmk.** *Perf. 13*

Design: 250fr, Mountain acanthus.

C8 AP4 100fr multicolored 4.00 1.75
C9 AP4 250fr multicolored 8.00 3.25

Brazzaville City Hall and Pres. Fulbert Youlou — AP4a

1963, Aug. **Photo.** *Perf. 13x12*

C10 AP4a 100fr multicolored 150.00 125.00

African Postal Union Issue
Common Design Type

1963, Sept. 8 *Perf. 12½*

C13 CD114 85fr pur, ocher & red 1.25 .75

Air Afrique Issue, 1963
Common Design Type

Perf. 13x12

1963, Nov. 19 **Unwmk.** **Photo.**

C14 CD115 50fr multicolored .85 .50

Liberty Place, Brazzaville — AP5

1963, Nov. 28

C15 AP5 25fr multicolored .55 .40

See No. 118.

Europafrica Issue
Common Design Type

1963, Nov. 30 *Perf. 12x13*
C16 CD116 50fr gray, yel & dk brn 1.25 .90

Timber Industry — AP6

1964, May 12 **Engr.** *Perf. 13*
C17 AP6 100fr grn, brn red & blk 2.10 .90

Chiefs of State Issue

Map and Presidents of Chad, Congo, Gabon and CAR AP6a

1964, June 23 **Photo.** *Perf. 12½*
C18 AP6a 100fr multicolored 1.40 .80

See note after Central African Republic No. C19.

Europafrica Issue, 1964

Sunburst, Wheat, Cogwheel and Globe — AP7

1964, July 20 *Perf. 12x13*
C19 AP7 50fr yel, Prus bl & mar 1.00 .75

See note after Cameroun No. 402.

Hammer Thrower, Olympic Flame and Stadium — AP8

50fr, 100fr, vert.

1964, July 30 **Engr.** *Perf. 13*
C20 AP8 25fr shown .45 .25
C21 AP8 50fr Weight lifter .80 .45
C22 AP8 100fr Volleyball 1.75 1.00
C23 AP8 200fr High jump 3.25 2.10
a. Min. sheet of 4, #C20-C23 8.00 8.00
Nos. C20-C23 (4) 6.25 3.80

18th Olympic Games, Tokyo, 10/10-25/64.

Communications Symbols — AP8a

1964, Nov. 2 **Litho.** *Perf. 12½x13*
C24 AP8a 25fr dl rose & dk brn .50 .30

See note after Chad No. C19.

Town Hall, Brazzaville — AP9

1965, Jan. 30 **Photo.** *Perf. 12½*
C25 AP9 100fr multicolored 1.25 .60

Coupling Hooks — AP10

1965, Feb. 27 **Photo.** *Perf. 13x12*
C26 AP10 50fr multicolored 1.00 .75

Economic Europe-Africa Association.

Breguet Dial Telegraph, ITU Emblem and Telstar — AP11

1965, May 17 **Engr.** *Perf. 13*
C27 AP11 100fr dk bl, ocher & brn 2.25 .75

Cent. of the ITU.

Pope John XXIII (1881-1963), St. Peter's Cathedral — AP12

Perf. 12½x13
1965, June 26 **Photo.** **Unwmk.**
C28 AP12 100fr gldn brn & multi 1.60 .75

Pres. John F. Kennedy — AP13

Log Rolling — AP14

Portraits: 25fr on 50fr, Patrice Lumumba, premier of Congo Republic (ex-Belgian). 50fr, Sir Winston Churchill. 80fr, Barthélémy Boganda, premier of Central African Republic.

1965, June *Perf. 12½*
C29 AP13 25fr on 50fr dk brn & red .50 .40
a. Surcharge omitted 35.00 35.00
C30 AP13 50fr dk brn & yel grn 1.10 1.00
C31 AP13 80fr dk brn & bl 2.00 1.50
C32 AP13 100fr dk brn & org yel 2.75 2.25
a. Min. sheet of 4, #C29-C32 6.25 6.25
Nos. C29-C32 (4) 6.35 5.15

A second miniature sheet contains one each of Nos. C29a, C30-C32. Value, $50.

Issued: 25fr, 80fr, 6/25; 50fr, 100fr, #C32a, 6/26.

1965, Aug. 14 **Engr.** *Perf. 13*
C33 AP14 50fr grn, brn & red brn .80 .50

Issued to publicize national unity.

World Map and Symbols of Agriculture and Industry — AP15

1965, Oct. 18 **Engr.** *Perf. 13*
C34 AP15 50fr dk bl, blk, brn & org 1.10 .75

International Cooperation Year, 1965.

Abraham Lincoln — AP16

1965, Dec. 15 **Photo.** *Perf. 13*
C35 AP16 90fr pink & multi 1.25 .60

Centenary of death of Abraham Lincoln.

Charles de Gaulle, Torch and Map of Africa — AP17

1966, Feb. 28 **Engr.** *Perf. 13*
C36 AP17 500fr dk red, dk grn & dk red brn 35.00 26.00

22nd anniv. of the Brazzaville Conf.

D-1 Satellite over Brazzaville Space Tracking Station — AP18

Grain, Atom Symbol and Map of Africa and Europe — AP19

1966, May 15 **Engr.** *Perf. 13*
C37 AP18 150fr blk, dl red & bl grn 2.25 1.25

1966, July 20 **Photo.** *Perf. 12x13*
C38 AP19 50fr multicolored .90 .50

See note after Gabon No. C46.

Pres. Massamba-Debat and President's Palace — AP20

3rd anniv. of the Revolution: 30fr, Robespierre and storming of the Bastille. 50fr, Lenin and storming of the Winter Palace.

1966, Aug. 15 **Photo.** *Perf. 12x12½*
C39 AP20 25fr multicolored .25 .20
C40 AP20 30fr multicolored .35 .25
C41 AP20 50fr multicolored 1.60 .35
a. Souv. sheet of 3, #C39-C41 2.25 2.25
Nos. C39-C41 (3) 2.20 .80

Air Afrique Issue, 1966
Common Design Type

1966, Aug. 31 **Photo.** *Perf. 13*
C42 CD123 30fr lilac, lemon & blk .60 .25

Dr. Albert Schweitzer — AP21

1966, Sept. 4 Photo. *Perf. 12½*
C43 AP21 100fr red, blk, bl & lilac 2.00 1.25

Issued to honor Dr. Albert Schweitzer (1875-1965), medical missionary.

AP22

AP23

1966, Dec. 26 Photo. *Perf. 13*
C44 AP22 100fr Crab, microscope and pagoda 1.50 1.00

9th Intl. Anticancer Cong., Tokyo. 10/23-29.

1967 Photo. *Perf. 13*

Birds: 50fr, Social Weaver. 75fr, European Bee-eater. 100fr, Lilac-breasted roller. 150fr, Regal sunbird. 200fr, Crowned cranes. 250fr, Secretary bird. 300fr, Knysna touraco.

C45 AP23 50fr multicolored 1.60 .75
C46 AP23 75fr multicolored 3.25 1.00
C47 AP23 100fr multicolored 3.25 1.00
C48 AP23 150fr multicolored 4.25 2.25
C49 AP23 200fr multicolored 7.50 2.50
C50 AP23 250fr multicolored 9.50 3.00
C51 AP23 300fr multicolored 13.50 5.00
Nos. C45-C51 (7) 42.85 15.50

Issued: #C45-C47, 2/13; others, 6/20.

Shackled Hands AP24

1967, May 24 Photo. *Perf. 12½x13*
C52 AP24 500fr multicolored 8.50 3.00

Issued for African Liberation Day.

Sputnik 1, Explorer 6 and Earth — AP25

Space Craft: 75fr, Ranger 6, Lunik 2 and moon. 100fr, Mars 1, Mariner 4 and Mars. 200fr, Gemini, Vostok and earth.

1967, Aug. 1 Engr. *Perf. 13*
C53 AP25 50fr multicolored .65 .30
C54 AP25 75fr multicolored 1.10 .35
C55 AP25 100fr multicolored 1.60 .60
C56 AP25 200fr multicolored 2.75 1.50
Nos. C53-C56 (4) 6.10 2.75

Space explorations.

African Postal Union Issue, 1967
Common Design Type

1967, Sept. 9 Engr. *Perf. 13*
C57 CD124 100fr ver, ol & emer 1.25 .60

Boy Scouts, Tents and Jamboree Emblem — AP26

Design: 70c, Borah Peak, Idaho; tents, Scout sign and Jamboree emblem.

1967, Sept. 29
C58 AP26 50fr multicolored 1.00 .30
C59 AP26 70fr multicolored 1.40 .50

12th Boy Scout World Jamboree, Farragut State Park, ID, Aug. 1-9.

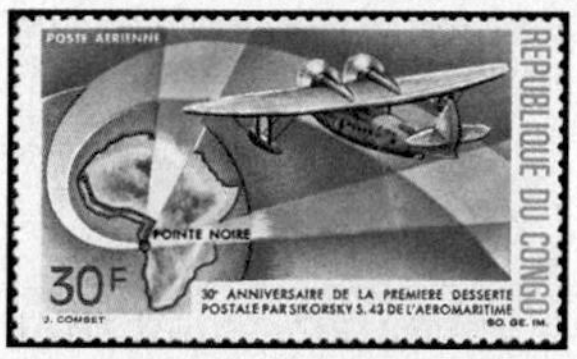

Sikorsky S-43 and Map of Africa — AP27

1967, Oct. 2 Photo. *Perf. 13*
C60 AP27 30fr multicolored .65 .30

30th anniv. of the 1st airmail connection by Aeromaritime Lines from Casablanca to Pointe-Noire.

Men of Four Races Dancing on Globe — AP28

1968, Feb 8 Engr. *Perf. 13*
C61 AP28 70fr dk brn, ultra & emer 1.00 .45

Friendship among peoples.

The Oath of the Horatii, by Jacques Louis David — AP29

Paintings: 25fr, On the Barricades, by Delacroix. No. C63, Grandfather and Grandson, by Ghirlandajo, vert. No. C64, The Demolition of the Bastille, by Hubert Robert. 200fr, Negro Woman Arranging Peonies, by Jean F. Bazille.

1968 Photo. *Perf. 12x12½, 12½x12*
C62 AP29 25fr multicolored 1.75 .35
C63 AP29 30fr multicolored .90 .30
C64 AP29 30fr multicolored 1.75 .50
C65 AP29 100fr multicolored 2.25 .90
C66 AP29 200fr multicolored 5.00 1.75
Nos. C62-C66 (5) 11.65 3.80

Issue dates: Nos. C62, C64, Aug. 15. Nos. C63, C65-C66, Mar. 20.
See Nos. C78-C81, C111-C115.

Early Automobile Type

1968, July 29 Photo. *Perf. 13x12½*
C67 A50 150fr Ford, 1915 3.50 1.75
C68 A50 200fr Citroen, 1922 5.25 1.75

Europafrica Issue

Square Knot — AP30

1968, July 20 Photo. *Perf. 13*
C69 AP30 50fr multicolored 1.00 .50

5th anniv. of the economic agreement between the European Economic Community and the African and Malgache Union.

Martin Luther King, Jr. — AP31

Robert F. Kennedy — AP32

1968, Aug. 5 *Perf. 12½*
C70 AP31 50fr lt grn, Prus grn & blk 1.10 .40

1968, Sept. 30 Photo. *Perf. 13x12½*
C71 AP32 50fr dp car, ap grn & blk .85 .40

Running — AP33

Olympic Rings and: 20fr, Soccer, vert. 60fr, Boxing, vert. 85fr, High jump.

1968, Dec. 27 Engr. *Perf. 13*
C72 AP33 5fr emer, brt bl & choc .25 .20
C73 AP33 20fr dk bl, brn & dk grn .45 .25
C74 AP33 60fr mar, brt grn & choc .90 .60
C75 AP33 85fr blk, car rose & choc 1.75 .85
Nos. C72-C75 (4) 3.35 1.90

19th Olympic Games, Mexico City, 10/12-27.

PHILEXAFRIQUE Issue

G. De Gueidan, by Nicolas de Largillière AP34

1968, Dec. 30 Photo. *Perf. 12½*
C76 AP34 100fr pink & multi 3.00 1.75

Issued to publicize PHILEXAFRIQUE, Philatelic Exhibition, in Abidjan, Feb. 14-23. Printed with alternating pink label.
See Nos. C89-C93.

2nd PHILEXAFRIQUE Issue
Common Design Type

Design: 50fr, Middle Congo No. 72 and Pointe-Noire harbor.

1969, Feb. 14 Engr. *Perf. 13*
C77 CD128 50fr car rose, sl grn & bis brn 1.75 1.75

Painting Type of 1968.

Paintings: 25fr, Battle of Rivoli, by Carle Vernet. 50fr, Battle of Marengo, by Jacques Augustin Pajou. 75fr, Battle of Friedland, by Horace Vernet. 100fr, Battle of Jena, by Charles Thevenin.

1969, May 20 Photo. *Perf. 12x12½*
C78 AP29 25fr vio bl & multi 1.25 .45
C79 AP29 50fr cop red & multi 1.75 .80
C80 AP29 75fr grn & multi 3.00 1.10
C81 AP29 100fr brn & multi 5.00 1.40
Nos. C78-C81 (4) 11.00 3.75

Bicentenary of birth of Napoleon I.

Ernesto Ché Guevara — AP35

1969, June 10 Photo. *Perf. 12½*
C82 AP35 90fr brn, org & blk 1.00 .50

Issued in memory of Ernesto Ché Guevara (1928-1967), Cuban revolutionist.

Doll, Train and Space Toy — AP36

1969, June 20 Engr. *Perf. 13*
C83 AP36 100fr mag, org & gray 1.50 .75

International Toy Fair, Nuremberg, Germany.

Europafrica Issue, 1969

Ribbon Tied Around Bar — AP37

1969, Aug. 5 Photo. *Perf. 13x12*

C84 AP37 50fr bl grn, lil & blk .90 .35

See note after Chad No. C11.

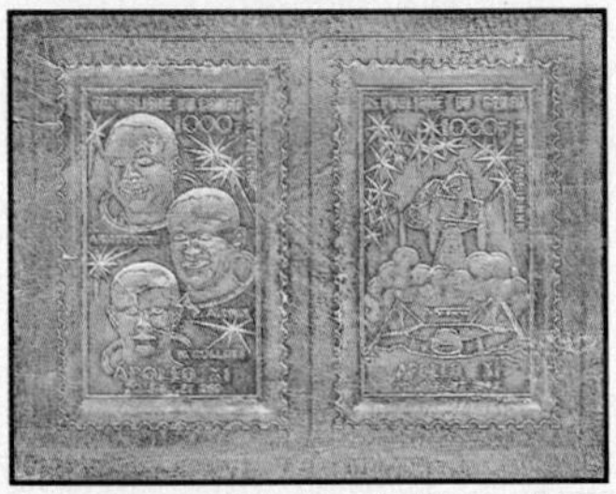

Armstrong, Aldrin and Collins — AP38

Souvenir Sheet

Design: No. C85b, Blast-off from Moon.

Embossed on Gold Foil

1969, Sept. 15 *Imperf.*

C85 AP38 1000fr #a-b 40.00 37.50

See note after Algeria No. 427. No. C85 contains one each of Nos. C85a and C85b with simulated perforations.

Painter, Poto-Poto School — AP39

150fr, Sculpture lesson (man, infant and sculpture). 200fr, Potter working on vase.

1970, Feb. 20 Engr. *Perf. 13*

C86 AP39 100fr multicolored 2.25 .60
C87 AP39 150fr multicolored 3.00 .95
C88 AP39 200fr multicolored 4.50 1.75
Nos. C86-C88 (3) 9.75 3.30

Painting Type (Philexafrique)

Paintings: 150fr, Child with Cherries, by John Russell. 200fr, Erasmus, by Hans Holbein the Younger. 250fr, "Silence" (head), by Bernardino Luini. 300fr, Scene from the Massacre of Scio, by Delacroix. 500fr, The Capture of Constantinople by the Crusaders, by Delacroix.

1970 Photo. *Perf. 12½*

C89 AP34 150fr lil & multi 4.50 1.50
C90 AP34 200fr multicolored 5.75 1.75
C91 AP34 250fr brn & multi 6.25 2.25
C92 AP34 300fr multicolored 8.00 3.25
C93 AP34 500fr brn & multi 13.50 4.50
Nos. C89-C93 (5) 38.00 13.25

Aurichalcite — AP40

1970, Mar. 20

C94 AP40 100fr shown 5.25 1.75
C95 AP40 150fr Dioptase 8.00 2.50

Lenin — AP41

Karl Marx — AP42

1970, June 25 Photo. *Perf. 12½*

C96 AP41 45fr shown 1.00 .35
C97 AP41 75fr Lenin, seated 1.75 .50

Centenary of the birth of Lenin (1870-1924), Russian communist leader.

1970, July 10 Engr. *Perf. 13*

Design: No. C99, Friedrich Engels.

C98 AP42 50fr emer, dk brn & dk red 1.50 .35
C99 AP42 50fr ultra, dk brn & dk red 1.50 .35

Karl Marx (1818-1883) and Friedrich Engels (1820-1895), German socialist writers.

Otto Lilienthal's Glider, 1891 — AP43

Designs: 50fr, "Spirit of St. Louis," Lindbergh's first transatlantic solo flight, 1927. 70fr, Sputnik 1, first satellite in space. 90fr, First man on the moon, Apollo 11, 1969.

1970, Sept. 5 Engr. *Perf. 13*

C100 AP43 45fr dp car, bl & ol bis 1.00 .30
C101 AP43 50fr emer, sl grn & brn 1.00 .35
C102 AP43 70fr brt bl, ol bis & dp car 1.25 .50
C103 AP43 90fr brn, bl & ol gray 1.90 .75
Nos. C100-C103 (4) 5.15 1.90

Forerunners of space exploration.

Saint on Horseback AP44

Marilyn Monroe and NYC — AP45

Designs from Stained Glass Windows, Brazzaville Cathedral: 150fr, Saint with staff. 250fr, The Elevation of the Host, from rose window.

1970, Dec. 10 Photo. *Perf. 12½*

C104 AP44 100fr multicolored 1.40 .50
C105 AP44 150fr multicolored 1.90 .85
C106 AP44 250fr multicolored 3.25 1.75
a. Souv. sheet of 3, #C104-C106 6.75 6.75
Nos. C104-C106 (3) 6.55 3.10

Christmas 1970.

1971, Mar. 16 Engr. *Perf. 13*

Portraits: 150fr, Martine Carol and Paris. 200fr, Erich von Stroheim and Vienna. 250fr, Sergei Eisenstein and Moscow.

C107 AP45 100fr brt grn, red brn & ultra 7.00 .50
C108 AP45 150fr brn, brt lil & ultra 7.00 .75
C109 AP45 200fr choc & ultra 7.00 1.10
C110 AP45 250fr brt grn, brn vio & ultra 7.00 1.25
Nos. C107-C110 (4) 28.00 3.60

History of motion pictures.

Painting Type of 1968

Paintings: 100fr, Christ Carrying Cross, by Paolo Veronese. 150fr, Christ on the Cross, Burgundian School, 1500, vert. 200fr, Descent from the Cross, by Rogier van der Weyden. 250fr, Christ Laid in the Tomb, Flemish School, 1500, vert. 500fr, Resurrection, by Hans Memling, vert.

1971, Apr. 26 Photo. *Perf. 13*

C111 AP29 100fr green & multi 1.75 .75
C112 AP29 150fr green & multi 2.75 .90
C113 AP29 200fr green & multi 4.00 1.10
C114 AP29 250fr green & multi 4.50 1.60
C115 AP29 500fr green & multi 10.00 3.00
Nos. C111-C115 (5) 23.00 7.35

Easter 1971.

Map of Africa and Telecommunications System — AP46

1971, June 18 Photo. *Perf. 12½*

C116 AP46 70fr bl, gray & dk brn .80 .30
C117 AP46 85fr bl, lil rose & dk brn 1.25 .35
C118 AP46 90fr grn, yel & dk brn 1.60 .70
Nos. C116-C118 (3) 3.65 1.35

Pan-African telecommunications system.

Globe and Waves — AP47

1971, June 19

C119 AP47 65fr lt bl & multi .70 .30

3rd World Telecommunications Day.

Japanese Mask and Play — AP48

Olympic Torch and Rings — AP49

Design: 150fr, Japanese and African women, symbolic leaves.

1971, June 28 Engr. *Perf. 13*

C120 AP48 75fr lil, blk & mag 1.00 .70
C121 AP48 150fr dk brn, brn red & red lil 1.60 1.10

PHILATOKYO '71 International Stamp Exhibition, Tokyo, Apr. 20-30.

13th World Boy Scout Jamboree, Japan, gold foil 1000fr airmail and silver foil souv. sheet of four 90fr, issued July 14. Nos. 71C01-71C02.

1971, July 20 Engr. *Perf. 13*

350fr, Olympic rings and various sports.

C122 AP49 150fr multi 1.90 .95
C123 AP49 350fr multi, horiz. 4.50 2.50

Pre-Olympic Year, 1971.

Scout Emblem, Japanese Dragon and African Carved Canoe — AP50

Designs (Boy Scout Emblem and): 90fr, Japanese mask and African boy, vert. 100fr, Japanese woman and African drummer, vert. 250fr, Congolese mask.

1971, Aug. 25

C124 AP50 85fr multicolored 1.10 .30
C125 AP50 90fr multicolored 1.25 .35
C126 AP50 100fr multicolored 1.60 .45
C127 AP50 250fr multicolored 3.25 .90
Nos. C124-C127 (4) 7.20 2.00

13th Boy Scout World Jamboree, Asagiri Plain, Japan, Aug. 2-10.

Olympic Rings and Running — AP51

Designs (Olympic Rings and): 85fr, Hurdles. 90fr, Weight lifting, boxing, discus, running, javelin. 100fr, Wrestling. 150fr, Boxing.

1971, Sept. 30

C128 AP51 75fr plum, bl & dk brn .75 .35
C129 AP51 85fr scar, sl & dk brn .85 .35
C130 AP51 90fr vio bl & dk brn 1.10 .60

C131 AP51 100fr brn & slate 1.40 .60
C132 AP51 150fr grn, red & dk brn 2.40 1.00
Nos. C128-C132 (5) 6.50 2.90

75th anniv. of the 1st modern Olympic Games.

Congo No. C36 and de Gaulle — AP52

Pres. Marien Ngouabi's Tribute to de Gaulle — AP53

Design: No. C135, Charles de Gaulle.

1971, Nov. 9
C133 AP52 500fr slate grn & multi 18.00 15.00

Lithographed; Gold Embossed
Perf. 12½

C134 AP53 1000fr gold, grn & red 27.50 20.00
C135 AP53 1000fr gold, grn & red 27.50 20.00
a. Pair, #C134-C135 55.00 55.00

Charles de Gaulle (1890-1970), president of France.

African Postal Union Issue, 1971
Common Design Type

Design: 100fr, Allegory of Congo Republic (woman) and UAMPT Building, Brazzaville.

1971, Nov. 13 Photo. *Perf. 13x13½*
C136 CD135 100fr bl & multi 1.40 .75

Flag of Congo Republic and "Revolution" — AP54

1971, Nov. 30
C137 AP54 100fr red & multi 1.75 .60

8th anniversary of revolution.

Workers and Flag — AP55

40fr, Flag of Congo Republic and sun.

1971, Dec. 31 Photo. *Perf. 13x12½*
C138 AP55 30fr multicolored .50 .25
C139 AP55 40fr red & multi 1.10 .40

2nd anniv. of founding of Congolese Labor Party (#C138), and adoption of red flag (#C139).

Book Year Emblem — AP56

1972, June 3 Litho. *Perf. 12½*
C140 AP56 50fr red, grn & yel .85 .40

International Book Year 1972.

Congolese Soccer Team — AP57

#C142, Captain of winning team and cup, vert.

1973, Feb. 22 Photo. *Perf. 13*
C141 AP57 100fr ultra, red & blk 1.50 .75
C142 AP57 100fr red, yel & blk 1.50 .75

Girl Holding Bird, Environment Emblem — AP58

1973, Mar. 5 Engr.
C143 AP58 85fr org, slate grn & bl 1.75 .90

UN Conference on Human Environment, Stockholm, Sweden, June 5-16, 1972.

Miles Davis AP59

Designs: 140fr, Ella Fitzgerald. 160fr, Count Basie. 175fr, John Coltrane.

1973, Mar. 5 Photo. *Perf. 13x13½*
C144 AP59 125fr multicolored 4.00 .95
C145 AP59 140fr multicolored 4.00 1.00
C146 AP59 160fr multicolored 5.00 1.50
C147 AP59 175fr multicolored 5.00 1.50
Nos. C144-C147 (4) 18.00 4.95

Black American jazz musicians.

Olympic Rings, Hurdling — AP60

1973, Mar. 15 Engr. *Perf. 13*
C148 AP60 100fr shown 1.10 .60
C149 AP60 150fr Pole vault, vert. 1.75 .90
C150 AP60 250fr Wrestling 2.75 1.50
Nos. C148-C150 (3) 5.60 3.00

20th Olympic Games, Munich, 8/26-9/11/72.

Refinery and Storage Tanks, Djéno — AP61

Designs: 230fr, Off-shore drilling platform, vert. 240fr, Workers assembling drill, vert. 260fr, Off-shore drilling installation.

1973, Mar. 20
C151 AP61 180fr red, bl & indigo 3.25 1.50
C152 AP61 230fr red, bl & blk 4.00 1.50
C153 AP61 240fr red, ind & brn 4.50 1.60
C154 AP61 260fr red, bl & blk 7.25 2.25
Nos. C151-C154 (4) 19.00 6.85

Oil installations, Pointe-Noire.

Astronauts, Landing Module and Lunar Rover on Moon — AP62

1973, Mar. 31
C155 AP62 250fr multicolored 4.50 1.75

Apollo 17 US moon mission, 12/7-19/72.

ITU Emblem, Symbols of Communications AP63

1973, May 24 Engr. *Perf. 13*
C156 AP63 120fr multicolored 2.25 .90

5th International Telecommunications Day.

White Horse, by Delacroix — AP64

Designs: Paintings by Eugene Delacroix.

1973, June 30 Photo. *Perf. 13*
C157 AP64 150fr shown 2.25 1.50
C158 AP64 250fr Lion sleeping 5.00 2.40
C159 AP64 300fr Lion and tiger 5.25 2.50
Nos. C157-C159 (3) 12.50 6.40

See Nos. C169-C171.

Copernicus and Heliocentric System — AP65

1973, June 30 Engr.
C160 AP65 50fr multicolored 1.00 .45

500th anniversary of the birth of Nicolaus Copernicus (1473-1543), Polish astronomer.

Plane, Ship, Rocket, Village, Sun and Clouds — AP66

1973, July
C161 AP66 50fr red & multi 1.40 .60

Cent. of intl. meteorological cooperation.

Pres. Marien Ngouabi — AP67

1973, Aug. 12 Photo. *Perf. 13*
C162 AP67 30fr multicolored .35 .20
C163 AP67 40fr aqua & multi .45 .20
C164 AP67 75fr red & multi 1.00 .35
Nos. C162-C164 (3) 1.80 .75

10th anniversary of independence.

Stamps, Album, African Woman AP68

40fr, #C167, Stamps in shape of map of Congo, album, globe. #C168, Like 30fr.

1973, Aug. 12
C165 AP68 30fr pur & multi 1.90 .30
C166 AP68 40fr multicolored .25 .20
C167 AP68 100fr dk brn & multi 3.75 .80
C168 AP68 100fr ocher & multi .90 .40
Nos. C165-C168 (4) 6.80 1.70

Nos. C165, C168 for the 10th anniv. of the revolution, Nos. C166-C167 the Intl. Philatelic Exhib., Brazzaville.

Painting Type of 1973 Inscribed "EUROPAFRIQUE"

Designs: Details from "Earth and Paradise," by Jan Brueghel, the Elder.

1973, Oct. 10 Photo. *Perf. 13*
C169 AP64 100fr Spotted hyena 3.00 1.50
C170 AP64 100fr Leopard and lion 3.00 1.50
C171 AP64 100fr Elephant and creatures 3.00 1.50
Nos. C169-C171 (3) 9.00 4.50

US and Russian Spacecraft Docking — AP69

Design: 80fr, US and USSR spacecraft docked in space and emblems of 1975 joint space mission.

1973, Oct. 15 Engr. *Perf. 13*
C172 AP69 40fr bl, red & brn .50 .35
C173 AP69 80fr red, grn & bl 1.10 .50

Planned joint US and Soviet space missions.

For overprint see No. C251.

UPU Monument, Satellites, Big Dipper — AP70

1973, Nov. 20 Engr. *Perf. 13*

C174 AP70 80fr vio bl & lt bl 1.00 .35

Universal Postal Union Day.

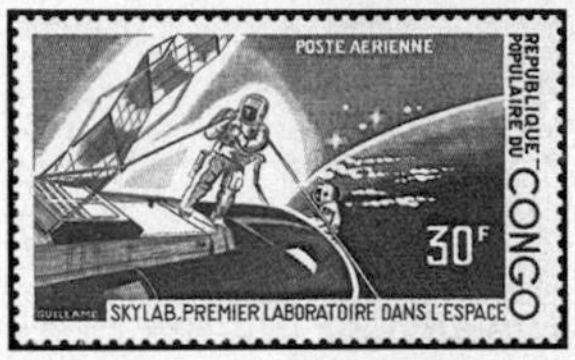

Astronauts Working in Space — AP71

40fr, Spacecraft & Skylab docking in space.

1973, Nov. 30

C175 AP71 30fr ultra, sl grn & choc .60 .20
C176 AP71 40fr mag, org & sl grn .60 .25

Skylab, first space laboratory.

Goalkeeper, Soccer — AP72

Design: 100fr, Soccer player kicking ball.

1973, Dec. 20

C177 AP72 40fr sl grn, sepia & brn .75 .25
C178 AP72 100fr pur, red & slate grn 1.90 .75

World Soccer Cup, Munich, 1974.

John F. Kennedy (1917-1963) AP73

1973, Dec. 20 Photo. *Perf. 12½*

C179 AP73 150fr ultra, gold & blk 1.75 .90

Runners — AP74

Flag over Map of Congo — AP75

1973, Dec. 20 Engr. *Perf. 13*

C180 AP74 40fr sl grn, red & brn .60 .25
C181 AP74 100fr red, sl grn, & brn 1.75 .75

2nd African Games, Lagos, Nigeria.

1973, Dec. 31 Photo.

C182 AP75 40fr dp grn & multi .50 .25

4th anniversary of Congolese Labor Party and of the Congo Red Flag.

Soccer and Games Emblem — AP76

1974, June 20 Photo. *Perf. 13*

C183 AP76 250fr multicolored 3.75 1.90

World Cup Soccer Championship, Munich, June 13-July 7.

Astronauts Yuri A. Gagarin and Alan B. Shepard — AP77

Designs: 30fr, Space, globe, Russian and American flags with names of astronauts who perished in space. 100fr, Alexei Leonov and Neil A. Armstrong in space and on moon.

1974, June 30 Engr. *Perf. 13*

C184 AP77 30fr red, ultra & brn .45 .20
C185 AP77 40fr red, bl & brn .60 .25
C186 AP77 100fr car, grn & brn 1.40 .90
Nos. C184-C186 (3) 2.45 1.35

For overprint see No. C254.

Soccer Game Superimposed on Ball — AP78

Link-up Emblem, Stages of Link-up — AP79

1974, July 31 Photo. *Perf. 13*

C187 AP78 250fr multicolored 3.50 1.75

Germany's victory in World Cup Soccer Championship.

1974, Aug. 8 Engr. *Perf. 13*

300fr, Spacecraft docking over globe.

C188 AP79 200fr pur, bl & red 2.25 1.10
C189 AP79 300fr multi, horiz. 3.50 1.50

Russo-American space cooperation.
For overprint see No. C255.

Symbols of Communications, UPU Emblem — AP80

1974, Aug. 10

C190 AP80 500fr blk & red 6.75 3.00

Centenary of Universal Postal Union.
For surcharge see No. C194.

Lenin and Pendulum Trace Pattern — AP81

1974, Sept. 16 Engr. *Perf. 13*

C191 AP81 150fr multicolored 2.10 1.10

Lenin (1870-1924).

Churchill and Order of the Garter AP82

Marconi and Wireless Telegraph AP83

1974, Oct. 1 Litho. *Perf. 13*

C192 AP82 200fr lt grn & multi 3.00 1.25
C193 AP83 200fr lt ultra & multi 3.00 1.25

No. C190 Surcharged in Violet Blue with New Value, 2 Bars and: "9 OCTOBER 1974"

1974, Oct. 9

C194 AP80 300fr on 500fr multi 3.50 1.75

Universal Postal Union Day.

UDEAC Issue

Presidents and Flags of Cameroun, CAR, Gabon and Congo — AP83a

1974, Dec. 8 Photo. *Perf. 13*

C195 AP83a 100fr gold & multi 1.00 .50

See note after Cameroun No. 595.

Regatta at Argenteuil, by Monet — AP84

Impressionist Paintings: 40fr, Seated Dancer, by Degas. 50fr, Girl on Swing, by Renoir. 75fr, Girl with Straw Hat, by Renoir. All vertical.

1974, Dec. 15

C196 AP84 30fr gold & multi 1.50 .35
C197 AP84 40fr gold & multi 2.00 .35
C198 AP84 50fr gold & multi 2.75 .50
C199 AP84 75fr gold & multi 3.25 .80
Nos. C196-C199 (4) 9.50 2.00

National Fair AP85

1974, Dec. 20

C200 AP85 30fr multicolored .90 .35

National Fair, Aug. 24-Sept. 8.

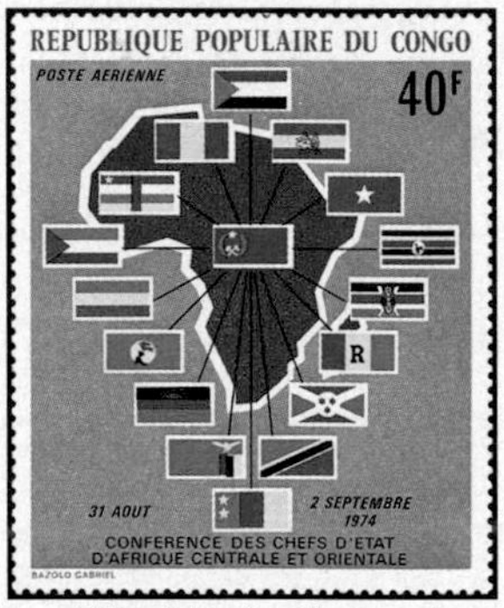

Flags of Participating Nations, Map of Africa — AP86

1974, Dec. 20 *Perf. 13*

C201 AP86 40fr ultra & multi .65 .35

Conference of Chiefs of State of Central and East Africa, Brazzaville, Aug. 31-Sept. 2.

"Five Weeks in a Balloon," by Jules Verne AP87

Design: 50fr, "Around the World in 80 Days," by Jules Verne.

1975, June 30 Litho. *Perf. 12½*

C202 AP87 40fr multicolored 1.40 .50
C203 AP87 50fr multicolored 1.75 1.00

Jules Verne (1828-1905), French science fiction writer, 70th death anniversary.

Paris-Brussels Train, 1890 — AP88

Design: 75fr, Santa Fe, 1880.

1975, June 30

C204	AP88	50fr ocher & multi	2.00	.75
C205	AP88	75fr lt bl & multi	4.25	.90

Soyuz and Apollo-Soyuz Emblem — AP89

Design: 100fr, Apollo and emblem.

1975, July 20 Litho. *Perf. 12½*

C206	AP89	95fr org, blk & mag	1.25	.50
C207	AP89	100fr vio, bl & blk	1.40	.60

Apollo Soyuz space test project (Russo-American space cooperation), launching July 15; link-up, July 17.

For overprints see Nos. C252-C253.

Bicycling and Montreal Olympic Emblem — AP90

Designs (Montreal Olympic Emblem and): 40fr, Boxing, vert. 50fr, Basketball, vert. 95fr, High jump. 100fr, Javelin. 150fr, Running.

Perf. 12½x13, 13x12½

1975, Oct. 30 Photo.

C208	AP90	40fr multicolored	.50	.25
C209	AP90	50fr red & multi	.60	.25
C210	AP90	85fr bl & multi	1.00	.35
C211	AP90	95fr org & multi	1.10	.45
C212	AP90	100fr multicolored	1.40	.50
C213	AP90	150fr multicolored	1.75	.80
		Nos. C208-C213 (6)	6.35	2.60

Pre-Olympic Year 1975.

Map of Africa, Sports and Flags — AP91

Workers and Flag — AP92

1975, Dec. 20 Litho. *Perf. 12½*

C214	AP91	30fr multicolored	.60	.35

1st African Games, Brazzaville, 10th anniv.

1975, Dec. 31 Litho. *Perf. 12½*

C215	AP92	60fr multicolored	.60	.25

Congolese Labor Party (P.C.T.), 6th anniv.

Alphonse Fondere — AP93

Historic Ships: 5fr, like 30fr. 10fr, 40fr, Hamburg, 1839. 15fr, 50fr, Gomer, 1831. 20fr, 60fr, Great Eastern, 1858. 95fr, J.M. White II, 1878.

1976 Engr. *Perf. 13*

C216	AP93	5fr multicolored	.25	.20
C217	AP93	10fr multicolored	.25	.20
C218	AP93	15fr multicolored	.30	.20
C219	AP93	20fr multicolored	.50	.20
C220	AP93	30fr multicolored	.75	.25
C221	AP93	40fr multicolored	1.00	.35
C222	AP93	50fr multicolored	1.25	.50
C223	AP93	60fr multicolored	1.75	.60
C224	AP93	95fr multicolored	2.50	1.00
		Nos. C216-C224 (9)	8.55	3.50

Issued: #C216-C219, May; #C220-C224, Mar. 7.

Europafrica Issue 1976

Peasant Family, by Louis Le Nain — AP94

Paintings: 80fr, Boy with Top, by Jean B. Chardin. 95fr, Venus and Aeneas, by Nicolas Poussin. 100fr, The Rape of the Sabine Women, by Jacques Louis David.

1976, Mar. 20 Litho. *Perf. 12½*

C225	AP94	60fr gold & multi	1.25	.45
C226	AP94	80fr gold & multi	1.40	.70
C227	AP94	95fr gold & multi	1.90	.70
C228	AP94	100fr gold & multi	2.10	.85
		Nos. C225-C228 (4)	6.65	2.70

Nos. C225-C228 printed in sheets of 8 stamps and horizontal gutter with commemorative inscription.

Telephone Type of 1976

1976, Apr. 25 Litho. *Perf. 12½x13*

C229	A107	60fr pink, mar & crim	.90	.30

Sports Type of 1976

Designs: 150fr, Runner and map of Central Africa. 200fr, Discus and map.

1976, Oct. 25 *Perf. 12½*

C230	A110	150fr multicolored	1.75	.75
C231	A110	200fr multicolored	2.75	1.10

Map of Africa, Flag and OAU Headquarters AP95

1976, Dec. 16 Typo. *Perf. 13x14*

C232	AP95	60fr multicolored	.70	.35

13th anniv. of the Organization for African Unity.

Europafrica Issue

Map of Europe and Africa — AP96

1977, June 28 Litho. *Perf. 13*

C233	AP96	75fr multicolored	.90	.45

Headdress Type of 1977

1977, June 30 *Perf. 12½*

250fr, Two straw caps. 300fr, Beaded cap.

C234	A118	250fr multicolored	2.75	1.50
C235	A118	300fr multicolored	3.00	1.75

Zeppelin Type of 1977

Souvenir Sheet

Design: 500fr, LZ 127 over US Capitol.

1977, Aug. 5 Litho. *Perf. 11*

C236	A120	500fr multicolored	6.75	2.00

No. C236 exists imperf.

Checkerboard AP97

1977, Aug. 20 Engr. *Perf. 13*

C237	AP97	60fr red & blk	.90	.35

Lomé Convention on General Agreement on Tariffs and Trade (GATT).

Newton, Intelsat Satellite and Classical "Planets" — AP98

1977, Aug. 25

C238	AP98	140fr multicolored	2.00	.90

Isaac Newton (1642-1727), natural philosopher and mathematician.

Elizabeth II Type of 1977

Souvenir Sheet

Design: 500fr, Royal family on balcony.

1977, Dec. 21 Litho. *Perf. 14*

C239	A128	500fr multicolored	5.75	1.75

For overprint see No. C244.

Mallard AP99

Birds: 75fr, Purple heron, vert. 150fr, Reed warbler, vert. 240fr, Hoopoe, vert.

1978, May 22 *Perf. 13x12½, 12½x13*

C240	AP99	65fr multicolored	1.10	.50
C241	AP99	75fr multicolored	1.40	.50
C242	AP99	150fr multicolored	3.25	1.00
C243	AP99	240fr multicolored	4.75	1.75
		Nos. C240-C243 (4)	10.50	3.75

Souvenir Sheet

No. C239 Overprinted in Silver: "ANNIVERSAIRE DU / COURONNEMENT / 1953-1978"

1978, Sept. Litho. *Perf. 14*

C244	A128	500fr multicolored	4.50	3.00

25th anniv. of coronation of Elizabeth II.

Philexafrique II-Essen Issue

Common Design Types

No. C245, Leopard and Congo No. C243. No. C246, Eagle and Wurttemberg No. 1.

1978, Nov. 1 Litho. *Perf. 12½*

C245	CD138	100fr multicolored	2.00	1.10
C246	CD139	100fr multicolored	2.00	1.10
a.		Pair, #C245-C246	5.25	5.25

Map of Africa, Satellites AP100

Map of Africa and People — AP101

1978, Nov. 25 Engr. *Perf. 13*

C247	AP100	100fr multicolored	1.25	.50

Pan-African Telecommunications Network, PANAFEL.

1979, Aug. 2 Litho. *Perf. 12½*

C248	AP101	45fr multicolored	.50	.25
C249	AP101	75fr multicolored	.85	.40

5th Conference of Panafrican Youth Movement, Brazzaville, Aug. 2-7.

Abala Peasant Woman AP102

1979, Aug. 20

C250	AP102	150fr multicolored	1.75	.90

Nos. C173, C206-C207, C186, C189 Overprinted "ALUNISSAGE APOLLO XI / JUILLET 1969" and Emblem

Perf. 13, 12½

1979, Nov. 5 Engr., Litho.

C251	AP69	80fr multicolored	1.00	.90
C252	AP89	95fr multicolored	1.50	1.00
C253	AP89	100fr multicolored	2.00	1.00
C254	AP77	100fr multicolored	2.00	1.00
C255	AP79	300fr multicolored	3.50	2.75
		Nos. C251-C255 (5)	10.00	6.65

Apollo 11 moon landing, 10th anniversary.

Runner, Olympic Rings — AP103

Pre-Olympic Year: 100fr, Boxing. 200fr, Fencing. 300fr, Soccer. 500fr, Moscow '80 emblem.

1979 **Litho.** ***Perf. 13½***

C256 AP103 65fr multi .50 .20
C257 AP103 100fr multi 1.00 .25
C258 AP103 200fr multi, vert. 2.00 .50
C259 AP103 300fr multi 2.50 .75
C260 AP103 500fr multi, vert. 5.00 1.25
Nos. C256-C260 (5) 11.00 2.95

Cross-Country Skiing — AP104

Lake Placid '80 Emblem and: 60fr, Slalom. 200fr, Ski jump, 350fr, Downhill skiing, horiz. 500fr, Woman skier.

1979, Dec ***Perf. 14½***

Size: 24x42mm, 42x24mm

C261 AP104 40fr multicolored .45 .20
C262 AP104 60fr multicolored .60 .20
C263 AP104 200fr multicolored 2.00 .45
C264 AP104 350fr multicolored 3.50 .90

Size: 31½x46½mm

Perf. 14

C265 AP104 500fr multicolored 5.00 1.40
Nos. C261-C265 (5) 11.55 3.15

13th Winter Olympic Games, Lake Placid, NY, Feb. 12-24, 1980.

Overprinted with Names of Winners

1980, Apr. 28

C266 AP104 40fr Zimiatov .40 .20
C267 AP104 60fr Moser-Proell .50 .25
C268 AP104 200fr Tomanen 1.90 .75
C269 AP104 350fr Stock 3.50 1.25
C270 AP104 500fr Stenmark-Wenzel 4.75 1.90
Nos. C266-C270 (5) 11.05 4.35

Long Jump, Olympic Rings — AP105

1980, May 2 **Litho.** ***Perf. 14½***

C271 AP105 75fr multi, vert. .90 .20
C272 AP105 150fr multi 1.40 .30
C273 AP105 250fr multi, vert. 2.25 .50
C274 AP105 350fr multi, vert. 3.25 .70
Nos. C271-C274 (4) 7.80 1.70

Souvenir Sheet

C275 AP105 500fr multi 5.00 1.60

22nd Summer Olympic Games, Moscow, July 19-Aug. 3.
For overprints see Nos. C292-C296.

Stadium, Mascot, Madrid Club Emblem — AP106

Stadium, Mascot and Club Emblem: 75fr, Zaragoza. 100fr, Madrid Athletic Club. 150fr, Valencia. 175fr, Spain. 250fr, Barcelona.

1980, June 23 **Litho.** ***Perf. 14x13½***

C276 AP106 60fr multicolored .60 .20
C277 AP106 75fr multicolored .60 .20
C278 AP106 100fr multicolored 1.00 .25
C279 AP106 150fr multicolored 1.40 .35
C280 AP106 175fr multicolored 1.60 .50
Nos. C276-C280 (5) 5.20 1.50

Souvenir Sheet

C281 AP106 250fr multicolored 2.75 1.25

World Soccer Cup 1982.
For overprints see Nos. C298-C303.

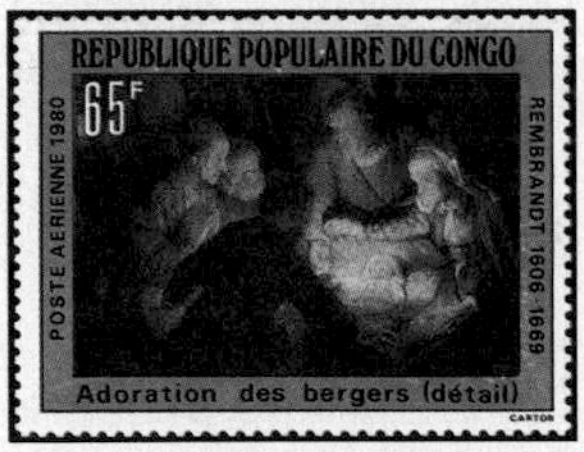

Adoration of the Shepherds — AP107

Rembrandt Paintings: 100fr, The Burial. 200fr, Christ at Emmaus. 300fr, Annunciation, vert. 500fr, Crucifixion, vert.

1980, July 4 ***Perf. 12½***

C282 AP107 65fr multicolored .60 .25
C283 AP107 100fr multicolored .90 .35
C284 AP107 200fr multicolored 1.60 .55
C285 AP107 300fr multicolored 2.50 .75
C286 AP107 500fr multicolored 5.25 1.25
Nos. C282-C286 (5) 10.85 3.15

Albert Camus (1913-1960), Writer — AP108

Design: 150fr, Jacques Offenbach (1819-1880), composer, vert.

1980, July 5 **Engr.** ***Perf. 13***

C287 AP108 100fr multicolored 1.25 .50
C288 AP108 150fr multicolored 2.25 1.25

Raffia Dancing Skirts — AP109

Traditional Dancing Costumes: 300fr, Tam-tam dancers, vert. 350fr, Masks.

1980, Aug. 6 **Litho.** ***Perf. 13½***

C289 AP109 250fr multicolored 2.75 .95
C290 AP109 300fr multicolored 3.25 1.50
C291 AP109 350fr multicolored 4.00 1.90
Nos. C289-C291 (3) 10.00 4.35

Nos. C271-C275 Overprinted with Winner and Country

1980, Nov. 14 **Litho.** ***Perf. 14½***

C292 AP105 75fr multicolored .70 .30
C293 AP105 150fr multicolored 1.40 .60
C294 AP105 250fr multicolored 2.25 .90
C295 AP105 350fr multicolored 3.25 1.50
Nos. C292-C295 (4) 7.60 3.30

Souvenir Sheet

C296 AP105 500fr multicolored 5.00 4.00

The Studio by Picasso — AP109a

1981, July 4 ***Perf. 12½***

C296A AP109a 100fr shown 1.10 .50
C296B AP109a 150fr Landscape 1.60 .75
C296C AP109a 200fr Cannes Studio 2.10 1.00
C296D AP109a 300fr Still Life 3.50 1.50
C296E AP109a 500fr Still Life, diff. 6.00 2.50
Nos. C296A-C296E (5) 14.30 6.25

1st Seminar on Petroleum, Gas and Energy Alternatives, Brazzaville AP109b

45fr, Emblem, oil platform, other energy sources. 100fr, Emblem, map, oil platforms. 150fr, Map, other energy sources. 200fr, Maps of Africa, Congo, oil worker.

1981 **Litho.** ***Perf. 12½***

C296F AP109b 45fr multi 20.00 13.00
C296G AP109b 75fr multi 32.50 19.00
C296H AP109b 100fr multi 45.00 27.50
C296I AP109b 150fr multi 65.00 40.00
C296J AP109b 200fr multi 90.00 50.00
Nos. C296F-C296J (5) 252.50 149.50

1350th Anniv. of Mohamed's Death at Medina — AP110

1982, July 17 **Litho.** ***Perf. 13***

C297 AP110 400fr Medina Mosque minaret 3.75 1.75

Nos. C276-C281 Overprinted with Finalists and/or Scores in Black on Silver

1982, Oct. 7 **Litho.** ***Perf. 14x13½***

C298 AP106 60fr multicolored .50 .25
C299 AP106 75fr multicolored .60 .30
C300 AP106 100fr multicolored .90 .45
C301 AP106 150fr multicolored 1.40 .60
C302 AP106 175fr multicolored 1.50 .60
Nos. C298-C302 (5) 4.90 2.20

Souvenir Sheet

C303 AP106 250fr multicolored 2.25 1.90

30th Anniv. of Amelia Earhart's Transatlantic Flight — AP111

1982, Dec. 4 **Engr.** ***Perf. 13***

C304 AP111 150fr multicolored 1.25 .75

Wind Surfing AP112

Various wind surfing scenes, 1984 Olympic Games, 100fr, 300fr, 400fr vert.

1983, June 4 **Litho.** ***Perf. 13***

C305 AP112 100fr multicolored .90 .25
C306 AP112 200fr multicolored 1.75 .50
C307 AP112 300fr multicolored 2.75 .70
C308 AP112 400fr multicolored 3.50 1.00
Nos. C305-C308 (4) 8.90 2.45

Souvenir Sheet

C309 AP112 500fr multicolored 5.00 2.50

For overprint see No. C336.

Manned Flight Bicentenary AP113

Various balloons.

1983, June 7

C310 AP113 100fr Montgolfiere, 1783 1.10 .20
C311 AP113 200fr Flesselles, 1784 2.10 .40
C312 AP113 300fr Auguste Piccard, 1931 3.00 .60
C313 AP113 400fr Don Piccard 4.50 .90
Nos. C310-C313 (4) 10.70 2.10

Souvenir Sheet

C314 AP113 500fr Mail transport balloon, 1870 5.75 1.60

For overprint see No. C337.

Christmas 1983 AP114

Various Virgin and Child Paintings by Botticelli.

1984, Jan. 21 **Litho.** ***Perf. 13***

C315 AP114 150fr multicolored 1.25 .50
C316 AP114 350fr multicolored 3.00 1.10
C317 AP114 500fr multicolored 4.50 1.50
Nos. C315-C317 (3) 8.75 3.10

Vase of Flowers, by Manet (1832-83) AP115

Paintings: 200fr, Small Holy Family, by Raphael. 300fr, La Belle Jardiniere, by Raphael. 400fr, Virgin of Loretto, by Raphael. 500fr, Portrait of Richard Wagner (1813-83), by Giuseppe Tivoli.

1984, Feb. 24 **Litho.** ***Perf. 13***

C318 AP115 100fr multicolored .90 .30
C319 AP115 200fr multicolored 1.90 .70
C320 AP115 300fr multicolored 2.75 1.00
C321 AP115 400fr multicolored 3.75 1.40
C322 AP115 500fr multicolored 5.00 1.50
Nos. C318-C322 (5) 14.30 4.90

1984 Summer Olympics — AP116

1984, Mar. 31 *Perf. 13*
C323 AP116 45fr Judo, vert. .45 .20
C324 AP116 75fr Judo, diff. .70 .25
C325 AP116 150fr Wrestling 1.40 .50
C326 AP116 175fr Fencing 1.60 .60
C327 AP116 350fr Fencing, diff. 3.25 1.10
Nos. C323-C327 (5) 7.40 2.65

Souvenir Sheet

C328 AP116 500fr Boxing 5.00 2.50

1984 Summer Olympic Gold Medalists — AP117

Sailing/yachting: 100fr, Stephan Van Den Berg, Netherlands, Windglider Class. 150fr, US, Soling Class. 200fr, Spain, 470 Class. 500fr, US, Flying Dutchman Class.

1984, Dec. 18 **Litho.** *Perf. 13*
C329 AP117 100fr multi, vert. 1.00 .45
C330 AP117 150fr multi 1.40 .65
C331 AP117 200fr multi 2.00 .90
C332 AP117 500fr multi, vert. 4.50 2.25
Nos. C329-C332 (4) 8.90 4.25

Virgin and Child, by Giovanni Bellini (c. 1430-1516) — AP118

Religious paintings: 100fr, Holy Family, by Andrea del Sarto (1486-1530). 400fr, Virgin with Angels, by Cimabue (c. 1240-1302).

1985, Feb. 12 **Litho.** *Perf. 13*
C333 AP118 100fr multi, vert. 1.00 .45
C334 AP118 200fr multi 2.00 .90
C335 AP118 400fr multi, vert. 3.75 1.75
Nos. C333-C335 (3) 6.75 3.10

Christmas 1984.

Souvenir Sheets

Nos. C309, C314 Ovptd. with Exhibition in Blue or Green

1985, Mar. 8 *Perf. 13*
C336 AP112 500fr OLYMPHILEX '85 / LAUSANNE (B) 5.00 4.00
C337 AP113 500fr MOPHILA '85 / HAMBURG (G) 5.00 4.00

Audubon Birth Bicentenary — AP119

Illustrations of North American bird species by Audubon. Nos. C338-C339 vert.

1985, Apr. 11 *Perf. 13½*
C338 AP119 100fr Passiformes fringillidae 1.00 .45
C339 AP119 150fr Eudocimus ruber 1.50 .65
C340 AP119 200fr Buteo jamaicensis 1.90 .90
C341 AP119 350fr Camptorhynchus labradorius 3.75 1.50
Nos. C338-C341 (4) 8.15 3.50

PHILEXAFRICA '85, Lome — AP120

Youths in public service activities.

1985, May 20 *Perf. 13*
C342 AP120 200fr Community health care 2.25 1.50
C343 AP120 200fr Agriculture 2.25 1.50
a. Pair, #C342-C343 + label 5.75 5.75

Admission to UN, 25th Anniv. — AP121

1985, Aug. 13
C344 AP121 190fr multicolored 1.75 .75

UN, 40th Anniv. — AP122

1985, Oct. 25 *Perf. 12½*
C345 AP122 180fr Rainbow, emblem 1.60 .65

Christmas — AP123

Paintings: 100fr, The Virgin and the Infant Jesus, by David. 200fr, Adoration of the Magi, by Hieronymus Bosch (1450-1516). 400fr, Virgin and Child, by Van Dyck.

1985, Dec. 20 **Litho.** *Perf. 13*
C346 AP123 100fr multicolored .90 .35
C347 AP123 200fr multicolored 1.90 .75
C348 AP123 400fr multicolored 3.50 1.75
Nos. C346-C348 (3) 6.30 2.85

Nos. C346-C347 vert.

Halley's Comet — AP124

1986, Feb. 17
C349 AP124 125fr Halley, comet 1.00 .50
C350 AP124 150fr West's Comet, 1976 1.25 .60
C351 AP124 225fr Ikeya Seki's Comet, 1965 1.75 .90
C352 AP124 300fr Trajectory diagram 2.25 1.25
C353 AP124 350fr Comet, Vega probe 2.75 1.50
Nos. C349-C353 (5) 9.00 4.75

Nos. C350-C351 vert.

Cosmos-Frantel Hotel — AP125

1986, May 1 *Perf. 13½*
C354 AP125 250fr multicolored 2.50 .90

1986 World Cup Soccer Championships, Mexico — AP126

Various soccer plays.

1986, July 22 **Litho.** *Perf. 13*
C355 AP126 150fr multicolored 1.25 .60
C356 AP126 250fr multicolored 2.00 1.00
C357 AP126 440fr multicolored 3.75 1.75
C358 AP126 600fr multicolored 6.50 2.50
Nos. C355-C358 (4) 13.50 5.85

Air Africa, 25th Anniv. — AP127

1986, Nov. 29 **Litho.** *Perf. 13½*
C359 AP127 200fr multicolored 1.75 .75

1988 Winter Pre-Olympics, Calgary — AP128

1986, Dec. 15 *Perf. 13*
C360 AP128 150fr Downhill skiing 1.25 .60
C361 AP128 250fr Bobsled 2.25 .95
C362 AP128 440fr Women's cross-country skiing 4.00 1.50
C363 AP128 600fr Ski jumping 5.75 2.40
Nos. C360-C363 (4) 13.25 5.45

Nos. C361-C362 vert.

Christmas AP129

Paintings by Rogier van der Weyden (c.1399-1464): 250fr, Virgin and Child. 440fr, The Nativity. 500fr, Virgin with Carnation.

1986, Dec. 23 *Perf. 13½*
C364 AP129 250fr multicolored 2.25 1.00
C365 AP129 440fr multicolored 4.50 1.75
C366 AP129 500fr multicolored 5.00 2.10
Nos. C364-C366 (3) 11.75 4.85

Crocodiles, World Wildlife Fund — AP130

1987, Jan. 22 *Perf. 13*
C367 AP130 75fr Osteolaemus tetraspis 2.75 1.10
C368 AP130 100fr Crocodylus cataphractus 3.25 1.25
C369 AP130 125fr Osteolaemus tetraspis, diff. 4.50 1.75
C370 AP130 150fr Crocodylus cataphractus, diff. 5.00 3.00
Nos. C367-C370 (4) 15.50 7.10

1988 Summer Olympics, Seoul — AP131

1987, July 11 **Litho.** *Perf. 13*
C371 AP131 100fr Backstroke .90 .35
C372 AP131 200fr Freestyle 1.75 .75
C373 AP131 300fr Breaststroke 2.75 1.10
C374 AP131 400fr Butterfly 3.50 1.40
Nos. C371-C374 (4) 8.90 3.60

Souvenir Sheet

C375 AP131 750fr Start of event 6.75 3.50

Launch of Sputnik, First Artificial Satellite, 30th Anniv. — AP132

1987, June 5 *Perf. 12½x12*
C376 AP132 60fr multicolored .50 .25
C377 AP132 240fr multicolored 2.25 1.10

Butterflies — AP133

1987, Sept. 4 *Perf. 12½*

C378 AP133 75fr Precis epicleli 1.00 .30
C379 AP133 120fr Deilephila nerii 1.75 .45
C380 AP133 450fr Euryphene senegalensis 5.25 1.75
C381 AP133 550fr Precis almanta 7.00 2.40
Nos. C378-C381 (4) 15.00 4.90

Coubertin, Eternal Flame and Greece No. 125 — AP134

Cameo portrait, athletes and stamps: 120fr, Runners, France No. 198. 350fr, Congo Republic No. C22, hurdler. 600fr, High jump, Congo Republic No. C75.

1987, Nov. 4

C382 AP134 75fr shown .80 .30
C383 AP134 120fr multicolored 1.10 .45
C384 AP134 350fr multicolored 3.50 1.25
C385 AP134 600fr multicolored 5.25 2.10
Nos. C382-C385 (4) 10.65 4.10

Pierre de Coubertin (1863-1937), promulgator of the modern Olympics.

Arrival of Schweitzer in Lambarene, 75th Anniv. — AP135

1988, Apr. 17 **Litho.** *Perf. 12½*

C386 AP135 240fr multicolored 2.75 1.25

Dr. Albert Schweitzer (1875-1965), Nobel Peace Prize winner of 1952, founded Lambarene Hospital, Gabon, in 1913.

1988 Summer Olympics, Seoul — AP136

Pentathlon: 75fr, Swimming. 170fr, Cross-country running, vert. 200fr, Shooting. 600fr, Equestrian. 700fr, Fencing.

1988, June 10 **Litho.** *Perf. 13*

C387 AP136 75fr multicolored .70 .25
C388 AP136 170fr multicolored 1.60 .60
C389 AP136 200fr multicolored 1.75 .70
C390 AP136 600fr multicolored 5.00 2.00
Nos. C387-C390 (4) 9.05 3.55

Souvenir Sheet

C391 AP136 750fr multicolored 6.75 3.75

Elimination Matches, 1990 World Cup Soccer Championships — AP137

Various athletes and cities in Italy.

1989, June 15 **Litho.** *Perf. 13*

C392 AP137 75fr Bari .60 .30
C393 AP137 120fr Rome 1.00 .45
C394 AP137 500fr Florence 4.75 1.90
C395 AP137 550fr Naples 5.25 2.00
Nos. C392-C395 (4) 11.60 4.65

PHILEXFRANCE '89 — AP138

Paintings: 300fr, Storming of the Bastille, July 14, 1789, from a gouache by J.P. Houel. 400fr, Eiffel Tower, by G. Seurat.

1989, June 22

C396 AP138 300fr multicolored 2.75 1.10
C397 AP138 400fr multicolored 3.75 1.50

French revolution, bicent. (300fr); Eiffel Tower, cent. (400fr).

First Moon Landing, 20th Anniv. AP139

Man's first step on the Moon: No. C398, Astronaut on ladder. No. C399, Conducting experiments on the Moon's surface.

1989, June 22

C398 AP139 400fr multicolored 3.75 1.50
C399 AP139 400fr multicolored 3.75 1.50

World Cup Soccer Championships, Italy — AP140

Various soccer plays and architecture.

1990, June 8 **Litho.** *Perf. 13*

C400 AP140 120fr multicolored 1.00 .50
C401 AP140 240fr multicolored 2.10 .95
C402 AP140 500fr multicolored 4.25 2.00
C403 AP140 600fr multicolored 5.25 2.40
Nos. C400-C403 (4) 12.60 5.85

Pan African Postal Union, 10th Anniv. AP141

1991, Jan. 10 **Litho.** *Perf. 13½*

C404 AP141 60fr shown .50 .25
C405 AP141 120fr Emblem .95 .50

1992 Winter Olympics, Albertville AP142

1991, June 8 **Litho.** *Perf. 13½*

C406 AP142 120fr Ice hockey 1.40 .60
C407 AP142 300fr Speed skating 3.00 1.50

Litho. & Embossed

C408 AP142 1500fr Slalom skiing 15.00 15.00

Numbers have been reserved for souvenir sheets in this set.

1992 Summer Olympics, Barcelona AP143

#C411, Equestrian. #C412, Long jump.

1992 **Litho. & Embossed** *Perf. 13½*

C411 AP143 1500fr gold & multi 16.00 16.00

Souvenir Sheet

C412 AP143 1500fr gold & multi 21.00 21.00

Anniversaries AP144

Designs: 90fr, Victor Schoelcher, missionary, death cent. 205fr, Martin Luther King, civil rights reformer, 25th death anniv. 300fr, Claude Chappe (1763-1805), bicent. of visual telegraph.

1993 **Litho.** *Perf. 14*

C413 AP144 90fr multicolored *1.00 .50*
C414 AP144 205fr multicolored *2.50 1.25*
C415 AP144 300fr multicolored *3.50 1.75*
Nos. C413-C415 (3) *7.00 3.50*

1994 Winter Olympics, Lillehammer AP145

1993, Apr. 26 **Litho.** *Perf. 13*

C416 AP145 400fr Ice dancing *3.50 1.40*
C417 AP145 600fr Ice hockey *6.00 1.75*

Souvenir Sheet

C418 AP145 750fr Downhill skiing *7.00 4.00*

Nos. C416-C417 exist in imperf. souvenir sheets of 1. Nos. C416-C418 exist imperf.

AIR POST SEMI-POSTAL STAMPS

Hathor Pillar — SPAP1

Unwmk.

1964, Mar. 9 **Engr.** *Perf. 13*

CB1 SPAP1 10fr + 5fr vio & chnt .45 .30
CB2 SPAP1 25fr + 5fr org brn & slate grn .70 .60
CB3 SPAP1 50fr + 5fr slate grn & brn red 1.90 1.60
Nos. CB1-CB3 (3) 3.05 2.50

UNESCO world campaign to save historic monuments in Nubia.

POSTAGE DUE STAMPS

Messenger — D6

MH. 1521 Broussard Plane — D7

Early Transportation: 1fr, Litter. 2fr, Canoe. 5fr, Bicyclist. 10fr, Steam locomotive. 25fr, Seaplane.

Unwmk.

1961, Dec. 4 **Engr.** *Perf. 11*

J34 D6 50c ultra, ol bis & red .20 .20
a. Pair, #J34, J40 .25
J35 D6 1fr red brn, red & grn .20 .20
a. Pair, #J35, J41 .30
J36 D6 2fr grn, ultra & brn .20 .20
a. Pair, #J36, J42 .40
J37 D6 5fr pur & gray brn .25 .25
a. Pair, #J37, J43 .50
J38 D6 10fr bl, grn & chocolate .70 .70
a. Pair, #J38, J44 1.40 1.40
J39 D6 25fr bl, dk grn & dk brn 1.60 1.60
a. Pair, #J39, J45 3.25

Modern transportation: 1fr, Land Rover. 2fr, River boat transporting barge. 5fr, Trailer-truck. 10fr, Diesel locomotive. 25fr, Boeing 707 jet plane.

J40	D7	50c ultra, olive bis & red	.20	.20
J41	D7	1fr red & grn	.20	.20
J42	D7	2fr ultra, grn & brn	.20	.20
J43	D7	5fr pur & gray brn	.25	.25
J44	D7	10fr dk grn & chocolate	.70	.70
J45	D7	25fr bl, dk grn & sepia	1.60	1.60
		Nos. J34-J45 (12)	6.30	6.30

Pairs printed tête bêche, se-tenant at the base.

Flowers — D8

Flowers: 2fr, Phaeomeria magnifica. 5fr, Millettia laurentii. 10fr, Tuberose. 15fr, Pyrostegia venusta. 20fr, Hibiscus.

1971, Mar. 25 Photo. *Perf. 12x12½*

J46	D8	1fr multi	.35	.35
J47	D8	2fr multi	.45	.45
J48	D8	5fr pink & multi	.55	.55
J49	D8	10fr dk grn & multi	.70	.70
J50	D8	15fr multi	1.10	1.10
J51	D8	20fr multi	1.40	1.40
		Nos. J46-J51 (6)	4.55	4.55

Flowers and Fruit — D9

1986, June 5 Litho. *Perf. 13*

J52	D9	5fr Passiflora quadrangulares	.25	.25
J53	D9	10fr Cannaceae, vert.	.45	.45
J54	D9	15fr Ananas comosus, vert.	.55	.55
		Nos. J52-J54 (3)	1.25	1.25

OFFICIAL STAMPS

Coat of Arms — O1

Perf. 14x13

1968-70 Unwmk. Typo.

O1	O1	1fr multi ('70)	.20	.20
O2	O1	2fr multi ('70)	.20	.20
O3	O1	5fr multi ('70)	.20	.20
O4	O1	10fr multi ('70)	.25	.20
O5	O1	25fr emer & multi	.45	.20
O6	O1	30fr red & multi	.60	.20
O7	O1	50fr multi ('70)	1.10	.50
O8	O1	85fr multi ('70)	2.25	.90
O9	O1	100frmulti ('70)	2.75	1.10
O10	O1	200frmulti ('70)	3.75	2.00
		Nos. O1-O10 (10)	11.75	5.70

COOK ISLANDS

'kuk 'ī-ləndz

(Rarotonga)

LOCATION — South Pacific Ocean, northeast of New Zealand
GOVT. — Internal self-government, linked to New Zealand
AREA — 91 sq. mi.
POP. — 19,103 (1996)
CAPITAL — Avarua

Fifteen islands in Northern and Southern groups extend over 850,000 square miles of ocean.

Separate stamp issues used by Aitutaki (1903-32 and 1972 onward) and Penrhyn Islands (1902-32 and 1973 onward). Niue is included geographically, but administered separately. It continues to issue separate stamps.

12 Pence = 1 Shilling
20 Shillings = 1 Pound
100 Cents = 1 Dollar (1967)

Catalogue values for unused stamps in this country are for Never Hinged items, beginning with Scott 127 in the regular postage section, Scott B1 in the semi-postal section, Scott C1 in the air post section, Scott CB1 in the air post semi-postal section and Scott O16 in the official section.

Watermarks

Wmk. 61 — Single-lined N Z and Star Close Together

Wmk. 62 — Single-lined N Z and Star Wide Apart

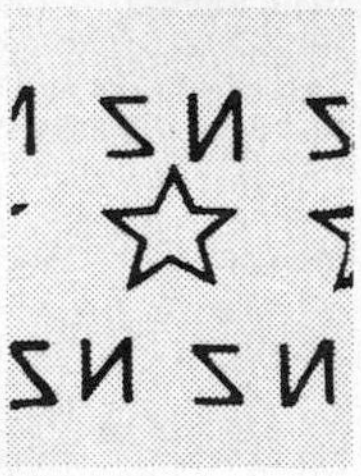

Wmk. 253 — Multiple N Z and Star

A1

1892 Unwmk. Typo. *Perf. 12½*

Toned Paper

1	A1	1p black	32.50	30.00
2	A1	1½p violet	47.50	45.00
a.		Imperf, pair	*19,000.*	
3	A1	2½p blue	47.50	45.00
4	A1	10p carmine	160.00	150.00
		Nos. 1-4 (4)	287.50	270.00

White Paper

5	A1	1p black	32.50	30.00
a.		Vert. pair, imperf. between	*11,000.*	
6	A1	1½p violet	47.50	45.00
7	A1	2½p blue	47.50	45.00
8	A1	10p carmine	160.00	150.00
		Nos. 5-8 (4)	287.50	270.00

Queen Makea Takau — A2

Wrybill (Torea) — A3

1893-94 Wmk. 62 *Perf. 12x11½*

9	A2	1p brown	47.50	*52.50*
10	A2	1p blue ('94)	13.00	2.50
11	A2	1½p brt violet	11.00	8.50
12	A2	2½p rose	47.50	27.50
13	A2	5p olive gray	22.50	16.00
14	A2	10p green	82.50	57.50
		Nos. 9-14 (6)	224.00	*164.50*

Perf. 12½ examples of Nos. 10, 12 are from a part of the normal perf. 12x11½ sheets. They were caused by a partial deviation of the original perforating.

1898-1900 *Perf. 11*

15	A3	½p blue ('00)	6.50	*9.00*
a.		"d" omitted at upper right	1,750.	
16	A2	1p brown	22.50	21.00
17	A2	1p blue	6.00	5.50
18	A2	1½p violet	10.50	7.50
19	A3	2p chocolate	10.50	8.25
20	A2	2½p car rose	22.50	10.50
21	A2	5p olive gray	27.50	21.00
22	A3	6p red violet	22.50	*29.00*
23	A2	10p green	21.00	*57.50*
24	A3	1sh car rose	57.50	57.50
		Nos. 15-24 (10)	207.00	226.75

No. 17 Surcharged in Black

1899

25	A2	½p on 1p blue	40.00	*50.00*
a.		Double surcharge	1,200.	1,050.
b.		Inverted surcharge	1,200.	*1,100.*

No. 16 Overprinted in Black

1901

26	A2	1p brown	210.00	160.00
a.		Inverted overprint	2,400.	1,900.
c.		Double overprint	1,900.	1,900.

Some single stamps were overprinted by favor. Other varieties could exist.

Forgeries exist.

Types of 1893-98

1902 Unwmk.

27	A3	½p green	5.25	5.00
a.		Vert. pair, imperf. horiz.	1,400.	
28	A2	1p rose	14.00	*12.50*
29	A2	2½p dull blue	15.00	*25.00*
		Nos. 27-29 (3)	34.25	*42.50*

1902 Wmk. 61 *Perf. 11*

30	A3	½p green	3.25	*3.75*
31	A2	1p rose	4.75	3.50
32	A2	1½p brt violet	4.75	*10.00*
33	A3	2p chocolate	6.50	*12.00*
a.		Figures of value omitted	*2,750.*	*3,600.*
b.		Perf. 11x14	*2,250.*	
34	A2	2½p dull blue	4.50	*8.25*
35	A2	5p olive gray	42.50	*57.50*
36	A3	6p purple	37.50	32.50
37	A2	10p blue green	55.00	*120.00*
38	A3	1sh car rose	55.00	*82.50*
a.		Perf. 11x14	*2,700.*	
		Nos. 30-38 (9)	213.75	*330.00*

1909-19 *Perf. 14, 14x14½, 14½x14*

39	A3	½p green, perf 14½x14 ('11)	7.00	*9.50*
a.		½p dp grn, wmk sideways, perf 14 ('15)	7.00	*17.50*
b.		As "a," wmk upright	9.00	*16.50*
40b	A2	1p red	6.50	7.25
41	A2	1½p purple ('15)	13.00	4.75
42	A3	2p dp brown ('19)	6.00	*57.50*
43	A2	10p dp green ('18)	22.50	*110.00*
44	A3	1sh car rose ('19)	32.50	*110.00*
		Nos. 39a,39-44 (7)	94.50	
		Nos. 39-44 (6)		*299.00*

Nos. 39-40 are on both ordinary and chalky paper; Nos. 41-44 on chalky paper.

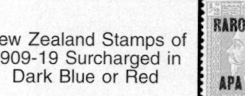

New Zealand Stamps of 1909-19 Surcharged in Dark Blue or Red

1919 Typo. *Perf. 14x13½, 14x14½*

48	A43	½p yel green (R)	.45	*1.25*
a.		Pair, one without surcharge		
49	A42	1p carmine	1.25	3.50
50	A47	1½p brown org (R)	.60	*.90*
51	A43	2p yellow (R)	1.75	*2.00*
52	A43	3p chocolate	3.25	*15.00*

Engr.

53	A44	2½p dull blue (R)	2.75	7.50
54	A45	3p violet brown	2.75	9.50
55	A45	4p purple	2.25	*6.50*
56	A44	4½p dark green	2.25	*9.50*
57	A45	6p car rose	3.50	*10.00*
58	A44	7½p red brown	2.10	*6.50*
59	A45	9p ol green (R)	3.75	*17.50*
60	A45	1sh vermilion	12.50	*35.00*
		Nos. 48-60 (13)	39.15	*124.65*

The Polynesian surcharge restates the denomination of the basic stamp.

Landing of Capt. Cook A4

Avarua Waterfront A5

Capt. James Cook — A6

Palm — A7

Houses at Arorangi — A8

Avarua Harbor — A9

1920 Unwmk. Engr. *Perf. 14*

61	A4	½p green & black	4.75	*25.00*
62	A5	1p car & black	5.50	*25.00*
a.		Center inverted	*600.00*	
63	A6	1½p blue & black	10.00	10.00
64	A7	3p red brn & blk	2.50	*6.50*
65	A8	6p org & red brn	3.50	*10.00*
66	A9	1sh vio & black	6.00	*20.00*
		Nos. 61-66 (6)	32.25	*96.50*

The stamps overprinted or inscribed "Rarotonga" were used throughout the Cook Islands.

For surcharges see Nos. 78, 79.

New Zealand Postal-Fiscal Stamps of 1906-13 Overprinted in Red or Dark Blue

a

Perf. 14, 14½, 14x14½

1921 Typo. Wmk. 61

67	PF1	2sh blue (R)	32.50	*65.00*
68	PF1	2sh6p brown	22.50	*60.00*
69	PF1	5sh green (R)	32.50	*77.50*
70	PF1	10sh claret	90.00	*140.00*
71	PF2	£1 rose	140.00	*240.00*
		Nos. 67-71 (5)	317.50	*582.50*

Types of 1920 Issue

1924-26 Engr. *Perf. 14*

72	A4	½p yel grn & black	5.25	10.00
73	A5	1p carmine & black	7.00	2.50

Issued: ½p, 5/13/26; 1p, 11/10/24.

New Zealand Stamps of 1926 Overprinted Type "a" in Red

1926-28 Typo. *Perf. 14, 14½x14*

74	A56	2sh blue ('27)	17.50	*47.50*
a.		2sh dark blue	12.00	*47.50*
75	A56	3sh violet ('28)	19.00	*50.00*

Rarotongan Chief (Te Po) — A10

Avarua Harbor — A11

1927, Oct. 15 **Engr.** ***Perf. 14***

76	A10	2½p dk bl & red brn	7.00	*29.00*
77	A11	4p dull vio & bl grn	10.00	*20.00*

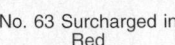

No. 63 Surcharged in Red

1931 **Unwmk.**

78	A6	2p on 1½p blue & blk	11.00	3.25

Same Surcharge on Type of 1920

Wmk. 61

79	A6	2p on 1½p blue & blk	5.50	*13.00*

No. 79 was not issued without surcharge.

New Zealand Postal-Fiscal Stamps of 1931-32 Overprinted Type "a" in Blue or Red

1931, Nov. 12 **Typo.**

80	PF5	2sh6p dp brn (Bl)	12.00	*26.00*
81	PF5	5sh green (R)	21.00	*65.00*
82	PF5	10sh dk car (Bl)	45.00	*110.00*
83	PF5	£1 pink (Bl) ('32)	105.00	*190.00*
		Nos. 80-83 (4)	183.00	391.00

See Nos. 103-108, 124A-126C.

Landing of Capt. Cook — A12

Capt. James Cook — A13

Double Canoe — A14

Islanders Unloading Ship — A15

View of Avarua Harbor — A16

R.M.S. Monowai — A17

King George V — A18

Unwmk.

1932, Mar. 16 **Engr.** ***Perf. 13***

Center in Black

84	A12	½p deep green	4.00	*19.00*
a.		Perf. 14	32.50	*105.00*
85	A13	1p brown lake	7.75	5.25
a.		Center inverted	*8,500.*	*8,500.*
b.		Perf. 14	17.50	*28.00*
86	A14	2p brown	3.50	6.50
b.		Perf. 14	10.00	*24.00*
87	A15	2½p dark ultra	18.00	*65.00*
b.		Perf. 14	18.00	*65.00*

Perf. 14

88	A16	4p ultra	12.00	*65.00*
a.		Perf. 13	25.00	*75.00*
b.		Perf. 14x13	35.00	*130.00*
89	A17	6p orange	5.00	*17.50*
a.		Perf. 13	30.00	*57.50*
90	A18	1sh deep violet	13.00	*26.00*
		Nos. 84-90 (7)	63.25	*204.25*

Nos. 84-90 were available for postage in Aitutaki, Penrhyn and Rarotonga and replaced the special issues for those islands.

Inverted centers of the 2p and 2½p are from printers waste.

1933-36 **Wmk. 61** ***Perf. 14***

91	A12	½p dp grn & blk	1.20	*5.25*
92	A13	1p dk car & black ('35)	1.50	*2.40*
93	A14	2p brn & blk ('36)	1.75	.60
94	A15	2½p dk ultra & blk	1.75	*2.50*
95	A16	4p blue & black	1.75	.60
96	A17	6p org & blk ('36)	2.00	*2.50*
97	A18	1sh dp vio & black ('36)	31.00	*42.50*
		Nos. 91-97 (7)	40.95	*56.35*

See Nos. 116-121.

Silver Jubilee Issue

Types of 1932 Overprinted in Black or Red

1935, May 7

98	A13	1p dk car & brn red	.40	*2.00*
99	A15	2½p dk ultra & bl (R)	1.00	*3.50*
100	A17	6p dull org & green	5.00	*8.50*
		Nos. 98-100 (3)	6.40	*14.00*
		Set, never hinged	12.50	

The vertical spacing of the overprint is wider on No. 100.

New Zealand Stamps of 1926 Overprinted in Black

b

1936, July 15 **Typo.** ***Perf. 14***

101	A56	2sh blue	15.00	*50.00*
102	A56	3sh violet	15.00	*80.00*

New Zealand Postal-Fiscal Stamps of 1931-35 Overprinted Type "b" in Black or Red

1932-36

103	PF5	2sh6p brown ('36)	21.00	*80.00*
104	PF5	5sh grn (R) ('36)	26.00	*100.00*
105	PF5	10sh dk car ('36)	55.00	*200.00*
106	PF5	£1 pink ('36)	85.00	*210.00*
107	PF5	£3 lt grn (R)	300.00	*550.00*
108	PF5	£5 dk blue (R)	210.00	*375.00*
		Nos. 103-108 (6)	697.00	*1,515.*

Issue dates: Mar. 1932, July 15, 1936.

New Zealand Stamps of 1937 Overprinted in Black

Perf. 14x13½

1937, June 1 **Engr.** **Wmk. 253**

109	A78	1p rose carmine	.20	.20
110	A78	2½p dark blue	.25	.20
111	A78	6p vermilion	.35	.30
		Nos. 109-111 (3)	.80	.70
		Set, never hinged	2.40	

King George VI A19

Village and Palms A20

Coastal Scene with Canoe — A21

1938, May 2 **Wmk. 61** ***Perf. 14***

112	A19	1sh dp violet & blk	7.50	*15.00*
113	A20	2sh dk red brn & blk	15.00	19.00
114	A21	3sh yel green & blue	37.50	*42.50*
		Nos. 112-114 (3)	60.00	76.50
		Set, never hinged	87.50	

See Nos. 122-124.

Mt. Ikurangi behind Avarua — A22

Perf. 13½x14

1940, Sept. 2 **Engr.** **Wmk. 253**

115	A22	3p on 1½p violet & blk	.70	.70

Issued only with surcharge. Stamps without surcharge are from the printer's archives.

Types of 1932-38

1944-46 **Engr.** ***Perf. 14***

116	A12	½p dk ol grn & blk ('45)	1.00	*4.50*
117	A13	1p dk car & blk ('45)	1.50	1.25
118	A14	2p brn & blk ('46)	.90	*7.00*
119	A15	2½p dk bl & blk ('45)	.60	*2.00*
120	A16	4p blue & black	2.50	*15.00*
121	A17	6p org & black	1.00	*2.50*
122	A19	1sh dp vio & blk	1.00	*3.50*
123	A20	2sh dk red brn & blk	27.50	*50.00*
124	A21	3sh yel green & blue ('45)	25.00	*40.00*
		Nos. 116-124 (9)	61.00	125.75
		Set, never hinged	100.00	

New Zealand Nos. AR76, AR78, AR85 and Type of 1931 Postal-Fiscal Stamps Overprinted Type "b" in Black or Red

1943-50 **Wmk. 253** **Typo.** ***Perf. 14***

124A	PF5	2sh6p brn ('46)	11.50	*22.50*
125	PF5	5sh green (R)	7.75	*22.50*
126	PF5	10sh dp pink ('48)	35.00	*90.00*
126A	PF5	£1 pink ('47)	40.00	*97.50*
126B	PF5	£3 lt grn (R) ('46)	47.50	*190.00*
126C	PF5	£5 dk bl (R) ('50)	175.00	*425.00*
		Nos. 124A-126C (6)	316.75	*847.50*
		Set, never hinged	525.00	

For surcharges see Nos. 192-194.

Catalogue values for unused stamps in this section, from this point to the end of the section, are for Never Hinged items.

Peace Issue

New Zealand Nos. 248, 250, 254 and 255 Overprinted in Black or Blue:

c

d

Perf. 13x13½, 13½x13

1946, June 1 **Engr.**

127	A94 (c)	1p emerald	.50	.20
128	A96 (d)	2p rose vio (Bl)	.50	.50
129	A100(c)	6p org red & red brn	1.00	.70
130	A101(c)	8p brn lake & blk (Bl)	.80	.70
		Nos. 127-130 (4)	2.80	2.10

Ngatangiia Channel, Rarotonga A23

Capt. James Cook Statue and Map of Cook Islands — A24

Designs: 1p, Cook and map of Hervey Isls. 2p, Rev. John Williams, his ship Messenger of Peace, and map of Rarotonga. 3p, Aitutaki map and palms. 5p, Mail plane landing at Rarotonga airport. 6p, Tongareva (Penrhyn) scene. 8p, Islander's house, Rarotonga. 2sh, Thatched house, mat weaver. 3sh, Steamer Matua offshore.

Perf. 13½x13, 13x13½

1949, Aug.1 **Engr.** **Wmk. 253**

131	A23	½p brown & violet	.20	*1.25*
132	A23	1p green & orange	3.75	2.50
133	A23	2p carmine & brn	2.25	*2.50*
134	A23	3p ultra & green	2.00	*2.50*
135	A23	5p purple & grn	6.50	2.00
136	A23	6p car rose & blk	6.50	3.25
137	A23	8p orange & olive	.65	*4.75*
138	A24	1sh chocolate & bl	6.00	4.75
139	A24	2sh rose car & brn	4.50	*16.00*
140	A24	3sh bl grn & lt ultra	11.50	*29.00*
		Nos. 131-140 (10)	43.85	*68.50*

For surcharge see No. 147.

Coronation Issue

Type of New Zealand

1953, May 25 **Photo.** ***Perf. 14x14½***

145	A113	3p brown	1.10	1.10
146	A114	6p slate black	2.10	2.10

No. 135 Surcharged with New Value and Two Dots

1960, Apr. 1 **Engr.** ***Perf. 13½x13***

147	A23	1sh6p on 5p purple & grn	.75	*.75*

Tiare Maori — A25

Fishing God — A26

Queen Elizabeth II — A27

Island Scene A28

3sh, Administration building, Mangaia. 5sh, Ship in Rarotonga harbor. 3p, 5p, 6p, 1sh, horiz.

Perf. 13½x13, 13x13½
Litho.; Engr.; (1sh6p)

1963, June 4

148	A25	1p shown	.50	*.65*
149	A25	2p shown	.20	*.65*
150	A25	3p Frangipani	.70	*.65*
151	A26	5p Fairy tern	8.25	1.60
152	A25	6p Hibiscus	1.00	.70
153	A26	8p Bonito	4.50	2.00
154	A25	1sh Oranges	.90	*.90*
155	A27	1sh6p shown	2.75	*2.75*
156	A28	2sh gray & brown	1.50	*1.10*
157	A28	3sh emer & black	1.75	*1.75*
158	A28	5sh ultra & brown	13.00	5.25
		Nos. 148-158 (11)	35.05	*18.00*

For overprints and surcharges see #167-169, 179-181, 183-184, 186-190.

Solar Eclipse and Palm Tree — A29

1965, May 31 Litho. *Perf. 13x13½*

159	A29	6p black, lt blue & yel	.40	.40

Observation of the solar eclipse on Manuae Island, May 30, 1965. Exists imperf.
For surcharge see No. 185.

Flag of New Zealand and Map of Cook Islands A30

Designs: 10p, London Missionary Society Church and graveyard. 1sh, Reading of Proclamation of Cession, Oct. 8, 1900, and Queen Elizabeth II. 1sh9p, Nikao School and flag of New Zealand.

Perf. 13½x13

1965, Sept. 16 Litho. Wmk. 253

160	A30	4p blue & red	.20	.20
161	A30	10p multicolored	.20	.20
162	A30	1sh multicolored	.20	.20
163	A30	1sh9p multicolored	.50	.50
		Nos. 160-163 (4)	1.10	1.10

Establishment of internal self-government.
For surcharges see Nos. 182, 191.

Nos. 160-162 and 156-158 Overprinted in Red: "In Memoriam / Sir Winston Churchill / 1874-1965"

1966, Jan. 24 Litho. Wmk. 253

164	A30	4p blue & red	.75	.30
165	A30	10p multicolored	2.25	.60
a.		Inverted overprint	*275.00*	
166	A30	1sh multicolored	2.25	.90
167	A28	2sh gray & brown	2.25	1.60
168	A28	3sh emer & black	2.25	1.60
169	A28	5sh ultra & brown	2.75	2.25
		Nos. 164-169 (6)	12.50	7.25

Statesman and WWII leader.

Adoration of the Wise Men, by Fra Angelico — A31

Paintings: 2p, Nativity, by Hans Memling, vert. 4p, Adoration of the Wise Men, by Velazquez. 10p, Adoration of the Wise Men, by Hieronymus Bosch. 1sh6p, Adoration of the Shepherds, by Jose Ribera, vert.

Perf. 13x14½, 14½x13

1966, Nov. 28 Photo. Unwmk.

170	A31	1p multicolored	.20	.20
171	A31	2p multicolored	.20	.20
172	A31	4p multicolored	.20	.20
173	A31	10p multicolored	.55	.55
174	A31	1sh6p multicolored	.65	.65
		Nos. 170-174 (5)	1.80	1.80

Christmas. Issued in sheets of 6 with ornamental gold border.

Perf. 13x12, 12x13

170a	A31	1p	.45	*.55*
171a	A31	2p	14.00	*11.50*
172a	A31	4p	1.10	*1.00*
173a	A31	10p	2.40	*4.50*
174a	A31	1sh6p	30.00	6.75
		Nos. 170a-174a (5)	47.95	24.30

Tennis and Queen Elizabeth A32

Sport: 1p, Women's basketball and Games' emblem. 4p, Boxing and team emblem. 7p, Soccer and Queen Elizabeth II.

1967, Jan. 12 *Perf. 13½*

175	A32	½p brt olive & multi	.20	.20
176	A32	1p brt blue & multi	.20	.20
177	A32	4p purple & multi	.20	.20
178	A32	7p red & multi	.20	.20
		Nos. 175-178,C10-C11 (6)	1.25	1.25

Second South Pacific Games, Noumea, New Caledonia, Dec. 8-18, 1966.

Nos. 148-155, 157-161 Surcharged with New Value or Black or Red

Pair (#181b), with Type I on left (#181) and Type II on right (#181a)

1967

179	A25	1c on 1p	.45	*1.75*
180	A26	2c on 2p	.20	.20
181	A25	2½c on 3p (I)	.20	.20
a.		Type II	.20	.20
b.		Pair, #181 and #181a	.45	.45
182	A30	3c on 4p	.20	.20
183	A26	4c on 5p	9.00	.40
184	A25	5c on 6p	.20	.20
185	A29	5c on 6p	5.00	1.25
186	A26	7c on 8p	.25	.20
187	A25	10c on 1sh	.20	.20
188	A27	15c on 1sh6p (R)	2.00	1.10
189	A28	30c on 3sh (R)	22.50	5.50
190	A28	50c on 5sh (R)	4.00	2.00
191	A30	$1 on 10p (R)	17.00	8.00
		Nos. 179-191 (13)	61.20	21.20

Issued: 2c, 2½c, 3c, 5c, 7c, 10c, 4/3; others 5/4.
No. 191 is surcharged "10/ $1.00" and 3 bars over old value.
Numerous varieties of surcharge include wrong-font "c," thin numerals, etc.

Nos. 126A, 126B and 126C Surcharged in Red

Wmk. 253

1967, June 6 Typo. *Perf. 14*

192	PF5	$2 on £1 pink	80.00	*200.00*
193	PF5	$6 on £3 lt green	140.00	*225.00*
194	PF5	$10 on £5 dk blue	250.00	*375.00*
		Nos. 192-194 (3)	470.00	800.00

Frequently found with stained gum.

Stamp of 1892, Village and Queen Victoria A33

Designs: 3c (4p), PO, Rarotonga, and Elizabeth II. 8c (10p), View of Avarua, Rarotonga, and 10p stamp of 1892. 18c (1sh9p), Map of Cook Islands, DC-3, S.S. Moana Roa and Capt. Cook.

Perf. 13½

1967, July 3 Photo. Unwmk.

195	A33	1c (1p) multi	.20	.20
196	A33	3c (4p) multi	.20	.20
197	A33	8c (10p) multi	.35	.35
198	A33	18c (1sh9p) multi	1.50	.80
a.		Souvenir sheet of 4, #195-198	3.50	3.50
		Nos. 195-198 (4)	2.25	1.55

75th anniv. of the 1st Cook Islands stamps. Issued in sheets of 8 stamps and 1 label with inscription in yellow margin.

Hibiscus — A34

Elizabeth II — A35

Elizabeth II and Flowers — A36

Flowers: 1c, Rose of Sharon. 2c, 15c, Frangipani. 2½c, Butterfly pea. 3c, Suva queen and Queen Elizabeth II. 4c, Water lily. 5c, Bauhania. 6c, Yellow hibiscus. 8c, Alamanda and Queen Elizabeth II. 9c, Stephanotis. 10c, Flaymboyant poinciana. 20c, Thunbergia. 25c, Canna lily and Queen Elizabeth II. 30c, Poinsettia. 50c, Gardenia.

1967-69 Photo. *Perf. 14x13½*

199	A34	½c gold & multi	.30	.20
200	A34	1c gold & multi	.30	.20
201	A34	2c gold & multi	.30	.20
202	A34	2½c gold & multi	.45	.20
203	A34	3c gold & multi	1.00	.20
204	A34	4c *Walter Lily*	1.40	*1.75*
205	A34	4c *Water Lily*	3.75	1.50
206	A34	5c gold & multi	.70	.20
207	A34	6c gold & multi	.75	.20
208	A34	8c gold & multi	.75	.20
209	A34	9c gold & multi	.75	.20
210	A34	10c gold & multi	.75	.20
211	A34	15c gold & multi	.75	.20
212	A34	20c gold & multi	8.50	.50
213	A34	25c gold & multi	1.50	.60
214	A34	30c gold & multi	1.25	.70
215	A34	50c gold & multi	1.90	1.00
216	A35	$1 gold & multi	4.00	2.25
217	A35	$2 gold & multi	9.00	3.50
218	A36	$4 multi ('68)	3.25	*5.50*
219	A36	$6 multi ('68)	3.75	*7.50*
219A	A36	$8 multi ('69)	11.00	*11.00*
220	A36	$10 multi ('68)	7.00	*12.00*
		Nos. 199-220 (23)	63.10	50.00

The $4 exists with "FOUR DOLLARS" in two widths: 32½mm and 33½mm.
Nos. 214-215 were surcharged "Plus 20c United Kingdom Special Mail Service" in 5 lines of capitals for use during the 1971 British mail strike. The strike ended Mar. 8, the day the 50c+20c, was released.
For surcharges see Nos. 290-291, 305-309, B1-B13, B17-B18, B20. For overprints see Nos. 277-283, 302-304, 315, 351-356, O1-O15.

Fluorescence

Since 1968 a number of stamps have been issued with a "fluorescent security underprinting" in a multiple coat of arms pattern. Some issues have this underprint, some do not.

Stamps issued both with and without the underprint are Nos. 199-203, 205-220, 283, 290-291.

From Nos. 292-296 onward, all stamps have this underprint unless otherwise noted.

Ia Orana Maria, by Gauguin A37

Gauguin Paintings: 3c, Riders on the Beach. 5c, Still Life with Flowers. 8c, Whispered Words. 15c, Maternity. 22c, Why Are You Angry?

1967, Oct. 23 Photo. *Perf. 13½*

221	A37	1c gold & multi	.25	.25
222	A37	3c gold & multi	.25	.25
223	A37	5c gold & multi	.25	.25
224	A37	8c gold & multi	.25	.25
225	A37	15c gold & multi	.40	.40
226	A37	22c gold & multi	.60	.60
a.		Souvenir sheet of 6, #221-226	3.50	3.50
		Nos. 221-226 (6)	2.00	2.00

#221-226 are printed in sheets of 6 (3x2).

Holy Family by Rubens — A38

Paintings: 3c, Adoration of the Magi, by Albrecht Durer. 4c, The Lucca Madonna, by Jan Van Eyck. 8c, Adoration of the Shepherds, by Jacopo da Bassano. 15c, Nativity, by El Greco. 25c, Madonna and Child, by Antonio Allegri da Correggio.

1967, Dec. 4 *Perf. 12x13*

227	A38	1c gold & multi	.20	.20
228	A38	3c gold & multi	.20	.20
229	A38	4c gold & multi	.20	.20
230	A38	8c gold & multi	.20	.20
231	A38	15c gold & multi	.30	.30
232	A38	25c gold & multi	.35	.35
		Nos. 227-232 (6)	1.45	1.45

Christmas.

Capt. Cook and Matavai Bay, Tahiti, by Sydney Parkinson A39

1c, Ships off Huahine Island, Tahiti, by John & James Clevely. 2c, town & harbor of Kamchatka, by John Webber, & Queen Elizabeth II. 4c, "The Ice Islands" (Antarctica), by William Hodges.

1968, Sept. 12 Photo. *Perf. 13*

233	A39	½c gold & multi	.20	.20
234	A39	1c gold & multi	.20	.20
235	A39	2c gold & multi	.20	.20
236	A39	4c gold & multi	.20	.20
		Nos. 233-236,C12-C15 (8)	6.45	6.45

Bicent. of Capt. Cook's 1st voyage of discovery. Printed in sheets of 10 stamps and 2 labels (3x4). Labels show portraits of Elizabeth II and Cook.

Gymnast A40

1968, Oct. 21

237	A40	1c Sailing	.20	.20
238	A40	5c shown	.20	.20
239	A40	15c High jump	.20	.20
240	A40	20c Woman diver	.35	.20
241	A40	30c Bicyclist	.70	.20
242	A40	50c Woman hurdler	.55	.30
		Nos. 237-242 (6)	2.20	1.30

19th Olympic Games, Mexico City, Oct. 12-27. Printed in sheets of 10 stamps and 2 labels (3x4).

Virgin and Child, by Titian — A41

Paintings: 4c, Holy Family, by Raphael. 10c, Madonna of the Rosary, by Murillo. 20c, Adoration of the Magi, by Memling. 30c, Adoration of the Magi, by Ghirlandajo.

1968, Dec. 2 Photo. *Perf. 13*

243	A41	1c gold & multi	.20	.20
244	A41	4c gold & multi	.20	.20
245	A41	10c gold & multi	.20	.20
246	A41	20c gold & multi	.30	.30
247	A41	30c gold & multi	.45	.45
a.		Souv. sheet, #243-247 + label	2.40	2.40
		Nos. 243-247 (5)	1.35	1.35

Issued in sheets of 6 (2x3).

Training on Ropeway A42

Designs: ½c, Boy Scouts cooking over campfire. 5c, Training with signal flags, and Queen Elizabeth II. 10c, Planting a tree. 20c, Erecting a hut. 30c, Lord Baden-Powell, lake and mountains (visit to Rarotonga in 1935).

1969, Feb. 6 Photo. *Perf. 13½*

248	A42	½c multicolored	.20	.20
249	A42	1c multicolored	.20	.20
250	A42	5c multicolored	.20	.20
251	A42	10c multicolored	.25	.25
252	A42	20c multicolored	.30	.30
253	A42	30c multicolored	.55	.55
		Nos. 248-253 (6)	1.70	1.70

5th Natl. Boy Scout Jamboree, Christchurch, New Zealand, Jan. 2-12.
Issued in sheets of 10 stamps and 2 labels (4x3).

Soccer — A43

#254b, Pole vault. #255a, Weight lifting. #255b, Basketball, Elizabeth II. #256a, Long jump. #256b, Tennis. #257a, Running. #257b, Javelin, Elizabeth II. #258a, Boxing. #258b, Golf.

Perf. 13½x13

1969, July 7 Photo. Unwmk.

254	A43	½c Pair, #a.-b.	.70	.70
255	A43	1c Pair, #a.-b.	.70	.70
256	A43	4c Pair, #a.-b.	1.50	1.50
257	A43	10c Pair, #a.-b.	2.10	2.10
258	A43	15c Pair, #a.-b.	3.50	3.50
c.		Souv. sheet, #254-258 + 2 labels	9.50	9.50
		Nos. 254-258 (5)	8.50	8.50

3rd South Pacifc Games, Port Moresby, Papua and New Guinea, Aug. 13-23.
Issued in sheets of 10.

Map of Cook Islands and Capt. Cook — A44

Map of Cook Islands and: 5c, Premier Albert Henry of New Zealand. 25c, Coat of arms of New Zealand. 30c, Queen Elizabeth II.

1969, Oct. 8 Photo. *Perf. 13*

264	A44	5c red & multi	.50	.50
265	A44	10c lemon & multi	1.50	1.50
266	A44	25c green & multi	.75	.75
267	A44	30c blue & multi	.75	.75
		Nos. 264-267 (4)	3.50	3.50

South Pacific Conf., Noumea, Oct. 1969.

Madonna and Child, by Filippo Lippi A45

Paintings: 4c, Holy Family, by Baccio della Porta. 10c, Madonna and Child, by Anton Raphael Mengs. 20c, Madonna and Child, by Le Maitre de Flemalle. 30c, Madonna and Child by Correggio.

1969, Nov. 21 Photo. *Perf. 13½*

268	A45	1c buff & multi	.20	.20
269	A45	4c buff & multi	.20	.20
270	A45	10c buff & multi	.20	.20
271	A45	20c buff & multi	.25	.25
272	A45	30c buff & multi	.25	.25
a.		Souv. sheet, #268-272 + label	2.00	2.00
		Nos. 268-272 (5)	1.10	1.10

Issued in sheets of 8 stamps, one label with portrait of Queen Elizabeth II.

Resurrection of Christ, by Raphael — A46

The Resurrection of Christ by: 8c, Dirk Bouts. 20c, Albert Altdorfer. 25c, Murillo.

1970, Mar. 12 Photo. *Perf. 13½*
Size: 25½x56mm

273	A46	4c gold & multi	.20	.20
274	A46	8c gold & multi	.20	.20
275	A46	20c gold & multi	.20	.20
276	A46	25c gold & multi	.25	.25
a.		Souv. sheet, #273-276 + 2 labels	1.50	1.50
		Nos. 273-276 (4)	.85	.85

Easter 1970.
Printed in sheets of 8 stamps and a label (3x3) showing portrait of Queen Elizabeth II and name of painting and painter.
See Nos. 316-318.

Nos. 205, 208, 211-212, 214, 217 Overpinted: "KIA ORANA / APOLLO 13 /ASTRONAUTS / Te Atua to / Tatou Irinakianga"

1970, Apr. *Perf. 14x13½*

277	A34	4c gold & multi	.30	.30
278	A34	8c gold & multi	.30	.30
279	A34	15c gold & multi	.30	.30
280	A34	20c gold & multi	.40	.40
281	A34	30c gold & multi	.55	.55
282	A35	$2 gold & multi	1.60	1.60

No. 218 Overprinted: "KIA ORANA / APOLLO 13 /ASTRONAUTS"

283	A36	$4 gold & multi	3.00	3.00
		Nos. 277-283 (7)	6.45	6.45

Splashdown of Apollo 13 west of Rarotonga, Apr. 17, 1970.
Issued: #277-282, 4/17; $4, 4/30.
Values for Nos. 283, 290-291 are for stamps with fluorescence. Stamps without fluorescence sell for more.

Queen Elizabeth II, Prince Philip, Princess Anne and Prince Charles — A47

Design: 30c, Wedgwood bust of Capt. Cook and "Endeavour." $1, Royal visit commemorative coin, obverse and reverse.

1970, June 12 Photo. *Perf. 13½*

284	A47	5c gold & multi	.50	.30
285	A47	30c gold & multi	1.75	1.50
286	A47	$1 gold & multi	5.00	4.50
a.		Souv. sheet, #284-286 + label	11.50	11.50
		Nos. 284-286 (3)	7.25	6.30

Visit of the British royal family.

Nos. 284-286 Overprinted in Silver or Black: "Fifth Anniversary Self-Government August 1970"

1970, Aug. 27 Photo. *Perf. 13½*

287	A47	5c gold & multi (S)	.50	.20
288	A47	30c gold & multi	1.50	1.00
289	A47	$1 gold & multi	2.50	1.40
		Nos. 287-289 (3)	4.50	2.60

5th anniv. of self-government. The overprint on No. 287 is arranged in one line around 3 sides of the design; the overprint on Nos. 288-289 is in 3 horizontal lines.

Nos. 219A-220 Surcharged

1970, Nov. 11 Photo. *Perf. 14x13½*

290	A36	$4 on $8 multi	*4.25*	*4.25*
291	A36	$4 on $10 multi	*3.00*	*3.00*

In each sheet of 15, 3 stamps have 2 surcharged bars instead of one. See second note after No. 283.

Nativity A48

Illuminations from 14th Century Robert de Lisle Psalter: 4c, Angel and shepherds. 10c, The Circumcision. 20c, The Adoration of the Kings. 30c, The Presentation at the Temple.

1970, Nov. 30 Photo. *Perf. 13½*

292	A48	1c gold & multi	.20	.20
293	A48	4c gold & multi	.20	.20
294	A48	10c gold & multi	.30	.30
295	A48	20c gold & multi	.35	.35
296	A48	30c gold & multi	.45	.45
a.		Souv. sheet, #292-296 + label	1.50	1.50
		Nos. 292-296 (5)	1.50	1.50

Christmas.
Issued in sheets of 5 stamps and a label (3x2) showing portrait of Queen Elizabeth II and source of design.

Queen Elizabeth II and Prince Philip — A49

Designs: 4c, Royal family at Balmoral. 10c, Prince Philip sailing. 15c, Prince Philip as polo player. 25c, Prince Philip and royal yacht.

1971, Mar. 11 Litho. *Perf. 13½*

297	A49	1c brt blue & multi	.20	.20
298	A49	4c brt blue & multi	.30	.30
299	A49	10c brt blue & multi	.75	.75
300	A49	15c brt blue & multi	1.10	1.10
301	A49	25c brt blue & multi	1.90	1.90
a.		Souv. sheet, #297-301 + 2 labels	5.75	5.75
		Nos. 297-301 (5)	4.25	4.25

Visit of Prince Philip, Duke of Edinburgh to Rarotonga, Feb. 27, 1971. Printed in sheets of 10 stamps and 2 labels showing Queen Elizabeth II commemorative coin and a portrait of Prince Philip.

Nos. 210, 213-214 Overprinted

1971, Sept. 8 Photo. *Perf. 14x13½*

302	A34	10c gold & multi	.65	.65
303	A34	25c gold & multi	.65	.65
304	A34	30c gold & multi	.65	.65
		Nos. 302-304 (3)	1.95	1.95

4th South Pacific Games, Papeete, French Polynesia, Sept. 8-19.

Nos. 202, 205, 208-209 and 211 Surcharged with New Value and Three Bars

1971, Oct. 20

305	A34	10c on 2½c multi	.20	.20
306	A34	10c on 4c multi	.20	.20
307	A34	10c on 8c multi	.20	.20
308	A34	10c on 9c multi	.20	.20
309	A34	10c on 15c multi	.20	.20
		Nos. 305-309 (5)	1.00	1.00

Madonna and Child, by Bellini — A50

Christmas: Paintings of the Madonna and Child, by Giovanni Bellini.

1971, Nov. 30 *Perf. 13½*

310	A50	1c gold & multi	.20	.20
311	A50	4c gold & multi	.20	.20
312	A50	10c gold & multi	.30	.30
313	A50	20c gold & multi	.60	.60
314	A50	30c gold & multi	.90	.90
a.		Souv. sheet, #310-314 + label	2.75	2.75
		Nos. 310-314 (5)	2.20	2.20

See No. B14.

No. 216 Overprinted: "SOUTH PACIFIC / COMMISSION / FEB. 1947-1972"

1972, Feb. 17 Photo. *Perf. 14x13½*

315 A35 $1 gold & multi .90 .90

South Pacific Commission, 25th anniv.

Easter Type of 1970

Illuminations from 14th century Robert de Lisle Psalter: 5c, St. John. 10c, Christ crucified. 30c, Virgin Mary.

1972, Mar. 6 Photo. *Perf. 13½*

Size: 21x68mm

316 A46 5c gold & multi .20 .20
317 A46 10c gold & multi .20 .20
318 A46 30c gold & multi .50 .50
a. Souvenir sheet of 3, #316-318 1.50 1.50
Nos. 316-318 (3) .90 .90

Printed in sheets of 12.
For surcharges see Nos. B15-B16, B19.

Rocket over Moon — A51

#319a, Shown. #319b, Earth over moon. #320a, Landing module and astronaut. #320b, Astronaut collecting moon rocks. #321a, Earth and rocket over moon. #321b, Lunar rover and astronaut. #322a, Helicopter over raft in Pacific. #322b, Capsule and parachutes.

1972, Apr. 17

319 A51 5c Pair, #a.-b. .20 .20
320 A51 10c Pair, #a.-b. .60 .60
321 A51 25c Pair, #a.-b. 1.75 1.75
322 A51 30c Pair, #a.-b. 2.25 2.25
c. Souvenir sheet of 8 7.50 7.50
Nos. 319-322 (4) 4.80 4.80

Apollo moon explorations.
No. 322c contains Nos. 319-322 arranged in 2 blocks of 4 divided by a map showing splashdown area of Apollo X, XII and XIII.
For surcharges see Nos. B21-B24.

High Jump, Olympic Rings — A52

Rest on Flight to Egypt, by Caravaggio — A53

1972, June 26

327 A52 10c shown .30 .30
328 A52 25c Running .65 .65
329 A52 30c Boxing .65 .65
a. Souv. sheet, #327-329 + label 2.50 2.50
Nos. 327-329 (3) 1.60 1.60

20th Olympic Games, Munich, Aug. 26-Sept. 10. Sheets of 8 stamps and label.
See No. B29.

1972, Oct. 11 Photo. *Perf. 13½*

Paintings: 5c, Virgin of the Swallows, by Guercino. 10c, Virgin with Green Cushion, by Andrea Solario. 20c, Virgin and Child, by Lorenzo di Credi. 30c, Virgin and Child, by Giovanni Bellini.

330 A53 1c gold & multi .30 .30
331 A53 5c gold & multi .30 .30
332 A53 10c gold & multi .40 .40
333 A53 20c gold & multi .75 .75
334 A53 30c gold & multi 1.25 1.25
a. Souv. sheet, #330-334 + label 4.50 4.50
Nos. 330-334 (5) 3.00 3.00

Christmas. See No. B30.

Princess Elizabeth and Prince Philip — A54

Designs: 5c, Wedding ceremony, Westminster Abbey. 15c, Bridal portrait. 30c, Official wedding picture of royal family.

1972, Nov. 20

Size: 29x40mm

335 A54 5c silver & multi .40 .40
336 A54 10c silver & multi .55 .55

Size: 40x40mm

337 A54 15c silver & multi .70 .70

Size: 66x40mm

338 A54 30c silver & multi .85 .85
Nos. 335-338 (4) 2.50 2.50

25th anniversary of the marriage of Queen Elizabeth II and Prince Philip.
Nos. 335-337 printed in sheets of 8 stamps and one label; No. 338 in sheets of 6.

1c Coin with Queen Elizabeth II and Taro Leaf A55

Queen Elizabeth II Coins: 2c, Pineapples. 5c, Hibiscus. 10c, Oranges. 20c, Fairy terns. 50c, Bonito. $1, Tangaroa, Polynesian god of creation, vert.

1973, Mar. 15 Photo. *Perf. 13x13½*

Size: 37x24mm

339 A55 1c dp car, blk & gold .20 .20
340 A55 2c blue, blk & gold .20 .20
341 A55 5c green, blk & gold .20 .20

Size: 46x30mm

342 A55 10c vio, blue, blk & sil .25 .25
343 A55 20c dk green, blk & sil .40 .40
344 A55 50c dp car, black & sil .60 .60

Size: 32x54½mm

345 A55 $1 blue, blk & silver .90 .90
Nos. 339-345 (7) 2.75 2.75

Coinage commemorating silver wedding anniversary of Queen Elizabeth II.
Printed in sheets of 20 stamps and label showing Westminster Abbey.

"Noli me Tangere," by Titian — A56

Paintings: 10c, Descent from the Cross, by Rubens. 30c, The Lamentation of Christ, by Dürer.

1973, Apr. 9

346 A56 5c gold & multi .20 .20
347 A56 10c gold & multi .40 .40
348 A56 30c gold & multi .50 .50
a. Souvenir sheet of 3, #346-348 1.40 1.40
Nos. 346-348 (3) 1.10 1.10

Easter. Printed in sheets of 15 stamps and one label.

See Nos. 378-380, B31-B33, B39-B41.

Queen Elizabeth II in Coronation Regalia — A57

1973, June 1 Photo. *Perf. 14x13½*

349 A57 10c gold & multi 1.25 1.25

Souvenir Sheet

Perf. 13½x14½

350 A57 50c gold & multi 3.50 3.50

20th anniv. of the coronation of Queen Elizabeth II. No. 349 printed in sheets of 5 stamps and one label.

Nos. 206, 208, 210, 212-214 Overprinted: "TENTH ANNIVERSARY / CESSATION OF / NUCLEAR TESTING / TREATY"

1973, July 25 Photo. *Perf. 14x13½*

351 A34 5c gold & multi .20 .20
352 A34 8c gold & multi .20 .20
353 A34 10c gold & multi .20 .20
354 A34 20c gold & multi .20 .20
355 A34 25c gold & multi .50 .50
356 A34 30c gold & multi .50 .50
Nos. 351-356 (6) 1.80 1.80

Nuclear Test Ban Treaty, 10th anniv. and as protest against French nuclear testing on Mururoa atoll.

Tipairua — A58

Historic South Pacific sailing vessels.

1973, Sept. 17 Photo. *Perf. 13½x13*

357 A58 ½c shown .30 .30
358 A58 1c Wa'a Kaulua .30 .30
359 A58 1½c Tainui .30 .30
360 A58 5c War canoe .85 .85
361 A58 10c Pahi 1.00 1.00
362 A58 15c Amatasi 1.25 1.25
363 A58 25c Vaka 1.75 1.75
Nos. 357-363 (7) 5.75 5.75

Annunciation A59

Princess Anne — A60

Designs from 15th Century Prayer Book: 5c, The Visitation. 10c, Adoration of the Shepherds. 20c, Adoration of the Kings. 30c, Slaughter of the Innocents.

1973, Oct. 30 Photo. *Perf. 13x13½*

364 A59 1c multicolored .20 .20
365 A59 5c multicolored .20 .20
366 A59 10c multicolored .20 .20
367 A59 20c multicolored .40 .40
368 A59 30c multicolored .65 .65
a. Souv. sheet, #364-368 + label 1.75 1.50
Nos. 364-368 (5) 1.65 1.65

Christmas. See Nos. B34-B38.

1973, Nov. 14 Photo. *Perf. 14*

369 A60 25c shown .40 .40
370 A60 30c Mark Phillips .60 .60
371 A60 50c Princess and Mark Phillips 1.00 1.00
a. Souv. sheet, #369-371 + label 2.50 2.50
Nos. 369-371 (3) 2.00 2.00

Wedding of Princess Anne and Capt. Mark Phillips.

Running and Games Emblem A61

1c, Diving. 3c, Boxing. 10c, Weight lifting. 30c, Bicycling. 50c, Discobolus.

1974, Jan. 24 Photo. *Perf. 14*

372 A61 1c multi, vert. .20 .20
373 A61 3c multi, vert. .20 .20
374 A61 5c multi .20 .20
375 A61 10c multi .25 .25
376 A61 30c multi .75 .75
Nos. 372-376 (5) 1.60 1.60

Souvenir Sheet

377 A61 50c multi, vert. 2.00 2.00

10th British Commonwealth Games, Christchurch, New Zealand, Jan. 24-Feb. 2. No. 377 contains one stamp 35x45mm.

Easter Type of 1973 Dated "1974"

Paintings: 5c, Jesus Carrying Cross, by Raphael. 10c, Jesus in the Arms of God, by El Greco. 30c, Descent from the Cross, by Caravaggio.

1974, Mar. 25 *Perf. 13½x13*

378 A56 5c gold & multi .20 .20
379 A56 10c gold & multi .25 .25
380 A56 30c gold & multi .65 .65
a. Souvenir sheet of 3, #378-380 2.00 2.00
Nos. 378-380 (3) 1.10 1.10

Easter. See Nos. B39-B41.

Phallicium Glaucum A62

Queen Elizabeth II — A63

Queen and Shells — A64

Cook Islands sea shells. The designs of the 2c, 5c, 10c, 30c include portrait of Queen Elizabeth II.

1974-75 Photo. *Perf. 13½*

381 A62 ½c shown .20 .20
382 A62 1c Vasum turbinellus .20 .20

383 A62 1½c Corculum cardissa .20 .20
384 A62 2c Terebellum terebellum .20 .20
385 A62 3c Aulica vespertilio .20 .20
386 A62 4c Strombus gibberulus .20 .20
387 A62 5c Cymatium pileare .20 .20
388 A62 6c Cyprae caputserpentis .20 .20
389 A62 8c Bursa granularis .20 .20
390 A62 10c Tenebra muscaria .20 .20
391 A62 15c Mitra mitra .40 .40
392 A62 20c Natica alapillonis roding .60 .60
393 A62 25c Gloripallium pallium .75 .75
394 A62 30c Conus miles .90 .90
395 A62 50c Conus textile 1.50 1.25
396 A62 60c Oliva sericea roding 2.25 1.25
397 A63 $1 multicolored 3.50 2.25
398 A63 $2 multi ('75) 7.00 4.50

Perf. 14x13½

399 A64 $4 multi ('75) 10.50 6.50
400 A64 $6 multi ('75) 17.00 10.50
401 A64 $8 multi ('75) 21.00 13.00
402 A64 $10 multi ('75) 27.50 18.00
Nos. 381-402 (22) 94.90 61.90

Issued: 50c, 60c, $1, 8/26; $2, 1/27; $4, 3/17; $6, 4/29; $8, 5/30; $10, 6/30; others, 5/17.

For surcharges & overprints see #488-498, 526-528, 991, O16-O26, O30-O31.

Soccer Player and Map of Oceania A65

50c, Munich stadium & map of Oceania. $1, Soccer player, Munich stadium & World Cup.

1974, July 5 Photo. *Perf. 13½*

Size: 31x29mm

403 A65 25c multicolored .45 .45
404 A65 50c multicolored .90 .90

Size: 68x28½mm

405 A65 $1 multicolored 1.75 1.75
a. Souvenir sheet of 3, #403-405 3.75 3.75
Nos. 403-405 (3) 3.10 3.10

World Cup Soccer Championship, Munich, June 13-July 7. Nos. 403-405 printed in sheets of 8 and commemorative label.

$2.50 Capt. Cook Silver Coin — A66

Commemorative Silver Coins: $7.50, $7.50 coin with Queen Elizabeth II on obverse; Capt. Cook, map of Islands and "Resolution" on reverse. $2.50 coin shows "Resolution," "Adventure" and globe on reverse.

1974, July 22 Photo. *Perf. 14*

406 A66 $2.50 sil, vio & blk 11.00 7.25
407 A66 $7.50 grn, sil & blk 29.00 22.50
a. Souvenir sheet of 2, #406-407 55.00 37.50

Bicentenary of Capt. Cook's 2nd voyage of discovery. Nos. 406-407 printed in sheets of 5 and commemorative label.

Cook Islands Nos. 1, 49, 62, 66, 77 — A67

Stamps of Cook Islands: 25c, DC-3 over old Rarotonga landing strip, and No. 19. 30c, Rarotonga Post Office, UPU emblem and No. 65. 50c, UPU emblem and Nos. 1, 19, 49, 62, 65-66 and 77.

1974, Sept. 16 Photo. *Perf. 13½x14*

408 A67 10c gold & multi .20 .20
409 A67 25c gold & multi .55 .55
410 A67 30c gold & multi .65 .65
411 A67 50c gold & multi 1.25 1.25
a. Souv. sheet, #408-411, perf. 13½ 2.75 2.75
Nos. 408-411 (4) 2.65 2.65

Cent. of UPU. Nos. 408-411 printed in sheets of 8 and commemorative label.

Virgin and Child, with St. John, by Raphael — A68

Paintings: 5c, Holy Family, by Andrea del Sarto. 10c, Nativity, by Correggio. 20c, Holy Family, by Rembrandt. 30c, Nativity, by Van der Weyden.

1974, Oct. 15 Photo. *Perf. 13½*

412 A68 1c multicolored .20 .20
413 A68 5c multicolored .20 .20
414 A68 10c multicolored .20 .20
415 A68 20c multicolored .65 .65
416 A68 30c multicolored .95 .95
a. Souv. sheet, #412-416 + label 2.50 2.50
Nos. 412-416 (5) 2.20 2.20

Christmas 1974. Nos. 412-416 printed in sheets of 15 and one label showing Queen Elizabeth II.

See Nos. B42-B46.

Churchill and Blenheim Palace A69

Sir Winston Churchill (1874-1965) and: 10c, Parliament. 25c, Chartwell. 30c, Buckingham Palace. 50c, St. Paul's Cathedral.

1974, Nov. 20 Photo. *Perf. 14*

417 A69 5c violet & multi .20 .20
418 A69 10c maroon & multi .25 .25
419 A69 25c dk blue & multi .65 .65
420 A69 30c brown & multi .85 .85
421 A69 50c multicolored 1.60 1.60
a. Souv. sheet, #417-421 + label 3.75 3.75
Nos. 417-421 (5) 3.55 3.55

Nos. 417-421 printed in sheets of 5 stamps and one label showing $100 commemorative gold coin.

Vasco Nunez de Balboa — A70

5c, Ferdinand Magellan & route around South America. 10c, Juan Sebastian del Cano & ship. 25c, Andres de Urdaneta & ship. 25c, Miguel Lopez de Legaspi & ship.

1975, Feb. 3 *Perf. 13½*

422 A70 1c multicolored .35 .20
423 A70 5c multicolored .35 .20
424 A70 10c multicolored 1.25 .35
425 A70 25c multicolored 3.00 1.10
426 A70 30c multicolored 3.50 1.25
Nos. 422-426 (5) 8.45 3.10

16th century explorers of the Pacific Ocean.

Apollo and Apollo-Soyuz Emblem — A71

Apollo-Soyuz Emblem &: #427b, Soyuz. #428a, Aleksei A. Leonov & Valery N. Kubasov. #428b, Donald K. Slayton, Vance D. Brand & Thomas P. Stafford. #429a, Cosmonaut inside Soyuz capsule. #429b, American astronauts inside Apollo capsule.

1975, July 15 Photo. *Perf. 13½*

427 A71 25c Pair, #a.-b. 1.00 1.00
428 A71 30c Pair, #a.-b. 1.25 1.25
429 A71 50c Pair, #a.-b. 2.00 2.00
c. Souvenir sheet of 6, #427-429 4.25 4.25
Nos. 427-429 (3) 4.25 4.25

Apollo Soyuz space test project (Russo-American space cooperation), launching July 15; link-up, July 17. Printed sheets of 18 stamps and 2 labels showing flags.

$100 Gold Commemorative Coin — A72

1975, Aug. 8 Photo. *Perf. 13½x13*

433 A72 $2 gold & dp violet 6.00 5.75

Bicentenary of the completion of Capt. Cook's second voyage of discovery.

Cook Islands' Flag, Map of Islands and New Zealand A73

Prime Minister Sir Albert Henry — A74

Design: 25c, View of Rarotonga and flag.

1975, Aug. 8 *Perf. 13½x13, 13x13½*

434 A73 5c gold & multi .60 .20
435 A74 10c gold & multi .75 .20
436 A73 25c gold & multi 1.90 .55
Nos. 434-436 (3) 3.25 .95

Tenth anniversary of self-government.

Virgin and Child, 15th Century, Flemish — A75

Paintings: 10c, Madonna in the Field, by Raphael. 15c, Holy Family, by Raphael. 20c, Adoration of the Shepherds, by J. B. Mayno. 35c, Annunciation, by Murillo.

1975, Dec. 1 Photo. *Perf. 13½*

437 A75 6c gold & multi .20 .20
438 A75 10c gold & multi .20 .20
439 A75 15c gold & multi .30 .30
440 A75 20c gold & multi .40 .40
441 A75 35c gold & multi .65 .65
a. Souv. sheet, #437-441 + label 1.75 1.75
Nos. 437-441 (5) 1.75 1.75

Christmas. See Nos. B47-B51.

Descent from the Cross, by Raphael A76

Paintings: 15c, Pieta, by Veronese. 35c, Pieta, by El Greco.

1976, Mar. 29 Photo. *Perf. 13½*

442 A76 7c gold & multi .20 .20
443 A76 15c gold & multi .60 .60
444 A76 35c gold & multi 1.40 1.40
a. Souvenir sheet of 3, #442-444 2.25 2.25
Nos. 442-444 (3) 2.20 2.20

Easter. Nos. 442-444 printed in sheets of 20 with label showing Queen Elizabeth II.

See Nos. B52-B54.

Benjamin Franklin and "Resolution" — A77

Designs: $2, Capt. James Cook and "Resolution." $3, Cook, "Resolution" and Franklin.

1976, May 29 Photo. *Perf. 13½*

445 A77 $1 gold & multi 5.50 3.00
446 A77 $2 gold & multi 11.50 6.25

Souvenir Sheet

Perf. 13

447 A77 $3 gold & multi 14.00 8.00

American Bicentennial. No. 447 contains one stamp 73x31mm. Nos. 445-446 printed in sheets of 5 and corner label with Franklin's request to assist Capt. Cook.

For overprint see No. O29.

Nos. 445-447 Overprinted "Royal Visit July 1976"

1976, July 6 Photo. *Perf. 13½*

448 A77 $1 gold & multi 2.50 2.00
449 A77 $2 gold & multi 6.25 5.75

Souvenir Sheet

Perf. 13

450 A77 $3 gold & multi 13.00 9.00

Visit of Queen Elizabeth II and Prince Philip to the United States.

High Hurdles — A78

15c, Field hockey. 30c, Fencing. 35c, Soccer.

1976, July 22 *Perf. 13½*

451 A78 7c Pair, #a.-b. .25 .25
452 A78 15c Pair, #a.-b. .50 .50
453 A78 30c Pair, #a.-b. 1.25 1.25
454 A78 35c Pair, #a.-b. 1.50 1.50
c. Souvenir sheet of 8, #451-454 4.50 4.50
Nos. 451-454 (4) 3.50 3.50

21st Olympic Games, Montreal, Canada, 7/17-8/1. Printed in sheets of 10 stamps + 2 labels.

The Visitation — A80

Designs: 10c, Virgin and Child. 15c, Adoration of the Shepherds. 20c, Adoration of the Kings. 35c, Holy Family. After painted Renaissance altar sculptures.

1976, Oct. 12 Photo. *Perf. 14x13½*

459	A80 6c gold & multi	.20	.20
460	A80 10c gold & multi	.20	.20
461	A80 15c gold & multi	.25	.25
462	A80 20c gold & multi	.35	.35
463	A80 35c gold & multi	.60	.60
a.	Souv. sheet, #459-463 + label	1.75	1.75
	Nos. 459-463 (5)	1.60	1.60

Christmas. Nos. 459-463 printed in sheets of 20 with label showing Queen Elizabeth II.
See Nos. B55-B59.

$5 Silver Coin, 1976 — A81

1976, Nov. 15 Photo. *Perf. 13½*

464	A81 $1 multicolored	3.00	2.25

National Wildlife and Conservation Day. Issued in sheets of 5 stamps and commemorative label.
See Nos. 502, 536.

A82

#465a, Crown. #465b, Elizabeth II in Coronation Vestments. #466a, Westminster Abbey. #466b, Coach in procession. #467a, Queen and Prince Philip after coronation. 467b, Investiture of Sir Albert Henry, Premier of Cook Islands, 1974.

1977, Feb. 7 Photo. *Perf. 13½x13*

465	A82 25c Pair, #a.-b.	1.00	.80
466	A82 50c Pair, #a.-b.	2.50	2.00
467	A82 $1 Pair, #a.-b.	5.00	4.00
c.	Souv. sheet, #465-467, perf. 13	8.75	7.50
	Nos. 465-467 (3)	8.50	6.80

Reign of Queen Elizabeth II, 25th anniv. Printed in sheets of 8.
For overprints see No. O27.

Crucifixion, by Rubens — A83

Virgin and Child, by Memling — A84

Paintings by Rubens: 15c, Christ Between the Thieves. 35c, Descent from the Cross.

1977, Mar. 28 Photo. *Perf. 14x13½*

471	A83 7c gold & multi	.50	.50
472	A83 15c gold & multi	.50	.50
473	A83 35c gold & multi	1.40	1.40
a.	Souv. sheet, #471-473, perf 13	2.50	2.50
	Nos. 471-473 (3)	2.40	2.40

Easter 1977, and 400th birth anniv. of Peter Paul Rubens (1577-1640), Flemish painter. Nos. 471-473 printed in sheets of 24 stamps and corner label with portrait of Queen Elizabeth II and description.
See Nos. B60-B62.

1977, Oct. 3 Photo. *Perf. 13½*

Virgin and Child by: 10c, Hans Memling. 15c, Geertgen Tot Sin Jans. 20c, Carlo Crivelli. 35c, School of Henry Blex.

474	A84 6c gold & multi	.25	.25
475	A84 10c gold & multi	.25	.25
476	A84 15c gold & multi	.25	.25
477	A84 20c gold & multi	.45	.45
478	A84 35c gold & multi	.80	.80
a.	Souv. sheet, #474-478 + label	2.25	2.25
	Nos. 474-478 (5)	2.00	2.00

Christmas. Nos. 474-478 printed in sheets of 24 and label. See Nos. B63-B67.

$5-silver Coin, 1977 — A85

1977, Nov. 15 Photo. *Perf. 13½*

479	A85 $1 silver & multi	3.50	1.60

National Wildlife Conservation Day. No. 479 issued in sheets of 5 and one label.

Capt. Cook, by Nathaniel Dance and "Resolution" — A86

$1, "Capt. Cook Landing at Owyhee" and Capt. Cook. $2, Cook Islands $200 commemorative coin, 1978, and Cook Monument, Hawaii, 1825.

1978, Jan. 20 Litho. *Perf. 13½*

480	A86 50c gold & multi	.90	.90
481	A86 $1 gold & multi	1.60	1.60
482	A86 $2 gold & multi	3.25	3.25
a.	Souvenir sheet of 3, #480-482	6.00	6.00
	Nos. 480-482 (3)	5.75	5.75

Bicentennial of Capt. Cook's arrival in Hawaii.
Nos. 480-482 issued in sheets of 5 with corner label showing ship off Hawaiian coast.
For overprints see Nos. 499-501a.

Pieta, by Rogier van der Weyden A87

Paintings, National Gallery, London: 35c, Burial of Jesus, by Michelangelo. 75c, Jesus at Emmaus, by Caravaggio.

1978, Mar. 20 Photo. *Perf. 13½x13*

483	A87 15c gold & multi	.20	.20
484	A87 35c gold & multi	.50	.50
485	A87 75c gold & multi	1.10	1.10
a.	Souv. sheet, #483-485 + label	1.75	1.75
	Nos. 483-485 (3)	1.80	1.80

Easter. Nos. 483-485 printed in sheets of 5 and corner label showing National Gallery.
See Nos. B68-B70.

A88

A89

Souvenir Sheets

1978, June 6 Photo. *Perf. 13*

486	Sheet of 4 + 2 labels	1.50	1.50
a.	A88 50c shown	.40	.40
b.	A88 50c Lion of England	.40	.40
c.	A88 50c Imperial State Crown	.40	.40
d.	A88 50c Tangaroa figure	.40	.40
487	Sheet of 4 + label	1.50	1.50
a.	A88 70c like 486a	.40	.40
b.	A88 70c Scepter with Cross	.40	.40
c.	A88 70c St. Edward's Crown	.40	.40
d.	A88 70c Rarotongan staff god	.40	.40
e.	Souv. sheet of 8, #486a-487d + label	3.00	3.00

Coronation of Queen Elizabeth II, 25th anniv.

Nos. 381, 383, 388-389, 393-396 Surcharged with New Value and Three Bars in Silver, Black or Gold

1978, Nov. 10 Photo. *Perf. 13½*

488	A62 5c on 1½c multi (S)	.25	.25
489	A62 7c on ½c multi	.35	.35
490	A62 10c on 6c multi (G)	.50	.50
491	A62 10c on 8c multi (G)	.50	.50
492	A62 15c on ½c multi	.80	.80
493	A62 15c on 25c multi (S)	.80	.80
494	A62 15c on 30c multi	.80	.80
495	A62 15c on 50c multi (S)	.80	.80
496	A62 15c on 60c multi (G)	.80	.80
497	A62 17c on ½c multi	.95	.95
498	A62 17c on 50c multi (S)	.95	.95
	Nos. 488-498 (11)	7.50	7.50

See Nos. 526-528.

Nos. 480-482a Overprinted in Black on Silver Panel: "1728--250th ANNIVERSARY OF COOK'S BIRTH--1978"

1978, Nov. 13 Litho. *Perf. 13½*

499	A86 50c gold & multi	1.00	1.00
500	A86 $1 gold & multi	2.00	2.00
501	A86 $2 gold & multi	4.00	4.00
a.	Souvenir sheet of 3, #499-501	18.00	18.00
	Nos. 499-501 (3)	7.00	7.00

250th anniv. of Capt. Cook's birth. Similar overprint in 4 lines was applied to labels. Label of No. 501a overprinted only with dates 1728, 1978.

Coin Type of 1976

$1, $5 Silver coin, 1978 (Polynesian warbler).

1978, Nov. 15 Photo. *Perf. 13½*

502	A81 $1 multicolored	2.25	2.00

National Wildlife and Conservation Day. Sheets of 24 containing 4 panes of 6.

1978, Dec. 8 Photo. *Perf. 13*

Virgin and Child by: 15c, Rogiervan der Weyden. 17c, Carlo Crivelli. 35c, Murillo.

503	A89 15c multicolored	.45	.45
504	A89 17c multicolored	.60	.60
505	A89 35c multicolored	.95	.95
a.	Souvenir sheet of 3, #503-505	2.10	2.10
	Nos. 503-505 (3)	2.00	2.00

Christmas. See Nos. B71-B73.

A90

A91

Descent from the Cross, by Gaspar de Crayer (Details): 10c, Pieta. 12c, St. John. 15c, Mary Magdalene. 20c, Cherubs.

1979, Apr. 5 Photo. *Perf. 13*

506	A90 10c multicolored	.30	.30
507	A90 12c multicolored	.30	.30
508	A90 15c multicolored	.35	.35
509	A90 20c multicolored	.75	.75
	Nos. 506-509 (4)	1.70	1.70

Easter. See No. B74.

1979, July 23 Photo. *Perf. 14x13½*

20c, Capt. Cook, by John Weber. 30c, Resolution, by Henry Roberts. 35c, Endeavour. 50c, Death of Capt. Cook, by George Carter.

510	A91 20c multicolored	.55	.55
511	A91 30c multicolored	.75	.75
512	A91 35c multicolored	.85	.85
513	A91 50c multicolored	1.10	1.10
a.	Souvenir sheet of 4	3.50	3.50
	Nos. 510-513 (4)	3.25	3.25

Capt. Cook (1728-1779), explorer. No. 513a contains 4 stamps similar to Nos. 510-513 with black frames.

Sir Rowland Hill, Originator of Penny Postage — A92

#514a, Postrider. #514b, Stagecoach. #514c, Automobile. #514d, Streamlined train. #515a, Cap-Horniers, sailing ship. #515b, River steamer. #515c, Liner Deutschland. #515d, Liner United States. #516a, Balloon Neptune. #516b, Junkers F13. #516c, Graf Zeppelin. #516d, Concorde.

1979, Sept. 10 *Perf. 14½*

514	A92 30c Block of 4, #a.-d.	1.40	1.40
515	A92 35c Block of 4, #a.-d.	1.60	1.60
516	A92 50c Block of 4, #a.-d.	2.50	2.50
e.	Souv. sheet of 12, #514-516	6.00	6.00
	Nos. 514-516 (3)	5.50	5.50

Nos. 381, 383, 396 Surcharged in Gold or Silver

1979, Sept. 12 Photo. *Perf. 13½*

526	A62	6c on ½c multi	.20	.20
527	A62	10c on 1½c multi (S)	.30	.30
528	A62	15c on 60c multi	.40	.40
		Nos. 526-528 (3)	.90	.90

Nos. 526-528 have 3 thick bars of equal length over old value.

Girl and Baby, IYC Emblem — A93

IYC Emblem and: 50c, Boy playing tree drum. 65c, Children dancing.

1979, Oct. 10 *Perf. 13*

529	A93	30c multicolored	.40	.40
530	A93	50c multicolored	.70	.70
531	A93	65c multicolored	.90	.90
		Nos. 529-531 (3)	2.00	2.00

See No. B75.

Apollo 11 Emblem A94

Christmas Tree Ornaments A95

50c, Apollo 11 crew, lunar map. 60c, Astronaut walking on moon. 65c, Splashdown.

1979, Nov. 7 *Perf. 14*

532	A94	30c multicolored	.40	.40
533	A94	50c multicolored	.60	.60
534	A94	60c multicolored	.75	.75
535	A94	65c multicolored	.85	.85
a.		Souv. sheet, #532-535, perf. 13	3.50	3.50
		Nos. 532-535 (4)	2.60	2.60

Apollo 11 moon landing, 10th anniv.

Coin Type of 1976

$1, $5 Silver coin, 1979 (Raratonga fruit dove).

Perf. 13½x14½

1979, Nov. 15 Photo.

536	A81	$1 multicolored	2.00	2.00

National Wildlife and Conservation Day.

1979, Dec. 14 *Perf. 14*

Christmas (Flowers and): 10c, Star. 12c, Bells and candle. 15c, Ancestral statue.

537	A95	6c multicolored	.20	.20
538	A95	10c multicolored	.20	.20
539	A95	12c multicolored	.20	.20
540	A95	15c multicolored	.20	.20
		Nos. 537-540,B76-B79 (8)	1.80	1.80

See also Nos. C16-C19, CB1-CB4.

A96

Bible illustrations by Gustave Dore, 1833-1883: #541a, Flagellation. #541b, Jesus Wearing Crown of Thorns. #542a, Jesus Mocked. #542b, Jesus Falls. #543a, The Crucifixion. #543b, Descent from the Cross.

1980, Mar. 31 Photo. *Perf. 13*

541	A96	20c Pair, #a.-b.	.60	.60
542	A96	30c Pair, #a.-b.	.90	.90
543	A96	35c Pair, #a.-b.	1.00	1.00
		Nos. 541-543 (3)	2.50	2.50

Easter. See Nos. 553, B80-B83.

Doves with Olive Branch, Rotary Emblem A97

1980, May 27 Photo. *Perf. 14*

547	A97	30c shown	.45	.45
548	A97	35c Flowers	.50	.50
549	A97	50c Flags, globe	.70	.70
		Nos. 547-549 (3)	1.65	1.65

Rotary Intl., 75th anniv. See No. B87

Easter Type of 1980 and:

New Zealand No. 1 — A98

#550a, Postrider. #550b, Coach. #550c, Automobile. #550d, Train.

New Zealand #2 and: #551a, Sailing ship. #551b, River steamer. #551c, Transatlantic liner (facing left). #551d, Transatlantic liner (facing right).

New Zealand #3 and: #552a, 1870-71 mail balloon. #552b, 1919 plane. #552c, Graf Zeppelin. #552d, Concorde.

1980, Aug. 22 Photo. *Perf. 14*

550	A98	30c Block of 4, #a.-d.	1.50	1.25
551	A98	35c Block of 4, #a.-d.	2.00	1.75
552	A98	50c Block of 4, #a.-d.	3.00	2.50
e.		Souvenir sheet of 12	7.50	6.50
		Nos. 550-552 (3)	6.50	5.50

Souvenir Sheet

Perf. 13

553	A96	Sheet of 6, #541-543	5.00	3.50

ZEAPEX '80, New Zealand Intl. Stamp Exhib., Auckland, Aug. 23-31. #552e contains of #550-552 arranged horizontally (4x3). #553 has black on gold overprint: "ZEAPEX / '80 / Auckland / +10c" in margin.

Queen Mother Elizabeth, 80th Birthday — A99

1980, Sept. 22 Photo. *Perf. 13*

554	A99	50c multicolored	1.50	1.00

Souvenir Sheet

555	A99	$2 multicolored	2.75	2.75

No. 554 issued in sheets of 9 (3x3).

Johannes Kepler, Spacecraft — A100

Designs: Nos. 556a, 559a, Kepler, spacecraft (diff.). No. 559b, Kepler, lunar rover, astronaut on moon. Nos. 557a-558b, Jules Verne, various scenes from From Earth to Moon, vert.

1980, Nov. 7 Photo. *Perf. 13*

556	A100	12c Pair, #a-b	.75	.75
557	A100	20c Pair, #a-b	.75	.75
558	A100	30c Pair, #a-b	2.00	2.00
a.		Souvenir sheet, #557-558	3.50	3.50
559	A100	50c Pair, #a-b	3.50	3.50
a.		Souv. sheet, #556, 559	4.50	4.50
		Nos. 556-559 (4)	7.00	7.00

Death anniversaries of Johannes Kepler, German astronomer and Jules Verne, French science fiction writer.

Burning Bush Coral — A101

Daisy Coral — A102

#564a, 570a, 576a, Siphonogorgia. #564b, 570b, 576b, Pavona practorta. #564c, 570c, 576c, Stylaster echinatus. #564d, 570d, 576d, Stylaster echinatus. #565a, 571a, 577a, Millepora alcicornis. #565b, 571b, 577b, Junceella gemmaea. #565c, 571c, 577c, Fungia fungites. #565d, 571d, 577d, Heliofungia actiniformis. #566a, 572a, 578a, Distichopora violacea. #566b, 572b, 578b, Stylaster. #566c, 572c, 578c, Gonipora. #566d, 572d, 578d, Caulastraea echinulata. #567a, 573a, 579a, Ptilosarcus gurneyi. #567b, 573b, 579b, Stylophora pistillata. #567c, 573c, 579c, Melithaea squamata. #567d, 573d, 579d, Porites andrewsi. #568a, 574a, 580a, Lobophyllia bemprichii. #568b, 574b, 580b, Palauastrea ramosa. #568c, 574c, 580c, Bellonella indica. #568d, 574d, 580d, Pectinia alcicornis. #569a, 575a, 581a, Sarcophyton digitatum. #569b, 575b, 581b, Melithaea albitincta. #569c, 575c, 581c, Plerogyra sinuosa. #569d, 575d, 581d, Dendrophyllia gracilis.

1980-82 *Perf. 13½x13*

Strips of 4

564	A101	1c	#a.-d.	.25	.25
565	A101	3c	#a.-d.	.30	.30
566	A101	4c	#a.-d.	.35	.35
567	A101	5c	#a.-d.	.45	.45
568	A101	6c	#a.-d.	.60	.60
569	A101	8c	#a.-d.	.70	.70
570	A101	10c	#a.-d.	.90	.90
571	A101	12c	#a.-d.	1.10	1.10
572	A101	15c	#a.-d.	1.40	1.40
573	A101	20c	#a.-d.	1.60	1.60
574	A101	25c	#a.-d.	2.25	2.25
575	A101	30c	#a.-d.	2.50	2.50
576	A101	35c	#a.-d.	3.00	3.00
577	A101	50c	#a.-d.	4.00	4.00
578	A101	60c	#a.-d.	5.25	5.25
579	A101	70c	#a.-d.	5.75	5.75
580	A101	80c	#a.-d.	6.25	6.25
581	A101	$1	#a.-d.	7.00	7.00

Perf. 14x13½

582	A102	$2	like #566c	5.50	5.50
583	A102	$3	like #565d	7.75	7.75
584	A102	$4	like #567b	10.00	10.00
585	A102	$6	like #564c	15.00	15.00
586	A102	$10	like #569b	22.50	22.50
			Nos. 564-586 (23)	104.40	104.40

Issued: 1-8c, 11/21/80; 10-30c, 12/19/80; 35-60c, 3/16/81; 70c, 80c, 4/13/81; $1, 5/20/81; $2, $3, 11/27/81; $4, $6, 1/11/82; $10, 3/5/82.

For surcharges see Nos. 710-714, 716, 738, 741, 811-815, 953-954, 956-957, 959, 961-962, 964, 978-979, 984-986, B109-B111, O50-O53. For overprints see Nos. 992, 1049.

Annunciation, 13th Century Prayerbook Illustration — A102a

1980, Dec. 1 Photo. *Perf. 14*

652	A102a	15c shown	.20	.20
653	A102a	30c Visitation	.40	.40
654	A102a	40c Nativity	.50	.50
655	A102a	50c Epiphany	.70	.70
a.		Souvenir sheet of 4, #652-655	2.00	2.00
		Nos. 652-655 (4)	1.80	1.80

Christmas. See Nos. B88-B91.

Crucifixion, 12th Cent. Prayerbook Illustration — A103

1981, Apr. 10 *Perf. 14*

656	A103	15c shown	.20	.20
657	A103	25c Placing in Tomb	.40	.40
658	A103	40c Marys at the Tomb	.60	.60
		Nos. 656-658 (3)	1.20	1.20

Easter. See Nos. B92-B95.

Prince Charles and Lady Diana — A104

1981, July 29 Photo. *Perf. 14*

659	A104	$1 Charles	1.75	1.75
660	A104	$2 shown	3.50	3.50
a.		Souv. sheet of 2, #659-660	5.25	5.25

Royal Wedding. Issued in sheets of 4.

For overprints and surcharges see Nos. 679-680, 715, 835, 980-981, B97-B98.

Soccer Players — A105

Designs: Various soccer players.

1981, Oct 20 Photo. *Perf. 14*

661	A105	20c Pair, #a.-b.	1.00	1.00
662	A105	30c Pair, #a.-b.	1.75	1.75
663	A105	35c Pair, #a.-b.	2.25	2.25
664	A105	50c Pair, #a.-b.	3.00	3.00
		Nos. 661-664 (4)	8.00	8.00

ESPANA '82 World Cup Soccer Championships. See No. B96.

Virgin and Child, by Rubens — A107

Christmas: Rubens Paintings.

1981, Dec. 14 Photo. ***Perf. 14x13½***

669 A107 8c shown .50 .50
670 A107 15c Coronation of St. Catherine .50 .50
671 A107 40c Adoration of the Shepherds 1.50 1.50
672 A107 50c Adoration of the Kings 1.75 1.75
Nos. 669-672 (4) 4.25 4.25

Souvenir Sheets

1982, Jan. 18

673 A107 75c +5c like #669 1.10 1.10
674 A107 75c +5c like #670 1.10 1.10
675 A107 75c +5c like #671 1.10 1.10
676 A107 75c +5c like #672 1.10 1.10

Surtax was for school children. See No. B99.

21st Birthday of Princess Diana A108

#677a, 21st Birthday. #677b, 1 July 1982. #678a, Wedding portrait. #678b, 1 July 1982. #678d, $1.25, #678e, $2.50, both inscribed "21st Birthday / 1 July 1982."

1982, June 21 Photo. ***Perf. 14***

677 A108 $1.25 Pair, #a.-b. 4.50 4.50
678 A108 $2.50 Pair, #a.-b. 9.50 9.50
c. Souv. sheet of 2, #d.-e. 9.50 9.50

Issued in sheets of 4.

See Nos. 681-682. For surcharges and overprints see Nos. 739-740, 833-834, 982.

Nos. 659-660a Overprinted: "ROYAL BIRTH 21 JUNE 1982" (a) or "PRINCE WILLIAM OF WALES" (b)

#680d, $1; #680e, $2, both inscribed "21 JUNE 1982 ROYAL BIRTH."

1982, July 12

679 A104 $1 Pair, #a.-b. 3.00 3.00
680 A104 $2 Pair, #a.-b. 5.50 5.50
c. Souv. sheet of 2, #d.-e. 6.00 6.00

Issued in sheets of 4.

For surcharges see Nos. 987-988.

Design A108 Inscribed: "Royal Birth" (a) or "21 June 1982" (b)

#682d, $1.25; #682e, $2.50, both inscribed "Royal Birth / June 1982."

1982, Aug. 3

681 A108 $1.25 Pair, #a.-b. 3.75 3.75
682 A108 $2.50 Pair, #a.-b. 7.25 7.25
c. Souv. sheet of 2, #d.-e. 7.50 7.50

Issued in sheets of 4.

Serenade, by Norman Rockwell (1894-1978) A109

1982, Sept. 10 Photo. ***Perf. 14***

683 A109 5c shown .20 .20
684 A109 10c The Hikers .20 .20
685 A109 20c The Doctor and the Doll .30 .30
686 A109 30c Home From Camp .45 .45
Nos. 683-686 (4) 1.15 1.15

Christmas A110

Princess Diana Holding Prince William. Various Details from Virgin with Garlands, by Rubens.

1982, Nov. 30 Photo. ***Perf. 14***

687 A110 35c multicolored 1.50 1.10
688 A110 48c multicolored 2.00 1.50
689 A110 60c multicolored 2.25 1.75
690 A110 $1.70 multicolored 6.75 6.75
Nos. 687-690 (4) 12.50 11.10

Souvenir Sheets

Perf. 13½

691 Sheet of 4 8.50 8.50
a. A110 60c like 35c 2.00 2.00
b. A110 60c like 48c 2.00 2.00
c. A110 60c like #689 2.00 2.00
d. A110 60c like $1.70 2.00 2.00
692 A110 75c + 5c like 35c 3.00 3.00
693 A110 75c + 5c like 48c 3.00 3.00
694 A110 75c + 5c like 60c 3.00 3.00
695 A110 75c + 5c like $1.70 3.00 3.00

No. 691 contains 4 stamps (27x32mm., showing only painting details) plus 2 labels showing Diana and William. Nos. 692-695 show Diana and William (27x39mm), multicolored margins show painting details. Surtax was for child welfare.

Commonwealth Day — A111

#696a, Tangaroa statue. #696b, Rarotonga oranges. #696c, Rarotonga Airport. #696d, Prime Minister Thomas Davis.

1983, Mar. 14 Photo. ***Perf. 14***

696 A111 60c Block of 4, #a.-d. 3.00 3.00

For overprints see No. O46.

Scouting Year — A112

1983, Apr. 5 Photo. ***Perf. 13x13½***

700 A112 12c Pair, #a.-b., shown .75 .75
701 A112 36c Pair, #a.-b., Camping 2.25 2.25
702 A112 48c Pair, #a.-b., Rope swing 2.75 2.75
703 A112 60c Pair, #a.-b., Tree planting 3.50 3.50
Nos. 700-703 (4) 9.25 9.25

Souvenir Sheet of 8

704 #a.-d. 8.00 8.00

#704 contains 2 each of #700-703 with 2c surtax.

Nos. 700-704 Overprinted: "XV WORLD JAMBOREE ALBERTA CANADA 1983"

1983, July 4 Photo. ***Perf. 13x13½***

705 A112 12c Pair, #a.-b. .50 .50
706 A112 36c Pair, #a.-b. 2.25 2.25
707 A112 48c Pair, #a.-b. 2.75 2.75
708 A112 60c Pair, #a.-b. 3.50 3.50
Nos. 705-708 (4) 9.00 9.00

Souvenir Sheet of 8

709 A112 #a.-d. 8.00 8.00

Nos. 569, 572, 574-575, 579, 587, 660 Surcharged in Black or Gold

Perf. 13½x13, 14x13½, 14

1983, Aug. 12 Photo.

Blocks of 4, #a.-d. (#710-714)

710 A101 18c on 8c #569 3.50 3.50
711 A101 36c on 15c #572 5.75 5.75
712 A101 36c on 30c #575 5.75 5.75
713 A101 48c on 25c #574 9.25 9.25
714 A101 72c on 70c #579 14.00 14.00
715 A104 96c on $2 #660 (G) 4.50 4.50
716 A102 $5.60 on $6 #587 (G) 29.00 29.00
Nos. 710-716 (7) 71.75 71.75

A114

A115

1983, Sept. 9 ***Perf. 14***

732 Pair .85 .85
a. A114 6c Gt. Britain .40 .40
b. A115 6c Cook Islds. Group Federal flag .40 .40
733 Pair 1.10 1.10
a. A114 12c Raratonga ensign .55 .55
b. A115 12c New Zealand .55 .55
734 Pair 1.25 1.25
a. A114 15c Cook Islds, 1973-79 .65 .65
b. A115 15c Cook Islds, 1983 .65 .65
c. Souvenir sheet of 6, #732-734 2.25 2.25
735 Pair 2.00 2.00
a. A114 20c like #732a .95 .95
b. A115 20c like #732b .95 .95
736 Pair 2.50 2.50
a. A114 30c like #733a 1.25 1.25
b. A115 30c like #733b 1.25 1.25
737 Pair 3.00 3.00
a. A114 35c like #734a 1.50 1.50
b. A115 35c like #734b 1.50 1.50
c. Souvenir sheet of 6, #735-737 4.75 4.75
Nos. 732-737 (6) 10.70 10.70

Nos. 732-737 have different background landscapes; Nos. 735-737 airmail with silver background. Nos. 734c, 737c perf. 13½.

Nos. 576, 586, 678 Surcharged in Black or Gold

Perf. 13½x13, 14x13½, 14

1983, Aug. 30 Photo.

Block of 4, #a.-d.

738 A101 36c on 35c #576 5.75 5.75

Pair, #a.-b. (#739)

739 A108 96c on $2.50 #678 (G) 9.25 9.25
740 A102 $5.60 on $10 #586 (G) 22.50 22.50
Nos. 738-740 (3) 37.50 37.50

Satellite Earth Station — A116

Designs: Various satellites in orbit.

1983, Oct. 10 Litho. ***Perf. 13½***

744 A116 36c multicolored 1.00 1.00
745 A116 48c multicolored 1.50 1.50
746 A116 60c multicolored 1.75 1.75
747 A116 96c multicolored 2.75 2.75
Nos. 744-747 (4) 7.00 7.00

Souvenir Sheet

748 A116 $2 multicolored 5.00 5.00

World Communications Year.

Christmas A117

Manned Flight Bicent. — A118

Raphael Paintings: 12c, La Belle Jardiniere. 18c, Madonna and Child with Five Saints. 36c, Madonna and Child with Saint John. 48c, Madonna of the Fish. 60c, Madonna of the Baldacchino.

1983 Photo. ***Perf. 14***

749 A117 12c multicolored 1.10 1.10
750 A117 18c multicolored 1.10 1.10
751 A117 36c multicolored 2.00 2.00
752 A117 48c multicolored 2.50 2.50
753 A117 60c multicolored 3.75 3.75
Nos. 749-753 (5) 10.45 10.45

Souvenir Sheets

Perf. 13½

754 Sheet of 5 4.00 4.00
a. A117 12c + 3c like #749 .30 .30
b. A117 18c + 3c like #750 .35 .35
c. A117 36c + 3c like #751 .70 .70
d. A117 48c + 3c like #752 .90 .90
e. A117 60c + 3c like #753 1.10 1.10
755 A117 85c + 5c like #749 1.60 1.60
756 A117 85c + 5c like #750 1.60 1.60
757 A117 85c + 5c like #751 1.60 1.60
758 A117 85c + 5c like #752 1.60 1.60
759 A117 85c + 5c like #753 1.60 1.60

Nos. 749-753 issued in sheets of 5 + label. Surtax was for children's charities.

Issued: #749-754, Nov. 14; others, Dec. 9.

1984, Jan. 16 Photo. ***Perf. 13***

Various balloons.

760 A118 36c 1st manned flight, 1783 .85 .85
761 A118 48c Ascent of Adorne, Strasbourg, 1784 1.00 1.00
762 A118 60c 1785 1.10 1.10
763 A118 72c Man on horse, 1785 1.60 1.60
764 A118 96c Godard's aerial acrobatics, 1850 1.75 1.75
Nos. 760-764 (5) 6.30 6.30

Souvenir Sheets

765 A118 $2.50 Blanchard & Jefferies, 1785 4.25 4.25
766 Sheet of 5 7.75 7.75
a. A118 36c + 5c like 36c .90 .90
b. A118 48c + 5c like 48c 1.10 1.10
c. A118 60c + 5c like 60c 1.50 1.50
d. A118 72c + 5c like 72c 1.75 1.75
e. A118 96c + 5c like 96c 2.25 2.25

#765 contains 1 stamp 30x48mm, perf. 13½.

Save the Whales Campaign A119

1984, Feb. 10 Photo. ***Perf. 13***

767 A119 10c Cuvier's beaked whale .40 .40
768 A119 18c Risso's dolphin .60 .60
769 A119 20c True's beaked whale .70 .70
770 A119 24c Long-finned pilot whale .90 .90
771 A119 30c Narwhal 1.10 1.10
772 A119 36c Beluga whale 1.25 1.25
773 A119 42c Common dolphin 1.60 1.60

774 A119 48c Commerson's dolphin 1.75 1.75
775 A119 60c Bottle-nosed dolphin 2.25 2.25
776 A119 72c Sowerby's whale 2.75 2.75
777 A119 96c Common porpoise 3.25 3.25
778 A119 $2 Boutu 7.25 7.25
Nos. 767-778 (12) 23.80 23.80

1984 Summer Olympics A120

Posters of Various Summer Olympics. 72c, 96c, $1.20 airmail.

1984, Mar. 8 Photo. *Perf. 13½*

779 A120 18c Athens, 1896 .35 .35
780 A120 24c Paris, 1900 .40 .40
781 A120 36c St. Louis, 1904 .65 .65
782 A120 48c London, 1948 .85 .85
783 A120 60c Tokyo, 1964 1.00 1.00
784 A120 72c Berlin, 1936 1.25 1.25
785 A120 96c Rome, 1960 1.75 1.75
786 A120 $1.20 Los Angeles, 1932 2.25 2.25
Nos. 779-786 (8) 8.50 8.50

For overprints see Nos. 826-828.

Nos. 582-586 Surcharged and:

Coral — A121

1c, Siphonogorgia. 2c, Millepora alcicornis. 3c, Distichopora violacea. 5c, Ptilosarcus gurneyi. 10c, Lobophyllia bemprichii. 12c, Sarcophyton digitatum. 14c, Pavona praetorta. 18c, Junceela gemmacea. 20c, Stylaster. 24c, Stylophora pistillata. 30c, Palauastrea ramosa. 36c, Melithaea albitincta. 40c, Stylaster echinatus. 42c, Fungia fungites. 48c, Gonipora. 50c, Melithaea squamata. 52c, Bellonella indica. 55c, Plerogyra sinuosa. 60c, Tubastraea. 70c, Heliofungia actinformis. 85c, Caulastraea echinulata. 96c, Porites andrewsi. $1.10, Pectinia alcicornis. $1.20, Dendrophyllia gracilis.

1984 *Perf. 13½x13*

787 A121 1c multi .20 .20
788 A121 2c multi .20 .20
789 A121 3c multi .20 .20
790 A121 5c multi .20 .20
791 A121 10c multi .20 .20
792 A121 12c multi .20 .20
793 A121 14c multi .30 .30
794 A121 18c multi .40 .40
795 A121 20c multi .40 .40
796 A121 24c multi .50 .50
797 A121 30c multi .60 .60
798 A121 36c multi .75 .75
799 A121 40c multi .80 .80
800 A121 42c multi .90 .90
801 A121 48c multi .95 .95
802 A121 50c multi 1.00 1.00
803 A121 52c multi 1.00 1.00
804 A121 55c multi 1.40 1.40
805 A121 60c multi 1.60 1.60
806 A121 70c multi 1.75 1.75
807 A121 85c multi 2.00 2.00
808 A121 96c multi 2.25 2.25
809 A121 $1.10 multi 3.00 3.00
810 A121 $1.20 multi 3.25 3.25

Perf. 14x13½

Size: 59½x38½mm

811 A102 $3.60 on $2 #582 8.00 8.00
812 A102 $4.20 on $3 #583 8.75 8.75
813 A102 $5 on $4 #584 10.50 10.50
814 A102 $7.20 on $6 #585 15.00 15.00
815 A102 $9.60 on $10 #586 17.50 17.50
Nos. 787-815 (29) 83.80 83.80

Issued: #787-801, 3/23; #802-810, 5/15; #811-813, 6/28; #814, 7/20; #815, 8/10.

For surcharges & overprints see #948-952, 955, 958, 960, 963, 965-967, B105-B108, O32-O45.

Nos. 784-786 Overprinted With Winners

1984, Aug. 24 Photo. *Perf. 13½*

826 A120 72c Team Dressage, Germany 1.00 1.00
827 A120 96c Daley Thompson, U.K. 1.50 1.50
828 A120 $1.20 Carl Lewis, USA 1.90 1.90
Nos. 826-828 (3) 4.40 4.40

1984 Summer Olympics. Nos. 826-828 airmail.

AUSIPEX '84 — A123

1984, Sept. 20

829 A123 36c Captain Cook's cottage 1.60 1.60
830 A123 48c The Endeavour 2.10 2.10
831 A123 60c Cook's landing 2.50 2.50
832 A123 $2 Portrait, by John Webber 8.50 8.50
a. Souv. sheet, #829-832, 90c ea 12.50 12.50
b. Sheet of 4, STAMPEX '86 emblem 10.50 10.50
Nos. 829-832 (4) 14.70 14.70

No. 832b issued Aug. 4, 1986, for STAMPEX '86, Adelaide, Aug. 4-10; margin ovptd. with exhibition emblem, stamp picturing James Cook ovptd. with gold circle and black "Stampex 86 / Adelaide."

Nos. 677-678 Ovptd.: "Commemorating -/15 Sept. 1984" or "Birth H.R.H./Prince Henry" and Surcharged in Gold.
No. 659 Ovptd. "Royal Birth/Prince Henry/15 Sept. 1984" and Surcharged in Silver.

1984, Oct. 15 Photo. *Perf. 14*

833 A108 $1.25 Pair, #a.-b. 3.50 3.50
834 A108 $2.50 Pair, #a.-b. 7.75 7.75
835 A104 $3 on $1 No. 659 4.75 4.75
Nos. 833-835 (3) 16.00 16.00

Nos. 833-835 printed in sheets of 4 stamps.

A124

A125

Christmas (Paintings): 36c, Virgin on Throne with Child, by Giovanni Bellini (c. 1430-1516). 48c, Virgin and Child, 15th century, artistunknown. 60c, Virgin and Child with Saints, by Alvise Vivarini (c. 1446-1505). 96c, Virgin and Child with Angels, by Hans Memling (c. 1435-1494). $1.20, Adoration of the Magi, by Giovanni Tiepolo (1696-1770).

1984

838 A124 36c multicolored .90 .90
839 A124 48c multicolored 1.25 1.25
840 A124 60c multicolored 1.60 1.60
841 A124 96c multicolored 2.50 2.50
842 A124 $1.20 multicolored 3.25 3.25
Nos. 838-842 (5) 9.50 9.50

Souvenir Sheets

Perf. 13½

843 Sheet of 5 5.75 5.75
a. A124 36c +5c like #838 .70 .70
b. A124 48c +5c like #839 .85 .85
c. A124 60c +5c like #840 1.00 1.00
d. A124 96c +5c like #841 1.50 1.50
e. A124 $1.20 +5c like #842 1.75 1.75
844 A124 95c + 5c like #838 1.75 1.75
845 A124 95c + 5c like #839 1.75 1.75
846 A124 95c + 5c like #840 1.75 1.75
847 A124 95c + 5c like #841 1.75 1.75
848 A124 95c + 5c like #842 1.75 1.75

Surtax of No. 843 for children's organizations, of Nos. 844-848 for youth education.
Issued: #838-843, 11/21; #844-848, 12/10.

1985, Apr. 23 *Perf. 13x13½*

Illustrations of North American bird species by artist, naturalist John J. Audubon.

849 A125 30c Downy woodpecker 1.50 1.50
850 A125 55c Black-throated blue warbler 2.75 2.75
851 A125 65c Yellow-throated warbler 3.00 3.00
852 A125 75c Chestnut-sided warbler 3.75 3.75
853 A125 95c Dickcissel 4.75 4.75
854 A125 $1.15 White-crowned sparrow 4.75 4.75
Nos. 849-854 (6) 20.50 20.50

Souvenir Sheets

855 A125 $1.30 Red-cockaded woodpecker 3.00 3.00
856 A125 $2.80 Seaside sparrow 5.25 5.25
857 A125 $5.30 Zenaida dove 10.75 10.75

Audubon birth bicentenary.

Locomotives — A126

1985, May 14 Litho. *Perf. 14x13½*

858 A126 20c Kingston Flyer, New Zealand .20 .20
859 A126 55c Class 640, Italy .50 .50
860 A126 65c Gotthard, Switzerland .60 .60
861 A126 75c Union Pacific 6900, US .70 .70
862 A126 95c Super Continental, Canada .90 .90
863 A126 $1.15 TGV, France 1.00 1.00
864 A126 $2.20 Flying Scotsman, U.K. 2.00 2.00
865 A126 $3.40 Orient Express, Europe 3.00 3.00
Nos. 858-865 (8) 8.90 8.90

Intl. Youth Year — A127

Paintings: 55c, Helena Fourment, by Rubens. 65c, Vigee-Lebrun and Daughter, by Elizabeth Vigee-Lebrun (1755-1842). 75c, On the Terrace, by Renoir. $1.30, Young Mother Sewing, by Mary Cassatt (1845-1926).

1985, June 6 Photo. *Perf. 13x13½*

866 A127 55c multicolored 3.50 3.50
867 A127 65c multicolored 4.00 4.00
868 A127 75c multicolored 4.50 4.50
869 A127 $1.30 multicolored 7.50 7.50
Nos. 866-869 (4) 19.50 19.50

Souvenir Sheet

870 Sheet of 4 11.00 11.00
a. A127 55c + 10c like #866 1.75 1.75
b. A127 65c + 10c like #867 2.10 2.10
c. A127 75c + 10c like #868 2.40 2.40
d. A127 $1.30 + 10c like #869 3.75 3.75

Surtax for youth organizations.

Queen Mother, 85th Birthday A128

Portraits: 65c, Lady Elizabeth, 1908, by Mable Hankey. 75c, Duchess of York, 1923, by Savely Sorine. $1.15, Duchess of York, 1925, by Philip De Laslo. $2.80, $5.30, Queen Elizabeth, 1938, by Sir Gerald Kelly.

1985, June 28

871 A128 65c multi .80 .80
872 A128 75c multi .95 .95
873 A128 $1.15 multi 1.50 1.50
874 A128 $2.80 multi 3.25 3.25
874A Sheet of 4 ('86) 6.50 6.50
b.-e. A128 55c, like #871-874 1.50 1.50
Nos. 871-874A (5) 13.00 13.00

Souvenir Sheet

875 A128 $5.30 multi 12.50 12.50

Nos. 871-874 printed in sheets of four.
#874A issued 8/4/86, for 86th birthday.
For surcharges see Nos. B114, B116, B122, B134, B140.

A129

A130

Portraits of prime ministers.

1985, July 29

876 A129 30c Albert Henry, 1965-78 1.25 1.25
877 A129 50c Sir Thomas Davis, 1978-83 2.50 2.50
878 A129 65c Geoffrey Henry, 1983 3.00 3.00
Nos. 876-878 (3) 6.75 6.75

Souvenir Sheet

879 Sheet of 3 11.50 11.50
a. A129 55c like #876 3.50 3.50
b. A129 55c like #877 3.50 3.50
c. A129 55c like #878 3.50 3.50

Self-government, 20th anniv.

1985, July 29 *Perf. 14*

880 A130 55c Golf 5.25 5.25
881 A130 65c Rugby 6.00 6.00
882 A130 75c Tennis 6.75 6.75
Nos. 880-882 (3) 18.00 18.00

Souvenir Sheet

883 Sheet of 3 18.00 18.00
a. A130 55c + 10c like #880 5.50 5.50
b. A130 65c + 10c like #881 5.50 5.50
c. A130 75c + 10c like #882 5.50 5.50

South Pacific Mini Games, Rarotonga, July 31-Aug. 10. Surtax for the benefit of the Mini Games.

A131

A132

Seahorse & conf. emblems: 55c, South Pacific Bureau for Economic Cooperation. 65c, No. 887b, South Pacific Forum. 75c, No. 887c, Pacific Islands Conf.

1985, July 29 ***Perf. 14***

884 A131 55c blk, scar & gold 1.75 1.75
885 A131 65c blk, vio & gold 2.00 2.00
886 A131 75c blk, brt grn & gold 2.25 2.25
Nos. 884-886 (3) 6.00 6.00

Souvenir Sheet

887 50c Sheet of 3, #a.-c. 3.50 3.50

Pacific islands conf., Rarotonga, 7/30-8/10.

1985

Virgin and Child paintings by Botticelli.

888 A132 55c Madonna of the Magnificent 2.25 2.25
889 A132 65c Madonna with Pomegranate 2.75 2.75
890 A132 75c Madonna with Child & Six Angels 3.50 3.50
891 A132 95c Madonna & Child with St. John 4.50 4.50
Nos. 888-891 (4) 13.00 13.00

Souvenir Sheets

Perf. 13½

892 A132 $2.75 Sheet of 4 8.00 8.00
a. A132 50c like #888 1.75 1.75
b. A132 50c like #888 1.75 1.75
c. A132 50c like #890 1.75 1.75
d. A132 50c like #891 1.75 1.75

Imperf

893 A132 $1.20 like #888 2.50 2.50
894 A132 $1.45 like #889 2.75 2.75
895 A132 $2.20 like #890 4.50 4.50
896 A132 $2.75 like #891 5.25 5.25

Christmas. Issue dates: Nos. 888-892, Nov. 18; Nos. 893-896, Dec. 9.

Halley's Comet — A133

Elizabeth II, 60th Birthday — A134

Paintings: 55c, No. 902a, The Eve of the Deluge, by John Martin (1789-1854). 65c, No. 902b, Lot and His Daughters, by Lucas van Leyden (1494-1533). 75c, No. 902c, Auspicious Comet, 1587, anonymous. $1.25, No. 902d, Events Following Charles I, by Herman Saftleven (1609-1658). $2, No. 902e, Ossian Receiving Napoleonic Officers, by Anne Louis Girodet-Trioson (1764-1824). $4, Halley's Comet over the Thames, 1759, by Samuel Scott (1702-1772).

1986, Mar. 13 **Photo.** ***Perf. 14***

897 A133 55c multicolored 1.40 1.40
898 A133 65c multicolored 1.75 1.75
899 A133 75c multicolored 2.10 2.10
900 A133 $1.25 multicolored 4.00 4.00
901 A133 $2 multicolored 5.75 5.75
Nos. 897-901 (5) 15.00 15.00

Souvenir Sheets

Perf. 13½

902 Sheet of 5 + label 8.00 8.00
a.-e. A133 70c, each single 1.50 1.50
903 A133 $4 multicolored 9.50 9.50

For surcharges see Nos. B113, B115, B117, B123, B129.

1986, Apr. 21 ***Perf. 13x13½***

Various portraits.

904 A134 95c multi 1.75 1.75
905 A134 $1.25 multi 2.10 2.10
906 A134 $1.50 multi 2.40 2.40
Nos. 904-906 (3) 6.25 6.25

Souvenir Sheets

907 A134 $1.10 like #904 2.75 2.75
908 A134 $1.95 like #905 5.00 5.00
909 A134 $2.45 like #906 7.25 7.25

For surcharges see Nos. 972-974, B118, B124, B127, B136-B137, B139.

AMERIPEX '86 — A135

Designs: $1, US No. 1, The Resolution, Rarotonga. $1.50, Downtown Chicago. $2, No. 398, Benjamin Franklin, The Resolution.

1986, May 21 **Photo.** ***Perf. 14***

910 A135 $1 multi 4.50 4.50
911 A135 $1.50 multi 6.50 6.50
912 A135 $2 multi 8.50 8.50
Nos. 910-912 (3) 19.50 19.50

For surcharges see Nos. B119, B128, B130.

Statue of Liberty, Cent. — A136

Wedding of Prince Andrew and Sarah Ferguson — A137

1986, July 4

913 A136 $1 Head 1.25 1.25
914 A136 $1.25 Torch 1.50 1.50
915 A136 $2.75 Liberty Is. 3.50 3.50
Nos. 913-915 (3) 6.25 6.25

For surcharges see Nos. B120, B125, B132.

1986, July 23

916 A137 $1 Sarah Ferguson 1.00 1.00
917 A137 $2 Prince Andrew 2.00 2.00

Size: 60x33½mm

Perf. 13½x13

918 A137 $3 Couple 3.00 3.00
Nos. 916-918 (3) 6.00 6.00

Nos. 916-918 each printed in sheets of 4.

For surch. see #975-977, B121, B131, B135.

Christmas A138

Paintings by Rubens: 55c, No. 922a, The Holy Family. $1.30, $6.40, No. 922b, Virgin with Garland. $2.75, No. 922c, Adoration of Magi.

1986, Nov. 17 **Litho.** ***Perf. 13½***

919 A138 55c multi 1.75 1.75
920 A138 $1.30 multi 4.00 4.00
921 A138 $2.75 multi 8.25 8.25
Nos. 919-921 (3) 14.00 14.00

Souvenir Sheets

922 Sheet of 3 18.00 18.00
a.-c. A138 $2.40, any single 5.75 5.75
923 A138 $6.40 multi 19.00 19.00

No. 922 contains 3 stamps 38½x49mm.
For surcharges see Nos. B100-B104, B112, B126, B133, B138, B141.

Stamps of 1980-84 Surcharged in Black

1987, Feb. **Litho.** ***Perfs. as before***

Blocks of 4, #a.-d.

(#953-954, 956-957, 959, 961-962, 964)

948 A121 5c on 1c #787 .20 .20
949 A121 5c on 2c #788 .20 .20
950 A121 5c on 3c #789 .20 .20
951 A121 5c on 12c #792 .20 .20
952 A121 5c on 14c #793 .20 .20
953 A101 10c on 15c #572 .55 .55
954 A101 10c on 25c #574 .55 .55
955 A121 18c on 24c #796 .20 .20
956 A101 18c on 12c #571 1.10 1.10
957 A101 18c on 20c #573 1.10 1.10
958 A121 55c on 52c #803 .90 .90
959 A101 55c on 35c #576 3.25 3.25
960 A121 65c on 42c #800 1.00 1.00
961 A101 65c on 50c #577 4.50 4.50
962 A101 65c on 60c #578 4.50 4.50
963 A121 75c on 48c #801 1.25 1.25
964 A101 75c on 70c #579 4.50 4.50
965 A121 95c on 96c #808 1.50 1.50
966 A121 95c on $1.10 #809 1.50 1.50
967 A121 95c on $1.20 #810 1.50 1.50

Stamps of 1981-86 Surcharged in Black (A102), Black and Gold (#969-970, A137) or Gold (#971, A134, A104, A108)

968 A123 $1.30 on 36c #829 1.90 1.90
969 A123 $1.30 on 48c #830 1.90 1.90
970 A123 $1.30 on 60c #831 1.90 1.90
971 A123 $1.30 on $2 #832 1.90 1.90
972 A134 $2.80 on 95c #904 4.25 4.25
973 A134 $2.80 on $1.25 #905 4.25 4.25
974 A134 $2.80 on $1.50 #906 4.25 4.25
975 A137 $2.80 on $1 #916 4.25 4.25
976 A137 $2.80 on $2 #917 4.25 4.25
977 A137 $2.80 on $3 #918 4.25 4.25
978 A102 $6.40 on $4 #584 9.25 9.25
979 A102 $7.20 on $6 #585 10.50 10.50
980 A104 $9.40 on $1 #659 14.50 14.50
981 A104 $9.40 on $2 #660 14.50 14.50

Pair, #a.-b.

982 A108 $9.40 on $2.50 #678 29.00 29.00
Nos. 948-982 (35) 139.75 139.75

Issued: 5c, #955, 958, 960, 963, 95c, $6.40, $7.20, 2/10; 10c, #956-957, 959, 961-962, 964, 2/11; $12.30, $2.80, $9.40, 2/12.
For surcharge see No. B111.

Stamps of 1980-82 Surcharged in Black (A102) or Gold (A104)

Perfs. as before

1987, June 17 **Photo.**

984 A102 $2.80 on $2 #582 3.25 3.25
985 A102 $5 on $3 #583 5.50 5.50
986 A102 $9.40 on $10 #586 10.00 10.00

Pairs, #a.-b.

987 A104 $9.40 on $1 #679 20.00 20.00
988 A104 $9.40 on $2 #680 20.00 20.00
Nos. 984-988 (5) 58.75 58.75

Souvenir Sheet

989 A104 $9.20 on #680c 19.00 19.00

Nos. 399 and 584 Ovptd. "ROYAL / WEDDING / FORTIETH / ANNIVERSARY" in Black on Gold Bar

1987, Nov. 20 **Photo.** ***Perf. 14x13½***

991 A64 $4 on #399 5.00 5.00
992 A102 $4 on #584 5.00 5.00

Christmas — A139

The Holy Family, religious paintings by Rembrandt in European museums: $1.25, No. 996a, The Louvre, Paris. $1.50, No. 996b, $6, The Holy Family with Angels, The Hermitage, Leningrad. $1.95, No. 996c, The Alte Pinakothek, Munich.

1987, Dec. 7 **Photo.** ***Perf. 13½***

993 A139 $1.25 multi 3.25 3.25
994 A139 $1.50 multi 4.50 4.50
995 A139 $1.95 multi 5.75 5.75
Nos. 993-995 (3) 13.50 13.50

Souvenir Sheets

996 Sheet of 3 12.00 12.00
a.-c. A139 $1.15 any single 3.75 3.75

Perf. 13x13½

997 A139 $6 multi 14.00 14.00

Size of Nos. 996a-996c: 49½x38½mm. No. 997 contains 1 stamp 39½x31½mm.

1988 Summer Olympics, Seoul A140

Designs: a, Cook Islands commemorative silver coin (obverse and reverse) issued on Aug. 20, 1987, for the '88 Summer Games. b, Seoul Olympic Park, torch and emblem. c, Steffi Graf, women's tennis champion, and '88 gold medal.

1988, Apr. 26 **Photo.** ***Perf. 13½x14***

998 Strip of 3 17.00 17.00
a.-c. A140 $1.50 multicolored 5.75 5.75

Souvenir Sheet

Perf. 13½

999 A140 $10 multi 19.00 19.00

Participation of national athletes in the Olympics for the first time, introduction of tennis as an Olympic gold-medal event.
No. 999 contains one stamp 114x47mm combining the designs of Nos. 998a-998c.

Nos. 998-999 Ovptd. for Olympic Winners

a. "MILOSLAV MECIR CZECHOSLOVAKIA GOLD MEDAL WINNER MEN'S TENNIS"
b. "TIM MAYOTTE UNITED STATES GABRIELA SABATINI ARGENTINA SILVER MEDAL WINNERS"
c. "GOLD MEDAL WINNER STEFFI GRAF WEST GERMANY"
d. "GOLD MEDAL WINNER SEOUL OLYMPIC GAMES STEFFI GRAF dash> WEST GERMANY"

1988, Oct. 12 **Photo.** ***Perf. 13½x14***

1000 Strip of 3 15.00 15.00
a.-c. A140 $1.50 multicolored 5.00 5.00

Souvenir Sheet

Perf. 13½

1001	A140(d)	$10 on No. 999	20.00	20.00

Margin of No. 1001 ovptd.: "STEFFI GRAF, WINNER OF AUSTRALIAN OPEN 24 JULY 1988, FRENCH OPEN / 4 JUNE 1988, WIMBLEDON 2 JULY 1988, U.S. OPEN 10 SEPTEMBER 1988. / FIRST GRAND SLAM WINNER IN 18 YEARS. GOLD MEDAL WINNER SEOUL / OLYMPICS 1 OCTOBER 1988."

Christmas A141

Paintings by Albrecht Durer: 70c, Virgin and Child. 85c, Virgin and Child, diff. 95c, Virgin and Child, diff. $1.25, Virgin and Child, diff. $6.40, The Nativity.

1988, Nov. 11 ***Perf. 13½***

1002	A141	70c multi	3.25	3.25
1003	A141	85c multi	3.75	3.75
1004	A141	95c multi	4.25	4.25
1005	A141	$1.25 multi	5.75	5.75
		Nos. 1002-1005 (4)	17.00	17.00

Souvenir Sheet

1006	A141	$6.40 multi	11.00	11.00

No. 1006 contains one stamp 45x60mm.

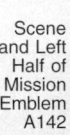

Scene and Left Half of Mission Emblem A142

1st Moon Landing, 20th Anniv. — A144

#1007a, Launch vehicle in space. #1007b, *Eagle* landing on Moon. #1008a, Astronaut descending ladder. #1008, Astronaut on Moon. #1009a, Seismic experiment. #1009b, Solar wind experiment. #1010a, Liftoff from Moon. #1010b, Splashdown and recovery.

The "b" stamps have the right half of the emblem.

1989, July 14 **Photo.** ***Perf. 13***

1007	A142	40c Pair, #a.-b.	3.25	3.25
1008	A142	55c Pair, #a.-b.	5.00	5.00
1009	A142	65c Pair, #a.-b.	6.00	6.00
1010	A142	75c Pair, #a.-b.	6.75	6.75
		Nos. 1007-1010 (4)	21.00	21.00

Souvenir Sheet

1011	A144	$4.20 Armstrong and Aldrin	11.00	11.00

Printed with continuous designs.

World Wildlife Fund A145

Endangered bird species.

1989, Oct. 4 **Photo.** ***Perf. 13½x13***

1016	A145	15c *Pomarea dimidiata*	1.50	1.50
1017	A145	20c *Pomarea dimidiata* (two)	2.25	2.25
1018	A145	65c *Ptilinopus rarotongensis* (two)	6.00	6.00
1019	A145	70c *Ptilinopus rarotongensis*	6.75	6.75
		Nos. 1016-1019 (4)	16.50	16.50

Souvenir Sheets Without WWF Emblem

Perf. 13½

1020	A145	$1 like 15c	3.25	3.25
1021	A145	$1.25 like 20c	3.75	3.75
1022	A145	$1.50 like 65c	4.25	4.25
1023	A145	$1.75 like 70c	4.75	4.75

World Wildlife Fund. #1020-1023 are airmail and contain one 52x34mm stamp; decorative margins continue the designs.

For overprints see Nos. C24-C27.

Christmas — A146

Details of *Adoration of the Magi*, by Rubens: 70c, Witnesses. 85c, Madonna. 95c, Christ child. $1.50, Attendant. $6.40, Entire painting.

1989, Nov. 24 **Photo.** ***Perf. 13½x13***

1024	A146	70c multicolored	2.25	2.25
1025	A146	85c multicolored	2.50	2.50
1026	A146	95c multicolored	3.00	3.00
1027	A146	$1.50 multicolored	4.75	4.75
		Nos. 1024-1027 (4)	12.50	12.50

Souvenir Sheet

Perf. 13½

1028	A146	$6.40 multicolored	19.00	19.00

No. 1028 contains one 45x60mm stamp.

Religious History A147

70c, John Williams, LMS Mission Church. 85c, Bernardine Castanie, Roman Catholic Church. 95c, Osborne J.P. Widstoe, Church of Jesus Christ of Latter Day Saints. $1.60, J.E. Caldwell, Seventh Day Adventist Church.

1990, Feb. 19 **Photo.** ***Perf. 13½x13***

1029	A147	70c multicolored	1.25	1.25
1030	A147	85c multicolored	1.50	1.50
1031	A147	95c multicolored	1.75	1.75
1032	A147	$1.60 multicolored	3.00	3.00
		Nos. 1029-1032 (4)	7.50	7.50

Souvenir Sheet

Perf. 13½

1033		Sheet of 4	8.50	8.50
a.		A147 90c like 70c	1.90	1.90
b.		A147 90c like 85c	1.90	1.90
c.		A147 90c like 95c	1.90	1.90
d.		A147 90c like $1.60	1.90	1.90

No. 1033 contains 4 36x36mm stamps.

Penny Black, 150th Anniv. — A148

Paintings: 85c, No. 1038a, *Woman Writing a Letter*, by Gerard Terborch (1617-1681). $1.15, No. 1038b, *Portrait of George Gisze,* by Hans Holbein the Younger. $1.55, No. 1038c, *Portrait of Mrs. John Douglas*, by Thomas Gainsborough. $1.85, No. 1038d, *Portrait of a Gentleman*, by Albrecht Durer.

1990, May 2 **Photo.** ***Perf. 13½***

1034	A148	85c multicolored	1.75	1.75
1035	A148	$1.15 multicolored	2.50	2.50
1036	A148	$1.55 multicolored	3.25	3.25
1037	A148	$1.85 multicolored	4.00	4.00
		Nos. 1034-1037 (4)	11.50	11.50

Souvenir Sheet

1038		Sheet of 4	15.00	15.00
a.-d.		A148 $1.05 any single	3.50	3.50

The margin of No. 1038 pictures the Stamp World '90 emblem and Great Britain #1-2.

1992 Olympics A149

Designs: a. Summer Games, Barcelona (runners). b. Eternal flame, commemorative coin obverse (Queen Elizabeth II) and reverse (athletes). c. Winter Games, Albertville (skier).

1990, June 15 **Photo.** ***Perf. 14***

1039		Strip of 3	19.00	19.00
a.-c.		A149 $1.85 any single	6.00	6.00

Queen Mother, 90th Birthday A150

1990, July 20 **Photo.** ***Perf. 13½***

1040	A150	$1.85 multicolored	8.00	8.00

Souvenir Sheet

1041	A150	$6.40 multicolored	14.00	14.00

Christmas A151

Paintings: 70c, Adoration of the Magi by Memling. 85c, The Holy Family by Lotto. 95c, Madonna and Child with Saints John and Catherine by Titian. $1.50, The Holy Family by Titian. $6.40, Madonna and Child Enthroned, Surrounded by Saints by Vivarini.

1990, Nov. 29 **Litho.** ***Perf. 14***

1042	A151	70c multicolored	2.00	2.00
1043	A151	85c multicolored	2.75	2.75
1044	A151	95c multicolored	3.00	3.00
1045	A151	$1.50 multicolored	4.75	4.75
		Nos. 1042-1045 (4)	12.50	12.50

Souvenir Sheet

1046	A151	$6.40 multicolored	18.00	18.00

Souvenir Sheet

1992 Olympic Games — A152

Illustration reduced.

1991, Feb. 12 ***Perf. 13½***

1047	A152	$6.40 multicolored	19.00	19.00

Discovery of America 500th Anniv. (in 1992) — A153

1991, Feb. 14 **Photo.** ***Perf. 13½x13***

1048	A153	$1 multicolored	4.25	4.25

No. 586 Ovptd. "65th BIRTHDAY" in Gold

1991, Apr. 22 **Litho.** ***Perf. 14x13½***

1049	A102	$10 multicolored	22.50	22.50

Christmas A154

Paintings: 70c, Adoration of the Child, by Delle Notti (Gerrit van Honthorst). 85c, Birth of the Virgin, by Murillo. $1.15, Adoration of the Shepherds, by Rembrandt. $1.50, Adoration of the Shepherds, by Le Nain. $6.40, Madonna and Child, by Fra Filippo Lippi, vert.

1991, Nov. 12 **Litho.** ***Perf. 14***

1050	A154	70c multicolored	2.00	2.00
1051	A154	85c multicolored	4.00	4.00
1052	A154	$1.15 multicolored	5.25	5.25
1053	A154	$1.50 multicolored	6.75	6.75
		Nos. 1050-1053 (4)	18.00	18.00

Souvenir Sheet

1054	A154	$6.40 multicolored	19.00	19.00

Marine Life — A155

A155a

5c, Red-breasted maori wrasse. 10c, Blue sea star. 15c, Black & gold angelfish. 20c, Spotted pebble crab. 25c, Black-tipped cod. 30c, Spanish dancer. 50c, Royal angelfish. 80c, Squirrel fish. 85c, Red pencil sea urchin. 90c, Red-spot rainbow fish. $1, Black-lined maori wrasse. $2, Longnose butterflyfish. $3, Red-spot rainbow fish. $5, Blue sea star. $7, Royal angelfish. $10, Spotted pebble crab. $15, Red pencil sea urchin.

1992-94 **Litho.** ***Perf. 14½x13½***

1058	A155	5c multi	.40	.40
1059	A155	10c multi	.40	.40
1062	A155	15c multi	.40	.40
1064	A155	20c multi	.50	.50
1065	A155	25c multi	.55	.55

1066	A155	30c	multi	.65	.65
1071	A155	50c	multi	1.10	1.10
1076	A155	80c	multi	1.75	1.75
1077	A155	85c	multi	1.75	1.75
1078	A155	90c	multi	1.75	1.75
1080	A155	$1	multi	2.00	2.00
1081	A155	$2	multi	4.25	4.25
1082	A155a	$3	multi	6.50	6.50
1083	A155a	$5	multi	10.00	10.00
1085	A155a	$7	multi	14.50	14.50
1087	A155a	$10	multi	21.00	21.00
1089	A155a	$15	multi	32.50	32.50
	Nos. 1058-1089 (17)			100.00	100.00

Issued: 85c, 90c, $1, $2, 3/23/92; $3, $5, 10/25/93; $7, 12/6/93; $10, 1/31/94; $15, 9/9/94; others, 1/22/92.

See Nos. 1154-1176 for stamps with buff border. For overprints see Nos. O54-O68.

This is an expanding set. Numbers may change.

Endangered Wildlife — A156

#1095, Tiger. #1096, Asiatic elephant. #1097, Grizzly bear. #1098, Black rhinoceros. #1099, Chimpanzee. #1100, Asian bighorn. #1101, Heavisides dolphin. #1102, Eagle owl. #1103, Bee hummingbird. #1104, Feliscon-color cougar. #1105, European otter. #1106, Red kangaroo.

1992 Litho. ***Perf. 14***

1095-1106 $1.15 Set of 12 30.00 30.00

Issued: #1095, 4/6; #1096, 4/7; #1097, 4/8; #1098, 4/9; #1099, 4/10; #1100, 4/11; #1101, 7/13; #1102, 7/14; #1103, 7/15; #1104, 7/16; #1105, 7/17; #1106, 7/18.

See Nos. 1119-1124, 1134-1138.

Discovery of America, 500th Anniv. — A157

1992, May 22 Litho. ***Perf. 14x14½***

1107 A157 $6 multicolored 11.00 11.00

Souvenir Sheet

Perf. 15x14

1107A A157 $10 Coming ashore 13.00 13.00

Issued: #1107, May 22. #1107A, Sept. 21.

No. 1107A contains one 40x30mm stamp.

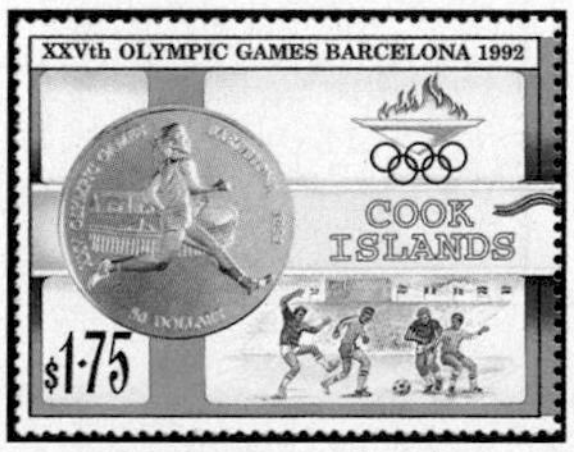

1992 Summer Olympics, Barcelona — A158

Designs: No. 1108a, $50 coin, soccer players. b, Flags of Spain, Cook Islands, Barcelona medal. c, $10 coin, basketball players. No. 1109a, Runners. b, $10, $50 coins. c, Cyclists. $6.40, Javelin.

1992, July 24 Litho. ***Perf. 13***

1108 A158 $1.75 Strip of 3, #a.-c. 12.00 12.00

1109 A158 $2.25 Strip of 3, #a.-c. 15.00 15.00

Souvenir Sheet

1110 A158 $6.40 multicolored 19.00 19.00

6th Festival of Pacific Arts, Rarotonga A159

80c, UNESCO poster. 85c, $1, $1.75, Different carvings of Rarotongan fertility god, Tangaroa.

1992, Oct. 16 Litho. ***Perf. 15x14***

1111	A159	80c	multicolored	2.25	2.25
1112	A159	85c	multicolored	2.50	2.50
1113	A159	$1	multicolored	3.00	3.00
1114	A159	$1.75	multicolored	4.75	4.75
	Nos. 1111-1114 (4)			12.50	12.50

For overprints see #1231-1234.

Ovptd. "ROYAL VISIT"

1992, Oct. 16

1115	A159	80c	on #1111	3.00	3.00
1116	A159	85c	on #1112	3.50	3.50
1117	A159	$1	on #1113	3.75	3.75
1118	A159	$1.75	on #1114	6.75	6.75
	Nos. 1115-1118 (4)			17.00	17.00

Endangered Wildlife Type of 1992

1992 Litho. ***Perf. 14***

1119	A156	$1.15	Jackass penguin	2.50	2.50
1120	A156	$1.15	Asian lion	2.50	2.50
1121	A156	$1.15	Peregrine falcon	2.50	2.50
1122	A156	$1.15	Persian fallow deer	2.50	2.50
1123	A156	$1.15	Key deer	2.50	2.50
1124	A156	$1.15	Alpine ibex	2.50	2.50
	Nos. 1119-1124 (6)			15.00	15.00

Issued: #1119, 11/2; #1120, 11/3; #1121, 11/4; #1122, 11/5; #1123, 11/6; #1124, 11/7.

Christmas A160

Paintings by El Parmigianino: 70c, Worship of Shepherds. 85c, $6.40, Virgin with Long Neck. $1.15, Virgin with Rose. $1.90, St. Margaret's Virgin.

1992, Nov. 20 Litho. ***Perf. 13½***

1125	A160	70c	multicolored	1.50	1.50
1126	A160	85c	multicolored	2.25	2.25
1127	A160	$1.15	multicolored	3.00	3.00
1128	A160	$1.90	multicolored	5.25	5.25
	Nos. 1125-1128 (4)			12.00	12.00

Souvenir Sheet

1129 A160 $6.40 multicolored 15.00 15.00

No. 1129 contains one 36x47mm stamp.

Queen Elizabeth II's Accession to the Throne, 40th Anniv. — A161

Various portraits of Queen Elizabeth II.

1992, Dec. 10 Litho. ***Perf. 14***

1130	A161	80c	multicolored	2.25	2.25
1131	A161	$1.15	multicolored	3.00	3.00
1132	A161	$1.50	multicolored	4.25	4.25
1133	A161	$1.95	multicolored	5.50	5.50
	Nos. 1130-1133 (4)			15.00	15.00

Endangered Wildlife Type of 1992

1993 Litho. ***Perf. 14***

1134	A156	$1.15	English mandrill	3.00	3.00
1135	A156	$1.15	Gorilla	3.00	3.00
1136	A156	$1.15	Vanessa atlanta	3.00	3.00
1137	A156	$1.15	Sichuan takin	3.00	3.00
1138	A156	$1.15	Ring tailed lemur	3.00	3.00
	Nos. 1134-1138 (5)			15.00	15.00

Issued: #1134, Feb. 1; #1135, Feb. 2; #1136, Feb. 3; #1137, Feb. 4; #1138, Feb. 5.

Coronation of Queen Elizabeth II, 40th Anniv. — A162

Designs: $1, Coronation ceremony. $2, Coronation portrait. $3, Queen, family on balcony, Buckingham Palace.

1993, June 2 Litho. ***Perf. 14***

1139	A162	$1	multicolored	2.50	2.50
1140	A162	$2	multicolored	5.25	5.25
1141	A162	$3	multicolored	8.25	8.25
	Nos. 1139-1141 (3)			16.00	16.00

Christmas A163

Paintings: 70c, Virgin with Child, by Filippo Lippi. 85c, Bargellini Madonna, by Lodovico Carracci. $1.15, Virgin of the Curtain, by Raphael. $2.50, Holy Family, by Il Bronzino. $4, Saint Zachary Virgin, by Il Parmigianino.

1993, Nov. 8 Litho. ***Perf. 14***

1142	A163	70c	multicolored	1.25	1.25
1143	A163	85c	multicolored	1.75	1.75
1144	A163	$1.15	multicolored	2.25	2.25
1145	A163	$2.50	multicolored	4.50	4.50

Size: 32x47mm

Perf. 13½

1146	A163	$4.00	multicolored	7.75	7.75
	Nos. 1142-1146 (5)			17.50	17.50

1994 Winter Olympics, Lillehammer — A164

Illustration reduced.

1994, Feb. 11 Litho. ***Perf. 13½x14***

1147 A164 $5 multicolored 11.00 11.00

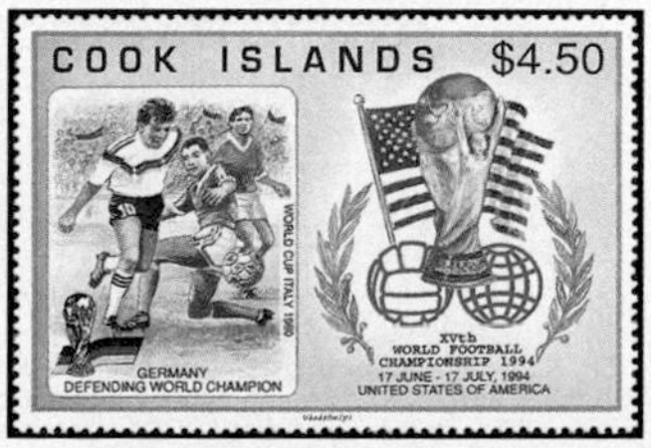

1994 World Cup Soccer Championships, US — A165

Illustration reduced.

1994, June 17 Litho. ***Perf. 14***

1148 A165 $4.50 multicolored 10.00 10.00

First Manned Moon Landing, 25th Anniv. — A166

Apollo 11 emblem and: No. 1149a, First step onto Moon, US flag. No. 1149b, Astronaut carrying experiment packs on Moon. No. 1150a, Astronaut, US flag. No. 1150b, Flag, reflection shown in astronaut's visor.

1994, July 20

1149 A166 $2.25 Pair, #a.-b. + label 11.50 11.50

1150 A166 $2.25 Pair, #a.-b. + label 11.50 11.50

Living Reef Type of 1992

1994 Litho. ***Perf. 14½x13½***

Size: 41x31mm

Buff & Multicolored

1154	A155	5c	like #1058	.60	.60
1158	A155	15c	like #1062	.60	.60
1160	A155	20c	like #1064	.75	.75
1161	A155	25c	like #1065	.85	.85
1162	A155	30c	like #1066	.95	.95
1167	A155	50c	like #1071	1.75	1.75
1172	A155	80c	like #1076	2.75	2.75
1173	A155	85c	like #1077	3.00	3.00
1174	A155	90c	like #1078	3.25	3.25
1176	A155	$1	like #1080	3.50	3.50
	Nos. 1154-1176 (10)			18.00	18.00

Issued: 5c, 15c, 20c, 25c, 30c, 50c, 80c, 85c, 90c, $1, 10/24/94. This is an expanding set. Numbers may change.

Miniature Sheet

The Return of Tommy Tricker — A167

Scenes from film: a, Three people in canoe. b, Traditional dancers. c, Couple walking on beach. d, Aerial view of island. e, Girls performing hand gestures. f, Girls walking along sand bar.

1994, Nov. 23 Litho. ***Perf. 14***

1191 A167 85c Sheet of 6, #a.-f. 16.00 16.00

See No. 1213.

Christmas — A168

Paintings: No. 1192a, The Virgin and Child, by Morales. b, Adoration of Kings, by Gerard David. c, Adoration of Kings, by Vinc Foppa. d, The Madonna & Child with St. Joseph & Infant Baptist, by Baroccio.

No. 1193a, Madonna with Iris, in style of Durer. b, Adoration of Shepherds, by Le Nain. c, The Virgin and Child, by follower of Leonardo. d, The Mystic Nativity, by Botticelli.

1994, Nov. 30 Litho. ***Perf. 14***

1192 A168 85c Block of 4, #a.-d. 7.75 7.75

1193 A168 $1 Block of 4, #a.-d. 8.75 8.75

Robert Louis Stevenson (1850-94), Writer — A169

Adventure scenes from books: a, "Treasure Island." b, "David Balfour." c, "Dr. Jekyll and Mr. Hyde." d, "Kidnapped."

1994, Dec. 12 *Perf. 14x15*

1194 A169 $1.50 Block of 4, #a.-d. 16.00 16.00

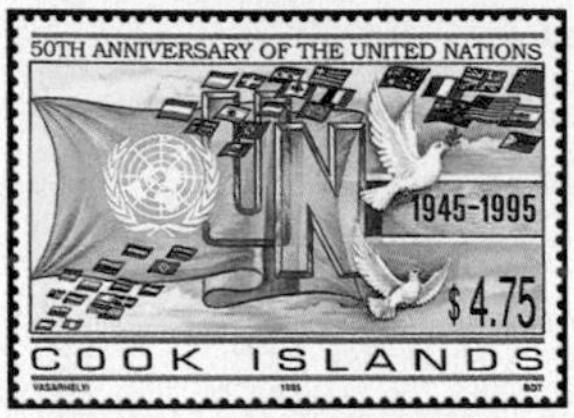

UN, 50th Anniv. — A170

$4.50, FAO, 50th anniv.

1995 **Litho.** *Perf. 13x13½*

1195 A170 $4.75 multicolored 8.50 8.50

Perf. 13½

1196 A170 $4.50 multicolored 8.00 8.00

Each issued in sheets of 4.
Issued: $4.75, 7/17; $4.50, 10/12.

Queen Mother, 95th Birthday — A172

1995, Aug. 31

1197 A172 $5 multicolored 15.00 15.00

End of World War II, 50th Anniv. — A173

Designs: a, German surrender, Rheims. b, Japanese surrender, Tokyo Bay.

1995, Sept. 4 *Perf. 13*

1198 A173 $3.50 Pair, #a.-b. 30.00 30.00

No. 1198 was issued in sheets of 4 stamps.

Year of the Sea Turtle A174

Designs: 85c, Green turtle in water. $1, Hawksbill turtle in water. $1.75, Green turtle nesting. $2.25, Hawksbill turtle hatchlings leaving nest.

1995, Nov. 20 **Litho.** *Perf. 14*

1199 A174 85c multicolored 2.50 2.50
1200 A174 $1 multicolored 3.50 3.50
1201 A174 $1.75 multicolored 5.25 5.25
1202 A174 $2.25 multicolored 7.25 7.25
Nos. 1199-1202 (4) 18.50 18.50

1996 Summer Olympics, Atlanta A175

1996, Jan. 12 **Litho.** *Perf. 14*

1203 A175 85c Discus 1.75 1.75
1204 A175 $1 Torch bearer 2.25 2.25
1205 A175 $1.50 Sprinting 3.25 3.25
1206 A175 $1.85 Gymnastics 4.25 4.25
1207 A175 $2.10 Archery 5.00 5.00
1208 A175 $2.50 Javelin 5.50 5.50
Nos. 1203-1208 (6) 22.00 22.00

Queen Elizabeth II, 70th Birthday — A176

Designs: $1.90, No. 1212a, In blue hat, coat. $2.25, No. 1212b, Wearing tiara. $2.75, No. 1212c, In robes of Order of the Garter.

1996, June 21 **Litho.** *Perf. 14*

1209 A176 $1.90 multicolored 4.00 4.00
1210 A176 $2.25 multicolored 5.00 5.00
1211 A176 $2.75 multicolored 5.50 5.50
Nos. 1209-1211 (3) 14.50 14.50

Sheet of 3

1212 A176 $2.50 #a.-c. + label 19.00 19.00

Nos. 1209-1211 were issued in sheets of 4.

"The Return of Tommy Tricker" Type of 1994

No. 1213a-1213f, like #1191a-1191f.

1997, Aug. 28 **Litho.** *Perf. 14*

1213 A167 90c Sheet of 6, #a.-f. 12.00 12.00

Nos. 1213a-1213f Overprinted in Silver

a

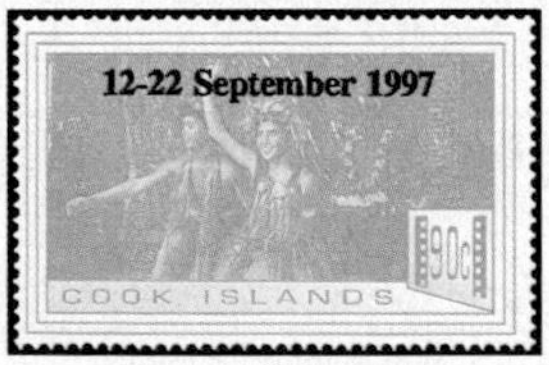

b

1997, Sept. 12 **Litho.** *Perf. 14*

1214 A167 90c Sheet 6, #a.-f. 9.00 9.00

#1214a, 1214d-1214e are overprinted type "a"; #1214b-1214c, 1214f type "b."

Butterflies A177

5c, Lampides boeticus (female). 10c, Vanessa atalanta. 15c, Lampides boeticus (male). 20c, Papilio godeffroyi. 25c, Danaus hamata. 30c, Xois sesara. 50c, Vagrans egista. 70c, Parthenos sylvia. 80c, Hyblaea sanguinea. 85c, Melanitis leda. 90c, Ascalapha odorata. $1, Precis villida. $1.50, Parthenos sylvia. $2, Lampides boeticus. $3, Precis villida. $4, Melanitis leda. $5, Vagrans egista. $7, Hyblaea sanguinea. $10, Vanessa atalanta. $15, Papilio godeffroyi.

1997-98 **Litho.** *Perf. 13*

1215 A177 5c multi .20 .20
1216 A177 10c multi .20 .20
1217 A177 15c multi .20 .20
1218 A177 20c multi .30 .30
1219 A177 25c multi .35 .35
1220 A177 30c multi .40 .40
1221 A177 50c multi .65 .65
1222 A177 70c multi .95 .95
1223 A177 80c multi 1.10 1.10
1224 A177 85c multi 1.10 1.10
1225 A177 90c multi 1.25 1.25
1226 A177 $1 multi 1.40 1.40

Perf. 13½

Size: 41x25mm

1226A A177 $1.50 multi 1.90 1.90
1226B A177 $2 multi 2.75 2.75
1226C A177 $3 multi 3.75 3.75
1226D A177 $4 multi 5.50 5.50
1226E A177 $5 multi 6.50 6.50
1226F A177 $7 multi 10.00 10.00
1226G A177 $10 multi 13.50 13.50
1226H A177 $15 multi 18.00 18.00
Nos. 1215-1226H (20) 70.00 70.00

Issued: 5c, 10c, 15c, 20c, 25c, 30c, 50c, 70c, 10/22/97; 80c, 85c, 90c, $1, 11/12/97; $1.50, $2, $3, 3/11/98; $4, $5, 6/19/98; $7, $10, 9/18/98; $15, 11/13/98.
For surcharges, see Nos. 1259-1264.

Queen Elizabeth II and Prince Philip, 50th Wedding Anniv. A178

1997, Nov. 20 *Perf. 14*

1227 A178 $2 multicolored 3.25 3.25

Souvenir Sheet

1228 A178 $5 like #1227, close-up 12.00 12.00

No. 1228 is a continuous design.

Diana, Princess of Wales (1961-97) — A179

1998, Mar. 18 **Litho.** *Perf. 14*

1229 A179 $1.15 shown 1.75 1.75

Souvenir Sheet

1230 A179 $3.50 like #1229 5.25 5.25

No. 1229 was issued in sheets of 5 + label.
See No. B142.

Nos. 1111-1114 Ovptd. "KIA ORANA / THIRD MILLENNIUM"

1231ovpt

Printing Methods and Perfs as before

1999, Dec. 31

1231 A159 80c on #1111 1.25 1.25
1232 A159 85c on #1112 1.25 1.25
1233 A159 $1 on #1113 1.50 1.50
1234 A159 $1.75 on #1114 2.50 2.50
Nos. 1231-1234 (4) 6.50 6.50

Queen Mother, 100th Birthday — A180

No. 1235: a, As child. b, As young woman. c, Wearing green hat. d, Wearing tiara.
Illustration reduced.

2000, Oct. 20 **Litho.** *Perf. 14*

1235 A180 $4.50 Sheet of 4, #a-d 20.00 20.00

Souvenir Sheet

1236 A180 $6 Wearing blue hat 7.00 7.00

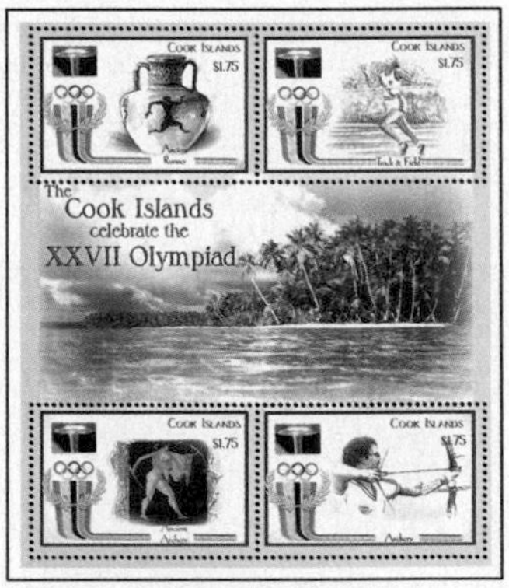

2000 Summer Olympics, Sydney — A181

No. 1237: a, Ancient runner. b, Track and field. c, Ancient archery. d, Archery.

2000, Nov. 14

1237 A181 $1.75 Sheet of 4, #a-d 11.00 11.00

Souvenir Sheet

1238 A181 $3.90 Torch bearer 4.50 4.50

Nos. 1095-1106 Surcharged in Gold

2001, Apr. 30 **Litho.** *Perf. 14*

1239 A156 80c on $1.15 #1101 1.00 1.00
1240 A156 80c on $1.15 #1102 1.00 1.00
1241 A156 80c on $1.15 #1103 1.00 1.00
1242 A156 80c on $1.15 #1104 1.00 1.00
1243 A156 80c on $1.15 #1105 1.00 1.00
1244 A156 80c on $1.15 #1106 1.00 1.00
1245 A156 90c on $1.15 #1095 1.25 1.25
1246 A156 90c on $1.15 #1096 1.25 1.25
1247 A156 90c on $1.15 #1097 1.25 1.25
1248 A156 90c on $1.15 #1098 1.25 1.25
1249 A156 90c on $1.15 #1099 1.25 1.25

1250 A156 90c on $1.15 #1100 1.25 1.25
Nos. 1239-1250 (12) 13.50 13.50

Nos. 1042-1045, 1050-1053 Surcharged or Overprinted in Black or Gold

2002, Nov. 11 Litho. *Perf. 14*

1251 A151 20c on 70c #1042 .20 .20
1252 A154 20c on 70c #1050 .20 .20
1253 A154 80c on $1.15 #1052 (G) 1.50 1.50
1254 A151 85c #1043 1.60 1.60
1255 A154 85c #1051 1.60 1.60
1256 A154 90c on $1.50 #1053 1.75 1.75
1257 A151 95c #1044 1.90 1.90
1258 A151 $1 on $1.50 #1045 2.25 2.25
Nos. 1251-1258 (8) 11.00 11.00

Nos. 1226A-1226F Surcharged

Methods and Perfs As Before

2003, June 30

1259 A177 20c on $1.50 #1226A .30 .30
1260 A177 80c on $2 #1226B 1.00 1.00
1261 A177 85c on $3 #1226C 1.25 1.25
1262 A177 85c on $4 #1226D 1.25 1.25
1263 A177 90c on $5 #1226E 1.50 1.50
1264 A177 90c on $7 #1226F 1.50 1.50
Nos. 1259-1264 (6) 6.80 6.80

Obliterator on Nos. 1260-1264 is a Moai head.

United We Stand — A182

2003, Sept. 30 Litho. *Perf. 14*

1265 A182 90c multi 2.50 2.50

Printed in sheets of 4.

2004 Summer Olympics, Athens A183

Designs: 40c, Poster for 1992 Barcelona Olympics. 60c, Pancration, horiz. $1, Cycling, horiz. $2, Gold medal, 1936 Berlin Olympics.

2004, Sept. 29 Litho. *Perf. 14¼*

1266-1269 A183 Set of 4 6.50 6.50

Worldwide Fund for Nature (WWF) — A184

Birds of Suwarrow National Park: 80c, Cook Islands reed warblers. 90c, Mangaia kingfishers. $1.15, Rarotonga starlings. $1.95, Atiu swiftlets.

2005, June 13 Litho. *Perf. 14*

1270-1273 A184 Set of 4 8.00 8.00

Each stamp printed in sheets of 4.

Pope John Paul II (1920-2005) A185

2005, Nov. 11

1274 A185 $1.35 multi 2.40 2.40

Printed in sheets of 5 + label.

A186

A187

A188

Designs: 5c, Black-lined Maori wrasse. 10c, Blue lorikeets. 20c, Daisy coral. 30c, Ocean sunfish. 40c, Female Lampides boeticus butterfly. 50c, Rarotonga starlings.

No. 1285: a, Mangaia kingfishers. b, Cook Islands reef warblers. c, Rarotonga starlings, diff. d, Matiu swiftlets.

No. 1286: a, Male Lampides boeticus. b, Vagrans egista. c, Melantis leda. d, Female Lampides boeticus, diff.

No. 1287: a, Daisy coral, diff. b, Hydroid coral. c, Sea star. d, Smooth sea star.

No. 1288: a, Black-tipped cod. b, Red spot rainbow fish. c, Black-lined Maori wrasse, diff. d, Fish (incorrectly identified as Smooth sea star).

No. 1289: a, Three Ocean sunfish, Latin name at LL. b, Three Ocean sunfish, large clump of seaweed, Latin name at LR. c, Two Ocean sunfish, diver. d, Three Ocean sunfish, small clump of seaweed at top, Latin name at LR.

No. 1290: a, Blue lorikeets on palm branch. b, Blue lorikeets in tree hollow. c, Blue lorikeets and white flowers. d, Blue lorikeets and pink flowers.

No. 1291 — Queen Elizabeth II and: a, Hawksbill turtle. b, Leatherback turtle. c, Green turtle. d, Olive ridley turtle.

No. 1292 — Queen Elizabeth II and: a, Sowerby's whales. b, Cuvier's beaked whales. c, Bottle-nosed dolphin. d, Commerson's dolphins.

$7.50, Queen Elizabeth II, fish and marine life. $10, Queen Elizabeth II, butterflies and flowers. $15, Queen Elizabeth II and birds. Illustrations A187 and A188 reduced.

2007 Litho. *Perf. 13¼*

1279 A186 5c multi .20 .20
1280 A186 10c multi .20 .20
1281 A186 20c multi .30 .30
1282 A186 30c multi .45 .45
1283 A186 40c multi .60 .60
1284 A186 50c multi .75 .75

Size: 48x27mm

Perf. 14x14¾

1285 Block of 4 4.75 4.75
a.-d. A186 80c Any single 1.10 1.10
1286 Block of 4 5.25 5.25
a.-d. A186 90c Any single 1.25 1.25
1287 Block of 4 5.75 5.75
a.-d. A186 $1 Any single 1.40 1.40
1288 Block of 4 6.50 6.50
a.-d. A186 $1.10 Any single 1.60 1.60
1289 Block of 4 7.00 7.00
a.-d. A186 $1.20 Any single 1.75 1.75
1290 Block of 4 11.50 11.50
a.-d. A186 $2 Any single 2.75 2.75

Perf. 13¾

1291 Block of 4 19.00 19.00
a.-d. A187 $3 Any single 4.75 4.75
1292 Block of 4 31.00 31.00
a.-d. A187 $5 Any single 7.75 7.75

Perf. 13¼

1293 A188 $7.50 multi 12.00 12.00
1294 A188 $10 multi 15.50 15.50
1295 A188 $15 multi 24.00 24.00
Nos. 1279-1295 (17) 144.75 144.75

Issued: Nos. 1279-1290, 3/20; No. 1291, 10/10; No. 1292, 11/13; Nos. 1293-1295, 12/10.

Miniature Sheet

2008 Summer Olympics, Beijing — A189

No. 1296: a, 40c, Weight lifting. b, 60c, High jump. c, $1, Swimming. d, $1.50, Running.

2008, July 28 Litho. *Perf. 14¾x14*

1296 A189 Sheet of 4, #a-d 5.25 5.25

SEMI-POSTAL STAMPS

Catalogue values for unused stamps in this section are for Never Hinged items.

Nos. 203-204, 223, 210, 213, 215-216 Surcharged

Perf. 14x13½, 13½

1968, Feb. 12 Photo.

B1 A34 3c + 1c multi .20 .20
B2 A34 4c + 1c multi .20 .20
B3 A37 5c + 2c multi .20 .20
B4 A34 10c + 2c multi .25 .25
B5 A34 25c + 5c multi .40 .40
B6 A34 50c + 10c multi .90 .90
B7 A35 $1 + 10c multi 1.75 1.75
Nos. B1-B7 (7) 3.90 3.90

Surtax for the victims of hurricane of Dec. 15-18, 1967. The surcharge on No. B3 is printed on a silver rectangle. The surcharge on No. B7 is in smaller type with serifs, measuring 7½mm in depth.

Nos. 210, 213-214 Surcharged in Ultramarine

1971, Sept. 8 Photo. *Perf. 14x13½*

B8 A34 10c + 1c multi .25 .25
B9 A34 10c + 3c multi .25 .25
B10 A34 25c + 1c multi .65 .65
B11 A34 25c + 3c multi .65 .65
B12 A34 30c + 1c multi .75 .75
B13 A34 30c + 3c multi .75 .75
Nos. B8-B13 (6) 3.30 3.30

4th South Pacific Games, Papeete, French Polynesia, Sept. 8-19.

Christmas Type of Regular Issue
Souvenir Sheet

50c+5c, Holy Family in a Garland of Flowers, by Jan Brueghel and Pieter van Avont.

1971, Nov. 30 Photo. *Perf. 13½*

B14 A50 50c + 5c gold & multi 1.75 1.75

No. B14 contains one stamp 45x40mm.

Nos. 316-318, 211, 213 and 215 Surcharged in Red or Black

a

b

1972, Mar. 30 Photo. *Perf. 13½*

B15 A46(a) 5c + 2c multi (R) .20 .20
B16 A46(a) 10c + 2c multi (R) .20 .20
B17 A34(b) 15c + 5c multi .35 .35
B18 A34(b) 25c + 5c multi .65 .65
B19 A46(a) 30c + 5c multi (R) .75 .75
B20 A34(b) 50c + 10c multi 1.40 1.40
Nos. B15-B20 (6) 3.55 3.55

Surtax for victims of hurricane of Mar. 22-26.

Nos. 319-322c with Surcharge Similar to Type "a"

1972, May 24 Photo. *Perf. 13½*

B21 A51 5c + 2c, pair, #a.-b. .25 .25
B22 A51 10c + 2c, pair, #a.-b. .45 .45
B23 A51 25c + 2c, pair, #a.-b. 1.00 1.00
B24 A51 30c + 2c, pair, #a.-b. 1.50 1.50
c. Souvenir sheet of 8 3.50 3.50
Nos. B21-B24 (4) 3.20 3.20

Surtax for victims of hurricane of Mar. 22-26. Stamps of No. B24c each surcharged 3c.

Olympic Type of Regular Issue
Souvenir Sheet

50c+5c, Pierre de Coubertin, Olympic rings.

1972, June 26

B29 A52 50c + 5c multi 3.25 3.25

Christmas Type of Regular Issue
Souvenir Sheet

Design: 50c+5c, Nativity, by Correggio.

1972, Oct. 11 Photo. *Perf. 13½*

B30 A53 50c + 5c multi 2.25 2.00

No. B30 contains one stamp 30x40mm.

POSTAL TAX STAMPS

Greece Nos. RA61-RA63, Overprinted Like Nos. N15-N34
Wmk., Unwmk.

1941, June 5 *Perf. 13½*

NRA1 PT7 10 l brt rose, *pale rose*	3.00	5.75
NRA2 PT7 50 l gray grn, *pale green*	3.75	*5.75*
NRA3 PT7 1d dull blue, *lt blue*	32.50	26.00
Nos. NRA1-NRA3 (3)	39.25	37.50
Set, never hinged	80.00	

Stamps overprinted "CORFU" were replaced by Italian stamps overprinted "Isole Jonie." See Ionian Islands.

COSTA RICA

ˌkäs-tə-ˈrē-kə

LOCATION — Central America between Nicaragua and Panama
GOVT. — Republic
AREA — 19,730 sq. mi.
POP. — 3,674,490 (1999 est.)
CAPITAL — San Jose

8 Reales= 100 Centavos= 1 Peso
100 Centimos= 1 Colon (1900)

Catalogue values for unused stamps in this country are for Never Hinged items, beginning with Scott 238 in the regular postage section, Scott C117 in the air post section, Scott CE1 in the air post special delivery section, Scott E1 in the special delivery section, and Scott RA1 in the postal tax section.

Watermarks

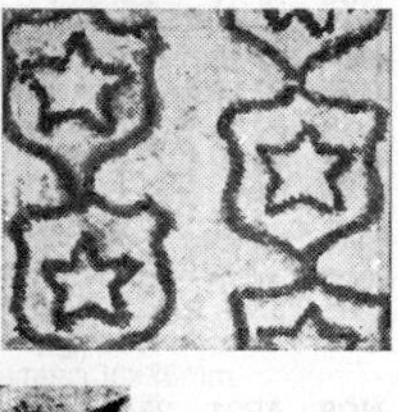
Wmk. 215 — Small Star in Shield, Multiple

Wmk. 229 — Wavy Lines

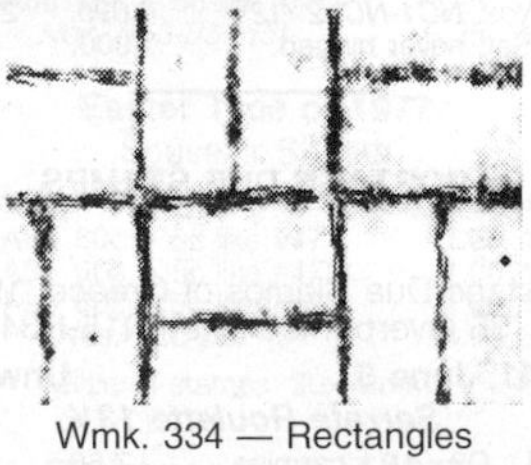
Wmk. 334 — Rectangles

Values for unused stamps are for examples with original gum as defined in the catalogue introduction. Very fine examples of Nos. 1-22 will have perforations just clear of the design on one or more sides due to the placement of the stamps on the plates and to imperfect perforating methods.

Coat of Arms — A1

1863 Unwmk. Engr. *Perf. 12*

1 A1 ½r blue	.40	*1.10*
a. ½r light blue	.40	1.10
b. Pair, imperf. horiz.	*1,500.*	
2 A1 2r scarlet	1.75	*2.25*
3 A1 4r green	16.00	*16.00*
4 A1 1p orange	42.50	*42.50*
Nos. 1-4 (4)	60.65	*61.85*

The ½r was printed from two plates. The second is in light blue with little or no sky over the mountains.

Imperforate examples of Nos. 1-2 are corner stamps from poorly perforated sheets.

Nos. 1-3 Surcharged in Red or Black:

a

b

c

d

e

1881-82
Red or Black Surcharge

7 A1(a) 1c on ½r ('82)	3.00	—
a. On No. 1a	15.00	
8 A1(b) 1c on ½r ('82)	18.00	—
9 A1(c) 2c on ½r, #1a	3.00	—
a. On No. 1	8.00	
12 A1(c) 5c on ½r	15.00	—
13 A1(d) 5c on ½r ('82)	55.00	—
14 A1(d) 10c on 2r (Bk) ('82)	70.00	—
15 A1(e) 20c on 4r ('82)	300.00	—

Overprints with different fonts and "OFICIAL" were never placed in use, and are said to have been surcharged to a dealer's order. The ½r surcharged "DOS CTS" is not a postage stamp. It probably is an essay.

Postally used examples of Nos. 7-15 are rare. Nos. 13-15 exist with a favor cancel having a hyphen between "San" and "Jose." Values same as unused. Fake cancellations exist.

Counterfeits exist of surcharges on Nos. 7-15.

Gen. Prospero Fernández
A6

President Bernardo Soto Alfaro
A7

1883, Jan. 1

16 A6 1c green	3.00	1.50
17 A6 2c carmine	3.00	1.50
18 A6 5c blue violet	30.00	2.00
19 A6 10c orange	150.00	12.00
20 A6 40c blue	3.00	*3.00*
Nos. 16-20 (5)	189.00	20.00

Unused examples of 40c usually lack gum.
For overprints see Nos. O1-O20, O24, Guanacaste 1-38, 44.

1887

21 A7 5c blue violet	7.00	.50
22 A7 10c orange	4.00	3.00

Unused examples of 5c usually lack gum.
For overprints see Nos. O22-O23, Guanacaste 42-43, 45.

A8

A9

1889
Black Overprint

23 A8 1c rose	5.00	3.00
24 A9 5c brown	7.00	3.00

Vertical and inverted overprints are fakes.
For overprints see Guanacaste Nos. 47-54.

President Soto Alfaro
A10 A11

A12

A13

A14

A15

A16

A17

A18

A19

1889 *Perf. 14-16 & Compound*

25 A10 1c brown	.35	*.45*
a. Horiz. pair, imperf. vert	*150.00*	
b. Imperf. pair	*100.00*	
c. Horiz. or vert. pair, imperf. btwn.	*150.00*	
26 A11 2c dark green	.35	*.45*
a. Imperf., pair	50.00	
b. Vert. pair, imperf. horiz.	125.00	
c. Horiz. pair, imperf. btwn.	125.00	
27 A12 5c orange	.45	.35
a. Imperf., pair		*250.00*
b. Horiz. pair, imperf. btwn.	*150.00*	
28 A13 10c red brown	.40	.35
a. Vert. or horiz. pair, imperf. btwn.	*150.00*	
29 A14 20c yellow green	.30	*.35*
a. Vert. pair, imperf. horiz.	*200.00*	
b. Horizontal pair, imperf. btwn.	*150.00*	
30 A15 50c rose red	1.00	
Telegram cancel		.75
31 A16 1p blue	1.25	
Telegram cancel		.75
32 A17 2p dull violet	6.00	
a. 2p slate	6.00	
Telegram cancel		4.00
33 A18 5p olive green	25.00	
Telegram cancel		10.00
34 A19 10p black	100.00	
Telegram cancel		60.00
Nos. 25-34 (10)	135.10	

Nos. 30-34 normally were used on telegrams, and most examples were removed from the forms and sold by the government.
For overprints see Nos. O25-O30, Guanacaste 55-67.

Arms of Costa Rica
A20 A21

A22

A23

A24

A25

A26

A27

A28

A29

1892 *Perf. 12-15 & Compound*

35 A20 1c grnsh blue	.30	*.40*
36 A21 2c yellow	.30	*.40*
37 A22 5c red lilac	.30	.25
a. 5c violet	60.00	.30
38 A23 10c lt green	.75	.35
a. Horiz. pair, imperf. btwn.	—	*100.00*
39 A24 20c scarlet	12.00	.20
a. Horiz. pair, imperf. btwn.	—	*100.00*
40 A25 50c gray blue	4.00	*4.25*
41 A26 1p green, *yel*	1.00	1.00
42 A27 2p brown red, *lilac*	3.00	1.00
a. 2p rose red, *pale lil*	12.00	1.00
43 A28 5p dk blue, *blue*	2.00	1.00
44 A29 10p brown, *pale buff*	35.00	5.00
a. 10p brown, *yellow*	8.00	
Nos. 35-44 (10)	58.65	13.85

Imperfs. of Nos. 35-44 are proofs.
For overprints see Nos. O31-O36.

Statue of Juan Santamaría
A30

Juan Mora Fernández
A31

View of Port Limón — A32

Braulio Carillo ("Branlio" on stamp) — A33

National Theater — A34

José M. Castro — A35

Birris Bridge — A36

Juan Rafael Mora — A37

Jesús Jiménez — A38

Coat of Arms — A39

1901, Jan. ***Perf. 12-15½***

45	A30	1c green & blk	3.25	.30
a.		Horiz. pair, imperf. btwn.	*150.00*	
46	A31	2c ver & blk	1.25	.30
47	A32	5c gray blue & blk	3.25	.30
a.		Vert. pair, imperf. btwn.	—	*150.00*
48	A33	10c ocher & blk	3.25	.35
49	A34	20c lake & blk	22.50	.25
a.		Vert. pair, imperf. btwn.	*150.00*	
50	A35	50c dull lil & dk bl	5.25	1.00
51	A36	1col ol bis & blk	110.00	3.50
52	A37	2col car rose & dk grn	16.00	3.00
53	A38	5col brown & blk	75.00	3.50
54	A39	10col yel grn & brn red	29.00	3.00
		Nos. 45-54 (10)	268.75	15.50

The 2c exists with center inverted. Value $77,500.

Nos. 45-57 in other colors are private reprints made in 1948. They have little value.

For surcharge and overprints see Nos. 58, 78, O37-O44.

Remainders

In 1914 the government sold a large quantity of stamps at very much less than face value. The lot included most regular issues from 1901 to 1911 inclusive, postage due stamps of 1903 and Official stamps of 1901-03. These stamps were canceled with groups of five thin parallel bars. The higher valued used stamps, such as Nos. 64, 65-68a, sell for much less than the values quoted, which are for stamps with regular postal cancellations. A few sell for much higher prices.

José M. Cañas — A40

Julián Volio — A41

Eusebio Figueroa Oreamuno — A42

1903 ***Perf. 13½, 14, 15***

55	A40	4c red vio & blk	1.75	.70
56	A41	6c olive grn & blk	7.25	4.00
57	A42	25c gray lil & brn	16.00	.30
		Nos. 55-57 (3)	25.00	5.00

See note on private reprints following #54. For overprints see Nos. 81, O45-O47.

No. 49 Surcharged in Black:

1905

58	A34	1c on 20c lake & blk	.60	.60
a.		Inverted surcharge	10.00	10.00
b.		Diagonal surcharge	.60	.60

Specimens surcharged in other colors are proofs.

Statue of Juan Santamaria A43

Juan Mora Fernández A44

José M. Cañas A45

Mauro Fernández A46

Braulio Carrillo — A47

Julián Volio — A48

Eusebio Figueroa Oreamuno A49

José M. Castro A50

Jesús Jiménez — A51

Juan Rafael Mora — A52

Perf. 11x14, 14 (1c, 5c, 10c, 25c)

1907 **Unwmk.**

59	A43	1c red brn & ind	8.00	.40
a.		Perf. 11x14	60.00	3.00
b.		Imperf pair	15.00	—
60	A44	2c yel grn & blk	3.00	.30
a.		Perf. 14	3.00	.30
b.		Imperf pair	15.00	—
61	A45	4c car & indigo	12.00	2.50
a.		Perf. 14	500.00	40.00
b.		Imperf pair	15.00	—
62	A46	5c yel & dull bl	3.00	.30
a.		Perf. 11x14	60.00	1.00
b.		Imperf pair	15.00	—
63	A47	10c blue & blk	10.00	.50
a.		Perf. 11x14	20.00	1.00
b.		Imperf pair	30.00	—
64	A48	20c olive grn & blk	25.00	6.00
a.		Perf. 14	25.00	6.00
		Remainder cancel		2.00
b.		Imperf pair		—
65	A49	25c gray lil & blk	3.00	3.00
		Remainder cancel		1.00
a.		Perf. 11x14	150.00	50.00
b.		Imperf pair		—
66	A50	50c red lil & blue	75.00	25.00
		Remainder cancel		2.00
a.		Perf. 14	175.00	50.00
b.		Imperf pair	100.00	
67	A51	1col brown & blk	25.00	20.00
a.		Perf. 14	25.00	20.00
		Remainder cancel		2.00
b.		Imperf pair	—	
68	A52	2col claret & grn	160.00	100.00
a.		Perf. 14	300.00	150.00
		Remainder cancel		3.00
b.		Imperf pair	200.00	
		Nos. 59-68 (10)	324.00	158.00

The remainder cancel value applies to both perforations.

The imperforate varieties of the above set are valued without gum. Ungummed stamps were probably placed on the market in London, while gummed stamps appear to have been sent to Costa Rica and accepted for postal use. There is a small premium for gummed stamps.

The 1c, 2c, 5c, 20c, 50c, 1 col and 2 col exist with center inverted. Value, set $62,500.

Nos. 59-68 exist with papermaker's watermark.

No. 65b with brown vignette is a proof. Value, pair $40. The actual No. 65b (black vignette) is worth much more.

For overprints see Nos. 77, 79-80, 82-84, O48-O55, O60-O64.

Statue of Juan Santamaria A53

Juan Mora Fernández A54

José M. Cañas A55

Mauro Fernández A56

Braulio Carrillo — A57

Julián Volio — A58

Eusebio Figueroa Oreamuno A59

Jesús Jiménez A60

1910 ***Perf. 12***

69	A53	1c brown	.20	.20
70	A54	2c dp green	.25	.20
71	A55	4c scarlet	.35	.35
72	A56	5c orange	1.00	.20
73	A57	10c deep blue	.25	.20
74	A58	20c olive grn	.50	.35
75	A59	25c dp violet	17.00	1.50
76	A60	1col dk brown	.50	.50
		Nos. 69-76 (8)	20.05	3.50

For overprints and surcharge see Nos. 111C-111J, B1, C2, O56-O59.

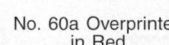

No. 60a Overprinted in Red

1911 ***Perf. 14***

77	A44	2c yel grn & blk	3.00	1.00
a.		Inverted overprint	6.00	5.00
b.		Double overprint, both inverted	45.00	

Stamps of 1901-07 Overprinted in Red or Black

78	A30	1c grn & blk (R)	3.00	1.00
a.		Black overprint	32.50	18.00
b.		Inverted overprint		
79	A43	1c red brn & ind (Bk)	1.00	.40
a.		Inverted overprint	4.50	3.50
b.		Double overprint	5.50	5.00
80	A44	2c yel grn & blk (Bk)	1.00	.40
a.		Inverted overprint	3.75	3.50
b.		Dbl. ovpt., one as on No. 77	40.00	27.50
c.		Double overprint, one inverted	15.00	15.00
d.		Pair, one stamp No. 77	25.00	18.00
e.		Perf. 11x14	30.00	10.00

No. 55 Overprinted in Black

81	A40	4c red vio & blk	1.50	.65

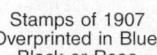

Stamps of 1907 Overprinted in Blue, Black or Rose

Perf. 14, 11x14 (#83, 84)

82	A46	5c yel & bl (Bl)	2.00	.20
a.		"Habilitada"	3.25	2.50
b.		"2911"	5.50	3.25
c.		Roman "I" in "1911"	4.00	2.50
d.		Double overprint	5.50	5.00
e.		Inverted overprint	6.00	3.75
f.		Black overprint	—	2.00
g.		Triple overprint	6.00	
h.		Vert. pair, imperf. horiz.	100.00	
83	A47	10c blue & blk (Bk)	5.00	1.40
a.		As #83, Roman "I" in "1911"	7.00	5.00
c.		As #83, double overprint	20.00	11.50
d.		Perf. 14	45.00	5.25
84	A47	10c blue & blk (R)	15.00	12.50
a.		Roman "I" in "1911"	*100.00*	*100.00*
c.		Perf. 14	*100.00*	*100.00*
		Nos. 77-84 (8)	31.50	17.55

Many counterfeits of overprint exist.

A61

A62

A63

Telegraph Stamps Surcharged in Rose, Blue or Black

1911 ***Perf. 12***

86	A61	1c on 10c bl (R)	.50	.20
a.		"Coereos"	7.75	5.50
b.		Inverted surcharge		
87	A61	1c on 10c bl (Bk)	*200.00*	*82.50*
88	A61	1c on 25c vio (Bk)	.50	.20
a.		"Coereos"	8.00	5.50
b.		Pair, one without surcharge	20.00	
c.		Double surcharge	9.00	
e.		Double surch., one inverted	12.50	
89	A61	1c on 50c red brn (Bl)	.50	.40
a.		Inverted surcharge	5.50	5.00
b.		Double surcharge	4.50	
90	A61	1c on 1col brn (R)	.50	.40
91	A61	1c on 5col red (Bl)	1.00	.55
92	A61	1c on 10col dk brn (R)	1.50	.70

Perf. 14

93	A62	2c on 5c brn org (Bk)	3.50	1.90
a.		Inverted surcharge	*9.00*	*3.75*
b.		"Correos" inverted	*17.50*	
c.		Double surcharge	9.00	

Perf. 14x11

94	A62	2c on 10c bl (R)	100.00	55.00
a.		Perf. 14	*300.00*	*75.00*
b.		"Correos" inverted		
c.		As "b," perf. 14		

95 A62 2c on 50c cl (Bk) 1.00 .50
a. Inverted surcharge 4.50 3.25
b. Double surcharge 12.50
c. Perf. 14 45.00 20.00
96 A62 2c on 1col brn (Bk) 1.25 .70
a. Inverted surcharge 12.50
b. Double surcharge 16.00
c. Perf. 14 2.00 .80
97 A62 2c on 2col car (Bk) 1.25 .60
a. Inverted surcharge 8.00 5.00
b. "Correos" inverted 10.00 5.50
c. Double surcharge
d. Perf. 14 26.00 15.00
98 A62 2c on 5col grn (Bk) 1.00 .65
a. Inverted surcharge 10.00 7.00
b. "Correos" inverted *16.00* *4.25*
c. Perf. 14 6.00 3.00
99 A62 2c on 10col mar (Bk) 1.50 .65
a. "Correos" inverted *400.00*
b. Perf. 14 6.00 3.00

Perf. 12

100 A63 5c on 5c org (Bl) .40 .25
a. Double surcharge 25.00 15.00
b. Inverted surcharge 25.00 8.50
c. Pair, one without surcharge 16.00

Counterfeits exist of Nos. 87, 94 and all minor varieties. Genuine used examples are rare and have a cancel only used on registered mail. Genuine "Coereos" errors do not exist on No. 87. Used examples of No. 94 with target cancels are counterfeits.

Nos. 93-99 exist with papermaker's watermark.

Coffee Plantation — A64

1921, June 17 Litho. *Perf. 11½*

103 A64 5c bl & blk 3.00 3.00
a. Tête bêche pair 15.00 6.50
b. Imperf., pair *40.00*
c. As "a," imperf. *125.00*

Centenary of coffee raising in Costa Rica.

Liberty with Torch of Freedom — A65

1921 Typo. *Perf. 11*

104 A65 5c violet 1.00 .40
a. Imperf, pair *100.00*

Cent. of Central American independence.

Beware of trimmed singles that look like No. 104a.

For overprint see No. 111.

Juan Mora and Julio Acosta — A66

1921, Sept. 15 *Perf. 11½*

105 A66 2c orange & blk 1.75 1.75
106 A66 3c green & blk 1.75 1.75
107 A66 6c scarlet & blk 3.00 3.00
108 A66 15c dk blue & blk 5.00 5.00
109 A66 30c orange brn & blk 6.50 6.50
Nos. 105-109 (5) 18.00 18.00

Centenary of Central American independence. Issue requested by Costa Rican Philatelic Society. Authorized by decree calling for 2,000 of 30c and 5,000 each of other values. Nos. 105-109 imperf were not regularly issued. Inverted centers exist of both perf and imperf. They are rare. Used values are for Independence commemorative cancel.

Each sheet of 20 (4x5) contains 5 tête-bêche pairs. Value, set of 5 pairs $37.50.

Simón Bolívar — A67

1921 Engr. *Perf. 12*

110 A67 15c deep violet .75 .20

For overprint No. 110a see set following No. 111. For surcharge see No. 148

No. 104 Overprinted

1922 *Perf. 11*

111 A65 5c violet .75 .40
a. Inverted overprint 10.00
b. Double overprint 15.00

Fakes of Nos. 111a and 111b are common.

Stamps of 1910-1921 Overprinted in Blue, Red, Black or Gold

1922 *Perf. 12*

111C A53 1c brown (Bl) .30 .20
111D A54 2c deep green (R) .40 .20
111E A55 4c scarlet .30 .20
111F A56 5c orange 2.00 .35
111G A57 10c deep blue (R) .75 .35
111H A67 15c deep violet (G) 3.50 2.00
Nos. 111C-111H (6) 7.25 3.30

Inverted overprints occur on all values. Counterfeits are very common for both normal and inverted overprints.

No. 72 Overprinted

1923

111J A56 5c orange 3.00 .75
k. "VD." for "UD." *75.00* *75.00*

Jesús Jiménez — A68

1923, June 18 Litho. *Perf. 11½*

112 A68 2c brown .40 .40
113 A68 4c green .40 .40
114 A68 5c blue .60 .40
115 A68 20c carmine .85 .50
116 A68 1col violet 1.10 1.25
Nos. 112-116 (5) 3.35 2.95

Pres. Jesús Jiménez (1823-98).

Nos. 112-116, imperf, were not regularly issued. Value, set $5.

For overprints see Nos. O65-O69.

National Monument A70

Harvesting Coffee — A71

Banana Growing — A73

General Post Office A74

Columbus Soliciting Aid of Isabella A75

Christopher Columbus A76

Columbus at Cariari A77

Map of Costa Rica — A78

Manuel M. Gutiérrez — A79

1923-26 Engr. *Perf. 12*

117 A70 1c violet .25 .20
118 A71 2c yellow .50 .20
119 A73 4c deep green .75 .30
120 A74 5c light blue 1.50 .20
121 A74 5c yellow grn ('26) .50 .20
122 A75 10c red brown 3.00 .20
123 A75 10c car rose ('26) .50 .20
124 A76 12c carmine rose 10.00 3.00
125 A77 20c deep blue 10.00 .60
126 A78 40c orange 11.00 3.00
127 A79 1col olive green 2.00 .65
Nos. 117-127 (11) 40.00 8.75

See #151-156. For surcharges & overprints see #136-140, 147, 189, 218, C2.

Rodrigo Arias Maldonado — A80

1924 *Perf. 12½*

128 A80 2c dark green .20 .20
a. Perf. 14 .50 .25

See No. 162.

Map of Guanacaste A81

Mission at Nicoya A82

1924 Litho. *Perf. 12*

129 A81 1c carmine rose .30 .20
130 A81 2c violet .30 .20
131 A81 5c green .30 .20
132 A81 10c orange 2.25 .50
133 A82 15c light blue 1.00 .45
134 A82 20c gray black 2.00 1.00
135 A82 25c light brown 3.00 1.50
Nos. 129-135 (7) 9.15 4.05

Centenary of annexation of Province of Guanacaste to Costa Rica.

Exist imperf. Value, set, $50.

Stamps of 1923 Surcharged:

a

b

1925

136 A74(a) 3c on 5c lt blue .30 .20
137 A75(a) 6c on 10c red brn .40 .25
138 A78(a) 30c on 40c orange 1.50 .40
139 A79(b) 45c on 1col ol grn 1.75 .50
a. Double surcharge *250.00*
Nos. 136-139 (4) 3.95 1.35

No. 124 Surcharged

1926

140 A76 10c on 12c car rose 1.50 .30

College of San Luis, Cartago A83

Chapui Asylum, San José — A84

Normal School, Heredia A85

Ruins of Ujarrás A86

1926 Unwmk. Engr. *Perf. 12½*
143 A83 3c ultra .50 .20
144 A84 6c dark brown .50 .20
145 A85 30c deep orange 2.00 .25
146 A86 45c black violet 4.00 1.00
Nos. 143-146 (4) 7.00 1.65

For surcharges see Nos. 190-190D, 217.

No. 124 Surcharged in Black:

1928, Jan. 7 *Perf. 12*
147 A76 10c on 12c car rose 4.50 4.50

Issued in honor of Col. Charles A. Lindbergh during his Good Will Tour of Central America.

The surcharge was privately reprinted using an original die. Reprints can be distinguished by distinct dots under the "10s." All errors and inverted surcharges are reprints.

No. 110 Surcharged

1928
148 A67 5(c) on 15c dp violet .25 .25
a. Inverted surcharge 35.00

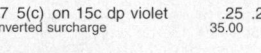

Type I — A88

Type II

Type III

Type IV

Type V

Surcharge Typo. (I-V) & Litho. (V)
1929 *Perf. 12½*
149 A88 5c on 2col car (I) .50 .20
a.-d. Types II-V (typo.) .60 .20
e. Type V (litho.) 3.00 3.00

Telegraph Stamp Surcharged for Postage as in 1929, Surcharge Lithographed

1929
150 A88 13c on 40c deep grn .35 .25
a. Inverted surcharge 1.00 1.00

Excellent counterfeits exist of No. 150a.

Types of 1923-26 Issues Dated "1929" Imprint of Waterlow & Sons

1930 Size: 26x21½mm *Perf. 12½*
151 A70 1c dark violet .70 .20
155 A74 5c green .70 .20
156 A75 10c carmine rose .70 .20
Nos. 151-156 (3) 2.10 .60

Juan Rafael Mora — A89

1931
157 A89 13c carmine rose .60 .20

For surcharge see No. 209.

Seal of Costa Rica Philatelic Society ("Octubre 12 de 1932") — A90

1932, Oct. 12 *Perf. 12*
158 A90 3c orange .25 .20
159 A90 5c dark green .40 .25
160 A90 10c carmine rose .50 .25
161 A90 20c dark blue .85 .30
Nos. 158-161 (4) 2.00 1.00

Phil. Exhib., Oct. 12, 1932. See #179-183.

Maldonado Type of 1924

1934 *Perf. 12½*
162 A80 3c dark green .20 .20

Red Cross Nurse — A91

1935, May 31 *Perf. 12*
163 A91 10c rose carmine 7.50 .25

50th anniv. of the founding of the Costa Rican Red Cross Society.

Air View of Cartago A92

Miraculous Statuette and View of Cathedral A93

Vision of 1635 — A94

1935, Aug. *Perf. 12½*
164 A92 5c green .20 .20
165 A93 10c carmine .30 .20
166 A92 30c orange .45 .20
167 A94 45c dark violet 1.10 .55
168 A93 50c blue black 1.75 1.00
Nos. 164-168 (5) 3.80 2.15

Tercentenary of the Patron Saint, Our Lady of the Angels, of Costa Rica.

Map of Cocos Island A95

1936, Jan. 29 *Perf. 14, 11½ (25c)*
169 A95 4c ocher .35 .20
170 A95 8c dark violet .50 .20
171 A95 25c orange .60 .20
172 A95 35c brown vio .75 .20
173 A95 40c brown 1.00 .20
174 A95 50c yellow 1.10 .60
175 A95 2col yellow grn 11.00 10.00
176 A95 5col green 30.00 25.00
Nos. 169-176 (8) 45.30 36.60

Exist imperf. Value, set, $50.
For surcharges see #196-200, C55-C56.

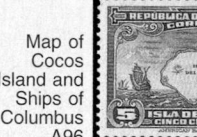

Map of Cocos Island and Ships of Columbus A96

1936, Dec. 5 *Perf. 12*
177 A96 5c green .30 .20
178 A96 10c carmine rose .45 .20

For overprints see Nos. 247, O80-O81.

Seal of Costa Rica Philatelic Society ("Diciembre 1937") — A97

1937
179 A97 2c dark brown .45 .20
180 A97 3c black .45 .20
181 A97 5c green .45 .20
182 A97 10c orange red .45 .20
Nos. 179-182 (4) 1.80 .80

Souvenir Sheet
Imperf
183 Sheet of 4 3.00 3.00
a. A97 2c dark brown .20 .20
b. A97 3c black .20 .20
c. A97 5c green .20 .20
d. A97 10c orange red .20 .20

Phil. Exhib., Dec. 1937.

Purple Guaria Orchid, National Flower — A98

Tuna — A99

Native with Donkey Carrying Bananas A101

3c, Cacao pod. 10c, Coffee harvesting.

1937-38 Wmk. 229 *Perf. 12½*
184 A98 1c green & vio ('38) .55 .20
185 A98 3c chocolate ('38) .35 .20

Unwmk. *Perf. 12*
186 A99 2c olive gray .40 .20
187 A101 5c dark green .55 .20
188 A101 10c carmine rose .90 .20
Nos. 184-188 (5) 2.75 1.00

National Exposition.

No. 125 Overprinted in Black

1938 Unwmk. *Perf. 12*
189 A77 20c deep blue 1.50 .20

No. 146 Surcharged in Red:

a

b

c

d

e

1940 *Perf. 12½*
190 A86(a) 15c on 45c blk vio .60 .30
190A A86(b) 15c on 45c blk vio .60 .30
190B A86(c) 15c on 45c blk vio .60 .30
190C A86(d) 15c on 45c blk vio .60 .30
190D A86(e) 15c on 45c blk vio .60 .30
Nos. 190-190D (5) 3.00 1.50

#190D exists with inverted surcharge. Value, $5.

Allegory A103

Overprinted "Dia Panamericano de la Salud / 2 Diciembre 1940" and Arc

1940, Dec. 2 Engr. *Perf. 12*
191 A103 5c green .20 .20
192 A103 10c rose carmine .35 .20
193 A103 20c deep blue .80 .50
194 A103 40c brown 1.50 1.50
195 A103 55c orange yellow 3.00 2.40
Nos. 191-195 (5) 5.85 4.80

Pan-American Health Day. See #C46-C54. Exist without overprint.

Stamps of 1936 Surcharged in Black:

1941 *Perf. 14, 11½*

196 A95 15c on 25c orange .50 .50
197 A95 15c on 35c brn vio .50 .50
198 A95 15c on 40c brown .50 .50
199 A95 15c on 2col yel grn .50 .50
200 A95 15c on 5col green 1.00 1.00
Nos. 196-200 (5) 3.00 3.00

Nos. 196-200 exist with surcharge inverted. Value, set of 5, $20.

National Stadium A104

Engr.; Flags Typo. in Natl. Colors

1941, May 8 *Perf. 12½*

201 A104 5c green .70 .20
a. Flags omitted 200.00
202 A104 10c orange .55 .30
203 A104 15c car rose .80 .40
204 A104 25c dk blue .85 .55
205 A104 40c chestnut 3.25 1.40
206 A104 50c purple 4.25 2.00
207 A104 75c red orange 6.75 5.75
208 A104 1col dk carmine 13.00 10.50
Nos. 201-208 (8) 30.15 21.10

Caribbean and Central American Soccer Championship. See #C57-C66, C121-C123.

No. 157 Surcharged in Black

1941 *Perf. 12*

209 A89 5c on 13c car rose .20 .20

Cleto González Viquez — A105

Design: 5c, José Rodriguez.

1941-45 Engr. *Perf. 12½*

210 A105 3c dp orange .25 .20
210A A105 3c dp plum ('43) .25 .20
210B A105 3c carmine ('45) .25 .20
211 A105 5c dp violet .25 .20
211A A105 5c brown blk ('43) .25 .20
Nos. 210-211A (5) 1.25 1.00

See No. 256.

Old University of Costa Rica A106

New National University A107

1941, Aug. 26 *Perf. 12*

212 A106 5c green .35 .20
213 A107 10c yellow org .40 .20
214 A106 15c lilac rose .75 .20
215 A107 25c dull blue 1.00 .35
216 A106 50c fawn 7.50 2.25
Nos. 212-216 (5) 10.00 3.20

National University, founded in 1940. See Nos. C74-C80.

Nos. 144, 189 Surcharged in Black or Red

1942 *Perf. 12½, 12*

217 A84 5c on 6c dk brn .35 .20
218 A77 15c on 20c dp bl (R) .65 .20

Nos. 217-218 exist with inverted surcharge. Value, each $10.

Torch of Freedom, "Victory" and Flags of American Nations A108

Juan Mora Fernández A109

1942, Sept. 25 *Perf. 12*

219 A108 5c rose .30 .20
220 A108 5c yellow grn .30 .20
221 A108 5c purple .30 .20
222 A108 5c dp blue .30 .20
223 A108 5c red orange .30 .20
Nos. 219-223 (5) 1.50 1.00

For overprints see Nos. 238-241.

1943-47 Engr.

Designs: 2c, Bruno Carranza. 3c, Tomas Guardia. 5c, Manuel Aguilar. 15c, Francisco Morazan. 25c, Jose M. Alfaro. 50c, Francisco M. Oreamuno. 1col, Jose M. Castro. 2col, Juan Rafael Mora.

224 A109 1c red lilac .20 .20
225 A109 2c black .20 .20
226 A109 3c deep blue .20 .20
227 A109 5c brt blue grn .20 .20
a. 5c bright green ('47) .20 .20
228 A109 15c scarlet .20 .20
229 A109 25c brt ultra 1.00 .20
230 A109 50c dp violet 3.00 .45
231 A109 1col black brown 4.00 2.00
232 A109 2col deep orange 5.00 3.00
Nos. 224-232 (9) 14.00 6.65

See Nos. 344-368, C81-C91A, C124-C127, C154-C158, C179-C181, C768-C772, C790-C794, C854-C858. For surcharges see Nos. C154-C158, C182, C184-C185.

View of San Ramón A118

1944, Jan. 19

233 A118 5c dark green .20 .20
234 A118 10c orange .20 .20
235 A118 15c rose pink .25 .20
236 A118 40c gray black 1.00 .80
237 A118 50c deep blue 2.40 1.60
Nos. 233-237 (5) 4.05 3.00

100th anniv. of the founding of the City of San Ramón. See Nos. C94-C102.

Catalogue values for unused stamps in this section, from this point to the end of the section, are for Never Hinged items.

Nos. 220-223 Overprinted in Red or Black

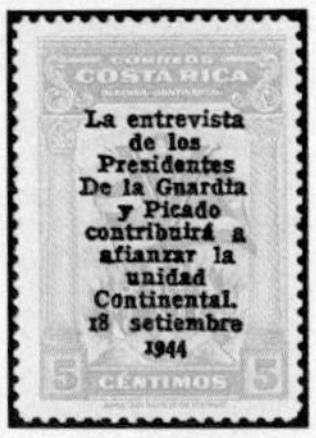

1944, Sept. 18

238 A108 5c yel green .30 .20
239 A108 5c purple (R) .30 .20
240 A108 5c dp blue (R) .30 .20
241 A108 5c red orange .30 .20
Nos. 238-241 (4) 1.20 .80

Amicable settlement of a boundary dispute with Panama. This overprint also exists on No. 219.

Mauro Fernández (1844-1905), Statesman — A119

Unwmk.

1945, July 21 Engr. *Perf. 14*

242 A119 20c deep green .30 .20

For surcharge see No. 246.

Coffee Harvesting — A120

1945, Oct. 9 *Perf. 12*

243 A120 5c dk green & blk .30 .20
244 A120 10c orange & blk .30 .20
245 A120 20c car rose & blk .40 .20
Nos. 243-245 (3) 1.00 .60

No. 242 Surcharged in Red Brown

1946 Unwmk. *Perf. 14*

246 A119 15c on 20c dp green .25 .20

Exists with inverted surcharge. Value, $6.

No. O80 Overprinted in Red

1947, Mar. 19 *Perf. 12*

247 A96 5c green .20 .20

Exist with inverted overprint. Value, $6.

Cervantes — A121

A122

Wmk. 215

1947, Nov. 10 Engr. *Perf. 14*

249 A121 30c deep blue .45 .20
250 A121 55c deep carmine .75 .35

Miguel de Cervantes Saavedra, novelist, playwright & poet, 400th birth anniv.

1947, Aug. 26 Unwmk. *Perf. 12*

251 A122 5c brt green .20 .20
252 A122 10c car rose .20 .20
253 A122 15c ultra .25 .20
254 A122 25c orange red .35 .25
255 A122 50c lilac .55 .30
Nos. 251-255,C160-C167 (13) 7.10 5.75

Franklin D. Roosevelt. For surcharges see Nos. C224-C226.

Small Portrait Type of 1941

Design: 3c, Bishop Bernardo A. Theil.

1948 *Perf. 12½*

256 A105 3c deep ultra .20 .20

Old University of Costa Rica A123

1953, June 25 Litho. *Perf. 12*

Black Surcharge

257 A123 5c on 10c green .35 .25

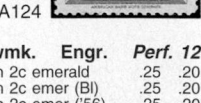

Revenue Stamp Surcharged in Red or Blue — A124

1955-56 Unwmk. Engr. *Perf. 12*

258 A124 5c on 2c emerald .25 .20
259 A124 15c on 2c emer (Bl) .25 .20
260 A124 15c on 2c emer ('56) .25 .20
Nos. 258-260,C341-C344 (7) 2.15 1.80

For surcharges see #C341-C344, C431-C433.

Justo A. Facio A125

Anglo-Costa Rican Bank A126

1960, Apr. 20 Photo. *Perf. 13½*

261 A125 10c brown red .40 .20

Centenary of the birth (in 1859) of Prof. Justo A. Facio. Exists imperf. Value, $35.

Nos. RA12-RA15 Surcharged in Red

1963, Mar.

262 PT3 10c on 5c dk car .35 .20
263 PT3 10c on 5c sepia .35 .20
264 PT3 10c on 5c dull grn .35 .20
265 PT3 10c on 5c blue .35 .20
Nos. 262-265 (4) 1.40 .80

1963 Unwmk. *Perf. 13½*

266 A126 10c gray .35 .25

Centenary of the Anglo-Costa Rican Bank.

Arms of San José — A127

Alberto M. Brenes Mora — A128

Coats of Arms: 35c, Cartago. 50c, Heredia. 55c, Alajuela. 65c, Guanacaste. 1col, Puntarenas. 2col, Limon.

1969, Sept. 14 Litho. *Perf. 14x13½*

267 A127 15c multicolored .30 .20
268 A127 35c multicolored .30 .20
269 A127 50c gray & multi .30 .20
270 A127 55c buff & multi .30 .20
271 A127 65c multicolored .75 .25
272 A127 1col pink & multi 2.50 .25
273 A127 2col multicolored 3.75 .60
Nos. 267-273 (7) 8.20 1.90

1976, Mar. 1 Litho. *Perf. 10½*

274 A128 1col violet blue .60 .20
Nos. 274,C653-C657 (6) 8.50 3.65

Prof. Alberto Manuel Brenes Mora, botanist, birth centenary.

Map of Costa Rica, Reader with Book — A129

1978, July 17 Litho. *Perf. 13½*

275 A129 50c multicolored .35 .20

National five-year literacy plan.

A130

A131

1983, May 17 Litho. *Perf. 13x13½*

276 A130 10c multicolored .35 .20
277 A130 50c multicolored .35 .20
278 A130 10col multicolored 1.25 .30
Nos. 276-278 (3) 1.95 .70

World Communications Year.

1983, May 30 Litho. *Perf. 10½*

279 A131 20col black 2.25 .55

1st World Cong. of Human Rights, 1982.

UPU Membership Centenary — A132

1983, June 30 Litho. *Perf. 16*

280 A132 3col #17, monument 1.10 .20
281 A132 10col #20, headquarters 2.25 .50

French Alliance Centenary — A133

1983, July 21 Litho. *Perf. 11*

282 A133 12col Scene in San Jose, by Christina Fournier 2.00 .50

Christmas 1983 — A134

Nativity tableau in continuous design. Illustration reduced.

1983, Dec. 5 Litho. *Perf. 13½*

283 1.50col multi .20 .20
284 1.50col multi .20 .20
285 1.50col multi .20 .20
a. A134 Strip of 3, #283-285 1.00 1.00

Costa Rican Gardens Association.

Fishery Development Administration A135

1983, Dec. 19 Litho. *Perf. 13½*

286 A135 8.50col multi .75 .30

Local Birds — A136

1984, Jan. 9 Litho. *Perf. 13½*

287 A136 10c Quetzal .50 .20
288 A136 50c Cyanerpes cyaneus .50 .20
289 A136 1col Turdus grayi .50 .20
290 A136 1.50col Momotus momota .50 .20
291 A136 3col Colibri thalassinus 1.40 .25
292 A136 10col Notiochelindon cyanoleuca 4.50 .30
Nos. 287-292 (6) 7.90 1.35

Dated 1983. 10c, 1.50col, 3col vert.

José Joaquin Mora, Hero of 1856 Independence Campaign — A137

Paintings, Juan Santamaria Museum, San José: 1.50col, Pancha Carrasco. 3 col, Death of Juan Santamaria, horiz. 8.50col, Juan Rafael Mora Porras.

1984, Apr. 10 Litho. *Perf. 10½*

293 A137 50c multi .20 .20
294 A137 1.50col multi .20 .20
295 A137 3col multi .25 .20
296 A137 8.50col multi .75 .50
Nos. 293-296 (4) 1.40 1.10

For surcharge see No. 440.

Jesus Bonilla Chavarria, Composer A138

Musicians and Composers: 5col, Benjamin Gutierrez (b. 1937). 12col, Pilar Jimenez (1835-1922). 13col, Jose Daniel Zuniga Zeledon (1889-1981).

1984, May 30 Litho. *Perf. 13½*

297 A138 3.50col black & lil .30 .20
298 A138 5col black & pink .40 .25
299 A138 12col black & grn 1.00 .75
300 A138 13col black & yel 1.10 .80
Nos. 297-300 (4) 2.80 2.00

Figurines, Jade Museum — A139

1984 Summer Olympics A140

1984, June 27 Litho. *Perf. 13½*

301 A139 4col Man (pendant) .75 .20
302 A139 7col Seated man 1.50 .35
303 A139 10col Dish, horiz. 2.00 .45
Nos. 301-303 (3) 4.25 1.00

1984, July 27

304 A140 1col Basketball .20 .20
305 A140 8col Swimming .60 .20
306 A140 11col Bicycling .80 .35
307 A140 14col Running 1.10 .60
308 A140 20col Boxing 1.60 1.00
309 A140 30col Soccer 2.50 1.25
Nos. 304-309 (6) 6.80 3.60

Public Street Lighting Centenary A141

1984, Aug. 9 Litho. *Perf. 10½*

310 A141 6col Street scene by Luis Chacon .50 .30

10th Natl. Stamp Exhibition, Sept. 10-16 — A142

1984, Sept. 10 Litho. *Perf. 10½*

311 A142 10col Natl. monument .80 .45
312 A142 10col Juan Mora Fernandez monument .80 .45
a. Min. sheet, 2 each #311-312 15.00 10.00

Natl. Arms — A143

1984, Oct. 29 Engr. *Perf. 14x13½*

313 A143 100col dk green 7.50 3.50
314 A143 100col yel org 7.50 3.50

Detail from Sistine Virgin by Raphael — A144

1984, Dec. 7 Litho. *Perf. 10½*

315 3col multicolored .25 .20
316 3col multicolored .25 .20
a. A144 Pair, #315-316 2.00 2.00

20th Intl. Bicycle Race, Costa Rica — A146

1984, Dec. 19 Litho. *Perf. 13½*

317 A146 6col multi .50 .30

Intl. Youth Year A147

1985, Jan. 31 *Perf. 10½*

322 A147 11col IYY emblem, #C476 1.50 .50

Scouting Movement, 75th anniv.

Labor Monument, San Jose — A148

Natl. values: 11col, Freedom of speech-wooden hand printing press. 13col, Neutrality-dove, natl. flag, outline map.

1985, Feb. 28

323 A148 6col shown .75 .30
324 A148 11col bl, blk & yel 1.25 .45
325 A148 13col multi 1.40 .50

Size: 68x38mm

326 A148 30col Nos. 323-325 4.00 1.10
Nos. 323-326 (4) 7.40 2.35

Natl. Red Cross Cent., UN 40th Anniv. A149

1985, May 3 *Perf. 10½*
327 A149 3col No. 163, horiz. 2.00 .20
328 A149 5col No. C120 3.00 .25

Club Emblem A150

1st Club Pres., Ricardo Saprissa Ayma A151

Design: No. 330, Hands holding soccer ball.

1985, July 16 *Perf. 10½*
329 A150 3col multi .50 .20
330 A150 3col multi .50 .20
a. Pair, #329-330 3.00 2.00
331 A151 6col multi 1.00 .30
Nos. 329-331 (3) 2.00 .70

Saprissa Soccer Club, 50th Anniv.

Orchids — A152

1985, Dec. 3
332 A152 6col Brassia arcuigera 3.25 .80
333 A152 6col Encyclia peraltensis 3.25 .80
334 A152 6col Maxillaria especie 3.25 .80
a. Strip of 3, #332-334 13.50 4.50
335 A152 13col Oncidium turialbae 3.25 1.40
336 A152 13col Trichopilia marginata 3.25 1.40
337 A152 13col Stanhopea ecornuta 3.25 1.40
a. Strip of 3, #335-337 13.50 4.50
Nos. 332-337 (6) 19.50 6.60

11th Natl. Philatelic Exposition A153

1985, Dec. 3 **Litho.** *Perf. 13½*
338 A153 20col No. C41 1.10 .50

Christmas 1985 — A153a

1985, Dec. 12 **Litho.** *Perf. 10½*
338A A153a 3col multi .35 .25

Compulsory Education, Cent. A154

Designs: 3col, Primary school, horiz. 30col, Mauro Fernandez Acuna, founder.

1986, Feb. 28 *Perf. 13½*
339 A154 3col pale yel & brn .20 .20
340 A154 30col pale pink & brn 1.50 .70

Agriculture Students — A155

1986, Mar. 21 *Perf. 10½*
341 10col Students on farm .40 .20
342 10col IDB emblem .40 .20
343 10col Capo Bianco fisherman .40 .20
a. A155 Strip of 3, #341-343 2.50 2.50
Nos. 341-343 (3) 1.20 .60

Inter-American Development Bank Annual Governors' Assembly, San Jose.

Presidents Type of 1943

Designs: Nos. 344, 349, 354, 359, 364, Francisco J. Orlich Bolmarcich, 1962-66.

Nos. 345, 350, 355, 360, 365, Jose Joaquin Trejos Fernandez, 1966-70.

Nos. 346, 351, 356, 361, 366, Daniel Oduber Quiros, 1974-78.

Nos. 347, 352, 357, 362, 367, Rodrigo Carazo Oido, 1978-82.

Nos. 348, 353, 358, 363, 368, Luis Alberto Monge Alvarez, 1982-86.

1986, May 12 **Litho.** *Perf. 10½*
344 A109 3col turq blue .35 .20
345 A109 3col turq blue .35 .20
346 A109 3col turq blue .35 .20
347 A109 3col turq blue .35 .20
348 A109 3col turq blue .35 .20
a. Strip of 5, #344-348 *2.00* *1.75*
349 A109 6col yel brn .60 .25
350 A109 6col yel brn .60 .25
351 A109 6col yel brn .60 .25
352 A109 6col yel brn .60 .25
353 A109 6col yel brn .60 .25
a. Strip of 5, #349-353 4.75 4.25
354 A109 10col brn org .90 .30
355 A109 10col brn org .90 .30
356 A109 10col brn org .90 .30
357 A109 10col brn org .90 .30
358 A109 10col brn org .90 .30
a. Strip of 5, #354-358 7.75 7.50
359 A109 11col slate gray 1.25 .40
360 A109 11col slate gray 1.25 .40
361 A109 11col slate gray 1.25 .40
362 A109 11col slate gray 1.25 .40
363 A109 11col slate gray 1.25 .40
a. Strip of 5, #359-363 10.00 9.00
364 A109 13col olive 1.50 .45
365 A109 13col olive 1.50 .45
366 A109 13col olive 1.50 .45
367 A109 13col olive 1.50 .45
368 A109 13col olive 1.50 .45
a. Strip of 5, #364-368 12.50 9.75
Nos. 344-368 (25) 23.00 8.00
Nos. 348a-368a (5) 25.00

1986 World Cup Soccer Championships, Mexico — A156

1986, May 30 **Litho.** *Perf. 13½*
369 A156 1col Players .30 .20
370 A156 1col Character trademark, vert. .30 .20
371 A156 4col as No. 370 1.25 .20
372 A156 6col as No. 369 1.75 .20
373 A156 11col Players, diff. 3.75 .35
Nos. 369-373 (5) 7.35 1.15

A second printing of No. 370 differs in paper and shade from the first printing, but the most obvious difference is in the absence of the initials "LIL" by the left foot of the soccer player. Unused stamps are rare. Value for used, $3.

Intl. Peace Year — A157

Gold Museum, Central Bank of Costa Rica — A158

Peace in many languages: a, "Hoa binh," etc. b, "Vrede," etc. c, "Pace," etc.

1986, July 31 **Litho.** *Perf. 10½*
374 Strip of 3 4.00 .20
a.-c. A157 5col, any single .50 .20

1986, Sept. 19 *Perf. 10½*

Designs: Various undescribed works of Pre-Columbian art.

375 Strip of 5 5.25 .90
a.-e. A158 6col any single .35 .25
376 Strip of 5 9.75 1.75
a.-e. A158 13col any single .75 .35

Exist perf 13½, value $10 for the two strips of 5 unused

A159

Fauna and Flora — A160

1986, Dec. 16 **Litho.** *Perf. 13x13½*
377 A159 2col Centurio senex .20 .20
378 A159 3col Glossophaga soricina .45 .20
379 A159 4col Ectophylla alba .60 .20
380 A159 5col Ectophylla alba, diff. .85 .20
381 A159 6col Agalychnis callidryas 1.00 .20
382 A159 10col Dendrobates pumilio 1.40 .20
383 A159 11col Hyla ebraccata 1.60 .20
384 A159 20col Phyllobates lugubris 2.40 .20
Nos. 377-384 (8) 8.50 1.60

Souvenir Sheet

Perf. 12½x12

385 A160 50col Agalychnis callidryas, diff. *60.00* *40.00*

Natl. Science and Technology Day — A161

Mural (detail), by Francisco Amighetti, Clorito Picado Social Security Clinic.

1987, July 31 **Litho.** *Perf. 10½*
386 A161 8col multi *6.00* .25

Natl. Museum, Cent. A162

Artifacts: No. 387a, Dowel-shaped figure of a man. No. 387b, Ape-like carved stone figurine. No. 387c, Polished stone ritual figure. No. 387d, Carved granite capital. No. 387e, Two-legged pot. No. 388a, Bowl. No. 388b, Sculpture. No. 388c, Water jar.

1987, Aug. 7
387 Strip of 5 3.75 1.90
a.-e. A162 8col any single, vert. .30 .20
388 Strip of 3 4.50 2.25
a.-c. A162 15col any single .60 .20
Nos. 387-388 (2) 8.25 4.15

Horse-drawn Wagon — A163

1987, Oct. 26
389 A163 20col shown .90 .45
390 A163 20col Street in old San Jose .90 .45
391 A163 20col Provincial coat of arms .90 .45
Nos. 389-391 (3) 2.70 1.35

City of San Jose, 250th anniv. Rotary Club, 60th anniv.

Columbus Day A164

1987, Oct. 26 *Perf. 10½*
392 A164 30col Map, 16th cent. 2.00 .50

Day of the Race; 495th anniv. of Columbus's departure from Palos, Spain, on first journey to the New World.

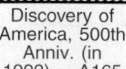

Discovery of America, 500th Anniv. (in 1992) — A165

Pres. Oscar Arias, 1987 Nobel Peace Prize Winner — A166

Maps of Honduras, Nicaragua, Costa Rica and Panama, believed to be Asia by Columbus: No. 393, Costa Rica, 16th cent. No. 394, Map of "Asia" by Bartholomeu Columbus (1461-1514).

1987, Nov. 20 **Litho.** *Perf. 13½*
393 A165 4col yel & dk red brn .20 .20
394 A165 4col yel & dk red brn .20 .20
a. Pair, #393-394 1.75 1.75

1987, Dec. 2 *Perf. 10½*
395 A166 10col multi *3.00* .20

Two Houses, a Watercolor by Fausto Pacheco (1899-1966)
A167

1987, Dec. 22 Litho. *Perf. 10½*

396	A167	1col multi	.50	.30

Intl. Year of Shelter for the Homeless.

17th General Conference for the Preservation of Natural Resources
A168

1988, Feb. 1 Litho. *Perf. 13½*

397	A168	5col Green turtle	.80	.25
398	A168	5col Emblem, golden toad	.80	.25
399	A168	5col Blue butterfly	.80	.25
a.		A168 Strip of 3, #397-399	2.50	2.50

Intl. Red Cross and Red Crescent Organizations, 125th Annivs. — A169

1988, Apr. 18 Litho. *Perf. 10½*

400	A169	30col lt blue & dark red	1.25	.50

North and South Campaign
A170

1988, June 6 Photo. *Perf. 11½*
Granite Paper

401	A170	18col Adult education	2.25	.20
402	A170	20col Cultural radio programs	2.25	.20

Cultural cooperation with Liechtenstein. See Liechtenstein #886-887. For overprint see #C921.

A171 A172

1988, June 27 Litho. *Perf. 10½*

403	A171	3col dk blue, dark red & yel	.35	.20

Anglo-Costa Rican Bank, 125th anniv.

1988, Sept. 16 Litho. *Perf. 13½*

404	A172	25col Character trademark	.95	.20
405	A172	25col Games emblem	.95	.20
a.		Pair, #404-405	2.25	2.25

1988 Summer Olympics, Seoul.

Girls' High School, Cent.
A173

1988, Oct. 17 Litho. *Perf. 10½*

406	A173	10col Student, courtyard	.50	.20

A174 A175

1988, Nov. 18

407	A174	10col gray, greenish bl & red brn	.35	.20

Educator Omar Dengo (1888-1928) and the Teachers' College, Heredia.

1988, Nov. 28 *Perf. 13½*

Indian glass-bead and lion-tooth necklace.

408	A175	4col multi	.20	.20

Discovery of America, 500th anniv. (in 1992).

A176 A177

1988, Dec. 26 Litho. *Perf. 10½*

409	A176	2col Observation tower	.60	.20

Natl. Meteorological Institute, cent. For surcharge see No. 439.

1989, Feb. 28

Designs: Indigenous flora.

410	A177	5col *Eschweilera costarricensis*	.50	.20
411	A177	10col *Heliconia wagneriana*	.95	.20
412	A177	15col *Heliconia lophocarpa*	1.25	.20
413	A177	20col *Aechmea magdalenae*	1.50	.20
414	A177	25col *Psammisia ramiflora*	1.75	.20
415	A177	30col *Passiflora vitifolia*	2.25	.20
		Nos. 410-415 (6)	8.20	1.20

A178

A179

1989, July 1 Litho. *Perf. 10½*

416	A178	30col Nation at Arms	1.25	.45

French Revolution, bicent.

1989, Aug. 28 Litho. *Perf. 13½*

417	A179	10col Sugar mill	.60	.20

Grecia County, 151st anniv.
For overprints see Nos. RA106-RA109.

America Issue — A180

UPAE emblem and pre-Columbian stone carvings: 50col, Three-footed bench for grinding corn. 100col, Sphere.

Litho. & Engr.
Perf. 12½x12

1989, Oct. 12 Wmk. 334

418	A180	50col multi	2.50	1.10
419	A180	100col multi	5.50	1.75

For overprint see No. C916.

A181 A182

Perf. 10½

1989, Oct. 23 Litho. Unwmk.

420	A181	10col Orchid	*2.00*	.20

"100 Years of Democracy" summit of Presidents.

Perf. 13½

1989, Nov. 27 Litho. Unwmk.

421	A182	18col Map, H.F. Pittier, emblem	.75	.20

Natl. Geographic Institute, cent.
For surcharge see No. 452.

America Issue — A183

Pre-Columbian gold frog figurine and facing portraits of Ferdinand V and Isabella I on gold coin struck by Spain from 1476 to 1516.

1989, Dec. 4 *Perf. 10½*

422	A183	4col multicolored	.25	.20

Discovery of America, 500th anniv. (in 1992).

Natl. Theater, Cent.
A184

Perf. 10½

1990, Feb. 27 Litho. Unwmk.

423	A184	5col *Coffee Allegory*	.60	.20

World Cup Soccer Championships, Italy — A185

1990, June 1 Litho. *Perf. 10½*

424	A185	5col multicolored	.25	.20

Univ. of Costa Rica, 50th Anniv.
A187

1990, Aug. 24 Litho. *Perf. 10½*

426	A187	18col multicolored	.75	.20

Education, Democracy, Peace — A188

Litho. & Engr.

1990, Oct. 31 *Perf. 12½*

427	A188	100col shown	2.25	1.10
428	A188	200col Flag as map	4.50	1.75
429	A188	500col National arms	12.00	6.00
		Nos. 427-429 (3)	18.75	8.85

"Invisible" security printing is sometimes visible.
For overprints see Nos. 448, C920.

Hospitals A190 America Issue A191

#431, St. Vincent de Paul Hospital, Heredia. #432, Natl. Psychiatric hospital.

1990, Dec. 18 Engr. *Perf. 13x12½*

431	A190	50col multicolored	1.10	.30
432	A190	100col multicolored	2.50	.55

1990, Dec. 21 Litho. *Perf. 10½*

433	A191	18col Ara macao	.90	.35
434	A191	18col Ara ambigua	.90	.35
a.		Pair, #433-434	5.50	5.50
435	A191	24col Cassia grandis	1.75	.35
436	A191	24col Tabebuia ochracea	1.75	.35
a.		Pair, #435-436	5.50	5.50
		Nos. 433-436 (4)	5.30	1.40

Costa Rica-Panama Border Treaty, 50th Anniv. — A192

Designs: a, Flags, national arms. b, Presidents. c, Map.

1991, May 24 Litho. *Perf. 10½*

437	A192	10col Strip of 3, #a.-c.	1.25	.50

Discovery of America, 500th Anniv. (in 1992) — A193

1991, Oct. 11 Litho. *Perf. 13½*

438	A193	4col multicolored	.70	.20

Nos. 409, 296 Surcharged

1991, Oct. 21 **Litho.** ***Perf. 10½***

439	A176	1col on 2col #409	.30	.20
440	A137	3col on 8.50col #296	.30	.20

Former Presidents, Supreme Court of Justice — A194

Designs: a, Benito Serrano Jimenez. b, Luis Davila Solera. c, Fernando Baudrit Solera. d, Alejandro Alvarado Garcia.

Perf. 14½x13½

1992, Feb. 28 **Litho.**

441	A194	5col Strip of 4, #a.-d.	1.75	.70

DINADECO, Natl. Directorate of Community Development, 25th Anniv. A195

1992, Apr. 28 **Litho.** ***Perf. 10½***

442	A195	15col multicolored	1.40	.35

Compare with No. C505.

A196

A197

1992, May 26 **Litho.** ***Perf. 13½***

443	A196	15col lake & black	1.25	.35

Dr. Solon Nunez Frutos, public health pioneer.

1992, July 17 **Litho.** ***Perf. 13***

Solar Eclipse: a, Total eclipse. b, Post Office Bldg. during eclipse. c, Partial eclipse.

444	A197	45col Strip of 3, #a.-c.	8.25	2.75

A198

A199

1992, Aug. 14 **Litho.** ***Perf. 13½***

445	A198	35col multicolored	1.25	.35

Interamerican Institute for Agricultural Cooperation, 50th anniv.

1992, Nov. 5 **Litho.** ***Perf. 10½***

446	A199	2col Waterfall	.25	.20
447	A199	15col Coastline	.35	.20

Cocos Island, 450th anniv. of discovery.

No. 427 Ovptd. "CENTENARIO / DE LIMON"

Litho. & Engr.

1992, Nov. 27 ***Perf. 12½***

448	A188	100col black & blue	2.10	1.00

America Issue A200

1992, Dec. 15 **Litho.** ***Perf. 10½***

449	A200	15col Anolis townsendi	*2.50*	.20
450	A200	35col Pinaroloxias inornata	*4.50*	.30

Natl. Theater A201

Detail from painting "Allegory of Fine Arts," by Roberto Fontana.

1993, Jan. 29 **Litho.** ***Perf. 10½***

451	A201	20col multicolored	.50	.20

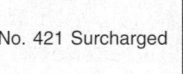

No. 421 Surcharged

1993, Mar. 26 **Litho.** ***Perf. 13½***

452	A182	5col on 18col multi	.50	.20

50,000 stamps originally were overprinted with a tiny block and four thin bars over the value, but this was considered unacceptable. So these stamps plus 1,550,000 unoverprinted stamps were overprinted with the large black square and surcharge, as shown.

Protection of the Dolphin A202

1993, May 17 **Litho.** ***Perf. 10½***

453	A202	10col Delphinus delphis	1.50	.30
454	A202	20col Stenella coeruleoalbus	3.00	.40

Costa Rican Civil Service, 40th Anniv. — A203

1993, May 28 **Litho.** ***Perf. 13½***

455	A203	5col multicolored	.45	.20

Costa Rican Chamber of Industries, 50th Anniv. A204

1993, July 15 ***Perf. 10½***

456	A204	45col multicolored	1.25	.75

School of Communication Sciences, University of Costa Rica, 25th Anniv. — A205

1993, Aug. 19 **Litho.** ***Perf. 13½***

457	A205	20col black, blue & red	.45	.25

Protection of the Tropical Rain Forest — A206

1993, Aug. 27 ***Perf. 10½***

458	A206	2col Passiflora vitifolia	.60	.20
459	A206	35col Gurania megistantha	1.40	.40

Social Guarantees and Labor Code, 50th Anniv. A207

1993, Sept. 14 **Litho.** ***Perf. 10½***

460	A207	20col multicolored	.45	.25

A208

A209

1993, Oct. 25 **Litho.** ***Perf. 13½***

461	A208	45col multicolored	1.00	.60

Intl. Assoc. of Professional Custom-House Agents, 15th Congress.

1993, Nov. 26 ***Perf. 10½***

462	A209	20col multicolored	.60	.25

Miguel Angel Castro Carazo (1893-1960), educator and humanitarian.

For surcharge see No. 481.

A211

A212

1993, Dec. 23 **Litho.** ***Perf. 10½***

464	A211	20col multicolored	.55	.25

Law School of Costa Rica, 150th anniv.

1994, Mar. 8 **Litho.** ***Perf. 13***

465	A212	20col Natl. Theater	.55	.25

Marine Life — A213

5col, Cyphoma gibbosum. 10col, Ophioderma rubicundum. 15col, Myripristis jacobus. 20col, Holocanthus passer. 35col, Paranthias furcifer. 45col, Tubastraea coccinea. 50col, Acanthaster planci. 55col, Ocypode. 70col, Arothron meleagris. 100col, Thalassoma lucasanum.

Litho. & Embossed

1994, Apr. 29 ***Perf. 12½x12***

466	A213	5col multicolored	.35	.20
467	A213	10col multicolored	.75	.20
468	A213	15col multicolored	1.10	.20
469	A213	20col multicolored	1.50	.35
470	A213	35col multicolored	2.50	.55
471	A213	45col multicolored	3.50	.75
472	A213	50col multicolored	3.75	.85
473	A213	55col multicolored	4.50	.95
474	A213	70col multicolored	5.50	1.25
		Nos. 466-474 (9)	23.45	5.30

Souvenir Sheet

Perf. 13

475	A213	100col multicolored	11.00	7.00

America Issue A214

Illustrations from 19th century Book of Figueroa: a, Man on horseback. b, Back of ox carrying bundles.

1994, Dec. 19 **Litho.** ***Perf. 10½***

476	A214	20col Pair, #a.-b. + label	1.75	1.00

No. 476 is a continuous design.

Rotary Intl., 90th Anniv. — A215

1995, Mar. **Litho.** ***Perf. 13½***

477	A215	20col multicolored	.80	.35

Antonio Jose de Sucre (1795-1830) A216

Guanacaste Institute, 50th Anniv. A217

Design: 30col, Jose Marti (1853-95).

1995, June Litho. *Perf. 10½*

478	A216	10col multicolored	.25	.20
479	A216	30col multicolored	.55	.25

1995, July 24 *Perf. 13½*

480	A217	50col grn, blk & bis	.95	.45

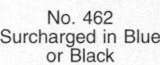

No. 462 Surcharged in Blue or Black

1995, Sept. 11 Litho. *Perf. 10½*

481	A209	5col on 20col multi	.30	.20

UN, 50th Anniv. — A218

13th Natl. Philatelic Expo — A219

1995, Oct. 24 Litho. *Perf. 10½*

482	A218	5col multicolored	.35	.25

1995, Dec. 1

Paintings by Lola Fernández: No. 483, Noviembre. No. 484, Enero.

483	A219	50col multicolored	.95	.45
484	A219	50col multicolored	.95	.45
a.		Pair, Nos. 483-484	2.75	2.75

America Issue A220

30col, Jabiru mycteria. #486, View of coast. #487, River, trees. 50col, Atta cephalotes.

1995, Dec. 25 Litho. *Rouletted 13½*

485	A220	30col multicolored	1.50	.75
486	A220	40col multicolored	1.50	1.00
487	A220	40col multicolored	1.50	1.00
a.		Pair, #486-487	3.50	2.75
488	A220	50col multicolored	2.00	.90
a.		Souvenir sheet, #485-488	12.00	7.00
		Nos. 485-488 (4)	6.50	3.65

Seaport City of Limón A221

Designs: a, Early picture of steam train. b, Photo of ship in port, 1922. c, Aerial view of seaport, 1995. d, Painting of fruit seller, by Diego Villalobos. e, Drawing of Calipso singers, by Jorge Esquivel.

1996, Jan. 31 Litho. *Perf. 10½*

489	A221	30col Strip of 5, #a.-e.	3.00	2.00

Jerusalem, 3000th Anniv. — A222

1996, May 17 Litho. *Perf. 13½*

490	A222	30col multicolored	.80	.55

1996 Summer Olympic Games, Atlanta A223

Olympic swimmers, coaches from Costa Rica: a, F. Rivas, M.M. Paris. b, S. Poll, R. Yglesias. c, C. Poll, A. Cruz.

1996, July 18 Litho. *Perf. 10½*

491	A223	5col Strip of 3, #a.-c.	1.50	1.00

No. 491 is a continuous design.

A224

A225

First lady, presidents: a, Juana del Castillo. b, Juan Mora Fernández. c, J.M. Castro Madriz. d, Pacífica Fernández.

1996, Sept. 13 Litho. *Perf. 10½*

492	A224	30col Block of 4, #a.-d.	3.00	1.00

Independence, 175th anniv. No. 492 was issued in sheets of 16 stamps.

1996, Oct. 4 Litho. *Perf. 13½*

493	A225	15col multicolored	.40	.20

Aqueducts and sewage systems, 35th anniv. Exists imperf.

A226

America issue (Paintings): No. 494, Black from Lemon, by Manuel da la Cruz González. No. 495, Peasant Women, by Gonzalo Morales Alvarado, vert.

1996, Dec. 16 *Perf. 10½*

494	A226	45col multicolored	1.10	.70
495	A226	45col multicolored	1.10	.70

A227

Entrance of the Saints at San Ramón, parade of people: a, Building with palm trees on top. b, Church on hill. c, Tree, holy family.

1997, Aug. 14 Litho. *Perf. 13½*

496	A227	30col Strip of 3, #a.-c.	3.00	1.25

Costa Rican traditions.

School of Fine Arts, Cent. A228

1997, Sept. 24 *Perf. 10½*

497	A228	50col multicolored	1.40	.60

Radio Netherlands, 50th Anniv. — A229

1997, Sept. 26 *Perf. 13½*

498	A229	45col multicolored	1.10	.55

Exists imperf.

14th Natl. Philatelic Exhibition A230

1997, Oct. 9 *Perf. 10½*

499	A230	30col Postmen	.65	.35

America Issue.

Church of the Immaculate Conception, Heredia, Bicent. — A231

1997, Nov. 10 Litho. *Perf. 10½*

502	A231	50col multicolored	1.25	.70

Second Republic, 50th Anniv. — A232

Former Pres. José Figueres demolishing wall of Fort Bellavista: 10col, 45col, Complete photo. 30col, Detail of Figueres' head. 50col, Hammer head hitting wall.

Litho. & Engr.

1998, Mar. 30 *Perf. 12½*

503	A232	10col multicolored	.60	.20
504	A232	30col multicolored	.90	.20
505	A232	45col multicolored	1.40	.20
506	A232	50col multicolored	1.50	.25
a.		Souvenir sheet of 2, #504, 506	3.25	3.25

Natl. University, 25th Anniv. — A233

1998, July 27 Litho. *Perf. 10½*

507	A233	50col multicolored	1.50	.75

Butterflies A234

10col, Caligo memnon. 15col, Morpho peleides. 20col, Papilio thoas. 30col, Siproeta stelenes. 35col, Ascia monuste. 40col, Parides iphidamas. 45col, Smyrna blonfildia. 50col, Callicore pitheas. 55col, Historis odius. 60col, Danaus plexippus.

1998, July

508	A234	10col multicolored	.75	.20
509	A234	15col multicolored	1.10	.30
510	A234	20col multicolored	1.50	.40
511	A234	30col multicolored	2.00	.60
512	A234	35col multicolored	2.40	.75
513	A234	40col multicolored	2.50	.85
514	A234	45col multicolored	3.00	1.00
515	A234	50col multicolored	3.50	1.10
516	A234	55col multicolored	3.75	1.25
517	A234	60col multicolored	4.50	1.25
		Nos. 508-517 (10)	25.00	7.70

1998 World Cup Soccer Championships, France — A235

1998, Feb. 27 Litho. *Perf. 10½*

518	A235	50col multicolored	1.25	.80

A236

A237

1998, Nov. 30 Litho. *Perf. 13½*

519	A236	50col brn, yel brn & lt yel	1.50	.55

Carmen Lyra (1888-1949), author.

1998, Dec. 11 Litho. *Perf. 13½*

520	A237	50col multicolored	1.25	.50

Gandhi (1869-1948).

Intl. Union for the Conservation of Nature, 50th Anniv. A238

Turtles: a, 70col, Rhinociemmys pulcherrima. b, 60col, Trachemys scripta. c, 70col, Chelydra serpentina.

1998, Dec. 1

521	A238	Strip of 3, #a.-c.	6.00	6.00

Mushrooms
A239

a, Morchella esculenta. b, Boletus edulis.

1999, July 2 Litho. *Perf. 10½*
522 A239 50col Pair, #a.-b. 3.75 3.75

SOS Children's Villages, 50th Anniv. — A240

1999, June Litho. *Perf. 10½*
523 A240 50col multicolored 1.25 .60

Costa Rican Institute of Electricity, 50th Anniv.
A241

1999, Sept. 21 Litho. *Perf. 13¼*
524 A241 75col multi .65 .45

A242

A243

1999, Oct. 7 Engr. *Perf. 13¾x14*
525 A242 300col violet 2.40 2.40

Archbishop Víctor M. Sanabria (1899-1952). See No. 538.

1999, Oct. 29 Litho. *Perf. 13¼*
526 A243 50col multi .60 .35

Intl. Year of Older Persons.

Supreme Election Tribunal, 50th Anniv.
A244

1999, Nov. 5 *Perf. 10½*
527 A244 70col multi .75 .45

UPU, 125th Anniv.
A245

Carmen Granados (1915-99), Humorist
A246

1999, Dec. 1 *Perf. 13¼*
528 A245 75col multi .70 .50

1999, Dec. 1
529 A246 50col multi .65 .40

America Issue, A New Millennium Without Arms — A247

1999, Dec. 1
530 A247 50col shown .75 .20
531 A247 70col Face, hands, diff. 1.00 .50

PhilexFrance '99 — A248

1999, Dec. 1
532 A248 300col shown 3.75 2.50
533 A248 300col Flower, Eiffel Tower 3.75 2.50

Natl. Bank, 50th Anniv. — A249

No. 534 — Pre-Columbian artifacts: a, Jaguar. b, Scorpion. c, Bat. d, Crab. e, Beast with horns.

No. 535 — Obverse and reverse of coins: a, Gold, from 1825. b, Gold, from 1850. c, Silver one-eighth peso. d, Gold 20-peso. e, 1935 1-colon.

2000, Jan. 28 Litho. *Perf. 13¼*
534 Vert. strip of 5 9.50 7.00
a.-e. A249 60col Any single 1.25 .60
535 Vert. strip of 5 22.50 12.50
a.-e. A249 90col Any single 3.00 1.50

2000 Summer Olympics, Sydney — A250

No. 536, 60col: a, Taekwando. b, Cycling. c, Swimming. d, Soccer.

No. 537, 70col: a, Running. b, Boxing. c, Men's rings. d, Tennis.

Illustration reduced.

2000, Aug. 31
Blocks of 4, #a-d
536-537 A250 Set of 2 7.50 7.50

There were two printings of Nos. 536-537. In the first printing, colors are paler, and the green Olympic ring is misregistered on Nos. 536a-536d. In the second, colors are more intense, and the green ring is properly registered. Values the same.

Famous Person Type of 1999

Pres. Rafael A. Calderón Guardia (1900-70).

2000 Engr. *Perf. 12½*
538 A242 100col deep blue 1.10 .50
a. Perf 13¾x14 3.25 1.50

Paintings by Max Jiménez — A251

No. 539: a, Fishermen in Cojimar. b, Adamant.
Illustration reduced.

2000, Nov. Litho. *Perf. 10½*
539 Horiz. pair 2.50 2.50
a.-b. A251 50col Either single 1.00 .50

America Issue, Fight Against AIDS — A252

Designs: 60col, Stylized people. 90col, Stylized person.

2000, Dec. *Perf. 13¼*
540-541 A252 Set of 2 1.75 1.50

Christmas — A253

2000, Dec.
542 A253 100col multi 1.25 .90

America Issue — UNESCO World Heritage
A254

Birds form Cocos Island Natl. Park: 95col, Coccyzus ferrugineus. 115col, Pinaroloxias inornata.

2001, Apr. 5 Litho. *Perf. 10½*
543-544 A254 Set of 2 3.50 2.50

Costa Rica — Netherlands Diplomatic Relations, 150th Anniv. — A255

2001, July
545 A255 65col multi .75 .50

No. 429 Surcharged

2001 Method and Perf. As Before
546 A188 65col on 500col multi .75 .50
547 A188 80col on 500col multi .90 .70
548 A188 95col on 500col multi 1.10 .80
Nos. 546-548 (3) 2.75 2.00

Issued: No. 846, 8/24. Nos. 547-548, 9/7.

Third Hispanic-Costa Rican Exposition — A256

Orchids: a, Guaria turrialba. b, Tricopilia.
Illustration reduced.

2001, Oct. 5 Litho. *Perf. 13¼*
549 A256 65col Horiz. pair, #a-b 2.00 2.00

Campaign Against Child Labor — A257

2001, Nov. 15 *Perf. 13¼*
550 A257 100col multi 1.25 .90

Pres. Tomás Guardia (1832-82) and Locomotive — A258

2001, Nov. 21
551 A258 65col multi 1.50 .60

A second printing of No. 551 was issued in 2002. It features a lighter beige and has yellow gum. This printing of 500 sheets of 15 stamps was made to complete the contract. Value, unused $25.

Costa Rican Team for 2002 World Cup Soccer Championships, Japan and Korea — A259

Illustration reduced.

2002, Mar. *Perf. 10½*
552 A259 65col multi .60 .40

No. 428 Surcharged in Red

Litho. & Engr.
2002, Jan. 24 *Perf. 12½*
553 A188 65col on 200col multi .75 .50

America Issue — Youth, Education and Literacy — A260

Designs: 65col, Children and globe. 100col, Blind person reading Braille.

Litho. & Embossed

2002, Mar. ***Perf. 10½***
554-555 A260 Set of 2 1.90 1.40

Taiwan Friendship Bridge A261

2002, Apr. 3 **Litho.**
556 A261 95col multi 1.00 .75

16th Rio Group Congress A262

2002, Apr. 10
557 A262 65col blue & green .75 .50

Pan-American Health Organization, Cent. — A263

No. 558: a, People (red denomination at UR). b, Emblem. c, Mother and child (black denomination at LR). d, Child and man (red denomination at LR).
50col, Emblem.

2002, July 5
558 A263 10col Block of 4, #a-d .60 .60
559 A263 50col multi .50 .40

In Remembrance of Sept. 11, 2001 Terrorist Attacks — A264

Litho. & Embossed

2002, Sept. 11
560 A264 110col multi 1.10 1.10

Marine Life of Uvita Island A265

Designs: No. 561, 75col, Gorgona flabellum. No. 562, 75col, Ulva lactuca. No. 563, 75col, Cittarium pica. No. 564, 75col, Liriope tetraphyla.

Litho & Embossed

2002, Sept. 25
561-564 A265 Set of 4 4.50 4.50

Space Exploration — A266

No. 565: a, Dr. Franklin Chang-Diaz, astronaut, and space shuttle. b, Phanaeus changdiazi and satellite.
Illustration reduced.

Litho. & Embossed

2003, June 15 ***Perf. 10½***
565 A266 115col Horiz. pair, #a-b 3.00 3.00

Coco Island National Park — A267

No. 566: a, Denomination at UR. b, Denomination at UL.
Illustration reduced.

2003, Aug. 1
566 A267 75col Horiz. pair, #a-b 2.25 2.25

America Issue - Fish — A268

No. 567: a, Archocentrus sajica. b, Astatheros diquis.
Illustration reduced.

2003
567 A268 110col Horiz. pair, #a-b 5.00 5.00

Scenes from Cocorí, by Joaquín Gutiérrez — A269

No. 568: a, Boy, turtle, monkey and bird. b, Boy looking at reflection in water. c, Toucan in tree, boy and monkey on ground. d, Sailor, girl and boy. e, Boy, bird on branch. f, Jaguar, turtle armadillo, monkey, boy and father. g, Boy and monkey pushing turtle. h, Monkey with open arms, turtle, boy. i, Mother and boy. j, Mother, boy, rose bush. k, Boy, father playing musical instrument (80x150mm).

Litho. & Embossed

2003, Sept. 3 ***Perf. 10½***
568 A269 Sheet of 11 7.00 7.00
a.-j. 25col Any single .35 .35
k. 225col multi 3.25 3.25

National Anthem, Cent. — A270

No. 569: a, Lyricist José Maria Zeledón (24x35mm). b, Flag, text of anthem (49x35mm).

2003, Sept. 10 **Litho.**
569 A270 75col Horiz. pair, #a-b 2.00 2.00

Election of Pope John Paul II, 25th Anniv. — A271

2003, Oct. 16 **Litho.** ***Perf. 13¼x13½***
570 A271 130col multi 1.75 1.75

Charles Lindbergh's Flight to Costa Rica, 75th Anniv. — A272

Litho. & Embossed

2003, Dec. 16 ***Perf. 13½x13¼***
571 A272 110col multi 1.50 1.50

Guayabo de Turrialba Archaeological Monument — A273

2003, Dec. 18
572 A273 110col multi 1.50 1.50

America Issue A274

Flora: No. 573, 75col, Ceiba pentandra. No. 574, 75col, Tetranema floribundum. 90col, Ceiba pentandra, diff. 110col, Tetranema gamboanum.

2004, Mar. 23 **Litho.** ***Perf. 10½***
573-576 A274 Set of 4 4.50 4.50

Volcanoes A275

Designs: 85col, Arenal. 120col, Irazú. 140col, Poás.

2004-05 ***Perf. 10½***
577-579 A275 Set of 3 4.50 4.50
577a Perf. 13¼ ('05) 1.10 1.10
578a Perf. 13¼ ('05) 1.50 1.50
579a Perf. 13¼ ('05) 1.75 1.75

Issued: Nos. 577-579, 6/24/04; 577a, 578a, 579a, 2005.
Nos. 577a, 578a and 579a have printer's inscription "LIL S.A."

2004 Summer Olympics, Athens A276

No. 580 — Various athletes in: a, Blue. b, Yellow orange. c, Green. d, Red.

2004, July 15
580 Horiz. strip of 4 6.00 6.00
a.-d. A276 120col Any single 1.50 1.50

Dr. Miguel Angel Rodríguez, Organization of American States President A277

2004, Sept. 15
581 A277 120col multi 1.50 1.50

FIFA (Fédération Internationale de Football Association), Cent. — A278

No. 582: a, Emblem (34x34mm). b, Soccer player and field (39x34mm).
Illustration reduced.

2004, Feb. 15 **Litho.** ***Perf. 10½***
582 A278 140col Horiz. pair, #a-b 3.75 3.75

Rotary International, Cent. — A279

No. 583: a, Emblem and frog. b, Centenary emblem. c, Emblem and butterfly.

2005, Feb. 23
583 Horiz. strip of 3 5.50 5.50
a.-c. A279 140col Any single 1.75 1.75

Souvenir Sheet

Popes — A280

No. 584: a, Pope John Paul II (1920-2005). b, Pope Benedict XVI.

2005, Aug. 22
584 A280 140col Sheet of 4, 2 each #a-b 7.00 7.00

An imperf. sheet lacking postal validity exists.

Intl. Year of Physics — A281

No. 585: a, Albert Einstein (1879-1955). b, Max Planck (1858-1947).

2005, June 7

585 Horiz. pair 2.50 2.50
a.-b. A281 95col Either single 1.25 1.25

Flora and Fauna in National Parks — A282

No. 586: a, Passiflora vitifolia. b, Dryas iulia moderata. c, Potos flavus.

2005, Oct. 11 Litho. *Perf. 10½*

586 Strip of 3 3.25 3.25
a.-c. A282 85col Any single 1.00 1.00

America Issue, Fight Against Poverty — A283

No. 587: a, Child at computer. b, Man sawing wood. c, Medical worker.

2005, Oct. 19

587 Strip of 3 4.50 4.50
a.-c. A283 120col Any single 1.60 1.60

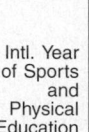

Intl. Year of Sports and Physical Education A284

2005, Dec. 6

588 A284 85col multi 1.00 1.00

Cartago Sport Club, Cent. — A285

Illustration reduced.

2006, Mar. 20

589 A285 85col multi 1.00 1.00

Miniature Sheet

National Campaign Against Nicaraguan Pres. William Walker, 150th Anniv. — A286

No. 590: a, Juan Rafael Mora, National Monument. b, Juan Santamaría Monument, barracks. c, Map (50x40mm). d, Gen. José María Cañas, Santa Rosa House. e, Luis Molina, Joaquín Bernardo Calvo.

2006, Apr. 7

590 A286 85col Sheet of 5, #a-e 5.00 5.00

2006 World Cup Soccer Championships, Germany — A287

2006, May 15

591 A287 120col multi 1.50 1.50

America Issue, Energy Conservation — A288

2006, July 31 Litho. *Perf. 10½*

592 A288 155col multi + label 2.00 2.00

Miniature Sheet

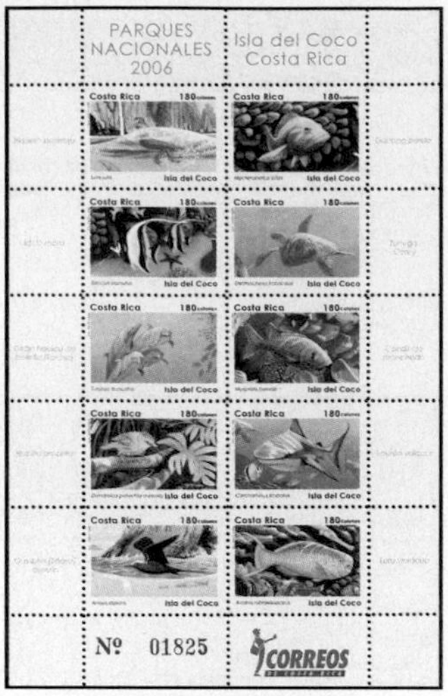

Birds and Marine Life of Cocos Island — A289

No. 593: a, Sula sula. b, Mycteroperca olfax. c, Zanclus cornutis. d, Eretmochely imbricaas. e, Tursiops truncatus. f, Myripristis berndti. g, Dendroica petechia aureola. h, Carcharhinus limbatus. i, Anous stolidus. j, Acarus rubroviolaceus.

2006, Aug. 25 Litho. *Perf. 10½*

593 A289 180col Sheet of 10, #a-j 25.00 25.00

Pres. José Figueres Ferrer (1906-90) — A290

2006, Sept. 25 *Perf. 10½*

594 A290 115col gray & multi + label 1.75 1.75

Souvenir Sheet

Imperf

595 A290 1000col tan & multi 15.00 15.00

Fruits A291

No. 596: a, Hymenaea courbaril. b, Bixa orellana. c, Garcinia intermedia.

2006, Oct. 12 *Perf. 10½*

596 Strip of 3 6.00 6.00
a.-c. A291 155col Any single 2.00 2.00

National Symbols — A292

No. 597: a, Flag. b, Coat of arms. Illustration reduced.

2006, Nov. 27

597 A292 155col Pair, #a-b 4.00 4.00

Printed in sheets containing two pairs.

Pres. Francisco J. Orlich (1907-69) — A293

2007, Mar. 7

598 A293 115col multi 1.50 1.50

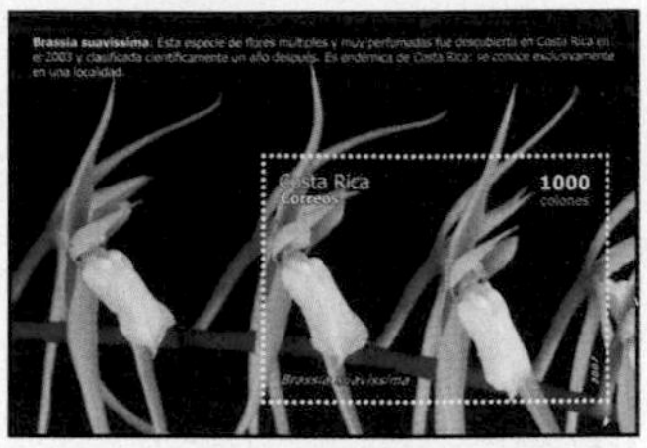

Orchids — A294

No. 599: a, Guarianthe skinneri (pink flowers). b, Galeandra arundinis. c, Encyclia ossenbachiana. d, Dracula inexperata. e, Guarianthe skinneri (white flowers). f, Kefersteinia retanae. g, Coryanthes kaiseriana. h, Psychopsis krameriana. i, Chondroscaphe yamilethae. j, Cattleya dowiana. 1000col, Brassia suavissima.

2007, Mar. 19 Litho. *Perf. 10½*

599 A294 180col Sheet of 10, #a-j 25.00 25.00

Souvenir Sheet

Imperf

600 A294 1000col multi 15.00 15.00

No. 599 contains ten 45x37mm stamps. No. 600 has simulated perforations.

Salesian Order in Costa Rica, Cent. — A295

2007, Apr. 30 *Perf. 10½*

601 A295 110col multi 1.50 1.50

Miniature Sheet

Pre-Columbian Art — A296

No. 602: a, Frog-shaped gold pendant (25x45mm). b, Bird-shaped jadeite pendant (25x45mm). c, Stone metate, horiz. (50x30mm). d, Ceramic censer with alligator (25x45mm). e, Stone figure of warrior (25x45mm).

2007, May 4
602 A296 155col Sheet of 5, #a-e 10.00 10.00

America Issue, Education For All — A297

No. 603: a, 115col, Teacher and students. b, 155col, Family around fire.
Illustration reduced.

2007, June 8
603 A297 Horiz. pair, #a-b 3.50 3.50

Plasma Technology — A298

No. 604: a, Astronaut and spacecraft's robot arm. b, Plasma containment vessel.
Illustration reduced.

2007, July 6
604 A298 240col Horiz. pair, #a-b 6.00 6.00

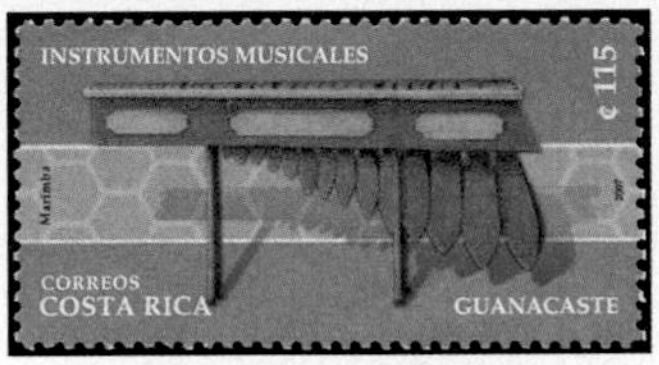

Guanacaste Musical Instruments — A299

Designs: No. 605, 115col, Marimba. No. 606, 115col, Quijongo, vert. (30x50mm).

2007, July 25
605-606 A299 Set of 2 2.75 2.75

Nos. 605-606 were printed in sheets containing two of each stamp + label.

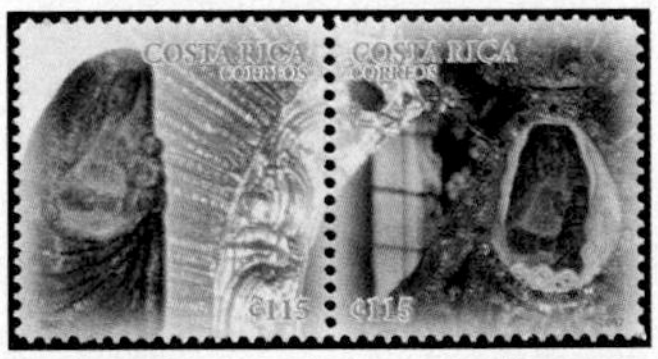

Virgin of the Angels Icon, 225th Anniv. as Patron of Cartago — A300

No. 607 — Icon with denomination at: a, LR. b, LL.
1000col, Interior of Cartago Basilica, vert.
Illustration reduced.

2007, July 27
607 A300 115col Horiz. pair, #a-b 2.75 2.75

Souvenir Sheet

608 A300 1000col multi 15.00 15.00

No. 608 contains one 75x115mm stamp.

Fauna of National Parks — A301

No. 609: a, Oxybelis fulgidus. b, Stagmomantis sp. c, Heliodoxa jacula. d, Pulsatrix perspicillata.

2007, Aug. 17 Litho. *Perf. 10½*
609 Horiz. strip of 4 3.75 3.75
a.-d. A301 235col Any single .90 .90

2007 Special Olympics, Shanghai — A302

No. 610: a, Cycling. b, Swimming. c, Running.

2007, Sept. 10
610 Horiz. strip of 3 2.75 2.75
a.-c. A302 240col Any single .90 .90

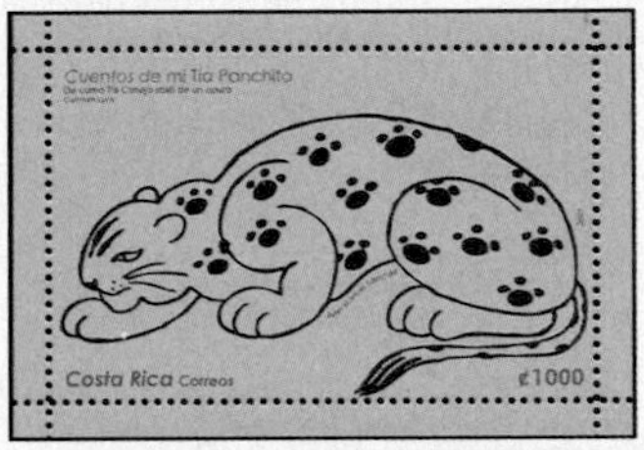

Accounts of My Aunt Panchita, Children's Book by Carmen Lyra — A303

No. 611, vert. — Text: a, Por qué Tío Conejo tiene las orejas tan largas. b, La Mica. c, Uvieta. d, Tío Conejo y los caites de su abuela.
1000col, De como Tío Conejo salió de un apuro.

2007, Oct. 18
611 A303 100col Sheet of 4, #a-d 1.60 1.60

Souvenir Sheet

612 A303 1000col multi 4.00 4.00

No. 611 contains four 37x50mm stamps.

Ox Cart Heritage — A304

No. 613: a, Man with oxen. b, Decorated wheel.

2007, Nov. 23
613 A304 180col Vert. pair, #a-b, + central label 1.50 1.50

Esquipulas II Central American Peace Accords, 20th Anniv. — A305

No. 614 — Nobel Peace medal of Pres. Oscar Arias Sánchez: a, Reverse (three men). b, Obverse (Alfred Nobel).

2007, Dec. 10
614 A305 135col Horiz. pair, #a-b 1.10 1.10

Dr. Fernando Centeno Güell (1907-93), Poet and Educator — A306

2008, Feb. 14
615 A306 115col multi .50 .50

Churches — A307

No. 616: a, Our Lord of Agony Chapel, Guanacaste. b, San Francisco Church, San José. c, Our Lady of Sorrow Church, San José. d, Santa Ana Church, San José. e, Our Lady of Carmel Cathedral, Puntarenas. f, San Bartolomé Apóstol Church, Heredia.
1000col, Our Lady of Mercy Parish Church, San José.

2008, Mar. 17
616 A307 230col Sheet of 6, #a-f 5.75 5.75

Souvenir Sheet

617 A307 1000col multi 4.00 4.00

No. 616 contains six 40x40mm stamps.

Souvenir Sheet

Women's Superior College, 120th Anniv. — A308

2008, Mar. 31
618 A308 1000col multi 4.00 4.00

Miniature Sheet

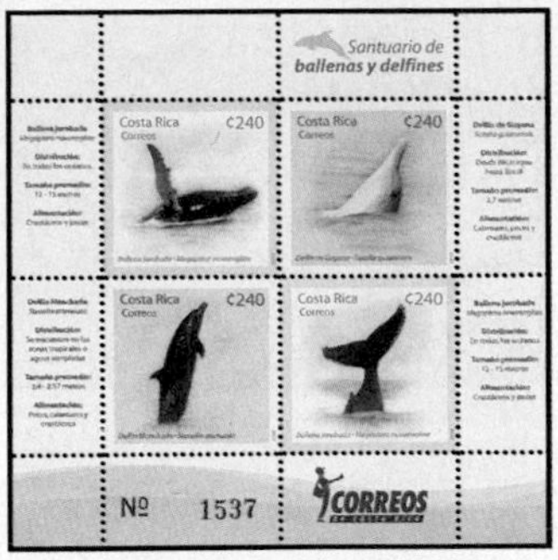

Marine Mammals — A309

No. 619: a, Megaptera novaeangliae, side view. b, Sotalia guianensis. c, Stenella attenuata. d, Megaptera novaeangliae flukes.

2008, June 16 Litho. *Perf. 10½*
619 A309 240col Sheet of 4, #a-d 3.75 3.75

Intl. Year of Planet Earth — A310

No. 620: a, San Vicente Cataracts. b, Santa Elena Peninsula.

2008, July 1
620 Pair 1.40 1.40
a.-b. A310 175col Either single .70 .70

Miniature Sheet

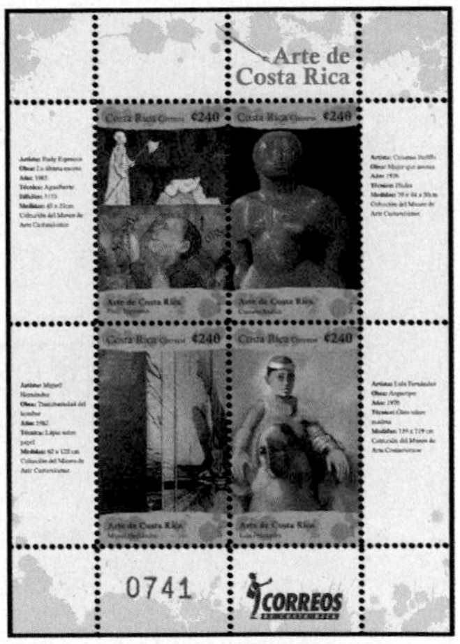

Art — A311

No. 621: a, La Ultima Escena, by Rudy Espinoza. b, Mujer que Avanza, sculpture by Crisanto Badilla. c, Transitoriedad del Hombre, by Miguel Hernández. d, Arquetipo, by Lola Fernández.

2008, July 3
621 A311 240col Sheet of 4, #a-d 3.75 3.75

Miniature Sheet

Ministry of Labor and Social Security, 80th Anniv. — A312

No. 622 — Details from mural "The Second Republic," by Luccio Ranucci: a, Man with hat, striped pole. b, Woman with basket of fruit. c, Man and woman embracing. d, Man carrying sack on head.

2008, Aug. 28 Litho. *Perf. 10½*
622 A312 240col Sheet of 4, #a-d 3.50 3.50

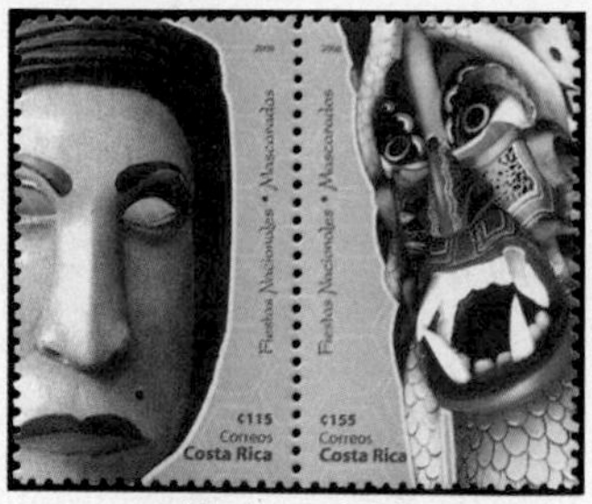

Masks — A313

No. 623 — Masks with background colors of: a, 115col, Brown orange. b, 155col, Green. Illustration reduced.

2008, Oct. 31

623	A313	Horiz. pair, #a-b	1.00	1.00

POSTAL-FISCAL STAMPS

From April 1884 through September 1889 revenue stamps were permitted for postal use, when post offices exhausted supplies of regular postage stamps.

Used values are for stamps with postal cancels.

PF1

PF2

1884 Engr. *Perf. 12*

AR1	PF1	1c rose	.50	*5.00*
AR2	PF1	2c light blue	*20.00*	5.00

1888

AR3	PF2	5c brown	.50	*3.00*
AR4	PF2	10c blue	.25	*3.00*

SEMI-POSTAL STAMPS

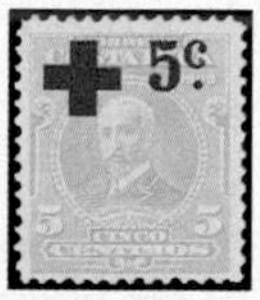

No. 72 Surcharged in Red

1922 Unwmk. *Perf. 12*

B1	A56	5c + 5c orange	1.00	.40

Issued for the benefit of the Costa Rican Red Cross Society. In 1928, owing to a temporary shortage of the ordinary 5c stamp, No. B1 was placed on sale as a regular 5c stamp, the surtax being disregarded.

Discus Thrower — SP1

Trophy — SP2

Parthenon SP3

1924 Litho. *Imperf.*

B2	SP1	5c dark green	1.50	*2.00*
B3	SP2	10c carmine	1.50	*2.00*
B4	SP3	20c dark blue	20.00	*20.00*
a.		Tête bêche pair	60.00	*60.00*

Perf. 12

B5	SP1	5c dark green	1.50	*2.00*
B6	SP2	10c carmine	1.50	*2.00*
B7	SP3	20c dark blue	3.00	*3.50*
a.		Tête bêche pair	14.00	*16.00*
		Nos. B2-B7 (6)	29.00	*31.50*

These stamps were sold at a premium of 10c each, to help defray the expenses of athletic games held at San José in Dec. 1924.

AIR POST STAMPS

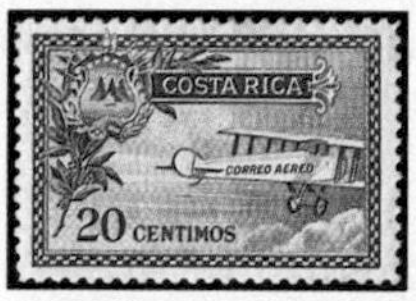

Airplane AP1

Perf. 12½

1926, June 4 Unwmk. Engr.

C1	AP1	20c ultramarine	3.00	.50

No. 123 Overprinted

1930, Mar. 14 *Perf. 12*

C2	A75	10c carmine rose	2.00	.25

Inverted or double overprints are fakes.

AP3

1930-32 *Perf. 12½*

C3	AP3	5c on 10c dk brn ('32)	.40	.25
C4	AP3	20c on 50c ultra	.50	.25
C5	AP3	40c on 50c ultra	.60	.25
		Nos. C3-C5 (3)	1.50	.75

The existence of genuine inverted or double surcharges of Nos. C3-C5 is in doubt.

Telegraph Stamp Overprinted

1930, Mar. 19

C6	AP3	1col orange	2.00	.50

No. O79 Surcharged in Red

1930, Mar. 11

C7	O7	8c on 1col lilac & blk	.65	.55
C8	O7	20c on 1col lilac & blk	1.00	.60
C9	O7	40c on 1col lilac & blk	2.00	1.50
C10	O7	1col on 1col lilac & blk	3.00	1.75
		Nos. C7-C10 (4)	6.65	4.40

AP6

AP7

Red Surcharge on Revenue Stamps

1931-32 *Perf. 12*

C11	AP6	2col on 2col gray grn	35.00	35.00
C12	AP6	3col on 5col lil brn	35.00	35.00
C13	AP6	5col on 10col gray blk	35.00	35.00
		Nos. C11-C13 (3)	105.00	105.00

There were two printings of this issue, which were practically identical in the colors of the stamps and the surcharges.

Nos. C11 and C13 have the date "1929" on the stamp, No. C12 has "1930."

Black Overprint on Telegraph Stamp

1932, Mar. 8 *Perf. 12½*

C14	AP7	40c green	3.00	.30
a.		Inverted overprint	30.00	

Unofficial "proofs," inverts and double overprints were made from a defaced plate.

Mail Plane about to Land AP8

Allegory of Flight AP9

1934, Mar. 14 *Perf. 12*

C15	AP8	5c green	.20	.20
C16	AP8	10c carmine rose	.20	.20
C17	AP8	15c chocolate	.35	.20
C18	AP8	20c deep blue	.40	.20
C19	AP8	25c deep orange	.50	.20
C20	AP8	40c olive blk	1.75	.20
C21	AP8	50c gray blk	.85	.20
C22	AP8	60c orange yel	1.50	.20
C23	AP8	75c dull violet	2.75	.45
C24	AP9	1col deep rose	1.50	.20
C25	AP9	2col lt blue	7.50	.90
C26	AP9	5col black	7.50	4.75
C27	AP9	10col red brown	10.00	8.00
		Nos. C15-C27 (13)	35.00	15.90

Nos. C15-C27 with holes punched through were for use of government officials.

See Nos. C216-C219. For overprints see Nos. C67-C73, C92-C93, C103-C116, CO1-CO13.

Airplane over Poás Volcano — AP10

1937, Feb. 10

C28	AP10	1c black	.45	.35
C29	AP10	2c brown	.45	.35
C30	AP10	3c dk violet	.45	.35
		Nos. C28-C30 (3)	1.35	1.05

First Fair of Costa Rica.

Puntarenas — AP11

National Bank AP12

Perf. 12, 12½

1937, Dec. 15 Unwmk.

C31	AP11	2c black gray	.20	.20
C32	AP11	5c green	.20	.20
C33	AP11	20c deep blue	.30	.20
C34	AP11	1.40col olive brn	2.50	2.50
		Nos. C31-C34 (4)	3.20	3.10

1938, Jan. 11 Wmk. 229 *Perf. 12½*

C35	AP12	1c purple	.20	.20
C36	AP12	3c red orange	.20	.20
C37	AP12	10c carmine rose	.30	.20
C38	AP12	75c brown	2.50	2.00
		Nos. C35-C38 (4)	3.20	2.60

Nos. C31-C38 for the Natl. Products Exposition held at San José, Dec. 1937.

Airport Administration Building, La Sabana — AP13

1940, May 2 Engr. Unwmk.

C39	AP13	5c green	.20	.20
C40	AP13	10c rose pink	.20	.20
C41	AP13	25c lt blue	.20	.20
C42	AP13	35c red brown	.20	.20
C43	AP13	60c red org	.30	.30
C44	AP13	85c violet	1.40	.90
C45	AP13	2.35col turq grn	6.00	5.50
		Nos. C39-C45 (7)	8.50	7.50

Opening of the Intl. Airport at La Sabana.

Duran Sanatorium AP14

Overprinted "Dia Panamericano de la Salud / 2 Diciembre 1940" and Bar in Black

1940, Dec. 2 *Perf. 12*

C46	AP14	10c scarlet	.20	.20
C47	AP14	15c purple	.20	.20
C48	AP14	25c lt blue	.35	.35
C49	AP14	35c bister brn	.65	.65
C50	AP14	60c pck green	.95	.95
C51	AP14	75c olive	2.50	2.50
C52	AP14	1.35col red org	8.00	8.00
C53	AP14	5col sepia	45.00	40.00
C54	AP14	10col red lilac	125.00	100.00
		Nos. C46-C54 (9)	182.85	152.85

Pan-American Health Day. Exist without overprint. Few examples of Nos. C53-C54 were sold for postal purposes, nearly all having been obtained by philatelic speculators.

No. 174 Surcharged in Black or Blue

1940, Dec. 17 *Perf. 14*

C55	A95	15c on 50c yel (Bk)	1.00	1.00
C56	A95	30c on 50c yel (Bl)	1.00	1.00

Pan-American Aviation Day, proclaimed by President F. D. Roosevelt.

The 15c surcharge exists normal and inverted on No. 171. Value, inverted, $30.

International Soccer Game at National Stadium — AP15

1941, May 8 *Perf. 12*

C57	AP15	15c red	.75	.20
C58	AP15	30c dp ultra	.85	.25
C59	AP15	40c red brn	.85	.35
C60	AP15	50c purple	1.25	.75
C61	AP15	60c brt green	1.50	.85
C62	AP15	75c yel org	2.50	1.40
C63	AP15	1col dull vio	4.50	4.25
C64	AP15	1.40col rose	9.00	8.75
C65	AP15	2col blue grn	20.00	17.50
C66	AP15	5col black	50.00	37.50
		Nos. C57-C66 (10)	91.20	71.80

Caribbean and Central American Soccer Championship. See Nos. C121-C123. For surcharges see Nos. C145-C147.

Air Post Stamps of 1934 Overprinted or Surcharged in Black with New Values and Bars

1941, June 2

C67	AP8	5c on 20c dp bl	.20	.20
C68	AP8	15c on 20c dp bl	.20	.20
C69	AP8	40c on 75c dl vio	.35	.20
C70	AP9	65c on 1col dp rose	.50	.50
C71	AP9	1.40col on 2col lt bl	3.25	3.00
C72	AP9	5col black	11.00	11.00
C73	AP9	10col red brn	14.50	12.50
		Nos. C67-C73 (7)	30.00	27.60

Issued in commemoration of the settlement of the Costa Rica-Panama border dispute.
Nos. C67-C73 are found with hyphen omitted in overprint.
Nos. C67-C69 exist with inverted overprint. Value, each, $35.

University Types of 1941

1941, Aug. 26 *Perf. 12*

C74	A107	15c salmon	.20	.20
C75	A106	30c lt blue	.30	.20
C76	A107	40c orange	.40	.30
C77	A106	60c turq green	.45	.40
C78	A107	1col violet	1.90	1.90
C79	A106	2col black	4.75	4.75
C80	A107	5col sepia	16.00	16.00
		Nos. C74-C80 (7)	24.00	23.75

Portrait Type of 1943-47

Designs: 40c, Manuel Aguilar. No. C83, Francisco Morazan. No. C83A, Jose R. De Gallegos. 50c, Jose M. Alfaro. 60c, Francisco M. Oreamuno. 65c, Jose M. Castro. 85c, Juan Rafael Mora. 1col, Jose M. Montealegre. 1.05col, Braulio Carrillo. 1.15col, Jesus Jimenez. 1.40col, Bruno Carranza. 2col, Tomas Guardia.

1943-45 **Engr.**

C81	A109	10c rose pink	.20	.20
C82	A109	40c blue	.20	.20
C82A	A109	40c car rose	.20	.20
C83	A109	45c magenta	.30	.20
C83A	A109	45c black	.20	.20
C84	A109	50c turq grn	1.60	.20
C84A	A109	50c red org	.30	.20
C85	A109	60c brt ultra	.60	.20
C85A	A109	60c brt green	.20	.20
C86	A109	65c scarlet	.90	.25
C86A	A109	65c brt ultra	.30	.20
C87	A109	85c dp org	1.10	.40
C87A	A109	85c dull pur	1.10	.40
C88	A109	1col black	1.50	.50
C88A	A109	1col scarlet	.60	.40
C88B	A109	1.05col bis brn	.80	.50
C89	A109	1.15col red brn	2.00	1.50
C89A	A109	1.15col green	2.75	1.25
C90	A109	1.40col dp vio	3.00	2.10
C90A	A109	1.40col org yel	1.60	1.40
C91	A109	2col black	4.75	1.25
C91A	A109	2col olive grn	1.50	.40
		Nos. C81-C91A (22)	25.70	12.35

Issued: Nos. C82A, C83A, C84A, C85A, C86A, C87A, C88A, C88B, C89A, C90A, C91A, 1945.

See Nos. C124-C127, C179-C181. For surcharges see Nos. C154-C158, C182, C184-C185.

Nos. C26-C27 Overprinted in Red or Blue

1943, Sept. 16

C92	AP9	5col black (R)	4.25	3.00
C93	AP9	10col red brown (Bl)	5.00	3.25

Mercury and Plane AP31

1944, Jan. 19

C94	AP31	10c red orange	.20	.20
C95	AP31	15c dk carmine	.20	.20
C96	AP31	40c brt ultra	.30	.20
C97	AP31	45c dp red lil	.35	.30
C98	AP31	60c turq green	.50	.40
C99	AP31	1col dk red brn	1.50	.80
C100	AP31	1.40col gray blk	8.25	5.00
C101	AP31	5col violet	22.50	15.00
C102	AP31	10col black	70.00	62.50
		Nos. C94-C102 (9)	103.80	84.60

City of San Ramón founding, 100th anniv.
Very few examples of the 5col or 10col stamps were sold for postal purposes, nearly all having been obtained by philatelic speculators.

No. CO10 With Additional Overprint in Black

1944, Nov. 22

C103	AP9	1col deep rose	2.00	.35
a.		Blue overprint	100.00	100.00

Nos. CO1-CO13 Overprinted in Carmine or Black

1945, Jan. 12 **Unwmk.** *Perf. 12*

C104	AP8	5c green	.60	.50
C105	AP8	10c car rose (Bk)	.60	.55
C106	AP8	15c chocolate	.60	.55
C107	AP8	20c deep blue	.50	.40
C108	AP8	25c dp org (Bk)	.60	.60
C109	AP8	40c olive blk	.35	.35
C110	AP8	50c gray blk	.60	.60
C111	AP8	60c org yel (Bk)	.90	.35
C112	AP8	75c dull violet	.75	.50
C113	AP9	1col dp rose (Bk)	.75	.35
C114	AP9	2col light blue	8.00	4.50
C115	AP9	5col black	8.00	5.50
C116	AP9	10col red brn (Bk)	11.00	8.25
		Nos. C104-C116 (13)	33.25	23.00

No. C104 exists inverted & overprinted in black. This is probably a trial color. Value, $50.

Catalogue values for unused stamps in this section, from this point to the end of the section, are for Never Hinged items.

AP32

Telegraph Stamps Overprinted in Black or Carmine

1945, Feb. 28 **Unwmk.** *Perf. 12½*

C117	AP32	40c green (C)	.25	.20
C118	AP32	50c ultra (C)	.30	.20
C119	AP32	1col orange (Bk)	1.00	.40
		Nos. C117-C119 (3)	1.55	.80

No. C117 exists with inverted overprint. Value, $10.

Florence Nightingale and Edith Cavell AP33

1945 **Engr.**

C120	AP33	1col black & car	1.00	.50

Costa Rican Red Cross Soc., 60th anniv
For surcharge see No. C183.

Soccer Type of 1941
Inscribed: "Febrero 1946"

1946, May 13 *Perf. 12*

C121	AP15	25c green	1.00	.60
C122	AP15	30c dull yellow	1.00	.60
C123	AP15	55c deep blue	1.40	.60
		Nos. C121-C123 (3)	3.40	1.80

Portrait Type of 1943-47

Designs: 25c, Aniceto Esquivel. 30c, Vicente Herrera. 55c, Prospero Fernandez. 75c, Bernardo Soto.

1946, May 12

C124	A109	25c blue	.20	.20
C125	A109	30c red brown	.25	.20
C126	A109	55c plum	.40	.30
C127	A109	75c blue green	.60	.40
		Nos. C124-C127 (4)	1.45	1.10

Hospital of St. John of God AP38

1946, June 24 **Unwmk.** *Perf. 12½*
Center in Black

C128	AP38	5c yellow grn	.30	.20
C129	AP38	10c dk brown	.35	.20
C130	AP38	15c carmine	.35	.20
C131	AP38	25c dk blue	.35	.20
C132	AP38	30c dp orange	.75	.25
C133	AP38	40c olive grn	.35	.20
C134	AP38	50c violet	.75	.25
C135	AP38	60c dk sl grn	1.50	.55
C136	AP38	75c brown	1.10	.40
a.		Horiz. pair, imperf. btwn.	100.00	
C137	AP38	1col blue	1.50	.35
C138	AP38	2col brn org	1.75	.70
C139	AP38	3col dk vio brn	3.75	1.75
C140	AP38	5col yellow	5.25	2.25
		Nos. C128-C140 (13)	18.05	7.50

Nos. C128, C129, C132 and C135 exist imperf.

Rafael Iglesias — AP39

3col, Ascensión Esquivel. 5col, Cleto González Viquez. 10col, Ricardo Jiménez Oreamuno.

1947, Jan. 15 **Wmk. 215** *Perf. 14*
Center in Black

C141	AP39	2col blue	1.50	1.00
C142	AP39	3col dp car	2.25	1.40
C143	AP39	5col dk green	3.75	1.90
C144	AP39	10col orange	6.50	4.50
		Nos. C141-C144 (4)	14.00	8.80

Nos. C141-C144 also exist in a souvenir sheet of 4. Value, $600. The sheet in sepia is a proof and worth less.

Nos. C121-C123 Surcharged in Black

1947, May 5 **Unwmk.** *Perf. 12*

C145	AP15	15c on 25c green	.90	.75
C146	AP15	15c on 30c dull yel	.90	.75
C147	AP15	15c on 55c dp blue	.90	.75
		Nos. C145-C147 (3)	2.70	2.25

Nos. C145-C147 exist with inverted surcharge.

Columbus in Cariari AP43

1947, May 19 **Engr.** *Perf. 12½*
Center in Black

C148	AP43	25c green	.25	.20
C149	AP43	30c dp ultra	.25	.20
C150	AP43	40c red orange	.35	.20
C151	AP43	45c violet	.55	.30
C152	AP43	50c brt carmine	.60	.20
C153	AP43	65c brown org	1.75	.80
		Nos. C148-C153 (6)	3.75	1.90

For surcharges see Nos. C178, C220-C223.

Nos. C84A, C85A, C127, C88A, and C88B Surcharged with New Value in Black or Red

1947, June 3 *Perf. 12*

C154	A109	15c on 50c red org	.30	.20
C155	A109	15c on 60c brt grn (R)	.30	.20
C156	A109	15c on 75c bl grn (R)	.30	.20
C157	A109	15c on 1col scar	.45	.20
C158	A109	15c on 1.05col bis brn	.30	.20
		Nos. C154-C158 (5)	1.65	1.00

No. C155 is known with black surcharge. Value, $10. No. C156 with inverted surcharge. Value, $10.

Early Steam Locomotive — AP44

1947, Nov. 10 *Perf. 12½*

C159	AP44	35c bl grn & blk	2.25	.50

Electric railroad to the Pacific coast, 50th anniv.

Roosevelt Type of Regular Issue

1947, Aug. 26 *Perf. 12*

C160	A122	15c green	.20	.20
C161	A122	30c car rose	.20	.20
C162	A122	45c red brown	.20	.20
C163	A122	65c orange yel	.25	.20
C164	A122	75c blue	.30	.20
C165	A122	1col olive grn	.50	.35
C166	A122	2col black	1.40	1.00
C167	A122	5col scarlet	2.50	2.25
		Nos. C160-C167 (8)	5.55	4.60

For surcharges see Nos. C224-C226.

National Theater AP46

Rafael Iglesias AP47

1948, Jan. 26 *Perf. 12½*

Center in Black

C168	AP46	15c brt ultra	.20	.20
C169	AP46	20c red	.20	.20
C170	AP47	35c dk green	.35	.20
C171	AP46	45c purple	.45	.25
C172	AP46	50c carmine	.45	.25
C173	AP46	75c red violet	1.00	.70
C174	AP46	1col olive	1.90	1.10
C175	AP46	2col red brn	3.00	1.50
C176	AP47	5col org yel	5.00	3.50
C177	AP47	10col brt blue	11.50	7.00
		Nos. C168-C177 (10)	24.05	14.90

50th anniversary of National Theater.

No. C150 Surcharged in Carmine

1948, Apr. 21

C178	AP43	35c on 40c	1.10	.45

Exists with surcharge inverted.

Portrait Type of 1943-47

5c, Salvador Lara. 15c, Carlos Duran.

1948 **Engr.** *Perf. 12*

C179	A109	5c sepia	.20	.20
C180	A109	10c olive brown	.20	.20
C181	A109	15c violet	.20	.20
		Nos. C179-C181 (3)	.60	.60

Nos. C88B, C120, C89A and C90A Surcharged in Carmine or Black

Perf. 12½, 12

1949, Aug. 28 **Unwmk.**

C182	A109	35c on 1.05col bis brn	.35	.20
C183	AP33	50c on 1col blk & car	.60	.45
a.		2nd & 3rd lines both read "125 Aniversario"	5.00	3.00
C184	A109	55c on 1.15col grn	.85	.70
C185	A109	55c on 1.40col org yel (Bk)	.90	.60
		Nos. C182-C185 (4)	2.70	1.95

125th anniv. of the annexation of the province of Guanacaste.

Overprint differs on No. C183, with "Guanacaste" in capitals, and lower case "a" in "Anexión."

The variety "l" for "i" in "Anexion" is found on Nos. C182, C184 and C185.

Symbols of UPU AP48

1950, Jan. 11 **Photo.** *Perf. 11½*

C186	AP48	15c lilac rose	.20	.20
C187	AP48	25c chalky blue	.35	.35
C188	AP48	1col gray green	.50	.50
		Nos. C186-C188 (3)	1.05	1.05

75th anniv. of the UPU.

Battle of El Tejar, Cartago AP49

Occupation of Limón — AP50

Bull (Cattle Raising) — AP51

25c, Lucha ranch. 35c, Trenches of San Isidro Battalion. 55c, 75c, Observation post. 80c, 1col, Dr. Carlos Luis Valverde.

Inscribed: "Guerra de Liberacion Nacional 1948"

Engraved; Center Photogravure

1950, July 20 *Perf. 12½*

Center in Black

C189	AP49	15c brt car	.20	.20
C190	AP50	20c dull green	.20	.20
C191	AP49	25c dull blue	.30	.20
C192	AP49	35c chestnut	.40	.20
C193	AP49	55c lilac	.70	.20
C194	AP49	75c red org	1.10	.30
C195	AP50	80c gray	1.10	.50
C196	AP50	1col org yel	1.50	.55
		Nos. C189-C196 (8)	5.50	2.35

2nd anniv. of the War for Natl. Liberation.

Inscribed: "Feria Nacional Agricola Ganadera e Industrial Cartago 1950"

1950, July 27

1c, 10c, 2col, Bull. 2c, 30c, 3col, Tuna fishing. 3c, 65c, Pineapple. 5c, 50c, 5col, Bananas. 45c, 80c, 10col, Coffee picker.

Center in Black

C197	AP51	1c brt green	.20	.20
C198	AP51	2c brt blue	.20	.20
C199	AP51	3c chocolate	.20	.20
C200	AP51	5c dp ultra	.20	.20
C201	AP51	10c green	.20	.20
C202	AP51	30c purple	.20	.20
C203	AP51	45c vermilion	.20	.20
C204	AP51	50c blue gray	.35	.20
C205	AP51	65c dk blue	.40	.20
C206	AP51	80c dp rose	.85	.60
C207	AP51	2col org yel	2.25	1.60
C208	AP51	3col blue	6.25	4.00
C209	AP51	5col carmine	7.25	6.00
C210	AP51	10col dp claret	7.25	6.00
		Nos. C197-C210 (14)	26.00	20.00

National Agricultural, Livestock and Industrial Fair, Cartago, 1950.

For surcharge see No. RA1.

Queen Isabella I and Caravels of Columbus AP52

Unwmk.

1952, Mar. 4 **Engr.** *Perf. 13*

C211	AP52	15c carmine	.25	.20
C212	AP52	20c orange	.45	.20
C213	AP52	25c ultra	.70	.20
C214	AP52	55c dp green	2.25	.25
C215	AP52	2col violet	4.75	.45
		Nos. C211-C215 (5)	8.40	1.30

Birth of Queen Isabella I of Spain, 500th anniv.

Mail Plane Type of 1934

1952-53 *Perf. 12*

C216	AP8	5c blue	.35	.20
C217	AP8	10c green	.35	.20
C218	AP8	15c car rose ('53)	.50	.20
C219	AP8	35c purple	1.40	.20
		Nos. C216-C219 (4)	2.60	.80

Nos. C216-C217 were reprinted in 1953 in different shades. Values the same.

Nos. C149-C151, C153 Surcharged in Red: "HABILITADO PARA CINCO CENTIMOS 1953"

1953, Apr. 24 *Perf. 12½*

Center in Black

C220	AP43	5c on 30c dp ultra	1.60	1.25
C221	AP43	5c on 40c red org	.30	.30
C222	AP43	5c on 45c vio	.30	.30
C223	AP43	5c on 65c brn org	.30	.30
		Nos. C220-C223 (4)	2.50	2.15

Nos. C161-C163 Surcharged in Black

1953, Apr. 11 *Perf. 12*

C224	A122	15c on 30c car rose	.30	.20
C225	A122	15c on 45c red brn	.30	.20
C226	A122	15c on 65c org yel	.30	.20
		Nos. C224-C226 (3)	.90	.60

Refinery of Vegetable Oils and Fats — AP53

Industries: 10c, Pottery. 15c, Sugar. 20c, Soap. 25c, Lumber. 30c, Matches. 35c, Textiles. 40c, Leather. 45c, Tobacco. 50c, Preserving. 55c, Canning. 60c, General. 65c, Metals. 75c, Pharmaceuticals. 80c, Pharmaceuticals. 1col, Paper. 2col, Rubber. 3col, Airplane maintenance. 5col, Marble. 10col, Beer.

Engraved; Center Photogravure

1954-59 **Unwmk.** *Perf. 13x12½*

Center in Black

C227	AP53	5c red	.20	.20
C228	AP53	10c dk blue	.20	.20
C229	AP53	15c green	.20	.20
C230	AP53	20c violet	.20	.20
C231	AP53	25c magenta	.20	.20
C232	AP53	30c purple	.50	.30
C233	AP53	35c red vio	.20	.20
C234	AP53	40c black	.50	.30
C235	AP53	45c dk green	.90	.30
C236	AP53	50c vio brown	.60	.20
C237	AP53	55c yellow	.45	.20
C238	AP53	60c brown	1.10	.55
C239	AP53	65c carmine	1.40	.80
C240	AP53	75c violet	2.10	.65
C240A	AP53	80c pur & gray	1.10	.65
C241	AP53	1col blue	.60	.30
a.		Imperf., pair	100.00	
C242	AP53	2col rose pink	1.90	1.00
C243	AP53	3col ol grn	2.75	1.50
C244	AP53	5col black	4.00	1.25
C245	AP53	10col yellow	12.00	8.00
		Nos. C227-C245 (20)	31.10	17.20

Issued: 30c, 35c, 60c, 65c, 75c, 2col, 3col, Oct. 20; 80c, Oct. 2, 1959; others, Sept. 1.

See Nos. C252-C255. For surcharges and overprint, see Nos. C314-C315, C334-C336, RA2, RA11.

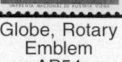

Globe, Rotary Emblem AP54

Map of Costa Rica AP55

25c, Hand protecting boy. 40c, 2col, Hospital. 45c, Globe & palm leaves. 60c, Lighthouse.

1956, Feb. 7 **Engr.** *Perf. 12*

C246	AP54	10c green	.20	.20
C247	AP54	25c dk blue	.20	.20
C248	AP54	40c dk brown	.35	.25
C249	AP54	45c brt red	.25	.20
C250	AP54	60c dk red vio	.30	.25
C251	AP54	2col yel org	1.25	.50
		Nos. C246-C251 (6)	2.55	1.60

50th anniv. of Rotary Intl. (in 1955).

Industries Type of 1954

Designs as in 1954.

Engraved; Center Photogravure

1956, Feb. 17 *Perf. 12*

Center in Black

C252	AP53	5c ultra	.30	.20
C253	AP53	10c violet blue	.35	.20
C254	AP53	15c orange yel	.45	.20
C255	AP53	75c red orange	.75	.30
		Nos. C252-C255 (4)	1.85	.90

1957, June 21 **Engr.** *Perf. 13½x13*

10c, Map of Guanacaste. 15c, Inn. 20c, House of Santa Rosa. 25c, Gen. Jose Manuel Quiros. 30c, Old Presidential Palace. 35c, Joaquin Bernardo Calvo. 40c, Luis Molina. 45c, Gen. Jose Joaquin Mora. 50c, Gen. Jose Maria Canas. 55c, Juan Santamaria monument. 60c, National monument. 65c, Antonio Vallerriestra. 70c, Ramon Castilla y Marquesado. 75c, San Carlos fortress. 80c, Francisco Maria Oreamuno. 1col, Pres. Juan Rafael Mora.

C256	AP55	5c lt blue	.20	.20
C257	AP55	10c green	.30	.20
C258	AP55	15c dp orange	.30	.20
C259	AP55	20c lt brown	.30	.20
C260	AP55	25c vio blue	.35	.20
C261	AP55	30c violet	.45	.20
C262	AP55	35c car rose	.50	.20
C263	AP55	40c slate	.50	.20
C264	AP55	45c rose red	.60	.20
C265	AP55	50c ultra	.65	.20
C266	AP55	55c ocher	1.00	.20
C267	AP55	60c brt car	.90	.30
C268	AP55	65c carmine	1.00	.30
C269	AP55	70c orange yel	1.10	.30
C270	AP55	75c emerald	1.25	.30
C271	AP55	80c dk brown	1.50	.35
C272	AP55	1col black	1.60	.35
		Nos. C256-C272 (17)	12.50	4.10

Centenary of War of 1856-57.

Cleto Gonzalez Viquez — AP56

Highway and Gonzalez Viquez AP57

Designs: 10c, Ricardo Jimenez Oreamuno. 20c, Puntarenas wharf and Jimenez. 35c, Post and Telegraph Bldg. and Jimenez. 55c, Pipeline and Gonzalez Viquez. 80c, National Library and Gonzalez Viquez. 1col, Electric train and Jimenez. 2col, Gonzales and Jimenez.

1959, Nov. 23 **Engr.** *Perf. 13½*

C274	AP56	5c car & ultra	.20	.20
C275	AP56	10c red & gray	.20	.20

Perf. 13½x13

C276	AP57	15c dk bl grn & blk	.20	.20
C277	AP57	20c car & brn	.50	.20
C278	AP57	35c rose lil & bl	.20	.20
C279	AP57	55c olive & vio	.50	.20
C280	AP57	80c ultra	.60	.35
C281	AP57	1col orange & mar	.85	.50
C282	AP57	2col gray & mar	2.00	1.60
		Nos. C274-C282 (9)	5.25	3.65

For surcharge and overprint see Nos. C337, C339.

Soccer AP58

Designs: Various soccer scenes.

Perf. 13½

1960, Mar. 7 **Unwmk.** **Photo.**

C283	AP58	10c black	.30	.25
C284	AP58	25c ultra	.30	.25
C285	AP58	35c red orange	.30	.25
C286	AP58	50c red brown	.35	.25
C287	AP58	85c Prus green	1.00	.75
C288	AP58	5col dp claret	2.40	2.40
		Nos. C283-C288 (6)	4.65	4.15

Souvenir Sheet
Imperf

C289 AP58 2col blue 5.50 5.50

3rd Pan-American Soccer Games, San José, Mar. 1960.
Nos. C283-C288 exist imperf. Value, pair $150.

WRY Uprooted Oak Emblem — AP59

1960, Apr. 7 Unwmk. *Perf. 11½*
Granite Paper

C290 AP59 35c vio bl, blk & yel .30 .25
C291 AP59 85c black & brt pink .60 .50

Refugee Year, July 1, 1959-June 30, 1960.

Banner and "OEA" — AP60

35c, "OEA" in oval. 55c, Clasped hands. 2col, "OEA" & map of Americas. 5col, Flags forming bird. 10col, Map of Costa Rica, flags & "OEA."

1960, Aug. 15 Litho. *Perf. 10*

C292 AP60 25c black & multi .20 .20
a. Multi, impression sideways 60.00
C293 AP60 35c multicolored .30 .30
a. Pair, imperf. between 60.00
C294 AP60 55c multicolored .50 .40
C295 AP60 5col multicolored 3.00 2.75
C296 AP60 10col black & multi 5.00 4.00
Nos. C292-C296 (5) 9.00 7.65

Souvenir Sheet
Imperf

C297 AP60 2col multicolored 2.75 2.75

Pan-American Conf., San Jose, Aug. 15.

St. Louisa de Marillac and Orphanage — AP61

St. Vincent de Paul — AP62

25c, St. Vincent & old seminary. 50c, St. Louisa & sickroom. 1col, St. Vincent & new seminary.

1960, Oct. 26 Engr. *Perf. 14x13½*

C298 AP61 10c green .20 .20
C299 AP61 25c carmine .20 .20
C300 AP61 50c dk blue .20 .20
C301 AP61 1col brown org .40 .30
C302 AP62 5col brown 2.00 1.60
Nos. C298-C302 (5) 3.00 2.50

St. Vincent (1581?-1660) and St. Louisa (1591-1660). Nos. C298-C302 exist imperf.

Runner AP63

Sports: 2c, Woman swimmer. 3c, Bicyclist. 4c, Weight lifter. 5c, Woman tennis player. 10c, Boxers. 25c, Soccer player. 85c, Basketball player. 1col, Baseball batter. 5col, Romulus and Remus statue. 10col, Pistol marksman.

Perf. 13½x14
1960, Dec. 14 Photo. Unwmk.
Designs in Black

C303 AP63 1c brt yellow .20 .20
C304 AP63 2c lt ultra .20 .20
C305 AP63 3c dp rose .20 .20
C306 AP63 4c yellow .20 .20
C307 AP63 5c brt yel grn .20 .20
C308 AP63 10c pink .20 .20
C309 AP63 25c lt bl grn .20 .20
C310 AP63 85c lilac 1.10 .75
C311 AP63 1col gray 1.25 .95
C312 AP63 10col lt violet 10.00 7.25
Nos. C303-C312 (10) 13.75 10.35

Souvenir Sheets
Perf. 14x13½

C313 AP63 5col multi 6.00 6.00

17th Olympic Games, Rome, 8/25-9/11.
Nos. C303-C313 exist imperf.

No. C255 Surcharged and Overprinted in Blue or Ultramarine: "XV Campeonato Mundial de Beisbol de Aficionados"

Engraved and Photogravure
1961, Apr. 21 *Perf. 12*
Center in Black

C314 AP53 25c on 75c red org (Bl) .25 .20
C315 AP53 75c red orange (U) .55 .20

15th Amateur Baseball Championships.

Alberto Brenes C. AP64

Miguel Obregon AP65

No. C317, Manuel Aguilar. No. C318, Agustin Gutierrez L. No. C319, Vicente Herrera.

1961, June 12 Photo. *Perf. 12*

C316 AP64 10c deep claret .25 .20
C317 AP64 10c blue .25 .20
C318 AP64 25c bright violet .25 .20
C319 AP64 25c gray .25 .20
Nos. C316-C319 (4) 1.00 .80

First Continental Congress of Lawyers, San José, June 11-15. Exist imperf.
See Nos. C330-C333.

1961, July 19 Litho. *Perf. 13½*

C320 AP65 10c Prussian green .30 .20

Birth centenary of Prof. Miguel Obregon L. Exists imperf. Value $50.

UN Food and Agriculture Organization AP66

UN day (UN Organizations): 20c, WHO. 25c, ILO. 30, ITU. 35c, World Meteorological Organization. 45c, UNESCO. 85c, ICAO. 5col, "United Nations" holding the world. 10col, Int. Bank for Reconstruction and Development.

Perf. 11½
1961, Oct. 24 Unwmk. Engr.

C321 AP66 10c lt green .20 .20
C322 AP66 20c orange .20 .20
C323 AP66 25c Prus grn .20 .20
C324 AP66 30c dk blue .20 .20
C325 AP66 35c carmine rose .85 .20
C326 AP66 45c violet .30 .20
C327 AP66 85c blue .65 .50
C328 AP66 10col dk sl grn 4.75 4.00
Nos. C321-C328 (8) 7.35 5.70

Souvenir Sheet
Imperf

C329 AP66 5col ultra 3.00 3.00

For overprint see No. C338.

Portrait Type of 1961

No. C330, Dr. José Maria Soto Alfaro. No. C331, Dr. Elias Rojas Roman. No. C332, Dr. Andres Saenz Llorente. No. C333, Dr. Juan José Ulloa Giralt.

1961 Photo. *Perf. 13½*

C330 AP64 10c blue green .25 .20
C331 AP64 10c violet .25 .20
C332 AP64 25c dark gray .25 .20
C333 AP64 25c deep claret .25 .20
Nos. C330-C333 (4) 1.00 .80

9th Congress of Physicians of Central America and Panama.

Nos. C229, C236 and C280 Surcharged in Black, Orange or Red

Engraved; Center Photogravure
1962 *Perf. 13x12½, 13½x13*

C334 AP53 10c ("10") on 15c .20 .20
C334A AP53 10c ("c0.10") on 15c (R) .20 .20
C335 AP53 25c on 15c .20 .20
C336 AP53 35c on 50c (O) .25 .20

Engr.

C337 AP57 85c on 80c (R) .90 .70
Nos. C334-C337 (5) 1.75 1.50

No. C336 exists with double surcharge. Value, $35.

Nos. C324 and C282 Overprinted in Red: "II CONVENCION FILATELICA CENTROAMERICANA SETIEMBRE 1962"

1962, Sept. 12 *Perf. 11½, 13½x13*

C338 AP66 30c dark blue .50 .40
C339 AP57 2col gray & mar 1.50 1.10

2nd Central American Phil. Convention.

Revenue Stamp Surcharged with New Values and "CORREO AEREO" in Red

1962 Engr. *Perf. 12*

C341 A124 25c on 2c emer .20 .20
C342 A124 35c on 2c emer .20 .20
C343 A124 45c on 2c emer .35 .30
C344 A124 85c on 2c emer .65 .50
Nos. C341-C344 (4) 1.40 1.20

Arms and Malaria Eradication Emblem AP67

1963, Feb. 14 Photo. *Perf. 11½*

C345 AP67 25c brt rose .20 .20
C346 AP67 35c brown org .25 .20
C347 AP67 45c ultra .30 .25
C348 AP67 85c blue grn .60 .40
C349 AP67 1col dk blue 1.00 .50
Nos. C345-C349 (5) 2.35 1.55

WHO drive to eradicate malaria.

Central American Tapir — AP68

Designs: 5c, Paca. 25c, Jaguar. 30c, Ocelot. 35c, Whitetail deer. 40c, Manatee. 85c, White-throated capuchin monkey. 5col, White-lipped peccary.

Perf. 13½
1963, May Unwmk. Photo.

C354 AP68 5c yel ol & brn .25 .20
C355 AP68 10c orange & sl .30 .20
C356 AP68 25c blue & yel .45 .35
C357 AP68 30c lt yel grn & brn .65 .35
C358 AP68 35c bis & red brn .95 .35
C359 AP68 40c emer & sl bl 1.25 .50
C360 AP68 85c green & blk 3.75 .50
C361 AP68 5col gray grn & choc 11.00 3.50
Nos. C354-C361 (8) 18.60 5.95

Stamp of 1863 and Packet "Monarch" — AP69

Issue of 1863 and: 2col, Recaredo Bonilla Carrillo, Postmaster, 1862-63. 3col, Burros, overland mail transport, 1839. 10col, Burro railway car.

1963, June 26 Litho.

C362 AP69 25c dl rose & chlky bl .25 .20
C363 AP69 2col gray bl & org 1.60 1.10
C364 AP69 3col bister & emer 2.75 1.75
C365 AP69 10col dl grn & ocher 9.75 5.00
Nos. C362-C365 (4) 14.35 8.05

Centenary of Costa Rica's stamps.
No. C362 is inscribed "William Le Lacheur," the builder and captain of the "Monarch."

Souvenir Sheets

Stamps of 1863 and San José Postmark — AP70

Perf. 13½, Imperf.
1963, June 26 Unwmk.

C366 AP70 5col bl, red, grn & org 4.25 4.25

Cent. of Costa Rica's stamps.
In 1968 examples of No. C366 were overprinted "2-4 Agosto 1968" and "III Exposicion Filatelica Nacional / 'Costa Rica 68'." Value, each, $10.

Animal Type of 1963 Surcharged in Red

No. C367, Little anteater. No. C368, Gray fox. No. C369, Armadillo. No. C370, Great anteater.

1963, Sept. 14 Photo. *Perf. 13½*

C367 AP68 10c on 1c brt grn & org brn 1.00 .30
C368 AP68 25c on 2c org yel & ol grn 1.00 .30
C369 AP68 35c on 3c bluish grn & brn 1.40 .30
C370 AP68 85c on 4c dp rose & dk brn 2.50 .55
Nos. C367-C370 (4) 5.90 1.45

Examples of #C370 exist without surcharge.

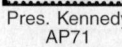

Pres. Kennedy
AP71

Ancestral Figure
AP72

Portraits- Presidents: 25c, Francisco J. Orlich, Costa Rica. 30c, Julio A. Rivera, El Salvador. 35c, Miguel Ydigoras F., Guatemala. 85c, Dr. Ramon Villeda M., Honduras. 1col, Luis A. Somoza, Nicaragua. 3col, Roberto F. Chiari, Panama.

1963, Dec. 7 Unwmk. *Perf. 14*

Portraits in Black Brown

C371 AP71 25c violet brn .30 .20
C372 AP71 30c brt lil rose .30 .20
C373 AP71 35c ocher .30 .20
C374 AP71 85c gray blue .45 .20
C375 AP71 1col orange brn .50 .30
C376 AP71 3col lt ol grn 2.40 1.50
C377 AP71 5col gray 3.00 2.25
Nos. C371-C377 (7) 7.25 4.85

Meeting of Central American Presidents with Pres. John F. Kennedy, San José, Mar. 18-20, 1963.

1963-64 Photo. *Perf. 12*

Ancient Art: 5c, Dog, horiz. 10c, Ornamental stool, horiz. 25c, Male figure. 30c, Ceremonial dancer. 35c, Ceramic vase. 50c, Frog. 55c, Bell. 75c, Six-limbed figure. 85c, Seated man. 90c, Bird-shaped jug. 1col, Twin human beaker, horiz. 2col, Alligator, horiz. 3col, Twin-tailed lizard. 5col, Figure under arch. 10col, Polished stone figure.

C378 AP72 5c lt yel grn & Prus grn .20 .20
C379 AP72 10c buff & dk grn .20 .20
C380 AP72 25c rose & dk brn .20 .20
C381 AP72 30c ocher & Prus grn ('64) .25 .20
C382 AP72 35c sal & sl grn .25 .20
C383 AP72 45c lt bl & dk brn .25 .20
C384 AP72 50c dl bl & dk brn .35 .20
C385 AP72 55c yel grn & dk brn .50 .20
C386 AP72 75c ocher & dk red brn .50 .20
C387 AP72 85c yel & red brn 1.25 1.25
C388 AP72 90c cit & red brn ('64) 1.60 1.60
C389 AP72 1col lt bl & dk brn ('64) .95 .30
C390 AP72 2col buff & dk grn ('64) 1.50 .60
C391 AP72 3col yel grn & dk brn ('64) 5.00 .90
C392 AP72 5col cit & sep ('64) 5.00 5.00
C393 AP72 10col rose lil & sl grn 8.25 8.25
Nos. C378-C393 (16) 26.25 19.70

For surcharges and overprint see Nos. C395, C397-C398, C400, C426-C428.

Flags of Central American States — AP73

Alfredo Gonzalez F. — AP74

1964 *Perf. 14*

C394 AP73 30c bl, gray, red & blk 1.00 .35

Central American Independence issue. For surcharge see No. C396.

Nos. C381, C394 and C387 Surcharged

1964, Oct. *Perf. 12, 14*

C395 AP72 5c on 30c .50 .25
C396 AP73 15c on 30c .50 .25
C397 AP72 15c on 85c .50 .25
Nos. C395-C397 (3) 1.50 .75

No. C388 Surcharged: "C 0.15 / CONFERENCIA POSTAL / DE PARIS — 1864"

1964 *Perf. 12*

C398 AP72 15c on 90c cit & red brn .45 .20

Paris Postal Conference.

1965, June Photo. *Perf. 12*

C399 AP74 35c dk blue green 3.00 .25

50th anniv. of the National Bank and honoring Alfredo Gonzalez Flores (1877-1962), 1st governor of the bank.

No. C390 Overprinted: "75 ANIVERSARIO / ASILO CHAPUI / 1890-1965"

1965, Aug. 14 Unwmk. *Perf. 12*

C400 AP72 2col buff & dk grn 1.25 .70

75th anniv. of Chapui Asylum, San José.

Girl, FAO Emblem and Hands Holding Grain — AP75

Church of Nicoya — AP76

FAO Emblem and: 15c, Map of Costa Rica and silos, horiz. 50c, World population chart and children. 1col, Plane over map of Costa Rica, horiz.

1965 Litho. *Perf. 14*

C401 AP75 15c lt brn & blk .25 .20
C402 AP75 35c black & yel .25 .20
C403 AP75 50c ultra & dk grn .25 .20
C404 AP75 1col grn, blk & sil .40 .25
Nos. C401-C404 (4) 1.15 .85

FAO "Freedom from Hunger" campaign.

1965, Dec. 20 *Perf. 13½x14*

5c, Leonidas Briceno B. 15c, Scroll dated "25 de Julio de 1964." 35c, Map of Guanacaste and Nicoya peninsula. 50c, Dancing couple. 1col, Map showing local products.

C405 AP76 5c red brn & blk .35 .20
C406 AP76 10c blue & gray .35 .20
C407 AP76 15c bis & slate .35 .20
C408 AP76 35c blue & slate .35 .20
C409 AP76 50c gray & vio bl .50 .20
C410 AP76 1col buff & slate 1.10 .35
Nos. C405-C410 (6) 3.00 1.35

Acquisition of the Nicoya territory.

Runner and Olympic Rings AP77

Pres. Kennedy Speaking in San José Cathedral AP78

Olympic Rings and Emblem: 10c, Bicyclists. 40c, Judo. 65c, Basketball. 80c, Soccer. 1col, Hands holding torches, and Mt. Fuji.

1965, Dec. 23 *Perf. 13x13½*

C411 AP77 5c bister & multi .20 .20
C412 AP77 10c lt lil & multi .20 .20
C413 AP77 40c multicolored .20 .20
C414 AP77 65c lemon & multi .25 .20
C415 AP77 80c tan & multi .35 .20
C416 AP77 1col multicolored .45 .30
a. Souvenir sheet of 2 6.00 3.00
Nos. C411-C416 (6) 1.65 1.30

18th Olympic Games, Tokyo, Oct. 10-25, 1964. No. C416a contains two 1col stamps, one like No. C416, the other with gray background replacing yellow orange.

No. C416a was issued both perf and imperf. Same values.

Nos. C411-C416 exist imperf.

Perf. 13½x13, 13x13½

1965, Dec. 23 Litho. Unwmk.

Designs: 45c, Friendship 7 capsule circling globe, and Kennedy, horiz. 85c, Kennedy and John, Jr. 1col, Curtis-Lee Mansion and flame from Kennedy grave, Arlington, Va.

C417 AP78 45c brt bl & lil .25 .20
C418 AP78 55c org & brt bl .30 .20
C419 AP78 85c gray, dk brn & red brn .50 .30
C420 AP78 1col multicolored .60 .40
a. Souvenir sheet of 2 1.10 1.10
Nos. C417-C420 (4) 1.65 1.10

President John F. Kennedy (1917-63). No. C420a contains two 1col stamps, one like No. C420, the other with green background replacing dark blue. Exists with light blue background instead of green; value $150.

No. C420a was issued both perf and imperf. Same values.

Nos. C417-C420 exist imperf.

For surcharges see Nos. C429-C430.

Firemen with Hoses — AP79

Designs: 5c, Fire engine "Knox," horiz. 10c, 1866 fire pump. 35c, Fireman's badge. 50c, Emblem and flags of Confederation of Central American Fire Brigades.

1966, Mar. 12 Litho. *Perf. 11*

C421 AP79 5c black & red .30 .20
C422 AP79 10c bister & red .35 .20
C423 AP79 15c blk, red brn & red .55 .20
C424 AP79 35c black & yel .90 .25
C425 AP79 50c dk blue & red 1.90 .35
Nos. C421-C425 (5) 4.00 1.20

Centenary of San José Fire Brigade.

Nos. C381, C383, C386 and C418-C419 Surcharged

a

b

1966 Photo. *Perf. 12*

C426 AP72(a) 15c on 30c .20 .20
C427 AP72(a) 15c on 45c .20 .20
C428 AP72(a) 35c on 75c .20 .20

Litho. *Perf. 13x13½*

C429 AP78(a) 35c on 55c .20 .20
C430 AP78(b) 50c on 85c .45 .20
Nos. C426-C430 (5) 1.25 1.00

Revenue Stamps (Basic Type of A124) Surcharged

1966, Dec. Engr. *Perf. 12*

C431 A124 15c on 5c blue .20 .20
C432 A124 35c on 10c claret .30 .20
C433 A124 50c on 20c rose red .45 .25
Nos. C431-C433 (3) .95 .65

Central Bank of Costa Rica — AP80

1967, Mar. Litho. *Perf. 11*

C434 AP80 5c brt green .35 .20
C435 AP80 15c brown .35 .20
C436 AP80 35c scarlet .35 .20
Nos. C434-C436 (3) 1.05 .60

Power Lines — AP81

Telecommunications Building, San Pedro — AP82

Electrification Program: 15c, Telephone Central. 25c, La Garita Dam. 35c, Rio Mache Reservoir. 50c, Cachi Dam.

1967, Apr. 24 Litho. *Perf. 11*

C437 AP81 5c dark gray .25 .20
C438 AP82 10c brt rose .25 .20
C439 AP81 15c brown org .25 .20
C440 AP82 25c brt ultra .25 .20
C441 AP82 35c brt green .30 .20
C442 AP82 50c red brown .40 .30
Nos. C437-C442 (6) 1.70 1.30

Chondrorhyncha Aromatica AP83

Institute Emblem AP84

Orchids: 10c, Miltonia endresii. 15c, Stanhopea cirrhata. 25c, Trichopilia suavis. 35c, Odontoglossum schlieperianum. 50c, Cattleya skinneri. 1col, Cattleya dowiana. 2col, Odontoglossum chiriquense.

1967, June 15 Engr. *Perf. 13x13½*

Orchids in Natural Colors

C443 AP83 5c multicolored .20 .20
C444 AP83 10c olive & multi .35 .25
C445 AP83 15c multicolored .50 .25
C446 AP83 25c multicolored .90 .25
C447 AP83 35c dull vio & multi 1.25 .25
C448 AP83 50c brown & multi 1.50 .25
C449 AP83 1col vio & multi 3.25 .75

C450 AP83 2col dk ol bis & multi 5.50 1.50
Nos. C443-C450 (8) 13.45 3.70

Issued for the University Library.

1967, Oct. 6 Litho. *Perf. 13x13½*

C451 AP84 50c vio bl, lt bl & bl .35 .20

Inter-American Agriculture Institute, 25th anniv.

Church of Solitude — AP85

LACSA Emblem — AP86

Costa Rican Churches: 10c, Basilica of Santo Domingo, Heredia. 15c, Cathedral of Tilaran. 25c, Cathedral of Alajuela. 30c, Mercy Church. 35c, Basilica of Our Lady of Angels. 40c, Church of St. Raphael, Heredia. 45c, Ujarras ruins. 50c, Ruins of parish church, Cartago. 55c, Cathedral of San José. 65c, Parish church, Puntarenas. 75c, Church of Orosi. 80c, Cathedral of St. Isidro, the General. 85c, St. Ramon Church. 90c, Church of the Abandoned. 1col, Coronado Church. 2col, Church of St. Teresita. 3col, Parish Church, Heredia. 5col, Carmelite Church. 10col, Limon Cathedral.

1967, Dec. 15 Engr. *Perf. 12½*

C452 AP85 5c green .20 .20
C453 AP85 10c blue .20 .20
C454 AP85 15c lilac .20 .20
C455 AP85 25c dull yel .20 .20
C456 AP85 30c orange brn .20 .20
C457 AP85 35c lt blue .25 .20
C458 AP85 40c dp orange .25 .20
C459 AP85 45c dl bl grn .25 .20
C460 AP85 50c olive .35 .20
C461 AP85 55c brown .35 .20
C462 AP85 65c car rose .60 .25
C463 AP85 75c sepia .65 .30
C464 AP85 80c yellow 1.25 .45
C465 AP85 85c violet blk 1.40 .45
C466 AP85 90c emerald 1.40 .65
C467 AP85 1col slate 1.10 .35
C468 AP85 2col brt green 5.00 1.75
C469 AP85 3col orange 7.25 3.00
C470 AP85 5col vio blue 7.25 3.00
C471 AP85 10col carmine 9.75 4.50
Nos. C452-C471 (20) 38.10 16.70

Nos. C452 and C454 exist imperf; Nos. C455 and C470 exist imperf horiz.

See Nos. C561-C576.

Perf. 13x13½, 13½x13

1967, Dec. 12 Litho. & Engr.

45c, LACSA emblem, jet, horiz. 50c, Decorated wheel, anniversary emblem.

C472 AP86 40c ultra, grnsh bl & gold .25 .20
C473 AP86 45c blk, pale grn, ultra & gold .30 .20
C474 AP86 50c blue & multi .35 .20
Nos. C472-C474 (3) .90 .60

20th anniv. (in 1966) of Lineas Aereas Costaricenses, LACSA, Costa Rican Airlines.

Scout Directing Traffic AP87

Runner AP88

Designs: 25c, Campfire under palm tree. 35c, Flag of Costa Rica, Scout flag and emblem. 50c, Encampment, horiz. 65c, Photograph of first Scout troop, horiz.

1968, Mar. 15 *Perf. 13*

C475 AP87 15c lt bl, blk & lt brn .20 .20
C476 AP87 25c lt ultra, vio bl & org .25 .20
C477 AP87 35c blue & multi .35 .20
C478 AP87 50c multicolored .60 .30
C479 AP87 65c sal, dk bl & brn .75 .35
Nos. C475-C479 (5) 2.15 1.25

Costa Rican Boy Scouts, 50th anniversary.

1968, Jan. 17 Litho. *Perf. 10x11*

Sports: 40c, Women's running. 55c, Boxing. 65c, Bicycling. 75c, Weight lifting. 1col, High diving. 3col, Rifle shooting.

C481 AP88 30c multi .20 .20
C482 AP88 40c multi .20 .20
C483 AP88 55c multi .25 .20
C484 AP88 65c lil & multi .30 .20
C485 AP88 75c multi .30 .20
C486 AP88 1col multi .35 .25
C487 AP88 3col multi 1.50 .90
Nos. C481-C487 (7) 3.10 2.15

19th Olympic Games, Mexico City, 10/12-27.

Philatelic Exhibition Emblem — AP89

1969, June 5 Litho. *Perf. 11x10*

C488 AP89 35c multicolored .20 .20
C489 AP89 40c pink & multi .20 .20
C490 AP89 50c lt blue & multi .25 .20
C491 AP89 2col multicolored .90 .50
Nos. C488-C491 (4) 1.55 1.10

4th Natl. Philatelic Exhib., San José, 6/5-8.

ILO Emblem AP90

1969, Oct. 29 Litho. *Perf. 10*

C492 AP90 35c bl grn & blk .25 .20
C493 AP90 50c scarlet & blk .25 .20

50th anniv. of the ILO.

Soccer — AP91

Stylized Crab — AP92

Designs: 65c, Soccer ball, map of North and Central America. 85c, Soccer player. 1col, Two players in action.

1969, Nov. 23 Litho. *Perf. 11x10*

C494 AP91 65c gray & multi .30 .20
C495 AP91 75c multicolored .30 .20
C496 AP91 85c multicolored .35 .30
C497 AP91 1col pink & multi .50 .35
Nos. C494-C497 (4) 1.45 1.05

Issued to publicize the 4th Soccer Championships (CONCACAF), Nov. 23-Dec. 7.

1970, May 14 Litho. *Perf. 12½*

C498 AP92 10c blk & lil rose .25 .20
C499 AP92 15c blk & yel .25 .20
C500 AP92 50c blk & brn org .25 .20
C501 AP92 1.10col blk & emer .50 .20
Nos. C498-C501 (4) 1.25 .80

10th Inter-American Cancer Cong., 5/22-29.

Costa Rica No. 124, Magnifying Glass and Stamps — AP93

2col, Father, son with stamps, album.

1970, Sept. 14 Litho. *Perf. 11*

C502 AP93 1col ultra, brn & car rose .95 .20
C503 AP93 2col blk, pink & ultra 1.10 .50

The 5th National Philatelic Exhibition.

EXPO Emblem and Costa Rican Cart — AP94

EXPO Emblem and: 10c, Japanese floral arrangement, vert. 35c, Pavilion and Tower of the Sun. 40c, Japanese tea ceremony. 45c, Woman picking coffee, vert. 55c, Earth seen from moon, vert.

1970, Oct. 22 Litho. *Perf. 13x13½*

C504 AP94 10c multicolored .20 .20
C505 AP94 15c green & multi .20 .20
C506 AP94 35c blue & multi .35 .20
C507 AP94 40c gray & multi .50 .20
C508 AP94 45c multicolored .50 .20
C509 AP94 55c black & multi 2.25 .30
Nos. C504-C509 (6) 4.00 1.30

EXPO '70 International Exhibition, Osaka, Japan, Mar. 15-Sept. 13.

Escazu Valley, by Margarita Bertheau — AP95

Paintings: 25c, "Irazu," by Rafael A. Garcia, vert. 80c, Shore landscape, by Teodorico Quiros. 1col, "The Other Face," by Cesar Valverde. 2.50col, Mother and Child, by Luis Daell, vert.

1970, Nov. 4 Litho. *Perf. 12½*

C510 AP95 25c multi .75 .30
C511 AP95 45c multi .75 .30
C512 AP95 80c multi 1.25 .55
C513 AP95 1col multi 1.25 .60
C514 AP95 2.50col multi 2.40 2.00
Nos. C510-C514 (5) 6.40 3.75

Arms of Costa Rica, 1964 — AP96

National Theater AP97

Various Coats of Arms, dated: 10c, Nov. 27, 1906. 15c, Sept. 29, 1848. 25c, Apr. 21, 1840. 35c, Nov. 22, 1824. 50c, Nov. 2, 1824. 1col, Mar. 6, 1824. 2col, May 10, 1823.

1971, Feb. 10 Litho. *Perf. 14x13½*

C515 AP96 5c buff & multi .35 .20
C516 AP96 10c multi .35 .20
C517 AP96 15c yel & multi .45 .20
C518 AP96 25c pink & multi .45 .20
C519 AP96 35c multi .60 .20
C520 AP96 50c rose & multi .70 .20
C521 AP96 1col beige & multi .75 .40
C522 AP96 2col multi 1.50 .80
Nos. C515-C522 (8) 5.15 2.40

1971, Apr. 14 Litho. *Perf. 11*

C523 AP97 2col plum .40 .30

Organization of American States meeting.

José Matias Delgado, Manuel José Arce AP98

Flag of Costa Rica — AP99

Independence Leaders: 10c, Miguel Larreinaga and Manuel Antonio de la Cerda, Nicaragua. 15c, José Cecilio del Valle, Dionisio de Herrera, Honduras. 35c, Pablo Alvarado and Florencio del Castillo, Costa Rica. 50c, Antonio Larrazabal and Pedro Molina, Guatemala. 2col, Costa Rica coat of arms.

1971, Sept. 14 *Perf. 13*

C524 AP98 5c multi .20 .20
C525 AP98 10c multi .20 .20
C526 AP98 15c gray, brn & blk .20 .20
C527 AP98 35c multi .20 .20
C528 AP98 50c multi .20 .20
C529 AP99 1col multi .20 .20
C530 AP99 2col multi .40 .40
Nos. C524-C530 (7) 1.60 1.60

Central American independence, sesqui.

Soccer Federation Emblem — AP100

Children of the World — AP101

1971, Dec. 6

C531 AP100 50c multi .30 .20
C532 AP100 60c multi .30 .20

50th anniv. of Soccer Federation of Costa Rica.

1972, Jan. 11 *Perf. 12½*

C533 AP101 50c multi .25 .20
C534 AP101 1.10col red & multi .40 .25

25th anniv. (in 1971) of UNICEF.

Tree of Guanacaste AP102

Designs: 40c, Hermitage, Liberia. 55c, Petroglyphs, Rincón Brujo. 60c, Painted head, sculpture from Curubandé, vert.

1972, Feb. 28 *Perf. 11*

C535 AP102 20c brn, ol & brt grn .35 .20
C536 AP102 40c brn & ol .35 .20
C537 AP102 55c blk & brn .35 .20
C538 AP102 60c blk, buff & ver .35 .20
Nos. C535-C538 (4) 1.40 .80

Bicentenary of the founding of the city of Liberia, Guanacaste.

Farm and Family — AP103

Inter-American Exhibitions AP104

Designs: 45c, Cattle, dairy products and meat, horiz. 50c, Kneeling figure with plant. 10col, Farmer and map of Americas.

1972, June 30 Litho. *Perf. 12½*

C539 AP103 20c multi .30 .20
C540 AP103 45c multi .30 .20
C541 AP103 50c dp yel, grn & blk .30 .20
C542 AP103 10col brn, org & blk 2.40 1.75
Nos. C539-C542 (4) 3.30 2.35

30th anniversary of the Inter-American Institute of Agricultural Sciences.

1972, Aug. 26 Litho. *Perf. 13*

C543 AP104 50c orange & brn .20 .20
C544 AP104 2col blue & vio .40 .30

4th Interamerican Philatelic Exhibition, EXFILBRA, Rio de Janeiro, Aug. 26-Sept. 2.

First Book Printed in Costa Rica — AP105

Intl. Book Year: 50c, 5col, Natl. Library, horiz.

1972, Dec. 7 Litho. *Perf. 12½*

C545 AP105 20c brt blue .35 .20
C546 AP105 50c gold & multi .35 .20
C547 AP105 75c multicolored .35 .20
C548 AP105 5col multicolored 1.75 .95
Nos. C545-C548 (4) 2.80 1.55

Road to Irazú Volcano AP106

1972-73 *Perf. 11x11½, 11½x11*

C549 AP106 5c like 20c .30 .20
C550 AP106 15c Coco-Culebra Bay .30 .20
C551 AP106 20c shown .30 .20
C552 AP106 25c like 15c .30 .20
C553 AP106 40c Manuel Antonio Beach .30 .20
C554 AP106 45c Tourist Office emblem .30 .20
C555 AP106 50c Lindora Lake .30 .20
C556 AP106 60c San Jose P.O., vert. .30 .20
C557 AP106 80c like 40c .35 .20
C558 AP106 90c like 45c .35 .20
C559 AP106 1col like 50c .35 .20
C560 AP106 2col like 60c .65 .45
Nos. C549-C560 (12) 4.10 2.65

Tourism year of the Americas.
Issued: 20c, 25c, 80c, 90c, 1col, 2col, 12/26; others, 3/21/73.
No. C555 exists with inverted center, used only. Value $10,000.

Church Type of 1967

Designs as before.

1973, July 16 Engr. *Perf. 12½*

C561 AP85 5c slate grn .20 .20
C562 AP85 10c olive .20 .20
C563 AP85 15c orange .20 .20
C564 AP85 25c brown .20 .20
C565 AP85 30c rose claret .20 .20
C566 AP85 35c violet .20 .20
C567 AP85 40c brt green .20 .20
C568 AP85 45c dull yellow .20 .20
C569 AP85 50c rose magenta .20 .20
C570 AP85 55c blue .25 .20
C571 AP85 65c black .30 .20
C572 AP85 75c rose red .40 .20
C573 AP85 80c yellow grn .45 .20
C574 AP85 85c lilac .50 .25
C575 AP85 90c brt pink .55 .25
C576 AP85 1col dark blue .65 .25
Nos. C561-C576 (16) 4.90 3.35

Human Rights Flame — AP107

OAS Emblem — AP108

1973, Dec. 10 Photo. *Perf. 10½*

C577 AP107 50c black & red .35 .20

25th anniversary of the Universal Declaration of Human Rights.

1973, Dec. 17 Litho. *Perf. 10½*

C578 AP108 20c dk bl & dp car .35 .20

25th anniv. of the OAS.

Joaquin Vargas Calvo — AP109

AP110

1974, Jan. 14

C579 AP109 20c shown .35 .20
C580 AP109 20c Alejandro Monestel .35 .20
C581 AP109 20c Julio Mata .35 .20
C582 AP109 60c Julio Fonseca .35 .20
C583 AP109 2col Rafael A. Chaves .80 .30
C584 AP109 5col Manuel M. Gutierrez 1.90 1.10
Nos. C579-C584 (6) 4.10 2.20

Costa Rican composers honored by the National Symphony Orchestra.

Revenue Stamps Overprinted "Habilitado para Correo Aereo"

1974, Apr. 5 Engr. *Perf. 12*

C585 AP110 50c brown .20 .20
C586 AP110 1col violet .30 .20
C587 AP110 2col orange .70 .35
C588 AP110 5col olive 1.60 1.60
Nos. C585-C588 (4) 2.80 2.35

Telephone Building, San Pedro — AP111

EXFILMEX 74 Emblem AP112

Designs: 65c, Rio Macho Control, horiz. 85c, Turbines, Rio Macho Center. 1.25col, Cachi Dam and reservoir, horiz. 2col, I.C.E. Headquarters.

1974, July 30 Litho. *Perf. 10½*

C589 AP111 50c gold & multi .20 .20
C590 AP111 65c gold & multi .25 .20
C591 AP111 85c gold & multi .30 .20
C592 AP111 1.25col gold & multi .35 .20
C593 AP111 2col gold & multi .75 .30
Nos. C589-C593 (5) 1.85 1.10

25th anniversary of Costa Rican Electrical Institute (I.C.E.).

1974, Aug. 22 *Perf. 13*

C594 AP112 65c green .20 .20
C595 AP112 3col lilac rose .60 .40

5th Inter-American Philatelic Exhibition, EXFILMEX-74 UPU, Mexico City, Oct. 26-Nov. 3.

Map of Costa Rica, 4-S Emblem AP113

50c, Young harvesters and 4-S emblem.

1974, Oct. 7 Litho. *Perf. 12x11*

C596 AP113 20c brt green .35 .20
C597 AP113 50c multicolored .35 .20

25th anniversary of 4-S Clubs of Costa Rica (similar to US 4-H Clubs).

Roberto Brenes Mesen — AP114

"Life Insurance" AP115

Designs: 85c, "Love and Death," manuscript. 5col, Hands of writer, horiz.

1974, Oct. 14 Litho. *Perf. 10½*

C598 AP114 20c black & brn .20 .20
C599 AP114 85c black & red .25 .20
C600 AP114 5col black & red brn 1.50 .85
Nos. C598-C600 (3) 1.95 1.25

Mesen, educator & writer, birth centenary.

1974, Oct. 30 *Perf. 14*

Designs: 20c, Ricardo Jiménez Oreamuno and Tomás Soley Güell, horiz. 50c, Harvest insurance (hand holding shovel), horiz. 85c, Maritime insurance (hand holding paper boat). 1.25col, INS emblem. 2col, Workers rehabilitation (arm with crutch). 2.50col, Workers' Compensation (hand holding wrench). 20col, Fire insurance (hands protecting house).

C601 AP115 20c multi .20 .20
C602 AP115 50c multi .20 .20
C603 AP115 65c multi .20 .20
C604 AP115 85c multi .20 .20
C605 AP115 1.25col multi .30 .20
C606 AP115 2col multi .55 .25
C607 AP115 2.50col multi .60 .40
C608 AP115 20col multi 4.00 4.00
Nos. C601-C608 (8) 6.25 5.65

Costa Rican Insurance Institute (Instituto Nacional de Seguros, INS), 50th anniversary.
For surcharges see Nos. C721-C722.

WPY Emblem — AP116

Oscar J. Pinto F. — AP117

1974, Nov. 13 Litho. *Perf. 11x11½*

C609 AP116 2col vio bl & red .45 .25

World Population Year.

1974, Dec. 2 *Perf. 13*

Designs: 50c, Alberto Montes de Oca D., champion sharpshooter. 1col, Eduardo Garnier, sports promoter. O. J. Pinto, introducer of soccer.

C610 AP117 20c gray & dk bl .20 .20
C611 AP117 50c gray & dk bl .20 .20
C612 AP117 1col gray & dk bl .45 .20
Nos. C610-C612 (3) .85 .60

First Central American Olympic Games, held in Guatemala, 1973.

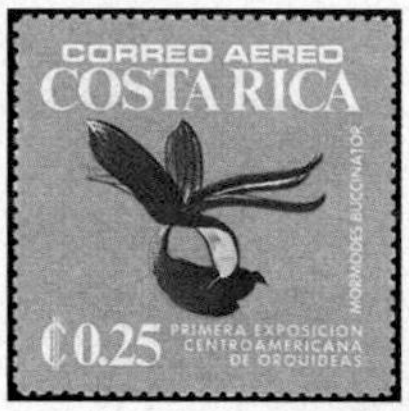

Mormodes Buccinator AP118

Masdevallia Ephippium AP119

Designs: Orchids.

1975, Mar. 7 Litho. *Perf. 10½, 13½*

C613 AP118 25c *shown* .60 .20
C614 AP118 25c *Gongora clavi-odora* .60 .20
C615 AP119 25c *shown* .60 .20
C616 AP119 25c *Encyclia spondiadum* .60 .20
a. Block of 4, #C613-C616 2.40 1.00
b. As "a," perf. 10½ 1.60
C617 AP118 65c *Lycaste skinneri alba* 1.50 .20
C618 AP118 65c *Peristeria elata* 1.50 .20
C619 AP119 65c *Miltonia roezelii* 1.50 .20
C620 AP119 65c *Brassavola digbyana* 1.50 .20
a. Block of 4, #C617-C620, perf. 13½ 6.00 2.00
b. As "a," perf. 10½ 16.00
C621 AP118 80c *Epidendrum mirabile* 2.10 .30
C622 AP118 80c *Barkeria lindleyana* 2.10 .30
C623 AP119 80c *Cattleya skinneri* 2.10 .30
C624 AP119 80c *Sobralia macrantha* 2.10 .30
a. Block of 4, #C621-C624 8.50 2.50
b. As "a," perf. 10½ 10.50
C625 AP118 1.40col *Lycaste cruenta* 2.50 .35
C626 AP118 1.40col *Oncidium obryzatum* 2.50 .35
C627 AP119 1.40col *Gongora armeniaca* 2.50 .35
C628 AP119 1.40col *Sievekingia suavis* 2.50 .35
a. Block of 4, #C625-C628 8.00 4.00

b. As "a," perf. 10½ 8.00

Perf. 13½

C629 AP118 1.75col *Hexisea imbricata* 1.50 .35
C630 AP118 2.15col *Warcewiczella discolor* 1.50 .50
C631 AP119 2.50col *Oncidium krameri-anum* 2.50 1.00
C632 AP119 3.25col *Cattleya dowiana* 3.00 1.25
Nos. C613-C632 (20) 35.30 7.30

5th National Orchid Exhibition.

Nos. C613-C628 were printed in both perforations on two different papers: dull finish and shiny. Nos. C629-C632 were printed on shiny paper.

Most examples of Nos. C617-C620, perf 10½, were surcharged.

For overprints and surcharges see Nos. C715-C720, C723-C728.

Radio Club Emblem AP120

Members' Flags and Emblem — AP121

Design: 2col, Federation emblem.

1975, Apr. 16 Litho. *Perf. 13½*

C633 AP120 1col blk & red lil .45 .20
C634 AP121 1.10col multi .55 .20
C635 AP120 2col black & bl .90 .25
Nos. C633-C635 (3) 1.90 .65

16th Central American Radio Amateurs' Convention, San José, May 2-4.

Nicoya Beach AP122

Designs: 75c, Driving cattle. 1col, Colonial Church, Nicoya. 3col, Savannah riders, vert.

1975, Aug. 1 Litho. *Perf. 13½*

C636 AP122 25c gray & multi .20 .20
C637 AP122 75c gray & multi .25 .20
C638 AP122 1col gray & multi .30 .20
C639 AP122 3col gray & multi .90 .75
Nos. C636-C639 (4) 1.65 1.35

Sesqui. of annexation of Nicoya District.

Costa Rica #158 AP123

Designs (Type A90 of 1932): No. C641, #159. No. C642, #160. No. C643, #161.

1975, Aug. 14 Litho. *Perf. 12*

C640 AP123 2.20col blk & org .40 .35
C641 AP123 2.20col blk & dk grn .40 .35
C642 AP123 2.20col blk & car rose .40 .35
C643 AP123 2.20col blk & dk bl .40 .35
a. Block of 4, #C640-C643 6.00 3.50

6th Natl. Phil. Exhib., San José, Aug. 14-17.

For surcharges see Nos. C885-C892.

IWY Emblem AP124

1975, Oct. 9 Litho. *Perf. 10½*

C644 AP124 40c vio bl & red .20 .20
C645 AP124 1.25col blk & ultra .35 .20

International Women's Year 1975.

UN Emblem AP125

UN, 30th Anniv.: 60c, UN General Assembly, horiz. 1.20col, UN Headquarters, NY.

1975, Oct. 24 *Perf. 12*

C646 AP125 10c bl & blk .20 .20
C647 AP125 60c multi .20 .20
C648 AP125 1.20col multi .40 .20
Nos. C646-C648 (3) .80 .60

The Visitation, by Jorge Gallardo AP126

"20-30" Club Emblem — AP127

Paintings by Jorge Gallardo: 1col, Nativity and Star. 5col, St. Joseph in his Workshop, Virgin and Child.

1975, Nov. 3 *Perf. 10½*

C649 AP126 50c multi .30 .20
C650 AP126 1col multi .45 .20
C651 AP126 5col multi 1.60 .70
Nos. C649-C651 (3) 2.35 1.10

Christmas 1975.

1976, Jan. 16 Litho. *Perf. 12*

C652 AP127 1col multi .35 .20

"20-30" Club of Costa Rica, 20th anniv.

Quercus Brenessi Trel — AP128

"Literary Development" AP129

Plants: 30c, Maxillaria albertii schecht. 55c, Calathea brenesii standl. 2col, Brenesia costaricensis schlecht. 10col, Philodendron brenesii standl.

1976, Mar. 1 *Perf. 10½*

C653 AP128 5c multi .45 .20
C654 AP128 30c multi .45 .20
C655 AP128 55c multi .75 .20
C656 AP128 2col tan & multi 1.00 .35
C657 AP128 10col multi 5.25 2.50
Nos. C653-C657 (5) 7.90 3.45

Prof. Alberto Manuel Brenes Mora, botanist, birth centenary.

1976, Apr. 9 Litho. *Perf. 16*

Designs: 1.10col, Man holding book, stylized. 5col, Costa Rican flag emanating from book, horiz.

C658 AP129 15c multi .20 .20
C659 AP129 1.10col multi .20 .20
C660 AP129 5col multi .90 .70
Nos. C658-C660 (3) 1.30 1.10

Publishing in Costa Rica.

Nos. C658-C660 exist imperf.

Postrider, 1839 — AP130

Costa Rica No. 13, Post Office AP131

Designs: 65c, Costa Rica No. 14 and Post Office. 85c, Costa Rica No. 15 and Post Office. 2col, UPU Monument, Bern, vert.

1976, May 24 *Perf. 10½*

C661 AP130 20c apple grn & blk .30 .20
C662 AP131 50c bister & multi .30 .20
C663 AP131 65c multi .30 .20
C664 AP131 85c multi .30 .20
C665 AP130 2col blk & lt bl .75 .40
Nos. C661-C665 (5) 1.95 1.20

Cent. of UPU (in 1974).

Nos. C662-C664 exist without the surcharges on reproductions of Nos. 13-15.

Telephones, 1876 and 1976 — AP132

Designs: 2col, Wall telephone. 5col, Alexander Graham Bell.

1976, June 28

C666 AP132 1.60col lt bl & blk .35 .20
C667 AP132 2col multicolored .45 .20
C668 AP132 5col yellow & blk 1.10 .90
Nos. C666-C668 (3) 1.90 1.30

Centenary of first telephone call by Alexander Graham Bell, Mar. 10, 1876.

Inverted Center Stamp of 1901 and Association Emblems — AP133

Design: 5col, 1901 stamp between Costa Rican Philatelic Society and Interamerican Philatelic Federation emblems.

1976, Nov. 11 Litho. *Perf. 10½*

C669 AP133 50c multi .20 .20
C670 AP133 1col multi .20 .20
C671 AP133 2col multi .35 .20
Nos. C669-C671 (3) .75 .60

Souvenir Sheet

Perf. 12

C672 AP133 5col multi 4.75 2.40

7th Natl. Phil. Exhib. and 9th Plenary Assembly of the Interamerican Phil. Fed. (FIAF), San José, Nov. 1976.

No. C670 exists in colors of No. C671.

No. C671 exists on thin dull paper, with bright gum. Value, mint, $25.

No. C672 was issued both perf and imperf. Same values.

"Seeing Eye" and Map of Costa Rica AP134

Amadeo Quiros Blanco — AP135

1976, Nov. 22 *Perf. 16*

C673 AP134 35c black & blue .20 .20
C674 AP135 2col multicolored .50 .35

General Audit Office, 25th anniversary.

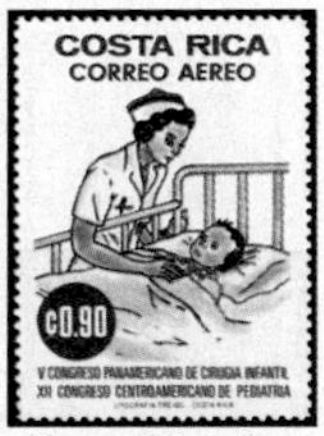

Nurse Attending Child — AP136

LACSA Circling Globe — AP137

1.10col, National Children's Hospital, horiz.

1976, Nov. 29

C675 AP136 90c multi .25 .20
C676 AP136 1.10col multi .35 .25

5th Panamerican Congress of Pediatric Surgery and 12th Congress of Pediatrics.

1976, Dec. 1 *Perf. 10½*

Designs: 1.20col, Route map. 3col, LACSA emblem and Costa Rican flag.

C677 AP137 1col multi .25 .20
C678 AP137 1.20col multi .35 .20
C679 AP137 3col multi 1.00 .60
Nos. C677-C679 (3) 1.60 1.00

Costa Rican Air Lines (LACSA), 30th anniversary.

Boston Tea Party AP138

US Bicent.: 5col, Declaration of Independence. 10col, Ringing Liberty Bell to announce Independence, vert.

1976, Dec. 24

C680 AP138 2.20col multi .35 .30
C681 AP138 5col multi .90 .70
C682 AP138 10col multi 1.75 1.40
Nos. C680-C682 (3) 3.00 2.40

Tree of Guanacaste AP139

Felipe J. Alvarado AP140

Designs (Rotary Emblem and): 60c, Dr. Paul Blanco Cervantes Hospital, horiz. 3col, Map of Costa Rica, horiz. 10col, Paul Harris.

1977, Mar. 31 Litho. *Perf. 16*

C683 AP139 40c multi .20 .20
C684 AP140 50c multi .20 .20
C685 AP139 60c multi .20 .20
C686 AP139 3col multi .90 .50
C687 AP140 10col multi 3.00 2.10
Nos. C683-C687 (5) 4.50 3.20

Rotary Club of San José, 50th anniversary.

Boruca Cloth AP141

Design: 1.50col, Painted wood ornament.

1977, Feb. 22

C688 AP141 75c multi .20 .20
C689 AP141 1.50col multi .30 .20

Natl. Artisan & Small Industry Program.

Juana Pereira AP142

Alonso de Anguciana de Gamboa AP143

Designs: 1col, First Church of Our Lady of the Angels, horiz. 1.10col, Our Lady of the Angels (gold sculpture). 1.25col, Crown of Our Lady of the Angels.

1977, June 6 Litho. *Perf. 10½*

C690 AP142 50c multi .20 .20
C691 AP142 1col multi .20 .20
C692 AP142 1.10col multi .20 .20
C693 AP142 1.25col multi .40 .20
Nos. C690-C693 (4) 1.00 .80

50th anniv. of the coronation of Our Lady of the Angels, patron saint of Costa Rica.

1977, July 4 Litho. *Perf. 10½*

Designs: 75c, Church of Esparza. 1col, Statue of Our Lady of Candlemas. 2col, Statue of Diego de Artieda y Chirino.

C694 AP143 35c multi .20 .20
C695 AP143 75c multi .20 .20
C696 AP143 1col multi .30 .20
C697 AP143 2col multi .60 .35
Nos. C694-C697 (4) 1.30 .95

400th anniv. of the founding of Esparza. For surcharge see No. C883.

CARE Emblem and Child — AP144

1col, CARE emblem and soybeans, horiz.

1977, Sept. 14 Litho. *Perf. 16*

C698 AP144 80c multi .25 .20
C699 AP144 1col multi .35 .20

20th anniversary of CARE (relief organization) in Costa Rica.

Institute's Emblem — AP145

First Map of Americas, 1540 — AP146

1977, Oct. 21 Litho. *Perf. 16*

C700 AP145 50c blk & multi .45 .20
C701 AP146 1.40col blk & multi .90 .35

Hispanic Cultural Institute of Costa Rica, 25th anniversary.

Mercy Church, by Ricardo Ulloa B. AP147

Health Ministry Emblem AP148

Paintings: 1col, Christ, by Floria Pinto de Herrero. 5col, St. Francis and the Birds, by Louisa Gonzalez Y Saenz.

1977, Nov. 9 Litho. *Perf. 10½*

C702 AP147 50c multi .35 .20
C703 AP147 1col multi .35 .20
C704 AP147 5col multi 1.60 .70
Nos. C702-C704 (3) 2.30 1.10

1977, Nov. 16 *Perf. 16*

C705 AP148 1.40col multi .35 .20

Creation of Ministry of Health.

Picnic — AP149

San Martin — AP150

Designs: 50c, Weaver. 2col, Beach scene. 5col, Fruit and vegetable market. 10col, Swans on lake.

1978, Mar. 21 Litho. *Perf. 10½*

C706 AP149 50c blk & multi .20 .20
C707 AP149 1col blk & multi .35 .20
C708 AP149 2col blk & multi 1.00 .20
C709 AP149 5col blk & multi 1.90 .75
C710 AP149 10col blk & multi 2.40 1.90
Nos. C706-C710 (5) 5.85 3.25

Conf. of Latin American Tourist Organizations.

1978, Aug. 7 Litho. *Perf. 10½*

C711 AP150 5col multi 1.25 .65

Gen. José de San Martin (1778-1850), soldier and statesman, fought for South American independence.

Geographical Institute Emblem — AP151

University Federation Emblem — AP152

1978, Aug. 28 Litho. *Perf. 12½*

C712 AP151 5col multi 1.10 .60

Pan-American Geography and History Institute, 50th anniversary. Exists imperf.

1978, Sept. 18 *Perf. 11*

C713 AP152 80c ultra .35 .20

Central American University Federation, 30th anniversary.

Emblems — AP153

1978, Oct. 24 *Perf. 16*

C714 AP153 2col aqua, blk & gold .50 .35

6th Interamerican Philatelic Exhibition, Argentina 78, Buenos Aires, Oct. 1978.

Nos. C629-C631 Overprinted: "50 Aniversario del / primer vuelo de PAN AM / en Costa Rica / 1928-1978"

1978, Nov. 1 Litho. *Perf. 13½*

C715 AP118 1.75col multi .45 .30
C716 AP118 2.15col multi .60 .30
C717 AP119 2.50col multi .80 .40
Nos. C715-C717 (3) 1.85 1.00

1st Pan Am flight in Costa Rica, 50th anniv.

Nos. C629-C631 Overprinted: "50 Aniversario de la / visita de Lindbergh a / Costa Rica 1928-1978"

1978, Nov. 1

C718 AP118 1.75col multi 1.25 .30
C719 AP118 2.15col multi 1.40 .35
C720 AP119 2.50col multi 1.90 .45
Nos. C718-C720 (3) 4.55 1.10

50th anniversary of Lindbergh's visit.

Nos. C603 and C607 Surcharged with New Value, 4 Bars and: "Centenario del / Asilo Carlos / Maria Ulloa / 1878-1978"

1978, Nov. 8 *Perf. 14*

C721 AP115 50c on 65c multi .20 .20
C722 AP115 2col on 2.50col multi .50 .25

Asilo Carlos Maria Ulloa, birth centenary.

No. C617-C620, C630-C631 Surcharged with New Value and 4 Bars

Perf. 10½, 13½

1978, Nov. 13 Litho.

C723 AP118 50c on 65c .60 .60
C724 AP118 50c on 65c .60 .60
C725 AP119 50c on 65c .60 .60
C726 AP119 50c on 65c .60 .60
a. Block of 4, #C723-C726 2.50 2.50
C727 AP118 1.20col on 2.15col 1.25 .50
C728 AP119 2col on 2.50col 1.25 .50
Nos. C723-C728 (6) 4.90 3.40

Nos. C723-C726, perf. 13½, value *$20*, unused, *$10*, used, each. No. C726a, unused, *$400*.

Star over Map of Costa Rica — AP154

"Flying Men," Chorotega AP155

1978, Nov. 13 *Perf. 10½*

C729 AP154 50c blue & blk .20 .20
C730 AP154 1col rose lil & blk .20 .20
C731 AP154 5col orange & blk 1.40 .60
a. Strip of 3, #C729-C731 1.90 1.90

Christmas 1978. Nos. C729-C731 printed in sheets of 100 and se-tenant in sheet of 15 (3x5). Value, se-tenant sheet, $20.

1978, Nov. 20 *Perf. 11½*

Designs: 1.20col, Oviedo giving his History of Indies to Duke of Calabria, horiz. 10col, Lord of Oviedo's coat of arms.

C732 AP155 85c multi .20 .20
C733 AP155 1.20col blk & lt bl .20 .20
C734 AP155 10col multi 1.90 1.90
Nos. C732-C734 (3) 2.30 2.30

500th birth anniv. of Gonzalo Fernandez de Oviedo, 1st chronicler of Spanish Indies.

Msgr. Domingo Rivas AP156

San José Cathedral AP157

1978, Dec. 6 *Perf. 16, 13½ (20col)*

C735 AP156 1col black & indigo .20 .20
C736 AP157 20col multicolored 3.50 3.25

Centenary of the Cathedral of San José.

View of Coco Island AP158

Designs: 2.10, 3, 5 col, various views of Coco Island. 10col, Installation of memorial plaque, people and flag. 5, 10col vert.

1979, Apr. 30 Litho. *Perf. 10½*

C737 AP158 90c multi .35 .20
C738 AP158 2.10col multi .90 .35
C739 AP158 3col multi 1.25 .45
C740 AP158 5col multi 1.90 1.75
C741 AP158 10col multi 3.75 3.75
a. Souv. sheet, #C737-C741 12.00 12.00
Nos. C737-C741 (5) 8.15 6.50

Visit of Pres. Rodrigo Carazo Odio to Coco Island, June 24, 1978, in the interest of national defense.

No. C741a exists imperf. Value $750.

Shrimp AP159

Designs: 85c, Mahogany snapper. 1.80col, Corvina. 3col, Crayfish. 10col, Tuna.

1979, May 14 Litho. *Perf. 13½*

C742	AP159	60c	multi	.20	.20
C743	AP159	85c	multi	.20	.20
C744	AP159	1.80col	multi	.60	.20
C745	AP159	3col	multi	1.00	.55
C746	AP159	10col	multi	5.00	3.50
	Nos. C742-C746 (5)			7.00	4.65

Marine life protection.

Hungry Nestlings, IYC Emblem AP160

Microwave Transmitters, Mt. Irazu AP161

1979, May 24 *Perf. 11*

C747	AP160	1col	multi	.75	.20
C748	AP160	2col	multi	2.00	1.25
C749	AP160	20col	multi	13.00	6.00
	Nos. C747-C749 (3)			15.75	7.45

International Year of the Child.

1979, June 28 Litho. *Perf. 14*

Design: 1col, Arenal Dam, horiz.

C750	AP161	1col	multi	.20	.20
C751	AP161	5col	multi	1.10	.60

Costa Rican Electricity Institute, 30th anniversary.

Costa Rica No. 1 and Rowland Hill AP162

Design: 10col, Penny Black and Hill.

1979, July 16 *Perf. 13*

C752	AP162	5col	lil rose & bl gray	1.10	.50
C753	AP162	10col	dl bl & blk	2.25	1.00

Sir Rowland Hill (1795-1879), originator of penny postage.

Poverty, by Juan Ramon Bonilla AP163

National Sculpture Contest: 60c, Hope, by Hernan Gonzalez. 2.10col, Cattle, by Victor M. Bermudez, horiz. 5col, Bust of Clorito Picado, by Juan Rafael Chacon. 20col, Mother and Child, by Francisco Zuniga.

1979, July 16 Litho. *Perf. 12*

C754	AP163	60c	multi	.20	.20
C755	AP163	1col	multi	.20	.20
C756	AP163	2.10col	multi	.50	.25
C757	AP163	5col	multi	1.40	1.10
C758	AP163	20col	multi	4.50	2.25
	Nos. C754-C758 (5)			6.80	4.00

Danaus Plexippus — AP164

Butterflies: 1col, Phoebis philea. 1.80col, Rothschildia. 2.10col, Prepona omphale. 2.60col, Marpesia marcella. 4.05col, Morpho cypris.

1979, Aug. 31 Litho. *Perf. 13½*

C759	AP164	60c	multi	*3.00*	.40
C760	AP164	1col	multi	*5.00*	.40
C761	AP164	1.80col	multi	*7.00*	.65
C762	AP164	2.10col	multi	*10.00*	1.25
C763	AP164	2.60col	multi	*10.00*	2.50
C764	AP164	4.05col	multi	*18.00*	3.50
	Nos. C759-C764 (6)			*53.00*	8.70

SOS Emblem, Houses AP165

Children's Drawings: 5col, 5.50col, Landscapes, diff.

1979, Sept. 18

C765	AP165	2.50col	multi	.50	.35
C766	AP165	5col	multi	1.10	.70
C767	AP165	5.50col	multi	1.50	1.10
	Nos. C765-C767 (3)			3.10	2.15

SOS Children's Villages, 30th anniversary.

President Type of 1943

Presidents of Costa Rica: 60c, Rafael Iglesias C. 85c, Ascension Esquivel Ibarra. 1col, Cleto Gonzalez Viquez. 2col, Ricardo Jimenez Oreamuno.

1979, Oct. 8 Litho. *Perf. 13½*

C768	A109	10c	dk blue	.20	.20
C769	A109	60c	dull purple	.20	.20
C770	A109	85c	red orange	.25	.20
C771	A109	1col	red orange	.30	.20
C772	A109	2col	brown	.60	.30
a.	Strip of 5, #C768-C772			1.75	1.40
	Nos. C768-C772 (5)			1.55	1.10

Printed in sheets of 100 and se-tenant in sheets of 25 (5x5).

See Nos. C790-C794.

Holy Family, Creche AP167

Reforestation AP168

1979, Nov. 16 Litho. *Perf. 12½*

C773	AP167	1col	multi	.25	.20
C774	AP167	1.60col	multi	.65	.25

Christmas 1979.

1980, Jan. 14 Litho. *Perf. 11*

C775	AP168	1col	multi	.20	.20
C776	AP168	3.40col	multi	.65	.50

Anatomy Lesson, by Rembrandt AP169

1980, Feb. 7 Litho. *Perf. 10½*

C777	AP169	10col	multi	3.75	1.50

Legal medicine teaching in Costa Rica, 50th anniversary.

Rotary Intl., 75th Anniv. — AP170

Gulf of Nicoya, Satellite Photo — AP171

1980, Feb. 26 *Perf. 16*

C778	AP170	2.10col	multi	.35	.25
C779	AP170	5col	multi	1.00	.60

1980, Mar. 10 Litho. *Perf. 12½*

C780	AP171	2.10col	Puerto Limon	.35	.25
C781	AP171	5col	shown	1.00	.60

14th Intl. Symposium on Remote Sensing of the Environment, San José, Apr. 23-30. Exist imperf.

Soccer, Moscow '80 Emblem — AP172

Poas Volcano AP173

1980, Apr. 16 Litho. *Perf. 10½*

C782	AP172	1col	shown	*1.00*	.20
C783	AP172	3col	Bicycling	*5.00*	.75
C784	AP172	4.05col	Baseball	*5.00*	1.00
C785	AP172	20col	Swimming	*6.00*	6.00
	Nos. C782-C785 (4)			*17.00*	7.95

22nd Summer Olympic Games, Moscow, July 19-Aug. 3.

1980, May 14 Litho. *Perf. 10½*

C786	AP173	1col	shown	.20	.20
C787	AP173	2.50col	Cahuita Beach	.50	.35

National Parks Service, 10th anniversary.

José Maria Zeledon Brenes, Score — AP174

Design: 10col, Manuel Maria Gutierrez.

1980, June 25 Litho. *Perf. 12½*

C788	AP174	1col	multi	.25	.20
C789	AP174	10col	multi	1.60	1.25

National anthem composed by Brenes (words) and Gutierrez (music). Nos. C788-C789 exist imperf.

President Type of 1943

1col, Alfredo Gonzalez F. 1.60col, Federico Tinoco G. 1.80col, Francisco Aguilar B. 2.10col, Julio Acosta G. 3col, Leon Cortes C.

1980, Aug. 14 Litho. *Perf. 11*

C790	A109	1col	dk red	.20	.20
C791	A109	1.60col	slate bl	.35	.20
C792	A109	1.80col	brown	.35	.20
C793	A109	2.10col	dull green	.45	.25
C794	A109	3col	dark purple	.75	.40
	Nos. C790-C794 (5)			2.10	1.25

8th Natl. Phil. Exhib. — AP175

Fruits — AP176

1980, Sept. 11 *Perf. 13½*

C795	AP175	5col	multi	.80	.60
C796	AP175	20col	multi	3.25	2.75

1980, Sept. 24 *Perf. 10½*

C797	AP176	10c	shown	.20	.20
C798	AP176	60c	Cacao	.40	.20
C799	AP176	1col	Coffee	.75	.20
C800	AP176	2.10col	Bananas	1.50	.25
C801	AP176	3.40col	Flowers	1.75	.40
C802	AP176	5col	Sugar cane	2.25	.80
	Nos. C797-C802 (6)			6.85	2.05

Giant Tree, by Jorge Carvajal AP177

Virgin and Child, by Raphael AP178

Paintings: 2.10col, Secret Look, by Rolando Cubero. 2.45col, Consuelo, by Fernando Carballo. 3col, Volcano, by Lola Fernandez. 4.05col, attending Mass, by Francisco Amighetti.

1980, Oct. 22 Litho. *Perf. 10½*

C803	AP177	1col	multi	.35	.20
C804	AP177	2.10col	multi	.50	.25
	Size: 28x30mm				
C805	AP177	2.45col	multi	.65	.30
	Size: 22x36mm				
C806	AP177	3col	multi	.75	.35
C807	AP177	4.05col	multi	1.10	.45
	Nos. C803-C807 (5)			3.35	1.55

1980, Nov. 11 *Perf. 13½*

Christmas 1980: 10col, Virgin and Child and St. John, by Raphael.

C808	AP178	1col	multi	.40	.40
C809	AP178	10col	multi	2.00	2.00

Juan Santamaria International Airport AP179

1980, Dec. 11 Litho. *Perf. 10½*

Sizes: 30x30mm, 31x25mm (1.30col), 25x32mm (2.60col)

C810	AP179	1col	Caldera Harbor	.25	.20
C811	AP179	1.30col	shown	.35	.20
C812	AP179	2.10col	Rio Frio Railroad Bridge	.75	.35
C813	AP179	2.60col	Highway to Colon	.75	.35
C814	AP179	5col	Huetar post office	1.25	.70
	Nos. C810-C814 (5)			3.35	1.80

Paying your taxes means progress.

For surcharge see No. C884.

Repertorio Americano Cover, J. Garcia Monge and Signature — AP180

1981, Jan. 2 Litho. *Perf. 10½*

C815 AP180 1.60col multi .30 .20
C816 AP180 3col multi .60 .35

Birth centenary of J. Garcia Monge, founder of Repertorio Americano journal.

Arms of Aserri (Site of Cornea Bank) AP181

Harpia Harpyja AP182

1981, Jan. 28 Litho. *Perf. 13½*

C817 AP181 1col shown .20 .20
C818 AP181 1.80col Eye .50 .20
C819 AP181 5col Rojas 1.50 .70
Nos. C817-C819 (3) 2.20 1.10

Establishment of human cornea bank, founded by Abelardo Rojas.

1980, Dec. 23 *Perf. 11*

C820 AP182 2.10col shown 1.40 .35
C821 AP182 2.50col Ara macao 2.00 .55
C822 AP182 3col Felis concolor 2.50 .65
C823 AP182 5.50col Ateles geoffrovi 5.25 1.10
Nos. C820-C823 (4) 11.15 2.65

Medical and Surgical Clinic AP183

10c, Physiology class. 50c, Medical school, A. Chavarria (1st dean). 1.30col, Music school. 3.40col, Carlos Monge Alfaro Library. 4.05col, R.F. Brenes, rector (1952-61).

1981, Apr. 8 Litho. *Perf. 10½*

C824 AP183 5c multi .20 .20
C825 AP183 10c multi .20 .20
C826 AP183 50c multi .20 .20
C827 AP183 1.30col multi .40 .20
C828 AP183 3.40col multi .50 .40
C829 AP183 4.05col multi, vert. .75 .50
Nos. C824-C829 (6) 2.25 1.70

University of Costa Rica, 40th anniversary.

Mail Transport by Horse — AP184

1981, May 6 Litho. *Perf. 10½*

C830 AP184 1col shown .20 .20
C831 AP184 2.10col Train, 1857 .50 .25
C832 AP184 10col Mail carriers, 1858 2.25 1.40
Nos. C830-C832 (3) 2.95 1.85

Heinrich von Stephan (1831-97), UPU founder.

13th World Telecommunications Day — AP185

1981, May 18 *Perf. 11*

C833 AP185 5col multi 3.00 .60
C834 AP185 25col multi 7.50 4.00

Bishop Bernardo Thiel AP186

Juan Santamaria AP187

1981, June 8 Litho. *Perf. 10½*

C835 Strip of 5, stained glass windows 2.50 2.50
a. AP186 1col Sts. Peter & Paul .20 .20
b. AP186 1col St. Vincent de Paul .20 .20
c. AP186 1col Death of St. Joseph .20 .20
d. AP186 1col Archangel Michael .20 .20
e. AP186 1col Holy Family .20 .20
C836 AP186 2col shown .60 .35

Consecration of Bernardo Augusto Thiel as Bishop of San Jose.

1981, June 26 *Perf. 13½*

C837 AP187 1col shown .20 .20
C838 AP187 2.45col Alajuela Cathedral, horiz. .45 .35

Alajuela province.

Potters — AP188

1981, July 10 Litho. *Perf. 10½*

C839 AP188 15c shown .20 .20
C840 AP188 1.60col Bricklayers .20 .20
C841 AP188 1.80col Farmers .20 .20
C842 AP188 2.50col Fishermen .25 .20
C843 AP188 3col Nurse, patient .35 .20
C844 AP188 5col Children, traffic policeman .65 .25
Nos. C839-C844 (6) 1.85 1.25

Model of New Natl. Archives AP189

Natl. Archives Centenary: 1.40col, Leon Fernandez Bonilla, founder, vert. 2col, Arms, vert. 3col, St. Thomas University, former headquarters.

1981, Aug. 24 Litho. *Perf. 13½*

C845 AP189 1.40col multi .25 .20
C846 AP189 2col multi .45 .20
C847 AP189 3col multi .60 .20
C848 AP189 3.50col multi .65 .20
Nos. C845-C848 (4) 1.95 .80

Men Reaching for Sun, Map AP190

1981, Sept. 9 Litho. *Perf. 11*

C849 AP190 1col Man in wheelchair, stairs, vert. .30 .20
C850 AP190 2.60col Man reaching for scale, vert. .75 .20
C851 AP190 10col shown 3.25 1.00
Nos. C849-C851 (3) 4.30 1.40

Intl. Year of the Disabled.

World Food Day — AP191

1981, Oct. 16 Litho. *Perf. 10½*

C852 AP191 5col multi .40 .25
C853 AP191 10col multi .75 .50

President Type of 1943

1col, Rafael A. Calderon Guardia, 1940. 2col, Teodoro Picado Michalski, 1944. 3col, José Figueres Ferrer, 1953. 5col, Otilio Ulate Blanco, 1949. 10col, Mario Echandi Jimenez, 1958.

1981, Dec. 7 Litho. *Perf. 13½*

C854 A109 1col pink .50 .50
C855 A109 2col orange .50 .50
C856 A109 3col green .65 .50
C857 A109 5col dk bl 1.25 .75
C858 A109 10col blue 2.40 1.75
Nos. C854-C858 (5) 5.30 4.00

Bar Assoc. of Costa Rica Centenary (1981) AP192

1982, Mar. 22 Litho. *Perf. 13½*

C859 AP192 1col Emblem, horiz. .20 .20
C860 AP192 2col E. Figueroa, 1st pres. .20 .20
C861 AP192 20col Bar building, horiz. 2.40 1.25
Nos. C859-C861 (3) 2.80 1.65

National Progress AP193

1982 *Perf. 10½*

C862 AP193 95c Housing .20 .20
C863 AP193 1.15col Agricultural fair .20 .20
C864 AP193 1.45col Education .20 .20
C865 AP193 1.65col Drinkable water .20 .20
C866 AP193 1.80col Rural medical care .20 .20
C867 AP193 2.10col Recreational areas .20 .20
C868 AP193 2.35col Natl. Theater Square .35 .20
C869 AP193 2.60col Communications .35 .20
C870 AP193 3col Electric railroad .50 .20
C871 AP193 4.05col Irrigation .50 .20
Nos. C862-C871 (10) 2.90 2.00

Issue dates: 1.80col, 2.10col, 2.60col, 3col, 4.05col, May 5; others, June 16.

City of Alajuela Bicentenary AP194

Perez Zeledon County, 50th Anniv. (1981) AP195

Designs: 5col, Central Park Fountain. 10col, Juan Santamaria Historical and Cultural Museum, horiz. 15col, Church of Christ of Esquipulas. 20col, Monsignor Esteban Lorenzo de Tristan, 25col, Father Juan Manuel Lopez del Corral.

1982, Aug. 9

C872 AP194 5col multi .50 .25
C873 AP194 10col multi 1.10 .50
C874 AP194 15col multi 1.60 1.10
C875 AP194 20col multi 2.25 1.10
C876 AP194 25col multi 2.75 1.40
Nos. C872-C876 (5) 8.20 4.35

1982, Aug. 30

Designs: 10c, Saint's Stone. 50c, Monument to Mothers. 1col, Pedro Perz Zeledon. 1.25col, St. Isidore Labrador Church. 3.50col, Municipal Building, horiz. 4.25col, Arms.

C877 AP195 10c multi .20 .20
C878 AP195 50c multi .20 .20
C879 AP195 1col multi .20 .20
C880 AP195 1.25col multi .20 .20
C881 AP195 3.50col multi .35 .20
C882 AP195 4.25col multi .50 .20
Nos. C877-C882 (6) 1.65 1.20

Nos. C695 and C813 Surcharged

1982, Oct. 28 Litho. *Perf. 10½*

C883 AP143 3col on 75c multi .35 .20
C884 AP179 5col on 2.60col multi .50 .20

Nos. C640-C643 Surcharged and Overprinted: "IX EXPOSICION FILATELICA - 1982"

1982, Oct. 28 *Perf. 12*

C885 AP123 8.40col on #C640 .50 .40
C886 AP123 8.40col on #C641 .50 .40
C887 AP123 8.40col on #C642 .50 .40
C888 AP123 8.40col on #C643 .50 .40
C889 AP123 9.70col on #C640 .60 .50
C890 AP123 9.70col on #C641 .60 .50
C891 AP123 9.70col on #C642 .60 .50
C892 AP123 9.70col on #C643 .60 .50
Nos. C885-C892 (8) 4.40 3.60

9th Natl. Stamp Exhibition.

TB Bacillus Centenary AP196

Pan-American Blood Donors' Society, 7th Cong. — AP197

1982, Nov. 19 *Perf. 13½*

C893 AP196 1.50col Koch .20 .20
C894 AP196 3col Koch, slide .35 .20
C895 AP196 3.30col Health Ministry .35 .20
Nos. C893-C895 (3) .90 .60

1982, Nov. 25 *Perf. 11*

C896 AP197 30col Natl. Blood Assoc. emblem 1.75 1.40
C897 AP197 50col Cong. emblem 3.00 2.00

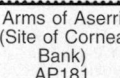

AP198

AP199

1982, Dec. 13 Litho. *Perf. 10½*

C898	AP198	8.40col Emblem, horiz.	.50	.20
C899	AP198	9.70col Emblem, diff.	.75	.35
C900	AP198	11.70col Handshake, horiz.	.75	.35
C901	AP198	13.05col Emblem, diff., horiz.	.90	.40
		Nos. C898-C901 (4)	2.90	1.30

Inter-Governmental Migration Committee, 30th anniv.

1983, Jan. 3 *Perf. 16*

4.80col, St. Francis of Assisi, by El Greco. 7.40col, Portrait, diff.

C902	AP199	4.80col multi	.50	.20
C903	AP199	7.40col multi	.75	.20

For surcharges see Nos. C908-C911.

Visit of Pope John Paul II AP200

Bolivar, by Francisco Zuniga Chavarria AP201

1983, Mar. 1 Litho. *Perf. 10½*

C904	AP200	5col multi	*2.75*	.20
C905	AP200	10col multi	*2.75*	.50
C906	AP200	15col multi	*6.00*	.75
		Nos. C904-C906 (3)	*11.50*	1.45

1983, July 22 Litho. *Perf. 16*

C907	AP201	10col multi	1.00	.20

Nos. C902-C903 Surcharged

1983, Sept. 23 Litho. *Perf. 16*

C908	AP199	10c on 4.80col	.20	.20
C909	AP199	50c on 4.80col	.20	.20
C910	AP199	1.50col on 7.40col	.20	.20
C911	AP199	3col on 7.40col	.20	.20
		Nos. C908-C911 (4)	.80	.80

LACSA Costa Rica Airlines, 40th Anniv. — AP202

Various childrens' drawings.

1986, Dec. 12 Litho. *Perf. 13½*

C912	AP202	1col Adriana E. Hidalgo	*.50*	.20
C913	AP202	7col Osvaldo A.G. Vega	*3.25*	.30
C914	AP202	16col David V. Rodriguez	*7.50*	.75
		Nos. C912-C914 (3)	*11.25*	1.25

Nos. C912-C913 exist perf 11. Unused examples are rare. Value used, $5 each.

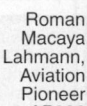

Roman Macaya Lahmann, Aviation Pioneer AP203

1988, Sept. 26 Litho. *Perf. 10½*

C915	AP203	10col multi	.50	.20

No. 418 Ovptd.

1990, Nov. 5

C916	A180	50col multicolored	1.50	.50

Bagging Coffee Beans — AP204

Perf. 10½

1990, Nov. 16 Litho. Unwmk.

C917	AP204	50col multicolored	2.00	.40

AP205

AP206

1990, Dec. 6

C918	AP205	50col blue & black	1.60	.40

First postage stamps, 150th anniv.

1991, Mar. 25 Litho. *Perf. 10½*

Banana Picker, 1897, by Alleardo Villa.

C919	AP206	30col multicolored	1.25	.35

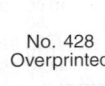

National Theater.

No. 428 Overprinted

Litho. & Engr.

1991, Sept. 13 *Perf. 12½*

C920	A188	200col	6.25	1.50

12th Natl. Philatelic Exposition.

No. 402 Overprinted

1991, Oct. 11 Litho. *Perf. 11½*

Granite Paper

C921	A170	20col multicolored	2.25	.75

Basketball, cent.

Social Security Administration, 50th Anniv. AP207

1991, Nov. 1 Litho. *Perf. 13½*

C922	AP207	15col multicolored	2.50	.30

La Poesia by Vespaciano Bignami — AP208

1992, Jan. 24 Litho. *Perf. 10½*

C923	AP208	35col multicolored	3.25	.65

National Theater.

Discovery of America, 500th Anniv. AP209

Columbus' ships: a, Nina. b, Santa Maria. c, Pinta.

1992, Oct. 8 Litho. *Perf. 13½*

C924	AP209	45col Strip of 3, #a.-c.	4.00	.75

Intl. Arts Festival — AP210

1993, Mar. 15 Litho. *Perf. 13½*

C925	AP210	45col multicolored	1.25	.35

Telecommunications Institute, 30th Anniv. — AP211

1993, Nov. 25 Litho. *Perf. 13½*

C926	AP211	45col multicolored	.95	.60

Ministry of the Interior, 150th Anniv. AP212

1994, Mar. 8 Litho. *Perf. 10½*

C927	AP212	45col multicolored	.95	.60

Intl. Year of the Family — AP213

1994, May 5 Litho. *Perf. 10½*

C928	AP213	45col multicolored	1.00	1.00

LACSA, 50th Anniv. AP214

1996, Mar. 29 Litho. *Perf. 10½*

C929	AP214	5col Douglas DC-3	.20	.20
C930	AP214	10col Curtiss C-46	.20	.20
C931	AP214	20col Beechcraft	.35	.35
C932	AP214	30col DC-6B	.60	.60
C933	AP214	35col BAC 1-11	.65	.65
C934	AP214	40col Convair CV 440	.80	.80
C935	AP214	45col Electra L-188	.90	.90
C936	AP214	50col Boeing 727-200	.95	.95
C937	AP214	55col Douglas DC-8	1.10	1.10
C938	AP214	60col Airbus A320	1.25	1.25
		Nos. C929-C938 (10)	7.00	7.00

No. C932 Surcharged

2001, Oct. 5 Litho. *Perf. 10½*

C939	AP214	5col on 30col multi	.35	.20

10th Intl. Art Festival — AP215

2006, Mar. 17 Litho. *Perf. 10½*

C940	AP215	120col multi	1.75	1.75

AIR POST SPECIAL DELIVERY STAMPS

Catalogue values for unused stamps in this section are for Never Hinged items.

Ivan Goran Kovacic (1913-1943), Author — A61

1993, Apr. 24
153 A61 200d multicolored .35 .35

59th PEN Congress, Dubrovnik A62

1993, Apr. 24
154 A62 800d multicolored 1.40 1.40

Ivan Kukuljevic (1816-89), Politician, Historian, Writer — A63

1993, May 2 Litho. *Perf. 14*
155 A63 500d multicolored .75 .75

Croatian Natl. Theatre, Split, Cent. — A64

Pag, 500th Anniv. — A65

1993, May 6 Litho. *Perf. 14*
156 A64 600d multicolored .75 .75

1993, May 18
157 A65 800d multicolored .90 .90

Croatian Membership in United Nations, 1st Anniv. — A66

1993, May 22
158 A66 500d multicolored .60 .60

Europa A67

Contemporary paintings by: 700d, Ivo Dulcic (1916-75). 1000d, Miljenko Stancic (1926-77). 1100d, Ljubo Ivancic (b. 1925).

1993, June 5
159 A67 700d multicolored *.90 .90*
160 A67 1000d multicolored *1.25 1.25*
161 A67 1100d multicolored *1.50 1.50*
a. Min. sheet, 2 each #159-161 *8.00 8.00*
Nos. 159-161 (3) 3.65 3.65

Intl. Art Biennial, Venice — A68

Works of art by: 250d, Milivoj Bijelic. 600d, Ivo Dekovic. 1000d, Zeljko Kipke.

1993, June 10 Litho. *Perf. 14*
162 A68 250d multicolored .25 .25
a. Souvenir sheet of 4 1.00 1.00
163 A68 600d multicolored .75 .75
a. Souvenir sheet of 4 3.00 3.00
164 A68 1000d multicolored 1.00 1.00
a. Souvenir sheet of 4 4.00 4.00
Nos. 162-164 (3) 2.00 2.00

1993 Mediterranean Games — A69

1993, June 15 Litho. *Perf. 14*
165 A69 700d multicolored .65 .65

Adolf Waldinger (1843-1904), Painter — A70

1993, June 16
166 A70 300d multicolored .30 .30

Famous Croatian Battles A71

1993, July 6 Litho. *Perf. 14*
167 A71 800d Krbavskom, 1493 .65 .65
168 A71 1300d Sisak, 1593 1.10 1.10

Miroslav Krleza (1893-1981), Writer — A72

1993, July 7
169 A72 400d multicolored .35 .35

Croatian Membership in UPU, 1st Anniv. — A73

1993, July 20 Litho. *Perf. 14*
170 A73 1800d multicolored 1.40 .80

Vlaho Paljetak (1893-1944), Composer A74

1993, Aug. 7
171 A74 500d multicolored .40 .40

Stamp Day — A75

1993, Sept. 9 Litho. *Perf. 14*
172 A75 600d multicolored .50 .50

Map of Istria, 1620 — A76

1993, Sept. 20
173 A76 2200d multicolored 1.25 1.25

Incorporation of Istria, Rijeka and Zadar into Croatia, 50th anniv.

Tadija Smiciklas (1843-1914), Historian — A77

1993, Oct. 1
174 A77 800d black, gold & red .50 .50

Archaelogical Museum, Split, Cent. — A78

1993, Oct. 27
175 A78 1000d multicolored .60 .60

A79

A80

1993, Nov. 17 Litho. *Perf. 14*
176 A79 3000d multicolored 1.50 1.50

Uprising of 13th Pioneer Battalion, Villefranche-de-Rouergue, France, 50th anniv.

1993, Nov. 18

900d, Josip Eugen Tomic (1843-1906), writer.

177 A80 900d multicolored .50 .50

Publication of De Esscentiis, by Hermana Dalmatin, 850th Anniv. — A81

1993, Nov. 30
178 A81 1000d multicolored .60 .50

Christmas A82

Paintings: 1000d, Christmas at the Front, by Miroslav Sutej. 4000d, Birth of Christ, 15th cent. fresco, Marienkirch of Dvigrad.

1993, Dec. 3
179 A82 1000d multicolored .60 .40
180 A82 4000d multicolored 2.25 1.50

Organized Skiing in Croatia, Cent. — A83

1993, Dec. 15
181 A83 1000d multicolored .55 .40

Croatian Natl. Guard, 125th Anniv. A84

1993, Dec. 22
182 A84 1100d multicolored .65 .45

Printers of Senj, 500th Anniv. — A85

1994, Jan. 29

183 A85 2200d multicolored 1.10 .75

1994 Winter Olympics, Lillehammer A86

1994, Feb. 12

184 A86 4000d multicolored 2.10 1.75

Dinosaurs from Western Istria — A87

a, 2400d, Iguanodons. b, 4000d, Map, skeleton.

1994, Mar. 7

185 A87 Pair, #a.-b. 3.50 3.50

Nos. 185a-185b are a continuous design.

Zora Dalmatinska Magazine, 150th Anniv. — A88

1994, Mar. 15

186 A88 800d multicolored .45 .30

Croatian University, Zagreb, 325th Anniv. — A89

Design: 2200d, University building, Emperor Leopold I's seal, vice-chancellor's chain.

1994, Apr. 19 **Litho.** ***Perf. 14***

187 A89 2200d multicolored 1.10 .70

Protect the Environment A90

ILO, 75th Anniv. — A91

1994, Apr. 22 **Litho.** ***Perf. 14***

188 A90 3800d Canis lupus 2.00 1.75

1994, May 2

189 A91 1000d multicolored .60 .40

A92

Europa — A93

European inventions, discoveries: 3800d, Faust Vrancic (1551-1617), parachute. 4000d, Slavoljub Penkala (1871-1922), fountain pen.

1994, May 16

190 A92 3800d multicolored *1.40 1.25*
191 A93 4000d multicolored *1.50 1.25*

A94

A95

1994, June 3

192 A94 2.40k Iris croatica 1.25 .60
193 A94 4k Colchicum visianii 2.00 1.25

1994, June 7

Drazen Petrovic (1964-93), basketball player.

194 A95 1k multicolored .50 .45

Tourism in Croatia, 150th Anniv. — A96

Designs: 80 l, Plitvice Lakes Natl. Park. 1k, Waterfalls, Krka River. 1.10k, Kornati Islands Natl. Park. 2.20k, Kopacki Trscak nature reserve. 2.40k Sailboats, Opatijska Riviera resort. 3.80k, Brijuni islands. 4k, Trakoscan castle, Zagorje.

1994, June 15 **Litho.** ***Perf. 14***

196 A96 80 l multicolored .45 .20
197 A96 1k multicolored .50 .25
198 A96 1.10k multicolored .55 .30
199 A96 2.20k multicolored 1.10 .35
200 A96 2.40k multicolored 1.25 .50
201 A96 3.80k multicolored 1.90 .65
202 A96 4k multicolored 2.00 .90
a. Min. sheet of 7, #196-202 + 2 labels 8.50 6.00
Nos. 196-202 (7) 7.75 3.15

Croatian Musicians A97

Designs: 1k, Kresimir Baranovic (1894-1975), composer, vert. 2.20k, Vatroslav Lisinski (1819-54), composer, vert. 2.40k, Pauline Liederbuch (b.1644), harpist.

1994, June 20

211 A97 1k multicolored .50 .35
212 A97 2.20k multicolored 1.10 .75
213 A97 2.40k multicolored 1.25 .85
Nos. 211-213 (3) 2.85 1.95

Croatian Fraternal Union, Cent. — A98

1994, Aug. 15 **Litho.** ***Perf. 14***

214 A98 2.20k multicolored 1.40 1.40

A99

A100

1994, Aug. 31

215 A99 80 l multicolored .50 .50

Intl. Year of the Family.

1994, Sept. 10

216 A100 1k multicolored .50 .50

Intl. Olympic Committee, cent.

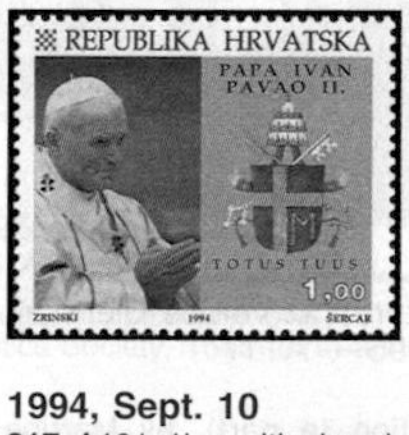

Visit of Pope John Paul II — A101

1994, Sept. 10

217 A101 1k multicolored .65 .55

No. 217 printed with se-tenant label.

Antoine de Saint-Exupery (1900-44), Aviator, Author A102

1994, Sept. 20

218 A102 3.80k multicolored 1.90 1.25

13th Intl. Congress on Early Christian Archeology A103

1994, Sept. 23

219 A103 4k multicolored 2.00 1.25

No. 219 printed with se-tenant label.

Modern Croatian Paintings A104

Designs: 2.40k, Still Life with Fruits and Basket, by Marino Tartaglia, 1926. 3.80k, In the Park, by Milan Steiner, c. 1918. 4k, Self-portrait, by Vilko Gecan, 1929.

1994, Oct. 12

220 A104 2.40k multicolored 1.25 .75
221 A104 3.80k multicolored 1.90 1.25
222 A104 4k multicolored 2.00 1.25
Nos. 220-222 (3) 5.15 3.25

Ivan Belostenec (1594-1675), Writer & Lexicographer A105

1994, Nov. 9

223 A105 2.20k multicolored 1.10 .90

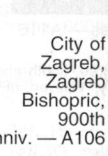

City of Zagreb, Zagreb Bishopric, 900th Anniv. — A106

Designs: No. 224a, 1k, Zagreb exchange building, designed by V. Kovacic, S. Penkala's airplane, Cibona office tower, designed by Hrzic, Pitesa and Serbetic. b, 1k, Maxi Cat, by Zlatko Grgic, Zagreb School of Animated Film. c, 1k, St. Mark's Church, Gradec; photo of gas lantern, by Toso Dabac. d, 4k, Late Gothic bishop's staff, Valvasor's view of Zagreb.

13.50k, Zagreb street scene, Penkala's airplane, vert.

1994, Nov. 16

224 A106 Strip of 4, #a.-d. *3.50 3.50*

Souvenir Sheet

225 A106 13.50k multicolored *6.50 6.50*

No. 224 is a continuous design. No. 225 contains one 24x48mm stamp.

Christmas A107

Design: 1k, Epiphany, by unknown sculptor.

1994, Dec. 1 **Litho.** ***Perf. 14***

226 A107 1k multicolored .60 .50

Kastel Stafilic Olive Trees, 1500th Anniv. — A249

2001, Apr. 20
450 A249 1.80k multi .75 .65

Europa — A250

No. 451: a, 3.50k, Denomination at R. b, 5k, Denomination at L.

2001, May 9
451 A250 Horiz. pair, #a-b *3.25 3.25*

World No Smoking Day — A251

2001, May 31
452 A251 2.50k multi 1.00 .80

Butterflies A252

Designs: 2.50k, Parnassius apollo. 2.80k, Maculinea teleius. 5k, Coenonympha oedippus.

2001, June 5
453-455 A252 Set of 3 4.50 4.50

Type of 1992 Redrawn

2001, June 21 Litho. ***Perf. 14***
456 A39 2.80k Eltz Castle, Vukovar 1.10 1.10
a. Perf. 14 syncopated 1.00 1.00

No. 456 has "1991-2001" inscription, and "HP" and post horn at LL. Issued: No. 456a, 6/19/06.

Souvenir Sheet

Trsteno Arboretum — A253

2001, July 12 Litho. ***Perf. 14***
457 A253 14.40k multi 6.00 6.00

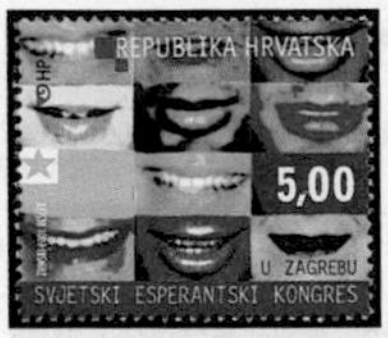

World Esperanto Congress, Zagreb — A254

2001, July 21
458 A254 5k multi 1.80 1.75

Refugee Organizations, 50th Annivs. A255

Designs: 1.80k, UN High Commissioner for Refugees. 5k, Intl. Organization for Migration.

2001, July 28
459-460 A255 Set of 2 2.75 2.75

Victory of Goran Ivanisevic at Wimbledon A256

2001, Aug. 31
461 A256 2.50k multi 1.50 1.25

Printed in sheets of 9 + label.

Stamp Day — A257

2001, Sept. 9
462 A257 2.50k multi .90 .80

Printed in sheets of 16 + 4 labels.

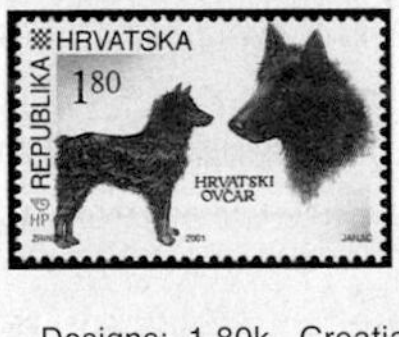

Native Dog Breeds A258

Designs: 1.80k, Croatian sheepdog. 5k, Dalmatian.

2001, Oct. 4
463-464 A258 Set of 2 2.50 2.50

Independence, 10th Anniv. — A259

2001, Oct. 8
465 A259 2.30k multi .80 .75

Printed in sheets of 25 + 5 labels.

Year of Dialogue Among Civilizations — A260

2001, Oct. 9
466 A260 5k multi 1.50 1.40

Fortresses — A261

Designs: 1.80k, Klis, 16th cent. 2.50k, Ston, 14th-15th cents. 3.50k, Sisak, 16th cent.

2001, Oct. 26 Litho. ***Perf. 14***
467-469 A261 Set of 3 3.00 3.00

See Nos. 499-501, 525-527, 565-567, 594-596.

Adoration of the Magi Altarpiece, Church of the Visitation of Mary, Cucerje — A262

2001, Nov. 22 Litho. ***Perf. 14***
470 A262 2.30k multi .90 .80
a. Booklet pane of 10 10.00 —
Complete booklet, #470a 10.00

Modern Art Type of 2000

Designs: No. 471, 2.50k, Maternité du Port-Royal, by Leo Junek. No. 472, 2.50k, Amphitheater Ruins, by Vjekoslav Parac. 5k, Nude with a Baroque Figure, by Slavko Sohaj, vert.

2001, Dec. 1
471-473 A242 Set of 3 4.50 4.50

Croatian Nobel Laureates — A263

Laureates: 2.80k, Lavoslav (Leopold) Ruzicka, Chemistry, 1939. 3.50k, Vladimir Prelog, Chemistry, 1975. 5k, Ivo Andric, Literature, 1961.

2001, Dec. 5
474-476 A263 Set of 3 5.00 5.00

Famous Croats and Events — A264

Designs: 1.80k, Ivan Gucetic (1451-1502), writer. 2.30k, Dobrisa Cesaric (1902-80), writer. 2.50k, Publishing of Juraj Rattkay's *History of Croatian Rulers,* 350th anniv. 2.80k, Franjo Vranjanin Laurana (c. 1420-1502), sculptor. 3.50k, Beatification of Bishop Augustin Kazotic (c. 1260-1323), 300th anniv. 5k, Matko Laginja (1852-1930), politician and writer.

2002, Jan. 24 Litho. ***Perf. 14***
477-482 A264 Set of 6 7.50 7.50

2002 Winter Olympics, Salt Lake City — A265

2002, Feb. 8
483 A265 5k multi 2.00 2.00

Croatian Chamber of Economy, 150th Anniv. — A266

2002, Feb. 16
484 A266 2.50k multi .90 .90

Souvenir Sheet

Trpimir's Deed of Gift, 1150th Anniv. — A267

2002, Mar. 4
485 A267 14.40k multi 6.00 6.00

Franjo Cardinal Kuharic (1919-2002) A268

2002, Mar. 25
486 A268 2.30k multi .90 .90

Divan, by Vlaho Bukovac — A269

Litho. & Engr.

2002, Apr. 23 ***Perf. 11¾***
487 A269 5k multi 2.00 2.00

See Czech Republic No. 3169.

Royal Borough of Krizevci, 750th Anniv. — A270

2002, Apr. 24 Litho. ***Perf. 14***
488 A270 1.80k multi .70 .70

Varazdin Post Office, Cent. — A271

2002, Apr. 26
489 A271 2.30k multi .85 .85

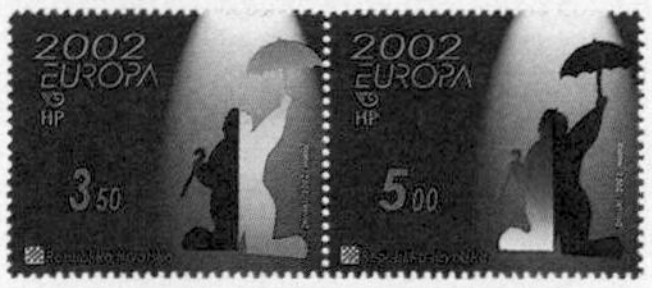

Europa — A272

Clown color: a, 3.50k, Orange. b, 5k, Blue. Illustration reduced.

2002, May 9 Litho. *Perf. 14*
490 A272 Horiz. pair, #a-b *3.00 3.00*

2002 World Cup Soccer Championships, Japan and Korea — A273

Stylized players facing: a, 3.50k, Left. b, 5k, Right.

2002, May 15
491 A273 Horiz. pair, #a-b 3.75 3.75

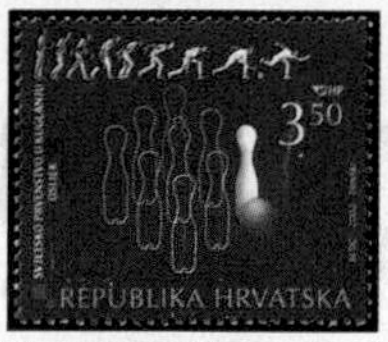

World Bowling Championships, Osijek — A274

2002, May 18
492 A274 3.50k multi 1.40 1.40

Oak Trees — A275

Designs: 1.80k, Quercus rober. 2.50k, Quercus petraea. 2.80k, Quercus ilex.

2002, June 5
493-495 A275 Set of 3 2.75 2.75
493a Booklet pane of 10 5.00 —
Complete booklet, #493a 5.25
494a Booklet pane of 10 10.00 —
Complete booklet, #494a 10.50
495a Booklet pane of 10 12.50 —
Complete booklet, #495a 13.00

15th World Animated Films Festival, Zagreb — A276

2002, June 18
496 A276 5k multi 1.90 1.90

Lace — A277

Lace from: 3.50k, Pag Island, Croatia. 5k, Liedekerke, Belgium.

2002, July 13 Photo. *Perf. 11½*
497-498 A277 Set of 2 3.25 3.25

See Belgium Nos. 1927-1928.

Fortresses Type of 2001

Designs: No. 499, 2.50k, Nehaj, 16th cent. No. 500, 2.50k, Skocibuha, 16th cent. 5k, Veliki Tabor, 16th cent.

2002, Sept. 20 Litho. *Perf. 14*
499-501 A261 Set of 3 3.75 3.75

Old Slavonic Academy, Krk, Cent. — A278

2002, Oct. 3 Litho. & Embossed
502 A278 4k red & black 1.75 1.75

Children's Help Line 48 26 051, 5th Anniv. — A279

2002, Oct. 15 Litho.
503 A279 2.30k multi .90 .90

Christmas A280

2002, Nov. 21
504 A280 2.30k multi .90 .90
a. Booklet pane of 10 9.00 —
Complete booklet, #504a 9.25

Modern Art Type of 2002

Designs: No. 505, 2.50k, Flowers on the Window, by Antun Motika (1902-92), vert. No. 506, 2.50k, The Girl in the Boat, by Milivoj Uzelac (1897-1977), vert. 5k, On the Drava River, by Krsto Hegedusic (1901-75).

2002, Dec. 2 Litho. *Perf. 14*
505-507 A242 Set of 3 4.25 4.25

Zagreb Bishopric, 150th Anniv. — A281

2002, Dec. 11
508 A281 2.80k multi 1.00 1.00

Printed in sheets of 19 + label.

Pavao Ritter Vitezovic (1652-1713), Writer — A282

2002, Dec. 13
509 A282 2.30k multi .90 .90

Pacta Conventa, 900th Anniv. — A283

2002, Dec. 14
510 A283 3.50k multi 1.10 1.10

Fairies From Stories by Ivana Brlic Mazuranic — A284

No. 511: a, 2.30k, Kosjenka, fairy character from *Regoc.* b, 2.80k, Tintilinic, fairy character from *Suma Striborova.*
Illustration reduced.

2003, Jan. 15
511 A284 Horiz. pair, #a-b 1.90 1.90

St. Valentine's Day — A285

Litho. With Foil Application

2003, Feb. 1
512 A285 2.30k multi .90 .90

Astronomy and Meteorology A286

No. 513: a, 1.80k, Zagreb Astronomical Observatory, cent. b, 3.50k, Meteorological measurements in Zagreb, 150th anniv.; Meteorological station on Zavizan, 50th anniv.

2003, Feb. 17 Litho.
513 A286 Pair, #a-b 2.00 2.00

Souvenir Sheet

Croatia, 2003 World Handball Champions — A287

No. 514: a, Five team members, one wearing red shirt. b, Eight team members, one with arm extended. c, Six team members. d, Four team members, one wearing blue shirt.

2003, Feb. 20
514 A287 4k Sheet of 4, #a-d 6.25 6.25

Paulist High School, Lepoglava, 500th Anniv. — A288

2003, Mar. 1
515 A288 5k multi 1.90 1.90

Missal of Hrvoje Vukcic Hrvatinic, 600th Anniv. — A289

2003, Mar. 25
516 A289 5k multi 1.90 1.90

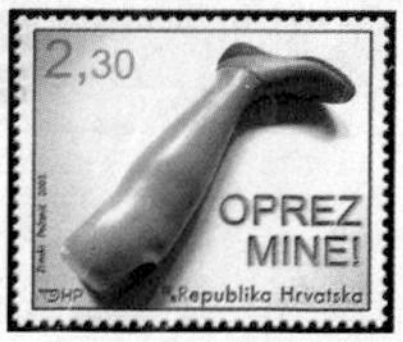

Land Mine Danger A290

2003, Apr. 8
517 A290 2.30k multi .90 .90

Alpine Skiing World Cup Victories of Janica and Ivica Kostelic A291

No. 518: a, Janica. b, Ivica.

2003, Apr. 16
518 A291 3.50k Pair, #a-b 5.00 5.00

Printed in sheets containing 4 vertical pairs and 2 labels.

Christian Institutions in Rome Founded by Croatian Roman Brotherhood of St. Jerome, 550th Anniv. — A292

2003, Apr. 22
519 A292 2.80k multi 1.10 1.10

Famous Croatians A293

Designs: 1.80k, Antun Soljan (1932-93), writer. 2.30k, Hanibal Lucic (1485-1553), writer. 5k, Federiko Benkovic (1667-1753), painter.

2003, Apr. 22
520-522 A293 Set of 3 3.50 3.50

Poster for Performance of Marya Delvard, by Tomislav Krizman, 1907 — A294

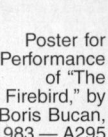

Poster for Performance of "The Firebird," by Boris Bucan, 1983 — A295

2003, May 9 Litho. *Perf. 14*
523 A294 3.50k multi *1.00 1.00*
524 A295 5k multi *1.40 1.40*

Europa.

Fortresses Type of 2001

Designs; 1.80k, Kostajnica, 15th-18th cent. 2.80k, Slavonski Brod, 18th cent. 5k, Minceta Tower, 15th cent., vert.

2003, May 13
525-527 A261 Set of 3 3.50 3.50

Visit of Pope John Paul II — A296

2003, June 2
528 A296 2.30k multi 1.40 1.40

Rodents A297

Designs: 2.30k, Sciuris vulgaris. 2.80k, Glis glis. 3.50k, Castor fiber.

2003, June 5
529-531 A297 Set of 3 3.50 3.50
531a Booklet pane, 6 #529, 2 each #530-531 11.50 —
Complete booklet, #531a 11.50

Souvenir Sheet

Robe of King Ladislaus, 11th Cent. — A298

2003, June 13
532 A298 10k multi 4.00 4.00

Stamp Day — A299

2003, Sept. 9 Litho. *Perf. 14*
533 A299 2.30k multi .90 .90

Souvenir Sheet

Primosten Vineyards — A300

Litho. with Foil Application

2003, Sept. 19
534 A300 10k multi 4.25 4.25

Ursuline Sisters in Croatia, 300th Anniv. — A301

2003, Oct. 20 Litho.
535 A301 2.50k multi .90 .90

Christmas A302

2003, Nov. 20 Litho. *Perf. 14*
536 A302 2.30k multi .90 .90

Self-Adhesive

Serpentine Die Cut 5¼
537 A302 2.30k multi 1.00 1.00

Modern Art A304

Designs: 1.80k, Flower Girl II, by Slavko Kopac, vert. No. 539, 3.50k, Dry Stone Wall 5-71, by Oton Gliha. No. 540, 3.50k, Pont des Arts, by Josip Racic.

2003, Nov. 21 *Perf. 14*
538-540 A304 Set of 3 3.75 3.75

See Nos. 568-570, 604-606, 636-638, 668-670, 712-714.

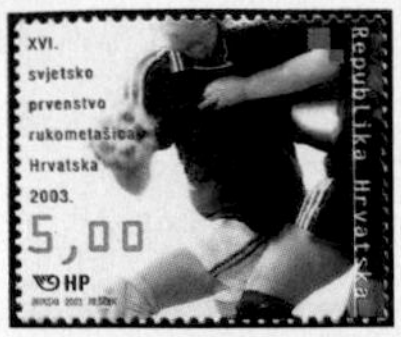

18th World Women's Handball Championships — A305

2003, Dec. 1
541 A305 5k multi 2.00 2.00

Musicians — A306

No. 542: a, Josip Hatze (1879-1959), composer. b, Zagreb Soloists, 50th anniv.

2004, Jan. 5 Litho. *Perf. 14*
542 A306 5k Horiz. pair, #a-b 4.00 4.00

Hval's Manuscript, 600th Anniv. — A307

2004, Jan. 22
543 A307 2.30k multi 1.10 1.10

European Boxing Championships, Pula — A308

2004, Feb. 19 Litho. *Perf. 14*
544 A308 2.80k multi 1.10 1.10

Worldwide Fund for Nature (WWF) — A309

Ardea purpurea: a, In grass. b, Standing with head extended. c, With young. d, In flight.

2004, Mar. 22
545 Strip or block of 4 7.75 7.75
a.-d. A309 5k Any single 1.75 1.75

Famous Croats — A310

Designs: 2.30k, Ivan Lucic (1604-79), historian. No. 547, 3.50k, Antun Vrancic (1504-75), archbishop, writer. No. 548, 3.50k, St. Jerome, sculpture by Andrija Alesi (c. 1425-1504). 10k, Printing of Croatian grammar book, by Bartol Kasic (1575-1650), 400th anniv.

2004, Apr. 22
546-549 A310 Set of 4 7.50 7.50

Souvenir Sheet

Risnjak National Park — A311

2004, Apr. 22
550 A311 10k multi 4.00 4.00

Martyrdom of St. Domnio, 1700th Anniv. — A312

2004, May 7
551 A312 3.50k multi 1.40 1.40

Europa A313

Designs: No. 552, 3.50k, Summer vacation items. No. 553, 3.50k, Winter vacation items.

2004, May 9
552-553 A313 Set of 2 *2.25 2.25*

FIFA (Fédération Internationale de Football Association), Cent. A314

2004, May 21 Litho. *Perf. 14*
554 A314 2.50k multi .95 .95

Medicinal Herbs — A315

Designs: 2.30k, Rosa canina. 2.80k, Viola odorata. 3.50k, Mentha piperita.

2004, June 5

555-557 A315 Set of 3 3.50 3.50
555a Booklet pane of 10 9.00 —
Complete booklet, #555a 9.25
556a Booklet pane of 10 11.00 —
Complete booklet, #556a 11.50
557a Booklet pane of 10 15.00 —
Complete booklet, #557a 15.50

Nos. 555-557 are impregnated with a floral scent.

Intl. Marionette Union Congress, Intl. Puppetry Art Festival, Rijeka A316

2004, June 6

558 A316 3.50k multi 1.25 1.25

European Soccer Championships, Portugal — A317

2004, June 12

559 A317 3.50k multi 1.40 1.40

Values are for stamps with surrounding selvage.

Restoration of Old Bridge, Mostar, Bosnia & Herzegovina A318

2004, July 23 **Litho.** ***Perf. 14***

560 A318 3.50k multi 1.40 1.40

2004 Summer Olympics, Athens — A319

2004, Aug. 13

561 A319 3.50k multi 1.25 1.25

Virovitica A320

2004, Aug. 16

562 A320 5k multi 2.00 2.00

Zagreb Post Office, Cent. A321

2004, Sept. 9

563 A321 2.30k multi .90 .90

Printed in sheets of 16 + 4 labels.

Father Andrija Kacic Miosic (1704-60), Poet — A322

2004, Sept. 15

564 A322 2.80k multi 1.10 1.10

Fortresses Type of 2001

Designs: No. 565, 3.50k, Dubovac, 15th-19th cent. No. 566, 3.50k, Gripe, 17th cent. No. 567, 3.50k, Valpovo, 15th-18th cent.

2004, Sept. 29

565-567 A261 Set of 3 4.25 4.25

Modern Art Type of 2003

Designs: No. 568, 2.30k, Self-portrait, by Miroslav Kraljevic, vert. No. 569, 2.30k, Noon in Supetar, by Jerolim Mise, vert. No. 570, 2.30k, Stari Grad, by Juraj Plancic, vert.

2004, Nov. 15 **Litho.** ***Perf. 14***

568-570 A304 Set of 3 2.75 2.75

Christmas A323

2004, Nov. 25

571 A323 2.30k multi .90 .90

Antun and Stjepan Radic and Plowman — A324

2004, Dec. 22 **Litho.** ***Perf. 14***

572 A324 7.20k multi 2.75 2.75

Croatian People's Peasant Party, Cent.

Fairy Tale Characters — A325

No. 573: a, Mermaid Halugica. b, Dwarf Pedalj Muza Lakat Brade. Illustration reduced.

2005, Jan. 14

573 A325 5k Horiz. pair, #a-b 4.25 4.25

World Conference on the Information Society, Tunis — A326

2005, Feb. 10

574 A326 2.80k multi 1.10 1.10

Values are for stamps with surrounding selvage.

Souvenir Sheet

Bust of Livia Drusilla — A327

2005, Feb. 24

575 A327 10k multi 5.25 5.25

Souvenir Sheet

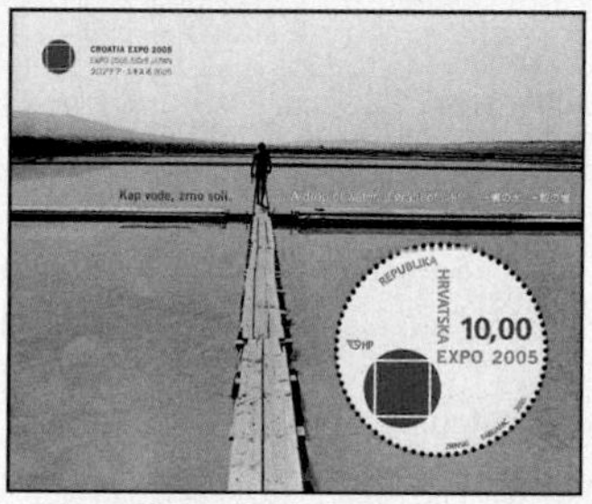

Expo 2005, Aichi, Japan — A328

2005, Mar. 25 ***Perf.***

576 A328 10k multi 5.25 5.25

Pope John Paul II (1920-2005) A329

2005, Apr. 8 ***Perf. 14***

577 A329 2.30k multi .95 .95

World Music Days, Zagreb A330

Stjepan Sulek (1914-86), Composer A331

2005, Apr. 15

578 A330 2.30k multi .95 .95
579 A331 2.30k multi .95 .95

Insects — A332

Designs: 1.80k, Coccinella septempunctata. 2.30k, Rosalia alpina. 3.50k, Lucanus cervus.

2005, Apr. 22

580-582 A332 Set of 3 3.25 3.25

Liberation of Western Slavonia, 10th Anniv. A333

2005, May 1

583 A333 1.80k multi .70 .70

Dr. Josip Buturac (1905-93), Historian — A334

2005, May 6

584 A334 2.80k multi 1.10 1.10

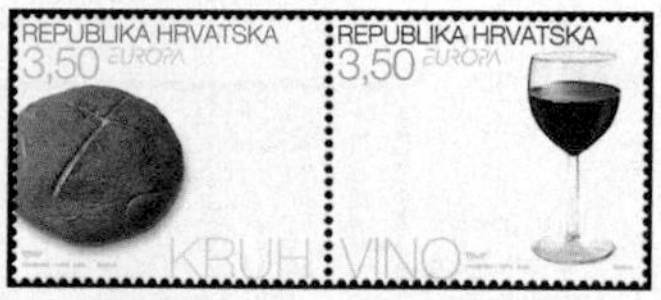

Europa — A335

No. 585: a, Loaf of bread. b, Glass of wine. Illustration reduced.

2005, May 9

585 A335 3.50k Horiz. pair, #a-b *2.75 2.75*

Coast of Hvar Island — A336

No. 586: a, Rock at L, tree tops at bottom. b, Tree tops at LL. c, Rock at R. d, Canoe, rock at R. e, Small rock in center. f, Rocks at UL, trees. g, Rocks at R, trees. h, Tree tops at LL corner, rock at UR corner. i, Rocks at UL and LL corners. j, Rocks at LL.

2005, May 24 **Litho.** ***Perf. 14***

586 A336 Booklet pane of 10 14.00 —
a.-e. 1.80k Any single 1.00 1.00
f.-j. 3.50k Any single 1.50 1.50
Complete booklet, #586 15.00

Kresimir Cosic (1948-95), Basketball Player — A337

2005, May 25

587 A337 3.50k multi 1.40 1.40

Printed in sheets of 9 + 1 label.

Krapanj Island Sponge and Coral Diving — A338

2005, June 2 **Litho.**

588 A338 3.50k multi 1.40 1.40

Portions of the design were applied by a thermographic process producing a shiny, raised effect.

Emperor Constantine's Bath, Varazdinske Toplice A339

2005, June 20 ***Perf. 14***

589 A339 1.80k multi .75 .75

Intl. Fire Brigade Olympics, Varazdin A340

2005, July 15

590 A340 2.30k multi 1.25 1.25

Printed in sheets of 8 + 2 labels.

European Philatelic Cooperation, 50th Anniv. (in 2006) A341

Designs: 7.20k, Vignette of #134. 8k, Stylized gull.

2005, Sept. 8

591-592 A341 Set of 2 *7.00 7.00*

592a Souvenir sheet, #591-592 *38.50 38.50*

Europa stamps, 50th anniv. (in 2006).

Telegraph A342

2005, Sept. 9

593 A342 2.30k multi .95 .95

First overhead telegraph lines in Croatia, 155th anniv., Stamp Day.

Fortresses Type of 2001

Designs: 1k, Ilok, 14th-15th cents. 2.30k, Motovun, 13th-15th cents., vert. 3.50k, St. Nicholas, 16th cent.

2005, Sept. 15

594-596 A261 Set of 3 2.75 2.75

Famous People — A343

Designs: 1k, Adam Baltazar Krcelic (1715-78), historian. No. 598, 2.30k, Dragutin Tadijanovic (b. 1905), poet. No. 599, 2.30k, Tin Ujevic (1891-1955), poet. 2.80k, Madonna and Child, by Juraj Culinovic (c.1433-1504).

2005, Nov. 4

597-600 A343 Set of 4 3.75 3.75

Clock Tower, Rijeka — A344

2005, Nov. 10 **Litho.** ***Perf. 14***

601 A344 3.50k multi 1.40 1.40

a. Perf. 14 syncopated 1.40 1.40

Issued: No. 601a, 6/12/06.

Christmas A345

2005, Nov. 22 ***Perf. 14***

602 A345 2.30k multi .95 .95

Booklet Stamp
Self-Adhesive
Serpentine Die Cut 5¼

603 A345 2.30k multi .95 .95

a. Booklet pane of 10 9.50 9.50

Complete booklet, #603a 9.50 9.50

Modern Art Type of 2003

Designs: 1.80k, Zadar, by Edo Murtic. 5k, Meander, by Julije Knifer. 10k, Drawing, by Miroslav Sutej, vert.

2005, Dec. 1 ***Perf. 14***

604-606 A304 Set of 3 7.25 7.25

Davis Cup and Members of Croatian Tennis Team — A346

2005, Dec. 22 **Litho.** ***Perf. 14***

607 A346 5k multi 2.00 2.00

Croatia, winners of 2005 Davis Cup. Printed in sheets of 9 + label.

Composers A347

Designs: 1.80k, Boris Papandopulo (1906-91). 2.30k, Milo Cipra (1906-85). 2.80k, Ivan Brkanovic (1906-87).

2006, Jan. 17

608-610 A347 Set of 3 2.75 2.75

2006 Winter Olympics, Turin — A348

2006, Feb. 10

611 A348 3.50k multi 1.40 1.40

Rembrandt (1606-69), Painter A349

2006, Mar. 7

612 A349 5k multi 2.25 2.25

Famous Men — A350

Designs: No. 613, 1k, Andrija Ljudevit Adamic (1766-1828), merchant. No. 614, 1k, Josip Kozarac (1858-1906), writer. 5k, Vanja Radaus (1906-75), sculptor. 7.20k, Ljubo Karaman (1886-1971), art historian.

2006, Mar. 21 ***Perf. 14 Syncopated***

613-616 A350 Set of 4 5.75 5.75

European Track and Field Championships, Göteborg, Sweden — A351

2006, Apr. 4

617 A351 2.30k multi .95 .95

2006 World Cup Soccer Championships, Germany A352

2006, Apr. 4

618 A352 2.80k multi 1.10 1.10

Flag and Crowd — A353

No. 619 — Location and placement of denomination: a, At left, with denomination above crowd. b, At right, with top of numerals over red in flag. c, At left, with top of "8" and "0" above white in flag. d, At left, with serif of "1" above red in flag. e, At left, with entire denomination above red in flag. f, At right, with parts of "5" and "0" above red in flag. g, At right, with entire denomination above red in flag. h, At right, with entire denomination above white in flag. i, At left, with entire denomination above red in flag. j, At right, with denomination above crowd.

2006, Apr. 25

619 A353 Booklet pane of 10 11.50 —

a.-e. 1.80k Any single .80 .80

f.-j. 3.50k Any single 1.50 1.50

Complete booklet, #619 12.50

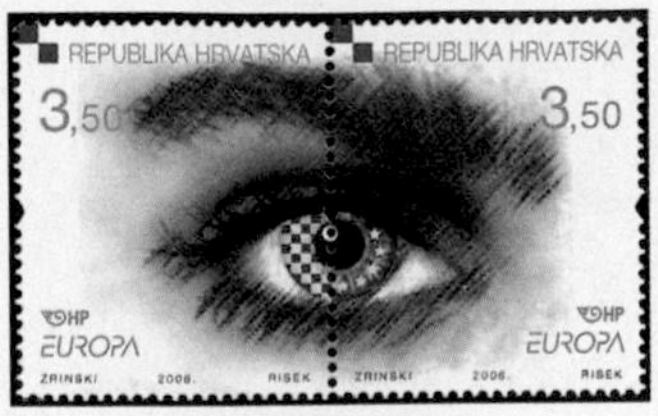

Europa — A354

No. 620: a, Denomination at left. b, Denomination at right.

2006, May 9

620 A354 3.50k Horiz. pair, #a-b *3.00 3.00*

Worldwide Fund for Nature (WWF) A355

No. 621 — Various views of Sterna albifrons with denomination in: a, Gray. b, Dull green. c, Yellow orange. d, Red.

2006, May 23

621 Strip of 4 8.50 8.50

a.-d. A355 5k Any single 2.00 2.00

Croatian Automobile Club, Cent. — A356

Perf. 13¾x14 Syncopated

2006, June 4

622 A356 5k multi 2.00 2.00

Aquatic Flowers A357

Designs: 2.30k, Nymphaea alba. 2.80k, Nuphar lutea. 3.50k, Menyanthes trifoliata.

2006, June 5 ***Perf. 14 Syncopated***

623-625 A357 Set of 3 3.50 3.50

623a Booklet pane of 10 9.50 9.50

Complete booklet, #623a 9.50

624a Booklet pane of 10 11.00 11.00

Complete booklet, #624a 11.00

625a Booklet pane of 10 14.00 14.00

Complete booklet, #625a 14.00

Nikola Tesla (1856-1943), Inventor — A358

Perf. 14x13½ Syncopated

2006, July 10 **Litho.**

626 A358 3.50k multi 1.40 1.40

Bjelovar, 250th Anniv. A359

Perf. 14 Syncopated

2006, Aug. 22 **Litho.**

627 A359 2.80k multi 1.10 1.10

Stamp Day — A360

2006, Sept. 9 **Litho. & Embossed**

628 A360 2.30k multi .95 .95

Jewish Community of Zagreb, 200th Anniv. — A361

Perf. 14¼x13¾ Syncopated

2006, Sept. 15 **Litho.**

629 A361 5k multi 2.00 2.00

Fortresses Type of 2001

Designs: No. 630, 1k, St. Mary of Mercy Church, Vrboska, 16th cent. No. 631, 1k, Church of the Holy Spirit, Sudurad, 16th cent. 7.20k, Frankapan Citadel, Ogulin, 16th cent.

Perf. 13¾x14¼ Syncopated

2006, Sept. 21

630-632 A261 Set of 3 3.75 3.75

White Cane Safety Day — A362

Perf. 14 Syncopated

2006, Oct. 15 **Litho. & Embossed**

633 A362 1.80k black & red .75 .75

Christmas A363

Perf. 14¼ Syncopated

2006, Nov. 27 **Litho.**

634 A363 2.30k multi .85 .85

Booklet Stamp

Self-Adhesive

Serpentine Die Cut 5¼

635 A363 2.30k multi .85 .85
a. Booklet pane of 10 8.50
Complete booklet, #635a 8.50

Modern Art Type of 2003

Designs: 1k, Still Life, by Vladimir Becic. 1.80k, Composition Tyma 3, by Ivan Picelj. 10k, Self-portrait as Hunter, by Nasta Rojc, vert.

2006, Dec. 1 ***Perf. 14 Syncopated***

636-638 A304 Set of 3 5.25 5.25

Classical Gymnasium, Zagreb, 400th Anniv. — A364

Perf. 14 Syncopated

2007, Jan. 9 **Litho.**

639 A364 5k multi 2.00 2.00

Fairy Tale Characters — A365

No. 640: a, Monster Orko. b, Devil Macic. Illustration reduced.

2007, Jan. 18

640 A365 2.30k Horiz. pair, #a-b 1.75 1.75

National and University Library, Zagreb, 400th Anniv. A366

2007, Feb. 22

641 A366 5k multi 2.00 2.00

Crustaceans A367

Designs: 1.80k, Palinurus elephas. 2.30k, Nephrops norvegicus. 2.80k, Astacus astacus.

2007, Mar. 15

642 A367 1.80k multi .80 .80
a. Booklet pane of 10 8.00 —
Complete booklet, #642a 8.00
643 A367 2.30k multi 1.00 1.00
a. Booklet pane of 10 10.00 —
Complete booklet, #643a 10.00
644 A367 2.80k multi 1.25 1.25
a. Booklet pane of 10 12.50 —
Complete booklet, #644a 12.50
Nos. 642-644 (3) 3.05 3.05

Native Breeds of Farm Animals A368

Designs: 2.80k, Istrian ox. 3.50k, Posavina horse. 5k, Dalmatian donkey.

2007, Mar. 20

645-647 A368 Set of 3 4.50 4.50

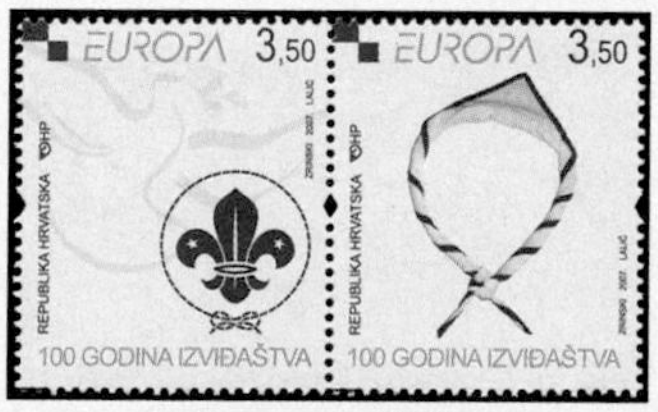

Europa — A369

No. 648: a, Scouting emblem and dove. b, Scout neckerchief.

2007, Apr. 16

648 A369 3.50k Horiz. pair, #a-b 2.60 2.60

Scouting, cent.

Scientists — A370

Designs: 5k, Andrija Mohorovicic (1857-1936), seismologist. 7.20k, Duro Baglivi (1668-1707), physician.

Perf. 14x13½ Syncopated

2007, Apr. 23

649-650 A370 Set of 2 5.00 5.00

Souvenir Sheet

World Championship Victory of Croatian Water Polo Team — A371

No. 651: a, Man with red shirt at right, denomination at UL. b, Man with red shirt at LR, denomination at UR. c, Man with red shirt at left, denomination at UR.

Litho. With Foil Application

2007, May 3 ***Perf. 14¼ Syncopated***

651 A371 5k Sheet of 3, #a-c 6.00 6.00

World Table Tennis Championships, Zagreb — A372

Perf. 14 Syncopated

2007, May 21 **Litho. & Embossed**

652 A372 3.50k multi 1.50 1.50

Starting with No. 652 some stamps have an imprinted wing-shaped tagging design that looks like a watermark.

Diplomatic Relations Between Croatia and People's Republic of China, 15th Anniv. — A373

No. 653: a, "China" in Glagolithic letters. b, "Croatia" in Chinese characters. Illustration reduced.

2007, May 30 **Litho.** ***Perf. 12***

653 A373 5k Horiz. pair, #a-b 4.25 4.25

Zagreb City Museum, Cent. — A374

2007, May 31 ***Perf. 14 Syncopated***

654 A374 2.30k multi .85 .85

Souvenir Sheet

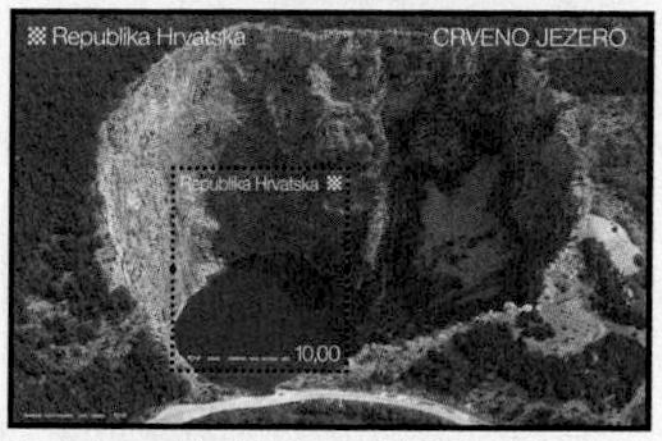

Red Lake — A375

2007, June 8

655 A375 10k multi 4.25 4.25

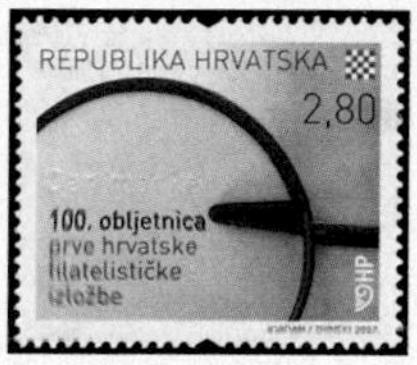

First Croatian Philatelic Exhibition, Cent. — A376

Perf. 14 Syncopated

2007, Sept. 9 **Litho. & Embossed**

656 A376 2.80k multi 1.10 1.10

Stamp Day.

Lighthouses — A377

Designs: No. 657, 5k, St. John on the Sea Lighthouse. No. 658, 5k, Porer Lighthouse. No. 659, 5k, Savudrija Lighthouse.

Perf. 13¾x14¼ Syncopated

2007, Sept. 14 **Litho.**

657-659 A377 Set of 3 6.25 6.25

Veprinac Statute, 500th Anniv. — A378

Perf. 14¼x13¾ Syncopated

2007, Oct. 2

660 A378 2.70k multi 1.10 1.10

City Views — A379

Designs: 1.80k, Omis. 2.30k, Koprivnica, horiz. 2.80k, Krk.

2007, Oct. 30 ***Perf. 14 Syncopated***

661	A379 1.80k multi		.75	.75
662	A379 2.30k multi		.90	.90
663	A379 2.80k multi		1.10	1.10
	Nos. 661-663 (3)		2.75	2.75

Blanka Vlasic, 2007 World Women's High Jump Champion A380

2007, Nov. 8

664	A380 2.30k multi	.95	.95

Christmas A381

Perf. 14¼ Syncopated

2007, Nov. 15 **Litho.**

665	A381 2.30k multi	.95	.95

Booklet Stamp

Self-Adhesive

Serpentine Die Cut 5¼

666	A381 2.30k multi	.95	.95
a.	Booklet pane of 10	9.50	
	Complete booklet, #666a	9.50	

Marija Juric Zagorka (1873-1957), Writer — A382

Perf. 14¼x13¾ Syncopated

2007, Nov. 16

667	A382 7.20k multi	3.00	3.00

Modern Art Type of 2003

Designs: 2.80k, Area by the Sava River, by Branko Senoa. No. 669, 5k, Pegasus's Garden, by Ferdinand Kulmer. No. 670, 5k, Bridgeport, by Ivan Benkovic.

Perf. 14 Syncopated

2007, Dec. 1 **Litho.**

668-670	A304 Set of 3	5.25	5.25

New Year 2008 — A383

2007, Dec. 5

671	A383 1.80k multi	.75	.75

Composers A384

Designs: No. 672, 2.30k, Igor Kuljeric (1938-2006). No. 673, 2.30k, Krsto Odak (1888-1965).

2008, Jan. 22

672-673	A384 Set of 2	1.90	1.90

Publication of *Arithmetika Horvatszka*, by Mijo Silobod Bolsic, 250th Anniv. — A385

Perf. 13¾x14 Syncopated

2008, Jan. 25

674	A385 3.50k multi	1.40	1.40

Steam Locomotives — A386

Designs: No. 675, 5k, MAV 601/JZ 32. No. 676, 5k, MAV 651/JZ 31.

2008, Feb. 15

675-676	A386 Set of 2	4.25	4.25

Nos. 675-676 were printed in sheets of 6 containing three of each stamp.

St. Nicholas Church, Cavtat A387

Perf. 14 Syncopated

2008, Mar. 8 **Litho.**

677	A387 7.20k multi	3.00	3.00

2008 Summer Olympics, Beijing A388

2008, Mar. 11

678	A388 5k multi	2.25	2.25

Printed in sheets of 9 + label.

Flowers — A389

Designs: 1.80k, Helleborus niger. 2.80k, Onosma stellulata. 3.50k, Lonicera glutinosa.

2008, Mar. 20

679	A389 1.80k multi	.80	.80
a.	Booklet pane of 10	8.00	—
	Complete booklet, #679a	8.00	
680	A389 2.80k multi	1.25	1.25
a.	Booklet pane of 10	12.50	—
	Complete booklet, #680a	12.50	
681	A389 3.50k multi	1.50	1.50
a.	Booklet pane of 10	15.00	—
	Complete booklet, #681a	15.00	
	Nos. 679-681 (3)	3.55	3.55

Famous Writers — A390

Designs: 2.30k, Petar Zoranic (1508-c. 1569), novelist. 2.80k, Silvije Strahimir Kranjcevic (1865-1908), poet. 7.20k, Marin Drzic (1508-67), dramatist.

Perf. 14 Syncopated

2008, Apr. 22 **Litho.**

682-684	A390 Set of 3	5.25	5.25

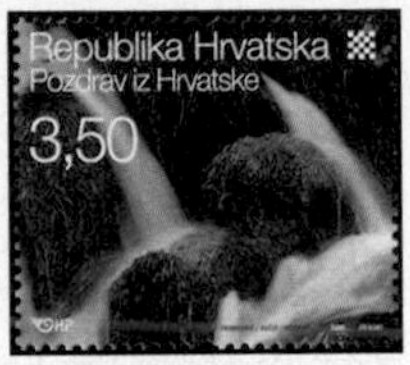

Waterfall, Plitvice Lakes National Park — A391

No. 685 — Part of waterfall with: a, Country name in white, denomination at UL, "HP" symbol in white at LL. b, Country name in white, denomination at UR, "HP" symbol in white at LL, green foliage at UL. c, Country name in black, denomination at UR. d, Country name in white, denomination at UR, "HP" symbol in black at LL. e, Country name in white, denomination at UR, "HP" symbol in white at LL, green foliage at UR. f, Country name in white, denomination in black at LR, "HP" symbol in black at LL, rock with foliage in center. g, Country name in white, denomination in black at LR, "HP" symbol in black at LL, all rocks covered by spray. h, Country name in black, denomination at LR. i, Country name in white, denomination in white at LR. j, Country name in white, denomination in black at LR, "HP" symbol in white at LL.

Perf. 14 Syncopated

2008, Apr. 25 **Litho.**

685	Booklet pane of 10	15.00	—
a.-j.	A391 3.50k Any single	1.50	1.50
	Complete booklet, #685	15.00	

2008 Volkswagen Beetle — A392

Illustration reduced.

2008, May 8

686	A392 2.30k multi + label	1.00	1.00

Europa A393

Designs: 3.50k, Insured envelope with wax seal. 5k, Airmail envelope.

2008, May 9 **Litho.**

687	A393 3.50k multi	1.50	1.50

Litho. & Embossed

688	A393 5k multi	2.25	2.25

Portions of the design of No. 687 were applied using a thermographic process producing a shiny raised effect.

UEFA Euro 2008 Soccer Championships, Austria and Switzerland — A394

2008, May 14 **Litho.** ***Perf. 14x13½***

689	A394 3.50k multi	1.60	1.60

Values are for stamps with surrounding selvage. Printed in sheets of 9 + label.

Adris Group — A395

Illustration reduced.

2008, May 16 ***Perf. 14 Syncopated***

690	A395 2.30k multi + label	1.00	1.00

Souvenir Sheet

Ivan Vucetic (1858-1925), Fingerprint Classifier — A396

2008, Apr. 20

691	A396 10k multi	4.50	4.50

Souvenir Sheet

Expo Zaragoza 2008 — A397

Litho. With Foil Application

2008, June 16

692	A397 10k multi	4.50	4.50

Souvenir Sheet

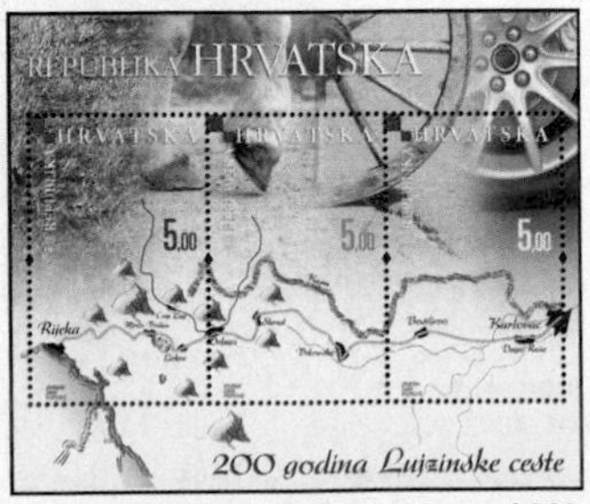

Lujzinske Road, 200th Anniv. — A398

No. 693 — Parts of map of Lujzinske Road with denomination in: a, Red. b, Green. c, White.

Perf. 14x13½ Syncopated

2008, June 17 **Litho.**

693	A398 5k Sheet of 3, #a-c	6.50	6.50

Western Union — A399

Illustration reduced.

2008, July 11 ***Perf. 14 Syncopated***
694 A399 3.50k multi + label 1.50 1.50

Postal Workers' Games — A400

Litho. With Foil Application
2008, Sept. 9 ***Perf. 14 Syncopated***
695 A400 2.80k multi 1.10 1.10

Stamp Day.

Lighthouses A401

Designs: No. 696, 5k, Pinida Lighthouse. No. 697, 5k, Vnetak Lighthouse. No. 698, 5k, Zaglav Lighthouse.

Perf. 14¼x13¾ Syncopated
2008, Sept. 12 **Litho.**
696-698 A401 Set of 3 6.00 6.00

Order of St. Clare, Split, 700th Anniv. — A402

2008, Sept. 16
699 A402 2.80k multi 1.10 1.10

Details From Native Costumes A403

Costume from: 10 l, Sunja. 20 l, Bistra. 50 l, Bizovac. 1k, Ravni Kotari. 10k, Pag.

2008, Sept. 30 ***Perf. 14 Syncopated***
700-704 A403 Set of 5 4.75 4.75
704a Sheet of 5, #700-704 + label 4.75 4.75

European Healthy Cities Movement, 20th Anniv. — A404

Illustration reduced.

2008, Oct. 17 ***Perf. 14¼ Syncopated***
705 A404 2.80k multi + label 1.00 1.00

Collegium Ragusinum, Dubrovnik, 350th Anniv. — A405

Perf. 14¼x13¾ Syncopated
2008, Nov. 7 **Litho. & Embossed**
706 A405 7.20k multi 2.60 2.60

Intl. Amateur Radio Union Region 1 Conference, Cavtat — A406

Perf. 13¾x14¼ Syncopated
2008, Nov. 14 **Litho.**
707 A406 3.50k multi 1.25 1.25

The Book on the Art of Trading, by Benedikt Kotruljevic, 550th Anniv. of Publication A407

Perf. 14¼x13¾ Syncopated
2008, Oct. 22 **Litho.**
708 A407 2.80k multi 1.00 1.00

New Year's Day — A408

Perf. 14 Syncopated
2008, Nov. 21 **Litho.**
709 A408 1.80k multi .65 .65

Christmas A409

2008, Nov. 27
710 A409 2.80k multi 1.00 1.00

Modern Art Type of 2003

Designs: 1.65k, Two Trees at the Foot of a Hill, by Oskar Herman. 1.80k, Carousel, by Nevenka Djordjevic. 6.50k, Still Life, by Ivo Rezek.

Perf. 14 Syncopated
2008, Dec. 1 **Litho.**
712-714 A304 Set of 3 3.50 3.50

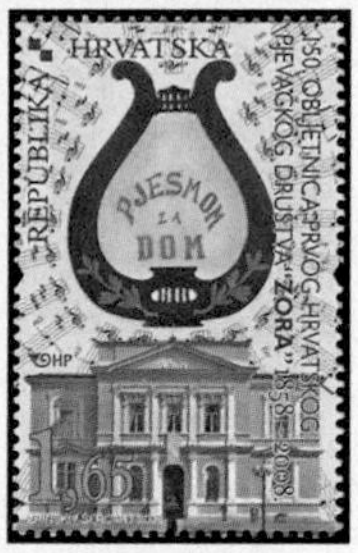

Zora Choral Society, 150th Anniv. — A410

Perf. 14x13¾ Syncopated
2008, Dec. 5
715 A410 1.65k multi .60 .60

SEMI-POSTAL STAMPS

Catalogue values for unused stamps in this section are for Never Hinged items.

Types of Yugoslavia, 1941, Overprinted in Gold "NEZAVISNA / DRZAVA / HRVATSKA"

Perf. 11½
1941, May 10 **Unwmk.** **Engr.**
B1 SP80 1.50d + 1.50d bl blk 16.00 16.00
B2 SP81 4d + 3d choc 16.00 16.00

Panes of 16 stamps and 9 labels.
This overprint exists on Yugoslavia No. B124. Value $2,500.

Five thousand sets of Yugoslavia Nos. 142-154 were overprinted "NEZAVISNA DRZAVA HRVATSKA 10. IV. 1941" and small shield in red or blue, in 1941. Sold for double face value. Value, set, $550.

Costume of Sinj, Dalmatia — SP1

Soldiers with Arms of the Axis States — SP4

Designs (Costumes): 2k+2k, Travnik, Bosnia. 4k+4k, Turopolje, Croatia.

1941, Oct. 12 **Photo.** ***Perf. 10½x10***
B3 SP1 1.50k + 1.50k Prus bl & red 1.00 1.00
B4 SP1 2k + 2k ol brn & red 1.25 1.25
B5 SP1 4k + 4k brn lake & red 2.25 2.25
Nos. B3-B5 (3) 4.50 *4.50*

The surtax aided the Croatian Red Cross.
Panes of 20 stamps and 5 labels.

1941, Dec. 3 ***Perf. 11***
B6 SP4 4k + 2k blue 3.00 *3.75*

The surtax was used for Croatian Volunteers in the East.
Issued in panes of 100 stamps.

Model Plane — SP5

Model Plane — SP6

Designs: 3k+3k, Boy with model plane. 4k+4k, Model seaplane in flight.

1942, Mar. 25
B7 SP5 2k + 2k sepia 1.75 1.75
B8 SP6 2.50k + 2.50k dl grn 1.75 1.75
B9 SP5 3k + 3k brn car 1.75 1.75
B10 SP6 4k + 4k dp bl 1.75 1.75
Nos. B7-B10 (4) 7.00 *7.00*

Nos. B7-B10 were issued both in panes of 25 and in panes of 24 plus label.

Values for used souvenir sheets are for those with special philatelic cancels. Faked postal cancellations on souvenir sheets are common, especially using cancellers stolen after WWII. Genuine postal cancellations are the exception and sell for much more. Expertization is recommended.

Souvenir Sheets
Perf. 11

B11 Sheet of 2 47.50 45.00
a. SP5 2k+8k brown carmine 12.00 *12.00*
b. SP5 3k+12k deep blue 12.00 *12.00*

Imperf

B12 Sheet of 2 55.00 52.50
a. SP5 2k+8k deep blue 14.00 *14.00*
b. SP5 3k+12k brown carmine 14.00 *14.00*

The sheets measure 125x110mm.
Aviation Exposition of Zagreb. The surtax aided society of Croatian Wings (Hrvatska Krila).
Nos. B11-B12 exist with colors of stamps and inscriptions transposed, with missing colors and with one stamp missing.

Boy Trumpeters SP10

Triumphal Arch — SP11

Mother and Child — SP12

1942, July 5 ***Perf. 11½***
B13 SP10 3k + 1k lake 1.50 1.50
B14 SP11 4k + 2k dk brn 1.50 1.50
B15 SP12 5k + 5k dp bl grn 1.50 1.50
Nos. B13-B15 (3) 4.50 *4.50*

The surtax was for national welfare.
Issued in panes of 25.

Matthew Gubec
SP13

Ante Starcevich
SP14

SP15

1942, Nov. 22 *Perf. 14½*

B16 SP13 3k + 6k dark red .80 .80
B17 SP14 4k + 7k sepia .80 .80

Souvenir Sheets

Perf. 12, Imperf.

B18 SP15 5k + 20k dull blue 20.00 *20.00*

Heroes of Senj, May 9, 1937. Nos. B16-B17 were printed in panes of 16 + 9 labels, each bearing a hero's name. The surtax aided the Natl. Youth Soc.

Sestine Peasant
SP16

Croatian Labor Corpsman
SP20

Designs: 3k+1k, Slavonian peasant. 4k+2k, Bosnian peasant. 10k+5k, Dalmatian peasant. 13k+6k, Sestine peasant.

1942, Oct. 4 *Perf. 11½*

B20 SP16 1.50k + 50b org brn & red 1.50 1.50
B21 SP16 3k + 1k dl pur & red 1.50 1.50
B22 SP16 4k + 2k dp bl & red 2.25 2.25
B23 SP16 10k + 5k dk ol bis & red 3.25 3.25
B24 SP16 13k + 6k rose lake & red 6.00 6.00
Nos. B20-B24 (5) 14.50 *14.50*

The surtax aided the Croatian Red Cross. Issued in panes of 24 stamps plus label.

1943, Jan. 17 **Wmk. 278** *Perf. 11*

Designs: 3k+3k, Corpsman with wheelbarrow. 7k+4k, Corpsman plowing.

B25 SP20 2k + 1k ol gray & sepia 4.00 *4.25*
B26 SP20 3k + 3k brn & sepia 4.00 *4.25*
B27 SP20 7k + 4k gray bl & sepia 4.00 *4.25*
Nos. B25-B27 (3) 12.00 *12.75*

The surtax aided the State Labor Service (Drzavna Radna Sluzba). Issued in panes of 9.

Arms of Zagreb and "Golden Bull" — SP23

1943, Mar. 21 **Unwmk.**

B28 SP23 3.50k (+ 6.50k) ultra 4.00 *4.25*

700th anniversary of Zagreb's "Golden Bull," a Magna Carta of civic rights and privileges granted to the city in 1242 by King Bela because the Croats annihilated Tartar hordes at Grobnik.

Issued in panes of 8 with marginal inscriptions.

Ante Pavelich — SP24

Sailor at Sea of Azov — SP26

1943, Apr. 10 *Perf. 13¾x14*

B29 SP24 5k + 3k copper red .60 .60
a. Sheetlet of 16 #B29 + 9 labels 11.00 11.00
B30 SP24 7k + 5k dark green .60 .60
a. Sheetlet of 16 #B30 + 9 labels 11.00 11.00

Surtax aided the National Youth Society.

Nos. B29-B30 were issued in panes of 100 stamps. Nos. B29a and B30a were issued Apr. 12 and are perf 14½.

Souvenir Sheets

1943, May 17 *Perf. 12, Imperf.*

B31 SP24 12k + 8k dp ultra 25.00 25.00

1943, July 1 *Perf. 11*

Designs: 2k+1k, Flier at Sevastopol and Rzhev. 3.50k+1.50k, Infantrymen at Stalingrad. 9k+4.50k, Panzer Division at Don River.

B33 SP26 1k + 50b grn .35 .25
B34 SP26 2k + 1k dk red .35 .25
B35 SP26 3.50k + 1.50k dk bl .35 .25
B36 SP26 9k + 4.50k chestnut .35 .25
Nos. B33-B36 (4) 1.40 *1.00*

Souvenir Sheets

Perf. 11, Imperf.

B37 Sheet of 4 7.00 7.00
a. SP26 1k+50b dark blue 1.25 *1.25*
b. SP26 2k+1k green 1.25 *1.25*
c. SP26 3.50k+1.50k dk red brown 1.25 *1.25*
d. SP26 9k+4.50k bluish black 1.25 *1.25*

Surtax aided the National Youth Society. Issued to honor the Croatian Legion which fought with the Germans in Russia. The surtax aided the Legion.

Issued in panes of 100.

St. Mary's Church and Cistercian Cloister, Zagreb, in 1650
SP31

1943, Sept. 12 **Engr.** *Perf. 14½*

B39 SP31 18k + 9k dl gray vio 5.00 *5.25*

Souvenir Sheet

Perf. 12½

B40 SP31 18k + 9k blk brn 15.00 15.00

Croatian Phil. Soc. Exhibition at Zagreb. No. B39 issued in pane of 40.

No. B39 Overprinted in Red

HRVATSKO MORE
8. IX.
1943.

1943, Sept. 12

B41 SP31 18k + 9k dl gray vio 10.00 *12.00*

Return to Croatia of the Dalmatian and Croatian coasts.

The overprint exists inverted, double, and double, one inverted.

Mother and Children — SP33

Nurse and Patient — SP34

1943, Oct. 3 **Litho.** *Perf. 11*

Cross in Red

B42 SP33 1k + 50b bl grn .75 .75
B43 SP33 2k + 1k bril car .75 .75
B44 SP33 3.50k + 1.50k brt bl .75 .75
B45 SP34 8k + 3k red brn .90 .90
B46 SP34 9k + 4k yel grn 1.00 1.00
B47 SP33 10k + 5k dp vio 1.00 1.00
B48 SP34 12k + 6k brt ultra 1.00 1.00
B49 SP33 12.50k + 6k dk brn 1.50 1.50
B50 SP34 18k + 8k brn org 1.50 1.50
B51 SP34 32k + 12k dk gray 1.50 1.50
Nos. B42-B51 (10) 10.65 *10.65*

The surtax aided the Croatian Red Cross. Issued in panes of 100.

Post Horn and Arms — SP35

Carrier Pigeon and Plane — SP36

Mercury — SP37

Winged Wheel — SP38

1944, Feb. 3

B52 SP35 7k + 3.50k ol bis & red .75 .75
B53 SP36 16k + 8k bl & dk bl .75 .75
B54 SP37 24k + 12k red & rose red .75 .75
B55 SP38 32k + 16k gray & red .75 .75
Nos. B52-B55 (4) 3.00 *3.00*

The surtax benefited communications and railway employees. Panes of 9.

St. Sebastian — SP39

War Invalids
SP40

Statue of Ancient Croatian King — SP41

Death of King Peter Svacic, 1097 — SP42

1944, Feb. 15

B56 SP39 7k + 3.50k org red & rose car .75 .75
B57 SP40 16k + 8k yel grn & dk grn .75 .75
B58 SP41 24k + 12k yel brn & red .75 .75
B59 SP42 32k + 16k bl & dk bl .75 .75
Nos. B56-B59 (4) 3.00 *3.00*

The surtax aided wounded war victims.

Issued in panes of eight stamps, with marginal inscriptions and a central label picturing St. Sebastian.

Black Legion in Combat — SP43

Guarding the Drina — SP44

Jure Francetic — SP45

1944, May 22 **Photo.** *Imperf.*

B60 SP43 3.50k + 1.50k brn red .20 .20
B61 SP44 12.50k + 6.50k slate bl .20 .20
B62 SP45 18k + 9k olive brn .20 .20
Nos. B60-B62 (3) .60 .60

Third anniversary of Croatian independence.

The surtax aided the National Youth Society. Panes of 20.

Perf. 14½

B63 SP45 12.50k + 287.50k int blk 11.00 11.00

Issued to commemorate Jure Francetic. Issued in pane of 30.

Labor Corpsmen Marching SP46

Corpsman Digging SP47

Designs: 18k+9k, Officer instructing corpsman. 32k+16k, Pavelich reviewing Labor Corps. Panes of 8 plus label.

Perf. 11½, 12½, 14½

1944, Aug. 20 **Engr.**

B65 SP46 3.50k + 1k dk red .50 .50
B66 SP47 12.50k + 6k sepia .50 .50
B67 SP47 18k + 9k dk bl .50 .50
B68 SP47 32k + 16k gray grn .50 .50
Nos. B65-B68 (4) 2.00 2.00

Nos. B68 exists only perf 12½, while B65-B67 exist perf 11½, 12½ or 14½. Values are for copies perf 11½ or 12½. Values Nos. B65-B67 perf 14½, $5 each unused or used.

Souvenir Sheet

Perf. 12½

B69 SP47 32k + 16k dk brn, *cr* 4.00 *4.50*

The surtax aided the State Labor Service (Drzavna Radna Sluzba).

Palm Leaf — SP51

1944, Nov. 12 **Litho.** ***Perf. 11***

B70 SP51 2k + 1k dl grn & red .40 .40
B71 SP51 3.50k + 1.50k car lake & red .40 .40
B72 SP51 12.50k + 6k ind & red .40 .40
Nos. B70-B72 (3) 1.20 1.20

The surtax aided the Croatian Red Cross. Panes of 16.

Men of Storm Division — SP52

70k+70k, Soldiers of Storm Division in action. 100k+100k, Storm Division emblem.

1944 **Unwmk.** **Litho.** ***Perf. 11***

B73 SP52 50k + 50k brick red 120.00 *125.00*
B74 SP52 70k + 70k sepia 120.00 *125.00*
B75 SP52 100k + 100k chlky, pale & dp bl 120.00 *125.00*
Nos. B73-B75 (3) 360.00 *375.00*

Nos. B73-B75 issued in panes of 20.

Souvenir Sheet

B76 Sheet of 3 1,450. 1,450.
a. SP52 50k + 50k brick red 400.00 400.00
b. SP52 70k + 70k sepia 400.00 400.00
c. SP52 100k + 100k chalky, pale & deep blue 400.00 400.00

Nos. B76a to B76c are inscribed "O. A." in brick red at right below design. The sheet measures 216x132mm. The surtax aided the First Croatian Storm Division. Counterfeits are plentiful.

Postman SP55

Telephone Line Repairman SP56

24k+12k, Switchboard operator. 50k+25k, 100k+50k, Postman delivering parcel.

1945 **Photo.**

B77 SP55 3.50k + 1.50k sl gray .30 *.30*
B78 SP56 12.50k + 6k brn car .30 *.30*
B79 SP56 24k + 12k dk grn .30 *.30*
B80 SP56 50k + 25k brn vio .30 .30
Nos. B77-B80 (4) 1.20 *1.20*

Souvenir Sheet

B81 SP56 100k + 50k dp brn 9.00 9.00

The surtax on #B77-B81 aided employees of the P.T.T. Panes of 8.

Famous Croatians SP60

#B100, Ban Josip Jelacic (1801-59). #B101, Dr. Ante Starcevic (1823-96). 7d + 3d, Stjepan Radic (1871-1928).

1992 **Litho.** ***Perf. 11x10½***

B100 SP60 4d +2d multi *.50 .50*
B101 SP60 4d +2d multi *.40 .35*

Perf. 14

B102 SP60 7d +3d multi *.35 .35*
Nos. B100-B102 (3) *1.25* 1.20

Issued: #B100, 2/1; #B101, 3/4; #B102, 4/2.

The surcharge on Nos. B100-B102 was initially an obligatory tax on all internal and overseas mail. From May 15, 1992, these stamps were valid for postage at their 6d or 10d face values.

AIR POST STAMPS

Catalogue values for unused stamps in this section are for Never Hinged items.

Airplane, Zagreb Cathedral and Port of Dubrovnik AP1

Airplane Over Ruins of Diocletian's Palace, Split — AP2

Coat of Arms, Aiplane, Zagreb Cathedral and Pula Amphitheatre AP3

Paper Airplane Made From Picture of Osijek Cathedral AP4

1991-92 **Litho.** ***Perf. 11x10½***

C1 AP1 1d multicolored *.30* .20
a. Perf. 14 *.20* .20
C2 AP2 2d multicolored *.90* .25
a. Perf. 14 *.20* .20
C3 AP3 3d multicolored *.45* .20
C4 AP4 4d multicolored *.40* .20
Nos. C1-C4 (4) 2.05

Issued: #C1, 9/9/91; #C1a, 6/24/92; #C2, 10/9/91; #C2a, 1992; #C3, 11/20/91; #C4, 2/14/92.

POSTAGE DUE STAMPS

Yugoslavia Nos. J28-J32 Overprinted in Black

1941, Apr. 26 **Unwmk.** ***Perf. 12½***

J1 D4 50p violet .30 *.50*
a. Double overprint 150.00
b. 50p rose violet 5.00 *10.00*
c. As "b," double overprint 200.00
J2 D4 1d deep magenta .30 *.50*
a. Inverted overprint 200.00
J3 D4 2d deep blue 8.50 *20.00*
a. Double overprint 300.00
J4 D4 5d orange .75 *1.75*
a. Double overprint 300.00
J5 D4 10d chocolate 4.50 *11.00*
Nos. J1-J5 (5) 14.35 *33.75*
Set, never hinged 32.50

Counterfeit overprints exist, particularly of Nos. J3 and J5.

D1

D2

1941, Sept. 12 **Litho.** ***Perf. 11***

J6 D1 50b carmine lake .20 *.45*
J7 D1 1k carmine lake .20 *.45*
J8 D1 2k carmine lake .25 *.60*
J9 D1 5k carmine lake .40 *.85*
J10 D1 10k carmine lake .75 *1.25*
Nos. J6-J10 (5) 1.80 *3.60*
Set, never hinged 3.50

1943 ***Perf. 11½, 12x12½, 12½***

Size: 24x24mm

J11 D2 50b lt blue & gray .20 *.25*
J12 D2 1k lt blue & gray .20 *.25*
J13 D2 2k lt blue & gray .20 *.25*
J14 D2 4k lt blue & gray .20 *.35*
J15 D2 5k lt blue & gray .20 *.40*
J16 D2 6k lt blue & gray .20 *.45*
J17 D2 10k blue & indigo .20 *.40*
J18 D2 15k blue & indigo .20 *1.10*
J19 D2 20k blue & indigo .65 *1.60*
Nos. J11-J19 (9) 2.25 *5.05*
Set, never hinged 4.50

1942, July 30 ***Perf. 10½, 11½***

Size: 25x24¼mm

J20 D2 50b lt blue & gray .20 *.40*
J21 D2 1k lt blue & gray .20 *.40*
J22 D2 2k lt blue & gray .20 *.50*
J23 D2 5k lt blue & gray .20 *.50*
J24 D2 10k lt blue & blue .55 *1.10*
J25 D2 20k lt blue & blue .85 *1.60*
Nos. J20-J25 (6) 2.20 *4.50*
Set, never hinged 5.25

Nos. J21-J25 exist both perf 10½ and 11½. No. J20 exists only perf 11½.

OFFICIAL STAMPS

Croatian Coat of Arms
O1 O2

Perf. 10½, 11½

1942-43 **Unwmk.** **Litho.**

Ordinary Paper

O1 O1 25b rose lake .20 .20
O2 O1 50b slate blk .20 .20
O3 O1 75b gray grn .20 .20
O4 O1 1k orange brn .20 .20
O5 O1 2k turq blue .20 *.40*
O6 O1 3k vermilion .20 .20
O7 O1 4k brown vio .20 .20
O8 O1 5k ultra .20 *.40*
a. Thin paper 4.50 *2.00*
O9 O1 6k brt violet .20 .20
O10 O1 10k lt green .20 .20
O11 O1 12k brown rose .20 *.30*
O12 O1 20k dark blue .20 *.30*
O13 O2 30k brn vio & gray .25 *.40*
O14 O2 40k vio blk & gray .30 *.50*
O15 O2 50k brn lake & gray .35 *.90*
O16 O2 100k black & pink .55 *1.00*
Nos. O1-O16 (16) 3.85 *5.80*
Set, never hinged 7.00

Nos. O1-O16 exist perf 10½ and 11½. No. O8a exists only perf 11½.

1943-44 **Thin Paper** ***Perf. 11½***

O17 O1 25b claret .20 .20
O18 O1 50b gray .20 .20
O19 O1 75b dull green .20 .20
O20 O1 1k orange brn .20 .20
O21 O1 2k slate blue .20 .20
O22 O1 3.50k car rose .20 .20
a. Ordinary paper 3.00 *3.00*
O23 O1 6k brt red vio .20 .20
O24 O1 12.50k deep orange .20 .20
a. Ordinary paper 2.00 *2.00*
Set, never hinged 1.50

POSTAL TAX STAMPS

Catalogue values for unused stamps in this section are for Never Hinged items.

Nurse and Soldier — PT1

Wounded Soldier — PT2

Unwmk.

1942, Oct. 4 **Litho.** ***Perf. 11***

RA1 PT1 1k olive grn & red .85 .80

The tax aided the Croatian Red Cross. Issued in sheets of 24 plus label.

No. RA1 can be found with a red cross printed on the nurse's hat. The original design included this element, but it was removed from the final approved design. Early printings of No. RA1, probably trial printings, included the red cross.

1943, Oct. 3

RA2 PT2 2k blue & red .85 .85

The tax aided the Croatian Red Cross.

Ruins — PT3

Wounded Soldier — PT4

1944, Jan. 1 Photo. *Perf. 12*

RA3 PT3 1k dk slate green .25 .25
RA4 PT4 2k carmine lake .30 .30
RA5 PT4 5k black .35 .35
RA6 PT4 10k deep blue .55 .35
RA7 PT4 20k brown 1.00 .55
Nos. RA3-RA7 (5) 2.45 1.80

Interior of Zagreb Cathedral PT10

1991, Apr. 1 Litho. *Perf. 14*

RA20 PT10 1.20d black & gold .60 .50
a. Perf. 11x10½ .70 .60
b. Perf. 11 15.00 12.00
c. Imperf .90 .90

Worker's Fund. Required on mail during April 1991.

For surcharges see Nos. 100, 100a.

Shrine of the Virgin, 700th Anniv. PT11

1991, May 16 *Perf. 10½x11*

RA21 PT11 1.70d multicolored .65 .55
a. Imperf .80 .70

Workers' Fund. Required on mail May 16-31.

Croatian Arms Type of 1992

1991, July 1 *Perf. 11x10½*

RA22 A37 2.20d multicolored .70 .60
a. Imperf .95 .75

Required on mail during July.

Members of Parliament PT12

1991, Aug. 1 *Perf. 11x10½*

RA23 PT12 2.20d multicolored .70 .60
a. Imperf .95 .80

Worker's Fund. Required on mail during Aug.

Red Cross and Tuberculosis PT13

1991, Sept 14 *Perf. 11*

RA24 PT13 2.20d blue & red .50 .45

Required on mail Sept. 14-21.

Re-erection of Ban Josip Jelacic Equestrian Statue, Zagreb PT14

1991, Nov. 1 *Perf. 11x10½*

RA25 PT14 2.20d multicolored .50 .45
a. Imperf. .65 .50

Worker's Fund. Required on mail during Nov.

New Constitution PT15

1991, Dec. 2 Litho. *Perf. 10¾x10½*

Language of Inscription

RA26 PT15 2.20d English *2.25* 2.00
RA27 PT15 2.20d Croatian *.80* .70
RA28 PT15 2.20d French *2.25* 2.00
RA29 PT15 2.20d German *2.25* 2.00
RA30 PT15 2.20d Russian *2.25* 2.00
RA31 PT15 2.20d Spanish *2.25* 2.00
a. Vert. strip, #RA26-RA31 *14.00* 14.00

Nos RA26-RA31 were printed in sheet containing 15 of No. RA27, 2 each of the other stamps and five labels. Obligatory on mail Dec. 2-31.

Sheet exists imperf. Value $225.

"VUKOVAR" with Barbed Wire — PT16

1992, Jan. 1 Litho. *Perf. 11x10½*

RA32 PT16 2.20d black & brown .70 .55
a. Imperf. 1.00 .90

Vukovar Refugee's Fund. Required on mail during Jan.

Red Cross PT17

Red Cross and Solidarity PT18

1992 *Perf. 11*

RA33 PT17 3d red & black .25 .20
RA34 PT18 3d red & black .25 .20

Issued: No. RA33, May 8. No. RA34, June 1.

No. RA33 was required on mail May 8-15; No. RA34, June 1-7.

Madonna of Bistrica — PT19

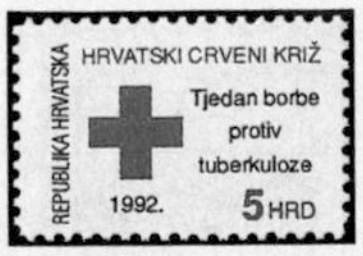

Red Cross — PT20

1992, Aug. 1 Litho. *Perf. 14*

RA35 PT19 5d blue & gold .45 .40

Required on mail, Aug. 1-8.

1992, Sept. 21 Litho. *Perf. 11*

RA36 PT20 5d black & red .30 .25

Required on mail Sept. 14-21.

St. George Slaying Dragon PT21

1992, Nov. 4 *Perf. 14*

RA37 PT21 15d multicolored .30 .25

Cancer Research League. Required on mail Nov. 4-11.

See No. RA43.

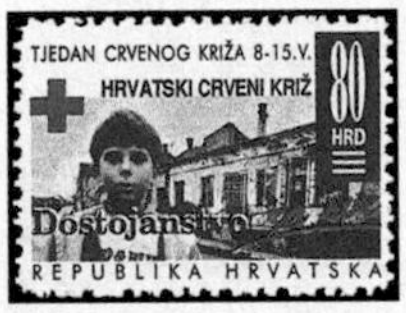

Red Cross — PT22

1993, May 8 Litho. *Rough Perf. 11*

RA38 PT22 80d black & red .30 .25

Required on mail May 8-15.

Red Cross and Solidarity PT23

1993, June 1

RA39 PT23 100d black & red .30 .25

Required on mail June 1-7.

Cardinal Stepinac (1898-1960) PT24

1993, July 15 Litho. *Perf. 14*

RA40 PT24 150d multicolored .30 .25

Required on mail July 15-22.

Zrinski-Frankopan Foundation — PT25

Design: 200d, Gen. Peter Zrinski (1621-1671), Politician and Fran Krsto Frankopan, Count of Tersat (1643-1671), Poet.

1993, Aug. 12 Litho. *Perf. 14*

RA41 PT25 200d gray & blue .35 .25

Required on mail Aug. 12-19.

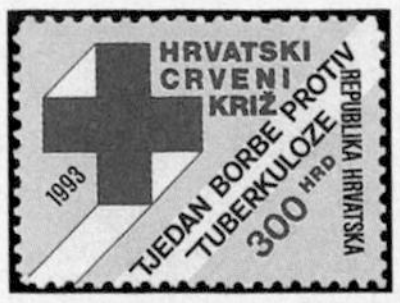

Red Cross Campaign Against Tuberculosis PT26

1993, Sept. 14 Litho. *Perf. 11*

RA42 PT26 300d gray, red & black .45 .40

Required on mail Sept. 14-21.

St. George Slaying Dragon Type of 1992

1993, Oct. 11 Litho. *Perf. 14*

RA43 PT21 400d multicolored .45 .40

Cancer Research League. Required on mail Oct. 11-31.

Save the Children of Croatia PT27

1993, Nov. 1 *Perf. 13½x14*

RA44 PT27 400d multicolored .45 .40

Required on mail Nov. 1-30.

Croatian Red Cross — PT28

1994, May 5 Litho. *Perf. 11*

RA45 PT28 500d multicolored .30 .25

Required on mail May 8-15.

Red Cross Solidarity PT29

Ludberg Church PT30

1994, May 5 Litho. *Perf. 11*

RA46 PT29 50 l multicolored .45 .40

Required on mail June 1-7.

1994, July 15 *Perf. 14*

RA47 PT30 50 l multicolored .30 .25

Required on mail July 15-22.

Save the Children of Croatia — PT31

St. George Slaying Dragon — PT32

1994, Aug. 16 Litho. *Perf. 14*

RA48 PT31 50 l multicolored .30 .25

Required on mail Aug. 16-29.

1994, Sept. 1

RA49 PT32 50 l multicolored .30 .25

Cancer Research League. Required on mail Sept. 1-8.

PT33 PT34

1994, Sept. 14 *Perf. 11*

RA50 PT33 50 l blk, grn & red .45 .40

Red Cross Campaign against Tuberculosis. Required on mail Sept. 14-21.

1994, Oct. 15 Litho. *Perf. 14*

RA51 PT34 50 l multicolored .30 .25

Town of Slavonski Brod, 750th anniv.

Homage to Olympia, by Ivan Lackovic PT35

Intl. Olympic Committee, Cent. — PT36

Designs: a, Tennis. b, Soccer. c, Basketball. d, Team handball. e, Canoeing, kayaking. f, Water polo. g, Track and field. h, Gymnastics.

1994, Nov. 2 Litho. *Perf. 14*

RA52 PT35 50 l Pair, #a.-b. 1.40 1.25

Miniature Sheets of 8

RA53 PT36 50 l #a.-h. 6.25 6.25

RA54 PT36 50 l #a.-h. 6.25 6.25

Nos. RA52b, RA53a, RA53d-RA53e, RA53h, RA54b-RA54c, RA54f-RA54g have IOC centennial emblem. Others have emblem of Croatian Olympic Committee.

Required on mail Nov. 2-15.

Natl. Olympic Committee PT37

Designs: a, Rowing. b, Pétanque. c, Monument to Drazen Petrovic, Olympic Park, Lausanne. d, Tennis. e, Basketball.

1995, Apr. 17 Litho. *Perf. 14*

RA55 PT37 50 l Strip of 5, #a.-e. 1.75 1.75

Required on mail Apr. 17-30.

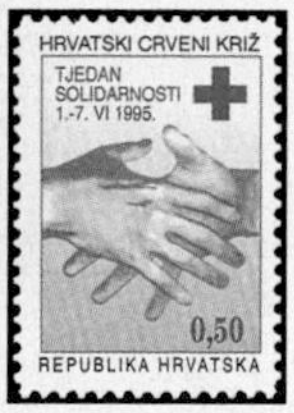

Red Cross Stamps

PT38 PT39

1995, May 8 *Perf. 11*

RA56 PT38 50 l multicolored .30 .25

Required on mail May 8-15.

1995, June 1

RA57 PT39 50 l multicolored .30 .25

Required on mail June 1-7.

Sts. Peter and Paul Cathedral, Osijek — PT40

1995, July 17 *Perf. 14*

RA58 PT40 65 l multicolored .45 .40

Required on mail July 17-30.

Holy Mother of Freedom PT41

Design: No. RA59, Like No. RA60, but with black surcharge on white panel. #RA60, Croatian Pieta, by Ivan Lackovic. #RA61, Gedenkstatte Church Project.

1995, Aug. 14 Litho. *Perf. 14*

RA59 PT41 65 l on 50 l multi 1.75 1.75

RA60 PT41 65 l multicolored .40 .35

RA61 PT41 65 l multicolored .40 .35

Nos. RA59-RA61 (3) 2.55 2.45

No. RA59 not issued without surcharge. Examples without surcharge are printer's waste. Required on mail Aug. 14-27.

Red Cross and Tuberculosis PT42

Save the Croatian Children PT43

1995, Sept. 14 Litho. *Perf. 11*

RA62 PT62 65 l multicolored .45 .40

Required on mail Sept. 14-21.

1995, Oct. 16 *Perf. 14*

RA63 PT43 65 l multicolored .45 .40

Required on mail Oct. 16-29.

PT44

PT45

Performance scene: a, Woman seated at top of steps. b, Gathering of people. c, People, large statue in background.

1995, Oct. 16

RA64 PT44 65 l Strip of 3, #a.-c. 1.40 1.40

Croatian Natl. Theater, Zagreb, cent. No. RA64 has continuous design. Required on mail 10/16-29.

1995, Nov. 6 Litho. *Perf. 14*

RA65 PT45 65 l multicolored .45 .35

Fight against drugs. Required on mail Nov. 20-30.

PT46

1995, Nov. 20 Litho. *Perf. 14x13¾*

RA66 PT46 65 l multicolored .45 .35

Croatian Anti-Cancer League. Required on mail Nov. 20-30.

PT47 PT48

1996, Feb. 15 Litho. *Perf. 14x13½*

RA67 PT47 65 l multicolored .45 .35

Croatian Anti-Cancer League. Required on mail Feb. 15-28.

1996, Mar. 18 Litho. *Perf. 14*

RA68 PT48 65 l multicolored .45 .35

Sanctuary of the Virgin Mary of Bistrica. Required on mail Mar. 18-31.

Croatian Olympic Committee PT49

1996, Apr. 17 Litho. *Perf. 14*

RA69 PT49 65 l multi .45 .35

No. RA69 exists imperf. and in booklets, which were not placed on sale. Required on mail Apr. 17-30.

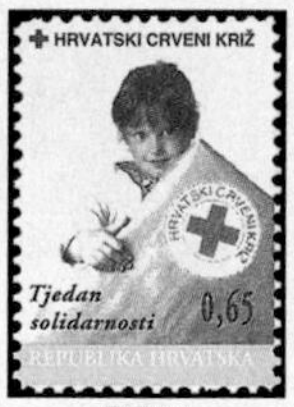

PT50 PT51

1996, May 8 Litho. *Perf. 11*

RA70 PT50 65 l multicolored .45 .35

Red Cross. Required on mail May 8-15.

1996, June 6 Litho. *Perf. 11*

RA71 PT51 65 l multicolored .45 .35

Red Cross Solidarity Week. Required on mail June 1-7.

PT52

1996, June 14 Litho. *Perf. 14x13½*

RA72 PT52 65 l multicolored .45 .35

For Croatian children. Required on mail 6/14-27.

PT53

1996, July 3 Litho. *Perf. 14*

RA73 PT53 65 l multicolored .45 .35

Osijek, 800th anniv. Required on mail July 3-16.

PT54

PT55

1996, July 17 Litho. *Perf. 14*

RA74 PT54 65 l multicolored .45 .35

Renovation of Dakovaska Cathedral. Required on mail July 17-30.

1996, Aug. 1 Litho. *Perf. 14*

RA75 PT55 65 l multicolored .45 .35

Split, 1700th anniv. Required on mail Aug. 1-14.

PT56

PT57

1996, Aug. 16 Litho. ***Perf. 14x13½***

RA76 PT56 65 l multicolored .45 .35

Aid to Vukovar. Required on mail 8/16-29.

1996, Sept. 1 Litho. ***Perf. 14***

RA77 PT57 65 l multicolored .45 .35

Fight against drugs. Required on mail Sept. 1-12.

PT58

1996, Sept. 14 Litho. ***Perf. 11***

RA78 PT58 65 l multicolored .45 .35

Red Cross Tuberculosis Week. Required on mail Sept. 14-21.

PT59

1996, Oct. 10 Litho. ***Perf. 14***

RA79 PT59 65 l multicolored .45 .35

Isolation of insulin, 75th anniv. Required on mail Oct. 10-17.

PT60

PT61

1996, Nov. 11 Litho. ***Perf. 14***

RA80 PT60 65 l multicolored .45 .35

Remete pilgrimage. Required on mail Nov. 11-24.

1997, Jan. 6 Litho. ***Perf. 14***

RA81 PT61 65 l multicolored .45 .35

Antun Mihanovic (1796-1861), natl. anthem lyricist. Required on mail Jan. 6-26.

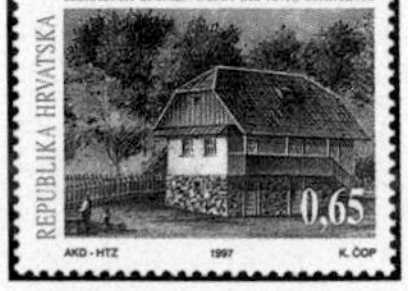

House of Dr. Ante Starcevic PT62

1997, Jan. 27 Litho. ***Perf. 14***

RA82 PT62 65 l multicolored .45 .35

Required on mail Jan. 27-Feb. 14.

PT63

PT64

1997, Feb. 15 Litho. ***Perf. 14***

RA83 PT63 65 l multicolored .45 .35

Croatian Anti-Cancer League. Required on mail Feb. 15-28.

1997, May 8 Litho. ***Perf. 10½x11***

RA84 PT64 65 l multicolored .70 .50

a. Perf 10½ .70 .50

b. Perf 11 *35.00*

Red Cross. Required on mail May 8-15.

Numerous charity stamps were issued between 1997 and 2001, but their use on mail was not obligatory.

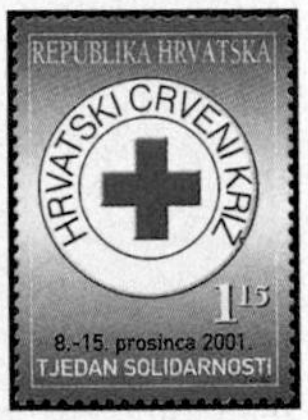

Red Cross Solidarity Week — PT65

2001, Dec. 8 Litho. ***Perf. 14***

RA85 PT65 1.15k red & black .60 .50

Obligatory on mail Dec. 8-15.

Red Cross Week — PT66

2002, May 8

RA86 PT66 1.15k multi .70 .60

Obligatory on mail May 8-15.

Red Cross Anti-Tuberculosis Week — PT67

2002, Sept. 14

RA87 PT67 1.15k multi .60 .50

Obligatory on mail Sept. 14-21.

Red Cross Solidarity Week — PT68

2002, Dec. 8

RA88 PT68 1.15k multi .60 .50

Obligatory on mail Dec. 8-15.

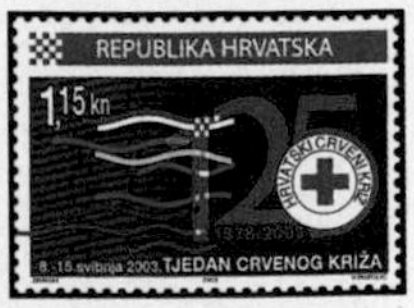

Red Cross Week — PT69

2003, May 8

RA89 PT69 1.15k multi .65 .55

Obligatory on mail May 8-15.

Red Cross Anti-Tuberculosis Week — PT70

2003, Sept. 14

RA90 PT70 1.15k multi .65 .55

Obligatory on mail Sept. 14-21.

Red Cross Solidarity Week — PT71

2003, Dec. 8

RA91 PT71 1.15k multi .65 .55

Obligatory on mail Dec. 8-15.

Red Cross Week — PT72

2004, May 8

RA92 PT72 1.15k multi .65 .55

Obligatory on mail May 8-15.

Red Cross Anti-Tuberculosis Week — PT73

2004, Sept. 14

RA93 PT73 1.15k multi .65 .55

Obligatory on mail Sept. 14-21.

Red Cross Solidarity Week — PT74

2004, Dec. 8

RA94 PT74 1.15k multi .65 .55

Obligatory on mail Dec. 8-15.

Red Cross Week — PT75

2005, May 8 Litho. ***Perf. 14***

RA95 PT75 1.15k multi .40 .40

Obligatory on mail May 8-15.

Red Cross Anti-Tuberculosis Week — PT76

2005, Sept. 14

RA96 PT76 1.15k multi .40 .40

Obligatory on mail Sept. 14-21.

Red Cross Solidarity Week — PT77

2005, Dec. 8

RA97 PT77 1.15k multi .40 .40

Obligatory on mail Dec. 8-15.

Red Cross Week — PT78

2006, May 8 Litho. ***Perf. 14***

RA98 PT78 1.15k multi .45 .45

Obligatory on mail May 8-15.

Red Cross Anti-Tuberculosis Week — PT79

2006, Sept. 14

RA99 PT79 1.15k multi .40 .40

Obligatory on mail Sept. 14-21.

Red Cross Solidarity Week — PT80

2006, Dec. 8

RA100 PT80 1.15k multi .45 .45

Obligatory on mail Dec. 8-15.

Issued under Administration of [the] United States
Puerto Principe Issue
Issues of Cuba of 1898 and 189[…] Surcharged:

HABILITADO 1 cent. — a
HABILIT[ADO] 1 cent[.] — b
HABILITADO 2 cents. — c
HABILIT[ADO] 2 cent[s.] — d
HABILITADO 3 cents. — e
HABILIT[ADO] 3 cent[s.] — f
HABILITADO 5 cents. — g
HABILIT[ADO] 5 cent[s.] — h
HABILITADO 5 cents. — i
HABILIT[ADO] 5 cent[s.] — j
HABILITADO 3 cents. — k
HABILIT[ADO] 3 cent[s.] — l
m
HABILIT[ADO] 10 cent[s.]

Types a, c, d, e, f, g and h are 17½mm h[igh] the others are 19½mm high.

Black Surcharge On Nos. 156, 15[7], 158 and 160

1898-99

#176-189 are Orange Brown

176	A19 (a)	1c on 1m	50.00	30
177	A19 (b)	1c on 1m	45.00	35
a.		Broken figure "l"	75.00	6
b.		Inverted surcharge		20
d.		As "a," inverted		25
178	A19 (c)	2c on 2m	24.00	20
a.		Inverted surcharge	250.00	5
179	A19 (d)	2c on 2m	40.00	35
a.		Inverted surcharge	350.00	10
179B	A19 (k)	3c on 1m	300.00	175
c.		Double surcharge	1,500.	75
179D	A19 (l)	3c on 1m	*1,500.*	*750*
e.		Double surcharge	—	
179F	A19 (e)	3c on 2m		*1,5*

Value is for copy with minor faults.

179G	A19 (f)	3c on 2m	—	*2,0*

Value is for copy with minor faults.

180	A19 (e)	3c on 3m	30.00	30
a.		Inverted surcharge		11
181	A19 (f)	3c on 3m	75.00	75
a.		Inverted surcharge		20
182	A19 (g)	5c on 1m	700.00	200
a.		Inverted surcharge		50
183	A19 (h)	5c on 1m	*1,300.*	*500*
a.		Inverted surcharge		70

CUBA

'kyü-bə

LOCATION — The largest island of the West Indies; south of Florida
GOVT. — Former Spanish possession
AREA — 44,206 sq. mi.
POP. — 11,096,395 (1999 est.)
CAPITAL — Havana

Formerly a Spanish possession, Cuba made several unsuccessful attempts to gain her freedom, which finally led to the intervention of the US in 1898. In that year under the Treaty of Paris, Spain relinquished the island to the US in trust for its inhabitants.

In 1902 a republic was established and the Cuban Congress took over the government from the military authorities.

8 Reales Plata = 1 Peso
100 Centesimos = 1 Escudo or Peseta (1867)
1000 Milesimas = 100 Centavos = 1 Peso

Catalogue values for unused stamps in this country are for Never Hinged items, beginning with Scott 402 in the regular postage section, Scott B3 in the semi-postal section, Scott C38 in the airpost section, Scott CB1 in the airpost semi-postal section, Scott E13 in the special delivery section, and Scott RA1 in the postal tax section.

Pen cancellations are common on the earlier stamps of Cuba. Stamps so canceled sell for very much less than those with postmark cancellations.

Watermarks

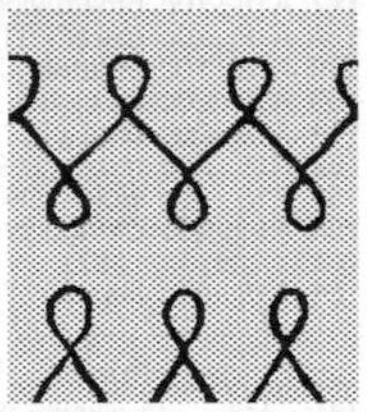

Wmk. 104 — Loops

Loops from different rows may or may not be directly opposite each other.

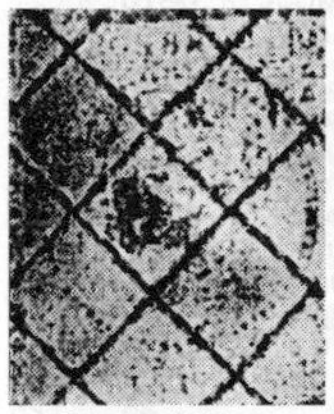

Wmk. 105 — Crossed Lines

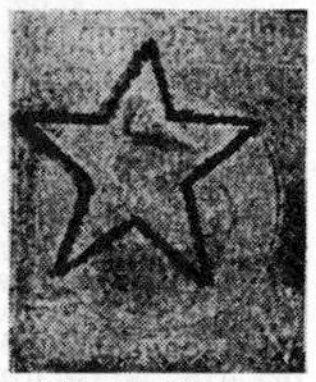

Wmk. 106 — Star

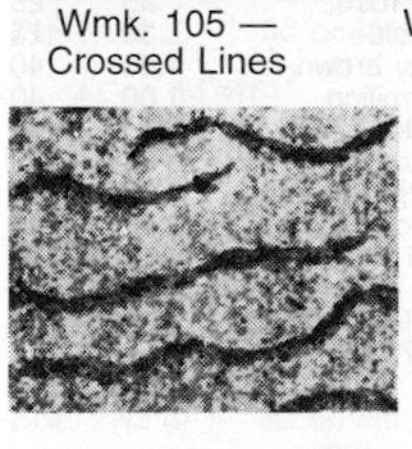

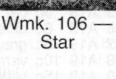

Wmk. 229 — Wavy Lines

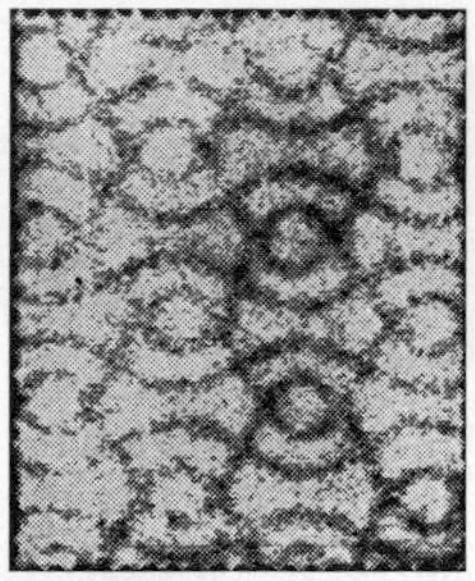

Wmk. 320

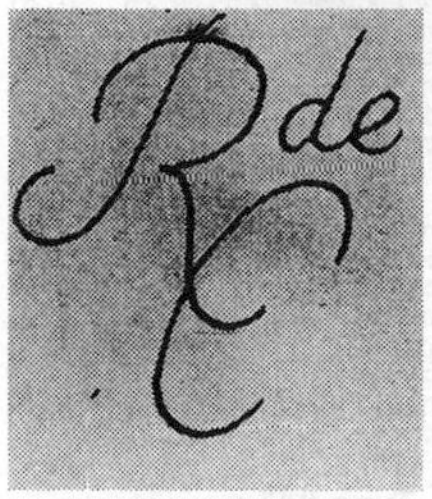

Wmk. 321 — "R de C"

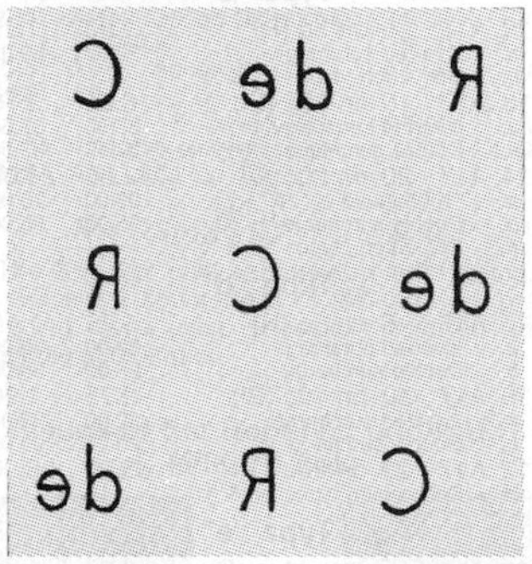

Wmk. 376 — "R de C"

Issued under Spanish Dominion

Used also in Puerto Rico: Nos. 1-3, 9-14, 17-21, 32-34, 35A-37, 39-41, 43-45, 47-49, 51-53, 55-57.

Used also in the Philippines: Nos. 2-3.

Identifiable cancellations of those countries will increase the value of the stamps.

Queen Isabella II — A1

Blue Paper

1855 Typo. Wmk. 104 *Imperf.*

1	A1	½r p blue green	70.00	6.00
a.		½r p blackish green	80.00	11.00
2	A1	1r p gray green	60.00	4.00
3	A1	2r p carmine	400.00	12.00
4	A1	2r p orange red	900.00	19.00
		Nos. 1-4 (4)	1,430.	41.00

See Nos. 9-14. For surcharges see Nos. 5-8, 15.

Counterfeit surcharges are plentiful.

Nos. 3-4 Surcharged

1855-56

5	A1	¼r p on 2r p car	775.00	210.00
a.		Without fraction bar	*1,700.*	625.00
6	A1	¼r p on 2r p org red	600.00	160.00

Surcharged

7	A1	¼r p on 2r p car	675.00	200.00
a.		Without fraction bar	*1,500.*	750.00
8	A1	¼r p on 2r p org red	1,050.	425.00
a.		Without fraction bar		1,200.

The "Y ¼" surcharge met the "Ynterior" rate for delivery within the city of Havana.

Rough Yellowish Paper

1856 Wmk. 105

9	A1	½r p grnsh blue	6.75	.85
10	A1	1r p green	800.00	18.00
a.		1r p emerald	*1,150.*	21.00
11	A1	2r p orange red	400.00	16.00

White Smooth Paper

1857 Unwmk.

12	A1	½r p blue	3.50	.70
13	A1	1r p gray green	3.25	.70
a.		1r p pale yellow green	3.00	.70
14	A1	2r p dull rose	18.50	3.25
		Nos. 12-14 (3)	25.25	4.65

Surcharged

1860

15	A1	¼r p on 2r p dl rose	240.00	85.00
a.		1 of ¼ inverted	350.00	150.00
b.		"1⅟" instead of 1 ¼		—

22 overprint varieties exist.

Queen Isabella II
A2 A3

1862-64 *Imperf.*

16	A2	¼r p black	18.00	14.00
17	A3	¼r p blk, *buff* ('64)	18.00	13.00
18	A3	½r p green ('64)	4.75	.70
19	A3	½r p grn, *pale rose* ('64)	11.00	2.00
20	A3	1r p bl, *sal* ('64)	4.75	1.00
a.		Diagonal half used as ½r p on cover		125.00
21	A3	2r p ver, *buff* ('64)	25.00	6.00
a.		2r p red, *buff*	30.00	6.75
		Nos. 16-21 (6)	81.50	36.70

No. 17 Overprinted in Black

1866

22	A3	¼r p black, *buff*	80.00	*85.00*

Exists with handstamped "1866."

A5

A6

1866

23	A5	5c dull violet	40.00	26.00
24	A5	10c blue	2.50	1.00
25	A5	20c green	1.50	1.00
a.		Diag. half used as 10c on cover		150.00
26	A5	40c rose	9.50	8.00
		Nos. 23-26 (4)	53.50	36.00

For the Type A5 20c in dull lilac, see Spain No. 87.

Stamps Dated "1867"

1867 *Perf. 14*

27	A5	5c dull violet	40.00	21.00
28	A5	10c blue	19.00	1.40
a.		Imperf., pair	110.00	6.50
b.		Diagonal half used as 5c on cover		140.00
29	A5	20c green	12.00	1.90
a.		Imperf., pair	110.00	70.00
b.		Diag. half used as 10c on cover		150.00
30	A5	40c rose	15.00	10.00
		Nos. 27-30 (4)	86.00	34.30

Stamps Dated "1868"

1868

31	A6	5c dull violet	17.00	7.75
32	A6	10c blue	3.75	1.75
a.		Diagonal half used as 5c on cover		140.00
33	A6	20c green	5.50	3.00
a.		Diag. half used as 10c on cover		140.00
34	A6	40c rose	14.00	8.00
a.		Diag. half used as 20c on cover		175.00
		Nos. 31-34 (4)	40.25	20.50

Nos. 31-34 Overprinted in Black

1868

35	A6	5c dull violet	62.50	29.00
35A	A6	10c blue	62.50	29.00
b.		Diag. half used as 5c on cover		*275.00*
36	A6	20c green	62.50	27.50
37	A6	40c rose	62.50	27.50
		Nos. 35-37 (4)	250.00	113.00

1869 Stamps Dated "1869"

38	A6	5c rose	37.50	12.00
39	A6	10c red brown	3.75	1.75
a.		Diag. half used as 5c on cover		125.00
40	A6	20c orange	6.50	2.25
41	A6	40c dull violet	30.00	9.50
		Nos. 38-41 (4)	77.75	25.50

Nos. 38-41 Ovptd. Like Nos. 35-37

42	A6	5c rose	150.00	42.50
43	A6	10c red brown	45.00	32.50
a.		Diag. half used as 5c on cover		—
44	A6	20c orange	37.50	32.50
a.		Diag. half used as 10c on cover		—
45	A6	40c dull violet	65.00	32.50
		Nos. 42-45 (4)	297.50	140.00

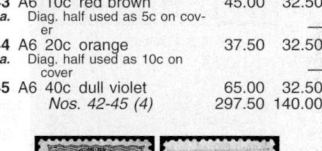

"Espana"
A8 A9

1870 *Perf. 14*

46	A8	5c blue	190.00	60.00
47	A8	10c green	2.75	.85
a.		Diagonal half used as 5c on cover		150.00
48	A8	20c red brown	2.75	.85
a.		Diag. half used as 10c on cover		225.00
49	A8	40c rose	225.00	30.00

1871

50	A9	12c red lilac	20.00	10.00
a.		Imperf., pair	85.00	—
51	A9	25c ultra	2.25	.85
a.		Imperf., pair	40.00	—
b.		Diagonal half used as 12c on cover		140.00
52	A9	50c gray green	2.25	.85
a.		Imperf., pair	15.00	—
b.		Diagonal half used as 25c on cover		140.00
53	A9	1p yel brown	27.50	9.00
a.		Imperf., pair	125.00	—
		Nos. 50-53 (4)	52.00	20.70

King Amadeo — A10

1873 *Perf. 14*

54	A10	12½c dark green	22.50	14.00
55	A10	25c gray	2.25	.85
a.		Diagonal half used as 12½c on cover		82.50
b.		25c lilac	6.00	1.10

c. As "b," half used as 12½c on cover
56 A10 50c brown 1.50
a. Imperf., pair 55.00
b. Half used as 25c on cover
57 A10 1p red brown 325.00
a. Diagonal half used as 50c on cover

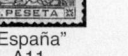

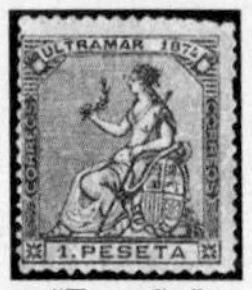
"España"
A11

Coat of A
A12

1874

58 A11 12½c brown 18.00
a. Half used as 5c on cover
59 A11 25c ultra .90
a. Diagonal half used as 12½c on cover
60 A11 50c dp violet 1.60
a. Diagonal half used as 25c on cover
61 A11 50c gray 1.60
a. Diagonal half used as 25c on cover
62 A11 1p carmine 210.00
a. Imperf., pair 600.00
Nos. 58-62 (5) 232.10

1875

63 A12 12½c lt violet .80
a. Imperf., pair 75.00
64 A12 25c ultra .40
a. Imperf., pair 75.00
b. Diagonal half used as 12½c on cover
65 A12 50c blue green .45
a. Imperf., pair 75.00
b. Diag. half used as 25c on cover
66 A12 1p brown 7.25
b. Diag. half used as 50c on cover
Nos. 63-66 (4) 8.90

King Alfonso XII
A13 A14

1876

67 A13 12½c green 1.75
a. 12½c emerald green 2.00
68 A13 25c gray .80
a. Diagonal half used as 12½c on cover
b. 25c pale violet 1.50
d. 25c bluish gray 2.25
69 A13 50c ultra .80
a. Imperf., pair 16.00
b. Diag. half used as 25c on cover
70 A13 1p black 8.50
a. Imperf., pair 40.00
b. Diag. half used as 50c on cover
Nos. 67-70 (4) 11.85

1877

71 A14 10c lt green 21.50
72 A14 12½c gray 5.75
a. Imperf., pair 32.50
b. Diagonal half used on cover
73 A14 25c dk green .50
a. Imperf., pair 32.50
b. Diagonal half used as 12½c on cover
74 A14 50c black .50
a. Imperf., pair 32.50
b. Half used as 25c on cover
75 A14 1p brown 24.00
Nos. 71-75 (5) 52.25

No. 71 was not placed in use.

Stamps Dated "1878"

1878

76 A14 5c blue .55
77 A14 10c black 62.50
78 A14 12½c brown bis 3.25
a. 12½c gray bister 4.00
c. Diagonal half used on cover
79 A14 25c yel green .20
b. No. 79 or 79c, diagonal half used as 12½c on cover
c. 25c deep green .20
80 A14 50c dk blue grn .35
b. Diagonal half used as 25c on cover
81 A14 1p carmine 10.00
b. 1p rose 6.75
Nos. 76-81 (6) 76.85

No. 77 was not placed in use.

Imperf., Pairs

76a A14 5c blue 22.50
77a A14 10c black 115.00
78b A14 12½c brown bister 22.50

Calixto García
A31

José M. Rodriquez y Rodriquez (Mayia)
A32

Carlos Roloff — A33

1910, Feb. 1

239 A27 1c grn & vio .85 .20
a. Center inverted 260.00 260.00
240 A28 2c car & grn 1.60 .20
a. Center inverted 575.00 575.00
241 A29 3c vio & bl 1.10 .20
242 A30 5c bl & grn 16.00 .80
243 A31 8c ol & vio 1.10 .30
244 A32 10c brn & bl 6.75 .65
a. Center inverted 850.00
245 A26 50c vio & blk 1.60 .50
246 A33 1p slate & blk 7.75 4.00
Nos. 239-246 (8) 36.75 6.85
Set, never hinged 50.00

1911-13

247 A27 1c green .55 .20
248 A28 2c car rose .70 .20
a. Booklet pane of 6 ('13) 82.50
250 A30 5c ultra 1.75 .20
251 A31 8c ol grn & blk 1.10 .60
252 A33 1p black 5.00 2.00
Nos. 247-252 (5) 9.10 3.20
Set, never hinged 16.00

Map of Cuba — A34

1914-15

253 A34 1c green .90 .20
a. Booklet pane of 6 100.00
254 A34 2c car rose 1.10 .20
a. Booklet pane of 6 100.00
255 A34 2c red ('15) 1.75 .20
a. Booklet pane of 6 100.00
256 A34 3c violet 5.50 .35
257 A34 5c blue 7.50 .20
258 A34 8c ol grn 6.00 .70
259 A34 10c brown 11.00 .35
260 A34 10c ol grn ('15) 13.00 .55
261 A34 50c orange 85.00 10.00
262 A34 1p gray 125.00 24.00
Nos. 253-262 (10) 256.75 36.75
Set, never hinged 450.00

Complete set of eight 1914 stamps, imperf. pairs, value $1,500.

Nos. 253, 254, 256 and E5 exist with "1917 GOB./CONSTITUCIONAL/CAMAGUEY" overprint. These were not authorized.

Gertrudis Gómez de Avellaneda, Cuban Poetess (1814-73)
A34a

1914

263 A34a 5c blue 14.00 5.00
Never hinged 22.50

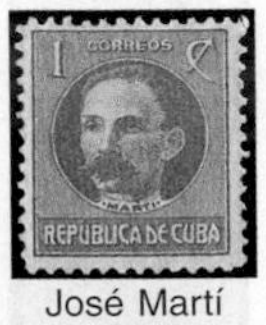
José Martí
A35

Máximo Gómez
A36

José de la Luz Caballero
A37

Calixto García
A38

Ignacio Agramonte
A39

Tomás Estrada Palma
A40

José A. Saco — A41

Antonio Maceo — A42

Carlos Manuel de Céspedes — A43

1917-18 Unwmk. *Perf. 12*

264 A35 1c bl grn .75 .20
a. Booklet pane of 6 40.00
b. Booklet pane of 30 250.00
265 A36 2c rose .75 .20
a. Booklet pane of 6 50.00
b. Booklet pane of 30 210.00
266 A36 2c lt red ('18) .60 .20
a. Booklet pane of 6 50.00
267 A37 3c violet .75 .20
a. Imperf. pair 275.00
b. Booklet pane of 6 50.00
268 A38 5c dp bl .75 .20
269 A39 8c red brn 3.50 .20
270 A40 10c yel brn 2.25 .20
271 A41 20c gray grn 14.00 1.60
272 A42 50c dl rose 14.00 .70
273 A43 1p black 14.50 .70
Nos. 264-273 (10) 51.85 4.40
Set, never hinged 75.00

1925-28 Wmk. 106 *Perf. 12*

274 A35 1c blue green 1.10 .20
a. Booklet pane of 6 350.00
275 A36 2c brt rose 1.20 .20
a. Booklet pane of 6 75.00
b. Booklet pane of 30 350.00
276 A38 5c dp bl 2.50 .20
277 A39 8c red brn ('28) 5.75 .60
278 A40 10c yel brn ('27) 7.00 .70
279 A41 20c olive grn 11.00 1.10
Nos. 274-279 (6) 28.55 3.00
Set, never hinged 40.00

1926 *Imperf.*

280 A35 1c blue green 1.40 1.00
281 A36 2c brt rose 1.40 1.00
282 A38 5c deep blue 1.75 1.40
Nos. 280-282 (3) 4.55 3.40
Set, never hinged 5.00

See Nos. 304-310. For overprint and surcharge see Nos. 317-318, 644.

Arms of Republic
A44

1927, May 20 Unwmk. *Perf. 12*

283 A44 25c violet 16.00 3.50
Never hinged 24.00

25th anniversary of the Republic.
For surcharges see Nos. 355, C3.

Tomás Estrada Palma
A45

Designs: 2c, Gen. Gerardo Machado. 5c, Morro Castle. 8c, Havana Railway Station. 10c, Presidential Palace. 13c, Tobacco Plantation. 20c, Treasury Building. 30c, Sugar Mill. 50c, Havana Cathedral. 1p, Galician Clubhouse, Havana.

1928, Jan. 2 Wmk. 106

284 A45 1c deep green .45 .20
285 A45 2c brt rose .50 .20
286 A45 5c deep blue .75 .30
287 A45 8c lt red brn 3.00 .90
288 A45 10c bister brn .75 .55
289 A45 13c orange 1.50 .55
290 A45 20c olive grn 1.75 .65
291 A45 30c dk violet 4.25 .55
292 A45 50c carmine rose 6.50 2.10
293 A45 1p gray black 13.00 5.00
Nos. 284-293 (10) 32.45 11.00
Set, never hinged 50.00

Sixth Pan-American Conference.

Capitol, Havana
A55

1929, May 18

294 A55 1c green .35 .35
295 A55 2c carmine rose .35 .30
296 A55 5c blue .50 .35
297 A55 10c bister brn 1.00 .50
298 A55 20c violet 3.50 2.75
Nos. 294-298 (5) 5.70 4.25
Set, never hinged 10.50

Opening of the Capitol, Havana.

Hurdler — A56

1930, Mar. 15 Engr.

299 A56 1c green .75 .35
300 A56 2c carmine .75 .40
301 A56 5c deep blue 1.00 .40
302 A56 10c bister brn 2.00 .85
303 A56 20c violet 12.00 3.00
Nos. 299-303 (5) 16.50 5.00
Set, never hinged 24.00

2nd Central American Athletic Games.

Types of 1917 Portrait Issue

Flat Plate Printing

1930-45 Wmk. 106 Engr. *Perf. 10*

304 A35 1c blue green .75 .25
a. Booklet pane of 6 50.00
b. Booklet pane of 30 —
305 A36 2c brt rose 75.00 —
a. Booklet pane of 6 1,200.
305B A37 3c dk rose vio ('42) 4.00 .75
c. Booklet pane of 6 42.50
306 A38 5c dk blue 2.75 .20
306A A39 8c red brn ('45) 2.75 .25
307 A40 10c brown 2.75 .25
a. 10c yellow brown ('35) 3.50 .75
307B A41 20c olive grn ('41) 4.75 .75
Nos. 304-307B (7) 92.75 2.45

Nos. 305 and 305B were printed for booklet panes and all copies have straight edges.

For surcharge see No. 644.

Rotary Press Printing

308 A35 1c blue grn 1.10 .20
309 A36 2c brt rose 1.10 .20
a. Booklet pane of 50
310 A37 3c violet 1.50 .20
a. 3c dull violet ('38) 1.10 .20
b. 3c rose violet ('41) 1.10 .20
c. Booklet pane of 50
Nos. 308-310 (3) 3.70 .60

Flat plate stamps measure 18½x21½mm; rotary press, 19x22mm.

The Mangos of Baragua — A57

War Memorial — A61

Battle of Mal Tiempo
A58

Battle of Coliseo
A59

Maceo, Gómez and Zayas
A60

Wmk. 229

1933, Apr. 23 Photo. *Perf. 12½*

312 A57 3c dk brown 1.40 .30
313 A58 5c dk blue 1.25 .35
314 A59 10c emerald 2.25 .35
315 A60 13c red 2.75 .90
316 A61 20c black 5.50 2.10
Nos. 312-316 (5) 13.15 4.00
Set, never hinged 22.50

War of Independence and dedication of the "Soldado Invasor" (the American Army that came to the aid of the revolution against Spain)monument.

Types of 1917 Issues with Carmine or Black Overprint Reading Up or Down

Rotary Press Printing

Wmk. 106

1933, Dec. 23 Engr. *Perf. 10*

317 A35 1c blue green (C) 1.75 .20

With Additional Surcharge of New Value and Bars

318 A37 2c on 3c vio (Bk) 1.75 .20

Establishment of a revolutionary junta.
Catalogue values for Nos. 317-318 unused are for examples with overprint reading up. Values for overprint reading down, $4.

Dr. Carlos J. Finlay — A62

1934, Dec. 3 Engr. *Perf. 10*

319 A62 2c dark carmine 1.00 .50
320 A62 5c dark blue 2.75 1.50
Set, never hinged 6.00

Cent. of the birth of Dr. Carlos J. Finlay (1833-1915), physician-biologist who found that a mosquito transmitted yellow fever.

Pres. José Miguel Gómez — A63

Gómez Monument A64

1936, May ***Perf. 10***

322	A63 1c green	1.50	.40
323	A64 2c carmine	2.25	.50
	Set, never hinged	7.00	

Unveiling of a monument to Gen. José Miguel Gómez, ex-president.

Matanzas Issue

Map of Cuba A65

2c, Map of Free Zone. 4c, S. S. "Rex" in Matanzas Bay. 5c, Ships in Matanzas Bay. 8c, Caves of Bellamar. 10c, Valley of Yumuri. 20c, Yumuri River. 50c, Ships Leaving Port.

Wmk. 229

1936, May 5 **Photo.** ***Perf. 12½***

324	A65	1c blue green	.40	.20
325	A65	2c red	.60	.20
326	A65	4c claret	1.00	.20
327	A65	5c ultra	1.50	.20
328	A65	8c orange brn	2.50	.55
329	A65	10c emerald	2.75	.55
330	A65	20c brown	5.25	2.10
331	A65	50c slate	9.75	3.00
		Nos. 324-331,C18-C21,CE1,E8 (14)	45.65	19.40
		Set, never hinged	60.00	

Issued both perf and imperf. Same values.

"Peace and Work" A73

Máximo Gómez Monument — A74

Torch — A75

"Independence" — A76

"Messenger of Peace" — A77

1936, Nov. 18 ***Perf. 12½***

332	A73 1c emerald	.50	.20
333	A74 2c crimson	.60	.20
334	A75 4c maroon	.70	.20
335	A76 5c ultra	2.75	.45
336	A77 8c dk green	4.00	1.00
	Nos. 332-336,C22-C23,E9 (8)	18.80	6.65
	Set, never hinged	35.00	

Maj. Gen. Máximo Gómez, birth centenary.

Issued both perf and imperf. Values for imperfs are approx. 400% higher.

Sugar Cane — A78

Primitive Sugar Mill — A79

Modern Sugar Mill — A80

Wmk. 106

1937, Oct. 2 **Engr.** ***Perf. 10***

337	A78 1c yellow green	1.25	.40
338	A79 2c red	.75	.25
339	A80 5c bright blue	1.75	.40
	Nos. 337-339 (3)	3.75	1.05
	Set, never hinged	6.00	

Cuban sugar cane industry, 400th anniv.

Argentine Emblem — A81

Mountain Scene (Bolivia) — A82

Arms of Brazil — A83

Canadian Scene — A84

Camilo Henriquez (Chile) A85

Gen, Francisco de Paula Santander (Colombia) A86

Natl. Monument (Costa Rica) — A87

Autograph of José Marti (Cuba) — A88

Columbus Lighthouse (Dominican Rep.) — A89

Juan Montalvo (Ecuador) — A90

Abraham Lincoln (US) A91

Quetzal and Scroll (Guatemala) A92

Arms of Haiti A93

Francisco Morazán (Honduras) A94

Fleet of Columbus — A95

Wmk. 106

1937, Oct. 13 **Engr.** ***Perf. 10***

340	A81	1c deep green	.60	.60
341	A82	1c green	.60	.60
342	A83	2c carmine	.60	.60
343	A84	2c carmine	.60	.60
344	A85	3c violet	1.60	1.60
345	A86	3c violet	1.60	1.60
346	A87	4c bister brown	1.90	1.90
347	A88	4c bister brown	3.50	3.50
348	A89	5c blue	1.75	1.75
349	A90	5c blue	1.75	1.75
350	A91	8c citron	6.25	6.25
351	A92	8c citron	3.00	3.00
352	A93	10c maroon	3.00	3.00
353	A94	10c maroon	3.00	3.00
354	A95	25c rose lilac	32.50	32.50
		Nos. 340-354,C24-C29,E10-E11 (23)	121.75	121.75
		Set, never hinged	160.00	

Nos. 340-354 were sold by the Cuban PO for 3 days, Oct. 13-15, during which no other stamps were sold. They were postally valid for the full face value. Proceeds from their three-day sale above 30,000 pesos were paid by the Cuban POD to the Assoc. of American Writers and Artists. Remainders were overprinted "SVP" (Without Postal Value).

No. 283 Surcharged in Green

1937, Nov. 19 **Unwmk.** ***Perf. 12***

355	A44 10c on 25c violet	12.50	3.50
	Never hinged	19.00	

Centenary of Cuban railroads.

Ciboney Indian and Cigar — A96

Cigar and Globe — A97

Tobacco Plant and Cigars — A98

1939, Aug. 28 **Wmk. 106** ***Perf. 10***

356	A96 1c yellow green	.35	.20
357	A97 2c red	.50	.20
358	A98 5c brt ultra	.90	.25
	Nos. 356-358 (3)	1.75	.65
	Set, never hinged	3.00	

General Calixto García A99 A100

1939, Nov. 6 ***Perf. 10, Imperf.***

359	A99 2c dark red	.75	.20
360	A100 5c deep blue	1.00	.30
	Set, never hinged	3.00	

Birth centenary of General Garcia.

Values are for perf examples. Value of imperfs approx. 20% higher.

Gonzalo de Quesada — A101

1940, Apr. 30 **Engr.** ***Perf. 10***

361	A101 2c rose red	1.25	.50
	Never hinged	2.00	

Pan American Union, 50th anniversary.

651 A241 1c Guaiacum 1.50 1.50
652 A241 1c Coffee 1.50 1.50
a. Block of 4, #649-652 7.00
653 A240 2c ultra 1.00 1.00
654 A241 2c Tobacco 3.00 3.00
655 A241 2c Mariposa 3.00 3.00
656 A241 2c Guaiacum 3.00 3.00
657 A241 2c Coffee 3.00 3.00
a. Block of 4, #654-657 14.00
658 A240 10c ocher 3.00 2.50
659 A241 10c Tobacco 10.00 6.00
660 A241 10c Mariposa 10.00 6.00
661 A241 10c Guaiacum 10.00 6.00
662 A241 10c Coffee 10.00 6.00
a. Block of 4, #659-662 27.50
Nos. 648-662 (15) 62.75 46.25

Issued for Christmas 1960.

Nos. 648-662 were printed in three sheets of 25. Nine stamps of type A240 form a center cross, stamps of type A241 form a block of four in each corner with the musical bars joined in an oval around the floral designs.

"Public Capital for Economic Benefit" — A242

Designs: 2c, Chart and symbols of agriculture and industry. 6c, Cogwheels.

Perf. 11½

1961, Jan. 10 Unwmk. Photo.
663 A242 1c yel, blk & org .40 .20
664 A242 2c bl, blk & red .40 .20
665 A242 6c yel, red org & blk 1.00 .25
Nos. 663-665,C215-C218 (7) 8.80 2.55

Issued to publicize the conference of underdeveloped countries, Havana.

Jesus Menéndez and Sugar Cane — A243

1961, Jan. 22 Litho. *Perf. 12½*
666 A243 2c dk grn & brn .50 .20

Jesus Menéndez, leader in sugar industry.

Same Overprinted in Red: "PRIMERO DE MAYO 1961 ESTAMOS VENCIENDO"

1961, May 2
667 A243 2c dk grn & brn 1.50 .25

Issued for May Day, 1961.

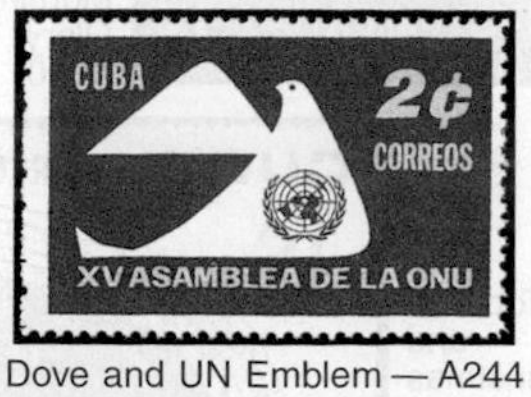

Dove and UN Emblem — A244

1961, Apr. 12 Litho. *Perf. 12½*
668 A244 2c red brn & yel grn .60 .20
669 A244 10c emer & rose lil 1.00 .20
a. Souv. sheet, #668-669, imperf. 5.00
Nos. 668-669,C222-C223 (4) 3.60 .95

15th anniv. (in 1960) of the UN.

Maceo Stamp of 1907 and 1902 Simulated Cancel A245

Stamp Day: 1c, Revolutionary 10c stamp of 1874, 1868 "cancel." 10c, #613, "cancel."

1961, Apr. 24 Unwmk.
670 A245 1c dull rose & dk grn .35 .20
671 A245 2c salmon & dk grn .40 .20
672 A245 10c pale grn, car rose & blk 2.00 .25
Nos. 670-672 (3) 2.75 .65

For overprint see No. 681.

Hand Releasing Dove — A246

1961, July 26 *Perf. 12½*
673 A246 2c blk, red, yel & gray 1.50 .20

26th of July (1953) movement, Castro's revolt against Fulgencio Batista.

Burelage on back consisting of wavy lines and diagonal rows of "CUBA CORREOS" in pale salmon.

Portrait Type of 1954

Designs: Same as before. On the 2c, "1833" is replaced by "?."

Wmk. 321 (Nos. 674, 676); Unwmkd.
Perf. 12½ (Nos. 674, 676); Rouletted

1961-69 Engr.
674 A184 1c brown red .50 .20
675 A184 1c lt blue ('69) .30 .20
676 A184a 2c slate green .50 .20
677 A184a 2c yel grn ('69) .30 .20
678 A184 3c org ('64) 1.50 .20
679 A184 13c brn ('64) 1.50 .30
680 A184 20c lilac ('69) .30 .20
Nos. 674-680 (7) 4.90 1.50

Issued: #674, 676, 8/1; #678-679, 12/764; others, 9/69.

For Nos. 675, 677-680, see embargo note following No. 702.

No. 672 Ovptd. in Red

Perf. 12½

1961, Oct. 7 Litho. Unwmk.
681 A245 10c pale grn, car rose & blk 2.00 .45

1st Official Phil. Exhib., Havana, Oct. 7-17.

Education Year — A247

Designs: One letter (per stamp) of "CUBA," book and various quotations by Jose Marti about the virtues of literacy.

1961, Nov. 22
682 A247 1c pale grn, red & blk .20 .20
683 A247 2c blue, red & blk .20 .20
684 A247 10c vio, red & blk .90 .25
685 A247 12c org, red & blk 1.75 .60
Nos. 682-685 (4) 3.05 1.25

A248

Christmas A249

1c, Snails. 2c, Birds, vert. 10c, Butterflies.

1961, Dec. 1
686 A248 1c Polymita flammulata .50 .20
687 A249 1c Polymita fulminata .50 .20
688 A249 1c Polymita nigrofasciata .50 .20
689 A249 1c Polymita fuscolimbata .50 .20
690 A249 1c Polymita roseolimbata .50 .20
a. Block of 5 + label, Nos. 686-690 2.50 1.50
691 A248 2c Cuban grassquit 2.00 .50
692 A249 2c Cuban macaw 2.00 .50
693 A249 2c Cuban trogon 2.00 .50
694 A249 2c Bee hummingbird 2.00 .50
695 A249 2c Ivory-billed woodpecker 2.00 .50
a. Block of 5 + label, Nos. 691-695 12.50 4.00
696 A248 10c Othreis toddi 3.00 1.00
697 A249 10c Uranidia boisduvalii 3.00 1.00
698 A249 10c Phoebis avellaneda 3.00 1.00
699 A249 10c Phaloe cubana 3.00 1.00
700 A249 10c Papilio gundlachianus 3.00 1.00
a. Block of 5 + label, Nos. 696-700 15.00 7.50
Nos. 686-700 (15) 27.50 8.50

Stamps of the same denomination printed se-tenant in sheets of 20 stamps plus 5 labels picturing bells and star. Stamps of Type A249 are arranged in blocks of 4; Type A248 stamps and labels form a cross in sheet.

See Nos. 760-774, 912-926, 1025-1039, 1179-1193, 1303-1317, 1464-1478, 1572-1586.

3rd Anniv. of the Revolution A250

1962, Jan. 3
701 A250 1c multi .85 .35
702 A250 2c multi 1.75 .45

See Nos. C226-C228.

Cuban goods have been embargoed by the United States since a Feb. 7, 1962 proclamation by President Kennedy, but according to the Office of Foreign Assets Control of the Treasury Department, used Cuban stamps can be imported and sold without limitation, and unused stamps may be imported for personal use, but not resold.

Natl. Militia A251

Silhouettes of militiamen and women and their peace-time occupations: 1c, Farmer. 2c, Welder. 3c, Seamstress.

1962, Feb. 26
703 A251 1c blue grn & blk .30 .20
704 A251 2c deep blue & blk .60 .25
705 A251 10c brt org & blk 2.10 .55
Nos. 703-705 (3) 3.00 1.00

Bay of Pigs Invasion, 1st Anniv. — A252

1962, Apr. 17
706 A252 2c multi .45 .20
707 A252 3c multi .45 .20
708 A252 10c multi 3.00 .65
Nos. 706-708 (3) 3.90 1.05

1st West Indies Packet A253

1962, Apr. 24
709 A253 10c red & gray 2.25 .90

Stamp Day. See No. E32.

Intl. Labor Day — A254

1962, May 1
710 A254 2c ocher & blk .35 .20
711 A254 3c ver & blk .75 .25
712 A254 10c greenish blue & blk 2.50 .70
Nos. 710-712 (3) 3.60 1.15

Natl. Sports Institute (INDER) Emblem and Athletes — A255

1962, July 25 Wmk. 321
713 A255 1c Judo .35 .20
714 A255 1c Discus .35 .20
715 A255 1c Gymnastics .35 .20
716 A255 1c Wrestling .35 .20
717 A255 1c Weight lifting .35 .20
718 A255 2c Roller skating .35 .20
719 A255 2c Equestrian .35 .20
720 A255 2c Archery .35 .20
721 A255 2c Bicycling .35 .20
722 A255 2c Bowling .35 .20
723 A255 3c Power boating 1.00 .20
724 A255 3c One-man kayak 1.00 .20
725 A255 3c Swimming 1.00 .20
726 A255 3c Sculling 1.00 .20
727 A255 3c Yachting 1.00 .20
728 A255 9c Soccer .90 .35
729 A255 9c Volleyball .90 .35
730 A255 9c Baseball .90 .35
731 A255 9c Basketball .90 .35
732 A255 9c Tennis .90 .35
733 A255 10c Boxing .90 .35
734 A255 10c Underwater fishing .90 .35
735 A255 10c Model-plane flying .90 .35
736 A255 10c Pistol shooting .90 .35
737 A255 10c Water polo .90 .35
738 A255 13c Paddleball 1.00 .50
739 A255 13c Fencing 1.00 .50
740 A255 13c Sports Palace 1.00 .50

741 A255 13c Chess 1.00 .50
742 A255 13c Jai alai 1.00 .50
Nos. 713-742 (30) 22.50 9.00

Stamps of the same denomination printed se-tenant in sheets of 25. Various combinations possible.

9th Anniv. of the Revolution A256

Attack on Moncada Barracks: Abel Santamaria and: 2c, Barracks under siege. 3c, Children at Moncada School.

1962, July 26

743 A256 2c brn car & dark ultra .65 .35
744 A256 3c dark ultra & brn car 1.10 .55

8th World Youth Festival for Peace and Friendship, Helsinki, July 28-Aug. 6 — A257

1962, July 28

745 A257 2c Dove, emblem 1.00 .25
746 A257 3c Hand grip, emblem 1.75 .55
a. Min. sheet of 2, Nos. 745-746, imperf. 6.50 6.50

9th Central American and Caribbean Games, Kingston, Jamaica, Aug. 11-25 A258

1962, Aug. 27

747 A258 1c Boxing .20 .20
748 A258 2c Tennis .20 .20
749 A258 3c Baseball .20 .20
750 A258 13c Fencing 2.40 .80
Nos. 747-750 (4) 3.00 1.40

A259

First Natl. Congress of the Federation of Cuban Women — A260

1962, Oct. 1

751 A259 9c rose, blk & grn 1.10 .25
752 A260 13c blk, grn & lt blue 2.40 .65

Latin American University Games — A261

1962, Oct. 13 **Wmk. 106**

753 A261 1c Running .40 .20
754 A261 2c Baseball .85 .20
755 A261 3c Basketball 1.25 .20
756 A261 13c World map 2.50 .55
Nos. 753-756 (4) 5.00 1.15

World Health Organization Campaign to Eradicate Malaria — A262

Designs: 1c, Magnified specimen of the parasitic protozoa, microscope. 2c, Swamp and mosquito. 3c, Chemist's structural formulas for quinine, cinchona plant.

1962, Dec. 14

757 A262 1c multi .50 .20
758 A262 2c multi .50 .20
759 A262 3c multi 1.75 .20
Nos. 757-759 (3) 2.75 .60

Christmas Type of 1961

2c, Reptiles. 3c, Insects, vert. 10c, Rodents.

1962, Dec. 21 **Unwmk.**

760 A248 2c Epicrates angulifer .65 .20
761 A249 2c Cricosaurus typica .65 .20
762 A249 2c Anolis equestris .65 .20
763 A249 2c Tropidophis wrighti .65 .20
764 A249 2c Cyclura macleayi .65 .20
a. Block of 5 + label, Nos. 760-764 3.50 1.50
765 A248 3c Cubispa turquino 1.00 .60
766 A249 3c Chrysis superba 1.00 .60
767 A249 3c Essostruta roberto 1.00 .60
768 A249 3c Hortensia conciliata 1.00 .60
769 A249 3c Lachnopus argus 1.00 .60
a. Block of 5 + label, Nos. 765-769 5.50 4.50
770 A248 10c Monophyllus cubanus 4.00 1.25
771 A249 10c Capromys pilorides 4.00 1.25
772 A249 10c Capromys prehensilis 4.00 1.25
773 A249 10c Solenodon cubensis 4.00 1.25
774 A249 10c Capromys pilorides (Blanca) 4.00 1.25
a. Block of 5 + label, Nos. 770-774 21.00 9.00
Nos. 760-774 (15) 28.25 10.25

Christmas 1962. See note after No. 700.

Around 1962 a 1ctv. label picturing Fidel Castro was used as a voluntary contribution stamp. It is not inscribed "Correos" and was not valid for postage.

Soviet Space Flights — A263

Spacecraft and cosmonauts: 1c, Vostok 1, Yuri A. Gagarin, Apr. 12, 1961. 2c, Vostok 2, Gherman S. Titov, Aug. 6-7, 1961. 3c, Vostok 3, Andrian G. Nikolaev, Aug. 11-15, 1962, and Vostok 4, Pavel R. Popovich, Aug. 12-15, 1962. 9c, Vostok 5, Valery F. Bykovsky, June 14-19, 1963. 13c, Vostok 6, Valentina V. Tereshkova, June 16-19, 1963.

1963-64 **Wmk. 321**

775 A263 1c ultra, red & yel .35 .20
776 A263 2c grn, yel & rose lake .65 .25
777 A263 3c yel, vio & ver .65 .25
778 A263 9c red, dark vio & yel 1.25 .45
779 A263 13c dark blue green, dull red brown & yel 3.25 .70
Nos. 775-779 (5) 6.15 1.85

Issued: 1c, 2c, 3c, 2/26/63; others, 8/15/64.

Attack of the Presidential Palace, 6th Anniv. — A264

9c, Guerillas attacking palace. 13c, Four student leaders. 30c, Jose A. Echeverria, Menelad Mora.

1963, Mar. 13

780 A264 9c dark red & blk 1.10 .20
781 A264 13c chalky blue & sep 1.40 .20
782 A264 30c org & grn 3.50 1.00
Nos. 780-782 (3) 6.00 1.40

4th Pan American Games, Sao Paulo, Brazil, Apr. 20-May 5 — A265

1963, Apr. 20

783 A265 1c Baseball 1.25 .35
784 A265 13c Boxing 3.25 .65

Stamp Day A266

3c, Mask mailbox, 19th cent. 10c, Mask mailbox at the Plaza de la Catedral, Havana.

1963, Apr. 25

785 A266 3c black & dark org 1.00 .20
786 A266 10c black & pur 2.50 .30

See Nos. 828-829, 956-957 and 1102-1103.

Labor Day — A267

1963, May 1

787 A267 3c shown .50 .20
788 A267 13c Four workers 1.75 .30

Intl. Children's Week, June 1-7 — A268

1963, June 1

789 A268 3c blue blk & bister brn .50 .20
790 A268 30c blue blk & red 2.75 .80

Ritual Effigy — A269

Broken Chains at Moncada A270

Taino Civilization artifacts: 3c, Wood-carved throne, horiz. 9c, Stone-carved figurine.

1963, June 29

791 A269 2c org & red brn .75 .20
792 A269 3c ultra & red brn .90 .25
793 A269 9c rose & gray 1.60 .45
Nos. 791-793 (3) 3.25 .90

Montane Anthropology Museum, 60th anniv.

1963, July 26

2c, Attack on the Presidential Palace. 3c, The insurrection. 7c, Strike of April 9. 9c, Triumph of the revolution. 10c, Agricultural reform and nationalization of industry. 13c, Bay of Pigs victory.

794 A270 1c pink & blk .20 .20
795 A270 2c lt blue & vio brn .20 .20
796 A270 3c lt vio & brn .20 .20
797 A270 7c apple green & rose .20 .20
798 A270 9c olive bister & rose vio .30 .20
799 A270 10c beige & sage grn .85 .30
800 A270 13c pale org & slate blue 1.25 .50
Nos. 794-800 (7) 3.20 1.80

Indigenous Fruit — A271

1963, Aug. 19

801 A271 1c Star apple .20 .20
802 A271 2c Cherimoya .20 .20
803 A271 3c Cashew nut .35 .20
804 A271 10c Custard apple 2.00 .25
805 A271 13c Mangoes 2.50 .40
Nos. 801-805 (5) 5.25 1.25

Geometric Shapes A272

View of a Town — A273

Designs: No. 806, Circle, triangle, square, vert. No. 807, Roof, window, vert. No. 808, View of a town. No. 809, View of a town in blue. No. 810, View of a town in olive bister and red. No. 811, Circle, triangle, vert. No. 812, House, roof and doorway, vert. No. 813, House, girders.

1963, Sept. 29 **Unwmk.**

806 A272 3c multi .50 .20
807 A272 3c multi .50 .20
808 A273 3c multi .50 .20
809 A273 3c multi .50 .20
810 A273 13c multi 1.50 .50
811 A272 13c multi 1.50 .50
812 A272 13c multi 1.50 .50
813 A272 13c multi 1.50 .50
Nos. 806-813 (8) 8.00 2.80

7th Intl. Congress of the Intl. Union of Architects.

10th Anniv. of Successful Revolution Campaigns — A338

Revolution leaders, scenes of the insurrection.

1966, Nov. 30

1166 A338 1c Antonio Fernandez .20 .20
1167 A338 2c Candido Gonzalez .20 .20
1168 A338 3c Jose Tey .20 .20
1169 A338 7c Tony Aloma .30 .20
1170 A338 9c Otto Parelleda .60 .20
1171 A338 10c Juan Manuel Marquez 2.00 .50
1172 A338 13c Frank Pais 1.90 .80
Nos. 1166-1172 (7) 5.40 2.30

Intl. Leisure Time and Recreation Seminar — A339

1966, Dec. 2

1173 A339 3c shown .20 .20
1174 A339 9c World map, stop-watch, eye 1.40 .20
1175 A339 13c Earth, clock, emblem 1.75 .60
Nos. 1173-1175 (3) 3.35 1.00

1st Natl. Telecommunications Forum — A340

1966, Dec. 12

1176 A340 3c shown .75 .20
1177 A340 10c Satellite in orbit 3.75 .20
1178 A340 13c Shell, satellite 5.50 .70
a. Souv. sheet of 3, #1176-1178, imperf. 15.00 15.00
Nos. 1176-1178 (3) 10.00 1.10

No. 1178a sold for 30c.

Christmas Type of 1961

1966, Dec. 20 **Unwmk.**

1179 A248 1c Cypripedium eurylochus .90 .20
1180 A249 1c Cattleya speciosissima .90 .20
1181 A249 1c Cattleya mendelii majestica .90 .20
1182 A249 1c Cattleya trianae amesiana .90 .20
1183 A249 1c Cattleya labiata macfarlanei .90 .20
a. Block of 5 + label, #1179-1183 5.00 1.00
1184 A248 3c Cypripedium morganiae burfordense 1.40 .20
1185 A249 3c Cattleya Countess of Derby 1.40 .20
1186 A249 3c Cypripedium hookerae volunteanum 1.40 .20
1187 A249 3c Cattleya warscewiczii reginae burfordense 1.40 .20
1188 A249 3c Cypripedium stonei cannartae 1.40 .20
a. Block of 5 + label, #1184-1188 8.00 1.00
1189 A248 13c Cattleya mendelii Duchess of Montrose 5.00 .50
1190 A249 13c Oncidium macranthum 5.00 .50
1191 A249 13c Cypripedium stonei platytoenium 5.00 .50
1192 A249 13c Cattleya dowiana aurea 5.00 .50
1193 A249 13c Laelia anceps 5.00 .50
a. Block of 5 + label, #1189-1193 27.50 2.75
Nos. 1179-1193 (15) 36.50 4.50

Christmas 1966. See note after No. 700.

8th Anniv. of the Revolution — A341

1967, Jan. 2

1194 A341 3c Liberation, 1959 .30 .20
1195 A341 3c Agrarian Reform, 1960 .30 .20
1196 A341 3c Education, 1961 .30 .20
1197 A341 3c Agriculture, 1965 .30 .20
a. Strip of 4, Nos. 1194-1197 1.25 .90
1198 A341 13c Rodin's Thinker, Planning, 1962 1.90 .45
1199 A341 13c Organization, 1963 1.90 .45
1200 A341 13c Economy, 1964 1.90 .45
1201 A341 13c Solidarity, 1966 1.90 .45
a. Strip of 4, Nos. 1198-1201 7.75 4.25
Nos. 1194-1201 (8) 8.80 2.60

Nos. 1198-1201 vert.

Spring, by Jorge Arche — A342

Paintings in the Natl. Museum: 1c, Coffee Machine, by Angel Acosta Leon, vert. 2c, Country People, by Eduardo Abela, vert. 13c, Still-life, by Amelia Pelaez, vert. 30c, Landscape, by Gonzalo Escalante.

1967, Feb. 27

1202 A342 1c multi .30 .20
1203 A342 2c multi .50 .20
1204 A342 3c multi .70 .20
1205 A342 13c multi 2.00 .30
1206 A342 30c multi 5.50 .60
Nos. 1202-1206 (5) 9.00 1.50

Natl. Events, Mar. 13, 1957 A343

1967, Mar. 13 **Wmk. 376**

1207 A343 3c Attack on Presidential Palace .20 .20

Size: 41x28mm

1208 A343 13c Landing of Corynthia 2.50 .70
1209 A343 30c Cienfuegos revolt 2.40 .80
Nos. 1207-1209 (3) 5.10 1.70

Evolution of Man — A344

Prehistoric men: 2c, Australopithecus. 3c, Pithecanthropus erectus. 4c, Sinanthropus pekinensis. 5c, Neanderthal man. 13c, Cro-magnon man carving tusk. 20c, Cro-magnon man painting petroglyph.

1967, Mar. 31 **Unwmk.**

1210 A344 1c multi .30 .20
1211 A344 2c multi .50 .20
1212 A344 3c multi .50 .20
1213 A344 4c multi .75 .20
1214 A344 5c multi 1.10 .20
1215 A344 13c multi 3.75 .30
1216 A344 20c multi 7.50 .45
Nos. 1210-1216 (7) 14.40 1.75

Stamp Day A345

Carriages.

1967, Apr. 24

1217 A345 3c Victoria .35 .20
1218 A345 9c Volante 2.00 .45
1219 A345 13c Quitrin 3.00 .80
Nos. 1217-1219 (3) 5.35 1.45

EXPO '67, Montreal, Apr. 28-Oct. 27 — A346

1967, Apr. 28

1220 A346 1c Cuban pavilion .40 .20
1221 A346 2c Space exploration .40 .20
1222 A346 3c Petroglyph, hieroglyph .55 .20
1223 A346 13c Agriculture, computer technology 3.00 .20
1224 A346 20c Athletes 3.50 .20
Nos. 1220-1224 (5) 7.85 1.00

Botanical Gardens, Sequicentennial A347

Flowering plants.

1967, May 30

1225 A347 1c Eugenia malaccencis .20 .20
1226 A347 2c Jacaranda filicifolia .20 .20
1227 A347 3c Coroupita guianensis .45 .20
1228 A347 4c Spathodea campanulata .45 .20
1229 A347 5c Cassia fistula .90 .20
1230 A347 13c Plumieria alba 2.75 .35
1231 A347 20c Erythrina poeppigiana 4.75 .40
Nos. 1225-1231 (7) 9.70 1.75

Natl. Ballet — A348

1967, June 15

1232 A348 1c Giselle .35 .20
1233 A348 2c Swan Lake .35 .20
1234 A348 3c Don Quixote .50 .20
1235 A348 4c Calaucan 1.00 .20
1236 A348 13c Swan Lake 2.75 .70
1237 A348 20c Nutcracker 4.00 1.25
Nos. 1232-1237 (6) 8.95 2.75

Intl. Ballet Festival, Havana.

5th Pan American Games, Winnipeg, Canada, July 22-Aug. 7 — A349

1st Conference of Latin American Solidarity Organization (OLAS) — A350

1967, July 22

1238 A349 1c Baseball, horiz. .20 .20
1239 A349 2c Swimming, horiz. .35 .20
1240 A349 3c Basketball .50 .20
1241 A349 4c Gymnastic rings .85 .20
1242 A349 5c Water polo 1.00 .20
1243 A349 13c Weight lifting, horiz. 3.00 .45
1244 A349 20c Javelin 4.75 .80
Nos. 1238-1244 (7) 10.65 2.25

1967, July 28 **Wmk. 376**

Portrait of representative, map of South American homeland: No. 1245, Camilo Torres, Colombia. No. 1246, Luis de la Puente Uceda, Peru. No. 1247, Luis A. Turcios Lima, Guatemala. No. 1248, Fabricio Ojeda, Venezuela.

1245 A350 13c pale grn, blk & red 2.00 .50
1246 A350 13c lil, blk & red 2.00 .50
1247 A350 13c dark chalky blue, blk & red 2.00 .50
1248 A350 13c golden brn, blk & red 2.00 .50
Nos. 1245-1248 (4) 8.00 2.00

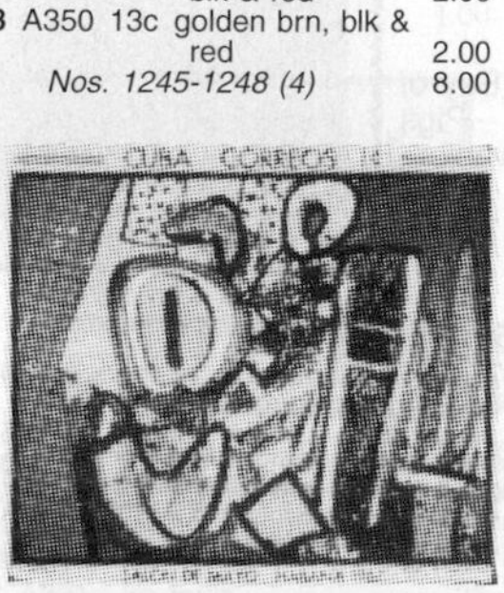

Portrait of Sonny Rollins, by Alan Davie — A351

Bathers, by Gustave Singier
A352

Modern Art: No. 1250, Twelve Selenities, by Felix Labisse. No. 1251, Night of the Drinker, by Friedensreich Hundertwasser. No. 1252, Figure, by Mariano. No. 1253, All-Souls, by Wilfredo Lam. No. 1254, Darkness and Cracks, by Antonio Tapies. No. 1256, Torso of a Muse, by Jean Arp. No. 1257, Figure, by M.W. Svanberg. No. 1258, Oppenheimer's Information, by Erro. No. 1259, Where Cardinals Are Born, by Max Ernst. No. 1260, Havana Landscape, by Portocarrero. No. 1261, EG 12, by Victor Vasarely. No. 1262, Frisco, by Alexander Calder. No. 1263, The Man with the Pipe, by Picasso. No. 1264, Abstract Composition, by Sergei Poliakoff. No. 1265, Painting, by Bram van Velde. No. 1266, Sower of Fires, by R. Matta. No. 1267, The Art of Living, by Rene Magritte. No. 1268, Poem, by Joan Miro. No. 1269, Young Tigers, by Jean Messagier. No. 1270, Painting, by M. Vieira da Silva. No. 1271, Live Cobra, by Pierre Alechinsky. No. 1272, Stalingrad, by Asger Jorn. 30c, Warriors, by Edouard Pignon. 50c, Cloister, a mural at the exhibition representing the Salon de Mayo pictures.

1967, July 29 **Unwmk.**

1249	A351	1c	shown	.30	.20
1250	A351	1c	multi	.30	.20
1251	A351	1c	multi	.30	.20
1252	A351	1c	multi	.30	.20
1253	A351	1c	multi	.30	.20
a.			Strip of 5, Nos. 1249-1253	1.75	1.50

Sizes: 36½x54mm, 36½x53mm, 36½x45mm, 36½x41mm

1254	A352	2c	multi	.60	.20
1255	A352	2c	shown	.60	.20
1256	A352	2c	multi	.60	.20
1257	A352	2c	multi	.60	.20
1258	A352	2c	multi	.60	.20
a.			Strip of 5, Nos. 1254-1258	3.50	2.50

Sizes: 36½x54mm, 36½x40mm, 36½x42mm, 36½x49mm

1259	A352	3c	multi	1.50	.20
1260	A352	3c	multi	1.50	.20
1261	A352	3c	multi	1.50	.20
1262	A352	3c	multi	1.50	.20
1263	A352	3c	multi	1.50	.20
a.			Strip of 5, Nos. 1259-1263	7.50	3.50

Sizes: 35x15mm, 35x67mm, 35x46½mm, 35x55mm

1264	A352	4c	multi	1.75	.80
1265	A352	4c	multi	1.75	.80
1266	A352	4c	multi	1.75	.80
1267	A352	4c	multi	1.75	.80
1268	A352	4c	multi	1.75	.80
a.			Strip of 5, Nos. 1264-1268	9.00	4.00

Sizes: 49x32mm, 49x35mm, 49x46mm

1269	A351	13c	multi	4.50	2.75
1270	A351	13c	multi	4.50	2.75
1271	A351	13c	multi	4.50	2.75
1272	A351	13c	multi	4.50	2.75
a.			Strip of 4, Nos. 1269-1272	19.00	11.00

Size: 54x32mm

1273	A351	30c	multi	17.50	11.00
			Nos. 1249-1273 (25)	56.25	29.00

Souvenir Sheet

Imperf

1274	A351	50c	multi	25.00	12.50

Salon de Mayo Art Exhibition, Havana. No. 1274 contains one 88x45mm stamp with simulated perforations. Issued Oct. 7.

World Underwater Fishing Championships — A353

1967, Sept. 5

1275	A353	1c	Green moray	.20	.20
1276	A353	2c	Octopus	.20	.20
1277	A353	3c	Great barracuda	.20	.20
1278	A353	4c	Blue shark	.75	.20
1279	A353	5c	Spotted jewfish	1.60	.20
1280	A353	13c	Sting ray	3.25	.35
1281	A353	20c	Green turtle	6.50	.45
			Nos. 1275-1281 (7)	12.70	1.80

Soviet Space Program
A354

1967, Oct. 4 **Wmk. 376**

1282	A354	1c	Sputnik 1	.20	.20
1283	A354	2c	Lunik 3	.20	.20
1284	A354	3c	Venusik	.20	.20
1285	A354	4c	Cosmos	.40	.20
1286	A354	5c	Mars 1	.65	.20
1287	A354	9c	Electron 1 & 2	.75	.20
1288	A354	10c	Luna 9	1.10	.25
1289	A354	13c	Luna 10	2.50	.30
a.			Souv. sheet of 8, #1282-1289, imperf.	15.00	15.00
			Nos. 1282-1289 (8)	6.00	1.75

Stamps in #1289a have simulated perfs.

50th Anniv. of the October Revolution, Russia
A355

Paintings: 1c, Storming the Winter Palace, by Sokolov, Skalia and Miasnikov. 2c, Lenin Addressing Congress, by W.A. Serov. 3c, Lenin, by H.D. Nalbandian. 4c, Lenin Explaining Electrification Map, by L.A. Schmatko. 5c, Dawn of the Five-Year Plan, by J.D. Romas. 13c, Kusnetzkroi Steel Furnace No. 1, by P. Kotov. 30c, Victory, by A. Krivonogov.

1967, Nov. 7 **Unwmk.**

1290	A355	1c	64x36mm	.20	.20
1291	A355	2c	48x36mm	.20	.20
1292	A355	3c		.45	.20
1293	A355	4c	48x36mm	.45	.20
1294	A355	5c	50x36mm	3.75	.20
1295	A355	13c	36x50mm	3.00	.20
1296	A355	30c	50x36mm	4.00	.25
			Nos. 1290-1296 (7)	12.05	1.45

Castle of the Royal Forces, Havana — A356

Historic architecture: 2c, Iznaga Tower, Trinidad, vert. 3c, Castle of Our Lady of the Angels, Cienfuegos. 4c, St. Francis de Paula Church, Havana. 13c, St. Francis Convent, Havana. 30c, Castle del Morro, Santiago de Cuba.

1967, Nov. 7 **Wmk. 376**

Sizes: 26x47mm (1c), 41x29mm (3c, 4c), 38½x31mm (13c)

1297	A356	1c	multi	.20	.20
1298	A356	2c	multi	.20	.20
1299	A356	3c	multi	.65	.20
1300	A356	4c	multi	.65	.20
1301	A356	13c	multi	3.25	.50
1302	A356	30c	multi	5.00	1.00
			Nos. 1297-1302 (6)	9.95	2.30

Christmas Type of 1961

Birds.

1967, Dec. 20

1303	A248	1c	Struthia camelus australis	1.75	.60
1304	A249	1c	Chysolophus pictus	1.75	.60
1305	A249	1c	Ciconia ciconia ciconia	1.75	.60
1306	A249	1c	Balearica pavonina	1.75	.60
1307	A249	1c	Dromiceius novaehollandiae	1.75	.60
a.			Block of 5 + label, Nos. 1303-1307	10.00	3.25
1308	A248	3c	Anodorhynchus hyacinthus	2.40	1.00
1309	A249	3c	Psittacus erithacus	2.40	1.00
1310	A249	3c	Domicella garrula	2.40	1.00
1311	A249	3c	Ramphastos sulfuratus	2.40	1.00
1312	A249	3c	Kakatoe galerita galerita	2.40	1.00
a.			Block of 5 + label, Nos. 1308-1312	14.00	5.50
1313	A248	13c	Phoenicopterus ruber	4.50	1.75
1314	A249	13c	Pelecanus erythrorhynchos	4.50	1.75
1315	A249	13c	Alopochen aegyptiacus	4.50	1.75
1316	A249	13c	Dendronessa galericulata	4.50	1.75
1317	A249	13c	Chenopsis atrata	4.50	1.75
a.			Block of 5 + label, Nos. 1313-1317	25.00	9.00
			Nos. 1303-1317 (15)	43.25	16.75

Christmas 1967. See note after No. 700.

Ernesto "Che" Guevara (1928-1967), Revolution Leader — A356a

1968, Jan. 3

1318	A356a	13c	blk, dark red & buff	2.50	.55

Cultural Congress, Havana — A357

Abstract designs: No. 1319, Independence fostering culture. No. 1320, Integral formation of man. No. 1321, Responsibility of intellectuals. No. 1322, Relationship between culture and the mass media. No. 1323, The arts versus science and technology.

1968, Jan. 4

1319	A357	3c	multi, vert.	.20	.20
1320	A357	3c	multi, vert.	.20	.20
1321	A357	13c	multi, vert.	1.50	.20
1322	A357	13c	multi, vert.	1.75	.20
1323	A357	30c	multi	2.40	.25
			Nos. 1319-1323 (5)	6.05	1.05

Canaries and Breeding Cycles
A358

1968, Apr. 13

1324	A358	1c	F.C.C. 4016	.20	.20
1325	A358	2c	A.C.C. 774	.20	.20
1326	A358	3c	A.C.C. 122	.40	.20
1327	A358	4c	F.C.C. 4477	.40	.25
1328	A358	5c	A.C.C 117	.75	.20
1329	A358	13c	A.N.R. 1175	4.00	.20
1330	A358	20c	A.C.C. 777	5.50	.25
			Nos. 1324-1330 (7)	11.45	1.50

Stamp Day
A359

Paintings: 13c, The Village Postman, by J. Harris. 30c, The Philatelist, by G. Sciltian.

1968, Apr. 24 **Unwmk.**

1331	A359	13c	multi	2.00	.20
1332	A359	30c	multi	3.00	.20

World Health Organization, 20th Anniv. — A360

1968, May 10 **Wmk. 376**

1333	A360	13c	Nurse, mother, child	1.60	.20
1334	A360	30c	Surgeons	2.10	.20
			Nos. 1333-1334 (2)	3.70	.40

Intl. Children's Day — A361

1968, June 1

1335	A361	3c	multi	1.25	.25

Seville Camaguey Flight, 35th Anniv. — A362

1968, June 20

1336	A362	13c	Plane Four Winds	2.25	.45
1337	A362	30c	Capt. Barberan, Lt. Collar, pilots	2.75	.60

Natl. Food Production — A363

1968, June 29

1338	A363	1c	Yellow tuna, can	.25	.20
1339	A363	2c	Cow, dairy products	.25	.20
1340	A363	3c	Rooster, eggs	.50	.20
1341	A363	13c	Rum, sugar cane	3.00	.20
1342	A363	20c	Crayfish, box	3.50	.30
			Nos. 1338-1342 (5)	7.50	1.10

Attack of Moncada Barracks, 15th Anniv. A364

1968, July 26

Size: 43x29mm (13c)

1343	A364	3c	Siboney farmhouse	.20	.20
1344	A364	13c	Assault route, Santiago de Cuba	1.75	.20
1345	A364	30c	Students, school	3.00	.20
			Nos. 1343-1345 (3)	4.95	.60

Committee for the Defense of the Revolution, 8th Anniv. — A365

1968, Sept. 28

1346	A365	3c	multi	2.00	.20

Guerilla Day A366

Che Guevara and: 1c, Rifleman and "En Cualquier Lugar..." 3c, Machine gunners and "Crear tres muchos Viet Nam." 9c, Silhouette of battalion and "Este Tipo De Lucha..." 10c, Guerillas cheering and "Hoy aquilatamos..." 13c, Map of Caribbean, So. America and "Hasta La Victoria Siempre."

1968, Oct. 8

1347	A366	1c	gold, brt blue grn & blk	.20	.20
1348	A366	3c	gold, org brn blk	.20	.20
1349	A366	9c	multi	.60	.20
1350	A366	10c	gold, lt olive grn & blk	1.40	.20
1351	A366	13c	gold, red org & blk	2.50	.70
			Nos. 1347-1351 (5)	4.90	1.50

Cuban War of Independence, Cent. — A367

Independence fighters and scenes.

1968, Oct. 10 **Unwmk.**

1352	A367	1c	C.M. de Cespedes, broken wheel	.20	.20
1353	A367	1c	E. Betances, horsemen, flag	.20	.20
1354	A367	1c	I. Agramonte, Clavellinas Monument	.20	.20
1355	A367	1c	A. Maceo, Baragua Protest	.20	.20
1356	A367	1c	J. Marti, horsemen	.20	.20
a.			Strip of 5, Nos. 1352-1356	1.00	1.00
1357	A367	3c	M. Gomez, The Invasion	.25	.20
1358	A367	3c	J.A. Mella, declaration	.25	.20
1359	A367	3c	A. Guiteras, El Morrillo monument	.25	.20
1360	A367	3c	A. Santamaria, attack on Moncada Barracks	.25	.20
1361	A367	3c	F. Paiz memorial	.25	.20
a.			Strip of 5, Nos. 1357-1361	1.75	1.00
1362	A367	9c	J. Echeverria, student protest	1.25	.20
1363	A367	13c	C. Cienfuegos, insurrection	3.00	.70
1364	A367	30c	Che Guevara, 1st Declaration of Havana	3.50	1.10
			Nos. 1352-1364 (13)	10.00	4.00

Souvenir Sheet

The Burning of Bayamo, by J.E. Hernandez Giro — A368

1968, Oct. 18 ***Imperf.***

1365	A368	50c	multi	9.00	4.00

Natl. Philatelic Exhibition, independence cent. Stamp in No. 1365 has simulated perforations.

19th Summer Olympics, Mexico City, Oct. 12-27 — A369

1968, Oct. 21 ***Perf. 12½***

1366	A369	1c	Parade of athletes	.20	.20
1367	A369	2c	Women's basketball, vert.	.20	.20
1368	A369	3c	Hammer throw, vert.	.20	.20
1369	A369	4c	Boxing	.20	.20
1370	A369	5c	Water polo	.45	.20
1371	A369	13c	Pistol shooting	3.00	.25

Size: 32x50mm

1372	A369	30c	Mexican flag, calendar stone	4.50	.40
			Nos. 1366-1372 (7)	8.75	1.65

Souvenir Sheet

Imperf

1373	A369	50c	Running	15.00	4.00

Stamp in #173 has simulated perforations.

Civilian Activities of the Armed Forces A370

1968, Dec. 2 **Wmk. 376** ***Perf. 12½***

1374	A370	3c	Crop dusting	.20	.20
1375	A370	9c	Che Guevara's Brigade	.60	.20
1376	A370	10c	Road building	1.00	.20
1377	A370	13c	Plowing, harvesting	2.10	.70
			Nos. 1374-1377 (4)	3.90	1.30

San Alejandro School of Painting, Sesquicentennial — A371

Paintings: 1c, Manrique de Lara's Family, by Jean Baptiste Vermay, vert. 2c, Seascape, by Leopoldo Romanach. 3c, Wild Cane, by Antonio Rodriguez, vert. 4c, Self-portrait, by Miguel Melero, vert. 5c, The Lottery List, by Jose Joaquin Tejada. 13c, Portrait of Nina, by Armando B. Menocal, vert. 30c, Landscape, by Esteban B. Chartrand. 50c, Siesta, by Guillermo Collazo.

1968, Dec. 30 **Unwmk.**

Sizes: 38x48mm (1c, 3c), 39x50mm (4c, 13c), 53x36mm (30c)

1378	A371	1c	multi	.20	.20
1379	A371	2c	multi	.20	.20
1380	A371	3c	multi	.30	.20
1381	A371	4c	multi	.30	.20
1382	A371	5c	multi	1.40	.20
1383	A371	13c	multi	4.00	.25
1384	A371	30c	multi	6.25	.40
			Nos. 1378-1384 (7)	12.65	1.65

Souvenir Sheet

Imperf

1385	A371	50c	multi	9.00	3.50

No. 1385 contains one 52x41½mm stamp that has simulated perforations.

10th Anniv. of the Revolution A372

1969, Jan. 3 **Wmk. 376** ***Perf. 12½***

1386	A372	13c	multi	2.00	.60

Villaclarenos Rebellion, Cent. — A373

1969, Feb. 6

1387	A373	3c	Gutierrez and Sanchez	1.00	.25

Women's Day — A374

Design: Mariana Grajales, rose and statue.

1969, Mar. 8

1388	A374	3c	multi	1.25	.20

Cuban Pioneers and Young Communists Unions — A375

1969, Apr. 4

1389	A375	3c	Pioneers	.40	.20
1390	A375	13c	Young Communists	2.25	.80

Guaimaro Assembly, Cent. — A376

1969, Apr. 10

1391	A376	3c	dark brn	1.00	.20

The Postman, by Jean C. Cazin A377

Paintings: 30c, Portrait of a Young Man, by George Romney.

1969, Apr. 24 **Unwmk.**

1392	A377	13c	multi	2.50	.20

Size: 35½x43½mm

1393	A377	30c	multi	4.00	.20

Stamp Day.

Agrarian Reform, 10th Anniv. A378

1969, May 17 **Wmk. 376**

1394	A378	13c	multi	2.25	.70

Marine Life A379

1969, May 20 **Unwmk.**

1395	A379	1c	Petrochirus bahamensis	.20	.20
1396	A379	2c	Stenopus hispidus	.40	.20
1397	A379	3c	Panulirus argus	.40	.20
1398	A379	4c	Callinectes sapidus	.50	.20
1399	A379	5c	Gecarcinus ruricola	.50	.20
1400	A379	13c	Macrobrachium carcinus	3.50	.45
1401	A379	30c	Carpilius coralinus	5.25	.80
			Nos. 1395-1401 (7)	10.75	2.25

Intl. Labor Organization, 50th Anniv. — A380

1969, June 6 **Wmk. 376**

1402 A380 3c shown .45 .20
1403 A380 13c Blacksmith breaking chains 2.25 .70

Paintings in the Natl. Museum — A381

Designs: 1c, Flowers, by Raul Milian, vert. 2c, Annunciation, by Antonia Eiriz. 3c, Factory, by Marcelo Pogolotti, vert. 4c, Territorial Waters, by Luis Martinez Pedro, vert. 5c, Miss Sarah Gale, by John Hoppner, vert. 13c, Two Women Wearing Mantilla, by Ignacio Zuloaga. 30c, Virgin and Child, by Francisco de Zurburan.

1969, June 15 **Unwmk.**

1404 A381 1c 39x59mm .20 .20
1405 A381 2c .20 .20
1406 A381 3c 39½x49mm 1.10 .20
1407 A381 4c 39½x43mm .30 .20
1408 A381 5c 39½x45½mm .30 .20
1409 A381 13c 38x41½mm 2.10 .70
1410 A381 30c 39x45mm 3.25 .90
Nos. 1404-1410 (7) 7.45 2.60

Broadcasting Institute — A382

1969, July 5 **Wmk. 376**

1411 A382 3c shown .40 .25
1412 A382 13c Hemispheres, tower 2.10 .80
1413 A382 1p Waves on graph 5.00 1.75
Nos. 1411-1413 (3) 7.50 2.80

Fish A383

1969, July 20 **Unwmk.**

1414 A383 1c Apogon maculatus .20 .20
1415 A383 2c Bodianus rufus .20 .20
1416 A383 3c Microspathodon chrysurus .40 .20
1417 A383 4c Gramma loreto .40 .20
1418 A383 5c Chromis marginatus .60 .20
1419 A383 13c Myripristis jacobus 3.75 .25
1420 A383 30c Nomeus gronovii, vert. 5.25 .40
Nos. 1414-1420 (7) 10.80 1.65

Natl. Film Industry, 10th Anniv. — A384

1969, Aug. 5 **Wmk. 376**

1421 A384 1c Poster .20 .20
1422 A384 3c Documentaries .20 .20
1423 A384 13c Cartoons 3.00 .20
1424 A384 30c Entertainers 3.50 .20
Nos. 1421-1424 (4) 6.90 .80

Napoleon in Milan, by Andrea Appiani — A385

Paintings in the Napoleon Museum, Havana: 2c, Hortensia de Beauharnais, by Francois Gerard. 3c, Napoleon as First Consul, by J.B. Regnault. 4c, Elisa Bonaparte, by Robert Lefevre. 5c, Napoleon Planning Coronation Ceremony, by J.G. Vibert, horiz. 13c, Napoleon as Cuirassier Corporal, by Jean Meissonier. 30c, Napoleon Bonaparte, by LeFevre.

1969, Aug. 20 **Unwmk.**

1425 A385 1c .20 .20
1426 A385 2c 41½x55mm .25 .20
1427 A385 3c 45½x56mm .25 .20
1428 A385 4c 43x62½mm .45 .20
1429 A385 5c 63x47½mm .70 .20
1430 A385 13c 43x62½mm 3.25 .40
1431 A385 30c 45x59½mm 4.25 .55
Nos. 1425-1431 (7) 9.35 1.95

See Nos. 2448-2453.

Cuba's Victory at the 17th World Amateur Baseball Championships, Santo Domingo — A386

1969, Sept. 11

1432 A386 13c multi 2.75 .20

No. 1432 printed se-tenant with inscribed label listing finalists.

Alexander von Humboldt (1769-1859), German Naturalist — A387

1969, Sept. 14

1433 A387 3c Surinam eel .20 .20
1434 A387 13c Night ape 2.50 .25
1435 A387 30c Condors 4.00 .25
Nos. 1433-1435 (3) 6.70 .70

World Fencing Championships, Havana — A388

Designs: 1c, Ancient Egyptians in combat. 2c, Roman gladiators. 2c, Viking and Norman. 4c, Medieval tournament. 5c, French musketeers. 13c, Japanese samurai. 30c, Mounted Cubans, War of Independence. 50c, Modern fencers.

1969, Oct. 2

1436 A388 1c multi .20 .20
1437 A388 2c multi .20 .20
1438 A388 3c multi .20 .20
1439 A388 4c multi .40 .20
1440 A388 5c multi .65 .20
1441 A388 13c multi 3.00 .30
1442 A388 30c multi 4.75 .50
Nos. 1436-1442 (7) 9.40 1.80

Souvenir Sheet

Imperf

1443 A388 50c multi 12.00 5.00

Stamp in No. 1443 has simulated perforations.

Natl. Revolutionary Militia, 10th Anniv. — A389

1969, Oct. 26 **Wmk. 376**

1444 A389 3c multi 1.25 .20

Disappearance of Maj. Camilo Cienfuegos, 10th Anniv. — A390

1969, Oct. 28

1445 A390 13c multi 2.50 .20

Agriculture — A391

1969, Nov. 2 **Unwmk.**

1446 A391 1c Strawberries, grapes .25 .20
1447 A391 1c Onions, asparagus .25 .20
1448 A391 1c Rice .25 .20
1449 A391 1c Banana .25 .20
a. Strip of 4, #1446-1449 1.00 .80
1450 A391 3c Pineapple, vert. .50 .50
1451 A391 3c Tobacco, vert. .50 .50
1452 A391 3c Citrus fruits, vert. .50 .50
1453 A391 3c Coffee, vert. .50 .50
1454 A391 3c Rabbits, vert. .50 .50
a. Strip of 5, #1450-1454 2.75 2.50
1455 A391 10c Pigs, vert. .50 .20
1456 A391 13c Sugar cane 2.75 .50
1457 A391 30c Bull 4.00 .65
Nos. 1446-1457 (12) 10.75 4.65

Sporting Events — A392

1969, Nov. 15

1458 A392 1c 2nd Natl. Games .25 .20
1459 A392 2c 11th Anniv. Games .25 .20
1460 A392 3c Barrientos Commemorative, vert. .25 .20
1461 A392 10c 2nd Olympic Trials, vert. .40 .20
1462 A392 13c 6th Socialist Bicycle Race, vert. 2.75 .20
1463 A392 30c 6th Capablanca Memorial Chess Championships, vert. 4.00 .30
Nos. 1458-1463 (6) 7.90 1.30

Christmas Type of 1961

Flowering plants.

1969, Dec. 1

1464 A248 1c Plumbago capensis .40 .20
1465 A249 1c Petrea volubilis .40 .20
1466 A249 1c Clitoria ternatea .40 .20
1467 A249 1c Duranta repens .40 .20
1468 A249 1c Ruellia tuberosa .40 .20
a. Block of 5 + label, Nos. 1464-1468 3.00 1.00
1469 A248 3c Turnera ulmifolia 1.00 .20
1470 A249 3c Thevetia peruviana 1.00 .20
1471 A249 3c Hibiscus elatus 1.00 .20
1472 A249 3c Allamanda cathartica 1.00 .20
1473 A249 3c Cosmos sulphureus 1.00 .20
a. Block of 5 + label, Nos. 1469-1473 6.00 1.00
1474 A248 13c Delonix regia 2.25 .50
1475 A249 13c Nerium oleander 2.25 .50
1476 A249 13c Cordia sebestena 2.25 .50
1477 A249 13c Lochnera rosea 2.25 .50
1478 A249 13c Jatropha integerrima 2.25 .50
a. Block of 5 + label, Nos. 1474-1478 11.00 2.50
Nos. 1464-1478 (15) 18.25 4.50

Christmas 1969. See note after No. 700.

Zapata Swamp Fauna — A393

1969, Dec. 15

1479 A393 1c Trelanorhynus variabilis .20 .20
1480 A393 2c Hyla insulsa .20 .20
1481 A393 3c Atractosteus tristoechus .20 .20
1482 A393 4c Capromys nana .20 .20
1483 A393 5c Crocodylus rhombifer .20 .20
1484 A393 13c Amazona leucocephala 4.50 .50
1485 A393 30c Agelaius phoeniceus assimilis 5.00 1.00
Nos. 1479-1485 (7) 10.50 2.50

Nos. 1482, 1484-1485 vert.

Tourism
A394

1970, Jan. 25 **Wmk. 376**

1486 A394 1c Jibacoa Beach .20 .20
1487 A394 3c Trinidad City .20 .20
1488 A394 13c Santiago de Cuba 1.90 .80
1489 A394 30c Vinales Valley 2.75 1.00
Nos. 1486-1489 (4) 5.05 2.20

Medicinal Plants — A395

1970, Feb. 10 **Unwmk.**

1490 A395 1c Guarea guara .20 .20
1491 A395 3c Ocimum sanctum .20 .20
1492 A395 10c Canella winterana .45 .20
1493 A395 13c Bidens pilosa 2.25 .60
1494 A395 30c Turnera ulmifolia 2.75 .75
1495 A395 50c Picramnia pentandra 4.00 .90
Nos. 1490-1495 (6) 9.85 2.85

11th Central American and Caribbean Games, Panama, Feb. 28-Mar. 14 — A396

1970, Feb. 28 **Wmk. 376**

1496 A396 1c Weight lifting .20 .20
1497 A396 3c Boxing .20 .20
1498 A396 10c Gymnastics .20 .20
1499 A396 13c Running 2.40 .65
1500 A396 30c Fencing 3.50 .90
Nos. 1496-1500 (5) 6.50 2.15

Souvenir Sheet

Imperf

1501 A396 50c Baseball 12.00 6.00

No. 1501 contains one 50x37mm stamp that has simulated perforations.

EXPO '70, Osaka, Japan, Mar. 15-Sept. 13 — A397

1970, Mar. 15

1502 A397 1c Enjoying life .20 .20
1503 A397 2c Improving on nature, vert. .40 .20
1504 A397 3c Better living standard .40 .20
1505 A397 13c Intl. cooperation, vert. 2.75 .55
1506 A397 30c Cuban pavilion 4.00 .80
Nos. 1502-1506 (5) 7.75 1.95

Speleological Soc., 30th Anniv. — A398

Petroglyphs in Cuban caves: 1c, Ambrosio Cave, Varadero Matanzas. 2c, Cave No. 1, Punta del Este, Isle of Pines. 3c, Pichardo Cave, Cubitas Camaguey Mountains. 4c, Ambrosio Cave, diff. 5c, Cave No. 1, diff. 13c, Garcia Ribiou Cave, Havana. 30c, Cave No. 2, Punta del Este.

1970, Mar. 28 **Unwmk.**

Sizes: 29x45mm (1c, 3c, 4c, 13c)

1507 A398 1c multi .20 .20
1508 A398 2c shown .20 .20
1509 A398 3c multi .20 .20
1510 A398 4c multi .20 .20
1511 A398 5c multi .20 .20
1512 A398 13c multi 2.25 .30
1513 A398 30c multi 4.75 .35
Nos. 1507-1513 (7) 8.00 1.65

Aviation Pioneers — A399

1970, Apr. 10

1514 A399 3c Jose D. Blino 1.00 .20
1515 A399 13c Adolfo Teodore 3.50 .70

Lenin Birth Centenary — A400

Paintings and quotes: 1c, Lenin in Kazan, by O. Vishniakov. 2c, Young Lenin, by V. Prager. 3c, Second Socialist Party Congress, by Y. Vinagradov. 4c, First Manifesto, by F. Golubkov. 5c, First Day of Soviet Power, by N. Babasiuk. 13c, Lenin in Smolny, by M. Sokolov. 30c, Autumn in Gorky, by A. Varlamov. 50c, Lenin at Gorky, by N. Bashkakov.

1970, Apr. 22

Sizes: 67½x46mm (1c, 4c, 5c)

1516 A400 1c multi .20 .20
1517 A400 2c shown .20 .20
1518 A400 3c multi .20 .20
1519 A400 4c multi .20 .20
1520 A400 5c multi .20 .20
1521 A400 13c multi 2.75 .35
1522 A400 30c multi 3.25 .45
Nos. 1516-1522 (7) 7.00 1.80

Souvenir Sheet

Imperf

1523 A400 50c multi 13.00 6.50

No. 1523 contains one 48x46mm stamp that has simulated perforations.

Stamp Day — A401

1970, Apr. 24

1524 A401 13c The Letter, by J. Arche 3.00 .25

Size: 30x44mm

1525 A401 30c Portrait of A Cadet, Anonymous 3.75 .30

Da Vinci's Anatomical Drawing, Earth, Moon — A402

1970, May 17 **Wmk. 376**

1526 A402 30c multi 3.50 .20

World Telecommunications Day.

Ho Chi Minh (1890-1969), President of North Viet Nam — A403

1970, May 19 **Unwmk.**

1527 A403 1c Vietnamese fisherman .20 .20

Size: 32x44mm

1528 A403 3c Two women .50 .20
1529 A403 3c Plowing field .50 .20

Size: 33x45mm

1530 A403 3c Teacher, students in air-raid shelter .50 .20
1531 A403 3c Nine women in paddy .70 .20

Size: 34x41½mm

1532 A403 3c Camouflaged machine shop .70 .20

Size: 34x39mm

1533 A403 13c shown 3.25 .70
Nos. 1527-1533 (7) 6.35 1.90

Cuban Cigar Industry A404

1970, July 5

1534 A404 3c Plantation, Eden cigar band .20 .20
1535 A404 13c Factory, El Mambi band 2.25 .70
1536 A404 30c Packing cigars, Lopez Hermanos band 3.25 1.00
Nos. 1534-1536 (3) 5.70 1.90

Projected Sugar Production: Over 10 Million Tons — A405

1970, July 26

1537 A405 1c Cane-crushing .20 .20
1538 A405 2c Sowing and crop dusting .20 .20
1539 A405 3c Cutting sugar cane .25 .20
1540 A405 10c Transporting cane 5.00 .45
1541 A405 13c Modern cutting machine 1.50 .25
1542 A405 30c Intl. Brigade, cane cutters, vert. 2.25 .70
1543 A405 1p Sugar warehouse 4.00 2.00
Nos. 1537-1543 (7) 13.40 4.00

Pedro Figueredo (d. 1870), Composer — A406

Versions of the Natl. Anthem.

1970, Aug. 17

1544 A406 3c 1868 Version .30 .20
1545 A406 20c 1898 Version 2.75 .60

Women's Federation, 10th Anniv. — A407

1970, Aug. 23

1546 A407 3c multi 1.00 .50

Militia, by Servando C. Moreno — A408

Paintings in the Natl. Museum: 2c, Washerwomen, by Aristides Fernandez. 3c, Puerta del Sol, Madrid, by L. Paret Y Alcazar. 4c, Fishermen's Wives, by Joaquin Sorolla. 5c, Portrait of a Woman, by Thomas de Keyser. 13c, Mrs. Edward Foster, by Sir Thomas Lawrence. 30c, Tropical Gypsy, by Victor M. Garcia.

1970, Aug. 31

1547 A408 1c shown .20 .20

Size: 45x41mm

1548 A408 2c multi .20 .20
1549 A408 3c multi .20 .20

Size: 40x41mm

1550 A408 4c multi .20 .20

Size: 38x45½mm

1551 A408 5c multi .20 .20
1552 A408 13c multi 2.50 .50
1553 A408 30c multi 4.00 .80
Nos. 1547-1553 (7) 7.50 2.30

See #1640-1646, 1669-1675, 1773-1779.

Havana Declaration, 10th Anniv. — A409

1970, Sept. 2

1554 A409 3c Jose Marti Square .75 .20

Committee for the Defense of the Revolution, 10th Anniv. A410

1970, Sept. 28

1555 A410 3c multi .40 .20

39th Sugar Technician's Assoc. (ATAC) Conference — A411

1970, Oct. 11

1556 A411 30c multi 3.25 .70

Wildlife — A412

1970, Oct. 20

1557 A412 1c Numida meleagris galeata .65 .20
1558 A412 2c Dendrocygna arborea .75 .20
1559 A412 3c Phasianus colchicus torquatus .90 .20
1560 A412 4c Zenaida macroura macroura 1.00 .20
1561 A412 5c Colinus virginianus cubanensis 1.10 .25
1562 A412 13c Sus scrofa 1.90 1.00
1563 A412 30c Odocoileus virginianus 3.00 1.50
Nos. 1557-1563 (7) 9.30 3.55

Black-magic Feast, by M. Puente — A413

Afro-Cuban folk paintings: 3c, Hat Dance, by V.P. Landaluze. 10c, Los Hoyos Conga Dance, by Domingo Ravenet. 13c, Climax of the Rumba, by Eduardo Abela.

1970, Nov. 5

Sizes: 36x48½mm (3c, 13c), 44½x44mm (10c)

1564 A413 1c shown .20 .20
1565 A413 3c multi .35 .20
1566 A413 10c multi .90 .45
1567 A413 13c multi 2.50 .70
Nos. 1564-1567 (4) 3.95 1.55

Road Safety Week A414

1970, Nov. 15

1568 A414 3c Zebra, road signs 1.10 .20
1569 A414 9c Prudence the Bear 1.60 .20

Intl. Education Year — A415

1970, Nov. 20

1570 A415 13c Abacus, "a" 2.50 .25
1571 A415 30c Cow, microscope 3.25 .70

Christmas Type of 1961

Birds.

1970, Dec. 1

1572 A248 1c Dives atroviolaceus .80 .20
1573 A249 1c Glaucidium siju siju .80 .20
1574 A249 1c Todus multicolor .80 .20
1575 A249 1c Xiphidiopicus percussus percussus .80 .20
1576 A249 1c Ferminia cerverai .80 .20
a. Block of 5 + label, Nos. 1572-1576 5.00 1.00
1577 A248 3c Teretistris fornsi 1.75 .35
1578 A249 3c Myadestes elisabeth elisabeth 1.75 .35
1579 A249 3c Polioptila lembeyei 1.75 .35
1580 A249 3c Vireo gundlachii gundlachii 1.75 .35
1581 A249 3c Teretistris fernandinae 1.75 .35
a. Block of 5 + label, Nos. 1577-1581 10.00 2.00
1582 A248 13c Torreornis inexpectata inexpectata 2.50 .90
1583 A249 13c Chondrohierax wilsonii 2.50 .90
1584 A249 13c Accipiter gundlachi 2.50 .90
1585 A249 13c Starnoenas cyanocephala 2.50 .90
1586 A249 13c Aratinga euops 2.50 .90
a. Block of 5 + label, Nos. 1582-1586 15.00 5.00
Nos. 1572-1586 (15) 25.25 7.25

Christmas 1970. See note after No. 700.

Camilo Cienfuegos Military Academy — A416

1970, Dec. 2

1587 A416 3c multi 1.25 .25

7th Congress of the Intl. Organization of Journalists — A417

1971, Jan. 4

1588 A417 13c multi 2.25 .50

World Meteorology Day — A418

1971, Feb. 16

Size: 39½x35½mm (3c)

1589 A418 1c Class, weather chart, computer, vert. .20 .20
1590 A418 3c Weather map .20 .20
1591 A418 8c Equipment, vert. 1.00 .25
1592 A418 30c shown 4.75 1.25
Nos. 1589-1592 (4) 6.15 1.90

6th Pan American Games, Cali, Colombia — A419

1971, Feb. 20

1593 A419 1c Emblem, vert. .20 .20
1594 A419 2c Women's running, vert. .20 .20
1595 A419 3c Rifle shooting .20 .20
1596 A419 4c Gymnastics, vert. .20 .20
1597 A419 5c Boxing, vert. .20 .20
1598 A419 13c Water polo 2.40 .30
1599 A419 30c Baseball 3.00 .50
Nos. 1593-1599 (7) 6.40 1.80

Porcelain and Mosaics in the Metropolitan Museum, Havana — A420

Designs: 1c, Parisian vase, 19th cent. 3c, Mexican bowl, 17th cent. 10c, Parisian vase, diff. 13c, Colosseum, Italian mosaic, 19th cent. 20c, Mexican bowl, 17th cent. 30c, St. Peter's Square, Italian mosaic, 19th cent.

1971, Mar. 11

Sizes: 34½x53mm (1c, 10c), 46x53mm (3c), 42x48mm (20c)

1600 A420 1c multi .20 .20
1601 A420 3c multi .20 .20
1602 A420 10c multi .40 .20
1603 A420 13c shown 2.25 .20
1604 A420 20c multi 2.25 .40
1605 A420 30c multi 2.75 .50
Nos. 1600-1605 (6) 8.05 1.70

See Nos. 1699-1705.

Natl. Child Centers, 10th Anniv. — A421

1971, Apr. 10

1606 A421 3c multi .75 .20

Manned Space Flight 10th Anniv. — A422

Cosmonauts in training.

1971, Apr. 12

1607 A422 1c multi .20 .20
1608 A422 2c multi, diff. .20 .20
1609 A422 3c multi, diff. .20 .20
1610 A422 4c multi, diff. .20 .20
1611 A422 5c multi, diff. .20 .20
1612 A422 13c multi, diff. 2.25 .30
1613 A422 30c multi, diff. 3.25 .60
Nos. 1607-1613 (7) 6.50 1.90

Souvenir Sheet

Imperf

1614 A422 50c multi 10.00 10.00

Stamp in #1614 has simulated perf.

Bay of Pigs Invasion, 10th Anniv. A423

1971, Apr. 17

1615 A423 13c multi 1.75 .60

Stamp Day — A424

Packets: 13c, Jeune Richard attacking the Windsor Castle, 1807. 30c, Orinoco.

1971, Apr. 24

1616 A424 13c multi 2.40 .25
1617 A424 30c multi 3.50 .35

Cuban Intl. Broadcast Service, 10th Anniv. — A425

1971, May 1 **Wmk. 376**

1618 A425 3c multi .40 .20
1619 A425 50c multi 4.50 .90

Orchids A426

1971, May 15

1620	A426	1c	Cattleya skinnerii	.20	.20
1621	A426	2c	Vanda hibrida	.20	.20
1622	A426	3c	Cypripedium collossum	.20	.20
1623	A426	4c	Cypripedium gloucophyllum	.20	.20
1624	A426	5c	Vanda tricolor	.25	.20
1625	A426	13c	Cypripedium mowgh	2.40	.45
1626	A426	30c	Cypripedium solum	4.75	.85
			Nos. 1620-1626 (7)	8.20	2.30

See Nos. 1677-1683 and 1780-1786.

Enrique Loynaz del Castillo (b. 1861), Composer — A427

1971, June 5 **Wmk. 376**

1627	A427	3c	Portrait, Invasion Hymn	.90	.25

Bee Keeping — A428

1971, June 20 **Unwmk.**

1628	A428	1c	Egg, larvae, pupa	.20	.20
1629	A428	3c	Worker	.20	.20
1630	A428	9c	Drone	.45	.20
1631	A428	13c	Defense of hive	2.25	.25
1632	A428	30c	Queen	3.50	.60
			Nos. 1628-1632 (5)	6.60	1.45

Children's Drawings — A429

1971, Aug. 30

Size: 45x39mm

1633	A429	1c	Sailboat	.20	.20
1634	A429	3c	The Little Train	.85	.20

Sizes: 45½x35½mm (9c, 13c), 47x37½mm (10c)

1635	A429	9c	Sugar Cane Cutter	.20	.20
1636	A429	10c	Return of the Fishermen	.40	.20
1637	A429	13c	The Zoo	1.60	.25

Size: 47x42mm

1638	A429	20c	House and Garden	2.50	.40

Size: 31½x50mm

1639	A429	30c	Landscape	2.75	.65

Art Type of 1970

Paintings in the Natl. Museum: 1c, St. Catherine of Alexandria, by F. Zurburan. 2c, The Cart, by Federico Americo. 3c, St. Christopher and Child, by J. Bassano. 4c, Little Devil, by Rene Portocarrero. 5c, Portrait of a Woman, by Nicolas Maes. 13c, Phoenix, by Raul Martinez. 30c, Sir William Pitt, by Thomas Gainsborough.

1971, Sept. 20

1640	A408	1c	31x55mm	.20	.20
1641	A408	2c	48x37mm	.20	.20
1642	A408	3c	31x55mm	.20	.20
1643	A408	4c	37x48mm	.25	.20
1644	A408	5c	37x48mm	.40	.20
1645	A408	13c	39x48½mm	2.25	.45
1646	A408	30c	39x48½mm	3.25	.75
			Nos. 1640-1646 (7)	6.75	2.20

Sport Fishing — A431

1971, Oct. 30

1647	A431	1c	Albula vulpes	.20	.20
1648	A431	2c	Seriola species	.20	.20
1649	A431	3c	Micropterus salmoides	.20	.20
1650	A431	4c	Coryphaena hippurus	.25	.20
1651	A431	5c	Megalops atlantica	.30	.20
1652	A431	13c	Acanthocybium solandri	2.00	.40
1653	A431	30c	Makaira ampla	3.25	.70
			Nos. 1647-1653 (7)	6.40	2.10

19th World Amateur Baseball Championships — A432

1971, Nov. 22 **Wmk. 376**

1654	A432	3c	shown	.25	.25
1655	A432	1p	Globe as baseball	6.25	1.00

Execution of Medical Students, Cent. A433

Paintings: 3c, Dr. Fermin Valdez Dominguez, anonymous. 13c, Execution of the Medical Students, by M. Mesa. 30c, Capt. Federico Capdevila, anonymous.

1971, Nov. 27 **Unwmk.**

Size: 61½x46mm (13c)

1656	A433	3c	multi	.35	.20
1657	A433	13c	multi	1.90	.25
1658	A433	30c	multi	3.00	.35
			Nos. 1656-1658 (3)	5.25	.80

Spindalis Zena Pretrei — A434

Birds: 1c, Falco sparverius sparverioides vigors. 2c, Glaucidium siju siju. 3c, Priotelus temnurus temnurus. 4c, Saurothera merlini merlini. 5c, Nesoceleus fernandinae. 30c, Mimocichla plumbea rubripes. 50c, Chlorostilbon ricordii ricordii and Archilochus colubris. Nos. 1659-1663 vert.

1971, Dec. 10

1659	A434	1c	multi	.35	.20
1660	A434	2c	multi	.35	.20
1661	A434	3c	multi	.60	.20
1662	A434	4c	multi	.65	.20
1663	A434	5c	multi	.80	.20
1664	A434	13c	shown	1.50	.50
1665	A434	30c	multi	3.00	1.00
			Nos. 1659-1665 (7)	7.25	2.50

Size: 55½x29mm

1666	A434	50c	multi	5.50	1.50

Death centenary of Ramon de la Sagra, naturalist.

Cuba's Victory at the World Amateur Baseball Championships — A435

1971, Dec. 8 **Wmk. 376**

1667	A435	13c	multi	2.00	.60

UNICEF, 25th Anniv. A436

1971, Dec. 11

1668	A436	13c	multi	2.50	.70

Art Type of 1970

Paintings in the Natl. Museum: 1c, Arrival of an Ambassador, by Vittore Carpaccio. 2c, Senora Malpica, by G. Collazo. 3c, La Chorrera Tower, by Esteban Chartrand. 4c, Creole Landscape, by Carlos Enriquez. 5c, Sir William Lemon, by George Romney. 13c, Landscape, by Henry Cleenewerk. 30c, Valencia Beach, by Joaquin Sorolla y Bastida.

1972, Jan. 25 **Unwmk.**

1669	A408	1c	50x33mm	.20	.20
1670	A408	2c	27½x52mm	.20	.20
1671	A408	3c	50x33mm	.20	.20
1672	A408	4c	35x43mm	.20	.20
1673	A408	5c	35x43mm	.20	.20
1674	A408	13c	43x33mm	2.00	.35
1675	A408	30c	43x33mm	3.50	.85
			Nos. 1669-1675 (7)	6.50	2.20

Academy of Sciences, 10th Anniv. — A437

1972, Feb. 20 **Wmk. 376**

1676	A437	13c	Capitol Type of 1929	2.00	.25

Orchid Type of 1971

1972, Feb. 25 **Unwmk.**

1677	A426	1c	Brasso cattleya sindorossiana	.20	.20
1678	A426	2c	Cypripedium doraeus	.20	.20
1679	A426	3c	Cypripedium exul	.20	.20
1680	A426	4c	Cypripedium rosy dawn	.20	.20
1681	A426	5c	Cypripedium champolliom	.20	.20
1682	A426	13c	Cypripedium bucolique	2.75	.65
1683	A426	30c	Cypripedium sullanum	3.50	.80
			Nos. 1677-1683 (7)	7.25	2.45

Eduardo Agramonte (1849-1872), Physicist A438

1972, Mar. 8

1684	A438	3c	Portrait by F. Martinez	.60	.20

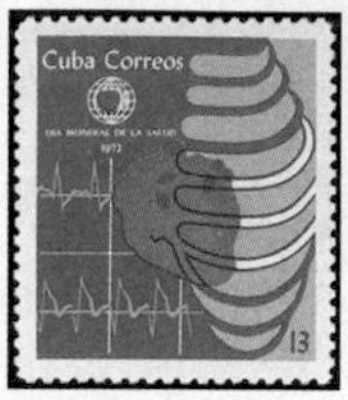

World Health Day — A439

1972, Apr. 7 **Wmk. 376**

1685	A439	13c	multi	2.00	.20

Soviet Space Program — A440

1972, Apr. 12 **Unwmk.**

1686	A440	1c	Sputnik 1	.20	.20
1687	A440	2c	Vostok 1	.20	.20
1688	A440	3c	Valentina Tereshkova	.20	.20
1689	A440	4c	Alexei Leonov	.20	.20
1690	A440	5c	Lunokhod 1, moon vehicle	.20	.20
1691	A440	13c	Linking Soyuz capsules	2.10	.40
1692	A440	30c	Victims of Soyuz 11 accident	2.50	.70
			Nos. 1686-1692 (7)	5.60	2.10

Stamp Day — A441

Designs: 13c, Postmaster-Gen. Vicente Mora Pera, by Ramon Loy. 30c, Soldier's Letter, Cuba to Venezuela, 1897.

1972, Apr. 24

1693	A441	13c	shown	1.75	.30

Size: 48x39mm

1694	A441	30c	multi	2.75	.35

Labor Day — A442

Jose Marti, Ho Chi Minh — A443

3rd Conference Against War in Indo-China, May 19 — A444

1972, May 1 **Wmk. 376**

1695 A442 3c multi .90 .20

1972, May 19

1696 A443 3c shown .40 .20
1697 A444 13c shown 1.60 .20
1698 A443 30c Roses, conference emblem 2.00 .20
Nos. 1696-1698 (3) 4.00 .60

Metropolitan Museum Type of 1971

Portraits: 1c, Salvador del Muro, by J. Del Rio. 2c, Luis de las Casas, by Del Rio. 3c, Cristopher Columbus, anonymous. 4c, Tomas Gamba, by V. Escobar. 5c, Maria Galarraga, by Escobar. 13c, Isabel II, by Federico Madrazo. 30c, Carlos III, by Miguel Melero.

1972, May 25 **Unwmk.**

Size: 34x43½mm

1699 A420 1c multi .20 .20
1700 A420 2c multi .20 .20
1701 A420 3c multi .20 .20
1702 A420 4c multi .40 .20
1703 A420 5c multi .40 .20

Size: 34x51½mm

1704 A420 13c multi 2.00 .40
1705 A420 30c multi 2.50 .70
Nos. 1699-1705 (7) 5.90 2.10

Children's Songs Competition, Natl. Library A445

1972, June 5 **Wmk. 376**

1706 A445 3c multi .80 .25

Thoroughbred Horses — A446

1972, June 30 **Unwmk.**

1707 A446 1c Tarpan .20 .20
1708 A446 2c Kertag .20 .20
1709 A446 3c Creole .20 .20
1710 A446 4c Andalusian .20 .20
1711 A446 5c Arabian .20 .20
1712 A446 13c Quarter horse 3.00 .55
1713 A446 30c Pursang 3.50 .80
Nos. 1707-1713 (7) 7.50 2.35

Frank Pais (d. 1957), Educator, Revolutionary — A447

1972, July 26 **Wmk. 376**

1714 A447 13c blk & red 1.75 .50

1972 Summer Olympics, Munich, Aug. 26-Sept. 10 — A448

1972, Aug. 26 **Unwmk.**

1715 A448 1c Athlete, emblems, vert. .20 .20
1716 A448 2c "M," boxing .20 .20
1717 A448 3c "U," weight lifting .20 .20
1718 A448 4c "N," fencing .20 .20
1719 A448 5c "I," rifle shooting .20 .20
1720 A448 13c "C," running 2.00 .35
1721 A448 30c "H," basketball 2.50 .65
Nos. 1715-1721 (7) 5.50 2.00

Souvenir Sheet

Imperf

1722 A448 50c Gymnastics 6.00 1.90

Stamp in No. 1722 has simulated perforations.

Intl. Hydrological Decade — A449

Landscapes: 1c, Tree Trunks, by Domingo Ramos. 3c, Cyclone, by Tiburcio Lorenzo. 8c, Vinales, by Ramos. 30c, Forest and Brook, by Antonio R. Morey, vert.

1972, Sept. 20

1723 A449 1c multi .20 .20
1724 A449 3c multi .20 .20
1725 A449 8c multi .80 .20
1726 A449 30c multi 2.50 .20
Nos. 1723-1726 (4) 3.70 .80

Butterflies from the Gundlach Collection — A450

1972, Sept. 25

1727 A450 1c Papilio thoas oviedo .20 .20
1728 A450 2c Papilio devilliers .20 .20
1729 A450 3c Papilio polixenes polixenes .20 .20
1730 A450 4c Papilio androgeus epidaurus .20 .20
1731 A450 5c Papilio cayguanabus .30 .20
1732 A450 13c Papilio andraemon hernandezi 3.25 .75
1733 A450 30c Papilio celadon 4.50 1.00
Nos. 1727-1733 (7) 8.85 2.75

A451

Miguel de Cervantes Saavedra (1547-1616), Spanish Author — A452

Paintings by A. Fernandez: 3c, In La Mancha, vert. 13c, Battle with Wine Skins. 30c, Don Quixote de La Mancha, vert. 50c, Scene from Don Quixote, by Jose Moreno Carbonero.

1972, Sept. 29

Size: 34½x46mm (3c, 30c)

1734 A451 3c multi .20 .20
1735 A451 13c shown 2.10 .30
1736 A451 30c multi 2.25 .35
Nos. 1734-1736 (3) 4.55 .85

Souvenir Sheet

Perf. 12½ on 3 Sides

1737 A452 50c shown 5.00 1.25

Guerrilla Day, 5th Anniv. — A453

1972, Oct. 8

1738 A453 3c Ernesto "Che" Guevara .20 .20
1739 A453 13c Tamara "Tania" Bunke 2.25 .50
1740 A453 30c Guido "Inti" Peredo 2.50 .60
Nos. 1738-1740 (3) 4.95 1.30

Traditional Musical Instruments A454

1972, Oct. 25

1741 A454 3c Abwe (rattles) .20 .20
1742 A454 13c Bonko enchemiya (drum) 2.25 .30
1743 A454 30c Iya (drum) 2.50 .35
Nos. 1741-1743 (3) 4.95 .85

MATEX '72, 3rd Natl. Philatelic Exhibition, Matanzas — A455

1972, Nov. 18 **Wmk. 376**

1744 A455 13c No. 467 2.50 .35
1745 A455 30c No. C49 3.00 .40

Nos. 1744-1745 printed se-tenant with insribed labels picturing Type A232, emblem of the Cuban Philatelic Federation.

Historic Ships A456

1972, Nov. 30 **Unwmk.**

1746 A456 1c Viking long boat, 6th-9th cent. .20 .20
1747 A456 2c Caravel, 15th cent., vert. .20 .20
1748 A456 3c Galleass, 16th cent. .20 .20
1749 A456 4c Galleon, 17th cent., vert. .30 .20
1750 A456 5c Clipper, 19th cent. .35 .20
1751 A456 13c Steam packet, 19th cent. 1.75 .75

Size: 52½x29mm.

1752 A456 30c Atomic icebreaker Lenin 3.50 1.00
Nos. 1746-1752 (7) 6.50 2.75

UNESCO Save Venice Campaign — A457

1972, Dec. 8

1753 A457 3c Lion of St. Mark .20 .20
1754 A457 13c Bridge of Sighs, vert. 1.75 .20
1755 A457 30c St. Mark's Cathedral 2.25 .35
Nos. 1753-1755 (3) 4.20 .75

Cuba, World Amateur Baseball Champion in 1972 — A458

Sport Events, 1972 — A459

1972, Dec. 15

1756 A458 3c Umpire 1.25 .30

1972, Dec. 22

1757 A459 1c shown .20 .20
1758 A458 2c Pole vault .20 .20
1759 A458 3c like No. 1756 .20 .20
1760 A458 4c Wrestling .20 .20
1761 A458 5c Fencing .20 .20
1762 A458 13c Boxing 1.75 .55
1763 A458 30c Marlin 2.50 .80
Nos. 1757-1763 (7) 5.25 2.35

Barrientos Memorial Athletics Championships, 11th Amateur Baseball Championships, Cerro Pelado Intl. Tournament, Central American and Caribbean Fencing Tournament,

Giraldo Cordova Tournament, Ernest Hemingway Natl. Fishing Contest.

No. 1759 inscribed "XI serie nacional de beisbol aficionado."

Medals Won by Cubans at the 1972 Summer Olympics, Munich A460

1c, Bronze, Women's 100-meter. 2c, Bronze, women's relay. 3c, Gold, 54kg boxing. 4c, Silver, 81kg boxing. 5c, Bronze, 51kg boxing. 13c, Gold, 87kg boxing. 30c, Gold, silver cup, heavyweight boxing. 50c, Bronze, basketball.

1973, Jan. 28

1764	A460	1c multi	.20	.20
1765	A460	2c multi	.20	.20
1766	A460	3c multi	.20	.20
1767	A460	4c multi	.20	.20
1768	A460	5c multi	.20	.20
1769	A460	13c multi	1.75	.60
1770	A460	30c multi	2.25	.90
		Nos. 1764-1770 (7)	5.00	2.50

Souvenir Sheet

Imperf

1771	A460	50c multi	6.00	1.25

Stamp in No. 1771 has simulated perforations.

A461

A462

Portrait by A.M. Esquivel.

1973, Feb. 10

1772	A461	13c multi	2.25	.30

Gertrudis Gomez de Avellaneda (1814-1873), poet.

Art Type of 1970

Paintings in the Natl. Museum: 1c, Bathers in the Lagoon, by C. Enriquez. 2c, Still-life, by W.C. Heda. 3c, Gallantry, by P. Landaluze. 4c, Return in the Late Afternoon, by C. Troyon. 5c, Elizabetta Mascagni, by F.X. Fabre. 13c, The Picador, by De Lucas Padilla, horiz. 30c, In the Garden, by Arburu Morell.

1973, Feb. 28

Sizes: 36x46mm, 46x36mm

1773	A408	1c multi	.20	.20
1774	A408	2c multi	.20	.20
1775	A408	3c multi	.20	.20
1776	A408	4c multi	.20	.20
1777	A408	5c multi	.20	.20
1778	A408	13c multi	1.60	.30
1779	A408	30c multi	2.25	.80
		Nos. 1773-1779 (7)	4.85	2.10

Orchid Type of 1971

1973, Mar. 26

1780	A426	1c Dendrobium hybrid	.20	.20
1781	A426	2c Cypripedium exul	.20	.20
1782	A426	3c Vanda miss. joaquin rose marie	.20	.20
1783	A426	4c Phalaenopsis schilleriana	.20	.20
1784	A426	5c Vanda gilbert tribulet	.40	.20
1785	A426	13c Dendrobium hybrid, diff.	3.00	.55
1786	A426	30c Arachnis catherine	3.50	.80
		Nos. 1780-1786 (7)	7.70	2.35

1973, Apr. 7 **Wmk. 376**

1787	A462	10c multi, *buff*	1.25	.25

World Health Day. World Health Organization, 25th anniv.

Anti-Polio Campaign — A463

1973, Apr. 9 **Unwmk.**

1788	A463	3c multi	.70	.20

Soviet Space Program — A464

1973, Apr. 12

1789	A464	1c Soyuz rocket launch, vert.	.20	.20
1790	A464	2c Luna 1, Moon	.20	.20
1791	A464	3c Luna 16 taking-off from Moon, vert.	.20	.20
1792	A464	4c Venus 7	.20	.20
1793	A464	5c Molnia 1, vert.	.20	.20
1794	A464	13c Mars 3	1.00	.55
1795	A464	30c Radar observation ship, Yuri Gagarin	3.00	.70
		Nos. 1789-1795 (7)	5.00	2.25

Stamp Day A465

Postmarks: 13c, Santiago de Cuba, 1760. 30c, Havana, 1760.

1973, Apr. 24

1796	A465	13c multi	1.90	.50
1797	A465	30c multi	2.10	.60

See Nos. 1888-1891.

Portrait by A. Espinosa A466

1973, May 11

1798	A466	13c multi	1.50	.25

Maj.-Gen. Ignacio Agramonte (1841-1873).

Birthplace, Torun, and Inventions — A467

Copernicus Monument, Warsaw — A468

1973, May 25

1799	A467	3c shown	.20	.20
1800	A467	13c Copernicus, spacecraft	1.60	.20
1801	A467	30c Manuscript, Frombork Tower	3.00	.25
		Nos. 1799-1801 (3)	4.80	.65

Souvenir Sheet

Perf. 12½ on 3 Sides

1802	A468	50c shown	6.50	1.90

500th anniversary of the birth of Nicolaus Copernicus (1473-1543), Polish astronomer.

Improvement of School Education — A469

1973, June 12 **Wmk. 376**

1803	A469	13c multi	1.50	.20

Cattle — A470

1973, June 28 **Unwmk.**

1804	A470	1c Jersey	.20	.20
1805	A470	2c Charolaise	.20	.20
1806	A470	3c Creole	.20	.20
1807	A470	4c Swiss	.25	.20
1808	A470	5c Holstein	.25	.20
1809	A470	13c Santa Gertrudis	1.60	.40
1810	A470	30c Brahman	3.25	.75
		Nos. 1804-1810 (7)	5.95	2.15

A471

A472

1973, July 10 **Wmk. 376**

1811	A471	13c multi	1.50	.30

10th Communist Festival of Youths and Students, East Berlin.

1973, July 26 **Unwmk.**

1812	A472	3c Siboney Farm, Santiago de Cuba	.35	.20
1813	A472	13c Moncada Barracks	1.50	.20
1814	A472	30c Revolution Plaza, Havana	2.25	.20
		Nos. 1812-1814 (3)	4.10	.60

20th anniv. of the Revolution.

10th Anniv. of the Revolutionary Navy — A473

1973, Aug. 3 **Wmk. 376**

1815	A473	3c Midshipman, missile frigate	.60	.30

Interior, by Manuel Vicens A474

Paintings in the Natl. Museum: 1c, Amalia of Saxony, by J.K. Rossler. 3c, Margarita of Austria, by J. Pantoja de la Cruz. 4c, City Hall Official, anonymous. 5c, View of Santiago de Cuba, by Hernandez Giro. 13c, The Catalan, by J.J. Tejada. 30c, Alley in Guayo, by Tejada.

1973, Aug. 30 **Unwmk.**

Sizes: 26½x41mm (1c, 3c), 28½x39mm (4c, 13c, 30c)

1816	A474	1c multi	.20	.20
1817	A474	2c multi	.20	.20
1818	A474	3c multi	.25	.20
1819	A474	4c multi	.25	.20
1820	A474	5c multi	.25	.20
1821	A474	13c multi	1.90	.60
1822	A474	30c multi	2.50	.70
		Nos. 1816-1822 (7)	5.55	2.30

WMO Emblem, Paintings by J. Madrazo A475

1973, Sept. 4

1823	A475	8c Spring	.75	.20
1824	A475	8c Summer	.75	.20
1825	A475	8c Fall	.75	.20
1826	A475	8c Winter	.75	.20
		Nos. 1823-1826 (4)	3.00	.80

World Meterogogical Organization, cent. Nos. 1823-1826 printed se-tenant in strips of 4; frame reversed on 2nd and 4th stamp in strip.

A476

A477

27th World and 1st Pan American Weight Lifting Championships: Various weightlifting positions.

1973, Sept. 12

1827	A476	1c multi, diff.	.20	.20
1828	A476	2c shown	.20	.20
1829	A476	3c multi, diff.	.20	.20
1830	A476	4c multi, diff.	.20	.20
1831	A476	5c multi, diff.	.20	.20
1832	A476	13c multi, diff.	1.60	.45
1833	A476	30c multi, diff.	2.75	.90
		Nos. 1827-1833 (7)	5.35	2.35

1973, Sept. 28

Flowering plants.

1834	A477	1c Erythrina standleyana	.20	.20
1835	A477	2c Lantana camara	.20	.20
1836	A477	3c Canavalia maritima	.20	.20
1837	A477	4c Dichromena colorata	.20	.20
1838	A477	5c Borrichia arborescens	.20	.20
1839	A477	13c Anguria pedata	2.10	.65
1840	A477	30c Cordia sebestena	3.25	.90
		Nos. 1835-1840 (6)	6.15	2.35

8th World Trade Union Congress, Varna, Bulgaria — A478

1973, Oct. 5 **Wmk. 376**

1841	A478	13c multi	1.50	.35

Cuban Natl. Ballet, 25th Anniv. — A479

Sea Shells — A480

1973, Oct. 28 **Unwmk.**

1842	A479	13c gold & brt ultra	2.00	.40

1973, Oct. 29

1843	A480	1c Liguus fasciatus fasciatus	.20	.20
1844	A480	2c Liguus fasciatus guitarti	.20	.20
1845	A480	3c Liguus fasciatus whartoni	.20	.20
1846	A480	4c Liguus fasciatus angelae	.20	.20
1847	A480	5c Liguus fasciatus trinidadense	.20	.20
1848	A480	13c Liguus blainianus	2.75	.55
1849	A480	30c Liguus vittatus	3.75	.65
		Nos. 1843-1849 (7)	7.50	2.20

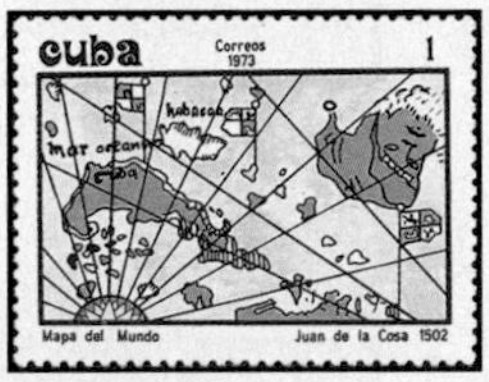

Maps of Cuba A481

1973, Oct. 29

1850	A481	1c Juan de la Cosa, 1502	.20	.20
1851	A481	3c Ortelius, 1572	.25	.20
1852	A481	13c Bellini, 1762	1.75	.25
1853	A481	40c 1973	2.10	.80
		Nos. 1850-1853 (4)	4.30	1.45

15th Anniversary of the Revolution — A482

1974, Jan. 2

1854	A482	1c No. 625	.20	.20
1855	A482	3c No. 626	.20	.20
1856	A482	13c No. C200	3.00	.35
1857	A482	40c No. C201	1.25	.50
		Nos. 1854-1857 (4)	4.65	1.25

Woman, by F. Ponce de Leon — A483

Amilcar Cabral — A484

Portraits in the Camaguey Museum: 3c, Mexican Girls, by J. Arche. 8c, Young Woman, by A. Menocal. 10c, Mulatto Woman Drinking from Coconut, by L. Romanach. 13c, Head of an Old Man, by J. Arburu.

1974, Jan. 10

1858	A483	1c multi	.20	.20
1859	A483	3c multi	.20	.20
1860	A483	8c multi	.35	.20
1861	A483	10c multi	1.10	.20
1862	A483	13c multi	1.60	.25
		Nos. 1858-1862 (5)	3.45	1.05

1974, Jan. 20

1863	A484	13c multi	1.40	.25

Amilcar Cabral, Guinea-Bissau freedom fighter, 1st death anniv.

Lenin, by I.V. Kosmin — A485

12th Central American and Caribbean Games, Santo Domingo — A486

1974, Jan. 21

1864	A485	30c multi	3.00	.30

50th death anniv. of Lenin.

1974, Feb. 8

1865	A486	1c Emblem	.25	.20
1866	A486	2c Javelin	.25	.20
1867	A486	3c Boxing	.25	.20
1868	A486	4c Baseball, horiz.	.25	.20
1869	A486	13c Basketball, horiz.	1.60	.20
1870	A486	30c Volleyball, horiz.	2.40	.70
		Nos. 1865-1870 (6)	5.00	1.70

Portrait by F. Martinez — A487

Portrait of a Man, by J.B. Vermay — A488

1974, Feb. 27

1871	A487	13c multi	1.40	.20

Carlos M. de Cespedes (d. 1874), patriot.

1974, Mar. 7

Paintings in the Natl. Museum: 2c, The Wet Nurse, by C.A. Van Loo. 3c, Cattle in River, by R. Morey. 4c, Village, by Morey. 13c, Faun and Bacchus, by Rubens. 30c, Young Woman Playing Cards, by R. Madrazo.

1872	A488	1c shown	.20	.20
1873	A488	2c multi	.20	.20
1874	A488	3c multi	.20	.20
1875	A488	4c multi	.20	.20
1876	A488	13c multi	1.40	.20
1877	A488	30c multi	2.50	.25
		Nos. 1872-1877 (6)	4.70	1.25

Council for Mutual Economic Assistance (COMECON), 25th Anniv. — A489

1974, Mar. 15

1878	A489	30c Comecon building, Moscow	2.00	.70

Visit of Leonid I. Brezhnev to Cuba, Jan. 28-Feb. 3 — A490

1974, Mar. 28

1879	A490	13c Jose Marti, Lenin, flags	2.00	.25
1880	A490	30c Brezhnev, Fidel Castro	2.10	.25
		Nos. 1879-1880 (2)	4.10	.50

Science Fiction A491

Paintings by A. Sokolov.

1974, Apr. 12

1881	A491	1c Martian Crater	.25	.20
1882	A491	2c Fiery Labyrinth	.25	.20
1883	A491	3c Amber Wave	.25	.20
1884	A491	4c Flight Through Space	.25	.20
1885	A491	13c Planet in Nebula	2.00	.25
1886	A491	30c World of Two Suns	3.25	.60
		Nos. 1881-1886 (6)	6.25	1.65

Cosmonauts Day.

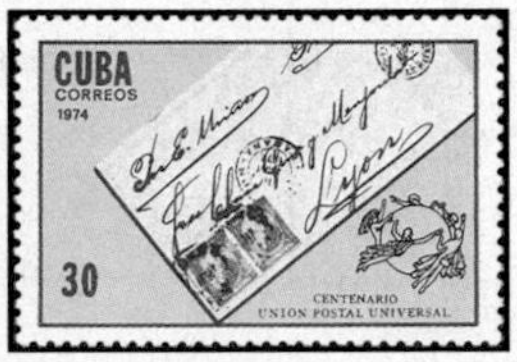

UPU, Cent. A492

1974, Apr. 15

1887	A492	30c Letter, 1874	2.50	.30

Stamp Day Type of 1973

Postmarks.

1974, Apr. 24

1888	A465	1c Havana	.25	.20
1889	A465	3c Matanzas	.40	.20
1890	A465	13c Trinidad	1.50	.20
1891	A465	20c Guana Vacoa	2.25	.35
		Nos. 1888-1891 (4)	4.40	.95

18th Sports Congress of Friendly Armies — A493

1974, May 5 **Wmk. 376**

1892	A493	3c multi	.80	.20

Felipe Poey (1799-1891), Naturalist — A494

Designs: 1c, 4c, Butterflies. 2c, 13c, Sea shells. 3c, 30c, 50c, Fish.

1974, May 26 *Perf. 12½x12*

1893 A494 1c Eumaeus atala atala .20 .20
1894 A494 2c Pineria terebra .20 .20
1895 A494 3c Chaetodon sedentarius .20 .20
1896 A494 4c Eurema dina dina .80 .20
1897 A494 13c Hemitrochus fus-colabiata 2.75 .35
1898 A494 30c Eupomacentrus partitus 3.50 .40
Nos. 1893-1898 (6) 7.65 1.55

Souvenir Sheet

Imperf

1899 A494 50c Apogon binotatus 7.00 1.25

Stamp in #1899 has simulated perforations.

Havana Philharmonic Orchestra, 50th Anniv. — A495

1c, Antonio Mompo, cello. 3c, Cesar Perez Sentenat, piano. 5c, Pedro Mercado, trumpet. 10c, Pedro Sanjuan, Havana Philharmonic emblem. 13c, Roberto Ondina, flute.

1974, June 8 *Perf. 12½*

1900 A495 1c multi .25 .20
1901 A495 3c multi .25 .20
1902 A495 5c multi .25 .20
1903 A495 10c multi 1.40 .25
1904 A495 13c multi 1.75 .25
Nos. 1900-1904 (5) 3.90 1.10

Garden Flowers — A496

1974, June 12

1905 A496 1c Heliconia humilis .20 .20
1906 A496 2c Anthurium andraeanum .20 .20
1907 A496 3c Canna generalis .20 .20
1908 A496 4c Alpinia purpurata .25 .20
1909 A496 13c Gladiolus grandiflorus 1.75 .20
1910 A496 30c Amomum capitatum 4.50 .40
Nos. 1905-1910 (6) 7.10 1.40

A497

A498

World Amateur Boxing Championships: Emblem and various boxers.

Perf. 12x12½

1974, Aug. 24 **Litho.** **Unwmk.**

1911 A497 1c multi .20 .20
1912 A497 3c multi .35 .20
1913 A497 13c multi 1.60 .20
Nos. 1911-1913 (3) 2.15 .60

1974, Aug. 28 *Perf. 13*

Extinct birds.

1914 A498 1c Dodo .20 .20
1915 A498 3c Ara de Cuba (parrot) .20 .20
1916 A498 8c Passenger pigeon .45 .20
1917 A498 10c Moa 1.40 .25
1918 A498 13c Great auk 1.75 .40
Nos. 1914-1918 (5) 4.00 1.25

Pres. Salvador Allende of Chile (d. 1973) A499

1974, Sept. 11

1919 A499 13c multi 1.25 .45

Wildflowers A500

Model Aircraft — A501

1974, Sept. 14 *Perf. 13x12½*

1920 A500 1c Suriana maritima .20 .20
1921 A500 3c Cassia ligustrina .20 .20
1922 A500 8c Flaveria linearis .30 .20
1923 A500 10c Stachytarpheta jamaicensis 2.10 .20
1924 A500 13c Bacopa monnieri 3.50 .40
Nos. 1920-1924 (5) 6.30 1.20

1974, Sept. 22 *Perf. 12½*

1925 A501 1c shown .20 .20
1926 A501 3c Sky diving .20 .20
1927 A501 8c Glider .45 .20
1928 A501 10c Crop dusting 1.25 .25
1929 A501 13c Commercial aviation 2.00 .25
Nos. 1925-1929 (5) 4.10 1.10

Civil Aeronautic Institute, 10th anniv. Nos. 1927-1929 horiz.

History of Cuban Baseball — A502

1974, Oct. 3 *Perf. 13*

1930 A502 1c Indians playing ball .20 .20
1931 A502 3c 1st Official game, 1874 .20 .20
1932 A502 8c Emilio Sabourin .40 .20
1933 A502 10c Umpire, players, 1974 1.25 .20
1934 A502 13c Latin-American Stadium, Havana 2.10 .25
Nos. 1930-1934 (5) 4.15 1.05

Nos. 1930-1932 vert.

Mambi 10c Stamp (Revolutionary Junta Issue), Cent. — A503

1974, Oct. 10

1935 A503 13c multi 1.50 .20

16th Conference of Customs Organizations of Socialist Countries — A504

1974, Oct. 15

1936 A504 30c Comecon Building, Moscow 2.00 .55

Disappearance of Major Camilo Cienfuegos, 15th Anniv. — A505

Wmk. 376

1974, Oct. 28 **Litho.** *Perf. 13*

1937 A505 3c multi .75 .20

8th World Mining Conference — A506

1974, Nov. 3

1938 A506 13c multi 1.50 .25

Petroleum Institute, 15th Anniv. — A507

1974, Nov. 20

1939 A507 3c multi .70 .20

Intersputnik Earth Station Opening — A508

1974, Nov. 30 **Unwmk.**

1940 A508 3c shown .25 .20
1941 A508 13c Satellite, satellite dish 1.25 .20
1942 A508 1p Satellite, flags 3.25 1.10
Nos. 1940-1942 (3) 4.75 1.50

Philatelic Federation, 10th Anniv. — A509

1974, Nov. 30 *Perf. 12½x13*

1943 A509 30c multi 2.40 .20

Souvenir Sheet

Mercury — A510

1974, Dec. 6 *Imperf.*

1944 A510 50c multi 6.00 .95

4th Natl. Phil. Exhib., Havana.

1st World Peace Congress, 25th Anniv. — A511

1974, Dec. 16 **Wmk. 376** *Perf. 13*

1945 A511 30c *F. Joliot-Curie,* by Picasso 3.00 .25

Ruben Martinez Villena (b. 1899), Revolutionary — A512

1974, Dec. 20 **Unwmk.**

1946 A512 3c red org & yel .75 .20

Souvenir Sheet

Cuban Victories, 1st Amateur Boxing Championships — A513

1975, Jan. 6 Litho. *Imperf.*

1947 A513 50c Trophy 6.00 .95

The World, by Marcelo Pogolotti A514

Paintings in the Natl. Museum: 2c, *The Silk-Cotton Tree,* by Henry Cleenewerk. 3c, *Landscape,* by Guillermo Collazo. 5c, *Still-life,* by Francisco Peralta. 13c, *Maria Wilson,* by Federico Martinez, vert. 30c, *The Couple,* by Mariano Fortuny.

1975, Jan. 20 *Perf. 13*

1948 A514 1c multi .20 .20
1949 A514 2c multi .20 .20
1950 A514 3c multi .20 .20
1951 A514 5c multi .25 .20
1952 A514 13c multi 1.50 .20
1953 A514 30c multi 2.75 .40
Nos. 1948-1953 (6) 5.10 1.40

Intl. Women's Year A515

1975, Feb. 6

1954 A515 13c multi 1.25 .25

Fishing Industry A516

Various fish and fishing vessels.

1975, Feb. 22

1955 A516 1c Long-finned tuna .20 .20
1956 A516 2c Tuna .20 .20
1957 A516 3c Mediterranean grouper .20 .20
1958 A516 8c Hake .20 .20
1959 A516 13c Prawn 1.10 .35
1960 A516 30c Lobster 3.25 .35
Nos. 1955-1960 (6) 5.15 1.50

Minerals — A517

1975, Mar. 15 Litho. *Perf. 13x12½*

1961 A517 3c Nickel .40 .20
1962 A517 13c Copper 1.60 .20
1963 A517 30c Chromium 2.75 .35
Nos. 1961-1963 (3) 4.75 .75

Cosmonaut's Day — A518

1975, Apr. 12 *Perf. 13x12½, 12½x13*

1964 A518 1c Cosmodrome .20 .20
1965 A518 2c Probe, vert. .20 .20
1966 A518 3c Eclipse .20 .20
1967 A518 5c Threshold to Space .40 .20
1968 A518 13c Midday on Mars 1.50 .25
1969 A518 30c Cosmonaut's view of Earth 2.50 .45
Nos. 1964-1969 (6) 5.00 1.50

The future of space.

Stamp Day A519

Various covers.

1975, Apr. 24 *Perf. 13*

1970 A519 3c multi .20 .20
1971 A519 13c multi 1.40 .20
1972 A519 30c multi 2.10 .25
Nos. 1970-1972 (3) 3.70 .65

Victory Over Fascism, 30th Anniv. — A520

Design: Raising red flag over Reichstag, Berlin.

1975, May 9 *Perf. 13x12½*

1973 A520 30c multi 2.00 .20

A521

Works in the Decorative Art Museum — A522

1c, Sevres porcelain vase, vert. 2c, Meissen porcelain statue *Shepherdess and Dancers,* vert. 3c, Chinese porcelain dish *Lady with Parasol.* 5c, Chinese screen detail *The Phoenix,* vert. 13c, *Allegory of Music,* by Francois Boucher (1703-70), vert. 30c, *Portrait of a Lady,* by L. Tocque, vert. 50c, *The Swing,* by Hubert Robert (1733-1808).

1975, May 10 *Perf. 12½x13, 13x12½*

1974 A521 1c multi .20 .20
1975 A521 2c multi .20 .20
1976 A521 3c shown .25 .20
1977 A521 5c multi .40 .20
1978 A521 13c multi 1.50 .20
1979 A521 30c multi 2.00 .40
Nos. 1974-1979 (6) 4.55 1.40

Souvenir Sheet

Perf. 13x12½ on 3 Sides

1980 A522 50c shown 5.50 .95

No. 1980 contains one 25x39mm stamp.

Intl. Children's Day — A523

Wmk. 376

1975, May 31 Litho. *Perf. 13*

1981 A523 3c multi .50 .20

Indigenous Birds — A524

1975, June 18 Unwmk.

1982 A524 1c *Vireo gundlachi* .20 .20
1983 A524 2c *Gymnoglaux lawrenci* .20 .20
1984 A524 3c *Aratingo eoups* .20 .20
1985 A524 5c *Staroenas cyanocephala* .35 .20
1986 A524 13c *Chondrohierax wilsoni* 1.60 .35
1987 A524 30c *Cyanolimnas cerverai* 2.50 .60
Nos. 1982-1987 (6) 5.05 1.75

See #2121-2125, 2180-2182, C276-C276.

Scientific Investigation Center, 10th Anniv. — A525

1975, July 1 *Perf. 12½*

1988 A525 13c multi 1.40 .20

Irrigation and Drainage Commission, 25th Anniv. — A526

1975, Aug. 2 *Perf. 13*

1989 A526 13c multi 1.40 .20

Afforestation A527

1975, Aug. 20

1990 A527 1c *Cedrela mexicana* .20 .20
1991 A527 3c *Swietenia mahagoni* .40 .20
1992 A527 5c *Calophyllum brasiliense* .40 .20
1993 A527 13c *Hibiscus tiliaceus* 1.10 .20
1994 A527 30c *Pinus caribaea* 1.75 .30
Nos. 1990-1994 (5) 3.85 1.10

Cuban Women's Federation, 15th Anniv. — A528

1975, Aug. 23

1995 A528 3c multi .50 .20

Intl. Conference on the Independence of Puerto Rico — A529

1975, Sept. 5 Litho.

1996 A529 13c multi 1.00 .20

A530

A531

7th Pan American Games, Mexico: Aztec calendar stone and various athletes.

1975, Sept. 20 ***Perf. 12½x13***

1997 A530 1c Baseball .25 .20
1998 A530 3c Boxing .25 .20
1999 A530 5c Basketball .25 .20
2000 A530 13c High jump 1.50 .25
2001 A530 30c Weight lifting 2.10 .25
Nos. 1997-2001 (5) 4.35 1.10

Souvenir Sheet

Imperf

2002 A530 50c Stone, emblem 4.00 .95

1975, Sept. 28 ***Perf. 12½x13***

2003 A531 3c multi .50 .20

Revolutionary Defense Committees (CDR), 15th anniv.

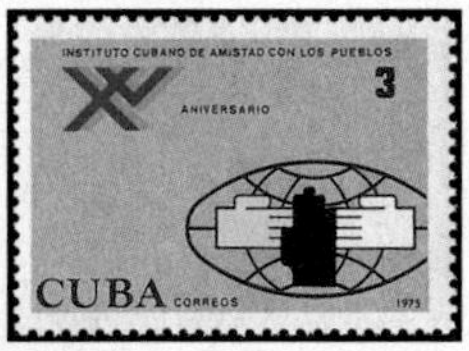

Friendship Among the Peoples Institute, 15th Anniv. A532

1975, Oct. 8 ***Perf. 12½x13***

2004 A532 3c multi .30 .20

Natl. Bank, 25th Anniv. A533

Designs: 1-peso coins and banknotes identified by serial numbers.

1975, Oct. 13 ***Perf. 13x12½***

2005 A533 13c Coin, 1915 1.10 .20
2006 A533 13c C882736A, 1934 1.10 .20
2007 A533 13c A000387A, 1946 1.10 .20
2008 A533 13c 933906, 1964 1.10 .20
2009 A533 13c K000000, 1976 1.10 .20
a. Strip of 5, Nos. 2005-2009 6.00 1.25
Nos. 2005-2009 (5) 5.50 1.00

Locomotives — A534

1975, Oct. 28 **Unwmk.** ***Perf. 12½***

2010 A534 1c *La Junta,* 1837 .20 .20
2011 A534 3c Steam engine 2-8-0 *No. 12* .30 .20
2012 A534 5c Diesel TEM 4 *No. 51010* .30 .20
2013 A534 13c Diesel DVM 9 *I-7 55* 2.50 .20
2014 A534 30c Diesel M 62K *No. 61601* 3.00 .30
Nos. 2010-2014 (5) 6.30 1.10

Railway history.

Development of the Textile Industry — A535

1975, Nov. 10 ***Perf. 13x12½***

2015 A535 13c Bobbins, flag, loom operator 1.25 .20

Veterinary Medicine — A536

Parasites and host species.

1975, Nov. 25 **Litho.** ***Perf. 13***

2016 A536 1c *Haemonchus,* lamb .25 .20
2017 A536 2c *Ancylostoma caninum,* dog .25 .20
2018 A536 3c *Dispharynx nasuta,* rooster .25 .20
2019 A536 5c *Gasterophilus intestinalis,* horse .25 .20
2020 A536 13c *Ascaris lumbricoides,* pig 1.40 .20
2021 A536 30c *Boophilus microplus,* bull 2.50 .40
Nos. 2016-2021 (6) 4.90 1.40

Manuel Ascunce Domenech Educational Detachment A537

1975, Nov. 27 **Litho.**

2022 A537 3c multi .40 .20

Development of Agriculture and Animal Husbandry — A538

1975, Dec. 15 **Litho.** ***Perf. 13x12½***

2023 A538 13c Irrigation 1.25 .20

1st Communist Party Congress — A539

1975, Dec. 17 ***Perf. 12½x13, 13x12½***

2024 A539 3c "1," revolutionaries, vert. .20 .20
2025 A539 13c shown 1.10 .20
2026 A539 30c Party leaders 1.50 .30
Nos. 2024-2026 (3) 2.80 .70

8th Latin-American Obstetrics and Gynecology Congress — A540

1976, Jan. 24 ***Perf. 13***

2027 A540 3c multi .60 .20

Paintings in Natl. Museums — A541

Designs: 1c, *Seated Woman,* by Victor Manuel, vert. 2c, *Garden,* by Santiago Rusinol. 3c, *Guadalquivir River,* by Manuel Barron y Carrillo. 5c, *Self-portrait,* by Jan Havicksz Steen, vert. 13c, *Portrait of a Woman,* by Louis Michel Van Loo, vert. 30c, *La Chula,* by Jose Arburu Morell, vert.

Perf. 13, 12½ (3c, 30c)

1976, Jan. 30

Sizes: 29x40mm (1c, 5c, 13c), 40x29mm (2c), 44x27mm (3c), 27x44mm (30c)

2028 A541 1c multi .20 .20
2029 A541 2c multi .20 .20
2030 A541 3c multi .25 .20
2031 A541 5c multi .25 .20
2032 A541 13c multi 1.40 .25
2033 A541 30c multi 2.25 .50
Nos. 2028-2033 (6) 4.55 1.55

10th Cong. of Ministers from Socialist Communications Organizations, Feb. 12, Havana — A542

1976, Feb. 12 **Litho.** ***Perf. 13***

2034 A542 13c multi 1.40 .20

Hunting Dogs A543

1976, Feb. 20

2035 A543 1c American foxhound .25 .20
2036 A543 2c Labrador retriever .25 .20
2037 A543 3c Borzoi .25 .20
2038 A543 5c Irish setter .25 .20
2039 A543 13c Pointer 2.25 .30
2040 A543 30c Cocker spaniel 3.00 .40
Nos. 2035-2040 (6) 6.25 1.50

Socialist Constitution — A544

1976, Feb. 24 ***Perf. 12½***

2041 A544 13c Natl. flag, arms, anthem 1.40 .20

Chess Champions — A545

Designs: 1c, Ruy Lopez Segura and chessboard. 2c, Francois Philidor and frontispiece of his book, *Analysis of the Game of Chess.* 3c, Wilhelm Steinitz and knight. 13c, Emanuel Lasker and king. 30c, Jose Raul Capablanca learning to play chess as a small boy.

1976, Mar. 15 ***Perf. 13x12½***

2042 A545 1c multi .20 .20
2043 A545 2c multi .20 .20
2044 A545 3c multi .25 .20
2045 A545 13c multi 1.75 .20
2046 A545 30c multi 1.90 .50
Nos. 2042-2046 (5) 4.30 1.30

Havana Radio Intl. Broadcasts, 15th Anniv. — A546

1976, Mar. 26

2047 A546 50c multi 2.00 .70

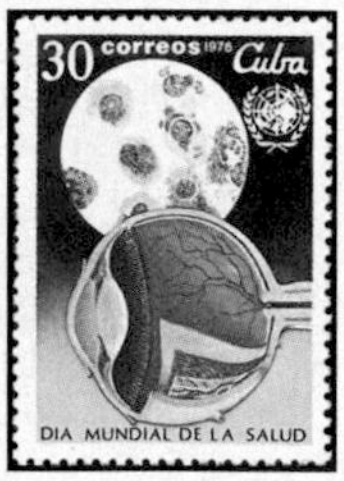

World Health Day — A547

Child Care Centers, 15th Anniv. — A548

1976, Apr. 7

2048 A547 30c multi 1.50 .45

1976, Apr. 10 ***Perf. 12½x13***

2049 A548 3c multi .60 .20

1st Manned Space Flight, 15th Anniv. A549

1976, Apr. 12 ***Perf. 13***

2050 A549 1c Gagarin, lift-off .20 .20
2051 A549 2c V. Tesreshkova, rockets .20 .20
2052 A549 3c A. Leonov's space walk, vert. .25 .20
2053 A549 5c Spacecraft, vert. .40 .20
2054 A549 13c Spacecraft, diff., vert. 1.10 .20
2055 A549 30c Space link-up 1.75 .35
Nos. 2050-2055 (6) 3.90 1.35

Bay of Pigs Invasion, 15th Anniv. — A550

1976, Apr. 17 ***Perf. 13x12½, 12½x13***

2056 A550 3c shown .25 .20
2057 A550 13c Bomber, pilot .95 .20
2058 A550 30c Soldiers exulting, vert. 1.75 .45
Nos. 2056-2058 (3) 2.95 .85

Natl. Militia, 17th anniv. (3c); Air Force, 15th anniv. (13c); proclamation of the socialist revolution, 15th anniv. (30c).

Nat. Assoc. of Small Farmers (ANAP), 15th Anniv. — A551

1976, May 17 ***Perf. 13x12½***

2059 A551 3c multi .60 .20

1976 Summer Olympics, Montreal — A552

1976, May 25 ***Perf. 12½x13***

2060 A552 1c Volleyball .20 .20
2061 A552 2c Basketball .20 .20
2062 A552 3c Long jump .20 .20
2063 A552 4c Boxing .25 .20
2064 A552 5c Weight lifting .25 .20
2065 A552 13c Judo 1.10 .20
2066 A552 30c Swimming 1.75 .45
Nos. 2060-2066 (7) 3.95 1.65

Souvenir Sheet

Imperf

2067 A552 50c Character trademark (beaver) 4.00 1.25

See Nos. 2106, 2112.

Modern Secondary Schools — A553

1976, June 12 **Litho.** ***Perf. 13***

2068 A553 3c red, pale grn & blk .60 .20

Indigenous Birds — A554

1976, June 15 ***Perf. 13x12½***

2069 A554 1c *Teretistris fornsi* .30 .20
2070 A554 2c *Glaucidium siju* .30 .20
2071 A554 3c *Nesoceleus fernandinae* .35 .25
2072 A554 5c *Todus mutlicolor* .65 .25
2073 A554 13c *Accipiter gundlachi* 1.25 .25
2074 A554 30c *Priotelus temnurus* 3.00 .80
Nos. 2069-2074 (6) 5.85 1.95

EXPO '76, USSR A555

1976, July 5 ***Perf. 12½x13, 13x12½***

2075 A555 1c Anatomical scanning device .20 .20
2076 A555 3c Child, doe .20 .20
2077 A555 10c Cosmonauts .50 .20
2078 A555 30c Tupolev supersonic jet 2.50 .55
Nos. 2075-2078 (4) 3.40 1.15

Public health and industrial safety (1c), environmental protection (3c), space exploration (10c) and modern transportation (30c). Nos. 2075-2077 vert.

Death Cent. of "El Inglesito" A556

1976, Aug. 4 ***Perf. 13***

2079 A556 13c Henry M. Reeve .70 .20

Portrait of G. Collazo, by Jean Dabour — A557

Paintings by Collazo: 2c, *The Art Lovers,* horiz. 3c, *The Patio.* 5c, *Coconut Tree.* 13c, *New York Studio,* horiz. 30c, *R. Emelina Collazo.*

Perf. 13, 12½x13 (5c, 30c), 13x12½ (13c)

1976, Sept. 2

Sizes: 33x44mm, 44x33mm (2c), 31x46mm (5c, 30c), 46x31mm (13c)

2080 A557 1c multi .20 .20
2081 A557 2c multi .20 .20
2082 A557 3c multi .20 .20
2083 A557 5c multi .20 .20
2084 A557 13c multi .65 .25
2085 A557 30c multi 2.10 .50
Nos. 2080-2085 (6) 3.55 1.55

Camilo Cienfuegos Military Schools, 10th Anniv. — A558

1976, Sept. 23 ***Perf. 13***

2086 A558 3c multi .40 .20

Development of the Merchant Marine — A559

Various cargo and passenger ships.

1976, Oct. 2 ***Perf. 12½***

2087 A559 1c multi .25 .20
2088 A559 2c multi .25 .20
2089 A559 3c multi .25 .20
2090 A559 5c multi .35 .20
2091 A559 13c multi 1.00 .20
2092 A559 30c multi 2.00 .35
Nos. 2087-2092 (6) 4.10 1.35

8th Intl. Health Film Festival of Socialist Countries, Havana — A560

1976, Oct. 4 ***Perf. 13x12½***

2093 A560 3c multi .40 .20

5th Intl. Ballet Festival, Havana A561

Scenes from ballets. 2c, 5c, 13c, 30c vert.

1976, Nov. 6 ***Perf. 13***

2094 A561 1c *Apollo* .20 .20
2095 A561 2c *The River and the Forest* .20 .20
2096 A561 3c *Giselle* .20 .20
2097 A561 5c *Oedipus Rex* .25 .20
2098 A561 13c *Carmen* 1.10 .20
2099 A561 30c *Vital Song* 2.10 .35
Nos. 2094-2099 (6) 4.05 1.35

3rd Military Games A562

1976, Nov. 25 ***Perf. 13***

2100 A562 3c multi .50 .20

Granma Landings, 20th Anniv. — A563

1976, Dec. 2 ***Perf. 13x12½***

2101 A563 1c Landing craft .20 .20
2102 A563 3c Landing force .20 .20
2103 A563 13c Castro, soldiers 1.00 .20
2104 A563 30c Globe, rifles 1.60 .55
Nos. 2101-2104 (4) 3.00 1.15

Souvenir Sheet

Cuban Landscape, by F. Cadava — A564

1976, Dec. 8 ***Perf. 13x13½***

2105 A564 50c multi 5.25 1.25

CIENFUEGOS '76, 5th natl. phil. exhib.

Summer Olympics Type of 1976 and

Victory of Cuban Athletes at the Montreal Games — A565

1976, Dec. 10 ***Perf. 12½x13***

2106 A565 1c Volleyball .20 .20
2107 A565 2c Hurdles .20 .20
2108 A565 3c Running (starting blocks) .20 .20
2109 A565 8c Boxing .25 .20
2110 A565 13c Running (finish line) .85 .20
2111 A565 30c Judo 1.75 .45
Nos. 2106-2111 (6) 3.45 1.45

Souvenir Sheet

Imperf

2112 A552 50c like No. 2063 5.00 .95

Paintings in the Natl. Museum A566

1c, *Golden Cross Inn,* by S. Scott. 3c, *Portrait of a Man,* by J.C. Verspronck, vert. 5c, *Venetian Landscape,* by Francesco Guardi. 10c, *Valley Corner,* by H. Cleenewerck, vert. 13c, *F. Xaviera Paula,* anonymous, vert. 30c, *F. de Medici,* by C. Allori, vert.

Perf. 13, 12½x13 (3c, 10c, 30c), 12½ (13c)

1977, Jan. 18

Sizes: 40x29mm, 27x42mm (3c, 10c, 30c), 27x43½mm (13c)

2113 A566 1c multi .20 .20
2114 A566 3c multi .20 .20
2115 A566 5c multi .20 .20
2116 A566 10c multi .55 .20
2117 A566 13c multi .85 .20
2118 A566 30c multi 2.10 .40
Nos. 2113-2118 (6) 4.10 1.40

Rural Transport A567

1977, Feb. 15 ***Perf. 13***

2119 A567 3c multi .80 .20

Constitution of Popular Government — A568

1976, Dec. 1 *Perf. 13x12½*
2120 A568 13c multi .70 .20

Bird Type of 1975

1977, Feb. 25 *Perf. 13*
2121 A524 1c *Xiphidiopicus percussus* .25 .20
2122 A524 4c *Tiaris canora* .30 .20
2123 A524 10c *Dives atroviolaceus* .60 .20
2124 A524 13c *Ferminia cerverai* .85 .20
2125 A524 30c *Mellisuga helenae* 1.75 .35
Nos. 2121-2125 (5) 3.75 1.15

Lenin Park Aquarium, Havana — A569

1977, Mar. 15
2126 A569 1c *Chichlasoma meeki* .20 .20
2127 A569 3c *Barbus tetrazona tetrazona* .20 .20
2128 A569 5c *Cyprinus carpio* .20 .20
2129 A569 10c *Betta splendens* .30 .20
2130 A569 13c *Pterophyllum scalare*, vert. 1.25 .25
2131 A569 30c *Hemigrammus caudovittatus* 2.50 .50
Nos. 2126-2131 (6) 4.65 1.55

Sputnik (1st Artificial Satellite), 20th Anniv. — A570

1c, DDR No. 370, *Sputnik.* 3c, Hungary No. 1216, *Luna 16.* 5c, North Korean Intl. Geophysical Year 10-won stamp of 1958, *Cosmos.* 10c, Poland No. 822, *Sputnik 3.* 13c, Yugoslavia No. 870, Earth, Moon. 30c, Cuba No. 866, Earth, Moon. 50c, Russia No. 2021, *Sputnik.*

1977, Apr. 12 *Perf. 13x12½*
2132 A570 1c multi .25 .20
2133 A570 3c multi .25 .20
2134 A570 5c multi .25 .20
2135 A570 10c multi .35 .20
2136 A570 13c multi 1.10 .20
2137 A570 30c multi 1.90 .35
Nos. 2132-2137 (6) 4.10 1.35

Souvenir Sheet

Imperf

2138 A570 50c multi 4.25 1.25

No. 2138 has simulated perfs.

Antonio Maria Romeu (1876-1955), Composer — A571

1977, May 10 **Litho.** *Perf. 13*
2139 A571 3c multi .35 .20

See No. C251.

Flowering Plants — A572

1977, May 31
2140 A572 1c *Hibiscus rosa sinensis* .20 .20
2141 A572 2c *Nerium oleander* .20 .20
2142 A572 5c *Allamanda cathartica* .20 .20
2143 A572 10c *Pelargonium zonale* .40 .20
Nos. 2140-2143 (4) 1.00 .80

Dr. Juan Tomas Roig (b. 1877), botanist. See Nos. C252-C254.

Fire Prevention Week — A573

1977, June 20
2144 A573 1c shown .20 .20
2145 A573 2c Horse-drawn fire pump, diff. .20 .20
2146 A573 6c Early motorized vehicle .25 .20
2147 A573 10c Modern truck .50 .20
2148 A573 13c Turntable-ladder truck .90 .20
2149 A573 30c Crane vehicle 1.90 .40
Nos. 2144-2149 (6) 3.95 1.40

Natl. Decorations (Ribbons and Medals of Honor) — A574

1977, July 26 *Perf. 12x12½*
2150 A574 1c shown .25 .20
2151 A574 3c multi, diff. .25 .20

See Nos. C255-C256.

Paintings by Jorge Arche — A575

Perf. 13x12½, 12½x13 (10c), 13 (5c)

1977, Aug. 25

Sizes: 26x38mm, 29x40mm (5c), 38x26mm (10c)

2152 A575 1c *Portrait of Mary* .20 .20
2153 A575 3c *Jose Marti* .20 .20
2154 A575 5c *Portrait of Aristides* .20 .20
2155 A575 10c *Bathers* .50 .20
Nos. 2152-2155 (4) 1.10 .80

Nos. 2152-2154 vert. See Nos. C257-C259.

4th Military Spartakiad (Summer Sports) — A576

1977, Sept. 10 *Perf. 13*
2156 A576 1c Boxing .20 .20
2157 A576 3c Volleyball .20 .20
2158 A576 5c Parachuting .20 .20
2159 A576 10c Running .35 .20
Nos. 2156-2159 (4) .95 .80

See Nos. C260-C261.

Intl. Airmail Service, 50th Anniv. A577

Designs: 1c, Biplane and No. C62. 2c, Three-engine plane and Cuba-Key West 1st flight cancel, Oct. 28, 1927. 5c, Flying boat and intl. airmail service 1st flight cachet. 10c, Jet aircraft and Havana-Madrid cachet, Apr. 26, 1948.

1977, Oct. 27 **Litho.** *Perf. 12x12½*
2160 A577 1c multi .20 .20
2161 A577 2c multi .20 .20
2162 A577 5c multi .20 .20
2163 A577 10c multi .50 .20
Nos. 2160-2163 (4) 1.10 .80

See Nos. C263-C264.

October Revolution, Russia, 60th Anniv. — A578

1977, Nov. 7 *Perf. 13x12½*
2164 A578 3c Cruiser *Aurora* .20 .20
2165 A578 13c Lenin, Flags .40 .20
2166 A578 30c Hammer, sickle, symbols of agriculture, technology 1.40 .25
Nos. 2164-2166 (3) 2.00 .65

Felines, Havana Zoo — A579

1977, Nov. 24 **Litho.** *Perf. 13*
2167 A579 1c Cat .20 .20
2168 A579 2c Black panther .20 .20
2169 A579 8c Puma .20 .20
2170 A579 10c Leopard .85 .20
Nos. 2167-2170 (4) 1.45 .80

See Nos. C266-C267.

Martyrs of the Revolution, 20th Death Annivs. — A580

1977, Dec. 2 *Perf. 12½x12*
2171 A580 3c Cienfuegos Uprising .20 .20
2172 A580 20c Siege on the Presidential Palace 1.00 .20

See No. C268.

Intl. Measurement System — A581

1977, Dec. 9
2173 A581 3c multi .40 .20

Havana University, 250th Anniv. — A582

1978, Jan. 5 *Perf. 13x12½*
2174 A582 3c multi .25 .20

See Nos. C270-C271.

Landscape with Figures, by J. Pilliment — A583

Paintings in the Natl. Museum of Art: 1c, *Seated Woman,* by R. Mandrazo, vert. 4c, *Girl,* by J. Sorolla, vert. 10c, *The Cow,* by E. Abela.

Perf. 12x12½, 13 (4c, 6c, 10c)

1978, Feb. 20

Sizes: 27x42mm, 29x40mm (4c), 40x29mm (6c, 10c)

2175 A583 1c multi .20 .20
2176 A583 4c multi .20 .20
2177 A583 6c shown .20 .20
2178 A583 10c multi .60 .20
Nos. 2175-2178 (4) 1.20 .80

See Nos. C273-C274.

Frontier Troops, 15th Anniv. — A584

1978, Mar. 5 *Perf. 13*
2179 A584 13c multi 1.50 .25

Bird Type of 1975

Perf. 13, 12½x12 (4c)

1978, Mar. 10 **Size: 42x27mm**

2180 A524 1c *Myadestes elisabeth* .35 .20
2181 A524 4c *Palioptila lembeyei* .40 .20
2182 A524 10c *Teretistris fernandinae* 1.00 .25
Nos. 2180-2182 (3) 1.75 .65

Name of bird inscribed below vignette. See Nos. C275-C276.

Cosmonaut's Day — A585

1978, Apr. 12 ***Perf. 13***

2183 A585 1c Intercosmos, vert. .20 .20
2184 A585 2c Luna 24 .20 .20
2185 A585 5c Venus 9, vert. .35 .20
2186 A585 10c Cosmos .35 .20
Nos. 2183-2186 (4) 1.10 .80

See Nos. C278-C279.

9th World Trade Unions Congress, Prague — A586

1978, Apr. 16

2187 A586 30c ver, deep brn & blk 1.00 .45

Cactus Flowers — A587

1978, May 15 ***Perf. 12½x13 (1c), 13***

2188 A587 1c *Melocactus guitarti* .25 .20
2189 A587 4c *Leptocereus wrightii* .25 .20
2190 A587 6c *Opuntia militaris* .25 .20
2191 A587 10c *Cylindropuntia hystrix* .65 .25
Nos. 2188-2191 (4) 1.40 .85

Natl. Botanical Gardens. See #C281-C282.

Lenin Park Aquarium, Havana — A588

1978, June 15 ***Perf. 13***

2192 A588 1c *Barbus arulios* .20 .20
2193 A588 4c *Hiphessobrycon flammeus* .20 .20
2194 A588 6c *Poecilia reticulata* .30 .20
2195 A588 10c *Colis lalia* .60 .20
Nos. 2192-2195 (4) 1.30 .80

See Nos. C286-C287.

MEDELLIN '78, 13th Central American and Caribbean Games — A589

1978, July 1

2196 A589 1c Basketball, vert. .25 .20
2197 A589 3c Boxing, vert. .25 .20
2198 A589 5c Weight lifting, vert. .25 .20
2199 A589 10c Fencing .45 .20
Nos. 2196-2199 (4) 1.20 .80

See Nos. C288-C289.

Attack on Moncada Barracks, 25th Anniv. — A590

1978, July 26

2200 A590 3c multi .25 .20

See Nos. C290-C291.

World Youth and Students Festival, Havana A591

Natl. flags and views of host cities.

1978, July 28

2201 A591 3c Prague, 1947 .25 .20
2202 A591 3c Budapest, 1949 .25 .20
2203 A591 3c Berlin, 1951 .25 .20
2204 A591 3c Bucharest, 1953 .25 .20
2205 A591 3c Warsaw, 1955 .25 .20
a. Strip of 5, Nos. 2201-2205 1.40 1.40
Nos. 2201-2205 (5) 1.25 1.00

See Nos. C292-C297.

Young Workers' Army, 5th Anniv. — A592

1978, Aug. 3

2206 A592 3c multi .30 .20

Tuna Industry A593

1978, Aug. 30 ***Perf. 12½x12***

2207 A593 1c Tuna boat .20 .20
2208 A593 2c Processing ship .20 .20
2209 A593 5c Shrimp boat .20 .20
2210 A593 10c Inshore stern trawler .35 .20
Nos. 2207-2210 (4) .95 .80

See Nos. C298-C299.

Paintings by Amelia Pelaez del Casal (1896-1968) — A594

Perf. 13x12½, 13 (3c, 6c), 12½x13

1978, Sept. 15

2211 A594 1c *The White Mantle* .20 .20
2212 A594 3c *Still-life with Flowers*, vert. .20 .20
2213 A594 6c *Women*, vert. .20 .20
2214 A594 10c *Fish*, vert. .45 .20
Nos. 2211-2214 (4) 1.05 .80

See Nos. C301-C303.

African Fauna, Havana Zoo A595

1978, Oct. 20 ***Perf. 13***

2215 A595 1c Rhinoceros .25 .20
2216 A595 4c Okapi, vert. .25 .20
2217 A595 6c Mandrill .25 .20
2218 A595 10c Giraffe, vert. .60 .20
Nos. 2215-2218 (4) 1.35 .80

See Nos. C307-C308.

Natl. Ballet, 30th Anniv. — A596

1978, Oct. 28 ***Perf. 13x12½***

2219 A596 3c *Grande Pas de Quatre* .25 .20

See Nos. C309-C310.

A597

A598

Flowers of the Pacific: Various species.

1978, Nov. 30 **Litho.** ***Perf. 13***

2220 A597 1c multi .20 .20
2221 A597 4c multi .20 .20
2222 A597 6c multi .25 .20
2223 A597 10c multi .50 .20
Nos. 2220-2223 (4) 1.15 .80

See Nos. C311-C312.

1979, Jan. 1 ***Perf. 12½x13 (3c), 13***

2224 A598 3c Castro, soldier .20 .20
2225 A598 13c Industry .50 .20
2226 A598 1p Flag, globe, flame 3.25 .75
Nos. 2224-2226 (3) 3.95 1.15

Triumph of the Revolution, 20th anniv.

Doves and Pigeons A599

1979, Jan. 30 ***Perf. 13***

2227 A599 1c *Starnoenas cyanocephala* .35 .20
2228 A599 3c *Geotrygon chysia* .40 .20
2229 A599 7c *Geotrygon caniceps* .40 .20
2230 A599 8c *Geotrygon montana* .50 .20
2231 A599 13c *Columba leucocephala* .90 .20
2232 A599 30c *Columba inornata* 1.90 .45
Nos. 2227-2232 (6) 4.45 1.45

Paintings in the Natl. Museum of Art A600

Designs: 1c, *Genre Scene*, by David Teniers. 3c, *Arrival of Spanish Troops*, by J. Louis Meissonier. 6c, *A Joyful Gathering*, by Sir David Wilkie. 10c, *A Robbery*, by E. De Lucas Padilla. 13c, *Tea Time*, by R. Madrazo, vert. 30c, *Peasants in Front of a Tavern*, by Adriaen van Ostade.

1979, Feb. 20

2233 A600 1c multi .20 .20
2234 A600 3c multi .20 .20
2235 A600 6c multi .30 .20
2236 A600 10c multi .45 .20
2237 A600 13c multi .80 .20
2238 A600 30c multi 1.75 .25
Nos. 2233-2238 (6) 3.70 1.25

See Nos. 2262-2267, C317.

Marine Flora — A601

1979, Mar. 20

2239 A601 3c *Nymphaea capensis* .20 .20
2240 A601 10c *Nymphaea ampla* .40 .20
2241 A601 13c *Nymphaea coerulea* .65 .25
2242 A601 30c *Nymphaea rubra* 1.50 .30
Nos. 2239-2242 (4) 2.75 .95

All are incorrectly inscribed "Nymphaca."

A602

A603

1979, Mar. 24

2243 A602 3c multi .25 .25

Cuban film industry, 20th anniv.

1979, Apr. 12

2244	A603	1c	Rocket launch	.20	.20
2245	A603	4c	Soyuz	.20	.20
2246	A603	6c	Salyut	.35	.20
2247	A603	10c	Link-up	.50	.20
2248	A603	13c	Soyuz, Salyut	.85	.20
2249	A603	30c	Parachute landing	1.90	.25
			Nos. 2244-2249 (6)	4.00	1.25

Cosmonaut's Day. See No. C315.

6th Summit Meeting of Non-Aligned Countries — A604

1979, Apr. 17

2250	A604	3c	Understanding, cooperation	.25	.20
2251	A604	13c	Fight colonialism	.50	.20
2252	A604	30c	New world economic order	1.40	.40
			Nos. 2250-2252 (3)	2.15	.80

House of the Americas Museum, 20th Anniv. — A605

1979, Apr. 28 ***Perf. 13x12½***

2253 A605 13c Cuna Indian tapestry .40 .20

Agrarian Reform, 20th Anniv. — A606

1979, May 17 ***Perf. 12½x12***

2254 A606 3c multi .40 .20

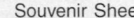

Souvenir Sheet

The Party, by Jules Pascin — A607

1979, May 18 ***Perf. 13***

2255 A607 50c multi 3.50 .90

PHILASERDICA '79 phil. exhib., Sofia.

Nocturnal Butterflies — A608

1979, May 25

2256	A608	1c	*Eulepidotis rectimargo*	.20	.20
2257	A608	4c	*Othreis materna*	.20	.20
2258	A608	6c	*Noropsis hieroglyphica*	.40	.20
2259	A608	10c	*Heterochroma*	.40	.20
2260	A608	13c	*Melanchroia regnatrix*	.80	.20
2261	A608	30c	*Attera gemmata*	2.00	.30
			Nos. 2256-2261 (6)	4.00	1.30

Art Type of 1979

Paintings by Victor Emmanuel Garcia (d. 1969): 1c, *Main Avenue, Paris.* 3c, *Portrait of Enmita.* 6c, *San Juan River, Matanzas.* 10c, *Woman Carrying Hay.* 13c, *Still-life with Vase.* 30c, *Street at Night.* Nos. 2262-2267 vert.

1979, June 15

2262	A600	1c	multi	.20	.20
2263	A600	3c	multi	.20	.20
2264	A600	6c	multi	.20	.20
2265	A600	10c	multi	.30	.20
2266	A600	13c	multi	.45	.20
2267	A600	30c	multi	1.60	.45
			Nos. 2262-2267 (6)	2.95	1.45

See No. C317.

World Peace Council, 30th Anniv. A609

1979, June 29 ***Perf. 12½x13***

2268 A609 30c multi 1.00 .35

1980 Summer Olympics, Moscow — A610

1979, July 30 ***Perf. 13x12½***

2269	A610	1c	Wrestling	.20	.20
2270	A610	4c	Boxing	.20	.20
2271	A610	6c	Women's volleyball	.20	.20
2272	A610	10c	Shooting	.25	.20
2273	A610	13c	Weight lifting	.55	.20
2274	A610	30c	High jump	1.50	.30
			Nos. 2269-2274 (6)	2.90	1.30

Roses — A611

A612

1979, Aug. 20 ***Perf. 13***

2275	A611	1c	*Rosa eglanteria*	.25	.20
2276	A611	2c	*Rosa centifolia anemonoides*	.25	.20
2277	A611	3c	*Rosa indica vulgaris*	.25	.20
2278	A611	5c	*Rosa eglanteria punicea*	.25	.20
2279	A611	10c	*Rosa sulfurea*	.25	.20
2280	A611	13c	*Rosa muscosa alba*	.45	.20
2281	A611	20c	*Rosa gallica purpurea velutina*	.90	.25
			Nos. 2275-2281 (7)	2.60	1.45

1979, Aug. 30

2282 A612 13c multi .50 .20

Council for Mutual Economic Assistance, 30th anniv.

Cubana Airlines, 50th Anniv. A613

Various aircraft.

1979, Oct. 8

2283	A613	1c	Ford trimotor	.20	.20
2284	A613	2c	Sikorsky S-38	.20	.20
2285	A613	3c	Douglas DC-3	.35	.20
2286	A613	4c	Brittania	.35	.20
2287	A613	13c	Ilyushin IL-14	.90	.20
2288	A613	40c	Tupolev TU-104	2.50	.30
			Nos. 2283-2288 (6)	4.50	1.30

Disappearance of Camilo Cienfuegos, 20th Anniv. — A614

1979, Oct. 28

2289 A614 3c multi .30 .20

Reinoso, Sugar Cane and Blossom A615

1979, Nov. 12

2290 A615 13c multi .75 .20

Sugar Cane Research Institute, 15th anniv., and sesquicentennial of the birth of Alvaro Reinoso.

Zoo Animals A616

1979, Nov. 15

2291	A616	1c	Chimpanzees	.20	.20
2292	A616	2c	Leopards	.20	.20
2293	A616	3c	Deer	.20	.20
2294	A616	4c	Lion cubs	.20	.20
2295	A616	5c	Bear cubs	.20	.20
2296	A616	13c	Squirrels	.30	.20
2297	A616	30c	Pandas	.70	.25
2298	A616	50c	Tiger cubs	1.40	.35
			Nos. 2291-2298 (8)	3.40	1.80

Insects A617

1980, Jan. 25

2299	A617	1c	*Rhina oblita*	.20	.20
2300	A617	5c	*Odontocera josemartii*, vert.	.20	.20
2301	A617	6c	*Pinthocoelium columbinum*	.20	.20
2302	A617	10c	*Calasoma splendida*, vert.	.45	.20
2303	A617	13c	*Homophileurus cubanus*, vert.	.90	.20
2304	A617	30c	*Heterops dimidiata*, vert.	1.90	.70
			Nos. 2299-2304 (6)	3.85	1.70

1980 Summer Olympics, Moscow — A618

1980, Feb. 20 ***Perf. 12½***

2305	A618	1c	Weight lifting	.20	.20
2306	A618	2c	Shooting	.20	.20
2307	A618	5c	Javelin	.20	.20
2308	A618	6c	Wrestling	.20	.20
2309	A618	8c	Judo	.25	.20
2310	A618	10c	Running	.25	.20
2311	A618	13c	Boxing	.55	.20
2312	A618	30c	Women's volleyball	1.40	.60
			Nos. 2305-2312 (8)	3.25	2.00

Souvenir Sheet

Imperf

2313 A618 50c Mischa character 3.00 1.60

No. 2313 contains one 32x40mm stamp.

Paintings in the Natl. Museum A619

Designs: 1c, *The Oak Trees,* by Henry Joseph Harpignies, vert. 4c, *Family Reunion,* by Willem van Mieris. 6c, *Domestic Fowl,* by Melchior De Hondecoeter, vert. 9c, *Innocence,* by William A. Bougereau, vert. 13c, *Venetial Scene II,* by Michele Marieschi. 30c, *Spanish Peasant Woman,* by Joaquin Dominguez Bequer, vert.

Perf. 12½, 13 (9c, 30c), 12½x13 (13c)

1980, Mar. 11

Sizes: 29x40mm, 40x29mm (4c), 28x42mm (9c, 30c), 38x26mm (13c)

2314	A619	1c	multi	.20	.20
2315	A619	4c	multi	.20	.20
2316	A619	6c	multi	.20	.20
2317	A619	9c	multi	.65	.20
2318	A619	13c	multi	.85	.20
2319	A619	30c	multi	1.90	.65
			Nos. 2314-2319 (6)	4.00	1.65

Souvenir Sheet

LONDON '80 — A620

1980, Apr. 1 ***Perf. 13***

2320	A620	50c	*Malvern Hall,* by John Constable	3.50	1.60

Intercosmos Program — A621

1980, Apr. 12

2321	A621	1c	Emblem, flags	.20	.20
2322	A621	4c	Astrophysics	.20	.20
2323	A621	6c	Satellite communications	.20	.20
2324	A621	10c	Meteorology	.45	.20
2325	A621	13c	Biology and medicine	.60	.20
2326	A621	30c	Surveying satellite	1.90	.65
			Nos. 2321-2326 (6)	3.55	1.65

Cuban Postage Stamps, 125th Anniv. — A622

1980, Apr. 24 ***Perf. 12½***

2327	A622	30c	Nos. 1, 7 and 613	1.25	.45

Orchids — A623

1980, May 20 ***Perf. 13***

2328	A623	1c	*Bletia purpurea*	.25	.20
2329	A623	4c	*Oncidium leiboldii*	.25	.20
2330	A623	6c	*Epidendrum cochieatum*	.25	.20
2331	A623	10c	*Cattleyopsis lindenii*	.45	.20
2332	A623	13c	*Encyclia fucata*	.80	.20
2333	A623	30c	*Encyclia phoenicea*	1.75	.60
			Nos. 2328-2333 (6)	3.75	1.60

Marine Mammals — A624

1980, June 20

2334	A624	1c	*Tursiops truncatus*	.45	.20
2335	A624	3c	*Megaptera novaeangliae,* vert.	.45	.20
2336	A624	13c	*Ziphius cavirostris*	1.40	.20
2337	A624	30c	*Monachus tropicalis*	3.25	.40
			Nos. 2334-2337 (4)	5.55	1.00

Urban Reform Campaign, 20th Anniv. — A625

Nationalization of Foreign Industry, 20th Anniv. — A626

1980, July 26 ***Perf. 13x12½, 12½x13***

2338	A625	3c	multi	.20	.20
2339	A626	13c	multi	.35	.20

Moncada Program.

Colonial Copperware A627

Perf. 12½, 12½x13 (13c)

1980, July 29

Sizes: 27x43½mm, 38x26mm (13c)

2340	A627	3c	Wine pitcher, 19th cent.	.20	.20
2341	A627	13c	Oil jar, 18th cent.	.70	.20
2342	A627	30c	Lidded pitcher, 19th cent.	1.40	.20
			Nos. 2340-2342 (3)	2.30	.60

Cuban Women's Federation, 20th Anniv. — A628

1980, Aug. 23 ***Perf. 13***

2343	A628	3c	multi	.40	.20

Souvenir Sheet

ESPAMER '80, Madrid — A629

Design: *Clotilde Passing Through the Country Garden,* by Joaquin Sorolla y Bastida.

1980, Aug. 29

2344	A629	50c	multi	3.50	1.60

Postage stamps of Spain, 130th anniv.

1st Havana Declaration, 20th Anniv. — A630

1980, Sept. 2

2345	A630	13c	multi	.50	.20

Construction of Naval Vessels in Cuba, 360th Anniv. — A631

Ships under construction: 1c, *Our Lady of Atocha,* galleon, 1620. 3c, *El Rayo,* warship, 1749. 7c, *Santisima Trinidad,* 1769. 10c, *Santisima Trinidad,* diff., 1805, vert. 13c, Steamships *Congreso* and *Colon,* 1851. 30c, Cardenas and Chullima shipyards.

1980, Sept. 15

2346	A631	1c	multi	.20	.20
2347	A631	3c	multi	.20	.20
2348	A631	7c	multi	.20	.20
2349	A631	10c	multi	.40	.20
2350	A631	13c	multi	.85	.20
2351	A631	30c	multi	1.40	.60
			Nos. 2346-2351 (6)	3.25	1.60

A633

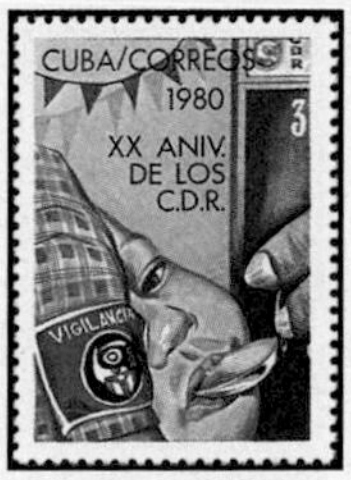

A634

1980, Sept. 26 ***Perf. 13***

2354	A633	13c	multi	.60	.20

Fidel Castro's 1st speech before the UN General Assembly, 20th anniv.

1980, Sept. 28 ***Perf. 13x12½***

2355	A634	3c	multi	.30	.20

Revolutionary defense committees, 20th anniv.

Souvenir Sheet

ESSEN '80, 49th Intl. Philatelic Federation Congress — A635

Painting: *Portrait of a Lady,* by Ludger Tom Ring The Younger.

1980, Oct. 2 **Litho.** ***Perf. 13***

2356	A635	50c	multi	3.75	1.25

Early Locomotives — A636

1980, Oct. 15

2357	A636	1c	Josefa	.25	.20
2358	A636	2c	Chaparra Sugar Co. No. 22	.25	.20
2359	A636	7c	Steam storage locomotive	.25	.20
2360	A636	10c	2-4-2 locomotive	.40	.20
2361	A636	13c	2-4-0 locomotive	.65	.20
2362	A636	30c	Oil combustion engine, 1909	1.60	.60
			Nos. 2357-2362 (6)	3.40	1.60

Lighthouses A637

1980, Oct. 30

2363	A637	3c	Roncali, San Antonio	.20	.20
2364	A637	13c	Jagua, Cienfuegos	.70	.20
2365	A637	30c	Maisi Point, Guantanamo	1.60	.20
			Nos. 2363-2365 (3)	2.50	.60

See Nos. 2440-2442, 2553-2555, 2614-2616.

Victory of Cuban Athletes at the 1980 Summer Olympics, Moscow — A638

1980, Nov. 10 Litho. ***Perf. 12½x12***

2366 A638 13c Bronze medals .50 .20
2367 A638 30c Silver medals 1.10 .25
2368 A638 50c Gold medals 2.25 .50
Nos. 2366-2368 (3) 3.85 .95

Nos. 2366-2368 each printed se-tenant with label containing statistical data.

Wildflowers A639

1980, Nov. 20 ***Perf. 13***

2369 A639 1c *Pancratium arenicolum* .20 .20
2370 A639 4c *Urechites lutea* .20 .20
2371 A639 6c *Solanum elaegnifolium* .25 .20
2372 A639 10c *Hamelia patens* .45 .20
2373 A639 13c *Morinda royoc* .70 .20
2374 A639 30c *Centrosema virginianum* 2.00 .30
Nos. 2369-2374 (6) 3.80 1.30

Souvenir Sheet

7th Natl. Stamp Exhibition — A640

1980, Nov. 22

2375 A640 50c Mail train 3.00 1.25

2nd Communist Party Congress A641

1980, Dec. 17

2376 A641 3c shown .20 .20
2377 A641 13c Industry, communication .40 .20
2378 A641 30c Athletics, elderly, education 1.10 .20
Nos. 2376-2378 (3) 1.70 .60

Paintings in the Natl. Museum of Art A642

Designs: 1c, *Lady Mayo,* by Anton Van Dyck, vert. 6c, *The Spinner,* by Giovanni Battista Piazzeta, vert. 10c, *Daniel Collyer,* by Francis Cotes, vert. 13c, *Gardens, Palma de Mallorca,* by Santiago Rusinol Prats. 20c, *Landscape with Roadway and Houses,* by Frederick Waters Watts. 50c, *Landscape with Sheep,* by Jean-Francois Millet.

1981, Jan. 20

2379 A642 1c multi .20 .20
2380 A642 6c multi .20 .20
2381 A642 10c multi .50 .20
2382 A642 13c multi .60 .20
2383 A642 20c multi 1.00 .30
2384 A642 50c multi 2.10 .60
Nos. 2379-2384 (6) 4.60 1.70

See Nos. 2510-2515.

Pelagic Fish A643

1981, Feb. 25

2385 A643 1c *Isurus oxyrhynchus* .25 .20
2386 A643 3c *Lampris regius* .25 .20
2387 A643 10c *Istiophorus platypterus* .45 .20
2388 A643 13c *Mola mola,* vert. 1.75 .20
2389 A643 30c *Coruphaena hippurus* 1.10 .30
2390 A643 50c *Tetrapturus albidus* 2.00 .70
Nos. 2385-2390 (6) 5.80 1.80

1982 World Cup Soccer Championships, Spain — A644

Globe and various soccer players.

1981, Mar. 20 ***Perf. 12½***

2391 A644 1c multi .20 .20
2392 A644 2c multi .20 .20
2393 A644 3c multi .20 .20
2394 A644 10c multi, vert. .45 .20
2395 A644 13c multi, vert. .45 .20
2396 A644 50c multi 1.75 .60
Nos. 2391-2396 (6) 3.25 1.60

Souvenir Sheet

Perf. 13

2397 A644 1p Soccer ball, flag 4.75 1.60

No. 2397 contains one 40x32mm stamp.

Opening of the 1st Kindergarten, 20th Anniv. — A645

1981, Apr. 10 ***Perf. 13***

2398 A645 3c multi .40 .20

1st Man in Space, 20th Anniv. A646

Designs: 1c, Jules Verne, Russian scientist Konstantin E. Tsiolkovski, and Sergei P. Korolev, designer of the 1st Soviet spacecraft, vert. 2c, Yuri Gagarin, 1st man in space. 3c, Valentina Tereshkova, 1st woman in space, and *Vostok 6.* 5c, Aleksei A. Leonov, 1st man to walk in space. 13c, Konstantin Feoktistov, Boris Yegorov and Vladimir Komarov, *Voskhod 1* crew, 1st 3-man orbital flight. 30c, Valeri Ryumen and Leonid Popov, set a space endurance record. 50c, Arnaldo Tamayo, 1st Cuban cosmonaut, and Soviet cosmonaut Yuri Romanenko on joint space flight, vert.

1981, Apr. 12 ***Perf. 12½***

2399 A646 1c multi .20 .20
2400 A646 2c multi .20 .20
2401 A646 3c multi .20 .20
2402 A646 5c multi .20 .20
2403 A646 13c multi .45 .20
2404 A646 30c multi 1.00 .35
2405 A646 50c multi 2.25 .60
Nos. 2399-2405 (7) 4.50 1.95

A647

Designs: 3c, Rocket, aircraft. 13c, Hand raising gun.

1981, Apr. 19 Litho. ***Perf. 13***

2406 A647 3c multi, vert. .20 .20
2407 A647 13c multi, vert. .40 .20
2408 A647 30c multi .95 .60
Nos. 2406-2408 (3) 1.55 1.00

Creation of armed forces (DAAFAR) (3c), Bay of Pigs Invasion, 20th Anniv. (13c), Proclamation of the socialist revolution (30c).

Attack on Goicuria Barracks, 25th Anniv. — A648

1981, Apr. 29

2409 A648 3c multi .30 .20

Natl. Assoc. of Small Farmers (ANAP), 20th Anniv. A649

1981, May 17

2410 A649 3c multi .50 .20

Souvenir Sheet

WIPA '81 — A650

1981, May 22 **Litho.**

2411 A650 50c Austria No. 643 2.50 .90

Fighting Cocks A651

1981, May 25 ***Perf. 12½x13, 13x12½***

2412 A651 1c Canelo, vert. .20 .20
2413 A651 3c Cenizo .20 .20
2414 A651 7c Blanco, vert. .25 .20
2415 A651 13c Pinto, vert. .50 .20
2416 A651 30c Giro 1.50 .35
2417 A651 50c Jabao, vert. 2.25 .60
Nos. 2412-2417 (6) 4.90 1.75

Ministry of the Interior, 20th Anniv. — A652

1981, June 6 ***Perf. 13***

2418 A652 13c multi .40 .20

Souvenir Sheet

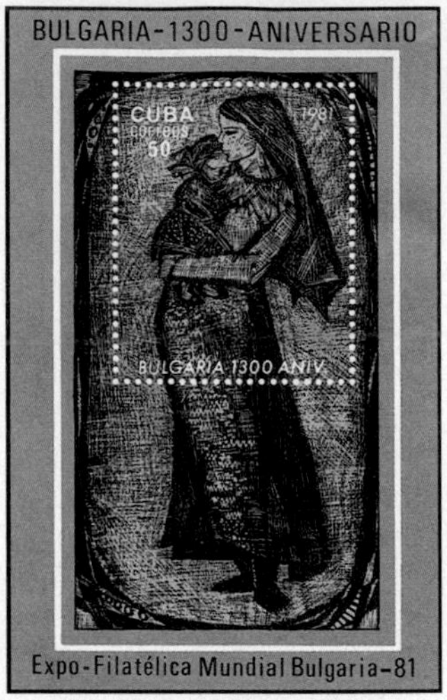

Mother and Child, by Zlatka Dabova — A653

1981, June 14

2419 A653 50c gold, sil & blk 2.25 .80

Bulgaria, 1300th anniv. BULGARIA '81 phil. exhib.

Horse-drawn Carriages — A654

1981, June 25

2420 A654 1c Streetcar .20 .20
2421 A654 4c Bus .20 .20
2422 A654 9c Breake .25 .20
2423 A654 13c Landau .40 .20
2424 A654 30c Phaeton 1.40 .45
2425 A654 50c Funeral coach 2.50 .75
Nos. 2420-2425 (6) 4.95 2.00

House in the Country, by Mario Caridad — A655

1981, July 15 ***Perf. 12½***

2426 A655 30c multi 1.25 .30

Intl. Year of the Disabled.

Sandinistas, 25th Anniv. — A656

1981, July 23 *Perf. 13*

2427 A656 13c multi .50 .20

State Institutions, 20th Annivs. — A657

1981, July 26 *Perf. 12½*

2428 A657 3c multi .20 .20
2429 A657 13c multi, diff. .45 .20
2430 A657 30c multi, diff. 1.25 .25
Nos. 2428-2430 (3) 1.90 .65

Institute for Sports, Physical Education and Recreation (3c); Radio Havana (13c); and Ministry of Foreign Trade (MINCEX) (30c).

Carlos J. Finlay and Cent. of His Theory of Biological Vectors — A658

1981, Aug. 14 *Perf. 13*

2431 A658 13c multi 1.00 .20

Nonaligned Countries Movement, 20th Anniv. — A659

1981, Sept. 1

2432 A659 50c multi 1.50 .80

Horses — A660

Illustration reduced. Nos. 2433-2437 vert.

1981, Sept. 15 *Perf. 13*

Size: 29x40mm

2433 A660 1c multi .20 .20
2434 A660 3c multi, diff. .20 .20
2435 A660 8c multi, diff. .20 .20
2436 A660 13c multi, diff. .35 .20
2437 A660 30c multi, diff. 1.10 .45
Nos. 2433-2437 (5) 2.05 1.25

Size: 68x27mm

Perf. 12½

2438 A660 50c Herd 1.75 .75

Souvenir Sheet

Idyll in a Tea House, by Kitagawa Utamaro — A661

1981, Oct. 9 *Perf. 13*

2439 A661 50c multi 2.75 1.25

PHILATOKYO '81.

Lighthouse Type of 1980

1981, Oct. 15 **Litho.**

2440 A637 3c North Rock .20 .20
2441 A637 13c Lucrecia Point .50 .20
2442 A637 40c East Guano 2.10 .30
Nos. 2440-2442 (3) 2.80 .70

Jose Marti Natl. Library, 80th Anniv. — A662

Sugar mills, lithographs from *Los Ingenios,* by Eduardo Laplante (b. 1818): 3c, Flor de Cuba, 1838. 13c, El Progreso, 1845. 30c, Santa Teresa, 1847.

1981, Oct. 18 *Perf. 12½x12*

2443 A662 3c multi .20 .20
2444 A662 13c multi .35 .20
2445 A662 30c multi 1.25 .55
Nos. 2443-2445 (3) 1.80 .95

Pablo Picasso (b. 1881) and No. 1263 A663

1981, Oct. 25 *Perf. 12½x13*

2446 A663 30c multi 1.25 .40

Souvenir Sheet

ESPAMER '81, Buenos Aires — A664

1981, Nov. 13 *Perf. 13*

2447 A664 1p Packet 4.00 1.60

Art Type of 1969

Paintings in the Napoleon Museum: 1c, *Napoleon in Coronation Costume,* anonymous. 3c, *Napoleon with Landscape in the Background,* by Jean Horace Vernet. 10c, *Bonaparte in Egypt,* by Edouard Detaille. 13c, *Napoleon on Horseback,* by Hippolyte Bellange. 30c, *Napoleon in Normandy,* by Bellange. 50c, *Death of Napoleon,* anonymous.

1981, Dec. 1 *Perf. 12½*

Sizes: 42x58mm, 58x42mm (3c, 13c, 30c, 50c)

2448 A385 1c multi .20 .20
2449 A385 3c multi, horiz. .20 .20
2450 A385 10c multi .40 .20
2451 A385 13c multi, horiz. .40 .20
2452 A385 30c multi, horiz. 1.25 .40
2453 A385 50c multi, horiz. 2.10 .70
Nos. 2448-2453 (6) 4.55 1.90

Napoleon Museum, 20th anniv.

25th Annivs. A665

1981, Dec. 2 *Perf. 13*

2454 A665 3c Revolutionaries, vert. .20 .20
2455 A665 20c Marksman .45 .20
2456 A665 1p Yacht *Granma* 5.25 1.40
Nos. 2454-2456 (3) 5.90 1.80

November 30th insurrection (3c); creation of the revolutionary armed forces (20c); and disembarking of revolutionary forces (1p).

Fauna — A666

1981, Dec. 14 **Litho.** *Perf. 12½x12*

2457 A666 1c Hummingbird .20 .20
2458 A666 2c Parakeet .20 .20
2459 A666 5c Hutia .20 .20
2460 A666 20c Almiqui .65 .20
2461 A666 35c Manatee 1.25 .25
2462 A666 40c Crocodile 1.00 .55
Nos. 2457-2462 (6) 3.50 1.60

Fernando Ortiz, Folklorist, Birth Cent. A667

1981, Dec. 20 *Perf. 12½x13*

2463 A667 3c Portrait by Jorge Arche y Silva .20 .20
2464 A667 10c Hanging idol .40 .20
2465 A667 30c Arara drum 1.50 .45
2466 A667 50c Chango statue 2.25 .70
Nos. 2463-2466 (4) 4.35 1.55

Literacy Campaign, 20th Anniv. — A668

1981, Dec. 25 *Perf. 12½x12*

2467 5c Conrado Benitez .30 .20
2468 5c Manuel Asunce .30 .20
a. A668 Pair, #2467-2468 .75 .25
Nos. 2467-2468 (2) .60 .40

A669

1982 World Cup Soccer Championships, Spain — A670

Various athletes.

1982, Jan. 15 *Perf. 13*

2469 A669 1c multi, vert. .20 .20
2470 A669 2c multi, vert. .20 .20
2471 A669 5c multi, vert. .20 .20
2472 A669 10c multi, vert. .30 .20
2473 A669 20c shown .70 .20
2474 A669 40c multi 1.25 .50
2475 A669 50c multi, vert. 1.60 .70
Nos. 2469-2475 (7) 4.45 2.20

Souvenir Sheet

2476 A670 1p shown 5.00 1.60

No. 2476 contains one 32x40mm stamp.

10th World Trade Unions Congress, Havana — A671

1982, Feb. 10 **Litho.**

2477 A671 30c Lazaro Pena, delegate 1.00 .25

Butterflies — A672

1982, Feb. 25 *Perf. 12½*

2478 A672 1c *Euptoieta hegesia* .20 .20
2479 A672 4c *Metamorpha stelenes insularis* .20 .20
2480 A672 5c *Heliconius charithonius ramsdeni* .20 .20
2481 A672 20c *Phoebis avellaneda* 1.40 .25
2482 A672 30c *Hamadryas ferox diasia* 2.25 .40
2483 A672 50c *Marpesia eleuchea* 4.00 .70
Nos. 2478-2483 (6) 8.25 1.95

Exports — A673

3c, Sugar (processing plant). 4c, Lobster (fishing boat). 6c, Canned fruits. 7c, Agricultural machinery. 8c, Nickel (passenger jet, industrial complex, car). 9c, Rum. 10c, Coffee. 30c, Fresh fruit. 50c, Tobacco. 1p, Cement. Nos. 2489-2493 vert.

1982, Feb. 26 *Perf. 12x12½, 12½x12*

2484	A673	3c	lt grn	.20	.20
2485	A673	4c	car rose	.20	.20
2486	A673	6c	dull blue	.25	.20
2487	A673	7c	brt org	.40	.20
2488	A673	8c	brt vio	.40	.20
2489	A673	9c	slate	.40	.20
2490	A673	10c	dull red brn	.50	.20
2491	A673	30c	bister	.75	.25
2492	A673	50c	orange	2.10	.40
2493	A673	1p	olive bister	4.00	1.25
			Nos. 2484-2493 (10)	9.20	3.30

Tulips A674

1982, Mar. 30 *Perf. 12½x13*

2494	A674	1c	Greenland	.20	.20
2495	A674	3c	Mariette	.25	.20
2496	A674	8c	Ringo	.25	.20
2497	A674	20c	La Tulipe Noire	.80	.20
2498	A674	30c	Jewel of Spring	1.40	.25
2499	A674	50c	Orange Parrot	1.90	.60
			Nos. 2494-2499 (6)	4.80	1.65

Communist Youth Organization, 20th Anniv. — A675

1982, Apr. 4 *Perf. 13*

2500	A675	5c	multi	.30	.20

2nd UN Congress on the Peaceful Use of Outer Space — A676

1982, Apr. 12

2501	A676	1c	*Mars*	.20	.20
2502	A676	3c	*Venera*	.20	.20
2503	A676	6c	*Salyut-Soyuz* link-up	.25	.20
2504	A676	20c	*Lunokhod* moon vehicle	.50	.20
2505	A676	30c	*Venera* with heat shield	1.40	.30
2506	A676	50c	*Intelsat-4a*	2.00	.60
			Nos. 2501-2506 (6)	4.55	1.70

Cover A677

1982, Apr. 24 *Perf. 12½x12*

2507	A677	20c	Havana-Veracruz	.75	.25
2508	A677	30c	Havana-Tampico	1.25	.25

Stamp Day. English post office, 1842-1877 (20c); and French post office, 1862-1877 (30c).

Broadcasting and Television Institute (ICRT), 20th Anniv. — A678

1982, May 24 *Perf. 12x12½*

2509	A678	30c	multi	1.00	.25

Art Type of 1981
With Larger Type

Paintings in the Natl. Museum of Art: 1c, *Portrait of a Youth* (girl), by Jean B. Greuze, vert. 3c, *Procession in Brittany,* by Jules Breton. 9c, *Landscape,* by Jean Piliment. 20c, *Late Afternoon,* by William A. Bourgueran, vert. 30c, *Tiger,* by Ferdinand V.E. Delacroix. 40c, *The Chair,* by Wilfredo Lam, vert.

Perf. 13, 13x12½ (3c), 12x12½ (20c, 40c), 12½x12 (30c)

1982, May 31 **Litho.**

2510	A642	1c	29x40mm	.20	.20
2511	A642	3c	46x36mm	.20	.20
2512	A642	9c	40x29mm	.25	.20
2513	A642	20c	27x42mm	.65	.25
2514	A642	30c	42x27mm	1.25	.40
2515	A642	40c	27x42mm	2.00	.40
			Nos. 2510-2515 (6)	4.55	1.65

Souvenir Sheet

PHILEXFRANCE '82 — A679

1982, June 7 *Perf. 13*

2516	A679	1p	Steamship *Louisiana* at St. Nazaire	5.00	1.60

DEPORFILEX '82 — A680

1982, June 10 *Perf. 13x12½*

2517	A680	20c	Hurdler, No. 300	1.50	.25

Reptiles A681

1982, June 15 *Perf. 13*

2518	A681	1c	*Pseudemys decussata*	.20	.20
2519	A681	2c	*Tropidophis pardalis*	.20	.20
2520	A681	3c	*Crocodylus rhombifer*	.25	.20
2521	A681	20c	*Cyclura nubila*	.85	.20
2522	A681	30c	*Anolis allisonis*	1.25	.30
2523	A681	50c	*Alsophis cantherigerus*	2.40	.50
			Nos. 2518-2523 (6)	5.15	1.60

George Dimitrov (1882-1949), Bulgarian Prime Minister — A682

1982, June 18

2524	A682	30c	multi	1.00	.25

Koch, Bacillus A683

1982, July 18

2525	A683	20c	multi	1.25	.25

Discovery of the tubercle bacillus by Dr. Robert Koch, cent.

14th Central American and Caribbean Games — A684

1982, Aug. 1

2526	A684	1c	Baseball	.20	.20
2527	A684	2c	Boxing	.20	.20
2528	A684	10c	Water polo	.35	.20
2529	A684	20c	Javelin	.80	.30
2530	A684	35c	Weight lifting	1.25	.45
2531	A684	50c	Volleyball	2.00	.55
			Nos. 2526-2531 (6)	4.80	1.90

Hydraulic Development Plan, 20th Anniv. — A685

5c, Fruit, *Eichornia crassipes,* ship. 20c, Arid soil, *Nymphaea alba,* irrigation & reservoir systems.

1982, Aug. 9

2532	A685	5c	multi	.35	.20
2533	A685	20c	multi	.90	.25

Souvenir Sheet

DEPORFILEX '82, Intl. Stamp and Coin Exhibition — A686

1982, Aug. 10 **Litho.**

2534	A686	1p	Cuco, character trademark	4.75	1.60

14th Central American and Caribbean Games.

Namibia Day — A687

1982, Aug. 26

2535	A687	50c	multi	1.75	.75

1982 World Cup Soccer Championships, Spain — A688

Various athletes.

1982, Aug. 30

2536	A688	5c	multi	.20	.20
2537	A688	20c	multi	.75	.30
2538	A688	30c	multi	1.10	.40
2539	A688	50c	multi	1.90	.80
			Nos. 2536-2539 (4)	3.95	1.70

Also exist in miniature sheets of 16 + 9 labels containing 4 each Nos. 2536-2539 in blocks of 4.

Natl. Folklore Ensemble, 20th Anniv. — A689

Paintings by V.P. Landaluze.

1982, Sept. 10

2540	A689	20c	*Little Devil,* vert.	.80	.25
2541	A689	30c	*Day of Kings*	1.10	.45

Prehistoric Fauna — A690

1982, Sept. 15 **Litho.**

2542	A690	1c	*Ornimegalonyx oteroi,* vert.	.60	.20
2543	A690	5c	*Crocodylus rhombifer*	.20	.20
2544	A690	7c	*Aquila borrasi,* vert.	2.50	.35
2545	A690	20c	*Geocapromys colombianus*	.60	.20
2546	A690	35c	*Megalocnus rodens,* vert.	1.00	.40
2547	A690	50c	*Nesophontes micrus*	1.40	.55
			Nos. 2542-2547 (6)	6.30	1.90

15th Death Anniv. of Che Guevara — A691

1982, Oct. 8 *Perf. 13x12½*

2548 A691 20c multi .70 .25

Discovery of America, 490th Anniv. — A692

1982, Oct. 12 *Perf. 13*

2549 A692 5c shown 1.10 .20
2550 A692 20c *Santa Maria,* vert. 1.25 .20
2551 A692 35c *Pinta,* vert. 1.90 .20
2552 A692 50c *Nina,* vert. 2.40 .30
Nos. 2549-2552 (4) 6.65 .90

Lighthouse Type of 1980

1982, Oct. 25

2553 A637 5c Jutias Caye 1.00 .20
2554 A637 20c Paredon Grande Caye 2.75 .20
2555 A637 30c Morro Santiago de Cuba 3.75 .45
Nos. 2553-2555 (3) 7.50 .85

George Washington, 250th Birth Anniv. — A693

Designs: Quotations and anonymous oil paintings, 18th-19th cent.

1982, Oct. 29 *Perf. 12x12½*

2556 A693 5c multi .25 .20
2557 A693 20c multi, diff. .75 .20

Souvenir Sheet

8th Natl. Philatelic Exposition, Ciego de Avila — A694

1982, Nov. 13

2558 A694 1p Paddle steamer *Almendares* 5.00 1.60

8th Congress of the Cuban Philatelic Federation, Nov. 13-22.

Lenin Natl. Park, 10th Anniv. A695

1982, Dec. 28

2559 A695 5c multi .40 .20

Chess Champion Jose Raul Capablanca and King — A696

1982, Dec. 29

2560 A696 5c shown .25 .20
2561 A696 20c Rook 1.10 .20
2562 A696 30c Knight 1.40 .30
2563 A696 50c Queen 2.25 .50
a. Bklt. pane of 4, Nos. 2560-2563 20.00 10.00
Nos. 2560-2563 (4) 5.00 1.20

Exist in sheets of 4+2 labels picturing chessmen.

USSR, 60th Anniv. — A697

1982, Dec. 30 *Perf. 13x12½*

2564 A697 30c multi 1.25 .25

World Communications Year — A698

1983, Jan. 24 **Litho.** *Perf. 13*

2565 A698 20c multi .75 .25

No. 507 and Birthplace — A699

1983, Jan. 28 *Perf. 13x12½*

2566 A699 5c multi .30 .20

Jose Marti (b. 1853), writer, revolution leader.

1984 Summer Olympics, Los Angeles A700

1983, Jan. 31 *Perf. 13*

2567 A700 1c Javelin .20 .20
2568 A700 5c Volleyball .25 .20
2569 A700 6c Basketball .25 .20
2570 A700 20c Weight lifting .80 .20
2571 A700 30c Wrestling 1.10 .40
2572 A700 50c Boxing 1.75 .60
a. Block of 6, #2567-2572 4.50 2.00
Nos. 2567-2572 (6) 4.35 1.80

Souvenir Sheet

Perf. 13½x13

2573 A700 1p Judo 5.00 2.50

No. 2573 contains one 32x40mm stamp.

Radio Rebelde, 25th Anniv. — A701

1983, Feb. 24 *Perf. 13*

2574 A701 20c multi .70 .20

Karl Marx, Death Cent. A702

1983, Mar. 14

2575 A702 30c multi 1.00 .40

1st Manned Balloon Flight, Bicent. — A703

Various balloons.

1983, Mar. 30

2576 A703 1c multi .20 .20
2577 A703 3c multi .20 .20
2578 A703 5c multi .20 .20
2579 A703 7c multi .35 .20
2580 A703 30c multi 2.10 .60
2581 A703 50c multi 2.10 .60
Nos. 2576-2581 (6) 5.15 2.00

Souvenir Sheet

2582 A703 1p Jose D. Blino 4.00 2.00

No. 2582 contains one 32x40mm stamp.

Cosmonauts' Day — A704

1983, Apr. 12 **Litho.**

2583 A704 1c *Vostok 1* .20 .20
2584 A704 4c Satellite *Frances D1* .20 .20
2585 A704 5c *Mars 2* .20 .20
2586 A704 20c *Soyuz* .75 .20
2587 A704 30c Meteorological satellite 1.10 .50
2588 A704 50c Intercosmos satellite 1.75 .70
Nos. 2583-2588 (6) 4.20 2.00

Stamp Day A705

1983, Apr. 24

2589 A705 20c Havana-Key West cover .75 .30
2590 A705 30c Spain-Havana cover 1.25 .30

1st Intl. airmail services.

Souvenir Sheet

TEMBAL '83, Basel — A706

1983, May 21 *Perf. 13½x13*

2591 A706 1p Weasel 5.00 2.50

Simon Bolivar, Liberator of South America A707

1983, July 24 *Perf. 12½x13*

2592 A707 5c Jose Rafael de las Heras .20 .20
2593 A707 20c Bolivar .60 .20

Attack of Moncada Barracks, 30th Anniv. — A708

Designs: 5c, Jose Marti, Moncada barracks. 20c, Abel Santamaria, Jose Luis Tasende and Boris Luis Santa Coloma, martyrs, vert. 30c, *History Will Absolve Me,* declaration of Fidel Castro, vert.

1983, July 26 *Perf. 13*

2594 A708 5c multi .20 .20
2595 A708 20c multi .70 .20
2596 A708 30c multi .90 .50
Nos. 2594-2596 (3) 1.80 .90

Souvenir Sheet

Alberto Santos-Dumont (1873-1932) — A709

1983, July 29 *Perf. 13x13½*

2597 A709 1p Dumont's aircraft 5.00 2.50

BRASILIANA '83, Rio; 140th anniv. of 1st stamp issued in the Americas.

9th Pan American Games, Caracas — A710

1983, Aug. 14 *Perf. 13x12½*

2598 A710 1c Weight lifting .20 .20
2599 A710 2c Volleyball .20 .20
2600 A710 3c Baseball .20 .20
2601 A710 20c High jump .75 .20
2602 A710 30c Basketball 1.10 .50
2603 A710 50c Boxing 1.75 .70
Nos. 2598-2603 (6) 4.20 2.00

Port, by Claude Joseph Vernet — A711

1983, Sept. 5

2604 A711 30c multi 1.40 .35

French alliance, cent.

Pres. Salvador Allende of Chile (d. 1973) — A712

1983, Sept. 12

2605 A712 20c multi .70 .20

1st Congress of Farmers at Arms, 25th Anniv. — A713

1983, Sept. 21 *Perf. 12½x12*

2606 A713 5c multi .25 .20

Raphael, 500th Birth Anniv. — A714

1983, Sept. 30 **Litho.** *Perf. 13*

2607 A714 1c *Girl with Veil* .20 .20
2608 A714 2c *The Cardinal* .20 .20
2609 A714 5c *Francesco M. Della Rovere* .20 .20
2610 A714 20c *Portrait of a Youth* .75 .20
2611 A714 30c *Magdalena Doni* 1.10 .25
2612 A714 50c *La Fornarina* 1.75 .65
Nos. 2607-2612 (6) 4.20 1.70

State Quality Seal A715

1983, Oct. 14

2613 A715 5c multi .25 .20

Lighthouse Type of 1980

1983, Oct. 20

2614 A637 5c Carapachibey .20 .20
2615 A637 20c Cadiz Bay .80 .30
2616 A637 30c Gobernadora Point 2.00 .50
Nos. 2614-2616 (3) 3.00 1.00

Turtles A716

1983, Nov. 15

2617 A716 1c *Eretmochelys imbricata* .20 .20
2618 A716 2c *Lepidochelys kempi* .20 .20
2619 A716 5c *Chrysemys decussata* .25 .20
2620 A716 20c *Caretta caretta* .80 .20
2621 A716 30c *Chelonia mydas* 1.40 .25
2622 A716 50c *Dermochelys coriacea* 2.75 .75
Nos. 2617-2622 (6) 5.60 1.80

World Communications Year — A717

1983, Nov. 23

2623 A717 1c Bell's Gallow Frame, telephone .20 .20
2624 A717 5c Telegram, airmail .20 .20
2625 A717 10c Satellite, satellite dish .45 .20
2626 A717 20c Television, radio .75 .20
2627 A717 30c 24th Communications conf. 1.10 .40
Nos. 2623-2627 (5) 2.70 1.20

Nos. 319 and 990 A718

1983, Dec. 3 *Perf. 13x12½*

2628 A718 20c multi .70 .25

See note after No. 320.

Flowers, Birds A719

Flowers A720

1983, Dec. 20 *Perf. 13*

2629 A719 5c *Opuntia dillenii* .40 .20
2630 A719 5c *Euphorbia podocarpifolia* .40 .20
2631 A719 5c *Dinema cubincola* .40 .20
2632 A719 5c *Guaiacum officinale* .40 .20
2633 A719 5c *Magnolia cubensis* .40 .20
a. Strip of 5, Nos. 2629-2633 3.00 2.00
2634 A719 5c *Jatropha angustifolia* .40 .20
2635 A719 5c *Cochlospermum vitifolium* .40 .20
2636 A719 5c *Tabebuia lepidota* .40 .20
2637 A719 5c *Kalmiella ericoides* .40 .20
2638 A719 5c *Jatropha integerrima* .40 .20
2639 A719 5c *Melocactus actinacanthus* .40 .20
2640 A719 5c *Cordia sebestana* .40 .20
2641 A719 5c *Tabernaemontana apoda* .40 .20
2642 A719 5c *Lantana camara* .40 .20
2643 A719 5c *Cordia gerascanthus* .40 .20
a. Block of 10, Nos. 2634-2643 5.00 4.00
2644 A719 5c *Tiaris canora* .40 .20
2645 A719 5c *Phaethon lepturus* .40 .20
2646 A719 5c *Myadestes elisabeth* .40 .20
2647 A719 5c *Saurothera merlini* .40 .20
2648 A719 5c *Polioptila lembeyei* .40 .20
a. Strip of 5, Nos. 2644-2648 3.00 2.00
2649 A719 5c *Mellisuga helenae* .40 .20
2650 A719 5c *Mimus polyglottos* .40 .20
2651 A719 5c *Todus multicolor* .40 .20
2652 A719 5c *Amazona leucocephala* .40 .20
2653 A719 5c *Ferminia cerverai* .40 .20
2654 A719 5c *Pelecanus occidentalis* .40 .20
2655 A719 5c *Melanerpes superciliaris* .40 .20
2656 A719 5c *Mimocichla plumbea* .40 .20
2657 A719 5c *Aratinga euops* .40 .20
2658 A719 5c *Sturnella magna* .40 .20
a. Block of 10, Nos. 2649-2658 5.00 4.00
Nos. 2629-2658 (30) 12.00 6.00

Souvenir Sheets

2658B A719 100c *Hedychium coronarium* 5.00 4.50
2658C A719 100c *Priotelus temnurus* 5.00 4.50

1983, Dec. 30 *Perf. 12½*

2659 A720 60c Tobacco 1.75 .55
2660 A720 70c Lily 2.25 .60
2661 A720 80c Mariposa 2.50 .70
2662 A720 90c Orchid 3.50 1.00
Nos. 2659-2662 (4) 10.00 2.85

25th Anniv. of the Revolution — A721

1983, Dec. 31 **Litho.** *Perf. 13*

2663 A721 5c shown .20 .20
2664 A721 20c Flags, Santa Clara Rlwy. tracks .80 .20

25th Anniv. of the Revolution — A722

1984, Jan. 8

2665 20c Guevara, Castro .70 .25
2666 20c Star .70 .25
2667 20c PCC emblem, workers 1.75 .80
a. A722 Strip of 3, #2665-2667 3.25 1.50
Nos. 2665-2667 (3) 3.15 1.30

Lenin, 60th Death Anniv. A723

1984, Jan. 21 *Perf. 12½x12*

2668 A723 30p Spasski Tower, Russia Nos. 295, 265 1.25 .25

Cuban Labor Union, 45th Anniv. A724

1984, Jan. 28 *Perf. 13*

2669 A724 5c multi .25 .20

Butterflies — A725

1984, Jan. 31 *Perf. 13x12½*

2670 A725 1c *Ixias balice* .20 .20
2671 A725 2c *Phoebis avellaneda* .20 .20
2672 A725 3c *Anthocaris sara* .20 .20
2673 A725 5c *Victorina* .20 .20

2674 A725 20c *Heliconius cydno cydnides* .75 .20
2675 A725 30c *Parides gundlachianus calzadillae* 1.40 .55
2676 A725 50c *Catagramma sorana* 2.25 .80
Nos. 2670-2676 (7) 5.20 2.35

Marine Mammals — A726

1984, Feb. 15 ***Perf. 12x12½, 12½x12***
2677 A726 1c *Grampus griseus*, vert. .20 .20
2678 A726 2c *Delphinus delphis*, vert. .20 .20
2679 A726 5c *Physeter catodon* .20 .20
2680 A726 6c *Stenella plagiodon*, vert. .20 .20
2681 A726 10c *Pseudorca crassidens* .65 .20
2682 A726 30c *Tursiops truncatus*, vert. 1.50 .35
2683 A726 50c *Megaptera novaeangliae* 2.50 .60
Nos. 2677-2683 (7) 5.45 1.95

Augusto C. Sandino (1893-1934), Nicaraguan Revolutionary — A727

1984, Feb. 21 ***Perf. 13***
2684 A727 20c multi .70 .25

Red Cross in Cuba, 75th Anniv. — A728

1984, Mar. 10
2685 A728 30c Flag, No. 404 1.25 .35

Cuban Film Industry, 25th Anniv. A729

1984, Mar. 24
2686 A729 20c multi .80 .20

Caribbean Flowers — A730

1984, Mar. 29
2687 A730 1c *Brownea grandiceps* .20 .20
2688 A730 2c *Couroupita guianensis* .20 .20
2689 A730 5c *Triplaris surinamensis* .20 .20
2690 A730 20c *Amherstia nobilis* .70 .25
2691 A730 30c *Plumieria alba* 1.00 .35
2692 A730 50c *Delonix regia* 1.75 .65
Nos. 2687-2692 (6) 4.05 1.85

Cosmonauts' Day — A731

1984, Apr. 12
2693 A731 2c *Electron 1*, 1964 .20 .20
2694 A731 3c *Electron 2*, 1964 .20 .20
2695 A731 5c *Intercosmos 1*, 1969 .20 .20
2696 A731 10c *Mars 5*, 1974 .40 .20
2697 A731 30c *Soyuz*, 1969 1.00 .35
2698 A731 50c USSR-Bulgaria space flight, 1979 1.90 .65
Nos. 2693-2698 (6) 3.90 1.80

Souvenir Sheet
Perf. 12½
2699 A731 1p *Luna 1*, 1959 4.00 1.60

No. 2699 contains one 32x40mm stamp.

Mothers' Day — A732

1984, Apr. 19 ***Perf. 13***
2700 A732 20c Red roses .75 .20
2701 A732 20c Pink roses .75 .20

Stamp Day — A733

Designs: Mural, by R. Rodriguez Radillo (details).

1984, Apr. 24 ***Perf. 13x12½***
2702 A733 20c Mexican runner .80 .20
2703 A733 30c Egyptian boatman 1.10 .35

See Nos. 2787-2788, 2860-2861, 3025-3026, 3122-3123, 3213-3214.

Souvenir Sheet

ESPANA '84, Madrid — A734

1984, Apr. 27 ***Perf. 13x13½***
2704 A734 1p Clipper ship 4.75 1.60

Women's Basketball, 1984 Summer Olympics A735

1984, May 5 ***Perf. 13***
2705 A735 20c multi 1.25 .35

Agrarian Reform Act, 25th Anniv. — A736

1984, May 17 ***Perf. 13½x13***
2706 A736 5c multi .40 .20

Banco Popular de Ahorro, 1st Anniv. — A737

1984, May 18 ***Perf. 13***
2707 A737 5c multi .40 .20

Early Locomotives — A738

1984, June 11 ***Perf. 12½x12***
2708 A738 1c multi .20 .20
2709 A738 4c multi, diff. .20 .20
2710 A738 5c multi, diff. .20 .20
2711 A738 10c multi, diff. .35 .20
2712 A738 30c multi, diff. 1.10 .35
2713 A738 50c multi, diff. 2.00 .70
Nos. 2708-2713 (6) 4.05 1.85

Souvenir Sheet

19th UPU Congress, HAMBURG '84 — A739

1984, June 19 ***Perf. 13x13½***
2714 A739 1p Nos. 73, 232 4.50 2.10

Intl. Olympic Committee, 90th Anniv. — A740

1984, June 23 ***Perf. 13***
2715 A740 30c Coubertin, torchbearer 1.40 .35

Children's Day A741

1984, July 15 ***Perf. 12½x13***
2716 A741 5c multi .25 .20

1984 Summer Olympics, Los Angeles A742

1984, July 28 ***Perf. 13***
2717 A742 1c Wrestling .20 .20
2718 A742 3c Discus .20 .20
2719 A742 5c Volleyball .20 .20
2720 A742 20c Boxing .80 .25
2721 A742 30c Basketball 1.10 .35
2722 A742 50c Weight lifting 2.00 .65
Nos. 2717-2722 (6) 4.50 1.85

Souvenir Sheet
Perf. 12½
2723 A742 1p Baseball 4.50 1.60

No. 2723 contains one 32x40mm stamp.

Emilio Roig de Leuchsenring (1889-1964), Historian A743

1984, Aug. 8 ***Perf. 13***
2724 A743 5c multi .25 .20

Friendship Games, Aug. 18-26, Havana — A744

1984, Aug. 18
2725 A744 3c Volleyball .20 .20
2726 A744 5c Women's volleyball .35 .20
2727 A744 8c Water polo .35 .20
2728 A744 30c Boxing 1.25 .35
Nos. 2725-2728 (4) 2.15 .95

Cattle Breeding A745

1984, Sept. 20

2729	A745	2c	Artificial pastures	.20	.20
2730	A745	3c	Cuban carib	.20	.20
2731	A745	5c	Charolaise, vert.	.20	.20
2732	A745	30c	Cuban cebu, vert.	1.25	.40
2733	A745	50c	White-udder	2.25	.75
			Nos. 2729-2733 (5)	4.10	1.75

Souvenir Sheet

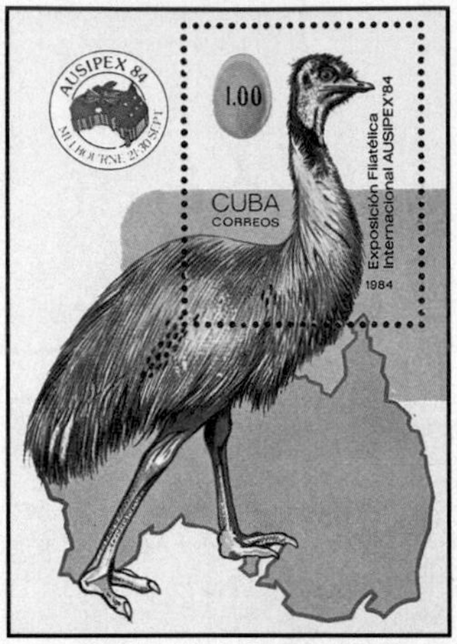

AUSIPEX '84, Sept. 21-30, Melbourne — A746

1984, Sept. 21 ***Perf. 12½***

2734 A746 1p Emu 5.00 2.75

Fauna — A747

1984, Oct. 10 ***Perf. 13***

2735	A747	1c	*Polymita*	.20	.20
2736	A747	2c	*Solenodon cubanus*	.20	.20
2737	A747	3c	*Alsophis cantherigerus*	.20	.20
2738	A747	4c	*Osteopilus septentrionalis*	.20	.20
2739	A747	5c	*Mellisuga helenae*	.50	.20
2740	A747	10c	*Capromys melanurus*	.30	.20
2741	A747	30c	*Todus multicolor*	2.25	.80
2742	A747	50c	Parrots (cotorra)	2.25	.60
			Nos. 2735-2742 (8)	6.10	2.60

Souvenir Sheet

ESPAMER '85, Havana A748

1984, Oct. 12

2743 Sheet of 4+2 labels 5.00 2.50
- *a.* A748 5c Ferdinand, Isabella .20 .20
- *b.* A748 20c Departure from Palos 1.50 .70
- *c.* A748 30c *Nina, Pinta, Santa Maria* 2.25 1.10
- *d.* A748 50c Landing in America 1.00 .50

Columbus Day.

Souvenir Sheet

9th Natl. Phil. Exhibition, Oct. 20-28, Santiago de Cuba — A749

1984, Oct. 20 ***Perf. 12½***

2744 A749 1p multicolored 4.50 1.60

Natl. Revolutionary Militia, 25th Anniv. — A750

1984, Oct. 26 ***Perf. 12½x13***

2745 A750 5c multi .30 .20

Disappearance of Camilo Cienfuegos, 25th Anniv. — A751

1984, Oct. 28 ***Perf. 13x12½***

2746 A751 5c multi .40 .20

UN Child Survival Campaign A752

1984, Nov. 11 ***Perf. 13***

2747 A752 5c Breast-feeding .40 .20

Classic Automobiles — A753

1984, Nov. 25

2748	A753	1c	1909 Morgan	.20	.20
2749	A753	2c	1922 Austin	.20	.20
2750	A753	5c	1903 De Dion-Bouton	.20	.20
2751	A753	20c	1908 Ford Model T	.95	.20
2752	A753	30c	1885 Benz	1.50	.35
2753	A753	50c	1910 Benz	2.75	.70
			Nos. 2748-2753 (6)	5.80	1.85

Postal Museum, 20th Anniv. — A754

1985, Jan. 2 ***Perf. 13x12½***

2754 A754 20c multi .75 .25

Portrait of Celia Sanchez, by E. Escobedo A755

1985, Jan. 11 ***Perf. 13***

2755 A755 5c multi .40 .20

Celia Sanchez (1920-1980), party leader.

PORTO '85, Intl. Pigeon Exhibition — A756

1985, Jan. 23

2756 A756 20c multi 1.25 .25

1986 World Cup Soccer Championships, Mexico — A757

Athletes and Flags of previous host nations.

1985, Jan. 25

2757	A757	1c	Chile, 1962	.20	.20
2758	A757	2c	Great Britain, 1966	.20	.20
2759	A757	3c	Mexico, 1970	.20	.20
2760	A757	4c	Federal Republic of Germany, 1974	.25	.20
2761	A757	5c	Argentina, 1978	.25	.20
2762	A757	30c	Spain, 1982	1.40	.35
2763	A757	50c	Sweden, 1958	2.25	.60
			Nos. 2757-2763 (7)	4.75	1.95

Souvenir Sheet

Perf. 12½

2764 A757 1p Mexico, 1986 4.00 2.00

No. 2764 contains one 40x32mm stamp.

Bacanao Natl. Park — A758

Dinosaurs.

1985, Feb. 14 ***Perf. 13x12½***

2765	A758	1c	Pteranodon	.30	.20
2766	A758	2c	Brontosaurus	.30	.20
2767	A758	4c	Iguanodontus	.30	.20
2768	A758	5c	Estegosaurus	.30	.20
2769	A758	8c	Monoclonius	.50	.20
2770	A758	30c	Corythosaurus	1.50	.35
2771	A758	50c	Tyrannosaurus	2.75	.55
			Nos. 2765-2771 (7)	5.95	1.90

13th Congress of the Postal Unions of the Americas, Havana — A759

Design: Uruguay #196, congress emblem and Brazil #287. Illustration reduced.

1985, Mar. 11 ***Perf. 12½x12***

2772 A759 20c multi .75 .25

ESPAMER '85 — A760

Indian activities: 1c, Playing ball. 2c, Medicine man preparing calumet and other ritual items. 5c, Net and spear fishing. 20c, Potter. 30c, Hunting. 50c, Hollowing-out canoe, decorating paddle. 1p, Cooking.

1985, Mar. 19 ***Perf. 12½x13***

2773	A760	1c	multi	.20	.20
2774	A760	2c	multi	.20	.20
2775	A760	5c	multi	.35	.20
2776	A760	20c	multi	.35	.20
2777	A760	30c	multi	.55	.30
2778	A760	50c	multi	2.50	.60
			Nos. 2773-2778 (6)	4.15	1.70

Souvenir Sheet

Perf. 12½

2779 A760 1p multi 5.00 1.60

No. 2779 contains one 32x40mm stamp.

An imperf. souvenir sheet exists containing Nos. 2773-2779.

Cosmonauts' Day — A761

Designs: 2c, Spacecraft orbiting Moon. 3c, Two spacecraft. 10c, Space walkers linked. 13c, Space walkers welding. 20c, *Vostok 2.* 50c, *Lunokhod 1* moon vehicle.

1985, Apr. 12 ***Perf. 13x12½***

2780	A761	2c	multi	.20	.20
2781	A761	3c	multi	.20	.20
2782	A761	10c	multi	.45	.20
2783	A761	13c	multi	.65	.20
2784	A761	20c	multi	.75	.25
2785	A761	50c	multi	2.50	.70
			Nos. 2780-2785 (6)	4.75	1.75

12th Youth and Students Festival, Moscow
A762

1985, Apr. 19 *Perf. 13*

2786 A762 30c Lenin Mausoleum .50 .35

Stamp Day Type of 1984

Mural, by R. Rodriguez Radillo (1967), details: 20c, Roman charioteer (courier of *Cursus Publicus*). 35c, Medieval nobleman, monks (monastic messenger mail).

1985, Apr. 24 *Perf. 13x12½*

2787 A733 20c multi .80 .20
2788 A733 35c multi 1.10 .30

Mothers' Day — A763

1985, May 2 *Perf. 13*

2789 A763 1c Peonies .20 .20
2790 A763 4c Carnations .20 .20
2791 A763 5c Dahlias .20 .20
2792 A763 13c Roses .45 .20
2793 A763 20c Roses, diff. .75 .20
2794 A763 50c Tulips 2.00 .50
Nos. 2789-2794 (6) 3.80 1.50

50th Death Anniv. of Antonio Guiteras and Carlos Aponte, Revolutionaries — A764

1985, May 9 *Perf. 12½x12*

2795 A764 5c multi .25 .25

End of WWII, 40th Anniv. A765

1985, May 10

2796 A765 5c shown .20 .20
2797 A765 20c Soviet memorial, Berlin-Treptow .65 .25
2798 A765 30c Dove 1.10 .35
Nos. 2796-2798 (3) 1.95 .80

Souvenir Sheet

ARGENTINA '85, Buenos Aires — A766

1985, June 5 *Perf. 13½x13*

2799 A766 1p *Vulture gryphus* 4.50 1.60

Motorcycle, Cent. — A767

1985, June 28 *Perf. 13*

2800 A767 2c 1885 Daimler .20 .20
2801 A767 5c 1910 Kaiser Tricycle .25 .20
2802 A767 10c 1925 Fanomobile .55 .20
2803 A767 30c 1926 Mars A20 1.50 .30
2804 A767 50c 1936 Simson BSW 2.75 .70
Nos. 2800-2804 (5) 5.25 1.60

Development of Health Care Since the Revolution — A768

1985, July 18 *Perf. 12½x12*

2805 A768 5c Hospitals .25 .20

Federation of Cuban Women (FMC), 25th Anniv. — A769

1985, Aug. 23

2806 A769 5c multi .25 .20

No. 2806 printed se-tenant with label picturing federation emblem.

Universiade Games, Japan — A770

1985, Aug. 27 *Perf. 13*

2807 A770 50c multi 1.75 .35

1st Havana Declaration, 25th Anniv. — A771

1985, Sept. 2

2808 A771 5c Jose Marti statue, revolutionaries .40 .20

Souvenir Sheet

ITALIA '85 — A772

1985, Sept. 25 *Perf. 12½*

2809 A772 1p Roman galley 5.00 1.60

Revolutionary Defense Committees (CDR), 25th Anniv. — A773

1985, Sept. 28 *Perf. 13*

2810 A773 5c multi .25 .20

Aquarium Fish — A774

1985, Sept. 30 **Litho.**

2811 A774 1c *Centropyge argi* .20 .20
2812 A774 3c *Holacanthus tricolor* .20 .20
2813 A774 5c *Chaetodon capistratus* .20 .20
2814 A774 10c *Chaetodon sedentarius* .35 .20
2815 A774 20c *Chaetodon ocellatus* .90 .40
2816 A774 50c *Holacanthus ciliaris* 2.25 1.40
Nos. 2811-2816 (6) 4.10 2.60

Communist Party Central Committee, 20th Anniv. — A775

1985, Oct. 1

2817 A775 5c multi .40 .20

Souvenir Sheet

EXFILNA '85 — A776

1985, Oct. 18

2818 A776 1p Spain No. C45, Cuba No. 387 5.00 2.50

UN, 40th Anniv. — A777

1985, Oct. 24

2819 A777 20c multi .90 .25

Sites on the UNESCO World Heritage List — A778

Designs: 2c, Plaza Vieja, 16th cent. 5c, Royal Army Castle, c. 1558. 20c, Havana Cathedral, c. 1748. 30c, Captains-General Palace (Havana City Museum), 1776. 50c, The Temple, 1827.

1985, Nov. 25

2820 A778 2c multi .25 .20
2821 A778 5c multi .25 .20
2822 A778 20c multi .95 .25
2823 A778 30c multi 1.50 .45
2824 A778 50c multi 2.40 .60
Nos. 2820-2824 (5) 5.35 1.70

1986 World Cup Soccer Championships, Mexico — A779

Various athletes.

1986, Jan. 20

2825 A779 1c multi .20 .20
2826 A779 4c multi .20 .20
2827 A779 5c multi .20 .20
2828 A779 10c multi .30 .20
2829 A779 30c multi 1.10 .25
2830 A779 50c multi 1.60 .40
Nos. 2825-2830 (6) 3.60 1.45

Souvenir Sheet

Perf. 13½x13

2831 A779 1p multi 4.50 2.25

No. 2831 contains one 32x40mm stamp.

3rd Communist Party Congress, Havana — A780

1986, Feb. 4 *Perf. 13*

2832 A780 5c shown .20 .20
2833 A780 20c Party and natl. flags, emblem 1.25 .25

Natl. Sports Institute (INDER), 25th Anniv. A781

1986, Feb. 23

2834 A781 5c multi .30 .20

A782 A783

1986, Feb. 23

2835 A782 5c multi .30 .20

Ministry of Domestic Trade, 25th anniv.

1986, Feb. 25 *Perf. 12½x12*

Exotic flowers in the Botanical Gardens.

2836 A783 1c *Tecomaria capensis* .20 .20
2837 A783 3c *Michelia champaca* .20 .20
2838 A783 5c *Thunbergia grandiflora* .20 .20
2839 A783 8c *Dendrobium phalaenopsis* .20 .20
2840 A783 30c *Allamanda violacea* .75 .25
2841 A783 50c *Rhodactus bleo* 1.10 .40
Nos. 2836-2841 (6) 2.65 1.45

Gundlach and Birds — A784

1986, Mar. 14 Litho. *Perf. 13½x13*

2842 A784 1c *Agelaius assimilis* .30 .20
2843 A784 3c *Dendroica pityophila* .30 .20
2844 A784 7c *Myiarchus sagrae* .50 .35
2845 A784 9c *Dendroica petechia gundlachi* .65 .40
2846 A784 30c *Geotrygon caniceps* 2.50 1.50
2847 A784 50c *Colaptes auratus chrysocaulosus* 4.00 2.50
Nos. 2842-2847 (6) 8.25 5.15

Juan Cristobal Gundlach (d. 1896), ornithologist.

Pioneers Youth Organization, 25th Anniv. — A785

1986, Apr. 3 *Perf. 13*

2848 A785 5c Induction .30 .20

150th Birth Anniv. of Maximo Gomez — A786

1986, Apr. 4

2849 A786 20c multi .90 .25

A787

A788

1986, Apr. 10 *Perf. 12½*

2850 A787 5c multi .40 .20

Kindergartens, 25th anniv.

1986, Apr. 12 *Perf. 13x13½*

1st Man in Space, 25th Anniv.: 1c, *Vostok* and rocket designer Sergei Korolev. 2c, Yuri Gagarin, *Vostok 1.* 5c, Valentina Tereshkova, *Vostok 6.* 20c, *Salyut-Soyuz* space link. 30c, Capsule landing. 50c, *Soyuz* rocket launch. 1p, Konstantin Tsiolkovski (1857-1935), rocket scientist.

2851 A788 1c multi .20 .20
2852 A788 2c multi .20 .20
2853 A788 5c multi .20 .20
2854 A788 20c multi .60 .20
2855 A788 30c multi .80 .20
2856 A788 50c multi 1.75 .35
Nos. 2851-2856 (6) 3.75 1.35

Souvenir Sheet

Perf. 12½

2857 A788 1p multi 4.50 1.60

No. 2857 contains one 32x40mm stamp.

Natl. Flag and No. 2407 A789

1986, Apr. 19 *Perf. 13*

2858 A789 5c shown .20 .20
2859 A789 20c Banners, natl. crest 1.10 .20

Bay of Pigs invasion, 25th anniv. (5c); Proclamation of Socialist Revolution, 25th anniv. (20c).

Stamp Day Type of 1984

Mural, by R. Rodriguez Radillo (1967), details.

1986, Apr. 24 *Perf. 13x12½*

2860 A733 20c Mail coach, 18th-19th cent. .75 .20
2861 A733 30c Pony Express 1.00 .25

Radio Havana, 25th Anniv. — A790

1986, May 1

2862 A790 5c multi .40 .20

EXPO '86, Vancouver — A791

Locomotives: 1c, *Stourbridge Lion,* 1829, US. 4c, Stephenson's *Rocket,* 1829, GB. 5c, 1st Russian locomotive, 1845. 8c, Seguin's locomotive, 1830, France. 30c, 1st Canadian locomotive, 1836. 50c, Urban locomotive, Belgian Grand Central Rlwy., 1872. 1p, US locomotive pulling Cuban sugar train, 1837.

1986, May 2 Litho. *Perf. 12½x12*

2863 A791 1c multi .20 .20
2864 A791 4c multi .20 .20
2865 A791 5c multi .20 .20
2866 A791 8c multi .20 .20
2867 A791 30c multi .50 .20
2868 A791 50c multi 1.25 .25
Nos. 2863-2868 (6) 2.55 1.25

Souvenir Sheet

Perf. 13x13½

2869 A791 1p multi 5.00 1.60

No. 2869 contains one 40x32mm stamp.

Assoc. of Small Farmers, (ANAP), 25th Anniv. — A792

1986, May 17 *Perf. 13*

2870 A792 5c multi .40 .20

Intl. Peace Year A793

1986, June 2

2871 A793 30c multi 1.00 .25

Ministry of the Interior (MININT), 25th Anniv. — A794

1986, June 6

2872 A794 5c multi .40 .20

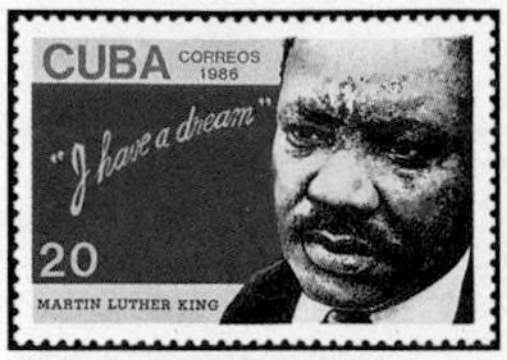

Martin Luther King, Jr. A795

1986, June 27 *Perf. 13½x13*

2873 A795 20c multi 1.00 .25

Bonifacio Byrne (d. 1936), Poet A796

1986, July 5 *Perf. 13*

2874 A796 5c multi .30 .20

Cuban Union of Writers and Artists (UNEAC), 25th Anniv. — A797

Sandinista Movement in Nicaragua (FSLN), 25th Anniv. — A798

1986, July 10 *Perf. 13x12½*

2875 A797 5c multi .30 .20

1986, July 23 *Perf. 13x12*

Augusto Cesar Sandino and Carlos Fonseca.

2876 A798 20c multi .75 .25

Ministry of Transportation, 25th Anniv. — A799

1986, Aug. 1 *Perf. 13*

2877 A799 5c multi .35 .20

7th University Games of Central America and the Caribbean
A800

1986, Aug. 9
2878 A800 20c multi 1.00 .25

Souvenir Sheet

STOCKHOLMIA '86 — A801

Designs: a, 2c Mambi Revolutionary stamp of 1897. b, Sweden Type A7, cancellation.

1986, Aug. 28 ***Perf. 12½***
2879 A801 Sheet of 2 4.50 1.60
a.-b. 50c multi

Nonaligned Countries Movement, 25th Anniv. — A802

1986, Sept. 1 ***Perf. 13½x13***
2880 A802 50c multi 2.00 .45

Orchids — A803

1986, Sept. 15 ***Perf. 12½***
2881 A803 1c *Cattleya hardyana* .20 .20
2882 A803 4c *Brassolaelio cattleya* .20 .20
2883 A803 5c *Phalaenopsis marget moses* .20 .20
2884 A803 10c *Laelio cattleya prism palette* .30 .20
2885 A803 30c *Phalaenopsis violacea* 1.10 .25
2886 A803 50c *Disa uniflora* 1.75 .45
Nos. 2881-2886 (6) 3.75 1.50

Latin American History — A804

Pre-Columbian artifacts: No. 2887, Mayan dwelling and votive jade sculpture. No. 2888, Inca vase and Tiahuanacu sun gate (Bolivia). No. 2889, Spain No. C47, discovery of America 500th anniv. emblem, scroll. No. 2890, Diaguitan duck-shaped pitcher and Pucara de Quitor ruins (Chile). No. 2891, San Agustin Archaeological Park megaliths and Quimbayan sculpture (Colombia). No. 2892, Moler grinding stone and Chorotega ceramic figurine. No. 2893, Tabaco idol and Indian dwelling (Cuba). No. 2894, Spain No. C38. No. 2895, Taino dwelling and chair (Dominica). No. 2896, Tolita statue and Ingapirca Castle ruins. No. 2897, Maya vase and Tikal Temple (Guatemala). No. 2898, Copan ruins and Maya idol. No. 2899, Spain No. C37. No. 2900, Chichen Itza Temple and Zapotecan urn (Mexico). No. 2901, Punta de Zapote megaliths and Ometepe ceramic figurine. No. 2902, Tonosi lidded ceramic bowl and Barriles monoliths. No. 2903, Ruins at Machu-Picchu and Inca statue (Peru). No. 2904, Spain No. C49. No. 2905, Teepees and triangular sculpture (Puerto Rico). No. 2906, Fertility statue from Santa Ana and Santo Domingo Cave.

1986, Oct. 12 ***Perf. 13***
2887 A804 1c multi .20 .20
2888 A804 1c multi .20 .20
2889 A804 1c multi .20 .20
2890 A804 1c multi .20 .20
2891 A804 1c multi .20 .20
a. Strip of 5, Nos. 2887-2891 1.00 1.00
2892 A804 5c multi .20 .20
2893 A804 5c multi .20 .20
2894 A804 5c multi .20 .20
2895 A804 5c multi .20 .20
2896 A804 5c multi .20 .20
a. Strip of 5, Nos. 2892-2896 1.00 1.00
2897 A804 10c multi .30 .20
2898 A804 10c multi .30 .20
2899 A804 10c multi .30 .20
2900 A804 10c multi .30 .20
2901 A804 10c multi .30 .20
a. Strip of 5, Nos. 2897-2901 1.50 1.00
2902 A804 20c multi .70 .30
2903 A804 20c multi .70 .30
2904 A804 20c multi .70 .30
2905 A804 20c multi .70 .30
2906 A804 20c multi .70 .30
a. Strip of 5, Nos. 2902-2906 3.50 1.50
Nos. 2887-2906 (20) 7.00 4.50

Discovery of America, 500th anniv. (in 1992). See Nos. 2966-2985, 3065-3084, 3253-3272, 3463-3466.

Intl. Brigades, Spain, 50th Anniv. — A805

1986, Oct. 14 ***Perf. 12½x12***
2907 A805 30c multi .75 .35

Paintings in the Natl. Museum
A806

Designs: 2c, *Two Children*, by Gutierrez de la Vega, vert. 4c, *Sed*, by Jean-Georges Vibert. 6c, *Virgin and Child*, by Niccolo Abbate, vert. 10c, *Bullfight*, by Eugenio de Lucas Velazquez. 30c, *The Five Senses*, anonymous. 50c, *Arrival at Thomops Castle*, by Jean Louis Ernest.

1986, Nov. 5 ***Perf. 13***
2908 A806 2c multi .25 .20
2909 A806 4c multi .25 .20
2910 A806 6c multi .25 .20
2911 A806 10c multi .40 .20
2912 A806 30c multi 1.10 .20
2913 A806 50c multi 1.90 .25
Nos. 2908-2913 (6) 4.15 1.25

Anniversaries — A807

1986, Dec. 2 **Litho.** ***Perf. 12½***
2914 A807 5c *Granma* .45 .20

Size: 26x38mm

2915 A807 20c Soldier, rifle, flag 1.50 .20

Granma Landings, 30th anniv. (5c); Revolutionary Armed Forces, 30th anniv. (20c).

Scholarship Program, 25th Anniv. — A808

1986, Dec. 22 ***Perf. 13***
2916 A808 5c Guevara, students .30 .20

Natl. Literacy Campaign, 25th Anniv. — A809

1986, Dec. 25 ***Perf. 13x12½***
2917 A809 5c Marti, man learning to write .30 .20

Siege of La Plata, 30th Anniv.
A810

1987, Jan. 17 ***Perf. 12½x12***
2918 A810 5c Map, revolutionaries .30 .20

Paintings in the Natl. Museum
A811

3c, *Gypsy*, by Joaquin Sorolla. 5c, *Sir Walter Scott*, by Sir John W. Gordon. 10c, *Farm Meadows*, by Alfred de Breanski. 20c, *Still-life*, by Isaac van Duynen. 30c, *Landscape with Figures*, by Francesco Zuccarelli. 40c, *The Failure* (defeated bullfighter), by Ignacio Zuloaga.

1987, Feb. 5 ***Perf. 13***
2919 A811 3c multi, vert. .25 .20
2920 A811 5c multi, vert. .25 .20
2921 A811 10c multi .40 .20
2922 A811 20c multi 1.00 .20
2923 A811 30c multi 1.10 .20
2924 A811 40c multi, vert. 1.60 .25
Nos. 2919-2924 (6) 4.60 1.25

Siege of the Presidential Palace, 30th Anniv. — A812

1987, Mar. 13 ***Perf. 12½x12***
2925 A812 5c Palace, van, Echeverra .30 .20

Lazarus Ludwig Zamenhof and Russia Type A77 — A813

1987, Mar. 16 ***Perf. 13½x13***
2926 A813 30c multi 1.00 .25

Esperanto, cent.

Souvenir Sheet

EXFILNA '87, 10th Natl. Stamp Exposition, Holguin — A814

1987, Mar. 28 ***Perf. 13x13½***
2927 A814 1p Nos. 552, C129 4.50 2.25

25th Anniv. and 5th Cong. of the Youth Communist League (U.J.C.) — A815

1987, Apr. 4 ***Perf. 13***
2928 A815 5c multi .30 .20

Intercosmos, 20th Anniv. — A816

1987, Apr. 12 **Litho.** ***Perf. 12½x12***
2929 A816 3c *Intercosmos 1* .20 .20
2930 A816 5c *Intercosmos 2* .20 .20
2931 A816 10c *TD* .30 .20
2932 A816 20c *Cosmos 93* .75 .20
2933 A816 30c *Prognoz* 1.00 .20
2934 A816 50c *Vostok 3* 1.60 .25
Nos. 2929-2934 (6) 4.05 1.25

Souvenir Sheet

Perf. 13½x13

2935 A816 1p Rocket, *Vostok 3* 4.50 2.25

No. 2935 contains one 32x40mm stamp.

Stamp Day
A817

Stamped covers and canceled stamps.

1987, Apr. 24 ***Perf. 13***
2936 A817 30c Havana, 1890 1.25 .30
2937 A817 50c Santiago de Cuba, 1869 2.10 .60

Souvenir Sheet

1992 Winter Olympics, Albertville — A914

1991, Sept. 25 Litho. *Perf. 12½*
3350 A914 1p multicolored 3.50 1.75

Cuban Communist Party, 4th Congress A915

1991, Oct. 10
3351 A915 5c shown .20 .20
3352 A915 50c Congress symbol 1.75 .50

Discovery of America, 500th Anniv. (in 1992) — A916

Designs: 5c, Columbus, Vicente and Martin Pinzon. 20c, Santa Maria, Nina and Pinta.

1991, Oct. 12
3353 A916 5c multicolored .25 .20
3354 A916 20c multicolored 1.25 .25

Jose Marti A917

1991, Oct. 15 *Perf. 13x12½*
3355 A917 50c multicolored 2.00 .40

Publication of "Simple Verses," cent.

Latin American History A918

Stamps or musicians and instruments: No. 3356, Julian Aguirre, Argentina, charango. No. 3357, Eduardo Caba, Bolivia, antara. No. 3358, Chile #2. No. 3359, Heitor Villalobos, Brazil, resonator trumpet. No. 3360, Guillermo Uribe-Holguin, Colombia, drum. No. 3361, Miguel Failde, Cuba, claves. No. 3362, Enrique Soro, Chile, drum. No. 3363, Chile #57. No. 3364, Segundo L. Moreno, Ecuador, xylophone. No. 3365, Ricardo Castillo, Guatemala, marimba. No. 3366, Carlos Chavez, Mexico, guitar. No. 3367, Luis A. Delgadillo, Nicaragua, maracas. No. 3368, Chile #69. No. 3369, Alfredo De Saint-Malo, Panama, mejorana. No. 3370, Jose Asuncion Flores, Paraguay, harp. No. 3371, Daniel Alomia, Peru, flute. No. 3372, Juan Morell y Campos, Puerto Rico, cuatro. No. 3373, Chile #72. No. 3374, Eduardo Farini, Uruguay, drums. No. 3375, Juan V. Lecuna, Venezuela, cuatro, diff.

1991, Oct. 27 *Perf. 13*
3356 A918 1c multicolored .20 .20
3357 A918 1c multicolored .20 .20
3358 A918 1c multicolored .20 .20
3359 A918 1c multicolored .20 .20
3360 A918 1c multicolored .20 .20
a. Strip of 5, #3356-3360 1.00 .50
3361 A918 5c multicolored .20 .20
3362 A918 5c multicolored .20 .20
3363 A918 5c multicolored .20 .20
3364 A918 5c multicolored .20 .20
3365 A918 5c multicolored .20 .20
a. Strip of 5, #3361-3365 1.00 .50
3366 A918 10c multicolored .40 .20
3367 A918 10c multicolored .40 .20
3368 A918 10c multicolored .40 .20
3369 A918 10c multicolored .40 .20
3370 A918 10c multicolored .40 .20
a. Strip of 5, #3366-3370 2.00 1.00
3371 A918 20c multicolored .80 .20
3372 A918 20c multicolored .80 .20
3373 A918 20c multicolored .80 .20
3374 A918 20c multicolored .80 .20
3375 A918 20c multicolored .80 .20
a. Strip of 5, #3371-3375 4.00 2.00
b. Sheet of 20, #3356-3375 8.00 —
Nos. 3356-3375 (20) 8.00 4.00

Discovery of America, 500th anniv. in 1992 (Nos. 3358, 3363, 3368, 3373).

Jose Marti Pioneers Organization, 1st Congress A919

1991, Oct. 29
3376 A919 5c multicolored .35 .20

Toussaint L'Ouverture (1743-1803) — A920

1991, Nov. 20 *Perf. 12½x13*
3377 A920 50c multicolored 2.00 .40

Haitian Revolution, Bicent.

Cuban Revolutionary Armed Forces, 35th Anniv. — A921

Design: 50c, Landing of the Granma expedition, 35th anniv., vert.

Perf. 12½x12, 12x12½
1991, Dec. 2 Litho.
3378 A921 5c multicolored .25 .20
3379 A921 50c multicolored 1.75 .40

Gen. Ignacio Agramonte (1841-1873), Revolutionary Hero — A922

1991, Dec. 23 Litho. *Perf. 12½x13*
3380 A922 5c multicolored .30 .20

Souvenir Sheet

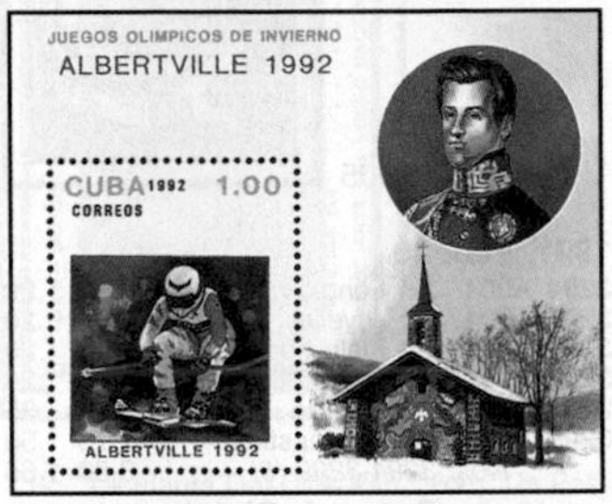

1992 Winter Olympics, Albertville — A923

1992, Jan. 15 *Perf. 13*
3381 A923 1p multicolored 3.50 1.75

1992 Summer Olympics, Barcelona — A924

1992, Jan. 20 Litho. *Perf. 13x12½*
3382 A924 3c Table tennis .20 .20
3383 A924 5c Handball .20 .20
3384 A924 10c Shooting .30 .20
3385 A924 20c Long jump, vert. .60 .20
3386 A924 35c Judo 1.25 .40
3387 A924 50c Fencing 1.60 .40
Nos. 3382-3387 (6) 4.15 1.60

Souvenir Sheet
Perf. 12½
3388 A924 100c Rhythmic gymnastics, vert. 3.50 1.75

No. 3388 contains one 32x40mm stamp.

Environmental Protection A925

1992, Feb. 10 *Perf. 13*
3389 A925 5c Terraced hillsides .25 .20
3390 A925 20c Save the whales .60 .25
3391 A925 35c Ozone hole over Antarctica 1.25 .40
3392 A925 40c Nuclear disarmament 1.40 .40
Nos. 3389-3392 (4) 3.50 1.25

Dogs A926

1992, Mar. 10 Litho. *Perf. 13x12½*
3393 A926 5c Boxer .20 .20
3394 A926 10c Great dane .20 .20
3395 A926 20c German shepherd .65 .20
3396 A926 30c Various breeds 1.10 .25
3397 A926 35c Doberman pinscher 1.10 .30
3398 A926 40c Fox terrier 1.40 .40
3399 A926 50c Poodle 1.75 .50
Nos. 3393-3399 (7) 6.40 2.05

Souvenir Sheet
Perf. 12½
3400 A926 1p Bichon frise, vert. 4.00 2.00

No. 3400 contains one 32x40mm stamp.
Nos. 3401-3404 will not be assigned.

Union of Young Communists, 30th Anniv. — A928

1992, Apr. 4 Litho. *Perf. 13*
3405 A928 5c multicolored .35 .20

Cuban Revolutionary Party, Cent. — A929

1992, Apr. 10 *Perf. 13x12½*
3406 A929 5c multicolored .25 .20
3407 A929 50c multicolored 1.75 .50

Discovery of America, 500th Anniv. — A930

1992, Apr. 14 *Perf. 12½*
3408 A930 5c Landing at Bariay .20 .20
3409 A930 20c Landing at San Salvador .55 .25

Granada '92 Philatelic Exhibition — A931

Views of the Alhambra, Granada: 5c, With Sierra Nevada mountains beyond. 10c, Arches at sunset. 20c, Interior architecture. 30c, Patio, fountain of lions. 35c, Bedroom. 50c, View of Albaicin.

1992, Apr. 17 *Perf. 13*

3410	A931	5c multicolored	.20	.20
3411	A931	10c multicolored	.25	.20
3412	A931	20c multicolored	.75	.20
3413	A931	30c multicolored	1.25	.25
3414	A931	35c multicolored	1.50	.40
3415	A931	50c multicolored	2.10	.50
		Nos. 3410-3415 (6)	6.05	1.75

La Bodeguita Del Medio Restaurant, 50th Anniv. — A932

1992, Apr. 26

3416 A932 50c multicolored 1.75 .50

Fish A933

1992, May 15 **Litho.** *Perf. 12½*

3417	A933	5c Holacanthus isabelita	.20	.20
3418	A933	10c Equetus lanceolatus	.20	.20
3419	A933	20c Acanthurus coeruleus	.65	.20
3420	A933	30c Abudefduf saxatilis	1.10	.25
3421	A933	50c Microspathodon chrysurus	1.90	.50
		Nos. 3417-3421 (5)	4.05	1.35

Orchids — A934

1992, June 20 **Litho.** *Perf. 12½*

3422	A934	3c Cattleya hibrida	.20	.20
3423	A934	5c Phalaenopsis	.20	.20
3424	A934	10c Cattleyopsis lindenii	.20	.20
3425	A934	30c Bletia purpurea	1.00	.25
3426	A934	35c Oncidium luridum	1.10	.30
3427	A934	40c Vanda hibrida	1.40	.40
		Nos. 3422-3427 (6)	4.10	1.55

Soroa Orchid Garden, 40th anniv.

Mellisuga Helenae — A935

1992, July 7 *Perf. 13*

3428	A935	5c Sitting on nest	.50	.40
3429	A935	10c Wings extended	.70	.50
3430	A935	20c Sitting on branch	1.50	.60
3431	A935	30c In flight	2.50	1.25
		Nos. 3428-3431 (4)	5.20	2.75

World Wildlife Fund.

Tourism A936

1992, July 15 **Litho.** *Perf. 12½*

3432	A936	10c Guardalavaca Beach	.30	.20
3433	A936	20c Bucanero Hotel	.70	.20
3434	A936	30c Sailing ship, Havana	1.25	.40
3435	A936	50c Varadero Beach	1.75	.50
		Nos. 3432-3435 (4)	4.00	1.30

Souvenir Sheet

Expo '92, Seville — A937

1992, July 27 **Litho.** *Perf. 13*

3436 A937 1.50p multicolored 4.00 2.00

1992 Summer Olympics, Barcelona A938

Athlete, sport: 5c, Eligio (Kid Chocolate) Sardinas, boxing. 35c, Ramon Fonst, fencing. 40c, Sergio Martinez, cycling. 50c, Martin Dihigo, baseball.

1992, July 20 **Litho.** *Perf. 12½x13*

3437	A938	5c multicolored	.20	.20
3438	A938	35c multicolored	1.10	.30
3439	A938	40c multicolored	1.25	.40
3440	A938	50c multicolored	1.75	.60
		Nos. 3437-3440 (4)	4.30	1.50

Olymphilex '92.

Discovery of America, 500th Anniv. — A939

5c, Alvarez Cabral. 10c, Alonso Pinzon. 20c, Alonso de Ojeda. 30c, Amerigo Vespucci. 35c, Prince Henry the Navigator. 40c, Bartolomeu Dias. 1p, Columbus' fleet.

1992, Sept. 18 **Litho.** *Perf. 12½*

3441	A939	5c multicolored	.20	.20
3442	A939	10c multicolored	.30	.20
3443	A939	20c multicolored	.70	.20
3444	A939	30c multicolored	1.10	.30
3445	A939	35c multicolored	1.25	.30
3446	A939	40c multicolored	1.50	.40
		Nos. 3441-3446 (6)	5.05	1.60

Souvenir Sheet

Perf. 13

3447 A939 1p multi, vert. 3.00 1.50

Genoa '92. No. 3447 contains one 32x40mm stamp.

1992 Summer Olympics Medal Winners, Barcelona — A940

Medals and participants in events: No. 3448, Bronze, 4x100-meter relay, women's high jump, and women's 800-meter. No. 3449, Gold, high jump, women's discus. No. 3450, Silver, 4x400-meter relay, bronze, discus. No. 3451, Gold and silver, boxing. No. 3452, Gold, baseball. No. 3453, Gold, women's volleyball. No. 3454, Gold, silver, and bronze, judo. No. 3455, Gold and bronze, Greco-Roman and freestyle wrestling. No. 3456, Silver and bronze, fencing, silver, weight lifting.

1992, Sept. 24 **Litho.** *Perf. 13*

3448	A940	5c multicolored	.20	.20
3449	A940	5c multicolored	.20	.20
3450	A940	5c multicolored	.20	.20
3451	A940	20c multicolored	.65	.20
3452	A940	20c multicolored	.65	.20
3453	A940	20c multicolored	.65	.20
3454	A940	50c multicolored	1.75	.50
3455	A940	50c multicolored	1.75	.50
3456	A940	50c multicolored	1.75	.50
		Nos. 3448-3456 (9)	7.80	2.70

6th World Track and Field Cup, Havana A941

1992, Sept. 24 **Litho.** *Perf. 13*

3457	A941	5c High jump	.20	.20
3458	A941	20c Javelin	.65	.20
3459	A941	30c Hammer throw	1.00	.25
3460	A941	40c Long jump, vert.	1.40	.40
3461	A941	50c Hurdles, vert.	1.75	.50
		Nos. 3457-3461 (5)	5.00	1.55

Souvenir Sheet

3462 A941 1p Women's relay 3.50 1.75

No. 3462 contains one 40x32mm stamp.

Latin American History Type of 1986

Discovery of America: No. 3463a, Columbus, Queen Isabella. b, Columbus at Rabida Monastery. c, Columbus, pointing up, outlining his plan. d, Columbus, with scroll, before Salamanca Council. e, Departure of Columbus' fleet from Palos.

No. 3464a, Three ships stopping at Canary Islands. b, Columbus speaking to crew. c, Land sighted, Oct. 12, 1492. d, Columbus landing in New World. e, Meeting natives.

No. 3465a, Grounding of Santa Maria at Hispanola. b, Arrival of Nina at Palos. c, Columbus welcomed in Barcelona. d, Columbus describes his voyage to Ferdinand and Isabella. e, Departure of fleet from Cadiz on second voyage.

No. 3466a, King and Queen welcome Columbus. b, Fleet on Columbus' third voyage. c, Columbus deported from Hispanola to Spain as prisoner. d, Columbus on ship, fourth voyage. e, Death of Columbus, May 20, 1506 in Valladolid.

1992, Oct. 3 *Perf. 13*

3463	A804	1c Strip of 5, #a.-e.	.65	.30
3464	A804	5c Strip of 5, #a.-e.	.65	.30
3465	A804	10c Strip of 5, #a.-e.	1.25	.75
3466	A804	20c Strip of 5, #a.-e.	4.00	1.50
		Nos. 3463-3466 (4)	6.55	2.85

Jose Maria Chacon y Calvo (1892-1969), Historian A942

1992, Oct. 29 *Perf. 13*

3467 A942 30c multicolored 1.25 .40

Churches A943

Designs: 5c, Basilica of Nuestra Senora de la Caridad del Cobre. 20c, Santa Maria del Rosario Church. 30c, Espiritu Santo Church. 50c, Santo Angel Custodio Church.

1992, Nov. 10 **Litho.** *Perf. 12½*

3468	A943	5c multicolored	.20	.20
3469	A943	20c multicolored	.90	.20
3470	A943	30c multicolored	1.25	.25
3471	A943	50c multicolored	2.40	.30
		Nos. 3468-3471 (4)	4.75	.95

Development of the Diesel Engine — A944

1993, Jan. 20 **Litho.** *Perf. 12½*

3472	A944	5c Truck	.20	.20
3473	A944	10c Automobile	.20	.20
3474	A944	30c Tugboat	.55	.40
3475	A944	40c Locomotive	2.50	1.25
3476	A944	50c Tractor	1.00	.65
		Nos. 3472-3476 (5)	4.45	2.70

Souvenir Sheet

3477 A944 1p Rudolf Diesel 3.50 1.75

No. 3477 contains one 40x32mm stamp. Rudolf Diesel, 80th anniv. of death (#3477).

Davis Cup Tennis Competition — A945

Various tennis players in action.

Perf. 12x12½, 12½x12

1993, Feb. 10 **Litho.**

3478	A945	5c multi, vert.	.20	.20
3479	A945	20c multi, vert.	.60	.20
3480	A945	30c multi, vert.	.90	.40
3481	A945	35c multicolored	1.00	.50
3482	A945	40c multicolored	1.25	.60
		Nos. 3478-3482 (5)	3.95	1.90

Souvenir Sheet

Perf. 12½

3483 A945 1p multicolored 2.50 1.25

No. 3483 contains one 40x32mm stamp.

Scientists A946

Designs: 3c, Pierre-Paul-Emile Roux (1853-1933), bacteriologist. 5c, Carlos J. Finlay (1833-1915), suggested mosquito as carrier of yellow fever. 10c, Ivan Petrovich Pavlov (1849-1936), physiologist, investigated conditioned reflexes. 20c, Louis Pasteur, chemist, developer of pasteurization. 30c, Santiago Ramon y Cajal (1852-1934), histologist, isolated the neuron. 35c, Sigmund Freud, psychoanalyst. 40c, Wilhelm Conrad Roentgen, physicist, discoverer of x-ray. 50c, Joseph Lister, surgeon, introduced principle of antisepsis. 1p, Robert Koch, bacteriologist, developer of tuberculin, vert.

1993, Mar. 3 Litho. *Perf. 12½*

3484	A946	3c multicolored	.20	.20
3485	A946	5c multicolored	.20	.20
3486	A946	10c multicolored	.25	.20
3487	A946	20c multicolored	.55	.25
3488	A946	30c multicolored	.80	.40
3489	A946	35c multicolored	.90	.50
3490	A946	40c multicolored	1.10	.60
3491	A946	50c multicolored	1.25	.65
		Nos. 3484-3491 (8)	5.25	3.00

Souvenir Sheet

3492	A946	1p multicolored	2.75	1.40

Bicycles — A947

Bicycles designed by: 3c, Leonardo da Vinci, 15th cent. 5c, Karl Von Drais de Sauerbrun, 1813. 10c, Ernest Michaux, 1856. 20c, James Starley, 1869. 30c, Harry Lawson, 1879. 35c, Guaso (Cuba), 1992.

1993, Apr. 14 *Perf. 13*

3493	A947	3c multicolored	.20	.20
3494	A947	5c multicolored	.20	.20
3495	A947	10c multicolored	.45	.20
3496	A947	20c multicolored	.90	.25
3497	A947	30c multicolored	1.40	.40
3498	A947	35c multicolored	1.50	.50
		Nos. 3493-3498 (6)	4.65	1.75

Cuban Natl. Museum, 80th Anniv. A948

Paintings by Joaquin Sorolla y Bastida (1863-1923): 3c, Child Eating Watermelon, 1920, vert. 5c, Valencian Fisherwomen, 1909. 10c, Regattas. 20c, Contadina, 1889. 40c, Summer, 1904. 50c, Boats on the Ocean, 1908.

1993, May 29 Litho. *Perf. 13x12½*

3499	A948	3c multicolored	.20	.20

Perf. 12½x13

3500	A948	5c multicolored	.30	.20
3501	A948	10c multicolored	.35	.20
3502	A948	20c multicolored	.65	.25
3503	A948	40c multicolored	1.25	.60
3504	A948	50c multicolored	1.75	.65
		Nos. 3499-3504 (6)	4.50	2.10

Water Birds A949

Perf. 12½, 13x12½ (5, 30c)

1993, June 15

3505	A949	3c Jacana spinosa	.20	.20
3506	A949	5c Ardea herodias, vert.	.20	.20
3507	A949	10c Himantopus mexicanus	.35	.20
3508	A949	20c Nycticorax nycticorax	.75	.25
3509	A949	30c Grus canadensis, vert.	1.10	.40
3510	A949	50c Aramus guarauna	2.10	.65
		Nos. 3505-3510 (6)	4.70	1.90

Brasiliana '93. Nos. 3506, 3510 are 27x44mm.

Anniversaries — A950

#3511, Jose Marti, Moncada Barracks. #3512, "History Will Absolve Me," declaration of Fidel Castro, Marti. #3513, Jose Marti, Rafael M. Mendive, vert. #3514, Carlos Manuel de Cespedes, gear wheels.

1993, July 26 Litho. *Perf. 13*

3511	A950	5c multicolored	.20	.20
3512	A950	5c multicolored	.20	.20
3513	A950	5c multicolored	.20	.20
3514	A950	5c multicolored	.20	.20
		Nos. 3511-3514 (4)	.80	.80

Attack on Moncada Barracks, 40th anniv. (#3511). Declaration of Fidel Castro, 40th anniv. (#3512). Birth of Jose Marti, 140th anniv. (#3513). Declaration of the Ten Years' War, 125th anniv. (#3514).

Flowers from Cienfuegos Botanical Gardens A951

1993, Aug. 20

3515	A951	3c Sedum allantoides	.20	.20
3516	A951	5c Heliconia caribaea	.20	.20
3517	A951	10c Anthurium andraeanum	.35	.20
3518	A951	20c Pseudobombax ellipticum	.70	.25
3519	A951	35c Ixora coccinea	1.10	.50
3520	A951	50c Callistemon speciosus	1.90	.65
		Nos. 3515-3520 (6)	4.45	2.00

Bangkok '93, Intl. Philatelic Exhibition A952

Butterflies: 3c, Battus devillievs. 5c, Anteos maerula. 20c, Ascia monuste evonima. 30c, Junonia coenia. 35c, Anartia jatrophae guantanamo. 50c, Hypolimnas misippus.

1993, Sept. 10 Litho. *Perf. 13*

3521	A952	3c multicolored	.20	.20
3522	A952	5c multicolored	.25	.20
3523	A952	20c multicolored	.70	.25
3524	A952	30c multicolored	1.00	.40
3525	A952	35c multicolored	1.10	.40
3526	A952	50c multicolored	1.60	.65
		Nos. 3521-3526 (6)	4.85	2.10

Endangered Species A953

1993, Oct. 12 Litho. *Perf. 13*

3527	A953	5c Phoenicopterus ruber	.25	.20
3528	A953	50c Ajaia ajaja	1.75	.65

Latin American Revolutionaries A954

Flags, map and: No. 3529, Simon Bolivar. No. 3530, Jose Marti. No. 3531, Benito Juarez, Mexican President. No. 3532, Ernesto "Che" Guevara.

1993, Oct. 27 Litho. *Perf. 13*

3529	A954	50c multicolored	1.40	.65
3530	A954	50c multicolored	1.40	.65
3531	A954	50c multicolored	1.40	.65
3532	A954	50c multicolored	1.40	.65
a.		Block of 4, #3529-3532	7.25	3.50
		Nos. 3529-3532 (4)	5.60	2.60

17th Central American and Caribbean Games, Ponce, Puerto Rico — A955

1993, Nov. 10 Litho. *Perf. 12½*

3533	A955	5c Swimming	.20	.20
3534	A955	10c Pole vault	.20	.20
3535	A955	20c Boxing	.70	.25
3536	A955	35c Gymnastics, vert.	1.10	.40
3537	A955	50c Baseball, vert.	1.60	.65
		Nos. 3533-3537 (5)	3.80	1.70

Souvenir Sheet

3538	A955	1p Basketball	3.75	1.75

No. 3538 contains one 40x32mm stamp.

Mariana Grajales (1808-93), Patriot — A956

Peter I. Tchaikovsky (1840-93), Composer A957

1993, Nov. 27 *Perf. 13*

3539	A956	5p multicolored	.30	.20

1993, Nov. 30

3540	A957	5c Portrait	.20	.20
3541	A957	20c Swan Lake Ballet	.65	.25
3542	A957	30c Statue	.90	.40
3543	A957	50c Museum, horiz.	1.25	.65
		Nos. 3540-3543 (4)	3.00	1.50

A958

A959

1994, Jan. 1 Litho. *Perf. 13*

3544	A958	5c multicolored	.30	.20

35th anniv. of the Revolution.

1994, Jan. 1

Various soccer players.

3545	A959	5c multicolored	.20	.20
3546	A959	20c multicolored	.60	.25
3547	A959	30c multicolored	.85	.40
3548	A959	35c multicolored	.95	.40
3549	A959	40c multicolored	1.25	.50
3550	A959	50c multicolored	1.40	.65
		Nos. 3545-3550 (6)	5.25	2.40

Souvenir Sheet

3551	A959	1p multicolored	3.00	1.50

1994 World Cup Soccer Championships, US. No. 3551 contains one 40x31mm stamp.

Cats A960

1994, Feb. 15 Litho. *Perf. 12½*

3552	A960	5c Blue Persian	.20	.20
3553	A960	10c Havana	.25	.20
3554	A960	20c Maine coon	.70	.25
3555	A960	30c Blue British shorthair	1.00	.40
3556	A960	35c Bicolor Persian	1.10	.40
3557	A960	50c Gold chinchilla	1.60	.65
		Nos. 3552-3557 (6)	4.85	2.10

Souvenir Sheet

Perf. 13

3558	A960	1p Abyssinian, vert.	4.00	2.00

No. 3558 contains one 30x38mm stamp.

Medicinal Plants — A961

Designs: 5c, Salvia officinalis. 10c, Aloe barbadensis. 20c, Helianthus annuus. 30c, Matricaria chamomilla. 40c, Calendula officinalis. 50c, Tilia platyphyllos.

1994, Mar. 30 Litho. *Perf. 12½*

3559	A961	5c multicolored	.25	.20
3560	A961	10c multicolored	.25	.20
3561	A961	20c multicolored	.65	.25
3562	A961	30c multicolored	.90	.40
3563	A961	40c multicolored	1.25	.50
3564	A961	50c multicolored	1.50	.65
		Nos. 3559-3564 (6)	4.80	2.20

Carriages — A962

Designs: 5c, Public coach, 1860. 10c, Coach of Ferdinand VII, Maria Louisa. 30c, Louis XV-style coach. 35c, Elizabeth II gala day's coach. 40c, Catalina II's summer coach. 50c, Volanta habanera.

1994, Apr. 20 *Perf. 12½x12*

3565	A962	5c multicolored	.20	.20
3566	A962	10c multicolored	.25	.20
3567	A962	30c multicolored	1.00	.40
3568	A962	35c multicolored	1.10	.40
3569	A962	40c multicolored	1.40	.50
3570	A962	50c multicolored	1.60	.65
		Nos. 3565-3570 (6)	5.55	2.35

No. 3570 is 68x37mm.

Aquaculture — A963

Designs: 5c, Crassostrea rhizophorae. 20c, Cardisoma guanhumi. 30c, Tilapia melanopleura. 35c, Hippospongia lachne. 40c, Panulirus argus. 50c, Cyprinus carpio.

1994, May 10 **Litho.** *Perf. 12½*

3571	A963	5c multicolored	.35	.20
3572	A963	20c multicolored	.60	.25
3573	A963	30c multicolored	.85	.40
3574	A963	35c multicolored	1.00	.40
3575	A963	40c multicolored	1.25	.50
3576	A963	50c multicolored	1.50	.65
		Nos. 3571-3576 (6)	5.55	2.40

Intl. Olympic Committee, Cent. — A964

1994, June 23 **Litho.** *Perf. 12½*

3577	A964	5c Flag, runners	.20	.20
3578	A964	30c Flag, world map	.85	.40
3579	A964	50c Flag, Olympic flame	1.50	.65
		Nos. 3577-3579 (3)	2.55	1.25

Scientists A965

Designs: 5c, Michael Faraday (1791-1867), physicist. 10c, Marie Curie (1867-1934), physical chemist. 20c, Pierre Curie (1859-1906), chemist. 30c, Albert Einstein (1879-1955), physicist, mathematician. 40c, Max Planck (1858-1947), theoretical physicist. 50c, Otto Hahn (1879-1968), physical chemist.

1994, July 20 **Litho.** *Perf. 12½*

3580	A965	5c multicolored	.20	.20
3581	A965	10c multicolored	.25	.20
3582	A965	20c multicolored	.70	.25
3583	A965	30c multicolored	1.00	.40
3584	A965	40c multicolored	1.40	.50
3585	A965	50c multicolored	1.75	.65
		Nos. 3580-3585 (6)	5.30	2.20

Cactus Flowers A966

Designs: 5c, Opuntia dillenii. 10c, Opuntia millspaughii, vert. 30c, Leptocereus santamarinae. 35c, Pereskia marcanoi. 40c, Dendrocereus nudiflorus, vert. 50c, Pilocereus robinii.

1994, Aug. 15 **Litho.** *Perf. 12½*

3586	A966	5c multicolored	.30	.20
3587	A966	10c multicolored	1.00	.40
3588	A966	30c multicolored	1.10	.40
3589	A966	35c multicolored	1.50	.50
3590	A966	40c multicolored	1.75	.65
3591	A966	50c multicolored		
		Nos. 3586-3591 (5)	5.65	2.15

Souvenir Sheet

2nd Spanish-Cuban Philatelic Exhibition, Havana — A967

Design: 1p, Cuban postal rocket, #C31.

1994, Sept. 18

3592	A967	1p multicolored	3.50	1.75

Experimental postal rocket flight, 55th anniv.

Dogs A968

1994, Sept. 20

3593	A968	5c Rough collie	.25	.20
3594	A968	20c American cocker spaniel	.70	.20
3595	A968	30c Dalmatian	.95	.25
3596	A968	40c Afghan hound	1.40	.40
3597	A968	50c English cocker spaniel	1.60	.65
		Nos. 3593-3597 (5)	4.90	1.70

Cayo Largo Island A969

Fauna: 15c, Carpilius corallinus. 65c, Cyclura nubila, vert. 75c, Pelecanus occidentalis. 4p, Chelonia mydas.

1994, Sept. 30 **Litho.** *Perf. 12½*

3598	A969	15c multicolored	.40	.20
3599	A969	65c multicolored	2.25	.90
3600	A969	75c multicolored	2.50	1.00
3601	A969	1p multicolored	3.50	1.25
		Nos. 3598-3601 (4)	8.65	3.35

A970

A971

1994, Oct. 28

3602	A970	15c multicolored	.80	.20

Camilo Cienfuegos Gorriaran, revolutionary, 35th anniv. of disappearance.

1994, Oct. 30

Fauna of the Caribbean: 10c, Epinephelus flavolimbatus, horiz. No. 3604, Phoenicopterus ruber. No. 3605, Aetobatus narinari. No. 3606, Istiophorus platypterus, horiz. No. 3607, Tursiops truncatus, horiz. No. 3608, Pelecanus occidentalis.

3603	A971	10c multicolored	.40	.20
3604	A971	15c multicolored	.40	.20
3605	A971	15c multicolored	.40	.20
3606	A971	15c multicolored	.40	.20
3607	A971	65c multicolored	2.25	.90
3608	A971	65c multicolored	2.25	.90
		Nos. 3603-3608 (6)	6.10	2.60

ICAO, 50th Anniv. A972

1994, Nov. 9

3609	A972	65c multicolored	2.00	.90

Zoological Garden, Havana, 55th Anniv. — A973

1994, Nov. 14 **Litho.** *Perf. 13*

3610	A973	15c Bronze monument	.20	.20
3611	A973	65c Ara chloroptera	1.10	.90
3612	A973	75c Carduelis carduelis	1.25	1.00
		Nos. 3610-3612 (3)	2.55	2.10

Cuban Philatelic Federation, 30th Anniv. — A974

1994, Nov. 20

3613	A974	15c multicolored	.50	.20

America Issue — A975

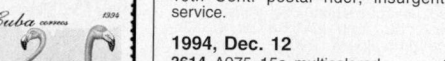

Postal transportation: 15c, 18th Cent. Spanish galleon, maritime postal service, vert. 65c, 19th Cent. postal rider, insurgent postal service.

1994, Dec. 12

3614	A975	15c multicolored	.25	.20
3615	A975	65c multicolored	1.75	.90

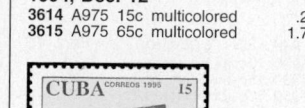

Postal Museum, 30th Anniv. — A976

1995, Jan. 2

3616	A976	15c multicolored	.50	.20

Lizards — A977

Designs: 15c, Anolis baracoae. 65c, Sphaerodactylus ramsdeni. 75c, Leiocephalus raviceps. 85c, Sphaerodactylus ruibali. 90c, Anolis ophiolepis. 1p, Sphaerodactylus armasi.

1994, Nov. 30 **Litho.** *Perf. 12½*

3617	A977	15c multicolored	.30	.20
3618	A977	65c multicolored	1.60	.90
3619	A977	75c multicolored	1.75	1.00
3620	A977	85c multicolored	2.00	1.25
3621	A977	90c multicolored	2.25	1.25
3622	A977	1p multicolored	2.50	1.40
		Nos. 3617-3622 (6)	10.40	6.00

Cuban War of Independence, Cent. — A978

1995, Feb. 24 **Litho.** *Perf. 12½*

3623	A978	15c Jose Marti, flag	.50	.20

Pan American Games, Mar del Plata, Argentina — A979

1995, Mar. 11 **Litho.** *Perf. 13*

3624	A979	10c Boxing, vert.	.20	.20
3625	A979	15c Weight lifting, vert.	.25	.20
3626	A979	65c Volleyball, vert.	1.10	.80
3627	A979	75c Wrestling	1.25	1.00
3628	A979	85c Baseball	1.50	1.00
3629	A979	90c High jump	1.60	1.10
		Nos. 3624-3629 (6)	5.90	4.30

National Aquarium, 35th Anniv. — A980

Fish: 10c, Holacanthus cillaris. 15c, Hypoplectrus guttavarius. 65c, Anisotremus virginicus. 75c, Amblycirrhitus pinos. 85c, Pomaacanthus paru. 90c, Acanthurus coeruleus.

1995, Apr. 28 Litho. *Perf. 13*

3630 A980 10c multicolored	.20	.20
3631 A980 15c multicolored	.25	.20
3632 A980 65c multicolored	1.00	.70
3633 A980 75c multicolored	1.10	.80
3634 A980 85c multicolored	1.90	1.10
3635 A980 90c multicolored	1.90	1.10
Nos. 3630-3635 (6)	6.35	4.10

FAO, 50th Anniv. A981

1995, Apr. 7 Litho. *Perf. 13*

3636 A981 75c multicolored	1.25	1.00

First Cuban Postage Stamp, 140th Anniv. — A982

65c, Ornamental letter drop, envelope.

1995. Apr. 24 Litho. *Perf. 12½*

3637 A982 15c black & blue green	.30	.20
3638 A982 65c multicolored	1.40	.75

Jose Marti, Death Cent. A983

Designs: 15c, Marti killed in combat, signature, portrait. 65c, Landing of Marti, Cuban patriots on Playitas beach. 75c, Montecristi Manifesto signed in Domincan Republic, Marti. 85c, Meeting of Marti, Maceo, Gomez at La Mejorana Farm. 90c, Marti's mausoleum, Santiago, Cuba, vert.

1995, May 19 *Perf. 12½x13, 13x12½*

3639 A983 15c multicolored	.25	.20
3640 A983 65c multicolored	1.25	.80
3641 A983 75c multicolored	1.40	1.00
3642 A983 85c multicolored	1.75	1.00
3643 A983 90c multicolored	1.75	1.10
Nos. 3639-3643 (5)	6.40	4.10

Antonio Maceo (1845-96), Revolutionary — A984

1995, June 14 Litho. *Perf. 12½*

3644 A984 15c multicolored	.60	.20

Butterflies — A985

Designs: 10c, Dione vanillae. 15c, Eunica tatila. 65c, Melete salacia. 75c, Greta cubana. 85c, Eurema daira. 90c, Phoebis sennae.

1995, June 20 *Perf. 12½x13*

3645 A985 10c multicolored	.25	.20
3646 A985 15c multicolored	.25	.20
3647 A985 65c multicolored	1.25	.80
3648 A985 75c multicolored	1.40	1.00
3649 A985 85c multicolored	1.75	1.00
3650 A985 90c multicolored	1.75	1.10
Nos. 3645-3650 (6)	6.65	4.30

World War II Combat Planes — A986

Designs: 10c, Supermarine "Spitfire," Great Britain. 15c, IL-2, Russia. 65c, Curtiss P-40, US. 75c, Messerschmitt Bf-109, Germany. 85c, Morane-Sauinier 406, France.

1995, July 30 Litho. *Perf. 12½*

3651 A986 10c multicolored	.30	.20
3652 A986 15c multicolored	.30	.20
3653 A986 65c multicolored	1.40	.80
3654 A986 75c multicolored	1.60	1.00
3655 A986 85c multicolored	1.90	1.00
Nos. 3651-3655 (5)	5.50	3.20

A987

A988

1995, Aug. 6 Litho. *Perf. 12½*

3656 A987 15c multicolored	.50	.20

Ernesto Lecuona, composer, pianist, birth cent.

1995, Aug. 10

Color of Horse or Horses

3657 A988 10c golden brown, white	.40	.20
3658 A988 15c white, horiz.	.40	.20
3659 A988 65c dark brown, white	1.75	.80
3660 A988 75c red brown	2.10	1.00
3661 A988 85c tan	2.50	1.00
3662 A988 90c white	2.50	1.10
Nos. 3657-3662 (6)	9.65	4.30

Singapore '95.

Souvenir Sheet

Beijing Intl. Stamp & Coin Expo '95 — A989

Illustration reduced.

1995, Aug. 28 *Perf. 13*

3663 A989 50c multicolored	1.25	.75

1996 Summer Olympics, Atlanta — A990

1995, Sept. 25 Litho. *Perf. 13*

3664 A990 10c Wrestling	.20	.20
3665 A990 15c Weight lifting	.25	.20
3666 A990 65c Women's volleyball	1.10	.80
3667 A990 75c Women's athletics	1.25	1.00
3668 A990 85c Baseball	1.50	1.00
3669 A990 90c Women's judo	1.60	1.10
Nos. 3664-3669 (6)	5.90	4.30

Souvenir Sheet

3670 A990 1p Boxing	3.00	1.50

No. 3670 contains one 30x36mm stamp.

Cuban Sugar Industry, 400th Anniv. A991

Paintings from "Los Ingenios," by Edouard Laplante, 1852: 15c, Steam train, sugar factory. 65c, Sugar factory, tower, bridge.

1995, Oct. 3

3671 A991 15c multicolored	1.25	.35
3672 A991 65c multicolored	.75	.70

UN, 50th Anniv. A992

1995, Oct. 24 Litho. *Perf. 13*

3673 A992 65c multicolored	1.00	.80

Zoological Gardens, Havana — A993

Designs: 10c, Panthera leo, vert. 15c, Equus grevyi. 65c, Pongo pygmaeus, vert. 75c, Elephas maximus. 85c, Sciurus vulgaris. 90c, Procyon lotor.

1995, Oct. 30 Litho. *Perf. 13*

3674 A993 10c multicolored	.25	.20
3675 A993 15c multicolored	.30	.20
3676 A993 65c multicolored	1.25	.80
3677 A993 75c multicolored	1.40	1.00
3678 A993 85c multicolored	1.75	1.00
3679 A993 90c multicolored	1.90	1.10
Nos. 3674-3679 (6)	6.85	4.30

UNESCO, 50th Anniv. — A994

UNESCO World Culture and National Heritage sites: 65c, Santa Clara de Asis Convent. 75c, San Francisco de Asis Minor Basilica.

1995, Nov. 4

3680 A994 65c multicolored	1.10	.80
3681 A994 75c multicolored	1.25	1.00

Orchids — A995

Designs: 5c, Epidendrum porpax. 10c, Cyrtopodium punctatum. 15c, Polyrrhiza lindeni. 40c, Bletia patula. 45c, Galeandra beyrichii. 50c, Vanilla dilloniana. 65c, Macradenia lutescens. 75c, Oncidium luridum. 85c, Ionopsis utricularioides.

1995, Nov. 10 *Perf. 12½*

3681A A995 5c multicolored	.20	.20
3681B A995 10c multicolored	.25	.20
3681C A995 15c multicolored	.25	.20
3682 A995 40c multicolored	.80	.55
3683 A995 45c multicolored	.90	.55
3684 A995 50c multicolored	1.00	.65
3685 A995 65c multicolored	1.25	.80
3686 A995 75c multicolored	1.40	1.00
3687 A995 85c multicolored	1.75	1.00
Nos. 3681A-3687 (9)	7.80	5.15

Issued: 40c-85c, 11/10/95; 5c-15c, 6/28/96.

Motion Pictures, Cent. — A996

1995, Dec. 7 *Perf. 13*

3688 A996 15c Lumiere Brothers	.30	.20
3689 A996 15c Marilyn Monroe	.30	.20
3690 A996 15c Marlene Dietrich	.30	.20
3691 A996 15c Vittorio DeSica	.30	.20
3692 A996 15c Charlie Chaplin	.30	.20
3693 A996 15c Greta Garbo	.30	.20
3694 A996 65c Humphrey Bogart	1.40	.80
3695 A996 75c Montaner	1.60	1.00
3696 A996 85c Cantinflas	1.90	1.00
Nos. 3688-3696 (9)	6.70	4.00

Souvenir Sheet

4th Cuban-Spanish Philatelic Exhibition, Havana — A997

Illustration reduced.

1995, Dec. 11 Litho. *Perf. 13*

3697 A997 1p multicolored	3.00	1.50

America Issue — A998

1995, Dec. 12

3698 A998 15c Centurus superciliaris	.35	.20
3699 A998 65c Todus multicolor	1.60	.80

Generals Who Died in 1895 War — A999

Designs: No. 3700, Alfonso Goulet Goulet, Francisco Adolfo Crombet Ballon. No. 3701, Jesus Calvar O, Jose Guillermo Moncada, Tomas Jordan. No. 3702, Francisco Borrero Lavadi, Francisco Inchaustegui Cabrera.

1995, Dec. 20 *Perf. 12½*

3700 A999 15c multicolored .35 .20
3701 A999 15c multicolored .35 .20
3702 A999 15c multicolored .35 .20
a. Strip of 3, #3700-3702 1.10 .90
Nos. 3700-3702 (3) 1.05 .60

See Nos. 3758-3760.

Island of Coco Cay, Jardines del Rey A1000

Bird, scenic view: 10c, Sterna antillarum, aerial view of island. 15c, Eudocimus albus, people on beach. 45c, Spindalis zena, couple on steps of resort complex. 50c, Turdus plumbeus, resort. 65c, Mimus polyglottos, resort. 75c, Phoenicopterus ruber, couple in pool at resort.

1995, Dec. 23

3703 A1000 10c multicolored .20 .20
3704 A1000 15c multicolored .30 .20
3705 A1000 45c multicolored 1.00 .55
3706 A1000 50c multicolored 1.10 .60
3707 A1000 65c multicolored 1.40 .80
3708 A1000 75c multicolored 1.60 1.00
Nos. 3703-3708 (6) 5.60 3.35

Patriots — A1001

Designs: 15c, Carlos M. de Céspedes (1819-74). 65c, José Marti (1853-95). 75c, Antonio Maceo (1845-96). 1.05p, Ignacio Agramonte (1841-73). 2.05p, Máximo Gómez (1836-1905). 3p, Calixto Garcia (1839-98).

1996, Jan. 10

3709 A1001 15c green .25 .20
3710 A1001 65c blue 1.10 .80
3711 A1001 75c carmine 1.25 1.00
3712 A1001 1.05p lilac 1.90 1.40
3713 A1001 2.05p brown 3.75 2.50
3714 A1001 3p light brown 5.25 3.75
Nos. 3709-3714 (6) 13.50 9.65

See Nos. 3755-3757.

Organization of Solidarity of the Peoples of Africa, Asia and Latin America (OSPAAAL), 30th Anniv. — A1002

1996, Jan. 14

3715 A1002 65c multicolored 1.50 .75

Scientists — A1003

10c, Leonardo da Vinci (1452-1519). 15c, Mikhail V. Lomonosov (1711-65), atmospheric scientist. 65c, James Watt (1736-1819), engineer, inventor. 75c, Guglielmo Marconi (1874-1937), physicist. 85c, Charles R. Darwin (1809-82), naturalist.

1996, Jan. 30 Litho. *Perf. 12½*

3716 A1003 10c multicolored .25 .20
3717 A1003 15c multicolored .25 .20
3718 A1003 65c multicolored 1.25 .80
3719 A1003 75c multicolored 1.40 1.00
3720 A1003 85c multicolored 1.75 1.00
Nos. 3716-3720 (5) 4.90 3.20

1996 Summer Olympics, Atlanta — A1004

1996, Feb. 15 Litho. *Perf. 12½*

3721 A1004 10c Athletics, vert. .30 .20
3722 A1004 15c Weight lifting, vert. .30 .20
3723 A1004 65c Judo, vert. 1.40 .80
3724 A1004 75c Wrestling 1.60 1.00
3725 A1004 85c Boxing 1.90 1.00
Nos. 3721-3725 (5) 5.50 3.20

Souvenir Sheet

3726 A1004 1p Baseball, vert. 3.00 1.50

No. 3726 contains one 40x32mm stamp.

Espamer '96, Aviation and Space, Philatelic Exhibition, Seville — A1005

1996, Mar. 4

3727 A1005 15c C-4 Autogiro .25 .20
3728 A1005 65c CASA C-352 1.25 .80
3729 A1005 75c Alcotan C-201 1.60 1.00
3730 A1005 85c CASA C-212 1.75 1.00
Nos. 3727-3730 (4) 4.85 3.00

Juan C. Gundlach (1810-1896), Ornithologist — A1006

Birds: 10c, Ceryle alcyon. 15c, Setophaga ruticilla. 65c, Geothlypis trichas. 75c, Passerina ciris. 85c, Bombycilla cedrorum.
1p, Vireo gundlachi.

1996, Mar. 15 *Perf. 12½*

3731 A1006 10c multicolored .30 .20
3732 A1006 15c multicolored .30 .20
3733 A1006 65c multicolored 1.40 .80
3734 A1006 75c multicolored 1.60 1.00
3735 A1006 85c multicolored 1.90 1.00
Nos. 3731-3735 (5) 5.50 3.20

Souvenir Sheet

3736 A1006 1p multicolored 3.75 1.90

No. 3736 contains one 40x32mm stamp.

Souvenir Sheet

ESPAMER '96, Stamp Exhibition of America and Europe, Seville — A1007

Illustration reduced.

1996, Mar. 14 Litho. *Perf. 12½*

3737 A1007 1p multicolored 3.00 1.50

First Man in Space, 35th Anniv. — A1008

Designs: 15c, Yuri A. Gagarin (1934-68). 65c, Spaceship, map showing orbital route.

1996, Apr. 12 Litho. *Perf. 12½*

3738 A1008 15c multi .25 .20
3739 A1008 65c multi, horiz. 1.10 .80

Bay of Pigs Invasion, 35th Anniv. — A1009

1996, Apr. 19

3740 A1009 15c shown .35 .20
3741 A1009 65c Natl. flags 1.60 .80

Cuban Sailing Ships A1010

Designs: 10c, Bahama. 15c, Santísima Trinidad. 65c, Principe de Asturias. 75c, San Pedro de Alcántara. 85c, Santa Ana.
1p, San Genaro.

1996, May 8 Litho. *Perf. 12½*

3742 A1010 10c multicolored .20 .20
3743 A1010 15c multicolored .30 .20
3744 A1010 65c multicolored 1.40 .80
3745 A1010 75c multicolored 1.60 1.00
3746 A1010 85c multicolored 1.75 1.00
Nos. 3742-3746 (5) 5.25 3.20

Souvenir Sheet

3747 A1010 1p multicolored 2.00 1.00

CAPEX '96. No. 3747 contains one 40x32mm stamp.

Fauna of the Caribbean A1011

Designs: 10c, Todus multicolor. No. 3749, Eulampis jugularis. No. 3750, Aix sponsa. No. 3751, Chaetodon ocellatus. No. 3752, Papilio cresphontes. No. 3753, Hypoplectrus indigo.

1996, June 18 Litho. *Perf. 12½*

3748 A1011 10c multicolored .30 .20
3749 A1011 15c multicolored .30 .20
3750 A1011 15c multicolored .30 .20
3751 A1011 15c multicolored .30 .20
3752 A1011 65c multicolored 1.40 .80
3753 A1011 65c multicolored 1.40 .80
Nos. 3748-3753 (6) 4.00 2.40

Jose M. Maceo Grajales (1849-96), Revolutionary War Leader — A1012

1996, July 5

3754 A1012 15c multicolored .50 .20

Patriot Type of 1996

Designs: 10c. Serafin Sánchez. 85c, Juan Gualberto Gomez. 90c, Quintin Bandera.

1996, July 10

3755 A1001 10c orange .20 .20
3756 A1001 85c olive 1.75 1.00
3757 A1001 90c olive brown 2.00 1.10
Nos. 3755-3757 (3) 3.95 2.30

Generals Who Died in 1895 War Type of 1995

#3758, Esteban Tamayo (1843-96), Angel Guerra (1842-96). #3759, Juan Fernández Ruz (1821-96), José Maria Aguirre (1843-96), Serafin Sánchez (1846-96). #3760, Juan Bruno Zayas (1867-96), Pedro Vargas Sotomayor (1868-96).

1996, July 30

3758 A999 15c multicolored .35 .20
3759 A999 15c multicolored .35 .20
3760 A999 15c multicolored .35 .20
a. Strip of 3, #3758-3760 1.70 .90
Nos. 3758-3760 (3) 1.05 .60

Santiago de Cuba — A1013

Flower, scenic view: 15c, Jacaranda arborea, beach. 65c, Begonia bissei, Fort San Pedro de la Roca. 75c, Byrsonima crassifolia, palm trees, mountains, vert. 85c, Pereskia zinniiflora, church, vert.

Perf. 13x12½, 12½x13

1996, Sept. 27 **Litho.**

3761 A1013 15c multicolored .30 .20
3762 A1013 65c multicolored 1.40 .80
3763 A1013 75c multicolored 1.60 1.00
3764 A1013 85c multicolored 1.75 1.00
Nos. 3761-3764 (4) 5.05 3.00

Steam Locomotives — A1014

Designs: 10c, Baldwin 0-4-2, 1878. 15c, American 2-6-0, 1904. 65c, Baldwin 4-6-0, 1906. 75c, Rogers 2-4-4, 1914. 90c, Baldwin 2-8-0, 1920.

1996, Sept. 30 *Perf. 12½*

3765 A1014 10c multicolored .25 .20
3766 A1014 15c multicolored .25 .20
3767 A1014 65c multicolored 1.40 .80
3768 A1014 75c multicolored 1.60 .90
3769 A1014 90c multicolored 1.75 1.00
Nos. 3765-3769 (5) 5.25 3.10

Traditional Costumes A1015

America Issue: 15c, Free black couple, 19th cent. 65c, Guayabera couple, 20th cent.

1996, Oct. 12 Litho. *Perf. 12½*

3770	A1015	15c multicolored	.35	.20
3771	A1015	65c multicolored	1.60	.80

UNICEF, 50th Anniv. — A1016

1996, Nov. 8 Litho. *Perf. 12½*

3772	A1016	15c multicolored	.50	.20

World Chess Championship Won by José Raúl Capablanca, 75th Anniv. — A1017

Designs: 15c, Portrait, chess board. 65c, Portrait, seated at chess board. 75c, Rook with top shaped as world, portrait. 85c, Playing chess as a child. 90c, In championship match, 1921.

1996, Nov. 30 Litho. *Perf. 12½*

3773	A1017	15c multicolored	.25	.20
3774	A1017	65c multicolored	1.25	.80
3775	A1017	75c multicolored	1.40	1.00
3776	A1017	85c multicolored	1.60	1.00
3777	A1017	90c multicolored	1.75	1.10
		Nos. 3773-3777 (5)	6.25	4.10

Revolutionary Armed Forces and Return of Castro from Mexico, 40th Anniv. — A1018

1996, Dec. 2

3778	A1018	15c Yacht Granma	.20	.20
3779	A1018	65c Armed forces	1.25	1.00

Maj. Gen. Antonio Maceo (1845-96) — A1019

Designs: 10c, Monument, Santiago, vert. No. 3781, Portrait, vert. No. 3782, Monument, Duaba. 65c, Detail of painting showing Maceo dying from combat wounds. 75c, Maceo, young man and monument, San Pedro.

1996, Dec. 7

3780	A1019	10c multicolored	.20	.20
3781	A1019	15c multicolored	.30	.20
3782	A1019	15c multicolored	.30	.20
3783	A1019	65c multicolored	1.50	1.10
3784	A1019	75c multicolored	1.75	1.40
		Nos. 3780-3784 (5)	4.05	3.10

Medals Won at 1996 Summer Olympic Games, Atlanta — A1020

Medal, sport: No. 3785a, Gold, judo. b, Bronze, wrestling.

No. 3786: a, Gold, weight lifting. b, Gold, wrestling. c, Silver, fencing. d, Silver, swimming.

No. 3787: a, Gold, women's volleyball. b, Gold, boxing. c, Silver, women's running. d, Gold, baseball.

1996, Dec. 10

3785	A1020	10c Pair, #a-b + 4 labels	.50	.25
3786	A1020	15c Block, #a-d + 2 labels	1.00	.50
3787	A1020	65c Block, #a-d + 2 labels	4.50	2.25
		Nos. 3785-3787 (3)	6.00	3.00

New Year 1996 (Year of the Rat) — A1021

1996, Dec. 28 Litho. *Perf. 12½*

3788	A1021	15c multicolored	.50	.25

Espamer '98 — A1022

Locomotives: 15c, Minho Douro 0-6-0, Portugal. No. 3790, Vulcan Iron Works 0-4-0, Brazil. No. 3791, Baldwin 2-6-0, Dominican Republic. No. 3792, American Locomotive Co. 2-6-4, Panama. No. 3793, Baldwin 0-4-0, Puerto Rico. No. 3794, Slaughter, Gruning Co. 0-4-0, Spain. No. 3795, Yorkshire Engine Co. 4-4-0, Argentina. No. 3796, 2-6-0 Paraguay. No. 3797, H.K. Porter Co. 2-8-2, Chile. No. 3798, 2-6-0, Mexico.

1p, Baldwin 0-4-2 (1884), Cuba.

1996, Dec. 30

3789	A1022	15c multicolored	.30	.20
3790	A1022	65c multicolored	1.50	.85
3791	A1022	65c multicolored	1.50	.85
3792	A1022	65c multicolored	1.50	.85
3793	A1022	65c multicolored	1.50	.85
3794	A1022	65c multicolored	1.50	.85
3795	A1022	75c multicolored	1.75	1.00
3796	A1022	75c multicolored	1.75	1.00
3797	A1022	75c multicolored	1.75	1.00
3798	A1022	75c multicolored	1.75	1.00
		Nos. 3789-3798 (10)	14.80	8.45

Souvenir Sheet

3799	A1022	1p multicolored	3.50	1.75

No. 3799 contains one 36x28mm.

Hong Kong '97, Intl. Philatelic Exhibition — A1023

Cats: 10c, Brown-point Siamese, vert. No. 3801, Japanese bobtail. No. 3802, Burmese, vert. No. 3803, Singapore. No. 3804, Korat.

1p, Blue-point Siamese.

1997, Jan. 15 Litho. *Perf. 12½*

3800	A1023	10c multicolored	.20	.20
3801	A1023	15c multicolored	.30	.20
3802	A1023	15c multicolored	.30	.20
3803	A1023	65c multicolored	1.60	1.00
3804	A1023	75c multicolored	2.00	1.10
		Nos. 3800-3804 (5)	4.40	2.70

Souvenir Sheet

3805	A1023	1p multicolored	4.00	2.00

No. 3805 contains one 40x31mm stamp.

Motion Pictures, Cent. A1024

Film scenes from: 15c, "El Romance del Palmar," directed by Ramón Peón. 65c, "Memorias del Subdesarrollo," directed by Tomás Gutiérrez Alea, vert.

1997, Jan. 24 Litho. *Perf. 13*

3806	A1024	15c multicolored	.30	.20
3807	A1024	65c multicolored	1.60	1.00

Zoo Animals A1025

Designs: 10c, Camelus dromedarius. No. 3809, Ailuropada melanoleuca. No. 3810, Cerothoterium simun. 75c, Pongo pygmaeus. 90c, Bison bonasus.

1997, Feb. 20 Litho. *Perf. 12½*

3808	A1025	10c multicolored	.20	.20
3809	A1025	15c multicolored	.30	.20
3810	A1025	15c multicolored	.30	.20
3811	A1025	75c multicolored	1.60	1.00
3812	A1025	90c multicolored	1.75	1.10
		Nos. 3808-3812 (5)	4.15	2.70

New Year 1997 (Year of the Ox) — A1026

1997, Feb. 22

3813	A1026	15c multicolored	.50	.25

Attack on the Presidential Palace, 40th Anniv. — A1027

1997, Mar. 13 Litho. *Perf. 12½*

3814	A1027	15c Menelao Mora Morales	.75	.20

1998 World Cup Soccer Championships, France — A1028

Action scenes: 10c, Three players. No. 3816, Player in green, player in blue & yellow. No. 3817, Player in yellow & black, player in green. 65c, Player in yellow & blue, player in blue and red. 75c, Player in red & blue, player in yellow & black.

1p, Player down.

1997, Mar. 25

3815	A1028	10c multicolored	.20	.20
3816	A1028	15c multicolored	.30	.20
3817	A1028	15c multicolored	.30	.20
3818	A1028	65c multicolored	1.60	1.00
3819	A1028	75c multicolored	1.90	1.10
		Nos. 3815-3819 (5)	4.30	2.70

Souvenir Sheet

3820	A1028	1p multicolored	2.25	1.10

No. 3820 contains one 40x31mm stamp.

Young Communist League (UJC), 35th Anniv. — A1029

1997, Apr. 4

3821	A1029	15c multicolored	.75	.20

Paddle Steamer Caledonia — A1030

Stamp Day: 15c, Maritime Postal Service, 170th anniv. 65c, Air Postal Service, 70th anniv.

1997, Apr. 24 Litho. *Perf. 12½*

3822	A1030	15c multicolored	.35	.25
3823	A1030	65c multicolored	1.40	.95

Death of Generals in War of 1895, 102nd Anniv. — A1031

#3824, Adolfo de Castillo, Enrique del Junco Cruz-Muñoz. #3825, Alberto Rodríguez Acosta, Mariano Sánchez Vaillant.

1997, May 18 Litho. *Perf. 12½*

3824	A1031	15c multicolored	.30	.20
3825	A1031	15c multicolored	.30	.20
a.		Pair, #3824-3825	.60	.20

Gen. Gregorio Luperon, Death Cent. — A1032

1997, May 20

3826	A1032 65c multicolored	1.50	1.00

Butterflies — A1033

Designs: 10c, Eurema nicippe. No. 3828, Eurema dina. No. 3829, Colobura dirce clementi. 65c, Vanesa atalanta. 85c, Kricogonia castalia.

1997, May 20

3827	A1033 10c multicolored	.20	.20
3828	A1033 15c multicolored	.30	.20
3829	A1033 15c multicolored	.30	.20
3830	A1033 65c multicolored	1.50	.90
3831	A1033 85c multicolored	1.75	1.00
	Nos. 3827-3831 (5)	4.05	2.50

Cuban Assoc. of the UN, 50th Anniv. A1034

1997, May 31

3832	A1034 65c multicolored	1.50	.95

Chinese In Cuba, 150th Anniv. — A1035

1997, May 29 *Perf. 13*

3833	A1035 15c multicolored	.80	.45

14th World Festival of Youth and Students A1036

Designs: 10c, Dove holding olive twig, rainbow. No. 3835, Children playing on playground equipment, vert. No. 3836, Monument with arms extended. 65c, Maj. Ernesto "Che" Guevara, revolutionary hero. 75c, Monument, diff.

1997, July 28 **Litho.** *Perf. 12½*

3834	A1036 10c multicolored	.20	.20
3835	A1036 15c multicolored	.30	.20
3836	A1036 15c multicolored	.30	.20
3837	A1036 65c multicolored	1.50	.95
3838	A1036 75c multicolored	1.75	1.00
	Nos. 3834-3838 (5)	4.05	2.55

Frank País (1934-57), Revolutionary Hero — A1037

1997, July 30

3839	A1037 15c multicolored	.50	.20

Seven Wonders of the Ancient World A1038

Designs: 10c, Lighthouse of Alexandria. No. 3841, Pyramids of Egypt. No. 3842, Gardens of Semiramis at Babylon. No. 3843, Colossus at Rhodes. No. 3844, Mausoleum of Halicarnassus. No. 3845, Statue of Zeus at Olympia. 75c, Temple of Artemis at Ephesus.

1997, July 30

3840	A1038 10c multicolored	.20	.20
3841	A1038 15c multicolored	.30	.20
3842	A1038 15c multicolored	.30	.20
3843	A1038 15c multicolored	.30	.20
3844	A1038 65c multicolored	1.50	.95
3845	A1038 65c multicolored	1.50	.95
3846	A1038 75c multicolored	1.60	1.00
	Nos. 3840-3846 (7)	5.70	3.70

Independence of India, 50th Anniv. — A1039

1997, Aug. 15

3847	A1039 15c Mahatma Gandhi	.50	.20

Caribbean Birds — A1040

#3848, Sicalis flaveola. #3849, Eubucco bourcierii. #3850, Trogon curucui. #3851, Amazona leucocephala. #3852, Amazona ochrocephala. #3853, Hylocharis eliciae. #3854, Carduelis carduelis.

1997, Aug. 15

3848	A1040 15c multicolored	.30	.20
3849	A1040 15c multicolored	.30	.20
3850	A1040 15c multicolored	.30	.20
3851	A1040 15c multicolored	.30	.20
3852	A1040 65c multicolored	1.60	1.00
3853	A1040 65c multicolored	1.60	1.00
3854	A1040 75c multicolored	1.75	1.10
	Nos. 3848-3854 (7)	6.15	3.90

Famous Composers — A1041

10c, Liszt. #3856, Chopin. #3857, Bach. #3858, Beethoven. 65c, Ignacio Cervantes (1847-1905). 75c, Mozart.

1997, Sept. 15 **Litho.** *Perf. 12½*

3855	A1041 10c multicolored	.45	.20
3856	A1041 15c multicolored	.45	.20
3857	A1041 15c multicolored	.45	.20
3858	A1041 15c multicolored	.45	.20
3859	A1041 65c multicolored	1.60	.80
3860	A1041 75c multicolored	1.75	.95
	Nos. 3855-3860 (6)	5.15	2.55

Tourism in Pinar del Rio — A1042

Bird, scene: 10c, Myadestes elisabeth, Viñales Valley. 15c, Corvus nasicus, Jutia Key. 65c, Dendroica pityophila, Soroa Falls. 75c, Tyrannus cubensis, San Juan River.

1997, Sept. 27 **Litho.**

3861	A1042 10c multi	.35	.20
3862	A1042 15c multi	.35	.20
3863	A1042 65c multi, vert.	1.50	.80
3864	A1042 75c multi, vert.	1.60	.95
	Nos. 3861-3864 (4)	3.80	2.15

Caribbean Flowers — A1043

Designs: No. 3865, Hibiscus elatus (majagua). No. 3866, Cordia sebestena (vomitel). No. 3867, Bidens pilosa (romerillo). No. 3868, Catharanthus roseus (vicaria). 65c, Reullia tuberosa (salta perico). 75c, Turnera ulmifolia (marilope).

1997, Sept. 30

3865	A1043 15c multicolored	.35	.20
3866	A1043 15c multicolored	.35	.20
3867	A1043 15c multicolored	.35	.20
3868	A1043 15c multicolored	.35	.20
3869	A1043 65c multicolored	1.50	.80
3870	A1043 75c multicolored	1.60	.95
	Nos. 3865-3870 (6)	4.50	2.55

Eastern University, 50th Anniv. — A1044

1997, Oct. 1 *Perf. 13*

3871	A1044 15c multicolored	.50	.20

Che Guevara (1928-67), 5th Cuban Communist Party Congress A1045

1997, Oct. 8

3872	A1045 15c Flags	.35	.20
3873	A1045 15c Text, Guevara	1.50	.80
3874	A1045 75c Portrait of Guevara	1.60	.80
	Nos. 3872-3874 (3)	3.45	1.80

America Issue — A1046

1997, Oct. 12 **Litho.** *Perf. 13*

3875	A1046 15c 19th cent. postman	.20	.20
3876	A1046 65c 20th cent. postman	.75	.55

Hominids — A1047

Designs: 10c, Australopithecus. No. 3878, Pithecanthropus (Java man). No. 3879, Sinanthropus (Peking man). No. 3880, Neanderthal. 65c, Cro-magnon man. 75c, Oberkassel man.

1997, Oct. 30 *Perf. 12½*

3877	A1047 10c multicolored	.30	.20
3878	A1047 15c multicolored	.45	.20
3879	A1047 15c multicolored	.45	.20
3880	A1047 15c multicolored	.45	.20
3881	A1047 65c multicolored	1.60	.90
3882	A1047 75c multicolored	1.75	.90
	Nos. 3877-3882 (6)	5.00	2.60

October Revolution, 80th Anniv. — A1048

1997, Nov. 7 *Perf. 12½*

3884	A1048 75c multicolored	1.75	1.00

Cuban Railroad, 160th Anniv. — A1049

10c, John Bull, 1830, UK. No. 3886, Old Ironsides, Baldwin, 1832, US. No. 3887, Baldwin Pacific Type 4-6-2, 1910-13, US. 65c, TE.M4:1 diesel electric, 1970, USSR. 75c, TE.114-K, diesel electric, 1975, USSR.

1997, Nov. 19 **Litho.** *Perf. 12½*

3885	A1049 10c multicolored	.20	.20
3886	A1049 15c multicolored	.30	.20
3887	A1049 15c multicolored	.30	.20
3888	A1049 65c multicolored	1.50	.90
3889	A1049 75c multicolored	1.60	.90
	Nos. 3885-3889 (5)	3.90	2.40

UN Conference on Commerce and Employment, Havana, 50th Anniv. — A1050

1997, Nov. 21

3890	A1050 65c multicolored		1.40	.80

Victor Manuel Garcia, Painter, Birth Cent. A1051

1997, Dec. 29 Litho. ***Perf. 12½***

3891	A1051 15c #1553, Garcia		.50	.25

Visit of Pope John Paul II A1052

Pope John Paul II, different coats of arms, and: 65c, Havana Cathedral. 75c, Basilica of Our Lady of Charity, Cobre, vert.

No. 3894, vert: a, Pope John Paul II greeting Fidel Castro. b, Pope waving.

1998, Jan. 18 Litho. ***Perf. 12½***

3892	A1052 65c multicolored		1.50	.80
3893	A1052 75c multicolored		1.75	.80

Souvenir Sheet of 2

3894	A1052 50c #a.-b.		3.00	1.50

Nos. 3894a-3894b are 32x40mm.

Assassination of Jesus Menendez, 50th Anniv. — A1053

1998, Jan. 22

3895	A1053 15c multicolored		.55	.20

1998 World Cup Soccer Championships, France — A1054

Various soccer plays: 10c, 2 players. #3897, Player in black & yellow. #3898, Player on ground, 1 in striped shirt. #3899, 3 players, 2 in striped shirts. #3900, 3 players, 2 in blue shirts.

1p, Player with #11 on sleeve.

1998, Feb. 10 Litho. ***Perf. 12½***

3896	A1054 10c multi, vert.		.50	.20
3897	A1054 15c multi, vert.		.60	.20
3898	A1054 15c multi, vert.		.60	.20
3899	A1054 65c multi		2.10	1.00
3900	A1054 65c multi		2.10	1.00
	Nos. 3896-3900 (5)		5.90	2.60

Souvenir Sheet

Perf. 13

3901	A1054 1p multicolored		3.00	1.50

No. 3901 contains one 40x32mm stamp.

Capt. Isabel Rubio Diaz, Medical Aide During Revolution, Death Cent. — A1055

1998, Feb. 15 ***Perf. 13***

3902	A1055 15c multicolored		.65	.25

Brig. Gen. Vidal Ducasse Reeve (1852-98) A1056

1998, Feb. 19 ***Perf. 12½***

3903	A1056 15c multicolored		.65	.25

No. 3903 inscribed "Revee."

"Radio Rebelde," 40th Anniv. — A1057

1998, Feb. 23

3904	A1057 15c multicolored		.65	.25

Fire Engines A1058

Designs: 10c, 1901 Shand Mason & Co., London. No. 3905, 1905 Horse-drawn municipal fire wagon, Havana, 1905. No. 3906, 1921 American-La France Fire Engine Co. 65c, 1952 Chevrolet 6400, US. 75c, 1956 American-La France Foamite Co., US.

1998, Mar. 10

3905	A1058 10c multicolored		.40	.20
3906	A1058 15c multicolored		.45	.20
3907	A1058 15c multicolored		.45	.20
3908	A1058 65c multicolored		1.50	.90
3909	A1058 75c multicolored		1.75	.90
	Nos. 3905-3909 (5)		4.55	2.40

Protest of Baragua, 120th Anniv. — A1059

1998, Mar. 15

3910	A1059 15c multicolored		.65	.25

Victory at Cuito Cuanavale, Angola, 10th Anniv. — A1060

1998, Mar. 23 Litho. ***Perf. 12½***

3911	A1060 15c multicolored		.65	.25

New Year 1998 (Year of the Tiger) — A1061

1998, Mar. 30

3912	A1061 15c multicolored		.65	.25

Dogs — A1062

1998, Apr. 15 Litho. ***Perf. 12½***

3913	A1062 10c Chihuahua		.40	.20
3914	A1062 15c Beagle		.45	.20
3915	A1062 15c Xoloitzcuintle		.45	.20
3916	A1062 65c German pointer		1.50	.90
3917	A1062 75c Chow chow		1.75	1.10
	Nos. 3913-3917 (5)		4.55	2.60

Evolution of the Chimpanzee A1063

Pan troglodytes and: 10c, Proconsul. No. 3919, Cranium. No. 3920, Right hand and foot. 65c, New-born chimpanzee. 75c, Map of Africa showing chimpanzee's range.

1998, May 15 Litho. ***Perf. 12½***

3918	A1063 10c multicolored		.40	.20
3919	A1063 15c multicolored		.40	.20
3920	A1063 15c multicolored		.40	.20
3921	A1063 65c multicolored		1.60	1.00
3922	A1063 75c multicolored		1.75	1.00
	Nos. 3918-3922 (5)		4.55	2.60

Lisbon '98, World Stamp Exhibition — A1064

Deep sea fish: No. 3923, Raja batis. No. 3924, Eurypharynx pelecanoides. 65c, Caulophryne. 75c, Chauliodus sloani.

1998, May 22 Litho. ***Perf. 12½***

3923	A1064 15c multicolored		.35	.25
3924	A1064 15c multicolored		.35	.25
3925	A1064 65c multicolored		1.60	1.10
3926	A1064 75c multicolored		1.80	1.25
	Nos. 3923-3926 (4)		4.10	2.85

Souvenir Sheet

Juvalux '98, World Stamp Exhibition for Youth Philately and Postal History, Luxembourg — A1065

Illustration reduced.

1998, May 20 Litho. ***Perf. 12½***

3927	A1065 1p Postman on bicycle		3.00	1.50

Federico Garcia Lorca (1898-1936), Poet — A1066

1998, June 2

3928	A1066 75c multicolored		2.25	1.00

Intl. Year of the Oceans A1067

#3929, Canarreos flower coral, coral crab, small fish. #3030, French angel fish, brain coral, gorgonia.

1998, June 5

3929	A1067 65c multicolored		1.50	.70
3930	A1067 65c multicolored		1.50	.70
a.	Pair, #3929-3930		3.50	1.75

Diana, Princess of Wales (1961-97) A1068

Various portraits, color of clothes: No. 3931, Pale yellow and pink. No. 3932, Black and white. No. 3933, Multicolored print. No. 3934, Red. No. 3935, Pink and black plaid. 65c, White. 75c, Blue.

1998, June 30 Litho. ***Perf. 13***

3931	A1068 10c multicolored		.30	.20
3932	A1068 10c multicolored		.30	.20
3933	A1068 10c multicolored		.30	.20
3934	A1068 15c multicolored		.40	.25
3935	A1068 15c multicolored		.40	.25
3936	A1068 65c multicolored		1.90	1.10
3937	A1068 75c multicolored		2.10	1.25
	Nos. 3931-3937 (7)		5.70	3.45

Expo 2000, Hanover A1069

#3938, Mascot, "Twipsy." #3939, Mascot in London, 1851. #3940, Mascot in Brussels, 1958. #3941, German flag, map of Germany. 65c, Mascot in Paris, 1889. 75c, Mascot on top of world, fireworks.

1998, July 31 *Perf. 12½*

3938 A1069 15c multi, vert. .40 .25
3939 A1069 15c multi .40 .25
3940 A1069 15c multi .40 .25
3941 A1069 15c multi .40 .25
3942 A1069 65c multi, vert. 1.90 1.00
3943 A1069 75c multi 2.10 1.25
Nos. 3938-3943 (6) 5.60 3.25

Maracaibo '98, 18th Central America and Caribbean Games — A1070

1998, Aug. 8

3944 A1070 15c multicolored .50 .20

Attack on Moncada Barracks, 45th Anniv. — A1071

Designs: 15c, Siboney farmhouse, Abel Santamaría. 65c, Barracks, José Martí.

1998, July 26 **Litho.** *Perf. 13*

3945 A1071 15c multicolored .40 .25
3946 A1071 65c multicolored 1.90 .80

Democratic Republic of Korea, 50th Anniv. — A1072

1998, Sept. 8 **Litho.** *Perf. 13*

3947 A1072 75c Kim Il Sung (1912-94) 2.25 1.00

Japanese Immigration to Cuba, Cent. — A1073

1998, Sept. 9 **Litho.** *Perf. 13*

3948 A1073 75c multicolored 2.25 1.00

Orchids A1074

10c, Coelogyne flaccida. #3950, Dendrobium fimbriatum. #3951, Arunding graminifolia. #3952, Bletia patula. #3953, Phaius tankervilliaea.

1998, Sept. 10

3949 A1074 10c multicolored .30 .20
3950 A1074 15c multicolored .50 .25
3951 A1074 15c multicolored .50 .25
3952 A1074 65c multicolored 1.90 1.00
3953 A1074 65c multicolored 1.90 1.00
Nos. 3949-3953 (5) 5.10 2.70

5th Congress of the Revolution Defense Committees A1075

1998, Sept. 25 **Litho.** *Perf. 13*

3954 A1075 15c multicolored .45 .20

World Tourism Day — A1076

Holguin Province, reptiles: 10c, Looking through gateway, city of Gibara, anolis equestris, vert. 15c, Mayabe Valley, anolis vermiculatus, vert. 65c, Guardalavaca Beach, anolis allisoni. 75c, Mayari pine forest, anolis mestrei.

1998, Sept. 27

3955 A1076 10c multicolored .30 .20
3956 A1076 15c multicolored .50 .25
3957 A1076 65c multicolored 1.90 .80
3958 A1076 75c multicolored 2.10 1.00
Nos. 3955-3958 (4) 4.80 2.25

Women Who Aided Cuban Revolutionary Movements A1077

America Issue: 65c, Bernarda Toro Pelegrin (1852-1911). 75c, Maria Magdalena Cabrales Issac (1842-1905).

1998, Oct. 12

3959 A1077 65c multicolored 1.90 .80
3960 A1077 75c multicolored 2.10 1.00

World Wildlife Fund Protected Fauna — A1078

Cuban Natl. Ballet, 50th Anniv. — A1079

Arantinga Euops: 10c, Two on tree branch. 15c, One looking out of nest. 65c, One on tree branch. 75c, One up close.

1998, Oct. 21

3961 A1078 10c multicolored .45 .30
3962 A1078 15c multicolored .65 .50
3963 A1078 65c multicolored 2.75 .90
3964 A1078 75c multicolored 3.25 1.10
Nos. 3961-3964 (4) 7.10 2.80

1998, Oct. 28

3965 A1079 15c Swan Lake .50 .25
3966 A1079 65c Giselle 1.90 .80

Massacre of O'Farrill and Goicuria, 40th Anniv. — A1080

Rogelio Perea, Angel Ameijeiras, Pedro Gutiérrez.

1998, Nov. 8

3967 A1080 15c multicolored .45 .20

Battle of Guisa, 40th Anniv. A1081

Design: Capt. Braulio Coroneaux, tank.

1998, Nov. 30 **Litho.** *Perf. 12½*

3968 A1081 15c multicolored .45 .20

A1082

A1083

1998, Dec. 10 **Litho.** *Perf. 12½*

3969 A1082 65c multicolored 1.90 .80

Universal Declaration of Human Rights, 50th anniv.

1998, Dec. 11 *Perf. 13*

Calixto Garcia Iñiguez (1839-98), revolutionary Major General.

3970 A1083 65c multicolored 1.90 .80

Padre Félix Varela (1788-1853) — A1084

1998, Dec. 16

3971 A1084 75c multicolored 2.25 1.00

War for Independence, Cent. — A1085

War heroes, historical scene: No. 3972, Carlos Manuel de Céspedes. No. 3973, Ignacio Agramonte. No. 3974, Máximo Gómez. No. 3975, José Maceo. No. 3976, Salvador Cisneros. No. 3978, Calixto Garcia. No. 3979, Adolfo Flor. No. 3980, Serafin Sánchez. 65c, José Martí. 75c, Antonio Maceo.

1998, Dec. 25 **Litho.** *Perf. 12½*

3972 A1085 15c multicolored .45 .20
3973 A1085 15c multicolored .45 .20
3974 A1085 15c multicolored .45 .20
3975 A1085 15c multicolored .45 .20
3976 A1085 15c multicolored .45 .20
3977 A1085 15c multicolored .45 .20
3978 A1085 15c multicolored .45 .20
3979 A1085 15c multicolored .45 .20
3980 A1085 65c multicolored 1.90 .80
3981 A1085 75c multicolored 2.10 1.00
a. Sheet of 10, #3972-3981 + 3 labels 8.00 8.00
Nos. 3972-3981 (10) 7.60 3.40

Battle for Palma Soriano, 40th Anniv. A1086

1998, Dec. 27 **Litho.** *Perf. 13*

3982 A1086 15c multicolored .45 .20

Cuban Revolution, 40th Anniv. — A1087

a, Boat, soldiers in water. b, Fidel Castro with soldier. c, Castro giving speech, pigeons.

1999, Jan. 1
3983 A1087 65c Strip of 3, #a.-c. 4.50 2.25

Natl. Revolutionary Police, 40th Anniv. — A1088

1999, Jan. 5
3984 A1088 15c multicolored .45 .20

Cuban Workers' Trade Union Organization, 60th Anniv. — A1089

1999, Jan. 28 Litho. ***Perf. 12½***
3985 A1089 15c multicolored .45 .20

New Year 1999 (Year of the Rabbit) — A1090

1999, Feb. 5 ***Perf. 13***
3986 A1090 75c multicolored 1.50 1.00

Lenin (1870-1924) — A1091

1999, Feb. 21 Litho. ***Perf. 12½***
3987 A1091 75c multicolored 1.50 1.00

Dinosaurs — A1092

1999, Mar. 10
3988 A1092 10c Ornithosuchus .30 .25
3989 A1092 15c Saltopus .50 .25
3990 A1092 15c Bactrosaurus .50 .25
3991 A1092 65c Protosuchus 1.90 .80
3992 A1092 75c Mussaurus 2.10 1.00
Nos. 3988-3992 (5) 5.30 2.55

Cuban Musicians — A1093

1999, Mar. 22 ***Perf. 13***
3993 A1093 5c Dámaso Pérez Prado .20 .20
3994 A1093 15c Benny Moré .50 .25
3995 A1093 15c Chano Pozo .50 .25
3996 A1093 35c Miguelito Valdés 1.25 .50
3997 A1093 65c Bola de Nieve 1.90 .80
3998 A1093 75c Rita Montaner 2.10 1.00
Nos. 3993-3998 (6) 6.45 3.00

Simón Bolivar's Visit to Cuba, Bicent. A1094

1999, Mar. 25
3999 A1094 65c Portrait 1.90 .80
4000 A1094 65c Monument 1.90 .80
a. Pair, #3999-4000 4.25 2.00

State Security Organization, 40th Anniv. — A1095

1999, Mar. 26 Litho. ***Perf. 12½***
4001 A1095 65c multicolored 1.90 .80

Souvenir Sheet

China '99 World Philatelic Exhibition — A1096

Illustration reduced.

1999, Apr. 10 Litho. ***Perf. 12½***
4002 A1096 1p Giant panda 3.00 1.50

Stamp Day A1097

1999, Apr. 24
4003 A1097 15c Postal rocket .50 .20
4004 A1097 65c Post rider 1.90 .80

Test of Cuban Postal Rocket, 60th anniv. Insurgent Postal Service, 130th anniv.

Casa de las Américas, 40th Anniv. — A1098

1999, Apr. 24
4005 A1098 65c multicolored 1.90 .80

Souvenir Sheet

IBRA '99, World Philatelic Exhibition, Nuremberg — A1099

Illustration reduced.

1999, Apr. 27
4006 A1099 1p Train 3.00 1.50

Agrarian Reform Law, 40th Anniv. A1100

1999, May 17
4007 A1100 65c multicolored 1.60 .80

Felipe Poey, Scientist, Birth Bicent. A1101

Fish: 5c, Gramma loreto Poey. 15c, Liopropoma rubre Poey. #4010, Hypoplectrus gummigutta. #74011, Stegastes dorsopunicans.
1p, Portrait of Poey, hypoplectrus guttavarius.

1999, May 26 Litho. ***Perf. 12½***
4008 A1101 5c multicolored .20 .20
4009 A1101 15c multicolored .40 .20
4010 A1101 65c multicolored 1.90 .80
4011 A1101 65c multicolored 1.90 .80
Nos. 4008-4011 (4) 4.40 2.00

Souvenir Sheet

Perf. 13¼x13

4012 A1101 1p multicolored 3.00 1.00

No. 4012 contains one 32x40mm stamp.

Souvenir Sheet

Philexfrance '99, World Philatelic Exhibition — A1102

Sculpture in sheet margin: "1814," by Jean Louis Meissonier (1815-1891). Illustration reduced.

1999, June 2 ***Perf. 13***
4013 A1102 1p multicolored 3.00 1.50

1999 Pan-American Games, Winnipeg — A1103

1999, June 25 Litho. ***Perf. 13***
4014 A1103 15c Baseball .40 .20
4015 A1103 65c Volleyball, vert 1.90 .80
4016 A1103 75c Boxing 2.10 .90
Nos. 4014-4016 (3) 4.40 1.90

People's Republic of China, 50th Anniv. A1104

5c, Victory at Wioming, by Gao Hong. 15c, Nanchang Insurrection, by Cai Lang. 40c, Red Army Crossing a Swamp, by Gao Quan. 65c, Occupation of the Presidential Palace, by Cheng Yifei and Wei Jingshan. 75c, Proclamation of the People's Republic of China, by Dong Xiwen.

1999, Aug. 21 Litho. ***Perf. 12¾***
4017 A1104 5c multicolored .20 .20
4018 A1104 15c multicolored .40 .20
4019 A1104 40c multicolored 1.10 .45
4020 A1104 65c multicolored 1.75 .70
4021 A1104 75c multicolored 2.00 .85
Nos. 4017-4021 (5) 5.45 2.40

China 1999 World Philatelic Exhibition, Beijing — A1105

No. 4022, Morning Glories, by Qi Baishi. No. 4023, Three Galloping Horses, by Xu Beihong. No. 4024, Hunan Woman, by Fu Baoshi. No. 4025, Birthplace of Luxun, by Wu Guanzhong. No. 4026, Horse Riders, by Huangzhou. 40c, Pine Tree, by He Xiangning. 65c, Sleep, by Jin Shangyi. 75c, Poetic Scene in Xun Yang, by Chen Yifei.

1999, Aug. 22 Litho. ***Perf. 13***
4022 A1105 5c multicolored .20 .20
4023 A1105 5c multicolored .20 .20
4024 A1105 15c multicolored .40 .20

4025 A1105 15c multicolored .40 .20
4026 A1105 15c multicolored .40 .20
4027 A1105 40c multicolored 1.10 .45
4028 A1105 65c multicolored 1.75 .70
4029 A1105 75c multicolored 2.00 .80
a. Sheet of 8, #4022-4029 + label 8.00 8.00
Nos. 4022-4029 (8) 6.45 2.95

UPU, 125th Anniv. A1106

1999, Sept. 16 Litho. ***Perf. 12¾***
4030 A1106 75c multicolored 1.50 .50

World Tourism Day A1107

Butterflies and Havana tourist sites: 10c, Antia numidia, Morro Castle. 15c, Papilio polyxenes, Havana Cathedral. 65c, Dryas julia, Convent of San Francisco. 75c, Eueides cleobaea, Capitol.

1999, Sept. 27 ***Perf. 12½x12¾***
4031 A1107 10c multicolored .25 .20
4032 A1107 15c multicolored .40 .20
4033 A1107 65c multicolored 1.75 .70
4034 A1107 75c multicolored 2.00 .80
Nos. 4031-4034 (4) 4.40 1.90

Expo 2000, Hanover, Germany A1108

5c, World map, Expo 2000 emblem. #4036, "Twipsy" mascot, vert. #4037, "Twipsy" and 1876 Philadelphia Exposition. #4038, "Twipsy" and 1970 Osaka Exposition. 65c, "Twipsy" and 2000 Exposition. 75c, "Twipsy" and 1967 Montreal Exposition.

1999, Oct. 1 ***Perf. 12¾***
4035 A1108 5c multicolored .20 .20
4036 A1108 15c multicolored .35 .20
4037 A1108 15c multicolored .35 .20
4038 A1108 15c multicolored .35 .20
4039 A1108 65c multicolored 1.60 .70
4040 A1108 75c multicolored 2.00 .80
Nos. 4035-4040 (6) 4.85 2.30

Cubana Airlines, 70th Anniv. — A1109

1999, Oct. 8 ***Perf. 12½x12¼***
4041 A1109 15c Fokker .35 .20
4042 A1109 15c DC-10 .35 .20
4043 A1109 65c A-320 1.60 .70
4044 A1109 75c DC-3 2.00 .80
Nos. 4041-4044 (4) 4.30 1.90

America Issue, A New Millennium Without Arms — A1110

1999, Oct. 12 ***Perf. 12¾***
4045 A1110 15c Pigeon, mushroom cloud .40 .20
4046 A1110 65c Dove, globe 1.60 .75

National Instiutions, 40th Anniv. — A1111

1999, Oct. 16 ***Perf. 12¾***
4047 A1111 15c MINFAR .35 .20
4048 A1111 65c Natl. Revolutionary Militia 1.50 .75

Disappearance of Camilo Cienfuegos, 40th Anniv. — A1112

1999, Oct. 28 Litho. ***Perf. 12¾***
4049 A1112 15c multicolored .50 .20

Souvenir Sheet

12th Congress of Cuban Philatelic Federation — A1113

Illustration reduced.

1999, Dec. 11 ***Perf. 13***
4050 A1113 1p multicolored 2.50 1.25

Ernest Hemingway (1899-1961), Writer — A1114

1999, Dec. 15 ***Perf. 12½x12¼***
4051 A1114 65c multicolored 1.50 .70

9th Summit of Ibero-American Heads of State and Government, Havana — A1115

Designs: 65c, Plaza Vieja. 75c, Plaza of St. Francis of Assisi.
1p, Plaza de Armas.

1999, Nov. 5 Litho. ***Perf. 12¾x12½***
4052 A1115 65c multi 1.50 .70
4053 A1115 75c multi 1.60 .80

Souvenir Sheet

Perf. 13

4054 A1115 1p multi 2.50 1.25

No. 4054 contains one 40x31mm stamp.

Rubén Martínez Villena (1899-1934), Revolutionary — A1116

1999, Dec. 20 ***Perf. 12½x12¾***
4055 A1116 15c multi .40 .20

Dr. Tomás Romay Chacón (1764-1849) A1117

1999, Dec. 21 ***Perf. 13***
4056 A1117 65c multi 1.40 .70

New Year 2000 (Year of the Dragon) — A1118

2000, Jan. 10 ***Perf. 12½***
4057 A1118 15c multi .40 .20

Folklore A1119

Paintings depicting Cuban folklore by Concepción Ferrant (1882-1968): 10c, Rumba Caliente. 15c, Cachumba. 65c, En Casa de un Babalao. 75c, Tata Cuñengue.

2000, Jan. 26 ***Perf. 12½x12¾***
4058 A1119 10c multi .25 .20
4059 A1119 15c multi .35 .20
4060 A1119 65c multi 1.40 .80
4061 A1119 75c multi 1.60 .90
Nos. 4058-4061 (4) 3.60 2.10

Butterflies — A1120

10c, Helcyra superba. No. 4063, Pantaporia punctata. No. 4064, Neptis themis. 65c, Curetis acuta. 75c, Chrysozephyrus ataxus.

2000, Feb. 25 ***Perf. 12¾***
4062 A1120 10c multi .30 .20
4063 A1120 15c multi .40 .20
4064 A1120 15c multi .40 .20
4065 A1120 65c multi 1.60 .80
4066 A1120 75c multi 1.90 .95
Nos. 4062-4066 (5) 4.60 2.35

Bangkok 2000 Stamp Exhibition.

Group of 77 South Summit, Havana — A1121

2000, Apr. 7 Litho. ***Perf. 13x12½***
4067 A1121 75c multi 2.00 .90

Lenin, 130th Anniv. of Birth — A1122

2000, Apr. 22 ***Perf. 12¾***
4068 A1122 75c multi 2.00 .90

Che Guevara in Congo, 35th Anniv. A1123

2000, Apr. 24
4069 A1123 65c multi 1.75 .80

Stamp Day — A1124

Designs: 65c, Cuba #2, building. 90c, Airplane, cover, Jaime Gonzáles, pilot of first experimental airmail flight in Cuba.

2000, Apr. 24
4070 A1124 65c multi 1.75 .80
4071 A1124 90c multi 2.25 1.10

Capt. San Luis (Elisio Reyes), Military Hero (1940-67) A1125

2000, Apr. 27
4072 A1125 65c multi 1.75 .80

The Stamp Show 2000, London A1126

Locomotives: 5c, 1882 Baldwin 0-6-0. 10c, 1895 Baldwin 2-8-0. 15c, 1912 Baldwin 2-8-0. 65c, 1919 Alco 2-8-0. 75c, 1925 Alco 2-8-2.
1p, 1920 Henschel 2-6-0.

2000, May 5 *Perf. 12¾*
4073 A1126 5c multi .20 .20
4074 A1126 10c multi .30 .20
4075 A1126 15c multi .40 .20
4076 A1126 65c multi 1.60 .80
4077 A1126 75c multi 1.90 .90
Nos. 4073-4077 (5) 4.40 2.30

Souvenir Sheet
Perf. 13

4078 A1126 1p multi 3.00 1.50

No. 4078 contains one 40x32mm stamp.

WIPA 2000 Philatelic Exhibition, Vienna — A1127

Airships of: 10c, Henri Giffart, 1852. 15c, Albert and Gaston Tissandier, 1883, vert. 50c, Charles Renard and Arthur Krebs, 1884. 65c, Pierre and Paul Lebaudy, 1903. 75c, August von Perseval, 1906.
1p, Ferdinand von Zeppelin.

Perf. 12½x12¼, 12¼x12½
2000, May 18
4079 A1127 10c multi .35 .20
4080 A1127 15c multi .50 .20
4081 A1127 50c multi 1.40 .60
4082 A1127 65c multi 1.90 .80
4083 A1127 75c multi 2.10 .90
Nos. 4079-4083 (5) 6.25 2.70

Souvenir Sheet
Perf. 12½

4084 A1127 1p multi 3.00 1.50

No. 4084 contains one 40x32mm stamp.

Second World Meeting of Friendship and Solidarity With Cuba — A1128

2000, June 23 **Litho.** ***Perf. 12¾***
4085 A1128 65c multi 1.50 1.10

José de la Luz y Caballero (1800-62), Educator — A1129

2000, July 11 ***Perf. 12½x12¼***
4086 A1129 65c multi 1.50 1.10

Amadeo Roldan (1900-39), Violinist — A1130

2000, July 12 ***Perf. 12¾***
4087 A1130 65c multi 1.50 1.10

La Edad de Oro, by José Marti — A1131

5c, Bebé y El Señor Don Pomposo. 10c, La Muñeca Negra. 15c, Nene Traviesa. 50c, Los Dos Ruiseñores. 65c, Frontispiece of La Edad de Oro. 75c, El Camarón Encantado.

2000, July 20
4088-4093 A1131 Set of 6 5.50 4.25
4093a Sheet of 6, #4088-4093 5.50 5.50

Latin American Association for Integration — A1132

2000, Aug. 12
4094 A1132 65c multi 1.50 1.10

Souvenir Sheet

Olymphilex 2000, Sydney — A1133

Illustration reduced.

2000, Aug. 17 ***Perf. 13***
4095 A1133 1p multi 2.00 1.00

2000 Summer Olympics, Sydney A1134

Designs: 5c, Runners. 15c, Soccer. 65c, Baseball. 75c, Cycling.

2000, Aug. 20 ***Perf. 12¾***
4096-4099 A1134 Set of 4 4.00 3.50

Dr. Pedro Kouri Esmeja (1900-64) A1135

2000, Aug. 21 **Litho.**
4100 A1135 65c multi 1.50 1.10

Federation of Cuban Women, 40th Anniv. — A1136

2000, Aug. 23
4101 A1136 15c multi .35 .25

España 2000 Intl. Philatelic Exhibition — A1137

Designs: 10c, 1851 Havana-Bilbao stampless cover, ship. No. 4103, 15c, Spain #1, Cibeles Fountain, Madrid. No. 4104, 15c, 1850 Zaragoza-Cadiz cover, Palacio de Cristal, Madrid. 65c, Spain #1-5, Palacio de Comunicaciones, Madrid. 75c, Cuba #1, Centro Gallego, Havana.

2000, Sept. 7 ***Perf. 12¾x12½***
4102-4106 A1137 Set of 5 4.50 2.75
4106a Sheet of 5, #4102-4106 + label 4.50 4.50

Souvenir Sheet
Perf. 12½

4107 A1137 100c Queen Isabella II, vert. 3.00 2.25

No. 4107 contains one 32x40mm stamp.

Beaches — A1138

#4108, Coconuts Bay, PRC. #4109, Varadero Beach, Cuba.

2000, Sept. 26 ***Perf. 12½x12¼***
4108-4109 A1138 15c Set of 2 .45 .40
4109a Pair, #4108-4109 .45 .40

See People's Republic of China No. 3052.

World Tourism Day — A1139

Marine life: 10c, Eretmochelys imbricata, vert. 15c, Epinephelus striatus, vert. 65c, Pomacanthus paru. 75c, Anisotremus surinamensis.

Perf. 12½x12¾, 12¾x12½
2000, Sept. 27
4110-4113 A1139 Set of 4 4.00 1.60

Committees of Defense of the Revolution, 40th Anniv. — A1140

2000, Sept. 28 ***Perf. 12¾***
4114 A1140 15c multi .35 .25

America Issue — AIDS Prevention A1141

Ribbon, heart-shaped map and: 15c, Family. 65c, Couple.

2000, Oct. 12
4115-4116 A1141 Set of 2 2.75 1.25

Cuban Military in Angola, 25th Anniv. — A1142

2000, Nov. 7
4117 A1142 75c multi 1.50 1.10

Visit by Alexander von Humboldt, Bicent. — A1143

Humboldt and: 15c, House in Trinidad. 65c, House in Havana, Political Essay on the Island of Cuba.

2000, Dec. 19 **Litho.** ***Perf. 12¾***
4118-4119 A1143 Set of 2 2.50 1.25

20th Pan-American Railway Congress A1144

2000, Sept. 18 **Litho.** ***Perf. 12¾***
4120 A1144 65c multi 1.50 1.10

Millennium — A1145

Snails: a, Polymita versicolor. b, Polymita picta iolimbata. c, Polymita picta roseolimbata. d, Polymita picta picta. e, Polymita picta nigrolimbata.
Illustration reduced.

2000, Dec. 20
4121 A1145 65c Block of 5, #a-e, + label 8.00 4.00

New Year 2001 (Year of the Snake) — A1146

Illustration reduced.

2001, Jan. 10
4122 A1146 15c multi .50 .20

Hong Kong 2001 Stamp Exhibition — A1147

Birds: 5c, Aix galericulata. 10c, Chrysolophus pictus. 15c, Ardea cinerea. 65c, Gallus gallus. 75c, Streptotelia decaocto.

2001, Jan. 25 ***Perf. 12¾***
4123-4127 A1147 Set of 5 4.00 3.25

Souvenir Sheet
Perf. 12½

4128 A1147 1p Grus grus 2.90 1.25

No. 4128 contains one 32x40mm stamp.

National Institute for Sport Physical Education and Recreation, 40th Anniv. — A1148

2001, Feb. 23 ***Perf. 12½x12¼***
4129 A1148 65c multi 1.50 .75

UN High Commissioner for Refugees, 50th Anniv. — A1149

2001, Mar. 15 ***Perf. 12¾x12½***
4130 A1149 65c multi 1.50 .60

Antique Locomotives — A1150

Locomotives from, 10c, 1863. 15c, 1876. 40c, 1885. 65c, 1914. 75c, 1932.

2001, Mar. 20 ***Perf. 12½x12¼***
4131-4135 A1150 Set of 5 4.50 2.40

105th Interparliamentary Union Congress, Havana — A1151

2001, Mar. 30 ***Perf. 12¾***
4136 A1151 65c multi 1.50 .70

Bay of Pigs Invasion, 40th Anniv. — A1152

2001, Apr. 19 ***Perf. 12¾x12½***
4137 A1152 65c multi 1.50 .70

Cats and Dogs A1153

Designs: 10c, Cats, emblem of Cat Aficionados Association. No. 4139, 15c, Dogs, Cats, emblem of Aniplant. No. 4140, 15c, Dogs, emblem of Cynological Federation of Cuba. 65c, Dogs, emblem of Sporting Dog Federation of Cuba. 75c, Dogs, cats.

2001, Apr. 25 ***Perf. 12½x12¾***
4138-4142 A1153 Set of 5 4.00 1.75

Radio Havana, 40th Anniv. — A1154

2001, May 1 ***Perf. 12½x12¼***
4143 A1154 65c multi 1.50 .70

Tourism Convention — A1155

2001, May 7 ***Perf. 12¾x12½***
4144 A1155 65c multi 1.50 .70

Belgica 2001 Intl. Stamp Exhibition, Brussels A1156

Designs: 5c, St. Michel Cathedral. 10c, Sablon Church, horiz. 15c, Royal Residence, horiz. 65c, Sacred Heart Basilica, horiz. 75c, Atomium.
1p, Royal Palace.

2001, May 10 ***Perf. 12¾***
4145-4149 A1156 Set of 5 4.00 1.75

Souvenir Sheet
Perf. 12½

4150 A1156 100c multi 2.40 1.25

No. 4150 contains one 32x40mm stamp.

Interior Ministry, 40th Anniv. A1157

2001, June 6 ***Perf. 12¾***
4151 A1157 65c multi 1.50 .70

Phila Nippon '01, Japan A1158

Japanese trains: 5c., JR 500. 10c, JR 700. 15c, MAX 1. 65c, MAX 2. 75c, 300.

2001, June 20 **Litho.** ***Perf. 12¾***
4152-4156 A1158 Set of 5 3.75 1.50

Souvenir Sheet
Perf. 12½

4157 A1158 100c Zero 2.40 1.25

No. 4157 contains one 40x32mm stamp.

Republic of San Marino, 1700th Anniv. — A1159

2001, July 20 **Litho.** ***Perf. 12½x12¼***
4158 A1159 75c multi 1.75 .75

Aquaculture — A1160

Designs: 5c, Tinca tinca. 10c, Rana temporaria. 15c, Cardisoma guanhumi. 65c, Mytius edulis. 75c, Tilapia mariae.
1p, Potamobius pallipes.

2001, Sept. 17 *Perf. 12¾*
4159-4163 A1160 Set of 5 3.75 1.50

Souvenir Sheet

Perf. 12½

4164 A1160 1p multi 2.40 1.25

No. 4164 contains one 40x32mm stamp.

Recovery of Raw Materials, 40th Anniv. — A1161

2001, Sept. 21 *Perf. 12¾x12½*
4165 A1161 65c multi 1.60 .65

Tourism — A1162

Designs: 10c, Valle de Viñales. 15c, Trinidad. 65c, Sirena Beach, Cayo Largo del Sur. 75c, Morro Castle, Havana.

2001, Sept. 27
4166-4169 A1162 Set of 4 3.75 1.60

Year of Dialogue Among Civilizations A1163

2001, Oct. 9 *Perf. 12¾*
4170 A1163 65c multi 1.50 .70

America Issue — UNESCO World Heritage A1164

Flora and fauna from Desembarco del Granma Natl. Park: 15c, Tetramicra malpighiarum. 65c, Liggus vittatus.

2001, Oct. 12 *Perf. 12½x12¾*
4171-4172 A1164 Set of 2 1.75 .85

José Marti National Library, Cent. A1165

2001, Oct. 18 *Perf. 12¾*
4173 A1165 15c multi .35 .20

Cuban Airliner Explosion Near Barbados, 25th Anniv. — A1166

Various details of painting.

2001, Oct. 22

4174	Horiz. strip of 5	3.25	1.60
a.	A1166 5c shown	.20	.20
b.	A1166 10c multi	.20	.20
c.	A1166 15c multi	.35	.20
d.	A1166 50c multi	1.10	.55
e.	A1166 65c multi	1.40	.90

Eduardo R. Chibas, Communist Leader, Cent. of Birth — A1167

2001, Nov. 27 **Litho.** *Perf. 13*
4175 A1167 65c multi 1.60 .70

Napoleonic Museum, 40th Anniv. — A1168

Equestrian statues of Napoleon and map of battle of: No. 4176, 10c, Eylau. No. 4177, 10c, Marengo. 65c, Waterloo. 75c, Aboukir.

2001, Dec. 1 *Perf. 12¾x12½*
4176-4179 A1168 Set of 4 3.75 1.50

Pablo de la Torriente Brau (1901-36), Poet — A1169

2001, Dec. 12 *Perf. 12¾*
4180 A1169 75c multi 1.75 .75

Cuban Federation of Pigeon Fanciers, 4th Congress A1170

Pigeons: No. 4181, 65c, Empedrado oscura 2021-61-ME. No. 4182, 65c, Empedrado claro 2241-55-ME. No. 4183, 65c, Mosaico 1561-66-HM. No. 4184, 65c, Mosaico, 3013-67-HM. No. 4185, 65c Bronceado, 338-59-HE.

2001, Dec. 14 *Perf. 12½*
4181-4185 A1170 Set of 5 7.00 3.00

Film Stars Who Never Won Academy Awards A1171

Designs: 5c, Tyrone Power. No. 4187, 10c, Ava Gardner. No. 4188, 10c, Steve McQueen. No. 4189, 15c, Rita Hayworth. No. 4190, 15c, Marilyn Monroe. No. 4191, 15c, James Dean. No. 4192, 65c, Rock Hudson. No. 4193, 65c, Natalie Wood. 75c, Richard Burton.

2001, Dec. 20
4186-4194 A1171 Set of 9 8.00 3.50
a. Sheet of 9, #4186-4194 8.00 3.50

New Year 2002 (Year of the Horse) — A1172

2002, Jan. 21 **Litho.** *Perf. 12½x12¾*
4195 A1172 15c multi .45 .20

Cigar Production — A1173

Cigars and: 5c, Hat, Cuba No. 358, tobacco leaf. 10c, Clock, cigar cylinder. 15c, Map of Cuba, Simon Bolivar. 65c, Cuba Nos. 356, 357, map, cigar smoker. 75c, Flag, tobacco field, man.
1p, Fidel Castro, map, star.

2002, Feb. 15 *Perf. 12¾*
4196-4200 A1173 Set of 5 4.00 1.75

Souvenir Sheet

Perf. 1313¼

4201 A1173 1p multi 2.50 .95

Fourth Havana Festival, Cohiba brand, 36th anniv. No. 4201 contains one 40x32mm stamp.

Second UPAEP Information Workshop — A1174

Illustration reduced.

2002, Feb. 21 *Perf. 12½x12¼*
4202 A1174 65c multi 1.50 .65

Explorers A1175

Explorers: 5c, Reading map. 15c, Tying knots. 50c, Starting campfire for cooking. 65c, Starting fire. 75c, Using orientation techniques.

2002, Mar. 20 *Perf. 12½*
4203-4207 A1175 Set of 5 5.00 2.10
a. Sheet of 5, #4203-4207, + label 7.00 3.00

Union of Young Communists, 40th Anniv. — A1176

2002, Apr. 4 *Perf. 12½x12¼*
4208 A1176 15c multi .30 .20

ExpoVid 2002 Wine Event — A1177

Designs: 15c, Cigar smokers, wine bottles and glasses, map of wine producing areas. 65c, Wine glass and barrels. 75c, Wine glass and vineyard.

2002, June 5 *Perf. 12¾x12½*
4209-4211 A1177 Set of 3 3.50 1.50

2002 World Cup Soccer Championships, Japan and Korea — A1178

Player and flag from: No. 4212, 15c, South Korea. No. 4213, 15c, France. No. 4214, 15c, Germany. No. 4215, 15c, Brazil. No. 4216, 15c, Spain. 65c, Argentina. 75c, Italy. 85c, Japan.

2002, Apr. 21 **Litho.** *Perf. 12½*
4212-4219 A1178 Set of 8 6.50 3.25
4219a Sheet, #4212-4219 8.50 4.25

Souvenir Sheet

Hispano-Cubano Philatelic Exposition — A1179

2002, Apr. 27 *Perf. 13*
4220 A1179 1p multi 2.25 1.10

Juan Tomas Roig, Botanist, 125th Anniv. of Birth A1180

Designs: 5c, Bust of Roig, experimental agronomic station, Santiago de las Vegas. 10c, Bust and house of Roig. 15c, Roig, laboratory glassware and Nicotiana tabacum. 50c, Building, Allophyllum roiggi, and sculpture of Roig. 65c, Roig, laboratory glassware and botanical dictionary.

2002, May 10 ***Perf. 12½x12¾***
4221-4225 A1180 Set of 5 3.25 1.50
4225a Sheet, #4221-4225, + label 5.00 2.40

Medi Cuba Suiza — A1181

2002, June 18 ***Perf. 12¾x12½***
4226 A1181 75c multi 1.60 .75

Mushrooms A1182

Designs: 5c, Amanita junquillea. 15c, Lepiota puellaris. 45c, Cortinarius cumatilis. 65c, Pholliota adiposa. 75c, Coprinus comatus.

2002, June 20 ***Perf. 12¾***
4227-4231 A1182 Set of 5 4.50 2.00
4231a Sheet, #4227-4231, + label 8.00 3.50

Nicolás Guillén (1902-89), Poet — A1183

2002, July 10 ***Perf. 12¾x12½***
4232 A1183 65c multi 1.75 .90

Dockers, By Marcelo Pogolotti (1902-88) A1184

2002, July 12 ***Perf. 12¾***
4233 A1184 15c multi .50 .25

Agostinho Neto (1922-79), Pres. of Angola — A1185

2002, Sept. 17 ***Perf. 12¾x12½***
4234 A1185 65c multi 1.75 .90

España 2002 Youth Philatelic Exposition, Salamanca — A1186

Birds: 5c, Calidris minutilla. 10c, Tringa melanoleucas. 15c, Charadius semipalmatus. 65c, Plurialis squatarola. 75c, Arenaria interpres.
1p, Porzana carolina.

2002, Sept. 20 ***Perf. 12½x12¼***
4235-4239 A1186 Set of 5 4.75 2.25
4239a Sheet, #4235-4239, + label 8.00 3.50

Souvenir Sheet

Perf. 13

4240 A1186 1p multi 2.50 1.25

No. 4240 contains one 40x31mm stamp.

Third Intl. Meeting of War Correspondents — A1187

2002, Oct. 7 ***Perf. 12¾***
4241 A1187 65c multi 1.75 .90

Ernesto "Che" Guevara (1928-67), Revolutionary Leader — A1188

Various depictions of Guevara: 5c, 10c, 15c, 50c, 65c, 75c.

2002, Oct. 8 **Litho.**
4242-4247 A1188 Set of 6 5.00 2.75
4247a Sheet, #4242-4247 16.00 3.25

America Issue — Youth, Education and Literacy — A1189

Designs: 15c, Emblem of Literacy Army, man with book, teacher with student. 65c, Building, flag, children at computer.

2002, Oct. 12 ***Perf. 12½x12¼***
4248-4249 A1189 Set of 2 2.00 1.00

Old Automobiles — A1190

Designs: No. 4250, 5c, 1956 Pontiac Catalina. No. 4251, 5c, 1957 Mercury Monterrey. 15c, 1959 Cadillac Fleetwood. 65c, Hudson Hornet. 75c, 1957 Chevrolet Bel Air. 85c, 1957 Mercedes-Benz 190SL.

2002, Oct. 19 ***Perf. 12¾***
4250-4255 A1190 Set of 6 6.00 3.50
a. Sheet, #4250-4255, + 6 labels 14.00 3.50

15th Intercontinental Baseball Cup — A1191

Baseball players: 5c, G. Mesa. 15c, A. Pacheco. 50c, O. Linares. 65c, O. Kindelan. 75c, L. Ulacia.

2002, Nov. 1
4256-4260 A1191 Set of 5 5.00 3.00
4260a Sheet of 5, #4256-4260 + 4 labels 11.00 3.50

20th Havana Intl. Fair — A1192

2002, Nov. 3
4261 A1192 65c multi 1.75 .90

Railroads, 165th Anniv. — A1193

Designs: 5c, Rocket. 15c, Miller. 50c, Vulcan. 65c, Consolidation. 75c, Mikado.

2002, Nov. 12 ***Perf. 12½x12¼***
4262-4266 A1193 Set of 5 5.00 3.00
a. Sheet, #4262-4266, + label 12.00 3.00

Camagüey Ballet, 35th Anniv. — A1194

Designs: 65c, Twelve dancers. 75c, Two dancers.

2002, Dec. 1 ***Perf. 12¾***
4267-4268 A1194 Set of 2 3.50 2.00

Pan-American Health Organization, Cent. — A1195

2002, Dec. 2
4269 A1195 65c multi 1.50 .90

Paintings of Wilfredo Lam (1902-82) A1196

Designs: 15c, Emi Cosinca, 1950. 45c, Yo Soy, 1949. 65c, Retrado de H.H., 1941-42. 75c, Mujer Sentada, 1951.

2002, Dec. 8 ***Perf. 12¾***
4270-4273 A1196 Set of 4 5.00 3.00
a. Sheet, #4270-4273, + 4 labels 14.00 3.00

Dulce M. Loynaz (1902-97), Writer A1197

Perf. 12½x12¾

2002, Dec. 19 **Litho.**
4274 A1197 65c multi 1.50 .90

Souvenir Sheet

Tursiops Truncatus — A1198

2002, Dec. 20 ***Perf. 12½***
4275 A1198 1p multi 3.00 1.50

Fifth National Philatelic Competition.

Prehistoric and Modern-Day Animals — A1199

Designs: 5c, Megaloceros, Cervus elaphus. 10c, Theropithecus, Papio anubis. 15c, Coelodonta, Diceros bicornis. 45c, Canis

dirus, Canis lupus. 65c, Ursus spelaeus, Ursus arctos. 75c, Smilodon, Panthera leo.
1p, Mammuthus primigenius.
Illustration reduced.

2002, Dec. 27 *Perf. 12½x12¼*
4276-4281 A1199 Set of 6 5.00 2.00

Souvenir Sheet
Perf. 13

4282 A1199 1p multi 2.75 1.10

No. 4282 contains one 40x32mm stamp.

New Year 2003 (Year of the Ram) A1200

Ram with background in: No. 4283, 15c, Green. No. 4284, 15c, Red.

2003, Jan. 6 *Perf. 12½*
4283-4284 A1200 Set of 2 .75 .40

San Alejandro Academy for Arts, 185th Anniv. — A1201

Paintings by: 5c, Amelia Pelaez. 15c, René Portocarrero. 65c, Mario Carreña, horiz. 75c, Servando Cabrera.

2003, Jan. 12 *Perf. 12¾*
4285-4288 A1201 Set of 4 4.00 2.00

José Martí (1853-95), Patriot — A1202

Designs: 15c, Birthplace. No. 4290, 65c, Martí and text. No. 4291, 65c, Martí, sky and text, horiz. 75c, Portrait.
1p, Martí, horiz.

2003, Jan. 28 *Perf. 12¾*
4289-4292 A1202 Set of 4 5.00 1.75

Souvenir Sheet
Perf. 12½

4293 A1202 1p multi 2.75 1.10

No. 4293 contains one 40x32mm stamp.

Arrival of Europeans at Havana, 510th Anniv. — A1203

Various Cuban stamps and: No. 4294, 15c, Woman with Cigar boxes, map of Cuba (diamond-shaped). No. 4295, 15c, Men at table holding cigars and drinks (diamond-shaped). 50c, Tobacco farmer, field, hands rolling cigar. 65c, Building, Trinidad. 75c, Cigar, building, palm tree, people in room.
1p, Indian lighting cigar, vert.

2003, Feb. 6 *Perf. 12½*
4294-4298 A1203 Set of 5 5.00 1.75

Souvenir Sheet

4299 A1203 1p multi 2.75 1.10

No. 4299 contains one 32x40mm stamp.

Radio Rebelde, 45th Anniv. A1204

2003, Feb. 13 *Perf. 12¾*
4300 A1204 65c multi 1.50 .85

Félix Varela (1788-1853), Priest — A1205

2003, Feb. 25 *Perf. 12½*
4301 A1205 65c multi 1.50 .85

Military Units, 45th Anniv. — A1206

Designs: No. 4302, 15c, 2nd Frank Pais Front. No. 4303, 15c, 3rd Mario Muñoz Front.

2003 *Perf. 12¾*
4302-4303 A1206 Set of 2 1.10 .40

Issued: No. 4302, 3/5; No. 4303, 3/11.

16th World Sexology Congress A1207

2003, Mar. 11
4304 A1207 65c multi 1.50 .85

Transportation and Shipping — A1208

Designs: 5c, Container ship. 10c, Truck. 15c, Train. 65c, Airplane and delivery van. 75c, Airplane and delivery van, diff.

2003, Apr. 10 *Perf. 12½*
4305-4309 A1208 Set of 5 4.00 1.50

Flora & Fauna — A1209

Designs: 5c, Nymphaea ampla, Lepisosteus tristoechus. 10c, Magnolia grandiflora, Spindalis zena pretrei. 15c, Lillium candidum, Polymita picta. 65c, Strelitzia regiae, Solenodon cubanus. 75c, Hibiscus rosasinensis, Mellysuga helenae.

2003, May 15
4310-4314 A1209 Set of 5 4.00 1.50

Pan American Games, Santo Domingo, Dominican Republic A1210

Designs: 5c, Kayaking. 15c, Judo. 50c, Track. 65c, Volleyball.

2003, June 27 *Perf. 12½x12¾*
4315-4318 A1210 Set of 4 3.00 1.10

Attack on Moncada Barracks, 50th Anniv. — A1211

Designs: 15c, Men and barracks. 65c, Fidel Castro, text.

2003, July 26 *Perf. 12¾*
4319-4320 A1211 Set of 2 1.75 .60

Railroads A1212

Designs: 5c, Three-wheeled handcar, 1930-35. 10c, Crane, 1920. 15c, B-B 120/120 E locomotive, 1925. 65c, DVM-9 Ganz Mavag locomotive, 1969. 75c, 2-6-0 locomotive, 1905.

2003, Aug. 7
4321-4325 A1212 Set of 5 4.00 1.40

UN Conference to Combat Desertification — A1213

Illustration reduced.

2003, Aug. 25 *Perf. 12½x12¼*
4326 A1213 65c multi 1.50 .85

Expo Bangkok A1214

Wildlife: 5c, Nyctea scandiaca. 10c, Fratercula arctica. 15c, Sula bassana. 65c, Ursus maritimus. 75c, Alopex lagopus.
1p, Pagolphilus groenlandicus.

2003, Aug. 28 *Perf. 12¾*
4327-4331 A1214 Set of 5 4.00 1.40

Souvenir Sheet
Perf. 12½

4332 A1214 1p multi 2.75 .90

No. 4332 contains one 32x40mm stamp.

Butterflies and Flowers — A1215

Designs: 5c, Dione juno, Gardenia jasminoides. 15c, Apatura ilia, Chrysanthemus sinence. 65c, Inachis io, Hibiscus rosasinensis. 75c, Marpesia iole, Althaea rosea.
1p, Danaus plexippus, Zantedeschia aethiopica, vert.

2003, Sept. 11 **Litho.** *Perf. 12½*
4333-4336 A1215 Set of 4 4.00 1.25

Souvenir Sheet

4337 A1215 1p multi 2.75 .90

No. 4337 contains one 32x40mm stamp.

Ecotourism — A1216

Bird and location: 10c, Aratinga eops, Baracoa. 15c, Xiphiopicus percussus, Valle de los Ingenios. 65c, Tiaris canora, Sierra Maestra. 75c, Priotelus temnurus, Granma.

2003, Sept. 27 *Perf. 12¾x12½*
4338-4341 A1216 Set of 4 4.00 1.25

Worldwide Fund for Nature (WWF) — A1217

Crocodylus rhombifer: No. 4342, 15c, Eggs and hatchling. No. 4343, 15c, Adult at water's edge. 65c, Capturing prey. 75c, With open mouth.

2003, Sept. 30 **Litho.** *Perf. 12¾*
4342-4345 A1217 Set of 4 5.00 1.75
4345a Sheet, 4 each #4342-4345 20.00 12.50

America Issue — Flora and Fauna — A1218

Designs: 15c, Xiphidiopicus percussus. 65c, Encyclia phoenicea.

2003, Oct. 12
4346-4347 A1218 Set of 2 1.75 .60

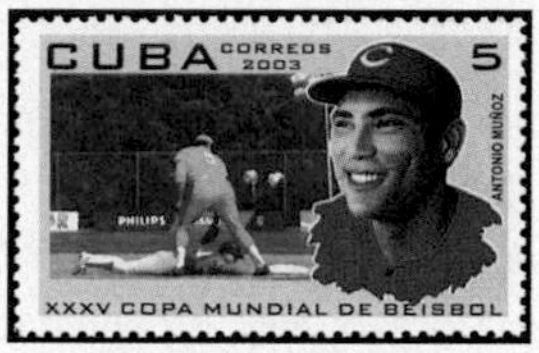

35th Baseball World Cup — A1219

Cuban players: 5c, Antonio Muñoz. 10c, Lourdes Gourriel. No. 4350, 15c, Jorge L. Valdes. No. 4351, 15c, Lazaro Vargas. 65c, Lazaro Valle. 75c, Javier Mendez.
1p, Players celebrating, vert.

2003, Oct. 17 ***Perf. 12½x12¼***
4348-4353 A1219 Set of 6 4.50 1.40

Souvenir Sheet

Perf. 12½

4354 A1219 1p multi 2.75 .90

No. 4354 contains one 32x40mm stamp.

Ballet — A1220

Designs: No. 4355, 65c, National Ballet of Cuba, 55th anniv. No. 4356, 65c, Alicia Alonso as Giselle, 60th anniv., vert.

Perf. 12¾x12½, 12½x12¾

2003, Oct. 28
4355-4356 A1220 Set of 2 3.00 1.10

Powered Flight, Cent. — A1221

Emblem and: 5c, Wright Brothers. 15c, Pitcairn PA-5. 65c, Stearman C-3MB. 75c, Douglas M-2.

2003, Dec. 17 ***Perf. 12½x12¼***
4357-4360 A1221 Set of 4 4.00 1.40

Cuban Revolution, 45th Anniv. — A1222

2004, Jan. 1 ***Perf. 12¾***
4361 A1222 65c multi 1.50 .85

Expocuba, 15th Anniv. — A1223

Illustration reduced.

2004, Jan. 4 ***Perf. 12½x12¼***
4362 A1223 65c multi 1.50 .85

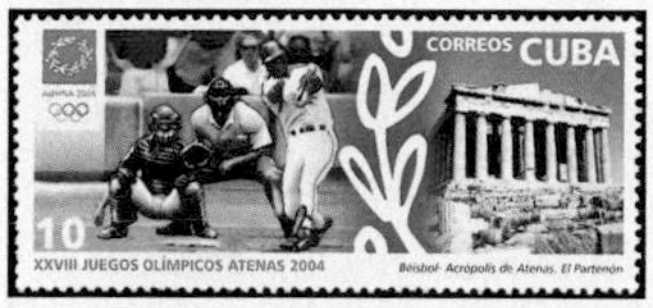

2004 Summer Olympics, Athens — A1224

Sports: 10c, Baseball. 15c (#4363A), Track. 65c, Boxing. 75c, Equestrian.
Illustration reduced.

2004, Jan. 6 **Litho.**
4363-4365 A1224 Set of 4 3.75 1.90

New Year 2004 (Year of the Monkey) A1225

Monkey with denomination in: No. 4366, 15c, Blue. No. 4367, 15c, Orange.

2004, Jan. 9 ***Perf. 12¾***
4366-4367 A1225 Set of 2 1.00 .30

Julio A. Mella (1903-29), Communist Leader A1226

2004, Jan. 10
4368 A1226 65c multi 1.50 1.10

José Martí (1853-95) — A1227

Designs: No. 4369, 5c, Martí in 1862, Colegio San Pablo, Prado No. 88. No. 4370, 5c, Martí's father, Mariano, Tapineria No. 16, Valencia. No. 4371, 5c, Martí's mother, Leonor Pérez, birthplace, Paula No. 41. No. 4372, 10c, Martí's high school, 1862, Martí, Fermín Valdés Domínguez, 1869. No. 4373, 10c, Martí in 1869, Havana Royal Jail. No. 4374, 15c, Martí in 1870, El Abra farm, Isle of Pines. No. 4375, 15c, Martí in 1870, Martí Forge. No. 4376, 15c, Martí and son, José Francisco, 1879, Guanabacoa Lyceum. 65c, Martí and son, 1879, Mercaderes Law Offices. 75c, Martí in 1895, La Jatía farm, Oriente.

2004, Jan. 28 ***Perf. 12½x12¼***
4369-4378 A1227 Set of 10 4.75 2.75

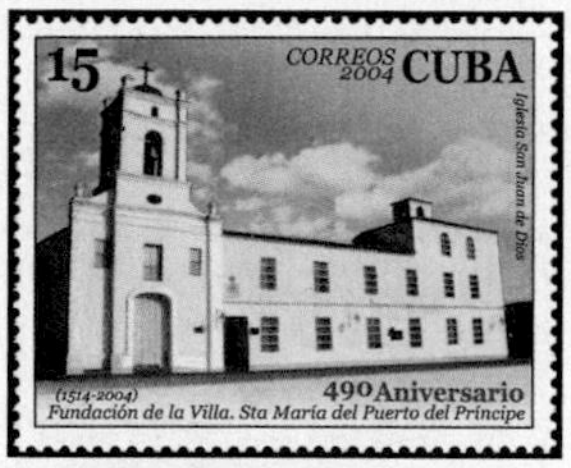

Town of Santa María de Puerto del Principe, 490th Anniv. — A1228

2004, Feb. 2 ***Perf. 12¾x12½***
4379 A1228 15c multi .50 .20

Trolleys A1229

Designs: 5c, Santiago. 10c, Havana. 15c, Camagüey. 65c, Matanzas. 75c, Camagüey, diff.
1p, Havana, diff.

2004, Feb. 20 ***Perf. 12¾***
4380-4384 A1229 Set of 5 3.75 1.90

Souvenir Sheet

Perf. 12½

4385 A1229 1p multi 2.50 1.25

No. 4385 contains one 40x32mm stamp.

Souvenir Sheet

Cuba — Mexico Binational Philatelic Exhibition — A1230

2004, Feb. 25 ***Perf. 12½***
4386 A1230 1p multi 2.50 1.25

EGREM Recording Co., 40th Anniv. — A1231

Recording artists: 10c, Cascarita, Julio Cuevas. 15c, Carlos Puebla. 65c, Benny Maré. 75c, Compay Segundo.

2004, Mar. 24 ***Perf. 12¾***
4387-4390 A1231 Set of 4 3.50 1.75

España 2004 Intl. Philatelic Exhibition — A1232

Dogs: 5c, Spanish pointer. 10c, Spanish hound. 15c, Mallorquin bulldog. 65c, Catalan sheepdog. 75c, Pyrenean mastiff.
1p, Spanish mastiff.

2004, Mar. 24 ***Perf. 12½x12¼***
4391-4395 A1232 Set of 5 3.75 1.90

Souvenir Sheet

Perf. 12½

4396 A1232 1p multi 2.50 1.25

No. 4396 contains one 40x32mm stamp.

National Police, 45th Anniv. — A1233

Illustration reduced.

2004, Mar. 26 ***Perf. 12½x12¼***
4397 A1233 15c multi + label .35 .20

Souvenir Sheet

Second Cuban Sports Olympiad — A1234

2004, Apr. 18 ***Perf. 12½***
4398 A1234 1p multi 2.50 1.25

Nature and Man Foundation, 10th Anniv. — A1235

2004, May 16 **Litho.** ***Perf. 12¼x12½***
4399 A1235 65c multi 1.50 .75

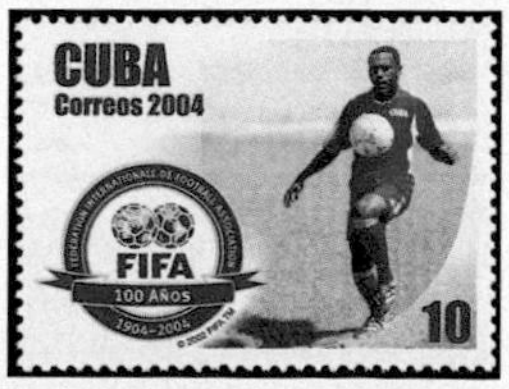

FIFA (Fédération Internationale de Football Association), Cent. — A1236

FIFA emblem and various players: 10c, 15c, 65c, 75c.

2004, May 21 ***Perf. 12¾***
4400-4403 A1236 Set of 4 3.50 1.75

Pets
A1237

Designs: 5c, Parakeets. 10c, Fish. 15c, Dogs. 65c, Cats. 75c, Finches.
1p, Horse, horiz.

2004, June 25 ***Perf. 12½x12¾***
4404-4408 A1237 Set of 5 3.75 1.90

Souvenir Sheet

Perf. 12½

4409 A1237 1p multi 2.50 1.25

No. 4409 contains one 40x32mm stamp.

Intl. Chess Federation, 80th Anniv. — A1238

Chess players: 15c, Maria Teresa Mora. 65c, José Raúl Capablanca, horiz. 75c, Ernesto "Che" Guevara.

2004, July 20 ***Perf. 12¾***
4410-4412 A1238 Set of 3 3.50 1.75

Minerals — A1239

Designs: 5c, Corundum. 10c, Thenardite. 15c, Uraninite. 65c, Realgar. 75c, Fluorite.
1p, Copper.

2004, July 30 ***Perf. 13***
4413-4417 A1239 Set of 5 3.50 1.75

Souvenir Sheet

Perf. 12½

4418 A1239 1p multi 2.50 1.25

No. 4418 contains one 40x32mm stamp.

Convention Hall, 25th Anniv. — A1240

2004, Sept. 3 ***Perf. 12¾***
4419 A1240 65c multi 1.50 1.25

Cuban Aviation, 75th Anniv. — A1241

Designs: 15c, Lockheed Constellation. 65c, IL-62M. 75c, Airbus 330.

2004, Oct. 8 ***Perf. 12½x12¼***
4420-4422 A1241 Set of 3 3.50 1.75

America Issue — A1242

Map of Cuba and: 15c, Bird over islands. 65c, Fish and marine life.

2004, Oct. 12
4423-4424 A1242 Set of 2 1.75 .90

Marine Mammals — A1243

Designs: 5c, Delphinus delphis. 10c, Lagenorhynchus obliquidens. 15c, Stenella attenuata. 65c, Grampus griseus. 75c, Tursiops truncatus.
1p, Orcinus orca.

2004, Oct. 20 ***Perf. 12½x12¼***
4425-4429 A1243 Set of 5 3.50 1.75

Souvenir Sheet

Perf. 13

4430 A1243 1p multi 2.50 1.25

No. 4430 contains one 40x32mm stamp.

Disappearance of Camilo Cienfuegos, 45th Anniv. A1244

2004, Oct. 28 ***Perf. 12¾***
4431 A1244 65c multi 1.50 .75

Railroad Stations, Cent. — A1245

Designs: 15c, Agramonte Station, 1906 ALCO No. 48 4-6-0. 65c, Aguacate Station, 1907 BLW No. 57 4-6-0. 75c, Guira de Melina Station, 1903 ALCO No. 7 4-4-0.

2004, Nov. 10 ***Perf. 13***
4432-4434 A1245 Set of 3 3.50 1.75

Souvenir Sheet

13th Philatelic Congress, Havana — A1245a

2004, Nov. 20 **Litho.** ***Perf. 12½***
4434A A1245a 1p multi 2.25 2.25

Founding of San Cristóbal de la Habana, 485th Anniv. A1246

Designs: 15c, Temple. 65c, Painting showing priest in red vestments at base of tree. 75c, Paintig showing group of men at base of tree.

Perf. 12½x12¾

2004, Nov. 30 **Litho.**
4435-4437 A1246 Set of 3 3.00 1.50

Latin American Parliament Foundation, 40th Anniv. — A1246a

2004, Nov. 30 **Litho.** ***Perf. 12¾***
4437A A1246a 65c multi 1.40 .70

Ministry of Foreign Affairs, 45th Anniv. — A1247

2004, Dec. 23 ***Perf. 12½x12¼***
4438 A1247 65c multi 1.40 .70

Alejo Carpentier (1904-80), Writer — A1248

2004, Dec. 26 ***Perf. 12¾***
4439 A1248 65c multi 1.40 .70

First Baseball Game in Cuba, 130th Anniv. — A1249

Baseball players: 5c, Rey Vicente Anglada. 10c, Braudilio Vinent. 15c, Rogelio Garcia. 65c, Luis G. Casanova. 75c, Victor Mesa.
1p, Martin Dihigo, vert.

2004, Dec. 27 ***Perf. 12½x12¼***
4440-4444 A1249 Set of 5 5.25 2.50

Souvenir Sheet

Perf. 12½

4445 A1249 1p multi 2.25 1.10

No. 4445 contains one 32x40mm stamp.

Jose L. Guerra Aguiar Cuban Postal Museum, 40th Anniv. — A1250

Designs:15c, Plaza Mayor, Trinidad and 1855 Trinidad to Barcelona cover. 65c, Charity Sanctuary, El Cobre and 1861 El Cobre to Santiago de Cuba cover. 85c, Matanzas Cathedral, Matanzas and 1848 Mantanzas to Havana cover.

2005, Jan. 2 ***Perf. 12¾x12½***
4446-4448 A1250 Set of 3 3.50 1.75

New Year 2005 (Year of the Rooster) A1251

Designs: No. 4449, 15c, Rooster in air. No. 4450, 15c, Rooster on ground.

2005, Jan. 4 ***Perf. 12¼x12½***
4449-4450 A1251 Set of 2 .60 .30

Ministry of Information Technology and Communications, 5th Anniv. — A1252

Illustration reduced.

2005, Jan. 12 *Perf. 12½x12¼*
4451 A1252 65c multi 1.40 .70

Dinosaurs — A1253

Designs: 5c, Carnotaurus. 10c, Oviraptor. 30c, Parasaurolophus. 65c, Sauropelta. 90c, Iguanodon.
1p, Velociraptor.

2005, Jan. 20 Litho. *Perf. 12½x12¼*
4452-4456 A1253 Set of 5 4.25 2.10

Souvenir Sheet

Perf. 13

4457 A1253 1p multi 2.25 1.10

No. 4457 contains one 40x32mm stamp.

Miguel de Cervantes and Title Page of *Don Quixote* — A1254

2005, Jan. 24 *Perf. 12¾x12½*
4458 A1254 65c multi 1.40 .70

Publication of *Don Quixote*, 400th anniv.

Bridges A1255

Designs: 10c, Bacunayagua Bridge. 15c, La Concordia Bridge. 50c, El Triunfo Bridge. 65c, Yayabo Bridge. 75c, Canimar Bridge.
1p, Plaza Bridge.

2005, Feb. 5 *Perf. 13x12¾*
4459-4463 A1255 Set of 5 4.75 2.40

Souvenir Sheet

Perf. 13

4464 A1255 1p multi 2.25 1.10

No. 4464 contains one 40x32mm stamp.

Cuban Telecommunications Enterprise, 10th Anniv. — A1256

2005, Feb. 24 *Perf. 12½x12¾*
4465 A1256 90c multi 1.90 .95

Parrots — A1257

Designs: 5c, Amazona ochrocephala, Amazona leucocephala. 10c, Agapornis personata, Agapornis fischeri. 15c, Cacatua galerita, Cacatua leadbeateri. 65c, Psittacula krameri, Psittacula himalayana, vert. 1.05p, Aratinga guarouba, Aratinga euops.
1p, Ara macao, Ara araruana, Anodorhynchus hyacythus.

Perf. 12½x12¼, 12¼x12½

2005, Feb. 23 **Litho.**
4466-4470 A1257 Set of 5 4.25 2.10

Souvenir Sheet

Perf. 13

4471 A1257 1p multi 2.25 1.10

No. 4471 contain one 32x40mm stamp.

Cats A1258

Various cats: 5c, 10c, 40c, 65c, 75c. 10c is vert.

2005, Mar. 15 *Perf. 12¾*
4472-4476 A1258 Set of 5 4.25 2.10

Perf. 13

4477 A1258 1p Two cats, vert. 2.25 1.10

No. 4477 contains one 32x40mm stamp.

Cuba — Canada Diplomatic Relations, 60th Anniv. — A1259

2005, Mar. 20 *Perf. 12¾x12½*
4478 A1259 65c multi 1.40 .70

Wildlife — A1260

2005, Mar. 21 *Perf. 12½x12¼*
4479 A1260 15c Manatee .30 .20
4480 A1260 65c Parrot 1.40 .70
4481 A1260 75c Crocodile 1.50 .75
4482 A1260 90c Hummingbird 1.90 .95
Nos. 4479-4482 (4) 5.10 2.60

World Water Day — A1261

2005, Mar. 22 *Perf. 13*
4483 A1261 90c multi 1.90 .95

Boats — A1262

Designs: 10c, Fishing boat, fish. 20c, Schooner, fish. 30c, Bonito boat, bonito. 45c, Shrimp boat, shrimp. 90c, Lobster boat, lobster.
1p, Cargo ship, horiz.

2005, Apr. 15 *Perf. 12½*
4484-4488 A1262 Set of 5 4.25 2.10

Souvenir Sheet

4489 A1262 1p multi 2.25 1.10

First Cuban Postage Stamps, 150th Anniv. — A1263

Designs: 15c, St. Francis of Assisi Convent, Cuba #1. 65c, Morro Lighthouse, Cuba #2. 75c, Colonial Post Office, Cuba #3.

2005, Apr. 24 *Perf. 12¾x12½*
4490-4492 A1263 Set of 3 3.50 1.75

Social Security For All — A1264

2005, May 5 **Litho.**
4493 A1264 65c multi 1.40 .70

Major General Máximo Gómez (1836-1905) — A1265

2005, June 17 *Perf. 12½*
4494 A1265 1.05p multi 2.25 1.10

Souvenir Sheet

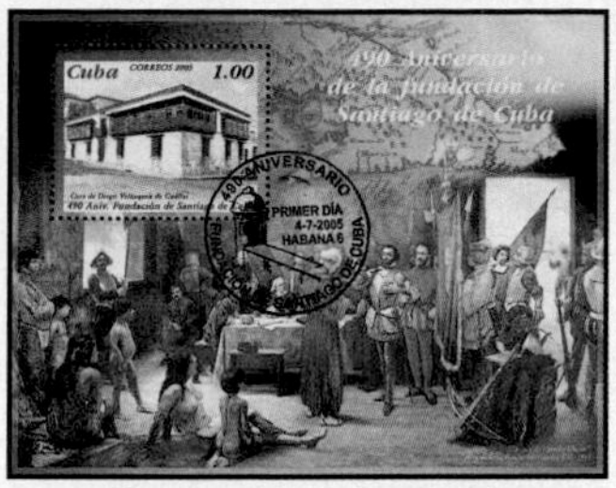

Santiago de Cuba, 490th Anniv. — A1266

2005, July 4 *Perf. 13*
4495 A1266 1p multi 2.25 1.10

16th World Youth and Student Festival, Venezuela — A1267

2005, July 29 *Perf. 12¾x12½*
4496 A1267 65c multi 1.40 .70

Dances A1268

Parrot and: No. 4497, 65c, Samba dancers and Brazilian flag. No. 4498, 65c, Son dancers, Cuban flag.

2005, Aug. 15 *Perf. 12¾*
4497-4498 A1268 Set of 2 2.75 1.50

See Brazil Nos. 2967-2968.

Cuban — Soviet Space Flight, 25th Anniv. — A1269

No. 4499: a, Cosmonaut Arnaldo Tamayo Mendez. b, Cosmonaut Yuri Romanenko.
Illustration reduced.

2005, Sept. 18 *Perf. 12½*
4499 A1269 90c Horiz. pair, #a-b 4.00 2.00

Albert Einstein's Visit to Cuba, 75th Anniv. — A1270

Designs: 65c, Caricature of Einstein. 75c, Equation for energy, Einstein writing.

2005, Sept. 21
4500-4501 A1270 Set of 2 4.00 2.00

Locomotives — A1271

Designs: 5c, DSB B40, 1869. 10c, Great Northern, 1902. No. 4504, 15c, Minaret, 1929. No. 4505, 15c, C. F. White, 1885. 2.05p, Western Pacific FP7A 805D.
1p, 14th No. 4 Krauss & Co., 1884.

2005, May 10 **Litho.** ***Perf. 12¾***
4502-4506 A1271 Set of 5 5.50 2.75

Souvenir Sheet
Perf. 13

4507 A1271 1p multi 2.25 1.10

No. 4507 contains one 40x32mm stamp.

Zoo Animals A1272

Designs: 10c, Loxodonta africana. 15c, Acunonyx jubatus, horiz. 50c, Synceros caffer, horiz. 65c, Giraffa camelopardalis. 75c, Panthera leo.
1p, Equus burchelli, horiz.

2005, July 21 ***Perf. 12¾***
4508-4512 A1272 Set of 5 4.75 2.40

Souvenir Sheet
Perf. 13

4513 A1272 1p multi 2.25 1.10

No. 4513 contains one 40x32mm stamp.

Santiago de Cuba, 490th Anniv. — A1273

2005, Sept. 22 ***Perf. 12¾x12½***
4514 A1273 75c multi 1.60 .80

Revolutionary Defense Committees, 45th Anniv. — A1274

Illustration reduced.

2005, Sept. 28 ***Perf. 12½x12¼***
4515 A1274 50c multi 1.10 .55

Diplomatic Relations Between Cuba and People's Republic of China, 45th Anniv. — A1275

No. 4516: a, Chinese General Secretary Hu Jintao and Cuban Pres. Fidel Castro. b, Great Wall of China and Morro Castle, Havana.
Illustration reduced.

2005, Sept. 28 ***Perf. 13x13¼***
4516 A1275 15c Horiz. pair, #a-b 1.00 .50

America Issue, Fight Against Poverty A1276

Designs: 50c, Starving children, map of Africa. 75c, Woman and child, map of South America.

2005, Oct. 12 ***Perf. 12¾***
4517-4518 A1276 Set of 2 2.75 1.40

Horses A1277

Breeds: 10c, Gelderlander. 20c, Arabian. 30c, Quarterhorse. 65c, Wild horses. 75c, Lipizzaner.
100c, Holsteiner, vert.

2005, Oct. 21 ***Perf. 12¾***
4519-4523 A1277 Set of 5 4.25 2.10

Souvenir Sheet
Perf. 12¾x12½

4524 A1277 100c multi 2.25 1.10

No. 4524 contains one 32x40mm stamp.

José Martí Type of 2004

Martí and: No. 4525, 5c, Central University, Madrid, 1871. No. 4526, 5c, Zaragoza University, 1871. No. 4527, 5c, F. Valdés Domínguez, Teatro Principal, Zaragoza, 1872. No. 4528, 10c, Victor Hugo House, Paris, 1872. No. 4529, 10c, Moneda No. 12, Mexico City, 1875. No. 4530, 15c, Normal School, Guatemala City, 1876. No. 4531, 15c, San Ildefonso No. 40, Mexico City, 1894. No. 4532, 15c, Plaza de Guardiola, Mexico City, 1894. 65c, Plaza Bolívar, Caracas, 1885. 75c, Santa María College, Caracas, 1893.
1p, Martínez Ibor Tobacco Factory, Tampa, 1892.

2005, Oct. 20 ***Perf. 12½x12¼***
4525-4534 A1227 Set of 10 4.75 2.40

Souvenir Sheet
Perf. 13

4535 A1227 1p multi 2.25 1.10

No. 4535 contains one 40x32mm stamp.

World Summit on the Information Society, Tunis — A1278

2005, Nov. 16 ***Perf. 12½x12¼***
4536 A1278 75c multi 1.60 .80

Establishment of Local Delivery of Mail in Havana, 150th Anniv. — A1279

Designs 15c, Cuba #7, cover to Havana. 65c, Cuba #16, Colonial Havana mailbox.

2005, Nov. 19 ***Perf. 12¾x12½***
4537-4538 A1279 Set of 2 1.60 .80

Cuban Men Convicted of Terrorism Imprisoned In the United States A1280

2005, Nov. 25 ***Perf. 12½x12¾***
4539 A1280 65c multi 2.00 1.00

Europa Stamps, 50th Anniv. (in 2006) A1281

Designs: 1.30p, Spain #1126, Castilla de la Fuerza, Havana. 2.05p, Spain #1010, Santisima Church, Trinidad, Cuba. 2.55p, Spain #1526, Morro Castle, Santiago de Cuba. 3.90p, Spain #1263, San Cristóbal Cathedral, Havana.

2005, Nov. 30 ***Perf. 12½***
4540-4543 A1281 Set of 4 20.00 10.00
4543a Souvenir sheet, #4540-4543 20.00 10.00

Nos. 4540-4543, 4543a exist imperf. Values, same.

Jewelry A1282

Jewelry by: 5c, Antonio Barcala. 10c, Raúl Valladares. 45c, Carlos de la Torre. 65c, J. Carlo Rafart. 75c, Osvaldo Castilla.
1p, 19th cent. jewelry in Gold Museum.

2005, Dec. 1 ***Perf. 12¾***
4544-4548 A1282 Set of 5 4.25 2.10

Souvenir Sheet
Perf. 12½

4549 A1282 1p multi 2.25 1.10

No. 4549 contains one 32x40mm stamp.

Friendship Among the Peoples Institute, 45th Anniv. — A1283

2005, Dec. 14 ***Perf. 12¾x12½***
4550 A1283 1.05p multi 2.25 1.10

Snails and Mushrooms A1284

Designs: 10c, Clathrus cancellatus. 20c, Polymita genus picta. 30c, Lepiota puellaris. 65c, Polymita genus muscarum. 75c, Clitocybe infundibuliformis.
1p, Polymita genus versicolor, horiz.

2005, Dec. 15 ***Perf. 12¾***
4551-4555 A1284 Set of 5 4.25 2.10

Souvenir Sheet
Perf. 13

4556 A1284 1p multi 2.25 1.10

No. 4556 contains one 40x32mm stamp.

Hotel Inglaterra, 130th Anniv. — A1285

2005, Dec. 23 ***Perf. 12¾x12½***
4557 A1285 65c multi 1.40 .70

New Year 2006 (Year of the Dog) — A1286

Designs: No. 4558, 15c, Shih tzu. No. 4559, 15c, Pug.

2006, Jan. 4 ***Perf. 12¼x12½***
4558-4559 A1286 Set of 2 .60 .30

Organization of Solidarity of the People of Asia, Africa and Latin America, 40th Anniv. A1287

2006, Jan. 16 *Perf. 12¾*
4560 A1287 65c multi 1.40 .70

Establishment of Cuban Postal Service, 250th Anniv. — A1288

Stampless cover and: 75c, Horse and rider. 2.05p, Ship.

2006, Mar. 1 *Perf. 12½x12¼*
4561-4562 A1288 Set of 2 6.00 3.00

OPEC Intl. Development Fund, 30th Anniv. — A1289

2006, Mar. 23 **Litho.**
4563 A1289 75c multi 1.60 .80

Souvenir Sheet

Havana '06 Intl. Philatelic Exhibition — A1290

2006, Mar. 25 *Perf. 12½*
4564 A1290 1p multi 2.25 1.10

Pope John Paul II (1920-2005) — A1291

Designs: 65c, Pope, Mass in Santa Clara. 75c, Mass in Camagüey (44x27mm). 90c, Mass in Santiago de Cuba (44x27mm). 1.05p, Pope, Mass in Havana.
Illustration reduced.

2006, Apr. 2 *Perf. 12½x12¼*
4565-4568 A1291 Set of 4 7.25 3.75

Bay of Pigs Invasion, 45th Anniv. — A1292

2006, Apr. 17 *Perf. 12¼x12½*
4569 A1292 65c multi 1.40 .70

José Martí Type of 2004

Martí and: No. 4570, Madame Griffou's Hotel, New York, 1890. No. 4571, Gonzalo de Quesada, 116 West 64th Street, New York, 1893. No. 4572, Son, José Francisco, 324 Classon Ave., New York, 1885. No. 4573, Masonic Temple, New York, 1888.

No. 4574: a, Cajobabo beach, Gomez monument. b, Martí monument, monument at Dos Ríos.

Martí and: 75c, Hardman Hall, New York, 1891. 85c, Office, 120 Front Street, New York, 1891. 90c, María Mantilla, Bath Beach, Long Island.

1p, Home of Teodoro Pérez, Cayo Hueso, 1893.

2006, May 19 **Litho.** *Perf. 12½x12¼*

4570	A1227	5c	multi	.20	.20
4571	A1227	5c	multi	.20	.20
4572	A1227	10c	multi	.20	.20
4573	A1227	10c	multi	.20	.20
4574	A1227	15c	Horiz. pair, #a-b	.65	.65
4575	A1227	75c	multi	1.60	1.60
4576	A1227	85c	multi	1.90	1.90
4577	A1227	90c	multi	1.90	1.90
	Nos. 4570-4577 (8)			6.85	6.85

Souvenir Sheet
Perf. 13

4578 A1227 1p multi 2.25 2.25

No. 4578 contains one 40x32mm stamp.

Prehistoric Animals — A1293

Designs: 5c, Dsungaripetrus, Yangchuanosaurus. 10c, Pterodactylus, Sprinosaurus. 30c, Pteranodon, Pachycephalosaurus. 35c, Scaphognathus, Muttaburrasaurus. 65c, Quetzalcoatlus, Stegosaurus. 1.05p, Sordes, Saichania.
1p, Stenonychosaurus, vert.

2006, May 24 *Perf. 12½x12¼*
4579-4584 A1293 Set of 6 5.50 5.50

Souvenir Sheet
Perf. 12½

4585 A1293 1p multi 2.25 2.25

No. 4585 contains one 32x40mm stamp.

Ministry of the Interior, 45th Anniv. — A1294

2006, June 6 *Perf. 12½x12¼*
4586 A1294 75c multi 1.60 1.60

Fowl — A1295

Designs: 5c, Chickens. No. 4588, 15c, Turkeys. No. 4589, 15c, Guinea fowl. 45c, Geese. 50c, Pheasants. 75c, Peafowl.
1p, Ducks.

2006, June 15 *Perf. 12½x12¼*
4587-4592 A1295 Set of 6 4.50 4.50

Souvenir Sheet
Perf. 13

4593 A1295 1p multi 2.25 2.25

No. 4593 contains one 40x32mm stamp.

Cerro Pelado Declaration, 40th Anniv. — A1296

Designs: 65c, Ship, man and crowd. 75c, People in cargo hoist. 85c, Men assisting woman down ship's stairs, flags of Cuba and Puerto Rico.

2006, June 25 *Perf. 12½x12¾*
4594-4596 A1296 Set of 3 4.75 4.75

2006 World Cup Soccer Championships, Germany — A1296a

Various Cuban soccer players: 15c, 45c, 65c, 75c.

2006, June **Litho.** *Perf. 12¾*
4596A-4596D A1296a Set of 4 4.00 4.00

Genetic Engineering and Biotechnology Center, 20th Anniv. — A1297

2006, July 1 *Perf. 12½x12¼*
4597 A1297 65c multi 1.40 1.40

Comic Strips by Virgilio Martinez — A1298

Designs: 15c, Pucho y Sus Perrerias. 65c, Cucho.

Illustration reduced.

2006, July 16 *Perf. 12¾x12¼*
4598-4599 A1298 Set of 2 1.75 1.75

Airplanes — A1299

Designs: 10c, Granville GeeBee R2. No. 4601, 15c, Bücker Jungmann. No. 4602, 15c, Comte AC-4 Gentleman. 50c, Mustang TF-51. 75c, Supermarine Spitfire. 85c, Lavochkin La-9.
1p, Bücker Jungmeister.

2006, July 20 *Perf. 12¾*
4600-4605 A1299 Set of 6 5.50 5.50

Souvenir Sheet
Imperf

4606 A1299 1p multi 2.25 2.25

No. 4606 contains one 36x28mm stamp.

Dogs — A1300

Designs: 5c, Bulldog. 10c, American cocker spaniel. 15c, Shar-pei. 20c, Airedale terrier. 35c, Pomeranian. 2.05p, Dalmatian.
1p, Whippet, vert.

2006, Aug. 18 *Perf. 12½x12¼*
4607-4612 A1300 Set of 6 6.25 6.25

Souvenir Sheet
Perf. 13

4613 A1300 1p multi 2.25 2.25

Recovery of Raw Materials, 45th Anniv. — A1301

Designs: 15c, Ernesto "Che" Guevara. 65c, Cuban and recovery program flags.

2006, Aug. 24 *Perf. 12¾*
4614-4615 A1301 Set of 2 1.75 1.75

14th Congress of Non-Aligned Countries, Havana A1302

2006, Sept. 10
4616 A1302 65c multi 1.40 1.40

Pedro Santacilia, Benito Juárez and Mexico House, Havana — A1303

Illustration reduced.

2006, Sept. 15 ***Perf. 12½x12¼***
4617 A1303 65c multi 1.40 1.40

Benito Juárez (1806-72), President of Mexico.

Souvenir Sheet

7th Hispano-Cuban Philatelic Exposition — A1304

No. 4618: a, Statue, arms of Cuba, denomination at LR. b, Statue, arms of Spain, denomination at LL.

2006, Sept. 20 ***Imperf.***
4618 A1304 50c Sheet of 2, #a-b 2.25 2.25

España 06 World Philatelic Exposition, Malaga, Spain — A1305

Designs: 5c, Rio Hanabanilla. 10c, Laguna Bacanao. 15c, Sierra de la Gran Piedra. 20c, Valle de los Ingenios. 50c, Laguna del Tesoro. 75c, Sierra Maestra.
1p, Valle de Viñales.

2006, Sept. 20 ***Perf. 12¾***
4619-4624 A1305 Set of 6 3.75 3.75

Souvenir Sheet

Perf. 13

4625 A1305 1p multi 2.25 2.25

No. 4625 contains one 40x32mm stamp.

America Issue, Energy Conservation — A1306

Equipment for harnessing energy source: No. 4626, 65c, Petroleum. No. 4627, 65c, Water. No. 4628, 65c, Solar. No. 4629, 65c, Wind.

2006, Oct. 12 ***Perf. 12¾***
4626-4629 A1306 Set of 4 5.50 5.50

Saiz Brothers Association, 20th Anniv. A1307

2006, Oct. 18
4630 A1307 75c multi 1.60 1.60

20th Intl. Ballet Festival, Havana A1308

Dancers: 75c, Alicia Alonso and Igor Youskévitch. 85c, Alonso.

2006, Oct. 28 ***Perf. 12¼x12½***
4631-4632 A1308 Set of 2 3.50 3.50

A1309

Belgica '06 Intl. Youth Philately Exposition, Belgium — A1310

Trains: 5c, Rocket and Intercity Diesel-electric. 10c, Turbine locomotive, Diesel-electric locomotive. 15c, Shinkasen and City of Los Angeles. 65c, Steam locomotive, Diesel locomotive. 75c, TEE Diesel-electric, TGV electric. 85c, Brisbane electric monorail, Wuppertal monorail.

No. 4639: a, Steam locomotive. b, Diesel locomotive.

2006, Nov. 2 ***Perf. 12¾***
4633-4638 A1309 Set of 6 5.50 5.50

Souvenir Sheet

Perf. 12½

4639 A1310 50c Sheet of 2, #a-b 2.25 2.25

TeleFood Emblem — A1311

2006, Nov. 11 ***Perf. 12¾***
4640 A1311 75c multi 1.60 1.60

Animals Serving Man — A1312

Designs: 5c, Equus caballus, Greek horse-drawn chariot. 15c, Camelus dromedarius, Ibn Battuta on camel. 30c, Capra aegagrus, Roman musician. 40c, Lama lama, Peruvian pre-Columbian ceramic llama. 50c, Felis catus, painting by Kuniyoshi Utagawa. 1.05p, Elephas maximus, elephant with Indian caparison.
1p, Canis familiaris, Grecian with dog.

2006, Oct. 1 Litho. ***Perf. 12½x12¼***
4641-4646 A1312 Set of 6 5.50 5.50

Souvenir Sheet

Perf. 12½

4647 A1312 1p multi 2.25 2.25

No. 4647 contains one 40x32mm stamp.

Fire Fighting and Rescue Equipment — A1313

Designs: 5c, 1899 Horse-drawn ambulance, Brazil, and megaphone. 10c, Fireman's hat, and 1898 Merryweather fire truck, England. 20c, 1910 Laurin & Klement fire truck, Bohemia, and fire hydrant. 30c, 1939 American La France ladder truck, US, and badge. 45c, 1925 Leyland Motors pumper motorcycle, United Kingdom, and portable hose and tank. 90c, Brussels fire badge and 1930 Magirus ladder truck, Germany.
1p, Fireman spraying water, vert.

2006, Nov. 13 ***Perf. 12¾***
4648-4653 A1313 Set of 6 4.50 4.50

Souvenir Sheet

Perf. 12½

4654 A1313 1p multi 2.25 2.25

No. 4654 contains one 32x40mm stamp.

Santiago Rebellion, 50th Anniv. — A1314

2006, Nov. 30 ***Perf. 12½x12¼***
4655 A1314 65c multi 1.40 1.40

Governmental Reorganization, 30th Anniv. — A1315

2006, Dec. 2
4656 A1315 75c multi 1.60 1.60

Granma Landings, 50th Anniv. — A1316

Revolutionary Armed Forces, 50th Anniv. — A1317

2006, Dec. 2 ***Perf. 13***
4657 A1316 65c multi 1.40 1.40
4658 A1317 65c multi 1.40 1.40

General Antonio Maceo Grajales (1845-96) — A1317a

2006, Dec. 7 Litho. ***Perf. 12½x12¼***
4658A A1317a 1.05p multi 2.10 2.10

Intl. Film and Television School, 20th Anniv. — A1318

2006, Dec. 15 ***Perf. 12¾***
4659 A1318 75c multi 1.60 1.60

Martí Forge Museum, 55th Anniv. — A1319

Illustration reduced.

2006, Dec. 15 ***Perf. 12½x12¼***
4660 A1319 90c multi 1.90 1.90

Literacy Campaign, 45th Anniv. A1320

2006, Dec. 19 ***Perf. 12¾***
4661 A1320 65c multi 1.40 1.40

Major General Ignacio Agramonte y Loinaz (1841-73) — A1321

2006, Dec. 23 ***Perf. 12½x12¼***
4662 A1321 65c multi 1.40 1.40

Special Education, 45th Anniv. — A1322

2007, Jan. 4 ***Perf. 12¾***
4663 A1322 85c multi 1.75 1.75

Francesa Pharmacy, 125th Anniv. A1323

2007, Jan. 18 **Litho.**
4664 A1323 65c multi 1.40 1.40

Electric Trains A1324

Designs: 5c, First American electric locomotive, 1895. 10c, Locomotive, Netherlands. 15c, Interurban train, Australia. 65c, High-speed train, Italy. 85c, Helensburgh-Bridgeton train, Great Britain. 1.05p, Lyon-St. Etienne interurban train, France.
1p, High-speed train, Germany.

2007, Jan. 18 ***Perf. 12¾***
4665-4670 A1324 Set of 6 6.00 6.00

Souvenir Sheet
Imperf

4671 A1324 1p multi 2.25 2.25

No. 4671 contains one 40x32mm stamp with simulated perforations.

12th Intl. Information Fair and Convention — A1325

Illustration reduced.

2007, Feb. 12 ***Perf. 12½x12¼***
4672 A1325 75c multi 1.60 1.60

Cats A1326

Designs: 10c, Two cats. No. 4674, 15c, Kitten with paw raised. No. 4675, 15c, Cat. 50c, Cat and telephone. 75c, Cat with ball. 90c, Cat, diff.
1p, Cat, diff.

2007, Feb. 14 ***Perf. 12¾***
4673-4678 A1326 Set of 6 5.50 5.50

Souvenir Sheet
Imperf

4679 A1326 1p multi 2.25 2.25

No. 4679 contains one 40x32mm stamp with simulated perforations.

Fifth Congress of Cuban Pigeon Fanciers Federation — A1327

2007, Feb. 24 ***Perf. 12¾***
4680 A1327 75c multi 1.60 1.60

Souvenir Sheet

Patria Newspaper, 115th Anniv. — A1328

Imperf. With Simulated Perforations

2007, Mar. 14
4681 A1328 1p multi 2.25 2.25

Animals in National Zoo — A1329

Designs: 5c, Ara ararauana. 10c, Tsetudo elephantopus. 15c, Balearica regulorum. 20c, Procyon lotor. 45c, Panthera pardus. 2.05p, Pongo pygmaeus.
1p, Giraffa camelopardalis, vert.

2007, Mar. 31 ***Perf. 12½x12¼***
4682-4687 A1329 Set of 6 6.50 6.50

Souvenir Sheet
Imperf

4688 A1329 1p multi 2.25 2.25

No. 4688 contains one 32x40mm stamp with simulated perforations.

Raúl Roa García (1907-82), Foreign Minister A1330

2007, Apr. 18 ***Perf. 12¾***
4689 A1330 65c multi 1.40 1.40

Union of Young Communists, 45th Anniv. — A1331

2007, Apr. 4 ***Perf. 12½x12¼***
4690 A1331 75c multi 1.60 1.60

José Martí Type of 2004

Martí and: No. 4691, 5c, Cuban High School, Tampa, 1892. No. 4692, 5c, Casa de los Pedrosa, Tampa, 1892. No. 4693, 10c, Hotel Duval, Cayo Hueso, 1891. No. 4694, 10c, Hotel Cherokee, Tampa, 1891. No. 4695, 15c, Cayo Hueso Committee, 1891 (68x28mm). No. 4696, 15c, F. Valdés Domínguez, Gato Brothers Cigar Factory, Cayo Hueso, 1894. 35c, Club San Carlos, Cayo Hueso, 1893. 40c, Hotel Myrtle Bank, Kingston, 1892. 50c, Gen. Francisco Gómez Toro, Friends of the Country Society Building, Santo Domingo, 1894. 65c, Máximo Gómez, Gómez's house, Montecristi.

2007, Apr. 10 ***Perf. 12½x12¼***
4691-4700 A1227 Set of 10 5.50 5.50

World Food Program Children's Art Exhibition, 10th Anniv. — A1332

2007, May 3 **Litho.** ***Perf. 12¾***
4701 A1332 65c multi 1.40 1.40

Folklore Union — A1333

2007, May 7 ***Perf. 12¼x12½***
4702 A1333 75c multi 1.60 1.60

Islands and Wildlife — A1334

Designs: 5c, Cayo Guillermo, pelican. No. 4704, 15c, Cayo Las Brujas, sea gull. No. 4705, 15c, Cayo Levisa, conches. 20c, Cayo Santa Maria, iguana. 50c, Cayo Ensenachos, plover. 85c, Cayo Largo, Carey turtle.
1p, Cayo Coco, flamingos.

2007, May 8 ***Perf. 12½x12¼***
4703-4708 A1334 Set of 6 4.25 4.25

Souvenir Sheet
Imperf

4709 A1334 1p multi 2.25 2.25

No. 4709 contains one 40x32mm stamp.

Singers and Songwriters A1335

Designs: 5c, Benny Moré. 10c, Ignacio Piñeiro. 30c, Arsenio Rodríguez. 35c, Miguelito Cuní. 65c, Pio Leyva. 75c, Ibrahim Ferrer.
1p, Miguel Matamoros.

2007, May 10 ***Perf. 12¾***
4710-4715 A1335 Set of 6 4.75 4.75

Souvenir Sheet
Imperf

4716 A1335 1p multi 2.25 2.25

No. 4716 contains one 32x40mm stamp with simulated perforations.

Souvenir Sheet

Martí Studies Youth Seminary, 35th Anniv. — A1336

2007, May 19 ***Imperf.***
4717 A1336 1p multi 2.25 2.25

Cuban Radio and Television Institute, 45th Anniv. — A1337

2007, May 24 ***Perf. 12½x12¼***
4718 A1337 3p multi 6.50 6.50

Integral Development Group of the Capital, 20th Anniv. — A1338

2007, May 25 **Litho.**
4719 A1338 65c multi 1.40 1.40

Cuban Admission to the United Nations, 60th Anniv. A1339

2007, May 29 *Perf. 12¾*
4720 A1339 65c multi 1.40 1.40

2007 Pan American Games, Rio de Janeiro — A1340

Designs: No. 4721, 15c, Fencing. No. 4722, 15c, Boxing. 20c, Wrestling. 45c, Running. 65c, Gymnastics. 75c, Cycling.
1p, Games emblem, vert.

2007, June 20 *Perf. 12¾*
4721-4726 A1340 Set of 6 5.00 5.00

Souvenir Sheet

Imperf

4727 A1340 1p multi 2.25 2.25

No. 4727 contains one 32x40mm stamp.

Third Technological Transfer and Intl. Trade Workshop — A1341

2007, July 3 *Perf. 12½x12¼*
4728 A1341 65c multi 1.40 1.40

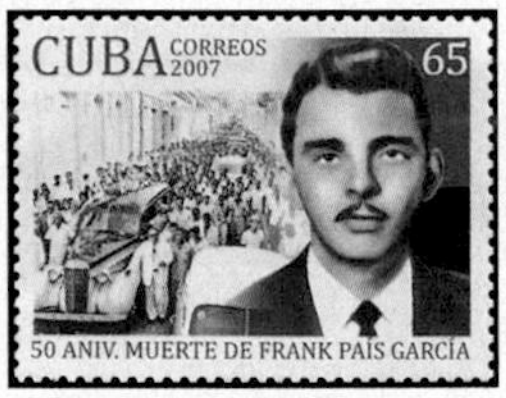

Frank País (1934-57), Revolutionary Hero — A1342

2007, July 30 *Perf. 12¾*
4729 A1342 65c multi 1.40 1.40

Radio Cubana, 85th Anniv. A1343

2007, Aug. 22 *Perf. 12¾*
4730 A1343 65c multi 1.40 1.40

Seven Wonders of the Modern World A1344

Designs: 10c, Great Wall of China. 15c, Petra, Jordan. 20c, Christ the Redeemer Statue, Brazil. 40c, Machu Picchu, Peru. 65c, Chichén Itzá Pyramids, Mexico. 75c, Roman Colosseum. 85c, Taj Mahal, India.

2007, Aug. 16 **Litho.** *Perf. 12¾*
4731-4737 A1344 Set of 7 6.25 6.25

Transportation — A1345

Designs: 10c, Cocotaxis (40x29mm). 15c, Lada 2105 taxi (40x29mm). 30c, Girón VI bus (40x29mm). 40c, Bus trailer on truck (44x27mm). 75c, DAF articulated bus (44x27mm). 85c, Yutong bus (44x27mm).
1p, La Gaviota train.

Perf. 12¾, 12½x12¼ (#4741-4743)

2007, Sept. 3
4738-4743 A1345 Set of 6 5.25 5.25

Souvenir Sheet

Imperf

4744 A1345 1p multi 2.00 2.00

No. 4744 contains one 40x32mm stamp with simulated perforations.

Central Youth Club, 20th Anniv. — A1346

2007, Sept. 8 *Perf. 12¼x12½*
4745 A1346 65c multi 1.40 1.40

Cubans Convicted of Espionage by United States A1347

Designs: No. 4746, 65c, Raised hand with "Cuban Five" emblem. No. 4747, 65c, Fernando González Liort. No. 4748, 65c, Gerardo Hernández Nordelo. No. 4749, 65c, Antonio Guerrero Rodriguez. No. 4750, 65c, Ramón Labañino Salazar. No. 4751, 65c, René González Schwerert.

2007, Sept. 12 *Perf. 12¾*
4746-4751 A1347 Set of 6 8.00 8.00

Tree Planting Campaign — A1348

2007, Oct. 24 *Perf. 12½x12¼*
4752 A1348 65c multi 1.40 1.40

Rose Varieties A1349

Designs: 5c, Pink Parfait. No. 4754, 15c, Alison Wheatcroft. No. 4755, 15c, Prima Ballerina. 45c, Fragrant Cloud. 50c, Blue Moon. 75c, Grandmère Jenny.
1p, Rosa highdownensis.

2007, Oct. 25 *Perf. 12¾*
4753-4758 A1349 Set of 6 4.25 4.25

Souvenir Sheet

Imperf

4759 A1349 1p multi 2.00 2.00

No. 4759 contains one 40x32mm stamp with simulated perforations.

International Design Conference — A1350

Designs: 75c, Electronic machine. 85c, Caricatures.

2007, Oct. 26 *Perf. 12½x12¼*
4760-4761 A1350 Set of 2 3.25 3.25

Souvenir Sheet

International Air Mail Service From Cuba, 80th Anniv. — A1351

2007, Oct. 27 ***Imperf.***
4762 A1351 1p multi 2.00 2.00

Seventh Natl. Philatelic Championship. No. 4762 has simulated perforations.

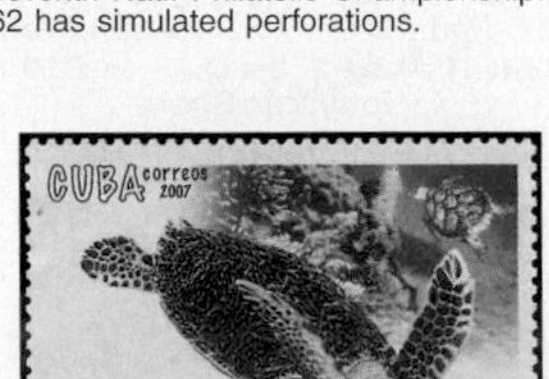

Protected Animals — A1352

Designs: 5c, Eretmochelys imbricata. 10c, Trichechus manatus. 20c, Mesocapromys sanfelipensis. 30c, Mesocapromys nanus. 45c, Epinephelus itajara. 85c, Balistes vetula.
1p, Chelonia mydas.

2007, Nov. 15 *Perf. 12½x12¼*
4763-4768 A1352 Set of 6 4.00 4.00

Souvenir Sheet

Imperf

4769 A1352 1p multi 2.00 2.00

No. 4769 contains one 40x32mm stamp with simulated perforations.

Cuban UNESCO Commission, 60th Anniv. — A1353

2007, Nov. 17 *Perf. 12½x12¼*
4770 A1353 65c multi 1.40 1.40

Cuban Railroads, 170th Anniv. — A1354

2007, Nov. 19 *Perf. 12¾*
4771 A1354 3p multi 6.00 6.00

Camagüey Ballet, 40th Anniv. — A1355

2007, Dec. 1 **Litho.**
4772 A1355 75c multi 1.50 1.50

Infomed Health Network, 15th Anniv. — A1356

2007, Dec. 15
4773 A1356 65c green & black 1.40 1.40

Federation of University Students, 85th Anniv. — A1357

2007, Dec. 20
4774 A1357 65c multi 1.40 1.40

Seven Marvels of Cuban Civil Engineering — A1358

Designs: 5c, White Aqueduct, Havana. 10c, Sewer system, Havana. 20c, Central Highway, Santiago. 30c La Bahia Tunnel, Havana. 85c, Bacunayagua Bridge, Matanzas. 90c, La Farola Viaduct, Guantánamo.
1p, FOSCA Building, Havana.

2007, Dec. 31 ***Perf. 12¾***
4775-4780 A1358 Set of 6 5.00 5.00

Souvenir Sheet
Imperf

4781 A1358 1p multi 2.00 2.00

No. 4781 contains one 40x32mm stamp with simulated perforations.

World Ozone Layer Protection Day, 20th Anniv. — A1359

2007 ***Perf. 12¾***
4782 A1359 65c multi 1.40 1.40

Tourism — A1360

No. 4783, 75c — El Yunque, Baracoa and: a, Atlantea perezi. b, Polymita picta.
No. 4784, 75c — Alexander von Humboldt National Park and: a, Eleutherodactylus iberia. b, Solenodon cubanus.
Illustration reduced.

2007 **Litho.**
Horiz. Pairs, #a-b
4783-4784 A1360 Set of 2 6.00 6.00

Miniature Sheet

America Issue, Education For All — A1361

No. 4785: a, Teacher and children, children in uniforms, girl at computer. b, Students at table. c, Students, flag, marchers. d, Artist, people sitting in front of building, man at computer.

2007
4785 A1361 75c Sheet of 4, #a-d 6.00 6.00

Ernesto "Che" Guevara (1928-67) — A1362

Designs: 65c, Guevara sitting with other men. 75c, Monument to Guevara, La Higuera, Bolivia. 85c, Guevara and text. 90c, Guevara and marchers.

2007 ***Perf. 12½x12¼***
4786-4789 A1362 Set of 4 6.50 6.50
4789a Miniature sheet, #4786-4789 6.50 6.50

Historic Central City of Cienfuegos — A1363

Buildings: 15c, City Hall. 65c, San Lorenzo and Santo Tomás College. 75c, Tomás Terry Theater. 85c, Ferrer Palace.
1p, Gazebo, José Martí Park.

2007 **Litho.** ***Perf. 12¾***
4790-4793 A1363 Set of 4 5.00 5.00

Souvenir Sheet
Imperf

4794 A1363 1p multi 2.00 2.00

No. 4794 contains one 40x32mm stamp with simulated perforations.

University of Havana, 280th Anniv. — A1364

2008, Jan. 5 **Litho.** ***Perf. 12½x12¼***
4795 A1364 65c multi 1.40 1.40

2008 Summer Olympics, Beijing — A1365

Designs: 15c, Baseball. 45c, Swimming. 65c, Discus. 75c, Volleyball.

2008, Jan. 18 ***Perf. 12¾***
4796-4799 A1365 Set of 4 4.00 4.00

José Martí Type of 2004

Designs: No. 4800, 15c, Martí at Twilight Park, New York, 1892, vert. No. 4801, 15c, Martí with members of Cuban Revolutionary Party, 1892, vert. 30c, Martí, and family of Carme Miyares, Sandy Hill, New York, 1893, vert. 40c, Mausoleum, Santa Ifigenia, vert. 45c, Martí, tomb of Félix Varela, San Agustín. 50c, Martí, Dellundé House, Cabo Haitiano. 65c, Hanábana Memorial, Matanzas. 85c, Cover from 1889 in Postal Museum.

2008, Jan. 28
4800-4807 A1227 Set of 8 7.00 7.00

Subway Trains and Stations — A1366

Trains and stations in: No. 4808, 15c, New York. No. 4809, 15c, Paris. 30c, Caracas. 65c, Madrid. 75c, Mexico City. 1.05p, Tokyo.
No. 4814: a, 1866 London Underground train. b, Modern London Underground train, Westminster station emblem.

2008, Feb. 15 ***Perf. 12½x12¼***
4808-4813 A1366 Set of 6 6.25 6.25

Souvenir Sheet
Imperf

4814 A1366 50c Sheet of 2, #a-b 2.00 2.00

No. 4814 contains two 39x24mm stamps with simulated perforations.

Radio Rebelde, 50th Anniv. A1367

2008, Feb. 24 ***Perf. 12¾***
4815 A1367 75c multi 1.50 1.50

Frontier Guards, 45th Anniv. A1368

2008, Mar. 3
4816 A1368 65c multi 1.40 1.40

Dr. Mario Muñoz Monroy Third Guerrilla Front, 50th Anniv. — A1369

2008, Mar. 6 **Litho.** ***Perf. 12¾***
4817 A1369 75c multi 1.50 1.50

Aquaculture — A1370

Designs: 65c, Penaeus vannamei. 75c, Ctenopharyngodon idella. 85c, Clarias gariepinus.
1p, Oreochromis aurea.

2008, Apr. 8 ***Perf. 12½x12¼***
4818-4820 A1370 Set of 3 4.50 4.50

Souvenir Sheet
Imperf

4821 A1370 1p multi 2.00 2.00

No. 4821 contains one 31x28mm stamp.

Souvenir Sheet

Cuban Postal Stationery, 130th Anniv. — A1371

2008, Apr. 24 ***Imperf.***
4822 A1371 1p multi 2.00 2.00

Bohemia Magazine, Cent. — A1372

2008, May 10 ***Perf. 12¾***
4823 A1372 65c multi 1.40 1.40

Second Frank Pais Front, 50th Anniv. — A1373

2008, Mar. 11 **Litho.** ***Perf. 12¾***
4824 A1373 65c multi 1.40 1.40

Birds — A1374

Designs: 5c, Cartacuba (Cuban tody). 10c, Ruiseñor (nightingale). 15c, Carpintero verde (green woodpecker). 50c, Tocororo (Cuban trogon). 65c, Catey (parakeet), horiz. 75c, Cabrerito de la Ciénaga (Zapata sparrow), horiz. 90c, Zunzuncito (hummingbird), horiz. 1.05p, Juan Chiví (Cuban vireo), horiz.

2008, May 22
4825-4832 A1374 Set of 8 8.50 8.50

"Wings of Liberty" Symposium, Cuban National Museum of Natural History.

Visit of Indonesian Pres. Sukarno, 48th Anniv. — A1375

Sukarno and: No. 4833, 65c, Fidel Castro (shown). No. 4834, 65c, Ernesto "Che" Guevara.

2008 Litho. *Perf. 12½x12¼*
4833-4834 A1375 Set of 2 2.60 2.60

SEMI-POSTAL STAMPS

Common Design Types pictured following the introduction.

Curie Issue
Common Design Type
Wmk. 106

1938, Nov. 23 Engr. *Perf. 10*
B1 CD80 2c + 1c salmon 4.00 1.00
B2 CD80 5c + 1c deep ultra 4.00 1.25
Set, never hinged 12.00

40th anniv. of the discovery of radium by Pierre and Marie Curie. Surtax for the benefit of the Intl. Union for the Control of Cancer.

Catalogue values for unused stamps in this section, from this point to the end of the section, are for Never Hinged items.

"Agriculture" Supporting "Industry" SP2

Engr., Center Typo.
1959, May 7 Wmk. 321 *Perf. 12½*
B3 SP2 2c + 1c car & ultra .65 .20

Agricultural reforms. See No. CB1. For surcharges see Nos. 624, C199.

Nurse — SP3

Wmk. 229
1959, Sept. 22 Photo. *Perf. 12½*
B4 SP3 2c + 1c crimson rose .35 .25

Exists imperf, value about double.

AIR POST STAMPS

Seaplane over Havana Harbor AP1

Wmk. 106
1927, Nov. 1 Engr. *Perf. 12*
C1 AP1 5c dark blue 5.00 1.00
Never hinged 8.00

For overprint see No. C30.

Type of 1927 Issue Overprinted

1928, Feb. 8
C2 AP1 5c carmine rose 4.00 1.60
Never hinged 6.00

No. 283 Surcharged in Red

1930, Oct. 27 Unwmk.
C3 A44 10c on 25c violet 3.50 1.60
Never hinged 4.75

Airplane and Coast of Cuba — AP3

For Foreign Postage

1931, Feb. 26 Wmk. 106 *Perf. 10*
C4 AP3 5c green .45 .20
C5 AP3 10c dk blue .45 .20
C6 AP3 15c rose .90 .30
C7 AP3 20c brown .90 .20
C8 AP3 30c dk violet 1.25 .20
C9 AP3 40c dp orange 2.75 .35
C10 AP3 50c olive grn 3.25 .35
C11 AP3 1p black 5.25 .90
Nos. C4-C11 (8) 15.20 2.70
Set, never hinged 25.00

See No. C40. For surcharges see Nos. C16-C17, C203, C225.

Airplane AP4

For Domestic Postage

1931-46
C12 AP4 5c rose vio ('32) .35 .20
a. 5c brown violet ('36) .35 .20
C13 AP4 10c gray blk .35 .20
C14 AP4 20c car rose 3.00 .85
C14A AP4 20c rose pink ('46) 1.10 .20
C15 AP4 50c dark blue 4.75 .90
Nos. C12-C15 (5) 9.55 2.35
Set, never hinged 17.00

See #C130. For overprints see #C31, E29-E30.

Type of 1931 Surcharged in Black

1935, Apr. 24 *Perf. 10*
C16 AP3 10c + 10c red 11.00 9.50
Never hinged 18.00
a. Double surcharge 110.00

Imperf
C17 AP3 10c + 10c red 25.00 *25.00*
Never hinged 35.00

Matanzas Issue

Air View of Matanzas AP5

10c, Airship "Macon." 20c, Airplane "The Four Winds." 50c, Air View of Fort San Severino.

Wmk. 229
1936, May 5 Photo. *Perf. 12½*
C18 AP5 5c violet .75 .25
C19 AP5 10c yellow orange .90 .40
C20 AP5 20c green 3.25 1.75
C21 AP5 50c greenish slate 8.00 3.00
Nos. C18-C21 (4) 12.90 5.40
Set, never hinged 20.00

Exist imperf. Value 20% more.

"Lightning" AP9

Allegory of Flight AP10

1936, Nov. 18
C22 AP9 5c violet 1.75 1.10
C23 AP10 10c orange brown 2.50 1.50
Set, never hinged 5.50

Major Gen. Maximo Gomez, birth cent.

Flat Arch (Panama) — AP11

Carlos Antonio López (Paraguay) — AP12

Inca Gate, Cuzco (Peru) — AP13

Atlacatl (Salvador) AP14

José Enrique Rodó (Uruguay) AP15

Simón Bolívar (Venezuela) AP16

Wmk. 106
1937, Oct. 13 Engr. *Perf. 10*
C24 AP11 5c red 7.00 7.00
C25 AP12 5c red 7.00 7.00
C26 AP13 10c blue 7.00 7.00
C27 AP14 10c blue 7.00 7.00
C28 AP15 20c green 9.50 9.50
C29 AP16 20c green 9.50 9.50
Nos. C24-C29 (6) 47.00 47.00
Set, never hinged 60.00

See note after No. 354.

Type of 1927 Overprinted in Black

1938, May Wmk. 106
C30 AP1 5c dark orange 5.00 1.50
Never hinged 7.00

1st airplane flight from Key West to Havana, made by Domingo Rosillo, 1913.

Type of 1931-32 Overprinted

1939, Oct. 15
C31 AP4 10c emerald 40.00 5.50
Never hinged 60.00

Issued in connection with an experimental postal rocket flight held at Havana.

Sir Rowland Hill, Map of Cuba and First Stamps of Britain, Spanish Cuba and Republic of Cuba — AP17

1940, Nov. 28 Engr. Wmk. 106
C32 AP17 10c brown 4.50 2.00
Never hinged 7.50

Souvenir Sheet

Unwmk. *Imperf.*
C33 Sheet of 4 15.00 11.00
Never hinged 25.00
a. AP17 10c light brown 2.75 1.25
Never hinged 3.50

Cent. of the 1st postage stamp.
Sheet sold for 60c.
No. C33 exists with each of the four stamps overprinted in black: "Exposicion de la ACNU/24 de Octubre de 1951/Dia de las Naciones" and "Historia de la Aviacion" in lower margin. Value, $80.
For overprints see Nos. C39, C211.

Poet José Heredia and Palms AP18

Heredia and Niagara Falls — AP19

1940, Dec. 30 Wmk. 106
C34 AP18 5c emerald 2.00 1.00
C35 AP19 10c greenish slate 3.00 1.50
Set, never hinged 7.50

Death cent. of José Maria Heredia y Campuzano (1803-39), poet and patriot.

First Cuban Land Sighted by Columbus AP20

Columbus Lighthouse AP21

1944, May 19

C36	AP20	5c olive green	.90	.30
C37	AP21	10c slate black	1.90	.50

450th anniv. of the discovery of America.

Catalogue values for unused stamps in this section, from this point to the end of the section, are for Never Hinged items.

Conference of La Mejorana (Meceo, Gomez and Marti) AP22

1948, May 21 Wmk. 229 *Perf. 12½*

C38	AP22	8c org yel & blk	3.00	.75

50th anniv. of the start of the War of 1895.

Souvenir Sheet
No. C33 Overprinted in Ultramarine

1948, May 21 Unwmk. *Imperf.*

C39	AP17	Sheet of 4	15.00	9.50

The overprint is applied in the center of the sheet, so that a part of the overprint falls on each stamp.

American Air Mail Soc. Convention, Havana, May 21 to 23, 1948. The sheets sold for 60c each.

Type of 1931

1948, June 15 Wmk. 106 *Perf. 10*

C40	AP3	8c orange brown	2.25	.70

Narciso Lopez Landing at Cárdenas AP23

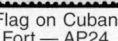

Flag on Cuban Fort — AP24

Flag on Morro Castle, Havana — AP25

Engraved and Lithographed

1951, July 3 Wmk. 229 *Perf. 13*

C41	AP23	5c ol grn, ultra & red	2.25	.30
C42	AP24	8c red brn, bl & red	3.50	.30
C43	AP25	25c gray blk, bl & red	5.00	1.90
		Nos. C41-C43 (3)	10.75	2.50

Centenary of adoption of Cuba's flag.

Souvenir Sheet
No. 365a Overprinted in Green

Illustration reduced.

1951, Aug. 24 Unwmk. *Imperf.*

C43A		Sheet of 4	12.00	9.00

50th anniv. of the discovery of the cause of yellow fever by Dr. Carlos J. Finlay, and to honor the martyrs of science.

Postage Type and

Resignation Play of Dr. Lasker AP26

Capablanca Making "The Exact Play" — AP27

Wmk. 229

1951, Nov. 1 Photo. *Perf. 13*

C44	AP26	5c shown	5.00	.80
C45	AP27	8c shown	9.00	1.25
C46	A165	25c Capablanca	15.00	3.25
		Nos. C44-C46 (3)	29.00	5.30

30th anniv. of the winning of the World Chess title by José Raul Capablanca.

Morrillo Types of Regular Issue

Wmk. 106

1951, Nov. 22 Engr. *Perf. 10*

C47	A167	5c violet	2.40	.50
C48	A168	8c deep green	3.25	.75
C49	A169	25c dark brown	6.50	1.50
a.		Souv. sheet of 6, black brown, perf. 13	50.00	35.00
b.		Souv. sheet of 6, green, imperf.	200.00	125.00
		Nos. C47-C49 (3)	12.15	2.75

Nos. C49a and C49b contain one each of the 1c, 2c and 5c of types A167-A169 and of the 5c, 8c and 25c airmail stamps of types A167-A169. Sheets are unwatermarked and measure 124x133mm.

Isabella Type of Regular Issue, 1952

1952, Feb. 22

C50	A172	25c purple	4.00	1.00
a.		Souv. sheet of 2, perf. 11	18.00	18.00
b.		Souv. sheet of 2, imperf.	22.50	22.50

Nos. C50a and C50b contain one each of a 2c of type A172 and a 25c air-mail stamp of type A172. In No. C50a, the 2c and marginal inscriptions are brown carmine; the 25c, dark blue. In No. C50b, the 2c and marginal inscriptions are dark blue; the 25c, brown carmine. Sheets measure 108x18mm.

Type of Regular Issue of 1951 Surcharged in Various Colors

1952, Mar. 18

Color: Yellow Brown

C51	A159	5c on 2c	.85	.25
C52	A159	8c on 2c (C)	1.75	.25
C53	A159	10c on 2c (Bl)	1.75	.25
C54	A159	25c on 2c (V)	2.75	1.00
C55	A159	50c on 2c (C)	8.50	1.50
C56	A159	1p on 2c (Bl)	19.00	6.00
		Nos. C51-C56 (6)	34.60	9.25

Country School AP32

Entrance, University of Havana — AP33

10c, Presidential Mansion. 25c, Banknote.

Wmk. 106

1952, May 27 Engr. *Perf. 12½*

Centers Various Shades of Green

C57	AP32	5c dark purple	.45	.20
C58	AP33	8c dark red	.70	.20
C59	AP32	10c deep blue	1.40	.20
C60	AP32	25c dark violet brn	2.40	1.00
		Nos. C57-C60 (4)	4.95	1.60

Foundation of the Republic of Cuba, 50th anniv.

Plane and Map — AP34

Agustín Parlá — AP35

1952, July 22 Engr. *Perf. 10*

C61	AP34	8c black	1.50	.55
a.		Souv. sheet, 8c deep blue	15.00	10.00
b.		Souv. sheet, 8c deep green	15.00	10.00
C62	AP35	25c ultra	4.00	1.60
a.		Souv. sheet, 25c deep blue	15.00	10.00
b.		Souv. sheet, 25c deep green	15.00	10.00

30th anniv. of the Key West-Mariel flight of Agustin Parla.

The four souvenir sheets are perf. 11.

Col. Charles Hernandes y Sandrino — AP36

1952, Oct. 7

C63	AP36	5c orange	.70	.20
C64	AP36	8c brt yel grn	.70	.20
C65	AP36	10c dk brown	.90	.20
C66	AP36	15c dk Prus grn	1.75	.50
C67	AP36	20c aqua	2.25	.65
C68	AP36	25c crimson	1.75	.65
C69	AP36	30c dk vio bl	4.50	1.60
C70	AP36	45c rose lilac	4.50	2.25
C71	AP36	50c indigo	2.75	1.60
C72	AP36	1p bister	10.00	3.25
		Nos. C63-C72 (10)	29.80	11.10

Three-fourths of the proceeds from the sale were used for the Communications Ministry Employees' Retirement Fund.

Entrance, University of Havana — AP37

F. V. Dominguez, M. Estebanez and F. Capdevila — AP38

Engr.; Center Typo.

1952, Nov. 27

C73	AP37	5c indigo & dk blue	1.75	.35
C74	AP38	25c org & dk grn	5.00	1.25

Execution of 8 medical students, 81st anniv.

AP39

Lockheed Constellation Airliners — AP40

1953, May 22 Engr.

C75	AP39	8c orange brn	1.25	.20
C76	AP39	15c scarlet	2.25	.70

Typographed and Engraved

C77	AP40	2p dp green & dk brn	27.50	10.00
C78	AP40	5p blue & dk brn	55.00	17.50
		Nos. C75-C78 (4)	86.00	28.40

See #C120-C121. For surcharge see #C224.

Page of Manifesto of Montecristi — AP42

House of Maximo Gomez AP43

#C79, Marti in Kingston, Jamaica, #C80, With Workers in Tampa, Florida. #C83, Marti addressing liberating army. #C84, Portrait. #C85, Dos Rios obelisk. #C86, Marti's first tomb. #C87, Present tomb. #C88, Monument in Havana. #C89, Martian forge.

1953 Engr. *Perf. 10*

C79	AP42	5c dk car & blk	.30	.20
C80	AP42	5c dk car & blk	.30	.20
C81	AP43	8c dk green & blk	.60	.20
C82	AP42	8c dk green & blk	.60	.20
C83	AP43	10c dk blue & dk car	1.75	.75
C84	AP42	10c dk blue & dk car	1.75	.75
C85	AP42	15c violet & gray	1.00	.90
C86	AP42	15c violet & gray	1.00	.90
C87	AP42	25c brown & car	3.75	1.25
C88	AP42	25c brown & car	3.75	1.25
C89	AP43	50c yellow & bl	5.00	2.50
		Nos. C79-C89 (11)	19.80	9.10

Cent. of the birth of José Marti.

Board of Accounts Building — AP44

25c, Plane above Board of Accounts Bldg.

1953, Nov. 3

C90 AP44 8c rose carmine 1.90 .60
C91 AP44 25c dk gray grn 3.50 1.00

1st Intl. Cong. of Boards of Account, Havana, Nov. 2-9, 1953.

Miguel Coyula Llaguno AP45

Antonio Ginard Rojas AP46

Designs: 10c, Gregorio Hernandez Saez. 1p, Communications Association Flag.

1954

C92 AP45 5c dark blue .60 .25
C93 AP46 8c red violet .75 .25
C94 AP46 10c orange 1.40 .35
C95 AP45 1p black 9.50 4.50
Nos. C92-C95 (4) 12.25 5.35

See note after No. C72.

Alvaro Reinoso — AP47

Plane and Harvesters Cutting Cane AP48

Designs in Lower Triangle: 5c, Four-engine Plane and Cane Field. 10c, Tractor pulling loaded wagons. 15c, Train of sugar cane. 20c, Modern mill. 25c, Evaporators. 30, Sacks of sugar. 40c, Loading sugar on ship. 45c, Ox cart. 50c, Primitive sugar mill.

1954, Apr. 27 **Engr.**

C96 AP47 5c yellow green .45 .20
C97 AP48 8c brown 1.25 .50
C98 AP48 10c dark green 1.25 .50
C99 AP48 15c henna brn 3.00 .50
C100 AP48 20c blue 1.25 .20
C101 AP48 25c scarlet .95 .20
C102 AP48 30c lilac rose 2.50 .95
C103 AP48 40c deep blue 5.00 1.25
C104 AP48 45c violet 4.00 2.50
C105 AP48 50c brt blue 4.00 1.60
C106 AP47 1p dk gray blue 11.00 3.25
Nos. C96-C106 (11) 34.65 11.65

For surcharges see Nos. C204.

Sanatorium Type of Regular Issue

1954, Sept. 21 Wmk. 106 *Perf. 10*

C107 A186 9c deep green 2.50 .50

Dolz Type of Regular Issue, 1954

1954, Dec. 23

C108 A188 12c carmine 2.00 .60

Rotary Type of Regular Issue, 1955

1955, Feb. 23

C109 A190 12c carmine 2.50 .50

Stamps of 1855 and 1905, Palace of Fine Arts AP52

Designs (including 2 stamps): 12c, Plaza de la Fraternidad. 24c, View of Havana. 30c, Plaza de la Republica.

1955, Apr. 24 ***Perf. 12½***

C110 AP52 8c dk grnsh bl & grn 1.00 .35
C111 AP52 12c dk ol grn & red 1.10 .35
C112 AP52 24c dk red & ultra 2.00 .90
C113 AP52 30c dp org & brn 4.25 1.50
Nos. C110-C113 (4) 8.35 3.10

Cent. of Cuba's 1st postage stamps.

Mariel Bay — AP53

Views: 12c, Varadero beach. 1p, Vinales valley.

1955, June 22 **Wmk. 106**

C114 AP53 8c dk car & dk grn .75 .25
C115 AP53 12c dk ocher & brt bl 1.75 .35
C116 AP53 1p dk grn & ocher 7.50 2.50
Nos. C114-C116 (3) 10.00 3.10

See note after No. C72.

Map of Crocier's 1914 Flight — AP54

Design: 30c, Crocier in plane.

1955, July 4 ***Perf. 10***

C117 AP54 12c red & dk grn 1.00 .25
C118 AP54 30c dk grn & mag 3.00 .60

35th anniv. of the death of Jaime Gonzalez Crocier, aviation pioneer.

Cuban Museum, Tampa, Fla. — AP55

1955, July 1 Engr. *Perf. 12½*

C119 AP55 12c red & dk brn 2.00 .50

Cent. of Tampa's incorporation as a town.

Lockheed Type of 1953

Typographed and Engraved

1955, Sept. 21 **Wmk. 106**

C120 AP40 2p bl & ol grn 20.00 6.00
C121 AP40 5p dp rose & ol grn 42.50 15.00

Wright Brothers' Plane and Stamps AP56

Designs: 12c, Spirit of St. Louis. 24c, Graf Zeppelin. 30c, Constellation passenger plane. 50c, Convair jet fighter.

Engraved and Photogravure

1955, Nov. 12 Wmk. 106 *Perf. 12½*

Inscription and Plane in Black

C122 AP56 8c car & bl 1.00 .35
C123 AP56 12c yel grn & car 2.25 .70
C124 AP56 24c vio & car 6.75 2.50
C125 AP56 30c bl & red org 5.75 3.25
C126 AP56 50c ol grn & red org 7.75 4.00
a. Souvenir sheet of 5 45.00 25.00
Nos. C122-C126 (5) 23.50 10.80

International Centenary Philatelic Exhibition in Havana, Nov. 12-19, 1955.

No. C126a is printed on thick paper and measures 140x178mm. It contains one each of Nos. C122-C126 with the background of each stamp printed in a different color from the perforated stamps.

"Three Friends" and Gen. Emilio Nuñez AP57

Design: 12c, Landing on the Cuban Coast.

1955, Dec. 27 Engr. Unwmk.

C127 AP57 8c ultra & dk car 2.00 .40
C128 AP57 12c grn & dk red brn 3.25 .50

Gen. Emilio Nuñez, Cuban revolutionary hero, birth cent.

Post Type of Regular Issue, 1956

Bishop P. A. Morell de Santa Cruz (1694-1768).

1956, Mar. 27 **Wmk. 106**

C129 A197 12c dk brn & grn 1.75 .40

Plane Type of 1931-46

1956 Engr. *Perf. 10*

C130 AP4 50c greenish blue 3.00 1.00

Portrait Type of Regular Issue, 1956

1956, May 2 ***Perf. 12½***

Portraits: 8c, Gen. Julio Sanguily. 12c, Gen. José Maria Aguirre. 30c, Col. Ernesto Fonts Sterling.

Portraits in Black

C131 A198 8c brown 1.10 .20
C132 A198 12c dull yellow 1.75 .25
C133 A198 30c indigo 3.00 1.50
Nos. C131-C133 (3) 5.85 1.95

See note after No. C72.

Mother and Child — AP60

Masonic Temple Havana — AP61

1956, May 13 Wmk. 106 *Perf. 12½*

C134 AP60 12c ultra & red 2.50 .25

Issued in honor of Mother's Day 1956.

1956, June 5

C135 AP61 12c olive green 2.75 .40

Pigeon AP62

Gundlach Hawk — AP63

Birds: 8c, Wood duck. 19c, Herring gulls. 24c, White pelicans. 29c, Common merganser. 30c, Quail. 50c, Herons (great white, great blue and Wurdemann's). 1p, Northern caracara. 2p, Middle American jacana. 5p, Ivory-billed woodpecker.

1956

C136 AP62 8c blue .50 .20
C137 AP62 12c gray blue 7.50 .20
C138 AP63 14c green 1.75 .25
C139 AP63 19c redsh brn 1.10 .55
C140 AP63 24c lilac rose 1.25 .55
C141 AP62 29c green 1.90 .55
C142 AP62 30c dk olive bis 2.25 .80
C143 AP63 50c slate blk 4.25 1.10
C144 AP63 1p dk car rose 6.50 2.25
C145 AP62 2p rose violet 13.00 4.25
C146 AP63 5p brt red 35.00 8.75
Nos. C136-C146 (11) 75.00 19.45

See Nos. C205, C235-C237. For surcharges and overprints see #C147, C151, C197, C209-C210

Type of 1956 Surcharged

Design: 24c, White pelicans.

1956, July 13

C147 AP63 8c on 24c deep org 2.50 .75

Opening of the new building of the Cuba Philatelic Club, Havana, July 14, 1956.

Hubert de Blanck — AP64

Church of Our Lady of Charity — AP65

1956, July 6

C148 AP64 12c ultra 2.00 .30

Hubert de Blanck (1856-1932), composer.

1956, Sept. 8

C149 AP65 12c green & carmine 2.75 .40
a. Souvenir sheet of 2, imperf. 14.00 8.00

Issued in honor of Our Lady of Charity of Cobre, patroness of Cuba.

No. C149a contains one each of Nos. 559 and C149. No. C149a exists with yellow of No. 559 omitted.

Benjamin Franklin AP66

1956, Oct. 5 Engr. *Perf. 12½*

C150 AP66 12c red brown 2.00 .40

Type of 1956 Surcharged in Blue

Design: 2p, Middle American jacana.

1956, Oct. 26 **Wmk. 106**

C151 AP62 12c on 2p dark gray 2.25 .85

Issued in honor of the 12th Inter-American Press Association Conference, Havana.

Lord Baden-Powell AP67

1957, Feb. 22

C152 AP67 12c slate 2.40 .50

Centenary of the birth of Lord Baden-Powell, founder of the Boy Scouts.

Hanabanilla Waterfall AP68

12c, Sierra de Cubitas. 30c, Puerto Boniato.

1957, Mar. 29

C153 AP68 8c blue & red .75 .20
C154 AP68 12c green & red 2.25 .30
C155 AP68 30c ol grn & dk pur 3.00 .50
Nos. C153-C155 (3) 6.00 1.00

See note after No. 457.

Philatelic Club, Havana AP69

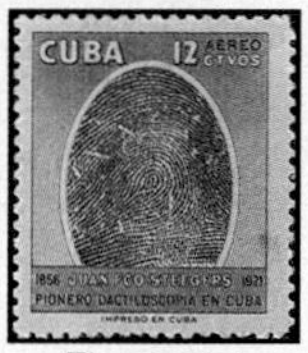

Fingerprint AP70

1957, Apr. 24 Wmk. 106 *Perf. 12½*

C156 AP69 12c yel, grn & brn 1.75 .30

Stamp Day, and the Natl. Phil. Exhib.

1957, Apr. 30

C157 AP70 12c claret brown 1.75 .30

Birth cent. (in 1856) of Juan Francisco Steegers y Perera, dactyloscopy pioneer.

Baseball Player — AP71

1957, May 17 Wmk. 106 *Perf. 12½*

C158 AP71 8c shown 1.10 .35
C159 AP71 12c Ballerina 1.90 .40
C160 AP71 24c Girl diver 2.75 1.00
C161 AP71 30c Boxers 3.75 1.50
Nos. C158-C161 (4) 9.50 3.25

Issued to honor young Cuban athletes.

Joaquin de Aguero AP72

Jeanette Ryder AP73

1957, July 4

C162 AP72 12c indigo 1.50 .25

Issued to honor Joaquin de Aguero, Cuban freedom fighter and patriot.

1957, July 17

C163 AP73 12c dk red brn 2.50 .40
a. Pair, #574, C163 7.00 3.50

Mrs. Jeanette Ryder, founder of the Humane Society of Cuba.

José M. de Heredia y Girard — AP74

John Robert Gregg — AP75

1957, Aug. 16 Engr. Wmk. 106

C164 AP74 8c dk blue vio 1.50 .25

José Maria de Heredia y Girard (1842-1905), Cuban born French poet.

Justice Type of Regular Issue, 1957

1957, Sept. 2 *Perf. 12½*

C165 A214 12c green 2.00 .50

1957, Oct. 1

C166 AP75 12c dark green 2.00 .50

90th anniv. of the birth of John Robert Gregg, inventor of the Gregg shorthand system.

D. Figarola Caneda — AP76

José Marti National Library AP77

1957, Oct. 18 Wmk. 106 *Perf. 12½*

C167 AP76 8c ultra .75 .25
C168 AP77 12c chocolate 2.00 .35

José Marti National Library.

Map of Cuba and UN Emblem AP78

1957, Oct. 24

C169 AP78 8c dk green & brn 1.00 .25
C170 AP78 12c car rose & grn 1.50 .40
C171 AP78 30c ind & brt pink 3.50 1.00
Nos. C169-C171 (3) 6.00 1.65

Issued for United Nations Day, 1957.

Map of Cuba and Florida AP79

1957, Oct. 28

C172 AP79 12c dk red brn & bl 1.75 .50

30th anniv. of airmail service from Key West to Havana.

Type of Regular Issue, 1957 and

Stairway and Bell Tower AP80

Design: 12c, Facade of Normal School.

1957, Nov. 19 Engr. *Perf. 12½*

C173 A217 12c indigo & ocher 1.40 .30
C174 AP80 30c dk car & gray 2.50 .60

View Types of Regular Issue, 1957

Views: 8c, El Viso Fort, El Caney. 12c, Sancti Spiritus Church. 30c, Concordia Bridge, Matanzas.

1957, Dec. 17 *Perf. 12½*

C175 A218 8c dk gray & red .75 .30
C176 A219 12c brown & gray 1.50 .30
C177 A218 30c red brn & bl gray 2.75 .75
Nos. C175-C177 (3) 5.00 1.35

See note after No. C72.

Hedges Types of Regular Issue, 1958

8c, Dayton Hedges & Matanzas rayon factory.

1958, Jan. 30 Wmk. 106 *Perf. 12½*

C178 A221 8c green 2.00 .50

Diario de la Marina Building — AP81

1958, Apr. 1

C179 AP81 29c black 3.50 1.00

Jose Ignacio Rivero y Alonso, editor of the newspaper, Diario de la Marina.

Map Showing Sea Mail Route, 1765 AP82

1958, Apr. 24 Wmk. 106 *Perf. 12½*

C180 AP82 29c dk bl aqua & buff 4.75 1.25

Issued for Stamp Day, Apr. 24, and the National Philatelic Exhibition.

Gen. Gomez in Battle — AP83

Snail (Polymita Picta) — AP84

1958, June 6 Engr.

C181 AP83 12c slate green 2.00 .35

Issued in honor of Maj. Gen. José Miguel Gomez, President of Cuba, 1909-13.

1958, Aug. 29 Wmk. 321 *Perf. 12½*

12c, Megalocnus Rodens. 30c, Ammonite.

C182 AP84 8c gray, red & yel 3.25 .90
C183 AP84 12c brn, *yel grn* 5.50 1.50
C184 AP84 30c grn, *pink* 8.00 2.00
Nos. C182-C184 (3) 16.75 4.40

Centenary of the birth of Dr. Carlos de la Torre, naturalist.

Papilio Caiguanabus AP85

Cuban Sea Bass — AP86

12c, Teria gundlachia. 14c, Teria ebriola. 19c, Nathalis felicia. 29c, Butter Hamlet. 30c, Tattler.

1958, Sept. 26 Wmk. 106 *Perf. 12½*

C185 AP85 8c multicolored 3.00 .50
C186 AP85 12c emer, blk & org 3.50 .50
C187 AP85 14c multicolored 5.25 .75
C188 AP85 19c bl, blk & yel 6.75 1.00
C189 AP86 24c multicolored 7.50 1.00
C190 AP86 29c blk, brn & ultra 11.00 1.25
C191 AP86 30c blk, yel grn & sep 16.00 1.75
Nos. C185-C191 (7) 53.00 6.75

Felipe Poey (1799-1891), naturalist.

Battle of San Juan Hill, 1898 — AP87

Wmk. 106

1958, Oct. 27 Engr. *Perf. 12½*

C192 AP87 12c black brown 2.75 .30

Birth centenary of Theodore Roosevelt.

UNESCO Building, Paris — AP88

Design: 30c, "UNESCO" and map of Cuba.

1958, Nov. 7

C193 AP88 12c dk slate grn 1.50 .40
C194 AP88 30c dp ultra 3.00 1.25

UNESCO Headquarters in Paris opening, Nov. 3.

Postal Notice of 1765 — AP89

Musical Arts Building — AP90

Design: 30c, Administrative postal book of St. Cristobal, Havana, 1765.

1959, Apr. 24 Wmk. 321 *Perf. 12½*

C195 AP89 12c Prus blue & sep 1.50 .25
C196 AP89 30c sepia & Prus bl 2.50 1.00

Issued for Stamp Day, Apr. 24, and the National Philatelic Exhibition.

Type of 1956 Surcharged with New Value, Bar and "ASTA" Emblem in Dark Blue

1959, Oct. 17 Wmk. 321 *Perf. 12½*

C197 AP63 12c on 1p emerald 2.25 1.10

Issued to publicize the meeting of the American Soc. of Travel Agents, Oct. 17-23.

Wmk. 106

1959, Nov. 11 Engr. *Perf. 12½*

C198 AP90 12c yellow green 3.00 .45

40th anniversary of the Musical Arts Society.

No. CB1 Surcharged in Red: "HABILITADO PARA / 12c"

Engr. & Typo.

1960 Wmk. 321 *Perf. 12½*

C199 SPAP1 12c on 12 + 3c car & grn 2.25 .75

Type of Regular Issue, 1960

8c, Battle of Santa Clara. 12c, Rebel forces entering Havana. 29c, Bank-note changing hands ("Clandestine activities in the cities").

Wmk. 320

1960, Jan. 28 Engr. *Perf. 12½*

C200 A236 8c bl, gray ol & sal 2.25 .25
C201 A236 12c gray ol & ocher 3.25 .25
C202 A236 29c gray & car 6.50 1.50
Nos. C200-C202 (3) 12.00 2.00

Nos. C9 and C104 Surcharged "12c" in Red

1960, Feb. 3 Wmk. 106

C203 AP3 12c on 40c dp org 1.10 .40
C204 AP48 12c on 45c vio 1.10 .40

Pigeon Type of 1956

1960, Feb. 12 Wmk. 321

C205 AP62 12c brt blue grn .70 .25

Statue Type of Regular Issue, 1960.

Statues: 8c, José Martí, Matanzas. 12c, Heroes of the Cacarajicara, Pinar del Rio. 30c, Cosme de la Torriente, Isle of Pines, horiz.

1960, Mar. 28 *Perf. 12½*

C206 A237 8c gray & car .65 .25
C207 A237 12c blue & car 1.10 .25
C208 A237 30c violet & brn 2.50 1.00
Nos. C206-C208 (3) 4.25 1.50

See note after No. 386.

Type of 1956 and No. C33 Overprinted in Dark Blue

1960, Apr. 24 Wmk. 321 *Perf. 12½*

C209 AP62 8c orange yel .60 .30
C210 AP62 12c cerise 1.60 .40

Souvenir Sheet

C211 AP17 Sheet of 4 20.00 20.00

Stamp Day, 4/24/60, and Natl. Phil. Exhib.
No. C211 has added marginal inscription in dark blue for cent. of the ¼r on 2r (No. 15).

Type of Olympic Games Issue, 1960

Wmk. 321

1960, Sept. 22 Engr. *Perf. 12½*

C212 A238 8c Boxer .75 .20
C213 A238 12c Runner 1.50 .40
a. Souvenir sheet of 4 5.00

17th Olympic Games, Rome, Aug. 25-Sept. 11. No. C213a contains one each imperf. of types of Nos. 645-646 and Nos. C212-C213 in dark blue.

No. C3 and Flight Symbols of 1930, 1960 — AP91

1960, Oct. 30 Litho. Unwmk.

C214 AP91 8c multicolored 3.25 1.75

30th anniv. of national air mail service.

Sword of Sheaf of Wheat — AP92

12c, Two workers, horiz. 30c, Three maps, horiz. 50c, Hand inscribed "Peace" in 5 languages.

1961, Jan. 10 Photo. *Perf. 11½*

Granite Paper

C215 AP92 8c multicolored .60 .20
C216 AP92 12c multicolored .90 .20
C217 AP92 30c black & red 2.50 .50
C218 AP92 50c blk, bl & red 3.00 1.00
Nos. C215-C218 (4) 7.00 1.90

Conf. of Underdeveloped Countries, Havana.

José Marti and "Declaration of Havana" — AP93

Background in Spanish, English or French.

1961, Jan. 28 Litho. *Perf. 12½*

C219 AP93 8c pale grn, blk & red 1.00 .60
C220 AP93 12c org yel, blk & pale vio 1.50 1.00
C221 AP93 30c pale bl, blk & pale brn 2.50 2.00
a. Souvenir sheet of 3 11.00 11.00
Nos. C219-C221 (3) 5.00 3.60

Declaration of Havana, Sept. 1, 1960.
Sheets of 25 are imprinted in margin "E" for Spanish, "I" for English or "F" for French.
No. C221a contains one each of Nos. C219-C221, imperf. The 8c has background in Spanish, the 12c in English and the 30e in French.

UN Type of 1961

1961, Apr. 12 Unwmk. *Perf. 12½*

C222 A244 8c dp car & yel .60 .20
C223 A244 12c brt ultra & org 1.40 .35
a. Souv. sheet of 2, #C222-C223, imperf. 10.00

Nos. C76 and C7 Surcharged

Wmk. 106

1961, Oct. 1 Engr. *Perf. 10*

C224 AP39 8c on 15c No. C76 1.00 .35
C225 AP3 8c on 20c No. C7 1.00 .35

Revolution Anniv. Type of 1962

Perf. 12½

1962, Jan. 3 Litho. Unwmk.

C226 A250 8c multi .85 .30
C227 A250 12c multi 1.90 .55
C228 A250 30c multi 2.50 .90
Nos. C226-C228 (3) 5.25 1.75

1st Sugarcane Harvest in Socialist Cuba, 1st Anniv. — AP94

1962, Jan. 16

C229 AP94 8c salmon pink & dark brn 1.00 .20
C230 AP94 12c bluish lil & blk 2.50 .45

Cuban goods have been embargoed by the United States since a Feb. 7, 1962 proclamation by President Kennedy, but according to the Office of Foreign Assets Control of the Treasury Department, used Cuban stamps can be imported and sold without limitation, and unused stamps may be imported for personal use, but not resold.

Intl. Radio Service AP95

1962, Mar. 26 Wmk. 321

C231 AP95 8c multi 1.10 .25
C232 AP95 12c multi 2.25 .55
C233 AP95 30c multi 3.25 1.25
C234 AP95 1p multi 7.00 3.25
Nos. C231-C234 (4) 13.60 5.30

Bird Type of 1956

1962, July 20 Engr. Wmk. 321

C235 AP63 1p like #C144, royal blue 5.75 5.75
C236 AP62 2p like #C145, dark red 17.00 15.00
C237 AP63 5p like #C146, rose lake 37.50 32.50
Nos. C235-C237 (3) 60.25 53.25

PRAGA '62 — AP96

1962, Aug. 18 Litho.

C238 AP96 31c Czechoslovakia No. 1080 3.50 1.50

Souvenir Sheet

Imperf

C239 AP96 31c like No. C238 17.50 12.00

No. C239 contains one 60x35½mm stamp.

Achievements of the Revolution — AP97

1966, July 26 Wmk. 376 *Perf. 12½*

C240 AP97 1c Agrarian reform .20 .20
C241 AP97 2c Industrialization .20 .20
C242 AP97 3c Urban reform .50 .20
C243 AP97 7c Eradication of unemployment .50 .20
C244 AP97 9c Education .95 .20
C245 AP97 10c Public health 2.10 .20
C246 AP97 13c Excerpt from *La Historia Me Absolvera,* by Castro 2.75 .45
Nos. C240-C246 (7) 7.20 1.65

Camaguey-Seville Flight, 35th Anniv. — AP98

1971, Jan. 12 Unwmk.

C247 AP98 13c Aircraft 2.75 .20
C248 AP98 30c Map, Lieut. Menendez Palaez 3.25 .40

Havana-Santiago de Chile Direct Air Service, 1st Anniv. — AP99

1972, June 26 Wmk. 376

C249 AP99 25c multi 3.00 .75

6th Congress of Latin American and Caribbean Exporters of Sugar, Havana — AP100

Perf. 12½x12

1977, Feb. 28 Unwmk.

C250 AP100 13c multi .75 .20

Composer Type of 1977

1977, May 10 *Perf. 13*

C251 A571 13c Jorge Ankerman and score 1.00 .20

Flower Type of 1977

1977, May 31

C252 A572 13c *Caesalpinia pulcherrima* .85 .20
C253 A572 30c *Catharanthus roseus* 1.75 .50

Souvenir Sheet

Perf. 13½x13

C254 A572 50c Juan Tomas Roig 4.00 .90

No. C254 contains one 32x40mm stamp.

Natl. Decorations Type of 1977

1977, July 26 *Perf. 12x12½*

C255 A574 13c multi, diff. .80 .20
C256 A574 30c multi, diff. 1.50 .45

Art Type of 1977

Paintings by Jorge Arche: 13c, *My Wife and I*, vert. 30c, *Domino Players.* 50c, *Self-portrait*, vert.

1977, Aug. 25 *Perf. 13x12½*

Size: 26x38mm

C257 A575 13c multi .65 .20

Size: 40x29mm

Perf. 13

C258 A575 30c multi 1.60 .40

Souvenir Sheet

Perf. 13½x13

C259 A575 50c multi 4.00 4.00

No. C259 contains one 32x40mm stamp.

Spartakiad Type of 1977

1977, Sept. 10 *Perf. 13*

C260 A576 13c Grenade-throwing .60 .20
C261 A576 30c Rifle-shooting, horiz. 1.50 .40

10th Heroic Guerrilla's Day AP101

1977, Oct. 8 *Perf. 12½x13*

C262 AP101 13c Guerrilla fighters 1.00 .20

Airmail Service Type of 1977

1977, Oct. 27 *Perf. 12x12½*

C263 A577 13c Havana-Mexico cachet .85 .20
C264 A577 30c Havana-Prague cachet 1.75 .35

Souvenir Sheet

Adoration of the Magi, by Rubens — AP102

1977, Nov. 18 *Perf. 13*

C265 AP102 50c multi 4.00 4.00

Ruben's 400th birth anniv.

Havana Zoo Type of 1977

1977, Nov. 24

C266 A579 13c Tiger 1.00 .20
C267 A579 30c Lion 1.40 .50

Revolution Martyrs Type of 1977

1977, Dec. 2 *Perf. 12½x12*

C268 A580 13c *Corynthia* landing .75 .20

Pan American Health Organization (OPS), 75th Anniv. — AP103

1977, Dec. 2

C269 AP103 13c multi .75 .20

Havana University Type of 1978

1978, Jan. 5 *Perf. 13x12½*

C270 A582 13c Crossed sabres, university .75 .20
C271 A582 30c University, statue, crowd 1.10 .50

Portrait of Jose Marti (b. 1853), by A. Menocal AP104

1978, Jan. 28

C272 AP104 13c multi .80 .20

Art Type of 1978

Paintings in the Nat. Museum of Art: 13c, *El Guadalquivir,* by M. Barron. 30c, *Portrait of H.E. Ridley,* by J.J. Masqueries, vert.

1978, Feb. 20 *Perf. 12½x12, 13*

Sizes: 42x27mm, 29x40mm

C273 A583 13c multi 1.00 .20
C274 A583 30c multi 1.10 .35

Bird Type of 1975

1978, Mar. 10 *Perf. 12½x12, 13*

Size: 42x27mm, 27x42mm

C275 A524 13c *Torreornis inexpectata,* horiz. 1.50 .50
C276 A524 30c *Ara tricolor* 2.25 1.10

Baragua Protest, Cent. — AP105

1978, Mar. 15 *Perf. 13x13½*

C277 AP105 13c *Antonio Maceo,* by A. Melero .70 .20

Cosmonaut's Day Type of 1978

1978, Apr. 12 *Perf. 13*

C278 A585 13c *Venus 10* .70 .20

Size: 36x46mm

Perf. 12½x13

C279 A585 30c *Lunokhod 2,* vert. 1.25 .50

SOCFILEX '78, Budapest — AP106

1978, May 7 *Perf. 13x12½*

C280 AP106 30c Parliament, Hungary No. 217 1.75 .55

Cactus Type of 1978

1978, May 15 *Perf. 13*

C281 A587 13c *Rhodocactus cubensis* .90 .25
C282 A587 30c *Harrisia taetra* 1.75 .35

World Telecommunications Day — AP107

1978, May 17

C283 AP107 30c multi 1.25 .45

Organization of African Unity, 15th Anniv. — AP108

1978, May 25 *Perf. 13x12½*

C284 AP108 30c multi 1.00 .45

Souvenir Sheet

CAPEX '78, Toronto — AP109

1978, June 9 *Perf. 13x13½*

C285 AP109 50c *Niven, Wales,* by G.H. Russell 3.50 2.25

Aquarium Type of 1978

1978, June 15 *Perf. 13*

C286 A588 13c *Carassias auratus,* vert. 1.25 .25
C287 A588 30c *Symphysodon aequifasciata axelrodi* 2.50 .50

MEDELLIN Games Type of 1978

1978, July 1

C288 A589 13c Volleyball .60 .20
C289 A589 30c Running 1.25 .45

Attack on Moncada Type of 1978

1978, July 26

C290 A590 13c Soldiers bearing rifles .45 .20
C291 A590 30c Stylized dove, banners 1.10 .35

Youth Festival Type of 1978

Natl. flags and views of host cities.

1978, July 28

C292 A591 13c Moscow, 1957 .70 .20
C293 A591 13c Vienna, 1959 .70 .20
C294 A591 13c Helsinki, 1962 .70 .20
C295 A591 13c Sofia, 1968 .70 .20
C296 A591 13c Berlin, 1973 .70 .20
a. Strip of 5, Nos. C292-C296 3.75 1.75
Nos. C292-C296 (5) 3.50 1.00

Size: 46x36mm

Perf. 13x12½

C297 A591 30c Havana, 1978 1.50 .35

Tuna Industry Type of 1978

1978, Aug. 30 *Perf. 12½x12*

C298 A593 13c Stern trawler .80 .20
C299 A593 30c Refrigerator ship 1.50 .60

Souvenir Sheet

PRAGA '78 — AP110

1978, Sept. 8 *Perf. 13*

C300 AP110 50c *Marina,* by A. Brandeis 3.75 .90

Art Type of 1978

Paintings by Amelia Pelaez del Casal (1896-1968).

1978, Sept. 15 *Perf. 12x12½, 13*

C301 A594 13c *Yellow Flowers,* vert. .55 .20
C302 A594 30c *Still-life in Blue,* vert. 1.25 .45

Souvenir Sheet

Perf. 13½x13

C303 A594 50c *Portrait of Amelia,* by L. Romanach, vert. 4.00 .90

No. C303 contains one 32x40mm stamp.

Socialist Communication Organizations Congress (OSS), 20th Anniv. — AP111

1978, Sept. 25 *Perf. 13*

C304 AP111 30c multi 1.25 .25

Souvenir Sheet

EXFILNA '78, 6th Natl. Philatelic Exposition — AP112

1978, Oct. 10 *Imperf.*

C305 AP112 50c 1st Postal Card, issued in 1878 3.25 .90

No. C305 has simulated perfs.

Intl. Anti-Apartheid Year — AP113

1978, Oct. 16 *Perf. 12½*

C306 AP113 13c multi .60 .20

Zoo Type of 1978

1978, Oct. 20 *Perf. 13*

C307 A595 13c *Acinonyx jubatos* .95 .25
C308 A595 30c *Loxodonta africana,* vert. 2.25 .65

Natl. Ballet Type of 1978

1978, Oct. 28 *Perf. 12½x13*

C309 A596 13c *Giselle,* vert. .85 .20
C310 A596 30c *Genesis,* vert. 1.60 .25

Pacific Flora Type of 1978

1978, Nov. 30 *Perf. 13*

C311 A597 13c multi, diff. .80 .20
C312 A597 30c multi, diff. 1.60 .30

25th Death Anniv. of Julius and Ethel Rosenberg, American Communists Executed for Espionage — AP114

1978, Dec. 20
C313 AP114 13c multi .60 .20

Julio A. Mella (d. 1929) AP115

1979, Jan. 10
C314 AP115 13c multi .60 .20

Cosmonaut's Day Type of 1979
Souvenir Sheet

1979, Apr. 12 ***Perf. 13½x13***
C315 A603 50c Orbital complex 3.75 .90

No. C315 contains one 32x40mm stamp.

Intl. Year of the Child — AP116

1979, June 1 ***Perf. 13x12½***
C316 AP116 13c multi 1.00 .20

Art Type of 1979

1979, June 15 ***Perf. 13½x13***
C317 A600 50c *Portrait of Victor Emmanuel Garcia,* by J. Arche, vert. 3.50 1.75

No. C317 contains one 32x40mm stamp.

CARIFESTA '79, Festival of Caribbean Peoples, Havana AP117

1979, July 16 ***Perf. 12½x13***
C318 AP117 13c multi .75 .20

10th World Universiade Games, Mexico City — AP118

1979, Sept. 1 ***Perf. 13x12½***
C319 AP118 13c grn, pale grn & gold .75 .20

6th Conference of Nonaligned Countries — AP119

1979, Sept. 3
C320 AP119 50c Convention Palace 1.75 .90

Sir Rowland Hill (d. 1879), Originator of Penny Postage — AP120

1979, Sept. 4 ***Perf. 13½x13***
C321 AP120 30c Hill, casket 1.50 .25

SOCFILEX '79, Bucharest — AP121

Illustration reduced.

1979, Oct. 25 ***Perf. 12½***
C322 AP121 30c Romania No. 683, flags 1.40 .40

Intl. Radio Consultative Committee (CCIR), 50th Anniv. — AP122

1979, Nov. 30 ***Perf. 12½x12***
C323 AP122 30c Ground receiving station 1.40 .40

1st Soviet-Cuban Joint Space Flight — AP123

1980, Sept. 23 ***Perf. 12½***
C324 AP123 13c multi .50 .20
C325 AP123 30c multi 1.50 .35

Capt. Mariano Barberan, Lt. Joaquin Collar, and Their Airplane Cuatro Vientos. — AP124

1993, June 11 **Litho.** ***Perf. 13***
C326 AP124 30c multicolored 1.00 .45

1st Flight Seville-Camaguey, 60th anniv.

AIR POST SEMI-POSTAL STAMP

Catalogue values for unused stamps in this section are for Never Hinged items.

Farm Couple and Factory SPAP1

Engr. & Typo.

1959, May 7 **Wmk. 321** ***Perf. 12½***
CB1 SPAP1 12c + 3c car & grn 2.00 .50

Agricultural reforms. See No. C199.

AIR POST SPECIAL DELIVERY STAMP

Matanzas Issue

Matanzas Harbor APSD1

Wmk. 229

1936, May 5 **Photo.** ***Perf. 12½***
CE1 ASPD1 15c light blue 4.50 3.50
Never hinged 7.00

Exists imperf. Value $6 unused, $4.50 used.

SPECIAL DELIVERY STAMPS

Issued under US Administration

US No. E5 Surcharged in Red

1899 **Wmk. 191** ***Perf. 12***
E1 SD3 10c on 10c blue 160.00 100.00
a. No period after "CUBA" 575.00 400.00

Issues of the Republic under US Military Rule

Special Delivery Messenger SD2

Inscribed: "Immediata"

1899 **Wmk. U S-C (191C)** **Engr.**
E2 SD2 10c orange 55.00 15.00

Issues of the Republic

Inscribed: "Inmediata"

1902 ***Perf. 12***
E3 SD2 10c orange 3.00 1.00

J. B. Zayas SD3

1910 **Unwmk.**
E4 SD3 10c orange & blue 20.00 3.25
Never hinged 30.00
a. Center inverted 1,250.

Airplane and Morro Castle SD4

1914, Feb. 24 ***Perf. 12***
E5 SD4 10c dark blue 15.00 1.25

Exists imperf. Value, pair $500.

1927 **Wmk. Star (106)**
E6 SD4 10c deep blue 12.00 .50
Never hinged 18.00

1935 ***Perf. 10***
E7 SD4 10c blue 12.00 .40
Never hinged 15.00

Matanzas Issue

Mercury SD5

Wmk. Wavy Lines (229)

1936, May 5 **Photo.** ***Perf. 12½***
E8 SD5 10c deep claret 4.50 3.50
Never hinged 7.00

Exists imperf. Value $7 unused, $5 used.

"Triumph of the Revolution" — SD6

1936, Nov. 18
E9 SD6 10c red orange 6.00 2.00
Never hinged 8.00

Maj. Gen. Máximo Gómez (1836-1905).

Temple of Quetzalcoatl (Mexico) SD7

Ruben Dario (Nicaragua) SD8

Wmk. 106

1937, Oct. 13 **Engr.** ***Perf. 10***
E10 SD7 10c deep orange 6.25 6.25
E11 SD8 10c deep orange 6.25 6.25
Set, never hinged 15.00

See note after No. 354.

Letter and Symbols of Transportation — SD9

1945, Oct. 30

E12 SD9 10c olive brown 1.40 .25
Never hinged 3.00

> **Catalogue values for unused stamps in this section, from this point to the end of the section, are for Never Hinged items.**

Governor's Building, Cárdenas SD10

Engraved and Lithographed

1951, July 3 Wmk. 229 *Perf. 13*

E13 SD10 10c henna brn, ultra & red 7.00 1.25

Cent. of the adoption of Cuba's flag.

Chess Type of Regular Issue, 1951

1951, Nov. 1 Photo.

E14 A166 10c dk grn & rose brn 21.00 4.50

Type of Regular Issue of 1951 Surcharged in Red Violet

Wmk. 106

1952, Mar. 18 Engr. *Perf. 10*

E15 A159 10c on 2c yel brn 6.00 1.00

Arms and Bars from National Hymn — SD12

Roseate Tern — SD13

1952, May 27 *Perf. 12½*

E16 SD12 10c dp org & bl 3.00 .75

Republic of Cuba founding, 50th anniv.

Type of Air Post Stamps of 1952 Inscribed: "Entrega Especial"

1952, Oct. 7 *Perf. 10*

E17 AP36 10c pale olive grn 4.50 2.00

Three-fourths of the proceeds from the sale of No. E17 were used for the Communications Ministry Employees' Retirement Fund.

1953, July 28

E18 SD13 10c blue 5.75 1.50

Gregorio Hernandez Saez SD14

Felix Varela SD15

1954, Feb. 23

E19 SD14 10c olive green 5.25 .90

1955, June 22 *Perf. 12½*

E20 SD15 10c brown car 3.00 .95

See note after No. E17.

Portrait Type of Regular Issue, 1956 Inscribed: "Entrega Especial"

Portrait: 10c, Jose Jacinto Milanes.

1956, May 2 Wmk. 106

E21 A198 10c dk car rose & blk 3.75 .75

See note after No. E17.

Painting Type of Regular Issue, 1957, Inscribed: "Entrega Especial"

10c, "Yesterday" by E. Garcia Cabrera.

1957, Mar. 15 Engr. *Perf. 12½*

E22 A207 10c dk brn & turq bl 3.50 1.10

See note after No. E17.

View Type of Regular Issue, 1957, Inscribed: "Entrega Especial."

10c, Independence square, Pino del Rio.

1957, Dec. 17

E23 A218 10c dk pur & brn 3.00 1.00

See note after No. E17.

View in Havana and Messenger SD16

1958, Jan. 10 Engr.

E24 SD16 10c blue 2.00 .75
E25 SD16 20c green 2.50 .75

See Nos. E28, E31.

Fish Type of Air Post Issue, 1958, Inscribed "Entrega Especial."

Fish: 10c, Blackfish snapper. 20c, Mosquitofish.

1958, Sept. 26 Wmk. 106 *Perf. 12½*

E26 AP86 10c blk, bl, pink & yel 6.00 2.50
E27 AP86 20c blk, ultra & pink 19.00 10.00

See note after No. C191.

Messenger Type of 1958

1960 Wmk. 321 *Perf. 12½*

E28 SD16 10c brt vio 3.50 .50

Plane Type of Air Post Issue, of 1931-46, Surcharged in Black or Red: "HABILITADO ENTREGA ESPECIAL 10¢"

1960 Wmk. 106 *Perf. 10*

E29 AP4 10c on 20c car rose 3.00 .50
E30 AP4 10c on 50c grnsh bl (R) 3.00 .50

Messenger Type of 1958

1961, June 28 Wmk. 321 *Perf. 12½*

E31 SD16 10c orange 3.50 .75

West Indies Packet Type of 1962

Perf. 12½

1962, Apr. 24 Litho. Unwmk.

E32 A253 10c buff, dull ultra & brn 5.00 1.75

POSTAGE DUE STAMPS

Issued under Administration of the United States

Postage Due Stamps of the US Nos. J38, J39, J41 and J42 Surcharged in Black like Nos. 221-226A

1899 Wmk. 191 *Perf. 12*

J1 D2 1c on 1c dp claret 45.00 5.25
J2 D2 2c on 2c dp claret 45.00 5.25
a. Inverted surcharge *4,000.*
J3 D2 5c on 5c dp claret 45.00 5.25
J4 D2 10c on 10c dp claret 27.50 2.50
Nos. J1-J4 (4) 162.50 18.25

Issues of the Republic

D1

1914 Unwmk. Engr. *Perf. 12*

J5 D1 1c carmine rose 7.50 1.50
J6 D1 2c carmine rose 9.75 1.10
J7 D1 5c carmine rose 14.00 2.25
Nos. J5-J7 (3) 31.25 4.85

1927-28

J8 D1 1c rose red 4.00 .75
J9 D1 2c rose red 6.25 .75
J10 D1 5c rose red 7.50 1.10
Nos. J8-J10 (3) 17.75 2.60

NEWSPAPER STAMPS

Issued under Spanish Dominion

N1

N2

1888 Unwmk. Typo. *Perf. 14*

P1 N1 ½m black .20 *.25*
P2 N1 1m black .20 *.30*
P3 N1 2m black .20 *.30*
P4 N1 3m black 1.50 1.00
P5 N1 4m black 1.90 *2.00*
P6 N1 8m black 7.25 *8.50*
Nos. P1-P6 (6) 11.25 12.35

1890

P7 N2 ½m red brown .50 *.65*
P8 N2 1m red brown .50 *.65*
P9 N2 2m red brown .80 *.95*
P10 N2 3m red brown 1.00 *1.10*
P11 N2 4m red brown 7.50 5.50
P12 N2 8m red brown 7.50 5.50
Nos. P7-P12 (6) 17.80 14.35

1892

P13 N2 ½m violet .20 *.30*
P14 N2 1m violet .20 *.30*
P15 N2 2m violet .20 *.30*
P16 N2 3m violet 1.00 .35
P17 N2 4m violet 3.75 1.90
P18 N2 8m violet 8.00 3.00
Nos. P13-P18 (6) 13.35 6.15

1894

P19 N2 ½m rose .20 *.30*
a. Imperf. pair 35.00 35.00
P20 N2 1m rose .45 .35
P21 N2 2m rose .50 .35
P22 N2 3m rose 1.90 1.40
P23 N2 4m rose 3.25 1.60
P24 N2 8m rose 5.50 4.00
Nos. P19-P24 (6) 11.80 8.00

1896

P25 N2 ½m blue green .20 *.30*
P26 N2 1m blue green .20 *.30*
P27 N2 2m blue green .20 *.30*
P28 N2 3m blue green 2.50 1.50
P29 N2 4m blue green 5.25 *7.00*
P30 N2 8m blue green 9.50 10.00
Nos. P25-P30 (6) 17.85 19.40

For surcharges see Nos. 190-193, 201-220.

POSTAL TAX STAMPS

> **Catalogue values for unused stamps in this section are for Never Hinged items.**

Mother and Child — PT1

Nurse with Child — PT2

Wmk. Star. (106)

1938, Dec. 1 Engr. *Perf. 10*

RA1 PT1 1c bright green 1.50 .20

The tax benefited the National Council of Tuberculosis fund for children's hospitals. Obligatory on all mail during December and January. This note applies also to Nos. RA2-RA4, RA7-RA10, RA12-RA15, RA17-RA21.

1939, Dec. 1

RA2 PT2 1c orange vermilion .90 .20

"Health" Protecting Children — PT3

1940, Dec. 1

RA3 PT3 1c deep blue .90 .20

Mother and Child — PT4

Victory — PT5

1941, Dec. 1

RA4 PT4 1c olive bister .90 .20

1942-44

RA5 PT5 ½c orange .35 .20
RA6 PT5 ½c gray ('44) .50 .20

Issued: No. RA5, 7/1/42; No. RA6, 10/3/44.

Type of 1941 Overprinted "1942" in Black

1942, Dec. 1

RA7 PT4 1c salmon 1.10 .25
a. Inverted overprint 70.00 55.00

As PT3 — PT6

As PT4 — PT7

1943, Dec. 1

RA8 PT6 1c brown .90 .20

1949, Dec. 9

RA9 PT7 1c blue .60 .20

Type of 1949 Inscribed: "1950"

1950, Dec. 1 Engr.

RA10 PT7 1c rose red .60 .20

Proposed Communications Building

PT8 PT10

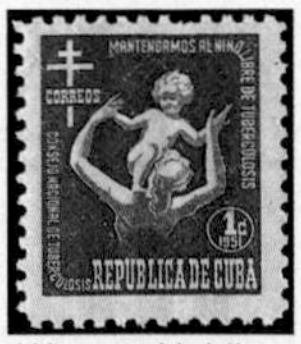
Woman Holding Child Aloft — PT9

Child — PT11

1951, June 5 Wmk. 106 *Perf. 10*

RA11	PT8	1c violet	.90	.20

The tax was to help build a new Communications Building. This note applies also to Nos. RA16, RA34, RA43.

1951, Dec. 1

RA12	PT9	1c violet blue	.50	.20
RA13	PT9	1c brown carmine	.50	.20
RA14	PT9	1c olive bister	.50	.20
RA15	PT9	1c deep green	.50	.20
		Nos. RA12-RA15 (4)	2.00	.80

1952, Feb. 8

RA16	PT10	1c slate blue	.35	.20

See Nos. RA34, RA43.

1952, Dec. 1

RA17	PT11	1c rose carmine	.90	.20
RA18	PT11	1c yellow green	.90	.20
RA19	PT11	1c blue	.90	.20
RA20	PT11	1c orange	.90	.20
		Nos. RA17-RA20 (4)	3.60	.80

Hands Reaching for Lorraine Cross PT12

Child's Head, Lorraine Cross PT13

1953, Dec. 1 *Perf. 9½*

RA21	PT12	1c rose carmine	.60	.20

1954, Nov. 1 *Perf. 9½x10*

RA22	PT13	1c rose red	.90	.20
RA23	PT13	1c violet	.90	.20
RA24	PT13	1c bright blue	.90	.20
RA25	PT13	1c emerald	.90	.20
		Nos. RA22-RA25 (4)	3.60	.80

The tax benefited the Natl. Council of Tuberculosis fund for children's hospitals. Obligatory on all mail during Nov., Dec., Jan. & Feb. This note also applies to Nos. RA26-RA33, RA35-RA42.

Rose and Watering Can PT14

Child and Protective Hands PT15

1955, Nov. 1

RA26	PT14	1c red orange	.90	.20
RA27	PT14	1c red lilac	.90	.20
RA28	PT14	1c bright blue	.90	.20
RA29	PT14	1c orange yellow	.90	.20
		Nos. RA26-RA29 (4)	3.60	.80

1956, Nov. 1

RA30	PT15	1c rose red	.90	.20
RA31	PT15	1c yellow brown	.90	.20
RA32	PT15	1c bright blue	.90	.20
RA33	PT15	1c emerald	.90	.20
		Nos. RA30-RA33 (4)	3.60	.80

Building Type of 1952

1957, Jan. 18 *Perf. 10*

RA34	PT10	1c rose red	.90	.20

Mother and Child by Silvia Arrojo Fernandez PT16

National Council of Tuberculosis PT17

Wmk. 321

1957, Nov. 1 Engr. *Perf. 10*

RA35	PT16	1c dull rose	.80	.20
RA36	PT16	1c bright blue	.80	.20
RA37	PT16	1c gray	.80	.20
RA38	PT16	1c emerald	.80	.20
		Nos. RA35-RA38 (4)	3.20	.80

1958

RA39	PT17	1c rose red	.45	.20
RA40	PT17	1c red brown	.45	.20
RA41	PT17	1c gray	.45	.20
RA42	PT17	1c emerald	.45	.20
		Nos. RA39-RA42 (4)	1.80	.80

Building Type of 1952

1958 Wmk. 321

RA43	PT10	1c rose red	.90	.20

CYPRUS

ˈsī-prəs

LOCATION — An island in the Mediterranean Sea off the coast of Turkey
GOVT. — Republic
AREA — 3,572 sq. mi.
POP. — 754,064 (1999 est.)
CAPITAL — Nicosia

The British Crown Colony of Cyprus became a republic in 1960.

Turkey invaded Cyprus in 1974 resulting in the the northern 40% of the island becoming the Turkish Republic of Northern Cyprus. No other country recognizes this division of the island.

See Turkey in Volume 6.

12 Pence = 1 Shilling
40 Paras = 1 Piaster
9 Piasters = 1 Shilling
20 Shillings = 1 Pound
1000 Milliemes = 1 Pound (1955)
100 Cents = 1 Cyprus Pound (1983)
100 Cents = 1 Euro (2008)

Catalogue values for unused stamps in this country are for Never Hinged items, beginning with Scott 156 in the regular postage section and Scott RA1 in the postal tax section.

Values for unused stamps are for examples with original gum as defined in the catalogue introduction. Very fine examples of Nos. 1, 2 and 7-10 will have perforations touching the design on at least one or more sides due to the narrow spacing of the stamps on the plates and to imperfect perforation methods. Stamps with perfs clear on all four sides are scarce and will command higher prices.

Watermark

Wmk. 344 — Map of Cyprus and KC/K Delta

Queen Victoria — A1

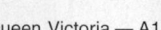

A2

A3

A4

A5

A6

A7

Various Watermarks as in Great Britain (#20, 23, 25, 27 & 29)

1880 Typo. *Perf. 14*

1	A1	½p rose (P 15)	125.00	115.00
		Plate 12	210.00	*300.00*
		Plate 19	5,750.	950.00
b.		Double overprint (P 15)		*20,000.*
2	A2	1p red (P 216)	19.00	*45.00*
		Plate 217	14.00	*57.50*
		Plate 174	1,400.	1,400.
		Plate 181	425.00	200.00
		Plate 184	14,500.	2,750.
		Plate 193	800.00	
		Plate 196	700.00	
		Plate 201	15.00	*57.50*
		Plate 205	65.00	57.50
		Plate 208	110.00	65.00
		Plate 215	13.00	*57.50*
		Plate 218	21.00	*65.00*
		Plate 220	550.00	475.00
b.		Double overprint (P 218)	5,400.	
		Double overprint (P 208)	*17,500.*	
c.		Pair, one without ovpt. (P 208)	*22,000.*	
3	A3	2½p claret (P 14)	2.75	*9.25*
		Plate 15	4.00	*27.50*
4	A4	4p lt ol grn (P 16)	140.00	*240.00*
5	A5	6p ol gray (P 16)	575.00	*750.00*
6	A6	1sh green (P 13)	750.00	525.00

Black Surcharge

7	A7	30 paras on 1p red (P 216)	115.00	*95.00*
		Plate 201	140.00	105.00
		Plate 217	200.00	200.00
		Plate 220	175.00	*190.00*
b.		Dbl. surch., one invtd. (P 220)	1,600.	*1,350.*
		Dbl. surch., one invtd. (P 216)	5,000.	

No. 2 Surcharged

18mm Long

1881

8	A2	½p on 1p (205, 216)	80.00	*100.00*
		Plate 174	175.00	*350.00*
		Plate 181	175.00	*200.00*
		Plate 201	110.00	*140.00*
		Plate 205	80.00	*100.00*
		Plate 208	190.00	*325.00*
		Plate 215	750.00	*800.00*
		Plate 217	925.00	825.00
		Plate 218	525.00	*640.00*
		Plate 220	300.00	*375.00*

16mm Long

9	A2	½p on 1p (P 201)	140.00	*190.00*
		Plate 216	400.00	*450.00*
		Plate 218		*11,500.*
a.		Double surcharge (P 201, 216)	3,200.	2,900.

13mm Long

10	A2	½p on 1p red (P 215)	52.50	*75.00*
		Plate 205	325.00	
		Plate 217	150.00	92.50
		Plate 218	80.00	*110.00*
c.		Double surcharge (P 215)	550.00	700.00
		Double surcharge (P 205)	800.00	
e.		Triple surcharge (P 215)	800.00	
		Triple surcharge (P 205)	*4,000.*	
		Triple surcharge (P 217)	—	
		Triple surcharge (P 218)	*4,000.*	
h.		Quadruple surch. (P 205, 215)	*5,500.*	
j.		"CYPRUS" double (P 218)	*5,500.*	

A8

1881, July Typo. Wmk. 1

11	A8	½pi emerald green	210.00	52.50
12	A8	1pi rose	425.00	37.50
13	A8	2pi ultramarine	525.00	37.50
14	A8	4pi olive green	1,050.	325.00
15	A8	6pi olive gray	1,750.	500.00

Postage and revenue stamps of Cyprus with "J.A.B." (the initials of Postmaster J.A. Bulmer) in manuscript, or with "POSTAL SURCHARGE" (with or without "J. A. B."), were not Postage Due stamps but were employed for accounting purposes between the chief PO at Larnaca and the sub-offices.

See Nos. 19-25, 28-37. For surcharges see Nos. 16-18, 26-27.

A9

A10

Black Surcharge

1882 Wmk. 1

16	A9	½pi on ½pi grn	750.00	92.50
17	A10	30pa on 1pi rose	1,900.	140.00

1884 Wmk. 2

18	A9	½pi on ½pi green	190.00	10.00
a.		Double surcharge		3,200.

See Nos. 26, 27.

1882-94 Die B

For description of Dies A and B see "Dies of British Colonial Stamps" in Table of Contents.

19	A8	½pi green	6.50	1.25
20	A8	30pa violet	6.50	8.50
21	A8	1pi rose	14.50	3.75
22	A8	2pi blue	17.50	2.10
23	A8	4pi pale ol grn	27.50	*29.00*
24a	A8	6pi	210.00	*675.00*
25a	A8	12pi	160.00	*400.00*
		Nos. 19-25a (7)	442.50	*1,119.*

Die A

19a	A8	½pi	20.00	2.00
b.		½pi emerald	*6,400.*	475.00
20a	A8	30pa lilac	77.50	25.00
21a	A8	1pi	110.00	2.50
22a	A8	2pi	150.00	2.50
23a	A8	4pi	450.00	30.00
24	A8	6pi olive gray	60.00	21.00
25	A8	12pi brown org	225.00	45.00
		Nos. 19a-25 (7)	1,092.	128.00

A11

Type I — Figures "½" 8mm apart.
Type II — Figures "½" 6mm apart.
The space between the fraction bars varies from 5½ to 8½mm but is usually 6 or 8mm.

Black Surcharge Type I

1886 Wmk. 2

26	A11	½pi on ½pi grn	400.00	15.00
a.		Type II	300.00	100.00

b. Double surcharge, type II

Wmk. 1

27	A11	½pi on ½pi grn		*8,750.*	500.00
a.		Type II		*19,500.*	

No. 27a probably is a proof.

1894-96 **Wmk. 2**

28	A8	½pi	grn & car rose	5.25	1.75
29	A8	30pa	violet & green	3.00	2.00
30	A8	1pi	rose & ultra	8.00	1.75
31	A8	2pi	ultra & mar	8.25	1.75
32	A8	4pi	ol green & vio	21.00	6.00
33	A8	6pi	ol gray & grn	16.00	*18.00*
34	A8	9pi	brown & rose	20.00	22.50
35	A8	12pi	brn org & blk	22.50	*70.00*
36	A8	18pi	slate & brown	60.00	60.00
37	A8	45pi	dk vio & ultra	125.00	*175.00*
			Nos. 28-37 (10)	289.00	*358.75*

King Edward VII A12

King George V A13

1903 **Typo.**

38	A12	½pi	grn & car rose	5.00	1.40
39	A12	30pa	violet & green	12.50	3.75
40	A12	1pi	carmine rose & ultra	24.00	4.25
41	A12	2pi	ultra & mar	70.00	12.50
42	A12	4pi	ol green & vio	37.50	22.50
43	A12	6pi	ol brown & grn	50.00	*140.00*
44	A12	9pi	brn & car rose	125.00	*225.00*
45	A12	12pi	org brn & blk	17.00	*62.50*
46	A12	18pi	black & brown	100.00	*175.00*
47	A12	45pi	dk vio & ultra	250.00	*600.00*
			Nos. 38-47 (10)	691.00	*1,246.*

1904-07 **Wmk. 3**

48	A12	5pa	bis & blk ('07)	1.25	.80
49	A12	10pa	org & grn ('07)	4.00	.55
50	A12	½pi	grn & car rose	5.75	.20
51	A12	30pa	violet & green	18.00	1.75
52	A12	1pi	car rose & ultra	7.25	1.10
53	A12	2pi	ultra & maroon	9.00	2.00
54	A12	4pi	ol grn & red vio	14.50	9.25
55	A12	6pi	ol brn & green	20.00	*17.00*
56	A12	9pi	brn & car rose	40.00	9.75
57	A12	12pi	org brn & blk	32.50	*45.00*
58	A12	18pi	black & brown	40.00	12.50
59	A12	45pi	dk vio & ultra	95.00	*175.00*
			Nos. 48-59 (12)	287.25	*274.90*

1912

61a	A13	10pa	org yellow & green	2.75	1.60
62	A13	½pi	grn & car rose	2.25	.25
63	A13	30pa	violet & green	3.25	.80
64	A13	1pi	car & ultra	5.00	2.25
65	A13	2pi	ultra & maroon	8.50	2.50
66	A13	4pi	ol grn & red vio	5.50	*6.25*
67	A13	6pi	ol brn & green	4.50	*11.00*
68	A13	9pi	brn & car rose	32.50	*35.00*
69	A13	12pi	org brn & blk	20.00	*47.50*
70	A13	18pi	black & brown	35.00	*40.00*
71	A13	45pi	dl vio & ultra	100.00	*160.00*
			Nos. 61a-71 (11)	219.25	*307.15*

1921-23 **Wmk. 4**

72	A13	10pa	orange & grn	9.00	*10.50*
73	A13	10pa	gray & yellow	16.00	9.50
74	A13	30pa	violet & grn	3.25	.50
75	A13	30pa	green	9.00	.50
76	A13	1pi	rose & ultra	22.50	*32.50*
77	A13	1pi	violet & car	4.00	*5.00*
78	A13	1½pi	orange & blk	7.00	*6.00*
79	A13	2pi	ultra & red vio	25.00	17.00
80	A13	2pi	rose & ultra	12.50	*27.50*
81	A13	2¾pi	ultra & red vio	9.00	*12.00*
82	A13	4pi	ol grn & red vio	16.00	*22.50*
83	A13	6pi	ol brn & green	21.00	*85.00*
84	A13	9pi	brn & carmine	32.50	*90.00*
85	A13	18pi	black & brn	77.50	*175.00*
86	A13	45pi	dl vio & ultra	225.00	*325.00*
			Nos. 72-86 (15)	489.25	*818.50*

Wmk. 3

87	A13	10sh	grn & red, *yel*	425.00	*875.00*
88	A13	£1	vio & black, *red*	1,150.	*2,200.*

Years of issue: Nos. 73, 75, 77-78, 80-81, 87-88, 1923; others, 1921.

A14

1924-28 **Chalky Paper** **Wmk. 4**

89	A14	¼pi	gray & brn org	1.10	.20
90	A14	½pi	gray blk & blk	3.00	*10.00*
91	A14	½pi	grn & dp grn ('25)	2.50	1.10
92	A14	¾pi	grn & dp grn	2.50	1.10
93	A14	¾pi	gray blk & blk ('25)	2.25	.20
94	A14	1pi	brn vio & org brown	2.25	.80
95	A14	1½pi	org & black	2.25	*8.50*
96	A14	1½pi	carmine ('25)	2.90	.35
97	A14	2pi	car & green	2.50	*15.00*
98	A14	2pi	org & black ('25)	8.00	4.25
99	A14	2½pi	ultra ('25)	3.50	.35
100	A14	2¾pi	ultra & dull vio	3.75	3.50
101	A14	4pi	ap grn & vio	3.75	3.75
102	A14	4½pi	black & yel, *emer*	4.00	4.00
103	A14	6pi	grn ol & grn	4.25	*6.25*
104	A14	9pi	brn & dk vio	7.00	5.00
105	A14	12pi	org brn & blk	10.50	*62.50*
106	A14	18pi	blk & org	22.50	5.75
			Revenue cancel		1.00
107	A14	45pi	gray vio & ultra	42.50	*42.50*
			Revenue cancel		1.50
108	A14	90pi	grn & red, *yel*	100.00	*200.00*
			Revenue cancel		3.00
109	A14	£5	blk, *yel* ('28)	3,200.	*7,000.*
			Revenue cancel		175.00

Wmk. 3

110	A14	£1	vio & black, *red*	350.00	*800.00*
			Revenue cancel		10.00
			Nos. 89-108 (20)	231.00	*375.10*

Nos. 96 and 99 are on ordinary paper.

Silver Coin of Amathus — A15

Philosopher Zeno — A16

Map of Cyprus — A17

Discovery of Body of St. Barnabas — A18

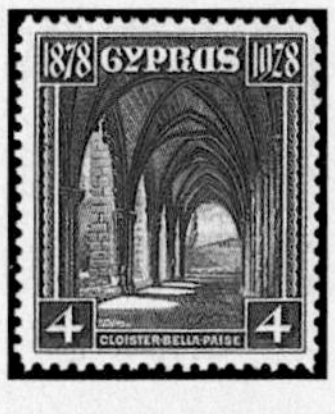

Cloisters of Bella Paise Monastery — A19

Badge of the Colony — A20

Hospice of Umm Haram at Larnaca — A21

Statue of Richard Coeur de Lion, London — A22

St. Nicholas Cathedral, Famagusta — A23

King George V — A24

Perf. 12

1928, Feb. 1 **Engr.** **Wmk. 4**

114	A15	¾pi	dark violet	3.50	1.25
115	A16	1pi	Prus bl & blk	4.00	2.00
116	A17	1½pi	red	6.00	2.50
117	A18	2½pi	ultramarine	4.75	*2.75*
118	A19	4pi	dp red brown	7.50	*8.00*
119	A20	6pi	dark blue	10.00	*27.50*
120	A21	9pi	violet brown	10.00	*14.00*
121	A22	18pi	dk brn & blk	25.00	*25.00*
122	A23	45pi	dp blue & vio	52.50	*62.50*
123	A24	£1	ol brn & deep blue	275.00	*400.00*
			Nos. 114-123 (10)	398.25	*545.50*

50th year of Cyprus as a British colony.

Ruins of Vouni Palace — A25

Columns at Salamis — A26

Peristerona Church — A27

Soli Theater — A28

Kyrenia Castle and Harbor — A29

Kolossi Castle — A30

St. Sophia Cathedral — A31

Bairakdar Mosque — A32

Queen's Window, St. Hilarion Castle — A33

Buyuk Khan, Nicosia — A34

Forest Scene — A35

1934, Dec. 1 **Engr.** ***Perf. 12½***

125	A25	¼pi	yel brn & ultra	1.25	.65
			Never hinged	1.75	
a.			Vert. pair, imperf. between	*37,500.*	*22,500.*
126	A26	½pi	green	1.90	1.25
			Never hinged	2.00	
a.			Vert. pair, imperf. between	*17,500.*	*17,500.*
127	A27	¾pi	violet & blk	2.25	.25
			Never hinged	3.25	
a.			Vert. pair, imperf. between	*40,000.*	
128	A28	1pi	brown & blk	1.60	1.10
			Never hinged	2.75	
a.			Vert. pair, imperf. between	*20,000.*	*20,000.*
b.			Horiz. pair, imperf. btwn.	*17,500.*	
129	A29	1½pi	rose red	3.25	.70
			Never hinged	4.75	
130	A30	2½pi	dark ultra	3.25	2.40
			Never hinged	5.00	
131	A31	4½pi	dk car & blk	4.00	*5.00*
			Never hinged	11.00	
132	A32	6pi	blue & black	11.50	*16.00*
			Never hinged	24.00	
133	A33	9pi	dl vio & blk brown	10.50	*6.50*
			Never hinged	21.00	
134	A34	18pi	ol grn & black	52.50	37.50
			Never hinged	110.00	
135	A35	45pi	blk & emer	87.50	*67.50*
			Never hinged	175.00	
			Nos. 125-135 (11)	179.50	*138.85*

Common Design Types pictured following the introduction.

Silver Jubilee Issue

Common Design Type

1935, May 6 ***Perf. 11x12***

136	CD301	¾pi	gray blk & ultra	2.25	.50
137	CD301	1½pi	car & dk bl	5.25	3.50

138 CD301 2½pi ultra & brn 4.75 *2.00*
139 CD301 9pi brn vio & ind 19.00 *21.00*
Nos. 136-139 (4) 31.25 *27.00*
Set, never hinged 50.00

Coronation Issue
Common Design Type

1937, May 12 ***Perf. 11x11½***

140 CD302 ¾pi dark gray .35 .20
141 CD302 1½pi dark carmine .60 *.85*
142 CD302 2½pi deep ultra 1.25 *1.40*
Nos. 140-142 (3) 2.20 2.45
Set, never hinged 4.75

Ruins of Vouni Palace — A36

Columns at Salamis — A37

Peristerona Church — A38

Soli Theater — A39

Kyrenia Castle and Harbor — A40

Kolossi Castle — A41

Map of Cyprus — A42

Bairakdar Mosque — A43

Citadel, Famagusta — A44

Buyuk Khan — A45

Forest Scene A46

King George VI A47

1938-44 **Wmk. 4** ***Perf. 12½***

143 A36 ¼pi yel brn & ultra .20 .20
144 A37 ½pi green .40 .20
145 A38 ¾pi violet & blk 9.00 .65
146 A39 1pi orange .50 .20
a. Perf. 13½x12½ ('44) 375.00 30.00
Never hinged 525.00
147 A40 1½pi rose car 3.25 1.90
147A A40 1½pi lt vio ('43) .35 .35
147B A38 2pi carmine & blk ('42) .45 .20
c. Perf. 12½x13½ ('44) 2.00 *7.50*
Never hinged 2.50
148 A41 2½pi ultramarine 13.00 4.25
148A A41 3pi dp ultra ('42) 1.00 .20
149 A42 4½pi gray .45 .20
150 A43 6pi blue & black .80 *1.25*
151 A44 9pi dk vio & blk 1.25 .20
152 A45 18pi ol grn & blk 2.50 1.10
153 A46 45pi blk & emer 11.50 3.25
154 A47 90pi blk & brt vio 21.00 6.50
155 A47 £1 ind & dl red 45.00 30.00
Nos. 143-155 (16) 110.65 50.65
Set, never hinged 290.00

See Nos. 164-166.

Catalogue values for unused stamps in this section, from this point to the end of the section, are for Never Hinged items.

Peace Issue
Common Design Type

1946, Oct. 21 **Engr.** ***Perf. 13½x14***

156 CD303 1½pi purple .20 .20
157 CD303 3pi deep blue .20 .20

Silver Wedding Issue
Common Design Types

1948, Dec. 20 **Photo.** ***Perf. 14x14½***

158 CD304 1½pi purple .70 .20

Engr.; Name Typo.
Perf. 11½x11

159 CD305 £1 dark blue 55.00 *70.00*

UPU Issue
Common Design Types
Perf. 13½, 11x11½

1949, Oct. 10 **Engr.** **Wmk. 4**

160 CD306 1½pi violet .45 *.75*
161 CD307 2pi deep carmine 1.75 1.75
162 CD308 3pi indigo .80 *1.10*
163 CD309 9pi rose violet 2.00 2.00
Nos. 160-163 (4) 5.00 5.60

Types of 1938-43

1951, July 2 **Engr.** ***Perf. 12½***

164 A37 ½pi purple 3.00 .20
165 A40 1½pi deep green 4.00 .65
166 A41 4pi deep ultra 4.25 .30
Nos. 164-166 (3) 11.25 1.15

Coronation Issue
Common Design Type

1953, June 2 ***Perf. 13½x13***

167 CD312 1½pi brt grn & black 1.40 .40

Carobs A48

Copper Pyrites Mine A49

St. Hilarion Castle A50

Queen Elizabeth II and Cyprian Coin Devices — A51

Designs: 3m, Grapes. 5m, Oranges. 15m, Troodos forest. 20m, Aphrodite beach. 25m, Coin of Paphos. 30m, Kyrenia. 35m, Harvest in Mesaoria. 40m, Famagusta harbor. 100m, Hala Sultan Tekke. 250m, Kanakaria church. £1, Queen Elizabeth II and devices of Byzantium, Lusignan, Ottoman Empire and Venice.

Perf. 11½

1955, Aug. 1 **Engr.** **Wmk. 4**

168 A48 2m chocolate .20 .50
169 A48 3m violet blue .20 .20
170 A48 5m orange 1.00 .20
171 A49 10m gray grn & chocolate 1.25 .20
172 A49 15m indigo & olive 3.00 .50
173 A49 20m ultra & brown 1.00 .25
174 A49 25m aquamarine 2.50 .70
175 A49 30m carmine & blk 2.00 .20
176 A49 35m aqua & orange .75 .50
177 A49 40m choc & dk grn 1.00 .75

Perf. 13½

178 A50 50m red brn & aqua 1.10 .25
179 A50 100m bl green & mag 12.50 .60
180 A50 250m vio brn & dk blue gray 10.50 7.50

Perf. 11x11½

181 A51 500m lilac rose & grnsh gray 27.50 10.00
182 A51 £1 grnsh gray & brn red 24.00 *35.00*
Revenue cancel 1.00
Nos. 168-182 (15) 88.50 57.35

Republic

Nos. 168-182 Overprinted in Dark Blue

1960, Aug. 16 **Ovpt. 10x6½mm**

183 A48 2m chocolate .20 .20
184 A48 3m violet blue .20 .20
185 A48 5m orange .20 .20

Overprint 12½x11mm

186 A49 10m gray grn & choc .25 .20
187 A49 15m indigo & ol .45 .20
188 A49 20m ultra & brn .50 .20
a. Double overprint *8,500.*
189 A49 25m aquamarine .60 .35
190 A49 30m car & black .75 .30
a. Double overprint *13,500.*
191 A49 35m aqua & org 1.00 .45
192 A49 40m choc & dk grn 1.10 .65

2-line overprint 2½mm apart

193 A50 50m red brown & aqua 1.25 .75
194 A50 100m bl grn & mag 3.00 2.00
195 A50 250m vio brn & dk blue gray 10.50 6.00

2-line overprint 22mm apart

196 A51 500m lil rose & grnsh gray 47.50 19.00
197 A51 £1 grnsh gray & brn red 87.50 47.50
Nos. 183-197 (15) 155.00 78.20

The overprint, in Greek and Turkish, reads "Republic of Cyprus."

Map of Cyprus — A52

Wmk. 314

1960, Aug. 16 **Engr.** ***Perf. 11½***

198 A52 10m brown & green .25 .20
199 A52 30m blue & brown 1.00 .70
200 A52 100m purple & black 2.75 2.25
Nos. 198-200 (3) 4.00 3.15

Independence of Republic of Cyprus.

Europa Issue, 1961

Nineteen Doves Flying as One CD4

Perf. 14x13½

1962, Mar. 19 **Litho.** **Unwmk.**

201 CD4 10m lilac *.30* *.20*
202 CD4 40m deep ultra *.90* *.35*
203 CD4 100m emerald *.90* *.60*
Nos. 201-203 (3) *2.10* *1.15*

Admission of Cyprus to Council of Europe.

Malaria Eradication Emblem A54

1962, May 14 ***Perf. 14x13½***

204 A54 10m gray green & blue .25 .20
205 A54 30m red brown & black .50 .50

WHO drive to eradicate malaria.

Iron Age Jug — A55

St. Barnabas Church, Salamis A56

Designs: 5m, Grapes. 10m, Head of Apollo. 15m, St. Sophia Church, Nicosia. 30m, Temple of Apollo. 35m, Head of Aphrodite. 40m, Skiing on Mt. Troodos. 50m, Ruins of Gymnasium, Salamis. 100m, Hala Sultan Tekke (sheep, Salt Lake Larnaca and tomb). 250m, Bella Paise Monastery. 500m, Cyprus mouflon. £1, St. Hilarion Castle.

Perf. 13½x14, 14x13½

1962, Sept. 17 **Wmk. 344**

206 A55 3m dk brn & sal .20 .30
207 A55 5m dull green & red lilac .20 .20
208 A55 10m dk slate grn & yel green .20 .20
209 A55 15m dk brn & rose vio .40 .20
210 A56 25m salmon & brn .45 .20
211 A56 30m lt bl & dk bl .25 .20
212 A55 35m dk bl & pale grn .45 .20
213 A56 40m vio bl & dk bl 1.50 1.75
214 A56 50m olive bis & dk grn .60 .20
215 A55 100m brn & yel brn 4.25 .30
216 A56 250m tan & black 11.00 2.40
217 A55 500m brown & olive 21.00 9.00
218 A56 £1 gray & green 22.50 *30.00*
Nos. 206-218 (13) 63.00 45.15

Wmk. 344 is found in two positions: normal or inverted on vertical stamps, and reading up or down on horizontal stamps.

For overprints see Nos. 232-236, 265-268. For surcharge see No. 273.

Europa Issue, 1962

Common Design Type

Perf. 14x13½

1963, Jan. 28 **Wmk. 344**

Size: 36x20mm

219	CD5	10m ultra & black	*2.50*	*.20*
220	CD5	40m red & black	*10.00*	*1.40*
221	CD5	150m green & black	*37.50*	*2.75*
		Nos. 219-221 (3)	*50.00*	*4.35*

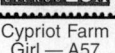

Cypriot Farm Girl — A57

Cub Scout and Tents — A58

75m, Statue of Demeter, goddess of agriculture.

1963, Mar. 21 *Perf. 13½x14*

222	A57	25m blk, ultra & ocher	.60	.45
223	A57	75m dk car, gray & blk	3.50	1.75

FAO "Freedom from Hunger" campaign.

1963, Aug. 21 **Wmk. 344**

20m, Sea Scout. 150m, Boy Scout & mouflon.

224	A58	3m multicolored	.20	.20
225	A58	20m multicolored	.40	.25
226	A58	150m multicolored	2.00	2.50
a.		Souvenir sheet of 3	150.00	150.00
		Nos. 224-226 (3)	2.60	2.95

Boy Scout movement in Cyprus, 50th anniv. #226a contains 3 imperf. stamps similar to #224-226 with simulated perforations. Sold for 250m.

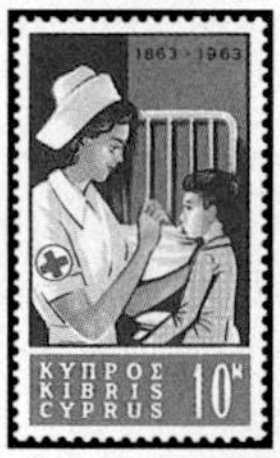

Red Cross Nurse — A59

Children's Home, Kyrenia A60

Perf. 13½x14, 14x13½

1963, Sept. 9 **Litho.** **Wmk. 344**

227	A59	10m multicolored	1.00	.20
228	A60	100m multicolored	4.00	4.00

Intl. Red Cross, cent.

Europa Issue, 1963

Stylized Links, Symbolizing Unity — CD6

1963, Nov. 4 *Perf. 14x13½*

229	CD6	20m multicolored	*4.75*	*.70*
230	CD6	30m multicolored	*5.25*	*.70*
231	CD6	150m multicolored	*35.00*	*3.75*
		Nos. 229-231 (3)	*45.00*	*5.15*

Nos. 208, 211, 213-215 Overprinted in Ultramarine

1964, May 5 *Perf. 13½x14, 14x13½*

232	A55	10m dk sl grn & yel grn	.20	.20
233	A55	30m lt blue & dk blue	.25	.20
234	A55	40m vio bl & dull bl	.35	.30
235	A55	50m ol bis & dk grn	.45	.35
236	A55	100m brn & yel brown	.75	.75
		Nos. 232-236 (5)	2.00	1.80

Decision by the UN and its Security Council to help restore the country to normality and to seek a solution of its problems.

Clay Mask and Soli Theater A62

Designs: 35m, Curium theater. 50m, Salamis theater. 100m, Performance of "Othello" in front of Othello Tower.

1964, June 15 *Perf. 13½x14*

237	A62	15m multicolored	.40	.20
238	A62	35m multicolored	.40	.25
239	A62	50m multicolored	.40	.25
240	A62	100m multicolored	1.60	1.90
		Nos. 237-240 (4)	2.80	2.60

400th anniversary of Shakespeare's birth.

Boxers A63

14th century B.C. art: 10m, Runners, vert. 75m, Chariot.

1964, July 6 *Perf. 13½x14, 14x13½*

241	A63	10m brn, bis & blk	.20	.20
242	A63	25m gray bl, bl & brn	.30	.25
243	A63	75m brick red, blk & brn	.75	.80
a.		Souvenir sheet of 3	10.00	*13.50*
		Nos. 241-243 (3)	1.25	1.25

18th Olympic Games, Tokyo, Oct. 10-25, 1964. No. 243a contains three imperf. stamps similar to Nos. 241-243 with gray marginal inscription. Sheet sold for 250m; the difference between face value and selling price went for the promotion of classical athletics in Cyprus.

Symbolic Daisy CD7

Satyr Drinking Wine, 5th Century B.C. Statuette A65

Modern Winery A66

Europa Issue, 1964

Perf. 13½x14

1964, Sept. 14 **Litho.** **Wmk. 344**

244	CD7	20m bis brn & red brn	*2.50*	*.35*
245	CD7	30m lt blue & dk blue	*3.25*	*.35*
246	CD7	150m grn & ol grn	*30.00*	*2.75*
		Nos. 244-246 (3)	*35.75*	*3.45*

CEPT, 5th anniv. The 22 petals of the flower symbolize the 22 members of the organization.

Perf. 14x13½, 13½x14

1964, Oct. 26 **Wmk. 344**

Cypriot Wine Industry: 10m, Dionysus and Acme drinking wine, 3rd century mosaic. 50m, Commandaria wine, Knight Templar and Kolossi Castle.

247	A66	10m multicolored	.50	.20
248	A65	40m multicolored	.95	1.25
249	A65	50m multicolored	.95	.30
250	A66	100m multicolored	2.50	2.00
		Nos. 247-250 (4)	4.90	3.75

Pres. John F. Kennedy (1917-1963) — A67

Perf. 14x13½

1965, Feb. 15 **Litho.** **Wmk. 344**

251	A67	10m violet blue	.20	.20
252	A67	40m green	.50	.45
253	A67	100m rose claret	.65	.45
a.		Souvenir sheet of 3	4.75	6.75
		Nos. 251-253 (3)	1.35	1.10

No. 253a contains 3 imperf. stamps similar to Nos. 251-253 with simulated perforations. Sold for 250m, 100m going to charitable organizations in Cyprus.

Old Couple — A68

Mother and Children by A. Diamantis — A69

45m, Man with broken leg (accident insurance).

1965, Apr. 12 *Perf. 13½x14*

254	A68	30m dull green & tan	.30	.20
255	A68	45m dk vio bl, bl & gray	.50	.30

Perf. 13½x12½

256	A69	75m buff & red brown	1.50	2.00
		Nos. 254-256 (3)	2.30	2.50

Introduction of Social Insurance Law.

ITU Emblem, Old and New Communication Equipment — A70

1965, May 17 **Litho.** *Perf. 14x13½*

257	A70	15m brn, yel & black	.75	.25
258	A70	60m grn, lt grn & black	8.50	3.25
259	A70	75m dk & lt bl & black	9.75	4.50
		Nos. 257-259 (3)	19.00	8.00

ITU, cent.

ICY Emblem A71

1965, May 17 **Wmk. 344**

260	A71	50m multicolored	1.25	.20
261	A71	100m multicolored	2.00	.90

International Cooperation Year.

Europa Issue, 1965

Leaves and Fruit CD8

Perf. 14x13½

1965, Sept. 27 **Litho.** **Wmk. 344**

262	CD8	5m org, org brn & black	1.10	*.25*
263	CD8	45m lt grn, org brn & black	*5.25*	*.80*
264	CD8	150m gray, org brn & black	*19.00*	*2.75*
		Nos. 262-264 (3)	*25.35*	*3.80*

Nos. 206, 208, 211 and 216 Overprinted in Dark Blue

1966, Jan. 31 *Perf. 13½x14, 14x13½*

265	A55	3m dk brn & salmon	.25	.30
266	A55	10m dk sl grn & yel green	.25	.20
267	A56	30m lt bl & dk blue	.25	.20
268	A56	250m tan & black	1.00	*2.40*
		Nos. 265-268 (4)	1.75	3.10

UN General Assembly's resolution to mediate the dispute between Greeks and Turks on Cyprus, Dec. 18, 1965.

St. Barnabas, Ancient Icon — A73

Chapel over Tomb of St. Barnabas A74

Bishop Anthemios of Constantine Dreaming of St. Barnabas, Discovering Tomb, etc. — A75

Design: 15m, Discovery of body of St. Barnabas (scene as in type A18).

Perf. 13x14, 14x13

1966, Apr. 25 Litho. Wmk. 344

269 A73 15m multicolored .20 .20
270 A74 25m multicolored .20 .20
271 A73 100m multicolored .90 *1.75*

Size: 110x91mm

Imperf

272 A75 250m multicolored 6.50 *12.00*
Nos. 269-272 (4) 7.80 14.15

1900th anniv. of the death of St. Barnabas.

No. 206 Surcharged with New Value and Three Bars

Perf. 13½x14

1966, May 30 Litho. Wmk. 344

273 A55 5m on 3m dk brn & sal .40 .25

Gen. K. S. Thimayya A76

1966, June 6 ***Perf. 14x13½***

274 A76 50m tan & black .40 .25

In memory of Gen. Kodendera Subayya Thimayya (1906-1965), commander of the UN Peace-keeping Force on Cyprus.

Europa Issue, 1966

Symbolic Sailboat — CD9

Perf. 13½x14

1966, Sept. 26 Litho. Wmk. 344

275 CD9 20m multicolored *.50 .20*
276 CD9 30m multicolored *.50 .25*
277 CD9 150m multicolored *3.75 1.40*
Nos. 275-277 (3) 4.75 1.85

Stavrovouni Monastery A78

St. Nicholas Cathedral, Famagusta A79

Ingot Bearer, Bronze Age — A80

Designs: 5m, St. James' Church, Tricomo, vert. 10m, Zeno of Citium, marble bust, vert. 15m, Ship from 7th cent. BC vase, horiz. 20m, Silver coin, 4th cent. BC (head of Hercules with lion skin). 25m, Sleeping Eros (1st cent. marble statue; horiz.). 35m, Hawks on 11th cent. gold and enamel scepter from Curium. 40m, Marriage of David (7th cent. silver disc). 50m, Silver coin of Alexander the Great showing Hercules and Zeus, horiz. 100m, Bird catching fish on 7th cent. BC jug. 500m, The Rape of Ganymede (3rd cent. mosaic). £1, Aphrodite (1st cent. marble statue).

Perf. 12x12½, 12½x12

1966, Nov. 21 Litho. Wmk. 344

278 A78 3m bl, dl yel, grn & black .60 .20
279 A78 5m dk bl, ol & blk .20 .20
280 A78 10m olive & black .25 .20

Perf. 14x13½, 13½x14

281 A79 15m org brn, blk & red brn .25 .20
282 A79 20m red brn & blk 1.75 1.40
283 A79 25m red brn, gray & black .55 .20
284 A79 30m aqua, tan & blk .75 .30
285 A79 35m dk car, yel & blk .75 .45
286 A79 40m brt bl, gray & blk 1.00 .45
287 A79 50m org brn, gray & blk 1.50 .20
288 A79 100m gray, buff, blk & red 5.00 .20

Perf. 13x14

289 A80 250m dull yel, grn & blk 1.50 .50
290 A80 500m multicolored 3.50 1.00
291 A80 £1 gray, lt gray & black 3.00 *7.00*
Nos. 278-291 (14) 20.60 12.50

Electric Power Station, Limassol — A81

Arghaka-Maghounda Dam — A82

Designs: 35m, Troodos Highway. 50m, Cyprus Hilton Hotel. 100m, Ships in Famagusta Harbor.

Perf. 14x13½, 13½x14

1967, Apr. 10 Litho. Wmk. 344

292 A81 10m lt brn, dark brn & yellow .20 .20
293 A82 15m lt bl, bl & grn .25 .25
294 A82 35m dark gray, indigo & dark grn .35 .35
295 A82 50m gray, olive & blue .35 .35
296 A82 100m gray, ind & bl .35 .35
Nos. 292-296 (5) 1.50 1.50

1st development program, 1962-66, completion.

Europa Issue, 1967

Common Design Type

1967, May 2 ***Perf. 13x14***

Size: 21x37mm

297 CD10 20m yel grn & olive *.50 .20*
298 CD10 30m rose vio & pur *.50 .25*
299 CD10 150m pale brn & brn *3.25 1.25*
Nos. 297-299 (3) 4.25 1.70

Javelin Thrower, Map of Eastern Mediterranean and "Victory" — A83

Map of Eastern Mediterranean, Victory Statue and: 35m, Runner. 100m, High jumper. 250m, Amphora, map of Eastern Mediterranean and Victory statue.

Perf. 13½x13

1967, Sept. 4 Litho. Wmk. 344

300 A83 15m multicolored .20 .20
301 A83 35m multicolored .35 .30
302 A83 100m multicolored .75 .75

Size: 97x77mm

Imperf

303 A83 250m multicolored 3.50 *6.50*
Nos. 300-303 (4) 4.80 7.75

Cyprus-Crete-Salonika Athletic Games.

Marble Forum at Salamis, Church of St. Barnabas and Bellapais Abbey A84

ITY Emblem and: 40m, Famagusta Beach. 50m, Plane and Nicosia International Airport. 100m, Youth Hostel and skiing on Mt. Troodos.

Perf. 13½x13

1967, Oct. 16 Litho. Wmk. 344

304 A84 10m multicolored .20 .20
305 A84 40m multicolored .20 *1.00*
306 A84 50m multicolored .30 .20
307 A84 100m multicolored .50 *1.00*
Nos. 304-307 (4) 1.20 2.40

Intl. Tourist Year, 1967.

St. Andrew, 6th Century Mosaic — A85

Crucifixion, 15th Century — A86

The Three Kings, 15th Century Fresco — A87

1967, Nov. 8 ***Perf. 13x13½***

308 A85 25m multicolored .20 .20
309 A86 50m multicolored .20 .20
310 A87 75m multicolored .20 .20
Nos. 308-310 (3) .60 .60

St. Andrew's Monastery, cent. (25m); Exhibition of Art of Cyprus, Paris, Nov. 7, 1967-Jan. 3, 1968 (50m); 20th anniv. of UNESCO (75m).

Human Rights Flame and Stars — A88

Designs: 90m, Human Rights flame and UN emblem. 250m, Scroll showing Article One of the Declaration of Human Rights.

Perf. 13½x14

1968, Mar. 18 Litho. Wmk. 344

311 A88 50m multicolored .20 .20
312 A88 90m multicolored .40 .60

Size: 110x90mm

Imperf

313 A88 250m multicolored 1.40 *4.50*
Nos. 311-313 (3) 2.00 5.30

Intl. Human Rights Year.

Europa Issue, 1968

Common Design Type

1968, Apr. 29 ***Perf. 14x13½***

314 CD11 20m multicolored *.40 .25*
315 CD11 30m dk car rose, gray brn & blk *.50 .25*
316 CD11 150m multicolored *2.00 1.25*
Nos. 314-316 (3) 2.90 1.75

Boy Holding Milk, UNICEF Emblem A89

Aesculapius and WHO Emblem — A90

Perf. 14x13½, 13½x14

1968, Sept. 2 Wmk. 344

317 A89 35m dk red, lt brn & blk .20 .20
318 A90 50m gray ol, blk & grn .20 .20

21st anniv. of UNICEF (No. 317), 20th anniv. of the WHO (No. 318).

Discus Thrower — A91

ILO Emblem — A92

25m, Runners. 100m, Stadium, Mexico City.

Perf. 13½x14, 14x13½

1968, Oct. 24 Litho.

319 A91 10m multicolored .20 .20
320 A91 25m vio blue & multi .20 .20
321 A91 100m blue & multi, horiz. .30 *1.00*
Nos. 319-321 (3) .70 1.40

19th Olympic Games, Mexico City, 10/12-27.

Perf. 12x13½

1969, Mar. 3 Wmk. 344

322 A92 50m bl, vio bl & org brn .20 .20
323 A92 90m gray, blk & org brn .25 .25

ILO, 50th anniv.

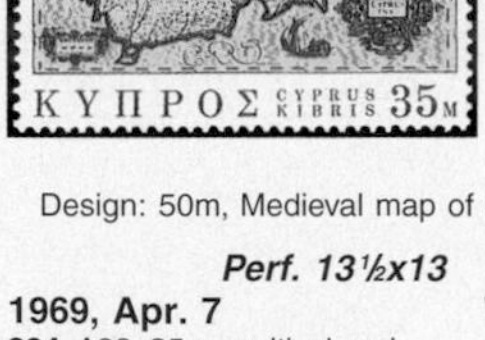

Ancient Map of Cyprus A93

Design: 50m, Medieval map of Cyprus.

Perf. 13½x13

1969, Apr. 7 Wmk. 344

324 A93 35m multicolored .25 .25
325 A93 50m olive & multi .25 .25

1st Intl. Congress of Cypriot Studies.

Europa Issue, 1969

"EUROPA" and "CEPT" CD12

1969, Apr. 28 Litho. *Perf. 14x13½*

326 CD12 20m bl, blk & gray *.55* .20
327 CD12 30m cop red, blk & ocher *.55* .20
328 CD12 150m grn, blk & yel *1.90* .85
Nos. 326-328 (3) *3.00* *1.25*

CEPT, 10th anniv.

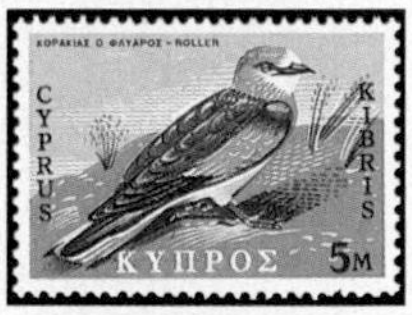

European Roller — A95

Birds: 15m, Audouin's gull. 20m, Cyprus warbler. 30m, Eurasian jay, vert. 40m, Hoopoe, vert. 90m, Eleonora's falcon, vert.

Perf. 13½x12, 12x13½

1969, July 7 Wmk. 344

329 A95 5m multicolored .55 .20
330 A95 15m multicolored .75 .20
331 A95 20m multicolored .75 .20
332 A95 30m multicolored .80 .25
333 A95 40m multicolored .95 .30
334 A95 90m multicolored 2.10 4.50
Nos. 329-334 (6) 5.90 5.65

Nativity, Mural, 1192 A96

Christmas: 45m, Nativity, mural in Church of Ayios Nicolaos tis Steghis, 14th century. 250m, Virgin and Child between Archangels Michael and Gabriel, mosaic in Church of Panayia Angeloktistos, 6th-7th centuries. Design of 20m is a mural in Church of Panayia tou Arakos, Lagoudhera.

1969, Nov. 24 Litho. *Perf. 13½x13*

335 A96 20m multicolored .20 .20
336 A96 45m multicolored .30 .25

Size: 109x89mm

Imperf

337 A96 250m dk blue & multi 5.00 *10.00*
Nos. 335-337 (3) 5.50 10.45

Mahatma Gandhi A97

1970, Jan. 26 *Perf. 14x13½*

338 A97 25m multicolored .25 .25
339 A97 75m multicolored .75 .85

Birth cent. of Mohandas K. Gandhi (1869-1948), leader in India's struggle for independence.

Europa Issue, 1970

Interwoven Threads CD13

1970, May 4 Litho. Wmk. 344

340 CD13 20m brn, yel & org *.40* .25
341 CD13 30m brt bl, yel & org *.40* .25
342 CD13 150m brt rose lil, yel & orange *1.90* *1.40*
Nos. 340-342 (3) *2.70* *1.90*

Landscape with Flowers — A99

Designs: Various landscapes with flowers.

Perf. 13x14

1970, Aug. 3 Litho. Wmk. 344

343 A99 10m multicolored .20 .20
344 A99 50m multicolored .20 .20
345 A99 90m multicolored .85 *1.10*
Nos. 343-345 (3) 1.25 1.50

European Nature Conservation Year.

Education Year Emblem — A100

Grapes and Partridge (Mosaic) A101

UN Emblem, Dove, Globe and Wheat A102

Perf. 13x14, 14x13

1970, Sept. 7 Litho. Wmk. 344

346 A100 5m tan, blk & brn .20 .20
347 A101 15m multicolored .20 .20
348 A102 75m multicolored .20 .20
Nos. 346-348 (3) .60 .60

Intl. Education Year (No. 346); 50th General Assembly of the Intl. Vine and Wine Office (No. 347); 25th anniv. of the UN (No. 348).

Virgin and Child, Mural from Podhithou Church, 16th Century — A103

Perf. 14x14½

1970, Nov. 23 Photo. Unwmk.

349 A103 Strip of three .45 .45
a. 25m Left angel .20 .20
b. 25m Virgin and Child .20 .20
c. 25m Right angel .20 .20
350 A103 75m multicolored .35 .35

Christmas.
Design of No. 349 is same as No. 350, but divided by perforation into 3 stamps with 25m denomination each. Size of No. 349: 71x46mm; size of No. 350: 42x31mm.

Cotton Napkin — A104

Festive Costume — A105

Drinking Cup, 7th Cent. B.C. A106

Mouflon from Mosaic Pavement, 3rd Century — A107

Cypriot Art: 5m, St. George, bas-relief on pine board, 19th cent. 20m, kneeling donors, painting, Church of St. Mamas, 1465. 25m, Mosaic head, 5th cent. A.D. 30m, Athena mounting horse-drawn chariot, terracotta figurine, 5th cent. B.C. 40m, Shepherd playing pipe, 14th cent. fresco. 50m, Woman's head, limestone, 3rd cent. B.C. 75m, Angel, mosaic, 6th cent. 90m, Mycenaean silver bowl, 14th cent. B.C. 500m, Woman and tree, decoration from amphora, 7th-6th cent. B.C. £1, God statue (horned helmet), from Enkomi, 12th cent. B.C., vert.

Perf. 12½x13½ (A104), 13x14 (A105), 14x13 (A106), 13½x13, 13x13½ (A107)

1971, Feb. 22 Litho. Wmk. 344

351 A104 3m blk, red & brn .40 .50
352 A104 5m citron, red brn & black .20 .20
353 A105 10m multicolored .20 .30
354 A106 15m bister brn, blk & slate .25 .20
355 A105 20m slate, red brn & black .45 .50
356 A105 25m multicolored .35 .20
357 A106 30m multicolored .35 .20
358 A105 40m gray & multi 1.25 1.10
359 A105 50m bl, bis & blk 1.00 .20
360 A105 75m cit & multi 2.25 1.25
361 A106 90m multicolored 2.50 2.50
362 A107 250m lt red brn, brn & black 1.90 .40
363 A107 500m tan & multi 1.00 .50
364 A107 £1 multicolored 1.90 .75
Nos. 351-364 (14) 14.00 8.80

For surcharges & overprints see #403, 424-427, 444, RA1.

Europa Issue, 1971

"Fraternity, Co-operation, Common Effort" — CD14

1971, May 3 Litho. *Perf. 14x13½*

Size: 36½x23½mm

365 CD14 20m lt bl, vio bl & blk *.30* *.20*
366 CD14 30m brt yel grn, grn & blk *.30* *.20*
367 CD14 150m yel, grn & blk *2.00* *1.25*
Nos. 365-367 (3) *2.60* *1.65*

Archbishop Kyprianos, 1821 — A109

Paintings: 30m, Young Greek Taking Oath, horiz. 100m, Bishop Germanòs of Patras Declaring Greek Independence.

Perf. 13x13½, 13½x13

1971, July 9 Wmk. 344

368 A109 15m multicolored .20 .20
369 A109 30m multicolored .20 .20
370 A109 100m multicolored .30 .30
Nos. 368-370 (3) .70 .70

150th anniversary of Greek independence.

Arch and Castle A110

Tourist Publicity: 25m, Decorated gourd and sun over shore, vert. 60m, Mountain road, vert. 100m, Village church.

Perf. 13½x13, 13x13½

1971, Sept. 20

371 A110 15m vio bl & multi .20 .20
372 A110 25m ocher & multi .20 .20
373 A110 60m green & multi .25 .25
374 A110 100m blue & multi .25 .25
Nos. 371-374 (4) .90 .90

Virgin and Child — A111

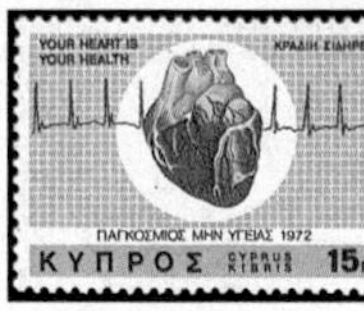

Heart and Electrocardiogram — A112

1971, Nov. 22 *Perf. 13½x14*

375 A111 10m shown .20 .20
376 A111 50m The Three Kings .20 .20
377 A111 100m Shepherds .30 .30
a. Strip of 3, Nos. 375-377 .75 .75

Christmas.

1972, Apr. 11 *Perf. 13½x12½*

378 A112 15m bister & multi .20 .20
379 A112 50m brown & multi .30 .30

"Your heart is your health," World Health Day.

Europa Issue 1972

Sparkles, Symbolic of Communications CD15

1972, May 22 *Perf. 12½x13½*

380 CD15 20m brn, org & fawn .60 .30
381 CD15 30m pur, org & lilac .60 .55
382 CD15 150m dk ol, org & brt green 4.75 1.60
Nos. 380-382 (3) 5.95 2.45

Archery, Olympic and Motion Emblems A114

1972, July 24 *Perf. 14x13½*

383 A114 10m shown .25 .20
384 A114 40m Wrestling .35 .25
385 A114 100m Soccer .65 1.25
Nos. 383-385 (3) 1.25 1.70

20th Olympic Games, Munich, 8/26-9/11.

Apollo, Silver Stater, Marion, 5th Century B.C. A115

Silver Staters of Cyprus: 30m, Eagle's head, Paphos, c. 460 B.C. 40m, Pallas Athena, Lapithos, 388-387 B.C. 100m, Sphinx (obverse) and lotus flower (reverse), Idalion, c. 460 B.C.

1972, Sept. 25 Litho. Wmk. 344

Coins in Silver

386 A115 20m lt grnsh bl & blk .20 .20
387 A115 30m pale bl & silver .20 .20
388 A115 40m ol bister & black .35 .30
389 A115 100m pale brn & blk 1.25 1.10
Nos. 386-389 (4) 2.00 1.80

Bathing the Christ Child — A116

Christmas: 20m, The Three Kings. 100m, Nativity. 250m, The Nativity, 1466, mural in Church of the Holy Cross, Platanistasa. The designs of the 10m, 20m, 100m, show details from mural shown entirely on 250m.

1972, Nov. 20 Litho. *Perf. 13½x14*

390 A116 10m multicolored .30 .30
391 A116 20m multicolored .30 .30
392 A116 100m multicolored .40 .40

Size: 110x90mm

Imperf

393 A116 250m multicolored 2.75 2.75
Nos. 390-393 (4) 3.75 3.75

Landscape, Troodos Mountains A117

100m, FIS Congress emblem and map of Cyprus.

Perf. 14x13½

1973, Mar. 13 Wmk. 344

394 A117 20m blue & multi .20 .20
395 A117 100m blue & multi .40 .40

29th Meeting of the Intl. Ski Fed. (FIS), Nicosia, June 1973.

Europa Issue 1973

Post Horn of Arrows CD16

1973, May 7 Size: 37x21mm

396 CD16 20m dl bl & multi .40 .25
397 CD16 30m multicolored .40 .35
398 CD16 150m multicolored 2.50 1.50
Nos. 396-398 (3) 3.30 2.10

Archbishop's Palace, Nicosia — A119

Traditional Architecture: 30m, Konak, Nicosia, 18th century, vert. 50m, House, Gourri, 1850, vert. 100m, House, Rizokarpaso, 1772.

1973, July 23 *Perf. 14x13, 13x14*

399 A119 20m multicolored .20 .20
400 A119 30m multicolored .20 .20
401 A119 50m multicolored .20 .20
402 A119 100m multicolored .50 .50
Nos. 399-402 (4) 1.10 1.10

No. 354 Surcharged

1973, Sept. 24 *Perf. 14x13*

403 A106 20m on 15m multi .40 .40

Cyprus Scout Emblem — A120

EEC Emblem A122

Cyprus Airways Emblem — A121

35m, FAO emblem. 100m, INTERPOL emblem.

1973, Sept. 24 *Perf. 13x14, 14x13*

404 A120 10m brn ol, ol & buff .40 .35
405 A121 25m pur, bl & plum .30 .30
406 A121 35m grn, gray grn & citron .30 .30
407 A122 50m black & blue .30 .30
408 A120 100m brown & fawn .60 .60
Nos. 404-408 (5) 1.90 1.85

60th anniv. of Cyprus Boy Scout Organ.; association of Cyprus with EEC; 10th anniv. of FAO; 25th anniv. of Cyprus Airways; 50th anniv. of Intl. Criminal Police Organization.

Archangel Gabriel — A123

Virgin and Child — A124

Christmas: 100m, Panaya tou Araka Church, horiz. Designs of 10m, 20m are from wall paintings in Arakas Church.

1973, Nov. 26 Wmk. 344

409 A123 10m multicolored .20 .20
410 A124 20m multicolored .20 .20
411 A124 100m multicolored .60 .60
Nos. 409-411 (3) 1.00 1.00

Grapes — A125

Rape of Europa — A126

1974, Mar. 18 Litho. *Perf. 13x14*

412 A125 25m shown .25 .20
413 A125 50m Grapefruit .30 .20
414 A125 50m Oranges .30 .20
415 A125 50m Lemons .30 .30
a. Strip of 3, #413-415 1.25 1.25
Nos. 412-415 (4) 1.15 .90

Europa Issue 1974

1974, Apr. 29

Design shows a silver stater of Marion, second half of 5th century B.C.

416 A126 10m org brn & multi .60 .30
417 A126 40m multicolored .60 .60
418 A126 150m dk car & multi 2.75 1.40
Nos. 416-418 (3) 3.95 2.30

Solon, 3rd Century Mosaic A127

Designs: 10m, Front page of "History of Cyprus," by Archimandrite Kyprianos, 1788, vert. 100m, St. Neophytos, mural, vert. 250m, Maps of Cyprus and Greek Islands, by Abraham Ortelius, 1584.

Perf. 13x14, 14x13

1974, July 22 Litho. Wmk. 344

419 A127 10m multicolored .20 .20
420 A127 25m multicolored .20 .20
421 A127 100m multicolored .85 .85

Size: 110x90mm

Imperf

422 A127 250m multicolored 3.00 *3.25*
Nos. 419-422 (4) 4.25 4.50

2nd Intl. Congress of Cypriot Studies, Nicosia, Sept. 15-21. No. 422 has simulated perforations.

Nos. 353, 358-359, 362 Overprinted

Perf. 13x14, 13½x13

1974, Oct. 14 Litho.

424 A105 10m multicolored .25 .25
425 A105 40m multicolored .35 .35
426 A105 50m multicolored .35 .35
427 A107 250m multicolored .80 .80
Nos. 424-427 (4) 1.75 1.75

UN Security Council Resolution No. 353 to end hostilities on Cyprus. Overprint is in 3 lines on No. 427.

Virgin and Child, 1466 A129

Adoration of the Kings, c. 1500 — A130

Christmas: 100m, Flight into Egypt, mural, Monastery Church of Ayios Meophytos, c. 1500. (50m is from same church). Mural on 10m is in Church of Stavros tou Ahiasmati.

Perf. 14x13, 13x14

1974, Dec. 2 Wmk. 344

429 A129 10m multicolored .20 .20
430 A130 50m multicolored .20 .20
431 A129 100m multicolored .40 .40
Nos. 429-431 (3) .80 .80

Disabled Persons, Emblem — A131

Council of Europe Flag — A132

1975, Feb. 17 Unwmk. *Perf. 14½*

432 A131 30m ocher & ultra .20 .20
433 A132 100m multicolored .70 .60

8th European Meeting of the Intl. Society for the Rehabilitation of Disabled Persons (30m; design shows society's emblem); 25th anniv. of Council of Europe (100m).

First Mail Coach in Cyprus A133

1975, Feb. 17

434 A133 20m multicolored .20 .20
435 A133 50m ultra & multi 1.10 .40

Centenary (in 1974) of UPU.

The Distaff, by Michael Kashalos — A134

Europa (Paintings): 30m, Still Life, by Christoforos Savva. 150m, Virgin and Child of Liopetri, by Georghios P. Georghiou.

Perf. 13½x14½

1975, Apr. 28 **Photo.**

436	A134	20m multicolored	.30	.20
437	A134	30m multicolored	.35	.20
438	A134	150m multicolored	1.00	.60
a.		Strip of 3, #436-438	1.75	1.75

Red Cross Flag over Cyprus — A135

Nurse and Nurses Emblem A136

Steatite Female Figure, c. 3000 B.C. — A137

Perf. 12½x13½, 13½x12½

1975, Aug. 4 **Litho.** **Wmk. 344**

439	A135	25m blue green & red	.25	.20
440	A136	30m dp blue & lt grn	.30	.25
441	A137	75m multicolored	.45	.40
		Nos. 439-441 (3)	1.00	.85

Cyprus Red Cross, 25th anniv.; Intl. Nurses' Day 1975; IWY.

Submarine Cable — A138

International Telephone A139

Perf. 12½x13½, 13½x12½

1975, Oct. 13 **Litho.**

442	A138	50m multicolored	.35	.20
443	A139	100m purple & org	.60	.45

Telecommunications achievements.

No. 351 Surcharged

1976, Jan. 5 *Perf. 12½x13½*

444	A104	10m on 3m multi	.40	.40

Vessel in Shape of Woman, 19th Century — A140

Composite Vessel, 2100-2000 B.C. — A141

Europa: 100m, Byzantine goblet, 15th cent.

Perf. 13x14

1976, May 3 **Litho.** **Wmk. 344**

445	A140	20m violet & multi	.35	.20
446	A141	60m gray & multi	.80	.70
447	A140	100m brown & multi	1.60	.95
		Nos. 445-447 (3)	2.75	1.85

Self-help Housing A142

Cyprus Airways Jet — A143

Designs: 25m, Women sewing in front of tents. 30m, Aforestation.

1976, May 3 *Perf. 14x13*

448	A142	10m multicolored	.20	.20
449	A142	25m multicolored	.20	.20
450	A142	30m multicolored	.20	.20
451	A143	60m multicolored	.40	.40
		Nos. 448-451 (4)	1.00	1.00

Re-activation of the economy.

Terracotta Statue, 7th-6th Centuries B.C. — A144

Bronze Plate with Inscription, Idalion, 5th Century B.C. A145

Designs: 10m, Limestone head of bearded man, 5th cent. B.C. 20m, Gold necklace, Lamboussa, 6th cent. A.D. 25m, Terracotta warrior on horseback, 7th cent. B.C. 30m, Limestone figure, priest of Aphrodite, 5th cent. B.C. 50m, Mycenaean crater, 13th cent. B.C. 60m, Limestone sarcophagus, Amathus, 550-500 B.C. 100m, Gold bracelet, Lamboussa, 6th cent. A.D. 250m, Silver dish, Lamboussa, 6th cent. A.D. 500m, Bronze stand, 12th cent. B.C. £1, Marble statue of Artemis, Larnaca, 4th cent. B.C.

Perf. 12x13½

1976, June 7 **Wmk. 344**

Size: 22x33mm

452	A144	5m brn & multi	.20	.75
453	A144	10m gray & multi	.20	.65

Size: 24x37mm, 37x24mm

Perf. 13x14, 14x13

454	A144	20m red & multi	.20	.60
455	A144	25m lt brn & blk	.20	.20
456	A144	30m green & multi	.20	.20
457	A145	40m bis gray & blk	.20	.60
458	A145	50m brn & multi	.20	.20
459	A145	60m dk brn & multi	.25	.20
460	A145	100m crim & multi	.40	.60

Size: 28x40mm

Perf. 13x12½

461	A144	250m dk bl & multi	.90	1.50
462	A144	500m yel & multi	1.75	1.75
463	A144	£1 slate & multi	3.75	3.50
		Nos. 452-463 (12)	8.45	10.75

George Washington A146

1976, July 5 *Perf. 13x13½*

464	A146	100m multicolored	.70	.60

American Bicentennial.

Montreal Olympic Games Emblem — A147

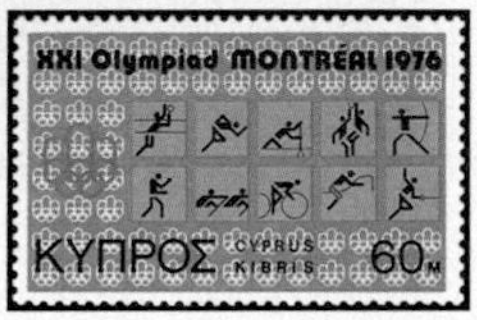

Various Sports A148

100m, like 60m, with different sports.

1976, July 5 **Unwmk.** *Perf. 14*

465	A147	20m yel, blk & dk car	.20	.20
466	A148	60m ultra & multi	.30	.30
467	A148	100m lilac & multi	.50	.50
		Nos. 465-467 (3)	1.00	1.00

21st Olympic Games, Montreal, Canada, July 17-Aug. 1.

Children in Library — A149

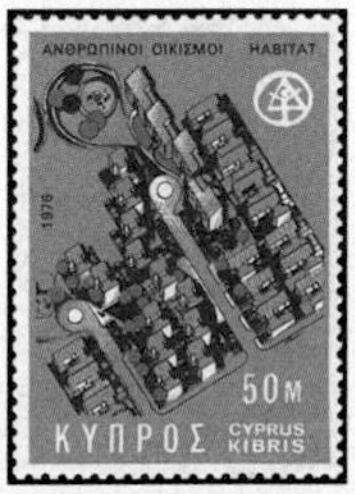

Low-cost Housing Development A150

Hands Shielding Eye — A151

Perf. 13½x14, 13x13½

1976, Sept. 27 **Litho.** **Wmk. 344**

468	A149	40m black & multi	.30	.30
469	A150	50m multicolored	.25	.20
470	A151	80m ultra & multi	.45	.35
		Nos. 468-470 (3)	1.00	.85

Books for Children (40m); Habitat, UN Conference on Human Settlements, Vancouver, Canada, May 31-June 11 (50m); World Health Day: Foresight prevents blindness (80m).

Archangel Michael — A152

Christmas: 15m, Archangel Gabriel. 150m, Nativity. Icons in Ayios Neophytis Monastery, 16th century.

1976, Nov. 15 **Unwmk.** *Perf. 12½*

471	A152	10m multicolored	.20	.20
472	A152	15m multicolored	.20	.20
473	A152	150m multicolored	.85	.75
		Nos. 471-473 (3)	1.25	1.15

Landscape, by A. Diamantis — A154

Europa (Paintings): 60m, Trees and Meadow, by T. Kanthos. 120m, Harbor, by V. Ioannides.

Perf. 13½x13

1977, May 2 **Litho.** **Unwmk.**

475	A154	20m multicolored	.30	.20
476	A154	60m multicolored	.70	.40
477	A154	120m multicolored	1.25	.90
		Nos. 475-477 (3)	2.25	1.50

Cyprus No. 196 — A155

Perf. 13x13½

1977, June 13 **Litho.** **Wmk. 344**

478	A155	120m multicolored	.55	.40

25th anniv. of reign of Queen Elizabeth II.

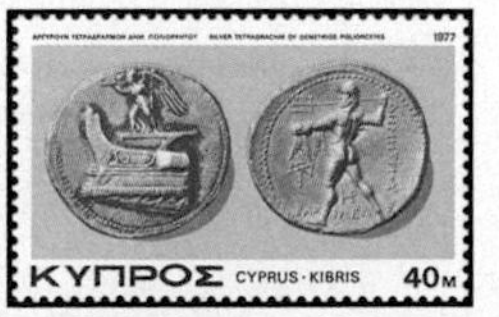

Silver Tetradrachm of Demetrios Poliorcetes — A156

Ancient Coins of Cyprus: 10m, Bronze coin of Emperor Trajan. 60m, Silver Tetradrachm of Ptolemy VIII. 100m, Gold octadrachm of Arsinoe II.

1977, June 13 **Unwmk.** *Perf. 14*

479	A156	10m multicolored	.20	.20
480	A156	40m multicolored	.25	.20
481	A156	60m multicolored	.35	.30
482	A156	100m multicolored	.50	.50
		Nos. 479-482 (4)	1.30	1.20

Archbishop Makarios (1913-1977), Pres. of Cyprus — A157

20m, Archbishop in full vestments. 250m, Head.

Perf. 13x14

1977, Sept. 10 Litho. Unwmk.

483	A157	20m multicolored	.20	.20
484	A157	60m multicolored	.25	.20
485	A157	250m multicolored	.95	.85
		Nos. 483-485 (3)	1.40	1.25

Handicrafts A158

Sputnik over Earth — A159

Designs: 40m, Map of Cyprus. 60m, Gold medals and sports emblems.

Perf. 13½x12

1977, Oct. 17 Wmk. 344

486	A158	20m multicolored	.20	.20
487	A158	40m multicolored	.20	.20
488	A158	60m multicolored	.25	.25
489	A159	80m multicolored	.35	.30
		Nos. 486-489 (4)	1.00	.95

Revitalization of handicrafts (20m); Man and the biosphere (40m); Gold medals won by secondary school students in France for long jump and 200 meter race (60m); 60th anniv. of Bolshevik Revolution (80m).

Nativity A160

Christmas (Children's Drawings): 10m, Three Kings following the star. 150m, Flight into Egypt.

Perf. 14x13½

1977, Nov. 21 Litho. Unwmk.

490	A160	10m multicolored	.20	.20
491	A160	40m multicolored	.20	.20
492	A160	150m multicolored	.60	.55
		Nos. 490-492 (3)	1.00	.95

Demetrios Libertis (1866-1937) — A161

150m, Vasilis Michaelides (1849-1917).

1978, Mar. 6 Wmk. 344 *Perf. 14x13*

493	A161	40m bister & olive	.20	.20
494	A161	150m gray, ver & blk	.60	.55

Cypriot poets.

Chrysorrhogiatissa Monastery — A162

Europa: 75m, Kolossi Castle. 125m, Municipal Library, Paphos.

Perf. 14½x13

1978, Apr. 24 Litho. Unwmk.

495	A162	25m multicolored	*.30*	*.20*
496	A162	75m multicolored	*.80*	*.40*
497	A162	125m multicolored	*1.40*	*.70*
		Nos. 495-497 (3)	*2.50*	*1.30*

Makarios as Archbishop 1950-1977 A163

"The Great Leader" — A164

Archbishop Makarios: 25m, Exiled, Seychelles, 1956-1957. 50m, President of Cyprus, 1960-1977. 75m, Soldier of Christ. 100m, Freedom fighter.

Perf. 14x14½

1978, Aug. 3 Litho. Unwmk.

498	A163	15m multicolored	.20	.20
499	A163	25m multicolored	.20	.20
500	A163	50m multicolored	.25	.25
501	A163	75m multicolored	.35	.35
502	A163	100m multicolored	.50	.50
a.		Strip of 5, #498-502	1.50	1.50

Size: 110x80mm

Imperf

503	A164	300m multicolored	3.50	2.50
		Nos. 498-503 (6)	5.00	4.00

Archbishop Makarios, President of Cyprus.

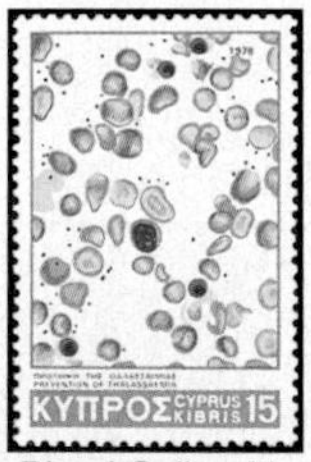

Blood Cells with Low Hemoglobin A165

Bust of Aristotle A166

Heads and Human Rights Emblem A167

Wilbur and Orville Wright, Flyer I A168

Perf. 13x14, 14x13

1978, Oct. 23 Unwmk. Litho.

504	A165	15m multicolored	.20	.20
505	A166	35m multicolored	.20	.20
506	A167	75m black	.35	.35
507	A168	125m multicolored	.50	.50
		Nos. 504-507 (4)	1.25	1.25

Anemia prevention (15m); 2300th birth anniv. of Aristotle (35m); 30th anniv. of Universal Declaration of Human Rights (75m); 75th anniv. of first powered flight (125m).

Kiti Icon Stand — A169

Christmas: 35m, Athienou icon stand. 150m, Omodhos icon stand.

1978, Dec. 4 *Perf. 14x14½*

508	A169	15m multicolored	.20	.20
509	A169	35m multicolored	.20	.20
510	A169	150m multicolored	.75	.75
		Nos. 508-510 (3)	1.15	1.15

Venus Statue from Soli A170

125m, Birth of Venus, by Botticelli (detail).

1979, Mar. 12 Litho. *Perf. 14x13½*

511	A170	75m multicolored	.35	.35
512	A170	125m multicolored	.55	.55

Mail Coach, Envelope and Truck A171

Europa: 75m, Old telephone, dish antenna and satellite. 125m, Steamship, jet and envelopes.

1979, Apr. 30 Litho. *Perf. 14x13½*

513	A171	25m multicolored	*.45*	*.25*
514	A171	75m multicolored	*.80*	*.40*
515	A171	125m multicolored	*2.50*	*1.00*
		Nos. 513-515 (3)	*3.75*	*1.65*

Peacock Wrasse A172

Designs: 50m, Black partridge, vert. 75m, Cyprus cedar, vert. 125m, Mule.

Perf. 13½x12½, 12½x13½

1979, June 25 Litho.

516	A172	25m multicolored	.25	.20
517	A172	50m multicolored	.50	.40
518	A172	75m multicolored	.50	.35
519	A172	125m multicolored	.75	.55
		Nos. 516-519 (4)	2.00	1.50

Children Holding Globe, UNESCO Emblem — A173

Dove, Magnifying Glass, Album A174

Lord Kitchener, Map of Cyprus A175

Smiling Child, IYC Emblem A176

Soccer A177

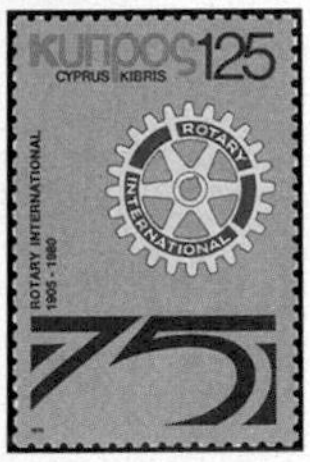

Rotary Emblem — A178

1979, Oct. 1 Litho. *Perf. 12½*

520	A173	15m multicolored	.20	.20
521	A174	25m multicolored	.20	.20
522	A175	50m multicolored	.25	.25
523	A176	75m multicolored	.30	.25
524	A177	100m multicolored	.50	.45
525	A178	125m multicolored	.55	.50
		Nos. 520-525 (6)	2.00	1.85

Intl. Bureau of Education, Geneva, 50th anniv.; Cyprus Philatelic Society, 20th anniv.; Horatio Herbert Kitchener's survey of Cyprus, cent.; IYC; European Soccer Assoc., 25th anniv.; Rotary Club of Cyprus, 75th anniv.

Jesus, Icon, 12th Century — A179

Christmas (Icons): 35m, Nativity, 16th cent. 150m, Virgin and Child, 12th cent.

Perf. 13½x14, 13x14

1979, Nov. 5 Litho.

Sizes: 24x37mm; 27x40mm (35m)

526	A179	15m multicolored	.20	.20
527	A179	35m multicolored	.20	.20
528	A179	150m multicolored	.50	.40
		Nos. 526-528 (3)	.90	.80

Cyprus No. 1, Nicosia Cancel A180

Cyprus Stamp Centenary: 125m, #3, Kyrenia cancel. 175m, #6, Larnaca cancel. 500m, #1-6.

1980, Mar. 17 Litho. *Perf. 14x13*

529	A180	40m multicolored	.20	.20
530	A180	125m multicolored	.50	.50

531 A180 175m multicolored .75 .75

Size: 105x85mm

Imperf

532 A180 500m multicolored 2.00 2.00
Nos. 529-532 (4) 3.45 3.45

Holy Cross, St. Barnabas Church, Ayiasmati — A181

Europa: 125m, Zenon of Citium, Ny Carsberg Glyptothek, Copenhagen.

1980, Apr. 28 ***Perf. 12½***

533 A181 40m multicolored *.25 .20*
534 A181 125m multicolored *.45 .30*

Sailing, Moscow '80 Emblem A182

1980, June 23 Litho. *Perf. 14x13*

535 A182 40m shown .20 .20
536 A182 125m Swimming .40 .40
537 A182 200m Gymnast .70 .70
Nos. 535-537 (3) 1.30 1.30

22nd Summer Olympic Games, Moscow, July 19-Aug. 3.

Gold Necklace — A183

Clay Amphora — A184

Archaeological finds on Cyprus, 12th cent. B.C. to 3rd cent. A.D. 15m, 40m, 150m, 500m, horiz.

Perf. 13½x14, 14x13½

1980, Sept. 15 Litho. Wmk. 344

538 A183 10m shown .30 .30
539 A184 15m Bronze cow .30 .30
540 A184 25m shown .30 .30
541 A184 40m Lion, gold ring .40 .40
542 A184 50m Bronze cauldron .40 .40
543 A184 75m Stele 1.25 1.25
544 A184 100m Clay jug .90 .90
545 A184 125m Warrior, terracotta bust .90 .90
546 A184 150m Lions attacking bull 1.50 1.50
547 A184 175m Faience and enamel vase 1.00 1.00
548 A184 200m Warrior god, bronze 1.00 1.00
549 A184 500m Stone bowl 1.00 1.00
550 A183 £1 Ivory plaque 1.25 1.25
551 A183 £2 Leda and the swan, mosaic 2.50 2.50
Nos. 538-551 (14) 13.00 13.00

For surcharges see Nos. 584, 600-611.

Cyprus Flag — A185

Archbishop Makarios — A187

Treaty Signing Establishing Republic, 20th Anniversary — A186

1980, Oct. 1 ***Perf. 13½x14, 14x13***

552 A185 40m multicolored .20 .20
553 A186 125m multicolored .45 .45
554 A187 175m multicolored .65 .65
Nos. 552-554 (3) 1.30 1.30

Dove and Woman A188

Perf. 14x13

1980, Nov. 29 Litho. Wmk. 344

555 A188 40m shown .20 .20
556 A188 125m Dove and man .60 .60
a. Pair, #555-556 .80 .80

Intl. Palestinian Solidarity Day.

Pulpit, Tripiotis Church, Nicosia — A189

Christmas: 100m, Iconostatis (Holy Door), Panayia Church, Paralimni. 125m, Pulpit, Ayios Lazaros Church, Larnaca.

1980, Nov. 29 ***Perf. 13½x14***

557 A189 25m multicolored .20 .20

Size: 24x37mm

558 A189 100m multicolored .35 .35

Size: 21x37mm

559 A189 125m multicolored .45 .45
Nos. 557-559 (3) 1.00 1.00

Europa Issue 1981

Folk Dance — A190

1981, May 4 Photo. *Perf. 14*

560 A190 40m shown *.35 .20*
561 A190 175m Dance, diff. *.75 .50*

Self-portrait, by Leonardo Da Vinci — A191

The Last Supper, by Da Vinci — A192

Perf. 13½x14, 12½x13½

1981, June 15 Wmk. 344 Litho.

562 A191 50m shown .40 .30
563 A192 125m shown .85 .70
564 A191 175m Lace pattern, Milan Cathedral 1.25 1.00
Nos. 562-564 (3) 2.50 2.00

Da Vinci's visit to Cyprus, 500th anniv.

Ophrys Kotschyi — A193

Designs: Orchids.

1981, July 6 ***Perf. 13½x14***

565 A193 25m shown .35 .35
566 A193 50m Orchis puntulata .65 .65
567 A193 75m Ophrys argolica elegantis .95 .95
568 A193 150m Epipactis veratrifolia 1.75 1.75
a. Block of 4, #565-568 4.00 4.00

Prince Charles and Lady Diana, St. Paul's Cathedral A194

Perf. 14x13

1981, Sept. 28 Wmk. 344

569 A194 200m multicolored 1.00 1.00

Royal wedding.

Heinrich von Stephan (1831-1897), UPU Founder — A195

World Food Day (Oct. 16) A196

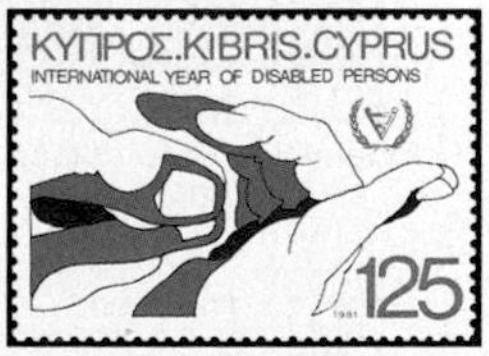

Intl. Year of the Disabled A197

European Campaign for Urban Renaissance — A198

1981, Sept. 28

570 A195 25m multicolored .20 .20
571 A196 40m multicolored .20 .20
572 A197 125m multicolored .55 .55
573 A198 150m multicolored .60 .60
Nos. 570-573 (4) 1.55 1.55

Our Lady of the Angels, Transfiguration Church, Palekhori A199

Christmas (Frescoes): 100m, Christ, Madonna of Arakas Church, Lagoudera, vert. 125m, Baptism of Christ, Our Lady of Assinou Church, Nikitari.

1981, Nov. 16 ***Perf. 12½***

574 A199 25m multicolored .25 .20
575 A199 100m multicolored .65 .35
576 A199 125m multicolored .80 .45
Nos. 574-576 (3) 1.70 1.00

Bathing Aphrodite, Sculpture, Soloi, 250 B.C. — A200

Design: 175m, Aphrodite Emerging from the Water, by Titian, 16th cent.

Perf. 13½x14

1982, Apr. 12 Litho. Wmk. 344

577 A200 125m multicolored .80 .65
578 A200 175m multicolored 1.10 1.00

Europa Issue 1982

Liberation by Emperor Nicephorus II Phocas, 965 A.D. A201

Perf. 12½

1982, May 3 Photo. Unwmk.

579 A201 40m shown *.50 .20*
580 A201 175m Conversion of Sergius Paulus, 45 A.D. *.85 .75*

Mosaic Chrismon A202

Cultural Heritage: 125m, King of Palaepaphos (High Priest of Aphrodite), sculpture, vert. 225m, Theseus Struggling with the Minotaur, mosaic.

1982, July 5 Litho. Wmk. 344

581 A202 50m multicolored .20 .20
582 A202 125m multicolored .60 .60
583 A202 225m multicolored 1.10 1.10
Nos. 581-583 (3) 1.90 1.90

No. 543 Surcharged

1982, Sept. 6 Litho. *Perf. 13½x14*

584 A184 100m on 75m multi .60 .60

Scouting Year A203

Christmas A204

Perf. 13½x12½, 12½x13½

1982, Nov. 8 Wmk. 344

585 A203 100m Emblem, horiz. .50 .50
586 A203 125m Baden-Powell .60 .60
587 A203 175m Camp site, horiz. .80 .80
Nos. 585-587 (3) 1.90 1.90

Perf. 12½, 13½x14 (100m)

1982, Dec. 6

Designs: 25m, 250m, Christ Giving Holy Communion (bread, 25m: wine, 250m) to the Apostles, St. Neophytos Monastery Church, Paphos, horiz. 100m, Chalice, Church of St. Savvas, Nicosia.

588 A204 25m multicolored .20 .20
589 A204 100m multicolored .40 .40
590 A204 250m multicolored 1.00 1.00
Nos. 588-590 (3) 1.60 1.60

A204a

1983, Mar. 14 ***Perf. 14x13½***

591 A204a 50m Cyprus Forest Industries, Ltd. .20 .20
592 A204a 125m Mosaic, 3rd cent. .35 .35
593 A204a 150m Dancers .45 .45
594 A204a 175m Royal Exhibition Building, Melbourne .50 .50
Nos. 591-594 (4) 1.50 1.50

Commonwealth Day.

Europa A205

50m, Cyprosyllabic script funerary stele, 6th cent. B.C. 200m, Copper ore, Enkomi ingot, 1400-1250 BC, bronze jug, 2nd cent.

1983, May 3 **Photo.** ***Perf. 14½x14***

595 A205 50m multicolored *.25* .20
596 A205 200m multicolored *.75* *.50*

Local Butterflies A206

Wmk. 344

1983, June 28 **Litho.** ***Perf. 12½***

597 A206 60m Pararge aegeria .45 .45
598 A206 130m Aricia medon .90 .90
599 A206 250m Glaucopsyche paphos 1.75 1.75
Nos. 597-599 (3) 3.10 3.10

Nos. 538-549 Surcharged

Perf. 13½x14, 14x13½

1983, Oct. 3 **Litho.** **Wmk. 344**

600 A183 1c on 10m multi .20 .20
601 A184 2c on 15m multi .20 .20
602 A184 3c on 25m multi .20 .20
603 A184 4c on 40m multi .20 .20
604 A184 5c on 50m multi .25 .25
605 A184 6c on 75m multi .25 .25
606 A184 10c on 100m multi .45 .45
607 A184 13c on 125m multi .65 .65
608 A184 15c on 150m multi .75 .75
609 A184 20c on 200m multi 1.00 1.00
610 A184 25c on 175m multi 1.40 1.40
611 A184 50c on 500m multi 2.40 2.40
Nos. 600-611 (12) 7.95 7.95

Electricity Authority of Cyprus, 30th Anniv. — A207

World Communications Year — A208

Intl. Maritime Org., 25th Anniv. — A209

Universal Declaration of Human Rights, 35th Anniv. — A210

Nicos Kazantzakis, 100th Birth Anniv. — A211

Archbishop Makarios III, 70th Birth Anniv. — A212

1983, Oct. 31 **Litho.** ***Perf. 13½x14***

612 A207 3c multicolored .20 .20
613 A208 6c multicolored .20 .20
614 A209 13c multicolored .40 .40
615 A210 15c multicolored .45 .45
616 A211 20c multicolored .65 .65
617 A212 25c multicolored .80 .80
Nos. 612-617 (6) 2.70 2.70

Christmas — A213

Designs: 4c, Belfry, St. Lazaros Church, Larnaca. 13c, Belfry, St. Varvara Church, Kaimakli, Nicosia. 20c, Belfry, St. Ioannis Church, Larnaca.

1983, Dec. 12 ***Perf. 12½x14***

618 A213 4c multicolored .20 .20
619 A213 13c multicolored .70 .70
620 A213 20c multicolored 1.00 1.00
Nos. 618-620 (3) 1.90 1.90

Waterside Cafe at the Marina, Larnaca — A214

19th Century engravings. Size of 6c: 41x27mm; 75c, 110x85mm.

Perf. 14½x14 (6c), 14, Imperf. (75c)

1984, Mar. 6

621 A214 6c shown .20 .20
622 A214 20c Bazaar, Larnaca .65 .65
623 A214 30c East Gate, Nicosia .95 .95
624 A214 75c St. Lazarus Church Interior, Larnaca 2.50 2.50
Nos. 621-624 (4) 4.30 4.30

Europa (1959-1984) — A215

1984, Apr. 30 **Wmk. 344** ***Perf. 12½***

625 A215 6c multicolored *.40* *.20*
626 A215 15c multicolored *.90* *.75*

1984 Summer Olympics A216

1984, June 18 **Litho.** ***Perf. 14***

627 A216 3c Running .20 .20
628 A216 4c Olympic column .20 .20
629 A216 13c Swimming .60 .60
630 A216 20c Gymnastics .90 .90
Nos. 627-630 (4) 1.90 1.90

Turkish Invasion, 10th Anniv. A217

1984, July 20 **Litho.** ***Perf. 14x13½***

631 A217 15c Prisoners, barbed wire .45 .45
632 A217 20c Map .60 .60

Cyprus Philatelic Society, 25th Anniv. — A218

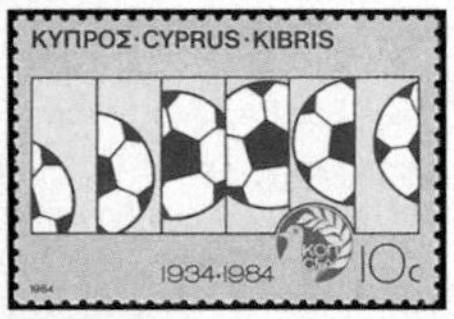

Cyprus Soccer Assoc., 50th Anniv. A219

George Papanicolaou (1883-1962), Cancer Researcher — A220

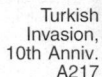

Medieval Map A221

1984, Oct. 15 **Wmk. 344** ***Perf. 12½***

633 A218 6c multicolored .25 .25
634 A219 10c multicolored .45 .45
635 A220 15c multicolored .80 .80
636 A221 25c multicolored 1.50 1.50
Nos. 633-636 (4) 3.00 3.00

Intl. Symposium of Cyprus Cartography and First Intl. Symposium on Medieval Paleography (25c).

Christmas — A222

1984, Nov. 26 **Litho.** ***Perf. 12½***

637 A222 4c St. Mark .30 .30
638 A222 13c Gospel page (St. Mark) 1.00 1.00
639 A222 20c St. Luke 1.50 1.50
Nos. 637-639 (3) 2.80 2.80

Landscapes — A223

Perf. 15x14, 14x15

1985, Mar. 18 **Litho.**

640 A223 1c Autumn at Platania .20 .65
641 A223 2c Ayia Napa Monastery .20 .65
642 A223 3c Phine Village .20 .65
643 A223 4c Kykko Monastery .20 .35
644 A223 5c Beach at Makronissos .20 .20
645 A223 6c Village Street, Omodhos, vert. .20 .20
646 A223 10c Sea view .35 .35
647 A223 13c Water sports .45 .45
648 A223 15c Beach at Protaras .55 .55
649 A223 20c Forestry, vert. .65 .65
650 A223 25c Sunrise at Protaras, vert. 1.00 .85
651 A223 30c Village houses, Pera Orinis 1.40 1.00
652 A223 50c Apollo Hylates Sanctuary 2.75 1.25
653 A223 £1 Troodos Mountain, vert. 5.50 2.25
654 A223 £5 Personification of Autumn, Dionyssos House, vert. 19.00 17.00
Nos. 640-654 (15) 32.85 27.05

For surcharges see Nos. 684-685, 712.

Europa A224

6c, Ceramic figures playing the double flute, lyre and tambourine, 7th-6th cent. B.C. 15c, Cypriot violin, lute, flute, the Fourth Women's Dance from the Cyprus Suite.

1985, May 6 **Litho.** ***Perf. 12½***

655 A224 6c multicolored *.60* *.40*
656 A224 15c multicolored *1.40* *1.10*

Republic of Cyprus, 25th Anniv. — A225

UN 40th Anniv. — A229

Natl. Liberation Movement, 30th Anniv. — A226

Intl. Youth Year A227

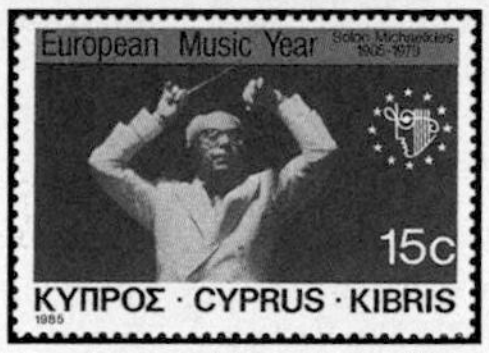

Solon Michaelides (1905-1979), Conductor, European Music Year — A228

Perf. 14½ (#657), 14½x14, 15 (#661)
1985, Sept. 23 — Litho.

657 A225 4c multicolored .30 .30
658 A226 6c multicolored .45 .45
659 A227 13c multicolored .95 .95
660 A228 15c multicolored 1.10 1.10
661 A229 20c multicolored 1.40 1.40
Nos. 657-661 (5) 4.20 4.20

Christmas — A230

Murals of the St. Ioannis Lampadistis Monastery, Kalopanyiotis: 4c, Virgin Mary's Visit to Elizabeth. 13c, The Nativity. 20c, The Candlemas, Church of Our Lady of Assinous, Nikitari.

1985, Nov. 18 — Litho. — *Perf. 12½*

662 A230 4c multicolored .35 .35
663 A230 13c multicolored 1.00 1.00
664 A230 20c multicolored 1.65 1.65
Nos. 662-664 (3) 3.00 3.00

Hellenistic Platinum Spoon A231

Designs: 20c, Ionian helmet, foot of a sculpture. 25c, Union of Eros and Intellect personified, abstract. 30c, Statue profile.

1986, Feb. 17 — *Perf. 15x14*

665 A231 15c multicolored .90 .90
666 A231 20c multicolored 1.25 1.25
667 A231 25c multicolored 1.60 1.60
668 A231 30c multicolored 2.00 2.00
a. Souv. sheet of 4, #665-668 17.50 17.50
Nos. 665-668 (4) 5.75 5.75

Construction of the New Archaeological Museum, Nicosia. Department of Antiquities, 50th anniv. No. 668a sold for £1.

Europa Issue

Mouflon, Cedar Trees A232

1986, Apr. 28 — Litho. — *Perf. 14x13*

669 A232 7c shown *.40 .35*
670 A232 17c Flamingos, Larnaca Salt Lake *1.50 1.25*

Seashells A233

1986, July 1 — *Perf. 14x13½*

671 A233 5c Chlamys pesfelis .45 .45
672 A233 7c Charonia variegata .55 .55
673 A233 18c Murex brandaris 1.40 1.40
674 A233 25c Cypraea spurca 1.90 1.90
Nos. 671-674 (4) 4.30 4.30

Overseas Cypriots Year A234

Halley's Comet A235

Anniversaries and events.

Perf. 13½x13
1986, Oct. 13 — Litho. — Wmk. 344

675 A234 15c multicolored 1.25 1.25
676 A235 18c shown 1.75 1.75
677 A235 18c Comet tail, Edmond Halley 1.75 1.75
a. Pair, #676-677 3.50 3.50
Nos. 675-677 (3) 4.75 4.75

No. 677a has continuous design.

Road Safety A236

1986, Nov. 10 — *Perf. 14x13*

678 A236 5c Pedestrian crossing .75 .75
679 A236 7c Helmet, motorcycle controls 1.25 1.25
680 A236 18c Seatbelt, rearview mirror 3.00 3.00
Nos. 678-680 (3) 5.00 5.00

Intl. Peace Year, Christmas A237

Nativity frescoes (details): 5c, Church of Panayia tou Araka. 15c, Church of Panayia tou Moutoulla. 17c, Church of St. Nicholaos tis Steyis.

1986, Nov. 24 — *Perf. 13½x14*

681 A237 5c multicolored .50 .50
682 A237 15c multicolored 1.50 1.50
683 A237 17c multicolored 1.90 1.90
Nos. 681-683 (3) 3.90 3.90

Nos. 645 and 647 Surcharged

Perf. 14x15, 15x14
1986, Oct. 13 — Litho. — Wmk. 344

684 A223 7c on 6c multi 1.00 1.00
685 A223 18c on 13c multi 2.00 2.00

Miniature Sheet

Troodos Churches on UNESCO World Heritage List — A238

Churches and frescoes: a, Assinou, Nikitari. b, Moutoulla, Moutoullas. c, Podithou, Galata. d, Ayios Ioannis Lampadistis, Kalopanayiotis. e, Timios Stavros, Pelentri. f, Stavros Ayiasmati, Platanistasa. g, Archangelos Pedoula, Pedoulas. h, Ayios Nicolaos tis Steyis, Kakopetria. i, Araka, Lagoudera.

Perf. 12½
1987, Apr. 22 — Photo. — Unwmk.

686 Sheet of 9 11.00 11.00
a.-i. A238 15c any single 1.10 1.10

Europa Issue

Modern Architecture A239

Perf. 14x13½
1987, May 11 — Litho. — Wmk. 344

687 A239 7c Central Bank of Cyprus *.50 .40*
688 A239 18c Cyprus Communications Authority *1.00 .90*

Ships Named Kyrenia A240

1987, Oct. 3

689 A240 2c The Kyrenia, Kyrenia Castle .50 .30
690 A240 3c Kyrenia II, Perama Shipyard .70 .75
691 A240 5c Kyrenia II, Paphos .90 .50
692 A240 17c Kyrenia II, NY Harbor 1.90 1.50
Nos. 689-692 (4) 4.00 3.05

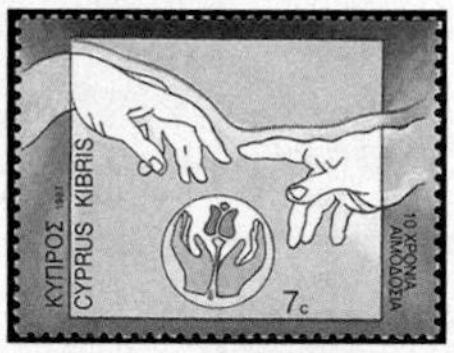

Blood Donation Coordinating Committee, 10th Anniv. — A241

European Campaign for Countryside — A242

TROODOS '87 — A243

Perf. 14x13½
1987, Nov. 2 — Litho. — Wmk. 344

693 A241 7c multicolored .60 .55
694 A242 15c multicolored 1.40 1.25
695 A243 20c multicolored 2.00 1.75
Nos. 693-695 (3) 4.00 3.55

Christmas A244

1987, Nov. 30 — *Perf. 14*

696 A244 5c Babe in a manger .40 .40
697 A244 15c Ornament 1.40 1.40
698 A244 17c Fruit bowl 1.75 1.75
Nos. 696-698 (3) 3.55 3.55

Cyprus Customs Union in Cooperation with the EEC — A245

Perf. 13x13½
1988, Jan. 11 — Wmk. 344

699 A245 15c Natl. and EEC flags 1.25 1.25
700 A245 18c Maps 1.60 1.60

A246

Europa (Communication and transportation): No. 701, Electronic mail (Intelpost). No. 702, Cellular telephone system. No. 703, Cyprus Airways, technology vs. ecology (jet, 3 flamingos). No. 704, Cyprus Airways (jet, 4 flamingos).

1988, May 9 — *Perf. 14x14½*

701 A246 7c multicolored *.55 .45*
702 A246 7c multicolored *.55 .45*
a. Pair, #701-702 *1.25 1.25*
703 A246 18c multicolored *2.00 1.50*
704 A246 18c multicolored *2.00 1.50*
a. Pair, #703-704 *5.00 5.00*
Nos. 701-704 (4) 5.10 3.90

1988 Summer Olympics, Seoul — A247

Unwmk.
1988, June 27 — Photo. — *Perf. 12*
Granite Paper

705 A247 5c Sailing .45 .30
706 A247 7c Track .50 .50
707 A247 10c Marksmanship .55 .55
708 A247 20c Judo 1.25 1.25
Nos. 705-708 (4) 2.75 2.60

Non-Aligned Foreign Minister's Conference — A248

Designs: 10c, Natl. coat of arms. 50c, Jawaharlal Nehru, Tito, Gamal Abdel Nasser and Makarios III (1913-77).

Perf. 14x13½

1988, Sept. 5 Litho. Wmk. 344

709	A248	1c shown	.20	.20
710	A248	10c multicolored	.50	.50
711	A248	50c multicolored	2.75	2.75
		Nos. 709-711 (3)	3.45	3.45

No. 643 Surcharged

1988, Oct. 3 Litho. *Perf. 15x14*

712 A223 15c on 4c multi 1.75 1.40

A249

A250

Christmas.

Perf. 13½x14

1988, Nov. 28 Litho. Wmk. 344

713	A249	5c Candlemas	.45	.25
714	A249	15c Madonna and child	.95	.30
715	A249	17c Adoration of the Magi	1.40	1.40
		Nos. 713-715 (3)	2.80	1.95

1988, Dec. 10

716 A250 25c lt ultra & int blue 1.25 1.25

UN Declaration of Human Rights, 40th anniv.

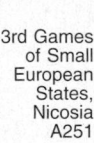

3rd Games of Small European States, Nicosia A251

Perf. 13½

1989, Apr. 10 Litho. Unwmk.

717	A251	1c Discus	.40	.30
718	A251	5c Javelin	.40	.30
719	A251	15c Wrestling	.90	.70
720	A251	18c Running	1.10	1.10

Size: 110x80mm

Imperf

721	A251	£1 Mythological woman, laurel, bird	8.00	8.00
		Nos. 717-721 (5)	10.80	10.40

Various Children's Games A252

Perf. 13x13½

1989, May 8 Litho. Unwmk.

722	A252	7c multi (5 boys)	*.85*	*.75*
723	A252	7c multi (6 boys)	*.85*	*.75*
a.		Pair, #722-723	*1.90*	*1.90*
724	A252	18c multi (6 boys)	*1.25*	*1.10*
725	A252	18c multi (5 boys)	*1.25*	*1.10*
a.		Pair, #724-725	*2.75*	*2.75*
		Nos. 722-725 (4)	4.20	3.70

Europa.

French Revolution, Bicent. — A253

Perf. 11½

1989, July 7 Litho. Unwmk.

Granite Paper

726 A253 18c multicolored 1.50 1.50

A254

A255

Perf. 13½

1989, Sept. 4

727	A254	15c multicolored	.70	.65
728	A255	30c multicolored	1.50	1.40

15c for Interparliamentary Union, cent. 30c for 9th Non-Aligned Summit Conf., Belgrade.

Apiculture A256

Annivs. & Events — A257

1989, Oct. 15 *Perf. 13½x14*

729	A256	3c Honeycomb	.55	.30
730	A256	10c Gathering nectar	1.00	.60
731	A256	15c Gathering nectar, diff.	1.25	.60
732	A256	18c Queen, worker bees	1.50	1.50
		Nos. 729-732 (4)	4.30	3.00

1989, Nov. 13

Designs: 3c, Armenian earthquake. 5c, Cyprus Philatelic Society. 7c, European Cancer Year. 17c, World Food Day.

733	A257	3c multicolored	.40	.40
734	A257	5c multicolored	.55	.30
735	A257	7c multicolored	.95	.95
736	A257	17c multicolored	1.40	1.40
		Nos. 733-736 (4)	3.30	3.05

A258

A259

Mosaics, 3rd-5th Cent. A260

Details: 1c, Winter, from *The Four Seasons,* House of Dionysos. 2c, Personification of Crete, from *Theseus Slaying the Minotaur,* Villa of Theseus. 3c, Centaur and Maenad, from *The Dionysiac Procession,* House of Aion, vert. 4c, *Poseidon and Amymone,* House of Dionysos. 5c, Leda, from *Leda and the Swan,* House of Aion. 7c, Apollon, from *Apollo and Marsyas,* House of Aion. 10c, Hermes and Dionysos, from *Hermes Presenting Dionysos to Tropheus,* House of Aion, vert. 15c, Cassiopeia, from *Cassiopeia and the Nereids,* House of Aion. 18c, *Orpheus Playing the Lyre,* House of Orpheus. 20c, Nymphs preparing bath, from *Hermes Presenting Dionysos to Tropheus,* vert. 25c, Amazon holding double ax and reins, House of Orpheus, vert. 40c, Doris, one of 3 Nereids in *Cassiopeia and the Nereids.* 50c, Hercules and the lion, from *The First Labor of Hercules,* House of Orpheus. £1, *Apollon and Daphne,* House of Dionysos. £3, Cupid hunting, Villa of Theseus.

Perf. 13, 13x13½ (2c, 4c, 18c, 40c), 13½x13 (3c, 10c, 20c, 25c)

1989, Dec. 29

737	A258	1c multicolored	.40	1.25
738	A259	2c multicolored	.50	1.25
739	A259	3c multicolored	.65	1.50
740	A259	4c multicolored	.85	1.50
741	A258	5c multicolored	.85	.30
742	A258	7c multicolored	1.00	.35
743	A259	10c multicolored	1.25	.40
744	A258	15c multicolored	2.10	.65
745	A259	18c multicolored	2.10	.70
746	A259	20c multicolored	2.50	1.10
747	A259	25c multicolored	2.50	1.10
748	A259	40c multicolored	3.50	2.25

Perf. 13½x14

749	A260	50c multicolored	2.75	2.25
750	A260	£1 multicolored	5.50	4.50
751	A260	£3 multicolored	12.50	12.00
		Nos. 737-751 (15)	38.95	31.10

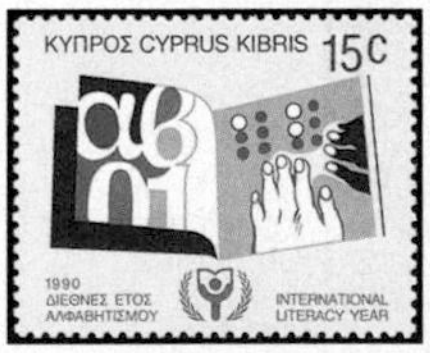

UNESCO World Literacy Year — A261

83rd Interparliamentary Conference, Nicosia — A262

Lions Europa Forum A263

Anniversaries & events.

1990, Apr. 3 *Perf. 14x13½*

752	A261	15c multicolored	.80	.80
753	A262	17c multicolored	.95	.95
754	A263	18c multicolored	1.25	1.25
		Nos. 752-754 (3)	3.00	3.00

Europa A264

Post Offices.

1990, May 10 Litho. *Perf. 13x13½*

755	A264	7c Paphos	*1.00*	*.45*
756	A264	18c Limassol City Center	*1.75*	*1.25*

European Year of Tourism — A265

Designs: 5c, Hotel and Catering Institute, 25th anniv. 7c, Holy Church of St. Lazarus, 1100th anniv. 15c, Female silhouette, butterflies. 18c, Male silhouette, birds.

1990, July 9 *Perf. 14*

757	A265	5c multicolored	.65	.60
758	A265	7c multicolored	.85	.80
759	A265	15c multicolored	2.25	1.75
760	A265	18c multicolored	2.60	2.60
		Nos. 757-760 (4)	6.35	5.75

Republic of Cyprus, 30th Anniv. A266

1990, Sept. 29 Photo. *Perf. 11½*

761	A266	15c Sun	.85	.60
762	A266	17c shown	1.10	.70
763	A266	18c Fish	1.40	.80
764	A266	40c Birds, flowers	3.00	3.00

Size: 90x90mm

Imperf

765	A266	£1 Stylized bird	6.50	6.50
		Nos. 761-765 (5)	12.85	11.60

Flowers — A267

Christmas — A268

1990, Nov. 5 Litho. *Perf. 13½x13*

766	A267	2c Chionodoxa lochiae	.40	*.70*
767	A267	3c Pancrayium maritimum	.60	*.70*
768	A267	5c Paeonia mascula	.85	.60
769	A267	7c Cyclamen cyprium	1.10	.90
770	A267	15c Tulipa cypria	2.25	2.00
771	A267	18c Crocus cyprius	2.50	2.50
		Nos. 766-771 (6)	7.70	7.40

1990, Dec. 3 *Perf. 13½x14*

772	A268	5c Nativity	.90	.30
773	A268	15c Virgin and Child	1.90	.45
774	A268	17c Nativity, diff.	2.25	1.90
		Nos. 772-774 (3)	5.05	2.65

Mosaics From Kanakaria Church — A269

1991, Mar. 28 Photo. *Perf. 12*
Granite Paper

775 A269 5c Archangel .80 .20
776 A269 15c Christ Child .85 .75
777 A269 17c St. James 1.75 1.75
778 A269 18c St. Matthew 2.00 2.00
Nos. 775-778 (4) 5.40 4.70

Europa A270

1991, May 6 Litho. *Perf. 13x13½*

779 A270 7c Spacecraft Ulysses *.75 .40*
780 A270 18c Spacecraft Giotto *1.60 1.10*

Oenanthe Cypriaca (Cyprus Wheatear) A271

1991, July 4 Litho. *Perf. 13½*

781 A271 5c Juvenile bird 1.10 .50
782 A271 7c Autumn plumage 1.25 .50
783 A271 15c Male bird 1.50 .75
784 A271 30c Female bird 2.50 2.50
Nos. 781-784 (4) 6.35 4.25

UN High Commissioner for Refugees, 40th Anniv. — A272

1991, Oct. 7 Litho. *Perf. 14x13½*

785 A272 5c shown .40 .25
786 A272 15c Legs 1.50 .75
787 A272 18c Faces 1.90 1.90
Nos. 785-787 (3) 3.80 2.90

Christmas A273

A274

1991, Nov. 25 Litho. *Perf. 13½*

788 A273 5c Nativity scene .40 .25
789 A273 15c St. Basil .95 .85
790 A273 17c Baptism of Jesus 1.25 1.25
a. Strip of 3, #788-790 3.00 3.00

Strips of 3 are from sheets of 9.

1992, Apr. 3 Litho. *Perf. 12*
Granite Paper

791 A274 10c Swimming .95 .50
792 A274 20c Long jump 1.50 1.00
793 A274 30c Running 2.10 2.10
794 A274 35c Discus 2.40 2.40
Nos. 791-794 (4) 6.95 6.00

1992 Summer Olympics, Barcelona.

Expo '92, Seville A275

10th Youth Under 16 European Soccer Tournament — A276

Opening of University of Cyprus A277

1992, Apr. 20 Litho. *Perf. 14*

795 A275 20c multicolored 2.00 .95
796 A276 25c multicolored 2.10 1.25
797 A277 30c multicolored 2.10 2.10
Nos. 795-797 (3) 6.20 4.30

Discovery of America, 500th Anniv. A278

1992, May 29 Litho. *Perf. 13x13½*

798 A278 10c Map *1.00 .90*
799 A278 10c Embarkation at Palos *1.00 .90*
a. Pair, #798-799 *2.25 2.25*
800 A278 30c Three ships *1.50 1.25*
801 A278 30c Columbus *1.50 1.25*
a. Pair, #800-801 *3.25 3.25*
Nos. 798-801 (4) 5.00 4.30

Europa.

Reptiles A279

Designs: 7c, Chamaeleo chamaeleon. 10c, Lacerta laevis troodica. 15c, Mauremys caspica. 20c, Coluber cypriensis.

1992, Sept. 14 Litho. *Perf. 14x13½*

802 A279 7c multicolored 1.10 .40
803 A279 10c multicolored 1.25 .65
804 A279 15c multicolored 1.75 1.10
805 A279 20c multicolored 2.00 2.00
Nos. 802-805 (4) 6.10 4.15

Intl. Maritime and Shipping Conference — A280

Unwmk.
1992, Nov. 9 Litho. *Perf. 14*

806 A280 50c multicolored 4.25 4.25

Christmas A281

Church wall paintings: 7c, , "Virgin Mary Greeting Elizabeth," Church of Timios Stavros, Pelendri. 15c, "The Virgin and Child," Church of Panayia tou Araka. 20c, "Holy Mother Odigitria," Church of Ayios Nicolaos tis Steyis.

1992, Nov. 9 *Perf. 13½x14*

807 A281 7c multicolored .65 .35
808 A281 15c multicolored 1.10 .75
809 A281 20c multicolored 1.75 1.75
Nos. 807-809 (3) 3.50 2.85

A282

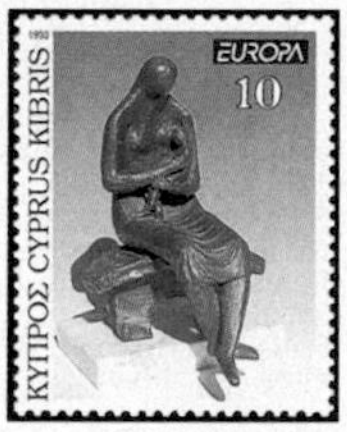

A283

1993, Feb. 15 Litho. *Perf. 14*

810 A282 10c multicolored 1.00 .80

Pancyprian Gymnasium, cent.

1993, Apr. 3 *Perf. 13½x14, 14x13½*

Europa: 10c, Bronze sculpture, Motherhood, by N. Dymiotis (1930-1990). 30c, Applique, Motherhood, by Savva (1924-1968), horiz.

811 A283 10c multicolored *.90 .65*
812 A283 30c multicolored *1.60 1.25*

13th European Cup for Women Athletes A284

Scouting in Cyprus, 80th Anniv. — A285

Water Skiing Moufflon Encouragement Cup — A286

Archbishop Makarios III, 80th Anniv. of Birth — A287

Perf. 13½x14, 14x13½
1993, May 24 Litho.

813 A284 7c multicolored .60 .40
814 A285 10c multicolored .80 .55
815 A286 20c multicolored 1.40 1.40
a. Inscribed "MUFFLON" 25.00
816 A287 25c multicolored 2.00 2.00
Nos. 813-816 (4) 4.80 4.35

Fish — A288

1993, Sept. 6 Litho. *Perf. 14x13½*

817 A288 7c Holocentrus ruber .60 .30
818 A288 15c Scorpaena scrofa .95 .60
819 A288 20c Serranus scriba 1.10 1.10
820 A288 30c Balistes capriscus 2.10 2.10
Nos. 817-820 (4) 4.75 4.10

Maritime Cyprus A289

1993, Oct. 4 *Perf. 14*

821 A289 25c multicolored 2.50 2.50

12th Commonwealth Summit Conference — A290

1993, Oct. 4 *Perf. 14x13½*

822 A290 35c red brown & tan 2.40 2.40
823 A290 40c olive brown & tan 3.00 3.00

Christmas A291

7c, Carved wooden cross, Stavrovouni Monastery. 20c, Crucifixion, cross from Lefkara Church. 25c, Nativity, cross from Pedoulas Church.

1993, Nov. 22 Litho. *Perf. 13½x14*

824 A291 7c multicolored .40 .30
825 A291 20c multicolored .95 .95

Perf. 14x13½

826 A291 25c multi, horiz. 1.40 1.40
Nos. 824-826 (3) 2.75 2.65

Copper Industry A292

Europa: 10c, Early smelting of copper. 30c, Map, boat, copper ingot.

1994, Mar. 1 Litho. *Perf. 13x13½*

827	A292	10c multicolored	*.45*	*.40*
828	A292	30c multicolored	*1.25*	*1.10*

Persons with Special Needs — A293

Intl. Olympic Committee, Cent. — A294

World Gymnasiade, Nicosia — A295

Intl. Year of the Family — A296

1994, May 9 Litho. *Perf. 13*

829	A293	7c multicolored	.65	.35
830	A294	15c multicolored	1.10	.65
831	A295	20c multicolored	1.40	1.40
832	A296	25c multicolored	1.75	1.75
		Nos. 829-832 (4)	4.90	4.15

Turkish Invasion and Occupation of Cyprus, 20th Anniv. — A297

1994, June 27 Litho. *Perf. 14*

833	A297	10c Human rights	.90	.40
834	A297	50c Cultural heritage	3.50	3.50

Trees — A298

7c, Pinus nigra. 15c, Cedrus libani. 20c, Quercus alnifolia. 30c, Arbutus andrachne.

1994, Oct. 10 Litho. *Perf. 13½*

835	A298	7c multicolored	.70	.40
836	A298	15c multicolored	1.10	.75
837	A298	20c multicolored	1.25	1.25
838	A298	30c multicolored	2.00	2.00
		Nos. 835-838 (4)	5.05	4.40

ICAO, 50th Anniv. A299

1994, Nov. 21 Litho. *Perf. 14*

839	A299	30c multicolored	3.00	3.00

Christmas A300

Designs: 7c, Virgin Mary (Vlahernitissa). 20c, Nativity. 25c, Archangel Michael.

1994, Nov. 21 *Perf. 13½*

840	A300	7c multicolored	.75	.40
841	A300	20c multicolored	1.75	1.10
842	A300	25c multicolored	2.00	2.00
		Nos. 840-842 (3)	4.50	3.50

Traditional Costumes — A301

Costumes: 1c, Female, Phapos. 2c, Bridal, Karpess. 3c, Female, Phapos, diff. 5c, Female, Messaoria. 7c, Bridegroom's. 10c, Shepherd's, Messaoria. 15c, Festive female, Nicosia. 20c, Festive female, Karpass. 25c, Female, Mountain-Pitsillia. 30c, Festive female, Karpass, diff. 35c, Rural male. 40c, Plain festive male, Messaoria. 50c, Urban male. £1, Urban festive female, Sarka.

1994, Dec. 27 Litho. *Perf. 13½x13*

843	A301	1c multicolored	.35	.35
844	A301	2c multicolored	.50	.50
845	A301	3c multicolored	.55	.55
846	A301	5c multicolored	.70	.70
847	A301	7c multicolored	.75	.75
848	A301	10c multicolored	1.00	1.00
849	A301	15c multicolored	1.75	1.75
850	A301	20c multicolored	1.75	1.75
851	A301	25c multicolored	2.00	2.00
852	A301	30c multicolored	2.00	2.00
853	A301	35c multicolored	2.00	2.00
854	A301	40c multicolored	2.25	2.25
855	A301	50c multicolored	3.50	3.50
856	A301	£1 multicolored	6.75	6.75
		Nos. 843-856 (14)	25.85	25.85

No. 856 exists inscribed "1998."

Third Intl. Congress of Cypriot Studies — A302

Excavations: 20c, Hearth room, Ashlar building, Paliotaverna. 30c, Hall, Agios Demetrios area, Kalavasos. £1, Old Nicosia Archbishorpic building, 18th cent.

1995, Feb. 27 Litho. *Perf. 14*

859	A302	20c multicolored	1.40	1.40
860	A302	30c multicolored	2.00	2.00

Size: 107x71mm

Imperf

861	A302	£1 multicolored	6.25	6.25
		Nos. 859-861 (3)	9.65	9.65

A303

A304

Liberation Monument, Nicosia: a, People walking left. b, Statue of Liberty, prisoners leaving prison. c, People walking right.

1995, Mar. 31 Litho. *Perf. 13x14*

862		Strip of 3	4.75	4.75
a.-c.		A303 20c any single	1.50	1.50

No. 862 is a continuous design.

Formation of EOKA (Natl. Organization of Cypriot Struggle), 40th anniv.

1995, May 8 Litho. *Perf. 13½*

Europa: 10c, Concentration camp prisoners, dove, rainbow, map of Europe. 30c, Prisoner, dove.

863	A304	10c multicolored	*1.00*	*.75*
864	A304	30c multicolored	*2.00*	*1.60*

Liberation of the concentration camps, 50th anniv.

Health A305

7c, Proper nutrition, exercise. 10c, Fight against AIDS. 15c, Fight against illegal drugs. 20c, Stop smoking campaign.

1995, June 26 Litho. *Perf. 13½*

865	A305	7c multi, vert.	.35	.30
866	A305	10c multi	.80	.80
867	A305	15c multi	.85	.85
868	A305	20c multi, vert.	1.25	1.25
		Nos. 865-868 (4)	3.25	3.20

European Cultural Month A306

1995, Sept. 18 Litho. *Perf. 13x13½*

869	A306	20c shown	.95	.95
870	A306	25c Map of Europe, building	1.25	1.25

Souvenir Sheet

Eurofilex '95 A307

Designs: a, Dove carrying letter, stars. b, Stars, exhibition emblem. Illustration reduced.

1995, Sept. 18 Litho. *Perf. 14*

871		Sheet of 2	9.50	9.50
a.-b.		A307 50c any single	4.25	4.25

A limited number were surcharged £5 on each stamp and sold at "Europhilex '95" on Oct. 27 and 28, 1995.

UN, 50th Anniv. A308

Volleyball, Cent. — A309

European Conservation Year — A310

World Clay Target Shooting Championships — A311

Perf. 13x13½, 13½x13

1995, Oct. 24 Litho.

872	A308	10c multicolored	.65	.65
873	A309	15c multicolored	1.00	.80
874	A310	20c multicolored	1.40	1.10
875	A311	25c multicolored	1.75	1.75
		Nos. 872-875 (4)	4.80	4.30

Christmas A312

Various reliquaries, Kykko Monastery.

1995, Nov. 27 Litho. *Perf. 13½x13*

876	A312	7c multicolored	.60	.45
877	A312	20c multicolored	1.40	1.10
878	A312	25c multicolored	1.75	1.75
		Nos. 876-878 (3)	3.75	3.30

A313

A314

A315

Anniversaries and Events — A316

1996, Jan. 4 Litho. *Perf. 13½x13*

879 A313 10c multicolored .90 .70
880 A314 20c multicolored 1.60 1.10
881 A315 35c multicolored 2.40 2.40
882 A316 40c multicolored 2.50 2.50
Nos. 879-882 (4) 7.40 6.70

Pancyprian Organization of Large Families, 25th anniv. (#879). Motion pictures, cent. (#880). UNICEF, 50th anniv. (#881). 13th Conf. of Commonwealth Speakers and Presiding Officers (#882).

Portraits of Women
A317 A318

1996, Apr. 8 Litho. *Perf. 14*

883 A317 10c multicolored *.75 .40*
884 A318 30c multicolored *1.50 1.10*

Europa.

1996 Summer Olympics, Atlanta
A319

1996, June 10 Litho. *Perf. 13*

885 A319 10c High jump .90 .35
886 A319 20c Javelin 1.25 .70
887 A319 25c Wrestling 1.75 1.00
888 A319 30c Swimming 2.10 2.10
Nos. 885-888 (4) 6.00 4.15

Mills of Cyprus — A320

1996, Sept. 23 Litho. *Perf. 13*

889 A320 10c Watermill .95 .70
890 A320 15c Olivemill 1.40 1.00
891 A320 20c Windmill 1.50 1.40
892 A320 25c Handmill 2.25 2.25
Nos. 889-892 (4) 6.10 5.35

Icons, Religious Landmarks
A321

Designs: No. 893, Icon of Our Lady of Iberia, Moscow. No. 894, Holy Monastery of Stavrovouni, Cyprus. No. 895, Icon of St. Nicholas, Cyprus. No. 896, Iveron Mother of God Resurrection Gate, Moscow.

1996, Nov. 13 Litho. *Perf. 11½*

893 A321 30c multicolored 2.40 2.40
894 A321 30c multicolored 2.40 2.40
895 A321 30c multicolored 2.40 2.40
896 A321 30c multicolored 2.40 2.40
a. Block of 4, #893-896 10.00 10.00

See Russia No. 6356.

Christmas
A322

Paintings from Church of the Virgin of Asinou: 7c, Detail from Nativity. 20c, Virgin Mary between Archangels Gabriel and Michael. 25c, Christ bestowing blessings, vert.

1996, Dec. 2 *Perf. 13x13½, 13½x13*

897 A322 7c multicolored 1.00 .50
898 A322 20c multicolored 2.25 1.25
899 A322 25c multicolored 2.75 2.75
Nos. 897-899 (3) 6.00 4.50

Easter
A323

1997, Mar. 24 Litho. *Perf. 13x13½*

900 A323 15c The Last Supper 1.25 .65
901 A323 25c The Crucifixion 1.75 1.75

A324

A325

1997, Mar. 24 *Perf. 13½x13*

902 A324 30c multicolored 4.00 3.75

European Men's Clubs Basketball Cup finals.

1997, May 5 Litho. *Perf. 13½x13*

Europa (Stories and Legends): 30c, Man in red cape fighting Death, eagle above.

903 A325 15c shown *.75 .45*
904 A325 30c multicolored *1.25 1.00*

Insects
A326

10c, Oedipoda miniata. 15c, Acherontia atropos. 25c, Daphnis nerii. 35c, Ascalaphus macaronius.

1997, June 30 Litho. *Perf. 13x13½*

905 A326 10c multicolored .95 .55
906 A326 15c multicolored 1.40 .75
907 A326 25c multicolored 1.90 1.50
908 A326 35c multicolored 2.40 2.40
Nos. 905-908 (4) 6.65 5.20

Archbishop Makarios III (1913-77), 1st Pres. of Cyprus Republic
A327

1997, Aug. 1 Litho. *Perf. 13x13½*

909 A327 15c multicolored 1.50 1.50

Christmas
A328

Frescoes from Church of Ayios Ioannis Lambadestis: 10c, Nativity. 25c, Magi on way to Bethlehem. 30c, Flight into Egypt.

1997, Nov. 17 Litho. *Perf. 13½x13*

910 A328 10c multicolored .95 .65
911 A328 25c multicolored 2.40 1.40
912 A328 30c multicolored 2.75 2.75
Nos. 910-912 (3) 6.10 4.80

Minerals
A329

1998, Mar. 9 Litho. *Perf. 13x13½*

913 A329 10c Green jasper .60 .40
914 A329 15c Iron pyrite .90 .65
915 A329 25c Gypsum 1.40 1.40
916 A329 30c Chalcedony 1.75 1.75
Nos. 913-916 (4) 4.65 4.20

1998 World Cup Soccer Championships, France — A330

1998, May 4 Litho. *Perf. 14*

917 A330 35c multicolored 3.00 1.75

Europa
A331

Festivals, holidays: 15c, "Katakklysmos" Larnaca. 30c, People watching proclamation of independence, 1960.

1998, May 4

918 A331 15c multicolored *.80 .50*
919 A331 30c multicolored *1.75 1.40*

Ovis Gmelini Ophion
A332

World Wildlife Fund: No. 920, Male, female, calf. No. 921, Group running. No. 922, Male up close. No. 923, Male with front legs up on rock, one grazing.

1998, June 22 Litho. *Perf. 13x13½*

920 A332 25c multicolored 1.50 1.50
921 A332 25c multicolored 1.50 1.50
922 A332 25c multicolored 1.50 1.50
923 A332 25c multicolored 1.50 1.50
a. Block of 4, #920-923 6.25 6.25

Issued in sheets of 16.

World Stamp Day
A333

1998, Oct. 9 Litho. *Perf. 14*

924 A333 30c multicolored 2.75 2.75
a. Booklet pane of 8 24.00
Complete booklet, #924a 26.00

A334 A335

1998, Oct. 9

925 A334 50c multicolored 2.25 2.25

Universal Declaration of Human Rights, 50th anniv.

1998, Nov. 16 Litho. *Perf. 14*

Christmas (Scenes from paintings in the Church of the Virgin of Théosképasti, Kalopanayiotis): 10c, The Annunciation. 25c, The Nativity. 30c, Baptism of Christ.

926 A335 10c multicolored .40 .40
927 A335 25c multicolored 1.10 1.10
928 A335 30c multicolored 3.25 3.25
a. Souvenir sheet, #926-928 4.75 4.75
Nos. 926-928 (3) 4.75 4.75

Mushrooms — A336

10c, Pleurotus eryngii. 15c, Lactarius deliciosus. 25c, Sparassis crispa. 30c, Morchella elata.

1999, Mar. 4 Litho. *Perf. 13½x13*

929 A336 10c multicolored .50 .50
930 A336 15c multicolored 1.00 .65
931 A336 25c multicolored 1.50 1.50
932 A336 30c multicolored 1.60 1.60
Nos. 929-932 (4) 4.60 4.25

Natl. Parks and Nature Preserves
A337

1999, May 6 Litho. *Perf. 14*

933 A337 15c Tripylos Reserve .80 .50
934 A337 30c Lara Reserve 1.40 1.00
a. Booklet pane, 4 each #933-934 *9.00*
Complete booklet, #934a *10.00*

Europa.

Council of Europe, 50th Anniv. A338

1999, May 6

935 A338 30c multicolored 2.00 2.00

4000 Years of Hellenism — A339

a, Sanctuary of Apollo Hylates, Kourion. b, Mycenaean "Krater of the Warriors," Athens. c, Mycenaean amphoral krater, Cyprus Museum. d, Sanctuary of Apollo Epikourios, Delphi.

1999, June 28 Litho. *Perf. 13½x13*

936 A339 25c Block of 4, #a.-d. 5.75 5.75

See Greece No. 1938.

UPU, 125th Anniv. A340

1999, Sept. 30 Litho. *Perf. 14*

937 A340 15c shown 1.10 .80
938 A340 35c "125" 2.50 1.90

Souvenir Sheet

Maritime Cyprus Shipping Conference A341

Cyprus flag and: a, Container ship. b, Binoculars, chart, cap. c, Ship with yellow stripe on tower. d, Tanker.

1999, Sept. 30

939 A341 25c Sheet of 4, #a.-d. 5.00 5.00

Souvenir Sheet

Turkish Invasion of Cyprus, 25th Anniv. — A342

Illustration reduced.

1999, Nov. 11 Litho. *Imperf.*

940 A342 30c multicolored 2.25 2.25

A343

A344

1999, Nov. 11 *Perf. 14*

941 A343 10c Angel .65 .50
942 A343 25c Magi 1.25 1.10
943 A343 30c Madonna and child 1.40 1.40
Nos. 941-943 (3) 3.30 3.00

Christmas.

Souvenir Sheet

2000, Mar. 30 Litho. *Perf. 13¼x13*

Miss Universe 2000: a, 15c, Woman, stars. b, 35c, Armless nude statue of woman.

944 A344 Sheet of 2, #a.-b. 2.00 2.00

Jewelry — A345

Various pieces of jewelry. #945-952 vert.

2000, Mar. 30 Litho. *Perf. 14*

945 A345 10c multi .40 .40
946 A345 15c multi .55 .55
947 A345 20c multi .75 .75
948 A345 25c multi .95 .95
949 A345 30c multi 1.10 1.10
950 A345 35c multi 1.25 1.25
951 A345 40c multi 1.50 1.50
952 A345 50c multi 2.00 2.00
953 A345 75c multi 2.75 2.75
954 A345 £1 multi 3.75 3.75
955 A345 £2 multi 7.50 7.50
956 A345 £3 multi 11.50 11.50
Nos. 945-956 (12) 34.00 34.00

Cyprus Red Cross, 50th Anniv. A346

2000, May 9 Litho. *Perf. 13x13¼*

957 A346 15c multi 2.00 2.00

Memorial to Heroes of 1955-59 Independence Struggle — A347

2000, May 9 *Perf. 13¼x13*

958 A347 15c multi 1.75 1.75

Europa, 2000
Common Design Type

2000, May 9 *Perf. 14*

959 CD17 30c multi *1.40 1.00*

World Meteorological Org., 50th Anniv. — A348

2000, May 9

960 A348 30c multi 2.00 2.00

European Convention of Human Rights, 50th Anniv. A349

2000, June 29 Litho. *Perf. 13x13¼*

961 A349 30c multi 2.75 2.75

Churches Damaged Under Turkish Occupation A350

Designs: 10c, Monastery of Antifonitis, Kalograia, vert. 15c, Church of St. Themonianos, Lysi, vert. 25c, Church of Panagia Kanakaria, Lytrhagkomi. 30c, Avgasida Monastery Church, Milia.

Perf. 13¼x13, 13x13¼

2000, June 29

962 A350 10c multi .80 .50
963 A350 15c multi 1.10 .70
964 A350 25c multi 1.50 1.40
965 A350 30c multi 1.75 1.75
Nos. 962-965 (4) 5.15 4.35

2000 Summer Olympics, Sydney A351

Designs: 10c, Archery. 15c, Pommel horse. 25c, Diving. 35c, Trampoline.

2000, Sept. 14 Litho. *Perf. 13x13½*

966-969 A351 Set of 4 5.25 5.25

Christmas — A352

Gospel covers: 10c, Annunciation. 25c, Nativity. 30c, Baptism of Jesus.

2000, Nov. 2 *Perf. 13½x13*

970-972 A352 Set of 3 4.25 4.25

Pavlos Liasides (1901-85), Poet — A353

2001, Mar. 12 Litho. *Perf. 13¼x13*

973 A353 13c multi 1.00 .55

Commonwealth Day, 25th Anniv. — A354

2001, Mar. 12 *Perf. 13x13¼*

974 A354 30c multi 2.25 2.25

UN High Commissioner for Refugees, 50th Anniv. — A355

2001, Mar. 12

975 A355 30c multi 2.25 2.25

Europa A356

Designs: 20c, Bridge over Diarizos River. 30c, Akaki River.

2001, May 3

976-977 A356 Set of 2 *2.25 1.40*
977a Booklet pane, 4 each #976-977 *9.50*
Booklet, #977a *10.50*

Crabs A357

Designs: 13c, Parthenope massena. 20c, Calappa granulata. 25c, Ocypode cursor. 30c, Pagurus bernhardus.

2001, June 7

978-981 A357 Set of 4 6.50 6.50

Loukis Akritas (1909-65), Writer A358

Christmas A359

2001, Oct. 25 Litho. *Perf. 13½x13*

982 A358 20c multi 1.50 .85

2001, Oct. 25

Holy Monastery of Macheras, 800th anniv.: 13c, Icon of Madonna. 25c, Monastery building. 30c, Crucifix.

983-985 A359 Set of 3 3.75 3.75

Cats — A360

No. 986, 20c: a, Red brown panel. b, Green panel.
No. 987, 25c: a, Dark brown panel. b, Orange brown panel.
Illustration reduced.

2002, Mar. 21 Litho. *Perf. 13x13½*
Horiz. Pairs, #a-b

986-987 A360 Set of 2 6.00 6.00

Europa — A361

Designs: 20c, Equestrian act. 30c, Tightrope walker.

2002, May 9 *Perf. 13½x13*

988-989 A361 Set of 2 2.25 1.40
a. Booklet pane, 4 each #988-989 9.50 —
Booklet, #989a 10.50

Medicinal Plants A362

Designs: 13c, Myrtus communis. 20c, Lavandula stoechas. 25c, Capparis spinosa. 30c, Ocimum basilicum.

2002, June 13 *Perf. 13x13½*

990-993 A362 Set of 4 6.00 6.00

Mother Teresa (1910-97) — A363

2002, Sept. 12 Litho. *Perf. 13½x13*

994 A363 40c multi 3.25 3.25

Intl. Teachers' Day — A364

No. 995: a, 13c, Blackboard and teachers. b, 30c, Computer and teachers.
Illustration reduced.

2002, Sept. 12 *Perf. 13x13½*

995 A364 Horiz. pair, #a-b 2.75 2.75

Cyprus-Europhilex 02 Philatelic Exhibition — A365

No. 996: a, Seal, 490-470 B.C. (red brown background). b, Silver coin of Timoharis, 5th-4th cent B.C. (blue background) c, Silver coin of Stasioikos, 449 B.C. (yellow background).
No. 997: a, Clay oil lamp, 2nd cent. A.D. (olive green background). b, Clay statue of Europa on a bull, 7th-6th cent. B.C. (yellow background). c, Clay oil lamp, 1st cent. B.C. (lilac background)
No. 998: a, 15th cent. map of eastern Crete and western Cyprus, and statue of Aphrodite, 1st cent. B.C. b, Map of eastern Cyprus, and Abduction of Europe, by Francesco di Giorgio.

2002, Sept. 22

996 Horiz. strip of 3 4.25 4.25
a.-c. A365 20c Any single 1.40 1.40
997 Horiz. strip of 3 6.00 6.00
a.-c. A365 30c Any single 2.00 2.00

Souvenir Sheet

998 Sheet of 2, #a-b 8.75 8.75
a.-b. A365 50c Any single 3.50 3.50

Christmas A366

Wall painting in Church of Metamorphosis Sotiros, Palechori: 13c, Nativity, detail. 25c, Angels, detail. 30c, Entire painting (37x37mm).

Perf. 13x13½, 13¾ (30c)

2002, Nov. 21

999-1001 A366 Set of 3 4.25 4.25

Antique Automobiles A367

No. 1002: a, 20c, 1946 Triumph Roadster 1800. b, 25c, 1917 Ford Model T. c, 30c, 1932 Baby Ford.

2003, Mar. 20 Litho. *Perf. 13x13½*

1002 A367 Vert. strip of 3, #a-c 5.25 5.25

Europa — A368

2003, May 8 *Perf. 13½x13*
Color of Triangles

1003 A368 20c yellow .85 .60
a. Perf. 13½x13¾ on 3 sides 1.50 1.00
1004 A368 30c red 1.25 .90
a. Perf. 13½x13¾ on 3 sides 2.50 1.50
b. Booklet pane, 4 each #1003a-1004a 17.50 —
Complete booklet, #1004b 20.00

European Ministers of Education, 7th Conference — A369

2003, June 12 Litho. *Perf. 13½x13*

1005 A369 30c multi 2.25 2.25

Worldwide Fund for Nature (WWF) — A370

Mediterranean horseshoe bat: a, In flight. b, Close-up. c, Hanging from rock. d, With open mouth.
Illustration reduced.

2003, June 12 *Perf. 13x13½*

1006 A370 25c Block of 4, #a-b 7.50 7.50

Birds of Prey — A371

No. 1007, 20c: a, Eleonora's falcon. b, Eleonora's falcons in flight.
No. 1008, 25c: a, Head of Imperial eagle. b, Imperial eagles in flight.
No. 1009, 30c: a, Owl on branch. b, Owl in flight, eggs.

2003, Sept. 25 Litho. *Perf. 14*
Horiz. pairs, #a-b

1007-1009 A371 Set of 3 8.00 8.00

Famous Men A372

Designs: No. 1010, 5c, Constantinos Spyridakis (1903-76), Education minister. No. 1011, 5c, Tefkros Anthias (1903-68), poet (23x31mm).

Perf. 13x13¼, 13¼x13

2003, Nov. 13

1010-1011 A372 Set of 2 1.00 1.00

Christmas A373

Details of Nativity icon from church in Kourdali: 13c, Angels. 30c, Three Magi on horses. 40c, Entire icon (37x60mm).

Perf. 13¾x13¼, 13¾x14 (40c)

2003, Nov. 13

1012-1014 A373 Set of 3 4.50 4.50

FIFA (Fédération Internationale de Football Association), Cent. — A374

Perf. 13¼x13¾

2004, Mar. 11 Litho.

1015 A374 30c multi 1.75 1.75

UEFA (European Soccer Union), 50th Anniv. — A375

2004, Mar. 11 *Perf. 13¼x13*

1016 A375 30c multi 1.75 1.75

Yiannos Kranidiotis (1947-99), Politician A376

2004, May 1 *Perf. 13¼x13½*

1017 A376 20c multi 1.00 1.00

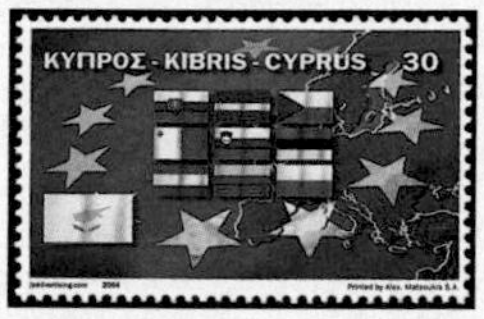

Admission to European Union — A377

2004, May 1 *Perf. 14¼x14*

1018 A377 30c multi 1.75 1.75

Europa A378

Cliff and: 20c, Amphitheater, ship. 30c, Family at seashore, sculpture

2004, May 1 *Perf. 13¾x13¼*

1019 A378 20c multi .80 .50
a. Perf. 13¾ on 3 sides 1.00 .60
1020 A378 30c multi 1.25 .80
a. Perf. 13¾ on 3 sides 1.50 1.00
b. Booklet pane, 4 each #1019a, 1020a 11.50 —
Complete booklet, #1020b 13.00

2004 Summer Olympics, Athens — A379

Designs: 13c, Equestrian. 20c, Runners. 30c, Swimmers. 40c, Athletes, man in robe.
Illustration reduced.

2004, June 10 Litho. *Perf. 13¼x13*

1021-1024 A379 Set of 4 5.25 5.25

Mammals — A380

No. 1025, 20c — Tursiops truncatus: a, Blue background. b, White background.
No. 1026, 30c — Vulpes vulpes indutus: a, Green background. b, White background.
No. 1027, 40c, Lepus europaeus cyprium: a, Orange brown background. b, White background.
Illustration reduced.

2004, Sept. 9 Litho. *Perf. 13¾x13½*
Horiz. Pairs, #a-b

1025-1027 A380 Set of 3 12.50 12.50

Georgios Philippou Pierides (1904-99), Writer — A381

Emilios Chourmouzios (1904-73), Writer — A382

2004, Nov. 11 *Perf. 13¼x13*

1028 A381	5c multi	.40	.40
1029 A382	5c multi	.40	.40

Christmas
A383

Details from icon depicting the birth of Christ, Monastery of Chrysoroyiatissa: 13c, Angels. 30c, Magi on horseback. 40c, Annunciation, vert. (37x60mm).
£1, Adoration of the Shepherds.

Perf. 13¾x13¼, 13¾x14 (40c)

2004, Nov. 11

1030-1032 A383	Set of 3	6.00	6.00

Souvenir Sheet

Perf. 13¾ on 3 Sides

1033 A383	£1 multi	7.00	7.00

No. 1033 contains one 37x38mm stamp.

Carolina Pelendritou, Swimming Gold Medalist at 2004 Paralympics
A384

2005, Mar. 3 **Litho.** *Perf. 13¼x13¾*

1034 A384	20c multi	1.40	1.40

Rotary International, Cent. — A385

2005, Mar. 3

1035 A385	40c multi	2.25	2.25

Natl. Organization of Cypriot Struggle (EOKA), 50th Anniv. — A386

2005, Mar. 3

1036 A386	50c multi	2.75	2.75

Europa — A387

Table with food and: 20c, Purple grapes, sailboat. 30c, Green grapes, steamship.

2005, May 5 *Perf. 13½x13*

White Frame All Around

1037 A387	20c multi	.90	.90
1038 A387	30c multi	1.40	1.40

Booklet Stamps

White Frame on 3 Sides

Perf. 13½ on 3 Sides

1039 A387	20c multi	1.25	.75
1040 A387	30c multi	1.75	1.25
a.	Horiz. pair, #1039-1040	3.25	2.25
b.	Booklet pane, 4 #1040a	13.50	—
	Complete booklet, #1040b	15.00	
	Nos. 1037-1040 (4)	5.30	4.30

Dogs — A388

Designs: 13c, German shepherd. 20c, Hungarian vizsla. 30c, Labrador retriever. 40c, Dalmatian.

2005, June 16 **Litho.** *Perf. 13¼*

1041-1044 A388	Set of 4	5.50	5.50
1044a	Booklet pane, #1041-1044	5.50	—
	Complete booklet, #1044a	5.50	

Christmas
A389

Icons: 13c, Annunciation to the Shepherds. 30c, Adoration of the Magi. 40c, Madonna and Child, vert. (38x60mm).

Perf. 13¼, 13¾x14 (40c)

2005, Nov. 10 **Litho.**

1045-1047 A389	Set of 3	4.25	4.25

Souvenir Sheet

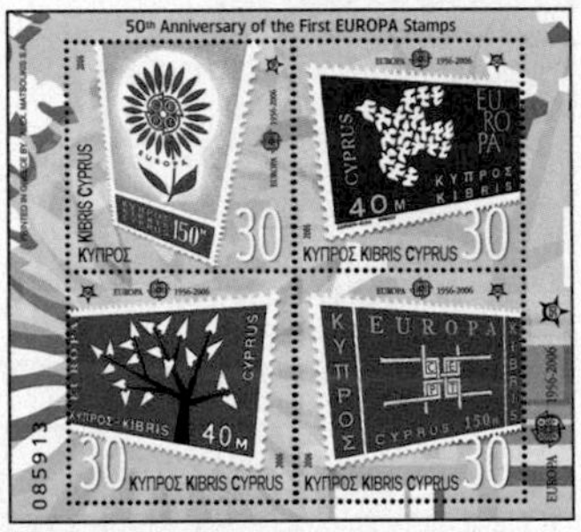

Europa Stamps, 50th Anniv. — A390

No. 1048: a, Cyprus #246. b, Cyprus #202. c, Cyprus #220. d, Cyprus #231.

2006, Feb. 23 **Litho.** *Perf. 13¾*

1048 A390	30c Sheet of 4, #a-d	6.00	6.00

Postal Museum, 25th Anniv.
A391

2006, Mar. 30 *Perf. 13¾x13¼*

1049 A391	25c multi	1.25	1.25

Rembrandt (1606-69), Painter
A392

2006, Mar. 30

1050 A392	40c multi	2.00	2.00

2006 World Cup Soccer Championships, Germany
A393

2006, Mar. 30 *Perf. 13¼x13¾*

1051 A393	50c multi	2.50	2.50

Souvenir Sheet

Folk Dances — A394

No. 1052 — Folk dancers from: a, Cyprus. b, India.

2006, Apr. 12 *Perf. 13x13½*

1052 A394	40c Sheet of 2, #a-b	4.00	4.00

See India No. 2151.

Europa — A395

2006, May 4 *Perf. 13½x13*

1053 A395	30c grn & multi	1.40	1.40
a.	Perf. 13½x13¾ on 3 sides	1.40	1.40
1054 A395	40c red & multi	1.75	1.75
a.	Perf. 13½x13¾ on 3 sides	1.75	1.75
b.	Booklet pane, 4 each #1053a-1054a	13.00	—
	Complete booklet, #1054b	13.00	

Organ Transplantation — A396

2006, June 15 **Litho.** *Perf. 13¼*

1055 A396	13c multi	.65	.65

Fruit — A397

Designs: 20c, Elaeagnus angustifolia. 25c, Mespilus germanica, horiz. 60c, Opuntia ficus barbarica.

Perf. 13¼x13½, 13½x13¼

2006, June 15

1056-1058 A397	Set of 3	5.25	5.25

Fire Trucks
A398

Designs: 13c, Bedford water carrier. 20c, Hino pump water tender. 50c, Bedford ladder truck.

2006, Sept. 14 *Perf. 13¾x13¼*

1059-1061 A398	Set of 3	4.25	4.25

Nicos Nicolaides (1884-1956), Writer — A399

2006, Nov. 16 **Litho.** *Perf. 13½x13*

1062 A399	5c multi	.25	.25

Christmas — A400

Items from Agiou Eleftheriou Church: 13c, Carved wood iconostasis. 30c, Cross. 40c, Bas-relief of cross, spear and sponge.

2006, Nov. 16 *Perf. 13¼x13¾*

1063-1065 A400	Set of 3	4.25	4.25

St. Xenon, the Postman — A401

Illustration reduced.

Litho. & Embossed

2007, Feb. 8 *Imperf.*

1066 A401	£1 multi	4.75	4.75

Echinoderms — A402

No. 1067: a, Antedon mediterranea. b, Centrostephanus longispinus. c, Astropecten jonstoni. d, Ophioderma longicadum.

2007, Feb. 8 **Litho.** *Perf. 13¾x13¼*

1067	Horiz. strip of 4	4.75	4.75
a.-d.	A402 25c Any single	1.10	1.10

Motorcycles A403

Designs: 13c, 1972 Triumph Daytona. 20c, 1941 Matchless. 40c, 1940 BSA. 60c, 1939 Ariel Red Hunter.

2007, Mar. 15
1068-1071 A403 Set of 4 6.25 6.25

Treaty of Rome, 50th Anniv. — A404

2007, May 3 ***Perf. 13¼x13¾***
1072 A404 30c multi 1.40 1.40

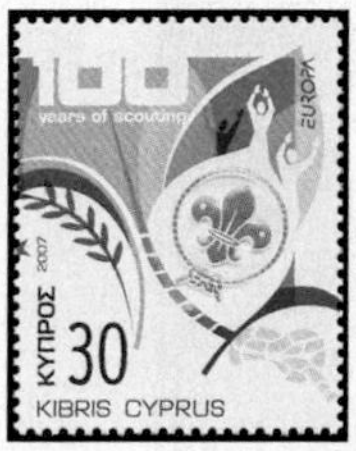

Europa — A405

Scouting emblem in gold, knot in: 30c, Light blue. 40c, Buff.

Litho. & Embossed With Foil Application
2007, May 3
1073-1074 A405 Set of 2 3.25 3.25
1074a Booklet pane, 4 each #1073-1074, perf. on 3 sides 13.00 —
Complete booklet, #1074a 13.00

Scouting, cent.

Social Insurance, 50th Anniv. — A406

No. 1075: a, Text in Greek. b, Text in English.
Illustration reduced.

2007, June 14 Litho. ***Perf. 13x13¼***
1075 A406 40c Horiz. pair, #a-b 3.75 3.75

Miniature Sheet

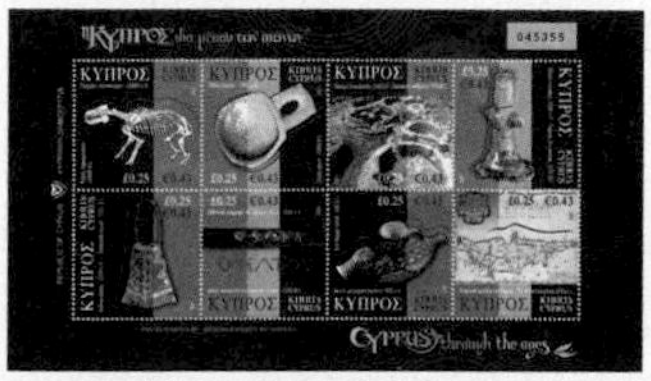

Cyprus Throughout the Ages — A407

No. 1076: a, Skeleton of pygmy hippopotamus, 10,000 B.C. b, Stone vessel, 7000 B.C. c, Choirokoitia Settlement, 7000 B.C. d, Female terracotta figurine, 3000 B.C. e, Terracotta vessel, 2000 B.C. f, Greek inscriptions on bronze skewer, 1000 B.C. g, Bird-shaped vessel, 800 B.C. h, Map of ancient kingdoms of Cyprus.

2007, Oct. 2 ***Perf. 13¾***
1076 A407 25c Sheet of 8, #a-h 9.75 9.75

Neoclassical Buildings A408

Designs: 13c, Limassol District Administration Building. 15c, National Bank of Greece Building, Nicosia. 20c, Archaeological Research Unit Building, Nicosia. 30c, National Art Gallery, Nicosia. 40c, Paphos Municipal Library. 50c, A. G. Leventis Foundation Office Building, Nicosia. £1, Limassol Municipal Library. £3, Phaneromeni Gymnasium, Nicosia.

2007, Oct. 2 ***Perf. 13¾x13½***

1077	A408	13c multi	.65	.65
1078	A408	15c multi	.75	.75
1079	A408	20c multi	1.00	1.00
1080	A408	30c multi	1.50	1.50
1081	A408	40c multi	2.00	2.00
1082	A408	50c multi	2.40	2.40
1083	A408	£1 multi	5.00	5.00
1084	A408	£3 multi	14.50	14.50
		Nos. 1077-1084 (8)	27.80	27.80

Christmas — A409

Murals from Chapel of St. Themonianus, Lysi: 13c, Virgin Mary. 30c, Archangel Gabriel. 40c, Christ Pantocrator (35x45mm).

Perf. 14x13¾, 13¾ (40c)
2007, Nov. 15
1085-1087 A409 Set of 3 4.25 4.25

100 Cents = 1 Euro

Souvenir Sheet

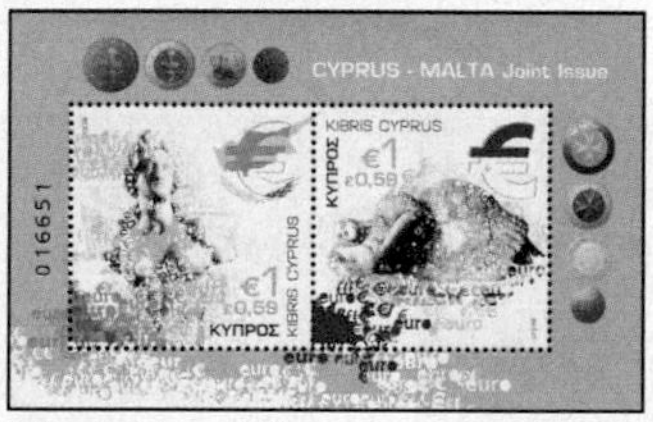

Introduction of Euro Currency — A410

No. 1088: a, Statue of Aphrodite, map of Cyprus. b, Sleeping Lady statue.

2008, Jan. 1 Litho. ***Perf. 13¾***
1088 A410 €1 Sheet of 2, #a-b 6.00 6.00

See Malta No. 1329.

Anemone Flowers — A411

Variously colored Anemone coronaria flowers with background colors of: 26c, Blue. 34c, Red. 51c, Green. 68c, Yellow orange.

2008, Mar. 6 ***Perf. 13¼x13¾***
1089-1092 A411 Set of 4 5.50 5.50

Europa — A412

Designs: 51c, Closed and open envelopes. 68c, Envelopes and mail boxes.

2008, May 2 Litho. ***Perf. 13¼x13¾***
1093-1094 A412 Set of 2 3.75 3.75
1094a Booklet pane, 4 each #1093-1094, perf. 13¼x13¾ on 3 sides 15.00 —
Complete booklet, #1094a 15.00

Souvenir Sheet

Fourth Intl. Congress of Cypriot Studies, Nicosia — A413

2008, May 2 ***Perf. 13¾ on 3 Sides***
1095 A413 85c multi 2.75 2.75

12th Francophone Summit, Quebec — A414

2008, June 5 Litho. ***Perf. 13¾***
1096 A414 85c multi 2.75 2.75

2008 Summer Olympics, Beijing A415

Designs: 22c, Sailboarding. 34c, High jump. 43c, Tennis. 51c, Shooting.

2008, June 5 ***Perf. 13x13¼***
1097-1100 A415 Set of 4 4.75 4.75

Cyprus Throughout the Years Type of 2007

Miniature Sheet

No. 1101: a, Coin from Archaic period, 750 B.C.-480 B.C. b, Ship from Archaic period. c, Bust of Kimon the Athenian and ship, Classical period, 480 B.C.-310 B.C. d, Tomb of the Kings, Hellenistic period, 310 B.C.-30 B.C. e, Coin from Hellenistic period. f, Painting of St. Paul from Roman period, 30 B.C.-A.D. 324. g, Bust of Septimus Severus from Roman period. h, Granting of church privileges from Early Byzantine period, 324-841.

2008, Oct. 2 Litho. ***Perf. 13¾***
1101 A407 43c Sheet of 8, #a-h 9.50 9.50

Christmas — A416

Icons from church, Pelendri: 22c, Archangel Gabriel. 51c, Archangel Michael. 68c, Madonna and Child.

2008, Nov. 13 ***Perf. 13¼x13***
1102-1104 A416 Set of 3 3.75 3.75

POSTAL TAX STAMPS

Catalogue values for unused stamps in this section are for Never Hinged items.

Unless otherwise stated, Cyprus postal tax stamps are for the Refugee Fund.

No. 352 Surcharged

Perf. 12x12½
1974, Dec. 2 **Wmk. 344**
RA1 A104 10m on 5m multi .30 .30

Old Woman and Child — PT1

Child and Barbed Wire — PT2

1974, Oct. 1 ***Perf. 12½x13½***
RA2 PT1 10m gray & black .30 .30

Perf. 13x12½
1977, Jan. 10 Litho. Wmk. 344
RA3 PT2 10m black .40 .40

Inscribed 1984

1984, June 18 ***Perf. 13x12½***
RA4 PT2 1c black .40 .40

There are two types of No. RA4.

Inscribed 1988 — PT3

1988-2006 ***Perf. 13x12½***

Design Size 22x28mm

RA5 PT3 1c black & pale gray .40 .40

Perf. 11½x12

RA6 PT3 1c Inscribed 1989 .40 .40
RA7 PT3 1c Inscribed 1990 .40 .40

Unwmk.

Perf. 13

RA8 PT3 1c Inscribed 1991 .40 .40
RA9 PT3 1c Inscribed 1992 .40 .40
RA10 PT3 1c Inscribed 1993 .40 .40
RA11 PT3 1c Inscribed 1994 .40 .40

Perf. 14½x13¾

Design Size 21x24.5mm

RA12	PT3 1c Inscribed 1995	.40	.40
RA13	PT3 1c Inscribed 1996	.40	.40
RA14	PT3 1c Inscribed 1997	.40	.40
RA15	PT3 1c Inscribed 1998	.40	.40
RA16	PT3 1c Inscribed 1999	.40	.40
RA17	PT3 1c Inscribed 2000	.40	.40
RA18	PT3 1c Inscribed 2001	.40	.40

Size: 22x27mm

Perf. 12¾

RA19	PT3 1c Inscribed 2002	.40	.40
RA20	PT3 1c Inscribed 2003	.40	.40

Perf. 12¾x13

RA21	PT3 1c Inscribed 2004	.40	.40
RA22	PT3 1c Inscribed 2005	.40	.40
RA23	PT3 1c Inscribed 2006	.40	.40

Perf. 13½x14

RA24	PT3 1c Inscribed 2007	.20	.20
	Nos. RA5-RA25 (21)	8.00	8.00

Issued: #RA5, 9/12/88; #RA6, 9/4/89; #RA7, 9/29/90; #RA8, 10/7/91; #RA9, 11/9/92; #RA10, 1993; #RA11, 11/21/94; #RA12, 10/24/95; #RA13, 6/10/96; #RA14, 6/30/97; #RA15, 1998; #RA16, 1999; #RA17, 2000; #RA18, 2001. #RA19, 2002. #RA19, 2003. #RA20, 2003. #RA21, 11/11/04. #RA22, 6/16/05. #RA23, 5/4/06. #RA24, 3/15/07.

Child and Barbed Wire With Denomination in Euro Currency — PT4

2008, Jan. 1 Litho. ***Perf. 13½x14***

RA25	PT4 2c dk gray & gray	.20	.20

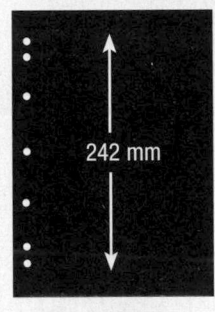

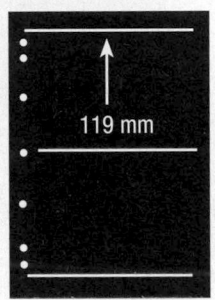

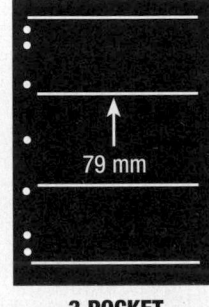

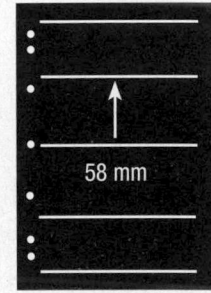

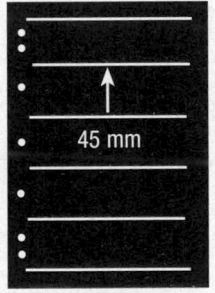

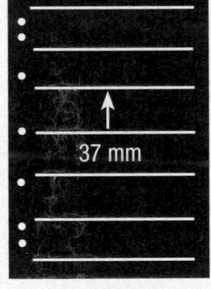

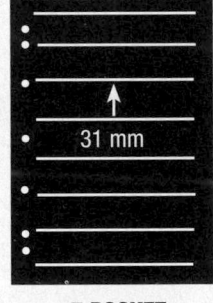

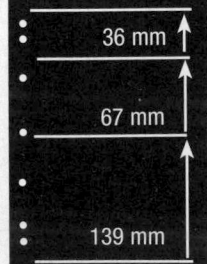

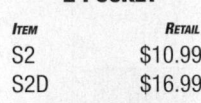

CYRENAICA

ˌsir-ə-ˈnā-ə-kə

LOCATION — In northern Africa bordering on the Mediterranean Sea
GOVT. — Italian colony
AREA — 75,340 sq. mi.
POP. — 225,000 (approx. 1934)
CAPITAL — Bengasi (Benghazi)

Cyrenaica was an Italian Colony. In 1949 Great Britain granted the Amir of Cyrenaica autonomy in internal affairs. Cyrenaica was incorporated into the kingdom of Libya in 1951.

100 Centesimi = 1 Lira
1000 Milliemes = 1 Pound (1950)

Catalogue values for unused stamps in this country are for Never Hinged items, beginning with Scott 65 in the regular postage section, Scott J1 in the postage due section.

Used values in italics are for postally used stamps. CTO's sell for about the same as unused, hinged stamps.

Watermark

Wmk. 140 — Crown

Propagation of the Faith Issue

Italy Nos. 143-146 Overprinted

1923, Oct. 24 Wmk. 140 *Perf. 14*

1	A68	20c ol grn & brn org	8.00	*40.00*
2	A68	30c claret & brn org	8.00	*40.00*
3	A68	50c vio & brn org	4.75	*47.50*
4	A68	1 l bl & brn org	4.75	*60.00*
		Nos. 1-4 (4)	25.50	*187.50*
		Set, never hinged	64.00	

Fascisti Issue

Italy Nos. 159-164 Overprinted in Red or Black

1923, Oct. 29 Unwmk. *Perf. 14*

5	A69	10c dk grn (R)	8.00	*14.50*
6	A69	30c dk vio (R)	8.00	*14.50*
7	A69	50c brn car	8.00	*16.00*

Wmk. 140

8	A70	1 l blue	8.00	*40.00*
9	A70	2 l brown	8.00	*47.50*
10	A71	5 l blk & bl (R)	8.00	*55.00*
		Nos. 5-10 (6)	48.00	*187.50*
		Set, never hinged	140.00	

Manzoni Issue

Italy Nos. 165-170 Overprinted in Red

1924, Apr. 1 *Perf. 14*

11	A72	10c brn red & blk	13.00	*52.50*
12	A72	15c bl grn & blk	13.00	*52.50*
13	A72	30c blk & slate	13.00	*52.50*
14	A72	50c org brn & blk	13.00	*52.50*
15	A72	1 l bl & blk	80.00	*300.00*
a.		Double overprint	975.00	
		Never Hinged	1,450.	
16	A72	5 l vio & blk	525.00	*2,250.*
		Nos. 11-16 (6)	657.00	*2,760.*
		Set, never hinged	1,600.	

Vertical overprints on Nos. 11-14 are essays. On Nos. 15-16 the overprint is vertical at the left.

All examples of #15a are poorly centered.

Victor Emmanuel Issue

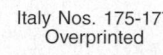

Italy Nos. 175-177 Overprinted

1925-26 Unwmk. *Perf. 11*

17	A78	60c brn car	.80	*8.00*
18	A78	1 l dark blue	.80	*8.00*
19	A78	1.25 l dk bl ('26)	3.25	*16.00*
a.		Perf. 13½	240.00	*600.00*
		Never hinged	475.00	
		Nos. 17-19 (3)	4.85	*32.00*
		Set, never hinged	12.00	

Issue dates: Nov. 1925, July 1926.

Saint Francis of Assisi Issue

Italian Stamps of 1926 Overprinted

1926, Apr. 12 Wmk. 140 *Perf. 14*

20	A79	20c gray green	2.40	*11.00*
21	A80	40c dark violet	2.40	*11.00*
22	A81	60c red brown	2.40	*20.00*

Overprinted in Red

Unwmk.

23	A82	1.25 l dk bl, perf. 11	2.40	*27.50*
24	A83	5 l + 2.50 l ol grn	6.50	*55.00*
		Nos. 20-24 (5)	16.10	*124.50*
		Set, never hinged	40.00	

Volta Issue

Type of Italy 1927, Overprinted

1927, Oct. 10 Wmk. 140 *Perf. 14*

25	A84	20c purple	6.50	*32.50*
26	A84	50c dp org	8.00	*20.00*
27	A84	1.25 l brt bl	13.00	*52.50*
		Nos. 25-27 (3)	27.50	*105.00*
		Set, never hinged	67.50	

#25 exists with overprint omitted. See Italy.

Monte Cassino Issue

Types of 1929 Issue of Italy, Overprinted in Red or Blue

1929, Oct. 14

28	A96	20c dk grn (R)	4.75	*17.50*
29	A96	25c red org (Bl)	4.75	*17.50*
30	A98	50c + 10c crim (Bl)	4.75	*20.00*
31	A98	75c + 15c ol brn (R)	4.75	*20.00*
32	A96	1.25 l + 25c dk vio (R)	11.00	*36.00*
33	A98	5 l + 1 l saph (R)	11.00	*40.00*

Overprinted in Red

Unwmk.

34	A100	10 l + 2 l gray brn	11.00	*55.00*
		Nos. 28-34 (7)	52.00	*206.00*
		Set, never hinged	130.00	

Royal Wedding Issue

Type of Italian Stamps of 1930 Overprinted

1930, Mar. 17 Wmk. 140

35	A101	20c yel grn	1.60	*4.75*
36	A101	50c + 10c dp org	1.25	*8.00*
37	A101	1.25 l + 25c rose red	1.25	*16.00*
		Nos. 35-37 (3)	4.10	*28.75*
		Set, never hinged	10.00	

#35 exists with overprint omitted. See Italy.

Ferrucci Issue

Types of Italian Stamps of 1930, Overprinted in Red or Blue

1930, July 26

38	A102	20c violet (R)	4.75	*4.75*
39	A103	25c dk grn (R)	4.75	*4.75*
40	A103	50c black (R)	4.75	*9.75*
41	A103	1.25 l dp bl (R)	4.75	*17.50*
42	A104	5 l + 2 l dp car	9.75	*32.50*
		Nos. 38-42 (5)	28.75	*69.25*
		Set, never hinged	70.00	

Virgil Issue

Types of Italian Stamps of 1930 Overprinted in Red or Blue

1930, Dec. 4

43	A106	15c vio blk	1.25	*8.00*
44	A106	20c org brn (Bl)	1.25	*3.25*
45	A106	25c dk grn	1.25	*3.25*
46	A106	30c lt brn (Bl)	1.25	*3.25*
47	A106	50c dl vio	1.25	*3.25*
48	A106	75c rose red (Bl)	1.25	*7.75*
49	A106	1.25 l gray bl	1.25	*8.00*

Unwmk.

50	A106	5 l + 1.50 l dk vio	3.50	*40.00*
51	A106	10 l + 2.50 l ol brn (Bl)	3.50	*60.00*
		Nos. 43-51 (9)	15.75	*136.75*
		Set, never hinged	39.00	

Saint Anthony of Padua Issue

Types of Italian Stamps of 1931 Overprinted in Blue or Red

1931, May 7 Wmk. 140

52	A116	20c brown (Bl)	1.60	*17.50*
53	A116	25c green (R)	1.60	*6.50*
54	A118	30c gray brn (Bl)	1.60	*6.50*
55	A118	50c dl vio (Bl)	1.60	*6.50*
56	A120	1.25 l slate bl (R)	1.60	*17.50*

Overprinted like Nos. 23-24 in Red or Black

Unwmk.

57	A121	75c black (R)	1.60	*32.50*
58	A122	5 l + 2.50 l dk brn	6.50	*67.50*
		Nos. 52-58 (7)	16.10	*154.50*
		Set, never hinged	40.00	

Carabineer
A1

1934, Oct. 16 Photo. Wmk. 140

59	A1	5c dk ol grn & brn	4.00	*20.00*
60	A1	10c brn & blk	4.00	*20.00*
61	A1	20c scar & indigo	4.00	*16.00*
62	A1	50c pur & brn	4.00	*16.00*
63	A1	60c org brn & ind	4.00	*24.00*
64	A1	1.25 l dk bl & grn	4.00	*40.00*
		Nos. 59-64 (6)	24.00	*136.00*
		Set, never hinged	60.00	

2nd Colonial Art Exhibition held at Naples. See Nos. C24-C29.

Catalogue values for unused stamps in this section, from this point to the end of the section, are for Never Hinged items.

Autonomous State

Senussi Warrior
A2 A3

Perf. 12½

1950, Jan. 16 Unwmk. Engr.

65	A2	1m dark brown	.65	*2.25*
66	A2	2m rose car	.85	*2.00*
67	A2	3m orange	.85	*2.00*
68	A2	4m dark green	4.00	*3.25*
69	A2	5m gray	1.10	*1.25*
70	A2	8m red orange	1.25	*1.50*
71	A2	10m purple	1.25	*1.50*
72	A2	12m red	1.25	*1.50*
73	A2	20m deep blue	1.25	*1.50*
74	A3	50m choc & ultra	6.00	*7.50*
75	A3	100m bl blk & car rose	17.50	*37.50*
76	A3	200m vio & pur	20.00	*60.00*
77	A3	500m dk grn & org	97.50	*120.00*
		Nos. 65-77 (13)	153.45	*241.75*

SEMI-POSTAL STAMPS

Many issues of Italy and Italian Colonies include one or more semipostal denominations. To avoid splitting sets, these issues are generally listed as regular postage unless all values carry a surtax.

Holy Year Issue

Italian Semi-Postal Stamps of 1924 Overprinted in Black or Red

1925, June 1 Wmk. 140 Perf. 12

B1 SP4 20c + 10c dk grn & brn 3.25 *20.00*
B2 SP4 30c + 15c dk brn & brn 3.25 *22.50*
B3 SP4 50c + 25c vio & brn 3.25 *20.00*
B4 SP4 60c + 30c dp rose & brn 3.25 *25.00*
B5 SP8 1 l + 50c dp bl & vio (R) 3.25 *32.50*
B6 SP8 5 l + 2.50 l org brn & vio (R) 3.25 *47.50*
Nos. B1-B6 (6) 19.50 *167.50*
Set, never hinged 48.00

Colonial Institute Issue

"Peace" Substituting Spade for Sword — SP1

1926, June 1 Typo. Perf. 14

B7 SP1 5c + 5c brown 1.00 *8.00*
B8 SP1 10c + 5c olive grn 1.00 *8.00*
B9 SP1 20c + 5c blue grn 1.00 *8.00*
B10 SP1 40c + 5c brown red 1.00 *8.00*
B11 SP1 60c + 5c orange 1.00 *8.00*
B12 SP1 1 l + 5c blue 1.00 *17.50*
Nos. B7-B12 (6) 6.00 *57.50*
Set, never hinged 15.00

Surtax for Italian Colonial Institute.

Types of Italian Semi-Postal Stamps of 1926 Overprinted like Nos. 17-19

1927, Apr. 21 Unwmk. Perf. 11

B13 SP10 40c + 20c dk brn & blk 2.40 *32.50*
B14 SP10 60c + 30c brn red & ol brn 2.40 *32.50*
B15 SP10 1.25 l + 60c dp bl & blk 2.40 *52.50*
B16 SP10 5 l + 2.50 l dk grn & blk 4.00 *72.50*
Nos. B13-B16 (4) 11.20 *190.00*
Set, never hinged 28.00

The surtax on these stamps was for the charitable work of the Voluntary Militia for Italian National Defense.

Allegory of Fascism and Victory — SP2

1928, Oct. 15 Wmk. 140 Perf. 14

B17 SP2 20c + 5c bl grn 2.40 *12.00*
B18 SP2 30c + 5c red 2.40 *12.00*
B19 SP2 50c + 10c purple 2.40 *20.00*
B20 SP2 1.25 l + 20c dk bl 3.25 *24.00*
Nos. B17-B20 (4) 10.45 *68.00*
Set, never hinged 25.00

46th anniv. of the Societa Africana d'Italia. The surtax aided that society.

Types of Italian Semi-Postal Stamps of 1926 Overprinted in Red or Black like Nos. 52-56

1929, Mar. 4 Unwmk. Perf. 11

B21 SP10 30c + 10c red & blk 4.00 *20.00*
B22 SP10 50c + 20c vio & blk 4.00 *24.00*
B23 SP10 1.25 l + 50c brn & bl 4.75 *40.00*
B24 SP10 5 l + 2 l ol grn & blk (Bk) 4.75 *72.50*
Nos. B21-B24 (4) 17.50 *156.50*
Set, never hinged 45.00

Surtax for the charitable work of the Voluntary Militia for Italian Natl. Defense.

Types of Italian Semi-Postal Stamps of 1926 Overprinted in Black or Red like Nos. 52-56

1930, Oct. 20 Perf. 14

B25 SP10 30c + 10c dk grn & bl grn (Bk) 21.00 *37.50*
B26 SP10 50c + 10c dk grn & vio 21.00 *47.50*
B27 SP10 1.25 l + 30c ol brn & red brn 21.00 *60.00*
B28 SP10 5 l + 1.50 l ind & grn 67.50 *175.00*
Nos. B25-B28 (4) 130.50 *320.00*
Set, never hinged 320.00

Surtax for the charitable work of the Voluntary Militia for Italian Natl. Defense.

Sower — SP3

1930, Nov. 27 Photo. Wmk. 140

B29 SP3 50c + 20c ol brn 4.00 *20.00*
B30 SP3 1.25 l + 20c dp bl 4.00 *20.00*
B31 SP3 1.75 l + 20c green 4.00 *22.50*
B32 SP3 2.55 l + 50c purple 6.50 *36.00*
B33 SP3 5 l + 1 l dp car 7.00 *52.50*
Nos. B29-B33 (5) 25.50 *151.00*
Set, never hinged 62.50

25th anniv. of the Italian Colonial Agricultural Institute. The surtax was for the aid of that institution.

AIR POST STAMPS

Air Post Stamps of Tripolitania, 1931, Overprinted in Blue like Nos. 38-42

1932, Jan. 7 Wmk. 140 Perf. 14

C1 AP1 50c rose car 1.60 .40
C2 AP1 60c dp org 4.75 *12.00*
C3 AP1 80c dl vio 4.75 *20.00*
Nos. C1-C3 (3) 11.10 *32.40*
Set, never hinged 28.00

Air Post Stamps of Tripolitania, 1931, Overprinted in Blue

1932, May 12

C4 AP1 50c rose car 1.60 2.00
C5 AP1 80c dull violet 4.75 *22.00*
Set, never hinged 16.00

This overprint was also applied to the 60c, Tripolitania No. C9. The overprinted stamp was never used in Cyrenaica, but was sold at Rome in 1943 by the Postmaster General for the Italian Colonies. Value $5.

Arab on Camel — AP2

Airplane in Flight AP3

1932, Aug. 8 Photo.

C6 AP2 50c purple 9.00 .20
C7 AP2 75c brn rose 9.00 *11.50*
C8 AP2 80c deep blue 9.00 *22.50*
C9 AP3 1 l black 3.75 .20
C10 AP3 2 l green 3.75 *11.50*
C11 AP3 5 l deep car 7.50 *22.50*
Nos. C6-C11 (6) 42.00 *68.40*
Set, never hinged 95.00

For surcharges and overprint see #C20-C23.

Graf Zeppelin Issue

Zeppelin and Clouds forming Pegasus AP4

Zeppelin and Ancient Galley AP5

Zeppelin and Giant Bowman AP6

1933, Apr. 15

C12 AP4 3 l dk brn 8.00 *120.00*
C13 AP5 5 l purple 8.00 *120.00*
C14 AP6 10 l dp grn 8.00 *220.00*
C15 AP5 12 l deep blue 8.00 *240.00*
C16 AP4 15 l carmine 8.00 *240.00*
C17 AP6 20 l black 8.00 *325.00*
Nos. C12-C17 (6) 48.00 *1,265.*
Set, never hinged 120.00

North Atlantic Crossing Issue

Airplane Squadron and Constellations — AP7

1933, June 1

C18 AP7 19.75 l grn & dp bl 16.00 *600.00*
C19 AP7 44.75 l red & indigo 16.00 *600.00*
Set, never hinged 80.00

Type of 1932 Overprinted and Surcharged

1934, Jan. 20

C20 AP3 2 l on 5 l org brn 3.25 *72.50*
C21 AP3 3 l on 5 l yel grn 3.25 *72.50*
C22 AP3 5 l ocher 3.25 *80.00*
C23 AP3 10 l on 5 l rose 4.85 *80.00*
Nos. C20-C23 (4) 14.60 *305.00*
Set, never hinged 32.50

For use on mail to be carried on a special flight from Rome to Buenos Aires.

Transport Plane AP8

Venus of Cyrene AP9

1934, Oct. 9

C24 AP8 25c sl bl & org red 4.00 *20.00*
C25 AP8 50c dk grn & ind 4.00 *16.00*
C26 AP8 75c dk brn & org red 4.00 *16.00*
a. Imperf. 2,000.
Never hinged 2,000.
C27 AP9 80c org brn & ol grn 4.00 *20.00*
C28 AP9 1 l scar & ol grn 4.00 *24.00*
C29 AP9 2 l dk bl & brn 4.00 *40.00*
Nos. C24-C29 (6) 24.00 *136.00*
Set, never hinged 60.00

2nd Colonial Arts Exhib. held at Naples.

AIR POST SEMI-POSTAL STAMPS

King Victor Emmanuel III SPAP1

Wmk. 104

1934, Nov. 5 Photo. Perf. 14

CB1 SPAP1 25c + 10c gray grn 6.50 *14.50*
CB2 SPAP1 50c + 10c brn 6.50 *14.50*
CB3 SPAP1 75c + 15c rose red 6.50 *14.50*
CB4 SPAP1 80c + 15c brn blk 6.50 *14.50*
CB5 SPAP1 1 l + 20c red brn 6.50 *14.50*
CB6 SPAP1 2 l + 20c brt bl 6.50 *14.50*
CB7 SPAP1 3 l + 25c pur 22.50 *72.50*
CB8 SPAP1 5 l + 25c org 22.50 *72.50*
CB9 SPAP1 10 l + 30c dp vio 22.50 *72.50*
CB10 SPAP1 25 l + 2 l dp grn 22.50 *72.50*
Nos. CB1-CB10 (10) 129.00 *377.00*
Set, never hinged 315.00

65th birthday of King Victor Emmanuel III and the non-stop flight, Rome-Mogadiscio.

AIR POST SEMI-POSTAL OFFICIAL STAMP

Type of Air Post Semi-Postal Stamps, 1934, Overprinted Crown and "SERVIZIO DI STATO" in Black

1934, Nov. 5 Wmk. 140 *Perf. 14*

CBO1	SPAP1	25 l + 2 l cop red		*2,750.*
		Never hinged		*4,250.*

POSTAGE DUE STAMPS

Catalogue values for unused stamps in this section are for Never Hinged items.

D1

Perf. 12½

1950, July 1 Unwmk. Engr.

J1	D1	2m dark brown	57.50	*110.00*
J2	D1	4m deep green	57.50	*110.00*
J3	D1	8m scarlet	57.50	*110.00*
J4	D1	10m vermilion	57.50	*120.00*
J5	D1	20m orange yel	57.50	*120.00*
J6	D1	40m deep blue	57.50	*160.00*
J7	D1	100m dark gray	57.50	*225.00*
		Nos. J1-J7 (7)	402.50	*955.00*

CZECHOSLOVAKIA

ˌche-kə-slō-ˈvä-kē-ə

LOCATION — Central Europe
GOVT. — Republic
AREA — 49,355 sq. mi.
POP. — 15,395,970 (1983 est.)
CAPITAL — Prague

The Czechoslovakian Republic consists of Bohemia, Moravia and Silesia, Slovakia and Ruthenia (Carpatho-Ukraine). In March 1939, a German protectorate was established over Bohemia and Moravia, as well as over Slovakia which had meanwhile declared its independence. Ruthenia was incorporated in the territory of Hungary. These territories were returned to the Czechoslovak Republic in 1945, except for Ruthenia, which was ceded to Russia. Czechoslovakia became a federal state on Jan. 2, 1969. On Jan. 1, 1993 Czechoslovakia separated into Slovakia and the Czech Republic. See Volume 5 for the stamps of Slovakia.

100 Haleru = 1 Koruna

Catalogue values for unused stamps in this country are for Never Hinged items, beginning with Scott 142 in the regular postage section, B144 in the semi-postal section, Scott C19 in the air post section, Scott EX1 in the personal delivery section, and Scott J58 in the postage due section, Scott O1 int he officials section, and Scott P14 in the newspaper section.

Watermarks

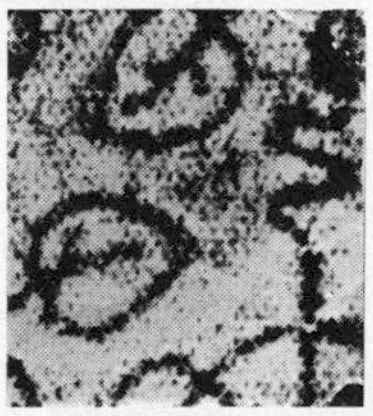
Wmk. 107 — Linden Leaves (Vertical)

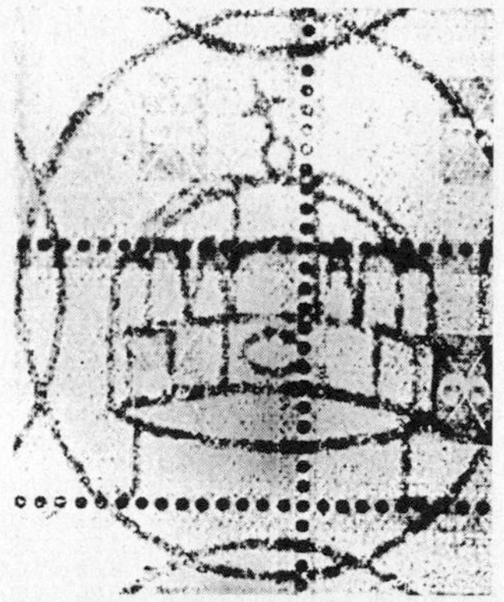
Wmk. 135 — Crown in Oval or Circle, Sideways

Wmk. 136

Wmk. 136a

Wmk. 341 — Striped Ovals

Stamps of Austria overprinted "Ceskoslovenska Republika," lion and "Cesko Slovensky Stat," "Provisorni Ceskoslovenska Vlada" and Arms, and "Ceskoslovenska Statni Posta" and Arms were made privately. A few of them were passed through the post but all have been pronounced unofficial and unauthorized by the Postmaster General.

During the occupation of part of Northern Hungary by the Czechoslovak forces, stamps of Hungary were overprinted "Cesko Slovenska Posta," "Ceskoslovenska Statni Posta" and Arms, and "Slovenska Posta" and Arms. These stamps were never officially issued though copies have passed the post.

Hradcany at Prague — A1

1918-19 Unwmk. Typo. *Imperf.*

1	A1	3h red violet	.20	.20
2	A1	5h yellow green	.20	.20
3	A1	10h rose	.20	.20
4	A1	20h bluish green	.20	.20
5	A1	25h deep blue	.25	.20
6	A1	30h bister	.45	.20
7	A1	40h red orange	.45	.20
8	A1	100h brown	1.25	.20
9	A1	200h ultra	2.25	.20
10	A1	400h purple	3.50	.20

On the 3h-40h "Posta Ceskoslovenska" is in white on a colored background; on the higher values the words are in color on a white background.

The 25h in ultramarine was not valid for postage.

Nos. 1-6 exist as tete-beche gutter pairs.

See #368, 1554, 1600. For surcharges see #B130, C1, C4, J15, J19-J20, J22-J23, J30.

Perf. 11½, 13½

13	A1	5h yellow green	.80	.20
a.		Perf. 11½x10¾	2.50	.55
14	A1	10h rose	.40	.20
15	A1	20h bluish green	.40	.20
a.		Perf. 11½	.40	.20
16	A1	25h deep blue	.60	.20
a.		Perf. 11½	1.50	.65
20	A1	200h ultra	4.25	.20
		Nos. 1-10,13-16,20 (15)	15.40	3.00

All values of this issue exist with various private perforations and copies have been used on letters.

The 3, 30, 40, 100 and 400h formerly listed are now known to have been privately perforated.

For overprints see Eastern Silesia Nos. 2, 5, 7-8, 14, 16, 18, 30.

A2

Type II — Sun behind cathedral. Colorless foliage in foreground.

Type III — Without sun. Shaded foliage in foreground.

Type IV — No foliage in foreground. Positions of buildings changed. Letters redrawn.

1919 *Imperf.*

23	A2	1h dark brown (II)	.20	.20
25	A2	5h blue green (IV)	.40	.20
27	A2	15h red (IV)	.85	.20
29	A2	25h dull violet (IV)	.65	.20
30	A2	50h dull violet (II)	.40	.20
31	A2	50h dark blue (IV)	.40	.20
32	A2	60h orange (III)	1.25	.20
33	A2	75h slate (IV)	.85	.20
34	A2	80h olive grn (III)	.95	.20
36	A2	120h gray black (IV)	2.50	.35
38	A2	300h dark green (III)	6.50	.65
39	A2	500h red brown (IV)	8.50	.50
40	A2	1000h violet (III)	19.00	1.20
a.		1000h bluish violet	42.50	1.75
		Nos. 23-40 (13)	42.45	4.50

For overprints see Eastern Silesia Nos. 1, 3-4, 6, 9-13, 15, 17, 20-21.

1919-20 *Perf. 11½, 13¾, 13¾x11½*

41	A2	1h dk brown (II)	.20	.20
42	A2	5h blue grn (IV), perf. 13½	.75	.20
a.		Perf. 11½	25.00	4.00
43	A2	10h yellow grn (IV)	.40	.20
a.		Imperf.	21.00	19.00
b.		Perf. 11¾	13.00	1.25
44	A2	15h red (IV)	.40	.20
a.		Perf. 11½x10¾	30.00	4.50
b.		Perf. 11½x13¾	85.00	22.50
c.		Perf. 13¾x10¾	125.00	26.00
45	A2	20h rose (IV)	.40	.20
a.		Imperf.	82.50	77.50
46	A2	25h dull vio (IV), perf. 11½	.65	.25
a.		Perf. 11½x10¾	5.00	1.10
b.		Perf. 13¾x10¾	175.00	40.00
47	A2	30h red violet (IV)	.35	.20
a.		Imperf.	190.00	190.00
b.		Perf. 13¾x13½	550.00	175.00
c.		30h deep violet	.70	.20
d.		As "c," perf. 13¾x13½	625.00	190.00
e.		As "c," imperf.	190.00	140.00
50	A2	60h orange (III)	.30	.20
a.		Perf. 13¾x13½	15.00	6.25
53	A2	120h gray black (IV)	3.75	.95
		Nos. 41-53 (9)	7.20	2.60

Nos. 43a, 45a, 47a and 47e were imperforate by accident and not issued in quantities as were Nos. 23 to 40.

Rouletted stamps of the preceding issues are said to have been made by a postmaster in a branch post office at Prague, or by private firms, but without authority from the Post Office Department.

The 50, 75, 80, 300, 500 and 1000h have been privately perforated.

Unlisted color varieties of types A1 and A2 were not officially released, and some are printer's waste.

For surcharges and overprints see Nos. B131, C2-C3, C5-C6, J16-J18, J21, J24-J29, J31, J42-J43, Eastern Silesia 22-29.

Pres. Thomas Garrigue Masaryk — A4

1920 *Perf. 13½*

61	A4	125h gray blue	1.50	.20
a.		125h ultramarine	30.00	19.00
62	A4	500h slate, *grysh*	4.75	2.50
63	A4	1000h blk brn, *brnsh*	8.00	5.00
		Nos. 61-63 (3)	14.25	7.70

#61-63 imperf were not regularly issued. Values, unused singles, #61, $15; #61a, $55; #62, $20; #63, $40.

For surcharge and overprints see Nos. B131, Eastern Silesia 31-32.

Carrier Pigeon with Letter — A5

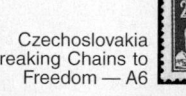

Czechoslovakia Breaking Chains to Freedom — A6

Hussite Priest — A7

Agriculture and Science — A8

Two types of 40h:
Type I: 9 leaves by woman's hip.
Type II: 10 leaves by woman's hip.

1920 *Perf. 14*

65	A5	5h dark blue	.20	.20
a.		Perf. 13¾	*325.00*	*150.00*
66	A5	10h blue green	.20	.20
a.		Perf. 13¾	*225.00*	110.00
67	A5	15h red brown	.20	.20
68	A6	20h rose	.20	.20
69	A6	25h lilac brown	.20	.20
70	A6	30h red violet	.20	.20
71	A6	40h red brown	.60	.20
a.		Tête bêche pair	6.75	2.00
b.		Perf. 13½	1.50	.20
c.		Type II	.25	.20
72	A6	50h carmine	.50	.20
73	A6	60h dark blue	.50	.20
a.		Tête bêche pair	6.00	3.00
b.		Perf. 13½	2.00	.25
		Photo.		
74	A7	80h purple	.20	.20
75	A7	90h black brown	.30	.20
		Typo.		
76	A8	100h dark green	1.00	.20
77	A8	200h violet	1.50	.20
78	A8	300h vermilion	3.50	.20
a.		Perf. 13¾x13½	7.00	.35
79	A8	400h brown	6.00	.45
80	A8	500h deep green	7.00	.45
a.		Perf. 13¾x13½	100.00	5.50
81	A8	600h deep violet	9.00	.45
a.		Perf. 13¾x13½	275.00	7.00
		Nos. 65-81 (17)	31.30	4.15

No. 69 has background of horizontal lines.

Imperfs. were not regularly issued.

Nos. 71 and 73 exist as tete-beche gutter pairs.

For surcharges and overprint see Nos. C7-C9, J44-J56.

1920-25 *Perf. 14*

Two types of 20h:
Type I: Base of 2 is long, interior of 0 is angular.
Type II: Base of 2 is short, interior of 0 is an oval.

Two types of 25h:
Type I: Top of 2 curves up.
Type II: Top of 2 curves down.

82	A5	5h violet	.20	.20
a.		Tête bêche pair	2.00	1.00
b.		Perf. 13½	1.00	.35
83	A5	10h olive bister	.20	.20
a.		Tête bêche pair	2.25	1.50
b.		Perf. 13½	.80	.20
84	A5	20h deep orange	1.00	.20
a.		Tête bêche pair	30.00	14.00
b.		Perf. 13½	6.00	.60
c.		Type II	.20	.20
85	A5	25h blue green	.20	.20
a.		Type II	.20	.20
86	A5	30h deep violet ('25)	3.00	.20
87	A6	50h yellow green	1.00	.20
a.		Tête bêche pair	60.00	27.50
b.		Perf. 13½	12.00	2.00
88	A6	100h dark brown	1.00	.20
a.		Perf. 13½	15.00	.25
89	A6	150h rose	4.50	.50
a.		Perf. 13½	80.00	1.10

90 A6 185h orange 3.00 .20
91 A6 250h dark green 5.00 .25
Nos. 82-91 (10) 19.10 2.35

Imperfs. were not regularly issued.
#82-84, 87 exist as tete-beche gutter pairs.

Type of 1920 Issue Redrawn

Type I — Rib of leaf below "O" of POSTA is straight and extends to tip. White triangle above book is entirely at left of twig. "P" has a stubby, abnormal appendage.

Type II — Rib is extremely bent; does not reach tip. Triangle extends at right of twig. "P" like Type I.

Type III — Rib of top left leaf is broken in two. Triangle like Type II. "P" has no appendage.

1923 ***Perf. 13¾, 13¾x13½***
92 A8 100h red, *yellow,* III, perf. 14x13½ 1.00 .20
a. Type I, perf. 13¾ 1.25 .20
b. Type I, perf. 13¾x13½ 1.25 .20
c. Type II, perf. 13¾ 1.50 .20
d. Type II, perf. 13¾x13½ 1.50 .20
e. Type III, perf. 13¾ 7.00 .20
93 A8 200h blue, *yellow,* II, perf. 14 5.00 .20
a. Type II, perf. 13¾x13½ 8.50 .25
b. Type III, perf. 13¾ 8.50 .25
c. Type III, perf. 13¾x13½ 52.50 .50
94 A8 300h violet, *yellow,* I, perf. 13¾ 3.75 .20
a. Type II, perf. 13¾ 35.00 .25
b. Type II, perf. 13¾x13½ 50.00 .50
c. Type III, perf. 13¾x13½ 7.00 .20
d. Type III, perf. 13¾ 24.00 .35
Nos. 92-94 (3) 9.75 .60

President Masaryk
A9 A10

Perf. 13¾x13½, 13¾
1925 Photo. Wmk. 107
Size: 19½x23mm
95 A9 40h brown orange .75 .20
96 A9 50h olive green 1.50 .20
97 A9 60h red violet 1.75 .20
Nos. 95-97 (3) 4.00 .60

Distinctive Marks of the Engravings.

I, II, III — Background of horizontal lines in top and bottom tablets. Inscriptions in Roman letters with serifs.

IV — Crossed horizontal and vertical lines in the tablets. Inscriptions in Antique letters without serifs.

I, II, IV — Shading of crossed diagonal lines on the shoulder at the right.

III — Shading of single lines only.

I — "T" of "Posta" over middle of "V" of "Ceskoslovenska." Three short horizontal lines in lower part of "A" of "Ceskoslovenska."

II — "T" over right arm of "V." One short line in "A."

III — "T" as in II. Blank space in lower part of "A."

IV — "T" over left arm of "V."

Engr.
I. First Engraving
Wmk. Horizontally (107)
Size: 19¾x22½mm
98 A10 1k carmine .85 .20
99 A10 2k deep blue 2.00 .25
100 A10 3k brown 4.00 .65
101 A10 5k blue green 1.40 .45
Nos. 98-101 (4) 8.25 1.55

Wmk. Vertically (107)
Size: 19¼x23mm
101A A10 1k carmine 100.00 4.00
101B A10 2k deep blue 100.00 12.50
101C A10 3k brown 250.00 12.50
101D A10 5k blue green 5.00 2.00
Nos. 101A-101D (4) 455.00 31.00

II. Second Engraving
Wmk. Horizontally (107)
Size: 19x21½mm
102 A10 1k carmine 42.50 .50
103 A10 2k deep blue 3.50 .25
104 A10 3k brown 3.50 .50
Nos. 102-104 (3) 49.50 1.25

III. Third Engraving
Size: 19-19½x21½-22mm
Perf. 10
105 A10 1k carmine rose 1.00 .20
a. Perf. 14 12.50 .20

IV. Fourth Engraving
Size: 19x22mm
1926 ***Perf. 10***
106 A10 1k carmine rose 1.00 .20
Perf. 14
108 A10 3k brown 4.50 .20

There is a 2nd type of No. 106: with long mustache. Same values. See No. 130, design SP3.

Karlstein Castle — A11

1926, June 1 Engr. ***Perf. 10***
109 A11 1.20k red violet .50 .30
110 A11 1.50k car rose .30 .20
111 A11 2.50k dark blue 3.00 .30
Nos. 109-111 (3) 3.80 .80

See Nos. 133, 135.

Karlstein Castle — A12

Pernstein Castle — A13

Orava Castle A14

Masaryk A15

Strahov Monastery — A16

Hradcany at Prague A17

Great Tatra — A18

1926-27 Engr. Wmk. 107
114 A13 30h gray green 1.25 .20
115 A14 40h red brown .50 .20
116 A15 50h deep green .50 .20
117 A15 60h red vio, *lil* .85 .20
118 A16 1.20k red violet 4.00 1.50
Perf. 13½
119 A17 2k blue .75 .20
a. 2k ultramarine 5.50 .75
120 A17 3k deep red 1.50 .20
121 A18 4k brn vio ('27) 3.50 .40
122 A18 5k dk grn ('27) 12.50 2.25
Nos. 114-122 (9) 25.35 5.35

No. 116 exists in two types. The one with short, straight mustache at left sells for several times as much as that with longer wavy mustache.
See Nos. 137-140.

Coil Stamps
Perf. 10 Vertically
123 A12 20h brick red .50 .40
a. Vert. pair, imperf. horiz. 100.00
124 A13 30h gray green .35 .20
a. Vert. pair, imperf. horiz. 100.00
125 A15 50h deep green .25 .20
Nos. 123-125 (3) 1.10 .80

See No. 141.

1927-31 Unwmk. ***Perf. 10***
126 A13 30h gray green .25 .20
127 A14 40h deep brown .70 .20
128 A15 50h deep green .20 .20
129 A15 60h red violet .70 .20
130 A10 1k carmine rose 1.10 .20
131 A15 1k deep red .75 .20
132 A16 1.20k red violet .40 .20
133 A11 1.50k carmine ('29) .55 .20
134 A13 2k dp grn ('29) .50 .20
135 A11 2.50k dark blue 5.50 .30
136 A14 3k red brown ('31) .60 .20
Nos. 126-136 (11) 11.25 2.30

No. 130 exists in two types. The one with longer mustache at left sells for several times as much as that with the short mustache.

1927-28 ***Perf. 13½***
137 A17 2k ultra .85 .20
138 A17 3k deep red ('28) 1.90 .65
139 A18 4k brown violet ('28) 6.00 1.00
140 A18 5k dark green ('28) 6.25 .50
Nos. 137-140 (4) 15.00 2.35

Coil Stamp
1927 ***Perf. 10 Vertically***
141 A12 20h brick red .50 .20

Catalogue values for unused stamps in this section, from this point to the end of the section, are for Never Hinged items.

Hradec Castle A19

Brno Cathedral A25

Masaryk — A27

10th anniv. of Czech. independence: 40h, Town Hall, Levoca. 50h, Telephone exchange, Prague. 60h, Town of Jasina. 1k, Hluboka Castle. 1.20k, Pilgrims' House, Velehrad. 2.50k, Great Tatra. 5k, Old City Square, Prague.

1928, Oct. 22 ***Perf. 13½***
142 A19 30h black .20 .20
143 A19 40h red brown .20 .20
144 A19 50h dark green .25 .20
145 A19 60h orange red .25 .20
146 A19 1k carmine .40 .40
147 A19 1.20k brown vio .80 .80
148 A25 2k ultra 1.00 1.00
149 A19 2.50k dark blue 2.25 2.25
150 A27 3k dark brown 1.50 1.50
151 A25 5k deep violet 3.50 3.50
Nos. 142-151 (10) 10.35 10.25

From one to three sheets each of Nos. 142-148, perf 12½, appeared on the market in the early 1950's.

Coat of Arms — A29

1929-37 ***Perf. 10***
152 A29 5h dark ultra ('31) .20 .20
153 A29 10h bister brn ('31) .20 .20
154 A29 20h red .20 .20
155 A29 25h green .20 .20
156 A29 30h red violet .20 .20
157 A29 40h dk brown ('37) 1.00 .20
a. 40h red brown ('29) 3.00 .20
Nos. 152-157 (6) 2.00 1.20

Coil Stamp
Perf. 10 Vertically
158 A29 20h red .20 .20

For overprints see Bohemia and Moravia Nos. 1-5, Slovakia 2-6.

St. Wenceslas A30

Founding St. Vitus' Cathedral A31

Design: 3k, 5k, St. Wenceslas martyred.

1929, May 14 ***Perf. 13½***
159 A30 50h gray green .40 .20
160 A30 60h slate violet .60 .20
161 A31 2k dull blue 1.25 .40
162 A30 3k brown 1.50 .40
163 A30 5k brown violet 5.50 3.50
Nos. 159-163 (5) 9.25 4.70

Millenary of the death of St. Wenceslas.

Statue of St. Wenceslas and National Museum, Prague — A33

1929 ***Perf. 10***
164 A33 2.50k deep blue .65 .20

Brno Cathedral A34

Tatra Mountain Scene A35

Design: 5k, Old City Square, Prague.

1929, Oct. 15 ***Perf. 13½***
165 A34 3k red brown 3.00 .20
166 A35 4k indigo 9.50 .50
167 A35 5k gray green 11.00 .45
Nos. 165-167 (3) 23.50 1.15

See No. 183.

A37

Type I 

Type II 

Two types of 50h:

I — A white space exists across the bottom of the vignette between the coat, shirt and tie and the "HALERU" frame panel.

II — An extra frame line has been added just above the "HALERU" panel which finishes off the coat and tie shading evenly.

1930, Jan. 2 ***Perf. 10***
168 A37 50h myrtle green (II) .20 .20
a. Type I 1.25 .20
169 A37 60h brown violet 1.00 .20
170 A37 1k brown red .40 .20
Nos. 168-170 (3) 1.60 .60

See No. 234.

Coil Stamp
1931 ***Perf. 10 Vertically***
171 A37 1k brown red 1.25 .65

President Masaryk — A38

St. Nicholas' Church, Prague — A39

1930, Mar. 1 *Perf. 13½*

175 A38 2k gray green 1.60 .40
176 A38 3k red brown 2.50 .40
177 A38 5k slate blue 6.50 1.50
178 A38 10k gray black 18.00 4.00
Nos. 175-178 (4) 28.60 6.30

Eightieth birthday of President Masaryk.

1931, May 15

183 A39 10k black violet 13.50 2.50

Krivoklat Castle — A40

Krumlov Castle — A42

Design: 4k, Orlik Castle.

1932, Jan. 2 *Perf. 10*

184 A40 3.50k violet 4.00 1.25
185 A40 4k deep blue 4.00 .65
186 A42 5k gray green 5.00 .65
Nos. 184-186 (3) 13.00 2.55

A43

A44

Miroslav Tyrs — A45

1932, Mar. 16

187 A43 50h yellow green .55 .20
188 A43 1k brown carmine 1.40 .20
189 A44 2k dark blue 10.00 .50
190 A44 3k red brown 15.00 .50
Nos. 187-190 (4) 26.95 1.40

1933, Feb. 1

191 A45 60h dull violet .30 .20

Miroslav Tyrs (1832-84), founder of the Sokol movement; and the 9th Sokol Congress (#187-190).

First Christian Church at Nitra
A46 A47

1933, June 20

192 A46 50h yellow green .40 .20
193 A47 1k carmine rose 8.00 .40

Prince Pribina who introduced Christianity into Slovakia and founded there the 1st Christian church in A.D. 833.

All gutter pairs are vertical. Values unused: No. 192 $350; No. 193 $10,000.

Bedrich Smetana, Czech Composer and Pianist, 50th Death Anniv. — A48

1934, Mar. 26 **Engr.** *Perf. 10*

194 A48 50h yellow green .40 .20

Consecration of Legion Colors at Kiev, Sept. 21, 1914 — A49

Ensign Heyduk with Colors A51

Legionnaires A52

1k, Legion receiving battle flag at Bayonne.

1934, Aug. 15 *Perf. 10*

195 A49 50h green .40 .20
196 A49 1k rose lake .55 .20
197 A51 2k deep blue 3.00 .40
198 A52 3k red brown 5.00 .50
Nos. 195-198 (4) 8.95 1.30

20th anniv. of the Czechoslovakian Legion which fought in WWI.

Antonin Dvorák, (1841-1904), Composer — A53

1934, Nov. 22

199 A53 50h green .40 .20

Pastoral Scene — A54

1934, Dec. 17 *Perf. 10*

200 A54 1k claret .65 .20
a. Souv. sheet of 15, perf. 13½ 200.00 *300.00*
b. As "a," single stamp 10.00 *12.50*
201 A54 2k blue 1.75 .65
a. Souv. sheet of 15, perf. 13½ 900.00 *1,000.*
b. As "a," single stamp 42.50 29.00

Centenary of the National Anthem.

Nos. 200-201 were each issued in sheets of 100 stamps and 12 blank labels.

Nos. 200a & 201a have thick paper, darker shades, no gum. Forgeries exist.

A55

President Masaryk — A56

1935, Mar. 1

202 A55 50h green, *buff* .35 .20
203 A55 1k claret, *buff* .40 .20
204 A56 2k gray blue, *buff* 2.00 .60
205 A56 3k brown, *buff* 3.25 .60
Nos. 202-205 (4) 6.00 1.60

85th birthday of President Masaryk. See No. 235.

Nos. 204-205 were each issued in sheets of 100 stamps and 12 blank labels. Value with attached labels: mint $30; used $10.

Monument to Czech Heroes at Arras, France — A57

1935, May 4

206 A57 1k rose .85 .20
207 A57 2k dull blue 3.00 .75

20th anniversary of the Battle of Arras.

Nos. 206-207 were each issued in sheets of 100 stamps and 12 blank labels. Value, set with attached labels: mint $22.50; used $10.

Gen. Milan Stefánik A58

Sts. Cyril and Methodius A59

1935, May 18

208 A58 50h green .20 .20

1935, June 22

209 A59 50h green .40 .20
210 A59 1k claret .55 .20
211 A59 2k deep blue 2.00 .50
Nos. 209-211 (3) 2.95 .90

Millenary of the arrival in Moravia of the Apostles Cyril and Methodius.

Masaryk — A60

Statue of Macha, Prague — A61

1935, Oct. 20 *Perf. 12½*

212 A60 1k rose lake .20 .20

No. 212 exists imperforate. See No. 256. For overprints see Bohemia and Moravia Nos. 9-10, Slovakia 12.

1936, Apr. 30

213 A61 50h deep green .20 .20
214 A61 1k rose lake .50 .20

Karel Hynek Macha (1810-1836), Bohemian poet.

Nos. 213-214 were each issued in sheets of 100 stamps and 12 blank labels. Value, with attached labels: mint $2; used 80c.

Jan Amos Komensky (Comenius) — A61a

Pres. Eduard Benes A62

Gen. Milan Stefánik A63

1936

215 A61a 40h dark blue .20 .20
216 A62 50h dull green .20 .20
217 A63 60h dull violet .20 .20
Nos. 215-217 (3) .60 .60

See #252, 255. For overprints see Bohemia and Moravia #6, 8, Slovakia 7, 9-11.

Castle Palanok near Mukacevo A64

Town of Banska Bystrica A65

Castle at Zvikov — A66

Ruins of Castle at Strecno — A67

Castle at Cesky Raj A68

Palace at Slavkov (Austerlitz) A69

Statue of King George of Podebrad A70

Town Square at Olomouc — A71

Castle Ruins at Bratislava A72

1936, Aug. 1

218 A64 1.20k rose lilac .20 .20
219 A65 1.50k carmine .20 .20
220 A66 2k dark blue green .20 .20
221 A67 2.50k dark blue .40 .20
222 A68 3k brown .40 .20
223 A69 3.50k dark violet 1.60 .55
224 A70 4k dark violet .65 .20
225 A71 5k green .65 .20
226 A72 10k blue 1.10 .55
Nos. 218-226 (9) 5.40 2.50

Nos. 224-226 were each issued in sheets of 100 stamps and 12 blank labels. Value, with attached labels: mint $7; used $2.75.

For overprints and surcharge see Nos. 237-238, 254A, Bohemia and Moravia 11-12, 14-19, Slovakia 13-14, 16-23.

President Benes — A73

Soldiers of the Czech Legion — A74

1937, Apr. 26 Unwmk. *Perf. 12½*

227 A73 50h deep green .20 .20

For overprints see Nos. 236, Slovakia 8.

1937, June 15

228 A74 50h deep green .20 .20
229 A74 1k rose lake .40 .20

20th anniv. of the Battle of Zborov.

Nos. 228-229 were each issued in sheets of 100 stamps and 12 blank labels. Value, set with attached labels: mint $4; used $2.

Cathedral at Prague — A75

Jan Evangelista Purkyne — A76

1937, July 1

230 A75 2k green 1.00 .20
231 A75 2.50k blue 1.50 .80

Founding of the "Little Entente," 16th anniv.

Nos. 230-231 were each issued in sheets with blank labels. Value, set with attached labels: mint $22.50; used $11.

1937, Sept. 2

232 A76 50h slate green .25 .20
233 A76 1k dull rose .30 .20

150th anniv. of the birth of Purkyne, Czech physiologist.

Masaryk Types of 1930-35

1937, Sept. *Perf. 12½*

234 A37 50h black .20 .20

With date "14.IX. 1937" in design

235 A56 2k black .30 .20

Death of former President Thomas G. Masaryk on Sept. 14, 1937.

No. 235 was issued in sheets of 100 stamps and 12 inscribed labels. Value, with attached label: mint $1.20; used 60c.

International Labor Bureau Issue

Stamps of 1936-37 Overprinted in Violet or Black

1937, Oct. 6 *Perf. 12½*

236 A73 50h dp green (Bk) .40 .25
237 A65 1.50k carmine (V) .40 .25
238 A66 2k dp green (V) .70 .50
Nos. 236-238 (3) 1.50 1.00

Bratislava Philatelic Exhibition Issue

Souvenir Sheet

A77

1937, Oct. 24 *Perf. 12½*

239 A77 Sheet of 2 2.50 *3.25*
a. 50h dark blue .80 1.20
b. 1k brown carmine .80 1.20

The stamps show a view of Poprad Lake (50h) and the tomb of General Milan Stefanik (1k).

No. 239 overprinted with the Czechoslovak arms and "Czecho-Slovak Participation New York World's Fair 1939, Czecho-Slovak Pavilion" were privately produced to finance Czechoslovak participation in the exhibition. The overprint exists in black, green, red, blue, gold and silver.

No. 239 overprinted "Liberation de la Tchechoslovaquie, 28-X-1945" etc., was sold at a philatelic exhibition in Brussels, Belgium.

St. Barbara's Church, Kutna Hora — A79

Peregrine Falcon, Sokol Emblem — A80

1937, Dec. 4

240 A79 1.60k olive green .20 .20

For overprints see Bohemia and Moravia Nos. 13, Slovakia 15.

1938, Jan. 21

241 A80 50h deep green .20 .20
242 A80 1k rose lake .25 .20

10th Intl. Sokol Games.

Nos. 241-242 were each issued in sheets of 100 stamps and 12 inscribed labels. Value, set with attached labels: mint $2; used $1.50.

Imperf. copies of No. 242 are essays.

Legionnaires

A81 A82

Legionnaire — A83

1938

243 A81 50h deep green .20 .20
244 A82 50h deep green .20 .20
245 A83 50h deep green .20 .20
Nos. 243-245 (3) .60 .60

20th anniv. of the Battle of Bachmac, Vouziers and Doss Alto.

Nos. 243-245 were each issued in sheets of 100 stamps and 12 inscribed labels. Value, set with attached labels $3, mint or used.

Jindrich Fügner, Co-Founder of Sokol Movement — A84

1938, June 18 *Perf. 12½*

246 A84 50h deep green .20 .20
247 A84 1k rose lake .20 .20
248 A84 2k slate blue .40 .20
Nos. 246-248 (3) .80 .60

10th Sokol Summer Games.

Nos. 246-248 were each issued in sheets of 100 stamps and 12 inscribed labels. Value, set with attached labels: mint $2.50; used $2.

View of Pilsen — A85

Cathedral of Kosice — A86

1938, June 24

249 A85 50h deep green .20 .20

Provincial Economic Council meeting, Pilsen.

No. 249 was issued in sheets of 150 stamps and 10 labels depicting a flower within a cogwheel. Value, with attached label 40c, mint or used.

For overprint see Bohemia & Moravia #7.

1938, July 15 *Perf. 12½*

250 A86 50h deep green .20 .20

Kosice Cultural Exhibition.

No. 250 was issued in sheets of 150 stamps and 10 labels bunches of grapes. Value, with attached label 40c, mint or used.

Prague Philatelic Exhibition Issue

Souvenir Sheet

Vysehrad Castle — Hradcany — A87

1938, June 26 *Perf. 12½*

251 A87 Sheet of 2 5.00 5.00
a. 50h dark blue 1.50 1.50
b. 1k deep carmine 1.50 1.50

See No. 3036.

Stefánik Type of 1936

1938, Nov. 21

252 A63 50h deep green .20 .20

Allegory of the Republic — A89

1938, Dec. 19 Unwmk.

253 A89 2k lt ultra .30 .20
254 A89 3k pale brown .50 .40

20th anniv. of Independence.

Nos. 253-254 were each issued in sheets of 100 stamps and 12 blank labels. Value, set with attached labels $2.50, mint or used.

See No. B153.

"Wir sind frei!"

Stamps of Czechoslovakia, 1918-37, overprinted with a swastika in black or red and "Wir sind frei!" were issued locally and unofficially in 1938 as Czech authorities were evacuating and German authorities arriving. They appeared in the towns of Asch, Karlsbad, Reichenberg-Maffersdorf, Rumburg, etc.

The overprint, sometimes including a surcharge or the town name (as in Karlsbad), exists on many values of postage, air post, semi-postal, postage due and newspaper stamps.

No. 226 Surcharged in Orange Red

1939, Jan. 18 Unwmk. *Perf. 12½*

254A A72 300h on 10k blue 1.25 *1.60*

Opening of the Slovakian Parliament.

View of Jasina — A89a

Perf. 12½

1939, Mar. 15 Engr. Unwmk.

254B A89a 3k ultra 25.00 *90.00*

Inauguration of the Carpatho-Ukraine Diet, Mar. 2, 1939.

Printed for use in the province of Carpatho-Ukraine but issued in Prague at the same time.

Used value is for red commemorative cancel.

Stefánik Type of 1936

1939 Engr. *Perf. 12½*

255 A63 60h dark blue 45.00 37.50

Used exclusively in Slovakia.

Masaryk Type of 1935 with hyphen in Cesko-Slovensko

1939, Apr. 23

256 A60 1k rose lake .20 .20

Linden Leaves and Buds — A90

1945 Photo. *Perf. 14*

256A A90 10h black .20 .20
257 A90 30h yellow brown .20 .20
258 A90 50h dark green .20 .20
258A A90 60h dark blue .20 .20

Engr.

(Buds Open)

Perf. 12½

259 A90 60h blue .20 .20
259A A90 80h orange ver .20 .20
260 A90 1.20k rose .20 .20
261 A90 3k violet brown .20 .20
262 A90 5k green .20 .20
Nos. 256A-262 (9) 1.80 1.80

Compare with Bohemia-Moravia type A1.

Thomas G. Masaryk — A91

Coat of Arms — A92

1945-46 Photo. *Perf. 12*

262A A91 5h dull violet ('46) .20 .20
262B A91 10h orange yel ('46) .20 .20
262C A91 20h dk brown ('46) .20 .20
263 A91 50h brt green .20 .20
264 A91 1k orange red .20 .20
265 A91 2k chalky blue .25 .25
Nos. 262A-265 (6) 1.25 1.25

1945 *Imperf.*

266	A92	50h	olive gray	.20	.20
267	A92	1k	brt red vio	.20	.20
268	A92	1.50k	dk carmine	.20	.20
269	A92	2k	deep blue	.20	.20
269A	A92	2.40k	henna brn	.30	.20
270	A92	3k	brown	.20	.20
270A	A92	4k	dk slate grn	.20	.20
271	A92	6k	violet blue	.25	.20
271A	A92	10k	sepia	.40	.20
			Nos. 266-271A (9)	2.15	1.80

Nos. 266, 268, 269, 270 and 271 exist in 2 printings. Stamps of the 1st printing have a coarse impression and are on thin, hard paper in sheets of 100; all values exist in the 2nd printing, with fine impressions on thick, soft wove paper in sheets of 200. Values are the same.

Staff Capt. Ridky (British Army) — A93

Dr. Miroslav Novak (French Army) — A94

Capt. Otakar Jaros (Russian Army) — A95

Staff Capt. Stanislav Zimprich (Foreign Legion) — A96

2nd Lt. Jiri Kral (French Air Force) A97

Josef Gabcik (Parachutist) A98

Staff Capt. Alois Vasatko (Royal Air Force) A99

Private Frantisek Adamek (British Colonial Service) A100

1945, Aug. 18 **Engr.** *Perf. 11½x12½*

272	A93	5h	intense blue	.20	.20
273	A94	10h	dark brown	.20	.20
274	A95	20h	brick red	.20	.20
275	A96	25h	rose red	.20	.20
276	A97	30h	purple	.20	.20
277	A98	40h	sepia	.20	.20
278	A99	50h	dark olive	.20	.20
279	A100	60h	violet	.20	.20
280	A93	1k	carmine	.20	.20
281	A94	1.50k	lake	.20	.20
282	A95	2k	ultra	.20	.20
283	A96	2.50k	deep violet	.20	.20
284	A97	3k	sepia	.20	.20
285	A98	4k	rose lilac	.20	.20
286	A99	5k	myrtle green	.20	.20
287	A100	10k	brt ultra	.65	.20
			Nos. 272-287 (16)	3.65	3.20

Flags of Russia, Great Britain, US and Czechoslovakia — A101

View of Banská Bystrica A102

Patriot Welcoming Russian Soldier, Turciansky A103

Ruins of Castle at Sklabina A104

Czech Patriot, Strecno A105

1945, Aug. 29 **Photo.** *Perf. 10*

288	A101	1.50k	brt carmine	.20	.20
289	A102	2k	brt blue	.20	.20
290	A103	4k	dark brown	.20	.20
291	A104	4.50k	purple	.25	.25
292	A105	5k	deep green	.50	.50
			Nos. 288-292 (5)	1.35	1.35

National uprising against the Germans.

A card contains one each of Nos. 288-292 on thin cardboard, ungummed. Size: 148x210mm. Sold for 50k. Value, $35 unused, $125 used.

A106

A107

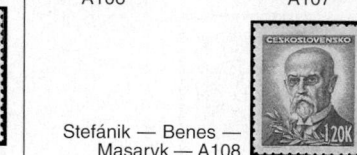

Stefánik — Benes — Masaryk — A108

1945-47 **Engr.** *Perf. 12, 12½*

293	A106	30h	rose violet	.20	.20
294	A107	60h	blue	.20	.20
294A	A106	1k	red org ('47)	.20	.20
295	A108	1.20k	car rose	.20	.20
295A	A108	1.20(k)	rose lil ('46)	.20	.20
296	A106	2.40(k)	rose	.20	.20
297	A107	3k	red violet	.20	.20
297A	A108	4k	dark blue ('46)	.20	.20
298	A108	5k	Prus green	.20	.20
299	A107	7k	gray	.20	.20
300	A106	10k	gray blue	.35	.20
300A	A106	20k	sepia ('46)	.75	.20
			Nos. 293-300A (12)	3.10	2.40

1945 **Photo.** *Perf. 14*

301	A108	50h	brown	.20	.20
302	A106	80h	dark green	.20	.20
303	A107	1.60(k)	olive green	.20	.20
304	A108	15k	red violet	.55	.20
			Nos. 301-304 (4)	1.15	.80

Statue of Kozina and Chod Castle, Domazlice A109

Red Army Soldier A110

1945, Nov. 28 **Engr.** *Perf. 12½*

305	A109	2.40k	rose carmine	.20	.20
306	A109	4k	blue	.25	.25

250th anniv. of the death of Jan Sladky Kozina, peasant leader.

1945, Mar. 26 **Litho.** *Imperf.*

307	A110	2k	crimson rose	.40	.40
308	A110	5k	slate black	1.25	1.25
309	A110	6k	ultramarine	1.25	1.25
			Nos. 307-309 (3)	2.90	2.90

Souvenir Sheet

1945, July 16

Gray Burelage

310		Sheet of 3	4.00	4.00
a.	A110	2k crimson rose	.75	.75
b.	A110	5k slate black	.75	.75
c.	A110	6k ultramarine	.75	.75

Return of Pres. Benes, Apr., 1945.

Clasped Hands — A112

Karel Havlícek Borovsky — A113

1945 *Rouletted 12½*

311	A112	1.50k	brown red	2.25	2.25
312	A112	9k	red orange	.50	.50
313	A112	13k	orange brown	.65	.65
314	A112	20k	blue	1.75	1.75
			Nos. 311-314 (4)	5.15	5.15

1946, July 5 **Engr.** *Perf. 12½*

315	A113	1.20k	gray black	.20	.20

Borovsky (1821-56), editor and writer.

Issued in sheets of 100 stamps and 12 inscribed labels. Value with attached label: $1.25.

Old Town Hall, Brno — A114

Hodonin Square — A115

Perf. 12½x12, 12x12½

1946, Aug. 3 **Engr.** **Unwmk.**

316	A114	2.40k	deep rose	.20	.20
317	A115	7.40k	dull violet	.30	.20

See No. B159.

President Eduard Benes — A116

1946, Oct. 28

318	A116	60h	indigo	.20	.20
319	A116	1.60k	dull green	.20	.20
320	A116	3k	red lilac	.20	.20
321	A116	8k	sepia	.25	.20
			Nos. 318-321 (4)	.85	.80

Flag, Symbols — A117

Saint Adalbert — A118

1947, Jan. 1 *Perf. 12½*

322	A117	1.20k	Prus green	.20	.20
323	A117	2.40k	deep rose	.20	.20
324	A117	4k	deep blue	.80	.25
			Nos. 322-324 (3)	1.20	.65

Czechoslovakia's two-year reconstruction and rehabilitation program.

Nos. 322-324 each issued in sheets of 100 stamps and 12 inscribed labels. Value, set with attached labels, $3.

1947, Apr. 23

326	A118	1.60k	gray	.50	.30
327	A118	2.40k	rose carmine	.80	.65
328	A118	5k	blue green	1.00	.40
			Nos. 326-328 (3)	2.30	1.35

950th anniv. of the death of Saint Adalbert, Bishop of Prague.

Nos. 326-328 each issued in sheets of 100 stamps and 12 monogrammed labels. Value, set with attached labels, $40.

Grief — A119

Allegorical Figure — A120

1947, June 10 **Engr.**

329	A119	1.20k	black	.30	.25
330	A119	1.60k	slate black	.40	.40
331	A120	2.40k	brown violet	.50	.50
			Nos. 329-331 (3)	1.20	1.15

Destruction of Lidice, 5th anniversary.

Nos. 329-331 each issued in sheets of 100 stamps and 12 inscribed labels. Value, set with attached labels, $10.

World Federation of Youth Symbol — A121

Thomas G. Masaryk — A122

1947, July 20

332	A121	1.20k	violet brown	.30	.20
333	A121	4k	slate	.35	.20

World Youth Festival held in Prague, July 20-Aug. 17.

1947, Sept. 14

334	A122	1.20k	gray blk, *buff*	.20	.20
335	A122	4k	blue blk, *cream*	.40	.20

Death of Masaryk, 10th anniv.

Nos. 334-335 each issued in sheets of 100 stamps and 12 inscribed labels. Value, set with attached labels, $7.50.

Msgr. Stefan Moyses A123

1947, Oct. 19

336	A123	1.20k	rose violet	.20	.20
337	A123	4k	deep blue	.35	.20

150th anniversary of the birth of Stefan Moyses, first Slovakian chairman of the Slavic movement.

Each issued in sheets of 100 stamps and 12 labels with "MOYSES" and floral decoration. Value, set with attached labels, $9.50.

"Freedom from Social Oppression" A124

1947, Oct. 26 Photo. *Perf. 14*

338 A124 2.40k brt carmine .20 .20
339 A124 4k brt ultra .35 .20

Russian revolution of Oct., 1917, 30th anniv.

Benes A125

"Czechoslovakia" Greeting Sokol Marchers A126

1948, Feb. 15 Photo.

Size: 17½x21½mm

340 A125 1.50k brown .20 .20

Size: 19x23mm

341 A125 2k deep plum .20 .20
342 A125 5k brt ultra .20 .20
Nos. 340-342 (3) .60 .60

1948, Mar. 7 Engr. *Perf. 12½*

343 A126 1.50k brown .20 .20
344 A126 3k rose carmine .20 .20
345 A126 5k blue .60 .20
Nos. 343-345 (3) 1.00 .60

The 11th Sokol Congress.
Nos. 343-345 each issued in sheets of 100 stamps and 12 labels depicting dates and bouquet. Values, set with attached labels: mint $2.50; used $1.50.

King Charles IV — A127

St. Wenceslas, King Charles IV — A128

1948, Apr. 7

346 A127 1.50k black brown .20 .20
347 A128 2k dark brown .20 .20
348 A128 3k brown red .20 .20
349 A127 5k dark blue .40 .20
Nos. 346-349 (4) 1.00 .80

600th anniv. of the foundation of Charles University, Prague.
Nos. 346-349 each issued in sheets of 100 stamps and 12 inscribed labels. Value, set with attached labels, $6.

Czech Peasants in Revolt A129

Jindrich Vanicek A130

Unwmk.

1948, May 14 Photo. *Perf. 14*

350 A129 1.50k dk olive brown .20 .20

Centenary of abolition of serfdom.

1948, June 10 Engr. *Perf. 12½*

Designs: 1.50k, 2k, Josef Scheiner.

351 A130 1k dark green .20 .20
352 A130 1.50k sepia .20 .20
353 A130 2k gray blue .20 .20
354 A130 3k claret .25 .20
Nos. 351-354 (4) .85 .80

11th Sokol Congress, Prague, 1948.
Nos. 351-354 each issued in sheets of 100 stamps and 12 labels depicting a sunflower. Values, set with attached labels: $3.75 mint; $3 used.

Frantisek Palacky & F. L. Rieger — A131

Miloslav Josef Hurban — A132

1948, June 20 Unwmk.

355 A131 1.50k gray .20 .20
356 A131 3k brown carmine .20 .20

Constituent Assembly at Kromeriz, cent.
Nos. 355-356 each issued in sheets of 100 stamps and 12 labels depicting a wreath. Value, set with attached labels, $1.50.

1948, Aug. 27 *Perf. 12½*

3k, Ludovit Stur. 5k, Michael M. Hodza.

357 A132 1.50k dark brown .20 .20
358 A132 3k carmine lake .20 .20
359 A132 5k indigo .25 .20
Nos. 357-359 (3) .65 .60

Cent. of 1848 insurrection against Hungary.
Nos. 357-359 each issued in sheets of 100 stamps and 12 labels depicting signatures. Values, set with attached labels: mint $3.50; used 1.50.

Eduard Benes A133

Czechoslovak Family A134

1948, Sept. 28

360 A133 8k black .20 .20

President Eduard Benes, 1884-1948.

1948, Oct. 28 *Perf. 12½x12*

361 A134 1.50k deep blue .20 .20
362 A134 3k rose carmine .20 .20

Czechoslovakia's Independence, 30th anniv.
Nos. 361-362 each issued in sheets of 100 stamps and 12 labels depicting dates, leaves. Value, set with attached labels, $1.50.

Pres. Klement Gottwald — A135

1948-49 *Perf. 12½*

Size: 18½x23½mm

363 A135 1.50k dk brown .20 .20
364 A135 3k car rose .40 .20
a. 3k rose brown 1.20 .20
365 A135 5k gray blue .25 .20

Size: 23½x29mm

366 A135 20k purple 1.10 .20
Nos. 363-366 (4) 1.95 .80

No. 366 was issued in sheets of 100 stamps and 12 monogrammed labels. Value, with attached label, $3.
See Nos. 373, 564, 600-604.

Souvenir Sheet

1948, Nov. 23 Unwmk. *Imperf.*

367 A135 30k rose brown 4.50 3.50

52nd birthday of Pres. Klement Gottwald (1896-1953).

Hradcany Castle Type of 1918
Souvenir Sheet

1948, Dec. 18

368 A1 10k dk blue violet 2.75 2.00

1st Czech postage stamp, 30th anniv.

Czechoslovak and Russian Workmen Shaking Hands — A138

Lenin — A139

1948, Dec. 12 *Perf. 12½*

369 A138 3k rose carmine .20 .20

5th anniv. of the treaty of alliance between Czechoslovakia and Russia.
No. 369 issued in sheets of 100 stamps and 12 labels depicting Czech and Soviet flags. Value with attached label 60c.

1949, Jan. 21 Engr. *Perf. 12½*

370 A139 1.50k violet brown .30 .20
371 A139 5k deep blue .30 .30

25th anniversary of the death of Lenin.
Nos. 370-371 each issued in sheets of 100 stamps and 12 labels depicting torch. Values, set with attached labels: mint $1.75; used $1.50.

Gottwald Type of 1948 Inscribed: "UNOR 1948" and

Gottwald Addressing Meeting A140

1949, Feb. 25 Photo. *Perf. 14*

372 A140 3k red brown .20 .20

Perf. 12½

Engr.

Size: 23½x29mm

373 A135 10k deep green .60 .25

1st anniv. of Gottwald's speech announcing the appointment of a new government. No. 372 exists in a souvenir sheet of 1. It was not sold to the public.
No. 373 issued in sheets of 100 stamps and 12 inscribed labels. Values with attached label: mint $3; used $2.

A141

A142

Writers: 50h, P. O. Hviezdoslav. 80h, V. Vancura. 1k, J. Sverma. 2k, Julius Fucik. 4k, Jiri Wolker. 8k, Alois Jirasek.

1949 Photo. *Perf. 14*

374 A141 50h violet brown .20 .20
375 A141 80h scarlet .20 .20
376 A141 1k dk olive green .20 .20
377 A141 2k brt blue .40 .20

Perf. 12½

Engr.

378 A141 4k violet brown .40 .20
379 A141 8k brown black .50 .20
Nos. 374-379 (6) 1.90 1.20

1949, May 20

3k, Stagecoach and Train. 5k, Postrider and post bus. 13k, Sailing ship and plane.

380 A142 3k brown carmine 1.25 1.25
381 A142 5k deep blue .80 .40
382 A142 13k deep green 1.25 .80
Nos. 380-382 (3) 3.30 2.45

75th anniv. of the UPU.

Reaping A143

Communist Emblem and Workers A144

Workman, Symbol of Industry — A145

Perf. 12½x12, 12x12½

1949, May 24 Unwmk.

383 A143 1.50k deep green .50 .45
384 A144 3k brown carmine .50 .45
385 A145 5k deep blue .50 .45
Nos. 383-385 (3) 1.50 1.35

No. 384 for the 9th meeting of the Communist Party of Czechoslovakia, 5/25/49.
Nos. 383-385 each issued in sheets of 100 stamps and 12 inscribed labels. Value, set with attached labels, $15.

Bedrich Smetana and Natl. Theater, Prague — A146

Aleksander Pushkin — A147

1949, June 4 *Perf. 12½x12*

386 A146 1.50k dull green .20 .20
387 A146 5k deep blue .55 .20

Birth of Bedrich Smetana, composer, 125th anniv.

1949, June 6 *Perf. 12x12½*

388 A147 2k olive gray .30 .25

Birth of Aleksander S. Pushkin, 150th anniv.

Frederic Chopin and Conservatory, Warsaw A148

1949, June 24 ***Perf. 12½x12***

389	A148	3k dark red	.40	.20
390	A148	8k violet brown	.75	.50

Cent. of the death of Frederic F. Chopin.

Globe and Ribbon — A149

Zvolen Castle — A150

1949, Aug. 20 ***Perf. 12½x12***

391	A149	1.50k violet brown	.35	.20
392	A149	5k ultra	.75	.75

50th Prague Sample Fair, Sept. 11-18, 1949.

Starting in October, 1949, some commemorative sets included one "blocked" value, which could be obtained only by purchasing the complete set. These restricted values were printed in smaller quantities than other stamps in the set and were typically sold for more than face value.

1949, Aug. 28 ***Perf. 12½***

393	A150	10k rose lake	.75	.20

Early Miners — A151

Miner of Today — A152

Design: 5k, Mining Machine.

1949, Sept. 11 ***Perf. 12½***

394	A151	1.50k sepia	.80	.60
395	A152	3k carmine rose	6.50	2.50
396	A151	5k deep blue	5.00	1.75
		Nos. 394-396 (3)	12.30	4.85

700th anniv. of the Czechoslovak mining industry; 150th anniv. of the miner's laws.

Construction Workers — A153

Joseph V. Stalin — A154

1949, Dec. 11 ***Perf. 12½***

397	A153	1k shown	2.50	.75
398	A153	2k Machinist	1.50	.40

2nd Trade Union Congress, Prague, 1949.

1949, Dec. 21 **Unwmk.**

Design: 3k, Stalin facing left.

Cream Paper

399	A154	1.50k greenish gray	1.25	.60
400	A154	3k claret	4.75	2.00

70th birthday of Joseph V. Stalin.

Skier — A155

Efficiency Badge — A156

Engr., Photo. (3k)

1950, Feb. 15 ***Perf. 12½, 13½***

401	A155	1.50k gray blue	3.00	1.50
402	A156	3k vio brn, *cr*	3.00	1.50
403	A155	5k ultramarine	2.25	1.25
		Nos. 401-403 (3)	8.25	4.25

51st Ski Championship for the Tatra cup, Feb. 15-26, 1950.

Vladimir V. Mayakovsky, Poet, 20th Death Anniv. — A157

1950, Apr. 14 **Engr.** ***Perf. 12½***

404	A157	1.50k dark brown	2.50	1.25
405	A157	3k brown red	2.50	1.25

See Nos. 414-417, 422-423, 432-433, 464-465, 477-478.

Soviet Tank Soldier and Hradcany A158

2k, Hero of Labor medal. 3k, Two workers (militiamen) and Town Hall, Prague. 5k, Text of government program and heraldic lion.

1950, May 5

406	A158	1.50k gray green	.40	.25
407	A158	2k dark brown	1.25	1.25
408	A158	3k brown red	.25	.20
409	A158	5k dark blue	.55	.25
		Nos. 406-409 (4)	2.45	1.95

5th anniv. of the Czechoslovak People's Democratic Republic.

Factory and Young Couple with Tools A159

Designs: 2k, Steam shovel. 3k, Farmer and farm scene. 5k, Three workers leaving factory.

1950, May 9 **Engr.**

410	A159	1.50k dark green	1.50	.75
411	A159	2k dark brown	1.50	.75
412	A159	3k rose red	1.00	.40
413	A159	5k deep blue	1.00	.40
		Nos. 410-413 (4)	5.00	2.30

Canceled to Order

The government philatelic department started about 1950 to sell canceled sets of new issues. Values in the second ("used") column are for these canceled-to-order stamps. Postally used copies are worth more.

Portrait Type of 1950

Design: S. K. Neumann.

1950, June 5 **Unwmk.** ***Perf. 12½***

414	A157	1.50k deep blue	.20	.20
415	A157	3k violet brown	.95	.75

Stanislav Kostka Neumann (1875-1947), journalist and poet.

1950, June 21

Design: Bozena Nemcova.

416	A157	1.50k deep blue	1.25	.75
417	A157	7k dark brown	.30	.20

Bozena Nemcova (1820-1862), writer.

Liberation of Colonies A160

Designs: 2k, Allegory, Fight for Peace. 3k, Group of Students. 5k, Marching Students with flags.

1950, Aug. 14

418	A160	1.50k dark green	.20	.20
419	A160	2k sepia	.85	.55
420	A160	3k rose carmine	.20	.20
421	A160	5k ultra	.40	.35
		Nos. 418-421 (4)	1.65	1.30

2nd International Students World Congress, Prague, Aug. 12-24, 1950.

Portrait Type of 1950

Design: Zdenek Fibich.

1950, Oct. 15

422	A157	3k rose brown	.90	.55
423	A157	8k gray green	.35	.20

Zdenek Fibich, musician, birth centenary.

Miner, Soldier and Farmer A161

Czech and Soviet Soldiers A162

1950, Oct. 6

424	A161	1.50k slate	.60	.60
425	A162	3k carmine rose	.30	.30

Issued to publicize Czech Army Day.

Prague Castle, 16th Century A163

Prague, 1493 A164

3k, Prague, 1606. 5k, Prague, 1794.

1950, Oct. 21 ***Perf. 14***

426	A163	1.50k black	4.50	3.00
427	A164	2k chocolate	4.50	3.00
428	A164	3k brown car	4.50	3.00
429	A164	5k gray	4.50	3.00
a.		Block of 4, #426-429	25.00	16.00

See Nos. 434-435.

Communications Symbols — A165

1950, Oct. 25 ***Perf. 12½***

430	A165	1.50k chocolate	.20	.20
431	A165	3k brown carmine	.85	.30

1st anniv. of the foundation of the Intl. League of P.T.T. Employees.

Portrait Type of 1950

Design: J. Gregor Tajovsky.

1950, Oct. 26

432	A157	1.50k brown	1.00	.60
433	A157	5k deep blue	*.65*	.30

10th anniversary of the death of J. Gregor Tajovsky (1874-1940), Slovakian writer.

Scenic Type of 1950

Design: Prague, 1950.

1950, Oct. 28

434	A164	1.50k indigo	.35	.20
a.		Souvenir sheet of 4, imperf.	40.00	20.00
435	A164	3k brown car	.65	.50

Czech and Soviet Steel Workers A166

1950, Nov. 4 **Unwmk.**

436	A166	1.50k chocolate	.40	.35
437	A166	5k deep blue	.90	.60

Issued to publicize the 2nd meeting of the Union of Czechoslovak-Soviet Friendship.

Dove by Picasso A167

1951, Jan. 20 **Photo.** ***Perf. 14***

438	A167	2k deep blue	4.75	3.00
439	A167	3k rose brown	3.25	1.50

1st Czechoslovak Congress of Fighters for Peace, held in Prague.

Julius Fucik — A168

1951, Feb. 17 **Engr.** ***Perf. 12½***

440	A168	1.50k gray	.65	.30
441	A168	5k gray blue	1.50	1.50

Drop Hammer — A169

Installing Gear — A170

1951, Feb. 24

442	A169	1.50k gray blk	.20	.20
443	A170	3k violet brn	.20	.20
444	A169	4k gray blue	.60	.50
		Nos. 442-444 (3)	1.00	.90

Women Machinists A171

Apprentice Miners A172

Designs: 3k, Woman tractor operator. 5k, Women of different races.

1951, Mar. 8 Photo. *Perf. 14*

445	A171	1.50k olive brown	.40	.30
446	A171	3k brown car	1.60	1.25
447	A171	5k blue	.80	.50
		Nos. 445-447 (3)	2.80	2.05

International Women's Day, Mar. 8.

1951, Apr. 12 Engr. *Perf. 12½*

448	A172	1.50k gray	.55	.50
449	A172	3k red brown	.20	.20

Plowing A173

Collective Cattle Breeding A174

1951, Apr. 28 Photo. *Perf. 14*

450	A173	1.50k brown	.65	.65
451	A174	2k dk green	1.50	1.50

Tatra Mountain Recreation Center — A175

Mountain Recreation Centers: 2k, Beskydy (Beskids). 3k, Krkonose (Carpathians).

1951, May 5 Engr. *Perf. 12½*

452	A175	1.50k deep green	.20	.20
453	A175	2k dark brown	.75	.50
454	A175	3k rose brown	.30	.20
		Nos. 452-454 (3)	1.25	.90

Issued to publicize the summer opening of trade union recreation centers.

Klement Gottwald and Joseph Stalin A176

Factory Militiaman A177

Red Army Soldier and Partisan A178

Marx, Engels, Lenin and Stalin A179

1951 Unwmk. *Perf. 12½*

455	A176	1.50k olive gray	.65	.25
456	A177	2k red brown	.25	.20
457	A178	3k rose brown	.25	.20
458	A176	5k deep blue	2.00	1.40
459	A179	8k gray	.60	.25
		Nos. 455-459 (5)	3.75	2.30

30th anniv. of the founding of the Czechoslovak Communist Party.

A180

A181

Design: 1k, 2k, Antonin Dvorák. 1.50k, 3k, Bedrich Smetana.

1951, May 30

460	A180	1k redsh brown	.35	.20
461	A180	1.50k olive gray	1.50	.75
462	A180	2k dk redsh brn	1.50	.75
463	A180	3k rose brown	.35	.20
		Nos. 460-463 (4)	3.70	1.90

International Music Festival, Prague.

Portrait Type of 1950

1951, June 21

Portrait: Bohumir Smeral (facing right).

464	A157	1.50k dark gray	.45	.35
465	A157	3k rose brown	.40	.20

10th anniv. of the death of Bohumir Smeral, political leader.

1951, June 21

466	A181	1k shown	.75	.35
467	A181	1.50k Discus	.75	.35
468	A181	3k Soccer	1.50	.35
469	A181	5k Skier	3.50	1.50
		Nos. 466-469 (4)	6.50	2.55

Issued to honor the 9th Congress of the Czechoslovak Sokol Federation.

Scene from "Fall of Berlin" A182

Scene from "The Great Citizen" A183

1951, July 14

470	A182	80h rose brown	.30	.20
471	A183	1.50k dark gray	.30	.20
472	A182	4k gray blue	1.25	.75
		Nos. 470-472 (3)	1.85	1.15

Intl. Film Festival, Karlovy Vary, July 14-29.

Alois Jirásek — A184

"Fables and Fate" A185

Design: 4k, Scene from "Reign of Tabor."

1951, Aug. 23 Engr. *Perf. 12½*

473	A184	1.50k gray	.55	.20
474	A184	5k dark blue	2.25	1.25

Photo.

Perf. 14

475	A185	3k dark red	.55	.20
476	A185	4k dark brown	.55	.20
		Nos. 473-476 (4)	3.90	1.85

Cent. of the birth of Alois Jirásek, author.

Portrait Type of 1950

Design: Josef Hybes (1850-1921), co-founder of Czech Communist Party.

1951, July 21 Engr.

477	A157	1.50k chocolate	.20	.20
478	A157	2k rose brown	.80	.65

"Ostrava Region" — A186

Mining Iron Ore — A187

1951, Sept. 9

479	A186	1.50k dk brown	.20	.20
480	A187	3k rose brown	.20	.20
481	A186	5k deep blue	1.25	1.00
		Nos. 479-481 (3)	1.65	1.40

Miner's Day, Sept. 9, 1951.

Soldiers on Parade — A188

1k, Gunner and field gun. 1.50k, Klement Gottwald. 3k, Tankman and tank. 5k, Aviators.

Photo. (80h, 5k), Engr.

1951, Oct. 6 *Perf. 14 (80h, 5k), 12½*

Inscribed: "Den CS Armady 1951"

482	A188	80h olive brown	.35	.30
483	A188	1k dk olive grn	.35	.30
484	A188	1.50k sepia	.35	.30
485	A188	3k claret	.75	.35
486	A188	5k blue	1.75	.75
		Nos. 482-486 (5)	3.55	2.00

Issued to publicize Army Day, Oct. 6, 1951.

Stalin and Gottwald — A189

Lenin, Stalin and Soldiers — A190

1951, Nov. 3 Engr. *Perf. 12½*

487	A189	1.50k sepia	.20	.20
488	A190	3k red brown	.20	.20
489	A189	4k deep blue	1.10	.40
		Nos. 487-489 (3)	1.50	.80

Issued to publicize the month of Czechoslovak-Soviet friendship, 1951.

Peter Jilemnicky A191

Ladislav Zapotocky A192

1951, Dec. 5 Unwmk.

491	A191	1.50k redsh brown	.25	.20
492	A191	2k dull blue	.80	.35

Peter Jilemnicky (1901-1949), writer.

1952, Jan. 12 *Perf. 11½*

493	A192	1.50k brown red	.20	.20
494	A192	4k gray	.75	.45

Centenary of the birth of Ladislav Zapotocky, Bohemian socialist pioneer.

Jan Kollar — A193

Lenin and Lenin Hall — A194

1952, Jan. 30 Unwmk. *Perf. 11½*

495	A193	3k dark carmine	.20	.20
496	A193	5k violet blue	1.25	.75

Jan Kollar (1793-1852), poet.

1952, Jan. 30 *Perf. 12½*

497	A194	1.50k rose carmine	.30	.20
498	A194	5k deep blue	1.25	.75

6th All-Russian Party Conf., 40th anniv.

Emil Holub and African — A195

Gottwald Metallurgical Plant — A196

1952, Feb. 21 *Perf. 11½*

499 A195 3k red brown .50 .30
500 A195 5k gray 1.75 1.10

Death of Emil Holub, explorer, 50th anniv.

1952, Feb. 25 Photo. *Perf. 14*

Designs: 2k, Foundry. 3k, Chemical plant.

501 A196 1.50k sepia .25 .20
502 A196 2k red brown 1.50 .75
503 A196 3k scarlet .25 .20
Nos. 501-503 (3) 2.00 1.15

Student, Soldier and Worker — A197

Youths of Three Races — A198

1952, Mar. 21 Unwmk. *Perf. 14*

504 A197 1.50k blue .20 .20
505 A198 2k olive black .25 .20
506 A197 3k lake .85 .50
Nos. 504-506 (3) 1.30 .90

International Youth Day, Mar. 25, 1952.

Similar to Type of 1951

Portrait: Otakar Sevcik.

1952, Mar. 22 Engr. *Perf. 12½*

507 A184 2k choc, *cr* .65 .45
508 A184 3k rose brn, *cr* .20 .20

Otakar Sevcik, violinist, birth cent.

Jan A. Komensky A199

Industrial and Farm Women A200

1952, Mar. 28

509 A199 1.50k dk brown, *cr* 1.25 .60
510 A199 11k dk blue, *cr* .25 .20

360th anniv. of the birth of Jan Amos Komensky (Comenius), teacher and philosopher.

1952, Mar. 8

511 A200 1.50k dp blue, *cr* 1.25 .50

International Women's Day Mar. 8, 1952.

Woman and Children A201

Antifascist A202

1952, Apr. 12

512 A201 2k chocolate, *cr* 2.00 1.25
513 A201 3k dp claret, *cr* .20 .20

Intl. Conf. for the Protection of Children, Vienna, Apr. 12-16, 1952.

1952, Apr. 11 Photo. *Perf. 14*

514 A202 1.50k red brown .20 .20
515 A202 2k ultra 1.25 .75

Day of International Solidarity of Fighters against Fascism, Apr. 11, 1952.

Harvester A203

Design: 3k, Tractor and Seeders.

1952, Apr. 30

516 A203 1.50k deep blue 2.50 1.40
517 A203 2k brown .30 .30
518 A203 3k brown red .30 .30
Nos. 516-518 (3) 3.10 2.00

Youths Carrying Flags — A204

1952, May 1

519 A204 3k brown red .45 .25
520 A204 4k dk red brown 2.00 1.75

Issued to publicize Labor Day, May 1, 1952.

Crowd Cheering Soviet Soldiers — A205

1952, May 9

521 A205 1.50k dark red .65 .50
522 A205 5k deep blue 2.50 2.00

Liberation of Czechoslovakia from German occupation, 7th anniversary.

Children A206

J. V. Myslbek — A207

Design: 3k, "Pioneer" teaching children.

1952, May 31 Engr. *Perf. 12½*

523 A206 1.50k dk brn, *cr* .20 .20
524 A206 2k Prus grn, *cr* 1.50 1.00
525 A206 3k rose brn, *cr* .25 .20
Nos. 523-525 (3) 1.95 1.40

International Children's Day May 31, 1952.

1952, June 2

Design: 8k, Allegory, "Music."

526 A207 1.50k red brown .30 .20
527 A207 2k dark brown 1.50 1.25
528 A207 8k gray green .25 .20
Nos. 526-528 (3) 2.05 1.65

Joseph V. Myslbek (1848-1922), sculptor.

Beethoven — A208

House of Artists — A209

1952, June 7 Unwmk. *Perf. 11½*

529 A208 1.50k sepia .35 .25
530 A209 3k red brown .40 .25
531 A208 5k indigo 1.25 .75
Nos. 529-531 (3) 2.00 1.25

International Music Festival, Prague, 1952.

Lidice, Symbol of a New Life — A210

1952, June 10 *Perf. 12½*

532 A210 1.50k dk violet brn .20 .20
533 A210 5k dark blue 1.25 .75

Destruction of Lidice, 10th anniversary.

Jan Hus — A211

Bethlehem Chapel — A212

1952, July 5

534 A211 1.50k brown .20 .20
535 A212 3k red brown .20 .20
536 A211 5k black *1.40 1.00*
Nos. 534-536 (3) 1.80 1.40

550th anniv. of the installation of Jan Hus as pastor of Bethlehem Chapel, Prague.

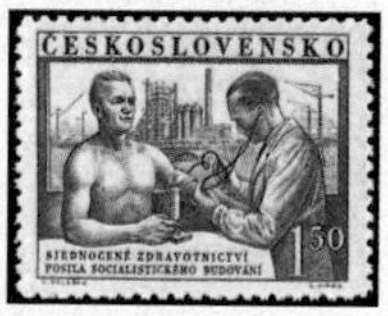

Doctor Examining Patient — A213

2k, Doctor, Nurse, Mother and child.

1952, July 31

537 A213 1.50k dark brown 1.50 1.00
538 A213 2k blue violet .35 .20
539 A213 3k rose brown .35 .20
Nos. 537-539 (3) 2.20 1.40

Czechoslovakia's Unified Health Service.

Relay Race — A214

1952, Aug. 2 *Perf. 11½*

540 A214 1.50k shown .85 .55
541 A214 2k Canoeing 2.50 1.00
542 A214 3k Cycling .55 .50
543 A214 4k Hockey *4.00 2.90*
Nos. 540-543 (4) 7.90 4.95

Issued to publicize Czechoslovakia's Unified Physical Education program.

F. L. Celakovski A215

Mikulas Ales A216

1952, Aug. 5 *Perf. 12½*

544 A215 1.50k dark brown .20 .20
545 A215 2k dark green 1.60 1.25

Centenary of the death of Frantisek L. Celakovski, poet and writer.

Perf. 11x11½

1952, Aug. 30 Engr. Unwmk.

546 A216 1.50k dk gray grn .35 .25
547 A216 6k red brown 2.50 1.75

Birth centenary of Mikulas Ales, painter.

17th Century Mining Towers — A217

Jan Zizka — A218

Designs: 1.50k, Coal Excavator. 2k, Peter Bezruc mine. 3k, Automatic coaling crane.

1952, Sept. 14 *Perf. 12½*

548 A217 1k sepia 1.25 .80
549 A217 1.50k dark blue .20 .20
550 A217 2k olive gray .20 .20
551 A217 3k violet brown .20 .20
Nos. 548-551 (4) 1.85 1.40

Miners' Day, Sept. 14, 1952. No. 550 also for the 85th anniv. of the birth of Peter Bezruc (Vladimir Vasek), poet.

1952, Oct. 5 Engr. *Perf. 11½*
Inscribed: ". . . . Armady 1952,"

Designs: 2k, Fraternization with Russians. 3k, Marching with flag.

552 A218 1.50k rose lake .20 .20
553 A218 2k olive bister .20 .20
554 A218 3k dk car rose .20 .20
555 A218 4k gray 1.10 .85
Nos. 552-555 (4) 1.70 1.45

Issued to publicize Army Day, Oct. 5, 1952.

Souvenir Sheet

Statues to Bulgarian Partisans and to Soviet Army — A219

1952, Oct. 18 Unwmk. *Perf. 12½*

556 A219 Sheet of 2 110.00 25.00
a. 2k deep carmine 35.00 7.50
b. 3k ultramarine 35.00 7.50

National Philatelic Exhibition, Bratislava, Oct. 18-Nov. 2, 1952.

Danube River, Bratislava
A220

1952, Oct. 18

557 A220 1.50k dark brown .20 .20

National Philatelic Exhibition, Bratislava.

Conference with Lenin and Stalin — A221

Worker and Nurse Holding Dove and Olive Branch — A222

1952, Nov. 7

558 A221 2k brown black 1.00 .75
559 A221 3k carmine .20 .20

35th anniv. of the Russian Revolution and to publicize Czechoslovak-Soviet friendship.

1952, Nov. 15 Photo. *Perf. 14*

560 A222 2k brown 1.20 .65
561 A222 3k red .20 .20

Issued to publicize the first State Congress of the Czechoslovak Red Cross.

Matej Louda, Hussite Leader, Painted by Mikulas Ales
A223

3k, Dragon-killer Trutnov, painted by Ales.

1952, Nov. 18 Engr. *Perf. 11½*

562 A223 2k red brown .40 .20
563 A223 3k grnsh gray .80 .25

Mikulas Ales, painter, birth cent.

Gottwald Type of 1948-49

1952, June 2 Unwmk. *Perf. 12½*
Size: 19x24mm

564 A135 1k dark green .60 .20

"Peace" Flags — A224

Dove by Picasso — A225

1952, Dec. 12 Photo. *Perf. 14*

565 A224 3k red brown .40 .20
566 A224 4k deep blue 1.50 1.00

Issued to publicize the Congress of Nations for Peace, Vienna, Dec. 12-19, 1952.

1953, Jan. 17

Design: 4k, Czech Family.

567 A225 1.50k dark brown .20 .20
568 A225 4k slate blue .75 .45

2nd Czechoslovak Peace Congress.

Smetana Museum — A226

Design: 4k, Jirásek Museum.

1953, Feb. 10 Engr. *Perf. 11½*

569 A226 1.50k dk violet brn .20 .20
570 A226 4k dark gray 1.50 .90

Prof. Zdenek Nejedly, 75th birth anniv.

Martin Kukucin — A227

Jaroslav Vrchlicky — A228

Designs: 2k, Karel Jaromir Erben. 3k, Vaclav Matej Kramerius. 5k, Josef Dobrovsky.

1953, Feb. 28

571 A227 1k gray .20 .20
572 A228 1.50k olive .20 .20
573 A228 2k rose lake .20 .20
574 A228 3k lt brown .75 .50
575 A228 5k slate blue 1.50 1.10
Nos. 571-575 (5) 2.85 2.20

Issued to honor Czech writers and poets: 1k, 25th anniv. of death of Kukucin. 1.50k, birth cent. of Vrchlicky. 2k, cent. of completion of "Kytice" by Erben. 3k, birth bicent. of Kramerius. 5k, birth bicent. of Dobrovsky.

Militia — A229

Gottwald — A230

Design: 8k, Portraits of Stalin and Gottwald and Peoples Assembly.

Perf. 13½x14

1953, Feb. 25 Photo. Unwmk.

576 A229 1.50k deep blue .20 .20
577 A230 3k red .20 .20
578 A229 8k dark brown 2.40 1.00
Nos. 576-578 (3) 2.80 1.40

5th anniv. of the defeat of the attempt to reinstate capitalism.

Book and Torch — A231

Design: 3k, Bedrich Vaclavek.

1953, Mar. 5 Engr. *Perf. 11½*

579 A231 1k sepia 1.50 .75
580 A231 3k orange brown .20 .20

Bedrich Vaclavek (1897-1943), socialist writer.

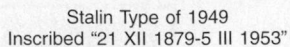

Stalin Type of 1949
Inscribed "21 XII 1879-5 III 1953"

1953, Mar. 12

581 A154 1.50k black .35 .25

Death of Joseph Stalin, Mar. 5, 1953.

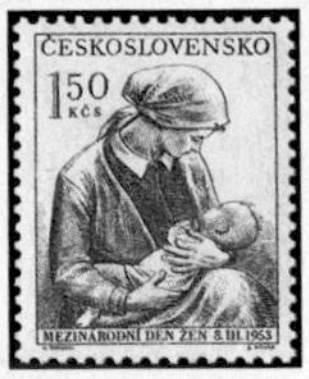

Mother and Child — A232

Girl Revolutionist
A233

1953, Mar. 8

582 A232 1.50k ultra .20 .20
583 A233 2k brown red 1.25 .75

International Women's Day.

Klement Gottwald — A234

1953, Mar. 19

584 A234 1.50k black .20 .20
585 A234 3k black .20 .20

Souvenir Sheet
Imperf

586 A234 5k black 5.75 4.00

Death of Pres. Klement Gottwald, 3/14/53.

Josef Pecka, Ladislav Zapotocky and Josef Hybes — A236

1953, Apr. 7 Unwmk. *Perf. 11½*

587 A236 2k lt violet brn .20 .20

75th anniversary of the first congress of the Czech Social Democratic Party.

Cyclists — A237

1953, Apr. 29

588 A237 3k deep blue .75 .35

6th International Peace Bicycle Race, Prague-Berlin-Warsaw.

Medal of "May 1, 1890"
A238

Designs: 1.50k, Lenin and Stalin. 3k, May Day Parade. 8k, Marx and Engels.

Engraved and Photogravure

1953, Apr. 30 *Perf. 11½x11, 14*

589 A238 1k chocolate 1.50 .75
590 A238 1.50k dark gray .20 .20
591 A238 3k carmine lake .20 .20
592 A238 8k dk gray green .35 .20
Nos. 589-592 (4) 2.25 1.35

Issued to publicize Labor Day, May 1, 1953.

Sowing Grain — A239

1953, May 8 Photo. *Perf. 14*

593 A239 1.50k shown .35 .20
594 A239 7k Reaper 1.60 1.40

Socialization of the village.

Dam — A240

Welder — A241

Design: 3k, Iron works.

1953, May 8 *Perf. 11½*

595 A240 1.50k gray 1.25 .60
596 A241 2k blue gray .20 .20
597 A240 3k red brown .20 .20
Nos. 595-597 (3) 1.65 1.00

Josef Slavik — A242

Leos Janacek — A243

1953, June 19 Photo.

598 A242 75h dp gray blue .75 .20
599 A243 1.60k dark brown 1.00 .20

Issued on the occasion of the International Music Festival, Prague, 1953.

Gottwald Type of 1948-49

Perf. 12½ (15h, 1k), 11½ (20h, 3k)

1953

600 A135 15h yellow green .35 .20
601 A135 20h dk violet brn .50 .20
602 A135 1k purple 1.25 .20
603 A135 3k brown car .20 .20
604 A135 3k gray .80 .20
Nos. 600-604 (5) 3.10 1.00

Nos. 600-604 vary slightly in size.

Pres. Antonin Zapotocky — A244

1953, June 19 *Perf. 14*

605 A244 30h violet blue .75 .20
606 A244 60h cerise 1.00 .20

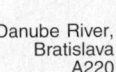

Julius Fucik
A245

Book and Carnation
A246

1953, Sept. 8 **Engr.** ***Perf. 12½***

607	A245 40h dk violet brn	.30	.20
608	A246 60h pink	.50	.30

10th anniv. of the death of Julius Fucik, Communist leader executed by the Nazis.

Miner and Flag — A247

Design: 60h, Oil field and workers.

1953, Sept. 10 ***Perf. 11½***

609	A247 30h gray	.25	.20
610	A247 60h brown vio	1.25	.50

Miner's Day, Sept. 10, 1953.

Volleyball Game — A248

Motorcyclist
A249

Design: 60h, Woman throwing javelin.

1953, Sept. 15

611	A248 30h brown red	5.25	1.50
612	A249 40h dk violet brn	3.25	1.00
613	A248 60h rose violet	2.75	1.00
	Nos. 611-613 (3)	11.25	3.50

Hussite Warrior
A250

Pres. Antonin Zapotocky
A251

Designs: 60h, Soldier presenting arms. 1k, Red army soldiers.

1953, Oct. 8

614	A250 30h brown	.30	.20
615	A250 60h rose lake	.65	.20
616	A250 1k brown red	1.50	1.25
	Nos. 614-616 (3)	2.45	1.65

Issued to publicize Army Day, Oct. 3, 1953.

1953 **Unwmk.** ***Perf. 11½, 12½***

617	A251 30h violet blue	.45	.20
618	A251 60h carmine rose	.80	.20

#617 is perf. 11½ & measures 19x23mm, #618 perf. 12½ & 18½x23½mm.
See No. 780.

Charles Bridge and Prague Castle — A252

Korean and Czech Girls — A253

1953, Aug. 15 **Engr.** ***Perf. 11½***

619	A252 5k gray	3.00	.20

1953, Oct. 11 ***Perf. 11x11½***

620	A253 30h dark brown	2.25	1.50

Czechoslovakia's friendship with Korea.

Flags, Hradcany Castle and Kremlin — A254

Designs: 60h, Lomonosov University, Moscow. 1.20k, Lenin Ship Canal.

1953, Nov. 7

621	A254 30h dark gray	.80	.55
622	A254 60h dark brown	1.25	1.00
623	A254 1.20k ultra	4.00	2.00
	Nos. 621-623 (3)	6.05	3.55

Czechoslovak-Soviet friendship month.

Emmy Destinn, Opera Singer — A255

National Theater, Prague — A256

Portrait: 2k, Eduard Vojan, actor.

1953, Nov. 18 ***Perf. 14***

624	A255 30h blue black	1.25	.75
625	A256 60h brown	.40	.40
626	A255 2k sepia	3.25	1.25
	Nos. 624-626 (3)	4.90	2.40

Natl. Theater founding, 70th anniv.

Josef Manes — A257

Vaclav Hollar — A258

1953, Nov. 28 ***Perf. 11x11½***

627	A257 60h brown carmine	.35	.20
628	A257 1.20k deep blue	1.50	.90

Issued to honor Josef Manes, painter.

1953, Dec. 5

Portrait: 1.20k, Head framed, facing right.

629	A258 30h brown black	.35	.20
630	A258 1.20k dark brown	1.50	.65

Vaclav Hollar, artist and etcher.

Leo N. Tolstoi — A259

1953, Dec. 29 **Unwmk.**

631	A259 60h dark green	.35	.20
632	A259 1k chocolate	1.50	.65

Leo N. Tolstoi, 125th birth anniv.

Locomotive — A260

Design: 1k, Plane loading mail.

Engraved, Center Photogravure

1953, Dec. 29 ***Perf. 11½x11***

633	A260 60h brn org & gray vio	1.50	.50
634	A260 1k org brn & brt bl	4.00	1.25

Lenin — A261

Lenin Museum, Prague — A262

1954, Jan. 21 **Engr.** ***Perf. 11½***

635	A261 30h dark brown	.45	.20
636	A262 1.40k chocolate	1.50	.90

30th anniversary of the death of Lenin.

Klement Gottwald — A263

Design: 2.40k, Revolutionist with flag.

1954, Feb. 18 ***Perf. 11x11½, 14x13½***

637	A263 60h dark brown	.30	.20
638	A263 2.40k rose lake	4.25	1.50

25th anniversary of the fifth congress of the Communist Party in Czechoslovakia.

Gottwald Mausoleum, Prague — A264

Gottwald and Stalin
A265

1.20k, Lenin & Stalin mausoleum, Moscow.

1954, Mar. 5 ***Perf. 11½, 14x13½***

639	A264 30h olive brown	.35	.20
640	A265 60h deep ultra	.35	.20
641	A264 1.20k rose brown	2.25	1.00
	Nos. 639-641 (3)	2.95	1.40

1st anniv. of the deaths of Stalin and Gottwald.

Two Runners — A266

Group of Hikers — A267

Design: 1k, Woman swimmer.

1954, Apr. 24 ***Perf. 11½***

642	A266 30h dark brown	2.25	1.00
643	A267 80h dark green	7.50	3.75
644	A266 1k dk violet blue	1.75	.75
	Nos. 642-644 (3)	11.50	5.50

Nurse — A268

Designs: 15h, Construction worker. 40h, Postwoman. 45h, Ironworker. 50h, Soldier. 75h, Lathe operator. 80h, Textile worker. 1k, Farm woman. 1.20k, Scientist and microscope. 1.60k, Miner. 2k, Physician and baby. 2.40k, Engineer. 3k, Chemist.

1954 ***Perf. 12½x12, 11½x11***

645	A268 15h dark green	.30	.20
646	A268 20h lt violet	.35	.20
647	A268 40h dark brown	.45	.20
648	A268 45h dk gray blue	.35	.20
649	A268 50h dk gray green	.45	.20
650	A268 75h deep blue	.45	.20
651	A268 80h violet brown	.45	.20
652	A268 1k green	.75	.20
653	A268 1.20k dk violet blue	.45	.20
654	A268 1.60k brown blk	1.10	.20
655	A268 2k orange brown	1.60	.20
656	A268 2.40k violet blue	1.50	.20
657	A268 3k carmine	1.50	.20
	Nos. 645-657 (13)	9.70	2.60

Antonin Dvorák — A269

Prokop Divis — A270

40h, Leos Janacek. 60h, Bedrich Smetana.

1954, May 22 ***Perf. 11x11½***

658	A269 30h violet brown	2.00	.25
659	A269 40h brick red	2.50	.30
660	A269 60h dark blue	1.00	.20
	Nos. 658-660 (3)	5.50	.75

"Year of Czech Music," 1954.

1954, June 15

661	A270 30h gray	.30	.20
662	A270 75h violet brown	1.20	.50

200th anniv. of the invention of a lightning conductor by Prokop Divis.

Slovak Insurrectionist A271

Anton P. Chekhov A272

Design: 1.20k, Partisan woman.

1954, Aug. 28 *Perf. 11½*

663 A271 30h brown orange .20 .20
664 A271 1.20k dark blue .80 .75

Slovak national uprising, 10th anniv.

1954, Sept. 24

665 A272 30h dull gray grn .25 .20
666 A272 45h dull gray brn 1.00 .65

50th anniv. of the death of Chekhov, writer.

Soviet Representative Giving Agricultural Instruction — A273

Designs: 60h, Soviet industrial instruction. 2k, Dancers (cultural collaboration).

1954, Nov. 6 *Perf. 11½x11*

667 A273 30h yellow brown .20 .20
668 A273 60h dark blue .20 .20
669 A273 2k vermilion 1.40 1.25
Nos. 667-669 (3) 1.80 1.65

Czechoslovak-Soviet friendship month.

Jan Neruda — A274

60h, Janko Jesensky. 1.60k, Jiri Wolker.

1954, Nov. 25 *Perf. 11x11½*

670 A274 30h dark blue .85 .20
671 A274 60h dull red 1.40 .50
672 A274 1.60k sepia .35 .20
Nos. 670-672 (3) 2.60 .90

Issued to honor Czechoslovak poets.

View of Telc A275

Views: 60h, Levoca. 3k, Ceske Budejovice.

1954, Dec. 10 **Engr. & Photo.**

673 A275 30h black & bis .35 .20
674 A275 60h brown & bis .35 .20
675 A275 3k black & bis 2.25 1.50
Nos. 673-675 (3) 2.95 1.90

Pres. Antonin Zapotocky A276

Attacking Soldiers A278

1954, Dec. 18 **Engr.** *Perf. 11½*

676 A276 30h black brown .45 .20
677 A276 60h dark blue .45 .20

Souvenir Sheet

Imperf

678 A276 2k deep claret 15.00 7.50

70th birthday of Pres. Antonin Zapotocky. See Nos. 829-831.

1954, Oct. 3 *Perf. 11½*

Design: 2k, Soldier holding child.

679 A278 60h dark green .30 .20
680 A278 2k dark brown 1.20 1.00

Army Day, Oct. 6, 1954.

Woman Holding Torch — A279

Comenius University Building A280

Design: 45h, Ski jumper.

1955, Jan. 20 **Engr.**

681 A279 30h red 2.25 .50

Engraved and Photogravure

682 A279 45h black & blue 3.75 .50

First National Spartacist Games, 1955.

1955, Jan. 28 **Engr.** *Perf. 11½*

Design: 75h, Jan A. Komensky medal.

683 A280 60h deep green .30 .20
684 A280 75h chocolate 1.20 .65

35th anniversary of the founding of Comenius University, Bratislava.

Czechoslovak Automobile A281

60h, Textile worker. 75h, Lathe operator.

1955, Mar. 15 **Unwmk.**

685 A281 45h dull green 1.50 .45
686 A281 60h dk violet blue .60 .20
687 A281 75h sepia .90 .20
Nos. 685-687 (3) 3.00 .85

Woman Decorating Soviet Soldier — A282

Stalin Memorial, Prague — A283

Designs: 35h, Tankman with flowers. 60h, Children greeting soldier.

1955, May 5 **Engr.** *Perf. 11½*

688 A282 30h blue .35 .20
689 A282 35h dark brown 1.50 .75
690 A282 60h cerise .35 .20

Photo.

691 A283 60h sepia .35 .20
Nos. 688-691 (4) 2.55 1.35

10th anniv. of Czechoslovakia's liberation.

Music and Spring — A284

Foundry Worker — A285

Design: 1k, Woman with lyre.

1955, May 12 **Engr. & Photo.**

692 A284 30h black & pale blue .35 .25
693 A284 1k black & pale rose 1.50 1.50

International Music Festival, Prague, 1955.

1955, May 12 **Engr.**

Design: 45h, Farm workers.

694 A285 30h violet .20 .20
695 A285 45h green 1.40 .75

Issued to publicize the third congress of the Trade Union Revolutionary Movement.

Woman Athlete — A286

Jakub Arbes — A287

60h, Dancing couple. 1.60k, Athlete.

1955, June 21

696 A286 20h violet blue 1.00 .50
697 A286 60h green .35 .20
698 A286 1.60k red .75 .30
Nos. 696-698 (3) 2.10 1.00

Issued to publicize the first National Spartacist Games, Prague, June-July, 1955.

1955

Portraits: 30h, Jan Stursa. 40h, Elena Marothy-Soltesova. 60h, Josef Vaclav Sladek. 75h, Alexander Stepanovic Popov. 1.40k, Jan Holly. 1.60k, Pavel Josef Safarik.

699 A287 20h brown .25 .20
700 A287 30h black .25 .20
701 A287 40h gray green .75 .20
702 A287 60h black .50 .20
703 A287 75h claret 1.75 .70
704 A287 1.40k black, *cr* .50 .20
705 A287 1.60k dark blue .50 .20
Nos. 699-705 (7) 4.50 1.90

Various anniversaries of prominent Slavs.

Girl and Boy of Two Races — A288

Costume of Ocova, Slovakia — A289

1955, July 20

706 A288 60h violet blue .75 .20

5th World Festival of Youth in Warsaw, July 31-Aug. 14.

1955, July 25

Regional Costumes: 75h, Detva man, Slovakia. 1.60k, Chodsko man, Bohemia. 2k, Hana woman, Moravia.

Frame and Outlines in Brown

707 A289 60h orange & rose 9.00 6.00
708 A289 75h orange & lilac 3.75 3.75
709 A289 1.60k blue & orange 11.00 6.75
710 A289 2k yellow & rose 11.00 6.75
Nos. 707-710 (4) 34.75 23.25

Carp A290

Designs: 30h, Beetle. 35h, Gray Partridge. 1.40k, Butterfly. 1.50k, Hare.

1955, Aug. 8 **Engr. & Photo.**

711 A290 20h sepia & lt bl 2.25 .35
712 A290 30h sepia & pink 1.50 .30
713 A290 35h sepia & buff 1.50 .75
714 A290 1.40k sepia & cream 7.50 4.50
715 A290 1.50k sepia & lt grn 2.50 1.00
Nos. 711-715 (5) 15.25 6.90

Tabor A291

45h, Prachatice. 60h, Jindrichuv Hradec.

1955, Aug. 26 **Engr.**

716 A291 30h violet brown .35 .20
717 A291 45h rose carmine 1.50 .75
718 A291 60h sage green .75 .20
Nos. 716-718 (3) 2.60 1.15

Issued to publicize the architectural beauty of the towns of Southern Bohemia.

Souvenir Sheet

Various Views of Prague — A292

1955, Sept. 10 **Engr.** *Perf. 14x13½*

719 A292 Sheet of 5 24.00 27.50
a. 30h gray black 4.50 5.25
b. 45h gray black 4.50 5.25
c. 60h rose lake 4.50 5.25
d. 75h rose lake 4.50 5.25
e. 1.60k gray black 4.50 5.25

International Philatelic Exhibition, Prague, Sept. 10-25, 1955. Size: 145x110mm. Exists imperf., value $40.

Motorcyclists A293

Workers, Soldier and Pioneer A294

1955, Aug. 28

720 A293 60h violet brown 3.00 .75

30th International Motorcycle Races at Gottwaldov, Sept. 13-18, 1955.

1955, Oct. 6 **Unwmk.** *Perf. 11½*

Army Day: 60h, Tanks and planes.

721 A294 30h violet brown .35 .20
722 A294 60h slate 1.75 1.25

Hans Christian Andersen — A295

Portraits: 40h, Friedrich von Schiller. 60h, Adam Mickiewicz. 75h, Walt Whitman.

1955, Oct. 27

723	A295	30h brown red	.35	.20
724	A295	40h dark blue	2.25	1.00
725	A295	60h deep claret	.35	.20
726	A295	75h greenish black	.75	.35
		Nos. 723-726 (4)	3.70	1.75

Issued in honor of these four poets and to mark the 100th anniversary of the publication of Walt Whitman's "Leaves of Grass."

Railroad Bridge A296

30h, Train crossing bridge. 60h, Train approaching tunnel. 1.60k, Miners' housing project.

Inscribed: "Stavba Socialismu"

1955, Dec. 15

727	A296	20h dull green	.40	.20
728	A296	30h violet brown	.80	.20
729	A296	60h slate	.80	.20
730	A296	1.60k carmine rose	.55	.20
		Nos. 727-730 (4)	2.55	.80

Issued to publicize socialist public works.

Hydroelectric Plant — A297

Jewelry — A298

2nd Five Year Plan: 10h, Miner with drill. 25h, Building construction. 30h, Harvester. 60h, Metallurgical plant.

Inscribed: "Druhy Petilety Plan 1956-1960."

1956, Feb. 20 *Perf. 11½x11*

731	A297	5h violet brown	.30	.20
732	A297	10h gray black	.30	.20
733	A297	25h dk car rose	.55	.20
734	A297	30h green	.35	.20
735	A297	60h violet blue	.55	.20
		Nos. 731-735 (5)	2.05	1.00

1956, Mar. 17 *Perf. 11x11½*

736	A298	30h shown	.55	.20
737	A298	45h Glassware	4.00	2.00
738	A298	60h Ceramics	.80	.20
739	A298	75h Textiles	.65	.30
		Nos. 736-739 (4)	6.00	2.70

Products of Czechoslovakian industries.

Karlovy Vary (Karlsbad) A299

"We Serve our People" A300

Various Spas: 45h, Marianske Lazne (Marienbad). 75h, Piestany. 1.20k, Tatry Vysne Ruzbachy (Tatra Mountains).

1956, Mar. 17

740	A299	30h olive green	1.50	.30
741	A299	45h brown	1.20	.30
742	A299	75h claret	6.00	4.00
743	A299	1.20k ultra	.80	.30
		Nos. 740-743 (4)	9.50	4.90

Issued to publicize Czechoslovakian spas.

1956, Apr. 9 Photo. *Perf. 11x11½*

Designs: 60h, Russian War Memorial, Berlin. 1k, Tank crewman with standard.

744	A300	30h olive brown	.75	.20
745	A300	60h carmine rose	.75	.20
746	A300	1k ultra	4.75	3.00
		Nos. 744-746 (3)	6.25	3.40

Exhibition: "The Construction and Defense of our Country," Prague, Apr., 1956.

Cyclists — A301

Girl Basketball Players — A302

Athletes and Olympic Rings — A303

Engraved and Photogravure

1956, Apr. 25 Unwmk. *Perf. 11½*

747	A301	30h green & lt blue	3.25	.30
748	A302	45h dk blue & car	1.25	.30
749	A303	75h brown & lemon	1.00	.65
		Nos. 747-749 (3)	5.50	1.25

9th Intl. Peace Cycling Race, Warsaw-Berlin-Prague, May 1-15, 1956 (No. 747). 5th European Womens' Basketball Championship (No. 748). Summer Olympics, Melbourne, Nov. 22-Dec. 8, 1956 (No. 749).

Mozart — A304

Home Guard — A305

45h, Josef Myslivecek. 60h, Jiri Benda. 1k, Bertramka House, Prague. 1.40k, Xaver Dusek (1731-99) and wife Josepha. 1.60k, Nostic Theater, Prague.

1956, May 12 Engr.

Design in Gray Black

750	A304	30h bister	1.50	.35
751	A304	45h gray green	13.50	9.00
752	A304	60h pale rose lilac	1.50	.35
753	A304	1k salmon	1.90	.35
754	A304	1.40k lt blue	4.50	.75
755	A304	1.60k lemon	3.00	.35
		Nos. 750-755 (6)	25.90	11.15

200th anniv. of the birth of Wolfgang Amadeus Mozart and to publicize the International Music Festival in Prague.

1956, May 25

756	A305	60h violet blue	.75	.20

Issued to commemorate the first meeting of the Home Guard, Prague, May 25-27, 1956.

Josef Kajetan Tyl — A306

River Patrol — A307

Portraits: 20h, Ludovit Stur. 30h, Frana Sramek. 1.40k, Karel Havlicek Borovsky.

1956, June 23

757	A306	20h dull purple	.75	.20
758	A306	30h blue	.45	.20
759	A306	60h black	.45	.20
760	A306	1.40k claret	3.00	1.75
		Nos. 757-760 (4)	4.65	2.35

Issued to honor various Czechoslovakian writers. See Nos. 781-784, 873-876.

1956, July 8 *Perf. 11x11½*

Design: 60h, Guard and dog.

761	A307	30h ultra	.85	.25
762	A307	60h green	.60	.20

Issued to honor men of Frontier Guard.

Type of 1956 and

Steeplechase — A308

1956, Sept. 8 Unwmk. *Perf. 11½*

763	A308	60h indigo & bister	2.75	.70
764	A308	80h brown vio & vio	1.50	.35
765	A303	1.20k slate & orange	2.75	1.50
		Nos. 763-765 (3)	7.00	2.55

Steeplechase, Pardubice, 1956 (No. 763). Marathon race, Kosice, 1956 (No. 764). Olympic Games, Melbourne, Nov. 22-Dec. 8 (No. 765).

Woman Gathering Grapes — A309

Fishermen — A310

35h, Women gathering hops. 95h, Logging.

1956, Sept. 20 Engr.

766	A309	30h brown lake	.35	.20
767	A309	35h gray green	.35	.20
768	A310	80h dark blue	.75	.20
769	A310	95h chocolate	2.25	1.00
		Nos. 766-769 (4)	3.70	1.60

Issued to publicize natural resources.

European Timetable Conf., Prague, Nov. 9-13 — A311

A312

Locomotives: 10h, 1846. 30h, 1855. 40h, 1945. 45h, 1952. 60h, 1955. 1k, 1954.

1956, Nov. 9 Unwmk. *Perf. 11½*

770	A311	10h brown	1.50	.30
771	A312	30h gray	3.00	.30
772	A312	40h green	4.50	.45
773	A312	45h brown car	13.50	6.75
774	A312	60h indigo	3.00	.30
775	A312	1k ultra	5.25	.45
		Nos. 770-775 (6)	30.75	8.55

Costume of Moravia — A313

Regional Costumes (women): 1.20k, Blata, Bohemia. 1.40k, Cicmany, Slovakia. 1.60k, Novohradsko, Slovakia.

1956, Dec. 15 *Perf. 13½*

776	A313	30h brn, ultra & car	1.50	1.50
777	A313	1.20k brn, car & ultra	2.50	.35
778	A313	1.40k brn, ocher & ver	7.50	2.50
779	A313	1.60k brn, car & grn	3.00	.75
		Nos. 776-779 (4)	14.50	5.10

See Nos. 832-835.

Zapotocky Type of 1953

1956, Oct. 7 Unwmk. *Perf. 12½*

780	A251	30h blue	.75	.20

Portrait Type of 1956

15h, Ivan Olbracht. 20h, Karel Toman. 30h, F. X. Salda. 1.60k, Terezia Vansova.

1957, Jan. 18 Engr. *Perf. 11½*

781	A306	15h dk red brn, *cr*	.30	.20
782	A306	20h dk green, *cr*	.30	.20
783	A306	30h dk brown, *cr*	.30	.20
784	A306	1.60k dk blue, *cr*	.60	.20
		Nos. 781-784 (4)	1.50	.80

Issued in honor of Czechoslovakian writers.

Kolin Cathedral — A315

Views: No. 786, Banska Stiavnica. No. 787, Uherske Hradiste. No. 788, Karlstein. No. 789, Charles Bridge, Prague. 1.25k, Moravska Trebova.

1957, Feb. 23

785	A315	30h dk blue gray	.30	.20
786	A315	30h rose violet	.45	.20
787	A315	60h deep rose	.45	.20
788	A315	60h gray green	.45	.20

789 A315 60h brown .60 .20
790 A315 1.25k gray 2.50 1.50
Nos. 785-790 (6) 4.75 2.50

Anniversaries of various towns and landmarks.

Komensky Mausoleum, Naarden A316

Jan A. Komensky A317

Farm Woman — A318

Old Prints: 40h, Komensky teaching. 1k, Sun, moon, stars and earth.

Perf. 11½x11, 14 (A317)

1957, Mar. 28 Engr. Unwmk.

791 A316 30h pale brown .45 .20
792 A316 40h dark green .45 .20
793 A317 60h chocolate 3.00 .75
794 A316 1k carmine rose .60 .20
Nos. 791-794 (4) 4.50 1.35

300th anniv. of the publication of "Didactica Opera Omnia" by J. A. Komensky (Comenius). No. 793 issued in sheets of four.

1957, Mar. 22 *Perf. 11½*

795 A318 30h lt blue green .75 .20

3rd Cong. of Agricultural Cooperatives.

Cyclists A319

Woman Archer A320

Boxers — A321

Rescue Team A322

1957, Apr. 30 *Perf. 11½x11, 11x11½*

796 A319 30h sepia & ultra .60 .20
797 A319 60h dull grn & bis 2.25 1.25
798 A320 60h gray & emer .45 .20
799 A321 60h sepia & org .45 .20
800 A322 60h violet & choc .75 .20
Nos. 796-800 (5) 4.50 2.05

10th Intl. Peace Cycling Race, Prague-Berlin-Warsaw (#796-797). Intl. Archery Championships (#798). European Boxing Championships, Prague (#799). Mountain Climbing Rescue Service (#800).

Jan V. Stamic — A323

Musicians: No. 802, Ferdinand Laub. No. 803, Frantisek Ondricek. No. 804, Josef B. Foerster. No. 805, Vitezslav Novak. No. 806, Josef Suk.

1957, May 12 *Perf. 11½*

801 A323 60h purple .35 .20
802 A323 60h black .35 .20
803 A323 60h slate blue .35 .20
804 A323 60h brown .35 .20
805 A323 60h dull red brn .90 .20
806 A323 60h blue green .35 .20
Nos. 801-806 (6) 2.65 1.20

Spring Music Festival, Prague.

Josef Bozek — A324

School of Engineering A325

60h, F. J. Gerstner. 1k, R. Skuhersky.

1957, May 25

807 A324 30h bluish black .20 .20
808 A324 60h gray brown .35 .20
809 A324 1k rose lake .35 .20
810 A325 1.40k blue violet .75 .20
Nos. 807-810 (4) 1.65 .80

School of Engineering in Prague, 250th anniv.

Pioneer and Philatelic Symbols A326

Design: 60h, Girl and carrier pigeon.

Engraved and Photogravure

1957, June 8 *Perf. 11½*

811 A326 30h olive grn & org .50 .20

Engr. *Perf. 13½*

812 A326 60h brn & vio bl 1.50 1.00

Youth Philatelic Exhibition, Pardubice.
No. 812 was printed in miniature sheets of 4. Value $12.

"Grief" A327

Motorcyclists A328

Design: 60h, Rose, symbol of new life.

1957, June 10

813 A327 30h black .35 .20
814 A327 60h blk & rose red 1.25 .45

Destruction of Lidice, 15th anniversary.

1957, July 5 *Perf. 11½*

815 A328 60h dk gray & blue 1.50 .30

32nd International Motorcycle Race.

Karel Klic — A329

Josef Ressel — A330

1957, July 5

816 A329 30h gray black .60 .20
817 A330 60h violet blue .60 .20

Klic, inventor of photogravure, and Ressel, inventor of the ship screw.

Chamois — A331

Gentian A332

Designs: 30h, Brown bear. 60h, Edelweiss. 1.25k, Tatra Mountains.

1957, Aug. 28 Engr. *Perf. 11½*

818 A331 20h emer & brnsh gray 1.00 .35
819 A331 30h lt blue & brn 1.00 .20
820 A332 40h gldn brn & vio bl 1.75 .35
821 A332 60h yellow & grn 1.00 .20

Size: 48x28½mm

822 A332 1.25k ol grn & bis 1.75 1.00
Nos. 818-822 (5) 6.50 2.10

Tatra Mountains National Park.

"Marycka Magdonova" A333

Man Holding Banner of Trade Union Cong. A334

Engraved and Photogravure

1957, Sept. 15 Unwmk. *Perf. 11½*

823 A333 60h black & dull red .45 .20

90th birthday of Petr Bezruc, poet and author of "Marycka Magdonova."

1957, Sept. 28 Engr.

824 A334 75h rose red .45 .20

4th Intl. Trade Union Cong., Leipzig, 10/4-15.

Television Transmitter and Antennas — A335

Design: 60h, Family watching television.

1957, Oct. 19 Engr. *Perf. 11½*

825 A335 40h dk blue & car .30 .20
826 A335 60h redsh brown & emer .45 .20

Issued to publicize the television industry.

Worker, Globe and Lenin A336

60h, Worker, factory, hammer and sickle.

1957, Nov. 7 *Perf. 12x11½*

827 A336 30h claret .20 .20
828 A336 60h gray blue .25 .20

Russian Revolution, 40th anniversary.

Zapotocky Type of 1954 dated: 19 XII 1884-13 XI 1957

1957, Nov. 18 Unwmk. *Perf. 11½*

829 A276 30h black .20 .20
830 A276 60h black .25 .20

Souvenir Sheet

Imperf

831 A276 2k black 4.00 2.00

Death of Pres. Antonin Zapotocky.

Costume Type of 1956

Regional Costumes: 45h, Pilsen woman, Bohemia. 75h, Slovacko man, Moravia. 1.25k, Hana woman, Moravia. 1.95k, Teshinsko woman, Silesia.

1957, Dec. 18 Engr. *Perf. 13½*

832 A313 45h brn, bl & dk red 4.25 1.50
833 A313 75h dk brn, red & grn 3.00 .80
834 A313 1.25k dk brn, scar & ocher 5.25 1.50
835 A313 1.95k sepia, bl & ver 6.00 3.75
Nos. 832-835 (4) 18.50 7.55

A337

A338

Designs: 30h, Radio telescope and observatory. 45h, Meteorological station in High Tatra. 75h, Sputnik 2 over Earth.

1957, Dec. 20 *Perf. 11½*

836 A337 30h violet brn & yel 1.75 .65
837 A338 45h sepia & lt bl .45 .35
838 A337 75h claret & blue 2.50 1.00
Nos. 836-838 (3) 4.70 2.00

IGY, 1957-58. No. 838 also for the launching of Sputnik 2, Nov. 3, 1957.

Girl Skater — A339

Litomysl Castle — A340

Designs: 40h, Canoeing. 60h, Volleyball. 80h, Parachutist. 1.60k, Soccer.

1958, Jan. 25 Engr. *Perf. 11½x12*

839 A339 30h rose violet 1.25 .25
840 A339 40h blue .25 .20
841 A339 60h redsh brown .25 .20
842 A339 80h violet blue 1.50 .50
843 A339 1.60k brt green .45 .20
Nos. 839-843 (5) 3.70 1.35

Issued to publicize various sports championship events in 1958.

1958, Feb. 10 *Perf. 11½*

Design: 60h, Bethlehem Chapel.

844 A340 30h green .30 .20
845 A340 60h redsh brown .30 .20

80th anniversary of the birth of Zdenek Nejedly, restorer of Bethlehem Chapel.

Giant Excavator A341

Jewelry — A342

Peace Dove and: 60h, Soldiers, flame and banner, horiz. 1.60k, Harvester and rainbow, horiz.

1958, Feb. 25

846 A341 30h gray violet & yel .20 .20
847 A341 60h gray brown & car .30 .20
848 A341 1.60k green & dull yel .50 .20
Nos. 846-848 (3) 1.00 .60

10th anniv. of the "Victorious February."

Engraved and Photogravure

1958 Unwmk. *Perf. 11½*

Designs: 45h, Dolls. 60h, Textiles. 75h, Kaplan turbine. 1.20k, Glass.

849 A342 30h rose car & blue .40 .20
850 A342 45h rose red & pale lil .40 .20
851 A342 60h violet & aqua .60 .20
852 A342 75h ultra & salmon 1.50 .75
853 A342 1.20k blue grn & pink .60 .20
Nos. 849-853 (5) 3.50 1.55

Issued for the Universal and International Exposition at Brussels.

King George of Podebrad — A343

Design: 60h, View of Prague, 1628.

1958, May 19 Engr.

854 A343 30h carmine rose .50 .20
855 A343 60h violet blue .30 .20

Issued to publicize the National Archives Exhibition, Prague, May 15-Aug. 15.

"Towards the Stars" — A344

Women of Three Races — A345

Boy, Girl and Globes A346

1958, May 26

856 A344 30h carmine rose .75 .35
857 A345 45h rose violet .20 .20
858 A346 60h blue .20 .20
Nos. 856-858 (3) 1.15 .75

The Soc. for Dissemination of Political and Cultural Knowledge (#856). 4th Cong. of the Intl. Democratic Women's Fed. (#857). 1st World Trade Union Conf. of Working Youths, Prague, July 14-20 (#858).

Grain, Hammer and Sickle A347

Atomic Reactor A348

45h, Map of Czechoslovakia, hammer & sickle.

1958, May 26

859 A347 30h dull red .25 .20
860 A347 45h green .25 .20
861 A348 60h dark blue .25 .20
Nos. 859-861 (3) .75 .60

11th Congress of the Czech Communist Party and the 15th anniv. of the Russo-Czechoslovakian Treaty.

Karlovy Vary A349

Various Spas: 40h, Podebrady. 60h, Marianske Lazne. 80h, Luhacovice. 1.20k, Strbske Pleso. 1.60k, Trencianske Teplice.

1958, June 25

862 A349 30h rose claret .45 .20
863 A349 40h redsh brown .45 .20
864 A349 60h gray green .30 .20
865 A349 80h sepia .45 .20
866 A349 1.20k violet blue .60 .20
867 A349 1.60k lt violet 1.20 .75
Nos. 862-867 (6) 3.45 1.75

Telephone Operator A350

Pres. Novotny A351

Design: 45h, Radio transmitter.

1958, June 20

868 A350 30h black & brn org .30 .20
869 A350 45h black & lt grn .45 .20

Conference of Postal Ministers of Communist Countries, Prague, June 30-July 9.

1958-59 *Perf. 12½*

870 A351 30h brt violet blue .60 .20
b. Perf. 11½ .60 .20
870A A351 30h lt violet ('59) 4.00 1.75
871 A351 60h carmine rose .50 .20

Perf. 11½

Redrawn

871A A351 60h rose red .50 .20
Nos. 870-871A (4) 5.60 2.35

On No. 871 the top of the "6" turns down; on No. 871A it is open.

Czechoslovak Pavilion, Brussels — A352

1958, July 15 Engr. & Photo.

872 A352 1.95k lt blue & bis brn .90 .20

Czechoslovakia Week at the Universal and International Exhibition at Brussels.

Portrait Type of 1956

30h, Julius Fucik. 45h, G. K. Zechenter 60h, Karel Capek. 1.40k, Svatopluk Cech.

1958, Aug. 20 Engr. *Perf. 11½*

873 A306 30h rose red .30 .20
874 A306 45h violet 1.50 .50
875 A306 60h dk blue gray .50 .20
876 A306 1.40k gray .50 .20
Nos. 873-876 (4) 2.80 1.10

Death anniversaries of four famous Czechs.

The Artist and the Muse — A353

1958, Aug. 20 *Perf. 14*

877 A353 1.60k black 3.50 1.25

85th birthday of Max Svabinsky, artist and engraver.

No. 877 was printed in miniature sheets of 4. Value $24.

Children's Hospital, Brno — A354

Designs: 60h, New Town Hall, Brno. 1k, St. Thomas Church. 1.60k, View of Brno.

1958, Sept. 6 Unwmk. *Perf. 11½*

Size: 40x23mm

878 A354 30h violet .20 .20
879 A354 60h rose red .20 .20
880 A354 1k brown .45 .20

Perf. 14

Size: 50x28mm

881 A354 1.60k dk slate grn 1.90 1.75
Nos. 878-881 (4) 2.75 2.35

Natl. Phil. Exhib., Brno, Sept. 9.

No. 881 sold for 3.10k, including entrance ticket to exhibition. Issued in sheets of four.

Lepiota Procera — A355

Children on Beach — A356

Mushrooms: 40h, Boletus edulis. 60h, Krombholzia rufescens. 1.40k, Amanita muscaria L. 1.60k, Armillariella mellea.

1958, Oct. 6 *Perf. 14*

882 A355 30h dk brn, grn & buff 1.50 .75
883 A355 40h vio brn & brn org 2.25 .75
884 A355 60h black, red & buff 3.00 .75
885 A355 1.40k brown, scar & grn 3.75 2.00
886 A355 1.60k blk, red brn & ol 12.00 5.25
Nos. 882-886 (5) 22.50 9.50

1958, Oct. 24 Unwmk. *Perf. 14*

45h, Mother, child and bird. 60h, Skier.

887 A356 30h blue, yel & red .30 .20
888 A356 45h ultra & carmine 1.25 .65
889 A356 60h brown, blue & yel .30 .20
Nos. 887-889 (3) 1.85 1.05

UNESCO Headquarters in Paris opening, Nov. 3.

Bozek's Steam Car of 1815 A357

Designs: 45h, "Präsident" car of 1897. 60h, "Skoda" sports car. 80h, "Tatra" sedan. 1k, "Autocar Skoda" bus. 1.25k, Trucks.

Engraved and Photogravure

1958, Dec. 1 *Perf. 11½x11*

890 A357	30h vio blk & buff	.75	.20
891 A357	45h ol & lt ol grn	.75	.30
892 A357	60h ol gray & sal	1.75	.20
893 A357	80h claret & bl grn	1.10	.30
894 A357	1k brn & lt yel grn	1.50	.30
895 A357	1.25k green & buff	2.25	.45
	Nos. 890-895 (6)	8.10	1.75

Issued to honor the automobile industry.

Stamp of 1918 and Allegory — A358

1958, Dec. 18 Engr. *Perf. 11x11½*

896 A358 60h dark blue gray 1.00 .25

1st Czechoslovakian postage stamp, 40th anniv.

Ice Hockey A359

30h, Girl throwing javelin. 60h, Ice hockey. 1k, Hurdling. 1.60k, Rowing. 2k, High jump.

1959, Feb. 14 *Perf. 11½x11*

897 A359	20h dk brown & gray	.65	.20
898 A359	30h red brn & org brn	.45	.20
899 A359	60h dk bl & pale grn	.80	.20
900 A359	1k maroon & citron	.65	.20
901 A359	1.60k dull vio & lt bl	.95	.20
902 A359	2k red brn & lt bl	2.00	1.00
	Nos. 897-902 (6)	5.50	2.00

Congress Emblem — A360

"Equality of All Races" — A361

60h, Industrial & agricultural workers, emblem.

1959, Feb. 27 *Perf. 11½*

903 A360	30h maroon & lt blue	.45	.20
904 A360	60h dk blue & yellow	.45	.20

4th Agricultural Cooperative Cong. in Prague.

1959, Mar. 23

Designs: 1k, "Peace." 2k, Mother and Child: "Freedom for Colonial People."

905 A361	60h gray green	.30	.20
906 A361	1k gray	.45	.20
907 A361	2k dk gray blue	1.50	.50
	Nos. 905-907 (3)	2.25	.90

10th anniversary of the signing of the Universal Declaration of Human Rights.

Girl Holding Doll — A362

Frederic Joliot Curie — A363

40h, Pioneer studying map. 60h, Pioneer with radio. 80h, Girl pioneer planting tree.

1959, Mar. 28 Engr. & Photo.

908 A362	30h violet bl & yel	.35	.20
909 A362	40h indigo & ultra	.35	.20
910 A362	60h black & lilac	.35	.20
911 A362	80h brown & lt green	.75	.20
	Nos. 908-911 (4)	1.80	.80

10th anniv. of the Pioneer organization.

1959, Apr. 17 Engr.

912 A363 60h sepia 1.50 .25

Frederic Joliot Curie and the 10th anniversary of the World Peace Movement.

"Reaching for the Moon" — A364

Town Hall Pilsen — A365

1959, Apr. 17

913 A364 30h violet blue .95 .25

2nd Cong. of the Czechoslovak Assoc. for the Propagation of Political and Cultural knowledge.

1959, May 2

Designs: 60h, Part of steam condenser turbine. 1k, St. Bartholomew's Church, Pilsen. 1.60k, Part of lathe.

914 A365	30h lt brown	.20	.20
915 A365	60h violet & lt grn	.25	.20
916 A365	1k violet blue	.30	.20
917 A365	1.60k black & yellow	1.25	.85
	Nos. 914-917 (4)	2.00	1.45

2nd Pilsen Stamp Exhib. in connection with the centenary of the Skoda (Lenin) armament works.

Factory and Emblem A366

Inscribed: "IV Vseodborovy sjezd, 1959"

1959, May 13

918 A366	30h shown	.35	.20
919 A366	60h Dam	.25	.20

4th Trade Union Congress.

Zvolen Castle A367

1959, June 13

920 A367 60h gray olive & yel .60 .20

Regional Stamp Exhibition, Zvolen, 1959.

Frantisek Benda — A368

Aurel Stodola — A369

30h, Vaclav Kliment Klicpera. 60h, Karel V. Rais. 80h, Antonin Slavicek. 1k, Peter Bezruc.

1959, June 22 *Perf. 11½x11*

921 A368	15h violet blue	.25	.20
922 A368	30h orange brown	.25	.20
923 A369	40h dull green	.25	.20
924 A369	60h dull red brn	.35	.20
925 A369	80h dull violet	.65	.20
926 A368	1k dark brown	.65	.25
	Nos. 921-926 (6)	2.40	1.25

View of the Fair Grounds A370

Designs: 60h, Fair emblem and world map. 1.60k, Pavilion "Z."

Inscribed: "Mezinarodni Veletrh Brne 6.-20.IX. 1959"

Engraved and Photogravure

1959, July 20 Unwmk. *Perf. 11½*

927 A370	30h lilac & yellow	.25	.20
928 A370	60h dull blue	.25	.20
929 A370	1.60k dk blue & bister	.75	.20
	Nos. 927-929 (3)	1.25	.60

International Fair at Brno, Sept. 6-20.

Revolutionist and Flag — A371

Slovakian Fighter — A372

1.60k, Linden leaves, sun and factory.

Perf. 11½

1959, Aug. 29 Unwmk. Engr.

930 A371	30h black & rose	.20	.20
931 A372	60h carmine rose	.25	.20
932 A371	1.60k dk blue & yel	.45	.20
	Nos. 930-932 (3)	.90	.60

Natl. Slovakian revolution, 15th anniv. and Slovakian Soviet Republic, 40th anniv.

Alpine Marmots A373

1959, Sept. 25 Engr. & Photo.

933 A373	30h shown	1.40	.25
934 A373	40h Bison	1.00	.40
935 A373	60h Lynx, vert.	2.75	.25
936 A373	1k Wolf	2.75	.25
937 A373	1.60k Red deer	2.40	.55
	Nos. 933-937 (5)	10.30	1.70

Tatra National Park, 10th anniv.

Lunik 2 Hitting Moon and Russian Flag A374

1959, Sept. 23 *Perf. 11½*

938 A374 60h dk red & lt ultra 1.50 .25

Issued to commemorate the landing of the Soviet rocket on the moon, Sept. 13, 1959.

Stamp Printing Works, Peking A375

1959, Oct. 1

939 A375 30h pale green & red .40 .20

10 years of Czechoslovakian-Chinese friendship.

Haydn — A376

Great Spotted Woodpecker A377

Design: 3k, Charles Darwin.

1959, Oct. 16 Engr. *Perf. 11½*

940 A376	60h violet black	.50	.20
941 A376	3k dark red brown	1.50	.70

150th death anniv. of Franz Joseph Haydn, Austrian composer, and 150th birth anniv. of Charles Darwin, English naturalist.

1959, Nov. 16 *Perf. 14*

Birds: 30h, Blue tits. 40h, Nuthatch. 60h, Golden oriole. 80h, Goldfinch. 1k, Bullfinch. 1.20k, European kingfisher.

942 A377	20h multicolored	1.50	.60
943 A377	30h multicolored	1.50	.60
944 A377	40h multicolored	6.50	1.50
945 A377	60h multicolored	1.50	.60
946 A377	80h multicolored	2.50	.90
947 A377	1k multicolored	2.75	.90
948 A377	1.20k multicolored	5.00	1.25
	Nos. 942-948 (7)	21.25	6.35

Nos. 942-948 were each issued in miniature sheets of 10. Value, set $250.

Nikola Tesla A378

Designs: 30h, Alexander S. Popov. 35h, Edouard Branly. 60h, Guglielmo Marconi. 1k, Heinrich Hertz. 2k, Edwin Howard Armstrong and research tower, Alpine, N. J.

Engraved and Photogravure

1959, Dec. 7 *Perf. 11½*

949 A378	25h black & pink	.50	.20
950 A378	30h black & orange	.20	.20
951 A378	35h black & lt vio	.20	.20
952 A378	60h black & blue	.20	.20
953 A378	1k black & lt grn	.25	.20
954 A378	2k black & bister	1.50	.40
	Nos. 949-954 (6)	2.85	1.40

Issued to honor inventors in the fields of telegraphy and radio.

Gymnast — A379

2nd Winter Spartacist Games: 60h, Skier. 1.60k, Basketball players.

1960, Jan. 20 *Perf. 11½*

955 A379 30h salmon pink & brn .95 .20
956 A379 60h lt blue & blk .95 .20
957 A379 1.60k bister & brn .85 .25
Nos. 955-957 (3) 2.75 .65

1960, June 15 **Unwmk.**

Designs: 30h, Two girls in "Red Ball" drill. 60h, Gymnast with stick. 1k, Three girls with hoops.

958 A379 30h lt grn & rose claret .65 .20
959 A379 60h pink & black .50 .20
960 A379 1k ocher & vio bl .85 .20
Nos. 958-960 (3) 2.00 .60

2nd Summer Spartacist Games, Prague, June 23-July 3.

River Dredge Boat A380

Ships: 60h, River tug. 1k, Tourist steamer. 1.20k, Cargo ship "Lidice."

1960, Feb. 22 *Perf. 11½*

961 A380 30h slate grn & sal 2.75 .30
962 A380 60h maroon & pale bl 1.40 .30
963 A380 1k dk violet & yel 2.40 .30
964 A380 1.20k lilac & pale grn 3.50 .90
Nos. 961-964 (4) 10.05 1.80

Ice Hockey Players — A381

Design: 1.80k, Figure skaters.

1960, Feb. 27

965 A381 60h sepia & lt blue 2.00 .40
966 A381 1.80k black & lt green 6.00 2.50

8th Olympic Winter Games, Squaw Valley, Calif., Feb. 18-29, 1960.

1960, June 15 **Unwmk.**

Designs: 1k, Running. 1.80k, Women's gymnastics. 2k, Rowing.

967 A381 1k black & orange .85 .30
968 A381 1.80k black & sal pink 1.40 .40
969 A381 2k black & blue 2.25 .95
Nos. 967-969 (3) 4.50 1.65

17th Olympic Games, Rome, 8/25-9/11.

Trencin Castle — A382

Castles: 10h, Bezdez. 20h, Kost. 30h, Pernstein. 40h, Kremnica. 50h, Krivoklát castle. 60h, Karlstein. 1k, Smolenice. 1.60k, Kokorin.

1960-63 **Engr.** *Perf. 11½*

970 A382 5h gray violet .25 .20
971 A382 10h black .25 .20
972 A382 20h brown org .35 .20
973 A382 30h green .25 .20
974 A382 40h brown .35 .20
974A A382 50h black ('63) 2.00 .20
975 A382 60h rose red .40 .20
976 A382 1k lilac .40 .20
977 A382 1.60k dark blue .80 .20
Nos. 970-977 (9) 5.05 1.80

1961, Oct. **Wmk. 341**

977A A382 30h green 2.75 .40

Lenin — A383

Soldier Holding Child — A384

1960, Apr. 22 **Unwmk.**

978 A383 60h gray olive 1.25 .20

90th anniversary of the birth of Lenin.

1960, May 5 **Engr. & Photo.**

Designs: No. 980, Child eating pie. No. 981, Soldier helping concentration camp victim. No. 982, Welder and factory, horiz. No. 983, Tractor driver and farm, horiz.

979 A384 30h maroon & lt blue .35 .20
980 A384 30h dull red .35 .20
981 A384 30h green & dull blue .40 .20
982 A384 60h dk blue & buff .35 .20
983 A384 60h redsh brn & yel grn .40 .20
Nos. 979-983 (5) 1.85 1.00

15th anniversary of liberation.

Steelworker — A385

Design: 60h, Farm woman and child.

1960, May 24

984 A385 30h maroon & gray .20 .20
985 A385 60h green & pale blue .30 .20

1960 parliamentary elections.

Red Cross Nurse Holding Dove A386

Fire Fighters A387

1960, May 26 **Unwmk.**

986 A386 30h brown car & bl .40 .20
987 A387 60h dk blue & pink .60 .20

3rd Congress of the Czechoslovakian Red Cross (No. 986), and the 2nd Fire Fighters' Congress (No. 987).

Hand of Philatelist with Tongs and Two Stamps — A388

Design: 1k, Globe and 1937 Bratislava stamp (shown in miniature on 60h).

1960, July 11 *Perf. 11½*

988 A388 60h black & dull yel .70 .20
989 A388 1k black & blue .80 .20

Issued to publicize the National Stamp Exhibition, Bratislava, Sept. 24-Oct. 9.
See Nos. C49-C50.

Stalin Mine, Ostrava-Hermanovice — A390

Viktorin Cornelius, Lawyer — A391

Designs: 20h, Power station, Hodonin. 30h, Gottwald iron works, Kuncice. 40h, Harvester. 60h, Oil refinery.

1960, July 25

992 A390 10h black & pale grn .30 .20
993 A390 20h maroon & lt bl .30 .20
994 A390 30h indigo & pink .30 .20
995 A390 40h green & pale lilac .30 .20
996 A390 60h dk blue & yel .30 .20
Nos. 992-996 (5) 1.50 1.00

Issued to publicize the new five-year plan.

1960, Aug. 23 **Engr.**

Portraits: 20h, Karel Matej Capek-Chod, writer. 30h, Hana Kvapilova, actress. 40h, Oskar Nedbal, composer. 60h, Otakar Ostrcil, composer.

997 A391 10h black .25 .20
998 A391 20h red brown .35 .20
999 A391 30h rose red .50 .20
1000 A391 40h dull green 1.25 .60
1001 A391 60h gray violet .35 .20
Nos. 997-1001 (5) 2.70 1.40

See Nos. 1037-1041.

Skoda Sports Plane Flying Upside Down A392

1960, Aug. 28 **Engr. & Photo.**

1002 A392 60h violet blue & blue 1.50 .30

1st aerobatic world championships, Bratislava.

Constitution and "Czechoslovakia" — A393

1960, Sept. 18

1003 A393 30h violet bl & pink .40 .20

Proclamation of the new socialist constitution.

Workers Reading Newspaper — A394

Man Holding Newspaper — A395

1960, Sept. 18

1004 A394 30h slate & ver .25 .20
1005 A395 60h black & rose .25 .20

Day of the Czechoslovak Press, Sept. 21, 1960, and 40th anniv. of the Rudé Právo paper.

Globes and Laurel A396

1960, Sept. 18 **Engr.**

1006 A396 30h dk blue & bister .40 .20

World Federation of Trade Unions, 15th anniv.

Black-crowned Night Heron — A397

Doronicum Clusii (Thistle) — A398

Birds: 30h, Great crested grebe. 40h, Lapwing. 60h, Gray heron. 1k, Graylag goose, horiz. 1.60k, Mallard, horiz.

Engraved and Photogravure

1960, Oct. 24 **Unwmk.** *Perf. 11½*

Designs in Black

1007 A397 25h pale vio blue .80 .20
1008 A397 30h pale citron .70 .20
1009 A397 40h pale blue .80 .30
1010 A397 60h pink .55 .20
1011 A397 1k pale yellow 1.50 .20
1012 A397 1.60k lt violet 4.00 1.25
Nos. 1007-1012 (6) 8.35 2.35

1960, Nov. 21 **Engr.** *Perf. 14*

Flowers: 30h, Cyclamen. 40h, Primrose. 60h, Hen-and-chickens. 1k, Gentian. 2k, Pasqueflower.

1013 A398 20h black, yel & grn .85 .85
1014 A398 30h black, car rose & grn .85 .85
1015 A398 40h black, yel & grn .85 .85
1016 A398 60h black, pink & grn .85 .85
1017 A398 1k black, bl, vio & grn 2.50 .85
1018 A398 2k black, lil, yel & grn 3.25 1.60
Nos. 1013-1018 (6) 9.15 5.85

Alfons Mucha — A399

1960, Dec. 18 **Engr.** *Perf. 11½x12*

1019 A399 60h dk blue gray 2.50 .20

Day of the Czechoslovak Postage Stamp and birth cent. of Alfons Mucha, designer of the 1st Czechoslovakian stamp (Type A1).

Rolling-mill Control Bridge — A400

Athletes with Flags — A401

Designs: 30h, Turbo generator. 60h, Ditch-digging machine.

1961, Jan. 20 Unwmk. *Perf. 11½*

1020	A400 20h blue		.30	.20
1021	A400 30h rose		.30	.20
1022	A400 60h brt green		.30	.20
	Nos. 1020-1022 (3)		.90	.60

Third Five-Year Plan.

Perf. 11x11½, 11½x11

1961, Feb. 20 Engr. & Photo.

Designs: No. 1024, Motorcycle race, horiz. 40h, Sculling, horiz. 60h, Ice skater. 1k, Rugby. 1.20k, Soccer. 1.60k, Long-distance runners.

1023	A401	30h rose red & bl	.20	.20
1024	A401	30h dk blue & car	.20	.20
1025	A401	40h dk gray & car	.35	.20
1026	A401	60h lilac & blue	.30	.20
1027	A401	1k ultra & yel	.30	.20
1028	A401	1.20k green & buff	.50	.20
1029	A401	1.60k sepia & salmon	2.00	1.00
		Nos. 1023-1029 (7)	3.85	2.20

Various sports events.

Exhibition Emblem A402

Rocket Launching A403

1961, Mar. 6 Engr. *Perf. 11½*

1030	A402	2k dk blue & red	2.00	.20

"Praga 1962" International Stamp Exhibition, Prague, Sept. 1962.

1961, Mar. 6 Engr. & Photo.

30h, Sputnik III, horiz. 40h, As 20h, but inscribed "Start Kosmicke Rakety k Venusi — 12.II.1961". 60h, Sputnik I, horiz. 1.60k, Interplanetary station, horiz. 2k, Similar to type A404, without commemorative inscription.

1031	A403	20h violet & pink	.35	.20
1032	A403	30h dk green & buff	.65	.20
1033	A403	40h dk red & yel grn	.65	.30
1034	A403	60h violet & buff	.80	.20
1035	A403	1.60k dk bl & pale grn	.50	.25
1036	A403	2k mar & pale bl	1.90	1.10
		Nos. 1031-1036 (6)	4.85	2.25

Issued to publicize Soviet space research.

Portrait Type of 1960

No. 1037, Jindrich Mosna. No. 1038, Pavol Orszagh Hviezdoslav. No. 1039, Alois Mrstik. No. 1040, Joza Uprka. No. 1041, Josef Hora.

1961, Mar. 27 *Perf. 11½*

1037	A391 60h green	.25	.20
1038	A391 60h dark blue	.45	.20
a.	"ORSZACH" instead of "ORSZAGH"	*400.00*	*100.00*
1039	A391 60h dull claret	.60	.20
1040	A391 60h gray	.45	.20
1041	A391 60h sepia	.25	.20
	Nos. 1037-1041 (5)	2.00	1.00

Man Flying into Space A404

1961, Apr. 13

1042	A404	60h car & pale bl	.50	.20
1043	A404	3k ultra & yel	*2.00*	*.60*

1st man in space, Yuri A. Gagarin, Apr. 12, 1961. See No. 1036.

Flute Player — A405

Blast Furnace and Mine, Kladno — A406

1961, Apr. 24 Engr.

1044	A405	30h shown	.45	.20
1045	A405	30h Dancer	.45	.20
1046	A405	60h Lyre player	.60	.20
		Nos. 1044-1046 (3)	1.50	.60

Prague Conservatory of Music, 150th anniv.

1961, Apr. 24

1047	A406	3k dull red	.75	.20

Marching Workers — A407

Woman with Hammer and Sickle — A408

Klement Gottwald Museum A409

Designs: No. 1050, Lenin Museum. No. 1051, Crowd with flags. No. 1053, Man saluting Red Star.

1961, May 10

1048	A407	30h dull violet	.30	.20
1049	A409	30h dark blue	.30	.20
1050	A409	30h redsh brown	.30	.20
1051	A407	60h vermilion	.30	.20
1052	A408	60h dark green	.30	.20
1053	A408	60h carmine	.30	.20
		Nos. 1048-1053 (6)	1.80	1.20

Czech Communist Party, 40th anniversary.

Puppet — A410

Designs: Various Puppets.

Engraved and Photogravure

1961, June 20 Unwmk. *Perf. 11½*

1054	A410	30h ver & yel	.20	.20
1055	A410	40h sepia & bluish grn	.20	.20
1056	A410	60h vio bl & sal	.20	.20
1057	A410	1k green & lt blue	.30	.20
1058	A410	1.60k mar & pale vio	1.10	.35
		Nos. 1054-1058 (5)	2.00	1.15

Woman, Map of Africa and Flag of Czechoslovakia — A411

1961, June 26

1059	A411	60h red & blue	.30	.20

Issued to publicize the friendship between the people of Africa and Czechoslovakia.

Map of Europe and Fair Emblem A412

Fair emblem and: 60h Horizontal boring machine, vert. 1k, Scientists' meeting and nuclear physics emblem.

1961, Aug. 14 *Perf. 11½*

1060	A412	30h dk bl & pale grn	.30	.20
1061	A412	60h green & pink	.30	.20
1062	A412	1k vio brn & lt bl	.60	.25
		Nos. 1060-1062 (3)	1.20	.65

International Trade Fair, Brno, Sept. 10-24.

Sugar Beet, Cup of Coffee and Bags of Sugar A413

Charles Bridge, St. Nicholas Church and Hradcany A414

1961, Sept. 18 Unwmk. *Perf. 11½*

1063	A413	20h shown	.20	.20
1064	A413	30h Clover	.20	.20
1065	A413	40h Wheat	.20	.20
1066	A413	60h Hops	.20	.20
1067	A413	1.40k Corn	.35	.20
1068	A413	2k Potatoes	1.25	.55
		Nos. 1063-1068 (6)	2.40	1.55

1961, Sept. 25

1069	A414	60h violet bl & car	1.20	.20

26th session of the Governor's Council of the Red Cross Societies League, Prague.

Orlik Dam and Kaplan Turbine A415

Designs: 30h, View of Prague, flags and stamps. 40h, Hluboká Castle, river and fish. 60h, Karlovy Vary and cup. 1k, Pilsen and beer bottle. 1.20k, North Bohemia landscape and vase. 1.60k, Tatra mountains, boots, ice pick and rope. 2k, Ironworks, Ostrava Kuncice and pulley. 3k, Brno and ball bearing. 4k, Bratislava and grapes. 5k, Prague and flags.

1961 Unwmk. *Perf. 11½*

Size: 41x23mm

1070	A415	20h gray & blue	*1.25*	*.50*
1071	A415	30h vio blue & red	.30	.20
1072	A415	40h dk blue & lt grn	1.25	.65
1073	A415	60h dk blue & yel	1.40	.65
1074	A415	1k mar & grn	1.00	.65
1075	A415	1.20k green & pink	1.40	.65
1076	A415	1.60k brn & vio bl	1.40	1.00
1077	A415	2k blk & ocher	1.60	1.00
1078	A415	3k ultra & yel	1.60	.50
1079	A415	4k purple & sal	2.40	1.10

Perf. 13½

Engr.

Size: 50x29mm

1080	A415	5k multicolored	27.00	17.50
		Nos. 1070-1080 (11)	40.60	24.40

"PRAGA 1962 World Exhib. of Postage Stamps," Aug. 18-Sept. 2, 1962. No. 1080 was printed in sheet of 4. Value $150.

Globe A416

Engraved and Photogravure

1961, Nov. 27 *Perf. 11½*

1081	A416	60h red & ultra	.50	.20

Issued to publicize the Fifth World Congress of Trade Unions, Moscow, Dec. 4-16.

Orange Tip Butterfly A417

Bicyclists A418

Designs (butterflies): 20h, Zerynthia hypsipyle Sch. 30h, Apollo. 40h, Swallowtail. 60h, Peacock. 80h, Mourning cloak (Camberwell beauty). 1k, Underwing (moth). 1.60k, Red admiral. 2k, Brimstone (sulphur).

1961, Nov. 27 Engr.

1082	A417	15h multicolored	.90	.30
1083	A417	20h multicolored	.90	.30
1084	A417	30h multicolored	.90	.30
1085	A417	40h multicolored	.90	.30
1086	A417	60h multicolored	.90	.30
1087	A417	80h multicolored	2.75	.90
1088	A417	1k multicolored	3.00	.90
1089	A417	1.60k multicolored	3.00	.90
1090	A417	2k multicolored	7.50	3.00
		Nos. 1082-1090 (9)	20.75	7.20

Printed in sheets of ten. Value, set $275.

Engraved and Photogravure

1962, Feb. 5 Unwmk. *Perf. 11½*

Sports: 40h, Woman gymnast. 60h, Figure skaters. 1k, Woman bowler. 1.20k, Goalkeeper, soccer. 1.60k, Discus thrower.

1091	A418	30h black & vio bl	.20	.20
1092	A418	40h black & yel	.20	.20
1093	A418	60h slate & grnsh bl	.35	.20
1094	A418	1k black & pink	.35	.20
1095	A418	1.20k black & green	.35	.20
1096	A418	1.60k blk & dull grn	1.75	.80
		Nos. 1091-1096 (6)	3.20	1.80

Various 1962 sports events.

No. 1095 does not have the commemorative inscription.

Karel Kovarovic — A419

Frantisek Zaviska and Karel Petr A420

20h, Frantisek Skroup. 30h, Bozena Nemcova. 60h, View of Prague & staff of Aesculapius. 1.60k, Ladislav Celakovsky. 1.80k, Miloslav Valouch & Juraj Hronec.

1962, Feb. 26 **Engr.**

1097	A419	10h red brown	.20	.20
1098	A419	20h violet blue	.20	.20
1099	A419	30h brown	.20	.20
1100	A420	40h claret	.20	.20
1101	A419	60h black	.20	.20
1102	A419	1.60k slate green	.50	.20
1103	A420	1.80k dark blue	.60	.20
		Nos. 1097-1103 (7)	2.10	1.40

Various cultural personalities and events.

Miner and Flag A421

1962, Mar. 19 **Engr. & Photo.**

1104	A421	60h indigo & rose	.25	.20

30th anniv. of the miners' strike at Most.

"Man Conquering Space" — A422

Soviet Spaceship Vostok 2 — A423

40h, Launching of Soviet space rocket. 80h, Multi-stage automatic rocket. 1k, Automatic station on moon. 1.60k, Television satellite.

1962, Mar. 26

1105	A422	30h dk red & lt blue	.25	.20
1106	A422	40h dk blue & sal	.25	.20
1107	A423	60h dk blue & pink	.25	.20
1108	A423	80h rose vio & lt grn	.60	.20
1109	A422	1k indigo & citron	.35	.20
1110	A423	1.60k green & buff	1.75	.75
		Nos. 1105-1110 (6)	3.45	1.75

Issued to publicize space research.

Polar Bear — A424

Zoo Animals: 30h, Chimpanzee. 60h, Camel. 1k, African and Indian elephants, horiz. 1.40k, Leopard, horiz. 1.60k, Przewalski horse, horiz.

1962, Apr. 24 **Unwmk.** ***Perf. 11½***

Design and Inscriptions in Black

1111	A424	20h grnsh blue	.75	.20
1112	A424	30h violet	.75	.20
1113	A424	60h orange	.75	.20
1114	A424	1k green	.90	.20
1115	A424	1.40k carmine rose	.90	.20
1116	A424	1.60k lt brown	2.00	1.25
		Nos. 1111-1116 (6)	6.05	2.25

Child and Grieving Mother — A425

Klary's Fountain, Teplice — A426

60h, Flowers growing from ruins of Lezáky.

1962, June 9 **Engr. & Photo.**

1118	A425	30h black & red	.35	.20
1119	A425	60h black & dull bl	.65	.20

20th anniversary of the destruction of Lidice and Lezáky by the Nazis.

1962, June 9

1120	A426	60h dull grn & yel	.40	.20

1,200th anniversary of the discovery of the medicinal springs of Teplice.

Malaria Eradication Emblem, Cross and Dove A427

Soccer Goalkeeper A428

3k, Dove and malaria eradication emblem.

1962, June 18

1121	A427	60h black & crimson	.20	.20
1122	A427	3k dk blue & yel	1.25	.60

WHO drive to eradicate malaria.

1962, June 20 **Unwmk.** ***Perf. 11½***

1123	A428	1.60k green & yellow	1.50	.20

Czechoslovakia's participation in the World Cup Soccer Championship, Chile, May 30-June 17. See No. 1095.

Soldier in Swimming Relay Race A429

"Agriculture" A430

Designs: 40h, Soldier hurdling. 60h, Soccer player. 1k, Soldier with rifle in relay race.

1962, July 20

1124	A429	30h green & lt ultra	.20	.20
1125	A429	40h dk purple & yel	.20	.20
1126	A429	60h brown & green	.20	.20
1127	A429	1k dk blue & sal pink	.35	.20
		Nos. 1124-1127 (4)	.95	.80

2nd Summer Spartacist Games of Friendly Armies, Prague, Sept., 1962.

1962 **Engr.** ***Perf. 13½***

Designs: 60h, Astronaut in capsule. 80h, Boy with flute, horiz. 1k, Workers of three races, horiz. 1.40k, Children dancing around tree. 1.60k, Flying bird, horiz. 5k, View of Prague, horiz.

1128	A430	30h multicolored	1.50	.90
1129	A430	60h multicolored	.70	.55
a.		Miniature sheet of 8	*20.00*	*20.00*
1130	A430	80h multicolored	2.00	1.40
1131	A430	1k multicolored	2.00	1.40
1132	A430	1.40k multicolored	2.00	1.40
1133	A430	1.60k multicolored	3.50	3.50
		Nos. 1128-1133 (6)	11.70	9.15

Souvenir Sheet

1134	A430	5k multicolored	12.00	10.00
a.		Imperf.	45.00	35.00

"PRAGA 1962 World Exhib. of Postage Stamps," 8/18-9/2/62. No. 1133 also for FIP Day, Sept. 1. Printed in sheets of 10. Value: Nos. 1128-1133 $150; No. 1134 $80.

No. 1129a contains 4 each of Nos. 1128-1129 and 2 labels arranged in 2 rows of 2 se-tenant pairs of Nos. 1128-1129 with label between. Sold for 5k, only with ticket.

No. 1134 contains one 51x30mm stamp. Sold only with ticket.

Children in Day Nursery and Factory A431

Sailboat and Trade Union Rest Home, Zinkovy — A432

Engraved and Photogravure

1962, Oct. 29 **Unwmk.** ***Perf. 11½***

1135	A431	30h black & lt blue	.20	.20
1136	A432	60h brown & yellow	.20	.20

Cruiser "Aurora" A433

1962, Nov. 7

1137	A433	30h black & gray bl	.20	.20
1138	A433	60h black & pink	.20	.20

Russian October revolution, 45th anniv.

Cosmonaut and Worker — A434

Lenin — A435

1962, Nov. 7

1139	A434	30h dark red & blue	.20	.20
1140	A435	60h black & dp rose	.20	.20

40th anniversary of the USSR.

Symbolic Crane — A436

40h, Agricultural products, vert. 60h, Factories.

1962, Dec. 4

1141	A436	30h dk red & yel	.20	.20
1142	A436	40h gray blue & yel	.20	.20
1143	A436	60h black & dp rose	.30	.20
		Nos. 1141-1143 (3)	.70	.60

Communist Party of Czechoslovakia, 12th cong.

Ground Beetle — A437

Table Tennis — A438

Beetles: 30h, Cardinal beetle. 60h, Stag beetle, vert. 1k, Great water beetle. 1.60k, Alpine longicorn, vert. 2k, Ground beetle, vert.

1962, Dec. 15 **Engr.** ***Perf. 14***

1144	A437	20h multicolored	1.00	.40
1145	A437	30h multicolored	1.00	.40
1146	A437	60h multicolored	1.00	.40
1147	A437	1k multicolored	2.00	.60
1148	A437	1.60k multicolored	4.00	.60
1149	A437	2k multicolored	6.00	2.00
		Nos. 1144-1149 (6)	15.00	4.40

Nos. 1144-1149 were each printed in sheets of 10. Value, set $200.

Engraved and Photogravure

1963, Jan. ***Perf. 11½***

Sports: 60h, Bicyclist. 80h, Skier. 1k, Motorcyclist. 1.20k, Weight lifter. 1.60k, Hurdler.

1150	A438	30h black & dp grn	.20	.20
1151	A438	60h black & orange	.20	.20
1152	A438	80h black & ultra	.20	.20
1153	A438	1k black & violet	.40	.20
1154	A438	1.20k blk & pale brn	.40	.20
1155	A438	1.60k blk & car	.85	.20
		Nos. 1150-1155 (6)	2.25	1.20

Various 1963 sports events.

Industrial Plant, Laurel and Star — A439

Symbol of Child Welfare Home — A440

Industrial Plant and Symbol of Growth — A441

1963, Feb. 25 **Unwmk.** ***Perf. 11½***

1156	A439	30h carmine & lt bl	.20	.20
1157	A440	60h black & car	.20	.20
1158	A441	60h black & red	.20	.20
		Nos. 1156-1158 (3)	.60	.60

15th anniv. of the "Victorious February" and 5th Trade Union Cong.

Artists' Guild Emblem — A442

Juraj Jánosik — A443

Eduard Urx — A444

National Theater, Prague — A445

#1163, Woman reading to children. #1164, Juraj Pálkovic. 1.60k, Max Svabinsky.

Engr. & Photo.; Engr. (A444)

1963, Mar. 25 Unwmk. ***Perf. 11½***

1159 A442 20h black & Prus bl .20 .20
1160 A443 30h car & lt bl .20 .20
1161 A444 30h carmine .20 .20
1162 A445 60h dl red brn & lt bl .20 .20
1163 A444 60h green .20 .20
1164 A444 60h black .25 .20
1165 A444 1.60k brown .50 .20
Nos. 1159-1165 (7) 1.75 1.40

Various cultural personalities and events.

Boy and Girl with Flag A446

Television Transmitter A447

Engraved and Photogravure

1963, Apr. 18 ***Perf. 11½***

1166 A446 30h slate & rose red .35 .20

The 4th Congress of Czechoslovak Youth.

1963, Apr. 25

40h, Television camera, mast and set, horiz.

1167 A447 40h buff & slate .40 .20
1168 A447 60h dk red & lt blue .40 .20

Czechoslovak television, 10th anniversary.

Rocket to the Sun A448

50h, Rockets & Sputniks leaving Earth. 60h, Spacecraft to & from Moon. 1k, 3k, Interplanetary station & Mars 1. 1.60k, Atomic rocket & Jupiter. 2k, Rocket returning from Saturn.

1963, Apr. 25

1169 A448 30h red brn & buff .20 .20
1170 A448 50h slate & bluish grn .20 .20
1171 A448 60h dk green & yel .25 .20
1172 A448 1k dk gray & sal .45 .20
1173 A448 1.60k gray brn & lt grn .75 .20
1174 A448 2k dk purple & yel *2.50 .75*
Nos. 1169-1174 (6) *4.35 1.75*

Souvenir Sheet

Imperf

1175 A448 3k Prus grn & org red *12.00 6.00*

No. 1175 issued for 1st Space Research Exhib., Prague, Apr. 1963.

Studio and Radio A449

1k, Globe inscribed "Peace" & aerial mast, vert.

1963, May 18 Unwmk. ***Perf. 11½***

1176 A449 30h choc & pale grn .40 .20
1177 A449 1k bluish grn & lilac .40 .20

40th anniversary of Czechoslovak radio.

Tupolev Tu-104B Turbojet A450

Design: 1.80k, Ilyushin Il-18 Moskva.

1963, May 25

1178 A450 80h violet & lt bl 1.00 .25
1179 A450 1.80k dk blue & lt grn 1.60 .25

40th anniversary of Czechoslovak airlines.

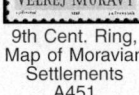

9th Cent. Ring, Map of Moravian Settlements A451

Woman Singing A452

1.60k, Falconer, 9th cent. silver disk.

1963, May 25

1180 A451 30h lt green & blk .25 .20
1181 A451 1.60k dull yel & blk .75 .20

1100th anniversary of Moravian empire.

1963, May 25 Engr.

1182 A452 30h bright red .60 .20

60th anniversary of the founding of the Moravian Teachers' Singing Club.

Kromeriz Castle and Barley — A453

Centenary Emblem, Nurse and Playing Child — A454

Engraved and Photogravure

1963, June 20 Unwmk. ***Perf. 11½***

1183 A453 30h slate grn & yel .40 .20

Natl. Agricultural Exhib. and 700th anniv. of Kromeriz.

1963, June 20

1184 A454 30h dk gray & car .40 .20

Centenary of the International Red Cross.

Bee, Honeycomb and Emblem A455

Liberec Fair Emblem — A456

1963, June 20

1185 A455 1k brown & yellow .75 .20

19th Intl. Beekeepers Cong., Apimondia, 1963.

1963, July 13

1186 A456 30h black & dp rose .40 .20

Liberec Consumer Goods Fair.

Town Hall, Brno — A457

Cave, Moravian Karst — A458

Design: 60h, Town Hall tower, Brno.

1963, July 29

1187 A457 30h lt blue & maroon .35 .20
1188 A457 60h pink & dk blue .35 .20

International Trade Fair, Brno.

1963, July 29

#1190, Trout, Hornad Valley. 60h, Great Hawk Gorge. 80h, Macocha mountains.

1189 A458 30h brown & lt bl .60 .20
1190 A458 30h dk bl & dull grn .70 .20
1191 A458 60h green & blue .60 .20
1192 A458 80h sepia & pink .60 .20
Nos. 1189-1192 (4) 2.50 .80

Blast Furnace A459

1963, Aug. 15 Unwmk. ***Perf. 11½***

1193 A459 60h blk & bluish grn .40 .20

30th Intl. Cong. of Iron Founders, Prague.

White Mouse A460

1963, Aug. 15

1194 A460 1k black & carmine .50 .20

2nd Intl. Pharmacological Cong., Prague.

Farm Machinery for Underfed Nations — A461

1963, Aug. 15 Engr.

1195 A461 1.60k black .50 .20

FAO "Freedom from Hunger" campaign.

Wooden Toys — A462

1963, Sept. 2 Engr. ***Perf. 13½***

Folk Art (Inscribed "UNESCO"): 80h, Cock and flowers. 1k, Flowers in vase. 1.20k, Janosik, Slovak hero. 1.60k, Stag. 2k, Postilion.

1196 A462 60h red & vio bl .75 .30
1197 A462 80h multi .75 .30
1198 A462 1k multi .75 .30
1199 A462 1.20k multi .75 .30
1200 A462 1.60k multi .75 .30
1201 A462 2k multi 3.25 1.75
Nos. 1196-1201 (6) 7.00 3.25

Nos. 1196-1201 were printed in sheets of 10. Value, set $150.

Canoeing A463

Tree and Star — A464

Sports: 40h, Volleyball. 60h, Wrestling. 80h, Basketball. 1k, Boxing. 1.60k, Gymnastics.

Engraved and Photogravure

1963, Oct. 26 ***Perf. 11½***

1202 A463 30h indigo & grn .35 .20
1203 A463 40h red brn & lt bl .35 .25
1204 A463 60h brn red & yel .40 .20
1205 A463 80h dk pur & dp org .50 .25
1206 A463 1k ultra & dp rose .70 .35
1207 A463 1.60k vio bl & ultra 2.25 1.00
Nos. 1202-1207 (6) 4.55 2.25

1964 Olympic Games, Tokyo.

1963, Dec. 11 Unwmk. ***Perf. 11½***

Design: 60h, Star, hammer and sickle.

1208 A464 30h bis brn & lt bl .30 .20
1209 A464 60h carmine & gray .30 .20

Russo-Czechoslovakian Treaty, 20th anniv.

Atom Diagrams Surrounding Head — A465

Chamois — A466

1963, Dec. 12 Engr.

1210 A465 60h dark purple .40 .20

3rd Congress of the Association for the Propagation of Scientific Knowledge.

1963, Dec. 14 ***Perf. 14***

40h, Alpine ibex. 60h, Mouflon. 1.20k, Roe deer. 1.60k, Fallow deer. 2k, Red deer.

1211	A466	30h multi	1.50	.35
1212	A466	40h multi	1.50	.35
1213	A466	60h brn, yel & grn	1.50	.35
1214	A466	1.20k multi	2.50	1.00
1215	A466	1.60k multi	3.00	1.25
1216	A466	2k multi	6.00	2.50
		Nos. 1211-1216 (6)	16.00	5.80

Figure Skating — A467

Ice Hockey — A468

80h, Skiing, horiz. 1k, Field ball player.

Engraved and Photogravure

1964, Jan. 20 **Unwmk.** ***Perf. 11½***

1217	A467	30h violet bl & yel	.30	.20
1218	A467	80h dk blue & org	.45	.20
1219	A467	1k brown & lilac	.75	.20
		Nos. 1217-1219 (3)	1.50	.60

Intl. University Games (30h, 80h) and the World Field Ball Championships (1k).

1964, Jan. 20

1220	A468	1k shown	.85	.35
1221	A468	1.80k Toboggan	1.00	.60
1222	A468	2k Ski jump	2.50	2.25
		Nos. 1220-1222 (3)	4.35	3.20

9th Winter Olympic Games, Innsbruck, Jan. 29-Feb. 9, 1964.

Magura Rest Home, High Tatra — A469

Design: 80h, Slovak National Insurrection Rest Home, Low Tatra.

1964, Feb. 19 **Unwmk.** ***Perf. 11½***

1223	A469	60h green & yellow	.30	.20
1224	A469	80h violet bl & pink	.30	.20

Skiers and Ski Lift A470

60h, Automobile camp, Telc. 1k, Fishing, Spis Castle. 1.80k, Lake & boats, Cesky Krumlov.

1964, Feb. 19 **Engr. & Photo.**

1225	A470	30h dk vio brn & bl	.40	.20
1226	A470	60h slate & car	.45	.20
1227	A470	1k brown & olive	.65	.20
1228	A470	1.80k slate grn & org	1.00	.35
		Nos. 1225-1228 (4)	2.50	.95

Moses, Day and Night by Michelangelo — A471

Designs: 60h, "A Midsummer Night's Dream," by Shakespeare. 1k, Man, telescope and heaven, vert. 1.60k, King George of Podebrad (1420-71).

1964, Mar. 20

1229	A471	40h black & yel grn	.35	.20
1230	A471	60h slate & car	.25	.20
1231	A471	1k black & lt blue	.90	.20
1232	A471	1.60k black & yellow	1.00	.20
a.		Souvenir sheet of 4 ('88)	9.00	6.00
		Nos. 1229-1232 (4)	2.50	.80

400th anniv. of the death of Michelangelo (40h); 400th anniv. of the birth of Shakespeare (60h); 400th anniv. of the birth of Galileo (1k); 500th anniv. of the pacifist efforts of King George of Podebrad (1.60k).

No. 1232a for PRAGA '88.

Yuri A. Gagarin — A472

Astronauts: 60h, Gherman Titov. 80h, John H. Glenn, Jr. 1k, Scott M. Carpenter, vert. 1.20k, Pavel R. Popovich and Andrian G. Nikolayev. 1.40k, Walter M. Schirra, vert. 1.60k, Gordon L. Cooper, vert. 2k, Valentina Tereshkova and Valeri Bykovski, vert.

1964, Apr. 27 **Unwmk.** ***Perf. 11½***

Yellow Paper

1233	A472	30h black & vio bl	.50	.25
1234	A472	60h dk grn & dk car	.25	.20
1235	A472	80h dk car & vio	.50	.20
1236	A472	1k ultra & rose vio	.25	.25
1237	A472	1.20k ver & ol gray	.50	.35
1238	A472	1.40k black & dl grn	1.25	.50
1239	A472	1.60k pale pur & Prus grn	3.00	1.50
1240	A472	2k dk blue & red	1.00	.40
		Nos. 1233-1240 (8)	7.25	3.65

World's first 10 astronauts.

Creeping Bellflower A473

Film "Flower" and Karlovy Vary Colonnade A474

Flowers: 80h, Musk thistle. 1k, Chicory. 1.20k, Yellow iris. 1.60k, Gentian. 2k, Corn poppy.

1964, June 15 **Engr.** ***Perf. 14***

1241	A473	60h dk grn, lil & org	1.25	.25
1242	A473	80h blk, grn & red lil	1.25	.25
1243	A473	1k vio bl, grn & pink	1.25	.45
1244	A473	1.20k black, yel & grn	1.25	.30
1245	A473	1.60k violet & grn	3.00	.40
1246	A473	2k vio, red & grn	7.00	2.00
		Nos. 1241-1246 (6)	*15.00*	*3.65*

Nos. 1241-1246 were each issued in sheets of 10. Value, set $225.

Engraved and Photogravure

1964, June 20 **Unwmk.** ***Perf. 13½***

1247	A474	60h black, blue & car	1.75	.30

14th Intl. Film Festival at Karlovy Vary, July 4-19.

Silesian Coat of Arms — A475

Young Miner of 1764 — A476

1964, June 20 ***Perf. 11½***

1248	A475	30h black & yel	.30	.20

150th anniv. of the Silesian Museum, Opava.

1964, June 20

1249	A476	60h sepia & lt grn	.30	.20

Mining School at Banska Stiavnica, bicent.

Skoda Fire Engine A477

1964, June 20

1250	A477	60h car rose & lt bl	1.25	.20

Voluntary fire brigades in Bohemia, cent.

Gulls, Hradcany Castle, Red Cross — A478

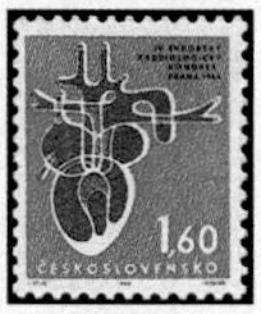

Human Heart — A479

1964, July 10

1251	A478	60h car & bluish gray	.45	.20

4th Czechoslovak Red Cross Congress at Prague.

1964, July 10

1252	A479	1.60k ultra & car	1.00	.20

4th European Cardiological Cong. at Prague.

Partisans, Girl and Factories A480

Battle Scene, 1944 — A481

Design: 60h, Partisans and flame.

Engraved and Photogravure

1964, Aug. 17 **Unwmk.** ***Perf. 11½***

1253	A480	30h brown & red	.20	.20
1254	A480	60h dk blue & red	.20	.20
1255	A481	60h black & red	.20	.20
		Nos. 1253-1255 (3)	.60	.60

20th anniv. of the Slovak Natl. Uprising; No. 1255, 20th anniv. of the Battles of Dukla Pass.

Hradcany at Prague — A482

Discus Thrower and Pole Vaulter — A483

Design: 5k, Charles Bridge and Hradcany.

1964, Aug. 30 ***Perf. 11½x12***

1256	A482	60h black & red	.50	.20

Souvenir Sheet

Engr. ***Imperf.***

1257	A482	5k deep claret	3.00	2.50

Millenium of the Hradcany, Prague.

No. 1257 stamp size: 30x50mm.

Engraved and Photogravure

1964, Sept. 2 ***Perf. 13½***

Designs: 60h, Bicycling, horiz. 1k, Soccer. 1.20k, Rowing. 1.60k, Swimming, horiz. 2.80k, Weight lifting, horiz.

1258	A483	60h multi	1.00	.30
1259	A483	80h multi	1.00	.30
1260	A483	1k multi	1.00	.30
1261	A483	1.20k multi	1.00	.30
1262	A483	1.60k multi	1.00	.30
1263	A483	2.80k multi	*5.00*	*2.00*
		Nos. 1258-1263 (6)	*10.00*	*3.50*

Issued to commemorate the 18th Olympic Games, Tokyo, Oct. 10-25.

Nos. 1258-1263 were issued in sheets of 10. Value, set $200.

Miniature Sheet

Space Ship Voskhod I, Astronauts and Globe — A484

1964, Nov. 12 **Unwmk.** ***Perf. 11½***

1264	A484	3k dk bl & dl lil, *buff*	6.00	4.00

Russian 3-man space flight of Vladimir M. Komarov, Boris B. Yegorov and Konstantin Feoktistov, Oct. 12-13.

Steam Engine and Atomic Power Plant — A485

Diesel Engine "CKD Praha" — A486

1964, Nov. 16 **Engr.**

1265	A485	30h dull red brown	.25	.20

Engraved and Photogravure

1266	A486	60h green & salmon	.75	.20

Traditions and development of engineering; No. 1265 for 150th anniv. of the First Brno Engineering Works, No. 1266 for the engineering concern CKD Praha.

European Redstart — A487

Birds: 60h, Green woodpecker. 80h, Hawfinch. 1k, Black woodpecker. 1.20k, European robin. 1.60k, European roller.

1964, Nov. 16 Litho. *Perf. 10½*

1267	A487	30h	multicolored	1.00	.30
1268	A487	60h	black & multi	1.00	.30
1269	A487	80h	multicolored	1.25	.35
1270	A487	1k	multicolored	1.75	.40
1271	A487	1.20k	lt vio bl & blk	1.75	.40
1272	A487	1.60k	yellow & blk	3.25	1.00
			Nos. 1267-1272 (6)	10.00	2.75

Dancer A488

"In the Sun" Preschool Children A489

Designs: 60h, "Over the Obstacles," teenagers. 1k, "Movement and Beauty," woman flag twirler. 1.60k, Runners at start.

Engraved and Photogravure

1965 Unwmk. *Perf. 11½*

1273	A488	30h	red & lt blue	.20	.20

Perf. 11½x12

1274	A489	30h	vio bl & car	.20	.20
1275	A489	60h	brown & ultra	.20	.20
1276	A489	1k	black & yellow	.25	.20
1277	A489	1.60k	maroon & gray	.60	.20
			Nos. 1273-1277 (5)	1.45	1.00

3rd Natl. Spartacist Games. Issue dates: No. 1273, Jan. 3; Nos. 1274-1277, May 24.

Mountain Rescue Service — A490

Arms and View, Beroun — A491

Designs: No. 1279, Woman gymnast. No. 1280, Bicyclists. No. 1281, Women hurdlers.

1965, Jan. 15 Unwmk. *Perf. 11½*

1278	A490	60h	violet & blue	.25	.20
1279	A490	60h	maroon & ocher	.25	.20
1280	A490	60h	black & carmine	.25	.20
1281	A490	60h	green & yellow	.25	.20
			Nos. 1278-1281 (4)	1.00	.80

Mountain Rescue Service (#1278); 1st World Championship in Artistic Gymnastics, Prague, Dec. 1965 (#1279); World Championship in Indoor Bicycling, Prague, Oct. 1965 (#1280); "Universiada 1965," Brno (#1281).

1965, Feb. 15

Designs: No. 1283, Town Square, Domazlice. No. 1284, Old and new buildings, Frydek-Mystek. No. 1285, Arms and view, Lipnik. No. 1286, Fortified wall, City Hall and Arms, Policka. No. 1287, View and hops, Zatek. No. 1288, Small fortress and rose, Terezin.

1282	A491	30h	vio bl & lt bl	.30	.20
1283	A491	30h	dull pur & yel	.30	.20
1284	A491	30h	slate & gray	.30	.20
1285	A491	30h	green & bis	.30	.20
1286	A491	30h	brown & tan	.30	.20
1287	A491	30h	dk blue & cit	.30	.20
1288	A491	30h	black & rose	.30	.20
			Nos. 1282-1288 (7)	2.10	1.40

Nos. 1282-1287 for 700th anniv. of the founding of various Bohemian towns; No. 1288 the 20th anniv. of the liberation of the Theresienstadt (Terezin) concentration camp.

Sun's Corona A492

Space Research: 30h, Sun. 60h, Exploration of the Moon. 1k, Twin space craft, vert. 1.40k, Space station. 1.60k, Exploration of Mars, vert. 2k, USSR and US Meteorological collaboration.

1965, Mar. 15 *Perf. 12x11½, 11½x12*

1289	A492	20h	rose & red lilac	.25	.20
1290	A492	30h	rose red & yel	.25	.20
1291	A492	60h	bluish blk & yel	.25	.20
1292	A492	1k	pur & pale bl	.50	.20
1293	A492	1.40k	black & salmon	.50	.20
1294	A492	1.60k	black & pink	.50	.20
1295	A492	2k	bluish blk & lt bl	*1.50*	*1.00*
			Nos. 1289-1295 (7)	*3.75*	*2.20*

Space research; Nos. 1289-1290 also for the Intl. Quiet Sun Year, 1964-65.

Frantisek Ventura, Equestrian; Amsterdam, 1928 — A493

Czechoslovakian Olympic Victories: 30h, Discus, Paris, 1900. 60h, Running, Helsinki, 1952. 1k, Weight lifting, Los Angeles, 1932. 1.40k, Gymnastics, Berlin, 1936. 1.60k, Double sculling, Rome, 1960. 2k, Women's gymnastics, Tokyo, 1964.

1965, Apr. 16 *Perf. 11½x12*

1296	A493	20h	choc & gold	.25	.20
1297	A493	30h	indigo & emer	.25	.20
1298	A493	60h	ultra & gold	.25	.20
1299	A493	1k	red brn & gold	.35	.25
1300	A493	1.40k	dk sl grn & gold	.75	.60
1301	A493	1.60k	black & gold	.80	.60
1302	A493	2k	maroon & gold	1.10	.45
			Nos. 1296-1302 (7)	3.75	2.50

Astronauts Virgil Grissom and John Young — A494

Designs: No. 1304, Alexei Leonov floating in space. No. 1305, Launching pad at Cape Kennedy. No. 1306, Leonov leaving space ship.

1965, Apr. 17 *Perf. 11x11½*

1303	A494	60h	slate bl & lil rose	.45	.20
1304	A494	60h	vio blk & blue	.45	.20
1305	A494	3k	slate bl & lil rose	1.75	1.00
a.			Pair, #1303, 1305	3.75	2.00
1306	A494	3k	vio blk & blue	1.75	1.00
a.			Pair, #1304, 1306	3.75	2.00
			Nos. 1303-1306 (4)	4.40	2.40

Issued to honor American and Soviet astronauts. Printed in sheets of 25; one sheet contains 20 No. 1303 and 5 No. 1305, the other sheet contains 20 No. 1304 and 5 No. 1306.

Russian Soldier, View of Prague and Guerrilla Fighters A495

Designs: No. 1308, Blast furnace, workers and tank. 60h, Worker and factory. 1k, Worker and new constructions. 1.60k, Woman farmer, new farm buildings and machinery.

1965, May 5 Engr. *Perf. 13½*

1307	A495	30h	dk red, blk & ol	.40	.20
1308	A495	30h	multicolored	.40	.20
1309	A495	60h	vio bl, red & blk	.40	.20
1310	A495	1k	dp org, blk & brn	.65	.20
1311	A495	1.60k	yel, red & blk	.70	.20
			Nos. 1307-1311 (5)	2.55	1.00

20th anniv. of liberation from the Nazis.

Nos. 1307-1311 were each printed in sheets of 10. Value, set $85.

Slovakian Kopov Dog A496

Dogs: 40h, German shepherd. 60h, Czech hunting dog with pheasant. 1k, Poodle. 1.60k, Czech terrier. 2k, Afghan hound.

1965, June 10 *Perf. 12x11½*

1312	A496	30h	black & red org	.50	.20
1313	A496	40h	black & yellow	.50	.20
1314	A496	60h	black & ver	.80	.20
1315	A496	1k	black & dk car rose	1.10	.30
1316	A496	1.60k	black & orange	1.50	.35
1317	A496	2k	black & orange	3.00	1.25
			Nos. 1312-1317 (6)	7.40	2.50

World Dog Show at Brno and the International Dog Breeders Congress, Prague.

UN Headquarters Building, NY — A497

Emblems: 60h, UN & inscription. 1.60k, ICY.

1965, June 24 *Perf. 12x11½*

1318	A497	60h	dk red brn & yel	.25	.20
1319	A497	1k	ultra & lt blue	.65	.25
1320	A497	1.60k	gold & dk red	.60	.35
			Nos. 1318-1320 (3)	1.50	.80

20th anniv. of the UN and the ICY, 1965.

Trade Union Emblem A498

1965, June 24 Engr.

1321	A498	60h	dk red & ultra	.40	.20

Intl. Trade Union Federation, 20th anniv.

Women and Globe — A499

1965, June 24 *Perf. 11½x12*

1322	A499	60h	violet blue	.40	.20

20th anniv. of the Intl. Women's Federation.

Children's House (Burgraves' Palace), Hradcany A500

Matthias Tower — A501

1965, June 25 *Perf. 11½*

1323	A500	30h	slate green	.30	.20
1324	A501	60h	dark brown	.30	.20

Issued to publicize the Hradcany, Prague.

Marx and Lenin — A502

1965, July 1 Engr. & Photo.

1325	A502	60h	car rose & gold	.30	.20

6th conf. of Postal Ministers of Communist Countries, Peking, June 21-July 15.

Joseph Navratil — A503

Jan Hus — A504

Gregor Johann Mendel A505

Costume Jewelry A506

Bohuslav Martinu A507

Seated Woman and University of Bratislava A508

ITU Emblem and Communication Symbols A509

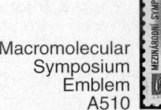

Macromolecular Symposium Emblem A510

Design: No. 1327, Ludovit Stur (diff. frame).

1965 Unwmk. *Perf. 11½*

1326	A503	30h	black & fawn	.20	.20
1327	A503	30h	black & dull grn	.20	.20
1328	A504	60h	black & crimson	.20	.20

1329 A505 60h vio bl & red .20 .20
1330 A506 60h purple & gold .20 .20
1331 A507 60h black & orange .20 .20
1332 A508 60h brn, *yel* .20 .20
1333 A509 1k orange & blue .35 .20
1334 A510 1k black & dp org .35 .20
Nos. 1326-1334 (9) 2.10 1.80

No. 1326, Navratil (1798-1865), painter; No. 1327, Stur (1815-56), Slovak author and historian; No. 1328, the 550th anniv. of the death of Hus, religious reformer;

No. 1329, cent. of publication of Mendel's laws of inheritance; No. 1330 publicizes the "Jablonec 1965" costume jewelry exhib.; No. 1331, Martinu (1890-1959), composer; No. 1332, 500th anniv. of the founding of the University of Bratislava as Academia Istropolitana; No. 1333, cent. of the ITU; No. 1334, Intl. Symposium on Macromolecular Chemistry, Prague, Sept. 1-8.

Issued: No. 1333, 7/10.

"Young Woman at her Toilette," by Titian — A512

Miniature Sheet

1965, Aug. 12
1336 A512 5k multicolored 6.00 4.00

Hradcany Art Gallery. #1336 contains one stamp.

Help for Flood Victims — A513

Rescue of Flood Victims A514

1965, Sept. 6 **Engr.**
1337 A513 30h violet blue .20 .20

Engraved and Photogravure
1338 A514 2k dk ol grn & ol .65 .45

Help for Danube flood victims in Slovakia.

Dotterel A515

Mountain Birds: 60h, Wall creeper, vert. 1.20k, Lesser redpoll. 1.40k, Golden eagle, vert. 1.60k, Ring ouzel. 2k, Eurasian nutcracker, vert.

1965, Sept. 20 **Litho.** ***Perf. 11***
1339 A515 30h multi 1.20 .20
1340 A515 60h multi 1.00 .20
1341 A515 1.20k multi 1.20 .20
1342 A515 1.40k multi 2.00 .40
1343 A515 1.60k multi 1.40 .50
1344 A515 2k multi 5.25 2.00
Nos. 1339-1344 (6) 12.05 3.50

Levoca — A516

Medicinal Plants — A517

Views of Towns: 10h, Jindrichuv Hradec. 20h, Nitra. 30h, Kosice. 40h, Hradec Králové. 50h, Telc. 60h, Ostrava. 1k, Olomouc. 1.20k, Ceske Budejovice. 1.60k, Cheb. 2k, Brno. 3k, Bratislava. 5k, Prague.

Engraved and Photogravure
1965-66 ***Perf. 11½x12***

Size: 23x19mm

1345 A516 5h black & yel .20 .20
1346 A516 10h ultra & ol bis .65 .20
1347 A516 20h black & lt bl .20 .20
1348 A516 30h vio bl & lt grn .20 .20
1348A A516 40h dk brn & lt bl ('66) .20 .20
1348B A516 50h black & ocher ('66) .50 .20
1348C A516 60h red & gray ('66) 1.00 .20
1348D A516 1k pur & pale grn ('66) .65 .20

Perf. 11½x11

Size: 30x23mm

1349 A516 1.20k slate & lt bl .55 .20
1350 A516 1.60k indigo & yel .80 .20
1351 A516 2k sl grn & pale yel .75 .20
1352 A516 3k brn & yel 1.00 .20
1353 A516 5k black & pink 1.40 .20
Nos. 1345-1353 (13) 8.10 2.60

1965, Dec. 3 **Engr.** ***Perf. 14***
1354 A517 30h Coltsfoot .40 .20
1355 A517 60h Meadow saffron .40 .20
1356 A517 80h Corn poppy 1.25 .20
1357 A517 1k Foxglove 1.25 .40
1358 A517 1.20k Arnica 1.75 .75
1359 A517 1.60k Cornflower 1.75 .75
1360 A517 2k Dog rose 4.25 2.00
Nos. 1354-1360 (7) 11.05 4.50

Nos. 1354-1360 were each printed in sheets of 10. Value, set $200.

Strip of "Stamps" — A518

Engraved and Photogravure
1965, Dec. 18 ***Perf. 11½***
1361 A518 1k dark red & gold 3.00 2.25

Issued for Stamp Day, 1965.

Romain Rolland (1866-1944), French Writer A519

Symbolic Musical Instruments & Names of Composers A520

Portraits: No. 1362, Stanislav Sucharda (1866-1916), sculptor. No. 1363, Ignac Josef Pesina (1766-1808), veterinarian. No. 1365, Donatello (1386-1466), Italian sculptor.

1966, Feb. 14 **Engr.** ***Perf. 11½***
1362 A519 30h deep green .20 .20
1363 A519 30h violet blue .20 .20
1364 A519 60h rose lake .20 .20
1365 A519 60h brown .20 .20
Nos. 1362-1365 (4) .80 .80

1966, Jan. 15 **Engr. & Photo.**
1366 A520 30h black & gold .50 .20

Czech Philharmonic Orchestra, 70th anniv.

Figure Skating Pair A521

#1368, Man skater. #1369, Volleyball player, spiking, vert. 1k, Volleyball player, saving, vert. 1.60k, Woman skater. 2k, Figure skating pair.

1966, Feb. 17
1367 A521 30h dk car rose .20 .20
1368 A521 60h green .20 .20
1369 A521 60h carmine & buff .20 .20
1370 A521 1k vio & lt bl .30 .20
1371 A521 1.60k brown & yellow .40 .20
1372 A521 2k blue & grnsh bl 2.00 .40
Nos. 1367-1372 (6) 3.30 1.40

#1367-1368, 1371-1372 for the European Figure Skating Championships, Bratislava; #1369-1370 for the World Volleyball Championships.

Souvenir Sheet

Girl Dancing — A522

1966, Mar. 21 **Engr.** ***Imperf.***
1373 A522 3k slate bl, red & bl 3.50 2.50

Cent. of the opera "The Bartered Bride" by Bedrich Smetana.

"Ajax" 1841 A523

Locomotives: 30h, "Karlstejn" 1865. 60h, Steam engine, 1946. 1k, Steam engine with tender, 1946. 1.60k, Electric locomotive, 1964. 2k, Diesel locomotive, 1964.

1966, Mar. 21 ***Perf. 11½x11***

Buff Paper

1374 A523 20h sepia 1.25 .20
1375 A523 30h dull violet 1.60 .20
1376 A523 60h dull purple 1.10 .20
1377 A523 1k dark blue 1.25 .40
1378 A523 1.60k dk blue grn 2.25 .30
1379 A523 2k dark red 4.50 2.00
Nos. 1374-1379 (6) 11.95 3.30

European Perch A524

30h, Brown trout, vert. 1k, Carp. 1.20k, Northern pike. 1.40k, Grayling. 1.60k, Eel.

Perf. 13x13½, 13½x13

1966, Apr. 22 **Litho.** **Unwmk.**
1380 A524 30h multi .70 .20
1381 A524 60h multi .70 .20
1382 A524 1k multi 1.40 .20
1383 A524 1.20k multi .70 .20
1384 A524 1.40k multi 1.00 .25
1385 A524 1.60k multi 2.75 1.10
Nos. 1380-1385 (6) 7.25 2.15

Intl. Fishing Championships, Svit, Sept. 3-5.

WHO Headquarters, Geneva — A525

Engraved and Photogravure
1966, Apr. 25 ***Perf. 12x11½***
1386 A525 1k dk blue & lt blue .50 .20

Opening of the WHO Headquarters, Geneva.

Symbolic Handshake and UNESCO Emblem A526

1966, Apr. 25 ***Perf. 11½***
1387 A526 60h bister & olive gray .30 .20

20th anniv. of UNESCO.

Prague Castle Issue

Belvedere Palace and St. Vitus' Cathedral A527

Crown of St. Wenceslas, 1346 — A528

Design: 60h, Madonna, altarpiece from St. George's Church.

1966, May 9 **Engr.** ***Perf. 11½***
1388 A527 30h dark blue .40 .20

Engraved and Photogravure
1389 A527 60h blk & yel bis .60 .20

Souvenir Sheet

Engr.
1390 A528 5k multi 6.50 3.25

See Nos. 1537-1539.

Tiger Swallowtail A529

Butterflies and Moths: 60h, Clouded sulphur. 80h, European purple emperor. 1k, Apollo. 1.20k, Burnet moth. 2k, Tiger moth.

1966, May 23 Engr. *Perf. 14*

1391 A529 30h multi .90 .25
1392 A529 60h multi .90 .25
1393 A529 80h multi 1.25 .40
1394 A529 1k multi 1.90 .60
1395 A529 1.20k multi 1.90 .50
1396 A529 2k multi 5.50 2.00
Nos. 1391-1396 (6) 12.35 4.00

Nos. 1391-1396 were issued in sheets of 10. Value, set $250.

Flags of Russia and Czechoslovakia — A530

Designs: 60h, Rays surrounding hammer and sickle "sun." 1.60k, Girl's head and stars.

Engraved and Photogravure

1966, May 31 *Perf. 11½*

1397 A530 30h dk bl & crim .20 .20
1398 A530 60h dk bl & red .20 .20
1399 A530 1.60k red & dk bl .30 .20
Nos. 1397-1399 (3) .70 .60

13th Congress of the Communist Party of Czechoslovakia.

Dakota Chief — A531

Model of Molecule — A532

Designs: 20h, Indians, canoe and tepee, horiz. 30h, Tomahawk. 40h, Haida totem poles. 60h, Kachina, good spirit of the Hopis. 1k, Indian on horseback hunting buffalo, horiz. 1.20k, Calumet, Dakota peace pipe.

1966, June 20

Size: 23x40mm

1400 A531 20h vio bl & dp org .25 .20
1401 A531 30h blk & dl org .25 .20
1402 A531 40h blk & lt bl .25 .20
1403 A531 60h grn & yel .25 .20
1404 A531 1k pur & emer .40 .20
1405 A531 1.20k vio bl & rose lil .65 .30

Perf. 14

Engr.

Size: 23x37mm

1406 A531 1.40k multi 1.60 .90
Nos. 1400-1406 (7) 3.65 2.20

Cent. of the Náprstek Ethnographic Museum, Prague, and "The Indians of North America" exhibition.

No. 1406 was issued in sheets of 10. Value $60.

Engraved and Photogravure

1966, July 4 Unwmk. *Perf. 11½*

1407 A532 60h blk & lt bl .20 .20

Czechoslovak Chemical Society, cent.

"Guernica" by Pablo Picasso — A533

1966, July 5

Size: 75x30mm

1408 A533 60h blk & pale bl 2.50 1.25

30th anniversary of International Brigade in Spanish Civil War.

Sheets of 15 stamps and 5 labels inscribed "Picasso-Guernica 1937." Values: with tab attached, $3.75; sheet $75.

Pantheon, Bratislava A534

Atom Symbol and Sun A535

Designs: No. 1410, Devin Castle and Ludovit Stur. No. 1411, View of Nachod. No. 1412, State Science Library, Olomouc.

1966, July 25 Engr.

1409 A534 30h dl pur .30 .20
1410 A534 60h dk bl .35 .20
1411 A534 60h green .35 .20
1412 A534 60h sepia .30 .20
Nos. 1409-1412 (4) 1.30 .80

No. 1409, Russian War Memorial, Bratislava; No. 1410, the 9th cent. Devin Castle as symbol of Slovak nationalism; No. 1411, 700th anniv. of the founding of Nachod; No. 1412, the 400th anniv. of the State Science Library, Olomouc.

Engraved and Photogravure

1966, Aug. 29 *Perf. 11½*

1413 A535 60h blk & red .40 .20

Issued to publicize Jachymov (Joachimsthal), where pitchblende was first discovered, "cradle of the atomic age."

Brno Fair Emblem — A536

Olympia Coin and Olympic Rings — A537

1966, Aug. 29

1414 A536 60h blk & red .40 .20

8th International Trade Fair, Brno.

1966, Aug. 29

Design: 1k, Olympic flame, Czechoslovak flag and Olympic rings.

1415 A537 60h blk & gold .30 .20
1416 A537 1k dk bl & red 1.00 .30

70th anniv. of the Olympic Committee.

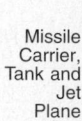

Missile Carrier, Tank and Jet Plane A538

1966, Aug. 31

1417 A538 60h blk & apple grn .40 .20

Issued to commemorate the maneuvers of the armies of the Warsaw Pact countries.

Mercury A539

30h, Moravian silver thaler, 1620, reverse & obverse, vert. 1.60k, Old & new buildings of Brno State Theater. 5k, Intl. Trade Fair Administration Tower & postmark, vert.

1966, Sept. 10

1418 A539 30h dk red & blk .40 .20
1419 A539 60h org & blk .40 .20
1420 A539 1.60k blk & brt grn .75 .25
Nos. 1418-1420 (3) 1.55 .65

Souvenir Sheet

1421 A539 5k multi 3.50 3.50

Brno Philatelic Exhibition, Sept. 11-25. No. 1421 contains one 30x40mm stamp.

First Meeting in Orbit — A540

30h, Photograph of far side of Moon & Russian satellite. 60h, Photograph of Mars & Mariner 4. 80th, Soft landing on Moon. 1k, Satellite, laser beam & binary code. 1.20k, Telstar over Earth & receiving station.

1966, Sept. 26 *Perf. 11½*

1422 A540 20h vio & lt grn .20 .20
1423 A540 30h blk & sal pink .20 .20
1424 A540 60h slate & lilac .25 .20
1425 A540 80h dk pur & lt bl .25 .20
1426 A540 1k blk & vio .30 .20
1427 A540 1.20k red & bl 1.60 .45
Nos. 1422-1427 (6) 2.80 1.45

Issued to publicize American and Russian achievements in space research.

Badger A541

Game Animals: 40h, Red deer, vert. 60h, Lynx. 80h, Hare. 1k, Red fox. 1.20k, Brown bear, vert. 2k, Wild boar.

1966, Nov. 28 Litho. *Perf. 13½*

1428 A541 30h multi .50 .20
1429 A541 40h multi .50 .20
1430 A541 60h multi .40 .20
1431 A541 80h multi (europaens) 1.00 .25
a. 80h multi *(europaeus)* 6.00 3.50
1432 A541 1k multi .75 .30
1433 A541 1.20k multi 1.00 .50
1434 A541 2k multi 2.50 1.25
Nos. 1428-1434 (7) 6.65 2.90

The sheet of 50 of the 80h contains 40 with misspelling "europaens" and 10 with "europaeus."

"Spring" by Vaclav Hollar, 1607-77 A542

Paintings: No. 1436, Portrait of Mrs. F. Wussin, by Jan Kupecky (1667-1740). No. 1437, Snow Owl by Karel Purkyne (1834-1868). No. 1438, Tulips by Vaclav Spála (1885-1964). No. 1439, Recruit by Ludovít Fulla (1902-1980).

1966, Dec. 8 Engr. *Perf. 14*

1435 A542 1k black 3.75 3.50
1436 A542 1k multicolored 5.25 1.90
1437 A542 1k multicolored 2.40 1.90
1438 A542 1k multicolored 2.40 1.90
1439 A542 1k multicolored 19.00 16.00
Nos. 1435-1439 (5) 32.80 25.20

Printed in sheets of 4 stamps and 2 labels. The labels in sheet of No. 1435 are inscribed "Vaclav Hollar 1607-1677" in fancy frame. Other labels are blank. Value, set $150.

See No. 1484.

Symbolic Bird — A543

Engraved and Photogravure

1966, Dec. 17 *Perf. 11½*

1440 A543 1k dp blue & yel 1.00 .65

Issued for Stamp Day.

Youth — A544

1967, Jan. 16 *Perf. 11½*

1441 A544 30h ver & lt bl .20 .20

5th Cong. of the Czechoslovak Youth Org.

Symbolic Flower and Machinery A545

1967, Jan. 16

1442 A545 30h carmine & yel .30 .20

6th Trade Union Congress, Prague.

Parents with Dead Child — A545a

1967, Jan. 16 *Perf. 11½*

1442A A545a 60h black & salmon .30 .20

"Peace and Freedom in Viet Nam."

View of Jihlava and Tourist Year Emblem A546

Views and Tourist Year Emblem: 40h, Spielberg Castle and churches, Brno. 1.20k, Danube, castle and churches, Bratislava. 1.60k, Vlatava River bridges, Hradcany and churches, Prague.

1967, Feb. 13 Engr. *Perf. 11½*

Size: 40x23mm

1443 A546 30h brown violet .20 .20
1444 A546 40h maroon .20 .20

Size: 75x30mm

1445 A546 1.20k violet blue .45 .20
1446 A546 1.60k black 1.50 .50
Nos. 1443-1446 (4) 2.35 1.10

International Tourist Year, 1967.

Black-tailed Godwit — A547

Birds: 40h, Shoveler, horiz. 60h, Purple heron. 80h, Penduline tit. 1k, Avocet. 1.40k, Black stork. 1.60k, Tufted duck, horiz.

1967, Feb. 20 Litho. *Perf. 13½*

1447	A547	30h	multi	.50	.30
1448	A547	40h	multi	.50	.30
1449	A547	60h	multi	.50	.30
1450	A547	80h	multi	.50	.30
1451	A547	1k	multi	.75	.30
1452	A547	1.40k	multi	1.00	.60
1453	A547	1.60k	multi	4.00	1.20
			Nos. 1447-1453 (7)	7.75	3.30

Solar Research and Satellite — A548

Space Research: 40h, Space craft, rocket and construction of station. 60h, Man on moon and orientation system. 1k, Exploration of solar system and rocket. 1.20k, Lunar satellites and moon photograph. 1.60k, Planned lunar architecture and moon landing.

Engraved and Photogravure

1967, Mar. 24 *Perf. 11½*

1454	A548	30h	yel & dk red	.25	.20
1455	A548	40h	vio bl & blk	.35	.20
1456	A548	60h	lilac & grn	.35	.20
1457	A548	1k	brt pink & sl	.35	.20
1458	A548	1.20k	lt violet & blk	.50	.20
1459	A548	1.60k	brn lake & blk	1.75	.60
			Nos. 1454-1459 (6)	3.55	1.60

Gothic Painting, by Master Theodoric A549

Designs: 40h, "Burning of Master Hus," from Litomerice Hymnal. 60h, Modern glass sculpture. 80h, "The Shepherdess and the Chimney Sweep," Andersen fairy tale, painting by J. Trnka. 1k, Section of pressure vessel from atomic power station. 1.20k, Three ceramic figurines, by P. Rada. 3k, Montreal skyline and EXPO '67 emblem.

1967, Apr. 10 Engr. *Perf. 14*

Size: 37x23mm

1460	A549	30h	multi	.20	.20
1461	A549	40h	multi	.20	.20
1462	A549	60h	multi	.20	.20
1463	A549	80h	multi	.25	.20
1464	A549	1k	multi	1.00	.25
1465	A549	1.20k	multi	1.25	.60
			Nos. 1460-1465 (6)	3.10	1.65

Souvenir Sheet

Perf. 11½

Size: 40x30mm

1466	A549	3k	multi	3.00	2.50

EXPO '67, International Exhibition, Montreal, Apr. 28-Oct. 27, 1967.

Canoe Race A550

Women Playing Basketball — A551

#1468, Wheels, dove & emblems of Warsaw, Berlin, Prague. 1.60k, Canoe slalom.

Perf. 12x11½, 11½x12

1967, Apr. 17 Engr. & Photo.

1467	A550	60h	black & brt bl	.20	.20
1468	A550	60h	black & salmon	.20	.20
1469	A551	60h	blk & grnsh bl	.20	.20
1470	A551	1.60k	black & brt vio	1.25	.50
			Nos. 1467-1470 (4)	1.85	1.10

No. 1467, 5th Intl. Wild-Water Canoeing Championships; No. 1468, 20th Warsaw-Berlin-Prague Bicycle Race: No. 1469, Women's Basketball Championships; No. 1470, 10th Intl. Water Slalom Championships.

"Golden Street" — A552

Designs: 60h, Interior of Hall of King Wenceslas. 5k, St. Matthew, from illuminated manuscript, 11th century.

1967, May 9 *Perf. 11½x11*

1471	A552	30h	rose claret	.25	.20
1472	A552	60h	bluish black	.50	.20

Souvenir Sheet

Perf. 11½

1473	A552	5k	multicolored	2.75	2.50

Issued to publicize the Castle of Prague.

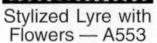

Stylized Lyre with Flowers — A553

Old-New Synagogue, Prague — A554

1967, May 10 *Perf. 11½*

1474	A553	60h	dull pur & brt grn	.30	.20

Prague Music Festival.

1967, May 22 *Perf. 11½*

30h, Detail from Torah curtain, 1593. 60h, Prague Printer's emblem, 1530. 1k, Mikulov jug, 1804. 1.40k, Memorial for Concentration Camp Victims 1939-45, Pincas Synagogue (menorah & tablet). 1.60k, Tombstone of David Gans, 1613.

1475	A554	30h	dull red & lt bl	.30	.20
1476	A554	60h	blk & lt grn	.20	.20
1477	A554	1k	dk bl & rose lil	.35	.20
1478	A554	1.20k	dk brn & mar	.65	.20
1479	A554	1.40k	black & yellow	.55	.20
1480	A554	1.60k	green & yel	4.50	2.75
			Nos. 1475-1480 (6)	6.55	3.75

Issued to show Jewish relics. The items shown on the 30h, 60h and 1k are from the State Jewish Museum, Prague.

"Lidice" A555

Prague Architecture A556

1967, June 9 Unwmk. *Perf. 11½*

1481	A555	30h	black & brt rose	.30	.20

Destruction of Lidice by the Nazis, 25th anniv.

1967, June 10 Engr. & Photo.

1482	A556	1k	black & gold	.45	.20

Issued to publicize the 9th Congress of the International Union of Architects, Prague.

Peter Bezruc A557

1967, June 21

1483	A557	60h	dull rose & blk	.30	.20

Peter Bezruc, poet & writer, birth cent.

Painting Type of 1966

2k, Henri Rousseau (1844-1910), self-portrait.
Issued in shhets of 4. Value $12.50.

1967, June 22 Engr. *Perf. 11½*

1484	A542	2k	multicolored	1.75	1.25

Praga 68, World Stamp Exhibition, Prague, June 22-July 7, 1968. Printed in sheets of 4 stamps (2x2), separated by horizontal gutter with inscription and picture of Natl. Gallery, site of Praga 68.

View of Skalitz — A558

#1486, Mining tower & church steeple, Pribram. #1487, Hands holding book & view of Presov.

1967, Aug. 21 Engr. *Perf. 11½*

1485	A558	30h	violet blue	.20	.20
1486	A558	30h	slate green	.20	.20
1487	A558	30h	claret	.20	.20
			Nos. 1485-1487 (3)	.60	.60

Towns of Skalitz, Pribram, Presov, annivs.

Colonnade and Spring, Karlovy Vary and Communications Emblem — A559

1967, Aug. 21 Engr. & Photo.

1488	A559	30h	violet bl & gold	.30	.20

5th Sports & Cultural Festival of the Employees of the Ministry of Communications, Karlovy Vary.

Ondrejov Observatory and Galaxy — A560

1967, Aug. 22 Engr.

1489	A560	60h	vio bl, rose lil & sil	1.50	.25

13th Cong. of the Intl. Astronomical Union.

Orchid — A561

Flowers from the Botanical Gardens: 30h, Cobaea scandens. 40h, Lycaste deppei. 60h, Glottiphyllum davisii. 1k, Anthurium. 1.20k, Rhodocactus. 1.40k, Moth orchid.

1967, Aug. 30 Litho. *Perf. 12½*

1490	A561	20h	multicolored	.35	.20
1491	A561	30h	pink & multi	.35	.20
1492	A561	40h	multicolored	.45	.20
1493	A561	60h	lt blue & multi	.45	.20
1494	A561	1k	multicolored	.65	.20
1495	A561	1.20k	lt yellow & multi	.75	.30
1496	A561	1.40k	multicolored	2.00	.70
			Nos. 1490-1496 (7)	5.00	2.00

Red Squirrel A562

Animals from the Tatra National Park: 60h, Wild cat. 1k, Ermine. 1.20k, Dormouse. 1.40k, Hedgehog. 1.60k, Pine marten.

Engraved and Photogravure

1967, Sept. 25 *Perf. 11½*

1497	A562	30h	black, yel & org	.25	.20
1498	A562	60h	black & buff	.25	.20
1499	A562	1k	black & lt blue	.30	.20
1500	A562	1.20k	brn, pale grn & yel	.50	.20
1501	A562	1.40k	blk, pink & yel	.60	.20
1502	A562	1.60k	black, org & yel	2.50	1.00
			Nos. 1497-1502 (6)	4.40	2.00

Rockets and Weapons — A563

1967, Oct. 6 Engr. *Perf. 11½*

1503	A563	30h	slate green	.30	.20

Day of the Czechoslovak People's Army.

Cruiser "Aurora" Firing at Winter Palace A564

Designs: 60h, Hammer and sickle emblems and Red Star, vert. 1k, Hands reaching for hammer and sickle, vert.

1967, Nov. 7 **Engr. & Photo.**

1504 A564 30h black & dk car .20 .20
1505 A564 60h black & dk car .20 .20
1506 A564 1k black & dk car .20 .20
Nos. 1504-1506 (3) .60 .60

Russian October Revolution, 50th anniv.

The Conjurer, by Frantisek Tichy A565

Paintings: 80h, Don Quixote, by Cyprian Majernik. 1k, Promenade in the Park, by Norbert Grund. 1.20k, Self-portrait, by Peter J. Brandl. 1.60k, Saints from Jan of Jeren Epitaph, by Czech Master of 1395.

1967, Nov. 13 **Engr.** ***Perf. 11½***

1507 A565 60h multi .30 .20
1508 A565 80h multi .40 .25
1509 A565 1k multi .65 .40
1510 A565 1.20k multi .65 .40
1511 A565 1.60k multi 2.75 2.25
Nos. 1507-1511 (5) 4.75 3.50

Nos. 1507-1511 were issued in sheets of 4. Value, set $27.50.

See Nos. 1589-1593, 1658-1662, 1711-1715, 1779-1783, 1847-1851, 1908-1913, 2043-2047, 2090-2093, 2147-2151, 2265-2269, 2335-2339, 2386-2390, 2437-2441, 2534-2538, 2586-2590, 2634-2638, 2810-2813, 2843-2847, 2872-2874, 2908-2910, 2936-2938, 2973-2975, 2995, 3001-3002, 3028-3030, 3054-3055, 3075-3076, 3105-3107, 3133-3135, 3160-3162, 3188-3190, 3224-3226, 3233, 3255-3257, 3287-3289, 3323-3325, 3359-3361.

Pres. Antonin Novotny — A566

1967, Dec. 9 **Engr.** ***Perf. 11½***

1512 A566 2k blue gray 1.25 .20
1513 A566 3k brown 1.25 .20

Czechoslovakia Nos. 65, 71 and 81 of 1920 — A567

1967, Dec. 18

1514 A567 1k maroon & silver 1.25 .75

Issued for Stamp Day.

Symbolic Flag and Dates — A568

1968, Jan. 15 **Engr.** ***Perf. 11½***

1515 A568 30h red, dk bl & ultra .60 .20

50th anniversary of Czechoslovakia.

Figure Skating and Olympic Rings — A569

Olympic Rings and: 1k, Ski course. 1.60k, Toboggan chute. 2k, Ice hockey.

1968, Jan. 29 **Engr. & Photo.**

1516 A569 60h blk, yel & ocher .25 .20
1517 A569 1k ol grn, lt bl & lem .50 .20
1518 A569 1.60k blk, lil & bl grn .65 .20
1519 A569 2k blk, ap grn & lt bl 1.10 .55
Nos. 1516-1519 (4) 2.50 1.15

10th Winter Olympic Games, Grenoble, France, Feb. 6-18.

Factories and Rising Sun — A570

Design: 60h, Workers and banner.

1968, Feb. 25 ***Perf. 11½x12***

1520 A570 30h car & dk bl .20 .20
1521 A570 60h car & dk bl .20 .20

20th anniversary of February Revolution.

Map of Battle of Sokolow A571

Human Rights Flame — A572

1968, Mar. 8 ***Perf. 11½***

1522 A571 30h blk, brt bl & car .40 .20

Engr.

1523 A572 1k rose carmine 1.00 .35

25th anniv. of the Battle of Sokolow, Mar. 8, 1943, against the German Army, No. 1522; Intl. Human Rights Year, No. 1523.

Janko Kral and Liptovsky Mikulas — A573

Karl Marx — A574

Girl's Head — A575

Arms and Allegory — A576

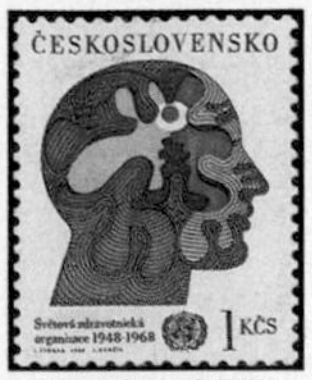

Head — A577

1968, Mar. 25 **Engr.**

1524 A573 30h green .30 .20
1525 A574 30h claret .25 .20

Engraved and Photogravure

1526 A575 30h dk red & gold .25 .20
1527 A576 30h dk blue & dp org .25 .20
1528 A577 1k multicolored .50 .20
Nos. 1524-1528 (5) 1.55 1.00

The writer Janko Kral and the Slovak town Liptovsky Mikulas (No. 1524); 150th anniv. of the birth of Karl Marx (No. 1525); cent. of the cornerstone laying of the Prague Natl. Theater (No. 1526); 150th anniv. of the Prague Natl. Museum (No. 1527); 20th anniv. of WHO (1k).

Symbolic Radio Waves A578

No. 1530, Symbolic television screens.

1968, Apr. 29 ***Perf. 11½***

1529 A578 30h blk, car & vio bl .20 .20
1530 A578 30h blk, car & vio bl .20 .20

45th anniv. of Czechoslovak broadcasting (#1529), 15th anniv. of television (#1530).

Olympic Rings, Mexican Sculpture and Diver — A579

Olympic Rings and: 40h, Runner and "The Sanctification of Quetzalcoatl." 60h, Volleyball and Mexican ornaments. 1k, Czechoslovak and Mexican Olympic emblems and carved altar. 1.60k, Soccer and ornaments. 2k, View of Hradcany, weather vane and key.

1968, Apr. 30

1531 A579 30h black, bl & car .20 .20
1532 A579 40h multi .20 .20
1533 A579 60h multi .20 .20
1534 A579 1k multi .35 .20
1535 A579 1.60k multi .35 .20
1536 A579 2k black & multi 1.75 .40
Nos. 1531-1536 (6) 3.05 1.40

19th Olympic Games, Mexico City, 10/12-27.

Prague Castle Types of 1966

Designs: 30h, Tombstone of Bretislav I. 60h, Romanesque door knocker, St. Wenceslas Chapel. 5k, Head of St. Peter, mosaic from Golden Gate of St. Vitus Cathedral.

1968, May 9 ***Perf. 11½***

1537 A527 30h multicolored .40 .20
1538 A527 60h black, red & cit .40 .20

Souvenir Sheet

Engr.

1539 A528 5k multicolored 2.50 2.50

Pres. Ludvik Svoboda — A580

1968-70 **Engr.** ***Perf. 11½***

1540 A580 30h ultramarine .20 .20
1540A A580 50h green ('70) .20 .20
1541 A580 60h maroon .20 .20
1541A A580 1k rose car ('70) .30 .20
Nos. 1540-1541A (4) .90 .80

Shades exist of No. 1541A.

"Business," Sculpture by Otto Gutfreund A581

Cabaret Performer, by Frantisek Kupka — A582

Designs (The New Prague): 40h, Broadcasting Corporation Building. 60h, New Parliament. 1.40k, Tapestry by Jan Bauch "Prague 1787." 3k, Presidential standard.

Engr. & Photo.; Engr. (2k)

1968, June 5

1542 A581 30h black & multi .20 .20
1543 A581 40h black & multi .20 .20
1544 A581 60h dk brn & multi .20 .20
1545 A581 1.40k dk brn & multi .40 .20
1546 A582 2k indigo & multi .85 .70
1547 A581 3k black & multi .85 .30
Nos. 1542-1547 (6) 2.70 1.80

1968, June 21 ***Perf. 11½***

Designs (The Old Prague): 30h, St. George's Basilica. 60h, Renaissance fountain. 1k, Villa America-Dvorak Museum, 18th cent. building. 1.60k, Emblem from the House of Three Violins, 18th cent. 2k, Josefina, by Josef Manes. 3k, Emblem of Prague, 1475.

1548 A581 30h green, gray & yel .20 .20
1549 A581 60h dk vio, ap grn & gold .20 .20
1550 A581 1k black, lt bl & pink .30 .20
1551 A581 1.60k slate grn & multi .55 .20
1552 A582 2k brown & multi 1.25 .60
1553 A581 3k blk, yel, bl & pink 1.25 .60
Nos. 1548-1553 (6) 3.75 2.00

Nos. 1542-1553 publicized the Praga 68 Philatelic Exhibition. Nos. 1542-1545, 1547-1551, 1553 issued in sheets of 15 + 15 labels with Praga 68 emblem and inscription.

Nos. 1546, 1552 issued in sheets of 4 (2x2) with one horizontal label between top and bottom rows showing Praga 68 emblem. Values for sheets of 4, each $8.

Souvenir Sheet

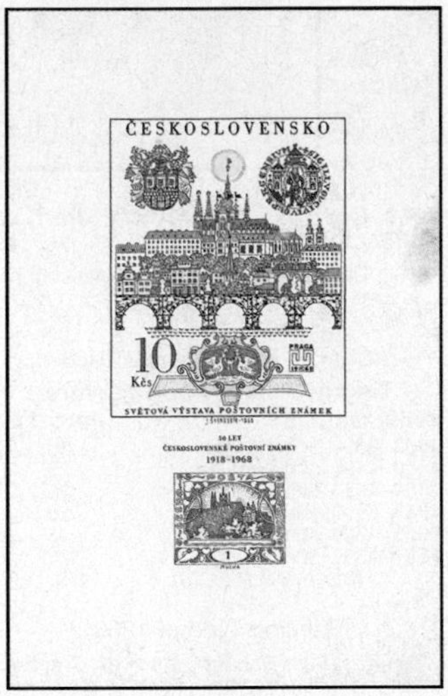

View of Prague and Emblems — A583

Engraved and Photogravure

1968, June 22 ***Imperf.***

1554	A583	10k	multicolored	3.00	2.50

Praga 68 and 50th anniv. of Czechoslovak postage stamps. Sold only together with a 5k admission ticket to the Praga 68 philatelic Exhibition. Value $20.

Madonna with the Rose Garlands, by Dürer — A584

1968, July 6 ***Perf. 11½***

1555	A584	5k	multicolored	3.00	1.75

FIP Day, July 6. Issued in sheets of 4 (2x2) with one horizontal label between, showing Praga 68 emblem.

Stagecoach on Rails — A585

Design: 1k, Steam and electric locomotives.

1968, Aug. 6

1556	A585	60h	multicolored	.35	.20
1557	A585	1k	multicolored	1.25	.45

No. 1556: 140th anniv. of the horse-drawn railroad Ceské Budejovice to Linz; No. 1557: cent. of the Ceské Budejovice to Plzen railroad.

6th Intl. Slavonic Cong. in Prague — A586

1968, Aug. 7 ***Perf. 11½***

1558	A586	30h	vio blue & car	.40	.20

Ardspach Rocks and Ammonite — A587

60h, Basalt formation & frog skeleton fossil. 80h, Rocks, basalt veins & polished agate. 1k, Pelecypoda (fossil shell) & Belanske Tatra mountains. 1.60k, Trilobite & Barrande rock formation.

1968, Aug. 8

1559	A587	30h	black & citron	.20	.20
1560	A587	60h	black & rose cl	.20	.20
1561	A587	80h	black, lt vio & pink	.30	.20
1562	A587	1k	black & lt blue	.40	.20
1563	A587	1.60k	black & bister	1.40	.65
			Nos. 1559-1563 (5)	2.50	1.45

Issued to publicize the 23rd International Geological Congress, Prague, Aug. 8-Sept. 3.

Raising Slovak Flag A588

60h, Slovak partisans, and mountain.

1968, Sept. 9 **Engr.** ***Perf. 11½***

1564	A588	30h	ultra	.20	.20
1565	A588	60h	red	.20	.20

No. 1564 for the Slovak Natl. Council, No. 1565 the 120th anniv. of the Slovak national uprising.

Flowerpot, by Jiri Schlessinger (age 10) — A589

Drawings by Children in Terezin Concentration Camp: 30h, Jew and Guard, by Jiri Beutler (age 10). 60h, Butterflies, by Kitty Brunnerova (age 11).

Engraved and Photogravure

1968, Sept. 30 ***Perf. 11½***

Size: 30x23mm

1566	A589	30h	blk, buff & rose lil	.25	.20
1567	A589	60h	black & multi	.25	.20

Perf. 12x11½

Size: 41x23mm

1568	A589	1k	black & multi	.80	.20
			Nos. 1566-1568 (3)	1.30	.60

30th anniversary of Munich Pact.

Arms of Regional Capitals A590

Arms of Prague — A591

1968, Oct. 21 ***Perf. 11½***

1569	A590	60h	Banská Bystrica	.20	.20
1570	A590	60h	Bratislava	.20	.20
1571	A590	60h	Brno	.20	.20
1572	A590	60h	Ceské Budejovice	.20	.20
1573	A590	60h	Hradec Králové	.20	.20
1574	A590	60h	Kosice	.20	.20
1575	A590	60h	Ostrava (horse)	.20	.20
1576	A590	60h	Plzen	.20	.20
1577	A590	60h	Ustí nad Labem	.20	.20

Perf. 11½x16

1578	A591	1k	shown	.75	.20
			Nos. 1569-1578 (10)	2.55	2.00

#1578 issued in sheets of 10. See #1652-1657, 1742-1747, 1886-1888, 2000-2001.

Flag and Linden Leaves A592

Bohemian Lion Breaking Chains (Type SP1 of 1919) — A593

Design: 60h, Map of Czechoslovakia, linden leaves, Hradcany in Prague and Castle in Bratislava.

1968, Oct. 28 ***Perf. 12x11½***

1579	A592	30h	dp blue & mag	.30	.20
1580	A592	60h	blk, gold, red & ultra	.30	.20

Souvenir Sheet

Engr.

Perf. 11½x12

1581	A593	5k	red	3.50	2.75

Founding of Czechoslovakia, 50th anniv.

Ernest Hemingway A594

Cinderlad A595

Caricatures: 30h, Karel Capek (1890-1938), writer. 40h, George Bernard Shaw. 60h, Maxim Gorki. 1k, Pablo Picasso. 1.20k, Taikan Yokoyama (1868-1958), painter. 1.40k, Charlie Chaplin.

Engraved and Photogravure

1968, Nov. 18 ***Perf. 11½x12***

1582	A594	20h	black, org & red	.20	.20
1583	A594	30h	black & multi	.30	.20
1584	A594	40h	blk, lic & car	.30	.20
1585	A594	60h	black, sky bl & grn	.20	.20
1586	A594	1k	black, brn & yel	.45	.20
1587	A594	1.20k	black, dp car & vio	.45	.20
1588	A594	1.40k	black, brn & dp org	1.75	.40
			Nos. 1582-1588 (7)	3.65	1.60

Cultural personalities of the 20th cent. and UNESCO. See Nos. 1628-1633.

Painting Type of 1967

Czechoslovakian Art: 60h, Cleopatra II, by Jan Zrzavy (1890-1977). 80h, Black Lake (man and horse), by Jan Preisler (1872-1918). 1.20k, Giovanni Francisci as a Volunteer, by Peter Michal Bohun (1822-1879). 1.60k, Princess Hyacinth, by Alfons Mucha (1860-1939). 3k, Madonna and Child, woodcarving, 1518, by Master Paul of Levoca.

1968, Nov. 29 **Engr.** ***Perf. 11½***

1589	A565	60h	multi	.75	.35
1590	A565	80h	multi	.75	.35
1591	A565	1.20k	multi	.75	.35
1592	A565	1.60k	multi	.75	.35
1593	A565	3k	multi	2.50	2.50
			Nos. 1589-1593 (5)	5.50	3.90

Nos. 1589-1593 were issued in sheets of 4. Value, set $30.

1968, Dec. 18 **Engr. & Photo.**

Slovak Fairy Tales: 60h, The Proud Lady. 80h, The Ruling Knight. 1k, Good Day, Little Bench. 1.20k, The Spellbound Castle. 1.80k, The Miraculous Hunter. The designs are from illustrations by Ludovit Fulla for "Slovak Stories."

1594	A595	30h	multi	.25	.20
1595	A595	60h	multi	.25	.20
1596	A595	80h	multi	.40	.20
1597	A595	1k	multi	.55	.20
1598	A595	1.20k	multi	.55	.20
1599	A595	1.80k	multi	1.50	.65
			Nos. 1594-1599 (6)	3.50	1.65

Czechoslovakia Nos. 2 and 3 — A596

1968, Dec. 18

1600	A596	1k	violet bl & gold	.75	.65

50th anniv. of Czechoslovakian postage stamps.

Crescent, Cross and Lion and Sun Emblems A597

ILO Emblem A598

60h, 12 crosses in circles forming large cross.

1969, Jan. 31 ***Perf. 11½***

1601	A597	60h	black, red & gold	.20	.20
1602	A597	1k	black, ultra & red	.35	.20

No. 1601: 50th anniv. of the Czechoslovak Red Cross. No. 1602: 50th anniv. of the League of Red Cross Societies.

1969, Jan. 31

1603	A598	1k	black & gray	.30	.20

50th anniv. of the ILO.

Cheb Pistol A599

Historical Firearms: 40h, Italian pistol with Dutch decorations, c. 1600. 60h, Wheellock rifle from Matej Kubik workshop c. 1720. 1k, Flintlock pistol, Devieuxe workshop, Liege, c. 1760. 1.40k, Duelling pistols, from Lebeda workshop, Prague, c. 1835. 1.60k, Derringer pistols, US, c. 1865.

1969, Feb. 18

1604	A599	30h	black & multi	.20	.20
1605	A599	40h	black & multi	.20	.20
1606	A599	60h	black & multi	.20	.20
1607	A599	1k	black & multi	.25	.20
1608	A599	1.40k	black & multi	.35	.20
1609	A599	1.60k	black & multi	1.00	.50
			Nos. 1604-1609 (6)	2.20	1.50

Bratislava Castle, Muse and Book — A600

#1611, Science symbols & emblem (Brno University). #1612, Harp, laurel & musicians' names. #1613, Theatrical scene. #1614, Arms of Slovakia, banner & blossoms. #1615, School, outstretched hands & woman with linden leaves.

1969, Mar. 24 Engr. *Perf. 11½*

1610	A600 60h violet blue	.20	.20

Engraved and Photogravure

1611	A600 60h blk, gold & slate	.20	.20
1612	A600 60h gold, blue, blk & red	.20	.20
1613	A600 60h black & rose red	.20	.20
1614	A600 60h rose red, sil & bl	.20	.20
1615	A600 60h black & gold	.20	.20
	Nos. 1610-1615 (6)	1.20	1.20

50th anniv. of: Komensky University in Bratislava (#1610); Brno University (#1611); Brno Conservatory of Music (#1612); Slovak Natl. Theater (#1613); Slovak Soviet Republic (#1614); cent. of the Zniev Gymnasium (academic high school) (#1615).

Baldachin-top Car and Four-seat Coupé of 1900-1905 — A601

Designs: 1.60k, Laurin & Klement Voiturette, 1907, and L & K touring car with American top, 1907. 1.80k, First Prague bus, 1907, and sectionalized Skoda bus, 1967.

1969, Mar. 25 Engr. & Photo.

1616	A601 30h blk, lil & lt grn	.55	.20
1617	A601 1.60k blk, org brn & lt bl	.70	.20
1618	A601 1.80k multi	1.25	.60
	Nos. 1616-1618 (3)	2.50	1.00

Peace, by Ladislav Guderna — A602

1969, Apr. 21 *Perf. 11*

1619	A602 1.60k multi	.50	.35

20th anniv. of the Peace Movement. Issued in sheets of 15 stamps and 5 tabs.

Horse and Rider, by Vaclav Hollar — A603

Old Engravings of Horses: 30h, Prancing Stallion, by Hendrik Goltzius, horiz. 80h, Groom Leading Horse, by Matthäus Merian, horiz. 1.80k, Horse and Soldier, by Albrecht Dürer. 2.40k, Groom and Horse, by Johann E. Ridinger.

1969, Apr. 24 *Perf. 11x11½, 11½x11*

Yellowish Paper

1620	A603 30h dark brown	.20	.20
1621	A603 80h violet brown	.20	.20
1622	A603 1.60k slate	.40	.20
1623	A603 1.80k sepia	.45	.20
1624	A603 2.40k multi	2.25	.60
	Nos. 1620-1624 (5)	3.50	1.40

M. R. Stefánik as Astronomy Professor and French General — A604

1969, May 4 Engr. *Perf. 11½*

1625	A604 60h rose claret	.40	.20

Gen. Milan R. Stefánik, 50th death anniv.

St. Wenceslas Pressing Wine, Mural by the Master of Litomerice — A605

Design: No. 1627, Coronation banner of the Estates, 1723, with St. Wenceslas and coats of arms of Bohemia and Czech Crown lands.

1969, May 9 Engr. *Perf. 11½*

1626	A605 3k multicolored	1.50	1.40
1627	A605 3k multicolored	1.50	1.40

Issued to publicize the art treasures of the Castle of Prague.

Issued in sheets of 4. Value, set $20.

See Nos. 1689-1690.

Caricature Type of 1968

Caricatures: 30h, Pavol Orszagh Hviezdoslav (1849-1921), Slovak writer. 40h, Gilbert K. Chesterton (1874-1936), English writer. 60h, Vladimir Mayakovski (1893-1930), Russian poet. 1k, Henri Matisse (1869-1954), French painter. 1.80k, Ales Hrdlicka (1869-1943), Czech-born American anthropologist. 2k, Franz Kafka (1883-1924), Austrian writer.

Engraved and Photogravure

1969, June 17 *Perf. 11½x12*

1628	A594 30h blk, red & bl	.20	.20
1629	A594 40h blk, bl & lt vio	.20	.20
1630	A594 60h blk, rose & yel	.20	.20
1631	A594 1k black & multi	.20	.20
1632	A594 1.80k blk, ultra & ocher	.20	.20
1633	A594 2k blk, yel & brt grn	1.50	.50
	Nos. 1628-1633 (6)	2.50	1.50

Issued to honor cultural personalities of the 20th century and UNESCO.

"Music," by Alfons Mucha — A606

Paintings by Mucha: 60h, "Painting." 1k, "Dance." 2.40k, "Ruby" and "Amethyst."

1969, July 14 *Perf. 11½x11*

Size: 30x49mm

1634	A606 30h black & multi	.80	.20
1635	A606 60h black & multi	.80	.20
1636	A606 1k black & multi	.90	.20

Size: 39x51mm

1637	A606 2.40k black & multi	2.00	1.25
	Nos. 1634-1637 (4)	4.50	1.85

Alfons Mucha (1860-1930), painter and stamp designer (Type A1).

No. 1637 was issued in sheets of 4. Value $18.

Pres. Svoboda and Partisans A607

No. 1639, Slovak fighters and mourners.

1969, Aug. 29 *Perf. 11*

1638	A607 30h ol grn & red, *yel*	.20	.20
1639	A607 30h vio bl & red, *yel*	.20	.20

25th anniversary of the Slovak uprising and of the Battle of Dukla.

Tatra Mountain Stream and Gentians — A608

Designs: 60h, Various views in Tatra Mountains. No. 1644, Mountain pass and gentians. No. 1645, Houses, Krivan Mountain and autumn crocuses.

1969, Sept. 8 Engr. *Perf. 11*

Size: 71x33mm

1640	A608 60h gray	.25	.20
1641	A608 60h dark blue	.25	.20
1642	A608 60h dull gray vio	.25	.20

Perf. 11½

Size: 40x23mm

1643	A608 1.60k multi	.35	.20
1644	A608 1.60k multi	1.50	.50
1645	A608 1.60k multi	.40	.20
	Nos. 1640-1645 (6)	3.00	1.50

20th anniv. of the creation of the Tatra Mountains Natl. Park.

Nos. 1640-1642 are printed in sheets of 15 (3x5) with 5 labels showing mountain plants. Value, set with tabs $2.50.

Nos. 1643-1645 were issued in sheets of 10. Value, $55.

Bronze Belt Ornaments A609

Archaeological Treasures from Bohemia and Moravia: 30h, Gilt ornament with 6 masks. 1k, Jeweled earrings. 1.80k, Front and back of lead cross with Greek inscription. 2k, Gilt strap ornament with human figure.

Engraved and Photogravure

1969, Sept. 30 *Perf. 11½x11*

1646	A609 20h gold & multi	.20	.20
1647	A609 30h gold & multi	.20	.20
1648	A609 1k red & multi	.25	.20
1649	A609 1.80k dull org & multi	.50	.20
1650	A609 2k gold & multi	1.50	.40
	Nos. 1646-1650 (5)	2.65	1.20

"Mail Circling the World" A610

1969, Oct. 1 Engr. *Perf. 12*

1651	A610 3.20k multi	.75	.50

16th UPU Cong., Tokyo, Oct. 1-Nov. 14. Issued in sheets of 4. Value $9.

Coat of Arms Type of 1968

Engraved and Photogravure

1969, Oct. 25 *Perf. 11½*

1652	A590 50h Bardejov	.25	.20
1653	A590 50h Hranice	.25	.20
1654	A590 50h Kezmarok	.25	.20
1655	A590 50h Krnov	.25	.20
1656	A590 50h Litomerice	.25	.20
1657	A590 50h Manetin	.25	.20
	Nos. 1652-1657 (6)	1.50	1.20

Painting Type of 1968

Designs: 60h, Requiem, 1944, by Frantisek Muzika. 1k, Resurrection, 1380, by the Master of the Trebon Altar. 1.60k, Crucifixion, 1950, by Vincent Hloznik. 1.80k, Girl with Doll, 1863, by Julius Bencur. 2.20k, St. Jerome, 1357-67, by Master Theodorik.

1969, Nov. 25 *Perf. 11½*

1658	A565 60h multi	1.00	.25
1659	A565 1k multi	1.00	.25
1660	A565 1.60k multi	1.10	.40
1661	A565 1.80k multi	1.40	.50
1662	A565 2.20k multi	3.00	2.00
	Nos. 1658-1662 (5)	7.50	3.40

Nos. 1658-1662 were each issued in sheets of 4. Value, set $40.

Symbolic Sheet of Stamps — A611

1969, Dec. 18 *Perf. 11½x12*

1663	A611 1k dk brn, ultra & gold	.30	.30

Issued for Stamp Day 1969.

Ski Jump — A612

Designs: 60h, Long distance skier. 1k, Ski jump and slope. 1.60k, Woman skier.

1970, Jan. 6 *Perf. 11½*

1664	A612 50h multi	.20	.20
1665	A612 60h multi	.20	.20
1666	A612 1k multi	.20	.20
1667	A612 1.60k multi	.60	.30
	Nos. 1664-1667 (4)	1.20	.90

Intl. Ski Championships "Tatra 1970."

Ludwig van Beethoven — A613

Portraits: No. 1669, Friedrich Engels (1820-95), German socialist. No. 1670, Maximilian Hell (1720-92), Slovakian Jesuit and astronomer. No. 1671, Lenin, Russian Communist leader. No. 1672, Josef Manes (1820-71), Czech painter. No. 1673, Comenius (1592-1670), theologian and educator.

1970, Feb. 17 Engr. *Perf. 11x11½*

1668	A613	40h black	.20	.20
1669	A613	40h dull red	.20	.20
1670	A613	40h yellow brn	.20	.20
1671	A613	40h dull red	.20	.20
1672	A613	40h brown	.20	.20
1673	A613	40h black	.20	.20
		Nos. 1668-1673 (6)	1.20	1.20

Anniversaries of birth of Beethoven, Engels, Hell, Lenin and Manes, 300th anniv. of the death of Comenius, and to honor UNESCO.

Bells A614

80h, Machine tools & lathe. 1k, Folklore masks. 1.60k, Angel & Three Wise Men, 17th cent. icon from Koniec. 2k, View of Orlik Castle, 1787, by F. K. Wolf. 3k, "Passing through Koshu down to Mishima" from Hokusai's 36 Views of Fuji.

Engraved and Photogravure

1970, Mar. 13 *Perf. 11½x11*

Size: 40x23mm

1674	A614	50h multi	.20	.20
1675	A614	80h multi	.20	.20
1676	A614	1k multi	.25	.20

Size: 50x40mm

Perf. 11½

1677	A614	1.60k multi	.45	.30
1678	A614	2k multi	.60	.35
1679	A614	3k multi	1.60	1.00
		Nos. 1674-1679 (6)	3.30	2.25

EXPO '70 Intl. Exhib., Osaka, Japan, Mar. 15-Sept. 13, 1970.

Nos. 1674-1676 issued in sheets of 50, Nos. 1677-1679 in sheets of 4. Value, set of 3 sheets, $28.

Kosice Townhall, Laurel and Czechoslovak Arms — A615

1970, Apr. 5 *Perf. 11*

1680	A615	60h slate, ver & gold	.30	.20

Government's Kosice Program, 25th anniv.

"The Remarkable Horse" by Josef Lada — A616

Lenin — A617

Paintings by Josef Lada: 60h, Autumn, 1955, horiz. 1.80k, "The Water Sprite." 2.40k, Children in Winter, 1943, horiz.

1970, Apr. 21 *Perf. 11½*

1681	A616	60h black & multi	.25	.20
1682	A616	1k black & multi	.40	.20
1683	A616	1.80k black & multi	.70	.20
1684	A616	2.40k black & multi	1.40	.40
		Nos. 1681-1684 (4)	2.75	1.00

1970, Apr. 22

Design: 60h, Lenin without cap, facing left.

1685	A617	30h dk red & gold	.20	.20
1686	A617	60h black & gold	.20	.20

Lenin (1870-1924), Russian communist leader.

Fighters on the Barricades — A618

No. 1688, Lilac, Russian tank and castle.

1970, May 5 *Perf. 11x11½*

1687	A618	30h dull pur, gold & bl	.20	.20
1688	A618	30h dull grn, gold & red	.20	.20

No. 1687: 25th anniv. of the Prague uprising. No. 1688: 25th anniv. of the liberation of Czechoslovakia from the Germans.

Prague Castle Art Type of 1969

#1689, Bust of St. Vitus, 1486. #1690, Hermes and Athena, by Bartholomy Springer (1546-1611), mural from White Tower.

1970, May 7 Engr. *Perf. 11½*

1689	A605	3k maroon & multi	1.75	1.50
1690	A605	3k lt blue & multi	1.75	1.50

Nos. 1689-1690 were issued in sheets of 4. Value, set of 2 sheets, $20.

Compass Rose, UN Headquarters and Famous Buildings of the World — A619

Engraved and Photogravure

1970, June 26 *Perf. 11*

1691	A619	1k black & multi	.40	.20

25th anniv. of the UN. Issued in sheets of 15 (3x5) and 5 labels showing UN emblem. Value of single with tab attached: unused 75c; used 40c.

Cannon from 30 Years' War and Baron Munchhausen — A620

Historical Cannons: 60h, Cannon from Hussite war and St. Barbara. 1.20k, Cannon from Prussian-Austrian war, and legendary cannoneer Javurek. 1.80k, Early 20th century cannon and spaceship "La Colombiad" (Jules Verne). 2.40k, World War I cannon and "Good Soldier Schweik."

1970, Aug. 31 *Perf. 11½*

1692	A620	30h black & multi	.20	.20
1693	A620	60h black & multi	.20	.20
1694	A620	1.20k black & multi	.20	.20
1695	A620	1.80k black & multi	.30	.20
1696	A620	2.40k black & multi	1.40	.65
		Nos. 1692-1696 (5)	2.30	1.45

"Rude Pravo" (Red Truth) A621

1970, Sept. 21 *Perf. 11½x11*

1697	A621	60h car, gold & blk	.20	.20

50th anniv. of the Rude Pravo newspaper.

"Great Sun" House Sign and Old Town Tower Bridge, Prague — A622

60h, "Blue Lion" & Town Hall Tower, Brno. 1k, Gothic corner stone & Town Hall Tower, Bratislava. 1.40k, Coat of Arms & Gothic Tower, Bratislava, & medallion. 1.60k, Moravian Eagle & Gothic Town Hall Tower, Brno. 1.80k, "Black Sun" & "Green Frog" house signs & New Town Hall, Prague.

1970, Sept. 23 *Perf. 11x11½*

1698	A622	40h black & multi	.20	.20
1699	A622	60h black & multi	.20	.20
1700	A622	1k black & multi	.20	.20
1701	A622	1.40k black & multi	1.10	.50
1702	A622	1.60k black & multi	.25	.20
1703	A622	1.80k black & multi	.80	.20
		Nos. 1698-1703 (6)	2.75	1.50

Germany-Uruguay Semifinal Soccer Match — A623

Designs: 20h, Sundisk Games' emblem and flags of participating nations. 60h, England-Czechoslovakia match and coats of arms. 1k, Romania-Czechoslovakia match and coats of arms. 1.20k, Brazil-Italy, final match and emblems. 1.80k, Brazil-Czechoslovakia match and emblems.

1970, Oct. 29 *Perf. 11½*

1704	A623	20h blk & multi	.20	.20
1705	A623	40h blk & multi	.20	.20
1706	A623	60h blk & multi	.20	.20
1707	A623	1k blk & multi	.30	.20
1708	A623	1.20k blk & multi	.35	.20
1709	A623	1.80k blk & multi	1.50	.30
		Nos. 1704-1709 (6)	2.75	1.30

9th World Soccer Championships for the Jules Rimet Cup, Mexico City, 5/30-6/21.

Congress Emblem — A624

1970, Nov. 9 Engr. & Photo.

1710	A624	30h blk, gold, ultra & red	.20	.20

Congress of the Czechoslovak Socialist Youth Federation.

Painting Type of 1967

Paintings: 1k, Seated Mother, by Mikulas Galanda. 1.20k, Bridesmaid, by Karel Svolinsky. 1.40k, Walk by Night, 1944, by Frantisek Hudecek. 1.80k, Banska Bystrica Market, by Dominik Skutecky. 2.40k, Adoration of the Kings, from the Vysehrad Codex, 1085.

1970, Nov. 27 Engr. *Perf. 11½*

1711	A565	1k multi	.60	.25
1712	A565	1.20k multi	.75	.40
1713	A565	1.40k multi	.60	.30
1714	A565	1.80k multi	1.00	.40
1715	A565	2.40k multi	3.00	2.00
		Nos. 1711-1715 (5)	5.95	3.35

Nos. 1711-1715 were each issued in sheets of 4. Value, set $30.

Radar A625

Designs: 40h, Interkosmos 3, geophysical satellite. 60h, Kosmos meteorological satellite. 1k, Astronaut and Vostok satellite. No. 1720, Interkosmos 4, solar research satellite. No. 1720A, Space satellite (Sputnik) over city. 1.60k, Two-stage rocket on launching pad.

1970-71 Engr. & Photo. *Perf. 11*

1716	A625	20h black & multi	.20	.20
1717	A625	40h black & multi	.20	.20
1718	A625	60h black & multi	.20	.20
1719	A625	1k black & multi	.20	.20
1720	A625	1.20k black & multi	.20	.20
1720A	A625	1.20k black & multi ('71)	.30	.20
1721	A625	1.60k black & multi	1.40	.35
		Nos. 1716-1721 (7)	2.70	1.55

"Interkosmos," the collaboration of communist countries in various phases of space research.

Issued: #1720A, 11/15/71; others, 11/30/70.

Face of Christ on Veronica's Veil — A626

Slovak Ikons, 16th-18th Centuries: 60h, Adam and Eve in the Garden, vert. 2k, St. George and the Dragon. 2.80k, St. Michael, vert.

1970, Dec. 17 Engr. *Perf. 11½*

Cream Paper

1722	A626	60h multi	.80	.35
1723	A626	1k multi	1.10	.50
1724	A626	2k multi	1.40	.60
1725	A626	2.80k multi	2.00	1.25
		Nos. 1722-1725 (4)	5.30	2.70

Nos. 1722-1725 were each issued in sheets of 4. Value, set $30.

Carrier Pigeon Type of 1920 — A627

Engraved and Photogravure

1970, Dec. 18 *Perf. 11x11½*

1726	A627	1k red, blk & yel grn	.40	.30

Stamp Day.

Song of the Barricades, 1938, by Karel Stika — A628

Czech and Slovak Graphic Art: 50h, Fruit Grower's Barge, 1941, by Cyril Bouda. 60h, Moon (woman) Searching for Lilies of the Valley, 1913, by Jan Zrzavy. 1k, At the Edge of Town (working man and woman), 1931, by Koloman Sokol. 1.60k, Summer, 1641, by Vaclav Hollar. 2k, Gamekeeper and Shepherd of Orava Castle, 1847, by Peter M. Bohun.

Engr. & Photo.; Engr. (40h, 60h, 1k)

1971, Jan. 28 *Perf. 11½*

1727 A628 40h brown .20 .20
1728 A628 50h black & multi .20 .20
1729 A628 60h slate .20 .20
1730 A628 1k black .25 .20
1731 A628 1.60k black & buff .25 .20
1732 A628 2k black & multi 1.25 .30
Nos. 1727-1732 (6) 2.35 1.30

Saris Church A629

Bell Tower, Hronsek A630

Designs: 1k, Roofs and folk art, Horácko. 2.40k, House, Jicin. 3k, House and folk art, Melnik. 3.60k, Church of St. Bartholomew, Chrudim. 5k, Watch Tower, Nachod. 5.40k, Baroque house, Posumavi. 6k, Cottage, Orava. 9k, Cottage, Turnov. 10k, Old houses, Liptov. 14k, House and wayside bell stand. 20k, Houses, Cicmany.

Engraved and Photogravure

1971-72 *Perf. 11½x11, 11x11½*

1733 A630 1k multi .20 .20
1734 A629 1.60k multi 1.25 .20
1735 A630 2k multi 1.90 .20
1736 A629 2.40k multi 1.10 .30
1736A A630 3k multi ('72) 1.90 .20
1737 A629 3.60k multi 1.50 .20
1737A A630 5k multi ('72) 1.90 .20
1738 A629 5.40k multi .95 .20
1739 A630 6k multi 3.00 .20
1740 A630 9k multi 1.25 .20
1740A A629 10k multi ('72) 2.75 .20
1741 A629 14k multi 3.00 .25
1741A A629 20k multi ('72) 3.25 .30
Nos. 1733-1741A (13) 23.95 2.85

Nos. 1736A, 1738, 1740 are horizontal.
See No. 2870.

Coat of Arms Type of 1968

1971, Mar. 26 *Perf. 11½*

1742 A590 60h Zilina .20 .20
1743 A590 60h Levoca .20 .20
1744 A590 60h Ceska Trebova .20 .20
1745 A590 60h Uhersky Brod .20 .20
1746 A590 60h Trutnov .20 .20
1747 A590 60h Karlovy Vary .20 .20
Nos. 1742-1747 (6) 1.20 1.20

"Fight of the Communards and Rise of the International" — A631

Design: No. 1749, World fight against racial discrimination, and "UNESCO."

1971, Mar. 18 *Perf. 11*

1748 A631 1k multicolored .30 .20
1749 A631 1k multicolored .30 .20

No. 1748 for cent. of the Paris Commune. No. 1749 for the Year against Racial Discrimination. Issued in sheets of 15 stamps and 5 labels. Value for single with attached tab, each 40c.

A632

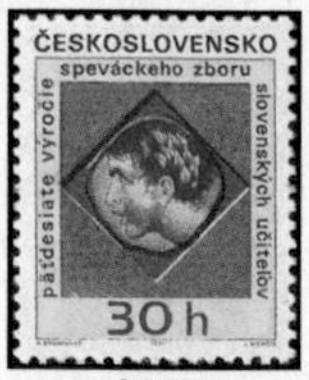

A633

Edelweiss, mountaineering map & equipment.

1971, Apr. 27 *Perf. 11½x11*

1750 A632 30h multicolored .25 .20

50th anniversary of Slovak Alpine Club.

1971, Apr. 27 *Perf. 11½*

1751 A633 30h Singer .25 .20

50th anniversary of Slovak Teachers' Choir.

Abbess' Crosier, 16th Century A634

#1753, Allegory of Music, 16th cent. mural.

1971, May 9

1752 A634 3k gold & multi 1.75 1.25
1753 A634 3k blk, dk brn & buff 2.25 1.25

Nos. 1752-1753 were each issued in sheets of 4. Value, set $22.50.

See Nos. 1817-1818, 1884-1885, 1937-1938, 2040-2041, 2081-2082, 2114-2115, 2176-2177, 2238-2239, 2329-2330, 2384-2385, 2420-2421.

Lenin A635

40h, Hammer & sickle allegory. 60h, Raised fists. 1k, Star, hammer & sickle.

1971, May 14 *Perf. 11*

1754 A635 30h blk, red & gold .20 .20
1755 A635 40h blk, ultra, red & gold .20 .20
1756 A635 60h blk, ultra, red & gold .20 .20
1757 A635 1k blk, ultra, red & gold .30 .20
Nos. 1754-1757 (4) .90 .80

Czechoslovak Communist Party, 50th anniv.

Star, Hammer-Sickle Emblems — A636

60h, Hammer-sickle emblem, fist & people, vert.

Perf. 11½x11, 11x11½

1971, May 24 **Engr. & Photo.**

1758 A636 30h blk, red, gold & yel .20 .20
1759 A636 60h blk, red, gold & bl .20 .20

14th Congress of Communist Party of Czechoslovakia.

Ring-necked Pheasant — A637

Designs: 60h, Rainbow trout. 80h, Mouflon. 1k, Chamois. 2k, Stag. 2.60k, Wild boar.

1971, Aug. 17 *Perf. 11½x11*

1760 A637 20h orange & multi .20 .20
1761 A637 60h lt blue & multi .20 .20
1762 A637 80h yellow & multi .20 .20
1763 A637 1k lt green & multi .35 .20
1764 A637 2k lilac & multi .50 .20
1765 A637 2.60k bister & multi 2.25 .65
Nos. 1760-1765 (6) 3.70 1.65

World Hunting Exhib., Budapest, Aug. 27-30.

Diesel Locomotive A638

Gymnasts and Banners A639

1971, Sept. 2 *Perf. 11x11½*

1766 A638 30h lt bl, blk & red .30 .20

Cent. of CKD, Prague Machine Foundry.

1971, Sept. 2 *Perf. 11½x11*

1767 A639 30h red brn, gold & ultra .20 .20

50th anniversary of Workers' Physical Exercise Federation.

Road Intersections and Bridge — A640

1971, Sept. 2 **Engr. & Photo.**

1768 A640 1k blk, gold, red & bl .30 .20

14th World Highways and Bridges Congress. Sheets of 25 stamps and 25 labels printed se-tenant with continuous design. Value, single with attached tab, 40c.

Chinese Fairytale, by Eva Bednarova A641

Designs: 1k, Tiger and other animals, by Mirko Hanak. 1.60k, The Miraculous Bamboo Shoot, by Yasuo Segawa, horiz.

Perf. 11½x11, 11x11½

1971, Sept. 10

1769 A641 60h multi .20 .20
1770 A641 1k multi .30 .20
1771 A641 1.60k multi .45 .20
Nos. 1769-1771 (3) .95 .60

Bratislava BIB 71 biennial exhibition of illustrations for children's books.

Apothecary Jars and Coltsfoot — A642

Intl. Pharmaceutical Cong.: 60h, Jars and dog rose. 1k, Scales and adonis vernalis. 1.20k, Mortars and valerian. 1.80k, Retorts and chicory. 2.40k, Mill, mortar and henbane.

1971, Sept. 20 *Perf. 11½x11*

Yellow Paper

1772 A642 30h multi .20 .20
1773 A642 60h multi .20 .20
1774 A642 1k multi .20 .20
1775 A642 1.20k multi .20 .20
1776 A642 1.80k multi .35 .20
1777 A642 2.40k multi 1.40 .45
Nos. 1772-1777 (6) 2.55 1.45

Painting Type of 1967

Paintings: 1k, "Waiting" (woman's head), 1967, by Imro Weiner-Král. 1.20k, Resurrection, by Master of Vyssi Brod, 14th century. 1.40k, Woman with Pitcher, by Milos Bazovsky. 1.80k, Veruna Cudova (in folk costume), by Josef Mánes. 2.40k, Detail from "Feast of the Rose Garlands," by Albrecht Dürer.

1971, Nov. 27 *Perf. 11½*

1779 A565 1k multi .35 .25
1780 A565 1.20k multi .80 .40
1781 A565 1.40k multi .65 .25
1782 A565 1.80k multi 1.20 .50
1783 A565 2.40k multi 2.00 .80
Nos. 1779-1783 (5) 5.00 2.20

Nos. 1779-1783 were each issued in sheets of 4. Value, set $27.

Workers Revolt in Krompachy, by Julius Nemcik — A643

1971, Nov. 28 *Perf. 11x11½*

1784 A643 60h multi .30 .20

History of the Czechoslovak Communist Party.

Wooden Dolls and Birds — A644

Folk Art and UNICEF Emblem: 80h, Jug handles, carved. 1k, Horseback rider. 1.60k, Shepherd carrying lamb. 2k, Easter eggs and rattle. 3k, "Zbojnik," folk hero.

1971, Dec. 11 *Perf. 11½*

1785 A644 60h multi .30 .20
1786 A644 80h multi .60 .20
1787 A644 1k multi .30 .20
1788 A644 1.60k multi .30 .20
1789 A644 2k multi .30 .40
1790 A644 3k multi 1.75 .55
Nos. 1785-1790 (6) 3.55 1.75

25th anniv. of UNICEF.

Nos. 1785-17903 were each issued in sheets of 10. Value, set $50.

Runners, Parthenon, Czechoslovak Olympic Emblem — A645

Designs: 40h, Women's high jump, Olympic emblem and plan for Prague Stadium. 1.60k, Cross-country skiers, Sapporo '72 emblem and ski jump in High Tatras. 2.60k, Discus thrower, Discobolus and St. Vitus Cathedral.

1971, Dec. 16 **Engr. & Photo.**

1791	A645	30h	multi	.20	.20
1792	A645	40h	multi	.20	.20
1793	A645	1.60k	multi	.25	.20
1794	A645	2.60k	multi	1.25	.65
	Nos. 1791-1794 (4)			1.90	1.25

75th anniversary of Czechoslovak Olympic Committee (30h, 2.60k); 20th Summer Olympic Games, Munich, Aug. 26-Sept. 10, 1972 (40h); 11th Winter Olympic Games, Sapporo, Japan, Feb. 3-13, 1972 (1.60k).

Post Horns and Lion — A646

1971, Dec. 17 ***Perf. 11x11½***

1795	A646 1k blk, gold, car & bl		.30	.20

Stamp Day.

Figure Skating — A647

"Lezáky" — A648

Olympic Emblems and: 50h, Ski jump. 1k, Ice hockey. 1.60k, Sledding, women's.

1972, Jan. 13 ***Perf. 11½***

1796	A647	40h	pur, org & red	.20	.20
1797	A647	50h	dk bl, org & red	.20	.20
1798	A647	1k	mag, org & red	.35	.20
1799	A647	1.60k	bl grn, org & red	1.25	.30
	Nos. 1796-1799 (4)			2.00	.90

11th Winter Olympic Games, Sapporo, Japan, Feb. 3-13.

1972, Feb. 16

No. 1801, Boy's head behind barbed wire, horiz. No. 1802, Hand rising from ruins. No. 1803, Soldier and banner, horiz.

1800	A648	30h	blk, dl org & red	.20	.20
1801	A648	30h	blk & brn org	.20	.20
1802	A648	60h	blk, yel & red	.20	.20
1803	A648	60h	sl grn & multi	.20	.20
	Nos. 1800-1803 (4)			.80	.80

30th anniv. of: destruction of Lezáky (No. 1800) and Lidice (No. 1802); Terezin concentration camp (No. 1801); Czechoslovak Army unit in Russia (No. 1803).

Book Year Emblem A649

Steam and Diesel Locomotives A650

1972, Mar. 17 ***Perf. 11½x11***

1804	A649 1k blk & org brn		.30	.20

International Book Year 1972.

1972, Mar. 17 ***Perf. 11½x11***

1805	A650 30h multi		.75	.20

Centenary of the Kosice-Bohumin railroad.

"Pasture," by Vojtech Sedlacek A651

Designs: 50h, Dressage, by Frantisek Tichy. 60th, Otakara Kubina, by Vaclav Fiala. 1k, The Three Kings, by Ernest Zmetak. 1.60k, Woman Dressing, by Ludovit Fulla.

1972, Mar. 27 ***Perf. 11½x11***

1806	A651	40h	multi	.20	.20
1807	A651	50h	multi	.20	.20
1808	A651	60h	multi	.20	.20
1809	A651	1k	multi	.30	.20
1810	A651	1.60k	multi	1.25	1.25
	Nos. 1806-1810 (5)			2.15	2.05

Czech and Slovak graphic art.
1.60k issued in sheets of 4. Value $12.
See #1859-1862, 1921-1924.

Ice Hockey A652

Design: 1k, Two players.

1972, Apr. 7 ***Perf. 11***

1811	A652	60h	blk & multi	.20	.20
1812	A652	1k	blk & multi	.40	.20

World and European Ice Hockey Championships, Prague.
For overprint see Nos. 1845-1846.

Bicycling, Olympic Rings and Emblem A653

1972, Apr. 7

1813	A653	50h	shown	.20	.20
1814	A653	1.60k	Diving	.40	.20
1815	A653	1.80k	Canoeing	.55	.20
1816	A653	2k	Gymnast	1.10	.40
	Nos. 1813-1816 (4)			2.25	1.00

20th Olympic Games, Munich, 8/26-9/11.

Prague Castle Art Type of 1971

Designs: No. 1817, Adam and Eve, column capital, St. Vitus Cathedral. No. 1818, Czech coat of arms (lion), c. 1500.

1972, May 9 ***Perf. 11½***

1817	A634 3k blk & multi		2.50	1.50
1818	A634 3k blk, red, sil & gold		1.25	.75

Nos. 1817-1818 were each issued in sheets of 4. Value, set $20.

Andrej Sladkovic (1820-1872), Poet — A654

#1820, Janko Kral (1822-1876), poet. #1821, Ludmilla Podjavorinska (1872-1951), writer. #1822, Antonin Hudecek (1872-1941), painter. #1823, Frantisek Bilek (1872-1941), sculptor. #1824, Jan Preisler (1872-1918), painter.

1972, June 14 ***Perf. 11***

1819	A654	40h	pur, ol & bl	.20	.20
1820	A654	40h	dk grn, bl & yel	.20	.20
1821	A654	40h	blk & multi	.20	.20
1822	A654	40h	brn, grn & bl	.20	.20
1823	A654	40h	choc, grn & org	.20	.20
1824	A654	40h	grn, sl & dp org	.20	.20
	Nos. 1819-1824 (6)			1.20	1.20

Men with Banners — A655

1972, June 14 ***Perf. 11x11½***

1825	A655 30h dk vio bl, red & yel		.20	.20

8th Trade Union Congress, Prague.

Art Forms of Wire A656

Ornamental Wirework: 60h, Plane and rosette. 80h, Four-headed dragon and ornament. 1k, Locomotive and loops. 2.60k, Tray and owl.

1972, Aug. 28 ***Perf. 11½x11***

1826	A656	20h	sal & multi	.20	.20
1827	A656	60h	multi	.20	.20
1828	A656	80h	pink & multi	.30	.20
1829	A656	1k	multi	.40	.20
1830	A656	2.60k	rose & multi	1.40	.45
	Nos. 1826-1830 (5)			2.50	1.25

"Jiskra" A657

Engr. & Photo.

1972, Sept. 27 ***Perf. 11½x11***

Size: 40x22mm

Multicolored Design on Blue Paper

1831	A657	50h	shown	.20	.20
1832	A657	60h	"Mir"	.20	.20
1833	A657	80h	"Republika"	.20	.20

Size: 48x29mm

Perf. 11x11½

1834	A657	1k	"Kosice"	.30	.20
1835	A657	1.60k	"Dukla"	.45	.20
1836	A657	2k	"Kladno"	1.40	.55
	Nos. 1831-1836 (6)			2.75	1.55

Czechoslovak sea-going vessels.

Hussar, 18th Century Tile — A658

1972, Oct. 24 ***Perf. 11½x11***

1837	A658	30h	shown	.20	.20
1838	A658	60h	Janissary	.20	.20
1839	A658	80h	St. Martin	.25	.20
1840	A658	1.60k	St. George	.45	.20
1841	A658	1.80k	Nobleman's guard	.70	.20
1842	A658	2.20k	Slovakian horseman	1.40	.60
	Nos. 1837-1842 (6)			3.20	1.60

Horsemen from 18th-19th century tiles or enamel paintings on glass.

Worker, Flag Hoisted on Bayonet A659

Star, Hammer and Sickle A660

1972, Nov. 7 ***Perf. 11x11½***

1843	A659	30h	gold & multi	.20	.20
1844	A660	60h	rose car & gold	.20	.20

55th anniv. of the Russian October Revolution (30h); 50th anniv. of the Soviet Union (60h).

Nos. 1811-1812 Overprinted in Violet Blue or Black

1972 ***Perf. 11***

1845	A652	60h	multi (VBl)	7.50	6.00
1846	A652	1k	multi (Bk)	7.50	6.00

Czechoslovakia's victorious ice hockey team. The overprint on the 60h (shown) is in Czech and reads CSSR/MISTREM/SVETA; the overprint on the 1k is in Slovak.

Painting Type of 1967

Designs: 1k, "Nosegay" (nudes and flowers), by Max Svabinsky. 1.20k, Struggle of St. Ladislas with Kuman nomad, anonymous, 14th century. 1.40k, Lady with Fur Hat, by Vaclav Hollar. 1.80k, Midsummer Night's Dream, 1962, by Josef Liesler. 2.40k, Pablo Picasso, self-portrait.

1972, Nov. 27 **Engr. & Photo.**

1847	A565	1k	multi	.55	.35
1848	A565	1.20k	multi	.70	.50
1849	A565	1.40k	blk & cream	.85	.65
1850	A565	1.80k	multi	1.10	1.00
1851	A565	2.40k	multi	2.50	2.50
	Nos. 1847-1851 (5)			5.70	5.00

Nos. 1847-1851 were each issued in sheets of 4. Value, set $30.

Goldfinch A661

Songbirds: 60h, Warbler feeding young cuckoo. 80h, Cuckoo. 1k, Black-billed magpie. 1.60k, Bullfinch. 3k, Song thrush.

1972, Dec. 15

Size: 30x48½mm

1852	A661	60h yel & multi	.20	.20
1853	A661	80h multi	.20	.20
1854	A661	1k lt bl & multi	.20	.20

Engr.

Size: 30x23mm

1855	A661	1.60k multi	1.40	.75
1856	A661	2k multi	1.40	.75
1857	A661	3k multi	1.40	.75
		Nos. 1852-1857 (6)	4.80	2.85

Post Horn and Allegory — A662

1972, Dec. 18 **Engr. & Photo.**

1858	A662	1k blk, red lil & gold	.30	.30

Stamp Day.

Art Type of 1972

Designs: 30h, Flowers in Window, by Jaroslav Grus. 60h, Quest for Happiness, by Josef Balaz. 1.60k, Balloon, by Kamil Lhotak. 1.80k, Woman with Viola, by Richard Wiesner.

1973, Jan. 25 ***Perf. 11½x11***

1859	A651	30h multi	.20	.20
1860	A651	60h multi	.20	.20
1861	A651	1.60k multi	.35	.20
1862	A651	1.80k multi	1.40	.35
		Nos. 1859-1862 (4)	2.15	.95

Czech and Slovak graphic art.

Tennis Player — A663

Figure Skater — A664

Torch and Star — A665

1973, Feb. 22 ***Perf. 11***

1863	A663	30h vio & multi	.20	.20
1864	A664	60h blk & multi	.20	.20
1865	A665	1k multi	.30	.20
		Nos. 1863-1865 (3)	.70	.60

80th anniversary of the tennis organization in Czechoslovakia (30h); World figure skating championships, Bratislava (60h); 3rd summer army Spartakiad of socialist countries (1k).

Star and Factories A666

Workers' Militia, Emblem and Flag — A667

1973, Feb. 23

1866	A666	30h multi	.20	.20
1867	A667	60h multi	.20	.20

25th anniversary of the Communist revolution in Czechoslovakia and of the Militia.

Capt. Jan Nalepka, Major Antonin Sochor and Laurel A668

Torch &: 40h, Evzen Rosicky, Mirko Nespor & ivy leaves. 60h, Vlado Clementis, Karol Smidke & linden leaves. 80h, Jan Osoha, Josef Molak & oak leaves. 1k, Marie Kuderikova, Jozka Jaburkova & rose. 1.60k, Vaclav Sinkule, Eduard Urx & palm leaf.

1973, Mar. 20 ***Perf. 11½x11***

Yellow Paper

1868	A668	30h blk, ver & gold	.20	.20
1869	A668	40h blk, ver & grn	.20	.20
1870	A668	60h blk, ver & gold	.20	.20
1871	A668	80h blk, ver & gold	.20	.20
1872	A668	1k blk, ver & grn	.30	.20
1873	A668	1.60k blk, ver & sil	.60	.20
		Nos. 1868-1873 (6)	1.70	1.20

Fighters against and victims of Fascism and Nazism during German Occupation.

Virgil I. Grissom, Edward H. White, Roger B. Chaffee — A669

Designs: 20h, Soviet planetary station "Venera." 30h, "Intercosmos" station. 40h, Lunokhod on moon. 3.60k, Vladimir M. Komarov, Georgi T. Dobrovolsky, Vladislav N. Volkov, Victor I. Patsayev. 5k, Yuri A. Gagarin.

Two types of 3.60k: type I, Cosmonaut on background of cross-hatched lines; type 2, Cosmonaut on background of parallel diagonal lines.

1973, Apr. 12 ***Perf. 11½x11***

Size: 40x22mm

1874	A669	20h multi	.20	.20
1875	A669	30h multi	.20	.20
1876	A669	40h multi	.20	.20

Engr.

Perf. 11½

Size: 49x30mm

1877	A669	3k multi	.80	.50
1878	A669	3.60k multi, type 1	1.25	1.10
a.		Type 2	25.00	15.00
1879	A669	5k multi	3.00	2.00
		Nos. 1874-1879 (6)	5.65	4.20

In memory of American and Russian astronauts.

Nos. 1877-1879 were each issued in sheets of 4. Values: set (with No. 1878) $30; mset (with No. 1878a) $120.

Radio — A670

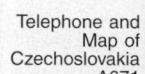

Telephone and Map of Czechoslovakia A671

Television A672

1973, May 1 ***Perf. 11½x11***

1880	A670	30h blk & multi	.20	.20
1881	A671	30h lt bl, pink & blk	.20	.20
1882	A672	30h dp bl & multi	.20	.20
		Nos. 1880-1882 (3)	.60	.60

Czechoslovak anniversaries: 50 years of broadcasting (No. 1880); 20 years of telephone service to all communities (No. 1881); 20 years of television (No. 1882).

Coat of Arms and Linden Branch — A673

1973, May 9 ***Perf. 11x11½***

1883	A673	60h red & multi	.20	.20

25th anniv. of the Constitution of May 9.

Prague Castle Art Type of 1971

No. 1884, Royal Legate, 14th century. No. 1885, Seal of King Charles IV, 1351.

1973, May 9 ***Perf. 11½***

1884	A634	3k blue & multi	1.00	.75
1885	A634	3k gold, grn & dk brn	2.00	1.50

Nos. 1884-1885 were each issued in sheets of 4. Value, set $16.

Coat of Arms Type of 1968

1973, June 20

1886	A590	60h Mikulov	.20	.20
1887	A590	60h Zlutice	.35	.20
1888	A590	60h Smolenice	.35	.20
		Nos. 1886-1888 (3)	.90	.60

Coats of arms of Czechoslovakian cities.

Heraldic Colors of Olomouc and Moravia — A674

Anthurium — A675

1973, Aug. 23 **Engr. & Photo.**

1889	A674	30h multi	.25	.20

University of Olomouc, 400th anniv.

1973, Aug. 23 ***Perf. 11½***

Sizes: 60h, 1k, 2k, 30x50mm; 1.60k, 1.80k, 3.60k, 23x39mm.

1890	A675	60h Tulips	.75	.35
1891	A675	1k Rose	.75	.35
1892	A675	1.60k shown	.40	.35
1893	A675	1.80k Iris	.40	.35
1894	A675	2k Chrysanthemum	1.90	1.00
1895	A675	3.60k Cymbidium	.75	.35
		Nos. 1890-1895 (6)	4.95	2.75

Flower Show, Olomouc, Aug. 18-Sept. 2. 60h, 1k, 2k issued in sheets of 4, others in sheets of 10. Value, set $100.

Hunting Dogs A676

1973, Sept. 5

1896	A676	20h Irish setter	.40	.20
1897	A676	30h Czech terrier	.40	.20
1898	A676	40h Bavarian hunting dog	.55	.20
1899	A676	60h German pointer	.55	.20
1900	A676	1k Cocker spaniel	.85	.20
1901	A676	1.60k Dachshund	2.00	.50
		Nos. 1896-1901 (6)	4.75	1.50

Czechoslovak United Hunting Org., 50th anniv.

St. John, the Baptist, by Svabinsky A677

Works by Max Svabinsky: 60h, "August Noon" (woman). 80h, "Marriage of True Minds" (artist and muse). 1k, "Paradise Sonata I" (Adam dreaming of Eve). 2.60k, Last Judgment, stained glass window, St. Vitus Cathedral.

1973, Sept. 17 **Litho. & Engr.**

1902	A677	20h blk & pale grn	.20	.20
1903	A677	60h black & buff	.20	.20

Engr.

1904	A677	80h black	.60	.20
1905	A677	1k slate green	.60	.25
1906	A677	2.60k multi	1.50	1.25
		Nos. 1902-1906 (5)	3.10	2.10

Centenary of the birth of Max Svabinsky (1873-1962), artist and stamp designer. 20h and 60h issued in sheets of 25; 80h and 1k se-tenant in sheets of 4 checkerwise (value $5); 2.60k in sheets of 4 (value $10).

Trade Union Emblem A678

1973, Oct. 15 **Engr. & Photo.**

1907	A678	1k red, bl & yel	.25	.20

8t (valueh Congress of the World Federation of Trade Unions, Varna, Bulgaria.

Painting Type of 1967

1k, Boy from Martinique, by Antonin Pelc. 1.20k, "Fortitude" (mountaineer), by Martin Benka. 1.80k, Rembrandt, self-portrait. 2k, Pierrot, by Bohumil Kubista. 2.40k, Ilona Kubinyiova, by Peter M. Bohun. 3.60k, Virgin and Child (Veveri Madonna), c. 1350.

1973, Nov. 27 ***Perf. 11½***

1908	A565	1k multi, vio bl inscriptions	2.50	1.25
a.		1k multi, black inscriptions	10.00	10.00
1909	A565	1.20k multi	*2.50*	*1.25*
1910	A565	1.80k multi	.80	.80
1911	A565	2k multi	.80	.80
1912	A565	2.40k multi	.80	.80
1913	A565	3.60k multi	.80	.80
		Nos. 1908-1913 (6)	8.20	5.70

Sheets of 4. Nos. 1910-1913 printed se-tenant with gold and black inscription on gutter. Value, set $35. No. 1908a in sheet of 4, value $45.

Central background bluish gray on No. 1908, light bluish green on No. 1908a.

Postilion — A679

1973, Dec. 18

1914	A679	1k gold & multi	.30	.20

Stamp Day 1974 and 55th anniversary of Czechoslovak postage stamps. Printed with 2 labels showing telephone and telegraph. Value of single with two labels, 60c.

Bedrich Smetana — A681

Pablo Neruda, Chilean Flag — A682

"CSSR" — A680

Comecon Building, Moscow — A683

1974, Jan. 1

1915	A680	30h red, gold & ultra	.20	.20

5th anniversary of Federal Government in the Czechoslovak Socialist Republic.

1974, Jan. 4 ***Perf. 11x11½***

1916	A681	60h shown	.20	.20
1917	A681	60h Josef Suk	.20	.20
1918	A682	60h shown	.20	.20
		Nos. 1916-1918 (3)	.60	.60

Smetana (1824-84), composer; Suk (1874-1935), composer, and Pablo Neruda (Neftali Ricardo Reyes, 1904-73), Chilean poet.

1974, Jan. 23

1919	A683	1k gold, red & vio bl	.25	.20

25th anniversary of the Council of Mutual Economic Assistance (COMECON).

Symbols of Postal Service — A684

1974, Feb. 20 ***Perf. 11½***

1920	A684	3.60k multi	.95	.45

BRNO '74 National Stamp Exhibition, Brno, June 8-23.

No. 1920 was issue both in normal sheets of 25 stamps and in sheets containing 16 stamps se-tenant with 9 labels depicting Brno. Values: single stamp with attached tab $2.25; full sheet of 16 stamps and 9 labels $85.

Art Type of 1972

Designs: 60h, Tulips 1973, by Josef Broz. 1k, Structures 1961 (poppy and building), by Orest Dubay. 1.60k, Bird and flowers (Golden Sun-Glowing Day), by Adolf Zabransky. 1.80k, Artificial flowers, by Frantisek Gross.

1974, Feb. 21 ***Perf. 11½x11***

1921	A651	60h multi	.20	.20
1922	A651	1k multi	.25	.20
1923	A651	1.60k multi	.35	.20
1924	A651	1.80k multi	.90	.30
		Nos. 1921-1924 (4)	1.70	.90

Czech and Slovak graphic art.

Oskar Benes and Vaclav Prochazka — A685

40h, Milos Uher, Anton Sedlacek. 60h, Jan Hajecek, Marie Sedlackova. 80h, Jan Sverma, Albin Grznar. 1k, Jaroslav Neliba, Alois Hovorka. 1.60k, Ladislav Exnar, Ludovit Kukorelli.

1974, Mar. 21 ***Perf. 11½x11***

1925	A685	30h indigo & multi	.20	.20
1926	A685	40h indigo & multi	.20	.20
1927	A685	60h indigo & multi	.20	.20
1928	A685	80h indigo & multi	.20	.20
1929	A685	1k indigo & multi	.25	.20
1930	A685	1.60k indigo & multi	.75	.25
		Nos. 1925-1930 (6)	1.80	1.25

Partisan commanders and fighters.

"Water, the Source of Energy" A686

Symbolic Designs: 1k, Importance of water for agriculture. 1.20k, Study of the oceans. 1.60k, "Hydrological Decade." 2k, Struggle for unpolluted water.

1974, Apr. 25 **Engr.** ***Perf. 11½***

1931	A686	60h multi	.55	.20
1932	A686	1k multi	.55	.20
1933	A686	1.20k multi	1.00	.40
1934	A686	1.60k multi	1.00	.40
1935	A686	2k multi	2.00	1.50
		Nos. 1931-1935 (5)	5.10	2.70

Hydrological Decade (UNESCO), 1965-1974.

Nos. 1931-1935 were each issued in sheets of 4. Value $30.

Allegory Holding "Molniya," and Ground Station — A687

Sousaphone A688

1974, Apr. 30 **Engr. & Photo.**

1936	A687	30h vio bl & multi	.25	.20

"Intersputnik," first satellite communications ground station in Czechoslovakia.

Prague Castle Art Type of 1971

#1937, Golden Cock, 17th century locket. #1938, Glass monstrance, 1840.

1974, May 9 **Engr.** ***Perf. 11½***

1937	A634	3k gold & multi	1.50	1.25
1938	A634	3k blk & multi	2.00	1.50

Nos. 1937-1938 werre each issued in sheets of 4. Value, set $18.

Engraved and Photogravure

1974, May 12 ***Perf. 11x11½***

1939	A688	20h shown	.20	.20
1940	A688	30h Bagpipe	.20	.20
1941	A688	40h Violin, by Martin Benka	.20	.20
1942	A688	1k Pyramid piano	.20	.20
1943	A688	1.60k Tenor quinton, 1754	.80	.20
		Nos. 1939-1943 (5)	1.60	1.00

Prague and Bratislava Music Festivals. The 1.60k also commemorates 25th anniversary of Slovak Philharmonic Orchestra.

Child — A689

1974, June 1 ***Perf. 11½***

1944	A689	60h multi	.20	.20

Children's Day. Design is from illustration for children's book by Adolf Zabransky.

Globe, People and Exhibition Emblems — A690

Design: 6k, Rays and emblems symbolizing "Oneness and Mutuality."

1974, June 1

1945	A690	30h multi	.20	.20
1946	A690	6k multi	1.20	.75

BRNO 74 Natl. Stamp Exhib., Brno, June 8-23.

Nos. 2171-2172 were each issued both in sheet of 50 stamps and in sheets of 16 stamps and 14 labels. Values: stamps with attached labels, $1.75; sheet of 16 stamps and 14 labels $75.

Resistance Fighter — A691

Actress Holding Tragedy and Comedy Masks — A692

1974, Aug. 29 ***Perf. 11½***

1947	A691	30h multi	.20	.20

Slovak National Uprising, 30th anniversary.

1974, Aug. 29

1948	A692	30h red, sil & blk	.20	.20

Bratislava Academy of Music and Drama, 25th anniversary.

Slovak Girl with Flower — A693

1974, Aug. 29

1949	A693	30h multi	.20	.20

SLUK, Slovak folksong and dance ensemble, 25th anniversary.

Hero and Leander A694

Design: 2.40k, Hero watching Leander swim the Hellespont. No. 1952, Leander reaching shore. No. 1953, Hero mourning over Leander's body. No. 1954, Hermione, Leander's sister. No. 1955, Mourning Cupid. Designs are from 17th century English tapestries in Bratislava Council Palace.

1974-76

1950	A694	2k multi	1.25	1.10
1951	A694	2.40k multi	1.50	1.25
1952	A694	3k multi	1.00	.45
1953	A694	3k multi	1.75	1.75
1954	A694	3.60k multi	2.50	1.10
1955	A694	3.60k multi	.85	.60
		Nos. 1950-1955 (6)	8.85	6.25

Issued: #1950-1951, 9/25/74; #1952, 1954, 8/29/75; #1953, 1955, 5/9/76.

Nos. 1950-1951 were each issued in sheets of 6, with 2 blank labels. Nos. 1952-1955 were issued in sheets of 4. Value, set $50.

Soldier Standing Guard, Target, 1840 — A695

Painted Folk-art Targets: 60h, Landscape with Pierrot and flags, 1828. 1k, Diana crowning champion marksman, 1832. 1.60k, Still life with guitar, 1839. 2.40k, Salvo and stag in flight, 1834. 3k, Turk and giraffe, 1831.

1974, Sept. 26 ***Perf. 11½***

Size: 30x50mm

1956	A695	30h black & multi	.20	.20
1957	A695	60h black & multi	.20	.20
1958	A695	1k black & multi	.25	.20

Engr.

Perf. 12

Size: 40x50mm

1959	A695	1.60k green & multi	.40	.35
1960	A695	2.40k sepia & multi	.70	.60
1961	A695	3k multi	*2.25*	*2.25*
		Nos. 1956-1961 (6)	*4.00*	*3.80*

Nos. 1959-1961 were each issued in sheets of 4. Value, set $25.

UPU Emblem and Postilion — A696

UPU Cent. (UPU Emblem and): 40h, Mail coach. 60h, Railroad mail coach, 1851. 80h, Early mail truck. 1k, Czechoslovak Airlines mail plane. 1.60k, Radar.

Engraved and Photogravure

1974, Oct. 9 *Perf. 11½*

1962	A696	30h multi	.20	.20
1963	A696	40h multi	.20	.20
1964	A696	60h multi	.20	.20
1965	A696	80h multi	.20	.20
1966	A696	1k multi	.30	.20
1967	A696	1.60k multi	1.00	.25
		Nos. 1962-1967 (6)	2.10	1.25

Sealed Letter — A697

Post Rider — A699

Stylized Bird — A698

Postal Code Symbol — A698a

20h, Post Horn, Old Town Bridge Tower. #1971, Carrier pigeon. #1979, Map of Czechoslovakia with postal code numbers.

1974, Oct. 31 *Perf. 11½x11*

1968	A699 20h multi	.20	.20
1969	A697 30h brn, bl & red	.20	.20
1970	A699 40h multi	.20	.20
1971	A697 60h bl, yel & red	.20	.20
	Nos. 1968-1971 (4)	.80	.80

Nos. 1968-1971 were reissued in 1979, printed on fluorescent paper. Value, set $15.

See No. 2675.

Coil Stamps

1975 **Photo.** *Perf. 14*

1976 A698	30h brt bl	.20	.20
1977 A698	60h carmine	.20	.20

1976 *Perf. 11½*

1978 A698a	30h emer	.20	.20
1979 A698a	60h scar	.20	.20

Nos. 1976-1979 have black control number on back of every fifth stamp.

Ludvik Kuba, Self-portrait, 1941 — A700

Paintings: 1.20k, Violinist Frantisek Ondricek, by Vaclav Brozik. 1.60k, Vase with Flowers, by Otakar Kubin. 1.80k, Woman with Pitcher, by Janko Alexy. 2.40k, Bacchanalia, c. 1635, by Karel Skreta.

1974, Nov. 27 **Engr.** *Perf. 11½*

1980	A700 1k multi	.40	.25
1981	A700 1.20k multi	.65	.30
1982	A700 1.60k multi	.65	.45
1983	A700 1.80k multi	.80	.30
1984	A700 2.40k multi	2.00	1.40
	Nos. 1980-1984 (5)	4.50	2.70

Czech and Slovak art.

Nos. 1980-194 were each issued in sheets of 4. Value, set $25.

See Nos. 2209-2211, 2678-2682, 2721-2723, 2743, 2766-2768.

Post Horn — A701

Engraved and Photogravure

1974, Dec. 18 *Perf. 11x11½*

1985	A701 1k multicolored	.30	.20

Stamp Day.

Still-life with Hare, by Hollar — A702

Designs: 1k, The Lion and the Mouse, by Vaclav Hollar. 1.60k, Deer Hunt, by Philip Galle. 1.80k, Grand Hunt, by Jacques Callot.

1975, Feb. 26 *Perf. 11½x11*

1988 A702	60h blk & buff	.20	.20
1989 A702	1k blk & buff	.20	.20
1990 A702	1.60k blk & yel	.20	.20
1991 A702	1.80k blk & buff	1.00	.50
	Nos. 1988-1991 (4)	1.60	1.10

Hunting scenes from old engravings.

Guns Pointing at Family A703

Young Woman and Globe — A704

Designs: 1k, Women and building on fire. 1.20k, People and roses. All designs include names of destroyed villages.

1975, Feb. 26 *Perf. 11*

1992 A703	60h multi	.20	.20
1993 A703	1k multi	.20	.20
1994 A703	1.20k multi	.30	.20
	Nos. 1992-1994 (3)	.70	.60

Destruction of 14 villages by the Nazis, 30th anniversary.

1975, Mar. 7 *Perf. 11½x11*

1995	A704 30h red & multi	.20	.20

International Women's Year 1975.

Little Queens, Moravian Folk Custom A705

Folk Customs: 1k, Straw masks (animal heads and blackened faces), Slovak. 1.40k, The Tale of Maid Dorothea (executioner, girl, king and devil). 2k, Drowning of Morena, symbol of death and winter.

1975, Mar. 26 **Engr.** *Perf. 11½*

1996 A705	60h blk & multi	.40	.20
1997 A705	1k blk & multi	.70	.40
1998 A705	1.40k blk & multi	.80	.55
1999 A705	2k blk & multi	1.00	.75
	Nos. 1996-1999 (4)	2.90	1.90

Nos. 1996-1999 were each issued in sheets of four. Value $15.

Coat of Arms Type of 1968

Engraved and Photogravure

1975, Apr. 17 *Perf. 11½*

2000	A590 60h Nymburk	.25	.20
2001	A590 60h Znojmo	.25	.20

Coats of arms of Czechoslovakian cities.

Czech May Uprising — A706

Liberation by Soviet Army — A707

Czechoslovak-Russian Friendship — A708

Engr. & Photo.; Engr. (A707)

1975, May 9

2002	A706 1k multi	.25	.20
2003	A707 1k multi	.25	.20
2004	A708 1k multi	.25	.20
	Nos. 2002-2004 (3)	.75	.60

30th anniv. of the May uprising of the Czech people and of liberation by the Soviet Army; 5th anniv. of the Czechoslovak-Soviet Treaty of Friendship, Cooperation and Mutual Aid.

Adolescents' Exercises — A709

Designs: 60th, Children's exercises. 1k, Men's and women's exercises.

Engraved and Photogravure

1975, June 15 *Perf. 12x11½*

2005	A709 30h lil & multi	.20	.20
2006	A709 60h multi	.20	.20
2007	A709 1k vio & multi	.25	.20
	Nos. 2005-2007 (3)	.65	.60

Spartakiad 1975, Prague, June 26-29. Nos. 2005-2007 each issued in sheets of 30 stamps and 40 labels, showing different Spartakiad emblems. Value, set with tabs, $1.

Datrioides Microlepis and Sea Horse — A710

Tropical Fish (Aquarium): 1k, Beta splendens regan and pterophyllum scalare. 1.20k, Carassius auratus. 1.60k, Amphiprion percula and chaetodon sp. 2k, Pomacanthodes semicirculatus, pomocanthus maculosus and paracanthorus hepatus.

1975, June 27 *Perf. 11½*

2008	A710 60h multi	.20	.20
2009	A710 1k multi	.35	.20
2010	A710 1.20k multi	.40	.20
2011	A710 1.60k multi	.55	.20
2012	A710 2k multi	1.75	.50
	Nos. 2008-2012 (5)	3.25	1.30

Pelicans, by Nikita Charushin — A711

Book Illustrations: 30h, The Dreamer, by Lieselotte Schwarz. 40h, Hero on horseback, by Val Muntenau. 60h, Peacock, by Klaus Ensikat. 80h, Man on horseback, by Robert Dubravec.

1975, Sept. 5

2013	A711 20h multi	.20	.20
2014	A711 30h multi	.20	.20
2015	A711 40h multi	.25	.20
2016	A711 60h multi	.25	.20
2017	A711 80h multi	.50	.20
	Nos. 2013-2017 (5)	1.40	1.00

Bratislava BIB 75 biennial exhibition of illustrations for children's books.

Nos. 2013-2017 issued in sheets of 25 stamps and 15 labels with designs and inscriptions in various languages. Value, set with attached labels, $2.50.

Strakonice, 1951 — A712

Designs: Motorcycles.

1975, Sept. 29 *Perf. 11½*

2018 A712	20h shown	.20	.20
2019 A712	40h Jawa 250, 1945	.20	.20
2020 A712	60h Jawa 175, 1935	.20	.20
2021 A712	1k ITAR, 1921	.20	.20
2022 A712	1.20k ORION, 1903	.25	.20
2023 A712	1.80k Laurin & Klement, 1898	1.40	.40
	Nos. 2018-2023 (6)	2.45	1.40

Study of Shortwave Solar Radiation — A713

Soyuz-Apollo Link-up in Space — A714

60h, Study of aurora borealis & Oréol satellite. 1k, Study ofionosphere & cosmic radiation. 2k, Copernicus, radio map of the sun & satellite.

1975, Sept. 30

2024	A713	30h multi	.20	.20
2025	A713	60h yel, rose red & vio	.20	.20
2026	A713	1k bl, yel & vio	.20	.20
2027	A713	2k red, vio & yel	.35	.20

Engr.

2028	A714	5k vio & multi	2.00	1.50
		Nos. 2024-2028 (5)	2.95	2.30

International cooperation in space research.
No. 2028 issued in sheets of 4. Value $15.
The design of No. 2026 appears to be inverted.

Slovnaft, Petrochemical Plant — A715

Designs: 60h, Atomic power station. 1k, Construction of Prague subway. 1.20k, Construction of Friendship pipeline. 1.40k, Combine harvesters. 1.60k, Apartment house construction.

Engraved and Photogravure

1975, Oct. 28

2029	A715	30h multi	.20	.20
2030	A715	60h multi	.20	.20
2031	A715	1k multi	.25	.20
2032	A715	1.20k multi	.25	.20
2033	A715	1.40k multi	.25	.20
2034	A715	1.60k multi	.75	.30
		Nos. 2029-2034 (6)	1.90	1.30

Socialist construction, 30th anniversary. Nos. 2029-2034 printed se-tenant with labels. Value, set with attached labels, $2.50.

Pres. Gustav Husak — A716

1975, Oct. 28 **Engr.**

2035	A716	30h ultra	.20	.20
2036	A716	60h rose red	.20	.20

Prague Castle Art Type of 1971

3k, Gold earring, 9th cent. 3.60k, Arms of Premysl Dynasty & Bohemia from lid of leather case containing Bohemian crown, 14th cent.

1975, Oct. 29

2040	A634	3k blk, grn, pur & gold	.75	.40
2041	A634	3.60k red & multi	1.50	1.25

Nos. 2040-2041 each issued in sheets of 4. Value, set $15.

Miniature Sheet

Ludvik Svoboda, Road Map, Buzuluk to Prague, Carnations — A717

1975, Nov. 25

2042	A717	10k multi	9.00	7.00

Pres. Ludvik Svoboda, 80th birthday.
Exists imperf. Value, $40 unused, $25 used.

Art Type of 1967

Paintings: 1k, "May 1975" (Woman and doves for 30th anniv. of peace), by Zdenek Sklenar. 1.40k, Woman in national costume, by Eugen Nevan. 1.80k, "Liberation of Prague," by Alena Cermakova, horiz. 2.40k, "Fire 1938" (woman raising fist), by Josef Capek. 3.40k, Old Prague, 1828, by Vincenc Morstadt.

1975, Nov. 27 **Engr.** ***Perf. 11½***

2043	A565	1k blk, buff & brn	.25	.20
2044	A565	1.40k multi	.50	.30
2045	A565	1.80k multi	.50	.30
2046	A565	2.40k multi	1.25	.75
2047	A565	3.40k multi	1.25	1.25
		Nos. 2043-2047 (5)	3.75	2.80

Nos. 2043-2047 were each issued in sheets of 4. Value, set $22.50.

Carrier Pigeon — A718

Engraved and Photogravure

1975, Dec. 18 ***Perf. 11½***

2048	A718	1k red & multi	.30	.20

Stamp Day 1975.

Frantisek Halas — A719

Wilhelm Pieck — A720

Frantisek Lexa — A721

Jindrich Jindrich — A722

Ivan Krasko — A723

1976, Feb. 25 ***Perf. 11½***

2049	A719	60h multi	.20	.20
2050	A720	60h multi	.20	.20
2051	A721	60h multi	.20	.20
2052	A722	60h multi	.20	.20
2053	A723	60h multi	.20	.20
		Nos. 2049-2053 (5)	1.00	1.00

Halas (1901-49), poet; Pieck (1876-1960), pres. of German Democratic Republic; Lexa (1876-1960), professor of Egyptology; Jindrich (1876-1967), composer and writer; Krasko (1876-1958), Slovak poet. No. 2051 printed in sheets of 10, others in sheets of 50. Value, No. 2051 sheet, $5.00.

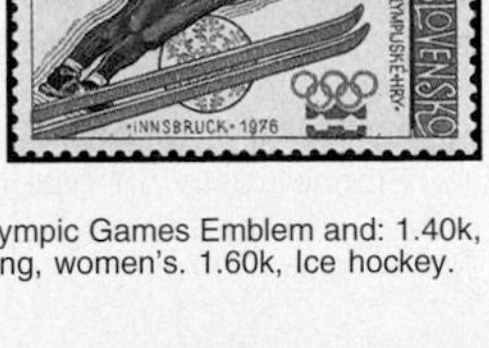

Ski Jump, Olympic Emblem A724

Winter Olympic Games Emblem and: 1.40k, Figure skating, women's. 1.60k, Ice hockey.

1976, Mar. 22 ***Perf. 12x11½***

2054	A724	1k gold & multi	.20	.20
2055	A724	1.40k gold & multi	.20	.20
2056	A724	1.60k gold & multi	1.00	.30
		Nos. 2054-2056 (3)	1.40	.70

12th Winter Olympic Games, Innsbruck, Austria, Feb. 4-15.

Javelin and Olympic Rings — A725

1976, Mar. 22 ***Perf. 11½***

2057	A725	2k shown	.25	.20
2058	A725	3k Relay race	.40	.20
2059	A725	3.60k Shot put	1.40	.90
		Nos. 2057-2059 (3)	2.05	1.30

21st Olympic Games, Montreal, Canada, July 17-Aug. 1.

Table Tennis — A726

1976, Mar. 22 ***Perf. 11x12***

2060	A726	1k multi	.30	.20

European Table Tennis Championship, Prague, Mar. 26-Apr. 4.

Symbolic of Communist Party — A727

Worker, Derrick, Emblem — A728

1976, Apr. 12 ***Perf. 11x12***

2061	A727	30h gold & multi	.20	.20
2062	A728	60h gold & multi	.20	.20

15th Congress of the Communist Party of Czechoslovakia.

Radio Prague Orchestra A729

Dancer, Violin, Tragic Mask — A730

Actors — A731

Folk Dancers A732

Film Festival — A733

1976, Apr. 26 ***Perf. 11½***

2063	A729	20h gold & multi	.20	.20
2064	A730	20h pink & multi	.20	.20
2065	A731	20h lt bl & multi	.20	.20
2066	A732	30h blk & multi	.20	.20
2067	A733	30h vio bl, rose & grn	.20	.20
		Nos. 2063-2067 (5)	1.00	1.00

Czechoslovak Radio Symphony Orchestra, Prague, 50th anniv. (No. 2063); Academy of Music and Dramatic Art, Prague, 50th anniv. (No. 2064); Nova Scena Theater Co., Bratislava, 30th anniv. (No. 2065); Intl. Folk Song and Dance Festival, Straznice, 30th anniv. (No. 2066); 20th Intl. Film Festival, Karlovy Vary (No. 2067).

Hammer and Sickle
A734 A735

Design: 6k, Hammer and sickle, horiz.

1976, May 14

2068	A734	30h gold, red & dk bl	.20	.20
2069	A735	60h gold, red & dp car	.20	.20

Souvenir Sheet

2070	A735	6k red & multi	1.75	1.75

Czechoslovak Communist Party, 55th anniv.
#2070 contains a 50x30mm stamp.

Ships in Storm, by Frans Huys (1522-1562) A736

Old Engravings of Ships: 60h, by Václav Hollar (1607-77). 1k, by Regnier Nooms Zeeman (1623-68). 2k, by Francois Chereau (1680-1729).

Engraved and Photogravure

1976, July 21 ***Perf. 11x11½***

2071	A736	40h buff & blk	.20	.20
2072	A736	60h gray, buff & blk	.20	.20
2073	A736	1k lt grn, buff & blk	.20	.20
2074	A736	2k lt bl, buff & blk	*1.10*	*.40*
		Nos. 2071-2074 (4)	*1.70*	*1.00*

"UNESCO"
A737

1976, July 30 ***Perf. 11½***
2075 A737 2k gray & multi .40 .45

30th anniversary of UNESCO. Issued in sheets of 10. Value $8.

Souvenir Sheet

Hands Holding Infant, Globe and Dove
A738

1976, July 30
2076 Sheet of 2 4.00 3.50
a. A738 6k multi 2.50 2.00

European Security and Cooperation Conference, Helsinki, Finland, 2nd anniv.

Merino Ram — A739

Couple Smoking, WHO Emblem and Skull — A740

Designs: 40h, Bern-Hana milk cow. 1.60k, Kladruby stallion Generalissimus XXVII.

1976, Aug. 28 ***Perf. 11½x12***
2077 A739 30h multi .20 .20
2078 A739 40h multi .20 .20
2079 A739 1.60k multi .35 .20
Nos. 2077-2079 (3) .75 .60

Bountiful Earth Exhibition, Ceske Budejovice, Aug. 28-Sept. 12.

1976, Sept. 7 ***Perf. 12x11½***
2080 A740 2k multi .50 .30

Fight against smoking, WHO drive against drug addiction.
Printed in sheets of 10 (2x5) with WHO emblems and inscription in margin. Value $10.

Prague Castle Art Type of 1971

Designs: 3k, View of Prague Castle, by F. Hoogenberghe, 1572. 3.60k, Faun and Satyr, sculptured panel, 16th century.

1976, Oct. 22 **Engr.** ***Perf. 11½***
2081 A634 3k multi 2.00 1.75
2082 A634 3.60k multi .75 .50

Nos. 2081-2082 were each issued in sheets of 4. Value $15.

Guernica 1937, by Imro Weiner-Kral
A741

1976, Oct. 22
2083 A741 5k multi .75 .35

40th anniv. of the Intl. Brigade in Spain.

Zebras
A742

20h, Elephants. 30h, Cheetah. 40h, Giraffes. 60h, Rhinoceros. 3k, Bongos.

Engraved and Photogravure

1976, Nov. 3 ***Perf. 11½x11, 11x11½***
2084 A742 10h multi .20 .20
2085 A742 20h multi, vert. .20 .20
2086 A742 30h multi .25 .20
2087 A742 40h multi, vert. .35 .20
2088 A742 60h multi .35 .20
2089 A742 3k multi, vert. 1.75 .50
Nos. 2084-2089 (6) 3.10 1.50

African animals in Dvur Kralove Zoo.

Art Type of 1967

Paintings of Flowers: 1k, by Peter Matejka. 1.40k, by Cyril Bouda. 2k, by Jan Breughel. 3.60k, J. Rudolf Bys.

1976, Nov. 27 **Engr.** ***Perf. 11½***
2090 A565 1k multi .65 .40
2091 A565 1.40k multi 1.25 .75
2092 A565 2k multi 1.00 .75
2093 A565 3.60k multi .75 .45
Nos. 2090-2093 (4) 3.65 2.35

Nos. 2090-2093 were each issued in sheets of 4, with emblem and name of Praga 1978 on horizontal gutter. Value, set $25.

Postrider, 17th Century, and Satellites — A743

1976, Dec. 18 **Engr. & Photo.**
2094 A743 1k multi .25 .20

Stamp Day 1976.

Ice Hockey — A744

Arms of Vranov — A745

1977, Feb. 11 ***Perf. 11½***
2095 A744 60h shown .20 .20
2096 A744 1k Biathlon .20 .20
2097 A744 1.60k Ski jump .95 .25
2098 A744 2k Downhill skiing .25 .20
Nos. 2095-2098 (4) 1.60 .85

6th Winter Spartakiad of Socialist Countries' Armies.

1977, Feb. 20

Coats of Arms of Czechoslovak towns.

2099 A745 60h shown .20 .20
2100 A745 60h Kralupy & Vltavou .20 .20
2101 A745 60h Jicin .20 .20
2102 A745 60h Valasske Mezirici .20 .20
Nos. 2099-2102 (4) .80 .80

See Nos. 2297-2300.

Window, Michna Palace — A746

Prague Renaissance Windows: 30h, Michna Palace. 40h, Thun Palace. 60h, Archbishop's Palace, Hradcany. 5k, St. Nicholas Church.

1977, Mar. 10
2103 A746 20h multi .20 .20
2104 A746 30h multi .20 .20
2105 A746 40h multi .20 .20
2106 A746 60h multi .20 .20
2107 A746 5k multi 1.50 .60
Nos. 2103-2107 (5) 2.30 1.40

PRAGA 1978 International Philatelic Exhibition, Prague, Sept. 8-17, 1978.

Children, Auxiliary Police
A747

1977, Apr. 21 ***Perf. 11½***
2108 A747 60h multi .25 .20

Auxiliary Police, 25th anniversary.

Warsaw, Polish Flag, Bicyclists
A748

Congress Emblem — A749

Designs: 60h, Berlin, DDR flag, bicyclists. 1k, Prague, Czechoslovakian flag, victorious bicyclist. 1.40k, Bicyclists on highways, modern views of Berlin, Prague and Warsaw.

1977, May 7
2109 A748 30h multi .20 .20
2110 A748 60h multi .20 .20
2111 A748 1k multi .50 .20
2112 A748 1.40k multi .35 .20
Nos. 2109-2112 (4) *1.25* *.80*

30th International Bicycle Peace Race Warsaw-Prague-Berlin.

1977, May 25 ***Perf. 11½***
2113 A749 30h car, red & gold .20 .20

9th Trade Union Congress, Prague 1977.

Prague Castle Art Type of 1971

Designs: 3k, Onyx footed bowl, 1350. 3.60k, Bronze horse, 1619.

1977, June 7 **Engr.**
2114 A634 3k multi .95 .90
2115 A634 3.60k multi .90 .90

Nos. 2114-2115 were each issued in sheets of 4. Value, set $13.

French Postrider, 19th Century, PRAGA '78 Emblem — A750

Postal Uniforms: 1k, Austrian, 1838. 2k, Austrian, late 18th century. 3.60k, Germany, early 18th century.

1977, June 8 **Engr. & Photo.**
2116 A750 60h multi .20 .20
2117 A750 1k multi .20 .20
2118 A750 2k multi .30 .20
2119 A750 3.60k multi 1.20 .60
Nos. 2116-2119 (4) 1.90 1.20

PRAGA 1978 International Philatelic Exhibition, Prague, Sept. 8-17, 1978.
Nos. 2116-2119 were each issued both in sheets of 50 and in sheets of 4 stamps with 4 inscribed labels and 2 blank labels. Value, set of sheets of 4, $16.

Coffeepots, Porcelain Mark — A751

Mlada Boleslav Costume — A752

Czechoslovak Porcelain and Porcelain Marks: 30h, Urn. 40h, Vase. 60h, Cup and saucer, jugs. 1k, Candlestick and plate. 3k, Cup and saucer, coffeepot.

1977, June 15
2120 A751 20h multi .20 .20
2121 A751 30h multi .20 .20
2122 A751 40h multi .20 .20
2123 A751 60h multi .20 .20
2124 A751 1k multi .20 .20
2125 A751 3k multi 1.10 .35
Nos. 2120-2125 (6) 2.10 1.35

1977, Aug. 31 **Engr.** ***Perf. 11½***

PRAGA Emblem and Folk Costumes from: 1.60k, Vazek. 3.60k, Zavadka. 5k, Belkovice.

2126 A752 1k multi 1.00 .80
2127 A752 1.60k multi 1.00 .80
2128 A752 3.60k multi 1.00 .80
2129 A752 5k multi 1.00 .80
Nos. 2126-2129 (4) *4.00* *3.20*

Issued in sheets of 10 and in sheets of 8 plus 2 labels showing PRAGA '78 emblem. Value, set: sheets of 10 $50; sheets of 8 $40.

Old Woman, Devil and Spinner, by Viera Bombova
A753

Book Illustrations: 60h, Bear and tiger, by Genadij Pavlisin. 1k, Coach drawn by 4 horses (Hans Christian Andersen), by Ulf Lovgren. 2k, Bear and flamingos (Lewis Carroll), by Nicole Claveloux. 3k, King with keys, and toys, by Jiri Trnka.

1977, Sept. 9 **Engr. & Photo.**
2130 A753 40h multi .20 .20
2131 A753 60h multi .20 .20
2132 A753 1k multi .20 .20
2133 A753 2k multi .25 .20
2134 A753 3k multi 1.00 .35
Nos. 2130-2134 (5) 1.85 1.15

Prize-winning designs, 6th biennial exhibition of illustrations for children's books, Bratislava.

Globe, Violin, Doves, View of Prague — A754

1977, Sept. 28 *Perf. 11½*

2135 A754 60h multi	.25	.20

Congress of International Music Council of UNESCO, Prague and Bratislava.

Souvenir Sheets

"For a Europe of Peace" A755

1.60k, "For a Europe of Cooperation." 2.40k, "For a Europe of Social Progress."

1977, Oct. 3

2136 Sheet of 2	.50	.50
a. A755 60h multi	.20	.20
2137 Sheet of 2	1.00	1.00
a. A755 1.60k multi	.25	.25
2138 Sheet of 2	2.00	1.75
a. A755 2.40k multi	.50	.50

2nd European Security and Cooperation Conference, Belgrade. Nos. 2136-2138 each contain 2 stamps and 2 blue on buff inscriptions and ornaments.

S. P. Korolev, Sputnik I Emblem — A756

Sailors, Cruiser Aurora — A757

30h, Yuri A. Gagarin & Vostok I. 40h, Alexei Leonov. 1k, Neil A. Armstrong & footprint on moon. 1.60k, Construction of orbital space station.

1977, Oct. 4

2139 A756 20h multi	.20	.20
2140 A756 30h multi	.20	.20
2141 A756 40h multi	.20	.20
2142 A756 1k multi	.20	.20
2143 A756 1.60k multi	.60	.20
Nos. 2139-2143 (5)	1.40	1.00

Space research, 20th anniv. of 1st earth satellite.

1977, Nov. 7

2144 A757 30h multi	.20	.20

60th anniv. of Russian October Revolution.

"Russia," Arms of USSR, Kremlin A758

"Science" A759

1977, Nov. 7

2145 A758 30h multi	.20	.20

55th anniversary of the USSR.

1977, Nov. 17

2146 A759 3k multi	.50	.20

Czechoslovak Academy of Science, 25th anniversary.

Art Type of 1967

Paintings: 2k, "Fear" (woman), by Jan Murdoch. 2.40k, Jan Francisci, portrait by Peter M. Bohun. 2.60k, Vaclav Hollar, self-portrait, 1647. 3k, Young Woman, 1528, by Lucas Cranach. 5k, Cleopatra, by Rubens.

1977, Nov. 27 **Engr.** *Perf. 11½*

2147 A565 2k multi	.70	.40
2148 A565 2.40k multi	1.10	1.00
2149 A565 2.60k multi	1.10	1.00
2150 A565 3k multi	.70	.60
2151 A565 5k multi	1.40	1.40
Nos. 2147-2151 (5)	5.00	4.40

Nos. 2147-2151 were each issued in sheets of 4. Value, set $28.

View of Bratislava, by Georg Hoefnagel — A760

Design: 3.60k, Arms of Bratislava, 1436.

1977, Dec. 6

2152 A760 3k multi	1.40	1.20
2153 A760 3.60k multi	.60	.40

Nos. 2152-21531 were each issued in sheets of 4. Value, set $12.50.

See Nos. 2174-2175, 2270-2271, 2331-2332, 2364-2365, 2422-2423, 2478-2479, 2514-2515, 2570-2571, 2618-2619.

Stamp Pattern and Post Horn — A761

1977, Dec. 18 **Engr. & Photo.**

2154 A761 1k multi	.25	.20

Stamp Day.

Zdenek Nejedly — A762

Karl Marx — A763

1978, Feb. 10 *Perf. 11½*

2155 A762 30h multi	.20	.20
2156 A763 40h multi	.20	.20

Zdenek Nejedly (1878-1962), musicologist and historian; Karl Marx (1818-1883), political philosopher.

Civilians Greeting Guardsmen — A764

Intellectual, Farm Woman and Steel Worker, Flag — A765

1978, Feb. 25

2157 A764 1k gold & multi	.20	.20
2158 A765 1k gold & multi	.20	.20

30th anniv. of "Victorious February" (No. 2157), and Natl. Front (No. 2158). See note after 2190.

Yuri A. Gagarin, Vostok I — A766

10k Coin, 1964, and 25k Coin, 1965 — A767

Design: 30h, 3.60k, like No. 2140.

Engraved; Overprint Photogravure (Blue and carmine on 30h, green and lilac rose on 3.60k)

1978, Mar. 2 *Perf. 11½x12*

2159 A766 30h dk red	.20	.20
2160 A766 3.60k vio bl	2.25	2.00

Capt. V. Remek, 1st Czechoslovakian cosmonaut on Russian spaceship Soyuz 28, Mar. 2-9.

1978, Mar. 14 **Engr. & Photo.**

40h, Medal for Culture, 1972. 1.40k, Charles University medal, 1948. 3k, Ferdinand I medal, 1568. 5k, Gold florin, 1335.

2161 A767 20h sil & multi	.20	.20
2162 A767 40h sil & multi	.20	.20
2163 A767 1.40k gold & multi	1.00	.20
2164 A767 3k gold & multi	.35	.20
2165 A767 5k gold & multi	.35	.20
Nos. 2161-2165 (5)	2.10	1.00

650th anniversary of Kremnica Mint.

Tire Tracks and Ball — A768

Congress Emblem — A769

1978, Mar. 15

2166 A768 60h multi	.25	.20

Road safety.

1978, Apr. 16 *Perf. 11½*

2167 A769 1k multi	.25	.20

9th World Trade Union Cong., Prague 1978.

Shot Put and Praha '78 Emblem A770

1k, Pole vault. 3.60k, Women runners.

1978, Apr. 26

2168 A770 40h multi	.20	.20
2169 A770 1k multi	.25	.20
2170 A770 3.60k multi	.60	.35
Nos. 2168-2170 (3)	1.05	.75

5th European Athletic Championships, Prague 1978.

Ice Hockey — A771

Designs: 30h, Hockey. 2k, Ice hockey play.

1978, Apr. 26

2171 A771 30h multi	.30	.25
2172 A771 60h multi	.20	.20
2173 A771 2k multi	.40	.20
Nos. 2171-2173 (3)	.90	.65

5th European Ice Hockey Championships and 70th anniversary of Bandy hockey.

Bratislava Type of 1977

Designs: 3k, Bratislava, 1955, by Orest Dubay. 3.60k, Fishpound Square, Bratislava, 1955, by Imro Weiner-Kral.

1978, May 9 **Engr.** *Perf. 11½*

2174 A760 3k multi	.90	.75
2175 A760 3.60k multi	1.10	.75

Nos. 2174-2175 were each issued in sheets of 4. Value, set $12.

Prague Castle Art Type of 1971

3k, King Ottokar II, detail from tomb. 3.60k, Charles IV, detail from votive panel by Jan Ocka.

1978, May 9

2176 A634 3k multi	.75	.50
2177 A634 3.60k multi	3.25	2.00

Nos. 2176-2177 were each issued in sheets of 4. Value, set $20.

Ministry of Post, Prague A772

Engraved and Photogravure

1978, May 29 *Perf. 12x11½*

2178 A772 60h multi		.25	.20

14th session of permanent COMECOM Commission (Ministers of Post and Telecommunications of Socialist Countries).

Palacky Bridge A773

Prague Bridges and PRAGA '78 Emblem: 40h, Railroad bridge. 1k, Bridge of May 1. 2k, Manes Bridge. 3k, Svatopluk Cech Bridge. 5.40k, Charles Bridge.

1978, May 30

2179 A773	20h blk & multi	.20	.20
2180 A773	40h blk & multi	.20	.20
2181 A773	1k blk & multi	.20	.20
2182 A773	2k blk & multi	.20	.20
2183 A773	3k blk & multi	.45	.20
2184 A773	5.40k blk & multi	1.50	.75
	Nos. 2179-2184 (6)	2.75	1.75

PRAGA 1978 International Philatelic Exhibition, Prague, Sept. 8-17.

St. Peter and Apostles, Clock Tower, and Emblem A774

Town Hall Clock, Prague, by Josef Manes, and PRAGA '78 Emblem: 1k, Astronomical clock. 2k, Prague's coat of arms. 3k, Grape harvest (September). 3.60k, Libra. 10k, Arms surrounded by zodiac signs and scenes symbolic of 12 months, horiz. 2k, 3k, 3.60k show details from design of 10k.

1978, June 20 *Perf. 11½x11*

2185 A774	40h multi	.20	.20
2186 A774	1k multi	.20	.20
2187 A774	2k multi	.25	.20
2188 A774	3k multi	1.50	.35
2189 A774	3.60k multi	.75	.25
	Nos. 2185-2189 (5)	2.90	1.20

Souvenir Sheet

Perf. 12x12

2190 A774	10k multi	10.00	7.50

PRAGA'78 Intl. Philatelic Exhibition, Prague, Sept. 8-17. No. 2190 contains one 50x40mm stamp. Sheet exists imperf. Value $30.

A non-valid souvenir sheet contains 4 imperf. copies of No. 2157. Sold only with PRAGA ticket.

Folk Dancers — A775

1978, July 7 *Perf. 11½x12*

2191 A775 30h multi		.20	.20

25th Folklore Festival, Vychodna.

Overpass and PRAGA Emblem — A776

1k, 2k, Modern office buildings, diff. 6k, Old & new Prague. 20k, Charles Bridge & Old Town, by Vincent Morstadt, 1828.

1978 *Perf. 12x11½*

2192 A776	60h blk & multi	.20	.20
2193 A776	1k blk & multi	.20	.20
2194 A776	2k blk & multi	.20	.20
2195 A776	6k blk & multi	1.50	.75
	Nos. 2192-2195 (4)	2.10	1.35

Souvenir Sheet

Engr.

2196 A776	20k multi	9.50	7.50

PRAGA 1978 Intl. Phil. Exhib., Prague, Sept. 8-17. No. 2196 also for 60th anniv. of Czechoslovak postage stamps. No. 2196 contains one 61x45mm stamp.

Issued: #2192-2195, 9/8; #2196, 9/10.

Souvenir Sheet

Apollo's Companion, by Titian — A777

#2197b, King Midas. Stamps show details from "Apollo Flaying Marsya" by Titian.

1978, Sept. 12 *Perf. 11½*

2197	Sheet of 2	10.00	8.00
a. A777 10k multi		4.25	3.50
b. A777 10k multi		4.25	3.50

Titian (1488-1576), Venetian painter. No. 2197 with dark blue marginal inscription "FIP" was sold only with entrance ticket to PRAGA Philatelic Exhibition. Value $25.

Exhibition Hall — A778

Engraved and Photogravure

1978, Sept. 13 *Perf. 11½x11*

2198 A778 30h multi		.20	.20

22nd International Engineering Fair, Brno.

Postal Newspaper Service — A779

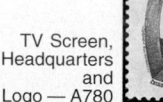

TV Screen, Headquarters and Logo — A780

Newspaper, Microphone A781

1978, Sept. 21 *Perf. 11½*

2199 A779 30h multi		.20	.20
2200 A780 30h multi		.20	.20
2201 A781 30h multi		.20	.20
	Nos. 2199-2201 (3)	.60	.60

Postal News Service, 25th anniv.; Czechoslovakian television, 25th anniv.; Press, Broadcasting and Television Day.

Sulky Race A782

Pardubice Steeplechase: 10h, Falling horses and jockeys at fence. 30h, Race. 40h, Horses passing post. 1.60k, Hurdling. 4.40k, Winner.

1978, Oct. 6 *Perf. 12x11½*

2202 A782	10h multi	.20	.20
2203 A782	20h multi	.20	.20
2204 A782	30h multi	.20	.20
2205 A782	40h multi	.20	.20
2206 A782	1.60k multi	.25	.20
2207 A782	4.40k multi	1.50	.65
	Nos. 2202-2207 (6)	2.55	1.65

Woman Holding Arms of Czechoslovakia A783

1978, Oct. 28 *Perf. 11½*

2208 A783 60h multi		.20	.20

60th anniversary of independence.

Art Type of 1974

2.40k, Flowers, by Jakub Bohdan (1660-1724). 3k, The Dream of Salas, by Ludovit Fulla, horiz. 3.60k, Apostle with Censer, Master of the Spissko Capitals (c. 1480-90).

1978, Nov. 27 **Engr.**

2209 A700	2.40k multi	.60	.45
2210 A700	3k multi	.70	.65
2211 A700	3.60k multi	2.50	2.00
	Nos. 2209-2211 (3)	3.80	3.10

Slovak National Gallery, 30th anniversary.

Nos. 2209-2211 were each issued in sheets of 4. Value, set $22.50.

Musicians, by Jan Könyves — A784

Slovak Ceramics: 30h, Janosik on Horseback, by Jozef Franko. 40h, Woman in Folk Costume by Michal Polasko. 1k, Three Girls Singing, by Ignac Bizmayer. 1.60k, Janosik Dancing, by Ferdis Kostka.

Engraved and Photogravure

1978, Dec. 5 *Perf. 11½x12*

2212 A784	20h multi	.20	.20
2213 A784	30h multi	.20	.20
2214 A784	40k multi	.20	.20
2215 A784	1k multi	.20	.20
2216 A784	1.60k multi	1.00	.30
	Nos. 2212-2216 (5)	1.80	1.10

Alfons Mucha and his Design for 1918 Issue — A785

1978, Dec. 18 *Perf. 11½*

2217 A785 1k multi		.25	.20

60th Stamp Day.

COMECON Building, Moscow — A786

1979, Jan. 1 *Perf. 11½*

2218 A786 1k multi		.25	.20

Council for Mutual Economic Aid (COMECON), 30th anniversary.

Woman's Head and Grain — A787

Woman, Workers, Child, Doves — A788

1979, Jan. 1

2219 A787 30h multi		.20	.20
2220 A788 60h multi		.20	.20

United Agricultural Production Assoc., 30th anniv. (30h); Czechoslovakian Federation, 10th anniv. (60h).

Soyuz 28, Rockets and Capsule — A789

60h, Astronauts Aleksei Gubarev and Vladimir Remek on launching pad, vert. 1.60k, Soviet astronauts J. Romanenko and G. Grecko, Salyut 6 and recovery ship. 2k, Salyut-Soyuz orbital complex, post office in space and Czechoslovakia No. 2153. 4k, Soyuz 28, crew after landing and trajectory map, vert. 10k, Gubarev and Remek, Intercosmos emblem, arms of Czechoslovakia and USSR.

1979, Mar. 2

2221 A789	30h multi	.20	.20
2222 A789	60h multi	.20	.20
2223 A789	1.60k multi	.20	.20
2224 A789	2k multi	1.25	.30
2225 A789	4k multi	.60	.25
	Nos. 2221-2225 (5)	2.45	1.15

Souvenir Sheet

2226 A789	10k multi	5.00	3.50

1st anniv. of joint Czechoslovak-Soviet space flight. Size of No. 2226: 76x93mm (stamp 39x55mm). No. 2226 has Cyrillic inscription, No. 2455a does not. No. 2226 exists imperf. Value, $22.50.

Alpine Bellflowers A790

Stylized Satellite, Dial, Tape A791

Mountain Flowers: 20h, Crocus. 30h, Pinks. 40h, Alpine hawkweed. 3k, Larkspur.

1979, Mar. 23 *Perf. 11½*

2227	A790	10h	multi	.20	.20
2228	A790	20h	multi	.20	.20
2229	A790	30h	multi	.20	.20
2230	A790	40h	multi	.20	.20

Perf. 14

2231	A790	3k	multi	1.50	.75
	Nos. 2227-2231 (5)			2.30	1.55

Mountain Rescue Service, 25th anniversary.
The 3k exists perf. 11½. Value, $40 unused, $20 used.
The 3k was issued in sheets of 10. Values: perf 14 (No. 2231), $25; perf 11½, $400.

1979, Apr. 2

2232	A791	10h	multi	.20	.20

Telecommunications research, 30th anniv.

Artist and Model, Dove, Bratislava Castle — A792

Cog Wheels, Transformer and Student — A793

Musical Instruments, Bratislava Castle — A794

Pioneer Scarf, IYC Emblem — A795

Red Star, Man, Child and Doves — A796

1979, Apr. 2

2233	A792	20h	multi	.20	.20
2234	A793	20h	multi	.20	.20
2235	A794	30h	multi	.20	.20
2236	A795	30h	multi	.20	.20
2237	A796	60h	multi	.20	.20
	Nos. 2233-2237 (5)			1.00	1.00

Fine Arts Academy, Bratislava, 30th anniv.; Slovak Technical University, 40th anniv.; Radio Symphony Orchestra, Bratislava, 30th anniv.; Young Pioneers, 30th anniv. and IYC; Peace Movement, 30th anniversary.

Prague Castle Art Type of 1971

3k, Burial crown of King Ottokar II. 3.60k, Portrait of Mrs. Reitmayer, by Karel Purkyne.

1979, May 9 *Perf. 11½*

2238	A634	3k	multi	1.75	1.40
2239	A634	3.60k	multi	.85	.50

Nos. 2238-2239 were each issued in sheets of 4. Value, set $15.

Arms of Vlachovo Brezi, 1538 — A797

Animals in Heraldry: 60h, Jesenik, 1509 (bear and eagle). 1.20k, Vysoke Myto, 1471 (St. George slaying dragon). 1.80k,Martin, 1854 (St. Martin giving coat to beggar). 2k, Zebrak, 1674 (mythological beast).

1979, May 25 *Perf. 11½x12*

2240	A797	30h	multi	.20	.20
2241	A797	60h	multi	.20	.20
2242	A797	1.20k	multi	.20	.20
2243	A797	1.80k	multi	*1.00*	*.30*
2244	A797	2k	multi	.60	.20
	Nos. 2240-2244 (5)			*2.20*	*1.10*

Forest, Thriving and Destroyed A798

Designs: 1.80k, Water. 3.60k, City. 4k, Cattle. All designs show good and bad environment, separated by exclamation point; Man and Biosphere emblem.

1979, June 22 **Engr.** *Perf. 11½*

2245	A798	60h	multi	.20	.20
2246	A798	1.80k	multi	.30	.25
2247	A798	3.60k	multi	*1.75*	*.75*
2248	A798	4k	multi	.75	.40
	Nos. 2245-2248 (4)			*3.00*	*1.60*

Man and Biosphere Program of UNESCO.

Blast Furnace — A799

Engraved and Photogravure

1979, Aug. 29 *Perf. 11x11½*

2249	A799	30h	multi	.20	.20

Slovak National Uprising, 35th anniversary.

Frog and Goat A800

Book Illustrations (IYC Emblem and): 40h, Knight on horseback. 60h, Maidens. 1k, Boy with sled following rooster. 3k, King riding flying beast.

1979, Apr. 2 *Perf. 11½x11*

2250	A800	20h	multi	.20	.20
2251	A800	40h	multi	.20	.20
2252	A800	60h	multi	.20	.20
2253	A800	1k	multi	.20	.20
2254	A800	3k	multi	*1.50*	*.50*
	Nos. 2250-2254 (5)			*2.30*	*1.30*

Prize-winning designs, 7th biennial exhibition of illustrations for children's books, Bratislava; International Year of the Child. Printed with labels showing story characters. Value, set with attached labels, $4.75.

"Bone Shaker" Bicycles, 1870 A801

Bicycles from: 20h, 1978. 40h, 1910. 60h, 1886. 3.60k, 1820.

1979, Sept. 14 *Perf. 12x11½*

2255	A801	20h	multi	.20	.20
2256	A801	40h	multi	.20	.20
2257	A801	60h	multi	.20	.20
2258	A801	2k	multi	.40	.20
2259	A801	3.60k	multi	1.50	.50
	Nos. 2255-2259 (5)			2.50	1.30

Bracket Clock, 18th Century A802

Designs: 18th century clocks.

1979, Oct. 1 *Perf. 11½*

2260	A802	40h	multi	.20	.20
2261	A802	60h	multi	.20	.20
2262	A802	80h	multi	.85	.20
2263	A802	1k	multi	.25	.20
2264	A802	2k	multi	.50	.20
	Nos. 2260-2264 (5)			2.00	1.00

Art Type of 1967

Paintings: 1.60k, Sunday by the River, by Alois Moravec. 2k, Self-portrait, by Gustav Mally. 3k, Self-portrait, by Ilia Yefimovic Repin. 3.60k, Horseback Rider, by Jan Bauch. 5k, Dancing Peasants, by Albrecht Dürer.

1979, Nov. 27 **Engr.** *Perf. 12*

2265	A565	1.60k	multi	.35	.30
2266	A565	2k	multi	.50	.45
2267	A565	3k	multi	.50	.45
2268	A565	3.60k	multi	1.75	1.50
2269	A565	5k	multi	1.40	1.10
	Nos. 2265-2269 (5)			4.50	3.80

Nos. 2265-2269 were each issued in sheets of 4. Value, set $25.

Bratislava Type of 1977

Designs: 3k, Bratislava Castle on the Danube, by L. Janscha, 1787. 3.60k, Bratislava Castle, stone engraving by Wolf, 1815.

1979, Dec. 5

2270	A760	3k	multi	.70	.65
2271	A760	3.60k	multi	1.80	1.50

Nos. 2270-2272 were each issued in sheets of 4. Value, set $15.

Stamp Day — A803

Engraved and Photogravure

1979, Dec. 18 *Perf. 11½x12*

2272	A803	1k	multi	.25	.20

Electronic Circuits — A804

Designs: 50h, Satellite dish. 2k, Airplane. 3k, Computer punch tape.

1979-80 **Photo.** *Perf. 11½x12*

Coil Stamps

2273	A804	50h	red	.20	.20
2274	A804	1k	brown	.25	.20
2275	A804	2k	green ('80)	.30	.20
2276	A804	3k	lake ('80)	.45	.25
	Nos. 2273-2276 (4)			1.20	.85

The 1k comes in two shades.

Runners and Dove A805

Engraved and Photogravure

1980, Jan. 29 *Perf. 12x11½*

2289	A805	50h	multi	.20	.20

50th Intl. Peace Marathon, Kosice, Oct. 4.

Downhill Skiing — A806

1980, Jan. 29 *Perf. 11½x12*

2290	A806	1k	shown	.25	.20
2291	A806	2k	Speed skating	.80	.30
2292	A806	3k	Four-man bobsled	.65	.30
	Nos. 2290-2292 (3)			1.70	.80

13th Winter Olympic Games, Lake Placid, NY, Feb. 12-24.

Basketball — A807

1980, Jan. 29 *Perf. 11½*

2293	A807	40h	shown	.20	.20
2294	A807	1k	Swimming	.30	.20
2295	A807	2k	Hurdles	1.25	.30
2296	A807	3.60k	Fencing	.95	.25
	Nos. 2293-2296 (4)			2.70	.95

22nd Olympic Games, Moscow, 7/19-8/3.

Arms Type of 1977

1980, Feb. 20 *Perf. 11½*

2297	A745	50h	Bystrice Nad Pernstejnem	.20	.20
2298	A745	50h	Kunstat	.20	.20
2299	A745	50h	Rozmital Pod Tremsinem	.20	.20
2300	A745	50h	Zlata Idka	.20	.20
	Nos. 2297-2300 (4)			.80	.80

Theatrical Mask — A808

Slovak National Theater, Actors — A809

1980, Mar. 1

2301 A808 50h multi .20 .20
2302 A809 1k multi .25 .20

50th Jiraskuv Hronov Theatrical Ensemble Review; Slovak National Theater, Bratislava, 60th anniversary.

Mouse in Space, Satellite — A810

Police Corps Banner, Emblem — A811

Intercosmos: 1k, Weather map, satellite. 1.60k, Intersputnik television transmission. 4k, Camera, satellite. 5k, Czech satellite station, 1978, horiz. 10k, Intercosmos emblem, horiz.

1980, Apr. 12 ***Perf. 11½x12, 12x11½***

2303 A810 50h multi .20 .20
2304 A810 1k multi .30 .20
2305 A810 1.60k multi 1.75 .20
2306 A810 4k multi .75 .40
2307 A810 5k multi 1.00 .50
Nos. 2303-2307 (5) 4.00 1.50

Souvenir Sheet

2308 A810 10k multi 3.25 2.50

Intercosmos cooperative space program.
No. 2308 exists imperf. Value, $30.

1980, Apr. 17 ***Perf. 11½***

2309 A811 50h multi .20 .20

National Police Corps, 35th anniversary.

Lenin's 110th Birth Anniversary — A812

Design: #2311, Engels's 160th birth anniv.

1980, Apr. 22

2310 A812 1k tan & brn .25 .20
2311 A812 1k lt grn & brn .25 .20

Old and Modern Prague, Czech Flag, Bouquet A813

Boy Writing "Peace" A814

Pact Members' Flags, Dove — A815

Czech and Soviet Arms, Prague and Moscow Views A816

1980, May 6 ***Perf. 12x11½***

2312 A813 50h multi .20 .20
2313 A814 1k multi .20 .20
2314 A815 1k multi .20 .20
2315 A816 1k multi .20 .20
Nos. 2312-2315 (4) .80 .80

Liberation by Soviet army, 35th anniv.; Soviet victory in WWII, 35th anniv.; Signing of Warsaw Pact (Bulgaria, Czechoslovakia, German Democratic Rep., Hungary, Poland, Romania, USSR), 25th anniv.; Czechoslovak-Soviet Treaty of Friendship, Cooperation and Mutual Aid, 10th anniv.

Souvenir Sheet

UN, 35th Anniv. A817

1980, June 3 **Engr.** ***Perf. 12***

2316 Sheet of 2 3.50 2.75
a. A817 4k multicolored 1.50 1.25

Athletes Parading Banners in Strahov Stadium, Prague, Spartakiad Emblem — A818

Engraved and Photogravure

1980, June 3 ***Perf. 12x11½***

2317 A818 50h shown .20 .20
2318 A818 1k Gymnast, vert. .20 .20

Spartakiad 1980, Prague, June 26-29.

Aechmea Fasciata — A819

A820

1980, Aug. 13 ***Perf. 12***

2319 A819 50h *Gerbera Jamesonii* .35 .20
2320 A819 1k *Aechmea fasciata* 1.75 .60
2321 A819 2k *Strelitzia reginae* .50 .20
2322 A819 4k *Paphiopedilum* 1.90 .30
Nos. 2319-2322 (4) 4.50 1.30

Olomouc and Bratislava Flower Shows.
Nos. 2319-2322 were each issued in sheets of 10. Value, set $70.

1980, Sept. 24 ***Perf. 11½x12***

Designs: Folktale character embroideries.

2323 A820 50h Chad girl .20 .20
2324 A820 1k Punch and dog .20 .20
2325 A820 2k Dandy and Posy .75 .20
2326 A820 4k Lion and moon 1.30 .75
2327 A820 5k Wallachian dance .65 .20
Nos. 2323-2327 (5) 3.10 1.55

National Census A821

1980, Sept. 24 ***Perf. 12x11½***

2328 A821 1k multi .25 .20

Prague Castle Type of 1971

Designs: 3k, Old Palace gateway. 4k, Armorial lion, 16th century.

1980, Oct. 28 ***Perf. 12***

2329 A634 3k multi 1.25 1.10
2330 A634 4k multi 1.00 .65

Nos. 2329-2330 were each issued in sheets of 4. Value, set $18.

Bratislava Type of 1977

3k, View across the Danube, by J. Eder, 1810. 4k, The Old Royal Bridge, by J.A. Lantz, 1820.

1980, Oct. 28

2331 A760 3k multi 1.25 1.10
2332 A760 4k multi .75 .65

Nos. 2331-2332 were each issued in sheets of 4. Value, set $14.

10th Anniversary of Socialist Youth Federation — A822

1980, Nov. 9 ***Perf. 12x11½***

2333 A822 50h multi .20 .20

No. 2137 Overprinted in Red: 3. / MEZINARODNI VELETRH ZNAMEK / ESSEN '80

1980, Nov. 18

2334 A755 1.60k multi 20.00 15.00

Czechoslovak Day/ ESSEN '80, 3rd International Stamp Exhibition, No. 2334 has overprinted red marginal inscription.

Art Type of 1967

Designs: 1k, Pavel Jozef Safarik, by Jozef B. Klemens. 2k, Peasant Revolt mosaic, Anna Podzemma. 3k, St. Lucia, 14th century statue. 4k, Waste Heaps, by Jan Zrzavy, horiz. 5k, Labor, sculpture by Jan Stursa.

1980, Nov. 27 **Engr.** ***Perf. 12***

2335 A565 1k multi .95 1.10
2336 A565 2k multi 1.10 .95
2337 A565 3k multi .55 .50
2338 A565 4k multi .65 .55
2339 A565 5k multi .65 .55
Nos. 2335-2339 (5) 3.90 3.65

Nos. 2335-2339 were each issued in sheets of 4. Value, set $27.

Stamp Day — A823

Engraved and Photogravure

1980, Dec. 18 ***Perf. 11½x12***

2340 A823 1k multi .25 .20

7th Five-year Plan, 1981-1985 A824

1981, Jan. 1 ***Perf. 11½***

2341 A824 50h multi .20 .20

International Year of the Disabled A825

1981, Feb. 24

2342 A825 1k multi .25 .20

Landau, 1800 A826

1981, Feb. 25 ***Perf. 12x11½***

2343 A826 50h shown .20 .20
2344 A826 1k Mail coach, 1830 .25 .20
2345 A826 3.60k Mail sled, 1840 1.25 .60
2346 A826 5k 4-horse mail coach, 1860 .85 .45
2347 A826 7k Open carriage, 1840 1.25 .85
a. Sheet of 4 13.00 10.00
Nos. 2343-2347 (5) 3.80 2.30

WIPA '81 Intl. Philatelic Exhibition, Vienna, Austria, May 22-31. #2347a issued May 10.

Wolfgang Amadeus Mozart — A827

Famous Men: #2348, Joesph Hlavka (1831-1908). #2349, Juraj Hronec (1881-1959). #2350, Jan Sverma (1901-44). #2351, Mikulas Schneider-Trnavsky (1881-1958). #2352, B. Bolzano (1781-1848). #2353, Dimitri Shostakovich, composer. #2354, George Bernard Shaw, playwright.

1981, Mar. 10 ***Perf. 11½***

2348 A827 50h multi .20 .20
2349 A827 50h multi .20 .20
2350 A827 50h multi .20 .20
2351 A827 50h multi .20 .20
2352 A827 1k multi .75 .35
2353 A827 1k multi .25 .20
2354 A827 1k multi .25 .20
2355 A827 1k multi .25 .20
Nos. 2348-2355 (8) 2.30 1.75

Souvenir Sheet

Yuri Gagarin A828

1981, Apr. 5 ***Perf. 12***

2356 Sheet of 2 3.75 3.00
a. A828 6k multicolored 1.75 1.10

20th anniv. of 1st manned space flight.

Workers and Banner A829

1981, Apr. 6 ***Perf. 12x11½***

2357 A829 50h shown .20 .20
2358 A829 1k Hands holding banner .25 .20

2359 A829 4k Worker holding banner, vert. .35 .25
Nos. 2357-2359 (3) .80 .65

Czechoslovakian Communist Party, 60th anniv.

Congress Emblem, View of Prague — A830

1981, Apr. 6
2360 A830 50h shown .20 .20
2361 A830 1k Bratislava .25 .20

16th Communist Party Congress.

Agriculture Museum, 90th Anniv. A831

Natl. Assembly Elections A832

1981, May 14 *Perf. 11½x12*
2362 A831 1k multi .25 .20

1981, June 1
2363 A832 50h multi .20 .20

Bratislava Type of 1977

Designs: 3k, Bratislava Castle, by G.B. Probst, 1760. 4k, Grassalkovic Palace, by C. Bschor, 1815.

1981, June 10 *Perf. 12*
2364 A760 3k multi 1.25 1.10
2365 A760 4k multi 1.00 .75

Nos. 2364-2365 were each issued in sheets of 4. Value, set $18.

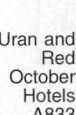

Uran and Red October Hotels A833

Successes of Socialist Achievements Exhibition: 1k, Brno-Bratislava Highway, Jihlava. 2k, Nuclear power station, Jaslovske Bohunice.

1981, June 10 *Perf. 12x11½*
2366 A833 80h multi .20 .20
2367 A833 1k multi .20 .20
2368 A833 2k multi .20 .20
Nos. 2366-2368 (3) .60 .60

Border Defense Units, 30th Anniv. A834

Civil Defense, 30th Anniv. A835

Army Cooperation, 30th Anniv. — A836

Rysy Youth Mountain Climbing Contest A837

Engraved and Photogravure

1981, July 11 *Perf. 11½*
2369 A834 40h multi .20 .20
2370 A835 50h multi .20 .20
2371 A836 1k multi .25 .20
2372 A837 3.60k multi .75 .30
Nos. 2369-2372 (4) 1.40 .90

30th Natl. Festival of Amateur Puppet Ensembles — A838

1981, July 2 *Perf. 11½*
2373 A838 2k Punch and Devil .50 .20

Souvenir Sheet

Guernica, by Pablo Picasso — A839

1981, July 2 **Engr.** *Perf. 11½x12*
2374 A839 10k multi 3.50 2.50

Picasso's birth centenary; 45th anniv. of Intl. Brigades in Spain.

Cat Holding Flower, by Etienne Delessert A840

8th Biennial Exhibition of Children's Book Illustrations (Designs by): 50h, Albin Brunovsky, vert. 1k, Adolf Born. 2k, Vive Tolli. 10k, Suekichi Akaba.

Engraved and Photogravure

1981, Sept. 5 *Perf. 11½*
2375 A840 50h multi .20 .20
2376 A840 1k multi .25 .20
2377 A840 2k multi .40 .20
2378 A840 4k multi .95 .40
2379 A840 10k multi 2.00 .75
Nos. 2375-2379 (5) 3.80 1.75

Prague Zoo, 50th Anniv. — A841

1981, Sept. 28 *Perf. 11½x12*
2380 A841 50h Gorillas .40 .20
2381 A841 1k Lions .75 .20
2382 A841 7k Przewalski's horses 2.10 .80
Nos. 2380-2382 (3) 3.25 1.20

Anti-smoking Campaign A842

1981, Oct. 27 *Perf. 12*
2383 A842 4k multi 1.00 .60

No. 2383 was issued in sheets of 10, containing 8 stamps and 2 labels. Values: single with label attached, $1.50; sheet, $14.

Prague Castle Art Type of 1971

Designs: 3k, Carved dragon, Palais Lobkovitz, 16th cent. 4k, St. Vitus Cathedral, by J. Sember and G. Dobler, 19th cent.

1981, Oct. 28
2384 A634 3k multi .75 .45
2385 A634 4k multi 1.75 1.40

Nos. 2384-2385 were each issued in sheets of 4. Value, set $13.

Art Type of 1967

Designs: 1k, View of Prague, by Vaclav Hollar (1607-1677). 2k, Czechoslovak Academy medallion, engraved by Otakar Spaniel (1881-1955). 3k, Jihoceska Vysivka, by Zdenek Sklenar (b. 1910). 4k, Still Life, by A.M. Gerasimov (1881-1963). 5k, Standing Woman, by Pablo Picasso (1881-1973).

1981, Nov. 27 **Engr.** *Perf. 12*
2386 A565 1k multi 1.90 1.25
2387 A565 2k multi .50 .25
2388 A565 3k multi .65 .40
2389 A565 4k multi .75 .50
2390 A565 5k multi 1.25 1.00
Nos. 2386-2390 (5) 5.05 3.40

Nos. 2386-2390 were each issued in sheets of 4. Value, set $35.

Sheets of No. 2390 exist with center gutter inscribed with Philexfrance 82 and FIP emblems. Value, $22.

Stamp Day — A843

Engraved and Photogravure

1981, Dec. 18 *Perf. 11½x12*
2391 A843 1k Engraver Edward Karel .25 .20

Russian Workers' Party, Prague Congress, 70th Anniv. — A844

1982, Jan. 18 *Perf. 12*
2392 A844 2k Lenin .50 .20
a. Sheet of 4 *5.00 4.00*

No. 2392 issued in sheet of 8. Value $5.

1982 World Cup Soccer A845

Designs: Various soccer players.

1982, Jan. 29 *Perf. 12x11½*
2393 A845 1k multi .25 .20
2394 A845 3.60k multi .70 .30
2395 A845 4k multi 1.40 .50
Nos. 2393-2395 (3) 2.35 1.00

10th World Trade Union Congress, Havana — A846

Arms of Hrob — A847

1982, Feb. 10 *Perf. 11½*
2396 A846 1k multi .25 .20

1982, Feb. 10 *Perf. 12x11½*

Arms of various cities.

2397 A847 50h shown .20 .20
2398 A847 50h Nove Mesto Nad Metuji .20 .20
2399 A847 50h Trencin .20 .20
2400 A847 50h Mlada Boleslav .20 .20
Nos. 2397-2400 (4) .80 .80

See Nos. 2499-2502, 2542-2544, 2595-2597, 2783-2786.

50th Anniv. of the Great Strike at Most — A848

1982, Mar. 23 *Perf. 11½*
2401 A848 1k multi .25 .20

60th Intl. Railway Union Congress — A849

1982, Mar. 23 *Perf. 12x11½*
2402 A849 6k Steam locomotive, 1922, electric, 1982 2.50 .75

10th Workers' Congress, Prague A850

George Dimitrov A851

1982, Apr. 15
2403 A850 1k multi .25 .20

1982, May 1
2404 A851 50h multi .20 .20

A852

10th Lidice Intl. Children's Drawing Contest — A853

Engravings: 40h, The Muse Euterpe Playing a Flute, by Crispin de Passe (1565-1637). 50h, The Lute Player, by Jacob de Gheyn (1565-1629). 1k, Woman Flautist, by Adriaen Collaert (1560-1618). 2k, Musicians in a Hostel, by Rembrandt (1606-1669). 3k, Hurdy-gurdy Player, by Jacques Callot (1594-1635).

1982, May 18 *Perf. 11½x12*

2405 A852 40h multi .20 .20
2406 A852 50h multi .20 .20
2407 A852 1k multi .20 .20
2408 A852 2k multi .30 .20
2409 A852 3k multi 1.10 .60
Nos. 2405-2409 (5) 2.00 1.40

1982, May 18

2410 A853 2k multi 1.25 1.00

Issued in sheets of 6. Value $10.

40th Anniv. of Destruction of Lidice and Lezaky — A854

1982, June 4 *Perf. 11½*

2411 A854 1k Girl, rose .45 .20
2412 A854 1k Hands, barbed wire .45 .20

Souvenir Sheet

UN Disarmament Conference — A855

1982, June 4 *Perf. 12*

2413 Sheet of 2 12.00 8.00
a. A855 6k Woman holding doves 5.00 3.50

Souvenir Sheet

2nd UN Conference on Peaceful Uses of Outer Space, Vienna, Aug. 9-21 — A856

1982, Aug. 9 **Engr. & Photo.**

2414 Sheet of 2 12.00 9.00
a. A856 5k multi 5.00 3.50

Krivoklat Castle A857

1982, Aug. 31 *Perf. 12x11½*

2415 A857 50h shown .25 .20
2416 A857 1k Statues (Krivoklat) .25 .20
2417 A857 2k Nitra Castle .30 .20
2418 A857 3k Pottery, lock (Nitra) .40 .35
a. Souv. sheet of 4, #2415-2418 1.60 1.25
Nos. 2415-2418 (4) 1.20 .95

50th Anniv. of Zizkov Hill Natl. Monument — A858

1982, Sept. 16

2419 A858 1k multi .25 .20

Prague Castle Art Type of 1971

Designs: 3k, St. George and the Dragon, 1373. 4k, Tomb of King Vratislav I, 10th cent.

1982, Sept. 28 *Perf. 12*

2420 A634 3k multi 1.40 1.00
2421 A634 4k multi .75 .75

Nos. 2420-2421 were each issued in sheets of 4. Value, set $13.

Bratislava Type of 1977

Designs: 3k, Paddle steamer, Parnik, 1818. 4k, View from Bridge, 19th cent.

1982, Sept. 29

2422 A760 3k multi 1.40 1.00
2423 A760 4k multi 1.10 1.00

Nos. 2422-2423 were each issued in sheets of 4. Value, set $18.

European Danube Commission — A859

1982, Sept. 29 *Perf. 11½x12*

2424 A859 3k Steamer, Bratislava Bridge .75 .35
a. Souvenir sheet of 4 5.00 4.00
2425 A859 3.60k Ferry, Budapest .95 .50
a. Souvenir sheet of 4 7.00 6.00

16th Communist Party Congress — A860

1982, Oct. 28 *Perf. 12x11½*

2426 A860 20h Agriculture .20 .20
2427 A860 1k Industry .20 .20
2428 A860 3k Engineering .35 .35
Nos. 2426-2428 (3) .75 .75

30th Anniv. of Academy of Sciences — A861

1982, Oct. 29 *Perf. 11½*

2429 A861 6k Emblem .90 .35

65th Anniv. of October Revolution — A862

Design: 1k, 60th anniv. of USSR.

1982, Nov. 7 *Perf. 12x11½*

2430 A862 50h multi .20 .20
2431 A862 1k multi .25 .20

Jaroslav Hasek, Writer, Sculpture by Josef Malejovsky — A863

Sculptures: 2k, Jan Zrzavy, freedom fighter, by Jan Simota. 4.40k, Leos Janacek, composer, by Milos Axman. 6k, Martin Kukucin, freedom fighter, by Jan Kulich. 7k, Peaceful Work, by Rudolf Pribis.

Engraved and Photogravure

1982, Nov. 26 *Perf. 11½x12*

2432 A863 1k multi .20 .20
2433 A863 2k multi .25 .20
2434 A863 4.40k multi .85 .20
2435 A863 6k multi 1.20 .30
2436 A863 7k multi 1.50 .75
Nos. 2432-2436 (5) 4.00 1.65

Nos. 2432-2436 were each issued in sheets of 4. Value, set $30.

Art Type of 1967

1k, Revolution in Spain, by Josef Sima (1891-1971). 2k, Woman Dressing, by Rudolf Kremlicka (1886-1932). 3k, The Girl Bride, by Dezider Milly (1906-1971). 4k, Performers, by Jan Zelibsky (b. 1907). 5k, The Complaint of the Birds, by Emil Filla (1882-1953).

1982, Nov. 27 *Perf. 12*

2437 A565 1k multi .70 .40
2438 A565 2k multi 1.40 1.10
2439 A565 3k multi .75 .75
2440 A565 4k multi .75 .75
2441 A565 5k multi 1.40 1.10
Nos. 2437-2441 (5) 5.00 4.10

Stamp Day — A864

1982, Dec. 8 *Perf. 11½*

2442 A864 1k Engraver Jaroslav Goldschmied (1890-1977) .25 .20

A865

A866

1983, Jan. 10 **Engr.** *Perf. 12x11½*

2443 A865 50h dark blue .20 .20

Pres. Gustav Husak, 70th birthday. See No. 2686.

1983, Feb. 24 **Engr. & Photo.**

Designs: 50h, Jaroslav Hasek (1882-1923), writer. 1k, Julius Fucik (1903-1943), antifascist martyr. 2k, Martin Luther (1483-1546). 5k, Johannes Brahms (1833-1897), composer.

2444 A866 50h multi .20 .20
2445 A866 1k multi .20 .20
2446 A866 2k multi .25 .20
a. Souvenir sheet of 4 20.00 10.00
2447 A866 5k multi .85 .20
Nos. 2444-2447 (4) 1.50 .80

Nordposta '83 Intl. Stamp Exhibition, Hamburg.
No. 2446a issued Nov. 1.

Workers Marching A867

Family — A868

1983, Feb. 25 *Perf. 11½*

2448 A867 50h multi .20 .20
2449 A868 1k multi .25 .20

35th anniv. of "Victorious February" (50h), and Natl. Front (1k).

World Communications Year — A869

Perf. 11½, 12x11½ (2k)

1983, Mar. 16

2450 A869 40h multi .20 .20
2451 A869 1k multi .20 .20
2452 A869 2k multi .30 .20
2453 A869 3.60k multi .60 .20
Nos. 2450-2453 (4) 1.30 .80

Various wave patterns. 2k, 40x23mm; 3.60k, 49x19mm.

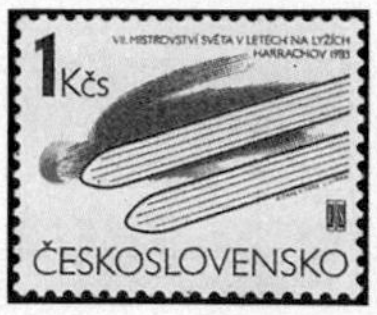

7th World Ski-jumping Championships A870

1983, Mar. 16 *Perf. 11½*

2454 A870 1k multi .25 .20

Souvenir Sheet

5th Anniv. of Czechoslovak-USSR Intercosmos Cooperative Space Program — A871

1983, Apr. 12 *Perf. 12*

2455 Sheet of 2 11.00 6.00
a. A871 10k multi 4.75 2.50

See No. 2226.

Protected Species — A872

1983, Apr. 28 *Perf. 12x11½*

2456 A872 50h Butterfly, violets .30 .20
2457 A872 1k Water lilies, frog .65 .20
2458 A872 2k Pine cones, crossbill .65 .30
2459 A872 3.60k Herons .80 .35
2460 A872 5k Gentians, lynx 1.10 .45
2461 A872 7k Stag 2.50 1.00
Nos. 2456-2461 (6) 6.00 2.50

A873

A874

Soviet Marshals.

1983, May 5 *Perf. 11½*

2462 A873 50h Ivan S. Konev .20 .20
2463 A873 1k Andrei I. Sheremenko .20 .20
2464 A873 2k Rodion J. Malinovsky .25 .20
Nos. 2462-2464 (3) .65 .60

30th anniv. of Czechoslovak-Soviet defense treaty.

1983, July 13 *Perf. 12*
2465 A874 2k multi .40 .25
a. Souvenir sheet of 4 6.00 5.00

World Peace and Life Congress, Prague. No. 2465 issued in sheets of 8. Value $10.

Emperor Rudolf II by Adrian De Vries (1560-1626) A875

Art treasures of the Prague Castle: 5k, Kinetic relief, Timepiece, Rudolf Svoboda.

1983, Aug. 25 *Perf. 11½*
2466 A875 4k multi .90 .60
2467 A875 5k multi .90 .60

Nos. 2466-2467 were each issued in sheets of 6. Value, set $15.

See Nos. 2518-2519, 2610-2611, 2654-2655, 2717-2718, 2744-2745, 2792-2793.

9th Biennial of Illustrations for Children and Youth — A876

Illustrators: 50h, Oleg K. Zotov, USSR. 1k, Zbigniew Rychlicki, Poland. 4k, Lisbeth Zwerger, Austria. 7k, Antonio Dominques, Angola.

1983, Sept. 9 **Engr. & Photo.**
2468 A876 50h multi .20 .20
2469 A876 1k multi .20 .20
2470 A876 4k multi .35 .20
2471 A876 7k multi .75 .30
a. Souv. sheet of 4, #2468-2471 5.00 3.00
Nos. 2468-2471 (4) 1.50 .90

World Communications Year — A877

Emblems and aircraft.

1983, Sept. 30 *Perf. 11½*
2472 A877 50h red & black .20 .20
2473 A877 1k red & black, vert. .20 .20
2474 A877 4k red & black .75 .25
Nos. 2472-2474 (3) 1.15 .65

60th anniv. of the Czechoslovak Airlines.

16th Party Congress Achievements — A878

1983, Oct. 20 *Perf. 12x11½*
2475 A878 50h Civil engineering construction .20 .20
2476 A878 1k Chemical industry .20 .20
2477 A878 3k Health services .40 .20
Nos. 2475-2477 (3) .80 .60

Bratislava Type of 1977

Designs: 3k, Two sculptures, Viktor Tilgner (1844-96). 4k, Mirbachov Palace, 1939, by Julius Schubert (1888-1947).

1983, Oct. 28 *Perf. 12*
2478 A760 3k multi 1.25 1.00
2479 A760 4k multi 1.00 .80

Nos. 2478-2479 were each issued in sheets of 4 stamps. Value, set $16.

Natl. Theater, Prague, Centenary — A879

1983, Nov. 8 **Engr.** *Perf. 11½*
2480 A879 50h Natl. Theater building .20 .20
2481 A879 2k State Theater, Natl. Theater .30 .20

Messenger of Mourning, by Mikolas Ales — A880

Designs: 2k, Genius, theater curtain by Vojtech Hynais (1854-1925). 3k, Music, Lyric drawings by Frantisek Zenisek (1849-1916). 4k, Symbolic figure of Prague, by Vaclay Brozik (1851-1901). 5k, Hradcany Castle, by Julius Marak (1832-1899).

1983, Nov. 18 **Engr.**
2482 A880 1k multi 1.20 .75
2483 A880 2k multi 1.50 1.10
2484 A880 3k multi .90 .45
2485 A880 4k multi 1.40 .45
2486 A880 5k multi 1.10 .60
Nos. 2482-2486 (5) 6.10 3.35

Nos. 2482-2486 were each issued in sheets of 4 stamps. Value, set $35.

Warrior with Sword and Shield, Engraving, 17th Cent. — A881

Engravings of Costumes: 50h, Bodyguard of Rudolf II, by Jacob de Gheyn (1565-1629). 1k, Lady with Lace Collar, by Jacques Callot (1592-1635). 4k, Lady, by Vaclav Hollar (1607-77). 5k, Man, by Antoine Watteau (1684-1721).

Engraved and Photogravure

1983, Dec. 2 *Perf. 11½x12*
2487 A881 40h multi .20 .20
2488 A881 50h multi .20 .20
2489 A881 1k multi .20 .20
2490 A881 4k multi .75 .20
2491 A881 5k multi 1.25 .75
Nos. 2487-2491 (5) 2.60 1.55

Stamp Day — A882

1983, Dec. 18
2492 A882 1k Karl Seizinger (1889-1978), #114 .25 .20

Czechoslovak Federation, 15th Anniv. — A883

1984, Jan. 1 *Perf. 11½*
2493 A883 50h Bratislava, Prague Castles .20 .20

35th Anniv. of COMECON A884

1984, Jan. 23
2494 A884 1k Headquarters, Moscow .25 .20

1984 Winter Olympics A885

1984, Feb. 7 *Perf. 12x11½*
2495 A885 2k Cross-country skiing .30 .20
2496 A885 3k Hockey .35 .20
a. Souvenir sheet of 4 3.75 3.00
2497 A885 5k Biathlon 1.00 .35
Nos. 2495-2497 (3) 1.65 .75

Intl. Olympic Committee, 90th Anniv. — A886

1984, Feb. 7 *Perf. 11½x12*
2498 A886 7k Rings, runners, torch 1.25 .35

City Arms Type of 1982

1984, Mar. 1 *Perf. 12x11½*
2499 A847 50h Kutna Hora .20 .20
2500 A847 50h Turnov .20 .20
2501 A847 1k Martin .25 .20
2502 A847 1k Milevsko .25 .20
Nos. 2499-2502 (4) .90 .80

Intercosmos Space Program — A887

Various satellites. Nos. 2503-2507 se-tenant with labels showing flags.

1984, Apr. 12 *Perf. 11½x12*
2503 A887 50h multi .20 .20
2504 A887 1k multi .20 .20
2505 A887 2k multi .35 .20
2506 A887 4k multi .75 .40
2507 A887 5k multi 1.40 .50
Nos. 2503-2507 (5) 2.90 1.50

Resistance Heroes — A888

Designs: 50h, Vendelin Opatrny (1908-44). 1k, Ladislav Novomesky (1904-44). 2k, Rudolf Jasiok (1919-44). 4k, Jan Nalepka (1912-43).

1984, May 9 *Perf. 11x11½*
2508 A888 50h multi .20 .20
2509 A888 1k multi .20 .20
2510 A888 2k multi .30 .20
2511 A888 4k multi .50 .20
Nos. 2508-2511 (4) 1.20 .80

Music Year — A889

1984, May 11 *Perf. 11½*
2512 A889 50h Instruments .20 .20
2513 A889 1k Organ pipes, vert. .30 .20

Bratislava Type of 1977

Designs: 3k, Vintners' Guild arms, 19th cent. 4k, View of Bratislava (painting commemorating shooting competition, 1827).

1984, June 1 *Perf. 12*
2514 A760 3k multi 1.00 .75
2515 A760 4k multi 1.50 1.00

Nos. 2514-2515 were each issued in sheets of 4 stamps. Value, set $15.

Central Telecommunications Building, Bratislava — A890

1984, June 1 *Perf. 11½*
2516 A890 2k multi .35 .20

A891

A893

1984, June 12 *Perf. 12*
2517 A891 5k UPU emblem, dove, globe 2.50 2.00

1984 UPU Congress. Issued in sheet of 4 with and without Philatelic Salon text. Values, $40 with text, $12 without text.

Prague Castle Type of 1983

Designs: 3k, Crowing rooster, St. Vitus Cathedral, 19th cent. 4k, King David from the Roundnice, Book of Psalms illuminated manuscript, Bohemia, 15th cent.

1984, Aug. 9 **Engr. & Photo.**
2518 A875 3k multi .65 .40
2519 A875 4k multi .90 .65

Nos. 2518-2519 were each issued in sheets of 6 stamps. Value, set $18.

1984, Aug. 28 *Perf. 11½x12*

Playing cards.

2520 A893 50h Jack of Spades, 16th cent. .20 .20
2521 A893 1k Queen of spades, 17th cent. .20 .20
2522 A893 2k 9 of hearts, 18th cent. .25 .20
2523 A893 3k Jack of clubs, 18th cent. .35 .20
2524 A893 5k King of hearts, 19th cent. 1.00 .20
Nos. 2520-2524 (5) 2.00 1.00

Slovak Natl. Uprising, 40th Anniv. A894

1984, Aug. 29 *Perf. 12x11½*
2525 A894 50h Family, factories, flowers .20 .20

Battle of Dukla Pass (Carpathians), 40th Anniv. — A895

1984, Sept. 8 *Perf. 11½x12*
2526 A895 2k Soldiers, flag .40 .20

1984 Summer Olympics A896

1984, Sept. 9 *Perf. 12x11½*
2527 A896 1k Pole vault .20 .20
2528 A896 2k Bicycling .40 .20
2529 A896 3k Rowing .60 .35
2530 A896 5k Weight lifting 1.00 .45
a. Souv. sheet of 4, #2527-2530 3.00 2.00
Nos. 2527-2530 (4) 2.20 1.20

16th Party Congress Goals and Projects — A897

1984, Oct. 28 *Perf. 12x11½*
2531 A897 1k Communications .20 .20
2532 A897 2k Transportation .25 .20
2533 A897 3k Transgas pipeline .35 .25
a. Souvenir sheet of 3 1.50 1.00
Nos. 2531-2533 (3) .80 .65

Art Type of 1967

1k, The Milevsky River, by Karel Stehlik (b. 1912). 2k, Under the Trees, by Viktor Barvitius (1834-1902). 3k, Landscape with Flowers, by Zolo Palugyay (1898-1935). 4k, King in Palace, Visehrad Codex miniature, 1085. 5k, View of Kokorin Castles, by Antonin Manes. #2534-2537 horiz.; issued in sheets of 4.

1984, Nov. 16 *Perf. 11½*
2534 A565 1k multi 2.50 .75
2535 A565 2k multi 2.50 .75
2536 A565 3k multi 1.80 .45
2537 A565 4k multi 2.50 .60
2538 A565 5k multi 2.50 .60
Nos. 2534-2538 (5) 11.80 3.15

Nos. 2534-2538 were each issued in sheets of 4 stamps. Value, set $60.

Students' Intl., 45th Anniv. A898

Birth Cent., Antonin Zapotocky A899

1984, Nov. 17
2539 A898 1k Head, dove .25 .20

Engr. & Photo.

1984, Dec. 18 *Perf. 11½*
2540 A899 50h multi .25 .20

Stamp Day — A900

1984, Dec. 18 *Perf. 11½x12*
2541 A900 1k Engraver Bohumil Heinz (1894-1940) .25 .20

City Arms Type of 1982

1985, Feb. 5 *Perf. 12x11½*
2542 A847 50h Kamyk nad Vltavou .20 .20
2543 A847 50h Havirov .20 .20
2544 A847 50h Trnava .20 .20
Nos. 2542-2544 (3) .60 .60

University of Applied Arts, Prague, Centenary — A901

1985, Feb. 6 *Perf. 11½x12*
2545 A901 3k Art and Pleasure, sculpture .40 .20

Trnava University, 350th Anniv. — A902

1985, Feb. 6 *Perf. 11½x12*
2546 A902 2k Town of Trnava .40 .20

Military Museum Exposition — A903

1985, Feb. 7 *Perf. 11½x12, 12x11½*
2547 A903 50h Armor, crossbow, vert. .20 .20
2548 A903 1k Medals, vert. .20 .20
2549 A903 2k Biplane, spacecraft .40 .20
Nos. 2547-2549 (3) .80 .60

Vladimir I. Lenin (1870-1924), 1st Chairman of Russia — A904

1985, Mar. 15 **Engr.** *Perf. 12*
2550 A904 2k multi .60 .30

No. 2550 printed in sheets of 6 stamps. Value $5.

UN 40th Anniv., Peace Year 1986 A905

1985, Mar. 15
2551 A905 6k UN, Peace Year emblems 2.25 1.75

Issued in sheets of 4 stamps. Value $12.

A906

A907

Engraved and Photogravure

1985, Apr. 5 *Perf. 11½*
2552 A906 4k Natl. arms, twig, crowd .60 .20

Kosice govt. plan, Apr. 5, 1945.

1985, Apr. 5
2553 A907 50h Natl. arms, flag, soldiers .20 .20

Natl. Security Forces, 40th anniv.

Halley's Comet, INTERCOSMOS Project Vega — A908

Design: Emblem, space platform, interstellar map, intercept data.

1985, Apr. 12 *Perf. 12x11½*
2554 Sheet of 2 12.00 8.00
a. A908 5k multicolored 3.50 2.25

Project Vega, a joint effort of the USSR, France, German Democratic Republic, Austria, Poland, Bulgaria and CSSR, was for the geophysical study of Halley's Comet, Dec. 1984-Mar. 1986.

European Ice Hockey Championships, Prague, Apr. 17-May 3 — A909

1985, Apr. 13
2555 A909 1k Hockey players, emblem .25 .20

No. 2555 Ovptd. "CSSR MISTREM SVETA" in Violet Blue

1985, May 31 *Perf. 12x11½*
2556 A909 1k multi 2.50 2.50

Natl. Chess Org., 80th Anniv. — A910

1985, Apr. 13 *Perf. 11½*
2557 A910 6k Emblem, game board, chessmen .90 .50

Anniversaries — A911

1985, May 5 *Perf. 11½x12*
2558 A911 1k May Uprising, 1945 .20 .20
2559 A911 1k Soviet Army in CSSR, 1945 .20 .20
2560 A911 1k Warsaw Treaty, 1950 .20 .20
2561 A911 1k Czech-Soviet Treaty, 1970 .20 .20
Nos. 2558-2561 (4) .80 .80

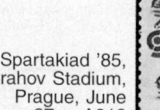

Spartakiad '85, Strahov Stadium, Prague, June 27 — A912

Designs: 50h, Gymnasts warming up with rackets and balls. 1k, Rhythmic gymnastics floor exercise, Prague Castle.

1985, June 3 *Perf. 11½, 11½x12*
2562 A912 50h multi .20 .20

Size: 53x22mm

2563 A912 1k multi .20 .20

WWII Anti-Fascist Political Art — A913

Drawings and caricatures: 50h, Fire, and From the Concentration Camp, by Joseph Capek (1887-1945). 2k, The Conference on Disarmament in Geneva, 1927 and The Prophecy of Three Parrots, 1933, by Frantisek Bidlo (1895-1945). 4k, The Unknown Warrior to Order, 1936, and The Almost Peaceful Dove, 1937, by Antonin Pelc (1895-1967).

1985, June 4 *Perf. 12x11½*
2564 A913 50h multi .20 .20
2565 A913 2k multi .30 .20
2566 A913 4k multi .60 .40
Nos. 2564-2566 (3) 1.10 .80

Helsinki Conference on European Security and Cooperation, 10th Anniv. — A914

1985, July 1 **Engr. & Photo.**
2567 A914 7k multi 2.25 1.50
a. Souvenir sheet of 4 12.00 8.00

An imperf. souv. sheet similar to No. 2567a was issued June 1, 1988 for FINLANDIA '88 and PRAGA '88. Value $40.

12th World Youth Festival, Moscow A915

1985, July 2
2568 A915 1k Kremlin, youths .20 .20

A916

A918

1985, Sept. 3 *Perf. 11½*
2569 A916 50h multi .20 .20

Federation of World Trade Unions, 40th anniv.

Bratislava Type of 1977

Designs: 3k, Castle and river, lace embroidery by Elena Holeczyova (1906-1983). 4k, Pottery cups and mugs, 1600-1500 B.C.

1985, Sept. 4 Engr. *Perf. 12*

2570 A760 3k multi 1.40 .45
2571 A760 4k multi 2.10 .60

Nos. 2570-2571 were each issued in sheets of 4 stamps. Value, set $15.

Engraved and Photogravure

1985, Sept. 5 *Perf. 11½*

Children's book illustrations: 1k, Rocking Horse, by Kveta Pacovska, USSR. 2k, Fairies, by Gennadij Spirin, USSR. 3k, Butterfly and Girl, by Kaarina Kaila, Finland. 4k, Boy and Animals, by Erick Ingraham, US.

2572 A918 1k multi .20 .20
2573 A918 2k multi .30 .20
2574 A918 3k multi .45 .25
2575 A918 4k multi .60 .35
a. Souv. sheet of 4, #2572-2575 4.00 3.00
Nos. 2572-2575 (4) 1.55 1.00

10th biennial of illustrations.

5-Year Development Plan — A919

1985, Oct. 28 *Perf. 12x11½*

2576 A919 50h Construction machinery .20 .20
2577 A919 1k Prague subway, map .20 .20
2578 A919 2k Modern textile spinning .20 .20
Nos. 2576-2578 (3) .60 .60

16th Communist Party Congress goals.

Prague Castle — A920

A921

Engr., Engr. & Photo. (3k)

1985, Oct. 28 *Perf. 12*

2579 A920 2k Presidential Palace Gate, 1768 .40 .40
2580 A920 3k St. Vitus' Cathedral .50 .50

Nos. 2579-2580 were each issued in sheets of 6 stamps. Value, set $9.

Engraved and Photogravure

1985, Nov. 23 *Perf. 11½x12*

Glassware: 50h, Pitcher, Near East, 4th cent. 1k, Venetian pitcher, 16th cent. 2k, Bohemian goblet, c. 1720. 4k, Harrachov Bohemian vase, 18th cent. 6k, Jablonec Bohemian vase, c. 1900.

2581 A921 50h multi .20 .20
2582 A921 1k multi .20 .20
2583 A921 2k multi .25 .20
2584 A921 4k multi .40 .20
2585 A921 6k multi .70 .35
Nos. 2581-2585 (5) 1.75 1.15

Arts and Crafts Museum, Prague, cent.

Art Type of 1967

Designs: 1k, Young Woman in a Blue Gown, by Jozef Ginovsky (1800-1857). 2k, Lenin on the Charles Bridge, Prague, 1952, by Martin Sladky (b. 1920). 3k, Avenue of Poplars, 1935, by Vaclav Rabas (1885-1954). 4k, The Martyrom of St. Dorothea, 1516, by Hans Baldung Grien (c. 1484-1545). 5k, Portrait of Jasper Schade van Westrum, 1645, by Frans Hals (c. 1581-1666).

1985, Nov. 27 Engr. *Perf. 12*

2586 A565 1k multi 1.60 .80
2587 A565 2k multi 1.10 .35
2588 A565 3k multi 1.50 .35
2589 A565 4k multi .90 .50
2590 A565 5k multi .90 .50
Nos. 2586-2590 (5) 6.00 2.50

Nos. 2586-2590 were each issued in sheets of 4 stamps. Value, set $30.

Bohdan Roule (1921-1960), Engraver — A922

Engraved and Photogravure

1985, Dec. 18 *Perf. 11½x12*

2591 A922 1k multicolored .25 .20

Stamp Day 1985.

Intl. Peace Year — A923

1986, Jan. 2

2592 A923 1k multi .25 .20

Philharmonic Orchestra, 90th Anniv. — A924

EXPO '86, Vancouver A925

1986, Jan. 2 *Perf. 11½*

2593 A924 1k Victory Statue, Prague .25 .20

1986, Jan. 23 *Perf. 11½*

Design: Z 50 LS monoplane, Cenyerth Prague-Kladno locomotive, Sahara Desert rock drawing, 5th-6th cent. B.C.

2594 A925 4k multicolored .75 .20

City Arms Type of 1982

1986, Feb. 10 *Perf. 12x11½*

Size: 42x54mm

2595 A847 50h Myjava .20 .20
2596 A847 50h Vodnany .20 .20
2597 A847 50h Zamberk .20 .20
Nos. 2595-2597 (3) .60 .60

17th Natl. Communist Party Congress, Prague, Mar. 24 — A926

1986, Mar. 20 *Perf. 11½*

2598 A926 50h shown .20 .20
2599 A926 1k Industry .20 .20

Natl. Communist Party, 65th Anniv. — A927

1986, Mar. 20 *Perf. 12x11½*

2600 A927 50h Star, man, woman .20 .20
2601 A927 1k Hammer, sickle, laborers .20 .20

Natl. Front Election Program A928

1986, Mar. 28

2602 A928 50h multi .20 .20

Karlovy Vary Intl. Film Festival, 25th Anniv. — A929

1986, Apr. 3 *Perf. 11½*

2603 A929 1k multi .25 .20

A930

A931

1986, Apr. 8 Engr. & Photo.

2604 A930 1k multi .25 .20

Spring of Prague Music Festival.

1986, Apr. 25

2605 A931 50h multi .40 .20

Prague-Moscow air service, 50th anniv.

Intl. Olympic Committee, 90th Anniv. — A932

1986, May 12 *Perf. 11½x12*

2606 A932 2k multi .30 .20

1986 World Cup Soccer Championships, Mexico — A933

1986, May 15 *Perf. 12x11½*

2607 A933 4k multi .60 .40

Women's World Volleyball Championships, Prague — A934

1986, May 19

2608 A934 1k multi .25 .20

Souvenir Sheet

Intl. Philatelic Federation, FIP, 60th Anniv. — A935

1986, June 3 Engr. *Perf. 12*

2609 A935 20k multi 6.00 5.00

Exists imperf and with perforations between stamps omitted. Values, $12 and $25, respectively.

Prague Castle Type of 1983

Designs: 2k, Jewelled funerary pendant, 9th cent. 3k, Allegory of Blossoms, sculpture by Jaroslav Horejc (1886-1983), St. Vitus' Cathedral.

1986, June 6 Engr. *Perf. 12*

2610 A875 2k multi .30 .30
2611 A875 3k multi .70 .45

Nos. 2610-2611 were each issued in sheets of 6 stamps. Value, set $10.

UN Child Survival Campaign — A937

Toys.

Engraved and Photogravure

1986, Sept. 1 *Perf. 11½*

2612 A937 10h Rooster .20 .20
2613 A937 20h Horse and rider .20 .20
2614 A937 1k Doll .25 .20
2615 A937 2k Doll, diff. .50 .20
2616 A937 3k Tin omnibus, c. 1910 .65 .30
Nos. 2612-2616 (5) 1.80 1.10

UNICEF, 40th anniv.

Registration, Cent. — A938

1986, Sept. 2 *Perf. 11½x12*

2617 A938 4k Label, mail coach .45 .20

Bratislava Type of 1977

1986, Sept. 11 Engr. *Perf. 12*

2618 A760 3k Sigismund Gate 1.00 .60
2619 A760 4k St. Margaret, bas-relief 1.00 .50

Nos. 2618-2619 were each issued in sheets of 4 stamps. Value, set $12.

Owls — A939

Engraved and Photogravure

1986, Sept. 18 *Perf. 11½*

2620 A939 50h Bubo bubo .70 .20
2621 A939 2k Asio otus .85 .30
2622 A939 3k Strix aluco 1.40 .30
2623 A939 4k Tyto alba 1.40 .40
2624 A939 5k Asio flammeus 2.00 6.00
Nos. 2620-2624 (5) 6.35 7.20

Souvenir Sheet

Intl. Brigades in Spain — A940

Theater curtain: Woman Savaged by Horses, 1936, by Vladimir Sychra (1903-1963), Natl Gallery, Prague.

1986, Oct. 1 **Engr.** *Perf. 12*

2625 Sheet of 2 4.50 3.50
a. A940 5k multi 2.00 1.25

Locomotives and Streetcars — A941

Engraved and Photogravure

1986, Oct. 6 *Perf. 12x11½*

2626 A941 50h KT-8 .20 .20
2627 A941 1k E458.1 .20 .20
2628 A941 3k T466.2 .75 .30
2629 A941 5k M152.0 .80 .20
Nos. 2626-2629 (4) 1.95 .90

Paintings in the Prague and Bratislava Natl. Galleries — A942

Designs: 1k, The Circus Rider, 1980, by Jan Bauch (b. 1898). 2k, The Ventriloquist, 1954, by Frantisek Tichy (1896-1961). 3k, In the Circus, 1946, by Vincent Hloznik (b. 1919). 6k, Clown, 1985, by Karel Svolinsky (1896-1986).

1986, Oct. 13 **Engr.** *Perf. 12*

2630 A942 1k multi 1.00 .50
2631 A942 2k multi 1.25 .65
2632 A942 3k multi 1.25 .65
2633 A942 6k multi 1.50 .75
Nos. 2630-2633 (4) 5.00 2.55

Nos. 2630-2633 were each issued in sheets of 4 stamps. Value, set $30.

Art Type of 1967

1k, The Czech Lion, May 1918, by Vratislav H. Brunner (1886-1928). 2k, Boy with Mandolin, 1945, by Jozef Sturdik (b. 1920). 3k, Metra Building, 1984, by Frantisek Gross (1909-1985). 4k, Portrait of Maria Maximiliana at Sternberk, 1665, by Karel Skreta (1610-1674). 5k, Adam & Eve, 1538, by Lucas Cranach (1472-1553).

1986, Nov. 3 **Engr.** *Perf. 12*

2634 A565 1k multi 3.00 2.25
2635 A565 2k multi 3.00 2.25
2636 A565 3k multi 3.00 2.25
2637 A565 4k multi 3.00 2.25
2638 A565 5k multi 3.00 2.25
Nos. 2634-2638 (5) 15.00 11.25

Nos. 2634-2638 were each issued in sheets of 4 stamps. Value, set $100.

Stamp Day — A943

Design: V.H. Brunner (1886-1928), stamp designer, and No. 88.

Photo. & Engr.

1986, Dec. 18 *Perf. 11½x12*

2639 A943 1k multicolored .25 .20

World Cyclocross Championships, Jan. 24-25, Central Bohemia — A944

1987, Jan. 22 *Perf. 11½*

2640 A944 6k multi .80 .20

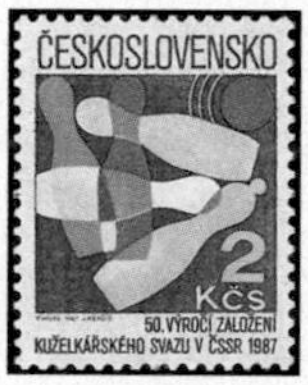

Czechoslovakian Bowling Union, 50th Anniv. — A945

1987, Jan. 22 *Perf. 11½*

2641 A945 2k multi .35 .20

State Decorations — A946

Designs: 50h, Gold Stars of Socialist Labor and Czechoslovakia. 2k, Order of Klement Gottwald. 3k, Order of the Republic. 4k, Order of Victorious February. 5k, Order of Labor.

1987, Feb. 4 *Perf. 12x11½*

2642 A946 50h multi .20 .20
2643 A946 2k multi .25 .20
2644 A946 3k multi .30 .20
2645 A946 4k multi .45 .20
2646 A946 5k multi .60 .40
Nos. 2642-2646 (5) 1.80 1.20

Butterflies — A947

1987, Mar. 4

2647 A947 1k Limenitis populi .70 .20
2648 A947 2k Smerinthus ocellatus 1.10 .25
2649 A947 3k Pericallia matronula 1.40 .40
2650 A947 4k Saturnia pyri 1.40 .40
Nos. 2647-2650 (4) 4.60 1.25

Natl. Nuclear Power Industry A948

1987, Apr. 6

2651 A948 5k multi .50 .20

11th Revolutionary Trade Union Movement Congress, Apr. 14-17, Prague — A949

1987, Apr. 7 *Perf. 11½*

2652 A949 1k multi .20 .20

Souvenir Sheet

INTERCOSMOS, 20th Anniv. — A950

Cosmonauts Alexei Gubarev of the USSR & Vladimir Remek of Czechoslovakia, rocket & emblem.

1987, Apr. 12 **Engr.** *Perf. 12*

2653 Sheet of 2 6.00 4.50
a. A950 10k multi 2.50 2.00
b. Souv. sheet of 4, litho. & engr., imperf. 8.00 8.00

No. 2653b issued Nov. 15, 1987.

Prague Castle Art Treasures Type of 1983

Designs: 2k, Three Saints, stained-glass window detail, c. 1870, St. Vitus Cathedral, by Frantisek Sequens (1830-1896). 3k, Coat of Arms, New Land Rolls Hall, 1605.

1987, May 9 *Perf. 11½*

2654 A875 2k multi .40 .30
2655 A875 3k dk red, slate gray & yel org .60 .45

Nos. 2634-2638 were each issued in sheets of 6 stamps. Value, set $9.

PRAGA '88 A951

Photo. & Engr.

1987, May 12 *Perf. 12x11½*

2656 A951 3k Telephone, 1894 .75 .20
2657 A951 3k Postal van, 1924 .75 .30
2658 A951 4k Locomotive tender, 1907 .75 .30
2659 A951 4k Tram, 1900 .75 .30
2660 A951 5k Steam roller, 1936 .75 .30
Nos. 2656-2660 (5) 3.75 1.40

Printed in sheets of 8 + 2 labels picturing telephone or vehicles. Value $40.

Nos. 2657-2658 were also printed in sheets of 4 + label picturing vehicles. Value, $30 for both sheets.

Destruction of Lidice and Lezaky, 45th Anniv. — A952

Drawings: No. 2661, When the Fighting Ended, 1945, by Pavel Simon. No. 2662, The End of the game, 1945, by Ludmila Jirincova.

1987, June *Perf. 11½*

2661 A952 1k blk, cerise & vio .20 .20
2662 A952 1k blk, gold, pale lil & cerise .20 .20

Union of Czechoslovakian Mathematicians and Physicists, 125th Anniv. — A953

Designs: No. 2663, Prague Town Hall mathematical clock, Theory of Functions diagram. No. 2664, J.M. Petzval (1807-1891), J. Strouhal (1850-1922) and V. Jarnik (1897-1970). No. 2665, Geographical measurement from A.M. Malletta's book, 1672, earth fold and Brownian motion diagrams.

1987, July 6 *Perf. 11½x12*

2663 A953 50h multi .20 .20
2664 A953 50h multi .20 .20
2665 A953 50h multi .20 .20
Nos. 2663-2665 (3) .60 .60

A954

A955

Award-winning illustrations.

1987, Sept. 3 *Perf. 11½*

2666 A954 50h Asun Balzola, Spain .20 .20
2667 A954 1k Frederic Clement, France .20 .20
2668 A954 2k Elzbieta Gaudasinska, Poland .40 .25
a. Souv. sheet of 2 + label 2.50 1.75
2669 A954 4k Marija Lucija Stupica, Yugoslavia .80 .50
Nos. 2666-2669 (4) 1.60 1.15

11th Biennial of Children's Book Illustration, Sept. 11-Oct. 30, Bratislava.

1987, Sept. 23

2670 A955 50h Eternal flame, flower .20 .20

Theresienstadt Memorial for the victims from 23 European countries who died in the Small Fortress, Terezin, a Nazi concentration camp.

Socialist Communications Organization, 30th Anniv. — A956

1987, Sept. 23

2671 A956 4k Emblem, satellite, dish receiver .40 .20

Jan Evangelista Purkyne (1787-1869), Physiologist A957

1987, Sept. 30

2672 A957 7k multicolored .80 .20

Views of Bratislava — A958

Designs: 3k, Male and female figures supporting an oriel, Arkier Palace, c. 1552. 4k, View of Bratislava from Ware Conterfactur de Stadt Presburg, from an engraving by Hans Mayer, 1563.

1987, Oct. 1 **Engr.** ***Perf. 12***

2673 A958 3k multicolored .50 .35
2674 A958 4k multicolored .70 .45

Each printed in sheets of 4 with Bratislava Castle (from Mayer's engraving) between. Value, set $6.50.

See #2719-2720, 2763-2764, 2800-2801.

Type of 1974

Photo. & Engr.

1987, Nov. 1 ***Perf. 12x11½***

2675 A699 1k Post rider .20 .20

PRAGA '88, Aug. 26-Sept. 4, 1988. No. 2675 printed se-tenant with label picturing exhibition emblem. Value for single with attached label 40c.

October Revolution, Russia, 70th Anniv. — A959

Establishment of the Union of Soviet Socialist Republics, 65th Anniv. — A960

1987, Nov. 6 ***Perf. 12x11½***

2676 A959 50h multicolored .20 .20
2677 A960 50h multicolored .20 .20

Art Type of 1974

Paintings in national galleries: 1k, Enclosure of Dreams, by Kamil Lhotak (b. 1912). 2k, Tulips, by Ester Simerova-Martincekova (b. 1909). 3k, Triptych with Bohemian Landscape, by Josef Lada (1887-1957). 4k, Accordion Player, by Josef Capek (1887-1945). 5k, Self-portrait, by Jiri Trnka (1912-1969).

1987, Nov. 18 **Engr.** ***Perf. 12***

2678 A700 1k multi 2.40 .60
2679 A700 2k multi 3.50 1.20
2680 A700 3k multi 3.00 .85
2681 A700 4k multi 2.10 .60
2682 A700 5k multi 3.25 1.00
Nos. 2678-2682 (5) 14.25 4.25

Czech and Slovak art.

Nos. 2678-2682 were each issued in sheets of 4. Value, set $75.

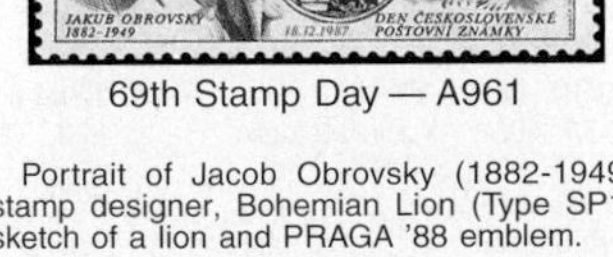

69th Stamp Day — A961

Portrait of Jacob Obrovsky (1882-1949), stamp designer, Bohemian Lion (Type SP1), sketch of a lion and PRAGA '88 emblem.

Photo. & Engr.

1987, Dec. 18 ***Perf. 11½x12***

2683 A961 1k multicolored .25 .20

No. 2683 printed in sheet of four with eight labels se-tenant with stamps, inscribed "100 Years of the National Philatelic Movement in Czechoslovakia" in Czech. The four labels between the "blocks of six" are blank. Value, sheet $3.

Czechoslovak Republic, 70th Anniv. — A962

1988, Jan. 1 ***Perf. 12x11½***

2684 A962 1k Woman, natl. arms, linden branch .25 .20

Natl. Front, 40th Anniv. — A963

1988, Feb. 25 ***Perf. 11½***

2685 A963 50h multicolored .25 .20

Husak Type of 1983

Photo. & Engr.

1988, Jan. 10 ***Perf. 12x11½***

2686 A865 1k brt rose & dk carmine .25 .20

Olympics — A965

1988, Feb. 1 ***Perf. 11½x12***

2687 A965 50h Ski jumping, ice hockey .20 .20
2688 A965 1k Basketball, soccer .20 .20
2689 A965 6k Discus, weight lifting .80 .40
Nos. 2687-2689 (3) 1.20 .80

Exist in souv. sheets of 2, imperf. between and in souv. sheets of 2, imperf.

Victorious February, 40th Anniv. — A966

Statue of Klement Gottwald by Rudolf Svoboda.

1988, Feb. 25 ***Perf. 11½***

2690 A966 50h multicolored .20 .20

No. 2690 exists in a souvenir sheet of two No. 2690 and two postally invalid imperf impressions of No. 637. Value $9. Sheet exists imperf. Value $12.

Classic Automobiles — A967

1988, Mar. 1 ***Perf. 12x11½***

2691 A967 50h 1914 Laurin & Klement .20 .20
2692 A967 1k 1902 Tatra NW Type B .20 .20
2693 A967 2k 1905 Tatra NW Type E .30 .20
2694 A967 3k 1929 Tatra 12 Normandie .60 .25
2695 A967 4k 1899 Meteor .80 .40
a. Bklt. pane, 2 3k, 3 4k + label 6.00 6.00
omplete booklet, #2695a 7.00
Nos. 2691-2695 (5) 2.10 1.25

Postal Museum, 70th Anniv. A968

Praga '88 emblem and: 50h, Postman, Malostranske Namesti Square p.o., Prague, c. 1742, and Velka Javorina television transmitter, 1979. 1k, Telecommunications Center, Mlada Boleslav, 1986, and Carmelite Street p.o., Prague, c. 1792. 2k, Prague 1 (1873) and Bratislava 56 (1984) post offices. 4k, Communications Center, Prachatice (1982), postman and Maltetske Nameski Square p.o., Prague, c. 1622.

1988, Mar. 10

2696 A968 50h multi .20 .20
2697 A968 1k multi .20 .20
2698 A968 2k multi .25 .20
2699 A968 4k multi .45 .25
a. Souv. sheet, 2 ea #2698-2699 2.25 1.25
Nos. 2696-2699 (4) 1.10 .85

In No. 2699a the top pair of Nos. 2698-2699 is imperf. at top and sides.

A969

A970

1988, Mar. 29 ***Perf. 11½***

2700 A969 50h multicolored .20 .20

Matice Slovenska Cultural Assoc., 125th anniv.

1988, May 12 **Photo. & Engr.**

PRAGA '88. (Exhibition emblem and aspects of the Museum of Natl. Literature, Prague): 1k, Gate and distant view of museum. 2k, Celestial globe, illuminated manuscript, bookshelves and ornately decorated ceiling. 5k, Illuminated "B" and decorated binder of a medieval Bible. 7k, Celestial globe, illuminated manuscript, Zodiacal signs (Aries and Leo), view of museum.

2701 A970 1k multicolored .25 .20
a. Souvenir sheet of 4 1.25 1.00
2702 A970 2k multicolored .50 .30
a. Souvenir sheet of 4 3.50 3.00
2703 A970 5k multicolored .75 .45
a. Souvenir sheet of 4 5.50 4.50
2704 A970 7k multicolored 1.60 .75
a. Souvenir sheet of 4 11.00 9.00
b. Souv. sheet of 4, imperf., #2701-2704 4.00 3.50
Nos. 2701-2704 (4) 3.10 1.70

PRAGA '88 — A971

Exhibition emblem and fountains, Prague.

1988, June 1 ***Perf. 11½x12***

2705 A971 1k Waldstein Palace .20 .20
2706 A971 2k Old town square .25 .20
2707 A971 3k Charles University .50 .25
2708 A971 4k Prague Castle .70 .30
a. Souv. sheet of 4, #2705-2708 3.00 2.00
Nos. 2705-2708 (4) 1.65 .95

Souvenir Sheet

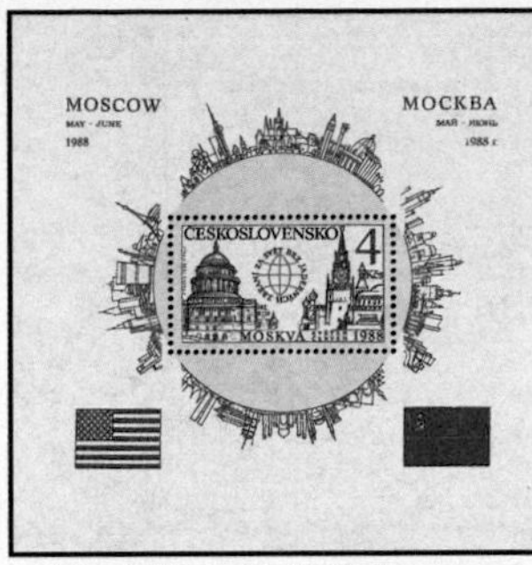

Soviet-US Summit Conference on Arms Reduction, Moscow — A972

Design: The capital, Washington, and the Kremlin, Moscow.

1988, June 1 ***Perf. 12x11½***

2709 A972 4k blue blk, dark red & gold 2.50 1.50

Exists imperf. Value $6.

PRAGA '88 A973

Exhibition emblem and modern architecture, Prague: 50h, Trade Unions Central Recreation Center. 1k, Koospol foreign trade company. 2k, Motol Teaching Hospital. 4k, Culture Palace.

1988, July 1 ***Perf. 12x11½***

2710 A973 50h multicolored .20 .20
2711 A973 1k blk, lt blue & bister .20 .20
2712 A973 2k multicolored .20 .20
a. Souv. sheet, 2 1k, 2 2k + 4 labels, imperf. 2.00 1.50
2713 A973 4k multicolored .50 .35
a. Souv. sheet, 2 50h, 2 4k + 4 labels, imperf. 2.00 1.50
Nos. 2710-2713 (4) 1.10 .95

Souvenir Sheet

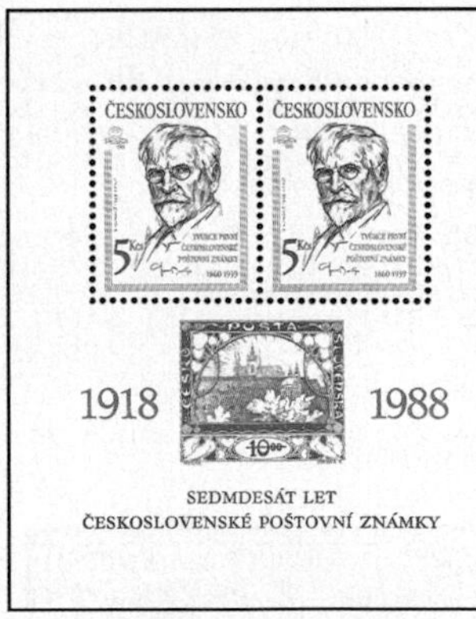

PRAGA '88 — A974

Design: Exhibition emblem and Alfons Mucha (1860-1939), designer of first Czech postage stamp.

1988, Aug. 18 **Engr.** ***Perf. 12***

2714 A974 Sheet of 2 4.50 2.50
a. 5k multicolored 2.00 .85

Czech postage stamps, 70th anniv.

Souvenir Sheets

PRAGA '88 A975

5k, *Turin, Monte Superga,* by Josef Navratil (1798-1865), Postal Museum, Prague.

Details of *Bacchus and Ariadne,* by Sebastiano Ricci (1659-1734), Natl. Gallery, Prague: No. 2716a, Ariadne. No. 2716b, Bacchus and creatures.

1988

2715 Sheet of 2 5.00 3.00
a. A975 5k multi 2.00 1.20
2716 Sheet of 2 8.50 5.00
a.-b. A975 10k any single 3.00 1.75

#2716 exists with emblem and inscription "DEN F.I.P. JOURNEE DE LA FEDERATION INTERNATIONALE DE PHILATELIE." Value $12.

Issue dates: 5k, Aug. 19; 10k, Aug. 26.

Prague Castle Type of 1983

2k, Pottery jug, 17th cent. 3k, *St. Catherine with Angel,* 1580, by Paolo Veronese.

1988, Sept. 28 Engr. *Perf. 12*

2717 A875 2k shown .50 .50
2718 A875 3k multi 1.25 .70

Nos. 2717-2718 were each issued in sheets of 6. Value, set $12.

Bratislava Views Type of 1987

3k, *Hlavne Square, circa 1840* an etching by R. Alt-Sandman, 1840. 4k, *Ferdinand House, circa 1850,* a pen-and-ink drawing by V. Reim.

1988, Oct. 19

2719 A958 3k multicolored .50 .50
2720 A958 4k multicolored 1.25 1.25

Nos. 2719-2720 were each issued in sheets of 4. Value, set $9.

Art Type of 1974

Paintings in natl. galleries: 2k, *With Bundles,* 1931, by Martin Benka (1888-1971). 6k, *Blue Bird,* 1903, by Vojtech Preissig (1873-1944). 7k, *A Jaguar Attacking a Rider,* c. 1850, by Eugene Delacroix (1798-1863).

1988, Nov. 17 Engr. *Perf. 12*

2721 A700 2k multicolored 2.75 1.40
2722 A700 6k multicolored 4.25 2.00
2723 A700 7k multicolored 4.25 2.00
Nos. 2721-2723 (3) 11.25 5.40

Czech and Slovak art.

Nos. 2721-2723 were each issued in sheets of 4. Value, set $50.

Stamp Day — A978

Design: 1k, Jaroslav Benda (1882-1970), illustrator and stamp designer.

Photo. & Engr.

1988, Dec. 18 *Perf. 11½x12*

2724 A978 1k multicolored .25 .20

Paris-Dakar Rally — A979

Trucks: 50h, Earth, Motokov Liaz. 1k, Liaz, globe. 2k, Earth, Motokov Tatra. No. 607. 4k, Map of racecourse, turban, Tatra.

1989, Jan. 2 *Perf. 12x11½*

2725 A979 50h multicolored .20 .20
2726 A979 1k multicolored .30 .20
2727 A979 2k multicolored .45 .20
2728 A979 4k multicolored .80 .30
Nos. 2725-2728 (4) 1.75 .90

Czechoslovakian Federation, 20th Anniv. — A980

1989, Jan. 1

2729 A980 50h multicolored .20 .20

Jan Botto (1829-1881) A981

Taras Grigorievich Shevchenko (1814-1861) A982

Jean Cocteau (1889-1963) A983

Charlie Chaplin (1889-1977) A984

Jawaharlal Nehru (1889-1964) and "UNESCO" — A985

Famous men: No. 2732, Modest Petrovich Musorgsky (1839-1881).

Photo. & Engr.

1989, Mar. 9 *Perf. 12x11½*

2730 A981 50h brn blk & lt blue green .20 .20
2731 A982 50h shown .20 .20
2732 A982 50h multicolored .20 .20
2733 A983 50h red brn, grnh blk & org brn .20 .20
2734 A984 50h blk, int blue & dark red .20 .20
2735 A985 50h brn blk & lt yel green .20 .20
Nos. 2730-2735 (6) 1.20 1.20

Shipping Industry A986

1989, Mar. 27

2736 A986 50h *Republika* .20 .20
2737 A986 1k *Pionyr,* flags .20 .20
2738 A986 2k *Brno,* flags .35 .20
2739 A986 3k *Trinec* .60 .20
2740 A986 4k Flags, mast, *Orlik* .80 .30
2741 A986 5k *Vltava,* communication hardware 1.00 .30
Nos. 2736-2741 (6) 3.15 1.40

Pioneer Organization, 40th Anniv. — A987

Photo. & Engr.

1989, Apr. 20 *Perf. 11½*

2742 A987 50h multi .20 .20

Art Type of 1974

Details of *Feast of Rose Garlands,* 1506, by Albrecht Durer, Natl. Gallery, Prague: a, Virgin and Child. b, Angel playing mandolin.

1989, Apr. 21 Engr. *Perf. 12*

Miniature Sheet

2743 Sheet of 2 10.00 5.00
a.-b. A700 10k any single 4.50 2.00

Prague Castle Art Type of 1983

2k, Bas-relief picturing Kaiser Karl IV, from Kralovske tomb by Alexander Colin (c. 1527-1612). 3k, Self-portrait, by V.V. Reiner (1689-1743).

1989, May 9 Photo. & Engr.

2744 A875 2k dark red, sepia & buff .40 .30
2745 A875 3k multi .60 .40

Nos. 2744-2745 were each issued in sheets of 6. Value, set $7.

Souvenir Sheet

PHILEXFRANCE '89, French Revolution Bicent. — A988

1989, July 14 Engr. *Perf. 12*

2746 A988 5k brt blue, blk & dk red 2.00 1.50

Haliaeetus albicilla — A989

Photo. & Engr.

1989, July 17 *Perf. 12x11½*

2747 A989 1k multicolored .50 .20

World Wildlife Fund — A990

Toads and newts.

1989, July 18 *Perf. 11½x12*

2748 A990 2k *Bombina bombina* 1.25 .30
2749 A990 3k *Bombina variegata* 1.50 .40
2750 A990 4k *Triturus alpestris* 1.75 .60
2751 A990 5k *Triturus montandoni* 2.00 .75
Nos. 2748-2751 (4) 6.50 2.05

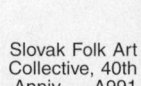

Slovak Folk Art Collective, 40th Anniv. — A991

1989, Aug. 29 *Perf. 12x11½*

2752 A991 50h multicolored .20 .20

Slovak Uprising, 45th Anniv. — A992

Photo. & Engr.

1989, Aug. 29 *Perf. 11½x12*

2753 A992 1k multicolored .20 .20

A993

A994

Award-winning illustrations.

1989, Sept. 4 *Perf. 11½*

2754 A993 50h Hannu Taina, Finland .20 .20
2755 A993 1k Aleksander Aleksov, Bulgaria .20 .20
2756 A993 2k Jurgen Spohn, West Berlin .25 .20
2757 A993 4k Robert Brun, Czechoslovakia .75 .20
a. Souvenir sheet of 2 1.75 .75
Nos. 2754-2757 (4) 1.40 .80

12th Biennial of Children's Book Illustration, Bratislava.

1989, Sept. 5 Engr. *Perf. 11½x12*

Poisonous mushrooms.

2758 A994 50h *Nolanea verna* .25 .20
2759 A994 1k *Amanita phalloides* .30 .30
2760 A994 2k *Amanita virosa* .45 .40
2761 A994 3k *Cortinarius orellanus* .70 .55
2762 A994 5k *Galerina marginata* .80 .55
Nos. 2758-2762 (5) 2.50 2.00

Nos. 2758-2762 were each issued in sheets of 10. Value, set $40.

Bratislava Views Type of 1987

Views of Devin, a Slavic castle above the Danube, Bratislava.

1989, Oct. 16 Engr. *Perf. 12*

2763 A958 3k Castle, flower .65 .65
2764 A958 4k Castle, urn .85 .85

Nos. 2763-2764 were each issued in sheets of 4. Value, set $7.

Jan Opletal (1915-39) — A996

Photo. & Engr.

1989, Nov. 17 *Perf. 12x11½*

2765 A996 1k multicolored .20 .20

Intl. Student's Day. Funeral of Opletal, a Nazi victim, on Nov. 15, 1939, sparked student demonstrations that resulted in the closing of all universities in occupied Bohemia and Moravia.

Art Type of 1974

Paintings in Natl. Galleries: 2k, *Nirvana,* c. 1920, by Anton Jasusch (1882-1965). 4k, *Winter Evening in Town,* c. 1907, by Jakub

Schikaneder (1855-1924), horiz. 5k, *The Bakers*, 1926, by Pravoslav Kotik (1889-1970), horiz.

1989, Nov. 27 Engr. *Perf. 12*

2766	A700	2k multicolored	.90	.55
2767	A700	4k multicolored	1.60	1.10
2768	A700	5k multicolored	1.50	1.10
		Nos. 2766-2768 (3)	4.00	2.75

Nos. 2766-2768 were each issued in sheets of 4. Value, set $17.

Stamp Day — A997

Design: Portrait of Cyril Bouda, stamp designer, art tools and falcon.

Photo. & Engr.

1989, Dec. 18 *Perf. 11½x12*

2769	A997	1k multicolored	.25	.20

A998

A999

Photo. & Engr.

1990, Jan. 8 *Perf. 11½x12*

2770	A998	1k multicolored	.60	.20

UNESCO World Literacy Year. Printed se-tenant with inscribed label picturing UN and UNESCO emblems. Value, single with label attached 75c.

1990, Jan. 9 *Perf. 11½*

Famous men: No. 2771, Karel Capek, writer. No. 2772, Thomas G. Masaryk. 1k, Lenin. 2k, Emile Zola, French writer. 3k, Jaroslav Heyrovsky (1890-1987), chemical physicist. 10k, Bohuslav Martinu (1890-1959), composer.

2771	A999	50h multicolored	.20	.20
2772	A999	50h multicolored	.20	.20
2773	A999	1k multicolored	.20	.20
2774	A999	2k multicolored	.30	.20
2775	A999	3k multicolored	.50	.30
2776	A999	10k multicolored	1.60	.90
		Nos. 2771-2776 (6)	3.00	2.00

#2771, 2775-2776 inscribed "UNESCO."

Pres. Vaclav Havel A1000

Handball Players A1001

1990, Jan. 9 *Perf. 12x11½*

2777	A1000	50h red, brt vio & bl	.30	.20

See Nos. 2879, 2948.

1990, Feb. 1 *Perf. 11½*

2778	A1001	50h multicolored	.20	.20

1990 Men's World Handball Championships, Czechoslovakia.

Flora — A1002

A1003

Photo. & Engr.

1990, Mar. 1 *Perf. 11½*

2779	A1002	50h *Antirrhinum majus*	.50	.20
2780	A1002	1k *Zinnia elegans*	.70	.20
2781	A1002	3k *Tigridia pavonia*	1.00	.25

Perf. 12x12½

2782	A1002	5k *Lilium candidum*	1.30	.70
		Nos. 2779-2782 (4)	3.50	1.35

City Arms Type of 1982

Photo. & Engr.

1990, Mar. 28 *Perf. 12x11½*

2783	A847	50h Prostejov	.20	.20
2784	A847	50h Bytca	.20	.20
2785	A847	50h Sobeslav	.20	.20
2786	A847	50h Podebrady	.20	.20
		Nos. 2783-2786 (4)	.80	.80

1990, Apr. 16 *Perf. 11½x12*

2787	A1003	1k brn vio, rose & buff	.60	.20

Visit of Pope John Paul II.

World War II Liberation A1004

Photo. & Engr.

1990, May 5 *Perf. 11½*

2788	A1004	1k multicolored	.25	.20

Souvenir Sheet

150th Anniv. of the Postage Stamp — A1005

1990, May 6 Engr. *Perf. 12*

2789	A1005	7k multicolored	3.50	1.50

Stamp World London 90.

A1006

A1007

Photo. & Engr.

1990, May 8 *Perf. 11½*

2790	A1006	1k multicolored	.60	.20

World Cup Soccer Championships, Italy.

1990, June 1

2791	A1007	1k multicolored	.50	.20

Free elections.

Prague Castle Type of 1983

1990, June 6, 1990 Engr.

2792	A875	2k Gold and jeweled hand	.60	.30
2793	A875	3k Medallion	.90	.45

Art treasures of Prague Castle.

Nos. 2792-2793 were each issued in sheets of 6. Value, set $12.

Helsinki Conference, 15th Anniv. — A1008

Photo & Engr.

1990, June 21 *Perf. 12x11½*

2794	A1008	7k multicolored	1.10	.60

Dr. Milada Horakova A1009

1990, June 25 *Perf. 12x11½*

2795	A1009	1k multicolored	.30	.20

Intercanis Dog Show, Brno — A1010

Designs: 50h, Poodles, 1k, Afghan hound, Irish wolfhound, greyhound. 4k, Czech terrier, bloodhound, Hannoverian hound. 7k, Cavalier King Charles Spaniel, cocker spaniel, American cocker spaniel.

1990, July 2

2796	A1010	50h multicolored	.55	.20
2797	A1010	1k multicolored	.85	.20
2798	A1010	4k multicolored	1.40	.40
2799	A1010	7k multicolored	2.00	.65
		Nos. 2796-2799 (4)	4.80	1.45

Bratislava Art Type of 1987

1990 Engr. *Perf. 12*

2800	A958	3k Ancient Celtic coin	.80	.40
2801	A958	4k Gen. Milan Stefanik	.80	.50

Issue dates: 3k, Sept. 29. 4k, July 21.

Nos. 2800-2801 were each issued in sheets of 4. Value, set $8.

Grand Pardubice Steeplechase, Cent. — A1011

Photo. & Engr.

1990, Sept. 7 *Perf. 12x11½*

2802	A1011	50h multicolored	.20	.20
2803	A1011	4k multi, diff.	.70	.35

Protected Animals — A1012

Litho. & Engr.

1990, Oct. 1 *Perf. 12x11*

2804	A1012	50h Marmota marmota	.85	.20
2805	A1012	1k Felis silvestris	1.40	.20
2806	A1012	4k Castor fiber	1.60	.40
2807	A1012	5k Plecotus auritus	2.00	.65
		Nos. 2804-2807 (4)	5.85	1.45

Conf. of Civic Associations, Helsinki — A1013

Litho. & Engr.

1990, Oct. 15 *Perf. 12x11½*

2808	A1013	3k blue, gold & yel	.50	.30

Christmas — A1014

Photo. & Engr.

1990, Nov. 15 *Perf. 11½x12*

2809	A1014	50h multicolored	.20	.20

Art Type of 1967

Works of art: 2k, Krucemburk by Jan Zrzavy (1890-1977), horiz. 3k, St. Agnes of Bohemia from the St. Wenceslas Monument, Prague by Josef V. Myslbek (1848-1922). 4k, The Slavs in their Homeland by Alfons Mucha (1860-1939). 5k, St. John the Baptist by Auguste Rodin (1840-1917).

1990, Nov. 27 Engr. *Perf. 11½*

2810	A565	2k multicolored	1.25	.45
2811	A565	3k multicolored	1.50	1.50
2812	A565	4k multicolored	1.80	.50
2813	A565	5k multicolored	2.10	.50
		Nos. 2810-2813 (4)	6.65	2.95

Nos. 2810-2813 were each issued in sheets of 4. Value, set $30.

Karel Svolinsky (1896-1986), Vignette from No. 1182 — A1016

1990, Dec. 18 Photo. & Engr.

2814	A1016	1k multicolored	.25	.20

Stamp Day.

A1017

A1018

1991, Jan. 10 *Perf. 11½*

2815	A1017	1k multicolored	.30	.20

European Judo Championships, Prague.

1991, Jan. 10

Design: A. B. Svojsik (1876-1938), Czech Scouting Founder.

2816	A1018	3k multicolored	1.00	.20

Scouting in Czechoslovakia, 80th Anniv.

Bethlehem Chapel, Prague, 600th Anniv. — A1019

1991, Feb. 4 ***Perf. 12x11½***
2817 A1019 50h multicolored .25 .20

Wolfgang Amadeus Mozart (1756-1791), Old Theatre — A1020

1991, Feb. 4
2818 A1020 1k multicolored .20 .20

Steamship Bohemia, 150th Anniv. — A1021

1991, Feb. 4 ***Perf. 11½x12***
2819 A1021 5k multicolored 1.00 .30

Famous Men A1022

Designs: No. 2820, Antonin Dvorak (1841-1904), composer. No. 2821, Andrej Kmet (1841-1908), botanist. No. 2822, Jaroslav Seifert (1901-1986), poet, Nobel laureate for Literature. No. 2823, Jan Masaryk (1886-1948), diplomat. No. 2824, Alois Senefelder (1771-1834), lithographer.

1991, Feb. 18 ***Perf. 12x11½***
2820 A1022 1k multicolored .20 .20
2821 A1022 1k multicolored .30 .20
2822 A1022 1k multicolored .40 .20
2823 A1022 1k multicolored .50 .20
2824 A1022 1k multicolored .60 .20
Nos. 2820-2824 (5) 2.00 1.00

#2820-2824 printed with se-tenant labels. See No. 2831.

Europa — A1023 A1024

Photo. & Engr.
1991, May 6 ***Perf. 11½x12***
2825 A1023 6k blk, bl & red 2.50 .75

Photo. & Engr.
1991, May 10 ***Perf. 11½x12***
2826 A1024 1k multicolored .25 .20

General Exhibition in Prague, cent.

Antarctic Treaty, 30th Anniv. A1025

1991, May 20 ***Perf. 12x11½***
2827 A1025 8k multicolored 1.75 .60

Castles — A1026 Scenic Views — A1027

1991, June 3 ***Perf. 11½***
2828 A1026 50h Blatna .40 .20
2829 A1026 1k Bouzov .50 .20
2830 A1026 3k Kezmarok .60 .20
Nos. 2828-2830 (3) 1.50 .60

Famous Men Type

Design: Jan Palach (1948-1969), Student.

Photo. & Engr.
1991, Aug. 9 ***Perf. 12x11½***
2831 A1022 4k black 2.00 .30

Printed se-tenant with label.

Photo. & Engr.
1991, Aug. 28 ***Perf. 11½***
2832 A1027 4k Krivan mountains 1.00 .60
2833 A1027 4k Rip mountain 1.00 .60

A1028 A1029

Illustrations by: 1k, Binette Schroeder, Germany. 2k, Stasys Eidrigevicius, Poland.

Photo. & Engr.
1991, Sept. 2 ***Perf. 11½***
2834 A1028 1k multicolored .40 .20
2835 A1028 2k multicolored .40 .20

13th Biennial Exhibition of Children's Book Illustrators, Bratislava.

1991, Sept. 27 **Engr.** ***Perf. 11½***

Design: Father Andrej Hlinka (1864-1938), Slovak nationalist.

2836 A1029 10k blue black 1.60 .30

Art of Prague and Bratislava A1030

Designs: No. 2837, Holy Infant of Prague. No. 2838, Blue Church of Bratislava.

1991, Sept. 30
2837 A1030 3k multicolored 1.00 .75
2838 A1030 3k multicolored 1.00 .75

Nos. 2837-2838 were each issued in sheets of 8. Value, set $20.

Flowers A1031 Christmas A1033

Photo. & Engr.
1991, Nov. 3 ***Perf. 12x11½***
2839 A1031 1k Gagea bohemica .30 .20
2840 A1031 2k Aster alpinus .60 .20
2841 A1031 5k Fritillaria meleagris 1.60 .25
2842 A1031 11k Daphne cneorum 2.50 .35
Nos. 2839-2842 (4) 5.00 1.00

Art Type of 1967

Paintings: 2k, Everyday Homelife by Max Ernst. 3k, Lovers by Auguste Renoir. 4k, Head of Christ by El Greco. 5k, Coincidence by Ladislav Guderna. 7k, Two Maidens by Utamaro.

1991, Nov. 3 **Engr.** ***Perf. 11½***
2843 A565 2k multicolored .80 .30
2844 A565 3k multicolored 1.00 .40
2845 A565 4k multicolored 1.50 .50
2846 A565 5k multicolored 1.50 .60
2847 A565 7k multicolored 2.00 1.00
Nos. 2843-2847 (5) 6.80 2.80

Nos. 2843-2847 were each issued in sheets of 4. Value, set $30.

1991, Nov. 19
2848 A1033 50h multicolored .30 .20

Stamp Day — A1034

Martin Benka (1888-1971), stamp engraver.

Photo. & Engr.
1991, Dec. 18 ***Perf. 11½x12***
2849 A1034 2k multicolored .45 .20

1992 Winter Olympics, Albertville — A1035

1992, Jan. 6 ***Perf. 11½***
2850 A1035 1k Biathlon .25 .20

Photo. & Engr.
1992, May 21 ***Perf. 11½***
2851 A1035 2k Tennis .30 .20

1992 Summer Olympics, Barcelona.

Souvenir Sheet

Jan Amos Komensky (Comenius), Educator — A1036

1992, Mar. 5 **Engr.**
2852 A1036 10k multicolored 4.50 3.00

World Ice Hockey Championships, Prague and Bratislava — A1037

1992, Mar. 31 **Photo. & Engr.**
2853 A1037 3k multicolored .75 .20

Traffic Safety A1038

1992, Apr. 2
2854 A1038 2k multicolored .50 .20

Expo '92, Seville — A1039

1992, Apr. 2
2855 A1039 4k multicolored .75 .20

Discovery of America, 500th Anniv. — A1040

1992, May 5 **Engr.**
2856 A1040 22k multicolored 2.75 2.75

Europa. Printed in sheets of 8. Value $25.

Czechoslovak Military Actions in WWII — A1041

Designs: 1k, J. Kubis and J. Gabcik, assassins of Reinhard Heydrich, 1942. 2k, Pilots flying for France and Great Britain. 3k, Defense of Tobruk. 6k, Capture of Dunkirk, 1944-45.

1992, May 21 Engr. *Perf. 12x11½*
2857 A1041 1k multicolored .50 .20
2858 A1041 2k multicolored .60 .20
2859 A1041 3k multicolored .75 .25
2860 A1041 6k multicolored 1.60 .35
Nos. 2857-2860 (4) 3.45 1.00

A1042

A1043

Photo. & Engr.
1992, June 10 *Perf. 11½*
2861 A1042 2k multicolored .30 .20

Czechoslovakian Red Cross.

1992, June 30
2862 A1043 1k multicolored .30 .20

Junior European Table Tennis Championships, Topolcany.

Beetles
A1044

1992, July 15
2863 A1044 1k Polyphylla fullo .65 .20
2864 A1044 2k Ergates faber .90 .30
2865 A1044 3k Meloe violaceus 1.80 .45
2866 A1044 4k Dytiscus latissimus 1.80 .60
Nos. 2863-2866 (4) 5.15 1.55

The 1k exists with denomination omitted.

Troja Castle
A1045

1992, Aug. 28 Engr. *Perf. 11½*
2867 A1045 6k shown 2.00 .75
2868 A1045 7k Statue of St. Martin, vert. 3.00 .80
2869 A1045 8k Lednice Castle 3.00 .95
Nos. 2867-2869 (3) 8.00 2.50

Nos. 2867-2869 were each issued in sheets of 8. Value, set $75.

Chrudim Church Type of 1971

Photo. & Engr.
1992, Aug. 28 *Perf. 11½x11*
2870 A629 50h multicolored .75 .20

Postal Bank — A1045a

Photo. & Engr.
1992, Aug. 28 *Perf. 11½x12*
2870A A1045a 20k multicolored 5.00 1.10

Antonius Bernolak, Georgius Fandly — A1046

Photo. & Engr.
1992, Oct. 6 *Perf. 12x11½*
2871 A1046 5k multicolored 1.50 .50

Slovakian Educational Society, bicent.

Cesky Krumlov — A1046a

Photo. & Engr.
1992, Oct. 19 *Perf. 11½x12*
2871A A1046a 3k brick red & brn .90 .20

See No. 2890.

Painting Type of 1967

6k Old Man on a Raft, by Koloman Sokol. 7k, Still Life of Grapes and Raisins, by Georges Braque, horiz. 8k, Abandoned Corset, by Toyen.

Perf. 11½x12, 12x11½
1992, Nov. 2 Engr.
2872 A565 6k multicolored 1.40 .55
2873 A565 7k multicolored 2.25 .65
2874 A565 8k multicolored 2.25 .75
Nos. 2872-2874 (3) 5.90 1.95

Nos. 2872-2874 were each issued in sheets of 4. Value, set $30.

Christmas — A1047

Photo. & Engr.
1992, Nov. 9 *Perf. 12x11½*
2875 A1047 2k multicolored .60 .20

Jindra Schmidt (1897-1984), Graphic Artist and Engraver — A1048

Photo. & Engr.
1992, Dec. 18 *Perf. 11½x12*
2876 A1048 2k multicolored .60 .20

Stamp Day.

On January 1, 1993, Czechoslovakia split into Czech Republic and Slovakia. Czech Republic listings continue here. Slovakia can be found in Volume 5.

CZECH REPUBLIC

AREA — 30,449 sq. mi.
POP. — 10,280,513 (1999 est.)

Natl. Arms
A1049

Photo. & Engr.
1993, Jan. 20 *Perf. 11*
2877 A1049 3k multicolored 1.00 .20

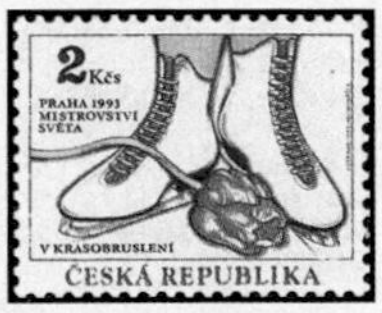
1993 World Figure Skating Championships, Prague
A1050

1993, Feb. 25 *Perf. 11½x11*
2878 A1050 2k multicolored .50 .20

Havel Type of 1990 Inscribed "Ceska Republika"

Photo. & Engr.
1993, Mar. 2 *Perf. 12x11½*
2879 A1000 2k vio, vio brn & blue .40 .20

St. John Nepomuk, Patron Saint of Czechs, 600th Death Anniv. — A1051

1993, Mar. 11
2880 A1051 8k multicolored 1.00 .35

See Germany No. 1776; Slovakia No. 158.

Holy Hunger, by Mikulas Medek — A1052

1993, Mar. 11 *Perf. 11½*
2881 A1052 14k multicolored *4.00 2.00*

Europa.

Sacred Heart Church, Prague
A1053

1993, Mar. 30 Engr. *Perf. 11½*
2882 A1053 5k multicolored 2.00 .35

Brevnov Monastery, 1000th Anniv. — A1054

Litho. & Engr.
1993, Apr. 12 *Perf. 12x11½*
2883 A1054 4k multicolored .65 .25

1993 Intl. Junior Weight Lifting Championships, Cheb — A1055

Photo. & Engr.
1993, May 12 *Perf. 11½*
2884 A1055 6k multicolored 1.00 .35

Clock Tower and Church, Brno — A1056

1993, June 16 Engr. *Perf. 12x11½*
2885 A1056 8k multicolored 1.20 1.20

Brno, 750th anniv.

Arrival of St. Cyril and St. Methodius, 1130th Anniv. — A1057

1993, June 22 Photo. & Engr.
2886 A1057 8k multicolored 1.00 .50

See Slovakia No. 167.

Souvenir Sheet

State Arms — A1058

1993, June 22 *Perf. 11½*
2887 A1058 8k Sheet of 2 3.00 3.00

Architecture Type of 1992 Inscribed "Ceska Republika" and

A1059

Cities: 1k, Ceske Budejovice. 2k, Usti Nad Labem. #2890, like #2871A. #2890A, Brno. 5k, Plzen. 6k, Slany. 7k, Ostrava. 8k, Olomouc. 10k, Hradec Kralove. 20k, Prague. 50k, Opava.

Perf. 12x11½, 11½x12
1993-94 Photo. & Engr.
2888 A1059 1k dp cl & org .20 .20
2889 A1059 2k red vio & bl .25 .20
2890 A1046a 3k gray bl & red .35 .20
Complete booklet, 5 #2890 6.00
2891 A1059 3k dk bl & red .35 .20
Complete booklet, 5 #2890A 5.00
2892 A1059 5k bluish green & brn .60 .25
2893 A1059 6k grn & org yel .75 .30
2894 A1059 7k blk brn & grn .85 .30
2895 A1059 8k dp vio & yel .95 .30
2896 A1059 10k olive gray & red 1.20 .40
2897 A1059 20k red & blue 2.50 .75
2898 A1059 50k brn & grn 6.00 1.75
Nos. 2888-2898 (11) 14.00 4.85

Issued: No. 2891, 3/30/94; 6k, 10/1/94; 7k, 11/23/94; others, 7/1/93.

World Rowing Championships, Racice
A1060

Photo. & Engr.

1993, Aug. 18 ***Perf. 11½***

2901 A1060 3k multicolored	.50	.20

A1061

Trees — A1062

Famous men: 2k, August Sedlacek (1843-1926), historian. 3k, Eduard Cech (1893-1960), mathematician.

1993, Aug. 26 ***Perf. 12x11½***

2902 A1061 2k multicolored	.25	.20
2903 A1061 3k multicolored	.35	.20

1993, Oct. 26 ***Perf. 11½***

2904 A1062 5k Quercus robur	.75	.30
2905 A1062 7k Carpinus betulus	1.00	.40
2906 A1062 9k Pinus silvestris	1.50	.50
Nos. 2904-2906 (3)	3.25	1.20

Christmas — A1063

A1064

Photo. & Engr.

1993, Nov. 8 ***Perf. 11½***

2907 A1063 2k multicolored	.30	.20

Art Type of 1967 Inscribed "CESKA REPUBLIKA"

Paintings: 9k, Strahovska Madonna, by "Bohemian Master" in the year 1350. 11k, Composition, by Miro, horiz. 14k, Field of Green, by Van Gogh, horiz.

1993 **Engr.** ***Perf. 11½x12***

2908 A565 9k multicolored	2.25	2.25

Perf. 12x11½

2909 A565 11k multicolored	2.25	2.25
2910 A565 14k multicolored	3.50	3.50
Nos. 2908-2910 (3)	8.00	8.00

Issued: 11k, 14k, Nov. 8; 9k, Dec. 15.

Nos. 2908-2910 were each issued in sheets of 4. Value $35.

Photo. & Engr.

1994, Jan. 19 ***Perf. 11½***

2911 A1064 2k multicolored	.30	.20

Intl. Year of the Family.

Jan Kubelik (1880-1940), Composer A1065

Photo. & Engr.

1994, Jan. 19 ***Perf. 11½***

2912 A1065 3k multicolored	.40	.25

UNESCO — A1065a

Designs: 2k, Voltaire (1694-1778), philosopher. 6k, Georgius Agricola (1494-1555), mineralogist, humanist.

1994, Feb. 2 ***Perf. 12x11½***

2913 A1065a 2k multicolored	.25	.20
2914 A1065a 6k multicolored	.80	.35

A1066

A1067

Photo. & Engr.

1994, Feb. 2 ***Perf. 11½***

2915 A1066 5k multicolored	.65	.35

1994 Winter Olympics, Lillehammer.

Photo. & Engr.

1994, May 4 ***Perf. 11½***

Europa (Marco Polo &): #2916, Stylized animals, Chinese woman. #2917, Stylized animals.

2916 A1067 14k multicolored	1.75	1.75
2917 A1067 14k multicolored	1.75	1.75
a. Pair, #2916-2917	3.50	3.50

A1068

A1070

Architectural Sights — A1069

1994, May 18

2918 A1068 5k Eduard Benes	.60	.20

1994, May 18

UNESCO: 8k, Houses at the square, Telc. 9k, Cubist house designed by Chochol, Prague.

2919 A1069 8k multicolored	1.00	.75
2920 A1069 9k multicolored	1.10	.75

Photo. & Engr.

1994, June 1 ***Perf. 11½***

2921 A1070 2k Children's Day	.40	.20

Dinosaurs — A1071

Perf. 11½x11, 11x11½

1994, June 1 **Litho.**

2922 A1071 2k Stegosaurus	.75	.20
2923 A1071 3k Apatosaurus	1.00	.25
2924 A1071 5k Tarbosaurus, vert.	1.25	.35
Nos. 2922-2924 (3)	3.00	.80

A1072

A1073

Photo. & Engr.

1994, June 1 ***Perf. 11½x11***

2925 A1072 8k multicolored	1.10	.50

1994 World Cup Soccer Championships, US.

1994, June 15 ***Perf. 11x11½***

2926 A1073 2k multicolored	.30	.20

12th Pan-Sokol Rally, Prague.

Intl. Olympic Committee, Cent. — A1074

1994, June 15

2927 A1074 7k multicolored	.85	.50

UPU, 120th Anniv. A1075

1994, Aug. 3 **Engr.** ***Perf. 11½***

2928 A1075 11k multicolored	1.50	1.00

Songbirds — A1076

Designs: 3k, Saxicola torquata. 5k, Carpodacus erythrinus. 14k, Luscinia svecica.

Photo. & Engr.

1994, Aug. 24 ***Perf. 11x11½***

2929 A1076 3k multicolored	.45	.25
2930 A1076 5k multicolored	.75	.30
2931 A1076 14k multicolored	1.80	.80
Nos. 2929-2931 (3)	3.00	1.35

Historic Race Cars — A1077

Photo. & Engr.

1994, Oct. 5 ***Perf. 11½***

2932 A1077 2k 1900 NW	.25	.20
Complete booklet, 10 #2932	3.00	
2933 A1077 3k 1908 L&K	.55	.20
Complete booklet, 5 #2933	3.50	
2934 A1077 9k 1912 Praga	1.40	.50
Nos. 2932-2934 (3)	2.20	.90

Christmas — A1078

Photo. & Engr.

1994, Nov. 9 ***Perf. 11½***

2935 A1078 2k multicolored	.45	.20

Art Type of 1967 Inscribed "CESKA REPUBLIKA"

Engraving or paintings: 7k, Stary Posetilec A Zena, by Lucas Van Leyden. 10k, Moulin Rouge, by Henri de Toulouse-Lautrec. 14k, St. Vitus Madonna, St. Vitus Cathedral, Prague.

1994, Nov. 9 **Engr.** ***Perf. 12***

2936 A565 7k multicolored	.85	.85
2937 A565 10k multicolored	1.20	1.20
2938 A565 14k multicolored	1.75	1.75
Nos. 2936-2938 (3)	3.80	3.80

Nos. 2936-2938 were each printed in sheets of 4. Value, set $14.

World Tourism Organization, 20th Anniv. A1079

Czech Stamp Production A1080

Photo. & Engr.

1995, Jan. 2 ***Perf. 11x12***

2939 A1079 8k green blue & red	.95	.50

1995, Jan. 20

2940 A1080 3k Design N1	.35	.25

Czech Republic & European Union Association Agreement A1081

1995, Jan. 20 **Litho.** ***Perf. 13½x12½***

2941 A1081 8k multicolored	.95	.65

Famous Men A1082

Designs: 2k, Johannes Marcus Marci (1595-1667). 5k, Ferdinand Peroutka (1895-1978). 7k, Premysl Pitter (1895-1976).

Photo. & Engr.

1995, Feb. 1 ***Perf. 12x11***

2942 A1082 2k multicolored	.25	.20
2943 A1082 5k multicolored	.60	.25
2944 A1082 7k multicolored	.85	.35
Nos. 2942-2944 (3)	1.70	.80

Theater Personalities — A1083

Designs: No. 2945, Jiri Voskovec (1905-81). No. 2946, Jan Werich (1905-80). No. 2947, Jaroslav Jezek (1906-42). 22k, Caricatures of Voskovec, Werich, and Jezek with piano.

1995 Photo. & Engr. *Perf. 12x11*

2945	A1083	3k multicolored	.50	.25
		Complete booklet, 3 #2945	2.00	
2946	A1083	3k multicolored	.50	.25
		Complete booklet, 3 #2946	2.00	
2947	A1083	3k multicolored	.50	.25
		Complete booklet, 3 #2947	2.00	
a.		Strip of 3, #2945-2947	1.75	1.50
		Complete booklet, 2 #2947a	4.00	
		Nos. 2945-2947 (3)	1.50	.75

Souvenir Sheet

Photo.

Perf. 12

2947B A1083 22k yellow & black 2.50 2.50

Issued: 3k, 3/15; 22k, 9/20.

Havel Type of 1990 Inscribed "Ceska Republika"

Photo. & Engr.

1995, Mar. 22 *Perf. 12x11½*

2948 A1000 3.60k bl, vio & mag .45 .20
Complete booklet, 5 #2948 4.00

Rural Architecture A1084

1995, Mar. 22 *Perf. 11½*

2949 A1084 40h shown .20 .20
2950 A1084 60h Homes, diff. .20 .20

European Nature Conservation Year — A1085

1995, Apr. 12

2951	A1085 3k Bombus terrestris	.35	.30
	Complete booklet, 5 #2951	4.00	
2952	A1085 5k Mantis religiosa	.60	.30
	Complete booklet, 5 #2952	4.50	
2953	A1085 6k Calopteryx splendens	.75	.30
	Complete booklet, 5 #2953	5.00	
	Nos. 2951-2953 (3)	1.70	.90

Peace & Freedom A1086

Photo. & Engr.

1995, May 3 *Perf. 11½*

2954 A1086 9k Rose, profiles 1.20 .35
2955 A1086 14k Butterfly, profiles 1.75 .75

Europa.

Natural Beauties in Czech Republic A1087

Designs: 8k, "Stone Organ" scenic mountain. 9k, Largest sandstone bridge in Europe.

Photo. & Engr.

1995, May 3 *Perf. 11½*

2956 A1087 8k multicolored .95 .95
2957 A1087 9k multicolored 1.00 1.00

Nos. 2956-2957 were each issued in sheets of 8. Value, set $17.50.

Children's Day — A1088

Photo. & Engr.

1995, June 1 *Perf. 11½*

2958 A1088 3.60k multicolored .60 .25

First Train from Vienna to Prague, 150th Anniv. A1089

3k, Chocen Tunnel. 9.60k, Entering Prague.

1995, June 21

2959	A1089 3k multicolored	.35	.25
	Complete booklet, 5 #2959	2.00	
2960	A1089 9.60k multicolored	1.15	.50

World Wrestling Championships, Prague A1090

Photo. & Engr.

1995, Sept. 6 *Perf. 11½*

2961 A1090 3k multicolored .35 .25

Cartoon Characters A1091

Designs: 3k, Man playing violin, woman washing, by Vladimir Rencin. 3.60k, Angel, naked man, by Vladimir Jiranek. 5k, Circus trainer holding ring for champagne cork to pop through, by Jiri Sliva.

1995, Sept. 6

2962	A1091 3k multicolored	.35	.25
	Complete booklet, 5 #2962	2.00	
2963	A1091 3.60k multicolored	.45	.25
	Complete booklet, 5 #2963	2.50	
2964	A1091 5k multicolored	.60	.30
	Complete booklet, 5 #2964	3.50	
	Nos. 2962-2964 (3)	1.40	.80

A1092

A1093

1995, Sept. 20 Litho. *Perf. 13½x13*

2965 A1092 3k multicolored .35 .20

SOS Children's Villages, 25th anniv.

Photo. & Engr.

1995-97 *Perf. 12x11½*

Designs: 2.40k, Gothic. 3k, Secession. 3.60k, Romance. 4k, Classic portal; 4.60k, Rococo. 9.60k, Renaissance Portal. 12.60k, Cubist. 14k, Baroque.

2966	A1093	2.40k red & green	.30	.20
2967	A1093	3k grn & bl	.35	.20
2967A	A1093	3.60k pur & grn	.45	.20
2968	A1093	4k blue & red	.50	.20
		Complete booklet, 5 #2967A	3.00	
2968A	A1093	4.60k multicolored	.55	.20
2969	A1093	9.60k blue & red	1.10	.45
2969A	A1093	12.60k red brn & bl	1.50	.45
2970	A1093	14k grn & pur	1.60	.60
		Nos. 2966-2970 (8)	6.35	2.50

Issued: 9.60k, 9/27; 2.40k, 14k, 10/11; 3k, 3.60k, 10/25; 4k, 6/12/96; 4.60k, 3/26/97; 12.60k, 6/25/97.

UN, 50th Anniv. A1094

1995, Oct. 11 Litho. *Perf. 12x11½*

2971 A1094 14k multicolored 1.60 .80

Wilhelm Röntgen (1845-1923), Discovery of the X-Ray, Cent. — A1095

1995, Oct. 11 Photo. & Engr.

2972 A1095 6k blk, buff & bl vio .75 .35

Art Type of 1967 Inscribed "CESKA REPUBLIKA"

Designs: 6k, Parisiene, by Ludek Marold. 9k, Vase of Flowers, by J.K. Hirschely. 14k, Portrait of J. Malinsky, by Antoinín Machek.

1995, Nov. 8 *Perf. 12*

2973	A565 6k multicolored	.75	.35
2974	A565 9k multicolored	1.00	.50
2975	A565 14k multicolored	1.60	.80
	Nos. 2973-2975 (3)	3.35	1.65

Nos. 2973-2975 were each printed in sheets of 4. Value, set $13.50.

Christmas — A1096

1995, Nov. 8 *Perf. 11½*

2976 A1096 3k multicolored .40 .20
Complete booklet, 3 #2976 1.50

Czech Philharmonic Orchestra, Cent. — A1097

Photo. & Engr.

1996, Jan. 2 *Perf. 12x11½*

2977 A1097 3.60k multicolored .45 .25

Tradition of Czech Stamp Production — A1098

Photo. & Engr.

1996, Jan. 20 *Perf. 11½x12*

2978 A1098 3.60k Design A5 of 1920 .45 .25

Vera Mencikova (1906-44), Chess Player — A1099

Photo. & Engr.

1996, Feb. 14 *Perf. 12x11½*

2979 A1099 6k multicolored .75 .35

Easter — A1100

1996, Mar. 13 *Perf. 11½x12*

2980 A1100 3k multicolored .35 .20
Complete booklet, 5 #2980 1.75

Josef Sudek (1896-1976), Photographer A1101

Photo. & Engr.

1996, Mar. 13 *Perf. 11*

2981 A1101 9.60k multicolored 1.10 .55

Rulers from House of Luxembourg — A1102

Designs: a, John of Luxembourg (1296-1346). b, Charles IV (1316-78). c, Wenceslas IV. (1361-1419). d, Sigismund (1368-1437).

1996, Mar. 27 Engr. *Perf. 11½*

2982 A1102 14k Sheet of 4, #a.-d. + label 6.75 6.75

Jiri Guth-Jurkovsky, Participant in First Modern Olympic Games, Athens A1103

Photo. & Engr.

1996, Mar. 27 *Perf. 11½*

2983 A1103 9.60k multicolored 1.10 .60

Modern Olympic Games, cent.

World Wildlife Fund — A1104

Ema Destinnova (1878-1930), Singer — A1105

Designs: a, 3.60k, Eliomys quercinus. b, 5k, Dryomys nitedula. c, 6k, Spermophilus citellus. d, 8k, Sicista betulina.

Photo. & Engr.

1996, Apr. 24 ***Perf. 11½x12***
2984 A1104 Block of 4, #a.-d. 3.00 3.00

Issued in sheets of 8 stamps. Value $9.

1996, May 2 ***Perf. 11½***
2985 A1105 8k multicolored .90 .40

Europa.

No. 2985 was issued in sheets of 10. Value $11.

A1106 A1107

Photo. & Engr.

1996, May 15 ***Perf. 11x11½***
2986 A1106 12k multicolored 1.40 .65

Jean Gaspart Deburau (1796-1846), mime.

1996, May 29
2987 A1107 3k multicolored .35 .20

1996 Summmer Olympic Games, Atlanta.

Intl. Children's Day — A1108

Photo. & Engr.

1996, May 29 ***Perf. 11½***
2988 A1108 3k multicolored .35 .20

Architectural Sites — A1109

UNESCO: 8k, St. Nepomuk Church, Zelena Hora. 9k, Loretta Tower, Prague.

1996, June 26 **Engr.** ***Perf. 11½***
2989 A1109 8k multicolored .95 .95
2990 A1109 9k multicolored 1.00 1.00

Nos. 2989-2990 were each issued in sheets of 8. Value, set $16.

See Nos. 3056-3057.

UNICEF, 50th Anniv. A1110

Photo. & Engr.

1996, Sept. 11 ***Perf. 12x11***
2991 A1110 3k multicolored .35 .20

Horses

A1111 A1112

Photo. & Engr.

1996, Sept. 25 ***Perf. 11x11½***
2992 A1111 3k multicolored .50 .20
2993 A1112 3k multicolored .50 .20
a. Pair, #2992-2993 1.00 .75
Complete booklet, 3 #2992, 2 #2993 3.00
Complete booklet, 2 #2992, 3 #2993 3.00

Souvenir Sheet

Vaclav Havel, 60th Birthday — A1113

Illustration reduced.

1996, Oct. 5
2994 A1113 Sheet of 2 1.40 1.40
a. 6k red & blue .80 .50

Art Type of 1967 Inscribed "CESKA REPUBLICA"

The Baroque Chair, by Endre Nemes (1909-85).

1996, Oct. 5 **Engr.** ***Perf. 11½***
2995 A565 20k multicolored 2.40 2.40

No. 2995 was issued in sheets of 4. Value $10.

See Slovakia No. 255; Sweden No. 2199.

Tycho Brahe (1546-1601), Astronomer — A1114

Photo. & Engr.

1996, Oct. 9 ***Perf. 11½x11***
2996 A1114 5k multicolored .60 .30

Biplanes A1115

1996, Oct. 9
2997 A1115 7k Letov S1 (1920) .85 .40
2998 A1115 8k Aero A11 (1925) .95 .45
2999 A1115 10k Avia BH21 (1925) 1.20 .55
Nos. 2997-2999 (3) 3.00 1.40

Christmas A1116

Photo. & Engr.

1996, Nov. 13 ***Perf. 11½***
3000 A1116 3k multicolored .45 .20
Complete booklet, 5 #3000 3.50

Art Type of 1967 Inscribed "CESKA REPUBLICA"

Designs: 9k, Garden of Eden, by Josef Váchal (1884-1969), horiz. 11k, Breakfast, by Georg Flegel (1566-1638).

1996, Nov. 13 **Engr.** ***Perf. 11½***
3001 A565 9k multicolored 1.00 1.00
3002 A565 11k multicolored 1.25 1.25

Nos. 3001-3002 were each issued in sheets of 4. Value, set $10.

Czech Stamp Production — A1117

Photo. & Engr.

1997, Jan. 20 ***Perf. 11½x12***
3003 A1117 3.60k #68, bl & red .40 .25

Easter — A1118 Flowers — A1119

Photo. & Engr.

1997, Mar. 12 ***Perf. 11½***
3004 A1118 3k multicolored .65 .20
Complete booklet, 5 #3004 4.00

1997, Mar. 12 ***Perf. 11x11½***

3.60k, Erythronium dens-canis. 4k, Calla palustris. 5k, Cypripedium calceolus. 8k, Iris pumila.

3005 A1119 3.60k multicolored .45 .20
Complete booklet, 5 #3005 2.50
3006 A1119 4k multicolored .45 .25
Complete booklet, 5 #3006 2.50
3007 A1119 5k multicolored .60 .30
Complete booklet, 5 #3007 3.50
3008 A1119 8k multicolored .95 .45
Complete booklet, 5 #3008 5.00
Nos. 3005-3008 (4) 2.45 1.20

A1120 A1121

Jewish Monuments in Prague: 8k, Altneuschul Synagogue. 10k, Tombstone of Rabbi Judah Loew MaHaRal.

1997, Apr. 30 ***Perf. 11½***
3009 A1120 8k multicolored .90 .45
3010 A1120 10k multicolored 1.10 .55
a. Sheet, 4 each #3009-3010 8.00 4.00

See Israel Nos. 1302-1303.

1997, Mar. 26 **Litho.** ***Perf. 13x13½***

Greetings stamp.

3011 A1121 4k Girl with cats .50 .25

A1122 A1123

1997, Apr. 23 **Engr.** ***Perf. 11½***
3012 A1122 7k deep violet .85 .40

St. Adalbert (956-97). See Germany No. 1964, Hungary No. 3569, Poland No. 3337, Vatican City No. 1040.

Photo. & Engr.

1997, Apr. 30 ***Perf. 11½x12***

Europa (Stories and Legends): No. 3013, Queen, knight with sword, lion, snakes. No. 3014, Man riding in chariot drawn by chickens, King looking through window.

3013 A1123 8k multicolored .95 .95
3014 A1123 8k multicolored .95 .95

Nos. 3013-3014 were each issued in sheets of 8. Value, set $16.

Souvenir Sheet

Collections of Rudolf II (1522-1612), Prague Exhibition A1124

Designs: a, 6k, Musical instruments, flowers, face of bearded man. b, 8k, Rudolf II wearing laurel wreath, holding rose, Muses. c, 10k, Rudolf II, skull, moth's wings, tree, flowers, leaves, fruit.

1997, May 14 **Engr.** ***Perf. 12***
3015 A1124 Sheet of 3, #a.-c. 2.75 2.75

Intl. Children's Day — A1125

Photo. & Engr.

1997, May 28 ***Perf. 11½***
3016 A1125 4.60k multicolored .55 .25

Frantisek Krizik (1847-1941), Electrical Engineer, Inventor of Arc Lamp — A1126

Photo. & Engr.

1997, June 25 *Perf. 12x11½*

3017 A1126 6k multicolored .70 .25

European Swimming & Diving Championships, Prague — A1127

Photo. & Engr.

1997, Aug. 27 *Perf. 11½*

3018 A1127 11k multicolored 1.50 .40

"The Good Soldier Schweik," by Jaroslav Hasek, 110th Anniv. — A1128

4k, Mrs. Müller, Schweik in wheelchair. 4.60k, Lt. Lukás, Col. Kraus von Zillergut, dog. 6k, Schweik smoking pipe, winter scene.

Photo. & Engr.

1997, Sept. 10 *Perf. 12x11½*

3019 A1128 4k multicolored .50 .20
a. Booklet pane of 8 + 4 labels 4.50
Complete booklet, #3019a 4.50
3020 A1128 4.60k multicolored .55 .20
a. Booklet pane of 8 + 4 labels 5.00
Complete booklet, #3020a 5.00
3021 A1128 6k multicolored .70 .30
a. Booklet pane of 8 + 4 labels 6.00
Complete booklet, #3021a 6.00
Nos. 3019-3021 (3) 1.75 .70

Praga 1998, Intl. Stamp Exhibition — A1129

#3022, Lesser Town, Prague Castle. #3023, Old Town, bridges over Vltava River.

Photo. & Engr.

1997, Sept. 24 *Perf. 11½*

3022 A1129 15k multicolored 1.80 .70
3023 A1129 15k multicolored 1.80 .70
a. Souvenir sheet, #3022-3023 + 2 labels 3.50 3.00

Historic Service Vehicles A1130

Designs: 4k, Postal bus, Prague. 4.60k, Sentinel truck, Skoda. 8k, Fire truck, Tatra.

1997, Oct. 8 *Perf. 12x11½*

3024 A1130 4k multicolored .45 .20
Complete booklet, 5 #3024 2.50
3025 A1130 4.60k multicolored .55 .25
Complete booklet, 5 #3025 3.50
3026 A1130 8k multicolored .95 .40
Complete booklet, 5 #3026 5.00
Nos. 3024-3026 (3) 1.95 .85

A1131

A1132

Photo. & Engr.

1997, Nov. 12 *Perf. 11½*

3027 A1131 4k multicolored .50 .20
Complete booklet, 5 #3027 2.75

Christmas.

Art Type of 1967 Inscribed "CESKA REPUBLIKA"

7k, Landscape with Chateau in Chantilly, by Antonín Chittussi (1847-91). 12k, The Prophets Came Out of the Desert, by Frantisek Bílek (1872-1941). 1 6k, Parisian Antiquarians, by T. F. Simon (1877-1942).

1997, Nov. 12 Engr. *Perf. 12*

3028 A565 7k multi, horiz. .85 .85
3029 A565 12k multi 1.40 1.40
3030 A565 16k multi 1.90 1.90
Nos. 3028-3030 (3) 4.15 4.15

Nos. 3028-3030 were each issued in sheets of 4. Value, set $17.

1998, Jan. 20 Litho. *Perf. 11½x12*

3031 A1132 7k multicolored .85 .30

1998 Winter Olympic Games, Nagano.

Tradition of Czech Stamp Production — A1133

Photo. & Engr.

1998, Jan. 20 *Perf. 12x11½*

3032 A1133 12.60k Type A8 1.50 .55
a. Booklet pane of 8 + 4 labels 12.50
Complete booklet, #3032a 12.50

Pres. Václav Havel A1134

Love A1135

1998, Jan. 22

3033 A1134 4.60k dark grn & red .55 .20

See No. 3114.

1998, Feb. 4 *Perf. 11½*

3034 A1135 4k multicolored .45 .20
Complete booklet, 5 #3034 2.50

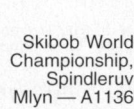

Skibob World Championship, Spindleruv Mlyn — A1136

1998, Feb. 25

3035 A1136 8k multicolored .95 .35

Prague Philatelic Exhibition Type of 1938

Souvenir Sheet

1998, Feb. 25 Engr. *Perf. 12x11½*

3036 A87 Sheet of 2 7.00 4.00
a. 30k like #251a 3.50 1.50

Prague '98, Intl. Philatelic Exhibition.

Easter — A1137

Photo. & Engr.

1998, Mar. 25 *Perf. 11x11½*

3037 A1137 4k multicolored .45 .20
Complete booklet, 5 #3037 2.25

Ondrejov Observatory, Cent. — A1138

1998, Mar. 25 *Perf. 12x11½*

3038 A1138 4.60k multicolored .55 .20

Czech Ice Hockey Team, Gold Medalists at Nagano Winter Olympic Games — A1139

1998, Apr. 1 Litho. *Perf. 11½x12*

3039 A1139 23k Dominik Hasek 2.75 2.00

No. 3039 was issued in a sheet with two labels.

Charles University and New Town, Prague, 650th Anniv. — A1140

Designs: a, 15k, Hands forming arch, University seal. b, 22k, Charles IV (1316-78), Holy Roman Emperor, King of Bohemia. c, 23k, Groin vault, St. Vitus Cathedral, Prague.

1998, Apr. 1 Engr. *Perf. 12*

3040 A1140 Sheet of 3, #a.-c. 7.00 5.00

World Book and Copyright Day — A1141

1998, Apr. 23 Litho. *Perf. 12x11½*

3041 A1141 10k multicolored 1.20 .45

Nature Conservation A1142

1998, Apr. 23 *Perf. 13x13½*

3042 A1142 4.60k Perdix perdix .55 .20
3043 A1142 4.60k Lyrurus tetrix .55 .20
a. Pair, #3042-3043 1.10 .60
3044 A1142 8k Cervus elaphus .95 .35
3045 A1142 8k Alces alces .95 .35
a. Pair, #3044-3045 1.90 1.10
Nos. 3042-3045 (4) 3.00 1.10

Natl. Festivals and Holidays A1143

Europa: 11k, King's Ride. 15k, Wearing masks for Carnival.

Litho. & Engr.

1998, May 5 *Perf. 11½*

3046 A1143 11k multicolored 1.25 .55
3047 A1143 15k multicolored 1.75 .75

Intl. Children's Day — A1144

Designs: 4k, Two satyr musicians. 4.60k, Character riding on fish.

Photo. & Engr.

1998, May 27 *Perf. 11½*

3048 A1144 4k multicolored .45 .20
a. Booklet of 6 +4 labels 3.00
Complete booklet, #3048a 3.00
3049 A1144 4.60k multicolored .55 .20
a. Booklet of 6 + 4 labels 3.50
Complete booklet, #3049a 3.50

Famous Men — A1145

Designs: 4k, Frantisek Kmoch (1848-1912), bandleader, composer. 4.60k, Frantisek Palacky (1798-1876), historian, politician. 6k, Rafael Kubelík (1914-96), composer, conductor.

1998, May 27 *Perf. 11½x12*

3050 A1145 4k multicolored .45 .20
3051 A1145 4.60k multicolored .55 .20
3052 A1145 6k multicolored .70 .25
Nos. 3050-3052 (3) 1.70 .65

Revolt of 1848, 150th Anniv. A1146

1998, May 27 *Perf. 12x11½*

3053 A1146 15k multicolored 1.75 .50

Art Type of 1967 Inscribed "CESKA REPUBLIKA"

Praga 1998 Intl. Stamp Exhibition, works of art: 22k, Amorfa Dvoubarevna Fuga, by Frantisek Kupka (1871-1957), horiz. 23k, Escape, by Paul Gauguin (1848-1903), horiz.

1998, June 17 Engr. *Perf. 12*

3054 A565 22k multicolored 2.50 1.75
3055 A565 23k multicolored 2.75 1.75

Nos. 3054-3055 were each issued in sheets of 4. Value, set $22.

UNESCO World Heritage Sites Type of 1996

8k, St. Barbara Cathedral, Kutná Hora, horiz. 11k, The Chateau of Valtice, horiz.

1998, Oct. 7 Engr. *Perf. 11½x12*

3056 A1109 8k multicolored .95 .40
3057 A1109 11k multicolored 1.25 .60

Nos. 3056-3057 were each issued in sheets of 8. Value, set $17.50.

Czechoslovak Republic, 80th Anniv. — A1147

Designs based on World War I recruitment posters by Vojtech Preissig (1873-1944): 4.60k, Soldiers holding flags, guns. 5k, Three soldiers marching. 12.60k, Flags waving from city buildings.

Perf. 11½x11¾

1998, Oct. 28 **Litho. & Engr.**

3058 A1147 4.60k multicolored .55 .25
3059 A1147 5k multicolored .60 .25
3060 A1147 12.60k multicolored 1.50 .60
Nos. 3058-3060 (3) 2.65 1.10

No. 3060 was issued in sheets of 6+2 labels. Value $25.

Christmas A1148

Designs: 4k, People following star. 6k, Angel blowing trumpet over town, vert.

Photo. & Engr.

1998, Nov. 18 ***Perf. 11½***

3061 A1148 4k multicolored .45 .20
Complete booklet, 5 #3061 2.50
3062 A1148 6k multicolored .70 .25
Complete booklet, 5 #3062 4.00

Signs of the Zodiac — A1149

1998-2000 ***Perf. 12x11½***

3063 A1149 1k Capricorn .20 .20
3064 A1149 10k Aquarius 1.20 .25
3065 A1149 9k Libra 1.00 .25
3066 A1149 8k Cancer .95 .25
3067 A1149 20k Sagittarius 2.25 .45

Photo. & Engr.

Perf. 11¾x11¼

3068 A1149 5k Taurus .55 .25
Booklet, 5 #3068 2.75
3069 A1149 5.40k Scorpio .60 .25
Booklet, 5 #3069 3.00
3070 A1149 2k Virgo .25 .20
3071 A1149 40h Pisces .20 .20
3072 A1149 12k Leo 1.40 .30
3073 A1149 17k Gemini 2.00 .65
3074 A1149 26k Aries 3.00 .95
Nos. 3063-3074 (12) 13.60 4.20

Issued: 1k, 10k, 11/18; 9k, 5/5/99; 8k, 20k, 9/8/99; 5k, 5.40k, 12/8/99; 2k, 5/9/00. 40h, 1/20/01. 12k, 2/21/01. 17k, 9/1/02. 26k, 2/12/03.

Art Type of 1967 Inscribed "CESKA REPUBLIKA"

15k, Painting from the Greater Cycle, 1902, by Jan Preisler (1872-1918), horiz. 16k, Spinner, by Josef Navrátil (1798-1865).

1998, Dec. 9 ***Perf. 12***

3075 A565 15k multicolored 1.75 1.00
3076 A565 16k multicolored 1.80 1.00

Nos. 3075-3076 were each issued in sheets of 4. Value, set $14.50.

A1150

A1151

Photo. & Engr.

1999, Jan. 20 ***Perf. 11½x11¾***

3077 A1150 4.60k #164 .50 .20
a. Booklet pane of 8 + 4 labels 4.00
Complete booklet, #3077a 4.00

Tradition of Czech stamp production.

Photo. & Engr.

1999, Feb. 17 ***Perf. 11½***

Domestic cats.

3078 A1151 4.60k shown .55 .20
Complete booklet, 5 #3078 2.75
3079 A1151 5k Adult, kitten .55 .25
Complete booklet, 5 #3079 2.75
3080 A1151 7k Two cats .80 .30
Complete booklet, 5 #3080 4.00
Nos. 3078-3080 (3) 1.90 .75

Easter — A1152

A1153

Photo. & Engr.

1999, Mar. 10 ***Perf. 11¼x11½***

3081 A1152 3k multicolored .35 .20

Perf. 12¾x13¼

1999, Mar. 10 **Litho.**

Protected birds: No. 3082, Merops apiaster. No. 3083, Upupa epops.

Protected butterflies: No. 3084, Catocala electa. No. 3085, Euphydryas maturna.

3082 A1153 4.60k multicolored .55 .20
3083 A1153 4.60k multicolored .55 .20
a. Pair, #3082-3083 1.10 .60
Complete booklet, 3 #3082, 2 #3083 2.75
3084 A1153 5k multicolored .55 .20
3085 A1153 5k multicolored .55 .20
a. Pair, #3084-3085 1.10 .60
Complete booklet, 3 #3084, 2 #3085 2.75

Nature conservation.

Czech Republic's Entry Into NATO — A1154

Photo. & Engr.

1999, Mar. 12 ***Perf. 12x11½***

3086 A1154 4.60k multicolored .55 .20

Council of Europe, 50th Anniv. A1155

Photo. & Engr.

1999, Apr. 14 ***Perf. 11¾x11¼***

3087 A1155 7k multicolored .80 .30

Natl. Olympic Committee, Cent. — A1156

Design: Josef Rössler-Orovsky (1869-1933), founder of Czech Olympic Committee.

1999, Apr. 14 ***Perf. 11¼x11¾***

3088 A1156 9k multicolored 1.00 .35

Europa A1157

Natl. Parks: 11k, Sumava. 17k, Podyji.

1999, May 5 ***Perf. 11¾x11¼***

3089 A1157 11k multicolored 1.25 .40
3090 A1157 17k multicolored 2.00 .65

Nos. 3089-3090 were each issued in sheets of 8. Value, set $27.

Ferda the Ant, Pytlik the Beetle and Ladybird A1158

Photo. & Engr.

1999, May 26 ***Perf. 11½x11¼***

3091 A1158 4.60k multicolored .55 .20
Complete booklet, 8 #3091 4.50

Bridges A1159

1999, May 26 **Engr.** ***Perf. 11¾***

3092 A1159 8k Stádlec, vert. .90 .40
3093 A1159 11k Cernvír 1.25 .60

Nos. 3092-3094 were each issued in sheets of 8. Value, set $17.50.

Souvenir Sheet

Paleontologist Joachim Barrande (1799-1883) and Trilobite Fossils — A1160

a, 13k, Barrande, fossils. b, 31k, Delphon forbesi, Ophioceras simplex, Carolicrinus barrandei.

1999, June 23 **Engr.** ***Perf. 11¾***

3094 A1160 Sheet of 2, #a.-b. + 2 labels 5.00 4.00

Jihlava Mining Rights, 750th Anniv. A1161

Photo. & Engr.

1999, June 23 ***Perf. 11¾x11¼***

3095 A1161 8k multicolored .90 .35
a. Bklt. pane of 8 + 4 labels 7.25
Complete booklet, #3095a 7.50

UPU, 125th Anniv. — A1162

Litho. & Engr.

1999, June 23 ***Perf. 11¾***

3096 A1162 9k multicolored 1.00 .40

Issued se-tenant with two labels.

Vincenc Preissnitz (1799-1851), Hydrotherapy Advocate A1163

Photo. & Engr.

1999, Sept. 8 ***Perf. 11¼***

3097 A1163 4.60k multicolored .50 .25

UNESCO.

Carved Beehives A1164

Cartoons by Miroslav Bartak A1165

Designs: 4.60k, Woman. 5k, St. Joseph and Infant Jesus. 7k, Chimney sweep.

Photo. & Engr.

1999, Sept. 29 ***Perf. 11¼x11½***

3098 A1164 4.60k multi .55 .25
Complete booklet, 5 #3098 2.75
3099 A1164 5k multi .60 .25
Complete booklet, 5 #3099 3.00
3100 A1164 7k multi .80 .30
Complete booklet, 5 #3100 4.00
Nos. 3098-3100 (3) 1.95 .80

1999, Oct. 20

Designs: 4.60k, Doctor in clown mask, infant. 5k, Dog with pipe. 7k, Night seeping through window sill.

3101 A1165 4.60k multi .55 .25
3102 A1165 5k multi .60 .25
3103 A1165 7k multi .80 .30
Nos. 3101-3103 (3) 1.95 .80

Souvenir Sheet

Beuron Art School — A1166

Designs: a, 11k, Mater Dei, 1898. b, 13k, Pantocrator, 1911.

Litho. & Engr.

1999, Oct. 20 *Perf. 11¾*
3104 A1166 Sheet of 2, #a.-b. 2.75 2.00

Art Type of 1967 Inscribed "CESKA REPUBLIKA"

Designs: 13k, Red Orchid, by Jindrich Styrsky (1899-1942). 17k, Landscape with Marsh, by Julius Marák (1832-99). 26k, Monument, by Frantisek Hudecek (1909-90).

1999, Nov. 10 **Engr.** *Perf. 11¾*
3105 A565 13k multi 1.50 1.00
3106 A565 17k multi 2.00 1.50
3107 A565 26k multi 3.00 2.00
Nos. 3105-3107 (3) 6.50 4.50

Nos. 3105-3107 were each issued in sheets of 4. Value, set $26.

A1167

A1168

Photo. & Engr.

1999, Nov. 10 *Perf. 11¼x11½*
3108 A1167 3k multi .35 .20

Christmas.

Photo. & Engr.

2000, Jan. 20 *Perf. 11¼x11¾*
3109 A1168 5.40k #B151 .60 .25
a. Bklt. pane of 8 + 4 labels 5.00
Booklet, #3109a 5.00

Tradition of Czech stamp production.

Brno 2000 Philatelic Exhibition — A1169

Designs: 5k, 1593 view of Brno. 50k, St. James's Church, vert.

2000, Jan. 20 *Perf. 11¾x11¼*
3110 A1169 5k multi .60 .20

Souvenir Sheet

Perf. 11¼x11¾
3111 A1169 50k multi 5.75 4.00

No. 3110 printed in sheets of 35 stamps and 30 labels.

Kutna Hora Royal Mining Law, 700th Anniv. — A1170

2000, Mar. 1 *Perf. 11¼x11¾*
3112 A1170 5k multi .60 .25
a. Booklet pane of 8 + 4 labels 5.00
Booklet, #3112a 5.00

Souvenir Sheet

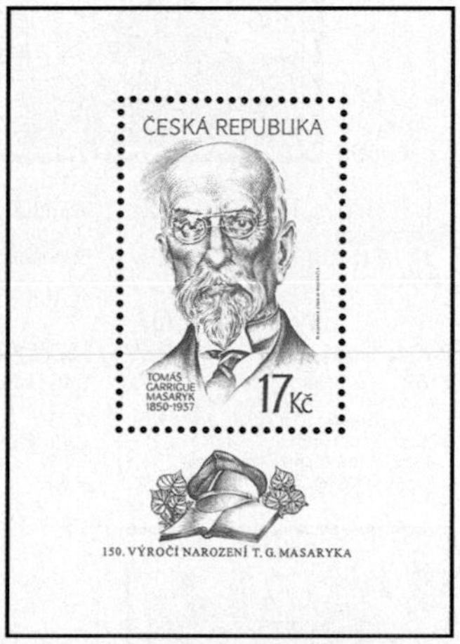

Pres. Thomas Garrigue Masaryk (1850-1937) — A1171

Illustration reduced.

2000, Mar. 1 **Engr.** *Perf. 11¾*
3113 A1171 17k multi 2.00 1.50

Pres. Havel Type of 1998

Photo. & Engr.

2000, Mar. 1 *Perf. 11¾x11¼*
3114 A1134 5.40k Prus bl & org brn .60 .25

Easter — A1172

Photo. & Engr.

2000, Apr. 5 *Perf. 11¼x11½*
3115 A1172 5k multi .60 .25

Souvenir Sheet

Prague, 2000 European City of Culture — A1173

No. 3116: a, 9k, Statue of man. b, 11k, Statue of harpist. c, 17k, Statue of King Charles IV.
Illustration reduced.

Litho. & Engr.

2000, Apr. 5 *Perf. 11¾*
3116 A1173 #a-c + 3 labels 4.25 4.25

Souvenir Sheet

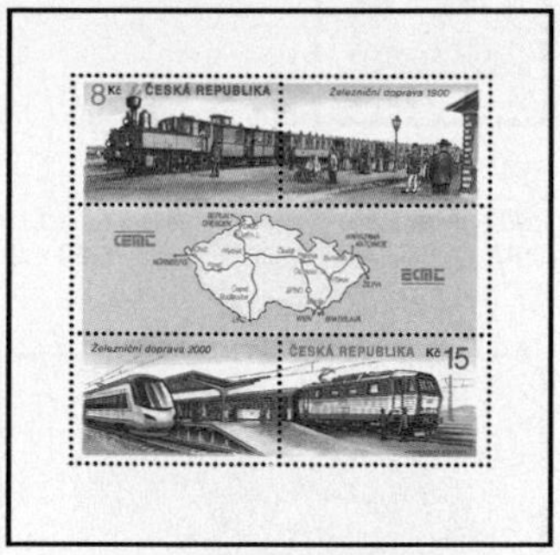

Trains — A1174

No. 3117: a, 8k, Train from 1900. b, 15k, Train from 2000.
Illustration reduced.

Litho. & Engr.

2000, May 5 *Perf. 11¾*
3117 A1174 Sheet of 2, #a-b, +3 labels 2.50 2.50

Czech Personalities A1175

5k, Vítezslav Nezval (1900-58), writer. 8k, Gustav Mahler (1860-1911), composer.

Photo. & Engr.

2000, May 5 *Perf. 11¼x11¾*
3118-3119 A1175 Set of 2 1.50 .45

Europa, 2000

Common Design Type

2000, May 5 **Litho.** *Perf. 12¾x13¼*
3120 CD17 9k multi 1.00 .40

Intl. Children's Year — A1176

Photo. & Engr.

2000, May 31 *Perf. 11½x11¼*
3121 A1176 5.40k multi .60 .20
a. Booklet pane of 8 + 2 labels 5.00
Booklet, #3121a 5.00

1995 Proof of Fermat's Last Theorem by Andrew Wiles A1177

2000, May 31 *Perf. 11¾x11¼*
3122 A1177 7k multi .80 .25

Intl. Mathematics Year.

Prague Landmarks — A1178

Designs: 9k, Charles Bridge tower. 11k, St. Nicholas's Church. 13k, Town Hall.

2000, June 28 **Engr.** *Perf. 11¾*
3123-3125 A1178 Set of 3 3.75 1.10

Mushrooms — A1179

No. 3126, 5k: a, Geastrum pouzarii. b, Boletus satanoides.
No. 3127, 5.40k: a, Morchella pragensis. b, Verpa bohemica.

Photo. & Engr.

2000, June 28 *Perf. 11¼x11½*

Pairs, #a-b

3126-3127 A1179 Set of 2 2.40 .70
Booklet, 3 #3126a, 2 #3126b 3.50
Booklet, 3 #3127b, 2 #3127a 3.50

Meeting of Intl. Monetary Fund and World Bank Group, Prague — A1180

2000, Aug. 30 *Perf. 11¾x11¼*
3128 A1180 7k multi .80 .25

Ancient Olympics A1181

2000, Aug. 30
3129 A1181 9k multi 1.00 .35

2000 Summer Olympics, Sydney — A1182

2000, Aug. 30
3130 A1182 13k multi 1.50 .45

Hunting — A1183

No. 3131: a, 5k, Falconry. b, 5k, Deer at feed trough.
No. 3132: a, 5.40k, Ducks and blind. b, 5.40k, Deer and blind.

Photo. & Engr.

2000, Oct. 4 *Perf. 11¼x11¾*

Horiz. Pairs, #a-b

3131-3132 A1183 Set of 2 2.40 .55
Booklet, 3 #3131a, 2 #3131b 3.50
Booklet, 3 #3132a, 2 #3132b 3.50

Art Type of 1967 Inscribed "CESKA REPUBLIKA"

Designs: 13k, St. Luke the Evangelist, by Master Theodoricus. 17k, Simeon With Infant

Jesus, by Petr Jan Brandl. 26k, Brunette, by Alfons Mucha.

2000, Nov. 15 Engr. *Perf. 11¾*
3133-3135 A565 Set of 3 6.50 4.00

Nos. 3133-3135 were each issued in sheets of 4. Value, set $27.

Christmas — A1184

Photo. & Engr.
2000, Nov. 15 *Perf. 11¼x11½*
3136 A1184 5k multi .55 .20

End of Millennium A1185

Advent of New Millennium A1186

2000, Nov. 22
3137 A1185 9k multi 1.00 .35

2001, Jan. 2
3138 A1186 9k multi 1.00 .35

Tradition of Czech Stamp Production A1187

2001, Jan. 20 *Perf. 11¼x11¾*
3139 A1187 5.40k #474 .60 .25
a. Booklet pane of 8 + 4 labels 5.00
Booklet, #3139a 5.00

Jan Amos Komensky (Comenius, 1592-1670), Theologian — A1188

Photo. & Engr.
2001, Mar. 14 *Perf. 11¼x11½*
3140 A1188 9k red & black 1.00 .35

Souvenir Sheet

Architecture — A1189

No. 3141: a, 13k, Church and decorations, Jakub. b, 17k, Arcade decorations, Bucovice Castle. c, 31k, Dance Hall, Prague.

2001, Mar. 28 Engr. *Perf. 11¾x11½*
3141 A1189 Sheet of 3, #a-c 7.00 4.00

Easter — A1190

Photo. & Engr.
2001, Mar. 28 *Perf. 11¼x11½*
3142 A1190 5.40k multi .60 .25

Souvenir Sheet

Allegory of Art, by Vaclav Vavrinec Reiner — A1191

Litho. & Engr.
2001, Apr. 18 *Perf. 11¾*
3143 A1191 50k multi 5.75 4.00

Europa A1192

Photo. & Engr.
2001, May 9 *Perf. 11¾x11¼*
3144 A1192 9k pur & lilac 1.00 .35

European Men's Volleyball Championships, Ostrova — A1193

Photo. & Engr.
2001, May 9 *Perf. 11¼x11½*
3145 A1193 12k multi 1.40 .40

Intl. Children's Day — A1194

Famous Men — A1195

Photo. & Engr.
2001, May 30 *Perf. 11¼x11½*
3146 A1194 5.40k multi .60 .25
a. Booklet pane of 8 + 2 labels 5.00 —
Booklet, #3146a 5.00

2001, May 30

Designs: 5.40k, Frantisek Skroup (1801-62), composer. 16k, Frantisek Halas (1901-49), writer.

3147-3148 A1195 Set of 2 2.50 .80

Congratulations A1196

2001, June 20
3149 A1196 5.40k multi .60 .25
Booklet, 5 #3149 3.00

Dogs — A1197

No. 3150: a, West Highland terrier. b, Beagle.
No. 3151: a, German shepherd. b, Golden retriever.

Photo. & Engr.
2001, June 20 *Perf. 11½x11¼*
3150 Pair 1.40 1.00
a.-b. A1197 5.40k Any single .65 .25
Booklet, 3 #3150a, 2 #3150b 3.25
Booklet, 3 #3150b, 2 #3150a 3.25
3151 Pair 1.40 1.00
a.-b. A1197 5.40k Any single .65 .25
Booklet, 3 #3151a, 2 #3151b 3.25

Zoo Animals A1198

No. 3152: a, Pongo pygmaeus. b, Panthera tigris altaica.
No. 3153: a, Ailurus fulgens. b, Fennecus zerda.

Photo. & Engr.
2001, Sept. 5 *Perf. 11¾x11¼*
3152 Pair 1.40 1.00
a.-b. A1198 5.40k Any single .65 .25
Booklet, 3 #3152b, 2 #3152a 3.25
3153 Pair 1.40 1.00
a.-b. A1198 5.40k Any single .65 .25
Booklet, 3 #3153b, 2 #3153a 3.25

UNESCO World Heritage Sites A1199

Designs: 12k, Kormeríz Castle and Gardens. 14k, Holasovice Historical Village Restoration.

2001, Oct. 9 Engr. *Perf. 11½x11¾*
3154-3155 A1199 Set of 2 3.00 1.25

See Nos. 3177-3178, 3267-3268.

Year of Dialogue Among Civilizations A1200

Photo. & Engr.
2001, Oct. 9 *Perf. 11¼x11½*
3156 A1200 9k multi 1.00 .35

Mills A1201

Christmas A1202

Designs: 9k, Windmill. 14.40k, Water mill.

2001, Oct. 9
3157-3158 A1201 Set of 2 2.75 .80

Photo. & Engr.
2001, Nov. 14 *Perf. 11¼x11½*
3159 A1202 5.40k multi .60 .30

Art Type of 1967 Inscribed "CESKA REPUBLIKA"

Designs: 12k, The Annunciation of the Virgin Mary, by Michael J. Rentz. 17k, The Sans Souci Bar in Nimes, by Cyril Bouda. 26k, The Goose Keeper, by Vaclav Brozík.

2001, Nov. 14 Engr. *Perf. 11¾*
3160-3162 A565 Set of 3 6.25 4.00

Nos. 3160-3162 were each issued in sheets of 4. Value, set $25.

Tradition of Czech Stamp Production — A1203

Photo. & Engr.
2002, Jan. 20 *Perf. 11¼x11¾*
3163 A1203 5.40k Type A89 .60 .25
a. Booklet pane of 8 + 4 labels 5.00 —
Booklet, #3163a 5.00

2002 Winter Olympics, Salt Lake City — A1204

2002, Jan. 30 *Perf. 11¼*
3164 A1204 12k multi 1.40 .45

For overprint, see No. 3168.

2002 Winter Paralympics, Salt Lake City — A1205

2002, Jan. 30 *Perf. 11¼x11½*
3165 A1205 5.40k multi .60 .25

Composers Jaromír Vejvoda (1902-88), Josef Poncar (1902-86) and Karel Vacek (1902-82) — A1206

2002, Mar. 6 *Perf. 11¾x11¼*
3166 A1206 9k multi 1.00 .35

Easter — A1207

2002, Mar. 6 *Perf. 11¼x11½*
3167 A1207 5.40k multi .60 .25

No. 3164 Overprinted in Blue

Photo. & Engr.

2002, Mar. 8 *Perf. 11¼*

3168 A1204 12k multi 1.40 .65

Divan, by Vlaho Bukovac (1855-1922) — A1208

Litho. & Engr.

2002, Apr. 23 *Perf. 11¾*

3169 A1208 17k multi 2.00 1.25

Printed in sheets of 4 + 2 labels. Value $9. See Croatia No. 487.

Europa A1209

Photo. & Engr.

2002, May 7 *Perf. 11¾x11¼*

3170 A1209 9k multi 1.00 .35

Souvenir Sheet

Czech Culture and France — A1210

No. 3171: a, 23k, Klávesy Piana-Jezero, by Frantisek Kupka. b, 31k, Man with Broken Nose, sculpture by Auguste Rodin.

Perf. 11¾x11½

2002, May 7 **Litho. & Engr.**

3171 A1210 Sheet of 2, #a-b 6.25 4.00

Intl. Children's Day — A1211

Photo. & Engr.

2002, May 29 *Perf. 11¼x11½*

3172 A1211 5.40k multi .60 .25

a. Booklet pane of 8 + 2 labels 5.00 —

Complete booklet, #3172a 5.00

Margaritifera Margaritifera A1212

2002, June 6

3173 A1212 9k multi 1.00 .35

Jan Hus (1372-1415), Religious Leader — A1213

2002, June 19

3174 A1213 9k multi + label 1.00 .35

Souvenir Sheet

Worldwide Fund for Nature (WWF) — A1214

Butterflies: a, 5.40k, Maculinea nausithous. b, 5.40k, Maculinea alcon. c, 9k, Maculinea teleius. d, 9k, Maculinea arion.

Litho. & Engr.

2002, June 19 *Perf. 11¾*

3175 A1214 Sheet of 4, #a-d + 4 labels 3.25 2.50

Pansy — A1215

Photo. & Engr.

2002, Sept. 1 *Perf. 11¾x11¼*

3176 A1215 6.40k multi .75 .25

See Nos. 3220-3221, 3262-3263, 3293-3294, 3340, 3345-3347, 3363-3366.

World Heritage Sites Type of 2001

Designs: 12k, Litomysl Castle. 14k, Holy Trinity Column, Olomouc, vert.

Perf. 11½x11¾, 11¾x11½

2002, Sept. 11 **Engr.**

3177-3178 A1199 Set of 2 2.75 2.00

Nos. 3177-3178 were each issued in sheets of 8. Value, set $25.

Emil Zátopek (1922-2000), Olympic Long Distance Runner — A1216

Photo. & Engr.

2002, Sept. 11 *Perf. 11¼x11¾*

3179 A1216 9k multi 1.00 .35

Pres. Havel Type of 1998

Photo. & Engr.

2002, Nov. 6 *Perf. 11¾x11¼*

3180 A1134 6.40k pur & blue .75 .25

St. Nicholas' Day A1217

Christmas A1218

2002, Nov. 6 *Perf. 11¼x11½*

3181 A1217 6.40k multi .75 .25

a. Booklet pane of 8 + 2 labels 6.00 —

Complete booklet, #3181a 6.00

2002, Nov. 13

3182 A1218 6.40k multi .75 .25

NATO Summit, Prague — A1219

2002, Nov. 14 *Perf. 11¼x11¾*

3183 A1219 9k multi 1.00 .30

Furniture — A1220

Designs: 6.40k, Armchair, 17th cent. 9k, Sewing table with hemispheric cover, 1820. 12k, Dressing table with mirror, 1860. 17k, Art deco amchair, 1923.

2003, Dec. 11

3184-3187 A1220 Set of 4 5.00 2.00

Art Type of 1967 Inscribed "CESKA REPUBLIKA"

Designs: 12k, The Abandoned, by Jaroslav Panuska, horiz. 20k, St. Wenceslas, by Mikolás Ales. 26k, Portrait of a Young Man with a Lute, by Jan Petr Molitor.

2002, Dec. 11 **Engr.** *Perf. 11¾*

3188-3190 A565 Set of 3 6.50 3.50

Nos. 3188-3190 were each issued in sheets of 4. Value, set $27.

Souvenir Sheet

Czech Republic, 10th Anniv. — A1221

Litho. & Engr.

2003, Jan. 1 *Perf. 11¾*

3191 A1221 25k multi 2.75 1.50

Tradition of Czech Stamp Production — A1222

Photo. & Engr.

2003, Jan. 20 *Perf. 11¼x11¾*

3192 A1222 6.40k Type A75 .75 .25

a. Booklet pane of 8 + 2 labels 6.00 —

Complete booklet, #3192a 6.00

Famous Men — A1223

Designs: 6.40k, Jaroslav Vrchlicky (1853-1912), poet. 8k, Josef Thomayer (1853-1927), physician and writer.

2003, Feb. 12 *Perf. 11½x11¼*

3193-3194 A1223 Set of 2 1.60 .50

Easter — A1224

2003, Mar. 26 *Perf. 11¼x11½*

3195 A1224 6.40k multi .75 .25

Roses Above Prague — A1225

Perf. 12¾x13¼

2003, Mar. 26 **Litho.**

3196 A1225 6.40k multi + label .75 .35

Labels could be personalized.

Issued in sheets of 9 stamps and 12 labels. Value $9.

Lace
A1226

Designs: 6.40k, Netted lace. 9k, Bobbin lace.

Photo. & Engr.

2003, Mar. 26 *Perf. 11¼*

3197 A1226 6.40k bl, dk bl & red	.75	.25
a. Booklet pane of 6 + 4 labels	4.50	—
Complete booklet, #3197a	4.50	
3198 A1226 9k dk bl, bl & red	1.00	.35
a. Booklet pane of 6 + 4 labels	6.00	—
Complete booklet, #3197a	6.00	

Europa — A1227

Litho. & Engr.

2003, May 7 *Perf. 11¾*

3199 A1227 9k multi 1.00 .65

Geologic Attractions — A1228

Designs: 12k, Sandstone towers, Hrubá Skála Region. 14k, Punkva Caves, Moravian karst area.

2003, May 7 **Engr.** *Perf. 11½x11¾*

3200-3201 A1228 Set of 2 3.00 1.75

Nos. 3200-3201 were each issued in sheets of 8. Value, set $25.

Mach and Sebestova, Children's Television Show Characters — A1229

Photo. & Engr.

2003, May 28 *Perf. 11¼x11½*

3202 A1229 6.40k multi .75 .35

First Electric Railway, Tábor — Bechyne, Cent.
A1230

2003, May 28 *Perf. 11¾x11¼*

3203 A1230 10k multi 1.10 .45

A1231

A1233

A1232

Observation towers: No. 3204, 6.40k, Klet. No. 3205, 6.40k, Slovanka.

2003, May 28 *Perf. 11¼x11½*

3204-3205 A1231 Set of 2 1.50 .50

2003, June 25 *Perf. 11¾x11¼*

3206 A1232 9k multi 1.00 .35

European Shooting Championships, Plzen and Brno.

2003, June 25 *Perf. 11¼x11½*

3207 A1233 9k multi 1.00 .35

Josef Dobrovsky (1753-1829), linguist.

Pres. Vaclav Klaus — A1234

Photo. & Engr.

2003 *Perf. 11¾x11¼*

3208 A1234 6.40k buff, red & vio bl	.75	.35
3209 A1234 6.50k Prus bl & pur	.75	.35

Issued: 6.40k, 7/30; 6.50k, 11/5.

See No. 3264.

Souvenir Sheet

Tropical Fish — A1235

No. 3210: a, 12k, Betta splendens (27x44mm). b, 14k, Pterophyllum scalare (27x44mm). c, 16k, Carassius auratus (54x44mm). d, 20k, Symphysodon aequifasciatus (54x44mm).

Litho. & Engr.

2003, Sept. 10 *Perf. 11¾*

3210 A1235 Sheet of 4, #a-d 7.00 4.50

Oriental Carpets
A1236

Designs: 9k, Turkish prayer carpet, 19th cent. 12k, Turkish carpet, 18th cent.

2003, Oct. 1 **Engr.** *Perf. 11¾*

3211-3212 A1236 Set of 2 2.40 1.50

Nos. 3211-3212 were each issued in sheets of 4. Value, set $10.

Tympanum, Porta Coeli Monastery, Predklásterí — A1237

Photo. & Engr.

2003, Oct. 15 *Perf. 11¾x11¼*

3213 A1237 6.50k multi	.75	.45
a. Booklet pane of 8 + 4 labels	6.00	—
Complete booklet, #3213a	6.00	

Birds of Prey — A1238

Designs: 6.50k, Milvus milvus. 8k, Falco peregrinus. 9k, Hieraaetus pennatus.

2003, Oct. 15 *Perf. 11¼x11½*

3214 A1238 6.50k multi	.75	.25
Booklet, 5 #3214	3.75	
3215 A1238 8k multi	.90	.30
Booklet, 5 #3215	4.50	
3216 A1238 9k multi	1.00	.30
Booklet, 5 #3216	5.00	
Nos. 3214-3216 (3)	2.65	.85

Czech Fire Fighters, 140th Anniv.
A1239

Fire engines: 6.50k, Wooden fire engine, 1822. 9k, Motorized fire engine, 1933. 12k, CAS 8/Avia Daewoo fire truck, 2002.

2003, Oct. 15 *Perf. 11¾x11¼*

3217-3219 A1239 Set of 3 3.00 1.00

Flower Type of 2002

Designs: 50h, Cornflower (chrpa). 6.50k, Dahlia (jirina).

2003, Oct. 22

3220 A1215 50h multi	.20	.20
3221 A1215 6.50k multi	.75	.25

Roses Over Prague Type of 2003 and

Prague Castle Lantern — A1240

2003, Oct. 22 **Litho.** *Perf. 12¾x13¼*

3222 A1225 6.50k multi + label	.75	.25
3223 A1240 9k multi + label	1.00	.30

Labels could be personalized.

Nos. 3222-3223 were each issued in sheets of 9 stamps and 12 labels. Value, set $17.50.

Art Type of 1967 Inscribed "CESKA REPUBLIKA"

Designs: 17k, Poor Countryside, by Max Svabinsky, horiz. 20k, Autumn in Veltrusy, by Antonín Slavícek. 26k, Eleanora de Toledo, by Agnolo Bronzino.

2003, Nov. 5 **Engr.** *Perf. 11¾*

3224-3226 A565 Set of 3 7.25 3.50

Nos. 3224-3226 were each issued in sheets of 4. Value, set $30.

Christmas
A1241

Photo. & Engr.

2003, Nov. 5 *Perf. 11¼x11½*

3227 A1241 6.50k multi .75 .35

Tradition of Czech Stamp Production
A1242

Photo. & Engr.

2004, Jan. 20 *Perf. 11¼x11¾*

3228 A1242 6.50k Vignette of #1703	.75	.35
a. Booklet pane of 8 + 4 labels	6.00	—
Complete booklet, #3228a	6.00	

Church of the Assumption of the Virgin Mary, Brno — A1243

2004, Feb. 18 **Engr.** *Perf. 11¾*

3229 A1243 17k multi 2.00 1.00

Brno 2005 Philatelic Exhibition.

No. 3229 was issued in sheets of 4. Value $8.

Industrial Building Historical Preservation
A1244

Designs: 6.50k, Busek's Water Forging Hammer, Lniste. 17k, Iron Furnace, Stará Hut u Adamova.

Photo. & Engr.

2004, Feb. 18 *Perf. 11½x11¼*

3230-3231 A1244 Set of 2 2.75 .90

Easter
A1245

2004, Mar. 17

3232 A1245 6.50k multi .75 .25

Art Type of 1967 Inscribed "CESKA REPUBLIKA"

Design: Prometheus, by Antonín Procházka.

2004, Mar. 17 **Engr.** *Perf. 11¾*

3233 A565 26k multi 3.00 1.50

Brno 2005 Philatelic Exhibition. No. 3233 was issued in sheets of 4. Value $12.

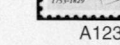

World Ice Hockey Championships, Prague and Ostrava — A1246

Photo. & Engr.

2004, Apr. 14 *Perf. 11¼x11¾*
3234 A1246 12k multi 1.40 .45

Admission to European Union A1247

Photo. & Engr.

2004, May 1 *Perf. 11¼*
3235 A1247 9k multi 1.00 .35

Admission to the European Union — A1248

2004, May 1 Litho. *Perf. 11¾x11¼*
3236 A1248 9k multi 1.00 .35

No. 3236 was issued in sheets of 10. Value $8.

Europa A1249

2004, May 5 *Perf. 11¼*
3237 A1249 9k multi 1.00 .35

Composers of Czech Operas — A1250

Designs: 6.50k, Dalibor, by Bedrich Smetana (1824-84). 8k, Jakobín, by Antonín Dvorák (1841-1904). 10k, Její Pastorkyna, by Leos Janácek (1854-1928).

Photo. & Engr.

2004, May 5 *Perf. 11¼x11¾*
3238-3240 A1250 Set of 3 2.75 .95

For Children A1251

Photo. & Engr.

2004, May 26 *Perf. 11½x11¼*
3241 A1251 6.50k multi .75 .25
a. Booklet pane of 8 + 2 labels 6.00 —
Complete booklet, #3241a 6.00

Statue of Radegast, by Albín Polásek — A1252

2004, May 26 *Perf. 11¼x11½*
3242 A1252 6.50k multi .75 .25

Brno 2005 Philatelic Exhibition.

Tourist Attractions — A1253

Designs: 12k, Holy Mountain, Príbram. 14k, Holy Shrine, Bystrice pod Hostynem.

2004, May 26 Engr. *Perf. 11½x11¾*
3243-3244 A1253 Set of 2 3.00 1.50

Nos. 3243-3244 were each issued in sheets of 8. Value, set $24.

A1254

A1255

Photo. & Engr.

2004, June 23 *Perf. 11¼x11¾*
3245 A1254 6.50k multi .75 .25

2004 Paralympics, Athens.

2004, June 23
3246 A1255 9k multi 1.00 .35

2004 Summer Olympics, Athens.

Petrarch (1304-74), Poet — A1256

2004, June 23 *Perf. 11¾x11¼*
3247 A1256 14k multi 1.60 .55

Famous Trees — A1257

Designs: 6.50k, Singing lime tree, Telecí. 8k, Jan Zizka oak tree, Podhradí.

Photo. & Engr.

2004, Sept. 8 *Perf. 11¼x11½*
3248 A1257 6.50k multi .75 .25
Complete booklet, 5 #3248 3.75
3249 A1257 8k multi .90 .30
Complete booklet, 5 #3249 4.50

Miniature Sheet

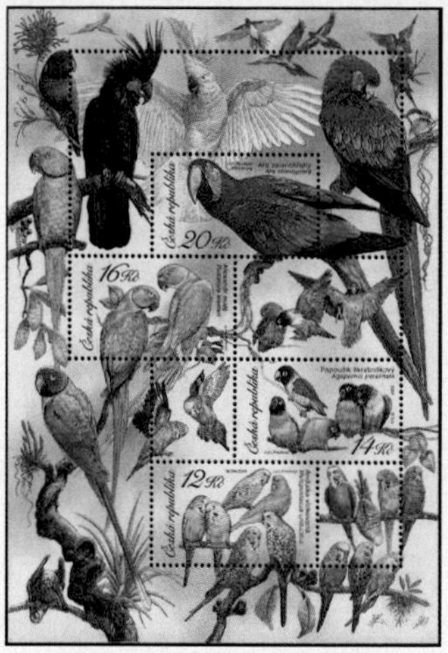

Parrots — A1258

No. 3250: a, 12k, Melopsittacus undulatus. b, 14k, Agapornis personata. c, 16k, Psittacula krameri. d, 20k, Ara chloroptera.

Litho. & Engr.

2004, Sept. 8 *Perf. 11¾*
3250 A1258 Sheet of 4, #a-d, + 4 labels 7.00 4.00

Compulsory School Attendance, 230th Anniv. — A1259

Photo. & Engr.

2004, Sept. 29 *Perf. 11¼x11½*
3251 A1259 6.50k multi .75 .25

Baby Carriages — A1260

Carriages made about: 12k, 1880. 14k, 1890. 16k, 1900.

2004, Oct. 20
3252-3254 A1260 Set of 3 4.75 1.75

Art Type of 1967 Inscribed "CESKA REPUBLIKA"

Designs: 20k, On the Outskirts of the Cesky Ráj Region, by Alois Bubák, horiz. 22k, The Long, the Broad and the Sharpsight, by Hanus Schwaiger. 26k, The Spring, by Vojtéch Hynais.

2004, Nov. 10 Engr. *Perf. 11¾*
3255-3257 A565 Set of 3 7.75 4.00

Nos. 3255-3257 were each issued in sheets of 4. Value, set $32.

Christmas — A1261

Photo. & Engr.

2004, Nov. 10 *Perf. 11¼x11½*
3258 A1261 6.50k multi .75 .25

Tradition of Czech Stamp Production A1262

2005, Jan. 18 *Perf. 11¼x11¾*
3259 A1262 6.50k Design of #975 .75 .30
a. Booklet pane of 8 + 4 labels 6.00 —
Complete booklet, #3259a 6.00

Peacock and Bugler Portal Decoration — A1263

2005, Jan. 18 Litho. *Perf. 12¾x13¼*
3260 A1263 7.50k multi + label .85 .30

Labels could be personalized for an additional fee.

Issued in sheets of 9 stamps and 12 labels. Value $8.

Souvenir Sheet

Moonscape, by Petr Ginz — A1264

Perf. 11¾x11½

2005, Jan. 18 Litho. & Engr.
3261 A1264 31k multi 3.50 2.00

Flower Type of 2002

Designs: 7.50k, Lily (lilie). 19k, Fuchsia (fuchsie).

Photo. & Engr.

2005 *Perf. 11¾x11¼*
3262 A1215 7.50k multi .85 .30
3263 A1215 19k multi 2.10 .85

Issued: 7.50k, 1/20; 19k, 3/2.

Pres. Vaclav Klaus Type of 2003

2005, Feb. 9
3264 A1234 7.50k claret & red .85 .30

Granny, by Bozena Nemcová, 150th Anniv. of Publication
A1265

2005, Feb. 9 *Perf. 11¼x11¾*
3265 A1265 7.50k multi .85 .30

Easter — A1266

Photo. & Engr.

2005, Mar. 2 *Perf. 11¼x11½*
3266 A1266 7.50k multi .85 .30

UNESCO World Heritage Sites Type of 2001

Designs: 14k, St. Prokop's Basilica, Trebíc, vert. 16k, Villa Tugendhat, Brno.

Perf. 11¾x11½, 11½x11¾

2005, Mar. 23 **Engr.**
3267-3268 A1199 Set of 2 3.50 1.90

Nos. 3267-32682 were each issued in sheets of 8. Value, set $28.

Famous Men — A1267

Designs: 7.50k, Bohuslav Brauner (1855-1935), chemist. 12k, Adalbert Stifter (1805-68), writer, painter. 19k, Mikulás Dacicky of Heslov (1555-1626), poet.

Photo. & Engr.

2005, Apr. 13 *Perf. 11¼x11¾*
3269-3271 A1267 Set of 3 4.50 1.60

Europa
A1268

2005, May 4 **Litho.** *Perf. 11¼*
3272 A1268 9k multi 1.00 .35

Battle of Austerlitz, Bicent. — A1269

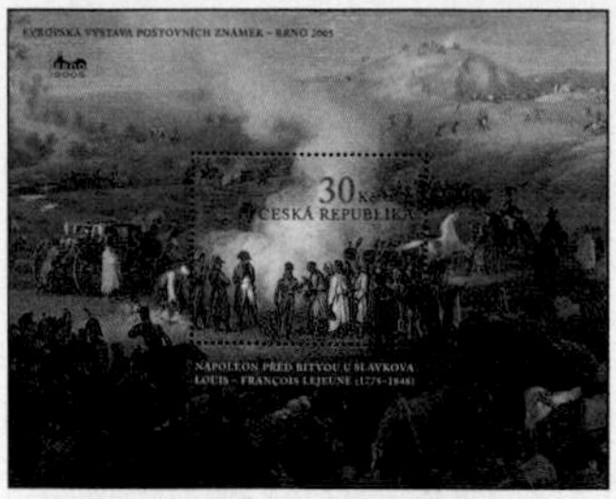

Napoleon Before the Battle of Austerlitz, by Louis-François Lejeune — A1270

Photo. & Engr.

2005, May 4 *Perf. 11¾x11¼*
3273 A1269 19k multi 2.10 .85

Souvenir Sheet

Litho. & Engr.

Perf. 11¾

3274 A1270 30k multi 3.50 2.25

Brno 2005 Stamp Exhibition (#3274). See France No. 3115.

Kremílek and Vochomurka, by Václav Ctvrtek — A1271

Photo. & Engr.

2005, May 25 *Perf. 11¼x11½*
3275 A1271 7.50k multi .85 .30
a. Booklet pane of 8 + 2 labels 7.00 —
Complete booklet, #3275a 7.00

A1272 A1273

2005, May 25 *Perf. 11¼x11¾*
3276 A1272 12k multi 1.00 .50

Intl. Year of Physics.

2005, June 22
3277 A1273 9k multi .75 .35

2005 European Baseball Championships.

Souvenir Sheet

Protected Flora and Fauna of the Krkonose Mountains — A1274

No. 3278: a, 12k, Viola lutea sudetica, Hedysarum hedysaroides (44x28mm). b, 14k, Cinclus cinclus, Leucojum vernum (44x28mm). c, 15k, Sorex alpinus, Salamandra salamandra, Primula minima (44x54mm). d, 22k, Mt. Snezka, Luscinia svecica svecica, Aeschna coerulea, Pneumonanthe asclepiadea (44x54mm).

Litho. & Engr.

2005, June 22 *Perf. 11¾*
3278 A1274 Sheet of 4, #a-d, + 4 labels 7.25 4.00

Church Bells — A1275

Bells from: 7.50k, Benesov, 1322, Havlíckuv Brod, 1335. 9k, Dobrs, 1561, 1596. 12k, Olomouc, 1827.

Photo. & Engr.

2005, Sept. 7 *Perf. 11½x11¾*
3279 A1275 7.50k multi .85 .30
Complete booklet, 5 #3279 4.25
3280 A1275 9k multi 1.00 .40
Complete booklet, 5 #3280 5.00
3281 A1275 12k multi 1.40 .50
Complete booklet, 5 #3281 7.00
Nos. 3279-3281 (3) 3.25 1.20

Tractors
A1276

Designs: 7.50k, 1923 John Deere 15/27. 9k, 1921 Lanz Bulldog HL-12, 1596. 18k, 1937 Skoda HT 40.

2005, Sept. 21 *Perf. 11½x11¼*
3282 A1276 7.50k multi .85 .30
Complete booklet, 5 #3282 4.25
3283 A1276 9k multi 1.00 .35
Complete booklet, 5 #3283 5.00
3284 A1276 18k multi 2.00 .75
Complete booklet, 5 #3284 10.00
Nos. 3282-3284 (3) 3.85 1.40

World Summit on the Information Society, Tunis
A1277

2005, Sept. 21 *Perf. 11¼*
3285 A1277 9k org & violet 1.00 .35

Curling
A1278

Photo. & Engr.

2005, Oct. 12 *Perf. 11¾x11¼*
3286 A1278 17k multi 2.00 .70

Art Type of 1967 Inscribed "CESKA REPUBLIKA"

Designs: 22k, Summer Landscape, by Adolf Kosárek. 25k, Deinotherium, by Zdenék Burian. 26k, Osiky Near Velké Nemcice, by Alois Kalvoda.

2005, Nov. 9 **Engr.** *Perf. 11¾*
3287-3289 A565 Set of 3 8.25 5.00

Nos. 3287-3289 were each issued in sheets of 4. Value, set $33.

A1279

Christmas
A1280

Photo. & Engr.

2005, Nov. 9 *Perf. 11¼x11½*
3290 A1279 7.50k multi .85 .30

Perf. 11½x11¼

3291 A1280 9k multi 1.00 .35

Tradition of Czech Stamp Production
A1281

Photo. & Engr.

2006, Jan. 20 *Perf. 11¼x11¾*
3292 A1281 7.50k Portion of #C59 .85 .30
a. Booklet pane of 8 + 2 labels 7.00 —
Complete booklet, #3292a 7.00

Flower Type of 2002

Designs: 11k, Marshmallow (ibisek). 24k, Daffodil (narcis).

2006 *Perf. 11¾x11¼*
3293 A1215 11k multi 1.25 .45
3294 A1215 24k multi 2.75 1.00

Issued: 11k, 2/1; 24k, 2/22.

Flowers — A1282

Flowers, Grapes, Glass of Wine — A1283

2006 **Litho.** *Perf. 12¾x13¼*
3295 A1282 10k multi + label 1.10 .60
3296 A1283 12k multi + label 1.40 .75

Issued: 10k, 2/1; 12k, 2/22. Labels could be personalized for an additional fee.

Nos. 3295-3296 were issued in sheets of 9 stamps and 12 labels. Value, set $22.50.

Madonna of Zbraslav — A1284

2006, Feb. 8 Engr. *Perf. 11¾*
3297 A1284 25k multi 2.75 1.50

Printed in sheets of 4. Value $11.

2006 Winter Paralympics, Turin — A1285

Photo. & Engr.
2006, Feb. 8 *Perf. 11¾x11¼*
3298 A1285 7.50k multi .85 .30

2006 Winter Olympics, Turin — A1286

2006 *Perf. 11¼x11¾*
3299 A1286 9k multi 1.00 .40

With "K. NEUMANNOVA / ZLATA MEDAILE" Overprinted in Red Reading Up
3300 A1286 9k multi 1.00 .40

Issued: No. 3299, 2/8; No. 3300, 3/15.

Famous Men — A1287

Designs: 11k, Frantisek Josef Gerstner (1756-1832), mathematician and educator. 12k, Jaroslav Jezek (1906-42), composer. 19k, Sigmund Freud (1856-1939), psychoanalyst.

2006, Feb. 22 *Perf. 11½x11¼*
3301-3303 A1287 Set of 3 4.75 1.75

Easter — A1288

2006, Mar. 22 *Perf. 11¼x11½*
3304 A1288 7.50k multi .85 .30

Osek Monastery — A1289

Kokorinsko Capstones — A1290

2006, Mar. 22 Engr. *Perf. 11½x11¾*
3305 A1289 12k multi 1.40 .65
3306 A1290 15k multi 1.75 .85

Nos. 3305-3306 were each issued in sheets of 8. Value, set $25.

Love — A1291

Photo. & Engr.
2006, Apr. 26 *Perf. 11¼x11½*
3307 A1291 7.50k multi .85 .35
Complete booklet, 5 #3307 4.25

Europa A1292

Silhouette of person and: 10k, Horse. 20k, Dog.

2006, May 3 *Perf. 11¾x11¼*
3308-3309 A1292 Set of 2 3.50 1.40

Rumcajs, Manka and Cipísek, by V. Ctvrtek — A1293

Photo. & Engr.
2006, May 31 *Perf. 11¼x11½*
3310 A1293 7.50k multi .85 .35
a. Booklet pane of 8 + 2 labels 7.00 —
Complete booklet, #3310a 7.00

A1294

A1295

2006, June 14 *Perf. 11¼x11¾*
3311 A1294 19k multi 2.10 .85

Kamenice Pass, Czech Switzerland National Park.

2006, June 14

Jewelry with garnets: 15k, Silver brooch with pearl, 1904. 18k, Gold pendant, 1930.

3312-3313 A1295 Set of 2 3.75 1.50

Miniature Sheet

Bohemian Kings of Premyslid Dynasty — A1296

No. 3314: a, 12k, Otakar I Premysl (c. 1155-1230). b, 14k, Václav (Wenceslas) I (1205-53). c, 15k, Otakar II Premysl (1230-78). d, 22k, Václav (Wenceslas) II (1271-1305). e, 28k, Václav (Wenceslas) III (1289-1306).

2006, June 14 Engr. *Perf. 11¾*
3314 A1296 Sheet of 5, #a-e, + label 10.50 6.00

Souvenir Sheet

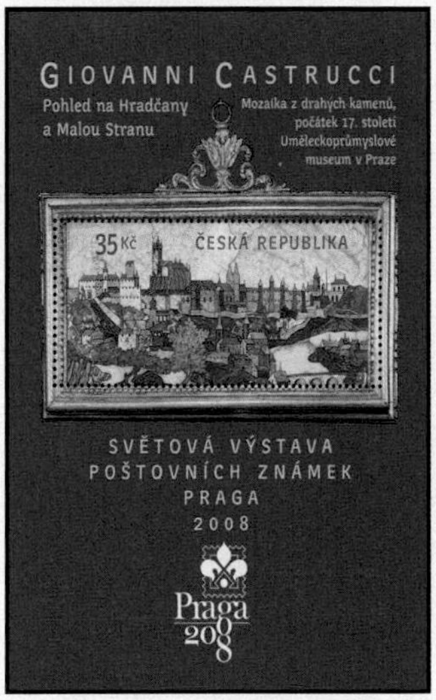

Mosaic of Prague Castle, by Giovanni Castrucci — A1297

Litho. & Engr.
2006, Sept. 13 *Perf. 11¾*
3315 A1297 35k multi 3.25 1.60

Cacti — A1298

No. 3316: a, Gymnocalycium denudatum. b, Obregonia denegrii.
No. 3317: a, Astrophytum asterias. b, Cintia knizei.

Perf. 11¼x11¾
2006, Sept. 13 Litho.
3316 A1298 7.50k Pair, #a-b 1.40 .70
Complete booklet, 2 #3316a, 3 #3316b 3.50
3317 A1298 10k Pair, #a-b 1.90 .95
Complete booklet, 2 #3317a, 3 #3317b 4.75

Ecology A1299

2006, Sept. 27 *Perf. 11¾x11¼*
3318 A1299 7.50k multi .70 .35

Christmas — A1300

2006, Oct. 11 *Perf. 12¾x13¼*
3319 A1300 7.50k multi + label .70 .35

Printed in sheets of 9 stamps + 12 labels. Labels could be personalized.

Vrtbovská Garden, Prague — A1301

Photo. & Engr.
2006, Oct. 11 *Perf. 11½x11¾*
3320 A1301 7.50k multi .70 .35
a. Booklet pane of 8 + 4 labels 5.75 —
Complete booklet, #3320a 5.75

Praga 2008 Intl. Philatelic Exhibition, Prague.

Wooden Churches — A1302

Designs: 7.50k, Church of the Virgin Mary, Broumov. 19k, Church of St. Andrew, Hodslavice.

Photo. & Engr.
2006, Oct. 11 *Perf. 11¾x11¼*
3321-3322 A1302 Set of 2 2.40 1.25

Art Type of 1967 Inscribed "CESKA REPUBLIKA"

Designs: 22k, Still Life with Fruit, by Jan Davidsz de Heem. 25k, Montenegrin Madonna, by Jaroslav Cermák. 28k, Pod Suchym Skalim, by Frantisek Kaván, horiz.

2006, Nov. 8 Engr. *Perf. 11¾*
3323-3325 A565 Set of 3 7.25 3.75

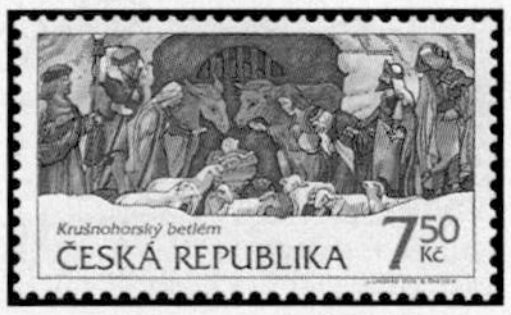

Christmas — A1303

Photo. & Engr.

2006, Nov. 8 *Perf. 11¾x11½*
3326 A1303 7.50k multi .75 .35

Emblem of Praga 2008 Intl. Philatelic Exhibition — A1304

2006, Dec. 1 **Litho.**
3327 A1304 7.50k multi .75 .35

See Nos. 3341, 3368.

Czech Technical University, Prague, 300th Anniv. — A1305

Photo. & Engr.

2007, Jan. 10 *Perf. 11¾x11½*
3328 A1305 9k multi .85 .40

Famous Men — A1306

Designs: 7.50k, Frána Srámek (1877-1952), writer. 19k, Karel Slavoj Amerling (1807-84), educator.

2007, Jan. 10 *Perf. 11½x11¼*
3329-3330 A1306 Set of 2 2.50 1.25

Tradition of Czech Stamp Production A1307

2007, Jan. 20 *Perf. 11½x11¾*
3331 A1307 7.50k Type A242 .70 .35
a. Booklet pane of 8 + 4 labels 5.75 —
Complete booklet, #3331a 5.75

Cancer Prevention A1308

Photo. & Engr.

2007, Feb. 21 *Perf. 11¼x11½*
3332 A1308 7.50k multi .70 .35

Snake — A1309

Perf. 11¼x11¾

2007, Feb. 21 **Litho.**
3333 A1309 12k multi 1.25 .60

Oriental Art A1310

Designs: 12k, Girl with a Puppet, by Kunisawa Utagawa. 24k, Siva, Parvati and Ganesa, 19th cent. Indian glass painting.

Litho. & Engr.

2007, Feb. 21 *Perf. 11¾*
3334-3335 A1310 Set of 2 3.50 1.75

Easter — A1311

Photo. & Engr.

2007, Mar. 14 *Perf. 11¼x11½*
3336 A1311 7.50k multi .75 .35

Model of Mala Strana Area of Prague, by Antonín Landweil — A1312

2007, Mar. 14 *Perf. 11¾x11¼*
3337 A1312 7.50k multi .75 .35

Praga 2008 Intl. Philatelic Exhibition, Prague.

Stoclet House, Brussels, Designed by Josef Hoffmann — A1313

Designs: 20k, Building interior. 35k, Building exterior.

2007, Mar. 26 *Perf. 11¼x11¾*
3338-3339 A1313 Set of 2 5.25 2.60

See Belgium Nos. 2228-2229.

Flowers Type of 2006

Perf. 12¾x13¼

2007, Mar. 26 **Litho.**
3340 A1282 11k multi + label 1.10 .55

Label could be personalized for an additional fee.

Praga 2008 Emblem Type of 2006

2007, Apr. 4 *Perf. 11¾x11½*
3341 A1304 11k blue & multi 1.10 .55

Spas A1314

Designs: 12k, Jurkovic House, Luhacovice. 15k, Gocár Pavillion, Lázne Bohdanec.

2007, Apr. 4 **Engr.** *Perf. 11½x11¾*
3342-3343 A1314 Set of 2 2.60 1.40

Europa A1315

Photo. & Engr.

2007, May 9 *Perf. 11¼*
3344 A1315 11k multi 1.10 .55

Scouting, cent.

Flowers Type of 2002

Designs: 1k, Cyclamen (bramborik). 15k, Tropaeolum (lichorerisnice). 23k, Geranium (pelargonie).

Photo. & Engr.

2007 *Perf. 11¾x11¼*
3345 A1215 1k multi .20 .20
3346 A1215 15k multi 1.50 .75
3347 A1215 23k multi 2.25 1.10
Nos. 3345-3347 (3) 3.95 2.05

Issued: 1k, 23k, 5/9. 15k, 9/5.

Fast Arrows, Comic Strip by Jaroslav Foglar A1316

Photo. & Engr.

2007, May 30 *Perf. 11¾x11¼*
3348 A1316 7.50k multi .75 .35
a. Booklet pane of 8 + 4 labels 6.00 —
Complete booklet, #3348a 6.00

Historic Stoves — A1317

Designs: 7.50k, Gothic era stove, Olomouc, and tile. 12k, Renaissance era stove, Rícany u Prahy and tile.

Photo. & Engr.

2007, June 20 *Perf. 11½x11¾*
3349 A1317 7.50k multi .70 .35
Complete booklet, 5 #3349 3.50
3350 A1317 12k multi 1.25 .60
Complete booklet, 5 #3350 6.25

Souvenir Sheet

Vaclav Hollar (1607-77), Engraver — A1318

Litho. & Engr.

2007, June 20 *Perf. 11¾*
3351 A1318 35k multi + 2 labels 3.50 1.75

Souvenir Sheet

Charles Bridge, Prague, 650th Anniv. — A1319

2007, June 20
3352 A1319 45k multi 4.25 2.10

Praga 2008 World Philatelic Exhibition.

First Movie Theater in Prague, Cent. A1320

Photo. & Engr.

2007, Sept. 5 *Perf. 11¾x11¼*
3353 A1320 7.50k multi .75 .35

Didactica Opera Omnia, by Comenius, 350th Anniv. — A1321

2007, Sept. 5
3354 A1321 12k multi 1.25 .60

Miniature Sheet

Flora and Fauna of the White Carpathians — A1322

No. 3355: a, 9k, Ophrys holosericea (27x44mm). b, 10k, Colias myrmidone, Anacamptis pyramidalis (27x44mm). c, 11k, Ophrys apifera (27x44mm). d, 12k, Coracias garrulus, Gymnadenia densiflora (54x44mm).

Litho. & Engr.

2007, Sept. 5 *Perf. 11¾*
3355 A1322 Sheet of 4, #a-d, + 4 labels 4.25 2.10

Emil Holub (1847-1902), Naturalist — A1323

Photo. & Engr.

2007, Oct. 3 *Perf. 11¾x11¼*
3356 A1323 11k multi 1.10 .55

Water Towers — A1324

Towers in: 7.50k, Karviná. 18k, Plzen.

2007, Oct. 3 *Perf. 11¼x11¾*
3357-3358 A1324 Set of 2 2.60 1.25

Art Type of 1967 Inscribed "CESKA REPUBLIKA"

Designs: 22k, Vrbicany Castle, by Amálie Mánesova, horiz. 25k, Way to Bechnye Castle, by Otakar Lebeda. 28k, Montmartre, by Sobeslav Hippolyt Pinkas, horiz.

2007, Nov. 7 **Engr.** *Perf. 11¾*
3359-3361 A565 Set of 3 8.50 4.25

Christmas — A1325

Photo. & Engr.

2007, Nov. 7 *Perf. 11¼x11½*
3362 A1325 7.50k multi .85 .40

Flower Type of 2002

Design: 2.50k, Gaillardia (kokarda); 3k, Azalea (azalka); 10k, Rose (ruze); 21k, Gerbera daisy (gerbera).

Photo. & Engr.

2007-08 *Perf. 11¾x11¼*
3363 A1215 2.50k multi .30 .20
3364 A1215 3k multi .40 .20
3365 A1215 10k multi 1.25 .60
3366 A1215 21k multi 2.60 1.40
Nos. 3363-3366 (4) 4.55 2.40

Issued: 2.50k, 12/12/07; 3k, 3/19/08; 10k, 1/30/08; 21k, 3/5/08.

Czech Republic's Entry Into Schengen Border-Free Zone A1326

2007, Dec. 19 **Litho.** *Perf. 11¼*
3367 A1326 10k multi 1.10 .55

Praga 2008 Emblem Type of 2006

2007, Dec. 19 *Perf. 11¾x11¼*
3368 A1304 18k bl grn & blue 2.00 1.00

Tradition of Czech Stamp Production A1327

Photo. & Engr.

2008, Jan. 20 *Perf. 11¼x11¾*
3369 A1327 10k Type A311 1.25 .60
a. Booklet pane of 8 + 4 labels 10.00 —
Complete booklet, #3369a 10.00

Famous Men — A1328

Designs: 11k, Karel Klostermann (1848-1923), writer. 14k, Josef Kajetán Tyl (1808-56), playwright.

2008, Jan. 20 *Perf. 11¼x11½*
3370-3371 A1328 Set of 2 3.00 1.50

Peacock and Bugler Type of 2005 and Flowers, Grapes and Glass of Wine Type of 2006 Redrawn

2008, Jan. 30 **Litho.** *Perf. 12¾x13¼*
3372 A1263 10k multi + label 1.25 .60
3373 A1283 17k multi + label 2.00 1.00

Nos. 3372-3373 were issued in sheets of 9 stamps and 12 labels. Labels could be personalized for an additional fee.

George of Podebrady (1420-71), King of Bohemia — A1329

Photo. & Engr.

2008, Feb. 20 *Perf. 11¼x11¾*
3374 A1329 12k multi 1.50 .75

Intl. Year of Planet Earth A1330

2008, Feb. 20 **Litho.** *Perf. 11¼*
3375 A1330 18k multi 2.25 1.10

Easter A1331

Photo. & Engr.

2008, Mar. 5 *Perf. 11½x11¼*
3376 A1331 10k multi 1.25 .60

Bath Servant Zuzana Carrying King Wenceslas IV Over the Vltava River, by J. Navrátil — A1332

2008, Mar. 5 *Perf. 11¾x11¼*
3377 A1332 10k multi 1.25 .60
a. Booklet pane of 8 + 4 labels 10.00 —
Complete booklet, #3377a 10.00

Praga 2008 Intl. Philatelic Exhibition, Prague.

Publication of Orbis Pictus, Children's Picture Book, by Comenius, 350th Anniv. — A1333

2008, Mar. 19 *Perf. 11¼x11¾*
3378 A1333 10k multi 1.25 .60

Mountaintop Hotel With Broadcast Tower, Jested — A1334

Hradec Kralové Buildings and Monuments A1335

2008, Mar. 19 **Engr.** *Perf. 11½*
3379 A1334 12k multi 1.50 .75
3380 A1335 15k multi 1.90 .95

Pres. Klaus Type of 2003

Photo. & Engr.

2008, Apr. 2 *Perf. 11¾x11¼*
3381 A1234 10k multi 1.25 .60

A1336

A1337

Items in National Technical Museum: 10k, Reichenbach-Ertel astronomical theodolite, c. 1830. 14k, 1935 Jawa 750 sports car, horiz. 18k, Märky, Bromovsky-Schulz gasoline combustion engine, c. 1889.

Perf. 11¼x11¾, 11¾x11¼

2008, Apr. 16 **Photo. & Engr.**
3382-3384 A1336 Set of 3 5.25 2.60

National Technical Museum, Prague, cent.

2008, Apr. 16 *Perf. 11¼x11¾*
3385 A1337 17k multi 2.10 1.10

Czech Hockey Association, cent.

Europa A1338

2008, May 7 **Litho.** *Perf. 11¾x11¼*
3386 A1338 17k multi 2.10 1.10

The Doggy's and Pussy's Tales, Children's Book by Josef Capek A1339

Photo. & Engr.

2008, May 28 *Perf. 11½x11¼*
3387 A1339 10k multi 1.40 .70
a. Booklet pane of 8 + 2 labels 11.50 —
Complete booklet, #3387a 11.50

Souvenir Sheet

Ledeburk Gardens, Prague — A1340

Litho. & Engr.

2008, May 28 *Perf. 11¾*
3388 A1340 51k multi 6.75 3.25

Praga 2008 World Philatelic Exhibition.

Miniature Sheet

Flora and Fauna of Trebon Basin UNESCO Biosphere Reservation — A1341

No. 3389: a, 10k, Alcedo atthis (28x44mm). b, 12k, Lutra lutra and Spiraea salicifolia (54x44mm). c, 14k, Haliaeetus albicilla (54x44mm). d, 18k, Netta rufina and Nymphaea alba (54x44mm).

2008, May 28
3389 A1341 Sheet of 4, #a-d, + 3 labels 7.00 3.50

2008 Paralympics, Beijing — A1342

Perf. 11¾x11¼

2008, June 18 **Litho.**
3390 A1342 10k multi 1.40 .70

2008 Summer Olympics, Beijing — A1343

2008, June 18
3391 A1343 18k multi 2.40 1.25

Explorers — A1344

Designs: 12k, Ferdinand Stolicka (1838-74), explorer of Himalayas. 21k, Alois Musil (1868-1944), explorer of Jordanian desert.

2008, June 18 **Photo. & Engr.**

3392-3393	A1344	Set of 2	4.50	2.25

Children's Book Illustration by Josef Palacek — A1345

2008, Sept. 3 **Litho.** ***Perf. 12¾x13¼***

3394	A1345	10k multi + label	1.25	.60

Printed in sheets of 9 stamps + 12 labels. Labels could be personalized.

Emmaus Monastery, Prague — A1346

Photo. & Engr.

2008, Sept. 3 ***Perf. 11¼x11¾***

3395	A1346	10k multi	1.25	.60

Praga 2008 World Philatelic Exhibition.

Applied Art Designers' Association, Cent. — A1347

2008, Sept. 3 ***Perf. 11¾x11¼***

3396	A1347	26k multi	3.00	1.50

Karel Plicka (1894-1987), Photographer — A1348

Litho. & Engr.

2008, Sept. 12 ***Perf. 11¾***

3397	A1348	35k multi + 2 labels	4.00	2.00

See Slovakia No. 548.

Souvenir Sheet

Mail Coach — A1349

2008, Sept. 12

3398	A1349	35k multi	4.00	2.00

Praga 2008 Intl. Stamp Exhibition, Prague, and 2008 Vienna Intl. Stamp Exhibition. See Austria No. 2172.

SEMI-POSTAL STAMPS

Nos. B1-B123 were sold at 1 ½ times face value at the Philatelists' Window of the Prague P.O. for charity benefit. They were available for ordinary postage.

Almost all stamps between Nos. B1-B123 are known with misplaced or inverted overprints and/or in pairs with one stamp missing the overprint.

The overprints of Nos. B1-B123 have been well forged.

Austrian Stamps of 1916-18 Overprinted in Black or Blue

a

1919 ***Perf. 12½***

B1	A37	3h brt violet	.20	*.25*
B2	A37	5h lt green	.20	*.25*
B3	A37	6h dp org (Bl)	.60	*.80*
B4	A37	6h dp org (Bk)	*2,000.*	*2,000.*
B5	A37	10h magenta	.80	*1.00*
B6	A37	12h lt blue	.80	.80
B7	A42	15h dull red	.20	*.25*
B8	A42	20h dark green	.20	*.25*
a.		20h green	55.00	40.00
B9	A42	25h blue	.35	.20
B10	A42	30h dull violet	.35	.25
B11	A39	40h olive grn	.40	.40
B12	A39	50h dk green	.40	.40
B13	A39	60h dp blue	.40	.40
B14	A39	80h orange brn	.40	.40
B15	A39	90h red violet	.80	.80
B16	A39	1k car, *yel* (Bl)	.60	.60
B17	A39	1k car, *yel* (Bk)	62.50	62.50
B18	A40	2k light blue	3.25	3.25
a.		2k dark blue	3,000.	2,000.
B19	A40	3k carmine rose	37.50	32.50
a.		3k claret	2,500.	900.00
B20	A40	4k yellow grn	20.00	15.00
a.		4k deep green	45.00	35.00
B21	A40	10k violet	300.00	160.00
a.		10k deep violet	375.00	275.00
b.		10k black violet	450.00	300.00

The used value of No. B18a is for copies which have only a Czechoslovakian cancellation. Some of the copies of Austria No. 160 which were officially overprinted with type "a" and sold by the post office, had previously been used and lightly canceled with Austrian cancellations. These canceled-before-overprinting stamps, which were postally valid, sell for about one-fourth as much.

Granite Paper

B22	A40	2k light blue	4.00	2.90
B23	A40	3k carmine rose	10.00	8.25

The 4k and 10k on granite paper with this overprint were not regularly issued.

Excellent counterfeits of Nos. B1-B23 exist.

Austrian Newspaper Stamps Overprinted

b

Imperf

On Stamp of 1908

B26	N8	10h carmine	*2,750.*	2,000.

On Stamps of 1916

B27	N9	2h brown	.20	.20
B28	N9	4h green	.40	.40
B29	N9	6h deep blue	.40	.40
B30	N9	10h orange	5.00	5.00
B31	N9	30h claret	1.60	1.60
		Nos. B27-B31 (5)	7.60	7.60

Austrian Special Handling Stamps Overprinted in Blue or Black Stamps of 1916 Overprinted

c

Perf. 12½

B32	SH1	2h claret, *yel* (Bl)	29.00	29.00
B33	SH1	5h dp grn, *yel* (Bk)	*1,600.*	*825.00*

Stamps of 1917 Overprinted

d

B34	SH2	2h cl, *yel* (Bl)	.25	*.35*
a.		Vert. pair, imperf. btwn.	*250.00*	
B35	SH2	2h cl, *yel* (Bk)	60.00	35.00
B36	SH2	5h grn, *yel* (Bk)	.25	.25

Austrian Air Post Stamps, #C1-C3, Overprinted Type "c" Diagonally

B37	A40	1.50k on 2k lil	200.00	200.00
B38	A40	2.50k on 3k ocher	200.00	200.00
B39	A40	4k gray	1,250.	900.00

1919

Austrian Postage Due Stamps of 1908-13 Overprinted Type "b"

B40	D3	2h carmine	*8,000.*	*2,750.*
B41	D3	4h carmine	25.00	15.00
B42	D3	6h carmine	12.50	8.00
B43	D3	14h carmine	90.00	35.00
B44	D3	25h carmine	45.00	20.00
B45	D3	30h carmine	600.00	300.00
B46	D3	50h carmine	1,200.	825.00

Austria Nos. J49-J56 Overprinted Type "b"

B47	D4	5h rose red	.20	*.30*
B48	D4	10h rose red	.20	*.30*
B49	D4	15h rose red	.20	*.30*
B50	D4	20h rose red	2.00	2.00
B51	D4	25h rose red	2.00	2.00
B52	D4	30h rose red	.65	.65
B53	D4	40h rose red	2.00	2.00
B54	D4	50h rose red	550.00	250.00

Austria Nos. J57-J59 Overprinted Type "a"

B55	D5	1k ultra	12.50	10.00
B56	D5	5k ultra	55.00	35.00
B57	D5	10k ultra	425.00	200.00

Austria Nos. J47-J48, J60-J63 Overprinted Type "c" Diagonally

B58	A22	1h gray	32.50	30.00
B59	A23	15h on 2h vio	150.00	110.00
B60	A38	10h on 24h blue	120.00	85.00
B61	A38	15h on 36h vio	1.00	1.00
B62	A38	20h on 54h org	90.00	85.00
B63	A38	50h on 42h choc	1.00	1.00

Hungarian Stamps Ovptd. Type "b"

1919 **Wmk. 137** ***Perf. 15***

On Stamps of 1913-16

B64	A4	1f slate	3,000.	1,600.
B65	A4	2f yellow	3.50	2.50
B66	A4	3f orange	45.00	25.00
B67	A4	6f olive green	4.50	4.50
B68	A4	50f lake, *bl*	1.25	1.00
B69	A4	60f grn, *sal*	50.00	20.00
B70	A4	70f red brn, *grn*	3,000.	1,600.

On Stamps of 1916

B71	A8	10f rose	475.00	175.00
B72	A8	15f violet	250.00	100.00

On Stamps of 1916-18

B73	A9	2f brown org	.20	.20
B74	A9	3f red lilac	.20	.20
B75	A9	5f green	.20	.20
B76	A9	6f grnsh blue	.60	.60
B77	A9	10f rose red	1.40	*2.25*
B78	A9	15f violet	.25	.25
B79	A9	20f gray brown	14.00	14.00
B80	A9	25f dull blue	1.00	.80
B81	A9	35f brown	10.00	10.00
B82	A9	40f olive green	3.25	2.50

Overprinted Type "d"

B83	A10	50f red vio & lil	1.25	*1.60*
B84	A10	75f brt bl & pale bl	1.25	1.60
B85	A10	80f yel grn & pale grn	1.25	1.60
B86	A10	1k red brn & cl	2.50	2.00
B87	A10	2k ol brn & bis	10.00	10.00
B88	A10	3k dk vio & ind	37.50	37.50
B89	A10	5k dk brn & lt brn	140.00	90.00
B90	A10	10k vio brn & vio	1,800.	800.00

Overprinted Type "b"

On Stamps of 1918

B91	A11	10f scarlet	.25	.25
B92	A11	20f dark brown	.30	.30
B93	A11	25f deep blue	1.40	1.25
B94	A12	40f olive grn	4.00	3.25
B95	A12	50f lilac	67.50	25.00

On Stamps of 1919

B96	A13	10f red	10.00	8.00
B97	A13	20f dk brn	*9,000.*	—

Same Overprint On Hungarian Newspaper Stamp of 1914

Imperf

B98	N5	(2f) orange	.20	*.30*

Same Overprint On Hungarian Special Delivery Stamp

Perf. 15

B99	SD1	2f gray grn & red	.25	*.35*

Same Ovpt. On Hungarian Semi-Postal Stamps

B100	SP3	10f + 2f rose red	.80	.80
B101	SP4	15f + 2f violet	1.25	1.25
B102	SP5	40f + 2f brn car	7.00	3.50
		Nos. B98-B102 (5)	9.50	6.20

Hungarian Postage Due Stamps of 1903-18 Overprinted Type "b"

1919 **Wmk. 135** ***Perf. 11½, 12***

B103	D1	50f green & black	*525.00*	*525.00*

Wmk. Crown (136, 136a)

Perf. 11½x12, 15

B104	D1	1f green & black	*1,200.*	*1,000.*
B105	D1	2f green & black	*1,000.*	*750.*
B106	D1	12f green & black	*4,250.*	*3,000.*
B107	D1	50f green & black	275.	150.

Wmk. Double Cross (137)

Perf. 15

On Stamps of 1914

B110	D1	1f green & black	1,250.	600.
B111	D1	2f green & black	700.	550.
B112	D1	5f green & black	1,325.	900.
B113	D1	12f green & black	*5,250.*	*4,000.*
B114	D1	50f green & black	275.	150.

On Stamps of 1915-18

B115	D1	1f green & red	175.00	140.00
B116	D1	2f green & red	1.00	.80
B117	D1	5f green & red	12.50	10.00
B118	D1	6f green & red	1.50	1.50
B119	D1	10f green & red	.60	.60
a.		Pair, one without overprint		
B120	D1	12f green & red	2.00	2.00
B121	D1	15f green & red	7.50	5.00
B122	D1	20f green & red	1.00	1.00
B123	D1	30f green & red	80.00	70.00
		Nos. B115-B123 (9)	281.10	230.90

Excellent counterfeits of Nos. B1-B123 exist.

Bohemian Lion Breaking its Chains — SP1

Mother and Child — SP2

Perf. 11½, 13¾ and Compound

1919 Typo. Unwmk.

Pinkish Paper

B124	SP1	15h gray green	.20	.20
B125	SP1	25h dark brown	.20	.25
a.		25h light brown	*5.00*	4.00
B126	SP1	50h dark blue	.20	.20

Photo.

Yellowish Paper

B127	SP2	75h slate	.20	.20
B128	SP2	100h brn vio	.20	.20
B129	SP2	120h vio, *yel*	.20	.20
		Nos. B124-B129 (6)	1.20	1.25

Nos. B124-B126 commemorate the 1st anniv. of Czechoslovak independence. Nos. B127-B129 were sold for the benefit of Legionnaires' orphans. Imperforates exist.

See No. 1581.

Regular Issues of Czechoslovakia Surcharged in Red:

a

b

1920 ***Perf. 13¾***

B130	A1(a)	40h + 20h bister	.50	*.80*
B131	A2(a)	60h + 20h green	.50	*.80*
B132	A4(b)	125h + 25h gray bl	2.00	*2.25*
		Nos. B130-B132 (3)	3.00	*3.85*

President Masaryk — SP3

Wmk. Linden Leaves (107)

1923 Engr. ***Perf. 13¾x14¾***

B133	SP3	50h gray green	.75	.50
B134	SP3	100h carmine	1.00	.80
B135	SP3	200h blue	3.00	2.75
B136	SP3	300h dark brown	3.25	4.00
		Nos. B133-B136 (4)	8.00	8.05

5th anniv. of the Republic.

The gum was applied through a screen and shows the monogram "CSP" (Ceskoslovenska Posta). These stamps were sold at double their face values, the excess being given to the Red Cross and other charitable organizations.

International Olympic Congress Issue

Semi-Postal Stamps of 1923 Overprinted in Blue or Red

1925

B137	SP3	50h gray green	10.00	8.50
B138	SP3	100h carmine	14.50	12.00
B139	SP3	200h blue (R)	72.50	55.00
		Nos. B137-B139 (3)	97.00	75.50
		Set, never hinged	175.00	

These stamps were sold at double their face values, the excess being divided between a fund for post office clerks and the Olympic Games Committee.

Sokol Issue

Semi-Postal Stamps of 1923 Overprinted in Blue or Red

1926

B140	SP3	50h gray green	1.60	*4.00*
B141	SP3	100h carmine	3.25	*4.00*
B142	SP3	200h blue (R)	15.00	12.50
a.		Double overprint		
B143	SP3	300h dk brn (R)	20.00	20.00
		Nos. B140-B143 (4)	39.85	40.50
		Set, never hinged	140.00	

These stamps were sold at double their face values, the excess being given to the Congress of Sokols, June, 1926.

Catalogue values for unused stamps in this section, from this point to the end of the section, are for Never Hinged items.

Midwife Presenting Newborn Child to its Father; after a Painting by Josef Manes

SP4 SP5

1936 Unwmk. Engr. ***Perf. 12½***

B144	SP4	50h + 50h green	.45	.20
B145	SP5	1k + 50h claret	.80	.65
B146	SP4	2k + 50h blue	2.25	1.60
		Nos. B144-B146 (3)	3.50	2.45

SP6

"Lullaby" by Stanislav Suchharda SP7

1937 ***Perf. 12½***

B147	SP6	50h + 50h dull green	.50	.20
B148	SP6	1k + 50h rose lake	.80	.60
B149	SP7	2k + 1k dull blue	2.25	1.25
		Nos. B147-B149 (3)	3.55	2.05

President Masaryk and Little Girl in Native Costume — SP8

1938 ***Perf. 12½***

B150	SP8	50h + 50h deep green	.65	.50
B151	SP8	1k + 50h rose lake	.85	.65

Souvenir Sheet

Imperf

B152	SP8	2k + 3k black	5.00	5.00

88th anniv. of the birth of Masaryk (1850-1937).

Nos. B150-B151 were each issued in sheets of 100 stamps and 12 blank labels. Value, set of singles with attached labels: mint $3.75; used $2.50.

Allegory of the Republic Type Souvenir Sheet

1938 ***Perf. 12½***

B153	A89	2k (+ 8k) dark blue	4.00	4.00

The surtax was devoted to national relief for refugees.

"Republic" and Congress Emblem SP10

St. George Slaying the Dragon SP11

1945 Engr.

B154	SP10	1.50k + 1.50k car rose	.20	.20
B155	SP10	2.50k + 2.50k blue	.25	.20

Students' World Cong., Prague, 11/17/45.

1946

B156	SP11	2.40k + 2.60k car rose	.20	.20
B157	SP11	4k + 6k blue	.45	.20

Souvenir Sheet

Imperf

B158	SP11	4k + 6k blue	1.50	1.50

1st anniv. of Czechoslovakia's liberation. The surtax aided WW II orphans.

Nos. B156-B157 were each issued in sheets of 100 stamps and 12 inscribed labels. Value for set of singles with attached labels, mint or used $4.

Old Town Hall Type of 1946 Souvenir Sheet

1946, Aug. 3 ***Imperf.***

B159	A114	2.40k rose brown	1.25	.80

Brno Natl. Stamp Exhib., Aug., 1946. The sheet was sold for 10k.

"You Went Away" — SP14

"You Remained Ours" — SP15

"You Came Back" — SP16

1946, Oct. 28 Photo. ***Perf. 14***

B160	SP14	1.60k + 1.40k red brn	.40	.40
B161	SP15	2.40k + 2.60k scarlet	.40	.40
B162	SP16	4k + 4k deep blue	.75	.75
		Nos. B160-B162 (3)	1.55	1.55

The surtax was for repatriated Slovaks.

Barefoot Boy — SP17

Woman and Child — SP18

2k+1k, Mother and child. 3k+1k, Little girl.

Perf. 12½

1948, Dec. 18 Unwmk. Engr.

B163	SP17	1.50k + 1k rose lilac	.35	.20
B164	SP17	2k + 1k dp blue	.20	.20
B165	SP17	3k + 1k rose car	.35	.20
		Nos. B163-B165 (3)	.90	.60

The surtax was for child welfare.

Nos. B163-B165 were each issued in sheets of 100 stamps and 12 inscribed labels. Value for set of singles with attached labels: mint $3.50; used $1.75.

1949, Dec. 18 ***Perf. 12½***

Design: 3k+1k, Man lifting child.

B166	SP18	1.50k + 50h gray	4.00	1.60
B167	SP18	3k + 1k claret	6.00	2.50

The surtax was for child welfare.

SP19

Dove Carrying Olive Branch — SP20

1949, Dec. 18

B168	SP19	1.50k + 50h claret	4.50	1.50
B169	SP20	3k + 1k rose red	4.50	1.50

The surtax was for the Red Cross.

AIR POST STAMPS

Nos. 9, 39-40, 20, and Types of 1919 Surcharged in Red, Blue or Green:

1920 Unwmk. ***Imperf.***

C1	A1	14k on 200h (R)	21.00	18.00
a.		Inverted surcharge	125.00	
C2	A2	24k on 500h (Bl)	50.00	30.00
a.		Inverted surcharge	225.00	
C3	A2	28k on 1000h (G)	32.50	30.00
a.		Inverted surcharge	150.00	
b.		Double surcharge	200.00	
		Nos. C1-C3 (3)	103.50	*78.00*

Perf. 13¾, 13¾x 13 ½ (#C6)

C4	A1	14k on 200h (R)	22.50	*30.00*
a.		Perf. 13¾x13½	95.00	95.00
C5	A2	24k on 500h (Bl)	45.00	*70.00*
a.		Perf. 13¾x13½	100.00	100.00
C6	A2	28k on 1000h (G)	20.00	27.50
a.		Inverted surcharge	400.00	—
b.		Perf. 13¾	475.00	700.00
c.		As "b," invtd. surcharge	350.00	—
		Nos. C4-C6 (3)	87.50	127.50
		Nos. C1-C6 (6)	191.00	*205.50*

Excellent counterfeits of the overprint are known.

Stamps of 1920 Surcharged in Black or Violet:

1922, June 15 ***Perf. 13¾***

C7	A8	50h on 100h dl grn	1.50	1.50
a.		Inverted surcharge	150.00	
b.		Double surcharge	160.00	
C8	A8	100h on 200h vio	4.00	3.25
a.		Inverted surcharge	150.00	

C9 A8 250h on 400h brn (V) 6.00 *7.50*
a. Inverted surcharge 275.00
Nos. C7-C9 (3) 11.50 *12.25*
Set, never hinged 20.00

Fokker Monoplane AP3

Smolik S 19 AP4

Smolik S 19 — AP5

Fokker over Prague AP6

1930, Dec. 16 Engr. *Perf. 13½*

C10 AP3 50h deep green .20 .20
C11 AP3 1k deep red .25 .25
C12 AP4 2k dark green .60 .55
C13 AP4 3k red violet 1.25 1.00
C14 AP5 4k indigo 1.00 .80
C15 AP5 5k red brown 1.50 1.50
C16 AP6 10k vio blue 3.50 3.50
a. 10k ultra 10.00 10.00
C17 AP6 20k gray violet 4.50 3.00
Nos. C10-C17 (8) 12.80 10.80

Two types exist of the 50h, 1k and 2k, and three types of the 3k, differing chiefly in the size of the printed area. A "no hill at left" variety of the 3k exists.

Imperf. copies of Nos. C10-C17 are proofs.

Perf. 12

C10a AP3 50h deep green 2.75 *4.75*
C11a AP3 1k deep red 18.00 *22.50*
C12a AP4 2k dark green 15.00 *22.50*
C14a AP5 4k indigo 2.25 *3.75*
C17a AP6 20k gray violet 3.00 *7.50*

Perf. 12x13½, 13½x12

C11b AP3 1k deep red 4.00 *7.50*
C12b AP4 2k dark green 11.00 *19.00*

Perf. 13¾x12¼

C17b AP6 20k gray violet *1,750.*

Perf. 12½

C15a AP5 5k red brown *2,000.*

Type of 1930 with hyphen in Cesko-Slovensko

1939, Apr. 22 *Perf. 13½*

C18 AP3 30h rose lilac .20 .20

Catalogue values for unused stamps in this section, from this point to the end of the section, are for Never Hinged items.

Capt. Frantisek Novak — AP7

Plane over Bratislava Castle — AP8

Plane over Charles Bridge, Prague — AP9

1946-47 *Perf. 12½*

C19 AP7 1.50k rose red .20 .20
C20 AP7 5.50k dk gray bl .40 .20
C21 AP7 9k sepia ('47) .75 .20
C22 AP8 10k dl grn .75 .35
C23 AP7 16k violet 1.40 .60
C24 AP8 20k light blue 1.50 1.10
C25 AP9 24k dk bl, *cr* .90 .65
C26 AP9 24k rose lake 1.50 1.00
C27 AP9 50k dk gray bl 3.00 2.60
Nos. C19-C27 (9) 10.40 6.90

No. C25 was issued June 12, 1946, for use on the first Prague-New York flight.

Nos. C22, C24-C27 were each issued in sheets of 100 stamps and 12 labels depicting airplane over globe. Values for singles with attached labels (mint/used): C22, $2/$1.50; C24, $4/$3; C25, $7.50/$4; C26, $5.50/$4.50; C27, $9/$7.50.

Nos. C19-C24, C26-C27 Surcharged with New Value and Bars in Various Colors

1949, Sept. 1 *Perf. 12½*

C28 AP7 1k on 1.50k (Bl) .20 .20
C29 AP7 3k on 5.50k (C) .35 .20
C30 AP7 6k on 9k (Br) .55 .20
C31 AP7 7.50k on 16k (C) .75 .25
C32 AP8 8k on 10k (G) .75 .75
C33 AP8 12.50k on 20k (Bl) 1.10 .55
C34 AP9 15k on 24k rose lake (Bl) 2.75 1.00
C35 AP9 30k on 50k (Bl) 2.00 .90
Nos. C28-C35 (8) 8.45 4.05

Karlovy Vary (Karlsbad) — AP10

1951, Apr. 2 Engr. *Perf. 13½*

C36 AP10 6k shown 3.00 1.50
C37 AP10 10k Piestany 3.00 1.50
C38 AP10 15k Marienbad 5.50 1.50
C39 AP10 20k Silac 8.50 4.00
Nos. C36-C39 (4) 20.00 8.50

View of Cesky Krumlov — AP11

Views: 1.55k, Olomouc. 2.35k, Banska Bystrica. 2.75k, Bratislava. 10k, Prague.

1955 *Perf. 11½*

Cream Paper

C40 AP11 80h olive green .80 .20
C41 AP11 1.55k violet brn 1.10 .35
C42 AP11 2.35k violet blue 1.50 .20
C43 AP11 2.75k rose brown 2.25 .35
C44 AP11 10k indigo 4.50 2.00
Nos. C40-C44 (5) 10.15 3.10

Issue dates: 10k, Feb. 20. Others, Mar. 28.

Airline: Moscow-Prague-Paris — AP12

2.35k, Airline: Prague-Cairo-Beirut-Damascus.

Engraved and Photogravure

1957, Oct. 15 Unwmk. *Perf. 11½*

C45 AP12 75h ultra & rose .75 .20
C46 AP12 2.35k ultra & org yel .75 .20

Planes at First Czech Aviation School, Pardubice — AP13

Design: 1.80k, Jan Kaspar and flight of first Czech plane, 1909.

1959, Oct. 15

C47 AP13 1k gray & yel .20 .20
C48 AP13 1.80k blk & pale bl .75 .20

50th anniv. of Jan Kaspar's 1st flight Aug. 25, 1909, at Pardubice.

Mail Coach, Plane and Arms of Bratislava — AP14

Design: 2.80k, Helicopter over Bratislava.

1960, Sept. 24 Unwmk. *Perf. 11½*

C49 AP14 1.60k dk bl & gray 1.50 .90
C50 AP14 2.80k grn & buff 2.00 1.10

Issued to publicize the National Stamp Exhibition, Bratislava, Sept. 24-Oct. 9.

AP15

AP16

Designs: 60h, Prague hails Gagarin. 1.80k, Gagarin, rocket and dove.

1961, June 22

C51 AP15 60h gray & car .25 .20
C52 AP15 1.80k gray & blue .45 .20

No. C51 commemorates Maj. Gagarin's visit to Prague, Apr. 28-29; No. C52 commemorates the first man in space, Yuri A. Gagarin, Apr. 12, 1961.

1962, May 14 Engr. *Perf. 14*

"PRAGA" emblem and: 80h, Dove & Nest of Eggs. 1.40k, Dove. 2.80k, Symbolic flower with five petals. 4.20k, Five leaves.

C53 AP16 80h multicolored .75 .35
C54 AP16 1.40k blk, dk red & bl 1.90 1.50
C55 AP16 2.80k multicolored 1.90 1.50
C56 AP16 4.20k multicolored 2.25 1.50
Nos. C53-C56 (4) 6.80 4.85

PRAGA 1962 World Exhibition of Postage Stamps, Aug. 18-Sept. 2, 1962.

Nos. C53-C56 were each issued in sheets of 10. Value, set $110.

Vostok 5 and Lt. Col. Valeri Bykovski AP17

2.80k, Vostok VI & Lt. Valentina Tereshkova.

1963, June 26

C57 AP17 80h slate bl & pink .45 .20
C58 AP17 2.80k dl red brn & lt bl 1.80 .25

Space flights of Valeri Bykovski, June 14-19, and Valentina Tereshkova, first woman astronaut, June 16-19, 1963.

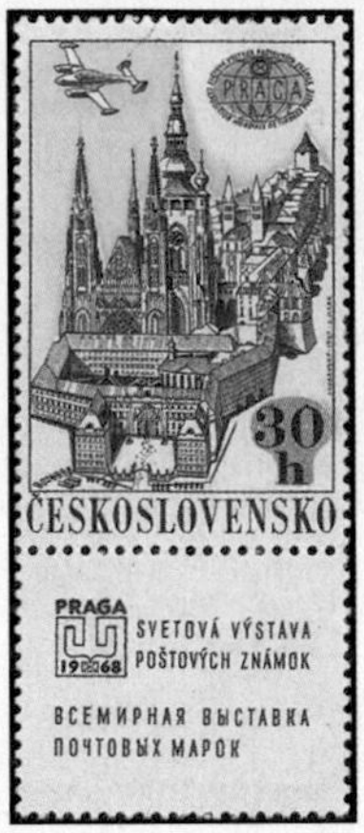

PRAGA 1962 Emblem, View of Prague and Plane — AP18

Designs: 60h, Istanbul '63 (Hagia Sophia). 1k, Philatec Paris 1964 (Ile de la Cité). 1.40k, WIPA 1965 (Belvedere Palace, Vienna). 1.60k, SIPEX 1966 (Capitol, Washington). 2k, Amphilex '67 (harbor and old town, Amsterdam). 5k, PRAGA 1968 (View of Prague).

Engraved and Photogravure

1967, Oct. 30 *Perf. 11½*

Size: 30x50mm

C59 AP18 30h choc, yel & rose .20 .20
C60 AP18 60h dk grn, yel & lil .20 .20
C61 AP18 1k blk, brick red & lt bl .35 .20
C62 AP18 1.40k vio, yel & dp org .40 .20
C63 AP18 1.60k ind, tan & lil .35 .20
C64 AP18 2k dk grn, org & red .40 .25

Size: 40x50mm

C65 AP18 5k multi 2.25 1.25
Nos. C59-C65 (7) 4.15 2.50

PRAGA 1968 World Stamp Exhibition, Prague, June 22-July 7, 1968. No. C59-C64 issued in sheets of 15 stamps and 15 bilingual labels. Values, set of singles with attached labels: mint $6.50; used $4.50. No. C65 issued in sheets of 4 stamps and one center label. Value $15.

Glider L-13 — AP19

Airplanes: 60h, Sports plane L-40. 80h, Aero taxi L-200. 1k, Crop-spraying plane Z-37. 1.60k, Aerobatics trainer Z-526. 2k, Jet trainer L-29.

1967, Dec. 11

C66 AP19 30h multi .20 .20
C67 AP19 60h multi .20 .20
C68 AP19 80h multi .20 .20
C69 AP19 1k multi .25 .20
C70 AP19 1.60k multi .40 .20
C71 AP19 2k multi 1.25 .55
Nos. C66-C71 (6) 2.50 1.55

Charles Bridge, Prague, and Balloon — AP20

Designs: 1k, Belvedere, fountain and early plane. 2k, Hradcany, Prague, and airship.

1968, Feb. 5 Unwmk. *Perf. 11½*

C72 AP20 60h multicolored .30 .20
C73 AP20 1k multicolored .45 .30
C74 AP20 2k multicolored .75 .30
Nos. C72-C74 (3) 1.50 .80

PRAGA 1968 World Stamp Exhibition, Prague, June 22-July 7, 1968.

Astronaut, Moon and Manhattan AP21

Design: 3k, Lunar landing module and J. F. Kennedy Airport, New York.

1969, July 21

C75	AP21	60h blk, vio, yel & sil	.20	.20
C76	AP21	3k blk, bl, ocher & sil	1.00	.50

Man's 1st landing on the moon, July 20, 1969, US astronauts Neil A. Armstrong and Col. Edwin E. Aldrin, Jr., with Lieut. Col. Michael Collins piloting Apollo 11.

Nos. C75-C76 printed with label inscribed with names of astronauts and European date of moon landing. Values for pair of singles with attached labels: mint $2; used $1.

TU-104A over Bitov Castle AP22

Designs: 60h, IL-62 over Bezdez Castle. 1.40k, TU-13A over Orava Castle. 1.90k, IL-18 over Veveri Castle. 2.40k, IL-14 over Pernstejn Castle. 3.60k, TU-154 over Trencin Castle.

1973, Oct. 24 Engr. *Perf. 11½*

C77	AP22	30h multi	.20	.20
C78	AP22	60h multi	.20	.20
C79	AP22	1.40k multi	.25	.20
C80	AP22	1.90k multi	.40	.20
C81	AP22	2.40k multi	1.50	.75
C82	AP22	3.60k multi	.70	.20
		Nos. C77-C82 (6)	3.25	1.75

50 years of Czechoslovakian aviation.

Nos. c77-c82 were each printed in sheets of 10. Values, set: mint $60; used $30.

Old Water Tower and Manes Hall — AP23

Designs (Praga 1978 Emblem, Plane Silhouette and): 1.60k, Congress Hall. 2k, Powder Tower, vert. 2.40k, Charles Bridge and Old Bridge Tower. 4k, Old Town Hall on Old Town Square, vert. 6k, Prague Castle and St. Vitus' Cathedral, vert.

Engraved and Photogravure

1976, June 23 *Perf. 11½*

C83	AP23	60h ind & multi	.20	.20
C84	AP23	1.60k ind & multi	.25	.20
C85	AP23	2k ind & multi	.35	.20
C86	AP23	2.40k ind & multi	.40	.20
C87	AP23	4k ind & multi	.80	.30
C88	AP23	6k ind & multi	2.00	.80
		Nos. C83-C88 (6)	4.00	1.90

PRAGA 1978 International Philatelic Exhibition, Prague, Sept. 8-17, 1978.

Zeppelin, 1909 and 1928 — AP24

PRAGA '78 Emblem and: 1k, Ader, 1890, L'Eole & Dunn, 1914. 1.60k, Jeffries-Blanchard balloon, 1785. 2k, Otto Lilienthal's glider, 1896. 4.40k, Jan Kaspar's plane, Pardubice, 1911.

1977, Sept. 15 *Perf. 11½*

C89	AP24	60h multi	.20	.20
C90	AP24	1k multi	.30	.20
C91	AP24	1.60k multi	.35	.20
C92	AP24	2k multi	.45	.20
C93	AP24	4.40k multi	2.25	.50
		Nos. C89-C93 (5)	3.55	1.30

History of aviation.

Nos. C89-C93 were each issued in sheets of 30 stamps, 15 labels depicting the exhibition emblem, and 5 blank labels. Values for set ofd singles with attached inscribed labels: mint $5; used $2.50.

SPECIAL DELIVERY STAMPS

Doves — SD1

1919-20 Unwmk. Typo. *Imperf.*

E1	SD1	2h red vio, *yel*	.20	.20
E2	SD1	5h yel grn, *yel*	.20	.20
E3	SD1	10h red brn, *yel* ('20)	.40	.40
		Nos. E1-E3 (3)	.80	.80

For overprints and surcharge see Nos. P11-P13, Eastern Silesia E1-E2.

1921 White Paper

E1a	SD1	2h red violet	8.00
E2a	SD1	5h yellow green	5.25
E3a	SD1	10h red brown	100.00
		Nos. E1a-E3a (3)	113.25

It is doubted that Nos. E1a-E3a were regularly issued.

PERSONAL DELIVERY STAMPS

Catalogue values for unused stamps in this section are for Never Hinged items.

PD1

Design: No. EX2, "D" in each corner.

1937 Unwmk. Photo. *Perf. 13½*

EX1	PD1	50h blue	.20	*.25*
EX2	PD1	50h carmine	.20	*.25*

PD3

1946 *Perf. 13½*

EX3	PD3	2k deep blue	.50	*.75*

POSTAGE DUE STAMPS

D1

1918-20 Unwmk. Typo. *Imperf.*

J1	D1	5h deep bister	.20	.20
J2	D1	10h deep bister	.20	.20
J3	D1	15h deep bister	.20	.20
J4	D1	20h deep bister	.30	.20
J5	D1	25h deep bister	.45	.20
J6	D1	30h deep bister	.45	.20
J7	D1	40h deep bister	.60	.20
J8	D1	50h deep bister	.75	.20
J9	D1	100h blk brn	1.50	.20
J10	D1	250h orange	11.00	1.40
J11	D1	400h scarlet	15.00	1.40
J12	D1	500h gray grn	7.50	.20
J13	D1	1000h purple	7.50	.25
J14	D1	2000h dark blue	22.50	.60
		Nos. J1-J14 (14)	68.15	5.65

For surcharges and overprints see Nos. J32-J41, J57, Eastern Silesia J1-J11.

Nos. 1, 33-34, 10 Surcharged in Blue

1922

J15	A1	20h on 3h red vio	.30	.20
J16	A2	50h on 75h slate	1.50	.20
J17	A2	60h on 80h olive grn	.80	.20
J18	A2	100h on 80h olive grn	3.00	.20
J19	A1	200h on 400h purple	4.00	.20
		Nos. J15-J19 (5)	9.60	1.00

Same Surcharge on Nos. 1, 10, 30-31, 33-34, 36, 40 in Violet

1923-26

J20	A1	10h on 3h red vio	.20	.20
J21	A1	20h on 3h red vio	.30	.20
J22	A1	30h on 3h red vio	.20	.20
J23	A1	40h on 3h red vio	.20	.20
J24	A2	50h on 75h slate	1.25	.20
J25	A2	60h on 50h dk vio ('26)	4.00	1.25
J26	A2	60h on 50h dk bl ('26)	4.00	1.50
J27	A2	60h on 75h slate	.50	.20
J28	A2	100h on 80h ol grn	27.50	.20
J29	A2	100h on 120h gray blk	1.00	.20
J30	A1	100h on 400h pur ('26)	1.00	.20
J31	A2	100h on 1000h dp vio ('26)	1.60	.20
		Nos. J20-J31 (12)	41.75	4.75

Postage Due Stamp of 1918-20 Surcharged in Violet

1924

J32	D1	50h on 400h scar	.75	.20
J33	D1	60h on 400h scar	2.75	.50
J34	D1	100h on 400h scar	1.75	.20
		Nos. J32-J34 (3)	5.25	.90

Postage Due Stamps of 1918-20 Surcharged with New Values in Violet as in 1924

1925

J35	D1	10h on 5h bister	.20	.20
J36	D1	20h on 5h bister	.20	.20
J37	D1	30h on 15h bister	.20	.20
J38	D1	40h on 15h bister	.20	.20
J39	D1	50h on 250h org	.95	.20
J40	D1	60h on 250h org	1.25	.50
J41	D1	100h on 250h org	1.90	.20
		Nos. J35-J41 (7)	4.90	1.70

Stamps of 1918-19 Surcharged with New Values in Violet as in 1922

1926 *Perf. 14, 11½*

J42	A2	30h on 15h red	.50	.30
J43	A2	40h on 15h red	.50	.30

On #J44-J49

On #J50-J56

1926 Violet Surcharge *Perf. 14*

J44	A8	30h on 100h dk grn	.20	.20
J45	A8	40h on 200h violet	.25	.20
J46	A8	40h on 300h ver	.95	.25
a.		Perf. 14x13½		60.00
J47	A8	50h on 500h dp grn	.50	.20
a.		Perf. 14x13½	2.75	
J48	A8	60h on 400h brown	1.00	.20
J49	A8	100h on 600h dp vio	2.50	.35
a.		Perf. 14x13½	30.00	1.25
		Nos. J44-J49 (6)	5.40	1.40

1927 Violet Overprint

J50	A6	100h dark brown	.55	.20
a.		Perf. 13½	*200.00*	10.00

Surcharged with New Value in Violet

J51	A6	40h on 185h org	.20	.20
J52	A6	50h on 20h car	.20	.20
a.		50h on 50h carmine (error)		*35,000.*
J53	A6	50h on 150h rose	.20	.20
a.		Perf. 13½	12.50	2.00
J54	A6	60h on 25h brown	.25	.20
J55	A6	60h on 185h orange	.55	.20
J56	A6	100h on 25h brown	.55	.20
		Nos. J50-J56 (7)	2.50	1.40

No. J52a is known only used.

No. J12 Surcharged in Violet

1927 *Imperf.*

J57	D1	200h on 500h gray grn	6.00	2.50

Catalogue values for unused stamps in this section, from this point to the end of the section, are for Never Hinged items.

D5

1928 *Perf. 14x13½*

J58	D5	5h dark red	.20	.20
J59	D5	10h dark red	.20	.20
J60	D5	20h dark red	.20	.20
J61	D5	30h dark red	.20	.20
J62	D5	40h dark red	.20	.20
J63	D5	50h dark red	.20	.20
J64	D5	60h dark red	.20	.20
J65	D5	1k ultra	.20	.20
J66	D5	2k ultra	.50	.20
J67	D5	5k ultra	.75	.20
J68	D5	10k ultra	1.90	.20
J69	D5	20k ultra	3.75	.30
		Nos. J58-J69 (12)	8.50	2.50

D6

1946-48 Photo. *Perf. 14*

J70	D6	10h dark blue	.20	.20
J71	D6	20h dark blue	.20	.20
J72	D6	50h dark blue	.35	.20
J73	D6	1k carmine rose	.35	.20
J74	D6	1.20k carmine rose	.35	.20
J75	D6	1.50k carmine rose ('48)	.35	.20
J76	D6	1.60k carmine rose	.35	.20
J77	D6	2k carmine rose ('48)	.35	.20
J78	D6	2.40k carmine rose	.35	.20
J79	D6	3k carmine rose	.70	.20
J80	D6	5k carmine rose	.70	.20
J81	D6	6k carmine rose ('48)	1.00	.20
		Nos. J70-J81 (12)	5.25	2.40

D7

D8

1954-55 Engr. *Perf. 12½, 11½*

J82	D7	5h	gray green ('55)	.20	.20
J83	D7	10h	gray green ('55)	.20	.20
J84	D7	30h	gray green	.20	.20
J85	D7	50h	gray green ('55)	.20	.20
J86	D7	60h	gray green ('55)	.20	.20
J87	D7	95h	gray green	.35	.20
J88	D8	1k	violet	.35	.20
J89	D8	1.20k	violet ('55)	.35	.20
J90	D8	1.50k	violet	.70	.20
J91	D8	1.60k	violet ('55)	.45	.20
J92	D8	2k	violet	.85	.20
J93	D8	3k	violet	1.10	.20
J94	D8	5k	violet ('55)	1.40	.25
			Nos. J82-J94 (13)	6.55	2.65

Perf. 11½ stamps are from a 1963 printing which lacks the 95h, 1.60k, and 2k.

Stylized Flower — D9

Designs: Various stylized flowers.

Engraved and Photogravure

1971-72 *Perf. 11½*

J95	D9	10h	vio bl & pink	.20	.20
J96	D9	20h	vio & lt bl	.20	.20
J97	D9	30h	emer & lil rose	.20	.20
J98	D9	60h	pur & emer	.20	.20
J99	D9	80h	org & vio bl	.20	.20
J100	D9	1k	dk red & emer	.25	.20
J101	D9	1.20k	grn & org	.20	.20
J102	D9	2k	blue & red	.40	.20
J103	D9	3k	blk & yel	.50	.20
J104	D9	4k	brn & ultra	.85	.20
J105	D9	5.40k	red & lilac	1.00	.20
J106	D9	6k	brick red & org	1.40	.20
			Nos. J95-J106 (12)	5.60	2.40

All except 5.40k issued in 1972.

OFFICIAL STAMPS

Catalogue values for unused stamps in this section are for Never Hinged items.

Coat of Arms — O1

1945 Unwmk. Litho. *Perf. 10½x10*

O1	O1	50h	dp slate grn	.20	.20
O2	O1	1k	dp bl vio	.20	.20
O3	O1	1.20k	plum	.20	.20
O4	O1	1.50k	crimson rose	.20	.20
O5	O1	2.50k	bright ultra	.20	.20
O6	O1	5k	dk vio brn	.30	.20
O7	O1	8k	rose pink	.30	.30
			Nos. O1-O7 (7)	1.60	1.50

Redrawn

1947 Photo. *Perf. 14*

O8	O1	60h	red	.20	.20
O9	O1	80h	dk olive grn	.20	.20
O10	O1	1k	dk lilac gray	.20	.20
O11	O1	1.20k	dp plum	.20	.20
O12	O1	2.40k	dk car rose	.20	.20
O13	O1	4k	brt ultra	.20	.20
O14	O1	5k	dk vio brn	.20	.20
O15	O1	7.40k	purple	.20	.20
			Nos. O8-O15 (8)	1.60	1.60

There are many minor changes in design, size of numerals, etc., of the redrawn stamps.

NEWSPAPER STAMPS

Windhover — N1

1918-20 Unwmk. Typo. *Imperf.*

P1	N1	2h	gray green	.20	.20
P2	N1	5h	green ('20)	.20	.20
a.		5h	dark green	.40	.20
P3	N1	6h	red	.30	.25
P4	N1	10h	dull violet	.20	.20
P5	N1	20h	blue	.20	.20
P6	N1	30h	gray brown	.20	.20
P7	N1	50h	orange ('20)	.30	.20
P8	N1	100h	red brown ('20)	.40	.20
			Nos. P1-P8 (8)	2.00	1.65

Nos. P1-P8 exist privately perforated.

For surcharges and overprints see Nos. P9-P10, P14-P16, Eastern Silesia P1-P5.

Stamps of 1918-20 Surcharged in Violet

1925-26

P9	N1	5h on 2h gray green	.50	.40
P10	N1	5h on 6h red ('26)	.25	*.40*

Special Delivery Stamps of 1918-20 Overprinted in Violet

1926

P11	SD1	5h apple grn, *yel*	.20	.20
a.		5h dull green, *yellow*	.50	.40
P12	SD1	10h red brn, *yel*	.20	.20

With Additional Surcharge of New Value

P13	SD1	5h on 2h red vio, *yel*	.35	.35
		Nos. P11-P13 (3)	.75	.75

Catalogue values for unused stamps in this section, from this point to the end of the section, are for Never Hinged items.

Newspaper Stamps of 1918-20 Overprinted in Violet

1934

P14	N1	10h dull violet	.20	.20
P15	N1	20h blue	.20	.20
P16	N1	30h gray brown	.20	.20
		Nos. P14-P16 (3)	.60	.60

Overprinted for use by commercial firms only.

Carrier Pigeon — N2

1937 *Imperf.*

P17	N2	2h	bister brown	.20	.20
P18	N2	5h	dull blue	.20	.20
P19	N2	7h	red orange	.20	.20
P20	N2	9h	emerald	.20	.20
P21	N2	10h	henna brown	.20	.20
P22	N2	12h	ultra	.20	.20
P23	N2	20h	dark green	.20	.20
P24	N2	50h	dark brown	.20	.20
P25	N2	1k	olive gray	.20	.20
			Nos. P17-P25 (9)	1.80	1.80

For overprint see Slovakia Nos. P1-P9.

Bratislava Philatelic Exhibition Issue

Souvenir Sheet

1937 *Imperf.*

P26	N2	10h	henna brn, sheet of 25	4.00	4.00

Newspaper Delivery Boy — N4

1945 Unwmk. Typo. *Imperf.*

P27	N4	5h	dull blue	.20	.20
P28	N4	10h	red	.20	.20
P29	N4	15h	emerald	.20	.20
P30	N4	20h	dark slate green	.20	.20
P31	N4	25h	bright red vio	.20	.20
P32	N4	30h	ocher	.20	.20
P33	N4	40h	red orange	.20	.20
P34	N4	50h	brown red	.20	.20
P35	N4	1k	slate gray	.20	.20
P36	N4	5k	deep vio blue	.20	.20
			Nos. P27-P36 (10)	2.00	2.00

CZECHOSLOVAK LEGION POST

The Czechoslovak Legion in Siberia issued these stamps for use on its mail and that of local residents. Forgeries exist.

For more detailed listings of Czechoslovak Legion Post issues, see the *Classic Specialized Catalogue of Stamps and Covers.*

Russia No. 79 Overprinted

1918 Typo. *Perf. 14x14½*

A1	A15	10k dark blue	2,100.	—

No. A1 was sold for a few days in Chelyabinsk. It was withdrawn because of a spelling error ("CZESZKJA," instead of "CZESZKAJA").

This overprint was also applied to Russia Nos. 73-78, 80-81, 83-85, 119-121, 123 and 130-131. These were trial printings, never sold to the public, although favor-cancelled covers exist.

Urn and Cathedral at Irkutsk — A1

Armored Railroad Car — A2

Sentinel — A3

Lion of Bohemia

1919-20 Litho. *Imperf.*

1	A1	25k	carmine	10.50
a.			Perf 11½ ('20)	10.50
2	A2	50k	yellow green	10.50
a.			Perf 11½ ('20)	10.50
3	A3	1r	red brown	14.00
a.			Perf 11½ ('20)	14.00

Originals of Nos. 1-3 and 1a-3a have a crackled yellow gum. Ungummed remainders, which were given a white gum, exist imperforate and perforated 11½ and 13¼. Value per set, $3.

Embossed

Perce en Arc in Blue

4	A4	(25k)	blue & rose	2.00

Two types: 1 — 6 points on star-like mace head at right of goblet; large saber handle; measures 20x25¼mm. 2 — 5 points on mace head; small saber handle; measures 19½x25mm.

No. 4 Overprinted

1920

5	A4	(25k)	bl & rose	10.00

Both types of No. 4 received overprint.

No. 5 Surcharged with New Values in Green

6	A4	2k	bl & rose	35.00
7	A4	3k	bl & rose	35.00
8	A4	5k	bl & rose	35.00
9	A4	10k	bl & rose	35.00
10	A4	15k	bl & rose	35.00
11	A4	25k	bl & rose	35.00
12	A4	35k	bl & rose	35.00
13	A4	50k	bl & rose	35.00
14	A4	1r	bl & rose	35.00
			Nos. 6-14 (9)	315.00

BOHEMIA AND MORAVIA

Catalogue values for unused stamps in this country are for never hinged items, beginning with Scott 20 in the regular postage section, Scott B1 in the semi-postal section, Scott J1 in the postage due section, Scott O1 in the official section, and Scott P1 in the newspaper section.

German Protectorate

Stamps of Czechoslovakia, 1928-39, Overprinted in Black

Perf. 10, 12½, 12x12½

1939, July 15 Unwmk.

1	A29	5h	dk ultra	.20	*1.25*
2	A29	10h	brown	.20	*1.25*
3	A29	20h	red	.20	*1.25*
4	A29	25h	green	.20	*1.25*
5	A29	30h	red vio	.20	*1.25*
6	A61a	40h	dk bl	2.50	*5.00*
7	A85	50h	dp grn	.20	*1.25*
8	A63	60h	dl vio	2.50	*5.00*
9	A60	1k	rose lake (212)	.75	*1.75*
10	A60	1k	rose lake (256)	.30	*1.25*
11	A64	1.20k	rose lilac	3.00	*5.00*
12	A65	1.50k	carmine	2.50	*5.75*
13	A79	1.60k	olive grn	3.75	*5.75*
a.			"Mähnen"	32.50	*75.00*
14	A66	2k	dk bl grn	1.10	*4.00*
15	A67	2.50k	dk bl	3.00	*5.00*
16	A68	3k	brown	3.00	*5.75*
17	A70	4k	dk vio	5.00	*6.50*

18	A71	5k green	3.50	10.00
19	A72	10k blue	4.75	15.00
		Nos. 1-19 (19)	36.85	83.25
		Set, never hinged	60.00	

Overprint size varies; #1-10 measure 17½x15½mm, #11-16 19x18mm, #17, 19 28x17½mm, #18 23½x23mm.

Catalogue values for unused stamps in this section, from this point to the end of the section, are for never hinged items.

Linden Leaves and Closed Buds — A1

1939-41 Photo. *Perf. 14*

20	A1	5h dark blue	.20	.30
21	A1	10h blk brn	.20	.40
22	A1	20h crimson	.20	.30
23	A1	25h dk bl grn	.20	.30
24	A1	30h dp plum	.20	.30
24A	A1	30h golden brn ('41)	.20	.30
25	A1	40h orange ('40)	.20	.20
26	A1	50h slate grn ('40)	.20	.20
		Nos. 20-26 (8)	1.60	2.30

See Nos. 49-51.

Castle at Zvikov — A2

Karlstein Castle — A3

St. Barbara's Church, Kutna Hora — A4

Cathedral at Prague — A5

Brno Cathedral — A6

Town Square, Olomouc — A7

1939 Engr. *Perf. 12½*

27	A2	40h dark blue	.20	.30
28	A3	50h dk bl grn	.20	.30
29	A4	60h dl vio	.20	.30
30	A5	1k dp rose	.20	.30
31	A6	1.20k rose lilac	.40	.60
32	A6	1.50k rose car	.20	.30
33	A7	2k dk bl grn	.20	.50
34	A7	2.50k dark blue	.20	.30
		Nos. 27-34 (8)	1.80	2.90

No. 31 measures 23½x29½mm, No. 42 measures 18½x23mm.

See #52-53, 53B. For overprints see #60-61.

Zlin — A8

Iron Works at Moravská Ostrava — A9

Prague — A10

1939-40

35	A8	3k dl rose vio	.20	.30
36	A9	4k slate ('40)	.20	.40
37	A10	5k green	.50	.80
38	A10	10k lt ultra	.40	1.00
39	A10	20k yel brn	1.25	2.00
		Nos. 35-39 (5)	2.55	4.50

Types of 1939 and

Neuhaus A11

Lainsitz Bridge near Bechyne A14

Pernstein Castle — A12

Samson Fountain, Budweis — A15

Pardubice Castle — A13

Kromeriz A16

Wallenstein Palace, Prague — A17

1940 Engr. *Perf. 12½*

40	A11	50h dk bl grn	.20	.20
41	A12	80h dp bl	.25	.40
42	A6	1.20k vio brn	.40	.25
43	A13	2k gray grn	.20	.20
44	A14	5k dk bl grn	.20	.20
45	A15	6k brn vio	.20	.50
46	A16	8k slate grn	.20	.30
47	A17	10k blue	.45	.30
48	A10	20k sepia	1.10	1.60
		Nos. 40-48 (9)	3.20	3.95

No. 42 measures 18½x23mm; No. 31, 23½x29½mm.

Types of 1939-40

1941

49	A1	60h violet	.20	.20
50	A1	80h red org	.20	.20
51	A1	1k brown	.20	.20
52	A5	1.20k rose red	.20	.20
53	A4	1.50k lil rose	.20	.25
53A	A13	2k light blue	.20	.20
53B	A6	2.50k ultra	.20	.20
53C	A12	3k olive	.20	.20
		Nos. 49-53C (8)	1.60	1.65

Nos. 49-51 show buds open. Nos. 52 and 53B measure 18¾x23½mm and have no inscriptions below design.

For overprints see Nos. 60-61.

Antonin Dvorák — A18

1941, Aug. 25 Engr. *Perf. 12½*

54	A18	60h dull lilac	.30	.50
55	A18	1.20k sepia	.30	.50

Antonin Dvorák (1841-1904), composer.

Nos. 54-55 were issued in sheets of 50 stamps and 50 alternating inscribed labels. Value for set of singles with attached labels, unused or used, $1.50.

Farming Scene — A19

Factories — A20

1941, Sept. 7 Photo. *Perf. 13½*

56	A19	30h dk red brn	.20	.30
57	A19	60h dark green	.20	.30
58	A20	1.20k dk plum	.20	.30
59	A20	2.50k sapphire	.25	.65
		Nos. 56-59 (4)	.85	1.55

Issued to publicize the Prague Fair.

Nos. 52 and 53B Overprinted in Blue or Red

1942, Mar. 15 *Perf. 12½*

60	A5	1.20k rose red (Bl)	.60	.65
61	A6	2.50k ultra (R)	.65	1.00

3rd anniv. of the Protectorate of Bohemia and Moravia.

Adolf Hitler A21

17th Century Messenger A22

1942 Photo. *Perf. 14*

Size: 17½x21½mm

62	A21	10(h) gray blk	.20	.25
63	A21	30(h) bister brn	.20	.25
64	A21	40(h) slate blue	.20	.25
65	A21	50(h) slate grn	.20	.25
66	A21	60(h) purple	.20	.25
67	A21	80(h) org ver	.20	.25

Perf. 12½

Engr.

Size: 18x21mm

68	A21	1k dl brn	.20	.25
69	A21	1.20(k) carmine	.20	.30
70	A21	1.50(k) claret	.20	.30
71	A21	1.60(k) Prus grn	.20	.30
72	A21	2k light blue	.20	.30
73	A21	2.40(k) fawn	.20	.30

Size: 18½x24mm

74	A21	2.50(k) ultra	.20	.30
75	A21	3k olive grn	.20	.30
76	A21	4k brt red vio	.20	.30
77	A21	5k myrtle grn	.20	.30
78	A21	6k claret brn	.20	.40
79	A21	8k indigo	.20	.40

Size: 23½x29¾mm

80	A21	10k dk gray grn	.25	1.00
81	A21	20k gray vio	.40	1.00
82	A21	30k red	.75	2.00
83	A21	50k deep blue	1.50	3.00
		Nos. 62-83 (22)	6.50	12.25

1943, Jan. 10 Photo. *Perf. 13½*

84	A22	60h dark rose violet	.40	.40

Stamp Day.

Scene from "Die Meistersinger" A23

Richard Wagner A24

Scene from "Siegfried" — A25

1943, May 22

85	A23	60h violet	.20	.20
86	A24	1.20k carmine rose	.20	.20
87	A25	2.50k deep ultra	.20	.20
		Nos. 85-87 (3)	.60	.60

Richard Wagner (1813-83).

St. Vitus' Cathedral, Prague — A26

Adolf Hitler — A27

1944, Nov. 21 Engr. *Perf. 12½*

88	A26	1.50k dull rose brn	.25	.25
89	A26	2.50k dull lilac blue	.25	.35

1944

90	A27	4.20k green	.50	.50

SEMI-POSTAL STAMPS

Catalogue values for unused stamps in this section are for never hinged items.

Nurse and Wounded Soldier — SP1

Perf. 13½

1940, June 29 Photo. Unwmk.

B1	SP1	60h + 40h indigo	.90	1.10
B2	SP1	1.20k + 80h deep plum	.90	1.25

Surtax for German Red Cross.

Nos. B1-B2 were issued in sheets of 50 stamps and 50 alternating inscribed labels. Value for set of singles with attached labels: unused $3; used $4.

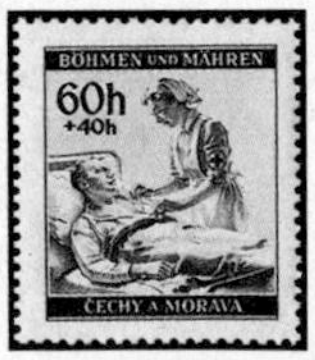

Red Cross Nurse and Patient — SP2

1941, Apr. 20

B3	SP2	60h + 40h indigo	.40	*.60*
B4	SP2	1.20k + 80h dp plum	.40	*.65*

Surtax for German Red Cross.

Nos. B3-B4 were issued in sheets of 50 stamps and 50 alternating inscribed labels. Value for set of singles with attached labels: unused $1.80; used $2.75.

Old Theater, Prague — SP3

Mozart — SP4

1941, Oct. 26

B5	SP3	30h + 30h brown	.20	.20
B6	SP3	60h + 60h Prus grn	.20	.20
B7	SP4	1.20k + 1.20k scar	.25	*.25*
B8	SP4	2.50k + 2.50k dk bl	.45	*.55*
		Nos. B5-B8 (4)	1.10	*1.20*

150th anniversary of Mozart's death.

Labels alternate with stamps in sheets of Nos. B5-B8. The labels with Nos. B5-B6 show two bars of Mozart's opera "Don Giovanni." Those with Nos. B7-B8 show Mozart's piano. Value for set of singles with attached labels: unused $2; used $3.25.

Adolf Hitler — SP5

Nurse and Soldier — SP6

1942, Apr. 20 Engr. *Perf. 12½*

B9	SP5	30h + 20h dl brn vio	.20	.20
B10	SP5	60h + 40h dl grn	.20	.20
B11	SP5	1.20k + 80h dp claret	.20	.25
B12	SP5	2.50k + 1.50k dl bl	.25	*.40*
		Nos. B9-B12 (4)	.85	*1.05*

Hitler's 53rd birthday.

Nos. B9-B12 were issued in sheets of 100 stamps and 12 blank labels. Value for set of singles with attached labels: unused $3; used $2.25.

1942, Sept. 4 *Perf. 13½*

B13	SP6	60h + 40h deep blue	.25	.25
B14	SP6	1.20(k) + 80(h) dp plum	.25	.25

The surtax aided the German Red Cross.

Emperor Charles IV SP7

Peter Parler SP8

John the Blind, King of Bohemia — SP9

Adolf Hitler — SP10

1943, Jan. 29

B15	SP7	60h + 40h violet	.20	.20
B16	SP8	1.20k + 80h carmine	.20	.20
B17	SP9	2.50k + 1.50k vio bl	.20	.20
		Nos. B15-B17 (3)	.60	*.60*

The surtax was for the benefit of the German wartime winter relief.

1943, Apr. 20 Engr. *Perf. 12½*

B18	SP10	60h + 1.40k dl vio	.25	*.30*
B19	SP10	1.20k + 3.80k carmine	.25	*.30*

Hitler's 54th birthday.

Nos. B18-B19 were issued in sheets of 100 stamps and 12 blank labels. Value for set of singles with attached labels: unused $1.10; used 60c.

Deathmask of Reinhard Heydrich — SP11

Eagle and Red Cross — SP12

1943, May 28 Photo. *Perf. 13½*

B20	SP11	60h + 4.40k black	.65	*1.60*

No. B20 exists in a miniature sheet containing a single copy. It was given to high Nazi officials attending a ceremony one year after Heydrich's assassination.

1943, Sept. 16 *Perf. 13*

B21	SP12	1.20k + 8.80k blk & car	.50	.50

The surtax aided the German Red Cross.

Native Costumes SP13

Nazi Emblem, Arms of Bohemia, Moravia SP14

1944, Mar. 15 *Perf. 13½*

B22	SP13	1.20(k) + 3.80(k) rose lake	.20	.20
B23	SP14	4.20(k) + 10.80(k) golden brn	.20	.20
B24	SP13	10k + 20k saph	.20	*.30*
		Nos. B22-B24 (3)	.60	*.70*

Fifth anniversary of protectorate.

Adolf Hitler — SP15

Bedrich Smetana — SP16

1944, Apr. 20

B25	SP15	60h + 1.40k olive blk	.25	.25
B26	SP15	1.20k + 3.80k slate grn	.25	.25

1944, May 12 Engr. *Perf. 12½*

B27	SP16	60h + 1.40k dk gray grn	.25	.25
B28	SP16	1.20k + 3.80k brn car	.25	.25

Bedrich Smetana (1824-84), Czech composer and pianist.

PERSONAL DELIVERY STAMPS

PD1

1939-40 Unwmk. Photo. *Perf. 13½*

EX1	PD1	50h indigo & blue ('40)	1.25	*2.00*
EX2	PD1	50h carmine & rose	1.60	*2.50*

POSTAGE DUE STAMPS

Catalogue values for unused stamps in this section are for never hinged items.

D1

1939-40 Unwmk. Typo. *Perf. 14*

J1	D1	5h dark carmine	.25	*.30*
J2	D1	10h dark carmine	.25	*.30*
J3	D1	20h dark carmine	.25	*.30*
J4	D1	30h dark carmine	.25	*.30*
J5	D1	40h dark carmine	.25	*.30*
J6	D1	50h dark carmine	.25	*.30*
J7	D1	60h dark carmine	.25	*.30*
J8	D1	80h dark carmine	.25	*.30*
J9	D1	1k bright ultra	.25	*.40*
J10	D1	1.20k brt ultra ('40)	.30	*.40*
J11	D1	2k bright ultra	1.00	*1.25*
J12	D1	5k bright ultra	1.10	*1.60*
J13	D1	10k bright ultra	1.60	*2.00*
J14	D1	20k bright ultra	3.25	*3.25*
		Nos. J1-J14 (14)	9.50	*11.30*

OFFICIAL STAMPS

Catalogue values for unused stamps in this section are for never hinged items.

Numeral O1

Eagle O2

Unwmk.

1941, Jan. 1 Typo. *Perf. 14*

O1	O1	30h ocher	.25	.20
O2	O1	40h indigo	.25	.20
O3	O1	50h emerald	.25	.20
O4	O1	60h slate grn	.25	.20
O5	O1	80h org red	.80	.20
O6	O1	1k red brn	.40	.20
O7	O1	1.20k carmine	.40	.20
O8	O1	1.50k dp plum	.65	.20
O9	O1	2k brt bl	.65	.20
O10	O1	3k olive	.65	.20
O11	O1	4k red vio	.80	.50
O12	O1	5k org yel	2.00	1.00
		Nos. O1-O12 (12)	7.35	3.50

1943, Feb. 15

O13	O2	30(h) bister	.20	*.30*
O14	O2	40(h) indigo	.20	*.30*
O15	O2	50(h) yel grn	.20	*.30*
O16	O2	60(h) dp vio	.20	*.30*
O17	O2	80(h) org red	.20	*.30*
O18	O2	1k chocolate	.20	*.30*
O19	O2	1.20(k) carmine	.20	*.30*
O20	O2	1.50(k) brn red	.20	*.30*
O21	O2	2k lt bl	.20	*.30*
O22	O2	3k olive	.20	*.30*
O23	O2	4k red vio	.20	*.30*
O24	O2	5k dk grn	.20	*.50*
		Nos. O13-O24 (12)	2.40	3.80

NEWSPAPER STAMPS

Catalogue values for unused stamps in this section are for never hinged items.

Carrier Pigeon — N1

1939 Unwmk. Typo. *Imperf.*

P1	N1	2h ocher	.20	*.30*
P2	N1	5h ultra	.20	*.30*
P3	N1	7h red orange	.20	*.30*
P4	N1	9h emerald	.20	*.30*
P5	N1	10h henna brown	.20	*.30*
P6	N1	12h dark ultra	.20	*.30*
P7	N1	20h dark green	.20	*.30*
P8	N1	50h red brown	.20	*.40*
P9	N1	1k greenish gray	.25	*.80*
		Nos. P1-P9 (9)	1.85	*3.30*

No. P5 Overprinted in Black

1940

P10	N1	10h henna brown	.40	*.65*

Overprinted for use by commercial firms.

N2

1943, Feb. 15

P11	N2	2(h) ocher	.20	.20
P12	N2	5(h) light blue	.20	.20
P13	N2	7(h) red orange	.20	.20
P14	N2	9(h) emerald	.20	.20
P15	N2	10(h) henna brown	.20	.20
P16	N2	12(h) dark ultra	.20	.20
P17	N2	20(h) dark green	.20	.20
P18	N2	50(h) red brown	.20	.20
P19	N2	1k slate green	.20	.20
		Nos. P11-P19 (9)	1.80	1.80

DAHOMEY

də-ˈhō-mē

LOCATION — West coast of Africa
AREA — 43,483 sq. mi.
POP. — 3,030,000 (est. 1974)
CAPITAL — Porto-Novo

Formerly a native kingdom including Benin, Dahomey was annexed by France in 1894. It became part of the colonial administrative unit of French West Africa in 1895. Stamps of French West Africa superseded those of Dahomey in 1945. The Republic of Dahomey was proclaimed Dec. 4, 1958.

The republic changed its name to the People's Republic of Benin on Nov. 30, 1975. See Benin for stamps issued after that date.

100 Centimes = 1 Franc

Catalog values for unused stamps in this country are for Never Hinged items, beginning with Scott 137 in the regular postage section, Scott B15 in the semi-postal section, Scott C14 in the airpost section, Scott CQ1 in the airpost parcel post section, Scott J29 in the postage due section, and Scott Q1 int he parcel post section.

See French West Africa No. 71 for stamp inscribed "Dahomey" and "Afrique Occidentale Francaise."

Navigation and Commerce — A1

Perf. 14x13½

1899-1905 Typo. Unwmk.

Name of Colony in Blue or Carmine

No.	Type	Description	Unused	Used
1	A1	1c black, *lil bl* ('01)	1.40	1.40
2	A1	2c brown, *buff* ('04)	2.25	1.40
3	A1	4c claret, *lav* ('04)	2.40	2.00
4	A1	5c yellow grn ('04)	6.00	4.00
5	A1	10c red ('01)	5.25	3.25
6	A1	15c gray ('01)	5.25	1.60
7	A1	20c red, *grn* ('04)	17.00	14.50
8	A1	25c black, *rose* ('99)	16.00	16.00
9	A1	25c blue ('01)	16.00	15.00
10	A1	30c brown, *bis* ('04)	21.00	12.00
11	A1	40c red, *straw* ('04)	22.50	14.50
12	A1	50c brn, *az* (name in red) ('01)	22.50	20.00
12A	A1	50c brn, *az* (name in bl) ('05)	32.50	22.50
13	A1	75c dp vio, *org* ('04)	80.00	55.00
14	A1	1fr brnz grn, *straw* ('04)	40.00	32.50
15	A1	2fr violet, *rose* ('04)	105.00	72.50
16	A1	5fr red lilac, *lav* ('04)	125.00	100.00
		Nos. 1-16 (17)	520.05	388.15

Perf. 13½x14 stamps are counterfeits.
For surcharges see Nos. 32-41.

Gen. Louis Faidherbe A2

Oil Palm — A3

Dr. Noel Eugène Ballay A4

1906-07 ***Perf. 13½x14***

Name of Colony in Red or Blue

No.	Type	Description	Unused	Used
17	A2	1c slate	1.40	1.40
18	A2	2c chocolate	1.75	1.40
19	A2	4c choc, *gray bl*	3.25	2.75
20	A2	5c green	8.75	2.50
21	A2	10c carmine (B)	21.00	3.75
22	A3	20c black, *azure*	13.50	11.00
23	A3	25c blue, *pnksh*	15.00	12.00
24	A3	30c choc, *pnksh*	15.00	12.50
25	A3	35c black, *yellow*	85.00	12.50
26	A3	45c choc, *grnsh* ('07)	20.00	14.50
27	A3	50c deep violet	20.00	17.00
28	A3	75c blue, *orange*	24.00	20.00
29	A4	1fr black, *azure*	27.50	24.00
30	A4	2fr blue, *pink*	105.00	105.00
31	A4	5fr car, *straw* (B)	95.00	100.00
		Nos. 17-31 (15)	456.15	340.30

#2-3, 6-7, 9-13 Surcharged in Black or Carmine

1912 ***Perf. 14x13½***

No.	Description	Unused	Used
32	5c on 2c brn, *buff*	1.60	1.75
33	5c on 4c claret, *lav* (C)	1.40	1.40
a.	Double surcharge	260.00	
34	5c on 15c gray (C)	1.60	1.75
35	5c on 20c red, *grn*	1.60	1.75
36	5c on 25c blue (C)	1.60	1.75
a.	Inverted surcharge	210.00	
37	5c on 30c brown, *bis* (C)	1.60	1.75
38	10c on 40c red, *straw*	1.60	1.60
a.	Inverted surcharge	310.00	
39	10c on 50c brn, *az*, name in bl (C)	2.25	2.40
40	10c on 50c brn, *az*, name in red (C)	1,050.	1,100.
41	10c on 75c violet, *org*	6.00	6.50
a.	Double surcharge	*5,250.*	
	Nos. 32-39,41 (9)	19.25	20.65

Two spacings between the surcharged numerals are found on Nos. 32 to 41. For detailed listings, see the *Scott Classic Specialized Catalogue of Stamps and Covers.*

Man Climbing Oil Palm — A5

1913-39 ***Perf. 13½x14***

No.	Type	Description	Unused	Used
42	A5	1c violet & blk	.25	.30
43	A5	2c choc & rose	.30	.40
44	A5	4c black & brn	.30	.40
45	A5	5c yel grn & bl grn	1.10	.55
46	A5	5c vio brn & vio ('22)	.50	.55
47	A5	10c org red & rose	1.20	.65
a.		Half used as 5c on wrapper or printed matter		—
48	A5	10c yel grn & bl grn ('22)	.75	.80
49	A5	10c red & ol ('25)	.25	.25
50	A5	15c brn org & dk vio ('17)	.75	.50
51	A5	20c gray & choc	.50	.50
52	A5	20c bluish grn & grn ('26)	.30	.30
53	A5	20c mag & blk ('27)	.30	.25
54	A5	25c ultra & dp blue	1.75	1.25
55	A5	25c vio brn & org ('22)	.95	.95
56	A5	30c choc & vio	2.60	2.10
57	A5	30c red org & rose ('22)	2.75	3.00
58	A5	30c yellow & vio ('25)	.30	.30
59	A5	30c dl grn & grn ('27)	.30	.25
60	A5	35c brown & blk	.80	.80
61	A5	35c bl grn & grn ('38)	.30	.25
62	A5	40c black & red org	.75	.75
63	A5	45c gray & ultra	.75	.75
64	A5	50c chocolate & brn	6.00	5.25
a.		Half used as 25c on cover		*500.00*
65	A5	50c ultra & bl ('22)	1.40	1.50
66	A5	50c brn red & bl ('26)	1.20	1.20
67	A5	55c gray grn & choc ('38)	.65	.50
68	A5	60c vio, *pnksh* ('25)	.30	.30
69	A5	65c yel brn & ol grn ('26)	1.20	1.20
70	A5	75c blue & violet	1.00	1.00
71	A5	80c henna brn & ultra ('38)	.30	.30
72	A5	85c dk bl & ver ('26)	1.40	1.40
73	A5	90c rose & brn red ('30)	.80	.75
74	A5	90c yel bis & red org ('39)	1.00	.55
75	A5	1fr blue grn & blk	1.00	.90
76	A5	1fr dk bl & ultra ('26)	1.50	1.50
77	A5	1fr yel brn & lt red ('28)	1.60	1.20
78	A5	1fr dk red & red org ('38)	.95	.90
79	A5	1.10fr vio & bis ('28)	5.25	4.75
80	A5	1.25fr dp bl & dk brn ('33)	17.00	8.75
81	A5	1.50fr dk bl & lt bl ('30)	1.25	.80
82	A5	1.75fr dk brn & dp buff ('33)	4.00	2.00
83	A5	1.75fr ind & ultra ('38)	1.40	.90
84	A5	2fr yel org & choc	1.00	1.20
85	A5	3fr red violet ('30)	2.75	1.75
86	A5	5fr violet & dp bl	2.10	2.40
		Nos. 42-86 (45)	72.80	56.85

The 1c gray and yellow green and 5c dull red and black are Togo Nos. 193a, 196a.

Nos. 47a and 64a were authorized for use in Paouignan during the last part of November 1921. Other values exist as bisects but were not authorized.

For surcharges see #87-96, B1, B8-B11.

Type of 1913 Surcharged

1922-25

No.	Type	Description	Unused	Used
87	A5	60c on 75c vio, *pnksh*	1.00	1.00
a.		Double surcharge	190.00	
88	A5	65c on 15c brn org & dk vio ('25)	1.60	1.60
89	A5	85c on 15c brn org & dk vio ('25)	1.60	1.60
		Nos. 87-89 (3)	4.20	4.20

Stamps and Type of 1913-39 Surcharged with New Value and Bars

1924-27

No.	Type	Description	Unused	Used
90	A5	25c on 2fr org & choc	1.10	1.10
91	A5	90c on 75c cer & brn red ('27)	1.60	1.60
92	A5	1.25fr on 1fr dk bl & ultra (R) ('26)	1.40	1.40
93	A5	1.50fr on 1fr dk bl & grnsh bl ('27)	2.10	2.10
94	A5	3fr on 5fr olvn & dp org ('27)	9.50	9.50
95	A5	10fr on 5fr bl vio & red brn ('27)	8.00	8.00
96	A5	20fr on 5fr ver & dl grn ('27)	8.00	8.00
		Nos. 90-96 (7)	31.70	31.70

Common Design Types pictured following the introduction.

Colonial Exposition Issue

Common Design Types

1931 Engr. ***Perf. 12½***

Name of Country in Black

No.	Type	Description	Unused	Used
97	CD70	40c deep green	5.50	5.50
98	CD71	50c violet	5.50	5.50
99	CD72	90c red orange	5.50	5.50
100	CD73	1.50fr dull blue	5.50	5.50
		Nos. 97-100 (4)	22.00	22.00

Paris International Exposition Issue

Common Design Types

1937 Engr. ***Perf. 13***

No.	Type	Description	Unused	Used
101	CD74	20c deep violet	1.75	1.75
102	CD75	30c dark green	1.75	1.75
103	CD76	40c carmine rose	1.75	1.75
104	CD77	50c dark brown	1.40	1.40
105	CD78	90c red	1.40	1.40
106	CD79	1.50fr ultra	1.75	1.75
		Nos. 101-106 (6)	9.80	9.80

Souvenir Sheet

Imperf

No.	Type	Description	Unused	Used
107	CD77	3fr dp blue & blk	8.00	*9.50*

Caillié Issue

Common Design Type

1939, Apr. 5 Engr. ***Perf. 12½x12***

No.	Type	Description	Unused	Used
108	CD81	90c org brn & org	1.00	1.00
109	CD81	2fr brt violet	1.40	1.40
110	CD81	2.25fr ultra & dk blue	1.40	1.40
		Nos. 108-110 (3)	3.80	3.80

New York World's Fair Issue

Common Design Type

1939 Engr.

No.	Type	Description	Unused	Used
111	CD82	1.25fr carmine lake	1.10	1.10
112	CD82	2.25fr ultra	1.10	1.10

Man Poling a Canoe — A7

Pile House A8

Sailboat on Lake Nokoué — A9

Dahomey Warrior — A10

1941 ***Perf. 13***

No.	Type	Description	Unused	Used
113	A7	2c scarlet	.25	.25
114	A7	3c deep blue	.25	.25
115	A7	5c brown violet	.65	.65
116	A7	10c green	.30	.30
117	A7	15c black	.25	.25
118	A8	20c violet brown	.30	.30
119	A8	30c dk violet	.30	.30
120	A8	40c scarlet	.65	.65
121	A8	50c slate green	.95	.95
122	A8	60c black	.30	.30
123	A8	70c brt red violet	1.00	1.00
124	A9	80c brown black	1.00	1.00
125	A9	1fr violet	1.00	1.00
126	A9	1.30fr brown violet	1.20	1.20
127	A9	1.40fr green	1.00	1.00
128	A9	1.50fr brt rose	1.00	1.00
129	A9	2fr brown orange	1.20	1.20
130	A10	2.50fr dark blue	1.20	1.20
131	A10	3fr scarlet	1.10	1.10
132	A10	5fr slate green	1.10	1.10
133	A10	10fr violet brown	1.75	1.75
134	A10	20fr black	2.25	2.25
		Nos. 113-134 (22)	19.00	19.00

Nos. 121, 122 without "RF," see Nos. 136A-136B.

Pile House and Marshal Pétain A11

1941 ***Perf. 12½x12***

No.	Type	Description	Unused	Used
135	A11	1fr green	.80	—
136	A11	2.50fr blue	.80	—

For surcharges see Nos. B14A-B14B.

Type of 1941 without "RF"

1944 *Perf. 13*

136A A8 50c slate green 1.00
136B A8 60c black 1.00

Nos. 136A-136B were issued by the Vichy government in France, but were not placed on sale in Dahomey.

Catalogue values for unused stamps in this section, from this point to the end of the section, are for Never Hinged items.

Republic

Village Ganvié — A12

Unwmk.

1960, Mar. 1 Engr. *Perf. 12*

137 A12 25fr dk blue, brn & red .55 .20

For overprint see No. 152.

Imperforates

Most Dahomey stamps from 1960 onward exist imperforate in issued and trial colors, and also in small presentation sheets in issued colors.

C.C.T.A. Issue

Common Design Type

1960, May 16

138 CD106 5fr rose lilac & ultra .45 .20

Emblem of the Entente — A13

Prime Minister Hubert Maga — A14

Council of the Entente Issue

1960, May 29 Photo. *Perf. 13x13½*

139 A13 25fr multicolored .55 .30

1st anniv. of the Council of the Entente (Dahomey, Ivory Coast, Niger and Upper Volta).

1960, Aug. Engr. *Perf. 13*

140 A14 85fr deep claret & blk 1.60 .90

Issued on the occasion of Dahomey's proclamation of independence, Aug. 1, 1960.
For surcharge see No. 149.

Weaver — A15

Doves, UN Building and Emblem — A16

2fr, 10fr, Wood sculptor. 3fr, 15fr, Fisherman and net, horiz. 4fr, 20fr, Potter, horiz.

1961, Feb. 17 Engr. *Perf. 13*

141 A15 1fr rose, org & red lilac .20 .20
142 A15 2fr bister brn & choc .20 .20
143 A15 3fr green & orange .20 .20
144 A15 4fr olive bis & claret .20 .20
145 A15 6fr rose, lt vio & ver .40 .20
146 A15 10fr blue & green .55 .40
147 A15 15fr red lilac & violet .75 .40
148 A15 20fr bluish vio & Prus bl .90 .55
Nos. 141-148 (8) 3.40 2.35

For surcharges see Nos. Q1-Q7.

No. 140 Surcharged with New Value, Bars and: "Président de la République"

1961, Aug. 1

149 A14 100fr on 85fr dp cl & blk 3.25 3.25

First anniversary of Independence.

1961, Sept. 20 Unwmk. *Perf. 13*

150 A16 5fr multicolored .35 .25
151 A16 60fr multicolored 1.10 .80

1st anniv. of Dahomey's admission to the UN. See #C16 and souvenir sheet #C16a.

No. 137 Overprinted: "JEUX SPORTIFS D'ABIDJAN 24 AU 31 DECEMBRE 1961"

1961, Dec. 24

152 A12 25fr dk blue, brn & red .55 .30

Abidjan Games, Dec 24-31.

Interior of Burned-out Fort Ouidah and Wrecked Car — A17

1962, July 31 Photo. *Perf. 12½*

153 A17 30fr multicolored .60 .45
154 A17 60fr multicolored 1.40 .60

Evacuation of Fort Ouidah by the Portuguese, and its occupation by Dahomey. 1st anniv.

African and Malgache Union Issue

Common Design Type

1962, Sept. 8 *Perf. 12½x12*

155 CD110 30fr red lil, bluish grn, red & gold .90 .90

Red Cross Nurses and Map — A18

1962, Oct. 5 Engr. *Perf. 13*

156 A18 5fr blue, choc & red .30 .20
157 A18 20fr blue, dk grn & red .60 .45
158 A18 25fr blue, brown & red .65 .45
159 A18 30fr blue, black & red .85 .70
Nos. 156-159 (4) 2.40 1.80

Ganvié Woman in Canoe — A19

Peuhl Herdsman and Cattle A20

Designs: 3fr, 65fr, Bariba chief of Nikki. 15fr, 50fr, Ouidah witch doctor, rock python. 20fr, 30fr, Nessoukoué women carrying vases on heads, Abomey. 25fr, 40fr, Dahomey girl. 60fr, Peuhl herdsman and cattle. 85fr, Ganvié woman in canoe.

1963, Feb. 18 Unwmk. *Perf. 13*

160 A19 2fr grnsh blue & vio .20 .20
161 A19 3fr blue & black .20 .20
162 A20 5fr brown, blk & grn .45 .20
163 A19 15fr brn, bl grn & red brn .45 .20
164 A19 20fr green, blk & car .35 .20
165 A20 25fr dk brn, bl & bl grn .45 .20
166 A19 30fr brn org, choc & mag .65 .40
167 A20 40fr choc, grn & brt bl 1.00 .40
168 A19 50fr blk, grn, brn & red brn 1.75 .55
169 A20 60fr choc, org red & ol 3.00 1.00
170 A19 65fr orange brn & choc 2.00 .65
171 A19 85fr brt blue & choc 3.00 1.00
Nos. 160-171 (12) 13.50 5.20

For surcharges see Nos. 211, 232, Benin 655A, 690F, 700, 722.

Boxers — A21

Designs: 1fr, 20fr, Soccer goalkeeper, horiz. 2fr, 5fr, Runners.

1963, Apr. 11 Engr.

172 A21 50c green & blue .20 .20
173 A21 1fr olive, blk & brn .20 .20
174 A21 2fr olive, blue & brn .20 .20
175 A21 5fr brown, crim & blk .20 .20
176 A21 15fr dk violet & brn .45 .20
177 A21 20fr multicolored .70 .55
Nos. 172-177 (6) 1.95 1.55

Friendship Games, Dakar, Apr. 11-21.
For surcharge & overprint see Benin #697, 704.

President's Palace, Cotonou — A22

1963, Aug. 1 Photo. *Perf. 12½x12*

178 A22 25fr multicolored .45 .20

Third anniversary of independence.

Gen. Toussaint L'Ouverture — A23

UN Emblem, Flame, "15" — A24

1963, Nov. 18 Unwmk. *Perf. 12x13*

179 A23 25fr multicolored .40 .20
180 A23 30fr multicolored .70 .20
181 A23 100fr ultra, brn & red 1.40 .80
Nos. 179-181 (3) 2.50 1.20

Pierre Dominique Toussaint L'Ouverture (1743-1803), Haitian gen., statesman and descendant of the kings of Allada (Dahomey).

1963, Dec. 10 *Perf. 12*

182 A24 4fr multicolored .20 .20
183 A24 6fr multicolored .20 .20
184 A24 25fr multicolored .45 .20
Nos. 182-184 (3) .85 .60

15th anniversary of the Universal Declaration of Human Rights.

Somba Dance — A25

Regional Dances: 3fr, Nago dance, Pobe-Ketou, horiz. 10fr, Dance of the baton. 15fr, Nago dance, Ouidah, horiz. 25fr, Dance of the Sakpatassi. 30fr, Dance of the Nessouhouessi, horiz.

1964, Aug. 8 Engr. *Perf. 13*

185 A25 2fr red, emerald & blk .20 .20
186 A25 3fr dull red, blue & grn .20 .20
187 A25 10fr purple, blk & red .40 .20
188 A25 15fr magenta, blk & grn .40 .20
189 A25 25fr Prus blue, brn & org .80 .30
190 A25 30fr dk red, choc & org 1.00 .40
Nos. 185-190 (6) 3.00 1.50

Runner — A26

1964, Oct. 20 Photo. *Perf. 11*

191 A26 60fr shown 1.90 1.00
192 A26 85fr Bicyclist 3.00 1.40

18th Olympic Games, Tokyo, Oct. 10-25.

Cooperation Issue

Common Design Type

1964, Nov. 7 Engr. *Perf. 13*

193 CD119 25fr org, vio & dk brn .80 .35

UNICEF Emblem, Mother and Child — A27

IQSY Emblem and Apollo — A28

25fr, Mother holding child in her arms.

1964, Dec. 11 Unwmk. *Perf. 13*

194 A27 20fr yel grn, dk red & blk .40 .20
195 A27 25fr blue, dk red & blk .60 .45

18th anniv. of UNICEF.

1964, Dec. 22 Photo. *Perf. 13x12½*

100fr, IQSY emblem, Nimbus weather satellite.

196 A28 25fr green & lt yellow .55 .20
197 A28 100fr deep plum & yellow 1.60 .95

International Quiet Sun Year, 1964-65.

Abomey Tapestry — A29

Designs (Abomey tapestries): 25fr, Warrior and fight scenes. 50fr, Birds and warriors, horiz. 85fr, Animals, ship and plants, horiz.

1965, Apr. 12 Photo. *Perf. 12½*

198 A29 20fr multicolored .75 .20
199 A29 25fr multicolored .85 .40
200 A29 50fr multicolored 1.40 .80
201 A29 85fr multicolored 2.75 1.10
a. Min. sheet of 4, #198-201 7.50 7.50
Nos. 198-201 (4) 5.75 2.50

Issued to publicize the local rug weaving industry.

Baudot Telegraph Distributor and Ader Telephone A30

1965, May 17 Engr. *Perf. 13*

202 A30 100fr lilac, org & blk 2.10 1.60

Cent. of the ITU.

Cotonou Harbor — A31

100fr, Cotonou Harbor, denomination at left.

1965, Aug. 1 Photo. *Perf. 12½*

203 A31 25fr multicolored .90 .20
204 A31 100fr multicolored 2.10 1.10
a. Pair, #203-204 3.75 2.10

The opening of Cotonou Harbor. No. 204a has a continuous design.
For surcharges see Nos. 219-220.

Cybium Tritor A32

Fish: 25fr, Dentex filosus. 30fr, Atlantic sailfish. 50fr, Blackish tripletail.

1965, Sept. 20 Engr. *Perf. 13*

205 A32 10fr black & brt blue .75 .20
206 A32 25fr brt blue, org & blk 1.00 .55
207 A32 30fr violet bl & grnsh bl 1.50 .80
208 A32 50fr black, gray bl & org 2.50 1.00
Nos. 205-208 (4) 5.75 2.55

For surcharge see Benin No. 911.

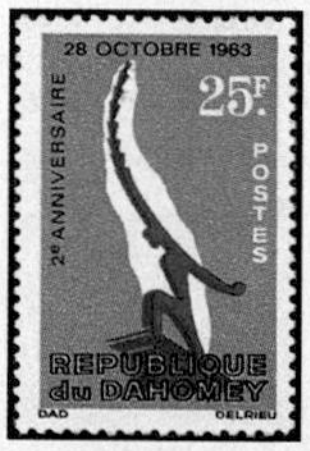

Independence Monument — A33

1965, Oct. 28 Photo. *Perf. 12x12½*

209 A33 25fr gray, black & red .40 .20
210 A33 30fr lt ultra, black & red .65 .20

October 28 Revolution, 2nd anniv.

No. 165 Surcharged

1965, Nov. Engr. *Perf. 13*

211 A20 1fr on 25fr .30 .20

Porto Novo Cathedral A34

Designs: 50fr, Ouidah Pro-Cathedral, vert. 70fr, Cotonou Cathedral.

1966, Mar. 21 Engr. *Perf. 13*

212 A34 30fr Prus bl, vio brn & grn .55 .20
213 A34 50fr vio brn, Prus bl & brn .70 .50
214 A34 70fr grn, Prus bl & vio brn 1.25 .75
Nos. 212-214 (3) 2.50 1.45

Jewelry — A35

Designs: 30fr, Architecture. 50fr, Musician. 70fr, Crucifixion, sculpture.

1966, Apr. 4 Engr. *Perf. 13*

215 A35 15fr dull red brn & blk .45 .20
216 A35 30fr dk brn, ultra & brn red .70 .45
217 A35 50fr brt blue & dk brn 1.10 .55
218 A35 70fr red brown & blk 2.25 .85
Nos. 215-218 (4) 4.50 2.05

International Negro Arts Festival, Dakar, Senegal, Apr. 1-24.

Nos. 203-204 Surcharged

1966, Apr. 24 Photo. *Perf. 12½*

219 A31 15fr on 25fr multi .55 .35
220 A31 15fr on 100fr multi .55 .35
a. Pair, #219-220 1.50 1.10

Fifth anniversary of the Cooperation Agreement between France and Dahomey.

WHO Headquarters from the East — A36

1966, May 3 *Perf. 12½x13*
Size: 35x22½mm

221 A36 30fr multicolored .55 .20

Inauguration of the WHO Headquarters, Geneva. See No. C32.

Boy Scout Signaling A37

Designs: 10fr, Patrol standard with pennant, vert. 30fr, Campfire and map of Dahomey, vert. 50fr, Scouts building foot bridge.

1966, Oct. 17 Engr. *Perf. 13*

222 A37 5fr dk brn, ocher & red .20 .20
223 A37 10fr black, grn & rose cl .20 .20
224 A37 30fr org, red brn & pur .55 .35
225 A37 50fr vio bl, grn & dk brn .95 .45
a. Min. sheet of 4, #222-225 2.75 2.75
Nos. 222-225 (4) 1.90 1.20

Clappertonia Ficifolia — A38

Lions Emblem, Dancing Children, Bird — A39

Flowers: 3fr, Hewittia sublobata. 5fr, Butterfly pea. 10fr, Water lily. 15fr, Commelina forskalaei. 30fr, Eremomastax speciosa.

1967, Feb. 20 Photo. *Perf. 12x12½*

226 A38 1fr multicolored .20 .20
227 A38 3fr multicolored .35 .20
228 A38 5fr multicolored .55 .20
229 A38 10fr multicolored .90 .35
230 A38 15fr multicolored 1.10 .55
231 A38 30fr multicolored 2.10 .90
Nos. 226-231 (6) 5.20 2.40

For surcharges see Benin Nos. 707, 715.

Nos. 170-171 Surcharged with New Value and Heavy Bar

1967, Mar. 1 Engr. *Perf. 13*

232 A19 30fr on 65fr .85 .60
a. Double surcharge 36.00
233 A19 30fr on 85fr .85 .60
a. Double surcharge 60.00
b. Inverted surcharge 60.00

1967, Mar. 20

234 A39 100fr dl vio, dp bl & grn 1.50 1.10

50th anniversary of Lions International.

EXPO '67 "Man in the City" Pavilion A40

Design: 70fr, "The New Africa" exhibit.

1967, June 12 Engr. *Perf. 13*

235 A40 30fr green & choc .70 .20
236 A40 70fr green & brn red 1.50 .65

EXPO '67, International Exhibition, Montreal, Apr. 28-Oct. 27, 1967. See No. C57 and miniature sheet No. C57a.
For surcharges see Benin No. 897.

Europafrica Issue, 1967

Trade (Blood) Circulation, Map of Europe and Africa — A41

1967, July 20 Photo. *Perf. 12x12½*

237 A41 30fr multicolored .55 .20
238 A41 45fr multicolored .80 .45

Scouts Climbing Mountain, Jamboree Emblem A42

70fr, Jamboree emblem, Scouts launching canoe.

1967, Aug. 7 Engr. *Perf. 13*

239 A42 30fr brt bl, red brn & sl .50 .20
240 A42 70fr brt bl, sl grn & dk brn 1.25 .65

12th Boy Scout World Jamboree, Farragut State Park, Idaho, Aug. 1-9. For souvenir sheet see No. C59a.
For surcharges see Benin Nos. 902, 912.

Rhone River and Olympic Emblems A43

Designs (Olympic Emblems and): 45fr, View of Grenoble, vert. 100fr, Rhone Bridge, Grenoble, and Pierre de Coubertin.

1967, Sept. 2 Engr. *Perf. 13*

241 A43 30fr bis, dp bl & grn .70 .40
242 A43 45fr ultra, grn & brn .90 .55
243 A43 100fr choc, grn & brt bl 1.90 1.00
a. Min. sheet of 3, #241-243 4.00 4.00
Nos. 241-243 (3) 3.50 1.95

10th Winter Olympic Games, Grenoble, Feb. 6-18, 1968.
For surcharge see Benin No. 903.

Monetary Union Issue
Common Design Type

1967, Nov. 4 Engr. *Perf. 13*

244 CD125 30fr grn, dk car & dk brn .65 .65

Animals from the Pendjari Reservation (I)

— A45

Designs: 15fr, Cape Buffalo. 30fr, Lion. 45fr, Buffon's kob. 70fr, African slender-snouted crocodile. 100fr, Hippopotamus.

1968, Mar. 18 Photo. *Perf. 12½x13*

245 A45 15fr multicolored .75 .20
246 A45 30fr purple & multi .90 .50
247 A45 45fr blue & multi 1.75 .60
248 A45 70fr multicolored 3.00 .75
249 A45 100fr multicolored 5.50 2.25
Nos. 245-249 (5) 11.90 4.30

See Nos. 252-256.
For surcharges see #310, Benin 655E, 725.

WHO Emblem A46

1968, Apr. 22 Engr. *Perf. 13*

250 A46 30fr multicolored .60 .20
251 A46 70fr multicolored 1.40 .70

20th anniv. of WHO.

Animals from the Pendjari Reservation (II) — A47

Animals: 5fr, Warthog. 30fr, Leopard. 60fr, Spotted hyena. 75fr, Anubius baboon. 90fr, Hartebeest.

1969, Feb. 10 Photo. *Perf. 12½x12*

252 A47 5fr dark brown & multi .25 .20
253 A47 30fr deep ultra & multi 1.00 .50
254 A47 60fr dark green & multi 1.75 .70
255 A47 75fr dark blue & multi 4.00 1.00
256 A47 90fr dark green & multi 5.50 2.25
Nos. 252-256 (5) 12.50 4.65

For surcharge, see Benin No. 708.

Heads, Symbols of Agriculture and Science, and Globe A48

1969, Mar. 10 Engr. *Perf. 13*

257 A48 30fr orange & multi .50 .20
258 A48 70fr maroon & multi 1.50 .70

50th anniv. of the ILO.
For surcharges see Benin Nos. 904, 913.

Arms of Dahomey — A49

1969, June 30 Litho. *Perf. 13½x13*

259 A49 5fr yellow & multi .35 .30
260 A49 30fr orange red & multi 1.25 .45

See No. C101.

Development Bank Issue

Cornucopia and Bank Emblem — A50

1969, Sept. 10 Photo. *Perf. 13*

261 A50 30fr black, grn & ocher .75 .55

African Development Bank, 5th anniv.
For surcharge see Benin No. 905.

Europafrica Issue

Ambary (Kenaf) Industry, Cotonou A51

Design: 45fr, Cotton industry, Parakou.

1969, Sept. 22 Litho. *Perf. 14*

262 A51 30fr multicolored 1.00 .50
263 A51 45fr multicolored 1.25 .75

See Nos. C105-C105a.

Sakpata Dance and Tourist Year Emblem — A52

Dances and Tourist Year Emblem: 30fr, Guelede dance. 45fr, Sato dance.

1969, Dec. 15 Litho. *Perf. 14*

264 A52 10fr multicolored .45 .30
265 A52 30fr multicolored .90 .45
266 A52 45fr multicolored 1.25 .55
Nos. 264-266 (3) 2.60 1.30

See No. C108. For surcharges see Benin Nos. 690J, 1054B.

UN Emblem, Garden and Wall — A53

1970, Apr. 6 Engr. *Perf. 13*

267 A53 30fr ultra, red org & slate .70 .20
268 A53 40fr ultra, brn & sl grn .90 .50

25th anniversary of the United Nations.
For surcharge see No. 294. For overprint, see Benin 647B.

ASECNA Issue

Common Design Type

1970, June 1 Engr. *Perf. 13*

269 CD132 40fr red & purple .90 .55

For surcharge see Benin No. 906.

Mt. Fuji, EXPO '70 Emblem, Monorail Train — A54

1970, June 15 Litho. *Perf. 13½x14*

270 A54 5fr green, red & vio bl .40 .20

EXPO '70 International Exhibition, Osaka, Japan, 3/15-9/13/70. See Nos. C124-C125.

Alkemy, King of Ardres — A55

40fr, Sailing ships "La Justice" & "La Concorde," Ardres, 1670. 50fr, Matheo Lopes, ambassador of the King of Ardres & his coat of arms. 200fr, Louis XIV & fleur-de-lis.

1970, July 6 Engr. *Perf. 13*

271 A55 40fr brt grn, ultra & brn .65 .20
272 A55 50fr dk car, choc & emer .90 .40
273 A55 70fr gray, lemon & choc 1.40 .65
274 A55 200fr Prus bl, dk car & choc 3.50 1.25
Nos. 271-274 (4) 6.45 2.50

300th anniv. of the mission from the King of Ardres to the King of France, and of the audience with Louis XIV on Dec. 19, 1670.
For surcharges see Benin Nos. 724, 914.

Star of the Order of Independence A56

Bariba Warrior A57

1970, Aug. 1 Photo. *Perf. 12*

275 A56 30fr multicolored .40 .20
276 A56 40fr multicolored .60 .20

10th anniversary of independence.
For surcharge see Benin No. 720.

1970, Aug. 24 *Perf. 12½x13*

Designs: 2fr, 50fr, Two horsemen. 10fr, 70fr, Horseman facing left.

277 A57 1fr yellow & multi .20 .20
278 A57 2fr gray grn & multi .30 .20
279 A57 10fr blue & multi .35 .20
280 A57 40fr yellow grn & multi 1.40 .35
281 A57 50fr gold & multi 1.75 .50
282 A57 70fr lilac rose & multi 2.10 .80
Nos. 277-282 (6) 6.10 2.25

For surcharges see Benin Nos. 350-351, 613, 703.

Globe and Heart A58

Design: 40fr, Hands holding heart, vert.

1971, June 7 Engr. *Perf. 13*

283 A58 40fr red, green & dk brn .90 .35
284 A58 100fr green, red & blue 1.75 .90

For surcharges see Benin Nos. 617, 647A, 712, 907.

Intl. year against racial discrimination.

Ancestral Figures and Lottery Ticket — A59

King Behanzin's Emblem (1889-1894) A60

1971, June 24 Litho. *Perf. 14*

285 A59 35fr multicolored .65 .20
286 A59 40fr multicolored .80 .35

4th anniv. of the National Lottery.
For overprint see Benin #710.

Photo.; Litho. (25fr, 135fr)

1971-72 *Perf. 12½*

Emblems of the Kings of Abomey: 25fr, Agoliagbo (1894-1900). 35fr, Ganyehoussou (1620-45), bird and cup, horiz. 100fr, Guezo (1818-58), bull, tree and birds. 135fr, Ouegbadja (1645-85), horiz. 140fr, Glèle (1858-89), lion and sword, horiz.

287 A60 25fr multicolored .55 .20
288 A60 35fr green & multi .90 .20
289 A60 40fr green & multi 1.25 .55
290 A60 100fr red & multi 2.25 .90
291 A60 135fr multicolored 3.25 1.40
292 A60 140fr brown & multi 3.75 1.90
Nos. 287-292 (6) 11.95 5.15

Issued: 25fr, 135fr, 7/17/72; others, 8/3/71.
For surcharges, see Benin #614, 634B, 791.

Kabuki Actor, Long-distance Skiing — A61

Brahms and "Soir d'été" — A62

1972, Feb. Engr. *Perf. 13*

293 A61 35fr dk car, brn & bl grn 1.60 .75

11th Winter Olympic Games, Sapporo, Japan, Feb. 3-13. See No. C153.

No. 268 Surcharged

1972

294 A53 35fr on 40fr multi .65 .35

1972, June 29 Engr. *Perf. 13*

65fr, Brahms, woman at piano & music, horiz.

295 A62 30fr red brn, blk & lilac 2.00 .80
296 A62 65fr red brn, blk & lilac 3.25 1.50

75th anniversary of the death of Johannes Brahms (1833-1897), German composer.
For surcharge see Benin Nos. 654B, 718.

The Hare and The Tortoise, by La Fontaine — A63

Fables: 35fr, The Fox and The Stork, vert. 40fr, The Cat, The Weasel and Rabbit.

1972, Aug. 28 Engr. *Perf. 13*

297 A63 10fr multicolored 1.75 .75
298 A63 35fr dark red & multi 3.25 1.25
299 A63 40fr ultra & multi 4.25 1.75
Nos. 297-299 (3) 9.25 3.75

Jean de La Fontaine (1621-1695), French fabulist.

West African Monetary Union Issue

Common Design Type

1972, Nov. 2 Engr. *Perf. 13*

300 CD136 40fr choc, ocher & gray .65 .20

Dr. Hansen, Microscope, Bacilli — A65

Design: 85fr, Portrait of Dr. Hansen.

1973, May 14 Engr. *Perf. 13*

301 A65 35fr ultra, vio brn & brn .50 .35
302 A65 85fr yel grn, bis & ver 1.10 .75

Centenary of the discovery by Dr. Armauer G. Hansen of the Hansen bacillus, the cause of leprosy.
For surcharges see Benin Nos. 655G, 1084.

Arms of Dahomey — A66

1973, June 25 Photo. *Perf. 13*

303 A66	5fr ultra & multi	.20	.20
304 A66	35fr ocher & multi	.40	.20
305 A66	40fr red orange & multi	.60	.20
	Nos. 303-305 (3)	1.20	.60

For overprint see Benin No. 690A.

INTERPOL Emblem and Spiderweb A67

Design: 50fr, INTERPOL emblem and communications symbols, vert.

1973, July Engr.

306 A67	35fr ver, grn & brn	.60	.30
307 A67	50fr green, brn & red	1.00	.45

50th anniversary of International Criminal Police Organization (INTERPOL).

For overprints see Benin Nos. 634A, 810.

Education in Hygiene and Nutrition A68

WHO, 25th Anniv.: 100fr, Prenatal examination and care, WHO emblem.

1973, Aug. 2 Photo. *Perf. 12½x13*

308 A68	35fr multicolored	.50	.30
309 A68	100fr multicolored	1.50	.65

For surcharge, see Benin No. 655B.

No. 248 Surcharged with New Value, 2 Bars, and Overprinted in Red: "SECHERESSE SOLIDARITE AFRICAINE"

1973, Aug. 16

310 A45	100fr on 70fr multi	2.10	1.00

African solidarity in drought emergency.

African Postal Union Issue

Common Design Type

1973, Sept. 12 Engr. *Perf. 13*

311 CD137	100fr red, purple & blk	1.25	.55

For surcharge see Benin No. 690I.

Epinephelus Aeneus — A69

Fish: 15fr, Drepane africana. 35fr, Pragus ehrenbergi.

1973, Sept. 18

312 A69	5fr slate blue & indigo	1.00	.30
313 A69	15fr black & brt blue	1.50	.35
314 A69	35fr emerald, ocher & sep	3.50	.60
	Nos. 312-314 (3)	6.00	1.25

Chameleon A70

40fr, Emblem over map of Dahomey, vert.

1973, Nov. 30 Photo. *Perf. 13*

315 A70	35fr olive & multi	.55	.30
316 A70	40fr multicolored	1.25	.35

1st anniv. of the Oct. 26 revolution.

The Chameleon in the Tree — A71

Designs: 5fr, The elephant, the hen and the dog, vert. 10fr, The sparrowhawk and the dog, vert. 25fr, The chameleon in the tree. 40fr, The eagle, the viper and the hen.

1974, Feb. 14 Photo. *Perf. 13*

317 A71	5fr emerald & multi	.40	.20
318 A71	10fr slate blue & multi	.50	.20
319 A71	25fr slate blue & multi	.90	.30
320 A71	40fr light blue & multi	1.40	.45
	Nos. 317-320 (4)	3.20	1.15

Folktales of Dahomey.

For surcharges see Benin Nos. 709, 908, 1363.

German Shepherd — A72

1974, Apr. 25 Photo. *Perf. 13*

321 A72	40fr shown	1.50	.35
322 A72	50fr Boxer	1.75	.35
323 A72	100fr Saluki	3.50	.80
	Nos. 321-323 (3)	6.75	1.50

Council Issue

Map and Flags of Members A73

1974, May 29 Photo. *Perf. 13x12½*

324 A73	40fr blue & multi	.80	.20

15th anniversary of the Council of Accord.

Locomotive 232, 1911 — A74

Designs: Locomotives.

1974, Sept. 2 Photo. *Perf. 13x12½*

325 A74	35fr shown	.75	.30
326 A74	40fr Freight, 1877	1.50	.30
327 A74	100fr Crampton, 1849	2.25	1.00
328 A74	200fr Stephenson, 1846	4.50	1.60
	Nos. 325-328 (4)	9.00	3.20

For surcharges see Benin Nos. 654E, 690K, 727, 909.

Globe, Money, People in Bank A75

1974, Oct. 31 Engr. *Perf. 13*

329 A75	35fr multicolored	.50	.35

World Savings Day.

Dompago Dance, Hissi Tribe — A76

Flags of Dahomey and Nigeria over Africa — A77

Folk Dances: 25fr, Fetish Dance, Vaudou-Tchinan. 40fr, Bamboo Dance, Agbehoun. 100fr, Somba Dance, Sandoua, horiz.

1975, Aug. 4 Litho. *Perf. 12*

330 A76	10fr yellow & multi	.50	.20
331 A76	25fr dk green & multi	1.00	.20
332 A76	40fr red & multi	1.25	.50
333 A76	100fr multicolored	2.25	.60
	Nos. 330-333 (4)	5.00	1.50

For surcharge and overprint see Benin Nos. 655D, 713.

1975, Aug. 11 Photo. *Perf. 12½x13*

Design: 100fr, Arrows connecting maps of Dahomey and Nigeria, horiz.

334 A77	65fr multicolored	.75	.25
335 A77	100fr green & multi	1.00	.45

Year of intensified cooperation between Dahomey and Nigeria.

For surcharges & overprint see Benin Nos. 690H, 701, 899, 901.

Map, Pylons, Emblem — A78

Benin Electric Community Emblem and Pylon — A79

1975, Aug. 18

336 A78	40fr multicolored	.75	.35
337 A79	150fr multicolored	2.00	1.00

Benin Electric Community and Ghana-Togo-Dahomey cooperation.

For surcharges see Benin #601, 900, 910.

Map of Dahomey, Rising Sun — A80

Albert Schweitzer, Nurse, Patient — A81

1975, Aug. 25 Photo. *Perf. 12½x13*

338 A80	35fr multicolored	.50	.20

Cooperation Year for the creation of a new Dahoman society.

For overprint see Benin No. 690E. For surcharge, see Benin No. 1362.

1975, Sept. 22 Engr. *Perf. 13*

339 A81	200fr olive, grn & red brn	5.00	1.50

Birth centenary of Albert Schweitzer (1875-1965), medical missionary and musician.

For surcharge see Benin No. 655F.

Woman Speaking on Telephone, IWY Emblem — A82

150fr, IWY emblem and linked rings.

1975, Oct. 20 Engr. *Perf. 12½x13*

340 A82	50fr Prus blue & lilac	.75	.35
341 A82	150fr emerald, brn & org	2.00	.80

International Women's Year 1975.

For surcharge see Benin No. 655C.

SEMI-POSTAL STAMPS

Regular Issue of 1913 Surcharged in Red

1915 Unwmk. *Perf. 14x13½*

B1 A5	10c + 5c orange red & rose	1.20	1.20

Curie Issue

Common Design Type

1938 *Perf. 13*

B2 CD80	1.75fr + 50c brt ultra	9.50	9.50

French Revolution Issue

Common Design Type

1939 Photo.

Name and Value Typo. in Black

B3 CD83	45c + 25c green	8.75	8.75
B4 CD83	70c + 30c brown	8.75	8.75
B5 CD83	90c + 35c red org	8.75	8.75
B6 CD83	1.25fr + 1fr rose pink	8.75	8.75
B7 CD83	2.25fr + 2fr blue	8.75	8.75
	Nos. B3-B7 (5)	43.75	43.75

Postage Stamps of 1913-38 Surcharged in Black

1941 *Perf. 13½x14*

B8 A5 50c + 1fr brn red & bl 2.75 2.75
B9 A5 80c + 2fr hn brn & ultra 6.75 6.75
B10 A5 1.50fr + 2fr dk bl & lt bl 7.25 7.25
B11 A5 2fr + 3fr yel org & choc 7.25 7.25
Nos. B8-B11 (4) 24.00 24.00

Common Design Type and

Radio Operator — SP1

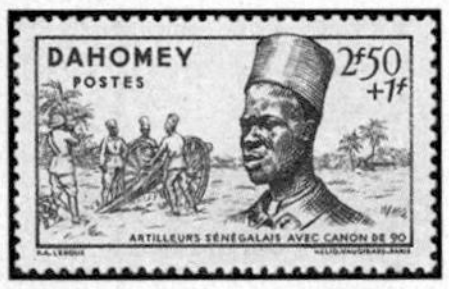

Senegalese Artillerymen SP2

1941 **Photo.** *Perf. 13½*

B12 SP1 1fr + 1fr red 1.20
B13 CD86 1.50fr + 3fr claret 1.20
B14 SP2 2.50fr + 1fr blue 1.20
Nos. B12-B14 (3) 3.60

Surtax for the defense of the colonies.

Nos. B12-B14 were issued by the Vichy government in France, but were not placed on sale in Dahomey.

Nos. 135-136 Surcharged in Black or Red

1944 **Engr.** *Perf. 12½x12*

B14A 50c + 1.50fr on 2.50fr deep blue (R) .80
B14B + 2.50fr on 1fr green .80

Colonial Development Fund.

Nos. B14A-B14B were issued by the Vichy government in France, but were not placed on sale in Dahomey.

Catalogue values for unused stamps in this section, from this point to the end of the section, are for Never Hinged items.

Republic

Anti-Malaria Issue

Common Design Type

1962, Apr. 7 **Engr.** *Perf. 12½x12*

B15 CD108 25fr + 5fr orange brn .55 .55

Freedom from Hunger Issue

Common Design Type

1963, Mar. 21 **Unwmk.** *Perf. 13*

B16 CD112 25fr + 5fr ol, brn red & brn .65 .65

AIR POST STAMPS

Common Design Type

1940 **Unwmk.** **Engr.** *Perf. 12½*

C1 CD85 1.90fr ultra .40 .40
C2 CD85 2.90fr dk red .55 .55
C3 CD85 4.50fr dk gray grn .80 .80
C4 CD85 4.90fr yel bister .95 .95
C5 CD85 6.90fr deep org 1.25 1.25
Nos. C1-C5 (5) 3.95 3.95

Common Design Types

1942

C6 CD88 50c car & bl .20
C7 CD88 1fr brn & blk .20
C8 CD88 2fr dk grn & red brn .35
C9 CD88 3fr dk bl & scar .80
C10 CD88 5fr vio & brn red .80

Frame Engr., Center Typo.

C11 CD89 10fr ultra, ind & org .80
C12 CD89 20fr rose car, mag & gray blk .80
C13 CD89 50fr yel grn, dl grn & dp bl 1.50 *3.25*
a. 50fr yellow green, dull green & pale blue 2.00 *3.75*
Nos. C6-C13 (8) 5.45

Nos. C6-C12 were issued by the Vichy government in France, but were not placed on sale in Dahomey.

Catalogue values for unused stamps in this section, from this point to the end of the section, are for Never Hinged items.

Republic

Somba House — AP4

Design: 500fr, Royal Court of Abomey.

Unwmk.

1960, Apr. 1 **Engr.** *Perf. 13*

C14 AP4 100fr multi 3.25 .80
C15 AP4 500fr multi 13.50 4.00

For overprint see Benin No. C419. For surcharge, see Benin No. C541.

Type of Regular Issue, 1961

1961, Sept. 20

C16 A16 200fr multi 3.00 2.25
a. Souv. sheet of 3, #150-151, C16 6.00 6.00

Air Afrique Issue

Common Design Type

1962, Feb. 17 *Perf. 13*

C17 CD107 25fr ultra, blk & org brn .70 .30

Palace of the African and Malgache Union, Cotonou — AP5

1963, July 27 **Photo.** *Perf. 13x12*

C18 AP5 250fr multi 4.00 2.00

Assembly of chiefs of state of the African and Malgache Union held at Cotonou in July.

African Postal Union Issue

Common Design Type

1963, Sept. 8 **Unwmk.** *Perf. 12½*

C19 CD114 25fr brt bl, ocher & red .60 .25

See note after Cameroun No. C47.

Boeing 707 — AP6

Boeing 707: 200fr, On the ground. 300fr, Over Cotonou airport. 500fr, In the air.

1963, Oct. 25 **Engr.** *Perf. 13*

C20 AP6 100fr multi 2.00 .60
C21 AP6 200fr multi 3.00 2.00
C22 AP6 300fr multi 5.00 2.00
C23 AP6 500fr multi 10.00 2.50
Nos. C20-C23 (4) 20.00 7.10

For surcharges see Nos. CQ1-CQ5.

Priests Carrying Funerary Boat, Isis Temple, Philae — AP7

1964, Mar. 9 **Unwmk.** *Perf. 13*

C24 AP7 25fr vio bl & brn 1.50 .75

UNESCO world campaign to save historic monuments in Nubia.

Weather Map and Symbols — AP8

1965, Mar. 23 **Photo.** *Perf. 12½*

C25 AP8 50fr multi .80 .55

Fifth World Meteorological Day.

ICY Emblem and Men of Various Races — AP9

1965, June 26 **Engr.** *Perf. 13*

C26 AP9 25fr dl pur, mar & grn .40 .20
C27 AP9 85fr dp bl, mar & sl grn .90 .65

International Cooperation Year, 1965

Winston Churchill — AP10

1965, June 15 **Photo.** *Perf. 12½*

C28 AP10 100fr multi 2.10 1.75

Abraham Lincoln — AP11

1965, July 15 *Perf. 13*

C29 AP11 100fr multi 1.65 1.00

Centenary of death of Lincoln

For surcharge see No. C55.

John F. Kennedy and Arms of Dahomey — AP12

1965, Nov. 22 **Photo.** *Perf. 12½*

C30 AP12 100fr dp grn & blk 2.25 1.10

President John F. Kennedy (1917-63).

For surcharge see No. C56.

Dr. Albert Schweitzer and Patients — AP13

1966, Jan. 17 **Photo.** *Perf. 12½*

C31 AP13 100fr multi 2.50 1.25

Dr. Albert Schweitzer (1875-1965), medical missionary, theologian and musician.

For surcharge see Benin No. C435.

WHO Type of Regular Issue

Design: WHO Headquarters from the West.

1966, May 3 **Unwmk.** *Perf. 13*

Size: 47x28mm

C32 A36 100fr ultra, yel & blk 1.75 1.50

Pygmy Goose — AP14

Broad-billed Rollers — AP15

Birds: 100fr, Fiery-breasted bush-shrike. 250fr, Emerald cuckoos. 500fr, Emerald starling.

1966-67 *Perf. 12½*

C33 AP14 50fr multi 2.00 .55
C34 AP14 100fr multi 3.00 .85
C35 AP15 200fr multi 10.00 2.25

C36 AP15 250fr multi 10.00 3.00
C37 AP14 500fr multi 15.00 6.00
Nos. C33-C37 (5) 40.00 12.65

Issued: 50fr, 100fr, 500fr, 6/13/66; others, 1/20/67.

For surcharges see Nos. C107, Benin C353-C355, C357, C368, C426, C436.

Industrial Symbols — AP16

1966, July 21 Photo. *Perf. 12x13*
C38 AP16 100fr multi 1.60 .80

Agreement between European Economic Community & the African & Malagache Union, 3rd anniv.

Pope Paul VI and St. Peter's, Rome — AP17

Pope Paul VI and UN General Assembly AP18

70fr, Pope Paul VI and view of NYC.

1966, Aug. 22 Engr. *Perf. 13*
C39 AP17 50fr multi .75 .45
C40 AP17 70fr multi .95 .55
C41 AP18 100fr multi 1.75 1.00
a. Min. sheet of 3, #C39-C41 4.50 4.50
Nos. C39-C41 (3) 3.45 2.00

Pope Paul's appeal for peace before the UN General Assembly, Oct. 4, 1965.

Air Afrique Issue, 1966

Common Design Type

1966, Aug. 31 Photo. *Perf. 12½*
C42 CD123 30fr dk vio, blk & gray .75 .20

"Science" — AP20

Designs: 45fr, "Art" (carved female statue), vert. 100fr, "Education" (book and letters).

1966, Nov. 4 Engr. *Perf. 13*
C43 AP20 30fr mag, ultra & vio brn .45 .20
C44 AP20 45fr mar & grn .80 .55
C45 AP20 100fr blk, mar & brt bl 1.90 1.00
a. Min. sheet of 3, #C43-C45 3.25 3.25
Nos. C43-C45 (3) 3.15 1.75

20th anniversary of UNESCO.

Madonna by Alessio Baldovinetti AP21

Christmas: 50fr, Nativity after 15th century Beaune tapestry. 100fr, Adoration of the Shepherds, by José Ribera.

1966, Dec. 25 Photo. *Perf. 12½x12*
C46 AP21 50fr multi 3.25 2.25
C47 AP21 100fr multi 4.50 3.25
C48 AP21 200fr multi 9.00 5.00
Nos. C46-C48 (3) 16.75 10.50

See Nos. C95-C96, C109-C115. For surcharge see No. C60.

1967, Apr. 10 *Perf. 12½x12*

Paintings by Ingres: No. C49, Self-portrait, 1804. No. C50, Oedipus and the Sphinx.

C49 AP21 100fr multi 3.00 1.50
C50 AP21 100fr multi 3.00 1.50

Jean Auguste Dominique Ingres (1780-1867), French painter.

Three-master Suzanne — AP22

Windjammers: 45fr, Three-master Esmeralda, vert. 80fr, Schooner Marie Alice, vert. 100fr, Four-master Antonin.

1967, May 8 *Perf. 13*
C51 AP22 30fr multi 1.00 .50
C52 AP22 45fr multi 1.25 .75
C53 AP22 80fr multi 2.25 1.25
C54 AP22 100fr multi 3.00 1.50
Nos. C51-C54 (4) 7.50 4.00

For overprint & surcharge see Benin Nos. C369, C420.

Nos. C29-C30 Surcharged

1967, May 29 Photo. *Perf. 13, 12½*
C55 AP11 125fr on 100fr 2.00 1.25
C56 AP12 125fr on 100fr 2.00 1.25

50th anniv. of the birth of Pres. John F. Kennedy.

EXPO '67 "Man In Space" Pavilion — AP23

1967, June 12 Engr. *Perf. 13*
C57 AP23 100fr dl red & Prus bl 2.25 .75
a. Min. sheet of 3, #235-236, C57 4.00 4.00

EXPO '67, International Exhibition, Montreal, Apr. 28-Oct. 27, 1967.

Europafrica Issue, 1967

Konrad Adenauer, by Oscar Kokoschká AP24

1967, July 19 Photo. *Perf. 12½x12*
C58 AP24 70fr multi 1.50 .75
a. Souv. sheet of 4 7.00 7.00

Konrad Adenauer (1876-1967), chancellor of West Germany (1949-1963).

Jamboree Emblem, Ropes and World Map — AP25

1967, Aug. 7 Engr. *Perf. 13*
C59 AP25 100fr lil, sl grn & dp bl 1.90 .75
a. Souv. sheet of 3, #239-240, C59 4.00 4.00

12th Boy Scout World Jamboree, Farragut State Park, Idaho, Aug. 1-9.

No. C48 Surcharged in Red

1967, Aug. 12 Photo. *Perf. 12½x12*
C60 AP21 150fr on 200fr 3.00 2.25
a. "150F" omitted 300.00 300.00

Riccione, Italy Stamp Exhibition.

African Postal Union Issue, 1967

Common Design Type

1967, Sept. 9 Engr. *Perf. 13*
C61 CD124 100fr red, brt lil & emer 1.25 .75

For surcharge see Benin No. C471.

Charles de Gaulle AP26

1967, Nov. 21 Photo. *Perf. 12½x13*
C62 AP26 100fr multi 3.25 2.00
a. Souv. sheet of 4 15.00 15.00

Pres. Charles de Gaulle of France on the occasion of Pres. Christophe Soglo's state visit to Paris, Nov. 1967.

Madonna, by Matthias Grunewald AP27

Paintings: 50fr, Holy Family by the Master of St. Sebastian, horiz. 100fr, Adoration of the Magi by Ulrich Apt the Elder. 200fr, Annunciation, by Matthias Grunewald.

1967, Dec. 11 Photo. *Perf. 12½*
C63 AP27 30fr multi .55 .45
C64 AP27 50fr multi 1.10 .60
C65 AP27 100fr multi 2.00 1.25
C66 AP27 200fr multi 5.00 2.00
Nos. C63-C66 (4) 8.65 4.30

Christmas 1967.

Venus de Milo and Mariner 5 — AP28

#C68, Venus de Milo and Venus 4 Rocket.

1968, Feb. 17 Photo. *Perf. 13*
C67 AP28 70fr grnsh bl & multi 1.50 .75
C68 AP28 70fr dp bl & multi 1.50 .75
a. Souv. sheet of 2, #C67-C68 3.50 3.50

Explorations of the planet Venus, Oct. 18-19, 1967.

For surcharges see Nos. C103-C104.

Gutenberg Monument, Strasbourg Cathedral AP29

1968, May 20 Litho. *Perf. 14x13½*

Design: 100fr, Gutenberg Monument, Mainz, and Gutenberg press.

C69 AP29 45fr grn & org 1.00 .40
C70 AP29 100fr dk & lt bl 2.00 1.00
a. Souv. sheet of 2, #C69-C70 3.75 3.75

500th anniv. of the death of Johann Gutenberg, inventor of printing from movable type.

For surcharge see Benin #C516.

Martin Luther King, Jr. — AP30

Designs: 30fr, "We must meet hate with creative love" in French, English and German. 100fr, Full-face portrait.

Perf. 12½, 13½x13

1968, June 17 **Photo.**

Size: 26x46mm

C71 AP30 30fr red brn, yel & blk .55 .35

Size: 26x37mm

C72 AP30 55fr multi .85 .45
C73 AP30 100fr multi 1.25 .90
a. Min. sheet of 3, #C71-C73 3.75 3.75
Nos. C71-C73 (3) 2.65 1.70

Martin Luther King, Jr. (1929-68), American civil rights leader.
For surcharge, see Benin No. C517.

Robert Schuman — AP31

45fr, Alcide de Gasperi. 70fr, Konrad Adenauer.

1968, July 20 **Photo.** ***Perf. 13***

C74 AP31 30fr dp yel, blk & grn .40 .40
C75 AP31 45fr org, dk brn & ol .85 .50
C76 AP31 70fr multi 1.40 .50
Nos. C74-C76 (3) 2.65 1.40

5th anniversary of the economic agreement between the European Economic Community and the African and Malgache Union.
For surcharge see Benin No. C462.

Battle of Montebello, by Henri Philippoteaux — AP32

Paintings: 45fr, 2nd Zouave Regiment at Magenta, by Riballier. 70fr, Battle of Magenta, by Louis Eugène Charpentier. 100fr, Battle of Solferino, by Charpentier.

1968, Aug. 12 ***Perf. 12½x12***

C77 AP32 30fr multi .90 .50
C78 AP32 45fr multi 1.25 .65
C79 AP32 70fr multi 2.50 1.25
C80 AP32 100fr multi 3.25 1.00
Nos. C77-C80 (4) 7.90 3.40

Issued for the Red Cross.

Mail Truck in Village — AP33

Designs: 45fr, Mail truck stopping at rural post office. 55fr, Mail truck at river bank. 70fr, Mail truck and train.

1968, Oct. 7 **Photo.** ***Perf. 13x12½***

C81 AP33 30fr multi .80 .50
C82 AP33 45fr multi 1.00 .55
C83 AP33 55fr multi 1.50 .55
C84 AP33 70fr multi 3.75 1.00
Nos. C81-C84 (4) 7.05 2.60

For surcharges see Benin Nos. C352, C357A.

Aztec Stadium, Mexico City — AP34

45fr, Ball player, Mayan sculpture, vert. 70fr, Wrestler, sculpture from Uxpanapan, vert. 150fr, Olympic Stadium, Mexico City.

1968, Nov. 20 **Engr.** ***Perf. 13***

C85 AP34 30fr dp cl & sl grn .60 .30
C86 AP34 45fr ultra & dk rose brn 1.10 .60
C87 AP34 70fr sl grn & dk brn 1.60 .65
C88 AP34 150fr dk car & dk brn 2.25 1.25
a. Min. sheet of 4, #C85-C88 5.50 5.50
Nos. C85-C88 (4) 5.55 2.80

19th Olympic Games, Mexico City, Oct. 12-27. No. C88a is folded down the vertical gutter separating Nos. C85-C86 se-tenant at left and Nos. C87-C88 se-tenant at right.
For overprint and surcharges see Benin Nos. C457, C461, C513.

The Annunciation, by Foujita — AP35

Paintings by Foujita: 30fr, Nativity, horiz. 100fr, The Virgin and Child. 200fr, The Baptism of Christ.

Perf. 12x12½, 12½x12

1968, Nov. 25 **Photo.**

C89 AP35 30fr multi .80 .55
C90 AP35 70fr multi 1.60 .80
C91 AP35 100fr multi 1.75 1.25
C92 AP35 200fr multi 4.00 2.75
Nos. C89-C92 (4) 8.15 5.35

Christmas 1968.

PHILEXAFRIQUE Issue

Painting: Diderot, by Louis Michel Vanloo.

1968, Dec. 16 ***Perf. 12½x12***

C93 AP35 100fr multi 3.50 3.50

PHILEXAFRIQUE, Philatelic Exhibition in Abidjan, Feb. 14-23. Printed with alternating label.
For surcharge, see Benin No. C522.

2nd PHILEXAFRIQUE Issue

Common Design Type

50fr, Dahomey #119 and aerial view of Cotonou.

1969, Feb. 14 **Engr.** ***Perf. 13***

C94 CD128 50fr bl, brn & pur 2.10 2.10

For surcharge see Benin No. C467.

Christmas Painting Type

Paintings: No. C95, Virgin of the Rocks, by Leonardo da Vinci. No. C96, Virgin with the Scales, by Cesare da Sesto.

1969, Mar. 17 **Photo.** ***Perf. 12½x12***

C95 AP21 100fr vio & multi 1.75 1.00
C96 AP21 100fr grn & multi 1.75 1.00

Leonardo da Vinci (1452-1519).

General Bonaparte, by Jacques Louis David AP36

Paintings: 60fr, Napoleon I in 1809, by Robert J. Lefevre. 75fr, Napoleon on the Battlefield of Eylau, by Antoine Jean Gros, horiz. 200fr, Gen. Bonaparte at Arcole, by Gros.

1969, Apr. 14 **Photo.** ***Perf. 12½x12***

C97 AP36 30fr multi 1.50 1.25
C98 AP36 60fr multi 2.75 1.75
C99 AP36 75fr multi 3.00 2.50
C100 AP36 200fr multi 7.25 5.50
Nos. C97-C100 (4) 14.50 11.00

Bicentenary of the birth of Napoleon I.

Arms Type of Regular Issue, 1969

1969, June 30 **Litho.** ***Perf. 13½x13***

C101 A49 50fr multi .55 .30

For overprint see Benin No. C417.

Apollo 8 Trip Around the Moon — AP37

Embossed on Gold Foil

1969, July ***Die-cut Perf. 10½***

C102 AP37 1000fr gold 20.00 20.00

US Apollo 8 mission, which put the 1st men into orbit around the moon, Dec. 21-27, 1968.

Nos. C67-C68 Surcharged

1969, Aug. 1 **Photo.** ***Perf. 13***

C103 AP28 125fr on 70fr, #C67 2.00 1.75
C104 AP28 125fr on 70fr, #C68 2.00 1.75

Man's 1st landing on the moon, July 20, 1969; US astronauts Neil A. Armstrong, Col. Edwin E. Aldrin, Jr., with Lieut. Col. Michael Collins piloting Apollo 11.

Europafrica Issue

Type of Regular Issue, 1969

Design: 100fr, Oil palm industry, Cotonou.

1969, Sept. 22 **Litho.** ***Perf. 14***

C105 A51 100fr multi 2.25 .35
a. Souv. sheet of 3, #262-263, C105 4.25 4.25

For surcharge see No. C523.

Dahomey Rotary Emblem — AP38

1969, Sept. 25 ***Perf. 14x13½***

C106 AP38 50fr multi 1.00 .75

For surcharge see Benin No. C468.

No. C33 Surcharged

1969, Nov. 15 **Photo.** ***Perf. 12½***

C107 AP14 10fr on 50fr multi .45 .20

Dance Type of Regular Issue

Design: Teke dance and Tourist Year emblem.

1969, Dec. 15 **Litho.** ***Perf. 14***

C108 A52 70fr multi 2.50 1.50

For surcharge see Benin No. C398.

Painting Type of 1966

Christmas: 30fr, Annunciation, by Vrancke van der Stockt. 45fr, Nativity, Swabian School, horiz. 110fr, Madonna and Child, by the Master of the Gold Brocade. 200fr, Adoration of the Kings, Antwerp School.

1969, Dec. 20 ***Perf. 12½x12, 12x12½***

C109 AP21 30fr multi .45 .40
C110 AP21 45fr red & multi .80 .65
C111 AP21 110fr multi 2.00 1.25
C112 AP21 200fr multi 3.50 2.25
Nos. C109-C112 (4) 6.75 4.55

For surcharges see Benin #C425, C463, C475, C532.

1969, Dec. 27 ***Perf. 12½x12***

Paintings: No. C113, The Artist's Studio (detail), by Gustave Courbet. No. C114, Self-portrait with Gold Chain, by Rembrandt. 150fr, Hendrickje Stoffels, by Rembrandt.

C113 AP21 100fr red & multi 2.25 1.25
C114 AP21 100fr grn & multi 2.25 1.25
C115 AP21 150fr multi 3.50 1.75
Nos. C113-C115 (3) 8.00 4.25

For overprint and surcharge see Benin Nos. C458, C472.

Franklin D. Roosevelt AP39

Astronauts, Rocket, US Flag — AP40

1970, Feb. Photo. *Perf. 12½*

C116 AP39 100fr ultra, yel grn & blk 1.60 .60

25th anniversary of the death of Pres. Franklin Delano Roosevelt (1882-1945).

1970, Mar. 9 Photo. *Perf. 12½*

Astronauts: 50fr, Riding rocket through space. 70fr, In landing module approaching moon. 110fr, Planting US flag on moon.

C117 AP40 30fr multi .65 .25

Souvenir Sheet

C118 Sheet of 4 8.00 8.00
- *a.* AP40 50fr violet blue & multi .75 .75
- *b.* AP40 70fr violet blue & multi 1.00 1.00
- *c.* AP40 110fr violet blue & multi 1.25 1.25

See note after No. C104. No. C118 contains Nos. C117, C118a, C118b and C118c.
For surcharge see No. C120.

Walt Whitman and Dahoman Huts — AP41

1970, Apr. 30 Engr. *Perf. 13*

C119 AP41 100fr Prus bl, brn & emer 1.25 .60

Walt Whitman (1818-92), American poet.

No. C117 Surcharged in Silver with New Value, Heavy Bar and: "APOLLO XIII / SOLIDARITE / SPATIALE / INTERNATIONALE"

1970, May 15 Photo. *Perf. 12½*

C120 AP40 40fr on 30fr multi 1.20 .75

The flight of Apollo 13.
For surcharge see Benin No. C464.

Soccer Players and Globe — AP42

Designs: 50fr, Goalkeeper catching ball. 200fr, Players kicking ball.

1970, May 19

C121 AP42 40fr multi .75 .40
C122 AP42 50fr multi .95 .50
C123 AP42 200fr multi 3.50 1.25
Nos. C121-C123 (3) 5.20 2.15

9th World Soccer Championships for the Jules Rimet Cup, Mexico City, May 30-June 21, 1970.
For surcharge see No. C126.

EXPO '70 Type of Regular Issue

EXPO '70 Emblems and: 70fr, Dahomey pavilion. 120fr, Mt. Fuji, temple and torii.

1970, June 15 Litho. *Perf. 13½x14*

C124 A54 70fr yel, red & dk vio 1.25 .60
C125 A54 120fr yel, red & grn 2.25 1.00

For surcharges see Benin Nos. C470, C477.

No. C123 Surcharged with New Value and Overprinted: "Bresil-Italie / 4-1"

1970, July 13 Photo. *Perf. 12½*

C126 AP42 100fr on 200fr multi 2.10 1.00

Brazil's victory in the 9th World Soccer Championships, Mexico City.
For surcharge see Benin No. C515.

Mercury, Map of Africa and Europe — AP43

Ludwig van Beethoven AP44

Europafrica Issue, 1970

1970, July 20 Photo. *Perf. 12x13*

C127 AP43 40fr multi .80 .40
C128 AP43 70fr multi 1.25 .60

For surcharges see Benin #C429, C488.

1970, Sept. 21 Litho. *Perf. 14x13½*

C129 AP44 90fr brt bl & vio blk 1.40 .45
C130 AP44 110fr yel grn & dk brn 1.75 .65

Bicentenary of the birth of Ludwig van Beethoven (1770-1827), composer.
For surcharge see Benin No. C476.

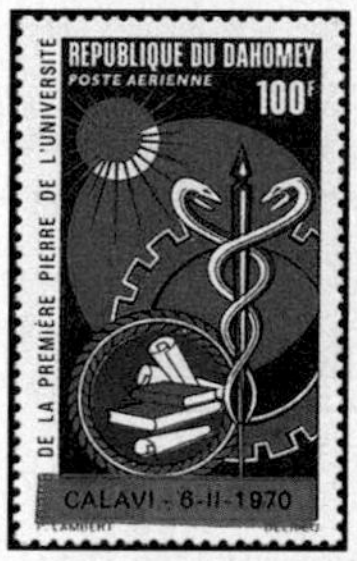

Symbols of Learning — AP45

1970, Nov. 6 Photo. *Perf. 12½*

C131 AP45 100fr multi 1.75 .75

Laying of the foundation stone for the University at Calavi.
For overprint see Benin No. C356.

Annunciation, Rhenish School, c.1340 — AP46

Paintings of Rhenish School, circa 1340: 70fr, Nativity. 110fr, Adoration of the Kings. 200fr, Presentation at the Temple.

1970, Nov. 9 *Perf. 12½x12*

C132 AP46 40fr gold & multi .55 .40
C133 AP46 70fr gold & multi 1.00 .55
C134 AP46 110fr gold & multi 2.40 1.25
C135 AP46 200fr gold & multi 4.00 2.00
Nos. C132-C135 (4) 7.95 4.20

Christmas 1970.
For surcharge see Benin No. C479.

Charles de Gaulle, Arc de Triomphe and Flag — AP47

Design: 500fr, de Gaulle as old man and Notre Dame Cathedral, Paris.

1971, Mar. 15 Photo. *Perf. 12½*

C136 AP47 40fr multi .80 .45
C137 AP47 500fr multi 6.50 3.25

Gen. Charles de Gaulle (1890-1970), President of France.
For surcharge see Benin No. C465.

L'Indifférent, by Watteau — AP48

Painting: No. C139, Woman playing stringed instrument, by Watteau.

1971, May 3 Photo. *Perf. 13*

C138 AP48 100fr red brn & multi 3.25 1.75
C139 AP48 100fr red brn & multi 3.25 1.75

For overprints see Nos. C151-C152, Benin C357D, C456.

1971, May 29 Photo. *Perf. 13*

Dürer Paintings: 100fr, Self-portrait, 1498. 200fr, Self-portrait, 1500.

C140 AP48 100fr bl grn & multi 2.25 1.25
C141 AP48 200fr dk grn & multi 4.50 2.25

Albrecht Dürer (1471-1528), German painter and engraver. See #C151-C152, C174-C175. For surcharge and overprint see Benin #C357B, C381.

Johannes Kepler and Diagram — AP49

200fr, Kepler, trajectories, satellite and rocket.

1971, July 12 Engr. *Perf. 13*

C142 AP49 40fr brt rose lil, blk & vio bl .90 .55
C143 AP49 200fr red, blk & dk bl 3.25 1.75

Kepler (1571-1630), German astronomer.
For overprints and surcharges see Benin Nos. C342, C348, C466, C480.

Europafrica Issue

Jet Plane, Maps of Europe and Africa — AP50

100fr, Ocean liner, maps of Europe and Africa.

1971, July 19 Photo. *Perf. 12½x12*

C144 AP50 50fr blk, lt bl & org 1.00 .60
C145 AP50 100fr multi 1.60 1.00

For surcharges see Benin #C374, C404, C421.

African Postal Union Issue, 1971
Common Design Type

Design: 100fr, Dahomey coat of arms and UAMPT building, Brazzaville, Congo.

1971, Nov. 13 *Perf. 13x13½*

C146 CD135 100fr bl & multi 1.40 .60

For overprint see Benin No. C357E.

Flight into Egypt, by Van Dyck — AP51

Paintings: 40fr, Adoration of the Shepherds, by the Master of the Hausbuch, c. 1500, vert. 70fr, Adoration of the Kings, by Holbein the Elder, vert. 200fr, The Birth of Christ, by Dürer.

1971, Nov. 22 *Perf. 13*

C147 AP51 40fr gold & multi .80 .45
C148 AP51 70fr gold & multi 1.25 .55
C149 AP51 100fr gold & multi 2.00 .80
C150 AP51 200fr gold & multi 4.75 1.75
Nos. C147-C150 (4) 8.80 3.55

Christmas 1971
For overprint and surcharges see Benin Nos. C394, C394A, C397, C403, C405, C481, C503.

Painting Type of 1971 Inscribed: "25e ANNIVERSAIRE DE L'UNICEF"

Paintings: 40fr, Prince Balthazar, by Velasquez. 100fr, Infanta Margarita Maria, by Velázquez.

1971, Dec. 11

C151 AP48 40fr gold & multi 1.00 .55
C152 AP48 100fr gold & multi 2.00 .85

25th anniv. of UNICEF.
For surcharges see Benin #C366, C418, C437.

Olympic Games Type

Design: 150fr, Sapporo '72 emblem, ski jump and stork flying.

1972, Feb. Engr. *Perf. 13*

C153 A61 150fr brn, dp rose lil & bl 3.00 1.25

11th Winter Olympic Games, Sapporo, Japan, Feb. 3-13.
For overprint and surcharge see Benin Nos. C347, C433.

Boy Scout and Scout Flag — AP52

Designs: 40fr, Scout playing marimba. 100fr, Scouts doing farm work.

1972, Mar. 19 Photo. *Perf. 13*

Size: 26x35mm

C154 AP52 35fr multi .50 .25
C155 AP52 40fr multi .85 .40

Size: 26x46mm

C156 AP52 100fr yel & multi 1.75 .85
- *a.* Souvenir sheet of 3, #C154-C156, perf. 12½ 4.25 4.25

Nos. C154-C156 (3) 3.10 1.50

World Boy Scout Seminar, Cotonou, Mar. 1972.
For overprint and surcharge see Benin Nos. C373, C414.

Workers Training Institute and Friedrich Naumann — AP53

Design: 250fr, Workers Training Institute and Pres. Theodor Heuss of Germany.

1972, Mar. 29 Photo. *Perf. 13x12*
C157 AP53 100fr brt rose, blk & vio 1.25 .65
C158 AP53 250fr bl, blk & vio 2.75 1.25

Laying of foundation stone for National Workers Training Institute.
For surcharges see Benin Nos. C380, C473, Q25A.

Mosaic Floor, St. Mark's, Venice — AP54

12th Century Mosaics from St. Mark's Basilica: 40fr, Roosters carrying fox on a pole. 65fr, Noah sending out dove.

1972, Apr. 10 *Perf. 13*
C159 AP54 35fr gold & multi 1.10 .75
C160 AP54 40fr gold & multi 1.25 .90
C161 AP54 65fr gold & multi 2.10 1.50
Nos. C159-C161 (3) 4.45 3.15

UNESCO campaign to save Venice.
For surcharge see Benin No. 690G.

Neapolitan and Dahoman Dancers — AP55

1972, May 3 *Perf. 13½x13*
C162 AP55 100fr multi 1.50 .65

12th Philatelic Exhibition, Naples.
For surcharge see Benin No. C395.

Running, German Eagle, Olympic Rings — AP56

85fr, High jump and Glyptothek, Munich. 150fr, Shot put and Propylaeum, Munich.

1972, June 12 Engr. *Perf. 13*
C163 AP56 20fr ultra, grn & brn .40 .25
C164 AP56 85fr brn, grn & ultra .95 .60
C165 AP56 150fr grn, brn & ultra 2.00 1.00
a. Min. sheet of 3, #C163-C165 4.00 4.00
Nos. C163-C165 (3) 3.35 1.85

20th Olympic Games, Munich, 8/26-9/10.
For overprints and surcharges see Nos. C170-C172, Benin C343, C346, C370, C404A.

Louis Blériot and his Plane — AP57

1972, June 26
C166 AP57 100fr vio, cl & brt bl 3.00 1.75

Birth centenary of Louis Blériot (1872-1936), French aviation pioneer.
For surcharge see Benin No. C386.

Adam, by Lucas Cranach — AP58

Design: 200fr, Eve, by Lucas Cranach.

1972, Oct. 24 Photo.
C167 AP58 150fr multi 1.90 .65
C168 AP58 200fr multi 3.25 1.25

Cranach (1472-1553), German painter.
For surcharges see Benin Nos. C402, C537.

Pauline Borghese, by Canova — AP59

1972, Nov. 8
C169 AP59 250fr multi 4.00 1.75

Antonio Canova (1757-1822), Italian sculptor.
For surcharge, see Benin No. 1366.

Nos. C163-C165 Overprinted:
a. 5.000m-10.000m. / VIREN / 2 MEDAILLES D'OR
b. HAUTEUR DAMES / MEYFARTH / MEDAILLE D'OR
c. POIDS / KOMAR / MEDAILLE D'OR

1972, Nov. 13 Engr. *Perf. 13*
C170 AP56(a) 20fr multi .45 .25
C171 AP56(b) 85fr multi 1.25 .60
C172 AP56(c) 150fr multi 2.25 1.25
a. Miniature sheet of 3 5.25 5.25
Nos. C170-C172 (3) 3.95 2.10

Gold medal winners in 20th Olympic Games: Lasse Viren, Finland, 5,000m. and 10,000m. races (20fr); Ulrike Meyfarth, Germany, women's high jump (85fr); Wladyslaw Komar, Poland, shot put (150fr).
For surcharge, see Benin No. C538.

Louis Pasteur — AP60

1972, Nov. 30
C173 AP60 100fr brt grn, lil & brn 2.25 1.00

Pasteur (1822-95), chemist and bacteriologist.
For surcharge see Benin No. C344.

Painting Type of 1971

Paintings by Georges de La Tour (1593-1652), French painter: 35fr, Vielle player. 150fr, The Newborn, horiz.

1972, Dec. 11 Photo.
C174 AP48 35fr multi .80 .40
C175 AP48 150fr multi 2.25 1.25

For surcharges see Benin #C364, C490.

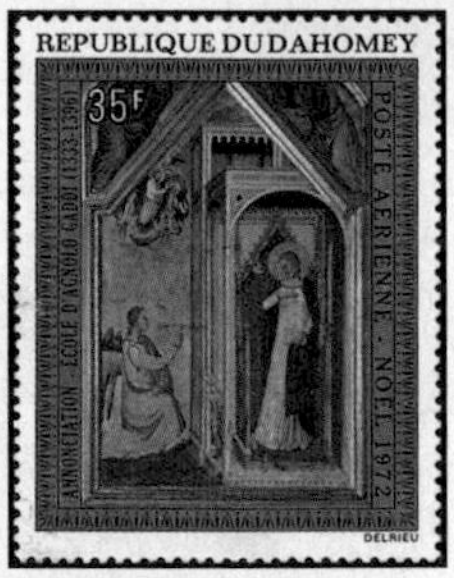

Annunciation, School of Agnolo Gaddi — AP61

Paintings: 125fr, Nativity, by Simone dei Crocifissi. 140fr, Adoration of the Shepherds, by Giovanni di Pietro. 250fr, Adoration of the Kings, by Giotto.

1972, Dec. 15
C176 AP61 35fr gold & multi .55 .25
C177 AP61 125fr gold & multi 1.50 .65
C178 AP61 140fr gold & multi 2.00 1.00
C179 AP61 250fr gold & multi 3.25 1.50
Nos. C176-C179 (4) 7.30 3.40

Christmas 1972. See Nos. C195-C198, C234, C251, C253-C254. For overprint and surcharges see Benin Nos. C384, C392, C401, C444.

Statue of St. Teresa, Basilica of Lisieux — AP62

100fr, St. Teresa, roses, and globe, vert.

1973, May 14 Photo. *Perf. 13*
C180 AP62 40fr blk, gold & lt ultra .75 .45
C181 AP62 100fr gold & multi 2.00 1.00

St. Teresa of Lisieux (Therese Martin, 1873-97), Carmelite nun.
For surcharge see Benin No. C390.

Scouts, African Scout Emblem — AP63

Designs (African Scout Emblem and): 20fr, Lord Baden-Powell, vert. 40fr, Scouts building bridge.

1973, July 2 Engr. *Perf. 13*
C182 AP63 15fr bl, grn & choc .45 .20
C183 AP63 20fr ol & Prus bl .75 .25
C184 AP63 40fr grn, Prus bl & brn .90 .35
a. Souvenir sheet of 3 3.00 3.00
Nos. C182-C184 (3) 2.10 .80

24th Boy Scout World Conference, Nairobi, Kenya, July 16-21. No. C184a contains 3 stamps similar to Nos. C182-C184 in changed colors (15fr in ultramarine, slate green and chocolate; 20fr in chocolate, ultramarine and indigo; 40fr in slate green, indigo and chocolate).
For surcharges see Nos. C217-C218, Benin C365, C409.

Copernicus, Venera and Mariner Satellites — AP64

125fr, Copernicus, sun, earth & moon, vert.

1973, Aug. 20 Engr. *Perf. 13*
C185 AP64 65fr blk, dk brn & org 1.25 .55
C186 AP64 125fr bl, slate grn & pur 2.00 1.00

For surcharges see Benin Nos. C345, C375.

Head and City Hall, Brussels AP64a

1973, Sept. 17 Engr. *Perf. 13*
C187 AP64a 100fr blk, Prus bl & dk grn 1.10 .60

African Weeks, Brussels, Sept. 15-30, 1973.
For surcharge see Benin No. C400.

WMO Emblem, World Weather Map — AP65

1973, Sept. 25
C188 AP65 100fr ol grn & lt brn 1.25 .75

Cent. of intl. meteorological cooperation.
For surcharge and overprint see Nos. C199, Benin C382.

Europafrica Issue

AP66

Design: 40fr, similar to 35fr.

1973, Oct. 1 Engr. *Perf. 13*
C189 AP66 35fr multi .55 .35
C190 AP66 40fr bl, sepia & ultra .70 .40

For overprint see Benin No. C411.

John F. Kennedy — AP67

1973, Oct. 18

C191 AP67 200fr bl grn, vio & sl grn 2.75 2.75
a. Souvenir sheet 5.00 5.00

Pres. John F. Kennedy (1917-63). No. C191a contains one stamp in changed colors (bright blue, magenta & brown).
For surcharge see Benin No. C377.

Soccer — AP68

40fr, 2 soccer players. 100fr, 3 soccer players.

1973, Nov. 19 Engr. *Perf. 13*

C192 AP68 35fr multi .55 .25
C193 AP68 40fr multi .65 .25
C194 AP68 100fr multi 1.25 .65
Nos. C192-C194 (3) 2.45 1.15

World Soccer Cup, Munich 1974.
For surcharges and overprint see Nos. C219-C220, Benin C396.

Painting Type of 1972

Christmas: 35fr, Annunciation, by Dirk Bouts. 100fr, Nativity, by Giotto. 150fr, Adoration of the Kings, by Botticelli. 200fr, Adoration of the Shepherds, by Jacopo Bassano, horiz.

1973, Dec. 20 Photo. *Perf. 13*

C195 AP61 35fr gold & multi .65 .40
C196 AP61 100fr gold & multi 1.25 .65
C197 AP61 150fr gold & multi 2.40 1.10
C198 AP61 200fr gold & multi 2.75 1.75
Nos. C195-C198 (4) 7.05 3.90

For surcharges see Benin Nos. C378, C388, C410, C434., C442

No C188 Surcharged in Violet with New Value and: "OPERATION SKYLAB / 1973-1974"

1974, Feb. 4 Engr. *Perf. 13*

C199 AP65 200fr on 100fr multi 2.10 1.25

Skylab US space missions, 1973-74.

Skiers, Snowflake, Olympic Rings — AP69

1974, Feb. 25 Engr. *Perf. 13*

C200 AP69 100fr vio bl, brn & brt bl 1.75 1.10

50th anniversary of first Winter Olympic Games, Chamonix, France.

Marie Curie AP70

1974, June 7 Engr. *Perf. 13*

C201 AP70 50fr Lenin 1.40 .65
C202 AP70 125fr shown 1.75 .90
C203 AP70 150fr Churchill 2.00 1.40
Nos. C201-C203 (3) 5.15 2.95

50th anniv. of the death of Lenin; 40th anniv. of the death of Marie Sklodowska Curie; cent. of the birth of Winston Churchill.
For surcharge see Benin No. C489.

Bishop, Persian, 18th Century — AP71

Frederic Chopin — AP72

200fr, Queen, Siamese chess piece, 19th cent.

1974, June 14 Photo. *Perf. 12½x13*

C204 AP71 50fr org & multi 2.50 1.00
C205 AP71 200fr brt grn & multi 6.00 2.50

21st Chess Olympiad, Nice, 6/6-30/74.
For surcharges and overprint see Benin Nos. C469, C482, Q11.

1974, June 24 Engr. *Perf. 13*

Design: No. C207, Ludwig van Beethoven.

C206 AP72 150fr blk & copper red 2.50 1.10
C207 AP72 150fr blk & copper red 2.50 1.10

Famous musicians: Frederic Chopin and Ludwig van Beethoven.
For surcharges see Benin #C376, C452, C459, C539.

Astronaut on Moon, and Earth AP73

1974, July 10 Engr. *Perf. 13*

C208 AP73 150fr multi 2.75 1.50

5th anniversary of the first moon walk.
For surcharge and overprint see Benin Nos. C391, C460.

Litho. & Embossed 'Gold Foil' Stamps
These stamps generally are of a different design format than the rest of the issue. Since there is a commemorative inscription tying them to the issue a separate illustration is not being shown.

There is some question as to the status of 4 sets, Nos. C209-C216, C225-C232, C238-C249.

World Cup Soccer Championships, Munich — AP74

World Cup trophy and players and flags of: 35fr, West Germany, Chile, Australia, DDR. 40fr, Zaire, Scotland, Brazil, Yugoslavia. 100fr, Sweden, Bulgaria, Uruguay, Netherlands. 200fr, Italy, Haiti, Poland, Argentina. 300fr, Stadium. 500fr, Trophy and flags.

Perf. 14x13, 13x14

1974, July 16 Litho.

C209 AP74 35fr multicolored .30 .20
C210 AP74 40fr multicolored .40 .25
C211 AP74 100fr multicolored .80 .70
C212 AP74 200fr multicolored 1.50 1.25
C213 AP74 300fr multi, horiz. 2.00 1.50

Souvenir Sheet

C215 AP74 500fr multi, horiz. 4.00 4.00

It is uncertain if this issue was valid for postage or recognized by the Dahomey government.

Nos. C182-C183 Surcharged and Overprinted in Black or Red: "XIe JAMBOREE PANARABE DE BATROUN-LIBAN"

1974, July 19

C217 AP63 100fr on 15fr multi 1.25 .60
C218 AP63 140fr on 20fr multi (R) 1.75 .90

11th Pan-Arab Jamboree, Batrun, Lebanon, Aug. 1974. Overprint includes 2 bars over old denomination; 2-line overprint on No. C217, 3 lines on No. C218.

Nos. C193-C194 Overprinted and Surcharged with New Value and Two Bars: "R F A 2 / HOLLANDE 1"

1974, July 26 Engr. *Perf. 13*

C219 AP68 100fr on 40fr 1.10 .65
C220 AP68 150fr on 100fr 1.60 1.00

World Cup Soccer Championship, 1974, victory of German Federal Republic.

Earth and UPU Emblem — AP75

Designs (UPU Emblem and): 65fr, Concorde in flight. 125fr, French railroad car, c. 1860. 200fr, African drummer and Renault mail truck, pre-1939.

1974, Aug. 5 Engr. *Perf. 13*

C221 AP75 35fr rose cl & vio .55 .40
C222 AP75 65fr Prus grn & cl 1.10 .95
C223 AP75 125fr multi 2.50 1.50
C224 AP75 200fr multi 2.50 2.00
Nos. C221-C224 (4) 6.65 4.85

Centenary of Universal Postal Union.
For surcharges, see Benin Nos. C422, C530, C540, Q17B.

UPU, Cent. — AP76

Communications and transportation: 50fr, Rocket, Indian shooting arrow. 100fr, Airplane, dog sled, vert. 125fr, Rocket launch, balloon. 150fr, Rocket re-entry into Earth's atmosphere, drum. 200fr, Locomotive, Pony Express rider. 500fr, UPU headquarters. No. C230, Train, 1829. No. C232, Astronaut canceling envelope on moon.

1974 Litho. *Perf. 13x14, 14x13*

C225 AP76 50fr multicolored .50 .30
C226 AP76 100fr multicolored .75 .60
C227 AP76 125fr multicolored 1.00 .85
C228 AP76 150fr multicolored 1.75 1.00
C229 AP76 200fr multicolored 2.00 1.25

Litho. & Embossed

Perf. 13½

Size: 48x60mm

C230 AP76 1000fr gold & multi 12.00 12.00

Souvenir Sheets

Litho.

Perf. 13x14

C231 AP76 500fr multicolored 4.50 4.50

Litho. & Embossed

Perf. 13½

C232 AP76 1000fr gold & multi 6.50 6.50

Issued: #C230, C232, Oct. 9; others, Aug. 5.
It is uncertain if this issue was valid for postage or recognized by the Dahomey government.

Painting Type of 1972 and

Lion of Belfort by Frederic A. Bartholdi — AP77

Painting: 250fr, Girl with Falcon, by Philippe de Champaigne.

1974, Aug. 20 Engr. *Perf. 13*

C233 AP77 100fr rose brn 2.50 1.00
C234 AP61 250fr multi 4.00 2.40

For surcharges see Benin Nos. C363, C387, C445.

Prehistoric Animals — AP78

1974, Sept. 23 Photo.

C235 AP78 35fr Rhamphorhynchus 1.50 .80
C236 AP78 150fr Stegosaurus 5.00 2.25
C237 AP78 200fr Tyrannosaurus 7.00 2.75
Nos. C235-C237 (3) 13.50 5.80

For surcharges see Benin #C349, C350.

Conquest of Space — AP79

Various spacecraft and: 50fr, Mercury. 100fr, Venus. 150fr, Mars. 200fr, Jupiter. 400fr, Sun.

1974, Oct. 31 Litho. *Perf. 13x14*

C238 AP79 50fr multicolored .40 .30
C239 AP79 100fr multicolored 1.00 .50
C240 AP79 150fr multicolored 1.50 .90
C241 AP79 200fr multicolored 2.00 1.25
Nos. C238-C241 (4) 4.90 2.95

Souvenir Sheet

C242 AP79 400fr multicolored 4.00 4.00

For surcharges, see Benin Nos. C407A, C424.

West Germany, World Cup Soccer Champions — AP80

Designs: 100fr, Team. 125fr, Paul Breitner. 150fr, Gerd Muller. 300fr, Presentation of trophy. 500fr, German team positioned on field.

1974, Nov. Litho. *Perf. 13x14*

C243 AP80 100fr multicolored .75 .50
C244 AP80 125fr multicolored 1.00 .75
C245 AP80 150fr multicolored 1.50 1.00
C246 AP80 300fr multicolored 3.25 2.00
Nos. C243-C246 (4) 6.50 4.25

Souvenir Sheet

C248 AP80 500fr multicolored 4.50 4.50

Europafrica Issue

Globe, Cogwheel, Emblem — AP81

1974, Dec. 20 Typo. *Perf. 13*

C250 AP81 250fr red & multi 3.25 2.75

Printed tête bêche in sheets of 10.
For surcharges see Benin Nos. C430, C509.

Christmas Type of 1972 and

Nativity, by Martin Schongauer — AP82

Paintings: 35fr, Annunciation, by Schongauer. 100fr, Virgin in Rose Arbor, by Schongauer. 250fr, Virgin and Child, with St. John the Baptist, by Botticelli.

1974, Dec. 23 Photo. *Perf. 13*

C251 AP61 35fr gold & multi .45 .30
C252 AP82 40fr gold & multi .45 .40
C253 AP61 100fr gold & multi 1.25 .55
C254 AP61 250fr gold & multi 3.25 1.75
Nos. C251-C254 (4) 5.40 3.00

For surcharges, see Benin Nos. C413, C431, C439, C446.

Apollo and Soyuz Spacecraft AP83

200fr, American and Russian flags, rocket take-off. 500fr, Apollo-Soyuz link-up.

1975, July 16 Litho. *Perf. 12½*

C255 AP83 35fr multi .50 .30
C256 AP83 200fr vio bl, red & bl 2.40 1.25
C257 AP83 500fr vio bl, ind & red 5.00 3.00
Nos. C255-C257 (3) 7.90 4.55

Apollo Soyuz space test project (Russo-American cooperation); launching July 15; link-up, July 17.
For surcharges see Benin #C406, C415-C416, C451.

Nos. C255-C256 Surcharged in Silver or Black:
"RENCONTRE / APOLLO-SOYOUZ / 17 Juil. 1975"

1975, July 17 Litho. *Perf. 12½*

C258 AP83 100fr on 35fr (S) 1.25 .60
C259 AP83 300fr on 200fr 3.25 1.40

Apollo-Soyuz link-up in space, July 17, 1975.

ARPHILA Emblem, "Stamps" and Head of Ceres — AP84

1975, Aug. 22 Engr. *Perf. 13*

C260 AP84 100fr blk, bl & lilac 1.25 .75

ARPHILA 75, International Philatelic Exhibition, Paris, June 6-16.
For surcharges see Benin Nos. C383, C474.

Holy Family, by Michelangelo AP85

Infantry and Stars — AP86

Europafrica Issue

1975, Sept. 29 Litho. *Perf. 12*

C261 AP85 300fr gold & multi 3.50 1.50

For surcharge see Benin No. C447.

1975, Nov. 18 Engr. *Perf. 13*

American bicentennial (Stars and): 135fr, Drummers and fifer. 300fr, Artillery with cannon. 500fr, Cavalry.

C262 AP86 75fr grn car & pur .85 .45
C263 AP86 135fr bl, mag & sep 1.50 .90
C264 AP86 300fr vio bl, ver & choc 2.75 1.75
C265 AP86 500fr ver, dk grn & brn 5.00 2.50
Nos. C262-C265 (4) 10.10 5.60

For overprint and surcharges see Benin Nos. C247-C249, C385, C412, C453, C478.

Diving and Olympic Rings AP87

Design: 250fr, Soccer and Olympic rings.

1975, Nov. 24

C266 AP87 40fr vio, grnsh bl & ol brn .55 .25
C267 AP87 250fr red, emer & brn 2.25 1.25

Pre-Olympic Year 1975.
For surcharge see Benin No. C341.

AIR POST SEMI-POSTAL STAMPS

Maternity Hospital, Dakar — SPAP1

Dispensary, Mopti — SPAP2

Nurse Weighing Baby — SPAP3

Perf. 13½x12½, 13 (#CB3)
Photo, Engr. (#CB3)

1942, June 22

CB1 SPAP1 1.50fr + 3.50fr green .55 *3.50*
CB2 SPAP2 2fr + 6fr brown .55 *3.50*
CB3 SPAP3 3fr + 9fr car red .55 *3.50*
Nos. CB1-CB3 (3) 1.65 *10.50*

Native children's welfare fund.

Colonial Education Fund
Common Design Type
Perf. 12½x13½

1942, June 22 Engr.

CB4 CD86a 1.20fr + 1.80fr blue & red .55 *3.50*

AIR POST PARCEL POST STAMPS

Catalogue values for unused stamps in this section are for Never Hinged items.

Nos. C20-C23, C14 Surcharged in Black or Red

1967-69 Engr. *Perf. 13*

CQ1 AP6 200fr on 200fr 4.75 3.50
CQ2 AP6 300fr on 100fr 5.25 4.25
CQ3 AP6 500fr on 300fr 10.00 8.00
CQ4 AP6 1000fr on 500fr 21.00 16.00
CQ5 AP4 5000fr on 100fr (R) ('69) 80.00 80.00
Nos. CQ1-CQ5 (5) 121.00 111.75

On No. CQ5, "Colis Postaux" is at top, bar at right.

POSTAGE DUE STAMPS

Dahomey Natives — D1

D2

1906 Unwmk. Typo. *Perf. 14x13½*

J1 D1 5c grn, *grnsh* 2.40 2.40
J2 D1 10c red brn 3.50 3.50
J3 D1 15c dark blue 7.25 7.25
J4 D1 20c blk, *yellow* 5.25 5.25
J5 D1 30c red, *straw* 8.00 8.00
J6 D1 50c violet 24.00 24.00
J7 D1 60c blk, *buff* 14.00 14.00
J8 D1 1fr blk, *pinkish* 40.00 35.00
Nos. J1-J8 (8) 104.40 99.40

1914

J9 D2 5c green .25 .25
J10 D2 10c rose .55 .55
J11 D2 15c gray .55 .55
J12 D2 20c brown 1.00 1.00
J13 D2 30c blue 1.25 1.25
J14 D2 50c black 1.50 1.50
J15 D2 60c orange 1.90 1.90
J16 D2 1fr violet 2.10 2.10
Nos. J9-J16 (8) 9.10 9.10

Type of 1914 Issue Surcharged

1927

J17 D2 2fr on 1fr lilac rose 5.50 5.50
J18 D2 3fr on 1fr org brn 5.50 5.50

Carved Mask — D3

1941 Engr. *Perf. 14x13*

J19 D3 5c black .20 .20
J20 D3 10c lilac rose .20 .20
J21 D3 15c dark blue .20 .20
J22 D3 20c bright yel green .20 .20
J23 D3 30c orange .35 .35
J24 D3 50c violet brown .55 .55
J25 D3 60c slate green .95 .95
J26 D3 1fr rose red 1.10 1.10
J27 D3 2fr yellow 1.25 1.25
J28 D3 3fr dark purple 1.60 1.60
Nos. J19-J28 (10) 6.60 6.60

Type D3 without "RF"

1944

J28A D3 10c lilac rose .20
J28B D3 15c dark blue .20
J28C D3 20c bright yel green .20
Nos. J28A-J28C (3) .60

Nos. J28A-J28C were issued by the Vichy government in France, but were not placed on sale in Dahomey.

Catalogue values for unused stamps in this section, from this point to the end of the section, are for Never Hinged items.

Republic

Panther and Man — D4

Perf. 14x13½

1963, July 22 Typo. Unwmk.

J29 D4	1fr green & rose	.20	.20
J30 D4	2fr brn & emerald	.20	.20
J31 D4	5fr org & vio bl	.20	.20
J32 D4	10fr magenta & blk	.50	.50
J33 D4	20fr vio bl & org	.75	.75
	Nos. J29-J33 (5)	1.85	1.85

Mail Boat — D5

No. J35, Heliograph. No. J36, Morse receiver. No. J37, Mailman on bicycle. No. J38, Early telephone. No. J39, Autorail. No. J40, Mail truck. No. J41, Radio tower. No. J42, DC-8F jet plane. No. J43, Early Bird communications satellite.

1967, Oct. 24 Engr. *Perf. 11*

J34 D5 1fr brn, dl pur & bl	.20	.20
J35 D5 1fr dl pur, brn & bl	.20	.20
a. Pair, #J34-J35	.25	
J36 D5 3fr dk brn, dk grn & org	.20	.20
J37 D5 3fr dk grn, dk brn & org	.20	.20
a. Pair, #J36-J37	.25	
J38 D5 5fr ol bis, lil & bl	.35	.35
J39 D5 5fr lil, ol bis & bl	.35	.35
a. Pair, #J38-J39	.75	
J40 D5 10fr brn org, vio & grn	.50	.50
J41 D5 10fr vio, brn org & grn	.50	.50
a. Pair, #J40-J41	1.10	
J42 D5 30fr Prus bl, mar & vio	1.00	1.00
J43 D5 30fr vio, Prus bl & mar	1.00	1.00
a. Pair, #J42-J43	2.25	
Nos. J34-J43 (10)	4.50	4.50

Pairs printed tete beche, se-tenant at the base.

PARCEL POST STAMPS

Catalogue values for unused stamps in this section are for Never Hinged items.

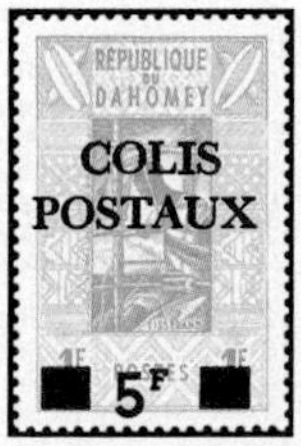

Nos. 141-146 and 148 Surcharged

1967, Jan. Unwmk. Engr. *Perf. 13*

Q1 A15 5fr on 1fr multi	.25	.25
Q2 A15 10fr on 2fr multi	.35	.35
Q3 A15 20fr on 6fr multi	.60	.60
Q4 A15 25fr on 3fr multi	.70	.70
Q5 A15 30fr on 4fr multi	.80	.80
Q6 A15 50fr on 10fr multi	1.25	1.25
a. "20" instead of "50"	100.00	
Q7 A15 100fr on 20fr multi	2.50	2.50
Nos. Q1-Q7 (7)	6.45	6.45

The surcharge is arranged to fit the shape of the stamp.
No. Q6a occurred once on the sheet.

DALMATIA

dal-'mă-sh͵ē-͵ə

LOCATION — A promontory in the northwestern part of the Balkan Peninsula, together with several small islands in the Adriatic Sea.
GOVT. — Part of the former Austro-Hungarian crownland of the same name.
AREA — 113 sq. mi.
POP. — 18,719 (1921)
CAPITAL — Zara.

Stamps were issued during Italian occupation. This territory was subsequently annexed by Italy.

100 Centesimi = 1 Corona = 1 Lira

Used values are for postally used copies.

Issued under Italian Occupation

Italy No. 87 Surcharged

1919, May 1 Wmk. 140 *Perf. 14*

1 A46 1cor on 1 l brn & grn	3.25	15.00
a. Pair, one without surcharge	*825.00*	*400.00*

Italian Stamps of 1906-08 Surcharged — a

1921-22

2 A48 5c on 5c green	1.60	3.00
3 A48 10c on 10c claret	1.60	3.00
a. Pair, one without surcharge	600.00	
4 A49 25c on 25c blue ('22)	2.40	6.00
5 A49 50c on 50c vio ('22)	2.40	6.00
a. Double surcharge		220.00
b. Pair, one without surcharge	825.00	

Italian Stamps of 1901-10 Surcharged — b

6 A46 1cor on 1 l brn & grn ('22)	4.00	18.50
7 A46 5cor on 5 l bl & rose ('22)	45.00	120.00
8 A51 10cor on 10 l gray grn & red ('22)	45.00	120.00
Nos. 2-8 (7)	102.00	276.50

Surcharges similar to these but differing in style or arrangement of type were used in Austria under Italian occupation.

SPECIAL DELIVERY STAMPS

Italian Special Delivery Stamp No. E1 Surcharged type "a"

1921 Wmk. 140 *Perf. 14*

E1 SD1 25c on 25c rose red	3.25	12.00
a. Double surcharge	350.00	525.00

Italian Special Delivery Stamp Surcharged **LIRE 1,20 DI CORONA**

1922

E2 SD2 1.20 l on 1.20 l	160.00
Never hinged	400.00

No. E2 was not placed in use.

POSTAGE DUE STAMPS

Italian Postage Due Stamps and Type Surcharged types "a" or "b"

1922 Wmk. 140 *Perf. 14*

J1 D3 (a) 50c on 50c buff & mag	1.60	6.00
J2 D3 (b) 1cor on 1 l bl & red	4.00	18.50
J3 D3 (b) 2cor on 2 l bl & red	47.50	110.00
J4 D3 (b) 5cor on 5 l bl & red	47.50	110.00
Nos. J1-J4 (4)	100.60	244.50

DANISH WEST INDIES

'dā-nish 'west 'in-dēs

LOCATION — A group of islands in the West Indies, lying east of Puerto Rico
GOVT. — A former Danish colony
AREA — 132 sq. mi.
POP. — 27,086 (1911)
CAPITAL — Charlotte Amalie

The US bought these islands in 1917 and they became the US Virgin Islands, using US stamps and currency.

100 Cents = 1 Dollar
100 Bit = 1 Franc (1905)

Watermarks

Wmk. 111 — Small Crown

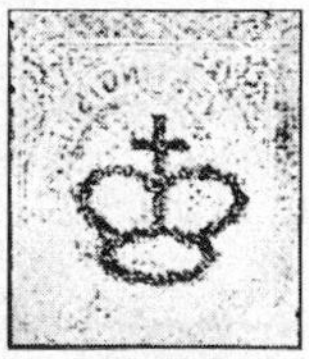

Wmk. 112 — Crown

Wmk. 113 — Crown

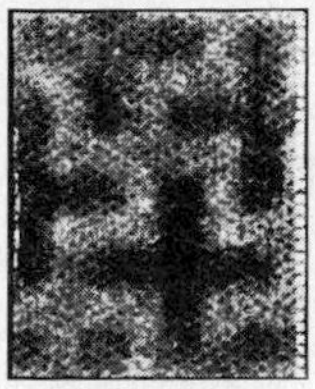

Wmk. 114 — Multiple Crosses

Coat of Arms — A1

Yellowish Paper
Yellow Wavy-line Burelage, UL to LR

1856 Wmk. 111 Typo. *Imperf.*

1 A1 3c dk car, brown gum	200.00	275.00
a. 3c dark carmine, yellow gum	220.00	275.00
b. 3c carmine, white gum	*4,250.*	—

Reprint: 1981, carmine, back-printed across two stamps ("Reprint by Dansk Post og Telegrafmuseum 1978"), value, pair, $10.

White Paper
Yellow Wavy-line Burelage, UR to LL

1866

2 A1 3c rose	40.00	75.00

No. 2 reprints unwatermarked: 1930 carmine, value $100. 1942 rose carmine, back-printed across each row ("Nytryk 1942 G. A. Hagemann Danmark og Dansk Vestindiens Friemaerker Bind 2"), value $50.

1872 *Perf. 12½*

3 A1 3c rose	92.50	275.00

1873

Without Burelage

4 A1 4c dull blue	250.00	475.00
a. Imperf., pair	775.00	—
b. Horiz. pair, imperf. vert.	575.00	—

#4 reprints, unwatermarked, imperf.: 1930, ultramarine, value $100. 1942, blue back-printed like 1942 reprint of #2, value $60.

A2

Normal Frame

Inverted Frame

The arabesques in the corners have a main stem and a branch. When the frame is in normal position, in the upper left corner the branch leaves the main stem half way between two little leaflets. In the lower right corner the branch starts at the foot of the second leaflet. When the frame is inverted the corner designs are, of course, transposed.

White Wove Paper, Varying from Thin to Thick

1874-79 Wmk. 112 *Perf. 14x13½*

5 A2 1c green & brn red 20.00 *30.00*
- *a.* 1c grn & rose lilac, thin paper 80.00 125.00
- *b.* 1c grn & red violet, medium paper 45.00 65.00
- *c.* 1c green & violet, thick paper 20.00 *30.00*
- *e.* Inverted frame 20.00 *30.00*
- *f.* As "a," inverted frame *475.00*

6 A2 3c blue & carmine 25.00 20.00
- *a.* 3c lt bl & rose car, thin paper 65.00 50.00
- *b.* 3c dp bl & dk car, medium paper 40.00 17.00
- *c.* 3c greenish blue & lake, thick paper 32.50 17.00
- *d.* Imperf., pair *375.00* —
- *e.* Inverted frame 21.00 15.00
- *f.* As "a," inverted frame *350.00*

7 A2 4c brn & dull blue 16.00 *19.00*
- *b.* 4c brown & ultramarine 190.00 *225.00*
- *c.* Diagonal half used as 2c on cover 140.00
- *d.* Inverted frame *825.00* *1,400.*

8 A2 5c green & gray ('76) 30.00 25.00
- *a.* 5c yel grn & dk gray, thin paper 55.00 37.50
- *b.* Inverted frame 27.50 25.00

9 A2 7c lilac & orange 32.50 *95.00*
- *a.* 7c lilac & yellow 90.00 *100.00*
- *b.* Inverted frame 60.00 150.00

10 A2 10c blue & brn ('76) 25.00 *30.00*
- *a.* 10c dk bl & blk brn, thin paper 70.00 45.00
- *b.* "cent.s" 30.00 30.00
- *c.* Inverted frame 27.50 *32.50*

11 A2 12c red lilac & yel green ('77) 42.50 *175.00*
- *a.* 12c lilac & deep green 150.00 *200.00*

12 A2 14c lilac & green 650.00 *1,100.*
- *a.* Inverted frame *2,500.* *3,500.*

13 A2 50c violet, thin paper ('79) 175.00 *300.00*
- *a.* 50c gray violet, thick porous paper ('85) 225.00 350.00

Nos. 5-13 (9) 1,016. 1,794.

The central element in the fan-shaped scrollwork at the outside of the lower left corner of Nos. 5a and 7b looks like an elongated diamond.

See Nos. 16-20. For surcharges see Nos. 14-15, 23-28, 40.

Nos. 9 and 13 Surcharged in Black

1887-95

14 A2 1c on 7c lilac & org 100.00 *200.00*
- *a.* 1c on 7c lilac & yellow 100.00 *225.00*
- *b.* Double surcharge 250.00 *500.00*
- *c.* Inverted frame 110.00 *350.00*

15 A2 10c on 50c violet ('95) 42.50 *67.50*

Type of 1873

1896-1901 *Perf. 13*

16 A2 1c green & red vio ('98) 13.00 *22.50*
- *a.* Normal frame 290.00 *425.00*

17 A2 3c blue & lake ('98) 12.00 *17.50*
- *a.* Normal frame 250.00 *425.00*

18 A2 4c bister & dull blue ('01) 17.50 15.00
- *a.* Diagonal half used as 2c on cover 100.00
- *b.* Inverted frame 55.00 *85.00*
- *c.* As "b," diagonal half used as 2c on cover 350.00

19 A2 5c green & gray 35.00 35.00
- *a.* Normal frame 750.00 *1,100.*

20 A2 10c blue & brown ('01) 80.00 *150.00*
- *a.* Inverted frame 925.00 *1,600.*
- *b.* "cent.s" 170.00 160.00

Nos. 16-20 (5) 157.50 240.00

Arms — A5

1900

21 A5 1c light green 3.00 3.00
22 A5 5c light blue 17.50 *25.00*

See Nos. 29-30. For surcharges see Nos. 41-42.

Nos. 6, 17, 20 Surcharged:

c

d

Surcharge "c" in Black

1902 *Perf. 14x13½*

23 A2 2c on 3c blue & car 575.00 *725.00*
- *a.* "2" in date with straight tail 650.00 *800.00*
- *b.* Normal frame *4,000.* —

Perf. 13

24 A2 2c on 3c blue & lake 10.00 *27.50*
- *a.* "2" in date with straight tail 12.00 *32.50*
- *b.* Dated "1901" 600.00 *650.00*
- *c.* Normal frame 175.00 *250.00*
- *d.* Dark green surcharge *2,000.*
- *e.* As "d" & "a" — —
- *f.* As "d" & "c" —

25 A2 8c on 10c blue & brn 25.00 *42.50*
- *a.* "2" with straight tail 30.00 *45.00*
- *b.* On No. 20b 32.50 *45.00*
- *c.* Inverted frame 250.00 *425.00*

Only one copy of No. 24f can exist.

Surcharge "d" in Black

27 A2 2c on 3c blue & lake 12.00 *40.00*
- *a.* Normal frame 240.00 *425.00*

28 A2 8c on 10c blue & brn 12.00 *14.00*
- *a.* On No. 20b 18.50 *25.00*
- *b.* Inverted frame 225.00 400.00

Nos. 23-28 (5) 634.00 849.00

1903 Wmk. 113

29 A5 2c carmine 8.00 *22.50*
30 A5 8c brown 27.50 *30.00*

King Christian IX — A8

St. Thomas Harbor — A9

1905 Typo. *Perf. 13*

31 A8 5b green 3.75 3.25
32 A8 10b red 3.75 3.25
33 A8 20b green & blue 8.75 8.25
34 A8 25b ultramarine 8.75 *10.50*
35 A8 40b red & gray 8.25 8.25
36 A8 50b yellow & gray 10.00 *12.00*

Frame Typo., Center Engr.

Wmk. Two Crowns (113)

Perf. 12

37 A9 1fr green & blue 17.50 *45.00*
38 A9 2fr org red & brown 30.00 *60.00*
39 A9 5fr yellow & brown 77.50 *275.00*

Nos. 31-39 (9) 168.25 425.50

Favor cancels exist on #37-39. Value 25% less.

Nos. 18, 22, 30 Surcharged in Black

1905 Wmk. 112 *Perf. 13*

40 A2 5b on 4c bis & dull blue 16.00 *45.00*
- *a.* Inverted frame 45.00 *82.50*

41 A5 5b on 5c light blue 14.00 *37.50*

Wmk. 113

42 A5 5b on 8c brown 14.00 *37.50*

Nos. 40-42 (3) 44.00 120.00

Frederik VIII A10

Christian X A11

Frame Typo., Center Engr.

1907-08 Wmk. 113 *Perf. 13*

43 A10 5b green 1.90 1.90
44 A10 10b red 1.90 1.90
45 A10 15b violet & brown 3.75 *4.50*
46 A10 20b green & blue 30.00 *27.50*
47 A10 25b blue & dk blue 1.90 *2.50*
48 A10 30b claret & slate 50.00 *52.50*
49 A10 40b ver & gray 5.75 *9.50*
50 A10 50b yellow & brown 5.75 *14.00*

Nos. 43-50 (8) 100.95 114.30

1915 Wmk. 114 *Perf. 14x14½*

51 A11 5b yellow green 4.00 *4.25*
52 A11 10b red 4.00 *42.50*
53 A11 15b lilac & red brown 4.00 *47.50*
54 A11 20b green & blue 4.00 *47.50*
55 A11 25b blue & dark blue 4.00 *12.50*
56 A11 30b claret & black 4.00 *85.00*
57 A11 40b orange & black 4.00 *85.00*
58 A11 50b yellow & brown 4.00 *85.00*

Nos. 51-58 (8) 32.00 409.25

Forged and favor cancellations exist.

POSTAGE DUE STAMPS

Royal Cipher, "Christian 9 Rex" D1

1902 Unwmk. Litho. *Perf. 11½*

J1 D1 1c dark blue 4.50 17.50
J2 D1 4c dark blue 11.50 22.50
J3 D1 6c dark blue 19.00 60.00
J4 D1 10c dark blue 18.00 65.00

Nos. J1-J4 (4) 53.00 165.00

There are five types of each value. On the 4c they may be distinguished by differences in the figures "4"; on the other values the differences are minute.

Used values of Nos. J1-J4 are for canceled stamps. Uncanceled examples without gum have probably been used. Value 60% of unused.

Counterfeits of Nos. J1-J4 exist.

D2

1905-13 *Perf. 13*

J5 D2 5b red & gray 4.50 *6.75*
J6 D2 20b red & gray 7.50 *14.00*
J7 D2 30b red & gray 6.75 *14.00*
J8 D2 50b red & gray 6.00 *35.00*
- *a.* Perf. 14x14½ ('13) 37.50 *140.00*
- *b.* Perf. 11½ 325.00

Nos. J5-J8 (4) 24.75 69.75

All values of this issue are known imperforate, but were not regularly issued.

Used values of Nos. J5-J8 are for canceled stamps. Uncanceled examples without gum have probably been used. Value 60% of unused.

Counterfeits of Nos. J5-J8 exist.

Danish West Indies stamps were replaced by those of the U.S. in 1917, after the U.S. bought the islands.

DANZIG

'dan‚t‚-sig

LOCATION — In northern Europe bordering on the Baltic Sea

AREA — 754 sq. mi.

POP. — 407,000 (approx. 1939)

CAPITAL — Danzig

Established as a "Free City and State" under the protection of the League of Nations in 1920, Danzig was seized by Germany in 1939. It became a Polish province in 1945.

100 Pfennig = 1 Gulden (1923)

100 Pfennig = 1 Mark

Watermarks

Wmk. 108 — Honeycomb

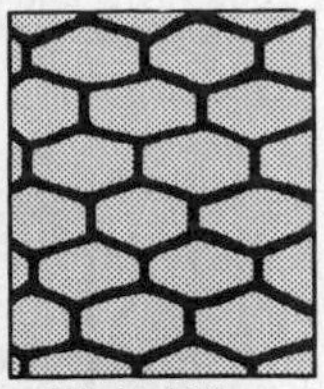

Wmk. 109 — Webbing

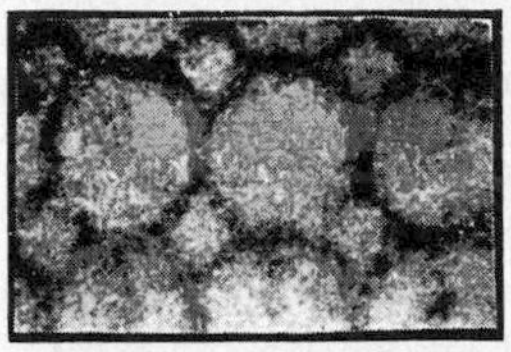

Wmk. 110 — Octagons

Wmk. 125 — Lozenges

Wmk. 237 — Swastikas

Used Values of 1920-23 are for favor-canceled stamps unless otherwise noted. Postally used copies bring much higher prices.

For additional varieties, see the *Scott Classic Catalogue*.

German Stamps of 1906-20 Overprinted in Black

Perf. 14, 14½, 15x14½

1920 Wmk. 125

1 A16 5pf green .30 .30
2 A16 10pf car rose .30 .30
3 A22 15pf violet brown .30 .30
4 A16 20pf blue violet .30 *1.10*
5 A16 30pf org & blk, *buff* .30 .30
6 A16 40pf car rose .30 .30
7 A16 50pf pur & blk, *buff* .50 .30
8 A17 1m red .50 .60
9 A17 1.25m yellow brn .50 .60
10 A17 1.50m yellow brn .90 .85
11 A21 2m blue 3.00 *4.75*
- *a.* Double overprint *375.00*
- Never hinged *825.00*

12 A21 2.50m lilac rose 1.75 *3.25*
13 A19 3m black violet 7.00 *10.00*
14 A16 4m black & rose 4.75 *6.00*
15 A20 5m slate & car 1.75 *2.00*
- *a.* Center & "Danzig" invtd. *15,000.*
- Never hinged —
- *b.* Inverted overprint *20,000.*

Nos. 1-15 (15) 22.45 30.95

Set, never hinged 100.00

The 5pf brown, 10pf orange and 40pf lake and black with this overprint were not regularly issued. Value for trio, $450.

Frame is inverted on No. 15a.

For surcharges see Nos. 19-23, C1-C3.

Issued: 40pf, 9/13; 1.50m, 3m 7/20; 4m, 12/21; others 6/14.

Nos. 5, 4 Surcharged in Various Sizes

1920

19 A16 5pf on 30pf (V) .20 .25
20 A16 10pf on 20pf (R) .20 .25
a. Double surcharge 110.00 —
Never hinged 250.00
21 A16 25pf on 30pf (G) .20 .25
a. Inverted surcharge 85.00 —
Never hinged 250.00
22 A16 60pf on 30pf (Br) .70 .85
a. Double surcharge 85.00 290.00
Never hinged 250.00
23 A16 80pf on 30pf (V) .70 .85

German Stamps Surcharged in Various Styles

Gray Burelage with Points Up

25 A16 1m on 30pf org & blk, *buff* (Bk) .85 1.50
a. Pair, one without surcharge
26 A16 1¼m on 3pf brn (R) 1.00 1.50
27 A22 2m on 35pf red brn (Bl) 1.50 1.50
d. Surcharge omitted 70.00 —
Never hinged 250.00
28 A22 3m on 7½pf org (G) 1.00 1.50
29 A22 5m on 2pf gray (R) 1.00 2.00
30 A22 10m on 7½pf org (Bk) 3.00 7.00
Nos. 19-30 (11) 10.35 17.45
Set, never hinged 60.00

Issued: #21, 8/10; #20, 8/17; #19, 22-23, 11/1.

Gray Burelage with Points Down

26a A16 1¼m on 3pf brown 36.00 42.50
27a A22 2m on 35pf red brn 300.00 325.00
28a A22 3m on 7½pf org 11.00 13.50
29a A22 5m on 2pf gray 11.50 30.00
30a A22 10m on 7½pf org 5.75 11.00
Nos. 26a-30a (5) 364.25 422.00
Set, never hinged 1,315.

Violet Burelage with Points Up

25b A16 1m on 30pf org & blk, *buff* 85.00 30.00
26b A16 1¼m on 3pf brown 4.50 6.50
27b A22 2m on 35pf red brown 11.50 37.50
28b A22 3m on 7½pf org 2.25 2.25
29b A22 5m on 2pf gray 1.10 2.10
30b A22 10m on 7½pf org 1.10 2.10
Nos. 25b-30b (6) 105.45 80.45
Set, never hinged 430.00

Violet Burelage with Points Down

25c A16 1m on 30pf org & blk, *buff* 1.10 2.50
26c A16 1¼m on 3pf brown 5.50 11.00
27c A22 2m on 35pf red brown 21.00 50.00
28c A22 3m on 7½pf org 40.00 85.00
29c A22 5m on 2pf gray 4.50 8.50
30c A22 10m on 7½pf org 13.50 29.00
Nos. 25c-30c (6) 85.60 186.00
Set, never hinged 350.00

Excellent counterfeits of the surcharges are known.

German Stamps of 1906-20 Overprinted in Blue

1920

31 A22 2pf gray 110.00 200.00
32 A22 2½pf gray 150.00 300.00
33 A16 3pf brown 11.00 17.00
a. Double overprint 75.00 —
Never hinged 180.00
34 A16 5pf green .55 .60
a. Double overprint 85.00
Never hinged 200.00
35 A22 7½pf orange 40.00 57.50
36 A16 10pf carmine 3.75 7.00
37 A22 15pf dk violet .55 .60
b. Double overprint 85.00
Never hinged 200.00
38 A16 20pf blue violet .55 .60

Overprinted in Carmine or Blue

39 A16 25pf org & blk, *yel* .55 .60
40 A16 30pf org & blk, *buff* 50.00 85.00
42 A16 40pf lake & blk 2.25 2.50
a. Inverted overprint 200.00
b. Double overprint —
43 A16 50pf pur & blk, *buff* 175.00 300.00
44 A16 60pf mag (Bl) 1,250. 2,100.
45 A16 75pf green & blk .55 .60
46 A16 80pf lake & blk, *rose* 2.40 4.25
47 A17 1m carmine 1,200. 2,100.
a. Double overprint 4,000.

Overprinted in Carmine

48 A21 2m gray blue 1,200. 2,100.

Counterfeit overprints of Nos. 31-48 exist.
Nos. 44, 47 and 48 were issued in small quantities and usually affixed directly to the mail by the postal clerk.
For surcharge see No. 62.

Hanseatic Trading Ship
A8 A9

Serrate Roulette 13½

1921, Jan. 31 Typo. Wmk. 108

49 A8 5pf brown & violet .20 .20
50 A8 10pf orange & dk vio .20 .20
51 A8 25pf green & car rose .50 .65
52 A8 40pf carmine rose 3.75 3.25
53 A8 80pf ultra .50 .50
54 A9 1m car rose & blk 1.60 1.60
55 A9 2m dk blue & dk grn 5.00 4.75
56 A9 3m blk & grnsh bl 1.75 2.25
57 A9 5m indigo & rose red 1.75 2.25
58 A9 10m dk grn & brn org 2.50 4.50
Nos. 49-58 (10) 17.75 20.15
Set, never hinged 80.00

Issued in honor of the Constitution.
Nos. 49 and 50 with center in red instead of violet and Nos. 49-51, 54-58 with center inverted are probably proofs. All values of this issue exist imperforate but are not known to have been regularly issued in that condition.

1921, Mar. 11 ***Perf. 14***

59 A8 25pf green & car rose .50 .85
60 A8 40pf carmine rose .50 .85
61 A8 80pf ultra 5.00 10.00
Nos. 59-61 (3) 6.00 11.70
Set, never hinged 30.00

No. 45 Surcharged in Black

1921, May 6 Wmk. 125

62 A16 60pf on 75pf .55 .90
Never hinged 3.25
a. Double surcharge 82.50 110.00
Never hinged 200.00

Arms — A11 Coat of Arms — A12

Wmk. 108 (Vert. or Horiz.)

1921-22 ***Perf. 14***

63 A11 5(pf) orange .20 .20
64 A11 10(pf) dark brown .20 .20
65 A11 15(pf) green .20 .20
66 A11 20(pf) slate .20 .20
67 A11 25(pf) dark green .20 .20
68 A11 30(pf) blue & car .25 .20
a. Center inverted 50.00
Never hinged 160.00
69 A11 40pf green & car .20 .20
a. Center inverted 50.00
Never hinged 140.00
70 A11 50pf dk green & car .20 .20
71 A11 60pf carmine .45 .45
72 A11 80pf black & car .35 .45

Paper With Faint Gray Network

73 A11 1m orange & car .25 .40
a. Center inverted 50.00
Never hinged 160.00
74 A11 1.20m blue violet 1.25 1.25
75 A11 2m gray & car 3.25 4.00
76 A11 3m violet & car 9.00 10.00

Serrate Roulette 13½

77 A12 5m grn, red & blk 1.25 2.90
78 A12 9m rose, red & org ('22) 2.90 8.50
79 A12 10m ultra, red & blk 1.25 2.90
80 A12 20m red & black 1.25 2.90
Nos. 63-80 (18) 22.85 35.35
Set, never hinged 85.00

In this and succeeding issues the mark values usually have the face of the paper covered with a gray network. This network is often very faint and occasionally is omitted.
Nos. 64-76 exist imperf. Value, each $16-$50 unused, $50-$150 never hinged.
See Nos. 81-93, 99-105. For surcharges and overprints see Nos. 96-98, O1-O33.

Type of 1921 and

A13

Coat of Arms — A13a

1922 Wmk. 108 ***Perf. 14***

81 A11 75(pf) deep violet .20 .25
82 A11 80(pf) green .20 .25
83 A11 1.25m violet & car .20 .25
84 A11 1.50m slate gray .20 .40
85 A11 2m car rose .20 .25
86 A11 2.40m dk brn & car .90 1.60
87 A11 3m car lake .20 .40
88 A11 4m dark blue .85 1.60
89 A11 5m deep green .20 .35
90 A11 6m car lake .20 .35
a. 6m car rose, wmk. 109 horiz. 1,800.
Never hinged 3,900.
91 A11 8m light blue .35 1.60
92 A11 10m orange .20 .35
93 A11 20m orange brn .20 .35
94 A13 50m gold & car 2.00 6.50
a. 50m gold & red 57.50 110.00
Never hinged 210.00
95 A13a 100m metallic grn & red 3.25 5.75
Nos. 81-95 (15) 9.35 20.25
Set, never hinged 35.00

No. 95 has buff instead of gray network.
Nos. 81-83, 85-86, 88 exist imperf. Value, each $12.50.
Nos. 94-95 exist imperf. Value, each $50

Nos. 87, 88 and 91 Surcharged in Black or Carmine

1922

96 A11 6m on 3m car lake .25 .55
a. Double surcharge
97 A11 8m on 4m dk blue .25 .60
a. Double surcharge 50.00 110.00
Never hinged 125.00
98 A11 20m on 8m lt bl (C) .25 .60
Nos. 96-98 (3) .75 1.75
Set, never hinged 2.50

1922-23 Wmk. 109 (Horiz.) ***Perf. 14***

99 A11 4m dark blue .20 .40
100 A11 5m dark green .20 .40
102 A11 10m orange .20 .40
103 A11 20m orange brn .20 .40

Paper Without Network

104 A11 40m pale blue .20 .60
105 A11 80m red .20 .60
Nos. 99-105 (6) 1.20 2.80
Set, never hinged 5.00

Nos. 100, 102 and 103 also exist with watermark vertical. Values slightly higher.
Nos. 104-105 exist imperf. Values: each $12.50 unused; $32.50 never hinged.

A15 A15a

Coat of Arms A16

1923 ***Perf. 14***

Paper With Gray Network

106 A15 50m pale bl & red .20 .40
107 A15a 100m dk grn & red .20 .40
108 A15a 150m violet & red .20 .40
109 A16 250m violet & red .25 .40
110 A16 500m gray blk & red .25 .40
111 A16 1000m brown & red .25 .40
112 A16 5000m silver & red 1.25 6.00

Paper Without Network

113 A15 50m pale blue .40 .60
114 A15a 100m deep green .40 .60
115 A15 200m orange .40 .60
Nos. 106-115 (10) 3.80 10.20
Set, never hinged 15.00

#108-112 exist imperf. Value, each $50 unused, $125 never hinged.
Nos. 113-115 exist imperf. Value, each $35 unused, $92.50 never hinged.
See Nos. 123-125. For surcharges and overprints see Nos. 126, 137-140, 143, 156-167, O35-O38.

A17

1923 ***Perf. 14***

Paper With Gray Network

117 A17 250m violet & red .20 .40
118 A17 300m blue grn & red .20 .40
119 A17 500m gray & red .20 .40
120 A17 1000m brown & red .20 .40

121 A17 3000m violet & red .20 *.40*
123 A16 10,000m orange & red .40 *.60*
124 A16 20,000m pale bl & red .40 *1.00*
125 A16 50,000m green & red .40 *1.00*
Nos. 117-125 (8) 2.20 *4.60*
Set, never hinged 10.00

#117, 119-121 exist imperf. Value, each $12.50 unused, $32.50 never hinged; #123-125 also exist imperf. Values each, $25 unused, $85 never hinged.

See #127-135. For surcharges & overprints see #141-142, 144-155, O39-O41.

No. 124 Surcharged in Red

1923, Aug. 14
126 A16 100,000m on 20,000m .60 *6.00*
Never hinged 3.75

No. 126 exists imperf. Value $40.00 unused, $100.00 never hinged.

1923 ***Perf. 14***

Paper Without Network

127 A17 1000m brown .20 *.40*
129 A17 5000m rose .20 *.40*
131 A17 20,000m pale blue .20 *.40*
132 A17 50,000m green .20 *.40*

Paper With Gray Network

133 A17 100,000m deep blue .20 *.40*
134 A17 250,000m violet .20 *.40*
135 A17 500,000m slate .20 *.40*
Nos. 127-135 (7) 1.40 2.80
Set, never hinged 4.50

Nos. 127, 129, 131-135 exist imperf. Value each, $40 unused, $100 never hinged.

Abbreviations: th=(tausend) thousand mil=million

Nos. 115, 114, 132, and Type of 1923 Surcharged

1923 ***Perf. 14***

Paper Without Network

137 A15 40th m on 200m .85 *2.00*
a. Double surcharge 85.00
Never hinged 160.00
138 A15 100th m on 200m .85 *2.00*
139 A15 250th m on 200m 6.25 *13.00*
140 A15a 400th m on 100m .40 *.40*
141 A17 500th m on 50,000m .40 *.40*
142 A17 1mil m on 10,000m org 3.75 *12.50*

The surcharges on Nos. 140-142 differ in details from those on Nos. 137-139.

Type of 1923 Surcharged

Paper With Gray Network

143 A16 10mil m on 1,000,000m org .40 *1.25*
Nos. 137-143 (7) 12.90 *31.55*
Set, never hinged 50.00

#142-143 exist imperf. Value: #142 unused $50; never hinged $125; #143 unused $25; never hinged $85.

Type of 1923 Surcharged

10,000m rose on paper without Network

144 A17 1mil m on 10,000m .25 *.40*
145 A17 2mil m on 10,000m .25 *.40*
146 A17 3mil m on 10,000m .25 *.40*
147 A17 5mil m on 10,000m .35 *.40*
b. Double surcharge 85.00
Never hinged 160.00

10,000m gray lilac on paper without Network

148 A17 10mil m on 10,000m .40 *.75*
149 A17 20mil m on 10,000m .40 *.75*
150 A17 25mil m on 10,000m .20 *.75*
151 A17 40mil m on 10,000m .20 *.75*
a. Double surcharge 52.50
Never hinged 160.00
152 A17 50mil m on 10,000m .20 *.75*

Type of 1923 Surcharged in Red

10,000m gray lilac on paper without Network

153 A17 100mil m on 10,000m .20 *.75*
154 A17 300mil m on 10,000m .20 *.75*
155 A17 500mil m on 10,000m .20 *.75*
Nos. 144-155 (12) 3.10 *7.60*
Set, never hinged 15.00

#144-147 exist imperf. Value, each $25 unused, $100 never hinged. #148-155 exist imperf. Value, each $32.50 unused, $85 never hinged.

Types of 1923 Surcharged

1923, Oct. 31 **Wmk. 110** ***Perf. 14***

156 A15 5pf on 50m rose .40 .40
157 A15 10pf on 50m rose .40 .40
158 A15a 20pf on 100m rose .40 .40
159 A15 25pf on 50m rose 3.25 *9.00*
160 A15 30pf on 50m rose 3.25 2.00
161 A15a 40pf on 100m rose 2.00 2.00
162 A15a 50pf on 100m rose 2.00 *3.00*
163 A15a 75pf on 100m rose 7.50 *16.00*

Type of 1923 Surcharged

1923, Nov. 5
164 A16 1g on 1mil m rose 4.00 *6.25*
165 A16 2g on 1mil m rose 11.50 *17.50*
166 A16 3g on 1mil m rose 20.00 *60.00*
167 A16 5g on 1mil m rose 25.00 *65.00*
Nos. 156-167 (12) 79.70 *181.95*
Set, never hinged 375.00

Coat of Arms — A19

1924-37 **Wmk. 109** ***Perf. 14***

168 A19 3pf brn, *yelsh* ('36) 1.25 *1.50*
a. 3pf dp brn, *white* ('27) 1.60 1.75
Never hinged 7.00
170 A19 5pf org, *yelsh* ('36) 3.25 .55
a. White paper 8.50 2.00
Never hinged 40.00
c. Tête bêche pair 325.00
Never hinged 750.00
d. Syncopated perf., #170 ('37) 10.50 9.00
Never hinged 29.00
e. Syncopated perf., #170a ('32) 21.00 10.50
Never hinged 110.00
171 A19 7pf yel grn ('33) 1.25 *2.50*
172 A19 8pf yel grn ('37) 1.60 *5.00*
173 A19 10pf grn, *yelsh* ('36) 5.50 .50
a. White paper 8.50 2.00
Never hinged 32.50
c. 10pf blue grn, *yellowish* ('37) 5.00 1.10
Never hinged 13.00
d. Tête bêche pair 325.00
Never hinged 750.00
e. Syncopated perf., #173 ('37) 18.00 10.50
Never hinged 52.50
f. Syncopated perf., #173a (132) 26.00 13.00
Never hinged 100.00
g. Syncopated perf., #173c ('37) 10.50 *14.50*
Never hinged 32.50
175 A19 15pf gray 3.75 .65
176 A19 15pf red, *yelsh* ('36) 2.10 1.10
a. White paper ('25) 4.00 1.10
Never hinged 20.00
177 A19 20pf carmine & red 13.00 .65
178 A19 20pf gray ('35) 1.75 1.75
179 A19 25pf slate & red 21.00 3.75
180 A19 25pf carmine ('35) 16.50 1.60
181 A19 30pf green & red 12.50 .85
182 A19 30pf dk violet ('35) 1.60 *4.25*
183 A19 35pf ultra ('25) 2.90 1.50
184 A19 40pf dk blue & blue 10.00 1.00
185 A19 40pf yel brn & red ('35) 6.50 *12.50*
186 A19 40pf dk blue ('35) 1.60 *3.75*
a. Imperf. 50.00
Never hinged 160.00
187 A19 50pf blue & red 14.00 8.50
a. Yellowish paper ('36) 25.00 11.50
Never hinged 57.50
188 A19 55pf plum & scar ('37) 5.00 *14.00*
189 A19 60pf dk grn & red ('35) 6.25 *26.00*
190 A19 70pf yel grn & red ('35) 2.10 *5.75*
191 A19 75pf violet & red, *yellowish* ('36) 7.50 *29.00*
a. White paper 10.00 *8.50*
Never hinged 32.50
192 A19 80pf dk org brn & red ('35) 2.10 *7.50*
Nos. 168-192 (23) 143.00 *134.15*
Set, never hinged 500.00

The 5pf and 10pf with syncopated perforations (Netherlands type C) are coils.

See Nos. 225-232. For overprints and surcharges see Nos. 200-209, 211-215, 241-252, B9-B11, O42-O52.

Oliva Castle and Cathedral A20

St. Mary's Church A23

Council Chamber on the Langenmarkt A24

2g, Mottlau River & Krantor. 3g, View of Zoppot.

1924-32 **Engr.** **Wmk. 125**

193 A20 1g yel grn & blk 20.00 *45.00*
Parcel post cancel 20.00
194 A20 1g org & gray blk ('25) 16.50 3.75
a. 1g red orange & blk ('32) 16.50 11.00
Never hinged 65.00
Parcel post cancel 1.00
195 A20 2g red vio & blk 45.00 *110.00*
Parcel post cancel 40.00
196 A20 2g rose & blk ('25) 3.75 *6.50*
Parcel post cancel 1.75
197 A20 3g dk blue & blk 4.00 *5.00*
Parcel post cancel 2.25
198 A23 5g brn red & blk 4.00 *8.50*
Parcel post cancel 1.90
199 A24 10g dk brn & blk 20.00 *100.00*
Parcel post cancel 18.00
Nos. 193-199 (7) 113.25 *278.75*
Set, never hinged 500.00

See No. 233. For overprints and surcharges see Nos. 210, 253-254, C31-C35.

Stamps of 1924-25 Overprinted in Black, Violet or Red

1930, Nov. 15 **Typo.** **Wmk. 109**

200 A19 5pf orange 2.50 *3.75*
201 A19 10pf yellow grn (V) 3.50 *4.50*
202 A19 15pf red 6.00 *10.50*
203 A19 20pf carmine & red 3.00 *5.75*
204 A19 25pf slate & red 4.25 *10.50*
205 A19 30pf green & red 8.50 *25.00*
206 A19 35pf ultra (R) 40.00 *100.00*
207 A19 40pf dk bl & bl (R) 11.50 *37.50*
208 A19 50pf dp blue & red 40.00 *85.00*
209 A19 75pf violet & red 40.00 *85.00*

Wmk. Lozenges. (125)

Engr.

210 A20 1g orange & blk (R) 40.00 *85.00*
Nos. 200-210 (11) 199.25 *452.50*
Set, never hinged 575.00

10th anniv. of the Free State. Counterfeits exist.

Nos. 171 and 183 Surcharged in Red Blue or Green:

Nos. 211-214

No. 215

1934-36
211 A19 6pf on 7pf (R) .85 *1.60*
212 A19 8pf on 7pf (Bl) ('35) 2.00 *2.25*
213 A19 8pf on 7pf (R) ('36) 1.25 *2.50*
214 A19 8pf on 7pf (G) ('36) .85 *2.50*
215 A19 30pf on 35pf (Bl) 12.00 *25.00*
Nos. 211-215 (5) 16.95 *33.85*
Set, never hinged 55.00

Bathing Beach, Brösen A25

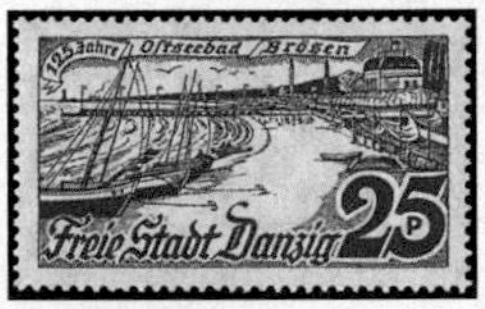

View of Brösen Beach A26

War Memorial at Brösen — A27

Skyline of Danzig — A28

1936, June 23 **Typo.** **Wmk. 109**

216 A25 10pf deep green .70 *.70*
217 A26 25pf rose red 1.00 *2.40*
218 A27 40pf bright blue 1.75 *4.50*
Nos. 216-218 (3) 3.45 *7.60*
Set, never hinged 11.50

Village of Brösen, 125th anniversary.

Exist imperf. Value each, $40 unused, $100 never hinged.

1937, Mar. 27
219 A28 10pf dark blue .50 *1.40*
220 A28 15pf violet brown 1.60 *2.00*
Set, never hinged 6.75

Air Defense League.

Danzig Philatelic Exhibition Issue

Souvenir Sheet

St. Mary's Church — A29

1937, June 6 Wmk. 109 *Perf. 14*

221	A29 50pf dark opal green	3.25	*20.00*
	Never hinged	10.75	

Danzig Philatelic Exhib., June 6-8, 1937.

Arthur Schopenhauer
A30 A31

Design: 40pf, Full-face portrait, white hair.

Unwmk.

1938, Feb. 22 Photo. *Perf. 14*

222	A30 15pf dull blue	1.25	*1.60*
223	A31 25pf sepia	3.00	*7.50*
224	A31 40pf orange ver	1.25	*3.25*
	Nos. 222-224 (3)	5.50	*12.35*
	Set, never hinged	18.00	

150th anniv. of the birth of Schopenhauer.

Type of 1924-35

1938-39 Typo. Wmk. 237 *Perf. 14*

225	A19 3pf brown	.90	*6.75*
226	A19 5pf orange	.90	*2.10*
b.	Syncopated perf.	1.40	*7.50*
	Never hinged	5.25	
227	A19 8pf yellow grn	4.00	*26.50*
228	A19 10pf blue green	.90	*1.60*
b.	Syncopated perf.	3.00	*10.00*
	Never hinged	13.00	
229	A19 15pf scarlet	1.60	*8.50*
230	A19 25pf carmine	2.10	*12.50*
231	A19 40pf dark blue	2.10	*29.00*
232	A19 50pf brt bl & red ('39)	2.10	*120.00*
	Engr.		
233	A20 1g red org & blk	6.00	*100.00*
	Nos. 225-233 (9)	20.60	*306.95*
	Set, never hinged	80.00	

Sizes: #233, 32½x21¼mm; #194, 31x21mm.

Nos. 226b and 228b are coils with Netherlands type C perforation.

Knights in Tournament, 1500 — A33

French Leaving Danzig, 1814 — A35

Stamp Day: 10pf, Signing of Danzig-Sweden neutrality treaty, 1630. 25pf, Battle of Weichselmünde, 1577.

Unwmk.

1939, Jan. 7 Photo. *Perf. 14*

234	A33 5pf dark green	.40	*2.10*
235	A33 10pf copper brown	.85	*2.50*
236	A35 15pf slate black	.85	*3.00*
237	A35 25pf brown violet	1.25	*4.00*
	Nos. 234-237 (4)	3.35	*11.60*
	Set, never hinged	12.50	

Gregor Mendel — A37

15pf, Dr. Robert Koch. 25pf, Wilhelm Roentgen.

1939, Apr. 29 Photo. *Perf. 13x14*

238	A37 10pf copper brown	.40	*.85*
239	A37 15pf indigo	.40	*2.00*
240	A37 25pf dark olive green	.85	*2.50*
	Nos. 238-240 (3)	1.65	*5.35*
	Set, never hinged	5.50	

Issued in honor of the achievements of Mendel, Koch and Roentgen.

Issued under German Administration

Stamps of Danzig, 1925-39, Surcharged in Black:

a

b

c

1939 Wmk. 109 *Perf. 14*

241	A19(b) 4rpf on 35pf ultra	.75	*2.10*
242	A19(b) 12rpf on 7pf yel grn	1.25	*2.10*
243	A19(a) 20rpf gray	2.75	*8.00*
	Wmk. 237		
244	A19(a) 3rpf brown	.75	*2.25*
245	A19(a) 5rpf orange	.65	*2.75*
246	A19(a) 8rpf yellow grn	1.10	*4.00*
247	A19(a) 10rpf blue grn	2.25	*4.00*
248	A19(a) 15rpf scarlet	6.00	*11.50*
249	A19(a) 25rpf carmine	4.50	*10.75*
250	A19(a) 30rpf dk violet	2.00	*4.50*
251	A19(a) 40rpf dk blue	2.75	*5.75*
252	A19(a) 50rpf brt bl & red	4.00	*7.00*
253	A20(c) 1rm on 1g red org & blk	14.00	*57.50*
	Wmk. 125		
254	A20(c) 2rm on 2g rose & blk	17.50	*45.00*
	Nos. 241-254 (14)	60.25	*167.20*
	Set, never hinged	180.00	

#241-254 were valid throughout Germany.

SEMI-POSTAL STAMPS

St. George and Dragon — SP1

Wmk. 108

1921, Oct. 16 Typo. *Perf. 14*

Size: 19x22mm

B1	SP1 30pf + 30pf grn & org	.45	.85
B2	SP1 60pf + 60pf rose & org	1.25	1.25

Size: 25x30mm

Serrate Roulette 13½

B3	SP1 1.20m + 1.20m dk bl & org	1.90	1.25
	Nos. B1-B3 (3)	3.60	3.35
	Set, never hinged	11.50	

Nos. B1-B3 exist imperf. Values: each, $40 unused; $125 never hinged.

Aged Pensioner SP2

1923, Mar. Wmk. 109 *Perf. 14*

Paper With Gray Network

B4	SP2 50m + 20m lake	.20	*.60*
B5	SP2 100m + 30m red violet	.20	*.60*
	Set, never hinged	1.60	

Nos. B4-B5 exist imperf. Values: each, $20 unused; $110 never hinged.

Philatelic Exhibition Issue

Neptune Fountain — SP3

Various Frames.

1929, July 7 Engr. Unwmk.

B6	SP3 10pf yel grn & gray	2.00	1.60
B7	SP3 15pf car & gray	2.00	1.60
B8	SP3 25pf ultra & gray	8.50	*13.00*
a.	25pf violet blue & black	25.00	*60.00*
	Never hinged	90.00	
	Nos. B6-B8 (3)	12.50	16.20
	Set, never hinged	40.00	

These stamps were sold exclusively at the Danzig Philatelic Exhibition, June 7-14, 1929, at double their face values, the excess being for the aid of the exhibition.

Regular Issue of 1924-25 Surcharged in Black

1934, Jan. 15 Wmk. 109

B9	A19 5pf + 5pf orange	8.50	*20.00*
B10	A19 10pf + 5pf yel grn	20.00	*50.00*
B11	A19 15pf + 5pf carmine	12.50	*37.50*
	Nos. B9-B11 (3)	41.00	*107.50*
	Set, never hinged	210.00	

Surtax for winter welfare. Counterfeits exist.

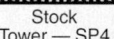

Stock Tower — SP4

George Hall — SP6

City Gate, 16th Century SP5

1935, Dec. 16 Typo. *Perf. 14*

B12	SP4 5pf + 5pf orange	.50	*1.50*
B13	SP5 10pf + 5pf green	.85	*2.25*
B14	SP6 15pf + 10pf scarlet	2.00	*3.75*
	Nos. B12-B14 (3)	3.35	*7.50*
	Set, never hinged	11.00	

Surtax for winter welfare.

Milk Can Tower SP7

Frauentor SP8

Krantor — SP9

Langgarter Gate — SP10

High Gate SP11

1936, Nov. 25

B15	SP7 10pf + 5pf dk bl	1.25	*3.25*
a.	Imperf.	75.00	
	Never hinged	180.00	
B16	SP8 15pf + 5pf dull green	1.25	*5.00*
B17	SP9 25pf + 10pf red brown	2.10	*6.50*
B18	SP10 40pf + 20pf brn & red brn	3.00	*10.50*
B19	SP11 50pf + 20pf bl & dk bl	5.00	*16.50*
	Nos. B15-B19 (5)	12.60	*41.75*
	Set, never hinged	52.50	

Surtax for winter welfare.

SP12

SP13

1937, Oct. 30

B20	SP12 25pf + 25pf dk car	2.50	*5.25*
B21	SP13 40pf + 40pf blue & red	2.50	*5.25*
a.	Souv. sheet of 2, #B20-B21	60.00	*100.00*
	Never hinged	110.00	
	Set, never hinged	20.00	

Founding of Danzig community at Magdeburg.

Madonna SP14

Mercury SP15

Weather Vane, Town Hall SP16

Neptune Fountain SP17

St. George and Dragon — SP18

1937, Dec. 13

B23	SP14	5pf + 5pf brt violet	2.50	*6.25*
B24	SP15	10pf + 10pf dk brn	2.50	*6.25*
B25	SP16	15pf + 5pf bl & yel brn	2.50	*6.25*
B26	SP17	25pf + 10pf bl grn & grn	3.25	*9.00*
B27	SP18	40pf + 25pf brt car & bl	5.75	*17.50*
		Nos. B23-B27 (5)	16.50	*45.25*
		Set, never hinged	52.50	

Surtax for winter welfare. Designs are from frieze of the Artushof.

"Peter von Danzig" Yacht Race — SP19

Ships: 10pf+5pf, Dredger Fu Shing. 15pf+10pf, S. S. Columbus. 25pf+10pf, S. S. City of Danzig. 40pf+15pf, Peter von Danzig, 1472.

1938, Nov. 28 Photo. Unwmk.

B28	SP19	5pf + 5pf dk blue grn	1.10	*1.60*
B29	SP19	10pf + 5pf gldn brown	1.40	*3.00*
B30	SP19	15pf + 10pf ol grn	1.60	*3.00*
B31	SP19	25pf + 10pf indigo	2.50	*4.00*
B32	SP19	40pf + 15pf vio brn	3.00	*7.00*
		Nos. B28-B32 (5)	9.60	*18.60*
		Set, never hinged	35.00	

Surtax for winter welfare.

AIR POST STAMPS

No. 6 Surcharged in Blue or Carmine

1920, Sept. 29 Wmk. 125 *Perf. 14*

C1	A16	40pf on 40pf	1.10	*2.90*
a.		Double surcharge	125.00	*250.00*
		Never hinged	325.00	
C2	A16	60pf on 40pf (C)	1.10	*2.90*
a.		Double surcharge	125.00	*250.00*
		Never hinged	325.00	
C3	A16	1m on 40pf	1.10	*2.90*
		Nos. C1-C3 (3)	3.30	*8.70*
		Set, never hinged	10.00	

Plane faces left on No. C2.

AP3

Plane over Danzig AP4

Wmk. Honeycomb (108)

1921-22 Typo. *Perf. 14*

C4	AP3	40(pf) blue green	.25	*.45*
C5	AP3	60(pf) dk violet	.25	*.45*
C6	AP3	1m carmine	.25	*.45*
C7	AP3	2m orange brown	.25	*.45*

Serrate Roulette 13½

Size: 34½x23mm

C8	AP4	5m violet blue	1.25	*2.25*
C9	AP4	10m dp grn ('22)	2.00	*4.50*
		Nos. C4-C9 (6)	4.25	*8.55*
		Set, never hinged	18.00	

Nos. C4-C9 exist imperf. Value, each $32.50 unused, $125 never hinged.

1923 Wmk. Webbing (109) *Perf. 14*

C10	AP3	40(pf) blue green	.40	*2.00*
C11	AP3	60(pf) dk violet	.40	*2.00*
a.		Double impression		—
C12	AP3	1m carmine	.40	*2.00*
C13	AP3	2m org brown	.40	*2.00*
C14	AP3	25m pale blue	.30	*.55*

Serrate Roulette 13½

Size: 34½x23mm

C15	AP4	5m violet blue	.40	*.85*
C16	AP4	10m deep green	.40	*.85*

Paper With Gray Network

C17	AP4	20m orange brown	.40	*.85*

Size: 40x23mm

C18	AP4	50m orange	.30	*.55*
C19	AP4	100m red	.30	*.55*
C20	AP4	250m dark brown	.30	*.55*
C21	AP4	500m carmine rose	.30	*.55*
		Nos. C10-C21 (12)	4.30	*13.30*
		Set, never hinged	17.00	

#C11, C12, C14-C21 exist imperf. Value, #C11, C12, C15-C17, each $8.50 unused, $32.50 never hinged. Value, #C14, C18-C21, each $40 unused, $125 never hinged.

Issued: #C10, C13, C15-C16, 1/3/23. #C14, C18, C20-C21, 4/27/23. #C17, 1/10/23. #C19, 2/5/23.

Nos. C18, C19 and C21 exist with wmk. sideways, both perf and imperf. Value each, $60 unused, $160 never hinged.

Post Horn and Airplanes — AP5

1923, Oct. 18 *Perf. 14*

Paper Without Network

C22	AP5	250,000m scarlet	.25	*1.10*
C23	AP5	500,000m scarlet	.25	*1.10*
		Set, never hinged	2.10	

Exist imperf. Value, each: $50 unused; $125 never hinged.

Surcharged

C24	AP5	2mil m on 100,000m	.25	*1.10*
C25	AP5	5mil m on 50,000m	.25	*1.10*
b.		Cliché of 10,000m in sheet of 50,000m	32.50	*125.00*
		Never hinged	110.00	
		Set, never hinged	2.10	

Exist imperf. Value, each $125 unused; $290 never hinged.

Nos. C24 and C25 were not regularly issued without surcharge, although copies have been passed through the post. Values: C24 unused $8.50, never hinged $32.50; C25 unused $12, never hinged $21.

AP6

Plane over Danzig — AP7

1924

C26	AP6	10(pf) vermilion	22.50	3.75
C27	AP6	20(pf) carmine rose	2.00	1.50
C28	AP6	40(pf) olive brown	3.00	1.75
C29	AP6	1g deep green	3.00	1.75
C30	AP7	2½g violet brown	17.50	*35.00*
		Nos. C26-C30 (5)	48.00	*43.75*
		Set, never hinged	150.00	

Exist imperf. Value #C26, C30, $85 unused, $200 never hinged; others, each $40 unused, $110 never hinged.

Nos. 193, 195, 197-199 Surcharged in Various Colors

1932 Wmk. 125

C31	A20	10pf on 1g (G)	8.50	*23.00*
C32	A20	15pf on 2g (V)	8.50	*23.00*
C33	A20	20pf on 3g (Bl)	8.50	*23.00*
C34	A23	25pf on 5g (R)	8.50	*23.00*
C35	A24	30pf on 10g (Br)	8.50	*23.00*
		Nos. C31-C35 (5)	42.50	*115.00*
		Set, never hinged	180.00	

Intl. Air Post Exhib. of 1932. The surcharges were variously arranged to suit the shapes and designs of the stamps. The stamps were sold at double their surcharged values, the excess being donated to the exhibition funds.

No. C31 exists with inverted surcharge and with double surcharge. Value each, $85 unused, $210 never hinged.

Airplane
AP8 AP9

1935 Wmk. 109

C36	AP8	10pf scarlet	1.60	.85
C37	AP8	15pf yellow	1.60	1.25
C38	AP8	25pf dark green	1.60	1.60
C39	AP8	50pf gray blue	6.50	*10.00*
C40	AP9	1g magenta	3.25	*13.00*
		Nos. C36-C40 (5)	14.55	*26.70*
		Set, never hinged	57.50	

Nos. C36 and C40 exist imperf. Values: C36 unused $20, never hinged $62.50; C40 unused $29, never hinged $85.

See Nos. C42-C45.

Souvenir Sheet

St. Mary's Church — AP10

1937, June 6 *Perf. 14*

C41	AP10	50pf dark grayish blue	3.50	*20.00*
		Never hinged	10.50	

Danzig Phil. Exhib., June 6-8, 1937.

Type of 1935

1938-39 Wmk. 237

C42	AP8	10pf scarlet	1.25	*3.25*
C43	AP8	15pf yellow ('39)	2.25	*13.00*
C44	AP8	25pf dark green	1.60	*5.75*
C45	AP8	50pf gray blue ('39)	4.00	*50.00*
		Nos. C42-C45 (4)	9.10	*72.00*
		Set, never hinged	35.00	

POSTAGE DUE STAMPS

Danzig Coat of Arms
D1 D2

Wmk. Honeycomb (108)

1921-22 Typo. *Perf. 14*

Paper Without Network

J1	D1	10(pf) deep violet	.25	*.50*
J2	D1	20(pf) deep violet	.25	*.50*
J3	D1	40(pf) deep violet	.25	*.50*
J4	D1	60(pf) deep violet	.25	*.50*
J5	D1	75(pf) dp violet ('22)	.25	*.50*
J6	D1	80(pf) deep violet	.25	*.50*
J7	D1	120(pf) deep violet	.25	*.50*
J8	D1	200(pf) dp violet ('22)	.85	*1.10*
J9	D1	240(pf) deep violet	.25	*1.10*
J10	D1	300(pf) dp violet ('22)	.85	*1.10*
J11	D1	400(pf) deep violet	.85	*1.10*
J12	D1	500(pf) deep violet	.85	*1.10*
J13	D1	800(pf) dp violet ('22)	.85	*1.10*
J14	D1	20m dp violet ('22)	.85	*1.10*
		Nos. J1-J14 (14)	7.10	*11.20*
		Set, never hinged	23.00	

Nos. J1-J14 exist imperf. Value, each $25 unused, $65 never hinged.

1923 Wmk. 109

J15	D1	100(pf) deep violet	.65	*.85*
J16	D1	200(pf) deep violet	2.50	*4.00*
J17	D1	300(pf) deep violet	.65	*.85*
J18	D1	400(pf) deep violet	.65	*.85*
J19	D1	500(pf) deep violet	.65	*.85*
J20	D1	800(pf) deep violet	1.40	*4.00*
J21	D1	10m deep violet	.65	*1.10*
J22	D1	20m deep violet	.65	*.85*
J23	D1	50m deep violet	.65	*.85*

Paper With Gray Network

J24	D1	100m deep violet	.65	*1.10*
J25	D1	500m deep violet	.65	*1.10*
		Nos. J15-J25 (11)	9.75	16.40
		Set, never hinged	24.00	

#J15, J17, J22-J25 exist imperf. Value each, $12.50 unused, $40 never hinged.

Nos. J22-J23 and Type of 1923 Surcharged

1923, Oct. 1

Paper without Network

J26	D1	5000m on 50m	.40	*.85*
J27	D1	10,000m on 20m	.40	*.85*
J28	D1	50,000m on 500m	.40	*.85*
J29	D1	100,000m on 20m	.85	*1.25*
		Nos. J26-J29 (4)	2.05	*3.80*
		Set, never hinged	8.25	

On No. J26 the numerals of the surcharge are all of the larger size.

A 1000(m) on 100m deep violet was prepared but not issued. Value, $145, never hinged $350.

Nos. J26-J28 exist imperf. Value each, $16.50 unused, $40 never hinged.

1923-28 Wmk. 110

J30	D2	5(pf) blue & blk	.85	.85
J31	D2	10(pf) blue & blk	.40	*.85*
J32	D2	15(pf) blue & blk	1.25	1.25
J33	D2	20(pf) blue & blk	1.25	*2.00*
J34	D2	30(pf) blue & blk	8.50	2.00
J35	D2	40(pf) blue & blk	2.00	*3.25*
J36	D2	50(pf) blue & blk	2.00	*2.50*
J37	D2	60(pf) blue & blk	13.00	*20.00*
J38	D2	100(pf) blue & blk	16.50	10.50

J39 D2 3g blue & car 7.50 *45.00*
- *a.* "Gulden" instead of "Gulden" 325.00 *1,050.*
- Never hinged 1,050.

Nos. J30-J39 (10) 53.25 *88.20*
Set, never hinged 170.00

Used values of Nos. J30-J39 are for postally used copies.

See Nos. J43-J47.

Postage Due Stamps of 1923 Issue Surcharged in Red

1932, Dec. 20
- **J40** D2 5pf on 40(pf) 2.50 *7.50*
- **J41** D2 10pf on 60(pf) 30.00 10.00
- **J42** D2 20pf on 100(pf) 2.50 *7.50*

Nos. J40-J42 (3) 35.00 *25.00*
Set, never hinged 110.00

Type of 1923

1938-39 Wmk. 237 *Perf. 14*
- **J43** D2 10(pf) bl & blk ('39) 1.25 *57.50*
- **J44** D2 30(pf) blue & black 2.10 *45.00*
- **J45** D2 40(pf) bl & blk ('39) 6.25 *85.00*
- **J46** D2 60(pf) bl & blk ('39) 6.25 *85.00*
- **J47** D2 100(pf) blue & black 10.00 *65.00*

Nos. J43-J47 (5) 25.85 *337.50*
Set, never hinged 100.00

OFFICIAL STAMPS

Regular Issues of 1921-22 Overprinted

a

1921-22 Wmk. 108 *Perf. 14x14½*
- **O1** A11 5(pf) orange .25 .20
- **O2** A11 10(pf) dark brown .25 .20
  - *a.* Inverted overprint 50.00
  - Never hinged 140.00
- **O3** A11 15(pf) green .25 .20
- **O4** A11 20(pf) slate .25 .20
- **O5** A11 25(pf) dark green .25 .20
- **O6** A11 30(pf) blue & car .60 .60
- **O7** A11 40(pf) green & car .25 .20
- **O8** A11 50(pf) dk grn & car .25 .20
- **O9** A11 60(pf) carmine .25 .20
- **O10** A11 75(pf) dp vio ('22) .20 *.40*
- **O11** A11 80(pf) black & car .85 .85
- **O12** A11 80(pf) green ('22) .20 *2.50*

Paper With Faint Gray Network
- **O14** A11 1m orange & car .25 .20
- **O15** A11 1.20m blue violet 1.25 1.25
- **O16** A11 1.25m vio & car ('22) .20 *.40*
- **O17** A11 1.50m sl gray ('22) .20 *.40*
- **O18** A11 2m gray & car 14.00 11.50
  - *a.* Inverted overprint 110.00
  - Never hinged 250.00
- **O19** A11 2m car rose ('22) .20 *.40*
- **O20** A11 2.40m dk brn & car ('22) 1.25 *2.50*
- **O21** A11 3m violet & car 8.50 *11.50*
- **O22** A11 3m car lake ('22) .20 *.40*
- **O23** A11 4m dk blue ('22) 1.25 .85
- **O24** A11 5m dp grn ('22) .20 *.40*
- **O25** A11 6m car lake ('22) .20 *.40*
- **O26** A11 10m orange ('22) .20 *.40*
- **O27** A11 20m org brn ('22) .20 *.40*

Nos. O1-O27 (26) 31.95 *36.95*
Set, never hinged 160.00

Double overprints exist on Nos. O1-O2, O5-O7, O10 and O12.

Same Overprint on No. 96
- **O28** A11 6m on 3m .20 *.75*
  - Never hinged .65
  - *a.* Inverted overprint 29.00
  - Never hinged 85.00

No. 77 Overprinted

1922 *Serrate Roulette 13½*
- **O29** A12 5m grn, red & blk 4.00 *10.50*
  - Never hinged 18.00

Nos. 99-103, 106-107 Overprinted Type "a"

1923 Wmk. 109 *Perf. 14*
- **O30** A11 4m dark blue .25 *.40*
- **O31** A11 5m dark green .25 *.40*
- **O32** A11 10m orange .25 *.40*
- **O33** A11 20m orange brn .25 *.40*
- **O34** A15 50m pale bl & red .25 *.40*
- **O35** A15a 100m dk grn & red .25 *.40*

Nos. 113-115, 118-120 Overprinted Type "a"
- **O36** A15 50m pale blue .25 *.50*
  - *a.* Inverted overprint 25.00
  - Never hinged 60.00
- **O37** A15a 100m dark green .20 *.50*
- **O38** A15 200m orange .20 *.50*
  - *a.* Inverted overprint 25.00
  - Never hinged 60.00

Paper With Gray Network
- **O39** A17 300m bl grn & red .25 *.40*
- **O40** A17 500m gray & red .20 *.50*
- **O41** A17 1000m brown & red .20 *.50*

Nos. O30-O41 (12) 2.80 *5.30*
Set, never hinged 11.00

Regular Issue of 1924-25 Overprinted

1924-25 *Perf. 14x14½*
- **O42** A19 5pf orange 2.10 *2.50*
- **O43** A19 10pf yellow grn 2.10 *2.50*
- **O44** A19 15pf gray 2.10 *2.50*
- **O45** A19 15pf red ('25) 18.00 10.00
- **O46** A19 20pf car & red 2.10 1.60
- **O47** A19 25pf slate & red 18.00 26.00
- **O48** A19 30pf green & red 2.90 *3.75*
- **O49** A19 35pf ultra ('25) 40.00 50.00
- **O50** A19 40pf dk bl & dull bl 6.50 *8.50*
- **O51** A19 50pf dp blue & red 21.00 *32.50*
- **O52** A19 75pf violet & red 32.50 *110.00*

Nos. O42-O52 (11) 147.30 *249.85*
Set, never hinged 500.00

Double overprints exist on Nos. O42-O44, O47, O50-O52.

DENMARK

'den-,märk

LOCATION — Northern part of a peninsula which separates the North and Baltic Seas, and includes the surrounding islands
GOVT. — Kingdom
AREA — 16,631 sq. mi.
POP. — 5,294,860 (1/1/1999)
CAPITAL — Copenhagen

96 Skilling = 1 Rigsbank Daler
100 Ore = 1 Krone (1875)

Catalogue values for unused stamps in this country are for Never Hinged items, beginning with Scott 297 in the regular postage section, Scott B15 in the semi-postal section, and Scott Q28 in the parcel post section.

Values for unused stamps are for examples with original gum as defined in the catalogue introduction. Very fine examples of Nos. 9-37 and O1-O9 will have perforations clear of the framelines but with the design noticeably off center. Well centered stamps are quite scarce and will command substantial premiums.

Watermarks

Wmk. 111 — Small Crown

Wmk. 112 — Crown

Wmk. 113 — Crown

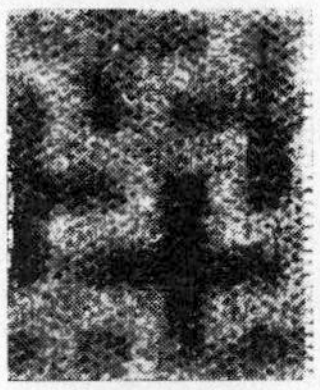

Wmk. 114 — Multiple Crosses

A1

Royal Emblems — A2

1851 Typo. Wmk. 111 *Imperf.*
With Yellow Brown Burelage
- **1** A1 2rs blue *3,000.* 1,200.
  - *a.* First printing *8,250.* *2,250.*
- **2** A2 4rs brown 500.00 40.00
  - *a.* First printing 600.00 65.00
  - *b.* 4rs yellow brown 875.00 55.00

The first printing of Nos. 1 and 2 had the burelage printed from a copper plate, giving a clear impression with the lines in slight relief. The subsequent impressions had the burelage typographed, with the lines fainter and not rising above the surface of the paper.

Nos. 1-2 were reprinted in 1885 and 1901 on heavy yellowish paper, unwatermarked and imperforate, with a brown burelage. No. 1 was also reprinted without burelage, on both yellowish and white paper. Value for least costly reprint of No. 1, $50.

No. 2 was reprinted in 1951 in 10 shades with "Colour Specimen 1951" printed on the back. It was also reprinted in 1961 in 2 shades without burelage and with "Farve Nytryk 1961" printed on the back. Value for least costly reprint of No. 2, $8.50.

Dotting in Spandrels A3

Wavy Lines in Spandrels A4

1854-57
- **3** A3 2s blue ('55) 75.00 60.00
- **4** A3 4s brown 325.00 15.00
  - *a.* 4s yellow brown 350.00 15.00
- **5** A3 8s green ('57) 300.00 67.50
  - *a.* 8s yellow green 300.00 72.50
- **6** A3 16s gray lilac ('57) 525.00 190.00

Nos. 3-6 (4) 1,225. 332.50

See No. 10. For denominations in cents see Danish West Indies Nos. 1-4.

1858-62

7 A4 4s yellow brown 65.00 9.00
a. 4s brown 67.50 9.50
b. Wmk. 112 ('62) 62.50 10.00
8 A4 8s green 800.00 95.00

Nos. 2 to 8 inclusive are known with unofficial perforation 12 or 13, and Nos. 4, 5, 7 and 8 with unofficial roulette 9½.

Nos. 3, 6-8 were reprinted in 1885 on heavy yellowish paper, unwatermarked, imperforate and without burelage. Nos. 4-5 were reprinted in 1924 on white paper, unwatermarked, imperforate, gummed and without burelage. Value for No. 3, $15; Nos. 4-5, each $110; No. 6, $20; Nos. 7-8, each $15.

1863 Wmk. 112 *Rouletted 11*

9 A4 4s brown 100.00 15.00
a. 4s deep brown 100.00 15.00
10 A3 16s violet 1,400. 650.00

Royal Emblems — A5

1864-68 *Perf. 13*

11 A5 2s blue ('65) 65.00 35.00
12 A5 3s red vio ('65) 80.00 75.00
13 A5 4s red 40.00 8.00
14 A5 8s bister ('68) 275.00 95.00
15 A5 16s olive green 475.00 175.00
Nos. 11-15 (5) 935.00 388.00

Nos. 11-15 were reprinted in 1886 on heavy yellowish paper, unwatermarked, imperforate and without gum. The reprints of all values except the 4s were printed in two vertical rows of six, inverted with respect to each other, so that horizontal pairs are always tête bêche. Value $12 each.

Nos. 13 and 15 were reprinted in 1942 with printing on the back across each horizontal row: "Nytryk 1942. G. A. Hagemann: Danmarks og Vestindiens Frimaerker, Bind 2." Value, $70 each.

Imperf

11a A5 2s blue 95.00 95.00
12a A5 3s red violet 140.00
13a A5 4s red 77.50 90.00
14a A5 8s bister 375.00
15a A5 16s olive green 450.00

1870 *Perf. 12½*

11b A5 2s blue 275.00 350.00
12b A5 3s red violet 475.00 650.00
14b A5 8s bister 475.00 475.00
15b A5 16s olive green 725.00 *1,450.*
Nos. 11b-15b (4) 1,950. 2,925.

A6

NORMAL FRAME

INVERTED FRAME

The arabesques in the corners have a main stem and a branch. When the frame is in normal position, in the upper left corner the branch leaves the main stem half way between two little leaflets. In the lower right corner the branch starts at the foot of the second leaflet. When the frame is inverted the corner designs are, of course, transposed.

1870-71 Wmk. 112 *Perf. 14x13½*

Paper Varying from Thin to Thick

16 A6 2s gray & ultra ('71) 70.00 27.50
a. 2s gray & blue 70.00 27.50
17 A6 3s gray & brt lil ('71) 100.00 110.00
18 A6 4s gray & car 40.00 10.00
19 A6 8s gray & brn ('71) 200.00 75.00
20 A6 16s gray & grn ('71) 275.00 175.00

Perf. 12½

21 A6 2s gray & bl ('71) 2,000. *3,250.*
22 A6 4s gray & car 150.00 125.00
24 A6 48s brn & lilac 450.00 275.00

Nos. 16-20, 24 were reprinted in 1886 on thin white paper, unwatermarked, imperforate and without gum. These were printed in sheets of 10 in which 1 stamp has the normal frame (value $32.50 each) and 9 the inverted (value $11 each).

Imperf

16b A6 2s *250.00*
17a A6 3s *240.00*
18a A6 4s *200.00*
19a A6 8s *250.00*
20a A6 16s *400.00*
24a A6 48s *425.00* —

Inverted Frame

16c A6 2s 1,000. 775.00
17b A6 3s 2,500. 2,000.
18b A6 4s 775.00 87.50
19b A6 8s 1,750. 900.00
20b A6 16s 2,000. 1,750.
24b A6 48s 2,750. 1,900.

1875-79 *Perf. 14x13½*

25 A6 3o gray blue & gray 18.00 15.00
a. 1st "A" of "DANMARK" missing 60.00 *150.00*
b. Imperf. *750.00*
c. Inverted frame 18.00 16.00
26 A6 4o slate & blue 25.00 .50
a. 4o gray & blue 25.00 1.10
b. 4o slate & ultra 90.00 17.00
c. 4o gray & ultra 75.00 16.00
d. Imperf 75.00 —
e. Inverted frame 25.00 .50
27 A6 5o rose & blue ('79) 30.00 72.50
a. Ball of lower curve of large "5" missing 125.00 300.00
b. Inverted frame 1,000. *2,250.*
28 A6 8o slate & car 22.50 .50
a. 8o gray & carmine 75.00 5.00
b. Imperf 150.00 —
c. Inverted frame 22.50 .50
29 A6 12o sl & dull lake 10.00 4.00
a. 12o gray & bright lilac 65.00 8.00
b. 12o gray & dull magenta 72.50 10.00
c. Inverted frame 10.00 4.00
30 A6 16o slate & brn 40.00 3.50
a. 16o light gray & brown 70.00 5.00
b. Inverted frame 32.50 4.25
31 A6 20o rose & gray 90.00 32.50
a. 20o carmine & gray 90.00 32.50
b. Inverted frame 90.00 32.50
32 A6 25o gray & green 65.00 40.00
a. Inverted frame 77.50 62.50
33 A6 50o brown & vio 70.00 37.50
a. 50o brown & blue violet 400.00 175.00
b. Inverted frame 70.00 32.50
34 A6 100o gray & org ('77) 110.00 60.00
a. Imperf 375.00
b. Inverted frame 150.00 60.00
Nos. 25-34 (10) 480.50 266.00
Set, never hinged 1,100.

The stamps of this issue on thin semi-transparent paper are far scarcer than those on thicker paper.

See Nos. 41-42, 44, 46-47, 50-52. For surcharges see Nos. 55, 79-80, 136.

Arms — A7

Two types of numerals in corners:

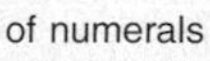

1882

Small Corner Numerals

35 A7 5o green 240.00 100.00
Never hinged 500.00
37 A7 20o blue 190.00 70.00
Never hinged 550.00

1884-88

Larger Corner Numerals

38 A7 5o green 15.00 3.50
a. Imperf. —
39 A7 10o carmine ('85) 16.00 2.50
a. Small numerals in corners ('88) 550.00 *725.00*
b. Imperf., single 175.00
c. Pair, Nos. 39, 39a 600.00 *875.00*
40 A7 20o blue 30.00 5.00
a. Pair, Nos. 37, 40 400.00 *875.00*
b. Imperf. —
Nos. 38-40 (3) 61.00 11.00
Set, never hinged 285.00

Stamps with large corner numerals have white line around crown and lower oval touches frame.

The plate for No. 39, was damaged and 3 clichés in the bottom row were replaced by clichés for post cards, which had small numerals in the corners.

Two clichés with small numerals were inserted in the plate of No. 40.

See Nos. 43, 45, 48-49, 53-54. For surcharge see No. 56.

1895-1901 Wmk. 112 *Perf. 13*

41 A6 3o blue & gray 10.00 7.25
42 A6 4o slate & bl ('96) 4.50 .40
43 A7 5o green 12.00 .75
44 A6 8o slate & car 4.50 .45
45 A7 10o rose car 24.00 .65
46 A6 12o sl & dull lake 7.00 4.00
47 A6 16o slate & brown 19.00 4.50
48 A7 20o blue 30.00 2.40
49 A7 24o brown ('01) 7.00 6.00
50 A6 25o gray & grn ('98) 110.00 19.50
51 A6 50o brown & vio ('97) 60.00 24.00
52 A6 100o slate & org 90.00 35.00
Nos. 41-52 (12) 378.00 104.90
Set, never hinged 860.00

Inverted Frame

41b A6 3o 12.00 7.00
42a A6 4o 4.50 .45
44a A6 8o 4.50 .50
46a A6 12o 14.00 4.50
47a A6 16o 30.00 5.00
50a A6 25o 60.00 27.50
51a A6 50o 95.00 32.50
52a A6 100o 90.00 57.50
Nos. 41b-52a (8) 310.00 134.95
Set, never hinged 635.00

1902-04 Wmk. 113

41c A6 3o blue & gray 2.75 3.00
42b A6 4o slate & blue 17.00 20.00
43a A7 5o green 2.00 .25
44d A6 8o slate & carmine 525.00 425.00
45a A7 10o rose carmine 3.00 .25
48a A7 20o blue 20.00 4.75
50b A6 25o gray & green 10.50 4.50
51b A6 50o brown & violet 27.50 20.00
52b A6 100o slate & orange 30.00 15.00
Nos. 41c-52b (9) 637.75 492.75
Set, never hinged 1,325.

Inverted Frame

41d A6 3o 75.00 130.00
42c A6 4o 140.00 130.00
50c A6 25o 210.00 60.00
51c A6 50o 260.00 240.00
52c A6 100o 225.00 240.00
Nos. 41d-52c (5) 910.00 800.00
Set, never hinged 2,500.

1902 Wmk. 113

53 A7 1o orange .75 .65
a. Imperf. — —
54 A7 15o lilac 11.00 .75
a. Imperf, single *4,250.*

Nos. 44d, 44, 49 Surcharged:

a

b

1904-12 Wmk. 113

55 A6(a) 4o on 8o sl & car 3.50 4.00
a. Wmk. 112 ('12) 21.00 *60.00*
Never hinged 42.50
b. As "a," inverted frame — 6,000.

Wmk. 112

56 A7(b) 15o on 24o brown 5.75 17.50
a. Short "15" at right 27.50 *75.00*
Never hinged 105.00
Set, never hinged 16.00

A10

King Christian IX
A11

King Frederik VIII
A12

1905-17 Wmk. 113 *Perf. 13*

57 A10 1o orange ('06) 1.75 .75
58 A10 2o carmine 2.75 .50
a. Perf. 14x14½ ('17) 3.00 *16.00*
59 A10 3o gray 6.00 .65
60 A10 4o dull blue 5.00 .65
a. Perf. 14x14½ ('17) 7.50 *37.50*
61 A10 5o dp green ('12) 3.50 .30
62 A10 10o dp rose ('12) 4.75 .30
63 A10 15o lilac 14.00 2.00
64 A10 20o dk blue ('12) 35.00 .80
Nos. 57-64 (8) 72.75 5.95
Set, never hinged 240.00

The three wavy lines in design A10 are symbolical of the three waters which separate the principal Danish islands. Compare with design A32.

See Nos. 85-96 and 1338-1342. For surcharges and overprints see Nos. 163, 181, J1, J38, Q1-Q2.

1904-05 Engr.

65 A11 10o scarlet 2.75 .55
66 A11 20o blue 18.00 2.40
67 A11 25o brown ('05) 24.00 7.00
68 A11 50o dull vio ('05) 100.00 *120.00*
69 A11 100o ocher ('05) 13.00 *60.00*
Nos. 65-69 (5) 157.75 *189.95*
Set, never hinged 425.00

1905-06 Re-engraved

70 A11 5o green 4.00 .25
71 A11 10o scarlet ('06) 14.00 .55
Set, never hinged 45.00

The re-engraved stamps are much clearer than the originals, and the decoration on the king's left breast has been removed.

1907-12

72 A12 5o green 1.10 .40
a. Imperf. —
73 A12 10o red 3.00 .30
a. Imperf. —
74 A12 20o indigo 14.00 .45
a. 20o bright blue ('11) 14.00 1.40
75 A12 25o olive brn 27.50 1.25
76 A12 35o dp org ('12) 6.00 *7.00*
77 A12 50o claret 32.00 6.75
78 A12 100o bister brn 85.00 5.00
Nos. 72-78 (7) 168.60 21.15
Set, never hinged 425.00

Nos. 47, 31 and O9 Surcharged:

c

d

Dark Blue Surcharge

1912 Wmk. 112 *Perf. 13*

79 A6(c) 35o on 16o 14.00 *50.00*
a. Inverted frame 175.00 *400.00*

Perf. 14x13½

80 A6(c) 35o on 20o 30.00 *80.00*
a. Inverted frame 75.00 *175.00*

Black Surcharge

81 O1(d) 35o on 32o 42.50 *120.00*
Nos. 79-81 (3) 86.50 *250.00*
Set, never hinged 150.00

General Post Office, Copenhagen — A15

1912 Engr. Wmk. 113 *Perf. 13*

82 A15 5k dark red 350.00 150.00
Never hinged 1,050.

See Nos. 135, 843.

Perf. 14x14½

1913-30 Typo. Wmk. 114

85 A10 1o dp org ('14) .30 .25
a. Bklt. pane, 2 ea #85, 91 + 2 labels 20.00
86 A10 2o car ('13) 3.00 .25
a. Imperf. 110.00 *225.00*
b. Booklet pane, 4 + 2 labels 27.50
87 A10 3o gray ('13) 5.25 .40
88 A10 4o blue ('13) 6.25 .45
a. Half used as 2o on cover 1,250.
89 A10 5o dk brown ('21) .65 .25
a. Imperf. 160.00
b. Booklet pane, 4 + 2 labels 14.00
90 A10 5o lt green ('30) 1.40 .25
a. Booklet pane, 4 + 2 labels 16.00
b. Booklet pane of 50
91 A10 7o apple grn ('26) 5.00 *6.75*
a. Booklet pane, 4 + 2 labels 20.00
92 A10 7o dk violet ('30) 14.00 5.75
93 A10 8o gray ('21) 7.00 3.00
94 A10 10o green ('21) .85 .25
a. Imperf. 175.00
b. Booklet pane, 4 + 2 labels 37.50

95 A10 10o bister brn ('30) 1.75 .25
a. Booklet pane, 4 + 2 labels 16.00
b. Booklet pane of 50
96 A10 12o violet ('26) 22.50 9.00
Nos. 85-96 (12) 67.95 26.85
Set, never hinged 160.00

No. 88a was used with No. 97 in Faroe Islands, Jan. 3-23, 1919.

See surcharge and overprint note following #64.

King Christian X
A16 A17

1913-28 Typo. Perf. 14x14½
97 A16 5o green 1.10 .25
a. Booklet pane of 4 11.00
98 A16 7o orange ('18) 2.25 2.50
99 A16 8o dk gray ('20) 8.00 6.00
100 A16 10o red 1.50 .25
a. Imperf. 200.00
b. Booklet pane of 4 11.00
101 A16 12o gray grn ('18) 6.50 10.00
102 A16 15o violet 2.00 .30
103 A16 20o dp blue 10.00 .25
104 A16 20o brown ('21) 1.00 .25
105 A16 20o red ('26) 1.25 .25
106 A16 25o dk brown 8.50 .45
107 A16 25o brn & blk ('20) 75.00 8.00
108 A16 25o red ('22) 3.25 .85
109 A16 25o yel grn ('25) 3.00 .45
110 A16 27o ver & blk ('18) 27.50 60.00
111 A16 30o grn & blk ('18) 35.00 2.75
112 A16 30o orange ('21) 2.25 1.75
113 A16 30o dk blue ('25) 1.50 .45
114 A16 35o orange 20.00 7.00
115 A16 35o yel & blk ('19) 7.50 7.00
116 A16 40o vio & blk ('18) 10.00 3.50
117 A16 40o gray bl & blk ('20) 27.50 5.00
118 A16 40o dk blue ('22) 4.00 1.40
119 A16 40o orange ('25) 1.75 .90
120 A16 50o claret 30.00 4.50
121 A16 50o claret & blk ('19) 50.00 2.00
122 A16 50o lt gray ('22) 7.50 .30
a. 50o dark gray ('21) 50.00 6.00
Never hinged 160.00
123 A16 60o brn & bl ('19) 40.00 4.00
a. 60o brown & ultra ('19) 160.00 10.00
Never hinged 600.00
124 A16 60o grn bl ('21) 8.00 .80
125 A16 70o brn & grn ('20) 20.00 2.00
126 A16 80o bl grn ('15) 40.00 20.00
127 A16 90o brn & red ('20) 15.00 3.75
128 A16 1k brn & bl ('22) 45.00 2.50
129 A16 2k gray & cl ('25) 57.50 13.00
130 A16 5k vio & brn ('27) 5.25 5.50
131 A16 10k ver & yel grn ('28) 250.00 55.00
Nos. 97-131 (35) 828.60 232.90
Set, never hinged 2,350.

#97 surcharged "2 ORE" is Faroe Islands #1.

Nos. 87 and 98, 89 and 94, 89 and 104, 90 and 95, 97 and 103, 100 and 102 exist se-tenant in coils for use in vending machines.

For surcharges and overprints see Nos. 161-162, 176-177, 182-184, J2-J8, M1-M2, Q3-Q10.

1913-20 Engr.
132 A17 1k yellow brown 65.00 1.00
133 A17 2k gray 75.00 6.00
134 A17 5k purple ('20) 11.00 9.00
Nos. 132-134 (3) 151.00 16.00
Set, never hinged 775.00

For overprint see No. Q11.

G.P.O. Type of 1912

Perf. 14x14½

1915 Wmk. 114 Engr.
135 A15 5k dark red ('15) 350.00 150.00
Never hinged 1,050.

Nos. 46 and O10 Surcharged in Black type "c" and:

e

1915 Wmk. 112 Typo. Perf. 13
136 A6 (c) 80o on 12o 42.50 110.00
a. Inverted frame 475.00 900.00
Never hinged 650.00
137 O1 (e) 80o on 8o 30.00 110.00
a. "POSTERIM" 47.50 260.00
Never hinged 85.00
Set, never hinged 140.00

Newspaper Stamps Surcharged

On Issue of 1907

1918 Wmk. 113 Perf. 13
138 N1 27o on 1o olive 85.00 225.00
139 N1 27o on 5o blue 85.00 225.00
140 N1 27o on 7o car 85.00 225.00
141 N1 27o on 10o dp lil 85.00 225.00
142 N1 27o on 68o yel brn 7.00 35.00
143 N1 27o on 5k rose & yel grn 5.00 22.50
144 N1 27o on 10k bis & bl 7.00 30.00
Nos. 138-144 (7) 359.00 987.50
Set, never hinged 750.00

On Issue of 1914-15

Wmk. Multiple Crosses (114)

Perf. 14x14½
145 N1 27o on 1o ol gray 3.25 14.50
146 N1 27o on 5o blue 8.00 24.00
147 N1 27o on 7o rose 3.25 8.00
148 N1 27o on 8o green 5.00 14.50
149 N1 27o on 10o dp lil 3.25 12.00
150 N1 27o on 20o green 4.50 10.50
151 N1 27o on 29o org yel 3.25 10.00
152 N1 27o on 38o orange 32.50 97.50
153 N1 27o on 41o yel brn 8.00 50.00
154 N1 27o on 1k bl grn & mar 3.25 13.00
Nos. 145-154 (10) 74.25 254.00
Set, never hinged 110.00

Kronborg Castle — A20

Sonderborg Castle — A21

Roskilde Cathedral — A22

Perf. 14½x14, 14x14½

1920, Oct. 5 Typo.
156 A20 10o red 3.75 .35
157 A21 20o slate 3.00 .35
158 A22 40o dark brown 12.50 4.50
Nos. 156-158 (3) 19.25 5.20
Set, never hinged 45.00

Reunion of Northern Schleswig with Denmark.

See #159-160. For surcharges see #B1-B2.

1921
159 A20 10o green 7.50 .50
160 A22 40o dark blue 57.50 11.00
Set, never hinged 155.00

Stamps of 1918 Surcharged in Blue

1921-22
161 A16 8o on 7o org ('22) 1.60 5.00
162 A16 8o on 12o gray grn 1.75 15.00
Set, never hinged 12.00

No. 87 Surcharged

1921
163 A10 8o on 3o gray 3.75 5.00
Never hinged 7.50

Christian X
A23

Christian IV
A24

A25

A26

1924, Dec. 1 Perf. 14x14½
164 A23 10o green 7.00 7.00
165 A24 10o green 7.00 7.00
166 A25 10o green 7.00 7.00
167 A26 10o green 7.00 7.00
a. Block of 4, #164-167 37.50 55.00
168 A23 15o violet 7.00 7.00
169 A24 15o violet 7.00 7.00
170 A25 15o violet 7.00 7.00
171 A26 15o violet 7.00 7.00
a. Block of 4, #168-171 37.50 55.00
172 A23 20o dark brown 7.00 7.00
173 A24 20o dark brown 7.00 7.00
174 A25 20o dark brown 7.00 7.00
175 A26 20o dark brown 7.00 7.00
a. Block of 4, #172-175 37.50 55.00
Nos. 164-175 (12) 84.00 84.00
Set, never hinged 175.00
#167a, 171a, 175a, never hinged 250.00

300th anniv. of the Danish postal service.

Stamps of 1921-22 Surcharged:

k

l

1926
176 A16 (k) 20o on 30o org 4.75 14.00
177 A16 (l) 20o on 40o dk bl 7.50 17.00
Set, never hinged 22.00

A27

A28

1926, Mar. 11 Perf. 14x14½
178 A27 10o dull green 1.10 .45
179 A28 20o dark red 1.50 .45
180 A28 30o dark blue 7.00 1.50
Nos. 178-180 (3) 9.60 2.40
Set, never hinged 13.00

75th anniv. of the introduction of postage stamps in Denmark.

Stamps of 1913-26 Surcharged in Blue or Black

No. 181

Nos. 182-184

1926-27 Perf. 14x14½
181 A10 7o on 8o gray (Bl) 1.40 4.00
182 A16 7o on 27o ver & blk 4.25 10.00
183 A16 7o on 20o red ('27) .65 .75
184 A16 12o on 15o violet 2.75 5.50

Surcharged on Official Stamps of 1914-23

185 O1 (e) 7o on 1o org 4.00 14.00
186 O1 (e) 7o on 3o gray 6.50 24.00
187 O1 (e) 7o on 4o blue 3.25 9.00
188 O1 (e) 7o on 5o grn 52.50 92.50
189 O1 (e) 7o on 10o grn 4.00 14.50
190 O1 (e) 7o on 15o vio 4.00 14.50
191 O1 (e) 7o on 20o ind 16.00 65.00
a. Double surcharge 600.00 750.00
Nos. 181-191 (11) 99.30 253.75
Set, never hinged 140.00

Caravel
A30

Christian X
A31

1927 Typo. Perf. 14x14½
192 A30 15o red 5.75 .30
193 A30 20o gray 10.50 2.25
194 A30 25o light blue 1.10 .40
195 A30 30o ocher 1.25 .40
196 A30 35o red brown 20.00 1.50
197 A30 40o yel green 19.00 .40
Nos. 192-197 (6) 57.60 5.25
Set, never hinged 170.00

See #232-238J. For surcharges & overprints see #244-245, 269-272, Q12-Q14, Q19-Q25.

1930, Sept. 26
210 A31 5o apple grn 2.25 .25
a. Booklet pane, 4 + 2 labels 18.00
211 A31 7o violet 6.50 2.75
212 A31 8o dk gray 22.50 30.00
213 A31 10o yel brn 4.25 .25
a. Booklet pane, 4 + 2 labels 29.00
214 A31 15o red 9.50 .25
215 A31 20o lt gray 25.00 8.50
216 A31 25o lt blue 8.25 1.25
217 A31 30o yel buff 8.75 1.75
218 A31 35o red brown 11.00 4.00
219 A31 40o dp green 9.50 1.25
Nos. 210-219 (10) 107.50 50.25
Set, never hinged 245.00

60th birthday of King Christian X.

Wavy Lines and Numeral of Value — A32

Type A10 Redrawn

1933-40 Unwmk. Engr. Perf. 13
220 A32 1o gray blk .20 .20
221 A32 2o scarlet .20 .20
222 A32 4o blue .30 .25
223 A32 5o yel grn 1.00 .25
a. 5o gray green 27.50 40.00
b. Tête bêche gutter pair 8.00 14.00
c. Booklet pane of 4 11.00
d. Bklt. pane, 1 #223a, 3 #B6 37.50
e. As "b," without gutter, never hinged 17.50
224 A32 5o rose lake ('38) .20 .20
a. Booklet pane of 4 .40
b. Booklet pane of 10 .90
224C A32 6o orange ('40) .30 .25
225 A32 7o violet 2.00 .25
226 A32 7o yel grn ('38) 1.10 .25
226A A32 7o lt brown ('40) .25 .25
227 A32 8o gray .45 .25
227A A32 8o yellow grn ('40) .25 .25
228 A32 10o yellow org 10.00 .25
a. Tête bêche gutter pair 35.00 35.00
b. Booklet pane of 4 110.00
c. As "a," without gutter, never hinged 45.00
229 A32 10o lt brown ('37) 9.50 .25
a. Booklet pane of 4 100.00
b. Booklet pane of 4, 1 #229, 3 #B7 30.00
230 A32 10o violet ('38) .60 .25
a. Booklet pane of 4 2.75
b. Bklt. pane, 2 #230, 2 #B10 4.50
Nos. 220-230 (14) 26.35 3.35
Set, never hinged 50.00

Design A10 was typographed. They had a solid background with groups of small hearts below the heraldic lions in the upper corners and below "DA" and "RK" of "DANMARK." The numerals of value were enclosed in single-lined ovals.

Design A32 is line-engraved and has a background of crossed lines. The hearts have been removed and the numerals of value are now in double-lined ovals. Two types exist of some values.

The 1ő, No. 220, was issued on fluorescent paper in 1969.

No. 230 with wide margins is from booklet pane No. 230b.

Surcharges of 20, 50 & 60öre on #220, 224 & 224C are listed as Faroe Islands #2-3, 5-6.

See Nos. 318, 333, 382, 416, 437-437A, 493-498, 629, 631, 688-695, 793-795, 883-886, 1111, 1114. For overprints and surcharges see Nos. 257, 263, 267-268, 355-356, Q15-Q17, Q31, Q43.

Certain Tête Bêche pairs of 1938-55 issues which reached the market in 1971, and were not regularly issued, are not listed. This group comprises 24 different major-number vertical pairs of types A32, A47, A61 and SP3 (13 with gutters, 11 without), and pairs of some minor numbers and shades. They were removed from booklet pane sheets.

Type of 1927 Issue

Type I

Type I — Two columns of squares between sail and left frame line.

1933-34 Engr. *Perf. 13*

232 A30 20o gray	13.50	.25
233 A30 25o blue	77.50	27.50
234 A30 25o brown ('34)	27.50	.25
235 A30 30o orange yel	1.10	1.00
236 A30 30o blue ('34)	1.00	.25
237 A30 35o violet	.40	.25
238 A30 40o yellow grn	5.00	.25
Nos. 232-238 (7)	126.00	29.75
Set, never hinged	265.00	

Type II

Type II — One column of squares between sail and left frame line.

1933-40

238A A30 15o deep red	2.25	.25
k. Booklet pane of 4	24.00	
l. Bklt. pane, 1 #238A, 3 #B8	37.50	
238B A30 15o yel grn ('40)	7.00	.25
238C A30 20o gray blk ('39)	4.50	.25
238D A30 20o red ('40)	.50	.25
238E A30 25o dp brown ('39)	.50	.25
238F A30 30o blue ('39)	1.75	.30
238G A30 30o orange ('40)	.50	.25
238H A30 35o violet ('40)	.60	.35
238I A30 40o yel grn ('39)	10.00	.25
238J A30 40o blue ('40)	1.00	.25
Nos. 238A-238J (10)	28.60	2.65
Set, never hinged	62.50	

Nos. 232-238J, engraved, have crosshatched background. Nos. 192-197, typographed, have solid background.

No. 238A surcharged 20 ore is listed as Faroe Islands No. 4.

See note on surcharges and overprints following No. 197.

King Christian X — A33

1934-41 *Perf. 13*

239 A33 50o gray	.90	.25
240 A33 60o blue grn	1.75	.25
240A A33 75o dk blue ('41)	.45	.25
241 A33 1k lt brown	3.25	.25
242 A33 2k dull red	6.00	.80
243 A33 5k violet	8.00	2.75
Nos. 239-243 (6)	20.35	4.55
Set, never hinged	60.00	

For overprints see Nos. Q26-Q27.

Nos. 233, 235 Surcharged in Black

1934, June 9

244 A30 4o on 25o blue	.40	*.50*
245 A30 10o on 30o org yel	1.90	*2.75*
Set, never hinged	5.75	

"The Ugly Duckling" A34

Andersen A35

"The Little Mermaid" — A36

1935, Oct. 4 *Perf. 13*

246 A34 5o lt green	2.50	.25
a. Tête bêche gutter pair	9.00	*9.50*
b. Booklet pane of 4	25.00	
c. As "a," without gutter, never hinged	20.00	
247 A35 7o dull vio	2.00	*2.50*
248 A36 10o orange	4.50	.25
a. Tête bêche gutter pair	12.00	*20.00*
b. Booklet pane of 4	45.00	
c. As "a," without gutter, never hinged	42.50	
249 A35 15o red	9.00	.25
a. Tête bêche gutter pair	32.50	*27.50*
b. Booklet pane of 4	95.00	
c. As "a," without gutter, never hinged	80.00	
250 A35 20o gray	10.00	1.25
251 A35 30o dl bl	2.50	.35
Nos. 246-251 (6)	30.50	*4.85*
Set, never hinged	115.00	

Centenary of the publication of the earliest installment of Hans Christian Andersen's "Fairy Tales."

Nikolai Church A37

Hans Tausen A38

Ribe Cathedral — A39

1936 *Perf. 13*

252 A37 5o green	1.10	.25
a. Booklet pane of 4	21.00	
253 A37 7o violet	1.25	*4.50*
254 A38 10o lt brown	1.60	.25
a. Booklet pane of 4	25.00	
255 A38 15o dull rose	2.40	.25
256 A39 30o blue	15.00	1.25
Nos. 252-256 (5)	21.35	6.50
Set, never hinged	55.00	

Church Reformation in Denmark, 400th anniv.

No. 229 Overprinted in Blue

1937, Sept. 17

257 A32 10o lt brown	1.40	*1.50*
Never hinged	2.00	

Jubilee Exhib. held by the Copenhagen Phil. Club on their 50th anniv. The stamps were on sale at the Exhib. only, each holder of a ticket of admission (1k) being entitled to purchase 20 stamps at face value; of a season ticket (5k), 100 stamps.

Yacht and Summer Palace, Marselisborg A40

Christian X in Streets of Copenhagen A41

Equestrian Statue of Frederik V and Amalienborg Palace — A42

1937, May 15 *Perf. 13*

258 A40 5o green	1.10	.25
a. Booklet pane of 4	15.00	
259 A41 10o brown	1.10	.25
a. Booklet pane of 4	15.00	
260 A42 15o scarlet	1.10	.25
a. Booklet pane of 4	17.00	
261 A41 30o blue	15.00	2.10
Nos. 258-261 (4)	18.30	2.85
Set, never hinged	47.50	

25th anniv. of the accession to the throne of King Christian X.

Emancipation Column, Copenhagen — A43

1938, June 20 *Perf. 13*

262 A43 15o scarlet	.50	.25
Never hinged	1.25	

Abolition of serfdom in Denmark, 150th anniv.

No. 223 Overprinted in Red on Alternate Stamps

1938, Sept. 2

263 A32 5o yellow grn, pair	3.00	*8.00*
Never hinged	5.00	

10th Danish Philatelic Exhibition.

Bertel Thorvaldsen A44

Statue of Jason A45

1938, Nov. 17 Engr. *Perf. 13*

264 A44 5o rose lake	.35	.25
265 A45 10o purple	.50	.25
266 A44 30o dark blue	1.40	.50
Nos. 264-266 (3)	2.25	1.00
Set, never hinged	4.50	

The return to Denmark in 1838 of Bertel Thorvaldsen, Danish sculptor.

Stamps of 1933-39 Surcharged with New Values in Black:

a

b

c

1940

267 A32 (a) 6o on 7o yel grn	.30	.25
268 A32 (a) 6o on 8o gray	.30	.25
269 A30 (b) 15o on 40o #238	.90	*4.00*
270 A30 (b) 15o on 40o #238I	.90	.80
271 A30 (c) 20o on 15o dp red	1.10	.25
272 A30 (b) 40o on 30o #238F	.90	.25
Nos. 267-272 (6)	4.40	*5.80*
Set, never hinged	6.00	

Bering's Ship — A46

1941, Nov. 27 Engr. *Perf. 13*

277 A46 10o dk violet	.30	.20
278 A46 20o red brown	.60	.25
279 A46 40o dk blue	.35	.30
Nos. 277-279 (3)	1.25	.75
Set, never hinged	2.10	

Death of Vitus Bering, explorer, 200th anniv.

King Christian X — A47

1942-46 Unwmk. *Perf. 13*

280 A47 10o violet	.25	.20
281 A47 15o yel grn	.35	.20
282 A47 20o red	.35	.20
283 A47 25o brown ('43)	.60	.30
284 A47 30o orange ('43)	.45	.20
285 A47 35o brt red vio ('44)	.40	.20
286 A47 40o blue ('43)	.45	.20
286A A47 45o ol brn ('46)	.35	.20
286B A47 50o gray ('45)	.45	.20
287 A47 60o bluish grn ('44)	.45	.20
287A A47 75o dk blue ('46)	.40	.20
Nos. 280-287A (11)	4.50	2.30
Set, never hinged	8.00	

For overprints see Nos. Q28-Q30.

Round Tower — A48

Condor Plane — A49

1942, Nov. 27

288 A48 10o violet	.25	.20
Never hinged	.40	

300th anniv. of the Round Tower, Copenhagen.

For surcharge see No. B14.

1943, Oct. 29

289 A49 20o red	.25	.20
Never hinged	.35	

25th anniv. of the Danish Aviation Company (Det Danske Luftfartsselskab).

Ejby Church — A50

15ö, Oesterlars Church. 20ö, Hvidbjerg Church.

1944 Engr. *Perf. 13*

290 A50 10o violet	.25	.20
291 A50 15o yellow grn	.30	.35
292 A50 20o red	.25	.20
Nos. 290-292 (3)	.80	.75
Set, never hinged	1.00	

Ole Roemer A53

Christian X A54

1944, Sept. 25

293 A53 20o henna brown	.30	.20
Never hinged	.65	

Birth of Ole Roemer, astronomer, 300th anniv.

1945, Sept. 26
294 A54 10o lilac .20 .20
295 A54 20o red .20 .20
296 A54 40o deep blue .40 .25
Nos. 294-296 (3) .80 .65
Set, never hinged 1.10

75th birthday of King Christian X.

> **Catalogue values for unused stamps in this section, from this point to the end of the section, are for Never Hinged items.**

Small State Seal — A55

Tycho Brahe — A56

1946-47 Unwmk. *Perf. 13*
297 A55 1k brown .85 .20
298 A55 2k red ('47) .70 .20
299 A55 5k dull blue 1.25 .20
Nos. 297-299 (3) 2.80 .60

Nos. 297-299 issued on ordinary and fluorescent paper. Values for ordinary paper are much higher.

See Nos. 395-400, 441A-444D, 499-506, 643-650, 716-720A, 804-815, 909. For overprints see Nos. Q35, Q40, Q46-Q48.

1946, Dec. 14 Engr.
300 A56 20o dark red .40 .20

Birth of Tycho Brahe, astronomer, 400th anniv.

First Danish Locomotive A57

Modern Steam Locomotive A58

Diesel Locomotive A59

1947, June 27
301 A57 15o steel blue .40 .35
302 A58 20o red .90 .30
303 A59 40o deep blue 3.50 1.50
Nos. 301-303 (3) 4.80 2.15

Inauguration of the Danish State Railways, cent.

Jacobsen A60

Frederik IX A61

1947, Nov. 10 *Perf. 13*
304 A60 20o dark red .30 .20

60th anniv. of the death of Jacob Christian Jacobsen, founder of the Glyptothek Art Museum, Copenhagen.

1948-50 Unwmk. *Perf. 13*

Three types among 15ö, 20ö, 30ö:
I — Background of horizontal lines. No outline at left for cheek and ear. King's uniform textured in strong lines.
II — Background of vertical and horizontal lines. Contour of cheek and ear at left. Uniform same.
III — Background and facial contour lines as in II. Uniform lines double and thinner.

306 A61 15(o) green (II) 2.25 .20
a. Type III ('49) 1.60 .20
307 A61 20(o) dk red (I) .85 .20
a. Type III ('49) 1.00 .20
308 A61 25(o) lt brown 1.25 .20
309 A61 30(o) org (II) 13.00 .20
a. Type III ('50) 16.00 .20
310 A61 40(o) dl blue ('49) 4.50 .50
311 A61 45(o) olive ('50) 1.75 .20
312 A61 50(o) gray ('49) 1.75 .20
313 A61 60(o) grnsh bl ('50) 2.50 .20
314 A61 75(o) lil rose ('50) 1.40 .20
Nos. 306-314 (9) 29.25 2.10

See Nos. 319-326, 334-341, 354. For surcharges see Nos. 357-358, 370, B20, B24-B25, Q32-Q34, Q36-Q39.

Legislative Assembly, 1849 — A62

Symbol of UPU — A63

1949, June 5
315 A62 20o red brown .30 .20

Adoption of the Danish constitution, cent.

1949, Oct. 9
316 A63 40o dull blue .65 .40

75th anniv. of the UPU.

Kalundborg Radio Station and Masts — A64

1950, Apr. 1 Engr. *Perf. 13*
317 A64 20o brown red .40 .20

Radio broadcasting in Denmark, 25th anniv.

Types of 1933-50

1950-51 Unwmk. *Perf. 13*
318 A32 10o green .30 .20
319 A61 15(o) lilac .75 .20
b. 15(o) gray lilac 3.75 .25
320 A61 20(o) lt brown .55 .20
321 A61 25(o) dark red 3.75 .20
322 A61 35(o) gray grn ('51) .75 .20
323 A61 40(o) gray .85 .20
324 A61 50(o) dark blue 3.00 .20
325 A61 55(o) brown ('51) 24.00 2.00
326 A61 70(o) deep green 2.75 .20
Nos. 318-326 (9) 36.70 3.60

Warship of 1701 — A65

Oersted — A66

1951, Feb. 26 Engr. *Perf. 13*
327 A65 25o dark red .50 .25
328 A65 50o deep blue 3.00 .75

250th anniv. of the foundation of the Naval Officers' College.

1951, Mar. 9 Unwmk.
329 A66 50o blue 1.40 .60

Cent. of the death of Hans Christian Oersted, physicist.

Post Chaise ("Ball Post") — A67

Marine Rescue — A68

1951, Apr. 1 *Perf. 13*
330 A67 15o purple .60 .25
331 A67 25o henna brown .60 .25

Cent. of Denmark's 1st postage stamp.

1952, Mar. 26
332 A68 25o red brown .45 .30

Cent. of the foundation of the Danish Life-saving Service.

Types of 1933-50

1952-53 *Perf. 13*
333 A32 12o lt yel grn .30 .20
334 A61 25(o) lt blue 1.00 .20
335 A61 30(o) brown red .55 .20
336 A61 50(o) aqua ('53) .55 .20
337 A61 60(o) dp blue ('53) .75 .20
338 A61 65(o) gray ('53) .55 .20
339 A61 80(o) orange ('53) .85 .20
340 A61 90(o) olive ('53) 3.00 .20
341 A61 95(o) red org ('53) 1.00 .25
Nos. 333-341 (9) 8.55 1.85

Jelling Runic Stone — A69

Designs: 15o, Vikings' camp, Trelleborg. 20o, Church of Kalundborg. 30o, Nyborg castle. 60o, Goose tower, Vordinborg.

1953-56 *Perf. 13*
342 A69 10o dp green .20 .20
343 A69 15o lt rose vio .20 .20
344 A69 20o brown .20 .20
345 A69 30o red ('54) .25 .20
346 A69 60o dp blue ('54) .40 .20

Designs: 10o, Manor house, Spottrup. 15o, Hammershus castle ruins. 20o, Copenhagen stock exchange. 30o, Statue of Frederik V, Amalienborg. 60o, Soldier statue at Fredericia.

347 A69 10o green ('54) .20 .20
348 A69 15o lilac ('55) .20 .20
349 A69 20o brown ('55) .20 .20
350 A69 30o red ('55) .25 .20
351 A69 60o deep blue ('56) .50 .20
Nos. 342-351 (10) 2.60 2.00

1000th anniv. of the Kingdom of Denmark. Each stamp represents a different century.

Telegraph Equipment of 1854 A70

Frederik V A71

1954, Feb. 2 *Perf. 13*
352 A70 30o red brown .40 .25

Cent. of the telegraph in Denmark.

1954, Mar. 31
353 A71 30o dark red .55 .30

200th anniv. of the founding of the Royal Academy of Fine Arts.

Type of 1948-50

1955, Apr. 27
354 A61 25o lilac .35 .20

Nos. 224C and 226A Surcharged with New Value in Black. Nos. 307 and 321 Surcharged with New Value and 4 Bars

1955-56
355 A32 5o on 6o org .25 .20
356 A32 5o on 7o lt brn .25 .20
357 A61 30(o) on 20(o) dk red (I) .30 .20
a. Type III .35 .20
b. Double surcharge 1,050. 1,050.
c. Inverted surcharge 650.00
358 A61 30(o) on 25(o) dk red ('56) .60 .20
a. Double surcharge 1,050.
Nos. 355-358 (4) 1.40 .80

A72

A73

1955, Nov. 11 Unwmk.
359 A72 30o dark red .30 .20

100th anniv. of the death of Sören Kierkegaard, philosopher and theologian.

1956, Sept. 12 Engr.
360 A73 30o Ellehammer's plane .50 .20

50th anniv. of the 1st flight made by Jacob Christian Hansen Ellehammer in a heavier-than-air craft.

Northern Countries Issue

Whooper Swans — A74

1956, Oct. 30 *Perf. 13*
361 A74 30o rose red 1.60 .20
362 A74 60o ultramarine 1.40 .65

Issued to emphasize the close bonds among the northern countries: Denmark, Finland, Iceland, Norway and Sweden.

Prince's Palace A75

Harvester A76

Design: 60ö, Sun God's Chariot.

1957, May 15 Unwmk.
363 A75 30o dull red .85 .20
364 A75 60o dark blue .85 .45

150th anniv. of the National Museum.

1958, Sept. 4 Engr. *Perf. 13*
365 A76 30o fawn .30 .20

Centenary of the Royal Veterinary and Agricultural College.

Frederik IX A77

Ballet Dancer A78

1959, Mar. 11

366 A77 30o rose red .40 .20
367 A77 35o rose lilac .40 .35
368 A77 60o ultra .40 .20
Nos. 366-368 (3) 1.20 .75

King Frederik's 60th birthday.

1959, May 16

369 A78 35o rose lilac .30 .20

Danish Ballet and Music Festival, May 17-31. See Nos. 401, 422.

No. 319 Surcharged

1960, Apr. 7

370 A61 30o on 15o lilac .30 .20

World Refugee Year, 7/1/59-6/30/60.

Seeder and Farm A79

30ö, Harvester combine. 60ö, Plow.

1960, Apr. 28 Engr. *Perf. 13*

371 A79 12o green .20 .20
372 A79 30o dull red .30 .20
373 A79 60o dk blue .50 .20
Nos. 371-373 (3) 1.00 .60

King Frederik IX and Queen Ingrid — A80

1960, May 24 Unwmk.

374 A80 30o dull red .45 .20
375 A80 60o blue .45 .20

25th anniversary of the marriage of King Frederik IX and Queen Ingrid.

Bascule Light — A81

Finsen — A82

1960, June 8 Engr.

376 A81 30o dull red .30 .20

400th anniv. of the Lighthouse Service.

1960, Aug. 1 *Perf. 13*

377 A82 30o dark red .30 .20

Centenary of the birth of Dr. Niels R. Finsen, physician and scientist.

Nursing Mother — A83

DC-8 Airliner — A84

1960, Aug. 16 Unwmk.

378 A83 60o ultra .55 .20

10th meeting of the regional committee for Europe of WHO, Copenhagen, Aug. 16-20.

Europa Issue, 1960

Common Design Type

1960, Sept. 19 *Perf. 13*

Size: 28x21mm

379 CD3 60o ultra .55 .45

1961, Feb. 24

380 A84 60o ultra .70 .50

10th anniv. of the Scandinavian Airlines System, SAS.

Landscape A85

Frederik IX A86

1961, Apr. 21 *Perf. 13*

381 A85 30o copper brown .30 .20

Denmark's Soc. of Nature Lovers, 50th anniv.

Fluorescent Paper

as well as ordinary paper, was used in printing many definitive and commemorative stamps, starting in 1962. These include No. 220, 224; the 15, 20, 25, 30, 35 (Nos. 386 and 387), 50 and 60ö, 1.20k, 1.50k and 25k definitives of following set, and Nos. 297-299, 318, 333, 380, 401-427, 429-435, 438-439, 493, 543, 548, B30.

Only fluorescent paper was used for Nos. 436-437, 437A and 440 onward; in semipostals from B31 onward.

1961-63 Engr. *Perf. 13*

382 A32 15o green ('63) .20 .20
383 A86 20o brown .50 .20
384 A86 25o brown ('63) .25 .20
385 A86 30o rose red .65 .20
386 A86 35o olive grn .65 .50
387 A86 35o rose red ('63) .25 .20
388 A86 40o gray 1.00 .20
389 A86 50o aqua .65 .20
390 A86 60o ultra .85 .20
391 A86 70o green 1.60 .20
392 A86 80o red orange 1.60 .20
393 A86 90o olive bister 4.25 .20
394 A86 95o claret ('63) 1.00 .70
Nos. 382-394 (13) 13.45 3.40

See Nos. 417-419, 438-441. For overprints see Nos. Q41-Q42, Q44-Q45.

State Seal Type of 1946-47

1962-65

395 A55 1.10k lilac ('65) 4.25 1.40
396 A55 1.20k gray 3.75 .20
397 A55 1.25k orange 3.75 .20
398 A55 1.30k green ('65) 4.25 1.40
399 A55 1.50k red lilac 1.25 .20
400 A55 25k yellow grn 8.00 .30
Nos. 395-400 (6) 25.25 3.70

Dancer Type of 1959 Inscribed "15-31 MAJ"

1962, Apr. 26

401 A78 60o ultra .30 .20

Issued to publicize the Danish Ballet and Music Festival, May 15-31.

Old Mill — A87

M.S. Selandia — A88

1962, May 10 Unwmk. *Perf. 13*

402 A87 10o red brown .30 .20

Cent. of the abolition of mill monopolies.

1962, June 14 Engr.

403 A88 60o dark blue 1.60 1.40

M.S. Selandia, the 1st Diesel ship, 50th anniv.

Violin Scroll, Leaves, Lights and Balloon A89

1962, Aug. 31

404 A89 35o rose violet .30 .20

150th anniv. of the birth of Georg Carstensen, founder of Tivoli amusement park, Copenhagen.

Cliffs on Moen Island — A90

Germinating Wheat — A91

1962, Nov. 22

405 A90 20o pale brown .30 .20

Issued to publicize preservation of natural treasures and landmarks.

1963, Mar. 21 Engr.

406 A91 35o fawn .30 .20

FAO "Freedom from Hunger" campaign.

Railroad Wheel, Tire Tracks, Waves and Swallow — A92

Sailing Vessel, Coach, Postilions and Globe — A93

1963, May 14 Unwmk. *Perf. 13*

407 A92 15o green .30 .20

Inauguration of the "Bird Flight Line" railroad link between Denmark and Germany.

1963, May 27

408 A93 60o dark blue .45 .20

Cent. of the 1st Intl. Postal Conf., Paris, 1863.

Niels Bohr and Atom Diagram — A94

Early Public School Drawn on Slate — A95

1963, Nov. 21 Engr.

409 A94 35o red brown .35 .20
410 A94 60o dark blue .65 .20

50th anniv. of Prof. Niels Bohr's (1885-1962) atom theory.

1964, June 19 Unwmk. *Perf. 13*

411 A95 35o red brown .30 .20

150th anniversary of the royal decrees for the public school system.

Fish and Chart — A96

Danish Watermarks and Perforations A97

1964, Sept. 7 Engr.

412 A96 60o violet blue .35 .20

Conference of the International Council for the Exploration of the Sea, Copenhagen.

1964, Oct. 10 *Perf. 13*

413 A97 35o pink .30 .20

25th anniv. of Stamp Day and to publicize the Odense Stamp Exhibition, Oct. 10-11.

Landscape A98

Calculator, Ledger and Inkwell — A99

1964, Nov. 12 Engr.

414 A98 25o brown .30 .20

Issued to publicize preservation of natural treasures and landmarks.

1965, Mar. 8 Unwmk.

415 A99 15o light olive green .20 .20

First Business School in Denmark, cent.

Types of 1933 and 1961

1965, May 15 Engr. *Perf. 13*

416 A32 25o apple green .35 .20
417 A86 40o brown .35 .20
418 A86 50o rose red .40 .20
419 A86 80o ultra .95 .20
Nos. 416-419 (4) 2.05 .80

For overprints see Nos. Q41-Q42.

ITU Emblem, Telegraph Key, Teletype Paper A100

Carl Nielsen (1865-1931), Composer A101

1965, May 17

420 A100 80o dark blue .40 .20

Cent. of the ITU.

1965, June 9 Engr.

421 A101 50o brown red .35 .20

Dancer Type of 1959 Inscribed "15-31 MAJ"

1965, Sept. 23

422 A78 50o rose red .30 .20

Issued to publicize the Danish Ballet and Music Festival, May 15-31.

Bogo Windmill A102

Mylius Dalgas Surveying Wasteland A103

1965, Nov. 10 **Engr.** ***Perf. 13***
423 A102 40o brown .30 .20

Issued to publicize the preservation of natural treasures and landmarks.

1966, Feb. 24
424 A103 25o olive green .30 .20

Cent. of the Danish Heath Soc. (reclamation of wastelands), founded by Enrico Mylius Dalgas.

Christen Kold (1816-70), Educator — A104

1966, Mar. 29 ***Perf. 13***
425 A104 50o dull red .30 .20

Poorhouse, Copenhagen A105

Holte Allée, Bregentved A106

Dolmen (Grave) in Jutland — A107

1966 **Unwmk.**
426 A105 50o dull red .25 .20
427 A106 80o dk blue .55 .20
428 A107 1.50k dk slate grn .80 .20
Nos. 426-428 (3) 1.60 .60

Publicizing preservation of national treasures and ancient monuments. Issued: 50o, May 12; 80o, June 16; 1.50k, Nov. 24.

George Jensen by Ejnar Nielsen A108

Music Bar and Instruments A109

1966, Aug. 31 **Engr.** ***Perf. 13***
429 A108 80o dark blue .85 .30

George Jensen, silversmith, birth cent.

1967, Jan. 9
430 A109 50o dark red .50 .20

Royal Danish Academy of Music, cent.

Cogwheels, and Broken Customs Duty Ribbon — A110

1967, Mar. 2
431 A110 80o dark blue .80 .20

European Free Trade Association. Industrial tariffs were abolished Dec. 31, 1966, among EFTA members: Austria, Denmark, Finland, Great Britain, Norway, Portugal, Sweden and Switzerland.

Windmill and Medieval Fortress — A111

Designs: 40ö, Ship's rigging and baroque house front. 50ö, Old Town Hall. 80ö, New building construction.

1967 **Engr.** ***Perf. 13***
432 A111 25o green .40 .20
433 A111 40o sepia .35 .20
434 A111 50o red brown .35 .20
435 A111 80o dk blue .90 .30
Nos. 432-435 (4) 2.00 .90

The 800th anniversary of Copenhagen. Issued: #432-433, 4/6; #434-435, 5/11.

Princess Margrethe and Prince Henri — A112

1967, June 10
436 A112 50o red .30 .20

Marriage of Crown Princess Margrethe and Prince Henri de Monpezat.

Types of 1933-1961

1967-71 **Engr.** ***Perf. 13***

437	A32	30o dk green	.35	.25
437A	A32	40o orange ('71)	.35	.25
438	A86	50o brown	.60	.25
439	A86	60o rose red	.60	.25
440	A86	80o green	.60	.25
441	A86	90o ultra	.60	.25
441A	A55	1.20k Prus grn ('71)	1.75	.30
442	A55	2.20k orange	2.50	.25
443	A55	2.80k gray	2.50	.25
444	A55	2.90k rose vio	4.25	.25
444A	A55	3k dk sl grn ('69)	.95	.25
444B	A55	3.10k plum ('70)	7.75	.25
444C	A55	4k gray ('69)	1.40	.25
444D	A55	4.10k olive ('70)	7.75	.25
		Nos. 437-444D (14)	31.95	3.55

Issued: #437-441, 6/30/67; #442-443, 7/8/67; #444, 4/29/68; #444A, 444C, 8/28/69; #444B, 444D, 8/27/70; #437A, 441A, 6/24/71.
For overprints see Nos. Q44-Q45.

Sonne — A113

Cross-anchor and Porpoise — A114

1967, Sept. 21
445 A113 60o red .30 .20

150th anniv. of the birth of Hans Christian Sonne, pioneer of the cooperative movement in Denmark.

1967, Nov. 9 **Engr.** ***Perf. 13***
446 A114 90o dk blue .35 .25

Centenary of the Danish Seamen's Church in Foreign Ports.

Esbjerg Harbor — A115

Koldinghus A116

1968, Apr. 24
447 A115 30o dk yellow grn .30 .20

Centenary of Esbjerg Harbor.

1968, June 13
448 A116 60o copper red .35 .20

700th anniversary of Koldinghus Castle.

Shipbuilding Industry A117

Sower A118

Designs: 50o, Chemical industry. 60o, Electric power. 90o, Engineering.

1968, Oct. 24 **Engr.** ***Perf. 13***
449 A117 30o green .25 .20
450 A117 50o brown .25 .20
451 A117 60o red brown .25 .20
452 A117 90o dark blue .60 .30
Nos. 449-452 (4) 1.35 .90

Issued to publicize Danish industries.

1969, Jan. 29
453 A118 30o gray green .30 .20

Royal Agricultural Soc. of Denmark, 200th anniv.

Five Ancient Ships A119

Frederik IX A120

Nordic Cooperation Issue

1969, Feb. 28 **Engr.** ***Perf. 13***
454 A119 60o brown red .80 .20
455 A119 90o blue 1.25 .70

50th anniv. of the Nordic Soc. and cent. of postal cooperation among the northern countries. The design is taken from a coin found at the site of Birka, an ancient Swedish town. See also Finland No. 481, Iceland Nos. 404-405, Norway Nos. 523-524 and Sweden Nos. 808-810.

1969, Mar. 11
456 A120 50o sepia .30 .20
457 A120 60o dull red .30 .20

70th birthday of King Frederik IX.

Common Design Types pictured following the introduction.

Europa Issue, 1969
Common Design Type

1969, Apr. 28
Size: 28x20mm
458 CD12 90o chalky blue .70 .55

Kronborg Castle — A121

Danish Flag — A122

1969, May 22 **Engr.** ***Perf. 13***
459 A121 50o brown .30 .20

Association of Danes living abroad, 50th anniv.

1969, June 12
460 A122 60o bluish blk, red & gray .30 .20

750th anniversary of the fall of the Dannebrog (Danish flag) from heaven.

Nexo A123

Stensen A124

1969, Aug. 28
461 A123 80o deep green .35 .20

Centenary of the birth of Martin Andersen Nexo (1869-1954), novelist.

1969, Sept. 25
462 A124 1k deep brown .40 .20

300th anniv. of the publication of Niels Stensen's geological work "On Solid Bodies."

Abstract Design — A125

Symbolic Design — A126

1969, Nov. 10 **Engr.** ***Perf. 13***
463 A125 60o rose, red & ultra .30 .20

1969, Nov. 20
464 A126 30o olive green .30 .20

Valdemar Poulsen (1869-1942), electrical engineer and inventor.

Post Office Bank — A127

School Safety Patrol — A128

1970, Jan. 15 **Engr.** ***Perf. 13***
465 A127 60o dk red & org .30 .20

50th anniv. of post office banking service.

1970, Feb. 19
466 A128 50o brown .30 .20

Issued to publicize road safety.

Candle in Window A129

Deer A130

1970, May 4 Engr. *Perf. 13*
467 A129 50o slate, dull bl & yel .30 .20

25th anniv. of liberation from the Germans.

1970, May 28
468 A130 60o yel grn, red & brn .30 .20

Tercentenary of Jaegersborg Deer Park.

Elephant Figurehead, 1741 A131

"The Homecoming" by Povl Christensen A132

1970, June 15 *Perf. 11½*
469 A131 30o multicolored .30 .20

Royal Naval Museum, tercentenary.

1970, June 15 *Perf. 13*
470 A132 60o org, dl vio & ol grn .30 .20

Union of North Schleswig and Denmark, 50th anniv.

Electromagnet A133

1970, Aug. 13 Engr.
471 A133 80o gray green .35 .20

150th anniversary of Hans Christian Oersted's discovery of electromagnetism.

Bronze Age Ship A134

Ships: 50o, Viking shipbuilding, from Bayeux tapestry. 60o, Thuroe schooner with topgallant. 90o, Tanker.

1970, Sept. 24
472 A134 30o ocher & brown .30 .20
473 A134 50o brn red & rose brn .30 .20
474 A134 60o gray ol & red brn .55 .20
475 A134 90o blue grn & ultra .85 .60
Nos. 472-475 (4) 2.00 1.20

UN Emblem A135

1970, Oct. 22 Engr. *Perf. 13*
476 A135 90o blue, grn & red 1.00 .75

25th anniversary of the United Nations.

Bertel Thorvaldsen A136

Mathide Fibiger A137

1970, Nov. 19
477 A136 2k slate blue .70 .20

Bicentenary of the birth of Bertel Thorvaldsen (1768-1844), sculptor.

1971, Feb. 25
478 A137 80o olive green .30 .20

Danish Women's Association centenary.

Refugees A138

Hans Egede A139

1971, Mar. 26 Engr. *Perf. 13*
479 A138 50o brown .25 .20
480 A138 60o brown red .35 .20

Joint northern campaign for the benefit of refugees.

1971, May 27
481 A139 1k brown .40 .20

250th anniversary of arrival of Hans Egede in Greenland and beginning of its colonization.

A140

A141

1971, Oct. 14
482 A140 30o Swimming .25 .20
483 A140 50o Gymnastics .40 .20
484 A140 60o Soccer .55 .20
485 A140 90o Sailing .80 .45
Nos. 482-485 (4) 2.00 1.05

1971, Nov. 11 Engr. *Perf. 13*
486 A141 90o dark blue .40 .20

Centenary of first lectures given by Georg Brandes (1842-1927), writer and literary critic.

A142

A143

1972, Jan. 27
487 A142 80o slate green .40 .20

Centenary of Danish sugar production.

1972, Mar. 11 Engr. *Perf. 13*
488 A143 60o red brown .30 .20

Frederik IX (1899-1972).

Abstract Design A144

1972, Mar. 11
489 A144 1.20k brt rose lil, bl gray & brn .60 .50

Danish Meteorological Institute, cent.

Nikolai F. S. Grundtvig A145

Locomotive, 1847, Ferry, Travelers A146

1972, May 4 Engr. *Perf. 13*
490 A145 1k sepia .50 .20

Nikolai Frederik Severin Grundtvig (1783-1872), theologian and poet.

1972, June 26
491 A146 70o rose red .35 .20

125th anniversary of Danish State Railways.

Rebild Hills A147

"Tinker Turned Politician" A148

1972, June 26
492 A147 1k bl, sl grn & mar .40 .20

Types of 1933-46

1972-78 Engr. *Perf. 13*
493 A32 20o slate bl ('74) .35 .20
494 A32 50o sepia ('74) .35 .20
a. Bklt. pane of 12 (4 #318, 4 #493, 4 #494) ('85) 3.50
495 A32 60o apple grn ('76) 1.75 .55
496 A32 60o gray ('78) .70 .60
497 A32 70o red .90 .20
498 A32 70o apple grn ('77) .35 .20
499 A55 2.50k orange 1.75 .20
500 A55 2.80k olive ('75) 1.25 .80
501 A55 3.50k lilac 2.00 .20
502 A55 4.5k olive 5.00 .20
503 A55 6k vio blk ('76) 1.75 .20
504 A55 7k red lilac ('78) 2.25 .20
505 A55 9k brown ol ('77) 3.25 .20
506 A55 10k lemon ('76) 3.00 .20
Nos. 493-506 (14) 24.65 4.15

1972, Sept. 14
507 A148 70o dark red .35 .20

250th anniv. of the comedies of Ludvig Holberg (1684-1754) on the Danish stage.

WHO Building, Copenhagen — A149

1972, Sept. 14
508 A149 2k bl, blk & lt red brn .70 .35

Opening of WHO Building, Copenhagen.

Bridge Across Little Belt A150

Aeroskobing House c. 1740 A151

Highway engineering (Diagrams): 60o, Hanstholm Harbor. 70o, Lim Fjord Tunnel. 90o, Knudshoved Harbor.

1972, Oct. 19 Engr. *Perf. 13*
509 A150 40o dk green .20 .20
510 A150 60o dk brown .30 .20
511 A150 70o dk red .30 .20
512 A150 90o dk blue grn .40 .20
Nos. 509-512 (4) 1.20 .80

1972, Nov. 23

Danish Architecture: 60o, East Bornholm farmhouse, 17th century, horiz. 70o, House, Christianshavn, c. 1710. 1.20k, Hvide Sande Farmhouse, c. 1810, horiz.

Size: 20x28mm, 27x20mm

513 A151 40o red, brn & blk .35 .25
514 A151 60o blk, vio bl & grn .35 .25

Size: 18x37mm, 36x20mm

515 A151 70o red, dk red & blk .45 .20
516 A151 1.20k dk brn, red & grn .60 .55
Nos. 513-516 (4) 1.75 1.25

Jensen A152

Guard Rails, Cogwheels A153

1973, Feb. 22 Engr. *Perf. 13*
517 A152 90o green .40 .20

Centenary of the birth of Johannes Vilhelm Jensen (1873-1950), lyric poet and novelist.

1973, Mar. 22
518 A153 50o sepia .30 .20

Centenary of first Danish Factory Act for labor protection.

Abildgaard A154

Rhododendron A155

1973, Mar. 22
519 A154 1k dull blue .60 .60

Bicentenary of Royal Veterinary College, Christianshaven, founded by Prof. P. C. Abildgaard.

1973, Apr. 26

Design: 70o, Dronningen of Denmark rose.

520 A155 60o brn, grn & vio .50 .25
521 A155 70o dk red, rose & grn .50 .25

Centenary of the founding of the Horticultural Society of Denmark.

Nordic Cooperation Issue 1973

Nordic House, Reykjavik A156

1973, June 26 Engr. *Perf. 13*

522 A156 70o multicolored .50 .20
523 A156 1k multicolored 1.50 1.00

A century of postal cooperation among Denmark, Finland, Iceland, Norway and Sweden, and in connection with the Nordic Postal Conference, Reykjavik.

Sextant, Stella Nova, Cassiopeia
A157

St. Mark, from 11th Cent. Book of Dalby
A158

1973, Oct. 18 Engr. *Perf. 13*

524 A157 2k dark blue .70 .20

400th anniversary of the publication of "De Nova Stella," by Tycho Brahe.

1973, Oct. 18 Photo. *Perf. 14x14½*

525 A158 120o buff & multi 1.00 .65

300th anniversary of Royal Library.

Devil and Gossips, Fanefjord Church, 1480 — A159

Frescoes: No. 527, Queen Esther and King Ahasuerus, Tirsted Church, c.1400. No. 528, Miraculous Harvest, Jetsmark Church, c.1474. No. 529, Jesus carrying cross, and wearing crown of thorns, Biersted Church, c.1400. No. 530, Creation of Eve, Fanefjord Church, c.1480.

1973, Nov. 28 Engr. *Perf. 13*

Cream Paper

526 A159 70o dk red, yel & grn 1.25 .30
527 A159 70o dk red, yel & grn 1.25 .30
528 A159 70o dk red, yel & grn 1.25 .30
529 A159 70o dk red, yel & grn 1.25 .30
530 A159 70o dk red, yel & grn 1.25 .30
a. Bklt. pane, 2 each #526-530 35.00
b. Strip of 5, #526-530 6.25

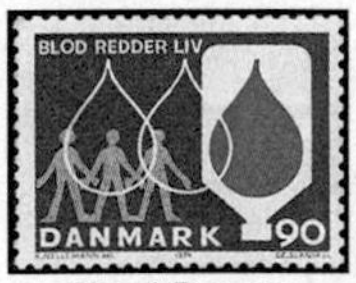

Blood Donors
A160

Queen Margrethe
A161

1974, Jan. 24

531 A160 90o purple & red .50 .20

"Blood Saves Lives."

1974-81 Engr. *Perf. 13*

532 A161 60o brown .50 .30
533 A161 60o orange .45 .20
534 A161 70o red .45 .20
535 A161 70o dk brown .45 .20
536 A161 80o green .50 .20
537 A161 80o dp brn ('76) .45 .20
538 A161 90o red lilac .50 .20
539 A161 90o dull red .45 .20
540 A161 90o slate grn ('76) .50 .20
541 A161 100o dp ultra .50 .20
542 A161 100o gray ('75) .50 .20
543 A161 100o red ('76) .50 .20
544 A161 100o brown ('77) .50 .20
a. Bklt. pane of 5 (#544, #494, 2 #493, #318) 1.75
545 A161 110o orange ('78) .55 .20
546 A161 120o slate .65 .40
547 A161 120o red ('77) .50 .20
548 A161 130o ultra ('75) 1.25 .95
549 A161 150o vio bl ('78) .65 .65
550 A161 180o slate grn ('77) .50 .30
551 A161 200o blue ('81) .85 .85
Nos. 532-551 (20) 11.20 6.25

See #630, 632-642. For overprint see #Q49.

Pantomime Theater — A162

Hverringe
A163

1974, May 16

552 A162 100o indigo .45 .20

Cent. of the Pantomime Theater, Tivoli.

1974, June 20 Engr. *Perf. 13*

Views: 60o, Norre Lyndelse, Carl Nielsen's childhood home. 70o, Odense, Hans Chr. Andersen's childhood home. 90o, Hesselagergaard, vert. 120o, Hindsholm.

553 A163 50o brown & multi .45 .20
554 A163 60o sl grn & multi .40 .25
555 A163 70o red brn & multi .40 .25
556 A163 90o dk green & mar .55 .20
557 A163 120o red org & dk grn .70 .45
Nos. 553-557 (5) 2.50 1.35

Emblem, Runner with Map — A164

Iris — A165

1974, Aug. 22 Engr. *Perf. 13*

558 A164 70o shown .45 .30
559 A164 80o Compass .45 .30

World Orienteering Championships 1974.

1974, Sept. 19

560 A165 90o shown .45 .20
561 A165 120o Purple orchid .65 .30

Copenhagen Botanical Garden centenary.

Mailman, 1624, and Postilion, 1780 — A166

Carrier Pigeon — A167

Design: 90o, Balloon and sailing ships.

1974, Oct. 9 Engr. *Perf. 13*

562 A166 70o lemon & dk brn .30 .35
563 A166 90o dull grn & sepia .40 .20
564 A167 120o dark blue .55 .30
Nos. 562-564 (3) 1.25 .85

350th anniv. of Danish PO (70o, 90o) and cent. of UPU (120o).

Souvenir Sheet

Ferslew's Essays, 1849 and 1852 — A168

Engraved and Photogravure

1975, Feb. 27 *Perf. 13*

565 A168 Sheet of 4 7.25 *8.50*
a. 70o Coat of arms 1.75 *2.00*
b. 80o King Frederik VII 1.75 *2.00*
c. 90o King Frederik VII 1.75 *2.00*
d. 100o Mercury 1.75 *2.00*

HAFNIA 76 Intl. Stamp Exhib., Copenhagen, Aug. 20-29, 1976. Sold for 5k.
See No. 585.

Early Radio Equipment
A169

Flora Danica Plate
A170

1975, Mar. 20 Engr. *Perf. 13*

566 A169 90o dull red .40 .20

Danish broadcasting, 50th anniversary.

1975, May 22

Danish China: 90o, Flora Danica tureen. 130o, Vase and tea caddy, blue fluted china.

567 A170 50o slate grn .30 .20
568 A170 90o brown red .60 .20
569 A170 130o violet bl .90 .90
Nos. 567-569 (3) 1.80 1.30

Church of Moravian Brethren, Christiansfeld
A171

120o, Kongsgaard farmhouse, Lejre. 150o, Anna Queenstraede, Helsingor, vert.

1975, June 19

570 A171 70o sepia .30 .25
571 A171 120o olive green 1.10 .30
572 A171 150o violet black .50 .20
Nos. 570-572 (3) 1.90 .75

European Architectural Heritage Year 1975.

Andersen
A172

Watchman's Square, Abenra
A173

Designs: 70o, Numbskull Jack, drawing by Vilh. Pedersen. 130o, The Marshking's Daughter, drawing by L. Frohlich.

1975, Aug. 28 Engr. *Perf. 13*

573 A172 70o brown & blk .60 .55
574 A172 90o brn red & dk brn 1.10 .30
575 A172 130o blue blk & sepia 1.40 1.40
Nos. 573-575 (3) 3.10 2.25

Hans Christian Andersen (1805-75), writer.

1975, Sept. 25

Designs: 90o, Haderslev Cathedral, vert. 100o, Mögeltönder Polder. 120o, Mouth of Vidaaen at Höjer Floodgates.

576 A173 70o multicolored .30 .25
577 A173 90o multicolored .40 .20
578 A173 100o multicolored .40 .25
579 A173 120o multicolored .65 .35
Nos. 576-579 (4) 1.75 1.05

European Kingfisher
A174

1975, Oct. 23 Engr. *Perf. 13*

580 A174 50o shown .45 .25
581 A174 70o Hedgehog .45 .25
582 A174 90o Cats .45 .20
583 A174 130o Avocets .85 .75
584 A174 200o Otter .70 .20
Nos. 580-584 (5) 2.90 1.65

Protected animals, and for the centenary of the Danish Society for the Prevention of Cruelty to Animals (90ö).

HAFNIA Type of 1974
Souvenir Sheet

1975, Nov. 20 Engr. & Photo.

585 A168 Sheet of 4 4.50 *6.00*
a. 50o buff & brown, No. 2 1.10 *1.40*
b. 70o buff, brown & blue, No. 1 1.10 *1.40*
c. 90o buff, blue & brown, No. 11 1.10 *1.40*
d. 130o olive, brown & buff, No. 19 1.10 *1.40*

HAFNIA 76 Intl. Stamp Exhib., Copenhagen, Aug. 20-29, 1976. Sold for 5k.

Copenhagen, Center — A175

View from Round Tower — A176

Copenhagen, Views: 100o, Central Station, interior. 130o, Harbor.

1976, Mar. 25 Engr. *Perf. 12½*

586 A175 60o multicolored .50 .20
587 A176 80o multicolored .50 .20
588 A176 100o multicolored .30 .20
589 A175 130o multicolored 1.50 1.50
Nos. 586-589 (4) 2.80 2.10

Postilion, by Otto Bache
A177

Emil Chr. Hansen, Physiologist, in Laboratory
A178

1976, June 17 Engr. *Perf. 12½*

590 A177 130o multicolored 1.25 1.25

Souvenir Sheet

591 A177 130o multicolored 9.25 *10.50*

HAFNIA 76 Intl. Stamp Exhib., Copenhagen, Aug. 20-29. No. 591 contains one stamp similar to No. 590 with design continuous into sheet margin. Sheet shows painting "A String of Horses Outside an Inn" of which No. 590

shows a detail. Sheet sold for 15k including exhibition ticket.

1976, Sept. 23 Engr. *Perf. 13*
592 A178 100o orange red .40 .20

Carlsberg Foundation (art and science), centenary.

Glass Blower Molding Glass — A179

Five Water Lilies — A180

Danish Glass Production: 80o, Finished glass removed from pipe. 130o, Glass cut off from foot. 150o, Glass blown up in mold.

1976, Nov. 18 Engr. *Perf. 13*
593 A179 60o slate .30 .25
594 A179 80o dk brown .35 .25
595 A179 130o dk blue 1.00 .90
596 A179 150o red brown .70 .25
Nos. 593-596 (4) 2.35 1.65

Photogravure and Engraved

1977, Feb. 2 *Perf. 12½*
597 A180 100o brt green & multi .50 .30
598 A180 130o ultra & multi 1.50 1.40

Nordic countries cooperation for protection of the environment and 25th Session of Nordic Council, Helsinki, Feb. 19.

Road Accident — A181

Europa — A182

1977, Mar. 24 Engr. *Perf. 12½*
599 A181 100o brown red .40 .20

Road Safety Traffic Act, May 1, 1977.

1977, May 2 Engr. *Perf. 12½*
600 A182 1k Allinge .50 *.45*
601 A182 1.30k View, Ringsted *2.25 2.25*

Kongeaen A183

Hammers and Horseshoes A184

Landscapes, Southern Jutland: 90o, Skallingen. 150o, Torskind. 200o, Jelling.

1977, June 30 Engr. *Perf. 12½*
602 A183 60o multicolored 1.00 .90
603 A183 90o multicolored .50 .30
604 A183 150o multicolored .60 .35
605 A183 200o multicolored .75 .25
Nos. 602-605 (4) 2.85 1.80

See Nos. 616-619, 655-658, 666-669.

1977, Sept. 22 Engr. *Perf. 12½*

Designs: 1k, Chisel, square and plane. 1.30k, Trowel, ceiling brush and folding ruler.

606 A184 80o dk brown .30 .25
607 A184 1k red .40 .20
608 A184 1.30k violet bl .70 .30
Nos. 606-608 (3) 1.40 .75

Danish crafts.

Globe Flower — A185

Handball — A186

Endangered Flora: 1.50k, Cnidium dubium.

1977, Nov. 17 Engr. *Perf. 12½*
609 A185 1k multicolored .50 .25
610 A185 1.50k multicolored 1.25 .65

1978, Jan. 19 *Perf. 12½*
611 A186 1.20k red .30 .20

Men's World Handball Championships.

Christian IV, Frederiksborg Castle A187

Frederiksborg Museum A188

1978, Mar. 16
612 A187 1.20k brown red .40 .20
613 A188 1.80k black .70 .30

Frederiksborg Museum, centenary.

Europa Issue

Jens Bang's House, Aalborg A189

Frederiksborg Castle, Ground Plan and Elevation A190

1978, May 11 Engr. *Perf. 12½*
614 A189 1.20k red *.55* .20
615 A190 1.50k dk bl & vio bl *1.25 .70*

Landscape Type of 1977

Landscapes, Central Jutland: 70o, Kongenshus Memorial Park. 120o, Post Office, Old Town in Aarhus. 150o, Lignite fields, Soby. 180o, Church wall, Stadil Church.

1978, June 15 Engr. *Perf. 12½*
616 A183 70o multicolored .30 .20
617 A183 120o multicolored .55 .20
618 A183 150o multicolored .70 .45
619 A183 180o multicolored .85 .40
Nos. 616-619 (4) 2.40 1.25

Boats in Harbor — A191

Edible Morel — A192

Danish fishing industry: 1k, Eel traps. 1.80k, Boats in berth. 2.50k, Drying nets.

1978, Sept. 7 Engr. *Perf. 12½*
620 A191 70o olive gray .45 .20
621 A191 1k redsh brown .45 .20
622 A191 1.80k slate .45 .20
623 A191 2.50k sepia 1.00 .35
Nos. 620-623 (4) 2.35 .95

1978, Nov. 16 Engr. *Perf. 12½*

Design: 1.20k, Satan's mushroom.

624 A192 1k sepia .60 .40
625 A192 1.20k dull red .90 .40

Telephones — A193

1979, Jan. 25 Engr. *Perf. 12½*
626 A193 1.20k dull red .45 .20

Centenary of Danish telephone.

University Seal A194

Pentagram: University Faculties A195

1979, Apr. 5 Engr. *Perf. 12½*
627 A194 1.30k vermilion .45 .20
628 A195 1.60k dk vio blue .60 .55

University of Copenhagen, 500th anniv.

Types of 1933-1974

1979-82 Engr. *Perf. 13*
629 A32 80o green .40 .20
630 A161 90o slate 2.00 1.75
631 A32 100o dp green ('81) .50 .20
632 A161 110o brown .65 .20
a. Bklt. pane, #493-494, 632, 2 #318 ('79) 1.50
633 A161 130o red .55 .20
a. Bklt. pane, 2 ea #494, 629, 632, 4 #633 ('79) 6.50
634 A161 130o brown ('81) .65 .40
635 A161 140o red org ('80) 1.40 1.40
636 A161 150o red org ('81) .70 .65
637 A161 160o ultra .95 .90
638 A161 160o red ('81) .65 .20
a. Bklt. pane, 2 ea #318, 634, 638, 8 #494) 12.00
639 A161 180o ultra ('80) 1.25 1.10
640 A161 210o gray ('80) 1.40 1.40
641 A161 230o ol grn ('81) 1.25 .40
642 A161 250o blue grn ('81) 1.25 .70
643 A55 2.80k dull grn .95 .20
644 A55 3.30k brn red ('81) 1.25 .55
645 A55 3.50k grnsh bl ('82) 2.00 2.00
646 A55 4.30k brn red ('80) 2.00 2.00
647 A55 4.70k rose lil ('81) 2.50 2.50
648 A55 8k orange 2.40 .20
649 A55 12k red brn ('81) 4.00 .55
650 A55 14k dk red brn ('82) 4.50 .70
Nos. 629-650 (22) 33.20 18.40

A196

A197

Europa: 1.30k, Mail cart, 1785. 1.60k, Morse key and amplifier.

1979, May 10 Engr. *Perf. 12½*
651 A196 1.30k red *.85* .20
652 A196 1.60k dark blue *1.25* .70

1979, June 14 Engr. *Perf. 13*

Viking Art: 1.10k, Gripping beast pendant. 2k, Key with gripping beast design.

653 A197 1.10k sepia .50 .20
654 A197 2k grnsh gray .90 .35

Landscape Type of 1977

Landscapes, Northern Jutland: 80o, Mols Bjerge. 90o, Orslev Kloster. 200o, Trans. 280o, Bovbjerg.

1979, Sept. 6 Engr. *Perf. 12½*
655 A183 80o multicolored .45 .45
656 A183 90o multicolored 1.10 .90
657 A183 200o multicolored .90 .35
658 A183 280o multicolored 1.10 .80
Nos. 655-658 (4) 3.55 2.50

Adam Oehlenschläger (1799-1850), Poet and Dramatist A198

1979, Oct, 4 Engr. *Perf. 13*
659 A198 1.30k dk carmine .50 .25

Score, Violin, Dancing Couple — A199

Ballerina — A200

1979, Nov. 8 Engr. *Perf. 13x12½*
660 A199 1.10k brown .35 .20
661 A200 1.60k ultra .65 .30

Jacob Gade (1879-63), composer; August Bournonville (1805-79), ballet master.

Royal Mail Guards' Office, Copenhagen, 1779 — A201

1980, Feb. 14 Engr. *Perf. 13*
662 A201 1.30k brown red .50 .25

National Postal Service, 200th anniversary.

Symbols of Occupation, Health and Education A202

1980, May 5 Engr. *Perf. 13*
663 A202 1.60k dark blue .65 .50

World Conference of the UN Decade for Women, Copenhagen, July 14-30.

Karen Blixen (1885-1962), Writer (Pen Name Isak Dinesen) — A203

Europa: 1.60k, August Krogh (1874-1949), physiologist.

1980, May 5
664 A203 1.30k red *.55* .20
665 A203 1.60k blue *1.10* .55

Landscape Type of 1977

Northern Jutland: 80o, Viking ship burial grounds, Lindholm Hoje. 110o, Lighthouse, Skagen, vert. 200o, Boreglum Monastery. 280o, Fishing boats, Vorupor Beach.

1980, June 19 Engr. *Perf. 13*
666 A183 80o multicolored .35 .35
667 A183 110o multicolored .45 .45
668 A183 200o multicolored .70 .30
669 A183 280o multicolored 1.50 1.50
Nos. 666-669 (4) 3.00 2.60

Nordic Cooperation Issue

Silver Tankard, by Borchardt Rollufse, 1641 — A204

1980, Sept. 9 Engr. *Perf. 13*
670 A204 1.30k shown .50 .35
671 A204 1.80k Bishop's bowl, Copenhagen faience, 18th cent. 1.10 *1.10*

Frisian Sceat Facsimile, Obverse and Reverse, 9th Century
A205

Coins: 1.40k Silver coin of Valdemar the Great and Absalom, 1157-1182, 1.80k, Gold 12-mark coin of Christian VII, 1781.

1980, Oct. 9 Engr. *Perf. 13*
672 A205 1.30k red & redsh brn .50 .45
673 A205 1.40k ol gray & sl grn 1.25 *1.25*
674 A205 1.80k dk bl & sl bl 1.10 *1.10*
Nos. 672-674 (3) 2.85 *2.80*

Tonder Lace Pattern, North Schleswig — A206

Designs: Tonder lace patterns.

1980, Nov. 13 Engr. *Perf. 13*
675 A206 1.10k brown .40 .45
676 A206 1.30k brown red .50 .30
677 A206 2k olive gray .70 .30
Nos. 675-677 (3) 1.60 1.05

Nyboder Development, Copenhagen, 350th Anniversary A207

Design: 1.30k, View of Nyboder, diff.

1981, Mar. 19
678 A207 1.30k dp org & ocher .80 .80
679 A207 1.60k dp org & ocher .55 .30

Tilting at a Barrel on Shrovetide A208

Design: 2k, Midsummer's Eve bonfire.

1981, May 4 Engr. *Perf. 13*
680 A208 1.60k brown red *.50* .20
681 A208 2k dk blue *.90* *.50*

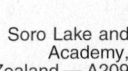

Soro Lake and Academy, Zealand — A209

Designs: Views of Zealand.

1981, June 18 Engr. *Perf. 13*
682 A209 100o shown .35 .35
683 A209 150o Poet N.F.S. Grundtvig's home, Udby .60 .60
684 A209 160o Kaj Munk's home, Opager .60 .30
685 A209 200o Gronsund .80 .80
686 A209 230o Bornholm Isld. .85 .80
Nos. 682-686 (5) 3.20 2.85

European Urban Renaissance Year — A210

1981, Sept. 10 Engr. *Perf. 12½x13*
687 A210 1.60k dull red .65 .25

Type of 1933

1981-85 Engr. *Perf. 13*
688 A32 30o orange .35 .35
a. Bklt. pane 10 (2 #318, 2 #688, 6 #494)('84) 2.75
689 A32 40o purple .35 .35
a. Bklt. pane of 10 (4 #318, 2 #689, 4 #494) ('89) 2.25
690 A32 80o ol bis ('85) .50 .50
691 A32 100o blue ('83) .70 .35
b. Bklt. pane of 8 (2 #494, 4 #691, 2 #706) ('83) 8.50
692 A32 150o dk green ('82) .50 .35
693 A32 200o green ('83) .70 .70
694 A32 230o brt yel grn ('84) .85 .35
695 A32 250o brt yel grn ('85) 1.10 .70
Nos. 688-695 (8) 5.05 3.65

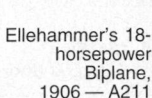

Ellehammer's 18-horsepower Biplane, 1906 — A211

1981, Oct. 8 Engr. *Perf. 13*
696 A211 1k shown .45 .45
697 A211 1.30k R-1 Fokker CV reconnaissance plane, 1926 1.00 1.00
698 A211 1.60k Bellanca J-300, 1931 .55 .30
699 A211 2.30k DC-7C, 1957 .85 .70
Nos. 696-699 (4) 2.85 2.45

Queen Margrethe II, 10th Anniv. of Accession — A212

1982-85 Engr. *Perf. 13*
700 A212 1.60k dull red .60 .25
701 A212 1.60k dk ol grn 2.10 2.10
702 A212 1.80k sepia .65 .45
703 A212 2k dull red .90 .25
b. Bklt. pane, 4 #494, 2 ea #493, 702, 703 12.00
704 A212 2.20k ol grn ('83) .85 .35
705 A212 2.30k violet .75 .25
706 A212 2.50k org red ('83) 2.75 2.75
707 A212 2.70k dk blue .85 .65
708 A212 2.70k cop red ('84) 1.25 .25
c. Booklet pane, 3 #688, 2 #494, 3 #708 ('84) 6.00
709 A212 2.80k cop red ('85) 1.00 .25
b. Booklet pane, 3 #493, 2 #494, 3 #709 ('85) 4.50
710 A212 3k violet ('83) 1.00 .25
711 A212 3.30k bluish blk ('84) 1.50 .60
712 A212 3.50k blue ('83) 2.10 2.10
713 A212 3.50k dk vio ('85) 1.75 .95
714 A212 3.70k dp blue ('85) 1.25 .35
715 A212 3.80k dk blue ('85) 1.50 .25

See Nos. 796-803, 887, 889, 896, 899.

Arms Type of 1946

Engr. *Perf. 13*
716 A55 4.30k dk ol grn ('84) 4.00 4.00
717 A55 5.50k dk bl grn ('84) 2.40 2.40
718 A55 16k cop red ('83) 4.75 .65
719 A55 17k cop red ('84) 6.75 1.40
720 A55 18k brn vio ('85) 6.75 1.00
720A A55 50k dk red ('85) 13.50 2.00
Nos. 700-720A (22) 58.95 23.50

World Figure Skating Championships A213

1982, Feb. 25
721 A213 2k dark blue .75 .30

A214

A215

1982, Feb. 25 Engr. *Perf. 12½*
722 A214 1.60k Revenue schooner Argus .60 .25

Customs Service centenary

1982, May 3 Engr. *Perf. 12½*
723 A215 2k Abolition of adscription, 1788 *1.00* .20
724 A215 2.70k Women's voting right, 1915 *1.25* *.60*

Europa.

Butter Churn, Barn, Hjedding — A216

Records Office, 400th Anniv. — A217

1982, June 10 Engr. *Perf. 13*
725 A216 1.80k brown .75 .75

Cooperative dairy farming centenary.

1982, June 10
726 A217 2.70k green 1.10 .40

Steen Steensen Blicher (1782-1848), Poet, by J.V. Gertner — A218

1982, Aug. 26 Engr. *Perf. 13*
727 A218 2k brown red .75 .30

Robert Storm Petersen (1882-1949), Cartoonist A219

Printing in Denmark, 500th Anniv. A220

Characters: 1.50k, Three little men and the number man. 2k, Peter and Ping the penguin, horiz.

1982, Sept. 23 Engr. *Perf. 12½*
728 A219 1.50k dk bl & red .70 .45
729 A219 2k red & ol grn .90 .40

1982, Sept. 23
730 A220 1.80k Press, text, ink balls .75 .75

A221

A222

1982, Nov. 4
731 A221 2.70k Library seal 1.00 .50

500th anniv. of University Library.

1983, Jan. 27 Engr. *Perf. 13*
732 A222 2k multicolored .80 .30

World Communications Year.

Amusement Park, 400th Anniv. A223

Badminton Championship A224

1983, Feb. 24
733 A223 2k multicolored .80 .30

1983, Feb. 24
734 A224 2.70k multicolored 1.10 .40

Nordic Cooperation Issue — A225

1983, Mar. 24
735 A225 2.50k Egeskov Castle 1.00 .40
736 A225 3.50k Troll Church, North Jutland 1.40 .60

50th Anniv. of Steel Plate Printed Stamps — A226

1983, Mar. 24 Engr. *Perf. 13*
737 A226 2.50k car rose 1.00 .30

Europa 1983 — A227

Weights and Measures Ordinance, 300th Anniv. — A228

2.50k, Kildekovshallen Recreation Center, Copenhagen. 3.50k, Salling Sound Bridge.

1983, May 5 Engr. *Perf. 13*
738 A227 2.50k multicolored *1.00* .20
739 A227 3.50k multicolored *1.25* *.45*

1983, June 16
740 A228 2.50k red 1.00 .30

A229

A230

1983, Sept. 8 **Engr.**
741 A229 5k Codex titlepage 1.75 .60

Christian V Danish law, 300th anniv.

1983, Oct. 6 **Engr.** ***Perf. 13***
742 A230 1k Car crash, police .40 .25
743 A230 2.50k Fire, ambulance service 1.00 .35
744 A230 3.50k Sea rescue 1.40 .75
Nos. 742-744 (3) 2.80 1.35

Life saving and salvage services.

Elderly in Society — A231

1983, Oct. 6
745 A231 2k Stages of life .80 .60
746 A231 2.50k Train passengers 1.00 .30

N.F.S. Grundtvig (1783-1872), Poet — A232

Street Scene, by C.W. Eckersberg (1783-1853) — A233

1983, Nov. 3 **Engr.**
747 A232 2.50k brown red 1.00 .30
748 A233 2.50k brown red 1.00 .30

A234

A235

1984, Jan. 26 **Litho. & Engr.**
749 A234 2.70k Shovel, sapling 1.10 .30

Plant a tree campaign.

1984, Jan. 26 **Engr.**
750 A235 3.70k Game 1.50 .45

1984 Billiards World Championships, Copenhagen, May 10-13.

Hydrographic Dept. Bicentenary A236

Pilotage Service, 300th Anniv. — A237

1984, Mar. 22 **Engr.** ***Perf. 13***
751 A236 2.30k Compass .90 .90
752 A237 2.70k Boat 1.10 .30

2nd European Parliament Elections A238

Scouts Around Campfire, Emblems A239

Litho. & Engr.

1984, Apr. 12 ***Perf. 13***
753 A238 2.70k org & dk bl 1.25 .30
754 A239 2.70k multi 1.10 .30

Europa (1959-84) A240

1984, May 3 **Engr.** ***Perf. 12½***
755 A240 2.70k red *1.10* .20
756 A240 3.70k blue *1.75* *.80*

Prince Henrik, 50th Birthday A241

D Day, 40th Anniv. A242

1984, June 6 **Engr.**
757 A241 2.70k brown red 1.10 .30
758 A242 2.70k War Memorial, Copenhagen 1.10 .30

See Greenland No. 160.

17th Cent. Inn — A243

1984, June 6
759 A243 3k multicolored 1.25 1.00

Fishing and Shipping A244

1984, Sept. 6 **Engr.**
760 A244 2.30k Research (Herring) .90 .90
761 A244 2.70k Sea transport 1.10 .60
762 A244 3.30k Deep-sea fishing 1.25 1.25
763 A244 3.70k Deep-sea, diff. 1.50 1.40
Nos. 760-763 (4) 4.75 4.15

A245

A246

1984, Oct. 5 **Litho. & Engr.**
764 A245 1k Post bird .35 .25

1984, Oct. 5

Holberg Meets with an Officer, by Wilhelm Marstrand (1810-73).

765 A246 2.70k multicolored 1.10 .30

Ludvig Holberg (1684-1754), writer.

Jewish Community in Copenhagen, 300th Anniv. — A247

1984, Oct. 5
766 A247 3.70k Woman blessing Sabbath candles 1.50 1.00

Carnival in Rome, by Christoffer W. Eckersberg (1783-1853) — A248

Paintings: 10k, Ymer and Odhumble (Nordic mythology figures), by Nicolai A. Abildgaard (1743-1809), vert.

Perf. 12½x13, 13x12½

1984, Nov. 22 **Litho. & Engr.**
767 A248 5k multicolored 2.75 2.75
768 A248 10k multicolored 5.25 5.25

German and French Reform Church, 300th Anniv. — A249

1985, Jan. 24 **Engr.** ***Perf. 13***
769 A249 2.80k magenta 1.10 .25

Bonn-Copenhagen Declaration, 30th Anniv. — A250

1985, Feb. 21 **Litho.** ***Perf. 14***
770 A250 2.80k Map, flags 1.40 .45

A251

A252

1985, Mar. 14 ***Perf. 13***
771 A251 3.80k multicolored 1.50 .75

Intl. Youth Year.

Souvenir Sheet

Early postal ordinances.

1985, Mar. 14 **Litho. & Engr.**
772 Sheet of 4 6.00 *6.00*
a. A252 1k Christian IV's Ordinance on Postmen, 1624 1.40 *1.50*
b. A252 2.50k Plague Mandate, 1711 1.40 *1.50*
c. A252 2.80k Ordinance on Prohibition of Mail by Means other than the Post, 1775 1.40 *1.50*
d. A252 3.80k Act on Postal Articles, 1831 1.40 *1.50*

HAFNIA '87 phil. exhib. Sold for 15k.

Europa 1985 — A253

1985, May 2
773 A253 2.80k Musical staff *1.25* *.35*
774 A253 3.80k Musical staff, diff. *1.50* *.90*

Arrival of Queen Ingrid in Denmark, 50th Anniv. — A254

1985, May 21
775 A254 2.80k Queen Mother, chrysanthemums 1.10 .25

See Greenland No. 163.

Opening of the Faro Bridges — A255

1985, May 21 **Litho.** ***Perf. 13***
776 A255 2.80k Faro-Falster Bridge 1.10 .25

St. Cnut's Land Grant to Lund Cathedral, 900th Anniv. — A256

Seal of King Cnut and: 2.80k, Lund Cathedral. 3k, City of Helsingdorg, Sweden.

1985, May 21 **Engr.**
777 A256 2.80k multi 1.10 .45
778 A256 3k multi 1.40 1.40

See Sweden Nos. 1538-1539.

UN Decade for Women A257

Sports A258

1985, June 27 **Litho. & Engr.**
779 A257 3.80k Cyclist 1.50 1.50

1985, June 27
780 A258 2.80k Women's floor exercise 1.10 .30
781 A258 3.80k Canoe & kayak 1.50 .80
782 A258 6k Cycling 2.40 1.60
Nos. 780-782 (3) 5.00 2.70

Kronborg Castle, Elsinore, 400th Anniv. — A259

UN 40th Anniv. — A260

1985, Sept. 5
783 A259 2.80k multi 1.10 .25

1985, Sept. 5
784 A260 3.80k Dove, emblem 1.50 .80

Niels Bohr (1885-1962), Physicist — A261

1985, Oct. 3 *Perf. 13x12½*

785 A261 2.80k With wife Margrethe 1.25 1.00

Winner of 1922 Nobel Prize in Physics for theory of atomic structure.

Hand Signing "D" — A262

Boat, by Helge Refn — A263

1985, Nov. 7 **Engr.** *Perf. 13*

786 A262 2.80k multicolored 1.10 .25

Danish Assoc. for the Deaf, 50th anniv.

1985, Nov. 7 **Litho.**

787 A263 2.80k multicolored 1.25 .25

Abstract Iron Sculpture by Robert Jacobsen A264

Lithographed and Engraved

1985, Nov. 7 *Perf. 13x12½*

788 A264 3.80k multicolored 2.75 3.00

Painting by Bjorn Wiinblad A265

1986, Jan. 23 **Litho.** *Perf. 13x12½*

789 A265 2.80k multicolored 1.25 1.25

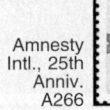

Amnesty Intl., 25th Anniv. A266

Lithographed and Engraved

1986, Jan. 23 *Perf. 13*

790 A266 2.80k multicolored 1.10 .25

Miniature Sheet

HAFNIA '87 — A267

1986, Feb. 20

791 Sheet of 4 8.00 9.00
- *a.* A267 100o Holstein carriage, c. 1840 1.75 2.00
- *b.* A267 250o Iceboat, c. 1880 1.75 2.00
- *c.* A267 280o 1st mail van, 1908 1.75 2.00
- *d.* A267 380o Airmail service 1919 1.75 2.00

Sold for 15k.

Changing of the Guard — A268

1986, Mar. 20 *Perf. 13*

792 A268 2.80k multicolored 1.10 .25

Royal Danish Life Guards barracks and Rosenborg Drilling Ground, bicent.

Types of 1933-82

1986-90		**Engr.**		*Perf. 13*
793	A32	5o brn org ('89)	.25	.25
794	A32	270o brt yel grn	1.00	.80
b.		Bklt. pane, 6 #318, 2 #691, 2 #794	4.75	
795	A32	300o brt yel grn	1.10	.35
796	A212	3k cop red	1.10	.25
797	A212	3.20k deep vio	1.25	.80
798	A212	3.20k carmine	1.25	.25
c.		Bklt. pane, 2 #693, 4 #798	7.00	
799	A212	3.40k dk grn	2.40	2.40
800	A212	3.80k dark vio	1.60	1.60
801	A212	4.10k dark blue	1.60	.40
802	A212	4.20k dk pur	2.40	2.00
803	A212	4.40k dp bl	1.60	.35
804	A55	4.60k gray	3.25	3.25
805	A55	6.50k dp grn	2.50	.80
806	A55	6.60k green	2.50	2.75
807	A55	7.10k brn vio	3.25	2.25
808	A55	7.30k green	3.50	3.50
809	A55	7.70k dk brn vio	3.00	1.40
810	A55	11k brown	3.50	2.75
811	A55	20k dp ultra	7.25	.70
812	A55	22k henna brn	7.25	1.60
813	A55	23k dark olive grn	8.00	1.10
814	A55	24k dark olive grn	8.00	.80
815	A55	26k dark olive grn	9.00	2.00
		Nos. 793-815 (23)	76.55	32.35

Issued: 6.50k, 20k, 1/9/86; 22k, 1/3/87; 270o, 3k, #797, 3.80k, 4.10k, 4.60k, 6.60k, 7.10k, 24k, 1/7/88; #794b, 1/28/88; 300o, #798, 3.40k, 4.20k, 4.40k, 7.30k, 7.70k, 11k, 26k, 1/26/89; 5o, 1989; 23k, 1/11/90.

No. 793 issued for use in lieu of currency of the same face value.

Soro Academy, 400th Anniv. — A269

1986, Apr. 28 **Litho. & Engr.**

816 A269 2.80k multi 1.10 .30

A270

A271

1986, Apr. 28

817 A270 3.80k multi 1.50 1.00

Intl. Peace Year.

1986, May 26 **Litho.**

818 A271 2.80k multi 1.50 .35

Crown Prince Frederik, 18th birthday.

Nordic Cooperation Issue 1986 — A272

Sister towns.

1986, May 27 **Engr.**

819 A272 2.80k Aalborg Harbor 1.00 .50

820 A272 3.80k Thisted Church and Town Hall 1.50 .80

Hoje Tastrup Train Station Opening, May 31 — A273

1986, May 27 **Litho.**

821 A273 2.80k multi 1.10 .25

Mailbox, Telegraph Lines, Telephone A274

Natl. Bird Candidates A275

1986, June 19 **Litho.** *Perf. 13*

822 A274 2.80k multi 1.10 .25

19th European Intl. PTT Congress, Copenhagen, Aug. 12-16.

1986, June 19 **Litho. & Engr.**

Finalists: a, Corvus corax. b, Sturnus vulgaris. c, Cygnus olor (winner). d, Vanellus vanellus. e, Alauda arvensis.

823 Strip of 5 9.00 10.00
- *a.-e.* A275 2.80k any single 1.75 1.00

A276

HAFNIA '87 — A277

1986, June 19

824 A276 2.80k multi 1.10 .25

Danish Rifle, Gymnastics and Sports Club, 125th anniv.

Souvenir Sheet

1986, Sept. 4

825 Sheet of 4 8.00 8.00
- *a.* A277 100o Mailcoach, c. 1841 1.60 1.60
- *b.* A277 250o Postmaster, c. 1840 1.60 1.60
- *c.* A277 280o Postman, c. 1851 1.60 1.60
- *d.* A277 380o Rural postman, c. 1893 1.90 1.90

Sold for 15k.

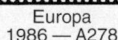

Europa 1986 — A278

Cupid — A279

1986, Sept. 4 **Engr.**

826 A278 2.80k Street sweeper *1.25* .20

827 A278 3.80k Garbage truck *1.60* *.70*

1986, Oct. 9 **Litho.**

828 A279 3.80k multi 1.50 .70

Premiere of The Whims of Cupid and the Ballet Master, by Vincenzo Galeotti, bicent.

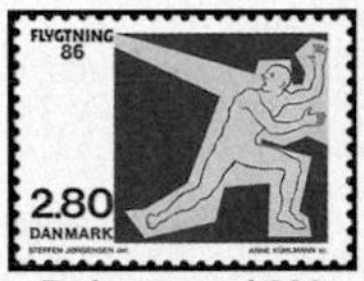

Refugee — A280

A281

1986, Oct. 9 **Litho. & Engr.**

829 A280 2.80k multi 1.10 .25

Danish Refugee Council Relief Campaign.

1986, Oct. 9 **Litho.** *Perf. 13*

Protestant Reformation in Denmark, 450th Anniv.: Sermon, altarpiece detail, 1561, Thorslunde Church, Copenhagen.

830 A281 6.50k multi 2.50 1.10

A282

Abstract by Lin Utzon — A283

1986, Nov. 6 **Litho. & Engr.**

831 A282 3.80k multi 1.75 1.75

Organization for Economic Cooperation and Development, 25th anniv.

1987, Jan. 22 **Litho.** *Perf. 13*

832 A283 2.80k multi 1.10 .25

Art appreciation.

A284

A285

1987, Feb. 26 **Engr.** *Perf. 13*

833 A284 2.80k lake & black 1.10 .25

Danish Consumer Council, 40th anniv.

1987, Apr. 9 **Litho.** *Perf. 13*

Religious art (details) from Ribe Cathedral.

834 A285 3k Fresco 1.25 .85

835 A285 3.80k Stained-glass window 1.75 1.40

836 A285 6.50k Mosaic 2.75 2.75

Nos. 834-836 (3) 5.75 5.00

Ribe Cathedral redecoration, 1982-1987, by Carl-Henning Pedersen.

A286

A287

Europa (Modern architecture): 2.80k, Central Library, Gentofte, 1985. 3.80k, Hoje Tastrup High School, 1985, horiz.

1987, May 4 Engr. *Perf. 13*
837 A286 2.80k rose claret *1.40 .35*
838 A286 3.80k bright ultra *1.90 .90*

1987, May 4
839 A287 2.50k dk red & bl blk 1.40 1.00

Danish Academy of Technical Sciences (ATV), 50th anniv.

8th Gymnaestrada, Herning, July 7-11 — A288

1987, June 18 Litho. & Engr.
840 A288 2.80k multi 1.10 .25

A289

A290

1987, June 18
841 A289 3.80k multi 1.50 1.00

Danish Cooperative Bacon Factories, cent.

1987, Aug. 27 Litho.
842 A290 3.80k Single-sculler 1.50 .90

World Rowing Championships, Aug. 23-30.

HAFNIA '87, Bella Center, Copenhagen, Oct. 16-25 — A291

Litho. & Engr.

1987, Aug. 27 *Perf. 13x12½*
843 A291 280o Type A15, mail train c. 1912 1.40 1.40

Souvenir Sheet

843A A291 280o like No. 843, green lawn and locomotive 24.00 24.00

Purchase of No. 843A included admission to the exhibition. Sold for 45k.

Abstact by Ejler Bille — A292

1987, Sept. 24 Litho. *Perf. 13*
844 A292 2.80k multi 1.10 .25

Rasmus Rask (1787-1832), Linguist — A293

1987, Oct. 15 Engr. *Perf. 13x12½*
845 A293 2.80k dark henna brown 1.10 .25

A294

A295

Emblem: Miraculous Catch (Luke 5:4-7), New Testament.

1987, Oct. 15 *Perf. 13*
846 A294 3k carmine lake 1.25 .30

Clerical Assoc. for the Home Mission in Denmark, 125th anniv.

Photo. & Engr., Litho. (4.10k)

1988, Feb. 18 *Perf. 13*

Designs: 3k, Two lions from the gate of Rosenburg Castle around the monogram of Christian IV. 4.10k, Portrait of the monarch painted by P. Isaacsz, vert.

847 A295 3k blue gray & gold 1.25 .30
848 A295 4.10k multi 1.60 .75

Accession of Christian IV (1577-1648), King of Denmark and Norway (1588-1648), 400th anniv.

Ole Worm (1588-1654), Archaeologist, and Runic Artifacts — A296

1988, Feb. 18 Engr.
849 A296 7.10k chocolate 2.75 2.75

Odense, 1000th Anniv. — A297

A298

Design: St. Cnut's Church and statue of Hans Christian Andersen, Odense.

1988, Mar. 10 Engr.
850 A297 3k multi 1.25 .25

1988, Apr. 7 Litho.
851 A298 2.70k multi 1.10 .70

Danish Civil Defense and Emergency Planning Agency, 50th Anniv.

WHO, 40th Anniv. — A299

Abolition of *Stavnsbaand,* 200th Anniv. — A300

1988, Apr. 7 Litho. & Engr.
852 A299 4.10k multi 1.60 .85

1988, May 5 Litho.

Painting: King Christian VII riding past the Liberty Memorial, Copenhagen, by C.W. Eckersberg (1783-1853).

853 A300 3.20k multi 1.25 .80

Stavnsbaand (adscription) provided that all Danish farmers' sons from age 4 to 40 would be bound as villeins to the estates on which they were born, thus providing landowners with free labor.

A301

A302

Europa: Transport and communication.

1988, May 5
854 A301 3k Postwoman on bicycle *1.00 .20*
855 A301 4.10k Mobile telephone *1.75 .70*

1988, June 16 Litho.
856 A302 4.10k multi 1.60 .75

1988 Individual Speedway World Motorcycle Championships, Denmark, Sept. 3.

Federation of Danish Industries, 150th Anniv. — A303

Painting (detail): *The Industrialists,* by P.S. Kroyer.

1988, June 16 *Perf. 13½x13*
857 A303 3k multi 1.25 .55

Danish Metalworkers' Union, Cent. — A304

1988, Aug. 18 Litho. *Perf. 13*
858 A304 3k Glass mosaic by Niels Winkel 1.25 .35

Tonder Teachers' Training College, 200th Anniv. — A305

1988, Aug. 18 Engr. *Perf. 13x12½*
859 A305 3k lake 1.25 .30

Homage to Leon Degand, Sculpture by Robert Jacobsen A306

1988, Sept. 22 *Perf. 11½x13*
860 A306 4.10k blk, lake & gray 2.50 *3.00*

Danish-French cultural exchange program, 10th anniv. See France No. 2130.

Preservation of Historic Sites — A307

1988, Oct. 13 Engr. *Perf. 13x12½*
861 A307 3k Lumby Windmill, 1818 1.40 .30
862 A307 7.10k Vejstrup Water Mill, 1837 2.75 1.60

Paintings in the State Museum of Art, Copenhagen — A308

4.10k, *Bathing Boys,* 1902, by Peter Hansen (1868-1928). 10k, *The Hill at Overkaerby,* 1917, by Fritz Syberg (1862-1939).

Litho. & Engr.

1988, Nov. 3 *Perf. 13*
863 A308 4.10k multi 3.00 *3.50*
864 A308 10k multi 6.00 *6.50*

See #881-882, 951-952, 972-973, 1018-1019.

The Little Mermaid, Sculpture by Edvard Eriksen — A309

1989, Feb. 16 Engr.
865 A309 3.20k dark green 1.25 .30

Tourism industry, cent.

Danish Soccer Assoc., Cent. — A310

NATO Membership, 40th Anniv. — A311

1989, Mar. 16 Litho.
866 A310 3.20k multi 1.25 .30

1989, Mar. 16
867 A311 4.40k dk blue, gold & lt blue 1.75 1.00

Nordic Cooperation Issue — A312

Folk costumes.

1989, Apr. 20 Litho. & Engr.
868 A312 3.20k Woman from Valby 1.25 .40
869 A312 4.40k Pork butcher 1.75 1.00

European Parliament 3rd Elections A313

1989, May 11 Litho.
870 A313 3k blue & yellow 1.25 1.25

Europa 1989 — A314

Children's toys.

1989, May 11 Litho. & Engr.
871 A314 3.20k Lego blocks *1.25* .20
872 A314 4.40k Wooden soldiers, by Kay Bojesen *1.75* *.55*

Agricultural Museum, Cent. A315

1989, June 15 Engr. *Perf. 13*
873 A315 3.20k Tractor, 1889 1.25 .30

Interparliamentary Union, Cent. — A316

1989, June 15 Litho. & Engr.
874 A316 3.40k Folketing Chamber layout 2.40 2.40

Danish Fishery and Marine Research Institute, Cent. A317

1989, Aug. 24 Litho. & Engr.
875 A317 3.20k multi 1.10 .30

Bernhard Severin Ingemann (1789-1862), Poet and Novelist — A318

1989, Aug. 24 Engr.
876 A318 7.70k dark green 2.75 1.25

A319

A320

Danish Film Office, 50th Anniv.: 3k, Scene from the short feature film *They Reached the Ferry*, 1948. 3.20k, Bodil Ipsen (d. 1964), actress. 4.40k, Carl Th. Dreyer (1889-1968), screenwriter and director.

1989, Sept. 28 Litho.
877 A319 3k multi 1.10 1.10
878 A319 3.20k multi 1.10 .50
879 A319 4.40k multi 1.60 .85
Nos. 877-879 (3) 3.80 2.45

1989, Nov. 10 Litho. & Engr.
880 A320 3.20k multi 1.25 .40

Stamp Day, 50th anniv.

Art Type of 1988

Paintings: 4.40k, *Part of the Northern Gate of the Citadel Bridge*, c. 1837, by Christen Kobke (1810-1848). 10k, *A Little Girl, Elise Kobke, With a Cup in Front of Her*, c. 1850, by Constantin Hansen (1804-1880).

1989, Nov. 10 *Perf. 12½x13*
881 A308 4.40k multi 2.40 *2.75*
882 A308 10k multi 5.75 *6.25*

Types of 1933-82 and:

A321

A321a Queen Margrethe II

Perf. 12½, 13 (A321a)

1990-98 Engr.
883 A32 25o bluish black .25 .25
a. Bklt. pane, 4 #691, 2 #883 1.90
884 A32 125o carmine lake .50 .25
885 A32 325o lt yel grn 1.25 1.25
886 A32 350o yellow green 1.40 .75
887 A212 3.50k dark red 1.40 .25
a. Bklt. pane, 2 each #691, 885, 887 6.00
888 A321 3.50k henna brown 1.40 .25
b. Bklt. pane, 4 each #883, #884, #888 ('91) 8.50
889 A212 3.75k dark green 1.50 1.50
890 A321 3.75k green 1.75 1.60
891 A321 3.75k red 1.50 .25
a. Bklt. pane, 4 each #884, #891 8.50
b. Booklet pane, 2 each #691, 883, 891 4.50
Complete booklet, #891b 4.50
892 A321a 3.75k red 1.50 .25
a. Booklet pane, 2 each #691, 883, 892 4.25
Complete booklet, #892a 4.25
b. Booklet pane, 2 #883, 4 #494, 2 #892 4.25
Complete booklet, #892b 4.25
893 A321 4k brown 1.60 .60
894 A321a 4k deep bl grn 1.60 .25
895 A321a 4.25k olive brown 1.75 .75
896 A212 4.50k brown violet 1.75 1.75
897 A321 4.50k violet 1.75 1.60
898 A321a 4.50k deep bl blk 1.75 .75
899 A212 4.75k dark blue 1.90 .30
900 A321 4.75k blue 1.90 .30
901 A321 4.75k violet 1.90 1.60
902 A321a 4.75k brown 1.90 1.50
903 A321a 5k violet 2.00 .25
904 A321 5k blue 2.00 .40
905 A321 5.25k black 2.10 1.50
906 A321a 5.25k deep blue 2.10 .25
907 A321 5.50k green 2.25 2.25
908 A321a 5.50k henna brown 2.25 2.10
909 A55 7.50k dark bl grn 3.00 2.50
Nos. 883-909 (27) 45.95 25.25

Queen Margrethe II's 50th birthday (No. 888).

Issued: #888, 4/5; #890, 897, 900, 1990; #888a, 2/14/91; #886, 891, 891a, 901, 904, 6/10/92; 5.50k, 1/13/94; 4k, 5.25k, 6/27/96; #892, 892a, 1/14/97; #894, 902, 903, 906, 8/28/97; #895, 898, 908, 909, 3/26/98; others, 1/11/90.

See Nos. 1120, 1127, 1135.

A322

A323

Design: Silver coffee pot designed by Axel Johannes Kroyer, Copenhagen, 1726.

1990, Feb. 15 Engr. *Perf. 13*
911 A322 3.50k dark blue & blk 1.40 .35

Museum of Decorative Art, cent.

1990, Feb. 15

Steam engine, 200th anniv.: Steam engine built by Andrew Mitchell, 1790.

912 A323 8.25k dull red brown 3.25 1.75

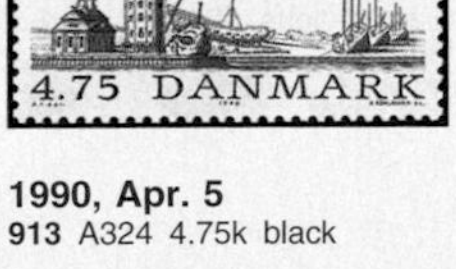

Nyholm, 300th Anniv. A324

1990, Apr. 5 Engr.
913 A324 4.75k black 1.90 1.00

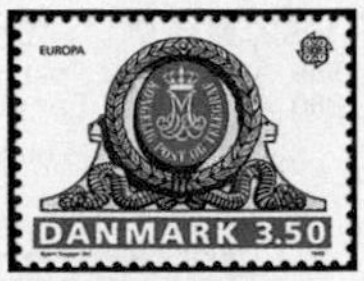

Europa 1990 — A325

1990, Apr. 5 Litho.
914 A325 3.50k Royal Monogram, Haderslev P.O. *1.75* .20
915 A325 4.75k Odense P.O. *2.75* *.70*

A326

A327

Pieces from the Flora Danica Banquet Service produced for King Christian VII.

1990, May 3 Litho.
916 A326 3.50k Bell-shaped lid, dish 1.50 1.75
917 A326 3.50k Gravy boat, dish 1.50 1.75
918 A326 3.50k Ice pot, casserole, lid 1.50 1.75
919 A326 3.50k Serving dish 1.50 1.75
a. Strip of 4, #916-919 6.50

Flora Danica porcelain, 200th anniv.

1990, June 14

Endangered plant species.

920 A327 3.25k Marshmallow 1.25 1.25
921 A327 3.50k Red helleborine 2.25 .40
922 A327 3.75k Purple orchis 1.60 1.60
923 A327 4.75k Lady's slipper 2.00 .95
Nos. 920-923 (4) 7.10 4.20

Village Churches, Jutland — A328

Perf. 13x12½, 12½x13

1990, Aug. 30 Engr.
924 A328 3.50k Gjellerup 1.40 .40
925 A328 4.75k Veng 1.90 .90
926 A328 8.25k Bredsten, vert. 3.25 2.10
Nos. 924-926 (3) 6.55 3.40

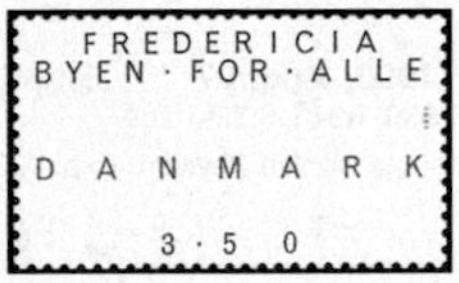

Fredericia, "The Town for Everybody" A329

Engr. & Embossed

1990, Oct. 5 *Perf. 13*
927 A329 3.50k black & red 1.40 .55

Tordenskiold (Peter Wessel, 1690-1720), Admiral — A330

1990, Oct. 5 Litho. *Perf. 13½x13*
928 A330 3.50k multicolored 1.40 .55

Prevent Bicycle Thefts — A331

Design: 3.50k, Stop drunk driving.

1990, Nov. 8 Litho. *Perf. 13x12½*
930 A331 3.25k shown 1.25 1.25
931 A331 3.50k Automobile, wine glass 1.40 .30

Locomotives — A332

1991, Mar. 14 Engr. *Perf. 13*
932 A332 3.25k IC3 1990 1.25 1.25
933 A332 3.50k Class A 1882 1.40 .70
934 A332 3.75k Class MY 1954 1.50 1.50
935 A332 4.75k Class P 1907 1.90 1.00
Nos. 932-935 (4) 6.05 4.45

Europa — A333

Jutland Law, 750th Anniv. — A334

Satellite photographs showing temperatures of Danish: 3.50k, Waters. 4.75k, Land.

1991, May 2 Litho. *Perf. 13*
936 A333 3.50k multicolored *1.10* *.25*
937 A333 4.75k multicolored *1.60* *.70*

1991, May 2
938 A334 8.25k multicolored 3.00 3.00

Danish Islands — A335

1991, June 6
939 A335 3.50k Fano 1.40 .30
940 A335 4.75k Christianso 1.90 .70

Decorative Art — A336

Keep Denmark Clean — A337

Designs: 3.25k, Earthenware bowl and jars by Christian Poulsen. 3.50k, Chair by Hans Wegner, vert. 4.75k, Silver cutlery by Kay Bojesen, vert. 8k, Lamp by Poul Henningsen.

1991, Aug. 22 Litho. *Perf. 13*
941 A336 3.25k multicolored 1.25 1.25
942 A336 3.50k multicolored 1.25 .40
943 A336 4.75k multicolored 1.90 1.00
944 A336 8.25k multicolored 3.25 3.25
Nos. 941-944 (4) 7.65 5.90

1991, Sept. 19 Engr. *Perf. 13*

Designs: 3.50k, Cleaning up after dog. 4.75k, Picking up litter.

945 A337 3.50k red 1.50 .30
946 A337 4.75k blue 2.00 1.00

Posters from Danish Museum of Decorative Arts — A338

Posters for: 3.50k, Nordic Advertising Congress, by Arne Ungermann (1902-1981).

4.50k, Poster Exhibition at Copenhagen Zoo (baboon), by Valdemar Andersen (1875-1928). 4.75k, Danish Air Lines, by Ib Andersen (1907-1969). 12k, The Sinner, by Sven Brasch (1886-1970).

1991, Sept. 19 **Litho.**

947 A338 3.50k multicolored 1.25 .40
948 A338 4.50k multicolored 2.25 2.25
949 A338 4.75k multicolored 1.75 1.75
950 A338 12k multicolored 4.25 2.50
Nos. 947-950 (4) 9.50 6.90

Art Type of 1988

Designs: 4.75k, Lady at her Toilet by Harald Giersing (1881-1927), vert. 14k, Road through a Wood by Edvard Weie (1879-1943), vert.

Litho. & Engr.

1991, Nov. 7 ***Perf. 13x12½***

951 A308 4.75k multicolored 1.90 1.90
952 A308 14k multicolored 5.50 5.50

A339 A340

Treasures of Natl. Museum: 3.50k, Earthenware bowl, Skarpsalling. 4.50k, Bronze dancer, Grevensvaenge. 4.75k, Bottom plate of silver cauldron, Gundestrup. 8.25k, Flint knife, Hindsgavl.

1992, Feb. 13 **Engr.** ***Perf. 13***

953 A339 3.50k dk vio & brown 1.40 .40
954 A339 4.50k dk bl & dk ol green 1.75 1.75
955 A339 4.75k brown & black 1.90 1.25
956 A339 8.25k dk ol grn & vio brown 3.25 3.25
Nos. 953-956 (4) 8.30 6.65

1992, Mar. 12 ***Perf. 13½x13***

957 A340 3.50k rose carmine 1.40 .50

Danish Society of Chemical, Civil, Electrical, and Mechanical Engineers, cent.

Souvenir Sheet

Queen Margaret I (1353-1412) — A341

Litho. & Engr.

1992, Mar. 12 ***Perf. 12½***

958 A341 Sheet of 2 5.50 6.00
a. 3.50k Fresco 2.10 2.10
b. 4.75k Alabaster bust 2.75 2.75

Nordia '94, Scandinavian Philatelic Exhibition. No. 958 sold for 12k to benefit the exhibition.

Discovery of America, 500th Anniv. — A342

1992, May 7 **Engr.** ***Perf. 12½***

959 A342 3.50k Potato plant *1.60 .40*
960 A342 4.75k Ear of corn *2.75 1.25*

Europa.

Protect the Environment — A343

Litho. & Engr.

1992, June 10 ***Perf. 13***

961 A343 3.75k Hare beside road 1.50 .30
962 A343 5k Fish, water pollution 2.00 .70
963 A343 8.75k Cut trees, vert. 3.50 2.00
Nos. 961-963 (3) 7.00 3.00

Queen Margrethe II and Prince Henrik, 25th Wedding Anniv. — A344

1992, June 10 **Litho.** ***Perf. 12½x13***

964 A344 3.75k multicolored 1.50 .85

See Greenland No. 253.

A345 A346

1992, July 16 ***Perf. 13***

965 A345 3.75k multicolored 1.50 .40

Denmark, European soccer champions.

1992, Aug. 27 **Engr.** ***Perf. 13***

966 A346 3.75k blue 1.50 .50

Danish Pavilion, Expo '92, Seville.

A347 A348

1992, Oct. 8 **Litho. & Engr.** ***Perf. 13***

967 A347 3.75k blue & org 1.50 .65

Single European market.

Litho. & Engr.

1992, Oct. 8 ***Perf. 12½***

Cartoon characters: 3.50k, A Hug, by Ivar Gjorup. 3.75k, Love Letter, by Phillip Stein Jonsson. 4.75k, Domestic Triangle, by Nikoline Werdelin. 5k, Poet and His Little Wife, by Jorgen Mogensen.

968 A348 3.50k multicolored 1.40 1.00

Engr.

969 A348 3.75k red & purple 1.50 .30
970 A348 4.75k blk & red brn 1.90 1.90
971 A348 5k blue & red brn 2.00 .70
Nos. 968-971 (4) 6.80 3.90

Art Type of 1988

5k, Landscape from Vejby, 1843, by John Thomas Lundbye. 10k, Motif from Halleby Brook, 1847, by Peter Christian Skovgaard.

Litho. & Engr.

1992, Nov. 12 ***Perf. 12½x13***

972 A308 5k multicolored 2.00 2.00
973 A308 10k multicolored 4.00 4.00

A349 A350

1992, Nov. 12 ***Perf. 13***

974 A349 3.75k Jacob's fight with angel 1.50 .30

Publication of new Danish bible.

Litho. & Engr.

1993, Feb. 4 ***Perf. 13***

Archaeological Treasures. Anthropomorphic gold foil figures found in: 3.75k, Lundeborg, horiz. 5k, Bornholm.

975 A350 3.75k multicolored 1.50 .30
976 A350 5k multicolored 2.00 .70

A351 A352

Butterflies.

1993, Mar. 11 **Litho.**

977 A351 3.75k Small tortoiseshell 1.40 .40
978 A351 5k Large blue 2.10 .80
979 A351 8.75k Marsh fritillary 4.25 2.50
980 A351 12k Red admiral 4.75 3.25
Nos. 977-980 (4) 12.50 6.95

1993, May 6 **Litho.** ***Perf. 12½***

Posters: 3.75k, Pierrot, by Thor Bogelund, 1947, horiz. 5k, Balloons, by Wilhelm Freddie, 1987.

981 A352 3.75k multicolored 1.50 .30
982 A352 5k multicolored 2.00 .80

Tivoli Gardens, 150th anniv.

A353

A354

Europa (Contemporary paintings by): 3.75k, Troels Worsel, horiz. 5k, Stig Brogger.

1993, May 6 ***Perf. 13***

983 A353 3.75k multicolored *.80 .50*
984 A353 5k multicolored *1.25 .60*

1993, June 17 **Engr.** ***Perf. 13***

985 A354 5k dark blue green 2.00 .70

Danish-Russian relations, 500th anniv. See Russia No. 6154.

Training Ships
A355 A356

Perf. 13, 13½x13 (#987)

1993, June 17 **Litho. & Engr.**

986 A355 3.75k Danmark 1.50 .30
987 A356 4.75k Jens Krogh 1.90 1.90
988 A355 5k Georg Stage, horiz. 2.00 .85

Size: 39x28mm

Perf. 13x13½

989 A356 9.50k Marilyn Anne, horiz. 3.75 4.00
Nos. 986-989 (4) 9.15 7.05

Child's Drawing of Viking Ships — A357

Letter Writing Campaign — A358

1993, Aug. 19 **Litho.** ***Perf. 13***

990 A357 3.75k multicolored 1.50 .30
991 A358 5k lt & dk bl & blk 2.00 .70

Ethnic Jewelry — A359

1993, Sept. 16 **Litho.** ***Perf. 13***

992 A359 3.50k Falster 1.40 .70
993 A359 3.75k Amager 1.50 .30
994 A359 5k Laeso 2.00 .60
995 A359 8.75k Romo 3.50 2.00
Nos. 992-995 (4) 8.40 3.60

Cubist Paintings A360

5k, Assemblage, by Vilhelm Lundstrom, 1929. 15k, Composition, by Franciska Clausen, 1929.

Litho. & Engr.

1993, Nov. 11 ***Perf. 12½***

996 A360 5k multicolored 2.25 2.25
997 A360 15k multicolored 6.00 6.00

See Nos. 1033-1034, 1080-1081.

Conservation — A361

1994, Jan. 27 **Litho.** ***Perf. 13***

998 A361 3.75k Save water 1.50 .30
999 A361 5k CO2 2.00 .45

Castles
A362

Castles: 3.50k, Marselisborg, Aarhus. 3.75k, Amalienborg, Copenhagen. 5k, Fredensborg, North Zealand. 8.75k, Graasten, South Jutland.

Litho. & Engr.

1994, Mar. 17 *Perf. 13x12½*
1000 A362 3.50k multicolored 1.40 .70
1001 A362 3.75k multicolored 1.50 .30
1002 A362 5k multicolored 2.00 .50
1003 A362 8.75k multicolored 3.50 3.50
a. Bklt. pane, #1000-1003 11.00 11.00

No. 1003a printed with 2 different labels. One shows a marching band, the other shows a ship.

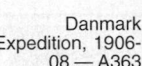

Danmark Expedition, 1906-08 — A363

Europa: 3.75k, Expedition ship, Danmark, Alfred Wegener's weather balloon. 5k, Theodolite, Johan Peter Koch, cartographer.

1994, May 5 **Engr.** *Perf. 13*
1004 A363 3.75k deep brn vio *.90 .20*
1005 A363 5k dp slate grn *1.25 .50*

Trams — A364

Designs: 3.75k, Copenhagen tram (Engelhardt). 4.75k, Aarhus car. 5k, Odense tram, vert. 12k, Horse-drawn tram.

Litho. & Engr.

1994, June 9 *Perf. 13*
1006 A364 3.75k multicolored 1.50 .30
1007 A364 4.75k multicolored 1.90 1.90
1008 A364 5k multicolored 2.00 .70

Size: 38x21mm

1009 A364 12k multicolored 4.75 4.25
Nos. 1006-1009 (4) 10.15 7.15

Children's Stamp Competition
A365

ILO, 75th Anniv.
A366

1994, Aug. 25 **Litho.** *Perf. 12½*
1010 A365 3.75k multicolored 1.50 .30

1994, Aug. 25 *Perf. 13*
1011 A366 5k multicolored 2.00 .40

A367

A368

Wild animals.

Litho. & Engr.

1994, Oct. 20 *Perf. 12½*
1012 A367 3.75k House sparrows 1.50 .35
1013 A367 4.75k Badger 1.90 1.50
1014 A367 5k Squirrel, vert. 2.00 .70
1015 A367 9.50k Black grouse 3.75 3.25

Size: 36x26mm

Perf. 13

1016 A367 12k Grass snake 4.75 4.00
Nos. 1012-1016 (5) 13.90 9.80

1994, Nov. 10 **Litho.** *Perf. 13*
1017 A368 3.75k multicolored 1.50 .30

Folk High Schools, 150th anniv.

Painting Type of 1988

Designs: 5k, Study of Italian Woman and Sleeping Child, by Wilhelm Marstrand. 15k, Interior from Amaliegade with the Artist's Brothers, by Wilhelm Bendz.

Litho. & Engr.

1994, Nov. 10 *Perf. 12½x13*
1018 A308 5k multicolored 2.00 2.00
1019 A308 15k multicolored 6.00 6.00

Aarhus Cathedral School, 800th Anniv. — A369

Litho. & Engr.

1995, Jan. 26 *Perf. 13*
1020 A369 3.75k multicolored 1.50 .30

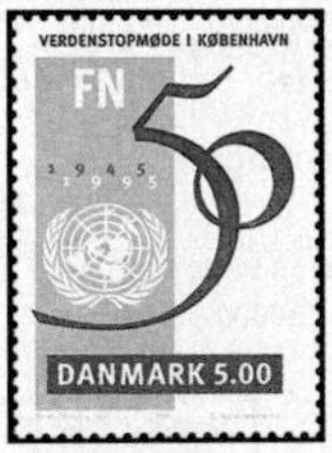

UN, 50th Anniv. — A370

Litho. & Engr.

1995, Jan. 26 *Perf. 13*
1021 A370 5k multicolored 2.00 .45
Complete booklet, 10 #1021 30.00

Danish Islands
A371

1995, Mar. 16 **Engr.** *Perf. 13*
1022 A371 3.75k Avernako 1.50 .30
Complete booklet, 10 #1022 15.00
1023 A371 4.75k Fejo 1.90 1.40
1024 A371 5k Fur 2.00 .75
1025 A371 9.50k Endelave 3.75 3.00
a. Booklet pane, #1022-1025 + 2 labels 10.00
Complete booklet, 2 #1025a 21.00
Nos. 1022-1025 (4) 9.15 5.45

No. 1025a printed with four different large labels. Labels with one pane are MF Faaborg II and MF Endelave. The other pane has MF Bukken-bruse and MF Fursund.

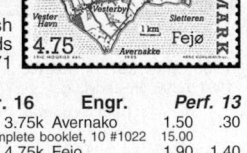

Liberation of Denmark, 50th Anniv. A372

Designs: 3.75k, Gen. Montgomery, Town Hall Square, vert. 5k, White busses returning from concentration camps. 8.75k, Airplane dropping supplies to resistance. 12k, Jews escape across the Sound to Sweden.

1995, May 4 **Litho.** *Perf. 13*
1026 A372 3.75k multicolored *.90 .20*
Complete booklet, 10 #1026 *11.00*
1027 A372 5k multicolored *1.25 .60*
1028 A372 8.75k multicolored *2.10 1.50*
1029 A372 12k multicolored *3.00 2.75*
Nos. 1026-1029 (4) *7.25 5.05*

Europa (Nos. 1026-1027).

A373

A374

1995, June 8 **Litho.** *Perf. 13*
1030 A373 3.50k multicolored 1.40 .60

Danish Rhymed Chronicle, 500th anniv.

1995, June 8

3.75k, Roskilde Festival. 5k, Tonder Festival.

1031 A374 3.75k multi, horiz. 1.50 .30
Complete booklet, 10 #1031 20.00
1032 A374 5k multi 2.00 .50

No. 1031 is 28x21mm.

Paintings
A375

Designs: 10k, "Sct. Hans Aften, 1955," by Jens Sondergaard. 15k, "Landskab-Gudhjem, 1939," by Niels Lergaard.

Litho. & Engr.

1995, Aug. 24 *Perf. 13x12½*
1033 A375 10k multicolored 4.00 4.00
1034 A375 15k multicolored 6.00 6.00

Tycho Brahe (1546-1601), Astronomer
A376

3.75k, Uranienborg Observatory. 5.50k, Sextant.

Litho. & Engr.

1995, Oct. 27 *Perf. 13*
1035 A376 3.75k multicolored 1.50 .30
1036 A376 5.50k multicolored 2.10 1.75

See Sweden Nos. 2149-2150.

Toys
A377

Designs: 3.75k, Tekno cars. 5k, Dolls, teddy bear. 8.75k, Model trains. 12k, Glud & Marstrand tin horse-drawn carriage & fire pumper.

1995, Nov. 9 *Perf. 13x12½*
1037 A377 3.75k multicolored 1.50 .30
Complete booklet, 10 #1037 16.00
1038 A377 5k multicolored 2.00 .75
1039 A377 8.75k multicolored 3.50 3.00
1040 A377 12k multicolored 4.75 4.75
Nos. 1037-1040 (4) 11.75 8.80

A378

A379

Cartoonlike views of Copenhagen: 3.75k, Round Tower as music box. 5k, Christiansborg Castle. 8.75k, Marble Church as top of balloon. 12k, The Little Mermaid statue on stage.

1996, Jan. 25 **Litho.** *Perf. 13*
1041 A378 3.75k multicolored 1.50 .30
Complete booklet, 10 #1041 16.00
1042 A378 5k multicolored 2.00 .70
1043 A378 8.75k multicolored 3.50 3.00
1044 A378 12k multicolored 4.75 4.25
Nos. 1041-1044 (4) 11.75 8.25

Copenhagen, 1996 cultural capital of Europe.

1996, Mar. 21 **Litho.** *Perf. 13*
1045 A379 3.75k Sports for disabled 1.50 .30
Complete booklet, 10 #1045 16.00
1046 A379 4.75k Swimming 1.90 1.50
1047 A379 5k Sailing 2.00 .50
1048 A379 9.50k Cycling 3.75 3.75
a. Bklt. pane of 4, #1045-1048 + 2 labels 10.00
Complete booklet, 2 #1048a 20.00

No. 1048a printed with two different large labels. One shows hands and soccer ball, second shows tennis racket and tennis balls.

Danish Federation for Sports for the Disabled (No. 1045). Modern Olympic Games, cent., Sports Confederation of Denmark, cent., 1996 Summer Olympics, Atlanta (Nos. 1046-1048).

A380

A381

1996, May 9 **Litho.** *Perf. 13*
1049 A380 3.75k multicolored 1.50 .30

Danish Employers' Confederation, cent.

1996, May 9

Famous Danish Women (Europa): 3.75k, Karen Blixen (1885-1962), writer. 5k, Asta Nielsen (1881-1972), silent screen actress.

1050 A381 3.75k lt brn & dk brn *.90 .20*
1051 A381 5k gray & dk blue *1.25 .40*
Complete booklet, 10 #1051 *16.00*

A382

A383

Wooden Dinghies: 3.50k, Roskilde Fjord sail boat. 3.75k, Limfjorden skiff. 12.25k, Two-masted smack, South Funen Archipelago.

Perf. 13, 12½ (#1053)

1996, June 13 **Engr.**
1052 A382 3.50k multicolored 1.40 .85
1053 A382 3.75k multicolored 1.50 .30
Complete booklet, 10 #1053 16.00
1054 A382 12.25k multicolored 4.75 3.25
Nos. 1052-1054 (3) 7.65 4.40

No. 1053 is 20x39mm.

Litho. & Engr.

1996, Sept. 12 *Perf. 13x12½*

Lighthouses.

1055 A383 3.75k Fornaes 1.50 .30
Complete booklet, 10 #1055 16.00
1056 A383 5k Blavandshuk 2.00 .40
a. Bklt. pane, 8 #1055, 2 #1056 17.50
Complete booklet, #1056a 20.00
1057 A383 5.25k Bovbjerg 2.10 1.50
1058 A383 8.75k Mon 3.50 2.25
Nos. 1055-1058 (4) 9.10 4.45

Art Works of Thorvald Bindesboll (1846-1908) — A384

Litho. & Engr.

1996, Oct. 10 *Perf. 13*

1059 A384 3.75k Pitcher 1.50 .30
Complete booklet, 10 #1059 16.00

Litho.

1060 A384 4k Portfolio cover 1.60 1.10

Paintings A385

Designs: 10k, "At Lunch," by P.S. Kroyer, 1893. 15k, "The Girl with Sunflowers," by Michael Ancher, 1889.

Litho. & Engr.

1996, Nov. 7 *Perf. 13x12½*

1061 A385 10k multicolored 4.00 2.00
1062 A385 15k multicolored 5.75 3.00

A386

A387

Queen Margrethe II: 3.50k, With Prince Henrik. 3.75k, With Crown Prince Frederik. 4k, Delivering New Year speech. 5.25k, Waving to crowd.

1997, Jan. 14 **Litho.** *Perf. 13*

1063 A386 3.50k multicolored 1.40 .50
1064 A386 3.75k multicolored 1.50 .30
Complete booklet, 10 #1064 16.00
1065 A386 4k multicolored 1.60 .50
1066 A386 5.25k multicolored 2.10 1.10
a. Sheet of 4, #1063-1066 + 2 labels 7.00 7.00
Nos. 1063-1066 (4) 6.60 2.40

Queen Margrethe II, 25th anniv. of coronation.

1997, Mar. 13 **Engr.** *Perf. 13*

Open Air Museum, Copenhagen, Cent.: 3.50k, Kalstrup post mill. 3.75k, Ellested water mill. 5k, Fjellerup manor barn. 8.75k, Romo farm.

1067 A387 3.50k multicolored 1.40 .30
1068 A387 3.75k multicolored 1.50 .30
Complete booklet, 10 #1068 16.00
1069 A387 5k multicolored 2.00 1.25
Complete booklet, 10 #1069 20.00
1070 A387 8.75k multicolored 3.50 3.00
a. Booklet pane, #1067-1070 + label 8.50
Complete booklet, 2 #1070a 17.00
Nos. 1067-1070 (4) 8.40 4.85

No. 1070a printed with two different large labels. One shows a view of Ellested water mill, the other shows a farm in Ejersted.

Great Belt Railway Link — A388

A389

1997, May 15 **Litho.** *Perf. 13*

1071 A388 3.75k East Tunnel 1.50 .30
Complete booklet, 10 #1071 15.00
1072 A388 4.75k West Bridge 1.90 .85

1997, June 12 **Litho.** *Perf. 13*

Kalmar Union, 600th Anniv.: No. 1073, Margrete I and Eric of Pomerania. No. 1074, The Three Graces symbolizing Denmark, Norway and Sweden.

1073 A389 4k multicolored 1.60 .60
1074 A389 4k multicolored 1.60 .60
a. Pair, #1073-1074 3.50 1.40

No. 1074a is a continuous design.

Copenhagen-Roskilde Railway, 150th Anniv. — A390

Designs: 3.75k, Two modern trains under Carlsberg Bridge. 8.75k, Early steam train going under Carlsberg Bridge.

Litho. & Engr.

1997, June 12 *Perf. 13*

1075 A390 3.75k multicolored 1.50 .30
Complete booklet, 10 #1075 15.00
1076 A390 8.75k multicolored 3.50 1.50

End of Railway Mail Service A391

1997, June 12 **Litho.**

1077 A391 5k multicolored 2.00 .70

Stories and Legends A392

Europa: 3.75k, Large cat on top of treasure chest, from "The Tinder Box." 5.25k, Butterfly, pond, frog, from "Thumbelina."

1997, Aug. 28 **Engr.** *Perf. 13*

1078 A392 3.75k multicolored *1.25* .20
1079 A392 5.25k multicolored *1.75* *.90*

Painting Type of 1993

Designs: 9.75k, "Dust Dancing in the Sun," by Vilhelm Hammershoi (1864-1916). 13k, "Woman Mountaineer," by J.F. Willumsen (1863-1958).

Litho. & Engr.

1997, Sept. 18 *Perf. 13x12½*

1080 A360 9.75k multicolored 3.75 1.60
1081 A360 13k multicolored 5.00 2.00

A393

Danish Design: 3.75k, Faaborg chair, vert. 4k, Margrethe bowl, vert. 5k, The Ant (chair). 12.25k, Georg Jensen silver bowl, vert.

1997, Nov. 6 **Litho.** *Perf. 13*

1082 A393 3.75k multicolored 1.50 .30
Complete booklet, 10 #1082 15.00
1083 A393 4k multicolored 1.60 .70
1084 A393 5k multicolored 2.00 .45
1085 A393 12.25k multicolored 4.75 2.25
Nos. 1082-1085 (4) 9.85 3.70

A394

A395

Danish Confederation of Trade Unions, Cent.: 3.50k, General Workers Union in Denmark (SiD). 3.75k, Danish Confederation of Trade Unions (LO). 4.75k, Danish Nurse's Organization. 5k, Union of Commercial and Clerical Employees in Denmark (HK).

1998, Jan. 22 **Litho.** *Perf. 13*

1086 A394 3.50k multicolored 1.40 .75
1087 A394 3.75k multicolored 1.50 .30
Complete booklet, 10 #1087 15.00
1088 A394 4.75k multicolored 1.90 1.10
1089 A394 5k multicolored 2.00 .45
Complete booklet, 10 #1089 20.00
Nos. 1086-1089 (4) 6.80 2.60

Litho. & Engr.

1998, Mar. 26 *Perf. 13*

1090 A395 3.75k multicolored 1.50 .65
Complete booklet, 10 #1090 15.00

City of Roskilde, 1000th anniv.

A396

A397

1998, Mar. 26 **Litho.** *Perf. 13*

1091 A396 5k Ladybug 2.00 .30

Reduce poison.

1998, May 28 **Litho.** *Perf. 13*

New Post & Tele Museum, Copenhagen: 3.75k, Postman, 1922. 4.50k, Morse code operator, c. 1910. 5.50k, Telephone operator, 1910. 8.75k, Modern postman.

1092 A397 3.75k multicolored 1.50 .30
Complete booklet, 10 #1092 15.00
a. Booklet pane, 2 each #1087, 1089, 3 ea. 1090, 1092 20.00
Complete booklet, #1092a 20.00
1093 A397 4.50k multicolored 1.75 .85
1094 A397 5.50k multicolored 2.10 1.00
1095 A397 8.75k multicolored 3.50 1.50
a. Booklet pane, #1092-1095 9.00
Complete booklet, 2 #1095a 18.00
Nos. 1092-1095 (4) 8.85 3.65

No. 1095a is printed with two backgrounds. One shows part of King Christian IV's "Order Concerning Postmen," 1624. The other shows part of Copenhagen c. 1923. Complete booklets contain panes with each background.

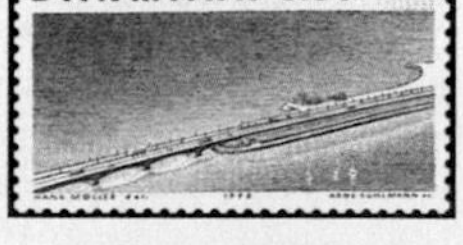

Bridges over Great Belt A398

1998, May 28 **Engr.** *Perf. 13*

1096 A398 5k West Bridge (shown) 2.00 .85
1097 A398 5k East Bridge (suspension) 2.00 .85
a. Pair, #1096-1097 + label 4.25 2.00

Nordic Stamps — A399

Shipping: No. 1098, Signal flags, harbor master with binoculars. No. 1099, Radar image of entrance to Copenhagen harbor, sextant.

1998, May 28 **Litho.** *Perf. 13*

1098 A399 6.50k multicolored 2.50 1.10
1099 A399 6.50k multicolored 2.50 1.10
a. Pair, #1098-1099 5.00 2.10
b. Souvenir sheet, #1099a 5.00 2.10

National Festivals — A400

Europa: 3.75k, Horse at Danish agricultural show. 4.50k, Theater, tents at Arhus Festival Week, Arhus.

Litho. & Engr.

1998, Sept. 3 *Perf. 13*

1100 A400 3.75k multicolored *1.25* *.60*
Complete booklet, 10 #1100 *12.50*
1101 A400 4.50k multicolored *1.50* *.70*

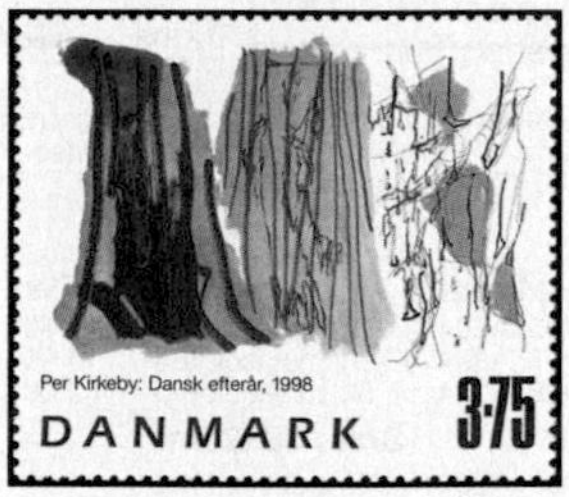

Contemporary Art — A401

Paintings: 3.75k, Danish Autumn, by Per Kirkeby. 5k, Alpha, by Mogens Andersen, vert. 8.75k, Imagery, by Ejler Bille, vert. 19k, Celestial Horse, by Carl-Henning Pedersen.

Perf. 12½x13, 13x12½

1998, Oct. 15 **Litho. & Engr.**

1102 A401 3.75k multicolored 1.50 .30

Litho.

1103 A401 5k multicolored 2.00 .70
1104 A401 8.75k multicolored 3.50 .70
1105 A401 19k multicolored 7.50 1.75
Nos. 1102-1105 (4) 14.50 3.45

See Nos. 1160-1161, 1190-1191, 1235-1236, 1282-1283, 1333-1336.

A402

Fossil, name of Danish geologist: 3.75k, Ammonite, Ole Worm (1588-1654). 4.50k, Shark's teeth, Niels Stensen (1638-86). 5.50k, Sea Urchin, Soren Abildgaard (1718-91). 15k, Slit-shell snail, Erich Pontoppidan (1698-1764).

1998, Nov. 5 **Engr.** *Perf. 13*

1106 A402 3.75k multicolored 1.50 .30
Complete booklet, 10 #1106 15.00
1107 A402 4.50k multicolored 1.75 .70
1108 A402 5.50k multicolored 2.10 .70
1109 A402 15k multicolored 5.75 1.75
a. Souvenir sheet, #1106-1109 11.50 5.25

Wavy Lines and Queen Types of 1933, 1997 and:

Queen Margrethe II — A402a

1999-2000 Engr. *Perf. 12¾*

1111 A32 150o purple .60 .25
1112 A32 375o green 1.50 .70
1113 A32 400o green 1.25 .65
1114 A321a 4k red 1.60 .25
a. Booklet pane, 4 #883, 2 #494, 2 #1114 4.00
Complete booklet, #1114a 4.00
1115 A402a 4k red 1.60 .25
b. Booklet pane, 4 #883, 2 #494, 2 #1115 2.50
Booklet, #1115b 2.50
c. Sheet of 8 + label 12.50
1116 A32 425o green 1.60 .30
1117 A402a 4.25k blue 1.60 .30
1118 A402a 4.25k red 1.50 .70
b. Booklet pane, 6 #883, 2 #1118 3.50
c. Sheet of 8 + central label 11.00 —
1119 A402a 4.50k orange 1.75 .30
a. Vert. strip of 10 + 10 etiquettes 17.50
1120 A402a 4.50k red 1.75 .30
a. Booklet pane, 2 #494, 2 #1120 4.00 —
Complete booklet, #1120a 4.00
b. Sheet of 8 + central label 13.50 —
1121 A402a 4.75k sepia 1.90 .65
1122 A402a 5k dk green 2.00 .25
a. Sheet of 8 + 8 etiquettes 11.00 —
1123 A402a 5.25k ultra 2.10 .40
1124 A402a 5.50k violet 2.25 .40
a. Sheet of 8 + label 14.00
b. Sheet of 8 + 8 etiquettes 15.00 15.00
1125 A321a 5.75k blue 2.25 .60
1126 A402a 5.75k emerald 2.25 .60
1127 A402a 6k bister 2.40 .50
a. Sheet of 10 + 10 etiquettes 22.50 —
1128 A402a 6.25k green 2.50 1.10
1129 A402a 6.50k slate grn 2.50 .85
a. Sheet of 8 + 8 etiquettes 20.00 20.00
b. Sheet of 8 + central label 17.00 —
1130 A321a 6.75k slate green 2.75 .60
1131 A402a 6.75k henna brn 2.75 1.00
1132 A402a 7k rose lilac 2.75 .50
1133 A402a 8.50k bright blue 3.25 1.50
1134 A55 10.50k dk bl gray 4.00 1.50
1135 A55 11.50k dk bl gray 4.50 1.90
1136 A55 12.50k gray 5.00 1.75
1137 A55 13k orange 5.00 1.90
1138 A55 15k blue 5.75 2.25
Nos. 1111-1138 (28) 70.65 22.25

Issued: 375o, #1118, 1130, 1/13/99; #1125, 1/3/00; #1119, 1119a, 4.25k, 4.50k, 5k, 5.25k, 5.50k, #1126, 1131, 4/12/00; No. 1119b, 6k, 7k, 5/9/01; Nos. 1119c, 1121a, 1124a, 4/17/01; 150o, 4.75k, 6.50k, 10.50k, 1/2/02. 400o, No. 1120, 6.25k, 8.50k, 11.50k, 1/2/03. No. 1120b, 3/12. Nos. 1124b, 1129a, 3/12/03. Nos. 1128b, 1/2/03; No. 1122a, 4/2/02; 425o, No. 1120, 12.50k, 13k, 15k, 1/2/04. Nos. 1120b, 1127a, 1/2/04.

A403

1999, Jan. 13 Litho. *Perf. 13*

1143 A403 4k Oersted Satellite 1.50 .55

Deciduous Trees A404

4k, Fagus sylvatica. 5k, Fraxinus excelsior, vert. 5.25k, Tilia cordata, vert. 9.25k, Quercus robur.

1999, Jan. 13 Litho. & Engr.

1144 A404 4k multicolored 1.60 .30
Complete booklet, 10 #1144 16.00
1145 A404 5k multicolored 2.00 .60
1146 A404 5.25k multicolored 2.10 .60
1147 A404 9.25k multicolored 3.50 1.25
Nos. 1144-1147 (4) 9.20 2.75

50th Anniversaries — A405

Litho. & Engr.

1999, Feb. 24 *Perf. 13*

1148 A405 3.75k Home Guard 1.50 .30
1149 A405 4.25k NATO 1.60 .60

A406

A407

Harbingers of spring.

1999, Feb. 24 Litho.

1150 A406 4k Lapwing in flight 1.60 .30
Complete booklet, 10 #1150 16.00
1151 A406 5.25k Geese 2.10 .90
a. Souvenir sheet, #1150-1151 5.50 1.75

Litho. & Engr.

1999, Apr. 28 *Perf. 13*

Nature Reserves.

1152 A407 4.50k Vejlerne *1.50 .40*
1153 A407 5.50k Langli *1.90 .60*

Europa.

Council of Europe, 50th Anniv. A408

1999, Apr. 28 Engr.

1154 A408 9.75k blue 3.75 1.25

Danish Constitution, 150th Anniv. — A409

1999, June 2 Litho. *Perf. 13*

1155 A409 4k red & black 1.60 .30

Danish Revue, 150th Anniv. A410

Performers: 4k, Kjeld Petersen and Dirch Passer, comedians. 4.50k, Osvald Helmuth, singer. 5.25k, Preben Kaas and Jorgen Ryg, comedians, singers. 6.75k, Liva Weel, singer.

1999, June 2 Engr. *Perf. 13*

1156 A410 4k deep red 1.60 .30
Complete booklet, 10 #1156 16.00
1157 A410 4.50k slate 1.75 .50
1158 A410 5.25k deep blue 2.10 .85
Complete booklet, 10 #1158 21.00
1159 A410 6.75k deep claret 2.75 1.10
a. Bklt. pane, #1156-1159 + 2 labels 8.50
Complete booklet, 2 #1159a 17.00
Nos. 1156-1159 (4) 8.20 2.75

No. 1159a printed with two different pairs of labels. One version has showgirl label at left, the second version has showgirl label at right. Complete booklets contain one of each pane.

Contemporary Paintings Type

9.25k, Fire Farver, by Thomas Kluge. 16k, Dreng, by Lise Malinovsky.

1999, Aug. 25 Litho. *Perf. 12¾*

1160 A401 9.25k multi, vert. 3.50 1.60
1161 A401 16k multi, vert. 6.25 2.50

Opening of New Extension of the Royal Library, "The Black Diamond" A411

1999, Aug. 25 Engr. *Perf. 13¾*

1162 A411 8.75k black 3.00 1.25

Migratory Birds — A412

Litho. & Engr.

1999, Sept. 29 *Perf. 12¾*

1163 A412 4k Swallows 1.60 .30
Complete booklet, 10 #1163 16.00
1164 A412 5.25k Gray-lag geese 2.10 .80
a. Souvenir sheet, #1163-1164 4.00 1.50
1165 A412 5.50k Common eider 2.25 .85
1166 A412 12.25k Arctic tern 4.75 2.10
a. Souvenir sheet, #1165-1166 7.50 3.00
Nos. 1163-1166 (4) 10.70 4.05

Stamps from Nos. 1164a and 1166a lack white border found on Nos. 1163-1166.

New Year 2000 — A413

1999, Nov. 10 Litho. *Perf. 13¼*

1167 A413 4k Hearts 1.60 .30
1168 A413 4k Wavy lines 1.60 .30
a. Bklt. pane, 5 ea #1167-1168 16.00
Complete booklet, #1168a 16.00

The 20th Century — A414

4k, Prof. J.H. Deuntzer on front page of newspaper, 1901. 4.50k, Newspaper illustration, 1903. 5.25k, Asta Nielsen and Poul Reumert in the film "The Abyss," 1910. 5.75k, Advertising sticker showing woman on telephone, 1914.

See sheet of 16, #1184a.

2000, Jan. 12 Litho. & Engr.

1169 A414 4k buff & blk 1.60 .30
Complete booklet, 10 #1169 16.00
1170 A414 4.50k multicolored 1.75 .50
1171 A414 5.25k multicolored 2.10 .85
Complete booklet, 10 #1171 21.00
1172 A414 5.75k multicolored 2.25 .90
Nos. 1169-1172 (4) 7.70 2.55

2000, May 9

4k, Allegory of women suffrage on front page of newspaper, 1915. 5k, Newspaper caricature of the Kanslergade Agreement, 1933. 5.50k, Film "Long and Short," 1927. 6.75k, Front page of Radio Weekly Review, 1925.

1173 A414 4k multi 1.60 .55
Booklet, 10 #1173 16.00
1174 A414 5k multi 2.00 .65
1175 A414 5.50k multi 2.25 .75
1176 A414 6.75k multi 2.75 .85
Nos. 1173-1176 (4) 8.60 2.80

2000, Aug. 23

4k, Liberation of Denmark on front page of newspaper, 1945. 5.75k, Newspaper caricature of new constitution, 1953. 6.75k, Poster for film "Café Paradise," 1950. 12.25k, Advertisement for Arena television, 1957.

1177 A414 4k multi 1.60 .55
Booklet, 10 #1177 16.00
1178 A414 5.75k multi 2.25 .80
1179 A414 6.75k multi 2.75 .85
1180 A414 12.25k multi 4.75 1.60
Nos. 1177-1180 (4) 11.35 3.80

2000, Nov. 8

4k, Entry of Denmark into European Community on front page of newspaper, 1972. 4.50k, Newspaper caricature of youth revolt, 1969. 5.25k, Poster for film "The Olsen Gang," 1968. 5.50k, Denmark Post website on Internet, 1999.

1181 A414 4k multi 1.60 .55
Booklet, 10 #1181 16.00
1182 A414 4.50k multi 1.75 .60
1183 A414 5.25k multi 2.10 .70
Booklet, 10 #1183 21.00
a. Booklet pane, #1171, 1175, 1179, 1183 + label 10.00
Booklet, 2 #1183a 20.00
1184 A414 5.50k multi 2.25 .75
a. Sheet of 16, #1169-1184 35.00 13.00
Nos. 1181-1184 (4) 7.70 2.60

No. 1183a comes with two different labels. Booklet contains one of each.

60th Birthday of Queen Margrethe II — A415

2000, Apr. 12 Litho. *Perf. 12¾*

1185 A415 4k blk & car 1.60 .60
Complete booklet, 10 #1185 16.00
1186 A415 5.25k blk & blue 2.10 .80
a. Souvenir sheet, #1185-1186 4.00 1.50

Oresund Bridge, Sweden-Denmark — A416

Illustration reduced.

Litho. & Engr.

2000, May 9 *Perf. 12¾*

1187 A416 4.50k shown 1.75 .60

Litho.

1188 A416 4.50k Map 1.75 .60
a. Pair, #1187-1188 3.50 1.25

See Sweden Nos. 2391-2393.

Europa, 2000

Common Design Type

2000, May 9 Litho. *Perf. 13*

1189 CD17 9.75k multi *3.25 1.10*

Contemporary Art Type of 1998

Designs: 4k, Pegasus, by Kurt Trampedach. 5.25k, Landscape, by Nina Sten-Knudsen.

2000, Sept. 27 *Perf. 12¾*

1190 A401 4k multi 1.60 .55
1191 A401 5.25k multi 2.10 .75

Royal Danish Air Force, 50th Anniv. A417

2000, Sept. 27 Engr.

1192 A417 9.75k black & red 3.75 1.25
a. Souvenir sheet of 1 3.75 1.25

Pasteur Institute, Cent. — A143

1987, Feb. 19 Litho. *Perf. 13*
624 A143 220fr multicolored 4.00 1.50

Natl. Vaccination Campaign.

Edible Mushrooms A144

1987, Apr. 16 Litho. *Perf. 13x12½*
625 A144 35fr Macrolepiota imbricata 1.25 .65
626 A144 50fr Lentinus squarrosulus 2.00 .85
627 A144 95fr Terfezia boudieri 2.75 1.50
Nos. 625-627 (3) 6.00 3.00

Wildlife A145

1987, May 14 *Perf. 12½x13*
628 A145 5fr Hare .25 .20
629 A145 30fr Dromedary 1.00 .30
630 A145 140fr Cheetah 4.50 1.00
Nos. 628-630 (3) 5.75 1.50

1988 Olympics, Seoul and Calgary — A146

85fr, Pierre de Coubertin (1863-1937), founder of the modern Olympics, & lighting of the flame. 135fr, Ski jumping. 140fr, Running.

1987, July 16 *Perf. 13*
631 A146 85fr multicolored 1.50 .55
632 A146 135fr multicolored 2.50 .95
633 A146 140fr multicolored 2.75 1.00
Nos. 631-633 (3) 6.75 2.50

Traditional Art — A147

UN Universal Immunization by 1990 Campaign A148

1988, Jan. 20 Litho. *Perf. 13*
634 A147 30fr Nomad's comb .60 .30
635 A147 70fr Wash jug 1.25 .60

1988, Apr. 10 *Perf. 12½*
636 A148 125fr multicolored 2.25 1.00

16th Africa Cup Soccer Championships, Morocco — A149

1988, Mar. 13 *Perf. 13*
637 A149 55fr Athletes, view of Rabat 1.10 .50

1988 Winter Olympics, Calgary — A150

1988, May 7 Litho. *Perf. 13*
638 A150 45fr Ski jump .90 .40

Campaign Against Thirst A151

1988, Sept. 10 Litho. *Perf. 12½x13*
639 A151 50fr multicolored 1.00 .40

Intl. Fund for Agricultural Development, 10th Anniv. — A152

1988, Nov. 14 *Perf. 13*
640 A152 135fr multicolored 2.25 1.00

Michel Lafoux Air Club, 40th Anniv. — A153

1988, Dec. 6
641 A153 145fr 1948 Tiger Moth, 1988 Tobago-10 2.75 1.00

Marine Life A154

1989, Jan. 20 Litho. *Perf. 12½*
642 A154 90fr *Lobophyllia costata* 1.75 .25
643 A154 160fr *Lambis truncata* 3.25 1.10

Colotis protomedia A155

1989, Feb. 15
644 A155 70fr multicolored 2.50 1.25

Nos. 573 and 547 Surcharged

1989 *Perf. 13*
646 A126 70fr on 2fr No. 573 2.25 .50
647 A118 70fr on 150fr No. 547 2.25 .50

Issued: 646, 12/20; 647, 12/29.

Folk Dances — A157

Francolin of Djibouti — A159

1989, Mar. 20
648 A157 30fr shown .50 .25
649 A157 70fr multicolored, diff. 1.40 .50

1989, Apr. 10 Litho. *Perf. 12½*
651 A159 35fr multicolored 1.40 .35

Rare Flora A160

1989, June 12
652 A160 25fr *Calotropis procera* .45 .20

A161

A162

1989, Aug. 10 Litho. *Perf. 13*
653 A161 70fr multicolored 1.25 .50

Interparliamentary Union, cent.

1989, Oct. 1
654 A162 145fr multicolored 2.75 1.10

Intl. Literacy Year.

Petroglyph — A163

1989, Nov. 18 Litho. *Perf. 13*
655 A163 5fr multicolored .35 .20

Girl — A164

1989, Dec. 6
656 A164 55fr multicolored 1.00 .40

Nos. 574, 576-577 Surcharged

1989-1990 Litho. *Perf. 13*
657 A126 30fr on 8fr multi .50 .30
658 A126 50fr on 40fr multi 2.00 .55
660 A126 120fr on 15fr multi 2.00 .80
Nos. 657-660 (3) 4.50 1.65

Issue dates: 30fr, 12/20/89; 50fr, 7/3/90; 120fr, 3/17/90.

Water Conservation — A165

1990, May 5 Litho. *Perf. 11½*
665 A165 120fr multicolored 1.75 .70

Traditional Jewelry A166

1990, Mar. 10
666 A166 70fr multicolored 1.25 .45

Commiphora — A167

1990, Feb. 20 ***Perf. 12***
667 A167 30fr multicolored .60 .35

Baskets — A168

1990, July 3
668 A168 30fr multicolored .50 .20

A169 A170

1990, June 12 ***Perf. 11½***
669 A169 100fr multicolored 1.50 .60

World Cup Soccer Championships, Italy.

1990, Apr. 16 ***Perf. 11½***
670 A170 55fr shown 1.00 .40

20 kilometer race of Djibouti.

Vaccination Campaign A171

1990, Aug. 22 Litho. ***Perf. 11½***
Granite Paper
671 A171 300fr multicolored 4.50 1.75

Charles de Gaulle — A172

African Tourism Year — A173

1990, Sept. 16
Granite Paper
672 A172 200fr multicolored 3.50 1.25

1991, Jan. 23 Litho. ***Perf. 13***
673 A173 115fr multicolored 2.00 .80

Corals — A174

Aquatic Birds — A175

1991, Jan. 28 ***Perf. 12½***
674 A174 40fr Acropora .80 .40
675 A174 45fr Seriatopora hytrise 1.00 .40

1991, Feb. 12
676 A175 10fr Pelecanus rufescens .60 .20
677 A175 15fr Egretta gularis 1.40 .25
678 A175 20fr Ardea goliath, horiz. 1.60 .30
679 A175 25fr Platalea leucorodia, horiz. 1.75 .35
Nos. 676-679 (4) 5.35 1.10

UNO Development Conference A176

Fossils A177

1990, Oct. 9 Litho. ***Perf. 11½x12***
Granite Paper
680 A176 45fr multicolored .90 .40

1990, Nov. 1
Granite Paper
681 A177 90fr pur, org & blk 5.25 1.75

Papio Hamadryas — A178

1990, Dec. 6
Granite Paper
682 A178 50fr multicolored .90 .30

Pandion Haliaetus A179

1991, Mar. 20 Litho. ***Perf. 12x11½***
683 A179 200fr multicolored 3.25 1.10

Traditional Game A180

1991, Apr. 4
684 A180 250fr multicolored 3.50 2.25

See No. 696.

Djibouti-Ethiopia Railroad — A181

1991, May 25 Litho. ***Perf. 11½***
685 A181 85fr multicolored 1.25 .70

World Environment Day — A182

1991, June 10
686 A182 110fr multicolored 2.00 .50

Philexafrique — A183

1991, Jul. 16 Litho. ***Perf. 11½***
687 A183 120fr Islands 1.75 1.00

A184

A185

1991, Sept. 25
688 A184 175fr Handball 2.25 1.60

Pre-Olympic year.

1991, Oct. 16 Litho. ***Perf. 11½x12***
689 A185 105fr multicolored 2.10 1.10

World Food Day.

Underwater Cable Network — A186

1991, Nov. 28 ***Perf. 12x11½***
690 A186 130fr multicolored 2.10 .80

Discovery of America, 500th Anniv. A187

1991, Dec. 19 Litho. ***Perf. 11½***
691 A187 145fr multicolored 2.25 1.40

Arthur Rimbaud (1854-1891) Poet and Merchant — A188

1991-92 ***Perf. 11½***
692 A188 90fr Young man, ship 2.00 .75
693 A188 150fr Old man, camels 2.25 .75

Issued: 90fr, 2/5/92; 150fr, 12/23/91.

Djibouti-Ethiopia Railroad — A189

Design: 250fr, Locomotive, map.

1992 Litho. ***Perf. 12x11½***
694 A189 70fr multicolored 1.50 .60

Souvenir Sheet
Perf. 13x12½
695 A189 250fr multicolored 4.50 4.50

Issue dates: 70fr, Feb. 2; 250fr, Jan. 30.

Traditional Game Type of 1991

1992, Feb. 10 ***Perf. 11½***
696 A180 100fr Boys playing Go 1.50 .60

Items commemorating the death of Pope John Paul II were declared as "fraudulent" by Djibouti Post.

Tanker in Port of Doraleh — A288

2006 **Litho.** ***Perf. 13***
845 A288 120fr multi *8.25 8.25*

Printed in sheets of 4.

Djibouti Chamber of Commerce, Cent. — A290

2007 **Litho.** ***Perf. 12¾***
847 A290 50fr multi — —
a. Souvenir sheet of 2 — —

Independence, 30th Anniv. — A291

2007 **Litho.** ***Perf. 13***
848 A291 75fr multi — —
a. Souvenir sheet of 2 — —

Mahamoud Harbi (1921-60), Politician — A292

2007 **Litho.** ***Perf. 13x12¾***
849 A292 165fr multi 11.50 11.50

AIR POST STAMPS

Afars and Issas Nos. C104-C105, C103 Overprinted with Bars and "REPUBLIQUE DE DJIBOUTI" in Brown or Black

1977 **Engr.** ***Perf. 13***
C106 AP37 55fr multi (Br) 1.75 1.75
C107 AP37 75fr multi 7.00 3.00

Litho. ***Perf. 12***
C108 AP36 500fr multi 13.50 13.50
Nos. C106-C108 (3) 22.25 18.25

Map of Djibouti, Dove, UN Emblem — AP38

1977, Oct. 19 **Photo.** ***Perf. 13***
C109 AP38 300fr multi 5.50 3.50

Djibouti's admission to the United Nations.

Marcel Brochet MB 101, 1955 — AP39

Djibouti Aero Club: 85fr, Tiger Moth, 1960. 200fr, Rallye-Commodore, 1973.

1978, Feb. 27 **Litho.** ***Perf. 13***
C110 AP39 60fr multi 1.10 .35
C111 AP39 85fr multi 1.60 .60
C112 AP39 200fr multi 3.50 1.00
Nos. C110-C112 (3) 6.20 1.95

Old Man, by Rubens AP40

500fr, Hippopotamus Hunt, by Rubens.

1978, Apr. 24 **Photo.** ***Perf. 13***
C113 AP40 50fr multi 1.00 .35
C114 AP40 500fr multi, horiz. 10.00 3.25

Peter Paul Rubens (1577-1640).

Player Holding Soccer Cup — AP41

Design: 300fr, Soccer player, map of South America with Argentina, Cup and emblem.

1978, June 20 **Litho.** ***Perf. 13***
C115 AP41 100fr multi 1.75 .35
C116 AP41 300fr multi 5.25 1.00

11th World Cup Soccer Championship, Argentina, June 1-25.
For overprints see Nos. C117-C118.

Nos. C115-C116 Overprinted:
a. ARGENTINE/CHAMPION 1978
b. ARGENTINE/HOLLANDE/3-1

1978, Aug. 20 **Litho.** ***Perf. 13***
C117 AP41 (a) 100fr multi 1.75 .40
C118 AP41 (b) 300fr multi 5.25 1.25

Argentina's victory in 1978 Soccer Championship.

Tahitian Women, by Gauguin — AP42

Young Hare, by Dürer AP43

Perf. 13x12½, 12½x13
1978, Sept. 25 **Litho.**
C119 AP42 100fr multi 2.25 .40
C120 AP43 250fr multi 5.25 1.50

Paul Gauguin (1848-1903) and Albrecht Dürer (1471-1528), painters.

Common Design Types pictured following the introduction.

Philexafrique II-Essen Issue
Common Design Types

Designs: No. C121, Lynx and Djibouti No. 456. No. C122, Jay and Brunswick No. 3.

1978, Dec. 13 **Litho.** ***Perf. 13x12½***
C121 CD138 90fr multi 3.00 1.25
C122 CD139 90fr multi 3.00 1.25
a. Pair, Nos. C121-C122 + label 6.25 6.25

UPU Emblem, Map of Djibouti, Dove — AP44

1978, Dec. 18 **Engr.** ***Perf. 13***
C123 AP44 200fr multi 3.00 1.10

Centenary of Congress of Paris.

Junkers JU-52 and Dewoitine D-338 — AP45

Powered Flight, 75th Anniversary: 250fr, Potez P63-11, 1941 and Supermarine Spitfire HF-VII, 1942. 500fr, Concorde, 1969 and Sikorsky S-40 "American Clipper," 1931.

1979, May 21 **Litho.** ***Perf. 13x12½***
C124 AP45 140fr multi 2.75 .60
C125 AP45 250fr multi 4.00 1.00
C126 AP45 500fr multi 8.50 1.75
Nos. C124-C126 (3) 15.25 3.35

The Laundress, by Honore Daumier AP46

1979, July 10 **Litho.** ***Perf. 12½x13***
C127 AP46 500fr multi 10.50 2.75

Olympic Emblem, Skis, Sleds — AP47

1980, Jan. 21 **Litho.** ***Perf. 13***
C128 AP47 150fr multi 2.75 .60

13th Winter Olympic Games, Lake Placid, N.Y., Feb. 12-24.
For surcharges see Nos. C133-C134.

Cathedral of the Archangel, Basketball, Moscow '80 Emblem — AP48

120fr, Lomonossov Univ., Moscow, soccer. 250fr, Cathedral of the Annunciation, running.

1980, Apr. 10 **Litho.** ***Perf. 13***
C129 AP48 60fr multi 1.00 .25
C130 AP48 120fr multi 2.00 .40
C131 AP48 250fr multi 4.00 1.00
Nos. C129-C131 (3) 7.00 1.65

22nd Summer Olympic Games, Moscow, July 18-Aug. 3.

Air Djibouti, 1st Anniversary — AP49

1980, Mar. 29 **Litho.** ***Perf. 13x12½***
C132 AP49 400fr multi 7.50 2.00

No. C128 Surcharged in Black and Blue or Purple:
80fr. A.M. MOSER-PROEL/ AUTRICHE / DESCENTE DAMES/ MEDAILLE D'OR
200fr. HEIDEN / USA / 5 MEDAIL-LES D'OR / PATINAGE DE VITESSE

1980, Apr. 5 **Litho.** ***Perf. 13***
C133 AP47 80fr on 150fr 1.40 .40
C134 AP47 200fr on 150fr (P) 3.50 1.25

Apollo 11 Moon Landing, 10th Anniversary — AP50

Space Conquests: 300fr, Apollo-Soyuz space project, 5th anniversary.

1980, May 8

C135	AP50	200fr multi	3.50	.60
C136	AP50	300fr multi	5.25	1.00

Satellite Earth Station Inauguration — AP51

1980, July 3 Litho. *Perf. 13*

C137	AP51	500fr multi	9.00	1.75

Graf Zeppelin — AP52

1980, Oct. 2 Litho. *Perf. 13*

C138	AP52	100fr shown	2.25	.40
C139	AP52	150fr Ferdinand von Zeppelin, blimp	2.75	.60

Zeppelin flight, 80th anniversary.

Voyager Passing Saturn — AP53

1980, Dec. 21 Litho. *Perf. 13*

C140	AP53	250fr multi	5.00	1.00

AP54

AP55

World Cup Soccer Preliminary Games: 200fr, Players, diff.

1981, Jan. 14

C141	AP54	80fr multi	1.40	.30
C142	AP54	200fr multi	3.50	.65

1981, Feb. 10 Litho. *Perf. 13*

C143	AP55	100fr multi	2.50	.50

European-African Economic Convention.

5th Anniversary of Viking I Take-off to Mars — AP56

20th Anniversary of Various Space Flights: 75fr, Vostok I, Yuri Gagarin, vert. 150fr, Freedom 7, Alan B. Shepard, vert.

1981, Mar. 9 Litho. *Perf. 13*

C144	AP56	75fr multi	1.40	.30
C145	AP56	120fr multi	2.00	.40
C146	AP56	150fr multi	2.75	.60
		Nos. C144-C146 (3)	6.15	1.30

Football Players, by Picasso (1881-1973) — AP57

Design: 400fr Man Wearing a Turban, by Rembrandt (1606-1669), vert.

Perf. 13x12½, 12½x13

1981, Aug. 3 Litho.

C147	AP57	300fr multi	6.25	1.40
C148	AP57	400fr multi	7.00	1.75

Columbia Space Shuttle — AP58

1981, Sept. 24 Litho. *Perf. 13*

C149	AP58	90fr Shuttle, diff., vert.	1.75	.40
C150	AP58	120fr shown	2.25	.60

Nos. C149-C150 Overprinted in Brown with Astronauts' Names and Dates

1981, Nov. 12 Litho. *Perf. 13*

C151	AP58	90fr multi	1.75	.50
C152	AP58	120fr multi	2.25	.75

1982 World Cup Soccer — AP59

Designs: Various soccer players.

1982, Jan. 20

C153	AP59	110fr multi	2.10	.60
C154	AP59	220fr multi	4.00	1.25

For overprints see Nos. C166-C167.

Space Anniversaries — AP60

Designs: 40fr, Luna 9 moon landing, 15th, vert. 60fr, John Glenn's flight, 20th, vert. 180fr, Viking I Mars landing, 5th.

1982, Feb. 15

C155	AP60	40fr multi	.70	.20
C156	AP60	60fr multi	1.10	.30
C157	AP60	180fr multi	3.00	1.00
		Nos. C155-C157 (3)	4.80	1.50

21st Birthday of Princess Diana of Wales AP61

1982, Apr. 29 Litho. *Perf. 12½x13*

C158	AP61	120fr Portrait	2.00	.75
C159	AP61	180fr Portrait, diff.	3.00	1.00

For overprints see Nos. C168-C169.

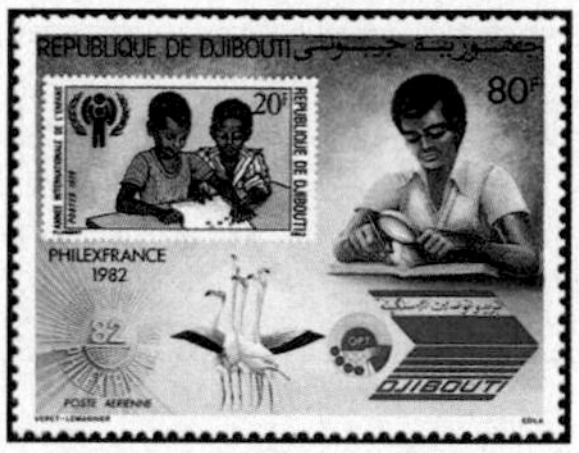

No. 489, Boy Examining Collection — AP62

1982, May 10 *Perf. 13x12½*

C160	AP62	80fr shown	1.40	.50
C161	AP62	140fr No. 495	2.75	.90
a.		Pair, Nos. C160-C161 + label	4.50	4.50

PHILEXFRANCE '82 Stamp Exhibition, Paris, June 11-21.

1350th Anniv. of Mohammed's Death at Medina — AP63

1982, June 8 Litho. *Perf. 13*

C162	AP63	500fr Medina Mosque	7.50	2.00

Scouting Year — AP64

1982, June 28

C163	AP64	95fr Baden-Powell	1.50	.50
C164	AP64	200fr Camp, scouts	3.50	1.25

2nd UN Conference on Peaceful Uses of Outer Space, Vienna, Aug. 9-21 — AP65

1982, Aug. 19

C165	AP65	350fr multi	3.00	1.40

Nos. C153-C154 Overprinted with Winner's Name and Scores

1982, July 21 Litho. *Perf. 13*

C166	AP59	110fr multi	2.00	.60
C167	AP59	220fr multi	4.00	1.10

Italy's victory in 1982 World Cup.

Nos. C158-C159 Overprinted in Blue or Red with Date, Name and Title

1982, Aug. 9 *Perf. 12½x13*

C168	AP61	120fr multi	2.25	.75
C169	AP61	180fr multi (R)	3.25	1.00

Birth of Prince William of Wales, June 21.

Franklin D. Roosevelt (1882-1945) AP66

1982, Oct. 7 Litho. *Perf. 13*

C170	AP66	115fr shown	1.75	.50
C171	AP66	250fr George Washington	4.50	1.00

Manned Flight Bicentenary AP67

Pre-olympic Year — AP68

1983, Jan. 20 Litho.

C172	AP67	35fr Montgolfiere, 1783	.65	.25
C173	AP67	45fr Giffard, Paris Exposition, 1878	1.10	.30
C174	AP67	120fr Double Eagle II, 1978	2.75	.80
		Nos. C172-C174 (3)	4.50	1.35

1983, Feb. 15

C175	AP68	75fr Volleyball	1.40	.50
C176	AP68	125fr Wind surfing	2.40	.80

50th Anniv. of Air France — AP69

1983, Mar. 20 Litho. *Perf. 13*

C177 AP69 25fr Bloch 220 .40 .20
C178 AP69 100fr DC-4 1.75 .70
C179 AP69 175fr Boeing 747 3.25 1.10
Nos. C177-C179 (3) 5.40 2.00

AP70

AP71

180fr, Martin Luther King, Jr. (1929-68), civil rights leader. 250fr, Alfred Nobel (1833-96)

1983, May 18 Litho. *Perf. 13*

C180 AP70 180fr multi 2.75 1.25
C181 AP70 250fr multi 3.75 2.00

1983, July 18 Litho. *Perf. 13*

Service Clubs: 90fr, Rotary Club Intl., Sailing Show, Toronto, June 5-9. 150fr, Lions Club Intl., Honolulu Meeting, June 22-24, Djibouti lighthouse.

C182 AP71 90fr multi 1.40 .60
C183 AP71 150fr multi 2.25 1.00
a. Pair, Nos. C182-C183 + label 5.00 1.75

Vintage Motor Cars — AP72

1983, Sep. 20 Litho. *Perf. 13x12½*

C184 AP72 60fr Renault, 1904 1.50 .40
C185 AP72 80fr Mercedes, 1910, vert. 2.00 .55
C186 AP72 110fr Lorraine-Dietrich, 1912 2.50 .75
Nos. C184-C186 (3) 6.00 1.70

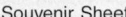

Souvenir Sheet

Air France, 50th Anniv. — AP73

Illustration reduced.

1983, Oct. 7 Litho. *Perf. 12½*
Self-Adhesive

C187 AP73 250fr multicolored 25.00 2.10

Printed on wood.

Vostok VI AP74

1983, Oct. 20 Litho. *Perf. 12*

C188 AP74 120fr shown 2.00 .80
C189 AP74 200fr Explorer I 3.50 1.10

1984 Winter Olympics — AP75

1984, Feb. 14 Litho. *Perf. 13*

C190 AP75 70fr Speed skating 1.40 .50
C191 AP75 130fr Figure skating 2.25 1.00

For overprints see Nos. C196-C197.

Souvenir Sheet

Ship — AP76

1984, Feb. 14 Litho. *Perf. 12½*

C192 AP76 250fr multi 11.00 1.75

Sea-Me-We (South-east Asia-Middle East-Western Europe) submarine cable construction agreement.

Motorized Hang Gliders — AP77

Various hang gliders.

1984, Mar. 12 *Perf. 13x12½*

C193 AP77 65fr multi 1.25 .50
C194 AP77 85fr multi 1.60 .60
C195 AP77 100fr multi 2.10 .75
Nos. C193-C195 (3) 4.95 1.85

Nos. C190-C191 Overprinted with Winners' Names and Country

1984, Mar. 28 *Perf. 13*

C196 AP75 70fr multi 1.25 .50
C197 AP75 130fr multi 2.40 1.00

Portrait of Marguerite Matisse, 1910, by Henri Matisse AP78

Design: 200fr, Portrait of Mario Varvogli, by Amedeo Modigliani.

1984, Apr. 15 Litho. *Perf. 12½x13*

C198 AP78 150fr multi 3.25 1.00
C199 AP78 200fr multi 4.00 1.40

1984 Summer Olympics — AP79

1984, May 24 *Perf. 13*

C200 AP79 50fr Running 1.00 .40
C201 AP79 60fr High jump 1.25 .40
C202 AP79 80fr Swimming 1.50 .60
Nos. C200-C202 (3) 3.75 1.40

Battle Scene — AP80

1984, June 16 Litho. *Perf. 13x12½*

C203 AP80 300fr multi 5.50 2.25

125th anniv. of Battle of Solferino and 120th anniv. of Red Cross.

Bleriot's Flight over English Channel, 75th Anniv. — AP81

1984, July 8

C204 AP81 40fr 14-Bis plans .80 .30
C205 AP81 75fr Britten-Norman Islander 1.40 .55
C206 AP81 90fr Air Djibouti jet 1.50 .65
Nos. C204-C206 (3) 3.70 1.50

375th Anniv., Galileo's Telescope AP82

1984, Oct. 7 Litho. *Perf. 13*

C207 AP82 120fr Telescopes, spacecraft 2.25 .80
C208 AP82 180fr Galileo, telescopes 3.25 1.10

1984 Soccer Events — AP83

1984, Oct. 20 Litho. *Perf. 13*

C209 AP83 80fr Euro Cup 1.75 .60
C210 AP83 80fr Los Angeles Olympics 1.75 .60
a. Pair, Nos. C209-C210 + label 4.25 1.25

Service Clubs — AP84

1985, Feb. 23 Litho. *Perf. 13*

C211 AP84 50fr Lions, World Leprosy Day 1.10 .40
C212 AP84 60fr Rotary, chess board, pieces 1.25 .45

#C211-C212 exist in souvenir sheets of 1.

Telecommunications Technology — AP85

No. C213, Technician, researchist, operator. No. C214, Offshore oil rig, transmission tower, government building.

1985, July 2 *Perf. 13x12½*

C213 AP85 80fr multi 2.00 .55
C214 AP85 80fr multi 2.00 .55
a. Pair, Nos. C213-C214 + label 4.50 1.10

PHILEXAFRICA '85, Lome.

Telecommunications Development — AP86

1985, Oct. 2 *Perf. 13*

C215 AP86 50fr Intl. transmission center .90 .35
C216 AP86 90fr Ariane rocket, vert. 1.60 .65
C217 AP86 120fr ARABSAT satellite 2.00 .90
Nos. C215-C217 (3) 4.50 1.90

Youths Windsurfing, Playing Tennis — AP87

No. C219, Tadjoura Highway construction.

1985, Nov. 13 *Perf. 13x12½*

C218 AP87 100fr multi 2.00 .70
C219 AP87 100fr multi 2.00 .70
a. Pair, Nos. C218-C219 + label 4.50 1.50

PHILEXAFRICA '85, Lome, Togo, 11/16-24.

1986 World Cup Soccer Championships, Mexico — AP88

1986, Feb. 24 **Litho.** *Perf. 13*

C220 AP88 75fr shown 1.50 .50
C221 AP88 100fr Players, stadium 2.00 .70

For overprints see Nos. C223-C224.

Statue of Liberty, Cent. — AP89

1986, May 21

C222 AP89 250fr multi 4.00 1.75

Nos. C220-C221 Ovptd. with Winners

1986, Sept. 15 **Litho.** *Perf. 13*

C223 75fr "FRANCE - BELGIQUE / 4-2" 1.10 .55
C224 100fr "3-2 ARGENTINE-RFA" 1.50 .70

1986 World Chess Championships, May 1-19 — AP89a

Malayan animal chess pieces.

1986, Oct. 13 **Litho.** *Perf. 13*

C225 AP89a 80fr Knight, bishops 1.75 .60
C226 AP89a 120fr Rook, king, pawn 2.75 .90

Yuri Gagarin, Sputnik Spacecraft — AP90

1986, Nov. 27 **Litho.** *Perf. 13*

C227 AP90 150fr shown 3.00 1.10
C228 AP90 200fr Space rendezvous, 1966 3.25 1.25

First man in space, 25th anniv.; Gemini 8-Agena link-up, 20th anniv.

Historic Flights — AP91

1987, Jan. 22 **Litho.** *Perf. 13*

C229 AP91 55fr Amiot 370 1.25 .40
C230 AP91 80fr Spirit of St. Louis 1.75 .55
C231 AP91 120fr Voyager 2.50 .90
Nos. C229-C231 (3) 5.50 1.85

First flight from Istria to Djibouti, 1942; Lindbergh's Transatlantic flight, 1927; nonstop world circumnavigation without refueling.
For surcharge see No. C240.

Souvenir Sheet

Fight Against Leprosy — AP91a

Design: Raoul Follereau (b. 1903), care giver to lepers, Gerhard Hansen (1841-1912), discoverer of bacillus of leprosy.
Illustration reduced.

1987, Mar. 23 **Litho.** *Perf. 13x12½*
Self-Adhesive

C231A AP91a 500fr multi 17.00 4.25

No. C231A printed on wood.

Pres. Aptidon, Natl. Crest and Flag AP92

1987, June 27 **Litho.** *Perf. 12½x13*

C232 AP92 250fr multi 4.00 1.50

Natl. independence, 10th anniv.

Telstar, 25th Anniv. — AP93

1987, Oct. 1 *Perf. 13*

C233 AP93 190fr shown 3.00 1.25
a. Souvenir sheet, 1 #C233 12.00 —
C234 AP93 250fr Samuel Morse, telegraph key 3.75 1.50
a. Souvenir sheet, 1 #C234 12.00 —

Invention of the telegraph, 150th anniv. (250fr).
Nos. C233a and C234a also exist imperf. Value, set of 2, $40.

City of Djibouti, Cent. — AP94

100fr, Djibouti Creek & quay, 1887. 150fr, Aerial view of city, 1987. 250fr, Somali Coast #6, 20, postmarks of 1898 & 1903.

1987, Nov. 15 **Litho.** *Perf. 13x12½*

C235 AP94 100fr blk & buff 2.00 1.10
C236 AP94 150fr multi 3.00 1.60
a. Pair, Nos. C235-C236 + label 6.00 2.75

Souvenir Sheet

237 AP94 250fr multi 5.50 2.75

No. C237 has decorative margin like design of 100fr.

Intl. Red Cross and Red Crescent Organizations, 125th Anniv. — AP95

1988, Feb. 17 **Litho.** *Perf. 13*

C238 AP95 300fr multi 6.00 3.25

1988 Summer Olympics, Seoul — AP96

1988, June 15 **Litho.** *Perf. 13*

C239 AP96 105fr multi 2.50 1.00

For overprint see No. C242.

No. C229 Surcharged in Black

1988, June 28

C240 AP91 70fr on 55fr multi 1.75 .70

Air race in memory of the Paris-Djibouti-St. Denis flight of French aviator Roland Garros (1888-1913).

World Post Day — AP97

1988, Oct. 9 **Litho.** *Perf. 13*

C241 AP97 1000fr multi 15.00 10.00

No. C239 Ovptd. "AHMED SALAH / 1re MEDAILLE OLYMPIQUE"

1988, Dec. 15 **Litho.** *Perf. 13*

C242 AP96 105fr multi 2.00 1.50

World Telecommunications Day — AP98

1989, May 17 **Litho.** *Perf. 12½*

C243 AP98 150fr multi 2.75 1.50

PHILEXFRANCE '89, Declaration of Human Rights and Citizenship Bicent. — AP99

1989, July 14 **Litho.** *Perf. 12½x13*

C244 AP99 120fr multi 2.25 1.25

Salt, Lake Assal — AP100

1989, Sept. 15 **Litho.** *Perf. 13*

C245 AP100 300fr multicolored 4.50 3.00

POSTAGE DUE STAMP

Urn for Milking Camel — D1

1988, Jan. 20 **Litho.** ***Perf. 13***

J1	D1	60fr multi	.90	.65

DOMINICA

ˌdä-mə-ˈnē-kə

LOCATION — The largest island of the Windward group in the West Indies. Southeast of Puerto Rico.
GOVT. — Republic in British Commonwealth
AREA — 290 sq. mi.
POP. — 64,881 (1999 est.)
CAPITAL — Roseau

Formerly a Presidency of the Leeward Islands, Dominica became a separate colony under the governor of the Windward Islands on January 1, 1940. Dominica joined the West Indies federation April 22, 1958. In 1968, Dominica became an associate state of Britain; in 1978, an independent nation.

12 Pence = 1 Shilling
20 Shillings = 1 Pound
100 Cents = 1 Dollar (1949)

Catalogue values for unused stamps in this country are for Never Hinged items, beginning with Scott 112.

Watermark

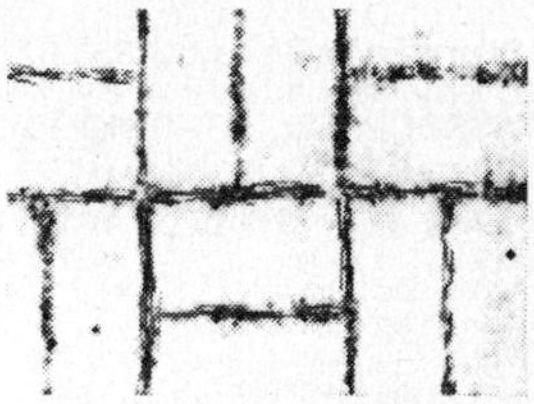

Wmk. 334 — Rectangles

Queen Victoria — A1

Perf. 12½

1874, May 4 Typo. Wmk. 1
1 A1 1p violet 170.00 55.00
a. Vertical half used as ½p on cover 8,000.
2 A1 6p green 625.00 115.00
3 A1 1sh deep lilac rose 375.00 80.00
Nos. 1-3 (3) 1,170. 250.00

During 1875-87 some issues were manuscript dated with village names. These are considered postally used. Stamps with entire village names sell for much more, starting at $100.

1877-79 *Perf. 14*
4 A1 ½p bister ('79) 16.00 60.00
5 A1 1p violet 8.25 2.50
a. Diagonal or vertical half used as ½p on cover 2,250.
6 A1 2½p red brown ('79) 260.00 32.50
7 A1 4p blue ('79) 125.00 4.00
8 A1 6p green 170.00 22.50
9 A1 1sh dp lilac rose 140.00 57.50
Nos. 4-9 (6) 719.25 179.00

For surcharges see Nos. 10-15.

No. 5 Bisected and Surcharged in Black or Red:

a b c

1882
10 A1(a) ½p on half of 1p 210.00 48.00
a. Inverted surcharge 1,150. 900.00
b. Surcharge tete beche pair 2,100. 1,750.
11 A1(b) ½p on half of 1p 72.50 27.50
a. Surch. reading downward 72.50 27.50
b. Double surcharge 900.00
12 A1(c) ½p on half of 1p (R) 35.00 19.00
a. Inverted surcharge 1,150. 550.00
b. Double surcharge 1,850. 750.00
Nos. 10-12 (3) 317.50 94.50

The existence of genuine examples of No. 10b has been questioned.

Nos. 8 and 9 Surcharged in Black

1886
13 A1 ½p on 6p green 6.50 6.00
14 A1 1p on 6p green 50,000. 12,500.
15 A1 1p on 1sh 16.00 19.00
a. Double surcharge 10,000. 3,750.

All examples of No. 14 may have small pin marks which may have been part of the surcharging process.

1883-88 Wmk. 2
16 A1 ½p bister ('83) 3.75 11.50
17 A1 ½p green ('86) 1.70 6.25
18 A1 1p violet ('86) 32.50 14.00
a. Half used as ½p on cover 2,200.
19 A1 1p dp carmine ('89) 3.25 8.00
a. 1p rose ('87) 18.00 20.00
b. Vert. half used as ½p on cover 2,100.
20 A1 2½p red brn ('84) 160.00 3.00
21 A1 2½p ultra ('88) 4.25 5.75
22 A1 4p gray ('86) 4.50 7.00
23 A1 6p orange ('88) 11.00 60.00
24 A1 1sh dp lil rose ('88) 180.00 325.00
Nos. 16-24 (9) 400.95 440.50

Roseau, Capital of Dominica — A6

King Edward VII — A7

1903 Wmk. 1 *Perf. 14*
25 A6 ½p gray green 5.25 3.25
26 A6 1p car & black 10.50 1.00
27 A6 2p brn & gray grn 3.25 5.75
28 A6 2½p ultra & blk 6.50 5.25
29 A6 3p black & vio 10.50 4.50
30 A6 6p org brn & blk 5.75 23.00
31 A6 1sh gray grn & red vio 35.00 52.50
32 A6 2sh red vio & blk 32.50 35.00
33 A6 2sh6p ocher & gray grn 23.00 92.50
34 A7 5sh brown & blk 125.00 175.00
Nos. 25-34 (10) 257.25 397.75

Nos. 25 to 29 and 31 are on both ordinary and chalky paper. For detailed listings, see the *Scott Classic Specialized Catalogue of Stamps & Covers.*

1907-20 Wmk. 3
Chalky Paper
35 A6 ½p gray green 4.25 4.00
36 A6 1p car & black 2.50 .55
37 A6 2p brn & gray grn 6.75 20.00
38 A6 2½p ultra & black 5.50 27.50
39 A6 3p black & vio 5.00 17.00
40 A6 3p vio, *yel* ('09) 3.75 5.25
41 A6 6p org brn & blk ('08) 65.00 100.00
42 A6 6p vio & dl vio ('09) 12.50 19.00
43 A6 1sh gray grn & red vio 4.75 67.50
44 A6 1sh blk, *green* ('10) 3.75 3.50
45 A6 2sh red vio & blk ('08) 30.00 40.00
46 A6 2sh ultra & vio, *bl* ('19) 32.50 110.00
47 A6 2sh6p ocher & gray grn ('08) 27.50 75.00
48 A6 2sh6p red & blk, *bl* ('20) 32.50 125.00
49 A7 5sh brn & blk ('08) 75.00 75.00
Nos. 35-49 (15) 311.25 689.30

Nos. 40, 42 and 44 are on both ordinary and chalky paper. For detailed listings, see the *Scott Classic Specialized Catalogue of Stamps & Covers.*
For type surcharged see No. 55.

1908-09 Ordinary Paper
50 A6 ½p green 3.50 3.00
51 A6 1p scarlet 1.75 .55
a. 1p carmine 3.50 .35
52 A6 2p gray ('09) 4.00 14.00
53 A6 2½p ultramarine 9.50 7.00
a. 2½p bright blue ('18) 5.75 10.50
Nos. 50-53 (4) 18.75 24.55

King George V — A8

1914 Chalky Paper *Perf. 14*
54 A8 5sh grn & scar, *yel* 70.00 92.50

Type of 1903 Surcharged

1920
55 A6 1½p on 2½p orange 4.50 5.25

1921 Wmk. 4
Ordinary Paper
56 A6 ½p green 3.50 21.00
57 A6 1p rose red 2.75 5.50
58 A6 1½p orange 4.75 15.00
59 A6 2p gray 4.25 4.75
60 A6 2½p ultra 2.75 12.00
61 A6 6p vio & dl vio 3.50 50.00
62 A6 2sh ultra & vio, *bl* 45.00 125.00
63 A6 2sh6p red & blk, *bl* 45.00 140.00
Nos. 56-63 (8) 111.50 373.25

No. 61 is on chalky paper.

Seal of Colony and George V — A9

1923-33 Chalky Paper Wmk. 4
65 A9 ½p green & blk 2.50 .85
66 A9 1p violet & blk 2.75 2.25
67 A9 1p scar & black 12.50 1.40
68 A9 1½p car & black 4.00 .90
69 A9 1½p dp brn & blk 12.50 .95
70 A9 2p gray & black 2.50 .65
71 A9 2½p org & black 2.00 12.00
72 A9 2½p ultra & black 5.50 2.75
73 A9 3p ultra & black 2.25 16.00
74 A9 3p red & blk, *yel* 2.25 1.40
75 A9 4p brown & blk 3.25 7.25
76 A9 6p red vio & blk 4.75 9.00
77 A9 1sh blk, *emerald* 3.00 3.75
78 A9 2sh ultra & blk, *bl* 14.00 27.50
79 A9 2sh6p red & blk, *bl* 25.00 27.50
80 A9 3sh vio & blk, *yel* 4.50 17.50
81 A9 4sh red & blk, *emer* 15.00 30.00
82 A9 5sh grn & blk, *yel* 30.00 62.50
Nos. 65-82 (18) 148.25 224.15

Issue years: Nos. 80, 82, 1927; Nos. 72, 74, 1928; Nos. 67, 69, 1933; others, 1923.

1923 Wmk. 3
83 A9 3sh vio & blk, *yel* 5.75 80.00
84 A9 5sh grn & blk, *yel* 13.50 65.00
85 A9 £1 vio & blk, *red* 300.00 450.00
Nos. 83-85 (3) 319.25 595.00

Common Design Types pictured following the introduction.

Silver Jubilee Issue
Common Design Type
Perf. 13½x14

1935, May 6 Wmk. 4 Engr.
90 CD301 1p car & blue .60 .35
91 CD301 1½p gray blk & ultra 2.00 2.00
92 CD301 2½p blue & brn 3.75 4.50
93 CD301 1sh brt vio & ind 3.75 7.00
Nos. 90-93 (4) 10.10 13.85
Set, never hinged 17.00

Coronation Issue
Common Design Type

1937, May 12 *Perf. 11x11½*
94 CD302 1p dark carmine .20 .20
95 CD302 1½p brown .20 .20
96 CD302 2½p deep ultra .35 .75
Nos. 94-96 (3) .75 1.15
Set, never hinged 1.50

Fresh-Water Lake — A10

Layou River — A11

Picking Limes — A12

Boiling Lake — A13

1938-47 Wmk. 4 *Perf. 12½*
97 A10 ½p grn & red brn .20 .20
98 A11 1p car & gray .20 .20
99 A12 1½p rose vio & grn .20 1.10
100 A13 2p brn blk & dp rose .55 1.50
101 A12 2½p ultra & rose vio 4.00 3.00
102 A11 3p red brn & ol .20 .60
103 A12 3½p red vio & brt ultra 1.40 2.50
104 A10 6p vio & yel grn .70 1.90
105 A10 7p org brn & grn 1.25 2.10
106 A13 1sh olive & vio 2.40 1.90
107 A11 2sh red vio & blk 5.50 12.00
108 A10 2sh6p scar ver & blk 12.00 7.75
109 A11 5sh dk brn & bl 6.75 12.00
110 A13 10sh dl org & blk 13.50 22.50
Nos. 97-110 (14) 48.85 69.25
Set, never hinged 60.00

Issued: 3½p, 7p, 2sh, 10sh, 10/15/47; others, 8/15/38.

King George VI — A14

1940, Apr. 15 Photo. *Perf. 14½x14*
111 A14 ¼p brown violet .40 .40

Catalogue values for unused stamps in this section, from this point to the end of the section, are for Never Hinged items.

Peace Issue
Common Design Type

1946, Oct. 14 Engr. *Perf. 13½x14*
112 CD303 1p carmine .25 .25
113 CD303 3½p deep blue .25 .25

Silver Wedding Issue
Common Design Types

1948, Dec. 1 Photo. ***Perf. 14x14½***

114	CD304	1p scarlet	.25	.25

Engraved; Name Typographed
Perf. 11½x11

115	CD305	10sh orange brn	18.00	*32.50*

UPU Issue
Common Design Types
Engr.: Name Typo. on 6c and 12c

1949, Oct. 10 ***Perf. 13½, 11x11½***

116	CD306	5c blue	.20	.20
117	CD307	6c chocolate	1.40	1.40
118	CD308	12c rose violet	.70	.70
119	CD309	24c olive	.45	.45
		Nos. 116-119 (4)	2.75	2.75

University Issue
Common Design Types

1951, Feb. 16 Engr. ***Perf. 14x14½***

120	CD310	3c purple & green	.70	.45
121	CD311	12c dp car & dk bl grn	.90	.70

George VI
A15

Drying Cocoa
A16

Picking
Oranges — A17

Designs: 2c and 60c, Carib Baskets. 3c and 48c, Lime Plantation. 4c, Picking Oranges. 5c, Bananas. 6c, Botanical Gardens. 8c, Drying Vanilla Beans. 12c and $1.20, Fresh Water Lake. 14c, Layou River. 24c, Boiling Lake.

Perf. 14½x14

1951, July 1 Photo. Wmk. 4

122	A15	½c brown	.20	.20

Perf. 13x13½
Engr.

123	A16	1c red org & blk	.20	.30
124	A16	2c dp grn & red brn	.20	.20
125	A16	3c red vio & bl grn	.20	.70
126	A16	4c dk brn & brn org	.45	.80
127	A16	5c rose red & blk	1.10	.30
128	A16	6c org brn & ol grn	1.10	.30
129	A16	8c dp bl & dp grn	.75	.70
130	A16	12c emer & gray	.60	1.90
131	A16	14c pur & blue	1.25	1.90
132	A16	24c rose car & red vio	1.00	.30
133	A16	48c red org & bl grn	3.50	*8.25*
134	A16	60c gray & car	3.50	*7.00*
135	A16	$1.20 gray & emer	5.50	*7.00*

Perf. 13½x13

136	A17	$2.40 gray & org	30.00	*40.00*
		Nos. 122-136 (15)	49.55	*69.85*

Nos. 125, 127, 129 and 131 Overprinted in Black or Carmine

1951, Oct. 15 ***Perf. 13x13½***

137	A16	3c red vio & bl green	.25	.25
138	A16	5c rose red & black	.50	.50
139	A16	8c dp blue & dp grn (C)	.65	.65
140	A16	14c purple & blue (C)	1.10	1.10
		Nos. 137-140 (4)	2.50	2.50

Adoption of a new constitution for the Windward Islands, 1951.

Coronation Issue
Common Design Type

1953, June 2 Engr. ***Perf. 13½x13***

141	CD312	2c dk green & black	.40	.40

Types of 1951 with Portrait of Queen Elizabeth II

1954, Oct. 1 Photo. ***Perf. 14½x14***

142	A15	½c brown	.20	.20

Perf. 13x13½
Engr.

143	A16	1c red org & blk	.20	.30
144	A16	2c dp grn & red brn	.90	.30
145	A16	3c red vio & bl grn	1.90	.70
146	A16	4c dk brn & brn org	.20	.30
147	A16	5c rose red & blk	1.90	.95
148	A16	6c org brn & ol grn	.55	.30
149	A16	8c dp bl & dp grn	1.25	.30
150	A16	12c emer & gray	.75	.30
151	A16	14c pur & bl	.30	.45
152	A16	24c rose car & red vio	.55	*.70*
153	A16	48c red org & bl grn	2.40	*3.25*
154	A16	60c gray & car	1.60	*2.75*
155	A16	$1.20 gray & emer	24.00	6.25

Perf. 13½x13

156	A17	$2.40 gray & org	24.00	14.00
		Nos. 142-156 (15)	60.70	31.05

Mat
Making — A18

5c, Canoe making. 10c, Bananas.

1957, Oct. 15 Wmk. 4 ***Perf. 13x13½***

157	A18	3c car rose & black	2.40	*2.50*
158	A18	5c brown & blue	7.50	1.10
159	A18	10c redsh brn & brt grn	4.00	2.25
160	A18	48c violet & brown	1.00	*1.10*
		Nos. 157-160 (4)	14.90	6.95

West Indies Federation
Common Design Type
Perf. 11½x11

1958, Apr. 22 Wmk. 314

161	CD313	3c green	.50	.50
162	CD313	6c blue	.50	.50
163	CD313	12c car rose	1.00	1.00
		Nos. 161-163 (3)	2.00	2.00

Sailing
Canoe — A19

Traditional
Costume — A20

Designs: 1c, Seashore, Rosalie. 2c, 5c, Queen Elizabeth II by Annigoni. 4c, Sulphur Springs. 6c, Road making. 8c, Dugout canoe. 10c, Frog (mountain chicken). 12c, Boats and Scotts Head. 15c, Bananas. 24c, Imperial parrot. 48c, View of Goodwill. 60c, Cacao tree. $1.20, Coat of Arms. $2.40, Trafalgar Falls. $4.80, Coconut palm.

Two types of 14c:

I — Mountain light violet. Girl's eyes look straight out.

II — Mountain blue. Eyes look sideways.

Perf. 14½x14, 14x14½

1963, May 16 Photo. Wmk. 314

164	A19	1c bl, brn & grn	.20	*1.10*
165	A20	2c ultramarine	.20	.20
166	A19	3c lt ultra & blk	1.10	1.40
167	A19	4c sl, grn & brn	.20	.20
168	A20	5c magenta	.20	.20
169	A19	6c lt grn, vio & buff	.20	.20
170	A19	8c tan, blk & lt grn	.20	.20
171	A19	10c pink & brn	.20	.20
172	A19	12c bl, blk, grn & brn	.70	.20
173	A20	14c multi (II)	*2.75*	*2.50*
a.		Type I	.55	.75
174	A19	15c grn, yel & brn	1.10	.20
175	A20	24c multicolored	8.25	.20
176	A19	48c bl, blk & grn	.75	.55
177	A19	60c blk, grn, org & brn	1.10	.95
178	A19	$1.20 multicolored	7.00	1.40
179	A20	$2.40 grn, bl, brn & blk	3.25	3.25
180	A20	$4.80 bl, brn & grn	9.25	*24.00*
		Nos. 164-180 (17)	36.65	36.95

For overprints see Nos. 211-232.

1966-67 Wmk. 314 Sideways

167a	A19	4c ('67)	.20	.30
169a	A19	6c	.25	.80
170a	A19	8c	.65	.90
171a	A19	10c ('67)	.70	.95
174a	A19	15c ('67)	1.25	1.50
		Nos. 167a-174a (5)	3.05	4.45

Freedom from Hunger Issue
Common Design Type

1963, June 4 ***Perf. 14x14½***

181	CD314	15c lilac	.30	.30

Red Cross Centenary Issue
Common Design Type
Wmk. 314

1963, Sept. 2 Litho. ***Perf. 13***

182	CD315	5c black & red	.20	.20
183	CD315	15c ultra & red	.70	*.90*

Shakespeare Issue
Common Design Type

1964, Apr. 23 Photo. ***Perf. 14x14½***

184	CD316	15c lilac rose	.30	.30

ITU Issue
Common Design Type

1965, May 17 Litho. ***Perf. 11x11½***

185	CD317	2c emerald & blue	.20	.20
186	CD317	48c grnsh blue & slate	.60	.60

Intl. Cooperation Year Issue
Common Design Type

1965, Oct. 25 ***Perf. 14½***

187	CD318	1c blue grn & claret	.20	.20
188	CD318	15c lt violet & grn	.40	.40

Churchill Memorial Issue
Common Design Type

1966, Jan. 24 Photo. ***Perf. 14***
Design in Black, Gold and Carmine Rose

189	CD319	1c bright blue	.20	.20
a.		Gold omitted	*775.00*	
190	CD319	5c green	.20	.20
191	CD319	15c brown	.45	.45
192	CD319	24c violet	.65	.65
		Nos. 189-192 (4)	1.50	1.50

Royal Visit Issue
Common Design Type

1966, Feb. 4 Litho. ***Perf. 11x12***

193	CD320	5c violet blue	.85	.20
194	CD320	15c dk car rose	2.40	.45

World Cup Soccer Issue
Common Design Type

1966, July 1 Litho. ***Perf. 14***

195	CD321	5c multicolored	.40	.20
196	CD321	24c multicolored	1.00	.60

WHO Headquarters Issue
Common Design Type

1966, Sept. 20 Litho. ***Perf. 14***

197	CD322	5c multicolored	.20	.20
198	CD322	24c multicolored	.60	.60

UNESCO Anniversary Issue
Common Design Type

1966, Dec. 1 Litho. ***Perf. 14***

199	CD323	5c "Education"	.35	.20
200	CD323	15c "Science"	.50	.20
201	CD323	24c "Culture"	.90	.20
		Nos. 199-201 (3)	1.75	.60

Carib, Negro and Caucasian Children — A21

10c, Columbus' ship Santa Maria & banderol. 15c, Hands with banderol. 24c, Belaire dancers.

Perf. 14½x14

1967, Nov. 3 Photo. Wmk. 314

202	A21	5c multicolored	.20	.20
203	A21	10c multicolored	.30	.20
204	A21	15c multicolored	.20	.20
205	A21	24c multicolored	.20	.20
		Nos. 202-205 (4)	.90	.80

Issued for National Day, Nov. 3.

John F. Kennedy and Human Rights Flame — A22

Human Rights Flame and: 10c, Cecil E. A. Rawle (1891-1938), Dominican crusader for human rights. 12c, Pope John XXIII. 48c, Florence Nightingale. 60c, Dr. Albert Schweitzer.

Wmk. 314 Sideways

1968, Apr. 20 Litho. ***Perf. 14***

206	A22	1c multicolored	.20	.20
207	A22	10c multicolored	.20	.20
208	A22	12c multicolored	.45	.20
209	A22	48c multicolored	.30	.25
210	A22	60c multicolored	.30	.25
		Nos. 206-210 (5)	1.45	1.10

International Human Rights Year.

Stamps and Types of 1963-67 Overprinted in Silver or Black: "ASSOCIATED / STATEHOOD"

Perf. 14½x14, 14x14½

1968, July 8 Photo. Wmk. 314

211	A19	1c multi	.20	.20
212	A20	2c ultra	.20	.20
213	A19	3c lt ultra & blk	.20	.20
214	A19	4c multi	.20	.20
215	A20	5c magenta	.20	.20
216	A19	6c multi (B)	.20	.20
217	A19	8c multi (B)	.20	.20
218	A19	10c pink & brn	.55	1.40
219	A19	12c multi	.20	.20
a.		Watermark upright	.20	.20
220	A20	14c multi (II)	.20	.20
221	A19	15c multi	.20	.20
222	A20	24c multi	3.25	.20
223	A19	48c multi	.55	1.25
a.		Watermark upright	.50	*1.25*
224	A19	60c multi (B)	.90	2.10
225	A19	$1.20 multi (B)	1.00	2.40
226	A20	$2.40 multi	1.00	2.40
227	A20	$4.80 multi	1.25	3.00
		Nos. 211-227 (17)	10.50	14.75

In this set, overprint was applied to 2c, 3c, 12c, 14c, 24c, 48c, 60c, $1.20, $2.40 and $4.80 with watermark upright. A reprinting of the 1c, 4c, 6c, 8c, 10c, 12c, No. 219, 15c and 48c, No. 223 on paper with watermark sideways was made. Same value.

Nos. 164-166, 173 and 178 Overprinted: "NATIONAL DAY / 3 NOVEMBER 1968"

Perf. 14½x14, 14x14½

1968, Nov. 3 Photo. Wmk. 314

228	A19	1c blue, brn & grn	.20	.20
229	A20	2c ultra	.20	.20
230	A19	3c lt ultra & blk	.20	.20
231	A20	14c multi (I)	.20	.20
232	A19	$1.20 multicolored	.70	.70
		Nos. 228-232 (5)	1.50	1.50

A23

#233a, 3 soccer players. #233b, Soccer player, goalie. #234a, Swimmers at start. #234b, Divers. #235a, Javelin thrower, hurdlers. #235b, Hurdlers. #236a, Basketball. #236b, 3 basketball players.

Perf. 11½

1968, Nov. 23 Unwmk. Litho.

233	A23	1c Pair, #a-b	.20	.20
234	A23	5c Pair, #a-b	.20	.20
235	A23	48c Pair, #a-b	.60	.60
236	A23	60c Pair, #a-b	1.75	1.75
		Nos. 233-236 (4)	2.75	2.75

19th Olympic Games, Mexico City, 10/12-27.

The Small Cowper Madonna, by Raphael A24

Perf. 12½x12

1968, Dec. 23 Photo. Unwmk.

241 A24 5c multicolored	.30	.30

Christmas. No. 241 printed in sheets of 20. Sheets of 6 (3x2) exist containing two each of 12c, 24c, and $1.20 stamps, each picturing a different madonna painting. Value $6.

Venus and Adonis, by Rubens — A25

Citrus Fruit Picker — A26

Paintings: 15c, The Death of Socrates, by Louis Jacques David. 24c, Christ at Emmaus, by Velazquez. 50c, Pilate Washing his Hands, by Rembrandt.

Perf. 14½x15

1969, Jan. 30 Litho. Wmk. 314

242 A25 5c lilac & multi	.25	.25
243 A25 15c emerald & multi	.35	.35
244 A25 24c lt blue & multi	.35	.35
245 A25 50c crimson & multi	.55	.55
Nos. 242-245 (4)	1.50	1.50

20th anniv. (in 1968) of the WHO.

1969, Mar. 10 *Perf. 14½*

#247, Woman and child. #248, Hotel. #249, Red-necked parrots. #250, Calypso band. #251, Women dancers. #252, Tropical fish and coelenterates. #253, Diver and turtle.

246 A26 10c multicolored	.20	.20
247 A26 10c multicolored	.20	.20
a. Pair, #246-247	.25	
248 A26 12c multicolored	.20	.20
249 A26 12c multicolored	.20	.20
a. Pair, #248-249	.25	
250 A26 24c multicolored	.35	.35
251 A26 24c multicolored	.35	.35
a. Pair, #250-251	.70	
252 A26 48c multicolored	1.00	1.00
253 A26 48c multicolored	1.00	1.00
a. Pair, #252-253	2.00	
Nos. 246-253 (8)	3.50	3.50

Tourist publicity.

Spinning, by Millet, Flags and ILO Emblem — A27

50th anniv. of the ILO (Etchings by Jean F. Millet, Flags and ILO Emblem): 30c, Threshing. 30c, Flax pulling.

1969, July Unwmk. *Perf. 13½*

254 A27 15c multicolored	.20	.20
255 A27 30c multicolored	.30	.30
256 A27 38c multicolored	.30	.30
Nos. 254-256 (3)	.80	.80

"Strength in Unity," Bananas and Cacao A28

"Strength in Unity" Emblem and: 8c, Map of Dominica and Hawker Siddeley 748. 12c, Map of Caribbean. 24c, Ships in harbor.

1969, July Litho.

257 A28 5c orange & multi	.30	.30
258 A28 8c gray & multi	.30	.30
259 A28 12c lilac & multi	.30	.30
260 A28 24c lt blue & multi	.60	.60
Nos. 257-260 (4)	1.50	1.50

Caribbean Free Trade Area (CARIFTA).

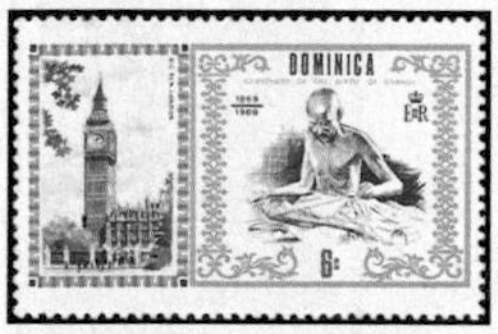

Gandhi at Spinning Wheel and Big Ben, London A29

38c, Gandhi, Nehru and Fatehpur Sikri Mausoleum. $1.20, Gandhi & Taj Mahal.

1969, Oct. Litho. *Perf. 14½*

261 A29 6c multicolored	.45	.20
262 A29 38c multicolored	.75	.25
263 A29 $1.20 multicolored	.80	.80
Nos. 261-263 (3)	2.00	1.25

Mohandas K. Gandhi (1869-1948), leader in India's fight for independence. "Gandhi" is misspelled "Ghandi" on Nos. 261-263.

St. Joseph — A30

Stained Glass Windows, from 17th Century French Churches: 8c, St. John. 12c, St. Peter. 60c, St. Paul.

1969, Nov. 10 Litho. *Perf. 14*

264 A30 6c black & multi	.20	.20
265 A30 8c black & multi	.20	.20
266 A30 12c black & multi	.20	.20
267 A30 60c black & multi	.40	.40
Nos. 264-267 (4)	1.00	1.00

National Day, Nov. 3. Issued in sheets of 16 (4x4) with control numbers and 4 tabs with a patriotic poem by W. O. M. Pond.

Queen Elizabeth II — A31

Purplethroated Carib (Hummingbird) — A32

2c, Poinsettia. 3c, Red-necked pigeon. 4c, Imperial parrot. 5c, Swallowtail butterfly. 6c, Brown Julia butterfly. 8c, Banana shipment. 10c, Portsmouth Harbor. 12c, Copra processing plant. 15c, Women with straw work. 25c, Timber plant. 30c, Mining pumice. 38c, Cricket, Grammar School. 50c, Roman Catholic Cathedral. 60c, Government headquarters. $1.20, Melville Hall Airport. $2.40, Coat of Arms. $4.80, Queen Elizabeth II.

Perf. 13½

1969, Nov. 26 Unwmk. Photo.

268 A31 ½c silver & multi	.20	.20
269 A32 1c yellow & multi	.20	.20
270 A32 2c yellow & multi	.20	.20
271 A32 3c yellow & multi	.20	.20
272 A32 4c yellow & multi	.20	.20
273 A32 5c yellow & multi	.20	.20
274 A32 6c brown & multi	.20	.20
275 A32 8c brown & multi	.20	.20
276 A32 10c yellow & multi	.20	.20
277 A32 12c citron & multi	.20	.20
278 A32 15c blue & multi	.30	.30
279 A32 25c pink & multi	.65	.65
280 A32 30c olive & multi	.80	.75
281 A32 38c multicolored	1.00	1.10
282 A32 50c brown & multi	1.10	1.25

Wmk. Rectangles (334)

Perf. 14

Size: 38x26mm, 26x38mm

283 A32 60c yel & multi	1.60	1.40
284 A32 $1.20 yel & multi	3.25	3.25
285 A32 $2.40 gold & multi	7.25	7.00
286 A31 $4.80 gold & multi	14.00	13.50
Nos. 268-286 (19)	31.95	31.20

Madonna and Child, by Filippino Lippi — A33

Paintings: 10c, Holy Family with Lamb, by Raphael. 15c, Virgin and Child, by Perugino. $1.20, Madonna of the Rose Hedge, by Botticelli.

Perf. 14½

1969, Dec. Unwmk. Litho.

287 A33 6c lt blue & multi	.20	.20
288 A33 10c multicolored	.20	.20
289 A33 15c lilac & multi	.20	.20
290 A33 $1.20 lt grn & multi	.60	.60
a. Souvenir sheet of 2	1.50	1.50
Nos. 287-290 (4)	1.20	1.20

Christmas. No. 290a contains 2 imperf. stamps with simulated perforations similar to Nos. 289-290.

Neil A. Armstrong, First Man on the Moon — A34

Designs: 5c, American flag and astronauts on moon. 8c, Astronauts collecting moon rocks. 30c, Landing module, moon and earth. 50c, Memorial tablet left on moon. 60c, Astronauts Armstrong, Aldrin and Collins.

1970, Feb. 2 Litho. *Perf. 12½*

291 A34 ½c lilac & multi	.20	.20
292 A34 5c lt blue & multi	.20	.20
293 A34 8c orange & multi	.20	.20
294 A34 30c blue & multi	.25	.25
295 A34 50c red brn & multi	.60	.60
296 A34 60c rose & multi	.80	.80
a. Souvenir sheet of 4	3.00	3.00
Nos. 291-296 (6)	2.25	2.25

See note after US No. C76. No. 296a contains 4 stamps similar to Nos. 293-296, but imperf. with simulated perforations.

Giant Green Turtle — A35

Designs: 24c, Flying fish. 38c, Anthurium lily. 60c, Imperial and red-necked parrots.

1970, Sept. 6 Litho. *Perf. 13½x13*

297 A35 6c lt green & multi	.65	.65
298 A35 24c multicolored	.85	.85
299 A35 38c green & multi	1.00	1.00
300 A35 60c yellow & multi	4.00	4.00
a. Souvenir sheet of 4, #297-300	10.00	10.00
Nos. 297-300 (4)	6.50	6.50

Women in 18th Century Dress A36

Natl. Day: 8c, Carib mace & wife leader, 18th cent. $1, Map & flag of Dominica.

1970, Nov. 3 Litho. *Perf. 14*

301 A36 5c yellow & multi	.20	.20
302 A36 8c green & multi	.20	.20
303 A36 $1 lt blue & multi	.60	.60
a. Souv. sheet of 3, #301-303 + 3 labels	1.75	2.00
Nos. 301-303 (3)	1.00	1.00

Marley's Ghost — A37

Designs (from A Christmas Carol, by Dickens): 15c, Fezziwig's Ball. 24c, Scrooge and his Nephew's Christmas Party. $1.20, The Ghost of Christmas Present.

1970, Nov. 23 Litho. *Perf. 14x14½*

304 A37 2c blue & multi	.20	.20
305 A37 15c multicolored	.30	.30
306 A37 24c red & multi	.30	.30
307 A37 $1.20 multicolored	1.00	1.00
a. Souvenir sheet of 4, #304-307	3.25	3.25
Nos. 304-307 (4)	1.80	1.80

Christmas; Charles Dickens (1812-1870).

Hands and Red Cross A38

Designs: 8c, The Doctor, by Sir Luke Fildes. 15c, Dominica flag and Red Cross. 50c, The Sick Child, by Edvard Munch.

1970, Dec. 28 *Perf. 14½x14*

308 A38 8c multicolored	.20	.20
309 A38 10c multicolored	.20	.20
310 A38 15c multicolored	.20	.20
311 A38 50c multicolored	.75	.75
a. Souvenir sheet of 4, #308-311	2.25	2.50
Nos. 308-311 (4)	1.35	1.35

Centenary of the British Red Cross Society.

Marigot Primary School — A39

Education Year Emblem and: 8c, Goodwill Junior High School. 14c, University of the West Indies. $1, Trinity College, Cambridge, England.

1971, Mar. 1 Litho. *Perf. 13½*

312 A39 5c multicolored .20 .20
313 A39 8c multicolored .20 .20
314 A39 14c multicolored .20 .20
315 A39 $1 multicolored .65 .65
a. Souvenir sheet of 2, #314-315 1.00 1.00
Nos. 312-315 (4) 1.25 1.25

International Education Year.

Waterfall and Bird-of-Paradise Flower — A40

Tourist Publicity: 10c, Boat building. 30c, Sailboat along North Coast. 50c, Speed boat and steamer.

1971, Mar. 22 *Perf. 13½x14*

316 A40 5c multicolored .20 .20
317 A40 10c multicolored .20 .20
318 A40 30c multicolored .25 .25
319 A40 50c multicolored .60 .60
a. Souvenir sheet of 4, #316-319 1.25 1.25
Nos. 316-319 (4) 1.25 1.25

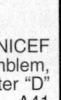

UNICEF Emblem, Letter "D" A41

1971, June 14 Litho. *Perf. 14*

320 A41 5c multicolored .20 .20
321 A41 10c multicolored .20 .20
322 A41 38c multicolored .20 .20
323 A41 $1.20 multicolored .50 .50
a. Souvenir sheet of 2, #321, 323 1.00 1.00
Nos. 320-323 (4) 1.10 1.10

25th anniv. of UNICEF.

Boy Scout, Jamboree Emblem, Torii, Camp and Mt. Fuji — A42

24c, British Scout, flag. 30c, Japanese Scout, flag. $1, Dominican Scout, flag.

1971, Oct. 18 Unwmk. *Perf. 11*

324 A42 20c bister & multi .25 .25
325 A42 24c green & multi .30 .30
326 A42 30c red lilac & multi .45 .45
327 A42 $1 blue & multi 1.75 1.75
a. Souvenir sheet of 2, #326-327 2.75 2.75
Nos. 324-327 (4) 2.75 2.75

13th Boy Scout World Jamboree, Asagiri Plain, Japan, Aug. 2-10.

Boats at Portsmouth — A43

15c, Carnival street scene. 20c, $1.20, Anthea Mondesire, Carifta Queen. 50c, Rock of Atkinson.

Perf. 13½x14, 14x13½

1971, Nov. 15 Litho.

328 A43 8c multi .20 .20
329 A43 15c multi .20 .20
330 A43 20c multi, vert. .20 .20
331 A43 50c multi, vert. .30 .30
Nos. 328-331 (4) .90 .90

Souvenir Sheet

Perf. 15

332 A43 $1.20 multi, vert. 1.00 1.00

National Day.

First Dominica Coin, 8 Reals, 1761 — A44

Early Dominica Coins: 30c, Eleven and 3-bit pieces, 1798. 35c, Two-real coin, 1770, vert. 50c, Three "mocos" and piece of 8, 1798.

1972, Feb. 7 Litho. *Perf. 14*

333 A44 10c violet, silver & blk .20 .20
334 A44 30c green, silver & blk .20 .20
335 A44 35c ultra, silver & blk .25 .25
336 A44 50c red, silver & blk .35 .35
a. Souvenir sheet of 2, #335-336 1.40 1.40
Nos. 333-336 (4) 1.00 1.00

Margin of #336a inscribed "Christmas 1971."

Common Opossum, Environment Emblem — A45

Environment Emblem and: 35c, Agouti. 60c, Oncidium papillo (orchid). $1.20, Hibiscus.

1972, June 5

337 A45 ½c yel grn & multi .20 .20
338 A45 35c org brn & multi .35 .35
339 A45 60c lt blue & multi 3.00 3.00
340 A45 $1.20 yellow & multi 2.50 2.50
a. Souvenir sheet of 4, #337-340 8.25 8.25
Nos. 337-340 (4) 6.05 6.05

UN Conf. on Human Environment, Stockholm, June 5-16.

100-meter Sprint, Olympic Rings — A46

Olympic Rings and: 35m, 400-meter hurdles. 58c, Hammer throw, vert. 72c, Broad jump, vert.

1972, Oct. 9 Litho. *Perf. 14*

341 A46 30c dp org & multi .20 .20
342 A46 35c blue & multi .30 .30
343 A46 58c lilac rose & multi .40 .40
344 A46 72c yel green & multi .85 .85
a. Souv. sheet, #343-344, perf. 15 1.50 1.50
Nos. 341-344 (4) 1.75 1.75

20th Olympic Games, Munich, Aug. 26-Sept. 11.

General Post Office — A47

1972, Nov. 1 *Perf. 13½*

345 A47 10c shown .20 .20
346 A47 20c Morne Diablotin Mountain .20 .20
347 A47 30c Rodney's Rock .20 .20
a. Souv. sheet, #346-347, perf. 15 .75 .75
Nos. 345-347 (3) .60 .60

National Day.

Adoration of the Shepherds, by Caravaggio A48

Paintings: 14c, Madonna and Child, by Rubens. 30c, Madonna and Child, with St. Anne by Orazio Gentileschi. $1, Adoration of the Kings, by Jan Mostaert. (On 8c, painting is mistakenly attributed to Boccaccino, according to Fine Arts Philatelist.)

1972, Dec. 4.

348 A48 8c gold & multi .20 .20
349 A48 14c gold & multi .20 .20
350 A48 30c gold & multi .20 .20
351 A48 $1 gold & multi .65 .65
a. Souvenir sheet of 2 1.50 1.50
Nos. 348-351 (4) 1.25 1.25

Christmas. No. 351a contains one each of Nos. 350-351 with simulated perforations.

Silver Wedding Issue, 1972

Common Design Type

Design: Queen Elizabeth II, Prince Philip, bananas, sisseron parrot.

Perf. 14x14½

1972, Nov. 13 Photo. Wmk. 314

352 CD324 5c olive & multi .20 .20
353 CD324 $1 multicolored .60 .60

See note after Antigua No. 296.

Launching of Tiros Weather Satellite — A49

1c, Nimbus satellite. 2c, Radiosonde balloon & equipment. 30c, Radarscope. 35c, General circulation of atmosphere. 50c, Picture of hurricane transmitted by satellite. $1, Computer weather map. 30c, 35c, 50c, $1, horiz.

Perf. 14½

1973, July 16 Unwmk. Litho.

354 A49 ½c black & multi .20 .20
355 A49 1c black & multi .20 .20
356 A49 2c black & multi .20 .20
357 A49 30c black & multi .20 .20
358 A49 35c black & multi .20 .20
359 A49 50c black & multi .40 .40
360 A49 $1 black & multi .80 .80
a. Souvenir sheet of 2, #359-360 2.00 2.00
Nos. 354-360 (7) 2.20 2.20

Intl. meteorological cooperation, cent.

Going to the Hospital A50

WHO Emblem and: 1c, Maternity and infant care. 2c, Inoculation against smallpox. 30c, Emergency service. 35c, Waiting patients. 50c, Examination. $1, Traveling physician.

1973, Aug. 20 Unwmk. *Perf. 14½*

361 A50 ½c lt blue & multi .20 .20
362 A50 1c gray grn & multi .20 .20
363 A50 2c yellow & multi .20 .20
364 A50 30c lt vio & multi .30 .30
365 A50 35c yel grn & multi .40 .40
366 A50 50c multicolored .50 .50
367 A50 $1 bister & multi .95 .95
a. Souvenir sheet of 2, #366-367, perf. 14x14½ 2.25 2.25
Nos. 361-367 (7) 2.75 2.75

WHO, 25th anniv. #367a exists perf. 14½.

Cyrique Crab — A51

1973, Oct.

368 A51 ½c shown .20 .20
369 A51 22c Blue land crab .35 .35
370 A51 25c Breadfruit .45 .45
371 A51 $1.20 Sunflower 2.00 2.00
a. Souvenir sheet of 4, #368-371 5.00 5.00
Nos. 368-371 (4) 3.00 3.00

Princess Anne and Mark Phillips — A52

1973, Nov. 14 *Perf. 13½*

372 A52 25c salmon & multi .20 .20
373 A52 $2 blue & multi .80 .80
a. Souv. sheet of 2 (75c, $1.20) 1.00 1.00

Wedding of Princess Anne and Capt. Mark Phillips.

#372-373 were issued in sheets of 5 + label.

No. 373a contains 2 stamps of type A52: 75c in colors of the 25c, and $1.20 in colors of the $2.

Nativity, by Brueghel A53

Paintings of the Nativity by: 1c, Botticelli. 2c, Dürer. 12c, Botticelli. 22c, Rubens. 35c, Dürer. $1, Giorgione (inscribed "Giorgeone").

1973 Unwmk. *Perf. 14½x15*

374 A53 ½c gray & multi .20 .20
375 A53 1c gray & multi .20 .20
376 A53 2c gray & multi .20 .20
377 A53 12c gray & multi .20 .20
378 A53 22c gray & multi .20 .20
379 A53 35c gray & multi .40 .40
380 A53 $1 gray & multi 1.10 1.10
a. Souvenir sheet of 2 1.75 1.75
Nos. 374-380 (7) 2.50 2.50

Christmas. No. 380a contains one each of Nos. 379-380 in changed colors.

Carib Basket Weaving — A54

Designs: 10c, Staircase of the Snake. 50c, Miss Caribbean Queen, Kathleen Telemacque, vert. 60c, Miss Carifta Queen, Esther Fadelle, vert. $1, La Jeune Etoille Dancers.

1973, Dec. 17 ***Perf. 13½x14, 14x13½***

381	A54	5c buff & multi	.20	.20
382	A54	10c multicolored	.20	.20
383	A54	50c multicolored	.25	.25
384	A54	60c multicolored	.25	.25
385	A54	$1 multicolored	.35	.35
a.		Souv. sheet of 3, #381-382, 385	1.10	1.10
		Nos. 381-385 (5)	1.25	1.25

National Day.

U.W.I. Center, Dominica — A55

30c, Graduation. $1, University coat of arms.

1974, Jan. 21 **Litho.** ***Perf. 13½x14***

386	A55	12c dp orange & multi	.20	.20
387	A55	30c violet & multi	.20	.20
388	A55	$1 multicolored	.50	.50
a.		Souvenir sheet of 3, #386-388	.85	*1.25*
		Nos. 386-388 (3)	.90	.90

University of the West Indies, 25th anniv.

Dominica No. 1 and Map of Island A56

Designs: 1c, 50c, No. 8 and post horn. 2c, $1.20, No. 9 and coat of arms. 10c, Like ½c.

1974, May 4 **Litho.** ***Perf. 14½***

389	A56	½c brt pur & multi	.20	.20
390	A56	1c salmon & multi	.20	.20
391	A56	2c ultra & multi	.20	.20
392	A56	10c violet & multi	.20	.20
393	A56	50c yel grn & multi	.55	.55
394	A56	$1.20 rose & multi	1.40	1.40
a.		Souv. sheet, #392-394, perf. 15	2.10	2.10
		Nos. 389-394 (6)	2.75	2.75

Centenary of Dominican postage stamps.

Soccer Player and Cup, Brazilian Flag — A57

Soccer cup, various players and flags.

1974, July **Litho.** ***Perf. 14½***

395	A57	½c shown	.20	.20
396	A57	1c Germany, Fed. Rep.	.20	.20
397	A57	2c Italy	.20	.20
398	A57	30c Scotland	.65	.65
399	A57	40c Sweden	.65	.65
400	A57	50c Netherlands	.85	.85
401	A57	$1 Yugoslavia	1.25	1.25
a.		Souvenir sheet of 2, #400-401, perf. 13½	1.60	1.60
		Nos. 395-401 (7)	4.00	4.00

World Cup Soccer Championship, Munich, June 13-July 7.

Indian Hole A58

40c, Teachers' Training College. $1, Petite Savane Co-operative Bay Oil Distillery.

1974, Nov. 1 **Litho.** ***Perf. 13½x14***

402	A58	10c multicolored	.20	.20
403	A58	40c multicolored	.35	.35
404	A58	$1 multicolored	.75	.75
a.		Souvenir sheet of 3, #402-404	1.00	1.00
		Nos. 402-404 (3)	1.30	1.30

Churchill at Race Track A59

Sir Winston Churchill (1874-1965): 1c, with Gen. Eisenhower. 2c, with Franklin D. Roosevelt. 20c, as First Lord of the Admiralty. 45c, painting outdoors. $2, giving "V" sign.

1974, Nov. 25 **Litho.** ***Perf. 14½***

405	A59	½c multicolored	.20	.20
406	A59	1c multicolored	.20	.20
407	A59	2c multicolored	.20	.20
408	A59	20c multicolored	.20	.20
409	A59	45c multicolored	.30	.30
410	A59	$2 multicolored	.75	.75
a.		Souvenir sheet of 2, #409-410, perf. 13½	1.75	1.75
		Nos. 405-410 (6)	1.85	1.85

Virgin and Child, by Oronzo Tiso — A60

Paintings (Virgin and Child): 1c, by Lorenzo Costa. 2c, by unknown Master. 10c, by G. F. Romanelli. 25c, Holy Family, by G. S. da Sermoneta. 45c, Adoration of the Shepherds, by Guido Reni. $1, Adoration of the Kings, by Cristoforo Caselli.

1974, Dec. 16 **Litho.** ***Perf. 14***

411	A60	½c multicolored	.20	.20
412	A60	1c multicolored	.20	.20
413	A60	2c multicolored	.20	.20
414	A60	10c multicolored	.35	.20
415	A60	25c multicolored	.50	.40
416	A60	45c multicolored	.65	.20
417	A60	$1 multicolored	.90	.50
a.		Souvenir sheet of 2, #416-417	2.00	2.00
		Nos. 411-417 (7)	3.00	1.90

Christmas.

Seamail, "Orinoco," 1851, and "Geesthaven," 1966 — A61

Cent. of UPU: $2, $2.40, Airmail, De Havilland 4, 1918, and Boeing 747, 1974.

1974, Dec. 4 **Litho.** ***Perf. 13½***

418	A61	10c multicolored	.20	.20
419	A61	$2 multicolored	1.75	1.75

Souvenir Sheet

419A		Sheet of 2	2.25	2.25
b.	A61	$1.20 multicolored	.75	.75
c.	A61	$2.40 multicolored	1.50	1.50

Oldwife A62

1975, June 2 **Litho.** ***Perf. 14½***

421	A62	½c shown	.20	.20
422	A62	1c Ocyurus chrysurus	.20	.20
423	A62	2c Blue marlin	.20	.20
424	A62	3c Swordfish	.20	.20
425	A62	20c Great barracuda	1.50	1.00
426	A62	$2 Grouper	5.25	2.75
a.		Souvenir sheet, perf. 13½	5.50	*5.25*
		Nos. 421-426 (6)	7.55	4.55

Myscelia Antholia A63

Designs: Butterflies.

1975, July 28 **Litho.** ***Perf. 14½***

427	A63	½c shown	.20	.20
428	A63	1c Lycorea ceres	.20	.20
429	A63	2c Siderone nemesis	.25	.25
430	A63	6c Battus polydamas	1.10	.95
431	A63	30c Anartia lytrea	3.00	1.00
432	A63	40c Morpho peleides	3.00	1.00
433	A63	$2 Dryas julia	4.25	*6.75*
a.		Souvenir sheet, perf. 13½	6.50	6.50
		Nos. 427-433 (7)	12.00	10.35

Royal Mail Ship Yare A64

Ships Tied in with Dominican History: 1c, Royal mail ship Thames. 2c, Canadian National S.S. Lady Nelson. 20c, C.N. S.S. Lady Rodney. 45c, Harrison Line M.V. Statesman. 50c, Geest Line M.V. Geestcape. $2, Geest Line M.V. Geeststar.

1975, Sept. 1 ***Perf. 14***

434	A64	½c black & multi	.45	.35
435	A64	1c black & multi	.45	.35
436	A64	2c black & multi	.50	.40
437	A64	20c black & multi	1.90	.85
438	A64	45c black & multi	2.25	1.00
439	A64	50c black & multi	2.25	1.25
440	A64	$2 black & multi	4.25	*4.75*
a.		Souvenir sheet of 2, #439-440	6.75	4.25
		Nos. 434-440 (7)	12.05	8.95

IWY Emblem, Farm Women A65

$2, IWY emblem, dressmaker & saleswoman.

1975, Oct. 30 **Litho.** ***Perf. 14***

441	A65	10c pink & multi	.20	.20
442	A65	$2 yellow & multi	1.10	1.10

International Women's Year.

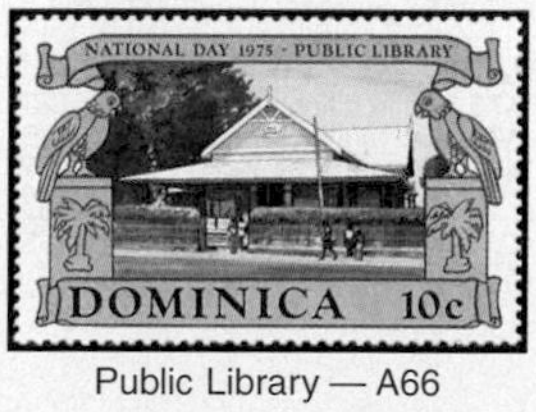

Public Library — A66

5c, Miss Caribbean Queen 1975. 30c, Citrus factory. $1, National Day Cup.

1975, Nov. 6

443	A66	5c multi, vert.	.30	.30
444	A66	10c multi	.30	.30
445	A66	30c multi	.30	.30
446	A66	$1 multi, vert.	.85	.85
a.		Souvenir sheet of 3	1.00	1.50
		Nos. 443-446 (4)	1.75	1.75

National Day. No. 446a contains 3 stamps similar to Nos. 444-446 with simulated perforations.

Virgin and Child, by Mantegna — A67

Christmas: Paintings of the Virgin and Child.

1975, Nov. 24

447	A67	½c shown	.20	.20
448	A67	1c Fra Filippo Lippi	.20	.20
449	A67	2c Bellini	.20	.20
450	A67	10c Botticelli	.20	.20
451	A67	25c Bellini	.25	.25
452	A67	45c Correggio	.30	.30
453	A67	$1 Durer	.65	.65
a.		Souvenir sheet of 2, #452-453	1.75	1.75
		Nos. 447-453 (7)	2.00	2.00

Hibiscus A68

Queen Elizabeth II — A69

Designs: 1c, African tulip. 2c, Castor oil tree. 3c, White cedar flower. 4c, Eggplant. 5c, Garfish. 6c, Okra. 8c, Zenaida doves. 10c, Screw pine. 20c, Mangoes. 25c, Crayfish. 30c, Manicou. 40c, Bay leaf groves. 50c, Tomatoes. $1, Lime factory. $2, Rum distillery. $5, Bay oil distillery.

1975, Dec. 8 **Litho.** ***Perf. 14½***

454	A68	½c ultra & multi	.20	*.50*
455	A68	1c lilac & multi	.25	*.50*
456	A68	2c orange & multi	.25	*.50*
457	A68	3c multicolored	.25	*.50*
458	A68	4c pink & multi	.25	*.50*
459	A68	5c multicolored	.30	*.50*
460	A68	6c gray & multi	.30	*.65*
461	A68	8c multicolored	4.00	.65
462	A68	10c violet & multi	.25	.20
463	A68	20c yellow & multi	.50	.20
464	A68	25c lemon & multi	.55	.20
465	A68	30c salmon & multi	1.50	.95
466	A68	40c multicolored	1.50	.95
467	A68	50c red & multi	.65	.55
468	A68	$1 citron & multi	.90	.65
469	A68	$2 multicolored	1.60	*3.75*
470	A68	$5 multicolored	2.00	*5.50*

Perf. 14

471	A69	$10 blue & multi	2.75	*16.00*
		Nos. 454-471 (18)	18.00	*33.25*

For overprints see Nos. 584-601, 640-643.

American Infantry — A70

Rowing — A71

Designs: 1c, English three-decker, 1782. 2c, George Washington. 45c, English sailors. 75c, English ensign with regimental flag. $2, Admiral Hood. All designs have old maps in background.

1976, Apr. 12 Litho. *Perf. 14½*

472	A70	½c green & multi	.20	.20
473	A70	1c purple & multi	.20	.20
474	A70	2c orange & multi	.20	.20
475	A70	45c brown & multi	.90	.20
476	A70	75c ultra & multi	1.50	1.00
477	A70	$2 red & multi	1.75	*3.00*
a.		Souvenir sheet of 2	4.50	*6.00*
		Nos. 472-477 (6)	4.75	4.80

American Bicentennial. No. 477a contains 2 stamps similar to Nos. 476-477, perf. 13.

1976, May 24 Litho. *Perf. 14½*

1c, Shot put. 2c, Swimming. 40c, Relay race. 45c, Gymnastics. 60c, Sailing. $2, Archery.

478	A71	½c ocher & multi	.20	.20
479	A71	1c ocher & multi	.20	.20
480	A71	2c ocher & multi	.20	.20
481	A71	40c ocher & multi	.20	.20
482	A71	45c ocher & multi	.20	.20
483	A71	60c ocher & multi	.30	.30
484	A71	$2 ocher & multi	.80	.80
a.		Souv. sheet, #483-484, perf 13	2.00	2.00
		Nos. 478-484 (7)	2.10	2.10

21st Olympic Games, Montreal, Canada, July 17-Aug. 1.

Ringed Kingfisher A72

Birds: 1c, Mourning dove. 2c, Green heron. 15c, Broad-winged hawk. 30c, Blue-headed hummingbird. 45c, Banana-quit. $2, Imperial parrot. 15c, 30c, 45c, $2, vert.

1976, June 28

485	A72	½c multicolored	.25	.25
486	A72	1c multicolored	.25	.25
487	A72	2c multicolored	.25	.25
488	A72	15c multicolored	1.25	1.25
489	A72	30c multicolored	2.00	2.00
490	A72	45c multicolored	2.25	2.25
491	A72	$2 multicolored	5.00	5.00
a.		Souv. sheet of 3, #489-491, perf. 13	9.50	9.50
		Nos. 485-491 (7)	11.25	11.25

Map of West Indies, Bats, Wicket and Ball A72a

Prudential Cup — A72b

1976, July 26 Litho. *Perf. 14*

492	A72a	15c lt blue & multi	.50	.50
493	A72b	25c lilac rose & black	1.00	1.00

World Cricket Cup, won by West Indies Team, 1975.

Viking Spacecraft — A73

Virgin and Child, by Giorgione — A74

1c, Titan launch center, horiz. 2c, Titan 3-D & Centaur D-IT. 3c, Orbiter & landing capsule. 45c, Capsule with closed parachute. 75c, Capsule with open parachute. $1, Landing capsule descending on Mars, horiz. $2, Viking on Mars, horiz.

1976, Sept. 20 Litho. *Perf. 15*

494	A73	½c multicolored	.20	.20
495	A73	1c multicolored	.20	.20
496	A73	2c multicolored	.20	.20
497	A73	3c multicolored	.20	.20
498	A73	45c multicolored	.35	.35
499	A73	75c multicolored	.45	.45
500	A73	$1 multicolored	.55	.55
501	A73	$2 multicolored	.85	.85
a.		Souvenir sheet of 2, #500, 501, perf. 13½	2.00	2.00
		Nos. 494-501 (8)	3.00	3.00

Viking mission to Mars.

1976, Nov. 1 Litho. *Perf. 14*

Virgin and Child by: 1c, Bellini. 2c, Mantegna. 6c, Mantegna. 25c, Memling. 45c, 50c, Correggio. $1, $3, Raphael.

502	A74	½c multicolored	.20	.20
503	A74	1c multicolored	.20	.20
504	A74	2c multicolored	.20	.20
505	A74	6c multicolored	.20	.20
506	A74	25c multicolored	.20	.20
507	A74	45c multicolored	.25	.25
508	A74	$3 multicolored	1.25	1.25
		Nos. 502-508 (7)	2.50	2.50

Souvenir Sheet

509		Sheet of 2	1.60	1.60
a.	A74	50c multicolored	.40	
b.	A74	$1 multicolored	.80	

Christmas.

Island Craft Co-operative — A75

National Day: 50c, Banana harvest, Castle Bruce Co-operative. $1, Banana shipping plant, Bourne Farmers' Co-operative.

1976, Nov. 22 Litho. *Perf. 13½x14*

510	A75	10c multicolored	.20	.20
511	A75	50c multicolored	.25	.25
512	A75	$1 multicolored	.55	.55
a.		Souvenir sheet of 3, #510-512	1.25	1.25
		Nos. 510-512 (3)	1.00	1.00

Common Sundial — A76

Sea Shells: 1c, Flame helmet. 2c, Mouse cone. 20c, Caribbean vase. 40c, West Indian fighting conch. 50c, Short coral shell. $2, Long-spined star shell. $3, Apple murex.

1976, Dec. 20 Litho. *Perf. 14*

513	A76	½c black & multi	.20	.20
514	A76	1c black & multi	.20	.20
515	A76	2c black & multi	.20	.20
516	A76	20c black & multi	.35	.20
517	A76	40c black & multi	.75	.55
518	A76	50c black & multi	.80	.65
519	A76	$3 black & multi	5.50	3.50
		Nos. 513-519 (7)	8.00	5.50

Souvenir Sheet

520	A76	$2 black & multi	3.00	3.00

Queen Enthroned — A77

Designs: 1c, Imperial crown. 45c, Elizabeth II and Princess Anne. $2, Coronation ring. $2.50, Ampulla and spoon. $5, Royal visit to Dominica.

1977, Feb. 7 *Perf. 14*

521	A77	½c multicolored	.20	.20
522	A77	1c multicolored	.20	.20
523	A77	45c multicolored	.25	.25
524	A77	$2 multicolored	1.10	1.10
525	A77	$2.50 multicolored	1.40	1.40
		Nos. 521-525 (5)	3.15	3.15

Souvenir Sheet

526	A77	$5 multicolored	2.50	2.50

25th anniv. of the reign of Elizabeth II.

Nos. 521-525 were printed in sheets of 40 (4x10), perf. 14, and sheets of 5 plus label, perf. 12, in changed colors.

For overprints see Nos. 549-554.

Joseph Haydn — A78

Designs: 1c, Fidelio, act I, scene IV. 2c, Dancer Maria Casentini. 15c, Beethoven working on Pastoral Symphony. 30c, "Wellington's Victory." 40c, Soprano Henriette Sontag. $2, Young Beethoven.

1977, Apr. 25 Litho. *Perf. 14*

527	A78	½c multicolored	.20	.20
528	A78	1c multicolored	.20	.20
529	A78	2c multicolored	.20	.20
530	A78	15c multicolored	.45	.45
531	A78	30c multicolored	.45	.45
532	A78	40c multicolored	.45	.45
533	A78	$2 multicolored	2.75	2.75
a.		Souvenir sheet of 3, #531-533	3.75	3.75
		Nos. 527-533 (7)	4.70	4.70

Ludwig van Beethoven (1770-1827), composer.

Boy Scouts on Hike A79

Saluting Boy Scout and: 1c, First aid. 2c, Scouts setting up camp. 45c, Rock climbing. 50c, Kayaking. 75c, Map reading. $2, Campfire. $3, Sailing.

1977, Aug. 8 Litho. *Perf. 14*

534	A79	½c multicolored	.20	.20
535	A79	1c multicolored	.20	.20
536	A79	2c multicolored	.20	.20
537	A79	45c multicolored	.50	.50
538	A79	50c multicolored	.60	.60
539	A79	$3 multicolored	2.50	2.50
		Nos. 534-539 (6)	4.20	4.20

Souvenir Sheet

540		Sheet of 2	2.50	2.50
a.	A79	75c multicolored	.75	
b.	A79	$2 multicolored	1.75	

6th Caribbean Jamboree, Kingston, Jamaica, Aug. 5-14.

Nativity A80

Christmas: 1c, Annunciation to the Shepherds. 2c, 45c, Presentation at the Temple (different). 6c, $2, $3, Flight into Egypt (different). 15c, Adoration of the Kings. 50c, Virgin and Child with Angels. ½c to 45c are illustrations from De Lisle Psalter, 14th century. 50c, $2, $3 are from other Psalters.

1977, Nov. 14 Litho. *Perf. 14*

541	A80	½c multicolored	.20	.20
542	A80	1c multicolored	.20	.20
543	A80	2c multicolored	.20	.20
544	A80	6c multicolored	.20	.20
545	A80	15c multicolored	.20	.20
546	A80	45c multicolored	.40	.40
547	A80	$3 multicolored	1.10	1.10
		Nos. 541-547 (7)	2.50	2.50

Souvenir Sheet

548		Sheet of 2	1.75	1.75
a.	A80	50c multicolored	.25	
b.	A80	$2 multicolored	1.50	

Nos. 521-526 Overprinted "ROYAL VISIT / W.I. 1977"

1977, Nov. 24 Litho. *Perf. 12, 14*

549	A77	½c multicolored	.20	.20
550	A77	1c multicolored	.20	.20
551	A77	45c multicolored	.20	.20
552	A77	$2 multicolored	.60	.60
553	A77	$2.50 multicolored	.65	.65
		Nos. 549-553 (5)	1.85	1.85

Souvenir Sheet

Perf. 14

554	A77	$5 multicolored	1.50	1.50

Caribbean visit of Queen Elizabeth II. #549-550 are perf. 12, others perf. 12 and 14.

Two types of No. 554: I. Overprinted only on stamp. II. Overprinted "W.I. 1977" on stamp and "Royal Visit W.I. 1977" on margin.

Masqueraders — A81

Designs: 1c, Sensay costume. 2c, Street musicians. 45c, Douiette band. 50c, Pappy Show wedding. $2, $2.50, Masquerade band.

1978, Jan. 9 *Perf. 14*

555	A81	½c multicolored	.20	.20
556	A81	1c multicolored	.20	.20
557	A81	2c multicolored	.20	.20
558	A81	45c multicolored	.30	.30
559	A81	50c multicolored	.35	.35
560	A81	$2 multicolored	1.40	1.40
		Nos. 555-560 (6)	2.65	2.65

Souvenir Sheet

561	A81	$2.50 multicolored	1.75	1.75

History of Carnival.

Lindbergh and Spirit of St. Louis A82

Designs: 10c, Spirit of St. Louis take-off, Long Island, May 20, 1927. 15c, Lindbergh and map of route New York to Paris. 20c, Lindbergh and plane in Paris. 40c, 1st Zeppelin, trial over Lake Constance. 50c, Spirit of St. Louis. 60c, Count Zeppelin and Zeppelin LZ-2, 1906. $2, Graf Zeppelin, 1928. $3, LZ-127, 1928.

1978, Mar. 13 — Litho. — *Perf. 14½*

562	A82	6c multicolored	.20	.20
563	A82	10c multicolored	.20	.20
564	A82	15c multicolored	.20	.20
565	A82	20c multicolored	.20	.20
566	A82	40c multicolored	.60	.60
567	A82	60c multicolored	.85	.85
568	A82	$3 multicolored	3.75	3.75
		Nos. 562-568 (7)	6.00	6.00

Souvenir Sheet

569	Sheet of 2	2.75	2.75
a.	A82 50c multicolored	.50	
b.	A82 $2 multicolored	2.00	

Charles A. Lindbergh's solo transatlantic flight from New York to Paris, 50th anniv., and flights of Graf Zeppelin.

Royal Family on Balcony — A83

Designs: 45c, Coronation. $2.50, Elizabeth II and Prince Philip. $5, Elizabeth II.

1978, June 2 — Litho. — *Perf. 14*

570	A83	45c multicolored	.20	.20
571	A83	$2 multicolored	.95	.95
572	A83	$2.50 multicolored	1.10	1.10
		Nos. 570-572 (3)	2.25	2.25

Souvenir Sheet

573	A83	$5 multicolored	2.00	2.00

Coronation of Queen Elizabeth II, 25th anniv. Nos. 570-572 were issued in sheets of 50, and in sheets of 3 stamps and label, in changed colors, perf. 12.

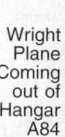

Wright Plane Coming out of Hangar A84

Designs: 40c, 1908 plane. 60c, Flyer I gliding. $2, Flyer I taking off. $3, Wilbur and Orville Wright and Flyer I.

1978, July 10 — Litho. — *Perf. 14½*

574	A84	30c multicolored	.20	.20
575	A84	40c multicolored	.30	.30
576	A84	60c multicolored	.40	.40
577	A84	$2 multicolored	1.60	1.60
		Nos. 574-577 (4)	2.50	2.50

Souvenir Sheet

578	A84	$3 multicolored	2.50	2.50

75th anniv. of first powered flight.

Two Apostles, by Rubens — A85

Rubens Paintings: 45c, Descent from the Cross. 50c, St. Ildefonso Receiving Chasuble. $2, Holy Family. $3, Assumption of the Virgin.

1978, Oct. 16 — Litho. — *Perf. 14*

579	A85	20c multicolored	.20	.20
580	A85	45c multicolored	.30	.30
581	A85	50c multicolored	.35	.35
582	A85	$3 multicolored	2.00	2.00
		Nos. 579-582 (4)	2.85	2.85

Souvenir Sheet

583	A85	$2 multicolored	1.50	1.50

Christmas.

Nos. 454-471 Overprinted: "INDEPENDENCE/ 3rd NOVEMBER 1978"

1978 Nov. 1 — Litho. — *Perf. 14½*

584	A68	½c ultra & multi	.20	.20
585	A68	1c lilac & multi	.20	.20
586	A68	2c orange & multi	.20	.20
587	A68	3c multicolored	.20	.20
588	A68	4c pink & multi	.20	.20
589	A68	5c multicolored	.20	.20
590	A68	6c gray & multi	.20	.20
591	A68	8c multicolored	.20	.20
592	A68	10c violet & multi	.20	.20
a.		Perf. 13½ ('79)	.20	.20
593	A68	20c yellow & multi	.20	.20
594	A68	25c lemon & multi	.20	.20
595	A68	30c salmon & multi	.30	.30
596	A68	40c multicolored	.40	.55
597	A68	50c red & multi	.55	.75
598	A68	$1 citron & multi	.95	1.40
599	A68	$2 multicolored	2.10	2.75
600	A68	$5 multicolored	4.25	5.50

Perf. 14

601	A69	$10 blue & multi	8.75	12.50
		Nos. 584-601 (18)	19.50	25.95

Map of Dominica with Parishes — A86

Rowland Hill — A87

25c, Sabinea carinalis, natl. flower, & map. 45c, New flag & map. 50c, Coat of arms & map. $2, Prime Minister Patrick John.

1978, Nov. 1 — *Perf. 14*

602	A86	10c multicolored	.20	.20
603	A86	25c multicolored	.20	.20
604	A86	45c multicolored	.65	.65
605	A86	50c multicolored	.75	.75
606	A86	$2 multicolored	3.25	3.25
		Nos. 602-606 (5)	5.05	5.05

Souvenir Sheet

607	A86	$2.50 multicolored	*3.00*	*3.25*

Dominican independence.

1979, Mar. 19

45c, Great Britain #2. 50c, Dominica #1. $2, Maltese Cross handstamps. $5, Penny Black.

608	A87	25c multicolored	.20	.20
609	A87	45c multicolored	.20	.20
610	A87	50c multicolored	.25	.25
611	A87	$2 multicolored	.95	.95
		Nos. 608-611 (4)	1.60	1.60

Souvenir Sheet

612	A87	$5 multicolored	2.50	2.50

Sir Rowland Hill (1795-1879), originator of penny postage.

Nos. 608-611 printed in sheets of 5 plus label, perf. 12x12½, in changed colors.

For overprints see Nos. 663A-663D.

Boys and Dugout Canoe A88

IYC Emblem and: 40c, Children carrying bananas. 50c, Boys playing cricket. $3, Child feeding rabbits. $5, Boy showing catch of fish.

1979, Apr. 23 — Litho. — *Perf. 14*

613	A88	30c multicolored	.30	.30
614	A88	40c multicolored	.45	.45
615	A88	50c multicolored	.50	.50
616	A88	$3 multicolored	2.75	2.75
		Nos. 613-616 (4)	4.00	4.00

Souvenir Sheet

617	A88	$5 multicolored	3.25	3.25

Grouper A89

30c, Striped dolphin. 50c, White-tailed tropic birds. 60c, Brown pelicans. $1, Pilot whale. $2, Brown booby. $3, Elkhorn coral.

1979, May 21 — Litho. — *Perf. 14*

618	A89	10c multicolored	.20	.20
619	A89	30c multicolored	1.00	1.00
620	A89	50c multicolored	1.75	1.75
621	A89	60c multicolored	2.10	2.10
622	A89	$1 multicolored	3.50	3.50
623	A89	$2 multicolored	7.00	7.00
		Nos. 618-623 (6)	15.55	15.55

Souvenir Sheet

624	A89	$3 multicolored	3.50	3.50

Wildlife protection.

Capt. Cook, Bark Endeavour — A90

Capt. Cook and: 50c, Resolution, map of 2nd voyage. 60c, Discovery, map of 3rd voyage. $2, Cook's map of New Zealand, 1770. $5, Portrait.

1979, July 16 — Litho. — *Perf. 14*

625	A90	10c multicolored	.20	.20
626	A90	50c multicolored	1.00	1.00
627	A90	60c multicolored	1.25	1.25
628	A90	$2 multicolored	3.75	3.75
		Nos. 625-628 (4)	6.20	6.20

Souvenir Sheet

629	A90	$5 multicolored	3.00	3.00

200th death anniv. of Capt. James Cook (1728-1779).

Girl Guides Cooking A91

Girl Guides: 20c, Setting up emergency rain tent. 50c, Raising flag of independent Dominica. $2.50, Playing accordion and singing. $3, Leader and Guides of different ages.

1979, July 30

630	A91	10c multicolored	.20	.20
631	A91	20c multicolored	.20	.20
632	A91	50c multicolored	.40	.40
633	A91	$2.50 multicolored	2.00	2.00
		Nos. 630-633 (4)	2.80	2.80

Souvenir Sheet

634	A91	$3 multicolored	2.25	2.25

50th anniv. of Dominican Girl Guides.

Colvillea — A92

Flowering Trees: 40c, Lignum vitae. 60c, Dwarf poinciana. $2, Fern tree. $3, Perfume tree.

1979, Sept. 3 — Litho. — *Perf. 14*

635	A92	20c multicolored	.20	.20
636	A92	40c multicolored	.25	.25
637	A92	60c multicolored	.40	.40
638	A92	$2 multicolored	1.40	1.40
		Nos. 635-638 (4)	2.25	2.25

Souvenir Sheet

639	A92	$3 multicolored	2.40	2.40

Nos. 459, 466, 470-471 Overprinted: "HURRICANE / RELIEF"

Perf. 14½, 13½, 13½x14, 14

1979, Oct. 29 — Litho.

640	A68	5c multicolored	.20	.20
641	A68	40c multicolored	.40	.40
642	A68	$5 multicolored	5.00	5.00
643	A68	$10 multicolored	10.00	10.00
		Nos. 640-643 (4)	15.60	15.60

Hurricane devastation, Aug. 29. Vertical overprint on No. 643, others horizontal.

Music Scenes A92a

1979, Nov. 2 — Litho. — *Perf. 11*

644	A92a	½c Mickey Mouse	.20	.20
645	A92a	1c Goofy playing guitar	.20	.20
646	A92a	2c Mickey Mouse and Goofy	.20	.20
647	A92a	3c Donald Duck	.20	.20
648	A92a	4c Minnie Mouse	.20	.20
649	A92a	5c Goofy playing accordion	.20	.20
650	A92a	10c Horace Horsecollar and Dale	.20	.20
651	A92a	$2 Huey, Dewey, Louie	3.00	3.00
652	A92a	$2.50 Donald and Huey	3.50	3.50
		Nos. 644-652 (9)	7.90	7.90

Souvenir Sheet

Perf. 13

653	A92a	$3 Mickey Mouse playing piano	4.50	4.50

Cathedral of the Assumption — A93

Cathedrals: 40c, St. Patrick's, New York. 45c, St. Paul's, London, vert. 60c, St. Peter's, Rome. $2, Cologne Cathedral. $3, Notre Dame, Paris, vert.

1979, Nov. 26 — Litho. — *Perf. 14*

654	A93	6c multicolored	.20	.20
655	A93	45c multicolored	.30	.30
656	A93	60c multicolored	.40	.40
657	A93	$3 multicolored	2.00	2.00
		Nos. 654-657 (4)	2.90	2.90

Souvenir Sheet

658	Sheet of 2	1.00	1.00
a.	A93 40c multicolored	.25	.25
b.	A93 $2 multicolored	.75	.75

Christmas.

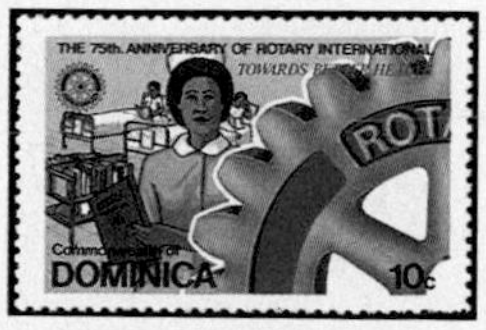

Nurse and Patients, Rotary Emblem A94

1980, Mar. 31 Litho. *Perf. 14*
659 A94 10c shown .20 .20
660 A94 20c Electrocardiogram machine .20 .20
661 A94 40c Mental hospital .30 .30
662 A94 $2.50 Paul Harris, founder 1.75 1.75
Nos. 659-662 (4) 2.45 2.45

Souvenir Sheet

663 A94 $3 Map of Africa and Europe 2.25 2.25

Rotary International, 75th anniv. Nos. 659-662 each contain quadrant of Rotary emblem.

Nos. 608-611 Overprinted "LONDON 1980"

1980, May 6 Litho. *Perf. 12*
663A A87 25c multicolored .25 .25
663B A87 45c multicolored .45 .45
663C A87 50c multicolored .50 .50
663D A87 $2 multicolored 2.00 2.00
Nos. 663A-663D (4) 3.20 3.20

London 80 Intl. Stamp Exhib., May 6-14.

Shot Put, Moscow '80 Emblem A95

1980, May 27 Litho. *Perf. 14*
664 A95 30c shown .20 .20
665 A95 40c Basketball .30 .30
666 A95 60c Swimming .40 .40
667 A95 $2 Gymnast 1.40 1.40
Nos. 664-667 (4) 2.30 2.30

Souvenir Sheet

668 A95 $3 Running 2.00 2.00

22nd Summer Olympic Games, Moscow, July 19-Aug. 3.

Embarkation for Cythera, by Watteau — A96

Paintings: 20c, Supper at Emmaus, by Caravaggio. 25c, Charles I Hunting, by Van Dyck, vert. 30c, The Maids of Honor, by Velazquez, vert. 45c, Rape of the Sabine Women, by Poussin. $1, Embarkation for Cythera, by Watteau. $3, Holy Family, by Rembrandt. $5, Girl before a Mirror, by Picasso, vert.

Perf. 14x13½, 13½x14
1980, July 22 Litho.
669 A96 20c multicolored .20 .20
670 A96 25c multicolored .20 .20
671 A96 30c multicolored .20 .20
672 A96 45c multicolored .25 .25
673 A96 $1 multicolored .65 .65
674 A96 $5 multicolored 2.40 2.40
Nos. 669-674 (6) 3.90 3.90

Souvenir Sheet

675 A96 $3 multicolored 1.50 1.50

Queen Mother Elizabeth, 80th Birthday A97

1980, Aug. 4 *Perf. 12, 14*
676 A97 40c multicolored .25 .25
677 A97 $2.50 multicolored 1.00 1.00

Souvenir Sheet

678 A97 $3 multicolored 1.25 1.75

Tinkerbell — A98

Designs: Scenes from Disney's Peter Pan.

1980, Oct. 1 Litho. *Perf. 11*
679 A98 ½c multicolored .20 .20
680 A98 1c multicolored .20 .20
681 A98 2c multicolored .20 .20
682 A98 3c multicolored .20 .20
683 A98 4c multicolored .20 .20
684 A98 5c multicolored .20 .20
685 A98 10c multicolored .20 .20
686 A98 $2 multicolored 3.25 1.60
687 A98 $2.50 multicolored 3.25 1.90
Nos. 679-687 (9) 7.90 4.90

Souvenir Sheet

688 A98 $4 multicolored 6.00 6.00

Christmas.

Douglas Bay A99

1981, Feb. 12 Litho. *Perf. 14*
689 A99 20c shown .20 .20
690 A99 30c Valley of Desolation .20 .20
691 A99 40c Emerald Pool, vert. .20 .20
692 A99 $3 Indian River, vert. 1.50 1.50
Nos. 689-692 (4) 2.10 2.10

Souvenir Sheet

693 A99 $4 Trafalgar Falls 2.00 2.00

Pluto and Fifi — A100

$4, Pluto in Blue Note (1947 cartoon).

1981, Apr. 30 Litho. *Perf. 13½x14*
694 A100 $2 multicolored 2.00 2.00

Souvenir Sheet

695 A100 $4 multicolored 4.00 4.00

50th anniversary of Walt Disney's Pluto.

Forest Thrush A101

1981, Apr. 30 *Perf. 14*
696 A101 20c shown .20 .20
697 A101 30c Stolid flycatcher .40 .40
698 A101 40c Blue-hooded euphonia .55 .55
699 A101 $5 Lesser antillean peewee 7.00 7.00
Nos. 696-699 (4) 8.15 8.15

Souvenir Sheet

700 A101 $3 Sisserou parrot 4.50 4.50

Royal Wedding Issue
Common Design Type

1981, June 16 Litho. *Perf. 14*
701 CD331a 45c Couple .25 .25
702 CD331a 60c Windsor Castle .30 .30
703 CD331a $4 Charles 2.00 2.00
Nos. 701-703 (3) 2.55 2.55

Souvenir Sheet

704 CD331 $5 Helicopter 2.00 2.00

Booklet

705 CD331 8.25
a. Pane of 6 (3x25c, Lady Diana, 3x$2, Charles) 4.75
b. Pane of 1, $5, Couple 3.50

No. 705 contains imperf., self-adhesive stamps.

Nos. 701-703 also printed in sheets of 5 plus label, perf. 12, in changed colors. Value, set of three sheets $10.

Elves Repairing Santa's Sleigh — A102

Christmas: Scenes from Walt Disney's Santa's Workshop.

1981, Nov. 2 Litho. *Perf. 14*
706 A102 ½c multicolored .20 .20
707 A102 1c multicolored .20 .20
708 A102 2c multicolored .20 .20
709 A102 3c multicolored .20 .20
710 A102 4c multicolored .20 .20
711 A102 5c multicolored .20 .20
712 A102 10c multicolored .20 .20
713 A102 45c multicolored .60 .60
714 A102 $5 multicolored 7.50 7.50
Nos. 706-714 (9) 9.50 9.50

Souvenir Sheet

715 A102 $4 multicolored 6.50 6.50

Ixora A103

1981, Dec. 1 Litho. *Perf. 14*
716 A103 1c shown .20 .20
717 A103 2c Flamboyant .20 .20
718 A103 4c Poinsettia .20 .20
719 A103 5c Sabinea carinalis .20 .20
720 A103 8c Annatto roucou .20 .20
721 A103 10c Passion fruit .20 .20
722 A103 15c Breadfruit .20 .20
723 A103 20c Allamanda buttercup .20 .20
724 A103 25c Cashew .20 .20
725 A103 35c Soursop .25 .25
726 A103 40c Bougainvillea .30 .65
727 A103 45c Anthurium .35 .70
728 A103 60c Cacao .45 .95
729 A103 90c Pawpaw tree .65 1.40
730 A103 $1 Coconut palm .70 1.50
731 A103 $2 Coffee tree 1.40 2.75
732 A103 $5 Lobster claw 3.50 7.00
a. Perf. 12½x12 ('85) 2.25 2.40
733 A103 $10 Banana fig 7.00 14.50
Nos. 716-733 (18) 16.40 31.50

Nos. 721-722, 728, 732 exist dated "1985." For overprints see Nos. 852-853.

1984 *Perf. 12*
721a A103 10c .80 .80
730a A103 $1 1.00 1.00
732a A103 $5 3.50 3.50
733a A103 $10 7.50 7.50

Dated "1984."

Intl. Year of the Disabled — A104

Bathers, by Picasso — A105

1981, Dec. 22 Litho. *Perf. 14*
734 A104 45c Ramp curb .35 .35
735 A104 60c Bus steps .50 .50
736 A104 75c Hand-operated car .65 .65
737 A104 $4 Bus lift 3.00 3.00
Nos. 734-737 (4) 4.50 4.50

Souvenir Sheet

738 A104 $5 Elevator buttons 6.00 6.00

1981, Dec. 30 *Perf. 14½*
739 A105 45c Olga in Armchair .35 .35
740 A105 60c shown .50 .50
741 A105 75c Woman in Spanish Costume .65 .65
742 A105 $4 Dog and Cock 3.00 3.00
Nos. 739-742 (4) 4.50 4.50

Souvenir Sheet

743 A105 $5 Sleeping Peasants 6.00 6.00

1982 World Cup Soccer — A106

Various Disney characters playing soccer.

1982, Jan. 29 *Perf. 14*
744 A106 ½c multicolored .20 .20
745 A106 1c multicolored .20 .20
746 A106 2c multicolored .20 .20
747 A106 3c multicolored .20 .20
748 A106 4c multicolored .20 .20
749 A106 5c multicolored .20 .20
750 A106 10c multicolored .20 .20
751 A106 60c multicolored 1.10 1.10
752 A106 $5 multicolored 8.50 8.50
Nos. 744-752 (9) 11.00 11.00

Souvenir Sheet

753 A106 $4 multicolored 6.50 6.50

Golden Days, by Norman Rockwell A107

1982, Mar. 10 Litho. *Perf. 14x13½*
754 A107 10c shown .20 .20
755 A107 25c The Morning News .20 .20
756 A107 45c The Marbles Champ .35 .35
757 A107 $1 Speeding Along .75 .75
Nos. 754-757 (4) 1.50 1.50

Intl. Decade for Women (1975-85) A108

Famous Women: 10c, Elma Napier (1890-1973), first woman elected to Legislative Council in British West Indies, 1940. 45c, Margaret Mead (1901-1978), anthropologist. $1, Mabel Caudiron (1909-1968), musician and folk historian. $3, Florence Nightingale, founder of modern nursing. $4, Eleanor Roosevelt.

1982, Apr. 15 Litho. *Perf. 14*

758 A108 10c multicolored .20 .20
759 A108 45c multicolored .35 .35
760 A108 $1 multicolored .75 .75
761 A108 $4 multicolored 3.25 3.25
Nos. 758-761 (4) 4.55 4.55

Souvenir Sheet

762 A108 $3 multicolored 3.50 3.50

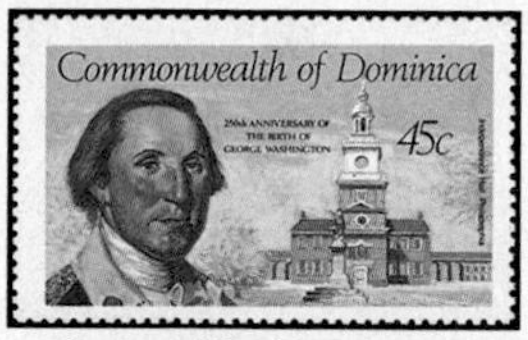

George Washington and Independence Hall, Philadelphia — A109

Washington or Roosevelt and: 60c, Capitol Building. 90c, The Surrender of Cornwallis, by John Trumbull. $2, Dam construction during New Deal (mural by William Gropper). $5, Washington, Roosevelt.

1982, May 1 *Perf. 14½*

763 A109 45c multicolored .35 .35
764 A109 60c multicolored .45 .45
765 A109 90c multicolored .70 .70
766 A109 $2 multicolored 1.75 1.75
Nos. 763-766 (4) 3.25 3.25

Souvenir Sheet

767 A109 $5 multicolored 3.50 3.50

George Washington's 250th birth anniv. and Franklin D. Roosevelt's birth cent.

Godman's Leaf Butterfly — A110

1982, June 1 Litho. *Perf. 14*

768 A110 15c shown .50 .50
769 A110 45c Zebra 2.25 2.25
770 A110 60c Mimic 2.50 2.50
771 A110 $3 Red rim 10.50 10.50
Nos. 768-771 (4) 15.75 15.75

Souvenir Sheet

772 A110 $5 Southern dagger tail 8.00 8.00

Princess Diana Issue

Common Design Type

1982, July 1 Litho. *Perf. 14½x14*

773 CD332 45c Buckingham Palace .35 .35
774 CD332 $2 Engagement portrait 1.50 1.50
775 CD332 $4 Wedding 3.00 3.00
Nos. 773-775 (3) 4.85 4.85

Souvenir Sheet

776 CD332 $5 Diana, diff. 4.25 4.25

Also issued in sheet of 5 plus label.
For overprints see Nos. 782-785.

Scouting Year A111

1982, July 1 Litho. *Perf. 14*

777 A111 45c Cooking .95 .95
778 A111 60c Meteorological study 1.50 1.50
779 A111 75c Sisserou parrot, cub scouts 1.75 1.75
780 A111 $3 Canoeing, Indian River 6.50 6.50
Nos. 777-780 (4) 10.70 10.70

Souvenir Sheet

781 A111 $5 Flagbearer 4.50 4.50

Nos. 773-776 Overprinted: "ROYAL BABY / 21.6.82"

1982, Sept. 1 Litho. *Perf. 14½x14*

782 CD332 45c multicolored .35 .35
783 CD332 $2 multicolored 1.50 1.50
784 CD332 $4 multicolored 3.00 3.00
Nos. 782-784 (3) 4.85 4.85

Souvenir Sheet

785 CD332 $5 multicolored 4.00 4.00

Birth of Prince William of Wales, June 21.
Also issued in sheet of 5 plus label.

Christmas — A112

Holy Family Paintings by Raphael.

1982, Oct. 18 Litho. *Perf. 14*

786 A112 25c multicolored .20 .20
787 A112 30c multicolored .20 .20
788 A112 90c multicolored .60 .60
789 A112 $4 multicolored 2.75 2.75
Nos. 786-789 (4) 3.75 3.75

Souvenir Sheet

790 A112 $5 multicolored 4.25 4.25

Goosebeak Whale Eating Squid — A113

1983, Feb. 15 Litho. *Perf. 14*

791 A113 45c shown 1.25 1.25
792 A113 60c Humpback whale 1.75 1.75
793 A113 75c Great right whale 2.25 2.25
794 A113 $3 Melonhead whale 9.25 9.25
Nos. 791-794 (4) 14.50 14.50

Souvenir Sheet

795 A113 $5 Pygmy sperm whale 8.00 8.00

A113a

1983, Mar. 14

796 A113a 25c Banana industry .20 .20
797 A113a 30c Road construction .20 .20
798 A113a 90c Community nursing .55 .55
799 A113a $3 Basket weavers 1.75 1.75
Nos. 796-799 (4) 2.70 2.70

Commonwealth Day.

World Communications Year — A114

1983, Apr. 18 Litho. *Perf. 14*

800 A114 45c Hurricane pattern, map .35 .35
801 A114 60c Air-to-ship communication .45 .45
802 A114 90c Columbia shuttle, dish antenna .70 .70
803 A114 $2 Walkie-talkie 1.50 1.50
Nos. 800-803 (4) 3.00 3.00

Souvenir Sheet

804 A114 $5 Satellite 3.50 3.50

Manned Flight Bicentenary — A115

1983, July 19 Litho. *Perf. 15*

805 A115 45c Mayo Composite .50 .50
806 A115 60c Macchi M-39 .65 .65
807 A115 90c Fairey Swordfish 1.00 1.00
808 A115 $4 Zeppelin LZ-3 4.25 4.25
Nos. 805-808 (4) 6.40 6.40

Souvenir Sheet

809 A115 $5 Double Eagle II, vert. 4.00 4.00

Duesenberg SJ, 1935 — A116

1983, Sept. 1 Litho. *Perf. 14*

810 A116 10c shown .20 .20
811 A116 45c Studebaker Avanti, 1962 .35 .35
812 A116 60c Cord 812, 1936 .45 .45
813 A116 75c MG-TC, 1945 .55 .55
814 A116 90c Camaro 350-SS, 1967 .70 .70
815 A116 $3 Porsche 356, 1948 2.25 2.25
Nos. 810-815 (6) 4.50 4.50

Souvenir Sheet

816 A116 $5 Ferrari 312-T, 1975 4.00 4.00

Christmas — A117

Raphael Paintings.

1983, Oct. 4 Litho. *Perf. 13½*

817 A117 45c multicolored .35 .35
818 A117 60c multicolored .50 .50
819 A117 90c multicolored .75 .75
820 A117 $4 multicolored 3.25 3.25
Nos. 817-820 (4) 4.85 4.85

Souvenir Sheet

821 A117 $5 multicolored 4.00 4.00

23rd Olympic Games, Los Angeles, July 28-Aug. 12 — A118

1984, Mar. Litho. *Perf. 14*

822 A118 30c Gymnastics .25 .25
823 A118 45c Javelin .35 .35
824 A118 60c Diving .50 .50
825 A118 $4 Fencing 3.25 3.25
Nos. 822-825 (4) 4.35 4.35

Souvenir Sheet

826 A118 $5 Equestrian 4.25 4.25

Local Birds A119

1984, May Litho.

827 A119 5c Plumbeous warbler 3.25 3.25
828 A119 45c Imperial parrot 8.50 8.50
829 A119 60c Blue-headed hummingbird 12.50 12.50
830 A119 90c Red-necked parrot 18.00 18.00
Nos. 827-830 (4) 42.25 42.25

Souvenir Sheet

831 A119 $5 Roseate flamingoes 13.00 13.00

Easter A120

Various Disney characters and Easter bunnies.

1984, Apr. 15 Litho. *Perf. 11*

832 A120 ½c multicolored .20 .20
833 A120 1c multicolored .20 .20
834 A120 2c multicolored .20 .20
835 A120 3c multicolored .20 .20
836 A120 4c multicolored .20 .20
837 A120 5c multicolored .20 .20
838 A120 10c multicolored .20 .20
839 A120 $2 multicolored 4.00 4.00
840 A120 $4 multicolored 8.00 8.00
Nos. 832-840 (9) 13.40 13.40

Souvenir Sheet

Perf. 14

841 A120 $5 multicolored 7.00 7.00

Ships A121

1984, June 14 Litho. *Perf. 14*

842 A121 45c Atlantic Star 1.10 1.10
843 A121 60c Atlantic 1.40 1.40
844 A121 90c Carib fishing pirogue 2.50 2.50
845 A121 $4 Norway 10.50 10.50
Nos. 842-845 (4) 15.50 15.50

Souvenir Sheet

846 A121 $5 Santa Maria 6.00 6.00

Local Plants — A122

Correggio & Degas — A122a

1984, Aug. 13

847 A122 45c Guzmania lingulata .45 .45
848 A122 60c Pitcairnia angustifolia .55 .55
849 A122 75c Tillandsia fasciculata .75 .75

850 A122 $3 Aechmea smithiorum 3.25 3.25
Nos. 847-850 (4) 5.00 5.00

Souvenir Sheet

851 A122 $5 Tillandsia utriculata 4.00 4.00

Ausipex Intl. Stamp Exhibition.

Nos. 721, 732 Overprinted: "19th UPU / CONGRESS HAMBURG"

1984 Litho. *Perf. 14*

852 A103 10c multicolored .20 .20
853 A103 $5 multicolored 5.00 5.00

1984, Nov. Litho. *Perf. 15*

Correggio: 25c, Virgin and Child with Young St. John. 60c, Christ Bids Farewell to the Virgin Mary. 90c, Do Not Touch Me. $4, The Mystical Marriage of St. Catherine. No. 862, Adoration of the Magi,

Degas, horiz.: 30c, Before the Start. 45c, On the Racecourse. $1, Jockeys at the Flagpole. $3, Racehorses at Longchamp. No. 863, Self-portrait.

854 A122a 25c multicolored .20 .20
855 A122a 30c multicolored .20 .20
856 A122a 45c multicolored .40 .40
857 A122a 60c multicolored .55 .55
858 A122a 90c multicolored .75 .75
859 A122a $1 multicolored .90 .90
860 A122a $3 multicolored 2.50 2.50
861 A122a $4 multicolored 3.50 3.50
Nos. 854-861 (8) 9.00 9.00

Souvenir Sheets

862 A122a $5 multicolored 3.75 3.75
863 A122a $5 multicolored 3.75 3.75

A123

A124

1984, Dec. *Perf. 14*

864 A123 30c Avro 748 .20 .20
865 A123 60c Twin Otter 1.40 1.40
866 A123 $1 Islander 2.40 2.40
867 A123 $3 Casa 7.00 7.00
Nos. 864-867 (4) 11.00 11.00

Souvenir Sheet

868 A123 $5 Boeing 747 7.50 7.50

Intl. Civil Aviation Org., 40th anniv.

1984, Nov. Litho.

Scenes from various Donald Duck movies.

869 A124 45c multicolored .95 .95
870 A124 60c multicolored 1.25 1.25
871 A124 90c multicolored 2.00 2.00
872 A124 $2 multicolored, perf. 12x12½ 4.00 4.00
873 A124 $4 multicolored 7.75 7.75
Nos. 869-873 (5) 15.95 15.95

Souvenir Sheet

Perf. 13½x14

874 A124 $5 multicolored 6.75 6.75

Christmas and 50th anniv. of Donald Duck.

Cats
A125

1984, Nov. 12 Litho. *Perf. 15*

875 A125 10c Tabby .20 .20
876 A125 15c Calico shorthair .20 .20
877 A125 20c Siamese .20 .20
878 A125 25c Manx .20 .20
879 A125 45c Abyssinian .45 .45
880 A125 60c Tortoise shell longhair .55 .55
881 A125 $1 Rex .90 .90
882 A125 $2 Persian 2.10 2.10
883 A125 $3 Himalayan 3.25 3.25
884 A125 $5 Burmese 5.00 5.00
Nos. 875-884 (10) 13.05 13.05

Souvenir Sheet

885 A125 $5 Gray Burmese, Persian, American shorthair 6.25 6.25

Girl Guides, 75th Anniv. A126

1985, Feb. 18 *Perf. 14*

886 A126 35c Lady Baden-Powell .50 .50
887 A126 45c Inspecting Dominican troop .75 .75
888 A126 60c With Dominican troop leaders 1.00 1.00
889 A126 $3 Lord and Lady Baden-Powell, vert. 4.50 4.50
Nos. 886-889 (4) 6.75 6.75

Souvenir Sheet

890 A126 $5 Flag ceremony 6.75 6.75

John James Audubon A127

1985, Apr. 4

891 A127 45c King rails 1.00 1.00
892 A127 $1 Black & white warbler, vert. 2.10 2.10
893 A127 $2 Broad-winged hawks, vert. 4.00 4.00
894 A127 $3 Ring-necked ducks 6.25 6.25
Nos. 891-894 (4) 13.35 13.35

Souvenir Sheet

895 A127 $5 Reddish egrets, vert. 7.00 7.00

Nos. 891-894 exist vertically se-tenant with labels showing additional bird species.

See Nos. 965-969.

Duke of Edinburgh Awards, 1984 — A128

1985, Apr. 30

896 A128 45c Woman at computer terminal .65 .65
897 A128 60c Medical staff, patient .85 .85
898 A128 90c Runners 1.25 1.25
899 A128 $4 Family jogging 5.25 5.25
Nos. 896-899 (4) 8.00 8.00

Souvenir Sheet

900 A128 $5 Duke of Edinburgh 5.50 5.50

Intl. Youth Year A129

1985, July 8 Litho. *Perf. 14*

901 A129 45c Cricket match 1.75 1.75
902 A129 60c Environmental study, parrot 2.25 2.25
903 A129 $1 Stamp collecting 3.25 3.25
904 A129 $3 Boating, leisure 11.50 11.50
Nos. 901-904 (4) 18.75 18.75

Souvenir Sheet

905 A129 $5 Youths join hands 4.75 4.75

Queen Mother, 85th Birthday — A130

Johann Sebastian Bach — A131

1985, July 15

906 A130 60c Visiting Sadlers Wells .55 .55
907 A130 $1 Fishing 1.25 1.25
908 A130 $3 At Clarence House, 1984 3.75 3.75
Nos. 906-908 (3) 5.55 5.55

Souvenir Sheet

909 A130 $5 Attending Windsor Castle Garter Ceremony 4.50 4.50

1985, Sept. 2

Portrait, signature, music from Explication and: 45c, Cornett 60c, Coiled trumpet. $1, Piccolo. $3, Violoncello piccolo.

910 A131 45c multicolored .85 .85
911 A131 60c multicolored 1.10 1.10
912 A131 $1 multicolored 1.75 1.75
913 A131 $3 multicolored 6.75 6.75
Nos. 910-913 (4) 10.45 10.45

Souvenir Sheet

914 A131 $5 Portrait 5.00 5.00

State Visit of Elizabeth II, Oct. 25 — A132

1985, Oct. 25 *Perf. 14½*

915 A132 60c Flags of UK, Dominica .55 .55
916 A132 $1 Elizabeth II, vert. .95 .95
917 A132 $4 HMS Britannia 4.50 4.50
Nos. 915-917 (3) 6.00 6.00

Souvenir Sheet

918 A132 $5 Map 4.50 4.50

Mark Twain — A133

Disney characters in Tom Sawyer.

1985, Nov. 11 Litho. *Perf. 14*

919 A133 20c multicolored .45 .45
920 A133 60c multicolored 1.10 1.10
921 A133 $1 multicolored 1.90 1.90
922 A133 $1.50 multicolored 3.50 3.50
923 A133 $2 multicolored 5.00 5.00
Nos. 919-923 (5) 11.95 11.95

Souvenir Sheet

924 A133 $5 multicolored 7.75 7.75

Christmas.

The Brothers Grimm — A134

Disney characters in Little Red Cap (Little Red Riding Hood).

1985, Nov. 11

925 A134 10c multicolored .45 .45
926 A134 45c multicolored .95 .95
927 A134 90c multicolored 1.75 1.75
928 A134 $1 multicolored 2.10 2.10
929 A134 $3 multicolored 6.25 6.25
Nos. 925-929 (5) 11.50 11.50

Souvenir Sheet

930 A134 $5 multicolored 9.25 9.25

Christmas.

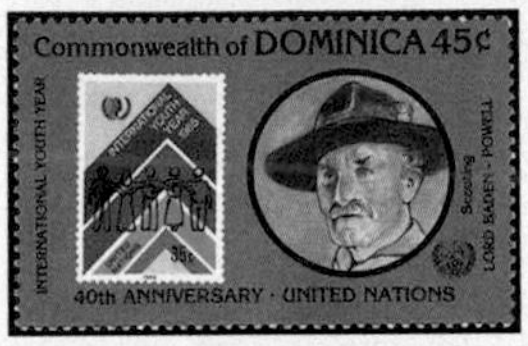

UN, 40th Anniv. A135

Stamps of UN, famous men and events: 45c, No. 442 and Lord Baden-Powell. $2, No. 157 and Maimonides (1135-1204) Judaic scholar. $3, No. 278 and Sir Rowland Hill. $5, Apollo-Soyuz Mission, 10th anniv.

1985, Nov. 22 *Perf. 14½*

931 A135 45c multicolored .50 .50
932 A135 $2 multicolored 3.00 3.00
933 A135 $3 multicolored 4.50 4.50
Nos. 931-933 (3) 8.00 8.00

Souvenir Sheet

934 A135 $5 multicolored 4.50 4.50

1986 World Cup Soccer Championships, Mexico — A136

Various soccer plays.

1986, Mar. 26 *Perf. 14*

935 A136 45c multicolored 1.00 1.00
936 A136 60c multicolored 1.40 1.40
937 A136 $1 multicolored 2.50 2.50
938 A136 $3 multicolored 7.50 7.50
Nos. 935-938 (4) 12.40 12.40

Souvenir Sheet

939 A136 $5 multicolored 10.00 10.00

For overprints see Nos. 974-978.

Statue of Liberty, Cent. A137

Statue and: 15c, New York police pursuing river pirates, c. 1890. 25c, Police patrol boat. 45c, Hoboken Ferry Terminal, c. 1890. $4, Holland Tunnel.

1986, Mar. 26

940 A137 15c multicolored .60 .60
941 A137 25c multicolored .60 .60
942 A137 45c multicolored .85 .85
943 A137 $4 multicolored 8.50 8.50
Nos. 940-943 (4) 10.55 10.55

Souvenir Sheet

944 A137 $5 Statue, vert. 6.50 6.50

Halley's Comet A138

5c, Jantal Mantar Observatory, Delhi, India, Nasir al Din al Tusi (1201-1274), astronomer. 10c, US Bell X-1 rocket plane breaking sound barrier. 45c, Astronomicum Caesareum, 1540, manuscript diagram of comet's trajectory, 1531. $4, Mark Twain, comet appeared at birth and death. $5, Comet.

1986, Apr. 17

945	A138	5c	multicolored	.20	.20
946	A138	10c	multicolored	.20	.20
947	A138	45c	multicolored	.60	.60
948	A138	$4	multicolored	5.00	5.00
			Nos. 945-948 (4)	6.00	6.00

Souvenir Sheet

949	A138	$5	multicolored	4.50	4.50

For overprints see Nos. 984-988.

Queen Elizabeth II, 60th Birthday
Common Design Type

1986, Apr. 21 Litho. *Perf. 14*

950	CD339	2c	Wedding, 1947	.25	.25
951	CD339	$1	With Pope John Paul II, 1982	.75	.75
952	CD339	$4	Royal visit, 1971	3.00	3.00
			Nos. 950-952 (3)	4.00	4.00

Souvenir Sheet

953	CD339	$5	Age 10	4.25	4.25

AMERIPEX '86 — A139

Walt Disney characters involved in stamp collecting.

1986, May 22 *Perf. 11*

954	A139	25c	Mickey Mouse and Pluto	.25	.25
955	A139	45c	Donald Duck	.80	.80
956	A139	60c	Chip-n-Dale	.95	.95
957	A139	$4	Donald, nephews	6.50	6.50
			Nos. 954-957 (4)	8.50	8.50

Souvenir Sheet
Perf. 14

958	A139	$5	Uncle Scrooge	7.25	7.25

British Monarchs — A140

1986, June 9 *Perf. 14*

959	A140	10c	William I	.20	.20
960	A140	40c	Richard II	.40	.40
961	A140	50c	Henry VIII	.50	.50
962	A140	$1	Charles II	1.00	1.00
963	A140	$2	Queen Anne	2.10	2.10
964	A140	$4	Queen Victoria	4.50	4.50
			Nos. 959-964 (6)	8.70	8.70

Audubon Type of 1985

Perf. 12½x12, 12x12½

1986, June 18

965	A127	25c	Black-throated diver	.45	.45
966	A127	60c	Great blue heron	1.10	1.10
967	A127	90c	Yellow-crowned night heron	1.75	1.75
968	A127	$4	Shoveler duck	8.00	8.00
			Nos. 965-968 (4)	11.30	11.30

Souvenir Sheet
Perf. 14

969	A127	$5	Goose	12.00	12.00

Nos. 966-967 vert.

Royal Wedding Issue, 1986
Common Design Type

1986, July 23 *Perf. 14*

970	CD340	45c	Couple	.40	.40
971	CD340	60c	Prince Andrew	.60	.60
972	CD340	$4	Prince, aircraft	3.00	3.00
			Nos. 970-972 (3)	4.00	4.00

Souvenir Sheet

973	CD340	$5	Couple, diff.	4.50	4.50

Nos. 935-939 Ovptd. "WINNERS / Argentina 3 / W. Germany 2" in Gold

1986, Sept. 15 Litho. *Perf. 14*

974	A136	45c	multicolored	.80	.80
975	A136	60c	multicolored	1.25	1.25
976	A136	$1	multicolored	2.10	2.10
977	A136	$3	multicolored	6.75	6.75
			Nos. 974-977 (4)	10.90	10.90

Souvenir Sheet

978	A136	$5	multicolored	10.50	10.50

Paintings by Albrecht Durer — A141

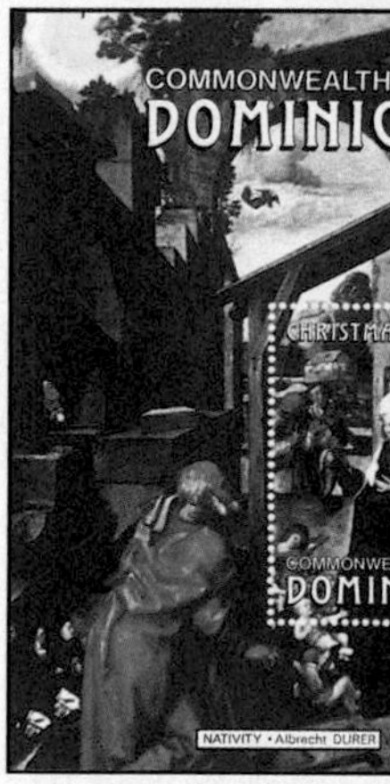

A142

1986, Dec. 2 Litho. *Perf. 14*

979	A141	45c	Virgin in Prayer	1.00	1.00
980	A141	60c	Madonna and Child	1.25	1.25
981	A141	$1	Madonna and Child, diff.	2.25	2.25
982	A141	$3	Madonna and Child with St. Anne	6.50	6.50
			Nos. 979-982 (4)	11.00	11.00

Souvenir Sheet

983	A142	$5	Nativity	10.50	10.50

Nos. 945-949 Printed with Halley's Comet Logo in Black or Silver

1986, Dec. 16

984	A138	5c	multicolored	.20	.20
985	A138	10c	multicolored	.20	.20
986	A138	45c	multicolored	.60	.60
987	A138	$4	multicolored	4.75	4.75
			Nos. 984-987 (4)	5.75	5.75

Souvenir Sheet

988	A138	$5	multi (S)	5.25	5.25

Birds — A143

1987, Jan. 20 Litho. *Perf. 15*

989	A143	1c	Broad-winged hawk	.20	.20
990	A143	2c	Ruddy quail dove	.20	.20
991	A143	5c	Red-necked pigeon	.20	.20
992	A143	10c	Green heron	.20	.20
993	A143	15c	Common gallinule	.20	.20
994	A143	20c	Ringed kingfisher	.20	.20
995	A143	25c	Brown pelican	.20	.20
996	A143	35c	White-tailed tropicbird	.30	.30
997	A143	45c	Red-legged thrush	.40	.40
998	A143	60c	Purple throated carib	.55	.55
999	A143	90c	Magnificent frigatebird	.75	.75
1000	A143	$1	Trembler	.85	.85
1001	A143	$2	Black-capped petrel	1.75	1.75
1002	A143	$5	Barn owl	4.25	4.25
1003	A143	$10	Imperial parrot	8.75	8.75
			Nos. 989-1003 (15)	19.00	19.00

Inscribed "1989" and "Questa"

1989, Aug. 31 Litho. *Perf. 14*

990a	A143	2c	.20	.20
991a	A143	5c	.20	.20
992a	A143	10c	.20	.20
993a	A143	15c	.20	.20
994a	A143	20c	.20	.20
995a	A143	25c	.30	.30
996a	A143	35c	.50	.50
997a	A143	45c	.60	.60
998a	A143	60c	.85	.85
1000a	A143	$1	1.40	1.40
1001a	A143	$2	2.75	2.75
1002a	A143	$5	6.75	6.75
1003a	A143	$10	14.00	14.00
		Nos. 990a-1003a (13)	28.15	28.15

Inscribed "1989" and "Questa"

1990 Litho. *Perf. 12*

990b	A143	2c	.20	.20
991b	A143	5c	.20	.20
992b	A143	10c	.20	.20
993b	A143	15c	.20	.20
994b	A143	20c	.20	.20
995b	A143	25c	.30	.30
996b	A143	35c	.50	.50
997b	A143	45c	.60	.60
998b	A143	60c	.85	.85
1000b	A143	$1	1.40	1.40
1001b	A143	$2	2.75	2.75
1002b	A143	$5	6.75	6.75
1003b	A143	$10	14.00	14.00
		Nos. 990b-1003b (13)	28.15	28.15

Inscribed "1989" and "Questa"

1991 Litho. *Perf. 13x11½*

990c	A143	2c	.20	.20
991c	A143	5c	.20	.20
992c	A143	10c	.20	.20
993c	A143	15c	.20	.20
994c	A143	20c	.20	.20
995c	A143	25c	.35	.35
996c	A143	35c	.55	.55
997c	A143	45c	.65	.65
998c	A143	60c	.95	.95
1000c	A143	$1	1.60	1.60
1001c	A143	$2	3.00	3.00
1002c	A143	$5	7.50	7.50
1003c	A143	$10	15.00	15.00
		Nos. 990c-1003c (13)	30.60	30.60

Paintings by Marc Chagall (1887-1985) A144

Designs: 25c, Artist and His Model. 35c, Midsummer Night's Dream. 45c, Joseph the Shepherd. 60c, the Cellist. 90c, Woman with Pigs. $1, the Blue Circus. $3, For Vava. $4, the Rider. No. 1012, Purim. No. 1013, Firebird design for the curtain of the Stravinsky Ballet production.

1987, Mar. 2 *Perf. 14*

1004	A144	25c	multicolored	.25	.25
1005	A144	35c	multicolored	.40	.40
1006	A144	45c	multicolored	.45	.45
1007	A144	60c	multicolored	.65	.65
1008	A144	90c	multicolored	.90	.90
1009	A144	$1	multicolored	1.00	1.00
1010	A144	$3	multicolored	3.00	3.00
1011	A144	$4	multicolored	4.25	4.25

Size: 110x95mm
Imperf

1012	A144	$5	multicolored	4.00	4.00
1013	A144	$5	multicolored	4.00	4.00
			Nos. 1004-1013 (10)	18.90	18.90

A145

Conch Shells — A147

America's Cup — A146

1987, Feb. 5 *Perf. 15*

1014	A145	45c	Reliance, 1903	.50	.45
1015	A145	60c	Freedom, 1980	.60	.55
1016	A145	$1	Mischief, 1881	1.10	1.00
1017	A145	$3	Australia, 1977	3.25	2.00
			Nos. 1014-1017 (4)	5.45	4.00

Souvenir Sheet

1018	A146	$5	Courageous, Australia, 1977	5.00	5.00

1987, Apr. 13 Litho.

Designs: 35c, Morch Poulsen's triton. 45c, Swainson globe purple sea snail. 60c, Banded tulip. No. 1022, Lamarck deltoid rock shell. No. 1023, Junoia volute.

1019	A147	35c	multicolored	.35	.35
1020	A147	45c	multicolored	.50	.50
1021	A147	60c	multicolored	.65	.65
1022	A147	$5	multicolored	4.25	4.25
			Nos. 1019-1022 (4)	5.75	5.75

Souvenir Sheet

1023	A147	$5	multicolored	5.25	5.25

CAPEX '87 A148

Mushrooms.

1987, June 15 Litho. *Perf. 14*

1024	A148	45c	Cantharellus cinnabarinus	.85	.85
1025	A148	60c	Boletellus cubenis	1.25	1.25
1026	A148	$2	Eccilia cystiophorus	4.50	4.50
1027	A148	$3	Xerocomus guadelupae	6.75	6.75
			Nos. 1024-1027 (4)	13.35	13.35

Souvenir Sheet

1028	A148	$5	Gymnopilus chrysopellus	12.00	12.00

A149

Discovery of America, 500th Anniv. (in 1992) — A150

Explorations of Christopher Columbus: 10c, Discovery of Dominica. 15c, Ships greeted by Carib Indians. 45c, Claiming New World for Spain. 60c, Wrecking of the Santa Maria. 90c, Fleet setting sail. $1, Sighting land. $3, Trading with the Indians. No. 1036, First settlement. No. 1037, Arrival of Second Fleet at Dominica, Nov. 3, 1493. No. 1038, Map of exploration of the Leeward Islands.

1987, July 27 *Perf. 15*

1029 A149 10c multicolored .25 .25
1030 A149 15c multicolored .25 .25
1031 A149 45c multicolored .50 .50
1032 A149 60c multicolored .65 .65
1033 A149 90c multicolored 1.00 1.00
1034 A149 $1 multicolored 1.10 1.10
1035 A149 $3 multicolored 3.25 3.25
1036 A149 $5 multicolored 5.50 5.50
Nos. 1029-1036 (8) 12.50 12.50

Souvenir Sheets

1037 A150 $5 multicolored 4.50 4.50
1038 A150 $5 multicolored 4.50 4.50

For overprints see Nos. 1083-1084.

Transportation — A151

10c, Warrior, 1st iron-clad warship. 15c, Maglev-MLU 001, fastest passenger train. 25c, Clipper Flying Cloud, fastest NYC-San Francisco voyage, 1852. 35c, 1st elevated railway, NYC. 45c, Tom Thumb, 1st US passenger train locomotive. 60c, Joshua Slocum, 1st solo circumnavigation of the world in a sloop. 90c, Se-Land Commerce, fastest Pacific crossing. $1, 1st cable car, San Francisco. $3, Orient Express. $4, The North River Steamboat of Clermont, invented by Robert Fulton, 1st successful commercial steamboat.

1987 **Litho.** *Perf. 14*

1039 A151 10c multicolored .20 .20
1040 A151 15c multicolored .20 .20
1041 A151 25c multi, vert. .45 .45
1042 A151 35c multi, vert. .55 .55
1043 A151 45c multicolored .70 .70
1044 A151 60c multi, vert. 1.00 1.00
1045 A151 90c multi, vert. 1.40 1.40
1046 A151 $1 multicolored 1.75 1.75
1047 A151 $3 multicolored 4.75 4.75
1048 A151 $4 multicolored 6.00 6.00
Nos. 1039-1048 (10) 17.00 17.00

Issued: 10c, 15c, 45c, 60c, $4, 9/28; others 8/1.

For overprints see Nos. 1081-1082.

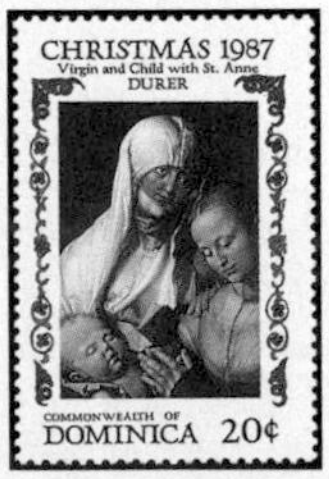

Christmas — A152

Paintings (details): 20c, Virgin and Child with St. Anne, by Durer. 25c, The Virgin and Child, by Murillo. $2, Madonna and Child, by Vincenzo Foppa (c. 1427-1516). $4, Madonna and Child, by Paolo Veronese (1528-1588). $5, Angel of the Annunciation, anonymous.

1987, Nov. 16

1049 A152 20c multicolored .30 .30
1050 A152 25c multicolored .30 .30
1051 A152 $2 multicolored 2.40 2.40
1052 A152 $4 multicolored 4.75 4.75
Nos. 1049-1052 (4) 7.75 7.75

Souvenir Sheet

1053 A152 $5 multicolored 4.50 4.50

Mickey Mouse, 60th Anniv. A153

Disney theme parks and trains: 20c, People Mover, Disney World. 25c, Horse-drawn Trolley, Disneyland. 45c, Roger E. Broggie, Disney World. 60c, Big Thunder Mountain, Disneyland. 90c, Walter E. Disney, Disneyland. $1, Monorail, Disney World. $3, Casey Jr. from Dumbo. $4, Lilly Belle, Disney World. No. 1062, Rainbow Caverns Mine Train, Disneyland, horiz. No. 1063, Toy train from movie Out of Scale, horiz.

1987, Dec. 7 **Litho.** *Perf. 14*

1054 A153 20c multicolored .45 .45
1055 A153 25c multicolored .45 .45
1056 A153 45c multicolored .80 .80
1057 A153 60c multicolored 1.10 1.10
1058 A153 90c multicolored 1.40 1.40
1059 A153 $1 multicolored 1.75 1.75
1060 A153 $3 multicolored 5.00 5.00
1061 A153 $4 multicolored 6.75 6.75
Nos. 1054-1061 (8) 17.70 17.70

Souvenir Sheets

1062 A153 $5 multicolored 4.75 4.75
1063 A153 $5 multicolored 4.75 4.75

40th Wedding Anniv. of Queen Elizabeth II and Prince Philip — A154

1988 Summer Olympics, Seoul — A155

1988, Feb. 15 **Litho.** *Perf. 14*

1064 A154 45c Couple, wedding party, 1947 .55 .55
1065 A154 60c Elizabeth, Charles, c. 1952 .70 .70
1066 A154 $1 Royal Family, c. 1952 1.25 1.25
1067 A154 $3 Queen with tiara, c. 1960 3.25 3.25
Nos. 1064-1067 (4) 5.75 5.75

Souvenir Sheet

1068 A154 $5 Elizabeth, 1947 4.00 4.00

1988, Mar. 15

1069 A155 45c Kayaking .75 .75
1070 A155 60c Tae kwon-do 1.00 1.00
1071 A155 $1 Diving 1.75 1.75
1072 A155 $3 Parallel bars 4.50 4.50
Nos. 1069-1072 (4) 8.00 8.00

Souvenir Sheet

1073 A155 $5 Soccer 4.00 4.00

For overprints see Nos. 1151-1155.

Reunion '88 Tourism Campaign A156

1988, Apr. 13 **Litho.** *Perf. 15*

1074 A156 10c Carib Indian, vert. .20 .20
1075 A156 25c Mountainous interior .20 .20
1076 A156 35c Indian River, vert. .25 .25
1077 A156 60c Belaire dancer, vert. .40 .40
1078 A156 90c The Boiling Lake, vert. .60 .60
1079 A156 $3 Coral reef 2.00 2.00
Nos. 1074-1079 (6) 3.65 3.65

Souvenir Sheet

1080 A156 $5 Belaire dancer, diff., vert. 3.50 3.50

Independence, 10th anniv.

Nos. 1046-1047, 1037-1038 Ovptd. for Philatelic Exhibitions in Black

a

b

c

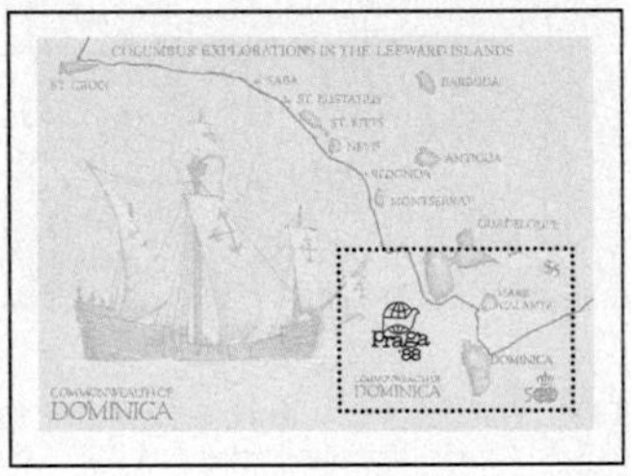

d

1988, June 1 **Litho.** *Perf. 14*

1081 A151(a) $1 multi 1.25 1.25
1082 A151(b) $3 multi 4.50 4.50

Souvenir Sheets

Perf. 15

1083 A150(c) $5 multi 4.75 4.75
1084 A150(d) $5 multi 4.75 4.75

Miniature Sheet

Rain Forest Flora and Fauna — A157

Designs: a, White-tailed tropicbirds. b, Blue-throated euphonia. c, Smooth-billed ani. d, Scaly-breasted thrasher. e, Purple-throated carib. f, Southern daggertail and Clench's hairstreak. g, Trembler. h, Imperial parrot. i, Mangrove cuckoo. j, Hercules beetle. k, Orion. l, Red-necked parrot. m, Tillandsia. n, Polystacha luteola and bananaquit. o, False chameleon. p, Iguana. q, Hypolimnas. r, Green-throated carib. s, Heliconia. t, Agouti.

1988, July 25 *Perf. 14½*

1085 Sheet of 20 17.50 17.50
a.-t. A157 45c any single .75 .75

Intl. Fund for Agricultural Development (IFAD), 10th Anniv. — A158

1988, Sept. 5 **Litho.** *Perf. 14*

1086 A158 45c Hen house .65 .65
1087 A158 60c Pig farm .80 .80
1088 A158 90c Cattle 1.25 1.25
1089 A158 $3 Black-belly sheep 4.25 4.25
Nos. 1086-1089 (4) 6.95 6.95

Souvenir Sheet

1090 A158 $5 Mixed crops, vert. 4.50 4.50

Entertainers A159

1988, Sept. 8

1091 A159 10c Gary Cooper .20 .20
1092 A159 35c Josephine Baker .40 .40
1093 A159 45c Maurice Chevalier .45 .45
1094 A159 60c James Cagney .55 .55
1095 A159 $1 Clark Gable .95 .95
1096 A159 $2 Louis Armstrong 2.00 2.00
1097 A159 $3 Liberace 2.75 2.75
1098 A159 $4 Spencer Tracy 3.75 3.75
Nos. 1091-1098 (8) 11.05 11.05

Souvenir Sheets

1099 A159 $5 Elvis Presley 5.00 5.00
1100 A159 $5 Humphrey Bogart 5.00 5.00

Flowering Trees and Shrubs A160

1988, Sept. 29 **Litho.** *Perf. 14*

1101 A160 15c Sapodilla .20 .20
1102 A160 20c Tangerine .20 .20
1103 A160 25c Avocado pear .20 .20
1104 A160 45c Amherstia .30 .30
1105 A160 90c Lipstick tree .60 .60
1106 A160 $1 Cannonball tree .65 .65
1107 A160 $3 Saman 2.10 2.10
1108 A160 $4 Pineapple 2.75 2.75
Nos. 1101-1108 (8) 7.00 7.00

Souvenir Sheets

1109 A160 $5 Lignum vitae 4.25 4.25
1110 A160 $5 Sea grape 4.25 4.25

Paintings by Titian A161

Designs: 25c, Jacopo Strada, c. 1567. 35c, Titian's Daughter Lavinia, c. 1565. 45c, Andrea Navagero, c. 1515. 60c, Judith with Head of Holoferenes, c. 1570. $1, Emilia di Spilimbergo, c. 1560. $2, Martyrdom of St. Lawrence, c. 1548. $3, Salome With the Head of St. John the Baptist, 1560. $4, St. John the

Baptist, c. 1540. No. 1119, Self-portrait, c. 1555. No. 1120, Sisyphus, 1549.

1988, Oct. 10 Litho. *Perf. 13½x14*

1111 A161 25c multicolored .20 .20
1112 A161 35c multicolored .30 .30
1113 A161 45c multicolored .45 .45
1114 A161 60c multicolored .55 .55
1115 A161 $1 multicolored 1.50 1.50
1116 A161 $2 multicolored 1.75 1.75
1117 A161 $3 multicolored 2.75 2.75
1118 A161 $4 multicolored 3.50 3.50
Nos. 1111-1118 (8) 11.00 11.00

Souvenir Sheets

1119 A161 $5 multicolored 4.00 4.00
1120 A161 $5 multicolored 4.00 4.00

A162

A163

1988, Oct. 31 Litho. *Perf. 14*

1121 A162 20c Imperial parrot .40 .40
1122 A162 45c No. 1, land-scape .60 .60
1123 A162 $2 No. 602, water-fall 2.50 2.50
1124 A162 $3 Carib wood 4.00 4.00
Nos. 1121-1124 (4) 7.50 7.50

Souvenir Sheet

1125 A162 $5 Natl. band per-forming 4.50 4.50

Independence, 10th Anniv. Nos. 1122-1123 horiz.

1988, Nov. 22

1126 A163 20c With Jackie .20 .20
1127 A163 25c Sailing Vicuna .20 .20
1128 A163 $2 Walking in Hyan-nis Port 1.10 1.10
1129 A163 $4 Berlin Wall speech 2.75 2.75
Nos. 1126-1129 (4) 4.25 4.25

Souvenir Sheet

1130 A163 $5 Portrait 4.25 4.25

John F. Kennedy. #1126-1128 horiz.

Miniature Sheet

Christmas, Mickey Mouse 60th Anniv. — A164

#1131: a, Huey, Dewey, Louie. b, Daisy Duck. c, Winnie-the-Pooh. d, Goofy. e, Donald Duck. f, Mickey Mouse. g, Minnie Mouse. h, Chip-n-Dale.

#1132, Mickey, Morty and Ferdy. #1133, Characters visiting shopping mall Santa.

1988, Dec. 1 *Perf. 13½x14*

1131 A164 Sheet of 8 7.75 7.75
a.-h. 60c any single .95 .95

Souvenir Sheets

1132 A164 $6 multi 6.00 6.00
1133 A164 $6 multi, horiz. 6.00 6.00

UN Declaration of Human Rights, 40th Anniv. — A165

Designs: $3, Flag of Sweden and Raoul Wallenberg, who helped save 100,000 Jews in Budapest from deportation to Nazi concentration camps. $5, Human Rights Flame.

1988, Dec. 12 *Perf. 14*

1134 A165 $3 multicolored 3.50 3.50

Souvenir Sheet

1135 A165 $5 multi, vert. 4.75 4.75

Coastal Game Fish A166

1988, Dec. 22 Litho. *Perf. 14*

1136 A166 10c Greater amberjack .30 .30
1137 A166 15c Blue marlin .30 .30
1138 A166 35c Cobia .50 .50
1139 A166 45c Dolphin .55 .55
1140 A166 60c Cero .75 .75
1141 A166 90c Mahogany snapper 1.10 1.10
1142 A166 $3 Yellowfin tuna 3.75 3.75
1143 A166 $4 Rainbow par-rotfish 5.25 5.25
Nos. 1136-1143 (8) 12.50 12.50

Souvenir Sheets

1144 A166 $5 Manta ray 6.00 6.00
1145 A166 $5 Tarpon 6.00 6.00

Caribbean Insects and Reptiles A167

1988, Dec. 29

1146 A167 10c Leatherback turtle .30 .30
1147 A167 25c Monarch but-terfly .70 .70
1148 A167 60c Green anole 1.75 1.75
1149 A167 $3 Praying mantis 9.25 9.25
Nos. 1146-1149 (4) 12.00 12.00

Souvenir Sheet

1150 A167 $5 Hercules bee-tle 6.25 6.25

Nos. 1069-1072 Ovptd. for Olympic Winners

a. "Men's c-1,500m O. Heukrodt DDR"
b. "Women's Flyweight N.Y. Choo S. Korea"
c. "Women's Platform Y. Xu China"
d. "V. Artemov USSR"
e. "USSR defeated Brazil 3-2 on penalty kicks after a 1-1 tie"

1989, Mar. 20 Litho. *Perf. 14*

1151 A155(a) 45c multi .40 .40
1152 A155(b) 60c multi .50 .50
1153 A155(c) $1 multi .95 .95
1154 A155(d) $3 multi 2.40 2.40
Nos. 1151-1154 (4) 4.25 4.25

Souvenir Sheet

1155 A155(e) $5 multi 4.50 4.50

Pre-Columbian Societies and Their Customs — A168

UPAE and discovery of America anniv. emblems and: 20c, Carib Indians canoeing. 35c, Bow hunting. $1, Canoe making. $3, Shield wrestling. $6, Dancing.

1989, May 8 Litho. *Perf. 14*

1156 A168 20c multicolored .30 .30
1157 A168 35c multicolored .45 .45
1158 A168 $1 multicolored 1.25 1.25
1159 A168 $3 multicolored 3.50 3.50
Nos. 1156-1159 (4) 5.50 5.50

Souvenir Sheet

1160 A168 $6 multicolored 5.50 5.50

Discovery of America 500th anniv. (in 1992).

Paintings by Yokoyama Taikan (1868-1958) A169

Designs: 10c, Lao-tzu. 20c, Red Maple Leaves (panels 1-2). 45c, King Wen Learns a Lesson from His Cook. 60c, Red Maple Leaves (panels 3-4). $1, Wild Flowers. $2, Red Maple Leaves (panels 5-6). $3, Red Maple Leaves (panels 7-8). $4, The Indian Ceremony of Floating Lamps on the River. No. 1169, Innocence. No. 1170, Red Maple Leaves (4 panels).

1989, Aug. 8 Litho. *Perf. 13½x14*

1161 A169 10c multicolored .20 .20
1162 A169 20c multicolored .20 .20
1163 A169 45c multicolored .40 .40
1164 A169 60c multicolored .55 .55
1165 A169 $1 multicolored .90 .90
1166 A169 $2 multicolored 1.60 1.60
1167 A169 $3 multicolored 2.40 2.40
1168 A169 $4 multicolored 3.25 3.25
Nos. 1161-1168 (8) 9.50 9.50

Souvenir Sheets

1169 A169 $5 multicolored 4.25 4.25
1170 A169 $5 multicolored 4.25 4.25

Hirohito (1901-89) and enthronement of Akihito as emperor of Japan.

PHILEXFRANCE '89, July 7-17, Paris — A170

Designs: 10c, Map of Dominica with French place names, 1766. 35c, French coin, 1688. $1, French ship, 1720. $4, Introduction of coffee to Dominica by the French, 1772. $5, Text.

1989, July 17 Litho. *Perf. 14*

1171 A170 10c multi, vert. .20 .20
1172 A170 35c shown .55 .55
1173 A170 $1 multicolored 1.25 1.25
1174 A170 $4 multicolored 4.50 4.50
Nos. 1171-1174 (4) 6.50 6.50

Souvenir Sheet

1175 A170 $5 multicolored 6.25 6.25

Butterflies A171

Designs: 10c, Homerus swallowtail. 15c, *Morpho peleides*. 25c, Julia. 35c, Gundlach's swallowtail. 60c, Monarch. $1, Gulf fritillary. $3, Red-splashed sulphur. $5, *Papilio andraemon*. No. 1184, *Heliconius doris, Adelpha cytherea, Calliona argenissa, Eurema proterpia*. No. 1185, *Adelpha iphicla, Dismorphia spio, Lucinia sida*.

1989, Sept. 11 Litho. *Perf. 14*

1176 A171 10c multicolored .20 .20
1177 A171 15c multicolored .20 .20
1178 A171 25c multicolored .45 .45
1179 A171 35c multicolored .65 .65
1180 A171 60c multicolored 1.10 1.10
1181 A171 $1 multicolored 1.75 1.75
1182 A171 $3 multicolored 4.50 4.50
1183 A171 $5 multicolored 8.00 8.00
Nos. 1176-1183 (8) 16.85 16.85

Souvenir Sheets

1184 A171 $6 multicolored 7.00 7.00
1185 A171 $6 multicolored 7.00 7.00

Misspellings: No. 1181, "Frittillary"; No. 1182, "Sulper."

Orchids — A172

1989, Sept. 28

1186 A172 10c *Oncidium pusil-lum* .20 .20
1187 A172 35c *Epidendrum cochleata* .55 .55
1188 A172 45c *Epidendrum ciliare* .60 .60
1189 A172 60c *Cyrtopodium andersonii* .90 .90
1190 A172 $1 *Habenaria pauciflora* 1.50 1.50
1191 A172 $2 *Maxillaria alba* 3.00 3.00
1192 A172 $3 *Selenipedium palmifolium* 4.50 4.50
1193 A172 $4 *Brassavola cucullata* 6.00 6.00
Nos. 1186-1193 (8) 17.25 17.25

Souvenir Sheets

1194 A172 $5 *Oncidium lanceanum* 7.00 7.00
1195 A172 $5 *Comparettia falcata* 7.00 7.00

1st Moon Landing, 20th Anniv. A173

1989, Oct. 31 Litho. *Perf. 14*

1196 A173 10c *Columbia* in lunar orbit .20 .20
1197 A173 60c Aldrin descending ladder .85 .85
1198 A173 $2 Aldrin, Sea of Tranquillity 2.75 2.75
1199 A173 $3 Flag raising 4.00 4.00
Nos. 1196-1199 (4) 7.80 7.80

Souvenir Sheet

1200 A173 $6 Liftoff 8.00 8.00

Souvenir Sheets

A174

1990 World Cup Soccer Championships, Italy — A175

Past championship match scenes, flags and soccer ball: a, Brazil vs. Italy, Mexico, 1970. b, England vs. West Germany, England, 1966. c, West Germany vs. Netherlands, West Germany, 1974. d, Italy vs. West Germany, Spain, 1982.

1989, Nov. 7 *Perf. 14*

1201 A174 Sheet of 4 9.50 9.50
a.-d. $1 any single 2.25 2.25

Perf. 14

1202 A175 $6 shown 7.00 7.00

Space Achievements — A471

No. 2578 — Viking I: a, Trenches dug by Viking I. b, Sunset at Viking I landing site. c, Chryse Planitia looking northwest over Viking I. d, First panoramic image of Chryse Planitia, country name and denomination in white. e, As "d," country name in black, denomination in white. f, As "d", country name and denomination in black.

No. 2579, $3, vert. — Luna 9: a, Flight apparatus. b, Modified SS-6 Sapwood rocket. c, Luna 9 Soft Lander. d, Tyuratam.

No. 2580, $3, vert. — Giotto Comet Probe: a, Launch of Giotto. b, Giotto during solar simulation test. c, Halley's Comet develops seven tails. d, Giotto and Comet Grigg-Skjellerup approach trajectories.

No. 2581, $6, Intl. Space Station. No. 2582, $6, Mars Reconnaissance Orbiter. No. 2583, $6, Venus Express Orbiter.

2006, June 6 Litho. *Perf. 14*

2578 A471 $2 Sheet of 6, #a-f 9.00 9.00

Sheets of 4, #a-d

2579-2580 A471 Set of 2 18.00 18.00

Souvenir Sheets

2581-2583 A471 Set of 3 13.50 13.50

Miniature Sheet

Wolfgang Amadeus Mozart (1756-91), Composer — A472

No. 2584: a, Oval portrait. b, Playing harpsichord. c, Wearing red coat. d, Head of Mozart.

2006, Sept. 1 *Perf. 13¼*

2584 A472 $3 Sheet of 4, #a-d 9.00 9.00

Miniature Sheet

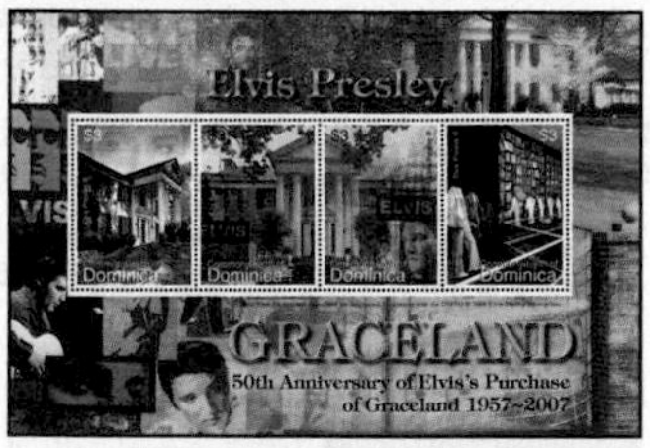

Purchase of Graceland by Elvis Presley, 50th Anniv. — A473

No. 2585: a, View of path leading to front door. b, Graceland, columns at right. c, Graceland, columns at left. d, Room with Presley's costumes.

2006, Sept. 1 *Perf. 13¼*

2585 A473 $3 Sheet of 4, #a-d 9.00 9.00

Miniature Sheets

Pres. John F. Kennedy (1917-63) — A474

No. 2586, $3: a, Supporters holding campaign sign. b, Kennedy campaigning. c, Kennedy waiting for concession. d, Kennedy addressing the nation.

No. 2587, $3: a, Kennedy on crutches from war injuries. b, Kennedy on stretcher. c, Dust jacket of *Profiles in Courage.* d, Kennedy as senator.

2006, Oct. 1 *Perf. 13¼*

Sheets of 4, #a-d

2586-2587 A474 Set of 2 18.00 18.00

Shells — A475

Designs: 5c, Turbinella angulata. 10c, Vasum muricatum. 15c, Fusinus closter. 20c, Crasispira gibbosa. 25c, Terebra strigata. 50c, Prunum carneum. 65c, Purpura patula. 90c, C. chrysostoma. $1, M. nodulosa. $2, Conus regius. $3.50, Conus hieroglyphus. $5, Anodontia alba, vert. $10, C. cassidiformis. $20, Strigilla carnaria, vert.

2006, Oct. 1 *Perf. 14x15, 15x14*

2588	A475	5c	multi	.20	.20
2589	A475	10c	multi	.20	.20
2590	A475	15c	multi	.20	.20
2591	A475	20c	multi	.20	.20
2592	A475	25c	multi	.20	.20
2593	A475	50c	multi	.35	.35
2594	A475	65c	multi	.50	.50
2595	A475	90c	multi	.65	.65
2596	A475	$1	multi	.75	.75
2597	A475	$2	multi	1.50	1.50
2598	A475	$3.50	multi	2.60	2.60
2599	A475	$5	multi	3.75	3.75
2600	A475	$10	multi	7.50	7.50
2601	A475	$20	multi	15.00	15.00
	Nos. 2588-2601 (14)			33.60	33.60

Souvenir Sheet

Ludwig Durr (1878-1956), Engineer — A476

2006, Nov. 15 Litho. *Perf. 12¾*

2602 A476 $5 multi 3.75 3.75

Betty Boop — A477

No. 2603, vert.: a, Betty Boop with black background and leg raised. b, Lips. c, Betty Boop with black background. d, Dog on leash, star. e, Betty Boop, white background. f, Dog, two stars.

No. 2604 — Betty Boop with: a, Light blue panel at top. b, Light yellow panel at top.

2006, Nov. 15

2603 A477 $2 Sheet of 6, #a-f 9.00 9.00

Souvenir Sheet

2604 A477 $3.50 Sheet of 2, #a-b 5.25 5.25

Christmas A478

Christmas stocking showing: No. 2605, 25c, No. 2609a, $2, Christmas tree. No. 2606, 50c, No. 2609b, $2, Bell. No. 2607, 90c, No. 2609c, $2, Candy canes. No. 2608, $1, No. 2609d, $2, Stars.

2006, Dec. 1 *Perf. 14¼*

2605-2608 A478 Set of 4 2.00 2.00

Souvenir Sheet

2609 A478 $2 Sheet of 4, #a-d 6.00 6.00

Souvenir Sheet

Christopher Columbus (1451-1506), Explorer — A479

2007, Jan. 10 *Perf. 12*

2610 A479 $5 brn & black 3.75 3.75

Scouting, Cent. — A480

2007, Jan. 10

2611 A480 $3.50 blue & multi 2.60 2.60

Souvenir Sheet

2612 A480 $5 org & multi 3.75 3.75

No. 2611 was printed in sheets of 3.

Concorde Prototype 001 F-WTSS — A481

No. 2613: a, $1, Airplane in hangar. b, $2, Airplane out of hangar.

Illustration reduced.

2007, Jan. 23 *Perf. 13¼*

2613 A481 Pair, #a-b 2.25 2.25

Printed in sheets containing 3 of each stamp.

Rembrandt (1606-69), Painter — A482

No. 2614, vert. — Details from Christ Driving the Money Changers from the Temple: a, Christ. b, Man with moustache looking up. c, Man with striped headdress. d, Man protecting face with hands.

$5, Jesus and His Disciples.

2007, Jan. 23 *Perf. 13¼*

2614 A482 $2 Sheet of 4, #a-d 6.00 6.00

Imperf

2615 A482 $5 shown 3.75 3.75

No. 2614 contains four 38x50mm stamps.

Cricket World Cup — A483

Designs: 90c, Cricket bats, ball and wicket, map and flag of Dominica. $1, Umpire Billy Doctrove.

$5, Cricket bats, ball and wicket.

2007, Apr. 11 *Perf. 14*

2616-2617 A483 Set of 2 1.50 1.50

Souvenir Sheet

2618 A483 $5 multi 3.75 3.75

Birds A484

Designs: 10c, Great frigatebird. 25c, Peruvian booby. 90c, Black stork, vert. No. 2622, $5, Lipkin, vert.

No. 2623: a, Antillean crested hummingbird. b, Rufous-breasted hermit. c, Cuban hummingbird. d, Blue-headed hummingbird.

No. 2624, $5, Red-capped manakin, vert.

2007, Apr. 11 *Perf. 12¾*

2619-2622 A484 Set of 4 4.75 4.75

2623 A484 $2 Sheet of 4, #a-d 6.00 6.00

Souvenir Sheet

2624 A484 $5 multi 3.75 3.75

Flowers — A485

Designs: 10c, Red jasmine. 25c, Bougainvillea. 90c, Portia tree. No. 2628, $5, Rose bay.

No. 2629 — Orchids: a, $1, Tolumnia urophylla. b, $1, Brassavola cucullata. c, $2, Isochilus linearis. d, Spathoglottis plicata.

No. 2630, horiz.: a, Red ginger. b, Baobab. c, Purple wreath. d, Thunbergia.

No. 2631, $5, Flamboyant. No. 2632, $5, Oncidium altissimum.

2007, Apr. 11 Litho. *Perf. 12¾*

2625-2628 A485 Set of 4 4.75 4.75
2629 A485 Sheet of 4, #a-d 4.50 4.50
2630 A485 $2 Sheet of 4, #a-d 6.00 6.00

Souvenir Sheets

2631-2632 A485 Set of 2 7.50 7.50

Princess Diana (1961-97) — A486

No. 2633: a, Holding flowers, wearing purple hat. b, Without hat. c, Not holding flowers, wearing purple hat. d, Close-up of #2633a, lines on face. e, Close-up of #2633b, lines on face. f, Close-up of #2633c, lines on face.
$5, Wearing purple sweater.

2007, June 11 *Perf. 13½*

2633 A486 $1 Sheet of 6, #a-f 4.50 4.50

Souvenir Sheet

2634 A486 $5 multi 3.75 3.75

No. 2633 contains six 28x42mm stamps.

Texas Rangers — A487

No. 2635, horiz.: a, Two Rangers on horses. b, Seven Rangers in front of building with pillars. c, Ten rangers showing rifles. d, Rangers on horses. e, Rangers around still. f, Three Rangers at Justice of the Peace office. g, Rangers and tents. h, Rangers and locomotive. i, Five Rangers on horses near house.
$5, Statue of Charles Goodnight.

2007, June 15 *Perf. 13½*

2635 A487 $1 Sheet of 9, #a-i 6.75 6.75

Souvenir Sheet

2636 A487 $5 multi 3.75 3.75

American Topical Association National Topical Stamp Show, Irving, TX.

Miniature Sheet

New Year 2007 (Year of the Pig) — A488

No. 2637 — Text in: a, Red. b, Green. c, Blue green. d, Purple.

2007, July 2

2637 A488 $2 Sheet of 4, #a-d 6.00 6.00

A489

A490

A491

Christmas A492

2007, Nov. 19 Litho. *Perf. 14¾x14*

2638 A489 25c multi .20 .20
2639 A490 50c multi .40 .40
2640 A491 90c multi .70 .70
2641 A492 $1 multi .75 .75
Nos. 2638-2641 (4) 2.05 2.05

New Year 2008 (Year of the Rat) — A493

2008, Feb. 28 *Perf. 12*

2642 A493 $1 multi .75 .75

Printed in sheets of 4.

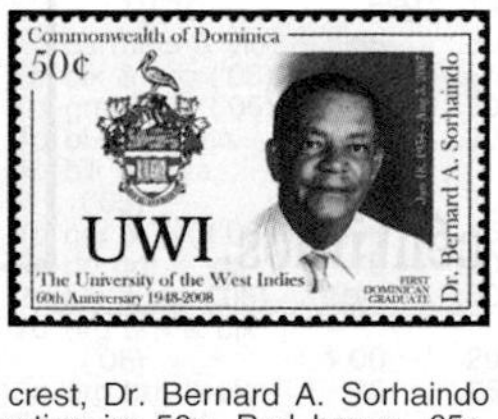

University of the West Indies, 60th Anniv. A494

University crest, Dr. Bernard A. Sorhaindo and denomination in: 50c, Red brown. 65c, Green. 90c, Brown.
No. 2646, $5, Crest, Sorhaindo, denomination in black. No. 2647, $5, Crest, Sorhaindo, denomination in blue. No. 2648, $5, Crest, diploma, 60th anniversary emblem.

2008, Apr. 8 *Perf. 13¼*

2643-2645 A494 Set of 3 1.60 1.60

Souvenir Sheets

2646-2648 A494 Set of 3 11.50 11.50

Miniature Sheet

2008 Summer Olympics, Beijing — A495

No. 2649: a, Archery. b, Men's gymnastics. c, Badminton. d, Boxing.

2008, Apr. 8 *Perf. 13¼x13*

2649 A495 $1.40 Sheet of 4, #a-d 4.25 4.25

Miniature Sheet

Visit of Pope Benedict XVI to New York — A496

No. 2650 — Pope and part of St. Patrick's Cathedral in background: a, Small circular window under spire. b, Large central circular window. c, Archway below spire. d, Archway above main door.

2008, June 16 Litho. *Perf. 13½*

2650 A496 $1.40 Sheet of 4, #a-d 4.25 4.25

Miniature Sheet

Wedding of Queen Elizabeth II and Prince Philip, 60th Anniv. — A497

No. 2651: a, Couple, denomination in white. b, Queen, denomination in red violet. c, Couple, denomination in black. d, Queen, denomination in white. e, Couple, denomination in red violet. f, Queen, denomination in black.

2008, June 16

2651 A497 $1 Sheet of 6, #a-f 4.50 4.50

Miniature Sheet

Elvis Presley (1935-77) — A498

No. 2652 — Presley and: a, Black and red background, Prussian blue denomination. b, Gray and black background, purple denomination. c, Blue and black background, Prussian blue denomination. d, Purple and black background, purple denomination. e, Gray and black background, Prussian blue denomination. f, Brown and black background, purple denomination.

2008, June 16

2652 A498 $1.50 Sheet of 6 #a-f 6.75 6.75

A499

Muhammad Ali, Boxer — A500

No. 2653 — Ali: a, Sweating, denomination in white. b, Smiling, denomination in black. c, Wearing headgear. d, With arms raised.
No. 2654 — Ali: a, Seated in corner of boxing ring. b, Speaking to the press. c, Punching bag. d, Wearing headgear and mouth guard.

2008, July 7

2653 A499 $2 Sheet of 4, #a-d 6.25 6.25
2654 A500 $2 Sheet of 4, #a-d 6.25 6.25

Convent High School, 150th Anniv. A501

Panel color: 50c, Red violet. 65c, Yellow orange. 90c, Blue. $1, Red.
$5, Denomination in LR corner.

2008, Oct. 1 *Perf. 12½*

2655-2658 A501 Set of 4 2.40 2.40

Souvenir Sheet

2659 A501 $5 multi 4.00 4.00

1939, Oct. 18

C34 AP14 10c green & dp green 1.40 .20
a. Pair, imperf. btwn. *450.00*

Proposed Columbus Lighthouse, Plane and Caravels — AP15

Christopher Columbus and Proposed Lighthouse — AP16

Proposed Lighthouse — AP17

Christopher Columbus — AP18

Caravel — AP19

1940, Oct. 12

C35 AP15 10c sapphire & lt bl .85 .45
C36 AP16 15c org brn & brn 1.10 .75
C37 AP17 20c rose red & red 1.10 .75
C38 AP18 25c brt red lil & red vio 1.10 .35
C39 AP19 50c green & lt green 2.25 1.25
Nos. C35-C39 (5) 6.40 3.55

Discovery of America by Columbus and proposed Columbus memorial lighthouse in Dominican Republic.

Posts and Telegraph Building, San Cristobal AP20

1941, Feb. 21

C40 AP20 10c brt red lil & pale lil rose .40 .20

Globe, Wing and Letter AP21

1942, Feb. 13

C41 AP21 10c dark violet brn .50 .25
C42 AP21 75c deep orange 2.75 1.75

Plane AP22

1943, Sept. 1

C43 AP22 10c brt red lilac .30 .20
C44 AP22 20c dp blue & blue .35 .20
C45 AP22 25c yellow olive 5.00 2.40
Nos. C43-C45 (3) 5.65 2.80

Plane, Flag, Coat of Arms and Torch of Liberty — AP23

1944, Feb. 27 *Perf. 11½*
Flag in Gray, Dark Blue, Carmine

C46 AP23 10c multicolored .35 .20
C47 AP23 20c multicolored .45 .20
C48 AP23 1p multicolored 2.00 1.50
Nos. C46-C48 (3) 2.80 1.90

Centenary of Independence. See No. 407 for souvenir sheet listing.

Communications Building, Ciudad Trujillo — AP24

1944, Nov. 12 **Litho.** *Perf. 12*

C49 AP24 9c yel grn & blue .20 .20
C50 AP24 13c dull brn & rose car .25 .20
C51 AP24 25c org & dull red .35 .20
b. Vert. pair, imperf. btwn. 45.00
C52 AP24 30c black & ultra .75 .65
Nos. C49-C52 (4) 1.55 1.25

Twenty booklets of 100 (25 panes of 4) of the 25c were issued. All booklets are still intact.

Communications Type

1945, Sept. 1
Center in Dark Blue and Carmine

C53 A92 7c deep yellow green .30 .25
C54 A92 12c red orange .35 .20
C55 A92 13c deep blue .45 .20
C56 A92 25c orange brown .80 .20
Nos. C53-C56 (4) 1.90 .85

AP26

Flags and National Anthem AP27

Unwmk.
1946, Feb. 27 **Litho.** *Perf. 12*
Center in Dark Blue, Deep Carmine and Black

C57 AP26 10c carmine .65 .30
C58 AP26 15c blue 1.50 .75
C59 AP26 20c chocolate 1.75 .75
C60 AP26 35c orange 2.10 .85
C61 AP27 1p grn, yel grn & cit 19.00 8.75
Nos. C57-C61 (5) 25.00 11.40

Nos. C57-C61 exist imperf.

Map Type of Regular Issue

1946, Aug. 4

C62 A94 10c multicolored .60 .20
C63 A94 13c multicolored 1.10 .20

Waterfall Type of Regular Issue

1947, Mar. 18 **Litho.**
Center Multicolored

C64 A95 18c light blue .75 .35
C65 A95 23c carmine 1.10 .55
C66 A95 50c red violet 1.50 .50
C67 A95 75c chocolate 2.10 1.00
Nos. C64-C67 (4) 5.45 2.40

Palace Type of Regular Issue

1948, Feb. 27

C68 A96 37c orange brown 1.50 .75
C69 A96 1p orange yellow 4.00 1.50

Ruins Type of Regular Issue

1949 **Unwmk.** *Perf. 11½*

C70 A97 7c ol grn & pale ol grn .30 .20
C71 A97 10c orange brn & buff .30 .20
C72 A97 15c brt rose & pale pink .90 .25
C73 A97 20c green & pale green 1.25 .45
Nos. C70-C73 (4) 2.75 1.10

Issue dates: 10c, Apr. 4; others, Apr. 13.

Las Carreras Monument — AP32

1949, Aug. 10

C74 AP32 10c red & pink .45 .20

Cent. of the Battle of Las Carreras.

Catalogue values for unused stamps in this section, from this point to the end of the section, are for Never Hinged items.

Hotel Type of Regular Issue

Hotels: 12c, Montana. 37c, San Cristobal.

1950, Sept. 8

C75 A100 12c dk blue & blue .50 .20
C76 A100 37c carmine & pink 3.00 2.00

Map, Plane and Caduceus AP34

1950, Oct. 2

C77 AP34 12c orange brn & yel .60 .20

13th Pan-American Health Conf. Exists imperf.

Hospital Type of Regular Issue

1952, Aug.

C78 A104 23c deep blue .85 .85
C79 A104 29c carmine 2.25 1.50

Columbus Lighthouse and Plane — AP36

Ano Mariano Initials in Monogram — AP37

1953, Jan. 6 **Engr.** *Perf. 13*

C80 AP36 12c ocher .30 .20
C81 AP36 14c dark blue .20 .20
C82 AP36 20c black brown .60 .45
C83 AP36 23c deep plum .35 .30
C84 AP36 25c dark blue .70 .55
C85 AP36 29c deep green .60 .50
C86 AP36 1p red brown 1.40 .80
a. Miniature sheet of 10 15.00 15.00
Nos. C80-C86 (7) 4.15 3.00

No. C86a is lithographed and contains Nos. 450-452 and C80-C86, in slightly different shades. Sheet measures 190x130mm and is imperf. with simulated perforations.

A miniature sheet similar to No. C86a, but measuring 200x163mm and in folder, exists. Value $100.

1954, Aug. 5 **Litho.** *Perf. 11½*

C87 AP37 8c claret .20 .20
C88 AP37 11c blue .20 .20
C89 AP37 33c brown orange .80 .50
Nos. C87-C89 (3) 1.20 .90

Marian Year. Nos. C87-C89 exist imperf.

Rotary Type of Regular Issue

1955, Feb. 23 *Perf. 12*

C90 A110 11c rose red .35 .20

Flags — AP39

Portraits of General Hector B. Trujillo: 25c, In civilian clothes. 33c, In uniform.

1955, May 16 **Engr.** *Perf. 13½x13*

C91 AP39 11c blue, yel & car .55 .20
C92 AP39 25c rose violet .90 .30
C93 AP39 33c orange brown 1.25 .50
Nos. C91-C93 (3) 2.70 1.00

The center of No. C91 is litho. 25th anniv. of the inauguration of the Trujillo era.

Fair Type of Regular Issue

1955, Dec. 20 **Unwmk.** *Perf. 13*

C94 A112 11c vermilion .35 .20

ICAO Type of Regular Issue

1956, Apr. 6 **Litho.** *Perf. 12½*

C95 A114 11c ultra .40 .20

Tree Type of Regular Issue

Design: 13c, Mahogany tree.

1956, Dec. 8 **Litho.** *Perf. 11½x12*

C96 A115 13c orange & green *1.60* .20

Type of Regular Issue, 1957

Olympic Winners and Flags: 11c, Paavo Nurmi, Finland. 16c, Ugo Frigerio, Italy. 17c, Mildred Didrikson ("Didrickson" on stamp), US.

Engraved and Lithographed
Perf. 11½, Imperf.

1957, Jan. 24 **Unwmk.**
Flags in National Colors

C97 A117 11c ultra & red org .25 .25
C98 A117 16c carmine & lt grn .25 .25
C99 A117 17c black, vio & red .25 .25
Nos. C97-C99 (3) .75 .75

16th Olympic Games, Melbourne, Nov. 22-Dec. 8, 1956.

Souvenir sheets of 3 exist, perf. and imperf., containing Nos. C97-C99. Value, 2 sheets, perf. & imperf., $15.

For surcharges see Nos. CB1-CB3, CB16-CB18.

Type of Regular Issue

Olympic Winners and Flags: 11c, Robert Morrow, US, 100 & 200 meter dash. 16c, Chris Brasher, England, steeplechase. 17c, A. Ferreira Da Silva, Brazil, hop, step and jump.

Perf. 13½, Imperf.

1957, July 18 **Photo.**
Flags in National Colors

C100 A118 11c yellow grn & dk bl .25 .25
C101 A118 16c lilac & dk blue .25 .25
C102 A118 17c brown & blue grn .25 .25
Nos. C100-C102 (3) .75 .75

1956 Olympic winners.

See note on miniature sheets following No. 483.

For surcharges see Nos. CB4-CB6.

Types of Regular Issue

Olympic Winners and Flags: 11c, Hans Winkler, Germany, individual jumping. 16c, Alfred Oerter, US, discus throw. 17c, Shirley Strickland, Australia, 800 meter hurdles.

Engraved and Lithographed
Perf. 13½, Imperf.
1957, Nov. 12 Unwmk.
Flags in National Colors

C103 A119 11c ultra .25 .25
C104 A120 16c rose carmine .25 .25
C105 A119 17c claret .25 .25
Nos. C103-C105 (3) .75 .75

1956 Olympic winners.
Miniature sheets of 3 exist, perf. and imperf., containing Nos. C103-C105. Value, 2 sheets, perf. and imperf., $5.50.
For surcharges see Nos. CB7-CB12.

Type of Regular Issue

Olympic Winners and Flags: 11c, Charles Jenkins, 400 & 800 meter run, and Thomas Courtney, 1,600 meter relay, US. 16c, Field hockey team, India. 17c, Yachting team, Sweden.

Perf. 13½, Imperf.
1958, Oct. 30 Unwmk. Photo.
Flags in National Colors

C106 A125 11c blue, olive & brn .25 .25
C107 A125 16c lt grn, org & dk bl .25 .25
C108 A125 17c ver, blue & yel .25 .25
Nos. C106-C108 (3) .75 .75

1956 Olympic winners.
Miniature sheets of 3 exist, perf. and imperf., containing Nos. C106-C108. Value, 2 sheets, perf. and imperf., $3.
For surcharges see Nos. CB13-CB15.

Fair Type of Regular Issue

1958, Dec. 9 Litho. *Perf. 12½*
C109 A127 9c gray .25 .20
C110 A127 25c lt violet .70 .40
a. Souv. sheet of 3, #C109-C110, 507, imperf. 1.75 1.75

Polo Type of Regular Issue

1959, May 15 *Perf. 12*
C111 A130 11c Dominican polo team .35 .30

"San Cristobal" Plane — AP42

Perf. 11½
1960, Feb. 25 Unwmk. Litho.
C112 AP42 13c org, bl, grn & gray .30 .20

Dominican Civil Aviation.

Children and WRY Emblem AP43

1960, Apr. 7 *Perf. 12½*
C113 AP43 10c plum, gray & grn .60 .30
C114 AP43 13c gray & green .80 .30

World Refugee Year, 7/1/59-6/30/60.
For surcharges see Nos. CB19-CB20.

Olympic Type of Regular Issue

Olympic Winners: 11c, Pat McCormick, US, diving. 16c, Mithat Bayrack, Turkey, welterweight wrestling. 17c, Ursula Happe, Germany, 200 meter breast stroke.

Perf. 13½, Imperf.
1960, Sept. 14 Photo.
Flags in National Colors

C115 A136 11c blue, gray & brn .20 .20
C116 A136 16c red, brown & ol .25 .25
C117 A136 17c black, blue & ocher .25 .25
Nos. C115-C117 (3) .70 .70

17th Olympic Games, Rome, 8/25-9/11.
Miniature sheets of 3 exist, perf. and imperf., containing Nos. C115-C117. Value, 2 sheets, perf. and imperf., $3.75.
For surcharges see Nos. CB21-CB23.

Coffee-Cacao Type of Regular Issue

1961, Dec. 30 Litho. *Perf. 12½*
C118 A140 13c orange ver .25 .25
C119 A140 33c brt yellow .50 .50

Nos. C118-C119 exist imperf.

Anti-Malaria Type of Regular Issue

1962, Apr. 29 Unwmk. *Perf. 12*
C120 A141 13c pink & red .40 .20
C121 A141 33c org & dp org .70 .45

See Nos. CB24-CB25.

Type of Regular Issue

Designs: 13c, Broken fetters and laurel. 50c, Flag, torch and inscription.

1962, May 30 *Perf. 12½*
C122 A142 13c brn, yel, ol, ultra & red .30 .25
C123 A142 50c rose lilac, ultra & red 1.10 .75

No. C122 exists imperf.

UPAE Type of Regular Issue

1962, Oct. 23 *Perf. 12½*
C124 A146 13c bright blue .25 .20
C125 A146 22c dull red brown .40 .40

Nos. C124-C125 exist imperf.

Nouel Type of Regular Issue

Design: Frame altered with rosary and cross surrounding portrait.

1962, Dec. 18
C126 A147 13c blue & pale blue .35 .20
C127 A147 25c vio & pale vio .50 .50
a. Souv. sheet, #C126-C127, imperf 1.00 1.00

Nos. C126-C127 exist imperf.

Sanchez, Duarte, Mella AP44

1963, July 7 Litho. *Perf. 11½x12*
C128 AP44 15c orange .30 .25

120th anniv. of separation from Haiti.

World Map AP45

1963, Oct. 25 Unwmk. *Perf. 12½*
C129 AP45 10c gray & carmine .30 .25

Cent. of Intl. Red Cross. Exists imperf.

Human Rights Type

1963, Dec. 10 Litho.
C130 A152 7c fawn & red brn .25 .20
C131 A152 10c lt blue & blue .25 .20

Nos. C130-C131 exist imperf.

Ramses II Battling the Hittites (from Abu Simbel) — AP46

1964, Mar. 8 *Perf. 12½*
C132 AP46 10c brt violet .25 .20
C133 AP46 13c yellow .25 .20

UNESCO world campaign to save historic monuments in Nubia.
Nos. C132-C133 exist imperf.
For surcharges see Nos. CB26-CB27.

Striated Woodpecker — AP47

1964, June 8 Litho.
C134 AP47 10c multicolored 4.25 .20

Type of Space Issue

Designs: 7c, Rocket leaving earth. 10c, Space capsule orbiting earth.

1964, July 28 Unwmk. *Perf. 12½*
C135 A156 7c brt green .25 .20
C136 A156 10c violet blue .30 .25
a. Souvenir sheet 3.00 3.00

No. C136a contains 7c and 10c stamps similar to Nos. C135-C136 with simulated perforations.

Pres. John F. Kennedy — AP48

1964, Nov. 22 *Perf. 11½*
C137 AP48 10c buff & dk brown .45 .25

President John F. Kennedy (1917-63). Sheets of 10 (5x2) and sheets of 50.

UPU Type of Regular Issue

1964, Dec. 5 Litho. *Perf. 12½*
C138 A157 7c blue .25 .20

ICY Type of Regular Issue

1965, Feb. 16 Unwmk. *Perf. 12½*
C139 A158 10c lilac & violet .30 .25

Basilica of Our Lady of Altagracia — AP49

1965, Mar. 18 Unwmk. *Perf. 12½*
C140 AP49 10c multicolored .30 .25

Fourth Mariological Congress and the Eleventh International Marian Congress.

Abraham Lincoln — AP50

1965, Apr. 15 Litho. *Perf. 12½*
C141 AP50 17c bright blue .45 .35

Cent. of the death of Abraham Lincoln.

Stamp Centenary Type of 1965

Design: Stamp of 1865, (No. 2).

1965, Dec. 28 Litho. *Perf. 12½*
C142 A161 7c violet, lt grn & blk .25 .20
C143 A161 10c yellow, lt grn & blk .25 .20

ITU Emblem, Old and New Communication Equipment — AP51

1966, Apr. 6 Litho. *Perf. 12½*
C144 AP51 28c pink & carmine .65 .65
C145 AP51 45c brt grn & grn 1.00 1.00

Cent. (in 1965) of the ITU.

Butterfly Type of Regular Issue

1966, Nov. 8 Litho. *Perf. 12½*
Various Butterflies in Natural Colors
Size: 35x24mm

C146 A164 10c lt violet & violet 5.25 .70
C147 A164 50c org & dp org 7.50 1.40
C148 A164 75c pink & rose red 10.00 2.25
Nos. C146-C148 (3) 22.75 4.35

For surcharges see Nos. CB28-CB30.

Altar Type of Regular Issue

1967, Jan. 18 Litho. *Perf. 11½*
C149 A165 7c lt olive green .20 .20
C150 A165 10c lilac .20 .20
C151 A165 20c yellow brown .30 .25
Nos. C149-C151 (3) .70 .65

Chess Type of Regular Issue

Design: 10c, Pawn and Bishop.

1967, June 23 Litho. *Perf. 12½*
C152 A167 10c ol, lt ol & blk 1.10 .25
a. Souvenir sheet 9.00 1.75

No. C152a contains 2 imperf. stamps similar to Nos. 636 and C152.

Alliance for Progress Type

1967, Sept. 16 Litho. *Perf. 12½*
C153 A168 8c gray .30 .25
C154 A168 10c blue .35 .25

Cornucopia and Emblem — AP52

Latin American Flags — AP53

1967, Oct. 7
C155 AP52 12c multicolored .45 .25

25th anniversary of the Inter-American Agriculture Institute.

Satellite Type of Regular Issue

1968, June 15 Typo. *Perf. 12*
C156 A170 10c dp blue & multi .25 .20
C157 A170 15c purple & multi .35 .30

Boxing Type of Regular Issue

Designs: Two views of boxing match.

1968, June 29
C158 A171 7c orange yel & grn .25 .20
C159 A171 10c gray & blue .30 .20

See note after No. 641.

Lions Type of Regular Issue

1968, Aug. 9 Litho. *Perf. 11½*
C160 A172 10c ultra & multi .25 .20

Olympic Type of Regular Issue

Designs (Olympic Emblem and): 10c, Weight lifting. 33c, Pistol shooting.

1968, Nov. 12 Litho. *Perf. 11½*
C161 A173 10c buff & multi .25 .25
C162 A173 33c pink & multi .75 .60

1969, Jan. 25 Litho. *Perf. 12½*
C163 AP53 10c pink & multi .25 .20

7th Inter-American Savings and Loan Conference, Santo Domingo, Jan. 25-31.

Taino Art Type of Regular Issue

7c, Various vomiting spoons with human heads, vert. 10c, Female torso forming drinking vessel. 20c, Vase with human head, vert.

1969, Jan. 31 Litho. *Perf. 12½*
C164 A175 7c lt bl, bl & lem .20 .20
C165 A175 10c pink, ver & brn .25 .20
C166 A175 20c yellow, org & brn .30 .30
Nos. C164-C166 (3) .75 .70

COTAL Type of Regular Issue

10c, Airport of the Americas and COTAL emblem.

1969, May 25 Litho. *Perf. 12½*
C167 A178 10c brown & pale fawn .25 .20

ILO Type of Regular Issue

1969, June 27 Litho. *Perf. 12½*
C168 A179 10c rose, red & black .25 .20

Baseball Type of Regular Issue

Designs: 7c, Bleachers, Tetelo Vargas Stadium, horiz. 10c, Batter, catcher and umpire. 1p, Quisqueya Stadium, horiz.

1969, Aug. 15 Litho. *Perf. 12½*
Size: 43x30mm (7c, 1p); 21x31mm (10c)
C169 A180 7c magenta & org .50 .30
C170 A180 10c mar & rose red .55 .30
C171 A180 1p violet blue & brn 4.25 3.00
Nos. C169-C171 (3) 5.30 3.60

Electrification Types of Regular Issue

Design: No. C172, Rio Haina steam plant. No. C173, Valdesa Dam.

1969 Litho. *Perf. 12*
C172 A181 10c orange ver .35 .20
C173 A182 10c multicolored .40 .20

Issued: #C172, Sept. 15; #C173, Oct. 15.

Duarte Type of Regular Issue

1970, Jan. 26 Litho. *Perf. 12*
C174 A183 10c brown & dk brown .45 .25

Census Type of Regular Issue

Design: 10c, Buildings and census emblem.

1970, Feb. 6 *Perf. 11*
C175 A184 10c lt blue & multi .45 .25

Sculpture Type of Regular Issue

Design: 10c, The Prisoner, by Abelardo Rodriguez Urdaneta, vert.

1970, Feb. 20 Litho. *Perf. 12½*
C176 A186 10c bluish gray .30 .20

Masonic Type of Regular Issue

1970, Mar. 2
C177 A187 10c brown .25 .20

Satellite Type of Regular Issue

1970, May 25 Litho. *Perf. 12½*
C178 A188 7c blue & gray .25 .20

UPU Type of Regular Issue

1970, June 5 *Perf. 11*
C179 A189 10c yellow & brown .25 .20

Education Year Type of Regular Issue

1970, June 26 Litho. *Perf. 12½*
C180 A190 15c bright pink .45 .25

Dancers
AP54

Album, Globe and Emblem — AP55

Design: 10c, UN emblem and wheel.

1970, Oct. 12 Litho. *Perf. 12½*
C181 AP54 7c blue & multi .25 .20
C182 AP54 10c pink & multi .30 .20

1st World Exhib. of Books and Culture Festival, Santo Domingo, Oct. 11-Dec. 11.

1970, Oct. 26 Litho. *Perf. 11*
C183 AP55 10c multicolored .30 .25

EXFILCA 70, 2nd Interamerican Philatelic Exhibition, Caracas, Venezuela, 11/27-12/6.

Basilica of Our Lady of Altagracia — AP56

1971, Jan. 20 Litho. *Perf. 12½*
C184 AP56 17c multicolored .65 .35

Inauguration of the Basilica of Our Lady of Altagracia.

Map of Dominican Republic, CARE Package
AP57

1971, May 28 Litho. *Perf. 12½*
C185 AP57 10c blue & green .25 .20

25th anniversary of CARE, a US-Canadian Cooperative for American Relief Everywhere.

Sports Type of Regular Issue

1971, Sept. 10 *Perf. 11*
C186 A195 7c Volleyball .25 .20

Animal Type of Regular Issue

Design: 25c, Cock and grain.

1971, Sept. 29 *Perf. 12½*
C187 A196 25c black & multi .50 .30

Independence Type

10c, Dominican-Colombian flag of 1821.

1971, Dec. 1 *Perf. 11*
C188 A197 10c vio bl, yel & red .50 .30

Christmas Type of Regular Issue

1971, Dec. 10 *Perf. 12½*
C189 A198 10c Bell, 1493 .25 .20

UNICEF Type of Regular Issue

Design: UNICEF emblem & child on beach.

1971, Dec. 14 *Perf. 11*
C190 A199 15c multicolored .45 .30

Book Year Type of Regular Issue

1972, Jan. 25 Litho. *Perf. 12½*
C191 A200 12c lilac, dk bl & red .30 .25

Magnifying Glass over Peru on Map of Americas — AP58

"Your Heart is your Health" — AP59

1972, Mar. 7 Litho. *Perf. 12*
C192 AP58 10c blue & multi .30 .25

EXFILIMA '71, 3rd Inter-American Philatelic Exposition, Lima, Peru, Nov. 6-14, 1971.

1972, Apr. 27 Litho. *Perf. 11*
C193 AP59 7c red & multi .25 .20

World Health Day.

Taino Art Type of 1972

Taino Art: 8c, Ritual vessel showing human figures. 10c, Trumpet (shell). 25c, Carved vomiting spoons. All horiz.

1972, May 10 Litho. *Perf. 11*
C194 A201 8c multicolored .40 .20
C195 A201 10c lt blue & multi .60 .20
C196 A201 25c multicolored 1.50 .45
Nos. C194-C196 (3) 2.50 .85

Telecommunications Type of Regular Issue

1972, May 17 *Perf. 12½*
C197 A202 21c yellow & multi .60 .30

Exhibition Type of Regular Issue

1972, June 3
C198 A203 33c orange & multi .60 .40

Olympic Type of Regular Issue

1972, Aug. 25 Litho. *Perf. 12½*
C199 A204 33c Running .75 .50

Club Type of Regular Issue

1972, Sept. 29 Litho. *Perf. 10½*
C200 A205 20c blue & multi .40 .25

Morel Type of Regular Issue

1972, Oct. 20 Litho. *Perf. 12½*
C201 A206 10c multicolored .25 .20

Bank Type of Regular Issue

25c, 1947 silver coin, entrance to the Mint.

1972, Oct. 23
C202 A207 25c ocher & multi .65 .45

"La Navidad" Fortress, 1492
AP60

1972, Nov. 21 Litho. *Perf. 12½*
C203 AP60 10c multicolored .45 .20

Christmas 1972.

Sports Type of Regular Issue

Various sports; a, UL. b, UR. c, LL. d, LR.

1973, Mar. 30 Litho. *Perf. 13½x13*
C204 A212 Block of 4 1.50 1.50
a.-d. 8c, any single .25 .25
C205 A212 Block of 4 2.50 2.50
a.-d. 10c, any single .50 .30

Easter Type 1973

10c, Belfry of Church of Our Lady of Help.

1973, Apr. 18 Litho. *Perf. 10½*
C206 A213 10c multicolored .40 .20

North and South America on Globe — AP61

1973, May 29 Litho. *Perf. 12*
C207 AP61 7c multicolored .25 .20

Pan-American Health Organization, 70th anniversary (in 1972).

WMO Type of Regular Issue

1973, Aug. 10 Litho. *Perf. 13½x13*
C208 A214 7c green & multi .25 .20

INTERPOL Emblem Police Scientist
AP62

1973, Sept. 28 Litho. *Perf. 10½*
C209 AP62 10c vio bl, bl & emer .35 .20

50th anniversary of International Criminal Police Organization.

Handicraft Type of Regular Issue

1973, Oct. 12
C210 A215 7c Sailing ship, mosaic .20 .20
C211 A215 10c Maracas rattles, horiz. .30 .20

Christmas Type of Regular Issue

Design: 10c, Angels adoring Christ Child.

1973, Nov. 26 Litho. *Perf. 13½x13*
C212 A216 10c multicolored .25 .20

Scout Type of Regular Issue

21c, Scouts cooking, Lord Baden-Powell.

1973, Dec. 7 Litho. *Perf. 12*
C213 A217 21c red & multi .65 .55

Sport Type of Regular Issue

10c, Olympic swimming pool and diver. 25c, Olympic Stadium, soccer and discus.

1974, Feb. 25 Litho. *Perf. 13½*
C214 A218 10c blue & multi .20 .20
C215 A218 25c multicolored .40 .20

The Last Supper
AP63

1974, June 27 Litho. *Perf. 13½*
C216 AP63 10c multicolored .30 .20

Holy Week 1974.

Bridge Type

Design: 10c, Higuamo Bridge.

1974, July 12 *Perf. 12*
C217 A221 10c multicolored .40 .20

Diabetes Type

Map of Dominican Republic, Diabetics' Emblem and: 7c, Kidney. 33c, Eye & heart.

1974, Aug. 22 Litho. *Perf. 13*
C218 A222 7c yellow & multi .25 .25
C219 A222 33c lt blue & multi 1.25 .75

UPU Type

1974, Oct. 9 Litho. *Perf. 13½*

C220	A223 7c Ships	.50	.25
C221	A223 33c Jet	1.50	.50
a.	Souvenir sheet of 4	4.50	4.50

No. C221a contains Nos. 727-728, C220-C221 forming continuous design.

Golfers and Championship Emblem — AP64

20c, Golfer and Golf Association emblem.

1974, Oct. 24 Litho. *Perf. 13x13½*

C222	AP64 10c green & multi	.40	.20
C223	AP64 20c green & multi	.75	.40

World Amateur Golf Championships.

Hand Holding Dove AP65

1974, Dec. 3 Litho. *Perf. 12*

C224	AP65 10c multicolored	.30	.20

Christmas 1974.

FAO Type

10c, Bee, beehive and barrel of honey.

1974, Dec. 5

C225	A227 10c multicolored	1.10	.20

Chrismon, Lamb, Candle and Palm — AP66

Spain No. 1, España 75 Emblem — AP67

1975, Mar. 26 Litho. *Perf. 13½*

C226	AP66 10c gold & multi	.30	.20

Holy Week 1975.

1975, Apr. 10

C227	AP67 12c red, yel & blk	.40	.25

Espana 75, International Philatelic Exhibition, Madrid, Apr. 4-13.

Development Bank Type

1975, May 19 Litho. *Perf. 10½x10*

C228	A230 10c rose car & multi	.30	.20

Three Satellites and Globe AP68

1975, June 21 Litho. *Perf. 13½*

C229	AP68 15c multicolored	.45	.35

Opening of first earth satellite tracking station in Dominican Republic.

Apollo Type

Design: 2p, Apollo-Soyuz link-up over earth.

1975, July 24 *Perf. 13*

Size: 42x28mm

C230	A232 2p multicolored	5.25	3.25

Indian Chief Type

7c, Mayobanex. 8c, Cotubanama & Juan de Esquivel. 10c, Enriquillo & Mencia.

1975, Sept. 27 Litho. *Perf. 12*

C231	A235 7c lt green & multi	.25	.25
C232	A235 8c orange & multi	.30	.25
C233	A235 10c gray & multi	.30	.25
	Nos. C231-C233 (3)	.85	.75

Volleyball AP69

10c, Weight lifting and Games' emblem.

1975, Oct. 24 Litho. *Perf. 12*

C234	AP69 7c blue & multi	.25	.20
C235	AP69 10c multicolored	.35	.25

7th Pan-American Games, Mexico City, Oct. 13-26.

Christmas Type

Design: 10c, Dove and peace message.

1975, Dec. 12 Litho. *Perf. 13x13½*

C236	A237 10c yellow & multi	.25	.20

Valdesia Dam — AP70

1976, Jan. 26 Litho. *Perf. 13*

C237	AP70 10c multicolored	.35	.20

Holy Week Type 1976

Design: 10c, Crucifixion, by Eliezer Castillo.

1976, Apr. 14 Litho. *Perf. 13½*

C238	A239 10c multicolored	.30	.25

Bicentennial Type and

George Washington, Independence Hall — AP71

Design: 10c, Hands holding maps of US and Dominican Republic.

1976, May 29 Litho. *Perf. 13½*

C239	A241 10c vio bl, grn & blk	.35	.20
C240	AP71 75c black & orange	1.10	1.10

American Bicentennial; No. C240 also for Interphil 76 International Philatelic Exhibition, Philadelphia, Pa., May 29-June 6.

King Juan Carlos I and Queen Sofia — AP72

1976, May 31

C241	AP72 21c multicolored	.60	.60

Visit of King Juan Carlos I and Queen Sofia of Spain.

Telephone Type

Design: 10c, Alexander Graham Bell and telephones, 1876 and 1976.

1976, July 15

C242	A243 10c multicolored	.30	.20

Duarte Types

10c, Scroll with Duarte letter and Dominican flag. 33c, Duarte return from Exile, by E. Godoy.

1976, July 20 Litho. *Perf. 13½*

C243	A245 10c blue & multi	.30	.20

Perf. 13x13½

C244	A244 33c brown & multi	1.10	.75

Fire Engine AP73

1976, Sept. 13 Litho. *Perf. 12*

C245	AP73 10c multicolored	.40	.20

Honoring firemen.

Radio Club Type

1976, Oct. 8 Litho. *Perf. 13½*

C246	A247 10c blue & black	.30	.20

Various People — AP74

1976, Oct. 22 Litho. *Perf. 13½*

C247	AP74 21c multicolored	.35	.35

Spanish heritage.

Olympic Games Type

1976, Oct. 22 *Perf. 12*

C248	A249 10c Running	.30	.20
C249	A249 25c Basketball	.85	.50

Christmas Type

Design: 10c, Angel with bells.

1976, Dec. 8 Litho. *Perf. 13½*

C250	A251 10c multicolored	.30	.25

Tourist Activities AP75

Tourist publicity: 12c, Angling and hotel. 25c, Horseback riding and waterfall, vert.

1977, Jan. 7

Size: 36x36mm

C251	AP75 10c multicolored	.25	.20

Size: 34x25½mm, 25½x34mm

C252	AP75 12c multicolored	.25	.20
C253	AP75 25c multicolored	.50	.30
	Nos. C251-C253 (3)	1.00	.70

Championship Type

1977, Mar. 4 Litho. *Perf. 13½*

C254	A253 10c yel grn & multi	.30	.20
C255	A253 25c lt brown & multi	.85	.50

Holy Week Type 1977

Design: 10c, Belfry and open book.

1977, Apr. 18 Litho. *Perf. 13½x13*

C256	A254 10c multicolored	.30	.20

Lions Type

1977, May 6 *Perf. 13½x13*

C257	A255 7c lt green & multi	.25	.20

Caravel under Sail — AP76

Melon Cactus — AP77

1977, July 16 Litho. *Perf. 13*

C258	AP76 10c multicolored	.45	.30

Miss Universe Contest, held in Dominican Republic.

1977, Aug. 19 Litho. *Perf. 12*

Design: 33c, Coccothrinax (tree).

C259	AP77 7c multicolored	.30	.25
C260	AP77 33c multicolored	1.10	.75

National Botanical Garden.

Chart and Factories — AP78

1977, Nov. 30 Litho. *Perf. 13x13½*

C261	AP78 28c multicolored	.50	.50

7th Interamerican Statistics Conference.

Animal Type

Congress Emblem and: 10c, "Dorado," red Roman stud bull. 25c, Flamingo, vert.

1977, Dec. 29 Litho. *Perf. 13*

C262	A259 10c multicolored	2.00	.30
C263	A259 25c multicolored	3.50	.50

Spanish Heritage Type

21c, Window, Casa del Tostado, 16th cent.

1978, Jan. 19 *Perf. 13x13½*

Size: 28x41mm

C264	A260 21c multicolored	.45	.35

Holy Week Type, 1978

7c, Facade, Santo Domingo Cathedral. 10c, Facade of Dominican Convent.

1978, Mar. 21 Litho. *Perf. 12*
Size: 27x36mm

C265 A261 7c multicolored .25 .25
C266 A261 10c multicolored .40 .25

Schooner Duarte AP79

1978, Apr. 15 Litho. *Perf. 13½*
C267 AP79 7c multicolored .35 .20

Dominican naval forces training ship.

Cardinal Type

1978, May 5 Litho. *Perf. 13*
C268 A262 10c multicolored .30 .20

Antenna AP80

1978, May 17 Litho. *Perf. 13½*
C269 AP80 25c silver & multi .55 .35

10th World Telecommunications Day.

No. C1 and Map AP81

1978, June 6
C270 AP81 10c multicolored .30 .20

1st Dominican Rep. airmail stamp, 50th anniv.

Globe, Soccer Ball, Emblem — AP82

Crown, Cross and Rosary Emblem — AP83

33c, Soccer field, Argentina '78 emblem, globe.

1978, June 29
C271 AP82 12c multicolored .40 .30
C272 AP82 33c multicolored .85 .85

11th World Cup Soccer Championship, Argentina, June 1-25.

1978, July 11 *Perf. 13x13½*
C273 AP83 21c multicolored .65 .65

Congregation of the Merciful Sisters of Charity, centenary.

Sports Type

1978, July 21 Litho. *Perf. 13½*
C274 A265 7c Baseball, vert. .40 .25
C275 A265 10c Basketball, vert. .45 .25

Wright Brothers and Glider, 1902 AP84

Designs: 7c, Diagrams of Flyer I and jet, vert. 13c, Diagram of air flow over wing. 45c, Flyer I over world map.

1978, Aug. 8 *Perf. 12*
C276 AP84 7c multicolored .25 .20
C277 AP84 10c multicolored .35 .20
C278 AP84 13c multicolored .55 .25
C279 AP84 45c multicolored 1.50 .95
Nos. C276-C279 (4) 2.65 1.60

75th anniversary of first powered flight.

Tourist Type

Designs: 7c, Sun and musical instruments. 10c, Sun and plane over Santo Domingo.

1978, Sept. 12 Litho. *Perf. 12*
C280 A266 7c multicolored .30 .20
C281 A266 10c multicolored .35 .20

People and Globe AP85

1978, Oct. 12 Litho. *Perf. 13½*
C282 AP85 21c multicolored .45 .45

Spanish heritage.

Dominican Republic and UN Flags AP86

1978, Oct. 23 *Perf. 12*
C283 AP86 33c multicolored .60 .60

33rd anniversary of the United Nations.

Statue of the Virgin — AP87

Pope John Paul II — AP88

1978, Dec. 5 Litho. *Perf. 12*
C284 AP87 10c multicolored .30 .25

Christmas 1978.

1979, Jan. 25 Litho. *Perf. 13½*
C285 AP88 10c multicolored 3.00 3.00

Visit of Pope John Paul II to the Dominican Republic, Jan. 25-26.

Map of Beata Island AP89

1979, Jan. 25 *Perf. 12*
C286 AP89 10c multicolored .50 .30

1st expedition of radio amateurs to Beata Is.

Year of the Child Type, 1979

Designs (ICY Emblem and): 7c, Children reading book. 10c, Symbolic head and protective hands. 33c, Hands and jars.

1979, Feb. 26
C287 A269 7c multicolored .20 .20
C288 A269 10c multicolored .30 .20
C289 A269 33c multicolored 1.10 .75
Nos. C287-C289 (3) 1.60 1.15

Pope John Paul II Giving Benediction AP90

Adm. Juan Bautista Cambiaso AP91

1979, Apr. 9 Litho. *Perf. 13½*
C290 AP90 10c multicolored 1.25 .90

Holy Week.

1979, Apr. 14 *Perf. 12*
C291 AP91 10c multicolored .30 .20

135th anniv. of the Battle of Tortuguero.

Map of Dominican Rep., Album, Magnifier AP92

1979, Apr. 18
C292 AP92 33c multicolored .60 .60

EXFILNA, 3rd National Philatelic Exhibition, Apr. 18-22.

Flower Type

Designs: 7c, Passionflower. 10c, Isidorea pungens. 13c, Calotropis procera.

1979, May 17 Litho. *Perf. 12*
C293 A271 7c multicolored .30 .30
C294 A271 10c multicolored .40 .25
C295 A271 13c multicolored .55 .45
Nos. C293-C295 (3) 1.25 1.00

Cardiology Type, 1979

10c, Figure of man showing blood circulation.

1979, June 2 Litho. *Perf. 13½*
C296 A272 10c multicolored, vert. .60 .40

Sports Type

7c, Runner and Games' emblem, vert.

1979, June 20
C297 A273 7c multicolored .30 .25

Soccer Type

1979, Aug. 9 Litho. *Perf. 12*
C298 A273 10c Tennis, vert. .30 .25

Rowland Hill, Dominican Republic No. 1 — AP93

1979, Aug. 21 *Perf. 13½*
C299 AP93 2p multicolored 3.00 2.50

Sir Rowland Hill (1795-1879), originator of penny postage.

Electric Light Type

Design: 10c, "100" and light bulb, horiz.

1979, Aug. 27 *Perf. 13½*
C300 A275 10c multicolored .30 .25

Bird Type

Birds: 7c, Phaenicophilus palmarum. 10c, Calyptophilus frugivorus tertius. 45c, Icterus dominicensis.

1979, Sept. 12 Litho. *Perf. 12*
C301 A277 7c multicolored 1.90 .25
C302 A277 10c multicolored 2.75 .25
C303 A277 45c multicolored 6.75 .90
Nos. C301-C303 (3) 11.40 1.40

Lions Type

10c, Melvin Jones, organization founder.

1979, Nov. 13 Litho. *Perf. 12*
C304 A278 10c multicolored .50 .30

Christmas Type

Christmas: 10c, Three Kings riding camels.

1979, Dec. 18 Litho. *Perf. 12*
C305 A279 10c multicolored .25 .25

Holy Week Type

1980, Mar. 27 Litho. *Perf. 12*
C306 A280 7c Crucifixion .20 .20
C307 A280 10c Resurrection .30 .25

Navy Day — AP94

1980, Apr. 15 Litho. *Perf. 13½*
C308 AP94 21c multicolored .45 .40

Dominican Philatelic Society, 25th Anniversary AP95

1980, Apr. 18
C309 AP95 10c multicolored .30 .25

Gold Type

1980, July 8 Litho. *Perf. 13½*
C310 A282 10c Drag line mining .45 .35
C311 A282 33c Mine .85 .55

Tourism Secretariat Emblem — AP96

1980, Aug. 26 Litho. *Perf. 13½*

C312 AP96 10c shown .30 .25
C313 AP96 33c Conf. emblem 1.10 .75

World Tourism Conf., Manila, Sept. 27.

Iguana Type

1980, Aug. 30 *Perf. 12*

C314 A284 7c American crocodile 1.60 .30
C315 A284 10c Cuban rat 1.75 .35
C316 A284 25c Manatee 2.75 .60
C317 A284 45c Turtle 3.75 .85
Nos. C314-C317 (4) 9.85 2.10

Painting Type

1980, Sept. 23 Litho. *Perf. 13½x13*

C318 A285 10c Abstract, by Paul Guidicelli, vert. .30 .25
C319 A285 17c Farmer, by Yoryi Morel, vert. .50 .35

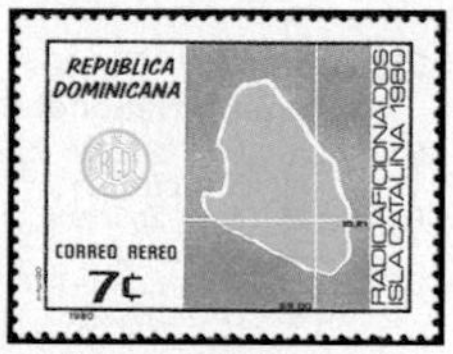

Visit of Radio Amateurs to Catalina Island AP97

1980, Oct. 3

C320 AP97 7c multicolored .50 .50

Rotary International, 75th Anniversary — AP98

1980, Oct. 23 Litho. *Perf. 12*

C321 AP98 10c Globe, emblem, vert. .40 .30
C322 AP98 33c shown .75 .75

Carrier Pigeons, UPU Emblem AP99

1980, Oct. 31 *Perf. 13½*

C323 AP99 33c shown .30 .25
C324 AP99 45c Pigeons, diff. .45 .30
C325 AP99 50c Pigeon, stamp .90 .45
Nos. C323-C325 (3) 1.65 1.00

Souvenir Sheet

Imperf

C326 AP99 1.10p UPU emblem 1.50 1.50

UPU cent. No. C326 contains one 48½x31mm stamp.

Christmas Type

1980, Dec. 5 Litho. *Perf. 13½*

C327 A286 10c Holy Family .30 .25

Christmas 1980.

Salcedo Type

Design: Map and arms of Salcedo.

1981, Jan. 14 Litho. *Perf. 13½*

C328 A287 10c multicolored .25 .25

AP100

AP101

Industrial Symbols, Seminar Emblem.

1981, Feb. 18 Litho. *Perf. 13½*

C329 AP100 10c shown .30 .25
C330 AP100 33c Seminar emblem .55 .25

CODIA Chemical Engineering Seminar.

National Games Type

1981, Mar. 31 Litho. *Perf. 13½*

C331 A289 10c Baseball .55 .35

1981, Apr. 15

Design: Admiral Juan Alejandro Acosta.

C332 AP101 10c multicolored .25 .20

Battle of Tortuguero anniversary.

13th World Telecommunications Day — AP102

1981, May 16 Litho. *Perf. 12*

C333 AP102 10c multicolored .25 .20

Heinrich von Stephan AP103

Worker in Wheelchair AP104

1981, July 15 Litho. *Perf. 13½*

C334 AP103 33c tan & lt red brn .75 .75

Birth sesquicentennial of UPU founder.

1981, July 24

C335 AP104 7c Stylized people .30 .30
C336 AP104 33c shown .75 .75

Intl. Year of the Disabled.

EXPURIDOM '81 Intl. Stamp Show, Santo Domingo, July 31-Aug. 2 — AP105

1981, July 31

C337 AP105 7c multicolored .50 .35

Bullet Holes in Target, Competition Emblem AP106

1981, Aug. 12

C338 AP106 10c shown .20 .20
C339 AP106 15c Riflemen .30 .25
C340 AP106 25c Pistol shooting .50 .40
Nos. C338-C340 (3) 1.00 .85

2nd World Sharpshooting Championship.

Exports — AP107

World Food Day — AP108

1981, Oct. 16 Litho. *Perf. 12*

C341 AP107 7c Jewelry .35 .25
C342 AP107 10c Handicrafts .45 .25
C343 AP107 11c Fruit .35 .30
C344 AP107 17c Vegetables .60 .40
Nos. C341-C344 (4) 1.75 1.20

1981, Oct. 16 Litho. *Perf. 13½*

C345 AP108 10c Fruits .45 .25
C346 AP108 50c Vegetables 1.10 1.00

5th Natl. Games AP109

1981, Dec. 5 Litho. *Perf. 13½*

C347 AP109 10c Javelin, vert. .30 .25
C348 AP109 50c Cycling 1.50 1.50

Orchids AP110

1981, Dec. 14

C349 AP110 7c Encyclia cochleata .55 .20
C350 AP110 10c Broughtonia domingensis .75 .25
C351 AP110 25c Encyclia truncata 1.10 .55
C352 AP110 75c Elleanthus capitatus 2.50 1.50
Nos. C349-C352 (4) 4.90 2.50

Christmas Type

1981, Dec. 23

C353 A294 10c Dove, sun .50 .30

Battle of Tortuguero Anniv. AP111

1982, Apr. 15 Litho. *Perf. 13½*

C354 AP111 10c Naval Academy, cadets .30 .25

1982 World Cup Soccer — AP112

American Air Forces Cooperation System — AP113

Designs: Various soccer players.

1982, Apr. 19

C355 AP112 10c multicolored .40 .30
C356 AP112 21c multicolored .40 .25
C357 AP112 33c multicolored .75 .75
Nos. C355-C357 (3) 1.55 1.30

1982, Apr. 12 *Perf. 12*

C358 AP113 10c multicolored .30 .25

Scouting Year AP114

1982, Apr. 30 Litho. *Perf. 13½*

C359 AP114 10c Baden-Powell, vert. .25 .20
C360 AP114 15c Globe .35 .25
C361 AP114 25c Baden-Powell, scout, vert. .50 .30
Nos. C359-C361 (3) 1.10 .75

Dancers — AP115

Espamer '82 Emblem — AP116

1982, June 1 Litho. *Perf. 13½*

C362 AP115 7c Emblem .20 .20
C363 AP115 10c Cathedral, Casa del Tostado, Santo Domingo .25 .20
C364 AP115 33c shown .85 .85
Nos. C362-C364 (3) 1.30 1.25

Tourist Org. of the Americas, 25th Congress (COTAL '82), Santo Domingo.

1982, July 5

Espamer '82 Intl. Stamp Exhibition, San Juan, Oct. 12-17: Symbolic stamps.

C365 AP116 7c multi .20 .20
C366 AP116 13c multi, horiz. .30 .25
C367 AP116 50c multi, horiz. 1.40 1.10
Nos. C365-C367 (3) 1.90 1.55

Sports Type

1982, Aug. 13 *Perf. 12, Imperf.*

C368 A300 10c Basketball .30 .20
C369 A300 13c Boxing .50 .25
C370 A300 25c Gymnast .65 .30
Nos. C368-C370 (3) 1.45 .75

Harbor, by Alejandro Bonilla — AP117

Paintings: 10c, Portrait of a Woman, by Leopoldo Navarro. 45c, Amelia Francasci, by Luis Desangles. 2p, Portrait, by Abelardo Rodriguez Urdaneta. 10c, 45c, 2p vert.

1982, Aug. 20 *Perf. 13, Imperf.*

C371 AP117 7c multicolored .25 .20
C372 AP117 10c multicolored .30 .25
C373 AP117 45c multicolored 1.50 1.00
C374 AP117 2p multicolored 6.75 4.00
Nos. C371-C374 (4) 8.80 5.45

San Pedro de Macoris Type

1982, Aug. 26

Size: 42x29mm

C375 A301 7c Lake .40 .30

35th Anniv. of Central Bank AP118

1982, Oct. 22 **Litho.** *Perf. 13½x13*

C376 AP118 10c multicolored .50 .35

490th Anniv. of Discovery of America AP119

1982, Oct. 7 **Litho.** *Perf. 13½*

C377 AP119 7c Map 1.00 .80
C378 AP119 10c Santa Maria, vert. 1.25 .90
C379 AP119 21c Columbus, vert. 1.50 .90
Nos. C377-C379 (3) 3.75 2.60

Christmas Type

1982, Dec. 8

C380 A303 10c multicolored .50 .35

French Alliance Centenary AP120

1983, Mar. 31 **Litho.** *Perf. 13½*

C381 AP120 33c multicolored .50 .45

Battle of Tortuguero Anniv. AP121

1983, Apr. 15 **Litho.** *Perf. 13½*

C382 AP121 15c Frigate Mella-451 .60 .25

World Communications Year — AP122

1983, May 6 **Litho.** *Perf. 13½*

C383 AP122 10c dk blue & blue .30 .25

AP123

AP124

1983, July 5 **Litho.** *Perf. 13½*

C384 AP123 9c multicolored .50 .35

Simon Bolivar (1783-1830).

1983, Aug. 22 **Litho.** *Perf. 12*

C385 AP124 7c Gymnast, basketball .35 .20
C386 AP124 10c Highjump, boxing .45 .20
C387 AP124 15c Baseball, weight lifting, bicycling .55 .25
Nos. C385-C387 (3) 1.35 .65

9th Pan American Games, Caracas, Aug. 13-28.

491st Anniv. of Discovery of America AP125

1983, Oct. 11 **Litho.** *Perf. 13½*

C388 AP125 10c Columbus' ships, map 1.10 .35
C389 AP125 21c Santa Maria (trophy) 1.60 .55
C390 AP125 33c Yacht Sotavento, vert. 1.75 .60
Nos. C388-C390 (3) 4.45 1.50

Size: 103x103mm

Imperf

C391 AP125 50c Ship models 10.00 10.00

10th Anniv. of Latin American Civil Aviation Commission AP126

1983, Dec. 7

C392 AP126 10c dark blue .50 .35

Funeral Procession, by Juan Bautista Gomez — AP127

Designs: 15c, Meeting of Maximo Gomez and Jose Marti in Guayubin, by Enrique Garcia Godoy. 21c, St. Francis, by Angel Perdomo, vert. 33c, Portrait of a Girl, by Adriana Billini, vert.

1983, Dec. 26 *Perf. 13½*

C393 AP127 10c multicolored .35 .20
C394 AP127 15c multicolored .35 .20
C395 AP127 21c multicolored .45 .25
C396 AP127 33c multicolored .70 .25
Nos. C393-C396 (4) 1.85 .90

Christmas 1983 — AP128

1983, Dec. 13 **Litho.** *Perf. 13½*

C397 AP128 10c Bells, ornaments .30 .20

AIR POST SEMI-POSTAL STAMPS

Catalogue values for unused stamps in this section are for Never Hinged items.

Nos. C97-C99 Surcharged in Red like Nos. B1-B5

Engraved and Lithographed

1957, Feb. 8 **Unwmk.** *Perf. 11½*

Flags in National Colors

CB1 A117 11c + 2c ultra & red org .30 .30
CB2 A117 16c + 2c car & lt grn .40 .40
CB3 A117 17c + 2c blk, vio & red .40 .40
Nos. CB1-CB3 (3) 1.10 1.10

The surtax was to aid Hungarian refugees. A similar 25c surcharge was applied to the souvenir sheets described in the footnote following No. C99. Value, 2 sheets, perf. and imperf., $17.50.

Nos. C100-C102 Surcharged in Red Orange like Nos. B6-B10

1957, Sept. 9 **Photo.** *Perf. 13½*

Flags in National Colors

CB4 A118 11c + 2c yel grn & dk bl .50 .45
CB5 A118 16c + 2c lilac & dk bl .60 .60
CB6 A118 17c + 2c brn & bl grn .65 .65
Nos. CB4-CB6 (3) 1.75 1.70

See note after No. B10.

A similar 5c surcharge was applied to the miniature sheets described in the footnote following No. 483. Value, 4 sheets, perf. & imperf., medal and flag, $40.

Types of Olympic Air Post Stamps, 1957, Surcharged in Carmine like Nos. B11-B20

1958, May 26 **Engr. & Litho.**

Flags in National Colors

Pink Paper

CB7 A119(a) 11c + 2c ultra .30 .30
CB8 A119(b) 11c + 2c ultra .30 .30
CB9 A120(a) 16c + 2c rose car .35 .35
CB10 A120(b) 16c + 2c rose car .35 .35
CB11 A119(a) 17c + 2c claret .40 .40
CB12 A119(b) 17c + 2c claret .40 .40
Nos. CB7-CB12 (6) 2.10 2.10

A similar 5c surcharge, plus marginal UN emblem and "UNRWA," was applied to the miniature sheets described in the footnote following No. C105. Value, 4 sheets, perf. and imperf., $20.

Nos. C106-C108 Surcharged like Nos. B21-B25

1959, Apr. 13 **Photo.** *Perf. 13½*

Flags in National Colors

CB13 A125 11c + 2c blue, ol & brn .50 .50
CB14 A125 16c + 2c lt grn, org & dk bl .70 .70
CB15 A125 17c + 2c ver bl & yel 1.00 1.00
Nos. CB13-CB15 (3) 2.20 2.20

A similar 5c surcharge was applied to the miniature sheets described in the footnote following No. C108. Value, 2 sheets, perf. and imperf., $25.

Type of Regular Issue 1957 Surcharged in Red like Nos. B26-B30

Engraved and Lithographed

1959, Sept. 10 ***Imperf.***

Flags in National Colors

CB16 A117 11c + 2c ultra & red org .45 .45
CB17 A117 16c + 2c carmine & lt grn .50 .50
CB18 A117 17c + 2c black, vio & red .55 .55
Nos. CB16-CB18 (3) 1.50 1.50

Nos. C113-C114 Surcharged in Red like Nos. B31-B33

1960, Apr. 7 **Litho.** *Perf. 12½*

CB19 AP43 10c + 5c plum, gray & grn .30 .30
CB20 AP43 13c + 5c gray & green .45 .45

World Refugee Year.

For souvenir sheets see note after No. B33.

Nos. C115-C117 Surcharged: "XV ANIVERSARIO DE LA UNESCO + 2c"

Perf. 13½

1962, Jan. 8 **Unwmk.** **Photo.**

Flags in National Colors

CB21 A136 11c + 2c blue, gray & brn .25 .25
CB22 A136 16c + 2c red, brn & ol .30 .30
CB23 A136 17c + 2c blk, bl & ocher .30 .30
Nos. CB21-CB23 (3) .85 .85

See note after No. B38.

A similar 5c surcharge was applied to the miniature sheets described in the footnote following No. C117. Value, 2 sheets, perf. and imperf., $7.50.

Anti-Malaria Type of 1962

1962, Apr. 29 **Litho.** *Perf. 12*

CB24 A141 13c + 2c pink & red .30 .25
CB25 A141 33c + 2c org & dp org .60 .40

Souvenir sheets exist, perf. and imperf. containing one each of Nos. B39-B40, CB24-CB25 and a 25c+2c pale grn and yel grn. Value, 2 sheets, perf. and imperf., $7.50.

Nos. C132-C133 Surcharged like Nos. B44-B46

1964, Mar. 8

CB26 AP46 10c + 2c brt violet .25 .20
CB27 AP46 13c + 2c yellow .25 .20

Nos. C146-C148 Surcharged like Nos. B47-B51

1966, Dec. 9 **Litho.** *Perf. 12½*

Size: 35x24mm

CB28 A164 10c + 5c multi *3.00* *1.00*
CB29 A164 50c + 10c multi *4.50* *3.00*
CB30 A164 75c + 10c multi *6.00* *3.75*
Nos. CB28-CB30 (3) *13.50* *7.75*

AIR POST OFFICIAL STAMPS

Nos. O13-O14 Overprinted in Blue

Unwmk.
1930, Dec. 3 Typo. *Perf. 12*
CO1 O3 10c light blue 11.50 *12.00*
a. Pair, one without ovpt. 900.00
CO2 O3 20c orange 11.50 *12.00*

SPECIAL DELIVERY STAMPS

Biplane SD1

Perf. 11½
1920, Apr. Unwmk. Litho.
E1 SD1 10c deep ultra 5.50 1.25
a. Imperf., pair

Special Delivery Messenger — SD2

1925
E2 SD2 10c dark blue 16.00 4.50

SD3

1927
E3 SD3 10c red brown 5.00 1.25
a. "E EXPRESO" at top 55.00 55.00

Type of 1927

1941 Redrawn
E4 SD3 10c yellow green 2.75 3.00
E5 SD3 10c dark blue green 2.40 .60

The redrawn design differs slightly from SD3.
Issue dates: No. E4, Mar. 27; No. E5, Aug. 7.

Emblem of Communications — SD4

1945, Sept. 1 *Perf. 12*
E6 SD4 10c rose car, car & dk bl .90 .20

Catalogue values for unused stamps in this section, from this point to the end of the section, are for Never Hinged items.

SD5

1950 Litho. Unwmk.
E7 SD5 10c multicolored .50 .20
Exists imperf.

Modern Communications System — SD6

1956, Aug. 18 *Perf. 11½*
E8 SD6 25c green 1.00 .30

Carrier Pigeon SD7

1967 Litho. *Perf. 11½*
E9 SD7 25c light blue .55 .25

Carrier Pigeon, Globe — SD8

Messenger, Plane — SD9

1978, Aug. 2 Litho. *Perf. 13½*
E10 SD8 25c multicolored .75 .30

1979, Nov. 30 *Perf. 13½*
E11 SD9 25c multicolored .45 .25

Motorcycling — SD10

1989, May Litho. *Perf. 13½*
E12 SD10 1p multicolored 2.50 1.10

Postman SD11

1999 Litho. *Perf. 13½x13¼*
E13 SD11 8p multicolored 2.75 2.75

INSURED LETTER STAMPS

Merino Issue of 1933 Surcharged in Red or Black

1935, Feb. 1 Unwmk. *Perf. 14*
G1 A35 8c on 7c ultra .60 .20
a. Inverted surcharge 18.00
G2 A35 15c on 10c org yel .65 .20
a. Inverted surcharge 18.00
G3 A35 30c on 8c dk green 1.75 .90
G4 A35 45c on 20c car rose (Bk) 3.00 1.00
G5 A36 70c on 50c lemon 6.00 1.25
Nos. G1-G5 (5) 12.00 3.55

Merino Issue of 1933 Surcharged in Red

1940
G6 A35 8c on ½c lt vio 2.00 2.00
G7 A35 8c on 7c ultra 3.25 3.25

Coat of Arms — IL1

1940-45 Litho. *Perf. 11½*
Arms in Black
G8 IL1 8c brown red .60 .25
a. 8c dk red, no shading on inner frame 1.00 .20
G9 IL1 15c dp orange ('45) 1.25 .20
G10 IL1 30c dk green ('41) 1.50 .20
a. 30c yellow green 1.50 .20
G11 IL1 45c ultra ('44) 1.50 .30
G12 IL1 70c olive brn ('44) 1.75 .30
Nos. G8-G12 (5) 6.60 1.25

See Nos. G13-G16, G24-G27.

Catalogue values for unused stamps in this section, from this point to the end of the section, are for Never Hinged items.

Redrawn Type of 1940-45

1952-53
Arms in Black
G13 IL1 8c car lake ('53) 2.40 .50
G14 IL1 15c red orange ('53) 1.75 .75
G15 IL1 70c dp brown car 5.25 1.50
Nos. G13-G15 (3) 9.40 2.75

Larger and bolder numerals on 8c and 15c. Smaller and bolder "70." There are many other minor differences in the design.

Type of 1940-45

1954
Arms in Black, 15x16mm
G16 IL1 10c carmine .75 .25

Coat of Arms — IL2

1955-69 Unwmk. Litho. *Perf. 11½*
Arms in Black, 13½x11½mm
G17 IL2 10c carmine rose .35 .20
G18 IL2 15c red orange ('56) 3.75 1.50
G19 IL2 20c red orange ('58) .90 .30
a. 20c orange ('69) .90 .30
b. 20c orange, retouched ('69) 3.50 1.25
G20 IL2 30c dark green ('55) 1.40 .30
G21 IL2 40c dark green ('58) 1.50 .90
a. 40c lt yellow grn ('62) 1.50 .45
G22 IL2 45c ultra ('56) 4.00 3.75
G23 IL2 70c dp brn car ('56) 5.00 2.00
Nos. G17-G23 (7) 16.90 8.95

On No. G19b the horizontal shading lines of shield are omitted.
See Nos. G28-G37.

Type of 1940-45
Second Redrawing

1963 *Perf. 12½*
Arms in Black, 17x16mm
G24 IL1 10c red orange 1.25 .30
G25 IL1 20c orange 1.50 .50

Third Redrawing

1966 Litho. *Perf. 12½*
Arms in Black, 14x14mm
G26 IL1 10c violet .40 .20
G27 IL1 40c orange 1.50 1.00

Type of 1955-62

1968 Litho. *Perf. 11½*
Arms in Black, 13½x11½mm
G28 IL2 20c red 2.00 .75
G29 IL2 60c yellow 1.50 1.50

1973-76 Litho. *Perf. 12½*
Arms in Black, 11x11mm
G30 IL2 10c car rose ('76) .50 .35
G31 IL2 20c yellow 1.40 .90
G32 IL2 20c orange ('76) 1.75 .50
G33 IL2 40c yel grn 1.60 1.00
a. 40c green ('76) 3.00 3.00
G34 IL2 70c blue 1.75 1.90
Nos. G30-G34 (5) 7.00 4.65

1973 *Perf. 11½*
Arms in Black, 13½x11½mm
G35 IL2 10c dark violet .90 .30

1978, Aug. 9 *Perf. 10½*
Arms in Black, 11x11mm
G36 IL2 10c rose magenta .35 .20
G37 IL2 40c bright green 1.50 1.50

IL3

1982-83 Litho. *Perf. 10½*
Arms in Black
G38 IL3 10c deep magenta .20 .20
G39 IL3 20c deep orange .35 .30
G40 IL3 40c bluish green .75 .50
Nos. G38-G40 (3) 1.30 1.00

IL4

1986 Litho. *Perf. 10½*
Arms in Black
G41 IL4 20c brt rose lilac .30 .25
G42 IL4 60c orange 1.00 .70
G43 IL4 1p light blue 1.60 1.10
G44 IL4 1.25p pink 2.10 1.40
G45 IL4 1.50p vermilion 2.50 1.50
G46 IL4 3p light green 5.00 3.25
G47 IL4 3.50p olive bister 6.00 3.75
G48 IL4 4p yellow 6.75 4.50
G49 IL4 4.50p lt blue grn 7.50 5.00
G50 IL4 5p brown olive 8.25 5.50
G51 IL4 6p gray 9.75 6.75
G52 IL4 6.50p lt ultra 11.00 7.50
Nos. G41-G52 (12) 61.75 41.20

Issue dates: Nos. G42-G43, G45, July 16. Nos. G46-G52, Sept. 2. Nos. G41, G44, Nov. 6.

Coat of Arms — IL5

Genciana A277

Designs: Ecuadorian plants.

Perf. 12x11½, 11½x12

1975, Nov. 18 **Litho.**

930 A277 20c Orchid, vert .25 .25
931 A277 30c shown .25 .25
932 A277 40c Bromeliaceae cactaceae, vert .30 .25
933 A277 50c Orchid .30 .25
934 A277 60c Orchid .35 .25
935 A277 80c Flowering cactus .35 .25
936 A277 1s Orchid .60 .25
Nos. 930-936,C559-C563 (12) 5.75 3.60

Venus, Chorrera Culture — A278

Female Mask, Tolita Culture — A279

Designs: 30c, Venus, Valdivia Culture. 40c, Seated man, Chorrera Culture. 50c, Man with poncho, Panzaleo Culture (late). 60c, Mythical head, Cashaloma Culture. 80c, Musician, Tolita Culture. No. 943, Chief Priest, Mantefia Culture. No. 945, Ornament, Tolita Culture. No. 946, Angry mask, Tolita Culture.

1976, Feb. 12 **Litho.** ***Perf. 11½***

937 A278 20c multicolored .30 .20
938 A278 30c multicolored .30 .20
939 A278 40c multicolored .30 .20
940 A278 50c multicolored .30 .20
941 A278 60c multicolored .30 .20
942 A278 80c multicolored .30 .20
943 A278 1s multicolored .30 .20
944 A279 1s multicolored .30 .20
945 A279 1s multicolored .30 .20
946 A279 1s multicolored .30 .20
Nos. 937-946,C568-C572 (15) 5.45 3.30

Archaeological artifacts.

Strawberries A280

Carlos Amable Ortiz (1859-1937) A281

1976, Mar. 30

947 A280 1s blue & multi .35 .20
Nos. 947,C573-C574 (3) 1.35 .60

25th Flower and Fruit Festival, Ambato.

1976, Mar. 15 **Litho.** ***Perf. 11½***

No. 949, Sixto Maria Duran (1875-1947). No. 950, Segundo Cueva Celi (1901-1969). No. 951, Cristobal Ojeda Davila (1910-1952). No. 952, Luis Alberto Valencia (1918-1970).

948 A281 1s ver & multi .25 .20
949 A281 1s orange & multi .25 .20
950 A281 1s lt green & multi .25 .20
951 A281 1s blue & multi .25 .20
952 A281 1s lt brn & multi .25 .20
Nos. 948-952 (5) 1.25 1.00

Ecuadorian composers and musicians.

Institute Emblem A282

1977, Aug. 15 **Litho.** ***Perf. 11½x12***

953 A282 2s multicolored .25 .20

11th General Assembly of Pan-American Institute of Geography and History, Quito, Aug. 15-30. See Nos. C597-C597a.

Hands Holding Rotary Emblem A283

José Peralta — A284

1977, Aug. 31 **Litho.** ***Perf. 12***

954 A283 1s multicolored .20 .20
955 A283 2s multicolored .30 .20

Souvenir Sheets

Imperf

956 A283 5s multicolored 1.10 1.10
957 A283 10s multicolored 1.40 1.40

Rotary Club of Guayaquil, 50th anniv.

1977 **Litho.** ***Perf. 11½***

Design: 2.40s, Peralta statue.

958 A284 1.80s multi .20 .20
959 A284 2.40s multi .25 .20
Nos. 958-959,C609 (3) .80 .65

José Peralta (1855-1937), writer.

Blue-faced Booby A285

Galapagos Birds: 1.80s, Red-footed booby. 2.40s, Blue-footed boobies. 3.40s, Gull. 4.40s, Galapagos hawk. 5.40s, Map of Galapagos Islands and boobies, vert.

Perf. 11½x12, 12x11½

1977, Nov. 29 **Litho.**

960 A285 1.20s multi .45 .20
961 A285 1.80s multi .60 .20
962 A285 2.40s multi 1.10 .20
963 A285 3.40s multi 1.60 .20
964 A285 4.40s multi 2.25 .35
965 A285 5.40s multi 3.00 .35
Nos. 960-965 (6) 9.00 1.50

Dr. Corral Moscoso Hospital, Cuenca A286

1978, Apr. 12 **Litho.** ***Perf. 11½x12***

966 A286 3s multicolored .25 .20
Nos. 966,C613-C614 (3) 1.75 1.00

Inauguration (in 1977) of Dr. Vicente Corral Moscoso Regional Hospital, Cuenca.

Surveyor Plane over Ecuador — A287

Latin-American Lions Emblem — A288

1978, Apr. 12 **Litho.** ***Perf. 11½***

967 A287 6s multicolored .55 .30
Nos. 967,C619-C620 (3) 2.85 2.20

Military Geographical Institute, 50th anniv.

1978

968 A288 3s multi .70 .25
969 A288 4.20s multi 1.00 .25
Nos. 968-969,C621-C623 (5) 4.75 2.55

7th meeting of Latin American Lions, Jan. 25-29.

70th Anniversary Emblem — A289

1978, Sept. **Litho.** ***Perf. 11½***

970 A289 4.20s gray & multi .45 .30

70th anniversary of Filanbanco (Philanthropic Bank). See No. C626.

Goalmouth and Net — A290

Designs: 1.80s, "Gauchito" and Games emblem, vert. 4.40s, "Gauchito," vert.

1978, Nov. 1 **Litho.** ***Perf. 12***

971 A290 1.20s multi .20 .20
972 A290 1.80s multi .20 .20
973 A290 4.40s multi .55 .20
Nos. 971-973,C627-C629 (6) 3.15 1.85

11th World Cup Soccer Championship, Argentina, June 1-25.

Symbols for Male and Female — A291

1979, Feb. 15 **Litho.** ***Perf. 12x11½***

974 A291 3.40s multi .45 .30

Inter-American Women's Commission, 50th anniversary.

Emblem A292

1979, June 21 **Litho.** ***Perf. 11½x12***

975 A292 4.40s multi .40 .30
976 A292 5.40s multi .50 .30

Ecuadorian Mortgage Bank, 16th anniv.

Street Scene, Quito — A293

Perf. 12x11½

1979, Aug. 3 **Litho.** **Unwmk.**

977 A293 3.40s multi .35 .20
Nos. 977,C651-C653 (4) 5.50 2.65

Natl. heritage: Quito & Galapagos Islands.

Jose Joaquin de Olmedo (1780-1847), Physician — A294

Chief Enriquillo, Dominican Republic — A295

1980, Apr. 29 **Litho.** ***Perf. 12x11½***

978 A294 3s multi .25 .25
979 A294 5s multi .45 .40
Nos. 978-979,C662 (3) 1.70 1.30

First Pres. of Free State of Guayaquil, 1820.

Wmk. 367, Unwmkd. (#981-983)

1980, May 12

Indo-American Tribal Chiefs: 3.40s, Guaycaypuro, Venezuela. No. 982, Abayuba, Uruguay. No. 983, Atlacatl, Salvador.

980 A295 3s multi .45 .20
981 A295 3.40s multi .75 .35
982 A295 5s multi 1.75 .55
983 A295 5s multi 1.75 .55
Nos. 980-983,C663-C678 (20) 40.95 9.90

King Juan Carlos and Queen Sofia, Visit to Ecuador A296

Perf. 11½x12

1980, May 18 **Unwmk.**

984 A296 3.40s multi .45 .30

See No. C679.

Cofan Indian, Napo Province — A297

1980, June 10 **Litho.** ***Perf. 12x11½***

985 A297 3s shown .45 .20
986 A297 3.40s Zuleta woman, Imbabura .45 .20
987 A297 5s Chota woman, Imbabura .65 .20
Nos. 985-987,C681-C684 (7) 7.25 4.90

Basilica, Our Lady of Mercy Church, Quito
A298

1980, July 7 Litho. *Perf. 11½*

988 A298 3.40s shown .45 .20
989 A298 3.40s Balcony .45 .20
989A A298 3.40s Dome and cupolas .45 .20

Sizes: 91x116mm, 116x91mm

Imperf

990 A298 5s multi 1.60 1.60
990A A298 5s multi, horiz. 1.60 1.60
990B A298 5s multi 1.60 1.60
Nos. 988-990B,C685-C691 (13) 14.25 9.40

Virgin of Mercy, patron saint of Ecuadorian armed forces. No. 990 contains designs of Nos. C686, C685, 989. No. 990A contains designs of Nos. C688, C691, C690. No. 990B contains designs of Nos. C689, C687, 989A, 988.

Olympic Torch and Rings — A299

Coronation of Virgin of Cisne, 50th Anniv. — A300

Perf. 12x11½

1980, July 19 Wmk. 395>

991 A299 5s multi .70 .20
992 A299 7.60s multi 1.25 .30
Nos. 991-992,C695-C696 (4) 3.65 1.70

Souvenir Sheet

Imperf

993 A299 30s multi 6.75 6.75

22nd Summer Olympic Games, Moscow, July 19-Aug. 3.

No. 993 contains vignettes in designs of Nos. 991 and C695.

1980 Litho. *Perf. 11½*

994 A300 1.20s shown .30 .30
995 A300 3.40s Different statue .40 .30

J.J. Olmeda, Father de Velasco, Flags of Ecuador and Riobamba, Constitution
A301

1980, Sept. 20 Litho. *Perf. 11½*

996 A301 3.40s multi .30 .30
997 A301 5s multi .70 .45
Nos. 996-997,C700-C701 (4) 2.70 1.60

Souvenir Sheet

Imperf

998 A301 30s multi 3.25 3.25

Constitutional Assembly of Riobamba sesquicentennial. #998 contains vignettes in designs of #996-997.

Young Indian Girl — A302

Perf. 12x11½

1980, Oct. 9 Litho. Wmk. 395

999 A302 1.20s multi .20 .20
1000 A302 3.40s multi .55 .20
Nos. 999-1000,C703-C704 (4) 3.00 1.55

Democratic government, 1st anniversary.

OPEC Emblem
A303

1980, Nov. 8 *Perf. 11½x12*

1001 A303 3.40s multi .45 .20

20th anniversary of OPEC. See No. C706.

Decorative Hedges, Capitol Gardens, Carchi
A304

1980, Nov. 21 *Perf. 13*

1002 A304 3s multi .50 .25
Nos. 1002,C707-C708 (3) 3.75 1.90

Carchi province centennial.

Cattleya Maxima
A305

Designs: Orchids.

1980, Nov. 22 *Perf. 11½x12*

1003 A305 1.20s *shown* .55 .20
1004 A305 3s *Comparattia speciosa* .95 .40
1005 A305 3.40s *Cattleya iricolor* 1.25 .45
Nos. 1003-1005,C709-C712 (7) 22.50 6.35

Souvenir Sheet

Imperf

1006 A305 20s multi 5.75 4.25

No. 1006 contains vignettes in designs of Nos. 1003-1005.

Pope John Paul II and Children — A306

1980, Dec. 27 *Perf. 12*

1007 A306 3.40s multi .60 .30
Nos. 1007,C715-C716 (3) 2.80 1.40

Christmas and visit of Pope John Paul II.

Carlos and Jorge Mantilla Ortega, Editors of El Comercio — A307

El Comercio Newspaper, 75th Anniv.: 3.40s, Editors Cesar & Carlos Mantilla Jacome.

1981, Jan. 6

1008 A307 2s multi .25 .25
1009 A307 3.40s multi .45 .25

Soldier on Map of Ecuador
A308

1981, Mar. 10 Litho. *Perf. 13*

1010 A308 3.40s shown .25 .25
1011 A308 3.40s Pres. Roldos .25 .25

National defense.

Theodore E. Gildred and Ecuador I
A309

1981, Mar. 31 Litho. *Perf. 13*

1012 A309 2s lt bl & blk .25 .25

Ecuador-US flight, 50th anniv.

A310

A311

1981, Apr. 10

1013 A310 2s multi .30 .20

Octavio Cordero Palacios (1870-1930), humanist.

1981 Litho. *Perf. 13*

1014 A311 2s multi .30 .30
Nos. 1014,C721-C722 (3) 2.70 1.55

Radio station HCJB, 50th anniv.

Virgin of Dolorosa
A312

1981, Apr. 30 Litho. *Perf. 12*

1015 A312 2s shown .20 .20
1016 A312 2s San Gabriel College Church .20 .20

Miracle of the painting of the Virgin of Dolorosa at San Gabriel College, 75th anniv.

Dr. Rafael Mendoza Aviles Bridge Inauguration
A313

1981, July 25 *Perf. 13*

1017 A313 2s multi .30 .20

Pablo Picasso (1881-1973), Painter — A313a

1981, Oct. 26 Litho. *Imperf.*

1017A A313a 20s multi 2.75 2.75
Nos. 1017A,C728-C731 (5) 7.35 6.30

No. 1017A contains design of No. C728, additional portrait.

World Food Day — A314

1981, Dec. 31 Litho. *Perf. 13½x13*

1018 A314 5s multi .45 .20

See No. C732

Transnave Shipping Co. 10th Anniv. — A315

Intl. Year of the Disabled — A316

1982, Jan. 21 Litho. *Perf. 13*

1019 A315 3.50s Freighter Isla Salango .45 .20

1982, Feb. 25

1020 A316 3.40s Man in wheelchair .40 .20
Nos. 1020,C733-C734 (3) 2.00 1.05

Arch — A317

Juan Montalvo Birth Sesqui. — A318

1982, May Litho. *Perf. 13*

1021 A317 2s shown .25 .25
1022 A317 3s Houses .45 .25

Miniature Sheet

Perf. 12½ on 2 Sides

1023 Sheet of 4, 18th cent. map of Quito 5.00 4.50
a.-d. A317 6s multi 1.10 .50

QUITEX '82, 4th Natl. Stamp Exhib., Quito, Apr. 16-22. #1023 contains 4 48x31mm stamps.

1982 *Perf. 13*

1024 A318 2s Portrait .25 .25
1025 A318 3s Mausoleum .25 .25
Nos. 1024-1025,C735 (3) 1.50 1.05

American Air Forces Cooperation System — A319

4th World Swimming Champ., Guayaquil A320

1982

1026 A319 5s Emblem .45 .35

1982, July 30

1027 A320 1.80s Stadium .20 .20
1028 A320 3.40s Water polo .35 .20
Nos. 1027-1028,C736-C737 (4) 2.50 1.25

A321 A322

1982, Dec. Litho. *Perf. 13*

1029 A321 5.40s shown .25 .25
1030 A321 6s Statue .35 .25

Juan L. Mera (1832-?), Writer, by Victor Mideros.

1983, Mar. 28 Litho. *Perf. 13*

1031 A322 2s multi .35 .25

St. Teresa of Jesus of Avila (1515-82).

Sea Lions A323 Flamingoes A324

1983, June 17 Litho. *Perf. 13*

1032 A323 3s multi .90 .20
1033 A324 5s multi 1.60 .20

Ecuadorian rule over Galapagos Islds., sesqui. (3s); Charles Darwin (1809-1882).

Pres. Rocafuerte A325 Simon Bolivar A326

Perf. 13x13½

1983, Aug. 26 Litho. Wmk. 395

1034 A325 5s Statue .30 .20
1035 A325 20s Portrait .85 .35
1036 A326 20s Portrait .85 .35
Nos. 1034-1036 (3) 2.00 .90

Vicente Rocafuerte Bejarano, president, 1833-39 (Nos. 1034-1035).

A327 A328

1983, Sept. 3

1037 A327 5s River .40 .20
1038 A327 10s Dam .70 .55

Size: 110x89mm

Imperf

1039 A327 20s Dam, river 2.75 2.75
Nos. 1037-1039 (3) 3.85 3.50

Paute hydroelectric plant opening. No. 1039 is airmail.

Wmk. 395

1983, Oct. 11 Litho. *Perf. 13*

1040 A328 2s multi .35 .25

World Communication Year.

A329 A330

1983, Sept. Litho. *Perf. 13*

1041 A329 3s multi .35 .25

Cent. of Bolivar and El Oro Provinces (1984).

1984, Mar. Litho. *Perf. 13*

1042 A330 15s Engraving .45 .30

Atahualpa (1497-1529), last Incan ruler.

A331

Christmas 1983 — A331a

Creche figures.

Perf. 13½x13, 13x13½

1984, July 7 Litho.

1043 A331 5s Jesus & the teachers .25 .20
1044 A331 5s Three kings .25 .20
1045 A331 5s Holy Family .25 .20
1046 A331a 6s Priest .25 .20
Nos. 1043-1046 (4) 1.00 .80

Foreign Policy of Pres. Hurtado A332

State visits.

1984, July 10 *Perf. 13½x13*

1047 A332 8s Brazil .40 .20
1048 A332 9s PRC .45 .20
1049 A332 24s UN 1.25 .90
1050 A332 28s US 1.60 .95
1051 A332 29s Venezuela 1.60 1.10
1052 A332 37s Latin American Economic Conf., Quito 2.00 1.40
Nos. 1047-1052 (6) 7.30 4.75

Miguel Diaz Cueva (1884-1942), Lawyer A333

1984, Aug. 8 Litho. *Perf. 13½x13*

1053 A333 10s multicolored .70 .35

1984 Winter Olympics A334 Manned Flight Bicentenary A335

Perf. 13x13½, 12x11½ (6s)

1984, Aug. 15

1054 A334 2s Emblem .20 .20
1055 A334 4s Ice skating .20 .20
1056 A334 6s Skating, diff. .20 .20
1057 A334 10s Skiing .80 .20
Nos. 1054-1057 (4) 1.40 .80

Size: 90x100mm

1057A A334 20s Figure skating 35.00 15.00

1984, Aug. 15 *Perf. 13x13½*

1058 A335 3s Montgolfier .20 .20
1059 A335 6s Charlier's balloon, Paris, 1789 .35 .20

Souvenir Sheet

1060 A335 20s Graf Zeppelin, Montgolfier 1.75 1.10

No. 1060 is airmail and contains one imperf. stamp (50x37mm).

SAN MATEO '83, Esmeraldas A336

1984 Litho. *Perf. 13*

1061 A336 8s La Marimba folk dance 1.75 .25

Size: 89x110mm

Imperf

1061A A336 15s La Marimba, diff. 1.10 1.10

No. 1061A is airmail.

Jose Maria de Jesus Yerovi (b. 1824), 4th Archbishop of Quito — A337

1984

1062 A337 5s multi .35 .25

Canonization of Brother Miguel A338

1984 Litho. *Perf. 13*

1063 A338 9s Academy of Languages .50 .20
1064 A338 24s Vatican City, vert. 1.00 .70

Imperf

Size: 110x90mm

1065 A338 28s Home of Brother Miguel 3.25 2.10
Nos. 1063-1065 (3) 4.75 3.00

No. 1065, airmail, has black control number.

State Visit of Pope John Paul II — A339 Beatification of Mercedes de Jesus Molina — A340

1985, Jan. 23 Litho. *Perf. 13x13½*

1066 A339 1.60s Papal arms 2.00 .25
1067 A339 5s Blessing crowd 2.00 .25
1068 A339 9s World map, itinerary 2.00 .25
1069 A339 28s Pope waving 4.50 .50
1070 A339 29s Portrait 5.00 .60

Size: 90x109mm

Imperf

1071 A339 30s Pope holding crosier 10.00 10.00
Nos. 1066-1071 (6) 25.50 11.85

1985, Jan. 23

Paintings, sculpture.

1072 A340 1.60s Portrait .30 .20
1073 A340 5s Czestochowa Madonna .30 .20
1074 A340 9s Alborada Madonna .75 .20

Size: 90x110mm

Imperf

1075 A340 20s Mercedes de Jesus, children 5.00 5.00
Nos. 1072-1075 (4) 6.35 5.60

Visit of Pope John Paul II, birth bimillennium of the Virgin Mary.

Samuel Valarezo Delgado, Naturalist, Politician — A341

1985, Feb.

1076 A341 2s Bird .20 .20
1077 A341 3s Swordfish, tuna .20 .20
1078 A341 6s Portrait .30 .20
Nos. 1076-1078 (3) .70 .60

ESPANA '84, Madrid A342

1985, Apr. 25 *Perf. 13½x13*

1079 A342 6s Emblem .20 .20
1080 A342 10s Spanish royal family .70 .20

Size: 110x90mm

Imperf

1081 A342 15s Retiro Park, exhibition site 1.50 1.50

Dr. Pio Jaramillo Alvarado (1884-1968), Historian A343

1985, May 17
1082 A343 6s multi .25 .20

Ingenio Valdez Sugar Refinery — A344

Designs: 50s, Sugar cane, emblem. 100s, Rafael Valdez Cervantes, founder.

1985, June **Litho.** ***Perf. 13***
1082A A344 50s multi 1.25 .65
1082B A344 100s multi 2.75 1.40

Size: 110x90mm

Imperf

1083 A344 30s multi 2.00 2.00
Nos. 1082A-1083 (3) 6.00 4.05

Chamber of Commerce, 10th Anniv. A345

50s, Natl. and American Statues of Liberty.

1985, Aug. 15 ***Perf. 13½x13***
1084 A345 24s multicolored .80 .45
1085 A345 28s multicolored 1.00 .65

Size: 110x90mm

Imperf

1086 A345 50s multicolored 2.75 2.75
Nos. 1084-1086 (3) 4.55 3.85

Natl. Philatelic Assoc., AFE, 50th Anniv. — A346

1985, Aug. 25 ***Perf. 12***
1087 A346 25s AFE emblem .60 .40
1088 A346 30s No. 357, horiz. 1.00 .65

Guayaquil Fire Dept., 150th Anniv. A347

1985, Oct. 10 ***Perf. 13½x13***
1089 A347 6s Steam fire pump, 1882 .20 .20
1090 A347 10s Fire Wagon, 1899 .50 .20
1091 A347 20s Anniv. emblem, natl. flag .90 .70
Nos. 1089-1091 (3) 1.60 1.10

Natl. Infant Survival Campaign A348

1st Natl. Phil. Cong., Quito, Nov. 25-28 A349

1985, Oct. ***Perf. 13x13½***
1092 A348 10s Boy, girl, tree .45 .30

1985, Nov. ***Perf. 13x13½, 13½x13***

20th cent. illustrations, natl. cultural collection: 5s, Supreme Court, Quito, by J. M. Roura. 10s, Riobamba Cathedral, by O. Munaz. 15s, House of 100 Windows, by J. M. Roura, horiz. 20s, Rural cottage near Cuenca, by J. M. Roura.

No. 1097: a, Stampless cover, 1779, Riobamba. b, Hand press, 1864, Quito. c, Postrider, 1880, Cuenca. d, Monoplane, 1st airmail flight, 1919, Guayaquil.

1093 A349 5s multi .20 .20
1094 A349 10s multi .50 .20
1095 A349 15s multi .65 .50
1096 A349 20s multi .90 .65
Nos. 1093-1096 (4) 2.25 1.55

Souvenir Sheet

1097 Sheet of 4 1.00 1.00
a.-d. A349 5s, any single .20 .20

AFE, 50th anniv. #1097 contains 53x42mm stamps, perf. 13x12½ on 2 sides.

10th Bolivarian Games, Cuenca A350

1985, Nov. ***Perf. 13½x13***
1098 A350 10s Boxing .50 .20
1099 A350 25s Women's gymnastics .65 .35
1100 A350 30s Discus .85 .40
Nos. 1098-1100 (3) 2.00 .95

BAE Calderon, Navy Cent. — A351

Military anniv.: #1102, Fighter plane, Air Force 65th anniv. #1103, Army & paratroops emblems, Special Forces 30th anniv.

1985, Dec. ***Perf. 13x13½***
1101 A351 10s multi .45 .20
1102 A351 10s multi .45 .20
1103 A351 10s multi .45 .20
Nos. 1101-1103 (3) 1.35 .60

UN, 40th Anniv. A352

1985, Oct. **Litho.** ***Perf. 13***
1104 A352 10s UN flag .45 .20
1105 A352 20s Natl. flag .45 .20

Size: 110x90mm

Imperf

1106 A352 50s UN Building 1.25 1.25
Nos. 1104-1106 (3) 2.15 1.65

Christmas A353

Indigenous Flowers A354

1985, Nov.
1107 A353 5s Child riding donkey .20 .20
1108 A353 10s Baked goods .45 .20
1109 A353 15s Riding donkey, diff. .60 .45

Size: 90x110mm

Imperf

1110 A353 30s like 5s 1.50 1.50
Nos. 1107-1110 (4) 2.75 2.35

1986, Feb.
1111 A354 24s Embotrium grandiforum 1.00 .45
1112 A354 28s Topobea sp. 1.75 .45
1113 A354 29s Befaria resinosa mutis 2.25 .50

Size: 110x90mm

Imperf

1114 A354 15s multi 7.25 5.00
Nos. 1111-1114 (4) 12.25 6.40

No. 1114 contains designs of Nos. 1111, 1113, 1112; black control number.

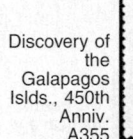

Discovery of the Galapagos Islds., 450th Anniv. A355

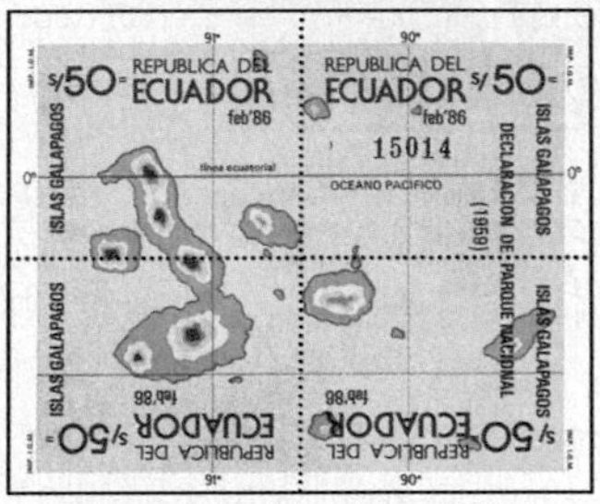
Map of the Islands — A356

1986, Feb. 12
1115 A355 10s Land iguana .45 .20
1116 A355 20s Sea lion .90 .45
1117 A355 30s Frigate birds 1.40 .70
1118 A355 40s Penguins 1.75 1.00
1119 A355 50s Sea turtle 2.25 1.10
1120 A355 100s Charles Darwin 4.50 2.50
1121 A355 200s Bishop Tomas de Berlenga, discoverer 8.75 4.50

Perf. 12½ on 2 Sides

1122 A356 Sheet of 4 11.00 11.00
a.-d. 50s, any single 1.50 1.50
Nos. 1115-1122 (8) 31.00 21.45

No. 1122 contains 53x42mm stamps.

Inter-American Development Bank, 25th Anniv. — A357

5s, Antonio Ortiz Mena, pres. 1971-88. 10s, Felipe Herrera, pres. 1960-71. 50s, Emblem.

1986, Mar. 6
1123 A357 5s multi .40 .20
1124 A357 10s multi .60 .20
1125 A357 50s multi 1.00 .80
Nos. 1123-1125 (3) 2.00 1.20

Guayaquil Tennis Club, 75th Anniv. A358

1986, Mar. 7
1126 A358 10s Emblem .45 .20
1127 A358 10s Francisco Segura Cano, vert. .45 .20
1128 A358 10s Andres Gomez Santos, vert. .45 .20
Nos. 1126-1128 (3) 1.35 .60

1986 World Cup Soccer Championships, Mexico — A359

1986, May 5
1129 A359 5s Shot .20 .20
1130 A359 10s Block .80 .20

An imperf. stamp exists picturing flags, player and emblem. Value $8.50.

Meeting of Presidents Cordero and Betancourt of Colombia, Feb. 1985 A360

1986 **Litho.** ***Perf. 13½x13***
1131 A360 20s Presidents .45 .20
1132 A360 20s Embracing .45 .20

Exports A361

35s, #1137c, Shrimp. 40s, #1137b, Tuna. 45s, #1137a, Sardines. #1137d, MICIP emblem.

1986, Apr. 12
1133 A361 35s ultra & ver 1.00 .55
1134 A361 40s red & yel grn 1.00 .55
1135 A361 45s car & dk yel 1.15 .75

Perf. 12½ on 2 Sides

1137 Sheet of 4 2.25 2.25
a.-d. A361 10s, any single .40 .40
Nos. 1133-1137 (4) 5.40 4.10

No. 1137 contains 4 53x42mm stamps.

A362

La Condamine's First Geodesic Mission, 250th Anniv. — A363

#1141a, Triangulation map for determining equatorial meridian, 1736. #1141b, Partial map of the Maranon & Amazon Rivers, by Samuel Fritz, 1743-1744. #1141c, Base of measurement, Yaruqui plains. #1141d, Caraburo & Dyambaru Pyramids near Quito. #1141 has a continuous design.

1986, July 10 Litho. *Perf. 13½x13*

1138 A362 10s La Condamine .35 .20
1139 A362 15s Maldonado .45 .20
1140 A362 20s Middle of the World, Quito .55 .20
Nos. 1138-1140 (3) 1.35 .60

Souvenir Sheet

Perf. 12½ on 2 Sides

1141 A363 Sheet of 4 2.75 2.75
a.-d. 10s any single .40 .40

Chambers of Commerce A364

1986 Litho. *Perf. 13½x13*

1142 A364 10s Pichincha .25 .20
1143 A364 10s Cuenca .25 .20
1144 A364 10s Guayaquil .25 .20
Nos. 1142-1144 (3) .75 .60

Civil Service and Communications Ministry, 57th Anniv. — A365

Organization emblems.

1986, Dec. Litho. *Perf. 13x13½*

1145 A365 5s State railway .20 .20
1146 A365 10s Post office .20 .20
1147 A365 15s Communications .55 .20
1148 A365 20s Ministry of Public Works .65 .40
Nos. 1145-1148 (4) 1.60 1.00

A366

A367

1987, Feb. 16 Litho. *Perf. 13x13½*

1149 A366 5s multi .35 .25

Chamber of Agriculture of the 1st Zone, 50th anniv.

Litho. & Typo.

1988, Jan. 6 *Perf. 13*

Col. Luis Vargas Torres (d. 1887): 50s, Portrait. #1151, Combat unit, c. 1885. #1152a, Torres & his mother, Delfina. #1152b, Letter to Delfina written by Torres during imprisonment, 1882. #1152c, Arms of Ecuador & combat unit.

1150 A367 50s yel grn, blk & gold 1.00 .80
1151 A367 100s ver, gold & ultra 2.25 1.40

Size: 95x140mm

Perf. 12 on One or Two Sides

1152 Block of 3 6.75 6.75
a.-c. A367 100s any single 1.50 1.50
Nos. 1150-1152 (3) 10.00 8.95

Sizes: #1152a, 1152c, 95x28mm, #1152b, 95x83mm.

Founding of Guayaquil, 450th Anniv. A368

15s, Street in Las Penas. 30s, Rafael Mendoza Aviles Bridge. 40s, Francisco de Orellana (c. 1490-1546), Spanish explorer, founder, & reenactment of landing, 1538.

1988, Feb. 19 Litho. *Perf. 13*

1153 A368 15s multi, vert. .20 .20
1154 A368 30s multi .45 .20
1155 A368 40s multi .60 .20
Nos. 1153-1155 (3) 1.25 .60

Social Security Foundation (IESS), 60th Anniv. A369

1988, Mar. 11

1156 A369 50s shown .75 .40
1157 A369 100s multi, diff. 1.50 1.00

Dr. Pedro Moncayo y Esparza (1807-1888), Author, Politician A370

1988, Apr. 28 Litho. *Perf. 14x13½*

1158 A370 10s Yaguarcocha Lake .20 .20
1159 A370 15s shown .20 .20
1160 A370 20s Residence .20 .20

Size: 89x110mm

Imperf

1161 A370 100s Full-length portrait 1.10 1.10
Nos. 1158-1161 (4) 1.70 1.70

A371

Avianca Airlines, 60th Anniv. — A372

1988, May 12 Litho. *Perf. 14x13½*

1162 A371 10s Junkers F-13 .20 .20
1163 A371 20s Dornier Wal seaplane .20 .20
1164 A371 30s Ford 5AT trimotor .35 .20
1165 A371 40s Boeing 247-D .45 .20
1166 A371 50s Boeing 720-059B .55 .35
1167 A371 100s Douglas DC-3 1.25 .55
1168 A371 200s Boeing 727-200 2.25 1.25
1169 A371 300s Sikorsky S-38 4.00 1.75

Perf. 13½x14

1170 A372 500s shown 6.25 3.00
Nos. 1162-1170 (9) 15.50 7.70

San Gabriel College, 125th Anniv. A373

1988, July 25 Litho. *Perf. 14x13½*

1171 A373 15s Contemporary facility .20 .20
1172 A373 35s College entrance, 19th cent. .50 .30

A374

Military Geographical Institute, 60th Anniv. A375

1988, July 25 *Perf. 12½ on 2 Sides*

Size of No. 1173: 110x90mm

1173 A374 Block of 4 1.75 1.75
a.-d. 5s any single .30 .30

Perf. 13½

1174 A375 25s Planetarium .45 .20
1175 A375 50s Zeiss projector .80 .20
1176 A375 60s Anniv. emblem 1.00 .35
1177 A375 500s Creation, mural by E. Kingman 6.25 3.25
Nos. 1173-1177 (5) 10.25 5.75

In 1996 Nos. 1174, 1183, 1265 were surcharged 800s, 2600s 400s respectively. Only a few sets were sold to the public. The balance were sold by postal employees at greatly inflated prices.

Salesian Brothers in Ecuador, Cent. A376

Designs: 10s, St. John Bosco (1815-88), vert. 50s, 1st Salesian Cong. in Ecuador. 100s, Bosco, Salesian Brothers monument and Andes Mountains.

1988, July 29 Litho. *Perf. 13½*

1178 A376 10s multi .25 .25
1179 A376 50s multi .75 .40

Size: 89x110mm

Imperf

1180 A376 100s multi 2.25 1.60
Nos. 1178-1180 (3) 3.25 2.25

Francisco Coello, Founder — A377

Social Services Council, Guayaquil, Cent. — A378

Flag: a, Emblem (upper left portion). b, Emblem (upper right portion). c, Emblem (lower left portion) and "100 ANOS." d, Emblem (lower right portion) and "DE TRADICION DE FE, AMPARO Y ESPERANZA."

1988, Nov. 24 Litho. *Perf. 13½x14*

1181 A377 15s shown .20 .20
1182 A377 20s Eduardo Arosemena, 1st Director .20 .20
1183 A377 45s Emblem .45 .20

Size: 110x90mm

Perf. 12½ on 2 Sides

1184 A378 Block of 4 1.25 1.25
a.-d. 10s any single .20 .20
Nos. 1181-1184 (4) 2.10 1.85

For surcharge see note following No. 1177.

A379

Azuay Bank, 75th Anniv. — A380

Perf. 14x13½, 13½x14

1989, Mar. 1 Litho.

1185 A379 20s shown .20 .20
1186 A379 40s multi, vert. .30 .20

Size: 90x110mm

Imperf

1187 A380 500s shown 9.00 2.40
Nos. 1185-1187 (3) 9.50 2.80

1988 Summer Olympics, Seoul — A381

Character trademark demonstrating sports.

1989, Mar. 20 *Perf. 13½x14*

1188 A381 10s Running .20 .20
1189 A381 20s Boxing .20 .20
1190 A381 30s Cycling .40 .20
1191 A381 40s Shooting .40 .20
1192 A381 100s Diving .90 .60
1193 A381 200s Weight lifting 1.75 1.25
1194 A381 300s Tae kwon do 2.75 1.75

Size: 90x110mm
Imperf

1195 A381 200s Emblems 2.75 2.75
Nos. 1188-1195 (8) 9.35 7.15

RUMINAHUI '88 — A382

Designs: 50s, *Bird*, by Joaquin Tinta, vert. 70s, Matriz Church, Sangolqui. 300s, Monument to Ruminahui in Sangolqui, Pichincha.

Perf. 14x13½, 13½x14

1989, May 2 Litho. Wmk. 395

1196 A382 50s multi .80 .20
1197 A382 70s multi 1.00 .20

Size: 90x111mm
Imperf

1198 A382 300s multi 5.75 1.10
Nos. 1196-1198 (3) 7.55 1.50

Cantonization, 50th anniv.

Benjamin Carrion Mora, Educator A383

Perf. 13½x14, 14x13½

1989, May 10 Litho.

1199 A383 50s Portrait, vert. .45 .20
1200 A383 70s Loja landscape .55 .20
1201 A383 1000s University 8.00 3.50

Size: 110x90mm
Imperf

1202 A383 200s Portrait, diff. 1.50 1.50
Nos. 1199-1202 (4) 10.50 5.40

2nd Intl. Art Biennial A384

Prize-winning art: 40s, *The Gilded Frame*, by Myrna Baez. 70s, *Paraguay III*, by Carlos Colorabino, vert. 100s, Ordinance establishing the art exhibition. 180s, *Modulation 892*, by Julio Le Parc, vert.

Perf. 14x13½, 13½x14, Imperf. (100s)

1989, June 2 Litho.

Size of No. 1205: 110x90mm

1203 A384 40s multi .45 .20
1204 A384 70s multi .90 .20
1205 A384 100s multi 1.75 .75
1206 A384 180s multi 1.50 .95
Nos. 1203-1206 (4) 4.60 2.10

Guayaquil Chamber of Commerce, Cent. A385

Perf. 13½x14, 14x13½, Imperf. (No. 1208)

1989, June 20 Litho.

Size of No. 1208: 110x91mm

1207 A385 50s Founder Ignacio Molestina, vert. .75 .35
1208 A385 200s Flags 3.25 2.00
1209 A385 300s Headquarters 2.25 2.25
1210 A385 500s Flags, diff. 1.50 1.50
Nos. 1207-1210 (4) 7.75 6.10

French Revolution, Bicent. A386

20s, French natl. colors, anniv. emblem. 50s, Cathedral fresco. 100s, Rooster. 200s, Symbols of the revolution. 600s, Story board showing events of the revolution.

1989, July 11 ***Perf. 13½x14, 14x13½***

1211 A386 20s multi, vert. .20 .20
1212 A386 50s multi .45 .20
1213 A386 100s multi, vert. .70 .45

Size: 90x110mm
Imperf

1214 A386 200s multi, vert. 1.50 1.50
1215 A386 600s multi, vert. 6.00 6.00
Nos. 1211-1215 (5) 8.85 8.35

A387

Ministry of Public Works and Communications A388

#1216a, MOP emblem, 2-lane roadway. #1216b, State railway emblem, train. #1216c, Postal service emblem, airmail cover. #1216d, Telecommunications (IETEL) emblem, wall telephone. #1217, MOP, IETEL, postal service & state railway emblems. 100s, IETEL emblem. 200s, MOP emblem.

1989, July 7 ***Perf. 12½ on 2 Sides***

1216 A387 Block of 4 2.00 2.00
a.-d. 50s any single .40 .40

Perf. 13½x14

1217 A388 50s shown .35 .20
1218 A388 100s multi .65 .40
1219 A388 200s multi 1.50 .85
Nos. 1216-1219 (4) 4.50 3.45

MOP, 60th anniv.; national communications, 105th anniv. (No. 1216d, 100s).

Natl. Red Cross, Intl. Red Cross and Red Crescent Societies, 125th Annivs. A389

1989, Sept. 14 Litho. ***Perf. 13½***

1220 A389 10s Medical volunteer, vert. .20 .20
1221 A389 30s shown .20 .20
1222 A389 200s Two volunteers 1.40 .85
Nos. 1220-1222 (3) 1.80 1.25

Juan Montalvo (1832-1889), Writer A390

1989, Nov. 11 Litho. ***Perf. 14x13½***

1223 A390 50s Mausoleum, Ambato .35 .20
1224 A390 100s Portrait (detail) .90 .55
1225 A390 200s Monument, Ambato 1.60 1.25

Size: 90x110mm
Imperf

1226 A390 200s Portrait 1.25 1.25
Nos. 1223-1226 (4) 4.10 3.25

America Issue A391

UPAE emblem and pre-Columbian pottery.

1990, Mar. 6 Litho. ***Perf. 13½***

1227 A391 200s La Tolita incensory, vert. 1.60 1.10
1228 A391 300s Warrior (plate) 2.50 1.60

Dated 1989.

Dr. Luis Carlos Jaramillo Leon, Founder A392

#1233a, Dr. Leon. #1230, 1233b, Federico Malo Andrade, honorary president. 130s, #1233c, Roberto Crespo Toral, 1st president. 200s, Alfonso Jaramillo Leon, founder.

1990, Jan. 17 Litho. ***Perf. 13½***

1229 A392 100s shown .80 .55
1230 A392 100s multicolored .80 .55
1231 A392 130s multicolored 1.10 .70
1232 A392 200s multicolored 1.60 1.10

Size: 91x38mm
Perf. 12½ Horiz. on 1 or 2 sides

1233 Block of 3 2.75 2.75
a.-c. A392 100s any single .50 .50
Nos. 1229-1233 (5) 7.05 5.65

Chamber of Commerce, 70th anniversary.

World Cup Soccer, Italy — A393

1990, July 12 Litho. ***Perf. 13½***

1234 A393 100s shown .55 .20
1235 A393 200s Soccer player 1.10 .55
1236 A393 300s Map of Italy, trophy 1.75 .80

Imperf
Size: 110x90mm

1237 A393 200s Player, flags 1.50 1.50

Size: 60x90mm

1238 A393 300s World Cup Trophy 2.25 2.25
Nos. 1234-1238 (5) 7.15 5.30

Nos. 1235-1236, 1238 vert.

A394

A396

A395

1990, June 12 ***Perf. 13½***

1239 A394 100s multi .60 .20
1240 A394 200s Church tower, book 1.00 .60

College of St. Mariana, cent.

1990, Sept. 7 Litho. ***Perf. 13½***

Tourism: No. 100s, No. 1244c, Iguana. 200s, No. 1244b, La Compania Church, Quito. 300s, No. 1244a, Old man from Vilcabamba. No. 1244d, Locomotive.

1241 A395 100s multi .70 .20
1242 A395 200s multi, vert. 1.40 .45
1243 A395 300s multi 1.90 .65

Size: 111x90mm
Perf. 12½ on 2 sides

1244 Block of 4 6.75 3.25
a.-d. A395 100s any single .35 .20
Nos. 1241-1244 (4) 10.75 4.55

1990, Sept. 1 ***Perf. 13½***

National Census: 100s, No. 1248a, People and house. 200s, No. 1248b, Map. 300s, No. 1248c, Census breakdown, pencil.

1245 A396 100s multicolored .45 .20
1246 A396 200s multicolored, horiz. 1.00 .45
1247 A396 300s multicolored 1.40 .65

Size: 109x88mm
Perf. 12½ on 2 sides

1248 Block of 3 1.50 1.50
a.-c. A396 100s any single .30 .30
Nos. 1245-1248 (4) 4.35 2.80

A397

A398

1990, Nov. 2 Litho. ***Perf. 14***

1249 A397 200s Flags .95 .35
1250 A397 300s shown 1.40 .50

Organization of Petroleum Exporting Countries (OPEC), 30th anniv.

1990, Oct. 31 ***Perf. 13½x14***

1251 A398 200s Emblem .95 .35
1252 A398 300s Wooden parrots 1.40 .50

Size: 92x110mm
Imperf

1253 A398 200s Wooden parrots, diff. 1.60 1.60
Nos. 1251-1253 (3) 3.95 2.45

Artisans' Organization, 25th anniv.

Flowers — A399

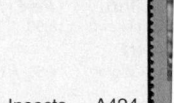

Wmk. 395

1994, June 22 Litho. *Perf. 13*

1350 A446 300s shown .50 .35
1351 A446 400s Stylized cyclist, vert. .75 .40

Postal Transportation A447

Christmas A448

America Issue: No. 1352, Van, airplane, ship, horiz. No. 1353, Airplane, mail bag.

1994

1352 A447 600s multicolored .70 .35
1353 A447 600s multicolored .90 .45

1994

#1354, Simulated stamp showing globe circled by envelope, horiz. #1355, Nativity.

1354 A448 600s multicolored 1.00 .75
1355 A448 900s multicolored 1.00 .75

Juan Leon Mera, Death Cent. A449 A450

Wmk. 395

1994, Dec. 21 Litho. *Perf. 13*

1356 A449 600s Mera's home .85 .65
1357 A450 900s multicolored 2.00 1.25

Gen. Antonio Jose de Sucre (1795-1830) — A451

Perf. 14x13½

1995, Mar. 14 Litho. Wmk. 395

1358 A451 1500s shown 2.50 1.50
1359 A451 2000s Portrait at right 3.75 2.00

Size: 80x105

Imperf

1360 A451 3000s In military uniform 4.00 4.00
Nos. 1358-1360 (3) 10.25 7.50

Beatification of Josemaria Escriva, 3rd Anniv. — A452

1995, May 17 *Perf. 13x13½*

1361 A452 900s multicolored 1.10 .80

Gen. Eloy Alfaro (1842-1912), Alfarista Revolution, Cent. A453

1995, June 5 *Perf. 13½x13*

1362 A453 800s multicolored 1.10 .80

A454

Conflict Between Ecuador & Peru — A455

Designs: 200s, Soldier writing to children. 400s, Hand holding flag of Ecuador. 800s, Soldier in wilderness.

1995, July *Perf. 13½, 13 (#1364)*

1363 A454 200s multicolored .35 .20
1364 A455 400s multicolored .75 .35
1365 A454 800s multicolored 1.25 .65
Nos. 1363-1365 (3) 2.35 1.20

CARE, 50th Anniv. — A456

1995, July 14 *Perf. 13½*

1366 A456 400s Girl, vert. .50 .30
1367 A456 800s shown 1.50 1.00

CAF (Andes Development Corporation), 25th Anniv. — A457

1995, Aug. 22 *Perf. 13*

1368 A457 1000s multicolored 2.10 .85

A458

A459

1995, Sept. 2 Litho. *Perf. 13*

1369 A458 500s Virgin of Cisne .60 .45

1995, Sept. 28

1370 A459 400s multicolored .70 .45

Natl. Institute of Children and Families (INNFA), 35th anniv.

UN, 50th Anniv. A460

Wmk. 395

1995, Oct. 6 Litho. *Perf. 13*

1371 A460 1000s bl, blk & bis 1.75 .90

Intl. Decade for Natural Disaster Reduction A461

Civil defense emblem and: No. 1372, House surrounded by flood waters. No. 1373, Family leaving site of erupting volcano. No. 1374, People under table during earthquake. No. 1375, Couple planting seedlings on hillside. No. 1376, Man reading instruction booklet for natural disaster preparation.

1995, Oct. 11

1372 A461 1000s multicolored 1.60 .85
1373 A461 1000s multicolored 1.60 .85
1374 A461 1000s multicolored 1.60 .85
1375 A461 1000s multicolored 1.60 .85
1376 A461 1000s multicolored 1.60 .85
Nos. 1372-1376 (5) 8.00 4.25

FAO, 50th Anniv. A462

1995, Oct. 16

1377 A462 1300s multicolored 2.25 1.25

Women's Culture Club, 50th Anniv. A463

1995, Oct. 20

1378 A463 1500s multicolored 2.00 1.50

29th Assembly of Inter-America Philatelic Federation, Quito — A464

1995, Nov. 11

1379 A464 1000s blue & red 1.25 .85

A465

A466

Christmas: 2000s, Santa, sleigh, reindeer on top of world. 2600s, Man on decorated horse, children.

Wmk. 395

1995, Dec. Litho. *Perf. 13*

1380 A465 2000s multicolored 4.00 2.40
1381 A465 2600s multicolored 4.50 2.40

1995, Dec.

Indigenous Birds: #1382, Aglaiocercus kingi.

#1383: a, Coeligena torquata. b, Phaethornis superciliosus. c, Ocreatus underwoodii. d, Oreotrochilus chimborazo. e, Aglaiocercus coelestis.

1382 A466 1000s multicolored 1.75 .85
1383 A466 1000s Strip of 5, #a.-e. 9.25 6.25

Ecuadoran Air Force, 75th Anniv. A467

1995, Dec.

1384 A467 1000s multicolored 1.75 .95

Year of Folk Music — A468

2000s, Julio Jaramillo (1935-78), musician, composer. 3000s, Jaramillo, wall.

1996, Jan. 16 Litho. *Perf. 13*

1385 A468 2000s multicolored 3.50 1.75

Imperf

1386 A468 3000s multicolored 4.50 4.00

Advancement of Ecuador, 4 Year Program A469

Designs show symbols for: 1500s, Mail delivery. 2000s, Customs crossing. 2600s, Telecommunications. 3000p, Ports.

Wmk. 395

1996, July 23 Litho. *Perf. 13*

1387 A469 1000s multicolored 1.60 .70
1388 A469 1500s multicolored 2.40 1.10
1389 A469 2000s multicolored 3.00 1.50
1390 A469 2600s multicolored 4.00 1.75
a. Pair, #1388, #1390 5.25 5.25
b. Pair, #1389, #1390 6.00 6.00
1391 A369 3000s multicolored 5.00 2.75
a. Pair, #1387, #1391 5.50 5.50
b. Pair, #1389, #1391 6.75 6.75
Nos. 1387-1391 (5) 16.00 7.80

Nos. 1387-1391 were issued in strips of 2 each.

Esmeraldas '96, 8th National Games A470

Mascot depicting two sports on each stamp: No. 1392, Tennis, boxing. No. 1393, Basketball, socccer. 600s, Racketball, swimming. 800s, Weight lifting, karate. 1000s, Volleyball, gymnastics. 1200s, Athletics, judo. No. 1398, Chess, wrestling.

No. 1399, Mascot holding flag, emblem, surrounded by flags.

1996, July 30

1392 A470 400s multicolored .50 .20
1393 A470 400s multicolored .50 .20
1394 A470 600s multicolored .80 .40
a. Pair, #1392, #1394 1.25 1.25
1395 A470 800s multicolored 1.10 .55
a. Pair, #1394-1395 1.75 1.75
1396 A470 1000s multicolored 1.50 .65
a. Pair, #1393, #1396 1.90 1.90
b. Pair, #1395-1396 2.40 2.40

1397 A470 1200s multicolored 1.60 .85
1398 A470 2000s multicolored 3.00 1.25
Nos. 1392-1398 (7) 9.00 4.10

Size: 120x100mm

1399 A470 2000s multicolored 3.00 3.00

Nos. 1392-1396 were printed in strips of 2 each.

Civil Aviation, 50th Anniv. A471

1996, Aug. 8
1400 A471 2000s multicolored 2.50 1.10

1996 Summer Olympic Games, Atlanta A472

Atlanta Games emblem and: 1000s, Mascot carrying torch. No. 1402, Emblem of Olympic Committee of Ecuador. 3000s, Jefferson Perez, vert.

No. 1404, Perez, gold medalist, 20-kilometer walk, walking.

1996
1401 A472 1000s multicolored 1.25 .55
1402 A472 2000s multicolored 3.00 1.75
a. Pair, #1401-1402 3.50 3.50
1403 A472 3000s multicolored 4.25 2.25
Nos. 1401-1403 (3) 8.50 4.55

Size: 100x120mm

Imperf

1404 A472 2000s multicolored 3.00 3.00

Fight Against Drug Abuse — A473

Dr. Eduardo Salazar Gomez, Birth Cent. — A474

1996 **Litho.** **Wmk. 395** ***Perf. 13***
1408 A473 2000s multicolored 3.75 2.00

1996
1409 A474 1000s multicolored 2.00 1.00

Catholic University, Quito, 50th Anniv. A475

Junior League Organization A476

Designs: 400s, Outside view of building, horiz. 800s, Entrance.

1996
1410 A475 400s multicolored .80 .45
1411 A475 800s multicolored 1.60 .85

1996
1412 A476 2000s Children's faces, horiz. 4.00 2.50
1413 A476 2600s shown 5.00 3.00

Catholic University, Quito, 50th Anniv. A477

1996, Nov.
1414 A477 2000s multicolored 3.75 2.00

The Universe Daily Newspaper, 75th Anniv. — A478

1996, Dec.
1415 A478 2000s multicolored 3.75 2.00

Private Technical University, Loja — A479

1996, Dec. 9
1416 A479 4700s multicolored 9.00 4.50

UNICEF, 50th Anniv. A480

1996, Dec. 11
1417 A480 2000s multicolored 3.75 2.00

Christmas A481

Children's paintings: 600s, Merry Chrismas All Over the World. 800s, World of Peace and Love. 2000s, Christmas.

1996, Dec. 19
1418 A481 600s multicolored 1.25 .75
1419 A481 800s multicolored 1.50 .90

Size: 51x31mm

Perf. 13½

1420 A481 2000s multicolored 3.50 1.90
Nos. 1418-1420 (3) 6.25 3.55

Preserving the Ecological System A482

America '95: 1000s, Voltur grypus. 1500s, Harpia harpyja, vert.

1996, Dec. 30 ***Perf. 13***
1421 A482 1000s multicolored 2.00 1.25
1422 A482 1500s multicolored 3.00 1.75

Typical Children's Costumes — A483

America '96: No. 1423, "Bordando" girl, Zuleta. No. 1424, Girl from Otavalo.

1996, Dec. 30
1423 A483 2600s multicolored 4.50 1.50
1424 A483 2600s multicolored 4.50 4.00
a. Pair, #1423-1424 11.00 11.00

Mejia Natl. Institute, Cent. A484

Design: Jose Mejia Lequerica, building.

1997, Jan. 10
1425 A484 1000s multicolored 2.00 1.00

Army Polytechnical School, 75th Anniv. A485

Wmk. 395

1997, June 16 **Typo.** ***Perf. 13***
1426 A485 400s multicolored .90 .50

Natl. Experimental College, Ambato, 50th Anniv. A486

1997, June 20
1427 A486 600s multicolored 1.10 .70

Vicente Rocafuerte (1783-1847), First Constitutional President of Ecuador — A487

1997, July 1
1428 A487 400s multicolored .90 .50

49th Intl. Congress of the Americanists A488

1997, July 3
1429 A488 2000s multicolored 3.75 1.90

Butterflies A489

Designs: 400s, Actinote equatoria. 600s, Dismorphia amphione. 800s, Marpesia corinna. 2000s, Marpesia berania. 2600s, Morpho helenor.

1997, July 21
1430 A489 400s multicolored .70 .30
1431 A489 600s multicolored .95 .35
1432 A489 800s multicolored 1.60 .65
1433 A489 2000s multicolored 3.75 1.60
1434 A489 2600s multicolored 5.50 2.00
Nos. 1430-1434 (5) 12.50 4.90

Air Club of Ecuador, 66th Anniv. A490

1997, July 23
1435 A490 2600s multicolored 5.25 2.10

Orchids — A491

400s, Epidendrum secundum. 600s, Epidendrum. 800s, Oncidium cultratrum. 2000s, Oncidium sp mariposa. 2600s, Pleurothalis corrulensis.

1997, Aug. 14 **Litho.** ***Perf. 13***
1436 A491 400s multicolored .70 .30
1437 A491 600s multicolored .95 .40
1438 A491 800s multicolored 1.60 .65
1439 A491 2000s multicolored 3.75 1.60
1440 A491 2600s multicolored 5.50 2.00
Nos. 1436-1440 (5) 12.50 4.95

Rocks and Minerals — A492

1997, Oct. 6 **Litho.** ***Perf. 13***
1441 A492 400s Quartz .70 .30
1442 A492 600s Chalcopyrite .95 .40
1443 A492 800s Gold 1.60 .65
1444 A492 2000s Petrified wood 3.75 1.60
1445 A492 2600s Pyrite 5.50 2.00
Nos. 1441-1445 (5) 12.50 4.95

A493

A494

Christmas (Children's designs): 400s, Santa as postman delivering letters over world. 2600s, Star on Christmas tree reaching for letters, airplane under tree. 3000s, Child dreaming of angels carrying letters.

1997, Dec. 22 **Litho.** ***Perf. 13***
1446 A493 400s multicolored .70 .30
1447 A493 2600s multicolored 5.25 2.00
1448 A493 3000s multicolored 6.50 2.50
Nos. 1446-1448 (3) 12.45 4.80

1997, Dec. 29
1449 A494 800s Life of a Postman 1.40 .70
1450 A494 2000s On bicycle 4.00 1.60

America issue.

A495

A496

City Gates, Loja — A579

2001 ***Perf. 13¼x13***
1584 A579 32c multi 2.10 .95

Quito Municipal District Directorate of Security A580

2001, Nov. 26
1585 A580 68c multi 4.00 2.00

Salvador Bustamante Celi (1876-1935), Musician A581

2001
1586 A581 68c multi 4.50 2.25

Marcel Laniado de Wind (1927-98), First Pres. of Natl. Modernization Council — A582

2001, Aug. 6 ***Perf. 13x13¼***
1587 A582 70c multi 4.50 2.25

Bernardino Cardinal Echeverria (1912-2000) A583

2001, Nov. 14
1588 A583 84c multi 5.50 2.50

José Joaquin Olmedo (1780-1847), Statesman and Poet — A584

2001, Nov. 8
1589 A584 84c multi 5.50 2.50

El Angel Ecological Reserve — A585

No. 1590: a, Paja de Paramo. b, Frailejón. Illustration reduced.

2001 ***Perf. 13¼x13***
1590 A585 16c Horiz. pair, #a-b 2.20 1.00

Yahuarcocha Race Track — A586

No. 1591: a, Race track and lake. b, Lake. Illustration reduced.

2001, Nov. 30
1591 A586 68c Horiz. pair, #a-b 8.00 4.00

World Food Day — A587

No. 1592: a, Wheat ears. b, Food baskets. Illustration reduced.

2001, Nov. 5
1592 A587 84c Horiz. pair, #a-b 11.00 5.50

Art of Voroshilov Bazante A588

No. 1593: a, Spatial composition. b, Abstract, artists name at LR. c, Urban landscape. d, Abstract, diff., "Abstracto" at UL, denomination at LL. e, Abstract, denomination at LR.

2001, Nov.
1593 Horiz. strip of 5 27.50 12.50
a.-e. A588 84c Any single 5.00 2.50

Wilson Popenoe Private Foundation A589

2001, Nov. 19 **Litho.** ***Perf. 13¼x13***
1594 A589 16c multi 1.10 .55

FAO Food Program A590

2001, Aug. 15
1595 A590 84c multi 5.50 2.50

Rotary District 4400, 75th Anniv. — A591

2001, Nov. 30 ***Perf. 13x13¼***
1596 A591 84c multi 5.50 2.50

Pres. Camilo Ponce Enriquez (1912-76) A592

Pedro Vicente Maldonado (1702-48), Geographer A593

2001
1597 A592 84c multi 5.50 2.50

2001, Dec. 12
1598 A593 84c multi 5.50 2.50

Otonga Foundation — A595

No. 1599: a, Frog on branch. b, Mustela frenata.

2001, Oct. 31
1599 A595 16c Horiz. pair, #a-b 2.20 1.10

Tourism in Zaruma — A596

No. 1600: a, Virgen del Carmen. b, Orchid. Illustration reduced.

2001, Dec. 12 ***Perf. 13¼x13***
1600 A596 68c Horiz. pair, #a-b 8.00 4.00

Radio HCJB, 70th Anniv. — A597

No. 1601: a, Microphone. b, Announcer. Illustration reduced.

2001, Dec. 21
1601 A597 68c Horiz. pair, #a-b 8.00 4.00

Tennis A598

No. 1602: a, Davis Cup. b, K. Lapentti, G. Lapentti, L.A. Morejón, A. Intriago and R. Viver. c, Francisco Guzman and Miguel Olvera. d, Pancho Segura. e, Andres Gomez.

2001, Nov. 1
1602 Horiz. strip of 5 21.00 10.50
a.-e. A598 68c Any single 4.00 2.00

Church Paintings of Wilfrido Martínez — A599

No. 1603: a, San Francisco (artist's name is vert.). b, Guapulo. c, San Francisco (artist's name is horiz.). d, La Compania. e, El Rosario.

2002, Apr. 9 ***Perf. 13¾***
1603 Horiz. strip of 5 24.00 12.00
a.-e. A599 90c Any single 4.50 2.25

First Judicial Summit of the Americas, Quito A600

Perf. 13¼x13
2002, Jan. 8 **Litho.** **Wmk. 395**
1604 A600 68c multi 4.00 2.00

Union Club, Guayaquil — A601

2002, Apr. 25 ***Perf. 13x13¼***
1605 A601 90c multi 5.50 2.75

South American Soccer Confederation A602

Designs: 25c, Confederation Pres. Nicolás Leoz. 40c, Confederation emblem, soccer players. 70c, Emblem of Emelec team.

2002, Jan. 29
1606-1608 A602 Set of 3 8.00 4.00

World Conservation Union — A603

Designs: 70c, Fish, man's head. 85c, Leopard, man, horiz.
$1, Bird, animals, women and children, horiz.

2002, Feb. 21 ***Perf. 13x13¼, 13¼x13***
1609-1610 A603 Set of 2 9.00 4.50

Imperf

Size: 100x70mm

1611 A603 $1 multi 6.25 3.00

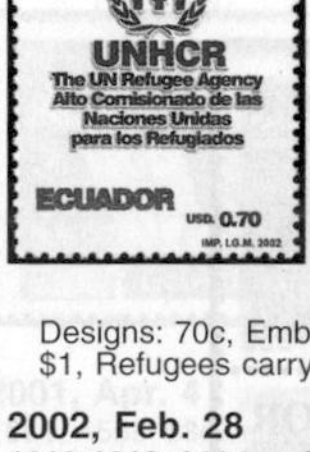

UN High Commissioner for Refugees — A604

Designs: 70c, Emblem. 85c, Child.
$1, Refugees carrying belongings, horiz.

2002, Feb. 28 ***Perf. 13x13¼***
1612-1613 A604 Set of 2 9.00 4.50

Imperf

Size: 100x70mm

1614 A604 $1 multi 6.25 3.00

Ecuadorian Educational Credit and Scholarship Institute — A605

No. 1615: a, Student using microscope. b, Emblem.

2002, Apr. 30 *Perf. 13x13¼*
1615 A605 25c Horiz. pair, #a-b 2.50 1.25

Cuenca Soccer Team — A606

No. 1616: a, Team photo. b, Emblem, player dribbling.
Illustration reduced.

2002, Apr. 19 *Perf. 13¼x13*
1616 A606 25c Horiz. pair, #a-b 2.50 1.25

Imbabura Province History — A607

No. 1617: a, Building. b, Statue.

2002, Mar. 27 *Perf. 13x13¼*
1617 A607 40c Horiz. pair, #a-b 5.00 2.40

Crucita — A608

No. 1618: a, Parachutist with sun on horizon. b, Prachutist above beach.
Illustration reduced.

2002, Mar. 28 *Perf. 13¼x13*
1618 A608 40c Horiz. pair, #a-b 5.00 2.40

Mountains A609

No. 1619: a, Mt. Altar (trees in foreground). b, Mt. Chimborazo. c, Mt. Carihuayrazo. d, Mt. Altar (lake in foreground). e, Mt. Cubillin.

2002, Apr. 19
1619 Horiz. strip of 5 29.00 15.00
a.-e. A609 90c Any single 5.00 2.25

Endangered Frogs A610

No. 1620: a, Atelopus bomolochos. b, Atelopus longirostris. c, Atelopus pachydermus. d, Atelopus arthuri. e, Atelopus sp.
$1, Atelopus ignescens.

2002, Mar. 25 *Perf. 13¼x13*
1620 Horiz. strip of 5 29.00 15.00
a.-e. A610 $1.05 Any single 5.00 2.25

Imperf

Size: 100x70mm

1621 A610 $1 multi 8.50 7.00

National Anti-narcotics Police — A611

No. 1622: a, Policeman and dog. b, Emblem.

Perf. 13x13¼

2002, Apr. 23 **Litho.** **Wmk. 395**
1622 A611 40c Horiz. pair, #a-b 5.00 2.50

2002 World Cup Soccer Championships, Japan and Korea — A612

Designs: 90c, Ecuadorian Soccer Federation emblem, vert. $1.05, $2, Emblem, team photo, players in action.

2002, Apr. 28 *Perf. 13x13¼, 13¼x13*
1623-1624 A612 Set of 2 7.25 3.50

Imperf

Size: 100x70mm

1625 A612 $2 multi 7.25 3.50

Dr. Servio Aguirre Villamagua, Forest Conservationist — A613

No. 1626: a, Aguirre. b, Plant.
Illustration reduced.

2002, May 22 *Perf. 13¼x13*
1626 A613 40c Horiz. pair, #a-b 3.00 1.50

Food and Agriculture Organization in Ecuador, 50th Anniv. A614

2002, May 30
1627 A614 $1.05 multi 4.00 2.00

Galapagos Islands Fauna A615

No. 1628: a, Grapsus grapsus. b, Conolophus subcristatus.
No. 1629, vert.: a, Sula sula websteri. b, Phoenicopterus ruber.
No. 1630, Amblyrhynchus cristatus.
No. 1631, vert.: a, Pair of Zalophus californianus wollebacki. b, One Zalophus californianus wollebacki.
No. 1632, Sula nebouxxi excisa, vert.
No. 1633, vert.: a, Sula dactylatra granti. b, Emblem of Iberoamerican Summit on Tourism and Environment.
$2, Bird, tourists, tourist ship.

2002, May 31 *Perf. 13¼x13, 13x13¼*
1628 A615 25c Horiz. pair, #a-b 2.50 1.50
1629 A615 40c Horiz. pair, #a-b 3.50 2.00
1630 A615 90c multi 4.25 3.00
1631 A615 90c Horiz. pair, #a-b 8.50 4.50
1632 A615 $1.05 multi 5.00 2.50
1633 A615 $1.05 Horiz. pair, #a-b 9.50 5.00
Nos. 1628-1633 (6) 33.25 18.50

Imperf

Size: 100x68mm

1634 A615 $2 multi 9.00 7.00

Ministry of Foreign Relations — A616

2002, June 5 *Perf. 13x13¼*
1635 A616 90c multi 3.50 1.60

Army Polytechnic School, 80th Anniv. A617

2002, June 13 *Perf. 13¼x13*
1636 A617 25c multi 1.25 .60

Military Engineers, Cent. A618

Designs: No. 1637, 40c, Castle of Engineering. No. 1638, 40c, Castle of Engineering, Military engineers in action, vert.
$2, Castle of Engineering, engineers in action, emblems of military groups.

Perf. 13¼x13, 13x13¼

2002, June 19
1637-1638 A618 Set of 2 3.20 1.60

Imperf

Size: 100x68mm

1639 A618 $2 multi 7.25 3.50

Dr. Alfredo Pérez Guerrero (1901-66), Academic — A619

2002, July 4 *Perf. 13x13¼*
1640 A619 25c multi 1.25 .60

20th Anniv. of Ecuador's Second Place Finish In World Taekwondo Championships — A620

2002, July 18 *Perf. 13¼x13*
1641 A620 40c multi 1.60 .80

Orellana Province — A621

No. 1642: a, Three native men. b, Man in tree.
Illustration reduced.

2002, July 30 **Wmk. 395**
1642 A621 25c Horiz. pair, #a-b 2.50 1.25

CARE in Ecuador, 40th Anniv. — A622

No. 1643: a, Two children. b, Boy.

2002, July 30 *Perf. 13x13¼*
1643 A622 90c Horiz. pair, #a-b 7.25 3.50

Macará Region A623

2002, Aug. 10 *Perf. 13¼x13*
1644 A623 40c multi 1.60 .80

Intl. Organization for Migration, 50th Anniv. — A624

Quito Philharmonic Society, 50th Anniv. — A625

2002, Aug. 18 *Perf. 13x13¼*
1645 A624 $1.05 multi 4.00 2.00

2002, Aug. 29
1646 A625 25c multi 1.25 .60

Comptroller General, 75th Anniv. — A625a

Perf. 13x13¼

2002, Sept. 26 **Litho.** **Wmk. 395**
1646A A625a 40c multi 1.60 .80

Second World Meeting of Mountain People — A626

No. 1647 — Emblem of World Meeting and: a, Mountain. b, Group of people. c, Houses in valley. d, Town. e, Other emblems.

2002, Sept. 18

1647 Horiz. strip of 5 18.00 9.00
a.-e. A626 90c Any single 3.50 1.60

Pujili Dancer — A627

Perf. 13x13¼

2002, Oct. 14 Litho. Wmk. 395

1648 A627 $1.05 multi 4.00 2.00

Paintings of Milton Estrella Gavidia — A628

No. 1649 — Various paintings with background colors of: a, Blue violet. b, Brown violet. c, Olive green. d, Blue. e, Gray lilac.

Wmk. 395

2002, May 17 Litho. ***Perf. 13¾***

1649 Horiz. strip of 5 18.00 9.00
a.-e. A628 90c Any single 3.50 1.60

Paintings of Leonardo Hidalgo A629

No. 1650: a, La Dolorosa. b, El Hombre Cargando su Fruto. c, Frida Kahlo. d, El Hombre Fuerte del Mar. e, Jesus.

Wmk. 395

2002, Oct. 3 Litho. ***Perf. 13¾***

1650 Horiz. strip of 5 18.00 9.00
a.-e. A629 90c Any single 3.50 1.60

Pan-American Health Organization, Cent. — A630

2002, Dec. 2 ***Perf. 13¼x12¾***

1651 A630 $1.05 multi 4.00 2.00

Lo Nuestro Art Exhibition — A631

No. 1652: a, Wall with six works of art. b, Walls with 16 works of art.
Illustration reduced.

2002, Dec. 15

1652 A631 25c Horiz. pair, #a-b 2.00 1.00

Catholic University, 40th Anniv. A632

2002, Dec. 18

1653 A632 40c multi 1.60 .80

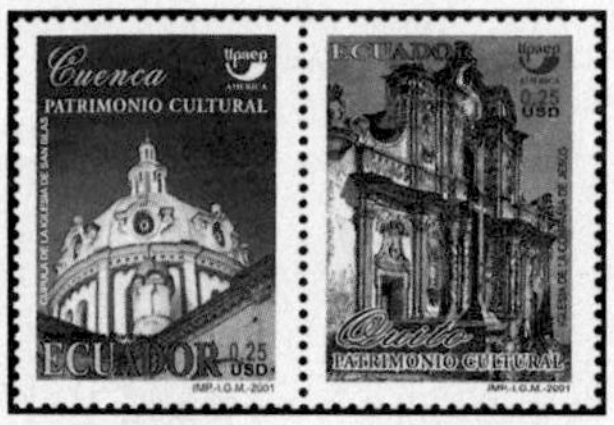

America Issue — UNESCO World Heritage Sites — A633

No. 1654: a, Cupola of San Blas Church, Cuenca. b, Society of Jesus Church, Quito.

2002, Dec. 18 ***Perf. 12¾x13¼***

1654 A633 25c Horiz. pair, #a-b 2.50 1.25

Dated 2001.

America Issue — Youth, Education and Literacy — A634

No. 1655: a, Students and blackboard. b, Toddler and books.
Illustration reduced.

2002, Dec. 18 ***Perf. 13¼x12¾***

1655 A634 25c Horiz. pair, #a-b 2.50 1.25

Second Meeting of South American Presidents, Guayaquil — A635

No. 1656: a, Meeting emblem. b, Emblem, presidents and flags.
Illustration reduced.

2003, Jan. 13

1656 A635 $1.05 Horiz. pair, #a-b 7.25 3.50

Papal Benediction for Ecuadorian Emigrants — A636

2003, Jan. 24 ***Perf. 12¾x13¼***

1657 A636 $1.05 multi 3.60 1.75

Size: 68x100mm

Imperf

1658 A636 $2 multi 7.25 3.50

World Vison — A637

2003, Feb. 6 ***Perf. 12¾x13¼***

1659 A637 40c multi 1.40 .70

Intl. Women's Day — A638

2003, Mar. 8 Wmk. 395

1660 A638 $1.05 multi 3.60 1.75

Agustin Cueva Vallejo (1820-73), Physician — A639

2003, Mar. 13 Litho.

1661 A639 40c multi 1.40 .70

Blasco Moscoso Cuesta, Founder of Pichincha Sports Writers Association — A640

2003, Mar. 14

1662 A640 25c multi .90 .45

Cuenca Artisan Products A641

No. 1663: a, Azuay University domes. b, Tinware. c, Jewelry. d, Fireworks. e, Saddles.
No. 1664: a, Engraving. b, Metallurgy. c, Baskets. d, Embroidery. e, Ceramics.
$2, Assorted products.

2003, Mar. 27 ***Perf. 13¼x12¾***

1663 Horiz. strip of 5 4.50 2.10
a.-e. A641 25c Any single .80 .40
1664 Horiz. strip of 5 18.00 8.75
a.-e. A641 $1.05 Any single 3.25 1.50

Size: 100x68mm

Imperf

1665 A641 $2 multi 7.25 3.50

Flora and Fauna A642

No. 1666: a, Curculionidae. b, Lycidae. c, Acridoidea. d, Aracnidae. e, Liliacea.

2003, Apr. 4 ***Perf. 13¼x12¾***

1666 Horiz. strip of 5 18.00 8.75
a.-e. A642 $1.05 Any single 3.50 1.60

Military Geographic Institute, 75th Anniv. A643

Designs: No. 1667, 40c, No. 1669, $2, Painting by Eduardo Kingman. No. 1668, 40c, Institute emblem, vert.

Perf. 13¼x12¾, 12¾x13¼

2003, Apr. 11

1667-1668 A643 Set of 2 2.90 1.40

Size: 100x68mm

Imperf

1669 A643 $2 multi 7.25 3.50

Galápagos Marine Reserve — A644

Designs: 40c, Stylized butterfly.
No. 1671, $1.05, horiz.: a, Sphyrna lewini. b, Chelonia mydas agassisi.
No. 1672, $1.05, horiz.: a, Xanthichthys mento. b, Zanclus cornutus.
$2, Tubastrea coccinea, horiz.

Perf. 12¾x13¼, 13¼x12¾

2003, May 9

1670 A644 40c multi 1.40 .70

Horiz. Pairs, #a-b

1671-1672 A644 Set of 2 14.50 7.25

Size: 100x68mm

Imperf

1673 A644 $2 multi 7.25 3.50

Intl. Tourism Trade Fair of Ecuador A645

No. 1674: a, Monkey in tree. b, Birds. c, Embroidery. d, Mountain. e, Hat seller on beach.

2003, May 14 ***Perf. 13¼x12¾***

1674 Vert. strip of 5 4.50 2.25
a.-e. A645 25c Any single .80 .40

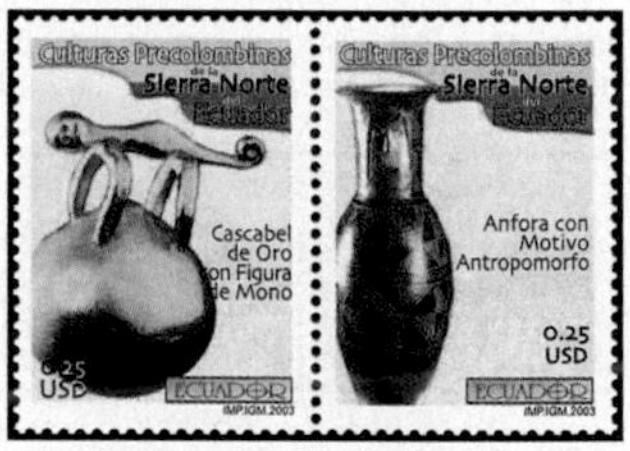

Artifacts of Pre-Columbian Cultures — A646

No. 1675, 25c: a, Gold bell with monkey. b, Amphora.
No. 1676, 25c: a, Sculpture of a man. b, Three-footed pot.

Perf. 13x13¼

2003, May 16 Litho. Wmk. 395

Horiz. pairs, #a-b

1675-1676 A646 Set of 2 3.50 1.75

Central Bank of Ecuador A647

No. 1677, vert.: a, Tolita Culture mask. b, Guayaquil Historic Park.
$1.05, Pumapungo Museum.

Perf. 13x13¼, 13¼x13

2003, June 5 Litho.

1677 A647 25c Horiz. pair, #a-b 1.00 .50
1678 A647 $1.05 multi 2.10 1.10

Philately and Guayaquil A648

No. 1679, horiz.: a, British consular cover to Veracruz with British stamp and cancel. b, Stampless cover.

No. 1680, horiz.: a, SCADTA first flight cover. b, French consular cover to Lima with French stamps and cancels.

$1.05, Philatelic magazines.

$2, Guayaquil Philatelic Club emblem, Ecuadoran stamps, horiz.

2003, July 22 *Perf. 13¾*

1679 A648	40c Vert. pair, #a-b	2.75	1.40
1680 A648	40c Vert. pair, #a-b	2.75	1.40
1681 A648	$1.05 multi	3.50	1.75
	Nos. 1679-1681 (3)	9.00	4.55

Size: 100x69mm

Imperf

1682 A648	$2 multi	4.00	2.00

Guayaquil Urban Renewal A649

No. 1683: a, Punta Cerro Santa Ana. b, Plaza Colón. c, Malecón Gardens. d, Crystal Palace. e, Plaza de San Francisco.

2003, July 26 *Perf. 13¼x13*

1683	Horiz. strip of 5	15.00	7.25
a.-e.	A649 90c Any single	2.75	1.40

World Bird Festival A650

Designs: No. 1684, $1.05, Geranoaetus melanoleucus. No. 1685, $1.05, Harpia harpyja, vert.

2003, Sept. 2 *Perf. 13¼x13, 13x13¼*

1684-1685 A650	Set of 2	7.25	3.50

Zamora-Chinchipe Province, 50th Anniv. — A651

No. 1686: a, Shown. b, Eira barbara. c, Boa constrictor. d, Tapirus terrestris. e, Psophia crepitans.

2003, Nov. 7 *Perf. 13¼x13*

1686	Vert. strip of 5	4.50	2.25
a.-e.	A651 25c Any single	.80	.40

America Issue — Flora and Fauna — A652

No. 1687: a, Semnornis ramphastinus. b, Bomarea glaucescens.

Perf. 13x13¼

2003, Nov. 1 **Litho.** **Wmk. 395**

1687 A652	$1.05 Horiz. pair, #a-b	6.25	3.00

Selection of Quito as World Heritage Site, 25th Anniv. A653

Churches: 40c, El Sagrario. No. 1689a, La Compañía de Jesus. No. 1689b, Santa Barbara. $1.05, San Francisco, vert.

2003, Nov. 1 *Perf. 13¼x13, 13x13¼*

1688 A653	40c multi	1.00	.50
1689 A653	90c Horiz. pair, #a-b	5.00	2.50
1690 A653	$1.05 multi	3.00	1.40
	Nos. 1688-1690 (3)	9.00	4.40

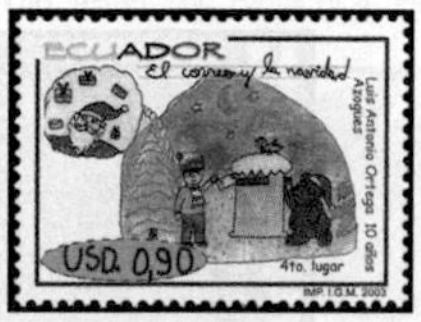

Christmas A654

Children's art by: No. 1691a, Stephanie Pacheco. No. 1691b, Sebastián Tejada. 40c, María Claudia Iturralde, vert. 90c, Luis Antonio Ortega. $1.05, Angel Andrés Castro, vert.

2003, Nov. 1

1691 A654	25c Horiz. pair, #a-b	1.50	.70
1692 A654	40c multi	1.25	.55
1693 A654	90c multi	2.75	1.25
1694 A654	$1.05 multi	3.00	1.50
	Nos. 1691-1694 (4)	8.50	4.00

Treasures of Guayaquil Municipal Museum A655

No. 1695: a, Santiago de Guayaquil Act of Independence. b, Punaes ceremonial stone. c, Proclamation of Mariano Donoso. d, Tzantzas. e, Manteño-Huancavilca totem.

2003, Dec. 1 *Perf. 13¼x13*

1695	Horiz. strip of 5	5.75	2.75
a.-e.	A655 40c Any single	1.10	.55

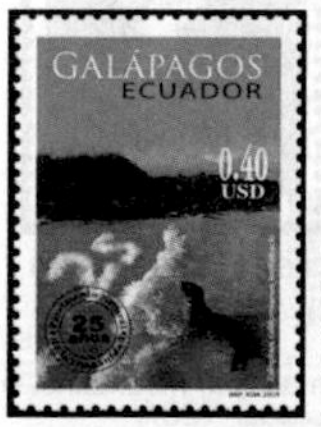

Selection of Galapagos Islands as World Heritage Site, 25th Anniv. — A656

No. 1696: a, Zalophus californianus wollebacki. b, Fregata minor palmerstoni. c, Sula nebouxxi excisa. d, Isla Bartolomé. e, Two Sula nebouxxi excisa shaped as "25."

2003, Nov. 26 *Perf. 13x13¼*

1696	Horiz. strip of 5	5.75	2.75
a.-e.	A656 40c Any single	1.10	.55

Army Aviation Instruction, 50th Anniv. — A657

No. 1697, 40c: a, Mountain, airplanes, emblem. b, Airplane in flight, men on ground.
No. 1698, 40c, horiz.: a, Helicopter and soldiers. b, Airplanes, mountain, people.

2004, Jan. 21 *Perf. 13x13¼, 13¼x13*

Horiz. pairs, #a-b

1697-1698 A657	Set of 2	4.50	2.25

Military Geographical Institute's Role in National Development — A658

2004, Apr. 14 *Perf. 13¼x13*

1699 A658	$1.05 multi	3.00	1.50

Commander Rafael Morán Valverde, Military Hero — A659

2004, Apr. 5 *Perf. 13x13¼*

1700 A659	$1.05 multi	3.00	1.50

Intl. Philately Day — A660

No. 1701: a, Ecuador #2, Greece #1. b, Cover with six stamps.

$2, Various stamps, tongs, magnifying glass, stamp catalogues.

Illustration reduced.

2004, May 6 *Perf. 13¼x13*

1701 A660	75c Horiz. pair, #a-b	5.00	2.50

Imperf

Size: 100x68mm

1702 A660	$2 multi	6.25	3.00

Ecuadorian Volleyball Federation A661

Perf. 13x13¼

2004, May 27 **Litho.** **Wmk. 395**

1703 A661	75c multi	2.50	1.10

2004 Miss Universe Pageant A662

2004, May 29 *Perf. 13¾*

1704 A662	75c multi	2.50	1.25

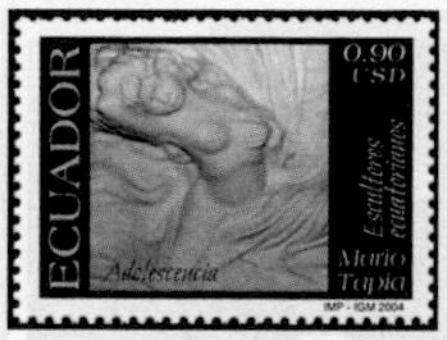

Sculpture by Mario Tapia A663

No. 1705: a, Adolescencia. b, Beato Chaminade. c, Delfin de Galapagos. d, Pelicano. e, Homenaje a Carlo Vidano.

$2, Similar to No. 1705b.

2004, June 1 *Perf. 13¼x13*

1705	Horiz. strip of 5	13.50	6.75
a.-e.	A663 90c Any single	1.80	.90

Imperf

Size: 100x69mm

1706 A663	$2 multi	7.25	3.75

Pedro Vicente Maldonado (1704-48), Cartographer A664

2004, June 25 *Perf. 13x13¼*

1707 A664	90c multi	2.50	1.25

Dr. Agustín Cueva Tamariz (1903-79) — A665

2004, June 30 **Litho.**

1708 A665	90c multi	2.50	1.25

34th General Assembly of the Organization of American States — A666

2004, July 4 **Wmk. 395**

1709 A666	75c multi	2.50	1.25

Dr. Angel Felicísmo Rojas (b. 1909), Writer — A667

2004, July 11

1710 A667	50c multi	1.60	.80

Ecuadoran and Spanish Postal Money Orders A668

2004, Aug. 3 *Perf. 13¼x13*

1711 A668	$1.05 multi	3.00	1.50

Straw Hat Makers A708

Designs: No. 1776, 40c, Hat maker. No. 1777, 40c, Hat maker wearing hat, vert.

2006, Apr. 8 ***Perf. 13¼x13, 13x13¼***
1776-1777 A708 Set of 2 1.60 .80

Federation of University Students — A709

2006, Apr. 21 ***Perf. 13x13¼***
1778 A709 30c multi .60 .30

Miracle of Colegio San Gabriel, Cent. — A710

2006, Apr. 21 **Wmk. 395**
1779 A710 80c multi 1.60 .80

Ibarra, 400th Anniv. A711

2006, Apr. 28 ***Perf. 13¼x13***
1780 A711 20c shown .40 .20

Size: 68x100mm

Imperf

1781 A711 $2.50 Painting, diff. 5.00 2.50

Baltazara Calderon — A712

2005, May 16 ***Perf. 13x13¼***
1782 A712 $1 multi 2.00 1.00

18th Cent. Military Uniforms A713

No. 1783: a, Compañia Fija de Quito. b, Dragones de Quito. c, Infanteria de Quito. d, Dragones de Guayaquil (gray horse). e, Dragones de Guayaquil (brown horse).

2006, May 18 ***Perf. 13¾***
1783 Horiz. strip of 5 2.00 1.00
a.-e. A713 20c Any single .40 .20

Mushrooms and Fauna of Podocarpus Park — A714

Designs: 20c, Basidiomicetes. 25c, Tremarctus ornatus. 90c, Harpya harpyja, vert.

Perf. 13¼x13, 13x13¼

2006, May 22 **Litho.** **Wmk. 395**
1784-1786 A714 Set of 3 2.75 1.40

Wolfgang Amadeus Mozart (1756-91), Composer A715

2006, May 31 ***Perf. 13¼x13***
1787 A715 20c multi .40 .20

UNICEF, 60th Anniv. A716

Designs: 75c, Child, butterfly, and sun. $1, Children and books.

Perf. 13¼x13

2006, June 1 **Litho.** **Wmk. 395**
1788-1789 A716 Set of 2 3.50 1.75

Eloy Alfaro Military School A717

2006, June 5
1790 A717 80c multi 1.60 .80

Banco Pichincha, Cent. A718

Designs: No. 1791, 1906 1-sucre banknote. No. 1792 — First bank building: a, Denomination at left. b, Denomination at right.

2006, June 8
1791 A718 40c shown .80 .40
1792 A718 40c Horiz. pair, #a-b 1.60 .80

2006 World Cup Soccer Championships, Germany — A719

FIFA emblem and: 40c, World Cup. 80c, 2006 World Cup emblem. $1, Mascot. $1.20, World Cup and flags of competing countries.

Perf. 13¼x13

2006, June 9 **Litho.** **Wmk. 395**
1793-1796 A719 Set of 4 7.00 3.50

Designs: No. 1797C, Like #1796. No. 1797D, Similar to #1796, but with scores of Ecuador team's first round victories.

2006 **Litho.** **Wmk. 395** ***Imperf.***

Size: 60x40mm

1797C A719 $2 multi 4.00 2.00
1797D A719 $2 multi 4.00 2.00

A720

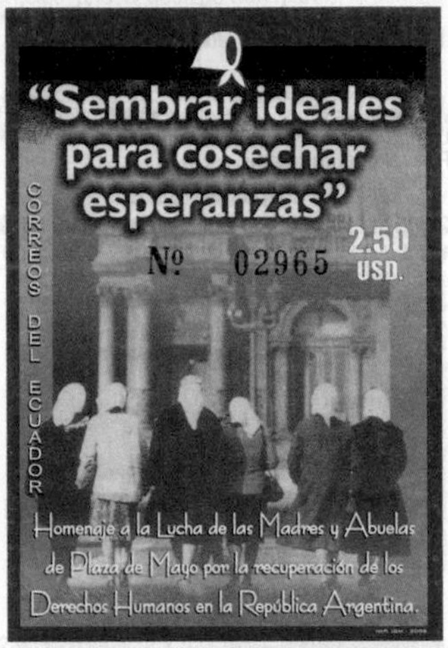

Plaza de Mayo Mothers of Argentina — A721

Illustration A721 reduced.

Perf. 13¼x13

2006, June 19 **Litho.** **Wmk. 395**
1798 A720 80c multi 1.60 .80

Imperf

1799 A721 $2.50 multi 5.00 2.50

Machala Canton, 182nd Anniv. A722

2006, June 20 ***Perf. 13¼x13***
1800 A722 30c multi .60 .30

Machala Canton, 182nd Anniv. — A723

Flags of 2006 World Cup Soccer Championship participants, FIFA emblem and: No. 1801, Flag of Ecuador. No. 1802, Soccer shoes and ball.

2006 **Litho.** **Wmk. 395** ***Imperf.***
1801 A723 $2 multi 4.00 2.00
1802 A723 $2 multi 4.00 2.00

2006 World Cup Soccer Championships, Germany.

Garibaldi Italian Assistance Society — A724

2006, July 7 ***Perf. 13x13¼***
1803 A724 90c multi 1.90 .95

Souvenir Sheet

Municipal Railroads — A726

Wmk. 395

2006, July 20 **Litho.** ***Imperf.***
1806 A726 $2 multi 4.00 2.00

Simón Bolívar Experimental College — A727

Bolívar A728

2006, July 25 **Litho.** ***Perf. 13x13¼***
1807 A727 20c multi .40 .20

Imperf

1808 A728 $10 multi 20.00 10.00

Spondylus Shell Carvings in National Institute of Cultural Heritage A729

Designs: 25c, Necklace.
No. 1810, vert.: a, Figurine of trader. b, Figurine of fishermen in boat.

2006, July 26 ***Perf. 13¼x13, 13x13¼***
1809 A729 25c multi .50 .25
1810 A729 $1 Horiz. pair, #a-b 4.00 4.00

Indian Postal Runner and Ecuador Post Emblem — A730

Background colors: 25c, White. 30c, Dark blue. 40c, Black. 60c, Beige. 80c, Olive green

2006, Aug. 5 *Perf. 13x13¼*
1811-1815 A730 Set of 5 4.75 2.75

Ecuadorian Olympic Committee A731

2006, Aug. 15 **Litho.**
1816 A731 30c multi .60 .30

Writers — A732

Designs: $1, Jorge Icaza (1906-78). $1.20, Pablo Palacio (1906-47).

2006, Sept. 18 **Wmk. 395**
1817-1818 A732 Set of 2 4.50 2.25

Ecuadorian Food — A733

No. 1819: a, Bandera Manabi. b, Viche de Manabi.
Illustration reduced.

2006, Sept. 23 *Perf. 13¼x13*
1819 A733 $1 Horiz. pair, #a-b 4.00 2.00

Orchids — A734

No. 1820: a, Caucaea olivaceum. b, Cyrtochilum macranthum. c, Miltoniopsis vexillaria. d, Odontoglossum harryanum. e, Cyrtochilum pastasae. f, Cyrtochilum loxense. g, Cyrtochilum eduardii. h, Odontoglossum epidendroides. i, Cyrtochilum retusum. j, Cyrtochilum geniculatum.
$2, Cyrtochilum macranthum, diff.

2006, Sept. 29 *Perf. 13x13¼*
1820 Block of 10 6.00 3.00
a.-j. A734 30c Any single .60 .30

Imperf
Size: 66x95mm

1821 A734 $2 multi 4.00 2.00

America Issue, Energy Conservation — A735

Background color: $1, Brown. $1.20, Blue.

2006, Oct. 4 *Perf. 13¼x13*
1822-1823 A735 Set of 2 4.50 2.25

Natural Fiber Art, by Giti Neuman — A736

Designs: No. 1824, En la Ventana.
No. 1825: a, Forma en Movimiento. b, Caminantes.
No. 1826, horiz.: a, Caminando. b, Cabezas Huecas.

2006, Oct. 4 *Perf. 13x13¼, 13¼x13*
1824 A736 30c multi .60 .30
1825 A736 30c Vert. pair, #a-b 1.25 .60
1826 A736 30c Horiz. pair, #a-b 1.25 .60
Nos. 1824-1826 (3) 3.10 1.50

Tourism in Otovalo A737

Designs: 25c, El Lechero tree. 30c, El Jordan Church. 75c, Young girl, vert. $1, Costume for El Coraza Festival, vert.

2006, Oct. 18 *Perf. 13¼x13, 13x13¼*
1827-1830 A737 Set of 4 4.75 2.40

Eruption of Tungurahua Volcano — A738

No. 1831: a, Ash cloud above volcano. b, Lava flowing down volcano.

2006, Oct. 20 *Perf. 13x13¼*
1831 A738 $1 Horiz. pair, #a-b 4.00 2.00

Urban Renewal of Guayaquil A739

No. 1832: a, Municipal Palace, denomination at left. b, Municipal Palace, denomination at right. c, Vulcan forge. d, José Joaquín de Olmedo Airport. e, Bus station.

2006, Oct. 24 *Perf. 13¼x13*
1832 Horiz. strip of 5 10.00 5.00
a.-e. A739 $1 Any single 2.00 1.00

Radio Station HCJB, 75th Anniv. A740

2006, Oct. 26 **Wmk. 395**
1833 A740 $1 multi 2.00 1.00

Millennium Development Objectives of the United Nations — A741

2006, Oct. 27 *Perf. 13¾*
1834 A741 $2 multi 4.00 2.00

Pres. Galo Plaza Lasso (1906-87) — A742

Designs: 40c, Photograph. 80c, Tree.

2006, Oct. 27 *Perf. 13x13¼*
1835-1836 A742 Set of 2 2.40 1.25

German Shepherd Breeding Association A743

2006, Oct. 28 **Litho.** *Perf. 13¼x13*
1837 A743 $1 multi 2.00 1.00

Military Parachuting, 50th Anniv. A744

Designs: 20c, Soldiers. 40c, Soldiers and airplane. 60c, Soldier and troop emblem. 80c, Paratrooper in air.

Perf. 13¼x13, 13x13¼
2006, Oct. 31 **Litho.** **Wmk. 395**
1838-1841 A744 Set of 4 4.00 2.00

Galapagos Islands Fauna — A745

No. 1842, horiz.: a, Sea turtle. b, Sea gull. c, Marine iguana. d, Blue-footed boobies. e, Sea lion.
80c, Flamingo. $1, Crab. $1.20, Fish.

2006, Nov. 1
1842 A745 30c Horiz. strip of 5, #a-e 3.00 1.50
1843 A745 80c multi 1.60 .80
1844 A745 $1 multi 2.00 1.00
1845 A745 $1.20 multi 2.40 1.25
Nos. 1842-1845 (4) 9.00 4.55

Christmas — A746

2006, Nov. 28 *Perf. 13x13¼*
1846 A746 80c multi 1.60 .80

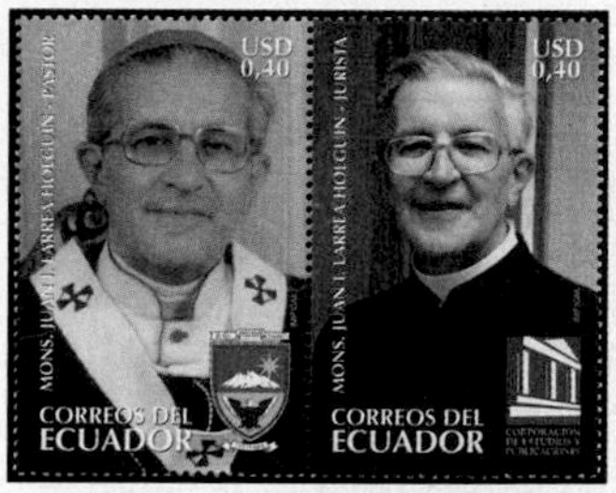

Monsignor Juan I. Larrea Holguín (1927-2006) — A747

No. 1847: a, In bishop's robes. b, In judicial robes.

2006, Dec. 8 *Perf. 13¾*
1847 A747 40c Horiz. pair, #a-b 1.60 .80

Freemasonry A748

Designs: 25c, Masonic altar, beehive. 40c, Compass and square.

2006, Dec. 11 *Perf. 13x13¼*
1848-1849 A748 Set of 2 1.40 .70

Quito Zoo Animals — A749

No. 1850: a, Parrot. b, Frog.
No. 1851: a, Harpy eagle. b, Jaguar.
$2, Parrot on branch.

2006, Dec. 11 *Perf. 13x13¼*
1850 A749 60c Horiz. pair, #a-b 2.40 1.25
1851 A749 80c Horiz. pair, #a-b 3.25 1.60

Imperf
Size: 40x65mm

1852 A749 $2 multi 4.00 2.00

Erotic and Fertility Figurines — A750

Designs: 10c, Nursing mother. 20c, Copulating couple. $1.20, Pregnant woman. $2, Man with erect penis.

2006, Dec. 12 *Perf. 13x13¼*
1853-1856 A750 Set of 4 7.00 3.50

Admiral Juan Illingworth Naval Museum — A751

Emblem of Ecuador Navy and Illingworth: 20c, On rope ladder, 1880. 25c, As Marine Guard, 1854.

2006, Dec. 15 **Litho.**
1857-1858 A751 Set of 2 .90 .45

Colors of Ecuador Flag — A752

2006, Dec. 15 **Wmk. 395**
1859 A752 $10 multi 20.00 10.00

Postmen and Bicycles A753

Color of photograph: 20c, Gray brown. 40c, Gray blue. 80c, Red.

2006, Dec. 17 ***Perf. 13¼x13***
1860-1862 A753 Set of 3 3.00 1.50

Pets A754

Designs: 25c, Puppy. 40c, Dog, vert. 50c, Cat with brown and blue eyes, vert. 80c, Dog running. $1, Cat with blue eyes, vert.

2006, Dec. 17 ***Perf. 13¼x13, 13x13¼***
1863-1867 A754 Set of 5 6.00 3.00

Cuenca Biennale A755

Art by: 5c, Alexander Apóstol. 15c, Ricardo González Elias, vert.

2006, Dec. 20
1868-1869 A755 Set of 2 .40 .20

Independence Monument, 50th Anniv. — A756

No. 1870: a, Head of statue. b, Entire statue.

Illustration reduced.

2006, Dec. 21 ***Perf. 13¾***
1870 A756 20c Horiz. pair, #a-b .80 .40

Quito Fair — A757

Designs: No. 1871, Matador Manolo Caena.
No. 1872 — Matadors: a, Sebastián Castella. b, El Juli.
No. 1873, horiz. — Quito Bull Ring: a, At right. b, At left.
$3, Sculpture of Jesus, horiz.

Perf. 13x13¼, 13¼x13

2006, Dec. 27 **Litho.**
1871 A757 50c multi 1.00 .50
1872 A757 50c Horiz. pair, #a-b 2.00 1.00
1873 A757 50c Horiz. pair, #a-b 2.00 1.00
Nos. 1871-1873 (3) 5.00 2.50

Litho. With Foil Application

Imperf

Size: 65x40mm

1874 A757 $3 multi 6.00 3.00

Pirates A758

No. 1875, vert.: a, Jolly Roger flag, ship, sea lions. b, Sea lions, ships. c, Ships, Jolly roger flag. d, Armed pirate on ship. e, Ship, Jolly Roger flag.
No. 1876: a, Map of Galapagos Islands, Jolly Roger flag, Sir Francis Drake. b, Ship, map, skull.
$1, Ship, map, skull, William Dampier.

Perf. 13x13¼, 13¼x13

2006, Dec. 27 **Litho.**
1875 A758 30c Horiz. strip of 5, #a-e 3.00 1.50
1876 A758 40c Horiz. pair, #a-b 1.60 .80
1877 A758 $1 multi 2.00 1.00
Nos. 1875-1877 (3) 6.60 3.30

SEK International University, Quito A759

Perf. 13¼x13

2006, Dec. 29 **Wmk. 395**
1878 A759 10c multi .20 .20

Scouting, Cent. — A760

Scout emblem and: 25c, Circles. $2, Scout and circles.

Perf. 13x13¼

2007, Mar. 29 **Litho.** **Wmk. 395**
1879-1880 A760 Set of 2 4.50 2.25

Hispanic-American Poetry Festival — A761

2007, Apr. 19
1881 A761 10c multi .20 .20

Cuenca, 450th Anniv. — A762

Designs: 40c, Casa de los Arcos (Arch House). 75c, Vergel Plaza. 80c, Tomebamba River Gorge, horiz. $3, Cathedral of the Immaculate Conception.

2007, Apr. 27 ***Perf. 13x13¼, 13¼x13***
1882-1885 A762 Set of 4 10.00 5.00

Prehistoric Animals — A763

Designs: No. 1886, 80c, Megatherium. No. 1887, 80c, Smilodon, horiz.

2007, May 10
1886-1887 A763 Set of 2 3.25 1.60

Beetles A764

Designs: No. 1888, Golopha eaucus.
No. 1889: a, Chrysophora chrysochlora. b, Dynastes hercules.

2007, May 10 ***Perf. 13¼x13***
1888 A764 40c multi .80 .40
1889 A764 40c Horiz. pair, #a-b 1.60 .80

Guayaquil Rotary Club, 80th Anniv. A765

2007, June 1 **Wmk. 395**
1890 A765 25c multi .50 .25

America Issue, Education For All — A766

Designs: 40c, Children on school bus. 80c, Girl doing geometry work. $1, Children flying kites, vert. $1.20, Student in wheelchair, vert. $2, Girl and handprints, vert.

2007, June 6 ***Perf. 13¼x13, 13x13¼***
1891-1894 A766 Set of 4 7.00 3.50

Imperf

Size: 40x65mm

1895 A766 $2 multi 4.00 2.00

Naval Institute of Oceanography, 75th Anniv. — A767

Antarctic research: 10c, Penguin, ship. $3, Scientists and scientific equipment, horiz.

2007, July 18 ***Perf. 13x13¼***
1896 A767 10c multi .20 .20

Perf. 12

Size: 52x32mm

1897 A767 $3 multi 6.00 3.00

Central Bank of Ecuador, 80th Anniv. — A768

2007, Aug. 28 ***Perf. 12***
1898 A768 $2 multi 4.00 2.00

Guayaquil Firefighters A769

Various firefighters at fires: 5c, 10c, 15c, 25c, $1. 25c and $1 are horiz.

2007, Oct. 10 ***Perf. 13x13¼, 13¼x13***
1899-1903 A769 Set of 5 3.25 1.60

Breast Cancer Prevention A770

2007, Oct. 15 ***Perf. 13¼x13***
1904 A770 $3 multi 6.00 3.00

Guayaquil Tourism — A771

Designs: 5c, Las Peñas. 10c, Lighthouse, Santa Ana Hill. 15c, El Velero Bridge. 25c, Mercado Sur, horiz. $1, June 5 Bridge, horiz.

2007, Oct. 23 ***Perf. 13x13¼, 13¼x13***
1905-1909 A771 Set of 5 3.25 1.60

Cuenca Chamber of Industries, 70th Anniv. A772

2007, Oct. 25 ***Perf. 13¼x13***
1910 A772 $1.20 multi 2.40 1.25

Operation Smile A773

2007, Nov. 16 **Litho.**
1911 A773 $1 multi 2.00 1.00

Vistazo Magazine, 50th Anniv. A774

2007, Nov. 29 ***Perf. 12***
1912 A774 20c multi .40 .20

Galapagos Islands Fauna A775

Designs: 40c, Sea turtle. 80c, Penguin. $1, Dolphin. $1.20, Tropicbird.

2007, Nov. 30 ***Perf. 13¼x13***
1913-1916 A775 Set of 4 7.00 3.50

Compare with type A780.

Comptroller General, 80th Anniv. A776

2007, Dec. 3 ***Perf. 12***
1917 A776 20c multi .40 .20

2007 Pan American Games, Rio de Janeiro — A777

No. 1918 — Athletes and text noting gold medalists: a, Alexandra Escobar. b, Seledina Nieve. c, Jefferson Perez. d, Xavier Moreno. e, Under-18 soccer team.

2007, Dec. 18 ***Perf. 13x13¼***
1918 Horiz. strip of 5 4.00 2.00
a.-e. A777 40c Any single .80 .40

Christmas — A778

No. 1919: a, The Annunciation. b, The Three Magi. c, Nativity. d, Flight into Egypt. Illustration reduced.

2007, Dec. 20 ***Perf. 13¼x13***
1919 A778 20c Block of 4, #a-d 1.60 .80

Guayas Province Transit Commission, 60th Anniv. — A779

Perf. 13x13¼
2008, Jan. 29 **Litho.** **Wmk. 395**
1920 A779 $1 multi 2.00 1.00

Galapagos Islands A780

Map of islands and: 40c, Pelecanus occidentalis. 80c, Aetobatus narinari. $1, Carcharhinus galapagensis. $1.20, San Cristóbal Windmill Project.

2008, Mar. 18 ***Perf. 13¼x13***
1921-1924 A780 Set of 4 7.00 3.50

Compare with Type A775.

Free Maternity and Infant Care — A781

2008, Mar. 28 ***Perf. 12***
1925 A781 $1 multi 2.00 1.00

Guayaquil Port Authority, 50th Anniv. A782

2008, Apr. 8
1926 A782 20c multi .40 .20

Tungurahua Chamber of Industry, 80th Anniv. — A783

Wmk. 395
2008, Apr. 24 **Litho.** ***Perf. 12***
1927 A783 $3 multi 6.00 3.00

Father Carlos Crespi (1891-1982) — A784

2008, Apr. 30
1928 A784 $2 multi 4.00 2.00

Santiago de Guayaquil Medallion A785

2008, June 3
1929 A785 30c multi .60 .30

Intl. Philately Day.

Jorge Pérez Concha, Historian and Diplomat, Birth Cent. — A786

2008, June 4
1930 A786 $3 multi 6.00 3.00

Los Pinos College, Quito, 40th Anniv. A787

2008, June 6
1931 A787 20c multi .40 .20

Guayaquil-Quito Railway, Cent. — A788

Ecuador No. 174 and: 56c, Steam locomotive. $5, Steam locomotives, Gabriel García Moreno and Gen. Eloy Alfaro.

2008, June 23 ***Perf. 12***
1932 A788 56c multi 1.25 .60

Imperf
Size: 100x70mm

1933 A788 $5 multi 10.00 5.00

Polytechnic School of the Coast, 50th Anniv. — A789

Wmk. 395
2008, July 28 **Litho.** ***Perf. 12***
1934 A789 32c multi .65 .30

Latin American Youth Year — A790

2008, Aug. 20
1935 A790 30c multi .60 .30

Ecuadorian Cacao — A791

No. 1936: a, Cacao pod, UL corner of #306. b, Cacao flower, UR corner of #306. c, Cacao processing, LL corner of #306. d, Cacao pods and beans, chocolate candy, LR corner of #306.

Illustration reduced.

2008, Oct. 1 ***Perf. 13¼x13***
1936 A791 56c Block of 4, #a-d 4.50 2.25

Meridiano Newspaper, 25th Anniv. — A792

2008, Oct. 22 ***Perf. 13x13¼***
1937 A792 60c multi 1.25 .60

No. C169 Overprinted in Carmine like No. 496 (MANANA reads up)

1948, Aug. 26 Unwmk. *Perf. 12*

C181 A185 1.30s deep blue .80 .25

National Fair of Today and Tomorrow, 1948.

Elia Liut and Telegrafo I
AP43

Teacher and Pupils
AP44

1948, Sept. 10 *Perf. 12½*

C182 AP43 60c rose red 1.00 .20
C183 AP43 1s green 1.00 .25
C184 AP43 1.30s deep claret 1.00 .25
C185 AP43 1.90s deep violet 1.00 .25
C186 AP43 2s dark brown 1.50 .30
C187 AP43 5s blue 2.75 .50
Nos. C182-C187 (6) 8.25 1.75

25th anniv. (in 1945) of the 1st postal flight in Ecuador.

1948, Oct. 12 *Perf. 14*

C188 AP44 50c violet 1.75 .60
C189 AP44 70c deep blue 1.75 .60
C190 AP44 3s dark green 3.50 1.60
C191 AP44 5s red 5.00 2.10
C192 AP44 10s brown 9.00 2.75
Nos. C188-C192 (5) 21.00 7.65

Campaign for adult education.

AP45

Franklin D. Roosevelt and Two of "Four Freedoms" — AP46

1948, Oct. 24 *Perf. 12½*

C193 AP45 60c emer & org brn .40 .25
C194 AP45 1s car rose & slate .40 .25
C195 AP46 1.50s grn & red brn .40 .25
C196 AP46 2s red & black 1.10 .25
C197 AP46 5s ultra & blk 2.25 .25
Nos. C193-C197 (5) 4.55 1.25

Maldonado Types

1948, Nov. 17

C198 A196 60c dp org & rose car .80 .20
C199 A197 90c red & gray blk .80 .20
C200 A196 1.30s pur & dp org 1.50 .20
C201 A197 2s dp bl & dull grn 1.50 .20
Nos. C198-C201 (4) 4.60 .80

See note after No. 519.

Juan Montalvo and Cervantes
AP47

Don Quixote — AP48

1949, May 2 Engr. *Perf. 12½x12*

C202 AP47 1.30s ol brn & ultra 5.00 2.50
C203 AP48 1.90s grn & rose car 1.20 .30
C204 AP47 3s vio & org brn 1.80 .30
C205 AP48 5s red & gray blk 3.00 .20
C206 AP47 10s red lil & aqua 5.00 .20
Nos. C202-C206 (5) 16.00 3.50

400th anniv. of the birth of Miguel de Cervantes Saavedra, novelist, playwright and poet, and the 60th anniv. of the death of Juan Montalvo (1832-89), Ecuadorean writer.

For surcharges see Nos. C225-C226.

No. C168 Surcharged in Blue

1949, June 15 *Perf. 12*

C207 A185 50c on 1.10s car rose .40 .20
C208 A185 60c on 1.10s car rose .40 .20
C209 A185 90c on 1.10s car rose .60 .20
Nos. C207-C209 (3) 1.40 .60

2nd Eucharistic Cong., Quito, June 1949.

No. C128 Surcharged in Black

1949, Oct. 11 *Perf. 11*

C210 A173 60c on 3s orange .90 .60
a. Double surcharge 30.00
C211 A173 90c on 3s orange .90 .20
C212 A173 1s on 3s orange 1.10 .60
C213 A173 2s on 3s orange 2.50 .60
Nos. C210-C213 (4) 5.40 2.00

"SUCRE(S)" in capitals on Nos. C212-C213.
75th anniv. of the UPU.

AP49

Black Surcharge

1950 Unwmk. *Perf. 12*

C214 AP49 60c on 50c gray .75 .20
a. Double surcharge 15.00

No. C170 Surcharged with New Value in Black

C215 A185 90c on 1.90s ol bis .75 .20

Nos. C168, C128-C129 and Type of 1944 Surcharged or Overprinted in Black or Carmine

1950, Feb. 10 *Perf. 12*

C216 A185 50c on 1.10s 1.75 1.75
C217 A185 70c on 1.10s 2.25 1.75

Perf. 11

C218 A173 3s orange 3.25 3.00
C219 A173 5s dark brown (C) 5.00 2.50
C220 A173 10s violet (C) 7.50 3.00
Nos. C216-C220 (5) 19.75 12.00

Issued to publicize adult education.
For overprint see No. 541.

Govt. Palace Type of 1944

1950, May 15 Engr. *Perf. 11*

C221 A173 10s violet 2.25 .20

For surcharges see Nos. C277-C279.

No. C169 Surcharged with New Value in Black

1950 *Perf. 12*

C222 A185 90c on 1.30s dp blue .40 .20

See No. C235.

Nos. C128-C129 Overprinted in Black

1951, July 28 Unwmk. *Perf. 11*

C223 A173 3s orange 1.90 .95
C224 A173 5s dark brown 3.75 1.75

20,000th crossing of the equator by Pan American-Grace Airways planes.

Nos. C202-C203 Surcharged in Black

1951 Unwmk. *Perf. 12½x12*

C225 AP47 60c on 1.30s .50 .20
C226 AP48 1s on 1.90s .50 .20
a. Inverted surcharge 20.00

Issued to publicize adult education.

St. Mariana de Jesus — AP50

1952, Feb. 15 Engr.

C227 AP50 60c plum & aqua 1.10 .40
C228 AP50 90c dk grn & lt ultra 1.30 .40
C229 AP50 1s car & dk grn 1.40 .40
C230 AP50 2s indigo & rose lil 1.40 .40
Nos. C227-C230 (4) 5.20 1.60

Canonization of Mariana de Jesus Paredes y Flores.

Plaza Visit to US Issue

3s, as No. 558. 5s, as No. 559.

1952, Mar. 26 *Perf. 12*

C231 A205 3s lilac & bl grn 1.00 .70
C232 A205 5s red brn & ol gray 2.00 2.00
a. Souv. sheet of 2, #C231-C232 4.50 *9.00*

Consular Service Stamps Surcharged "AEREO" and New Value in Black

1952 Unwmk. *Perf. 12*

C233 R2 60c on 1s green .50 .20
C234 R2 1s on 1s green .50 .20

Type R2 illustrated above No. 545.

No. C169 Surcharged with New Value in Carmine

C235 A185 90c on 1.30s dp bl .50 .20
Nos. C233-C235 (3) 1.50 .60

See No. C222.

Pres. José M. Urvina and Allegory of Freedom
AP52

Torch of Knowledge
AP53

Hyphen-hole Perf. 7x6½

1952, Nov. 18 Litho.

C236 AP52 60c rose red & blue 6.00 1.20
C237 AP52 90c lilac & red 6.00 1.40
C238 AP52 1s orange & green 6.00 .40
C239 AP52 2s red brn & blue 6.00 .80
Nos. C236-C239 (4) 24.00 3.80

Centenary of abolition of slavery in Ecuador. Counterfeits exist.

Unwmk.

1953, Apr. 13 Engr. *Perf. 12*

Design: 2s, Aged couple studying alphabet.

C240 AP53 1s dark blue 1.75 .20
C241 AP53 2s red orange 2.25 .20

1952 adult education campaign.

Globe Showing Part of Western Hemisphere
AP54

1953, June 5 *Perf. 12½x12*

C242 AP54 60c orange yellow .40 .20
C243 AP54 90c dark blue .70 .35
C244 AP54 3s carmine 1.10 .45
Nos. C242-C244 (3) 2.20 1.00

Issued to publicize the crossing of the equator by the Pan-American highway.

Consular Service Stamps Surcharged in Black

a

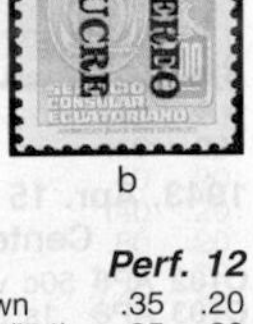

b

1953-54 *Perf. 12*

C245 R1 (a) 60c on 2s brown .35 .20
C246 R2 (a) 60c on 5s sep ('54) .35 .20
C247 R2 (a) 70c on 5s sep ('54) .35 .20
C248 R2 (a) 90c on 50c car rose ('54) .35 .20
C249 R1 (b) 1s on 2s brown .35 .20
C250 R1 (a) 1s on 2s brn ('54) .35 .20

C251 R1 (a) 2s on 2s brn ('54) .65 .20
C252 R1 (a) 3s on 5s vio ('54) .90 .20
Nos. C245-C252 (8) 3.65 1.60

Surcharge is horizontal on Nos. C245, C247 and C248.

Carlos Maria Cardinal de la Torre — AP55

Queen Isabella I — AP56

1954, Jan. 13 Photo. *Perf. 8½*
Center in Black

C253 AP55 60c rose lilac .75 .60
C254 AP55 90c green 1.00 .60
C255 AP55 3s orange 1.50 .60
Nos. C253-C255 (3) 3.25 1.80

1st anniv. of the elevation of Archbishop de la Torre to Cardinal.

1954, Apr. 22

C256 AP56 60c dk grn & grn .60 .60
C257 AP56 90c lil rose .60 .60
C258 AP56 1s blk & pale lil .60 .60
C259 AP56 2s blk brn & pale bl 1.20 .60
C260 AP56 5s blk brn & buff 3.00 .60
Nos. C256-C260 (5) 6.00 3.00

See note with No. 585.

Post Office, Guayaquil AP57

1954, May 19 Engr. *Perf. 12½x12*
Black Surcharge

C261 AP57 80c on 20c red .30 .20
C262 AP57 1s on 20c red .30 .20

25th anniversary of Pan American-Grace Airways' operation in Ecuador.

Plane, Gateway and Wheel — AP58

Unwmk.
1954, Aug. 2 Litho. *Perf. 11*

C263 AP58 80c blue .35 .20

Day of the Postal Employee.

San Pablo Lagoon AP59

1954, Sept. 24 Photo.

C264 AP59 60c orange .30 .20
C265 AP59 70c rose pink .30 .20
C266 AP59 90c dp grn .30 .20
C267 AP59 1s dk gray grn .30 .20
C268 AP59 2s blue .40 .20
C269 AP59 3s yel brn .65 .20
Nos. C264-C269 (6) 2.25 1.20

Glorification of Abdon Calderon Garaicoa AP60

Capt. Calderon — AP61

1954, Oct. 1

C270 AP60 80c rose pink .55 .20
C271 AP61 90c blue .55 .20

150th anniversary of the birth of Capt. Abdon Calderon Garaicoa.

El Cebollar College AP62

Brother Miguel Instructing Boys — AP63

Designs: 90c, Francisco Febres Cordero (Brother Miguel). 2.50s, Tomb of Brother Miguel. 3s, Monument to Brother Miguel.

1954, Dec. 3 Unwmk. *Perf. 11*

C272 AP62 70c dk grn .25 .20
C273 AP63 80c dk brn .25 .20
C274 AP63 90c dk gray bl .25 .20
C275 AP63 2.50s indigo .45 .20
C276 AP62 3s lil rose .65 .35
Nos. C272-C276 (5) 1.85 1.15

Centenary of the birth of Francisco Febres Cordero (Brother Miguel).

No. C221 Surcharged in Various Colors

1955, May 25

C277 A173 1s on 10s vio (Bk) .30 .20
C278 A173 1.70s on 10s vio (C) .50 .20
C279 A173 4.20s on 10s vio (Br) .80 .35
Nos. C277-C279 (3) 1.60 .75

Denomination in larger type on No. C279.
National Exhibition of Daily Periodicals.

"La Rotonda," Guayaquil, and Rotary Emblem AP64

Design: 90c, Eugenio Espejo hospital, Quito, and Rotary emblem.

1955, July 9 Engr. *Perf. 12½*

C280 AP64 80c dark brown .25 .25
C281 AP64 90c dark grown .35 .35

50th anniv. of the founding of Rotary Intl.

José Abel Castillo AP65

2s, 5s, José Abel Castillo, Map of Ecuador.

1955, Oct. 19 *Perf. 11x11½*

C282 AP65 60c chocolate 1.60 .20
C283 AP65 90c light olive green 1.60 .20
C284 AP65 1s lilac 2.50 .20
C285 AP65 2s vermilion 2.75 .70
C286 AP65 5s ultra 5.75 .55
Nos. C282-C286 (5) 14.20 1.85

See note after No. 595.

No. C29 Surcharged in Black

1955, Oct. 24 *Perf. 12*

C287 AP1 1s on 5s purple 1.00 .20

A similar surcharge on No. C29, set in two lines with letters 5mm high and no X's or black-out line of squares, was privately applied.

San Pablo, Imbabura — AP66

50s, Rumichaca Caves. 1.30s, Virgin of Quito. 1.50s, Cotopaxi Volcano. 1.70s, Tungurahua Volcano, Tungurahua. 1.90s, Guanacos. 2.40s, Mat market. 2.50s, Ruins at Incapirca. 4.20s, El Carmen, Cuenca, Azuay. 4.80s, Santo Domingo Church.

1956, Jan. 2 Photo. *Perf. 13*

C288 AP66 50c slate blue 2.75 .20
C289 AP66 1s ultra 2.75 .20
C290 AP66 1.30s crimson 4.25 .20
C291 AP66 1.50s dp grn 2.75 .20
C292 AP66 1.70s yel brn 1.75 .20
C293 AP66 1.90s olive 3.50 .20
C294 AP66 2.40s red org 3.75 .20
C295 AP66 2.50s violet 3.75 .20
C296 AP66 4.20s black 4.75 .20
C297 AP66 4.80s yel org 7.50 .30
Nos. C288-C297 (10) 37.50 2.10

See Nos. C310-C311. For surcharges see Nos. 766A, 766G.

Honorato Vazquez — AP67

Title Page of First Book — AP68

1956, May 28 Engr.
Various Portraits

C298 AP67 1s yellow green .50 .20
C299 AP67 1.50s red .50 .20
C300 AP67 1.70s bright blue .50 .20
C301 AP67 1.90s slate blue .50 .20
Nos. C298-C301 (4) 2.00 .80

Birth centenary (in 1955) of Honorato Vazquez, statesman.

1956, Aug. 27 Unwmk. *Perf. 13½*

C302 AP68 1s black .60 .20
C303 AP68 1.70s slate bl .60 .20
C304 AP68 2s blk brn .60 .20
C305 AP68 3s redsh brn .60 .20
Nos. C302-C305 (4) 2.40 .80

Bicentenary of printing in Ecuador.

Hands Reaching for UN Emblem AP69

1956, Oct. 24 *Perf. 14*

C307 AP69 1.70s red org 1.00 .20

10th anniv. of the UN (in 1955).
See No. C319. For overprint see No. C426.

Coat of Arms and Basketball Player — AP70

Designs: 1.70s, Map of South America with flags and girl basketball players.

1956, Dec. 28 Photo. *Perf. 14½x14*

C308 AP70 1s red lilac .50 .20
C309 AP70 1.70s deep green .75 .20

6th South American Women's Basketball Championship, Aug. 1956.

Scenic Type of 1956

1957, Jan. 2 *Perf. 13*

C310 AP66 50c bl grn 1.75 .20
C311 AP66 1s orange 1.75 .20

Type of Regular Issue, 1957

Designs: 50c, Map of Cuenca, 16th century. 80c, Cathedral of Cuenca. 1s, Modern City Hall.

Unwmk.
1957, Apr. 7 Photo. *Perf. 12*

C312 A219 50c brn, *cr* .20 .20
a. Souvenir sheet of 4 1.00 1.00
C313 A219 80c red, *bluish* .25 .20
C314 A219 1s pur, *yel* .30 .20
a. Souvenir sheet of 3 2.00 2.00
Nos. C312-C314 (3) .75 .60

No. C312a contains 4 imperf. 50c stamps similar to No. 613, but inscribed "AEREO" and printed in green. The sheet is printed on white ungummed paper.

No. C314a contains 3 imperf. stamps in designs similar to Nos. C312-C314, but with colors changed to orange (50c), brown (80c), violet (1s). The sheet is printed on white ungummed paper.

Gabriela Mistral — AP71

Arms of Espejo, Carchi — AP72

Unwmk.
1957, Sept. 18 Litho. *Perf. 14*

C315 AP71 2s lt bl, blk & red .40 .20

Issued to honor Gabriela Mistral (1889-1957), Chilean poet and educator.
See Nos. C406-C407.

1957, Nov. 16 *Perf. 14½x13½*

Arms of Cantons: 2s, Montufar. 4.20s, Tulcan.

Coat of Arms Multicolored

C316 AP72 1s carmine .40 .20
C317 AP72 2s black .40 .20
C318 AP72 4.20s ultra .75 .20
Nos. C316-C318 (3) 1.55 .60

Province of Carchi.
See Nos. C334-C337, C355-C364, C392-C395. For surcharge see No. 766.

Redrawn UN Type of 1956

1957, Dec. 10 Engr. *Perf. 14*
C319 AP69 2s greenish blue .40 .25

Honoring the UN. Dates, as on No. C307, are omitted; inscribed: "Homenaje a las Naciones Unidas."

Mater Dolorosa, San Gabriel College — AP73

Rafael Maria Arizaga — AP74

#C321, 1s, Door of San Gabriel College, Quito.

1958, Apr. 27 Engr. *Perf. 14*
C320 AP73 30c rose cl, *dp rose* .25 .20
C321 AP73 30c rose cl, *dp rose* .25 .20
a. Pair, #C320-C321 .60 .60
C322 AP73 1s dk bl, *lt bl* .25 .20
C323 AP73 1.70s dk bl, *lt bl* .25 .20
a. Pair, #C322-C323 .60 .60

Miracle of San Gabriel College, Quito, 50th anniv.

1958, July 21 Litho.
C324 AP74 1s multi .30 .20

Rafael Maria Arizaga (1858-1933), writer.
See Nos. C343, C350, C412.

Daule River Bridge AP75

1958, July 25 Engr. *Perf. 13½x14*
C325 AP75 1.30s green .35 .20

Issued to commemorate the opening of the River Daule bridge in Guayas province.
See Nos. C367-C369.

Basketball Player — AP76

Symbolical of the Eucharist — AP77

1958, Sept. 1 Photo. *Perf. 14x13½*
C326 AP76 1.30s dk grn & lt brn .35 .30

South American basketball championships.
For surcharge see No. 774A.

1958, Sept. 25 Litho. Unwmk.

Design: 60c, Cathedral of Guayaquil.

C327 AP77 10c vio & buff .35 .20
C328 AP77 60c org & vio brn .35 .20
C329 AP77 1s brn & lt bl .35 .20
Nos. C327-C329 (3) 1.05 .60

Souvenir Sheet

Symbolical of the Eucharist — AP78

Perf. 13½x14
C330 AP78 Sheet of 4 1.75 1.50
a.-d. 40c dark blue, any single .20 .20

3rd National Eucharistic Congress.

Stamps of 1865 and 1920 — AP79

Designs: 2s, Stamps of 1920 and 1948. 4.20s, Municipal museum and library.

1958, Oct. 8 Photo. *Perf. 11½*
Granite Paper
C331 AP79 1.30s grn & brn red .20 .20
C332 AP79 2s bl & vio .50 .30
C333 AP79 4.20s dk brn .60 .40
Nos. C331-C333 (3) 1.30 .90

National Philatelic Exposition (EXFIGUA), Guayaquil, Oct. 4-14.
For surcharge see No. 774.

Coat of Arms Type of 1957
Province of Imbabura

Arms of Cantons: 50c, Cotacachi. 60c, Antonio Ante. 80c, Otalvo. 1.10s, Ibarra.

1958, Nov. 9 Litho. *Perf. 14½x13½*
Coats of Arms Multicolored
C334 AP72 50c blk & red .35 .20
C335 AP72 60c blk, bl & red .35 .20
C336 AP72 80c blk & yel .35 .20
C337 AP72 1.10s blk & red .35 .20
Nos. C334-C337 (4) 1.40 .80

Charles V — AP80

Paul Rivet — AP81

Engr. & Photo.
1958, Dec. 12 *Perf. 14x13½*
C338 AP80 2s brn red & dk brn .30 .20
C339 AP80 4.20s dk gray & red brn .40 .30

400th anniv. of the death of Charles V, Holy Roman Emperor.

1958, Dec. 29 Photo. *Perf. 11½*
Granite Paper
C340 AP81 1s brown .30 .20

Issued in honor of Paul Rivet (1876-1958), French anthropologist.

1959, May 6

Portrait: 2s, Alexander von Humboldt.

C341 AP81 2s slate .25 .20

Cent. of the death of Alexander von Humboldt, German naturalist and geographer.

Front Page of "El Telegrafo" — AP82

1959, Feb. Litho. *Perf. 13½*
C342 AP82 1.30s bl grn & blk .25 .20

75th anniv. of Ecuador's oldest newspaper.

Portrait Type of 1958

José Luis Tamayo (1858-1947), lawyer.

1959, June 26 Unwmk. *Perf. 14*
Portrait Multicolored
C343 AP74 1.30s lt grn, bl & sal .30 .20

El Sagrario & House of Manuela Canizares AP83

Condor — AP84

Designs: 80c, Hall at San Agustin. 1s, First words of the constitutional act. 2s, Entrance to Cuartel Real. 4.20s, Allegory of Liberty.

Unwmk.
1959, Aug. 28 Photo. *Perf. 14*
C344 AP83 20c ultra & lt brn .25 .20
C345 AP83 80c brt bl & dp org .25 .20
C346 AP83 1s dk red & dk ol .25 .20
C347 AP84 1.30s brt bl & org .25 .20
C348 AP84 2s ultra & org brn .25 .20
C349 AP84 4.20s scar & brt bl .40 .30
Nos. C344-C349 (6) 1.65 1.30

Sesquicentennial of the revolution.

Portrait Type of 1958

1s, Alfredo Baquerizo Moreno (1859-1951), statesman.

1959, Sept. 26 Litho. *Perf. 14*
C350 AP74 1s gray, red & salmon .30 .20

Pope Pius XII — AP85

1959, Oct. 9 Unwmk. *Perf. 14½*
C351 AP85 1.30s multi .35 .20

Issued in memory of Pope Plus XII.

Flags of Argentina, Bolivia, Brazil, Guatemala, Haiti, Mexico and Peru — AP86

Flags of: 80c, Chile, Costa Rica, Cuba, Dominican Republic, Panama, Paraguay, United States. 1.30s, Colombia, Ecuador, Honduras, Nicaragua, Salvador, Uruguay, Venezuela.

1959, Oct. 12 *Perf. 13½.*
C352 AP86 50c multi .20 .20
C353 AP86 80c yel, red & bl .20 .20
C354 AP86 1.30s multi .35 .20
Nos. C352-C354 (3) .75 .60

Organization of American States.
For overprints see #C423-C425, CO19-CO21.

Arms of the Cantons Type of 1957
Province of Pichincha

10c, Rumiñahui. 40c, Pedro Moncayo. 1s, Mejia. 1.30s, Cayambe. 4.20s, Quito.

Perf. 14½x13½
1959-60 Unwmk. Litho.
Coat of Arms Multicolored
C355 AP72 10c blk & dk red ('60) .35 .20
C356 AP72 40c blk & yel .35 .20
C357 AP72 1s blk & brn ('60) .35 .20
C358 AP72 1.30s blk & grn ('60) .35 .20
C359 AP72 4.20s blk & org .35 .20
Nos. C355-C359 (5) 1.75 1.00

Province of Cotopaxi

40c, Pangua. 60c, Pujili. 70c, Saquisili. 1s, Salcedo. 1.30s, Latacunga.

1960
Coat of Arms Multicolored
C360 AP72 40c blk & car .25 .20
C361 AP72 60c blk & bl .25 .20
C362 AP72 70c blk & turq .25 .20
C363 AP72 1s blk & red org .25 .20
C364 AP72 1.30s blk & org .30 .20
Nos. C360-C364 (5) 1.30 1.00

Flags of American Nations — AP87

1960, Feb. 23 *Perf. 13x12½*
C365 AP87 1.30s multi .20 .20
C366 AP87 2s multi .25 .20

11th Inter-American Conference, Feb. 1960.

Bridge Type of 1958.

Bridges: No. C367, Juntas. No. C368, Saracay. 2s, Railroad bridge, Ambato.

1960 Litho. *Perf. 13½*
C367 AP75 1.30s chocolate .25 .20

Photo. *Perf. 12½*
C368 AP75 1.30s emerald .25 .20
C369 AP75 2s brown .35 .20
Nos. C367-C369 (3) .85 .60

Building of three new bridges.

Bahia-Chone Road — AP88

Pres. Camilo Ponce Enriquez AP89

Designs: 4.20s, Public Works Building, Cuenca. 5s, El Coca airport. 10s, New Harbor, Guayaquil.

1960, Aug. Litho. *Perf. 14*
C370 AP88 1.30s blk & dl yel .20 .20
C371 AP88 4.20s rose car & lt grn .30 .30
C372 AP88 5s dk brn & yel .45 .35
C373 AP88 10s dk bl & bl 1.00 .35

Perf. 11x11½

C374 AP89 2s org brn & blk 1.40 .25
Nos. C370-C374 (5) 3.35 1.45

Nos. C370-C374 publicize the achievements of Pres. Camilo Ponce Enriquez (1956-1960).
Issued: #C370-C373, 8/24; #C374, 8/31.

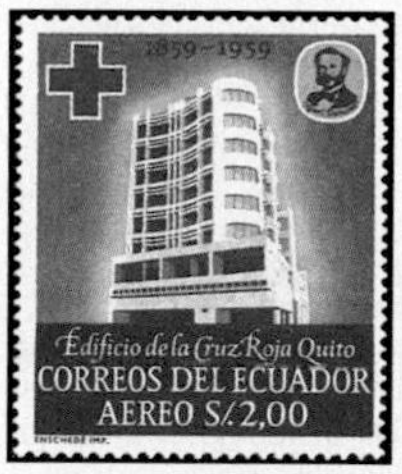

Red Cross Building, Quito and Henri Dunant AP90

1960, Oct. 5 Unwmk. *Perf. 13x14*
C375 AP90 2s rose vio & car .45 .20

Centenary (in 1959) of Red Cross idea.
For overprint see No. C408.

El Belen Church, Quito — AP91

1961, Jan. 14 *Perf. 12½*
C376 AP91 3s multi .40 .20

Ecuador's participation in the 1960 Barcelona Philatelic Congress.

Map of Ecuador and Amazon River System AP92

1961, Feb. 27 Litho. *Perf. 10½*
C377 AP92 80c salmpn, claret & grn .25 .20
C378 AP92 1.30s gray, slate & grn .35 .20
C379 AP92 2s beige, red & grn .50 .20
Nos. C377-C379 (3) 1.10 .60

Amazon Week, and the 132nd anniversary of the Battle of Tarqui against Peru.

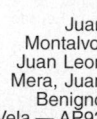

Juan Montalvo, Juan Leon Mera, Juan Benigno Vela — AP93

Hugo Ortiz G. — AP94

1961, Apr. 13 Unwmk. *Perf. 13*
C380 AP93 1.30s salmon & blk .35 .20

Centenary of Tungurahua province.

1961, May 25 *Perf. 14x14½*

Design: No. C382, Ortiz monument.

C381 AP94 1.30s grnsh bl, blk & yel .25 .20
C382 AP94 1.30s grnsh bl, pur, ol & brn .25 .20

Lt. Hugo Ortiz G., killed in battle 8/2/41.

Condor and Airplane Stamp of 1936 AP95

1.30s, Map of South America and stamp of 1865. 2s, Bolivar monument stamp of 1930.

Perf. 10½

1961, May 25 Litho. Unwmk.

Size: 41x28mm

C383 AP95 80c org & vio .20 .20

Size: 41x34mm

C384 AP95 1.30s bl, yel, ol & car .30 .25

Size: 40½x37mm

C385 AP95 2s car rose & blk .45 .25
Nos. C383-C385 (3) .95 .70

Third National Philatelic Exhibition, Quito, May 25-June 3, 1961.

Arms of Los Rios and Egret — AP96

1961, May 27 *Perf. 14½x13½*

Coat of Arms Multicolored

C386 AP96 2s bl & blk .35 .30

Centenary (in 1960) of Los Rios province.

Gabriel Garcia Moreno — AP97

Remigio Crespo Toral — AP98

1961, Sept. 24 Unwmk. *Perf. 12*
C387 AP97 1s bl, brn & buff .30 .20

Centenary of the restoration of national integrity.

1961, Nov. 3 Unwmk. *Perf. 14*
C388 AP98 50c multi .30 .20

Centenary of the birth of Remigio Crespo Toral, poet laureate of Ecuador.

Galapagos Islands Nos. LC1-LC3 Overprinted in Black or Red: "Estacion de Biologia Maritima de Galapagos" and "UNESCO 1961" (Similar to #684-686)

1961, Oct. 31 Photo. *Perf. 12*
C389 A1 1s dp bl .35 .20
a. "de Galapagos" on top line 2.00 2.00
C390 A1 1.80s rose vio .60 .30
a. UNESCO emblem omitted 1.25 1.25
C391 A1 4.20s blk (R) .75 .55
Nos. C389-C391 (3) 1.70 1.05

Establishment of maritime biological stations on Galapagos Islands by UNESCO.

Arms of the Cantons Type of 1957

Province of Tungurahua

50c, Pillaro. 1s, Pelileo. 1.30s, Baños. 2s, Ambato.

Perf. 14½x13½

1962, Mar. 30 Litho. Unwmk.

Coats of Arms Multicolored

C392 AP72 50c black .20 .20
C393 AP72 1s black .20 .20
C394 AP72 1.30s black .25 .20
C395 AP72 2s black .45 .20
Nos. C392-C395 (4) 1.10 .80

Pres. Arosemena and Prince Philip, Arms of Ecuador and Great Britain and Equator Monument AP99

Perf. 14x13½

1962, Feb. 17 Wmk. 340
C396 AP99 1.30s bl, sepia, red & yel .20 .20
C397 AP99 2s multi .35 .20

Visit of Prince Philip, Duke of Edinburgh, to Ecuador, Feb. 17-20, 1962.

Mountain Farming — AP100

Perf. 12½

1963, Mar. 21 Unwmk. Litho.
C398 AP100 30c emer, yel & blk .20 .20
C399 AP100 3s dl red, grn & org .50 .20
C400 AP100 4.20s bl, blk & yel .70 .45
Nos. C398-C400 (3) 1.40 .85

FAO "Freedom from Hunger" campaign.
Exist imperf. Value $32.50.

Mosquito and Malaria Eradication Emblem AP101

1963, Apr. 17 Unwmk. *Perf. 12½*
C401 AP101 50c multi .20 .20
C402 AP101 80c multi .20 .20
C403 AP101 2s multi .30 .20
Nos. C401-C403 (3) .70 .60

WHO drive to eradicate malaria.

Stagecoach and Jet Plane AP102

1963, May 7 Litho.
C404 AP102 2s org & car rose .30 .20
C405 AP102 4.20s claret & ultra .50 .35

1st Intl. Postal Conference, Paris, 1863.

Type of 1957 Inscribed "Islas Galapagos," Surcharged with New Value and Overprinted "Ecuador" in Black or Red

1963, June 19 Unwmk. *Perf. 14*
C406 AP71 5s on 2s gray, dk bl & red .80 .60
C407 AP71 10s on 2s gray, dk bl & red (R) 1.40 1.40

The basic 2s exists without surcharge and overprint. No. C407 exists with "ECUADOR" omitted, and with both "ECUADOR" and "10 SUCRES" double.

No. C375 Overprinted: "1863-1963/Centenario/de la Fundación/ de la Cruz Roja/Internacional"

1963, June 21 Photo. *Perf. 13x14*
C408 AP90 2s rose vio & car .30 .20

Intl. Red Cross, centenary.

Type of Regular Issue, 1963

Arosemena and: 70c, Flags of Ecuador. 2s, Flags of Ecuador, Panama. 4s, Flags of Ecuador, US.

1963, July 1 Litho. *Perf. 14*
C409 A238 70c pale bl & multi .25 .20
C410 A238 2s pink & multi .50 .20
C411 A238 4s lt bl & multi 1.25 .35
Nos. C409-C411 (3) 2.00 .75

Imperfs exist. Value $15.

Portrait Type of 1958

Portrait: 2s, Dr. Mariano Cueva (1812-82).

Unwmk.

1963, July 4 Litho. *Perf. 14*
C412 AP74 2s lt grn & multi .35 .20

Social Insurance Symbol — AP103

Mother and Child — AP104

1963, July 9 Litho.
C413 AP103 10s brn, bl, gray & ocher .90 .70

25th anniversary of Social Insurance.
Exists imperf. Value $9.

1963, July 28 *Perf. 12½*
C414 AP104 1.30s org, dk bl & blk .20 .20
C415 AP104 5s gray, red & brn .45 .45

7th Pan-American and South American Pediatrics Congresses, Quito.

Simon Bolivar Airport, Guayaquil AP105

1963, July 25 *Perf. 14*
C416 AP105 60c gray .20 .20
C417 AP105 70c dl grn .20 .20
C418 AP105 5s brn vio .50 .35
Nos. C416-C418 (3) .90 .75

Opening of Simon Bolivar Airport, Guayaquil, July 15, 1962.
Exist imperf. Value $4.50.

Nos. 638, 640-641 Overprinted "AEREO"

1964 *Perf. 12*

Flags in National Colors

C419 A223 1.80s dl vio .50 .35
C420 A224 2s dk brn .50 .35
C421 A223 2.20s blk brn .50 .35
Nos. C419-C421 (3) 1.50 1.05

On 1.80s and 2.20s, "AEREO" is vertical, reading down.

No. 650 Overprinted in Gold: "FARO DE COLON / AEREO"

1964 Photo. *Perf. 14x13½*
C422 A229 1.80s dk bl 2.50 1.50

Nos. C352-C354 Overprinted

Illustration reduced.

1964 Litho. *Perf. 13½*
C423 AP86 50c bl & multi .65 .45
C424 AP86 80c yel & multi .65 .45
C425 AP86 1.30s pale grn & multi .65 .45
Nos. C423-C425 (3) 1.95 1.35

No. C307 Overprinted: "DECLARACION / DERECHOS HUMANOS / 1964 / XV-ANIV"

Unwmk.

1964, Sept. 29 Engr. *Perf. 14*

C426 AP69 1.70s red org .35 .20

15th anniversary (in 1963) of the Universal Declaration of Human Rights.

Banana Type

1964, Oct. 26 Litho. *Perf. 12½x12*

C427 A241 4.20s blk, bis & gray ol .30 .20
C428 A241 10s blk, scar & gray ol .50 .40
a. Souv. sheet of 4 2.10 2.10

No. C428a contains imperf. stamps similar to Nos. 720-721 and C427-C428.

John F. Kennedy, Flag-draped Coffin and John Jr. — AP106

1964, Nov. 22 Litho. *Perf. 14*

C429 AP106 4.20s multi .85 .65
C430 AP106 5s multi 1.10 .80
C431 AP106 10s multi 2.00 1.10
a. Souv. sheet of 3 7.00 7.00
Nos. C429-C431 (3) 3.95 2.55

President John F. Kennedy (1917-63).
No. C431a contains stamps similar to Nos. C429-C431, imperf.

Olympic Type

1.30s, Gymnast, vert. 1.80s, Hurdler. 2s, Basketball.

Perf. 13½x14, 14x13½

1964, Dec. 16 Unwmk.

C432 A243 1.30s vio bl, ver & brn .25 .20
C433 A243 1.80s vio bl & multi .25 .20
C434 A243 2s red & multi .25 .20
a. Souv. sheet of 4 2.90 2.90
Nos. C432-C434 (3) .75 .60

No. C434a contains stamps similar to Nos. 725 and C432-C434, imperf.

Sports Type

Torch and Athletes: 2s, 3s, Diver, gymnast, wrestlers and weight lifter. 2.50s, 4s, Bicyclists. 3.50s, 5s, Jumpers.

1965, Nov. 20 Litho. *Perf. 12x12½*

C435 A247 2s bl, gold & blk .50 .20
C436 A247 2.50s org, gold & blk .50 .20
C437 A247 3s brt pink, gold & blk .50 .20
C438 A247 3.50s lt vio, gold & bl .55 .55
C439 A247 4s brt yel grn, gold & blk .55 .20
C440 A247 5s red org, gold & blk .60 .30
a. Souv. sheet of 12 8.00 8.00
Nos. C435-C440 (6) 3.20 1.65

No. C440a contains 12 imperf. stamps similar to Nos. 738-743 and C435-C440.
For surcharges see Nos. 766B, C449.

Bird Type

Birds: 1s, Yellow grosbeak. 1.30s, Black-headed parrot. 1.50s, Scarlet tanager. 2s, Sapphire quail-dove. 2.50s, Violet-tailed sylph. 3s, Lemon-throated barbet. 4s, Yellow-tailed oriole. 10s, Collared puffbird.

1966, June 17 Litho. *Perf. 13½*

Birds in Natural Colors

C441 A249 1s lt red brn & blk 1.10 .20
C442 A249 1.30s pink & blk 1.10 .20
C443 A249 1.50s pale grn & blk 1.10 .20
C444 A249 2s sal & blk 2.25 .40
C445 A249 2.50s lt yel grn & blk 2.25 .40
C446 A249 3s sal & blk 3.25 .45
C447 A249 4s gray & blk 4.25 .70
C448 A249 10s beige & blk 6.50 1.75
Nos. C441-C448 (8) 21.80 4.30

For surcharges see Nos. 766E-766F, C450, C455-C457.

Nos. C436 and C443 Surcharged

1967

C449 A247 80c on 2.50s multi .45 .35
C450 A249 80c on 1.50s multi .45 .20

Old denomination on No. C449 is obliterated with heavy bar; the surcharge on No. C450 includes "Resello" and an ornament over old denomination.

Peñaherrera Monument, Quito — AP107

Design: 2s, Peñaherrera statue.

1967, Dec. 29 Litho. *Perf. 12x12½*

C451 AP107 1.30s blk & org .25 .20
C452 AP107 2s blk & lt ultra .25 .20

See note after No. 763.

Arosemena Type

1.30s, Inauguration. 2s, Pres. Arosemena speaking in Punta del Este.

1968, May 9 Litho. *Perf. 13½x14*

C453 A251 1.30s multi .25 .20
C454 A251 2s multi .25 .20

No. C448 Surcharged in Plum, Dark Blue or Green

1969, Jan. 9 Litho. *Perf. 13½*

Bird in Natural Colors

C455 A249 80c on 10s beige (P) .50 .25
C456 A249 1s on 10s beige (DBl) .50 .25
C457 A249 2s on 10s beige (G) .50 .25
Nos. C455-C457 (3) 1.50 .75

"Operation Friendship" AP108

1969-70 Typo. *Perf. 13½*

C458 AP108 2s yel, blk, red & lt bl .25 .20
a. Perf. 12½ .25 .20
C459 AP108 2s bl, blk, car & yel ('70) .25 .20

Friendship campaign. Medallion background on Nos. C458 and C458a is blue; on No. C459, yellow.
No. C459 exists imperf. Value $5.

No. 639 Surcharged in Gold "S/. 5 AEREO" and Bar

1969, Nov. 25 Litho. *Perf. 12*

C460 A224 5s on 2s multi 1.60 .50

Butterfly Type

Butterflies: 1.30s, Morpho peleides. 1.50s, Anartia amathea.

1970 Litho. *Perf. 12½*

C461 A255 1.30s multi 3.50 .25
C462 A255 1.50s pink & multi 3.50 .25

Same, White Background

1970 *Perf. 13½*

C463 A255 1.30s multi 3.50 .25
C464 A255 1.50s multi 3.50 .25

Arms Type

Provincial Arms and Flags: 1.30s, El Oro. 2s, Loja. 3s, Manabi. 5s, Pichincha. 10s, Guayas.

1971 Litho. *Perf. 10½*

C465 A258 1.30s pink & multi .30 .20
C466 A258 2s multi .35 .20
C467 A258 3s multi .55 .30
C468 A258 5s multi .75 .35
C469 A258 10s multi 1.25 .40
Nos. C465-C469 (5) 3.20 1.45

Presentation of the Virgin — AP109

Pres. Allende and Chilean Flag AP110

Art of Quito: 1.50s, Blessed Anne at Prayer. 2s, St. Theresa de Jesus. 2.50s, Altar of Carmen, horiz. 3s, Descent from the Cross. 4s, Christ of St. Mariana de Jesus. 5s, Shrine of St. Anthony. 10s, Cross of San Diego.

1971 *Perf. 11½*

Inscriptions in Black

C473 AP109 1.30s multi .20 .20
C474 AP109 1.50s multi .25 .20
C475 AP109 2s multi .30 .20
C476 AP109 2.50s multi .40 .20
C477 AP109 3s multi .55 .20
C478 AP109 4s multi .65 .20
C479 AP109 5s multi .65 .35
C480 AP109 10s multi 1.50 .65
Nos. C473-C480 (8) 4.50 2.20

1971, Aug. 24 *Perf. 12½*

2.10s, Pres. José M. Velasco Ibarra of Ecuador, Pres. Salvador Allende of Chile, national flags.

C481 AP110 2s multi .25 .20
C482 AP110 2.10s multi .25 .20

Visit of Pres. Salvador Allende of Chile, Aug. 24.

Globe and Emblem AP111

1971

C483 AP111 5s black 1.00 .35
C484 AP111 5.50s dl pur & blk 1.00 .35

Opening of Postal Museum, Aug. 24, 1971.
Exist imperf. Value $7.50.

Pazmiño Type

1971, Sept. 16 *Perf. 12x11½*

C485 A260 1.50s grn & multi .25 .20
C486 A260 2.50s grn & multi .40 .20

AP112

AP113

Designs: 5s, Map of Americas. 10s, Converging roads and map. 20s, Map of Americas and Equator. 50s, Mountain road and monument on Equator.

1971 *Perf. 11½*

C487 AP112 5s org & multi .85 .45
C488 AP112 10s org & blk 1.25 1.00
C489 AP112 20s blk, bl & brt rose 2.40 1.60
C490 AP112 50s bl, blk & gray 3.50 2.50
Nos. C487-C490 (4) 8.00 5.55

11th Pan-American Road Congress.
Issued: 5s, 10s, 50s, 11/15; 20s, 11/22.
No. C488 exists imperf. Value $8.

1972

Design: 3s, Arms of Ecuador and Argentina. 5s, Presidents José M. Velasco Ibarra and Alejandro Agustin Lanusse.

C491 AP113 3s blk & multi .25 .20
C492 AP113 5s blk & multi .45 .30

Visit of Lt. Gen. Alejandro Agustin Lanusse, president of Argentina, Jan. 25.

Flame, Scales, Map of Americas AP114

1972, Apr. 24 Litho. *Perf. 12½*

C493 AP114 1.30s bl & red .30 .20

17th Conference of the Interamerican Federation of Lawyers, Quito, Apr. 24.

Religious Paintings Type of Regular Issue

Ecuadorian Paintings: 3s, Virgin of the Flowers, by Miguel de Santiago. 10s, Virgin of the Rosary, by Quito School.

1972, Apr. 24 *Perf. 14x13½*

C494 A263 3s blk & multi .35 .35
C495 A263 10s blk & multi 1.25 .60
a. Souv. sheet of 2, #C494-C495 1.50 1.50

1972, May 4

Ecuadorian Statues: 3s, St. Dominic, Quito School. 10s, St. Rosa of Lima, by Bernardo de Legarda.

C496 A263 3s blk & multi .35 .35
C497 A263 10s blk & multi 1.25 .60
a. Souv. sheet of 2, #C496-C497 2.50 2.10

Letters of "Ecuador" 3mm high on #C496-C497, 7mm high on #C494-C495.

Portrait Type

Designs (Generals, from Paintings): 1.30s, José Maria Saenz. 3s, Tomás Wright. 4s, Antonio Farfan. 5s, Antonio José de Sucre. 10s, Simon Bolivar. 20s, Arms of Ecuador.

1972, May 24

C498 A264 1.30s bl & multi .40 .40
C499 A264 3s bl & multi .50 .40
C500 A264 4s bl & multi .60 .40
C501 A264 5s bl & multi 1.00 .60
C502 A264 10s bl & multi 1.75 1.00
C503 A264 20s bl & multi 3.50 1.75
Nos. C498-C503 (6) 7.75 4.55

Artisan Type

Handicraft of Ecuador: 2s, Woman wearing flowered poncho. 3s, Striped poncho. 5s, Poncho with roses. 10s, Gold sunburst sculpture.

1972, July Photo. *Perf. 13*

C504 A265 2s multi .45 .40
C505 A265 3s multi .70 .45
C506 A265 5s multi 1.10 .50
C507 A265 10s org red & multi 2.00 1.25
a. Souv. sheet of 4, #C504-C507 4.75 4.75
Nos. C504-C507 (4) 4.25 2.60

Epidendrum Orchid — AP115

1972 Photo. *Perf. 12½*
C508 AP115 4s shown 1.40 1.25
C509 AP115 6s Canna 1.75 1.50
C510 AP115 10s Jimson weed 3.25 3.00
a. Souv. sheet of 3, #C508-C510 10.00 8.25
Nos. C508-C510 (3) 6.40 5.75

Exists imperf.

Oil Drilling Towers — AP116

Coat of Arms — AP117

1972, Oct. 17 Litho. *Perf. 11½*
C511 AP116 1.30s bl & multi .25 .20

Ecuadorian oil industry.

1972, Nov. 18 Litho. *Perf. 11½*
Arms Multicolored
C512 AP117 2s black .25 .20
C513 AP117 3s black .25 .20
C514 AP117 4s black .30 .20
C515 AP117 4.50s black .30 .20
C516 AP117 6.30s black .65 .30
C517 AP117 6.90s black .65 .30
Nos. C512-C517 (6) 2.40 1.40

Pichincha Type

Designs: 2.40s, Corridor, San Agustin. 4.50s, La Merced Convent. 5.50s, Column base. 6.30s, Chapter Hall, San Agustin. 6.90s, Interior, San Agustin. 7.40s, Crucifixion, Cantuña Chapel. 7.90s, Decorated ceiling, San Agustin.

1972, Dec. 6 Wmk. 367
C518 A266 2.40s yel & multi .30 .20
C519 A266 4.50s yel & multi .45 .20
C520 A266 5.50s yel & multi .55 .20
C521 A266 6.30s yel & multi .60 .40
C522 A266 6.90s yel & multi .65 .40
C523 A266 7.40s yel & multi .75 .40
C524 A266 7.90s yel & multi .80 .40
Nos. C518-C524 (7) 4.10 2.20

UN Emblem — AP118

OAS Emblem — AP119

1973, Mar. 23 Unwmk.
C525 AP118 1.30s lt bl & blk .25 .20

25th anniversary of the Economic Committee for Latin America (CEPAL).

1973, Apr. 14 Wmk. 367
C526 AP119 1.50s multi .30 .20
a. Unwatermarked .30 .20

Day of the Americas and "Philately for Peace."

Bird Type

1973 Unwmk. *Perf. 11½x11*
C527 A268 1.30s Blue-footed booby 2.10 .20
C528 A268 3s Brown pelican 2.10 .20

Presidents Lara and Caldera AP120

1973, June 15 Wmk. 367
C529 AP120 3s multi .35 .20

Visit of Venezuela Pres. Rafael Caldera, Feb. 5-7.

Silver Coin, 1934 — AP121

Globe, OPEC Emblem, Oil Derrick — AP122

Ecuadorian Coins: 10s, Silver coin, obverse. 50s, Gold coin, 1928.

Unwmk.
1973, Dec. 14 Photo. *Perf. 14*
C530 AP121 5s multi .50 .35
C531 AP121 10s multi .85 .55
C532 AP121 50s multi 4.00 2.25
a. Souvenir sheet of 3 6.00 6.00
Nos. C530-C532 (3) 5.35 3.15

No. C532a contains one each of Nos. C530-C532; Dated "1972." Exists imperf. Value, same.

A gold marginal overprint was applied in 1974 to No. C532a (perf. and imperf.): "X Campeonato Mundial de Football / Munich - 1974." Value, each $60.

A carmine overprint was applied in 1974 to No. C532a (perf. and imperf.): "Seminario de Telecommunicaciones Rurales, / Septiembre-1974 / Quito-Ecuador" and ITU emblem. Value, each $8.50.

1974, June 15 Litho. *Perf. 11½*
C533 AP122 2s multi .30 .20

Meeting of Organization of Oil Exporting Countries, Quito, June 15-24.

Ecuadorian Flag, UPU Emblem — AP123

1974, July 15 Litho. *Perf. 11½*
C534 AP123 1.30s multi .25 .20

Centenary of Universal Postal Union.

Two 25s souvenir sheets exist. These were sold on a restricted basis. Value, each $40.

Teodoro Wolf AP124

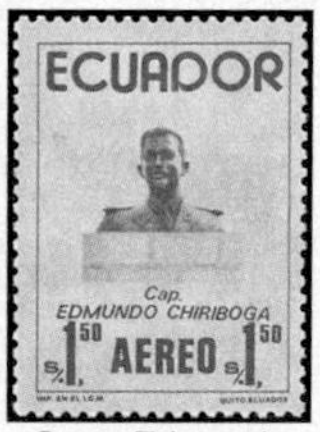

Capt. Edmundo Chiriboga AP125

1974 Litho. *Perf. 12x11½*
C535 AP124 1.30s blk & ultra .20 .20
C536 AP125 1.50s gray .25 .20

Teodoro Wolf, geographer; Edmundo Chiriboga, national hero.

Issued: #C535, Nov. 29; #C536, Dec. 4.

Congress Emblem AP126

1974, Dec. 8 Litho. *Perf. 11½x12*
C537 AP126 5s bl & multi .35 .20

8th Inter-American Postmasters' Cong., Quito.

Map of Americas and Coat of Arms AP127

Prominent Ecuadorians AP128

1975, Feb. 1 *Perf. 12x11½*
C538 AP127 3s bl & multi .35 .20

EXFIGUA Stamp Exhibition and 5th General Assembly of Federation Inter-Americana de Filatelia, Guayaquil, Nov. 1973.

1975 *Perf. 12x11½*

#C539, Manuel J. Calle, Journalist. #C540, Leopoldo Benites V., president of UN General Assembly, 1973-74; #C541, Adofo H. Simmonds G. (1892-1969), journalists; #C542, Juan de Dios Martinez Mera, President of Ecuador, birth centenary.

C539 AP128 5s lilac rose .45 .20
C540 AP128 5s gray .45 .20
C541 AP128 5s violet .45 .30
C542 AP128 5s blk & rose red .45 .20
Nos. C539-C542 (4) 1.80 .90

Pres. Guillermo Rodriguez Lara — AP129

1975 Unwmk. *Perf. 12*
C546 AP129 5s vermilion & blk .50 .30

State visit of Pres. Guillermo Rodriguez Lara to Algeria, Romania and Venezuela.

Meeting Type of 1975

1.50s, Rafael Rodriguez Palacio & Argelino Duran Quintero meeting at border in Ruichacha. 2s, Signing border agreement.

1975, Apr. 1 Litho. *Perf. 12x11½*
C547 A273 1.50s multi .25 .20
C548 A273 2s multi .25 .20

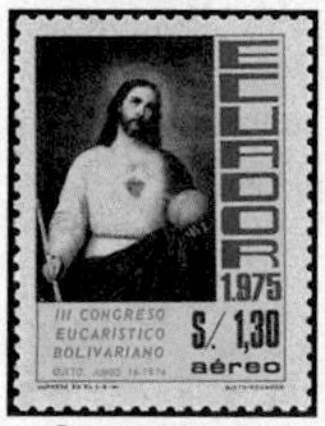

Sacred Heart (Painting) AP130

Quito Cathedral AP131

Design: 2s, Monstrance.

1975, Apr. 28 Litho. *Perf. 12x11½*
C549 AP130 1.30s yel & multi .20 .20
C550 AP130 2s bl & multi .20 .20
C551 AP131 3s multi .30 .20
Nos. C549-C551 (3) .70 .60

3rd Bolivarian Eucharistic Congress, Quito, June 9-16, 1974.

J. Delgado Panchana with Trophy — AP132

J. Delgado Panchana Swimming AP133

Perf. 12x11½, 11½x12
1975, June 12 Unwmk.
C552 AP132 1.30s bl & multi .20 .20
C553 AP133 3s blk & multi .30 .20

Jorge Delgado Panchana, South American swimming champion, 1971 and 1974.

Sports Type of 1975

1975, Sept. 11 Litho. *Perf. 11½*
C554 A276 1.30s Tennis .45 .25
C555 A276 2s Target shooting .45 .25
C556 A276 2.80s Volleyball .55 .25
C557 A276 3s Raft with sails .55 .25
C558 A276 5s Mask .80 .25
Nos. C554-C558 (5) 2.80 1.25

Flower Type of 1975

1975, Nov. 18 Litho. *Perf. 11½x12*
C559 A277 1.30s Pitcairnia pungens .25 .25
C560 A277 2s Scarlet sage .40 .25
C561 A277 3s Amaryllis .60 .35
C562 A277 4s Opuntia quitense .85 .40
C563 A277 5s Amaryllis 1.25 .60
Nos. C559-C563 (5) 3.35 1.85

Tail Assemblies and Emblem — AP134

Planes over Map of Ecuador — AP135

1975, Dec. 17 Litho. *Perf. 11½*
C564 AP134 1.30s bl & multi .30 .20
C565 AP135 3s multi .35 .20

TAME, Military Transport Airline, 13th anniv.

Benalcázar Statue — AP136

1976, Feb. 6 Litho. *Perf. 11½*
C566 AP136 2s multi .25 .20
C567 AP136 3s multi .25 .20

Sebastián de Benalcázar (1495-1550), Spanish conquistador, founder of Quito.

Archaeology Type of 1975

1.30s, Seated man, Carchi Culture. 2s, Funerary urn, Tuncahuan Culture. 3s, Priest, Bahia de Caraquez Culture. 4s, Snail's shell, Cuasmal Culture. 5s, Bowl supported by figurines, Guangala Culture.

1976, Feb. 12 Litho. *Perf. 11½*
C568 A278 1.30s multi .20 .20
C569 A278 2s multi .30 .20
C570 A278 3s multi .45 .30
C571 A278 4s multi .65 .30
C572 A278 5s multi .85 .30
Nos. C568-C572 (5) 2.45 1.30

Fruit Type of 1976

1976, Mar. 30

C573 A280 2s Apples .40 .20
C574 A280 5s Rose .60 .20

Lufthansa Jet — AP137

1976, June 25 Litho. *Perf. 12*
C575 AP137 10s bl & multi 1.50 .35

Lufthansa, 50th anniversary.

An imperf. 20s miniature sheet exists, similar to No. C575 enlarged, with overprinted black bar covering line below "Lufthansa." Size: 90x115mm.

Projected PO, Quito — AP138

Fruit Peddler — AP139

1976, Aug. 10 Litho. *Perf. 12*
C576 AP138 5s blk & multi .30 .20

Design for new General Post Office, Quito.

1976, July 25

#C578, Longshoreman. #C579, Cerros del Carmen & Santa Ana, hills of Guayaquil, horiz. #C580, Sebastián de Belalcázar. #C581, Francisco de Orellana. #C582, Chief Guayas & his wife Quila.

C577 AP139 1.30s red & multi .20 .20
C578 AP139 1.30s red & multi .20 .20
C579 AP139 1.30s red & multi .20 .20
C580 AP139 2s red & multi .20 .20
C581 AP139 2s red & multi .20 .20
C582 AP139 2s red & multi .20 .20
Nos. C577-C582 (6) 1.20 1.20

Founding of Quayaquil, 441st anniversary.

Emblem and Laurel AP140

1976, Aug. 9
C583 AP140 1.30s yel & multi .25 .20

Bolivarian Soc. of Ecuador, 50th anniv.

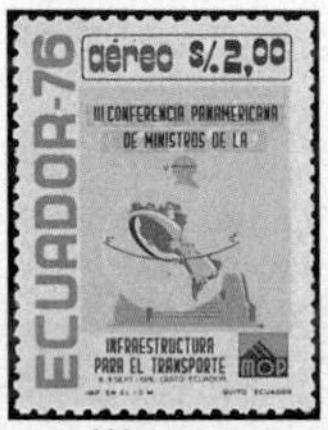

Western Hemisphere and Equator Monument AP141

Congress Emblem AP142

1976, Sept. 6
C584 AP141 2s multi .25 .20

Souvenir Sheet

Imperf

C585 AP141 5s multi 2.75 2.75

3rd Conf. of Pan-American Transport Ministers, Quito, Sept. 6-11. No. C585 contains design similar to No. C584 with black denomination and red control number in margin.

1976, Sept. 27 Litho. *Perf. 11½*
C586 AP142 1.30s bl & multi .30 .20
C587 AP142 3s bl & multi .40 .30

Souvenir Sheet

Imperf

C588 AP142 10s bl & multi 1.50 1.00

10th Inter-American Congress of the Construction Industry, Quito, Sept. 27-30.

George Washington AP143

American Bicentennial: 5s, Naval battle, Sept. 23, 1779, in which the Bonhomme Richard, commanded by John Paul Jones, defeated and captured the Serapis, British man-of-war, off Yorkshire coast, horiz.

1976, Oct. 18 Litho. *Perf. 12*
C589 AP143 3s blk & multi .60 .30
C590 AP143 5s red brn & yel .90 .45

Dr. Hideyo Noguchi — AP144

Luis Cordero — AP145

1976 Litho. *Perf. 11½*
C591 AP144 3s yel & multi .35 .20

Dr. Hideyo Noguchi (1876-1928), bacteriologist (at Rockefeller Institute). A 10s imperf. miniature sheet in same design exists without "Aereo." Size: 95x114mm.

1976, Dec. Litho. *Perf. 11½*
C592 AP145 2s multi .25 .20

Luis Cordero (1833-1912), president of Ecuador.

Mariuxi Febres Cordero — AP146

1976, Dec. *Perf. 11½*
C593 AP146 3s multi .25 .20

Mariuxi Febres Cordero, South American swimming champion.

Flags and Monument AP147

1976, Nov. 9 *Perf. 12*
C594 AP147 3s multi .25 .20

Miniature Sheet

Imperf

C595 AP147 5s multi 1.60 .50

2nd Meeting of the Agriculture Ministers of the Andean Countries, Quito, Nov. 8-10.

Sister Catalina — AP148

Congress Hall, Quito — AP149

1977, June 17 Litho. *Perf. 12x11½*
C596 AP148 1.30s blk & pale salmon .30 .20

Sister Catalina de Jesus Herrera (1717-1795), writer.

1977, Aug. 15 Litho. *Perf. 12x11½*
C597 AP149 5s multi .45 .20
a. 10s souvenir sheet 1.50 1.50

11th General Assembly of Pan-American Institute of Geography and History, Quito, Aug. 15-30. No. C597a contains the designs of types A282 and AP149 without denominations and with simulated perforations.

Pres. Alfonso López Michelsen, Flag of Colombia — AP150

Designs: 5s, Pres. López M. of Colombia, Pres. Alfredo Povedo B. of Ecuador and aide. 7s, as 5s, vert. 9s, 10s, Presidents with aides.

1977 *Perf. 12*
C598 AP150 2.60s multi .45 .20
C599 AP150 5s multi .65 .25
C600 AP150 7s multi .70 .35
C601 AP150 9s multi 1.10 .55

Imperf

C602 AP150 10s multi .85 .70
Nos. C598-C602 (5) 3.75 2.05

Meeting of the Presidents of Ecuador and Colombia and Declaration of Putumayo, Feb. 25, 1977. Nos. C598-C602 are overprinted in multiple fluorescent, colorless rows: INSTITUTO GEOGRAFICO MILITAR GOBIERNO DEL ECUADOR.

Ceramic Figure, Tolita Culture AP151

9s, Divine Shepherdess, sculpture by Bernardo de Legarda. 11s, The Fruit Seller, sculpture by Legarda. 20s, Sun God, pre-Columbian gold mask.

1977, Aug. 24 *Perf. 12*
C603 AP151 7s gold & multi 1.25 .40
C604 AP151 9s gold & multi 1.60 .45
C605 AP151 11s gold & multi 2.10 1.00
Nos. C603-C605 (3) 4.95 1.85

Souvenir Sheet

Gold Embossed

Imperf

C606 AP151 20s vio, bl, blk & gold 8.00 4.25

Central Bank of Ecuador, 50th anniversary. Nos. C603-C605 overprinted like Nos. C598-C602.

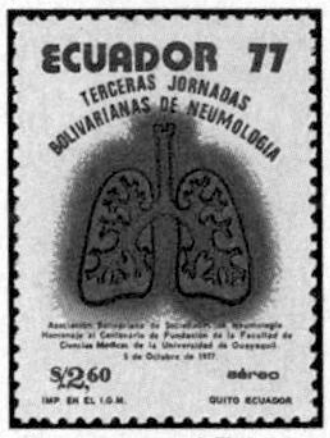

Lungs — AP152

Brother Miguel, St. Peter's, Rome — AP153

1977, Oct. 5 Litho. *Perf. 12x11½*
C607 AP152 2.60s multi .30 .25

3rd Cong. of the Bolivarian Pneumonic Soc. and cent. of the founding of the medical faculty of the University of Guayaquil.

1977
C608 AP153 2.60s multi .25 .20

Beatification of Brother Miguel.

Peralta Type

2.60s, Titles of works by Peralta & his bookmark.

1977 *Perf. 11½*
C609 A284 2.60s multi .35 .25

Broadcast Tower — AP154

Remigio Romero y Cordero — AP155

1977, Dec. 2 Litho. *Perf. 12x11½*
C610 AP154 5s multi .35 .35

9th World Telecommunications Day.

1978, Mar. 2 Litho. *Perf. 12½x11½*
C611 AP155 3s multi .30 .20
C612 AP155 10.60s multi .45 .25

Imperf

C612A AP155 10s multi 1.10 1.10
Nos. C611-C612A (3) 1.85 1.55

Remigio Romero y Cordero (1895-1967), poet.

No. C612A contains a vignette similar to Nos. C611-C612.

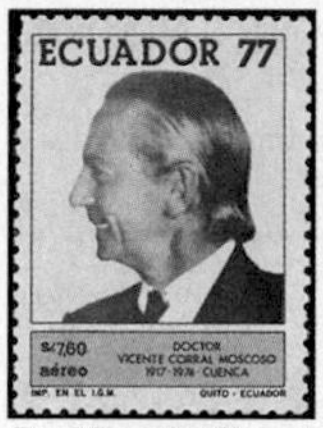

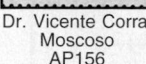

Dr. Vicente Corral Moscoso AP156

Faces AP157

5s, Hospital emblem with Caduceus.

1978, Apr. 12 Litho. *Imperf.*

C613	AP156	5s multi	.55	.30

Perf. 12x11½

C614	AP156	7.60s multi	.95	.50

Inauguration (in 1977) of Dr. Vicente Corral Moscoso Regional Hospital, Cuenca.

1978, Mar. 17

Designs: 9s, Emblems and flags of Ecuador. 10s, 11s, Hands reaching for light.

C615	AP157	7s multicolored	.60	.20
C616	AP157	9s multicolored	.85	.20
C617	AP157	11s multicolored	1.00	.20

Imperf

C618	AP157	10s multicolored	1.00	1.00
		Nos. C615-C618 (4)	3.45	1.60

Ecuadorian Social Security Institute, 50th anniv.

Geographical Institute Type

7.60s, Plane over map of Ecuador with mountains.

1978, Apr. 12 Litho. *Perf. 11½*

C619	A287	7.60s multi	.90	.50

Imperf

C620	A287	10s multi	1.40	1.40

No. C620 contains 2 vignettes with simulated perforations in designs of Nos. 967 and C619.

Lions Type

1978 *Perf. 11½*

C621	A288	5s multi	.65	.25
C622	A288	6.20s multi	1.00	.40

Imperf

C623	A288	10s multi	1.40	1.40
		Nos. C621-C623 (3)	3.05	2.05

No. C623 contains a vignette similar to Nos. C621-C622.

San Martin — AP158

1978, Apr. 13 Litho. *Perf. 12*

C624	AP158	10.60s multi	1.40	.50

Imperf

C625	AP158	10s multi	1.40	1.40

Gen. José de San Martin (1778-1850), soldier and statesman. No. C625 contains a vignette similar to No. C624.

Bank Type

Design: 5s, Bank emblem.

1978, Sept. Litho. *Perf. 11½*

C626	A289	5s gray & multi	.30	.20

Soccer Type

Designs: 2.60s, "Gauchito" and Games' emblem. 5s, "Gauchito." 7s, Soccer ball. 9s, Games' emblem, vert. 10s, Games' emblem.

1978, Nov. 1 *Perf. 12*

C627	A290	2.60s multi	.30	.20
C628	A290	7s multi	.80	.40
C629	A290	9s multi	1.10	.65

Imperf

C630	A290	5s blk & bl	5.25	5.25
C631	A290	10s blk & bl	5.25	5.25
		Nos. C627-C631 (5)	12.70	11.75

Bernardo O'Higgins AP159

Old Men of Vilcabamba AP160

1978, Nov. 11 Litho. *Perf. 12x11½*

C632	AP159	10.60s multi	.70	.30

Imperf

C633	AP159	10s multi	1.25	.75

Gen. Bernardo O'Higgins (1778-1842), Chilean soldier and statesman. No. C633 contains a vignette similar to No. C632.

1978, Nov. 11 *Perf. 12x11½*

C634	AP160	5s multi	.40	.25

Vilcabamba, valley of longevity.

Humphrey AP161

Virgin and Child AP162

1978, Nov. 27 Litho. *Perf. 12x11½*

C635	AP61	5s multi	.40	.25

Hubert H. Humphrey (1911-1978), Vice President of the US.

1978

Children's Drawings: 4.60s, Holy Family. 6.20s, Candle and children.

C636	AP162	2.20s multi	.20	.20
C637	AP162	4.60s multi	.45	.25
C638	AP162	6.20s multi	.75	.35
		Nos. C636-C638 (3)	1.40	.80

Christmas 1978.

Village, by Anibal Villacis AP163

Ecuadorian Painters: No. C640, Mountain Village, by Gilberto Almeida. No. C641, Bay, by Roura Oxandaberro. No. C642, Abstract, by Luis Molinari. No. C643, Statue, by Oswaldo Viteri. No. C644, Tools, by Enrique Tabara.

1978, Dec. 9 *Perf. 12*

C639	AP163	5s multi	.50	.25
C640	AP163	5s multi	.50	.25
C641	AP163	5s multi	.50	.25
C642	AP163	5s multi	.50	.25
C643	AP163	5s multi	.50	.25
C644	AP163	5s multi	.50	.25
		Nos. C639-C644 (6)	3.00	1.50

House and Monument AP164

Design: 3.40s, Monument, vert.

1979, Feb. 27 Litho. *Perf. 12*

C645	AP164	2.40s multi	.30	.20
C646	AP164	3.40s multi	.30	.20

Imperf

C647	AP164	10s multi	1.00	1.00
		Nos. C645-C647 (3)	1.60	1.40

Sesquicentennial of Battle of Portete and Tarqui. #C647 contains vignettes similar to #C645-C646.

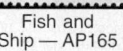

Fish and Ship — AP165

Flags of Ecuador and U.S. — AP166

7s, Map of Ecuador & Galapagos showing territorial waters. 9s, Map of South America with west-coast territorial waters.

Perf. 12x11½, 11½x12

1979, July 23 Litho. Wmk. 367

C648	AP165	5s multi	.75	.25
C649	AP165	7s multi, horiz.	1.00	.35
C650	AP165	9s multi	1.40	.50
		Nos. C648-C650 (3)	3.15	1.10

Declaration of 200-mile territorial limit, 25th anniversary.

1979, Aug. 3 *Perf. 12x11½*

Designs: 10.60s, Bells in Quito clock tower, horiz. 13.60s, Aerial view of Galapagos coast.

C651	A293	10.60s multi	1.25	.60
C652	A293	13.60s multi	1.40	.75

Size: 115x91mm

Imperf

Unwmk.

C653	A293	10s multi	2.50	1.10
		Nos. C651-C653 (3)	5.15	2.45

National heritage: Quito and Galapagos Islands. No. C653 contains vignettes similar to Nos. 977, C651-C652.

1979, Aug. Wmk. 367 *Perf. 11½x12*

C654	AP166	7.60s multi	.40	.40
C655	AP166	10.60s multi	.60	.60

Size: 115x91mm

Imperf

Unwmk.

C656	AP166	10s multi	1.00	.65
		Nos. C654-C656 (3)	2.00	1.65

5th anniv. of Ecuador-US Chamber of Commerce. No. C656 contains vignettes similar to Nos. C654-C655.

Smiling Girl, IYC Emblem — AP167

Perf. 12x11½

1979, Sept. 7 Litho. Wmk. 367

C657	AP167	10s multi	.70	.40

International Year of the Child.

Citizens and Flag of Ecuador AP168

Design: 10.60s, Pres. Jaime Roldas Aguilera, flag of Ecuador, vert.

Perf. 11½

1979, Sept. 27 Litho. Unwmk.

C658	AP168	7.60s multi	.85	.35

Wmk. 367

C659	AP168	10.60s multi	1.00	.30

Restoration of democracy to Ecuador.

Ecuador Coat of Arms, Olympic Rings and Eagle — AP169

Perf. 12x11½

1979, Nov. 23 Unwmk.

C660	AP169	28s multi	2.00	1.25

5th National Games, Cuenca.

CIESPAL Building, Quito AP170

Perf. 11½x12½

1979, Dec. 26 Wmk. 367

C661	AP170	10.60s multi	.70	.40

Opening of Ecuadorian Institute of Engineers building.

Olmedo Type

Perf. 12x11½

1980, Apr. 29 Litho. Unwmk.

C662	A294	10s multi	1.00	.65

Tribal Chief Type

Indo-American Tribal Chiefs: #C663, Cuauhtemoc, Mexico. #C664, Lempira, Honduras. #C665, Nicaragua. #C666, Lambaré, Paraguay. #C667, Urraca, Panama. #C668, Anacaona, Haiti. #C669, Caupolican, Chile. #C670, Tacun-Uman, Guatemala. #C671, Calarca, Colombia. #C672, Garabito, Costa Rica. #C673, Hatuey, Cuba. #C674, Cmarao, Brazil. #C675, Tehuelche, Argentina. #C676, Tupaj Katri, Bolivia. 17.80s, Sequoyah, US. 22.80s, Ruminahui, Ecuador.

Wmk. 367 (#C663, C667), Unwmkd.

1980, May 12

C663	A295	7.60s multi	1.75	.35
C664	A295	7.60s multi	1.75	.35
C665	A295	7.60s multi	1.75	.35
C666	A295	10s multi	1.90	.40
C667	A295	10s multi	1.90	.40
C668	A295	10.60s multi	1.90	.40
C669	A295	10.60s multi	1.90	.40
C670	A295	10.60s multi	1.90	.40
C671	A295	12.80s multi	2.50	.55
C672	A295	12.80s multi	2.50	.55
C673	A295	12.80s multi	2.50	.55
C674	A295	13.60s multi	2.50	.55
C675	A295	13.60s multi	2.50	.55
C676	A295	13.60s multi	2.50	.55
C677	A295	17.80s multi	3.00	.65
C678	A295	22.80s multi	3.50	1.25
		Nos. C663-C678 (16)	36.25	8.25

Royal Visit Type

Perf. 11½x12

1980, May 18 Unwmk.

C679	A296	10.60s multi	.65	.40

Pichincha Provincial Development Council Building — AP171

1980, June 1 *Perf. 12x11½*

C680	AP171	10.60s multi	1.10	.50

Progress in Pichincha Province.

Indian Type

1980, June 10 Litho. *Perf. 12x11½*

C681 A297 7.60s Salasaca boy, Tungurahua 1.10 .85
C682 A297 10s Amula woman, Chimborazo 1.25 .95
C683 A297 10.60s Canar woman, Canar 1.60 1.10
C684 A297 13.60s Colorado Indian, Pichincha 1.75 1.40
Nos. C681-C684 (4) 5.70 4.30

Virgin of Mercy Type

1980, July 7 Litho. *Perf. 11½*

C685 A298 7.60s Cupola, cloisters .90 .50
C686 A298 7.60s Gold screen .90 .50
C687 A298 7.60s Quito from basilica tower .90 .50
C688 A298 10.60s Retable 1.10 .50
C689 A298 10.60s Pulpit 1.10 .50
C690 A298 13.60s Cupola 1.60 .75
C691 A298 13.60s Statue of Virgin 1.60 .75
Nos. C685-C691 (7) 8.10 4.00

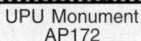

UPU Monument AP172

Marshal Sucre, by Marco Sales AP173

Design: 17.80s, Mail box, 1880.

1980, July 7 *Perf. 12*

C692 AP172 10.60s multi 1.25 .65
C693 AP172 17.80s multi 2.25 1.00

Souvenir Sheet

C694 AP172 25s multi 3.00 2.50

UPU membership cent. No. C694 contains designs of C692 and C693, horiz., perf. 11½.

Olympic Type.

Design: 10.60s, 13.60s, Moscow '80 emblem, Olympic rings.

Perf. 12x11½

1980, July 19 Wmk. 395

C695 A299 10.60s multi .70 .50
C696 A299 13.60s multi 1.00 .70

Souvenir Sheet

C697 A299 30s multi 6.75 6.75

No. C697 contains vignettes in designs of Nos. 991 and C695.

1980

C698 AP173 10.60s multi .70 .50

Marshal Antonio Jose de Sucre, death sesquicentennial.

Rotary International, 75th Anniversary AP174

1980, Aug. 4 *Perf. 11½*

C699 AP174 10s multi 1.10 .50

Riobamba Type

Design: 7.60s, 10.60s, Monstrance, Riobamba Cathedral, vert.

1980, Sept. 20 Litho. *Perf. 11½*

C700 A301 7.60s multi .70 .40
C701 A301 10.60s multi 1.00 .45

Souvenir Sheet
Imperf

C702 A301 30s multi 1.90 1.90

No. C702 contains vignettes in designs of Nos. 996-997.

Democracy Type

7.60s, 10.60s, Pres. Aguilera and voter.

Perf. 12x11½

1980, Oct. 9 Litho. Wmk. 395

C703 A302 7.60s multi 1.00 .55
C704 A302 10.60s multi 1.25 .60

Souvenir Sheet
Imperf

C705 A302 15s multi 1.10 1.10

No. C705 contains vignettes in designs of Nos. 999 and C703.

OPEC Type

20th Anniversary of OPEC: 7.60s, Men holding OPEC emblem, vert.

1980, Nov. 8 *Perf. 11½x12*

C706 A303 7.60s multi .55 .45

Carchi Province Type

10.60s, Governor's Palace, vert. 17.80s, Victory Museum, Central Square, vert.

1980, Nov. 21 *Perf. 13*

C707 A304 10.60c multi 1.25 .65
C708 A304 17.80s multi 2.00 1.00

Orchid Type

Perf. 12x11½, 11½x12

1980, Nov. 22

C709 A305 7.60s *Anguloa uniflora* 2.75 .70
C710 A305 10.60s *Scuticaria salesiana* 3.50 .45
C711 A305 50s *Helcia sanguinolenta*, vert. 5.75 1.40
C712 A305 100s *Anguloa virginalis* 7.75 2.75
Nos. C709-C712 (4) 19.75 5.30

Souvenir Sheets
Imperf

C713 A305 20s multi 4.50 3.25
C714 A305 20s multi 4.50 3.25

Nos. C713-C714 contain vignettes in designs of Nos. C709, C711 and C710, C712 respectively.

Christmas Type

7.60s, Pope blessing crowd. 10.60s, Portrait.

1980, Dec. 27 *Perf. 12*

C715 A306 7.60s multi, vert. .95 .50
C716 A306 10.60s multi, vert. 1.25 .60

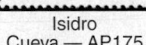

Isidro Cueva — AP175

Simon Bolivar, by Marco Salas — AP176

1980, Nov. 20 *Perf. 13*

C717 AP175 18.20s multi 2.25 1.10

Dr. Isidro Ayora Cueva, former president, birth centenary.

1980, Dec. 17 *Perf. 11½*

C718 AP176 13.60s multi 1.75 .90

Simon Bolivar death sesquicentennial.

Turtle, Galapagos Islands AP177

100s, Oldest Ecuadorian mail box, 1793.

1981, Feb. 12 Litho. *Perf. 13*

C719 AP177 50s multi 6.50 4.25
C720 AP177 100s multi, vert. 8.00 5.50

HCJB Type

1981 Litho. *Perf. 13*

C721 A311 7.60s Emblem, horiz. 1.00 .55
C722 A311 10.60s Emblem, diff. 1.40 .70

Soccer Players — AP178

1981, July 8

C723 AP178 7.60s Emblem 1.00 .60
C724 AP178 10.60s shown 1.25 .60
C725 AP178 13.60s World Cup 1.60 .90
Nos. C723-C725 (3) 3.85 2.10

Souvenir Sheets

C726 AP178 20s multi 3.25 3.25
C727 AP178 20s multi 3.25 3.25

1982 World Cup Soccer Championship. Nos. C726-C727 contain vignettes in designs of Nos. C723 and C724 respectively.

Picasso Type

1981, Oct. 26 Litho. *Perf. 13*

C728 A313a 7.60s Still-life .70 .35
C729 A313a 10.60s First Communion, vert. .85 .45
C730 A313a 13.60s Las Meninas, vert. .95 .65

Size: 110x90mm
Imperf

C731 A313a 20s multi 2.10 2.10
Nos. C728-C731 (4) 4.60 3.55

No. C731 contains designs of Nos. C730, C729.

World Food Day Type

1981, Dec. 31 Litho. *Perf. 13x13½*

C732 A314 10.60s Farming, vert. 1.00 .50

IYD Type

1982, Feb. 25 Litho. *Perf. 13*

C733 A316 7.60s Emblem .70 .40
C734 A316 10.60s Man with crutch .90 .45

Montalvo Type

1982 Litho. *Perf. 13*

C735 A318 5s Home, horiz. 1.00 .55

Swimming Type

1982, July 30

C736 A320 10.20s Emblem, vert. .85 .40
C737 A320 14.20s Diving, vert. 1.10 .45

Pres. Jaime Roldos, (1940-81), Mrs. Martha Roldos, Independence Monument, Quito — AP179

1983, May 25 Litho. *Perf. 12*

C738 AP179 13.60s multi .55 .40

Souvenir Sheet
Imperf

C739 AP179 20s multi .85 .85

AIR POST SEMI-POSTAL STAMPS

Nos. C119-C123 Surcharged in Blue or Red:

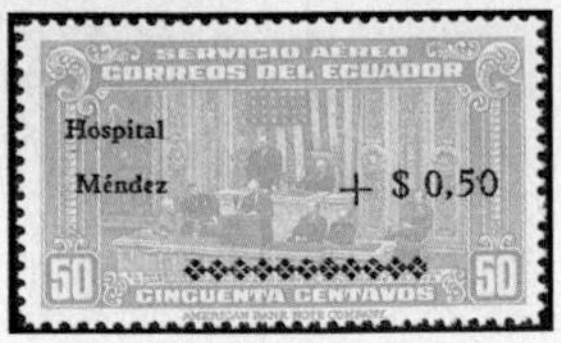

1944, May 9 Unwmk. *Perf. 12*

CB1 AP26 50c + 50c 6.50 3.25
CB2 AP26 70c + 30c 6.50 3.25
CB3 AP26 3s + 50c (R) 6.50 3.25
CB4 AP26 5s + 1s (R) 6.50 3.25
CB5 AP26 10s + 2s 6.50 3.25
Nos. CB1-CB5 (5) 32.50 16.25

The surtax aided Mendez Hospital.

AIR POST REGISTRATION STAMPS

Issued by Sociedad Colombo-Alemana de Transportes Aereos (SCADTA)

Nos. C3 and C3a Overprinted "R" in Carmine

1928-29 Wmk. 116 *Perf. 14x14½*

CF1 AP6 1s on 20c (#C3) 140.00 110.00
a. 1s on 20c (#C3a) ('29) 175.00 140.00

No. C18 Overprinted "R" in Black

1929, Apr. 1 Wmk. 127 *Perf. 14*

CF2 AP2 1s rose 75.00 60.00

AIR POST OFFICIAL STAMPS

Nos. C8-C15 Overprinted in Red or Black

1929, May Unwmk. *Perf. 12*

CO1 AP1 2c black (R) 1.00 .50
CO2 AP1 5c carmine rose 1.00 .50
CO3 AP1 10c deep brown 1.00 .50
CO4 AP1 20c dark violet 1.00 .50
CO5 AP1 50c deep green 4.00 2.00
CO6 AP1 1s dark blue 4.00 2.00
a. Inverted overprint 240.00
CO7 AP1 5s orange yellow 18.00 7.75
CO8 AP1 10s orange red 210.00 75.00
Nos. CO1-CO8 (8) 240.00 88.75

Establishment of commercial air service in Ecuador.

Counterfeits of No. CO8 exist.

See Nos. CO9-CO12. For overprints and surcharges see Nos. C35-C38.

1930, Jan. 9

CO9 AP1 50c olive brown 3.50 1.75
CO10 AP1 1s carmine lake 4.50 2.25
CO11 AP1 5s olive green 11.00 5.50
CO12 AP1 10s black 21.00 10.50
Nos. CO9-CO12 (4) 40.00 20.00

For surcharges & overprint see #C36-C38.

Air Post Stamps of 1937 Overprinted in Black

1937, Aug. 19

CO13 AP7 10c chestnut .50 .20
CO14 AP7 20c olive black .50 .20
CO15 AP7 70c black brown .60 .25
CO16 AP7 1s gray black .70 .25
CO17 AP7 2s dark violet .70 .35
Nos. CO13-CO17 (5) 3.00 1.25

For overprints see Nos. 463-464.

No. C79 Overprinted in Black

1940, Aug. 1 *Perf. 12½x13*

CO18	AP15	5s emerald	1.75	.65

Catalogue values for unused stamps in this section, from this point to the end of the section, are for Never Hinged items.

Nos. C352-C354 Overprinted: "1961 oficial"

1964 *Perf. 13½*

CO19	AP86	50c multi	1.75	.85
CO20	AP86	80c multi	1.75	.85
CO21	AP86	1.30s multi	1.75	.85
		Nos. CO19-CO21 (3)	5.25	2.55

SPECIAL DELIVERY STAMPS

SD1

1928 **Unwmk.** *Perf. 12*

E1	SD1	2c on 2c blue	8.00	9.00
E2	SD1	5c on 2c blue	7.00	9.00
E3	SD1	10c on 2c blue	7.00	6.00
a.		"10 CTVOS" inverted	21.00	25.00
E4	SD1	20c on 2c blue	10.00	9.00
E5	SD1	50c on 2c blue	12.00	9.00
		Nos. E1-E5 (5)	44.00	42.00

No. RA49A Surcharged in Red

1945

E6	PT18	20c on 5c green	3.00	2.00

LATE FEE STAMP

No. RA49A Surcharged in Black

1945 **Unwmk.** *Perf. 12*

I1	PT18	10c on 5c green	1.00	1.00

POSTAGE DUE STAMPS

Numeral — D1

Coat of Arms — D2

1896 **Engr.** **Wmk. 117** *Perf. 12*

J1	D1	1c blue green	6.00	6.50
J2	D1	2c blue green	6.00	6.50
J3	D1	5c blue green	6.00	6.50
J4	D1	10c blue green	6.00	6.50
J5	D1	20c blue green	6.00	8.50
J6	D1	50c blue green	6.00	13.00
J7	D1	100c blue green	6.00	17.00
		Nos. J1-J7 (7)	42.00	64.50

Reprints are on very thick paper with distinct watermark and vertical paper-weave direction. Value 20c each.

Unwmk.

J8	D1	1c blue green	5.00	6.00
J9	D1	2c blue green	5.00	6.00
J10	D1	5c blue green	5.00	6.00
J11	D1	10c blue green	5.00	6.00
J12	D1	20c blue green	5.00	7.50
J13	D1	50c blue green	5.00	10.50
J14	D1	100c blue green	5.00	15.00
		Nos. J8-J14 (7)	35.00	57.00

1929

J15	D2	5c deep blue	.40	.40
J16	D2	10c orange yellow	.40	.40
J17	D2	20c red	.60	.60
		Nos. J15-J17 (3)	1.40	1.40

Numeral — D3

Perf. 13½

1958, Nov. **Unwmk.** **Litho.**

J18	D3	10c bright lilac	.50	.40
J19	D3	50c emerald	.50	.40
J20	D3	1s maroon	.60	.40
J21	D3	2s red	.70	.40
		Nos. J18-J21 (4)	2.30	1.60

OFFICIAL STAMPS

Regular Issues of 1881 and 1887 Handstamped in Black

1886 **Unwmk.** *Perf. 12*

O1	A5	1c yellow brown	2.50	2.50
O2	A6	2c lake	3.00	3.00
O3	A7	5c blue	6.75	8.75
O4	A8	10c orange	5.25	3.25
O5	A9	20c gray violet	5.25	5.25
O6	A10	50c blue green	15.00	11.50
		Nos. O1-O6 (6)	37.75	34.25

1887

O7	A12	1c green	3.25	2.50
O8	A13	2c vermilion	3.25	3.25
O9	A14	5c blue	5.25	2.50
O10	A15	80c olive green	17.50	10.00
		Nos. O7-O10 (4)	29.25	18.25

Nos. O1-O10 are known with red handstamp but these are believed to be speculative.

The overprint on the 1886-87 issues is handstamped and is found in various positions.

Flores — O1

Arms — O1a

1892

Carmine Overprint

O11	O1	1c ultramarine	.20	.40
O12	O1	2c ultramarine	.20	.40
O13	O1	5c ultramarine	.20	.40
O14	O1	10c ultramarine	.20	.60
O15	O1	20c ultramarine	.20	.60
O16	O1	50c ultramarine	.20	.90
O17	O1	1s ultramarine	.35	1.00
		Nos. O11-O17 (7)	1.55	4.30

1894

O18	O1a	1c slate green (R)	15.00	
O19	O1a	2c lake (Bk)	20.00	

Nos. O18 and O19 were not placed in use.

Rocafuerte O20ovpt

Dated 1894

1894

Carmine Overprint

O20	O2	1c gray black	.60	1.00
O21	O2	2c gray black	.60	.60
O22	O2	5c gray black	.60	.60
O23	O2	10c gray black	.75	1.00
O24	O2	20c gray black	1.00	1.00
O25	O2	50c gray black	3.75	3.75
O26	O2	1s gray black	6.00	6.00
		Nos. O20-O26 (7)	13.30	13.95

Dated 1895

1895

Carmine Overprint

O27	O2	1c gray black	5.25	5.25
O28	O2	2c gray black	7.50	7.50
O29	O2	5c gray black	1.50	1.50
O30	O2	10c gray black	7.50	7.50
O31	O2	20c gray black	11.00	10.50
O32	O2	50c gray black	75.00	75.00
O33	O2	1s gray black	3.75	3.75
		Nos. O27-O33 (7)	111.50	111.00

Reprints of 1894-95 issues are on very thick paper with paper weave found both horizontal and vertical for all denominations. Values: Nos. O20-O26, 35c each; O27-O33, 20c each. Generally they are blacker than originals.

For overprints see Nos. O50-O91.

Types of 1896 Overprinted in Carmine

1896 **Wmk. 117**

O34	A21	1c olive bister	1.00	1.00
O35	A22	2c olive bister	1.00	1.00
O36	A23	5c olive bister	1.00	1.00
O37	A24	10c olive bister	1.00	1.00
O38	A25	20c olive bister	1.00	1.00
O39	A26	50c olive bister	1.00	1.00
O40	A27	1s olive bister	3.00	3.00
O41	A28	5s olive bister	6.00	6.00
		Nos. O34-O41 (8)	15.00	15.00

Reprints of Nos. O34-O41 are on thick paper with vertical paper weave direction. Value 20 cents each.

Unwmk.

O42	A21	1c olive bister	3.00	3.00
O43	A22	2c olive bister	3.00	3.00
O44	A23	5c olive bister	3.00	3.00
O45	A24	10c olive bister	3.00	3.00
O46	A25	20c olive bister	3.00	3.00
O47	A26	50c olive bister	3.00	3.00
O48	A27	1s olive bister	7.50	7.50
O49	A28	5s olive bister	10.50	10.50
		Nos. O42-O49 (8)	36.00	36.00

Reprints of Nos. O42-O49 all have overprint in black. Value 20 cents each.

#O20-O26 Overprinted 1897 1898

1897-98

O50	O2	1c gray black	20.00	20.00
O51	O2	2c gray black	35.00	35.00
O52	O2	5c gray black	200.00	200.00
O53	O2	10c gray black	30.00	30.00
O54	O2	20c gray black	20.00	20.00
O55	O2	50c gray black	35.00	35.00
O56	O2	1s gray black	55.00	55.00
		Nos. O50-O56 (7)	395.00	395.00

#O20-O26 Overprinted 1897 1898

O57	O2	1c gray black	4.00	4.00
O58	O2	2c gray black	9.00	9.00
O59	O2	5c gray black	90.00	90.00
O60	O2	10c gray black	100.00	100.00
O61	O2	20c gray black	25.00	25.00
O62	O2	50c gray black	15.00	15.00
O63	O2	1s gray black	165.00	165.00
		Nos. O57-O63 (7)	408.00	408.00

#O20-O26 Overprinted **1897 Y 1898**

O64	O2	1c gray black	40.00	40.00
O65	O2	2c gray black	40.00	40.00
O66	O2	5c gray black	40.00	40.00
O67	O2	10c gray black	40.00	40.00
O68	O2	20c gray black	40.00	40.00
O69	O2	50c gray black	40.00	40.00
O70	O2	1s gray black	40.00	40.00
		Nos. O64-O70 (7)	280.00	280.00

#O27-O33 Overprinted in Black like Nos. O50-O56

O71	O2	1c gray black	20.00	20.00
O72	O2	2c gray black	20.00	20.00
O73	O2	5c gray black	20.00	20.00
O74	O2	10c gray black	20.00	20.00
O75	O2	20c gray black	30.00	30.00
O76	O2	50c gray black	275.00	275.00
O77	O2	1s gray black	100.00	100.00
		Nos. O71-O77 (7)	485.00	485.00

#O27-O33 Overprinted like #O57-O63

O78	O2	1c gray black	35.00	35.00
O79	O2	2c gray black	30.00	30.00
O80	O2	5c gray black	30.00	30.00
O81	O2	10c gray black	32.50	32.50
O82	O2	20c gray black	42.50	42.50
O83	O2	50c gray black	30.00	30.00
O84	O2	1s gray black	30.00	30.00

#O27-O33 Overprinted like #O64-O70

O85	O2	1c gray black	90.00	90.00
O86	O2	2c gray black	20.00	20.00
O87	O2	5c gray black	80.00	80.00
O88	O2	10c gray black	80.00	80.00
O89	O2	20c gray black	140.00	140.00
O90	O2	50c gray black	85.00	85.00
O91	O2	1s gray black	165.00	165.00
		Nos. O85-O91 (7)	660.00	660.00

Many forged overprints of Nos. O50-O91 exist, made on the original stamps and reprints.

O3

Black Surcharge

1898-99 *Perf. 15, 16*

O92	O3	5c on 50c lilac	10.00	10.00
a.		Inverted surcharge	25.00	25.00
O93	O3	10c on 20s org	15.00	15.00
a.		Double surcharge	40.00	30.00
O94	O3	10c on 50c lilac	140.00	140.00
O95	O3	20c on 50c lilac	30.00	30.00
O96	O3	20c on 50s green	30.00	30.00
		Nos. O92-O96 (5)	225.00	225.00

Green Surcharge

O97	O3	5c on 50c lilac	10.00	10.00
a.		Double surcharge	5.00	
b.		Double surcharge, blk and grn	12.00	
c.		As "b," blk surch. invtd.	5.00	

Red Surcharge

1899

O98	O3	5c on 50c lilac	10.00	10.00
a.		Double surcharge	20.00	
b.		Dbl. surch., blk and red	25.00	
O99	O3	20c on 50s green	15.00	15.00
a.		Inverted surcharge	40.00	
b.		Dbl. surch., red and blk	60.00	

Similar Surcharge in Black Value in Words in Two Lines

O100	O3	1c on 5c blue	650.00	

Red Surcharge

O101	O3	2c on 5c blue	1,150.	
O102	O3	4c on 20c blue	800.00	

Types of Regular Issue of 1899 Overprinted in Black

1899 ***Perf. 14, 15***

O103 A37 2c orange & blk .70 *1.60*
O104 A39 10c orange & blk .70 *1.60*
O105 A40 20c orange & blk .50 *2.50*
O106 A41 50c orange & blk .50 *3.25*
Nos. O103-O106 (4) 2.40 *8.95*

For overprint see No. O167.

The above overprint was applied to remainders of the postage stamps of 1904 with the idea of increasing their salability. They were never regularly in use as official stamps.

Regular Issue of 1911-13 Overprinted in Black

1913 ***Perf. 12***

O107 A71 1c scarlet & blk 3.50 3.50
O108 A72 2c blue & blk 3.50 3.50
O109 A73 3c orange & blk 2.25 2.25
O110 A74 5c scarlet & blk 4.50 4.50
O111 A75 10c blue & blk 4.50 4.50
Nos. O107-O111 (5) 18.25 18.25

Regular Issue of 1911-13 Overprinted

Overprint 22x3½mm

1916-17

O112 A72 2c blue & blk 25.00 18.00
O113 A74 5c scarlet & blk 25.00 18.00
O114 A75 10c blue & blk 15.00 12.00
Nos. O112-O114 (3) 65.00 48.00

Overprint 25x4mm

O115 A71 1c scarlet & blk 1.10 1.10
O116 A72 2c blue & blk 1.60 1.60
a. Inverted overprint 5.00 5.00
O117 A73 3c orange & blk 1.00 1.00
O118 A74 5c scarlet & blk 1.60 1.60
O119 A75 10c blue & blk 1.60 1.60
Nos. O115-O119 (5) 6.90 6.90

Same Overprint On Regular Issue of 1915-17

O120 A71 1c orange 1.40 1.40
O121 A72 2c green 1.40 1.40
O122 A73 3c black 2.25 2.25
O123 A78 4c red & blk 2.25 2.25
a. Inverted overprint 15.00
O124 A74 5c violet 1.40 1.40
O125 A75 10c blue 2.75 2.75
O126 A79 20c green & blk 15.00 15.00
Nos. O120-O126 (7) 26.45 26.45

Regular Issues of 1911-17 Overprinted in Black or Red

O127 A71 1c orange .90 .90
O128 A72 2c green .70 .70
O129 A73 3c black (Bk) .90 .90
O130 A73 3c black (R) .90 .70
a. Inverted overprint
O131 A78 4c red & blk .90 .90
O132 A74 5c violet 1.75 .70
O133 A75 10c blue & blk 4.50 1.75
O134 A75 10c blue .90 .90
O135 A79 20c green & blk 4.50 1.75
Nos. O127-O135 (9) 15.95 9.20

Regular Issue of 1920 Overprinted

1920

O136 A86 1c green 1.25 1.25
a. Inverted overprint 17.00 —
O137 A86 2c carmine 1.00 1.00
O138 A86 3c yellow brn 1.25 1.25
O139 A86 4c dark green 2.00 2.00
a. Inverted overprint 17.00 —
O140 A86 5c blue 2.00 2.00
O141 A86 6c orange 1.25 1.25
O142 A86 7c brown 2.00 2.00
O143 A86 8c yellow green 2.50 2.50
O144 A86 9c red 3.25 3.25
O145 A95 10c blue 2.00 2.00
O146 A86 15c gray 11.00 11.00
O147 A86 20c deep violet 14.50 14.50
O148 A86 30c violet 17.00 17.00
O149 A86 40c dark brown 21.00 21.00
O150 A86 50c dark green 14.50 14.50
O151 A86 60c dark blue 17.00 17.00
O152 A86 70c gray 17.00 17.00
O153 A86 80c yellow 21.00 21.00
O154 A104 90c green 21.00 21.00
O155 A86 1s blue 45.00 45.00
Nos. O136-O155 (20) 217.50 217.50

Cent. of the independence of Guayaquil.

Stamps of 1911 Overprinted

1922

O156 A71 1c scarlet & blk 9.00 9.00
O157 A72 2c blue & blk 4.50 4.50

Revenue Stamps of 1919-1920 Overprinted like Nos. O156 and O157

1924

O158 PT3 1c dark blue 2.00 2.00
O159 PT3 2c green 12.50 12.50

Regular Issues of 1911-17 Overprinted

OFICIAL

1924

O160 A71 1c orange 7.00 7.00
a. Inverted overprint 15.00

Overprinted in Black or Red

O161 A72 2c green .60 .60
O162 A73 3c black (R) .80 .80
O163 A78 4c red & blk 1.25 1.25
O164 A74 5c violet 1.25 1.25
O165 A75 10c deep blue 1.25 1.25
O166 A76 1s green & blk 7.00 7.00
Nos. O160-O166 (7) 19.15 19.15

No. O106 with Additional Overprint

1924 ***Perf. 14, 15***

O167 A41 50c orange & blk 2.25 2.25

#O160-O167 exist with inverted overprint.

No. 199 Overprinted

1924 ***Perf. 12***

O168 A71 1c orange 5.50 5.50

Regular Issues of 1911-25 Overprinted

1925

O169 A71 1c scarlet & blk 10.00 4.25
a. Inverted overprint 15.00
O170 A71 1c orange .60 .60
a. Inverted overprint 4.00
O171 A72 2c green .60 .60
a. Inverted overprint 4.00
O172 A73 3c black (Bk) .60 .60
O173 A73 3c black (R) 1.10 1.10
O174 A78 4c red & blk .60 .60
O175 A74 5c violet .80 .80
O176 A74 5c rose .80 .80
O177 A75 10c deep blue .60 .60
Nos. O169-O177 (9) 15.70 9.95

Regular Issues of 1916-25 Overprinted Vertically Up or Down

1927, Oct.

O178 A71 1c orange 2.00 2.00
O179 A86 2c carmine 2.00 2.00
O180 A86 3c yellow brown 2.00 2.00
O181 A86 4c myrtle green 2.00 2.00
O182 A86 5c pale blue 2.00 2.00
O183 A75 10c yellow green 2.00 2.00
Nos. O178-O183 (6) 12.00 12.00

Regular Issues of 1920-27 Overprinted

1928

O184 A71 1c lt blue 1.25 1.25
O185 A86 2c carmine 1.25 1.25
O186 A86 3c yellow brown 1.25 1.25
a. Inverted overprint 5.00
O187 A86 4c myrtle green 1.25 1.25
O188 A86 5c lt blue 1.25 1.25
O189 A75 10c yellow green 1.25 1.25
O190 A109 20c violet 11.00 2.50
a. Overprint reading up 3.50 2.25
Nos. O184-O190 (7) 18.50 10.00

The overprint is placed vertically reading down on No. O190.

Regular Issue of 1936 Overprinted in Black

1936 ***Perf. 14***

O191 A131 5c olive green 1.50 .50
O192 A132 10c brown 1.50 .50
O193 A133 20c dark violet 1.90 .70
O194 A134 1s dark carmine 2.25 1.10
O195 A135 2s dark blue 2.50 1.75
Nos. O191-O195 (5) 9.65 4.55

Regular Postage Stamps of 1937 Overprinted in Black

1937 ***Perf. 11½***

O196 A139 2c green .40 .40
O197 A140 5c deep rose .40 .40
O198 A141 10c blue .40 .40
O199 A142 20c deep rose .40 .40
O200 A143 1s olive green .40 .40
Nos. O196-O200 (5) 2.00 2.00

Catalogue values for unused stamps in this section, from this point to the end of the section, are for Never Hinged items.

Tobacco Stamp, Overprinted in Black

CORRESPONDENCIA OFICIAL

1946 **Unwmk.** ***Rouletted***

O201 PT7 1c rose red 1.75 1.75

Communications Building, Quito — O4

1947 **Unwmk.** **Litho.** ***Perf. 11***

O202 O4 30c brown .60 .40
O203 O4 30c greenish blue .60 .40
a. Imperf., pair
O204 O4 30c purple .60 .40
Nos. O202-O204 (3) 1.80 1.20

Nos. O202 to O204 overprinted "Primero la Patria!" and plane in dark blue are said to be essays.

No. 719 with Additional Diagonal Overprint

Illustration reduced.

1964 ***Perf. 14x13***

O205 A231 80c block of 4 6.00 6.00

The "OEA" overprint covers four stamps, the "oficial" overprint is applied to every stamp.

A set of 20 imperforate items in the above Roosevelt design, some overprinted with the initials of various government ministries, was released in 1949. Later that year a set of 8 miniature sheets, bearing the same design plus a marginal inscription, "Presidencia (or Vicepresidencia) de la Republica," and a frame-line were released. In the editors' opinion, information justifying the listing of these issues has not been received.

POSTAL TAX STAMPS

Roca — PT1

1920 **Unwmk.** ***Perf. 12***
RA1 PT1 1c orange .60 .30

PT2 PT3

RA2 PT2 1c red & blue 1.10 .20
a. "de" inverted 10.50 5.25
b. Double overprint 10.00 .60
c. Inverted overprint 10.00 .60
RA3 PT3 1c deep blue 1.25 .20
a. Inverted overprint 6.00 1.00
b. Double overprint 6.00 1.00

For overprints see Nos. O158-O159.

PT4 PT5

Red or Black Surcharge or Overprint

Stamp Dated 1911-1912

RA4 PT4 20c deep blue — 30.00

Stamp Dated 1913-1914

RA5 PT4 20c deep blue (R) 2.25 .35

Stamp Dated 1917-1918

RA6 PT4 20c olive green (R) 6.50 .55
a. Dated 1919-20 *25.00*
RA7 PT5 1c on 2c green .90 .20

Stamp Dated 1911-1912

RA8 PT5 1c on 5c green .90 .20
a. Double surcharge

Stamp Dated 1913-1914

RA9 PT5 1c on 5c green 8.00 .55
a. Double surcharge 12.00 4.00

On Nos. RA7, RA8 and RA9 the surcharge is found reading upward or downward.
For surcharges see Nos. RA15-RA16.

Post Office — PT6

1920-24 **Engr.**
RA10 PT6 1c olive green .40 .20
RA11 PT6 2c deep green .40 .20
RA12 PT6 20c bister brn ('24) 1.75 .20
RA13 PT6 2s violet 11.50 3.25
RA14 PT6 5s blue 20.00 5.75
Nos. RA10-RA14 (5) 34.05 9.60

For overprints and surcharge see Nos. 259, 266-268, 273, 302, RA17.

Revenue Stamps of 1917-18 Surcharged Vertically in Red reading up or down

1921-22
RA15 PT5 20c on 1c dk blue 55.00 6.50
RA16 PT5 20c on 2c green 55.00 6.50

No. RA12 Surcharged in Green

1924
RA17 PT6 2c on 20c bis brn .60 .20
a. Inverted surcharge 12.00 5.00
b. Double surcharge 4.00 2.00

PT7

1924 ***Rouletted 7***
RA18 PT7 1c rose red .90 .20
a. Inverted overprint 3.50

Similar Design, Eagle at left

Perf. 12

RA19 PT7 2c blue .90 .20
a. Inverted overprint 3.50 1.75

For overprints & surcharges see #346, O201, RA32, RA34, RA37, RA44-RA45, RA47.

PT8

Inscribed "Timbre Fiscal"

1924
RA20 PT8 1c yellow 4.50 .85
RA21 PT8 2c dark blue 1.40 .35

Inscribed "Region Oriental"

RA22 PT8 1c yellow .70 .30
RA23 PT8 2c dark blue 1.40 .35
Nos. RA20-RA23 (4) 8.00 1.85

Overprint on No. RA22 reads down or up.

Revenue Stamp Overprinted in Blue

1934
RA24 2c green .40 .20
a. Blue overprint inverted 3.50 1.75
b. Blue ovpt. dbl., one invtd. 4.00 1.25

No. 310 Overprinted in Red

Perf. 12½

RA25 A119 20c ultra & yel .50 .20

Telegraph Stamp Overprinted in Red, like No. RA24, and Surcharged diagonally in Black

1934 ***Perf. 14***
RA26 2c on 10c olive brn .70 .20
a. Double surcharge 5.50

Overprint Blue, Surcharge Red

RA27 2c on 10c olive brn .70 .20

PT9 PT10

Symbols of Post and Telegraph Service
PT11

1934-36 ***Perf. 12***
RA28 PT9 2c green .60 .20
a. Both overprints in red ('36) .60 .20

Postal Tax stamp of 1920-24, overprinted in red "POSTAL" has been again overprinted "CASA de Correos y Teleg. de Guayaquil" in black.

Perf. 14½x14

1934 **Photo.** **Wmk. 233**
RA29 PT10 2c yellow green .40 .20

For the rebuilding of the GPO at Guayaquil.
For surcharge see No. RA31.

1935
RA30 PT11 20c claret .50 .20

For the rebuilding of the GPO at Guayaquil.

No. RA29 Surcharged in Red and Overprinted in Black

1935
RA31 PT10 3c on 2c yel grn .40 .20
a. Double surcharge

Social and Rural Workers' Insurance Fund.

Tobacco Stamp Surcharged in Black

1936 **Unwmk.** ***Rouletted 7***
RA32 PT7 3c on 1c rose red .60 .20
a. Lines of words reversed 2.00 .20
b. Horiz. pair, imperf. vert.

Issued for the Social and Rural Workers' Insurance Fund.

No. 310 Overprinted in Black

1936 ***Perf. 12½***
RA33 A119 20c ultra & yel .60 .20
a. Double overprint

Tobacco Stamp Surcharged in Black

1936 ***Rouletted 7***
RA34 PT7 3c on 1c rose red .60 .20

Social and Rural Workers' Insurance Fund.

Worker — PT12

1936 **Engr.** ***Perf. 13½***
RA35 PT12 3c ultra .40 .20

Social and Rural Workers' Insurance Fund.
For surcharges see Nos. C64, RA36, RA53-RA54.

Surcharged in Black

1936
RA36 PT13 5c on 3c ultra .60 .20

This combines the 2c for the rebuilding of the post office with the 3c for the Social and Rural Workers' Insurance Fund.

National Defense Issue

Tobacco Stamp, Surcharged in Black

1936 ***Rouletted 7***
RA37 PT7 10c on 1c rose .90 .20
a. Double surcharge

Symbolical of Defense — PT14

1937-42 ***Perf. 12½***
RA38 PT14 10c deep blue .90 .20

A 1s violet and 2s green exist in type PT14.
For surcharge see No. RA40.

PT15

Overprinted or Surcharged in Black

Perf. 13½, 11½

1937 **Engr. & Typo.**
RA39 PT15 5c lt brn & red 2.00 .25
d. Inverted overprint 20.00

1942 ***Perf. 12, 11½***
RA39A PT15 20c on 5c rose pink & red 75.00 20.00
RA39B PT15 20c on 1s yel brn & red 75.00 20.00
RA39C PT15 20c on 2s grn & red 75.00 20.00
Nos. RA39A-RA39C (3) 225.00 60.00

A 50c dark blue and red exists.

No. RA38 Surcharged in Red

1937 **Engr.** ***Perf. 12½***

RA40 PT14 5c on 10c dp blue 1.10 .20

Map of Ecuador — PT16

1938 ***Perf. 14x13½***

RA41 PT16 5c carmine rose .70 .20

Social and Rural Workers' Insurance Fund.

No. C42 Surcharged in Red

1938 ***Perf. 12½***

RA42 AP5 20c on 70c black 1.10 .20

No. 307 Surcharged in Red

1938

RA43 A116 5c on 6c yel & red .40 .20

This stamp was obligatory on all mail from Nov. 23rd to 30th, 1938. The tax was for the Intl. Union for the Control of Cancer.

Tobacco Stamp, Surcharged in Black

1939 ***Rouletted***

RA44 PT7 5c on 1c rose .70 .20
- *a.* Double surcharge
- *b.* Triple surcharge

Tobacco Stamp, Surcharged in Blue

1940

RA45 PT7 5c on 1c rose red 1.00 .20
- *a.* Double surcharge 3.50 3.50

No. 370 Surcharged in Carmine

1940 ***Perf. 11½***

RA46 A144 20c on 50c blk & multi .50 .20
- *a.* Double surcharge, one inverted

Tobacco Stamp, Surcharged in Black

TIMBRE PATRIOTICO
VEINTE CENTAVOS

1940 ***Rouletted***

RA47 PT7 20c on 1c rose red 6.00 .50

Farmer Plowing PT17

Communication Symbols PT18

1940 ***Perf. 13x13½***

RA48 PT17 5c carmine rose .70 .20

1940-43 ***Perf. 12***

RA49 PT18 5c copper brown .70 .20

RA49A PT18 5c green ('43) .70 .20

For overprint & surcharges see #534, E6, I1.

Pursuit Planes PT19

Warrior Shielding Women PT20

1941 ***Perf. 11½x13***

RA50 PT19 20c ultra 1.10 .20

The tax was used for national defense.

1942-46 **Engr.** ***Perf. 12***

RA51 PT20 20c dark blue 1.10 .20

RA51A PT20 40c black brown ('46) 1.10 .20

The tax was used for national defense.

A 20c carmine, 20c brown and 30c gray exist lithographed in type PT20.

No. 370 Surcharged in Carmine

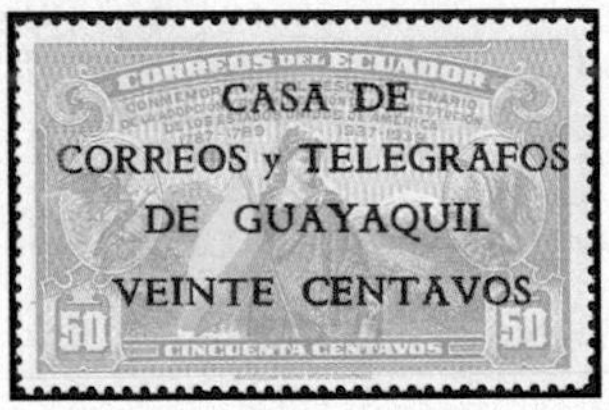

1942 ***Perf. 11½***

RA52 A144 20c on 50c multi 1.10 .20
- *a.* Double surcharge 10.00

No. RA35 Surcharged in Red

ADICIONAL
CINCO
CENTAVOS

1943 ***Perf. 13½***

RA53 PT12 5c on 3c ultra .60 .20

No. RA53 with Additional Surcharge in Black

1943

RA54 PT12 5c on 5c on 3c ultra 1.10 .20

Peons — PT21

Coat of Arms — PT22

1943 ***Perf. 12***

RA55 PT21 5c blue .90 .20

The tax was for farm workers.

For overprint & surcharge see #535, C135.

Revenue Stamp (as No. RA64) Overprinted or Surcharged in Black

TIMBRE
PATRIOTICO

No. RA56

No. RA57

1943 ***Perf. 12½***

RA56 20c red orange *75.00* 1.50

1943 ***Perf. 12***

RA57 20c on 10c orange 2.25 .25
- *a.* Double surcharge

1943 ***Perf. 12½***

RA58 PT22 20c orange red .70 .20

The tax was for national defense.

No. RA58 Surcharged in Black

1944

RA59 PT22 30c on 20c org red .70 .20
- *a.* Double surcharge

Catalogue values for unused stamps in this section, from this point to the end of the section, are for Never Hinged items.

Consular Service Stamps Surcharged in Black

1951 **Unwmk.** ***Perf. 12***

RA60 R1 20c on 1s red .60 .20

RA61 R1 20c on 2s brown .60 .20

RA62 R1 20c on 5s violet .60 .20

Nos. RA60-RA62 (3) 1.80 .60

Teacher and Pupils in Schoolyard — PT23

PT24

1952 **Engr.** ***Perf. 13***

RA63 PT23 20c blue green .60 .20

Revenue Stamp Overprinted "PATRIOTICO / SANITARIO"

1952 ***Perf. 12***

RA64 PT24 40(c) olive green 1.10 .20

For overprints & surcharges see #RA56-RA57

Woman Holding Flag — PT25

PT26

1953 ***Perf. 12½***

RA65 PT25 40c ultra 1.25 .20

Telegraph Stamp Surcharged "ESCOLAR 20 Centavos" in Black

1954 **Unwmk.** ***Perf. 13***

RA66 PT26 20c on 30c red brn 1.00 .20

PT26a

PT26b

PT26c

Revenue Stamps Surcharged or Overprinted Horizontally in Black "PRO TURISMO 1954"

1954 **Unwmk.** ***Perf. 12***

RA67 PT26a 10c on 25c blue 1.25 .20

RA68 PT26b 10c on 50c org red 1.25 .20

RA69 PT26c 10c carmine 1.25 .20

Nos. RA67-RA69 (3) 3.75 .60

PT27

Telegraph Stamp Surcharged "Pro-Turismo 1954 10 ctvs. 10"

1954 ***Perf. 13***

RA70 PT27 10c on 30c red brn 2.25 .20

Revenue Stamp Overprinted in Black

1954 ***Perf. 12***

RA71 R3 20c olive black 1.75 .20

Consular Service Stamp Surcharged in Black

1954

RA72 R1 20c on 10s gray 1.75 .20

Young Student at Desk PT28

Globe, Ship, Plane PT29

Imprint: "Heraclio Fournier.-Vitoria"

1954 **Photo.** ***Perf. 11***

RA73 PT28 20c rose pink 1.10 .20

See No. RA76.

1954 **Engr.** ***Perf. 12***

RA74 PT29 10c dp magenta 1.60 .20

Soldier Kissing Flag — PT30

1955 **Photo.** ***Perf. 11***

RA75 PT30 40c blue 2.25 .20

See No. RA77.

Types of 1954-55 Redrawn.
Imprint: "Thomas de la Rue & Co. Ltd."

1957 **Unwmk.** ***Perf. 13***

RA76 PT28 20c rose pink 1.10 .20

Perf. 14x14½

RA77 PT30 40c blue 2.25 .20

No. RA77 is inscribed "Republica del Ecuador."

The above stamp is believed to have been used only for fiscal purposes.

AIR POST POSTAL TAX STAMPS

No. 438 Surcharged in Black or Carmine

1945 **Unwmk.** ***Perf. 11***

RAC1 A173 20c on 10c dk grn .75 .20
a. Pair, one without surcharge 90.00

RAC2 A173 20c on 10c dk grn (C) .75 .20

Obligatory on letters and parcel post carried on planes in the domestic service.

Liberty, Mercury and Planes PTAP1

1946 **Engr.** ***Perf. 12***

RAC3 PTAP1 20c orange brown .75 .20

GALAPAGOS ISLANDS

Issued for use in the Galapagos Islands (Columbus Archipelago), a province of Ecuador, but were commonly used throughout the country.

Catalogue values for unused stamps in this section are for Never Hinged items.

Sea Lions — A1

Map — A2

Design: 1s, Marine iguana.

Unwmk.

1957, July 15 **Photo.** ***Perf. 12***

L1 A1 20c dark brown 1.25 .25
L2 A2 50c violet .80 .25
L3 A1 1s dull olive green 4.25 .65
Nos. L1-L3 (3) 6.30 1.15
Nos. L1-L3,LC1-LC3 (6) 16.00 3.10

125th anniv. of Ecuador's possession of the Galapagos Islands, and publicizing the islands.

See Nos. LC1-LC3. For overprints see Nos. 684-686, C389-C391.

GALAPAGOS AIR POST STAMPS

Type of Regular Issue

1s, Santa Cruz Island. 1.80s, Map of Galapagos archipelago. 4.20s, Galapagos giant tortoise.

Unwmk.

1957, July 19 **Photo.** ***Perf. 12***

LC1 A1 1s deep blue 1.10 .25
LC2 A1 1.80s rose violet 2.10 .60
LC3 A1 4.20s black 6.50 1.10
Nos. LC1-LC3 (3) 9.70 1.95

For overprints see Nos. C389-C391.

Redrawn Type of Ecuador, 1956

1959, Jan. 3 **Engr.** ***Perf. 14***

LC4 AP69 2s lt olive green .85 .50

Issued to honor the United Nations. See note after No. C407.

EGYPT

'ē-jəpt

LOCATION — Northern Africa, bordering on the Mediterranean and the Red Sea
GOVT. — Republic
AREA — 386,900 sq. mi.
POP. — 61,404,000 (1997 est.)
CAPITAL — Cairo

Modern Egypt was a part of Turkey until 1914 when a British protectorate was declared over the country and the Khedive was deposed in favor of Hussein Kamil under the title of sultan. In 1922 the protectorate ended and the reigning sultan was declared king of the new monarchy. Egypt became a republic on June 18, 1953. Egypt merged with Syria in 1958 to form the United Arab Republic. Syria left this union in 1961. In 1971 Egypt took the name of Arab Republic of Egypt.

40 Paras = 1 Piaster
1000 Milliemes = 100 Piasters = 1 Pound (1888)
1000 Milliemes = 1 Pound (1953)
1000 Milliemes = 100 Piasters = 1 Pound (1982)

Catalogue values for unused stamps in this country are for Never Hinged items, beginning with Scott 241 in the regular postage section, Scott B1 in the semi-postal section, Scott C38 in the airpost section, Scott CB1 in the airpost semi-postal section, Scott E5 in the special delivery section, Scott J40 in the postage due section, Scott M16 in the military stamps section, Scott O60 in the officials section, Scott N1 in the occupation section, Scott NC1 in the occupation airpost section, Scott NE1 in the occupation special delivery section, and Scott NJ1 in the occupation postage due section.

Watermarks

Wmk. 118 — Pyramid and Star

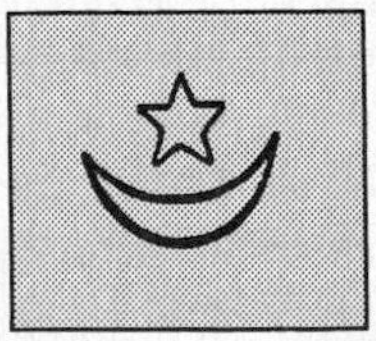
Wmk. 119 — Crescent and Star

Wmk. 120 — Triple Crescent and Star

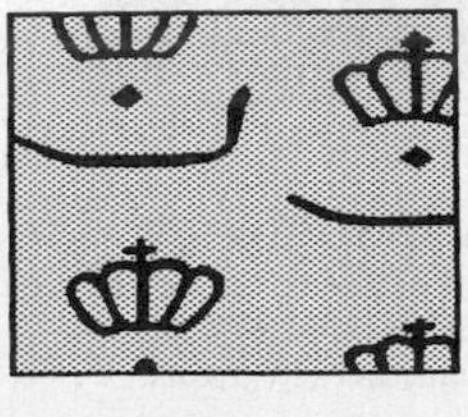
Wmk. 195 — Multiple Crown and Arabic F

"F" in watermark stands for Fuad.

Wmk. 315 — Multiple Eagle

Wmk. 318 — Multiple Eagle and "Misr"

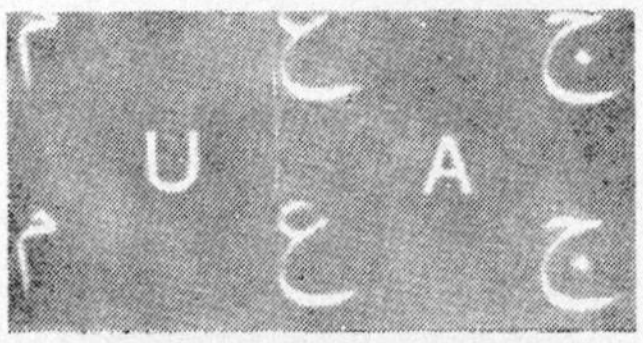

Wmk. 328 — U A R

Wmk. 342 — Coat of Arms, Multiple

Values for unused stamps are for examples with original gum as defined in the catalogue introduction. Very fine examples of Nos. 1-15 will have perforations that are clear of the framelines but with the design noticeably off center. Well centered stamps are extremely scarce and will command substantial premiums.

Turkish Suzerainty

A1

A2

A3

A4

A5

A6

A7

Surcharged in Black

Wmk. 118

1866, Jan. 1 Litho. *Perf. 12½*

1	A1 5pa greenish gray	50.00	30.00
a.	Imperf., pair	225.00	
b.	Pair, imperf. between	350.00	
c.	Perf. 12½x13	57.50	55.00
d.	Perf. 13	300.00	*350.00*
2	A2 10pa brown	75.00	32.50
a.	Imperf., pair	190.00	
b.	Pair, imperf. between	400.00	
c.	Perf. 13	200.00	*210.00*
d.	Perf. 12½x15	300.00	*325.00*
e.	Perf. 12½x13	92.50	55.00
3	A3 20pa blue	95.00	35.00
a.	Imperf., pair	275.00	
b.	Pair, imperf. between	450.00	
c.	Perf. 12½x13	110.00	95.00
d.	Perf. 13	475.00	275.00
4	A4 2pi yellow	110.00	47.50
a.	Imperf.	*125.00*	*125.00*
b.	Imperf. vert. or horiz., pair	400.00	400.00
c.	Perf. 12½x15	150.00	
d.	Diagonal half used as 1pi on cover		*2,600.*
e.	Perf. 12½x13, 13x12½	140.00	55.00
5	A5 5pi rose	300.00	250.00
a.	Imperf.	400.00	375.00
b.	Imperf. vert. or horiz., pair	*1,200.*	
d.	Inscription of 10pi, imperf.	950.00	850.00
e.	Perf. 12½x13, 13x12½	350.00	275.00
f.	As "d," perf. 12½x15	1,000.	850.00
6	A6 10pi slate bl	350.00	325.00
a.	Imperf.	*550.00*	450.00
b.	Pair, imperf. between	*2,250.*	
c.	Perf. 12½x13, 13x12½	550.00	550.00
d.	Perf. 13	*1,850.*	

Unwmk.

Typo.

7	A7 1pi rose lilac	72.50	5.50
a.	Imperf.	110.00	
b.	Horiz. pair, imperf. vert.	500.00	
c.	Perf. 12½x13, 13x12½	100.00	25.00
d.	Perf. 13	350.00	210.00
	Nos. 1-7 (7)	1,052.	725.50

Single imperforates of types A1-A10 are sometimes simulated by trimming wide-margined examples of perforated stamps.

No. 4d must be dated between July 16 and July 31, 1867.

Proofs of Nos. 1-7 are on smooth white paper, unwatermarked and imperforate. Proofs of No. 7 are on thinner paper than No. 7a.

Sphinx and Pyramid — A8

Perf. 15x12½

1867-69 Litho. Wmk. 119

8	A8 5pa orange	25.00	11.00
a.	Imperf.	250.00	—
b.	Horiz. pair, imperf between	175.00	
c.	Vert. pair, imperf between	—	
9	A8 10pa lilac ('69)	62.50	11.00
a.	10pa violet	82.50	14.00
b.	Half used as 5pa on newspaper piece		850.00
11	A8 20pa yel grn ('69)	110.00	11.00
a.	20pa blue green	125.00	17.00
13	A8 1pi rose red	11.00	1.10
a.	Imperf, pair	150.00	
b.	Pair, imperf. between	300.00	
d.	Rouletted	70.00	
e.	1pi lake red	130.00	32.50
14	A8 2pi blue	150.00	17.00
a.	Imperf.	250.00	
b.	Horiz. pair, imperf. vert.	500.00	
d.	Perf. 12½	250.00	
15	A8 5pi brown	375.00	200.00
	Nos. 8-15 (6)	733.50	251.10

There are 4 types of each value, so placed that any block of 4 contains all types.

A9

A10

Clear Impressions

Thick Opaque Paper

Typographed by the Government at Boulac

Perf. 12½x13½ Clean-cut

1872 Wmk. 119

19	A9 5pa brown	9.25	5.00
20	A9 10pa lilac	9.00	3.75
21	A9 20pa blue	50.00	4.00
22	A9 1pi rose red	57.50	2.25
h.	Half used as 20pa on cover		700.00
23	A9 2pi dull yellow	97.50	15.00
j.	Half used as 1p on cover		1,200.
24	A9 2½pi dull violet	82.50	11.00
25	A9 5pi green	325.00	35.00
i.	Tête bêche pair		
	Nos. 19-25 (7)	630.75	76.00

Perf. 13½ Clean-cut

19a	A9 5pa brown	27.50	9.25
20a	A9 10pa dull lilac	9.00	4.25
21a	A9 20pa blue	90.00	20.00
22a	A9 1pi rose red	82.50	8.00
23a	A9 2pi dull yellow	55.00	8.00
24a	A9 2½pi dull violet	1,200.	225.00
25a	A9 5pi green	375.00	75.00

Litho.

21m	A9 20pa blue, perf. 12½x13½	150.00	50.00
21n	A9 20pa blue, perf. 13½	225.00	80.00
21p	A9 20pa blue, imperf.	250.00	
22m	A9 1pi rose red, perf. 12½x13½	550.00	20.00
22n	A9 1pi rose red, perf. 13½	875.00	50.00

Typographed

Blurred Impressions

Thinner Paper

Perf. 12½ Rough

1874-75 Wmk. 119

26	A10 5pa brown ('75)	8.50	3.50
e.	Imperf.	200.00	200.00
f.	Vert. pair, imperf. horiz.	1,000.	—
g.	Tête bêche pair	40.00	40.00
20b	A9 10pa gray lilac	10.00	3.50
g.	Tête bêche pair	225.00	225.00
21b	A9 20pa gray blue	90.00	4.00
k.	Half used as 10pa on cover		—
22b	A9 1pi vermilion	7.50	1.75
f.	Imperf.	—	150.00
g.	Tête bêche pair	150.00	125.00
23b	A9 2pi yellow	75.00	5.75
i.	Tête bêche pair	600.00	600.00
24b	A9 2½pi deep violet	9.25	3.50
e.	Imperf.	—	—
f.	Tête bêche pair	600.00	600.00
25b	A9 5pi yellow green	60.00	22.50
e.	Imperf.	400.00	—

No. 26f normally occurs tête-bêche.

Perf. 13½x12½ Rough

26c	A10 5pa brown	7.50	4.50
i.	Tête bêche pair	62.50	62.50
20c	A9 10pa gray lilac	12.00	3.25
i.	Tête bêche pair	225.00	225.00
21c	A9 20pa gray blue	8.50	3.75
h.	Pair, imperf. between	350.00	
22c	A9 1pi vermilion	55.00	3.25
i.	Tête bêche pair	500.00	500.00
23c	A9 2pi yellow	10.00	6.00
g.	Tête bêche pair	500.00	500.00
k.	Half used as 1pi on cover		*2,800.*

Perf. 12½x13½ Rough

23d	A9 2pi yellow ('75)	62.50	10.00
h.	Tête bêche pair	*1,250.*	
24d	A9 2½pi dp violet ('75)	45.00	12.50
i.	Tête bêche pair	*1,150.*	*1,000.*
25d	A9 5pi yel green ('75)	350.00	225.00

Nos. 24b, 24d Surcharged in Black

1879, Jan. 1 *Perf. 12½ Rough*

27	A9 5pa on 2½pi dull vio	8.75	8.75
a.	Imperf.	400.00	400.00
b.	Tête bêche pair	*7,500.*	
c.	Inverted surcharge	125.00	75.00
d.	Perf. 12½x13½ rough	11.00	*11.00*
e.	As "d," tête bêche pair	7,500.	
f.	As "d," inverted surcharge	140.00	95.00
28	A9 10pa on 2½pi dull vio	11.00	11.00
a.	Imperf.	400.00	400.00
b.	Tête bêche pair	*2,500.*	
c.	Inverted surcharge	125.00	82.50
d.	Perf. 12½x13½ rough	17.00	17.00
e.	As "d," tête bêche pair	3,000.	
f.	As "d," inverted surcharge	150.00	125.00

A11

A12

A13

A14

A15

A16

1879-93 Typo. *Perf. 14x13½*

29	A11	5pa brown	1.50	.60
30	A12	10pa violet	45.00	5.00
31	A12	10pa lil rose ('81)	65.00	6.25
32	A12	10pa gray ('82)	13.25	1.60
33	A12	10pa green ('84)	.80	.65
34	A13	20pa ultra	62.50	2.25
35	A13	20pa rose ('84)	17.00	1.25
36	A14	1pi rose	25.00	.30
37	A14	1pi ultra ('84)	3.50	.20
38	A15	2pi orange yel	32.50	1.50
39	A15	2pi orange brn	25.00	1.50
40	A16	5pi green	70.00	8.75
41	A16	5pi gray ('84)	22.00	.50
		Nos. 29-41 (13)	383.05	30.35

Nos. 29-31, 35-41 imperf, are proofs.

Nos. 37, 39, 41, exist on both ordinary and chalky paper. See *Scott Classic Specialized Catalogue of Stamps & Covers* for detailed listings.

For overprints see Nos. 42, O6-O7.

A17

1884, Feb. 1

42	A17 20pa on 5pi green	15.00	2.25
a.	Inverted surcharge	70.00	62.50

A18

A19

A20

A21

A22

A23

1888-1906

43a	A18	1m brown	.65	.20
44a	A19	2m green	.90	.20
45	A20	3m maroon ('92)	7.00	1.25
46a	A20	3m orange ('93)	2.75	.20
47	A21	4m brown red ('06)	1.60	.20
48	A22	5m carmine rose	2.00	.20
49	A23	10p purple ('89)	35.00	1.00
		Nos. 43a-49 (7)	49.90	3.25

Nos. 43-44, 47-48 imperf, are proofs.

Nos. 43-44, 46, 48-49 exist on both ordinary and chalky paper, No. 47 only on chalky-surfaced paper. See *Scott Classic Specialized Catalogue of Stamps & Covers* for detailed listings.

For overprints, see O2-O5, O8-O10, O14-O15.

Boats on Nile
A24

Cleopatra
A25

Ras-el-Tin Palace
A26

Giza Pyramids
A27

Sphinx
A28

Colossi of Thebes
A29

Pylon of Karnak and Temple of Khonsu — A30

Citadel at Cairo — A31

Rock Temple of Abu Simbel — A32

Aswan Dam — A33

Perf. 13½x14

1914, Jan. 8 Wmk. 119

Chalk-surfaced Paper

50	A24	1m olive brown	.60	*.80*
51	A25	2m dp green	1.10	.20
52	A26	3m orange	1.40	.50
53	A27	4m red	2.00	.75
54	A28	5m lake	1.60	.20
a.		Booklet pane of 6	225.00	
55	A29	10m dk blue	4.00	.40

Perf. 14

56	A30	20m olive grn	6.75	.70
57	A31	50m red violet	13.50	1.10
58	A32	100m black	35.00	1.40
59	A33	200m plum	42.50	3.75
		Nos. 50-59 (10)	108.45	9.80

All values of this issue exist imperforate on both watermarked and unwatermarked paper but are not known to have been issued in that condition.

See Nos. 61-69, 72-74. For overprints and surcharge see Nos. 60, 78-91, O11-O13, O16-O27, O30.

British Protectorate

No. 52 Surcharged

1915, Oct. 15

60	A26 2m on 3m orange	1.75	1.75
a.	Inverted surcharge	225.00	225.00

Scenic Types of 1914 and

Statue of Ramses II
A34 A35

1921-22 Wmk. 120 *Perf. 13½x14*

Chalk-surfaced Paper

61	A24	1m olive brown	.60	*.80*
62	A25	2m dp green	2.50	1.75
63	A25	2m red ('22)	2.00	.60
64	A26	3m orange	1.50	.70
65	A27	4m green ('22)	3.75	*4.00*
66	A28	5m lake	2.25	.20
67	A28	5m pink	2.50	.20
68	A29	10m dp blue	2.75	.20
69	A29	10m lake ('22)	2.25	.50
70	A34	15m indigo ('22)	3.00	.20
71	A35	15m indigo ('22)	16.00	2.50

Perf. 14

72	A30	20m olive green	10.00	.40
73	A31	50m maroon	12.00	.50
74	A32	100m black	55.00	6.75
		Nos. 61-74 (14)	116.10	19.30

For overprints see Nos. O28-O29.

Independent Kingdom

Stamps of 1921-22 Overprinted

1922, Oct. 10

78	A24	1m olive brown	.95	.70
a.		Inverted overprint	350.00	450.00
b.		Double overprint	200.00	—
79	A25	2m red	.70	.40
a.		Double overprint	200.00	—
80	A26	3m orange	1.50	.95
81	A27	4m green	.90	.60
b.		Inverted overprint	225.00	—
82	A28	5m pink	2.10	.20
83	A29	10m lake	2.10	.20
84	A34	15m indigo	4.75	.90
85	A35	15m indigo	3.75	.90

Perf. 14

86	A30	20m olive green	5.00	.60
a.		Inverted overprint	200.00	—
b.		Double overprint	300.00	—
87	A31	50m maroon	8.00	.60
a.		Inverted overprint	400.00	500.00
88	A32	100m black	20.00	1.25
a.		Inverted overprint	500.00	160.00
b.		Double overprint	400.00	150.00
		Nos. 78-88 (11)	49.75	7.30

Same Overprint on Nos. 58-59

Wmk. Crescent and Star (119)

90	A32	100m black	80.00	50.00
91	A33	200m plum	27.50	1.50

Proclamation of the Egyptian monarchy.

The overprint signifies "The Egyptian Kingdom, March 15, 1922." It exists in four types, one lithographed and three typographed on Nos. 78-87, but lithographed only on Nos. 88-91.

King Fuad
A36 A37

Wmk. 120

1923-24 Photo. *Perf. 13½*

Size 18x22½mm

92	A36	1m orange	.20	.20
93	A36	2m black	.50	.20
94	A36	3m brown	.75	.40
a.		Imperf., pair	200.00	
95	A36	4m yellow grn	.65	.50
96	A36	5m orange brn	.20	.20
a.		Imperf., pair	50.00	
97	A36	10m rose	1.10	.20
98	A36	15m ultra	2.75	.20

Perf. 14

Size: 22x28mm

99	A36	20m dk green	5.50	.20
100	A36	50m myrtle grn	8.25	.20
101	A36	100m red violet	21.00	.55
102	A36	200m violet ('24)	42.50	1.75
a.		Imperf., pair	300.00	
103	A37	£1 ultra & dk vio ('24)	175.00	25.00
a.		Imperf., pair	1,600.	
		Nos. 92-103 (12)	258.40	29.60

For overprints & surcharge see No. 167, O31-O38.

Thoth Carving Name of King Fuad — A38

1925, Apr. Litho. *Perf. 11*

105	A38	5m brown	7.50	4.75
106	A38	10m rose	11.00	8.00
107	A38	15m ultra	13.50	9.50
		Nos. 105-107 (3)	32.00	22.25

International Geographical Congress, Cairo.

Nos. 106-107 exist with both white and yellowish gum.

Oxen Plowing
A39

1926 Wmk. 195 *Perf. 13x13½*

108	A39	5m lt brown	2.25	1.00
109	A39	10m brt rose	2.00	.90
110	A39	15m dp blue	2.25	.90
111	A39	50m Prus green	12.00	3.00
112	A39	100m brown vio	17.50	5.00
113	A39	200m brt violet	27.50	15.00
		Nos. 108-113 (6)	63.50	25.80

12th Agricultural and Industrial Exhibition at Gezira.

For surcharges see Nos. 115-117.

King Fuad — A40

Perf. 14x14½

1926, Apr. 2 Photo. Wmk. 120

114 A40 50p brn vio & red vio 135.00 22.50

58th birthday of King Fuad.

For overprint and surcharge see Nos. 124, 166.

Nos. 111-113 Surcharged

Perf. 13x13½

1926, Aug. 24 Wmk. 195

115 A39 5m on 50m Prus grn 2.25 2.25
116 A39 10m on 100m brn vio 2.25 2.25
117 A39 15m on 200m brt vio 2.25 2.25
a. Double surcharge 300.00
Nos. 115-117 (3) 6.75 6.75

Ship of Hatshepsut — A41

1926, Dec. 9 Litho. *Perf. 13x13½*

118 A41 5m brown & blk 2.25 1.40
119 A41 10m dp red & blk 3.25 1.50
120 A41 15m dp blue & blk 3.25 1.50
Nos. 118-120 (3) 8.75 4.40

International Navigation Congress, Cairo.

For overprints see Nos. 121-123.

Nos. 118-120, 114 Overprinted

1926, Dec. 21

121 A41 (a) 5m 250.00 150.00
122 A41 (a) 10m 250.00 150.00
123 A41 (a) 15m 250.00 150.00

Perf. 14x14½

Wmk. 120

124 A40 (b) 50p 1,500. 875.00

Inauguration of Port Fuad opposite Port Said.

Nos. 121-123 have a block over "Le Caire" at lower left.

Forgeries of Nos. 121-124 exist.

Branch of Cotton A42

Perf. 13x13½

1927, Jan. 25 Wmk. 195

125 A42 5m dk brown & sl grn 1.25 .80
126 A42 10m dp red & slate grn 2.00 1.50
127 A42 15m dp blue & slate grn 2.00 1.50
Nos. 125-127 (3) 5.25 3.80

International Cotton Congress, Cairo.

A43

King Fuad — A44

A45

A46

Perf. 13x13½

1927-37 Wmk. 195 Photo.

128 A43 1m orange .35 .20
129 A43 2m black .35 .20
130 A43 3m olive brn .35 .20
131 A43 3m dp green ('30) .65 .20
132 A43 4m yellow grn .85 .40
133 A43 4m brown ('30) 1.00 .40
134 A43 4m dp green ('34) .85 .40
135 A43 5m dk red brn ('29) .95 .40
b. 5m chestnut .95 .20
136 A43 10m dk red ('29) 1.25 .20
a. 10m orange red 1.25 .20
137 A43 10m purple ('34) 2.75 .20
138 A43 13m car rose ('32) 1.50 .40
139 A43 15m ultra 2.50 .20
140 A43 15m dk violet ('34) 5.25 .20
141 A43 20m ultra ('34) 9.25 .30

Early printings of Nos. 128, 129, 130, 132, 135, 136 and 139 were from plates with screen of vertical dots in the vignette; later printings show screen of diagonal dots.

Perf. 13½x14

142 A44 20m olive grn 3.25 .40
143 A44 20m ultra ('32) 4.00 .20
144 A44 40m olive brn ('32) 3.25 .20
145 A44 50m Prus green 3.50 .20
a. 50m greenish blue 5.50 .20
146 A44 100m brown vio 6.00 .20
a. 100m claret 9.00 .20
147 A44 200m deep violet 6.00 .50

Printings of Nos. 142, 145 and 146, made in 1929 and later, were from new plates with stronger impressions and darker colors.

Lithographed; Center Photogravure

Perf. 13x13½

148 A45 500m choc & Prus bl ('32) 125.00 11.50
a. Entirely photogravure 125.00 25.00
149 A46 £1 dk grn & org brn ('37) 140.00 7.00
a. Entirely photogravure 140.00 8.25
Nos. 128-149 (22) 318.85 24.10

Statue of Amenhotep, Son of Hapu — A47

1927, Dec. 29 Photo. *Perf. 13½x13*

150 A47 5m orange brown 1.25 .45
151 A47 10m copper red 1.50 .50
152 A47 15m deep blue 2.75 .55
Nos. 150-152 (3) 5.50 1.50

Statistical Congress, Cairo.

Imhotep — A48

Mohammed Ali Pasha — A49

1928, Dec. 15

153 A48 5m orange brown 1.10 .50
154 A49 10m copper red 1.25 .50

Intl. Congress of Medicine at Cairo and the cent. of the Faculty of Medicine at Cairo.

Prince Farouk — A50

1929, Feb. 11 Litho.

155 A50 5m choc & gray 1.60 1.10
156 A50 10m dull red & gray 1.90 1.25
157 A50 15m ultra & gray 1.90 1.25
158 A50 20m Prus blue & gray 1.90 1.25
Nos. 155-158 (4) 7.30 4.85

Ninth birthday of Prince Farouk.

Nos. 155-158 with black or brown centers are trial color proofs. They were sent to the UPU, but were never placed on sale to the public, although some are known used.

Tomb Fresco at El-Bersheh — A51

1931, Feb. 15 *Perf. 13x13½*

163 A51 5m brown .90 .55
164 A51 10m copper red 1.60 1.25
165 A51 15m dark blue 2.25 1.50
Nos. 163-165 (3) 4.75 3.30

14th Agricultural & Industrial Exhib., Cairo.

Nos. 114 and 103 Surcharged with Bars and

1932 Wmk. 120 *Perf. 14x14½*

166 A40 50m on 50p 20.00 2.75

Perf. 14

167 A37 100m on £1 250.00 190.00

Locomotive of 1852 — A52

Perf. 13x13½

1933, Jan. 19 Litho. Wmk. 195

168 A52 5m shown 13.00 5.25
169 A52 13m 1859 19.00 9.00
170 A52 15m 1862 19.00 9.00
171 A52 20m 1932 19.00 9.00
Nos. 168-171 (4) 70.00 32.25

International Railroad Congress, Heliopolis.

Commercial Passenger Airplane — A56

Dornier Do-X A57

Graf Zeppelin A58

1933, Dec. 20 Photo.

172 A56 5m brown 6.00 2.10
173 A56 10m brt violet 14.00 8.50
174 A57 13m brown car 17.00 11.00
175 A57 15m violet 17.00 10.50
176 A58 20m blue 22.50 19.00
Nos. 172-176 (5) 76.50 51.10

International Aviation Congress, Cairo.

A59

Khedive Ismail Pasha — A60

1934, Feb. 1 *Perf. 13½*

177 A59 1m dp orange .50 *1.00*
178 A59 2m black .55 *1.00*
179 A59 3m brown .60 *1.25*

180	A59	4m blue green	.90	.40
181	A59	5m red brown	.95	.20
182	A59	10m violet	2.00	.20
183	A59	13m copper red	3.00	1.25
184	A59	15m dull violet	3.00	1.10
185	A59	20m ultra	2.00	.30
186	A59	50m Prus blue	7.00	.60
187	A59	100m olive grn	16.50	1.00
188	A59	200m dp violet	55.00	5.50

Perf. 13½x13

189	A60	50p brown	175.00	75.00
190	A60	£1 Prus blue	285.00	125.00
		Nos. 177-190 (14)	552.00	213.80

10th Congress of UPU, Cairo.

King Fuad — A61

1936-37 ***Perf. 13½***

191	A61	1m dull orange	.50	.80
192	A61	2m black	1.60	.20
193	A61	4m dk green	1.75	.20
194	A61	5m chestnut	1.25	.20
195	A61	10m purple ('37)	2.25	.20
196	A61	15m brown violet	2.50	.50
197	A61	20m sapphire	3.00	.20
		Nos. 191-197 (7)	12.85	2.30

Entrance to Agricultural Building — A62

Agricultural Building — A63

Design: 15m, 20m, Industrial Building.

1936, Feb. 15 ***Perf. 13½x13***

198	A62	5m brown	1.00	.85

Perf. 13x13½

199	A63	10m violet	1.25	.95
200	A63	13m copper red	1.50	2.00
201	A63	15m dark violet	1.10	1.00
202	A63	20m blue	2.25	2.00
		Nos. 198-202 (5)	7.10	6.80

15th Agricultural & Industrial Exhib., Cairo.

Signing of Treaty — A65

1936, Dec. 22 ***Perf. 11***

203	A65	5m brown	.65	.60
204	A65	15m dk violet	.75	.75
205	A65	20m sapphire	2.00	1.00
		Nos. 203-205 (3)	3.40	2.35

Signing of Anglo-Egyptian Treaty, 8/26/36.

King Farouk — A66

Medal for Montreux Conf. — A67

1937-44 **Wmk. 195** ***Perf. 13x13½***

206	A66	1m brown org	.30	.20
207	A66	2m vermilion	.30	.20
208	A66	3m brown	.30	.20
209	A66	4m green	.30	.20
210	A66	5m red brown	.50	.20
211	A66	6m lt yel grn ('40)	.60	.20
212	A66	10m purple	.30	.20
213	A66	13m rose car	.60	.35
214	A66	15m dk vio brn	.50	.20
215	A66	20m blue	.75	.35
216	A66	20m lil gray ('44)	.75	.20
		Nos. 206-216 (11)	5.20	2.50

For overprints see Nos. 301, 303, 345, 348, 360E, N3, N6, N8, N22, N25, N27.

1937, Oct. 15 ***Perf. 13½x13***

217	A67	5m red brown	.80	.55
218	A67	15m dk violet	1.25	1.10
219	A67	20m sapphire	1.25	1.25
		Nos. 217-219 (3)	3.30	2.90

Intl. Treaty signed at Montreux, Switzerland, under which foreign privileges in Egypt were to end in 1949.

Eye of Ré — A68

1937, Dec. 8 ***Perf. 13x13½***

220	A68	5m brown	.90	.75
221	A68	15m dk violet	1.00	.75
222	A68	20m sapphire	1.50	1.00
		Nos. 220-222 (3)	3.40	2.50

15th Ophthalmological Congress, Cairo, December, 1937.

King Farouk, Queen Farida — A69

1938, Jan. 20 ***Perf. 11***

223	A69	5m red brown	7.00	4.25

Royal wedding of King Farouk and Farida Zulficar.

Inscribed: "11 Fevrier 1938"

1938, Feb. 11

224	A69	£1 green & sepia	175.00	110.00

King Farouk's 18th birthday.

Cotton Picker — A70

1938, Jan. 26 ***Perf. 13½x13***

225	A70	5m red brown	.50	.50
226	A70	15m dk violet	2.00	.85
227	A70	20m sapphire	1.50	.75
		Nos. 225-227 (3)	4.00	2.10

18th International Cotton Congress at Cairo.

Pyramids of Giza and Colossus of Thebes A71

1938, Feb. 1 ***Perf. 13x13½***

228	A71	5m red brown	1.00	.65
229	A71	15m dk violet	1.50	.80
230	A71	20m sapphire	1.75	.80
		Nos. 228-230 (3)	4.25	2.25

Intl. Telecommunication Conf., Cairo.

Branch of Hydnocarpus — A72

1938, Mar. 21 ***Perf. 13x13½***

231	A72	5m red brown	1.00	.50
232	A72	15m dk violet	1.60	.60
233	A72	20m sapphire	1.60	.60
		Nos. 231-233 (3)	4.20	1.70

International Leprosy Congress, Cairo.

King Farouk and Pyramids — A73

King Farouk
A74 A75

Backgrounds: 40m, Hussan Mosque. 50m, Cairo Citadel. 100m, Aswan Dam. 200m, Cairo University.

1939-46 **Photo.** ***Perf. 14x13½***

234	A73	30m gray	.75	.20
a.		30m slate gray	.75	.20
234B	A73	30m ol grn ('46)	.80	.20
235	A73	40m dk brown	.85	.20
236	A73	50m Prus green	1.00	.20
237	A73	100m brown vio	1.40	.20
238	A73	200m dk violet	4.25	.20

Perf. 13½x13

239	A74	50p green & sep	11.00	3.00
240	A75	£1 dp bl & dk brn	25.00	5.75
		Nos. 234-240 (8)	45.05	9.95

For £1 with A77 portrait, see No. 269D. See Nos. 267-269D. For overprints see Nos. 310-314, 316, 355-358, 360, 363-364, N13-N19, N32-N38.

Catalogue values for unused stamps in this section, from this point to the end of the section, are for Never Hinged items.

King Fuad A76

King Farouk A77

1944, Apr. 28 ***Perf. 13½x13***

241	A76	10m dk violet	.50	.20

8th anniv. of the death of King Fuad.

1944-50 **Wmk. 195** ***Perf. 13x13½***

242	A77	1m yellow brn ('45)	.45	.20
243	A77	2m red org ('45)	.45	.20
244	A77	3m sepia ('46)	.50	.40
245	A77	4m dp green ('45)	.45	.20
246	A77	5m red brown ('46)	.45	.20
247	A77	10m dp violet	.45	.20
247A	A77	13m rose red ('50)	12.00	4.25
248	A77	15m dk violet ('45)	.45	.20
249	A77	17m olive grn	.50	.20
250	A77	20m dk gray ('45)	.75	.20
251	A77	22m dp blue ('45)	.75	.20
		Nos. 242-251 (11)	17.20	6.45

For overprints see Nos. 299-300, 302, 304-309, 343-344, 346-347, 349-354, 360B, 361-362, N1-N2, N4-N5, N7, N9-N12, N20-N21, N23-N24, N26, N28-N31.

King Farouk — A78

Khedive Ismail Pasha — A79

1945, Feb. 10 ***Perf. 13½x13***

252	A78	10m deep violet	.40	.20

25th birthday of King Farouk.

1945, Mar. 2 **Photo.**

253	A79	10m dark olive	.35	.20

50th anniv. of death of Khedive Ismail Pasha.

Flags of Arab Nations — A80

1945, July 29

254	A80	10m violet	.35	.20
255	A80	22m dp yellow grn	.50	.20

League of Arab Nations Conference, Cairo, Mar. 22, 1945.

Flags of Egypt and Saudi Arabia A81

Perf. 13x13½

1946, Jan. 10 **Wmk. 195**

256	A81	10m dp yellow grn	.35	.20

Visit of King Ibn Saud, Jan. 1946.

Citadel, Cairo A82

1946, Aug. 9

257 A82 10m yel brn & dp yel grn .40 .20

Withdrawal of British troops from Cairo Citadel, Aug. 9, 1946.

King Farouk and Inchas Palace, Cairo A83

2m, Prince Abdullah, Yemen. 3m, Pres. Bechara el-Khoury, Lebanon. 4m, King Abdul Aziz ibn Saud, Saudi Arabia. 5m, King Faisal II, Iraq. 10m, Amir Abdullah ibn Hussein, Jordan. 15m, Pres. Shukri el Kouatly, Syria.

1946, Nov. 9

258	A83	1m dp yellow grn	.60	.20
259	A83	2m sepia	.60	.20
260	A83	3m deep blue	.60	.20
261	A83	4m brown orange	.60	.20
262	A83	5m brown red	.60	.20
263	A83	10m dark gray	.75	.20
264	A83	15m deep violet	.75	.20
		Nos. 258-264 (7)	4.50	1.40

Arab League Cong. at Cairo, May 28, 1946.

Parliament Building, Cairo — A84

1947, Apr. 7 **Photo.**

265 A84 10m green .35 .20

36th conf. of the Interparliamentary Union, Apr. 1947.

Raising Egyptian Flag over Kasr-el-Nil Barracks — A85

King Farouk — A85a

1947, May 6 ***Perf. 13½x13***

266 A85 10m dp plum & yel grn .40 .20

Withdrawal of British troops from the Nile Delta.

Farouk Types 1939 Redrawn

1947-51 **Wmk. 195** ***Perf. 14x13½***

267	A73	30m olive green	.50	.20
268	A73	40m dk brown	.60	.20
269	A73	50m Prus grn ('48)	.90	.20
269A	A73	100m dk brn vio ('49)	5.75	.75
269B	A73	200m dk violet ('49)	11.00	1.25

Perf. 13½x13

269C	A85a	50p green & sep ('51)	25.00	8.50
269D	A75	£1 dp bl & dk brn ('50)	36.00	3.75
		Nos. 267-269D (7)	79.75	14.85

The king faces slightly to the left and clouds have been added in the sky on Nos. 267-269B. Backgrounds as in 1939-46 issue. Portrait on £1 as on type A77.

For overprints see Nos. 315, 359.

Field and Branch of Cotton — A86

Map and Infantry Column — A87

Perf. 13½x13

1948, Apr. 1 **Wmk. 195**

270 A86 10m olive green .40 .20

Intl. Cotton Cong. held at Cairo in Apr. 1948.

1948, June 15 ***Perf. 11½x11***

271 A87 10m green .40 .20

Arrival of Egyptian troops at Gaza, 5/15/48.

Ibrahim Pasha (1789-1848) — A88

1948, Nov. 10 ***Perf. 13x13½***

272 A88 10m brn red & dp grn .40 .20

Statue, "The Nile" A89

Protection of Industry and Agriculture — A90

Perf. 13x13½

1949, Mar. 1 **Photo.** **Wmk. 195**

273	A89	1m dk green	.40	.20
274	A89	10m purple	1.00	.20
275	A89	17m crimson	1.00	.20
276	A89	22m deep blue	1.00	.40

Perf. 11½x11

277	A90	30m dk brown	1.50	.50
		Nos. 273-277 (5)	4.90	1.50

Souvenir Sheets

Photo. & Litho.

Imperf

278	Sheet of 4	3.25	3.25
a.	A89 1m red brown	.60	.60
b.	A89 10m dark brown	.60	.60
c.	A89 17m brown orange	.60	.60
d.	A89 22m dark Prussian green	.60	.60
279	Sheet of 2	3.25	3.25
a.	A90 10m violet gray	1.50	1.50
b.	A90 30m red orange	1.50	1.50

16th Agricultural & Industrial Expo., Cairo.

Mohammed Ali and Map — A93

Globe — A94

Perf. 11½x11

1949, Aug. 2 **Photo.** **Wmk. 195**

280 A93 10m orange brn & grn .60 .20

Centenary of death of Mohammed Ali.

1949, Oct. 9 ***Perf. 13½x13***

281	A94	10m rose brown	.85	.60
282	A94	22m violet	1.75	.85
283	A94	30m dull blue	2.40	1.10
		Nos. 281-283 (3)	5.00	2.55

75th anniv. of the UPU.

Scales of Justice A95

1949, Oct. 14 ***Perf. 13x13½***

284 A95 10m deep olive green .40 .20

End of the Mixed Judiciary System, 10/14/49.

Desert Scene A96

1950, Dec. 27

285 A96 10m violet & red brn .45 .20

Opening of the Fuad I Institute of the Desert.

Fuad I University A97

1950, Dec. 27

286 A97 22m dp green & claret .60 .25

Founding of Fuad I University, 25th anniv.

Globe and Khedive Ismail Pasha A98

1950, Dec. 27

287 A98 30m claret & dp grn .55 .25

75th anniv. of Royal Geographic Society of Egypt.

Picking Cotton — A99

1951, Feb. 24

290 A99 10m olive green .35 .20

International Cotton Congress, 1951.

King Farouk and Queen Narriman — A100

1951, May 6 **Photo.** ***Perf. 11x11½***

291	A100	10m green & red brn	3.50	2.75
a.		Souvenir sheet	12.00	*16.00*

Marriage of King Farouk and Narriman Sadek, May 6, 1951.

Stadium Entrance A101

Arms of Alexandria and Olympic Emblem — A102

King Farouk A103

1951, Oct. 5 ***Perf. 13x13½, 13½x13***

292	A101	10m brown	.75	.60
293	A102	22m dp green	.95	.95
294	A103	30m blue & dp grn	.95	.95
a.		Souvenir sheet of 3, #292-294	12.00	*16.00*
		Nos. 292-294 (3)	2.65	2.50

Issued to publicize the first Mediterranean Games, Alexandria, Oct. 5-20, 1951.

Winged Figure and Map — A105

Designs: 22m, King Farouk and Map. 30m, King Farouk and Flag.

Dated "16 Oct. 1951"

1952, Feb. 11 ***Perf. 13½x13***

296	A105	10m dp green	.55	.25
297	A105	22m plum & dp grn	.85	.45
298	A105	30m green & brown	1.10	.55
a.		Souvenir sheet of 3, #296-298	9.00	9.00
		Nos. 296-298 (3)	2.50	1.25

Abrogation of the Anglo-Egyptian treaty.

Stamps of 1937-51 Overprinted in Various Colors

Perf. 13x13½

1952, Jan. 17 **Wmk. 195**

299	A77	1m yellow brown	.35	.20
300	A77	2m red org (Bl)	.35	.20
301	A66	3m brown (Bl)	.35	.50
302	A77	4m dp green (RV)	.35	.20
303	A66	6m lt yel grn (RV)	.90	.70
304	A77	10m dp vio (C)	.35	.25
305	A77	13m rose red (Bl)	1.75	.75
306	A77	15m dk violet (C)	2.00	.75
307	A77	17m olive grn (C)	1.90	.30
308	A77	20m dk gray (RV)	1.40	.30
309	A77	22m dp blue (C)	2.50	1.50

No. 244, the 3m sepia, exists with this overprint but was not regularly issued or used.

Same Overprint, 24½mm Wide, on Nos. 267 to 269B

Perf. 14x13½

310	A73	30m olive grn (DkBl)	1.25	.20
a.		Black overprint	1.50	.20
311	A73	40m dk brown (G)	.90	.20
312	A73	50m Prus grn (C)	1.25	.25
313	A73	100m dk brn vio (C)	2.75	.40
314	A73	200m dk violet (C)	13.00	1.25

Same Overprint, 19mm Wide, on Nos. 269C-269D

Perf. 13½x13

315	A85a	50p grn & sep (C)	25.00	4.75
316	A75	£1 dp bl & dk brn (Bl)	40.00	5.25
		Nos. 299-316 (18)	96.35	17.95

The overprint translates: King of Egypt and the Sudan, Oct. 16, 1951.

Overprints in colors other than as listed are color trials.

Egyptian Flag — A106

Perf. 13½x13

1952, May 6 **Photo.** **Wmk. 195**

317	A106	10m org yel, dp bl & dp grn	.40	.20
a.		Souvenir sheet of 1	5.25	5.25

Issued to commemorate the birth of Crown Prince Ahmed Fuad, Jan. 16, 1952.

"Dawn of New Era" A107

Symbolical of Egypt Freed — A108

Designs: 10m, "Egypt" with raised sword. 22m, Citizens marching with flag.

Perf. 13x13½, 13½x13

1952, Nov. 23

Dated: "23 Juillet 1952"

318	A107	4m dp green & org	.35	.25
319	A107	10m dp grn & cop brn	.35	.50
320	A108	17m brn org & dp grn	.75	.60
321	A108	22m choc & dp grn	1.00	.45
		Nos. 318-321 (4)	2.45	1.80

Change of government, July 23, 1952.

Republic

Farmer A109

Soldier A110

Mosque of Sultan Hassan — A111

Queen Nefertiti — A112

1953-56 *Perf. 13x13½*

322	A109	1m red brown	.35	.20
323	A109	2m dk lilac	.35	.20
324	A109	3m brt blue	.35	.40
325	A109	4m dk green	.35	.20
326	A110	10m dk brown *("Defence")*	.40	.40
327	A110	10m dk brown *("Defense")*	.55	.20
328	A110	15m gray	.35	.20
329	A110	17m dk grnsh blue	.45	.20
330	A110	20m purple	.35	.20

Perf. 13½

331	A111	30m dull green	.35	.20
332	A111	32m brt blue	.70	.20
333	A111	35m violet ('55)	.90	.20
334	A111	37m gldn brn ('56)	1.75	.60
335	A111	40m red brown	.70	.20
336	A111	50m violet brn	1.20	.20
337	A112	100m henna brn	1.50	.20
338	A112	200m dk grnsh blue	3.75	.50
339	A112	500m purple	11.00	1.00
340	A112	£1 dk grn, blk & red	25.00	3.25
		Nos. 322-340 (19)	50.35	8.75

Nos. 327-330 are inscribed "Defense."

See No. 490. For overprints and surcharges see Nos. 460, 500, N44-N56, N72.

Stamps of 1939-51 Overprinted in Black with Three Bars to Obliterate Portrait

1953 *Perf. 13x13½, 13½x13*

343	A77	1m yellow brn	.35	.20
344	A77	2m red orange	.35	.20
345	A66	3m brown	.50	.50
346	A77	3m sepia	.35	.20
347	A77	4m dp green	.35	.20
348	A66	6m lt yellow grn	.35	.20
349	A77	10m dp violet	.35	.20
350	A77	13m rose red	.50	.20
351	A77	15m dk violet	.35	.20
352	A77	17m olive grn	.35	.20
353	A77	20m dk gray	.50	.20
354	A77	22m deep blue	.55	.20
355	A73	30m ol grn (#267)	.60	.20
356	A73	50m Prus grn (#269)	1.00	.25
357	A73	100m dk brn vio (#269A)	1.50	.40
358	A73	200m dk violet (#269B)	4.50	1.00
359	A85a	50p grn & sepia	15.00	5.00
360	A75	£1 dp bl & dk brn (#269D)	30.00	4.75
		Nos. 343-360 (18)	57.45	14.30

No. 206 with this overprint is a forgery.

Same Overprint on Nos. 300, 303-305, 311 and 314

360B	A77	2m red orange	.40	.20
360E	A66	6m lt yel grn	*50.00*	
361	A77	10m dp violet	4.00	4.00
362	A77	13m rose red	1.25	.75
363	A73	40m dk brown	6.00	.75
364	A73	200m dk violet	4.00	.90
		Nos. 360B,361-364 (5)	15.65	6.60

Practically all values of Nos. 343-364 exist with double overprint. Other values of the 1952 overprinted issue are known with counterfeit bars.

Symbols of Electronic Progress A113

1953, Nov. 23 **Photo.** ***Perf. 13x13½***

365	A113	10m brt blue	.50	.20

Electronics Exposition, Cairo, Nov. 23.

Crowd Acclaiming the Republic A114

Farmer A115

Design: 30m, Crowd, flag and eagle.

Perf. 13½x13

1954, June 18 **Wmk. 195**

366	A114	10m brown	.55	.25
367	A114	30m deep blue	.90	.60

Proclamation of the republic, 1st anniv.

1954-55 ***Perf. 13x13½***

368	A115	1m red brown	.35	.20
369	A115	2m dark lilac	.35	.20
370	A115	3m brt blue	.35	.20
371	A115	4m dk green ('55)	.70	.45
372	A115	5m dp car ('55)	.35	.20
		Nos. 368-372 (5)	2.10	1.25

For overprints see Nos. N39-N43.

Egyptian Flag, Map — A116

Globe — A117

Design: 35m, Bugler, soldier and map.

1954, Nov. 4 ***Perf. 13½x13***

373	A116	10m rose vio & grn	.45	.25
374	A116	35m ver, blk & bl grn	.65	.55

Agreement of Oct. 19, 1954, with Great Britain for the evacuation of the Suez Canal zone by British troops.

Arab Postal Union Issue

1955, Jan. 1

375	A117	5m yellow brn	.45	.20
376	A117	10m green	.45	.20
377	A117	37m violet	.90	.80
		Nos. 375-377 (3)	1.80	1.20

Founding of the Arab Postal Union, 7/1/54. For overprints see Nos. 381-383.

Paul P. Harris and Rotary Emblem — A118

35m, Globe, wings and Rotary emblem.

Perf. 13½x13

1955, Feb. 23 **Wmk. 195**

378	A118	10m claret	.95	.30
379	A118	35m blue	1.25	.40

50th anniv. of the founding of Rotary Intl.

Nos. 375-377 Overprinted

1955, Nov. 1

381	A117	5m yellow brown	.70	.60
382	A117	10m green	.85	.35
383	A117	37m violet	1.00	.80
		Nos. 381-383 (3)	2.55	1.75

Arab Postal Union Congress held at Cairo, Mar. 15, 1955.

Map of Africa and Asia, Olive Branch and Rings A119

Globe, Torch, Dove and Olive Branch — A120

1956, July 29 ***Perf. 13x13½, 13½x13***

384	A119	10m chestnut & green	.40	.25
385	A120	35m org yel & dull pur	.80	.70

Afro-Asian Festival, Cairo, July, 1956.

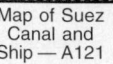

Map of Suez Canal and Ship — A121

Queen Nefertiti — A122

Perf. 11½x11

1956, Sept. 26 **Wmk. 195**

386 A121 10m blue & buff .55 .55

Nationalization of the Suez Canal, July 26, 1956. See No. 393.

1956, Oct. 15 ***Perf. 13½x13***

387 A122 10m dark green .90 .90

Intl. Museum Week (UNESCO), Oct. 8-14.

Egyptians Defending Port Said — A123

1956, Dec. 20 **Litho.** ***Perf. 11x11½***

388 A123 10m brown violet 1.00 .60

Honoring the defenders of Port Said.

No. 388 Overprinted in Carmine Rose

1957, Jan. 14

389 A123 10m brown violet .60 .60

Evacuation of Port Said by British and French troops, Dec. 22, 1956.

Old and New Trains A124

1957, Jan. 30 **Photo.** ***Perf. 13x13½***

390 A124 10m red violet & gray 1.00 .90

100th anniv. of the Egyptian Railway System (in 1956).

Mother and Children A125

1957, Mar. 21

391 A125 10m crimson .50 .35

Mother's Day, 1957.

Battle Scene A126

Perf. 13x13½

1957, Mar. 28 **Wmk. 195**

392 A126 10m bright blue .40 .30

Victory over the British at Rosetta, 150th anniv.

Type of 1956; New Inscriptions in English

1957, Apr. 15 ***Perf. 11½x11***

393 A121 100m blue & yel grn 1.25 1.00

Reopening of the Suez Canal.

No. 393 is inscribed: "Nationalisation of Suez Canal Co. Guarantees Freedom of Navigation" and "Reopening 1957."

Map of Gaza Strip — A127

Perf. 13½x13

1957, May 4 **Photo.** **Wmk. 195**

394 A127 10m Prus blue .95 .70

"Gaza Part of Arab Nation."

For overprint see No. N57.

Al Azhar University A128

1957, Apr. 27 ***Perf. 13x13½***

New Arabic Date in Red

395 A128 10m brt violet .40 .40

396 A128 15m violet brown .55 .35

397 A128 20m dark gray .95 .70

Nos. 395-397 (3) 1.90 1.45

Millenary of Al Azhar University, Cairo.

Shepheard's Hotel, Cairo — A129

Gate, Palace and Eagle — A130

Perf. 13½x13

1957, July 20 **Wmk. 195**

398 A129 10m brt violet .40 .20

Reopening of Shepheard's Hotel, Cairo.

Perf. 11½x11

1957, July 22 **Wmk. 315**

399 A130 10m yellow & brown .40 .20

First meeting of New National Assembly.

Amasis I in Battle of Avaris, 1580 B.C. A131

Designs: No. 401, Sultan Saladin, Hitteen, 1187 A. D. No. 402, Louis IX of France in chains, Mansourah, 1250, vert. No. 403, Map of Middle East, Ein Galout, 1260. No. 404, Port Said, 1956.

Inscribed:

"Egypt Tomb of Aggressors 1957"

1957, July 26 ***Perf. 13x13½, 13½x13***

400 A131 10m carmine rose 1.00 1.00

401 A131 10m dk olive grn 1.00 1.00

402 A131 10m brown violet 1.00 1.00

403 A131 10m grnsh blue 1.00 1.00

404 A131 10m yellow brown 1.00 1.00

Nos. 400-404 (5) 5.00 5.00

No. 400 exists with Wmk. 195.

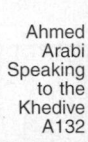

Ahmed Arabi Speaking to the Khedive A132

Perf. 13x13½

1957, Sept. 16 **Wmk. 315**

405 A132 10m deep violet .40 .20

75th anniversary of Arabi Revolution.

Hafez Ibrahim — A133

Portrait: No. 407, Ahmed Shawky.

1957, Oct. 14 ***Perf. 13½x13***

406 A133 10m dull red brn .30 .20

407 A133 10m olive green .30 .20

a. Pair, #406-407 .70 .70

25th anniv. of the deaths of Hafez Ibrahim and Ahmed Shawky, poets.

MiG and Ilyushin Planes A134

Design: No. 409, Viscount plane.

1957, Dec. 19 ***Perf. 13x13½***

408 A134 10m ultra .50 .20

409 A134 10m green .50 .20

a. Pair, #408-409 1.20 1.20

25th anniv. of the Egyptian Air Force and of Misrair, the Egyptian airline.

Pyramids, Dove and Globe A135

1957, Dec. 26 **Photo.** **Wmk. 315**

410 A135 5m brown orange .40 .25

411 A135 10m green .40 .20

412 A135 15m brt violet .40 .20

Nos. 410-412 (3) 1.20 .65

Afro-Asian Peoples Conf., Cairo, 12/26-1/2.

Farmer's Wife A136

Ramses II A137

"Industry" — A138

1957-58 **Wmk. 315** ***Perf. 13½***

413 A136 1m blue green ('58) .30 .20

414 A137 10m violet .30 .20

1958 **Wmk. 318**

415 A136 1m lt blue green .30 .20

416 A138 5m brown .35 .20

417 A137 10m violet .45 .20

Nos. 413-417 (5) 1.70 1.00

See Nos. 438-444, 474-488, 535. For overprints see Nos. N58-N63, N66-N68, N75, N77-N78.

Cyclists — A139

Mustafa Kamel — A140

Perf. 13½x13

1958, Jan. 12 **Wmk. 315**

418 A139 10m lt red brown .50 .30

5th Intl. Bicycle Race, Egypt, Jan. 12-26.

1958, Feb. 10 **Photo.** **Wmk. 318**

419 A140 10m blue gray .50 .20

50th anniversary of the death of Mustafa Kamel, orator and politician.

United Arab Republic

Linked Maps of Egypt and Syria — A141

Cotton — A142

Perf. 11½x11

1958, Mar. 22 **Wmk. 318**

436 A141 10m yellow & green .50 .20

Birth of United Arab Republic. See No. C90. See also Syria-UAR Nos. 1 and C1.

1958, Apr. 5 ***Perf. 13½x13***

437 A142 10m Prussian blue .40 .20

Intl. Fair for Egyptian Cotton, Apr., 1958.

Types of 1957-58 Inscribed "U.A.R. EGYPT" and

Princess Nofret — A143

Designs: 1m, Farmer's wife. 2m, Ibn-Tulun's Mosque. 4m, 14th century glass lamp (design lacks "1963" of A217). 5m, "Industry" (factories and cogwheel). 10m, Ramses II. 35m, "Commerce" (eagle, ship and cargo).

1958 *Perf. 13½x14*

438	A136	1m crimson	.20	.20
439	A138	2m blue	.20	.20
440	A143	3m dk red brown	.20	.20
441	A217	4m green	.20	.20
442	A138	5m brown	.20	.20
443	A137	10m violet	.55	.30
444	A138	35m lt ultra	2.00	.40
		Nos. 438-444 (7)	3.55	1.70

See Nos. 474-488, 532-533, N62-N68, N75-N78.

Qasim Amin — A144

Doves, Broken Chain and Globe — A145

1958, Apr. 23 *Perf. 13½x13*
445 A144 10m deep blue .40 .20

50th anniversary of the death of Qasim Amin, author of "Emancipation of Women."

1958, June 18
446 A145 10m violet .40 .20

5th anniv. of the republic and to publicize the struggle of peoples and individuals for freedom.
For overprint see No. N69.

Cement Industry — A146

UAR Flag — A147

Industries: No. 448, Textile. No. 449, Iron & steel. No. 450, Petroleum (Oil). No. 451, Electricity and fertilizers.

Perf. 13½x13
1958, July 23 **Photo.** **Wmk. 318**

447	A146	10m red brown	.40	.25
448	A146	10m blue green	.40	.25
449	A146	10m bright red	.40	.25
450	A146	10m olive green	.40	.25
451	A146	10m dark blue	.40	.25
a.		Strip of 5, #447-451	2.75	2.75

Souvenir Sheet
Imperf

452 A147 50m grn, dp car & blk 16.00 14.00

Revolution of July 23, 1952, 6th anniv.

Sayed Darwich A148

Hand Holding Torch, Broken Chain and Flag A149

1958, Sept. 15 *Perf. 13½x13*
453 A148 10m violet brown .40 .20

35th anniv. of the death of Sayed Darwich, Arab composer.

1958, Oct. 14 **Photo.** **Wmk. 318**
454 A149 10m carmine rose .40 .20

Establishment of the Republic of Iraq.
See Syria-UAR No. 13.

Maps and Cogwheels — A150

1958, Dec. 8 *Perf. 13x13½*
455 A150 10m blue .40 .20

Issued to publicize the Economic Conference of Afro-Asian Countries, Cairo, Dec. 8.

Overprinted in Red in English and Arabic in 3 Lines: "Industrial and Agricultural Production Fair"

1958, Dec. 9
456 A150 10m lt red brown .40 .20

Issued to publicize the Industrial and Agricultural Production Fair, Cairo, Dec. 9.

Dr. Mahmoud Azmy and UN Emblem A151

1958, Dec. 10
457 A151 10m dull violet .35 .20
458 A151 35m green .75 .40

10th anniv. of the signing of the Universal Declaration of Human Rights.
For overprints see Nos. N70-N71.

University Building, Sphinx, "Education" and God Thoth — A152

1958, Dec. 21 **Photo.** **Wmk. 318**
459 A152 10m grnsh black .40 .20

50th anniversary of Cairo University.

No. 337 Surcharged

1959, Jan. 20 **Wmk. 195** *Perf. 13½*
460 A112 55m on 100m henna brn 3.00 .75

For overprint see No. N72.

Emblem A153

1959, Feb. 2 *Perf. 13x13½*
461 A153 10m lt olive green .40 .20

Afro-Asian Youth Conf., Cairo, Feb. 2.

See Syria UAR issues for stamps of designs A141, A149, A154, A156, A157, A162, A170, A172, A173, A179 with denominations in piasters (p).

Arms of UAR — A154

Perf. 13½x13
1959, Feb. 22 **Photo.** **Wmk. 318**
462 A154 10m green, blk & red .40 .20

First anniversary, United Arab Republic.
See Syria UAR No. 17.

Nile Hilton Hotel A155

1959, Feb. 22 *Perf. 13x13½*
463 A155 10m dark gray .40 .20

Opening of the Nile Hilton Hotel, Cairo.

Globe, Radio and Telegraph A156

1959, Mar. 1
464 A156 10m violet .40 .20

Arab Union of Telecommunications.
See Syria-UAR Nos. C20-C21.

United Arab States Issue

Flags of UAR and Yemen A157

1959, Mar. 8
465 A157 10m sl grn, car & blk .40 .20

First anniversary of United Arab States.
See Syria-UAR No. 16.

Oil Derrick and Pipe Line — A158

Perf. 13½x13
1959, Apr. 16 **Litho.** **Wmk. 318**
466 A158 10m lt bl & dk bl .45 .20

First Arab Petroleum Congress, Cairo.

Railroad A159

Designs: No. 468, Bus on highway. No. 469, River barge. No. 470, Ocean liner. No. 471, Telecommunications on map. No. 472, Stamp printing building, Heliopolis. No. 472A, Ship, train, plane and motorcycle mail carrier.

1959, July 23 **Photo.** *Perf. 13x13½*
Frame in Gray

467	A159	10m maroon	.85	.30
468	A159	10m green	.85	.30
469	A159	10m violet	.85	.30
470	A159	10m dark blue	.85	.30
471	A159	10m dull purple	.85	.30
472	A159	10m scarlet	.85	.30
		Nos. 467-472 (6)	5.10	1.80

Souvenir Sheet
Imperf

472A A159 50m green & red *12.00 12.00*

No. 472A for the 7th anniv. of the Egyptian revolution of 1952 and was sold only with 5 sets of Nos. 467-472.

Globe, Swallows and Map — A160

1959, Aug. 8 *Perf. 13½x13*
473 A160 10m maroon .40 .20

Convention of the Assoc. of Arab Emigrants in the US.

Types of 1953-58 without "Egypt" and

St. Simon's Gate, Bosra, Syria — A161

Designs: 1m, Farmer's wife. 2m, Ibn-Tulun's Mosque. 3m, Princess Nofret. 4m, 14th century glass lamp (design lacks "1963" of A217). 5m, "Industry" (factories and cogwheel). 10m, Ramses II. 15m, Omayyad Mosque, Damascus. 20m, Lotus vase, Tutankhamen treasure. 35m, Eagle, ship and cargo. 40m, Scribe statue. 45m, Saladin's citadel, Aleppo. 55m, Eagle, cotton and wheat. 60m, Dam and factory. 100m, Eagle, hand, cotton and grain. 200m, Palmyra ruins, Syria. 500m, Queen Nefertiti, inscribed "UAR" (no ovpt.).

Perf. 13½x14, 14x13½
1959-60 **Wmk. 328** **Photo.**

474	A136	1m vermilion	.20	.20
475	A138	2m dp blue ('60)	.20	.20
476	A143	3m maroon	.20	.20
477	A217	4m green ('60)	.20	.20
478	A138	5m black ('60)	.20	.20
479	A137	10m dk ol grn	.30	.20
480	A138	15m deep claret	.30	.20
481	A138	20m crimson ('60)	.30	.20
482	A161	30m brown vio	.35	.20

483	A138	35m	lt vio bl ('60)	.50	.20
484	A143	40m	sepia	.55	.20
485	A161	45m	lil gray ('60)	.90	.20
486	A138	55m	brt blue grn	1.00	.20
487	A138	60m	dp purple ('60)	1.25	.20
488	A138	100m	org & sl grn ('60)	2.25	.30
489	A161	200m	lt blue & mar	4.00	.50
490	A112	500m	dk gray & red ('60)	12.00	1.25
			Nos. 474-490 (17)	24.70	4.85

See Nos. 532-535.

Shield and Cogwheel — A162

Perf. 13½x13

1959, Oct. 20 Photo. Wmk. 328

491 A162 10m brt car rose .40 .20

Issued for Army Day, 1959.
See Syria-UAR No. 32.

Cairo Museum A163

1959, Nov. 18 *Perf. 13x13½*

492 A163 10m olive gray .40 .20

Centenary of Cairo museum.

Abu Simbel Temple of Ramses II — A164

1959, Dec. 22 *Perf. 11x11½*

493 A164 10m lt red brn, *pnksh* .50 .25

Issued as propaganda to save historic monuments in Nubia threatened by the construction of Aswan High Dam.

Postrider, 12th Century A165

1960, Jan. 2 *Perf. 13x13½*

494 A165 10m dark blue .40 .20

Issued for Post Day, Jan. 2.

Hydroelectric Power Station, Aswan Dam — A166

1960, Jan. 9

495 A166 10m violet blk .40 .20

Inauguration of the Aswan Dam hydroelectric power station, Jan. 9.

A167

10m, Arabic and English Description of Aswan High Dam. 35m, Architect's Drawing of Aswan High Dam.

1960, Jan. 9 *Perf. 11x11½*

496	10m claret	.60	.30
497	35m claret	.95	.30
a.	A167 Pair, #496-497	1.60	1.60

Start of work on the Aswan High Dam.

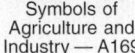

Symbols of Agriculture and Industry — A169

Arms and Flag — A170

1960, Jan. 16 *Perf. 13½x13*

498 A169 10m gray grn & sl grn .35 .20

Industrial and Agricultural Fair, Cairo.

1960, Feb. 22 Photo. Wmk. 328

499 A170 10m green, blk & red .35 .20

2nd anniversary of the proclamation of the United Arab Republic.
See Syria-UAR No. 38.

No. 340 Overprinted "UAR" in English and Arabic in Red

Perf. **13½ Wmk. 195**

1960

500 A112 £1 dk grn, blk & red 19.00 5.00

"Art" — A171

Perf. 13½x13

1960, Mar. 1 Wmk. 328

501 A171 10m brown .40 .20

Issued to publicize the 3rd Biennial Exhibition of Fine Arts in Alexandria.

Arab League Center, Cairo A172

1960, Mar. 22 Photo. *Perf. 13x13½*

502 A172 10m dull grn & blk .35 .20

Opening of Arab League Center and Arab Postal Museum, Cairo.
See Syria-UAR No. 40.

Refugees Pointing to Map of Palestine A173

1960, Apr. 7

503	A173	10m	orange ver	.40	.20
504	A173	35m	Prus blue	.60	.20

World Refugee Year, 7/1/59-6/30/60.
See Nos. N73-N74. See also Syria-UAR Nos. 43-44.

Weight Lifter — A174

Stadium, Cairo — A175

Sports: No. 506, Basketball. No. 507, Soccer. No. 508, Fencing. No. 509, Rowing. 30m, Steeplechase, horiz. 35m, Swimming, horiz.

Perf. 13½x13

1960, July 23 Photo. Wmk. 328

505	A174	5m	gray	.45	.20
506	A174	5m	brown	.45	.20
507	A174	5m	dp claret	.45	.20
508	A174	10m	brt carmine	.45	.20
509	A174	10m	gray green	.45	.20
a.			Vert. or horiz. strip, #505-509	2.50	
510	A174	30m	purple	.60	.20
511	A174	35m	dark blue	.70	.20
			Nos. 505-511 (7)	3.55	1.40

Souvenir Sheet

Imperf

512 A175 100m car & brown 3.00 3.00

Nos. 505-511 for the 17th Olympic Games, Rome, Aug. 25-Sept. 11.

Dove and UN Emblem — A176

35m, Lights surrounding UN emblem, horiz.

Perf. 13½x13

1960, Oct. 24 Wmk. 328

513	A176	10m	purple	.25	.20
514	A176	35m	brt rose	.35	.20

15th anniversary of United Nations.

Abu Simbel Temple of Queen Nefertari — A177

Perf. 11x11½

1960, Nov. 14 Photo. Wmk. 328

515 A177 10m ocher, *buff* .55 .20

Issued as propaganda to save historic monuments in Nubia and in connection with the UNESCO meeting, Paris, Nov. 14.

Model Post Office A178

1961, Jan. 2 *Perf. 13x13½*

516 A178 10m brt car rose .35 .20

Issued for Post Day, Jan. 2.

Eagle, Fasces and Victory Wreath — A179

Wheat and Globe Surrounded by Flags — A180

1961, Feb. 22 *Perf. 13½x13*

517 A179 10m dull violet .35 .20

3rd anniversary of United Arab Republic.
See Syria-UAR No. 50.

1961, Mar. 21 Wmk. 328

518 A180 10m vermilion .35 .20

Intl. Agricultural Exhib., Cairo, 3/21-4/20.

Patrice Lumumba and Map A181

Reading Braille and WHO Emblem A182

1961, Mar. 30 *Perf. 13½x13*

519 A181 10m black .35 .20

Africa Day, Apr. 15 and 3rd Conf. of Independent African States, Cairo, Mar. 25-31.

1961, Apr. 6 Photo.

520 A182 10m red brown .35 .20

WHO Day. See Nos. B21, N80.

Tower of Cairo — A183

Arab Woman and Son, Palestine Map — A184

1961, Apr. 11 ***Perf. 13½x13***
521 A183 10m grnsh blue .35 .20

Opening of the 600-foot Tower of Cairo, on island of Gizireh. See No. C95.

1961, May 15 **Wmk. 328**
522 A184 10m brt green .40 .20

Issued for Palestine Day.
See No. N79.

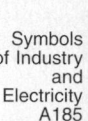

Symbols of Industry and Electricity A185

Chart and Workers — A186

#524, New buildings and family. #525, Ship, train, bus and radio. #526, Dam, cotton and field. #527, Hand holding candle and family.

1961, July 23 **Photo.** ***Perf. 13x13½***

523	A185	10m	dp carmine	.45	.20
524	A185	10m	brt blue	.45	.20
525	A185	10m	dk vio brown	.45	.20
526	A185	35m	dk green	.55	.20
527	A185	35m	brt purple	.55	.20
		Nos. 523-527 (5)		2.45	1.00

Souvenir Sheet

Imperf

528 A186 100m red brown 3.00 2.25

9th anniv. of the revolution.

Map of Suez Canal and Ships — A187

Perf. 11½x11

1961, July 26 **Unwmk.**
529 A187 10m olive .40 .20

Suez Canal Co. nationalization, 5th anniv.

Various Enterprises of Misr Bank — A188

Perf. 13x13½

1961, Aug. 22 **Wmk. 328**
530 A188 10m red brn, *pnksh* .35 .20

The 41st anniversary of Misr Bank.

Flag, Ship's Wheel and Battleship — A189

1961, Aug. 29 **Photo.** ***Perf. 13½x13***
531 A189 10m deep blue .40 .20

Issued for Navy Day.

Type A136 Redrawn, Type A138, Type A217 and:

Eagle of Saladin over Cairo — A190

Designs: 1m, Farmer's wife. 4m, 14th cent. glass lamp. 35m, "Commerce."

1961, Aug. 31 **Unwmk.** ***Perf. 11½***

532	A136	1m	blue	.25	.20
533	A217	4m	olive	.25	.20
534	A190	10m	purple	.25	.20
535	A138	35m	slate blue	.30	.20
		Nos. 532-535 (4)		1.05	.80

Smaller of two Arabic inscriptions in new positions: 1m, at right above Egyptian numeral; 4m, upward to spot beside waist of lamp; 35m, upper left corner below "UAR." On 4m, "UAR" is 2mm deep instead of 1mm. "Egypt" omitted as in 1959-60.

UN Emblem, Book, Cogwheel, Corn — A191

Perf. 13½x13

1961, Oct. 24 **Photo.** **Wmk. 328**

Design: 35m, Globe and cogwheel, horiz.

536 A191 10m black & ocher .25 .20
537 A191 35m blue grn & brn .45 .20

UN Technical Assistance Program and 16th anniv. of the UN.
See Nos. N81-N82.

Trajan's Kiosk, Philae — A192

1961, Nov. 4 **Unwmk.** ***Perf. 11½***
Size: 60x27mm
538 A192 10m dp vio blue .75 .30

15th anniv. of UNESCO, and to publicize UNESCO's help in safeguarding the monuments of Nubia.

Palette, Brushes, Map of Mediterranean A193

Atom and Educational Symbols A194

1961, Dec. 14 **Wmk. 328** ***Perf. 13½***
539 A193 10m dk red brown .35 .20

Issued to publicize the 4th Biennial Exhibition of Fine Arts in Alexandria.

1961, Dec. 18
540 A194 10m dull purple .35 .20

Issued to publicize Education Day.
See No. N83.

Arms of UAR A195

1961, Dec. 23 **Unwmk.** ***Perf. 11½***
541 A195 10m brt pink, brt grn & blk .35 .20

Victory Day. See No. N84.

Sphinx at Giza — A196

1961, Dec. 27 ***Perf. 11x11½***
542 A196 10m black .45 .30

Issued to publicize the "Sound and Light" Project, the installation of floodlights and sound equipment at the site of the Pyramids and Sphinx.

Post Office Printing Plant, Nasser City A197

1962, Jan. 2 **Photo.** ***Perf. 11½x11***
543 A197 10m dk brown .35 .20

Issued for Post Day, Jan. 2.

Map of Africa, King Mohammed V of Morocco and Flags — A198

1962, Jan. 4 ***Perf. 11x11½***
544 A198 10m indigo .35 .20

African Charter, Casablanca, 1st anniv.

Girl Scout Saluting and Emblem A199

Perf. 13x13½

1962, Feb. 22 **Wmk. 328**
545 A199 10m bright blue 1.25 .30

Egyptian Girl Scouts' 25th anniversary.

Arab Refugees, Flag and Map — A200

Mother and Child — A201

1962, Mar. 7 ***Perf. 13½x13***
546 A200 10m dark slate green .35 .20

5th anniv. of the liberation of the Gaza Strip.
See No. N85.

1962, Mar. 21 **Photo.**
547 A201 10m dk violet brn 1.00 .20

Issued for Arab Mother's Day, Mar. 21.

Map of Africa and Post Horn — A202

1962, Apr. 23 **Wmk. 328**
548 A202 10m crimson & ocher .30 .20
549 A202 50m dp blue & ocher .60 .20

Establishment of African Postal Union.

Cadets on Parade and Academy Emblem A203

1962, June 18 ***Perf. 13x13½***
550 A203 10m green .35 .20

Egyptian Military Academy, 150th anniv.

Malaria Eradication Emblem — A204

Theodor Bilharz — A205

1962, June 20 *Perf. 13½x13*

551 A204 10m dk brown & red .25 .20
552 A204 35m dk green & blue .30 .20

WHO drive to eradicate malaria.
See Nos. N87-N88.

1962, June 24 *Perf. 11x11½*

553 A205 10m brown orange .35 .20

Dr. Theodor Bilharz (1825-1862), German physician who first described bilharziasis, an endemic disease in Egypt.

Patrice Lumumba and Map of Africa — A206

Hand on Charter — A207

1962, July 1 **Photo.** **Wmk. 342**

554 A206 10m rose & red .35 .20

Issued in memory of Patrice Lumumba (1925-61), Premier of Congo.

1962, July 10 *Perf. 11x11½*

555 A207 10m brt blue & dk brn .35 .20

Proclamation of the National Charter.

"Birth of the Revolution" A208

Symbolic Designs: #557, Proclamation (Scroll and book). #558, Agricultural Reform (Farm and crescent). #559, Bandung Conference (Dove, globe and olive branch). #560, Birth of UAR (Eagle and flag). #561, Industrialization (cogwheel, factory, ship and bus). #562, Aswan High Dam. #563, Social Revolution (Modern buildings and emblem). 100m, Arms of UAR, emblems of Afro-Asian and African countries and UN.

1962, July 23 *Perf. 11½*

556	A208	10m brn, dk red brn & pink	.20	.20
557	A208	10m dk blue & sepia	.20	.20
558	A208	10m sepia & brt bl	.20	.20
559	A208	10m olive & dk ultra	.20	.20
560	A208	10m grn, blk & red	.20	.20
561	A208	10m brn org & indigo	.20	.20
562	A208	10m brn org & vio blk	.20	.20
563	A208	10m orange & blk	.20	.20
		Nos. 556-563 (8)	1.60	1.60

Souvenir Sheets

Perf. 11½

564 A208 100m grn, pink, red & blk 2.50 2.25

10th anniv. of the revolution.
No. 564 exists imperf. Same value.

Mahmoud Moukhtar, Museum and Sculpture A209

1962, July 24 *Perf. 11½x11*

565 A209 10m lt vio bl & olive .35 .20

Opening of the Moukhtar Museum, Island of Gezireh. The sculpture is "La Vestale de Secrets" by Moukhtar.

Flag of Algeria and Map of Africa Showing Algeria — A210

1962, Aug. 15 *Perf. 11x11½*

566 A210 10m multicolored .35 .20

Algeria's independence, July 1, 1962.

Rocket, Arms of UAR and Atom Symbol — A211

1962, Sept. 1 **Photo.** **Wmk. 342**

567 A211 10m brt grn, red & blk .40 .20

Launching of UAR rockets.

Rifle and Target — A212

Map of Africa, Table Tennis Paddle, Net and Ball — A213

1962, Sept. 18 *Perf. 11½*

568	A212	5m green, blk & red	.45	.25
569	A213	5m green, blk & red	.45	.25
a.		Pair, #568-569	1.00	1.00
570	A212	10m bister, bl & dk grn	.55	.40
571	A213	10m bister, bl & dk grn	.55	.40
a.		Pair, #570-571	1.25	1.25
572	A212	35m dp ultra, red & blk	1.25	.85
573	A213	35m dp ultra, red & blk	1.25	.85
a.		Pair, #572-573	2.75	2.75
		Nos. 568-573 (6)	4.50	3.00

38th World Shooting Championships and the 1st African Table Tennis Tournament. Types A212 and A213 are printed se-tenant at the base.

Dag Hammarskjold and UN Emblem — A214

Perf. 11½x11

1962, Oct. 24 **Photo.** **Wmk. 342**

Portrait in Slate Blue

574	A214	5m deep lilac	.40	.20
575	A214	10m olive	.50	.20
576	A214	35m deep ultra	.65	.20
		Nos. 574-576 (3)	1.55	.60

Dag Hammarskjold, Secretary General of the UN, 1953-61, and 17th anniv. of the UN.
See Nos. N89-N91.

Queen Nefertari Crowned by Isis and Hathor — A215

1962, Oct. 31 *Perf. 11½*

577 A215 10m blue & ocher 1.00 .40

Issued to publicize the UNESCO campaign to safeguard the monuments of Nubia.

Jet Trainer, Hawker Hart Biplane and College Emblem A216

1962, Nov. 2 *Perf. 11½x11*

578 A216 10m bl, dk bl & crim .35 .20

25th anniversary of Air Force College.

14th Century Glass Lamp and "1963" — A217

Yemen Flag and Hand with Torch — A218

1963, Feb. 20 *Perf. 11x11½*

579 A217 4m dk brn, grn & car .35 .20

Issued for use on greeting cards.
See Nos. 441, 477, 533, N76, N92. For overprint see No. N65.

1963, Mar. 14 **Photo.** **Wmk. 342**

580 A218 10m olive & brt car .35 .20

Establishment of Yemen Arab Republic.

Tennis Player, Pyramids and Globe A219

Perf. 11½x11

1963, Mar. 20 **Unwmk.**

581 A219 10m gray, blk & brn .50 .20

Intl. Lawn Tennis Championships, Cairo.

Cow, UN and FAO Emblems A220

Designs: 10m, Corn, wheat and emblems, vert. 35m, Wheat, corn and emblems.

Perf. 11½x11, 11x11½

1963, Mar. 21 **Wmk. 342**

582	A220	5m violet & dp org	.40	.25
583	A220	10m ultra & yel	.45	.25
584	A220	35m blue, yel & blk	.55	.40
		Nos. 582-584 (3)	1.40	.90

FAO "Freedom from Hunger" campaign.
See Nos. N93-N95.

Centenary Emblem — A221

Design: 35m, Globe and emblem.

1963, May 8 **Unwmk.** *Perf. 11x11½*

585 A221 10m lt blue, red & mar .30 .20
586 A221 35m lt blue & red .60 .20

Centenary of the Red Cross.
See Nos. N96-N97.

Arab Socialist Union Emblem A222

50m, Tools, torch & symbol of National Charter.

Wmk. 342

1963, July 23 **Photo.** *Perf. 11½*

587 A222 10m slate & rose pink .35 .20

Souvenir Sheets

Perf. 11½

588 A222 50m vio bl & org yel 1.90 1.60

11th anniv. of the revolution and to publicize the Arab Socialist Union.
No. 588 exists imperf. Same value.

Television Station, Cairo, and Screen A223

1963, Aug. 1 *Perf. 11½x11*

589 A223 10m dk blue & yel .35 .20

2nd Intl. Television Festival, Alexandria, 9/1-10.

Queen Nefertari A224

Swimmer and Map of Suez Canal A225

Designs: 10m, Great Hypostyle Hall, Abu Simbel. 35m, Ramses in moonlight.

Wmk. 342

1963, Oct. 1 Photo. *Perf. 11*
Size: 25x42mm (5m, 35m); 28x61mm (10m)

590 A224 5m brt vio blue & yel .40 .25
591 A224 10m gray, blk & red org .60 .30
592 A224 35m org yel & blk 1.00 .35
Nos. 590-592 (3) 2.00 .90

UNESCO world campaign to save historic monuments in Nubia.
See Nos. N98-N100.

1963, Oct. 15
593 A225 10m blue & sal rose .35 .20

Intl. Suez Canal Swimming Championship.

Ministry of Agriculture — A226

Perf. 11½x11

1963, Nov. 20 Wmk. 342
594 A226 10m multicolored .35 .20

50th anniv. of the Ministry of Agriculture.

Modern Building and Map of Africa and Asia A227

1963, Dec. 7
595 A227 10m multicolored .35 .20

Afro-Asian Housing Congress, Dec. 7-12.

Scales, Globe, UN Emblem A228

1963, Dec. 10
596 A228 5m dk green & yel .30 .20
597 A228 10m blue, gray & blk .35 .20
598 A228 35m rose red, pink & red .40 .30
Nos. 596-598 (3) 1.05 .70

15th anniv. of the Universal Declaration of Human Rights.
See Nos. N101-N103.

Sculpture, Arms of Alexandria and Palette with Flags — A229

1963, Dec. 12 *Perf. 11x11½*
599 A229 10m pale bl, dk bl & brn .35 .20

Issued to publicize the 5th Biennial Exhibition of Fine Arts in Alexandria.

Lion and Nile Hilton Hotel — A230

Vase, 13th Century — A231

Pharaoh Userkaf (5th Dynasty) A232

Designs: 1m, Vase, 14th century. 2m, Ivory headrest. 3m, Pharaonic calcite boat. 4m, Minaret and gate. 5m, Nile and Aswan High Dam. 10m, Eagle of Saladin over pyramids. 15m, Window, Ibn Tulun's mosque. No. 608, Mitwalli Gate, Cairo. 35m, Nefertari. 40m, Tower Hotel. 55m, Sultan Hassan's Mosque. 60m, Courtyard, Al Azhar University. 200m, Head of Ramses II. 500m, Funerary mask of Tutankhamen.

1964-67 Unwmk. Photo. *Perf. 11*
Size: Nos. 608, 612, 19x24mm; others, 24x29mm

600 A231 1m citron & ultra .20 .20
601 A230 2m magenta & bis .20 .20
602 A230 3m sal, org & bl .20 .20
603 A235 4m och, blk & ultra .35 .20
604 A230 5m brn & brt blue .20 .20
a. 5m brown & dark blue .50 .20
605 A231 10m green, dk brn & lt brn .30 .20
606 A230 15m ultra & yel .30 .20
607 A230 20m brn org & blk .70 .20
608 A231 20m lt olive grn ('67) 1.50 .20
609 A230 30m yellow & brown .70 .20
610 A231 35m sal, och & ultra .60 .20
611 A231 40m ultra & yellow 1.50 .40
612 A231 55m brt red lil ('67) 2.00 .20
613 A231 60m grnsh bl & yel brn .80 .30

Wmk. 342

614 A232 100m dk vio brn & sl 5.00 .85
615 A232 200m bluish blk & yel brn 8.00 1.00
616 A232 500m ultra & dp org 17.50 3.00
Nos. 600-616 (17) 40.05 7.95

Nos. 603 & N107 lack the vertically arranged dates which appear at lower right on No. 619.
See Nos. N104-N116.

HSN Commission Emblem — A233

Perf. 11x11½

1964, Jan. 10 Wmk. 342
617 A233 10m dull bl, dk bl & yel .35 .20

1st conf. of the Commission of Health, Sanitation and Nutrition.

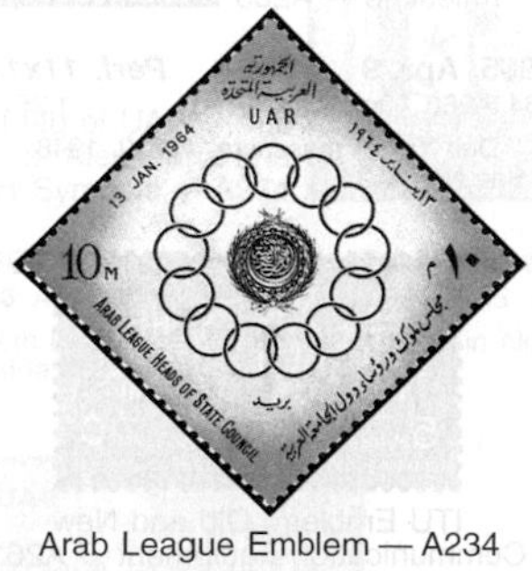

Arab League Emblem — A234

1964, Jan. 13 *Perf. 11*
618 A234 10m brt green & blk .35 .20

1st meeting of the Heads of State of the Arab League, Cairo, January.
See No. N117.

Minaret at Night — A235

1964 Unwmk. *Perf. 11*
619 A235 4m emerald, blk & red .35 .20

Issued for use on greeting cards.
See Nos. 603, N107, N118.

Old and New Dwellings and Map of Nubia A236

Perf. 11½x11

1964, Feb. 27 Photo. Wmk. 342
620 A236 10m dull vio & yel .35 .20

Resettlement of Nubian population.

Map of Africa and Asia and Train A237

1964, Mar. 21
621 A237 10m dull bl, dk bl & yel .90 .50

Asian Railway Conference, Cairo, Mar. 21.

Ikhnaton and Nefertiti with Children — A238

1964, Mar. 21 *Perf. 11x11½*
622 A238 10m dk brown & ultra .50 .30

Issued for Arab Mother's Day, Mar. 21.

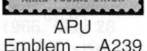

APU Emblem — A239

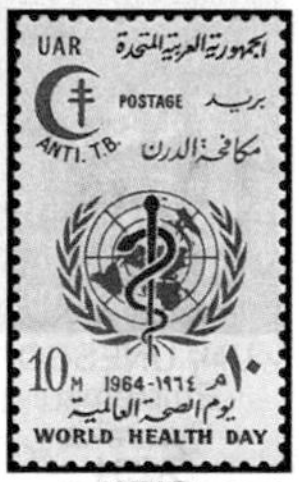

WHO Emblem — A240

1964, Apr. 1 Photo. Wmk. 342
623 A239 10m org brn & bl, *sal* .35 .20

Permanent Office of the APU, 10th anniv.
See No. N119.

1964, Apr. 7
624 A240 10m dk blue & red .35 .20

World Health Day (Anti-Tuberculosis).
See No. N120.

Statue of Liberty, World's Fair Pavilion and Pyramids A241

1964, Apr. 22 *Perf. 11½x11*
625 A241 10m brt green & ol, *grysh* .35 .20

New York World's Fair, 1964-65.

Nile and Aswan High Dam A242

1964, May 15 Unwmk. *Perf. 11½*
626 A242 10m black & blue .35 .20

The diversion of the Nile.

"Land Reclamation" — A243

Design: No. 628, "Electricity," Aswan High Dam hydroelectric station.

1964, July 23 *Perf. 11½*
627 A243 10m yellow & emer .35 .20
628 A243 10m green & blk .35 .20

Land reclamation and hydroelectric power due to the Aswan High Dam.

An imperf. souvenir sheet, issued July 23, contains two 50m black and blue stamps showing Aswan High Dam before and after diversion of the Nile. Value $2.

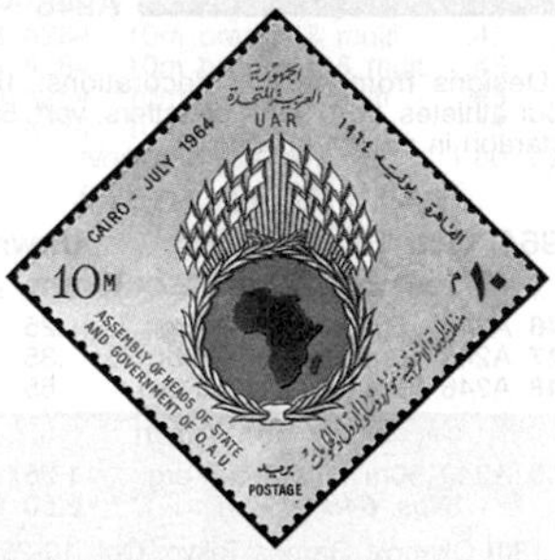

Map of Africa and 34 Flags — A244

1964, July 17 Photo.
629 A244 10m brn, brt bl & blk .35 .20

Assembly of Heads of State and Government of the Organization for African Unity at Cairo in July.

Jamboree Emblem — A245

Design: No. 631, Emblem of Air Scouts.

1964, Aug. 28 Unwmk. *Perf. 11½*
630 A245 10m red, grn & blk .50 .40
631 A245 10m green & red .50 .40
a. Pair, #630-631 1.25 1.25

The 6th Pan Arab Jamboree, Alexandria.

Flag of Algeria A246

Human Rights Flame
A415

Taha Hussein
A416

Perf. 11x11½

1973, Dec. 8 Photo. Wmk. 342
948 A415 20m yel grn, dk bl & car .45 .20

25th anniversary of the Universal Declaration of Human Rights.

1973, Dec. 10
949 A416 20m dk blue, brn & emer .35 .20

Dr. Taha Hussein (1893-1973), "Father of Education" in Egypt, writer, philosopher.

Pres. Sadat, Flag and Battle of Oct. 6 — A417

1973, Dec. 23 ***Perf. 11x11½***
950 A417 20m yellow, blk & red 1.50 1.00

October War against Israel (crossing of Suez Canal by Egyptian forces, Oct. 6, 1973). See No. 959.

WPY Emblem and Chart — A418

Cairo Fair Emblem — A419

1974, Mar. 21 Wmk. 342 ***Perf. 11***
951 A418 55m org, grn & dk bl .85 .30

World Population Year.

1974, Mar. 21 Photo.
952 A419 20m blue & multi .40 .20

Cairo International Fair.

Nurse and Medal of Angels of Ramadan 10 — A420

1974, May 15 ***Perf. 11½***
953 A420 55m multicolored 1.40 .35

Nurses' and World Hospital Day.

Workers, Relief Carving from Queen Tee's Tomb, Sakhara — A421

1974, May 15 ***Perf. 11***
954 A421 20m yellow, blue & brn .60 .20

Workers' Day.

Pres. Sadat, Troops Crossing Suez Canal — A422

"Reconstruction," Map of Suez Canal and New Building — A423

Sheet of Aluminum
A424

Design: 110m, Pres. Sadat's "October Working Paper," symbols of science and development.

1974, July 23 Photo. ***Perf. 11x11½***
955 A422 20m multicolored .70 .35
956 A423 20m blue, gold & blk .70 .35

Perf. 11½

957 A424 20m plum & silver .70 .35
Nos. 955-957 (3) 2.10 1.05

Souvenir Sheet

Imperf

958 A424 110m green & multi 3.50 3.00

22nd anniv. of the revolution establishing the republic and for the end of the October War. No. 958 contains one 52x59mm stamp.

Pres. Sadat and Flag — A425

Perf. 11x11½

1974, Oct. 6 Wmk. 342
959 A425 20m yellow, blk & red 1.25 .60

1st anniv. of Battle. See No. 950.

Palette and Brushes
A426

1974, Oct. 6 ***Perf. 11½***
960 A426 30m purple, yel & blk .70 .20

6th Exhibition of Plastic Art.

Teachers and Pupils — A427

1974, Oct. 6 ***Perf. 11x11½***
961 A427 20m multicolored .55 .20

Teachers' Day.

Souvenir Sheet

UPU Monument, Bern — A428

1974, Oct. 6 ***Imperf.***
962 A428 110m gold & multi 5.00 4.25

Cent. of the UPU.

Emblems, Cogwheel and Calipers — A429

Refugee Camp under Attack and UN Refugee Organization Emblem — A430

Child and UNICEF Emblem
A431

Temple of Philae — A432

1974, Oct. 24 ***Perf. 11½, 11x11½***
963 A429 10m black, bl & yel .40 .20
964 A430 20m dp org, bl & blk .75 .20
965 A431 30m green, bl & brn 1.00 .40
966 A432 55m black, bl & yel 2.40 .85
Nos. 963-966 (4) 4.55 1.65

UN Day. World Standards Day (10m); Palestinian refugee repatriation (20m); Family Planning (30m); Campaign to save Temple of Philae (55m).

Calla Lily — A433

1974, Nov. 7 ***Perf. 11***
967 A433 10m ultra & multi .40 .20

For use on greeting cards.

10m-coins, Smokestacks and Grain — A434

1974, Nov. 7 ***Perf. 11½x11***
968 A434 20m yel grn, dk bl & sil .40 .20

International Savings Day.

Organization Emblem and Medical Services — A435

1974, Nov. 7 ***Perf. 11½***
969 A435 30m vio, red & gold .65 .20

Health Insurance Organization, 10th anniv.

Mustafa Lutfy El Manfalouty
A436

Abbas Mahmoud El Akkad
A437

Perf. 11x11½

1974, Dec. 8 Photo. Wmk. 342

970 A436 20m blue blk & brn .40 .25
971 A437 20m brown & bl blk .40 .25
a. Pair, #970-971 1.00 .80

Arab writers; El Manfalouty (1876-1924) and El Akkad (1889-1964).

Goddess Maat Facing God Thoth — A438

Fish-shaped Vase — A439

Pharaonic Golden Vase — A440

Sign of Life, Mirror — A441

Wmk. 342

1975, Jan. 2 Photo. *Perf. 11½*

972 A438 20m silver & multi .75 .25
973 A439 30m multicolored 1.00 .25
974 A440 55m multicolored 1.40 .65
975 A441 110m blue & multi 2.25 1.25
Nos. 972-975 (4) 5.40 2.40

Post Day 1975. Egyptian art works from 12th-5th centuries B.C.

Om Kolthoum — A442

Perf. 11½

1975, Mar. 3 Photo. Unwmk.

976 A442 20m brown .70 .20

In memory of Om Kolthoum, singer.

Crescent, Globe, Al Aqsa and Kaaba — A443

Cairo Fair Emblem — A444

1975, Mar. 25

977 A443 20m multicolored .70 .20

Mohammed's Birthday.

Perf. 11x11½

1975, Mar. 25 Wmk. 342

978 A444 20m multicolored .40 .20

International Cairo Fair.

Kasr El Ainy Hospital WHO Emblem
A445

Perf. 11½x11

1975, May 7 Photo. Wmk. 342

979 A445 20m dk brown & blue .60 .20

World Health Organization Day.

Children Reading Book — A446

Children and Line Graph — A447

1975, May 7 *Perf. 11x11½*

980 A446 20m multicolored .70 .20
981 A447 20m multicolored .70 .20

Science Day.

Suez Canal, Globe, Ships, Pres. Sadat — A448

1975, June 5 *Perf. 11½*

982 A448 20m blue, brn & blk 1.00 .30
Nos. 982,C166-C167 (3) 5.00 2.00

Reopening of the Suez Canal, June 5.

Belmabgoknis Flowers — A449

1975, July 30 Photo. Wmk. 342

983 A449 10m green & blue .40 .20

For use on greeting cards.

Sphinx and Pyramids Illuminated — A450

Rural Electrification — A451

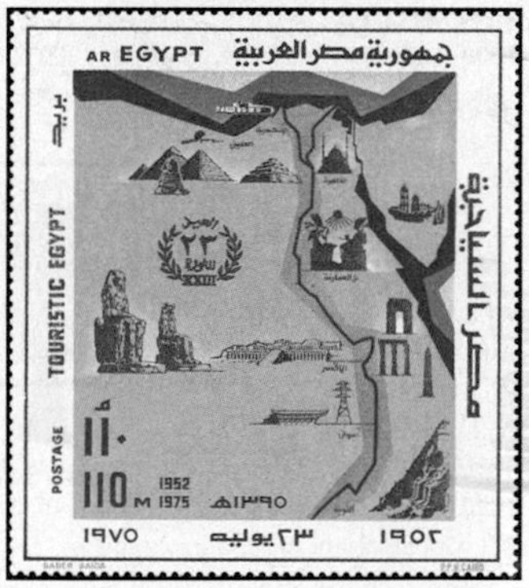

Map of Egypt with Tourist Sites — A452

Illustration A452 is reduced.

1975, July 23

984 A450 20m black, org & grn .55 .25
985 A451 20m dk blue & brown .55 .25

Perf. 11

986 A452 110m multicolored 5.50 4.75
Nos. 984-986 (3) 6.60 5.25

23rd anniversary of the revolution establishing the republic. No. 986 printed in sheets of 6 (2x3). Size: 71x80mm.

Volleyball — A453

1975, Aug. 2 Photo. *Perf. 11x11½*

987 A453 20m shown .70 .25
988 A453 20m Running .70 .25
989 A453 20m Torch and flag bearers .70 .25
990 A453 20m Basketball .70 .25
991 A453 20m Soccer .70 .25
a. Strip of 5, #987-991 4.00 3.50

6th Arab School Tournament.

Egyptian Flag and Tanks
A454

1975 Photo. Unwmk. *Perf. 11½*

992 A454 20m multicolored 1.25 .40

Two-line Arabic Inscription in Bottom Panel, "M" over "20"

992A A454 20m multicolored 1.25 .40

No. 992 for 2nd anniv. of October War against Israel, "The Spark;" No. 992A, the Intl. Symposium on October War against Israel 1973, Cairo University, Oct. 27-31.

Issue dates: No. 992, Oct. 6; No. 992A, Oct. 24.

Arrows Pointing to Fluke, and Emblems
A455

Submerged Wall and Sculpture, UNESCO Emblem
A456

Perf. 11x11½

1975, Oct. 24 Wmk. 342

993 A455 20m multicolored .65 .30
994 A456 55m multicolored 1.90 .50

UN Day. 20m for Intl. Conf. on Schistosomiasis (Bilharziasis); 55m for UNESCO help in saving temples at Philae. See Nos. C169-C170.

Pharaonic Gate, University Emblem — A457

Al Biruni — A458

1975, Nov. 15 Photo. Wmk. 342

995 A457 20m multicolored .35 .20

Ain Shams University, 25th anniversary.

1975, Dec. 23 Photo. *Perf. 11x11½*

Arab Philosophers: No. 997, Al Farabi and lute. No. 998, Al Kanady, book and compass.

996 A458 20m blue, brn & grn 1.10 .30
997 A458 20m blue, brn & grn 1.10 .30
998 A458 20m blue, brn & grn 1.10 .30
Nos. 996-998 (3) 3.30 .90

Ibex (Prow) — A459

Post Day (from Tutankhamen's Tomb): 30m, Lioness. 55m, Cow's head (Goddess Hawthor). 110m, Hippopotamus' head (God Horus).

1976, Jan. 2 Unwmk. *Perf. 11½*

999	A459	20m multicolored	3.25	1.25

Wmk. 342

1000	A459	30m brown, gold & ultra	5.25	1.50
1001	A459	55m multicolored	9.50	3.25
1002	A459	110m multicolored	13.00	8.00
		Nos. 999-1002 (4)	31.00	14.00

Lake, Aswan Dam, Industry and Agriculture — A460

Perf. 11½x11

1976, Jan. 27 Photo. Wmk. 342

1003 A460 20m multicolored .60 .20

Filling of lake formed by Aswan High Dam.

Fair Emblem — A461

Commemorative Medal — A462

1976, Mar. 15 *Perf. 11x11½*

1004 A461 20m orange & purple .35 .20

9th International Cairo Fair, Mar. 8-27.

1976, Mar. 15 Wmk. 342

1005 A462 20m olive, yel & blk .35 .20

11th Biennial Exhibition of Fine Arts, Alexandria.

Hands Shielding Invalid A463

1976, Apr. 7 Photo. *Perf. 11½*

1006 A463 20m dk grn, lt grn & yel .40 .20

Founding of Faithfulness and Hope Society.

Eye and WHO Emblem A464

1976, Apr. 7

1007 A464 20m dk brn, yel & grn .60 .20

World Health Day: "Foresight prevents blindness."

Pres. Sadat, Legal Department Emblem — A465

Perf. 11½x11

1976, May 15 Photo. Wmk. 342

1008 A465 20m olive & multi .75 .25

Centenary of State Legal Department.

Scales of Justice — A466

1976, May 15 *Perf. 11x11½*

1009 A466 20m carmine, blk & grn .60 .20

5th anniversary of Rectification Movement.

Al-Ahram Front Page, First Issue A467

Perf. 11½x11

1976, June 25 Photo. Wmk. 342

1010 A467 20m bister & multi .45 .20

Centenary of Al-Ahram newspaper.

World Map, Pres. Sadat and Emblems — A468

1976, July 23 *Perf. 11x11½*

1011 A468 20m bl, blk & yel .55 .30

Size: 240x216mm

Imperf

1012 A468 110m bl, brn & yel 5.50 4.75

24th anniv. of the revolution. No. 1012 design is similar to No. 1011.

Scarborough Lily — A469

1976, Sept. 10 Photo. *Perf. 11*

1013 A469 10m multicolored .35 .20

For use on greeting cards.

Reconstruction of Sinai by Irrigation — A470

Abu Redice Oil Wells and Refinery — A471

Unknown Soldier, Memorial Pyramid for October War — A472

1976, Oct. 6 *Perf. 11x11½*

1014	A470	20m multicolored	.65	.35
1015	A471	20m multicolored	.65	.35

Size: 65x77mm

1016 A472 110m grn, bl & blk 6.00 5.00

October War against Israel, 3rd anniv.

Papyrus with Children's Animal Story — A473

Al Aqsa Mosque, Palestinian Refugees — A474

55m, Isis, from Philae Temple, UNESCO emblem, vert. 110m, UNESCO emblem & "30."

Perf. 11½, 11½x11

1976, Oct. 24 Photo. Wmk. 342

1017	A473	20m dk bl, bis & brn	.55	.20
1018	A474	30m brn, grn & blk	.75	.30
1019	A473	55m dk blue & bister	1.25	.45
1020	A474	110m lt grn, vio bl & red	2.25	1.25
		Nos. 1017-1020 (4)	4.80	2.20

30th anniversary of UNESCO.

Census Chart A475

1976, Nov. 22 Photo. *Perf. 11½x11*

1021 A475 20m multicolored .40 .20

10th General Population and Housing Census.

A476

A477

Design: Nile and commemorative medal.

1976, Nov. 22 *Perf. 11x11½*

1022 A476 20m green & brown .45 .20

Geographical Soc. of Egypt, cent. (in 1975).

1977, Jan. 2 Photo. *Perf. 11x11½*

Post Day: 20m, Ikhnaton. 30m, Ikhnaton's daughter. 55m, Nefertiti, Ikhnaton's wife. 110m, Ikhnaton, front view.

1023	A477	20m multicolored	.30	.20
1024	A477	30m multicolored	.30	.20
1025	A477	55m multicolored	.65	.25
1026	A477	110m multicolored	2.75	.60
		Nos. 1023-1026 (4)	4.00	1.25

Policeman, Emblem and Emergency Car — A478

Perf. 11½x11

1977, Feb. 25 Photo. Wmk. 342

1027 A478 20m multicolored .85 .20

Police Day.

Map of Africa, Arab League Emblem — A479

1977, Mar 7 *Perf. 11x11½*

1028 A479 55m multicolored .70 .20

First Afro-Arab Summit Conference, Cairo.

Fair Emblem, Pharaonic Ship A480

1977, Mar. 7 ***Perf. 11½x11***
1029 A480 20m green, blk & red .45 .20

10th International Cairo Fair.

King Faisal — A481

Healthy and Crippled Children — A482

1977, Mar. 22 Photo. ***Perf. 11x11½***
1030 A481 20m indigo & brown .45 .20

King Faisal Ben Abdel-Aziz Al Saud of Saudi Arabia (1906-1975).

1977, Apr. 12 **Wmk. 342**
1031 A482 20m multicolored .50 .20

National campaign to fight poliomyelitis.

APU Emblem, Members' Flags A483

1977, Apr. 12 ***Perf. 11½***
1032 A483 20m blue & multi .25 .20
1033 A483 30m gray & multi .25 .20

25th anniv. of Arab Postal Union (APU).

Children's Village A484

Perf. 11½x11
1977, May 7 Photo. Wmk. 342
1034 A484 20m multicolored .25 .20
1035 A484 55m multicolored .75 .40

Inauguration of Children's Village, Cairo.

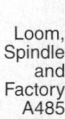

Loom, Spindle and Factory A485

1977, May 7
1036 A485 20m multicolored .35 .20

Egyptian Spinning and Weaving Company, El Mehalla el Kobra, 50th anniv.

Satellite, Globe, ITU Emblem — A486

1977, May 17 ***Perf. 11x11½***
1037 A486 110m dk blue & multi 1.25 .50

World Telecommunications Day.

Flag and "25" A487

Egyptian Flag and Eagle — A488

Perf. 11½x11
1977, July 23 Photo. Wmk. 342
1038 A487 20m silver, car & blk .50 .20

Perf. 11x11½
1039 A488 110m multicolored 2.50 1.00

25th anniversary of July 23rd Revolution. No. 1039 printed in sheets of six. Size: 75x83mm.

Saad Zaghloul A489

Archbishop Capucci, Map of Palestine A490

Perf. 11x11½
1977, Aug. 23 Photo. Wmk. 342
1040 A489 20m dk green & dk brn .20 .20

Saad Zaghloul, leader of 1919 Revolution, 50th death anniversary.

1977, Sept. 1
1041 A490 45m emerald & blue 1.00 .40

Palestinian Archbishop Hilarion Capucci, jailed by Israel in 1974.

Bird-of-Paradise Flower — A491

1977, Sept. 3
1042 A491 10m multicolored .20 .20

For use on greeting cards.

Proclamation Greening the Land — A492

Perf. 11x11½
1977, Sept. 25 Photo. Wmk. 342
1043 A492 20m multicolored .20 .20

Agrarian Reform Law, 25th anniversary.

Soldier, Tanks, Medal of Oct. 6 A493

Anwar Sadat — A494

1977, Oct. 6 ***Perf. 11½x11***
1044 A493 20m multicolored .30 .20

Unwmk.
Perf. 11
1045 A494 140m dk brn, gold & red 4.75 4.75

October War against Israel, 4th anniv. No. 1045 printed in sheets of 16.

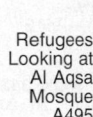

Refugees Looking at Al Aqsa Mosque A495

Goddess Taueret and Spirit of Flight (Horus) A496

Mural Relief, Temple of Philae — A497

Wmk. 342
1977, Oct. 24 Photo. ***Perf. 11***
1046 A495 45m green, red & blk .40 .20
1047 A496 55m dp blue & yellow .60 .25
1048 A497 140m ol bis & dk brn 1.50 .80
Nos. 1046-1048 (3) 2.50 1.25

United Nations Day.

Electric Trains, First Egyptian Locomotive — A498

1977, Oct. 22
1049 A498 20m multicolored 1.00 .20

125th anniversary of Egyptian railroads.

Film and Eye A499

1977, Nov. 16 ***Perf. 11½x11***
1050 A499 20m gray, blk & gold .35 .20

50th anniversary of Egyptian cinema.

Natural Gas Well and Refinery — A500

1977, Nov. 17 **Photo.**
1051 A500 20m multicolored .40 .20

National Oil Festival, celebrating the acquisition of Sinai oil wells.

Pres. Sadat and Dome of the Rock A501

Perf. 11½x11
1977, Dec. 31 Photo. Wmk. 342
1052 A501 20m green, brn & blk .60 .20
1053 A501 140m green, blk & brn 2.25 .80

Pres. Sadat's peace mission to Israel.

Ramses II — A502

Post Day: 45m, Queen Nefertari, bas-relief.

1978, Jan. 2 ***Perf. 11½***
1054 A502 20m green, blk & gold .60 .20
1055 A502 45m orange, blk & ol 1.25 .70

Post Day 1978.

Water Wheels, Fayum — A503

Flying Duck, from Floor in Ikhnaton's Palace
A504

5m, Birdhouse, 10m, Statue of Horus. 20m, 30m, Al Rifa'i Mosque, Cairo. 50m, Monastery, Wadi al-Natrun. 55m, Ruins of Edfu Temple. 70m, 80m, Bridge of Oct. 6. 85m, Medum pyramid. 100m, Facade, El Morsi Mosque, Alexandria. 200m, Column, Alexandria, Sphinx. 500m, Arabian stallion.

Wmk. 342, Unwmkd. (30m, 70m, 80m)

1978-85 ***Perf. 11½***

1056	A503	1m slate blue	.20	.20
a.		Unwmkd. ('79)	.20	.20
b.		1m gray ('83)	.20	.20
c.		1m gray, unwmkd. ('83)	.20	.20
1057	A503	5m bister brn	.20	.20
a.		5m dull brn, unwmkd. ('79)	.20	.20
1058	A503	10m brt green	.20	.20
a.		Unwmkd. ('79)	.20	.20
1059	A503	20m dk brown	.20	.20
b.		Unwmkd. ('79)	.20	.20
1059A	A503	30m sepia	.20	.20
1060	A503	50m Prus blue	.25	.20
a.		Unwmkd. ('79)	.25	.20
b.		Unwmkd., brt blue ('87)	.25	.20
1061	A503	55m olive	.25	.20
1062	A503	70m olive ('79)	.30	.20
1062A	A503	80m olive ('82)	.35	.20
1063	A503	85m dp purple	.40	.20
a.		Unwmkd. ('85)	.40	.20
1064	A503	100m brown	.45	.20
a.		Unwmkd. ('85)	.65	.25
1065	A503	200m bl & indigo	2.00	.60
1066	A504	500m multicolored	5.00	1.50
1067	A504	£1 multicolored	7.50	2.00
		Nos. 1056-1067 (14)	17.50	6.30

Issued: 500m, £1, 2/27/78; 70m, 8/22/79; others, 7/23/78.

Fair Emblem and Wheat
A505

1978, Mar. 15 ***Perf. 11½***
1072 A505 20m multicolored .20 .20

11th Cairo International Fair, Mar. 11-25.

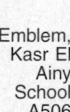

Emblem, Kasr El Ainy School
A506

1978, Mar. 18 ***Perf. 11½x11***
1073 A506 20m lt blue, blk & gold .20 .20

Kasr El Ainy School of Medicine, 150th anniv.

A507

#1074, Soldiers and Emblem. #1075, Youssef El Sebai.

1978, Mar. 30 ***Perf. 11x11½***

1074		20m multicolored	.30	.20
1075		20m bister brown	.30	.20
a.	A507	Pair, #1074-1075	.60	.20

Youssef El Sebai, newspaper editor, assassinated on Cyprus and in memory of the commandos killed in raid on Cyprus.

Biennale Medal, Statue for Entrance to Port Said
A509

1978, Apr. 1 ***Perf. 11½***
1076 A509 20m blue, grn & blk .25 .25

12th Biennial Exhibition of Fine Arts, Alexandria.

Child with Smallpox, UN Emblem
A510

1978, Apr. 7 **Photo.** ***Perf. 11½***
1077 A510 20m multicolored .20 .20

Eradication of smallpox.

Heart & Arrow, UN Emblem — A511

Anwar Sadat — A512

1978, Apr. 7 **Wmk. 342**
1078 A511 20m multicolored .20 .20

Fight against hypertension.

1978, May 15 **Photo.** ***Perf. 11½x11***
1079 A512 20m green, brn & gold .35 .20

7th anniversary of Rectification Movement.

Social Security Emblem — A513

1978, May 16 ***Perf. 11***
1080 A513 20m lt green & dk brn .20 .20

General Organization of Insurance and Pensions (Social Security), 25th anniversary.

New Cities on Map of Egypt — A514

Map of Egypt and Sudan, Wheat — A515

Wmk. 342

1978, July 23 **Photo.** ***Perf. 11½***

1081	A514	20m multicolored	.50	.20
1082	A515	45m multicolored	1.00	.20

26th anniversary of July 23rd revolution.

Symbols of Egyptian Ministries — A516

1978, Aug. 28 **Photo.** ***Perf. 11½x11***
1083 A516 20m multicolored .35 .20

Centenary of Egyptian Ministerial System.

Pres. Sadat and "Spirit of Egypt" Showing Way — A517

1978, Oct. 6 **Photo.** ***Perf. 11x11½***
1084 A517 20m multicolored .50 .20

October War against Israel, 5th anniv.

Human Rights Emblem — A518

Dove and Human Rights Emblem — A520

Kobet al Sakra Mosque, Refugee Camp
A519

UN Day: 55m, Temple at Biga and UNESCO emblem, horiz.

Perf. 11, 11½ (45m)

1978, Oct. 24 **Photo.** **Wmk. 342**

1085	A518	20m multicolored	.30	.20
1086	A519	45m multicolored	.85	.20
1087	A518	55m multicolored	.40	.20
1088	A520	140m multicolored	2.10	.30
		Nos. 1085-1088 (4)	3.65	.90

Pilgrims, Mt. Arafat and Holy Kaaba — A521

1978, Nov. 7 **Photo.** ***Perf. 11***
1089 A521 45m multicolored .80 .20

Pilgrimage to Mecca.

Tahtib Horse Dance — A522

1978, Nov. 7

1090	A522	10m multicolored	.45	.20
1091	A522	20m multicolored	.45	.20

UN Emblem, Globe and Grain
A523

1978, Nov. 11 **Photo.** ***Perf. 11½***
1092 A523 20m green, dk bl & yel .30 .20

Technical Cooperation Among Developing Countries Conf., Buenos Aires, Sept. 1978.

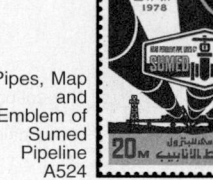

Pipes, Map and Emblem of Sumed Pipeline A524

1978, Nov. 11
1093 A524 20m brown, bl & yel .45 .20

Inauguration of Sumed pipeline from Suez to Alexandria, 1st anniversary.

Mastheads A525

Abu el Walid A526

1978, Dec. 24 ***Perf. 11x11½***
1094 A525 20m brown & black .45 .20

El Wakea el Masriya newspaper, 150th anniv.

1978, Dec. 24
1095 A526 45m brt green & indigo .55 .20

800th death anniv. of Abu el Walid ibn Rashid.

Helwan Observatory and Sky — A527

1978, Dec. 30 **Wmk. 342**
1096 A527 20m multicolored .60 .20

Helwan Observatory, 75th anniversary.

Second Daughter of Ramses II A528

Ramses Statues, Abu Simbel, and Cartouches — A529

1979, Jan. 2 **Photo.** ***Perf. 11***
1097 A528 20m brown & yellow .50 .25

Perf. 11½x11

1098 A529 140m multicolored 1.75 .35

Post Day 1979.

Book, Reader and Globe A530

Perf. 11½x11

1979, Feb. 1 **Photo.** **Wmk. 342**
1099 A530 20m yellow grn & brown .35 .20

Cairo 11th International Book Fair.

Wheat, Globe, Fair Emblem — A531

Perf. 11x11½

1979, Mar. 17 **Photo.** **Unwmk.**
1100 A531 20m blue, org & blk .35 .20

12th Cairo International Fair, Mar.-Apr.

Skull, Poppy, Agency Emblem — A532

1979, Mar. 20 ***Perf. 11***
1101 A532 70m multicolored 1.25 .35

Anti-Narcotics General Administration, 50th anniv.

Isis Holding Horus — A533

1979, Mar. 21
1102 A533 140m multicolored 2.10 .50

Mother's Day.

World Map and Book — A534

Perf. 11x11½

1979, Mar. 22 **Wmk. 342**
1103 A534 45m yellow, bl & brn .45 .25

Cultural achievements of the Arabs.

Pres. Sadat's Signature, Peace Doves A535

Wmk. 342

1979, Mar. 31 **Photo.** ***Perf. 11½***
1104 A535 70m brt green & red 1.00 .25
1105 A535 140m yellow grn & red 2.00 .60

Signing of Peace Treaty between Egypt and Israel, Mar. 26.

1979, May 26 **Photo.** ***Perf. 11½***
1106 A535 20m yellow & dk brn .40 .20

Return of Al Arish to Egypt.

Honeycomb with Food Symbols A536

1979, May 15
1107 A536 20m multicolored .30 .20

8th anniversary of movement to establish food security.

Coins, 1959, 1979 A537

Perf. 11½x11

1979, June 1 **Wmk. 342** **Photo.**
1108 A537 20m yellow & gray .35 .20

25th anniversary of the Egyptian Mint.

Egypt No. 1104 under Magnifying Glass — A538

1979, June 1 ***Perf. 11***
1109 A538 20m green, blk & brn .40 .20

Philatelic Society of Egypt, 50th anniversary.

Book, Atom Symbol, Rising Sun — A539

"23 July," "Revolution" and "Peace" — A540

Perf. 11½x11

1979, July 23 **Wmk. 342**
1110 A539 20m multicolored .35 .20

Miniature Sheet

Imperf

1111 A540 140m multicolored 3.00 1.50

27th anniversary of July 23rd revolution.

Musicians — A541

1979, Aug. 22 ***Perf. 11½***
1112 A541 10m multicolored .20 .20

For use on greeting cards.

Dove over Map of Suez Canal A542

Wmk. 342

1979, Oct. 6 **Photo.** ***Perf. 11½***
1113 A542 20m blue & brown .40 .20

October War against Israel, 6th anniv.

Prehistoric Mammal Skeleton, Map of Africa — A543

Perf. 11½x11

1979, Oct. 9 **Photo.** **Wmk. 342**
1114 A543 20m multicolored 1.25 .25

Egyptian Geological Museum, 75th anniv.

T Square on Drawing Board — A544

1979, Oct. 11 ***Perf. 11***
1115 A544 20m multicolored .50 .20

Engineers Day.

Human Rights Emblem Over Globe — A545

Boy Balancing IYC Emblem — A546

Perf. 11½

1979, Oct. 24 Photo. Unwmk.

1116 A545 45m multicolored .50 .25
1117 A546 140m multicolored 1.25 .50

UN Day and Intl. Year of the Child.

International Savings Day — A547

1979, Oct. 31

1118 A547 70m multicolored .75 .30

A548 A549

Design: Shooting championship emblem.

1979, Nov. 16

1119 A548 20m multicolored .40 .20

20th International Military Shooting Championship, Cairo.

1979, Nov. 29 ***Perf. 11x11½***

1120 A549 45m multicolored .75 .25

International Palestinian Solidarity Day.

Dove Holding Grain, Rotary Emblem, Globe A550

1979, Dec. 3 Photo. ***Perf. 11½***

1121 A550 140m multicolored 1.25 .60

Rotary Intl., 75th anniv,; Cairo Rotary Club, 50th anniv.

Arms Factories, 25th Anniversary — A551

Perf. 11½x11

1979, Dec. 23 Photo. Wmk. 342

1122 A551 20m lt olive grn & brn .35 .20

Aly El Garem (1881-1949) A552

Pharaonic Capital A553

Poets: No. 1124, Mahmoud Samy El Baroudy (1839-1904).

1979, Dec. 25 ***Perf. 11x11½***

1123 A552 20m dk brn & yel brn .40 .20
1124 A552 20m brown & dk brown .40 .20
a. Pair, #1123-1124 .80 .80

1980, Jan. 2 Unwmk. ***Perf. 11½***

Post Day: Various Pharaonic capitals.

1125 A553 20m multicolored .35 .25
1126 A553 45m multicolored .50 .35
1127 A553 70m multicolored .70 .25
1128 A553 140m multicolored 2.00 .40
a. Strip of 4, #1125-1128 4.75 2.40

Golden Goddess of Writing, Fair Emblem — A554

Exhibition Catalogue and Medal — A555

1980, Feb. 2 Photo. ***Perf. 11½***

1129 A554 20m multicolored .60 .20

12th Cairo Intl. Book Fair, Jan. 24-Feb. 4.

1980, Feb. 2

1130 A555 20m multicolored .45 .20

13th Biennial Exhibition of Fine Arts, Alexandria.

13th Cairo International Fair — A556

1980, Mar. 8 Photo. ***Perf. 11x11½***

1131 A556 20m multicolored .45 .20

Kiosk of Trajan — A557

a, Kiosk of Tratan. b, Temple of Korasy, entry at right. c, Temple of Ksalabsha, carvings on frame. d, Temple of Philae, 5 columns..

1980, Mar. 10 ***Perf. 11½***

1132 Strip of 4 + label 5.00 5.00
a.-d. A557 70m, any single 1.00 .60

UNESCO campaign to save Nubian monuments, 20th anniversary. Shown on stamps are Temples of Philae, Kalabsha, Korasy.

Physicians' Day — A558

1980, Mar. 18 ***Perf. 11x11½***

1133 A558 20m multicolored .45 .20

Rectification Movement, 9th Anniversary — A559

Perf. 11½x11

1980, May 15 Photo. Wmk. 342

1134 A559 20m multicolored .45 .20

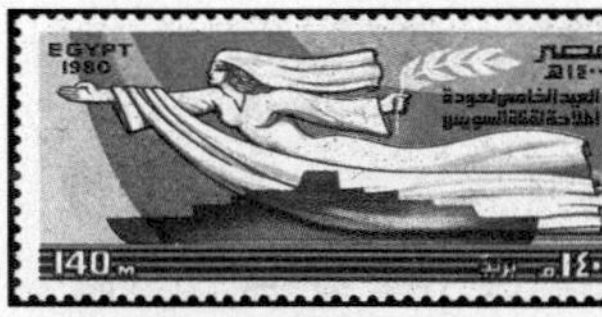

Re-opening of Suez Canal, 5th Anniversary — A560

1980, June 5 ***Perf. 11½***

1135 A560 140m multicolored 1.40 .50

Prevention of Cruelty to Animals Week A561

1980, June 5

1136 A561 20m lt yel grn & gray .70 .20

Industry Day A562

Perf. 11½x11

1980, July 12 Photo. Wmk. 342

1137 A562 20m multicolored .35 .20

Leaf with Text A563

Family Protection Emblem — A564

1980, July 23 ***Perf. 11½***

1138 A563 20m multicolored .45 .20

Souvenir Sheet

Imperf

1139 A564 140m multicolored 2.75 .55

July 23rd Revolution, 28th anniv.; Social Security Year.

Erksous Seller and Nakrazan Player — A565

Perf. 11½

1980, Aug. 8 Unwmk. Photo.

1140 A565 10m multicolored .30 .20

For use on greeting cards.

October War Against Israel, 7th Anniv. — A566

1980, Oct. 6 **Litho.**

1141 A566 20m multicolored .75 .20

Islamic and Coptic Columns A567

International Telecommunications Union Emblem — A568

Wmk. 342

1980, Oct. 24 **Photo.** ***Perf. 11½***

1142 A567 70m multicolored .70 .55
1143 A568 140m multicolored 1.40 .85

UN Day. Campaign to save Egyptian monuments (70m), Intl. Telecommunications Day (140m).

Hegira (Pilgrimage Year) A569

1980, Nov. 9 **Litho.** ***Perf. 11x11½***

1144 A569 45m multicolored .60 .25

Opening of Suez Canal Third Branch A570

Perf. 11½x11

1980, Dec. 16 **Photo.** **Wmk. 342**

1145 A570 70m multicolored .80 .30

Mustafa Sadek El-Rafai (1880-1927), Writer — A571

No. 1147, Ali Mustafa Mousharafa (1898-1950), mathematician (with glasses). No. 1148, Ali Ibrahim (1880-1947), surgeon.

1980, Dec. 23 ***Perf. 11x11½***

1146 A571 20m green & brown .45 .25
1147 A571 20m green & brown .45 .25
1148 A571 20m green & brown .45 .25
a. Strip of 3, #1146-1148 1.90 .75

See Nos. 1178-1179.

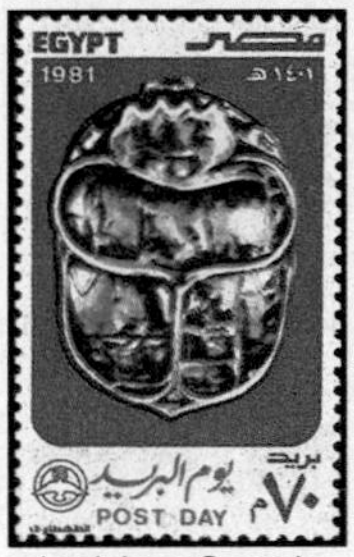

Ladybug Scarab Emblem — A572

von Stephan, UPU — A573

Perf. 11½

1981, Jan. 2 **Photo.** **Unwmk.**

1149 A572 70m shown .90 .25
1150 A572 70m Scarab, reverse .90 .25

Post Day.

Perf. 11x11½

1981, Jan. 7 **Wmk. 342**

1151 A573 140m grnsh bl & dk brn 1.75 .70

Heinrich von Stephan (1831-97), founder of UPU.

13th Cairo International Book Fair — A574

1981, Feb. 1 ***Perf. 11½x11***

1152 A574 20m multicolored .40 .20

14th Cairo International Fair, Mar. 14-28 — A575

Perf. 11x11½

1981, Mar. 14 **Photo.** **Wmk. 342**

1153 A575 20m multicolored .40 .20

Rural Electrification Authority, 10th Anniversary — A576

1981, Mar. 18

1154 A576 20m multicolored .45 .20

Veterans' Day — A577

Intl. Dentistry Conf., Cairo — A578

1981, Mar. 26

1155 A577 20m multicolored .50 .20

Perf. 11x11½

1981, Apr. 14 **Photo.** **Wmk. 342**

1156 A578 20m red & olive .50 .20

Trade Union Emblem — A579

Nurses' Day — A580

Perf. 11x11½

1981, May 1 **Photo.** **Wmk. 342**

1157 A579 20m brt blue & dk brn .40 .20

International Confederation of Arab Trade Unions, 25th anniv.

1981, May 12

1158 A580 20m multicolored .40 .20

Irrigation Equipment (Electrification Movement) — A581

1981, May 15 ***Perf. 11½***

1159 A581 20m multicolored .40 .20

Air Force Day — A582

Perf. 11x11½

1981, June 30 **Photo.** **Wmk. 342**

1160 A582 20m multicolored .50 .20

Flag Surrounding Map of Suez Canal — A583

Wmk. 342

1981, July 23 **Photo.** ***Perf. 11½***

1161 A583 20m multicolored .45 .20
1162 A583 20m Emblems .45 .20

July 23rd Revolution, 29th anniv.; Social Defense Year.

1981 Feasts — A584

Wmk. 342

1981, July 29 **Photo.** ***Perf. 11***

1163 A584 10m multicolored .40 .20

A585

A586

1981, Aug. 10 ***Perf. 11x11½***

1164 A585 140m Kemal Ataturk 2.00 .80

Perf. 11x11½

1981, Sept. 9 **Photo.** **Wmk. 342**

1165 A586 20m Arabi Pasha, Leader of Egyptian Force .40 .20

Orabi Revolution centenary.

A587

A588

1981, Sept. 14

1166 A587 45m Athlete, Pyramids, Sphinx .80 .20

World Muscular Athletics Championships, Cairo.

Perf. 11x11½

1981, Sept. 26 **Photo.** **Wmk. 342**

1167 A588 45m multicolored .60 .20

Ministry of Industry and Mineral Resources, 25th anniv.

20th Intl. Occupational Health Congress, Cairo — A589

1981, Sept. 28 ***Perf. 11½x11***

1168 A589 20m multicolored .50 .20

October War Against Israel, 8th Anniv. A590

1981, Oct. 6

1169 A590 20m multicolored .70 .20

World Food Day A591

13th World Telecommunications Day — A592

Intl. Year of the Disabled — A593

Fight Against Apartheid A594

Perf. 11½x11, 11x11½

1981, Oct. 24 Photo. Wmk. 342

1170 A591 10m multicolored .30 .20
1171 A592 20m multicolored .30 .20
1172 A593 45m multicolored .50 .25
1173 A594 230m multicolored 3.00 1.10
Nos. 1170-1173 (4) 4.10 1.75

United Nations Day.

Pres. Anwar Sadat (1917-81) — A595

Perf. 11x11½

1981, Nov. 14 Unwmk.

1174 A595 30m multicolored 1.40 .65
1175 A595 230m multicolored 3.50 2.50

Establishment of Shura Family Council — A596

Perf. 11½x11

1981, Dec. 12 Photo. Wmk. 342

1176 A596 45m purple & yellow .50 .20

Agricultural Credit and Development Bank, 50th Anniv. — A597

1981, Dec. 15 ***Perf. 11x11½***

1177 A597 20m multicolored .40 .20

Famous Men Type of 1980

30m, Ali el-Ghayati (1885-1956), journalist. 60m, Omar Ebn sl-Fared (1181-1234), Sufi poet.

Perf. 11x11½

1981, Dec. 21 Photo. Wmk. 342

1178 A571 30m green & brown .40 .20
1179 A571 60m green & brown .60 .20
a. Pair, #1178-1179 1.00 .50

20th Anniv. of African Postal Union A598

1981, Dec. 21 ***Perf. 11½x11***

1180 A598 60m multicolored .90 .30

14th Cairo Intl. Book Fair — A599

Arab Trade Union of Egypt, 25th Anniv. — A600

1982, Jan. 28

1181 A599 3p brown & yellow .60 .20

1982, Jan. 30

1182 A600 3p multicolored .40 .20

Khartoum Branch of Cairo University, 25th Anniv. A601

Perf. 11½x11

1982, Mar. 4 Wmk. 342

1183 A601 6p blue & green .80 .35

15th Cairo Intl. Fair — A602

1982, Mar. 13 ***Perf. 11x11½***

1184 A602 3p multicolored .40 .20

50th Anniv. of Al-Ghardaka Marine Biological Station — A603

Fish of the Red Sea.

1982, Apr. 24 Litho. ***Perf. 11½x11***

1185 10m Lined butterfly fish .65 .45
1186 30m Blue-banded sea perch .95 .50
1187 60m Batfish 1.10 .75
1188 230m Blue-spotted boxfish 3.00 1.40
a. A603 Block of 4, #1185-1188 6.00 2.00

Liberation of the Sinai — A604

1982, Apr. 25 Photo. ***Perf. 11x11½***

1189 A604 3p multicolored .60 .20

50th Anniv. of Egypt Air A605

1982, May 7 Photo. ***Perf. 11½x11***

1190 A605 23p multicolored 2.50 1.40

Minaret — A606

Al Azhar Mosque — A607

a, shown. b, Two terraces. c, Three terraces. d, Two turrets at top.

Perf. 11x11½

1982, June 28 Photo. Wmk. 342

1191 Strip of 4 + label 3.50 3.50
a.-d. A606 6p any single, multi .55 .30

Souvenir Sheet

Unwmk. ***Imperf.***

1192 A607 23p multicolored 6.00 3.00

Al Azhar Mosque millennium.
No. 1192 airmail.

Dove — A608

Flower in Natl. Colors — A609

Perf. 11x11½

1982, July 23 Photo. Wmk. 342

1193 A608 3p multicolored .40 .20

Souvenir Sheet

Imperf

1194 A609 23p multicolored 4.25 2.10

30th anniv. of July 23rd Revolution.

World Tourism Day A610

Design: Sphinx, pyramid of Cheops, St. Catherine's Tower.

Perf. 11½x11

1982, Sept. 27 Photo. Wmk. 342

1195 A610 23p multicolored 2.75 1.40

October War Against Israel, 9th Anniv. A611

1982, Oct. 6

1196 A611 3p Memorial, map .60 .20

Biennale of Alexandria Art Exhibition — A612

1982, Oct. 17 ***Perf. 11x11½***

1197 A612 3p multicolored .45 .20

10th Anniv. of UN Conference on Human Environment — A613

2nd UN Conference on Peaceful Uses of Outer Space, Vienna, Aug. 9-21 — A614

Scouting Year A615

TB Bacillus Centenary A616

Perf. 11½x11, 11½ (A615)

1982, Oct. 24

1198	A613	3p multicolored	.40	.20
1199	A614	6p multicolored	.70	.20
1200	A615	6p multicolored	.70	.20
1201	A616	8p multicolored	.80	.20
		Nos. 1198-1201 (4)	2.60	.80

United Nations Day.

50th Anniv. of Air Force A617

1982, Nov. 2 ***Perf. 11½x11***

1202 A617 3p Jet, plane .60 .20

Ahmed Chawki (1868-1932) and Hafez Ibrahim (1871-1932), Poets — A618

Perf. 11½x11

1982, Nov. 25 Photo. Wmk. 342

1203 A618 6p multicolored .60 .20

Natl. Research Center, 25th Anniv. — A619

1982, Dec. 12 Photo. ***Perf. 11x11½***

1204 A619 3p red & blue .65 .20

50th Anniv. of Arab Language Society A620

1982, Dec. 25 ***Perf. 11½x11***

1205 A620 6p multicolored .65 .20

Year of the Aged — A621

Post Day A622

1982, Dec. 25 ***Perf. 11x11½***

1206 A621 23p multicolored 2.50 1.40

1983, Jan. 2 ***Perf. 11½***

1207 A622 3p multicolored .50 .20

15th Cairo Intl. Book Fair — A623

Perf. 11x11½

1983, Jan. 25 Photo. Wmk. 342

1208 A623 3p blue & red .50 .20

Police Day A624

1983, Jan. 25 ***Perf. 11½x11***

1209 A624 3p multicolored .60 .20

16th Cairo Intl. Fair — A625

5th UN African Map Conf., Cairo — A626

Perf. 11x11½

1983, Mar. 2 Photo. Wmk. 342

1210 A625 3p multicolored .50 .20

1983, Mar. 2

1211 A626 3p lt green & blue .60 .20

African Ministers of Transport, Communications and Planning, 3rd Conference — A627

1983, Mar. 8 ***Perf. 11½x11***

1212 A627 23p green & blue 1.75 1.00

A628

A629

1983, Mar. 20 ***Perf. 11x11½***

1213	A628	3p Heading	.50	.20
1214	A628	3p Kick	.50	.20
	a.	Pair, #1213-1214	1.25	1.25

Victory in African Soccer Cup.

Perf. 11x11½

1983, Apr. 2 Photo. Wmk. 342

1215 A629 3p olive & red .70 .20

World Health Day and Natl. Blood Donation Campaign.

Org. of African Trade Union Unity A630

Perf. 11½x11

1983, Apr. 21 Photo. Wmk. 342

1216 A630 3p multicolored .50 .20

1st Anniv. of Sinai Liberation A631

75th Anniv. of Entomology Society A632

1983, Apr. 25 ***Perf. 11x11½***

1217 A631 3p multicolored .75 .20

1983, May 23

1218 A632 3p Emblem (Holy Scarab) .75 .20

Flowers — A633

1983, June 11 Photo. ***Perf. 11½x11***

1219 A633 20m green & org red .40 .20

5th African Handball Championship, Cairo — A634

Perf. 11½x11

1983, July 22 Photo. Wmk. 342

1220 A634 6p brown & dk grn .60 .20

31st Anniv. of Revolution A635

Simon Bolivar (1783-1830) A636

1983, July 23 ***Perf. 11½***

1221 A635 3p multicolored .40 .20

1983, Aug. ***Perf. 11x11½***

1222 A636 23p brown & dull grn 1.25 .80

Centenary of Arrival of Natl. Hero Orabi in Ceylon A637

Perf. 11½x11

1983, Aug. 25 Photo. Wmk. 342

1223 A637 3p Map, Orabi, El-Zahra School .40 .20

Islamic Vase, Museum Building A638

1983, Sept. 14 Photo. ***Perf. 11½x11***

1224 A638 3p yel brn & dk brn .70 .20

Reopening of Islamic Museum.

October War Against Israel, 10th Anniv. — A639

2nd Pharaonic Race — A640

1983, Oct. 6 ***Perf. 11½***

1225 A639 3p multicolored .70 .20

1983, Oct. 17 ***Perf. 11½***

1226 A640 23p multicolored 2.00 1.25

United Nations Day — A641

1983, Oct. 24 Photo. ***Perf. 11***

1227	A641	3p IMO, ships, horiz.	.40	.20
1228	A641	6p ITU, UPU	.40	.20
1229	A641	6p FAO, UN, grain	.40	.20
1230	A641	23p UN, ocean	2.00	.60
		Nos. 1227-1230 (4)	3.20	1.20

4th World Karate Championship, Cairo — A642

1983, Nov. Photo. *Perf. 13*

1231	A642 3p multicolored	.60	.20

Intl. Palestinian Cooperation Day — A643

1983, Nov. 29 Photo. *Perf. 13x13½*

1232	A643 6p Dome of the Rock	1.00	.20

75th Anniv. of Faculty of Fine Arts, Cairo A644

1983, Nov. 30 *Perf. 13*

1233	A644 3p multicolored	.40	.20

75th Anniv. of Cairo University — A645

1983, Nov. 30 *Perf. 11x11½*

1234	A645 3p multicolored	.40	.20

Intl. Egyptian Society of Mother and Child Care A646

1983, Nov. 30 *Perf. 11½x11*

1235	A646 3p multicolored	.40	.20

Org. of African Unity, 20th Anniv. — A647

World Heritage Convention, 10th Anniv. — A648

Perf. 11x11½

1983, Dec. 20 Photo. Wmk. 342

1236	A647 3p multicolored	.40	.20

1983, Dec. 24

1237	Strip of 3	2.50	2.50
a.	A648 3p Wood carving, Islamic	.75	.40
b.	A648 3p Coptic tapestry	.75	.40
c.	A648 3p Ramses II Thebes	.75	.40

Post Day A649

Restored Forts: 6p, Quatbay. 23p, Mosque, Salah El-Din.

1984, Jan. 2 *Perf. 13*

1238	A649 6p multicolored	.50	.20
1239	A649 23p multicolored	2.00	1.25

Misr Insurance Co., 50 Anniv. A650

1984, Jan. 14 *Perf. 11½x11*

1240	A650 3p multicolored	.35	.20

16th Cairo Intl. Book Fair — A651

Perf. 13½x13

1984, Jan. 26 Photo. Wmk. 342

1241	A651 3p multicolored	.40	.20

17th Cairo Intl. Fair A652

Perf. 11½x11

1984, Mar. 10 Photo. Wmk. 342

1242	A652 3p multicolored	.45	.20

25th Anniv. of Asyut University A653

75th Anniv. of Cooperative Unions A654

1984, Mar. 10 *Perf. 11x11½*

1243	A653 3p multicolored	.40	.20

1984, Mar. 17

1244	A654 3p multicolored	.40	.20

World Theater Day — A655

Mahmoud Mokhtar (1891-1934), Sculptor — A656

Perf. 11x11½, 11½x11

1984, Mar. 27 Photo. Unwmk.

1245	A655 3p Masks	.45	.20
1246	A656 3p Pride of the Nile	.45	.20

World Health Day and Fight Against Polio — A657

Perf. 11½x11

1984, Apr. 7 Photo. Wmk. 342

1247	A657 3p Polio vaccine	.60	.20

2nd Anniv. of Sinai Liberation — A658

1984, Apr. 25

1248	A658 3p Doves, map	.50	.20

Africa Day A659

Perf. 12½x13½

1984, May 25 Photo. Wmk. 342

1249	A659 3p Map, UN emblem	.40	.20

Satellite, Waves — A660

Flower — A661

1984, May 31 *Perf. 11x11½*

1250	A660 3p multicolored	.50	.20

Radio broadcasting in Egypt, 50th anniv.

1984, June 1

1251	A661 2p red & green	.35	.20

Intl. Cairo Arab Arts Biennale — A662

1984, June 1 *Perf. 13½x12½*

1252	A662 3p multicolored	.50	.20

July Revolution, 32nd Anniv. — A663

Wmk. 342

1984, July 23 Photo. *Perf. 11*

1253	A663 3p Atomic energy, agriculture	.50	.20

A664

A665

1984 Summer Olympics: a, Boxing. b, Basketball. c, Volleyball. d, Soccer.

1984, July 28

1254	Strip of 4 + label	4.50	4.50
a.-d.	A664 3p any single	.40	.40

Size: 130x80mm

Imperf

1255	A664 30p like No. 1254	4.25	4.25

Wmk. 342

1984, Aug. 13 Photo. *Perf. 11*

1256	A665 3p bl & multi	.45	.20
1257	A665 23p grn & multi	1.90	.90

2nd Genl. Conference of Egyptians Abroad, Aug. 11-15, Cairo.

Youth Hostels, 30th Anniv. — A666

Egypt Tour Co., 50th Anniv. — A667

Perf. 11x11½

1984, Sept. 22 Photo. Wmk. 342

1258	A666 3p Youths, emblem	.40	.20

1984, Sept. 27

1259	A667 3p Emblem, sphinx	.50	.20

October War Against Israel, 11th Anniv. — A668

Egypt-Sudan Unity — A669

1984, Oct. 6
1260 A668 3p Map, eagle .40 .20

1984, Oct. 12
1261 A669 3p Map of Nile, arms .50 .20

UN Day — A670

Tanks, Emblem — A671

Perf. 13½x12½
1984, Oct. 24 Photo. Wmk. 342
1262 A670 3p UNICEF Emblem, child .40 .20

UN campaign for infant survival.

1984, Nov. 10
1263 A671 3p multicolored .50 .20

Military Equipment Exhibition, Cairo, Nov. 10-14.

Tolon Mosque, Egypt A672

1984, Dec. 23 Photo. *Perf. 11½x11*
1264 A672 3p multicolored .60 .20

Ahmed Ebn Tolon (A.D. 835-884), Gov. of Egypt, founder of Kataea City.

A673

A674

1984, Dec. 23 *Perf. 11x11½*
1265 A673 3p multicolored .40 .20

Kamel el-Kilany (1897-1959), author.

Perf. 11x11½
1984, Dec. 26 Photo. Wmk. 342

Globe and congress emblem.

1266 A674 3p lt blue, ver & blk .60 .20

29th Intl. Congress on the History of Medicine, Dec. 27, 1984-Jan. 1, 1985, Cairo.

Academy of the Arts, 25th Anniv. A675

1984, Dec. 31 *Perf. 13*
1267 A675 3p Emblem in spotlights .60 .20

Pharaoh Receiving Message, Natl. Postal Museum, Cairo A676

1985, Jan. 2 *Perf. 11½x11*
1268 A676 3p brown, lt bl & ver .60 .20

Postal Museum, 50th anniv.

Intl. Union of Architects, 15th Conference, Jan. 14-Feb. 15 — A677

1985, Jan. 20
1269 A677 3p multicolored .60 .20

Seated Pharaonic Scribe — A678

Wheat, Cogwheels, Fair Emblem — A679

1985, Jan. 22 *Perf. 11x11½*
1270 A678 3p brt org & dk blue grn .60 .20

17th Intl. Book Fair, Jan. 22-Feb. 3, Cairo.

1985, Mar. 9 *Perf. 13½x13*
1271 A679 3p multicolored .60 .20

18th Intl. Fair, Mar. 9-22, Cairo.

Return of Sinai to Egypt, 3rd Anniv. — A680

1985, Apr. 25 Wmk. 342 Litho.
1272 A680 5p multicolored .60 .20

Ancient Artifacts — A681

A681a

Designs: 1p, God Mout, limestone sculpture, 360-340 B.C. 2p, No. 1281, Five wading birds, bas-relief. 3p, No. 1276, Seated statue, Ramses II, Temple of Luxor. No. 1276A, Vase. 8p, 15p, Slave bearing votive fruit offering, mural. 10p, Double-handled flask. 11p, Sculpted head of woman. No. 1282, Pitcher. 30p, 50p, Decanter. 35p, Temple of Karnak carved capitals. £1, Mosque.

1985-90 Photo. Unwmk. *Perf. 11½*

1273	A681	1p	brown olive	.40	.20
1274	A681	2p	brt grnsh bl	.40	.20
1275	A681	3p	yellow brown	.40	.20
1276	A681	5p	dk violet	.40	.20
1276A	A681	5p	lemon	.40	.20
1277	A681	8p	pale ol grn, sep & brn	.50	.20
1278	A681	10p	dk vio & bl	.60	.20
1279	A681	11p	dk violet	.60	.30
1280	A681	15p	pale yel, sep & brn	.60	.30
1281	A681	20p	yellow green	.60	.30
1282	A681	20p	dk grn & yel	.60	.30
1283	A681	30p	ol bis & buff	.70	.50
1284	A681	35p	sep & pale yel	1.00	.60
1285	A681	50p	purple & buff	1.40	.80
1285A	A681a	£1	brown & buff	3.75	3.75
1286	A681a	£2	sepia & yel	6.00	6.00
			Nos. 1273-1286 (16)	18.35	14.25

Issued: 1p, 2p, 3p, No. 1276, 8p, 11p, 15p, 5/1/85; 35p, 7/7/85; No. 1281, 4/1/86; 10p, 10/1/89; £2, 12/1/89; No. 1282, 2/1/90; 30p, 50p, 2/5/90; £1, 2/8/90; No. 1276A, 12/15/90.
Nos. 1276A, 1278 are 18x23mm.
No. 1278 exists dated "1990."
See Nos. 1467, 1470, 1472.

Helwan University School of Music, 50th Anniv. A682

1985, May 15
1287 A682 5p multicolored .50 .20

El-Moulid Bride, Folk Doll — A683

1985
1288 A683 2p orange & multi .40 .20
1289 A683 5p red & multi .40 .20

Festivals 1985. Issued: 2p, 6/11; 5p, 8/10.

A684

A685

Winning teams: a, b, Cairo Sports Stadium. c, El-Mokawiloon Club, white uniform, 1983. d, Natl. Club, red uniform, 1984. e, El-Zamalek Club, orange uniform, 1984.

1985, June 17 *Perf. 13½x13*
1290 Strip of 5 5.00 5.00
a.-e. A684 5p any single 1.00 1.00

1985 Africa Cup Soccer Championships. Cairo Sports Stadium, 25th anniv. Nos. 1290a-1290b have continuous design.

1985, July 23 *Perf. 11½x11*
1291 A685 5p blue, brn & yel .65 .20

Egyptian Television, 25th anniv. Egyptian Revolution, 33rd anniv.

Suez Canal Reopening, 10th Anniv. — A686

Perf. 13x13½
1985, July 23 Litho. Wmk. 342
1292 A686 5p multicolored .65 .20

Egyptian Revolution, 33rd anniv.

Ahmed Hamdi Memorial Underwater Tunnel — A687

1985, July 23 *Perf. 13½x13*
1293 A687 5p blue, vio & org .50 .20

Egyptian Revolution, 33rd anniv.

Souvenir Sheet

Aswan High Dam, 25th Anniv. — A688

Wmk. 342
1985, July 23 Photo. *Imperf.*
1294 A688 30p multicolored 3.50 2.75

Heart, Map, Olive Laurel, Conference Emblem — A689

1985, Aug. 10 Litho. *Perf. 13½x13*
1295 A689 15p multicolored 1.25 .85

Egyptian Emigrants, 3rd general conference, Aug. 10-14, Cairo.

Natl. Tourism Ministry, 50th Anniv. — A690

1985, Sept. 10 *Perf. 13x13½*
1296 A690 5p multicolored .45 .20

October War Against Israel, 12th Anniv. — A691

1985, Oct. 6
1297 A691 5p multicolored .45 .20

Air Scouts Assoc., 30th Anniv. — A692

1985, Oct. 15 Photo. *Perf. 11½*
1298 A692 5p Emblem .55 .20

A693

UN, 40th Anniv. — A694

1985, Oct. 24
1299 A693 5p UN emblem, weather map .45 .20

UN Day, Meteorology Day.

1985, Oct. 24
1300 A694 15p multicolored 1.25 .85

Intl. Youth Year — A695

A696

1985, Oct. 24
1301 A695 5p multicolored .45 .20

1985, Oct. 24
1302 A696 15p blue & int blue 1.25 .85

Intl. Communications Development Program.

A697

A698

Emblem, hieroglyphics of Hassi Raa, 1st known dentist.

1985, Oct. 29 *Perf. 11x11½*
1303 A697 5p beige & pale bl vio .75 .25

2nd Intl. Dentistry Conference.

1985, Nov. 18 Photo. *Perf. 11½*
1304 A698 5p Emblem, squash player .45 .20

1985 World Squash Championships, Nov. 18-Dec. 4.

A699

A700

1985, Nov. 2 Litho. *Perf. 13½x13*
1305 A699 5p multicolored .45 .20

4th Intl. Conference on the Biography and Sunna of Mohammed.

1985, Dec. 1 Photo. *Perf. 11x11½*
1306 A700 5p multicolored .45 .20

1st Conference on the Development of Vocational Training.

Natl. Olympic Committee, 75th Anniv. — A701

18th Intl. Book Fair, Cairo — A702

1985, Dec. 28 Photo. *Perf. 13x13½*
1307 A701 5p multicolored .50 .20

1986, Jan. 21 *Perf. 11x11½*
1308 A702 5p Pharaonic scribe .45 .20

CODATU III — A703

1986, Jan. 26 *Perf. 11½*
1309 A703 5p lt ol grn, ver & grnsh bl .40 .20

3rd Intl. Conference on Urban Transportation in Developing Countries, Cairo.

Central Bank, 25th Anniv. — A704

1986, Jan. 30 *Perf. 13x13½*
1310 A704 5p multicolored .40 .20

Cairo Postal Traffic Center Inauguration — A705

1986, Jan. 30 *Perf. 11½x11*
1311 A705 5p blue & dk brown .40 .20

Pharaonic Mural, Btah Hotteb's Tomb at Saqqara A706

1986, Feb. 27 Photo. *Perf. 11½x11*
1312 A706 5p yel, gldn brn & brn .60 .25

Faculty of Commerce, Cairo Univ., 75th anniv.

Cairo Intl. Fair, Mar. 8-21 — A707

1986, Mar. 8 Litho. *Perf. 13½x13*
1313 A707 5p multicolored .40 .20

Queen Nefertiti, Sinai — A708

Perf. 13x13½
1986, Apr. 25 Litho. Wmk. 342
1314 A708 5p multicolored .50 .20

Return of the Sinai to Egypt, 4th anniv.

Ministry of Health, 50th Anniv. — A709

1986, Apr. 10 *Perf. 13½x13*
1315 A709 5p multicolored .45 .20

1986 Census — A710

1986, May 26 Photo. *Perf. 11½*
1316 A710 15p brn, grnsh bl & yel bis 1.00 1.00

Egypt, Winner of African Soccer Cup — A711

Festivals, Roses — A712

1986, May 31 *Perf. 13½x13*
1317 A711 5p English inscription below cup .50 .50
1318 A711 5p Arabic .50 .50
a. Pair, #1317-1318 1.00 1.00

1986, June 2 *Perf. 11½*
1319 A712 5p multicolored .40 .20

World Environment Day — A713

1986, June 5 ***Perf. 13½x13***
1320 A713 15p Emblem, smoke-stacks 1.10 1.10

July 23rd Revolution, 34th Anniv. A714

1986, July 23 **Litho.** ***Perf. 13***
1321 A714 5p gray grn, scar & yel bis .40 .20

6th African Roads Conference, Cairo, Sept. 22-26 — A715

Perf. 13½x13
1986, Sept. 21 **Litho.** **Wmk. 342**
1322 A715 15p multicolored 1.00 1.00

October War Against Israel, 13th Anniv. A716

1986, Oct. 6 **Litho.** ***Perf. 13***
1323 A716 5p multicolored .70 .25

Engineers' Syndicate, 40th Anniv. A717

1986, Oct. 11 **Photo.** ***Perf. 11½***
1324 A717 5p lt blue, brn & pale grn .40 .20

Workers' Cultural Education Assoc., 25th Anniv. — A718

Intl. Peace Year — A719

1986, Oct. 11 ***Perf. 11x11½***
1325 A718 5p orange & rose vio .40 .20

1986, Oct. 24
1326 A719 5p blue, grn & pale sal .35 .20

First Oil Well in Egypt, Cent. — A720

1986, Nov. 7 **Photo.** ***Perf. 11½***
1327 A720 5p dull grn, blk & pale yel .60 .25

UN Child Survival Campaign A721

1986, Nov. 20 **Litho.** ***Perf. 13***
1328 A721 5p multicolored .60 .25

Ahmed Amin, Philosopher A722

National Theater, 50th Anniv. — A723

1986, Dec. 20 ***Perf. 11½***
1329 A722 5p pale grn, pale yel & brn .40 .20

1986, Dec. 20 ***Perf. 13½x13***
1330 A723 5p multicolored .45 .20

Post Day A724

Step Pyramid, Saqqara, King Zoser.

Perf. 13x13½
1987, Jan. 2 **Litho.** **Wmk. 342**
1331 A724 5p multicolored .60 .25

19th Intl. Book Fair, Cairo A725

1987, Jan. 25 **Litho.** ***Perf. 13***
1332 A725 5p multicolored .40 .20

5th World Conference on Islamic Education A726

Wmk. 342
1987, Mar. 8 **Litho.** ***Perf. 13***
1333 A726 5p multicolored .45 .20

20th Intl. Fair, Cairo — A727

1987, Mar. 21 **Photo.** ***Perf. 11½***
1334 A727 5p Good workers medal .40 .20

Veteran's Day A728

1987, Mar. 26
1335 A728 5p multicolored .40 .20

Intl. Gardens Inauguration, Nasser City — A729

1987, Mar. 30 **Litho.** ***Perf. 13***
1336 A729 15p multicolored 1.00 1.00

World Health Day A730

1987, Apr. 7 **Photo.** ***Perf. 11½***
1337 A730 5p Mother feeding child .45 .20

Litho.
Perf. 13
1338 A730 5p Oral rehydration therapy .45 .20

A731

Natl. Team Victory at 1986 Intl. Soccer Championships — A732

Trophies: No. 1339a, Al Ahly Cup. No. 1339b, National Cup. No. 1339c, Al Zamalek Cup. No. 1340, Natl. flag, Cairo Stadium and trophies pictured on No. 1339.

1987, Apr. 19 **Litho.** ***Perf. 13½x13***
1339 Strip of 3 1.50 1.50
a.-c. A731 5p any single .50 .50

Size: 115x85mm
Imperf
1340 A732 30p multicolored 3.50 3.50

A733

A734

Salah El Din Citadel, Pharoah's Is., Sinai.

1987, Apr. 25
1341 A733 5p sky blue & lt brown .50 .20

Return of the Sinai to Egypt, 5th anniv.

1987, May 21 Photo. *Perf. 11½*

Festivals.

1342 A734 5p Dahlia .40 .20

Cultural Heritage Exhibition — A735

1987, June 17 Litho. *Perf. 13x13½*
1343 A735 15p multicolored 1.00 1.00

Tourism Year — A736

a, Column and Sphinx, Alexandria. b, St. Catherine's Monastery, Mt. Sinai. c, Colossi of Thebes. d, Temple of Theban Triad, Luxor.

1987, June 18
1344 Block of 4 4.00 4.00
a.-d. A736 15p any single 1.00 1.00

See No. C187.

National Day A737

1987, June 26 *Perf. 13*
1345 A737 5p multicolored .40 .20

Industry-Agriculture Exhibition — A738

1987, July 23 Photo. *Perf. 11½*
1346 A738 5p grn, dull org & blk .40 .20

Intl. Year of Shelter for the Homeless A739

1987, Sept. 2 Litho. *Perf. 13*
1347 A739 5p multicolored .40 .20

World Architects' Day.

Aida, Performed at Al Ahram Pyramid, Giza A740

Radamis and troops returning from Ethiopia.

1987, Sept. 21
1348 A740 15p multicolored 1.25 1.25

Size: 70x70mm

Imperf

1349 A740 30p multicolored 5.00 5.00

Greater Cairo Subway Inauguration — A741

1987, Sept. 27 *Perf. 13x13½*
1350 A741 5p multicolored .85 .25

Industry Day A742

1987, Oct. 1 *Perf. 13*
1351 A742 5p multicolored .40 .20

Battle of Hettin, 700th Anniv. — A743

1987, Oct. 6 Photo. *Perf. 11x11½*
1352 A743 5p multicolored .50 .20

UPU Emblem A744

Perf. 11½

1987, Oct. 24 Unwmk. Photo.
1353 A744 5p multicolored .45 .20

UN Executive Council, 40th anniv.; UPU Consultative Council, 30th anniv.

16th Art Biennial of Alexandria A745

1987, Nov. 7 Litho. *Perf. 13½x13*
1354 A745 5p multicolored .45 .20

Second Intl. Defense Equipment Exhibition, Cairo, Nov. 9-13 — A746

Perf. 13x13½

1987, Nov. 9 Litho. Unwmk.
1355 A746 5p multicolored .45 .20

2nd Pan-Arab Congress on Anaesthesia and Intensive Care — A747

Unwmk.

1987, Dec. 1 Litho. *Perf. 13*
1356 A747 5p multicolored .50 .20

Intl. Orthopedic and Traumatology Conference A748

1987, Dec. 1 *Perf. 13½x13*
1357 A748 5p gray, red brn & bl .50 .20

Selim Hassan (1887-1961), Egyptologist, and Hieroglyphs A749

Abdel Hamid Badawi (1887-1965), Jurist, and Scales of Justice — A750

Perf. 13½x13

1987, Dec. 30 Litho. Unwmk.
1358 A749 5p multicolored .45 .20
1359 A750 5p multicolored .45 .20

Stamp Day 1988 — A751

Pyramids of the Pharaohs and: a, Cheops. b, Chefren. c, Mycerinus. No. 1360 has a continuous design.

1988, Jan. 2
1360 A751 Strip of 3 4.00 4.00
a.-c. 15p, any single 1.25 1.25

Afro-Asian Peoples Solidarity Organization, 30th Anniv. — A752

1988, Jan. 10 *Perf. 13x13½*
1361 A752 15p multicolored 1.00 1.00

20th Intl. Book Fair, Cairo — A753

1988, Jan. 26 *Perf. 13½x13*
1362 A753 5p multicolored .40 .20

Martrans (Natl. Shipping Line), 25th Anniv. A754

Unwmk.

1988, Mar. 3 Litho. *Perf. 13*
1363 A754 5p multicolored .60 .25

Cairo Intl. Fair A755

1988, Mar. 12 Photo. ***Perf. 11½x11***
1364 A755 5p multicolored .40 .20

World Health Day 1988: Diabetes A756

1988 Festivals A757

Perf. 11x11½
1988, Apr. 7 Photo. Unwmk.
1365 A756 5p multicolored .45 .20

1988, Apr. 17 ***Perf. 11½***
1366 A757 5p grn, brn org & brn .45 .20

African Postal Union, 25th Anniv. — A758

1988, Apr. 23 Litho. ***Perf. 13x13½***
1367 A758 15p brt blue 1.00 1.00

Oppose Racial Discrimination — A759

1988, May 25 Photo. ***Perf. 11½***
1368 A759 5p multicolored .40 .20

Taw Fek-Hakem (1902-1987), Playwright, Novelist — A760

1988, Aug. 5 Photo. ***Perf. 11½***
1369 A760 5p brt grn bl & org brn .60 .25

See Nos. 1383-1384, 1479-1480, 1486, 1500-1502, 1543-1546.

Faculty of Art Education, 50th Anniv. A761

Perf. 11½
1988, Sept. 10 Photo. Unwmk.
1370 A761 5p multicolored .50 .20

A762

1988 Summer Olympics, Seoul — A763

1988, Sept. 17 Litho. ***Perf. 13***
1371 A762 15p multicolored 1.25 1.25

Size: 96x91mm
Imperf.
1372 A763 30p multicolored 5.00 5.00

No. 1371 is airmail.

October War Against Israel, 15th Anniv. — A764

Perf. 13x13½
1988, Oct. 6 Litho. Unwmk.
1373 A764 5p multicolored .50 .20

A765

Opening of the Opera House — A766

1988, Oct. 10 ***Perf. 11½***
1374 A765 5p multicolored .50 .20

Size: 112x75mm
Imperf
1375 A766 50p multicolored 3.50 3.50

Intl. Red Cross and Red Crescent Organizations, 125th Annivs. — A767

Perf. 11½
1988, Oct. 24 Photo. Unwmk.
1376 A767 5p green, blk & red .40 .20

WHO, 40th Anniv. — A768

1988, Oct. 24 ***Perf. 11x11½***
1377 A768 20p multicolored 1.10 1.10

Naguib Mahfouz, 1988 Nobel Prize Winner for Literature — A769

1988, Nov. 7 Litho. ***Perf. 13x13½***
1378 A769 5p multicolored .60 .25

See No. C190.

Arab Scouting Organization, 75th Anniv. — A770

1988, Nov. 10
1379 A770 25p multicolored 1.10 1.10

Return of Taba to Egypt — A771

1988, Nov. 15
1380 A771 5p multicolored .40 .20

Intl. Conference on Orthopedic Surgery, Cairo, Nov. 15-18 — A772

1988, Nov. 15 Photo. ***Perf. 11½x11***
1381 A772 5p buff, brt yel grn & brn .40 .20

A773

1988, Dec. 3 ***Perf. 11½***
1382 A773 5p multicolored .40 .20

Ministry of Agriculture, 75th anniv.

A774

Perf. 13½x13
1988, Dec. 29 Litho. Unwmk.

Famous Men: No. 1383, Mohamed Hussein Hekal (1888-1956), author, politician. No. 1384, Ahmed Lotfi El Sayed (1872-1963), educator, politician.

1383 A774 5p green & red brn .40 .20
1384 A774 5p green & red brn .40 .20
a. Pair, #1383-1384 .80 .40

A775

A776

Statues: 5p, Statue of K. Abr, a priest, 5th cent. No. 1386, Queen Nefert, 4th Dynasty. No. 1387, King Ra Hoteb, 4th Dynasty.

1989, Jan. 2
1385 A775 5p multicolored .40 .20
1386 A775 25p multicolored 1.40 1.40
1387 A775 25p multicolored 1.40 1.40
a. Pair, #1386-1387 3.25 3.25
Nos. 1385-1387 (3) 3.20 3.00

Stamp Day.

1989, Jan. 10
1388 A776 5p dull green .50 .20

Jawaharlal Nehru (1889-1964), 1st Prime Minister of independent India.

Nile Hilton Hotel, 30th Anniv. — A777

1989, Feb. 22 Litho. ***Perf. 13x13½***
1389 A777 5p multicolored .50 .20

Return of Taba to Egypt A778

Unwmk.
1989, Mar. 15 Litho. ***Perf. 13***
1390 A778 5p multicolored .40 .20

2nd Stage of Cairo Subway A779

1989, Apr. 12 Litho. ***Perf. 13***
1391 A779 5p multicolored .50 .20

Festivals — A780

1989, May 4 Photo. ***Perf. 11½***
1392 A780 5p multicolored .40 .20

1st Arab Olympic Day A781

1989, May 24
1393 A781 5p tan, blk & dull grn .50 .20

Interparliamentary Union, Cent. — A782

Pyramids and the Parliament Building, Cairo.

1989, June 29 Litho. ***Perf. 13x13½***
1394 A782 25p shown 1.25 1.25

Size: 87x76mm

Imperf
1395 A782 25p multi, diff. 2.75 2.75

French Revolution, Bicent. — A783

1989, July 14 Photo. ***Perf. 11½***
1396 A783 25p multicolored 1.25 1.25

African Development Bank, 25th Anniv. — A784

Perf. 11½
1989, Oct. 1 Photo. Unwmk.
1397 A784 10p multicolored .40 .20

A785

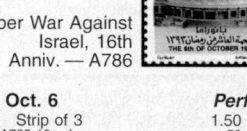

October War Against Israel, 16th Anniv. — A786

1989, Oct. 6 ***Perf. 13***
1398 Strip of 3 1.50 1.50
a. A785 10p shown .50 .50
b. A786 10p shown .50 .50
c. A785 10p Battle scene .50 .50

See No. 1424.

Aga Khan Award for Architecture A788

Perf. 11½
1989, Oct. 15 Photo. Unwmk.
1400 A788 35p multicolored 1.00 1.00

Natl. Health Insurance Plan, 25th Anniv. A789

1989, Oct. 24
1401 A789 10p blk, gray & ver .45 .20

World Post Day — A790

1989, Oct. 24 ***Perf. 11x11½***
1402 A790 35p blue, blk & brt yel .90 .90

Statues of Memnon, Thebes — A791

Perf. 11½
1989, Nov. 12 Photo. Unwmk.
1403 A791 10p lt vio, blk & brt yel grn .40 .20

Intl. Cong. & Convention Assoc. (ICCA) annual convention, Nov. 11-18, Cairo.

Cairo University School of Agriculture, Cent. — A792

1989, Nov. 15
1404 A792 10p pale grn, blk & brt yel .35 .20

Cairo Intl. Conference Center — A793

1989, Nov. 20 ***Perf. 11½x11***
1405 A793 5p multicolored .35 .20

Road Safety Soc., 20th Anniv. — A794

1989, Nov. 20 ***Perf. 11½***
1406 A794 10p multicolored .40 .20

Alexandria University, 50th Anniv. — A795

1989, Nov. 30 ***Perf. 11x11½***
1407 A795 10p pale blue & tan .35 .20

Portrait of Pasha, Monument in Opera Square, Cairo A796

Perf. 11½x11
1989, Dec. 31 Photo. Unwmk.
1408 A796 10p multicolored .45 .20

Ibrahim Pasha (d. 1838), army commander from 1825 to 1828.

Famous Men
A797 A798

1989, Dec. 31 ***Perf. 11x11½***
1409 A797 10p grn & dk ol grn .40 .20
1410 A798 10p golden brown .40 .20

Abd El-Rahman El-Rafei (b. 1889), historian (No. 1409); Abdel Kader El Mazni (b. 1889), man of letters (No. 1410).

See Nos. 1431-1432.

Statue of Priest Ranofr — A799

Relief Sculpture of Betah Hoteb — A800

1990, Jan. 2 ***Perf. 13½x13***
1411 A799 30p multicolored .90 .90
1412 A800 30p multicolored .90 .90
a. Pair, #1411-1412 2.00 2.00

Stamp Day.

Arab Cooperation Council, 1st Anniv. — A801

Perf. 13x13½
1990, Feb. 16 Photo. Unwmk.
1413 A801 10p multicolored .40 .20
1414 A801 35p multicolored 1.00 1.00

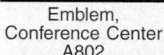

Emblem, Conference Center
A802

Road Safety Emblems
A803

Perf. 13½x13

1990, Mar. 10 Litho. Unwmk.

1415 A802 10p brt yel grn, red & blk .50 .20

Size: 80x59mm

Imperf

1416 A802 30p multicolored 1.25 1.25

African Parliamentary Union 13th general conference, Mar. 10-15.

1990, Mar. 19 Photo. *Perf. 11x11½*

1417 A803 10p multicolored .60 .25

Intl. Conference on Road Safety & Accidents in Developing Countries, Mar. 19-22.

Festivals 1990 — A804

1990, Apr. 24 *Perf. 11½*

1418 A804 10p multicolored .40 .20

Sinai Liberation, 8th Anniv. A805

1990, Apr. 25

1419 A805 10p blue, blk & yel grn .50 .20

World Cup Soccer Championships, Italy — A806

1990, May 26 Litho. *Perf. 13½x13*

1420 A806 10p multicolored .40 .20

Souvenir Sheet

Imperf

1421 A806 50p Flags, trophy 1.75 1.75

World Basketball Championships, Argentina — A807

1990, Aug. 8 *Perf. 13x13½*

1422 A807 10p multicolored .50 .20

Natl. Population Council, 5th Anniv. — A808

1990, Sept. 15 *Perf. 13½x13*

1423 A808 10p brown & yel grn .50 .20

October War Against Israel Type

1990, Oct. 6 Litho. *Perf. 13x13½*

1424 Strip of 3 1.75 1.75
- *a.* A785 10p Bunker, tank .55 .55
- *b.* A786 10p like #1398b .55 .55
- *c.* A785 10p Troops with flag, flame thrower .55 .55

Egyptian Postal Service, 125th Anniv. — A809

1990, Oct. 9

1425 A809 10p lt blue, blk & red .50 .20

Dar El Eloum Faculty, Cent. A810

1990, Oct. 13 Litho. *Perf. 13*

1426 A810 10p multicolored .40 .20

UN Development Program, 40th Anniv. — A811

ITU, 125th Anniv. — A812

1990, Oct. 24 *Perf. 11½*

1427 A811 30p yel, bl grn & yel grn .75 .75

Perf. 13

1428 A812 30p multicolored .75 .75

UN Day.

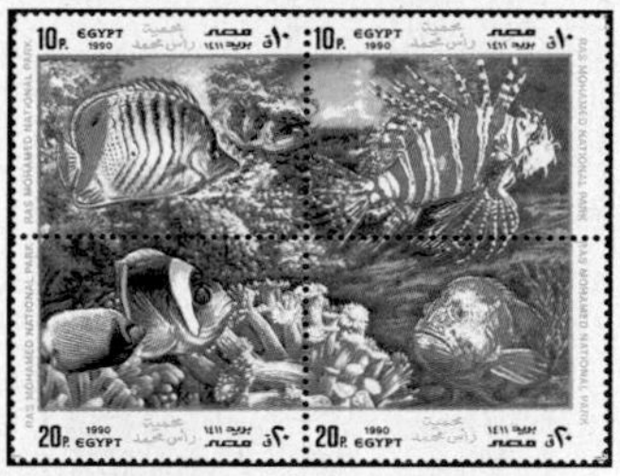

Ras Mohammed Natl. Park — A813

Various tropical fish and coral reefs.

1990, Dec. 22 Litho. *Perf. 13*

1429 A813 Block of 4 3.50 3.50
- *a.-b.* 10p any single .75 .75
- *c.-d.* 20p any single 1.00 1.00

Day of the Disabled — A814

1990. Dec. 15 Photo. *Perf. 11*

1430 A814 10p multicolored .60 .25

Mohamed Fahmy Abdel Meguid Bey, Medical Reformer A815

Nabaweya Moussa (1890-1951), Educator A816

Perf. 11x11½

1990, Dec. 30 Unwmk.

1431 A815 10p Prus bl, brn & org .40 .20
1432 A816 10p grn, org brn & blk .40 .20

Stamp Day — A817

1991, Jan. 1 Litho. *Perf. 13½x13*

1433 A817 5p No. 1 .40 .20
1434 A817 10p No. 2 .40 .20
1435 A817 20p No. 3 .60 .60
- *a.* Strip of 3, #1433-1435 1.40 1.40

See Nos. 1443-1446, 1459-1460.

Veterinary Surgeon Syndicate, 50th Anniv. — A818

1991, Feb. 28 Photo. *Perf. 11½*

1436 A818 10p multicolored .40 .20

Syndicate of Journalists, 50th Anniv. — A819

1991, Apr. Photo. *Perf. 11½*

1437 A819 10p multicolored .40 .20

Festivals — A820

1991, Apr. 13

1438 A820 10p multicolored .40 .20

Giza Zoo, Cent. — A821

1991, June 15 Litho. *Imperf.*

Size: 80x63mm

1439 A821 50p multicolored 3.00 3.00

Mahmoud Mokhtar (1891-1934), Sculptor — A822

Mohamed Nagi (1888-1956), Painter — A823

Perf. 13x13½, 13½x13

1991, June 11 Litho.

1440 A822 10p multicolored .40 .20
1441 A823 10p multicolored .40 .20

Faculty of Engineering — A824

1991, June 30 *Perf. 13x13½*
1442 A824 10p multicolored .40 .20

Stamp Day Type

Designs: No. 1443, No. 5. No. 1444, No. 4. No. 1445, No. 7. No. 1446, Sphinx, pyramid, No. 6.

1991, July 23 *Perf. 13*
1443 A817 10p orange & blk .40 .20
1444 A817 10p yellow & blk .40 .20
1445 A817 10p lilac & blk .40 .20
a. Strip of 3, #1443-1445 1.25 1.25

Size: 80x60mm

Imperf

1446 A817 50p multicolored 1.75 1.75
Nos. 1443-1446 (4) 2.95 2.35

Mohamed Abdel el Wahab, Musician A825

1991, Aug. 28 *Perf. 13*
1447 A825 10p multicolored .40 .20

5th Africa Games, Cairo — A826

No. 1448, Karate, judo. No. 1449, Table tennis, field hockey, tennis. No. 1450, Running, gymnastics, swimming. No. 1451, Soccer, basketball, shooting. No. 1452, Boxing, wrestling, weightlifting. No. 1453, Handball, cycling, volleyball. No. 1454, Games mascot, vert. No. 1455, Mascot, emblem, torch.

Perf. 13x13½

1991, Sept. Litho. Unwmk.
1448 A826 10p multicolored .45 .20
1449 A826 10p multicolored .45 .20
a. Pair, #1448-1449 .90 .90
1450 A826 10p multicolored .45 .20
1451 A826 10p multicolored .45 .20
a. Pair, #1450-1451 .90 .90
1452 A826 10p multicolored .45 .20
1453 A826 10p multicolored .45 .20
a. Pair, #1452-1453 .90 .90

Perf. 13½x13

1454 A826 10p multicolored .45 .20

Size: 80x60mm

Imperf

1455 A826 50p multicolored 1.75 1.75
Nos. 1448-1455 (8) 4.90 3.15

Intl. Statistics Institute, 48th Session A827

1991, Sept. 9
1456 A827 10p multicolored .40 .20

Opening of Dar Al Eftaa Religious Center — A828

1991, Oct. 1 Litho. *Perf. 13*
1457 A828 10p multicolored .40 .20

October War Against Israel, 18th Anniv. — A829

1991, Oct. 6 *Perf. 13x13½*
1458 A829 10p multicolored .50 .20

Stamp Day Type

Designs: 10p, No. 6. £1, Stamp exhibition emblem, hieroglyphics, pyramids, sphinx.

1991, Oct. 7 *Perf. 13*
1459 A817 10p blue & black .50 .20

Size: 90x60mm

Imperf

1460 A817 £1 multicolored *5.00 5.00*

Natl. Philatelic Exhibition, Cairo, 10/7-12 (No. 1460). No. 1460 sold with £1 at exhibition.

Ancient Artifacts Type of 1985

Perf. 11½x11

1990-92 Unwmk. Photo.

Size: 18x23mm

1467 A681 10p like #1278 .60 .25
1470 A681 30p like #1283 1.00 1.00
1472 A681 50p like #1285 1.75 1.75
Nos. 1467-1472 (3) 3.35 3.00

Issued: 10p, 1/20/90; 30p, 9/1/91; 50p, 7/11/92.

United Nations Day — A830

No. 1477, Brick hands housing people. No. 1478, Woman learning to write, fingerprint, vert.

Perf. 13x13½, 13½x13

1991, Oct. 24 Litho.
1476 A830 10p shown .40 .20
1477 A830 10p multicolored .40 .20
1478 A830 10p multicolored .40 .20
Nos. 1476-1478 (3) 1.20 .60

Famous Men Type of 1988

Inscribed "1991"

Designs: No. 1479, Dr. Zaki Mubarak (1891-1952), writer and poet. No. 1480, Abd El Kader Hamza (1879-1941), journalist.

1991, Dec. 23 Photo. *Perf. 13½x13*
1479 A760 10p olive brown .40 .20
1480 A760 10p gray .40 .20

A831

Post Day — A832

1992, Jan. 2 Litho. *Perf. 13*
1481 A831 10p shown .40 .25
1482 A831 45p Bird mosaic 1.00 1.00

Perf. 14

1483 A832 70p shown 1.75 1.75
Nos. 1481-1483 (3) 3.15 3.00

Nos. 1482-1483 are airmail.

Police Day — A833

1992, Jan. 25 *Perf. 14*
1484 A833 10p multicolored .40 .20

25th Cairo Intl. Fair A834

1992, Feb. 15 Litho. *Perf. 14*
1485 A834 10p multicolored .40 .20

Famous Men Type of 1988

Inscribed "1992"

10p, Sayed Darwish (1882-1923), musician.

1992, Mar. 17 Photo. *Perf. 14x13½*
1486 A760 10p dull org & olive .40 .20

Festivals — A835

1992, Mar. 18 *Perf. 11½*
1487 A835 10p Egyptian hoopoe .40 .20

World Health Day A836

1992, Apr. 20 Litho. *Perf. 13*
1488 A836 10p multicolored .50 .20

Aswan Dam, 90th Anniv. A837

1992, July Litho. *Perf. 13*
1489 A837 10p No. 487 .50 .20

20th Arab Scout Jamboree — A838

1992, July 10 *Perf. 13x13½*
1490 A838 10p multicolored .50 .20

A839

A840

1992, July 20 *Perf. 13½x13*
1491 A839 10p multicolored .40 .20

Size: 80x60mm

Imperf

1492 A839 70p Summer Games' emblem 1.75 1.75

1992 Summer Olympics, Barcelona.

1992, Sept. 14 Litho. *Perf. 13½x13*
1493 A840 10p multicolored .40 .20

El Helal Magazine, cent.

Alexandria World Festival — A841

1992, Sept. 27 *Perf. 13x13½*

1494 A841 70p multicolored 1.60 1.60

Congress of Federation of World and American Travel Companies, Cairo — A842

1992, Sept. 20

1495 A842 70p multicolored 1.50 1.50

World Post Day A843

1992, Oct. 9 **Litho.** *Perf. 13*

1496 A843 10p dk bl, lt bl & blk .40 .20

Children's Day — A844

1992, Oct. 24 **Litho.** *Perf. 13½x13*

1497 A844 10p multicolored .50 .20

Intl. Conference on Food, Agriculture and World Health A845

1992, Oct. 24 *Perf. 13*

1498 A845 70p multicolored 1.50 1.50

A846

A847

1992, Nov. 21 *Perf. 13½x13*

1499 A846 10p multicolored .50 .20

20th Arab Scout Conference, Cairo.

Famous Men Type of 1988 Inscribed "1992"

No. 1500, Talaat Harb, economist. No. 1501, Mohamed Taymour, writer. No. 1502, Dr. Ahmed Zaki Abu Shadi (with glasses), physician & poet.

1992, Dec. 23 **Photo.** *Perf. 13½x13*

1500	A760 10p blue & brown		.40	.20
1501	A760 10p citron & blue gray		.40	.20
1502	A760 10p citron & blue gray		.40	.20
a.	Pair, #1501-1502		.80	.80
	Nos. 1500-1502 (3)		1.20	.60

1993, Jan. 2 **Litho.** *Perf. 13½x13*

Pharaohs: 10p, Sesostris I. 45p, Amenemhet III. 70p, Hur I.

1503	A847 10p brown & yellow	.45	.20
1504	A847 45p brown & yellow	.65	.65
1505	A847 70p brown & yellow	1.00	1.00
a.	Strip of 3, #1503-1505	2.10	2.10

Post Day.

Intl. Book Fair, Cairo — A848

1993, Jan. 26 **Litho.** *Perf. 13½x13*

1506 A848 15p multicolored .40 .20

A849

A849a

A849b

A849c

A849d

A849e

A849f

A849g

A849h

Artifacts: A849, Bust. A849a, Sphinx. A849b, Bust of princess. A849c, Ramses II. A849d, Queen Ti. A849e, Horemheb. A849f, As A849b. A849g, Amenhotep III. £1, Head of a woman. £2, Woman wearing headdress. £5, Pharaonic capital.

Photo., Litho. (#1511)

1993-99 **Unwmk.** *Perf. 11½x11,*

1507	A849	5p multi	.30	.20
1508	A849a	15p brn & bis	.30	.20
1509	A849a	15p brn & bis	.30	.20
1510	A849b	25p brn & org brn	.30	.25
1511	A849c	55p blk & bl	.65	.65

Size: 21x25mm

Perf. 11¼

1512	A849	5p dp cl & brick red	.30	.20
1513	A849d	5p brown	.30	.20
a.		Wmk. 342	.30	.20
1514	A849a	15p brn & bis	.30	.20
1515	A849e	20p blk & gray	.30	.20
a.		Wmk. 342	.30	.20
1516	A849f	25p brn & org brn	.35	.30
1517	A849f	25p black brown	.30	.20
1518	A849c	55p blk & lt bl	.60	.60
1519	A849g	75p blk & brn	.80	.80

Perf. 11½

1520	A849h	£1 slate & blk	2.25	2.25
1521	A849h	£2 brn & grn	5.00	5.00
1521A	A849h	£5 brn & gold	10.00	10.00
		Nos. 1507-1521A (16)	22.35	21.45

Warning: Avoid using watermark fluid on Nos. 1513-1513a and 1515-1515a. Images will be adversely affected.

Body of Sphinx on Nos. 1509, 1514 stops above value, and extends through value on No. 1508.

Issued: Nos. 1507-1508, 2/1; No. 1509, 3/10; £1, £2, 4/1; No. 1511, 7/1/93; £5, 8/1/93; Nos. 1512, 1514, 1518, 10/30/94; No. 1516, 6/25/94; 20p, 2/1/97; 75p, 3/25/97; No. 1517, 1998; Nos. 1513a, 1515a, 1999.

See Nos. C204-C206.

Architects' Association, 75th Anniv. — A850

1993, Feb. 28 **Litho.** *Perf. 13x13½*

1522 A850 15p multicolored .40 .20

New Building for Ministry of Foreign Affairs A851

1993, Mar. 15 *Perf. 13*

1523 A851 15p multicolored .40 .20

1524 A851 80p multicolored 1.10 1.10

Diplomacy Day (No. 1523). No. 1524 is airmail.

Feasts — A852

1993, Mar. 20 **Litho.** *Perf. 13x13½*

1525 A852 15p Opuntia .40 .20

Newspaper, Le Progres Egyptien, Cent. — A853

1993, Apr. 15 **Litho.** *Perf. 13x13½*

1526 A853 15p multicolored .40 .20

A854 A855

1993, May 15 **Litho.** *Perf. 13½x13*

1527 A854 15p multicolored .50 .20

World Telecommunications Day.

1993, June 15 **Litho.** *Perf. 13½x13*

1528 A855 15p multicolored .40 .20

UN Conference on Human Rights, Vienna.

Organization of African Unity — A856

1993, June 26 *Perf. 13*

1529 A856 15p yel grn & multi .40 .20

1530 A856 80p red violet & multi 1.10 1.10

No. 1530 is airmail.

World PTT Conference, Cairo — A857

1993, Sept. 4 **Litho.** *Perf. 13*

1531 A857 15p multicolored .40 .20

Salah El-Din El Ayubi (1137-1193), Dome of the Rock — A858

1993, Sept. 4

1532 A858 55p multicolored 1.10 1.10

A859

A860

1993, Oct. 6

1533 A859 15p multicolored .50 .20

October War Against Israel, 20th Anniv.

1993, Oct. 12 ***Perf. 13½x13***

1534 A860 15p cream & multi .40 .20
1535 A860 55p silver & multi 1.10 1.10
1536 A860 80p gold & multi 1.50 1.50

Imperf

Size: 90x70mm

1537 A860 80p multicolored 3.00 3.00
Nos. 1534-1537 (4) 6.00 5.80

Pres. Mohamed Hosni Mubarak, Third Term.

Reduction of Natural Disasters A861

1993, Oct. 24 **Litho.** ***Perf. 13***

1538 A861 80p multicolored 1.10 1.10

Electricity in Egypt, Cent. — A862

1993, Oct. 24 ***Perf. 13½x13***

1539 A862 15p multicolored .40 .20

Intl. Conference on Big Dams, Cairo — A863

1993, Nov. 19 **Litho.** ***Perf. 13***

1540 A863 15p multicolored .40 .20

35th Military Intl. Soccer Championship — A864

1993, Dec. 1 **Litho.** ***Perf. 13x13½***

1541 A864 15p orange & multi .40 .20
1542 A864 15p Trophy, emblem .40 .20

9th Men's Junior World Handball Championship (No. 1542).

Famous Men Type of 1988

Inscribed "1993"

No. 1543, A. Al. Bishry. No. 1544, M.F. Abu Hadeed. No. 1545, M.B. Al. Tunisy. No. 1546, Ali Moubarak.

1993, Dec. 25 ***Perf. 13½x13***

1543 A760 15p blue .40 .20
1544 A760 15p blue black .40 .20
1545 A760 15p light violet .40 .20
1546 A760 15p green .40 .20
Nos. 1543-1546 (4) 1.60 .80

Post Day — A865

1994, Jan. 2

1547 A865 15p Amenhotep III .40 .20
1548 A865 55p Queen Hatshepsut 1.00 1.00
1549 A865 80p Thutmose III 1.10 1.10
Nos. 1547-1549 (3) 2.50 2.30

Congress of Egyptian Sedimentary Geology Society — A866

1994, Jan. 4 **Litho.** ***Perf. 13x13½***

1550 A866 15p multicolored .40 .20

Birds A867

1994, Mar. 3 **Litho.** ***Perf. 13***

1551 A867 Block of 4, #a.-d. 1.60 1.60
a. 15p Egyptian swallow .40 .40
b. 15p Fire crest .40 .40
c. 15p Rose-ringed parrot .40 .40
d. 15p Goldfinch .40 .40

Festivals 1994.

A868

A869

1994, Mar. 25 ***Perf. 13½x13***

1552 A868 15p multicolored .40 .20

Arab Scouting, 40th anniv.

1994, Apr. 9 **Litho.** ***Perf. 13½x13***

1553 A869 15p multicolored .40 .20

27th Cairo Intl. Fair.

A870

A871

1994, Apr. 15 **Litho.** ***Perf. 13***

1554 A870 15p green & brown .40 .20

1994 African Telecommunications Exhibition, Cairo.

1994, Apr. 30 **Litho.** ***Perf. 13***

1555 A871 15p grn, blk & blue .40 .20

Natl. Afforestation Campaign.

5th Arab Energy Conference, Cairo. — A872

Litho.

Perf. 13

1994, July 5

1556 A872 15p multicolored .40 .20

Signing of Washington Accord for Palestinian Self-Rule in Gaza and Jericho — A873

1994, May 4 **Litho.** ***Perf. 13***

1557 A873 15p multicolored .60 .25

18th Biennial Art Exhibition, Alexandria — A874

1994, May 21

1558 A874 15p yel, blk & gray .40 .20

Organization of African Unity — A875

1994, May 25

1559 A875 15p multicolored .40 .20

Natl. Reading Festival — A876

1994, June 15

1560 A876 15p multicolored .40 .20

ILO, 75th Anniv. — A877

1994, June 28 Litho. ***Perf. 13½x13***

1561 A877 15p multicolored .60 .25

Intl. Conference on Population and Development, Cairo — A878

15p, Conference, UN emblems. 80p, Drawings, hieroglyphics, conference emblem.

1994, Sept. 5 Litho. ***Perf. 13***

1562 A878 15p multi .40 .20

1563 A878 80p multi, vert. 1.10 1.10

No. 1563 is airmail.

World Junior Squash Championships — A879

1994, Sept. 14 Litho. ***Perf. 13***

1564 A879 15p multicolored .40 .20

World Post Day A880

1994, Oct. 9 Litho. ***Perf. 13***

1565 A880 15p multicolored .50 .20

Intl. Red Cross & Red Crescent Societies, 75th Anniv. — A881

1994, Oct. 24

1566 A881 80p multicolored 1.50 1.50

Akhbar El-Yom Newpaper, 50th Anniv. — A882

1994, Nov. 11

1567 A882 15p multicolored .40 .20

African Field Hockey Club Championships — A883

1994, Nov. 14 Litho. ***Perf. 13***

1568 A883 15p multicolored .40 .20

A884

Opera Aida, by Verdi — A885

1994, Nov. 26

1569 A884 15p multicolored .40 .20

Imperf

Size: 58x69mm

1570 A885 80p multicolored 2.50 2.50

No. 1570 is airmail.

Intl. Olympic Committee, Cent. — A886

Egyptian Youth Hostels Assoc., 40th Anniv. — A887

1994, Dec. 10 ***Perf. 13***

1571 A886 15p multicolored .40 .20

1994, Dec. 24

1572 A887 15p multicolored .40 .20

Intl. Speed Ball Federation, 10th Anniv. — A888

1994, Dec. 25

1573 A888 15p multicolored .40 .20

African Development Bank, 30th Anniv. — A889

1994, Dec. 26

1574 A889 15p multicolored .40 .20

Opening of Suez Canal, 125th Anniv. — A890

Design: 80p, Map, inaugural ceremony.

1994, Dec. 27

1575 A890 15p multicolored .40 .20

1576 A890 80p multicolored 1.25 1.25

No. 1576 is airmail.

Famous Men — A891

Post Day — A892

1994, Dec. 29

1577 A891 15p Hassan Fathy, engineer .40 .20

1578 A891 15p Mahmoud Taimour, writer .40 .20

1995, Jan. 2 Litho. ***Perf. 13½x13***

15p, Statue of Akhenaton. 55p, Golden mask of King Tutankhamen. 80p, Statue of Nefertiti.

1579 A892 15p multicolored .40 .20

1580 A892 55p multicolored 1.00 1.00

1581 A892 80p multicolored 1.25 1.25

Nos. 1579-1581 (3) 2.65 2.45

World Tourism Organization, 20th Anniv. — A893

1995, Jan. 2 ***Perf. 13x13½***

1582 A893 15p multicolored .40 .20

Festivals — A894

1995, Feb. 25 Litho. ***Perf. 13x13½***

1583 A894 15p multicolored .40 .20

Egyptian Women's Day — A895

1995, Mar. 16 Litho. ***Perf. 13x13½***

1584 A895 15p multicolored .40 .20

Arab League, 50th Anniv. — A896

1995, Mar. 22 ***Perf. 13½x13***

1585 A896 15p blue & multi .40 .20

1586 A896 55p green & multi .75 .75

Sheraton Hotel, Cairo, 25th Anniv. — A897

1995, Mar. 28 *Perf. 13x13½*
1587 A897 15p multicolored .40 .20

Misr Bank, 75th Anniv. — A898

1995, May 7 **Litho.** *Perf. 13½x13*
1588 A898 15p multicolored .60 .25

World Telecommunications Day — A899

1995, May 31 *Perf. 13x13½*
1589 A899 80p multicolored 1.00 1.00

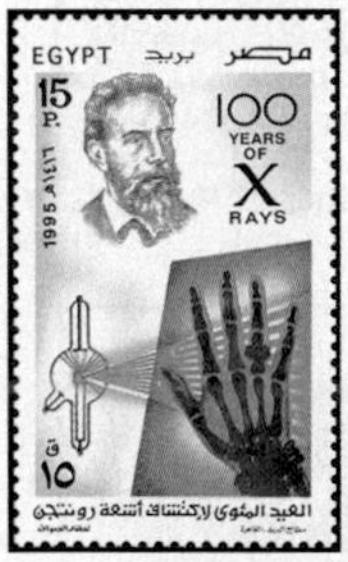

Wilhelm Roentgen (1845-1923), Discovery of the X-Ray, Cent. — A900

1995, May **Litho.** *Perf. 13½x13*
1590 A900 15p multicolored .60 .25

Membership in World Heritage Committee, 20th Anniv. (in 1994) — A901

Artifacts from the Shaft of Luxor: No. 1591, Goddess Hathor. No. 1592, God Atoum. 80p, God Amon and Horemheb.

1995, July 23 **Litho.** *Perf. 13½x13*
1591 15p multicolored .40 .20
1592 15p multicolored .40 .20
a. A901 Pair, #1591-1592 .80 .80
1593 A901 80p multicolored 1.10 1.10
Nos. 1591-1593 (3) 1.90 1.50

No. 1592a is a continuous design. No. 1593 is airmail.

21st Intl. Conference on Pediatrics, Cairo A902

1995, Sept. 10 **Litho.** *Perf. 13*
1594 A902 15p multicolored .60 .25

Intl. Ozone Day — A903

1995, Sept. 16 **Litho.** *Perf. 13x12½*
1595 A903 15p green & multi .40 .20
1596 A903 55p brown & multi .85 .85
1597 A903 80p blue & multi 1.10 1.10
Nos. 1595-1597 (3) 2.35 2.15

See Nos. 1622-1623.

World Tourism Day A904

1995, Sept. 25 *Perf. 12½x13*
1598 A904 15p multicolored .40 .20

Government Printing House, 175th Anniv. — A905

1995, Sept. 27
1599 A905 15p multicolored .40 .20

Sun Verticality on Abu Simbel Temple A906

1995, Oct. 22 **Litho.** *Perf. 12½x13*
1600 A906 15p multicolored .75 .30

Opening of New Esna Dam — A907

1995, Nov. 25 *Perf. 12½*
1601 A907 15p multicolored .75 .30

Egyptian Engineers Assoc., 75th Anniv. A908

1995, Dec. 20 *Perf. 13*
1602 A908 15p multicolored .40 .20

A909

A910

Famous artists.

1995, Dec. 9 **Litho.** *Perf. 13x12½*
1603 A909 15p A. Hafez .40 .20
1604 A909 15p Y. Wahby .40 .20
1605 A909 15p N. El. Rihany .40 .20
Nos. 1603-1605 (3) 1.20 .60

1995, Dec. 23 **Litho.** *Perf. 13x12½*
1606 A910 15p multicolored .40 .20

Motion Pictures, cent.

Post Day A911

Ancient paintings: 55p, Man facing right. 80p, Man facing left. 100p, Playing flute, dancers.

1996, Jan. 2 **Litho.** *Perf. 13½x13*
1607 55p multicolored .60 .60
1608 80p multicolored .90 .90
a. A911 Pair, Nos. 1607-1608 1.50 1.50

Imperf

Size: 88x72mm

1609 A911 100p multicolored 1.25 1.25

Nos. 1607-1608 are airmail.

Feasts — A912

1996, Feb. 15 *Perf. 12½*
1610 A912 15p blue flowers .30 .20
1611 A912 15p red flowers .30 .20
a. Pair, No. 1610-1611 .60 .60

A913

A914

1996, Mar. 13 **Litho.** *Perf. 13x12½*
1612 A913 15p pink & multi .40 .20
1613 A913 80p brown & multi .90 .90

Summit of Peace Makers, Sharm al-Sheikh. No. 1613 is airmail.

1996, Mar. 16
1614 A914 15p multicolored .40 .20

29th Intl. Fair, Cairo.

Egyptian Geological Survey, Cent. A915

1996, Mar. 18 *Perf. 12½x13*
1615 A915 15p multicolored .40 .20

A916

A917

1996, Apr. 11 **Litho.** *Perf. 13x12½*
1616 A916 15p blue & multi .40 .20
1617 A916 80p pink & multi .90 .90

Signing of African Nuclear Weapon-Free Zone Treaty.

1996, Apr. 20 **Litho.** *Perf. 13x12½*
1618 A917 15p multicolored .40 .20

Egyptian Society of Accountants and Auditors, 50th anniv.

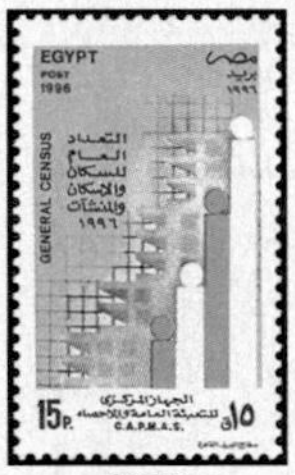

A918

A919

1996, May 4
1619 A918 15p multicolored .40 .20

General census.

1996, July 15 **Litho.** *Perf. 13x12½*

1996 Summer Olympics, Atlanta: 15p, Atlanta 1996 emblem. £1, Emblem surrounded by sports pictograms.

1620 A919 15p lilac & multi .40 .20

Size: 63x103mm

Imperf

1621 A919 £1 black & multi 1.60 1.60

No. 1621 is airmail.

Intl. Ozone Day Type of 1995

1996, Sept. 16 **Litho.** *Perf. 13x12½*
1622 A903 15p pink & multi .40 .20
1623 A903 80p gray & multi 1.10 1.10

No. 1623 is airmail.

A920

A921

1996, Sept. 19
1624 A920 80p multicolored 1.00 1.00
2nd Alexandriate World Festival.

1996, Sept. 21
1625 A921 15p grn, blk & bl .50 .20
Scientific Research and Technology Academy, 25th anniv.

Opening of 2nd Line of Greater Cairo Subway System
A922

1996, Oct. 7 ***Perf. 12½x13***
1626 A922 15p multicolored .50 .20

Rowing Festival
A923

1996
1627 A923 15p multicolored .40 .20

Courts of the State Council, 50th Anniv.
A924

1996, Nov. 2 Litho. ***Perf. 12½x13***
1628 A924 15p blue & claret .40 .20

A925

A926

1996, Nov. 4 ***Perf. 13x12½***
1629 A925 15p yel, blk & blue .40 .20
Intl. Federation Training Development Organization World Conf.

1996, Nov. 12 Litho. ***Perf. 13x12½***
Cairo Economic Summit (MENA): £1, Graph, earth, gear, olive branch, wheat.
1630 A926 15p shown .75 .30

Size: 65x45mm

Imperf

1631 A926 £1 multicolored 1.75 1.75
No. 1631 is airmail.

A927

A928

1996, Nov. 13 ***Perf. 13x12½***
1632 A927 15p multicolored .40 .20
1996 World Food Summit, Rome.

1996, Nov. 16
National Day of El-Gharbia Governorate: Al Sayd Ahmed El-Badawy mosque, Tanta.
1633 A928 15p multicolored .40 .20

A929

A930

Famous artists.

1996, Dec. 28 Litho. ***Perf. 13x12½***
1634 A929 20p Ali El-Kassar .45 .20
1635 A929 20p George Abyad .45 .20
1636 A929 20p Mohamed Kareem .45 .20
1637 A929 20p Fatma Roshdi .45 .20
Nos. 1634-1637 (4) 1.80 .80
See Nos. 1666-1669.

1997, Jan. 2
1638 A930 20p multicolored .45 .20

Size: 61x80mm

Imperf

1639 A930 £1 multicolored 2.00 2.00
Discovery of Tutankhamen's tomb, 75th anniv.
No. 1639 is airmail.

Police Day
A931

1997, Jan. 25 Litho. ***Perf. 13x13½***
1640 A931 20p multicolored .40 .20

Feasts — A932

1997, Feb. 1 ***Perf. 13***
1641 A932 20p pink flowers .40 .20
1642 A932 20p white fowers .40 .20
a. Pair, #1641-1642 .80 .80

World Civil Defense Day
A933

1997, Mar. 10 Litho. ***Perf. 13x13½***
1643 A933 20p multicolored .40 .20

30th Cairo Intl. Fair — A934

1997, Mar. 19 ***Perf. 13½x13***
1644 A934 20p multicolored .40 .20

Mahmoud Said, Photographer, Artist, Birth Cent. — A935

The City, By Mahmoud Said — A936

Illustration reduced (A936).

1997, Apr. 12 Litho. ***Perf. 12½***
1645 A935 20p multicolored .40 .20

Size: 80x60mm

Imperf

1646 A936 £1 multicolored 1.25 1.25
No. 1646 is airmail.

Institute of African Research and Studies, 50th Anniv. — A937

1997, May 27 Litho. ***Perf. 13***
1647 A937 75p multicolored .65 .65

New Headquarters of State Information Service — A938

1997, Aug. 16 Litho. ***Perf. 12½***
1648 A938 20p multicolored .40 .20

A939

A940

£1, Mascot, soccer ball, playing field, emblems.

1997, Sept. 4 ***Perf. 13x12½***
1649 A939 20p multicolored .40 .20
1650 AP81 75p multicolored .65 .65

Size: 75x55mm

Imperf

1651 A939 £1 multicolored 1.75 1.75
Nos. 1650-1651 are airmail. Under 17 FIFA World Soccer Championships, Egypt.

1997, Sept. 16 ***Perf. 13***
1652 A940 20p lt bl grn & multi .40 .20
1653 A940 £1 pink & multi 1.25 1.25
Montreal Protocol on Substances that Deplete the Ozone Layer, 10th anniv. No. 1653 is airmail.

Completion of Second Stage of Metro Line No. 2 — A941

1997, Sept. 27 ***Perf. 12½x13***
1654 A941 20p multicolored .40 .20

Premiere in Egypt of Opera Aida, by Verdi, 125th Anniv.
A942

1997, Oct. 12 ***Perf. 13***
1655 A942 20p multicolored .50 .20

Size: 80x75mm

Imperf

1656 A942 £1 like #1655 1.75 1.75
No. 1656 is airmail.

Queen Nefertari — A943

1997, Oct. 25 Litho. ***Perf. 13***
1657 A943 £1 multicolored 1.25 1.25

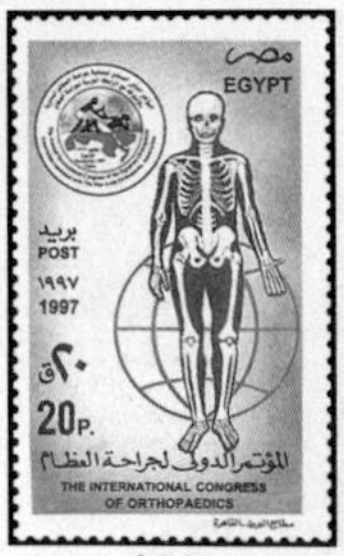

A944

A945

1997, Nov. 17 Litho. *Perf. 13*

1658 A944 20p multicolored .40 .20

Intl. Congress of Orthopedics, Cairo.

1997, Nov. 22 *Perf. 13x12½*

Designs: 20p, Goddess Selket. £1, Scarab, baboon pendant.

1659 A945 20p black & gold .40 .20

Size: 73x62mm

Imperf

1660 A945 £1 multicolored 1.25 1.25

No. 1660 is airmail. Discovery of King Tutanhkamen's tomb, 75th anniv.

Inauguration of Nubia Monument Museum — A946

1997, Nov. 23 *Perf. 13*

1661 A946 20p multicolored .60 .25

Arab Land Bank, 50th Anniv. — A947

1997, Dec. 10 *Perf. 12½*

1662 A947 20p multicolored .60 .25

5th Pan Arab Congress on Anesthesia and Intensive Care — A948

1997, Dec. 9 Litho. *Perf. 13*

1663 A948 20p multicolored .60 .25

El Salaam Canal — A949

1997, Dec. 28

1664 A949 20p multicolored .60 .25

Liberation of Sinai, 15th anniv.

A950

A951

Famous Artists Type of 1996 and A950

1997, Dec. 23 Litho. *Perf. 13x12½*

1665 A950 20p blue .40 .20
1666 A929 20p Zaky Tolaimat .40 .20
1667 A929 20p Ismael Yassen .40 .20
1668 A929 20p Zaky Roustom .40 .20
1669 A929 20p Soliman Naguib .40 .20
a. Strip of 5, #1665-1669 2.00 2.00

1998, Jan. 2 *Perf. 13*

Stamp Day: 20p, King Tutankhamen's guard. 75p, King Ramses III. £1, Cover of King Tutankhamen's coffin.

1670 A951 20p multicolored .50 .20
1671 A951 75p multicolored 1.10 1.10

Size: 26x43mm

1672 A951 £1 multicolored 2.25 2.25

Nos. 1671-1672 are airmail.

Feasts — A952

1998, Jan. 20

1673 20p multicolored .40 .20
1674 20p multicolored .40 .20
a. A952 Pair, #1673-1674 .80 .80

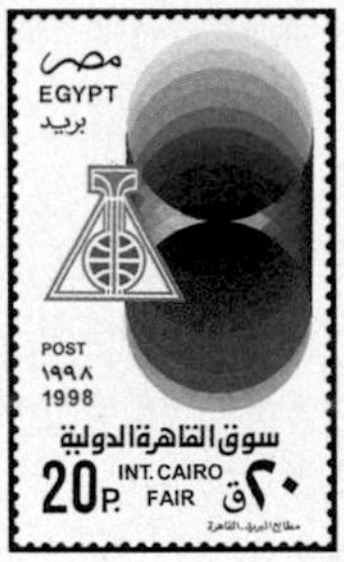

Intl. Cairo Fair — A954

Natl. Bank of Egypt, Cent. — A955

1998, Mar. 11 Litho. *Perf. 13*

1675 A954 20p multicolored .50 .20

1998, Mar. 12

1676 A955 20p multicolored .50 .20

Tutankhamen
A956

Thutmose IV
A957

1998 Litho. *Perf. 13½x12½*

1677 A956 £2 multicolored 1.75 1.75
1678 A957 £5 purple & black 4.25 4.25

Issued: £2, 4/23; £5, 3/23.

A958

A959

1998, Apr. 14 *Perf. 13*

1679 A958 20p green & multi .40 .20
1680 A958 75p blue & multi 1.10 1.10

Size: 70x52mm

Imperf

1681 A958 £1 Natl. flags, map, trophy 2.25 2.25

Egypt, winners of 21st African Cup of Nations soccer competition.
Nos. 1680-1681 are airmail.

1998, May 30 Litho. *Perf. 13*

1682 A959 20p Egyptian Satellite "Nile Sat" .50 .20

World Environment Day — A960

1998, June 5

1683 A960 20p shown .60 .25

Size: 43x62mm

Imperf

1684 A960 £1 Fauna, emblems 2.00 2.00

No. 1684 is airmail.

A961

A962

1998, June 14

1685 A961 20p blue & black .40 .20
1686 A961 £1 yellow, green & black 1.10 1.10

Dr. Ahmed Zewail, winner of Franklin Institute award.
No. 1686 is airmail.

1998, July 15

Imam Sheikh Mohamed Metwalli Al-Shaarawi.

1687 A962 20p buff & multi .40 .20
1688 A962 £1 green & multi 1.10 1.10

No. 1688 is airmail.

A963

A964

1998, Sept. 12 Litho. *Perf. 13*

1689 A963 20p multicolored .50 .20

Day of the Nile Flood.

1998, Sept. 30 Litho. *Perf. 13*

1690 A964 20p multicolored .50 .20

Chemistry Administration, cent.

October War Against Israel, 25th Anniv. — A965

1998, Oct. 6 Litho. *Perf. 13*

1691 A965 20p multicolored .60 .25

Size: 50x70mm

Imperf

1692 A965 £2 like No. 1691 4.00 4.00

No. 1692 is airmail.

Egyptian Survey Authority, Cent. — A966

1998, Oct. 15 *Perf. 13*

1693 A966 20p multicolored .50 .20

Cairo University, 90th Anniv. — A967

1998, Dec. 7 Litho. *Perf. 13*

1694 A967 20p multicolored .50 .20

A968

A970

1998, Dec. 17 Litho. *Perf. 13*

1695 A968 20p multicolored .40 .20

Egyptian trade unions, cent.

1999, Jan. 2 Litho. *Perf. 13*

Post Day (19th Dynasty): 20p, Queen Nefertari, Goddess Isis. 125p, God Osiris, Goddess Isis.

1696 A970 20p multicolored .50 .20

Size: 41x61mm

Imperf

1697 A970 125p multicolored 2.00 2.00

No. 1697 is airmail.

Feasts — A971

1999, Jan. 5 *Perf. 13*

1698 20p multicolored .40 .20

1699 20p multicolored .40 .20

a. A971 Pair, #1698-1699 .80 .80

Intl. Women's Day — A973

1999, Mar. 7 Litho. *Perf. 13*

1700 A973 20p multicolored .50 .20

Cairo Intl. Fair — A974

1999, Mar. 9

1701 A974 20p multicolored .50 .20

Opening of Metro Line Beneath Nile River — A975

1999, Apr. Litho. *Perf. 13*

1702 A975 20p multicolored .60 .25

A976

UPU, 125th Anniv. — A977

1999, Apr. 21

1703 A976 20p shown .40 .20

1704 A976 £1 multi 1.00 1.00

1705 A977 125p shown 1.10 1.10

Size: 50x70mm

Imperf

1706 A977 125p multi 2.25 2.25

Nos. 1703-1706 (4) 4.75 4.55

Nos. 1704-1706 are airmail.

A978

A980

1999, May 8 *Perf. 13*

1707 A978 20p green & multi .40 .20

1708 A978 125p buff, red & multi 1.25 1.25

Geneva Conventions, 50th anniv. No. 1708 is airmail.

1999, May 20 Litho. *Perf. 13x12¾*

1710 A980 20p green & multi .40 .20

1711 A980 £1 buff & multi 1.10 1.10

African Development Bank, 35th Meeting, Cairo. No. 1711 is airmail.

16th Men's Handball World Championship — A981

20p, Stylized player with ball, pyramids. 1£, Mascot with ball, Sphinx, pyramids, globe. 125p, Mascot with ball, goalie, pyramids.

1999, June 1 *Perf. 13*

1712 A981 20p multicolored .40 .20

1713 A981 £1 multicolored 1.00 1.00

1714 A981 125p multicolored 1.10 1.10

Nos. 1712-1714 (3) 2.50 2.30

Nos. 1713-1714 are airmail.

Goddess Selket — A982

1999, June 23 Litho. *Perf. 13*

1715 A982 25p multicolored .60 .25

See Nos. 1750, 1754.

SOS Children's Village, 50th Anniv. — A983

1999, June 23 *Perf. 12¾x13¼*

1716 A983 20p grn, blk & blue .40 .20

1717 A983 125p buff, blk & bl 1.10 1.10

No. 1717 is airmail.

A984

A985

No. 1718, Sameera Moussa (1917-52), Physicist. No. 1719, Aisha Abdul Rahman (1913-98), writer. No. 1720, Ahmed Eldemerdash Touny (1907-97), member of Intl. Olympic Committee.

1999 Litho. *Perf. 13x12¾*

1718 A984 20p multicolored .45 .20

1719 A984 20p multicolored .45 .20

1720 A984 20p multicolored .45 .20

Nos. 1718-1720 (3) 1.35 .60

Issued: Nos. 1718-1719, 7/23; No. 1720, 8/13.

See Nos. 1730-1733.

1999, Oct. 5 Litho. *Perf. 13x12¾*

1721 A985 20p org & multi .40 .20

1722 A985 £1 silver & multi 1.00 1.00

1723 A985 125p gold & multi 1.10 1.10

Imperf

1724 A985 125p multicolored 2.25 2.25

Nos. 1721-1724 (4) 4.75 4.55

Pres. Hosni Mubarak, 4th term.

Nos. 1722-1724 are airmail.

A986

A987

1999, Nov. 15 Litho. *Perf. 13¼x13*

Background Color

1725 A986 20p green .40 .20

1726 A986 £1 red vio 1.00 1.00

1727 A986 125p purple 1.10 1.10

Nos. 1725-1727 (3) 2.50 2.30

Intl. Year of the Elderly. Nos. 1726-1727 are airmail.

1999, Nov. 20

1728 A987 20p multi .50 .20

Children's Day.

Famous People Type of 1999

No. 1730, Farid El Attrash (1913-76), singer, movie star. No. 1731, Laila Mourad (1918-95), singer, movie star. No. 1732, Anwar Wagdi (1911-55), actor, director. No. 1733, Asia Dagher (1901-86), actor, producer.

1999, Dec. 30 Litho. ***Perf. 13x12¾***

1730	A984	20p lt bl & blk		.40	.20
1731	A984	20p lt bl & blk		.40	.20
1732	A984	20p lt bl & blk		.40	.20
1733	A984	20p lt bl & blk		.40	.20
		Nos. 1730-1733 (4)		1.60	.80

Millennium
A989

20p, "1999" & "2000." 125p, Countdown of years. £2, Holy Family, Virgin Tree.

2000, Jan. 1 ***Perf. 13x12¾***

1734	A989	20p multi	.40	.20
1735	A989	125p multi	1.10	1.10

Size: 70x50mm

Imperf

1736	A989	£2 multi, horiz.	4.00	4.00
		Nos. 1734-1736 (3)	5.50	5.30

Nos. 1735-1736 are airmail.

A990

Post Day — A991

2000, Jan. 2 ***Perf. 13¼x12¾***

1737	A990	20p multi	.50	.20
1738	A991	20p multi	.50	.20
a.		Pair, #1737-1738	1.00	1.00

Size: 70x50mm

Imperf

1739	A991	125p Chariot, horiz.	2.00	2.00
		Nos. 1737-1739 (3)	3.00	2.40

Ain Shams University, 50th Anniv. — A992

2000, Jan. 3 ***Perf. 13¼x13***

1740	A992	20p multi	.50	.20

Feasts

A993 A994

2000, Jan. 5 ***Perf. 13x13¼***

1741	A993	20p multi	.35	.20
1742	A994	20p multi	.35	.20
a.		Pair, #1741-1742	.70	.70

A995

A996

2000, Jan. 20 ***Perf. 13¼x13***

1743	A995	20p multi	.50	.20

Islamic Development Bank, 25th anniv.

2000, Feb. 28 ***Perf. 13¼x12¾***

1744	A996	125p multi	1.10	1.10

Common Market for Eastern and Southern Africa Economic Conference.

Death of Om Kolthoum, 25th Anniv. — A997

Europe-Africa Summit, Cairo — A999

8th Intl. Congress of Egyptologists — A998

2000, Mar. 11 ***Perf. 13¼x13***

1745	A997	20p multi	.50	.20

2000, Mar. 28 ***Perf. 13x13¼***

1746	A998	20p multi	.50	.20

2000, Apr. 3 ***Perf. 13¼x13***

1747	A999	125p multi	1.25	1.25

Group of 15 Developing Nations, 10th Summit, Cairo — A1000

Perf. 12¾x13¼

2000, June 19 Litho.

1748	A1000	125p multi	1.25	1.25

Goddess Selket Type of 1999 and

Scene from 20th Dynasty
A1003

Nofret, Wife of Rahotep
A1004

King Seostris
A1005

Princess Merit Aton
A1006

20th Dynasty — A1007

Pyramid at Snefru
A1008

Wife of Sheikh-el-Balad
A1009

King Psusennes I
A1010

King Tutankhamen
A1011

Obelisk of Ramses II
A1011a

Temple of Karnak
A1012

Perf. 12¾x13¼, 11¼ (1752-1755, 1757), 11x11½ (1758-1760), 13¼x12¾ (1756, 1761, 1763)

Photo., Litho. (1751, 1761, 1763)

2000-2002

1750	A982	10p multi	.40	.20
1750A	A982	10p multi, Type II	*3.00*	*3.00*
1751	A1003	10p multi	.40	.20
1752	A1004	20p multi	.40	.20
1753	A1005	25p multi	.40	.20
1754	A982	30p multi	.50	.20
1755	A1006	30p multi	.40	.20
1756	A1007	50p multi	.40	.20
1757	A1008	£1 multi	.60	.60
1758	A1009	110p multi	.65	.65
1759	A1010	125p multi	.75	.75
1760	A1011	150p multi	.85	.85
1761	A1011a	225p multi	1.50	1.50
1763	A1012	£5 multi	4.25	4.25
		Nos. 1750-1763 (14)	14.50	13.00

Issued: 20p, 6/25; No. 1750, 3/25/01; No. 1750A, 2001 (?); 30p, 6/11/01. Nos. 1751, 1755, 225p, 5/25/02; 110p, 6/4/02; 125p, 6/20/02; 150p, 6/15/02; £5, 6/1/02. 30p, 50p, #1, 6/30/02.

Type I (No. 1750), has "Goddess" in smaller type than "Silakht." Type II (No. 1750A), has "Goddess" and "Silakht" in type the same height.

Intl. Day Against Drug Abuse — A1013

Perf. 12¾x13¼

2000, June 26 Litho.

1764	A1013	20p multi	.50	.20

See No. 1796.

Natl. Insurance Company, Cent. — A1014

Perf. 13¼x12¾

2000, Aug. 20 Litho.

1765	A1014	20p shown	.50	.20

Imperf
Size: 96x75mm

1766 A1014 125p Emblem, building, horiz. 2.25 2.25

2000 Summer Olympics, Sydney
A1015

Background colors: 20p, Light blue. 125p, Pink.

2000, Sept. 9 ***Perf. 13¼x12¾***
1767-1768 A1015 Set of 2 1.40 1.40

No. 1768 is airmail.

Productive Cooperative Union, 25th Anniv. — A1016

2000, Sept. 15 ***Perf. 12¾x13¼***
1769 A1016 20p multi .50 .20

Opening of Fourth Stage of Second Cairo Subway Line — A1017

2000, Oct. 7
1770 A1017 20p multi .50 .20

World Post Day — A1018

2000, Oct. 9
1771 A1018 125p multi 1.10 1.10

Solidarity with Palestinians — A1019

Palestinian Authority flag and: 20p, Dome of the Rock, Jerusalem, vert. No. 1773, 125p, shown. No. 1774, 125p, Dome of the Rock, father and boy, vert.

Perf. 13¼x12¾, 12¾x13¼
2000, Nov. 29
1772-1774 A1019 Set of 3 2.75 2.75

No. 1774 is airmail.

Opening of El-Ferdan Railway Bridge — A1020

2000, Dec. 2 ***Perf. 12¾x13¼***
1775 A1020 20p multi .50 .20

Disabled Person's Day — A1021

2000, Dec. 9 ***Perf. 13¼x12¾***
1776 A1021 20p multi .50 .20

Opening of Al-Azhar Professorial Building — A1022

2000, Dec. 10 ***Perf. 12¾x13¼***
1777 A1022 20p multi .50 .20

Famous Egyptians
A1023

No. 1778: a, Karem Mahmoud, artist (yellow background). b, Mahmoud El-Miligi, artist (green background). c, Mohamed Fawzi, musician (pink background). d, Hussein Riyad, artist (lilac background). e, Abdel Wares Asser, artist (light blue background).

2000, Dec. 24 ***Perf. 13¼x12¾***
1778 Horiz. strip of 5 2.00 2.00
a.-e. A1023 20p Any single .40 .20

Feasts — A1024

a, Red and yellow flowers. b, Purple flowers.

Perf. 12¾x13¼
2000, Dec. 23 **Litho.**
1779 A1024 20p Pair, #a-b .80 .80

Jerusalem, City of Peace — A1025

Illustration reduced.

2001, Jan. 1 ***Imperf.***
1780 A1025 £2 multi 2.75 2.75

Post Day — A1026

Ancient Egyptian art: 20p, 8 standing figures. No. 1782, 125p, 3 large standing figures.

2001, Jan. 2 ***Perf. 12¾x13¼***
1781-1782 A1026 Set of 2 1.40 1.40

Imperf
Size: 80x60mm

1783 A1026 125p Chariot 2.25 2.25

No. 1782 is airmail.

Arab Labor Organization, 36th Anniv. — A1027

Perf. 13¼x12¾
2001, Feb. 10 **Litho.**
1784 A1027 20p multi .50 .20

Postal Savings Bank, Cent. — A1028

2001, Mar. 1
1785 A1028 20p multi .50 .20

Natl. Council for Women, 1st Anniv. — A1029

Background colors: 30p, Pink. 125p, Blue.

2001, Mar. 16 ***Perf. 12¾x13¼***
1786-1787 A1029 Set of 2 2.00 1.60

No. 1787 is airmail.

Cairo Intl. Fair — A1030

2001, Mar. 21 ***Perf. 13¼x12¾***
1788 A1030 30p multi .50 .20

Helwan University, 25th Anniv. — A1031

2001, May 4 ***Perf. 12¾x13¼***
1789 A1031 30p multi .50 .20

Inauguration of Alexandria Library — A1032

2001, May 20
1790 A1032 125p multi 1.10 1.10

African Conference on the Future of Children
A1033

Background color: 30p, Blue. 125p, Red.

2001, May 28 ***Perf. 13¼x12¾***
1791-1792 A1033 Set of 2 2.00 1.60

No. 1792 is airmail.

World Environment Day — A1034

2001, June 5 **Litho.** ***Perf. 13¼x12¾***
1793 A1034 125p multi 1.25 1.25

World Military Soccer Championships A1035

Designs: 30p, Emblem. 125p, Emblem and map.

Perf. 13¼x12¾

2001, June 21 **Litho.**
1794-1795 A1035 Set of 2 2.00 1.60

Intl. Day Against Drug Abuse Type of 2000

2001, June 26 ***Perf. 12¾x13¼***
1796 A1013 30p multi .50 .20

Egypt's Victory in World Military Soccer Championships — A1036

Illustration reduced.

2001, July 6 **Litho.** ***Imperf.***
1797 A1036 125p multi 2.25 2.25

Egyptian Railways, 150th Anniv. — A1037

2001, July 12 ***Perf. 12¾x13¼***
1798 A1037 30p multi .60 .25

Poets — A1038

No. 1799: a, Aziz Abaza Pasha (1898-73), blue background. b, Ahmed Rami (1892-1981), pink background.

2001, July 28 ***Perf. 13¼x12¾***
1799 A1038 30p Horiz. pair, #a-b .70 .70

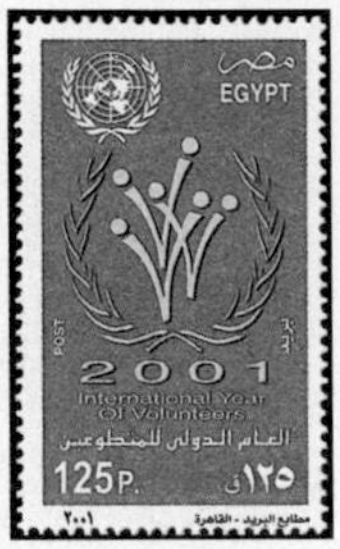

Intl. Volunteers Year — A1039

2001, Aug. 18
1800 A1039 125p multi 1.10 1.10

Ismailia Folklore Festival — A1040

2001, Aug. 20
1801 A1040 30p multi .60 .25

Satellite Telecommunications Ground Stations, 25th Anniv. — A1041

2001, Sept. 8 ***Perf. 12¾x13¼***
1802 A1041 30p multi .60 .25

Year of Dialogue Among Civilizations A1042

Designs: No. 1803, 125p, Emblem. No. 1804, 125p, UN emblem, globe, symbols of various civilizations, horiz.

Perf. 13¼x12¾, 12¾x13¼

2001, Oct. 9
1803-1804 A1042 Set of 2 3.00 2.50

Opening of Suez Canal Bridge — A1043

No. 1805: a, 30p, Bridge, ship. b, 125p, Bridge, road.

No. 1806, Bridge, ship and flags of Egypt and Japan.

Illustration reduced.

2001, Oct. 10 ***Perf. 12¾x13¼***
1805 A1043 Horiz. pair, #a-b 1.50 1.50

Imperf

Size: 81x60mm

1806 A1043 125p multi 2.25 2.25

Ancient Gold Masks — A1044

Designs: No. 1807, 30p, Mask of San Xing Dui, China, green background. No. 1808, 30p, Funerary mask of King Tutankhamun, brown background.

2001, Oct. 12 ***Perf. 12¾x13¼***
1807-1808 A1044 Set of 2 .75 .75

See People's Republic of China 3141-3142.

Opening of Azhar Tunnels, Cairo — A1045

2001, Oct. 28 ***Perf. 13¼x12¾***
1809 A1045 30p multi .60 .25

El-Menoufia University, 25th Anniv. — A1046

2001, Nov. 25
1810 A1046 30p multi .60 .25

Feasts — A1047

No.1811: a, Black and white bird on branch. b, Sea gulls. c, Parrot. d, Blue bird on branch.

2001, Dec. 5
1811 A1047 30p Block of 4, #a-d 2.00 1.10

Musicians — A1048

No. 1812: a, Zakaria Ahmed (1896-1961) with scarf around neck (4). b, Riyadh El-Sonbati (1908-81) with glasses with rectangular lenses (3). c, Mahmoud El-Sherif (1912-90) (2). d, Mohamed El-Kasabgi (1898-1966) with glasses with round lenses (1). Stamp numbers, shown in parentheses, are found at the bottom center in Arabian script. Illustration reduced.

2001, Dec.
1812 A1048 30p Horiz. strip of 4 2.00 1.10

Painting From Tomb of Anhur Khawi — A1049

Painting from Tomb of Irinefer — A1050

Illustration A1050 reduced.

2002, Jan. 2 **Litho.** ***Perf. 12¾x13¼***
1813 A1049 30p multi .60 .25

Imperf

Size: 79x60mm

1814 A1050 125p multi 2.25 2.25

Stamp Day.

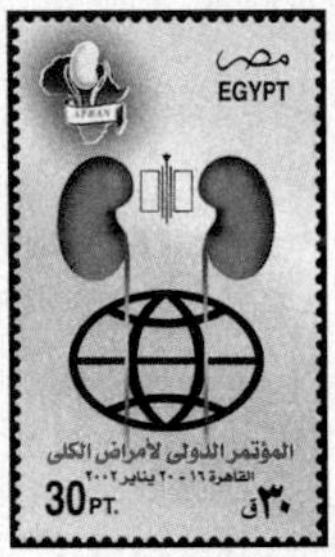

Intl. Nephrology Congress A1051

2002, Jan. 16 **Litho.** ***Perf. 13¼x12¾***
1815 A1051 30p multi .60 .25

Police Day, 50th Anniv. A1052

2002, Jan. 25 ***Perf. 12¾x13¼***
1816 A1052 30p multi .60 .25

Imperf

Size: 79x50mm

1817 A1052 30p multi 1.75 1.75

Return of Sinai to Egypt, 20th Anniv. — A1053

2002, Apr. 25 ***Perf. 13¼x12¾***
1818 A1053 30p multi .60 .25

Cairo Bank, 50th Anniv. — A1054

2002, May 15
1819 A1054 30p multi .60 .25

Weight Lifters — A1055

No. 1820: a, Ibrahim Shams, 1948 (weights over head). b, Khidre el Touney, 1936 (weights at knees).

2002, June 1
1820 A1055 30p Horiz. pair, #a-b .60 .25

Al Akhbar Newspaper, 50th Anniv. — A1056

2002, June 15 ***Perf. 12¾x13¼***
1821 A1056 30p multi .60 .25

Nos. 318-321 and Egyptian Arms — A1057

Illustration reduced.

2002, July 23 **Litho.** ***Imperf.***
1822 A1057 125p multi 1.60 1.60
July 23rd Revolution, 50th anniv.

Aswan Dam, Cent. — A1058

No. 1823: a, Dam. b, Dam and buildings. Illustration reduced.

2002, Aug. 15 ***Perf. 12¾x13¼***
1823 A1058 30p horiz. pair, #a-b .60 .60

Intl. Day for Preservation of the Ozone Layer — A1059

2002, Sept. 16 ***Perf. 13¼x12¾***
1824 A1059 125p multi 1.25 1.25

18th Intl. Conference on Road Safety, Cairo — A1060

2002, Sept. 22
1825 A1060 30p multi .60 .25

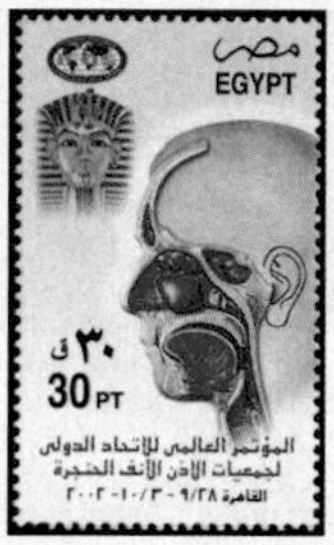

17th Congress of Intl. Federation of Otorhinolaryngological Societies, Cairo — A1061

2002, Sept. 28
1826 A1061 30p multi .60 .25

World Post Day — A1062

2002, Oct. 9
1827 A1062 125p multi 1.10 1.10

Opening of Alexandria Library — A1063

Ancient Alexandria Library — A1064

Designs: 30p, Library exterior. 125p, Pillar, sun on horizon, vert.

Perf. 12¾x13¼, 13¼x12¾
2002, Oct. 16
1828-1829 A1063 Set of 2 1.50 1.50

Size: 60x80mm
Imperf
1830 A1064 125p multi 1.60 1.60

Hassan Faek, Actor — A1065

Aziza Amir, Actress — A1066

Farid Shawki, Actor — A1067

Mary Mounib, Actress — A1068

2002, Nov. 23 ***Perf. 13¼x12¾***
1831 Horiz. strip of 4 1.60 1.60
a. A1065 30p tan & black .40 .20
b. A1066 30p tan & black .40 .20
c. A1067 30p tan & black .40 .20
d. A1068 30p tan & black .40 .20

A1069

A1070

A1071

Birds — A1072

2002, Dec. 3 ***Perf. 13¼x12¾***
1832 Block of 4 1.60 1.60
a. A1069 30p multi .40 .20
b. A1070 30p multi .40 .20
c. A1071 30p multi .40 .20
d. A1072 30p multi .40 .20

Egyptian Museum, Cent. — A1073

2002, Dec. 11 ***Perf. 12¾x13¼***
1833 A1073 30p shown .60 .25

Size: 80x60mm
Imperf
1834 A1073 125p Entrance, statue of Cheops 1.75 1.75

Opening of Aswan Suspension Bridge — A1074

No. 1835: a, Bridge and support cables. b, Bridge towers.
Illustration reduced.

2002, Dec. 17 ***Perf. 12¾x13¼***
1835 A1074 30p Horiz. pair, #a-b .75 .75

Suez Canal University, 25th Anniv. — A1075

2002, Dec. 29 ***Perf. 13¼x12¾***
1836 A1075 30p multi .50 .20

Toshka Land Reclamation Project — A1076

2002, Dec. 31 ***Perf. 12¾x13¼***
1837 A1076 30p multi .50 .20

A1077

A1078

Post Day — A1079

2003, Jan. 2
1838 A1077 30p multi .40 .20
1839 A1078 30p multi .40 .20
1840 A1079 125p multi 1.10 1.10
Nos. 1838-1840 (3) 1.90 1.50

Cairo Intl. Communications and Information Technology Fair — A1080

2003, Jan. 12 Litho. ***Perf. 13¼x12¾***
1841 A1080 30p multi .60 .25

Intl. Nile Children's Song Festival — A1081

Background color: 30p, Brown. 125p, Green.

2003, Jan. 28 ***Perf. 12¾x13¼***
1842-1843 A1081 Set of 2 1.25 1.25

Intl. Table Tennis Championships — A1082

Background color: 30p, Blue. 125p, Orange.

2003, Feb. 3
1844-1845 A1082 Set of 2 1.25 1.25

Tenth Intl. Building and Construction Conference A1083

Background color: 30p, Orange. 125p, Blue.

2003, Apr. 1 ***Perf. 13¼x12¾***
1846-1847 A1083 Set of 2 1.10 1.10

Arab Lawyer's Union, 60th Anniv. — A1084

Background color: 30p, Blue. 125p, Lilac.

2003, Apr. 25 ***Perf. 12¾x13¼***
1848-1849 A1084 Set of 2 1.10 1.10

Inauguration of First Phase of Smart Village Project — A1085

Denomination color: 30p, White. 125p, Yellow. £1, White.

2003, July 1 ***Perf. 12¾x13¼***
1850-1851 A1085 Set of 2 1.10 1.10

Size: 79x59mm

Imperf

1852 A1085 £1 multi 2.00 2.00

Writers — A1086

No. 1853: a, Ihsan Abdul Qudous (1919-90) (wearing checked tie). b, Youssef Idris (1927-91) (wearing solid tie).

2003, July 28 ***Perf. 13¼x12¾***
1853 A1086 30p Horiz. pair, #a-b .75 .75

African Men's Basketball Championships A1087

Background color: 30p, Black. 125p, Blue.

2003, Aug. 12
1854-1855 A1087 Set of 2 1.10 1.10

Natl. Institute of Astronomical and Geophysical Research, Cent. — A1088

2003, Sept. 7 ***Perf. 12¾x13¼***
1856 A1088 30p multi .75 .30

World Tourism Day — A1089

Denomination color: 30p, White. 125p, Red.

Perf. 12¾x13¼

2003, Sept. 27 **Litho.**
1857-1858 A1089 Set of 2 1.10 1.10

Egypt's Bid for Hosting 2010 World Cup Soccer Championships — A1090

Designs: 30p, Emblem, vert. 125p, Emblem, funerary mask of King Tutankhamen.

Perf. 13¼x12¾, 12¾x13¼

2003, Sept. 27
1859-1860 A1090 Set of 2 1.10 1.10

October War Against Israel, 30th Anniv. — A1091

2003, Oct. 6 ***Perf. 13¼x12¾***
1861 A1091 30p multi .75 .30

World Post Day — A1092

2003, Oct. 9
1862 A1092 125p multi .80 .80

National Bar Association, 91st Anniv. — A1093

2003, Oct. 30
1863 A1093 30p multi .50 .20

Festivals — A1094

No. 1864: a, Pink orchids. b, White rose. c, Red rose. d, Sunflower.

2003, Nov. 23 ***Perf. 14***
1864 A1094 30p Block of 4, #a-d 1.25 1.25

Film Directors — A1095

No. 1865: a, Salah Abou Seif (balding man with open collar). b, Kamal Selim (round eyeglasses) c, Henri Barakat (square eyeglasses). d, Hassan El Emam.
Illustration reduced.

2003, Dec. 1 ***Perf. 13¼x12¾***
1865 A1095 30p Horiz. strip of 4, #a-d 1.25 1.25

El Gomhoreya Newspaper, 50th Anniv. — A1096

2003, Dec. 7
1866 A1096 30p multi .50 .20

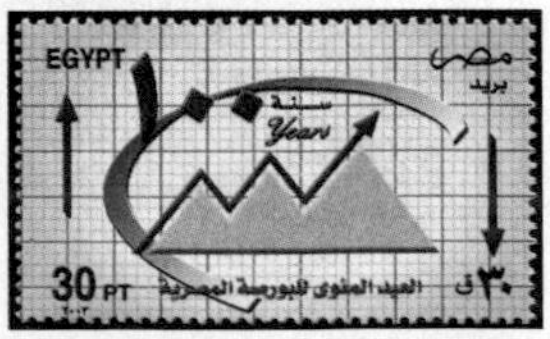

Cairo Bourse, Cent. — A1097

2003, Dec. 7 ***Perf. 12¾x13¼***
1867 A1097 30p multi .50 .20

Mrs. Suzanne Mubarak, Emblems of Fifth E-9 Ministerial Review Meeting and UNESCO — A1098

Background color: 30p, Blue. 125p, Orange. £2, Blue.

Perf. 12¾x13¼

2003, Dec. 18 **Litho.**

1868-1869 A1098 Set of 2 1.10 1.10

Imperf

Size: 79x60mm

1870 A1098 £2 multi 2.25 2.25

Delta International Bank, 25th Anniv. — A1099

Background color: 30p, Green. 125p, Blue. £2, Green and blue, horiz.

2004, Jan. 1 ***Perf. 12¾x13¼***

1871-1872 A1099 Set of 2 1.00 1.00

Imperf

Size: 80x60mm

1873 A1099 £2 multi 2.25 2.25

Post Day A1100

Denominations: 30p, 125p.

2004, Jan. 2 ***Perf. 12¾x13¼***

1874-1875 A1100 Set of 2 1.00 1.00

Eighth Intl. Telecommunications Conference — A1101

2004, Jan. 17

1876 A1101 30p multi .70 .30

Treasures of Egypt A1102

No. 1877: a, Sinai. b, Pyramids at dusk. c, Egyptian Bedouin. d, Red Sea corals. e, Suez Canal, Ferdinand-Marie de Lesseps, Khedive Ismail. f, Ramadan lanterns. g, Nile felucca. h, White Western Desert. i, Maydum Pyramid.

No. 1878: a, St. Catherine Monastery, Sinai. b, Icon of Sts. Paul and Anthony. c, Mosque of Muhammad Ali. d, Lamp, Old Cairo. e, Emblem of Sultan Qaytbay. f, Minaret, Cairo. g, Mosque of al-Azhar. h, Coptic priest and icon, Cairo. i, Ben Ezra Synagogue.

No. 1879: a, Ankh. b, Rosetta Stone. c, Sarcophagus of Ahmes Meritamun. d, Stela of Amenmhat. e, Sphinx. f, Udjat. g, Canopic jars of Tutankhamun. h, Cartouche of Tutankhamun. i, Egyptian scribe.

No. 1880: a, Sphinx, diff. b, Queen Nefertiti. c, Tutankhamun.

2004, Jan. 22 **Litho.** ***Perf. 13x13¼***

1877		Booklet pane of 9	2.25	—
a.-i.	A1102	30p Any single	.40	.20
1878		Booklet pane of 9	11.00	—
a.-i.	A1102	125p Any single	1.25	1.25

Litho. & Embossed, Litho. & Embossed With Foil Application (£10)

1879		Booklet pane of 9	17.50	—
a.-i.	A1102	£2 Any single	1.90	1.90

Perf. 13¼

1880		Booklet pane of 3	19.00	—
a.-b.	A1102	£5 Either single, 38x51mm	4.50	4.50
c.	A1102	£10 gold & multi, 38x51mm	9.00	9.00
		Complete booklet, #1877-1880	50.00	

Complete booklet sold for £80.

Morkos Hanna — A1103

Ahmed Lotfi — A1104

Mahmoud Abu el Nasr — A1105

Abd el Aziz Fahmy — A1106

Ibrahim el Helbawi — A1107

Makram Ebeid — A1108

Mohammad Naguib el Gharabli — A1109

Mohammad Bassiouni A1110

Mohammad Hafez Ramadan A1111

Mohammad Abu Shadi — A1112

Mahmoud Fahmi Goundia — A1113

Kamel Youssof Saleh — A1114

Abd el Hamid Abd el Hakk — A1115

Mohammad Ali Allouba — A1116

Kamel Sedki Beck — A1117

Bar Association Emblem — A1118

Abd el Rahman el Rafei — A1119

Abd el Fattah el Shalkany
A1120

Mohammad Sabri Abu Alam — A1121

Omar Omar — A1122

Sameh Ashour — A1123

Ahmed el Khawaga
A1124

Abd el Aziz el Shorgabi
A1125

Mostafa el Baradei — A1126

2004, Feb. **Litho.** ***Perf. 13¼x12¾***

1881	Block of 25	10.00	10.00
a.	A1103 30p bright blue & black	.40	.20
b.	A1104 30p bright blue & black	.40	.20
c.	A1105 30p bright blue & black	.40	.20
d.	A1106 30p bright blue & black	.40	.20
e.	A1107 30p bright blue & black	.40	.20
f.	A1108 30p pink & black	.40	.20
g.	A1109 30p pink & black	.40	.20
h.	A1110 30p pink & black	.40	.20
i.	A1111 30p pink & black	.40	.20
j.	A1112 30p pink & black	.40	.20
k.	A1113 30p orange & black	.40	.20
l.	A1114 30p orange & black	.40	.20
m.	A1115 30p orange & black	.40	.20
n.	A1116 30p orange & black	.40	.20
o.	A1117 30p orange & black	.40	.20
p.	A1118 30p green & multi	.40	.20
q.	A1119 30p green & black	.40	.20
r.	A1120 30p green & black	.40	.20
s.	A1121 30p green & black	.40	.20
t.	A1122 30p green & black	.40	.20
u.	A1118 30p dark blue & multi	.40	.20
v.	A1123 30p dark blue & black	.40	.20
w.	A1124 30p dark blue & black	.40	.20
x.	A1125 30p dark blue & black	.40	.20
y.	A1126 30p dark blue & black	.40	.20

National Bar Association, 92nd anniv.

IBM Corporation in Egypt, 50th Anniv. — A1127

2004, Feb. 24
1882 A1127 30p multi .50 .20

Cairo Rotary Club, 75th Anniv. — A1128

2004, Mar. 11
1883 A1128 30p multi .50 .20

Egyptian Victory in Regional Computer Programming and Information Technology Competition
A1129

2004, Mar. 15
1884 A1129 30p multi .60 .25

National Women's Day — A1130

Background colors: 30p, Blue. 125p, Red orange.

2004, Mar. 16 **Litho.**
1885-1886 A1130 Set of 2 1.00 1.00

Anti-Narcotics General Administration, 75th Anniv. — A1131

2004, Mar. 20 ***Perf. 12¾x13¼***
1887 A1131 30p multi .75 .30

Imperf

Size: 80x60mm

1888 A1131 125p multi 2.00 2.00

Orphan's Day — A1132

2004, Apr. 2 ***Perf. 13¼x12¾***
1889 A1132 30p multi .60 .25

Compare with Types A1169 and A1199.

Telecom Africa Fair and Conference, Cairo — A1133

2004, May 4 ***Perf. 12¾x13¼***
1890 A1133 30p multi .60 .25

Egyptian Philatelic Society, 75th Anniv. — A1134

Designs: 30p, Emblem. 125p, Emblem, stamp, magnifying glass, tongs.

2004, May 20 ***Perf. 13¼x12¾***
1891 A1134 30p multi .60 .25

Imperf

Size: 80x60mm

1892 A1134 125p multi 2.00 2.00

State Information Service, 50th Anniv. — A1135

2004, May 30 ***Perf. 12¾x13¼***
1893 A1135 30p multi .50 .20

Tenth Radio and Television Festival, Cairo — A1136

Designs: 30p, Festival emblem, green background. £1, Fesitval emblem, brown background. 125p, Sphinx, festival emblem, film, horiz.
£2, Like 125p, horiz.

Perf. 13¼x12¾, 12¾x13¼

2004, June 1
1894-1896 A1136 Set of 3 1.75 1.75

Imperf

Size: 80x60mm

1897 A1136 £2 multi 2.25 2.25

Pres. Hosni Mubarak, "Education for All" Arab Regional Conference Emblem — A1137

Stylized Children, Emblems
A1138

Perf. 12¾x13¼, 13¼x12¾

2004, June 1

1898	A1137 30p yel & multi	.35	.20
1899	A1137 125p red org & multi	.60	.60
1900	A1138 125p multi	.60	.60
	Nos. 1898-1900 (3)	1.55	1.40

Imperf

Size: 80x60mm

1901 A1137 £2 blue & multi 2.25 2.25

Construction and Housing Bank, 25th Anniv. — A1139

2004, June 24 ***Perf. 13¼x12¾***

1902 A1139 30p multi .60 .25

2004 Summer Olympics, Athens — A1140

Background color: 30p, Gray. 150p, Orange yellow.

Perf. 13¼x12¾

2004, Aug. 13 **Litho.**

1903-1904 A1140 Set of 2 1.40 1.40

Scouting in Egypt, 90th Anniv. — A1141

2004, Aug. 15 ***Perf. 12¾x13¼***

1905 A1141 30p multi .70 .30

14th Intl. Folklore Festival, Ismailia — A1142

2004, Aug. 24 ***Perf. 13¼x12¾***

1906 A1142 30p multi .60 .25

Administrative Attorneys, 50th Anniv. — A1143

2004, Sept. 16 ***Perf. 13¼x12¾***

1907 A1143 30p multi .60 .25

Imperf

Size: 60x80mm

1908 A1143 £1 multi 3.00 3.00

Egyptian National Archives, 50th Anniv. — A1144

2004, Sept. 20 ***Perf. 12¾x13¼***

1909 A1144 30p multi .60 .25

Light and Hope Society, 50th Anniv. — A1145

2004, Sept. 26

1910 A1145 30p multi .60 .25

General Arab Journalists Union, 10th Conference A1146

2004, Oct. 2 ***Perf. 13¼x12¾***

1911 A1146 125p multi .80 .80

Telecom Egypt, 150th Anniv. A1146a

2004, Oct. 3 **Litho.** ***Perf. 12¾x13¼***

1911A A1146a 30p multi *9.00 9.00*

No. 1911A was withdrawn from sale after a few days as anniversary emblem was incorrect.

Military Production Day, 50th Anniv. — A1147

2004, Oct. 6 ***Perf. 12¾x13¼***

1912 A1147 30p multi .70 .30

World Post Day — A1148

2004, Oct. 9

1913 A1148 150p multi 1.00 1.00

Egyptian Youth Hostels Association, 50th Anniv. — A1149

2004, Oct. 20 ***Perf. 13¼x12¾***

1914 A1149 30p multi .60 .25

Rose — A1150

Songbird A1151

Perf. 12¾x13¼

2004, Nov. 10 **Litho.**

1915 A1150 30p multi .50 .20

Perf. 13¼x12¾

1916 A1151 30p multi .50 .20

24th Arab Scouting Congress — A1152

2004, Nov. 27 ***Perf. 12¾x13¼***

1917 A1152 30p multi .65 .25

Arab Scouting Organization, 50th Anniv. — A1153

2004, Dec. 4

1918 A1153 30p multi .65 .25

Islamic Art Museum Foundation, Cent. — A1154

2004, Dec. 15 ***Perf. 13¼x12¾***

1919 A1154 30p multi .65 .25

FIFA (Fédération Internationale de Football Association), Cent. — A1155

2004, Dec. 15 ***Perf. 12¾x13¼***

1920 A1155 150p multi 1.00 1.00

Fekri Abaza (1896-1979), Journalist A1156

Abd El Rahman El Sharqawi (1920-87), Journalist A1157

2004, Dec. 28 ***Perf. 13¼x12¾***

1921 A1156 30p multi .40 .20

1922 A1157 30p multi .40 .20

Telecom Egypt, 150th Anniv. — A1158

Color of central panel: 30p, White. 125p, Gray.

2004, Dec. 30 ***Perf. 12¾x13¼***

1923-1924 A1158 Set of 2 1.10 1.10

First Sale of Natural Gas to Jordan — A1159

2005, Jan. 1

1925 A1159 30p multi .70 .30

Post Day — A1160

2005, Jan. 2 ***Perf. 13¼x12¾***

1926 A1160 30p multi .60 .25

Opening of Om El Massrean — El Moneib Subway Line, Cairo — A1161

2005, Jan. 16 ***Perf. 12¾x13¼***

1927 A1161 30p multi .60 .25

Imperf

Size: 80x59mm

1928 A1161 150p multi 1.75 1.75

Police Day — A1162

Pres. Hosni Mubarak and flag stripes aligned: 30p, Vertically. £1, Horizontally.

2005, Jan. 25 ***Perf. 13¼x12¾***

1929 A1162 30p multi .50 .20

Imperf

Size: 80x59mm

1930 A1162 £1 multi 1.50 1.50

El Mohandes Insurance Company, 25th Anniv. — A1163

2005, Jan. 26 ***Perf. 13¼x12¾***

1931 A1163 30p multi .60 .25

9th Intl. Telecommunications and Information Conference, Cairo — A1164

2005, Feb. 1

1932 A1164 30p multi .60 .25

7th University Youth Week — A1165

2005, Feb. 5

1933 A1165 30p multi .60 .25

Rotary International, Cent. — A1166

2005, Feb. 23 **Litho.**

1934 A1166 30p multi .70 .30

38th Intl. Fair, Cairo — A1167

2005, Mar. 15

1935 A1167 30p multi .40 .20

Arab League, 60th Anniv. — A1168

2005, Mar. 22

1936 A1168 30p multi .50 .20

Orphan's Day — A1169

2005, Apr. 2

1937 A1169 30p multi .50 .20

Heliopolis Foundation, Cent. — A1170

2005, May 5 ***Perf. 12¾x13¼***

1938 A1170 30p multi .60 .25

National Center of Social and Criminological Research, 50th Anniv. — A1171

2005, May 22 **Litho.** ***Perf. 13¼x12¾***

1939 A1171 30p multi .60 .25

Egyptian-European Association Agreement, 1st Anniv. — A1172

2005, June 1

1940 A1172 150p multi .80 .80

World Environment Day — A1173

2005, June 5 ***Perf. 12¾x13¼***

1941 A1173 30p multi .75 .30

World Summit on the Information Society, Tunis — A1174

2005, July 31 **Litho.** ***Perf. 13¼x12¾***

1942 A1174 150p multi 1.25 1.25

Ministry of Youth, 50th Anniv. — A1175

Background colors: 30p, Green. 125p, Olive green.

2005, Aug. 13

1943-1944 A1175 Set of 2 1.00 1.00

Presidential Elections A1176

2005, Sept. 7

1945 A1176 30p multi .60 .25

13th World Psychiatry Congress, Cairo — A1177

Designs: 30p, Emblem. 150p, Emblem and funerary mask of King Tutankhamen, horiz.

2005, Sept. 10 ***Perf. 13¼x12¾***

1946 A1177 30p multi .60 .25

Imperf

Size: 80x60mm

1947 A1177 150p multi 1.75 1.75

World Literacy Day — A1178

2005, Sept. 24 ***Perf. 12¾x13¼***

1948 A1178 30p multi .50 .20

Re-election of Pres. Hosni Mubarak A1179

2005, Sept. 27 ***Perf. 13¼x12¾***

1949 A1179 30p multi .50 .20

Mohamed El-Baradei, Director General of Intl. Atomic Energy Agency — A1180

Background colors: 30p, Blue green. 150p, Rose lilac.

2005, Oct. 8

1950-1951 A1180 Set of 2 1.50 1.50

Awarding of 2005 Nobel Peace Prize to El-Baradei and IAEA.

World Post Day — A1181

Denominations: 30p, 150p.

2005, Oct. 9

1952-1953 A1181 Set of 2 1.25 1.25

Intl. Year of Sports and Physical Education A1182

2005, Oct. 24

1954 A1182 150p multi 1.00 1.00

United Nations, 60th Anniv. — A1183

2005, Oct. 24 ***Perf. 12¾x13¼***

1955 A1183 150p multi 1.00 1.00

Festivals A1184

2005, Nov. 1 ***Perf. 13¼x12¾***

1956 A1184 30p multi .65 .25

Alexandria Biennale, 50th Anniv. — A1185

2005, Dec. 1

1957 A1185 30p multi .60 .25

K-8 Training Airplane — A1186

Denominations: 30p, 150p.

Perf. 12¾x13¼

2005, Dec. 26 **Litho.**

1958-1959 A1186 Set of 2 1.00 1.00

Saved Mekawi, Musician A1187

Mohamed El Mogi (1923-95), Musician A1188

Kamal El Taweel, Composer A1189

Ali Ismael (1921-75), Composer A1190

Mohamed Roshdi, Folk Singer — A1191

2005, Dec. 31 ***Perf. 13¼x12¾***

1960 Horiz. strip of 5 1.25 1.25
- *a.* A1187 30p green & multi .25 .20
- *b.* A1188 30p blue & multi .25 .20
- *c.* A1189 30p lilac & black .25 .20
- *d.* A1190 30p org & black .25 .20
- *e.* A1191 30p brt org & black .25 .20

Post Day — A1192

2006, Jan. 2

1961 A1192 30p multi .40 .20

25th Africa Cup of Nations Soccer Tournament A1193

2006, Jan. 20

1962 A1193 30p multi .40 .20

Arab University Youth Week — A1194

2006, Feb. 4 ***Perf. 12¾x13¼***

1963 A1194 30p multi .40 .20

Intl. Telecommunications, Information and Networking Exhibition, Cairo — A1195

2006, Feb. 5 ***Perf. 13¼x12¾***

1964 A1195 30p multi .40 .20

Pres. Hosni Mubarak Holding African Cup of Nations — A1196

2006, Feb. 10 ***Perf. 12¾x13¼***

1965 A1196 30p multi .40 .20

Size: 80x60mm

Imperf

1966 A1196 150p multi 1.10 1.10

Information and Decision Support Center, 20th Anniv. — A1197

2006, Mar. 27 ***Perf. 13¼x12¾***

1967 A1197 30p multi .40 .20

Total Solar Eclipse of March 29, 2006 — A1198

2006, Mar. 29 ***Perf. 12¾x13¼***

1968 A1198 30p multi .40 .20

Size: 82x60mm

Imperf

1969 A1198 150p multi 1.10 1.10

Orphan's Day — A1199

2006, Apr. 2 ***Perf. 13¼x12¾***

1970 A1199 30p multi .40 .20

Compare with types A1132 and A1169.

Gamal Hemdan (1928-93), Geographical Historian A1200

2006, Apr. 16

1971 A1200 30p lilac & black .40 .20

Abd El-Rahman ibn Khaldun (1332-1406), Historian
A1201

2006, May 27

1972 A1201 30p multi .40 .20

World Environment Day — A1202

Designs: 30p, Stone pillar in White Desert. 150p, Trees in desert.

2006, June 5 ***Perf. 12¾x13¼***

1973-1974 A1202 Set of 2 1.25 1.25

Diplomatic Relations Between Egypt and People's Republic of China, 50th Anniv. — A1203

No. 1975: a, Abu Simbel Temple, Egypt. b, South Gate Pavilion, China.
Illustration reduced.

2006, July 13 **Litho.** ***Perf. 12***

1975 A1203 £1.50 Horiz. pair, #a-b, + central label 1.40 1.40

c. Souvenir sheet, #1975 1.10 1.10

Military Academy Headquarters, Heliopolis, 50th Anniv. — A1204

2006, July 19 ***Perf. 12¾x13¼***

1976 A1204 30p multi .40 .20

Nationalization of the Suez Canal, 50th Anniv. — A1205

2006, July 26 ***Perf. 13¼x12¾***

1977 A1205 30p multi .40 .20

World Post Day — A1206

Denominations: 30p, 150p.

2006, Oct. 9

1978-1979 A1206 Set of 2 1.25 1.25

China - Africa Summit — A1206a

No. 1979A: b, Chinese mask. c, African mask.

2006, Nov. 5 **Litho.** ***Perf. 12***

1979A Horiz. pair with central label 1.10 1.10

b.-c. A1206a £1.50 Either single .55 .55

National Housing Census — A1207

2006, Nov. 21 **Litho.** ***Perf. 13¼x13***

1980 A1207 30p multi .20 .20

Al-Ahram Newspaper — A1208

No. 1981: a, Newspaper headquarters. b, Newspaper emblem.
150p, Headquarters and emblem.
Illustration reduced.

2006, Nov. 26 ***Perf. 13x13¼***

1981 A1208 30p Horiz. pair, #a-b, + central label .20 .20

Imperf

Size: 80x60mm

1982 A1208 150p multi .55 .55

Natl. Council for Childhood and Motherhood — A1209

2006, Dec. 27 ***Perf. 13x13¼***

1983 A1209 150p multi .55 .55

Feasts — A1210

2006, Dec. 30

1984 A1210 30p multi .20 .20

Post Day — A1211

2007, Jan. 2

1985 A1211 30p multi .20 .20

Ali El Kassar (1888-1957), Artist — A1212

2007, Jan. 15 ***Perf. 13¼x13***

1986 A1212 30p multi .20 .20

Automobile and Touring Club of Egypt — A1213

2007, Jan. 14 **Litho.** ***Perf. 12¾x13¼***

1987 A1213 30p multi .20 .20

Imperf

Size: 80x60mm

1988 A1213 150p multi .55 .55

Police Day — A1214

2007, Jan. 25 ***Perf. 12¾x13¼***

1989 A1214 30p multi .20 .20

Imperf

Size: 80x60mm

1990 A1214 150p multi .55 .55

Rededication of National Library — A1215

2007, Feb. 25 ***Perf. 12¾x13¼***

1991 A1215 30p multi .20 .20

Arabic Language Academy, 75th Anniv. — A1216

2007, Mar. 17 ***Perf. 13¼x12¾***

1992 A1216 30p multi .20 .20

World Health Day — A1217

2007, Apr. 7 **Litho.** ***Perf. 12¾x13¼***

1993 A1217 30p multi .20 .20

Egyptian Trade Union Federation, 50th Anniv. — A1218

2007, May 1 ***Perf. 13¼x12¾***

1994 A1218 30p multi .20 .20

Egypt Air, 75th Anniv. — A1219

Anniversary emblem and: 30p, Biplane. 150p, Biplane and jet.

2007, May 7 ***Perf. 12¾x13¼***

1995-1996 A1219 Set of 2 .65 .65

Return of Sinai to Egypt, 25th Anniv. — A1220

No. 1997: a, Monastery of St. Catherine. b, Salah el Din Castle. c, Sharm el-Sheikh. d, Oasis of Nabq.
Illustration reduced.

2007, Apr. 25 **Litho.** ***Perf. 12¾x13¼***

1997 A1220 30p Block of 4, #a-d .45 .45

Mevlana Jalal ad-Din ar-Rumi (1207-73), Islamic Philosopher
A1221

2007, May 8 ***Perf. 13¼x12¾***
1998 A1221 150p multi .55 .55

World Environment Day — A1222

Designs: 30p, Sinai baton blue butterfly. 150p, Melting ice, horiz.

Perf. 13¼x12¾, 12¾x13¼

2007, June 5
1999-2000 A1222 Set of 2 .65 .65

Scouting, Cent. — A1223

2007, June 6 ***Perf. 12¾x13¼***
2001 A1223 150p multi .55 .55

EuroMed Postal Conference, Marseille, France — A1224

2007, July 9
2002 A1224 150p multi .55 .55

Diplomatic Relations Between Egypt and Nepal, 50th Anniv. — A1225

2007, July 16
2003 A1225 150p multi .55 .55

Egyptian Air Force, 75th Anniv. — A1226

2007, Oct. 14 Litho. ***Perf. 13x13¼***
2004 A1226 30p multi .20 .20

A1227

11th Arab Games — A1228

Illustration A1228 reduced.

2007, Oct. 26 Litho. ***Perf. 13¼x12¾***
2005 A1227 150p multi .55 .55

Imperf

Size: 95x75mm

2006 A1228 150p multi .55 .55

Assiut University, 50th Anniv. — A1229

2007, Nov. 27 ***Perf. 13¼x12¾***
2007 A1229 30p brn & blk .20 .20

Hafez Ibrahim (1872-1932), Poet — A1230

Ahmed Shawky (1868-1932), Poet — A1231

2007, Dec. 16
2008 A1230 30p multi .20 .20
2009 A1231 30p multi .20 .20

Egyptian Handball Federation, 50th Anniv. — A1232

2007, Dec. 30
2010 A1232 30p multi .20 .20

Musicians — A1233

2008, Jan. 1 ***Perf. 12¾x13¼***
2011 A1233 30p multi .20 .20

Post Day — A1234

Illustration reduced.

2008, Feb. 7 Litho. ***Imperf.***
2012 A1234 150p multi .55 .55

Africa Cup of Nations Soccer Championships, Ghana — A1235

2008, Feb. 10 ***Perf. 13¼x13***
2013 A1235 30p multi .20 .20

Wadi El-Hitan UNESCO World Heritage Site — A1236

No. 2014: a, Whale bones on ground. b, Whale skeleton.

2008, Feb. 10 ***Perf. 13x13¼***
2014 Horiz. pair with central label .25 .25
a.-b. A1236 30p Either single .20 .20

Cairo University, Cent. — A1237

2008, Apr. 14 ***Perf. 13¼x13***
2015 A1237 30p multi .20 .20

Land Mine Clearance in Northwest Egypt — A1238

No. 2016 — Map and: a, Amputee surrounded by land mines. b, Hand, "no land mines" symbol, vert.

Perf. 13x13¼, 13¼x13 (#2016b)

2008, Apr. 22
2016 A1238 150p Pair, #a-b 1.10 1.10

Telecom Africa Conference
A1239

2008, May 12 ***Perf. 13¼x13***
2017 A1239 30p multi .20 .20

World Environment Day — A1240

Background colors: 30p, Blue. 150p, Lilac.

2008, June 5
2018-2019 A1240 Set of 2 .70 .70

Faculty of Fine Arts, Cent. — A1241

No. 2020 — Background color: a, 30p, Blue. b, 150p, Green.

2008, June 21 Litho. ***Perf. 13¼x13***
2020 A1241 Horiz. pair, #a-b .70 .70

Pan African Postal Union Plenipotentiary Conference, Cairo — A1242

2008, June 28 ***Perf. 13x13¼***
2021 A1242 150p multi .60 .60

Egypt Air Joining Star Alliance — A1243

2008, July 11
2022 A1243 150p multi .60 .60

Alexandria, 2008 Islamic Cultural Capital — A1244

2008, July 26
2023 A1244 150p multi .60 .60

Arab Post Day — A1245

No. 2024 — Emblem and: a, World map, pigeon. b, Camel caravan.
Illustration reduced.

2008, Aug. 3
2024 Horiz. pair 1.25 1.25
a.-b. A1245 150p Either single .60 .60

Men's Sports Education Faculty, 50th Anniv. — A1247

2008, Oct. 15 Litho. ***Perf. 13¼x13***
2026 A1247 30p multi .20 .20

SEMI-POSTAL STAMPS

Catalogue values for unused stamps in this section are for Never Hinged items.

Princess Ferial — SP1

Perf. 13½x14
1940, May 17 Photo. Wmk. 195
B1 SP1 5m + 5m copper brown 2.50 .75

No. B1 Overprinted in Green

1943, Nov. 17
B2 SP1 5m + 5m 9.00 6.00
a. Arabic date "1493" 200.00 200.00

The surtax on Nos. B1 and B2 was for the children's fund.

First Postage Stamp of Egypt SP2

Khedive Ismail Pasha SP3

No. B5, King Fuad. No. B6, King Farouk.

Perf. 13x13½
1946, Feb. 28 Wmk. 195
B3 SP2 1m + 1m gray .30 .25
B4 SP3 10m + 10m violet .40 .25
B5 SP3 17m + 17m brown .40 .25
B6 SP3 22m + 22m yel grn .40 .25
a. Souv. sheet, #B3-B6, perf. 8½ 35.00 35.00
b. As "a," imperf. 35.00 35.00
Nos. B3-B6 (4) 1.50 1.00

80th anniv. of Egypt's 1st postage stamp.
Nos. B6a, B6b measure 129x171mm.

Goddess Hathor, King Men-kau-Re (Mycerinus) and Jackalheaded Goddess — SP7

Ramesseum, Thebes — SP8

Queen Nefertiti SP9

Funerary Mask of King Tutankhamen SP10

Perf. 13½x13
1947, Mar. 9 Wmk. 195
B9 SP7 5m + 5m slate 2.00 .50
B10 SP8 15m + 15m dp blue 2.00 .70
B11 SP9 30m + 30m henna brn 2.00 1.00
B12 SP10 50m + 50m brown 3.00 1.10
Nos. B9-B12 (4) 9.00 3.30

Intl. Exposition of Contemporary Art, Cairo.

Boy Scout Emblem — SP11

Scout Emblems: 20m+10m, Sea Scouts. 35m+15m, Air Explorers.

1956, July 25 Photo. ***Perf. 13½x13***
B13 SP11 10m + 10m green 1.00 .40
B14 SP11 20m + 10m ultra 1.50 .60
B15 SP11 35m + 15m blue 2.00 .70
Nos. B13-B15 (3) 4.50 1.70

2nd Arab Scout Jamboree, Alexandria-Aboukir, 1956.
Souvenir sheets, perf. and imperf., contain one each of Nos. B13-B15. Size: 118x158mm. Value $750 each.

Ambulance — SP12

1957, May 13 ***Perf. 13x13½***
B16 SP12 10m + 5m rose red .40 .20

50th anniv. of the Public Aid Society.

United Arab Republic

Eye and Map of Africa, Europe and Asia SP13

Postal Emblem SP14

Perf. 13½x13
1958, Mar. 1 Photo. Wmk. 318
B17 SP13 10m + 5m orange 1.00 .40

1st Afro-Asian Cong. of Ophthalmology, Cairo.
The surtax was for centers to aid the blind.

1959, Jan. 2
B18 SP14 10m + 5m bl grn, red & blk .40 .20

Post Day. The surtax went to the social fund for postal employees.
See Syria UAR issues No. B1 for similar stamp with denominations in piasters (p).

Children and UN Emblem SP15

Arab League Building, Cairo, and Emblem SP16

1959, Oct. 24 Wmk. 328
B19 SP15 10m + 5m brown lake .30 .20
B20 SP15 35m + 10m dk blue .50 .20

Issued for International Children's Day and to honor UNICEF.

Braille Type of Regular Issue, 1961

1961, Apr. 6 ***Perf. 13½x13***
B21 A182 35m + 15m yel & brn .75 .25

1962, Mar. 22 Photo. Wmk. 328
B22 SP16 10m + 5m gray .40 .20

Arab Publicity Week, Mar. 22-28.
See No. N86.

Postal Emblem — SP17

Stamp of 1866 — SP18

1963, Jan. 2 Wmk. 342 *Perf. 11½*

B23	SP17 20m +10m brt grn, red & blk	.80	.60
B24	SP18 40m +20m blk & brn org	1.50	.90
B25	SP18 40m +20m brn org & blk	1.50	.90
a.	Pair, #B24-B25	3.50	3.00
	Nos. B23-B25 (3)	3.80	2.40

Post Day, Jan. 2 and 1966 exhibition of the FIP.

Arms of UAR and Pyramids SP19

1964, Jan. 2 Wmk. 342 *Perf. 11*

B26	SP19 10m + 5m org yel & grn	1.40	.80
B27	SP19 80m + 40m grnsh bl & blk	2.75	1.25
B28	SP19 115m + 55m org brn & blk	3.25	1.75
	Nos. B26-B28 (3)	7.40	3.80

Issued for Post Day. Jan. 2.

Type of 1963 and

SP20

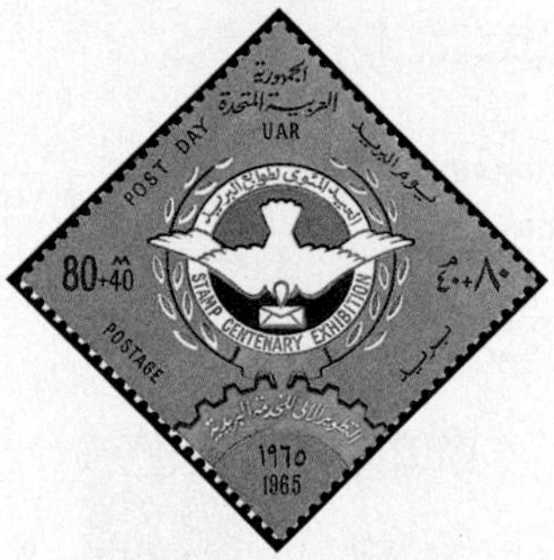

Postal Emblem — SP20a

No. B30, Emblem of Postal Secondary School. 80m+40m, Postal emblem, gearwheel, laurel wreath.

Perf. 11½

1965, Jan. 2 Unwmk. Photo.

B29	SP20 10m + 5m lt grn & car	.60	.40
B30	SP20 10m + 5m ultra, car & blk	.60	.40
a.	Pair, #B29-B30	1.50	1.25
B31	SP20a 80m + 40m rose, brt grn & blk	2.50	1.50
	Nos. B29-B31 (3)	3.70	2.30

Issued for Post Day, Jan. 2. No. B31 also publicizes the Stamp Centenary Exhibition.

Souvenir Sheet

Stamps of Egypt, 1866 — SP21

1966, Jan. 2 Wmk. 342 *Imperf.*

B32	SP21 140m + 60m blk, sl bl & rose	3.75	3.25

Post Day, 1966, and cent. of the 1st Egyptian postage stamps.

Pharaonic "Mediator" — SP22

Design: 115m+40m, Pharaonic guard.

1967, Jan. 2 Wmk. 342 *Perf. 11½*

B33	SP22 80m + 20m multi	3.00	2.00
B34	SP22 115m + 40m multi	4.75	3.00

Issued for Post Day, Jan. 2.

Grand Canal, Doges' Palace, Venice, and Santa Maria del Fiore, Florence — SP23

115m+30m, Piazetta and Campanile, Venice, and Palazzo Vecchio, Florence.

Perf. 11½x11

1967, Dec. 9 Photo. Wmk. 342

B35	SP23 80m + 20m grn, yel & brn	1.50	1.00
B36	SP23 115m + 30m ol, yel & sl bl	2.25	1.75

The surtax was to help save the cultural monuments of Venice and Florence, damaged in the 1966 floods.

Boy and Girl — SP24

Emblem and Flags of Arab League — SP25

Design: No. B38, Five children and arch.

Wmk. 342

1968, Dec. 11 Photo. *Perf. 11*

B37	SP24 20m + 10m car, bl & lt brn	.75	.50
B38	SP24 20m + 10m vio bl, sep & lt grn	.75	.50

Children's Day & 22nd anniv. of UNICEF.

1969, Mar. 22 *Perf. 11x11½*

B39	SP25 20m + 10m multi	.45	.25

Arab Publicity Week, Mar. 22-28.

Refugee Family SP26

1969, Oct. 24 Photo. *Perf. 11½*

B40	SP26 30m + 10m multi	.70	.40

Issued for United Nations Day.

Men of Three Races, Human Rights Emblem SP27

1970, Mar. 21 *Perf. 11½x11*

B41	SP27 20m + 10m multi	.95	.70

Issued to publicize the International Day for the Elimination of Racial Discrimination.

Arab League Type

1970, Mar. 22 Wmk. 342

B42	A344 20m + 10m bl, grn & brn	.70	.55

Map of Palestine and Refugees SP28

Perf. 11½x11

1970, Oct. 24 Photo. Wmk. 342

B43	SP28 20m + 10m multi	.75	.60

25th anniv. of the UN and to draw attention to the plight of the Palestinian refugees.

Arab Republic of Egypt

Blind Girl, WHO and Society Emblems — SP29

1973, Oct. 24 Photo. *Perf. 11x11½*

B44	SP29 20m + 10m blue & gold	.65	.50

25th anniv. of WHO and for the Light and Hope Soc., which educates and helps blind girls.

Map of Africa, OAU Emblem SP30

Social Work Day Emblem SP31

Perf. 11x11½

1973, Dec. 8 Photo. Wmk. 342

B45	SP30 55m + 20m multi	1.75	1.00

Organization for African Unity, 10th anniv.

1973, Dec. 8

B46	SP31 20m + 10m multi	.75	.65

Social Work Day.

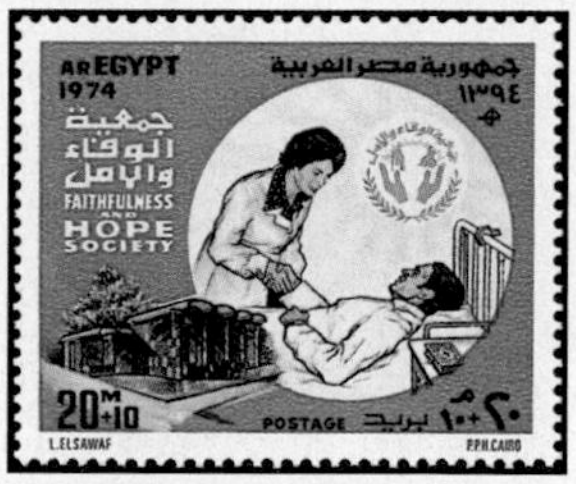

Jihan al Sadat Consoling Wounded Man — SP32

1974, Mar. 21 Wmk. 342 *Perf. 11*

B47	SP32 20m + 10m multi	.90	.70

Faithfulness and Hope Society.

Afghan Solidarity SP33

Wmk. 342

1981, July 15 Photo. *Perf. 11½*

B48	SP33 20m + 10m multi	1.25	1.25

Size: 30x25mm

1981 Photo. *Perf. 11½*

B49	SP33 20m + 10m multi	4.00	3.50

Map of Sudan, Dunes, Dead Tree — SP34

1986, Mar. 25 Photo. *Perf. 13x13½*

B50	SP34 15p + 5p multi	1.60	1.00

Fight against drought and desertification of the Sudan. Surtax for drought relief.

Organization of African Unity, 25th Anniv. — SP35

1988, May 25 Litho. *Perf. 13*

B51	SP35 15p +10p multi	.90	.90

AIR POST STAMPS

Mail Plane in Flight AP1

Perf. 13x13½

1926, Mar. 10 Wmk. 195 Photo.

C1	AP1 27m deep violet	17.00	15.00

1929, July 17

C2	AP1 27m orange brown	4.50	2.25

Zeppelin Issue

No. C2 Surcharged in Blue or Violet

1931, Apr. 6

C3	AP1	50m on 27m (Bl)	52.50	52.50
a.		"1951" instead of "1931"	57.50	57.50
C4	AP1	100m on 27m (V)	52.50	*62.50*

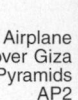

Airplane over Giza Pyramids AP2

1933-38 Litho. *Perf. 13x13½*

C5	AP2	1m orange & blk	.40	.25
C6	AP2	2m gray & blk	.80	.55
C7	AP2	2m org red & blk ('38)	2.00	.75
C8	AP2	3m ol brn & blk	.60	.20
C9	AP2	4m green & blk	.90	.45
C10	AP2	5m dp brown & blk	.40	.20
C11	AP2	6m dk green & blk	1.50	.65
C12	AP2	7m dk blue & blk	1.00	.55
C13	AP2	8m violet & blk	.60	.20
C14	AP2	9m dp red & blk	2.50	.75
C15	AP2	10m violet & brn	.75	.25
C16	AP2	20m dk green & brn	.60	.20
C17	AP2	30m dull blue & brn	.75	.20
C18	AP2	40m dp red & brn	15.00	.60
C19	AP2	50m orange & brn	12.00	.25
C20	AP2	60m gray & brn	3.75	.55
C21	AP2	70m dk blue & bl grn	3.50	.50
C22	AP2	80m ol brn & bl grn	3.50	.50
C23	AP2	90m org & bl grn	4.00	.50
C24	AP2	100m vio & bl grn	7.00	.50
C25	AP2	200m dp red & bl grn	10.00	1.00
		Nos. C5-C25 (21)	71.55	9.60

See Nos. C34-C37. For overprint see No. C38.

Type of 1933

1941-43 Photo.

C34	AP2	5m copper brn ('43)	.25	.25
C35	AP2	10m violet	.50	.25
C36	AP2	25m dk vio brn ('43)	.50	.25
C37	AP2	30m green	.65	.25
		Nos. C34-C37 (4)	1.90	1.00

Catalogue values for unused stamps in this section, from this point to the end of the section, are for Never Hinged items.

No. C37 Overprinted in Black

1946, Oct. 1

C38	AP2	30m green	.50	.35
a.		Double overprint	400.00	—
b.		Inverted overprint	400.00	—

Middle East Intl. Air Navigation Congress, Cairo, Oct. 1946.

King Farouk, Delta Dam and DC-3 Plane AP3

Perf. 13x13½

1947, Feb. 19 Photo. Wmk. 195

C39	AP3	2m red orange	.25	*.55*
C40	AP3	3m dk brown	.25	*.60*
C41	AP3	5m red brown	.25	.20
C42	AP3	7m dp yellow org	.45	.20
C43	AP3	8m green	.45	*.70*
C44	AP3	10m violet	.40	.20
C45	AP3	20m brt blue	.50	.20
C46	AP3	30m brown violet	.60	.20
C47	AP3	40m carmine rose	1.50	.60
C48	AP3	50m Prus green	1.75	.70
C49	AP3	100m olive green	3.25	.75
C50	AP3	200m dark gray	7.00	2.75
		Nos. C39-C50 (12)	16.65	7.65

For overprints see Nos. C51-C64, C67-C89, NC1-NC30.

Nos. C49 and C50 Surcharged in Black

1948, Aug. 23

C51	AP3	13m on 100m	.50	.40
C52	AP3	22m on 200m	.60	*.75*
a.		Date omitted		

Inaugural flights of "Services Aeriens Internationaux d'Egypte" from Cairo to Athens and Rome, Aug. 23, 1948.

Nos. C39 to C50 Overprinted in Various Colors

Overprint 27mm Wide

1952, Jan. Wmk. 195 *Perf. 13x13½*

C53	AP3	2m red orange (Bl)	.35	.20
C54	AP3	3m dark brown (RV)	.80	.80
C55	AP3	5m red brown	.35	.35
C56	AP3	7m dp yel org (Bl)	.70	.40
C57	AP3	8m green (RV)	1.00	.80
C58	AP3	10m violet (G)	.80	.80
C59	AP3	20m brt blue (RV)	3.25	1.00
C60	AP3	30m brown vio (G)	1.00	.40
C61	AP3	40m carmine rose	4.00	3.00
C62	AP3	50m Prus green (RV)	1.50	1.25
C63	AP3	100m olive green	5.00	2.00
C64	AP3	200m dark gray (RV)	10.00	4.00
		Nos. C53-C64 (12)	28.75	15.00

See notes after No. 316.

Delta Dam and Douglas DC-3 AP4

1953 Photo.

C65	AP4	5m red brown	.50	.50
C66	AP4	15m olive green	1.00	1.00

For overprints see Nos. NC31-NC32.

Nos. C39-C49 Overprinted in Black with Three Bars to Obliterate Portrait

1953

C67	AP3	2m red orange	1.50	1.50
C68	AP3	3m dk brown	1.20	1.20
C69	AP3	5m red brown	.80	.80
C70	AP3	7m dp yellow org	.50	.50
C71	AP3	8m green	1.20	1.20
C72	AP3	10m violet	*35.00*	
C73	AP3	20m brt blue	1.50	.30
C74	AP3	30m brown violet	1.75	.90
C75	AP3	40m carmine rose	1.75	1.00
C76	AP3	50m Prus green	3.25	1.75
C77	AP3	100m olive green	4.25	2.75
C77A	AP3	200m gray	*60.00*	

Nos. C72 and C77A are in question. They are not known postally used.

Nos. C53-C64 Overprinted in Black with Three Bars to Obliterate Portrait

1953

C78	AP3	2m red orange	.60	.35
C79	AP3	3m dark brown	1.10	.80
C80	AP3	5m red brown	.40	.25
C82	AP3	8m green	.80	*1.50*
C83	AP3	10m violet	.70	*1.25*
C85	AP3	30m brown violet	1.50	1.25
C87	AP3	50m Prus green	4.00	2.00
C88	AP3	100m olive green	6.00	3.00
C89	AP3	200m dark gray	10.00	10.00
		Nos. C78-C89 (9)	25.10	20.40

Practically all values of Nos. C67-C89 exist with double overprint. The 7m, 20m and 40m with this overprint are forgeries.

United Arab Republic
Type of Regular Issue

Perf. 11½x11

1958, Mar. 22 Photo. Wmk. 318

C90	A141	15m ultra & red brn	.40	.25

Pyramids at Giza AP5

Al Azhar University AP6

Designs: 15m, Colossi of Memnon, Thebes. 90m, St. Catherine Monastery, Mt. Sinai.

1959-60 Wmk. 328 *Perf. 13x13½*

C91	AP5	5m bright red	.25	.20
C92	AP5	15m dk dull violet	.35	.30
C93	AP6	60m dk green	.75	.50
C94	AP5	90m brown car ('60)	1.50	1.00
		Nos. C91-C94 (4)	2.85	2.00

Nos. C91-C93 exist imperf. See Nos. C101, C105, NC33.

Tower of Cairo Type, Redrawn

1961, May 1 *Perf. 13½x13*

C95	A183	50m bright blue	.90	.45

Top inscription has been replaced by two airplanes.

Weather Vane, Anemometer and UN World Meteorological Organization Emblem — AP7

Perf. 11½x11

1962, Mar. 23 Photo. Unwmk.

C96	AP7	60m yellow & dp blue	1.50	.90

2nd World Meteorological Day, Mar. 23.

Patrice Lumumba and Map of Africa — AP8

Perf. 13½x13

1962, July 1 Wmk. 328

C97	AP8	35m multicolored	.65	.35

Patrice Lumumba (1925-61), Premier of Congo.

Maritime Station, Alexandria — AP9

Designs: 30m, International Airport, Cairo. 40m, Railroad Station, Luxor.

1963, Mar. 18 *Perf. 13x13½*

C98	AP9	20m dark brown	.60	.20
C99	AP9	30m carmine rose	.85	.35
C100	AP9	40m black	1.50	.90
		Nos. C98-C100 (3)	2.95	1.45

Type of 1959-60 and

Temple of Queen Nefertari, Abu Simbel AP10

Arch and Tower of Cairo — AP11

Designs: 80m, Al Azhar University seen through arch. 140m, Ramses II, Abu Simbel.

Perf. 11½x11, 11x11½

1963-65 Photo. Wmk. 342

C101	AP6	80m vio blk & brt bl	3.75	1.50
C102	AP10	115m brown & yel	2.75	1.25
C103	AP10	140m pale vio, blk & org red	2.75	1.25

Unwmk.

C104	AP11	50m yel brn & brt bl	2.25	1.00
C105	AP6	80m vio bl & lt bl	3.50	1.50
		Nos. C101-C105 (5)	15.00	6.50

Issued: 50m, 11/2/64; No. C105, 2/13/65; others, 10/24/63.

See Nos. NC34-NC36.

Weather Vane, Anemometer and WMO Emblem — AP12

Perf. 11½x11

1965, Mar. 23 Wmk. 342

C106	AP12	80m dk blue & rose lil	2.50	1.25

Fifth World Meteorological Day.

See No. NC37.

Game Board from Tomb of Tutankhamen — AP13

1965, July 1 Photo. Unwmk.

C107	AP13	10m yellow & dk blue	1.25	.40

See No. NC38.

Temples at Abu Simbel — AP14

1966, Apr. 28 Wmk. 342 Perf. 11½

C108 AP14 20m multicolored 1.00 .40
C109 AP14 80m multicolored 2.00 1.10

Issued to commemorate the transfer of the temples of Abu Simbel to a hilltop, 1963-66.

Scout Camp and Jamboree Emblem AP15

1966, Aug. 10 Perf. 11½x11

C110 AP15 20m olive & rose 1.40 .45

7th Pan-Arab Boy Scout Jamboree, Good Daim, Libya, Aug. 12.

St. Catherine Monastery, Mt. Sinai — AP16

1966, Nov. 30 Photo. Wmk. 342

C111 AP16 80m multicolored 2.10 1.25

St. Catherine Monastery, Sinai, 1400th anniv.

Cairo Airport AP17

1967, Apr. 26 Perf. 11½x11

C112 AP17 20m sky bl, sl grn & lt brn .85 .35

Hotel El Alamein and Map of Nile Delta AP18

Intl. Tourist Year: 80m, The Virgin's Tree, Virgin Mary and Child. 115m, Fishing in the Red Sea.

1967, June 7 Wmk. 342 Perf. 11½

C113 AP18 20m dull pur, sl grn & dl org .75 .25
C114 AP18 80m blue & multi 2.25 1.00
C115 AP18 115m brown, org & bl 4.00 2.00
Nos. C113-C115 (3) 7.00 3.25

Oil Derricks, Map of Egypt AP19

1967, July 23 Photo.

C116 AP19 50m org & bluish blk 1.10 .75

15th anniversary of the revolution.

Type of Regular Issue, 1967

Design: 80m, Back of Tutankhamen's throne and UNESCO emblem.

1967, Oct. 24 Wmk. 342 Perf. 11½

C117 A301 80m blue & yellow 1.25 .85

Koran — AP20

1968, Mar. 25 Wmk. 342 Perf. 11½

C118 AP20 30m lilac, bl & yel .75 .60
C119 AP20 80m lilac, bl & yel 1.50 .80
a. Pair, #C118-C119 + label 3.00 2.50

1400th anniv. of the Koran. Nos. C118-C119 are printed in miniature sheets of 4 containing 2 each of Nos. C118-C119.

St. Mark and St. Mark's Cathedral — AP21

1968, June 25 Wmk. 342 Perf. 11½

C120 AP21 80m brt grn, dk brn & dp car 1.50 .70

Martyrdom of St. Mark, 1900th anniv. and the consecration of St. Mark's Cathedral, Cairo.

Map of United Arab Airlines and Boeing 707 AP22

Design: No. C122, Ilyushin 18 and routes of United Arab Airlines.

1968-69 Photo. Perf. 11½x11

C121 AP22 55m blue, ocher & car 1.25 .65
C122 AP22 55m bl, yel & vio blk ('69) 1.10 .65

1st flights of a Boeing 707 and an Ilyushin 18 for United Arab Airlines.

Mahatma Gandhi, Arms of India and UAR AP23

Imam El Boukhary AP24

1969, Sept. 10 Perf. 11x11½

C123 AP23 80m lt blue, ocher & brn 3.25 1.50

Mohandas K. Gandhi (1869-1948), leader in India's fight for independence.

1969, Dec. 27 Photo. Wmk. 342

C124 AP24 30m lt olive & dk brown .70 .20

1100th anniv. of the death of the Imam El Boukhary (824-870), philosopher and writer.

Azzahir Beybars Mosque AP25

1969, Dec. 27 Engr. Perf. 11½x11

C125 AP25 30m red lilac .50 .20

700th anniv. of the founding of the Azzahir Beybars Mosque, Cairo.

Lenin (1870-1924) — AP26

Perf. 11x11½

1970, Apr. 22 Photo. Wmk. 342

C126 AP26 80m lt green & brown 1.75 1.00

Phantom Fighters and Destroyed Factory AP27

1970, May 1 Perf. 11½x11

C127 AP27 80m yel, grn & dk vio brn 1.50 .90

Issued to commemorate the destruction of the Abu-Zaabal factory by Israeli planes.

UPU Type of Regular Issue

1970, May 20 Photo. Wmk. 342

C128 A350 80m multicolored 1.20 .85

Nasser and Burial Mosque — AP28

1970, Nov. 6 Wmk. 342 Perf. 11

C129 AP28 30m olive & blk .75 .30
C130 AP28 80m brown & blk 1.75 .80

Gamal Abdel Nasser (1918-70), Pres. of Egypt.

Postal Congress Type

Perf. 11½x11

1971, Mar. 6 Photo. Wmk. 342

C131 A365 30m lt ol, org & sl grn .80 .40

Nasser, El Rifaei and Sultan Hussein Mosques AP29

Designs: 85m, Nasser and Ramses Square, Cairo. 110m, Nasser, Sphinx and pyramids.

Perf. 11½x11

1971, July 1 Photo. Wmk. 342

C132 AP29 30m multicolored 2.50 .75
C133 AP29 85m multicolored 4.00 1.00
C134 AP29 110m multicolored 5.50 1.50
Nos. C132-C134 (3) 12.00 3.25

APU Type of Regular Issue

1971, Aug. 3 Wmk. 342 Perf. 11½

C135 A373 30m brown, yel & bl .85 .40

Arab Republic of Egypt Confederation Type

Perf. 11½x11

1971, Sept. 28 Photo. Wmk. 342

C136 A374 30m gray, sl grn & dk pur .80 .40

Al Aqsa Mosque and Woman AP30

Wmk. 342

1971, Oct. 24 Photo. Perf. 11½

C137 AP30 30m bl, yel, brn & grn 1.60 .40

25th anniv. of the UN (in 1970) and return of Palestinian refugees.

Postal Union Type

30m, African Postal Union emblem & letter.

1971, Dec. 2 Perf. 11½x11

C138 A384 30m green, blk & bl 1.40 .40

Aida, Triumphal March AP31

1971, Dec. 23 Wmk. 342 Perf. 11½

C139 AP31 110m dk brn, yel & sl grn 5.50 2.75

Centenary of the first performance of the opera Aida, by Giuseppe Verdi.

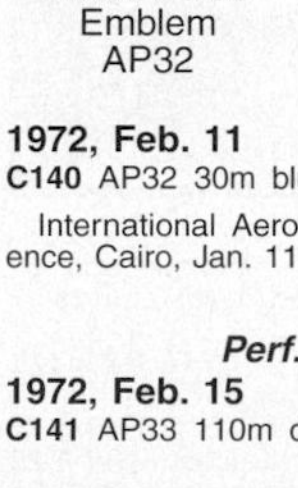

Globe, Glider, Rocket Club Emblem AP32

St. Catherine's Monastery on Fire AP33

1972, Feb. 11 Perf. 11x11½

C140 AP32 30m blue, ocher & yel 1.25 .40

International Aerospace Education Conference, Cairo, Jan. 11-13.

Perf. 11½x11

1972, Feb. 15 Unwmk.

C141 AP33 110m dp car, org & blk 4.25 3.00

The burning of St. Catherine's Monastery in Sinai Desert, Nov. 30, 1971.

Tutankhamen in Garden — AP34

Tutankhamen, from 2nd Sarcophagus — AP35

Design: No. C143, Ankhesenamun.

1972, May 22 Photo. *Perf. 11½*

C142	AP34	110m brn org, bl & grn	8.50	4.00
C143	AP34	110m brn org, bl & grn	8.50	4.00
a.		Pair, #C142-C143	24.00	20.00

Souvenir Sheet

Imperf

C144	AP35	200m gold & multi	30.00	27.50

50th anniv. of the discovery of the tomb of Tutankhamen. No. C143a has continuous design.

Souvenir Sheet

Flag of Confederation of Arab Republics — AP36

1972, July 23 Photo. *Imperf.*

C145	AP36	110m gold, dp car & blk	4.25	4.00

20th anniversary of the revolution.

Temples at Abu Simbel AP37

Designs: 30m, Al Azhar Mosque and St. George's Church. 110m, Pyramids at Giza.

1972 Wmk. 342 *Perf. 11½x11*

C146	AP37	30m blue, brn & buff	2.00	.35
C147	AP37	85m bl, brn & ocher	3.00	1.25
C148	AP37	110m multicolored	4.75	1.25
		Nos. C146-C148 (3)	9.75	2.85

Issued: Nos. C146, C148, 11/22; No. C147, 8/1.

Olympic Type of Regular Issue

Olympic and Motion Emblems and: No. C149, Handball. No. C150, Weight lifting. 50m, Swimming. 55m, Gymnastics. All vertical.

1972, Aug. 17 *Perf. 11x11½*

C149	A396	30m multicolored	.75	.35
C150	A396	30m yellow & multi	.75	.35
C151	A396	50m blue & multi	1.50	.80
C152	A396	55m multicolored	1.75	.90
		Nos. C149-C152 (4)	4.75	2.40

Champollion, Rosetta Stone, Hieroglyphics — AP38

1972, Oct. 16

C153	AP38	110m gold, grn & blk	7.50	2.50

Sesquicentennial of the deciphering of Egyptian hieroglyphics by Jean-François Champollion.

World Map, Telephone, Radar, ITU Emblem — AP39

1973, Mar. 21 Photo. *Perf. 11*

C154	AP39	30m lt bl, dk bl & blk	.90	.25

5th World Telecommunications Day.

Karnak Temple, Luxor — AP40

Hand Dripping Blood and Falling Plane — AP41

1973, Mar. 21

C155	AP40	110m dp ultra, blk & rose	4.75	2.25

Sound and light at Karnak.

1973, May 1 *Perf. 11x11½*

C156	AP41	110m multicolored	6.00	1.75

Israeli attack on Libyan civilian plane, Feb. 1973.

WMO Emblem, Weather Vane — AP42

1973, Oct. 24 *Perf. 11x11½*

C157	AP42	110m blue, gold & pur	2.75	1.75

Cent. of intl. meteorological cooperation.

Refugees, Map of Palestine AP43

1973, Oct. 24 *Perf. 11½*

C158	AP43	30m dk brn, yel & bl	1.60	.50

Plight of Palestinian refugees.

INTERPOL Emblem AP44

Postal and UPU Emblems AP45

Perf. 11x11½

1973, Dec. 8 Photo. Wmk. 342

C159	AP44	110m black & multi	3.50	1.75

Intl. Criminal Police Organization, 50th anniv.

1974, Jan. 2 Unwmk. *Perf. 11*

Post Day (UPU Emblems and): 30m, APU emblem. 55m, African Postal Union emblem. 110m, UPU emblem.

Size: 26x46½mm

C160	AP45	20m gray, red & blk	.40	.20
C161	AP45	30m sal, blk & pur	.60	.20
C162	AP45	55m emerald, blk & brt mag	1.25	.50

Size: 37x37½mm

Perf. 11½

C163	AP45	110m lt bl, blk & gold	1.50	1.00
		Nos. C160-C163 (4)	3.75	1.90

Solar Bark of Khufu (Cheops) — AP46

Wmk. 342

1974, Mar. 21 Photo. *Perf. 11½*

C164	AP46	110m blue, gold & brn	3.00	2.10

Solar Bark Museum.

Hotel Meridien AP47

1974, Oct. 6 *Perf. 11½x11*

C165	AP47	110m multicolored	2.00	1.10

Opening of Hotel Meridien, Cairo.

Suez Canal Type of 1975

1975, June 5 *Perf. 11½*

C166	A448	30m bl, yel grn & ind	1.50	.45
C167	A448	110m indigo & blue	2.50	1.25

Irrigation Commission Emblem — AP48

1975, July 20

C168	AP48	110m orange & dk grn	2.00	1.00

9th Intl. Congress on Irrigation and Drainage, Moscow, and 25th anniv. of the Intl. Commission on Irrigation and Drainage.

Refugees and UNWRA Emblem — AP49

Woman and IWY Emblem — AP50

Perf. 11x11½

1975, Oct. 24 Photo. Wmk. 342

C169	AP49	30m multicolored	1.25	.40

Unwmk.

C170	AP50	110m olive, org & blk	3.00	1.75

UN Day. 30m publicizes UN help for refugees; 110m is for Intl. Women's Year 1975.

Step Pyramid, Sakhara, and Entrance Gate AP51

Designs: 45m, 60m, Plane over Giza Pyramids. 140m, Plane over boats on Nile.

Perf. 11½x11

1978-82 Photo. Wmk. 342

C171	AP51	45m yel & brown	.55	.20
C171A	AP51	60m olive	1.25	.75
C172	AP51	115m blue & brown	.85	.50
C173	AP51	140m blue & purple	1.90	.85
C173A	AP51	185m bl, sep & gray brn	4.50	1.75
		Nos. C171-C173A (5)	9.05	4.05

Issued: 60m, 1/15/82; 185m, 1982; others, 1/1/78.

Flyer and UN ICAO Emblem — AP52

Perf. 11x11½

1978, Dec. 30 Photo. Wmk. 342

C174	AP52	140m blue, blk & brn	1.90	.95

75th anniversary of 1st powered flight.

Seeing Eye Medallion AP53

Perf. 11½x11

1981, Oct. 1 Photo. Wmk. 342

C175 AP53 230m multicolored 2.25 1.00

Hilton Ramses Hotel Opening — AP54

Perf. 11x11½

1982, Mar. 15 Photo. Wmk. 342

C176 AP54 18½p multi 1.75 .75

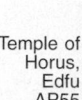

Temple of Horus, Edfu AP55

Designs: 15p, like 6p. 18½p, 25p, Statue of Akhnaton, Thebes, hieroglyphics, vert. 23p, 30p, Giza pyramids.

1985 Photo. *Perf. 11½x11, 11x11½*

C177 AP55 6p lt blue & dk bl grn .75 .30
C178 AP55 15p grnsh bl & brn 1.25 .45
C179 AP55 18½p grn, sep & dp yel 1.60 .90
C180 AP55 23p grnsh bl, sep & yel bis 2.00 1.10
C181 AP55 25p lt bl, sep & yel bis 1.75 .80
a. Unwmkd. ('87) 2.25 1.00
C182 AP55 30p grnsh bl, sep & org yel 1.75 .70
a. Unwmkd. ('87) 2.25 1.00
Nos. C177-C182 (6) 9.10 4.25

Issued: 6p, 18½p, 23p, 3/1; 15p, 25p, 30p, 5/1.

See No. C236.

Post Day — AP56

Narmer Board, oldest known hieroglyphic inscriptions: No. C183a, Tablet obverse. No. C183b, Reverse.

1986, Jan. 2 Photo. *Perf. 13½x13*

C183 AP56 Pair 2.00 2.00
a.-b. 15p any single 1.00 1.00

Map, Jet, AFRAA Emblem AP57

1986, Apr. 7 Photo. *Perf. 11½*

C184 AP57 15p blue, yel & blk 1.00 1.00

African Airlines Assoc., 18th General Assembly, Cairo, Apr. 7-10.

World Food Day AP58

UNESCO, 40th Anniv. — AP59

Perf. 13½x13, 13x13½

1986, Oct. 24 Litho.

C185 AP58 15p multicolored .80 .80
C186 AP59 15p multicolored .80 .80

UN Day.

Tourism Year — AP60

Design: Column and Sphinx in Alexandria, St. Catherine's Monastery in Mt. Sinai, Colossi of Thebes and Temple of Theban Triad in Luxor.

Unwmk.

1987, Sept. 30 Litho. *Imperf.*

Size: 140x90mm

C187 AP60 30p multicolored 4.00 4.00

Palestinian Uprising — AP61

1988, Sept. 28 Litho. *Perf. 12x13½*

C188 AP61 25p multicolored 1.25 1.25

UN Day AP62

1988, Oct. 20 Litho. *Perf. 13x13½*

C189 AP62 25p multicolored 1.25 1.25

Nobel Prize Type of 1988

1988, Nov. 7

C190 A769 25p multicolored 1.25 1.25

Arab Cooperation Council — AP63

Architecture and Art — AP64

1989, May 10 Litho. *Perf. 13½x13*

C191 AP63 25p Flags 1.00 1.00

Size: 89x80mm

Imperf

C192 AP63 50p Flags, seal 3.25 3.25

1989-91 Photo. *Perf. 11x11½*

C193 AP64 20p Balcony .60 .60
C194 AP64 25p Brazier .80 .80
C195 AP64 35p shown 1.00 1.00
C196 AP64 45p Tapestry 1.40 1.40
C197 AP64 45p like #C195 1.40 1.40
C198 AP64 50p Stag (dish) 1.50 1.50
C199 AP64 55p 4 animals (plate) 1.75 1.75
C200 AP64 60p like #C198 2.00 2.00
C201 AP64 65p like #C198 2.25 2.25
C202 AP64 70p like #C193 2.40 2.40
C203 AP64 85p like #C199 2.75 2.75
Nos. C193-C203 (11) 17.85 17.85

Issued: 35p, 60p, 10/1/89; 55p, 1/1/90; No. C197, C202, 1/25/91; 65p, 85p, 7/20/91; others, 4/1/89.

AP65

Funerary Mask of King Tutankhamen — AP66

King Tutankhamen AP66a

1993-99 Litho. *Perf. 11½*

C204 AP65 55p multicolored 1.75 .95
C205 AP66 80p multicolored 3.00 1.25

Photo.

Perf. 11x11¼

C206 AP66a £1 black & brown 1.25 1.25
b. Wmk. 342 1.25 1.25
Nos. C204-C206 (3) 6.00 3.45

Issued: 55p, 80p, 3/1/93; £1, 1997; No. C206b, 1999.

See No. C231.

ICAO, 50th Anniv. — AP67

1994, Sept. 16 Litho. *Perf. 13*

C207 AP67 80p multicolored 1.00 1.00

Intl. Year of the Family — AP68

1994, Oct. 24 Litho. *Perf. 13*

C208 AP68 80p multicolored 1.00 1.00

Arab League for Education, Culture, & Science Organization — AP69

1995, July 25 Litho. *Perf. 13x13½*

C209 AP69 55p multicolored .70 .70

UN Organizations, 50th Anniv. — AP70

Perf. 12½x13, 13x12½

1995, Oct. 24 Litho.

C210 AP70 80p UN 1.75 1.75
C211 AP70 80p FAO 1.75 1.75
C212 AP70 80p UNESCO, vert. 1.75 1.75
Nos. C210-C212 (3) 5.25 5.25

Arab Summit, Cairo — AP71

1996, June 21 Litho. *Perf. 13x12½*

C213 AP71 55p multicolored .60 .60

16th Intl. Conference on Irrigation and Drainage, Cairo — AP72

1996, Sept. 15 Litho. *Perf. 12½x13*

C214 AP72 80p multicolored 1.10 1.10

Intl. Tourism Day — AP73

1996, Sept. 27 *Perf. 13*

C215 AP73 80p multicolored .90 .90

Arabian Horse Day — AP74

World Post Day — AP75

1996 *Perf. 13x12½*
C216 AP74 55p grn, blk & gray .60 .60

1996, Oct. 9 Litho. *Perf. 13x12½*
C217 AP75 80p multicolored 1.10 1.10

AP76

AP77

1996, Oct. 24
C218 AP76 55p multicolored .60 .60

Cairo, Arab cultural capital of 1996.

1996, Oct. 24
C219 AP77 80p multicolored 1.00 1.00

UNICEF, 50th anniv.

World Meteorological Day — AP78

Thutmose III — AP79

1997, Mar. 23 Litho. *Perf. 13x12½*
C220 AP78 £1 multicolored 1.25 1.25

1997, Mar. 25 Photo. *Perf. 11x11½*
C221 AP79 75p blk, bl & gray 1.10 1.10

Heinrich von Stephan (1831-97) — AP80

1997, Apr. 15 Litho. *Perf. 13*
C222 AP80 £1 multicolored 1.25 1.25

AP81

1997, Sept. 11
C223 AP81 £1 multicolored .90 .90

98th Intl. Parliamentary Conference, Cairo.

AP82

AP83

1997, Sept. 10 Litho. *Perf. 13*
C224 AP82 75p multicolored .90 .90

1997 Egyptian Team, top medal winners of 8th Pan Arab Games, Beirut, Lebanon.

1997, Sept. 27 *Perf. 13x12½*
C225 AP83 £1 multicolored 1.25 1.25

Sarabas (180-211), mumified Egyptian.

World Book and Copyright Day AP84

1997, Oct. 24 Litho. *Perf. 12½x13*
C226 AP84 £1 multicolored 1.25 1.25

African Ministries of Transport and Communications, 11th Conference — AP85

1997, Nov. 22 Litho. *Perf. 13x12½*
C227 AP85 75p multicolored .90 .90

Arab Scout Movement, 85th Anniv. — AP86

1997, Nov. 24 *Perf. 12½x13*
C228 AP86 75p multicolored .90 .90

8th G-15 Summit Meeting — AP87

Lighthouse of Alexandria AP88

1998, May 11 Litho. *Perf. 13*
C229 AP87 £1 multicolored 1.00 1.00

1998, May 20 Litho. *Perf. 13*
C230 AP88 £1 multicolored 1.25 1.25

King Tut Type of 1997

1998, July 25 Litho. *Perf. 11x11¼*
C231 AP66a 125p Tutankhamen 1.50 1.50
a. Wmk. 342 ('99) 1.50 1.50

AP90

AP91

1998, Aug. 3 *Perf. 13*
C232 AP90 £1 multicolored 1.10 1.10

Arab Post Day.

1998, Oct. 9 Litho. *Perf. 13*
C233 AP91 125p multicolored 1.25 1.25

World Post Day.

AP92

AP93

1998, Oct. 22
C234 AP92 125p multicolored 1.25 1.25

67th Interpol Meeting, Cairo.

1998, Oct. 24
C235 AP93 125p multicolored 1.25 1.25

Universal Declaration of Human Rights, 50th anniv.

Statue of Akhnaton Type of 1985

1998 Litho. *Perf. 13*
C236 AP55 25p lt bl, brn & tan 1.00 1.00

AP94

AP95

1999, Oct. 12 Litho. *Perf. 13x12¾*
C237 AP94 125p multicolored 1.75 1.75

Performance of opera "Aida" at the Pyramids.

1999, Oct. 16
C238 AP95 125p multicolored 1.75 1.75

Discovery of the Rosetta Stone, bicent.

World Tourism Day — AP96

Perf. 13¼x12¾

2000, Sept. 27 Litho.
C239 AP96 125p multi 1.50 1.50

Awarding of Nobel Prize for Chemistry to Dr. Ahmed Zewail — AP97

Illustration reduced.

1999, Dec. 10 ***Imperf.***
C240 AP97 125p multi 1.50 1.50

UN High Commissioner for Refugees, 50th Anniv. — AP98

2000, Dec. 13
C241 AP98 125p multi 1.75 1.75

AIR POST SEMI-POSTAL STAMPS

Catalogue values for unused stamps in this section are for Never Hinged items.

United Arab Republic

Pharaonic Mail Carriers and Papyrus Plants SPAP1

Design: 115m+55m, Jet plane, world map and stamp of Egypt, 1926 (No. C1).

Wmk. 342
1966, Jan. 2 Photo. ***Perf. 11½***
CB1 SPAP1 80m + 40m multi 2.50 2.00
CB2 SPAP1 115m + 55m multi 3.00 2.25
a. Pair, #CB1-CB2 7.50 7.00

Post Day, Jan. 2.

SPECIAL DELIVERY STAMPS

Motorcycle Postman — SD1

Perf. 13x13½
1926, Nov. 28 Photo. Wmk. 195
E1 SD1 20m dark green 30.00 8.50

1929, Sept.
E2 SD1 20m brown red & black 4.50 1.50

Inscribed "Postes Expres"

1943-44 Litho.
E3 SD1 26m brn red & gray blk 4.00 *6.00*
E4 SD1 40m dl brn & pale gray ('44) 2.50 1.00

For overprints see Nos. E5, NE1.

Catalogue values for unused stamps in this section, from this point to the end of the section, are for Never Hinged items.

No. E4 Overprinted in Black

Overprint 27mm Wide

1952, Jan.
E5 SD1 40m dl brn & pale gray 2.00 2.00

See notes after No. 316.

POSTAGE DUE STAMPS

D1

D2

Wmk. Crescent and Star (119)
1884, Jan. 1 Litho. ***Perf. 10½***
J1 D1 10pa red 40.00 9.00
a. Horiz. pair, imperf. vert. 150.00
J2 D1 20pa red 175.00 50.00
J3 D1 1pi red 125.00 40.00
J4 D1 2pi red 225.00 11.00
J5 D1 5pi red 20.00 *60.00*
Nos. J1-J5 (5) 585.00 170.00

1886, Aug. 1 Unwmk.
J6 D1 10pa red 52.50 7.00
a. Horiz. pair, imperf. vert. 135.00
J7 D1 20pa red 225.00 30.00
J8 D1 1pi red 26.00 5.00
a. Pair, imperf. between 200.00
J9 D1 2pi red 26.00 5.00
a. Pair, imperf. between 175.00
Nos. J6-J9 (4) 329.50 47.00

1888, Jan. 1 ***Perf. 11½***
J10 D2 2m green 10.00 *15.00*
a. Horiz. pair, imperf. between 225.00
J11 D2 5m rose red 35.00 14.00
J12 D2 1pi blue 140.00 40.00
a. Pair, imperf. between 300.00
J13 D2 2pi yellow 150.00 20.00
J14 D2 5pi gray 210.00 190.00
a. Period after "PIASTRES" 275.00 250.00
Nos. J10-J14 (5) 545.00 279.00

Excellent counterfeits of Nos. J1-J14 are plentiful.

There are 4 types of each of Nos. J1-J14, so placed that any block of 4 contains all types.

D3

Perf. 14x13½
1889 Wmk. 119 Typo.
J15 D3 2m green 7.00 .55
a. Half used as 1m on cover 275.00
J16 D3 4m maroon 2.50 .55
J17 D3 1pi ultra 6.25 .55
J18 D3 2pi orange 6.00 .80
a. Half used as 1p on cover —
Nos. J15-J18 (4) 21.75 2.45

Nos. J15-J18 exist on both ordinary and chalky paper. Imperf. examples of Nos. J15-J17 are proofs.

Black Surcharge

D4

1898
J19 D4 3m on 2pi orange .65 *2.75*
a. Inverted surcharge 65.00 *82.50*
c. Pair, one without surcharge —
f. Double surcharge 225.00 —

There are two types of this surcharge. In type I, the spacing between the last two Arabic characters at the right is 2mm. In type II, this spacing is 3mm, and there is an added sign on top of the second character from the right. See *Scott Classic Specialized Catalogue of Stamps & Covers* for detailed listing.

D5

D6

1921 Wmk. 120 ***Perf. 14x13½***
J20 D5 2m green .25 .25
J21 D5 4m vermilion 1.10 .90
J22 D6 10m deep blue 1.25 1.00
Nos. J20-J22 (3) 2.60 2.15

1921-22
J23 D5 2m vermilion .25 .20
J24 D5 4m green .25 .20
J25 D6 10m lake ('22) .50 .40
Nos. J23-J25 (3) 1.00 .80

Nos. J18, J23-J25 Overprinted

1922, Oct. 10 Wmk. 119
J26 D3 2pi orange 5.00 *5.00*
a. Overprint right side up 25.00 *25.00*

Wmk. 120
J27 D5 2m vermilion .60 *.90*
J28 D5 4m green .90 *.90*
J29 D6 10m lake 1.25 .90
Nos. J27-J29 (3) 2.75 2.70

Overprint on Nos. J26-J29 is inverted.

Arabic Numeral — D7

Perf. 13x13½
1927-56 Litho. Wmk. 195
Size: 18x22½mm
J30 D7 2m slate .60 .40
J31 D7 2m orange ('38) .80 .50
J32 D7 4m green .60 .45
J33 D7 4m ol brn ('32) 6.25 4.25
J34 D7 5m brown 3.50 .80
J35 D7 6m gray grn ('41) 1.50 1.50
J36 D7 8m brn vio 1.00 .40
J37 D7 10m brick red ('29) 1.00 .30
a. 10m deep red 1.10 .35
J38 D7 12m rose lake ('41) 1.50 1.50
J38A D7 20m dk red ('56) 2.00 2.00

Perf. 14
Size: 22x28mm
J39 D7 30m purple 4.25 2.25
Nos. J30-J39 (11) 23.00 14.35

See Nos. J47-J59. For overprints see Nos. J40-J46, NJ1-NJ7.

Catalogue values for unused stamps in this section, from this point to the end of the section, are for Never Hinged items.

Postage Due Stamps and Type of 1927 Overprinted in Various Colors

1952, Jan. 16 ***Perf. 13x13½***
J40 D7 2m orange (Bl) 1.25 1.00
J41 D7 4m green 1.25 1.00
J42 D7 6m gray grn (RV) 1.50 1.25
J43 D7 8m brn vio (Bl) 2.00 1.75
J44 D7 10m dl rose (Bl) 3.50 2.75
a. 10m brown red (Bk) 3.00 3.00
J45 D7 12m rose lake (Bl) 1.75 1.75

Perf. 14
J46 D7 30m purple (C) 2.75 2.75
Nos. J40-J46 (7) 14.00 12.25

See notes after No. 316.

United Arab Republic

1960 Wmk. 318 ***Perf. 13x13½***
Size: 18x22½mm
J47 D7 2m orange .50 .25
J48 D7 4m light green 1.00 .25
J49 D7 6m green 1.50 .50
J50 D7 8m brown vio 3.00 1.25
J51 D7 12m rose brown 5.00 1.65
J52 D7 20m dull rose brn 1.00 .25

Perf. 14
Size: 22x28mm
J53 D7 30m violet 5.00 1.50
Nos. J47-J53 (7) 17.00 5.65

1962 Wmk. 328 ***Perf. 13x13½***
Size: 18x22½mm
J54 D7 2m salmon .50 .50
J55 D7 4m light green .75 .75
J56 D7 10m red brown 1.50 1.50
J57 D7 12m rose brown 3.50 3.50
J58 D7 20m dull rose brn 7.50 7.50

Perf. 14
Size: 22x28mm
J59 D7 30m light violet 10.00 10.00
Nos. J54-J59 (6) 23.75 23.75

D8

1965 Unwmk. Photo. ***Perf. 11***
J60 D8 2m org & vio blk .60 .50
J61 D8 8m lt bl & dk bl 1.00 .60
J62 D8 10m yel & emer 1.50 .75
J63 D8 20m lt bl & vio blk 2.00 1.25
J64 D8 40m org & emer 3.75 2.00
Nos. J60-J64 (5) 8.85 5.10

MILITARY STAMPS

The "British Forces" and "Army post" stamps were special issues provided at a reduced rate for the purchase and use by the British military forces in Egypt and their families for ordinary letters sent to Great Britain and Ireland by a concessionary arrangement made with the Egyptian government. From Nov. 1, 1932 to Feb. 29, 1936, in order to take advantage of the concessionary rate, it was mandatory to use Nos. M1-M11 by affixing them to the backs of envelopes. An "Egypt Postage Prepaid" handstamp was applied to the face of the envelopes. Envelopes bearing these stamps were to be posted only at British military post boxes. Envelopes bearing the 1936-39 "Army Post" stamps (Nos. M12-M15, issued by the Egyptian Postal Administration), also were sold at the concessionary rate and also were to be posted only at British military post boxes. The "Army Post" stamps were withdrawn in 1941, but the concession continued without the use of special stamps. The concession was finally canceled in 1951.

Imperf examples of Nos. M1-M4, M6, M9 (without overprint) and M10 are proofs.

sheets, perf., imperf., 500e, issued Jan. 17. Nos. 7828-7839.

1980 Summer Olympic Water Games, Tallinn, set of five, 5e, 10e, 20e, 25e, airmail 70e, two airmail souv. sheets, perf. 150e, imperf. 250e, and two embossed gold foil airmail souv. sheets, perf., imperf., 500e, issued Jan. 17. Nos. 7840-7848.

Eliz. II Coronation, 25th Anniv., set of eight, 2e, 5e, 8e, 10e, 12e, 15e, airmail 30e, 50e, and two airmail souv. sheets, perf. 150e, imperf. 250e, issued Apr. 25. Nos. 7849-7858.

English Knights of 1200-1350 A.D., set of seven, 5e, 10e, 15e, 20e, 25e, airmail 15e, 70e, and two airmail souv. sheets, perf. 130e, imperf. 250e, issued Apr. 25. Nos. 7859-7867.

Old Locomotives, set of seven, 1e, 2e, 3e, 5e, 10e, airmail 25e, 70e, and two airmail souv. sheets, perf. 150e, imperf. 250e, issued Aug. Nos. 7868-7876.

Prehistoric Animals, set of seven, 30e, 35e, 40e, 45e, 50e, airmail 25e, 60e, and airmail souv. sheet, 130e, issued Aug. Nos. 7877-7884.

Francisco Goya, "Maja Vestida," airmail souv. sheet, 150e, issued Aug. No. 7885.

Peter Paul Rubens — UNICEF, airmail souv. sheet, 250e, issued Aug. No. 7886.

Europa — CEPT — Europhila '78, airmail souv. sheet, 250e, issued Aug. No. 7887.

30th Intl. Stamp Fair, Riccione, airmail souv. sheet, 150e, issued Aug. Nos. 7888.

Eliz. II Coronation, 25th anniv., airmail souv. sheet of three, 150e, issued

CEPT, airmail souv. sheet, 250e, issued Aug. Nos. 7890.

World Cup Soccer Championships, Argentina '78 and Spain '82, airmail souv. sheet, 150e, issued Aug. Nos. 7891.

Christmas, Titian painting, "The Virgin," airmail souv. sheet, 150e, issued Aug. Nos. 7892.

Natl. Independence, 5th Anniv. (in 1973) — A7

1979 *Perf. 13x13½*

26 A7 1e Ekuele coin 1.10 .25

Natl. Independence, 5th Anniv. (in 1973) — A8

1979

27 A8 1e Port Bata .20 .20
28 A8 1.50e State Palace .25 .25
29 A8 2b Central Bank, Bata .30 .30
30 A8 2.50b Nguema Biyogo Bridge .35 .35
31 A8 3b Port, palace, bank, bridge .60 .60
Nos. 27-31 (5) 1.70 1.70

Pres. Nguema — A9

Independence Martyrs — A10

1979 *Perf. 13½x13*

32 A9 1.50e multi .50 .35

United Natl. Workers's Party (PUNT), 3rd Congress.

1979

33 A10 1e Enrique Nvo .20 .20
34 A10 1.50e Salvador Ndongo Ekang .30 .30
35 A10 2b Acacio Mane .40 .40
Nos. 33-35 (3) .90 .90

Agricultural Experiment Year A11

1979 *Perf. 13x13½*

36 A11 1e multi .65 .25
37 A11 1.50e multi, diff. .95 .35

Independence Martyrs — A12

Natl. Coat of Arms — A13

1981, Mar. **Photo.** *Perf. 13½x12½*

38 A12 5b Obiang Esono Nguema .55 .20
39 A12 15b Fernando Nvara Engonga .55 .20
40 A12 25b Ela Edjodjomo Mangue .55 .20
41 A12 35b Obiang Nguema Moasogo, president .75 .20
42 A12 50b Hipolito Micha Eworo 1.10 .20
43 A13 100b multi 2.25 .35
Nos. 38-43 (6) 5.75 1.35

Dated 1980.

Christmas 1980 A14

1981, Mar. 30 *Perf. 13½*

44 A14 8b Cathedral, infant .25 .20
45 A14 25b Bells, youth .30 .20

Dated 1980.

Souvenir Sheet

Pres. Obiang Nguema Mbasogo — A15

1981, Aug. 30 **Litho.** *Imperf.*

46 A15 400b multi 7.75 2.25

State Visit of King Juan Carlos of Spain — A16

Perf. 13x13½, 13½x13

1981, Nov. 30

47 A16 50b Government reception .95 .20
48 A16 100b Arrival at airport 1.75 .35
49 A16 150b King, Pres. Mbasogo, vert. 2.75 .60
Nos. 47-49 (3) 5.45 1.15

State Visit of Pope John Paul II — A17

1982, Feb. 18

50 A17 100b Papal and natl. arms 1.90 .70
51 A17 200b Pres. Mbasogo greeting Pope 3.50 1.40
52 A17 300b Pope, vert. 5.25 2.10
Nos. 50-52 (3) 10.65 4.20

Christmas 1981 A18

1982, Feb. 25 **Photo.**

53 A18 100b Carolers, vert. 1.25 .35
54 A18 150b Magi, African youth 1.90 .60

Dated 1981.

1982 World Cup Soccer Championships, Spain — A19

1982, June 13 *Perf. 13½*

55 A19 40b Emblem .55 .25
56 A19 60b Naranjito character trademark .80 .35
57 A19 100b World Cup trophy 1.40 .60
58 A19 200b Players, palm tree, emblem 2.75 1.10
Nos. 55-58 (4) 5.50 2.30

Fauna A20

1983, Feb. 4 **Litho.**

59 A20 40b Gorilla .65 .20
60 A20 60b Hippopotamus 1.10 .25
61 A20 80b Atherurus africanus 1.50 .35
62 A20 120b Felis pardus 2.25 .50
Nos. 59-62 (4) 5.50 1.30

Dated 1982.

Christmas 1982 A21

1983, Feb. 25 **Photo.**

63 A21 100b Stars .95 .35
64 A21 200b King offering frankincense 2.25 .75

Dated 1982.

World Communications Year — A22

1983, July 18 **Litho.**

65 A22 150b Postal runner 1.00 .45
66 A22 200b Microwave station, drummer 2.40 1.00

Banana Trees A23

1983, Oct. 8

67 A23 300b shown 3.25 1.00
68 A23 400b Forest, vert. 4.50 1.40

Christmas 1983 A24

1984

69 A24 80b Folk dancer, musical instruments .90 .30
70 A24 100b Holy Family 1.10 .50

Dated 1983.

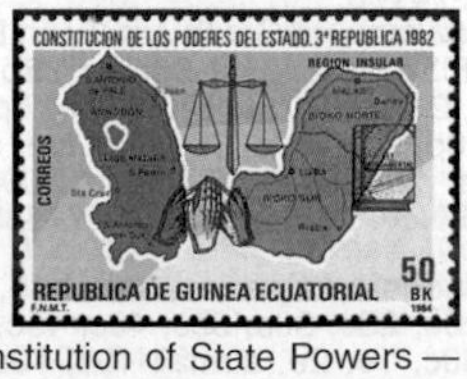

Constitution of State Powers — A25

Scales of justice, fundamental lawbook and various maps.

1984, Feb. 15

71 A25 50b Annobon and Bioko .60 .25
72 A25 100b Mainland regions 1.10 .50

Turtle Hunting, Rio Muni — A26

World Food Day — A27

1984, May 1

73	A26	125b	Hunting Whales, horiz.	1.25	.50
74	A26	150b	shown	1.50	.60

1984, Sept.

75	A27	60b	Papaya	1.00	.40
76	A27	80b	Malanga	1.25	.50

Abstract Wood-Carved Figurines and Art — A28

Designs: 25b, *Black Gazelle* and *Anxiety.* 30b, *Black Gazelle,* diff., and *Woman.* 60b, *Man and woman,* vert. 75b, *Poster,* vert. 100b, *Mother and Child,* vert. 150b, *Man and Woman,* diff., and *Bust of a Woman.*

1984, Nov. 15

77	A28	25b	multi	.25	.20
78	A28	30b	multi	.35	.20
79	A28	60b	multi	.65	.25
80	A28	75b	multi	.85	.30
81	A28	100b	multi	1.10	.40
82	A28	150b	multi	1.60	.60
			Nos. 77-82 (6)	4.80	1.95

Christmas A29

1984, Dec. 24

83	A29	60b	Mother and child, vert.	.70	.25
84	A29	100b	Musical instruments	1.00	.40

Immaculate Conception Missions, Cent. — A30

50fr, Emblem, vert. 60fr, Map, nun and youths, vert. 80fr, First Guinean nuns. 125fr, Missionaries landing at Bata Beach, 1885.

1985, Apr. *Perf. 14*

85	A30	50fr	multi	.45	.20
86	A30	60fr	multi	.50	.20
87	A30	80fr	multi	.60	.20
88	A30	125fr	multi	1.10	.40
			Nos. 85-88 (4)	2.65	1.00

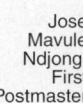

Jose Mavule Ndjong, First Postmaster A31

1985, July *Perf. 13½*

89	A31	50fr	Postal emblem, vert.	.85	.20
90	A31	80fr	shown	1.50	.35

Equatorial Guinea Postal Service.

Christmas A32

1985, Dec.

91	A32	40fr	Nativity	.55	.20
92	A32	70fr	Folk band, dancers, mother and child	.90	.35

Nature Conservation — A33

1985

93	A33	15fr	Crab, snail	.75	.20
94	A33	35fr	Butterflies, bees, birds	1.40	.25
95	A33	45fr	Flowering plants	2.10	.35
96	A33	65fr	Spraying and harvesting cacao	3.25	.50
			Nos. 93-96 (4)	7.50	1.30

Folklore — A34

A35

1986, Apr. 15

97	A34	10fr	Ndowe dance, Mekuyo, horiz.	.25	.20
98	A34	50fr	Fang dance, Mokom	.50	.20
99	A34	65fr	Cacha Bubi, Bisila	.65	.25
100	A34	80fr	Fang dance, Ndong-Mba	.80	.35
			Nos. 97-100 (4)	2.20	1.00

1986, June 25

1986 World Cup Soccer Championships, Mexico: Various soccer plays.

101	A35	50fr	multi, horiz.	.25	.20
102	A35	100fr	multi, horiz.	.75	.25
103	A35	150fr	multi	1.10	.40
104	A35	200fr	multi	1.40	.55
			Nos. 101-104 (4)	3.50	1.40

Christmas — A36

Conf. of the Union of Central African States — A37

1986, Dec. 12

105	A36	100fr	Musical instruments, horiz.	.85	.35
106	A36	150fr	Holy Family, lamb	1.40	.50

1986, Dec. 29

107	A37	80fr	Flags, map	.80	.35
108	A37	100fr	Emblem, map, horiz.	1.00	.40

Campaign Against Hunger A38

1987, June 5

109	A38	60fr	Chicken	.65	.25
110	A38	80fr	Fish	.95	.35
111	A38	100fr	Wheat	1.10	.40
			Nos. 109-111 (3)	2.70	1.00

Intl. Peace Year A39

1987, July 15 **Litho.** *Perf. 13½*

112	A39	100fr	shown	.75	.40
113	A39	200fr	Hands holding dove	1.60	.80

Stamp Day 1987 A40

1987, Oct. 5 **Litho.** *Perf. 13½*

114	A40	150fr	shown	1.25	.50
115	A40	300fr	Posting envelope	2.75	.85

Christmas 1987 — A41

Mother and child (wood carvings).

1987, Dec. 22 **Litho.** *Perf. 13½*

116	A41	80fr	multi	.95	.35
117	A41	100fr	multi, diff.	1.40	.50

Climbing Palm Tree — A42

Democratic Party — A43

1988, May 4 **Litho.** *Perf. 13½*

118	A42	50fr	shown	.50	.20
119	A42	75fr	Woman carrying fish	.60	.30
120	A42	150fr	Chopping down trees	1.25	.60
			Nos. 118-120 (3)	2.35	1.10

1988, Nov. 16

121	A43	40fr	Crest	.35	.20
122	A43	75fr	Torch, motto, horiz.	.60	.30
123	A43	100fr	Torch, flag, weaving, horiz.	.85	.40
			Nos. 121-123 (3)	1.80	.90

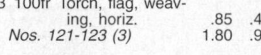

Cultural Revolution Day — A44

Geometric shapes.

1988, June 4

124	A44	35fr	shown	.25	.20
125	A44	50fr	Squares, sphere	.35	.20
126	A44	100fr	Bird	.75	.50
			Nos. 124-126 (3)	1.35	.90

Christmas — A45

1988, Dec. 22

127	A45	50fr	shown	.40	.20
128	A45	100fr	Mother and child	.95	.40

Natl. Independence, 20th Anniv. — A46

Designs: 10fr, Lumber on truck. 35fr, Folk dancers. 45fr, Officials on dais.

1989, Apr. 14 **Litho.** *Perf. 14*

129	A46	10fr	multicolored	.25	.20
130	A46	35fr	multicolored	.30	.20
131	A46	45fr	multicolored	.35	.20
			Nos. 129-131 (3)	.90	.60

Youths Bathing, Ilachi Falls — A47

25fr, Waterfall in the jungle. 60fr, Boy drinking from fruit, boys swimming at Luba Beach.

1989, July 7 *Perf. 13½*

132	A47 15fr shown		.20	.20
133	A47 25fr multicolored		.25	.20
134	A47 60fr multicolored		.45	.25
	Nos. 132-134 (3)		.90	.65

1st Congress of the Democratic Party of Equatorial Guinea A48

1989, Oct. 23 **Litho.** *Perf. 13½*

135	A48 25fr shown	.30	.20
136	A48 35fr Torch, vert.	.50	.20
137	A48 40fr Pres. Nguema, vert.	.60	.20
	Nos. 135-137 (3)	1.40	.60

Christmas — A49

1989, Dec. 18 **Litho.** *Perf. 13½*

138	A49 150fr shown	1.60	.75
139	A49 300fr Nativity, horiz.	2.00	1.00

Boy Scouts A50

1990, Mar. 23 **Litho.** *Perf. 13*

140	A50 100fr Lord Baden-Powell	1.75	.50
141	A50 250fr Salute	4.00	1.10
142	A50 350fr Bugler	5.25	1.50
	Nos. 140-142 (3)	11.00	3.10

World Cup Soccer Championships, Italy — A51

1990, June 8 **Litho.** *Perf. 13*

143	A51 100fr Soccer player, map	.75	.35
144	A51 250fr Goalkeeper	1.50	.65
145	A51 350fr Trophy	2.25	1.00
	Nos. 143-145 (3)	4.50	2.00

Musical Instruments of the Ndowe People — A52

Instruments of the: 250fr, Fang. 350fr, Bubi.

1990, June 19

146	A52 100fr multicolored	.60	.20
147	A52 250fr multicolored	1.25	.55
148	A52 350fr multicolored	1.60	.85
	Nos. 146-148 (3)	3.45	1.60

Discovery of America, 500th Anniv. (in 1992) A53

1990, Oct. 10

149	A53 170fr Arrival in New World	1.00	.35
150	A53 300fr Columbus' fleet	1.75	.55

Christmas — A54

1990, Dec. 23 **Litho.** *Perf. 13½*

151	A54 170fr shown	1.00	.45
152	A54 300fr Bubi tribesman	1.75	.75

1992 Summer Olympics, Barcelona A55

1991, Apr. 22 **Litho.** *Perf. 13½x14*

153	A55 150fr Tennis	2.10	.75
154	A55 250fr Cycling	3.25	1.10

Souvenir Sheet

155	A55 500fr Equestrian	14.50	6.00

La Maja Desnuda by Goya A56

Designs: 250fr, Eve by Durer, vert. 350fr, The Three Graces by Rubens, vert.

1991, May 6 **Litho.** *Perf. 14*

156	A56 100fr shown	1.75	.50
157	A56 250fr multicolored	3.75	1.10
158	A56 350fr multicolored	5.00	1.50
	Nos. 156-158 (3)	10.50	3.10

Madrillus Sphinx — A57

1991, July 1 **Litho.** *Perf. 13½x14*

159	A57 25fr shown	2.50	1.10
160	A57 25fr Face	2.50	1.10
161	A57 25fr Seated	2.50	1.10
162	A57 25fr Walking, horiz.	2.50	1.10
	Nos. 159-162 (4)	10.00	4.40

World Wildlife Fund.

Discovery of America, 500th Anniv. A58

Captains, ships: 150fr, Vicente Yanez Pinzon, Nina. 260fr, Martin Alonso Pinzon, Pinta. 350fr, Christopher Columbus, Santa Maria.

1991 **Litho.** *Perf. 13½x14*

163	A58 150fr multicolored	1.10	.40
164	A58 250fr multicolored	2.00	.75
165	A58 350fr multicolored	2.75	1.25
	Nos. 163-165 (3)	5.85	2.40

Locomotives — A59

150fr, Electric, Japan, 1932. 250fr, Steam, US, 1873. 500fr, Steam, Germany, 1841.

1991, Sept. 10

166	A59 150fr multicolored	1.25	.50
167	A59 250fr multicolored	2.00	.75

Souvenir Sheet

168	A59 500fr multicolored	12.50	6.00

1992 Summer Olympics, Barcelona A60

1992, Feb. 12 **Litho.** *Perf. 13½x14*

169	A60 200fr Basketball	1.75	.75
170	A60 300fr Swimming	2.50	1.10

Souvenir Sheet

171	A60 400fr Baseball	22.50	12.50

Souvenir Sheet

Discovery of America, 500th Anniv. — A61

Columbus: a, 300fr, Departing from Palos, Spain. b, 500fr, Landing in New World.

1992, Apr. 8

172	A61 Sheet of 2, #a.-b.	22.50	12.50

Motion Pictures, Cent. A61a

Scenes from movies: 100fr, Humphrey Bogart, Ingrid Bergman, Dooley Wilson in "Casablanca," 1942. 250fr, "Viridiana," 1961. 350fr, Laurel and Hardy in "Sons of the Desert," 1933.

1992, Sept. **Litho.** *Perf. 14*

172C	A61a 100fr multicolored	.90	.20
172D	A61a 250fr multicolored	1.75	.45
172E	A61a 350fr multicolored	2.75	.60
	Nos. 172C-172E (3)	5.40	1.25

A62

A62a

Mushrooms: 75fr, Termitomyces globulus. 125fr, Termitomyces le testui. 150fr, Termitomyces robustus.

1992, Nov. **Litho.** *Perf. 14x13½*

173	A62 75fr multicolored	.75	.20
174	A62 125fr multicolored	1.10	.35
175	A62 150fr multicolored	1.50	.45
	Nos. 173-175 (3)	3.35	1.00

1992 **Litho.** *Perf. 14x13½*

Wildlife Protection: 150fr, Halcyon malimbicus. 250fr, Corythaeola cristata. 500fr, Mariposa nymphalidae, horiz.

175A	A62a 150fr multicolored	1.75	.50
175B	A62a 250fr multicolored	3.25	1.00

Souvenir Sheet

Perf. 13½x14

175C	A62a 500fr multicolored	14.50	6.50

Virgin and Child with Virtuous Saints, by Claudio Coello (c. 1635-1693) — A63

Paintings, by Jacob Jordaens (1593-1678): 300fr, Apollo Conquering Marsias. 400fr, Meleager and Atalanta.

1993, Mar. **Litho.** *Perf. 13½x14*

176	A63 200fr multicolored	2.50	.75
177	A63 300fr multicolored	3.50	1.25

Souvenir Sheet

178	A63 400fr multicolored	17.00	8.00

1992 Olympic Gold Medalists A64

Designs: 100fr, Quincy Watts, 400-meter dash, US. 250fr, Martin Lopez Zubero, swimming, Spain. 350fr, Petra Kronberger, women's slalom, Austria. 400fr, Flying Dutchman class yachting, Spain.

1993 **Litho.** *Perf. 13½x14*

179	A64 100fr multicolored	.90	.35
180	A64 250fr multicolored	1.90	.75
181	A64 350fr multicolored	2.50	1.00
182	A64 400fr multicolored	3.00	1.25
	Nos. 179-182 (4)	8.30	3.35

Scene from Romeo and Juliet, by Tchaikovsky — A65

Design: 200fr, Scene from Faust, by Charles-Francois Gounod (1818-93).

1993, June Litho. *Perf. 13½x14*

183 A65 100fr multicolored .85 .40
184 A65 200fr multicolored 1.50 .75

First Ford Gasoline Engine, Cent. A66

1993 *Perf. 13½x14, 14x13½*

185 A66 200fr First Ford vehicle 3.50 1.00
186 A66 300fr Ford Model T 5.50 1.50
187 A66 400fr Henry Ford, vert. 7.75 2.10
Nos. 185-187 (3) 16.75 4.60

25th Anniv. of Independence — A67

Designs: 150fr, Pres. Obiang Nguema Mbasogo, vert. 250fr, Cargo ship, map, communications . 300fr, Hydroelectric plant, Riaba. 350fr, Bridge.

Perf. 14x13½, 13½x14

1993, Oct. 12 Litho.

188 A67 150fr multicolored 1.25 .50
189 A67 250fr multicolored 2.00 .75
190 A67 300fr multicolored 2.50 1.00
191 A67 350fr multicolored 2.75 1.10
Nos. 188-191 (4) 8.50 3.35

1994 World Cup Soccer Championships, US — A68

Designs: 200fr, German team, 1990 champions. 300fr, Rose Bowl Stadium, Pasadena, Calif. 500fr, Player kicking ball, vert.

1994 Litho. *Perf. 13½x14, 14x13½*

192 A68 200fr multicolored 1.25 .45
193 A68 300fr multicolored 1.75 .65
194 A68 500fr multicolored 3.25 1.10
Nos. 192-194 (3) 6.25 2.20

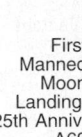

First Manned Moon Landing, 25th Anniv. A69

Designs: 500fr, Lunar module, Eagle. 700fr, "Buzz" Aldrin, Michael Collins, Neil Armstrong. 900fr, Footprint on moon, astronaut.

1994 *Perf. 13½x14*

195 A69 500fr multicolored 2.75 .70
196 A69 700fr multicolored 4.25 1.00
197 A69 900fr multicolored 6.50 1.75
Nos. 195-197 (3) 13.50 3.45

Dinosaurs A70

Designs: 300fr, Chasmosaurus. 500fr, Tyrannosaurus rex. 700fr, Triceratops. 800fr, Styracosaurus, deinonychus.

1994

198 A70 300fr multicolored 1.50 .65
199 A70 500fr multicolored 2.75 1.10
200 A70 700fr multicolored 3.75 1.60
Nos. 198-200 (3) 8.00 3.35

Souvenir Sheet

201 A70 800fr multicolored 16.00 16.00

Famous Men A71

Designs: 300fr, Jean Renoir (1894-1979), French film director. 500fr, Ferdinand de Lesseps (1805-94), French diplomat, promoter of Suez Canal. 600fr, Antoine de Saint Exupery (1900-44), French aviator, writer. 700fr, Walter Gropius (1883-1969), architect.

1994 Litho. *Perf. 13½x14*

202 A71 300fr multicolored 2.00 .75
203 A71 500fr multicolored 3.25 1.25
204 A71 600fr multicolored 3.75 1.50
205 A71 700fr multicolored 4.50 1.75
Nos. 202-205 (4) 13.50 5.25

Establishment of The Bauhaus, 75th anniv. (#205).

Minerals A72

1994 Litho. *Perf. 13½x14*

206 A72 300fr Aurichalcite 2.00 1.00
207 A72 400fr Pyromorphite 2.50 1.40
208 A72 600fr Fluorite 3.25 1.90
209 A72 700fr Halite 4.25 2.25
Nos. 206-209 (4) 12.00 6.55

Domestic Animals A73

Designs: a, Cat. b, Dog. c, Pig.

1995 Litho. *Perf. 13½x14*

210 Strip of 3, #a.-c. 8.50 8.50
a.-c. A73 500fr Any single 1.50 1.50

Butterflies & Orchids A74

a, Hypolimnas salmacis. b, Myrina silenus. c, Palla ussheri. d, Pseudacraea boisduvali.

1995

211 Strip of 4, #a.-d. 8.50 8.50
a.-d. A74 400fr Any single 1.50 1.50

Anniversaries — A75

Designs: a, 350fr, End of World War II, 50th Anniv. b, 450fr, UN, 50th anniv. c, 600fr, Sir Rowland Hill, birth bicent.

1995 Litho. *Perf. 13½x14*

212 Strip of 3, #a.-c. 8.50 8.50
a. A75 350fr multi 1.25 1.25
b. A75 450fr multi 1.50 1.50
c. A75 600fr multi 2.25 2.25

Trains A76

Designs: No. 213a, English steam engine. b, German diesel engine. c, Japanese Shinkansen train.

800fr, Swiss electric locomotive.

1995

213 Strip of 3, #a.-c. 12.50 12.50
a.-c. A76 500fr Any single 2.00 2.00

Souvenir Sheet

214 A76 800fr multicolored 9.00 9.00

Formula 1 Driving Champions A77

Designs: a, Juan Manuel Fangio. b, Ayrton Senna. c, Jim Clark. d, Jochen Rindt.

1995 Litho. *Perf. 14*

215 Strip of 4, #a.-d. 10.00 10.00
a.-d. A77 400fr Any single 1.50 1.50

Motion Pictures, Cent. A78

Designs: a, Marilyn Monroe. b, Elvis Presley. c, James Dean. d, Vittorio de Sica.

1996 Litho. *Perf. 14*

216 Strip of 4, #a.-d. 9.00 9.00
a.-d. A78 350fr Any single 1.50 1.50

Famous People A79

Designs: a, Alfred Nobel (1833-96), inventor, philanthropist. b, Anton Bruckner (1824-96), composer. c, Abraham and Three Angels, by Giovanni B. Tiepolo (1696-1770).

800fr, Family of Charles IV, by Francisco de Goya, (1746-1828).

1996

217 Strip of 3, #a.-c. 12.50 12.50
a.-c. A79 500fr Any single 2.00 2.00

Souvenir Sheet

218 A79 800fr multicolored 7.75 7.75

Chess A80

Designs: a, World Chess Festival for youth and children, Minorca, Spain. b, Women's World Chess Championship, Jaén, Spain. c, Men's World Chess Championship, Karpov versus Kamsky, Elista, Kalmyk. d, Chess Olympiad, Yerevan, Armenia.

1996 Litho. *Perf. 14*

219 Strip of 4, #a.-d. 10.00 10.00
a.-d. A80 400fr Any single 1.50 1.50

1996 Summer Olympic Games, Atlanta A81

Designs: a, Olympic Stadium, Athens, 1896. b, Cycling. c, Tennis. d, Equestrian show jumping.

1996 Litho. *Perf. 14*

220 Strip of 4, #a.-d. 10.00 10.00
a.-d. A81 400fr Any single 1.50 1.50

Ships A82

Designs: a, Paddle steamer with sails, 19th cent. b, Bark "Galatea," 1896. c, Modern ferry.

1996

221 Strip of 3, #a.-c. 11.00 11.00
a.-c. A82 500fr Any single 2.00 2.00

Franz Schubert (1797-1828), Composer — A83

Miguel de Cervantes (1547-1616), Novelist — A84

Designs: a, shown. b, Chinese Lunar New Year, 1997, (Year of the Ox). c, Johannes Brahms (1833-97), composer.

Illustration A84 reduced.

1997, Apr. 23 Litho. *Perf. 14*

222 Strip of 3, #a.-c. 9.00 9.00
a.-c. A83 500fr Any single 2.00 2.00

Souvenir Sheet

223 A84 800fr multicolored 5.50 5.50

Mushrooms — A85

a, Sparassis laminosa. b, Amanita pantherina. c, Morchella esculenta. d, Aleuria aurantia.

1997

224 Strip of 4, #a.-d. 11.00 11.00
a.-d. A85 400fr Any single 1.75 1.75

1998 World Cup Soccer Championships, France — A86

Designs: a, Players with ball on field. b, Stadium. c, Kicking ball.

1997 Litho. *Perf. 14*

225 Strip of 3, #a.-c. 6.00 6.00
a.-c. A86 300fr Any single 1.10 1.10

Fauna A88

a, Snake. b, Snail. c, Turtle. d, Monitor lizard.

1998 Litho. *Perf. 14*

230 Strip of 4, #a.-d. 10.00 10.00
a.-d. A88 400fr Any single 1.50 1.50

A89 A90

Military Uniforms: a, Alsace Regiment, French Infantry, 18th cent. b, English Marine, 18th cent. c, Georgian Hussars Regiment, Russian Calvary, 18th cent. d, Prussian Artillery, 19th cent.

1998

231 Strip of 4, #a.-d. 10.00 10.00
a.-d. A89 400fr Any single 1.50 1.50

1999 Litho. *Perf. 14*

Easter (Museum paintings): a, Crucifixion of Christ, by Velázquez. b, Adoration of the Magi, by Rubens. c, Holy Family, by Michelangelo.

232 Strip of 3, #a.-c. 10.00 10.00
a.-c. A90 500fr Any single 2.00 2.00

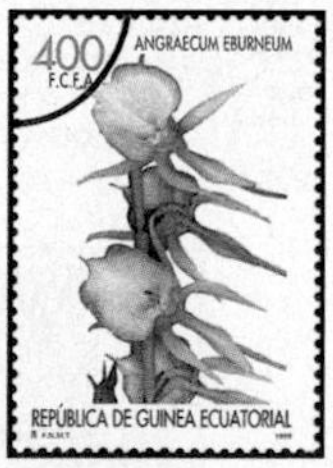

Orchids — A91

Designs: a, Angraecum eburneum. b, Paphiopedilum insigne. c, Ansellia africana. d, Cattleya leopoldii.

1999

233 Strip of 4, #a.-d. 10.00 10.00
a.-d. A91 400fr Any single 1.50 1.50

Birth and Death Anniversaries A92

No. 234: a, 750fr, Portrait of Frederic Chopin (1810-49), by Eugene Delacroix. b, 100fr, Christ Crowned With Thorns, by Anthony Van Dyck (1599-1641). c, 250fr, Portrait of Johann Wolfgang von Goethe (1749-1832), by Joseph Carl Stieler. d, 500fr, Jacques-Etienne Montgolfiere (1745-1799) and balloon.

1999 Litho. *Perf. 14x13¾*

234 Horiz. strip of 4, #a-d 10.00 10.00
a. A92 750fr multi 3.00 3.00
b. A92 100fr multi .35 .35
c. A92 250fr multi 1.10 1.10
d. A92 500fr multi 2.00 2.00

Parrots — A93

No. 235: a, Aratinga guarouba. b, Ara ambigua. c, Anodorhynchus hyacinthinus. 800fr, Alisterus amboinensis.

1999

235 Vert. strip of 3, #a-c 9.00 9.00
a.-c. A93 500fr any single 2.00 2.00

Souvenir Sheet

236 A93 800fr multi 6.00 6.00

Economic and Monetary Community of Central Africa Week — A93a

Designs: 100fr, Map of Africa, flags of member nations.

1999 Litho. *Perf. 14½*

236A A93a 100fr multi —

An additional stamp was issued in this set. The editors would like to examine any example.

Locomotives — A94

No. 237: a, Swiss. b, German. c, Japanese.

2000 Litho. *Perf. 13¾x14*

237 Horiz. strip of 3 7.00 7.00
a.-c. A94 500fr Any single 2.25 2.25

Souvenir Sheet

238 A94 800fr AVE Train 3.50 3.50

Butterflies A95

a, Fabriciana niobe. b, Palaeochrysophanus hippothoe. c, Inachis io. d, Apatura iris.

2000

239 Horiz. strip of 4 7.50 7.50
a.-d. A95 400fr Any single 1.75 1.75

UPU, 125th Anniv. (in 1999) A96

2000 Litho. *Perf. 13¾*

240 A96 400fr multi 1.75 1.75

Mushrooms A97

No. 241: a, Gyroporus cyanescens. b, Terfezia arenaria. c, Battarrea stevenii. d, Amanita muscaria.

2001 Litho. *Perf. 13¾*

241 Horiz. strip of 4 6.75 6.75
a.-d. A97 400fr Any single 1.60 1.60

Fire Trucks A98

No. 242: a, Truck, 1915. b, Tanker, 1943. c, Ladder truck, 1966. d, Merryweather pumper, 1888.

2001

242 Horiz. strip of 4 6.75 6.75
a.-d. A98 400fr Any single 1.60 1.60

Soldiers — A99

No. 243: a, Infantry officer, 1700. b, Harquebusier, 1534. c, Musketeer, 17th cent. d, Fusilier, 1815.

2001 Litho. *Perf. 14x13¾*

243 Horiz. strip of 4 6.75 6.75
a.-d. A99 400fr Any single 1.60 1.60

Prehistoric Animals A100

No. 244: a, Carnotaurus sastrei. b, Iberomesornis romerali. c, Troodon.
800fr, Diplodocus carnegiei.

2001 *Perf. 13¾x14*

244 Horiz. strip of 3 6.25 6.25
a.-c. A100 500fr Any single 2.00 2.00

Souvenir Sheet

245 A100 800fr multi 3.50 3.50

Millennium A101

Designs: No. 246, 200fr, Intl. Conference Center. No. 247, 200fr, Offshore petroleum exploration. No. 248, 200fr, Women's Plaza, Malabo.
400fr, Statue at Intl. Conference Center, vert.

2001 Litho. *Perf. 13¾x14*

246-248 A101 Set of 3 3.50 3.50

Souvenir Sheet

Perf. 14x13¾

249 A101 400fr multi 1.75 1.75

Flora — A102

No. 250: a, Alstonia congensis. b, Harongana madagascariensis. c, Caloncoba glauca. d, Cassia occidentalis.

2002 *Perf. 14x13¾*

250 Horiz. strip of 4 6.75 6.75
a.-d. A102 400fr Any single 1.60 1.60

Automobiles — A103

No. 251: a, 1924 Rochet Schneider 20,000. b, 1930 Bugatti T49. c, 1931 Ford Model A. d, 1925 Alfa Romeo RLSS.

2002 *Perf. 13¾x14*

251 Vert. strip of 4 6.75 6.75
a.-d. A103 400fr Any single 1.60 1.60

Butterflies A104

No. 252: a, Papilio menestheus canui. b, Papilio policenes. c, Papilio tynderaeus. d, Papilio zalmoxis.

2002

252 Strip of 4 6.75 6.75
a.-d. A104 400fr Any single 1.60 1.60

Famous Men A105

No. 253: a, Victor Hugo (1802-85), writer. b, Santiago Ramón y Cajal (1852-1934), histologist. c, Emile Zola (1840-1902), writer.

2002

253 Horiz. strip of 3 5.25 5.25
a.-c. A105 400fr Any single 1.60 1.60

2002 World Cup Soccer Championships, Japan and Korea — A106

No. 254: a, Player with yellow shirt with knee on ground. b, Stadium. c, Player with yellow shirt on ground.

2002

254 Horiz. strip of 3 6.75 6.75
a.-c. A106 500fr Any single 2.10 2.10

Souvenir Sheet

2002 Chess Olympiad, Bled, Slovenia — A107

2002

255 A107 800fr multi 3.50 3.50

Anniversaries and Events — A108

No. 256: a, Painting by Henri de Toulouse-Lautrec (1864-1901). b, Year of Dialogue Among Civilizations. c, Giuseppe Verdi (1813-1901), composer.

2004 ? Litho. ***Perf. 14x13¾***

256 Vert. strip of 3 5.50 5.50
a.-c. A108 400fr Any single 1.75 1.75

Dated 2001. Stamps did not appear in philatelic market until 2004.

Anniversaries and Events — A109

No. 257: a, Tour de France bicycle race, cent. b, Painting by Vincent van Gogh (1853-90). c, Wright Brothers and Wright Flyer.

2004 ? ***Perf. 13¾x14***

257 Horiz. strip of 3 8.50 8.50
a. A109 400fr multi 2.25 2.25
b. A109 500fr multi 2.75 2.75
c. A109 600fr multi 3.50 3.50

Dated 2003. Stamps did not appear in philatelic market until 2004.

Minerals A110

2004 ?

258 Vert. strip of 4 8.50 8.50
a. A110 400fr Realgar 1.75 1.75
b. A110 450fr Gypsum 2.00 2.00
c. A110 550fr Red quartz 2.25 2.25
d. A110 600fr Chrysoberyl 2.50 2.50

Dated 2003. Stamps did not appear in philatelic market until 2004.

Lighthouses A111

Designs: a, Marina Lighthouse, Luba, Equatorial Guinea. b, La Plata Lighthouse, Spain. c, Prodecao Lighthouse, Luba. d, Torre de Hércules, Spain.

2004 ? ***Perf. 14x13¾***

259 Horiz. strip of 4 11.00 11.00
a. A111 400fr multi 2.25 2.25
b. A111 450fr multi 2.50 2.50
c. A111 550fr multi 2.75 2.75
d. A111 600fr multi 3.50 3.50

Dated 2003. Stamps did not appear in philatelic market until 2004.

Space Shuttle Columbia Accident — A112

No. 260: a, Rocket lift-off. b, Rocket on launch pad. c, Flight crew patch.
1000fr, View of earth from outer space.

2004 ?

260 Vert. strip of 3 8.00 8.00
a. A112 500fr multi 2.25 2.25
b. A112 600fr multi 2.50 2.50
c. A112 700fr multi 3.00 3.00

Souvenir Sheet

261 A112 1000fr multi 4.50 4.50

Dated 2003. Stamps did not appear in philatelic market until 2004.

Motorcycles — A113

No. 262: a, 1944-47 Soriano Tigre. b, 1970 Derbi 50 Grand Prix. c, 1938 DKW 250 with sidecar.
1000fr, Harley-Davidson VRSCA V-Rod.

2004 ? ***Perf. 13¾x14***

262 Horiz. strip of 3 7.00 7.00
a. A113 450fr multi 1.90 1.90
b. A113 500fr multi 2.25 2.25
c. A113 550fr multi 2.75 2.75

Souvenir Sheet

263 A113 1000fr multi 5.50 5.50

Dated 2003. Stamps did not appear in philatelic market until 2004.

Souvenir Sheet

Wedding of Spanish Prince Felipe and Letizia Ortiz Rocasolano — A114

2004 Litho. ***Perf. 13¾x14***

264 A114 1400fr multi 5.75 5.75

2004 Summer Olympics, Athens A115

2004

265 Horiz. strip of 4 8.25 8.25
a. A115 400fr Basketball 1.60 1.60
b. A115 450fr Track 1.90 1.90
c. A115 550fr Tennis 2.25 2.25
d. A115 600fr Cycling 2.50 2.50

2004 Anniversaries A116

No. 266: a, FIFA (Fédération Internationale de Football Association), cent. b, Pablo Neruda (1904-73), poet. c, Anton Dvorak (1841-1904), composer.

2005 ? Litho. ***Perf. 14x13¾***

266 Vert. strip of 3 6.75 6.75
a. A116 450fr multi 1.90 1.90
b. A116 500fr multi 2.10 2.10
c. A116 550fr multi 2.40 2.40

Dated 2004. Stamps did not appear in philatelic marketplace until 2005.

Airplanes A117

No. 267: a, Concorde. b, Airbus A340-600. c, Boeing 747-400. d, Eurofighter C-16 Typhoon.

2005 ? ***Perf. 13¾x14***

267 Vert. strip of 4 8.50 8.50
a. A117 400fr multi 1.60 1.60
b. A117 450fr multi 1.90 1.90
c. A117 500fr multi 2.10 2.10
d. A117 600fr multi 2.50 2.50

Dated 2004. Stamps did not appear in philatelic marketplace until 2005.

Churches — A118

No. 268: a, Cathedral, Pisa, Italy. b, Notre-Dame-la-Grande Church, Poitiers, France. c, Speyer Cathedral, Germany. d, Cathedral, Santiago de Compostela, Spain.

2005 ***Perf. 14x13¾***

268 Horiz. strip of 4 9.00 9.00
a. A118 400fr multi 1.60 1.60
b. A118 450fr multi 1.90 1.90
c. A118 550fr multi 2.40 2.40
d. A118 600fr multi 2.50 2.50

Paintings by Salvador Dali (1904-89) — A119

Various unnamed paintings.

2005 ***Perf. 14x13¾***

269 Vert. strip of 3 8.00 8.00
a. A119 500fr multi 2.00 2.00
b. A119 600fr multi 2.50 2.50
c. A119 700fr multi 2.75 2.75

Souvenir Sheet

270 A119 1000fr multi 4.50 4.50

Art and Architecture — A120

No. 271: a, Statue of African Woman, Malabo. b, Building, Bioko Sur. c, Eyi Muan Ndong, troubador.

2005 Litho. ***Perf. 13¾x14***

271 Horiz. strip of 3 7.25 7.25
a. A120 450fr multi 2.00 2.00
b. A120 550fr multi 2.40 2.40
c. A120 600fr multi 2.75 2.75

Trains A121

No. 272: a, Tren Basculante. b, Tren Talgo Pendular. c, Tren Electrotrén. d, Tren T. A. F.

2005

272 Strip of 4 9.00 9.00
a. A121 400fr multi 1.75 1.75
b. A121 450fr multi 1.90 1.90
c. A121 550fr multi 2.40 2.40
d. A121 600fr multi 2.50 2.50

Publication of Don Quixote, 400th Anniv. — A122

No. 273: a, Emblem. b, Don Quixote and Sancho Panza riding. c, Quixote catching falling Panza. d, Quixote on horse, windmill.

2005 ***Perf. 14x13¾***

273 Horiz. strip of 4 9.00 9.00
a. A122 400fr multi 1.75 1.75
b. A122 450fr multi 1.90 1.90
c. A122 550fr multi 2.40 2.40
d. A122 600fr multi 2.50 2.50

Famous People A123

No. 274: a, Christopher Columbus (1451-1506), explorer. b, Federico García Lorca (1898-1936), poet. c, Wolfgang Amadeus Mozart (1756-91), composer.

2006 ***Perf. 13¾x14***

274 Horiz. strip of 3 7.25 7.25
a. A123 450fr multi 2.00 2.00
b. A123 550fr multi 2.25 2.25
c. A123 600fr multi 2.50 2.50

Pope Benedict XVI A124

No. 275: a, Coat of Arms. b, St. Peter's Basilica.
1000fr, Pope Benedict XVI.

2006

275 Vert. pair 4.50 4.50
a. A124 450fr multi 2.00 2.00
b. A124 550fr multi 2.40 2.40

Souvenir Sheet

276 A124 1000fr multi 4.50 4.50

Tourism A125

No. 277: a, Road from Boloko to Luba. b, Malabo Intl. Airport Terminal. c, Sculpture, Avenida de Juan Pablo II. d, National Parliament.

2006 Litho. *Perf. 13¾x14*

277	Strip of 4	8.00	8.00
a.	A125 400fr multi	1.60	1.60
b.	A125 450fr multi	1.75	1.75
c.	A125 550fr multi	2.25	2.25
d.	A125 600fr multi	2.40	2.40

Spain, 2006 World Basketball Champions A126

No. 278: a, Emblem of Spanish Basketball Federation. b, Basketball and hoop. c, Players.

2006 *Perf. 14x13¾*

278	Vert. strip of 3	6.50	6.50
a.	A126 450fr multi	1.75	1.75
b.	A126 550fr multi	2.25	2.25
c.	A126 600fr multi	2.40	2.40

Christmas A127

No. 279 — Baby and: a, People and drummer. b, People. c, People and airplane.

2006 *Perf. 13¾x14*

279	Horiz. strip of 3	6.50	6.50
a.	A127 450fr multi	1.75	1.75
b.	A127 550fr multi	2.25	2.25
c.	A127 600fr multi	2.40	2.40

European Economic Community, 50th Anniv. — A128

No. 280: a, Orchard, Spain. b, Mountain, France. c, Farm fields, Italy. d, Village, Germany.

2007 Litho. *Perf. 13¾x14*

280	Horiz. strip of 4	9.25	9.25
a.	A128 400fr multi	1.75	1.75
b.	A128 500fr multi	2.25	2.25
c.	A128 550fr multi	2.50	2.50
d.	A128 600fr multi	2.75	2.75

Locomotives in Madrid Train Museum — A129

No. 281: a, Steam locomotive 242F-2009. b, Diesel locomotive 1615. c, Electric locomotive 6101. d, Talgo II train.

1000fr, Steam locomotive, diff.

2007

281	Strip of 4	10.50	10.50
a.	A129 400fr multi	2.00	2.00
b.	A129 550fr multi	2.50	2.50
c.	A129 600fr multi	2.75	2.75
d.	A129 650fr multi	3.00	3.00

Souvenir Sheet

282	A129 1000fr multi	4.50	4.50

Native Toys A130

2007 Litho. *Perf. 13¾x14*

283	Horiz. strip of 4	8.50	8.50
a.	A130 400fr Airplane	1.75	1.75
b.	A130 450fr Car	2.00	2.00
c.	A130 500fr Scooter	2.25	2.25
d.	A130 550fr Songo game	2.50	2.50

Flora A131

No. 284: a, Artocarpus communis. b, Hibiscus sabdariffa. c, Spathodea campanulata. d, Theobroma cacao.

2007 Litho. *Perf. 13¾x14*

284	Horiz. strip of 4	9.00	9.00
a.	A131 400fr multi	1.75	1.75
b.	A131 450fr multi	2.00	2.00
c.	A131 550fr multi	2.50	2.50
d.	A131 600fr multi	2.75	2.75

African Children A132

No. 285: a, Child and basket. b, Five children and toy cars. c, Six children and net.

2008 Litho. *Perf. 13¾*

285	Horiz. strip of 3	6.50	6.50
a.	A132 400fr multi	1.90	1.90
b.	A132 450fr multi	2.10	2.10
c.	A132 500fr multi	2.40	2.40

2008 African Cup of Nations Soccer Championships, Ghana — A133

No. 286 — Emblem and: a, Soccer ball and player's foot. b, Soccer ball being caught. c, Goalie. d, Goalie, diff.

2008

286	Horiz. strip of 4	9.25	9.25
a.	A133 400fr multi	1.90	1.90
b.	A133 450fr multi	2.10	2.10
c.	A133 500fr multi	2.40	2.40
d.	A133 600fr multi	2.75	2.75

Flora and Fauna A134

No. 287: a, Sitatunga. b, Passiflora quadrangularis. c, Pachylobus edulis.

2008

287	Horiz. strip of 3	6.25	6.25
a.	A134 450fr multi	1.75	1.75
b.	A134 500fr multi	2.00	2.00
c.	A134 600fr multi	2.40	2.40

Intl. Year of Planet Earth A135

No. 288: a, Seedlings. b, Parched earth. c, Waterfall.

2008

288	Horiz. strip of 3	5.50	5.50
a.	A135 400fr multi	1.60	1.60
b.	A135 450fr multi	1.75	1.75
c.	A135 550fr multi	2.10	2.10

SPECIAL DELIVERY STAMPS

Archer with Crossbow — SD1

1971, Oct. 12 Photo. *Perf. 12½x13*

E1	SD1 4p blue & multi	.75	.20
E2	SD1 8p rose & multi	1.25	.20

3rd anniversary of independence.

ERITREA

ˌer-ə-ˈtrē-ə

LOCATION — In northeast Africa, bordering on the Red Sea, Sudan, Ethiopia and Djibouti.
GOVT. — Independent state
AREA — 45,300 (?) sq. mi.
POP. — 3,984,723 (1999 est.)
CAPITAL — Asmara

Formerly an Italian colony, Eritrea was incorporated as a State of Italian East Africa in 1936.

Under British occupation (1941-52) until it became part of Ethiopia as its northernmost region. Eritrea became independent May 24, 1993.

100 Centesimi = 1 Lira
100 cents = 1 birr (1991)
100 cents = 1 nakfa (1997)

Catalogue values for unused stamps in this country are for Never Hinged items, beginning with Scott 200 in the regular postage section.

All used values to about 1916 are for postally used stamps. From 1916-1934, used values in italics are for postally used stamps. CTO's, for stamps valued postally used, sell for about the same as unused, hinged stamps.

Watermark

Wmk. 140 — Crown

Stamps of Italy Overprinted

a

b

1892 Wmk. 140 *Perf. 14*

Overprinted Type "a" in Black

1	A6 1c bronze grn	8.00	8.00
a.	Inverted overprint	525.00	475.00
b.	Double overprint	1,450.	
	Never hinged	1,850.	
c.	Vert. pair, one without overprint	*2,850.*	
	Never hinged	*3,500.*	
2	A7 2c orange brn	4.00	4.00
a.	Inverted overprint	475.00	450.00
b.	Double overprint	1,450.	
	Never hinged	1,850.	
3	A33 5c green	120.00	12.00
a.	Inverted overprint	*5,750.*	*3,250.*
	Never hinged	*7,000.*	

Overprinted Type "b" in Black

4	A17 10c claret	165.00	12.00
5	A17 20c orange	300.00	8.00
6	A17 25c blue	1,050.	40.00
7	A25 40c brown	9.75	*24.00*
8	A26 45c slate green	9.75	*28.00*
9	A27 60c violet	9.75	*55.00*
10	A28 1 l brown & yel	37.50	*55.00*
11	A38 5 l blue & rose	525.00	400.00
	Nos. 1-11 (11)	2,238.	*646.00*
	Set, never hinged	5,350.	

1895-99

Overprinted type "a" in Black

12	A39 1c brown ('99)	15.00	9.75
13	A40 2c org brn ('99)	2.40	1.60
14	A41 5c green	2.40	1.60
a.	Inverted overprint	400.00	*3,250.*

Overprinted type "b" in Black

15	A34 10c claret ('98)	2.40	1.60
16	A35 20c orange	3.25	2.00
17	A36 25c blue	3.25	4.00
18	A37 45c olive grn	24.00	*22.50*
	Nos. 12-18 (7)	52.70	*43.05*
	Set, never hinged	130.00	

1903-28

Overprinted type "a" in Black

19	A42 1c brown	.80	*1.25*
a.	Inverted overprint	127.50	127.50
20	A43 2c orange brn	.80	.60
21	A44 5c blue green	40.00	.60
22	A45 10c claret	47.50	.60
23	A45 20c orange	3.25	1.25
24	A45 25c blue	350.00	16.00
a.	Double overprint	750.00	—
25	A45 40c brown	400.00	24.00
26	A45 45c olive grn	4.00	*8.00*
27	A45 50c violet	110.00	27.50
28	A46 75c dk red & rose ('28)	65.00	5.75
29	A46 1 l brown & grn	4.00	.80
30	A46 1.25 l bl & ultra ('28)	32.50	3.25
31	A46 2 l dk grn & org ('25)	52.50	*72.50*
32	A46 2.50 l dk grn & org ('28)	140.00	52.50
33	A46 5 l blue & rose	27.50	*40.00*
	Nos. 19-33 (15)	1,277.	254.60
	Set, never hinged	3,250.	

Surcharged in Black

1905

34	A45 15c on 20c orange	47.50	12.00
	Never hinged	120.00	

1908-28

Overprinted type "a" in Black

35	A48 5c green	1.00	.95
36	A48 10c claret ('09)	1.00	.95
37	A48 15c slate ('20)	16.00	9.50
38	A49 20c green ('25)	16.00	11.00
39	A49 20c lilac brn ('28)	4.75	3.25
40	A49 25c blue ('09)	4.50	2.25
41	A49 30c gray ('25)	16.00	16.00
42	A49 40c brown ('16)	36.00	*34.00*
43	A49 50c violet ('16)	12.00	2.00
44	A49 60c brn car ('18)	20.00	*22.50*
a.	Printed on both sides		*1,250.*

45 A49 60c brn org ('28) 80.00 *160.00*
46 A51 10 l gray grn & red ('16) 325.00 *600.00*
Nos. 35-46 (12) 532.25 *862.40*
Set, never hinged 1,300.

See No. 53.

A1

Government Building at Massaua — A2

1910-29 Unwmk. Engr. *Perf. 13½*
47 A1 15c slate 240.00 22.00
a. Perf. 11 ('29) 32.50 47.50
Never hinged 82.50
48 A2 25c dark blue 4.75 *14.00*
a. Perf. 12 600.00 600.00

For surcharges see Nos. 51-52.

A3

Farmer Plowing — A4

1914-28
49 A3 5c green .80 *2.40*
a. Perf. 11 ('28) 160.00 60.00
Never hinged 400.00
50 A4 10c carmine 4.00 *4.25*
a. Perf. 11 ('28) 12.00 *40.00*
Never hinged 30.00
b. Perf. 13½x14 60.00 60.00

No. 47 Surcharged in Red or Black

1916
51 A1 5c on 15c slate (R) 6.50 *14.50*
52 A1 20c on 15c slate 2.40 4.00
a. "CEN" for "CENT" 32.50 32.50
b. "CENT" omitted 175.00 *175.00*
c. "ENT" 47.50 *47.50*
Set, never hinged 22.00

Italy No. 113 Overprinted in Black — f

1921 Wmk. 140 *Perf. 14*
53 A50 20c brown orange 4.00 *12.00*
Never hinged 10.00

Victory Issue

Italian Victory Stamps of 1921 Overprinted type "f" 13mm long

1922
54 A64 5c olive green 2.00 *7.25*
55 A64 10c red 2.00 *7.50*
56 A64 15c slate green 2.00 *11.00*
57 A64 25c ultra 2.00 *11.00*
Nos. 54-57 (4) 8.00 *36.75*
Set, never hinged 20.00

Somalia Nos. 10-16 Overprinted In Black and Bars over Original Values

g

1922 Wmk. 140
58 A1 2c on 1b brn 4.75 *16.00*
59 A1 5c on 2b bl grn 4.75 *11.00*
60 A2 10c on 1a claret 4.75 2.40
61 A2 15c on 2a brn org 4.75 2.40
62 A2 25c on 2½a blue 4.75 2.40
63 A2 50c on 5a yellow 16.00 11.00
a. "ERITREA" double 1,050.
64 A2 1 l on 10a lilac 16.00 20.00
a. "ERITREA" double 1,050. 1,050.
Nos. 58-64 (7) 55.75 *65.20*
Set, never hinged 132.50

See Nos. 81-87.

Propagation of the Faith Issue

Italy Nos. 143-146 Overprinted

1923
65 A68 20c ol grn & brn org 8.00 *40.00*
66 A68 30c claret & brn org 8.00 *40.00*
67 A68 50c vio & brn org 4.75 *47.50*
68 A68 1 l bl & brn org 4.75 *60.00*
Nos. 65-68 (4) 25.50 *187.50*
Set, never hinged 62.50

Fascisti Issue

Italy Nos. 159-164 Overprinted in Red or Black — j

1923 Unwmk. *Perf. 14*
69 A69 10c dk green (R) 8.00 *14.50*
70 A69 30c dk violet (R) 8.00 *14.50*
71 A69 50c brown carmine 8.00 *16.00*

Wmk. 140
72 A70 1 l blue 8.00 *40.00*
73 A70 2 l brown 8.00 *47.50*
74 A71 5 l black & blue (R) 8.00 *65.00*
Nos. 69-74 (6) 48.00 *197.50*
Set, never hinged 120.00

Manzoni Issue

Italy Nos. 165-170 Overprinted in Red

1924 *Perf. 14*
75 A72 10c brn red & blk 13.00 *40.00*
76 A72 15c blue grn & blk 13.00 *40.00*
77 A72 30c black & slate 13.00 *40.00*
78 A72 50c org brn & blk 13.00 *40.00*
79 A72 1 l blue & blk 80.00 *275.00*
80 A72 5 l violet & blk 525.00 *2,200.*
Nos. 75-79 (5) 132.00 *435.00*

On Nos. 79 and 80 the overprint is placed vertically at the left side.

Somalia Nos. 10-16 Overprinted type "g" in Blue or Red

1924

Bars over Original Values

81 A1 2c on 1b brn 13.00 *27.50*
82 A1 5c on 2b bl grn (R) 13.00 *17.50*
83 A2 10c on 1a rose red 8.00 *16.00*
84 A2 15c on 2a brn org 8.00 *16.00*
a. Pair, one without "ERITREA" 1,650.
Never hinged 2,100.
85 A2 25c on 2½a bl (R) 8.00 *11.00*
a. Double surcharge 825.00
86 A2 50c on 5a yellow 8.00 *20.00*
87 A2 1 l on 10a lil (R) 8.00 *27.50*
Nos. 81-87 (7) 66.00 *135.50*
Set, never hinged 160.00

Stamps of Italy, 1901-08 Overprinted type "j" in Black

1924
88 A42 1c brown 8.00 *9.75*
a. Inverted overprint 275.00
89 A43 2c orange brown 4.75 *8.00*
90 A48 5c green 8.00 *9.00*
Nos. 88-90 (3) 20.75 *26.75*
Set, never hinged 50.00

Victor Emmanuel Issue

Italy Nos. 175-177 Overprinted — k

1925-26 Unwmk. *Perf. 11*
91 A78 60c brown car 1.60 *6.50*
a. Perf. 13½ 10.00 *24.00*
92 A78 1 l dark blue 1.60 *9.75*
a. Perf. 13½ *21,000.* *6,000.*
Never hinged *26,000.*

Perf. 13½
93 A78 1.25 l dk blue ('26) 3.25 *20.00*
a. Perf. 11 6.50 *28.00*
Nos. 91-93 (3) 6.45 *36.25*
Set, never hinged 16.00

Saint Francis of Assisi Issue

Italian Stamps of 1926 Overprinted

1926 Wmk. 140 *Perf. 14*
94 A79 20c gray green 2.40 *11.00*
95 A80 40c dark violet 2.40 *11.00*
96 A81 60c red violet 2.40 *20.00*

Overprinted in Red

Unwmk. *Perf. 11*
97 A82 1.25 l dark blue 2.40 *28.00*

Perf. 14
98 A83 5 l + 2.50 l ol grn 6.50 *55.00*
Nos. 94-98 (5) 16.10 *125.00*
Set, never hinged 40.00

Italian Stamps of 1926 Overprinted type "f" in Black

1926 Wmk. 140 *Perf. 14*
99 A46 75c dk red & rose 55.00 16.00
a. Double overprint 325.00
100 A46 1.25 l blue & ultra 32.50 16.00
101 A46 2.50 l dk grn & org 110.00 45.00
Nos. 99-101 (3) 197.50 77.00
Set, never hinged 495.00

Volta Issue

Type of Italy, 1927, Overprinted — o

1927
102 A84 20c purple 6.50 *32.50*
103 A84 50c deep orange 8.00 *20.00*
a. Double overprint 175.00
104 A84 1.25 l brt blue 12.50 *52.50*
Nos. 102-104 (3) 27.00 *105.00*
Set, never hinged 65.00

Italian Stamps of 1925-28 Overprinted type "a" in Black

1928-29
105 A86 7½c lt brown ('29) 16.00 *65.00*
106 A86 50c brt violet 55.00 55.00
Set, never hinged 180.00

Italian Stamps of 1927-28 Overprinted type "f"

1928-29
107 A86 50c brt violet 47.50 *47.50*
Never hinged 120.00

Unwmk. *Perf. 11*
107A A85 1.75 l deep brown 72.50 32.50
Never hinged 180.00

Italy No. 192 Overprinted type "o"

1928 Wmk. 140 *Perf. 14*
108 A85 50c brown & slate 16.00 8.00
Never hinged 40.00

Monte Cassino Issue

Types of 1929 Issue of Italy Overprinted in Red or Blue

1929 *Perf. 14*
109 A96 20c dk green (R) 4.75 *17.50*
110 A96 25c red orange (Bl) 4.75 *17.50*
111 A98 50c + 10c crim (Bl) 4.75 *20.00*
112 A98 75c + 15c ol brn (R) 4.75 *20.00*
113 A96 1.25 l + 25c dl vio (R) 11.00 *40.00*
114 A98 5 l + 1 l saph (R) 11.00 *60.00*

Overprinted in Red

Unwmk.
115 A100 10 l + 2 l gray brn 11.00 *55.00*
Nos. 109-115 (7) 52.00 *230.00*
Set, never hinged 130.00

Royal Wedding Issue

Type of Italian Stamps of 1930 Overprinted

1930 Wmk. 140
116 A101 20c yellow green 1.60 *4.75*
117 A101 50c + 10c dp org 1.25 *8.00*
118 A101 1.25 l + 25c rose red 1.25 *16.00*
Nos. 116-118 (3) 4.10 *28.75*
Set, never hinged 10.00

Lancer — A5

Scene in Massaua A6

2c, 35c, Lancer. 5c, 10c, Postman. 15c, Lineman. 25c, Askari (infantryman). 2 l, Railroad viaduct. 5 l, Asmara Deghe Selam. 10 l, Camels.

1930 Wmk. 140 Litho. *Perf. 14*

119	A5	2c brt bl & blk	3.00	*13.50*
120	A5	5c dk vio & blk	4.00	2.40
121	A5	10c yel brn & blk	4.00	1.25
122	A5	15c dk grn & blk	4.00	1.60
123	A5	25c gray grn & blk	4.00	1.25
124	A5	35c red brn & blk	10.50	*24.00*
125	A6	1 l dk bl & blk	4.00	1.25
126	A6	2 l choc & blk	10.50	*26.50*
127	A6	5 l ol grn & blk	15.00	*37.50*
128	A6	10 l dl bl & blk	22.50	*67.50*
		Nos. 119-128 (10)	81.50	*176.75*
		Set, never hinged	190.00	

Ferrucci Issue

Types of Italian Stamps of 1930 Overprinted type "f" in Red or Blue

1930

129	A102	20c violet (R)	4.75	*4.75*
130	A103	25c dk green (R)	4.75	*4.75*
131	A103	50c black (R)	4.75	*9.75*
132	A103	1.25 l dp blue (R)	4.75	*17.50*
133	A104	5 l + 2 l dp car (Bl)	9.75	*32.50*
		Nos. 129-133 (5)	28.75	*69.25*
		Set, never hinged	72.00	

Virgil Issue

Types of Italian Stamps of 1930 Overprinted in Red or Blue

1930 Photo.

134	A106	15c violet black	1.25	*8.00*
135	A106	20c orange brown	1.25	*3.25*
136	A106	25c dark green	1.25	*3.25*
137	A106	30c lt brown	1.25	*3.25*
138	A106	50c dull violet	1.25	*3.25*
139	A106	75c rose red	1.25	*6.50*
140	A106	1.25 l gray blue	1.25	*8.00*

Unwmk. Engr.

141	A106	5 l + 1.50 l dk vio	3.75	*40.00*
142	A106	10 l + 2.50 l ol brn	3.75	*60.00*
		Nos. 134-142 (9)	16.25	*135.50*
		Set, never hinged	40.00	

Saint Anthony of Padua Issue

Types of Italian Stamps of 1931 Overprinted type "f" in Blue, Red or Black

1931 Photo. Wmk. 140

143	A116	20c brown (Bl)	1.60	*17.50*
144	A116	25c green (R)	1.60	*6.50*
145	A118	30c gray brn (Bl)	1.60	*6.50*
146	A118	50c dl violet (Bl)	1.60	*6.50*
147	A120	1.25 l slate bl (R)	1.60	*17.50*

Unwmk. Engr.

148	A121	75c black (R)	1.60	*32.50*
149	A122	5 l + 2.50 l dk brn (Bk)	6.50	*67.50*
		Nos. 143-149 (7)	16.10	*154.50*
		Set, never hinged	40.00	

Victor Emmanuel III — A13

1931 Photo. Wmk. 140

150	A13	7½c olive brown	1.25	*4.00*
151	A13	20c slate bl & car	1.25	.20
152	A13	30c ol grn & brn vio	1.25	.20
153	A13	40c bl & yel grn	1.60	.20
154	A13	50c bis brn & ol	.80	.20
155	A13	75c carmine rose	3.25	.20
156	A13	1.25 l violet & indigo	4.00	4.00
157	A13	2.50 l dull green	4.00	9.75
		Nos. 150-157 (8)	17.40	18.75
		Set, never hinged	42.50	

Camel A14

Temple Ruins — A18

Designs: 2c, 10c, Camel. 5c, 15c, Shark fishery. 25c, Baobab tree. 35c, Pastoral scene. 2 l, African elephant. 5 l, Eritrean man. 10 l, Eritrean woman.

1934 Photo. Wmk. 140

158	A14	2c deep blue	1.60	*4.75*
159	A14	5c black	3.25	.40
160	A14	10c brown	3.25	.35
161	A14	15c orange brn	4.00	*1.60*
162	A14	25c gray green	3.25	.35
163	A14	35c purple	6.50	*9.75*
164	A18	1 l dk blue gray	.80	.35
165	A14	2 l olive black	19.00	3.25
166	A18	5 l carmine rose	9.75	6.50
167	A18	10 l red orange	15.00	*22.50*
		Nos. 158-167 (10)	66.40	*49.80*
		Set, never hinged	155.00	

Abruzzi Issue

Types of 1934 Issue Overprinted in Black or Red

1934

168	A14	10c dull blue (R)	13.00	*20.00*
169	A14	15c blue	9.75	*20.00*
170	A14	35c green (R)	5.75	*20.00*
171	A18	1 l copper red	5.75	*20.00*
172	A14	2 l rose red	17.50	*20.00*
173	A18	5 l purple (R)	9.75	*32.50*
174	A18	10 l olive grn (R)	9.75	*40.00*
		Nos. 168-174 (7)	71.25	*172.50*
		Set, never hinged	175.00	

Grant's Gazelle A22

1934 Photo.

175	A22	5c ol grn & brn	4.00	*20.00*
176	A22	10c yel brn & blk	4.00	*20.00*
177	A22	20c scar & indigo	4.00	*16.00*
178	A22	50c dk vio & brn	4.00	*16.00*
179	A22	60c org brn & ind	4.00	*24.00*
180	A22	1.25 l dk bl & grn	4.00	*40.00*
		Nos. 175-180 (6)	24.00	*136.00*
		Set, never hinged	60.00	

Second Colonial Arts Exhibition, Naples. See Nos. C1-C6.

Between 1981 and 1986 unofficial labels appeared showing such non-Eritrean subjects as the British royal weddings, Queen Mother, Queen's birthday, and the Duke & Duchess of York. These labels are not listed.

In 1978, two sets of stamps were issued for use within liberated areas of Eritrea and to publicize the liberation effort. A May 26 set of 5c, 10c, 80c and 1b commemorated the 8th anniv. of the Eritrean People's Liberation Front (EPLF). An August 1 set of 80c, 1b, 1.50b featured the Future of Eritrea theme. A September 1, 1991 set of 5c, 15c and 20c was issued with a Freedom Fighter design in orange and black almost identical to design A24. Although the 80c from the 1st 1978 issue was available at the Asmara post office in late 1992 and early 1993, there is no evidence that any of these stamps were available at the time of independence. Thus these stamps are more properly considered locals and provisionals.

Freedom Fighter with EPLF Flags
A23 A24

1991, Jan. 16 Typo. *Perf. 11 rough*

192	A23	5c lt bl, blk & org		—
193	A23	15c pale green, blk & org		—
194	A23	20c pale yel, blk & org		—
195	A23	3b silver, blk & org	*25.00*	*25.00*
196	A23	5b gold, blk & org	*25.00*	*25.00*

See footnotes following #199.

1993, Feb. 1 Litho. *Perf. 10*

197	A24	5c lt bl, blk & org	*4.50*	*4.50*
198	A24	15c pale grn, blk & org	*4.50*	*4.50*
199	A24	20c pale yel, blk & org	*4.50*	*4.50*

Nos. 192-199 commemorate 30 years of the war for national liberation.

Nos. 192-199 were issued for local use, and became valid for international mail on Sept. 13, 1993.

Catalogue values for unused stamps in this section, from this point to the end of the section, are for Never Hinged items.

Referendum for Independence A25

Designs: 15c, Placing ballot in box. 60c, Group of arrows pointing right, one pointing left. 75c, Signs indicating "yes" & "no." 1b, Candle burning. 2b, Peace dove, horn over country map.

Perf. 14x15

1993, Apr. 22 Litho. Wmk. 373

200	A25	15c multicolored	*1.00*	*1.00*
201	A25	60c multicolored	*2.00*	*2.00*
202	A25	75c multicolored	*3.00*	*3.00*
203	A25	1b multicolored	*5.00*	*5.00*
204	A25	2b multicolored	*7.00*	*7.00*
		Nos. 200-204 (5)	*18.00*	*18.00*

Natl. Flag — A26

1993 Litho. *Perf. 11 rough*

Blue Border

205	A26	5c multicolored	*3.00*	*.50*
206	A26	20c multicolored	—	—
207	A26	35c multicolored	*5.00*	*2.00*
208	A26	50c multicolored	*7.50*	*2.50*
209	A26	70c multicolored	*4.00*	*3.50*
210	A26	80c multicolored	*4.00*	*4.00*

The border of the 40c, No. 215, is similar to that of this issue but it was issued with next set. And the type face of the "0.40" matches that set.

1994 Litho. *Perf. 11 rough*

Color of Border

211	A26	5c brown	*1.50*	*1.50*
212	A26	15c red	*1.50*	*1.50*
213	A26	20c gold	*15.00*	—
214	A26	25c lt blue	*1.50*	*1.50*
215	A26	40c blue	*15.00*	*15.00*
216	A26	60c yellow	*2.00*	*2.00*
217	A26	70c purple	*2.25*	*2.25*
218	A26	3b light green	*6.00*	*6.00*
219	A26	5b silver	*6.00*	*6.00*

Flag & Map — A27

1994, Sept. 2 Litho. *Perf. 13½x14*

Color of Border

220	A27	5c deep yellow	*.45*	*.40*
221	A27	10c yellow green	*.50*	*.45*
222	A27	20c salmon	*.70*	*.65*
223	A27	25c red	*1.25*	*1.25*
224	A27	40c lilac rose	*1.40*	*1.25*
225	A27	60c blue green	*1.50*	*1.25*
226	A27	70c dark green	*1.60*	*1.50*
227	A27	1b yellow	*1.60*	*1.50*
228	A27	2b orange	*1.75*	*1.50*
229	A27	3b blue violet	*1.90*	*1.75*
230	A27	5b red lilac	*2.25*	*2.00*
231	A27	10b pale violet	*3.75*	*3.50*
		Nos. 220-231 (12)	*18.65*	*17.00*

World Tourism Organization, 20th Anniv. — A29

Perf. 14x13½, 13½x14

1995, Jan. 2 Litho.

232	A29	10c Fishing from boat	*1.50*	*1.50*
233	A29	35c Monument, vert.	*1.50*	*1.50*
234	A29	85c Winding road	*3.00*	*3.00*
235	A29	2b Stone dwelling, vert.	*5.00*	*5.00*
		Nos. 232-235 (4)	*11.00*	*11.00*

Fish — A30

Designs: 30c, Horned butterflyfish. 55c, Gonochaetodon larvatus. 70c, Shrimp lobster. 1b, Bluestripe snapper.

1995, Apr. 1 *Perf. 14x13½*

236	A30	30c multicolored	*.60*	*.60*
237	A30	55c multicolored	*.85*	*.85*
238	A30	70c multicolored	*1.25*	*1.25*
239	A30	1b multicolored	*1.50*	*1.50*
		Nos. 236-239 (4)	*4.20*	*4.20*

Independence Day — A31

Designs: 25c, Breaking chains, mountain, buildings, animals. 40c, Raising natl. flag, vert. 70c, Three men, holding natl. flag, sword, vert. 3b, Natl. flag, fireworks, vert.

Perf. 14x13½, 13½x14

1995, May 23 **Litho.**

240	A31	25c multicolored	*.40*	*.40*
241	A31	40c multicolored	*.45*	*.45*
242	A31	70c multicolored	*.70*	*.70*
243	A31	3b multicolored	*1.40*	*1.40*
		Nos. 240-243 (4)	*2.95*	*2.95*

Future Development Plan — A32

1995, Aug. 28 **Litho.** ***Perf. 13***

244	A32	60c Building bridge	*.40*	*.40*
245	A32	80c Trees	*.55*	*.55*
246	A32	90c Rural village	*.65*	*.65*
247	A32	1b Camels	*.70*	*.70*
		Nos. 244-247 (4)	*2.30*	*2.30*

A33

A34

1995, Oct. 23 ***Perf. 13½x14***

248	A33	40c shown	*.25*	*.25*
249	A33	60c Tree, emblem	*.35*	*.35*
250	A33	70c Dove, "50," emblem	*.45*	*.45*
251	A33	2b like No. 248	*2.00*	*2.00*
		Nos. 248-251 (4)	*3.05*	*3.05*

UN, 50th anniv.

1995, Oct. 2 ***Perf. 13½x14, 14x13½***

COMESA, Committee for Economic Growth and Development in Southern Africa: 40c, Map of African member countries. 50c, Tree with country names on branches. 60c, Emblem, 3b, Emblem surrounded by country flags, horiz.

252	A34	40c multicolored	*.25*	*.25*
253	A34	50c multicolored	*.45*	*.45*
254	A34	60c multicolored	*.45*	*.45*
255	A34	3b multicolored	*1.75*	*1.75*
		Nos. 252-255 (4)	*2.90*	*2.90*

FAO, 50th Anniv. — A35

5c, Food bowl with world map on it, spoon. 25c, Men with tractor. 80c, Mother bird feeding chicks. 3b, Vegetables in horn of plenty.

1995, Dec. 18 **Litho.** ***Perf. 13x14***

256	A35	5c multicolored	*.40*	*.40*
257	A35	25c multicolored	*.40*	*.40*
258	A35	80c multicolored	*.80*	*.80*
259	A35	3b multicolored	*2.50*	*2.50*
		Nos. 256-259 (4)	*4.10*	*4.10*

Endangered Fauna — A36

No. 260: a, Green monkey. b, Aardwolf. c, Dugong. d, Maned rat.

Beisa oryx: No. 261: a, With young. b, One facing left. c, Two with heads together. d, One facing right.

White-eyed gull: No. 262: a, Preening. b, In flight. c, Two standing. d, One facing right.

1996, July 15 **Litho.** ***Perf. 14***

260-262 A36 3b Set of 3 strips 24.00 24.00

Nos. 260-262 were each issued in sheets of 12 stamps, containing three strips of four stamps, #a.-d. No. 261 for World Wildlife Fund.

Martyrs Day — A37

1996, June 17 **Litho.** ***Perf. 13½x14***

263	A37	40c People, flag	.40	.40
264	A37	60c At grave	.40	.40
265	A37	70c Mother, child	.80	.80
266	A37	80c Planting crops	1.00	1.00
		Nos. 263-266 (4)	2.60	2.60

1996 Summer Olympic Games, Atlanta A38

No. 267, Cycling. No. 268, Basketball, vert. No. 269, Volleyball, vert. No. 270, Soccer.

No. 271, vert: a, Volleyball. b, Laurel wreath. c, Basketball. d, Torch. e, Cycling, yellow shirt. f, Torch, diff. g, Cycling, green shirt. h, Gold medal. i, Soccer.

Each 10b: #272, Soccer, vert. #273, Cycling, vert.

1996, Nov. 20 **Litho.** ***Perf. 14***

267-270	A38	3b Set of 4	7.50	7.50
271	A38	2b Sheet of 9, #a.-i.	11.00	11.00

Souvenir Sheets

272-273	A38	Set of 2	11.00	11.00

UNICEF, 50th Anniv. A39

UNICEF emblem and: 40c, Mother with child. 55c, Nurse helping child. 60c, Weighing baby. 95c, Boy with one leg walking with crutch.

1996 **Litho.** ***Perf. 14x13½***

274	A39	40c multicolored	.25	.25
275	A39	55c multicolored	.25	.25
276	A39	60c multicolored	.40	.40
277	A39	95c multicolored	.40	.40
		Nos. 274-277 (4)	1.30	1.30

Revival of Eritrea Railway A40

Designs: 40c, Repairing track. 55c, Steam train arriving at station. 60c, Train shuttle transporting people. 95c, Train tunnel.

1996

278	A40	40c multicolored	.45	.45
279	A40	55c multicolored	.45	.45
280	A40	60c multicolored	.45	.45
281	A40	95c multicolored	.90	.90
		Nos. 278-281 (4)	2.25	2.25

National Service A41

40c, Service members, speaker's platform, flags, vert. 55c, People looking over mountainside, vert. 60c, People digging ditches. 95c, Man standing on mountain top, overlooking valley, lake.

1996 ***Perf. 13½x14, 14x13½***

282	A41	40c multicolored	.45	.45
283	A41	55c multicolored	.45	.45
284	A41	60c multicolored	.85	.85
285	A41	95c multicolored	1.25	1.25
		Nos. 282-285 (4)	3.00	3.00

Butterflies and Moths A42

1b, Pieris napi. 2b, Heliconius melpomerie. 4b, Ornithoptera goliath. 8b, Heliconius astraea.

No. 290, vert, each 3b: a, Psaphis eusehemoides. b, Papilio brookiana. c, Parnassius charitonius. d, Morpho cypris. e, Dariaus plexippus. f, Precis octavia. g, Teinopalpus imperialis. h, Samia gloreri. i, Automeris nyctimene.

No. 291, each 3b: a, Papilio polymnestar. b, Ornithoptera paradiseo. c, Graphium marcellus. d, Panaxia quadripunctaria. e, Cardui japonica. f, Papilio childrence. g, Philosamea cynthis. h, Actias luna. i, Heticopis acit.

Each 10b: No. 292, Papilio glaucus. No. 293, Parnassius phoebus.

1997, June 16 **Litho.** ***Perf. 14***

286-289	A42	Set of 4	8.50	8.50

Sheets of 9

290-291	A42	3b Set of 2 Sheets, #a.-i.	24.00	24.00

Souvenir Sheets

292-293	A42	10b Set of 2 Sheets	9.00	9.00

Environmental Protection — A43

1997 **Litho.** ***Perf. 14x13½***

294	A43	60c Irrigation	.60	.60
295	A43	90c Reforestation	.60	.60
296	A43	95c Preventing erosion	1.25	1.25
		Nos. 294-296 (3)	2.45	2.45

Marine Life A44

No. 297, each 3n: a, Sergeant major, white tipped reef shark. b, Hawksbill turtle, devil ray (e). c, Surgeonfish. d, Red sea houndfish, humpback whale (a, g). e, Devil ray (b, f, h). f, Devil ray (e, c), two-banded clownfish. g, Long-nosed butterflyfish. h, Red sea houndfish (g), yellow sweetlips (i). i, White moray eel.

No. 298, each 3n: a, Masked butterflyfish. b, Suckerfish (a), whale shark (a). c, Sunrise dottyback, bluefin trevally. d, Moon wrasse (a), purple moon angel (a), two-banded anemonefish. e, Lionfish (b, f). f, White tipped shark, sand diver fish. g, Golden jacks (d), lunar tailed grouper. h, Batfish (e, i). i, Black triggerfish.

Each 10n: No. 299, Powder-blue surgeonfish. No. 300, Twin-spot wrasse.

1997, Dec. 29 **Litho.** ***Perf. 14***

Sheets of 9

297-298	A44	Set of 2 Sheets, #a.-i.	20.00	20.00

Souvenir Sheets

299-300	A44	Set of 2 Sheets	12.50	12.50

A45

A46

Natl. Constitution: 10c, Speaker, crowd seated beneath tree. 40c, Dove, scales of justice. 85c, Hands holding constitution.

1997 **Litho.** ***Perf. 13½x14***

301-303	A45	Set of 3	1.25	1.25

1998, Mar. 16 **Litho.** ***Perf. 14***

Birds — No. 304, each 3n: a, African darter (b, d, e). b, White-headed vulture (e). c, Egyptian vulture (f). d, Yellow-billed hornbill (g). e, Helmeted guineafowl (d, f). f, Secretary bird (d, e, i). g, Martial eagle (h). h, Bateleur eagle (i). i, Red-billed queleas.

No. 305, each 3n: a, Black-headed weaver. b, Abyssinian roller (c, f). c, Abyssinian ground hornbill (b, e, f). d, Lichtenstein's sandgrouse. e, Erckel's francolin (d, g, h). f, Arabian bustard (e, i). g, Chestnut-backed finch-lark. h, Desert lark. i, Bifasciated lark.

Each 10n: #306, Peregrine falcon. #307, Hoopoe.

Sheets of 9

304-305	A46	Set of 2 Sheets, #a.-i.	22.00	22.00

Souvenir Sheets

306-307	A46	Set of 2 Sheets	8.00	8.00

Dwellings — A47

Traditional Hair Styles — A48

1998, July 1 Litho. *Perf. 13½x14*

308 A47 50c Highlanders .50 .50
309 A47 60c Lowlanders .50 .50
310 A47 85c Danakils (Afars) .75 .75
Nos. 308-310 (3) 1.75 1.75

1998 Litho. *Perf. 13½x14*

311 A48 10c Cunama .30 .30
312 A48 50c Tignnys .35 .35
313 A48 85c Bllen .65 .65
314 A48 95c Tigre .75 .75
Nos. 311-314 (4) 2.05 2.05

Dated 1997.

A49

A50

Traditional Musical Instruments: 15c, Chirawata. 60c, Imbilta, malaket, shambeko. 75c, Kobero. 85c, K'rar.

1998, Dec. 28 Litho. *Perf. 13½x14*

315 A49 15c multicolored .35 .35
316 A49 60c multicolored .45 .45
317 A49 75c multicolored .65 .65
318 A49 85c multicolored .75 .75
Nos. 315-318 (4) 2.20 2.20

1999 Litho. *Perf. 13¼x14*

319 A50 60c green & multi .45 .45
320 A50 1n red & multi .70 .70
321 A50 3n blue & multi 2.25 2.25
Nos. 319-321 (3) 3.40 3.40

Independence, 8th Anniv.

1997 Introduction of Nakfa Currency — A51

Bank notes: 10c, 1 Nakfa. 60c, 5 Nakfa. 80c, 10 Nakfa. 1n, 20 Nakfa. 2n, 50 Nakfa. 3n, 100 Nakfa.

1999, Nov. 8 Litho. *Perf. 13¼*

322 A51 10c multicolored .45 .45
323 A51 60c multicolored .45 .45
324 A51 80c multicolored .45 .45
325 A51 1n multicolored .70 .70
326 A51 2n multicolored 1.40 1.40
327 A51 3n multicolored 2.00 2.00
Nos. 322-327 (6) 5.45 5.45

Natl. Union of Eritrean Women, 20th Anniv. A52

Designs: 5c, Woman and child, vert. 10c, Three women. 25c, Women and flag. 1n, Woman with binoculars.

1999 *Perf. 13¼x14, 14x13¼*

328 A52 5c multicolored .25 .25
329 A52 10c multicolored .25 .25
330 A52 25c multicolored .25 .25
331 A52 1n multicolored .40 .40
Nos. 328-331 (4) 1.15 1.15

A53

Marine Life A54

No. 332, each 3n: a, Coachwhip ray. b, Sulfur damselfish. c, "Gray moray." d, Sabre squirrelfish. e, Rusty parrotfish. f, "Striped eel catfish."

No. 333, each 3n: a, Spangled emperor. b, Devil scorpionfish. c, Crown squirrelfish. d, Vanikoro sweeper. e, Sergeant major. f, Giant manta.

No. 334, each 3n: a, Chilomycterus spilostylus. b, Dascyllus marginatus. c, Balistapus undulatus. d, Pomacanthus semicirculatus. e, Rhinecanthus assasi. f, Millepora.

No. 335, each 3n: a, Epinephalus fasciata. b, Pygoplites diacanthus. c, Cephalopholis miniata. d, Centropyge eibli. e, Ostracion cubicus. f, Heniochus acuminatus.

Each 10n: No. 336, Centropyge flavissimus. No. 337, Larabicus quadrilineatus. No. 338, Anthias squamipinnis. 15n, Pomacanthus maculosus.

2000, Apr. 17 Litho. *Perf. 14*

Sheets of 6, #a.-f.

332-333 A53 Set of 2 13.50 13.50
334-335 A54 Set of 2 13.50 13.50

Souvenir Sheets

336-338 A54 Set of 3 12.00 12.00
339 A54 15n multi 4.50 4.50

Illustrations on Nos. 332c and 332f were switched.

A55

Flag and: 5c, Man with sword. 10c, Ship Denden Assab. 25c, Independence Day festivities. 60c, Soldiers and barracks. 1n, Finger, heart and map. 2n, People under tree. 3n, Ballot box. 5n, Eritrean seal, military plane, tank, ship. 7n, Seal. 10n, Ten-nakfa note.

Perf. 13¾x13¼

2000, Mar. 17 Litho.

340-349 A55 Set of 10 11.00 11.00

See Nos. 363A, 363E.

Worldwide Fund for Nature (WWF) — A56

Proteles cristatus: a, Laying down. b. Pair in den. c, Walking. d, Close-up.

Illustration reduced.

2001, Oct. 1 Litho. *Perf. 14*

350 A56 3n Block or strip of 4, #a-d 4.50 4.50

Wild Animals — A57

No. 351, 3n: a, Salt's dik-dik. b, Klipspringer. c, Greater kudu. d, Soemmering's gazelle. e, Dorcas gazelle. f, Somali wild ass.

No. 352, 3n: a, Aardvark. b, Black-backed jackal. c, Striped hyena. d, Spotted hyena. e, East African leopard. f, African elephant.

2001, Oct. 29

Sheets of 6, #a-f

351-352 A57 Set of 2 10.00 10.00

Struggle for Independence, 10th Anniv. — A58

Designs: 20c, Women, flag, jewelry. 60c, Doves, stylized flag, vert. 1n, Bees, honeycomb, flag, vert. 3n, Men with sticks, vert.

Perf. 13x13¼, 13¼x13

2001, May 23 Litho.

353-356 A58 Set of 4 2.50 2.50

Liberation of Nakfa, 25th Anniv. A59

Designs: 50c, Denden. 1n, Town of Nakfa, 1977 (77x27mm). 3n, First Organizational Congress of the Eritrean People's Liberation Front (77x27mm).

2002, Mar. 23 Litho. *Perf. 14x13¼*

357-359 A59 Set of 3 1.50 1.50

Martyr's Day — A60

Designs: 1n, People and map. 2n, Hand, map of Badma area, and flag. 3n, Map and ship. 5n, Dove, map and dead man (49x29mm, triangular).

Perf. 14x13¼, 13½ (5n)

2002, June 20

360-363 A60 Set of 4 4.00 4.00

Type of 2000 Redrawn

Flag and: 30c, People under tree. 75c, Ship Denden Assab.

2002, Oct. 21 Litho. *Perf. 13¼x14¼*

363A A55 30c multi —
363E A55 75c multi —

Four additional stamps were issued in this set. The editors would like to examine any examples.

Dr. Fred C. Hollows (1929-93), Ophthalmologist A61

Designs: 50c, Portrait. 1n, Hollows wearing ophthalmological equipment. 2n, Hollows with man.

2003, Feb. 10 *Perf. 13¼x14*

364-366 A61 Set of 3 1.25 1.25

Eritrea — People's Republic of China Diplomatic Relations, 10th Anniv. A62

2003, May 24 *Perf. 12*

367 A62 4.50n multi 1.50 1.50

Eritrean postal authorities have declared "illegal" the following items:

Sheetlet of nine 5n stamps depicting Trains;

Sheetlets of nine 3n stamps depicting Marilyn Monroe (two different), Dogs, The Beatles "Yellow Submarine," September 11 firefighters, Brigitte Bardot, Grace Kelly, Sophia Loren, Golf etiquette, Sexy actresses, Sexy models, Boris Vallejo nudes, Dorian Cleavenger, Michael Möbius, Olivia, Ricky Carralero, Concorde;

Sheetlets of six stamps with various denominations depicting Lighthouses (with Rotary emblem) (two different), Hopper paintings (two different), Vettriano paintings (two different), Marilyn Monroe (two different), Elvgren pin-ups (two different), Teddy bears (two different);

Sheetlets of six 3n stamps depicting Van Gogh paintings, Paintings of nudes;

Sheetlets of five 3n stamps depicting Corot paintings, Pisarro paintings, Renoir paintings, Elvis Presley, Marilyn Monroe;

Sheetlets of four stamps with various denominations depicting Pandas (with Scouting emblem), Crocodiles (with Scouting emblem), Buffalos (with Rotary emblem), Elephants (with Rotary emblem), Monkeys (with Scouting emblem), Lizards (with Scouting emblem), Snakes (with Scouting Emblem), Turtles (with Rotary emblem), Wild cats (with Scouting emblem), Birds of prey (with Rotary emblem), Fowl (with Rotary emblem), Parrots (with Scouting emblem), Penguins (with Rotary emblem), Fish (with Rotary emblem), Marine life (with Scouting emblem), Mushrooms (with Rotary emblem), Butterflies (with Scouting emblem), Bees (with Scouting emblem), Spiders (with Scouting emblem);

Sheetlets of four 3n stamps depicting Dinosaurs (with Scouting emblem), Dinosaurs (with Rotary emblem) Elephants (with Scouting emblem), Elephants (with Rotary emblem), Horses (with Scouting emblem), Horses (with Rotary emblem), Birds (with Scouting emblem), Birds (with Rotary emblem), Penguins (with Scouting emblem), Penguins (with Scouting emblem), Orchids (with Scouting emblem), Orchids (with Rotary emblem), Butterflies (with Scouting emblem), Butterflies (with Rotary emblem), Cars (with Scouting emblem), Cars (with Rotary emblem), Motorcycles (with Scouting emblem), Motorcycles (with Rotary emblem), Trains (with Scouting emblem), Trains (with Rotary emblem);

Sheetlets of three 5n stamps depicting Dinosaurs (with Rotary emblem) (two different), Pandas;

Strips of three 5n stamps depicting Steam trains (four different);

Souvenir sheet with one 8n stamp depicting Steam Trains (with Rotary emblem) (two different), Dinosaurs (with Rotary emblem), Pandas (with Scouting emblem), Elephants (with Scouting emblem), Tigers (with Scouting emblem), Birds of prey (with Scouting emblem);

Souvenir sheets with one 5n stamp depicting Marilyn Monroe (six different), Lighthouses (with Rotary emblem) (four different), Teddy bears (four different), Hopper paintings (two different), Vettriano paintings (two different).

Eritrean Railway — A63

Independence Celebrations A63a

Massawa A63b

2003 **Litho.** ***Perf. 14x13¼***

Denomination Color

368	A63	5c Prussian blue	.20	.20
369	A63	10c greenish blk	.20	.20
370	A63	15c lilac	.20	.20
371	A63	35c violet	.20	.20
372	A63	50c orange	.20	.20
373	A63	90c olive green	.25	.25
374	A63	1n red	.25	.25
375	A63	2n blue violet	.55	.55
376	A63	10n red	2.75	2.75
376A	A63a	50n white	12.00	12.00
376B	A63b	75n white	18.00	18.00
376C	A63	100n white	24.00	24.00
		Nos. 368-376C (12)	58.80	58.80

Issued: 50n, 75n, 100n, 8/29.

Liberation of Massawa, 14th Anniv. A64

Designs: 40c, Tanks as fountains. 50c, Boat with soldiers.

No. 379: a, 3n, Crashed airplane, people, soldiers in shallow water. b, 3n, Tank, soldier, flag, boat. c, 4n, People, buildings at shore.

2004

377-378	A64	Set of 2	.40	.40

Miniature Sheet

379	A64	Sheet of 3, #a-c	3.00	3.00

Man and Camels — A65

Man and Cattle A66

Highland Woman, Child and Camel — A67

2004, July 12 **Litho.** ***Perf. 12***

Frame Color

380	A65	20c violet blue	.20	.20
381	A65	25c red violet	.20	.20
382	A65	40c brown	.20	.20
383	A66	50c red	.20	.20
384	A66	55c green	.20	.20
385	A66	60c light blue	.20	.20
386	A67	80c olive green	.35	.35
387	A67	1n orange	.35	.35
388	A67	4.50n blue	1.10	1.10
		Nos. 380-388 (9)	3.00	3.00

A68

A69

Monuments and Statues — A70

Perf. 13¼x14, 14x13¼

2006, Jan. 5 **Litho.**

389	A68	1.50n multi	.20	.20
390	A69	6n multi	.80	.80
391	A70	25n multi	3.50	3.50
		Nos. 389-391 (3)	4.50	4.50

China - Africa Cooperation Forum, Beijing — A71

2006, Nov. 3 **Litho.** ***Perf. 12***

392	A71	7n multi	.95	.95

African Soccer Confederation, 50th Anniv. — A72

Anniversary emblem and: 3n, Eritrean soccer players and flags. 5n, Soccer field. 10n, Soccer players in action.

2007, May 29 **Litho.** ***Perf. 13x13¼***

393-395	A72	Set of 3	2.40	2.40

SEMI-POSTAL STAMPS

Many issues of Italy and Italian Colonies include one or more semipostal denominations. To avoid splitting sets, these issues are generally listed as regular postage, airmail, etc., unless all values carry a surtax.

Italy Nos. B1-B3 Overprinted type "f"

1915-16 **Wmk. 140** ***Perf. 14***

B1	SP1	10c + 5c rose	4.00	*16.00*
a.		"EPITREA"	28.00	*40.00*
b.		Inverted overprint	525.00	525.00
B2	SP2	15c + 5c slate	16.00	*28.00*
B3	SP2	20c + 5c orange	4.75	*32.50*
a.		"EPITREA"	32.50	*52.50*
b.		Inverted overprint	525.00	525.00
c.		Pair, one without ovpt.	1,350.	*2,800.*
		Nos. B1-B3 (3)	24.75	*76.50*
		Set, never hinged	62.50	

No. B2 Surcharged

1916

B4	SP2	20c on 15c+5c slate	16.00	*32.50*
		Never hinged	40.00	
a.		"EPITREA"	57.50	*95.00*
b.		Pair, one without overprint	1,300.	
		Never hinged	1,600.	

Counterfeits exist of the minor varieties of Nos. B1, B3-B4.

Holy Year Issue

Italy Nos. B20-B25 Overprinted in Black or Red

1925 ***Perf. 12***

B5	SP4	20c + 10c dk grn & brn	3.25	*20.00*
B6	SP4	30c + 15c dk brn & brn	3.25	*22.50*
a.		Double overprint		
B7	SP4	50c + 25c vio & brn	3.25	*20.00*
B8	SP4	60c + 30c dp rose & brn	3.25	*25.00*
a.		Inverted overprint		
B9	SP8	1 l + 50c dp bl & vio (R)	3.25	*32.50*
B10	SP8	5 l + 2.50 l org brn & vio (R)	3.25	*47.50*
		Nos. B5-B10 (6)	19.50	*167.50*
		Set, never hinged	47.50	

The existence of Nos. B6a, B8a has been questioned.

Colonial Institute Issue

"Peace" Substituting Spade for Sword — SP1

1926 **Typo.** ***Perf. 14***

B11	SP1	5c + 5c brown	1.00	*8.00*
B12	SP1	10c + 5c olive grn	1.00	*8.00*
B13	SP1	20c + 5c blue grn	1.00	*8.00*
B14	SP1	40c + 5c brown red	1.00	*8.00*
B15	SP1	60c + 5c orange	1.00	*8.00*
B16	SP1	1 l + 5c blue	1.00	*17.50*
		Nos. B11-B16 (6)	6.00	*57.50*
		Set, never hinged	15.00	

The surtax of 5c on each stamp was for the Italian Colonial Institute.

Types of Italian Semi-Postal Stamps of 1926 Overprinted type "k"

1927 **Unwmk.** ***Perf. 11½***

B17	SP10	40c + 20c dk brn & blk	2.40	*32.50*
B18	SP10	60c + 30c brn red & ol brn	2.40	*32.50*
B19	SP10	1.25 l + 60c dp bl & blk	2.40	*52.50*

B20 SP10 5 l + 2.50 l dk grn & blk 4.00 *72.50*
Nos. B17-B20 (4) 11.20 *190.00*
Set, never hinged 28.00

The surtax on these stamps was for the charitable work of the Voluntary Militia for Italian National Defense.

Fascism and Victory
SP2

Agriculture
SP3

1928 Wmk. 140 Typo. *Perf. 14*

B21 SP2 20c + 5c blue grn 2.40 *12.00*
B22 SP2 30c + 5c red 2.40 *12.00*
B23 SP2 50c + 10c purple 2.40 *20.00*
B24 SP2 1.25 l + 20c dk blue 3.25 *24.00*
Nos. B21-B24 (4) 10.45 *68.00*
Set, never hinged 25.00

The surtax was for the Society Africana d'Italia, whose 46th anniv. was commemorated by the issue.

Types of Italian Semi-Postal Stamps of 1928 Overprinted type "f"

1929 Unwmk. *Perf. 11*

B25 SP10 30c + 10c red & blk 4.00 *20.00*
B26 SP10 50c + 20c vio & blk 4.00 *24.00*
B27 SP10 1.25 l + 50c brn & bl 4.75 *40.00*
B28 SP10 5 l + 2 l olive grn & blk 4.75 *72.50*
Nos. B25-B28 (4) 17.50 *156.50*
Set, never hinged 45.00

Surtax for the charitable work of the Voluntary Militia for Italian Natl. Defense.

Types of Italian Semi-Postal Stamps of 1929 Overprinted type "f" in Black or Red

1930 *Perf. 14*

B29 SP10 30c + 10c dk grn & bl grn (Bk) 21.00 *32.50*
B30 SP10 50c + 10c dk grn & vio 21.00 *45.00*
B31 SP10 1.25 l + 30c ol brn & red brn 21.00 *55.00*
B32 SP10 5 l + 1.50 l ind & grn 65.00 *160.00*
Nos. B29-B32 (4) 128.00 *292.50*
Set, never hinged 300.00

Surtax for the charitable work of the Voluntary Militia for Italian Natl. Defense.

1930 Photo. Wmk. 140

B33 SP3 50c + 20c ol brn 4.00 *20.00*
B34 SP3 1.25 l + 20c dp bl 4.00 *20.00*
B35 SP3 1.75 l + 20c green 4.00 *22.50*
B36 SP3 2.55 l + 50c purple 6.50 *36.00*
B37 SP3 5 l + 1 l dp car 6.50 *52.50*
Nos. B33-37 (5) 25.00 *151.00*
Set, never hinged 62.00

Italian Colonial Agricultural Institute, 25th anniv. The surtax aided that institution.

AIR POST STAMPS

Desert Scene
AP1

Design: 80c, 1 l, 2 l, Plane and globe.

Wmk. Crowns (140)

1934 Photo. *Perf. 14*

C1 AP1 25c sl bl & org red 4.00 *20.00*
C2 AP1 50c grn & indigo 4.00 *16.00*
C3 AP1 75c brn & org red 4.00 *16.00*
C4 AP1 80c org brn & ol grn 4.00 *20.00*
C5 AP1 1 l scar & ol grn 4.00 *24.00*
C6 AP1 2 l dk bl & brn 4.00 *40.00*
Nos. C1-C6 (6) 24.00 *136.00*
Set, never hinged 60.00

Second Colonial Arts Exhibition, Naples.

Plowing
AP3

Plane and Cacti
AP6

25c, 1.50 l, Plowing. 50c, 2 l, Plane over mountain pass. 60c, 5 l, Plane and trees. 75c, 10 l, Plane and cacti. 1 l, 3 l, Bridge.

1936 Photo.

C7 AP3 25c deep green 3.25 *4.00*
C8 AP3 50c dark brown 2.40 .35
C9 AP3 60c brown orange 4.00 *12.00*
C10 AP6 75c orange brown 3.25 1.60
C11 AP3 1 l deep blue 1.60 .35
C12 AP3 1.50 l purple 4.00 .80
C13 AP3 2 l gray blue 4.00 *3.25*
C14 AP3 3 l copper red 19.50 22.50
C15 AP3 5 l green 15.00 6.50
C16 AP6 10 l rose red 34.00 22.50
Nos. C7-C16 (10) 91.00 73.85
Set, never hinged 220.00

AIR POST SEMI-POSTAL STAMPS

King Victor Emmanuel III — SPAP1

1934 Wmk. 140 Photo. *Perf. 14*

CB1 SPAP1 25c + 10c 6.50 *14.50*
CB2 SPAP1 50c + 10c 6.50 *14.50*
CB3 SPAP1 75c + 15c 6.50 *14.50*
CB4 SPAP1 80c + 15c 6.50 *14.50*
CB5 SPAP1 1 l + 20c 6.50 *14.50*
CB6 SPAP1 2 l + 20c 6.50 *14.50*
CB7 SPAP1 3 l + 25c 22.50 *72.50*
CB8 SPAP1 5 l + 25c 22.50 *72.50*
CB9 SPAP1 10 l + 30c 22.50 *72.50*
CB10 SPAP1 25 l + 2 l 22.50 *72.50*
Nos. CB1-CB10 (10) 129.00 *377.00*
Set, never hinged 300.00

65th birthday of King Victor Emmanuel III and the nonstop flight from Rome to Mogadiscio. Used values are for stamps canceled to order.

AIR POST SEMI-POSTAL OFFICIAL STAMP

Type of Air Post Semi-Postal Stamps, 1934, Overprinted Crown and "SERVIZIO DI STATO" in Black

1934 Wmk. 140 *Perf. 14*

CBO1 SPAP1 25 l + 2 l cop red *2,800.*
Never hinged *4,200.*

SPECIAL DELIVERY STAMPS

Special Delivery Stamps of Italy, Overprinted type "a"

1907 Wmk. 140 *Perf. 14*

E1 SD1 25c rose red 20.00 20.00
Never hinged 50.00
a. Double overprint — —

1909

E2 SD2 30c blue & rose 110.00 *190.00*
Never hinged 275.00

1920

E3 SD1 50c dull red 2.40 *22.00*
Never hinged 6.00

"Italia"
SD1

1924 Engr. Unwmk.

E4 SD1 60c dk red & brn 5.50 *22.50*
a. Perf. 13½ 14.00 *35.00*
E5 SD1 2 l dk blue & red 14.00 *26.00*
Set, never hinged 49.00

For surcharges see Nos. E6-E8.

Nos. E4 and E5 Surcharged in Dark Blue or Red:

v

w

1926

E6 SD1 70c on 60c (Bl) 5.50 *14.00*
E7 SD1 2.50 l on 2 l (R) 14.00 *25.00*
Set, never hinged 49.00

Type of 1924 Surcharged in Blue or Black:

1927-35 *Perf. 11*

E8 SD1 1.25 l on 60c dk red & brn (Bl) 11.00 3.25
Never hinged 28.00
a. Perf. 14 (Bl) ('37) 100.00 20.00
Never hinged 200.00
b. Perf. 11 (Bk) ('35) *9,000.* 750.00
Never hinged *11,500.*
c. Perf. 14 (Bk) ('35) 275.00 47.50
Never hinged 575.00

AUTHORIZED DELIVERY STAMP

Authorized Delivery Stamp of Italy, No. EY2, Overprinted Type "f" in Black

1939-41 Wmk. 140 *Perf. 14*

EY1 AD2 10c dk brown ('41) .65
a. 10c reddish brown 17.50 *40.00*
Never hinged 45.00

On No. EY1a, which was used in Italian East Africa, the overprint hits the figures "10." On No. EY1, which was sold in Rome, the overprint falls above the 10's.

POSTAGE DUE STAMPS

Postage Due Stamps of Italy Overprinted type "a" at Top

1903 Wmk. 140 *Perf. 14*

J1 D3 5c buff & mag 22.50 *40.00*
a. Double overprint 500.00
J2 D3 10c buff & mag 17.50 *40.00*
J3 D3 20c buff & mag 17.50 *27.50*
J4 D3 30c buff & mag 25.00 *32.50*
J5 D3 40c buff & mag 65.00 *65.00*
J6 D3 50c buff & mag 87.50 65.00
J7 D3 60c buff & mag 25.00 *65.00*
J8 D3 1 l blue & mag 17.50 *36.00*
J9 D3 2 l blue & mag 175.00 160.00
J10 D3 5 l blue & mag 300.00 275.00
J11 D3 10 l blue & mag 3,000. 600.00
Never hinged 4,500.
Set #J1-J10, never hinged 1,100.

Same with Overprint at Bottom

1920-22

J1b D3 5c buff & magenta 4.75 *13.00*
c. Numeral and ovpt. invtd. 525.00 525.00
J2a D3 10c buff & magenta 8.00 *13.00*
J3a D3 20c buff & magenta 900.00 375.00
J4a D3 30c buff & magenta 60.00 36.00
J5a D3 40c buff & magenta 52.50 40.00
J6a D3 50c buff & magenta 28.00 *36.00*
J7a D3 60c buff & magenta 28.00 *36.00*
J8a D3 1 l blue & magenta 47.50 36.00
J9a D3 2 l blue & magenta 1,650. 900.00
J10a D3 5 l blue & magenta 425.00 300.00
J11a D3 10 l blue & magenta 57.50 *82.50*
Set, never hinged 4,750.

1903 Wmk. 140

J12 D4 50 l yellow 725.00 260.00
J13 D4 100 l blue 475.00 140.00
Set, never hinged 1,800.

1927

J14 D3 60c buff & brown 120.00 *150.00*
Never hinged 180.00

Postage Due Stamps of Italy, 1934, Overprinted type "j" in Black

1934

J15 D6 5c brown .80 *12.00*
J16 D6 10c blue .80 *2.40*
J17 D6 20c rose red 2.40 *4.00*
a. Inverted overprint — —
J18 D6 25c green 2.40 *4.75*
J19 D6 30c red orange 2.40 *12.00*
J20 D6 40c black brown 2.40 *12.00*
J21 D6 50c violet 2.40 1.60
J22 D6 60c black 5.00 *20.00*
J23 D7 1 l red orange 2.40 2.40
J24 D7 2 l green 14.50 *45.00*
J25 D7 5 l violet 25.00 *52.50*
J26 D7 10 l blue 30.00 *55.00*
J27 D7 20 l carmine rose 40.00 *65.00*
Nos. J15-J27 (13) 130.50 *288.65*
Set, never hinged 325.00

The existence of No. J17a has been questioned.

PARCEL POST STAMPS

These stamps were used by affixing them to the way bill so that one half remained on it following the parcel, the other half staying on the receipt given the sender. Most used halves are right halves. Complete stamps were obtainable canceled, probably to order. Both unused and used values are for complete stamps.

Parcel Post Stamps of Italy, 1914-17, Overprinted type "j" in Black on Each Half

1916 Wmk. 140 *Perf. 13½*

Q1 PP2 5c brown 120.00 *180.00*
Q2 PP2 10c deep blue *2,500.* *3,400.*
Never hinged *3,800.*
Q3 PP2 25c red 275.00 *275.00*
Q4 PP2 50c orange 65.00 *180.00*
Q5 PP2 1 l violet 120.00 *180.00*
Q6 PP2 2 l green 87.50 *180.00*
Q7 PP2 3 l bister 825.00 *500.00*
Q8 PP2 4 l slate 825.00 *500.00*
Set #Q1, Q3-Q8, never hinged 3,500.

Halves Used, Each

Q1	4.00
Q2	85.00
Q3	5.25
Q4	2.75
Q5	2.75
Q6	8.00
Q7	18.00
Q8	18.00

Overprinted type "f" on Each Half

1917-24

Q9 PP2 5c brown 3.25 *8.00*
Q10 PP2 10c deep blue 3.25 *8.00*
Q11 PP2 20c black 3.25 *8.00*
Q12 PP2 25c red 3.25 *8.00*
Q13 PP2 50c orange 6.50 *12.00*
Q14 PP2 1 l violet 6.50 *12.00*
Q15 PP2 2 l green 6.50 *12.00*
Q16 PP2 3 l bister 6.50 *12.00*
Q17 PP2 4 l slate 6.50 *20.00*
Q18 PP2 10 l rose lil ('24) 105.00 *160.00*
Q19 PP2 12 l red brn ('24) 225.00 *325.00*
Q20 PP2 15 l olive grn ('24) 225.00 *325.00*
Q21 PP2 20 l brn vio ('24) 300.00 *425.00*
Nos. Q9-Q21 (13) 900.50 *1,335.*
Set, never hinged 1,300.

Halves Used, Each

Q9	1.20
Q10	1.20

Q11	1.20
Q12	1.20
Q13	1.20
Q14	1.20
Q15	1.60
Q16	4.00
Q17	4.00
Q18	8.00
Q19	12.00
Q20	12.00
Q21	16.00

Parcel Post Stamps of Italy, 1927-39, Overprinted type "f" on Each Half

1927-37

Q21A	PP3	10c dp bl ('37)	*8,250.*	750.00
		Never hinged	*10,500.*	
Q22	PP3	25c red ('37)	525.00	52.50
Q23	PP3	30c ultra ('29)	4.00	*16.50*
Q24	PP3	50c orange ('36)	675.00	34.00
Q25	PP3	60c red ('29)	4.00	*16.50*
Q26	PP3	1 l brn vio ('36)	300.00	34.00
a.		1 l lilac	350.00	34.00
Q27	PP3	2 l green ('36)	300.00	34.00
Q28	PP3	3 l bister	9.50	*30.00*
Q29	PP3	4 l gray	9.50	*30.00*
Q30	PP3	10 l rose lil ('36)	525.00	600.00
Q31	PP3	20 l lil brn ('36)	525.00	600.00
		Nos. Q22-Q31 (10)	2,877.	
		Set, never hinged	4,200.	
		Nos. Q21A-Q31 (11)		2,197.

Halves Used, Each

Q21A	26.00
Q22	1.20
Q23	.65
Q24	.80
Q25	1.20
Q26	1.20
Q26a	1.20
Q27	1.20
Q28	1.20
Q292	.40
Q30	37.50
Q31	37.50

ESTONIA

e-ˈstō-nē-ə

LOCATION — Northern Europe, bordering on the Baltic Sea and the Gulf of Finland
GOVT. — Independent republic
AREA — 17,462 sq. mi.
POP. — 1,408,523 (1999 est.)
CAPITAL — Tallinn

Formerly a part of the Russia empire, Estonia declared its independence in 1918. In 1940 it was incorporated in the Union of Soviet Socialist Republics.

Estonia declared the restoration of its independence from the USSR on Aug. 20, 1991. Estonian independence was recognized by the Soviet Union on Sept. 6, 1991.

100 Kopecks = 1 Ruble (1918, 1991)
100 Penni = 1 Mark (1919)
100 Sents = 1 Kroon (1928, 1992)

Catalogue values for unused stamps in this country are for Never Hinged items, beginning with Scott 200 in the regular postage section, Scott B60 in the semi-postal section, and Scott F1 in the registration section.

Watermark

Wmk. 207 — Arms of Finland in the Sheet

Illustration reduced. Watermark covers a large part of sheet.

A1

A2

1918-19 Unwmk. Litho. *Imperf.*

1	A1	5k pale red	.90	.85
2	A1	15k bright blue	.90	.85
3	A2	35p brown ('19)	1.00	.90
a.		Printed on both sides	*150.00*	
b.		35p olive	55.00	55.00
4	A2	70p olive grn ('19)	1.50	1.25
		Nos. 1-4 (4)	4.30	3.85

Nos. 1-4 exist privately perforated.

Russian Stamps of 1909-17 Handstamped in Violet or Black

1919, May 7 *Perf. 14, 14½x15, 13½*

8	A14	1k orange	*2,100.*	*2,100.*
9	A14	2k green	30.00	*30.00*
10	A14	3k red	35.00	*32.50*
11	A14	5k claret	30.00	*27.50*
12	A15	10k dk bl (Bk)	55.00	*50.00*
13	A15	10k dk bl	175.00	*175.00*
14	A14	10k on 7k lt bl	*475.00*	*475.00*
15	A11	15k red brn & bl	42.50	*42.50*
16	A11	25k grn & vio	47.50	*45.00*
17	A11	35k red brn & grn	*1,750.*	*1,750.*
18	A8	50k vio & grn	100.00	100.00
19	A9	1r pale brn, brn & org	175.00	175.00
20	A13	10r scar, yel & gray	*4,000.*	*4,000.*

Imperf

21	A14	1k orange	27.50	*27.50*
22	A14	2k green	*400.00*	*400.00*
23	A14	3k red	50.00	50.00
24	A9	1r pale brn, brn & red org	*250.00*	*250.00*
25	A12	3½r maroon & grn	*475.00*	*475.00*
26	A13	5r dk bl, grn & pale bl	*600.00*	*600.00*

Provisionally issued at Tallinn. This overprint has been extensively counterfeited. Values are for genuine examples competently expertized.

No. 20 is always creased.

Gulls — A3

1919, May 13 *Imperf.*

27	A3	5p yellow	2.25	*3.25*

A4

A5

A6

A7

Viking Ship — A8

1919-20 *Perf. 11½*

28	A4	10p green	.25	.25

Imperf

29	A4	5p orange	.20	.20
30	A4	10p green	.20	.20
31	A5	15p rose	.20	.20
32	A6	35p blue	.25	.20
33	A7	70p dl vio ('20)	.25	.20
34	A8	1m bl & blk brn	1.25	.55
a.		Gray granite paper ('20)	.65	.40
35	A8	5m yel & blk	3.00	.95
a.		Gray granite paper ('20)	1.00	.50
36	A8	15m yel grn & vio ('20)	3.25	.65
37	A8	25m ultra & blk brn ('20)	4.75	2.50
		Nos. 28-37 (10)	13.60	5.90
		Set, never hinged	16.50	

The 5m exists with inverted center. Not a postal item.

See #76-77. For surcharges see #55, 57.

Skyline of Tallinn — A9

1920-24 *Imperf.*

Pelure Paper

39	A9	25p green	.35	.25
40	A9	25p yellow ('24)	.35	.30
41	A9	35p rose	.35	.25
42	A9	50p green ('21)	.35	.25
43	A9	1m vermilion	.95	.25
44	A9	2m blue	.80	.25
45	A9	2m ultramarine	.65	.25
46	A9	2.50m blue	.95	.25
		Nos. 39-46 (8)	4.75	2.05
		Set, never hinged	13.50	

Nos. 39-46 with sewing machine perforation are unofficial.

For surcharge see No. 56.

Stamps of 1919-20 Surcharged

1920 *Imperf.*

55	A5	1m on 15p rose	.50	.50
56	A9	1m on 35p rose	.70	.50
57	A7	2m on 70p dl vio	.85	.60
		Nos. 55-57 (3)	2.05	1.60
		Set, never hinged	4.00	

Weaver A10

Blacksmith A11

1922-23 Typo. *Imperf.*

58	A10	½m orange ('23)	2.00	*3.00*
59	A10	1m brown ('23)	2.75	2.25
60	A10	2m yellow green	2.00	2.00
61	A10	2½m claret	5.00	3.00
62	A11	5m rose	5.00	3.00
63	A11	9m red ('23)	8.00	6.00
64	A11	10m deep blue	6.00	5.00
		Nos. 58-64 (7)	30.75	24.25
		Set, never hinged	75.00	

1922-25 *Perf. 14*

65	A10	½m orange ('23)	.65	.20
66	A10	1m brown ('23)	.80	.20
67	A10	2m yellow green	1.40	.20
68	A10	2½m claret	1.40	.20
69	A10	3m blue green ('24)	1.50	.20
70	A11	5m rose	5.00	.20
71	A11	9m red ('23)	3.00	1.00
72	A11	10m deep blue	4.00	.20
73	A11	12m red ('25)	4.00	.90
74	A11	15m plum ('25)	4.00	.25
75	A11	20m ultra ('25)	15.00	.20
		Nos. 65-75 (11)	40.75	3.75
		Set, never hinged	90.00	

See No. 89. For surcharges see Nos. 84-88.

Viking Ship Type of 1920

1922, June 8 *Perf. 14x13½*

76	A8	15m yel grn & vio	6.00	.60
77	A8	25m ultra & blk brn	10.00	2.00
		Set, never hinged	25.00	

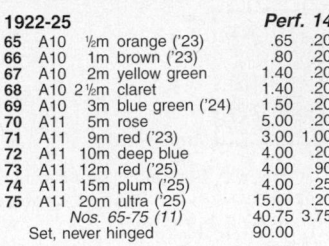

Map of Estonia — A13

1923-24

Paper with Lilac Network

78	A13	100m ol grn & bl	20.00	2.75

Paper with Buff Network

79	A13	300m brn & bl ('24)	50.00	12.50
		Set, never hinged	175.00	

For surcharges see Nos. 106-107.

National Theater, Tallinn — A14

1924, Dec. 9 *Perf. 14x13½*

Paper with Blue Network

81	A14	30m violet & blk	10.00	2.75

Paper with Rose Network

82	A14	70m car rose & blk	15.00	5.00
		Set, never hinged	45.00	

For surcharge see No. 105.

Vanemuine Theater, Tartu — A15

1927, Oct. 25

Paper with Lilac Network

83	A15	40m dp bl & ol brn	10.00	2.75
		Never hinged	18.00	

Stamps of 1922-25 Surcharged in New Currency in Red or Black

1928 *Perf. 14*

84	A10	2s yellow green	1.50	.20
85	A11	5s rose red (B)	1.50	.20
86	A11	10s deep blue	2.00	.20
a.		Imperf., pair	*900.00*	—
87	A11	15s plum (B)	6.50	.25
88	A11	20s ultra	4.50	.30
		Nos. 84-88 (5)	16.00	1.15
		Set, never hinged	35.00	

10th anniversary of independence.

3rd Philatelic Exhibition Issue

Blacksmith Type of 1922-23

1928, July 6

89	A11	10m gray	5.00	*7.50*
		Never hinged	10.00	

Sold only at Tallinn Philatelic Exhibition. Exists imperf.

Arms — A16

Paper with Network in Parenthesis

1928-40 ***Perf. 14, 14½x14***

90	A16 1s dk gray (bl)	.40	.20
a.	Thick gray-toned laid paper ('40)	10.00	6.00
91	A16 2s yel grn (org)	.50	.20
92	A16 4s grn (brn) ('29)	.65	.20
93	A16 5s red (grn)	3.75	.20
a.	5 feet on lowest lion	45.00	32.50
94	A16 8s vio (buff) ('29)	2.00	.20
95	A16 10s lt bl (lilac)	2.50	.20
96	A16 12s crimson (grn)	1.90	.20
97	A16 15s yel (blue)	2.25	.20
98	A16 15s car (gray) ('35)	7.50	.45
99	A16 20s slate bl (red)	3.50	.20
100	A16 25s red vio (grn) ('29)	7.50	.20
101	A16 25s bl (brn) ('35)	7.50	.40
102	A16 40s red org (bl) ('29)	9.00	.30
103	A16 60s gray (brn) ('29)	12.50	.50
104	A16 80s brn (bl) ('29)	12.50	1.00
	Nos. 90-104 (15)	73.95	4.65
	Set, never hinged	125.00	

Types of 1924 Issues Surcharged:

1930, Sept. 1 ***Perf. 14x13½***

Paper with Green Network

105	A14 1k on 70m car & blk	8.50	3.00

Paper with Rose Network

106	A13 2k on 300m brn & bl	17.50	7.50

Paper with Blue Network

107	A13 3k on 300m brn & bl	42.50	18.00
	Nos. 105-107 (3)	68.50	28.50
	Set, never hinged	150.00	

University Observatory A17

University of Tartu A18

Paper with Network as in Parenthesis

1932, June 1 ***Perf. 14***

108	A17 5s red (yellow)	6.50	.60
109	A18 10s light bl (lilac)	1.75	.60
110	A17 12s car (blue)	9.50	2.75
111	A18 20s dk bl (green)	7.25	1.10
	Nos. 108-111 (4)	25.00	5.05
	Set, never hinged	65.00	

University of Tartu tercentenary.

Narva Falls — A19

Ancient Bard Playing Harp — A20

1933, Apr. 1 **Photo.** ***Perf. 14x13½***

112	A19 1k gray black	7.00	1.00
	Never hinged	15.00	

See No. 149.

Paper with Network as in Parenthesis

1933, May 29 **Typo.** ***Perf. 14***

113	A20 2s green (orange)	1.60	.30
114	A20 5s red (green)	2.75	.30
115	A20 10s blue (lilac)	3.50	.30
	Nos. 113-115 (3)	7.85	.90
	Set, never hinged	15.00	

Tenth National Song Festival.
Nos. 113-115 exist imperf. Value $125.

Woman Harvester A21

Pres. Konstantin Päts A22

1935, Mar. 1 **Engr.** ***Perf. 13½***

116	A21 3k black brown	.50	*1.00*
	Never hinged	1.25	

1936-40 **Typo.** ***Perf. 14***

117	A22 1s chocolate	.40	.25
118	A22 2s yellow green	.40	.25
119	A22 3s dp org ('40)	10.00	7.50
120	A22 4s rose vio	.75	.25
121	A22 5s lt blue grn	.75	.30
122	A22 6s rose lake	.90	.25
123	A22 6s dp green ('40)	25.00	25.00
124	A22 10s greenish blue	.80	.25
125	A22 15s crim rose ('37)	1.25	.25
126	A22 15s dp bl ('40)	4.00	2.25
127	A22 18s dp car ('39)	25.00	9.00
128	A22 20s brt vio	1.25	.35
129	A22 25s dk bl ('38)	6.00	.35
130	A22 30s bister ('38)	4.25	.35
131	A22 30s ultra ('39)	20.00	5.00
132	A22 50s org brn	7.00	.85
133	A22 60s brt pink	12.50	4.50
	Nos. 117-133 (17)	120.25	56.95
	Set, never hinged	225.00	

St. Brigitta Convent Entrance A23

Ruins of Convent, Pirita River A24

Front View of Convent — A25

Seal of Convent — A26

Paper with Network as in Parenthesis

1936, June 10 ***Perf. 13½***

134	A23 5s green (buff)	.35	.20
135	A24 10s blue (lil)	.55	.20
136	A25 15s red (org)	.85	1.25
137	A26 25s ultra (brn)	1.25	*1.75*
	Nos. 134-137 (4)	3.00	*3.40*
	Set, never hinged	7.00	

St. Brigitta Convent, 500th anniversary.

Harbor at Tallinn — A27

1938, Apr. 11 **Engr.** ***Perf. 14***

138	A27 2k blue	.90	*1.25*
	Never hinged	1.75	

Friedrich R. Faehlmann A28

Friedrich R. Kreutzwald A29

1938, June 15 **Typo.** ***Perf. 13½***

139	A28 5s dark green	.70	.50
140	A29 10s deep brown	.70	.50
141	A29 15s dark carmine	1.00	.90
142	A28 25s ultra	1.60	1.40
a.	Sheet of 4, #139-142	10.00	*20.00*
	Nos. 139-142 (4)	4.00	3.30
	Set, never hinged	9.00	

Society of Estonian Scholars centenary.

Hospital at Pärnu — A30

Beach Hotel — A31

1939, June 20 **Typo.** ***Perf. 14x13½***

144	A30 5s dark green	.70	.35
145	A31 10s deep red violet	.50	.40
146	A30 18s dark carmine	1.50	1.50
147	A31 30s deep blue	1.75	1.75
a.	Sheet of 4, #144-147	15.00	*25.00*
	Nos. 144-147 (4)	4.45	4.00
	Set, never hinged	10.00	

Cent. of health resort and baths at Pärnu.

Narva Falls Type of 1933

1940, Apr. 15 **Engr.**

149	A19 1k slate green	1.40	*2.50*
	Never hinged	2.50	

The sky consists of heavy horizontal lines and the background consists of horizontal and vertical lines.

Carrier Pigeon and Plane — A32

1940, July 30 **Typo.**

150	A32 3s red orange	.25	.25
151	A32 10s purple	.25	.25
152	A32 15s rose brown	.25	.25
153	A32 30s dark blue	1.60	1.25
	Nos. 150-153 (4)	2.35	2.00
	Set, never hinged	4.00	

Centenary of the first postage stamp.
The 15s exists imperf. Value $6.25.

Catalogue values for unused stamps in this section, from this point to the end of the section, are for Never Hinged items.

Natl. Arms — A40

A41

1991, Oct. 1 **Litho.** ***Perf. 13x12½***

200	A40 5k salmon & red	.30	.30
201	A40 10k lt grn & dk bl grn	.30	.30
202	A40 15k lt bl & dk bl	.30	.30
203	A40 30k vio & gray	.45	.45
204	A40 50k org & brn	.60	.60
205	A40 70k pink & purple	.75	.75
206	A40 90k pur & rose lilac	.90	.90

Size: 20½x27mm

Engr.

Perf. 12½ Horiz.

207	A40 1r dark brown	1.10	1.10
208	A40 2r lt bl & dk bl	2.25	2.25
	Nos. 200-208 (9)	6.95	6.95

See Nos. 211-213, 215, 216, 230, 299-301, 314-314A, 317, 333-334, 339-340. For surcharge, see No. 217.

Perf. 13½x14, 14x13½

1991, Nov. 1 **Litho.**

209	A41 1.50r Flag, vert.	1.75	1.75
210	A41 2.50r shown	2.75	2.75

National Arms — A42

1992, Mar. 16 **Litho.** ***Perf. 13x12½***

211	A42 E (1r) lemon	.20	.20
212	A42 I (20r) blue green	1.25	1.25
213	A42 A (40r) blue	2.75	2.75
	Nos. 211-213 (3)	4.20	4.20

No. 211 was valid for postage within Estonia. No. 212 was valid for postage within Europe. No. 213 was valid for overseas mail. See Nos. 214, 219, 220, 224-229.

No. 202 Surcharged and Arms Types of 1991-1992

And

Natl. Arms — A42a

Perf. 14, 13x12½ (#214, 217, 219-220)

1992-96

214	A42 E (10s) orange	.25	.25
215	A40 10s blue & gray	.25	.25
216	A40 50s gray & brt bl	.25	.25
217	A40 60s on 15k #202	.25	.25
218	A40 60s lilac & olive	.25	.25
219	A42 I (1k) emerald	.75	.75
220	A42 A (2k) violet blue	1.50	1.50
221	A42a 5k bis & red vio	1.25	1.25
a.	5k yel orange & red violet	2.50	2.50
222	A42a 10k blue & olive	2.50	2.50
223	A42a 20k pale lilac & slate grn	4.25	4.25
	Nos. 214-223 (10)	11.50	11.50

Coil Stamps

Engr.

Size: 20½x27mm

Perf. 12½ Horiz.

224	A42 X (10s) brown	.30	.30
225	A42 X (10s) olive	.30	.30
226	A42 X (10s) black	.30	.30
227	A42 Z (30s) red lilac	.30	.30
228	A42 Z (30s) red	.30	.30
229	A42 Z (30s) dark blue	.30	.30

Litho.

230	A40 60s lilac brown	.30	.30
	Nos. 224-230 (7)	2.10	2.10

Issued: #214, 219-220, 6/22; #224, 8/29; #225, 9/25; #226, 10/31; #227, 11/16; #228, 12/1; #229, 12/22; #230, 1/8/93; #217, 3/5/93; 10s, 50s, 3/23 1993; 10k, 5/25/93; 5k, 7/7/93; #218, 8/5/93; 20k, 9/8/93; #221a, 9/19/96.

See note after No. 213. Nos. 224-229 were valid for postage within Estonia.

See No. F1.

A44

A45

Birds of the Baltic shores.

1992, Oct. 3 Litho. & Engr. *Perf. 13*

Booklet Stamps

231 A44 1k Pandion haliaetus .25 .25
232 A44 1k Limosa limosa .25 .25
233 A44 1k Mergus merganser .25 .25
234 A44 1k Tadorna todorna .25 .25
a. Booklet pane of 4, #231-234 1.50

See Latvia Nos. 332-335a, Lithuania Nos. 427-430a and Sweden Nos. 1975-1978a.

1992, Dec, 15 Litho. *Perf. 14*

235 A45 30s gray & multi .30 .30
236 A45 2k light brown & multi .70 .70

Christmas.

Exist on ordinary and fluorescent paper. Values are for former.

Friendship A46

1993, Feb. 8 Litho. *Perf. 14*

237 A46 1k multicolored .25 .25
a. Booklet pane of 6 1.50

See Finland No. 906.

A47 A48

1993, Feb. 16 *Perf. 13x13½*

238 A47 60s black & multi .25 .25
239 A47 1k violet & multi .30 .30
240 A47 2k blue & multi .40 .40
Nos. 238-240 (3) .95 .95

First Republic, 75th anniv.

1993, June 9 Litho. *Perf. 13½x14*

241 A48 60s Wrestling .25 .25
242 A48 1k +25s Viking ship, map .30 .30
243 A48 2k Shot put with rock .45 .45
Nos. 241-243 (3) 1.00 1.00

First Baltic sea games.

Tallinn Castle — A49

Designs: 1k, Toolse Castle. #245, Paide Castle, vert. #245A, Purtse Castle. 2.70k, Narva Fortress. 2.90k, Haapsalu Cathedral. 3k, Monks' Tower, Kiiu. 3.20k, Rakvere Castle. 4k, Kuressaare Castle. 4.80k, Viljandi Castle.

1993-97 Litho. *Perf. 14*

244 A49 1k gray & black .20 .20
245 A49 2k tan & brown .35 .35
246 A49 2.50k lt vio & dk vio .45 .45
247 A49 2.50k gray .45 .45
248 A49 2.70k lt blue & dk blue .45 .45
249 A49 2.90k lt grn & dk grn .50 .50
250 A49 3k rose & brown .50 .50
251 A49 3.20k lt grn & dk grn .75 .75
252 A49 4k lt gray vio & gray vio .75 .75
253 A49 4.80k dull org & brn .80 .80
Nos. 244-253 (10) 5.20 5.20

Issued: 1k, 2/22/94; 2k, 10/12/93; 2.70k, 12/10/93; 2.90k, 12/23/93; 3k, 3/31/94; 3.20, 12/28/94; 4k, 9/20/94; #246, 1/25/96; 247, 7/25/96; 4.80k, 1/21/97.

First Estonian Postage Stamp, 75th Anniv. — A50

1993, Nov. 13 Litho. *Perf. 14*

259 A50 1k multicolored .30 .30

Souvenir Sheet

Imperf

260 A50 4k multicolored 3.00 3.00
a. Ovptd. in sheet margin 15.00 15.00

No. 260 sold for 5k. Overprint on No. 260a reads "FILATEELIANAITUS / MARE BALTICUM '93 / 24.-28. NOVEMBER 1993".

Christmas A51

80s, Haapsalu Cathedral. 2k, Tallinn Church.

1993, Nov. Litho. *Perf. 14*

261 A51 80s red .20 .20
262 A51 2k blue, vert. .35 .35

See Nos. 279-280.

Lydia Koidula — A52

1993, Dec. 14 Litho. *Perf. 14*

263 A52 1k multicolored .25 .25

A53 A54

1994, Jan. 26

264 A53 1k +25s Ski jumping .45 .45
265 A53 2k Speed skating .55 .55

1994 Winter Olympics, Lillehammer.

1994, May 31 Litho. *Perf. 13½x14*

Festival badges: 1k+25s, Tartu, 1869. 2k, Tallinn, 1923. 3k, Tallinn, 1969. 15k, Anniversary badge.

266 A54 1k +25s olive & multi .25 .25
267 A54 2k blue & brown .45 .45
268 A54 3k brown, buff & bister .55 .55
Nos. 266-268 (3) 1.25 1.25

Souvenir Sheet

269 A54 15k multicolored 3.00 3.00

All Estonian Song Festival, 125th anniv.

Flying Squirrel — A55

A56

1994, June 27 Litho. *Perf. 13½x14*

270 A55 1k shown .40 .40
271 A55 2k On leafy branch .50 .50
272 A55 3k In fir tree .85 .85
273 A55 4k With young 1.10 1.10
Nos. 270-273 (4) 2.85 2.85

World Wildlife Fund.

1994, July 19

Europa (Estonian Inventions): 1k, Rotating horizontal millstones, by Aleksander Mikiver. 2.70k, First mini-camera, by Walter Zapp.

274 A56 1k multicolored *.30 .30*
275 A56 2.70k multicolored *.55 .55*

A57 A58

Folk Costumes.

1994, Aug. 23 Litho. *Perf. 14*

276 A57 1k Jamaja .25 .25
277 A57 1k Mustjala .25 .25

See Nos. 286-287, 303-304, 325-326, 347-348, 369-370.

1994, Sept. 27 Litho. *Perf. 13½*

278 A58 1.70k multicolored .35 .35

Estonian Art Museum, 75th anniv.

Christmas Type of 1993

Designs: 1.20k, Ruhnu Church, vert. 2.50k, Urvaste Church.

1994, Nov. 15 Litho. *Perf. 14*

279 A51 1.20k brown .30 .30
280 A51 2.50k green .55 .55

For surcharge see No. B63.

A59 A60

1994, Oct. 18

281 A59 1.70k multicolored .35 .35

Intl. Year of the Family.

1994, Dec. 9

Gustavus II Adolphus (1594-1632), King of Sweden.

282 A60 2.50k lilac .75 .75

A61 A62

1995, Jan. 26 Litho. *Perf. 14*

283 A61 1.70k Branta leucopsis .35 .35
284 A61 3.20k Anser anser .60 .60

Matsalu Nature Reserve.

1995, Feb. 28 Litho. *Perf. 14*

Farm Laborer's Family at Table, by Efraim Allsalu.

285 A62 2.70k multicolored .50 .50

FAO, 50th anniv.

Folk Costumes Type of 1994

1995, Mar. 30 Litho. *Perf. 14*

286 A57 1.70k Muhu couple .50 .50
287 A57 1.70k Three Muhu girls .50 .50

A63

A64

Via Baltica Highway Project: #288, 289a, Beach Hotel, Parnu. #289b, Castle, Bauska, Latvia. #289c, Kaunas, Lithuania.

1995, Apr. 20 Litho. *Perf. 14*

288 A63 1.70k multicolored .45 .45

Souvenir Sheet

289 A63 3.20k Sheet of 3, #a.-c. 2.00 2.00

See Latvia Nos. 394-395, Lithuania Nos. 508-509.

1995, Apr. 20 Litho. *Perf. 14*

290 A64 2.70k multicolored *.85 .85*

Europa. Liberation of Nazi Concentration Camps, 50th anniv.

UN, 50th Anniv. — A65

1995, June 1 Litho. *Perf. 14*

291 A65 4k multicolored .85 .85

Pakri Lighthouse A66

1995, July 5 Litho. *Perf. 14*

292 A66 1.70k multicolored .40 .40

See Nos. 309, 318, 338, 356, 388-389, 408.

Vanemuine Theater, 125th Anniv. — A67

1995, Aug. 14 Litho. *Perf. 14*
293 A67 1.70k multicolored .40 .40

Louis Pasteur (1822-95) A68

1995, Sept. 20 Litho. *Perf. 14*
294 A68 2.70k multicolored .60 .60

Finno-Ugric Peoples A69

Aleksander Kunileid (1845-75), Composer A70

Ethnographic object, languages: a, 2.50k, Drawing on shaman's drum, Saami. b, 3.50k, Duck-shaped brooch, Mordva, Mari. c, 4.50k, Duck-feet necklace pendant, Udmurdi, Komi. d, 2.50k, Khanty band ornament, Ungari, Mansi, Handi. e, 3.50k, Bronze amulet, Neenetsi, Eenetsi, Nganassaani, Solkupi, Kamassi. f, 4.50k, Karelian writing on birchbark, Eesti, Vadia, Soome, Liivi, Isuri, Karjala, Vespa.

1995, Oct. 17 Litho. *Perf. 14*
Miniature Sheet
295 A69 Sheet of 6, #a.-f. 3.75 3.75

1995, Nov. 1 Engr. *Perf. 12½ Horiz.*
296 A70 2k dark blue black .40 .40

Christmas — A71

Churches: 2k, St. Martin's, Türi. 3.50k, Charles' Church of the Toompea Congregation, Tallinn.

1995, Nov. 15 Litho. *Perf. 14*
297 A71 2k yellow orange .50 .50
298 A71 3.50k dull carmine .90 .90

See Nos. 315-316, 331.

Natl. Arms Type of 1991

1995, Oct. 26 Litho. *Perf. 14*
299 A40 20s blue green & black .20 .20
300 A40 30s gray & magenta .20 .20
301 A40 80s lilac & blue black .25 .25
a. Perf. 13 .25 .25
Nos. 299-301 (3) .65 .65

No. 301a issued in 1996.

Submarine *Lembit* — A72

1996, Feb. 29 Litho. *Perf. 14*
302 A72 2.50k multicolored .45 .45

See No. 308, 328.

Folk Costume Type of 1994

1996, Mar. 26 Litho. *Perf. 14*
303 A57 2.50k Emmaste .60 .60
304 A57 2.50k Reigi .60 .60

A73

A74

Designs: a, 2.50k, First gold medal, 1896. b, 3.50k, Alfred Neuland, weight lifter, first to win gold medal for Estonia, 1920. c, 4k, Cyclist.

1996, Apr. 25 Litho. *Perf. 14*
305 A73 Sheet of 3, #a.-c. 1.90 1.90

Modern Olympic Games, Cent. & 1996 Summer Olympics, Atlanta.

1996, May 10

Europa: Marie Under (1883-1980), poet.

306 A74 2.50k multicolored *.85 .85*

Radio, Cent. — A75

1996, June 27 Litho. *Perf. 14*
307 A75 3.50k Guglielmo Marconi .75 .75

Ship Type of 1996

Design: Icebreaker, Suur Toll.

1996, Aug. 30 Litho. *Perf. 14*
308 A72 2.50k multicolored .60 .60

Lighthouse Type of 1995

1996, Sept. 25 Litho. *Perf. 14*
309 A66 2.50k Vaindloo .65 .65

Estonian Narrow Gauge Railway, Cent. — A76

Designs: 3.20k, Class Gk steam locomotive. 3.50k, DeM 1 diesel motor wagon. 4.50k, Class Sk steam locomotive.

1996, Oct. 17 Litho. *Perf. 14*
310 A76 3.20k multicolored .55 .55
311 A76 3.50k multicolored .60 .60
312 A76 4.50k multicolored .75 .75
Nos. 310-312 (3) 1.90 1.90

See No. 397.

Christmas A77

1996, Nov. 27 Litho. *Perf. 14*
313 A77 2.50k multicolored .45 .45

Natl. Arms Type of 1991

1996-97 *Perf. 14*
314 A40 3.30k lilac and claret .55 .55

Perf. 13x13¼
314A A40 3.30k blue & lt claret .60 .60

Issued: #314, 12/2; #314A, 12/10/97.

Church Type of 1995

Christmas: 3.30k, Harju-Madise Church. 4.50k, Holy Spirit Church, Tallinn.

1996, Dec. 12
315 A71 3.30k blue .55 .55
316 A71 4.50k pink .75 .75

Natl. Arms Type of 1991

1996, Oct. 24 Litho. *Perf. 13½*
317 A40 2.50k grn & dark grn .45 .45

Lighthouse Type of 1995

1997, Feb. 11 Litho. *Perf. 14*
318 A66 3.30k Ruhnu .75 .75

Tallinn Zoo — A78

a, Haliaeetus pelagicus. b, Mustela lutreola. c, Aegypius monachus. d, Panthera pardus orientalis. e, Diceros bicornis. f, Capra cylindricornis.

1997, Mar. 26 Litho. *Perf. 14*
319 A78 3.30k Sheet of 6, #a.-f. 3.50 3.50

Heinrich von Stephan (1831-97), Founder of UPU — A79

1997, Apr. 8 Litho. *Perf. 14*
320 A79 7k black & bister 1.25 1.25

A80

A81

1997, May 5 Litho. *Perf. 14*
321 A80 4.80k Goldspinners Fairy Tale *1.10 1.10*

Europa.

1997, May 10

No. 323: a, like #322. b, Linijkugis, 17th cent. c, Kurenas, 16th cent.

322 A81 3.30k multicolored *.70 .70*

Perf. 14x14½
323 A81 4.50k Sheet of 3, #a.-c. 3.50 3.50

Maasilinn ship, 16th cent.

See Latvia Nos. 443-444, Lithuania Nos. 571-572.

Folk Costume Type of 1994

1997, June 10 Litho. *Perf. 14*
325 A57 3.30k Ruhnu .60 .60
326 A57 3.30k Vormsi .60 .60

One Kroon Coin — A82

1997, June 12 Litho. *Perf. 14*
327 A82 50k bl grn, blk & gray 8.50 8.50

See Nos. 345, 363, 391.

Ship Type of 1996

Design: Four-masted barkentine, Tormilind.

1997, July 2
328 A72 5.50k multicolored 1.00 1.00

Stone Bridge, Tartu — A83

1997, Sept. 16 Litho. *Perf. 14*
329 A83 3.30k multicolored .60 .60

Wastne Testament, Estonian Bible Translation, 1686 — A84

1997, Oct. 14 Litho. *Perf. 14*
330 A84 3.50k multicolored .60 .60

Church Type of 1995

Christmas: St. Anne's, Halliste.

1997, Nov. 27 Litho. *Perf. 14*
331 A71 3.30k brown .60 .60

Christmas A85

1997, Dec. 3
332 A85 2.90k Elves .50 .50

Natl. Arms Type of 1991

1998, Jan. 19 Litho. *Perf. 13x13½*
333 A40 3.10k lt violet & rose .55 .55
334 A40 3.60k lt blue & ultra .60 .60
a. 3.60k gray & vio bl .60 .60

Issued: #334a, 8/4/98.

1998 Winter Olympic Games, Nagano — A86

1998, Jan. 28 Litho. *Perf. 14*
335 A86 3.60k multicolored .65 .65

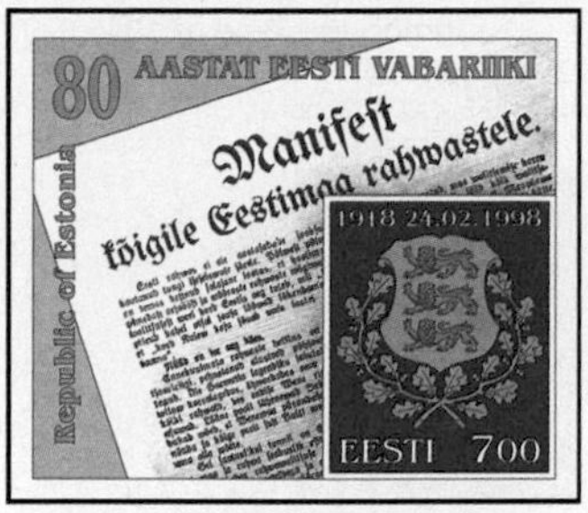

Republic of Estonia, 80th Anniv. — A87

Illustration reduced.

1998, Feb. 6 Litho. *Imperf.*
336 A87 7k Proclamation, arms 1.25 1.25

Eduard Viiralt (1898-1954), Print Artist — A88

Various sections of print, "Hell," showing faces: a, 3.60k, shown. b, 3.60k, Explosion coming from center figure. c, 5.50k, Cat on top of one figure's head. d, 5.50k, Faces within faces.

1998, Feb. 18 *Perf. 14*
337 A88 Sheet of 4, #a.-d. 3.50 3.50

Lighthouse Type of 1995

1998, Mar. 12 Litho. *Perf. 14*
338 A66 3.60k Kunda .65 .65

Natl. Arms Type of 1991

1998, Mar. 16 *Perf. 13*
339 A40 10s grn bl & brn blk .20 .20
340 A40 4.50k pale orange & brick red .75 .75

Issued: 10s, 3/25/97; 4.50k, 3/16/98.

A88a

A89

1998, Apr. 16 Litho. *Perf. 14*
341 A88a 7k multicolored 1.25 1.25

1998 World Cup Soccer Championship, France.

1998, May 5 Litho. *Perf. 14*
342 A89 5.20k St. John's Day *1.10 1.10*

Europa.

Use of Lübeck Charter in Tallinn, 750th Anniv. — A90

1998, June 1
343 A90 4.80k multicolored .90 .90

Beautiful Homes Year — A91

1998, June 16 Litho. *Perf. 14*
344 A91 3.60k multicolored .70 .70

One Kroon Coin Type of 1997

1998, June 18
345 A82 25k green, gray & black 4.75 4.75

A92

A93

1998, Aug. 4 Litho. *Perf. 14*
346 A92 5.50k multicolored .95 .95

470 Class World Yachting Championships.

Folk Costume Type of 1994

1998, Aug. 21 Litho. *Perf. 14*
347 A57 3.60k Kihnu couple .70 .70
348 A57 3.60k Kihnu family .70 .70

1998, Sept. 3
349 A93 3.60k yel, blue & blk .70 .70

Juhan Jaik (1899-1948), author.

Tallinn Zoo — A94

Design: Panthera tigris altaica.

1998, Sept. 17
350 A94 3.60k multicolored .70 .70

See No. 357.

Estonian Post, 80th Anniv. — A95

1998, Oct. 22 Litho. *Perf. 14*
351 A95 3.60k multicolored .75 .75

Military Aid from Finland, 90th Anniv. — A96

1998, Nov. 5 Litho. *Perf. 14*
352 A96 4.50k Freedom Cross .85 .85

Christmas A97

1998, Nov. 26 Litho. *Perf. 14*
353 A97 3.10k Santa, child, vert. .60 .60
354 A97 5k shown .90 .90

Friedrich Robert Faehlmann, Founder of Learned Estonian Society, Birth Bicent. — A98

1998, Dec. 2
355 A98 3.60k multicolored .70 .70

Lighthouse Type of 1995

1999, Jan. 20 Litho. *Perf. 14*
356 A66 3.60k Vilsandi .70 .70

Tallinn Zoo Type of 1998

1999, Feb. 18 Litho. *Perf. 14*
357 A94 3.60k Uncia uncia .65 .65

Council of Europe, 50th Anniv. — A99

1999, Mar. 24 Litho. *Perf. 14*
358 A99 5.50k multicolored 1.00 1.00

Estonian Pres. Lennart Meri, 70th Birthday A100

1999, Mar. 29
359 A100 3.60k multicolored .70 .70

Tolkuse Bog — A101

1999, Apr. 27 Litho. *Perf. 14*
360 A101 5.50k multicolored *1.10 1.10*

Europa.

Bank of Estonia, 80th Anniv. — A102

1999, May 3 Litho. *Perf. 14*
361 A102 5k multicolored .95 .95

Olustvere Manor — A103

1999, June 1
362 A103 3.60k multicolored .70 .70

See Nos. 395, 414, 433, 456, 490, 520, 551, 562, 603.

One Kroon Coin Type of 1997

1999, June 18 Litho. *Perf. 14*
363 A82 100k bl, bister & blk 17.50 17.50

Estonian Natl. Anthem — A104

1999, June 30 Litho. *Perf. 14*
364 A104 3.60k multicolored .65 .65

No. 364 is printed se-tenant with label.

Tower on Suur Munamägi, Highest Point in Baltic Countries A105

1999, July 17
365 A105 5.20k multicolored .95 .95

A106

A107

Families holding hands and: 3.60k, Estonian flag.

No. 367: a, like #366. b, Latvian flag. c, Lithuanian flag.

1999, Aug. 23 Litho. *Perf. 14*
366 A106 3.60k multicolored .70 .70

Souvenir Sheet

367 A106 5.50k Sheet of 3, #a.-c. 3.00 3.00

Baltic Chain, 10th Anniv.
See Latvia #493-494, Lithuania #639-640.

1999, Sept. 23 Litho. *Perf. 14x13¾*
368 A107 7k multicolored 1.25 1.25

UPU, 125th Anniv.

Folk Costumes Type of 1994

1999, Oct. 12 Litho. *Perf. 13¾x14*
369 A57 3.60k Setu couple .65 .65
370 A57 5k Setu man, boy .90 .90

Three Lions — A108

Perf. 13x13¼, 13¾x14 (#371, 373, 374, 378-382)

1999-2002 Litho.

371	A108	10s	brn & dk brn	.20	.20
372	A108	30s	lt bl & dk bl	.20	.20
a.			Perf. 13¾x14	.20	.20
373	A108	30s	blue & slate blue, dated 2003	.20	.20
374	A108	50s	olive & dk grn	.20	.20
375	A108	1k	brown & fawn	.20	.20
376	A108	2k	gray	.40	.40
377	A108	3.60k	sky bl & dk bl	.65	.65
a.			Bright blue green ('00)	.65	.65

378 A108 4.40k grn & bl grn .80 .70
379 A108 4.40k bl grn & brt bl grn, wide 2001 date .80 .25
380 A108 4.40k Prus bl & lt bl, narrow 2001 date .80 .25
381 A108 4.40k green & lt grn, dated 2002 .80 .25
382 A108 4.40k grn & apple grn, dated 2002 .80 .25
382A A108 4.40k ol grn & apple grn, dated 2003 .80 .30
382B A108 5k grn & lt grn .90 .90
382C A108 6k bis & yel 1.10 1.10
382D A108 6.50k bis & org 1.25 1.25
382E A108 8k lake & pink 1.50 1.50
Nos. 371-382E (17) 11.60 8.80

Issued: 30s, 2k, 11/4; 3.60k (378), 10/22; #377a, 3/31/00; No. 378, 8/21/00; 6k, 10/12/00; 6.50k, 10/5/00; 8k, 10/19/00; No. 372a: 4/17/01; 1k, 5k, 8/28/01; 10s, 2/2/02. 50s, 1/7/03; No. 373, 3/11/03; No. 379, 4/17/01; No. 380, 9/24/01; No. 381, 2/2/02; No. 382, 11/14/02; No. 382A, 3/11/03.

No. 378 exists dated 2001 and 2002. No. 382B exists dated 2002.

The background color of No. 379 is bolder than that on No. 380.

Christmas A109

1999, Nov. 25 Litho. ***Perf. 14x13¾***
383 A109 3.10k multicolored .60 .60

A110 A111

1999, Nov. 25 ***Perf. 13¾x14***
384 A110 7k multicolored 1.25 1.25

1st public Christmas tree in Tallinn, 1441.

Christmas Lottery A110a

1999, Dec. 1 Litho. ***Perf. 14x13¾***
384A A110a 3.10k + 1.90k multi 1.00 1.00

1999, Dec. 14 Litho. ***Perf. 13¾x14***
385 A111 5.50k Millennium 1.00 1.00

2000 Census — A112

2000, Jan. 5
386 A112 3.60k multicolored .70 .70

Tartu Peace Treaty, 80th Anniv. — A113

2000, Feb. 2 Litho. ***Perf. 14x13¾***
387 A113 3.60k multi .70 .70

Lighthouse Type of 1995

2000, Feb. 25
388 A66 3.60k Ristna .70 .70
389 A66 3.60k Kopu .70 .70
a. Pair, #388-389 1.40 1.40

Congress, 10th Anniv. — A114

2000, Mar. 9 ***Perf. 13¾x14***
390 A114 3.60k multi .65 .65

One Kroon Coin Type of 1997

2000, Mar. 14 ***Perf. 14x13¾***
391 A82 10k red, sil & blk 1.75 1.75

Cornflower (Natl. Flower) — A115

2000, Apr. 7
392 A115 4.80k multi .85 .85

Natl. Book Year — A116

2000, Apr. 22 ***Perf. 13¾x14***
393 A116 3.60k multi .60 .60

First book printed in Estonian language, 475th anniv.

Europa, 2000

Common Design Type

2000, May 9
394 CD17 4.80k multi *1.00 1.00*

Manor Type of 1999

2000, May 23 Litho. ***Perf. 14x13¾***
395 A103 3.60k Palmse Hall .65 .65

Tallinn Zoo — A117

2000, June 13 Litho. ***Perf. 14x13¾***
396 A117 3.60k Naemorhedus caudatus .70 .70

Railway Type of 1996

4.50k, Viljandi-Tallinn Railway, cent.

2000, June 30
397 A76 4.50k multi .80 .80

9th Intl. Finno-Ugric Congress A118

2000, Aug. 1
398 A118 5k multi .85 .85

2000 Summer Olympics, Sydney — A119

2000, Sept. 5 Litho. ***Perf. 13¾x14***
399 A119 8k multi 1.40 1.40

Folk Costume Type of 1994

Designs: 4.40k, Hargla. 8k, Polva.

2000, Sept. 12
400-401 A57 Set of 2 2.10 2.10

August Mälk (1900-87), Writer — A120

2000, Sept. 20 ***Perf. 14x13¾***
402 A120 4.40k multi .75 .75

Lake Peipus Fish — A121

No. 403: a, Osmerus eperlanus spirinchus. b, Stizostedion lucioperka.

2000, Oct. 25
403 Horiz. pair + central label 2.50 2.50
a.-b. A121 6.50k Any single 1.10 1.10

See Russia No. 6607.

Souvenir Sheet

Estonian Bookplates, Cent. — A122

Various bookplates. Denominiations in: a, LR. b, UR.
Illustration reduced.

2000, Nov. 11 ***Perf. 13¾x14***
404 A122 6k Sheet of 2, #a-b 2.10 2.10

Christmas A123

3.60k, Horn and bow. 6k, Ornament.

2000, Nov. 29 ***Perf. 14x13¾***
405-406 A123 Set of 2 1.60 1.60

Erki Nool, Olympic Decathlon Champion A124

2001, Jan. 10 Litho. ***Perf. 14x13¾***
407 A124 4.40k multi 1.00 1.00

Lighthouse Type of 1995

2001, Jan. 24
408 A66 4.40k Mohni .80 .80

Valentine's Day — A125

2001, Feb. 6 Litho. ***Perf. 13¾x14***
409 A125 4.40k multi .80 .80

Stenbock House, Seat of Government A126

2001, Feb. 20 ***Perf. 14x13¾***
410 A126 6.50k multi 1.10 1.10

Souvenir Sheet

Paintings of Johann Köler (1826-99) — A127

No. 411: a, Girl on the Spring, 1858-62. b, Eve of the Pomegranate, 1879-80.

2001, Feb. 27
411 A127 4.40k Sheet of 2, #a-b 1.75 1.75

European Year of Languages A128

2001, Mar. 6
412 A128 4.40k multi .75 .75

Vanellus Vanellus A129

2001, Apr. 4 ***Perf. 12¾x13***
413 A129 4.40k multi .75 .75

Manor Type of 1999

2001, Apr. 17 ***Perf. 14x13¾***
414 A103 4.40k Laupa Hall .75 .75

Europa — A130

2001, May 9 *Perf. 13¾x14*
415 A130 6.50k multi *1.25 1.25*

Kalev Sports Association, Cent. — A131

2001, May 24
416 A131 6.50k multi 1.10 1.10

Pärnu, 750th Anniv. — A132

2001, June 5 Litho. *Perf. 14x13¾*
417 A132 4.40k multi .75 .75

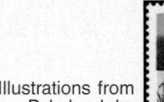

Illustrations from Pokuland, by Edgar Valter — A133

Characters and — No. 418: a, Lake. b, Owl. c, Crane. d, Bird in nest.
No. 419: a, Fence. b, Flowers. c, Dog. d, Moon.

2001, June 19

418	Booklet pane of 4	2.50	
a.-d.	A133 3.60k Any single	.75	.75
419	Booklet pane of 4	3.50	
a.-d.	A133 4.40k Any single	.90	.90
	Booklet, #418-419	6.75	

Entire booklet sold for 35k, 3k of which went to the Pokuland Project of the Estonian Nature Fund.

Restoration of Independence, 10th Anniv. — A134

2001, Aug. 7 *Perf. 13¾x14*
420 A134 4.40k multi .75 .75

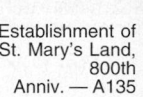

Establishment of St. Mary's Land, 800th Anniv. — A135

2001, Aug. 15 *Perf. 14x13¾*
421 A135 6.50k multi 1.10 1.10

Resumption of Issuing Stamps, 10th Anniv. — A136

2001, Sept. 4 *Perf. 13¾x14*
422 A136 4.40k #200 .75 .75

Baltic Coast Landscapes A137

Designs: 4.40k, No. 424a, Lahemaa. No. 424b, Vidzeme. No. 424c, Palanga.

2001, Sept. 15 *Perf. 14x13¾*
423 A137 4.40k multi .75 .75

Souvenir Sheet

Perf. 13¼x13½

424	Sheet of 3	3.00	3.00
a.-c.	A137 6k Any single	1.00	1.00

No. 424 contains three 35x29mm stamps. See Lithuania Nos.
See Latvia Nos. 534-535, Lithuania Nos. 698-699.

Tallinn Zoo — A138

2001, Oct. 4 *Perf. 14x13¾*
425 A138 4.40k Alligator sinensis .85 .85

Estonia 26/9 Racing Car — A139

2001, Oct. 23
426 A139 6k multi 1.10 1.10

Folk Costume Type of 1994

Designs: 4.40k, Paistu woman. 7.50k, Tarvastu man.

2001, Nov. 7 Litho. *Perf. 13¾x14*
427-428 A57 Set of 2 2.25 2.25

A140

Christmas A141

Perf. 13¾x14, 14x13¾

2001, Nov. 22
429 A140 3.60k multi .60 .60
430 A141 6.50k multi 1.10 1.10

Radio Broadcasting in Estonia, 75th Anniv. — A142

2001, Dec. 4 *Perf. 14x13¾*
431 A142 4.40k multi .80 .80

2002 Winter Olympics, Salt Lake City — A143

2002, Jan. 10 Litho. *Perf. 14x13¾*
432 A143 8k multi 1.40 1.40

Manor Type of 1999

2002, Jan. 22
433 A103 4.40k Sangaste Hall .75 .75

Lighthouse Type of 1995

2002, Feb. 20
434 A66 4.40k Laidunina .85 .85

Bird Type of 2001

Design: Passer domesticus and Passer montanus.

2002, Mar. 7 *Perf. 12¾x13*
435 A129 4.40k multi .75 .75

Spring Flowers — A144

2002, Mar. 20 *Perf. 14x13¾*
436 A144 4.40k multi .85 .85

Estonian Puppet Theater, 50th Anniv. — A145

2002, Mar. 27 *Perf. 13¾x14*
437 A145 4.40k multi + label .75 .75

PTO-4 Training Airplane — A146

2002, Apr. 10 *Perf. 14x13¾*
438 A146 6k multi 1.00 1.00

Andrus Veerpalu, Gold Medalist at 2002 Winter Olympics A147

2002, Apr. 12
439 A147 4.40k multi .75 .75

Tartu University Anniversaries — A148

No. 440: a, Main building, 1806-09, founding act of 1632. b, University Library, 1982, text from Biblia Latina.

2002, Apr. 24
440 A148 4.40k Horiz. pair, #a-b, + central label 2.00 2.00

Europa A149

2002, May 9 *Perf. 12¾x13*
441 A149 6.50k multi *1.40 1.40*

Re-adoption of Constitution, 10th Anniv. — A150

2002, May 23 *Perf. 13¾x14*
442 A150 4.40k multi .75 .75

Adoption of Lübeck Charter by Town of Rakvere, 700th Anniv. — A151

2002, June 5
443 A151 4.40k multi .75 .75

Souvenir Sheet

Re-introduction of the Kroon, 10th Anniv. — A152

No. 444 — Portraits from bank notes: a, Lydia Koidula, poet. b, Carl Rober Jakobson, journalist.

2002, June 10 *Perf. 14x13¾*
444 A152 4.40k Sheet of 2, #a-b 1.75 1.75

Souvenir Sheet

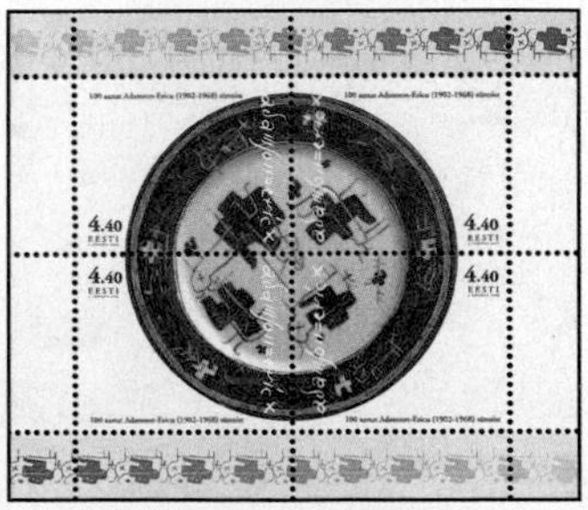

Adamson-Eric (1902-68), Painter — A153

Denomination at: a, LL. b, LR. c, UL. d, UR.

2002, Aug. 8 Litho. ***Perf. 14x13¾***
445 A153 4.40k Sheet of 4, #a-d 3.00 3.00

Sus Scrofa A154

2002, Aug. 21 ***Perf. 12¾x13***
446 A154 4.40k multi .75 .75

Limestone, Estonia's National Stone A155

2002, Sept. 18
447 A155 4.40k multi .75 .75

Folk Costume Type of 1994

Designs: 4.40k, Kolga-Jaani women. 5.50k, Suure-Jaani boy and girl.

2002, Oct. 1 ***Perf. 13¾x14***
448-449 A57 Set of 2 1.75 1.75

A156

Christmas — A157

Perf. 14x13¾, 13¾x14
2002, Nov. 20 Litho.
450 A156 3.60k Reindeer .60 .60
451 A157 6.50k Christmas tree 1.10 1.10

Lighthouse Type of 1995

2003, Jan. 15 ***Perf. 14x13¾***
452 A66 4.40k Keri .75 .75

Anton Hansen Tammsaare (1878-1940), Novelist — A158

2003, Jan. 30 Litho. ***Perf. 14x13¾***
453 A158 4.40k multi .75 .75

Pica Pica A159

2003, Feb. 13 ***Perf. 12¾x13***
454 A159 4.40k multi .75 .75

See Nos. 485, 509, 540, 566, 595.

Spring Flowers — A160

No. 455: a, Tulips. b, Helleborus purpurascens. c, Narcissus poeticus. d, Crocus vernus.

2003, Mar. 20 ***Perf. 13¾x14***
455 A160 4.40k Sheet of 4, #a-d 5.25 5.25
e. Booklet pane, like #455, without date in margin 3.00 —
Complete booklet, #455e 3.00

Manor Type of 1999

2003, Apr. 9 ***Perf. 14x13¾***
456 A103 4.40k Alatskivi Hall .75 .75

Pres. Arnold Rüütel, 75th Birthday — A161

2003, Apr. 24
457 A161 4.40k multi + label .75 .75

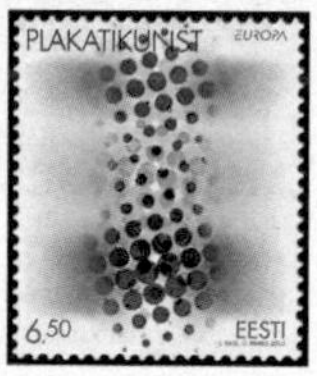

Europa — A162

2003, May 8 ***Perf. 13¾x14***
458 A162 6.50k multi *1.40 1.40*

Tartu University Botanical Gardens, Bicent. — A163

2003, June 11 Litho. ***Perf. 14x13¾***
459 A163 4.40k multi .75 .75

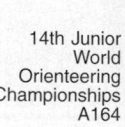

14th Junior World Orienteering Championships A164

2003, June 27
460 A164 7.50k multi 1.25 1.25

Circumnavigation of Adam Johann von Krusenstern (1770-1846) — A165

2003, Aug. 6 ***Perf. 12½***
461 A165 8k multi 1.40 1.40

Phoca Hispida A166

2003, Aug. 27 ***Perf. 12¾x13***
462 A166 4.40k multi .75 .75

Adm. Fabian Gottlieb von Bellingshausen (1778-1852) — A167

2003, Sept. 10
463 A167 8k multi 1.40 1.40

Ancient Trade Routes — A168

Map and: No. 464, 6.50k, Silver coin of Prince Volodymyr Sviatoslavovych, Slavic warship with sail. No. 465, 6.50k, Arrival of Scandinavian Seamen, coin of Danish King Svend Estridsen.

2003, Sept. 10 ***Perf. 11½***
464-465 A168 Set of 2 2.25 2.25

See Ukraine No. 524.

Three Lions Type of 1999-2002

2003-04 Litho. ***Perf. 13¾x14***
467 A108 20s blk & gray .20 .20
472 A108 4.40k ol grn & apple grn .75 .75
473 A108 5k dk grn & apple grn, dated 2004 .80 .80
474 A108 5.50k dk grn & yel grn .85 .85

Issued: 20s, 4.40k, 8/22; 5k, 1/20/04; 5.50k, 3/25/04.

Folk Costume Type of 1994

Designs: 4.40k, Aksi woman and girl. 6.50k, Otepää man, woman and girl.

2003, Oct. 9 Litho. ***Perf. 13¾x14***
476-477 A57 Set of 2 1.90 1.90

A169

Christmas A170

2003, Nov. 26 ***Perf. 14x13¾***
478 A169 3.60k multi .60 .60
479 A170 6k multi 1.00 1.00

Souvenir Sheet

Friedrich Reinhold Kreutzwald (1803-82), Writer — A171

No. 480: a, 4.40k, Illustration by Kristjan Raud of "Voyage to the End of the World," from "Kalevipoeg," by Kreutzwald. b, 6.50k, Portrait of Kreutzwald.

2003, Dec. 4 ***Perf. 13x12¾***
480 A171 Sheet of 2, #a-b 1.90 1.90

Lighthouse Type of 1995

2004, Jan. 7 Litho. ***Perf. 14x13¾***
481 A66 4.40k Sorgu .75 .75

Canis Lupus A172

2004, Feb. 3 ***Perf. 12¾x13***
482 A172 4.40k multi .75 .75

Voyage Around Cape Horn of the Hioma, 150th Anniv. — A173

2004, Feb. 18 ***Perf. 13¾x14***
483 A173 8k multi 1.25 1.25

Spring Flowers Type of 2003

No. 484: a, Viola riviniana. b, Anemone nemorosa. c, Hepatica nobilis. d, Trollius europaeus.

2004, Mar. 17
484 A160 4.40k Sheet of 4, #a-d 3.00 3.00
e. Booklet pane, like #484 without date in margin 3.00 —
Complete booklet, #484e 3.00

Bird Type of 2003

2004, Apr. 6 ***Perf. 12¾x13***
485 A159 4.40k Ciconia ciconia .75 .75

Admission to European Union A174

2004, May 1 ***Perf. 13¼x13***
486 A174 6.50k multi 1.10 1.10

Europa — A175

Illustration reduced.

2004, May 4 ***Perf. 13***
487 A175 6.50k multi *1.10 1.10*

Tallinn Town Hall, 600th Anniv. A176

2004, May 13 Litho. ***Perf. 12¾x13***
488 A176 4.40k multi .75 .75

Consecration of Estonian Flag, 120th Anniv. — A177

2004, June 4 ***Perf. 13¾x14***
489 A177 4.40k multi .75 .75

Manor Type of 1999

2004, June 15 ***Perf. 14x13¾***
490 A103 4.40k Vasalemma Hall .75 .75

Admission to NATO — A178

2004, June 28 ***Perf. 13¾x14***
491 A178 6k multi 1.00 1.00

2004 Summer Olympics, Athens — A179

2004, July 15 Litho. ***Perf. 13¾x14***
492 A179 8k multi 1.40 1.40

Dragon Class Yachting European Championships — A180

2004, Aug. 17 ***Perf. 14x13¾***
493 A180 6k multi 1.00 1.00

Taraxacum Officinale — A181

Serpentine Die Cut 12½
2004, Sept. 14
Self-Adhesive
494 A181 30s multi .20 .20

See Nos. 547, 560, 572, 588.

County Arms — A182

2004, Sept. 28 Self-Adhesive
495 A182 4.40k Harjumaa .75 .75
496 A182 4.40k Hiiumaa .75 .75

See Nos. 506-507, 518-519, 532-533, 536, 552, 561, 573, 594, 608.

Folk Costumes Type of 1994

Designs: 4.40k, Viru-Jaagupi boy and girl. 7.50k, Jõhvi woman and girl.

2004, Oct. 5 Litho. ***Perf. 13¾x14***
497-498 A57 Set of 2 2.10 2.10

A183

Christmas A184

2004, Nov. 23 ***Perf. 13¾x14***
499 A183 4.40k multi .80 .80
Perf. 14x13¾
500 A184 6.50k multi 1.10 1.10

Lighthouse Type of 1995

Norrby Lighthouse with: 4.40k, White top, vert. 6.50k, Red top, vert.

2005, Jan. 11 Litho. ***Perf. 14***
501-502 A66 Set of 2 1.90 1.90

Castor Fiber A185

2005, Jan. 25 ***Perf. 12¾x13***
503 A185 4.40k multi .75 .75

Rotary International, Cent. — A186

2005, Feb. 11 ***Perf. 13¾x14***
504 A186 8k multi 1.40 1.40

Flag Over Pikk Hermann Tower, Tallinn — A187

Serpentine Die Cut 12½
2005, Feb. 22
Self-Adhesive
505 A187 5k multi .85 .85

See Nos. 530, 559.

County Arms Type of 2004
2005 Litho.
Self-Adhesive
506 A182 4.40k Ida-Virumaa .75 .75
507 A182 4.40k Järvamaa .75 .75

Issued: No. 506, 3/8; No. 507, 3/15.

Souvenir Sheet

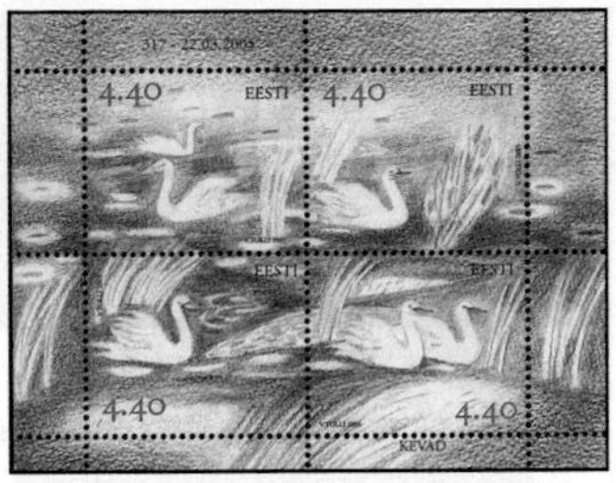

Spring — A188

No. 508: a, Two swans, denomination at UL. b, One swan, denomination at UL. c, One swan, denomination at LL. d, Two swans, denomination at LR.

2005, Mar. 22 Litho. ***Perf. 14x13¾***
508 A188 4.40k Sheet of 4, #a-d 3.00 3.00

Bird Type of 2003

2005, Apr. 5 ***Perf. 12¾x13***
509 A159 4.40k Accipiter gentilis .75 .75

Mother's Day — A189

2005, Apr. 20 ***Perf. 14x13¾***
510 A189 4.40k multi .75 .75

Europa — A190

Designs: 6k, Vegetable wrap. 6.50k, Tomato, carrots, egg yolk, parsley, fish, onion, beet.

2005, May 3
511-512 A190 Set of 2 *2.25 2.25*

Eduard Tubin (1905-82), Composer A191

2005, May 18
513 A191 6k multi .95 .95

Intl. Children's Day — A192

No. 514: a, Birds. b, Butterflies. Illustration reduced.

2005, June 1 ***Perf. 13¼x13¾***
514 A192 4.40k Horiz. pair, #a-b, + central label 1.50 1.50

Orchids — A193

Designs: 4.40k, Epipactis palustris. 8k, Epipogium aphyllum.

2005, June 16 Litho. ***Perf. 13¾x14***
515-516 A193 Set of 2 2.25 2.25

Restoration of St. John's Cathedral, Tartu — A194

2005, June 29
517 A194 4.40k multi .70 .70

Tartu, 975th anniv.

County Arms Type of 2004
Serpentine Die Cut 12½
2005 Litho.
Self-Adhesive
518 A182 4.40k Jõgevamaa .70 .70
519 A182 4.40k Läänemaa .70 .70

Issued: No. 518, 7/5; No. 519, 7/8.

Manor Type of 1999

2005, July 12 ***Perf. 14x13¾***
520 A103 4.40k Kiltsi Hall .70 .70

St. Catherine's Church, Karja — A195

2005, Sept. 20
521 A195 4.40k multi .70 .70

Souvenir Sheet

Sculptures by Amandus Adamson (1855-1929) — A196

No. 522: a, Igavesti Voidutsev Armastus, 1889. b, Lüüriline Muusika, 1891. c, Memento Mori, 1907. d, Koit ja Hämarik, 1895.

2005, Oct. 12 ***Perf. 13½***
522 A196 650s Sheet of 4, #a-d 4.50 4.50

Dogs — A197

No. 523: a, Kazakh hound (Kasaahi hurt). b, Estonian hound (Eesti hagijas).

2005, Oct. 19 ***Perf. 14x13¾***
523 A197 6.50k Horiz. pair, #a-b 2.25 2.25

See Kazakhstan No. 495.

Folk Costumes Type of 1994

Designs: 4.40k, Ambla man, woman and girl. 8k, Türi women.

2005, Oct. 28 ***Perf. 13¾x14***
524-525 A57 Set of 2 2.25 2.25

New Year's Goat — A198

Adoration of the Magi — A199

"110" and Lenin House Museum
A198

Lenin, 110th "Birthday" (Paintings): 15c, In hiding. 20c, As a young man. 40c, Returning to Russia. 1b, Speaking on the Goelro Plan.

1980, Apr. 22 Litho. ***Perf. 12x12½***

964 A198 5c multicolored .35 .30
965 A198 15c multicolored .40 .35
966 A198 20c multicolored .50 .45
967 A198 40c multicolored .95 .80
968 A198 1b multicolored 2.25 2.00
Nos. 964-968 (5) 4.45 3.90

Grévy's Zebras
A199

1980, June 10 Litho. ***Perf. 12½x12***

969 A199 10c shown .75 .75
970 A199 15c Gazelles 1.00 1.00
971 A199 25c Wild hunting dogs 1.50 1.50
972 A199 60c Swayne's hartebeests 2.75 2.75
973 A199 70c Cheetahs 3.50 3.50
Nos. 969-973 (5) 9.50 9.50

Runner, Moscow '80 Emblem — A200

1980, July 19 Photo. ***Perf. 11½x12***

974 A200 30c shown 1.00 1.00
975 A200 70c Gymnast 2.25 2.25
976 A200 80c Boxing 3.00 3.00
Nos. 974-976 (3) 6.25 6.25

22nd Summer Olympic Games, Moscow, July 19-Aug. 3.

Removing Blindfold — A201

Bamboo Folk Craft — A202

1980, Sept. 11 Photo. ***Perf. 14x13½***

977 A201 30c shown .75 .50
978 A201 40c Revolutionary 1.00 .65
979 A201 50c Woman breaking chain 1.50 1.00
980 A201 70c Russian & Ethiopian flags 2.25 1.25
Nos. 977-980 (4) 5.50 3.40

6th anniversary of revolution.

1980, Oct. 23 Litho. ***Perf. 14***

981 A202 5c Bamboo food basket .30 .25
982 A202 15c Lamp shade .40 .35
983 A202 25c Stool .75 .60
984 A202 35c Fruit basket 1.25 1.00
985 A202 1b Lamp shade 2.75 1.75
Nos. 981-985 (5) 5.45 3.95

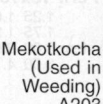

Mekotkocha (Used in Weeding)
A203

Traditional Harvesting Tools: 15c, Layda (grain separator). 40c, Mensh (fork). 45c, Mededekia (soil turner). 70c, Mofer & Kenber (plow and yoke).

1980, Dec. 18 Litho. ***Perf. 12½x12***

986 A203 10c multicolored .30 .25
987 A203 15c multicolored .35 .30
988 A203 40c multicolored .90 .75
989 A203 45c multicolored 1.25 1.00
990 A203 70c multicolored 2.50 1.75
Nos. 986-990 (5) 5.30 4.05

Baro River Bridge Opening
A204

1981, Feb. 28 Photo. ***Perf. 13½x13***

991 A204 15c Canoes and ferry .50 .40
992 A204 65c Bridge construction 1.75 1.25
993 A204 1b shown 3.00 2.25
Nos. 991-993 (3) 5.25 3.90

Semien National Park — A205

World Heritage Year: 5c, Wawel Castle, Poland. 15c, Quito Cathedral, Ecuador. 20c, Old Slave Quarters, Goree Island, Senegal. 30c, Mesa Verde Indian Village, US. 1b, L'Anse aux Meadows excavation, Canada.

Perf. 11x11½, 11½x11

1981, Mar. 10 Photo.

994 A205 5c multicolored .40 .30
995 A205 15c multicolored .55 .45
996 A205 20c multicolored .70 .55
997 A205 30c multicolored 1.00 .75
998 A205 80c multicolored 2.25 1.50
999 A205 1b multicolored 3.00 2.25
Nos. 994-999 (6) 7.90 5.80

1981, June 16 Photo.

10c, Biet Medhanialem Church, Ethiopia. 15c, Nahanni Natl. Park, Canada. 20c, Yellowstone River Lower Falls, U.S. 30c, Aachen Cathedral, Germany. 80c, Kicker Rock, San Cristobal Island, Ecuador. 1b, The Lizak corridor, Holy Cross Chapel, Cracow, Poland.

1000 A205 10c multi .45 .30
1001 A205 15c multi .55 .45
1002 A205 20c multi .75 .60
1003 A205 30c multi .95 .80
1004 A205 80c multi 3.25 2.25
1005 A205 1b multi, vert. 4.50 2.75
Nos. 1000-1005 (6) 10.45 7.15

Ancient Drinking Vessel
A206

1981, May 5 Litho. ***Perf. 12½x12***

1006 A206 20c shown .40 .30
1007 A206 25c Spice container .50 .40
1008 A206 35c Jug 1.00 .75
1009 A206 40c Cooking pot holder 1.50 1.10
1010 A206 60c Animal figurine 2.25 1.60
Nos. 1006-1010 (5) 5.65 4.15

Intl. Year of the Disabled — A207

7th Anniv. of Revolution
A208

1981, July 16 Photo. ***Perf. 11½x12***

1011 A207 5c Prostheses .30 .20
1012 A207 15c Boys writing .35 .25
1013 A207 20c Activities .65 .50
1014 A207 40c Knitting 1.25 1.00
1015 A207 1b Weaving 3.00 2.25
Nos. 1011-1015 (5) 5.55 4.20

1981, Sept. 10 ***Perf. 14***

1016 A208 20c Children's Center .65 .35
1017 A208 60c Heroes' Center 1.25 1.00
1018 A208 1b Serto Ader (state newspaper) 2.25 1.75
Nos. 1016-1018 (3) 4.15 3.10

World Food Day — A209

1981, Oct. 15 Litho. ***Perf. 13½x12½***

1019 A209 5c Wheat airlift .20 .20
1020 A209 15c Plowing .30 .25
1021 A209 20c Malnutrition .40 .30
1022 A209 40c Agriculture education .85 .70
1023 A209 1b Cattle, corn 2.25 1.75
Nos. 1019-1023 (5) 4.00 3.20

Ancient Bronze Type of 1978

1981, Dec. 15 Litho. ***Perf. 14x13½***

1024 A180 15c Pitcher .35 .35
1025 A180 45c Tsenatsil (musical instrument) 1.00 1.00
1026 A180 50c Pitcher, diff. 1.25 1.25
1027 A180 70c Pot 1.50 1.50
Nos. 1024-1027 (4) 4.10 4.10

Horn Artifacts — A210

1982, Feb. 18 Photo. ***Perf. 12x12½***

1028 A210 10c Tobacco containers .25 .20
1029 A210 15c Cup .35 .30
1030 A210 40c Container, diff. .90 .70
1031 A210 45c Goblet 1.25 .95
1032 A210 70c Spoons 1.75 1.25
Nos. 1028-1032 (5) 4.50 3.40

Coffee Cultivation
A211

1982, May, 6 Photo. ***Perf. 13½***

1033 A211 5c Plants .20 .20
1034 A211 15c Bushes .35 .30
1035 A211 25c Mature bushes .60 .50
1036 A211 35c Picking beans 1.00 .75
1037 A211 1b Drinking coffee 2.25 1.75
Nos. 1033-1037 (5) 4.40 3.50

1982 World Cup — A212

Various soccer plays.

Perf. 13½x12½

1982, June 10 Litho.

1038 A212 5c multicolored .25 .20
1039 A212 15c multicolored .40 .30
1040 A212 20c multicolored .55 .50
1041 A212 40c multicolored 1.25 1.10
1042 A212 1b multicolored 2.50 2.25
Nos. 1038-1042 (5) 4.95 4.35

TB Bacillus Centenary
A213

1982, July 12 Litho. ***Perf. 13½x12½***

1043 A213 15c Cow .50 .40
1044 A213 20c Magnifying glass .60 .50
1045 A213 30c Koch, microscope .80 .70
1046 A213 35c Koch 1.00 .85
1047 A213 80c Man coughing 2.00 1.75
Nos. 1043-1047 (5) 4.90 4.20

8th Anniv. of Revolution — A214

Designs: Symbols of justice.

1982, Sept. 10 ***Perf. 12½x13½***

1048 A214 80c multicolored 2.00 1.50
1049 A214 1b multicolored 2.25 1.75

World Standards Day — A215

1982, Oct. 14 Litho. ***Perf. 13½x12½***

1050 A215 5c Hand, foot, square .20 .20
1051 A215 15c Scales .40 .30
1052 A215 20c Rulers .50 .40
1053 A215 40c Weights 1.00 .80
1054 A215 1b Emblem 2.50 1.75
Nos. 1050-1054 (5) 4.60 3.45

10th Anniv. of UN Conference on Human Environment
A216

1982, Dec. 13 Litho. ***Perf. 12***

1055 A216 5c Wildlife conservation .20 .20
1056 A216 15c Environmental health and settlement .40 .35
1057 A216 20c Forest protection .60 .45
1058 A216 40c Natl. literacy campaign 1.00 .90
1059 A216 1b Soil and water conservation 2.50 2.00
Nos. 1055-1059 (5) 4.70 3.90

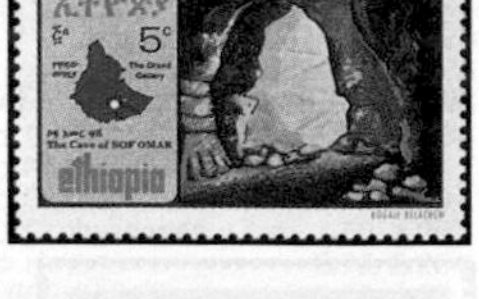

Cave of Sof Omar
A217

Various views.

1983, Feb. 10 Photo. ***Perf. 13½***

1060 A217 5c multicolored .20 .20
1061 A217 10c multicolored .30 .25
1062 A217 15c multicolored .40 .35
1063 A217 70c multicolored 1.50 1.10
1064 A217 80c multicolored 1.75 1.50
Nos. 1060-1064 (5) 4.15 3.40

A218

A219

1983, Apr. 29 **Photo.** ***Perf. 14***

1065	A218	80c	multicolored	2.00	1.50
1066	A218	1b	multicolored	2.25	2.00

25th Anniv. of Economic Commission for Africa.

Perf. 12½x11½

1983, June 3 **Photo.**

1067	A219	85c	Emblem	1.60	1.25
1068	A219	1b	Lighthouse, ship	3.25	2.25

25th Anniv. of Intl. Maritime Org.

WCY
A220

9th Anniv. of Revolution
A221

1983, July 22 **Litho.**

1069	A220	25c	UPU emblem	.70	.60
1070	A220	55c	Dish antenna, emblems	1.40	1.25
1071	A220	1b	Bridge, tunnel	3.25	2.50
			Nos. 1069-1071 (3)	5.35	4.35

1983, Sept. 10 **Litho.** ***Perf. 14½***

1072	A221	25c	Dove	.50	.40
1073	A221	55c	Star	1.40	1.00
1074	A221	1b	Emblems	2.00	1.60
			Nos. 1072-1074 (3)	3.90	3.00

Musical Instruments — A222

Charaxes Galawadiwosi
A223

1983, Oct. 17 **Litho.** ***Perf. 12½x13½***

1075	A222	5c	Hura	.25	.20
1076	A222	15c	Dinke	.45	.40
1077	A222	20c	Meleket	.75	.65
1078	A222	40c	Embilta	1.25	1.00
1079	A222	1b	Tom	2.25	2.00
			Nos. 1075-1079 (5)	4.95	4.25

1983, Dec. 13 **Photo.** ***Perf. 14***

1080	A223	10c	shown	1.25	1.00
1081	A223	15c	Epiphora elianae	1.75	1.50
1082	A223	55c	Batuana rougeoti	4.75	3.00
1083	A223	1b	Achaea saboeareginae	9.00	7.50
			Nos. 1080-1083 (4)	16.75	13.00

Intl. Anti-Apartheid Year (1983) — A224

Perf. 13½x12½

1984, Feb. 10 **Litho.**

1084	A224	5c	multicolored	.35	.30
1085	A224	15c	multicolored	.55	.50
1086	A224	20c	multicolored	.75	.65
1087	A224	40c	multicolored	1.25	1.00
1088	A224	1b	multicolored	2.50	2.00
			Nos. 1084-1088 (5)	5.40	4.45

Local Flowers — A225

Traditional Houses — A226

1984, Apr. 13 **Litho.** ***Perf. 13½***

1089	A225	5c	Protea gaguedi	.30	.25
1090	A225	25c	Sedum epidendrum	1.25	.90
1091	A225	50c	Echinops amplexicaulis	2.25	1.75
1092	A225	1b	Canarina eminii	4.25	3.25
			Nos. 1089-1092 (4)	8.05	6.15

1984, Aug. 3 **Photo.**

1093	A226	15c	Konso	.55	.40
1094	A226	65c	Dorze	1.75	1.40
1095	A226	1b	Harer	3.00	2.50
			Nos. 1093-1095 (3)	5.30	4.30

10th Anniv. of the Revolution
A227

1984, Sept. 10 **Photo.** ***Perf. 11½***

1096	A227	5c	Sept. 12, 1974	.25	.20
1097	A227	10c	Mar. 4, 1975	.35	.25
1098	A227	15c	Apr. 20, 1976	.45	.35
1099	A227	20c	Feb. 11, 1977	.60	.50
1100	A227	25c	Mar. 1978	.75	.60
1101	A227	40c	July 8, 1980	1.10	.80
1102	A227	45c	Dec. 17, 1980	1.40	1.00
1103	A227	50c	Sept. 15, 1980	1.75	1.25
1104	A227	70c	Sept. 18, 1981	2.00	1.50
1105	A227	1b	June 6, 1983	2.75	2.00
			Nos. 1096-1105 (10)	11.40	8.45

Traditional Sports
A228

1984, Dec. 7 **Photo.** ***Perf. 14***

1106	A228	5c	Gugs	.25	.20
1107	A228	25c	Tigil	.55	.50
1108	A228	50c	Genna	1.25	1.00
1109	A228	1b	Gebeta	2.25	1.75
			Nos. 1106-1109 (4)	4.30	3.45

Birds — A229

1985, Jan. 4 **Photo.** ***Perf. 14½***

1110	A229	5c	Francolinus harwoodi	.50	.40
1111	A229	15c	Rallus rougetti	1.00	.75
1112	A229	80c	Merops pusillus	3.50	3.00
1113	A229	85c	Malimbus rubriceps	4.00	3.50
			Nos. 1110-1113 (4)	9.00	7.65

Indigenous Fauna
A230

1985, Feb. 4 **Litho.** ***Perf. 12½x12***

1114	A230	20c	Hippopotamus amphibius	.90	.75
1115	A230	25c	Litocranius walleri	1.25	1.00
1116	A230	40c	Sylvicapra grimmia	2.00	1.50
1117	A230	1b	Rhynchotragus guentheri	4.50	3.25
			Nos. 1114-1117 (4)	8.65	6.50

Freshwater Fish — A231

1985, Apr. 3 ***Perf. 13½***

1118	A231	10c	Barbus degeni	.45	.40
1119	A231	20c	Labeo cylindricus	.75	.60
1120	A231	55c	Protopterus annectens	1.75	1.50
1121	A231	1b	Alestes dentex	3.75	3.25
			Nos. 1118-1121 (4)	6.70	5.75

Medicinal Plants
A232

1985, May 23 ***Perf. 11½x12½***

1122	A232	10c	Securidaca longepedunculata	.40	.30
1123	A232	20c	Plumbago zeylanicum	.65	.45
1124	A232	55c	Brucea antidysenteric	1.50	1.25
1125	A232	1b	Dorstenia barminiana	3.50	2.75
			Nos. 1122-1125 (4)	6.05	4.75

Ethiopian Red Cross Soc., 50th Anniv. — A233

1985, Aug. 6 **Litho.** ***Perf. 13½x13***

1126	A233	35c	multicolored	.90	.75
1127	A233	55c	multicolored	1.50	1.25
1128	A233	1b	multicolored	3.00	2.50
			Nos. 1126-1128 (3)	5.40	4.50

Ethiopian Revolution, 11th Anniv.
A234

10c, Kombolcha Mills, Welo Region. 80c, Muger Cement Factory, Mokoda, Shoa. 1b, Relocating famine and drought victims.

1985, Sept. 10 **Litho.** ***Perf. 13½***

1129	A234	10c	multicolored	.30	.25
1130	A234	80c	multicolored	2.25	2.00
1131	A234	1b	multicolored	3.00	2.50
			Nos. 1129-1131 (3)	5.55	4.75

UN 40th Anniv. — A235

1985, Nov. 22 **Litho.** ***Perf. 13½x14***

1132	A235	25c	multicolored	.90	.75
1133	A235	55c	multicolored	1.75	1.50
1134	A235	1b	multicolored	3.25	2.50
			Nos. 1132-1134 (3)	5.90	4.75

Anti-Polio Campaign
A236

1986, Jan. 10 **Litho.** ***Perf. 11½x12½***

1135	A236	5c	Boy, prosthesis	.25	.20
1136	A236	10c	Boy on crutches	.35	.30
1137	A236	20c	Nurse, boy	.65	.50
1138	A236	55c	Man, sewing machine	1.75	1.25
1139	A236	1b	Nurse, mother, child	3.00	2.50
			Nos. 1135-1139 (5)	6.00	4.75

Indigenous Trees
A237

1986, Feb. 10 ***Perf. 13½x14½***

1140	A237	10c	Millettia ferruginea	.40	.35
1141	A237	30c	Syzyigum guineense	1.00	.75
1142	A237	50c	Cordia africana	1.50	1.25
1143	A237	1b	Hagenia abyssinica	3.25	2.75
			Nos. 1140-1143 (4)	6.15	5.10

Spices — A238

1986, Mar. 10 ***Perf. 13½***

1144	A238	10c	Zingiber officinale rosc	.50	.40
1145	A238	15c	Ocimum bacilicum	.75	.50
1146	A238	55c	Sinapsis alba	1.75	1.50
1147	A238	1b	Cuminum cyminum	3.50	3.00
			Nos. 1144-1147 (4)	6.50	5.40

Current Coins, Obverse and Reverse
A239

1986, May 9 **Litho.** ***Perf. 13½x14***

1148	A239	5c	1-cent	.25	.20
1149	A239	10c	25-cent	.40	.35
1150	A239	35c	5-cent	1.25	1.00
1151	A239	50c	50-cent	1.50	1.25
1152	A239	1b	10-cent	3.00	2.50
			Nos. 1148-1152 (5)	6.40	5.30

Discovery of 3.5 Million Year-old Hominid Skeleton, "Lucy" — A240

1986, July 4 *Perf. 13½*

1153	A240	2b multicolored	7.00	7.00

Ethiopian Revolution, 12th Anniv. — A241

Designs: 20c, Military service. 30c, Tiglachin monument. 55c, Delachin Exhibition emblem. 85c, Food processing plant, Merti.

1986, Sept. 10 **Litho.** *Perf. 14*

1154	A241	20c multicolored	.50	.40
1155	A241	30c multicolored	.75	.60
1156	A241	55c multicolored	1.50	1.00
1157	A241	85c multicolored	2.00	1.75
		Nos. 1154-1157 (4)	4.75	3.75

Ethiopian Airlines, 40th Anniv. — A242

Intl. Peace Year — A243

1986, Oct. 14

1158	A242	10c DC-7	.40	.30
1159	A242	20c DC-3	.60	.50
1160	A242	30c Personnel, jet tail	1.00	.75
1161	A242	40c Engine	1.25	1.00
1162	A242	1b DC-7, map	2.75	2.25
		Nos. 1158-1162 (5)	6.00	4.80

1986, Nov. 13 *Perf. 13½*

1163	A243	10c multicolored	.40	.30
1164	A243	80c multicolored	2.25	2.00
1165	A243	1b multicolored	3.00	2.50
		Nos. 1163-1165 (3)	5.65	4.80

UN Child Survival Campaign — A244

1986, Dec. 11 *Perf. 12½*

1166	A244	10c Breast feeding	.35	.30
1167	A244	35c Immunization	1.00	.75
1168	A244	50c Hygiene	1.25	1.00
1169	A244	1b Growth monitoring	2.50	2.00
		Nos. 1166-1169 (4)	5.10	4.05

Umbrellas A245

1987, Feb. 10 *Perf. 13½*

1170	A245	35c Axum	1.00	.85
1171	A245	55c Negele-Borena	1.50	1.25
1172	A245	1b Jimma	3.00	2.50
		Nos. 1170-1172 (3)	5.50	4.60

Artwork by Afewerk Tekle (b. 1932) A246

Designs: 50c, Defender of His Country — Afar, stained glass window. 2b, Defender of His Country — Adwa, painting.

1987, Mar. 19 **Litho.** *Perf. 13½*

1173	A246	50c multicolored	1.50	1.00
1174	A246	2b multicolored	5.25	4.50

Stained Glass Windows by Afewerk Tekle — A247

1987, June 16 **Photo.** *Perf. 11½x12*

Granite Paper

1175	A247	50c multicolored	*6.00*	*4.00*

Size: 26x38mm

1176	A247	80c multicolored	*8.00*	*5.50*
1177	A247	1b multicolored	*12.00*	*8.00*
		Nos. 1175-1177 (3)	*26.00*	*17.50*

Struggle of the African People.
Sold out in Addis Ababa on date of issue.

Simien Fox A248

1987, June 29 **Litho.** *Perf. 13½*

1178	A248	5c multicolored	.25	.20
1179	A248	10c multicolored	.40	.25
1180	A248	15c multicolored	.60	.40
1181	A248	20c multicolored	.75	.50
1182	A248	25c multicolored	1.00	.75
1183	A248	45c multicolored	1.50	1.00
1184	A248	55c multicolored	1.75	1.50
		Nos. 1178-1184 (7)	6.25	4.60

For overprints see Nos. 1234-1237. For similar design see A294a.

Ethiopian Revolution, 13th Anniv. A249

1987, Sept. 10 *Perf. 12½*

1185	A249	5c Constitution, freedom of press	.35	.30
1186	A249	10c Popular elections	.45	.40
1187	A249	80c Referendum	1.75	1.50
1188	A249	1b Bahir Dar Airport, map	2.50	2.00
		Nos. 1185-1188 (4)	5.05	4.20

Addis Ababa, Cent. A251

"100" and views: 5c, Emperor Menelik II, Empress Taitu and city. 10c, Traditional buildings. 80c, Central Addis Ababa. 1b, Aerial view of city.

1987, Sept. 7 *Perf. 13½*

1193	A251	5c multicolored	.50	.30
1194	A251	10c multicolored	.65	.40
1195	A251	80c multicolored	2.00	1.50
1196	A251	1b multicolored	2.50	2.00
		Nos. 1193-1196 (4)	5.65	4.20

Wooden Spoons A252

1987, Nov. 30

1197	A252	85c Hurso, Harerge	1.75	1.75
1198	A252	1b Borena, Sidamo	2.25	2.25

Intl. Year of Shelter for the Homeless A253

1988, Jan. **Litho.** *Perf. 13*

1199	A253	10c Village revitalization program	.50	.40
1200	A253	35c Resettlement program	1.00	.90
1201	A253	50c Urban improvement	1.25	1.00
1202	A253	1b Cooperative and government housing	2.00	1.50
		Nos. 1199-1202 (4)	4.75	3.80

October Revolution, Russia, 70th Anniv. (in 1987) — A254

Painting: 1b, Lenin receiving Workers' Council delegates in the Smolny Institute.

1988, Feb. 17 *Perf. 12½x12*

1203	A254	1b multicolored	2.50	1.75

Traditional Hunting Methods and Prey — A255

1988, Mar. 30 **Litho.** *Perf. 13½*

1204	A255	85c Bow and arrow	2.50	2.25
1205	A255	1b Double-pronged spear	3.75	3.50

A256

A257

1988, May 6

1206	A256	85c multicolored	1.75	1.50
1207	A256	1b multicolored	2.25	1.75

Intl. Red Cross and Red Crescent Organizations, 125th annivs.

1988, June 7 **Photo.** *Perf. 11½x12*

1208	A257	2b multicolored	3.50	2.25

Organizaton of African Unity, 25th anniv.

Ethiopian Revolution, 14th Anniv. A258

Design: Various details of *The Victory of Ethiopia*, six-panel mural by Afewerk Tekle (b. 1932) in the museum of the Heroes Center, Debre Zeit.

1988, June 28 **Litho.** *Perf. 13½x13*

1209	A258	10c Jet over farm, vert.	.35	.30
1210	A258	20c Farm workers on road, vert.	.45	.35
1211	A258	35c Allegory of unity, vert.	.75	.50
1212	A258	55c Jet over industry	1.25	1.00
1213	A258	80c Steel works	1.75	1.25
1214	A258	1b Weaving	2.25	2.00
		Nos. 1209-1214 (6)	6.80	5.40

Nos. 1209-1211 vert.

Women, Bracelets and Maps A259

1988, July 27 **Litho.** *Perf. 13x13½*

1215	A259	15c Sidamo	.40	.30
1216	A259	85c Arsi	1.75	1.25
1217	A259	1b Harerge	2.50	2.00
		Nos. 1215-1217 (3)	4.65	3.55

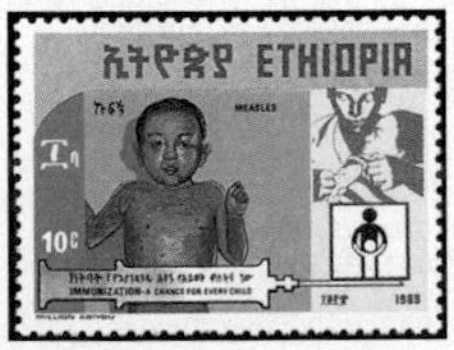

Immunize Every Child A260

1988, June 14 **Litho.** *Perf. 13x13½*

1218	A260	10c Measles	.35	.25
1219	A260	35c Tetanus	.75	.60
1220	A260	50c Whooping cough	1.25	1.00
1221	A260	1b Diphtheria	2.25	1.75
		Nos. 1218-1221 (4)	4.60	3.60

Intl. Fund for Agricultural Development (IFAD), 10th Anniv. — A261

1988, Aug. 16 *Perf. 13½*

1222 A261 15c Monetary aid .30 .25
1223 A261 85c Farming activities 1.50 1.10
1224 A261 1b Harvest 2.25 1.25
Nos. 1222-1224 (3) 4.05 2.60

People's Democratic Republic of Ethiopia, 1st Anniv. — A262

5c, 1st Session of the natl. Shengo (congress). 10c, Mengistu Haile-Mariam, 1st president of the republic. 80c, Natl. crest, flag & crowd. 1b, State assembly building.

1988, Sept. 9 *Perf. 14*

1225 A262 5c multicolored .20 .20
1226 A262 10c multicolored .30 .25
1227 A262 80c multicolored 1.75 1.50
1228 A262 1b multicolored 2.25 2.00
Nos. 1225-1228 (4) 4.50 3.95

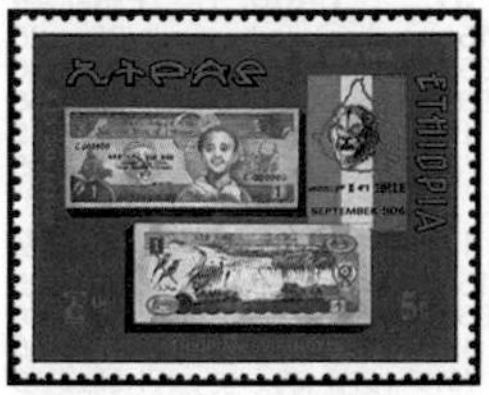

Bank Notes A263

1988, Nov. 10 Photo. *Perf. 13*

1229 A263 5c 1-Birr .20 .20
1230 A263 10c 5-Birr .35 .30
1231 A263 20c 10-Birr .75 .50
1232 A263 75c 50-Birr 1.75 1.50
1233 A263 85c 100-Birr 2.25 2.00
Nos. 1229-1233 (5) 5.30 4.50

Nos. 1181-1184 Overprinted "WORLD AIDS DAY" in Two Languages

1988, Dec. 1 Litho. *Perf. 13½*

1234 A248 20c multicolored *4.75 4.50*
1235 A248 25c multicolored *6.25 5.50*
1236 A248 45c multicolored *12.50 10.50*
1237 A248 55c multicolored *13.00 11.00*
Nos. 1234-1237 (4) *36.50 31.50*

Intl. Day for the Fight Against AIDS.

WHO, 40th Anniv. A264

1988, Dec. 30 Litho. *Perf. 14*

1238 A264 50c multicolored 1.00 .80
1239 A264 65c multicolored 1.40 1.00
1240 A264 85c multicolored 1.75 1.50
Nos. 1238-1240 (3) 4.15 3.30

Traditional Musical Instruments A265

1989, Feb. 9 *Perf. 13x13½*

1241 A265 30c Gere .75 .45
1242 A265 40c Fanfa 1.00 .65
1243 A265 50c Chancha 1.25 .90
1244 A265 85c Negareet 1.75 1.25
Nos. 1241-1244 (4) 4.75 3.25

Ethiopian Shipping Lines, 25th Anniv. A266

1989, Mar. 27 Litho. *Perf. 14*

1245 A266 15c *Abyot* .40 .30
1246 A266 30c *Wolwol* .75 .60
1247 A266 55c *Queen of Sheba* 1.40 1.25
1248 A266 1b *Abbay Wonz* 2.75 2.25
Nos. 1245-1248 (4) 5.30 4.40

Birds — A267

1989, May 18 Litho. *Perf. 13½x13*

1249 A267 10c Yellow-fronted parrot .40 .30
1250 A267 35c White-winged cliff chat 1.25 1.00
1251 A267 50c Yellow-throated seed eater 1.75 1.25
1252 A267 1b Black-headed forest oriole 2.75 2.25
Nos. 1249-1252 (4) 6.15 4.80

Production of Early Manuscripts — A268

1989, June 16 Litho. *Perf. 13½*

1253 A268 5c Preparing vellum .20 .20
1254 A268 10c Ink horns, pens .30 .25
1255 A268 20c Scribe .50 .40
1256 A268 75c Book binding 1.50 1.25
1257 A268 85c Illuminated manuscript 2.00 1.75
Nos. 1253-1257 (5) 4.50 3.85

Indigenous Wildlife — A269

1989, July 18

1258 A269 30c Greater kudu 1.00 .75
1259 A269 40c Lesser kudu 1.25 1.00
1260 A269 50c Roan antelope 1.50 1.25
1261 A269 85c Nile lechwe 2.50 2.00
Nos. 1258-1261 (4) 6.25 5.00

People's Democratic Republic of Ethiopia, 2nd Anniv. A270

Designs: 15c, Melka Wakana Hydroelectric Power Station. 75c, Adea Berga Dairy Farm. 1b, Pawe Hospital.

1989, Sept. 8

1262 A270 15c multicolored .35 .25
1263 A270 75c multicolored 1.50 1.25
1264 A270 1b multicolored 2.50 2.00
Nos. 1262-1264 (3) 4.35 3.50

African Development Bank, 25th Anniv. — A271

1989, Nov. 10 Litho. *Perf. 13½x13*

1265 A271 20c multicolored .35 .30
1266 A271 80c multicolored 1.50 1.25
1267 A271 1b multicolored 2.75 2.00
Nos. 1265-1267 (3) 4.60 3.55

Pan-African Postal Union, 10th Anniv. — A272

1990, Jan. 18 Litho. *Perf. 13½*

1268 A272 50c multicolored 1.00 .75
1269 A272 70c multicolored 1.50 1.25
1270 A272 80c multicolored 2.00 1.75
Nos. 1268-1270 (3) 4.50 3.75

UNESCO World Literacy Year — A273

15c, Illiterate man holding newspaper upside down. 85c, Adults learning alphabet in school. 1b, Literate man holding newspaper upright.

1990, Mar. 13

1271 A273 15c multicolored .50 .40
1272 A273 85c multicolored 1.75 1.50
1273 A273 1b multicolored 2.50 2.25
Nos. 1271-1273 (3) 4.75 4.15

Abebe Bikila, Marathon Runner A274

1990, Apr. 17

1274 A274 5c Race .20 .20
1275 A274 10c Flag bearer, Olympic team .30 .25
1276 A274 20c Race, Rome Olympics .60 .50
1277 A274 75c Race, Tokyo Olympics 1.75 1.50
1278 A274 85c Bikila, trophies, vert. 2.25 2.00
Nos. 1274-1278 (5) 5.10 4.45

Flag — A275

1990, Apr. 30 Litho. *Perf. 13½x13*

1279 A275 5c multicolored .20 .20
1280 A275 10c multicolored .20 .20
1281 A275 15c multicolored .30 .20
1282 A275 20c multicolored .40 .30
1283 A275 25c multicolored .45 .35
1284 A275 30c multicolored .55 .40
1285 A275 35c multicolored .65 .45
1286 A275 40c multicolored .80 .50
1287 A275 45c multicolored .90 .65
1288 A275 50c multicolored 1.00 .65
1289 A275 55c multicolored 1.10 .70
1290 A275 60c multicolored 1.20 .80
1291 A275 70c multicolored 1.25 .90
1292 A275 80c multicolored 1.40 1.00
1293 A275 85c multicolored 1.50 1.10
1294 A275 90c multicolored 1.60 1.25
1295 A275 1b multicolored 1.75 1.25
1296 A275 2b multicolored 3.75 2.75
1297 A275 3b multicolored 5.50 4.00
Nos. 1279-1297 (19) 24.50 17.65

Dated 1989.

Sowing of Teff A276

1990, May 18 Litho. *Perf. 13½*

1298 A276 5c shown .20 .20
1299 A276 10c Harvesting .25 .20
1300 A276 20c Threshing .50 .40
1301 A276 75c Storage, preparation 1.75 1.50
1302 A276 85c Consumption 2.25 2.00
Nos. 1298-1302 (5) 4.95 4.30

Walia Ibex — A277

1990, June 18 *Perf. 14x13½*

1303 A277 5c multi .75 .50
1304 A277 15c multi 1.75 1.00
1305 A277 20c multi 2.50 1.50
1306 A277 1b multi, horiz. 10.00 5.75
Nos. 1303-1306 (4) 15.00 8.75

World AIDS Day A278

1991, Jan. 31 Litho. *Perf. 14*

1307 A278 15c Stages of disease .40 .30
1308 A278 85c Education 1.75 1.50
1309 A278 1b Causes, preventatives 2.25 2.00
Nos. 1307-1309 (3) 4.40 3.80

Intl. Decade for Natural Disaster Reduction A279

Map of disaster-prone African areas and: 5c, Volcano. 10c, Earthquake. 15c, Drought. 30c, Flood. 50c, Red Cross health education. 1b, Red Cross assisting fire victims.

1991, Apr. 9 Litho. *Perf. 14*

1310 A279 5c multicolored .20 .20
1311 A279 10c multicolored .25 .20
1312 A279 15c multicolored .30 .25
1313 A279 30c multicolored .60 .50
1314 A279 50c multicolored 1.25 1.00
1315 A279 1b multicolored 2.25 2.00
Nos. 1310-1315 (6) 4.85 4.15

The Cannon of Tewodros A280

Designs: 15c, Villagers receiving cannon. 85c, Warriors leaving with cannon. 1b, Hauling cannon up mountainside.

Convair Plane over Mountains AP5

Engraved and Lithographed

1955, Dec. 30 Unwmk. *Perf. 12½*

Center Multicolored

C38	AP5	10c gray green	.40	.20
C39	AP5	15c carmine	.50	.25
C40	AP5	20c violet	.75	.40
		Nos. C38-C40 (3)	1.65	.85

10th anniversary of Ethiopian Airlines.

Promulgating the Constitution — AP6

Perf. 14x13½

1956, July 16 Engr. Wmk. 282

C41	AP6	10c redsh brn & ultra	.25	.30
C42	AP6	15c dk car rose & ol grn	.40	.45
C43	AP6	20c blue & org red	.60	.45
C44	AP6	25c purple & green	.75	.70
C45	AP6	30c dk grn & red brn	1.00	1.10
		Nos. C41-C45 (5)	3.00	3.00

25th anniversary of the constitution.

Aksum AP7

Ancient Capitals: 10c, Lalibela. 15c, Gondar. 20c, Mekele. 25c, Ankober.

1957, Feb. 7 *Perf. 14*

Centers in Green

C46	AP7	5c red brown	.50	.25
C47	AP7	10c rose carmine	.50	.25
C48	AP7	15c red orange	.60	.30
C49	AP7	20c ultramarine	.85	.45
C50	AP7	25c claret	1.25	.65
		Nos. C46-C50 (5)	3.70	1.90

Amharic "A" — AP8

Designs: Various Amharic characters and views of Addis Ababa. The characters, arranged by values, spell Addis Ababa.

1957, Feb. 14 Engr.

Amharic Letters in Scarlet

C51	AP8	5c ultra, *sal pink*	.20	.20
C52	AP8	10c ol grn, *pink*	.25	.20
C53	AP8	15c dl pur, *yel*	.40	.20
C54	AP8	20c grn, *buff*	.50	.25
C55	AP8	25c plum, *pale bl*	.75	.30
C56	AP8	30c red, *pale grn*	.90	.35
		Nos. C51-C56 (6)	3.00	1.50

70th anniversary of Addis Ababa.

Map, Rock Church at Lalibela and Obelisk AP9

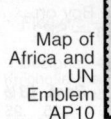

1958, Apr. 15 Wmk. 282 *Perf. 13½*

C57	AP9	10c green	.20	.20
C58	AP9	20c rose red	.30	.20
C59	AP9	30c bright blue	.50	.25
		Nos. C57-C59 (3)	1.00	.65

Conf. of Independent African States, Accra, Apr. 15-22.

Map of Africa and UN Emblem AP10

1958, Dec. 29 *Perf. 13*

C60	AP10	5c emerald	.20	.20
C61	AP10	20c carmine rose	.25	.20
C62	AP10	25c ultramarine	.30	.25
C63	AP10	50c pale purple	.60	.35
		Nos. C60-C63 (4)	1.35	1.00

1st session of the UN Economic Conf. for Africa, opened in Addis Ababa Dec. 29.

Nos. C23-C29 Overprinted

Perf. 13x13½

1959, Aug. 16 Engr. Wmk. 282

C64	AP3	8c purple brown	.30	.25
C65	AP3	10c brt green	.40	.30
C66	AP3	25c dull purple	.60	.35
C67	AP3	30c orange yellow	.65	.50
C68	AP3	35c blue	.85	.55
C69	AP3	65c purple	1.25	.85
C70	AP3	70c red	1.60	1.10
		Nos. C64-C70 (7)	5.65	3.90

30th anniv. of Ethiopian airmail service.

Ethiopian Soldier and Map of Congo — AP11

Globe with Map of Africa — AP12

Perf. 11½

1962, July 23 Unwmk. Photo.

Granite Paper

C71	AP11	15c org, bl, brn & grn	.20	.20
C72	AP11	50c pur, bl, brn & grn	.40	.30
C73	AP11	60c red, bl, brn & grn	.70	.35
		Nos. C71-C73 (3)	1.30	.85

2nd anniv. of the Ethiopian contingent of the UN forces in the Congo and in honor of the 70th birthday of Emperor Haile Selassie.

1963, May 22

Granite Paper

C74	AP12	10c magenta & blk	.20	.20
C75	AP12	40c emerald & blk	.40	.25
C76	AP12	60c blue & blk	.70	.35
		Nos. C74-C76 (3)	1.30	.80

Conf. of African heads of state for African Unity, Addis Ababa.

Bird Type of Regular Issue

Birds: 10c, Black-headed forest oriole. 15c, Broad-tailed paradise whydah, vert. 20c, Lammergeier, vert. 50c, White-checked touraco. 80c, Purple indigo bird.

1963, Sept. 12 *Perf. 11½*

Granite Paper

C77	A74	10c multicolored	.25	.20
C78	A74	15c multicolored	.30	.20
C79	A74	20c blue, blk & ocher	.60	.25
C80	A74	50c lemon & multi	.95	.45
C81	A74	80c ultra, blk & brn	1.90	.75
		Nos. C77-C81 (5)	4.00	1.85

Swimming AP13

Sport: 10c, Basketball, vert. 15c, Javelin. 80c, Soccer game in stadium.

Perf. 14x13½

1964, Sept. 15 Litho. Unwmk.

C82	AP13	5c multicolored	.20	.20
C83	AP13	10c multicolored	.20	.20
C84	AP13	15c multicolored	.35	.30
C85	AP13	80c multicolored	1.25	.60
		Nos. C82-C85 (4)	2.00	1.30

18th Olympic Games, Tokyo, Oct. 10-25.

Queen Elizabeth II and Emperor Haile Selassie — AP14

1965, Feb. 1 Photo. *Perf. 11½*

Granite Paper

C86	AP14	5c multicolored	.20	.20
C87	AP14	35c multicolored	.50	.30
C88	AP14	60c multicolored	.85	.50
		Nos. C86-C88 (3)	1.55	1.00

Visit of Queen Elizabeth II, Feb. 1-8.

Koka Dam and Power Plant — AP15

Designs: 15c, Sugar cane field. 50c, Blue Nile bridge. 60c, Gondar castles. 80c, Coffee tree. $1, Cattle at water hole. $3, Camels at well. $5, Ethiopian Air Lines jet plane.

1965, July 19 Unwmk. *Perf. 11½*

Granite Paper

Portrait in Black

C89	AP15	15c vio brn & buff	.20	.20
C90	AP15	40c vio bl & lt bl	.45	.30
C91	AP15	50c grn & lt bl	.60	.35
C92	AP15	60c claret & yel	.75	.45
C93	AP15	80c grn, yel & red	.90	.50
C94	AP15	$1 brn & lt bl	1.10	.60
C95	AP15	$3 claret & pink	3.50	1.60
C96	AP15	$5 ultra & lt bl	7.50	3.00
		Nos. C89-C96 (8)	15.00	7.00

Bird Type of Regular Issue

Birds: 10c, White-collared kingfisher. 15c, Blue-breasted bee-eater. 25c, African paradise flycatcher. 40c, Village weaver. 60c, White-collared pigeon.

1966, Feb. 15 Photo. *Perf. 11½*

Granite Paper

C97	A74	10c dull yel & multi	.25	.20
C98	A74	15c lt blue & multi	.35	.20
C99	A74	25c gray & multi	.70	.35
C100	A74	40c pink & multi	1.40	.50
C101	A74	60c multicolored	1.60	.75
		Nos. C97-C101 (5)	4.30	2.00

Black Rhinoceros — AP16

Animals: 10c, Leopard. 20c, Black-and-white colobus (monkey). 30c, Mountain nyala. 60c, Nubian ibex.

1966, June 20 Litho. *Perf. 13*

C102	AP16	5c dp grn, blk & gray	.20	.20
C103	AP16	10c grn, blk & ocher	.25	.20
C104	AP16	20c cit, blk & grn	.50	.20
C105	AP16	30c yel grn, blk & ocher	.75	.20
C106	AP16	60c yel grn, blk & dk brn	1.50	.30
		Nos. C102-C106 (5)	3.20	1.10

Bird Type of Regular Issue

Birds: 10c, Blue-winged goose, vert. 15c, Yellow-billed duck. 20c, Wattled ibis. 25c, Striped swallow. 40c, Black-winged lovebird, vert.

1967, Sept. 29 Photo. *Perf. 11½*

Granite Paper

C107	A74	10c lt ultra & multi	.20	.20
C108	A74	15c green & multi	.35	.20
C109	A74	20c yellow & multi	.40	.20
C110	A74	25c salmon & multi	.65	.20
C111	A74	40c pink & multi	1.40	.50
		Nos. C107-C111 (5)	3.00	1.30

SPECIAL DELIVERY STAMPS

Catalogue values for unused stamps in this section are for Never Hinged items.

Motorcycle Messenger — SD1

Addis Ababa Post Office SD2

Unwmk.

1947, Apr. 24 Engr. *Perf. 13*

E1	SD1	30c orange brown	3.00	.75
E2	SD2	50c blue	5.00	2.00

1954-62 Wmk. 282

E3	SD1	30c org brown ('62)	3.00	2.00
E4	SD2	50c blue	2.00	.75

POSTAGE DUE STAMPS

Very Fine examples of Nos. J1-J42 will have perforations touching the design on one or more sides.

Nos. 1-4 and unissued values Overprinted

1895 Unwmk. *Perf. 14x13½*

Black Overprint

J1	A1	¼g green	1.25
J2	A1	½g red	1.25
J3	A1	4g lilac brown	.90
a.		Without overprint	.90

J4	A1	8g violet	.90	
a.		Without overprint	.90	

Red Overprint

J5	A1	1g blue	1.25	
J6	A1	2g dark brown	1.25	
J7	A1	16g black	.90	
a.		Without overprint	.90	
		Nos. J1-J7 (7)	7.70	

Nos. J1-J7 were not issued.

Nos. 1-7 Handstamped in Various Colors:

a

b

1905, Apr.

J8	A1 (a)	¼g green	42.50	42.50
J9	A1 (a)	½g red	42.50	42.50
J10	A1 (a)	1g blue	42.50	42.50
J11	A1 (a)	2g dk brown	42.50	42.50
J12	A2 (a)	4g lilac brown	42.50	42.50
J13	A2 (a)	8g violet	42.50	42.50
J14	A2 (a)	16g black	42.50	42.50
		Nos. J7-J14 (8)	298.40	297.50

1905, June 1

J15	A1 (b)	¼g green	42.50	42.50
J16	A1 (b)	½g red	42.50	42.50
J17	A1 (b)	1g blue	42.50	42.50
J18	A1 (b)	2g dark brown	42.50	42.50
J19	A2 (b)	4g lilac brown	42.50	42.50
J20	A2 (b)	8g violet	42.50	42.50
J21	A2 (b)	16g black	42.50	42.50
		Nos. J15-J21 (7)	297.50	297.50

Excellent forgeries of Nos. J8-J42 exist.

Nos. 1-7 Handstamped in Blue or Violet

1905, Dec.

J22	A1	¼g green	10.00	10.00
J23	A1	½g red	10.00	10.00
J24	A1	1g blue	10.00	10.00
J25	A1	2g dark brown	10.00	10.00
J26	A2	4g lilac brown	10.00	10.00
J27	A2	8g violet	15.00	15.00
J28	A2	16g black	21.00	21.00
		Nos. J22-J28 (7)	86.00	86.00

Nos. J22-J27 exist with inverted overprint, also No. J22 with double overprint.
Forgeries exist.

With Additional Surcharge of Value Handstamped as on Nos. 71-77

1907, July 1

J29	A1 (e)	¼ on ¼g grn	14.00	14.00
J30	A1 (e)	½ on ½g red	14.00	14.00
J31	A1 (f)	1 on 1g blue	14.00	14.00
J32	A1 (f)	2 on 2g dk brown	14.00	14.00
J33	A2 (f)	4 on 4g lilac brn	14.00	14.00
J34	A2 (f)	8 on 8g violet	14.00	14.00
J35	A2 (f)	16 on 16g blk	22.50	22.50
		Nos. J29-J35 (7)	106.50	106.50

Many errors exist, most of them are unofficial reproductions.

Nos. 1-7 Handstamped in Black

1908, Dec. 1

J36	A1	¼g green	1.00	.90
J37	A1	½g red	1.00	.90
J38	A1	1g blue	1.00	.90
J39	A1	2g dark brown	1.25	1.10
J40	A2	4g lilac brown	1.75	1.75
J41	A2	8g violet	4.00	4.50
J42	A2	16g black	12.50	14.00
		Nos. J36-J42 (7)	22.50	24.05

Nos. J36 to J42 exist with inverted overprint and Nos. J36, J37, J38 and J40 with double overprint.
Forgeries of Nos. J36-J56 exist.

Same Handstamp on Nos. 87-93

1912, Dec. 1 *Perf. 11½*

J43	A3	¼g blue green	1.25	.85
J44	A3	½g rose	1.25	1.10

1913, July 1

J45	A3	1g green & org	4.25	3.00
J46	A4	2g blue	5.00	4.25
J47	A4	4g green & car	7.50	5.00
J48	A5	8g ver & dp grn	10.00	8.00
J49	A5	16g ver & car	25.00	19.00
		Nos. J43-J49 (7)	54.25	41.20

Nos. J43-J49, all exist with inverted, double and double, one inverted overprint.

Same Handstamp on Nos. 120-124 in Blue Black

1925-27 *Perf. 11½*

J50	A6	⅛g violet & brn	*18.00*	*18.00*
J51	A6	¼g bl grn & db	*18.00*	*18.00*
J52	A6	½g scar & ol grn	*20.00*	*20.00*
J53	A9	1g rose lil & gray grn	*20.00*	*20.00*
J54	A9	2g dp ultra & fawn	*20.00*	*20.00*
		Nos. J50-J54 (5)	*96.00*	*96.00*

Same Handstamp on Nos. 110, 112

1930 (?)

J55	A3	1g green & orange	*30.00*	*30.00*
J56	A4	2g blue	*30.00*	*30.00*

The status of Nos. J55-J56 is questioned.

Catalogue values for unused stamps in this section, from this point to the end of the section, are for Never Hinged items.

D2

Perf. 11½

1951, Apr. 2 **Unwmk.** **Litho.**

J57	D2	1c emerald	.35	.20
J58	D2	5c rose red	.55	.20
J59	D2	10c violet	.75	.30
J60	D2	20c ocher	1.10	.65
J61	D2	50c bright ultra	2.00	1.50
J62	D2	$1 rose lilac	4.25	2.00
		Nos. J57-J62 (6)	9.00	4.85

OCCUPATION STAMPS

Issued under Italian Occupation
100 Centesimi = 1 Lira

OS1

Emperor Victor Emmanuel III — OS2

1936 **Wmk. 140** *Perf. 14*

N1	OS1	10c orange brown	8.25	5.50
N2	OS1	20c purple	7.75	1.75
N3	OS2	25c dark green	3.75	.35
N4	OS2	30c dark brown	3.75	.85
N5	OS2	50c rose carmine	1.00	.20
N6	OS1	75c deep orange	15.00	4.00
N7	OS1	1.25 l deep blue	16.00	6.25
		Nos. N1-N7 (7)	55.50	18.90
		Set, never hinged	135.00	

Issued: #N3-N5, May 22; others Dec. 5.
For later issues see Italian East Africa.

FALKLAND ISLANDS

'fol-klənd 'ī-ləndz

LOCATION — A group of islands about 300 miles east of the Straits of Magellan at the southern limit of South America
GOVT. — British Crown Colony
AREA — 4,700 sq. mi.
POP. — 2,607 (1996)
CAPITAL — Stanley

Dependencies of the Falklands are South Georgia and South Sandwich. In March 1962, three other dependencies — South Shetland Islands, South Orkneys and Graham Land—became the new separate colony of British Antarctic Territory. In 1985 South Georgia and the South Sandwich Islands became a separate colony.

12 Pence = 1 Shilling
20 Shillings = 1 Pound
100 Pence = 1 Pound (1971)

Catalogue values for unused stamps in this country are for Never Hinged items, beginning with Scott 97 in the regular postage section, Scott B1 in the semi-postal section, Scott J1 in the postage due section, Scott 1L1 in Falkland Island Dependencies regular issues, Scott 1LB1 in Falkland Island Dependencies semi-postals, and Scott 2L1, 3L1, 4L1, 5L1 in the Issues for Separate Islands.

Values for unused stamps are for examples with original gum as defined in the catalogue introduction.

Nos. 1-4, 7-8, and some printings of Nos. 5-6, exist with straight edges on one or two sides, being the imperforate margins of the sheets. This occurs in 24 out of 60 stamps. Catalogue values are for stamps with perforations on all sides.

Queen Victoria — A1

1878-79 **Unwmk.** **Engr.** *Perf. 14*

1	A1	1p claret	850.00	500.00
2	A1	4p dark gray ('79)	1,400.	200.00
3	A1	6p green	100.00	85.00
4	A1	1sh bister brown	80.00	80.00

1883-95 **Wmk. 2**

5	A1	1p brt claret ('94)	130.00	95.00
a.		1p claret	425.00	175.00
b.		Horiz. pair, imperf. vert.	*65,000.*	
c.		1p red brown ('91)	240.00	90.00
d.		Diag. half of #5c used as ½p on cover		*3,500.*
6	A1	4p olive gray ('95)	14.00	27.50
a.		4p gray black	500.00	100.00
b.		4p olive gray black ('89)	180.00	65.00
c.		4p brownish black ('94)	900.00	400.00

No. 6c has watermark reversed.
For surcharge see No. 19E.

1886 **Wmk. 2 Sideways**

7	A1	1p claret	95.00	65.00
a.		1p brownish claret	125.00	60.00
b.		Diagonal half of #7a used as ½p on cover		*3,250.*
8	A1	4p olive gray	525.00	60.00
a.		4p pale gray black	825.00	90.00

For surcharge see No. 19.

1891-1902 **Wmk. 2**

9	A1	½p green ('92)	19.00	*18.00*
a.		½p blue green	27.50	*32.50*
10	A1	½p yel green ('99)	2.25	*3.50*
11	A1	1p orange brown	100.00	80.00
a.		Diagonal half used as ½p on cover		*2,750.*
11B	A1	1p pale red ('99)	9.00	5.00
12	A1	1p org red ('02)	16.00	4.75
a.		1p Venetian red ('95)	32.50	20.00
13	A1	2p magenta ('96)	7.00	14.00
14	A1	2½p deep blue ('94)	275.00	160.00
15	A1	2½p ultra ('94)	37.50	14.00
a.		2½p pale ultra ('98)	40.00	20.00
b.		2½p dull blue	190.00	30.00
c.		2½p deep ultra ('01)	45.00	40.00
d.		2½p pale chalky ultra	190.00	60.00
16	A1	6p yellow ('96)	42.50	55.00
a.		6p orange ('92)	100.00	75.00
17	A1	9p ver ('96)	50.00	*65.00*
a.		9p salmon	57.50	*70.00*
18	A1	1sh gray brn ('95)	67.50	65.00
a.		1sh bister brown ('96)	65.00	55.00
		Nos. 9-18 (11)	625.75	484.25

Nos. 7 and 5a Surcharged in Black

1891 **Wmk. 2 Sideways**

19	A1	½p on half of 1p, #7	725.00	360.00
d.		Unsevered pair	3,500.	1,350.

Wmk. 2

19E	A1	½p on half of 1p, #5a	825.00	325.00
f.		Unsevered pair	4,500.	1,800.

Genuine used bisects should be canceled with a segmented circular cork cancel. Any other cancel must be linked by date to known mail ship departures. This surcharge exists on "souvenir" bisects, including examples of No. 11, and can be found inverted, double and sideways.

A3 A4

1898 **Wmk. 1**

20	A3	2sh6p dark blue	300.00	300.00
21	A4	5sh brown red	240.00	275.00

King Edward VII
A5 A6

1904-07 **Wmk. 3** ***Perf. 14***

22	A5	½p yellow green	5.25	1.80
23	A5	1p red, wmk. sideways ('07)	1.20	*2.50*
a.		Wmk. upright ('04)	15.00	*1.80*
24	A5	2p dull vio ('05)	20.00	*32.50*
25	A5	2½p ultramarine	35.00	10.00
a.		2½p deep blue	300.00	200.00
26	A5	6p orange ('05)	50.00	*57.50*
27	A5	1sh bis brn ('05)	50.00	40.00
28	A6	3sh gray green	175.00	160.00
29	A6	5sh dull red ('05)	240.00	180.00
		Nos. 22-29 (8)	576.45	484.30

King George V
A7 A8

1912-14

30	A7	½p yellow green	3.00	3.25
31	A7	1p red	5.50	2.75
32	A7	2p brown violet	9.50	19.00
33	A7	2½p deep ultra	9.50	*19.00*
34	A7	6p orange	17.50	*22.50*
35	A7	1sh bister brown	40.00	*37.50*
36	A8	3sh dark green	100.00	*95.00*
37	A8	5sh brown red	95.00	*120.00*
38	A8	5sh plum ('14)	250.00	*250.00*
39	A8	10sh red, *green*	200.00	*300.00*
40	A8	£1 black, *red*	525.00	*600.00*
		Nos. 30-40 (11)	1,255.	*1,469.*

For overprints see Nos. MR1-MR3.

1921-29 **Wmk. 4**

41	A7	½p yellow green	3.50	*4.50*
42	A7	1p red ('24)	6.00	1.50
43	A7	2p brown vio ('23)	9.50	8.50
44	A7	2½p dark blue	9.00	*20.00*
a.		2½p Prussian blue ('29)	375.00	*550.00*
45	A7	2½p vio, *yel* ('23)	6.00	*42.50*
46	A7	6p orange ('25)	9.50	*45.00*
47	A7	1sh bister brown	20.00	*57.50*
48	A8	3sh dk green ('23)	100.00	*190.00*
		Nos. 41-48 (8)	163.50	*369.50*

No. 43 Surcharged

1928

52	A7	2½p on 2p brn vio	*1,200.*	*1,200.*
a.		Double surcharge	*45,000.*	

Beware of forged surcharges.

King George V — A9

1929-31 ***Perf. 14***

54	A9	½p green	1.40	*3.25*
55	A9	1p scarlet	4.00	.90
56	A9	2p gray	3.25	3.00
57	A9	2½p blue	3.25	2.50
58	A9	4p deep orange	20.00	15.00
59	A9	6p brown violet	20.00	15.00
60	A9	1sh black, *green*	25.00	*37.50*
a.		1sh black, *emerald*	*26.00*	*30.00*
61	A9	2sh6p red, *blue*	60.00	60.00
62	A9	5sh green, *yel*	100.00	*120.00*
63	A9	10sh red, *green*	190.00	*225.00*

Wmk. 3

64	A9	£1 black, *red*	350.00	425.00
		Nos. 54-64 (11)	776.90	907.15

Issue dates: 4p, 1931, others, Sept. 2.

Romney Marsh Ram — A10

Iceberg A11

Whaling Ship — A12

Port Louis A13

Map of the Islands A14

South Georgia A15

Blue Whale A16

Government House A17

Battle Memorial — A18

King Penguin — A19

Coat of Arms — A20

King George V — A21

1933, Jan. 2 **Wmk. 4** ***Perf. 12***

65	A10	½p green & blk	2.25	*6.50*
66	A11	1p dl red & blk	4.00	2.50
67	A12	1½p lt bl & blk	19.00	*20.00*
68	A13	2p ol brn & blk	12.50	*25.00*
69	A14	3p dl vio & blk	20.00	*22.50*
70	A15	4p orange & blk	20.00	*20.00*
71	A16	6p gray & black	57.50	*75.00*
72	A17	1sh ol grn & blk	50.00	*85.00*
73	A18	2sh6p dp vio & blk	200.00	200.00
74	A19	5sh yellow & blk	700.00	*1,000.*
a.		5sh yellow orange & black	2,000.	*2,500.*
75	A20	10sh lt brn & blk	725.00	*1,100.*
76	A21	£1 rose & black	2,000.	*2,500.*
		Nos. 65-76 (12)	3,810.	*5,056.*

Cent. of the permanent occupation of the islands as a British colony.

Common Design Types pictured following the introduction.

Silver Jubilee Issue
Common Design Type

1935, May 7 ***Perf. 11x12***

77	CD301	1p carmine & blue	2.00	.50
78	CD301	2½p ultra & brown	4.25	2.10
79	CD301	4p indigo & grn	8.75	5.50
80	CD301	1sh brn vio & ind	20.00	4.75
		Nos. 77-80 (4)	35.00	12.85
		Set, never hinged	52.50	

Coronation Issue
Common Design Type

1937, May 12 ***Perf. 11x11½***

81	CD302	½p deep green	.20	.20
82	CD302	1p dark carmine	.35	*.50*
83	CD302	2½p deep ultra	.60	*.80*
		Nos. 81-83 (3)	1.15	1.50
		Set, never hinged	3.50	

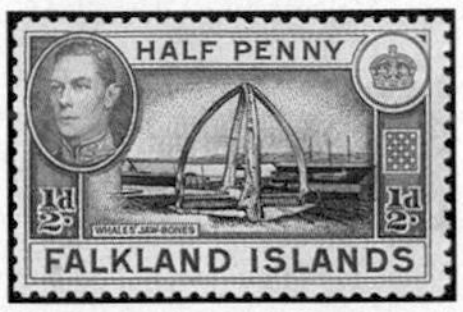

Whale Jawbones (Centennial Monument) — A22

#85, 86A, Black-necked swan. #85B, 86, Battle memorial. 2½p, 3p, Flock of sheep. 4p, Upland goose. 6p, R.R.S. "Discovery II." 9p, R.R.S. "William Scoresby." 1sh, Mt. Sugar Top. 1sh3p, Turkey vultures. 2sh6p, Gentoo penguins. 5sh, Sea lions. 10sh, Deception Island. £1, Arms of Colony.

1938-46 ***Perf. 12***

84	A22	½p green & blk	.20	.20
85	A22	1p red & black	2.50	2.75
a.		1p rose carmine & black	16.00	1.75
85B	A22	1p dk vio & blk	.20	.20
86	A22	2p dk vio & blk	1.75	1.90
86A	A22	2p rose car & black	.25	.30
87	A22	2½p ultra & blk	1.50	1.40
87A	A22	3p dp bl & blk	.75	.80
88	A22	4p rose vio & blk	1.75	1.90
89	A22	6p brown & blk	5.00	4.75
90	A22	9p sl bl & blk	1.75	1.60
91	A22	1sh dull blue	7.75	3.25
92	A22	1sh3p car & blk	1.75	*3.25*
93	A22	2sh6p gray black	37.50	22.50
94	A22	5sh org brown & ultra	55.00	47.50
a.		5sh yel brown & indigo	625.00	300.00
95	A22	10sh org & blk	60.00	47.50
96	A22	£1 dk vio & blk	125.00	92.50
		Nos. 84-96 (16)	302.65	232.30
		Set, never hinged	550.00	

Issued: #85B, 86A, 3p, 7/14/41; 1sh3p, 12/10/46; No. 94a, 1942; others, 1/3/38.

See Nos. 101-102. For overprints see Nos. 2L1-2L8, 3L1-3L8, 4L1-4L8, 5L1-5L8.

Catalogue values for unused stamps in this section, from this point to the end of the section, are for Never Hinged items.

Peace Issue
Common Design Type
Perf. 13½x14

1946, Oct. 7 **Engr.** **Wmk. 4**

97	CD303	1p purple	.35	.25
98	CD303	3p deep blue	.55	.25

Silver Wedding Issue
Common Design Types

1948, Nov. 1 **Photo.** ***Perf. 14x14½***

99	CD304	2½p bright ultra	1.25	.70

Engr.; Name Typo.
Perf. 11½x11

100	CD305	£1 purple	110.00	82.50

Types of 1938-46

2½p, Upland goose. 6p, R.R.S. "Discovery II."

Perf. 12

1949, June 15 **Engr.** **Wmk. 4**

101	A22	2½p dp blue & black	5.50	*7.25*
102	A22	6p gray black	4.75	3.50

UPU Issue
Common Design Types

Engr.; Name Typo. on 3p, 1sh3p

1949, Oct. 10 *Perf. 13½, 11x11½*

103	CD306	1p violet	.60	.60
104	CD307	3p indigo	1.50	1.50
105	CD308	1sh3p green	5.00	4.50
106	CD309	2sh blue	11.00	9.50
		Nos. 103-106 (4)	18.10	16.10

Sheep A35

Arms of the Colony — A36

Designs: 1p, R.M.S. Fitzroy. 2p Upland goose. 2½p, Map. 4p, Auster plane. 6p, M.S.S. John Biscoe. 9p, "Two Sisters" peaks. 1sh, Gentoo penguins. 1sh 3p, Kelp goose and gander. 2sh 6p, Sheep shearing. 5sh, Battle memorial. 10sh, Sea lion and clapmatch. £1, Hulk of "Great Britain."

Perf. 13½x13, 13x13½

1952, Jan. 2 **Engr.** **Wmk. 4**

107	A35	½p green	1.00	*1.40*
108	A35	1p red	2.10	.70
109	A35	2p violet	4.75	*4.50*
110	A35	2½p ultra & blk	1.25	.95
111	A36	3p deep ultra	1.40	*1.75*
112	A35	4p claret	10.00	2.75
113	A35	6p yellow brn	16.00	1.75
114	A35	9p orange yel	12.50	3.50
115	A36	1sh black	29.00	1.50
116	A35	1sh3p red orange	18.00	*9.25*
117	A36	2sh6p olive	22.50	*20.00*
118	A36	5sh red violet	14.00	*15.00*
119	A35	10sh gray	30.00	*25.00*
120	A35	£1 black	37.50	*32.50*
		Nos. 107-120 (14)	200.00	*120.55*

Coronation Issue
Common Design Type

1953, June 4 *Perf. 13½x13*

121	CD312	1p car & black	.95	1.25

Types of 1952 with Portrait of Queen Elizabeth II

1955-57 *Perf. 13½x13, 13x13½*

122	A35	½p green ('57)	.75	*1.50*
123	A35	1p red ('57)	1.25	1.25
124	A35	2p violet ('56)	3.50	*6.25*
125	A35	6p light brown	8.75	.70
126	A35	9p ocher ('57)	13.00	*21.00*
127	A36	1sh black	7.75	1.40
		Nos. 122-127 (6)	35.00	*32.10*

Marsh Starling A37

Birds: ½p, Falkland Islands Thrush. 1p, Dominican gull. 2p, Gentoo penguins. 3p, Upland geese. 4p, Steamer ducks. 5½p, Rock-hopper penguin. 6p, black-browed albatross. 9p, Silver grebe. 1sh, Pied oystercatchers. 1sh3p, Yellow-billed teal. 2sh, Kelp geese, 5sh, King shag. 10sh, Guadelupe caracara. £1, Black-necked swan.

Perf. 13½x13

1960, Feb. 10 **Engr.** **Wmk. 314**

Center in Black

128	A37	½p green	3.75	.50
a.		Wmk. sideways ('66)	.45	.30
129	A37	1p rose red	1.40	.80
130	A37	2p blue	3.75	1.00
131	A37	2½p bister brn	1.25	.30
132	A37	3p olive	.70	.30
133	A37	4p rose car	1.00	1.00
134	A37	5½p violet	1.75	*2.25*
135	A37	6p sepia	2.00	.30
136	A37	9p orange	1.75	1.25
137	A37	1sh dull purple	.65	.30
138	A37	1sh3p ultra	9.50	*13.00*
139	A37	2sh brown car	27.50	2.50
140	A37	5sh grnsh blue	27.50	11.00
141	A37	10sh rose lilac	47.50	13.00
142	A37	£1 yellow org	50.00	32.50
		Nos. 128-142 (15)	180.00	80.00

Morse Key — A38

1962, Oct. 5 **Photo.** *Perf. 11½x11*

143	A38	6p dp org & dk red	1.00	.60
144	A38	1sh brt ol grn & dp green	1.10	1.00
145	A38	2sh brt ultra & violet	1.90	1.90
		Nos. 143-145 (3)	4.00	3.50

Falkland Islands radio station, 50th anniv.

Freedom from Hunger Issue
Common Design Type

1963, June 4 *Perf. 14x14½*

146	CD314	1sh ultramarine	13.50	5.00

Red Cross Centenary Issue
Common Design Type

Wmk. 314

1963, Sept.2 **Litho.** *Perf. 13*

147	CD315	1p black & red	3.00	1.00
148	CD315	1sh ultra & red	20.00	6.00

Shakespeare Issue
Common Design Type

1964, Apr. 23 **Photo.** *Perf. 14x14½*

149	CD316	6p black	1.75	.50

H.M.S. Glasgow A39

6p, H.M.S. Kent. 1sh, H.M.S. Invincible. 2sh, Falkland Islands Battle Memorial, vert.

1964, Dec. 8 **Engr.** *Perf. 13*

150	A39	2½p ver & black	9.75	3.75
151	A39	6p blue & black	.45	.30
a.		"Glasgow" vignette	*27,500.*	
152	A39	1sh carmine & blk	.45	*1.10*

Perf. 13x14

153	A39	2sh dk blue & blk	.35	.85
		Nos. 150-153 (4)	11.00	6.00

Battle of the Falkland Islands between the British and German navies, 50th anniv.

ITU Issue
Common Design Type

Perf. 11x11½

1965, May 26 **Litho.** **Wmk. 314**

154	CD317	1p blue & dl dk bl	.65	.40
155	CD317	2sh lilac & dl yel	9.50	3.25

Intl. Cooperation Year Issue
Common Design Type

1965, Oct. 25 *Perf. 14½*

156	CD318	1p blue grn & claret	1.00	.25
157	CD318	1sh lt violet & grn	7.50	1.75

Churchill Memorial Issue
Common Design Type

1966, Jan. 24 **Photo.** *Perf. 14*

Design in Black, Gold and Carmine Rose

158	CD319	½p bright blue	.40	.20
159	CD319	1p green	1.60	.30
160	CD319	1sh brown	4.00	1.75
161	CD319	2sh violet	8.50	4.25
		Nos. 158-161 (4)	14.50	6.50

Human Rights Flame and Globe A40

Perf. 14x14½

1968, July 4 **Photo.** **Wmk. 314**

162	A40	2p brt rose & multi	.20	.20
163	A40	6p brt green & multi	.40	.40
164	A40	1sh orange & multi	.65	.65
165	A40	2sh ultra & multi	1.25	1.25
		Nos. 162-165 (4)	2.50	2.50

International Human Rights Year.

Dusty Miller — A41

Falkland Islands flora: 1½p, Pig vine, horiz. 2p, Pale maiden. 3p, Dog orchard. 3½p, Sea cabbage, horiz. 4½p, Vanilla daisy. 5½p, Arrowleaf marigold, horiz. 6p, Diddle-dee, horiz. 1sh, Scurvy grass, horiz. 1sh6p, Prickly burr. 2sh, Fachine. 3sh, Lavender. 5sh, Felton's flower, horiz. £1, Yellow orchid.

1968, Oct. 9 **Photo.** *Perf. 14*

166	A41	½p multicolored	.20	.20
167	A41	1½p multicolored	.45	.20
168	A41	2p multicolored	.60	.20
169	A41	3p multicolored	6.00	.40
170	A41	3½p multicolored	.35	*.55*
171	A41	4½p multicolored	1.75	.75
172	A41	5½p multicolored	1.75	1.00
173	A41	6p multicolored	.85	*1.25*
174	A41	1sh multicolored	.85	*2.40*
175	A41	1sh6p multicolored	4.75	*11.00*
176	A41	2sh multicolored	6.00	5.50
177	A41	3sh multicolored	8.50	8.00
178	A41	5sh multicolored	30.00	15.00
179	A41	£1 multicolored	13.25	8.75
		Nos. 166-179 (14)	75.30	55.20

See #210-222. For surcharges see #197-209.

Beaver DHC 2 Seaplane A42

Designs: 6p, Norseman seaplane. 1sh, Auster plane. 2sh, Falkland Islands arms.

1969, Apr. 8 **Litho.** *Perf. 14*

180	A42	2p multicolored	.20	.20
181	A42	6p multicolored	.35	.35
182	A42	1sh multicolored	.70	.70
183	A42	2sh multicolored	1.75	1.25
		Nos. 180-183 (4)	3.00	2.50

21st anniv. of Government Air Service.

Bishop Stirling A43

2p, Holy Trinity Church, 1869. 6p, Christ Church Cathedral, 1969. 2sh, Bishop's miter.

1969, Oct. 30 *Perf. 14*

184	A43	2p emerald & black	.60	.60
185	A43	6p red orange & black	.60	.60
186	A43	1sh lilac & black	.60	.60
187	A43	2sh yellow & multi	.70	.70
		Nos. 184-187 (4)	2.50	2.50

Consecration of Waite Hocking Stirling (1829-1923), as first Bishop of the Bishopric of the Falkland Islands, cent.

Gun Emplacement — A44

2p, Volunteer on horseback, vert. 1sh, Volunteer in dress uniform, vert. 2sh, Defense Force badge.

Perf. 13½x13, 13x13½

1970, Apr. 30 **Litho.** **Wmk. 314**

188	A44	2p ultra & multi	.65	.30
189	A44	6p multicolored	1.25	.75
190	A44	1sh buff & multi	2.50	1.25
191	A44	2sh yellow & multi	5.25	2.50
		Nos. 188-191 (4)	9.65	4.80

Falkland Islands Defense Force, 50th anniv.

The Great Britain, 1843 A45

The Great Britain in: 4p, 1845. 9p, 1876. 1sh, 1886. 2sh, 1970.

1970, Oct. 30 **Litho.** *Perf. 14½*

192	A45	2p lemon & multi	.35	.20
193	A45	4p lilac & multi	.70	.50
194	A45	9p bister & multi	1.40	1.10
195	A45	1sh org brn & multi	2.25	1.75
196	A45	2sh multicolored	4.75	3.75
		Nos. 192-196 (5)	9.45	7.30

Nos. 166-178 Surcharged with New Value (Decimal Currency) and Bar

1971, Feb. 15 **Photo.** *Perf. 14*

197	A41	½p on ½p multi	1.00	1.00
198	A41	1p on 1½p multi	.20	.20
199	A41	1½p on 2p multi	.35	.35
200	A41	2p on 3p multi	.40	.40
201	A41	2½p on 3½p multi	.60	.60
202	A41	3p on 4½p multi	.65	.65
203	A41	4p on 5½p multi	.90	.90
204	A41	5p on 6p multi	1.25	1.25
205	A41	6p on 1sh multi	1.90	1.60
206	A41	7½p on 1sh6p multi	2.25	2.10
207	A41	10p on 2sh multi	3.50	3.00
208	A41	15p on 3sh multi	6.50	5.25
209	A41	25p on 5sh multi	13.50	11.00
		Nos. 197-209 (13)	33.00	28.30

Flower Type of 1968 "p" instead of "d"

Designs as before. 1p, 2½p, 4p, 5p, 6p, 25p, horizontal.

Wmk. 314, Sideways on Vert. Stamps

1972, June 1 *Perf. 14*

210	A41	½p Dusty miller	1.25	1.00
a.		Wmk. upright ('74)	*12.50*	*22.50*
b.		Wmk. 373 ('75)	3.25	*3.50*
211	A41	1p Pig vine	.40	.30
212	A41	1½p Pale maiden	.55	.40
213	A41	2p Dog orchid	3.50	3.00
a.		Wmk. upright ('74)	27.50	3.50
214	A41	2½p Sea cabbage	.95	.70
215	A41	3p Vanilla daisy	.95	.85
216	A41	4p Arrowleaf marigold	1.25	.85
217	A41	5p Diddle-dee	1.50	1.00
218	A41	6p Scurvy grass	17.00	12.50
a.		Wmk. sideways ('74)	1.90	*2.25*
219	A41	7½p Prickly burr	3.50	3.00
220	A41	10p Fachine	7.25	6.50
221	A41	15p Lavender	6.25	5.50
222	A41	25p Felton's flower	11.50	11.50
		Nos. 210-222 (13)	55.85	47.10

No. 213 has watermark sideways.

Silver Wedding Issue, 1972
Common Design Type

Design: Queen Elizabeth II, Prince Philip, Romney Marsh sheep and giant sea lions.

1972, Nov 20 **Photo.** *Perf. 14x14½*

223	CD324	1p sl grn & multi	.30	.30
224	CD324	10p ultra & multi	1.00	1.00

Princess Anne's Wedding Issue
Common Design Type

1973, Nov. 14 **Litho.** *Perf. 14*

225	CD325	5p lilac & multi	.20	.20
226	CD325	15p citron & multi	.70	.70

Fur Seals A46

Tourist Publicity: 4p, Trout fishing. 5p, Rockhopper penguins. 15p, Military starling.

1974, Mar. 6 Litho. Wmk. 314

227	A46	2p lt ultra & multi	2.50	.95
228	A46	4p brt blue & multi	3.50	1.40
229	A46	5p yellow & multi	11.50	1.40
230	A46	15p lt ultra & multi	13.50	3.00
		Nos. 227-230 (4)	31.00	6.75

Early 19th Cent. Mail Coach, UPU Emblem — A47

UPU Cent.: 5p, Packet, 1841. 8p, First British mail planes, 1911. 16p, Catapult mail, 1920's.

1974, July 31 Perf. 14

231	A47	2p multicolored	.25	.25
232	A47	5p multicolored	.40	.40
233	A47	8p multicolored	.45	.45
234	A47	16p multicolored	.65	.65
		Nos. 231-234 (4)	1.75	1.75

Churchill, Parliament and Big Ben A48

Design: 20p, Churchill and warships.

1974, Nov. 30 Perf. 13x13½

235	A48	16p multicolored	1.50	1.50
236	A48	20p multicolored	2.00	2.00
	a.	Souvenir sheet of 2, #235-236	8.50	8.50

Sir Winston Churchill (1874-1965).

HMS Exeter A49

Battleships: 6p, HMNZS Achilles. 8p, Admiral Graf Spee. 16p, HMS Ajax.

1974, Dec. 13 Perf. 14

237	A49	2p multicolored	2.25	.85
238	A49	6p multicolored	3.75	2.00
239	A49	8p multicolored	4.75	3.00
240	A49	16p multicolored	12.00	8.00
		Nos. 237-240 (4)	22.75	13.85

35th anniv. of the Battle of the River Plate between British ships and the German battleship Graf Spee.

Seal and Flag Badge — A50

7½p, Coat of arms, 1925. 10p, Arms, 1948. 16p, Arms (Falkland Islands Dependencies), 1952.

1975, Oct. 28 Litho. Wmk. 373

241	A50	2p multicolored	1.00	1.00
242	A50	7½p multicolored	1.90	1.90
243	A50	10p multicolored	2.10	2.10
244	A50	16p multicolored	3.00	3.00
		Nos. 241-244 (4)	8.00	8.00

Falkland Islands heraldic arms, 50th anniv.

½p-Coin and Trout A51

New Coinage: 5½p, 1p-coin and gentoo penguins, 8p, 2p-coin and upland geese. 10p, 5p-coin and black-browed albatross. 16p, 10p-coin and sea lions.

1975, Dec. 31 Litho. Wmk. 373

245	A51	2p copper & multi	.20	.20
246	A51	5½p copper & multi	.65	.65
247	A51	8p copper & multi	1.25	1.25
248	A51	10p silver & multi	1.90	1.90
249	A51	16p silver & multi	5.50	5.50
		Nos. 245-249 (5)	9.50	9.50

Gathering Sheep — A52

Sheep Farming: 7½p, Shearing. 10p, Dipping sheep. 20p, Motor Vessel Monsunen collecting wool.

1976, Apr. 28 Litho. Perf. 13½

250	A52	2p multicolored	.50	.25
251	A52	7½p multicolored	1.00	.50
252	A52	10p multicolored	1.50	.75
253	A52	20p multicolored	3.50	1.90
		Nos. 250-253 (4)	6.50	3.40

Prince Philip, 1957 Visit A53

11p, Queen, ampulla and spoon. 33p, Queen awaiting anointment, and Knights of the Garter.

1977, Feb. 7 Perf. 13½x14

254	A53	6p multicolored	.35	.35
	a.	Booklet pane of 4, wmk. 314	9.00	
	b.	Single stamp from #254a	2.25	
255	A53	11p multicolored	.60	.60
	a.	Booklet pane of 4	3.50	
256	A53	33p multicolored	1.50	1.50
	a.	Booklet pane of 4	8.00	
		Nos. 254-256 (3)	2.45	2.45

25th anniv. of the reign of Elizabeth II.

Map of West and East Falkland with Communications Centers — A54

Telecommunications: 11p, Ship to shore communications at Fox Bay. 40p, Globe with Telex tape and telephone.

1977, Oct. 24 Litho. Perf. 14½x14

257	A54	3p yel brown & multi	.40	.25
258	A54	11p lt ultra & multi	1.00	.60
259	A54	40p rose & multi	4.25	3.00
		Nos. 257-259 (3)	5.65	3.85

A.E.S., 1957-1974 — A55

Designs: Mail ships.

1978, Jan. 25 Wmk. 373 Perf. 14

260	A55	1p shown	.25	.25
261	A55	2p Darwin, 1957-75	.25	.25
262	A55	3p Merak-N 1951-53	.25	.25
263	A55	4p Fitzroy, 1936-57	.25	.25
264	A55	5p Lafonia 1936-41	.30	.40
265	A55	6p Fleurus, 1924-33	.35	.50
266	A55	7p S.S. Falkland, 1914-34	.50	.70
267	A55	8p Oravia, 1900-12	.55	.75
268	A55	9p Memphis, 1890-97	.60	.85
269	A55	10p Black Hawk, 1873-80	.75	1.00
270	A55	20p Foam, 1963-72	.95	1.40
271	A55	25p Fairy, 1857-61	1.25	1.75
272	A55	50p Amelia, 1852-54	2.00	2.75
273	A55	£1 Nautilus, 1846-48	4.25	6.00
274	A55	£3 Hebe, 1842-46	12.00	14.00
		Nos. 260-274 (15)	24.50	31.10

The 1p, 3p, 5p, 6p and 10p were also issued in booklet panes of 4.

Nos. 260-274 also issued inscribed 1982.

For overprints see Nos. 352-353.

Elizabeth II Coronation Anniversary Issue

Souvenir Sheet

Common Design Type

1978, June 2 Unwmk. Perf. 15

275		Sheet of 6	4.00	4.00
	a.	CD326 25p Red Dragon of Wales	.60	.60
	b.	CD327 25p Elizabeth II	.60	.60
	c.	CD328 25p Hornless ram	.60	.60

No. 275 contains 2 se-tenant strips of Nos. 275a-275c, separated by horizontal gutter with commemorative and descriptive inscriptions.

Short Sunderland Mark III — A56

Design: 33p, Pane in flight and route Southampton to Stanley.

1978, Apr. 28 Wmk. 373 Perf. 14

276	A56	11p multicolored	2.40	1.90
277	A56	33p multicolored	5.00	3.25

First direct flight Southampton, England to Stanley, Falkland Islands, 26th anniv.

First Fox Bay PO and No. 1 — A57

Macrocystis Pyrifera — A58

Designs: 11p, Second Stanley Post Office and #2. 15p, New Island Post Office and #3. 22p, 1st Stanley Post Office and #4.

1978, Aug. 8 Litho. Perf. 13½x13

278	A57	3p multicolored	.20	.20
279	A57	11p multicolored	.40	.40
280	A57	15p multicolored	.55	.55
281	A57	22p multicolored	.85	.85
		Nos. 278-281 (4)	2.00	2.00

Falkland Islands postage stamps, cent.

1979, Feb. 19 Litho. Perf. 14

Kelp: 7p, Durvillea. 11p, Lessoniae, horiz. 15p, Callophyllis, horiz. 25p, Iridea.

282	A58	3p multicolored	.20	.20
283	A58	7p multicolored	.40	.40
284	A58	11p multicolored	.60	.60
285	A58	15p multicolored	.75	.75
286	A58	25p multicolored	1.25	1.25
		Nos. 282-286 (5)	3.20	3.20

Britten-Norman Islander over Map — A59

Opening of Stanley Airport: 11p, Fokker F27 over map. 15p, Fokker F28 over Stanley. 25p, Cessna 172 Skyhawk, Islander and Fokkers F27, F28 over runway.

1979, May 1 Litho. Perf. 13½

287	A59	3p multicolored	.20	.20
288	A59	11p multicolored	.75	.75
289	A59	15p multicolored	1.00	1.00
290	A59	25p multicolored	1.75	1.75
		Nos. 287-290 (4)	3.70	3.70

Rowland Hill and No. 121 A60

Sir Rowland Hill (1795-1879), originator of penny postage, and: 11p, Falkland Islands No. 1, vert. 25p, Penny Black. 33p, Falkland Islands No. 37, vert.

1979, Aug. 27 Perf. 14

291	A60	3p multicolored	.20	.20
292	A60	11p multicolored	.45	.45
293	A60	25p multicolored	.90	.90
		Nos. 291-293 (3)	1.55	1.55

Souvenir Sheet

294	A60	33p multicolored	1.40	1.40

Mail Delivery by Air, UPU Emblem A61

UPU Membership Cent. (Modes of Mail Delivery): 11p, Horseback. 25p, Schooner Gwendolin.

1979, Nov. 26

295	A61	3p multicolored	.20	.20
296	A61	11p multicolored	.45	.45
297	A61	25p multicolored	.95	.95
		Nos. 295-297 (3)	1.60	1.60

Commerson's Dolphin — A62

1980, Feb. 25 Wmk. 373 Perf. 14

298	A62	3p Peale's porpoise, vert.	.20	.20
299	A62	6p shown	.30	.30
300	A62	7p Hour-glass dolphin	.35	.35
301	A62	11p Spectacled porpose, vert.	.55	.55
302	A62	15p Dusky dolphin	.90	.90
303	A62	25p Killer whale	1.60	1.60
		Nos. 298-303 (6)	3.90	3.90

Miniature Sheet

Falkland Islands Cancel, 1878 A63

Designs: b, New Islds., 1915. c, Falklands Islds., 1901. d, Port Stanley, 1935. e, Port Stanley airmail, 1952. f, Fox Bay, 1934.

1980, May 6 Litho. *Perf. 14*
304 Sheet of 6 2.25 2.25
a.-f. A63 11p any single .35 .35

London 1980 Intl. Stamp Exhib., May 6-14.

Queen Mother Elizabeth Birthday
Common Design Type

1980, Aug. 4 Litho. *Perf. 14*
305 CD330 11p multicolored .50 .50

Striated Caracara A64

1980, Aug. 11 Wmk. 373 *Perf. 13½*
306 A64 3p shown .35 .20
307 A64 11p Red-backed buzzard .70 .60
308 A64 15p Crested caracara .85 .70
309 A64 25p Cassin's falcon 1.60 1.40
Nos. 306-309 (4) 3.50 2.90

Port Egmont, Early Settlement — A65

1980, Dec. 22 Litho. *Perf. 14*
310 A65 3p Stanley .20 .20
311 A65 11p shown .45 .45
312 A65 25p Port Louis .95 .50
313 A65 33p Mission House, Keppel Island 1.10 .95
Nos. 310-313 (4) 2.70 2.10

Polwarth Sheep A66

1981, Jan. 19 Litho. *Perf. 14*
314 A66 3p shown .20 .20
315 A66 11p Frisian cow and calf .40 .40
316 A66 25p Horse .85 .85
317 A66 33p Welsh collies 1.10 1.10
Nos. 314-317 (4) 2.55 2.55

Map of Falkland Islands, Bowles and Carver, 1779 A67

1981, May 22 Litho. *Perf. 14*
318 A67 3p shown .20 .20
319 A67 10p Hawkin's Mainland, 1773 .30 .25
320 A67 13p New Isles, 1747 .40 .35
321 A67 15p French & British Islands .50 .40
322 A67 25p Falklands, 1771 .75 .60
323 A67 26p Falklands, 1764 .85 .65
Nos. 318-323 (6) 3.00 2.45

Royal Wedding Issue
Common Design Type

1981, July 22 Litho. *Perf. 13½x13*
324 CD331 10p Bouquet .25 .25
325 CD331 13p Charles .35 .35
326 CD331 52p Couple 1.10 1.10
Nos. 324-326 (3) 1.70 1.70

Duke of Edinburgh's Awards, 25th Anniv. — A68

1981, Sept. 28 Litho. *Perf. 14*
327 A68 10p Spinning .30 .30
328 A68 13p Camping .35 .35
329 A68 15p Kayaking .45 .45
330 A68 26p Duke of Edinburgh .80 .80
Nos. 327-330 (4) 1.90 1.90

The Holy Virgin, by Guido Reni (1575-1642) A69

Rock Cod — A70

Christmas: 3p, Adoration of the Holy Child, 16th cent. Dutch. 13p, Holy Family in an Italian Landscape, 17th cent. Italian.

1981, Nov. 2 Litho. *Perf. 14*
331 A69 3p multicolored .20 .20
332 A69 13p multicolored .45 .45
333 A69 26p multicolored .80 .80
Nos. 331-333 (3) 1.45 1.45

1981, Dec. 7

Designs: Shelf fish. 5p, 15p, 25p horiz.

334 A70 5p Falkland herring .20 .20
335 A70 13p shown .40 .40
336 A70 15p Patagonian hake .50 .50
337 A70 25p Southern blue whiting .80 .80
338 A70 26p Gray-tailed skate .80 .80
Nos. 334-338 (5) 2.70 2.70

Shipwrecks — A71

1982, Feb. 15 Wmk. 373 *Perf. 14½*
339 A71 5p Lady Elizabeth, 1913 .20 .20
340 A71 13p Capricorn, 1882 .45 .45
341 A71 15p Jhelum, 1870 .55 .55
342 A71 25p Snowsquall, 1864 .75 .75
343 A71 26p St. Mary, 1890 .75 .75
Nos. 339-343 (5) 2.70 2.70

Sesquicentennial of Charles Darwin's Visit — A72

1982, Apr. 19 Litho. *Perf. 14*
344 A72 5p Darwin .20 .20
345 A72 17p Microscope .65 .65
346 A72 25p Warrah 1.00 1.00
347 A72 34p Beagle 1.25 1.25
Nos. 344-347 (4) 3.10 3.10

Princess Diana Issue
Common Design Type

1982, July 5 Wmk. 373 *Perf. 13*
348 CD333 5p Arms .40 .20
349 CD333 17p Diana 1.40 .50
350 CD333 37p Wedding 2.75 1.00
351 CD333 50p Portrait 3.75 1.40
Nos. 348-351 (4) 8.30 3.10

Nos. 264, 271 Overprinted: "1st PARTICIPATION / COMMONWEALTH GAMES 1982"

1982, Oct. 7 Litho. *Perf. 14*
352 A55 5p multicolored .20 .20
353 A55 25p multicolored .65 .65

12th Commonwealth Games, Brisbane, Australia, Sept. 30-Oct. 9.

Tussock Bird — A73

1982, Dec. 6 *Perf. 15x14½*
354 A73 5p shown .20 .20
355 A73 10p Black-chinned siskin .25 .25
356 A73 13p Grass wren .45 .45
357 A73 17p Black-throated finch .60 .60
358 A73 25p Falkland-correndera pipit 1.00 1.00
359 A73 34p Dark-faced ground-tyrant 1.10 1.10
Nos. 354-359 (6) 3.60 3.60

British Occupation Sesquicentennial — A74

1p, Raising the Standard, Port Louis, 1833. 2p, Chelsea pensioners & barracks, 1849. 5p, Wool trade, 1874. 10p, Ship repairing trade, 1850-90. 15p, Government House, early 20th cent. 20p, Battle of the Falkland Islands, 1914. 25p, Whalebone Arch centenary, 1933. 40p, Contribution to World War II effort, 1939-45. 50p, Visit of Duke of Edinburgh, 1957. £1, Royal Marines, 1933, 1983, vert. £2, Queen Elizabeth II.

1983, Jan. 1 Litho. *Perf. 14*
360 A74 1p multi, vert. .25 .30
361 A74 2p multi .25 .30
362 A74 5p multi, vert. .25 .30
363 A74 10p multi .25 .30
364 A74 15p multi .30 .40
365 A74 20p multi, vert. .45 .60
366 A74 25p multi .60 .70
367 A74 40p multi, vert. .90 1.10
368 A74 50p multi 1.10 1.40
369 A74 £1 multi 1.75 3.00
370 A74 £2 multi, vert. 4.00 6.50
Nos. 360-370 (11) 10.10 14.90

For surcharges see Nos. 402-403.

A75

1983, Mar. 14
371 A75 5p No. 69 .25 .25
372 A75 17p No. 65 .50 .50
373 A75 34p No. 75, vert. .75 1.00
374 A75 50p No. 370, vert. .90 1.00
Nos. 371-374 (4) 2.40 2.75

Commonwealth Day.

First Anniv. of Liberation A76

1983, June 14 Wmk. 373 *Perf. 14*
375 A76 5p Army .20 .20
376 A76 13p Merchant Navy .30 .30
377 A76 17p Royal Air Force .45 .45
378 A76 50p Royal Navy 1.25 1.25
a. Souvenir sheet of 4, #375-378 3.25 3.25
Nos. 375-378 (4) 2.20 2.20

Local Fruit A77

1983, Oct. 10 Litho. *Perf. 14*
379 A77 5p Diddle dee .20 .20
380 A77 17p Tea berries .40 .40
381 A77 25p Mountain berries .60 .60
382 A77 34p Native strawberries .80 .80
Nos. 379-382 (4) 2.00 2.00

Britten-Norman Islander — A78

1983, Nov. 14 Litho. *Perf. 14*
383 A78 5p shown .25 .20
384 A78 13p DHC-2 Beaver .40 .25
385 A78 17p Noorduyn Norseman .50 .30
386 A78 50p Auster 1.25 .85
Nos. 383-386 (4) 2.40 1.60

Green Spider A79

Insects and Spiders.

1984, Jan. 1 Litho. *Perf. 14*
387 A79 1p shown .20 .20
388 A79 2p Ichneumon-Fly .20 .20
389 A79 3p Brocade Moth .20 .20
390 A79 4p Black Beetle .20 .20
391 A79 5p Fritillary .20 .20
392 A79 6p Green Spider, diff. .30 .30
393 A79 7p Ichneumon-Fly, diff. .30 .30
394 A79 8p Ochre Shoulder .30 .30
395 A79 9p Clocker Weevil .30 .45
396 A79 10p Hover Fly .30 .45
397 A79 20p Weevil .60 1.00
398 A79 25p Metallic Beetle .80 1.25
399 A79 50p Camel Cricket 1.50 2.50
400 A79 £1 Beauchene Spider 3.25 5.50
401 A79 £3 Southern Painted Lady 9.75 15.00
Nos. 387-401 (15) 18.40 28.05

No. 388 exists inscribed "1986." Value $4.

Nos. 364, 366 Surcharged

1984, Jan. 3 Litho. *Perf. 14*
402 A74 17p on 15p multi .45 .45
403 A74 22p on 25p multi .55 .55

Lloyd's List Issue
Common Design Type

1984, May 7 Wmk. 373 *Perf. 14½*
404 CD335 6p Wavertree .25 .25
405 CD335 17p Port Stanley, 1910 .65 .65
406 CD335 22p Oravia .80 .80
407 CD335 52p Cunard Countess 2.00 2.00
Nos. 404-407 (4) 3.70 3.70

Great Grebe — A80

1984, Aug. 6 *Perf. 14½x14*

408 A80 17p shown 1.10 1.10
409 A80 22p Silver grebe 1.40 1.40
410 A80 52p Rolland's grebe 4.00 4.00
Nos. 408-410 (3) 6.50 6.50

See Nos. 450-453.

1984 UPU Congress A81

1984, June 22 Litho. *Perf. 14*

411 A81 22p Emblem, jet, ship .60 .60

Wildlife Conservation A82

1984, Nov. 5 Litho. *Perf. 14½*

412 A82 6p Birds .60 .40
413 A82 17p Plants 1.25 .90
414 A82 22p Mammals 1.40 1.00
415 A82 52p Marine Life 3.00 2.25
a. Souvenir sheet of 4, #412-415 8.50 6.00
Nos. 412-415 (4) 6.25 4.55

Camber Railway, 1915-1927 A83

1985, Feb. 18 Litho. *Perf. 14*

416 A83 7p multicolored .35 .30
417 A83 22p multicolored .85 .75
418 A83 27p multicolored .90 1.00

Size: 77x26mm

419 A83 54p multicolored 1.90 1.90
Nos. 416-419 (4) 4.00 3.95

Queen Mother 85th Birthday
Common Design Type

Designs: 7p, Commonwealth Visitor's Reception. 22p, With Prince Charles, Mark Phillips, Princess Anne. 27p, 80th birthday celebration. 54p, Holding Prince Henry. £1, In coach with Princess Diana.

Perf. 14½x14

1985, June 7 Litho. **Wmk. 384**

420 CD336 7p multicolored .20 .20
421 CD336 22p multicolored .85 .85
422 CD336 27p multicolored 1.10 1.10
423 CD336 54p multicolored 2.10 2.10
Nos. 420-423 (4) 4.25 4.25

Souvenir Sheet

424 CD336 £1 multicolored 4.50 4.50

Mount Pleasant Airport Opening A84

1985, May 12 Litho. *Perf. 14½*

425 A84 7p Pioneer camp, docked ship .40 .40
426 A84 22p Construction site 1.25 1.25
427 A84 27p Runway layout 1.60 1.60
428 A84 54p Aircraft landing 3.00 3.00
Nos. 425-428 (4) 6.25 6.25

Captain J. McBride, HMS Jason, 1765 — A85

18th-19th century naval explorers: 22p, Commodore J. Byron, HMS Dolphin and Tamar, 1765. 27p, Vice-Adm. R. Fitzroy, HMS Beagle, 1831. 54p, Adm. Sir B.J. Sulivan, HMS Philomel, 1842.

1985, Sept. 23

429 A85 7p multicolored .50 .50
430 A85 22p multicolored 1.40 1.40
431 A85 27p multicolored 1.50 1.50
432 A85 54p multicolored 3.25 3.25
Nos. 429-432 (4) 6.65 6.65

Philibert Commerson (1727-1773), Commerson's Dolphin — A86

Naturalists, endangered species: 22p, Rene Primevere Lesson (1794-1849), kelp. 27p, Joseph Paul Gaimard (1796-1858), diving petrel. 54p, Charles Darwin (1803-1882), Calceolaria darwinii.

1985, Nov. 4 *Perf. 14½*

433 A86 7p multicolored .50 .35
434 A86 22p multicolored 1.50 1.10
435 A86 27p multicolored 1.75 1.25
436 A86 54p multicolored 3.50 2.50
Nos. 433-436 (4) 7.25 5.20

Seashells A87

1986, Feb. 10 **Wmk. 384** *Perf. 14½*

437 A87 7p Painted keyhole limpet .40 .40
438 A87 22p Magellanic volute 1.50 1.50
439 A87 27p Falkland scallop 2.00 2.00
440 A87 54p Rough thorn drupe 4.00 4.00
Nos. 437-440 (4) 7.90 7.90

Queen Elizabeth II 60th Birthday
Common Design Type

Designs: 10p, With Princess Margaret at St. Paul's, Waldenbury, 1932. 24p, Christmas broadcast from Sandringham, 1958. 29p, Order of the Thistle, St. Giles Cathedral, Edinburgh, 1962. 45p, Royal reception on the Britannia, US visit, 1976. 58p, Visiting Crown Agents' offices, 1983.

1986, Apr. 21 Litho. *Perf. 14x14½*

441 CD337 10p scar, blk & sil .30 .30
442 CD337 24p ultra, blk & sil .65 .65
443 CD337 29p green & multi .85 .85
444 CD337 45p violet & multi 1.40 1.40
445 CD337 58p rose vio & multi 1.75 1.75
Nos. 441-445 (5) 4.95 4.95

AMERIPEX '86 — A88

SS Great Britain's arrival in the Falkland Isls., Cent.: 10p, Maiden voyage, crossing the Atlantic, 1845. 24p, Wreck in Sparrow Cove, 1937. 29p, Refloating wreck, 1970. 58p, Restored vessel, Bristol, 1986.

1986, May 22

446 A88 10p multicolored .25 .25
447 A88 24p multicolored .75 .75
448 A88 29p multicolored 1.00 1.00
449 A88 58p multicolored 2.00 2.00
a. Souvenir sheet of 4, #446-449 4.00 4.00
Nos. 446-449 (4) 4.00 4.00

Bird Type of 1984

Rockhopper Penguins.

1986, Aug. 25 **Wmk. 373** *Perf. 14½*

450 A80 10p Adult .65 .50
451 A80 24p Adults swimming 1.50 1.25
452 A80 29p Adults, diff. 2.00 1.75
453 A80 58p Adult and young 4.00 3.50
Nos. 450-453 (4) 8.15 7.00

Wedding of Prince Andrew and Sarah Ferguson — A90

Various photographs: 17p, Presenting Queen's Polo Cup, Windsor, 1986. 22p, Open carriage, wedding. 29p, Andrew wearing military fatigues.

1986, Nov. 10 **Wmk. 384** *Perf. 14½*

454 A90 17p multicolored .80 .80
455 A90 22p multicolored 1.00 1.00
456 A90 29p multicolored 1.40 1.40
Nos. 454-456 (3) 3.20 3.20

Royal Engineers, 200th Anniv. A91

1987, Feb. 9 Litho. *Perf. 14½*

457 A91 10p Surveying Sapper Hill .55 .55
458 A91 24p Explosives disposal 1.90 1.90
459 A91 29p Boxer Bridge, Pt. Stanley 2.25 2.25
460 A91 58p Postal services, Stanley Airport 5.00 5.00
Nos. 457-460 (4) 9.70 9.70

Seals A92

1987, Apr. 27

461 A92 10p Southern sea lion .80 .80
462 A92 24p Falkland fur seal 2.25 2.25
463 A92 29p Southern elephant seal 2.40 2.40
464 A92 58p Leopard seal 4.25 4.25
Nos. 461-464 (4) 9.70 9.70

Hospitals A93

Designs: 10p, Victorian Cottage Home, c. 1912. 24p, King Edward VII Memorial Hospital, c. 1914. 29p, Churchill Wing, 1953. 58p, Prince Andrew Wing, 1987.

1987, Dec. 8 *Perf. 14*

465 A93 10p multicolored .50 .50
466 A93 24p multicolored 1.10 1.10
467 A93 29p multicolored 1.40 1.40
468 A93 58p multicolored 2.50 2.50
Nos. 465-468 (4) 5.50 5.50

Fungi — A94

1987, Sept. 14 Litho. *Perf. 14½*

469 A94 10p Suillus luteus 1.50 1.50
470 A94 24p Mycena 2.75 2.75
471 A94 29p Camarophyllus adonis 3.75 3.75
472 A94 58p Gerronema schusteri 8.00 8.00
Nos. 469-472 (4) 16.00 16.00

1940 Morris Truck, Fitzroy A95

Classic automobiles: 24p, 1929 Citroen Kegresse, San Carlos. 29p, 1933 Ford 1-Ton Truck, Port Stanley. 58p, 1935 Ford Model T Saloon, Darwin.

1988, Apr. 11 Litho. *Perf. 14*

473 A95 10p multicolored .45 .45
474 A95 24p multicolored 1.10 1.10
475 A95 29p multicolored 1.40 1.40
476 A95 58p multicolored 2.50 2.50
Nos. 473-476 (4) 5.45 5.45

Geese A96

1988, July 25

477 A96 10p Kelp 1.50 .35
478 A96 24p Upland 3.00 .85
479 A96 29p Ruddy-headed 3.75 1.00
480 A96 58p Ashy-headed 7.75 2.25
Nos. 477-480 (4) 16.00 4.45

Lloyds of London, 300th Anniv.
Common Design Type

Designs: 10p, Lloyd's Nelson Collection silver service. 24p, Hydroponic Gardens, horiz. 29p, Supply ship A.E.S., horiz. 58p, Wreck of the Charles Cooper near the Falklands, 1866.

1988, Nov. 14 Litho. **Wmk. 373**

481 CD341 10p multicolored .50 .50
482 CD341 24p multicolored 1.00 1.00
483 CD341 29p multicolored 1.25 1.25
484 CD341 58p multicolored 2.50 2.50
Nos. 481-484 (4) 5.25 5.25

Ships of Cape Horn A97

1989, Feb. 28 *Perf. 373*

485 A97 1p Padua .45 .25
486 A97 2p Priwall, vert. .45 .25
a. Wmk. 384 .60 .45
487 A97 3p Passat .45 .25
a. Wmk. 384 .60 .45
488 A97 4p Archibald Russell, vert. .45 .25
489 A97 5p Pamir, vert. .45 .25
490 A97 6p Mozart .45 .25
a. Wmk. 384 .60 .45
491 A97 7p Pommern .45 .25
492 A97 8p Preussen .60 .45
493 A97 9p Fennia .65 .50
a. Wmk. 384 1.00 .75
494 A97 10p Cassard .75 .60
495 A97 20p Lawhill 1.60 1.25
496 A97 25p Garthpool 1.90 1.40
497 A97 50p Grace Harwar 3.75 2.75
498 A97 £1 Criccieth Castle 8.50 5.50
a. Wmk. 384 7.75 6.00

499 A97 £3 Cutty Sark, vert. 29.00 18.00
500 A97 £5 Flying Cloud 40.00 22.50
Nos. 485-500 (16) 89.90 54.70

Nos. 486a, 487a, 490a, 493a, 498a are dated "1991."

Whales — A98

1989, May 15 Wmk. 384 *Perf. 14*
501 A98 10p Southern right .90 .90
502 A98 24p Minke 2.10 2.10
503 A98 29p Humpback 2.75 2.75
504 A98 58p Blue 5.75 5.75
Nos. 501-504 (4) 11.50 11.50

Sports Assoc. Activities A99

Children's drawings.

1989, Sept. 16
505 A99 5p Gymkhana .20 .20
506 A99 10p Steer Riding .25 .25
507 A99 17p Sheep shearing .55 .55
508 A99 24p Dog trial .70 .70
509 A99 29p Horse racing .95 .95
510 A99 45p Sack race 1.50 1.50
Nos. 505-510 (6) 4.15 4.15

Battles — A100

Commanders, ships and ship crests: 10p, Vice-Adm. Sturdee, HMS *Invincible*. 24p, Vice-Adm. Von Spee, SMS *Scharnhorst*. 29p, Commodore Harwood, HMS *Ajax*. 58p, Capt. Langsdorff, *Admiral Graff Spee*.

1989, Dec. 8 *Perf. 14x13½*
511 A100 10p multicolored .55 .55
512 A100 24p multicolored 1.60 1.60
513 A100 29p multicolored 2.10 2.10
514 A100 58p multicolored 3.75 3.75
Nos. 511-514 (4) 8.00 8.00

Battle of the Falklands, 75th anniv. (10p, 24p); Battle of the River Plate, 50th anniv. (29p, 58p).

Emblems and Presentation Spitfires, 1940 — A101

1990, May 3 Wmk. 373 *Perf. 14*
515 A101 12p No. 92 Squadron .60 .60
516 A101 26p No. 611 Squadron 1.40 1.40
517 A101 31p No. 92 Squadron, diff. 1.75 1.75
518 A101 62p Spitfires scramble 3.25 3.25
Nos. 515-518 (4) 7.00 7.00

Souvenir Sheet

519 A101 £1 Battle of Britain 7.50 7.50

Stamp World London '90.

For souvenir sheet similar to #519, see #530.

A102

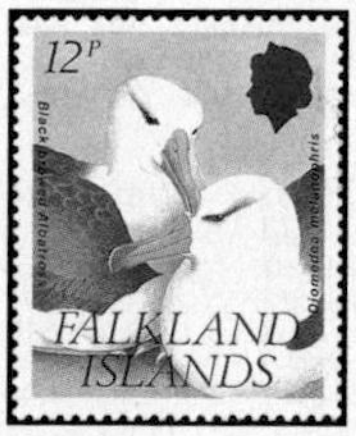

A103

1990, Apr. 1 Wmk. 384 *Perf. 14½*
520 A102 12p Kidney Is. .50 .50
521 A102 26p Beauchene Is. 1.25 1.25
522 A102 31p Bird Is. 1.50 1.50
523 A102 62p Elephant Jason Is. 3.00 3.00
Nos. 520-523 (4) 6.25 6.25

Nature reserves and bird sanctuaries.

Queen Mother, 90th Birthday
Common Design Types

1990, Aug. 4 Wmk. 384 *Perf. 14x15*
524 CD343 26p Queen Mother in Dover 1.00 1.00

Perf. 14½
525 CD344 £1 Steering the "Queen Elizabeth," 1946 4.25 4.25

Wmk. 384
1990, Oct. 3 Litho. *Perf. 14*
526 A103 12p Black browed albatross .75 .75
527 A103 26p Adult bird 1.75 1.75
528 A103 31p Adult, chick 2.25 2.25
529 A103 62p Bird in flight 4.50 4.50
Nos. 526-529 (4) 9.25 9.25

Battle of Britain Type of 1990 inscribed "SECOND VISIT OF / HRH THE DUKE OF EDINBURGH"
Souvenir Sheet

1991, Mar. 7
530 A101 £1 multicolored 10.50 10.50

Orchids — A104

King Penguin — A105

1991, Mar. 18 Wmk. 373
531 A104 12p Gavilea australis .70 .70
532 A104 26p Codonorchis lessonii 1.60 1.60
533 A104 31p Chlorea gaudichaudii 2.00 2.00
534 A104 62p Gavilea littoralis 4.00 4.00
Nos. 531-534 (4) 8.30 8.30

1991, Aug. 26 Wmk. 384
535 A105 2p Two adults crossing bills 1.00 1.00
536 A105 6p Two adults, one brooding 2.00 1.50
537 A105 12p Adult with two young 3.00 1.75
538 A105 20p Adult swimming 4.00 2.00
539 A105 31p Adult feeding young 2.00 2.00
540 A105 62p Two adults, diff. 3.00 3.00
Nos. 535-540 (6) 15.00 11.25

World Wildlife Fund.

Falkland Islands Bisects, Cent. A106

1991, Sept. 10 Wmk. 384 *Perf. 14½*
541 A106 12p #9, #15 .65 .65
542 A106 26p On cover 1.50 1.50
543 A106 31p Unsevered pair 1.60 1.60
544 A106 62p S.S. Isis 3.25 3.25
Nos. 541-544 (4) 7.00 7.00

Discovery of America, 500th Anniv. (in 1992) — A107

Sailing ships: 14p, STV Eye of the Wind. 29p, STV Soren Larsen. 34p, Nina, Santa Maria, Pinta. 68p, Columbus and Santa Maria.

1991, Dec. 12 Wmk. 373 *Perf. 14*
545 A107 14p multicolored .85 .85
546 A107 29p multicolored 1.75 1.75
547 A107 34p multicolored 2.25 2.25
548 A107 68p multicolored 4.25 4.25
Nos. 545-548 (4) 9.10 9.10

World Columbian Stamp Expo '92, Chicago and Genoa '92 Intl. Philatelic Exhibitions.

Queen Elizabeth II's Accession to the Throne, 40th Anniv.
Common Design Type

1992, Feb. 6
549 CD349 7p multicolored .40 .40
550 CD349 14p multicolored .65 .65
551 CD349 29p multicolored 1.25 1.25
552 CD349 34p multicolored 1.50 1.50
553 CD349 68p multicolored 3.00 3.00
Nos. 549-553 (5) 6.80 6.80

Christ Church Cathedral, Cent. — A108

1992, Feb. 21 Wmk. 384 *Perf. 14½*
554 A108 14p Laying foundation stone .70 .70
555 A108 29p Interior, 1920 1.60 1.60
556 A108 34p Bishop's chair 2.10 2.10
557 A108 68p Without tower c. 1900, horiz. 4.00 4.00
Nos. 554-557 (4) 8.40 8.40

First Sighting of Falkland Islands by Capt. John Davis, 400th Anniv. A109

Designs: 22p, Capt. John Davis using backstaff. 29p, Capt. Davis working on chart. 34p, Queen Elizabeth I, Queen Elizabeth II. 68p, The Desire sights Falkland Islands.

1992, Aug. 14 Wmk. 373
558 A109 22p multicolored 1.25 1.25
559 A109 29p multicolored 1.50 1.50
560 A109 34p multicolored 1.75 1.75
561 A109 68p multicolored 3.50 3.50
Nos. 558-561 (4) 8.00 8.00

Falkland Islands Defense Force and West Yorkshire Regiment — A110

7p, Private, Falkland Islands Volunteers, 1892. 14p, Officer, Falkland Islands Defense Corps, 1914. 22p, Officer, Falkland Islands Defense Force, 1920. 29p, Private, Falkland Islands Defense Force, 1939-45. 34p, Officer, West Yorkshire Regiment, 1942. 68p, Private, West Yorkshire Regiment, 1942.

1992, Oct. 1 *Perf. 14*
562 A110 7p multicolored .35 .35
563 A110 14p multicolored .70 .70
564 A110 22p multicolored 1.10 1.10
565 A110 29p multicolored 1.50 1.50
566 A110 34p multicolored 1.60 1.60
567 A110 68p multicolored 3.25 3.25
Nos. 562-567 (6) 8.50 8.50

Gulls and Terns A111

Perf. 14x14½
1993, Jan. 2 Litho. Wmk. 384
568 A111 15p South American tern .85 .85
569 A111 31p Pink breasted gull 1.75 1.75
570 A111 36p Dolphin gull 2.00 2.00
571 A111 72p Dominican gull 4.00 4.00
Nos. 568-571 (4) 8.60 8.60

Souvenir Sheet

Visit of Liner QE II to Falkland Islands — A112

Wmk. 373
1993, Jan. 22 Litho. *Perf. 14*
572 A112 £2 multicolored 10.00 10.00

Royal Air Force, 75th Anniv.
Common Designs Type

Designs: No. 573, Lockheed Tristar. No. 574, Lockheed Hercules. No. 575, Boeing Vertol Chinook. No. 576, Avro Vulcan.

No. 577a, Hawker Siddeley Andover. b, Westland Wessex. c, Panavia Tornado F3. d, McDonnell Douglas Phantom.

Wmk. 373
1993, Apr. 3 Litho. *Perf. 14*
573 CD350 15p multicolored 1.25 1.25
574 CD350 15p multicolored 1.25 1.25
575 CD350 15p multicolored 1.25 1.25
576 CD350 15p multicolored 1.25 1.25
Nos. 573-576 (4) 5.00 5.00

Souvenir Sheet of 4

577 CD350 36p #a.-d. 6.25 6.25

Fisheries A113

Designs: 15p, Short-finned squid. 31p, Stern haul of whiptailed hake. 36p, Fishery Patrol Vessel Falkalnds Protector. 72p, Aerial surveillance by Britten-Norman Islander.

Wmk. 384

1993, July 1 Litho. *Perf. 14*
578 A113 15p multicolored .85 .85
579 A113 31p multicolored 1.60 1.60
580 A113 36p multicolored 2.10 2.10
581 A113 72p multicolored 3.75 3.75
Nos. 578-581 (4) 8.30 8.30

Launch of SS Great Britain, 150th Anniv. — A114

Perf. 14x13½

1993, July 19 Litho. Wmk. 384
582 A114 8p In drydock, Bristol .40 .40
583 A114 £1 At sea 5.00 5.00

Cruise Ships and Penguins A115

Wmk. 373

1993, Oct. 1 Litho. *Perf. 14*
584 A115 16p Explorer 1.00 1.00
585 A115 34p Rockhopper penguins 2.25 2.25
586 A115 39p World Discoverer 2.50 2.50
587 A115 78p Columbus Caravelle 5.25 5.25
Nos. 584-587 (4) 11.00 11.00

Pets — A116

Perf. 14x14½

1993, Dec. 1 Litho. Wmk. 384
588 A116 8p Pony .50 .35
589 A116 16p Lamb .90 .65
590 A116 34p Puppy, kitten 2.10 1.50

Perf. 14½x14

591 A116 39p Kitten, vert. 2.50 1.75
592 A116 78p Collie, vert. 5.00 3.50
Nos. 588-592 (5) 11.00 7.75

Ovptd. with Hong Kong '94 Emblem

1994, Feb. 18
593 A116 8p on #588 .65 .65
594 A116 16p on #589 1.10 1.10
595 A116 34p on #590 2.25 2.25
596 A116 39p on #591 2.50 2.50
597 A116 78p on #592 5.00 5.00
Nos. 593-597 (5) 11.50 11.50

Inshore Marine Life A117

Wmk. 384

1994, Apr. 4 Litho. *Perf. 14*
598 A117 1p Goose barnacles, vert. .30 .30
599 A117 2p Painted shrimp .30 .30
600 A117 8p Common limpet .30 .30
601 A117 9p Mullet .35 .35
602 A117 10p Sea anemones .40 .40
603 A117 20p Rock eel .85 .85
604 A117 25p Spider crab 1.10 1.10
605 A117 50p Lobster krill, vert. 2.50 2.50
606 A117 80p Falkland skate 3.75 3.75
607 A117 £1 Centollon crab 5.00 5.00
a. Souv. sheet of 1, wmk. 373 8.00 8.00
608 A117 £3 Rock cod 13.00 13.00
609 A117 £5 Octopus, vert. 22.50 22.50
Nos. 598-609 (12) 50.35 50.35

No. 607a for return of Hong Kong to China. Issued 7/1/97.
See No. 671.

Founding of Stanley, 150th Anniv. A118

9p, Blacksmith's shop, dockyard, Sir James Clark Ross, explorer. 17p, James Leith Mody, 1st colonial chaplain, home at 21 Fitzroy Road. 30p, Stanley cottage, Dr. Henry J. Hamblin, 1st colonial surgeon. 35p, Pioneer row, Sergeant Major Henry Felton. 40p, Government House, Governor R. C. Moody R.E. 65p, View of Stanley, Edward Stanley, 14th Earl of Derby, Secretary of State for Colonies.

Wmk. 373

1994, July 1 Litho. *Perf. 14*
610 A118 9p multicolored .50 .50
611 A118 17p multicolored .95 .95
612 A118 30p multicolored 1.75 1.75
613 A118 35p multicolored 1.90 1.90
614 A118 40p multicolored 2.40 2.40
615 A118 65p multicolored 3.50 3.50
Nos. 610-615 (6) 11.00 11.00

Methods of Transportation — A119

17p, Tristar over Gypsy Cove. 35p, Cruise ship, Sea Lion Island. 40p, FIGAS Islander, Pebble Island Beach. 65p, Land Rover, Volunteer Beach.

Wmk. 384

1994, Oct. 24 Litho. *Perf. 14*
616 A119 17p multicolored .95 .55
617 A119 35p multicolored 2.00 1.10
618 A119 40p multicolored 2.40 1.25
619 A119 65p multicolored 3.25 2.00
Nos. 616-619 (4) 8.60 4.90

South American Missionary Society, 150th Anniv. — A120

Designs: 5p, Mission House, Keppel Island. 17p, Thomas Bridges, compiler of Yahgan dictionary. 40p, Fuegian Indians. 65p, Schooner Allen Gardiner, Capt. Allen Gardiner.

1994, Dec. 1
620 A120 5p multicolored .25 .25
621 A120 17p multicolored .75 .75
622 A120 40p multicolored 1.75 1.75
623 A120 65p multicolored 2.75 2.75
Nos. 620-623 (4) 5.50 5.50

Flowering Shrubs — A121

Designs: 9p, Lupinus arboreus. 17p, Boxwood. 30p, Fuchsia magellanica. 35p, Berberis ilicifolia. 40p, Gorse. 65p, Veronica.

Perf. 14½x14

1995, Jan. 3 Litho. Wmk. 384
624 A121 9p multicolored .35 .35
625 A121 17p multicolored .70 .70
626 A121 30p multicolored 1.60 1.60
627 A121 35p multicolored 2.10 2.10
628 A121 40p multicolored 2.25 2.25
629 A121 65p multicolored 4.00 4.00
Nos. 624-629 (6) 11.00 11.00

Shore Birds A122

Designs: 17p, Magellanic oystercatcher. 35p, Rufous chested dotterel. 40p, Black oystercatcher. 65p, Two banded plover.

Wmk. 373

1995, Mar. 1 Litho. *Perf. 13½*
630 A122 17p multicolored 1.00 1.00
631 A122 35p multicolored 2.40 2.40
632 A122 40p multicolored 2.75 2.75
633 A122 65p multicolored 4.25 4.25
Nos. 630-633 (4) 10.40 10.40

End of World War II, 50th Anniv.

Common Design Types

17p, Falkland Islands Victory Parade contingent. 35p, Governor Sir Alan Wolsey Cardinall on Bren gun carrier. 40p, HMAS Esperance Bay, 1942. 65p, HMS Exeter, 1939.
£1, Reverse of War Medal 1939-45.

Wmk. 373

1995, May 8 Litho. *Perf. 14*
634 CD351 17p multicolored 1.10 1.10
635 CD351 35p multicolored 2.25 2.25
636 CD351 40p multicolored 2.75 2.75
637 CD351 65p multicolored 4.25 4.25
Nos. 634-637 (4) 10.35 10.35

Souvenir Sheet

638 CD352 £1 multicolored 5.00 5.00

Transporting Peat — A123

Wmk. 384

1995, Aug. 1 Litho. *Perf. 14*
639 A123 17p Ox, cart .70 .70
640 A123 35p Horse, cart 2.10 2.10
641 A123 40p Tractor, sledge 2.10 2.10
642 A123 65p Truck, peat bank 3.50 3.50
Nos. 639-642 (4) 8.40 8.40

Miniature Sheet of 6

Wildlife — A124

Designs: a, Kelp geese. b, Albatross. c, Cormorants. d, Magellanic penguins. e, Fur seals. f, Rockhopper penguins.

1995, Sept. 11
643 A124 35p #a.-f. 12.50 12.50

No. 643 is a continuous design.

Wild Animals A125

1995, Nov. 6 Wmk. 373
644 A125 9p Rabbit .60 .60
645 A125 17p Hare 1.00 1.00
646 A125 35p Guanaco 2.40 2.40
647 A125 40p Fox 2.75 2.75
648 A125 65p Otter 4.25 4.25
Nos. 644-648 (5) 11.00 11.00

Visit by Princess Anne A126

Princess Anne and: 9p, Government House. 19p, San Carlos Cemetery. 30p, Christ Church Cathedral. 73p, Goose Green.

1996, Jan. 30 *Perf. 14½*
649 A126 9p multicolored .50 .50
650 A126 19p multicolored 1.50 1.50
651 A126 30p multicolored 2.50 2.50
652 A126 73p multicolored 5.50 5.50
Nos. 649-652 (4) 10.00 10.00

Queen Elizabeth II, 70th Birthday

Common Design Type

Various portraits of Queen, scenes from Falkland Islands: 17p, Steeple Jason. 40p, Ship, KV Tamar. 45p, New Island with shipwreck on beach. 65p, Community School.
£1, Queen in formal dress at Sandringham Ball.

1996, Apr. 21 *Perf. 13½*
653 CD354 17p multicolored .65 .65
654 CD354 40p multicolored 1.75 1.75
655 CD354 45p multicolored 2.10 2.10
656 CD354 65p multicolored 3.00 3.00
Nos. 653-656 (4) 7.50 7.50

Souvenir Sheet

657 CD354 £1 multicolored 4.25 4.25

CAPEX '96 A127

Mail delivery: 9p, Horseback, 1890. 40p, Norseman floatplane. 45p, Inter-island ship. 76p, Beaver floatplane.
£1, LMS Jubilee Class 4-6-0 locomotive.

1996, June 8 Wmk. 384 *Perf. 14*
658 A127 9p multicolored .50 .50
659 A127 40p multicolored 1.75 1.75
660 A127 45p multicolored 2.00 2.00
661 A127 76p multicolored 3.75 3.75
Nos. 658-661 (4) 8.00 8.00

Souvenir Sheet

662 A127 £1 multicolored 4.00 4.00

No. 662 contains one 48x32mm stamp.

Beaked Whales — A128

Designs: 9p, Southern bottlenose whale. 30p, Cuvier's beaked whale. 35p,

Straptoothed beaked whale. 75p, Gray's beaked whale.

Wmk. 373

1996, Sept. 2 Litho. *Perf. 14*

663	A128	9p multicolored	.50	.50
664	A128	30p multicolored	1.75	1.75
665	A128	35p multicolored	1.75	1.75
666	A128	75p multicolored	4.25	4.25
		Nos. 663-666 (4)	8.25	8.25

Magellanic Penguins — A129

Designs: 17p, Two adults. 35p, Young in nest. 40p, Chick, adult. 65p, Swimming.

Wmk. 373

1997, Jan. 2 Litho. *Perf. 14*

667	A129	17p multicolored	1.00	1.00
668	A129	35p multicolored	2.50	2.50
669	A129	40p multicolored	2.75	2.75
670	A129	65p multicolored	4.50	4.50
		Nos. 667-670 (4)	10.75	10.75

Fish Type of 1994

Souvenir Sheet

Wmk. 373

1997, Feb. 3 Litho. *Perf. 14*

671	A117	£1 Smelt	5.00	5.00

Hong Kong '97.

Ferns — A130

Perf. 14½x14

1997, Mar. 3 Litho. Wmk. 373

672	A130	17p Coral	1.00	1.00
673	A130	35p Adder's tongue	2.25	2.25
674	A130	40p Fuegian tall	2.50	2.50
675	A130	65p Small fern	4.25	4.25
		Nos. 672-675 (4)	10.00	10.00

Lighthouses — A131

Wmk. 373

1997, July 1 Litho. *Perf. 14*

676	A131	9p Bull Point	1.25	1.25
677	A131	30p Cape Pembroke	2.50	2.50
678	A131	£1 Cape Meredith	9.25	9.25
		Nos. 676-678 (3)	13.00	13.00

Queen Elizabeth II and Prince Philip, 50th Wedding Anniv. — A132

#679, Queen holding flowers. #680, Prince with horse. #681, Queen riding in open carriage. #682, Prince in uniform. #683, Queen in red coat & hat, Prince. #684, Princes William and Harry on horseback.

£1.50, Queen, Prince riding in open carriage.

1997 Wmk. 384 *Perf. 14½x14*

679		9p multicolored	.75	.75
680		9p multicolored	.75	.75
a.		A132 Pair, #679-680	1.75	1.75
681		17p multicolored	1.50	1.50
682		17p multicolored	1.50	1.50
a.		A132 Pair, #681-682	3.50	3.50
683		40p multicolored	3.25	3.25
684		40p multicolored	3.25	3.25
a.		A132 Pair, #683-684	7.25	7.25
		Nos. 679-684 (6)	11.00	11.00

Souvenir Sheet

685	A132	£1.50 multicolored	10.00	10.00

Endangered Species — A133

Designs: 17p, Phalcoboenus australis. 19p, Otaria flavescens. 40p, Calandrinia feltonii. 73p, Aplochiton zebra.

Wmk. 373

1997, Oct. 16 Litho. *Perf. 14½*

686	A133	17p multicolored	1.50	1.50
687	A133	19p multicolored	2.00	2.00
688	A133	40p multicolored	4.00	4.00
689	A133	73p multicolored	7.50	7.50
		Nos. 686-689 (4)	15.00	15.00

Fire Service in Falkland Islands, Cent. — A134

Equipment, manufacturer: 9p, Greenwich Gem, Merryweather & Son. 17p, Hatfield trailer pump, Merryweather & Son. 40p, Godiva trailer pump, Coventry Climax. 65p, Water tender type B, Carmichael Bedford.

Wmk. 384

1998, Feb. 26 Litho. *Perf. 14½*

690	A134	9p multicolored	1.00	1.00
691	A134	17p multicolored	2.25	2.25
692	A134	40p multicolored	6.00	6.00
693	A134	65p multicolored	9.75	9.75
		Nos. 690-693 (4)	19.00	19.00

Diana, Princess of Wales (1961-97)

Common Design Type

Portraits: a, Looking left. b, In red dress. c, Hand on cheek. d, Investigating land mines.

Perf. 14½x14

1998, Mar. 31 Wmk. 373

694	CD355	30p Sheet of 4, #a-d	6.00	6.00

No. 694 sold for £1.20 + 20p, with surtax from international sales being donated to the Princess Diana Memorial Fund and surtax from national sales being donated to designated local charity.

Birds A135

1p, Tawny-throated dotterel. 2p, Hudsonian godwit. 5p, Eared dove. #698, Great grebe. #699, Roseate spoonbill. 10p, Southern lapwing. 16p, Buff-necked ibis. 17p, Astral parakeet. 30p, Ashy-headed goose. 35p, American kestrel. 65p, Red-legged shag. 88p, Red shoveler. £1, Red-fronted coot. £3, Chilean flamingo. £5, Fork-tailed flycatcher.

Wmk. 373

1998, July 14 Litho. *Perf. 14*

695	A135	1p multicolored	.30	.30
696	A135	2p multicolored	.30	.30
697	A135	5p multicolored	.30	.30
698	A135	9p multicolored	.45	.45
699	A135	9p multicolored	.45	.45
700	A135	10p multicolored	.50	.50
701	A135	16p multicolored	.70	.70
702	A135	17p multicolored	.80	.80
a.		Booklet pane, 2 #699, 8 #702 + 2 labels	7.25	
		Complete booklet, #702a	7.25	
703	A135	30p multicolored	1.40	1.40
704	A135	35p multicolored	1.60	1.60
		Complete booklet, 6 #704	9.75	
705	A135	65p multicolored	3.00	3.00
706	A135	88p multicolored	4.00	4.00
707	A135	£1 multicolored	4.50	4.50
708	A135	£3 multicolored	15.00	15.00
709	A135	£5 multicolored	24.00	22.50
		Nos. 695-709 (15)	57.30	55.80

Boats — A136

Boat, country flag, year: 17p, Penelope, Germany, 1926. 35p, Ilen, Italy, 1926. 40p, Weddell, Chile, 1940. 65p, Lively, Scotland, 1940.

Wmk. 373

1998, Sept. 30 Litho. *Perf. 14*

710	A136	17p multicolored	1.25	1.25
711	A136	35p multicolored	2.50	2.50
712	A136	40p multicolored	2.75	2.75

Size: 29x18mm

713	A136	65p multicolored	4.50	4.50
		Nos. 710-713 (4)	11.00	11.00

FIGAS (First Medivac Air Ambulance Service), 50th Anniv. — A137

17p, Man carrying patient, airplane. £1, Airplane, map of Islands, float plane.

Wmk. 373

1998, Dec. 1 Litho. *Perf. 14*

714	A137	17p multicolored	1.75	1.75
715	A137	£1 multicolored	12.00	12.00

Military Uniforms — A138

Uniform, background location: 17p, Marine Private, 1776, The Block House at Port Egmont, Saunders Island. 30p, Marine Officer, 1833, Port Louis, East Falkland. 35p, Royal Marine Corporal, 1914, HMS Kent. 65p, Royal Marine Bugler, 1976, Government House.

Wmk. 373

1998, Dec. 8 Litho. *Perf. 14½*

716	A138	17p multicolored	2.00	2.00
717	A138	30p multicolored	4.00	4.00
718	A138	35p multicolored	4.25	4.25
719	A138	65p multicolored	8.75	8.75
		Nos. 716-719 (4)	19.00	19.00

St. Mary's Church, Cent. A139

Wmk. 373

1999, Feb. 12 Litho. *Perf. 14*

720	A139	17p Inside view	1.25	1.25
721	A139	40p Outside view	4.00	4.00
722	A139	75p Laying corner-stone, 1899	7.75	7.75
		Nos. 720-722 (3)	13.00	13.00

Australia '99, World Stamp Expo A140

25p, HMS Beagle. 35p, HMAS Australia. 40p, SS Canberra. #726, SS Great Britain. #727, All-England Eleven visit Australia, 1861-62.

1999, Mar. 5 Wmk. 384

723	A140	25p multicolored	2.50	2.50
724	A140	35p multicolored	3.50	3.50
725	A140	40p multicolored	4.00	4.00
726	A140	50p multicolored	4.75	4.75
727	A140	50p multicolored	4.75	4.75
a.		Pair, #726-727	9.50	9.50
		Nos. 723-727 (5)	19.50	19.50

1999 Visit of HRH Prince of Wales — A141

Perf. 14x13½

1999, Mar. 13 Litho. Wmk. 384

728	A141	£2 multicolored	14.50	14.50

Wedding of Prince Edward and Sophie Rhys-Jones

Common Design Type

Perf. 13¾x14

1999, June 15 Litho. Wmk. 384

729	CD356	80p Separate portraits	5.25	5.25
730	CD356	£1.20 Couple	8.25	8.25

PhilexFrance '99, World Philatelic Exhibition — A142

Designs: 35p, French cruiser, Jeanne d'Arc, Port Stanley, 1931. 40p, CAMS 37/11 Flying Boat's first flight.

£1, CAMS 37 Flying Boat over Port Stanley, 1931.

1999, June 21 Wmk. 373 *Perf. 14*

731	A142	35p multicolored	3.75	3.75
732	A142	40p multicolored	4.25	4.25

Souvenir Sheet

733	A142	£1 multicolored	12.00	12.00

No. 733 contains one 48x31mm stamp.

Queen Mother's Century

Common Design Type

Queen Mother: 9p, With King George VI at Port of London. 20p, With Queen Elizabeth at Women's Institute, Sandringham. 30p, With Princes Charles, William and Harry at Clarence House, 95th birthday. 67p, As Colonel-in-Chief of the Queen's Royal Hussars.

£1.40, With Ernest Shackleton, Robert F. Scott and Edward A. Wilson.

Wmk. 384

1999, Aug. 18 Litho. *Perf. 13½*

734	CD358	9p multi	1.00	1.00
735	CD358	20p multi	2.10	2.10
736	CD358	30p multi	3.25	3.25
737	CD358	67p multi	7.50	7.50
		Nos. 734-737 (4)	13.85	13.85

Souvenir Sheet

738	CD358	£1.40 multi	15.00	15.00

For overprint see #767.

Waterfowl A143

Perf. 14¼x14½

1999, Sept. 9 Litho. Wmk. 384

739	A143	9p Chiloe wigeon	.85	.85
740	A143	17p Crested duck	1.90	1.90
741	A143	30p Brown pintail	3.50	3.50
742	A143	35p Silver teal	4.00	4.00
743	A143	40p Yellow billed teal	5.25	5.25
744	A143	65p Flightless steamer duck	7.50	7.50
		Nos. 739-744 (6)	23.00	23.00

California Gold Rush A144

Designs: 9p, Vicar of Bray, 1999. 35p, Gold panning, 1849. 40p, Gold rocking cradle, 1849. 80p, Vicar of Bray, 1849.

£1, Vicar of Bray in San Francisco Harbor, 1849.

Wmk. 373

1999, Nov. 3 Litho. *Perf. 14*

745	A144	9p multicolored	1.00	1.00
746	A144	35p multicolored	3.75	3.75
747	A144	40p multicolored	4.25	4.25
748	A144	80p multicolored	9.00	9.00
		Nos. 745-748 (4)	18.00	18.00

Souvenir Sheet

Perf. 13¾

749	A144	£1 multicolored	12.00	12.00

No. 749 contains one 48x31mm stamp.

Millennium A145

Designs: No. 750, Kelp gull. No. 751, Upland goose. No. 752, Christchurch Cathedral. No. 753, Night heron. No. 754, King penguin. No. 755, Christmas at home.

1999, Dec. 6 *Perf. 14x14½*

750	A145	9p multicolored	1.00	1.00
751	A145	9p multicolored	1.00	1.00
752	A145	9p multicolored	1.00	1.00
753	A145	30p multicolored	4.25	4.25
754	A145	30p multicolored	4.25	4.25
755	A145	30p multicolored	4.25	4.25
		Nos. 750-755 (6)	15.75	15.75

Visit of Princess Alexandra A146

Designs: 9p, Princess in blue dress, trees. £1, Princess in patterned dress, trees.

Perf. 13¼x13¾

2000, Feb. 1 Litho. Wmk. 373

756	A146	9p multi	1.00	1.00
757	A146	£1 multi	10.00	10.00

Sir Ernest Shackleton (1874-1922), Polar Explorer — A147

17p, Ship Endurance, discovery of the Caird Coast. 45p, Endurance trapped in pack ice. 75p, Shackleton, Chilean tugboat Yelcho.

2000, Feb. 10 Wmk. 373 *Perf. 14*

758	A147	17p multi	2.00	2.00
759	A147	45p multi	7.00	7.00
760	A147	75p multi	12.00	12.00
		Nos. 758-760 (3)	21.00	21.00

See British Antarctic Territory Nos. 285-287, South Georgia and South Sandwich Islands Nos. 254-256.

British Monarchs — A148

a, Elizabeth I. b, James II. c, George I. d, William IV. e, Edward VIII. f, Elizabeth II.

2000, Feb. 29 Wmk. 373 *Perf. 14*

761	A148	40p Sheet of 6, #a.-f.	15.00	15.00

The Stamp Show 2000, London.

Prince William, 18th Birthday

Common Design Type

William: 10p, As toddler with fireman's helmet, vert. 20p, In checked suit and in navy suit, vert. 37p, With blue shirt. 43p, In gray suit and in navy suit holding flowers. 50p, As child with dog.

Perf. 13¾x14¼, 14¼x13¾

2000, June 21 Litho. Wmk. 373

Stamps with White Border

762	CD359	10p multi	.65	.65
763	CD359	20p multi	1.60	1.60
764	CD359	37p multi	3.00	3.00
765	CD359	43p multi	3.25	3.25
		Nos. 762-765 (4)	8.50	8.50

Souvenir Sheet

Stamps Without White Border

Perf. 14¼

766		Sheet of 5	12.00	12.00
a.		CD359 10p multi	.60	.60
b.		CD359 20p multi	1.25	1.25
c.		CD359 37p multi	2.25	2.25
d.		CD359 43p multi	2.50	2.50
e.		CD359 50p multi	3.00	3.00

No. 738 Ovptd. in Gold

Wmk. 384

2000, Aug. 4 Litho. *Perf. 13½*

767	CD358	£1.40 multi	14.00	14.00

Gold overprint in sheet margin reads "100TH BIRTHDAY OF HM QUEEN / ELIZABETH THE QUEEN MOTHER."

Bridges A149

Bridges over: 20p, Malo River. 37p, Bodie Creek. 43p, Fitzroy River.

2000, Oct. 16 *Perf. 14¼x14½*

768-770	A149	Set of 3	15.00	15.00

Christmas — A150

Designs: 10p, Shepherd, sheep. 20p, Shepherds, sheep, angel. 33p, Holy family, shepherds, Magus, donkey, sheep. 43p, Angel, two Magi. 78p, Camel.

2000, Nov. 1 Wmk. 373

771-775	A150	Set of 5	14.00	14.00
775a		Souvenir sheet, #771-775	17.00	17.00

Sunrises and Sunsets A151

Various photos: 10p, 20p, 37p, 43p.

2001, Jan. 10 *Perf. 14½x14¼*

776-779	A151	Set of 4	12.00	12.00

Souvenir Sheet

New Year 2001 (Year of the Snake) — A152

Birds: a, Striated caracara. b, Mountain hawk eagle.

Perf. 14½x14¼

2001, Feb. 1 Litho. Wmk. 373

780	A152	37p Sheet of 2, #a-b	8.00	8.00

Hong Kong 2001 Stamp Exhibition.

Age of Victoria — A153

Designs: 3p, Falkland Islands #1. 10p, S.S. Great Britain, horiz. 20p, Stanley Harbor, 1888, horiz. 43p, Cape Pembroke Lighthouse, telephones, 1897. 93p, Royal Marines, 1900. £1.50, Queen Victoria, by Franz Xavier Winterhalter, 1859.

£1, Funeral procession for Queen Victoria.

2001, May 24 *Perf. 14*

781-786	A153	Set of 6	22.50	22.50

Souvenir Sheet

787	A153	£1 multi	9.00	9.00

Royal Navy Connections to Falkland Islands — A154

Designs: 10p, Welfare, ship that made first recorded landing, 1690. 17p, HMS Invincible, ship in Battle of the Falklands, 1914. 20p, HMS Exeter, ship in Battle of the River Plate, 1939. 37p, SN.R6 Hovercraft, 1967. 43p, Antarctic patrol ship HMS Protector and Wasp helicopter, 1955. 68p, Desire, ship that made first sighting, 1592.

2001, July 24

788-793	A154	Set of 6	18.00	18.00

Carcass Island and its Flora and Fauna — A155

No. 794, 37p: a, Yellow violet. b, Tussac bird.

No. 795, 43p: a, Carcass Island settlement. b, Black-crowned night heron.

Wmk. 373

2001, Sept. 28 Litho. *Perf. 13¾*

Pairs, #a-b

794-795	A155	Set of 2	11.00	11.00

Gentoo Penguins — A156

Designs: 10p, Birds flapping wings. 33p, Feeding young. 37p, Bird with beak open. 43p, Four birds walking.

2001, Oct. 26 *Perf. 14½x14¼*

796-799	A156	Set of 4	9.00	9.00

Falkland Islands Company, 150th Anniv. A157

Designs: 10p, Company coat of arms, and gathering of cattle. 20p, Company flag, and ship Amelia. 43p, Manager F. E. Cobb, and company buildings. £1, Sheep farmer William Wickham Bertrand, sheep dip.

Wmk. 373

2002, Jan. 10 Litho. *Perf. 14*

800-803	A157	Set of 4	12.00	12.00

Reign Of Queen Elizabeth II, 50th Anniv. Issue

Common Design Type

Designs: Nos. 804, 808a, 20p, Princess Elizabeth reading, 1945. Nos. 805, 808b, 37p, In 1977. Nos. 806, 808c, 43p, Holding Prince Charles, 1949. Nos. 807, 808d, 50p, At Garter ceremony, 1994. No. 808e, 50p, 1955 portrait by Annigoni (38x50mm).

Perf. 14¼x14½, 13¾ (#808e)

2002, Feb. 6 Litho. Wmk. 373

With Gold Frames

804-807	CD360	Set of 4	7.00	7.00

Souvenir Sheet

Without Gold Frames

808	CD360	Sheet of 5, #a-e	9.50	9.50

Falkland Islands War, 20th Anniv. — A158

No. 809, 22p: a, HMS Hermes, 1982. b, Fishery patrol vessel, 2002.

No. 810, 40p: a, Troops landing, 1982. b, Mine clearing, 2002.

No. 811, 45p: a, RAF Harrier on HMS Hermes, 1982. b, RAF Tristar, 2002.
Illustration reduced.

Wmk. 373
2002, June 14 Litho. *Perf. 14*
Horiz. pairs, #a-b
809-811 A158 Set of 3 12.00 12.00

Queen Mother Elizabeth (1900-2002)
Common Design Type

Designs: 22p, Wearing hat and scarf (black and white photograph). 25p, Wearing blue hat with polka dots. Nos. 814, 816a, 95p, Wearing feathered hat (black and white photograph). Nos. 815, 816b, £1.20, Wearing blue hat.

Wmk. 373
2002, Aug. 5 Litho. *Perf. 14¼*
With Purple Frames
812-815 CD361 Set of 4 11.50 11.50
Souvenir Sheet
Without Purple Frames
Perf. 14½x14¼
816 CD361 Sheet of 2, #a-b 11.50 11.50

Worldwide Fund for Nature (WWF) — A159

Penguins: 36p, Rockhopper. 40p, Magellanic. 45p, Gentoo. 70p, Macaroni.

Wmk. 373
2002, Aug. 30 Litho. *Perf. 14¼*
817-820 A159 Set of 4 9.50 9.50
a. Horiz. strip of 4, #817-820 9.50 9.50

West Point Island and its Flora and Fauna — A160

No. 821, 40p: a, Felton's flower. b, Black-browed albatross.
No. 822, 45p: a, Rockhopper penguin. b, Island settlement.
Illustration reduced.

Perf. 14¼x14½
2002, Oct. 31 Litho. Wmk. 373
Horiz. Pairs, #a-b
821-822 A160 Set of 2 10.00 10.00

Visit of Prince Andrew — A161

No. 823: a, 22p, In uniform. b, £1.52, In suit and tie.

2002, Nov. 11 *Perf. 13¼x13½*
823 A161 Horiz. pair, #a-b 9.50 9.50

Shepherds' Houses — A162

Designs: 10p, Gun Hill shanty, Little Chartres. 22p, Paragon House, Lafonia. 45p, Dos Lomas, Lafonia. £1, Old House, Shallow Bay Farm.

Wmk. 373
2003, Mar. 31 Litho. *Perf. 14*
824-827 A162 Set of 4 9.00 9.00

Head of Queen Elizabeth II
Common Design Type
Wmk. 373
2003, June 2 Litho. *Perf. 13¾*
828 CD362 £2 multi 8.00 8.00

Prince William, 21st Birthday
Common Design Type

Color photographs: a, In suit at right. b, With Prince Harry at left.

Wmk. 373
2003, June 21 Litho. *Perf. 14¼*
829 Horiz. pair 10.00 10.00
a.-b. CD364 95p Either single 4.50 4.50

Birds — A163

Designs: 1p, Chiloe widgeon. 2p, Dolphin gull, vert. 5p, Falkland flightless steamer duck. 10p, Black-throated finch, vert. 22p, White-tufted grebe. 25p, Rufous-chested dotterel, vert. 45p, Upland goose. 50p, Dark-faced ground-tyrant, vert. 95p, Black-crowned night heron. £1, Red-backed hawk, vert. £3, Black-necked swan. £5, Short-eared owl, vert.

Perf. 13x13¼, 13¼x13
2003, July 21 Litho. Wmk. 373

830	A163	1p multi	.20	.20
831	A163	2p multi	.20	.20
832	A163	5p multi	.20	.20
833	A163	10p multi	.35	.35
834	A163	22p multi	.80	.80
835	A163	25p multi	.90	.90
836	A163	45p multi	1.60	1.60
837	A163	50p multi	1.90	1.90
838	A163	95p multi	3.50	3.50
839	A163	£1 multi	3.75	3.75
840	A163	£3 multi	11.00	11.00
841	A163	£5 multi	19.00	19.00
		Nos. 830-841,C1 (13)	44.65	44.65

Bird Life International A164

Black-browed albatross: No. 842, Adult on nest, facing right. No. 843, Chick. 40p, Heads of two adults, vert. £1, Adult on nest, facing left, vert.
16p, In flight.

Perf. 14¼x13¾, 13¾x14¼
2003, Sept. 26

842	A164 22p multi		1.10	1.10
	a.	Perf. 14¼x14½	1.10	1.10
843	A164 22p multi		1.10	1.10
	a.	Perf. 14¼x14½	1.10	1.10
844	A164 40p multi		2.00	2.00
	a.	Perf. 14½x14¼	1.90	1.90
845	A164 £1 multi		5.25	5.25
	a.	Perf. 14½x14¼	4.75	4.75
	Nos. 842-845 (4)		9.45	9.45

Souvenir Sheet
846 Sheet, #842a-846a 9.00 9.00
a. A164 16p multi, perf. 14¼x14½ .50 .50

New Island and its Flora and Fauna A165

No. 847, 40p: a, Striated caracara. b, Lady's slipper.
No. 848, 45p: a, Stone Cottage. b, King penguin.

Wmk. 373
2003, Oct. 24 Litho. *Perf. 13¾*
Pairs, #a-b
847-848 A165 Set of 2 8.50 8.50

Christmas — A166

Various depictions of Pale maiden flower: 16p, 30p, 40p, 95p.

2003, Nov. 3 *Perf. 14x14¼*
849-852 A166 Set of 4 8.75 8.75

Sheep Farming A167

Designs: 19p, Traditional hand shearing. 22p, Driving the sheep. 45p, Big House, Hill Cove. 70p, The early years. £1, Wool collection, SS Fitzroy.

Unwmk.
2004, Apr. 30 Litho. *Perf. 14*
853-857 A167 Set of 5 9.25 9.25

Wildlife Conservation in Falkland Islands, 25th Anniv. — A168

Designs: 20p, Man planting tussac grass. 24p, People cleaning beach. 50p, Satellite tracking of rockhopper penguins. £1, Weighing of albatross chick.

2004, June 17 Litho. *Perf. 14*
858-861 A168 Set of 4 8.00 8.00

Sir Rowland Hill (1795-1879) and Falkland Islands Postage Stamps — A169

Hill and: 24p, #20. 50p, #74. 75p, #94. £1, #151a.

2004, Aug. 31 Litho. *Perf. 13¼*
862-865 A169 Set of 4 9.00 9.00

Sea Lion Island and its Flora and Fauna — A170

No. 866, 42p: a, King cormorant. b, Dog orchid.
No. 867, 50p: a, Magellanic penguin. b, Sea Lion Lodge.
Illustration reduced.

2004, Sept. 15 *Perf. 13¾*
Pairs, #a-b
866-867 A170 Set of 2 7.50 7.50

Owls — A171

Designs: 18p, Head of short-eared owl. 45p, Short-eared owl. 50p, Barn owl in flight. £1.50, Barn owl.
£2, Barn owl in flight, horiz.

2004, Oct. 25
868-871 A171 Set of 4 10.50 10.50
Souvenir Sheet
872 A171 £2 multi 7.50 7.50

Battle of the Falkland Islands, 90th Anniv. A172

No. 873: a, HMS Kent, HMS Inflexible, half of HMS Carnarvon, half of HMS Cornwall. b, British Navy flag, HMS Glasgow, half of HMS Carnarvon, half of HMS Cornwall, half of HMS Invincible. c, Medals, half of HMS Invincible.
No. 874: a, Medals, half of SMS Scharnhorst. b, German imperial war ensign, SMS Dresden, half of SMS Scharnhorst, half of SMS Leipzig. c, SMS Nürnberg, SMS Gneisenau, half of SMS Leipzig.

2004, Dec. 8 Litho. *Perf. 14*
873 Horiz. strip of 3 3.50 3.50
a.-c. A172 24p Any single 1.00 1.00
874 Horiz. strip of 3 7.50 7.50
a.-c. A172 50p Any single 2.00 2.00

Camber Railway, 90th Anniv. — A173

Designs: 3p, Old track bed. 24p, Kerr Stuart Wren Class locomotive at Camber Depot, horiz. 50p, Kerr Stuart Wren Class locomotive Falkland Islands Express, horiz. £2, Camber sailing wagon.

2005, Feb. 28 *Perf. 13¾*
875-878 A173 Set of 4 11.00 11.00

Wedding of Prince Charles and Camilla Parker Bowles A174

Designs: 24p, Couple. 50p, Couple in formal wear, vert.
£2, Couple, Windsor Castle.

2005, Apr. 29 *Perf. 14*
879-880 A174 Set of 2 3.00 3.00
Souvenir Sheet
881 A174 £2 multi 7.75 7.75

End of World War II, 60th Anniv. — A175

No. 882, 24p: a, Walrus reconnaissance seaplane. b, Presentation Spitfire X4616.
No. 883, 80p: a, HMS Exeter at Port Stanley. b, Governor, King Edward Memorial Hospital staff, Rear Admiral Harwood and Capt. Bell.
No. 884, £1: a, Fitzroy. b, HMS William Scoresby.
Illustration reduced.

Perf. 13¼x13½

2005, June 29 Litho.
Horiz. Pairs, #a-b

882-884 A175 Set of 3 14.50 14.50

Maritime Heritage A176

Designs: 24p, Snow Squall escaping CSS Tuscaloosa, 1863. No. 886, 55p, Jhelum, 1870. No. 887, 55p, Charles Cooper, 1866. £1.20, SS Imo colliding with the Mont Blanc, Halifax Harbor, 1917.

2005, Aug. 29 Litho. ***Perf. 14***
885-888 A176 Set of 4 10.50 10.50

Pebble Island and its Flora and Fauna — A177

No. 889, 45p: a, Gentoo penguin. b, Falkland lavender.
No. 890, 55p: a, Pebble Island Lodge. b, Black-necked swan.
Illustration reduced.

2005, Sept. 12 ***Perf. 13¾***
Pairs, #a-b
889-890 A177 Set of 2 8.25 8.25

Souvenir Sheet

The Fall of Nelson, Battle of Trafalgar, 21 October 1805, by Denis Dighton — A178

2005, Oct. 21
891 A178 £2 multi 8.50 8.50

Battle of Trafalgar, bicent.

Hans Christian Andersen (1805-75), Author — A179

Stories: 18p, The Little Mermaid. 30p, The Snowman. 45p, The Ugly Duckling. £1, Thumbelina.

2005, Oct. 28 ***Perf. 14***
892-895 A179 Set of 4 8.25 8.25

Stanley Infant and Junior School, 50th anniv.

Black-crowned Night Heron — A180

Designs: 24p, Head. 55p, Bird on one leg. 80p, Juvenile standing. £1, Head of juvenile.

2006, Feb. 10 Litho. ***Perf. 13¾***
896-899 A180 Set of 4 9.00 9.00

Queen Elizabeth II, 80th Birthday — A181

Queen wearing: 24p, Yellow hat. 55p, Green hat. 80p, Blue hat. £1, Red hat.
£2, Tiara and white hat, horiz.

2006, Apr. 21 ***Perf. 14***
900-903 A181 Set of 4 9.75 9.75

Souvenir Sheet

904 A181 £2 multi 7.50 7.50

SS Great Britain — A182

View of: 24p, Bow. 55p, Stern. £1.50, Deck and masts.

2006, May 19 ***Perf. 13¾x13¼***
905-907 A182 Set of 3 8.75 8.75

Birds A183

Designs: No. 908, 25p, Gentoo penguin chicks. No. 909, 25p, King cormorants. No. 910, 60p, King penguin. No. 911, 60p, Wandering albatross.

2006, Aug. 30 Litho. ***Perf. 14¼x14***
908-911 A183 Set of 4 6.50 6.50

Bleaker Island and its Flora and Fauna — A184

No. 912, 50p: a, Woolly Falkland ragwort. b, Macaroni penguin.
No. 913, 60p: a, The Outlook and sheep. b, Long-tailed meadowlark.
Illustration reduced.

2006, Sept. 18 ***Perf. 13¼x13***
Pairs, #a-b
912-913 A184 Set of 2 8.25 8.25

Victoria Cross, 150th Anniv. — A185

Designs: Nos. 914, 916a, 60p, Lt. Col. H. Jones. Nos. 915, 916b, 60p, Sgt. Ian McKay. No. 916c, £1, Victoria Cross.

2006, Nov. 11 ***Perf. 13¼***
Stamps With White Frames
914-915 A185 Set of 2 4.75 4.75

Souvenir Sheet
Stamps Without White Frames
916 A185 Sheet of 3, #a-c 8.75 8.75

Bird Type of 2003

Designs: 20p, Black-browed albatross, vert. 25p, Rufous-chested dotterel, vert. £5, Short-eared owl, vert.

Perf. 13¼x13

2006, Nov. 15 Litho. Unwmk.
917 A163 20p multi .80 .80
918 A163 25p multi 1.00 1.00
919 A163 £5 multi 20.00 20.00
Nos. 917-919 (3) 21.80 21.80

Nos. 918-919 differ from Nos. 835 and 841 by having less color around the Queen's head. Nos. 917-919 are dated "2006."

Worldwide Fund for Nature (WWF) A186

Striated caracara: 25p, Heads of two birds. 50p, Bird in flight. 60p, Bird standing. 85p, Bird eating shellfish.

2006, Dec. 20 Litho. ***Perf. 13¾***
920-923 A186 Set of 4 8.50 8.50
923a Miniature sheet, 4 each #920-923 34.00 34.00

Fisheries, 20th Anniv. A187

Designs: 3p, Fishermen at sea. 11p, Fishing boat at night. 25p, Fishermen leaving boat. 30p, Japanese jigger. 60p, Fishery protection boat Dorada. £1.05, Trawler transferring fish to a freezer container ship.

2007, Feb. 24 ***Perf. 14¼***
924-929 A187 Set of 6 9.25 9.25

HMS Plymouth A188

HMS Plymouth: 25p, Joining Falkland Islands Task Force. 40p, Supporting SBS. 60p, Under attack by Argentine fighters. £1.05, Docked at Port Stanley.

2007, Mar. 27
930-933 A188 Set of 4 9.25 9.25

Souvenir Sheet

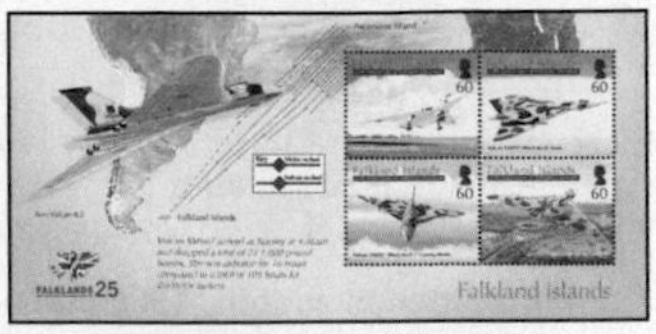

Falkland Islands War, 25th Anniv. — A189

No. 934: a, Avro Vulcan prototype VX770. b, Avro Vulcan XM597. c, Avro Vulcan XM607. d, Vulcan in the Sky Project.

2007, May 25 Litho. ***Perf. 13¼***
934 A189 60p Sheet of 4, #a-d 9.50 9.50

Miniature Sheets

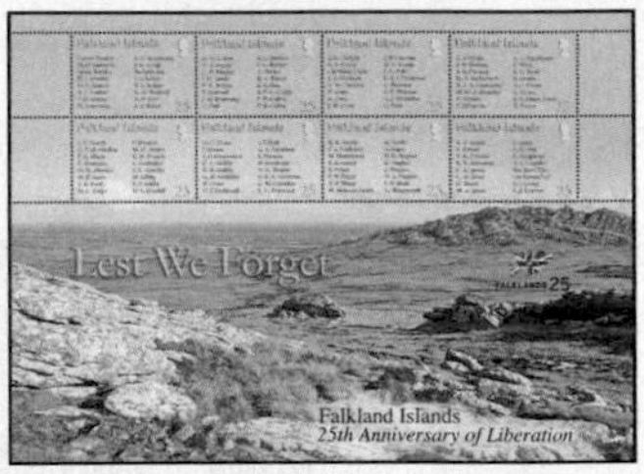

British and Falkland Islander Casualties of the Falkland Islands War — A190

No. 935, 25p — Casualties beginning with: a, Doreen Bonner. b, G. W. J. Batt. c, J. R. Carlyle. d, S. J. Dixon. e, I. R. Farrell. f, G. C. Grace. g, R. R. Heath. h, A. S. James.
No. 936, 60p: a, D. Lee. b, P. B. McKay. c, G. T. Nelson. d, J. B. Pashley. e, M. Sambles. f, D. A. Strickland. g, R. G. Thomas. h, P. A. West.

2007, June 14 Litho. ***Perf. 14¼***
Sheets of 8, #a-h
935-936 A190 Set of 2 27.00 27.00

Scouting, Cent. — A191

Designs: 10p, Scouts on ladder of RRS Discovery. 20p, Dignitaries on ship's deck. 25p, Dignitaries, diff. £2, RRS Discovery.

2007, July 23 Litho. ***Perf. 13½x13¼***
937-940 A191 Set of 4 10.50 10.50

Voyage of RRS Discovery from Falkland Islands for presentation to British Scout Association, 70th anniv.

Princess Diana (1961-97) — A192

2007, Aug. 31 ***Perf. 14***
941 A192 60p multi 2.50 2.50

Printed in sheets of 8 stamps + 21 labels.

Saunders Island and its Flora and Fauna — A193

No. 942, 50p: a, Rockhopper penguin. b, Dusty miller.
No. 943, 55p: a, Crested caracara. b, Earliest British settlement at Port Egmont.
Illustration reduced.

2007, Sept. 28 Litho. *Perf. 13¾*
Pairs, #a-b

942-943 A193 Set of 2 8.75 8.75

Wedding of Queen Elizabeth II and Prince Philip, 60th Anniv. A194

2007, Nov. 20 Litho. *Perf. 14*

944 A194 £1 multi 4.25 4.25

Polar Explorers and Their Ships A195

Explorers and ships: 4p, James Weddell (1787-1834), and Jane. 25p, James Clark Ross (1800-62), and HMS Erebus. 85p, William Spiers Bruce (1867-1921), and Scotia. £1.61, James Marr (1902-65), and Discovery II.

2008, Apr. 7

945-948 A195 Set of 4 11.00 11.00

Southern Elephant Seals A196

Designs: 27p, Seal pup. 55p, Male and female. 65p, Seals play fighting. £1.10, Seal and tussock bird.

2008, July 15 Litho. *Perf. 14*

949-952 A196 Set of 4 10.50 10.50

Aircraft A197

Designs: 1p, Taylorcraft Auster Mk 5. 2p, Boeing 747-300. 5p, De Havilland Canada DHC-6 Twin Otter. 10p, Lockheed C-130 Hercules. 27p, De Havilland Canada DHC-2 Beaver. 55p, Airbus A320. 65p, Lockheed L-1011-385-3 Tristar C2. 90p, Avro Vulcan B2. £1, Britten-Norman BN-2 Islander. £2, Panavia Tornado F3. £3, De Havilland Canada DHC-7-110 Dash 7. £5, BAE Sea Harrier.

2008, Aug. 1 Litho. *Perf. 14*

953 A197 1p multi .20 .20
954 A197 2p multi .20 .20
955 A197 5p multi .20 .20
956 A197 10p multi .40 .40
957 A197 27p multi 1.10 1.10
958 A197 55p multi 2.25 2.25
959 A197 65p multi 2.60 2.60
960 A197 90p multi 3.50 3.50
961 A197 £1 multi 4.00 4.00
962 A197 £2 multi 8.00 8.00
963 A197 £3 multi 12.00 12.00
964 A197 £5 multi 20.00 20.00
Nos. 953-964 (12) 54.45 54.45

Souvenir Sheet

Stamps With Royal Air Force 90th Anniv. Emblem Added

965 Sheet of 4 14.50 14.50
a. A197 10p Like #956 .40 .40
b. A197 65p Like #959 2.60 2.60
c. A197 90p Like #960 3.50 3.50
d. A197 £2 Like #962 8.00 8.00

Port Louis, 175th Anniv. — A198

Designs: 27p, Sailor raising British flag. 65p, Royal Marines, British flag.
£2, Capt. Onslow of HMS Clio, British flag.

2008, Sept. 22 Litho. *Perf. 14*

966-967 A198 Set of 2 3.25 3.25

Souvenir Sheet

968 A198 £2 multi 7.25 7.25

Islands and Rocks A199

Designs: 22p, The Slipper. 40p, Kidney Island. 60p, Stephens Bluff and Castle Rock. £1, The Colliers.

2008, Oct. 1 Litho. *Perf. 13¾*

969-972 A199 Set of 4 8.00 8.00

Retirement of Queen Elizabeth 2 as Ocean Liner — A200

Designs: 23p, Launch of Queen Elizabeth 2. 27p, Service of Queen Elizabeth 2 as troop ship in Falkland Islands War. 65p, Queen Elizabeth 2, Palm Jumeirah, Dubai. £2, Queen Elizabeth 2 (70x34mm).

2008, Nov. 21 Litho. *Perf. 13¼*

973-976 A200 Set of 4 9.50 9.50

SEMI-POSTAL STAMPS

Catalogue values for unused stamps in this section are for Never Hinged items.

Rebuilding after Conflict with Argentina — SP1

Wmk. 373

1982, Sept. 13 Litho. *Perf. 11*

B1 SP1 £1 + £1 Battle sites 3.00 3.00

Liberation of Falkland Islands, 10th Anniv. — SP2

Designs: 14p+6p, San Carlos Cemetery. 29p+11p, 1982 War Memorial, Port Stanley. 34p+16p, South Atlantic Medal. 68p+32p, Government House, Port Stanley.

Wmk. 373

1992, June 14 Litho. *Perf. 14*

B2 SP2 14p + 6p multicolored .75 .75
B3 SP2 29p + 11p multicolored 1.50 1.50
B4 SP2 34p + 16p multicolored 2.00 2.00
B5 SP2 68p + 32p multicolored 3.75 3.75
a. Souvenir sheet of 4, #B2-B5 9.50 9.50
Nos. B2-B5 (4) 8.00 8.00

Surtax for Soldiers', Sailors' and Airmen's Families Association.

AIR POST STAMPS

Bird Type of 2003

Design: Rockhopper penguins, vert.

Serpentine Die Cut 6x6½ Syncopated

2003, Sept. 19 Litho.

Booklet Stamp

Self-Adhesive

C1 A163 (40p) multi 1.25 1.25
a. Booklet pane of 8 10.00

Penguins — AP1

Designs: No. C2, (55p), King penguin. No. C3, (55p), Macaroni penguin. No. C4, (55p), Magellanic penguin. No. C5, (55p), Rockhopper penguin. No. C6, (55p), Gentoo penguin. No. C7, (55p), Albino rockhopper penguin.

2008, Dec. 1 Litho. *Perf. 13¼*

C2-C7 AP1 Set of 6 9.75 9.75
C7a Souvenir sheet, #C2-C7 9.75 9.75

POSTAGE DUE STAMPS

Catalogue values for unused stamps in this section are for never hinged items.

Penguin — D1

Perf. 14½x14

1991, Jan. 7 Litho. Wmk. 373

J1 D1 1p lilac rose & lake .20 .50
J2 D1 2p buff & brown org .20 .50
J3 D1 3p yel & orange yel .20 .50
J4 D1 4p lt bl grn & dk bl grn .25 .50
J5 D1 5p sky blue & Prus bl .25 .50
J6 D1 10p lt blue & dk blue .35 .70
J7 D1 20p lt violet & dk vio .90 1.50
J8 D1 50p brt yel grn & dk yel green 2.00 3.25
Nos. J1-J8 (8) 4.35 7.95

Penguins D2

Various penguins.

2005, Dec. 2 Litho. *Perf. 13¾*

J9 D2 1p multi .20 .20
J10 D2 3p multi .20 .20
J11 D2 5p multi .20 .20
J12 D2 10p multi .50 .50
J13 D2 20p multi .90 .90
J14 D2 50p multi 2.00 2.00
J15 D2 £1 multi 4.00 4.00
J16 D2 £2 multi 8.00 8.00
J17 D2 £3 multi 12.00 12.00
J18 D2 £5 multi 20.00 20.00
Nos. J9-J18 (10) 48.00 48.00

WAR TAX STAMPS

Regular Issue of 1912-14 Overprinted

1918, Oct. 7 Wmk. 3 *Perf. 14*

MR1 A7 ½p yellow green .55 *7.25*
MR2 A7 1p red .55 *4.00*
a. Double overprint *2,750.*
MR3 A7 1sh bister brown 6.50 *52.50*
a. Pair, one without overprint 10,000.
Nos. MR1-MR3 (3) 7.60 *63.75*

No. MR3a probably is caused by a foldover and is not constant.

FALKLAND ISLANDS DEPENDENCIES

Catalogue values for unused stamps in this section are for Never Hinged items.

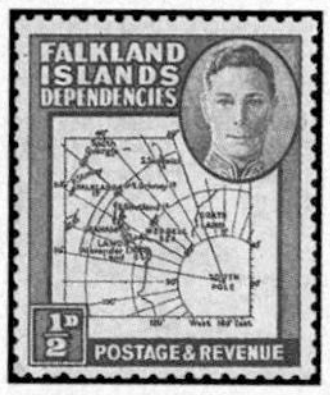

Map of Falkland Islands — A1

Engr., Center Litho. in Black

1946, Feb. 1 Wmk. 4 *Perf. 12*

1L1 A1 ½p yellow green .95 *1.50*
1L2 A1 1p blue violet .95 *1.90*
1L3 A1 2p deep carmine .95 *1.90*
1L4 A1 3p ultramarine 1.90 *1.90*
1L5 A1 4p deep plum 1.90 *3.00*
1L6 A1 6p orange yellow 3.00 *3.50*
1L7 A1 9p brown 3.00 *3.50*
1L8 A1 1sh rose violet 5.75 *7.50*
Nos. 1L1-1L8 (8) 18.40 *24.70*

Nos. 1-8 were reissued in 1948, printed on more opaque paper with the lines of the map finer and clearer. Value for set, unused or used $120.
See No. 1L13.

Common Design Types pictured following the introduction.

Peace Issue
Common Design Type

1946, Oct. 4 *Perf. 13½x14*

1L9 CD303 1p purple .60 .20
1L10 CD303 3p deep blue 1.10 .20

Silver Wedding Issue
Common Design Types

1948, Dec. 6 Photo. *Perf. 14x14½*

1L11 CD304 2½p brt ultra 1.25 1.25

Perf. 11½x11

Engr.

1L12 CD305 1sh blue violet 5.75 5.75

Type of 1946

1949, Mar. 6 *Perf. 12*

Center Litho. in Black

1L13 A1 2½p deep blue 12.50 12.00

UPU Issue
Common Design Types

Engr.; Name Typo. on 2p, 3p

1949, Oct. 10 ***Perf. 13½, 11x11½***

1L14 CD306 1p violet 1.60 1.90
1L15 CD307 2p deep carmine 4.25 1.90
1L16 CD308 3p indigo 6.50 4.25
1L17 CD309 6p red orange 11.00 8.50
Nos. 1L14-1L17 (4) 23.35 16.55

Coronation Issue
Common Design Type

1953, June 4 ***Perf. 13½x13***

1L18 CD312 1p purple & black 1.50 1.50

John Biscoe — A2

Trepassey — A3

Ships: 1½p, Wyatt Earp. 2p, Eagle. 2½p, Penola. 3p, Discovery II. 4p, William Scoresby. 6p, Discovery. 9p, Endurance. 1sh, Deutschland. 2sh, Pourquoi-pas? 2sh6p, Français. 5sh, Scotia. 10sh, Antarctic. £1, Belgica.

1954, Feb. 1 **Engr.** ***Perf. 12½***
Center in Black

1L19 A2 ½p blue green .20 *2.00*
1L20 A3 1p sepia 1.75 1.50
1L21 A3 1½p olive 2.00 1.75
1L22 A3 2p rose red 1.25 .20
1L23 A3 2½p yellow 1.25 .20
1L24 A3 3p ultra 1.25 .20
1L25 A3 4p red violet 3.00 .45
1L26 A2 6p rose violet 3.50 .45
1L27 A2 9p black 3.50 1.25
1L28 A3 1sh org brown 3.50 1.00
1L29 A3 2sh lilac rose 18.00 10.00
1L30 A2 2sh6p blue gray 19.00 6.25
1L31 A2 5sh violet 40.00 6.75
1L32 A3 10sh brt blue 55.00 18.00
1L33 A2 £1 black 87.50 50.00
Nos. 1L19-1L33 (15) 240.70 100.00

Nos. 20, 23-24, 26 Overprinted in Black

1956, Jan 30 **Center in Black**

1L34 A3 1p sepia .20 .20
1L35 A3 2½p yellow .50 .50
1L36 A3 3p ultramarine .60 .60
1L37 A2 6p rose violet .70 .70
Nos. 1L34-1L37 (4) 2.00 2.00

Trans-Antarctic Expedition, 1955-1958.

A4

Wmk. 373

1980, May 5 **Litho.** ***Perf. 13½***

1L38 A4 1p Map of Dependencies .20 .25
1L39 A4 2p Shag Rocks .20 .25
1L40 A4 3p Bird and Willis Islds. .20 .25
1L41 A4 4p Gulbrandsen Lake .20 .25
1L42 A4 5p King Edward Point .20 .25
1L43 A4 6p Shackleton's Memorial Cross .20 .25
1L44 A4 7p Shackleton's grave .20 .25
1L45 A4 8p Grytviken Church .20 .25
1L46 A4 9p Coaling Hulk "Louise" .25 .30
1L47 A4 10p Clerke Rocks .25 .30
1L48 A4 20p Candlemas Island .45 .55
1L49 A4 25p Twitcher Rock, Cook Island .60 .70
1L50 A4 50p "John Biscoe" 1.10 1.25
1L51 A4 £1 "Bransfield" 2.25 2.75
1L52 A4 £3 "Endurance" 7.50 9.00
Nos. 1L38-1L52 (15) 14.00 16.85

Nos. 38-50 exist dated 1984; issued May 3, 1984. Value, set $10.

1985, Nov. 18 **Wmk. 384**

1L48a A4 20p .75 1.10
1L49a A4 25p 1.00 1.25
1L50a A4 50p 2.75 3.50
1L51a A4 £1 4.00 5.00
1L52a A4 £3 12.50 16.00
Nos. 1L48a-1L52a (5) 21.00 26.85

Magellanic Clubmoss — A5

1981, Feb. 5 **Litho.** ***Perf. 14***

1L53 A5 3p shown .25 .25
1L54 A5 6p Alpine cat's-tail .25 .25
1L55 A5 7p Greater burnet .25 .25
1L56 A5 11p Antarctic bedstraw .35 .35
1L57 A5 15p Brown rush .50 .50
a. Brown missing —
1L58 A5 25p Antarctic hair grass .75 .75
Nos. 1L53-1L58 (6) 2.35 2.35

Royal Wedding Issue
Common Design Type

1981, July 22 **Litho.** ***Perf. 14***

1L59 CD331 10p Bouquet .25 .25
1L60 CD331 13p Charles .35 .35
1L61 CD331 52p Couple .85 .85
Nos. 1L59-1L61 (3) 1.45 1.45

Reindeer in Spring — A6

1982, Jan. 29 **Litho.** ***Perf. 14***

1L62 A6 5p shown .20 .20
1L63 A6 13p Autumn .45 .45
1L64 A6 25p Winter .80 .80
1L65 A6 26p Late winter .85 .85
Nos. 1L62-1L65 (4) 2.30 2.30

Gamasellus Racovitzai — A7

1982, Mar. 16 **Litho.** ***Perf. 14***

1L66 A7 5p shown .20 .20
1L67 A7 10p Alaskozetes antarcticus .25 .25
1L68 A7 13p Cryptopygus antarcticus .30 .30
1L69 A7 15p Notiomaso australis .40 .40
1L70 A7 25p Hydromedion sparsutum .60 .60
1L71 A7 26p Parochlus steinenii .65 .65
Nos. 1L66-1L71 (6) 2.40 2.40

Princess Diana Issue
Common Design Type

1982, July 1 **Litho.** ***Perf. 14x14½***

1L72 CD333 5p Arms .45 .20
1L73 CD333 17p Diana 1.40 .60
a. Perf. 14 9.00 9.00
1L74 CD333 37p Wedding 3.25 1.40
1L75 CD333 50p Portrait 4.25 1.75
Nos. 1L72-1L75 (4) 9.35 3.95

Crustacea — A8

Perf. 14½x14

1984, Mar. 23 **Wmk. 373**

1L76 A8 5p Euphausia superba .20 .20
1L77 A8 17p Glyptonotus antarcticus .65 .65
1L78 A8 25p Epimeria monodon 1.00 1.00
1L79 A8 34p Serolis pagenstecheri 1.40 1.40
Nos. 1L76-1L79 (4) 3.25 3.25

Manned Flight Bicentenary — A9

1983, Dec. 23 **Litho.** ***Perf. 14***

1L80 A9 5p Westland Whirlwind .20 .20
1L81 A9 13p Westland Wasp .45 .45
1L82 A9 17p Saunders-Roe Walrus .65 .65
1L83 A9 50p Auster 2.00 2.00
Nos. 1L80-1L83 (4) 3.30 3.30

South Sandwich Islds. Volcanoes — A10

1984, Nov. 8 **Wmk. 373** ***Perf. 14½***

1L84 A10 6p Zavodovski Isld. .60 .60
1L85 A10 17p Mt. Michael, Saunders Isld. 1.40 1.40
1L86 A10 22p Bellingshausen Isld. 2.00 2.00
1L87 A10 52p Bristol Isld. 4.75 4.75
Nos. 1L84-1L87 (4) 8.75 8.75

Albatrosses — A11

1985, May 5 **Wmk. 384** ***Perf. 14½***

1L88 A11 7p Diomedea chrysostoma .80 .80
1L89 A11 22p Diomedea melanophris 2.50 2.50
1L90 A11 27p Diomedea exulans 2.75 2.75
1L91 A11 54p Phoebetria palpebrata 5.75 5.75
Nos. 1L88-1L91 (4) 11.80 11.80

Queen Mother 85th Birthday
Common Design Type

Designs: 7p, 14th birthday celebration. 22p, With Princess Anne, Lady Sarah Armstrong-Jones, Prince Edward. 27p, Queen Mother. 54p, Holding Prince Henry. £1, On the Britannia.

1985, June 23 ***Perf. 14½x14***

1L92 CD336 7p multicolored .25 .25
1L93 CD336 22p multicolored .75 .75
1L94 CD336 27p multicolored 1.00 1.00
1L95 CD336 54p multicolored 2.00 2.00
Nos. 1L92-1L95 (4) 4.00 4.00

Souvenir Sheet

1L96 CD336 £1 multicolored 3.75 3.75

Falkland Islands Naturalists Type of 1985

Naturalists, endangered species: 7p, Dumont d'Urville (1790-1842), kelp. 22p, Johann Reinhold Forster (1729-1798), king penguin. 27p, Johann Georg Adam Forster (1754-1794), tussock grass. 54p, Sir Joseph Banks (1743-1820), dove prion.

1985, Nov. 4 ***Perf. 13½x14***

1L97 A86 7p multicolored .65 .65
1L98 A86 22p multicolored 1.60 1.60
1L99 A86 27p multicolored 2.40 2.40
1L100 A86 54p multicolored 4.75 4.75
Nos. 1L97-1L100 (4) 9.40 9.40

SEMI-POSTAL STAMP

Rebuilding Type of Falkland Islands

Wmk. 373

1982, Sept. 13 **Litho.** ***Perf. 11***

1LB1 SP1 £1 Map of So. Georgia 3.00 3.00

ISSUES FOR THE SEPARATE ISLANDS

Graham Land

Nos. 84, 85B, 86A, 87A, 88-91 Overprinted in Red

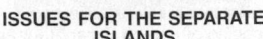

1944, Feb. 12 **Wmk. 4** ***Perf. 12***

2L1 A22 ½p green & black .55 .50
2L2 A22 1p dk vio & black .60 .60
2L3 A22 2p rose car & blk .90 .85
2L4 A22 3p deep bl & blk 1.25 1.10
2L5 A22 4p rose vio & blk 2.00 1.50
2L6 A22 6p brown & black 10.00 3.50
2L7 A22 9p slate bl & blk 3.00 3.00
2L8 A22 1sh dull blue 3.00 2.75
Nos. 2L1-2L8 (8) 21.30 13.80

South Georgia

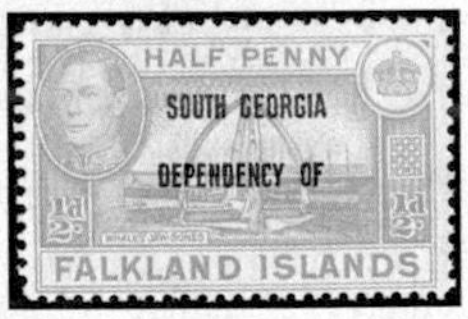

1944, Apr. 3 **Wmk. 4** ***Perf. 12***

3L1 A22 ½p green & black .60 .50
3L2 A22 1p dark vio & blk .65 .60
3L3 A22 2p rose car & blk 1.00 .85
3L4 A22 3p deep bl & blk 1.40 1.10
3L5 A22 4p rose vio & blk 2.00 1.50
3L6 A22 6p brown & black 10.00 4.00
3L7 A22 9p slate bl & blk 3.25 3.00
3L8 A22 1sh dull blue 3.25 3.00
Nos. 3L1-3L8 (8) 22.15 14.55

South Orkneys

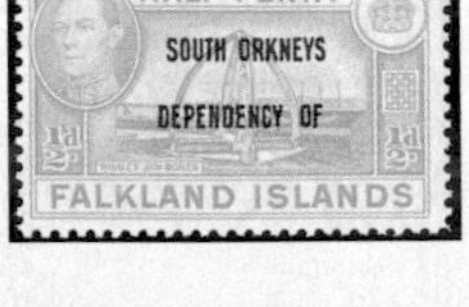

1944, Feb. 21 **Wmk. 4** ***Perf. 12***

4L1 A22 ½p green & black .55 .50
4L2 A22 1p dark vio & blk .60 .60
4L3 A22 2p rose car & blk .90 .85
4L4 A22 3p deep bl & blk 1.25 1.10
4L5 A22 4p rose vio & blk 2.00 1.50
4L6 A22 6p brown & black 10.00 3.50

4L7 A22 9p slate bl & blk 3.00 3.00
4L8 A22 1sh dull blue 3.00 2.75
Nos. 4L1-4L8 (8) 21.30 13.80

South Shetlands

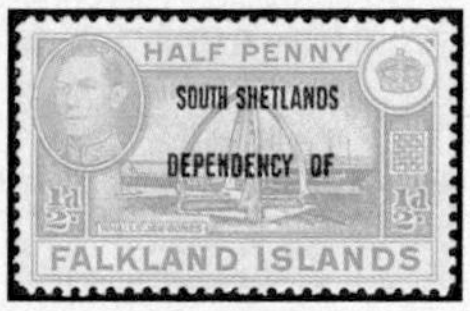

1944 Wmk. 4 *Perf. 12*
5L1 A22 ½p green & black .50 .50
5L2 A22 1p dark vio & blk .60 .60
5L3 A22 2p rose car & blk .90 .85
5L4 A22 3p deep bl & blk 1.25 1.10
5L5 A22 4p rose vio & blk 2.00 1.50
5L6 A22 6p brown & black 10.00 3.50
5L7 A22 9p slate bl & blk 3.00 3.00
5L8 A22 1sh dull blue 3.00 2.75
Nos. 5L1-5L8 (8) 21.25 13.80

FAR EASTERN REPUBLIC

ˈfär ˈē-stərn ri-ˈpə-blik

LOCATION — In Siberia east of Lake Baikal
GOVT. — Republic
AREA — 900,745 sq. mi.
POP. — 1,560,000 (approx. 1920)
CAPITAL — Chita

A short-lived independent government was established here in 1920.

100 Kopecks = 1 Ruble

Watermark

Wmk. 171 — Diamonds

Vladivostok Issue

Russian Stamps Surcharged or Overprinted:

a

b

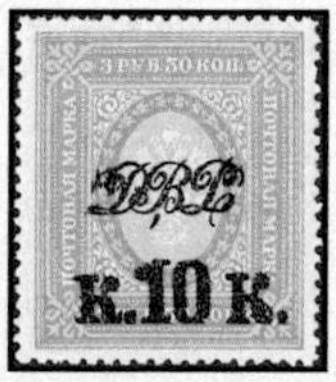

c

On Stamps of 1909-17
Perf. 14, 14½x15, 13½

1920 Unwmk.
2 A14(a) 2k green 10.00 *10.00*
3 A14(a) 3k red 10.00 *10.00*
4 A11(b) 3k on 35k red brn & grn 30.00 50.00
5 A15(a) 4k carmine 10.00 *12.00*
6 A11(b) 4k on 70k brn & org 10.00 *8.00*
8 A11(b) 7k on 15k red brn & bl 2.00 2.00
a. Inverted surcharge 100.00
b. Pair, one ovptd. "DBP" only *100.00*
9 A15(a) 10k dark blue 50.00 *55.00*
a. Overprint on back 80.00
10 A12(c) 10k on 3½r mar & lt grn 25.00 *25.00*
11 A11(a) 14k blue & rose 35.00 35.00
12 A11(a) 15k red brn & bl 25.00 25.00
13 A8(a) 20k blue & car 75.00 *100.00*
14 A11(b) 20k on 14k bl & rose 10.00 *8.00*
a. Surcharge on back 30.00
15 A11(a) 25k green & vio 25.00 15.00
16 A11(a) 35k red brn & grn 35.00 35.00
17 A8(a) 50k brn vio & grn 10.00 *12.00*
18 A9(a) 1r pale brn, dk brn & org *750.00 750.00*

On Stamps of 1917
Imperf
21 A14(a) 1k orange 10.00 *10.00*
22 A14(a) 2k gray grn 10.00 5.00
23 A14(a) 3k red 10.00 *10.00*
25 A11(b) 7k on 15k red brn & dp bl 2.00 *5.00*
a. Pair, one without surcharge *100.00*
b. Pair, one ovptd. "DBP" only *100.00*
26 A12(c) 10k on 3½r mar & lt grn 15.00 *15.00*
27 A9(a) 1r pale brn, brn & red org 20.00 *20.00*

On Stamps of Siberia 1919
Perf. 14, 14½x15
30 A14(a) 35k on 2k green 5.00 *8.00*
a. "DBP" on back 25.00 *50.00*

Imperf
31 A14(a) 35k on 2k green 25.00 25.00
32 A14(a) 70k on 1k orange 10.00 *10.00*

Counterfeit surcharges and overprints abound, including digital forgeries.

Postal Savings Stamps Surcharged for Postal Use

A1

Perf. 14½x15
Wmk. 171
35 A1(b) 1k on 5k green, *buff* 20.00 15.00
36 A1(b) 2k on 10k brown, *buff* 35.00 35.00

The letters on these stamps resembling "DBP," are the Russian initials of "Dalne Vostochnaya Respublika" (Far Eastern Republic).

Chita Issue

A2

A2a

1921 Unwmk. Typo. *Imperf.*
38 A2 2k gray green 1.50 1.50
39 A2a 4k rose 3.00 3.00
40 A2 5k claret 3.00 3.00
41 A2a 10k blue 2.50 2.50
Nos. 38-41 (4) 10.00 10.00

For overprints see Nos. 62-65.

Blagoveshchensk Issue

A3

1921 Litho. *Imperf.*
42 A3 2r red 2.75 2.00
43 A3 3r dark green 2.75 2.00
44 A3 5r dark blue 2.75 2.00
a. Tête bêche pair 30.00 *50.00*
45 A3 15r dark brown 2.75 2.00
46 A3 30r dark violet 2.75 2.00
a. Tête bêche pair 35.00 *60.00*
Nos. 42-46 (5) 13.75 10.00

Remainders of Nos. 42-46 were canceled in colored crayon or by typographed bars. These sell for half of foregoing values.

Chita Issue

A4

A5

1922 Litho. *Imperf.*
49 A4 1k orange .55 *.85*
50 A4 3k dull red .30 *.45*
51 A5 4k dp rose & buff .30 *.45*
52 A4 5k orange brown .65 .45
53 A4 7k light blue .65 *1.25*
a. Perf. 11½ 1.00 2.00
b. Rouletted 9 2.00 2.00
c. Perf. 11½x rouletted 4.00 3.00
54 A5 10k dk blue & red .40 *.65*
55 A4 15k dull rose .55 *.85*
56 A5 20k blue & red .55 *.85*
57 A5 30k green & red org .65 *1.10*
58 A5 50k black & red org 1.25 *1.75*
Nos. 49-58 (10) 5.85 *8.65*

The 4k exists with "4" omitted. Value $100.

Vladivostok Issue

Stamps of 1921 Overprinted in Red

1922 *Imperf.*
62 A2 2k gray green 35.00 25.00
a. Inverted overprint 250.00
63 A2a 4k rose 35.00 25.00
a. Inverted overprint 250.00
b. Double overprint 250.00
64 A2 5k claret 35.00 35.00
a. Inverted overprint 100.00
b. Double overprint 350.00
65 A2a 10k blue 35.00 35.00
a. Inverted overprint 100.00
Nos. 62-65 (4) 140.00 120.00

Russian revolution of Nov. 1917, 5th anniv.
Once in the setting the figures "22" of 1922 have the bottom stroke curved instead of straight. Value, each $75.

Vladivostok Issue

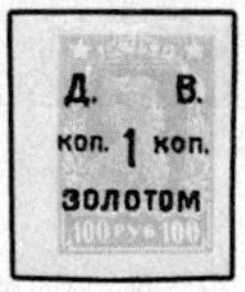

Russian Stamps of 1922-23 Surcharged in Black or Red

1923 *Imperf.*
66 A50 1k on 100r red .40 *1.00*
a. Inverted surcharge 60.00
67 A50 2k on 70r violet .40 *.75*
68 A49 5k on 10r blue (R) .40 *.75*
69 A50 10k on 50r brown .90 *1.25*
a. Inverted surcharge 150.00

Perf. 14½x15
70 A50 1k on 100r red .90 *1.25*
Nos. 66-70 (5) 3.00 *5.00*

OCCUPATION STAMPS

Issued under Occupation of General Semenov
Chita Issue

Russian Stamps of 1909-12 Surcharged:

р. 1 р.
a

2р.50к.
b

c

1920 Unwmk. *Perf. 14, 14x15½*
N1 A15 (a) 1r on 4k car 100.00 *100.00*
N2 A8 (b) 2r50k on 20k bl & car 20.00 *40.00*
N3 A14 (c) 5r on 5k claret 20.00 *50.00*
a. Double surcharge 65.00
N4 A11 (a) 10r on 70k brn & org 20.00 *40.00*
Nos. N1-N4 (4) 160.00 *230.00*

FAROE ISLANDS

ˈfar-ˌō ˈī-lənds

(The Faroes)

LOCATION — North Atlantic Ocean
GOVT. — Self-governing part of Kingdom of Denmark
AREA — 540 sq. mi.
POP. — 41,059 (1999 est.)
CAPITAL — Thorshavn

100 Ore = 1 Krone

Catalogue values for unused stamps in this country are for Never Hinged items, beginning with Scott 7.

Denmark No. 97 Handstamp Surcharged

1919, Jan. **Typo.** ***Perf. 14x14½***

1 A16 2o on 5o green 1,400. 400.00

Counterfeits of surcharge exist.
Denmark No. 88a, the bisect, was used with Denmark No. 97 in Faroe Islands Jan. 3-23, 1919.

Denmark Nos. 220, 224, 238A, 224C Surcharged in Blue or Black

Nos. 2, 5-6

No. 3

No. 4

1940-41 **Engr.** ***Perf. 13***

2 A32 20o on 1o ('41) 45.00 110.00
3 A32 20o on 5o ('41) 45.00 35.00
4 A30 20o on 15o (Bk) 60.00 22.50
5 A32 50o on 5o (Bk) 300.00 90.00
6 A32 60o on 6o (Bk) 125.00 *250.00*
Nos. 2-6 (5) 575.00 507.50
Set, never hinged 900.00

Issued during British administration.

Catalogue values for unused stamps in this section, from this point to the end of the section, are for Never Hinged items.

Map of Islands, 1673 — A1

Map of North Atlantic, 1573 — A2

West Coast, Sandoy — A3

Vidoy and Svinoy, by Eyvindur Mohr — A4

Designs: 200o, like 70o. 250o, 300o, View of Streymoy and Vagar. 450o, Houses, Nes, by Ruth Smith. 500o, View of Hvitanes and Skalafjordur, by S. Joensen-Mikines.

Unwmk.

1975, Jan. 30 **Engr.** ***Perf. 13***

7 A1 5o sepia .20 .20
8 A2 10o emer & dark blue .20 .20
9 A1 50o graysh green .20 .20
10 A2 60o brown & dark blue 1.00 1.00
11 A3 70o vio bl & slate grn 1.00 1.00
12 A2 80o ocher & dark blue .40 .50
13 A1 90o red brown 1.00 1.00
14 A2 120o brt bl & dark bl .45 .45
15 A3 200o vio bl & slate grn .45 .50
16 A3 250o multicolored .40 .45
17 A3 300o multicolored 5.50 2.25

Photo.

Perf. 12½x13

18 A4 350o multicolored .80 .80
19 A4 450o multicolored .80 .80
20 A4 500o multicolored .95 .95
Nos. 7-20 (14) 13.35 10.30

Faroe Boat — A5

Faroe Flag — A6

Faroe Mailman — A7

Perf. 12½x13, 12 (A6)

1976, Apr. 1 **Engr.; Litho. (A6)**

21 A5 125o copper red 2.00 1.25
22 A6 160o multicolored .40 .30
23 A7 800o olive 2.25 1.25
Nos. 21-23 (3) 4.65 2.80

Faroe Islands independent postal service, Apr. 1, 1976.

Motor Fishing Boat — A8

Faroese Fishing Vessels and Map of Islands: 125o, Inland fishing cutter. 160o, Modern seine fishing vessel. 600o, Deep-sea fishing trawler.

1977, Apr. 28 **Photo.** ***Perf. 14½x14***

24 A8 100o green & black 6.00 5.50
25 A8 125o carmine & black 1.75 1.75
26 A8 160o blue & black .55 .55
27 A8 600o brown & black .85 .85
Nos. 24-27 (4) 9.15 8.65

Common Snipe A9

Photogravure & Engraved

1977, Sept. 29 ***Perf. 14½x14***

28 A9 70o shown .25 .20
29 A9 180o Oystercatcher .50 .40
30 A9 250o Whimbrel .90 .65
Nos. 28-30 (3) 1.65 1.25

North Coast, Puffins — A10

Mykines Village — A11

Mykines Island: 140o, Tilled fields and coast. 150o, Aerial view. 180o, Map.

Perf. 13x13½, 13½x13

1978, Jan. 26 **Photo.**

Size: 21x28mm, 28x21mm

31 A10 100o multicolored .25 .25
32 A11 130o multicolored .35 .35
33 A11 140o multicolored .55 .55
34 A10 150o multicolored .55 .55

Size: 37x26mm

Perf. 14½x14

35 A11 180o multicolored .55 .55
Nos. 31-35 (5) 2.25 2.25

Sea Birds — A12

Old Library — A13

Lithographed and Engraved

1978, Apr. 13 ***Perf. 12x12½***

36 A12 140o Gannets .90 .90
37 A12 180o Puffins 1.25 1.25
38 A12 400o Guillemots .90 .90
Nos. 36-38 (3) 3.05 3.05

1978, Dec. 7 ***Perf. 13***

39 A13 140o shown .60 .55
40 A13 180o New library .60 *.65*

Completion of New Library Building.

Girl Guide, Tent and Fire — A14

Ram — A15

1978, Dec. 7 **Photo.** ***Perf. 13½***

41 A14 140o multicolored .70 .70

Faroese Girl Guides, 50th anniversary.

Lithographed and Engraved

1979, Mar. 19 ***Perf. 12***

42 A15 25k multicolored 6.25 5.75

Denmark No. 88a — A16

Europa: 180o, Faroe Islands No. 1.

1979, May 7 ***Perf. 12½***

43 A16 140o yellow & blue *.40 .40*
44 A16 180o rose, grn & blk *.40 .40*

Girl Wearing Festive Costume — A17

Children's Drawings and IYC Emblem: 150o, Fisherman. 200o, Two friends.

1979, Oct. 1 ***Perf. 12***

45 A17 110o multicolored .30 .30
46 A17 150o multicolored .45 .45
47 A17 200o multicolored .55 .55
Nos. 45-47 (3) 1.30 1.30

International Year of the Child.

Sea Plantain — A18

1980, Mar. 17 **Photo.** ***Perf. 12x11½***

48 A18 90o *shown* .30 .30
49 A18 110o *Glacier buttercup* .30 .30
50 A18 150o *Purple saxifrage* .45 .45
51 A18 200o *Starry saxifrage* .60 .60
52 A18 400o *Lady's mantle* 1.00 1.00
Nos. 48-52 (5) 2.65 2.65

Jakob Jakobsen (1864-1918), Linguist — A19

Coat of Arms, Virgin and Child, Gothic Pew Gable — A20

Europa: 200o, Vensel Ulrich Hammershaimb (1819-1909), theologian, linguist and folklorist.

1980, Oct. 6 **Engr.** ***Perf. 11½***

53 A19 150o dull green *.30 .30*
54 A19 200o dull red brown *.50 .50*

Photo. & Engr.

1980, Oct. 6 ***Perf. 13½***

Kirkjubour Pew Gables, 15th Century: 140o, Norwegian coat of arms, John the Baptist. 150o, Christ's head, St. Peter. 200o, Hand in halo, Apostle Paul.

55 A20 110o multicolored .25 .25
56 A20 140o multicolored .45 .45
57 A20 150o multicolored .45 .45
58 A20 200o multicolored .60 .60
Nos. 55-58 (4) 1.75 1.75

See Nos. 102-105.

A21

Sketches of Old Torshavn by Ingalzur Reyni.

1981, Mar. 2 **Engr.**

59	A21	110o dark green	.25	.25
60	A21	140o black	.45	.45
61	A21	150o dark brown	.45	.45
62	A21	200o dark blue	.55	.55
		Nos. 59-62 (4)	1.70	1.70

The Ring Dance A22

Europa: 200o, The garter dance.

1981, June 1 **Engr.** ***Perf. 13x14***

63	A22	150o pale rose & grn	*.30*	*.30*
64	A22	200o pale yel grn & dk brn	*.45*	*.45*

Rune Stones, 800-1000 AD — A23

Historic Writings: 1k, Folksong, 1846. 3k, Sheep Letter excerpt, 1298. 6k, Seal and text, 1533. 10k, Titlepage from Faeroae et Faeroa, by Lucas Jacobson Debes, library.

Photo. & Engr.

1981, Oct. 19 ***Perf. 11½***

65	A23	10o multicolored	.20	.20
66	A23	1k multicolored	.30	.30
67	A23	3k multicolored	.75	.70
68	A23	6k multicolored	1.50	1.25
69	A23	10k multicolored	2.50	2.50
		Nos. 65-69 (5)	5.25	4.95

Nos. 70-80 not assigned.

Europa 1982 — A24

1982, Mar. 15 **Engr.** ***Perf. 13½***

81	A24	1.50k Viking North Atlantic routes	.35	.35
82	A24	2k Viking house foundation	.50	.50

View of Gjogv, by Ingalvur av Reyni A25

1982, June 7 **Litho.** ***Perf. 12½x13***

83	A25	180o shown	.35	.35
84	A25	220o Hvalvik	1.40	1.10
85	A25	250o Kvivik	.50	.50
		Nos. 83-85 (3)	2.25	1.95

Ballad of Harra Paetur and Elinborg — A26

Scenes from the medieval ballad of chivalry.

1982, Sept. 27 **Litho.**

86	A26	220o multicolored	.55	.55
87	A26	250o multicolored	.65	.65
88	A26	350o multicolored	.90	.90
89	A26	450o multicolored	1.40	1.40
		Nos. 86-89 (4)	3.50	3.50

Cargo Ships A27

1983, Feb. 21 **Litho.** ***Perf. 14x14½***

90	A27	220o Arcturus, 1856	.75	.75
91	A27	250o Laura, 1882	.80	.80
92	A27	700o Thyra, 1866	2.25	2.25
		Nos. 90-92 (3)	3.80	3.80

Chessmen, by Pol i Buo (1791-1857) — A28

1983, May 2 **Engr.** ***Perf. 13 Vert.***

Booklet Stamps

93		250o King	3.00	3.00
94		250o Queen	3.00	3.00
a.		Bklt. pane of 6, 3 each #93-94	17.50	
b.	A28	Pair, #93-94	6.00	6.00

Europa 1983 — A29

Nobel Prizewinners in Medicine: 250o, Niels R. Finsen (1860-1903), ultraviolet radiation pioneer. 400o, Alexander Fleming (1881-1955), discoverer of penicillin.

1983, June 6 **Engr.** ***Perf. 12x11½***

95	A29	250o dark blue	*.55*	*.55*
96	A29	400o red brown	*.95*	*.95*

A30

1983, Sept. 19 **Litho.** ***Perf. 12½x13***

97	A30	250o Tusk	.90	.90
98	A30	280o Haddock	1.25	1.25
99	A30	500o Halibut	1.50	1.50
100	A30	900o Catfish	2.75	2.75
		Nos. 97-100 (4)	6.40	6.40

Souvenir Sheet

Traditional Costumes — A31

Various national costumes.

1983, Nov. 4 **Litho.** ***Perf. 12***

101	A31	Sheet of 3	9.25	9.25
a.-c.		250o multicolored	2.10	2.10

Nordic House Cultural Center opening. Margin shows Scandinavian flags.

Pew Gables Type of 1980

Designs: 250o, John, shield with three crowns. 300o, St. Jacob, shield with crossed keys. 350o, Thomas, shield with crossbeam. 400o, Judas Taddeus, Toulouse cross halo.

Photo. & Engr.

1984, Jan. 30 ***Perf. 14x13½***

102	A20	250o lil, pur & dk brn	.75	.75
103	A20	300o red brn, dk buff & dk brn	.90	.90
104	A20	350o blk, lt gray & dk brn	1.10	1.10
105	A20	400o ol grn, pale yel & dk brn	1.25	1.25
		Nos. 102-105 (4)	4.00	4.00

Europa (1959-84) A33

1984, Apr. 2 **Engr.** ***Perf. 13½***

106	A33	250o red	*.60*	*.60*
107	A33	500o dark blue	*1.40*	*1.40*

Sverri Patursson (1871-1960), Writer — A34

Poets: 2.50k, Joannes Patursson (1866-1946). 3k, J. H. O. Djurhuus (1881-1948). 4.50k, H.A. Djurhuus (1883-1951).

1984, May 28 **Engr.** ***Perf. 13½***

108	A34	2k olive green	.60	.60
109	A34	2.50k red	.75	.75
110	A34	3k dark blue	.90	.90
111	A34	4.50k violet	1.50	1.50
		Nos. 108-111 (4)	3.75	3.75

Faroese Smack (Fishing Boat) — A35

Perf. 12½x13, 13x12½

1984, Sept. 10 **Engr.**

112	A35	280o shown	.95	.95
113	A35	300o Fishermen, vert.	1.10	1.10
114	A35	12k Helmsman, vert.	4.00	4.00
		Nos. 112-114 (3)	6.05	6.05

Fairytale Illustrations by Elinborg Lutzen — A36

1984, Oct. 29 **Litho.** ***Perf. 13 Vert.***

Booklet Stamps

115	A36	140o Beauty of the Veils	5.00	5.00
116	A36	280o Veils, diff.	5.00	5.00
117	A36	280o Girl Shy Prince	5.00	5.00
118	A36	280o The Glass Sword	5.00	5.00
119	A36	280o Little Elin	5.00	5.00
120	A36	280o The Boy and the Ox	5.00	5.00
a.		Booklet pane of 6, #115-120	32.50	

View of Torshavn and the Forts, by Edward Dayes A37

Dayes' Landscapes, 1789: 280o, Skaeling. 550o, View Towards the North Seen from the Hills Near Torshavn in Stremoy, Faroes. 800o, The Moving Stones in Eysturoy, Faroes.

Litho. & Engr.

1985, Feb. 4 ***Perf. 13***

121	A37	250o multicolored	.75	.75
122	A37	280o multicolored	.85	.75
123	A37	550o multicolored	2.00	1.90
124	A37	800o multicolored	2.75	2.75
		Nos. 121-124 (4)	6.35	6.15

Europa 1985 — A38

Children taking music lessons.

1985, Apr. 1 **Litho.** ***Perf. 13½x14½***

125	A38	280o multicolored	*.85*	*.85*
126	A38	550o multicolored	*1.90*	*1.90*

Paintings, Faroese Museum of Art A39

Designs: 550o, Winter's Day in Nolsoy, 1959, by Steffan Danielsen (1922-76). 450o, Self-Portrait, 1952, by Ruth Smith (1913-58), vert. 280o, The Garden, Hoyvik, 1973, by Thomas Arge (1942-78).

Litho. & Engr.

1985, June 3 ***Perf. 12½***

127	A39	280o multicolored	1.25	1.25
128	A39	450o multicolored	1.75	1.75
129	A39	550o multicolored	2.50	2.10
		Nos. 127-129 (3)	5.50	5.10

Lighthouses — A40

1985, Sept. 23 **Litho.** ***Perf. 13½x14***

130	A40	270o Nolsoy, 1893	1.00	.90
131	A40	320o Thorshavn, 1909	1.40	1.25
132	A40	350o Mykines, 1909	1.50	1.40
133	A40	470o Map of locations	2.10	1.90
		Nos. 130-133 (4)	6.00	5.45

Passenger Aviation in the Faroes, 22nd Anniv. A41

Perf. 13½ Horiz.

1985, Oct. 28 **Photo.**

Booklet Stamps

134	A41	300o Douglas DC-3	2.75	2.75
135	A41	300o Fokker Friendship	2.75	2.75
136	A41	300o Boeing 737	2.75	2.75
137	A41	300o Interisland LM-IKB	2.75	2.75
138	A41	300o Helicopter Snipan	2.75	2.75
a.		Booklet pane of 5, #134-138	14.50	14.50

Skrimsla, Ancient Folk Ballad — A42

1986, Feb. 3 **Litho.** ***Perf. 12½x13***

139	A42	300o Peasant in woods	1.00	1.00
140	A42	420o Meets Giant	1.40	1.40
141	A42	550o Giant loses game	1.75	1.75

142 A42 650o Giant grants Peasant's wish 2.00 1.75
Nos. 139-142 (4) 6.15 5.90

Europa 1986 — A43

Amnesty Intl., 25th Anniv. — A44

1986, Apr. 7 Litho. *Perf. 13½*

143 A43 3k shown *1.00 1.00*
144 A43 5.50k Sea pollution *1.75 1.75*

1986, June 2 *Perf. 14x13½*

Winning design competition artwork.

145 A44 3k Olivur vid Neyst 1.00 .75
146 A44 4.70k Eli Smith 1.75 1.25
147 A44 5.50k Ranna Kunoy 2.25 1.75
Nos. 145-147 (3) 5.00 3.75

Nos. 145-146 horiz.

Souvenir Sheet

HAFNIA '87, Copenhagen — A45

Design: East Bay of Torshavn, watercolor, 1782, by Christian Rosenmeyer (1728-1802).

1986, Aug. 29 Litho. *Perf. 13x13½*

148 A45 Sheet of 3 9.00 9.00
a. 3k multicolored 3.00 3.00
b. 4.70k multicolored 3.00 3.00
c. 6.50k multicolored 3.00 3.00

Sold for 20k.

Old Stone Bridges A46

2.70k, Glyvrar on Eysturoy. 3k, Leypanagjogv on Vagar, vert. 13k, Skaelinger on Streymoy.

Perf. 13½x14½, 14½x13½

1986, Oct. 13 Engr.

149 A46 2.70k dp brown vio 1.90 1.60
150 A46 3k bluish blk 1.60 1.40
151 A46 13k gray green 3.50 3.00
Nos. 149-151 (3) 7.00 6.00

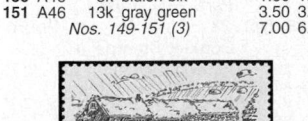

Farmhouses — A47

Traditional architecture: 300o, Depil on Borooy, 1814. 420o, Depil, diff. 470o, Frammi vio Gjonna on Streymoy, c. 1814. 650o, Frammi, diff.

1987, Feb. 9 Engr. *Perf. 13x14½*

152 A47 300o pale blue & blue 1.00 .90
153 A47 420o buff & brown 1.60 1.40
154 A47 470o pale grn & dp grn 2.00 1.60
155 A47 650o pale gray & black 2.50 2.25
Nos. 152-155 (4) 7.10 6.15

Europa 1987 — A48

Nordic House.

1987, Apr. 6 *Perf. 13x14*

156 A48 300o Exterior *.85 .85*
157 A48 550o Interior *1.90 1.60*

Fishing Trawlers A49

1987, June 1 Litho. *Perf. 14x13½*

158 A49 3k Joannes Patursson .90 .80
159 A49 5.50k Magnus Heinason 1.90 1.75
160 A49 8k Sjurdarberg 4.00 3.75
Nos. 158-160 (3) 6.80 6.30

Hestur (Horse) Island A50

Litho. & Engr.

1987, Sept. 7 *Perf. 13*

161 A50 270o Map .90 .85
162 A50 300o Seaport .70 .60
163 A50 420o Bird cliff 1.60 1.40
164 A50 470o Pasture, sheep 1.90 1.75
165 A50 550o Seashore 1.90 1.75
Nos. 161-165 (5) 7.00 6.35

Nos. 161, 163 and 165 vert.

Collages by Zacharias Heinesen A51

West Bay of Torshavn, Watercolor by Rosenmeyer — A52

1987, Oct. 16 Litho. *Perf. 13½x14*

166 A51 4.70k Eystaravag 1.75 1.60
167 A51 6.50k Vestarvag 2.25 2.00

Souvenir Sheet

Perf. 13½x13

168 A52 3k multicolored 3.50 3.50

HAFNIA '87. Sold for 4k.

Flowers — A53

Europa — A54

1988, Feb. 8 Litho. *Perf. 11½*

Granite Paper

169 A53 2.70k Bellis perennis 1.40 1.40
170 A53 3k Dactylorchis maculata .75 .75
171 A53 4.70k Potentilla erecta 2.10 2.10
172 A53 9k Pinguicula vulgaris 3.00 3.00
Nos. 169-172 (4) 7.25 7.25

1988, Apr. 11 Photo. *Perf. 11½*

Communication and transport.

173 A54 3k Satellite dish, satellite *1.10 1.10*
174 A54 5.50k Fork lift, crane, ship *1.90 1.90*

A55

A56

Writers: 270o, Jorgen-Frantz Jacobsen (1900-38). 300o, Christian Matras (b. 1900). 470o, William Heinesen (b. 1900). 650o, Hedin Bru (1901-87).

1988, June 6 Engr. *Perf. 13½*

175 A55 270o myrtle green 1.40 1.40
176 A55 300o rose lake 1.25 1.25
177 A55 470o dark blue 1.90 1.90
178 A55 650o brown black 2.10 2.10
Nos. 175-178 (4) 6.65 6.65

1988, Sept. 5 Photo. *Perf. 12*

Text, illustrations and cameo portraits of organizers: 3k, Announcement and Djoni Geil, Enok Baerentsen and H.H. Jacobsen. 3.20k, Meeting, Rasmus Effersoe, C.L. Johannesen and Samal Krakusteini. 12k, Oystercatcher and lyrics of *Now the Hour Has Come,* by poet Sverri Patursson (1871-1960), Just A. Husum, Joannes Patursson and Jens Olsen.

Granite Paper

179 A56 3k multicolored 1.25 1.25
180 A56 3.20k multicolored 1.25 1.25
181 A56 12k multicolored 4.50 4.50
Nos. 179-181 (3) 7.00 7.00

1888 Christmas meeting to preserve cultural traditions and the natl. language, cent.

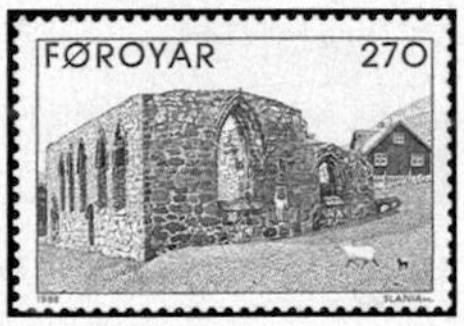

Kirkjubour Cathedral Ruins A57

270o, Exterior. 300o, Arch. 470o, Crucifixion, bas-relief. 550o, Interior.

1988, Oct. 17 Engr. *Perf. 13*

182 A57 270o dark green 1.60 1.60
183 A57 300o dark bl, vert. 1.25 1.25
184 A57 470o dark brn, vert. 1.75 1.75
185 A57 550o dark violet 1.90 1.90
Nos. 182-185 (4) 6.50 6.50

Havnar Church, Torshavn, 200th Anniv. A58

Designs: 350o, Church exterior. 500o, Crypt, vert. 15k, Bell, vert.

1989, Feb. 6 Engr. *Perf. 13*

186 A58 350o dark green 1.25 1.25
187 A58 500o dark brown 2.25 2.25
188 A58 15k deep blue 4.50 4.50
Nos. 186-188 (3) 8.00 8.00

Folk Costumes — A59

Photo. & Engr.

1989, Apr. 10 *Perf. 13½*

189 A59 350o Man 1.25 1.25
190 A59 600o Woman 2.50 2.50

Europa 1989 — A60

Wooden children's toys.

1989, Apr. 10 Photo. *Perf. 12x11½*

Granite Paper

191 A60 3.50k Boat *1.25 1.25*
192 A60 6k Horse *2.00 2.00*

Island Games, July 5-13 — A61

1989, June 5 Photo. *Perf. 12½*

Granite Paper

193 A61 200o Rowing .75 .75
194 A61 350o Handball 1.50 1.50
195 A61 600o Soccer 2.25 2.25
196 A61 700o Swimming 2.50 2.50
Nos. 193-196 (4) 7.00 7.00

A62

A63

Bird cliffs of Suduroy.

1989, Oct. 2 Engr. *Perf. 14x13½*

197 A62 320o Tvoran 1.10 1.10
198 A62 350o Skuvanes 1.40 1.40
199 A62 500o Beinisvord 1.90 1.90
200 A62 600o Asmundarstakkur 2.10 2.10
Nos. 197-200 (4) 6.50 6.50

1990, Feb. 5 Litho. *Perf. 14x13½*

Modern fish factory (filleting station).

201 A63 3.50k Unloading fish 1.00 1.00
202 A63 3.70k Cleaning and sorting 1.75 1.75
203 A63 5k Filleting 2.00 2.00
204 A63 7k Packaged frozen fish 2.25 2.25
Nos. 201-204 (4) 7.00 7.00

Europa 1990 — A64

Post offices.

1990, Apr. 9 Litho. *Perf. 13½x14*

205 A64 3.50k Gjogv *1.10 1.10*
206 A64 6k Klaksvik *2.00 2.00*

Souvenir Sheet

Recognition of the Merkid, Flag of the Faroes, by the British, 50th Anniv. — A65

Designs: a, Flag. b, Fishing trawler *Nyggjaberg,* disappeared, 1942. c, Sloop *Saana,* sunk by the Germans, 1942.

1990, Apr. 9 Photo. *Perf. 12*
Granite Paper

207 A65 Sheet of 3 4.50 4.50
a.-c. 3.50k any single 1.50 1.50

Whales A66

1990, June 6 Photo. *Perf. 11½*
Granite Paper

208 A66 320o *Mesoplodon bidens* 1.50 1.25
209 A66 350o *Balaena mysticetus* 2.00 1.75
210 A66 600o *Eubalaena glacialis* 3.25 2.00
211 A66 700o *Hyperoodon ampullatus* 5.25 2.50
Nos. 208-211 (4) 12.00 7.50

Nolsoy Island by Steffan Danielsen A67

1990, Oct. 8 Photo. *Perf. 11½*
Granite Paper

212 A67 50o shown .25 .25
213 A67 350o Coastline 1.40 1.40
214 A67 500o Town 1.75 1.75
215 A67 1000o Coastline, cliffs 3.75 3.75
Nos. 212-215 (4) 7.15 7.15

Flora and Fauna — A68

Europa — A69

1991, Feb. 4 Litho. *Perf. 13*

216 A68 3.70k Plantago lanceolata 1.40 1.40
217 A68 4k Rumex longifolius 1.40 1.40
218 A68 4.50k Amara aulica 1.75 1.75
219 A68 6.50k Lumbricus terrestris 3.00 3.00
Nos. 216-219 (4) 7.55 7.55

1991, Apr. 4 Litho. *Perf. 13*

Designs: 3.70k, Weather satellite. 6.50k, Celestial navigation.

220 A69 3.70k multicolored *1.00 1.00*
221 A69 6.50k multicolored *2.00 2.00*

Town of Torshavn, 125th Anniv. — A70

1991, Apr. 4 *Perf. 14x13½*

222 A70 3.70k Town Hall 1.25 1.25
223 A70 3.70k View of town 1.50 1.50

Birds — A71

1991, June 3 Litho. *Perf. 13½*

224 A71 3.70k Rissa tridactyla 1.50 1.50
225 A71 3.70k Sterna paradisaea 1.50 1.50
a. Bklt. pane, 3 each #224-225 9.00

Village of Saksun A72

1991, June 3

226 A72 370o shown 1.50 1.50
227 A72 650o Cliffs of Vestmanna 2.50 2.50

Samal Joensen-Mikines (1906-1979), Painter — A73

1991, Oct. 7 Litho. *Perf. 13½*

228 A73 340o Funeral Procession 1.25 1.25
229 A73 370o The Farewell 1.40 1.40
230 A73 550o Handanagarthur 2.00 2.00
231 A73 1300o Winter morning 4.50 4.50
Nos. 228-231 (4) 9.15 9.15

Mail Boats A74

1992, Feb. 10 Litho. *Perf. 13½x14*

232 A74 200o Ruth .75 .75
233 A74 370o Ritan 1.25 1.25
234 A74 550o Sigmundur 1.90 1.90
235 A74 800o Masin 2.75 2.75
Nos. 232-235 (4) 6.65 6.65

Europa A75

Designs: 3.70k, Map of North Atlantic, Viking ship. 6.50k, Map of Central Atlantic region, one of Columbus' ships.

1992, Apr. 6 Litho. *Perf. 13½x14*

236 A75 3.70k multicolored *.90 .90*
237 A75 6.50k multicolored *2.10 2.10*

Souvenir Sheet

238 A75 Sheet of 2, #236-237 *9.00 4.75*

First landing in the Americas by Leif Erikson (#236). Discovery of America by Christopher Columbus, 500th anniv. (#237).

Seals A76

1992, June 9 Litho. *Perf. 14x13½*

239 A76 3.70k Halichoerus grypus 1.50 1.50
240 A76 3.70k Phoca vitulina 1.50 1.50
a. Bklt. pane, 3 #239, 3 #240 *19.00*

Minerals — A77

1992, June 9 Photo. *Perf. 12*
Granite Paper

241 A77 370o Stilbite 1.75 1.75
242 A77 650o Mesolite 2.25 2.25

Traditional Houses A78

1992, Oct. 5 Litho. *Perf. 13½*

243 A78 3.40k Hja Glyvra Hanusi 1.25 1.25
244 A78 3.70k I Nordragotu 1.90 1.90
245 A78 6.50k Blasastova 2.25 2.25
246 A78 8k Jakupsstova 2.50 2.50
Nos. 243-246 (4) 7.90 7.90

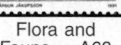

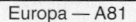

Nordic House Entertainers — A79

1993, Feb. 8 Litho. *Perf. 13½*

247 A79 400o Dancers 1.50 1.50
248 A79 400o Pianist 1.50 1.50
249 A79 400o Trio 1.50 1.50
a. Souv. sheet, #247-249, perf 12½ 4.50 4.50
Nos. 247-249 (3) 4.50 4.50

Village of Gjogv A80

1993, Apr. 5

250 A80 4k View toward sea 1.75 1.75
251 A80 4k Ravine, village 1.75 1.75
a. Booklet pane, 3 each #250-251 10.50

Europa — A81

Horses — A82

Sculptures by Hans Pauli Olsen: 4k, Movement. 7k, Reflection.

1993, Apr. 5

252 A81 4k multicolored *1.00 1.00*
253 A81 7k multicolored *2.00 2.00*

Perf. 13½x13, 13x13½

1993, June 7 Engr.

254 A82 400o shown 1.50 1.50
255 A82 20k Mare, foal, horiz. 7.50 7.50

Butterflies A83

1993, Oct. 4 Litho. *Perf. 14½*

256 A83 350o Apamea zeta 1.50 1.50
257 A83 400o Hepialus humuli 1.75 1.75
258 A83 700o Vanessa atalanta 2.40 2.40
259 A83 900o Perizoma albulata 3.25 3.25
Nos. 256-259 (4) 8.90 8.90

Fish — A84

1994, Feb. 7 Litho. *Perf. 14½*

260 A84 10o Gasterosteus aculeatus .50 .50
261 A84 4k Neocyttus helgae 1.75 1.75
262 A84 7k Salmo trutta fario 2.25 2.25
263 A84 10k Hoplostethus atlanticus 3.50 3.50
Nos. 260-263 (4) 8.00 8.00

Voyages of St. Brendan (484-577) A85

Europa: 4k, St. Brendan on island with sheep, Irish monks in boat. 7k, St. Brendan, monks sailing past volcano.

1994, Apr. 18 Litho. *Perf. 14½x14*

264 A85 4k multicolored *1.10 1.10*
265 A85 7k multicolored *2.25 1.90*
a. Miniature sheet of 2, #264-265 *4.00 4.00*

Nos. 264-265 have designers name below the design. Stamps in No. 265a do not.

See Iceland Nos. 780-781; Ireland Nos. 923-924.

Sheepdogs — A86

School of Navigation A87

Design: No. 267, Dog watching over sheep.

1994, June 6 Litho. *Perf. 13½*

266 A86 4k multicolored 1.50 1.50

Size: 39x25mm

267 A86 4k multicolored 1.50 1.50
a. Booklet pane, 3 each #266-267 9.00
Complete booklet, #267a 10.00

1994, June 6

Designs: 3.50k, Man using sextant, schooner. 7k, Ship, man at computer.

268 A87 3.50k multicolored 1.25 1.25
269 A87 7k multicolored 2.75 2.75

Brusajokil's Lay — A88

Scenes, verses of the ballad: 1k, Ship at sea. 4k, Asbjorn entering Brasajokil's cave. 6k, Ormar with cat, trolls. 7k, Ormar pulling Brusajokil's beard.

1994, Sept. 19 Litho. *Perf. 14*

270 A88 1k multicolored .30 .30
271 A88 4k multicolored 1.75 1.75
272 A88 6k multicolored 2.25 2.25
273 A88 7k multicolored 2.75 2.75
Nos. 270-273 (4) 7.05 7.05

Twelve Days of Christmas A89

#274, Goats, men, deer, hides. #275, Ducks, cattle, sheep, horses, banners, barrels.

1994, Oct. 31 Litho. *Perf. 14x13*

274 A89 4k multicolored 1.50 1.50
275 A89 4k multicolored 1.50 1.50
a. Bklt. pane, 3 each #274-275 9.00
Complete booklet, #275a 9.00

Leafhoppers — A90

Designs: 50o, Ulopa reticulata. 4k, Streptanus sordidus. 5k, Anoscopus flavostriatus. 13k, Macrosteles alpinus.

1995, Feb. 6 Litho. *Perf. 14*

276 A90 50o multicolored .25 .25
277 A90 4k multicolored 1.60 1.60
278 A90 5k multicolored 1.60 1.60
279 A90 13k multicolored 5.00 5.00
Nos. 276-279 (4) 8.45 8.45

Tourism A91

1995, Apr. 10 Litho. *Perf. 13½x14*

280 A91 4k Village of Famjin 1.50 1.50
281 A91 4k Vatnsdalur valley 1.50 1.50

Peace & Freedom A92

Europa: 4k, Island couple, "Vidar, vali og baldur." 7k, Couple looking toward sun, "Liv og livtrasir."

1995, Apr. 10 *Perf. 13x14*

282 A92 4k multicolored *1.25 1.25*
283 A92 7k multicolored *2.25 2.25*

Nordic Art — A93

Designs: 2k, Museum of Art, Torshavn. 4k, Woman, by Frimod Joensen, vert. 5.50k, Self-portrait, by Joensen, vert.

Perf. 13½x14, 14x13½

1995, June 12 Litho.

284 A93 2k multicolored .75 .75
285 A93 4k multicolored 1.50 1.50
286 A93 5.50k multicolored 2.00 2.00
Nos. 284-286 (3) 4.25 4.25

Corvus Corax A94

1995, June 12 *Perf. 13½x14*

287 A94 4k Black raven 1.60 1.60
288 A94 4k White-speckled raven 1.60 1.60
a. Booklet pane, 5 each #287-288 16.00
Complete booklet, #288a 16.00

Saint Olaf (955?-1030), Patron Saint of Faroe Islands — A95

Litho. & Engr.

1995, Sept. 12 *Perf. 13½x13*

289 A95 4k multicolored 1.60 1.60

See Aland Islands No. 119.

Early Folk Life — A95a

4k, Dairy maids carrying buckets. 6k, Peasants fleecing sheep. 15k, Schooners, saltfish being brought ashore, vert.

1995, Sept. 12 Engr. *Perf. 12½*

290 A95a 4k dark green 1.50 1.50
291 A95a 6k dark brn, vert. 2.25 2.25
292 A95a 15k dark blue 5.50 5.50
Nos. 290-292 (3) 9.25 9.25

Church of Mary Catholic Church — A96

Designs: No. 293, Stained glass window. No. 294, Exterior view of church.

1995, Nov. 9 Litho. *Perf. 13½*

293 A96 4k multicolored 1.60 1.60
294 A96 4k multicolored 1.60 1.60
a. Booklet pane, 5 ea #293-294 16.00
Complete booklet, #294a 16.00

Rocky Coastline — A97

Seaweed — A98

1996, Jan. 1 Litho. *Perf. 14*

295 A97 4.50k multicolored 1.75 1.75

1996, Feb. 12 *Perf. 15*

4k, Ptilota plumosa. 5.50k, Fucus spiralis. 6k, Ascophyllum nodosum. 9k, Laminaria hyperborea.

296 A98 4k multicolored 1.40 1.40
297 A98 5.50k multicolored 2.00 2.00
298 A98 6k multicolored 2.00 2.00
299 A98 9k multicolored 3.25 3.25
Nos. 296-299 (4) 8.65 8.65

Birds — A99

A100

1996, Apr. 15 Litho. *Perf. 14x15*

300 A99 4.50k Laxia curvirostra 1.60 1.60
301 A99 4.50k Bombycilla garrulus 1.60 1.60
a. Booklet pane, 5 each #300-301 17.00
Complete booklet, #301a 17.00

See Nos. 313-314.

1996, Apr. 15 *Perf. 15x14½, 14½x15*

Europa (Wives of Faroese Seamen): 4.50k, Woman standing beside sea coast. 7.50k, Portrait of a woman, vert.

302 A100 4.50k multicolored *1.50 1.50*
303 A100 7.50k multicolored *2.50 2.50*

A101

Nordatlantex '96 (Children's drawings): a, Boy playing with hoop, stick, by Bugvi. b, Two girls on steet, road sign, by Gudrid. c, Girl on bicycle, car on street, by Herborg.

1996, June 7 Litho. *Perf. 14½*

Souvenir Sheet of 3

304 A101 4.50k #a.-c. 5.00 5.00

A102

Litho. & Engr.

1996, June 7 *Perf. 13*

Sea bed off the Faroes.

305 A102 10k violet & multi 3.50 3.50
306 A102 16k green & multi 5.50 5.50

See Nos. 319-320, 343, 377-378.

James Kamban (b. 1913), Sculptor, Graphic Artist A103

Works of art: 4.50k, Flock of Sheep. 6.50k, Fisherman on the Way Home. 7.50k, View from Tórshavn's Old Quarter.

1996, Sept. 16 Litho. *Perf. 14*

307 A103 4.50k multicolored 1.60 1.60
308 A103 6.50k multicolored 2.40 2.40
309 A103 7.50k multicolored 2.75 2.75
Nos. 307-309 (3) 6.75 6.75

A104

Christianschurch, Klaksvík — A105

1996, Nov. 4 Litho. *Perf. 14x15*

310 A104 4.50k Exterior 1.60 1.60
311 A105 4.50k Interior, altar fresco 1.60 1.60
a. Booklet pane, 6 #310, 4 #311 16.00
Complete booklet, #311a 16.00

Christmas.

Souvenir Sheet

Reign of Queen Margaret II, 25th Anniv. — A106

Illustration reduced.

1997, Jan. 14 Litho. *Perf. 14½*

312 A106 4.50k multicolored 2.25 2.25

Bird Type of 1996

1997, Feb. 27 Litho. *Perf. 14x15*

313 A99 4.50k Pyrrhula pyrrhula 1.60 1.60
314 A99 4.50k Carduelis flammea 1.60 1.60
a. Booklet pane, 5 each #313-314 16.00 —
Complete booklet, #314a 16.00

Mushrooms — A107

Designs: 4.50k, Hygrocybe helobia. 6k, Hygrocybe chlorophana. 6.50k, Hygrocybe virginea. 7.50k, Hygrocybe psittacina.

1997, Feb. 17 *Perf. 14½*

315 A107 4.50k multicolored 1.50 1.50
316 A107 6k multicolored 2.10 2.10
317 A107 6.50k multicolored 2.40 2.40
318 A107 7.50k multicolored 2.75 2.75
Nos. 315-318 (4) 8.75 8.75

Map Type of 1996

Litho. & Engr.

1997, May 20 *Perf. 13*

319 A102 11k red & multi 3.75 3.75
320 A102 18k claret & multi 6.00 6.00

Europa — A108

Kalmar Union, 600th Anniv. — A109

Legends illustrated by William Heinesen: 4.50k, The Temptations of Saint Anthony. 7.50k, The Merman sitting at bottom of sea eating fish bait.

1997, May 20 **Litho.** *Perf. 14½*

321 A108 4.50k multicolored *1.40 1.25*
322 A108 7.50k multicolored *2.40 2.25*

1997, May 20 **Engr.** *Perf. 12½*

323 A109 4.50k deep blue violet 1.75 1.75

A110

A111

Barbara, Film Shot in Faroe Islands (Scenes from film): 4.50k, Danish theologian Poul Aggerso arriving at Faroe Islands. 6.50k, Barbara and Poul. 7.50k, Barbara with men on boat. 9k, Barbara in row boat, sailing ship.

1997, Sept. 15 **Litho.** *Perf. 14*

324 A110 4.50k multicolored 1.50 1.50
325 A110 6.50k multicolored 2.25 2.25
326 A110 7.50k multicolored 2.50 2.50
327 A110 9k multicolored 3.00 3.00
Nos. 324-327 (4) 9.25 9.25

1997, Sept. 15

Hvalvík church.

328 A111 4.50k Interior 1.60 1.60
329 A111 4.50k Exterior 1.60 1.60
a. Booklet pane, 5 each #328-329 16.00 —
Complete booklet, #329a 16.00

Birds — A112

A113

1998, Feb. 23 **Litho.** *Perf. 14x14½*

330 A112 4.50k Sturnus vulgaris 1.60 1.60
331 A112 4.50k Turdus merula 1.60 1.60
a. Bklt. pane, 5 each #330-331 16.00
Complete booklet, #331a 16.00

1998, Feb. 23 *Perf. 14*

Scenes from the Sigurd poem "Brynhild's Ballad": 4.50k, King Buole, daughter Brynhild. 6.50k, Sigurd riding through wall of fire on horseback. 7.50k, Sigurd, Brynhild together. 10k, Guthrun alone leading horse.

332 A113 4.50k multicolored 1.50 1.50
333 A113 6.50k multicolored 2.25 2.25
334 A113 7.50k multicolored 2.50 2.50
335 A113 10k multicolored 3.50 3.50
Nos. 332-335 (4) 9.75 9.75

Europa — A114

A115

1998, May 18 **Litho.** *Perf. 14*

336 A114 4.50k Parade *1.40 1.25*
337 A114 7.50k Processional *2.40 1.75*

Olavsoka, Natl. Festival of Faroe Islands.

1998, May 18 *Perf. 14½*

338 A115 7.50k multicolored 2.50 2.50

UN Declaration of Human Rights, 50th anniv.

Intl. Year of the Ocean A116

Toothed whales: 4k, Lagenorhynchus acutus. 4.50k, Orcinus orca. 7k, Tursiops truncatus. 9k, Delphinapterus leucas.

1998, May 18 *Perf. 14½x14*

339 A116 4k multicolored 1.40 1.40
340 A116 4.50k multicolored 1.50 1.50
341 A116 7k multicolored 2.40 2.40
342 A116 9k multicolored 3.00 3.00
Nos. 339-342 (4) 8.30 8.30

Map Type of 1996

Litho. & Engr.

1998, Sept. 14 *Perf. 13*

343 A102 14k multicolored 4.50 4.50

Frederickschurch A117

1998, Sept. 14 **Litho.** *Perf. 14*

344 A117 4.50k Exterior, coast-line 1.60 1.60
345 A117 4.50k Interior 1.60 1.60
a. Bklt. pane, 5 each #344-345 16.00
Complete booklet, #345a 16.00

A118

A119

Paintings by Hans Hansen (1920-70): 4.50k, Fell-field, 1966. 5.50k, Village Interior, 1965. 6.50k, Portrait of Farmer Ólavur í Utistovu from Mikladalur, 1968. 8k, Self-portrait, 1968.

Perf. 13½x14, 14x13½

1998, Sept. 14

346 A118 4.50k multi 1.50 1.50
347 A118 5.50k multi 1.90 1.90
348 A118 6.50k multi, vert. 2.25 2.25
349 A118 8k multi, vert. 2.75 2.75
Nos. 346-349 (4) 8.40 8.40

1999, Feb. 22 **Litho.** *Perf. 13½*

Birds.

350 A119 4.50k Passer domesticus 1.60 1.60
351 A119 4.50k Troglodytes troglodytes 1.60 1.60
a. Bklt. pane, 5 each #350-351 16.00
Complete booklet, #351a 16.00

Ships Named "Smyril" A120

1999, Feb. 22 *Perf. 14½x14*

352 A120 4.50k 1895 1.50 1.50
353 A120 5k 1932 1.75 1.75
354 A120 8k 1967 2.75 2.75
355 A120 13k 1975 4.50 4.50
Nos. 352-355 (4) 10.50 10.50

Northern Islands A121

1999, May 25 **Litho.** *Perf. 13½*

356 A121 50o Kalsoy .20 .20
357 A121 100o Vithoy .35 .35
358 A121 400o Svinoy 1.40 1.40
359 A121 450o Fugloy 1.50 1.50
360 A121 600o Kunoy 2.10 2.10
361 A121 800o Borthoy 3.00 3.00
Nos. 356-361 (6) 8.55 8.55

See Nos. 383-386.

Waterfalls — A122

Europa: 6k, Svartifossur. 8k, Foldarafossur.

1999, May 25 *Perf. 14x14½*

362 A122 6k multicolored *2.00 2.00*
363 A122 8k multicolored *2.75 2.75*

Abstract Paintings of Ingálvur av Reyni — A123

1999, Sept. 27 **Litho.** *Perf. 12½*

364 A123 4.50k Bygd 1.50 1.50
365 A123 6k Húsavik 2.00 2.00
366 A123 8k Reytt regn 2.75 2.75
367 A123 20k Genta 6.75 6.75
Nos. 364-367 (4) 13.00 13.00

Bible Stories — A124

1999, Sept. 27 *Perf. 14½x14*

368 A124 450o John 1:1-5 1.50 1.50
a. Booklet pane of 6 9.00
Complete booklet, #368a 9.00
369 A124 600o Luke 1:26-28 2.00 2.00
a. Booklet pane of 6 12.00
Complete booklet, #369a 12.00

See Nos. 387-388.

A125

A126

Christianity in the Faroes, 1000th Anniv.: 4.50k, Man on rocks in ocean. 5.50k, Monk with cross, man with sword. 8k, People, flags. 16k, Cross in sky.

Perf. 13½x13¼

2000, Feb. 21 **Litho.**

370 A125 4.50k multi 1.50 1.50
371 A125 5.50k multi 1.90 1.90
372 A125 8k multi 2.75 2.75
373 A125 16k multi 5.50 5.50
Nos. 370-373 (4) 11.65 11.65

2000, Feb. 21

School and: No. 374, Sanna av Skarthi, Anna Suffia Rasmussen, wives of founders. No. 375, Rasmus Rasmussen (1871-1962), Símun av Skarthi (1872-1942), school founders.

374 A126 4.50k multi 1.50 1.50
375 A126 4.50k multi 1.50 1.50
a. Bklt. pane, 4 ea #374-375 12.00
Complete booklet, #375a 12.00

Faroese Folk High School, cent.

Europa, 2000

Common Design Type

2000, May 9 **Litho.** *Perf. 13¼x13*

376 CD17 8k multi *3.00 3.00*

Map Type of 1996

Litho. & Engr.

2000, May 22 *Perf. 13¼x13*

377 A102 15k multi 5.00 5.00
378 A102 22k multi 7.50 7.50

Stampin' The Future Children's Stamp Design Contest Winners A127

Art by: 4k, Katrin Mortensen. 4.50k, Sigga Andreassen. 6k, Steingrímur Joensen. 8k, Dion Dam Frandsen.

2000, May 22 **Litho.** *Perf. 13x13¼*

379 A127 4k multi 1.40 1.40
380 A127 4.50k multi 1.50 1.50
381 A127 6k multi 2.00 2.00
382 A127 8k multi 2.75 2.75
Nos. 379-382 (4) 7.65 7.65

Island Type of 1999

2000, Sept. 18 **Litho.** *Perf. 13½*

383 A121 200o Skúvoy .70 .70
384 A121 650o Hestoy 2.25 2.25
385 A121 750o Koltur 2.50 2.50
386 A121 1000o Nólsoy 3.50 3.50
Nos. 383-386 (4) 8.95 8.95

Bible Story Type of 1999

2000, Sept. 18 **Litho.** *Perf. 13x13¼*

387 A124 4.50k Micah 5:1 1.50 1.50
a. Booklet pane of 6 9.00
Booklet, #387a 9.00
388 A124 6k John 1:14 2.00 2.00
a. Booklet pane of 6 12.00
Booklet, #388a 12.00

Pew Gables Type of 1980

Kirkjubour pew gables: 430o, St. Andrew with cross. 650o, St. Bartholomew. 800o, Unknown apostle. 18k, Unknown apostle, diff.

Photo. & Engr.

2001, Feb. 12 *Perf. 12¾x12½*

389 A20 450o multi 1.50 1.50
390 A20 650o multi 2.25 2.25
391 A20 800o multi 2.75 2.75
392 A20 18k multi 6.00 6.00
Nos. 389-392 (4) 12.50 12.50

Faroese Red Cross, 75th Anniv. A128

Designs: 4.50k, Old person. 6k, Relief worker.

2001, Feb. 12 Litho. ***Perf. 14½x14***

393	A128 4.50k multi		1.50	1.50
a.	Booklet pane of 6		9.00	
	Booklet, #393a		9.00	
394	A128 6k multi		2.00	2.00
a.	Booklet pane of 6		12.00	
	Booklet, #394a		12.00	

Souvenir Sheet

Faroe Islands Postal Service, 25th Anniv. — A129

No. 395: a, Boat for interisland mail transport, 19th cent. b, Tórshavn post office, 1906. c, Simon Pauli Poulsen (Morkabóndin), mail carrier.

Photo. & Engr.

2001, Apr. 1 ***Perf. 13x13¼***

395 A129 4.50k Sheet of 3, #a-c 4.50 4.50

Nordic Myths and Legends About Light and Darkness — A130

No. 396: a, The Death of Hogni. b, The Tree of the Year. c, The Harp. d, Gram and Grane. e, The Ballad of Nornagest. f, Gudrun's Evil Magic.

Litho. with Foil Application

2001, Apr. 1 ***Perf. 13½x13¼***

396 A130 6k Sheet of 6, #a-f 12.00 12.00

Hafnia 2001 Philatelic Exhibition, Copenhagen.

Paintings by Zacharias Heinesen A131

Designs: 4k, The Artist's Mother, 1992. 4.50k, Uti á Reyni, 1974. 10k, Ur Vágunum, 2000. 15k, Sunrise, 1975.

2001, June 11 Litho. ***Perf. 13¼x13***

397	A131 4k multi	1.40	1.40
398	A131 4.50k multi	1.50	1.50
399	A131 10k multi	3.50	3.50
400	A131 15k multi	5.00	5.00
	Nos. 397-400 (4)	11.40	11.40

Europa A132

Hydroelectric power stations: 6k, Fossáverkith. 8k, Eithisverkith.

2001, June 11 ***Perf. 13x13½***

401	A132 6k multi	*2.00*	*2.00*
402	A132 8k multi	*2.75*	*2.75*

Whales — A133

Designs: 4.50k, Physeter macrocephalus. 6.50k, Balaenoptera physalus. 9k, Balaenoptera musculus. 20k, Balaenoptera borealis.

Perf. 13¾x13¼

2001, Sept. 17 Litho.

403	A133 4.50k multi	1.50	1.50
404	A133 6.50k multi	2.25	2.25
405	A133 9k multi	3.00	3.00
406	A133 20k multi	6.75	6.75
	Nos. 403-406 (4)	13.50	13.50

Bible Stories Type of 1999

2001, Sept. 17 ***Perf. 13***

407	A124 5k Luke 2:34-35	1.75	1.75
a.	Booklet pane of 6	8.50	—
	Booklet, #407a	8.50	
408	A124 6.50k Matthew 2:18	2.25	2.25
a.	Booklet pane of 6	11.50	—
	Booklet, #408a	11.50	

Mollusks — A134

Designs: 5k, Sepiola atlantica. 7k, Modiolus modiolus. 7.50k, Polycera faeroensis. 18k, Buccinum undatum.

2002, Feb. 11 Litho. ***Perf. 13***

409	A134 5k multi	1.75	1.75
410	A134 7k multi	2.40	2.40
411	A134 7.50k multi	2.50	2.50
412	A134 18k multi	6.00	6.00
	Nos. 409-412 (4)	12.65	12.65

Portions of the designs were applied by a thermographic process producing a shiny, raised effect.

Souvenir Sheet

Viking Voyages — A135

No. 413: a, Navigation tool. b, Viking sailor on boat. c, Viking boat.

Litho. & Engr.

2002, Feb. 11 ***Perf. 13***

413 A135 6.50k Sheet of 3, #a-c 6.75 6.75

Europa A136

Designs: 6.50k, Clowns. 8k, Various circus performers.

2002, Apr. 8 Litho. ***Perf. 13¼x13½***

414	A136 6.50k multi	*2.25*	*2.25*
415	A136 8k multi	*2.75*	*2.75*

Art by Tróndur Patursson A137

Designs: 5k, Bládypi. 6.50k, Kosmiska Rúmith.

2002, Apr. 8

416	A137 5k multi	1.75	1.75
417	A137 6.50k multi	2.25	2.25
a.	Booklet pane of 8, 4 each #416-417	16.00	—
	Booklet, #417a	16.00	

Eggs and Chicks — A138

Designs: 5k, Numenius phaeopus. 7.50k, Gallinago gallinago. 12k, Haematopus ostralegus. 20k, Pluvialis apricaria.

2002, June 17 ***Perf. 14x14½***

418	A138 5k multi	1.75	1.75
419	A138 7.50k multi	2.50	2.50
420	A138 12k multi	4.00	4.00
421	A138 20k multi	6.75	6.75
	Nos. 418-421 (4)	15.00	15.00

Souvenir Sheet

Faroese Representative Council, 150th Anniv. — A139

Designs: 5k, Royal book and seal. 6.50k, Royal book, Protocol of 1852.

2002, June 17 ***Perf. 14***

422 A139 Sheet of 2, #a-b 4.00 4.00

Falco Columbarius Subaesalon — A140

Litho. & Embossed

2002, Sept. 23 ***Perf. 13¼***

423 A140 30k multi 10.00 10.00

Gota Church — A141

2002, Sept. 23 Litho. ***Perf. 12½***

424	A141 5k Exterior	1.75	1.75
425	A141 6.50k Interior	2.25	2.25
a.	Booklet pane, 5 each #424-425	20.00	—
	Booklet, #425a	20.00	

Souvenir Sheet

Intl. Council for the Exploration of the Sea, Cent. — A142

No. 426: a, Micromesistius poutassou and island. b, Exploration ship Magnus Heinason and fish.

Litho. & Engr.

2002, Sept. 23 ***Perf. 13***

426 A142 8k Sheet of 2, #a-b 5.50 5.50

See Denmark Nos. 1237-1238, Greenland Nos. 401-402.

Opening of Vagár-Streymoy Tunnel, Nov. 2002 — A143

Designs: No. 427, Wheeled tunneling machine at right. No. 428, Workers in red uniforms at left.

2003, Feb. 24 Litho. ***Perf. 13¼x13***

427	A143 5k multi	1.50	1.50
428	A143 5k multi	1.50	1.50
a.	Booklet pane, 5 each #427-428	15.00	—
	Complete booklet, #428a	15.00	

Voluspá, Ancient Norse Poem — A144

No. 429: a, Seeress Heid holding staff. b, Heid sees animal and man in vision. c, Nude man and woman. d, Scribe and horseman. e, Battle between group with swords and man with hammer. f, Horseman and warriors. g, Men, large sword. h, Longboat. i, Attack on man holding spear, fire. j, Two figures with staffs, winged serpent.

2003, Feb. 24 ***Perf. 14***

429	A144 Sheet of 10	21.00	21.00
a.-j.	6.50k Any single	2.10	2.10

Europa — A145

Poster art for Nordic House: 6.50k, Fish Tree, by Astrid Andreasen, 1991. 8k, Ceramics by Guthrith Poulsen, 1997.

2003, Apr. 14 *Perf. 13½x13¼*
430 A145 6.50k multi *1.90 1.90*
431 A145 8k multi *2.25 2.25*

Children's Songs — A146

No. 432: a, Woman playing hopscotch (26x44mm). b, Boy on rocks, moon (26x44mm). c, Girl with missing teeth (26x26mm). d, Boy with toy sailboat (26x26mm). e, Cat, horse and girl (26x26mm). f, Butterfly and fly (26x26mm). g, Girl in bed, boy with stars (44x26mm). h, Cat on stairs, mouse (26x36mm). i, Man playing drums (26x26mm). j, King and queen in longboat (44x26mm).

Perf. 13¼, 13¼x13¼x13¼x14 (#432g, 432j), 13¼x14 (#432h)

2003, Apr. 14
432 A146 Sheet of 10 15.00 15.00
a.-j. 5k Any single 1.50 1.50

Small Towns A147

2003, June 10 Litho. *Perf. 13x13¼*
433 A147 5k Bour 1.60 1.60
434 A147 5k Gásadalur 1.60 1.60

Communities With Post Offices 100 Years Old — A148

No. 435: a, Fuglafjorthur. b, Strendur. c, Sandur. d, Eithi. e, Vestmanna. f, Vágur. g, Mithvágur. h, Hvalba.

2003, June 10 *Perf. 13¼x13*
435 A148 Sheet of 8 13.00 13.00
a.-h. 5k Any single 1.60 1.60

Theologians — A149

Designs: 5k, Jesper Rasmussen Brochmand (1585-1652). 6.50k, Thomas Kingo (1634-1703).

2003, Sept. 22 *Perf. 13x13¼*
436 A149 5k multi 1.50 1.50
437 A149 6.50k multi 2.00 2.00
a. Booklet pane, 5 each #436-437 17.50 —
Complete booklet, #437a 17.50

Souvenir Sheet

Dancing in the Inn's Smoking Room, by Emil Krause — A150

Litho. & Engr.

2003, Sept. 22 *Perf. 12¼*
438 A150 25k multi 9.00 9.00

100th Faroese stamp engraved by Czeslaw Slania.

Islands Type of 1999

2004, Jan. 26 Litho. *Perf. 13½*
439 A121 550o Stóra Dímun 1.90 1.90
440 A121 700o Lítla Dímun 2.40 2.40

Suthuroy Island — A151

No. 441: a, Sigmundargjogv, Sandvik. b, Fiskieithi, Hvalba. c, A Hamri, Frothba. d, Tjaldavíkshólmur, Oravík. e, Fossurin Stóri, Fámjin. f, Hovsfjorthur, Hov. g, I Eystrum, Porkeri. h, A Okrum. i, I Horg, Sumba. j, I Akrabergi.

2004, Jan. 26 *Perf. 13x13¼*
441 A151 5k Sheet of 10, #a-j 17.00 17.00

1854 Cruise of Yacht "Maria" — A152

No. 442: a, Gáshólmur and Tindhólmur. b, Framvith "Diamantunum." c, Hús av tí betra slagnum. d, Mylingur sunnanífrá. e, Mylingur northanífrá. f, Kalsoyggin northanífrá. g, Raetha teir infoddu. h, Sunnari endi av Kunoynni.

2004, Mar. 26 Litho. *Perf. 13*
442 A152 6.50k Sheet of 8, #a.-h. 18.00 18.00

Souvenir Sheet

Norse Gods — A153

No. 443: a, Thor, in boat, fighting Midgard serpent. b, Ran in fishing net.

2004, Mar. 26
443 A153 6.50k Sheet of 2, #a.-b. 4.50 4.50

Souvenir Sheet

Wedding of Crown Prince Frederik and Mary Donaldson — A154

Litho. & Photo.

2004, May 14 *Perf. 13¼*
444 A154 Sheet of 2 + central label 4.00 4.00
a. 5k Couple facing right 1.60 1.60
b. 6.50k Couple facing left 2.10 2.10

Soccer Organization Centenaries A155

Soccer players and emblems of: 5k, Klaksvík and Tórshavn teams. 6.50k, FIFA (Fédération Internationale de Football Association).

2004, May 24 Litho. *Perf. 13¼x13*
445 A155 5k multi 1.75 1.75
446 A155 6.50k multi 2.25 2.25
a. Booklet pane, 4 each #445-446 16.00 —
Complete booklet, #446a 16.00

Europa A156

Designs: 6.50k, Tourists in gorge, Hestur. 8k, Tourists at shore, Stóra Dímun.

2004, May 24 *Perf. 13x13¼*
447 A156 6.50k multi *2.10 2.10*
448 A156 8k multi *2.60 2.60*

Churches A157

2004, Sept. 20 Litho. *Perf. 13¼x13*
449 A157 5.50k Vágur 1.90 1.90
450 A157 7.50k Tvoroyri 2.50 2.50
a. Booklet pane, 4 each #449-450 18.00 —
Complete booklet, #450a 18.00

Poems by Janus Djurhuus (1881-1948) — A158

No. 451: a, Atlantis. b, Grímur Kamban. c, Gandkvaethi Tróndar. d, Til Foroya I-III. e, Mín sorg. f, Loki. g, I búri og Slatur. h, Heimferth Nólsoyar Páls. i, Móses á Sinai fjalli. j, Cello.

2004, Sept. 20 *Perf. 13*
451 A158 Sheet of 10 26.00 26.00
a.-j. 7.50k Any single 2.60 2.60

Souvenir Sheet

Life of the Vikings — A159

No. 452: a, Men tending sheep. b, Men with farm implements. c, Women weaving and woman milking cow.

Litho. & Engr.

2005, Feb. 7 *Perf. 13*
452 A159 Sheet of 3 8.00 8.00
a.-c. 7.50k Any single 2.60 2.60

Miniature Sheet

Vágar Island — A160

No. 453: a, Víkar. b, Gásadalur. c, Bour. d, Slaettanes. e, Kvígandalsá. f, Sorvágur. g, Sandavágur. h, Vatnsoyrar. i, Fjallavatn. j, Mithvágur.

2005, Feb. 7 Litho. *Perf. 13x13¼*
453 A160 Sheet of 10 19.00 19.00
a.-j. 5.50k Any single 1.90 1.90

Lepus Timidus — A161

2005, Apr. 18 *Perf. 13¼x13½*
454 A161 5.50k shown 1.90 1.90
455 A161 5.50k Brown fur 1.90 1.90
a. Booklet pane, 4 each #454-455 15.50 —
Complete booklet, #455a 15.50

Europa — A162

Various traditional foods with: 7.50k, Brown panel. 10k, Green panel.
Illustration reduced.

2005, Apr. 18 *Perf. 13¼x13*
456 A162 7.50k multi *2.60 2.60*
457 A162 10k multi *3.50 3.50*

Worldwide Fund for Nature (WWF) A163

Petrels: 8.50k, Oceanodroma leucorhoa. 9k, Hydrobates pelagicus. 12k, Oceanodroma leucorhoa on ground. 20k, Hydrobates pelagicus on ground.

2005, June 6 *Perf. 13*
458 A163 8.50k multi 2.75 2.75
459 A163 9k multi 3.25 3.25
460 A163 12k multi 4.25 4.25
461 A163 20k multi 6.75 6.75
Nos. 458-461 (4) 17.00 17.00

Miniature Sheet

Landscapes by Jógvan Waagstein (1879-1949) — A164

No. 462: a, Path and wall at LL, denomination in red, year date in black in grass. b, Path and wall at LL, denomination in white, year date in black on wall. c, Stone hut at left, denomination in red, year date in black. d, Path at right, denomination in red, year date in black. e, Two large rocks at right, denomination in red, year date in black. f, Rocks at LL, denomination in red, year date in white. g, Path at center, denomination in white, year date in black on path. h, Buildings at LL, denomination in red, year date in black in path. i, Churches, denomination in white, year date in black in water.

2005, Sept. 19 Litho. *Perf. 14x14¼*
462 A164 Sheet of 9 22.00 22.00
a.-i. 7.50k Any single 2.40 2.40

End of British Occupation In World War II, 60th Anniv. A165

Soldiers with: 5.50k, Arms. 9k, Children.

2005, Sept. 19 *Perf. 14*
463 A165 5.50k blue & blk 2.00 2.00
464 A165 9k yel & blk 3.25 3.25

Christmas — A166

Ballads: 5.50k, Jólavísan. 7.50k, Rudisar Vísa.

2005, Nov. 7 *Perf. 13½x13¼*
465 A166 5.50k multi 1.75 1.75
466 A166 7.50k multi 2.40 2.40
466a Booklet pane, 5 each #465-466 16.00 —
Complete booklet, #466a 16.00

Villages A167

2006, Feb. 13 Litho. *Perf. 13¾*
467 A167 7k Sythrugota 2.25 2.25
468 A167 12k Fuglafjorthur 4.25 4.25
469 A167 20k Leirvík 6.75 6.75
Nos. 467-469 (3) 13.25 13.25

Miniature Sheet

Fish — A168

No. 470: a, Himantolophus groenlandicus. b, Gonostoma elongatum. c, Sebastes mentella. d, Neoraja caerulea. e, Rhinochimaera atlantica. f, Linophryne lucifer. g, Ceratias holboelli. h, Lampris guttatus. i, Argyropelecus olfersi. j, Lophius piscatorius.

2006, Feb. 13 *Perf. 14*
470 A168 Sheet of 10 19.00 19.00
a.-j. 5.50k Any single 1.90 1.90

Souvenir Sheet

Norse Folklore — A169

No. 471: a, Norns surrounding sleeping child. b, Sea ghost.

2006, Mar. 29 *Perf. 13*
471 A169 7.50k Sheet of 2, #a-b 5.00 5.00

Miniature Sheet

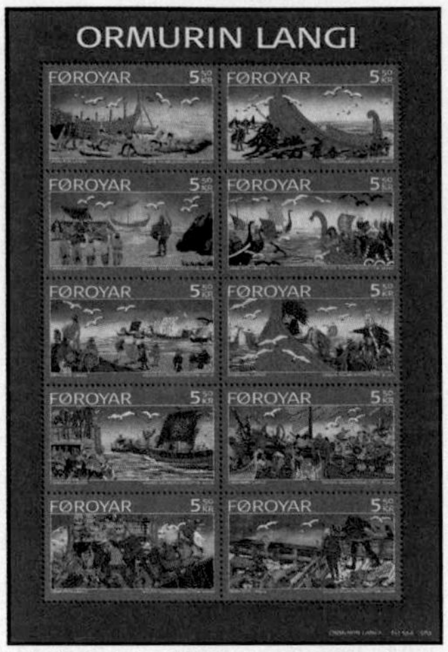

Ballad of the Long Serpent, by Jens Christian Djurhuus — A170

No. 472: a, Building of ship. b, Launch of ship. c, King on throne. d, King's fleet at sea (brown ship at LL, blue ship at LR). e, King and sailors on shore. f, King pointing. g, Ship with red sail at R. h, Battle scene (injured men falling into water). i, Battle scene (men with shields jumping from ship to ship). j, Dead men on ship's deck.

2006, Mar. 29 *Perf. 13¼x13*
472 A170 Sheet of 10 18.00 18.00
a.-j. 5.50k Any single 1.75 1.75

Opening of Northoy Tunnel — A171

Tunnel and: No. 473, Fish. No. 474, Canoe.

2006, June 12 *Perf. 13¼*
473 A171 5.50k multi 1.90 1.90
474 A171 5.50k multi 1.90 1.90
a. Booklet pane, 4 each #473-474 15.50 —
Complete booklet, #474a 15.50

Europa A172

2006, June 12 *Perf. 13¾*
475 A172 7.50k shown 2.60 2.60
476 A172 10k Hands, diff. 3.50 3.50

Miniature Sheet

Sandoy Island — A173

No. 477: a, Sunnan fyri Skopun. b, Dalur. c, Soltuvík. d, Skálavík. e, Skopun. f, Sandur. g, Skarvanes. h, Húsavík.

2006, Sept. 18 Litho. *Perf. 13x13¼*
477 A173 Sheet of 8 20.00 20.00
a.-h. 7.50k Any single 2.50 2.50

Sandur Church A174

Designs: 5.50k, Building exterior, steeple cross. 7.50k, Interior.

2006, Sept. 18 *Perf. 14*
478 A174 5.50k multi 1.90 1.90
479 A174 7.50k multi 2.60 2.60
a. Booklet pane, 4 each #478-479 18.00 —
Complete booklet, #479a 18.00

Wave Energy A175

2007, Feb. 12 Litho. *Perf. 12½x13*
480 A175 7.50k multi 2.60 2.60

Art From 1838 La Recherche Expedition A176

Art by Barthélemy Lauvergne: 5.50k, La Recherche off Nólsoy. 7.50k, Skaelingsfjall.

2007, Feb. 12
481 A176 5.50k multi 1.90 1.90
482 A176 7.50k multi 2.60 2.60
a. Booklet pane, 4 each #481-482 18.00 —
Complete booklet, #482a 18.00

Miniature Sheet

Legend of the Seal Woman — A177

No. 483: a, Man, head of white seal. b, Woman and seals in ring. c, Man, nude woman, seals. d, Man and nude woman seated on chest. e, Ship and two seals. f, Children, seal woman nursing child. g, Seal woman and man. h, Sleeping man and seal woman with hands open. i, Man and dead seals. j, Seal woman.

2007, Feb. 12 *Perf. 14*
483 A177 Sheet of 10 19.00 19.00
a.-j. 5.50k Any single 1.90 1.90

Miniature Sheet

The Old Man and His Sons, Novel by Hethin Brú — A178

No. 484: a, Ketil cutting whale's throat. b, Men carrying injured Klávus on log. c, Kálvur and fiancee, Klávusardóttir with pot and kettle.

d, Ketil and Kálvur in fishing boat. e, Ketil's wife arguing with daughter-in-law. f, Ketil catching flying northern fulmars. g, Kálvur and stone fence. h, Ketil, Kálvur and cow.

2007, Apr. 10 Litho. *Perf. 13x12½*
484 A178 Sheet of 8 22.00 22.00
a.-h. 7.50k Any single 2.75 2.75

Europa — A179

Design: 5.50k, Scout holding bird. 10k, Tent.

2007, Apr. 10
485 A179 5.50k multi 2.00 2.00
486 A179 10k multi 3.75 3.75

Scouting, cent.

Souvenir Sheet

Bible Translators — A180

No. 487: a, Jákup Dahl (1878-1944). b, Kristian O. Videro (1906-91). c, Victor Danielsen (1894-1961).

2007, June 11 Litho. *Perf. 13x12½*
487 A180 Sheet of 3 6.00 6.00
a.-c. 5.50k Any single 2.00 2.00

Domesticated Birds — A181

Designs: 9k, Chickens and rooster. 20k, Ducks. 25k, Geese.

2007, June 11 *Perf. 12½x13*
488 A181 9k multi 3.25 3.25
489 A181 20k multi 7.25 7.25
490 A181 25k multi 9.25 9.25
Nos. 488-490 (3) 19.75 19.75

Hoyvík — A182

Illustration reduced.

2007, Oct. 1 *Perf. 13½*
491 A182 7.50k multi 2.75 2.75

Wooden Religious Statues of Kirkjubour Cathedral — A183

2007, Oct. 1 *Perf. 13x12½*
492 A183 5.50k Jesus 2.10 2.10
493 A183 7.50k Mary 2.75 2.75
a. Booklet pane, 4 each #492-493 19.50 —
Complete booklet, #493a 19.50

Miniature Sheet

Stone Fence and Wildlife — A184

No. 494: a, Bird, worm. b, Two red beetles, fern. c, Mouse, purple flowers. d, Mosquito, pink flowers. e, Large black and white bird, dandelions. f, Bird with black wings, buttercups. g, Earwigs, grass. h, Bird and eggs.

2007, Oct. 1 *Perf. 13½x14¼*
494 A184 Sheet of 8 17.00 17.00
a.-h. 5.50k Any single 2.10 2.10

Klaksvík, Cent. — A185

Litho. & Embossed

2008, Feb. 11 *Perf. 14*
495 A185 5.50k multi 2.25 2.25

Tinganes A186

2008, Feb. 11 Litho. *Perf. 13¼*
496 A186 14k multi 5.75 5.75

Hoydalar Tuberculosis Sanatorium, Cent. — A187

Lungs and: 5.50k, Patients, buildings. 9k, Dr. Vilhelm Magnussen examining patient, child.

2007, Feb. 11 *Perf. 12½x13*
497 A187 5.50k multi 2.25 2.25
498 A187 9k multi 3.75 3.75
a. Booklet pane, 4 each #497-498 24.00
Complete booklet, #498a 24.00

Miniature Sheet

Prints by Elinborg Lützens — A188

No. 499: a, Houses below mountain. b, Milk maids (30x30mm). c, Houses. d, Underwater scene. e, Chicken (30x30mm). f, Person and bird near wooden bucket.

2008, Feb. 11 *Perf. 13¼*
499 A188 Sheet of 6 24.00 24.00
a.-f. 10k Any single 4.00 4.00

Souvenir Sheet

Mythical Places — A189

No. 500: a, Alvheyggur. b, Klovningasteinur.

2008, Mar. 27 Litho. *Perf. 12½x13*
500 A189 Sheet of 2 6.50 6.50
a.-b. 7.50k Either single 3.25 3.25

Caltha Palustris A190

2008, May 19 *Perf. 13¼*
501 A190 30k multi 13.00 13.00

Europa A191

Designs: 550o, Heart and "Teg." 750o, Posthorn with "@" symbol and "Hey."

2008, May 19 *Perf. 13¼x13*
502 A191 550o multi 2.25 2.25
503 A191 750o multi 3.25 3.25

Miniature Sheet

Famous People — A192

No. 504: a, Niels Winther (1822-92), politician and newspaper publisher. b, Súsanna Helena Patursson (1864-1916), writer and newspaper publisher. c, Rasmus C. Effersoe (1857-1916), writer and newspaper editor. d, Jógvan Poulsen (1854-1941), religious and school book writer. e, Frithrikur Petersen (1853-1917), poet. f, Andreas Christian Evensen (1874-1917), magazine publisher and school book writer.

2008, May 19 *Perf. 13½x13¼*
504 A192 Sheet of 6 14.00 14.00
a.-f. 5.50k Any single 2.25 2.25

Miniature Sheet

Ferns — A193

No. 505: a, Gymnocarpium dryopteris. b, Polypodium vulgare. c, Dryopteris dilatata. d, Asplenium adiantum-nigrum. e, Athyrium filix-femina. f, Dryopteris filix-mas. g, Cystopteris fragilis. h, Phegopteris connectilis. i, Polystichum lonchitis. j, Asplenium trichomanes.

2008, Sept. 22 Litho. *Perf. 13x13½*
505 A193 Sheet of 10 30.00 30.00
a.-j. 800o Any single 3.00 3.00

Christmas — A194

2008, Sept. 22 *Perf. 13x12½*
506 A194 6k shown 2.25 2.25
507 A194 10k Wooden cross 3.75 3.75
a. Booklet pane of 8, 4 each #506-507 24.00 —
Complete booklet, #507a 24.00

FERNANDO PO

fər-ˈnan-ˌdō ˈpō

LOCATION — An island in the Gulf of Guinea off west Africa.
GOVT. — Former province of Spain
AREA — 800 sq. mi.
POP. — 62,612 (1960)
CAPITAL — Santa Isabel

Together with the islands of Elobey, Annobon and Corisco, Fernando Po came under the administration of Spanish Guinea. Postage stamps of Spanish Guinea were used until 1960.

The provinces of Fernando Po and Rio Muni united Oct. 12, 1968, to form the Republic of Equatorial Guinea.

100 Centimos = 1 Escudo = 2.50 Pesetas
100 Centimos = 1 Peseta
1000 Milesimas = 100 Centavos = 1 Peso (1882)

Catalogue values for unused stamps in this country are for Never Hinged items, beginning with Scott 181 in the regular postage section and Scott B1 in the semi-postal section.

Isabella II — A1

Alfonso XII — A2

1868 Unwmk. Typo. *Perf. 14*

1	A1	20c brown	500.00	140.00
a.		20c red brown	525.00	140.00

No. 1 is valued in the grade of fine, as illustrated. Examples with very fine centering are uncommon and sell for more.
Forgeries exist.

1879

Centimos de Peseta

2	A2	5c green	60.00	15.00
3	A2	10c rose	30.00	15.00
4	A2	50c blue	105.00	15.00
		Nos. 2-4 (3)	195.00	45.00

1882-89

Centavos de Peso

5	A2	1c green	9.50	5.50
6	A2	2c rose	18.00	8.75
7	A2	5c gray blue	60.00	12.00
8	A2	10c dk brown ('89)	82.50	6.75
		Nos. 5-8 (4)	170.00	33.00

Nos. 5-7 Handstamp Surcharged Type "a" in Blue, Black or Violet

a

1884-95

9	A2	50c on 1c green ('95)	95.00	19.00
11	A2	50c on 2c rose	29.00	6.00
12	A2	50c on 5c blue ('87)	105.00	25.00
		Nos. 9-12 (3)	229.00	50.00

Values above are for examples surcharged in black. Stamps surcharged in violet or blue are worth about 25% more.
Inverted and double surcharges exist. No. 12 exists overprinted in carmine. Value $90.

King Alfonso XIII — A4

1894-97 *Perf. 14*

13	A4	⅛c slate ('96)	20.00	2.75
14	A4	2c rose ('96)	14.50	2.25
15	A4	5c blue grn ('97)	15.00	2.25
16	A4	6c dk violet ('96)	12.00	2.75
17	A4	10c blk vio ('94)	375.00	100.00
18	A4	10c lake ('95)	45.00	8.25
19	A4	10c org brn ('96)	9.50	2.25
20	A4	12½c dk brown ('96)	10.50	2.75
21	A4	20c slate bl ('96)	10.50	2.75
22	A4	25c claret ('96)	21.00	2.75
		Nos. 13-22 (10)	533.00	128.75

Stamps of 1894-97 Handstamped in Blue, Black or Red

b

c

Type "b" Surcharge

1896-98

23	A4	5c on 2c rose (Bl)	40.00	5.75
24	A4	5c on 10c brn vio (Bl)	120.00	16.00
25	A4	5c on 12½c brn (Bl)	27.50	4.75
a.		Black surcharge	27.50	4.75
		Nos. 23-25 (3)	187.50	26.50

Type "c" Surcharge

26	A4	5c on ⅛c slate (Bk)	25.00	6.25
27	A4	5c on 2c rose (Bl)	25.00	6.25
a.		Black surcharge	25.00	6.25
28	A4	5c on 5c green (R)	110.00	20.00
29	A4	5c on 6c dk vio (R)	19.00	12.50
a.		Violet surcharge	20.00	14.00
30	A4	5c on 10c org brn (Bk)	135.00	25.00
31	A4	5c on 12½c brn (R)	55.00	10.00
32	A4	5c on 20c sl bl (R)	30.00	9.50
33	A4	5c on 25c claret (Bk)	30.00	10.00
a.		Blue surcharge	30.00	12.00
		Nos. 26-33 (8)	429.00	99.50

Exist surcharged in other colors.

Type "a" Surch. in Blue or Black

1898-99

34	A4	50c on 2c rose	77.50	9.50
35	A4	50c on 10c brn vio	175.00	27.50
36	A4	50c on 10c lake	190.00	27.50
37	A4	50c on 10c org brn	175.00	27.50
38	A4	50c on 12½c brn (Bk)	165.00	18.00

The "a" surch. also exists on ⅛c, 5c & 25c. Values, $325, $225 and $210, respectively.

Arms

A5 A6

Revenue Stamps Handstamped in Blue

1897-98 *Imperf.*

39	A5	5c on 10c rose	28.00	12.50
40	A6	10c rose	24.00	11.00

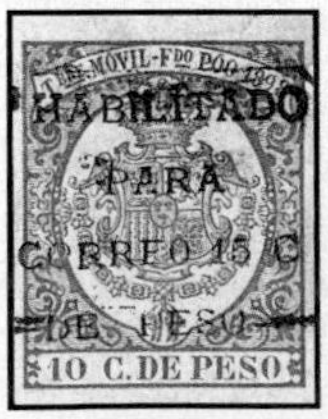

A7

A8

A9

Arms — A9a

Revenue Stamps Handstamped in Black or Red

1899 *Imperf.*

41	A7	15c on 10c green	42.50	22.50
a.		Blue surcharge, vertical	37.50	20.00
42	A8	10c on 25c green	115.00	62.50
43	A9	15c on 25c green	185.00	115.00
43A	A9a	15c on 25c green (R)	*1,700.*	*1,050.*
b.		Black surcharge	*1,700.*	*1,050.*

Surcharge on No. 41 is either horizontal, inverted or vertical.
On No. 42 "CORREOS" is ovptd. in red.

King Alfonso XIII — A10

Double-lined shaded letters at sides.

1899 *Perf. 14*

44	A10	1m orange brn	2.00	.40
45	A10	2m orange brn	2.00	.40
46	A10	3m orange brn	2.00	.40
47	A10	4m orange brn	2.00	.40
48	A10	5m orange brn	2.00	.40
49	A10	1c black vio	2.00	.40
50	A10	2c dk blue grn	2.00	.40
51	A10	3c dk brown	2.00	.40
52	A10	4c orange	12.00	1.00
53	A10	5c carmine rose	2.00	.40
54	A10	6c dark blue	2.00	.40
55	A10	8c gray brn	7.50	.40
56	A10	10c vermilion	4.75	.40
57	A10	15c slate grn	4.75	.40
58	A10	20c maroon	12.50	1.00
59	A10	40c violet	87.50	17.50
60	A10	60c black	87.50	17.50
61	A10	80c red brown	87.50	17.50
62	A10	1p yellow grn	325.00	85.00
63	A10	2p slate blue	325.00	87.50
		Nos. 44-63 (20)	974.00	232.20

Nos. 44-63 exist imperf. Value for set, $1,275.
See Nos. 66-85. For surcharges see Nos. 64-65, 88-88B.

1900

Surcharged type "a"

64	A10	50c on 20c maroon	15.00	2.25
a.		Blue surcharge	30.00	4.50

Surcharged type "b"

64B	A10	5c on 20c maroon	200.00	10.00

Surcharged type "c"

65	A10	5c on 20c maroon	8.50	2.25
		Nos. 64-65 (3)	223.50	14.50

Dated "1900"

Solid letters at sides.

1900

66	A10	1m black	3.00	.50
67	A10	2m black	3.00	.50
68	A10	3m black	3.00	.50
69	A10	4m black	3.00	.50
70	A10	5m black	3.00	.50
71	A10	1c green	3.00	.50
72	A10	2c violet	3.00	.50
73	A10	3c rose	3.00	.50
74	A10	4c black brn	3.00	.50
75	A10	5c blue	3.00	.50
76	A10	6c orange	3.00	.50
77	A10	8c bronze grn	3.00	.50
78	A10	10c claret	3.00	.50
79	A10	15c dk violet	3.00	.50
80	A10	20c olive brn	3.00	.50
81	A10	40c brown	7.75	2.25
82	A10	60c green	16.50	2.50
83	A10	80c dark blue	17.50	3.75
84	A10	1p red brown	100.00	30.00
85	A10	2p orange	175.00	62.50
		Nos. 66-85 (20)	361.75	108.50
		Set, never hinged	525.00	

Nos. 66-85 exist imperf. Value, set $1,750.

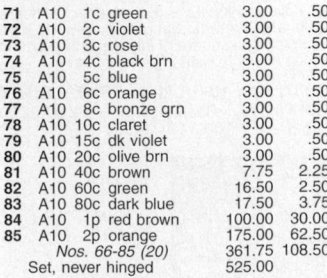

A11

A12

Revenue Stamps Overprinted or Surcharged with Handstamp in Red or Black

1900 *Imperf.*

86	A11	10c blue (R)	35.00	16.00
87	A12	5c on 10c blue	90.00	37.50
		Set, never hinged	165.00	

Nos. 52 and 80 Surcharged type "a" in Violet or Black

1900

88	A10	50c on 4c orange (V)	14.00	4.00
a.		Green surcharge	22.50	12.00
88B	A10	50c on 20c ol brn	14.00	3.50
		Set, never hinged	37.50	

A13

A14

1901 *Perf. 14*

89	A13	1c black	2.75	.90
90	A13	2c orange brn	2.75	.90
91	A13	3c dk violet	2.75	.90
92	A13	4c lt violet	2.75	.90
93	A13	5c orange red	1.75	.90
94	A13	10c violet brn	1.75	.90
95	A13	25c dp blue	1.75	.90
96	A13	50c claret	2.75	.90
97	A13	75c dk brown	2.00	.90
98	A13	1p blue grn	62.50	6.00
99	A13	2p red brown	39.00	9.00
100	A13	3p olive grn	39.00	12.00
101	A13	4p dull red	38.00	12.00
102	A13	5p dk green	47.50	12.00
103	A13	10p buff	105.00	35.00
		Nos. 89-103 (15)	352.00	94.10
		Set, never hinged	625.00	

Dated "1902"

1902

Control Numbers on Back

104	A13	5c dk green	2.25	.40
105	A13	10c slate	2.40	.45
106	A13	25c claret	5.50	.85
107	A13	50c violet brn	13.00	2.75
108	A13	75c lt violet	13.00	2.75
109	A13	1p car rose	16.00	3.50
110	A13	2p olive grn	34.00	8.00
111	A13	5p orange red	50.00	17.50
		Nos. 104-111 (8)	136.15	36.20
		Set, never hinged	200.00	

Exist imperf. Value for set, $850.

1903 *Perf. 14*

Control Numbers on Back

112	A14	¼c dk violet	.45	.25
113	A14	½c black	.45	.25
114	A14	1c scarlet	.45	.25
115	A14	2c dk green	.45	.30
116	A14	3c blue grn	.45	.30
117	A14	4c violet	.45	.30
118	A14	5c rose lake	.50	.30
119	A14	10c orange buff	.60	.45
120	A14	15c blue green	2.50	1.00
121	A14	25c red brown	2.75	1.25
122	A14	50c black brn	4.50	2.00
123	A14	75c carmine	16.50	3.50
124	A14	1p dk brown	25.00	6.00
125	A14	2p dk olive grn	32.50	7.50
126	A14	3p claret	32.50	7.50
127	A14	4p dark blue	40.00	12.50
128	A14	5p dp dull blue	60.00	16.00
129	A14	10p dull red	130.00	27.50
		Nos. 112-129 (18)	350.05	87.15
		Set, never hinged	500.00	

Dated "1905"

1905

Control Numbers on Back

136	A14	1c dp violet	.40	.30
137	A14	2c black	.40	.30
138	A14	3c vermilion	.40	.30
139	A14	4c dp green	.40	.30
140	A14	5c blue grn	.45	.35
141	A14	10c violet	1.60	.75
142	A14	15c car lake	1.60	.75
143	A14	25c orange buff	12.50	2.25
144	A14	50c green	8.00	2.75
145	A14	75c red brown	11.00	7.50
146	A14	1p dp gray brn	12.50	7.50
147	A14	2p carmine	20.00	12.50
148	A14	3p deep brown	32.50	14.00
149	A14	4p bronze grn	40.00	18.00
150	A14	5p claret	62.50	25.00
151	A14	10p deep blue	90.00	35.00
		Nos. 136-151 (16)	294.25	127.55
		Set, never hinged	525.00	

King Alfonso XIII — A15

1907

Control Numbers on Back

152	A15	1c blue black	.25	.20
153	A15	2c car rose	.25	.20
154	A15	3c dp violet	.25	.20
155	A15	4c black	.25	.20
156	A15	5c orange buff	.30	.20
157	A15	10c maroon	1.75	.75
158	A15	15c bronze grn	.50	.30
159	A15	25c dk brown	27.50	10.00
160	A15	50c blue green	.30	.25
161	A15	75c vermilion	.40	.25
162	A15	1p dull blue	2.50	.55
163	A15	2p brown	10.00	3.25
164	A15	3p lake	10.00	3.25
165	A15	4p violet	10.00	3.25
166	A15	5p black brn	10.00	3.25
167	A15	10p orange brn	10.00	3.25
		Nos. 152-167 (16)	84.25	29.35
		Set, never hinged	142.50	

No. 157 Handstamp Surcharged in Black or Blue

1908

168	A15	5c on 10c mar (Bk)	2.75	2.00
169	A15	5c on 10c mar (Bl)	10.00	5.50
		Set, never hinged	16.00	

The surcharge on Nos. 168-169 exist inverted, double, etc. The surcharge also exists on other stamps. A 25c on 10c also exists.

Seville-Barcelona Issue of Spain, 1929, Overprinted in Blue or Red

1929 *Perf. 11*

170	A52	5c rose lake	.20	.20
171	A53	10c green (R)	.20	.20
a.		Perf. 14	.65	.65
172	A50	15c Prus bl (R)	.25	.20
173	A51	20c purple (R)	.25	.20
174	A50	25c brt rose	.25	.20
175	A52	30c black brn	.25	.20
176	A53	40c dk blue (R)	.70	.70
177	A51	50c dp orange	1.50	1.50
178	A52	1p blue blk (R)	5.75	5.75
179	A53	4p deep rose	27.50	27.50
180	A53	10p brown	35.00	35.00
		Nos. 170-180 (11)	71.85	71.65
		Set, never hinged	135.00	

Catalogue values for unused stamps in this section, from this point to the end of the section, are for Never Hinged items.

Virgin Mary — A16

1960 Unwmk. Photo. *Perf. 13x12½*

181	A16	25c dull gray vio	.25	.20
182	A16	50c brown olive	.25	.20
183	A16	75c violet brn	.25	.20
184	A16	1p orange ver	.25	.25
185	A16	1.50p lt blue grn	.25	.25
186	A16	2p red lilac	.25	.25
187	A16	3p dark blue	3.00	.80
188	A16	5p lt red brn	.45	.25
189	A16	10p lt olive grn	.45	.30
		Nos. 181-189 (9)	5.20	2.70

Tricorn and Windmill from "The Three-Cornered Hat" by Falla — A17

Manuel de Falla A18

1960 *Perf. 13x12½, 12½x13*

190	A17	35c slate green	.50	.50
191	A18	80c Prus green	.60	.60

Issued to honor Manuel de Falla (1876-1946), Spanish composer.

See Nos. B1-B2.

Map of Fernando Po — A19

General Franco A20

Designs: 70c, Santa Isabel Cathedral.

Perf. 13x12½, 12½x13

1961, Oct. 1 Photo. Unwmk.

192	A19	25c gray violet	.25	.25
193	A20	50c olive brown	.25	.25
194	A19	70c brt green	.30	.30
195	A20	1p red orange	.35	.35
		Nos. 192-195 (4)	1.15	1.15

25th anniv. of the nomination of Gen. Francisco Franco as Chief of State.

Ocean Liner A21

Design: 50c, S.S. San Francisco.

1962, July 10 *Perf. 12½x13*

196	A21	25c dull violet	.25	.25
197	A21	50c gray olive	.25	.25
198	A21	1p orange brn	.25	.25
		Nos. 196-198 (3)	.75	.75

Mailman — A22

Mail Transport Symbols A23

Perf. 13x12½, 12½x13

1962, Nov. 23 Unwmk.

199	A22	15c dark green	.25	.25
200	A23	35c lilac rose	.25	.25
201	A22	1p brown	.25	.25
		Nos. 199-201 (3)	.75	.75

Issued for Stamp Day.

Fetish — A24

1963, Jan. 29 *Perf. 13x12½*

202	A24	50c olive gray	.25	.25
203	A24	1p deep magenta	.25	.25

Issued to help victims of the Seville flood.

Nuns A25

Design: 50c, Nun and child, vert.

Perf. 12½x13, 13x12½

1963, July 6 Photo. Unwmk.

204	A25	25c bright lilac	.25	.25
205	A25	50c dull green	.25	.25
206	A25	1p red orange	.25	.25
		Nos. 204-206 (3)	.75	.75

Issued for child welfare.

Child and Arms A26

1963, July 12 *Perf. 12½x13*

207	A26	50c brown olive	.25	.25
208	A26	1p carmine rose	.25	.25

Issued for Barcelona flood relief.

Governor Chacon A27

Orange Blossoms A28

Men in Dugout Canoe A29

1964, Mar. 6 *Perf. 12½x13, 13x12½*

209	A27	25c violet black	.25	.25
210	A28	50c dark olive	.25	.25
211	A27	1p brown red	.25	.25
		Nos. 209-211 (3)	.75	.75

Issued for Stamp Day 1963.

1964, June 1 Photo. *Perf. 13x12½*

Design: 50c, Pineapple.

212	A29	25c purple	.25	.25
213	A28	50c dull olive	.25	.25
214	A29	1p deep claret	.25	.25
		Nos. 212-214 (3)	.75	.75

Issued for child welfare.

Ring-necked Francolin — A30

Designs: 15c, 70c, 3p, Ring-necked francolin. 25c, 1p, 5p, Two mallards. 50c, 1.50p, 10p, Head of great blue touraco.

1964, July 1

215	A30	15c chestnut	.25	.25
216	A30	25c dull violet	.25	.25
217	A30	50c dk olive grn	.25	.25
218	A30	70c green	.25	.25
219	A30	1p brown orange	.30	.25
220	A30	1.50p grnsh blue	.35	.25
221	A30	3p violet blue	.65	.25
222	A30	5p dull purple	1.50	.30
223	A30	10p bright green	2.25	.85
		Nos. 215-223 (9)	6.05	2.90

The Three Kings A31

Designs: 50c, 1.50p, Caspar, vert.

Perf. 13x12½, 12½x13

1964, Nov. 23 Unwmk.

224	A31	50c green	.25	.25
225	A31	1p orange ver	.25	.25
226	A31	1.50p deep green	.30	.25
227	A31	3p ultra	1.50	.90
		Nos. 224-227 (4)	2.30	1.65

Issued for Stamp Day, 1964.

Boy — A32

Woman Fruit Picker — A33

1.50p, Girl learning to write, and church.

1964, Mar. 1 Photo. *Perf. 13x12½*

228	A32	50c indigo	.25	.25
229	A33	1p dark red	.25	.25
230	A33	1.50p grnsh blue	.30	.25
		Nos. 228-230 (3)	.80	.75

Issued to commemorate 25 years of peace.

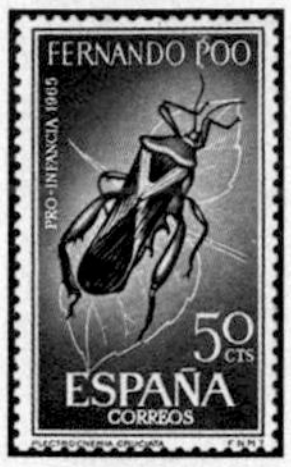

Plectrocnemia Cruciata — A34

Design: 1p, Metopodontus savagei, horiz.

Perf. 13x12½, 12½x13

1965, June 1 Photo. Unwmk.

231	A34	50c slate green	.30	.25
232	A34	1p rose red	.30	.25
233	A34	1.50p Prus blue	.35	.30
		Nos. 231-233 (3)	.95	.80

Issued for child welfare.

Pole Vault A35

Arms of Fernando Po — A36

Perf. 12½x13, 13x12½

1965, Nov. 23 Photo. Unwmk.

234	A35	50c yellow green	.25	.25
235	A36	1p brt org brn	.25	.25
236	A35	1.50p brt blue	.30	.25
		Nos. 234-236 (3)	.80	.75

Issued for Stamp Day, 1965.

Children Reading A37

1.50p, St. Elizabeth of Hungary, vert.

Perf. 12½x13, 13x12½

1966, June 1 Photo. Unwmk.

237	A37	50c dark green	.25	.25
238	A37	1p brown red	.25	.25
239	A37	1.50p dark blue	.25	.25
		Nos. 237-239 (3)	.75	.75

Issued for child welfare.

White-nosed Monkey — A38

Stamp Day: 40c, 4p, Head of moustached monkey, vert.

1966, Nov. 23 Photo. *Perf. 13*

240	A38	10c dk blue & yel	.30	.25
241	A38	40c lt brn, bl & blk	.30	.25
242	A38	1.50p ol bis, brn org & blk	.35	.30
243	A38	4p sl grn, brn org & blk	.45	.35
		Nos. 240-243 (4)	1.40	1.15

Flowers — A39

Designs: 40c, 4p, Six flowers.

1967, June 1 Photo. *Perf. 13*

244	A39	10c brt car & pale grn	.25	.25
245	A39	40c red brn & org	.25	.25
246	A39	1.50p red lil & lt red brn	.30	.25
247	A39	4p dk blue & lt grn	.35	.30
		Nos. 244-247 (4)	1.15	1.05

Issued for child welfare.

Linsang — A40

Stamp Day: 1.50p, Needle-clawed galago, vert. 3.50p, Fraser's scaly-tailed flying squirrel.

1967, Nov. 23 Photo. *Perf. 13*

248	A40	1p black & bister	.30	.25
249	A40	1.50p brown & olive	.30	.25
250	A40	3.50p rose lake & dl grn	.40	.30
		Nos. 248-250 (3)	1.00	.80

Stamp of 1868, No. 1, and Arms of San Carlos A41

Fernando Po No. 1 and: 1.50p, Arms of Santa Isabel. 2.50p, Arms of Fernando Po.

1968, Feb. 4 Photo. *Perf. 13*

251	A41	1p brt plum & brn org	.25	.25
252	A41	1.50p dp blue & brn org	.30	.25
253	A41	2.50p brn & brn org	.40	.30
		Nos. 251-253 (3)	.95	.80

Centenary of the first postage stamp.

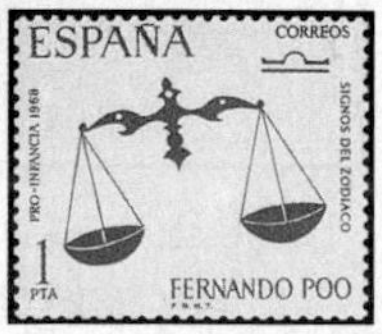

Signs of the Zodiac — A42

1968, Apr. 25 Photo. *Perf. 13*

254	A42	1p Libra	.25	.25
255	A42	1.50p Leo	.30	.25
256	A42	2.50p Aquarius	.40	.30
		Nos. 254-256 (3)	.95	.80

Issued for child welfare.

SEMI-POSTAL STAMPS

Catalogue values for unused stamps in this section are for Never Hinged items.

Types of Regular Issue, 1960

Designs: 10c+5c, Manuel de Falla. 15c+5c, Dancers from "Love, the Magician."

Perf. 12½x13, 13x12½

1960 Photo. Unwmk.

B1	A18	10c + 5c maroon	.25	.25
B2	A17	15c + 5c dk brn & bister	.25	.25

The surtax was for child welfare.

Whale SP1

Design: Nos. B4, B6, Harpooning whale.

1961 *Perf. 12½x13*

B3	SP1	10c + 5c rose brown	.30	.25
B4	SP1	20c + 5c dk slate grn	.30	.25
B5	SP1	30c + 10c olive brn	.30	.25
B6	SP1	50c + 20c dark brn	.30	.25
		Nos. B3-B6 (4)	1.20	1.00

Issued for Stamp Day, 1960.

Hand Blessing Woman — SP2

Design: 25c+10c, Boy making sign of the cross, and crucifix.

1961, June 21 *Perf. 13x12½*

B7	SP2	10c + 5c rose brn	.30	.25
B8	SP2	25c + 10c gray vio	.30	.25
B9	SP2	80c + 20c dk grn	.35	.30
		Nos. B7-B9 (3)	.95	.80

The surtax was for child welfare.

Ethiopian Tortoise SP3

Stamp Day: 25c+10c, 1p+10c, Native carriers, palms and shore.

1961, Nov. 23 *Perf. 12½x13*

B10	SP3	10c + 5c rose red	.30	.25
B11	SP3	25c + 10c dk pur	.30	.25
B12	SP3	30c + 10c vio brn	.30	.25
B13	SP3	1p + 10c red org	.35	.30
		Nos. B10-B13 (4)	1.25	1.05

FIJI

ˈfē-ˌjē

LOCATION — Group of 332 islands (106 inhabited) in the South Pacific Ocean east of Vanuatu

GOVT. — Independent nation in British Commonwealth

AREA — 7,078 sq. mi.

POP. — 812,918 (1999 est.)

CAPITAL — Suva

A British colony since 1874, Fiji became fully independent in 1970.

12 Pence = 1 Shilling

20 Shillings = 1 Pound

100 Cents = 1 Dollar (1872-74, 1969)

Syncopated Perforations

Type A (1st stamp #873): On shorter sides, the seventh hole from the larger side is an oval hole equal in width to three holes.

Catalogue values for unused stamps in this country are for Never Hinged items, beginning with Scott 137 in the regular postage section and Scott B1 in the semi-postal section.

Values for unused stamps are for examples with original gum as defined in the catalogue introduction except for Nos. 1-10 which are valued without gum. Additionally, Nos. 1-10 are valued with roulettes showing on two or more sides, but expect small faults which do not detract from the appearance of the stamps. Very few examples of Nos. 1-10 will be found free of faults and these will command substantial premiums.

Watermark

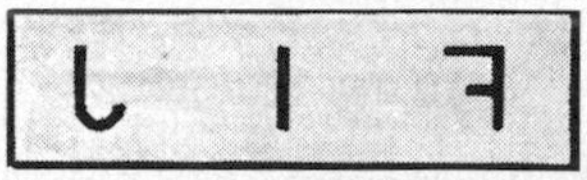

Wmk. 17 — FIJI POSTAGE Across Center Row of Sheet

A1

1870 Unwmk. Typeset *Rouletted*

Quadrille Paper

1	A1	1p black, *pink*	3,750.	*4,000.*
2	A1	3p black, *pink*	4,000.	4,000.
3	A1	6p black, *pink*	2,350.	*2,750.*
5	A1	1sh black, *pink*	1,750.	*2,250.*

1871 Laid Batonne Paper

6	A1	1p black, *pink*	1,000.	*2,000.*
7	A1	3p black, *pink*	1,750.	*3,250.*
8	A1	6p black, *pink*	1,400.	*2,000.*
9	A1	9p black, *pink*	2,300.	*3,500.*
10	A1	1sh black, *pink*	1,500.	1,600.

This service was established by the *Fiji Times,* a weekly newspaper, for the delivery of the newspaper. Since there was no postal service to the other islands, delivery of letters to agents of the newspaper on the islands was offered to the public.

Nos. 1-5 were printed in the same sheet, one horizontal row of 6 of each (6p, 1sh, 1p, 3p). Nos. 6-10 were printed from the same plate with three 9p replacing three 3p.

Most used examples have pen cancels.

Up to three sets of imitations exist. One on pink laid paper, pin-perforated, measuring 22½x16mm. Originals measure 22½x18½mm. A later printing was made on pink wove paper.

Forgeries also exist plus fake cancellations.

Crown and "CR" (Cakobau Rex)

A2 A3

A4

1871 Typo. Wmk. 17 *Perf. 12½*

Wove Paper

15	A2	1p blue	62.50	*140.00*
16	A3	3p green	125.00	*400.00*
17	A4	6p rose	150.00	*325.00*
		Nos. 15-17 (3)	337.50	*865.00*

Sheets of 50 (10x5).

For overprints and surcharges see #18-39.

Stamps of 1871 Surcharged in Black

1872, Jan. 13

18	A2	2c on 1p blue	37.50	*57.50*
19	A3	6c on 3p green	75.00	75.00
20	A4	12c on 6p rose	100.00	85.00
		Nos. 18-20 (3)	212.50	217.50

Nos. 18-20 with Additional Overprint in Black:

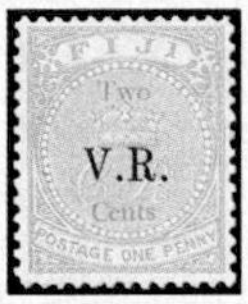
b

c

1874, Oct. 10

21	A2(b)	2c on 1p blue	1,150.	325.00
22	A2(c)	2c on 1p blue	1,000.	300.00
a.		Invtd. "A" instead of "V"	2,600.	1,500.
b.		Period after "R" is a Maltese Cross	2,600.	1,500.
23	A3(b)	6c on 3p green	2,100.	1,000.
24	A3(c)	6c on 3p green	1,650.	775.00
a.		Inverted "A"	4,250.	1,850.
b.		Period after "R" is a Maltese Cross	4,250.	1,850.
25	A4(b)	12c on 6p rose	900.00	250.00
a.		"V.R." inverted	5,750.	
26	A4(c)	12c on 6p rose	725.00	275.00
a.		Inverted "A"	2,250.	1,350.
b.		Period after "R" is a Maltese Cross	2,250.	1,350.
c.		"V.R." inverted	—	5,000.

Types "b" and "c" were in the same sheet.

Nos. 23-26 with Additional Surcharge in Black or Red

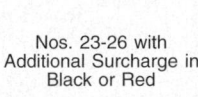

1875

27	A3(b)	2p on 6c on 3p	1,950.	750.00
a.		Period btwn. "2" and "d"	3,500.	1,400.
b.		"V.R." double	4,000.	3,750.
28	A3(b)	2p on 6c on 3p (R)	750.00	325.00
a.		Period btwn. "2" and "d"	1,750.	750.00
29	A3(c)	2p on 6c on 3p	1,650.	525.00
a.		Inverted "A"	3,750.	1,400.
b.		Period after "R" is a Maltese Cross	3,750.	1,400.
c.		No period after "2d"	3,750.	1,400.
30	A3(c)	2p on 6c on 3p (R)	600.00	225.00
a.		Inverted "A"	1,750.	750.00
b.		Period after "R" is a Maltese Cross	1,750.	750.00
c.		No period after "2d"	1,850.	750.00
31	A4(b)	2p on 12c on 6p	2,250.	950.00
a.		Period btwn. "2" and "d"		
b.		No period after "2d"		
c.		"2d, VR" double		4,250.
32	A4(c)	2p on 12c on 6p	2,100.	900.00
a.		Inverted "A"	2,750.	1,250.
b.		No period after "2d"		
c.		"2d, VR" double		4,250.

Types of 1871 Overprinted or Surcharged in Black:

e

f

1876, Jan. 31 **Unwmk.**

Wove Paper

33	A2(e)	1p ultramarine	57.50	57.50
a.		Inverted surcharge		
b.		Dbl. impression of stamp	1,000.	
c.		Horiz. pair, imperf vert.	1,000.	
34	A3(e+f)	2p on 3p dk grn	52.50	*60.00*
a.		Dbl. surch. "Two Pence"		
35	A4(e)	6p rose	70.00	65.00
b.		Surcharge inverted		
c.		Dbl. impression of stamp	2,850.	
		Nos. 33-35 (3)	180.00	182.50

1877 **Laid Paper**

36	A2(e)	1p ultramarine	20.00	*32.50*
a.		Horiz. pair, imperf. vert.	1,100.	
37	A3(e+f)	2p on 3p dk grn	65.00	*75.00*
38	A3(e+f)	4p on 3p lilac	95.00	30.00
a.		Horiz. pair, imperf. vert.	1,000.	
39	A4(e)	6p rose	55.00	32.50
a.		Horiz. pair, imperf. vert.	800.00	
		Nos. 36-39 (4)	235.00	*170.00*

Many of the preceding stamps are known imperforate. They are printer's waste and were never issued.

A12

A13

Queen Victoria
A14 A15

Perf. 10-13½ & Compound

1878-90 **Wove Paper** **Typo.**

40	A12	1p ultra ('79)	10.00	7.50
a.		1p blue	60.00	3.75
41	A12	2p green	15.00	1.10
b.		2p ultramarine (error)	*28,500.*	
42	A12	4p brt vio ('90)	8.50	7.00
a.		4p mauve	11.50	8.50
43	A13	6p brt rose ('80)	7.50	4.25
a.		Printed on both sides	1,150.	975.00
44	A14	1sh yel brn ('99)	40.00	10.00
a.		1sh deep brown ('81)	95.00	22.50

Litho.

45	A15	5sh blk & red brn ('82)	62.50	37.50
		Nos. 40-45 (6)	143.50	67.35

Official facsimiles of the 5sh were officially made in 1900, differing in shades and detail of design from No. 45. They exist imperf., perf. 10 and 12; are all canceled "SUVA" and usually dated "15 Dec., 00."

No. 41b was not put on sale. All copies were supposed to be destroyed.

For surcharges see Nos. 46-52.

Surcharged type "f" in Black

1878-90 **Typo.**

46	A12	2p on 3p green	6.50	*22.50*
47	A12	4p on 1p vio ('90)	47.50	30.00
48	A12	4p on 2p lilac ('83)	85.00	12.50
		Nos. 46-48 (3)	139.00	65.00

Nos. 40-43 Surcharged in Black:

g

h

j

k

1891-92 ***Perf. 10***

49	A12(g)	½p on 1p ('92)	50.00	*75.00*
50	A12(h)	2½p on 2p	50.00	*57.50*
a.		Wider space (2mm) between "2" and "½"	150.00	*160.00*
51	A12(j)	5p on 4p ('92)	57.50	*75.00*
52	A13(k)	5p on 6p ('92)	62.50	*80.00*
a.		"FIVE" and "PENCE" 3mm apart	75.00	*80.00*
		Nos. 49-52 (4)	220.00	*287.50*

A18

Fijian Canoe — A19

A20

1891-96 ***Perf. 10-12 & Compound***

53	A18	½p grnsh blk ('92)	4.50	*5.50*
a.		½p gray	3.50	*10.00*
54	A19	1p black ('93)	22.50	6.00
55	A19	1p lilac rose ('96)	7.50	1.00
56	A19	2p green ('93)	17.00	7.00
a.		Perf. 10x12 ('94)	700.00	425.00
57	A20	2½ red brown	12.00	12.00
58	A19	5p ultra ('93)	15.00	8.50
		Nos. 53-58 (6)	78.50	40.00

Edward VII
A22

George V
A23

1903, Feb. 1 **Wmk. 2** ***Perf. 14***

59	A22	½p pale green & gray green	2.60	2.25
60	A22	1p black & violet, *red*	15.00	.65
61	A22	2p orange & violet	4.50	1.40
62	A22	2½p ultramarine & violet, *blue*	16.00	4.00
63	A22	3p red violet & violet	1.75	*4.50*
64	A22	4p black & violet	1.75	*2.75*
65	A22	5p green & violet	1.75	*3.00*
66	A22	6p carmine rose & violet	1.75	*3.00*
67	A22	1sh carmine rose & green	12.50	*70.00*
68	A22	5sh black & green	62.50	*150.00*
69	A22	£1 ultramarine & gray	400.00	*550.00*
		Revenue cancel		70.00
		Nos. 59-68 (10)	120.10	*241.55*

Numerals of 2p, 4p, 6p and 5sh of type A22 are in color on plain tablet.

1904-12 **Wmk. 3**

Ordinary Paper

70	A22	½p pale green & green ('04)	15.00	3.50
70A	A22	½p green ('08)	12.50	3.50
71	A22	1p black & violet, *red* ('04)	30.00	.20
72	A22	1p carmine ('06)	11.00	.20
73	A22	2½p ultramarine ('10)	7.50	*8.50*

Chalky Paper

74	A22	6p violet ('10)	15.00	*30.00*
75	A22	1sh carmine rose & green ('09)	30.00	*45.00*
76	A22	1sh black, *green* ('11)	5.00	*11.00*
77	A22	5sh scarlet & green, *yellow* ('11)	65.00	*75.00*
78	A22	£1 black & violet, *red* ('12)	375.00	*325.00*
		Nos. 70-77 (9)	191.00	*176.90*

Die I

For description of Dies I and II see "Dies of British Colonial Stamps" in Table of Contents.

1912-23

Ordinary Paper

79	A23	¼p brown ('16)	1.50	.45
80	A23	½p green	1.40	.55
81	A23	1p scarlet	2.25	.75
a.		1p carmine ('16)	2.25	.25
82	A23	2p gray ('14)	2.00	.20
83	A23	2½p ultramarine ('14)	3.50	4.00
84	A23	3p violet, *yellow*	2.25	*4.00*
a.		Die II ('21)	2.75	*25.00*
85	A23	4p red & black, *yellow* ('14)	3.75	*15.00*
a.		Die II ('23)	3.75	*27.50*

Chalky Paper

86	A23	5p ol green & dl violet ('14)	5.50	*12.50*
87	A23	6p red violet & dl violet ('14)	2.40	*6.00*
88	A23	1sh black, *green*	1.10	*14.00*
a.		1sh blk, *blue green*, olive back	4.50	*11.00*
b.		1sh black, *emerald* ('21)	6.25	*45.00*
c.		Die II ('22)	3.25	*27.50*
89	A23	2sh 6p red & black, *blue*	37.50	*35.00*
90	A23	5sh scarlet & green, *yellow*	37.50	*45.00*
91	A23	£1 black & violet, *red*	300.00	*325.00*
a.		Die II ('21)	300.00	*325.00*
		Revenue cancel		52.50

Surface-colored Paper

92	A23	1sh black, *green*	1.25	*12.50*
		Nos. 79-90,92 (13)	101.90	*149.95*

Numerals of ¼p, 1½p, 2p, 4p, 6p, 2sh, 2sh6p and 5sh of type A23 are in color on plain tablet.

For overprints see Nos. MR1-MR2.

Die II

1922-27 **Wmk. 4**

Ordinary Paper

93	A23	¼p dark brown	3.00	*27.50*
94	A23	½p green	.85	*2.40*
95	A23	1p rose red	2.75	*1.25*
96	A23	1p violet ('27)	1.40	.20
97	A23	1½p rose red ('27)	4.50	2.00
98	A23	2p gray	1.40	.20
99	A23	3p ultramarine ('23)	3.00	1.20
100	A23	4p red & black, *yellow*	5.75	*7.50*
101	A23	5p ol green & dl violet	1.75	*2.25*
102	A23	6p red violet & dull violet	2.40	1.50

Chalky Paper

103	A23	1sh black, *emerald*	5.50	*6.75*
104	A23	2sh ultra & violet, *blue* ('27)	30.00	*67.50*
105	A23	2sh6p red & black, *blue*	12.50	*35.00*
106	A23	5sh scarlet & green, *yellow*	37.50	*75.00*
		Nos. 93-106 (14)	112.30	*230.25*

Common Design Types pictured following the introduction.

Silver Jubilee Issue

Common Design Type

1935, May 6 ***Perf. 13½x14***

110	CD301	1½p carmine & blue	1.10	*8.50*
111	CD301	2p gray blk & ultra	1.75	*.50*
112	CD301	3p blue & brown	3.00	*4.00*
113	CD301	1sh brt vio & indigo	7.50	*10.00*
		Nos. 110-113 (4)	13.35	*23.00*
		Set, never hinged	22.50	

Coronation Issue

Common Design Type

1937, May 12 ***Perf. 11x11½***

114	CD302	1p dark violet	.45	1.25
115	CD302	2p gray black	.45	*2.25*
116	CD302	3p indigo	.45	*2.25*
		Nos. 114-116 (3)	1.35	5.75
		Set, never hinged	2.00	

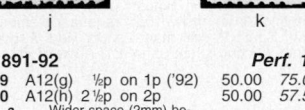

Outrigger Canoe — A24

Fijian Village — A25

Outrigger Canoe A26

Map of Fiji Islands A27

Canoe and Arms of Fiji — A28

Sugar Cane — A29

Spear Fishing at Night — A30

Arms of Fiji — A31

Suva Harbor — A32

River Scene — A33

Fijian House — A34

Papaya Tree — A35

Bugler — A36

Designs: No. 121, Government buildings. 8p, 1sh5p, 1sh6p, Arms of Fiji.

Perf. 13½, 12½ (1p)

1938-55 Engr. Wmk. 4

117	A24	½p green	.25	1.00
c.		Perf. 14 ('41)	16.00	4.50
d.		Perf. 12 ('48)	.80	*4.00*
118	A25	1p blue & brn	.40	.25
119	A26	1½p rose car (empty canoe)	12.00	2.00
120	A27	2p grn & org brn (no "180 degree")	30.00	.50
121	A27	2p mag & grn	.45	.80
a.		Perf. 12 ('46)	.45	.90

Perf. 12½, 13x12 (6p), 14 (8p)

122	A28	3p dp ultra	.80	.40
123	A29	5p rose red & bl	32.50	13.00
124	A29	5p rose red & yel grn	.25	*.40*
125	A27	6p blk (no "180 degree")	50.00	16.00
126	A31	8p rose car	.80	3.00
a.		Perf. 13 ('50)	.55	*3.50*
127	A30	1sh black & yel	.60	*.90*

Perf. 14

128	A31	1sh5p car & black	.20	.20
128A	A31	1sh6p ultra	2.75	3.50
b.		Perf. 13 ('55)	1.10	*20.00*

Perf. 12½

129	A32	2sh vio & org	2.00	.55
130	A33	2sh6p brn & grn	2.25	2.00
131	A34	5sh dk vio & grn	2.25	2.25
131A	A35	10sh emer & brn org	27.50	*52.50*
131B	A36	£1 car & ultra	37.50	*65.00*
		Nos. 117-131B (18)	202.50	*164.25*

Issued: 1sh5p, 6/13/40; 5p, 10/1/40; #121, 5/19/42; 8p, 11/15/48; 10sh, £1, 3/13/50; 1sh6p, 8/1/50; others, 4/5/38.

Types of 1938-40 Redrawn

Perf. 13½ (1½p, 2p, 6p), 14 (2½p)

1940-49 Wmk. 4

132	A26	1½p rose car (man in canoe)	1.00	*1.00*
a.		Perf. 12 ('49)	.80	*1.60*
b.		Perf. 14 ('42)	14.50	*25.00*
133	A27	2p grn & org brn ("180 degree")	12.50	*21.00*
134	A27	2½p grn & org brn	.50	*1.25*
a.		Perf. 12 ('48)	.80	.60
b.		Perf. 13½ ('42)	.55	*1.00*
135	A27	6p blk ("180 degree")	2.50	3.00
a.		Perf. 12 ('47)	1.40	2.00
		Nos. 132-135 (4)	16.50	*26.25*

No. 132, type A26, has a man sitting in the canoe.

Nos. 133-135, type A27, have 180 degree added to the lower right hand corner of the design.

Issued: 2½p, 1/6/42; others 10/1/40.

No. 133 Surcharged in Black

1941, Feb. 10 ***Perf. 13½***

136	A27	2½p on 2p grn & org brn	1.50	.40
		Never hinged	2.50	

Catalogue values for unused stamps in this section, from this point to the end of the section, are for Never Hinged items.

Peace Issue

Common Design Type

1946, Aug. 17 ***Perf. 13½***

137	CD303	2½p bright green	.20	*1.50*
138	CD303	3p deep blue	.20	.20

Silver Wedding Issue

Common Design Types

1948, Dec. 17 Photo. ***Perf. 14x14½***

139	CD304	2½p dark green	.70	*1.75*

Engr.; Name Typo.

Perf. 11½x11

140	CD305	5sh blue violet	22.50	16.00

UPU Issue

Common Design Types

Engr.; Name Typo. on 3p, 8p

Perf. 13½, 11x11½

1949, Oct. 10 Wmk. 4

141	CD306	2p red violet	.65	.75
142	CD307	3p indigo	4.00	3.75
143	CD308	8p dp carmine	.65	*3.75*
144	CD309	1sh6p blue	.70	*1.60*
		Nos. 141-144 (4)	6.00	9.85

Coronation Issue

Common Design Type

1953, June 2 ***Perf. 13½x13***

145	CD312	2½p dk green & blk	1.75	.60

Type of 1938-40 with Portrait of Queen Elizabeth II Inscribed: "Royal Visit 1953"

1953, Dec. 16 ***Perf. 13***

146	A31	8p carmine lake	.65	.35

Visit of Queen Elizabeth II and the Duke of Edinburgh, 1953.

Types of 1938-50 with Portrait of Queen Elizabeth II, and:

A39

Loading Copra A40

Designs: 1sh6p, Sugar cane train. 2sh, Bananas for export. 5sh, Gold industry.

Perf. 11½, 11½x11, 12, 12½, 13

1954-56 Engr.

147	A24	½p green	.20	*1.25*
148	A39	1p grnsh blue	2.00	.20
149	A39	1½p brown	1.10	.65
150	A27	2p mag & green	1.40	.40
151	A39	2½p blue vio	2.75	.20
152	A40	3p purple & brn	3.00	.20
154	A27	6p black	3.00	.85
155	A31	8p carmine lake	4.25	1.25
156	A30	1sh black & yel	2.75	.20
157	A40	1sh6p grn & dp ultra	21.00	1.00
158	A40	2sh brt car & black	6.25	.50
159	A33	2sh6p brn & bl grn	1.40	.20
160	A40	5sh dp ultra & yel	17.00	1.25
161	A35	10sh emer & brn org	8.00	*20.00*
162	A36	£1 car & ultra	42.50	19.00
		Nos. 147-162 (15)	116.60	47.15

Issued: 2p, 1sh, 2sh6p, 2/1/54; ½p, 6p, 8p, 10sh, £1, 7/1/54; 1p, 6/1/56; 1½p, 2½p, 3p, 1sh6p, 2sh, 5sh, 10/1/56.

Types of 1954-56 and:

Nautilus Shells — A41

Hibiscus — A42

Kandavu Parrot A43

½p, 2p, 2½p, Queen Elizabeth II (A39). 1p, Queen, turtles in bottom panels. 6p, Fijian beating drum (lali). 10p, Yaqona ceremony. 1sh, South Pacific map. 2sh6p, Nadi Airport. 10sh, Cutting sugar cane. £1, Arms of Fiji.

Perf. 11½ (A39, A41); 11½x11 (A40); 14½x14 (A42); 14x14½ (A43)

Engr. (A39, A40, A41); others Photo.

1959-63 Wmk. 4

163	A39	½p green ('61)	.25	*2.75*
164	A41	1p dk blue ('62)	4.00	2.75
165	A41	1½p dk brown ('62)	3.25	2.00
166	A39	2p crim rose ('61)	.90	.20
167	A39	2½p brown org ('62)	2.75	4.25
168	A40	6p blk & car rose ('61)	2.25	.20
169	A42	8p gray, red, yel & grn ('61)	.90	.40
170	A40	10p car & brn ('63)	1.10	.80
171	A40	1sh dk bl & bl ('61)	2.75	.75
172	A40	2sh6p pur & blk ('61)	4.50	1.40
173	A43	4sh dk grn, red, bl & emer	3.25	2.40
174	A40	10sh sep & emer ('61)	8.00	8.00
175	A40	£1 org & blk ('61)	24.00	10.00
		Nos. 163-175 (13)	57.90	35.90

Issued: 4sh, 7/13; 8p, 8/1; ½p, 2p, 6p, 1sh, 2sh6p, 10sh, £1, 11/14; 1p, 1½p, 2½p, 12/3; 10p, 4/1.

For type overprinted see No. 205.

Types of 1954-63 and:

Elizabeth II — A44

1sh6p, 180th meridian and Intl. Date Line. 2sh, White orchids. 5sh, Orange dove.

Perf. 11½ (A41); 12½ (A44); 11½x11 (A40); 14x14½ (A43)

Engr. (A40, A41); others Photo.

1962-67 Wmk. 314

176	A41	1p dark blue ('64)	.75	*4.25*
177	A39	2p crim rose ('65)	.95	.20
178	A44	3p rose cl & multi	.20	.20
179	A40	6p blk & car rose ('64)	1.10	.20
180	A42	9p ultra, red, yel & grn ('63)	1.10	1.00
181	A40	10p car & brn ('64)	1.10	.85
182	A40	1sh dk bl & bl ('66)	1.90	.75
183	A43	1sh6p dk bl & multi	2.25	1.60
184	A42	2sh gold, yel grn & grn	11.00	5.75
185	A40	2sh6p pur & blk ('65)	2.25	1.25
186	A43	4sh grn & multi, wmk. sideways ('67)	4.75	3.25
a.		As #186, wmk. upright ('64)	3.50	6.50
b.		4sh dark green & multi ('66)	4.00	5.25
187	A43	5sh dk gray, yel & red	8.00	1.00
188	A40	10sh sep & emer ('64)	5.50	5.75
189	A40	£1 org & blk ('64)	21.00	15.00
		Nos. 176-189 (14)	61.85	41.05

Issued: 3p, 1sh6p, 2sh, 5sh, 12/3; 9p, #186a, 4/1; 1p, 10p, 10sh, 1/14; 6p, £1, 6/9; 2p, 2sh6p, 8/3; #186b, 3/1; #186, 2/16.

Nos. 178 and 171 Overprinted: "ROYAL VISIT 1963"

1963, Feb. 1

196	A44	3p multicolored	.50	.35
197	A40	1sh dark blue & blue	.50	.35

Visit of Elizabeth II & Prince Philip, Feb. 3.

Freedom from Hunger Issue

Common Design Type

1963, June 4 Photo. ***Perf. 14x14½***

198	CD314	2sh ultramarine	6.00	3.25

Running A45

9p, Throwing the discus, vert. 1sh, Field hockey, vert. 2sh6p, Women's high jump.

Perf. 14½x14, 14x14½

1963, Aug. 6 Wmk. 314

199	A45	3p yel, blk & brn	.75	.20
200	A45	9p violet, blk & brn	.75	1.50
201	A45	1sh green, blk & brn	.75	.25
202	A45	2sh6p blue, blk & brn	1.75	1.75
		Nos. 199-202 (4)	4.00	3.70

1st So. Pacific Games, Suva, 8/29-9/7.

Red Cross Centenary Issue
Common Design Type

1963, Sept. 2 Litho. *Perf. 13*

203	CD315	2p black & red	1.50	.30
204	CD315	2sh ultra & red	4.50	4.50

Type of 1959-63 Overprinted

1963, Dec. 2 Engr. *Perf. 11½x11*

205	A40	1sh dark blue & blue	1.00	.35

Opening of the Commonwealth Pacific (telephone) Cable service, COMPAC.

Fiji Scout Badge — A46

Scouts of India, Fiji and Europe Tying Knot — A47

1964, Aug. 3 Photo. *Perf. 12½*

206	A46	3p multicolored	.65	.50
207	A47	1sh ocher & purple	1.00	.75

50th anniv. of the founding of the Fiji Boy Scouts.

Amphibian "Aotearoa," 1939 — A48

Map of Fiji and Tonga Islands and Plane A49

Design: 6p, Heron plane.

1964, Oct. 24 *Perf. 12½, 14½*

208	A48	3p brt red & black	.65	.35
209	A48	6p ultra & red	1.10	1.10
210	A49	1sh grnsh blue & black	1.10	1.10
		Nos. 208-210 (3)	2.85	2.55

Fiji-Tonga airmail service, 25th anniv.

ITU Issue
Common Design Type
Perf. 11x11½

1965, May 17 Litho. Wmk. 314

211	CD317	3p blue & rose red	.50	.30
212	CD317	2sh yel & bister	3.50	3.50

Intl. Cooperation Year Issue
Common Design Type

1965, Oct. 25 *Perf. 14½*

213	CD318	2p blue grn & claret	.40	.40
214	CD318	2sh6p lt vio & grn	2.60	2.10

Churchill Memorial Issue
Common Design Type

1966, Jan. 24 Photo. *Perf. 14*
Design in Black, Gold and Carmine Rose

215	CD319	3p brt blue	1.25	.35
216	CD319	9p green	1.75	1.75
217	CD319	1sh brown	1.75	.35
218	CD319	2sh6p violet	2.00	2.00
		Nos. 215-218 (4)	6.75	4.45

World Cup Soccer Issue
Common Design Type

1966, July 1 Litho. *Perf. 14*

219	CD321	2p multicolored	.60	.30
220	CD321	2sh multicolored	1.75	.90

H.M.S. Pandora and Split Island, Rotuma A50

Designs: 10p, Rotuma chiefs, Pandora, and Rotuma's position in Pacific. 1sh6p, Rotuma islanders welcoming Pandora.

1966, Aug. 29 Photo. *Perf. 14x13*

221	A50	3p multicolored	.60	.25
222	A50	10p multicolored	.75	.40
223	A50	1sh6p multicolored	1.00	1.00
		Nos. 221-223 (3)	2.35	1.65

175th anniv. of the discovery of Rotuma, a group of eight islands forming part of the colony of Fiji.

WHO Headquarters Issue
Common Design Type

1966, Sept. 20 Litho. *Perf. 14*

224	CD322	6p multicolored	2.10	.50
225	CD322	2sh6p multicolored	4.50	4.00

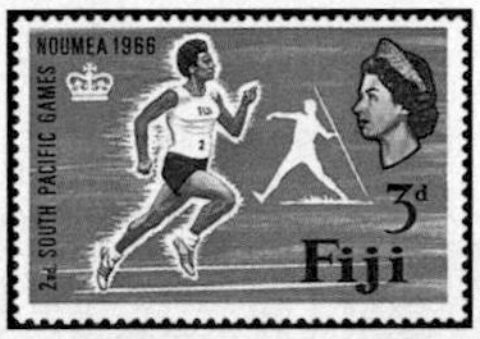

Woman Runner A51

Designs: 9p, Shot put, vert. 1sh, Diver.

1966, Dec. 8 Photo. *Perf. 14x14½*

226	A51	3p ol, black & lt brn	.40	.40
227	A51	9p brt blue, blk & brn	.65	.65
228	A51	1sh blue green & multi	.65	.65
		Nos. 226-228 (3)	1.70	1.70

2nd South Pacific Games, Noumea, New Caledonia, Dec. 8-18.

Military Band A52

Intl. Tourist Year: 9p, Reef diving. 1sh, Beqa fire walkers. 2sh, Liner Oriana and Mt. Rama volcano.

1967, Oct. 20 *Perf. 14x13*

229	A52	3p multi & gold	.90	.20
230	A52	9p multi & silver	.35	.25
231	A52	1sh multi & gold	.35	.35
232	A52	2sh multi & silver	.90	.60
		Nos. 229-232 (4)	2.50	1.40

Admiral Bligh, H.M.S. Providence and Old Map of "Feejee" A53

Designs: 1sh, Bligh's longboat being chased by double canoe and map of Fiji Islands. 2sh6p, Bligh's tomb, St. Mary's Cemetery, Lambeth, London.

Perf. 15x14, 12½x13 (1sh)
1967, Dec. 7 Photo. Wmk. 314
Size: 35x21mm

233	A53	4p emer, blk & yel	.30	.30

Size: 54x20mm

234	A53	1sh brt bl, brn org & blk	.45	.45

Size: 35x21mm

235	A53	2sh6p sepia & multi	1.25	1.25
		Nos. 233-235 (3)	2.00	2.00

150th anniv. of the death of Adm. William Bligh (1754-1817), captain of the Bounty and principal discoverer of the Fiji Islands.

Simmonds "Spartan" Seaplane — A54

Designs: 6p, Fiji Airways Hawker-Siddeley H748 and emblems of various airlines. 1sh, Fokker "Southern Cross," Capt. Charles Kingsford-Smith, his crew and Southern Cross constellation. 2sh, Lockheed Altair "Lady Southern Cross."

Perf. 14x14½
1968, June 5 Wmk. 314

236	A54	2p green & black	.30	.30
237	A54	6p brt blue, car & blk	.30	.30
238	A54	1sh dp violet & green	.50	.50
239	A54	2sh orange brn & dk blue	.90	.90
		Nos. 236-239 (4)	2.00	2.00

40th anniv. of the first Trans-Pacific Flight through Fiji under Capt. Charles Kingsford-Smith.

Fijian Bures — A55

Eastern Reef Heron — A56

1p, Passion fruit flowers. 2p, Nautilus pompilius shell. 4p, Hawk moth. 6p, Reef butterflyfish. 9p, Bamboo raft (bilibili). 10p, Tiger moth. 1sh, Black marlin. 1sh6p, Orange-breasted honey eaters. 2sh, Ringed sea snake, horiz. 2sh6p, Outrigger canoes (takia), horiz. 3sh, Golden cowrie shell. 4sh, Emperor gold mine and gold ore. 5sh, Bamboo orchids, horiz. 10sh, Tabua (ceremonial whale's tooth). £1, Coat of Arms and Queen Elizabeth II, horiz.

Perf. 13½ (A55), 14 (A56)
1968, July 15 Photo. Wmk. 314

240	A55	½p multicolored	.20	.20
241	A55	1p multicolored	.20	.20
242	A55	2p multicolored	.20	.20
243	A56	3p multicolored	.30	.20
244	A55	4p multicolored	.65	.20
245	A55	6p multicolored	.25	.30
246	A55	9p multicolored	.20	.45
247	A55	10p multicolored	1.00	.60
248	A56	1sh multicolored	1.25	.65
249	A56	1sh6p multicolored	2.75	.75
250	A56	2sh multicolored	1.50	1.50
251	A56	2sh6p multicolored	1.50	1.50
252	A55	3sh multicolored	3.00	2.00
253	A56	4sh multicolored	5.25	1.75
254	A56	5sh multicolored	2.60	2.25
255	A56	10sh multicolored	4.00	3.50
256	A56	£1 red & multi	5.00	4.00
		Nos. 240-256 (17)	29.85	20.25

See Nos. 260-276.

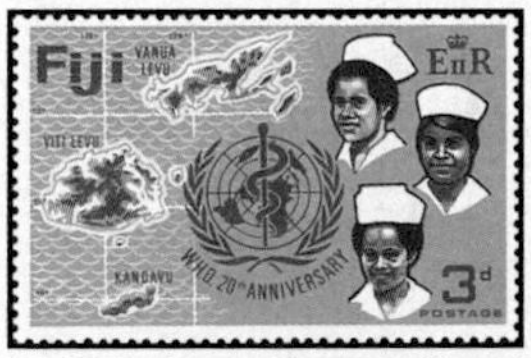

WHO Emblem, Map of Fiji and Nurses — A57

WHO Emblem and: 9p, Medical team loading patient on stretcher on dinghy and medical ship "Vuniwai." 3sh, People playing on beach.

1968, Dec. 9 Litho. *Perf. 14*

257	A57	3p blue green & multi	.20	.20
258	A57	9p brt blue & multi	.30	.30
259	A57	3sh dk blue & multi	.90	.90
		Nos. 257-259 (3)	1.40	1.40

WHO, 20th anniv.

Types of 1968
Values in Cents and Dollars

Designs: 1c, Passion fruit flowers. 2c, Nautilus pompilius shell. 3c, Reef heron. 4c, Hawk moth. 5c, Reef butterflyfish. 6c, Fijian bures. 8c, Bamboo raft. 9c, Tiger moth. 10c, Black marlin. 15c, Orange-breasted honey-eater. 20c, Ringed sea snake, horiz. 25c, Outrigger canoes (takia), horiz. 30c, Golden cowrie shell. 40c Emperor gold mine and gold ore. 50c, Bamboo orchids, horiz. $1, Tabua (ceremonial whale's tooth). $2, Coat of Arms and Queen Elizabeth II, horiz.

Perf. 13½ (A55), 14 (A56)
1969, Jan. 13 Photo. Wmk. 314

260	A55	1c multicolored	.20	.20
261	A55	2c multicolored	.20	.20
262	A56	3c multicolored	.50	.35
263	A55	4c multicolored	1.25	.35
264	A55	5c multicolored	.20	.20
265	A55	6c multicolored	.20	.20
266	A55	8c multicolored	.20	.20
267	A55	9c multicolored	1.25	*1.60*
268	A56	10c multicolored	.20	.20
269	A56	15c multicolored	7.25	3.50
270	A56	20c multicolored	.90	.65
271	A56	25c multicolored	.90	.25
272	A55	30c multicolored	5.25	1.40
273	A56	40c multicolored	6.00	3.25
274	A56	50c multicolored	3.50	.25
275	A56	$1 multicolored	5.00	2.00
276	A56	$2 red & multi	6.00	5.00
		Nos. 260-276 (17)	39.00	19.80

For overprints & surcharges see #286-288, B5-B6.

Fiji Soldiers and Map of Solomon Islands A58

Designs: 10c, Flags of Fiji Military Force, soldiers in full and battle dress. 25c, Cpl. Sefanaia Sukanaivalu and Victoria Cross.

1969, June 23 Wmk. 314 *Perf. 14*

277	A58	3c emerald & multi	.80	.80
278	A58	10c red & multi	.95	.95
279	A58	25c black & multi	1.25	1.25
		Nos. 277-279 (3)	3.00	3.00

25th anniv. of the Fiji Military Forces campaign in the Solomon Islands and of the posthumous award of the Victoria Cross to Cpl. Sefanaia Sukanaivalu.

Yachting — A59

Designs: 4c, Javelin. 20c, Winners and South Pacific Games medal.

1969, Aug. 18 Photo. *Perf. 14½x14*

280	A59	4c red, brown & blk	.45	.45
281	A59	8c blue & black	.60	.60
282	A59	20c olive grn, blk & ocher	1.25	1.25
		Nos. 280-282 (3)	2.30	2.30

3rd South Pacific Games, Port Moresby, Papua New Guinea, Aug. 13-23.

Students in Laboratory — A60

2c, Map of South Pacific and mortarboard. 8c, Site of University at Royal New Zealand Air Force Seaplane Station, Laucala Bay, RNZAF badge and Sunderland flying boat.

1969, Nov. 10 *Perf. 14x14½*

283	A60	2c multicolored	.30	.30
284	A60	8c red & multi	.50	.50
285	A60	25c dk green & multi	1.40	1.40
		Nos. 283-285 (3)	2.20	2.20

Inauguration of the University of the South Pacific, Laucala Bay, Suva.

Nos. 261, 268 and 271 Overprinted: "ROYAL VISIT / 1970"

1970, Mar. 4 *Perf. 13½, 14*

286	A55	2c multicolored	.30	.30
287	A56	10c multicolored	.40	.40
288	A55	25c multicolored	1.75	1.75
		Nos. 286-288 (3)	2.45	2.45

Visit of Queen Elizabeth II, Prince Philip and Princess Anne, Mar. 4-5.

Nuns Sitting under Chaulmoogra Tree, and Chaulmoogra Fruit — A61

Designs: 10c, Paintings by Semisi Maya (former patient). No. 290, Cascade, vert. No. 291, Sea urchins, vert. 30c, Aerial view of Makogai Hospital.

Perf. 14x14½, 14½x14

1970, May 25 Photo. Wmk. 314

289	A61	2c brt pink & multi	.50	.50
290	A61	10c gray green & blk	.75	.75
291	A61	10c blue, car & blk	.75	.75
a.		Pair, #290-291	1.50	1.50
292	A61	30c orange & multi	2.00	2.00
		Nos. 289-292 (4)	4.00	4.00

Closing of the Leprosy Hospital on Makogai Island in 1969.

Abel Tasman and Ship's Log, 1643 — A62

3c, Capt. James Cook & "Endeavour." 8c, Capt. William Bligh & longboat, 1789. 25c, Man of Fiji & Fijian ocean-going canoe.

1970, Aug. 18 Litho. *Perf. 13x12½*

293	A62	2c blue green & multi	1.00	1.00
294	A62	3c gray green & multi	1.25	1.25
295	A62	8c multicolored	1.50	1.50
296	A62	25c dull lilac & multi	2.25	2.25
		Nos. 293-296 (4)	6.00	6.00

Discoverers and explorers of Fiji Islands.

King Cakobau and Cession Stone at Lavuka A63

Designs: 3c, Chinese, Fijian, Indian and European children. 10c, Prime Minister Ratu Sir Kamisese Mara and flag of Fiji. 25c, Fijian male dancer and Indian female dancer.

1970, Oct. 10 Wmk. 314 *Perf. 14*

297	A63	2c multicolored	.25	.25
298	A63	3c multicolored	.35	.35
299	A63	10c multicolored	.55	.55
300	A63	25c multicolored	1.60	1.60
		Nos. 297-300 (4)	2.75	2.75

Fijian independence.

Fiji Nos. 1 and 3 — A64

15c, Fiji #15, 44, 59, 81, 127, 166. 20c, Fiji Times Office, Levuka, & G. P. O., Suva.

1970, Nov. 2 Photo. *Perf. 14½x14*

Size: 35x21mm

301	A64	4c multicolored	.40	.40

Size: 60x21½mm

302	A64	15c multicolored	1.10	1.10

Size: 35x21mm

303	A64	20c multicolored	1.50	1.50
		Nos. 301-303 (3)	3.00	3.00

Centenary of first postage stamps of Fiji.

Gray- backed White Eyes — A65

Yellow- breasted Musk Parrots — A66

Designs: 1c, Cirrhopetalum umbellatum. 2c, Cardinal honey eaters. 3c, Calanthe furcata.4c, Bulbophyllum. 6c, Phaius tancarvilliae. 8c,Blue-crested broadbills. 10c, Acanthephippiumvitiense. 15c, Dendrobium tokai. 20c, Slaty flycatchers. 25c, Kandavu honey eaters. 30c, Dendrobium gordonii. 50c, White-throated pigeon. $1, Collared lories (kula). $2, Dendrobium platygastrium. (Orchids shown on 1c, 3c, 4c, 6c, 10c, 15c, 30c, $2.)

Wmk. 314 Upright

1971-72 Litho. *Perf. 13½x14*

305	A65	1c blk & multi ('72)	.20	.20
306	A65	2c carmine & multi	.20	.20
307	A65	3c multi ('72)	.85	.20
308	A65	4c blk & multi ('72)	.75	1.50
309	A65	5c brown & multi	2.75	.25
310	A65	6c lt bl & multi ('72)	.45	.30
311	A65	8c black & multi	.50	.35
312	A65	10c multi ('72)	.55	.40
313	A65	15c multi ('72)	2.50	.55
314	A65	20c gray & multi	1.50	.60

Perf. 14

315	A66	25c sepia & multi	1.50	.95
316	A66	30c grn & multi ('72)	3.00	1.10
317	A66	40c blue & multi	3.50	1.50
318	A66	50c gray & multi	4.00	1.90
319	A66	$1 red & multi	6.25	3.75
320	A66	$2 multi ('72)	12.50	7.25
		Nos. 305-320 (16)	41.00	21.00

Issued: 5c, 20c, 40c, 50c, 8/6; 2c, 8c, 25c, $1, 11/22; 1c, 10c, 30c, $2, 1/4; 3c, 4c, 6c, 15c, 6/23.

1972-74 Wmk. 314 Sideways

306c	A65	2c ('73)	.70	*11.00*
307a	A65	3c ('73)	2.00	.60
308a	A65	4c ('73)	6.50	.90
309a	A65	5c ('73)	6.50	4.25
310a	A65	6c ('73)	8.75	1.60
311a	A65	8c ('73)	4.25	1.00
313a	A65	15c ('73)	3.75	2.75
314a	A65	20c	14.00	2.50
315a	A66	25c ('73)	2.00	1.10
317a	A66	40c ('74)	3.25	*8.75*
318a	A66	50c ('74)	3.25	*4.25*
319a	A66	$1	3.25	*6.50*
320a	A66	$2	4.25	*7.00*
		Nos. 306c-320a (13)	62.45	52.20

Issued: 20c, $1, $2, 11/17; 3c, 5c, 3/8; 4c, 6c, 8c, 15c, 25c, 4/11; 2c, 12/12; 40c, 50c, 3/15.

1975-77 Wmk. 373

305b	A65	1c	1.00	*4.75*
306d	A65	2c	1.00	*4.75*
307b	A65	3c	.50	*4.75*
308b	A65	4c ('76)	4.50	.20
309b	A65	5c	1.60	*4.75*
310b	A65	6c ('76)	3.75	.20
311b	A65	8c ('76)	.45	.20
312b	A65	10c	.50	*2.25*
313b	A65	15c ('76)	3.25	.50
314b	A65	20c ('77)	4.75	.65
316b	A66	30c ('76)	6.75	1.10
317b	A66	40c ('76)	3.75	.70
318b	A66	50c ('76)	3.75	.80
319b	A66	$1 ('76)	3.75	1.75
320b	A66	$2 ('76)	1.90	1.75
		Nos. 305b-320b (15)	41.20	29.10

Issued: 1c, 2c, 3c, 5c, 10c, 4/9; 20c, 7/15; others, 9/3.

Women's Basketball — A67

Community Education — A68

1971, Sept. 6 Wmk. 314 *Perf. 14*

321	A67	8c shown	.50	.50
322	A67	10c Running	.75	.75
323	A67	25c Weight lifting	1.50	1.50
		Nos. 321-323 (3)	2.75	2.75

4th South Pacific Games, Papeete, French Polynesia, Sept. 8-19.

1972, Feb. 7

Designs: 4c, Public health. 50c, Economic growth (farm scenes).

324	A68	2c bright rose & multi	.20	.20
325	A68	4c gray & multi	.30	.30
326	A68	50c bright blue & multi	2.00	2.00
		Nos. 324-326 (3)	2.50	2.50

South Pacific Commission, 25th anniv.

Arts Festival Emblem — A69

Rugby — A70

1972, Apr. 10

327	A69	10c blue, org & black	.50	.50

South Pacific Festival of Arts, May 6-20.

Silver Wedding Issue, 1972

Common Design Type

Queen Elizabeth II, Prince Philip, flowers, shells.

1972, Nov. 20 Photo. *Perf. 14x14½*

328	CD324	10c slate grn & multi	.40	.40
329	CD324	25c red lilac & multi	.60	.60

1973, Mar. 9 Litho. *Perf. 14*

330	A70	2c shown	.40	.40
331	A70	8c Tackle	.80	.80
332	A70	25c Kicking ball	1.25	1.25
		Nos. 330-332 (3)	2.45	2.45

60th anniversary of Fiji Rugby Union.

Forestry Development — A71

Development projects: 8c, Irrigation of rice field. 10c, Low income housing. 25c, Highway construction.

1973, July 23 *Perf. 14*

333	A71	5c multicolored	.30	.30
334	A71	8c multicolored	.40	.40
335	A71	10c multicolored	.45	.45
336	A71	25c multicolored	1.25	1.25
		Nos. 333-336 (4)	2.40	2.40

Holy Family — A72

Runners — A73

Festivals: 10c, Diwali (Candles; Indian New Year). 20c, Id-Ul-Fitar (Friendly greeting and mosque; Moslem, Ramadan). 25c, Chinese New Year (dragon dance).

1973, Oct. 26 *Perf. 14x14½*

337	A72	3c blue & multi	.45	.45
338	A72	10c purple & multi	.45	.45
339	A72	20c emerald & multi	.75	.75
340	A72	25c red & multi	.75	.75
		Nos. 337-340 (4)	2.40	2.40

Festivals celebrated by various groups in Fiji.

1974, Jan. 7

341	A73	3c shown	.60	.35
342	A73	8c Boxing	.60	.35
343	A73	50c Lawn bowling	2.25	2.25
		Nos. 341-343 (3)	3.45	2.95

10th British Commonwealth Games, Christchurch, N.Z., Jan. 24-Feb. 2.

Centenary of Cricket in Fiji — A74

Designs: 3c, Bowler. 25c, Batsman and wicketkeeper. 40c, Fielder, horiz.

Perf. 14x14½, 14½x14

1974, Feb. 21 Litho.

344	A74	3c multicolored	1.00	1.00
345	A74	25c multicolored	1.40	1.40
346	A74	40c multicolored	1.60	1.60
		Nos. 344-346 (3)	4.00	4.00

Mailman and UPU Emblem A75

UPU Emblem and: 8c, Loading mail on ship. 30c, Post office and truck. 50c, Jet.

1974, May 22 Wmk. 314 *Perf. 14*

347	A75	3c orange & multi	.40	.40
348	A75	8c multicolored	.45	.45
349	A75	30c lt blue & multi	.75	.75
350	A75	50c multicolored	1.40	1.40
		Nos. 347-350 (4)	3.00	3.00

Centenary of the Universal Postal Union.

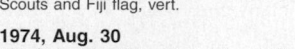

Cub Scouts A76

Designs: 10c, Boy Scouts reading map. 40c, Scouts and Fiji flag, vert.

1974, Aug. 30

351	A76	3c multicolored	.25	.25
352	A76	10c multicolored	.75	.75
353	A76	40c multicolored	2.00	2.00
		Nos. 351-353 (3)	3.00	3.00

First National Boy Scout Jamboree, Lautoka, Viti Levu Island.

Cakobau Club and Flag — A77

King Cakobau, Queen Victoria A78

Design: 50c, Signing ceremony at Levuka.

1974, Oct. 9 Litho. *Perf. 13½x13*

354 A77 3c multicolored .20 .20
355 A78 8c multicolored .40 .40
356 A78 50c multicolored 1.10 1.10
Nos. 354-356 (3) 1.70 1.70

Deed of Cession, cent. and 4th anniv. of independence.

Diwali, Hindu Festival of Lights — A79

Designs: 15c, Id-Ul-Fitar (women exchanging greetings under moon). 25c, Chinese New Year (girl twirling streamer, and fireworks). 30c, Christmas (man and woman singing hymns, and star).

1975, Oct. 31 Wmk. 373 *Perf. 14*

357 A79 3c black & multi .20 .20
358 A79 15c black & multi .45 .45
359 A79 25c black & multi .90 .90
360 A79 30c black & multi 1.10 1.10
a. Souvenir sheet of 4, #357-360 7.00 7.00
Nos. 357-360 (4) 2.65 2.65

Festivals celebrated by various groups in Fiji.

Steam Locomotive No. 21 — A80

Sugar mill trains: 15c, Diesel locomotive No. 8. 20c, Diesel locomotive No. 1. 30c, Free passenger train.

1976, Jan. 26 Litho. *Perf. 14½*

361 A80 4c yellow & multi .45 .45
362 A80 15c salmon & multi 1.10 1.10
363 A80 20c multicolored 1.50 1.50
364 A80 30c blue & multi 2.25 2.25
Nos. 361-364 (4) 5.30 5.30

Fiji Blind Society and Rotary Emblems A81

Rotary Intl. of Fiji, 40th Anniv.: 25c, Ambulance and Rotary emblems.

Perf. 13x13½

1976, Mar. 26 Wmk. 373

365 A81 10c lt green, brn, ultra .40 .40
366 A81 25c multicolored 1.00 1.00

De Havilland Drover — A82

Planes: 15c, BAC One-Eleven. 25c, Hawker-Siddeley 748. 30c, Britten Norman Trislander.

1976, Sept. 1 Litho. *Perf. 14*

367 A82 4c multicolored .20 .20
368 A82 15c multicolored .80 .80
369 A82 25c multicolored 2.00 2.00
370 A82 30c multicolored 2.25 2.25
Nos. 367-370 (4) 5.25 5.25

Fiji air service, 25th anniversary.

Queen's Visit, 1970 — A83

Designs: 25c, King Edward's Chair. 30c, Queen wearing cloth-of-gold supertunica.

1977, Feb. 7 Litho. *Perf. 14x13½*

371 A83 10c silver & multi .25 .25
372 A83 25c silver & multi .75 .75
373 A83 30c silver & multi .90 .90
Nos. 371-373 (3) 1.90 1.90

25th anniv. of reign of Elizabeth II.

World Map, Sinusoidal Projection — A84

Design: 30c, Map showing Fiji Islands.

Wmk. 373

1977, Apr. 12 Litho. *Perf. 14½*

374 A84 4c multicolored .20 .20
375 A84 30c multicolored 1.10 1.10

First Joint Council of Ministers Conference of the European Economic Community (EEC) and of African, Caribbean and Pacific States (ACP).

Hibiscus A85

1977, Aug. 27 Wmk. 373 *Perf. 14*

376 A85 4c red .20 .20
377 A85 15c orange .40 .35
378 A85 30c pink .90 .70
379 A85 35c yellow 1.10 .90
Nos. 376-379 (4) 2.60 2.15

Fiji Hibiscus Festival, 21st anniversary.

Drua, Double Canoe A86

Canoes: 15c, Tabilai. 25c, Takia, dugout outrigger canoe. 40c, Camakau.

1977, Nov. 7 Litho. *Perf. 14½*

380 A86 4c multicolored .20 .20
381 A86 15c multicolored .40 .30
382 A86 25c multicolored .70 .60
383 A86 40c multicolored .90 *.90*
Nos. 380-383 (4) 2.20 2.00

Elizabeth II Coronation Anniversary Issue

Common Design Types

Souvenir Sheet

Unwmk.

1978, Apr. 21 Litho. *Perf. 15*

384 Sheet of 6 3.25 3.25
a. CD326 25c White hart of Richard II .60 .60
b. CD327 25c Elizabeth II .60 .60
c. CD328 25c Banded iguana .60 .60

No. 384 contains 2 se-tenant strips of Nos. 348a-348c, separated by horizontal gutter.

Southern Cross on Naselai Beach — A87

4c, Fiji Defence Force surrounding Southern Cross. 25c, Wright Flyer. 30c, Bristol F2B.

1978, June 26 Wmk. 373 *Perf. 14½*

385 A87 4c multicolored .20 .20
386 A87 15c multicolored .40 .30
387 A87 25c multicolored .75 .60
388 A87 30c multicolored 1.10 .75
Nos. 385-388 (4) 2.45 1.85

50th anniv. of Kingsford-Smith's Trans-Pacific flight, May 31-June 10, 1928 (4c, 15c); 75th anniv. of Wright brothers' first powered flight, Dec. 17, 1903 (25c); 60th anniv. of Royal Air Force, Apr. 1, 1918 (30c).

Necklace of Sperm Whale Teeth A88

Fiji artifacts: 4c, Wooden oil dish in shape of man, vert. 25c, Twin water bottles. 30c, Carved throwing club (Ula), vert.

1978, Aug. 14 Litho. *Perf. 14*

389 A88 4c multicolored .30 .30
390 A88 15c multicolored .35 .35
391 A88 25c multicolored .60 .60
392 A88 30c multicolored .75 .75
Nos. 389-392 (4) 2.00 2.00

Christmas Wreath and Candles A89

Festivals: 15c, Diwali (oil lamps). 25c, Id-Ul-Fitr (fruit, coffeepot and cups). 40c, Chinese New Year (paper dragon).

1978, Oct. 30 *Perf. 14*

393 A89 4c multicolored .25 .25
394 A89 15c multicolored .35 .35
395 A89 25c multicolored .55 .55
396 A89 40c multicolored .85 .85
Nos. 393-396 (4) 2.00 2.00

Banded Iguana A90

Endangered species and Wildlife Fund emblem: 15c, Tree frog. 25c, Long-legged warbler. 30c, Pink-billed parrot finch.

1979, Mar. 19 Litho. Wmk. 373

397 A90 4c multicolored *2.00 2.00*
398 A90 15c multicolored *5.00 5.00*
399 A90 25c multicolored *8.00 8.00*
400 A90 30c multicolored *10.00 10.00*
Nos. 397-400 (4) *25.00 25.00*

Indian Women Making Music A91

15c, Indian men sitting around kava bowl. 30c, Indian sugar cane, houses. 40c, Sailing ship Leonidas, map of South Pacific.

1979, May 11 Wmk. 373 *Perf. 14*

401 A91 4c multicolored .20 .20
402 A91 15c multicolored .25 .25
403 A91 30c multicolored .45 .45
404 A91 40c multicolored .65 .65
Nos. 401-404 (4) 1.55 1.55

Arrival of Indians as indentured laborers, cent.

Soccer A92

Games Emblem and: 15c, Rugby. 30c, Tennis. 40c, Weight lifting.

1979, July 2 Litho. *Perf. 14*

405 A92 4c multicolored .30 .30
406 A92 15c multicolored .45 .45
407 A92 30c multicolored .90 .90
408 A92 40c multicolored 1.25 1.25
Nos. 405-408 (4) 2.90 2.90

6th South Pacific Games.

Old Town Hall, Suva A93

2c, Dudley Church, Suva. 3c, Telecommunications building, Suva. 4c, 5c, Lautoka Mosque. 6c, GPO, Suva. 8c, 12c, Levuka Public School. 10c, Visitors' Bureau, Suva. 15c, Colonial War Memorial Hospital Suva. 18c, Labasa Sugar Mill. 20c, Rewa Bridge, Nausori. 30c Sacred Heart Cathedral, Suva. 35c Grand Pacific Hotel, Suva. 45c, Shiva Temple, Suva. 50c Serua Island Village. $1, Solo Lighthouse. $2, Baker memorial Hall, Nausori. $5, Government House.

1979-91 Wmk. 373 *Perf. 14*

409 A93 1c multi .20 .20
410 A93 2c multi .20 .20
411 A93 3c multi .20 .20
411B A93 4c multi .20 .20
412 A93 5c multi .20 .20
413 A93 6c multi .20 .20
414 A93 10c multi .20 .20
415 A93 12c multi .20 .20
416 A93 15c multi .20 .20
417 A93 18c multi .25 .25
418 A93 20c multi .30 .30
419 A93 30c multi, vert. .35 .35
420 A93 35c multi .40 .40
421 A93 45c multi .45 .45
422 A93 50c multi .60 .60

Perf. 14x13½, 13½x14

Size: 45x29mm, 29x45mm (#423)

423 A93 $1 multi, vert. 1.10 1.10
424 A93 $2 multi 2.25 2.25
425 A93 $5 multi 5.50 5.50
Nos. 409-425 (18) 13.00 13.00

All denominations except 4c issued without inscribed dates. 4c inscribed 1991. Reissues include: 1c inscribed 1994; 2c inscribed 1983, 1986, 1991, 1993 and 1994; 3c inscribed 1993; 4c inscribed 1993 and 1994; 10c inscribed 1991; 12c inscribed 1993 and 1994; 15c inscribed 1991; 20c inscribed 1993 and 1994; 50c inscribed 1994.

Issued: 5c, 6c, 12c, 18c, 35c-$2, 12/22/80; #411B, 11/1991; others, 11/11/79.

1986-91 **Wmk. 384**

409a	A93	1c	.75	.75
410a	A93	2c	.75	.75
411a	A93	3c	.75	.75
411c	A93	4c	.75	.75
413A	A93	8c	1.00	1.00
414a	A93	10c	.75	.75
416a	A93	15c	.75	.75
418a	A93	20c	1.25	1.25
420a	A93	35c	1.50	*1.75*
422a	A93	50c	2.25	*2.50*
423a	A93	$1	3.75	*4.75*
		Nos. 409a-423a (11)	14.25	15.75

1c inscribed 1991, reissued inscribed 1992; 2c inscribed 1986, reissued inscribed 1988 and 1991; 3c inscribed 1988, reissued inscribed 1991 and 1992; 4c inscribed 1988, reissued inscribed 1991 and 1992; 8c inscribed 1986; 10c inscribed 1990, reissued inscribed 1991; 15c inscribed 1991, reissued inscribed 1992; 20c inscribed 1988, reissued inscribed 1990 and 1992; 35c, 50c and $1 each inscribed 1991, each reissued inscribed 1992.

Issued: 2c, 4/86; 8c, 12/1/86; 3c, 4c, 20c, 6/1/88; 10c, 3/1/90; 1c, 15c, 35c, 50c, $1, 3/11/90.

Southern Cross, 1873, London 1980 Emblem A94

1980, Apr. 28 **Wmk. 373** ***Perf. 13½***

426	A94	6c shown	.25	.25
427	A94	20c Levuka, 1910	.30	.30
428	A94	45c Matua, 1936	.70	.70
429	A94	50c Oronsay, 1951	.75	.75
		Nos. 426-429 (4)	2.00	2.00

London 80 Intl. Stamp Exhib., May 6-14.

Sovi Bay A95

1980, Aug. 18 ***Perf. 13½x14***

430	A95	6c shown	.20	.20
431	A95	20c Yanuca Island, evening scene	.25	.25
432	A95	45c Dravuni Beach	.55	.55
433	A95	50c Wakaya Island	.65	.65
		Nos. 430-433 (4)	1.65	1.65

Opening of Parliament, 1979 — A96

1980, Oct. 6 **Litho.** ***Perf. 13***

434	A96	6c shown	.20	.20
435	A96	20c Coat of arms, vert.	.25	.25
436	A96	45c Fiji flag	.50	.50
437	A96	50c Elizabeth II, vert.	.60	.60
		Nos. 434-437 (4)	1.55	1.55

Independence, 10th anniversary.

Coastal Scene, by Semisi Maya A97

Intl. Year of the Disabled: Paintings and portrait of disabled artist Semisi Maya.

1981, Apr. 21 **Wmk. 373** ***Perf. 14***

438	A97	6c shown	.20	.20
439	A97	35c Underwater Scene	.45	.45
440	A97	50c Maya Painting, vert.	.60	.60
441	A97	60c Peacock, vert.	.75	.75
		Nos. 438-441 (4)	2.00	2.00

Royal Wedding Issue

Common Design Type

1981, July 22 **Wmk. 373** ***Perf. 14***

442	CD331	6c Bouquet	.20	.20
443	CD331	45c Charles	.50	.50
444	CD331	$1 Couple	1.10	1.10
		Nos. 442-444 (3)	1.80	1.80

Operator Assistance Center — A98

1981, Aug. 7 **Litho.** ***Perf. 14***

445	A98	6c shown	.25	.20
446	A98	35c Microwave station, map	.60	.55
447	A98	50c Satellite earth station	1.00	.75
448	A98	60c Cableship Retriever	1.10	.90
		Nos. 445-448 (4)	2.95	*2.40*

World Food Day — A99

1981, Sept. 21 **Litho.** ***Perf. 14½x14***

449	A99	20c multicolored	.50	.50

Ratu Sir Lala Sukuna, First Legislative Council Speaker — A100

1981, Oct. 19 **Litho.** ***Perf. 14***

450	A100	6c shown	.20	.20
451	A100	35c Mace, flag	.55	.55
452	A100	50c Suva Civic Center	.75	.75
		Nos. 450-452 (3)	1.50	1.50

Souvenir Sheet

453	A100	60c Emblem, participants' flags	.90	.90

27th Commonwealth Parliamentary Assoc. Conf., Suva.

World War II Aircraft A101

1981, Dec. 7 **Litho.** ***Perf. 14***

454	A101	6c Bell P-39 Aircobra	1.10	.20
455	A101	18c Consolidated PBY-5 Catalina	2.40	.30
456	A101	35c Curtiss P-40 Warhawk	4.00	.65
457	A101	60c Short Singapore	4.50	1.00
		Nos. 454-457 (4)	12.00	2.15

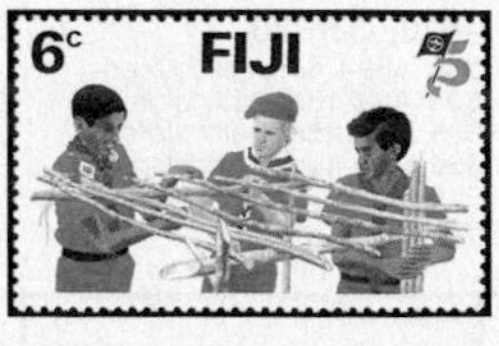

Scouting Year A102

1982, Feb. 22 **Litho.** ***Perf. 14½***

458	A102	6c Building	.25	.25
459	A102	20c Sailing, vert.	.50	.50
460	A102	45c Campfire	1.10	1.10
461	A102	60c Baden-Powell, vert.	1.25	1.25
		Nos. 458-461 (4)	3.10	3.10

Disciplined Forces — A103

1982, May 10 **Wmk. 373** ***Perf. 14***

462	A103	12c UN checkpoint	.50	.20
463	A103	30c Construction project	1.25	.50
464	A103	40c Police, car	2.00	.65
465	A103	70c Navy ship	2.25	*1.25*
		Nos. 462-465 (4)	6.00	2.60

1982 World Cup A104

1982, June 15 **Litho.** ***Perf. 14***

466	A104	6c Fiji Soccer Assoc. emblem	.20	.20
467	A104	18c Flag, ball	.35	.35
468	A104	50c Stadium	.90	.90
469	A104	90c Emblem	1.75	1.75
		Nos. 466-469 (4)	3.20	3.20

Princess Diana Issue

Common Design Type

1982, July 1 ***Perf. 14½x14***

470	CD333	20c Arms	.50	.50
471	CD333	35c Diana	.80	.80
472	CD333	45c Wedding	1.10	1.10
473	CD333	$1 Portrait	2.50	2.50
		Nos. 470-473 (4)	4.90	4.90

October Royal Visit — A105

1982, Nov. 1 **Litho.** ***Perf. 14***

474	A105	6c Duke of Edinburgh	.20	.20
475	A105	45c Elizabeth II	.80	.80

Souvenir Sheet

476		Sheet of 3	3.75	3.75
c.		A105 $1 Britannia	1.60	1.60

No. 476 contains Nos. 474-475 and 476c.

Christmas A106

1982, Nov. 22 ***Perf. 14x14½***

477	A106	6c Holy Family	.20	.20
478	A106	20c Adoration of the Kings	.40	.40
479	A106	35c Carolers	.75	.75
		Nos. 477-479 (3)	1.35	1.35

Souvenir Sheet

480	A106	$1 Faith, from The Three Virtues, by Raphael	2.00	2.00

Red-throated Lory — A107

Parrots.

1983, Feb. 14 **Litho.** ***Perf. 14***

481	A107	20c shown	1.50	1.50
482	A107	40c Blue-crowned lory	2.25	2.25
483	A107	55c Sulphur-breasted musk parrot	3.50	3.50
484	A107	70c Red-breasted musk parrot	4.25	4.25
		Nos. 481-484 (4)	11.50	11.50

A108

1983, Mar. 14

485	A108	8c Traditional house	.20	.20
486	A108	25c Barefoot firewalkers	.35	.35
487	A108	50c Sugar cane crop	.70	.70
488	A108	80c Kava Yagona ceremony	1.10	1.10
		Nos. 485-488 (4)	2.35	2.35

Commonwealth Day.

Manned Flight Bicentenary — A109

1983, July 18 **Wmk. 373** ***Perf. 14***

489	A109	8c Montgolfiere, 1783	.45	.20
490	A109	20c Wright Flyer	.55	.35
491	A109	25c DC-3	.65	.40
492	A109	40c DeHavilland Comet	1.00	.70
493	A109	50c Boeing 747	1.25	.85
494	A109	58c Columbia space shuttle	1.60	1.00
		Nos. 489-494 (6)	5.50	3.50

Cordia Subcordata A110

Earth Satellite Station, Fijian Playing Lali A111

Flowers.

1983, Sept. 26 **Litho.** ***Perf. 14***

495	A110	8c shown	.20	.20
496	A110	25c Gmelina vitiensis	.35	.35
497	A110	40c Carruthersia scandens	.60	.60
498	A110	$1 Amylotheca insularum	1.50	1.50
		Nos. 495-498 (4)	2.65	2.65

See Nos. 505-508.

Perf. 14x13½

1983, Nov. 7 **Wmk. 373**

499	A111	50c multicolored	.85	.85

Dacryopinax Spathularia A112

Various fungi.

1984, Jan. 9 *Perf. 14x13½, 13½x14*
500 A112 8c shown .65 .20
501 A112 15c Podoscypha involuta 1.10 .45
502 A112 40c Lentinus squarrosulus 2.25 1.10
503 A112 50c Scleroderma flavidum 3.50 1.50
504 A112 $1 Phillipsia domingensis 6.50 2.75
Nos. 500-504 (5) 14.00 6.00

Flower Type of 1983

1984 Litho. *Perf. 14x14½*
505 A110 15c Pseuderanthemum laxiflorum .25 .25
506 A110 20c Storkiella vitiensis .30 .30
507 A110 50c Paphia vitiensis .80 .80
508 A110 70c Elaeocarpus storkii 1.10 1.10
Nos. 505-508 (4) 2.45 2.45

Lloyd's List Issue
Common Design Type
Perf. 14½x14

1984, May 7 **Wmk. 373**
509 CD335 8c Tui Lau on reef .40 .40
510 CD335 40c Tofua 1.50 1.50
511 CD335 55c Canberra 2.00 2.00
512 CD335 60c Suva Wharf 2.25 2.25
Nos. 509-512 (4) 6.15 6.15

Souvenir Sheet

1984 UPU Congress — A113

1984, June 14 Litho. *Perf. 14½*
513 A113 25c Map 2.25 2.25

Ausipex '84 — A114

1984, Sept. 17 Wmk. 373 *Perf. 14*
514 A114 8c Yalavou cattle .20 .20
515 A114 25c Wailoa Power Station, vert. .55 .55
516 A114 40c Boeing 737 .95 .95
517 A114 $1 Cargo ship Fua Kavenga 2.50 2.50
Nos. 514-517 (4) 4.20 4.20

Christmas A115

1984, Nov. 5 Litho. *Perf. 14*
518 A115 8c Church on hill .20 .20
519 A115 20c Sailing .35 .35
520 A115 25c Santa, children, tree .40 .40
521 A115 40c Going to church .65 .65
522 A115 $1 Family, tree, vert. 1.75 1.75
Nos. 518-522 (5) 3.35 3.35

Butterflies A116

1985, Feb. 4 *Perf. 14*
523 A116 8c Monarch 1.00 .25
524 A116 25c Common eggfly 2.50 .80
525 A116 40c Long-tailed blue, vert. 4.00 1.40
526 A116 $1 Meadow argus, vert. 10.50 3.50
Nos. 523-526 (4) 18.00 5.95

EXPO '85, Tsukuba, Japan — A117

1985, Mar. 18 Litho. *Perf. 14*
527 A117 20c Outrigger canoe, Toberua Isl. .55 .50
528 A117 25c Wainivula Falls .60 .55
529 A117 50c Mana Island 1.60 1.40
530 A117 $1 Sawa-I-Lau Caves 2.75 2.50
Nos. 527-530 (4) 5.50 4.95

Queen Mother 85th Birthday Issue
Common Design Type
Perf. 14½x14

1985, June 7 **Wmk. 384**
531 CD336 8c Holding Prince Andrew .20 .20
532 CD336 25c With Prince Charles .60 .60
533 CD336 40c On Oaks Day, Epsom Races .95 .95
534 CD336 50c Holding Prince Henry 1.25 1.25
Nos. 531-534 (4) 3.00 3.00

Souvenir Sheet

535 CD336 $1 In Royal Wedding Cavalcade, 1981 4.00 4.00

Shallow Water Fish A118

1985, Sept. 23 *Perf. 14½*
536 A118 40c Horned squirrel fish 1.50 1.10
537 A118 50c Yellow-banded goatfish 2.25 1.40
538 A118 55c Fairy cod 2.25 1.50
539 A118 $1 Peacock rock cod 4.00 2.75
Nos. 536-539 (4) 10.00 6.75

Sea Birds — A119

1985, Nov. 4 *Perf. 14*
540 A119 15c Collared petrel 1.25 .45
541 A119 20c Lesser frigate bird 2.25 .70
542 A119 50c Brown booby 6.00 1.75
543 A119 $1 Crested tern 11.50 4.25
Nos. 540-543 (4) 21.00 7.15

Queen Elizabeth II 60th Birthday Issue
Common Design Type

20c, With the Duke of York at the Royal Tournament, 1936. 25c, On Buckingham Palace balcony, wedding of Princess Margaret and Anthony Armstrong-Jones, 1960. 40c, Inspecting the Guard of Honor, Suva, 1982. 50c, State visit to Luxembourg, 1976. $1, Visiting Crown Agents' offices, 1983.

Perf. 14x14½

1986, Apr. 21 **Wmk. 384**
544 CD337 20c scar, blk & sil .40 .40
545 CD337 25c ultra & multi .45 .45
546 CD337 40c green & multi .75 .75
547 CD337 50c violet & multi .95 .95
548 CD337 $1 rose vio & multi 1.90 1.90
Nos. 544-548 (5) 4.45 4.45

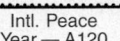

Intl. Peace Year — A120

Halley's Comet — A121

1986, June 23 Wmk. 373 *Perf. 14½*
549 A120 8c shown .20 .20
550 A120 40c Dove 1.10 1.10

1986, July 7 *Perf. 13½*
551 A121 25c Newton's reflector telescope .90 .60
552 A121 40c Comet over Lomaiviti 1.10 .95
553 A121 $1 Comet nucleus, Giotto probe 6.00 2.50
Nos. 551-553 (3) 8.00 4.05

Reptiles and Amphibians — A122

1986, Aug. 1 *Perf. 14½*
554 A122 8c Ground frog .40 .20
555 A122 20c Burrowing snake .65 *.70*
556 A122 25c Spotted gecko .70 *.90*
557 A122 40c Crested iguana 1.10 *1.25*
558 A122 50c Blotched skink 3.00 1.60
559 A122 $1 Speckled skink 6.00 3.50
Nos. 554-559 (6) 11.85 8.15

Ancient War Clubs — A123

Cone Shells — A124

1986, Nov. 10 Wmk. 384 *Perf. 14*
560 A123 25c Gatawaka .90 .80
561 A123 40c Siriti 1.25 1.00
562 A123 50c Bulibuli 1.60 1.40
563 A123 $1 Culacula 3.25 2.75
Nos. 560-563 (4) 7.00 5.95

1987, Feb. 26 Litho. *Perf. 14x14½*
564 A124 15c Weasel .60 .35
565 A124 20c Pertusus .65 .45
566 A124 25c Admiral 1.10 .60
567 A124 40c Leaden 1.40 .95
568 A124 50c Imperial 2.75 1.25
569 A124 $1 Geography 5.50 2.50
Nos. 564-569 (6) 12.00 6.10

Souvenir Sheet

Tagimoucia Flower — A125

1987, Apr. 23 Wmk. 373 *Perf. 14½*
570 A125 $1 multicolored 5.50 3.75

No. 570 Overprinted with CAPEX '87 Emblem

1987, June 13
571 A125 $1 multicolored 35.00 35.00

Intl. Year of Shelter for the Homeless A126

1987, July 20 *Perf. 14*
572 A126 55c Hut .70 .70
573 A126 70c Government housing .95 .95

Beetles — A127

1987, Sept. 7 **Wmk. 384**
574 A127 20c Bulbogaster ctenostomoides 1.00 .45
575 A127 25c Paracupta flaviventris 1.75 .65
576 A127 40c Cerambyrhynchus schoenherri 2.25 1.00
577 A127 50c Rhinoscapha lagopyga 3.75 1.25
578 A127 $1 Xixuthrus heros 8.25 2.50
Nos. 574-578 (5) 17.00 5.85

Christmas — A128

1987, Nov. 19
579 A128 8c Holy Family, vert. .25 .20
580 A128 40c Shepherds see star 1.00 .65
581 A128 50c Three Kings follow star 2.75 .75
582 A128 $1 Adoration of the Magi 5.75 1.50
Nos. 579-582 (4) 9.75 3.10

World Expo '88, Apr. 30-Oct. 30, Brisbane, Australia A129

1988, Apr. 27 Litho. *Perf. 14*
583 A129 30c Windsurfing 1.75 1.75

Intl. Council of Women, Cent. A130

1988, June 14
584 A130 45c Fiji Nouna 1.25 1.25

Pottery A131

Wmk. 384, 373 (69c)

1988, Aug. 29 Litho. *Perf. 13½*

585	A131	9c	Lapita (bowl)	.25	.20
586	A131	23c	Kuro (cooking pot)	.50	.40
587	A131	58c	Saqa (ritual drinking vessel)	1.00	.90
588	A131	63c	Saqa, diff.	1.50	1.25
589	A131	69c	Ramarama (oil lamp)	1.75	1.50
590	A131	75c	Kuro, diff., vert.	2.50	2.00
			Nos. 585-590 (6)	7.50	6.25

Fiji Tree Frog — A132

Indigenous Flowering Plants — A133

1988, Oct. 3 Wmk. 384 *Perf. 14*

591	A132	18c	multi	5.00	5.00
592	A132	23c	multi, diff.	5.75	5.75
593	A132	30c	multi, diff.	7.25	7.25
594	A132	45c	multi, diff.	12.00	12.00
			Nos. 591-594 (4)	30.00	30.00

World Wildlife Fund.

1988, Nov. 21 Wmk. 373

595	A133	9c	Dendrobium mohlianum	.35	.25
596	A133	30c	Dendrobium cattilare	1.25	1.00
597	A133	45c	Degeneria vitiensis	2.00	1.50
598	A133	$1	Degeneria roseiflora	4.00	3.00
			Nos. 595-598 (4)	7.60	5.75

Intl. Red Cross and Red Crescent Orgs., 125th Anniv. — A134

1989, Feb. 6 Wmk. 384

599	A134	58c	Battle of Solferino, 1859	1.75	1.10
600	A134	63c	Jean-Henri Dunant, vert.	2.00	1.10
601	A134	69c	Medicine	2.25	1.25
602	A134	$1	Anniv. emblem, vert.	5.00	1.90
			Nos. 599-602 (4)	11.00	5.35

Epic Voyage of William Bligh A135

Designs: 45c, Plans (line drawing) of the Bounty's launch. 58c, Diary and inscription on artifacts "The cup I eat my miserable allowance out of." 80c, Silhouette, lightning, quote "O Almighty God, relieve us. . ." $1, Map of Bligh's Islands, launch and compass rose.

1989, Apr. 28 *Perf. 14½*

603	A135	45c	multicolored	2.10	.70
604	A135	58c	multicolored	2.50	.95
605	A135	80c	multicolored	4.50	1.25
606	A135	$1	multicolored	6.00	1.50
			Nos. 603-606 (4)	15.10	4.40

Coral A136

1989, Aug. 21 Wmk. 373 *Perf. 14*

607	A136	46c	Platygyra daedalea	2.50	2.50
608	A136	60c	Caulastrea furcata	3.25	3.25
609	A136	75c	Acropora echinata	4.00	4.00
610	A136	90c	Acropora humilis	5.25	5.25
			Nos. 607-610 (4)	15.00	15.00

Nos. 609-610 vert.

1990 World Cup Soccer Championships, Italy — A137

Various Fijian soccer players.

1989, Sept. 25 Wmk. 384 *Perf. 14½*

611	A137	35c	shown	1.60	1.60
612	A137	63c	multi, diff.	2.50	2.50
613	A137	70c	multi, diff.	3.00	3.00
614	A137	85c	multi, diff.	3.50	3.50
			Nos. 611-614 (4)	10.60	10.60

Christmas A138

1989, Nov. 1 Wmk. 373

615	A138	9c	Church service	.35	.35
616	A138	45c	*Delonix regia* tree	1.10	1.10
617	A138	$1	Holy family	2.10	2.10
618	A138	$1.40	Tree, Fijian children	3.00	3.00
			Nos. 615-618 (4)	6.55	6.55

Fish A139

1990, Apr. 23 Litho. Wmk. 384

619	A139	50c	Mangrove jack	3.00	3.00
620	A139	70c	Orange-spotted therapon perch	4.50	4.50
621	A139	85c	Spotted scat	5.00	5.00
622	A139	$1	Flagtail	6.00	6.00
			Nos. 619-622 (4)	18.50	18.50

Souvenir Sheet

Stamp World London '90 — A140

1990, May 1

623	A140		Sheet of 2	13.50	6.00
a.			$1 No. 243	4.25	1.75
b.			$2 No. 249	8.50	4.25

Soil Conservation — A141

50c, Vertiver grass contours. 70c, Mulching. 90c, Contour cultivation. $1, Proper land use.

1990, July 23 Litho. Wmk. 373

625	A141	50c	multi	1.10	1.10
626	A141	70c	multi	1.60	1.60
627	A141	90c	multi	2.10	2.10
628	A141	$1	multi, vert.	2.25	2.25
			Nos. 625-628 (4)	7.05	7.05

Trees — A142

1990, Oct. 2

629	A142	25c	Dacrydium nidulum	.90	.90
630	A142	35c	Decussocarpus vitiensis	1.10	1.10
631	A142	$1	Agathis vitiensis	3.50	3.50
632	A142	$1.55	Santalum yasi	5.00	5.00
			Nos. 629-632 (4)	10.50	10.50

Christmas — A143

Christmas carols: 10c, Hark! The Herald Angels Sing. 35c, Silent Night. 65c, Joy to the World! $1, The Race that Long in Darkness Pined.

1990, Nov. 26 Wmk. 373 *Perf. 14*

633	A143	10c	multicolored	.40	.40
634	A143	35c	multicolored	1.10	1.10
635	A143	65c	multicolored	2.00	2.00
636	A143	$1	multicolored	3.00	3.00
			Nos. 633-636 (4)	6.50	6.50

Scenic Views — A144

1991, Feb. 25 Wmk. 384

637	A144	35c	Sigatoka sand dunes	1.50	1.50
638	A144	50c	Monu, Monuriki Islands	2.75	2.75
639	A144	65c	Ravilevu Nature Reserve	3.25	3.25
640	A144	$1	Colo-I-Suva Forest Park	5.50	5.50
			Nos. 637-640 (4)	13.00	13.00

Discovery of Rotuma Island, Bicent. A145

1991, Aug. 8 Wmk. 373 *Perf. 14*

641	A145	54c	HMS Pandora	2.75	2.75
642	A145	70c	Map of Rotuma Island	3.50	3.50
643	A145	75c	Natives	3.75	3.75
644	A145	$1	Mt. Solroroa, Uea Island	5.00	5.00
			Nos. 641-644 (4)	15.00	15.00

Crabs A146

Designs: 38c, Scylla serrata. 54c, Metopograpsus messor. 96c, Parasesarma erythrodactyla. $1.65, Cardisoma carnifex.

1991, Sept. 26 *Perf. 14½x14*

645	A146	38c	multicolored	1.10	1.10
646	A146	54c	multicolored	1.75	1.75
647	A146	96c	multicolored	2.75	2.75
648	A146	$1.65	multicolored	5.50	5.50
			Nos. 645-648 (4)	11.10	11.10

Christmas A147

Designs: 11c, Mary, Joseph travelling to Bethlehem. 75c, Manger scene. 96c, Jesus being blessed at temple in Jerusalem. $1, Baby Jesus.

1991, Oct. 31 Wmk. 384 *Perf. 14*

649	A147	11c	multicolored	.45	.45
650	A147	75c	multicolroed	2.10	2.10
651	A147	96c	multicolored	2.50	2.50
652	A147	$1	multicolored	2.50	2.50
			Nos. 649-652 (4)	7.55	7.55

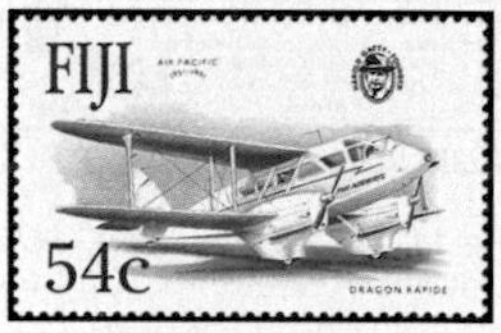

Air Pacific, 40th Anniv. A148

Airplanes: 54c, Dragon Rapide, Harold Gatty, founder. 75c, Douglas DC3. 96c, ATR 42. $1.40, Boeing 767.

1991, Nov. 18 *Perf. 14½*

653	A148	54c	multicolored	3.00	3.00
654	A148	75c	multicolored	3.25	3.25
655	A148	96c	multicolored	4.25	4.25
656	A148	$1.40	multicolored	6.50	6.50
			Nos. 653-656 (4)	17.00	17.00

Expo '92, Seville A149

Designs: 27c, Traditional dance and costumes. 75c, Faces of people. 96c, Train and gold bars. $1.40, Cruise ship in port.

Perf. 14½x14

1992, Mar. 23 Litho. Wmk. 373

657	A149	27c	multicolored	1.50	1.50
658	A149	75c	multicolored	4.00	4.00
659	A149	96c	multicolored	5.75	5.75
660	A149	$1.40	multicolored	7.75	7.75
			Nos. 657-660 (4)	19.00	19.00

Inter-Islands Shipping — A150

1992, June 22 *Perf. 14*

661	A150	38c	Tabusoro	2.00	2.00
662	A150	54c	Degei II	2.75	2.75
663	A150	$1.40	Dausoko	6.25	6.25
664	A150	$1.65	Nivanga	7.00	7.00
			Nos. 661-664 (4)	18.00	18.00

1992 Summer Olympics, Barcelona — A151

1992, July 30 *Perf. 13½*

665	A151 20c Running	.65	.65
666	A151 86c Yachting	2.75	2.75
667	A151 $1.34 Swimming	4.00	4.00
668	A151 $1.50 Judo	5.00	5.00
	Nos. 665-668 (4)	12.40	12.40

Levuka A152

30c, European War Memorial. 42c, Map. 59c, Beach Street. 77c, Sacred Heart Church, vert. $2, Deed of Cession Site, vert.

1992, Sept. 21 *Perf. 14½*

669	A152 30c multicolored	.75	.75
670	A152 42c multicolored	1.00	1.00
671	A152 59c multicolored	1.50	1.50
672	A152 77c multicolored	2.00	2.00
673	A152 $2 multicolored	4.75	4.75
	Nos. 669-673 (5)	10.00	10.00

Intl. Planned Parenthood Federation, 40th Anniv. — A153

1992, Nov. 2 *Perf. 15x14½*

674	A153 77c Globe	1.50	1.50
675	A153 $2 Family	3.75	3.75

Christmas — A154

Bible interpretations: 12c, "God so loved the world..." 77c, "We love because God first loved us." 83c, "It is more blessed to give..." $2, "Every good gift..."

1992, Nov. 17

676	A154 12c multicolored	.35	.35
677	A154 77c multicolored	1.90	1.90
678	A154 83c multicolored	2.25	2.25
679	A154 $2 multicolored	5.50	5.50
	Nos. 676-679 (4)	10.00	10.00

Peace Corps in Fiji, 25th Anniv. A155

Designs: 59c, Voluntary service. 77c, Fiji/US friendship. $1, Education. $2, Income generating business through volunteer help.

Wmk. 373

1993, Feb. 22 **Litho.** *Perf. 14½*

680	A155 59c multicolored	1.25	1.25
681	A155 77c multicolored	1.60	1.60
682	A155 $1 multicolored	2.00	2.00
683	A155 $2 multicolored	4.25	4.25
	Nos. 680-683 (4)	9.10	9.10

Hong Kong Rugby Sevens — A156

Designs: 77c, Players performing traditional Cibi Dance. $1.06, Two players, map of Fiji, Hong Kong, and Australia. $2, Stadium, players in scrum.

Perf. 14x15

1993, Mar. 26 **Litho.** **Wmk. 384**

684	A156 77c multicolored	1.75	1.75
685	A156 $1.06 multicolored	2.50	2.50
686	A156 $2 multicolored	4.50	4.50
	Nos. 684-686 (3)	8.75	8.75

Royal Air Force, 75th Anniv.

Common Design Type

Designs: 59c, Gloster Gauntlet. 77c, Armstrong Whitworth Whitley. 83c, Bristol F2b. $2, Hawker Tempest.

No. 691: a, Vickers Vildebeest. b, Handley Page Hampden. c, Vickers Vimy. d, British Aerospace Hawk.

1993, Apr. 1 *Perf. 14*

687	CD350 59c multicolored	1.25	1.25
688	CD350 77c multicolored	1.60	1.60
689	CD350 83c multicolored	1.60	1.60
690	CD350 $2 multicolored	4.50	4.50
	Nos. 687-690 (4)	8.95	8.95

Souvenir Sheet of 4

691	CD350 $1 #a.-d.	10.00	10.00
a.	Overprinted in sheet margin	10.00	10.00

Overprint on No. 691a is exhibition emblem for Hong Kong '94.

Nudibranchs A157

Wmk. 373

1993, July 27 **Litho.** *Perf. 14*

692	A157 12c Chromodoris fidelis	.50	.50
693	A157 42c Halgerda carlsoni	1.25	1.25
694	A157 53c Chromodoris lochi	1.75	1.75
695	A157 83c Glaucus atlanticus	2.75	2.75
696	A157 $1 Phyllidia bourguini	3.25	3.25
697	A157 $2 Hexabranchus sanguineus	6.50	6.50
	Nos. 692-697 (6)	16.00	16.00

Tropical Fruit — A158

Wmk. 373

1993, Oct. 25 **Litho.** *Perf. 13½*

698	A158 30c Mango	1.25	1.25
699	A158 42c Guava	2.25	2.25
700	A158 $1 Lemon	4.50	4.50
701	A158 $2 Soursop	9.00	9.00
	Nos. 698-701 (4)	17.00	17.00

Souvenir Sheet

Hong Kong '94 — A159

Butterflies: a, Caper white. b, Blue branded king crow. c, Vagrant. d, Glasswing.

Perf. 14½x13

1994, Feb. 18 **Litho.** **Wmk. 373**

702	A159 $1 Sheet of 4, #a.-d.	11.00	11.00

Easter A160

59c, The Last Supper. 77c, The Crucifixion. $1, The Resurrection. $2, Jesus showing his wounds to his disciples.

Perf. 14x15, 15x14

1994, Mar. 31 **Litho.** **Wmk. 373**

703	A160 59c multi	1.25	1.25
704	A160 77c multi, vert.	1.75	1.75
705	A160 $1 multi	2.00	2.00
706	A160 $2 multi, vert.	4.25	4.25
	Nos. 703-706 (4)	9.25	9.25

Edible Seaweeds A161

42c, Codium bulbopilum. 83c, Coulerpa racemosa. $1, Hypnea pannosa. $2, Gracilaria.

Wmk. 384

1994, June 6 **Litho.** *Perf. 14*

707	A161 42c multicolored	1.25	.95
708	A161 83c multicolored	2.25	1.90
709	A161 $1 multicolored	2.75	2.40
710	A161 $2 multicolored	5.75	4.75
	Nos. 707-710 (4)	12.00	10.00

Souvenir Sheet

White-Collared Kingfisher — A162

Designs: a, On branch. b, In flight.

Wmk. 373

1994, Aug. **Litho.** *Perf. 13½*

711	A162 $1.50 Sheet of 2, #a.-b.	12.50	12.50
c.	Overprinted in sheet margin	12.00	12.00

Overprint on No. 711c consists of exhibition emblem and "JAKARTA '95."

Issued: #711, 8/16; #711c, 8/19.

Souvenir Sheet

Singpex '94 — A163

Neoveitchia storckii: a, Complete tree. b. Fruits, inflorescence.

1994, Aug. 31 **Wmk. 384** *Perf. 14*

712	A163 $1.50 Sheet of 2, #a.-b.	11.00	11.00

First Catholic Missionaries in Fiji, 150th Anniv. — A164

Wmk. 373

1994, Dec. 16 **Litho.** *Perf. 14*

713	A164 23c Father Ioane Batita	.60	.60
714	A164 31c Local catechist	.70	.70
715	A164 44c Sacred Heart Cathedral	.95	.95
716	A164 63c Lomary Church	1.25	1.25
717	A164 81c Pope Gregory XVI	1.75	1.75
718	A164 $2 Pope John Paul II	4.00	4.00
	Nos. 713-718 (6)	9.25	9.25

Souvenir Sheet

Ecotourism in Fiji — A165

Designs: a, Waterfalls, banded iguana. b, Mountain trekking, Fiji tree frog. c, Bilibili River trip, kingfisher. d, Historic sites, flying fox.

Wmk. 373

1995, Mar. 27 **Litho.** *Perf. 14*

719	A165 81c Sheet of 4, #a.-d.	9.00	9.00

End of World War II, 50th Anniv.

Common Design Types

Designs: 13c, Fijian regiment guarding crashed Japanese Zero Fighter. 63c, Kameli Airstrip, Solomon Islands, built by Fijian regiment. 87c, Corp. Sukanaivalu VC, Victoria Cross. $1.12, HMS Fiji.

$2, Reverse side of War Medal 1939-45.

Wmk. 373

1995, May 8 **Litho.** *Perf. 13½*

720	CD351 13c multicolored	.50	.50
721	CD351 63c multicolored	2.75	2.75
722	CD351 87c multicolored	3.75	3.75
723	CD351 $1.12 multicolored	5.00	5.00
	Nos. 720-723 (4)	12.00	12.00

Souvenir Sheet

Perf. 14

724	CD352 $2 multicolored	5.00	5.00

Birds — A166

1995 **Litho.** **Wmk. 373** *Perf. 13*

725	A166 1c Red-headed parrotfinch	.20	.20
726	A166 2c Golden whistler	.20	.20

727 A166 3c Ogea flycatcher .20 .20
728 A166 4c Peale's pigeon .20 .20
729 A166 6c Blue-crested broadbill .20 .20
730 A166 13c Island thrush .20 .20
731 A166 23c Many-colored fruit dove .40 .40
732 A166 31c Mangrove heron .55 .55
733 A166 44c Purple swamphen 1.00 1.00
734 A166 63c Fiji goshawk 1.25 1.25
735 A166 81c Kadavu fantail 1.60 1.60
736 A166 87c Collared lory 1.75 1.75
737 A166 $1 Scarlet robin 2.00 2.00
738 A166 $2 Peregrine falcon 4.00 4.00
739 A166 $3 Barn owl 5.75 5.75
739A A166 $5 Yellow-breasted musk parrot 10.50 10.50
Nos. 725-739A (16) 30.00 30.00

Issued: 13c, 23c, 31c, 44c, 63c, 81c, $2, $3, 7/25; 1c, 2c, 3c, 4c, 6c, 87c, $1, $5, 11/7.
See No. 1011.

Souvenir Sheet

Singapore '95 — A167

Orchids: a, Arundina graminifolia. b, Phaius tankervilliae.

Wmk. 373
1995, Sept. 1 Litho. ***Perf. 14***
740 A167 $1 Sheet of 2, #a.-b. 9.00 9.00

Independence, 25th Anniv. — A168

Designs: 81c, Pres. Kamisese Mara, Parliament Building. 87c, Fijian youth. $1.06, Playing rugby. $2, Air Pacific Boeing 747.

Wmk. 373
1995, Oct. 4 Litho. ***Perf. 14***
741 A168 81c multicolored 1.60 1.60
742 A168 87c multicolored 1.90 1.90
743 A168 $1.06 multicolored 2.25 2.25
744 A168 $2 multicolored 4.25 4.25
Nos. 741-744 (4) 10.00 10.00

Christmas — A169

Paintings: 10c, Praying Madonna with the Crown of Stars, from Correggio Workshop. 63c, Madonna and Child with Crowns on porcelain. 87c, The Holy Virgin with the Holy Child and St. John, after Titian. $2, The Holy Family and St. John, from Rubens Workshop.

Wmk. 373
1995, Nov. 22 Litho. ***Perf. 13***
745 A169 10c multicolored .25 .25
746 A169 63c multicolored 1.25 1.25
747 A169 87c multicolored 1.75 1.75
748 A169 $2 multicolored 4.00 4.00
Nos. 745-748 (4) 7.25 7.25

Arrival of Banabans in Fiji, 50th Anniv. A170

Perf. 14x14½, 14½x14
1996, Jan. 24 Litho. Wmk. 373
749 A170 81c Trolling lure 2.25 2.25
750 A170 87c Canoes 2.50 2.50
751 A170 $1.12 Warrior, vert. 2.75 2.75
752 A170 $2 Frigate bird, vert. 5.25 5.25
Nos. 749-752 (4) 12.75 12.75

A171

A172

Radio, Cent.: 44c, L2B portable tape recorder. 63c, Fiji Broadcasting Center. 81c, Communications satellite in orbit. $3, Marconi.

Wmk. 373
1996, Mar. 11 Litho. ***Perf. 14½***
753 A171 44c multicolored .90 .90
754 A171 63c multicolored 1.25 1.25
755 A171 81c multicolored 1.60 1.60
756 A171 $3 multicolored 6.25 6.25
Nos. 753-756 (4) 10.00 10.00

Wmk. 384
1996, Apr. 25 Litho. ***Perf. 13½***

Ancient Chinese artifacts: 63c, Bronze monster mask and ring, c. 450 BC. 81c, Archer, 210 BC. $1, Plate, Hsuan Te Period, 1426-35. $2, Central Asian horseman, dated 706.
30c, Yan Deng Mountain.

757 A172 63c multicolored 1.25 1.25
758 A172 81c multicolored 1.50 1.50
759 A172 $1 multicolored 2.00 2.00
760 A172 $2 multicolored 4.25 4.25
Nos. 757-760 (4) 9.00 9.00

Souvenir Sheet
Perf. 13½x13
761 A172 30c multicolored 2.50 2.50

No. 761 contains one 48x76mm stamp.
CHINA '96, 9th Asian Intl. Philatelic Exhibition.

A173

A174

Wmk. 373
1996, June 18 Litho. ***Perf. 14***
762 A173 31c Hurdling .65 .65
763 A173 63c Judo 1.50 1.50
764 A173 87c Sailboarding 2.10 2.10
765 A173 $1.12 Swimming 2.50 2.50
Nos. 762-765 (4) 6.75 6.75

Souvenir Sheet
766 A173 $2 Athlete, 1896 4.00 4.00

Modern Olympic Games, cent.

1996, July 1

31c, Computerized telephone exchange, horiz. 44c, Mail being unloaded, horiz. 81c, Manual switchboard operator. $1, Mail delivery.
No. 771: a, #117. b, #527.

767 A174 31c multicolored .60 .60
768 A174 44c multicolored .80 .80
769 A174 81c multicolored 1.40 1.40
770 A174 $1 multicolored 1.90 1.90
Nos. 767-770 (4) 4.70 4.70

Souvenir Sheet of 2
771 A174 $1.50 #a.-b. 5.00 5.00

Creation of independent Postal, Telecommunications Companies.

UNICEF, 50th Anniv. A175

Designs: 81c, "Our children, our future." 87c, Village scene. $1, "Living in harmony the world over." $2, "Their future."

Wmk. 384
1996, Aug. 13 Litho. ***Perf. 14***
772 A175 81c multicolored 2.00 2.00
773 A175 87c multicolored 2.00 2.00
774 A175 $1 multicolored 2.25 2.25
775 A175 $2 multicolored 4.50 4.50
Nos. 772-775 (4) 10.75 10.75

Nadi Intl. Airport, 50th Anniv. A176

Designs: 31c, First airplane in Fiji, 1921. 44c, Nadi Airport commences Commercial Operations, 1946. 63c, First jet in Fiji, 1959. 87c, Airport entrance. $1, Control tower, 1996. $2, Global positioning system, first commercial use, 1994.

Wmk. 373
1996, Oct. 1 Litho. ***Perf. 14***
776 A176 31c multicolored .75 .75
777 A176 44c multicolored 1.00 1.00
778 A176 63c multicolored 1.50 1.50
779 A176 87c multicolored 2.00 2.00
780 A176 $1 multicolored 2.25 2.25
781 A176 $2 multicolored 4.50 4.50
Nos. 776-781 (6) 12.00 12.00

Christmas — A177

Scene from the Christmas story and native story or scene: 13c, Angel Gabriel & Mary, beating of Lali. 81c, Shepherds with sheep, Fijian canoe. $1, Wise men on camels, multiracial Fiji. $3, Mary, Christ Child in stable, blowing of conch shell.

1996, Nov. 20 Wmk. 373
782 A177 13c multicolored .30 .30
783 A177 81c multicolored 2.00 2.00
784 A177 $1 multicolored 2.40 2.40
785 A177 $3 multicolored 7.25 7.25
Nos. 782-785 (4) 11.95 11.95

Hong Kong '97 A178

Cattle: a, Brahman. b, Freisian (Holstein). c, Hereford. d, Fiji draught bullock.

1997, Feb. 12
786 A178 $1 Sheet of 4, #a.-d. 9.00 9.00

Souvenir Sheet

Black-Faced Shrikebill — A179

Illustration reduced.

1997, Feb. 21 ***Perf. 14x15***
787 A179 $2 multicolored 4.50 4.50

Singpex '97.

Orchids — A180

Designs: 81c, Dendrobium biflorum. 87c, Dendrobium dactylodes. $1.06, Spathoglottis pacifica. $2, Dendrobium macropus.

Wmk. 384
1997, Apr. 22 Litho. ***Perf. 14***
788 A180 81c multicolored 1.75 1.75
789 A180 87c multicolored 1.75 1.75

Wmk. 373
790 A180 $1.06 multicolored 2.25 2.25
791 A180 $2 multicolored 4.00 4.00
Nos. 788-791 (4) 9.75 9.75

Souvenir Sheet

Hawksbill Turtle A181

Designs: a, 63c, Female laying eggs. b, 81c, Baby turtles emerging from nest. c, $1.06 Young turtles in water. d, $2, One adult in water, coral.

1997, May 26 Wmk. 373
792 A181 Sheet of 4, #a.-d. 11.00 11.00

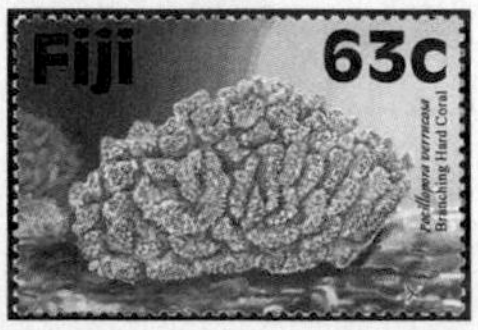

Coral A182

Designs: 63c, Branching hard coral 87c, Massive hard coral. $1, Soft coral, sinularia. $3, Soft coral, dendronephthya.

Wmk. 373

1997, July 16 Litho. *Perf. 14*

793 A182 63c multicolored 1.40 1.40
794 A182 87c multicolored 1.90 1.90
795 A182 $1 multicolored 2.25 2.25
796 A182 $3 multicolored 6.75 6.75
Nos. 793-796 (4) 12.30 12.30

Fijian Monkey-faced Bat — A183

63c, With nose pointed downward. 81c, Hanging below flower. $2, Between leaves on tree branch.

Perf. 13½

1997, Oct. 15 Litho. Unwmk.

797 A183 44c multicolored 1.25 1.00
798 A183 63c multicolored 1.75 1.50
799 A183 81c multicolored 2.25 1.75
800 A183 $2 multicolored 4.75 4.25
a. Sheet, 2 each #797-800 21.00 21.00
Nos. 797-800 (4) 10.00 8.50

World Wildlife Fund.

Christmas A184

Designs: 13c, Angel, shepherd. 31c, Birth of Jesus. 87c, Magi. $3, Madonna and Child.

Perf. 14x14½

1997, Nov. 18 Wmk. 373

801 A184 13c multicolored .20 .20
802 A184 31c multicolored .60 .60
803 A184 87c multicolored 1.60 1.60
804 A184 $3 multicolored 5.50 5.50
Nos. 801-804 (4) 7.90 7.90

A185

A186

1997 Rugby World Cup Sevens Champions: a, 50c, Waisale Serevi, captain, highest point scorer. b, 50c, Taniela Qauqau. c, 50c, Jope Tuikabe. d, 50c, Leveni Duvuduvukula. e, 50c, Inoke Maraiwai. f, 50c, Aminiasi Naituyaga. g, 50c, Lemeki Koroi. h, 50c, Marika Vunibaka, highest try scorer. i, 50c, Luke Erenavula. j, 50c, Manasa Bari. k, $1, Entire team.

Wmk. 373

1997, Oct. 30 Litho. *Perf. 14*

805 A185 Sheet of 11, #a.-k. 13.00 13.00

No. 805k is 53x39mm.

Wmk. 373

1998, Jan. 20 Litho. *Perf. 14*

Chief's Traditional Costumes: 81c, War dress. 87c, Formal dress. $1.12, Presentation dress. $2, Highland war dress.

806 A186 81c multicolored 1.25 1.25
807 A186 87c multicolored 1.25 1.25
808 A186 $1.12 multicolored 1.75 1.75
809 A186 $2 multicolored 3.00 3.00
Nos. 806-809 (4) 7.25 7.25

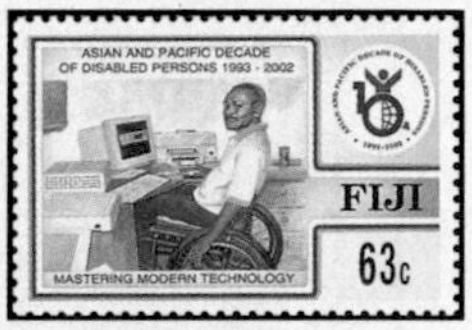

Asian and Pacific Decade of Disabled Persons, 1993-2000 A187

63c, Mastering modern technology. 87c, Assisting the will to overcome. $1, Using natural born skills. $2, Competing to win.

Wmk. 373

1998, Mar. 18 Litho. *Perf. 13*

810 A187 63c multicolored 1.00 1.00
811 A187 87c multicolored 1.40 1.40
812 A187 $1 multicolored 1.50 1.50
813 A187 $2 multicolored 3.00 3.00
Nos. 810-813 (4) 6.90 6.90

Royal Air Force, 80th Anniv.

Common Design Type of 1993 Re-Inscribed

Designs: 44c, R34 Airship. 63c, Handley Page Heyford. 87c, Supermarine Swift FR.5. $2, Westland Whirlwind.

No. 818: a, Sopwith Dolphin. b, Avro 504K. c, Vickers Warwick V. d, Shorts Belfast.

1998, Apr. 1 *Perf. 13½x14*

814 CD350 44c multicolored 1.00 1.00
815 CD350 63c multicolored 1.25 1.25
816 CD350 87c multicolored 1.75 1.75
817 CD350 $2 multicolored 4.00 4.00
Nos. 814-817 (4) 8.00 8.00

Souvenir Sheet of 4

818 CD350 $1 #a.-d. 7.50 7.50

Diana, Princess of Wales (1961-97)

Common Design Type

Design: No. 819, Wearing plaid jacket.

No. 820: a, Wearing blue jacket. b, In high-collared blouse. c, Holding flowers.

1998, Mar. 31 Litho. *Perf. 14x14½*

819 CD355 81c multicolored .75 .75
820 CD355 81c Sheet of 4, #819, a.-c. 5.25 5.25

No. 820 sold for $3.24 + 50c, with surtax from international sales being donated to the Princess Diana Memorial Fund and surtax from national sales being donated to designated local charity.

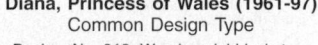

Sperm Whale A188

Wmk. 373

1998, June 22 Litho. *Perf. 14*

821 A188 63c shown 1.40 1.40
822 A188 81c Adult, calf 1.90 1.90
823 A188 87c Breaching 1.90 1.90
824 A188 $2 Sperm whale tooth 4.50 4.50
a. Souvenir sheet 7.25 7.25
Nos. 821-824 (4) 9.70 9.70

16th Commonwealth Games, Kuala Lumpur, Malaysia — A189

Wmk. 384

1998, Sept. 11 Litho. *Perf. 14*

825 A189 44c Athletics .70 .70
826 A189 63c Lawn bowls 1.00 1.00
827 A189 81c Javelin 1.40 1.40
828 A189 $1.12 Weight lifting 1.90 1.90
Nos. 825-828 (4) 5.00 5.00

Souvenir Sheet

829 A189 $2 Waisale Serevi, rugby sevens 4.00 4.00

Maritime Heritage A190

Designs: 13c, Takia, hollowed-out log with outrigger. 44c, Camakau, sailing canoe. 87c, Drua, twin-hulled sailing canoe. $3, MV Pioneer motor yacht.

$1.50, Camakau, map of Fiji.

Wmk. 384

1998, Oct. 26 Litho. *Perf. 13½*

830 A190 13c multicolored .30 .30
831 A190 44c multicolored .85 .85
832 A190 87c multicolored 1.60 1.60
833 A190 $3 multicolored 5.25 5.25
Nos. 830-833 (4) 8.00 8.00

Souvenir Sheet

834 A190 $1.50 multicolored 4.75 4.75

Australia '99, World Stamp Expo (#834). See Nos. 843-847.

Christmas A191

Children's drawings: 13c, "Jesus in a Manger." 50c, "A Time for Family and Friends." $1, "What Christmas Means to Me," vert. $2, "The Joy of Christmas," vert.

1998, Nov. 23 Wmk. 373

835 A191 13c multicolored .25 .25
836 A191 50c multicolored .80 .80
837 A191 $1 multicolored 1.60 1.60
838 A191 $2 multicolored 3.25 3.25
Nos. 835-838 (4) 5.90 5.90

Traditional Dances — A192

Designs: 13c, Vakamalolo (women's sitting dance). 81c, Mekeiwau (club dance). 87c, Seasea (women's fan dance). $3, Meke ni yaqona (Kava serving dance).

Wmk. 373

1999, Jan. 20 Litho. *Perf. 14½*

839 A192 13c multicolored .25 .25
840 A192 81c multicolored 1.60 1.60
841 A192 87c multicolored 1.90 1.90
842 A192 $3 multicolored 5.75 5.75
Nos. 839-842 (4) 9.50 9.50

Maritime Heritage Type of 1998

Designs: 63c, SS Toufua, 1920-30's. 81c, MF Adi Beti, 1920-30's. $1, SS Niagara, 1920-30's. $2, MV Royal Viking Sun, 1990's.

$1.50, SS. Makatea, 1920's.

1999, Mar. 19 Wmk. 384 *Perf. 13½*

843 A190 63c multicolored 1.10 1.10
844 A190 81c multicolored 1.90 1.90
845 A190 $1 multicolored 2.25 2.25
846 A190 $2 multicolored 4.50 4.50
Nos. 843-846 (4) 9.75 9.75

Souvenir Sheet

847 A190 $1.50 multicolored 4.50 4.50

Australia '99, World Stamp Exhibition (#847).

Souvenir Sheet

Ducks — A193

a, Wandering whistling. b, Pacific black.

1999, Apr. 27 Wmk. 373

848 A193 $2 Sheet of 2, #a.-b. 8.00 8.00

IBRA '99, Intl. Philatelic Exhibition, Nuremberg.

Orchids — A194

Designs: 44c, Calanthe ventilabrum. 63c, Dendrobium prasinum. 81c, Dendrobium macrophyllum. $3, Dendrobium tokai.

1999, June 28

849 A194 44c multicolored .75 .75
850 A194 63c multicolored 1.00 1.00
851 A194 81c multicolored 1.25 1.25
852 A194 $3 multicolored 5.00 5.00
Nos. 849-852 (4) 8.00 8.00

1st Manned Moon Landing, 30th Anniv.

Common Design Type

13c, Astronaut waves goodbye. 87c, Stage 3 fires towards moon. $1, Aldrin walks on lunar surface. $2, Command module fires towards earth.

$2, Looking at earth from moon.

Perf. 14x13¾

1999, July 20 Wmk. 384

853 CD357 13c multicolored .25 .25
854 CD357 87c multicolored 1.50 1.50
855 CD357 $1 multicolored 1.75 1.75
856 CD357 $2 multicolored 3.50 3.50
Nos. 853-856 (4) 7.00 7.00

Souvenir Sheet

Perf. 14

857 CD357 $2 multicolored 4.00 4.00

No. 857 contains one circular stamp 40mm in diameter.

Queen Mother's Century

Common Design Type

Queen Mother: 13c, Visiting Hull to see bomb damage. 63c, With Prince Charles. 81c, As Colonel-in-Chief of Light Infantry. $3, With Prince Charles at Clarence House.

$2, With crowd on Armistice Day.

Wmk. 384

1999, Aug. 18 Litho. *Perf. 13½*

858 CD358 13c multicolored .50 .50
859 CD358 63c multicolored 1.25 1.25
860 CD358 81c multicolored 1.75 1.75
861 CD358 $3 multicolored 5.50 5.50
Nos. 858-861 (4) 9.00 9.00

Souvenir Sheet

862 CD358 $2 multicolored 6.00 6.00

UPU, 125th Anniv. A195

Sugar Mills rolling stock: 50c, Diesel locomotive. 87c, Steam locomotive. $1, Diesel locomotive, diff. $2, Free passenger train.

Wmk. 373

1999, Oct. 26 Litho. ***Perf. 13¾***

863 A195 50c multicolored	.60	.60
864 A195 87c multicolored	1.25	1.25
865 A195 $1 multicolored	1.40	1.40
866 A195 $2 multicolored	2.75	2.75
Nos. 863-866 (4)	6.00	6.00

Christmas — A196

Designs: 13c, Giving gifts. 31c, Angels and star. 63c, Bible, Magi, Holy family. 87c, Joseph, mary, donkey, vert. $1, Mary, Jesus, animals, vert. $2, Children, Santa, vert.

Perf. 13¼x13

1999, Nov. 29 Litho. Wmk. 373

867 A196 13c multicolored	.20	.20
868 A196 31c multicolored	.45	.45
869 A196 63c multicolored	.90	.90
870 A196 87c multicolored	1.25	1.25
871 A196 $1 multicolored	1.40	1.40
872 A196 $2 multicolored	2.75	2.75
Nos. 867-872 (6)	6.95	6.95

Millennium A197

Designs: No. 873, Outstretched hands, islands (arch at top). No. 874, Map, flag (arch at right). No. 875, Globe, warrior beating lali, temple (arch at bottom). No. 876, Globe, drua, red line (arch at left).

No. 877: a, Fiji petrel (arch at top). b, Crested iguana, islands (arch at top). c, Red prawns (arch at bottom). d, Tagimaucia (arch at bottom).

Perf. 13¼ Syncopated Type A

Litho. with Foil Application

2000, Jan. 1 Unwmk.

873 A197 $5 gold & multi	8.00	8.00
874 A197 $5 gold & multi	8.00	8.00
875 A197 $5 gold & multi	8.00	8.00
876 A197 $5 gold & multi	8.00	8.00
Nos. 873-876 (4)	32.00	32.00

Souvenir Sheet

877 A197 $10 Sheet of 4, #a-d	65.00	65.00

Beetles — A198

Designs: 15c, Paracupta sulcata. 87c, Agrilus sp. $1.06, Cyphogastra abdominalis. $2, Paracupta sp.

Perf. 13¾x14

2000, Mar. 14 Litho. Wmk. 373

878 A198 15c multi	.25	.25
879 A198 87c multi	1.50	1.50
880 A198 $1.06 multi	1.75	1.75
881 A198 $2 multi	3.00	3.00
Nos. 878-881 (4)	6.50	6.50

Sesame Street — A199

No. 882: a, Big Bird. b, Oscar the Grouch. c, Cookie Monster. d, Grover. e, Elmo. f, Ernie. g, Zoe. h, The Count. i, Bert.

No. 883, Big Bird, Elmo and Ernie, horiz. No. 884, Cookie Monster, Bert and Ernie, horiz.

Illustration reduced.

Perf. 14½x14¾

2000, Apr. 20 Litho. Wmk. 373

882 A199 50c Sheet of 9, #a-i	7.50	7.50

Souvenir Sheets

Perf. 14¾x14½

883 A199 $2 multi	3.50	3.50
884 A199 $2 multi	3.50	3.50

The Stamp Show 2000, London (#882).

Pres. Ratu Sir Kamisese Mara, 80th Birthday — A200

President with: 15c, Lumberjack, timber truck. 81c, Women. $1, Workers in cane field. $3, Ships.

2000, May 13 ***Perf. 14x13¾***

885 A200 15c multi	.25	.25
886 A200 81c multi	1.25	1.25
887 A200 $1 multi	1.50	1.50
888 A200 $3 multi	5.50	5.50
Nos. 885-888 (4)	8.50	8.50

Prince William, 18th Birthday

Common Design Type

William: Nos. 889, 893a, As child, wearing fireman's helmet, vert. Nos. 890, 893b, Wearing navy suit, vert. Nos. 891, 893c, Wearing scarf. Nos. 892, 893d, Wearing suit and wearing blue shirt. No. 893e, As child, wearing camouflage and beret.

Perf. 13¾x14¼, 14¼x13¾

2000, June 21 Wmk. 373

Stamps With White Border

889 CD359 $1 multi	1.50	1.50
890 CD359 $1 multi	1.50	1.50
891 CD359 $1 multi	1.50	1.50
892 CD359 $1 multi	1.50	1.50
Nos. 889-892 (4)	6.00	6.00

Souvenir Sheet

Stamps Without White Border

Perf. 14¼

893 CD359 $1 Sheet of 5, #a-e	9.00	9.00

2000 Summer Olympics, Sydney — A201

Wmk. 373

2000, Aug. 8 Litho. ***Perf. 13¾***

894 A201 44c Swimming, vert.	.50	.50
895 A201 87c Judo, vert.	1.25	1.25
896 A201 $1 Running	1.50	1.50
897 A201 $2 Windsurfing	2.75	2.75
Nos. 894-897 (4)	6.00	6.00

Souvenir Sheet

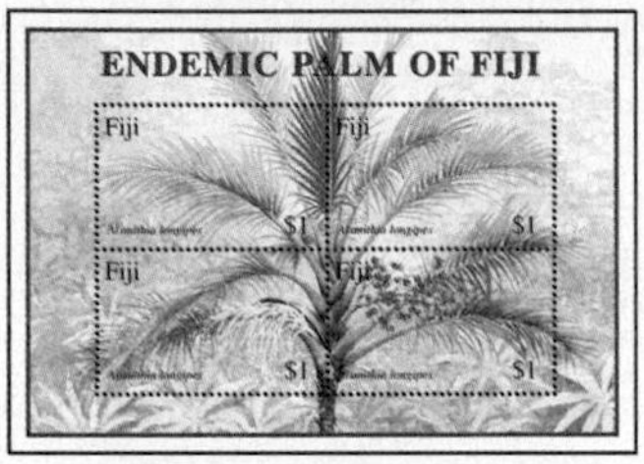

Alsmithia Longipes — A202

No. 898: a, Red frond at R. b, Red frond at L. c, Yellow frond. d, Fruit.

Illustration reduced.

Wmk. 373

2000, Sept. 12 Litho. ***Perf. 13½***

898 A202 $1 Sheet of 4, #a-d	7.50	7.50

Lapita Pottery Shards and Discovery Sites — A203

44c, Yanuca Island. 63c, Mago Island. $1, Ugaga Island. $2, Sigatoka sand dunes.

2000, Oct. 24 ***Perf. 13¾***

899-902 A203 Set of 4	7.00	7.00

Christmas A204

Designs: 15c, Jungle. 81c, Cliffside trail. 87c, Coastal village. $3, Outrigger canoe.

2000, Nov. 21

903-906 A204 Set of 4	8.00	8.00

Souvenir Sheet

Taveuni Rain Forest — A205

Designs: a, Orange dove. b, Xixuthrus heyrovskyi.

Perf. 13¾x13½

2001, Feb. 1 Litho. Unwmk.

907 A205 $2 Sheet of 2, #a-b	6.25	6.25

Moths A206

Designs: 17c, Macroglossum hirundo vitiensis. 48c, Hippotion celerio. 69c, Gnathothlibus erotus eras. 89c, Theretra pinastrina intersecta. $1.17, Deilephila placida torenia. $2, Psilogramma jordana.

2001, Mar. 20 ***Perf. 13¼x13***

908-913 A206 Set of 6	8.00	8.00

Souvenir Sheet

Gallus Gallus — A207

Designs: a, Hen. b, Rooster.

2001, May 22 ***Perf. 13¾x14***

914 A207 $2 Sheet of 2, #a-b	6.50	6.50

Society for Prevention of Cruelty — A208

Designs: 34c, Girl, cat. 96c, Boy, dogs. $1.23, Girl, cat, diff. $2, Boy, dog.

Perf. 14x13¾

2001, June 26 Litho. Unwmk.

915-918 A208 Set of 4	6.25	6.25

Pigeons — A209

Designs: 69c, White-throated. 89c, Pacific, vert. $1.23, Peal's, vert. $2, Rock.

2001, July 20 ***Perf. 14x14¾, 14¾x14***

919-922 A209 Set of 4	7.25	7.25

Westpac Pacific Bank, 100th Anniv. in Fiji — A210

Bank office in: 48c, 1901. 96c, 1916. $1, 1934. $2, 2001.

2001, Aug. 10 *Perf. 13¼x13¾*
923-926 A210 Set of 4 6.00 6.00

Fish A211

Designs: 50c, Yellowfin tuna. 96c, Wahoo. $1.17, Dolphin fish. $2, Pacific blue marlin.

2001, Aug. 23
927-930 A211 Set of 4 6.50 6.50

Christmas A212

Designs: 17c, Angel appears to Mary. 34c Nativity. 48c, Adoration of the shepherds. 69c, Adoration of the Magi. 89c, Flight to Egypt. $2, Fijian Chirst child.

2001, Oct. 29 Litho. *Perf. 13¾x13¼*
931-936 A212 Set of 6 7.00 7.00

Colonial Financial Services Group, 125th Anniv. in Fiji — A213

Designs: 17c, Bank office. 48c, Women using automatic teller machine. $1, Suva Private Hospital. $3, Hoisting of British flag.

2001, Nov. 16 Litho. *Perf. 13¼*
937-940 A213 Set of 4 7.00 7.00

Air Pacific, 50th Anniv. — A214

No. 941: a, De Havilland Drover. b, Hawker Siddley HS-748. c, Douglas DC-10-30. d, Boeing 747-200.

2001, Nov. 30 Litho. *Perf. 13*
941 Horiz. strip of 4 7.25 7.25
a. A214 89c multi 1.25 1.00
b. A214 96c multi 1.40 1.10
c. A214 $1 multi 1.50 1.25
d. A214 $2 multi 3.00 1.50

Spices — A215

Designs: 69c, Pepper. 89c, Nutmeg. $1, Vanilla. $2, Cinnamon.

2002, Mar. 12 Litho. *Perf. 13¼*
942-945 A215 Set of 4 6.25 6.25

Souvenir Sheet

Balaka Palm — A216

Palm and: a, Bird, butterfly, beetle. b, Lizard, butterfly

2002, Apr. 29
946 A216 $2 Sheet of 2, #a-b 5.25 5.25

Freshwater Fish — A217

Designs: 48c, Redigobius sp. 96c, Spotted flagtail. $1.23, Silverstripe mudskipper. $2, Snakehead gudgeon.

2002, May 13
947-950 A217 Set of 4 7.00 7.00

Fruit — A218

Designs: 25c, Breadfruit. 34c, Wi. $1, Jakfruit. $3, Avocado.

2002, July 25 Litho. *Perf. 13¾x13¼*
951-954 A218 Set of 4 6.25 6.25

Murex Shells — A219

Designs: 69c, Saul's murex. 96c, Caltrop murex. $1, Purple Pacific drupe. $2, Ramose murex.

2002, Aug. 20 *Perf. 13¾*
955-958 A219 Set of 4 6.25 6.25

Fiji Goshawk A220

Designs: 48c, Goshawk and eggs. 89c, Chicks in nest. $1, Juvenile on branch. $3, Adult.

2002, Sept. 10
959-962 A220 Set of 4 7.25 7.25

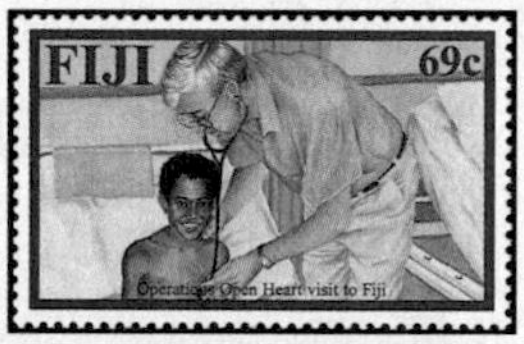

2002 Operation Open Heart Visit to Fiji — A221

Designs: 34c, Doctors performing operation, vert. 69c, Doctor listening to patient's heart with stethoscope. $1.17, Technician administering echocardiogram. $2, Administration of anesthesia to patient, vert.

2002, Oct. 30 *Perf. 13¼*
963-966 A221 Set of 4 5.50 5.50

Fiji Natural Artesian Water — A222

Designs: 25c, Bottle of water, flowers, vert. 48c, Bottling plant. $1, Delivery truck. $3, Children with bottled water, vert.

2002, Nov. 5
967-970 A222 Set of 4 7.00 7.00

Christmas — A223

Designs: 17c, Christian church. 89c, Mosque. $1, Hindu temple. $3, Christian church, diff.

2002, Nov. 20
971-974 A223 Set of 4 6.50 6.50

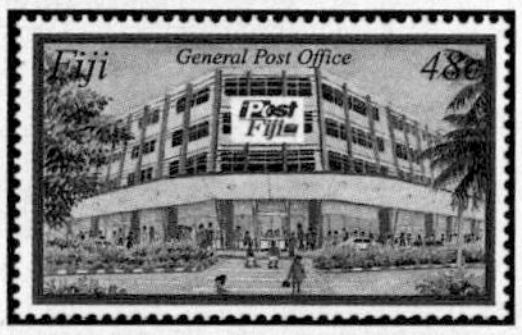

Post Fiji, Ltd. Improvements — A224

Designs: 48c, General Post Office. 96c, Post Fiji Mail Center. $1, Post Fiji Logistics Center. $2, Smart Mail.

2003, Mar. 19 Litho. *Perf. 13¼*
975-978 A224 Set of 4 6.50 6.50

Souvenir Sheet

Intl. Year of Fresh Water — A225

No. 979: a, Top of waterfall, flowers. b, Base of waterfall, butterfly.

2003, Apr. 22
979 A225 $2 Sheet of 2, #a-b 6.50 6.50

2003 South Pacific Games, Suva — A226

Designs: 10c, Track athlete with arms raised. 14c, Baseball. 20c, Netball. No. 983, $5, Shot put.

No. 984, $5, Flags of participating nations, venues, volleyball players.

2003 *Perf. 13¼*
980-983 A226 Set of 4 6.50 6.50

Size: 120x85mm

Imperf

984 A226 $5 multi 8.00 8.00

Issued: Nos. 980-983, 5/26; No. 984, 6/28.

Fish A227

Siganus uspi: 58c, Fish, crab and coral. 83c, Two fish and coral. $1.15, Two fish, coral, and other fish species. $3, Fish and coral.

2003, Aug. 12 *Perf. 13¼*
985-988 A227 Set of 4 8.00 8.00

Bird Life International A228

Designs: 41c, Long-legged warbler. 60c, Silktail. $1.07, Red-throated lorikeet. $3, Pink-billed parrot finch.

2003, Sept. 16
989-992 A228 Set of 4 8.00 8.00

Geckos A229

Designs: 83c, Pacific slender-toed gecko. $1.07, Indopacific tree gecko. $1.15, Mann's gecko. $2, Voracious gecko.

2003, Oct. 21 **Litho.** ***Perf. 13¼***
993-996 A229 Set of 4 9.00 9.00

Christmas — A230

Children's art: 18c, Children, Christmas tree. 41c, Children, flag of Fiji. 58c, Children, Santa Claus, reindeer pulling sleighs, vert. 83c, Santa Claus on chimney, gifts, children, Christmas tree, vert. $1.07, Children with candles, Christmas tree, vert. $1.15, Santa Claus, children, bell, rainbow, vert.
$1.41, Handshake.

2003, Nov. 26 **Litho.** ***Perf. 13¼***
997-1002 A230 Set of 6 7.50 7.50

Souvenir Sheet

1003 A230 $1.41 multi 3.50 3.50

Tagimoucia — A231

2003, Dec. 1 **Litho.** ***Perf. 14½x14***
1004 A231 50c multi + label 1.75 1.75

Sold in sheets of 10 stamps + 10 labels that could be personalized for $15 per sheet.

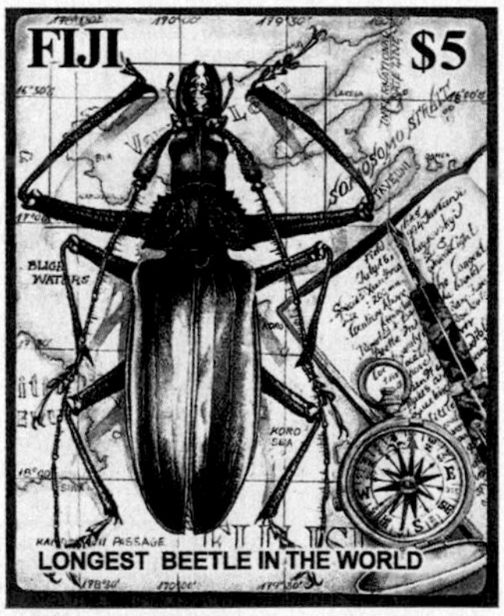

Xixuthrus Heyrovskyi, Longest Beetle in the World — A232

Illustration reduced.

2003, Feb. 27 ***Imperf.***
1005 A232 $5 multi 8.50 8.50

Miniature Sheet

Worldwide Fund for Nature (WWF) — A233

No. 1006: a, 58c, Skipjack tuna. b, 83c, Albacore tuna. c, $1.07, Yellowfin tuna. d, $3, Bigeye tuna.

2004, Apr. 7 ***Perf. 13¼***
1006 A233 Sheet of 4, #a-d 8.50 8.50
e. Like #1006, with artist's name at LL of each stamp 8.50 8.50

Land Snails A234

Designs: 18c, Malleated placostyle. 41c, Kandavu placostyle. $1.15, Fragile orpiella. $3, Thin Fijian placostyle.

2004, May 28
1007-1010 A234 Set of 4 8.50 8.50

Bird Type of 1995
Perf. 13¼x13

2004, June 26 **Unwmk.**
1011 A166 18c Island thrush .20 .20

Coral Reef Shrimp — A235

Designs: 58c, Boxer shrimp. 83c, Bumblebee shrimp. $1.07, Mantis shrimp. $3, Anemone shrimp.

2004, June 30 ***Perf. 13¼***
1012-1015 A235 Set of 4 8.00 8.00

Birds A236

Designs: 41c, Wandering tattler. 58c, Whimbrel. $1.15, Pacific golden plover. $3, Bristle-thighed curlew.

2004, July 28
1016-1019 A236 Set of 4 10.00 10.00

2004 Summer Olympics, Athens A237

Designs: 41c, Swimming. 58c, Judo, vert. $1.40, Weight lifting, vert. $2, Makelesi Bulikiobo, runner.

2004, Aug. 12
1020-1023 A237 Set of 4 8.75 8.75

Musket Cove to Port Vila Yacht Race, 25th Anniv. — A238

Various yachts: 83c, $1.07, $1.15, $2. $1.07 and $2 are vert.

2004, Sept. 18 ***Perf. 14¼***
1024-1027 A238 Set of 4 10.00 10.00
1027a Souvenir sheet of 1 5.00 5.00

See Vanuatu Nos. 858-861.

Souvenir Sheet

Coconut Crab — A239

2004, Oct. 20 **Litho.** ***Perf. 14***
1028 A239 $5 multi 10.00 10.00

Papilio Schmeltzii — A240

Designs: 58c, Newly-emerged adult, vert. 83c, Larva. $1.41, Adult. $3, Pupa, vert.

Perf. 14x14½, 14½x14

2004, Nov. 10
1029-1032 A240 Set of 4 11.00 11.00

Christmas A241

Designs: 18c, Annunciation. 58c, Infant in manger. $1.07, Madonna and child. $3, Adoration of the Shepherds.

2004, Dec. 1 **Litho.** ***Perf. 13¼***
1033-1036 A241 Set of 4 10.00 10.00

Birds — A242

No. 1037: a, Little heron. b, Great white egret. c, White-faced heron. d, Pacific reef heron.

2005, Jan. 26
1037 Horiz. strip of 4 11.00 11.00
a.-d. A242 $1 Any single 2.75 2.75

Flowers For Perfume — A243

Designs: 58c, Cananga odorata. $1.15, Euodia hortensis. $1.41, Pandanus tecorius. $2, Santalum yasi.

2005, Feb. 20 ***Perf. 14x14½***
1038-1041 A243 Set of 4 10.00 10.00

Peregrine Falcons — A244

Designs: 41c, Head of falcon. 83c, Adult at nest. $1.07, Chicks. $3, Adult on rock.

2005, Mar. 14 **Litho.** ***Perf. 14½x14***
1042-1045 A244 Set of 4 12.00 12.00

Triggerfish — A245

Designs: 58c, Whitebanded triggerfish. 83c, Yellow-spotted triggerfish. $1.15, Orange-lined triggerfish. $2, Clown triggerfish.

2005, Apr. 27
1046-1049 A245 Set of 4 9.00 9.00

European Philatelic Cooperation, 50th Anniv. (in 2006) — A246

Color of arches: 58c, Red. 83c, Blue green. $1.41, Purple. $4, Yellow bister.

2005, June 1 ***Perf. 13¾***
1050-1053 A246 Set of 4 11.00 11.00
1053a Souvenir sheet, #1050-1053 11.00 11.00

Europa stamps, 50th anniv. (in 2006).

Miniature Sheet

End of World War II, 60th Anniv. — A247

No. 1054: a, HMNZS Achilles. b, Japanese Yokosuka E14Y "Glen" over Suva Harbor. c, Fijian South Pacific Scouts in Solomon Islands. d, USS Chicago. e, Patrol vessel HMS

Viti. f, British Prime Minister Winston Churchill. g, HMS Hood. h, Dambusters Raid. i, German King Tiger tank in Ardennes. j, Gen. Dwight D. Eisenhower.

2005, June 27 Litho. *Perf. 13¾*
1054 A247 83c Sheet of 10, #a-j 13.00 13.00

Game Fish A248

Designs: 41c, Great barracuda. 58c, Narrow-barred Spanish mackerel. $1.07, Giant trevally. $3, Indo-Pacific sailfish.

2005, July 27 Litho. *Perf. 14½x14*
1055-1058 A248 Set of 4 10.00 10.00

Pope John Paul II (1920-2005) A249

2005, Aug. 18 *Perf. 14*
1059 A249 $1 multi 2.75 2.75

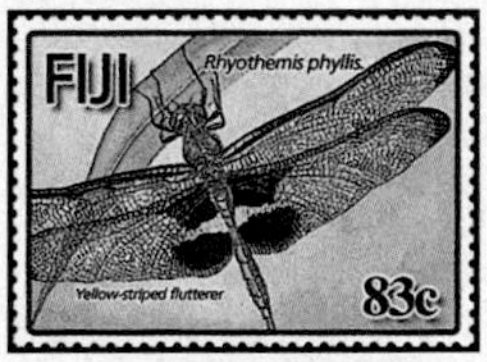
Dragonflies — A250

Designs: 83c, Yellow-striped flutterer. $1.07, Agrionoptera insignis. $1.15, Green skimmer. $2, Common percher.

2005, Aug. 30 Litho. *Perf. 13¼*
1060-1063 A250 Set of 4 9.75 9.75

Albert Einstein (1879-1955), Physicist — A251

Einstein: 83c, As a child. $1.07, In 1905. $1.15, And blackboard. $2, And galaxies.

2005, Sept. 27 Litho. *Perf. 14¼x14*
1064-1067 A251 Set of 4 6.00 6.00

Intl. Year of Physics.

Root Crops — A252

Designs: 41c, Manihot utilissima. 83c, Ipomoea satatas. $1.41, Colocasia esculenta. $2, Dioscorea sativa.

2005, Oct. 13 *Perf. 13¼*
1068-1071 A252 Set of 4 5.50 5.50

Tall Ships A253

Designs: 83c, Eliza of Province. $1.15, Elbe. $1.41, HMS Rosario. $2, L'Astrolabe.

2005, Nov. 21 Litho. *Perf. 14x14¼*
1072-1075 A253 Set of 4 7.50 7.50

Barn Owls — A254

Owl: 18c, And eggs. $1.15, Juvenile. $1.41, With prey. $2, Perched.

2006, Jan. 10 Litho. *Perf. 14¼x14*
1076-1079 A254 Set of 4 7.00 7.00

Platymantis Vitianus — A255

Various depictions: 50c, 83c, $1.15, $2.

2006, Feb. 8 Litho. *Perf. 14x14¼*
1080-1083 A255 Set of 4 6.00 6.00

Skinks A256

Designs: 18c, Pygmy snake-eyed skink. 58c, Brown-tailed copper striped skink. $1.15, Pacific black skink. $3, Pacific blue-tailed skink.

2006, Mar. 22
1084-1087 A256 Set of 4 6.25 6.25

Queen Elizabeth II, 80th Birthday A257

Designs: 50c, As child. 65c, Wearing tiara. 90c, Wearing blue hat. $3, Wearing blue hat, diff.

No. 1092: a, Like 65c. b, Like 90c.

2006, Apr. 21 Litho. *Perf. 14*
With White Frames
1088-1091 A257 Set of 4 6.00 6.00
Souvenir Sheet
Without White Frames
1092 A257 $2 Sheet of 2, #a-b 5.50 5.50

Nos. 725 and 729 Surcharged

Methods and Perfs. As Before

2006 Wmk. 373

1093	A166	2c on 1c #725	.20	.20
1094	A166	3c on 1c #725	.20	.20
1095	A166	4c on 1c #725	.20	.20
1096	A166	18c on 6c #729	.20	.20
		Nos. 1093-1096 (4)	.80	.80

Issued: No. 1093, 4/3; No. 1094, 3/13; No. 1095, 6/27; No. 1096, 6/8.

Miniature Sheet

Vijay Singh, Golfer — A258

No. 1097 — Singh: a, Head. b, With arm raised. c, Leaning on golf club. d, Hitting ball from sand trap. e, Holding trophy (60x87mm).

Perf. 14x14¼
2006, May 26 Litho. Unwmk.
1097 A258 $1 Sheet of 5, #a-e 5.75 5.75

2006 World Cup Soccer Championships, Germany — A259

Various players: 65c, 90c, $1.20, $2.

2006, June 9 *Perf. 14¼x14*
1098-1101 A259 Set of 4 5.50 5.50

Souvenir Sheet

Purple Swamphen — A260

No. 1102: a, Swamphen and flowers. b, Swamphen on nest.

2006, July 20 *Perf. 14½x14*
1102 A260 $2 Sheet of 2, #a-b 4.75 4.75

Extinct Species A261

Designs: 50c, Brachylophus vitiensis. $1.10, Natunaornis gigoura, vert. $1.20, Vitirallus watlingi, vert. $1.50, Platymantis megabotoniviti.

Perf. 14x14¼, 14¼x14
2006, Aug. 15 Litho.
1103-1106 A261 Set of 4 5.00 5.00

Phasmids — A262

Designs: 10c, Hermarchus apollonius. $1.10, Cotylosoma dipneusticum. $1.20, Chitoniscus feejeeanus. $2, Graeffea crouanii.

2006, Sept. 7 *Perf. 14½x14*
1107-1110 A262 Set of 4 5.25 5.25

Honey Production A263

Designs: 18c, Bees and honeycomb. 40c, Apiarist examining honeycomb, horiz. $1, Woman and beehives, horiz. $3, Man and bottle of honey.

2006, Oct. 16 *Perf. 14x14½, 14½x14*
1111-1114 A263 Set of 4 5.50 5.50

Christmas A264

Flowering plants: 18c, Decaspermum vitiense. 65c, Quisqualis indica. 90c, Mussaendra raiateensis. $3, Delonix regia.

2006, Dec. 5 *Perf. 14x14½*
1115-1118 A264 Set of 4 5.75 5.75

Anemonefish — A265

Designs: 18c, Spine-cheek anemonefish. 60c, Pink anemonefish. 90c, Orange-fin anemonefish. $3, Dusky anemonefish.

Perf. 14½x14, 14x14½
2006, Nov. 7 Litho.
1119-1122 A265 Set of 4 5.75 5.75

Souvenir Sheet

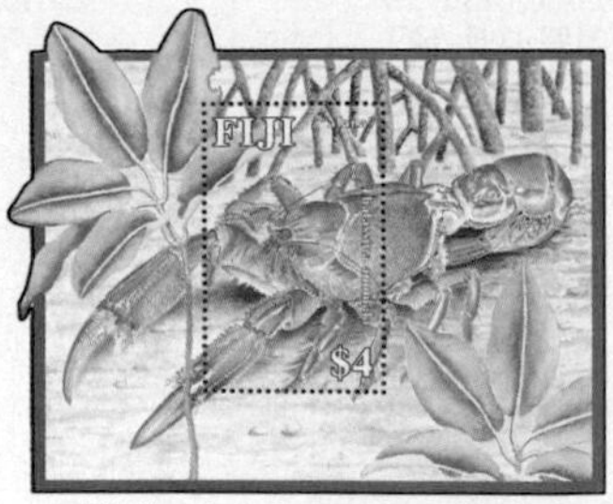

Thalassina Anomala — A266

2007, Jan. 24 *Perf. 13½*
1123 A266 $4 multi 4.75 4.75

Traditional Architecture — A267

Designs: 20c, Coastal dwelling. 65c, Inland dwelling. $1.10, Temple, Bau. $3, Lauan-style house.

2007, Mar. 20 **Litho.** *Perf. 13¼*
1124-1127 A267 Set of 4 6.00 6.00

Freshwater Gobies — A268

Designs: 20c, Sicyopterus lagocephalus. $1.10, Stiphodon rutilaureus. $1.20, Sicyopus zosterophorum. $2, Stiphodon sp.

2007, Apr. 5 **Litho.** *Perf. 13¼*
1128-1131 A268 Set of 4 5.50 5.50

Birds Introduced to Fiji — A269

Designs: 50c, Red-vented bulbul. 65c, Spotted dove, horiz. $1.50, Australian magpie, horiz. $2, Java sparrow.

2007, May 22
1132-1135 A269 Set of 4 5.75 5.75

Scouting, Cent. A270

Designs: 50c, Scout in kayak, hand holding compass. 90c, Three Scouts wearing helmets, hands tying knot. No. 1138, $1.50, Scout in harness climbing, Scout saluting. $2, Scout writing observation notes, hands tying neckerchief.

No. 1140, $1.50, vert.: a, Scout emblem. b, Lord Robert Baden-Powell.

2007, July 9 *Perf. 13¾*
1136-1139 A270 Set of 4 6.25 6.25

Souvenir Sheet

1140 A270 $1.50 Sheet of 2, #a-b 3.75 3.75

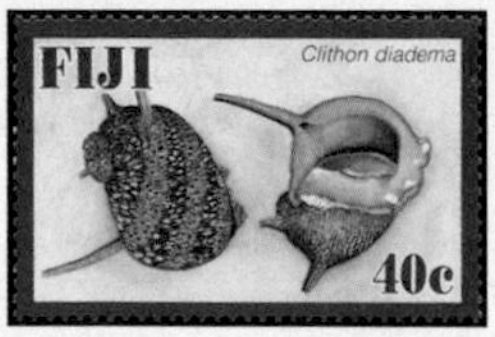

Snails A271

Designs: 40c, Clithon diadema. 90c, Neritina variegata. $1.20, Fijidoma maculata. $2, Neritina squamaepicta.

2007, Aug. 18 *Perf. 14x14¼*
1141-1144 A271 Set of 4 5.50 5.50

Orchids — A272

Designs: 20c, Liparis layardii. 65c, Dendrobium catillare, horiz. $1.10, Dendrobium mohlianum, horiz. $3, Glomera montana.

Perf. 14¼x14, 14x14¼

2007, Aug. 21
1145-1148 A272 Set of 4 6.25 6.25

Nos. 725 and 729 Surcharged

l — Large "XX"

m — Small "XX"

n — Small "2," Small "XX"

o — Large "2," Small "XX"

Methods, Types and Watermarks As Before

2006-08

1149	A166(l)	1c on 6c #729	*2.00*	*2.00*
1150	A166(m)	1c on 6c #729	*6.00*	*6.00*
1151	A166(n)	2c on 1c #725	*2.00*	*2.00*
1152	A166(o)	2c on 1c #725	*4.00*	*4.00*
1153	A166(l)	2c on 6c #729	*2.00*	*2.00*
a.		5mm between "c" and obliterator	2.00	2.00
1154	A166(m)	3c on 1c #725	*2.00*	*2.00*
1155	A166(m)	4c on 1c #725	*2.00*	*2.00*
1156	A166(l)	4c on 6c #729	*2.00*	*2.00*
a.		5mm between "c" and obliterator	2.00	2.00
1157	A166(m)	18c on 6c #729	*3.00*	*3.00*
1158	A166(l)	18c on 6c #729	*8.00*	*8.00*
a.		4mm between "c" and obliterator	12.00	12.00
1159	A166(m)	20c on 6c #729	*3.00*	*3.00*
a.		4mm between "c" and obliterator	12.00	12.00
1160	A166(l)	20c on 6c #729	*8.00*	*8.00*
a.		1½mm between "c" and obliterator	15.00	15.00
		Nos. 1149-1160 (12)	*44.00*	*44.00*

Issued: No. 1149, 5/30/07; No. 1150, 9/19/07; No. 1151, 4/3; No. 1152, 11/13; No. 1153, 2/19/07; No. 1154, 3/13; No. 1155, 6/27; No. 1156, 6/6/07; No. 1157, 6/8; No. 1158, 9/8; No. 1159, 1/19/07; No. 1160, 3/8/07. No. 1153a, 2/27/08; No. 1156a, 2/19/08; No. 1158a, Aug. 2007, No. 1159a, Jan. 2007; No. 1160a, 4/12/08.

On Nos. 1153, 1156 and 1160, 4mm separates "c" and obliterator. On Nos. 1158 and 1159, 3mm separates "c" and obliterator.

Fish A273

Designs: 50c, Coronation trout. 90c, Roving coral trout. $1.50, Squaretail coral trout. $2, Chinese footballer.

2007, Oct. 15 **Litho.** *Perf. 13¼*
1161-1164 A273 Set of 4 6.50 6.50

Butterflies — A274

Designs: 20c, Polyura caphontis. $1.10, Hypolimnas bolina, horiz. $1.20, Doleschallia bisaltide, horiz. $2, Danaus hamata.

2007, Nov. 20 **Litho.** *Perf. 13¼*
1165-1168 A274 Set of 4 6.00 6.00

Souvenir Sheet

Barred-winged Rail — A275

No. 1169: a, Head of adult. b, Chick.

2007, Dec. 3
1169 A275 $2 Sheet of 2, #a-b 5.25 5.25

National Medals — A276

Designs: 50c, Medal of the Order of Fiji. 65c, Member of the Order of Fiji. $1.20, Officer of the Order of Fiji. $2, Companion of the Order of Fiji.

2008, Feb. 20 **Litho.** *Perf. 13¼*
1170-1173 A276 Set of 4 6.00 6.00

Souvenir Sheet

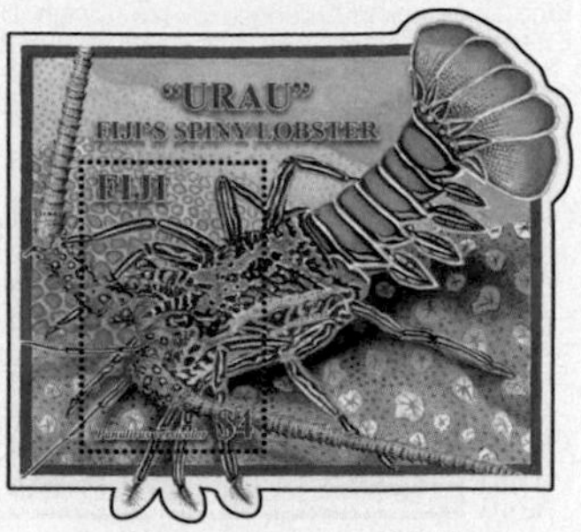

Spiny Lobster — A277

2008, Apr. 22 **Litho.** *Perf. 14x14½*
1174 A277 $4 multi 5.50 5.50

First Trans-Pacific Flight of the Southern Cross, 80th Anniv. — A278

Southern Cross: 20c, Over Fiji. 90c, In Albert Park, Suva. $1.50, Surrounded by police guard. $2, With crew.

2008, June 13 *Perf. 13½*
1175-1178 A278 Set of 4 6.25 6.25

2008 Summer Olympics, Beijing A279

Designs: 20c, Bamboo, Running. 65c, Dragon, Judo. 90c, Lanterns, Shooting. $1.50, Carp, Swimming.

2008, May 5 **Litho.** *Perf. 13¼*
1179-1182 A279 Set of 4 4.50 4.50

Red-breasted Musk Parrot Varieties — A280

Prosopeia tabuensis: 65c, Koroensis. 90c, Atrogularis, horiz. $1.50, Taviunensis, horiz. $2, Splendens.

2008, Mar. 25 **Litho.** *Perf. 13½*
1183-1186 A280 Set of 4 6.75 6.75

Humpback Whales — A281

Humpback whale: 20c, Pair underwater. 50c, Breaching water's surface. $1.10, Reentering water. $3, Flukes.

2008, July 17 **Litho.** *Perf. 14½x14*
1187-1190 A281 Set of 4 6.50 6.50

Nos. 729-731 Surcharged Like Nos. 1149-1160

Methods, Perfs and Watermarks As Before

2007-08

1191	A166(l)	1c on 13c #730	2.00	2.00
1192	A166(o)	2c on 6c #729, "==" instead of "xx"	*75.00*	*75.00*
1193	A166(l)	2c on 13c #730	2.00	2.00
1194	A166(l)	4c on 13c #730	2.00	2.00
1195	A166(n)	20c on 6c #729, "xxx" instead of "xx"	*85.00*	*25.00*
1196	A166(n)	20c on 23c #731, "xxx" instead of "xx"	2.00	2.00
1197	A166(l)	20c on 23c #731	*40.00*	*40.00*
		Nos. 1191-1197 (7)	*208.00*	*148.00*

Issued: No. 1191, 8/22/08; No. 1192, Feb. 2007; Nos. 1193, 1194, 8/20/08; No. 1195, 4/28/08; No. 1196, 4/12/08; No. 1197, Apr. 2008.

Bananas — A282

Various banana varieties: 65c, $1.10, $1.20, $2.

2008, Sept. 23 Litho. *Perf. 14x14½*

1198-1201	A282	Set of 4	6.00	6.00

Eels A283

Designs: 50c, Anguilla obscura. 90c, Anguilla marmorata. $1.50, Anguilla obscura, diff. $2, Gymnothorax potyuranodon.

2008, Oct. 15 *Perf. 14½x14*

1202-1205	A283	Set of 4	5.50	5.50

SEMI-POSTAL STAMPS

Catalogue values for unused stamps in this section are for Never Hinged items.

Children at Play — SP1

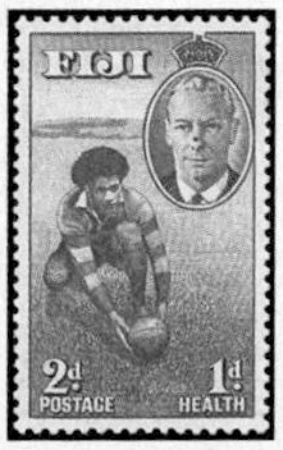

Rugby Player — SP2

Perf. 13x13½

1951, Sept. 17 Engr. Wmk. 4

B1	SP1	1p + 1p brown	.25	.25
B2	SP2	2p + 1p deep green	.30	.30

Bamboo River Raft — SP3

Design: 2½p+ ½p, Cross of Lorraine.

1954, Apr. 1 *Perf. 11x11½*

B3	SP3	1½p + ½p green & brn	.25	.25
B4	SP3	2½p + ½p black & org	.30	.30

Nos. 269 and 272 Surcharged

1972, Dec. 4 Photo. *Perf. 14, 13½*

B5	A56	15c + 5c multi	.50	.50
B6	A55	30c + 10c multi	1.10	1.10

Indian Boy, Map of Fiji SP4

Map of Fiji and: 15c+2c, European girl. 30c+3c, Chinese girl. 40c+4c, Fijian boy.

Wmk. 373

1979, Sept. 17 Litho. *Perf. 14½*

B7	SP4	4c + 1c multicolored	.20	.20
B8	SP4	15c + 2c multicolored	.25	.25
B9	SP4	30c + 3c multicolored	.50	.50
B10	SP4	40c + 4c multicolored	.70	.70
		Nos. B7-B10 (4)	1.65	1.65

The surtax was for IYC fund.

POSTAGE DUE STAMPS

D1

D2

D3

1917 Unwmk. Typeset *Perf. 11*
Laid Papers; Without Gum

J1	D1	½p black	1,300.	475.00
J2	D2	½p black	550.00	300.00
J3	D3	1p black	400.00	125.00
J4	D3	2p black	325.00	80.00
J5	D3	3p black	400.00	110.00
J6	D3	4p black	950.00	550.00
a.		Strip of 8, 3 #J3, 1 ea. #J1 and #J6, and 3 #J5	*16,000.*	
		Nos. J1-J6 (6)	3,925.	1,640.

There were two printings of this issue. In the first printing, the 2d was printed in sheets of 84 (7x12), and the other four values were printed together in sheets of 96 (8x12), with each row consisting of three 1p, one ½p, one 4p and three 3p values. Setenant multiples exist. Sheets were not perforated on the margins, so that marginal stamps were not perforated on the outer edge. Examples from the first printing are 25mm wide (including margins).

In the second printing, the ½p, 1p and 2p were printed in separate sheets of 84 (7x12). The clichés were set a little closer, and so that examples of this printing are 23mm wide.

D4

D5

Perf. 14

1918, June 1 Typo. Wmk. 3

J7	D4	½p black	4.25	*20.00*
J8	D4	1p black	4.25	*15.00*
J9	D4	2p black	5.50	*22.50*
J10	D4	3p black	7.00	*27.50*
J11	D4	4p black	8.25	*40.00*
		Nos. J7-J11 (5)	29.25	*125.00*

1940 Wmk. 4 *Perf. 12½*

J12	D5	1p bright green	4.75	*62.50*
J13	D5	2p bright green	8.50	*62.50*
J14	D5	3p bright green	11.00	*77.50*
J15	D5	4p bright green	12.00	*82.50*
J16	D5	5p bright green	15.00	*82.50*
J17	D5	6p bright green	8.00	*87.50*
J18	D5	1sh dk carmine	20.00	*140.00*
J19	D5	1sh6p dk carmine	20.00	*200.00*
		Nos. J12-J19 (8)	99.25	*795.00*
		Set, never hinged	140.00	

WAR TAX STAMPS

Regular Issue of 1912-16 Overprinted

Die I

1916 Wmk. 3 *Perf. 14*

MR1	A23	½p green	.85	*3.00*
a.		Inverted overprint	700.00	
b.		Double overprint		
MR2	A23	1p scarlet	2.00	.75
a.		1p carmine	30.00	26.00
b.		Pair, one without ovpt.	*9,000.*	
c.		Inverted overprint	800.00	

Most examples of #MR2b are within horiz. strips of 12.

FINLAND

ˈfin-lənd

(Suomi)

LOCATION — Northern Europe bordering on the Gulfs of Bothnia and Finland
GOVT. — Republic
AREA — 130,119 sq. mi.
POP. — 5,147,349 (1997)
CAPITAL — Helsinki

Finland was a Grand Duchy of the Russian Empire from 1809 until December 1917, when it declared its independence.

100 Kopecks = 1 Ruble
100 Pennia = 1 Markka (1866)
100 Cents = 1 Euro (2002)

Catalogue values for unused stamps in this country are for Never Hinged items, beginning with Scott 220 in the regular postage section, Scott B39 in the semi-postal section, Scott C2 in the air-post section, Scott M1 in the military stamp section, and Scott Q6 in the parcel post section.

Unused stamps are valued with original gum as defined in the catalogue introduction except for Nos. 1-3B which are valued without gum. Used values for Nos. 1-3B are for pen-canceled examples. Very fine examples of the serpentine rouletted issues, Nos. 4-13c, will have roulettes cutting the design slightly on one or more sides and will have all "teeth" complete and intact. Stamps with roulettes clear of the design on all four sides are extremely scarce and sell for substantial premiums.

Watermarks

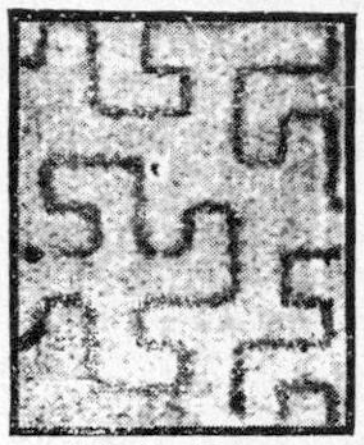
Wmk. 121 — Multiple Swastika

Wmk. 208 — Post Horn

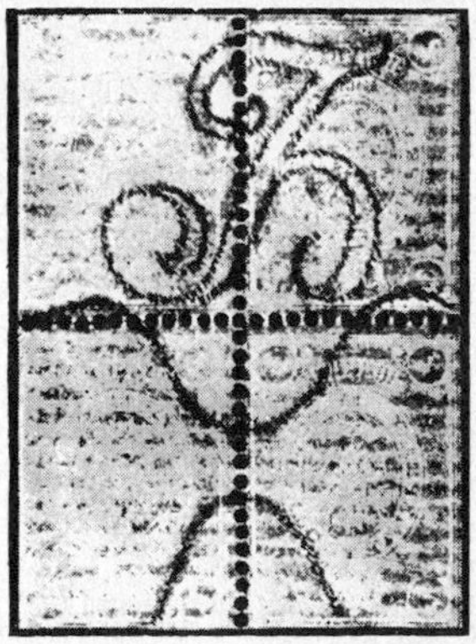
Wmk. 168 — Wavy Lines and Letters

Wmk. 273 — Roses

Wmk. 363 — Tree Stump

Syncopated Perforations

Type A (1st stamp #1065): On one longer side, groups of five holes are separated by an oval hole equal in width to eight holes.

Type B (1st stamp, #1142): On the top groups of 3 holes at left and right and a middle group of 4 holes separated by rectangular perforations equal in width to 4 holes.

Issues under Russian Empire

Coat of Arms — A1

1856 Unwmk. Typo. *Imperf.*

Small Pearls in Post Horns

Wove Paper

1 A1 5k blue *6,750.* 1,500.
Cut to shape 150.00
Pen and town cancellation 1,900.
Cut to shape 200.00
Town cancellation 3,250.
Cut to shape 250.00
a. Tête bêche pair *80,000.* *65,000.*
Pen and town cancellation *90,000.*
2 A1 10k rose 8,750. 400.00
Cut to shape 65.00
Pen and town cancellation 575.00
Cut to shape 90.00
Town cancellation 925.00
Cut to shape 100.00
a. Tête bêche pair *80,000.* *60,000.*
Pen and town cancellation *75,000.*

1858

Wide Vertically Laid Paper

2C A1 10k rose — 1,400.
Cut to shape 225.
Pen and town cancellation 1,800.
Cut to shape 275.
Town cancellation 2,500.
Cut to shape 350.
d. Tête bêche pair —

The wide vertically laid paper has 13-14 distinct lines per 2cm. The 10k rose also exists on a narrow laid paper with lines sometimes indistinct. Value, about 45 per cent of that for a wide laid paper example.

A 5k blue with small pearls exists on narrow vertically laid paper. It is rare.

Stamps on diagonally laid paper are envelope cut squares.

Large Pearls in Post Horns

Wove Paper

3 A1 5k blue *8,500.* 1,400.
Cut to shape 125.
Pen and town cancellation 1,550.
Cut to shape 175.
Town cancellation 2,500.
Cut to shape 225.
a. Tête bêche pair *60,000.*
Pen and town cancellation *65,000.*

1859 Wide Vertically Laid Paper

3B A1 5k blue — *18,000.*
Cut to shape 2,400.
Pen and town cancellation *25,000.*
Cut to shape *3,500.*

Reprints of Nos. 2 and 3, made in 1862, are on brownish paper, on vertically laid paper, and in tête bêche pairs on normal and vertically laid paper. Reprints of 1871, 1881 and 1893 are on yellowish or white paper. Value for least costly of each, $85.

In 1956, Nos. 2 and 3 were reprinted for the Centenary with post horn watermark and gum. Value, $85 each.

Coat of Arms — A2

1860 *Serpentine Roulette 7½, 8*

Four types of indentation are noted:

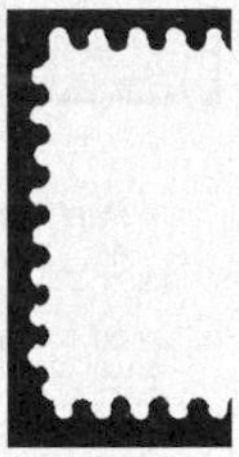
I — Depth 1-1¼mm

II — Depth 1½-1¾mm

III — Depth 2-2¼mm

IV — Shovel-shaped teeth. Depth 1¼-1½mm

Wove Paper

4 A2 5k blue, *bluish*, I 725.00 200.00
a. Roulette II 875.00 275.00
b. Perf. vert.
5 A2 10k rose, *pale rose*, I 625.00 65.00
a. Roulette II 1,300. 190.00

A3

A4

1866-74 *Serpentine Roulette*

6 A3 5p pur brn, *lil*, I ('73) 450.00 200.00
a. Roulette II 4,500.
b. 5p red brn, *lil*, III ('71) 400.00 200.00
7 A3 8p blk, *grn*, III ('67) 325.00 200.00
a. Ribbed paper, III ('72) 1,300. 1,000.
b. Roulette II ('74) 400.00 300.00
c. As "b," ribbed paper ('74) 400.00 275.00
d. Roulette I ('73) 575.00 375.00
e. As "d," ribbed paper 1,100. 475.00
f. Serpentine roulette 10½ ('67) *15,000.*
8 A3 10p blk, *yel*, III ('70) 750.00 400.00
a. 10p blk, *buff*, II 850.00 450.00
b. 10p blk, *buff*, I ('73) 800.00 425.00
9 A3 20p bl, *bl*, III 650.00 67.50
a. Roulette II 650.00 97.50
b. Roulette I ('73) 750.00 150.00
c. Roulette IV ('74) — *1,300.*
d. Perf. horiz. —
e. Printed on both sides (40p blue on back) —
10 A3 40p rose, *lil rose*, III 575.00 77.50
a. Ribbed paper, III ('73) 750.00 250.00
b. Roulette II 575.00 92.50
c. As "b," ribbed paper ('73) 750.00 200.00
d. Roulette I 800.00 200.00
e. As "d," ribbed paper 750.00 150.00
f. Roulette IV — *2,500.*
g. As "f," ribbed paper — —
h. Serpentine roulette 10½ —
11 A4 1m yel brn, III ('67) 2,500. 900.00
a. Roulette II 3,100. 1,900.

Nos. 7f and 10h are private roulettes and are also known in compound serpentine roulette 10½ and 7½.

Nos. 4-11 were reprinted in 1893 on thick wove paper. Colors differ from originals. Roulette type IV. Value for Nos. 4-5, each $40, Nos. 6-10, each $50. Value for No. 11, $55.

Thin or Thick Laid Paper

12 A3 5p red brn, *lil*, III 300.00 160.00
a. Roulette II 325.00 325.00
b. Roulette I 300.00 325.00
d. 5p blk, *buff*, roul. III (error) *22,500.*
e. Tête bêche pair —
13 A3 10p black, *buff*, III 750.00 300.00
a. 10p black, *yel*, II 900.00 300.00
b. 10p black, *yel*, I 1,300. 800.00
c. 10p red brown, *lil*, III (error) *8,500.* *7,750.*

Forgeries of No. 13c exist.

A5

1875 *Perf. 14x13½*

16 A5 32p lake 2,400. 500.00

1875-81 *Perf. 11*

17 A5 2p gray 55.00 65.00
18 A5 5p orange 140.00 15.00
a. 5p yellow 140.00 15.00
19 A5 8p blue green 275.00 75.00
a. 8p yellow green 275.00 85.00
20 A5 10p brown ('81) 625.00 67.50
21 A5 20p ultra 160.00 3.75
a. 20p blue 175.00 6.00
b. 20p Prussian blue 350.00 40.00
c. Tête bêche pair 3,500.
22 A5 25p carmine ('79) 300.00 16.00
a. 25p rose 425.00 65.00
23 A5 32p carmine 410.00 57.50
a. 32p rose 500.00 160.00
24 A5 1m violet ('77) 875.00 175.00
Nos. 17-24 (8) 2,840. 474.75

A souvenir card issued in 1974 for NORDIA 1975 reproduced a block of four of the unissued "1 MARKKAA" design.

Nos. 19, 23 were reprinted in 1893, perf. 12½. Value $17.50 each.

1881-83 *Perf. 12½*

25 A5 2p gray 15.00 17.00
a. Imperf., pair 575.00
26 A5 5p orange 57.50 7.00
a. Tête bêche pair 7,500. 4,500.
b. Imperf. vert., pair —
c. Imperf. horiz., pair —
27 A5 10p brown 100.00 20.00
28 A5 20p ultra 60.00 2.00
a. 20p blue 60.00 2.00
b. Tête bêche pair 3,000. 2,400.
c. Imperf., pair —
29 A5 25p rose 50.00 10.00
a. 25p carmine 67.50 20.00
b. Tête bêche pair *15,000.* —
30 A5 1m violet ('82) 400.00 50.00
Nos. 25-30 (6) 682.50 106.00

Nos. 27-29 were reprinted in 1893 in deeper shades, perf. 12½. Value $35 each.

Most examples of No. 28c are from printer's waste.

1881 *Perf. 11x12½*

26d A5 5p orange 500.00 100.00
27a A5 10p brown 1,000. 275.00
28d A5 20p ultra 650.00 50.00
28e A5 20p blue 650.00 50.00
29c A5 25p rose 750.00 200.00
29d A5 25p carmine 650.00 125.00
30a A5 1m violet *1,600.*

1881 *Perf. 12½x11*

26e A5 5p orange 500.00 100.00
27b A5 10p brown — 350.00
28f A5 20p ultra 650.00 50.00
28g A5 20p blue 650.00 50.00
29e A5 25p rose — 300.00
29f A5 25p carmine 650.00 125.00

1885 *Perf. 12½*

31 A5 5p emerald 19.00 .65
a. 5p yellow green 21.00 1.25
b. Tête bêche pair — *10,000.*
32 A5 10p carmine 29.00 3.00
a. 10p rose 29.00 3.00
33 A5 20p orange 32.50 .50
a. 20p yellow 37.50 1.75
b. Tête bêche pair — 3,500.
34 A5 25p ultra 62.50 3.50
a. 25p blue 57.50 3.00
35 A5 1m gray & rose 35.00 20.00
36 A5 5m green & rose 500.00 375.00
37 A5 10m brown & rose 625.00 625.00

A6

1889-92 *Perf. 12½*

38 A6 2p slate ('90) .65 *1.00*
39 A6 5p green ('90) 32.50 .40
40 A6 10p carmine ('90) 62.50 .55
a. 10p rose ('90) 77.50 .60
b. Imperf. 100.00 100.00
41 A6 20p orange ('92) 72.50 .35
a. 20p yellow ('90) 77.50 1.25
42 A6 25p ultra ('91) 72.50 1.00
a. 25p blue 77.50 1.25
43 A6 1m slate & rose ('92) 4.75 3.75
a. 1m brnsh gray & rose ('90) 27.50 4.00
44 A6 5m green & rose ('90) 27.50 *72.50*
45 A6 10m brown & rose ('90) 40.00 *100.00*
Nos. 38-45 (8) 312.90 *179.55*

The 2p slate, perf. 14x13, is believed to be an essay.

See Nos. 60-63.

See Russia for types similar to A7-A18.

Finnish stamps have "dot in circle" devices or are inscribed "Markka," "Markkaa," "Pen." or "Pennia."

Imperial Arms of Russia
A7 A8 A9

A10

A11

Laid Paper

1891-92 Wmk. 168 *Perf. 14½x15*

46 A7 1k orange yel 5.25 *11.00*
47 A7 2k green 6.25 *9.50*
48 A7 3k carmine 12.50 *17.50*
49 A8 4k rose 15.00 15.00
50 A7 7k dark blue 6.25 2.50
51 A8 10k dark blue 15.00 *16.00*
52 A9 14k blue & rose 21.00 *27.50*
53 A8 20k blue & car 19.00 18.00
54 A9 35k violet & grn 26.00 *57.50*
55 A8 50k violet & grn 35.00 40.00

Perf. 13½

56 A10 1r brown & org 90.00 90.00
57 A11 3½r black & gray 325.00 *475.00*
a. 3½r black & yellow (error) *14,000.* *17,000.*
58 A11 7r black & yellow 225.00 *300.00*
Nos. 46-58 (13) 801.25 *1,079.*

Forgeries of Nos. 57, 57a, 58 exist.

Type of 1889-90
Wove Paper

1895-96 Unwmk. *Perf. 14x13*

60	A6	5p green	.60	.40
61	A6	10p rose	.70	.50
62	A6	20p orange	.60	.25
a.		Imperf.	150.00	—
63	A6	25p ultra	1.00	.70
a.		25p blue	1.75	.75
b.		Imperf.	100.00	—
		Nos. 60-63 (4)	2.90	1.85

A12

A13

A14

A15

1901 Litho. *Perf. 14½x15*
Chalky Paper

64	A12	2p yellow	5.25	5.25
65	A12	5p green	10.00	1.00
66	A13	10p carmine	27.50	1.25
67	A12	20p dark blue	62.50	.85
68	A14	1m violet & grn	325.00	9.25

Perf. 13½

69	A15	10m black & gray	300.00	300.00
		Nos. 64-69 (6)	730.25	317.60

Imperf sheets of 10p and 20p, stolen during production, were privately perforated 11½ to defraud the P.O. Uncanceled imperfs. of Nos. 65-68 are believed to be proofs.
See Nos. 70-75, 82.

Types of 1901 Redrawn

No. 64

No. 70

2p. On No. 64, the "2" below "II" is shifted slightly leftward. On No. 70, the "2" is centered below "II."

No. 65

No. 71

5p. On No. 65, the frame lines are very close. On No. 71, a clear white space separates them.

Nos. 66, 67

Nos. 72, 73

10p, 20p. On Nos. 66-67, the horizontal central background lines are faint and broken. On Nos. 72-73, they are clear and solid, though still thin.
20p. On No. 67, "H" close to "2" with period midway. On No. 73 they are slightly separated with period close to "H."

No. 68

Nos. 74, 74a

1m. On No. 68, the "1" following "MARKKA" lacks serif at base. On Nos. 74-74a, this "1" has serif.

No. 69

No. 75

10m. On No. 69, the serifs of "M" and "A" in top and bottom panels do not touch. On No. 75, the serifs join.

Perf. 14¼x14¾ (#70-73), 14¼x14 (#74)

1901-14 Typo.
Ordinary Paper

70	A12	2p orange ('03)	.60	1.10
71	A12	5p green	1.75	.50
a.		Perf 14¼x14 ('06)	1.75	.50
72	A13	10p carmine	10.00	.50
a.		Perf 14¼x14 ('07)	55.00	.50
b.		Background inverted	16.00	2.50
c.		Background inverted, perf 14¼x14	62.50	2.50
73	A12	20p dark blue	5.25	.50
a.		Perf 14¼x14 ('06)	70.00	.65
74	A14	1m lil & grn, perf. 14¼x14 ('14)	1.40	.65
a.		1m violet & blue green, perf. 14¼x14¾ ('02)	10.00	1.00
		Nos. 70-74 (5)	19.00	3.25

Perf. 13½

75	A15	10m blk & drab ('03)	150.00	52.50

Imperf Pairs

70a	A12	2p	290.00	*410.00*
71b	A12	5p	77.50	*160.00*
72a	A13	10p	90.00	*160.00*
73a	A12	20p	160.00	*160.00*
74b	A14	1m	150.00	*160.00*
		Nos. 70a-74b (5)	767.50	1,050.

A16

A17

A18

1911-16 *Perf. 14¼x14*

77	A16	2p orange	.30	.25
78	A16	5p green	.35	.25
a.		Imperf.	410.00	
b.		Perf. 14¼x14¾	425.00	75.00
79	A17	10p rose	.30	.25
a.		Imperf.	77.50	*160.00*
80	A16	20p deep blue	.30	.25
a.		Imperf.	150.00	1.10
81	A18	40p violet & blue	.30	.25
a.		Perf. 14¼x14¾	4,000.	4,000.
		Nos. 77-81 (5)	1.55	1.25

There are three minor types of No. 79.

Perf. 14½

82	A15	10m blk & grnsh gray ('16)	125.00	175.00
a.		Horiz. pair, imperf. vert.	3,750.	

Republic
Helsinki Issue

Arms of the Republic
A19 A20

Two types of the 40p.
Type I — Thin figures of value.
Type II — Thick figures of value.

1917-29 Unwmk. *Perf. 14*

83	A19	5p green	.25	.20
84	A19	5p gray ('19)	.25	.20
85	A19	10p rose	.30	.20
a.		Imperf., pair	240.00	375.00
86	A19	10p green ('19)	2.00	.50
a.		Perf. 14½x15		*2,600.*
87	A19	10p lt blue ('21)	.30	.20
88	A19	20p buff	.30	.20
89	A19	20p rose ('20)	.60	.20
90	A19	20p brown ('24)	.60	.50
a.		Perf 14¼x14¾	.60	*32.50*
91	A19	25p blue	.25	.20
92	A19	25p lt brown ('19)	.25	.20
93	A19	30p green ('23)	.30	.20
94	A19	40p violet (I)	.25	.20
a.		Perf 14¼x14¾	350.00	19.00
95	A19	40p bl grn (II) ('29)	.35	*1.25*
a.		Type I ('24)	12.00	5.00
b.		Perf 14¼x14¾	1.10	16.00
96	A19	50p orange brn	.25	.20
97	A19	50p dp blue ('19)	3.50	.20
a.		Perf 14¼x14¾		1,400.
98	A19	50p green ('21)	4.50	.30
a.		Perf 14¼x14¾	.30	*2.50*
99	A19	60p red vio ('21)	.35	.20
a.		Imperf., pair	75.00	*100.00*
100	A19	75p yellow ('21)	.25	*.45*
101	A19	1m dull rose & blk	13.00	.20
102	A19	1m red org ('25)	7.00	*22.50*
103	A19	1⅓m bl grn & red vio ('29)	.25	*1.25*
a.		Perf 14¼x14¾	.25	*1.10*
104	A19	2m grn & blk ('21)	2.75	.70
105	A19	2m dk blue & ind ('22)	2.00	.30
a.		Perf 14¼x14¾	.60	*2.25*
106	A19	3m bl & blk ('21)	70.00	.20
107	A19	5m red vio & blk	17.00	.20
108	A19	10m brn & gray blk, perf. 14	.90	*1.25*
a.		10m light brown & black, perf. 14¼x14¾ ('29)	3.75	*450.00*
110	A19	25m dull red & yel ('21)	.90	*27.50*
		Nos. 83-108,110 (27)	128.65	*59.70*

Examples of a 2½p gray of this type exist. They are proofs from the original die which were distributed through the UPU. No plate was made for this denomination.
See Nos. 127-140, 143-152. For surcharge and overprints see Nos. 119-126, 153-154.

Vasa Issue

1918 Litho. *Perf. 11½*

111	A20	5p green	.35	*.90*
112	A20	10p red	.35	*.90*
113	A20	30p slate	.80	*2.25*
114	A20	40p brown vio	.30	*.90*
115	A20	50p orange brn	.40	*2.25*
116	A20	70p gray brown	2.40	*17.50*
117	A20	1m red & gray	.45	*1.40*
118	A20	5m red violet & gray	40.00	*80.00*
		Nos. 111-118 (8)	45.05	*106.10*

Nos. 111-118 exist imperforate but were not regularly issued in that condition.
Sheet margin examples, perf. on 3 sides, imperf. on margin side, were sold by post office.

Stamps and Type of 1917-29 Surcharged

1919 *Perf. 14*

119	A19	10p on 5p green	.35	.60
120	A19	20p on 10p rose	.35	.60
121	A19	50p on 25p blue	.90	.35
122	A19	75p on 20p orange	.35	.60
		Nos. 119-122 (4)	1.95	2.15

Stamps and Type of 1917-29 Surcharged:

Nos. 123-125

No. 126

1921

123	A19	30p on 10p grn	.65	.90
124	A19	60p on 40p red violet	3.75	1.10
125	A19	90p on 20p rose	.40	.30
126	A19	1½m on 50p blue	1.40	.40
a.		Thin "2" in "½"	11.00	8.00
b.		Imperf., pair	250.00	*375.00*
		Nos. 123-126 (4)	6.20	2.70

Arms Type of 1917-29
Perf. 14, 14½x15

1925-29 Wmk. 121

127	A19	10p ultra ('27)	.50	*2.00*
128	A19	20p brown	.50	*1.40*
129	A19	25p brn org ('29)	.80	*75.00*
130	A19	30p yel green	.25	.20
a.		Perf. 14¼x14¾	.25	
131	A19	40p blue grn (I)	2.75	.40
a.		Perf. 14¼x14¾ ('26)	4.00	.60
b.		Type II ('28)	*125.00*	*55.00*
c.		As "b," perf. 14¼x14¾ ('28)	4.00	.60
132	A19	50p gray grn ('27)	1.00	.50
a.		Perf. 14¼x14¾ ('26)	.35	*.50*
133	A19	60p red violet	.25	.25
134	A19	1m dp orange	4.75	.20
a.		Perf. 14¼x14¾	100.00	.60
135	A19	1⅓m blue grn & red vio, perf. 14¼x14¾ ('26)	5.00	.45
a.		Perf. 14 ('26)	50.00	.45
136	A19	2m dk bl & ind	1.00	.45
a.		Perf. 14¼x14¾	.60	.45
137	A19	3m chlky blue & blk	1.00	.45
138	A19	5m red vio & blk	1.10	.45
139	A19	10m lt brn & blk ('27)	4.00	*18.00*
140	A19	25m dp org & yel ('27)	20.00	*275.00*
		Nos. 127-140 (14)	42.90	*374.75*

A21

Wmk. 208
1927, Dec. 6 Typo. *Perf. 14*

141	A21	1⅓m deep violet	.20	*.35*
142	A21	2m deep blue	.25	*1.75*

10th anniv. of Finnish independence.

Arms Type of 1917-29

1927-29 Wmk. 208 *Perf. 14½x15*

143	A19	20p lt brown ('29)	1.60	*15.00*
144	A19	40p bl grn (II) ('28)	.20	.20
145	A19	50p gray grn ('28)	.20	.20
146	A19	1m dp orange	.20	*1.00*
a.		Imperf., pair	125.00	*200.00*
b.		Perf. 14	1.00	1.00
147	A19	1⅓m bl grn & red vio ('28)	2.50	.65
a.		Perf. 14	900.00	19.00
148	A19	2m dk bl & ind ('28)	.40	.35
149	A19	3m chlky bl & blk	.40	.35
a.		Perf. 14	1.75	*4.50*
150	A19	5m red vio & blk ('28)	.60	.60
151	A19	10m lt brown & blk	1.40	*37.50*
152	A19	25m brown org & yel	1.60	*175.00*
		Nos. 143-152 (10)	9.10	*230.85*

Nos. 146-147 Overprinted

1928, Nov. 10 Litho. Wmk. 208

153	A19	1m deep orange	7.75	*19.00*
154	A19	1⅓m bl grn & red vio	7.75	*19.00*

Nos. 153 and 154 were sold exclusively at the Helsinki Philatelic Exhibition, Nov. 10-18, 1928, and were valid only during that period.

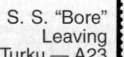

S. S. "Bore" Leaving Turku — A23

Turku Cathedral — A24

Turku Castle — A25

Wmk. 208
1929, May 22 Typo. *Perf. 14*

155	A23	1m olive green	1.50	*4.00*
156	A24	1⅓m chocolate	2.40	*4.00*
157	A25	2m dark gray	.85	*4.50*
		Nos. 155-157 (3)	4.75	*12.50*

Founding of the city of Turku (Abo), 700th anniv.

A26

1930-46 Unwmk. *Perf. 14*

158	A26	5p	chocolate	.20	.20
159	A26	10p	dull violet	.20	.20
160	A26	20p	yel grn	.30	*.35*
161	A26	25p	yel brn	.20	.20
162	A26	40p	bl grn	1.90	.35
163	A26	50p	yellow	.50	.35
164	A26	50p	blue grn ('32)	.20	.20
b.			Imperf., pair	140.00	140.00
165	A26	60p	dark gray	.35	.45
165A	A26	75p	dp org ('42)	.20	.20
166	A26	1m	red org	.45	.20
166B	A26	1m	yel grn ('42)	.20	.20
167	A26	1.20m	crimson	.35	*.60*
168	A26	1.25m	yel ('32)	.20	.20
169	A26	1½m	red vio	2.10	.20
170	A26	1½m	car ('32)	.20	.20
170A	A26	1½m	sl ('40)	.20	.20
170B	A26	1.75m	org yel ('40)	.60	.20
171	A26	2m	indigo	.30	.20
172	A26	2m	dp vio ('32)	6.25	.20
173	A26	2m	car ('36)	.20	.20
			Complete booklet, panes of 4 #161, 164, 166, 168, 173	5.50	
173B	A26	2m	yel org ('42)	.30	.20
173C	A26	2m	blue grn ('45)	.20	.20
174	A26	2½m	brt bl ('32)	3.00	.35
174A	A26	2½m	car ('42)	.20	.20
174B	A26	2.75m	rose vio ('40)	.20	.20
175	A26	3m	olive blk	26.00	.20
175B	A26	3m	car ('45)	.20	.20
175C	A26	3m	yel ('45)	.35	*.60*
176	A26	3½m	brt bl ('36)	8.50	.35
176A	A26	3½m	olive ('42)	.20	.20
176B	A26	4m	olive ('45)	.35	.20
176C	A26	4½m	saph ('42)	.20	.20
176D	A26	5m	saph ('45)	.35	.20
176E	A26	5m	pur ('45)	.35	.20
j.			Imperf., pair	150.00	150.00
176F	A26	5m	yel ('46)	.70	.20
k.			Imperf., pair	150.00	*190.00*
176G	A26	6m	car ('45)	.35	.20
m.			Imperf., pair	190.00	*225.00*
176H	A26	8m	pur ('46)	.20	.20
176I	A26	10m	saph ('45)	1.00	.20
			Nos. 158-176I (38)	57.75	9.40

See #257-262, 270-274, 291-296, 302-304. For surcharges & overprints see #195-196, 212, 221-222, 243, 250, 275, M2-M3.

Stamps of types A26-A29 overprinted "ITA KARJALA" are listed under Karelia, Nos. N1-N15.

Castle in Savonlinna A27

Lake Saima — A28

Woodchopper A29

1930 Engr.

177	A27	5m	blue	.20	.20
178	A28	10m	gray lilac	60.00	4.75
179	A29	25m	black brown	.95	.20
			Nos. 177-179 (3)	61.15	5.15

See #205, 305. For overprint see #C1.

Elias Lönnrot — A30

Seal of Finnish Literary Society — A31

1931, Jan. 1 Typo.

180	A30	1m olive brown	2.75	*6.00*
181	A31	1½m dull blue	14.00	6.00

Centenary of Finnish Literary Society.

A32

1931, Feb. 28

182	A32	1½m red	2.75	*10.00*
183	A32	2m blue	2.75	*11.00*

1st use of postage stamps in Finland, 75th anniv.

Nos. 162-163 Surcharged

1931, Dec.

195	A26	50p on 40p blue grn	1.40	.60
196	A26	1.25m on 50p yellow	4.25	1.75

Svinhufvud A33

Alexis Kivi A34

1931, Dec. 15

197	A33	2m gray blue & blk	1.50	*3.50*

Pres. Pehr Eyvind Svinhufvud, 70th birthday.

Lake Saima Type of 1930

1932-43 Re-engraved

205	A28	10m red violet ('43)	.35	.20
a.		10m dark violet	21.00	.75

On Nos. 205 and 205a the lines of the islands, the clouds and the foliage are much deeper and stronger than on No. 178.

1934, Oct. 10 Typo.

206	A34	2m red violet	2.25	2.25
		Never hinged	5.00	

Alexis Kivi, Finnish poet (1834-1872).

Bards Reciting the "Kalevala" A35

Goddess Louhi, As Eagle Seizing Magic Mill — A36

Kullervo — A37

1935, Feb. 28 Engr.

207	A35	1¼m brown lake	1.25	1.25
208	A36	2m black	3.50	1.50
209	A37	2½m blue	3.00	2.25
		Nos. 207-209 (3)	7.75	5.00
		Set, never hinged	17.00	

Cent. of the publication of the "Kalevala" (Finnish National Epic).

No. 170 Surcharged in Black

1937, Feb.

212	A26	2m on 1½m car	4.75	.90
		Never hinged	10.00	

Gustaf Mannerheim — A38

Swede-Finn Co-operation in Colonization A39

1937, June 4 Photo. *Perf. 14*

213	A38	2m ultra	.60	*1.25*
		Never hinged	1.50	

70th birthday of Field Marshal Baron Carl Gustaf Mannerheim, June 4th, 1937.

1938, June 1

214	A39	3½m dark brown	1.25	*3.25*
		Never hinged	2.75	

Tercentenary of the colonization of Delaware by Swedes and Finns.

Early Post Office — A40

Designs: 1¼m, Mail delivery in 1700. 2m, Modern mail plane. 3½m, Helsinki post office.

1938, Sept. 6 Photo. *Perf. 14*

215	A40	50p green	.35	.75
216	A40	1¼m dk blue	1.25	*3.50*
217	A40	2m scarlet	1.50	1.25
218	A40	3½m slate black	4.00	*7.00*
		Nos. 215-218 (4)	7.10	12.50
		Set, never hinged	14.00	

300th anniv. of the Finnish Postal System.

Margin strips of each denomination (3 of #215, 2 each of #216, 217, 218) were pasted on to advertising sheets and stapled into a booklet. Value, $110.

Post Office, Helsinki — A44

1939-42 Photo.

219	A44	4m brown black	.20	.20

Engr.

219A	A44	7m black brn ('42)	.35	.20
219B	A44	9m rose lake ('42)	.35	.20
		Nos. 219-219B (3)	.90	.60
		Set, never hinged	2.75	

See No. 248.

Catalogue values for unused stamps in this section, from this point to the end of the section, are for Never Hinged items.

University of Helsinki — A45

1940, May 1 Photo.

220	A45	2m dp blue & blue	.60	*1.00*

300th anniv. of the founding of the University of Helsinki.

Nos. 168 and 173 Surcharged in Black

1940, June 16 Typo.

221	A26	1.75m on 1.25m yel	1.90	1.90
222	A26	2.75m on 2m carmine	6.00	.70

President Kallio Reviewing Military Band — A46

1941, May 24 Engr.

223	A46	2.75m black	.60	*.90*

Pres. Kyösti Kallio (1873-1940).

Castle at Viborg — A47

1941, Aug. 30 Typo.

224	A47	1.75m yellow orange	.60	*.85*
225	A47	2.75m rose violet	.60	*.85*
226	A47	3.50m blue	.90	*1.75*

Field Marshal Mannerheim A48

Pres. Risto Ryti A49

1941, Dec. 31 Engr. Wmk. 273

227	A48	50p dull green	1.10	1.50
228	A48	1.75m deep brown	1.10	*1.50*
229	A48	2m dark red	1.10	1.50
230	A48	2.75m dull vio brn	1.10	*1.50*
231	A48	3.50m deep blue	1.10	*1.50*
232	A48	5m slate blue	1.10	*1.50*
		Nos. 227-232 (6)	6.60	*9.00*
233	A49	50p dull green	1.10	1.50
234	A49	1.75m deep brown	1.10	*1.50*
235	A49	2m dark red	1.10	1.50
236	A49	2.75m dull vio brn	1.10	*1.50*
237	A49	3.50m deep blue	1.10	*1.50*
238	A49	5m slate blue	1.10	*1.50*
		Nos. 233-238 (6)	6.60	*9.00*

Types A48-A49 overprinted "ITA KARJALA" are listed under Karelia, Nos. N16-N27.

Häme Bridge, Tampere A50

South Harbor, Helsinki — A51

1942 **Unwmk.**

239 A50 50m dull brown vio 3.00 .20
240 A51 100m indigo 4.00 .20

See No. 350.

Altar and Open Bible — A52

17th Century Printer — A53

1942, Oct. 10

241 A52 2.75m dk brown .50 *1.10*
242 A53 3.50m violet blue .90 *1.75*

300th anniv. of the printing of the 1st Bible in Finnish.

No. 174B Surcharged in Black

1943, Feb. 1

243 A26 3.50m on 2.75m rose vio .35 .35

Minna Canth (1844-96), Author and Playwright — A54

1944, Mar. 20

244 A54 3.50m dk olive grn .60 *1.00*

Pres. P. E. Svinhufvud A55

K. J. Stahlberg A56

1944, Aug. 1

245 A55 3.50m black .40 *1.00*

Death of President Svinhufvud (1861-1944).

1945, May 16 **Engr.** ***Perf. 14***

246 A56 3.50m brown vio .35 *.60*

80th birthday of Dr. K. J. Stahlberg.

Castle in Savonlinna A57

Jean Sibelius — A58

1945, Sept. 4

247 A57 15m lilac rose 1.75 .20
248 A44 20m sepia 1.75 .20

For a 35m of type A57, see No. 280.

1945, Dec. 8

249 A58 5m dk slate green .40 .40

Jean Sibelius (1865-1957), composer.

No. 176E Surcharged with New Value and Bars in Black

1946, Mar. 16

250 A26 8(m) on 5m purple .45 .20

Victorious Athletes — A59

Lighthouse at Uto — A60

1946, June 1 **Engr.** ***Perf. 13½***

251 A59 8m brown violet .35 *.60*

3rd Sports Festival, Helsinki, June 27-30, 1946.

1946, Sept. 19

252 A60 8m deep violet .45 *.60*

250th anniv. of the Finnish Department of Pilots and Lighthouses.

Post Bus — A61

1946-47 **Unwmk.** ***Perf. 14***

253 A61 16m gray black .75 .75
253A A61 30m gray black ('47) 2.25 .20

Issue dates: 16m, Oct. 16, 30m, Feb. 10.

Old Town Hall, Porvoo — A62

Cathedral, Porvoo — A63

1946, Dec. 3

254 A62 5m gray black .35 *.60*
255 A63 8m deep claret .45 *.60*

600th anniv. of the founding of the city of Porvoo (Borga).

Waterfront, Tammisaari A64

1946, Dec. 14

256 A64 8m grnsh black .35 *.60*

400th anniv. of the founding of the town of Tammisaari (Ekenas).

Lion Type of 1930

1947 **Typo.** ***Perf. 14***

257 A26 2½m dark green .35 .20
258 A26 3m slate gray .35 .20
259 A26 6m deep orange 1.75 .50
260 A26 7m carmine .80 .20
261 A26 10m purple 3.25 .20
262 A26 12m deep blue 2.50 .20
Nos. 257-262 (6) 9.00 1.50

Issued: 3m, 6/9; 7m, 12m, 2/10; others, 1/20.

Pres. Juho K. Paasikivi — A65

Postal Savings Emblem — A66

1947, Mar. 15 **Engr.**

263 A65 10m gray black .35 *.50*

1947, Apr. 1

264 A66 10m brown violet .35 *.50*

60th anniv. of the foundation of the Finnish Postal Savings Bank.

Ilmarinen, the Plowman A67

Girl and Boy Athletes A68

1947, June 2

265 A67 10m gray black .35 *.50*

2nd year of peace following WW II.

1947, June 2

266 A68 10m bright blue .35 *.50*

Finnish Athletic Festival, Helsinki, June 29-July 3, 1947.

Wheat and Savings Bank Assoc. Emblem — A69

Sower — A70

1947, Aug. 21

267 A69 10m red brown .35 *.75*

Finnish Savings Bank Assoc., 125th anniv.

1947, Nov. 1

268 A70 10m gray black .35 *.60*

150th anniv. of Finnish Agricultural Societies.

Koli Mountain and Lake Pielisjärvi A71

Statue of Michael Agricola — A72

1947, Nov. 1

269 A71 10m indigo .35 *.60*

60th anniv. of the Finnish Touring Assoc.

Lion Type of 1930

1948 **Typo.** ***Perf. 14***

270 A26 3m dark green 3.00 .20
271 A26 6m yellow green 1.25 .65
272 A26 9m carmine 1.10 .20
273 A26 15m dark blue 4.50 .20
274 A26 24m brown lake 1.40 .20
Nos. 270-274 (5) 11.25 1.45

Issued: 3m, 2/9; 24m, 4/26; others, 9/13.

No. 261 Surcharged with New Value and Bars in Black

1948, Feb. 9

275 A26 12(m) on 10m purple 1.10 .20

1948, Oct. 2 **Engr.** ***Perf. 14***

12m, Agricola translating New Testament.

276 A72 7m rose violet 1.00 *1.75*
277 A72 12m gray blue 1.00 *1.75*

400th anniv. of publication of the Finnish translation of the New Testament, by Michael Agricola.

Sveaborg Fortress A73

Post Rider — A74

1948, Oct. 15

278 A73 12m deep green 1.40 *2.25*

200th anniv. of the construction of Sveaborg Fortress on the Gulf of Finland.

1948, Oct. 27

279 A74 12m green 9.00 *20.00*

Helsinki Philatelic Exhibition. Sold only at exhibition for 62m, of which 50m was entrance fee.

Castle Type of 1945

1949

280 A57 35m violet 8.00 .20

Sawmill and Cellulose Plant — A75

Pine Tree and Globe — A76

Woman with Torch — A77

1949, June 15
281 A75 9m brown 2.75 *3.25*
282 A76 15m dull green 2.75 *3.25*

Issued to publicize the Third World Forestry Congress, Helsinki, July 10-20, 1949.

1949, July 16 Engr. *Perf. 14*
283 A77 5m dull green 5.50 *9.00*
284 A77 15m red *(Worker)* 5.50 *9.00*

50th anniv. of the Finnish labor movement.

Harbor of Lappeenranta (Willmanstrand) — A78

Raahe (Brahestad) — A79

1949
285 A78 5m dk blue grn .75 .70
286 A79 9m brown carmine .95 .95
287 A78 15m brt blue *(Kristiinankaupunki)* 1.75 *2.50*
Nos. 285-287 (3) 3.45 4.15

300th anniv. of the founding of Willmanstrand, Brahestad and Kristinestad (Kristiinankaupunki).
Issued: 5m, 8/6; 9m, 8/13; 15m, 7/30.

Technical High School Badge — A80

Hannes Gebhard — A81

1949, Sept. 13
288 A80 15m ultra .95 *1.00*

Founding of the technical school, cent.

1949, Oct. 2
289 A81 15m dull green .95 *1.00*

Establishment of Finnish cooperatives, 50th anniv.

Finnish Lake Country — A82

1949, Oct. 8
290 A82 15m blue 1.25 1.10

75th anniv. of the UPU.

Lion Type of 1930

1950, Jan. 9 Typo. *Perf. 14*
291 A26 8m brt green 3.00 3.00
292 A26 9m red orange 2.10 .50
293 A26 10m violet brown 7.25 .20
294 A26 12m scarlet 1.40 .20
295 A26 15m plum 17.00 .20
296 A26 20m deep blue 8.50 .20
Nos. 291-296 (6) 39.25 4.30

Forsell's Map of Old Helsinki — A83

J. A. Ehrenstrom and C. L. Engel — A84

City Hall — A85

1950, June 11 Engr.
297 A83 5m emerald .50 *.70*
298 A84 9m brown .75 *1.00*
299 A85 15m deep blue .60 *.75*
Nos. 297-299 (3) 1.85 2.45

400th anniv. of the founding of Helsinki.

J. K. Paasikivi — A86

View of Kajaani — A87

1950, Nov. 27
300 A86 20m deep ultra .60 .35

80th birthday of Pres. J. K. Paasikivi.

1951, July 7 Unwmk. *Perf. 14*
301 A87 20m red brown .60 .50

Tercentenary of Kajaani.

Lion and Chopper Types of 1930

1952, Jan. 18 Typo.
302 A26 10m emerald 4.00 .20
303 A26 15m red 4.25 .20
304 A26 25m blue 4.25 .20

Engr.
305 A29 40m black brown 4.25 .20
Nos. 302-305 (4) 16.75 .80

Arms of Pietarsaari A88

Rooftops of Vaasa A89

1952, June 19 Unwmk. *Perf. 14*
306 A88 25m blue .90 .90

300th anniv. of the founding of Pietarsaari (Jacobstad).

1952, Aug. 3
307 A89 25m brown .90 .90

Centenary of the burning of Vaasa.

Chess Symbols — A90

Torch Bearers — A91

1952, Aug. 10
308 A90 25m gray 2.00 *2.25*

10th Chess Olympics, Helsinki, 8/10-31/52.

1953, Jan. 27
309 A91 25m blue 1.10 1.00

Temperance movement in Finland, cent.

Air View of Hamina (Fredrikshamn) A92

Ivar Wilskman — A93

1953, June 20
310 A92 25m dk gray green .90 .80

Tercentenary of Hamina.

1954, Feb. 26
311 A93 25m blue .80 .80

Centenary of the birth of Prof. Ivar Wilskman, "father of gymnastics in Finland."

Arms of Finland A94

"In the Outer Archipelago" A95

1954-59 *Perf. 11½*
312 A94 1m red brown ('55) .50 .20
313 A94 2m green ('55) .50 .20
314 A94 3m deep orange .50 .20
314A A94 4m gray ('58) .45 .20
315 A94 5m violet blue .85 .20
316 A94 10m blue green 1.25 .20
a. Bklt. pane of 5 (vert. strip) 22.50 22.50
Complete booklet, #316a 25.00
317 A94 15m rose red 3.75 .20
318 A94 15m yellow org ('57) 8.50 .20
319 A94 20m rose lilac 12.00 .20
320 A94 20m rose red ('56) 2.75 .20
321 A94 25m deep blue 4.00 .20
322 A94 25m rose lilac ('59) 13.00 .20
323 A94 30m lt ultra ('56) 2.75 .20
Nos. 312-323 (13) 50.80 2.60

See Nos. 398, 400-405A, 457-459, 461A-462, 464-464B.

1954, July 21 *Perf. 14*
324 A95 25m black .75 .60

Cent. of the birth of Albert Edelfelt, painter.

J. J. Nervander A96

1955, Feb. 23
325 A96 25m blue .90 .70

150th anniv. of the birth of J. J. Nervander, astronomer and poet.

Composite of Finnish Public Buildings A97

Bishop Henrik with Foot on Lalli, his Murderer A98

1955, Mar. 30 Engr. *Perf. 14*
326 A97 25m gray 12.50 *15.00*

Sold for 125m, which included the price of admission to the Natl. Postage Stamp Exhibition, Helsinki, Mar. 30-Apr. 3, 1955.

1955, May 19

25m, Arrival of Bishop Henrik and monks.

327 A98 15m rose brown 1.00 .75
328 A98 25m green 1.00 .75

Adoption of Christianity in Finland, 800th anniv.

Conference Hall, Helsinki — A99

1955, Aug. 25
329 A99 25m bluish green 1.25 *1.40*

44th conf. of the Interparliamentarian Union, Helsinki, Aug. 25-31, 1955.

Sailing Vessel and Merchant A100

1955, Sept. 2
330 A100 25m sepia 1.50 1.50

350th anniv. of founding of Oulu.

Town Hall, Lahti — A101

Radio Sender, Map of Finland — A102

1955, Nov. 1 *Perf. 14x13½*
331 A101 25m violet blue 1.25 1.25

50th anniversary of founding of Lahti.

1955, Dec. 10 *Perf. 14*

Designs: 15m, Otto Nyberg. 25m, Telegraph wires and pines under snow.

Inscribed: Lennatin 1855-1955 Telegrafen

332 A102 10m green 1.50 1.50
333 A102 15m dull violet 1.50 1.50
334 A102 25m lt ultra 1.50 1.50
Nos. 332-334 (3) 4.50 4.50

Cent. of the telegraph in Finland.

A103

A104

1956, Jan. 26 Unwmk. *Perf. 14*
335 A103 25m Lighthouse, Porkkala Peninsula .80 .60

Return of the Porkkala Region to Finland by Russia, Jan. 1956.

1956-57 *Perf. 11½*

30m, 50m, Church at Lammi. 40m, House of Parliament. 60m, Fortress of Olavinlinna (Olofsborg).

336 A104 30m gray olive 1.25 .20
337 A104 40m dull purple 3.00 .20
338 A104 50m gray ol ('57) 7.50 .20
338A A104 60m pale pur ('57) 13.00 .20
Nos. 336-338A (4) 24.75 .80

Issued: 30m, 3/4; 40m, 3/11; 50m, 3/3; 60m, 4/7. See Nos. 406-408A.

Johan V. Snellman A105

Gymnast and Athletes A106

1956, May 12 Engr. *Perf. 14*
339 A105 25m dk violet brn .80 .65

Johan V. Snellman (1806-81), statesman.

1956, June 28
340 A106 30m violet blue 1.00 .70

Finnish Gymnastic and Sports Games, Helsinki, June 28-July 1, 1956.

A107

Wmk. 208

1956, July 7 Typo. *Rouletted*
341 A107 30m deep ultra 4.00 *6.00*
a. Tête bêche pair 8.50 *12.50*
b. Pane of 10 42.50 *65.00*

Issued to publicize the FINLANDIA Philatelic Exhibition, Helsinki, July 7-15, 1956.

Printed in sheets containing four 2x5 panes, with white margins around each group. The stamps in each double row are printed tete-beche, making the position of the watermark differ in the vertical row of each pane of ten.

Sold for 155m, price including entrance ticket to exhibition.

Town Hall at Vasa — A108

Unwmk.

1956, Oct. 2 Engr. *Perf. 14*
342 A108 30m bright blue .85 .60

350th anniversary of Vasa.

Northern Countries Issue

Whooper Swans — A108a

1956, Oct. 30 *Perf. 12½*
343 A108a 20m rose red 2.75 1.25
344 A108a 30m ultra 10.00 1.10

See footnote after Denmark No. 362.

University Clinic, Helsinki A109

Scout Sign, Emblem and Globe — A110

1956, Dec. 17 *Perf. 11½*
345 A109 30m dull green 2.25 .75

Public health service in Finland, bicent.

1957, Feb. 22 *Perf. 14*
346 A110 30m ultra 2.00 .90

50th anniversary of Boy Scouts.

Arms Holding Hammers and Laurel — A111

"Lex" from Seal of Parliament — A112

Design: 20m, Factories and cogwheel.

1957 Engr. *Perf. 13½*
347 A111 20m dark blue .90 .55
348 A111 30m carmine .90 .70

50th anniv.: Central Fed. of Finnish Employers (20m, issued 9/27); Finnish Trade Union Movement (30m, issued 4/15).

1957, May 23 *Perf. 14*
349 A112 30m olive gray 1.00 .60

50th anniv. of the Finnish parliament.

Harbor Type of 1942

1957 Unwmk. *Perf. 14*
350 A51 100m grnsh blue 15.00 .20

Ida Aalberg — A114

Arms of Finland A115

1957, Dec. 4 *Perf. 14*
351 A114 30m vio gray & mar .80 .65

Birth cent. of Ida Aalberg, Finnish actress.

1957, Dec. 6 *Perf. 11½*
352 A115 30m blue .85 .65

40th anniv. of Finland's independence.

Jean Sibelius — A116

Ski Jump — A117

1957, Dec. 8 *Perf. 14*
353 A116 30m black 1.25 .55

Jean Sibelius (1865-1957), composer.

1958, Feb. 1 Engr. *Perf. 11½*

Design: 30m, Skier, vert.

354 A117 20m slate green .75 *.95*
355 A117 30m blue .85 .55

Nordic championships of the Intl. Ski Federation, Lahti.

"March of the Bjorneborgienses," by Edelfelt — A118

1958, Mar. 8
356 A118 30m violet gray 1.25 .65

400th anniv. of the founding of Pori (Bjorneborg).

South Harbor, Helsinki A119

1958, June 2 Unwmk. *Perf. 11½*
357 A119 100m bluish green 22.00 .20

See No. 410.

Seal of Jyväskylä Lyceum A120

1958, Oct. 1 *Perf. 11½*
358 A120 30m rose carmine 1.60 .85

Cent. of the founding of the 1st Finnish secondary school.

Chrismon and Globe — A121

Diet at Porvoo, 1809 — A122

1959, Jan. 19
359 A121 30m dull violet .85 .60

Finnish Missionary Society, cent.

1959, Mar. 22 *Perf. 11½*
360 A122 30m dk blue gray .85 .60

150th anniv. of the inauguration of the Diet at Porvoo.

Saw Cutting Log — A123

Pyhakoski Power Station — A124

1959, May 13 Engr.
361 A123 10m shown .60 .60
362 A123 30m Forest .85 *.85*

No. 361 for the cent. of the establishment of the 1st steam saw-mill in Finland; No. 362, the cent. of the Dept. of Forestry.

1959, May 24
363 A124 75m gray 4.50 .20

See No. 409.

Oil Lamp — A125

Woman Gymnast A126

1959, Dec. 19
364 A125 30m blue .85 .50

Cent. of the liberation of the country trade.

1959, Nov. 14 Unwmk.
365 A126 30m rose lilac .95 .60

Finnish women's gymnastics and the cent. of the birth of Elin Oihonna Kallio, pioneer of Finnish women's physical education.

Arms of Six New Towns — A127

1960, Jan. 2 *Perf. 14*
366 A127 30m light violet .85 .50

Issued to commemorate the founding of new towns in Finland: Hyvinkaa, Kouvola, Riihimaki, Rovaniemi, Salo and Seinajoki.

Type of 1860 Issue
A128

1960, Mar. 25 Typo. ***Rouletted 4½***
367 A128 30m blue & gray 7.50 8.75

Cent. of Finland's serpentine roulette stamps, and in connection with HELSINKI 1960, 40th anniv. exhib. of the Federation of Philatelic Societies of Finland, Mar. 25-31. Sold only at the exhibition for 150m including entrance ticket.

Mother and Child, Waiting Crowd and Uprooted Oak Emblem
A129

1960, Apr. 7 Engr. ***Perf. 11½***
368 A129 30m rose claret .75 .65
369 A129 40m dark blue .75 .65

World Refugee Year, 7/1/59-6/30/60.

Johan Gadolin
A130

Hj. Nortamo
A131

1960, June 4 ***Perf. 11½***
370 A130 30m dark brown .80 .80

Bicent. of the birth of Gadolin, chemist.

1960, June 13 Unwmk.
371 A131 30m gray green .80 .50

Cent. of the birth of Hj. Nortamo (Hjalmar Nordberg), writer.

Symbolic Tree and Cuckoo
A132

1960, June 18
372 A132 30m vermilion .85 .50

Karelian Natl. Festival, Helsinki, June 18-19.

Geodetic Instrument
A133

Urho Kekkonen — A134

Design: 30m, Aurora borealis and globe.

1960, July 26 Unwmk. ***Perf. 13½***
373 A133 10m blue & pale brn .50 .40
374 A133 30m ver & rose car .85 .50

12th General Assembly of the Intl. Union of Geodesy and Geophysics, Helsinki.

1960, Sept. 3 Engr. ***Perf. 11½***
375 A134 30m violet blue .90 .50

Issued to honor President Urho Kekkonen on his 60th birthday.

Common Design Types pictured following the introduction.

Europa Issue, 1960
Common Design Type

1960, Sept. 19 ***Perf. 13½***
Size: 30½x21mm.
376 CD3 30m dk bl & Prus bl *.60 .60*
377 CD3 40m dk brn & plum *.60 .60*

A 30m gray similar to No. 376 was printed with simulated perforations in a non-valid souvenir sheet privately released in London for STAMPEX 1961.

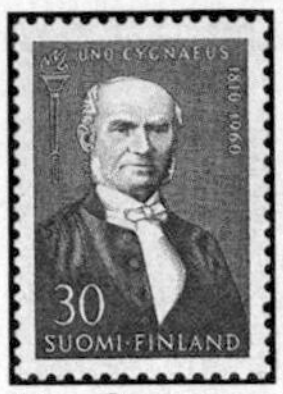

Uno Cygnaeus
A135

"Pommern" and Arms of Mariehamn
A136

1960, Oct. 13 ***Perf. 11½***
378 A135 30m dull violet 1.00 .50

150th anniv. of the birth of Pastor Uno Cygnaeus, founder of elementary schools.

1961, Feb. 21 ***Perf. 11½***
379 A136 30m grnsh blue 3.25 1.40

Centenary of the founding of Mariehamn.

Lake and Rowboat
A137

Turku Castle — A138

1961 Engr. Unwmk.
380 A137 5m green .40 .20
381 A138 125m slate green 20.00 .40

See Nos. 399, 411.

Postal Savings Bank Emblem — A139

Symbol of Standardization — A140

1961, May 24
382 A139 30m Prus green .85 .50

75th anniv. of Finland's Postal Savings Bank.

1961, June 5 Litho. ***Perf. 14x13½***
383 A140 30m dk sl grn & org .85 .50

Meeting of the Intl. Organization for Standardization (ISO), Helsinki, June 5.

Juhani Aho
A141

Various Buildings
A142

Perf. 11½
1961, Sept. 11 Unwmk. Engr.
384 A141 30m red brown .85 .50

Juhani Aho (1861-1921), writer.

1961, Oct. 16 ***Perf. 11½***
385 A142 30m slate .85 .50

150 years of the Central Board of Buildings.

Arvid Jarnefelt
A143

1961, Nov. 16
386 A143 30m deep claret .85 .50

Cent. of the birth of Arvid Jarnefelt, writer.

Bank of Finland — A144

First Finnish Locomotive — A145

1961, Dec. 12 Engr. ***Perf. 11½***
387 A144 30m brown violet .85 .50

150th anniversary of Bank of Finland.

1962, Jan. 31 Unwmk. ***Perf. 11½***

30m, Steam locomotive & timber car. 40m, Diesel locomotive & passenger train.

388 A145 10m gray green 1.50 .65
389 A145 30m violet blue 2.25 .65
390 A145 40m dull red brown 5.25 .90
Nos. 388-390 (3) 9.00 2.20

Centenary of the Finnish State Railways.

Mora Stone — A146

1962, Feb. 15
391 A146 30m gray brown .85 .50

Issued to commemorate 600 years of political rights of the Finnish people.

Senate Place, Helsinki
A147

1962, Apr. 8 Unwmk. ***Perf. 11½***
392 A147 30m violet brown .85 .50

Sesquicentennial of the proclamation of Helsinki as capital of Finland.

Customs Emblem
A148

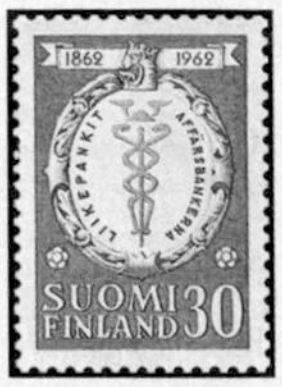

Staff of Mercury — A149

1962, Apr. 11
393 A148 30m red .85 .50

Finnish Board of Customs, sesquicentennial.

1962, May 21 Engr.
394 A149 30m bluish green .85 .50

Cent. of the 1st commercial bank in Finland.

Santeri Alkio — A150

Finnish Labor Emblem and Conveyor Belt — A151

1962, June 17 Unwmk. ***Perf. 11½***
395 A150 30m brown carmine .85 .50

Cent. of the birth of Santeri Alkio, writer and pioneer of the young people's societies in Finland.

1962, Oct. 19
396 A151 30m chocolate .85 .50

National production progress.

Survey Plane and Compass — A152

1962, Nov. 14
397 A152 30m yellow green 1.00 .60

Finnish Land Survey Board, 150th anniv.

Types of 1954-61 and

House of Parliament — A152a

Church at Lammi — A152b

Fortress of Olavinlinna — A152c

Log Floating
A153

Parainen Bridge — A154

Farm on Lake Shore — A155

Aerial View of Punkaharju — A155a

Ristikallio in Kuusamo A156

1963-67 Engr. *Perf. 11½*

398	A94	5p	violet blue	.40	.20
a.			Booklet pane of 2 (vert. pair)	22.50	20.00
b.			Bklt. pane of 2 (horiz. pair)	12.00	10.00
399	A137	5p	green	.30	.20
400	A94	10p	blue green	.45	.20
a.			Booklet pane of 2 (vert. pair)	22.50	20.00
401	A94	15p	yellow org	1.10	.20
402	A94	20p	rose red	.70	.20
a.			Booklet pane of 2 (vert. pair)	24.00	
			Complete booklet, #398a, 400a, 402a	75.00	
b.			Bklt. pane, 2 #400, 1 #402 + label; horiz. strip	45.00	35.00
			Complete booklet, #398b, 402b	97.50	
c.			Bklt. pane, 2 #398, 2 #400, 1 #402; horiz. strip	3.50	3.50
			Complete booklet, #402c	4.50	
403	A94	25p	rose lilac	1.10	.20
404	A94	30p	lt ultra	6.00	.20
404A	A94	30p	blue gray ('65)	.70	.20
405	A94	35p	blue	1.10	.20
405A	A94	40p	ultra ('67)	1.50	.20
406	A152a	40p	dull purple	3.50	.20
407	A152b	50p	gray olive	5.00	.20
408	A152c	60p	pale purple	8.50	.20
408A	A152c	65p	pale pur ('67)	1.10	.20
409	A124	75p	gray	1.75	.20
410	A119	1m	bluish grn	.50	.20
411	A138	1.25m	slate grn	1.60	.20
412	A153	1.50m	dk grnsh gray	1.60	.20
413	A154	1.75m	blue	1.50	.20
414	A155	2m	green ('64)	14.00	.20
414A	A155a	2.50m	ultra & yel grn ('67)	7.00	.20
415	A156	5m	dk slate grn ('64)	17.00	.30
			Nos. 398-415 (22)	76.40	4.50

Pennia denominations expressed: "0.05," "0.10," etc.

Four stamps of type A94 (5p, 10p, 20p, 25p) come in two types: I. Four vertical lines in "O" of SUOMI. II. Three lines in "O."

For similar designs see #457-470A.

Mother and Child — A157

1963, Mar. 21 Unwmk. *Perf. 11½*
416 A157 40p red brown .70 .45

FAO "Freedom from Hunger" campaign.

"Christ Today" — A158

Design: 10p, Crown of thorns and medieval cross of consecration.

1963, July 30 Engr. *Perf. 11½*
417 A158 10p maroon .50 .45
418 A158 30p dark green .75 .60

4th assembly of the Lutheran World Federation, Helsinki, July 30-Aug. 8.

Europa Issue, 1963
Common Design Type

1963, Sept. 16
Size: 30x20mm
419 CD6 40p red lilac *1.60 .50*

Assembly Building, Helsinki A159

1963, Sept. 18
420 A159 30p violet blue .80 .40

Representative Assembly of Finland, cent.

Convair Metropolitan A160 | M. A. Castrén A161

Design: 40p, Caravelle jetliner.

1963, Nov. 1
421 A160 35p slate green 1.00 .45
422 A160 40p brt ultra 1.00 .45

40th anniversary of Finnish air traffic.

1963, Dec. 2 Unwmk.
423 A161 35p violet blue .90 .40

Matthias Alexander Castrén (1813-52), ethnologist and philologist.

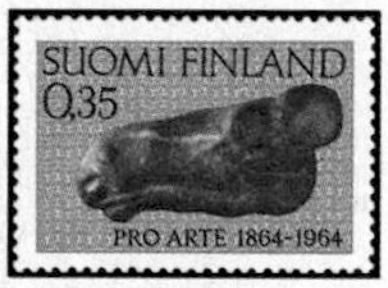

Stone Elk's Head, 2000 B.C. — A162

Emil Nestor Setälä — A163

1964, Feb. 5 Litho. *Perf. 11½*
424 A162 35p ocher & slate grn .90 .40

Cent. of the Finnish Artists' Association. The soapstone sculpture was found at Huittinen.

1964, Feb. 27 Engr.
425 A163 35p dk red brown .90 .40

Emil Nestor Setälä (1864-1946), philologist, minister of education and foreign affairs and chancellor of Abo University.

Staff of Aesculapius A164

1964, June 13 Unwmk. *Perf. 11½*
426 A164 40p slate green 1.25 .50

18th General Assembly of the World Medical Association, Helsinki, June 13-19, 1964.

Ice Hockey — A165

1965, Jan. 4 Engr.
427 A165 35p dark blue .85 .40

World Ice Hockey Championships, Finland, March 3-14, 1965.

Design from Centenary Medal — A166

1965, Feb. 6 Unwmk. *Perf. 11½*
428 A166 35p olive gray .85 .40

Centenary of communal self-government in Finland.

K. J. Stahlberg and "Lex" by W. Runeberg A167

1965, Mar. 22 Engr.
429 A167 35p brown .85 .40

Kaarlo Juho Stahlberg (1865-1952), 1st Pres. of Finland.

International Cooperation Year Emblem A168

1965, Apr. 2 Litho. *Perf. 14*
430 A168 40p bis, dull red, blk & grn .85 .40

UN International Cooperation Year.

"Fratricide" by Gallen-Kallela A169

Sibelius, Piano and Score — A170

35p, Girl's Head by Akseli Gallen-Kallela.

1965, Apr. 26 *Perf. 13½x14*
431 A169 25p multicolored 1.25 .45
432 A169 35p multicolored 1.25 .45

Centenary of the birth of the painter Aksell Gallen-Kallela.

1965, May 15 Engr. *Perf. 11½*

Design: 35p, Musical score and bird.

433 A170 25p violet .85 .45
434 A170 35p dull green .85 .45

Jean Sibelius (1865-1957), composer.

Antenna for Satellite Telecommunication — A171

"Winter Day" by Pekka Halonen — A172

1965, May 17
435 A171 35p blue .80 .40

Cent. of the ITU.

Perf. 14x13½
1965, Sept. 23 Litho. Unwmk.
436 A172 35p gold & multi .90 .45

Centenary of the birth of the painter Pekka Halonen.

Europa Issue, 1965
Common Design Type
Engraved and Lithographed

1965, Sept. 27 *Perf. 13½x14*
437 CD8 40p bister, red brn, dk bl & grn *1.10 .40*

"Growth" — A173

Old Post Office — A174

1966, May 11 Litho. *Perf. 14*
438 A173 35p vio blue & blue .80 .40

Centenary of the promulgation of the Elementary School Decree.

1966, June 11 Litho. *Perf. 14*
439 A174 35p ocher, yel, dk bl & blk 7.00 *8.00*

Cent. of the 1st postage stamps in Finnish currency, and in connection with the NORDIA Stamp Exhibition, Helsinki, June 11-15. The stamp was sold only to buyers of a 1.25m exhibition entrance ticket.

UNESCO Emblem and World Map — A175

Finnish Police Emblem — A176

Lithographed and Engraved
1966, Oct. 9 *Perf. 14*
440 A175 40p grn, yel, blk & brn org .80 .40

20th anniv. of UNESCO.

1966, Oct. 15
441 A176 35p dp ultra, blk & sil .80 .40

Issued to honor the Finnish police.

Insurance Sesquicentennial Medal — A177

1966, Oct. 28 **Engr. & Photo.**
442 A177 35p maroon, olive & blk .80 .40

150th anniv. of the Finnish insurance system.

UNICEF Emblem A178

1966, Nov. 14
443 A178 15p lt ultra, pur & grn .40 .30

Activities of UNICEF.

"FINEFTA," Finnish Flag and Circle — A179

1967, Feb. 15 **Engr.** ***Perf. 14***
444 A179 40p ultra 1.00 .30

European Free Trade Association, EFTA. See note after Denmark No. 431.

Windmill and Arms of Uusikaupunki A180

Mannerheim Monument by Aimo Tukiainen A181

Lithographed and Engraved

1967, Apr. 19 ***Perf. 14***
445 A180 40p multicolored .80 .40

350th anniv. of Uusikaupunki (Nystad).

1967, June 4 ***Perf. 14***
446 A181 40p violet & multi .80 .40

Cent. of the birth of Field Marshal Carl Gustav Emil Mannerheim.

Double Mortise Corner — A182

Watermark of Thomasböle Paper Mill — A183

1967, June 16 **Litho. & Photo.**
447 A182 40p multicolored .70 .35

Issued to honor Finnish settlers in Sweden.

1967, Sept. 6 ***Perf. 14***
448 A183 40p olive & black .70 .35

300th anniv. of the Finnish paper industry.

Martin Luther, by Lucas Cranach A184

Photogravure and Engraved

1967, Nov. 4 ***Perf. 14***
449 A184 40p bister & brown .70 .35

450th anniversary of the Reformation.

"Wood and Water" Globe and Flag — A185

Designs (Globe, Flag and): 25p, Flying swan. 40p, Ear of wheat.

1967, Dec. 5 ***Perf. 11½***

450	A185	20p green & blue	.85	.35
451	A185	25p ultra & blue	.85	.35
452	A185	40p magenta & bl	.85	.35
		Nos. 450-452 (3)	2.55	1.05

50th anniv. of Finland's independence.

Zachris Topelius and Blue Bird — A186

1968, Jan. 14 **Litho.** ***Perf. 14***
453 A186 25p blue & multi .70 .35

Topelius (1818-98), writer and educator.

Skiers and Ski Lift — A187

1968, Feb. 19 **Photo.** ***Perf. 14***
454 A187 25p multicolored .70 .35

Winter Tourism in Finland.

Paper Making, by Hannes Autere — A188

1968, Mar. 12 **Litho.** **Wmk. 363**
455 A188 45p dk red, brn & org .70 .35

Finnish paper industry and 150th anniv. of the oldest Finnish paper mill, Tervakoski, whose own watermark was used for this stamp.

World Health Organization Emblem A189

Lithographed and Photogravure

1968, Apr. 6 **Unwmk.** ***Perf. 14***
456 A189 40p red org, dk blue & gold .70 .35

To honor World Health Organization.

Lion Type of 1954-58 and

Market Place and Mermaid Fountain, Helsinki A190

Keuru Wooden Church, 1758 — A191

Häme Bridge, Tampere A192

Finnish Arms from Grave of King Gustav Vasa, 1581 — A194

25p, Post bus. 30p, Aquarium-Planetarium, Tampere. No. 463, P.O., Tampere. #465, National Museum, Helsinki, vert. #467A, like 70p. 1.30m, Helsinki railroad station.

Engr. (type A94, except #459A); Litho. (#459A, 465 & type A190); Engr. & Litho. (others)

Perf. 11½; 12½ (type A190); 14 (#465, 470A); 13½ (#470)

1968-78

457	A94	1p lt red brn	.40	.20
458	A94	2p gray green	.40	.20
459	A94	4p gray	.40	.20
459A	A94	5p violet blue	.40	.20
460	A192	25p multi ('71)	.40	.20
461	A191	30p multi ('71)	1.25	.20
461A	A94	35p dull org ('74)	.40	.20
b.		Bklt. pane of 4, #459A, 461A, 400, 464A + label	2.50	2.50
		Complete booklet, #461b	3.00	
462	A94	40p orange ('73)	.80	.20
a.		Bklt. pane of 3, #462, 2 #404A + 2 labels	5.50	5.50
		Complete booklet, #462a	7.00	
463	A192	40p multi ('73)	1.00	.20
464	A94	50p lt ultra ('70)	2.25	.20
c.		Bklt. pane of 5, #401, 403, 464, 2 #459A + 5 labels	11.00	10.50
		Complete booklet, #464c	12.00	
464A	A94	50p rose lake ('74)	.80	.20
d.		Bklt. pane of 4, #400, 464A, 2 #402 + label	1.75	1.75
		Complete booklet, #464Ad	2.00	
464B	A94	60p blue ('73)	.70	.20
465	A191	60p multi ('73)	.75	.20
466	A190	70p multi ('73)	.90	.20
467	A191	80p multi ('70)	5.00	.20
467A	A190	80p multi ('76)	.45	.20
468	A192	90p multicolored	2.00	.20
469	A191	1.30m multi ('71)	1.00	.20
470	A194	10m multi ('74)	5.00	.50
470A	A194	20m multi ('78)	10.00	.85
		Nos. 457-470A (20)	34.30	4.95

Issued: 5p, 6/72.

Infantry Monument, Vaasa — A195

Camping Ground A196

Designs: 25p, War Memorial (cross), Hietaniemi Cemetery. 40p, Soldier, 1968.

1968, June 4 **Photo.** ***Perf. 14***

471	A195	20p lt violet & multi	.80	.35
472	A195	25p lt blue & multi	.80	.35
473	A195	40p orange & multi	.80	.35
		Nos. 471-473 (3)	2.40	1.05

To honor Finnish national defense.

1968, June 10 **Litho.**
474 A196 25p multicolored .70 .35

Issued to publicize Finland for summer vacations.

Paper, Pulp and Pine — A197

Mustola Lock, Saima Canal — A198

Lithographed and Embossed

1968, July 2 **Unwmk.** ***Perf. 14***
475 A197 40p multicolored .70 .35

Finnish wood industry.

1968, Aug. 5 **Litho.** ***Perf. 14***
476 A198 40p multicolored .70 .35

Opening of the Saima Canal.

Oskar Merikanto and Pipe Organ — A199

1968, Aug. 5 **Unwmk.**
477 A199 40p vio, silver & lt brn .70 .35

Centenary of the birth of Oskar Merikanto, composer.

Ships in Harbor and Emblem of Central Chamber of Commerce A200

Welder — A201

1968, Sept. 13 **Litho.** ***Perf. 14***
478 A200 40p lt bl, brt bl & blk .70 .35

Publicizing economic development and for the 50th anniv. of the Central Chamber of Commerce of Finland.

1968, Oct. 11 **Litho.** ***Perf. 14***
479 A201 40p blue & multi .70 .35

Finnish metal industry.

Lyre, Students' Emblem — A202

Five Ancient Ships — A203

Lithographed and Engraved

1968, Nov. 24 ***Perf. 14***
480 A202 40p ultra, vio bl & gold .70 .35

Issued to publicize the work of the student unions in Finnish social life.

Nordic Cooperation Issue

1969, Feb. 28 Engr. ***Perf. 11½***
481 A203 40p lt ultra 2.00 .40

50th anniv. of the Nordic Society and centenary of postal cooperation among the northern countries. The design is taken from a coin found at the site of Birka, an ancient Swedish town. See also Denmark Nos. 454-455, Iceland Nos. 404-405, Norway Nos. 523-524 and Sweden Nos. 808-810.

Town Hall and Arms of Kemi — A203a

1969, Mar. 5 Photo. ***Perf. 14***
482 A203a 40p multicolored .70 .35

Centenary of the town of Kemi.

Europa Issue, 1969

Common Design Type

1969, Apr. 28 Photo. ***Perf. 14***

Size: 30x20mm

483 CD12 40p dl rose, vio bl & dk bl *3.75 1.00*

ILO Emblem A204

Armas Järnefelt — A205

Lithographed and Engraved

1969, June 2 ***Perf. 11½***
484 A204 40p dp rose & vio blue .70 .35

50th anniv. of the ILO.

1969, Aug. 14 Photo. ***Perf. 14***
485 A205 40p multicolored .70 .35

Järnefelt (1869-1958), composer and conductor. Portrait on stamp by Vilho Sjöström.

Emblems and Flag — A206

Johannes Linnankoski — A207

1969, Sept. 19 Photo. ***Perf. 14***
486 A206 40p lt bl, blk, grn & lil .70 .35

Publicizinge the importance of National and International Fairs in Finnish economy.

1969, Oct. 18 Litho.
487 A207 40p dk brn red & multi .70 .35

Linnankoski (1869-1913), writer.

Educational Symbols A208

Lithographed and Engraved

1969, Nov. 24 ***Perf. 11½***
488 A208 40p gray, vio & grn .70 .35

Centenary of the Central School Board.

DC-8-62 CF Plane and Helsinki Airport — A209

1969, Dec. 22 Photo. ***Perf. 14***
489 A209 25p sky blue & multi 1.00 .40

Golden Eagle — A210

1970, Feb. 10 Litho. ***Perf. 14***
490 A210 30p multicolored 3.00 .75

Year of Nature Conservation, 1970.

Swatches in Shape of Factories A211

1970, Mar. 9 Litho. ***Perf. 14***
491 A211 50p multicolored .75 .35

Finnish textile industry.

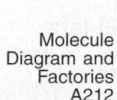

Molecule Diagram and Factories A212

UNESCO Emblem and Lenin — A213

Atom Diagram and Laurel — A214

UN Emblem and Globe — A215

1970, Mar. 26 Photo. ***Perf. 14***
492 A212 50p multicolored .75 .35

Finnish chemical industry.

1970 Litho. and Engr.
493 A213 30p gold & multi .75 .30
494 A214 30p red & multi .75 .30

Photogravure and Gold Embossed

495 A215 50p bl, vio bl & gold .75 .30
Nos. 493-495 (3) 2.25 .90

25th anniv. of the UN. No. 493 also publicizes the UNESCO-sponsored Lenin Symposium, Tampere, Apr. 6-10. No. 494 also publicizes the Nuclear Data Conf. of the Atomic Energy Commission, Otaniemi (Helsinki), June 15-19.

Issued: #493, 4/6; #494, 6/15; #495, 10/24.

Handicapped Volleyball Player — A216

Meeting of Auroraseura Society — A217

1970, June 27 Litho. ***Perf. 14***
496 A216 50p orange, red & blk .80 .35

Issued to publicize the position of handicapped civilians and war veterans in society and their potential contributions to it.

1970, Aug. 15 Photo. ***Perf. 14***
497 A217 50p multicolored .70 .35

200th anniv. of the Auroraseura Soc., dedicated to the study of Finnish history, geography, economy and language. The design of the stamp is after a painting by Eero Jarnefelt.

Uusikaarlepyy Arms, Church and 17th Cent. Building A218

Design: No. 499, Arms of Kokkola, harbor, Sports Palace and 17th century building.

1970 ***Perf. 14***
498 A218 50p multicolored .75 .35
499 A218 50p multicolored .75 .35

Towns of Uusikaarlepyy and Kokkola, 350th anniv.

Issued: #498, Aug. 21; #499, Sept. 17.

Urho Kekkonen, Medal by Aimo Tukiainen — A219

1970, Sept. 3 Litho. & Engr.
500 A219 50p ultra, sil & blk .80 .35

70th birthday of Pres. Urho Kekkonen.

Globe, Maps of US, Finland, USSR A220

Pres. Paasikivi by Essi Renavall A221

Lithographed and Gold Embossed

1970, Nov. 2
501 A220 50p blk, bl, pink & gold .75 .35

Strategic Arms Limitation Talks (SALT) between the US & USSR, Helsinki, 11/2-12/18.

1970, Nov. 27 Photo. ***Perf. 14***
502 A221 50p gold, brt bl & slate .85 .35

Centenary of the birth of Juho Kusti Paasikivi (1870-1956), President of Finland.

Cogwheels A222

1971, Jan. 28 Litho. ***Perf. 14***
503 A222 50p multicolored .75 .35

Finnish industry.

Europa Issue, 1971

Common Design Type

1971, May 3 Litho. ***Perf. 14***

Size: 30x20mm

504 CD14 50p dp rose, yel & blk *3.75 .55*

Tornio Church — A223

Front Page, January 15, 1771 — A224

1971, May 12 Litho. ***Perf. 14***
505 A223 50p multicolored .90 .35

350th anniversary of the town of Tornio.

1971, June 1 Litho. ***Perf. 14***
506 A224 50p multicolored .70 .35

Bicentenary of the Finnish press.

Athletes in Helsinki Stadium A225

50p, Running & javelin in Helsinki Stadium.

1971, July 5 Litho. ***Perf. 14***
507 A225 30p multicolored 1.00 .45
508 A225 50p multicolored 2.00 .45

European Athletic Championships.

Sailboats A226

1971, July 14

509 A226 50p multicolored 1.10 .35

International Lightning Class Championships, Helsinki, July 14-Aug. 1.

Silver Tea Pot, Guild's Emblem, Tools — A227

1971, Aug. 6

510 A227 50p lilac & multi .75 .35

600th anniv. of Finnish goldsmiths' art.

"Plastic Buttons and Houses" A228

Photogravure and Embossed

1971, Oct. 20 ***Perf. 14***

511 A228 50p multicolored .80 .35

Finnish plastics industry.

Europa Issue 1972

Common Design Type

1972, May 2 Litho. *Perf. 14*

Size: 20x30mm

512 CD15 30p dk red & multi *2.50 .50*

513 CD15 50p lt brn & multi *3.50 .50*

Finnish National Theater A229

1972, May 22. Litho. *Perf. 14*

514 A229 50p lt violet & multi .75 .35

Centenary of the Finnish National Theater, founded by Kaarlo and Emilie Bergbom.

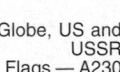

Globe, US and USSR Flags — A230

1972, June 2

515 A230 50p multicolored 1.40 .35

Strategic Arms Limitation Talks (SALT), final meeting, Helsinki, Mar. 28-May 26; treaty signed, Moscow, May 26.

Map and Arms of Aland — A231

Training Ship Suomen Joutsen — A232

1972, June 9

516 A231 50p multicolored 4.00 .75

1st Provincial Meeting of Aland, 50th anniv.

1972, June 19

517 A232 50p orange & multi 1.25 .40

Tall Ships' Race 1972, Helsinki, Aug. 20.

Costume from Perni, 12th Cent. — A233

Circle Surrounding Map of Europe — A234

1972, Nov. 19 Litho. *Perf. 13*

518 A233 50p shown 2.50 .65

519 A233 50p Couple, Tenhola, 18th cent. 2.50 .65

520 A233 50p Girl, Nastola, 19th cent. 2.50 .65

521 A233 50p Man, Voyni, 19th cent. 2.50 .65

522 A233 50p Lapps, Inari, 19th cent. 2.50 .65

a. Strip of 5, #518-522 12.50 14.50

Complete booklet, 2 each #518-522 30.00

Regional costumes.

See Nos. 533-537.

1972, Dec. 11 ***Perf. 14x13½***

523 A234 50p multicolored 2.50 .50

Preparatory Conference on European Security and Cooperation.

Book, Finnish and Soviet Colors — A235

Litho.; Gold Embossed

1973, Apr. 6 ***Perf. 14***

524 A235 60p gold & multi .65 .35

Soviet-Finnish Treaty of Friendship, 25th anniv.

Kyösti Kallio (1873-1940), Pres. of Finland — A236

1973, Apr. 10 Litho. *Perf. 13*

525 A236 60p multicolored .65 .35

Europa Issue 1973

Common Design Type

1973, Apr. 30 Photo. *Perf. 14*

Size: 31x21mm

526 CD16 60p bl, brt bl & emer 1.40 *.40*

Nordic Cooperation Issue

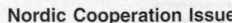

Nordic House, Reykjavik A236a

1973, June 26 Engr. *Perf. 12½*

527 A236a 60p multicolored .90 .30

528 A236a 70p multicolored .90 .30

A century of postal cooperation among Denmark, Finland, Iceland, Norway and Sweden, and in connection with the Nordic Postal Conference, Reykjavik.

Map of Europe, "EUROPA" as a Maze — A237

Litho. & Embossed

1973, July 3 ***Perf. 13***

529 A237 70p multicolored .85 .35

Conference for European Security and Cooperation, Helsinki, July 1973.

Paddling A238

Radiosonde, WMO Emblem — A239

1973, July 18 Litho. *Perf. 14*

530 A238 60p multicolored .65 .35

Canoeing World Championships, Tampere, July 26-29.

1973, Aug. 6 Litho. *Perf. 14*

531 A239 60p multicolored .65 .35

Cent. of intl. meteorological cooperation.

Eliel Saarinen and Design for Parliament, Helsinki A240

1973, Aug. 20 ***Perf. 12½x13***

532 A240 60p multicolored .65 .35

Eliel Saarinen (1873-1950), architect.

Costume Type of 1972

1973, Oct. 10 Litho. *Perf. 13*

533 A233 60p Woman, Kaukola 5.25 .65

534 A233 60p Woman, Jaaski 5.25 .65

535 A233 60p Married couple, Koivisto 5.25 .65

536 A233 60p Mother and son, Sakyla 5.25 .65

537 A233 60p Girl, Hainavesi 5.25 .65

a. Strip of 5, #533-537 27.50 14.00

Regional costumes.

DC10-30 Jet — A241

1973, Nov. 1 Litho. *Perf. 14*

538 A241 60p multicolored .80 .40

50th anniv. of regular air service, Finnair.

Santa Claus in Reindeer Sleigh — A242

1973, Nov. 15 Litho. *Perf. 14*

539 A242 30p multicolored .80 .30

Christmas 1973.

"The Barber of Seville" A243

1973, Nov. 21

540 A243 60p multicolored .75 .35

Centenary of opera in Finland.

Production of Porcelain Jug — A244

Nurmi, by Waino Aaltonen — A245

1973, Nov. 23

541 A244 60p blue & multi .75 .35

Finnish porcelain.

1973, Dec. 11

542 A245 60p multicolored .80 .40

Paavo Nurmi (1897-1973), runner, Olympic winner, 1920-1924-1928.

Arms, Map and Harbor of Hanko — A246

1974, Jan. 10 Litho. *Perf. 14*

543 A246 60p blue & multi .75 .35

Centenary of the town of Hanko.

Ice Hockey A247

1974, Mar. 5 Litho. *Perf. 14*

544 A247 60p multicolored .75 .35

European and World Ice Hockey Championships, held in Finland.

Seagulls (7 Baltic States) A248

1974, Mar. 18 *Perf. 12½*
545 A248 60p multicolored .75 .35

Protection of marine environment of the Baltic Sea.

Goddess of Freedom, by Waino Aaltonen — A249

Ilmari Kianto and Old Pine — A250

1974, Apr. 29 **Litho.** *Perf. 13x12½*
546 A249 70p multicolored *4.00 .35*

Europa.

1974, May 7 *Perf. 13*
547 A250 60p multicolored .70 .35

Ilmari Kianto (1874-1970), writer.

Society Emblem, Symbol A251

Lithographed and Embossed

1974, June 12 *Perf. 13½x14*
548 A251 60p gold & multi .70 .35

Centenary of Adult Education.

Grid A252

UPU Emblem A253

1974, June 14 **Litho.** *Perf. 14x13½*
549 A252 60p multicolored .70 .35

Rationalization Year in Finland, dedicated to economic and business improvements.

1974, Oct. 10 **Litho.** *Perf. 13½x14*
550 A253 60p multicolored .70 .35
551 A253 70p multicolored .70 .35

Centenary of Universal Postal Union.

Elves Distributing Gifts — A254

1974, Nov. 16 **Litho.** *Perf. 14x13½*
552 A254 35p multicolored 1.25 .40

Christmas 1974.

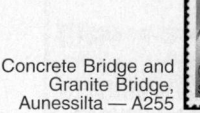

Concrete Bridge and Granite Bridge, Aunessilta — A255

Litho. & Engr.

1974, Dec. 17 *Perf. 14*
553 A255 60p multicolored .70 .35

Royal Finnish Directorate of Roads and Waterways, 175th anniversary.

Coat of Arms, 1581 — A256

Chimneyless Log Sauna — A256a

Carved Wooden Distaffs A258

Kirvu Weather Vane A258a

Cheese Frames A257

1.50m, Wood-carved high drinking bowl, 1542.

1975-90 **Engr.** *Perf. 11½; 14 (2m)*

555	A256	10p red lilac ('78)	.25	.20
a.		Bklt. pane of 4 (#555, 2 #556, #559) + label	2.25	2.25
		Complete booklet, #555a	2.50	
b.		Bklt. pane of 5 (2 #555, #557, #563, #564)	2.50	2.25
		Complete booklet, #555b	3.00	
c.		As "a," no label	2.50	2.50
		Complete booklet, #555c	3.00	
d.		Perf. 13x12½	.35	.20
556	A256	20p olive ('77)	.25	.20
a.		20p yellow bister ('87)	.25	.20
b.		As "a," perf. 13x12½	.25	.20
557	A256	30p carmine ('77)	.25	.20
557A	A256	30p car, litho.	.25	.20
558	A256	40p orange	.25	.20
a.		Perf. 13x12½, litho. & engr.	1.25	.20
559	A256	50p green ('76)	.25	.20
a.		Perf. 13x12½	.25	.20
560	A256	60p blue	.30	.20
a.		Perf. 13x12½	.35	.20
561	A256	70p sepia	.40	.20
562	A256	80p dl red & bl grn ('76)	.50	.20
a.		Perf. 13x12½	1.20	1.20
563	A256	90p vio bl ('77)	.50	.20
564	A256	1.10m yellow ('79)	.60	.20
565	A256	1.20m dk blue ('79)	.60	.20
566	A258	1.50m multi ('76)	.75	.20

Litho.

567	A256a	2m multi ('77)	.90	.20

Lithographed and Engraved

568	A257	2.50m multi ('76)	1.25	.20
a.		Perf. 14	2.25	.20
569	A258	4.50m multi ('76)	2.25	.20
a.		Perf. 14	3.25	.20
570	A258a	5m multi ('77)	2.50	.20
		Nos. 555-570 (17)	12.05	3.40

No. 562a was only issued within the booklet pane No. 715a.

Issued: #557A, 6/3/80; #560a, 7/25/88; #555d, 7/25/89; #562a, 3/1/90; #558a, 8/18/94; #568a, 12/28/88; #569a, 9/26/88; No. 556b, 4/3/98.

See Nos. 629, 631-633, 711-715, 861.

Finland No. 16 — A259

Girl Combing Hair, by Magnus Enckell — A260

Lithographed and Typographed

1975, Apr. 26 *Perf. 13*
571 A259 70p multicolored 3.75 4.00

Nordia 75 Philatelic Exhibition, Helsinki, Apr. 26-May 1. Sold only at exhibition for 3m including entrance ticket.

1975, Apr. 28 **Litho.** *Perf. 13x12½*

Europa: 90p, Washerwoman, by Tyko Sallinen (1879-1955).

572 A260 70p gray & multi *2.25 .35*
573 A260 90p tan & multi *2.25 .35*

Balance of Justice, Sword of Legality — A261

Rescue Boat and Sinking Ship — A262

1975, May 7 *Perf. 14*
574 A261 70p vio blue & multi .60 .30

Sesquicentennial of State Economy Comptroller's Office.

1975, June 2 **Litho.** *Perf. 14*
575 A262 70p multicolored .75 .35

12th Intl. Salvage Conf., Finland, stressing importance of coordinating sea, air and communications resources in salvage operations.

Safe and Unsafe Levels of Drugs — A263

1975, July 21 **Litho.** *Perf. 14*
576 A263 70p multicolored .60 .30

Importance of pharmacological studies and for the 6th Intl. Pharmacology Cong., Helsinki.

Olavinlinna Castle A264

1975, July 29 *Perf. 13*
577 A264 70p multicolored .65 .30

500th anniversary of Olavinlinna Castle.

Swallows over Finlandia Hall — A265

"Men and Women Working for Peace" — A266

1975, July 30
578 A265 90p multicolored .90 .30

European Security and Cooperation Conference, Helsinki, July 30-Aug. 1. (The swallows of the design represent freedom, mobility and continuity.) See No. 709.

1975, Oct. 24 **Litho.** *Perf. 13x12½*
579 A266 70p multicolored .65 .30

International Women's Year 1975.

"Continuity and Growth" — A267

Boys as Three Kings and Herod — A268

1975, Oct. 29 *Perf. 13*
580 A267 70p brown & multi .65 .30

Industrial Art and for the centenary of the Finnish Society of Industrial Art.

1975, Nov. 8 *Perf. 14*
581 A268 40p blue & multi 1.00 .25

Christmas 1975.

Top Border of State Debenture A269

Lithographed and Engraved

1976, Jan. 9 *Perf. 11½*
582 A269 80p multicolored .65 .30

Centenary of State Treasury.

Glider over Lake Region A270

1976, Jan. 13 **Litho.** *Perf. 14*
583 A270 80p multicolored .90 .30

15th World Glider Championships, Rayskala, June 13-27.

Prof. Heikki Klemetti (1876-1953), Musician & Writer — A271

1976, Feb. 14 **Litho.** ***Perf. 13***
584 A271 80p green & multi .65 .30

Map with Areas of Different Dialects — A272

Aino Ackté, by Albert Edelfelt — A273

1976, Mar. 10 **Litho.** ***Perf. 13***
585 A272 80p multicolored .65 .30

Finnish Language Society, centenary.

1976, Apr. 23
586 A273 70p yellow & multi .80 .30

Aino Ackté (1876-1944), opera singer.

Europa Issue 1976

Knife from Voyri, Sheath and Belt — A274

1976, May 3 **Litho.** ***Perf. 13***
587 A274 80p violet bl & multi *3.75 .55*

Radio and Television A275

1976, Sept. 9 **Litho.** ***Perf. 13***
588 A275 80p multicolored .65 .30

Radio broadcasting in Finland, 50th anniv.

Christmas Morning Ride to Church A276

1976, Oct. 23 **Litho.** ***Perf. 14***
589 A276 50p multicolored .85 .25

Christmas 1976.

Turku Chapter Seal (Virgin and Child) A277

1976, Nov. 1 **Litho.** ***Perf. 12½***
590 A277 80p buff, brn & red .65 .30

Cathedral Chapter of Turku, 700th anniv.

Alvar Aalto, Finlandia Hall, Helsinki A278

1976, Nov. 4
591 A278 80p multicolored .65 .30

Hugo Alvar Henrik Aalto (1898-1976), architect.

Ice Dancers — A280

Five Water Lilies — A281

1977, Jan. 25 **Litho.** ***Perf. 13***
592 A280 90p multicolored .65 .30

European Figure Skating Championships, Finland, Jan. 25-29.

Photogravure and Engraved

1977, Feb. 2 ***Perf. 12½***
593 A281 90p brt green & multi .80 .30
594 A281 1m ultra & multi .80 .30

Nordic countries cooperation for protection of the environment and 25th Session of Nordic Council, Helsinki, Feb. 19.

Icebreaker Rescuing Merchantman A282

1977, Mar. 2 **Litho.** ***Perf. 13***
595 A282 90p multicolored .70 .30

Winter navigation between Finland and Sweden, centenary.

Nuclear Reactor A283

1977, Mar. 3 ***Perf. 12½x13***
596 A283 90p multicolored .60 .30

Opening of nuclear power station on Hästholmen Island.

Europa Issue 1977

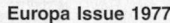

Autumn Landscape, Northern Finland — A284

1977, May 2 **Litho.** ***Perf. 12½x13***
597 A284 90p multicolored *3.25 .35*

Tree, Birds and Nest — A285

Orthodox Church, Valamo Cloister — A286

1977, May 4 ***Perf. 13x12½***
598 A285 90p multicolored .65 .30

75th anniversary of cooperative banks.

1977, May 31 **Litho.** ***Perf. 14***
599 A286 90p multicolored .60 .30

Consecration festival of new Orthodox Church at Valamo Cloister, Heinävesi; 800th anniversary of introduction of orthodoxy in Karelia and of founding of Valamo Cloister.

Paavo Ruotsalainen (1777-1852), Lay Leader of Pietists in Finland — A287

1977, July 8 **Litho.** ***Perf. 13***
600 A287 90p multicolored .60 .30

People Fleeing Fire and Water — A288

Volleyball — A289

1977, Sept. 14 **Litho.** ***Perf. 14***
601 A288 90p multicolored .55 .30

Civil defense for security.

1977, Sept. 15
602 A289 90p multicolored .65 .30

European Women's Volleyball Championships, Finland, Sept. 29-Oct. 2.

Children Bringing Water for Sauna — A290

1977, Oct. 25
603 A290 50p multicolored .75 .25

Christmas 1977.

Finnish Flag — A291

Wall Telephone, 1880, New Telephone — A292

1977, Dec. 5 **Litho.** ***Perf. 14***

Size: 31x21mm

604 A291 80p multicolored .65 .25

Size: 37x25mm

Perf. 13

605 A291 1m multicolored .95 .25

Finland's declaration of independence, 60th anniv.

1977, Dec. 9 ***Perf. 14***
606 A292 1m multicolored .60 .30

Centenary of first telephone in Finland.

Harbor, Sunila Factory, Kotka Arms — A293

1978, Jan. 2 **Litho.** ***Perf. 14***
607 A293 1m multicolored .65 .30

Centenary of founding of Kotka.

Paimio Sanitarium by Alvar Aalto — A294

Europa: 1.20m, Hvittrask studio house, 1902, horiz.

1978, May 2 **Litho.** ***Perf. 13***
608 A294 1m multicolored *6.00 .70*
609 A294 1.20m multicolored *6.00 3.75*

Rural Bus Service A295

1978, June 8 **Litho.** ***Perf. 14***
610 A295 1m multicolored .65 .30

Eino Leino and Eagle — A296

1978, July 6 **Litho.** ***Perf. 13***
611 A296 1m multicolored .65 .30

Eino Leino (1878-1926), poet.

Function Theory and Rhythmical Lines — A297

1978, Aug. 15 Litho. *Perf. 14*

612 A297 1m multicolored .65 .30

ICM 78, International Congress of Mathematicians, Helsinki, Aug. 15-23.

Child Feeding Birds — A298

1978, Oct. 23 Litho. *Perf. 14*

613 A298 50p multicolored .75 .25

Christmas 1978.

A299

A300

1979, Jan. 2 Litho. *Perf. 13*

614 A299 1.10m multicolored 2.00 .30

International Year of the Child.

1979, Feb. 7 Litho. *Perf. 14*

615 A300 1.10m Runner .80 .30

8th Orienteering World Championships, Finland, Sept. 1-4.

Old School, Hamina, Academy Flag — A301

1979, Mar. 20 Litho. *Perf. 14*

616 A301 1.10m multicolored .60 .30

200th anniv. of Finnish Military Academy.

A302

A303

Design: Turku Cathedral and Castle, Prinkkala house, Brahe statue.

1979, Mar. 31

617 A302 1.10m multicolored .60 .30

1979, May 2 Litho. *Perf. 14*

618 A303 1.10m Streetcar, Helsinki .65 .30

Non-polluting urban transportation.

View of Tampere, 1779 — A304

View of Tampere, 1979 — A305

1979, May 2

619 A304 90p multicolored .60 .30

1979, Oct. 1 *Perf. 13*

620 A305 1.10m multicolored .65 .30

Bicentenary of founding of Tampere.

Optical Telegraph, 1796, Map of Islands A306

Europa: 1.10m, Letter of Queen Christina to Per Brahe, 1638, establishing postal service.

1979, May 2 *Perf. 13*

621 A306 1.10m multi *2.00 .35*

622 A306 1.30m multi, vert *4.50 .85*

Shops and Merchants' Signs — A307

1979, Sept. 26 *Perf. 14*

623 A307 1.10m multicolored .60 .30

Business and industry regulation centenary.

Old and New Cars, Street Crossing A308

1979, Oct. 1

624 A308 1.10m multicolored .65 .30

Road safety.

Elves Feeding Horse — A309

1979, Oct. 24

625 A309 60p multicolored .90 .25

Christmas 1979.

Korppi House, Lapinjarvi A310

Farm houses, First Row: Syrjala House, Tammela, 2 stamps in continuous design; Murtovaara House, Valtimo; Antila House, Lapua. Second row: Lofts, Pohjanmaa; Courtyard gate, Kanajarvi House, Kalvola; Main door, Havuselka House, Kauhajoki; Makirasinpera House and dinner bell tower; Gable and eaves, Rasula Kuortane granary.

1979, Oct. 27 Litho. *Perf. 13*

626 Booklet pane of 10 6.00 6.00

a.-j. A310 1.10m single stamp .60 .35

Complete booklet, #626 6.00

See design A349a.

Type of 1975 and

Kauhaneva Swamp A315

Hame Castle, Hameenlinna A316

Windmill, Harrstrom A318

Multiharju Forest, Seitseminen Natl. Park — A319

Shuttle, Raanu Designs A322

Kaspaikka Towel Design — A323

Bridal Rug, Teisko, 1815 — A324

Iron-forged Door, Hollola Church — A325

Iron Fish Spear c. 1100 — A326

Design: 1.80m, Eastern Gulf natl. park.

Litho. & Engr., Litho., Engr.

1979-98 *Perf. 14, 11½ (A256, A318)*

627	A315	70p	multicolored	.35	.20
628	A316	90p	brown red	.30	.20
629	A256	1m	red brown	.90	.40
a.			Perf. 13x12½ ('98)	.90	.20
630	A318	1m	bl & red brn	.30	.20
631	A256	1.30m	dk green	.65	.20
631A	A256	1.30m	dk green, litho.	.65	.25
b.			Booklet pane, #555-556, 557A, 560, 631A	2.00	2.00
			Complete booklet, #631Ab	2.25	
632	A256	1.40m	purple	.65	.20
633	A256	1.50m	grnsh blue	.70	.20
634	A319	1.60m	multicolored	.75	.20
635	A315	1.80m	multicolored	1.40	.20
636	A322	3m	multicolored	1.40	.20
637	A323	6m	multicolored	2.75	.20
638	A324	7m	multicolored	3.25	.75
639	A325	8m	multicolored	3.75	.25
640	A326	9m	blk & dk bl	4.25	.30
			Nos. 627-640 (15)	22.05	3.95

Coil Stamps

Perf. 11½ Vert.

641 A316 90p brown red .45 .25

Perf. 12½ Horiz.

642 A318 1m blue & red brn .55 .25

Issued: 3m, 10/27/79; 6m, 4/9/80; #629, 1/2/81; 70p, 1/12/81; 90p, 9/1/82; 1.60m, 2/8/82; 7m, 2/15/82; #631, 1/3/83; #630, 642, 1/12/83; 1.80m, 8m, 2/10/83; 1.40m, 9m, 1/2/84; 1.50m, 1/2/85; #631A, 11/1/85.

Maria Jotuni (1880-1943), Writer — A327

1980, Apr. 9 Litho.

643 A327 1.10m multicolored .60 .25

Frans Eemil Sillanpaa (1888-1964), Writer — A328

Europa: 1.30m, Artturi Ilmari Virtanen (1895-1973), chemist, vert.

1980, Apr. 28 *Perf. 13*

644 A328 1.10m multicolored *1.25 .40*

645 A328 1.30m multicolored *1.50 .70*

Pres. Urho Kekkonen, 80th Birthday — A329

1980, Sept. 3 Litho. *Perf. 13*

646 A329 1.10m multicolored .65 .25

Nordic Cooperation Issue

Back-piece Harness, 19th century A330

1980, Sept. 9 *Perf. 14*

647 A330 1.10m shown .60 .30

648 A330 1.30m Collar harness, vert. .60 .40

Biathlon A331

1980, Oct. 17 Litho. *Perf. 14*

649 A331 1.10m multicolored .60 .25

World Biathlon Championship, Lahti, Feb. 10-15, 1981.

Pull the Roller, Weighing out the Salt — A332

Christmas 1980 (Traditional Games): 1.10m, Putting out the shoemaker's eye.

1980, Oct. 27
650 A332 60p multicolored .90 .25
651 A332 1.10m multicolored .90 .25

Boxing Match — A333

Glass Blowing A334

1981, Feb. 28 Litho. *Perf. 14*
652 A333 1.10m multicolored .60 .25

European Boxing Championships, Tampere, May 2-10.

1981, Mar. 12
653 A334 1.10m multicolored .60 .25

Glass industry, 300th anniversary.

Mail Boat Furst Menschikoff, 1836 — A335

Litho & Engr.

1981, May 6 *Perf. 13*
654 A335 1.10m brown & tan 3.50 3.25

Nordia '81 Stamp Exhibition, Helsinki, May 6-10. Sold only at exhibition for 3m including entrance ticket.

Europa Issue 1981

Rowing to Church A336

1981, May 18 Litho. *Perf. 13*
655 A336 1.10m shown *.75 .30*
656 A336 1.50m Midsummer's Eve dance *1.50 .50*

Traffic Conference Emblem — A337

Boy and Girl Riding Pegasus A338

1981, May 26 Litho. *Perf. 14*
657 A337 1.10m multicolored .50 .25

European Conference of Ministers of Transport, May 25-28.

1981, June 11
658 A338 1m multicolored .50 .25

Youth associations centenary.

Intl. Year of the Disabled — A339

1981, Sept. 2 Litho. *Perf. 13*
659 A339 1.10m multicolored .60 .25

Christmas 1981 — A340

1981, Oct. 27 Litho. *Perf. 14*
660 A340 70p Children, Christmas tree .90 .20
661 A340 1.10m Decorating tree, vert. .90 .30

"Om Konsten att Ratt Behaga" First Issue (Periodicals Bicentenary) A341

1982, Jan. 15
662 A341 1.20m multicolored .60 .25

Kuopio Bicentenary A343

Score, String Instrument Neck A344

1982, Mar. 4 Litho. *Perf. 14*
664 A343 1.20m multicolored .60 .25

1982, Mar. 11 *Perf. 13*
665 A344 1.20m multicolored .70 .25

Centenaries of Sibelius Academy of Music and Helsinki Orchestra.

Electric Power Plant Centenary A345

1982, Mar. 15 *Perf. 14*
666 A345 1.20m multicolored .60 .25

Gardening A346

1982, Apr. 16 Litho. *Perf. 14*
667 A346 1.10m multicolored .55 .25

Europa — A347

1.20m, Publication of Abckiria (1st Finnish book), 1543 (Sculpture of Mikael Agricola, translator, by Oskari Jauhiainen, 1951). 1.50m, Turku Academy, 1st Finnish university (Turku Academy Inaugural Procession, 1640, after Albert Edelfelt).

1982, Apr. 29 Litho. *Perf. 13x12½*
668 A347 1.20m multicolored *1.50 .45*

Size: 47x31mm

Perf. 12½
669 A347 1.50m multicolored *1.60 .45*

Intl. Monetary Fund and World Bank Emblems A348

1982, May 12 *Perf. 14*
670 A348 1.60m multicolored .75 .30

IMF Interim Committee and IMF-WB Joint Development Committee Meeting, Helsinki, May 12-14.

75th Anniv. of Unicameral Parliament A349

1982, May 25
671 A349 2.40m Future, by Waino Aaltonen, Parliament 1.10 .45

Manor Houses A349a

1st Row: a, Kuitia, Parainen, 1490. b, Louhisaari, Askainen, 1655. c, Frugard, Joroinen, 1780. d, Jokioinen, 1798. e, Moisio, Elimaki, 1820.
2nd Row: f, Sjundby, Siuntio, 1560. g, Fagervik, Inkoo, 1773. h, Mustio, Karjaa, 1792. i, Fiskars, Pohja, 1818. j, Kotkaniemi, Vihti, 1836.

1982, June 14 Litho. *Perf. 13x13½*
672 Booklet pane of 10 8.50 8.50
a.-j. A349a 1.20m single stamp .85 .45
Complete booklet, #672 9.50 9.50

See design A310.

Christmas 1982 — A350

1982, Oct. 25
673 A350 90p Feeding forest animals .80 .25
674 A350 1.20m Children eating porridge .80 .25

Nordic Cooperation A351

1983, Mar. 24 Litho. *Perf. 14*
675 A351 1.20m Panning for gold .55 .25
676 A351 1.30m Kitkajoki River rapids .65 .25

World Communications Year — A352

1983, Apr. 9 Litho. *Perf. 13*
677 A352 1.30m Postal services .65 .25
678 A352 1.70m Sound waves, optical cables .80 .40

Europa 1983 A353

1983, May 2 Litho. *Perf. 12½x13*
679 A353 1.30m Flash smelting method *5.00 .45*
680 A353 1.70m Temppeliaukio Church *6.00 .90*

Pres. Lauri Kristian Relander (1883-1942) A354

Running A355

1983, May 31 Litho. *Perf. 14*
681 A354 1.30m multicolored .65 .30

1983, June 6
682 A355 1.20m Javelin, horiz. .65 .40
683 A355 1.30m shown .70 .30

First World Athletic Championships, Helsinki, Aug. 7-14.

Toivo Kuula (1883-1918), Composer — A356

1983, July 7 *Perf. 14*
684 A356 1.30m multicolored .65 .30

Christmas 1983 — A357

Childrens drawings: 1m, Santa, reindeer, sled and gifts by Eija Myllyviita. 1.30m, Two candles by Camilla Lindberg.

Engr., Litho.

1983, Nov. 4 *Perf. 12, 14*
685 A357 1m dark blue .80 .30
686 A357 1.30m multi, vert. .80 .30

A358

A360

1983, Nov. 25 Litho. *Perf. 14*
687 A358 1.30m brt blue & blk .65 .30

President Mauno Henrik Koivisto, 60th birthday.

1984, Mar. 1 Engr. *Perf. 12*
689 A360 1.10m Letters (2nd class rate) .50 .20

Photo. & Engr.
690 A360 1.40m Automated sorting (1st class rate), vert. .65 .20

Inauguration of Nordic postal rates.

Museum Pieces — A361

Work and Skill — A362

Designs: No. 691, Pottery, 3200 B.C.; Silver chalice, 1416; Crossbow, 16th cent. No. 692, Kaplan hydraulic turbine.

1984, Apr. 30 Litho. *Perf. 13½*
691 A361 1.40m multicolored .65 .30
692 A362 1.40m multicolored .65 .30

Europa (1959-84) A363

1984, May 7 *Perf. 12½x13*
693 A363 1.40m multicolored *4.00* *.25*
694 A363 2m multicolored *4.00* *.80*

Dentistry — A364

1984, Aug. 27 Litho. *Perf. 14*
695 A364 1.40m Dentist, teeth .70 .30

Astronomy A365

1984, Sept. 12
696 A365 1.10m Observatory, planets, sun .50 .25

Aleksis Kivi (1934-72), Writer — A366

1984, Oct. 10 Litho. *Perf. 14*
697 A366 1.40m Song of my Heart .65 .30

Christmas 1984 — A367

Litho. & Engr.
1984, Nov. 30 *Perf. 12*
698 A367 1.10m Father Christmas, brownie .90 .30

Common Law of 1734 — A368

1984, Dec. 6 *Perf. 14*
699 A368 2m Statute Book .95 .40

25th Anniv. of EFTA — A369

1985, Feb. 2 Litho.
700 A369 1.20m multicolored .60 .25

100th Anniv. of Society of Swedish Literature in Finland A370

1985, Feb. 5 Litho.
701 A370 1.50m Johan Ludvig Runeberg .70 .30

A371

A372

1985, Feb. 18 Litho. *Perf. 11½x12*
702 A371 1.50m Icon .70 .30

Order of St. Sergei and St. Herman, 100th anniv.

Litho. & Engr.
1985, Feb. 28 *Perf. 13x12½*
703 A372 1.50m Pedri Semeikka .70 .30
704 A372 2.10m Larin Paraske 1.00 .45

150th anniv. of Kalevala.

A373

A374

Litho. & Engr.
1985, May 15 *Perf. 13*
705 A373 1.50m Mermaid and sea lions 5.00 *6.25*

NORDIA 1985 philatelic exhibition, May 15-19. Sold for 10m, which included admission ticket.

Photo. & Engr.
1985, May 18 *Perf. 11½*

Finnish Banknote Cent.: banknotes of 1886, 1909, 1922, 1945 and 1955.

706 Booklet pane of 8 7.50 8.50
a.-h. A374 1.50m any single .90 .40
Complete booklet, #706 8.00

A375

A376

Europa: 1.50m, Children playing the recorder. 2.10m, Excerpt "Ramus Virens Olivarum" from the "Piae Cantiones," 1582.

1985, June 17 Litho. *Perf. 13*
707 A375 1.50m multicolored *5.50* *.25*
708 A375 2.10m multicolored *6.50* *.85*

Security Conference Type of 1975

1985, June 19 Litho.
709 A265 2.10m multicolored 1.00 .45

European Security and Cooperation Conference, 10th Anniv.

1985, Sept. 5 Litho. *Perf. 14*
710 A376 1.50m Provincial arms, Count's seal .85 .30

Provincial Administration Established by Count Per Brahe, 350th Anniv.

Arms Type of 1975 and

Kerimaki Church A376a

Urho Kekkonen Natl. Park — A376b

Tulip Damask Table Cloth, 18th Cent. A377

Postal Service A377a

Brown Bear — A377b

Perf. 11½, 13x12½ (2m)
1985-90 Engr., Litho. (2m)
711 A256 1.60m vermilion .75 .20
712 A256 1.70m black .80 .20
a. Bklt. pane, #558, 560, 2 each #555, 556a, 712 + 2 labels 6.00 6.00
Complete booklet, #712a 8.50
713 A256 1.80m olive green .85 .20
a. Bklt. pane, 2 ea #555d, 560a, 713b 2.50 2.50
Complete booklet, #713a 2.75
b. Perf. 13x12½ .80 .30
714 A256 1.90m brt orange .90 .25
715 A256 2m blue grn, bklt. stamp 1.10 .75
a. Bklt. pane, #562a, 2 ea #715, 555d 5.00 5.50
Complete booklet, #715a 5.50

Litho. *Perf. 14*
716 A376a 2.20m multi 1.00 .25
717 A376b 2.40m multi 1.10 .25
718 A377 12m multi 5.75 .75

Litho. & Engr.
Perf. 13x12½
719 A377b 50m blk, grn & lt red brn 24.00 5.50
Nos. 711-719 (9) 36.25 8.35

No. 712a contains two labels inscribed to publicize FINLANDIA '88.

Issued: 12m, 9/13/85; 1.60m, 1/2/86; 1.70m, 1/2/87; #712a, 8/10/87; 1.80m, 1/4/88; 2.20m, 2.40m, 1/20/88; #713b, 7/25/88; 1.90m, 1/2/89; 2m, 1/19/90; 50m, 8/30/89.

Booklet Stamps

#720, Telephone, mailbox. #721, Postal truck, transport plane. #722, Transport plane, fork lift. #723, Postman delivering letter. #724, Woman accepting letter.

Perf. 12½ on 3 Sides

1988, Feb. 1 **Litho.**

720 A377a 1.80m multicolored .85 .35
721 A377a 1.80m multicolored .85 .35
722 A377a 1.80m multicolored .85 .35
723 A377a 1.80m multicolored .85 .35
724 A377a 1.80m multicolored .85 .35
a. Bklt. pane, 2 each #720-724 9.50 8.50
Complete booklet, #724a 9.50
Nos. 720-724 (5) 4.25 1.75

Nos. 721-722 and 723-724 printed se-tenant in continuous designs. No. 724c sold for 14m to households on mainland Finland. Each household entitled to buy 2 booklets at discount price from Feb. 1 to May 31, with coupon.

Miniature Sheet

Postal Map, 1698 A378

Designs: a, Postman on foot. c, Sailing vessel, diff. d, Postrider, vert.

Litho. & Engr.

1985, Oct. 16 *Perf. 14*

728 Sheet of 4 10.00 10.00
a.-d. A378 1.50m any single 2.50 2.50

FINLANDIA '88, 350th anniv. of Finnish Postal Service, founded in 1638 by Gov.-Gen. Per Brahe. Sheet sold for 8m.

Intl. Youth Year — A379

Christmas 1985 — A380

1985, Nov. 1 **Litho.** *Perf. 13*

729 A379 1.50m multicolored .70 .30

1985, Nov. 29 *Perf. 14*

730 A380 1.20m Bird, tulips .90 .30
731 A380 1.20m Cross of St. Thomas, hyacinths .90 .30

Natl. Geological Society, Cent. — A390

1986, Feb. 8 **Litho.** *Perf. 14*

732 A390 1.30m Orbicular granite .70 .30
733 A390 1.60m Rapaviki .85 .55
734 A390 2.10m Veined gneiss 1.10 .55
Nos. 732-734 (3) 2.65 1.40

Europa 1986 A391

1986, Apr. 10 *Perf. 12½x13*

735 A391 1.60m Saimaa ringed seal *5.00 .25*
736 A391 2.20m Environmental conservation *5.50 .80*

Conference Palace, Baghdad, 1982 — A392

Natl. Construction Year. b, Lahti Theater, 1983. c, Kuusamo Municipal Offices, 1978. d, Hamina Court Building, 1983. e, Finnish Embassy, New Delhi, 1986. f, Western Sakyla Daycare Center, 1980.

1986, Apr. 19 *Perf. 14*

737 Booklet pane of 6 5.00 4.50
a.-f. A392 1.60m, any single .80 .50
Complete booklet, #737 5.00

Nordic Cooperation Issue 1986 — A393

Sister towns.

1986, May 27 **Litho.** *Perf. 14*

738 A393 1.60m Joensuu .75 .40
739 A393 2.20m Jyvaskyla 1.00 .50

Souvenir Sheet

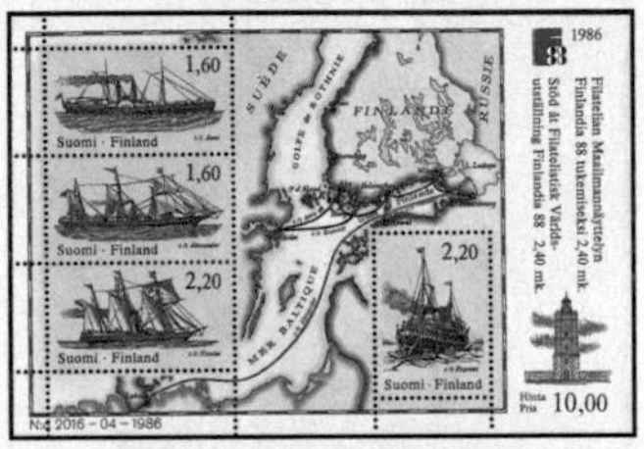

FINLANDIA '88 — A394

Postal ships: a, Iron paddle steamer Aura, Stockholm-St. Petersburg, 1858. b, Screw vessel Alexander, Helsinki-Tallinn-Lubeck, 1859. c, Steamship Nicolai, Helsinki-Tallinn-St. Petersburg, 1858. d, 1st Ice steamship Express II, Helsinki-Stockholm, 1877-98, vert.

Litho. & Engr.

1986, Aug. 29 *Perf. 13*

740 A394 Sheet of 4 12.00 *12.00*
a.-b. 1.60m, any single 3.00 *3.25*
c.-d. 2.20m, any single 3.00 *3.25*

Sold for 10k.

Pierre-Louis Moreau de Maupertuis (1698-1759) — A395

1986, Sept. 5 **Litho.** *Perf. 12½x13*

741 A395 1.60m multicolored .80 .30

Lapland Expedition, 250th anniv., proved Earth's poles are flattened.
See France No. 2016.

Urho Kaleva Kekkonen (1900-86), Pres. — A396

Intl. Peace Year — A397

1986, Sept. 30 **Engr.** *Perf. 14*

742 A396 5m black 2.50 2.25

1986, Oct. 13 **Litho.** *Perf. 13*

743 A397 1.60m multicolored .75 .30

A398

Christmas A399

Photo. & Engr.

1986, Oct. 31 *Perf. 12*

744 1.30m Denomination at L .80 .35
745 1.30m Denomination at R .80 .35
a. A398 Pair, #744-745 1.60 .85
746 A399 1.60m Elves 1.10 .45
Nos. 744-746 (3) 2.70 1.15

No. 745a has a continuous design.

Postal Savings Bank, Cent. — A400

1987, Jan. 2 **Litho.** *Perf. 14*

747 A400 1.70m multicolored .80 .40

Natl. Tourism, Cent. — A401

1987, Feb. 4 **Litho.** *Perf. 14*

748 A401 1.70m Winter .80 .40
749 A401 2.30m Summer 1.10 .55

A402

A403

1987, Feb. 4 *Perf. 14*

750 A402 1.40m multicolored .65 .30

Metric system in Finland, cent.

1987, Feb. 17 **Litho.** *Perf. 14*

751 A403 2.10m multicolored 1.00 .50

Leevi Madetoja (1887-1947), composer.

European Wrestling Championships A404

1987 World Bowling Championships A405

1987, Feb. 17

752 A404 1.70m multicolored .80 .40

1987, Apr. 13

753 A405 1.70m multicolored .80 .40

Mental Health — A406

1987, Apr. 13

754 A406 1.70m multicolored .80 .40

Souvenir Sheet

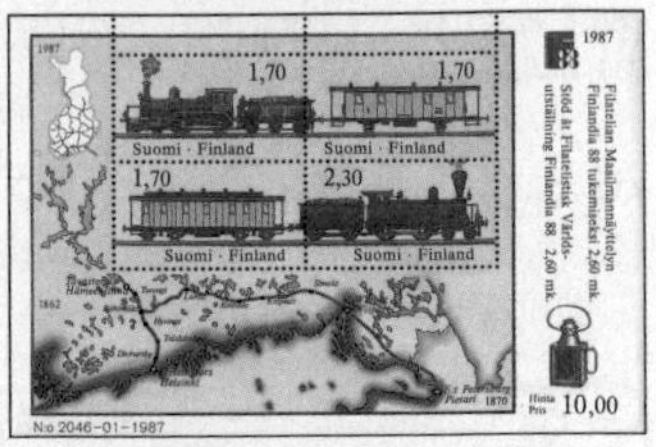

FINLANDIA '88 — A407

Locomotives and mail cars: a, Steam locomotive, 6-wheeled tender. b, 4-window mail car. c, 7-window mail car.

Litho. & Engr.

1987, May 8 *Perf. 12½x13*

755 A407 Sheet of 4 15.00 15.00
a.-c. 1.70m any single 4.00 4.00
d. 2.30m multicolored 4.00 4.00

Sold for 10m.

Europa 1987 A408

Modern architecture: 1.70m, Tampere Main Library, 1986, designed by Raili and Reima Pietila. 2.30m, Stoa Monument, Helsinki, c. 1981, by sculptor Hannu Siren.

1987, May 15 **Litho.** *Perf. 13*

756 A408 1.70m multicolored *5.25* .25
757 A408 2.30m multicolored *5.25* *.90*

Natl. Art Museum, Ateneum, Cent. — A409

Paintings: a, Strawberry Girl, by Nils Schillmark (1745-1804). b, Still-life on a Lady's Work Table, by Ferdinand von Wright (1822-1906). c, Old Woman with Basket, by Albert Edelfelt (1854-1906). d, Boy and Crow, by Akseli Gallen-Kallela (1865-1931). e, Late Winter, by Tyko Sallinen (1879-1955).

1987, May 15

758 Booklet pane of 5 8.00
a.-e. A409 1.70m any single 1.50 .50
Complete booklet, #758 8.00

A410

A411

1987, Aug. 12 *Perf. 14*

759 A410 1.70m multicolored .80 .25

European Physics Soc. 7th gen. conf., Helsinki, Aug. 10-14.

1987, Oct. 12

760 A411 1.70m ultra, sil & pale lt gray .80 .25

Size: 30x41mm

761 A411 10m dark ultra, lt blue & sil 5.00 1.75

Natl. independence, 70th anniv.

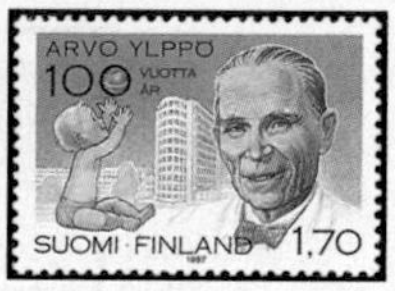

Ylppo, Child and Lastenlinna Children's Hospital A412

1987, Oct. 27

762 A412 1.70m multicolored .80 .25

Arvo Ylppo (b. 1887), pediatrics pioneer.

Christmas A413

Finnish News Agency (STT), Cent. A414

1987, Oct. 30

763 A413 1.40m Santa Claus, youths, horiz. .75 .20
764 A413 1.70m shown .85 .20

1987, Nov. 1

765 A414 2.30m multicolored 1.10 .70

Lauri "Tahko" Pihkala (1888-1981), Promulgator of Sports and Physical Education A415

1988, Jan. 5 Litho. *Perf. 14*

766 A415 1.80m blk, chalky blue & brt blue .85 .25

A416

1988, Mar. 14 Litho.

767 A416 1.40m multicolored .65 .20

Meteorological Institute, 150th anniv.

Settlement of New Sweden in America, 350th Anniv. — A417

Design: 17th Century European settlers negotiating with 3 American Indians, map of New Sweden, the Swedish ships Kalmar Nyckel and Fogel Grip, based on an 18th cent. illustration from a Swedish book about the American Colonies.

Litho. & Engr.

1988, Mar. 29 *Perf. 13*

768 A417 3m multicolored 1.50 .70

See US No. C117 and Sweden No. 1672.

FINLANDIA '88, June 1-12, Helsinki Fair Center — A418

Agathon Faberge (1876-1951), famed philatelist, & rarities from his collection.

Booklet Stamp

1988, May 2 Litho. *Perf. 13*

769 A418 5m Pane of 1+2 labels 14.00 16.00
Complete booklet, #769 14.00

350th Anniv. of the Finnish Postal Service. No. 769 sold for 30m to include the price of adult admission to the exhibition.

Achievements of Finnish Athletes at the 1988 Winter Olympics, Calgary — A419

Design: Matti Nykanen, gold medalist in all 3 ski jumping events at the '88 Games.

1988, Apr. 6 *Perf. 14*

770 A419 1.80m multicolored .85 .25

Europa 1988 A420

Communication and transport.

1988, May 23 Litho. *Perf. 13*

771 A420 1.80m shown *5.00 .25*
772 A420 2.40m Horse-drawn tram, 1890 *5.00 .90*

Souvenir Sheet

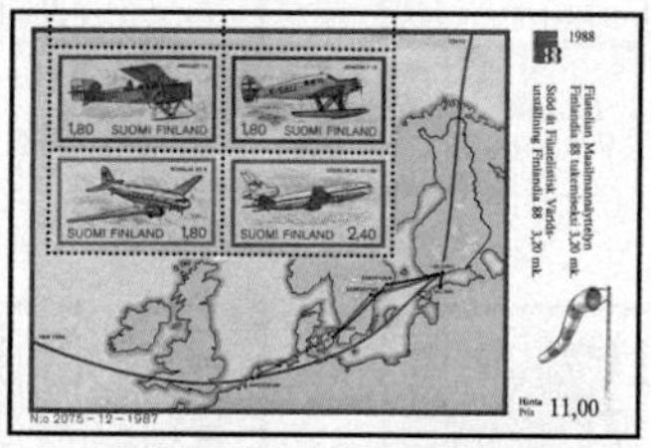

FINLANDIA '88 — A421

1st airmail flights: a, Finnish air force Breguet 14 biplane transporting mail from Helsinki to Tallinn, Feb. 12, 1920. b, AERO Junkers F-13 making 1st airmail night flight from Helsinki to Copenhagen, May 15, 1930. c, AERO Douglas DC-3, 1st intl. route, Helsinki-Norrkoping-Copenhagen-Amsterdam, 1947. d, Douglas DC 10-30, 1975-88, inauguration of Helsinki-Beijing route, June 2, 1988.

Litho. & Engr.

1988, June 2 *Perf. 13½*

773 Sheet of 4 15.00 15.00
a.-c. A421 1.80m any single 3.75 3.75
d. A421 2.40m multicolored 3.75 3.75

Sold for 11m.

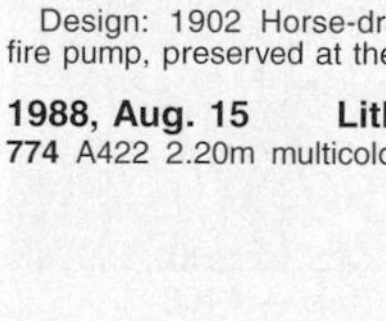

Turku Fire Brigade, 150th Anniv. — A422

Design: 1902 Horse-drawn, steam-driven fire pump, preserved at the brigade.

1988, Aug. 15 Litho. *Perf. 14*

774 A422 2.20m multicolored 1.10 .60

A423

A424

Missale Aboense, the 1st printed book in Finland, 500th anniv.

1988, Aug. 17

775 A423 1.80m multicolored .85 .25

Booklet Stamps

1988, Sept. 6 Litho. *Perf. 13*

Finnish Postal Service, 350th Anniv.: #776, Postal tariff issued by Queen Christina of Sweden, Sept. 6, 1638. #777, Postal cart, c. 1880. #778, Leyland Sherpa 185 mail van, 1976. #779, Malmi P.O. interior. #780, Skier using mobile telephone, c. 1970. #781, Telecommunications satellite in orbit.

776 A424 1.80m multicolored 1.00 .50
777 A424 1.80m multicolored 1.00 .50
778 A424 1.80m multicolored 1.00 .50
779 A424 1.80m multicolored 1.00 .50
780 A424 1.80m multicolored 1.00 .50
781 A424 1.80m multicolored 1.00 .50
a. Booklet pane of 6, #776-781 6.25 6.25
Complete booklet, #781a 6.50

Children's Playgroups (Preschool) A425

1988, Oct. 10 *Perf. 14*

782 A425 1.80m multicolored .85 .25

Christmas A426

1988, Nov. 4 Litho.

783 A426 1.40m multicolored .85 .20
784 A426 1.80m multicolored .85 .20

Hameenlinna Township, 350th Anniv. — A427

Design: Market square, coat of arms and 17th century plan of the town.

1989, Jan. 19 Litho.

785 A427 1.90m multicolored .90 .25

1989 Nordic Ski Championships, Lahti, Feb. 17-26 — A428

1989, Jan. 25

786 A428 1.90m multicolored .90 .25

Salvation Army in Finland, Cent. — A429

Photography, 150th Anniv. — A430

1989, Feb. 6 Litho.

787 A429 1.90m multicolored .90 .25

1989, Feb. 6

788 A430 1.50m Photographer, box camera, c.1900 .70 .30

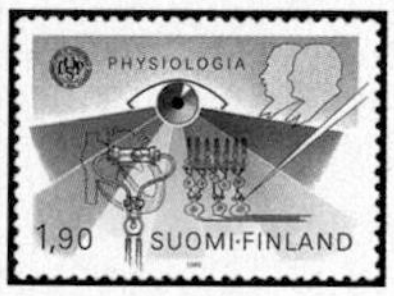

31st Intl. Physiology Congress, Basel, July 9-14 — A431

Design: Congress emblem, silhouettes of Robert Tigerstedt and Ragnar Granit, eye, flowmeter measuring flow of blood through heart, color-sensitive retinal cells and microelectrode.

1989, Mar. 2

789 A431 1.90m multicolored .90 .25

Sports — A432

1989, Mar. 10 Booklet Stamps

790 A432 1.90m Skiing .90 .30
791 A432 1.90m Jogging .90 .30
792 A432 1.90m Cycling .90 .30
793 A432 1.90m Canoeing .90 .30
a. Booklet pane of 4, #790-793 3.75 3.50
Complete booklet, #793a 4.00

Souvenir Sheet

Finnish Kennel Club, Cent. — A433

Dogs: a, Lapponian herder. b, Finnish spitz. c, Karelian bear dog. d, Finnish hound.

1989, Mar. 17 Litho. *Perf. 14*

794 A433 Sheet of 4 5.00 5.00
a.-d. 1.90m any single 1.25 .70

Europa — A434

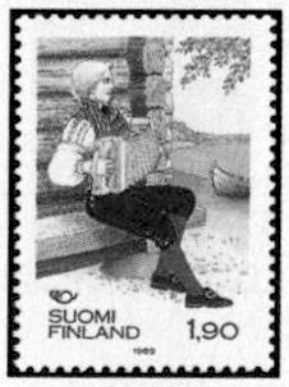

A435

1989, Mar. 31 *Perf. 13*

795 A434 1.90m Hopscotch *2.50 .25*
796 A434 2.50m Sledding *2.50 .65*

1989, Apr. 20 *Perf. 14*

Nordic Cooperation Year: Folk Costumes.

797 A435 1.90m Sakyla (man) .90 .25
798 A435 2.50m Veteli (woman) 1.25 .60

Finnish Pharmacies, 300th Anniv. — A436

Foxglove, distilling apparatus, mortar, flask.

1989, June 2 **Litho.**
799 A436 1.90m multicolored .90 .25

A437

A438

1989, June 2
800 A437 1.90m multicolored .90 .25

Savonlinna Municipal Charter, 350th anniv.

1989, June 12
801 A438 1.90m *Panthera uncia* .90 .25
802 A438 2.50m *Capra falconeri* 1.25 .80

Helsinki Zoo, cent.

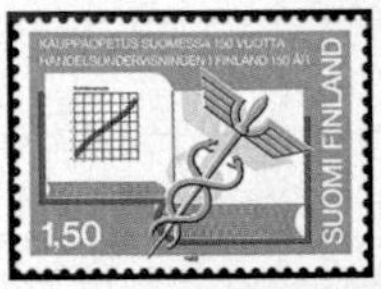

Vocational Training, 150th Anniv. — A439

Interparliamentary Union, Cent. — A440

Council of Europe, 40th Anniv. — A441

1989, Sept. 4 **Litho.** ***Perf. 14***
803 A439 1.50m multicolored .70 .30
804 A440 1.90m multicolored .90 .25
805 A441 2.50m multicolored 1.25 .55
Nos. 803-805 (3) 2.85 1.10

Admission of Finland to the Council of Europe (2.50m).

A442

A443

1989, Oct. 9 **Litho.**
806 A442 1.90m multicolored .90 .25

Hannes Kolehmainen (1889-1966) winning the 5000-meter race at the Stockholm Olympics, 1912.

1989, Oct. 20
807 A443 1.90m multicolored .90 .25

Continuing Education in Finland, cent.

A444

A445

Christmas: 1.90m, Sodankyla Church, Siberian jays in snow.

1989, Nov. 3
808 A444 1.50m shown .90 .20
809 A444 1.90m multicolored .90 .20

1990, Jan. 19 **Litho.** ***Perf. 13x13½***
810 A445 1.90m multicolored 1.00 1.00
811 A445 2.50m multicolored 1.25 1.10

Incorporation of the State Posts and Telecommunications Services.
Emblem of the corporation was produced by holography. Soaking may affect the design.

Musical Soc. of Turku and Finnish Orchestras, 200th Annivs. A446

1990, Jan. 26 ***Perf. 14***
812 A446 1.90m multicolored .90 .25

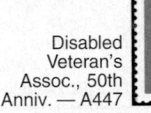

Disabled Veteran's Assoc., 50th Anniv. — A447

1990, Mar. 13 **Litho.**
813 A447 2m multicolored .95 .25

End of the Winter (Russo-Finnish) War, 50th Anniv. — A448

1990, Mar. 13
814 A448 2m blue .95 .25

University of Helsinki, 350th Anniv. — A449

University crest and: 2m, Queen Christina on horseback. 3.20m, Degree ceremony procession in front of the main university building.

1990, Mar. 26 **Litho.** ***Perf. 13***
815 A449 2m multicolored .95 .25
816 A449 3.20m multicolored 1.50 .75

Europa 1990 A450

Post Offices: 2m, Lapp man, P.O. at Nuvvus, Mt. Nuvvus Ailigas. 2.70m, Turku main P.O.

1990, Mar. 26 ***Perf. 12½x13***
817 A450 2m multicolored *6.00* *.25*
818 A450 2.70m multicolored *6.00* *.65*

Rural Postal Service and Address Reform, Cent. — A451

1990, Apr. 19 **Litho.** ***Perf. 13***
819 A451 2m multicolored .95 .25

"Ali Baba and the Forty Thieves" A452

"Story of the Great Musician" A453

"Story of the Giants, the Witches and the Daughter of the Sun" A454

"The Golden Bird, the Golden Horse and the Princess" A455

"Lamb Brother" A456

"The Snow Queen" A457

Fairy tale illustrations by Rudolf Koivu.

Booklet Stamps

Perf. 14 on 3 sides

1990, Aug. 29 **Litho.**
820 A452 2m multicolored 1.25 .30
821 A453 2m multicolored 1.25 .30
822 A454 2m multicolored 1.25 .30
823 A455 2m multicolored 1.25 .30
824 A456 2m multicolored 1.25 .30
825 A457 2m multicolored 1.25 .30
a. Booklet pane of 6, #820-825 8.00 9.00
Complete booklet, #825a 9.00

Souvenir Sheet

Horse Care — A458

a, Feeding. b, Riding. c, Watering. d, Currying.

1990, Oct. 10 **Litho.** ***Perf. 14***
826 A458 Sheet of 4 4.00 3.00
a.-d. 2m any single .95 .45

Christmas A459

1990, Nov. 2
827 A459 1.70m Santa's elves 1.10 .20
828 A459 2m Santa, reindeer 1.25 .20

Provincial Flowers

A460

A460a

A460b

A460c

A460d

A460e

A460f

A460g

A460h

A460i

A460j

A460k

1990-99 ***Perf. 13x12½***
829 A460 2m Wood anemone .95 .20
830 A460 2.10m Rowan 1.00 .20
831 A460 2.70m Heather 1.25 .35
832 A460 2.90m Sea buckthorn 1.40 .35
833 A460 3.50m Oak 1.75 .45
834 A460a 2 Globeflower 1.40 .30
835 A460b 1 Hepatica 1.60 .20
Nos. 829-835 (7) 9.35 2.05

Self-Adhesive

Die Cut

836 A460c 2 Iris 1.40 .20
a. Booklet pane of 20 28.00 15.00
837 A460 2.10m like #830 1.00 .20
838 A460d 1 Rosebay willowherb 1.60 .20
839 A460e 1 Labrador tea 1.60 .20
a. Booklet pane of 10 16.00 12.50
840 A460f 1 Karelian rose 1.60 .20
841 A460g 1 Daisy 1.60 .20
842 A460h 1 Water lily 1.60 .20
843 A460i 1 Bird cherry 1.60 .20

844 A460j 1 Harebell 1.60 .20
845 A460k 1 Cowslip 1.75 .20
Nos. 836-845 (10) 15.35 2.00

Issued: 2m, 2.70m, 1/19/90; 2.90m, 3.50m, 2/5/90; 2.10m, 1991; #834-835, 3/2/92; #838, 10/9/92; #836, 3/1/93; #839, 6/14/93; #840, 5/5/94; #841, 3/15/95; #842, 6/3/96; #843, 3/18/97; #844, 3/12/98; #845, 4/28/99.

#834 sold for 1.60m, #836 sold for 1.90m, #835, 838 for 2.10m, #839-840 for 2.30m, #841-844 sold for 2.80m, #845 sold for 3m at time of release.

#837-838, 840-845 issued in sheets of 10. Nos. 836a and 839a were issued as complete booklets. The peelable backing serves as a booklet cover.

The numbers on the stamps represent the class of mail for which each was intended at time of release.

A461

A462

1991, Mar. 1 ***Perf. 14***
846 A461 2.10m multicolored 1.00 .25

World Hockey Championships, Turku.

1991, Mar. 1
847 A462 2.10m Cooking class 1.00 .25

Home economics teacher education, cent.

Sauna Type of 1977 and:

Birds — A463

Perf. 13x12½, 14 (#861)

1991-99 **Litho.**

Booklet Stamps (#848-859)

848 A463 10p Great tit .50 .20
849 A463 10p Wagtail .25 .20
850 A463 10p Aegolius funereus .40 .60
850A A463 20p Phoenicurus phoenicurus 1.75 .70
851 A463 60p Chaffinches 1.75 .40
852 A463 60p Robin 1.75 .60
856 A463 2.10m Bullfinch 1.25 .20
a. Bklt. pane, #851, 2 each #848, 856 4.00 4.00
Complete booklet, #856a 4.25
857 A463 2.10m Waxwing 1.25 .25
a. Bklt. pane, #852, 2 each #849, 857 4.00 4.00
Complete booklet, #857a 4.25
859 A463 2.30m Dendrocopos leucotos 1.40 .40
a. Booklet pane of #850A, 2 each #850, #859 + 1 label 5.00 5.00
Complete booklet, #859a 5.25

Sheet Stamp

861 A256a 4.80m multicolored 2.50 .75
Nos. 848-861 (10) 12.80 4.30

Issued: #848, 851, 856, 3/20/91; #849, 852, 857, 4/22/92; #850, 850A, 859, 6/4/93. 861, 7/1/99.

"SUOMI" is in upper left on #849, 852, 857.

Fishing
A464

Tourism
A465

Designs: a, Fly fisherman, trout. b, Perch, bobber. c, Crayfish, trap. d, Trawling for herring. e, Stocking powan.

1991, Mar. 20 ***Perf. 14***
863 Booklet pane of 5 5.25 5.50
a.-e. A464 2.10m any single 1.00 .35
Complete booklet, #863 5.50

1991, June 4 **Litho.** ***Perf. 14***
864 A465 2.10m Seurasaari Island 1.00 .25
865 A465 2.90m Steamship, Lake Saimaa 1.40 .70

Europa
A466

European map and: 2.10m, Human figures. 2.90m, Satellites, dish antennae.

1991, June 7 **Litho.** ***Perf. 12½x13***
866 A466 2.10m multicolored *5.50* .25
867 A466 2.90m multicolored *5.50* .70

Alfred W. Finch (1854-1930)
A467

Designs: 2.10m, Iris, ceramic vase. 2.90m, Painting, The English Coast at Dover.

1991, Sept. 7 **Litho.** ***Perf. 13***
868 A467 2.10m multicolored 1.50 .25
869 A467 2.90m multicolored 1.50 .60

See Belgium No. 1410.

Finnish Candy Industry, Cent. — A468

1991, Sept. 17 **Photo.** ***Perf. 11½***
870 A468 2.10m multicolored 1.00 .25

Souvenir Sheets

Children's Stamp Designs — A469

a, Sun. b, Rainbow. c, Cows grazing.

1991, Sept. 17 **Litho.** ***Perf. 13½***
871 A469 Sheet of 3 3.00 2.25
a.-c. 2.10m any single 1.00 .55

Skiing — A470

1991, Oct. 4 ***Perf. 14***

Color of skisuit: a, red. b, green. c, yellow. d, blue.

872 A470 Sheet of 4 4.00 3.25
a.-d. 2.10m any single 1.00 .55

Town Status for Iisalmi, Cent. — A471

1991, Oct. 18 **Litho.** ***Perf. 14***
873 A471 2.10m multicolored 1.00 .60

Christmas
A472

1.80m, Santa, animals carrying candles. 2.10m, Reindeer pulling Santa's sleigh.

1991, Nov. 1 **Litho.** ***Perf. 14***
874 A472 1.80m multi 1.10 .25
875 A472 2.10m multi, vert. 1.10 .25

Chemists' Club, Finnish Chemists' Society, Cent. — A473

1991, Nov. 1
876 A473 2.10m multi 1.00 .25
877 A473 2.10m multi, diff. 1.00 .25
a. Pair, #876-877 + label 2.50 2.50

Second and third vertical branches merge while second and third branches below almost touch in the upper left part of camphor molecular structure on No. 877. Nos. 876-877 are designed to produce a three dimensional effect when viewed together.

1992 Olympic Games
A474

Designs: No. 878, Skier, Albertville. No. 879, Swimmer, Barcelona.

1992, Feb. 4 **Litho.** ***Perf. 14***
878 A474 2.10m multicolored 1.10 .25
879 A474 2.90m multicolored 1.50 .55

Expo '92, Seville — A475

1992, Mar. 20 **Litho.** ***Perf. 14***
880 A475 3.40m multicolored 1.60 .80

Conference on Security and Cooperation in Europe, Helsinki
A476

1992, Mar. 20 ***Perf. 14½x15***
881 A476 16m multicolored 7.75 2.75

Town of Rauma, 550th Anniv. — A477

1992, Mar. 27 ***Perf. 14***
882 A477 2.10m multicolored 1.00 .25

Healthy Brains — A478

1992, Mar. 27
883 A478 3.50m multicolored 1.75 .95

Discovery of America, 500th Anniv.
A479

1992, May 8 **Litho.** ***Perf. 12½x13***
884 A479 2.10m Santa Maria, map *2.25* .30
885 A479 2.10m Map, Columbus *2.25* .30
a. Pair, #884-885 *5.00* *4.00*

Europa.

Finnish Technology
A480

Hologram of trees and: 2.10m, Drawing of blowing machine. 2.90m, Schematic of electronic circuits. 3.40m, Triangles and grid.

1992, May 8 ***Perf. 13x12½***
886 A480 2.10m multicolored 1.10 .35
887 A480 2.90m multicolored 1.50 .60
888 A480 3.40m multicolored 1.75 1.00
Nos. 886-888 (3) 4.35 1.95

First Finnish patent granted, sesqui. (#886), Finnish chairmanship of Eureka (#887), Government Technology Research Center, 50th anniv. (#888).

Nos. 886-888 have holographic images. Soaking in water may affect the hologram.

Natl. Board of Agriculture, Cent. — A481

1992, June 4 **Litho.** ***Perf. 14***
889 A481 2.10m Currant harvesting 1.00 .25

Finnish Women
A482

#890, Aurora Karamzin (1808-1902), founder of Deaconesses' Institution of Helsinki. #891, Baroness Sophie Mannerheim (1863-1928), reformer of nursing education. #892, Laimi Leidenius (1877-1938), physician and educator. #893, Miina Sillanpaa (1866-1952), Minister for social affairs. #894, Edith Sodergran (1892-1923), poet. #895, Kreeta Haapasalo (1813-1893), folk singer.

Litho. & Engr.

1992, June 8 ***Perf. 14***

Booklet Stamps

890 A482 2.10m multicolored 1.00 .45
891 A482 2.10m multicolored 1.00 .45
892 A482 2.10m multicolored 1.00 .45
893 A482 2.10m multicolored 1.00 .45
894 A482 2.10m multicolored 1.00 .45
895 A482 2.10m multicolored 1.00 .45
a. Booklet pane of 6, #890-895 6.00 5.50
Complete booklet, #895a 6.00 5.50

Child's Painting
A483

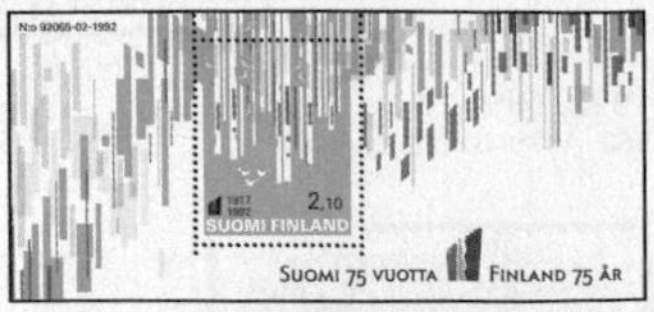
Independence, 75th Anniv. — A484

1992, Oct. 5 Litho. *Perf. 13*
896 A483 2.10m multicolored 1.00 .25

Souvenir Sheet
Perf. 13½

897 A484 2.10m multicolored 1.00 .80

Nordia '93 — A485

A486

Illustrations depicting "Moomin" characters, by Tove Jansson: No. 898, Winter scene, ice covered bridges. No. 899, Winter scene in forest. No. 900, Boats in water. No. 901, Characters on beach.

Perf. 13 on 3 Sides
1992, Oct. 9 Litho.
Booklet Stamps

898 A485 2.10m multicolored 1.75 .45
899 A485 2.10m multicolored 1.75 .45
900 A485 2.10m multicolored 1.75 .45
901 A485 2.10m multicolored 1.75 .45
a. Booklet pane of 4, #898-901 7.50 7.50
Complete booklet, #901a 7.75

1992, Oct. 20 Litho. *Perf. 13*
902 A486 2.10m multicolored 1.00 .25

Printing in Finland, 350th anniv.

Christmas
A487

Designs: 1.80m, Church of St. Lawrence, Vantaa. 2.10m, Stained glass window of nativity scene, Karkkila Church, vert.

1992, Oct. 30 Litho. *Perf. 14*
903 A487 1.80m multicolored 1.10 .20
904 A487 2.10m multicolored 1.10 .20

Central Chamber of Commerce, 75th Anniv. — A488

1993, Feb. 8 Litho. *Perf. 14*
905 A488 1.60m multicolored .75 .30

Friendship
A489

1993, Feb. 8 Litho. *Perf. 14*
906 A489 1 multicolored 1.60 .30
a. Booklet pane of 5 + label 8.00 8.00
Complete booklet, 2 #906a 16.00

No. 906 sold for 2m at time of release. See note following No. 845.
See Estonia No. 237.

Alopex Lagopus — A490

a, Adult with winter white coat. b, Face, full view, winter white coat. c, Mother, kits, summer coat. d, Two on rock, summer coat.

1993, Mar. 19 Litho. *Perf. 12½x13*
907 A490 2.30m Block of 4, #a-d 5.75 5.75

World Wildlife Fund.

Sculptures
A491

Europa: 2m, Rumba, by Martti Aiha. 2.90m, Complete Works, by Kari Caven.

1993, Apr. 26 *Perf. 13*
908 A491 2m multicolored *1.90 .25*
909 A491 2.90m multicolored *1.40 .60*

Organized Philately in Finland, Cent. — A492

1993, May 6 *Perf. 13x12½*
910 A492 2.30m Rosa pimpinellifolia 1.10 .45

Vyborg Castle, 700th Anniv.
A493

1993, May 6 *Perf. 13½*
911 A493 2.30m multicolored 1.10 .25

Tourism
A494

1993, May 7 *Perf. 13x12½*
912 A494 2.30m Naantali 1.10 .25
913 A494 2.90m Imatra 1.40 .45

550th anniv. of Naantali (#912).

A495

A496

Independent Finland Defense Forces, 75th Anniv.: 2.30m, Finnish landscape in form of soldier's silhouette. 3.40m, UN checkpoint of Finnish battalion, Middle East.

1993, June 4 Litho. *Perf. 14*
914 A495 2.30m multicolored 1.10 .25
915 A495 3.40m multicolored 1.60 .95

1993, June 14 Litho. *Perf. 12½x13*

Art by Martta Wendelin (1893-1986): #916, Boy on skis, 1936. #917, Mother, daughter knitting, 1931. #918, Children building snowman, 1931. #919, Mother, children at fence, 1935. #920, Girl with lamb, 1936.

Booklet Stamps

916 A496 2.30m multicolored 1.25 .50
917 A496 2.30m multicolored 1.25 .50
918 A496 2.30m multicolored 1.25 .50
919 A496 2.30m multicolored 1.25 .50
920 A496 2.30m multicolored 1.25 .50
a. Booklet pane of 5, #916-920 6.25 6.25
Complete booklet, #920a 6.50

Water Birds — A497

#921, Flock of gavia arctica. #922, Pair of gavia arctica. #923, Mergus merganser. #924, Anas platyrhynchos. #925, Mergus serrator.

Perf. 12½x13 on 3 or 4 Sides
1993, Sept. 20 Litho.
Booklet Stamps

921 A497 2.30m multicolored 1.25 .35
922 A497 2.30m multicolored 1.25 .35

Size: 26x40mm

923 A497 2.30m multicolored 1.25 .35
924 A497 2.30m multicolored 1.25 .35
925 A497 2.30m multicolored 1.25 .35
a. Booklet pane of 5, #921-925 6.25 6.25
Complete booklet, #925a 6.50

Physical Education in Finnish Schools, 150th Anniv. — A498

1993, Oct. 8 *Perf. 14*
926 A498 2.30m multicolored 1.10 .25

Souvenir Sheet

New Opera House, Helsinki
A499

Operas and ballet: a, 2.30m, Ostrobothnians, by Leevi Madetoja. b, 2.30m, The Faun (four dancers), by Claude Debussy. c, 2.90m, Giselle, by Adolphe Adam. d, 3.40m, The Magic Flute, by Wolfgang Amadeus Mozart.

1993, Oct. 8 *Perf. 13*
927 A499 Sheet of 4, #a.-d. 5.25 5.25

Christmas
A500

Pres. Mauno Koivisto, 70th Birthday
A501

1993, Nov. 5 Litho. *Perf. 14*
928 A500 1.80m Christmas tree, elves .85 .25
a. Booklet pane of 10 12.00 12.00
Complete booklet, #928a 12.00
929 A500 2.30m Three angels 1.10 .25

1993, Nov. 25
930 A501 2.30m multicolored 1.10 .25

Friendship — A502

Moomin characters: No. 931, Two standing. No. 932, Seven running.

1994, Jan. 27 Litho. *Perf. 12½x13*
Booklet Stamps

931 A502 1 multicolored 1.60 .25
932 A502 1 multicolored 1.60 .25
a. Bklt. pane, 4 each #931-932 13.50 12.00
Complete booklet, #932a 13.50

Nos. 931-932 each sold for 2.30m at time of release. See note following No. 845.

Souvenir Sheet

Intl. Olympic Committee, Cent. — A503

Winter Olympics medalists from Finland: a, Marja-Liisa Kirvesniemi, Marjo Matikainen, cross-country skiing. b, Clas Thunberg, speed skating. c, Veikko Kankkonen, ski jumping. d, Veikko Hakulinen, cross-country skiing.

1994, Jan. 27 *Perf. 13*
933 A503 4.20m Sheet of 4, #a-d 8.00 8.00

See No. 939.

A504

Waino Aaltonen (1894-1966), Sculptor — A505

1994, Mar. 8
934 A504 2m "Peace" .95 .25
935 A505 2m "Muse" .95 .25
a. Pair, #934-935 2.00 1.50

Postal Service Civil Servants' Federation, Cent. — A506

1994, Mar. 11

936 A506 2.30m multicolored 1.10 .25

Finnish Technology A507

Europa: 2.30m, Paper roll, nitrogen fixation, safety lock, ice breaker MS Fennica. 4.20m, Radiosonde, fishing lure, mobile phone, wind power plant.

1994, Mar. 18

937 A507 2.30m multicolored *1.40 .25*
938 A507 4.20m multicolored *1.90 1.10*

Olympic Athlete Type of 1994

Souvenir Sheet

Finnish athletes: a, Riitta Salin, Pirjo Haggman, runners. b, Lasse Viren, runner. c, Tiina Lillak, javelin thrower. d, Pentti Nikula, pole vaulter.

1994, May 5 Litho. *Perf. 13*

939 A503 4.20m Sheet of 4, #a-d 8.00 8.00

European Track & Field Championships, Finlandia '95.

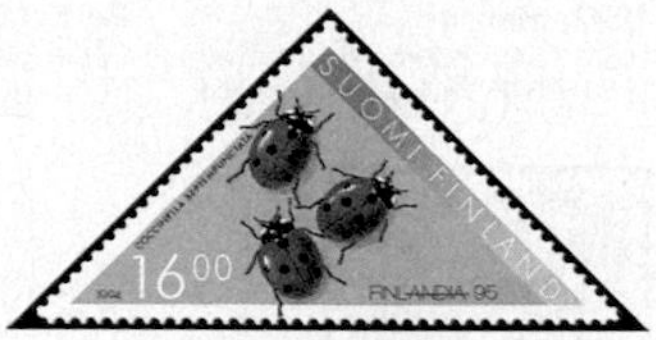

Finlandia '95, Helsinki — A508

1994, May 10 *Perf. 13½x13*

940 A508 16m Coccinella septempunctata 7.75 7.75

See Nos. 962, 1009.

Miniature Sheet

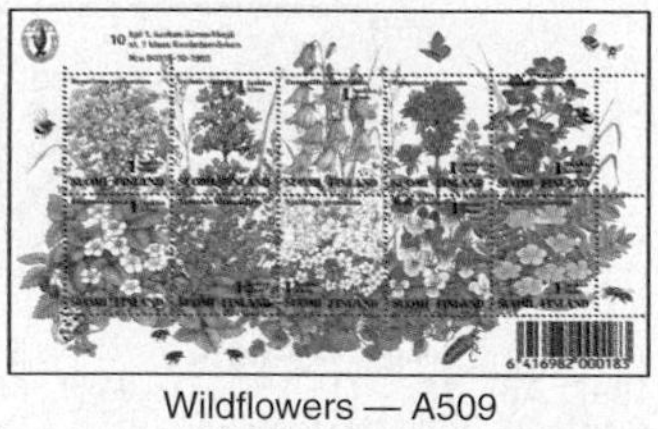

Wildflowers — A509

Designs: a, Hypericum perforatum (b). b, Lychnis viscaria. c, Campanula rotundifolia. d, Campanula glomerata. e, Geranium sanguineum (d). f, Fragaria vesca. g, Veronica chamaedrys (f, h). h, Saxifraga granulata (c, i). i, Viola tricolor (j). j, Potentilla anserina.

1994, June 1 *Perf. 12*

941 A509 1 Sheet of 10, #a.-j. 17.50 12.50

No. 941 sold for 23m at time of release. See note following No. 845.

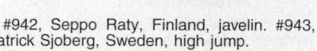

Finland-Sweden Track and Field Meet — A510

#942, Seppo Raty, Finland, javelin. #943, Patrick Sjoberg, Sweden, high jump.

1994, Aug. 26 Litho. *Perf. 12½*

Booklet Stamps

942 A510 2.40m multicolored 1.10 .25
943 A510 2.40m multicolored 1.10 .25
a. Booklet pane, 2 each #942-943 4.75 3.50
Complete booklet, #943a 4.75

See Sweden Nos. 2091-2092.

Population Registers, 450th Anniv. — A511

1994, Sept. 1

944 A511 2.40m multicolored 1.10 .25

Intl. Year of the Family — A512

1994, Sept. 1

945 A512 3.40m multicolored 1.60 .70

Souvenir Sheet

Letter Writing Day — A513

Dog Hill Kids in the Post Office: a, At Post Office window. b, Standing in doorway, mail cart. c, Blowing horn, pig. d, Putting letters in mailbox.

1994, Oct. 7 Litho. *Perf. 14*

946 A513 2.80m Sheet of 4, #a-d 5.50 5.50

Christmas A514

2.10m, Reindeer, bullfinches on antlers. 2.80m, Elves among snow-covered trees.

1994, Nov. 4

947 A514 2.10m multi 1.00 .25
a. Booklet pane of 10 10.00 11.00
Complete booklet, #947a 10.00
948 A514 2.80m multi, vert. 1.40 .45

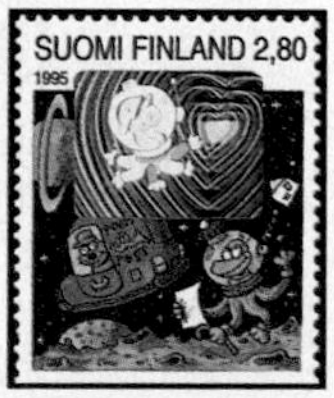

Greetings — A515

"Dog Hill Kids," sending/receiving greetings: No. 949, Delivering mail to Moon, spaceman. No. 950, Cat writing letter, clown. No. 951, Receiving mail from postman, baby. No. 952, Writing in bed, friend. No. 953, Winter scene at mailbox, characters at beach. No. 954, On bus, girl friend. No. 955, Standing at microphone with guitar, fan. No. 956, Baby in play pen, teddy bear.

Perf. 13 on 3 Sides

1995, Jan. 30 Litho.

Booklet Stamps

949 A515 2.80m multicolored 1.50 .60
950 A515 2.80m multicolored 1.50 .60
951 A515 2.80m multicolored 1.50 .60
952 A515 2.80m multicolored 1.50 .60
953 A515 2.80m multicolored 1.50 .60
954 A515 2.80m multicolored 1.50 .60
955 A515 2.80m multicolored 1.50 .60
956 A515 2.80m multicolored 1.50 .60
a. Booklet pane, #949-956 12.00
Complete booklet, 956a 12.00

Nos. 949-952 are printed tete beche with Nos. 953-956. Soaking in water may affect the holographic images on Nos. 949-956.

Souvenir Sheet

Team Sports — A516

a, Paivi Ikola, pesapallo. b, Jari Kurri, ice hockey. c, Jari Litmanen, soccer. d, Lea Hakala, basketball.

1995, Jan. 30 *Perf. 13*

957 A516 3.40m Sheet of 4, #a-d 6.50 6.50

See No. 961.

Membership in European Union — A517

1995, Jan. 30 *Perf. 14*

958 A517 3.50m multicolored 1.75 .85

Peace & Liberty — A518

Europa: 2.90m, Stylized parachutists.

1995, Mar. 1 Litho. *Perf. 14*

959 A518 2.90m multicolored *1.40 .45*

Endangered Species — A519

Designs: a, Felis lynx. b, Lake, forest. c, Rocks, lake. d, Pusa hispida.

1995, Mar. 1 *Perf. 13*

960 A519 2.90m Block of 4, #a-d 5.50 5.50

Nos. 960a-960b, 960c-960d are continuous designs. See Russia No. 6249.

Athlete Type of 1995

Souvenir Sheet

Motor sports drivers in cars, on motorcycles: a, Timo Makinen. b, Juha Kankkunen. c, Tommi Ahvala. d, Heikki Mikkola.

1995, May 10 Litho. *Perf. 13*

961 A516 3.50m Sheet of 4, #a.-d. 6.75 6.75

Insect Type of 1994

1995, May 11

962 A508 19m Geotrupes stercorarius 9.25 9.25

Tourism — A520

Designs: 2.80m, Linnanmaki amusement park, Helsinki. 2.90m, Town of Mantyharju.

1995, May 12

963 A520 2.80m multicolored 1.25 .55
964 A520 2.90m multicolored 1.25 .65

Town of Loviisa, 250th Anniv. — A521

1995, June 30 Litho. *Perf. 14*

965 A521 3.20m multicolored 1.50 1.10

Intl. Union of Forestry Research Organizations, 20th World Congress, Tampere — A522

Designs: No. 966, Betula pendula. No. 967, Pinus sylvestris. No. 968, Picea abies. No. 969, Research, tree grown from needle.

Perf. 14 on 2 or 3 Sides

1995, Aug. 8 Litho.

Booklet Stamps

966 A522 2.80m multicolored 1.25 .50
967 A522 2.80m multicolored 1.25 .50
968 A522 2.80m multicolored 1.25 .50
969 A522 2.80m multicolored 1.25 .50
a. Booklet pane of 4, #966-969 5.00 4.25
Complete booklet, #969a 5.00 4.25

Wilhelm Roentgen (1845-1923), Discovery of the X-Ray, Cent. — A523

1995, Aug. 8 *Perf. 14*

970 A523 4.30m multicolored 2.10 1.25

Cats — A525

1995, Oct. 9 Litho. *Perf. 13½*

972 A525 2.80m Somali 1.40 .60
973 A525 2.80m Siamese 1.40 .60
974 A525 2.80m Norwegian forest 1.40 .60
975 A525 2.80m Persian 1.40 .60

Size: 59x35mm

976 A525 2.80m European domestic female 1.40 .60
977 A525 2.80m Three kittens, frog 1.40 .60
a. Booklet pane of 6, #972-977 8.50
Complete booklet, #977a 8.50

UN, 50th Anniv. — A526

1995, Oct. 20 *Perf. 14*
978 A526 3.40m multicolored 1.60 1.00

A527

Christmas A528

1995, Nov. 3 **Litho.** *Perf. 14*
979 A527 2m Santa on skates .95 .20
980 A528 2.80m Poinsettias 1.40 .70

Letter Stamps A529

UNICEF, 50th Anniv. A530

1996, Feb 2 **Litho.** *Perf. 13½x14*
Booklet Stamps

981 A529 1m "M" .50 .35
982 A529 1m "O" .50 .35
983 A529 1m "I" .50 .35
984 A529 1m "H" .50 .35
985 A529 1m "E" .50 .35
986 A529 1m "J" .50 .35
987 A529 1m "A" .50 .35
988 A529 1m "N" .50 .35
989 A529 1m "T" .50 .35
990 A529 1m "P" .50 .35
991 A529 1m "U" .50 .35
992 A529 1m "S" .50 .35
a. Booklet pane of 12, #981-992 6.00
Complete booklet, No. 992a 6.00

1996, Feb. 2 *Perf. 14*
993 A530 2.80m multicolored 1.40 .50

Women's Gymnastics in Finland, Cent. — A531

1996, Feb. 26 **Litho.** *Perf. 13*
994 A531 2.80m multicolored 1.40 .55

Woman Suffrage, 90th Anniv. A532

Litho. & Engr.
1996, Mar. 8 *Perf. 13*
995 A532 3.20m multicolored *1.25 .75*

Europa.

Cinema, Cent. — A533

Finnish films: No. 996, "Juha," 1937. No. 997, "Laveata Tieta," 1931. No. 998, "Tuntematon Sotilas," 1935. No. 999, Oldest known photo of a motion picture show, 1896. No. 1000, "Jäniksen Vuosi," 1977. No. 1001, "Valkoinen Peura," 1952. No. 1002, "Kaikki Rakastavat," 1935. No. 1003, "Varjoja Paratiisissa," 1986.

1996, Apr. 1 **Litho.** *Perf. 14x13½*
Booklet Stamps

996 A533 2.80m multicolored 1.40 .55
997 A533 2.80m multicolored 1.40 .55
998 A533 2.80m multicolored 1.40 .55
999 A533 2.80m multicolored 1.40 .55
1000 A533 2.80m multicolored 1.40 .55
1001 A533 2.80m multicolored 1.40 .55
1002 A533 2.80m multicolored 1.40 .55
1003 A533 2.80m multicolored 1.40 .55
a. Bklt. pane of 8, #996-1003 11.50
Complete booklet, #1003a 11.50

Radio, Cent. — A534

1996, Apr. 25 *Perf. 14*
1004 A534 4.30m multicolored 2.10 1.10

1996 Summer Olympic Games, Atlanta — A535

1996, June 3 **Litho.** *Perf. 12 Vert.*
Booklet Stamps

1005 A535 3.40m Kayaking 1.60 1.00
1006 A535 3.40m Sailing 1.60 1.00
1007 A535 3.40m Rowing 1.60 1.00
1008 A535 3.40m Swimming 1.60 1.00
a. Booklet pane of 4, #1005-1008 6.50
Complete booklet, #1008a 6.50

Insect Type of 1994

1996, July 1 **Litho.** *Perf. 13*
1009 A508 19m Dytiscus marginalis 8.25 9.00

Shore Birds — A536

#1010, Gallinago gallinago. #1011, Haematopus ostralegus. #1012, Scolopax rusticola. #1013, Vanellus vanellus. #1014, Numenius arquata.

Perf. 13½ on 3 Sides
1996, Sept. 6 **Litho. & Engr.**

1010 A536 2.80m multicolored 1.40 .55
1011 A536 2.80m multicolored 1.40 .55
1012 A536 2.80m multicolored 1.40 .55
1013 A536 2.80m multicolored 1.40 .55

Size: 30x52mm

1014 A536 2.80m multicolored 1.40 .55
a. Sheet of 5, #1010-1014 7.00 6.00

Finnish Comic Strips — A537

#1015, "Professor Itikainen" examining plant with magnifying glass, by Ilmari Vainio. #1016, "Pekka Puupää (Peter Blockhead)" taking letter from mailbox, by Ola Fogelberg. #1017, "Joonas" holding drawing pencil, by Veikko Savolainen. #1018, "Mämmilä" wearing helmet, by Tarmo Koivisto. #1019, "Rymy-Eetu" smoking pipe, by Erkki Tanttu. #1020, "Kieku" writing letter, by Asmo Alho. # 1021, "Pikku Risunen" with animal, by Riitta Uusitalo. # 1022, "Kiti" holding up pencil, by Kati Kovács.

1996, Oct. 9 **Litho.** *Perf. 13½*
Booklet Stamps

1015 A537 2.80m black & red 1.40 .55
1016 A537 2.80m black & red 1.40 .55
1017 A537 2.80m red & black 1.40 .55
1018 A537 2.80m black & red 1.40 .55
1019 A537 2.80m black & red 1.40 .55
1020 A537 2.80m red & black 1.40 .55
1021 A537 2.80m red & black 1.40 .55
1022 A537 2.80m red & black 1.40 .55
a. Bklt. pane of 8, #1015-1022 11.50
Complete booklet, #1022a 11.50

Christmas A538

2m, Snowman, Santa, gnome playing muscical instruments. 2.80m, Rabbit, reindeer watching northern lights. 3.20m, Santa reading letters.

1996, Nov. 1 **Litho.** *Perf. 14*
1023 A538 2m multi 1.00 .20
1024 A538 2.80m multi 1.40 .55
1025 A538 3.20m multi, vert. 1.50 .65
Nos. 1023-1025 (3) 3.90 1.40

Greetings Stamps — A539

End of 19th cent.: #1026, Two angels. #1027, Flowers in basket. #1028, Hand reaching through garland, bluebird. #1029, Boy, girl dancing. #1030, Boy, envelope, shamrocks. #1031, Clasping hands through heart-shaped garlands. #1032, Roses. #1033, Angel.

Perf. 13x12½ on 3 Sides
1997, Jan. 30 **Litho.**
Booklet Stamps

1026 A539 1 multicolored 1.60 .50
1027 A539 1 multicolored 1.60 .50
1028 A539 1 multicolored 1.60 .50
1029 A539 1 multicolored 1.60 .50
1030 A539 1 multicolored 1.60 .50
1031 A539 1 multicolored 1.60 .50
1032 A539 1 multicolored 1.60 .50
1033 A539 1 multicolored 1.60 .50
a. Bklt. pane of 8, #1026-1033 13.50
Complete booklet, #1033a 13.50

Nos. 1026-1033 sold for 2.80m on day of issue.
Number on stamp represents class of mail.

Mail Order Sales in Finland, Cent. — A540

1997, Jan. 30 *Perf. 13½x14*
1034 A540 2.80m multicolored 1.40 .25

1997 Ice Hockey World Championships, Helsinki — A541

1997, Jan. 30
1035 A541 2.80m multicolored 1.40 .25

On each stamp from the right vertical row of the sheet, No. 1035 exists without the thin, curved black line at the center right edge of the stamp.

Lepus Timidus A542

1997, Mar. 4 **Litho.** *Perf. 14*
1036 A542 2.80m multicolored 1.40 .25

Saami Folktale, "Girl Who Turned into a Golden Merganser" — A543

Europa: 3.20m, Duck, girl, prince. 3.40m, Girl falling into crevice.

1997, Mar. 4 *Perf. 13*
1037 A543 3.20m multicolored *1.50 .50*
1038 A543 3.40m multicolored *1.60 .60*

Paavo Nurmi (1897-1973), Winner of 9 Olympic Gold Medals — A544

1997, Mar. 18 *Perf. 14*
1039 A544 3.40m multicolored 1.60 .90

Southwest Archipelago Natl. Park — A545

Litho. & Engr.
1997, Apr. 25 *Perf. 14*
1040 A545 4.30m multicolored 2.10 1.10

Tango — A546

A547

1997, May 19 **Litho.**
1041 A546 1 multicolored 1.60 .25
Complete booklet of 5 8.25

No. 1041 sold for 2.80m on day of release.
Number on stamp represents class of mail.

1997, May 19 ***Perf. 13½***

Sailing Ships: #1042, Astrid. #1043, Jacobstads Wapen. #1044, Tradewind. #1045, Merikokko. #1046, Suomen Joutsen. #1047, Sigyn.

Booklet Stamps

1042 A547 2.80m multicolored 1.40 .55
1043 A547 2.80m multicolored 1.40 .55
1044 A547 2.80m multicolored 1.40 .55
1045 A547 2.80m multicolored 1.40 .55

Size: 48x25½mm

1046 A547 2.80m multicolored 1.40 .55
1047 A547 2.80m multicolored 1.40 .55
a. Booklet pane of 6, #1042-1047 8.50
Complete booklet, #1047a 8.50

Pres. Martti Ahtisaari, 60th Birthday A548

1997, June 23 **Litho.** ***Perf. 14***
1048 A548 2.80m multicolored 1.40 .25

Independence, 80th Anniv. — A549

Four seasons: No. 1049, Spring, lily-of-the-valley (natl. flower). No. 1050, Summer, white clouds. No. 1051, Fall, colorful leaves. No. 1052, Winter, snow crystals.

Perf. 13x12½ on 2 or 3 Sides
1997, June 23

Booklet Stamps

1049 A549 2.80m multicolored 1.40 .55
1050 A549 2.80m multicolored 1.40 .55
1051 A549 2.80m multicolored 1.40 .55
1052 A549 2.80m multicolored 1.40 .55
a. Booklet pane, #1049-1052 5.75
Complete booklet, #1052a 5.75

Souvenir Sheet

A550

Grus Grus (Cranes): a, With young. b, With frog. c, Performing mating dance. d, In flight.

1997, Aug. 19 **Litho.** ***Perf. 14***
1053 A550 2.80m Sheet of 4, #a.-d. 5.50 5.50

A551

1997, Oct. 9 **Litho.** ***Perf. 14¼, 14½***

Finnish Writers Assoc. (Covers from books): No. 1054, "Seven Brothers," by Aleksis Kivi. No. 1055, "Sinuhe the Egyptian," by Mika Waltari. No. 1056, "Täällä Pohjantähden alla I," by Väinö Linna. No. 1057, "Hyvästi lijoki," by Kalle Päätalo. No. 1058, "Haukka, minum rakkaani," by Kaari Utrio. No. 1059, "Juhannustanssit," by Hannu Salama. No. 1060, "Manillaköysi," by Veijo Meri. No. 1061, "Uppo-Nalle ja Kumma," by Elina Karjalainen.

Booklet Stamps

1054 A551 2.80m multicolored 1.40 .55
1055 A551 2.80m multicolored 1.40 .55
1056 A551 2.80m multicolored 1.40 .55
1057 A551 2.80m multicolored 1.40 .55
1058 A551 2.80m multicolored 1.40 .55
1059 A551 2.80m multicolored 1.40 .55
1060 A551 2.80m multicolored 1.40 .55
1061 A551 2.80m multicolored 1.40 .55
a. Booklet pane, #1054-1061 11.50
Complete booklet, #1061a 11.50

No. 1056 exists perf 14½x14¼. The other values also should exist thus. The editors would like to examine such stamps.

Christmas A552

1997, Oct. 31
1062 A552 2m Village .95 .20
1063 A552 2.80m Candelabra, vert. 1.40 .55
1064 A552 3.20m Church, vert. 1.50 .65
Nos. 1062-1064 (3) 3.85 1.40

Wildlife A553

2nd, Stizostedion lucioperca. 1st, Turdus merula.

Die Cut 10 Horiz., Syncopated Type A

1998, Jan. 15 **Litho.**

Self-Adhesive

Coil Stamps

1065 A553 2 multicolored 1.50 .25
1066 A553 1 multicolored 1.60 .25

Nos. 1065-1066 were valued at 2.40m and 2.80m, respectively, on date of issue. Number on stamp represents class of mail.
See Nos. 1099-1100.

A554

A555

Moomin Cartoon Characters, by Tove Jansson: No. 1067, Boy Moomin drawing with pad and pencil. No. 1068, Girl Moomin in sunshine. No. 1069, Organ grinder. No. 1070, Boy Moomin giving flower to girl Moomin.

1998, Jan. 15 ***Perf. 13 (on 3 Sides)***

Booklet Stamps

1067 A554 1 multicolored 1.60 .50
1068 A554 1 multicolored 1.60 .50
1069 A554 1 multicolored 1.60 .50
1070 A554 1 multicolored 1.60 .50
a. Booklet pane, #1067-1070 6.50
Complete booklet, #1070a 6.50

Nos. 1067-1070 each sold for 2.80m on day of issue. Number on stamp represents class of mail.
See No. 1127.

1998, Feb. 3 ***Perf. 14***
1071 A555 2.80m multicolored 1.40 .25

Finnish Federation of Nurses, cent.

A556

A557

Valentine's Day Surprise Stamps. (Designs beneath scratch-off heart): a, Musical notes, two dogs. b, Elephant, mouse and flowers. c, Puppy, sealed envelope. d, Kittens, kittens hugging. e, Dog with nose in air, bouquet of flowers. f, Flowers, two rodents.

1998, Feb. 3 ***Perf. 12***
1072 1 Sheet of 6 10.00 6.25
a.-f. A556 Any single, unscratched 1.60 .50

Nos. 1072a-1072f were each valued at 2.80m on day of issue. Number on stamp represents class of mail. Unused values are for singles with attached selvage. Inscriptions are shown in selvage above or below each stamp.
Each stamp bears a heart-shaped, golden scratch-off overlay. Values are for unscratched examples. Scratched stamps, with hearts partially or fully removed, sell for about 20 percent less.

1998, Mar. 27 **Litho.** ***Perf. 14***
1073 A557 2.80m Tussilago farfara 1.40 .25

National Festivals A558

Europa: 3.20m, Boy and girl, balloons, "Vappu" (May Day). 3.40m, Boy and girl in a dream floating over water, Midsummer Festival.

1998, Mar. 27 ***Perf. 14x14½***
1074 A558 3.20m multicolored *1.50 .50*
1075 A558 3.40m multicolored *1.60 .60*

Finnish Marine Research Institute, 80th Anniv. — A559

Designs: 2.80m, Research vessel, "Aranda." 3.20m, "Vega," chart showing route of Nils Adolf Erik Nordenskjold's expedition.

Litho. & Engr.

1998, May 7 ***Perf. 14x13***
1076 A559 2.80m multicolored 1.40 .55
1077 A559 3.20m multicolored 1.50 .65

First Performance of National Anthem, 150th Anniv. — A560

1998, May 7 ***Perf. 13***
1078 A560 5m multicolored 2.40 .30

Puppies A561

#1079, Bernese Mountain dog. #1080, Puli. #1081, Boxer. #1082, Bichon Frisé. #1083, Finnish lapphound. #1084, Wire-haired dachshund. #1085, Scottish cairn terrier. #1086, Labrador retriever.

Perf. 13½x13 on 2 or 3 Sides
1998, June 4 **Litho.**

Booklet Stamps

1079 A561 1 multicolored 1.60 .50
1080 A561 1 multicolored 1.60 .50
1081 A561 1 multicolored 1.60 .50
1082 A561 1 multicolored 1.60 .50
1083 A561 1 multicolored 1.60 .50
1084 A561 1 multicolored 1.60 .50
1085 A561 1 multicolored 1.60 .50
1086 A561 1 multicolored 1.60 .50
a. Booklet pane, #1079-1086 13.50
Complete booklet, #1086a 13.50

Nos. 1079-1086 each sold for 2.80m on day of issue. Number on stamp represents class of mail.

Owls — A562

Cycling — A563

Designs: a, Bubo bubo. b, Wing of bubo bubo. c, Bubo bubo, aegolius funereus. d, Strix nebulosa. e, Nyctea scandiaca.

1998, Sept. 4 **Litho.** ***Perf. 13½***
1087 Sheet of 5 + label 7.25 7.25
a.-e. A562 3m any single 1.40 .55

#1087b is 52x27mm; #1087c-1087d, 26x44mm; #1087e, 30x44mm.
See No. 1113.

1998, Sept. 4 ***Perf. 14***
1088 A563 3m multicolored 1.25 .25

Finnish Design — A564

#1089, Savoy vases, by Alvar Aalto. #1090, Karuselli chair, by Yrjö Kukkapuro. #1091, Tasaraita knitwear, designed by Annika Rimala for Marimekko. #1092, Kilta tableware set, by Kaj Franck. #1093, Cast iron pot, by Timo Sarpaneva. #1094, Carelia cutlery set, by Bertel Gardberg.
Illustration reduced.

Perf. 13½ on 3 Sides
1998, Oct. 9 **Litho.**

Booklet Stamps

1089 A564 3m multicolored 1.40 .55
1090 A564 3m multicolored 1.40 .55
1091 A564 3m multicolored 1.40 .55
1092 A564 3m multicolored 1.40 .55
1093 A564 3m multicolored 1.40 .55
1094 A564 3m multicolored 1.40 .55
a. Booklet pane, #1089-1094 8.50
Complete booklet, #1094a 8.50

Nos. 1090-1091, 1093-1094 are 29x34mm.

Christmas A565

Designs: 2m, Christmas tree, children, vert. 3m, Children, dog riding sled. 3.20m, Winter scene of cottage in center of island.

1998, Oct. 30 ***Perf. 14***
1095 A565 2m multicolored .95 .20
1096 A565 3m multicolored 1.40 .55
1097 A565 3.20m multicolored 1.50 .65
Nos. 1095-1097 (3) 3.85 1.40

Souvenir Sheet

Mika Häkkinen, Formula 1 Driving Champion — A566

Illustration reduced.

1999, Jan. 15 *Perf. 13½*
1098 A566 3m multicolored 1.40 1.40

Native Wildlife Type of 1998

2nd, Salmo salar. 1st, Luscinia svecica.

1999, Jan. 27 Litho. *Die Cut*

Coil Stamps

Self-Adhesive

1099 A553 2 multi 1.50 .25

Die Cut

1100 A553 1 multi, vert. 1.60 .25

Nos. 1099-1100 were valued at 2.40m and 3m, respectively, on day of issue. Number on stamp represents class of mail.

Friendship A567

Animals' tails: No. 1101, Zebra, lion. No. 1102, Dog, cat.

Serpentine Die Cut Perf. 13xDie Cut

1999, Jan. 27

Booklet Stamps

Self-Adhesive

1101 A567 3m multicolored 1.40 .55
1102 A567 3m multicolored 1.40 .55
a. Bklt. pane, 3 each #1101-1102 8.50

No. 1102a is a complete booklet.

Finnish Labor Movement, Cent. — A568

1999, Jan. 27 *Perf. 13½*
1103 A568 4.50m multicolored 2.10 1.10

Finland's Roads — A569

#1104, Snow-covered landscape, Arctic Ocean Road. #1105, Freeway interchanges, Jyväsjtkä Lakeshore Road. #1106, Raippaluoto Bridge. #1107, Wooded drive, Kitee.

1999, Feb. 15 Litho. *Perf. 14 Horiz.*

Booklet Stamps

1104 A569 3m multicolored 1.40 .55
a. Perf. 12¾ horiz. 6.00 .55
1105 A569 3m multicolored 1.40 .55
a. Perf. 12¾ horiz. 6.00 .55
1106 A569 3m multicolored 1.40 .55
a. Perf. 12¾ horiz. 6.00 .55
1107 A569 3m multicolored 1.40 .55
a. Booklet pane, #1104-1107 5.75
Complete booklet, #1107a 6.75
b. Perf. 12¾ horiz. 6.00 .55
c. Booklet pane, #1104a, 1105a, 1106a, 1107b 24.00
Complete booklet, #1107c 25.00

A570

A571

Women's Kalevala-style brooches: a, Horse clasp. b, Bird clasp. c, Virusmäki clasp.

1999, Feb. 15 *Perf. 13½x14*
1108 Sheet of 3 4.25 3.25
a.-c. A570 3m any single 1.40 .55

1st Publication of Legend of the Kalevala, 150th Anniv.

1999, Mar. 15 *Perf. 13x13½*
1109 A571 3m Crocus vernus 1.40 .55

Martha Organization, Cent. — A572

1999, Mar. 15 *Perf. 13½x13*
1110 A572 3m multicolored 1.40 .55

Europa A573

1999, Mar. 15 *Perf. 13½x14*
1111 A573 2.70m Esplanade Park *1.25 .50*
1112 A573 3.20m Ruissalo Park *1.50 .60*

Bird Type of 1998

Designs: a, Luscinia luscinia. b, Cuculus canorus. c, Botaurus stellaris. d, Caprimulgus europaeus. e, Crex crex.

1999, May 18 *Perf. 13½*
1113 Sheet of 5 + label 7.00 7.00
a.-e. A562 3m any single 1.40 .55

No. 1113b is 25x43mm. No. 1113c is 45x30mm. No. 1113d-1113e are 26x37mm.

Finland's Presidency of European Union — A574

1999, July 1 Litho. *Perf. 13¾x13½*
1114 A574 3.50m multicolored 1.60 .65

Finnish Entertainers A575

a, Harmony Sisters, Vera (1914-97), Maire (1916-95) & Raija (1918-97) Valtonen. b, Olavi Virta (1915-72), singer. c, Georg Malmstén (1902-81), composer, conductor. d, Topi Kärki (1915-22), composer, and Reino (Repe) Helismaa (1913-65), lyricist. e, Tapio Rautavaara (1915-79), singer. f, Esa Parkarinen (1911-89), musician, actor.

Perf. 13¼ on 3 Sides

1999, Sept. 6 **Litho.**
1115 Booklet pane of 6 9.75
a.-f. A575 3.50m any single 1.60 .65
Complete booklet, #1115 9.75

Nos. 1115a, 1115d are each 60x34mm.

Finnish Commercial Product Design — A576

a, Fiskars cutting tools. b, Zoel/Versoul guitars. c, Ergo II/Silenta hearing protectors. d, Ponsse Cobra HS 10 tree harvester. e, Suunto compass. f, Exel Avanti QLS ski pole.
Illustration reduced.

Perf. 13¼ on 3 sides

1999, Oct 8 **Litho.**
1116 Booklet pane of 6 9.75
a.-f. A576 3.50m any single 1.60 .65
Complete booklet, #1116 9.75

Size of b, c, e, f: 30x35mm.

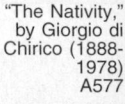

"The Nativity," by Giorgio di Chirico (1888-1978) A577

Rabbits, Birds — A578

1999, Nov. 5 *Perf. 14*
1117 A578 2.50m Santa Claus, vert. 1.25 .20
1118 A577 3m multicolored 1.40 .55
1119 A578 3.50m multicolored 1.60 .65
Nos. 1117-1119 (3) 4.25 1.40

Christmas. See Italy Nos. 2314-2315.

Sveaborg Fortress — A579

2000, Jan. 12 Litho. *Perf. 13¾x13½*
1120 A579 7.20m multi 3.50 .65

Helsinki, 450th Anniv. A580

Designs: No. 1121, Baltic herring market (designer's name at UL).
No. 1122: a, Museum of Contemporary Art (blue building), vert. b, Cathedral, Senate Square (green building). c, Finlandia Hall (orange building). d, Glass Palace Film and Media Center (red building), vert.
No. 1123: a, Quest for the Lost Crown, Sveaborg Fortress (children and arch), vert. b, Like No. 1121, no designer's name. c, Forces of Light City Festival. d, Cellist at outdoor concert, Kaivopuisto Park.

2000, Jan. 12 *Perf. 14*
1121 A580 3.50m multi 1.60 .65

Perf. 14½x14¾ (vert. stamps), 14¾x14½

1122 Booklet pane of 4 6.50
a.-d. A580 3.50m Any single 1.60 .65
1123 Booklet pane of 4 6.50
a.-d. A580 3.50m Any single 1.60 .65
Complete booklet, #1122-1123 13.00

Valentine's Day — A581

Designs: a, Earth as backpack. b, Painters on ladder. c, Birds in balloon. d, Alien with magnet. e, Boy with heart-shaped balloon. f, Polar bear and igloo.

Perf. 13x12¾ on 3 sides

2000, Jan. 12
1124 Bklt. pane of 6 + 4 labels 8.75
a.-f. A581 3.50m Any single 1.60 .65
Complete booklet, #1124 8.75

Souvenir Sheet of 2

Tommi Mäkinen, 1999 Rally World Champion — A582

a, Mäkinen behind wheel. b, Race car.
Illustration reduced.

2000, Mar. 3 *Perf. 13x13¼*
1125 A582 3.50m #a.-b. 3.25 3.25

Easter — A583

2000, Mar. 15 *Perf. 13¾x13¼*
1126 A583 3.50m Caltha palustris 1.60 .65

Moomin Type of 1998

a, Rat with broom looking at Moomins. b, Moomin with uniform, figures sprouting from ground. c, Moomin with hat in forest. d, Moomin with hat, children, in front of stove.

Perf. 13x12¾ on 3 sides

2000, Mar. 15
1127 Booklet pane of 4 6.75
a.-d. A554 1 Any single 1.60 .65
Complete booklet, #1127 6.75
e. As #1127, perf. 13¼ on 3 sides 6.75
f.-i. As #a-d, perf. 13¼ on 3 sides 1.60 .65
Booklet, #1127e 6.75

Nos. 1127a-1127d sold for 3.50m on day of issue. Number on stamp represents class of mail.
Issued: No. 1127e, 7/10/00.

Jubilee Year — A584

Turku Cathedral: a, Nave. b, Woman, votive candles. c, Christ on the Mount of Transfiguration, alterpiece. d, Infant baptism.

2000, Mar. 15 Litho. *Perf. 14 Vert.*
1128 Booklet pane of 4 6.50
a.-d. A584 3.50m Any single 1.60 .65
Complete booklet, #1128 6.50

Europa, 2000

Common Design Type

2000, May 9 *Perf. 13¼x13*
1129 CD17 3.50m multi 1.60 .65

Provincial Flowers

Spring Anemone A585

Blue Cornflower A586

Pulsatilla Patens — A587

Die Cut Perf. 13x12½

2000-2001 Litho.

Self-Adhesive

1130 A585 1 multi 1.60 .20
1131 A586 1 multi 1.60 .20
1132 A587 1 multi 1.60 .20
a. Pane, 5 each #1131-1132 17.00

Number on stamp represents class of mail. No. 1130 sold for 3.50m at time of release and was issued in sheets of 10. Nos. 1131-1132 each sold for 3.60m on day of issue.

Issued: No. 1130, 5/9. Nos. 1131-1132, 5/16/01.

Souvenir Sheet

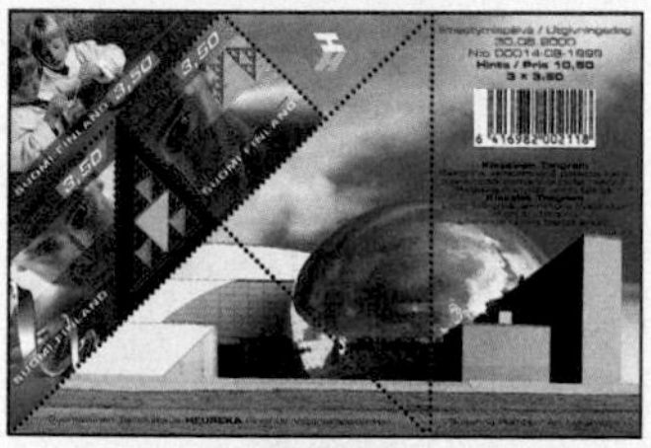
Science — A595

Designs: a, Children, molecuar model (triangular stamp). b, Man's face, DNA strand (rhomboid stamp). c, Man's face, Sierpinski triangles (square stamp).

Illustration reduced.

2000, May 30 *Perf. 14¼*
1140 A595 3.50m Sheet of 3, #a.-c. 5.00 5.00

No. 1140 has holographic image. Soaking in water may affect the hologram.

Finnish Design — A596

No. 1141: a, Rug, by Akseli Gallen-Kallela (1865-1931). b, Pearl Bird, by Birger Kaipiainen (1915-88). c, Pot, by Kyllikki Salmenhaara (1915-81). d, Leaf, by Tapio Wirkkala (1915-85). e, Detail from damask, by Dora Jung (1906-80). f, Glass vase, by Valter Jung (1879-1946).

Illustration reduced.

Perf. 13¼ on 3 sides

2000, Sept. 5 Litho.
1141 Booklet pane of 6 9.75
a.-f. A596 3.50m Any single 1.60 .65
Booklet, #1141 9.75

Size of b, c, e, f: 30x35mm.

Coregonus Lavaretus A597

Lagopus Lagopus A598

Die Cut 10 Horiz. Sync. Type B

2000, Sept. 5

Self-Adhesive

Coil Stamps

1142 A597 2 multi 1.50 .25

Die Cut 10 Horiz. Sync. Type A

1143 A598 1 multi 1.60 .25

Nos. 1142-1143 sold for 3m and 3.50m respectively on day of sale.

On modern stamps bearing the "denominations" "1" or "2," the number represents the class of mail.

Christmas A599

2.50m, Costumed Tiernapojat carol singers. 3.50m, Bullfinch on door ornament, vert.

Serpentine Die Cut 14¼

2000, Nov. 3 Photo.

Self-Adhesive

1144-1145 A599 Set of 2 2.75 .85

Christmas Type of 2000

Design: No. 1146, Like #1145.

Serpentine Die Cut 13¾

2000, Nov. 3 Litho.

Self-Adhesive

1146 A599 3.50m multi + label 3.50 3.50

No. 1146 issued in sheets of 20 that sold for 120m, together with a separate sheet of stickers that could be affixed on the label. The labels attached to the stamps are separated by a row of interrupted serpentine die cutting. Labels could be personalized with photographs taken at some sale sites.

European Year of Languages A600

2001, Jan. 17 **Litho.** *Perf. 13¼*
1147 A600 1 multi 1.60 .65

No. 1147 sold for 3.50m on day of sale.

World Ski Championships, Lahti — A601

No. 1148: a, Ski jumper Janne Ahonen (yellow helmet). b, Skier Mika Myllylä.

Illustration reduced.

2001, Jan. 17
1148 A601 3.50m Horiz. pair, #a-b 3.25 3.25

Valentine's Day — A602

No. 1149: a, Oval wreath. b, Basket of flowers, letter. c, Heart-shaped wreath. d, Bouquet of flowers, letter. e, Flowers, tea set. f, Flowers, heart-shaped pastry.

Serpentine Die Cut 11½x11¾ on 3 Sides

2001, Jan. 17 Photo.

Self-Adhesive

1149 Booklet pane of 6 10.00
a.-f. A602 1 Any single 1.60 .65
Booklet, #1149 10.00

Nos. 1149a-1149f each sold for 3.50m on day of issue.

Souvenir Sheet

Donald Duck Comics in Finland, 50th Anniv. — A603

No. 1150: a, Mickey Mouse, Donald Duck, Santa Claus, Goofy. b, First comics, silhouette of boy. c, Tin soldier with Finnish flag, Chip and Dale (25x30mm). d, Finnish epic hero Väinämöinen, silhouette of Donald Duck. e, Helsinki Cathedral, Donald Duck.

Perf. 7¾ on 3 or 4 Sides

2001, Mar. 13 Litho.
1150 A603 1 Sheet of 5, #a-e 8.50 5.25

Nos. 1150a-1150e sold for 3.50m each on day of issue.

Santa Claus and Sleigh — A604

2001-04 *Serpentine Die Cut 14½x14*

Self-Adhesive

1151 A604 1 multi 1.60 .65
a. Serpentine die cut 13¾x13¼ ('04) 1.75 1.75

No. 1151 sold for 3.60m on day of issue. No. 1151a sold for 65c on day of issue.

No. 1151, 4/2/01. No. 1151a, 12/04.

Europa A605

2001, Apr. 2 *Perf. 13x13½*
1152 A605 5.40m multi *2.50 1.25*

Easter — A606

No. 1153: a, Chick. b, Decorated egg.

Illustration reduced.

2001, Apr. 2 *Perf. 13¼*
1153 A606 3.60m Horiz. pair, #a-b 3.25 3.25

Souvenir Sheet

Verla Mill, UNESCO World Heritage Site — A607

Denominations in: a, UL. b, UR. c, LL. d, LR.

2001, Apr. 2
1154 A607 3.60m Sheet of 4, #a-d 7.00 7.00

Orienteering World Championships, Tampere — A608

2001, May 16
1155 A608 3.60m multi 1.60 .65

Values are for stamps with surrounding selvage.

Souvenir Sheet

Woodpeckers — A609

No. 1156: a, Dendrocopos minor (32x36mm). b, Picoides tridactylus (29x36mm). c, Dendrocopos leucotos (32x42mm). d, Dendrocopos major (29x42mm). e, Picus canus (32x41mm). f, Dryocopus martius (29x41mm).

Perf. 14½x14¼ on 2, 3 or 4 Sides

2001, May 16
1156 A609 3.60m Sheet of 6, #a-f 9.00 9.00

Marine Life — A610

No. 1157: a, Lampetra fluviatilis. b, Aspius aspius. c, Coregonus albula.

Type C Syncopation (1st stamp, #1157): On the top, groups of 3 holes at left and right and a central group of four holes, separated by 2 oval holes equal in width to 4 holes.

Perf. 10 Horiz. Sync. Type C

2001, Sept. 6 **Photo.**

Self-Adhesive

Coil Stamps

1157 Horiz. strip of 3 4.75
a.-c. A610 2 Any single 1.50 .50

Nos. 1157a-1157c were sold in boxes of 100 stamps that sold at a discount price of 270m on day of sale. The franking value on the day of sale for each stamp was 3m.

Birds
A611

No. 1158: a, Parus caeruleus. b, Motacilla alba. c, Oriolus oriolus.

Perf. 10 Horiz. Sync. Type B

2001, Sept. 6 **Photo.**

Self-Adhesive

Coil Stamps

1158 Horiz. strip of 3 5.00 3.50
a.-c. A611 1 Any single 1.60 .65

Nos. 1158a-1158c were sold in boxes of 100 stamps that sold at a discount price of 330m on day of sale. The franking value on the day of sale for each stamp was 3.60m.

History of Gulf of Finland
A612

No. 1159: a, Utö Lighthouse. b, Wreck of the St. Mikael. c, Diver exploring St. Mikael. d, Opossum shrimp, isopod. e, Ship's cabin and nautical chart (32x55mm).

Perf. 13¼x13¾ on 2 or 3 Sides

2001, Sept. 6 **Litho.**

1159 Booklet pane of 5 9.00 —
a.-e. A612 1 Any single 1.75 .70
Booklet, #1159 9.00

Nos. 1159a-1159e each sold for 3.60m on day of sale.

Christmas
A613

Designs: 2.50m, Elf reading Santa's book, candle. 3.60m, Elf delivering package on sled, horiz.

Serpentine Die Cut 14¼

2001, Oct. 26 **Photo.**

Self-Adhesive

1160 A613 2.50m multi 1.25 .50
1161 A613 3.60m multi 1.75 .70

Slightly larger examples of Nos. 1160-1161 serpentine die cut 14 are known on first day and other covers produced by the postal service. They were not sold unused to the public.

100 Cents = 1 Euro (€)

Flowers — A614

National Symbols
A615

Heraldic Lion — A616

Type A614 — No. 1162, Myosotis scorpioides: a, Forty-one flowers. b, Four flowers, five buds. c, One flower, four buds. d, Entire plant. e, Five flowers.

No. 1163, Convallaria majallis: a, Leaf, stem with five flowers. b, Two leaves, stem with eight flowers. c, Two flowers. d, Two leaves, stem with five flowers. e, Entire plants.

Type A615: 50c, Swan, vert. 60c, Birch. 1, Flag and bird. 90c, Kymintehtaalta, by Victor Westerholm. €1.30, Granite cliff. €2.50, Spruce. €3.50, Pine.

Die Cut Perf. 15

2002, Jan. 1 **Photo.**

Self-Adhesive

1162 Vert. strip of 5 .75 .75
a.-e. A614 5c Any single .20 .20
f. As #1162, die cut perf 14 .75
g.-k. A614 5c Any single, die cut perf 14 .20 .20
1163 Vert. strip of 5 1.50 1.50
a.-e. A614 10c Any single .30 .20

Die Cut Perf. 14

1164 A615 50c multi 1.40 .95
1165 A615 60c multi 1.75 1.25

Die Cut Perf. 13¾

1166 A615 1 multi 1.75 1.25
a. Booklet pane of 8 14.50
Booklet, #1166a 14.50

Die Cut Perf. 14¾x15

1167 A615 90c multi 2.50 1.75

Die Cut Perf. 12 Syncopated

1168 A616 €1 blue & multi 3.00 2.10

Die Cut Perf. 14¾x15

1169 A615 €1.30 multi 3.75 2.75
a. Die cut perf 14 ('04) 3.75 2.75

Die Cut Perf. 14

1170 A615 €2.50 multi 7.25 5.25
1171 A615 €3.50 multi 10.00 7.00

Die Cut Perf. 12 Syncopated

1172 A616 €5 red & multi 14.50 10.50
Nos. 1162-1172 (11) 48.15 35.05

No. 1166 sold for 60c on day of issue.

Die cut perf 14 examples of No. 1167 exist on first day and other covers produced by the postal service. They were not sold unused to the public.

No. 1169a issued 7/04. No. 1169a has a duller blue panel and a duller black denomination than that found on No. 1169, and a die cut perf. 14 version of No. 1169 that was available only on first day covers with 1/1/02 cancels, and which was not made available to the public unused. Nos. 1169 and 1169a were produced by different printers.

Nos. 1162f-1162k were printed and put on first day and other covers in 2002 but were not sold to the public until 2006.

Easter — A617

Die Cut Perf. 14

2002, Mar. 6 **Photo.**

Self-Adhesive

1173 A617 60c multi 1.75 1.75

Souvenir Sheet

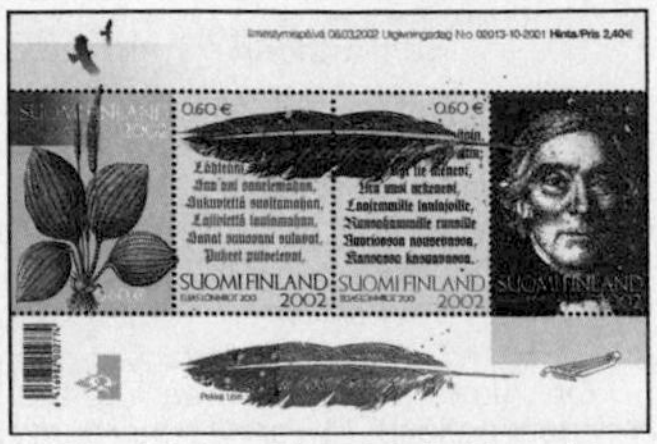

Elias Lönnrot (1802-84), Botanist, Linguist — A618

No. 1174: a, Plantain. b, Opening lines of "Kalevala" (denomination at UL). c, Closing lines of "Kalevala" (denomination at UR). d, Portrait.

Perf. 13¼ on 3 or 4 Sides

2002, Mar. 6 **Litho.**

1174 A618 60c Sheet of 4, #a-d 7.00 7.00

Souvenir Sheet

Old Rauma, UNESCO World Heritage Site — A619

Denominations at: a, UL. b, UR. c, LL. d, LR.

2002, Mar. 6 ***Perf. 13½***

1175 A619 60c Sheet of 4, #a-d 7.00 7.00

Europa — A620

2002, Apr. 15 ***Perf. 13***

1176 A620 60c multi *1.75 1.75*

Gulf of Finland Type of 2001

No. 1177: a, Birds, fish. b, Sailboat, plankton. c, Flounder on sea bed. d, Shrimp, herring. e, Tvärminne Zoological Station, ship, isopod, oceanographic equipment, mussels (32x55mm).

Perf. 13¼x13¾ on 2 or 3 Sides

2002, Apr. 15

1177 Booklet pane of 5 8.75 —
a.-e. A612 1 Any single 1.75 1.10
Booklet, #1177 8.75

Nos. 1177a-1177e each sold for 60c on day of issue.

Sibelius Monument, Helsinki, by Eila Hiltunen
A621

2002, May 3 ***Perf. 13***

1178 A621 60c multi 1.75 1.75

National Symbols Type of 2002 Without Finland Post Emblem

Designs: 60c, Juniperus communis. 1, Reindeer in Lapland.

Die Cut Perf. 14

2002, Oct. 9 **Photo.**

Self-Adhesive

1179 A615 60c multi 1.75 1.25
1180 A615 1 multi 1.75 1.25

No. 1180 sold for 60c on day of issue.

Christmas
A622

Designs: 45c, Horse-drawn sleigh. 60c, Angel with trumpet, vert.

Serpentine Die Cut 14¼

2002, Nov. 1

Self-Adhesive

1181-1182 A622 Set of 2 3.00 3.00

Fish — A623

No. 1183: a, Abramis brama. b, Salmo trutta lacustris. c, Esox lucius.

Syncopated Die Cut Perf. 10 Horiz.

2003, Jan. 15

Self-Adhesive

Coil Stamps

1183 Horiz. strip of 3 4.75 3.00
a.-c. A623 2 Any single 1.50 1.00

Nos. 1183a-1183c were sold in boxes of 100 that sold at a discount price of €47 on day of issue. The franking value on the day of issue for each stamp was 50c.

Birds — A624

No. 1184: a, Cuculus canorus. b, Alauda arvensis. c, Perisoreus infaustus.

Syncopated Die Cut Perf. 10 Horiz.

2003, Jan. 15

Self-Adhesive

Coil Stamps

1184 Horiz. strip of 3 5.25 3.75
a.-c. A624 1 Any single 1.75 1.25

Nos. 1184a-1184c were sold in boxes of 100 that sold at a discount price of €57 on day of issue. The franking value on the day of issue for each stamp was 60c.

Viivi and Wagner, by Jussi Tuomola — A625

No. 1185: a, Viivi and Wagner running. b, Viivi and Wagner dancing. c, Viivi writing love letter. d, Wagner and Viivi in bed. e, Viivi and Wagner kissing. f, Wagner reading love letter.

Serpentine Die Cut 11½x11¾ on 3 Sides

2003, Jan. 15

Self-Adhesive

1185 Booklet pane of 6 11.00
a.-f. A625 1 Any single 1.75 1.25
Booklet, #1185 11.00

Nos. 1185a-1185f each sold for 60c on day of issue.

Ice Hockey World Championships — A626

2003, Mar. 3 Litho. ***Perf. 13¼x13¾***
1186 A626 65c multi 1.90 1.90

St. Bridget (1303-73) A627

Viola Wittrockiana A628

2003, Mar. 3 ***Perf. 13***
1187 A627 65c multi 1.90 1.90

Die Cut Perf. 13¾x14
2003, Mar. 3 Photo.
Self-Adhesive
1188 A628 65c multi 1.90 1.90

Fighting Wood Grouses, by Ferdinand von Wright — A629

2003, Mar. 3 ***Die Cut Perf. 13¾***
Self-Adhesive
1189 A629 90c multi 2.50 2.50

Airplanes A630

No. 1190: a, Super Caravelle. b, Airbus 320. c, Junkers Ju 52/3m. d, Douglas DC-3.

Perf. 14x14½ on 3 Sides
2003, Mar. 3
1190 Booklet pane of 4 + 4 etiquettes 7.75 —
a.-d. A630 65c Any single 1.90 1.90
Complete booklet, #1190 7.75

Finnair, 80th anniv.; Powered flight, cent.

Europa A631

No. 1191 — Posters by Lasse Hietala: a, Woman with newspaper. b, Hearts.

2003, May 7 Litho. ***Perf. 13¾x13¼***
1191 A631 65c Pair, #a-b *3.75 3.75*

Souvenir Sheet

Flora and Fauna Seen in Summer — A632

No. 1192: a, Moth, flowers (35x29mm). b, Dragonfly, grasshopper (44x35mm). c, Grasshopper, caterpillar, thistle (35x25mm). d, Frog, flowers, butterfly, insects (44x36mm). e, Magpie, snail, flowers (35x46mm). f, Hedgehog, bee, ant, spider, flowers (44x29mm).

Perf. 14½ on 2 or 3 Sides
2003, May 7
1192 A632 65c Sheet of 6, #a-f 11.50 11.50

Moomins A633

No. 1193: a, Moomin ancestors. b, Moomins around stove. c, Moomin standing on hands in water. d, Moomin and fox. e, Moomin looking at film negative. f, Moomin with hat, flowers.

Serpentine Die Cut 11½x11¾ on 3 Sides
2003, May 7 Photo.
Self-Adhesive
1193 Booklet pane of 6 11.50
a.-f. A633 1 Any single 1.90 1.90
Complete booklet, #1193 11.50

Nos. 1193a-1193f each sold for 65c on day of issue.

Cupid A634

Serpentine Die Cut 11½ Syncopated
2003, May 14 Litho.
Self-Adhesive
1194 A634 1 multi 1.90 1.90

No. 1194 could be personalized. It sold for 65c on day of issue.

Lingonberries — A635

Serpentine Die Cut 14
2003, Sept. 10 Photo.
Self-Adhesive
1195 A635 65c multi 1.90 1.90

Philanthropists A636

No. 1196: a, Juho (1852-1913) and Maria (1858-1923) Lallukka. b, Emil Aaltonen (1869-1949), vert. c, Heikki Huhtamäki (1900-70), vert. d, Antti (1883-1962) and Jenny Wihuri. e, Alfred Kordelin (1868-1917), vert. f, Amos Anderson (1878-1961), vert.

Perf. 13¼x13¾, 13¾x13¼ on 3 Sides
2003, Sept. 10 Litho.
1196 Booklet pane of 6 11.50 —
a.-f. A636 65c Any single 1.90 1.90
Complete booklet, #1196 11.50

Lighthouses — A637

No. 1197: a, Bengtskär. b, Russarö. c, Rönnskär. d, Harmaja Grahara. e, Söderskär.

2003, Sept. 10 ***Perf. 13¼x13¾***
1197 A637 Sheet of 5 9.50 9.50
a.-e. 1 Any single 1.90 1.90

Nos. 1197a-1197e sold for 65c on day of issue. Size of No. 1197a, 28x45mm; Nos. 1197b-1197e, 21x36mm.

Christmas A638

Designs: 45c, Elf mailing letter. 65c, Elf with ginger biscuit on baking pan, vert.

Serpentine Die Cut 14x14¼, 14¼x14
2003, Oct. 31 Photo.
Self-Adhesive
1198-1199 A638 Set of 2 3.25 3.25

Slightly larger versions of No. 1198 with a serpentine die cutting of 13¼x13¾ and of No. 1199 with a serpentine die cutting of 13¾x13¼ exist only on first day and other covers produced by the postal service. They were not sold unused to the public.

Apples A639

Serpentine Die Cut 11½ Syncopated
2003, Oct. 31 Litho.
Self-Adhesive
1200 A639 1 multi 1.90 1.90

No. 1200 could be personalized. It sold for 65c on day of issue.

Pres. Tarja Halonen, 60th Birthday — A640

2003, Dec. 1 Litho. ***Perf. 13***
1201 A640 65c multi 1.90 1.90

Linnaea Borealis — A641

Die Cut Perf. 14
2004, Jan. 14 Photo.
Self-Adhesive
1202 A641 30c multi .85 .85

Souvenir Sheet

Johan Ludvig Runeberg (1804-77), Poet — A642

No. 1203: a, Title page of *Tales of Ensign Stahl.* b, Sven Dufva with gun. c, Illustration for "Our Country." d, Sculpture of Runeberg.

Perf. 13½x13¼ on 3 or 4 Sides
2004, Jan. 14 Litho.
1203 A642 65c Sheet of 4, #a-d 7.50 7.50

Jean Sibelius (1865-1957), Composer A643

No. 1204: a, Satu, and Sibelius, paintings by Akseli Gallen-Kallela. b, Hands of Sibelius on piano keyboard. c, Swans, musical score by Sibelius.

No. 1205: a, Sibelius' house, Ainola. b, Sibelius and wife, Aino. c, Score of "Voces Intimae."

Die Cut Perf. 10 Horiz., Syncopated at Top
2004, Jan. 14 Photo.
Coil Stamps
Self-Adhesive
1204 Horiz. strip of 3 5.00
a.-c. A643 2 Any single 1.60 1.60
1205 Horiz. strip of 3 5.75
a.-c. A643 1 Any single 1.90 1.90

Nos. 1204a-1204c each sold for 55c on day of issue and have two short syncopations; Nos. 1205a-1205c each sold for 65c on day of issue, and have one large syncopation.

Love — A644

Text and: a, Rose. b, Man kissing. c, Woman's eye. d, Man and woman embracing. e, Elderly woman. f, Hand pulling petal from daisy.

Serpentine Die Cut 11½x11¾ on 3 Sides
2004, Jan. 14
Self-Adhesive
1206 Booklet pane of 6 11.50
a.-f. A644 1 Any single 1.90 1.90

Nos. 1206a-1206f each sold for 65c on day of issue.

Ursus Arctos — A645

2004, Mar. 1 ***Die Cut Perf. 14***

Self-Adhesive

1207 A645 2 multi 1.60 1.60

No. 1207 sold for 55c on day of issue.

Rose — A646

2004, Mar. 1 **Booklet Stamp**

Self-Adhesive

1208 A646 1 multi 1.90 1.90
a. Booklet pane of 10 19.00

No. 1208 sold for 65c on day of issue. Booklet pane was sold folded.

Easter Flowers — A647

Die Cut Perf. 14

2004, Mar. 1 **Litho.**

Self-Adhesive

1209 A647 65c multi 1.90 1.90

Heraldic Lion Type of 2002

Die Cut Perf. 12 Syncopated

2004, Mar. 1

Self-Adhesive

1210 A616 €3 multi 8.75 8.75

Swallows A648

Orchid A649

Serpentine Die Cut 11½ Syncopated

2004, Mar. 26

Self-Adhesive

1211 A648 1 multi 1.90 1.90
1212 A649 1 multi 1.90 1.90

Nos. 1211-1212 each sold for 65c on day of issue, and they could be personalized.

Souvenir Sheet

Norse Gods — A650

No. 1213: a, Head of Luonnotar (33x30mm). b, Luonnotar with arms extended (22x42mm).

Perf. 14¼x14½ (#1213a), 14½x14 (#1213b)

2004, Mar. 26

1213 A650 65c Sheet of 2, #a-b 3.75 3.75

Forest Animals — A651

No. 1214: a, Red squirrel (40x40mm). b, Raven (40x31mm). c, Variable hare (40x34mm). d, Stoat (40x37mm). e, Lizard (40x34mm). f, Red fox (40x40mm).

Perf. 13¼x14 on 2 or 3 Sides

2004, Apr. 28

1214 A651 65c Sheet of 6, #a-f 11.50 11.50

Fragaria Vesca — A652

Die Cut Perf. 14

2004, Apr. 28 **Photo.**

Self-Adhesive

1215 A652 65c multi 1.90 1.90

Luxembourg Gardens, by Albert Edelfelt (1854-1905) A653

2004, Apr. 28 **Self-Adhesive**

1216 A653 1 multi 1.90 1.90

No. 1216 sold for 65c on day of issue.

Europa — A654

No. 1217: a, People around campfire. b, Family in rowboat.

2004, Apr. 28 **Litho.** ***Perf. 13***

1217 A654 65c Horiz. pair, #a-b *3.75 3.75*

Snufkin and Moomintroll A655

Litho. & Embossed

2004, Sept. 8 ***Perf. 13***

Flocked Paper

1218 A655 1 multi 1.90 1.90

No. 1218 sold for 65c on day of issue.

Shipwreck Treasures A656

No. 1219: a, Tankard. b, Fabric seal. c, Gold watch. d, Powder keg. e, Figurehead (23x40mm).

Perf. 14¼x13 on 3 or 4 Sides

2004, Sept. 8

1219 Booklet pane of 5 9.50 —
a.-e. A656 1 Any single 1.90 1.90
Complete booklet, #1219 9.50

Stamps sold for 65c each on day of issue.

Souvenir Sheet

Sammallahdenmäki, UNESCO World Heritage Site — A657

No. 1220: a, Stone wall and trees. b, Lichen-covered rocks.

2004, Sept. 8 **Litho.** ***Perf. 14¾x14¼***

1220 A657 65c Sheet of 2, #a-b 3.75 3.75

Rights of the Child — A658

No. 1221: a, Two girls. b, Boy painting. Illustration reduced

2004, Oct. 29 ***Perf. 13***

1221 A658 65c Horiz. pair, #a-b 4.00 4.00

Christmas A659

Designs: 45c, Boy writing Santa Claus. 65c, Christmas tree branch, candle, ornaments, vert.

Serpentine Die Cut 13¼x13¾, 13¾x13¼

2004, Oct. 29 **Photo.**

Self-Adhesive

1222-1223 A659 Set of 2 3.25 3.25

Rotary International, Cent. — A660

2005, Jan. 14 **Litho.** ***Perf. 13***

1224 A660 65c blue & gold 1.90 1.90

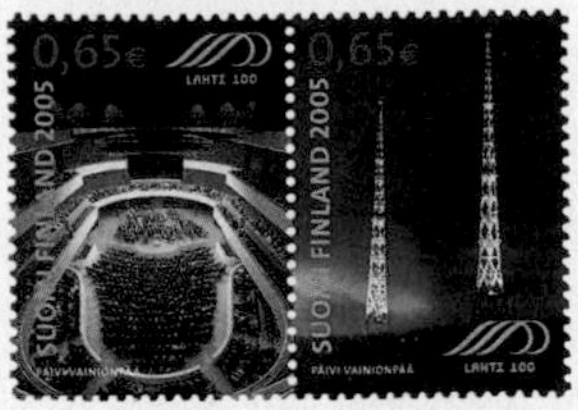

Lahti, Cent. — A661

No. 1225: a, Sibelius Concert Hall. b, Illuminated radio towers.

2005, Jan. 14

1225 A661 65c Pair, #a-b 3.75 3.75

Oulo, 400th Anniv. — A662

No. 1226: a, Child with pail and shovel. b, Woman riding bicycle.
Illustration reduced.

2005, Jan. 14

1226 A662 65c Horiz. pair, #a-b 3.75 3.75

Publishing of First Finnish Almanac, 300th Anniv. — A663

Die Cut Perf. 14

2005, Jan. 14 **Photo.**

Self-Adhesive

1227 A663 65c multi 1.90 1.90

Children's Toys — A664

No. 1228: a, Stuffed lion and tiger. b, Stuffed elephant and dog. c, Airplane, train and car. d, Stuffed bear and rabbit.

Serpentine Die Cut 9¼x8½ on 3 Sides

2005, Jan. 14

Self-Adhesive

1228 Booklet pane of 4 7.75
a.-d. A664 1 Any single 1.90 1.90

Stamps sold for 65c each on day of issue.

End of Winter War, 65th Anniv. — A665

2005, Mar. 2 **Litho.** ***Perf. 13***

1229 A665 65c multi 1.90 1.90

Easter — A666

2005, Mar. 2 ***Serpentine Die Cut 14***

Self-Adhesive

1230 A666 65c multi 1.90 1.90

Apple Blossom — A667

Die Cut Perf. 14

2005, Mar. 2 **Photo.**

Self-Adhesive

Booklet Stamp

1231 A667 1 multi 1.90 1.90
a. Booklet pane of 10 19.00

No. 1231 sold for 65c on day of issue.

Door Decoration, by Eliel Saarinen A668

Copper Stove Door — A669

Chair Back — A670

Stained Glass Window, by Olga Gummerus-Ehrström — A671

Dining Room — A672

Exterior of Hvitträsk A673

Die Cut Perf. 10 Horiz., Syncopated at Top

2005, Mar. 2 **Litho.**

Self-Adhesive

Coil Stamps

1232 Horiz. strip of 3 5.00
a. A668 2 multi 1.60 1.60
b. A669 2 multi 1.60 1.60
c. A670 2 multi 1.60 1.60

1233 Horiz. strip of 3 5.75
a. A671 1 multi 1.90 1.90
b. A672 1 multi 1.90 1.90
c. A673 1 multi 1.90 1.90

Hvitträsk, home and studio of architects Eliel Saarinen, Armas Lindgren and Herman Gesellius. Nos. 1232a-1232c each sold for 55c on day of issue and have two short syncopations. Nos. 1233a-1233c each sold for 65c on day of issue and have one large syncopation.

Miniature Schnauzer A674

Serpentine Die Cut 11½ Syncopated

2005, Apr. 6

1234 A674 1 multi 1.90 1.90

Sold for 65c on day of issue. Sheets could be personalized.

Europa — A675

No. 1235 — Plates with: a, Whitefish and beetroot tartare on lettuce. b, Sauteed reindeer and grouse breast.

2005, May 11 ***Perf. 13***

1235 A675 65c Pair, #a-b *3.75 3.75*

Souvenir Sheet

Golf — A676

No. 1236: a, Man driving ball (44x31mm). b, Boy holding flag, vert. (30x44mm). c, Boy putting, vert. (33x44mm). d, Putter and golf ball (44x32mm).

Perf. 13¼ on 3 or 4 Sides

2005, May 11

1236 A676 65c Sheet of 4, #a-d 7.50 7.50

World Track Championships, Helsinki — A677

Serpentine Die Cut 12½

2005, May 11

Self-Adhesive

1237 A677 65c multi 1.90 1.90

Buses in Finland, Cent. A678

Die Cut Perf. 14

2005, May 11 **Photo.**

Self-Adhesive

1238 A678 65c brown & black 1.90 1.90

Horses — A679

No. 1239: a, Icelandic horse with saddle. b, White Welsh Mountain pony. c, New Forest pony with blanket. d, Shetland Pony.

Serpentine Die Cut 9¼x8½ on 3 Sides

2005, May 11

Self-Adhesive

1239 Booklet pane of 4 7.50
a.-d. A679 1 Any single 1.90 1.90

Stamps sold for 65c each on day of issue.

Cloudberries — A680

Die Cut Perf. 14

2005, Sept. 7 **Photo.**

Self-Adhesive

1240 A680 1 multi 1.90 1.90

Sold for 65c on day of issue.

Fruits I, by Kari Huhtamo A681

Die Cut Perf. 11½ Syncopated

2005, Sept. 7 **Litho.**

Self-Adhesive

1241 A681 90c multi 2.50 2.50

Sheets could be personalized.

Souvenir Sheet

Petäjävesi Church, UNESCO World Heritage Site — A682

No. 1242: a, Bell tower (26x47mm). b, Church (34x39mm). c, Angel (26x39mm). d, Chandelier (27x39mm).

2005, Sept. 7 **Litho.** ***Perf. 13***

1242 A682 65c Sheet of 4, #a-d 7.50 7.50

Icebreakers — A683

No. 1243: a, Urho, 1975. b, Otso, 1986. c, Fennica, 1993. d, Botnica, 1998.

2005, Sept. 7 ***Perf. 13¼ Horiz.***

1243 Booklet pane of 4 7.50 —
a.-d. A683 1 Any single 1.90 1.90

Each stamp sold for 65c on day of issue.

Souvenir Sheet

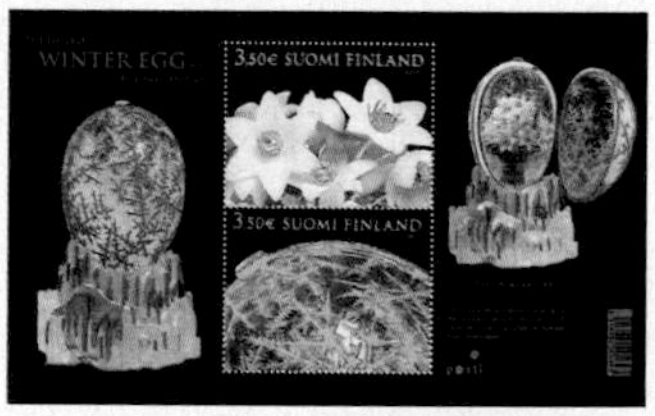

Imperial Winter Egg, by Carl Fabergé — A684

No. 684: a, Flowers in egg. b, Frost detail of egg.

Litho. & Embossed with Foil Application

2005, Oct. 28 ***Perf. 13***

1244 A684 €3.50 Sheet of 2, #a-b 20.00 20.00

A limited quantity of 2,500 numbered sheets, which sold for €30, exist. Value, $100.

Christmas — A685

Designs: 50c, Santa Claus reading letters. 1, Santa Claus and wife dancing, horiz.

Serpentine Die Cut 13¾x13¼, 13¼x13¾

2005, Oct. 28 **Photo.**

Self-Adhesive

1245-1246 A685 Set of 2 3.75 3.75

No. 1246 sold for 65c on day of issue.

Postal Employees Union, Cent. — A686

2006, Jan. 11 Litho. *Perf. 13*

1247 A686 65c multi 1.90 1.90

Heart — A687

2006, Jan. 11 *Die Cut*

Self-Adhesive

1248 A687 65c bright pink 1.90 1.90

Renaming of Helsinki University Library as National Library of Finland — A688

2006, Jan. 11 *Die Cut Perf. 14x13¾*

Self-Adhesive

1249 A688 1 multi 1.90 1.90

Sold for 65c on day of issue.

Forest in Winter — A689

2006, Jan. 11 Photo.

Self-Adhesive

1250 A689 1 multi 1.90 1.90

Sold for 65c on day of issue.

Taxis, Cent. — A690

No. 1251: a, Women passengers in taxi, 1906. b, Driver standing in front of 1929 Chevrolet taxi. c, Driver leaning on 1957 Pobeda taxi. d, Driver on phone at taxi stand next to Mercedes-Benz taxi.

Serpentine Die Cut 11¼ Vert.

2006, Jan. 11 Litho.

Self-Adhesive

1251 Booklet pane of 4 7.50
a.-d. A690 65c Any single 1.90 1.90

Souvenir Sheet

Johan Vilhelm Snellman (1806-81), Philosopher — A691

No. 1252: a, Caricature of Snellman, masthead of his newspaper "Saima." b, Snellman's portrait on 1940 five thousand mark note. c, Snellman and European railway map. d, Ilmarinen, first Finnish locomotive, and European railway map.

2006, Jan. 11 *Perf. 13¼x13¾*

1252 A691 65c Sheet of 4, #a-d 7.50 7.50

Parliament, Cent. — A692

Serpentine Die Cut 14

2006, Feb. 3 Litho.

Self-Adhesive

1253 A692 1 multi 1.90 1.90

Sold for 65c on day of sale.

Flag — A693

2006, Mar. 1

Self-Adhesive

1254 A693 1 multi 1.90 1.90

Sold for 65c on day of sale.

Lilacs — A694

Die Cut Perf. 13¾x14

2006, Mar. 1 Photo.

Self-Adhesive

1255 A694 1 multi 1.90 1.90

Sold for 65c on day of sale.

Easter — A695

2006, Mar. 1 Litho. *Die Cut*

Self-Adhesive

1256 A695 65c multi 1.90 1.90

Fortune Teller, by Helene Schjerfbeck — A696

Die Cut Perf. 13¾x14

2006, Mar. 1 Photo.

Self-Adhesive

1257 A696 95c multi 2.75 2.75

Bil-Bol Poster A697

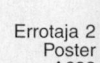

Errotaja 2 Poster A698

Concert Finnois Poster A699

Madonna A700 Self-Portrait A701

Home of Artist Akseli Gallen-Kallela, Tarvaspää — A702

Die Cut Perf. 10 Horiz., Syncopated at Top

2006, Mar. 1

Coil Stamps

Self-Adhesive

1258 Horiz. strip of 3 5.00
a. A697 2 multi 1.60 1.60
b. A698 2 multi 1.60 1.60
c. A699 2 multi 1.60 1.60

Die Cut Perf. 10, Syncopated at Right

1259 Vert. strip of 3 5.75
a. A700 1 multi 1.90 1.90
b. A701 1 multi 1.90 1.90
c. A702 1 multi 1.90 1.90

Akseli Gallen-Kallela (1865-1931), artist. Nos. 1258a-1258c each sold for 55c and Nos. 1259a-1259c each sold for 65c on day of issue.

Souvenir Sheet

Norse Mythology — A703

No. 1260 — Fairy tale book cover illustrations by Rudolf Koivu: a, Fairy. b, Fairy dancing with Santa Claus, vert.

Perf. 13½x13¼, 13¼x13½ (#1260b)

2006, Mar. 29 Litho.

1260 A703 65c Sheet of 2, #a-b 3.75 3.75

Europa A704

2006, May 4 *Perf. 13*

1261 A704 65c multi 1.90 1.90

Vaasa, 400th Anniv. — A705

2006, May 4

1262 A705 1 multi 1.90 1.90

Sold for 65c on day of issue.

A706

Serpentine Die Cut 10 Syncopated

2006, May 4

Booklet Stamp

Self-Adhesive

1263 A706 1 multi 1.90 1.90
a. Booklet pane of 8 15.00

No. 1263 sold for 65c on day of issue. Design portion of stamp could be personalized.

Summer Activities A707

No. 1264: a, Woman fishing. b, Children making flower garlands. c, Man making sauna whisk. d, Woman weeding flower garden.

Serpentine Die Cut 11¼ Vert.

2006, May 4

Self-Adhesive

1264 Booklet pane of 4 7.50
a.-d. A707 1 Any single 1.90 1.90

Nos. 1264a-1264d each sold for 65c on day of issue.

Cats — A708

No. 1265: a, Striped house cat. b, British shorthair (gray cat). c, Ragdoll cat (brown and white). d, Chocolate Persian cat.

2006, May 4

Self-Adhesive

1265 Booklet pane of 4 7.50
a.-d. A708 1 Any single 1.90 1.90

Nos. 1265a-1265d each sold for 65c on day of issue.

Suomenlinna (Sveaborg) Fortress, Helsinki — A709

No. 1266: a, Ship without oars. b, Ship with oars facing fortress. c, Ship with oars, windmill.

Litho. & Engr.

2006, May 4 ***Perf. 13x12¾***

1266 A709 Booklet pane of 3 5.75 —
a.-c. 1 Any single 1.90 1.90
Complete booklet, #1266 5.75

Nos. 1266a-1266c each sold for 65c on day of issue. See Sweden No. 2530.

Blueberries and Blueberry Pie — A710

Die Cut Perf. 14

2006, Aug. 24 **Photo.**

Self-Adhesive

1267 A710 1 multi 2.00 2.00

Sold for 70c on day of issue.

Miniature Sheet

Family Life — A711

No. 1268: a, Family watching television. b, Woman writing letter to husband.

2006, Aug. 24 ***Die Cut***

Self-Adhesive

1268 A711 1 Sheet of 2, #a-b 4.00 4.00

Nos. 1268a-1268b each sold for 70c on day of issue.

Newspaper Journalism — A712

Die Cut Perf. 14

2006, Sept. 22 **Litho.**

Self-Adhesive

1269 A712 70c multi 2.00 2.00

Points, Textile Art by Ritva Puotila — A713

Serpentine Die Cut 11½ Syncopated

2006, Sept. 22

Self-Adhesive

1270 A713 1 multi 2.00 2.00

Sold for 70c on day of issue.

Dryas Octopetala A714

Serpentine Die Cut 14

2006, Sept. 22 **Photo.**

Self-Adhesive

1271 A714 1 multi 2.00 2.00

Sold for 70c on day of issue.

Art of Snow and Ice — A715

No. 1272: a, Horse. b, Kemi Snow Castle. c, Wall of ice tiles. d, Snowball lantern.

Serpentine Die Cut 11¾ Vert.

2006, Sept. 22

Self-Adhesive

1272 Booklet pane of 4 8.00
a.-d. A715 1 Any single 2.00 2.00

Nos. 1272a-1272d each sold for 70c on day of issue. Denominations are printed in thermographic ink that changes color when warmed.

Miniature Sheet

Finnish Postage Stamps, 150th Anniv. — A716

No. 1273: a, 70c, Heraldic lion and fleurons in white. b, 95c, Part of vignette of type A1. c, €1.40, Heraldic lion in gold, fleurons in red.

Litho. & Embossed With Foil Application

2006, Oct. 27 ***Perf. 13½x13***

1273 A716 Sheet of 3, #a-c 8.75 8.75

A717

Christmas — A718

Serpentine Die Cut 13¼x13¾

2006, Oct. 27 **Photo.**

Self-Adhesive

1274 A717 50c multi 1.40 1.40

Serpentine Die Cut 13¾x13¼

1275 A718 1 multi 2.00 2.00

No. 1275 sold for 70c on day of issue.

Television Broadcasting in Finland, 50th Anniv. — A719

Die Cut Perf. 14

2007, Jan. 24 **Litho.**

Self-Adhesive

1276 A719 70c multi 1.90 1.90

Faces — A720

2007, Jan. 24

Self-Adhesive

1277 A720 70c multi 1.90 1.90

Winter Landscape, Haminalahti, by Ferdinand von Wright A721

2007, Jan. 24 **Photo.**

Self-Adhesive Booklet Stamp

1278 A721 1 multi 1.90 1.90
a. Booklet pane of 10 19.00

Sold for 70c on day of issue.

Sun Setting Over Flower Field — A722

2007, Jan. 24 **Litho.**

Self-Adhesive

1279 A722 €1.40 multi 3.75 3.75

Souvenir Sheet

Intl. Polar Year — A723

No. 1280: a, Snowflake. b, Aurora borealis.

Perf. 13 Syncopated (#1280a), 13 (#1280b)

Litho. With Hologram Affixed

2007, Jan. 24

1280 A723 70c Sheet of 2, #a-b + label 3.75 3.75

Truck Transport — A724

No. 1281: a, Log truck. b, Milk truck. c, Dump truck. d, Tractor trailer.

Serpentine Die Cut 12¼ Horiz.

2007, Jan. 24 **Litho.**

Self-Adhesive

1281 Booklet pane of 4 7.75
a.-d. A724 70c Any single 1.90 1.90

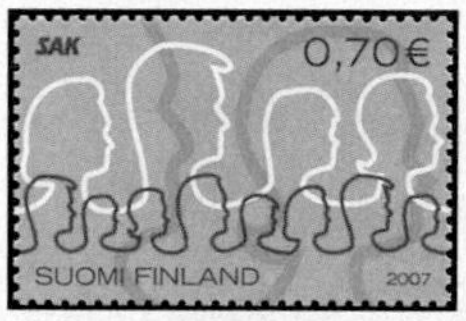

Central Organization of Finnish Trade Unions — A725

2007, Mar. 7 ***Perf. 13***

1282 A725 70c multi 1.90 1.90

Soccer Association of Finland, Cent. — A726

2007, Mar. 7 ***Die Cut***

Self-Adhesive

1283 A726 70c multi 1.90 1.90

Easter — A727

2007, Mar. 7 ***Die Cut Perf. 14***

Self-Adhesive

1284 A727 1 multi 1.90 1.90

Sold for 70c on day of issue. Portions of design were applied by a thermographic process producing a shiny, raised effect.

Lilium Enchantment A728

2007, Mar. 7 **Litho.**

Booklet Stamp

Self-Adhesive

1285 A728 1 multi 1.90 1.90
a. Booklet pane of 10 19.00

No. 1285 sold for 70c on day of issue.

Souvenir Sheet

Bishop Michael Agricola (1509-57) — A729

No. 1286: a, Text and open book. b, Agricola preaching.

2007, Mar. 7 ***Perf. 13½***

1286 A729 70c Sheet of 2, #a-b 3.75 3.75

Tampere Cathedral, Cent. — A730

2007, May 9 ***Perf. 13¼***

1287 A730 70c multi 1.90 1.90

Europa — A731

No. 1288: a, Scouts on sailboat. b, Scouts around campfire.
Illustration reduced.

2007, May 9 ***Perf. 12½x13***

1288 A731 Horiz. pair 3.80 3.80
a.-b. 70c Either single 1.90 1.90

Scouting, cent.

Helsinki Public Transportation — A732

No. 1289: a, Commuter train in station. b, Tram on street. c, Subway train on bridge. d. People in Kamppi Bus Station.

Serpentine Die Cut 12¼ Horiz.

2007, May 9

Self-Adhesive

1289 Booklet pane of 4 7.75
a.-d. A732 1 Any single 1.90 1.90

Nos. 1289a-1289d each sold for 70c on day of issue.

Moomins A733

No. 1290: a, Little My in water. b, Moomintroll running across rocks. c, Moominpappa at typewriter. d, Snork Maiden picking flowers. e, Moominmamma making pancakes. f, Snufkin amid flowers.

Serpentine Die Cut 11¾ Vert.

2007, May 9 **Photo.**

Self-Adhesive

1290 Booklet pane of 6 11.50
a.-f. A733 1 Any single 1.90 1.90

Nos. 1290a-1290f each sold for 70c on day of issue.

Souvenir Sheet

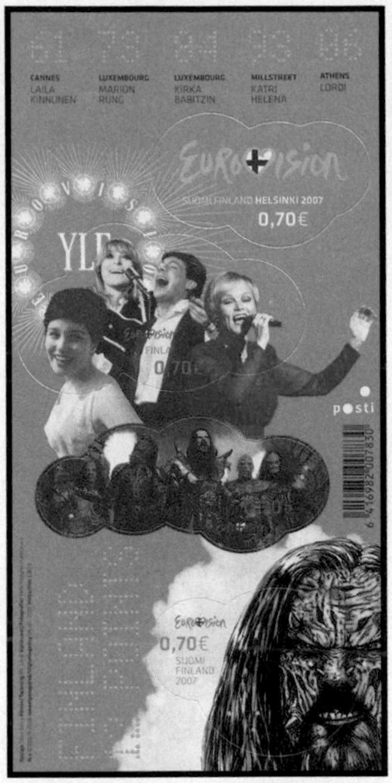

2007 Eurovision Song Contest, Helsinki — A734

No. 1291: a, Eurovision Song Contest emblem. b, Finnish singers Laila Kinnunen, Marion Rung, Kirka Babitzin and Katri Helena. c, 2006 Finnish contest-winning band, Lordi. d, Lead singer of Lordi.

Litho. With Foil Application

2007, May 9 ***Die Cut***

Self-Adhesive

1291 A734 70c Sheet of 4, #a-d 7.75 7.75

A735

Serpentine Die Cut 11½ Syncopated

2007, Aug. 24 **Litho.**

Self-Adhesive

1292 A735 1 multi 1.90 1.90

No. 1292 sold for 70c on day of issue. Design portion of stamp could be personalized.

Home Furnishings — A736

No. 1293 — Picture frame and: a, Empire-style chair, "Porvoo Garland" wallpaper, 19th cent. (country name at LR). b, Paimio chair, "2+3" wallpaper, 20th cent. (country name at LL).

Die Cut Perf. 14

2007, Aug. 24 **Litho.**

Self-Adhesive

1293 Pair 3.80
a.-b. A736 1 Either single 1.90 1.90

Nos. 1293a-1293b each sold for 70c on day of issue.

Raspberries and Raspberry Cake — A737

Die Cut Perf. 14

2007, Aug. 24 **Photo.**

Self-Adhesive

Booklet Stamp

1294 A737 1 multi 1.90 1.90

No. 1294 sold for 70c on day of issue.

Finnish Olympic Committee, Cent. — A738

2007, Aug. 24 **Litho.**

Self-Adhesive

Booklet Stamp

1295 A738 1 multi 1.90 1.90

No. 1295 sold for 70c on day of issue.

Butterflies — A739

No. 1296: a, Apatura iris. b, Scolitantides orion. c, Colias palaeno.

Die Cut Perf. 10 Vert., Syncopated at Right

2007, Aug. 24

Self-Adhesive

Coil Stamps

1296 Vert. strip of 3 5.75
a.-c. A739 1 Any single 1.90 1.90

Nos. 1296a-1296c had a franking value of 70c on day of issue. A roll of 100 stamps sold for €68.

Miniature Sheet

Independence, 90th Anniv. — A740

No. 1297 — Photographs of people at work and play: a, Man and horse hauling wood. b, Girl blowing horn. c, Four boys with skis. d, People at coffee break. e, People near bonfire. f, Boy ski jumping. g, Boy diving. h, Ice fisherman. Nos. 1297a-1297d are black and white photos.

2007, Nov. 2 ***Perf. 13¼***

1297 A740 Sheet of 8 16.50 16.50
a.-h. 70c Any single 2.00 2.00

Souvenir Sheet

Woodwork — A741

No. 1298: a, Zitan armchair with dragon design, China (denomination at left). b, Modern Finnish bowls (denomination at right).

2007, Nov. 2 ***Perf. 13¼x14¼***

1298 A741 Sheet of 2 4.25 4.25
a.-b. 70c Either single 2.00 2.00

See Hong Kong Nos. 1298-1299.

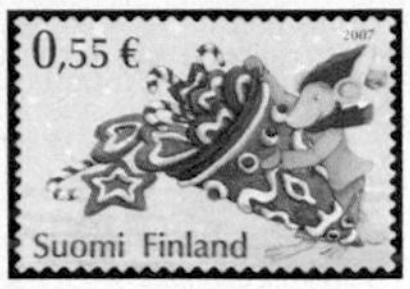

A742

Christmas — A743

Serpentine Die Cut 13¼x13¾

2007, Nov. 2 **Photo.**

Self-Adhesive

1299 A742 55c multi 1.60 1.60

Serpentine Die Cut 13¾x13¼

1300 A743 1 multi 2.00 2.00

No. 1300 sold for 70c on day of issue.

A744 A745

Water — A746

A747 A748

Islands — A749

2008, Jan. 24 **Photo.** ***Die Cut***

Self-Adhesive

1301 Horiz. strip of 3 .45
a. A744 5c multi .20 .20
b. A745 5c multi .20 .20
c. A746 5c multi .20 .20

1302 Horiz. strip of 3 .90
a. A747 10c multi .30 .30
b. A748 10c multi .30 .30
c. A749 10c multi .30 .30

Souvenir Sheet

Helsinki University of Technology, Cent. — A750

No. 1303: a, Robot. b, University building.

2008, Jan. 24 Litho. *Perf. 13½x13¼*

1303	A750	Sheet of 2	4.25	4.25
a.-b.		1 Any single	2.10	2.10

Nos. 1303a-1303b each sold for 70c on day of issue.

Miniature Sheet

Love — A751

No. 1304: a, Airplane pulling heart banner. b, Carrier pigeon with envelope. c, Heart-shaped smoke signals. d, Heart and cell phone. e, Bottle with hearts.

2008, Jan. 24 *Die Cut*

Self-Adhesive

1304	A751	Sheet of 5	10.50	
a.-e.		1 Any single	2.10	2.10

Nos. 1304a-1304e each sold for 70c on day of issue.

Miniature Sheet

Snow Sports — A752

No. 1305: a, Matti Räty in yellow ski suit. b, Antti Autti (snowboarder) in air in red ski suit. c, Tapio Saarimaki in red ski suit. d, Tanja Poutiainen in white and green ski suit.

Litho. With Three-Dimensional Plastic Affixed

Serpentine Die Cut 9 Syncopated

2008, Jan. 24

Self-Adhesive

1305	A752	Sheet of 4	8.50	
a.-d.		1 Any single	2.10	2.10

Nos. 1305a-1305d each sold for 70c on day of issue.

Clock and Lamp on Desk — A753

Die Cut Perf. 13¾

2008, Feb. 27 Litho.

Self-Adhesive

1306	A753	€1.05 multi	3.25	3.25
a.		Booklet pane of 10	32.50	

Finnish Book Publishers Association, 150th Anniv. — A754

Serpentine Die Cut 13¼

2008, Feb. 27

Self-Adhesive

1307	A754	1 multi	2.10	2.10

No. 1307 sold for 70c on day of issue.

Lathyrus Odoratus — A755

Die Cut Perf. 13¾

2008, Feb. 27 Photo.

Self-Adhesive

1308	A755	1 multi	2.10	2.10

No. 1308 sold for 70c on the day of issue and has Braille dots applied by a thermographic process.

Easter — A756

Litho. With Foil Application

Serpentine Die Cut 13¾

2008, Feb. 27

Self-Adhesive

1309	A756	1 multi	2.10	2.10

No. 1309 sold for 70c on day of issue.

Fauna Associated With Weather Forecasting Folk Beliefs — A757

No. 1310: a, Perch. b, Lambs. c, Frogs. d, Swallows. e, Snail.

Serpentine Die Cut 12¼ Horiz.

2008, Feb. 27 Litho.

Self-Adhesive

1310		Booklet pane of 5	10.50	
a.-e.	A757	1 Any single	2.10	2.10

Nos. 1310a-1310e each sold for 70c on day of issue.

Souvenir Sheet

Mythical Places — A758

No. 1311: a, Cliff resembling human face, Astuvansalmi. b, Amber carving of head found at Astuvansalmi.

2008, Mar. 27 *Perf. 13½*

1311	A758	Sheet of 2	4.50	4.50
a.-b.		70c Either single	2.25	2.25

Europa — A759

No. 1312 — Handwritten letters and portraits by Pekka Halonen of: a, Himself. b, His wife, Maija.

2008, May 9 *Perf. 13*

1312	A759	Horiz. pair	4.50	4.50
a.-b.		70c Either single	2.25	2.25

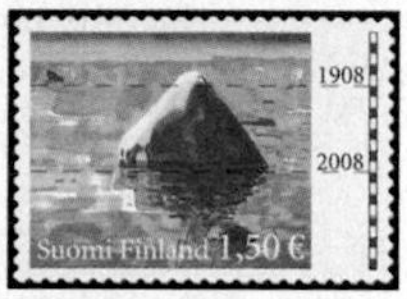

Kvarken Archipelago UNESCO World Heritage Site — A760

Serpentine Die Cut 13¾

2008, May 9

Self-Adhesive

1313	A760	€1.50 blk & red	4.75	4.75

Moths — A761

No. 1314: a, Arctia caja. b, Aglia tau. c. Deilephila elpenor.

Die Cut Perf. 10 Syncopated

2008, May 9 Photo.

Coil Stamps

Self-Adhesive

1314		Vert. strip of 3	6.75	
a.-c.	A761	1 Any single	2.25	2.25

Nos. 1314a-1314c each sold for 70c on day of issue.

Psychedelic Art — A762

No. 1315: a, Melting mushrooms and teardrops. b, Guitars. c, Flying fish. d, Flowers and woman's legs in high heels. e, Six balloons.

Serpentine Die Cut 12½ Horiz.

2008, May 9 Litho.

Self-Adhesive

1315		Booklet pane of 5	11.50	
a.-e.	A762	1 Any single	2.25	2.25

Nos. 1315a-1315e each sold for 70c on day of issue.

Modern Art — A763

No. 1316: a, Sinistä ja Punaista, by Sam Vanni. b, Merirosvolaiva, by Kimmo Kaivanto. c, Hiljaisuuden Kuuntelija, by Juhani Linnovaara. d, Odotan Kevään Tuloa, by Göran Augustson. e, Minä, by Carolus Enckell. f, Pöytä, by Reino Hietanen.

Serpentine Die Cut 11¾ Vert.

2008, May 9

Self-Adhesive

1316		Booklet pane of 6	13.50	
a.-f.	A763	1 Any single	2.25	2.25

Nos. 1316a-1316f each sold for 70c on day of issue.

Personalized Stamp — A764

Serpentine Die Cut 10

2008, Sept. 5 Litho.

Self-Adhesive

1317	A764	1 multi	2.40	2.40

No. 1317 sold for 80c on day of issue. The generic design portion of the stamp shown could be personalized.

Dogs — A765

No. 1318: a, Spitz with open mouth, facing forward. b, Rough collie, with open mouth, facing right. c, Boxer, facing left. d, Finnish hound, facing left. e, Cavalier King Charles spaniel, facing right. f, Jack Russell terrier, looking over shoulder.

Serpentine Die Cut 11¾ Vert.

2008, Sept. 5

Self-Adhesive

1318		Booklet pane of 6	14.50	
a.-f.	A765	1 Any single	2.40	2.40

Nos. 1318a-1318f each sold for 80c on day of issue.

Souvenir Sheet

Mika Waltari (1908-79), Writer — A766

No. 1319: a, Waltari. b, Cover of Waltari's book, *Komisario Palmun Erehyds.*

2008, Sept. 5 *Perf. 14x13½*

1319	A766	Sheet of 2	5.00	5.00
a.-b.		80c Either single	2.40	2.40

Souvenir Sheet

Kimi Räikkönen, 2007 Formula 1 Racing Champion — A767

No. 1320: a, Räikkönen (24x30mm). b, Räikkönen's Ferrari Formula 1 race car (74x30mm).

Die Cut Perf. 11x11½ on 2 Sides (#1320a), 11½ Vert. (#1320b)

2008, Sept. 5

Self-Adhesive

1320 A767 Sheet of 2 5.00 5.00
a.-b. 1 Either single 2.40 2.40

Nos. 1320a-1320b each sold for 80c on day of issue.

Souvenir Sheet

Adolf Erik Nordenskiöld (1832-1901), Arctic Explorer — A768

No. 1321: a, Nordenskiöld (29x34mm). b, Ship Sofia (58x34mm).

Litho. & Engr.

2008, Oct. 20 ***Perf. 13x13¼***

1321 A768 Sheet of 2 4.50 4.50
a.-b. 1 Either single 2.25 2.25

Nos. 1321a-1321b each sold for 80c on day of issue. See Greenland Nos. 527-528.

A769

A770

Christmas A771

Die Cut Perf. 14

2008, Nov. 6 **Litho.**

Self-Adhesive

1322 A769 60c multi 1.60 1.60

Serpentine Die Cut 13¼x13¾

Photo.

1323 A770 1 multi 2.10 2.10

Booklet Stamp

Printed On Plastic

Die Cut Perf. 13¾

1324 A771 1 multi 2.10 2.10
Nos. 1322-1324 (3) 5.80 5.80

On day of issue, Nos. 1323 and 1324 each sold for 80c.

Pres. Martti Ahtisaari, 2008 Nobel Peace Laureate A772

2008, Dec. 10 **Litho.** ***Perf. 13***

1325 A772 80c light blue 2.10 2.10

Hospital Work — A773

2009, Jan. 22 **Litho.** ***Perf. 13***

1326 A773 80c multi 2.25 2.25

Pallas-Yllästunturi National Park — A774

2009, Jan. 22 ***Die Cut Perf. 14***

Self-Adhesive

1327 A774 1 multi 2.25 2.25

No. 1327 sold for 80c on day of issue and has Braille dots applied in varnish.

Peony — A775

Die Cut Perf. 14

2009, Jan. 22 **Photo.**

Self-Adhesive

1328 A775 €1.10 multi 3.00 3.00

Children's Dream Occupations A776

No. 1329 — Child dressed as: a, Policeman. b, Doctor. c, Firefighter. d, Skier. e, Construction worker.

Serpentine Die Cut 12¼ Vert.

2009, Jan. 22 **Litho.**

Self-Adhesive

1329 Booklet pane of 5 11.50
a.-e. A776 1 Any single 2.25 2.25

Nos. 1329a-1329e each sold for 80c on day of issue.

Miniature Sheet

Finland as Grand Duchy of Russia, 200th Anniv. — A777

No. 1330: a, Tsar Alexander I (1777-1825), facing left with blue sash. b, Count Georg Magnus Sprengtporten (1740-1819), with red sash and gold epaulets. c, Count Carl Erik Mannerheim (1759-1837), without epaulets. d, Count Gustaf Mauritz Armfelt (1757-1814), facing right, with blue sash. Names are on sheet margin.

Litho. & Embossed With Foil Application

2009, Jan. 22 ***Perf. 13¾***

1330 A777 80c Sheet of 4, #a-d 9.00 9.00

Miniature Sheet

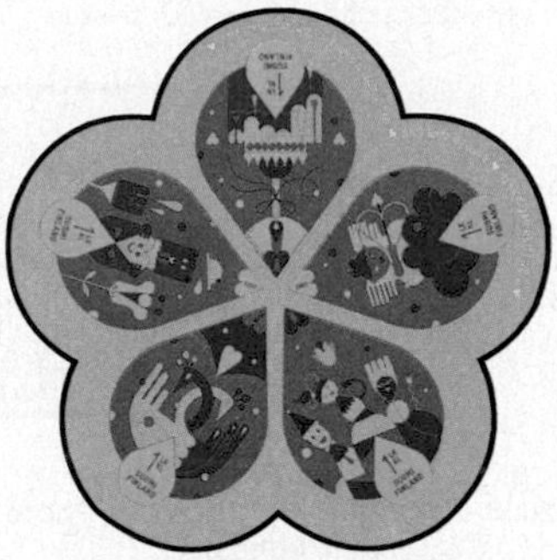

St. Valentine's Day — A778

No. 1331: a, Birthday cake and candle. b, Cupid. c, Three people, flower. d, Swans. e, Teddy bear hugging heart.

2009, Jan. 22 **Litho.** ***Die Cut***

Self-Adhesive

1331 A778 1 Sheet of 5, #a-e 11.50 11.50

Nos. 1331a-1331e each sold for 80c on day of issue.

SEMI-POSTAL STAMPS

Arms — SP1

Unwmk.

1922, May 15 **Typo.** ***Perf. 14***

B1 SP1 1m + 50p gray & red .80 *8.50*
Never hinged 1.75
a. Perf. 13x13½ 8.00
Never hinged 12.00

Red Cross Standard SP2

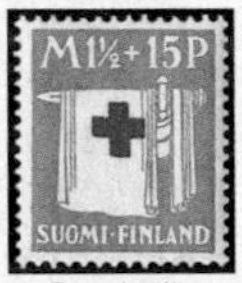

Symbolic SP3

Ship of Mercy — SP4

1930, Feb. 6

B2 SP2 1m + 10p red org & red 1.75 *9.00*
B3 SP3 1½m + 15p grysh grn & red 1.50 *9.00*
B4 SP4 2m + 20p dk bl & red 3.75 *42.50*
Nos. B2-B4 (3) 7.00 *60.50*
Set, never hinged 10.00

The surtax on this and subsequent similar issues was for the benefit of the Red Cross Society of Finland.

Church in Hattula — SP5

SP8

Designs: 1½m+15p, Castle of Hameenlinna. 2m+20p, Fortress of Viipuri.

1931, Jan. 1 **Engr.**

Cross in Red

B5 SP5 1m + 10p gray grn 1.60 *11.00*
B6 SP5 1½m + 15p lil brn 9.00 *14.00*
B7 SP5 2m + 20p dull bl 1.60 *30.00*
Nos. B5-B7 (3) 12.20 *55.00*
Set, never hinged 30.00

1931, Oct. 15 **Typo.** ***Rouletted 4, 5***

B8 SP8 1m + 4m black 15.00 *30.00*
Never hinged 22.50

The surtax was to assist the Postal Museum of Finland in purchasing the Richard Granberg collection of entire envelopes.

Helsinki University Library — SP9

Nikolai Church at Helsinki — SP10

2½m+25p, Parliament Building, Helsinki.

1932, Jan. 1 ***Perf. 14***

B9 SP9 1¼m + 10p ol bis & red 1.60 *11.00*
B10 SP10 2m + 20p dp vio & red .75 *7.00*
B11 SP9 2½m + 25p lt blue & red 1.25 *27.50*
Nos. B9-B11 (3) 3.60 *45.50*
Set, never hinged 7.00

Bishop Magnus Tawast SP12

Michael Agricola SP13

Design: 2½m+25p, Isacus Rothovius.

1933, Jan. 20 **Engr.**

B12 SP12 1¼m + 10p blk brn & red 2.75 *9.50*
B13 SP13 2m + 20p brn vio & red .75 *3.50*
B14 SP13 2½m + 25p indigo & red .80 *6.00*
Nos. B12-B14 (3) 4.30 *19.00*
Set, never hinged 8.50

Evert Horn — SP15

Designs: 2m+20p, Torsten Stalhandske. 2½m+25p, Jakob (Lazy Jake) de la Gardie.

1934, Jan.

Cross in Red

B15 SP15 1¼m + 10p brown .80 *3.00*
B16 SP15 2m + 20p gray lil 1.40 *5.00*
B17 SP15 2½m + 25p gray .80 *3.50*
Nos. B15-B17 (3) 3.00 *11.50*
Set, never hinged 4.75

Mathias Calonius SP18

Robert Henrik Rehbinder SP21

Designs: 2m+20p, Henrik C. Porthan. 2½m+25p, Anders Chydenius.

1935, Jan. 1

Cross in Red

B18 SP18 1¼m + 15p brown .80 *2.75*
B19 SP18 2m + 20p gray lil 1.75 *5.00*
B20 SP18 2½m + 25p gray bl .65 *3.00*
Nos. B18-B20 (3) 3.20 *10.75*
Set, never hinged 4.75

1936, Jan. 1

2m+20p, Count Gustaf Mauritz Armfelt. 2½m+25p, Count Arvid Bernard Horn.

Cross in Red

B21 SP21 1¼m + 15p dk brn .65 *2.75*
B22 SP21 2m + 20p vio brn 2.75 *6.50*
B23 SP21 2½m + 25p blue .65 *3.00*
Nos. B21-B23 (3) 4.05 *12.25*
Set, never hinged 8.00

Type "Uusimaa" SP24

Type "Turunmaa" — SP25

Design: 3½m+35p, Type "Hameenmaa."

1937, Jan. 1

Cross in Red

B24 SP24 1¼m + 15p brown .65 *2.50*
B25 SP24 2m + 20p brn lake 12.00 7.00
B26 SP24 3½m + 35p indigo .65 *3.00*
Nos. B24-B26 (3) 13.30 12.50
Set, never hinged 37.50

Aukuste Makipeska SP27

Skiing SP31

Designs: 1¼m+15p, Robert Isidor Orn. 2m+20p, Edward Bergenheim. 3½m+35p, Johan Mauritz Nordenstam.

1938, Jan. 5 **Engr.**

Cross in Red

B27 SP27 50p + 5p dk grn .50 *1.25*
B28 SP27 1¼m + 15p dk brn .90 *2.50*
B29 SP27 2m + 20p rose lake 6.75 6.75
B30 SP27 3½m + 35p dk blue .60 *2.75*
Nos. B27-B30 (4) 8.75 *13.25*
Set, never hinged 17.50

1938, Jan. 18

Designs: #B32, Skijumper. #B33, Skier.

B31 SP31 1.25m + 75p sl grn 3.00 *11.00*
B32 SP31 2m + 1m dk car 3.00 *11.00*
B33 SP31 3.50m + 1.50m dk blue 3.00 *11.00*
Nos. B31-B33 (3) 9.00 *33.00*
Set, never hinged 17.50

Ski championships held at Lahti.

Soldier — SP34

Battlefield at Solferino SP35

1938, May 16

B34 SP34 2m + ½m blue 1.25 *4.00*
Never hinged 3.25

Victory of the White Army over the Red Guards. The surtax was for the benefit of the members of the Union of the Finnish Front.

1939, Jan. 2

Cross in Scarlet

B35 SP35 50p + 5p dk grn .65 *1.40*
B36 SP35 1¼m + 15p dk brn .75 *2.25*
B37 SP35 2m + 20p lake 11.00 *11.00*
B38 SP35 3½m + 35p dk bl .65 *2.50*
Nos. B35-B38 (4) 13.05 17.15
Set, never hinged 30.00

Intl. Red Cross Soc., 75th anniv.

Catalogue values for unused stamps in this section, from this point to the end of the section, are for Never Hinged items.

Soldiers with Crossbows SP36

Arms of Finland SP40

1¼m+15p, Cavalryman. 2m+20p, Soldier of Charles XII of Sweden. 3½m+35p, Officer and soldier of War with Russia, 1808-1809.

1940, Jan. 3

Cross in Red

B39 SP36 50p + 5p dk grn 1.10 *1.60*
B40 SP36 1¼m + 15p dk brn 2.25 *2.40*
B41 SP36 2m + 20p lake 4.00 2.75
B42 SP36 3½m + 35p dp ultra 3.00 *3.75*
Nos. B39-B42 (4) 10.35 10.50

The surtax aided the Finnish Red Cross.

1940, Feb. 15 **Litho.**

B43 SP40 2m +2m indigo .50 *1.25*

The surtax was given to a fund for the preservation of neutrality.

Mason SP41

Soldier's Emblem SP45

1.75m+15p, Farmer plowing. 2.75m+25p, Mother and child. 3.50m+35p, Finnish flag.

1941, Jan. 2 **Engr.**

Cross in Red

B44 SP41 50p + 5p green .55 *.70*
B45 SP41 1.75m + 15p brown 1.40 *2.00*
B46 SP41 2.75m + 25p brn car 7.00 *8.00*
B47 SP41 3.50m + 35p dp ultra 1.60 *2.75*
Nos. B44-B47 (4) 10.55 13.45

See Nos. B65-B68.

1941, May 24 **Unwmk.**

B48 SP45 2.75m + 25p brt ultra .80 .80

The surtax was for the aid of the soldiers who fought in the Russo-Finnish War.

Aland Arms — SP46

Lapland Arms — SP51

Coats of Arms: 1.75m+15p, Nyland. 2.75m+25p, Finland's first arms. 3.50m+35p, Karelia. 4.75m+45p, Satakunta.

1942, Jan. 2 ***Perf. 14***

Cross in Red

B49 SP46 50p + 5p green 1.25 1.25
B50 SP46 1.75m + 15p brown 1.40 *2.25*
B51 SP46 2.75m + 25p dark red 1.40 *2.25*
B52 SP46 3.50m + 35p deep ultra 1.40 *2.25*
B53 SP46 4.75m + 45p dk sl grn 1.10 *2.75*
Nos. B49-B53 (5) 6.55 *10.75*

The surtax aided the Finnish Red Cross.

1943, Jan. 6 **Inscribed "1943"**

Coats of Arms: 2m+20p, Hame. 3.50m+35p, Eastern Bothnia. 4.50m+45p, Savo.

Cross in Red

B54 SP51 50p + 5p green .40 *1.00*
B55 SP51 2m + 20p brown 1.00 *2.00*
B56 SP51 3.50m + 35p dark red 1.00 *2.00*
B57 SP51 4.50m + 45p brt ultra 2.25 *5.50*
Nos. B54-B57 (4) 4.65 *10.50*

The surtax aided the Finnish Red Cross.

Soldier's Helmet and Sword — SP55

Mother and Children — SP56

1943, Feb. 1 ***Perf. 13***

B58 SP55 2m + 50p dk brown .50 *.85*
B59 SP56 3.50m + 1m brown red .50 *.85*

The surtax was for national welfare.

Red Cross Train — SP57

2m+50p, Ambulance. 3.50m+75p, Red Cross Hospital, Helsinki. 4.50m+1m, Hospital plane.

1944, Jan. 2 ***Perf. 14***

Cross in Red

B60 SP57 50p + 25p green .30 .30
B61 SP57 2m + 50p sepia .50 *.80*
B62 SP57 3.50m + 75p ver .50 *.80*
B63 SP57 4.50m + 1m brt ultra 1.10 *2.75*
Nos. B60-B63 (4) 2.40 *4.65*

The surtax aided the Finnish Red Cross.

Symbols of Peace SP61

Wrestling SP62

1944, Dec. 1

B64 SP61 3.50m + 1.50m dk red brn .40 *.85*

The surtax was for national welfare.

Type of 1941 Inscribed "1945"

1945, May 2 **Photo. & Engr.**

Cross in Red

B65 SP41 1m + 25p green .20 *.50*
B66 SP41 2m + 50p brown .20 *.65*
B67 SP41 3.50m + 75p brn car .20 *.65*
B68 SP41 4.50m + 1m dp ultra .60 *1.25*
Nos. B65-B68 (4) 1.20 3.05

The surtax was for the Finnish Red Cross.

1945, Apr. 16 **Engr.** ***Perf. 13½***

2m+1m, Gymnast. 3.50m+1.75m, Runner. 4.50m+2.25m, Skier. 7m+3.50m, Javelin thrower.

B69 SP62 1m + 50p bluish grn .20 *.80*
B70 SP62 2m + 1m dp red .20 *.80*
B71 SP62 3.50m + 1.75m dull vio .20 *.80*
B72 SP62 4.50m + 2.25m ultra .50 *1.00*
B73 SP62 7m + 3.50m dull brn .80 *2.00*
Nos. B69-B73 (5) 1.90 5.40

Fishing SP67

Nurse and Children SP71

Designs: 3m+75p, Churning. 5m+1.25m, Reaping. 10m+2.50m, Logging.

Engraved; Cross Typo. in Red

1946, Jan. 7

B74 SP67 1m + 25p dull grn .40 *.60*
B75 SP67 3m + 75p lilac brn .30 *.40*
B76 SP67 5m + 1.25m rose red .40 *.60*
a. Red cross omitted *650.00*
B77 SP67 10m + 2.50m ultra .50 *1.10*
Nos. B74-B77 (4) 1.60 *2.70*

The surtax was for the Finnish Red Cross.

1946, Sept. 2 **Engr.**

Design: 8m+2m, Doctor examining infant.

B78 SP71 5m + 1m green .40 *.60*
B79 SP71 8m + 2m brown vio .40 *.60*

The surtax was for the prevention of tuberculosis.

Nos. B78 and B79 Surcharged with New Values in Black

1947, Apr. 1

B80 SP71 6m + 1m on 5m + 1m .40 *.70*
B81 SP71 10m + 2m on 8m + 2m .40 *.70*

The surtax was for the prevention of tuberculosis.

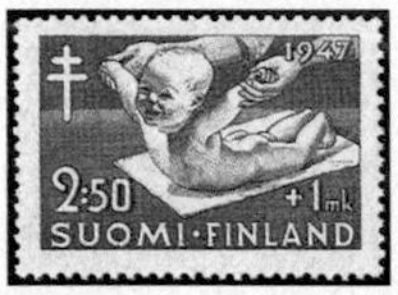

SP73

Medical Examination of Infants — SP74

Designs: 10m+2.50m, Infant held by the feet. 12m+3m, Mme. Alli Paasikivi and a child. 20m+5m, Infant standing.

1947, Sept. 15 **Engr.**

B82 SP73 2.50m + 1m green .50 *1.00*
B83 SP74 6m + 1.50m dk red .60 *1.50*
B84 SP74 10m + 2.50m red brn .70 *1.50*
B85 SP73 12m + 3m dp blue 1.10 *2.10*
B86 SP74 20m + 5m dk red vio 1.50 *3.25*
Nos. B82-B86 (5) 4.40 *9.35*

The surtax was for the prevention of tuberculosis.

For surcharges see Nos. B91-B93.

Zachris Topelius — SP78

7m+2m, Fredrik Pacius. 12m+3m, Johan L. Runeberg. 20m+5m, Fredrik Cygnaeus.

Engraved; Cross Typo. in Red

1948, May 10 **Unwmk.** ***Perf. 14***

B87 SP78 3m + 1m green .50 *.80*
B88 SP78 7m + 2m rose red .60 *.85*
B89 SP78 12m + 3m brt blue .65 *.95*
B90 SP78 20m + 5m dk vio .75 *1.25*
Nos. B87-B90 (4) 2.50 3.85

The surtax was for the Finnish Red Cross.

Nos. B83, B84 and B86 Surcharged with New Values and Bars in Black

1948, Sept. 13 **Engr.** ***Perf. 13½***

B91 SP74 7m + 2m on #B83 1.40 *3.00*
B92 SP74 15m + 3m on #B84 1.40 *3.00*
B93 SP74 24m + 6m on #B86 2.00 *3.75*
Nos. B91-B93 (3) 4.80 9.75

The surtax was for the prevention of tuberculosis.

Tying Birch Boughs SP79

Wood Anemone SP83

9m+3m, Bathers in Sauna house. 15m+5m, Rural bath house. 30m+10m, Cold plunge in lake.

Engraved; Cross Typo. in Red

1949, May 5 ***Perf. 13½x14***

B94 SP79 5m + 2m dull grn .45 *.75*
B95 SP79 9m + 3m dk car .70 *1.10*
B96 SP79 15m + 5m dp blue .70 *1.10*
B97 SP79 30m + 10m dk vio brn 1.90 *3.25*
Nos. B94-B97 (4) 3.75 6.20

The surtax was for the Finnish Red Cross.

1949, June 2 **Engr.**

Inscribed: "1949"

B98 SP83 5m + 2m shown .60 *.85*
B99 SP83 9m + 3m Wild rose .65 *1.00*
B100 SP83 15m + 5m Coltsfoot .75 *1.50*
Nos. B98-B100 (3) 2.00 3.35

The surtax was for the prevention of tuberculosis.

Similar to Type of 1949

Designs: 5m+2m, Water lily. 9m+3m, Pasqueflower. 15m+5m, Bell flower cluster.

1950, Apr. 1

Inscribed: "1950"

B101 SP83 5m + 2m emer 2.25 2.25
B102 SP83 9m + 3m rose car 2.10 2.10
B103 SP83 15m + 5m blue 2.10 2.10
Nos. B101-B103 (3) 6.45 6.45

The surtax was for the prevention of tuberculosis.

Hospital Entrance, Helsinki SP84

Blood Donor's Medal SP86

Design: 12m+3m, Giving blood.

Engraved; Cross Typo. in Red

1951, Mar. 17 **Unwmk.** ***Perf. 14***

B104 SP84 7m + 2m chocolate 1.10 *1.50*
B105 SP84 12m + 3m bl vio 1.10 *1.50*
B106 SP86 20m + 5m car 2.00 *3.00*
Nos. B104-B106 (3) 4.20 *6.00*

The surtax was for the Finnish Red Cross.

Capercaillie — SP87

Designs: 12m+3m, European cranes. 20m+5m, Caspian terns.

1951, Oct. 26 **Engr.**

B107 SP87 7m + 2m dk grn 1.90 *2.50*
B108 SP87 12m + 3m rose brn 1.90 *2.50*
B109 SP87 20m + 5m blue 1.90 *2.50*
Nos. B107-B109 (3) 5.70 *7.50*

The surtax was for the prevention of tuberculosis.

Diver — SP88

Soccer Players SP89

#B112, Stadum, Helsinki. #B113, Runners.

1951-52

B110 SP88 12m + 2m rose car 1.10 *1.60*
B111 SP89 15m + 2m grn ('52) 1.10 *1.60*
B112 SP88 20m + 3m deep blue 1.10 *1.60*
B113 SP89 25m + 4m brn ('52) 1.10 *1.60*
Nos. B110-B113 (4) 4.40 *6.40*

XV Olympic Games, Helsinki, 1952. The surtax was to help finance the games.

Issued: B110, B112, 11/16; B111, B113, 2/15/52.

Margin blocks of four of each denomination were cut from regular or perf-through-margin sheets and pasted by the selvage, overlapping, in a printed folder to create a kind of souvenir booklet. Value $60.

Field Marshal Mannerheim SP90

Great Titmouse SP91

Engraved; Cross Typo. in Red

1952, Mar. 4

B114 SP90 10m + 2m gray 1.50 *2.10*
B115 SP90 15m + 3m rose vio 1.50 *2.10*
B116 SP90 25m + 5m blue 1.50 *2.10*
Nos. B114-B116 (3) 4.50 *6.30*

The surtax was for the Red Cross.

1952, Dec. 4 **Engr.**

Designs: 15m+3m, Spotted flycatchers and nest. 25m+5m, Swift.

B117 SP91 10m + 2m green 2.00 *2.50*
B118 SP91 15m + 3m plum 2.00 *2.50*
B119 SP91 25m + 5m deep blue 2.00 *2.50*
Nos. B117-B119 (3) 6.00 *7.50*

The surtax was for the prevention of tuberculosis.

European Red Squirrel SP92

#B121, Brown bear. #B122, European elk.

Unwmk.

1953, Nov. 16 **Engr.** ***Perf. 14***

B120 SP92 10m + 2m red brown 2.25 *2.50*
B121 SP92 15m + 3m violet 2.25 *2.50*
B122 SP92 25m + 5m dark grn 2.25 *2.50*
Nos. B120-B122 (3) 6.75 *7.50*

Surtax for the prevention of tuberculosis.

Children Receiving Parcel from Welfare Worker — SP93

Designs: 15m+3m, Aged woman knitting. 25m+5m, Blind basket-maker and dog.

Engraved; Cross Typo. in Red

1954, Mar. 8 ***Perf. 11½***

B123 SP93 10m + 2m dk ol grn 1.25 *1.40*
B124 SP93 15m + 3m dk blue 1.40 *1.75*
B125 SP93 25m + 5m dk brown 1.40 *1.75*
Nos. B123-B125 (3) 4.05 *4.90*

The surtax was for the Finnish Red Cross.

Bumblebees, Dandelions — SP94

European Perch — SP95

15m+3m, Butterfly. 25m+5m, Dragonfly.

Engraved; Cross Typo. in Red

1954, Dec. 7 ***Perf. 14***

B126 SP94 10m + 2m brown 2.00 1.40
B127 SP94 15m + 3m carmine 2.00 1.60
B128 SP94 25m + 5m blue 2.00 1.60
Nos. B126-B128 (3) 6.00 4.60

The surtax was for the prevention of tuberculosis.

Engraved; Cross Typo. in Red

1955, Sept. 26 ***Perf. 14***

Designs: 15m+3m, Northern pike. 25m+5m, Atlantic salmon.

B129 SP95 10m + 2m dl grn 2.00 1.40
B130 SP95 15m + 3m vio brn 2.00 1.60
B131 SP95 25m + 5m dk bl 2.00 1.60
Nos. B129-B131 (3) 6.00 4.60

Surtax for the Anti-Tuberculosis Society.

Gen. von Dobeln in Battle of Juthas, 1808 SP96

Waxwing SP97

Illustrations by Albert Edelfelter from J. L. Runeberg's "Tales of Ensign Stal": 15m+3m, Col. J. Z. Duncker holding flag. 25m+5m, Son of fallen Soldier.

Engraved; Cross Typo. in Red

1955, Nov. 24

B132 SP96 10m + 2m dp ultra 1.25 1.25
B133 SP96 15m + 3m dk red brn 1.50 1.50
B134 SP96 25m + 5m green 1.50 1.50
Nos. B132-B134 (3) 4.25 4.25

The surtax was for the Red Cross.

Engraved; Cross Typo. in Red

1956, Sept. 25 ***Perf. 11½***

Birds: 20m+3m, Eagle owl. 30m+5m, Mute swan.

B135 SP97 10m + 2m dl red brn 1.90 1.25
B136 SP97 20m + 3m bl grn 2.10 1.75
B137 SP97 30m + 5m blue 2.10 1.90
Nos. B135-B137 (3) 6.10 4.90

Surtax for the Anti-Tuberculosis Society.

Pekka Aulin SP98

Wolverine (Glutton) SP99

Portraits: 10m+2m, Leonard von Pfaler. 20m+3m, Gustaf Johansson. 30m+5m, Viktor Magnus von Born.

Engraved; Cross Typo. in Red

1956, Nov. 26 **Unwmk.**

B138	SP98	5m + 1m grysh grn	.80	.75
B139	SP98	10m + 2m brown	1.40	1.40
B140	SP98	20m + 3m magenta	2.00	2.00
B141	SP98	30m + 5m lt ultra	2.00	2.00
		Nos. B138-B141 (4)	6.20	6.15

The surtax was for the Red Cross.

Engraved; Cross Typo. in Red

1957, Sept. 5 ***Perf. 11½***

20m+3m, Lynx. 30m+5m, Reindeer.

B142	SP99	10m + 2m dull purple	1.75	1.40
B143	SP99	20m + 3m sepia	1.90	1.75
B144	SP99	30m + 5m dark blue	2.00	1.75
		Nos. B142-B144 (3)	5.65	4.90

The surtax was for the Anti-Tuberculosis Society. See Nos. B160-B165.

Red Cross Flag SP100

Raspberry SP101

1957, Nov. 25 **Engr.** ***Perf. 14***

Cross in Red

B145	SP100	10m + 2m ol grn	1.75	1.50
B146	SP100	20m + 3m maroon	1.75	1.50
B147	SP100	30m + 5m dull blue	1.75	1.50
		Nos. B145-B147 (3)	5.25	4.50

80th anniv. of the Finnish Red Cross.

Type of 1952

Flowers: 10m+2m, Lily of the Valley. 20m+3m, Red clover. 30m+5m, Hepatica.

Engraved; Cross Typo. in Red

1958, May 5 **Unwmk.** ***Perf. 14***

B148	SP91	10m + 2m green	1.75	1.25
B149	SP91	20m + 3m lilac rose	2.25	1.60
B150	SP91	30m + 5m ultra	2.25	1.60
		Nos. B148-B150 (3)	6.25	4.45

Surtax for the Anti-Tuberculosis Society.

Engraved; Cross Typo. in Red

1958, Nov. 20 ***Perf. 11½***

20m+3m, Cowberry. 30m+5m, Blueberry.

B151	SP101	10m + 2m orange	1.25	1.00
B152	SP101	20m + 3m red	1.75	1.40
B153	SP101	30m + 5m dk blue	1.75	1.40
		Nos. B151-B153 (3)	4.75	3.80

The surtax was for the Red Cross.

Daisy — SP102

Reindeer SP103

20m+5m, Primrose. 30m+5m, Cornflower.

Engraved; Cross Typo. in Red

1959, Sept. 7 **Unwmk.**

B154	SP102	10m + 2m green	2.50	1.75
B155	SP102	20m + 3m lt brown	3.50	2.25
B156	SP102	30m + 5m blue	3.50	2.25
		Nos. B154-B156 (3)	9.50	6.25

Surtax for the Anti-Tuberculosis Society.

Engraved; Cross Typo. in Red

1960, Nov. 24 ***Perf. 11½***

#B158, Lapp & lasso. #B159, Mountains.

B157	SP103	10m + 2m dk gray	1.40	1.40
B158	SP103	20m + 3m gray vio	2.00	1.75
B159	SP103	30m + 5m rose vio	2.00	1.75
		Nos. B157-B159 (3)	5.40	4.90

The surtax was for the Red Cross.

Animal Type of 1957

Designs: 10m+2m, Muskrat. 20m+3m, Otter. 30m+5m, Seal.

Engr.; Cross at right, Typo. in Red

1961, Sept. 4

B160	SP99	10m + 2m brn car	1.75	1.50
B161	SP99	20m + 3m slate bl	2.25	2.00
B162	SP99	30m + 5m bl grn	2.25	2.00
		Nos. B160-B162 (3)	6.25	5.50

Surtax for the Anti-Tuberculosis Society.

Animal Type of 1957.

Designs: 10m+2m, Hare. 20m+3m, Pine marten. 30m+5m, Ermine.

Engraved; Cross Typo. in Red

1962, Oct. 1

B163	SP99	10m + 2m gray	2.00	1.25
B164	SP99	20m + 3m dl red brn	2.50	1.75
B165	SP99	30m + 5m vio bl	2.50	1.75
		Nos. B163-B165 (3)	7.00	4.75

The surtax was for the Anti-Tuberculosis Society.

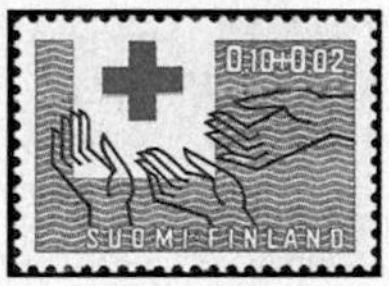

Cross and Outstretched Hands SP104

Engraved; Cross Typo. in Red

1963, May 8 **Unwmk.** ***Perf. 11½***

B166	SP104	10p + 2p red brn	.90	.90
B167	SP104	20p + 3p violet	1.10	1.10
B168	SP104	30p + 5p green	1.10	1.10
		Nos. B166-B168 (3)	3.10	3.10

The surtax was for the Red Cross.

Attending the Wounded SP105

Red Cross Activities: 25p+4p, Hospital ship. 35p+5p, Prisoner-of-war health examination. 40p+7p, Gift parcel distribution.

Engraved; Cross Typo. in Red

1964, May 26 ***Perf. 11½***

B169	SP105	15p + 3p vio bl	.75	.75
B170	SP105	25p + 4p green	1.00	.85
B171	SP105	35p + 5p vio brn	1.00	.85
B172	SP105	40p + 7p dk ol grn	1.00	.85
		Nos. B169-B172 (4)	3.75	3.30

The surtax was for the Red Cross.

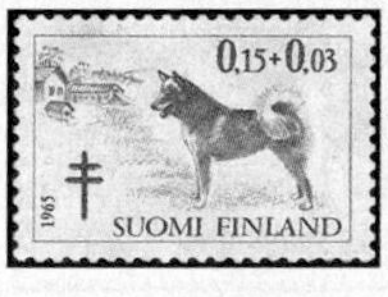

Finnish Spitz — SP106

Artificial Respiration — SP107

Designs: 25p+4p, Karelian bear dog. 35p+5p, Finnish hunting dog.

Engraved; Cross Typo. in Red

1965, May 10 ***Perf. 11½***

B173	SP106	15p + 3p org brn	2.00	1.40
B174	SP106	25p + 4p black	2.25	1.75
B175	SP106	35p + 5p gray brn	2.25	1.75
		Nos. B173-B175 (3)	6.50	4.90

Surtax for Anti-Tuberculosis Society.

1966, May 7 **Litho.** ***Perf. 14***

First Aid: 25p+4p, Skin diver rescuing occupants of submerged car. 35p+5p, Helicopter rescue in winter.

B176	SP107	15p + 3p multi	1.00	.90
B177	SP107	25p + 4p multi	1.00	.90
B178	SP107	35p + 5p multi	1.00	.90
		Nos. B176-B178 (3)	3.00	2.70

The surtax was for the Red Cross.

Birch — SP108

Horse-drawn Ambulance SP109

Trees: 25p+4p, Pine. 40p+7p, Spruce.

1967, May 12 **Litho.** ***Perf. 14***

B179	SP108	20p + 3p multi	.75	.75
B180	SP108	25p + 4p multi	.75	.75
B181	SP108	40p + 7p multi	.75	.75
		Nos. B179-B181 (3)	2.25	2.25

Surtax for Anti-Tuberculosis Society. See Nos. B185-B187.

1967, Nov. 24 **Litho.** ***Perf. 14***

25p+4p, Ambulance, 1967. 40p+7p, Red Cross.

Cross in Red

B182	SP109	20p + 3p dl yel, grn & blk	.75	.75
B183	SP109	25p + 4p vio & blk	.75	.75
B184	SP109	40p + 7p dk grn, blk & dk ol	.75	.75
		Nos. B182-B184 (3)	2.25	2.25

The surtax was for the Red Cross.

Tree Type of 1967

Trees: 20p+3p, Juniper. 25+4p, Aspen. 40p+7p, Chokecherry.

1969, May 12 **Litho.** ***Perf. 14***

B185	SP108	20p + 3p multi	.75	.75
B186	SP108	25p + 4p multi	.75	.75
B187	SP108	40p + 7p multi	.75	.75
		Nos. B185-B187 (3)	2.25	2.25

Surtax for Anti-Tuberculosis Society.

"On the Lapp's Magic Rock" SP110

Designs: 30p+6p, Juhani blowing horn on Impivaara Rock, vert. 50p+10p, The Pale Maiden. The designs are from illustrations by Askeli Gallen-Kallelas for "The Seven Brothers" by Aleksis Kivi.

1970, May 8 **Litho.** ***Perf. 14***

B188	SP110	25p + 5p multi	.70	.60
B189	SP110	30p + 6p multi	.70	.60
B190	SP110	50p + 10p multi	.70	.60
		Nos. B188-B190 (3)	2.10	1.80

The surtax was for the Red Cross.

Cutting and Loading Timber SP111

Designs: 30p+6p, Floating logs downstream. 50p+10p, Sorting logs at sawmill.

1971, Apr. 25 **Litho.** ***Perf. 14***

B191	SP111	25p + 5p multi	.70	.60
B192	SP111	30p + 6p multi	.70	.60
B193	SP111	50p + 10p multi	.70	.60
		Nos. B191-B193 (3)	2.10	1.80

Surtax for Anti-Tuberculosis Society.

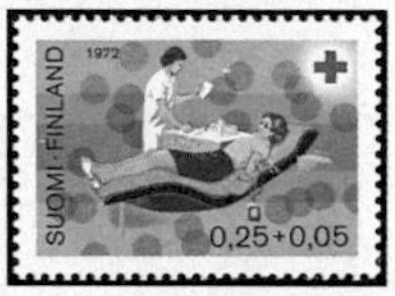

Blood Donor and Nurse SP112

30p+6p, Blood research (microscope, slides), vert. 50p+10p, Blood transfusion.

1972, Oct. 23

B194	SP112	25p + 5p multi	.65	.65
B195	SP112	30p + 6p multi	.65	.65
B196	SP112	50p + 10p multi	.65	.65
		Nos. B194-B196 (3)	1.95	1.95

Surtax was for the Red Cross.

Girl with Lamb, by Hugo Simberg — SP113

Paintings: 40p+10p, Summer Evening, by Vilho Sjöström. 60p+15p, Woman at Mountain Fountain, by Juho Rissanen.

1973, Sept. 12 **Litho.** ***Perf. 13x12½***

B197	SP113	30p + 5p multi	.90	.90
B198	SP113	40p + 10p multi	1.40	1.40
B199	SP113	60p + 15p multi	1.40	1.40
		Nos. B197-B199 (3)	3.70	3.70

Surtax for the Finnish Anti-Tuberculosis Assoc. Birth centenaries of featured artists.

Morel SP114

Mushrooms: 50p+10p, Chanterelle. 60p+15p, Boletus edulis.

1974, Sept. 24 **Litho.** ***Perf. 12½x13***

B200	SP114	35p + 5p multi	1.75	1.25
B201	SP114	50p + 10p multi	1.75	1.25
B202	SP114	60p + 15p multi	1.75	1.25
		Nos. B200-B202 (3)	5.25	3.75

Finnish Red Cross.

Echo, by Ellen Thesleff (1869-1954) SP115

Paintings: 60p+15p, Hilda Wiik, by Maria Wiik (1853-1928). 70p+20p, At Home (old woman in chair), by Helene Schjerfbeck (1862-1946).

1975, Sept. 30 Litho. ***Perf. 13x12½***
B203 SP115 40p + 10p multi .80 .75
B204 SP115 60p + 15p multi 1.10 1.00
B205 SP115 70p + 20p multi 1.10 1.00
Nos. B203-B205 (3) 3.00 2.75

Finnish Red Cross. In honor of International Women's Year paintings by women artists were chosen.

Disabled Veterans' Emblem SP116

Lithographed and Photogravure
1976, Jan. 15 ***Perf. 14***
B206 SP116 70p + 30p multi 1.00 .95

The surtax was for hospitals for disabled war veterans.

Wedding Procession SP117

Designs: 70p+15p, Wedding dance, vert. 80p+20p, Bride, groom, matron and pastor at wedding dinner.

1976, Sept. 15 Litho. ***Perf. 13***
B207 SP117 50p + 10p multi .55 .55
B208 SP117 70p + 15p multi .70 .70
B209 SP117 80p + 20p multi .75 .75
Nos. B207-B209 (3) 2.00 2.00

Surtax for Anti-Tuberculosis Society.

Disaster Relief SP118

Designs: 80p+15p, Community work. 90p+20p, Blood transfusion service.

1977, Jan. 19 Litho. ***Perf. 14***
B210 SP118 50p + 10p multi .50 .50
B211 SP118 80p + 15p multi .70 .70
B212 SP118 90p + 20p multi .70 .70
Nos. B210-B212 (3) 1.90 1.90

Finnish Red Cross centenary.

Long-distance Skiing SP119

Design: 1m+50p, Ski jump.

1977, Oct. 5 Litho. ***Perf. 13***
B213 SP119 80p + 40p multi 2.50 2.50
B214 SP119 1m + 50p multi 1.50 1.50

Surtax was for World Ski Championships, Lahti, Feb. 17-26, 1978.

Saffron Milkcap SP120

Edible Mushrooms: 80p+15p, Parasol, vert. 1m+20p, Gypsy.

1978, Sept. 13 Litho. ***Perf. 13***
B215 SP120 50p + 10p multi 1.00 .80
B216 SP120 80p + 15p multi 1.25 1.25
B217 SP120 1m + 20p multi 1.25 1.25
Nos. B215-B217 (3) 3.50 3.30

Surtax was for Red Cross. See Nos. B221-B223.

Pehr Kalm, 1716-1779 SP121

Finnish Scientists: 90p+15p, Title page of Pehr Adrian Gadd's (1727-97) book, vert. 1.10m+20p, Petter Forsskal (1732-63).

Perf. 12½x13, 13x12½
1979, Sept. 26 Litho.
B218 SP121 60p + 10p multi .40 .40
B219 SP121 90p + 15p multi .65 .65
B220 SP121 1.10m + 20p multi .65 .65
Nos. B218-B220 (3) 1.70 1.70

Surtax for Finnish Anti-Tuberculosis Assoc.

Mushroom Type of 1978

Edible Mushrooms: 60p+10p, Woolly milk-cap. 90p+15p, Orange-cap boletus, vert. 1.10m+20p, Russula paludosa.

1980, Apr. 19 Litho. ***Perf. 13***
B221 SP120 60p + 10p multi .70 .50
B222 SP120 90p + 15p multi .90 .70
B223 SP120 1.10m + 20p multi .90 .70
Nos. B221-B223 (3) 2.50 1.90

Surtax was for Red Cross.

Fuchsia — SP122

1981, Aug. 24 Litho. ***Perf. 13***
B224 SP122 70p + 10p shown .55 .55
B225 SP122 1m + 15p African violet .75 .75
B226 SP122 1.10m + 20p Geranium .95 .95
Nos. B224-B226 (3) 2.25 2.25

Surtax for Finnish Anti-Tuberculosis Assoc.

Garden Dormouse SP123

1982, Aug. 16 Litho. ***Perf. 13***
B227 SP123 90p + 10p shown .75 .65
B228 SP123 1.10m + 15p Flying squirrels 1.10 .75
B229 SP123 1.20m + 20p European minks 1.25 .95
Nos. B227-B229 (3) 3.10 2.35

Surtax was for Red Cross. No. B228 vert.

Forest and Wetland Plants SP124

1m+20p, Chickweed wintergreen. 1.20m+25p, Marsh violet. 1.30m+30p, Marsh marigold.

1983, July 7 Litho. ***Perf. 13***
B230 SP124 1m + 20p multi .70 .50
B231 SP124 1.20m + 25p multi .90 .70
B232 SP124 1.30m + 30p multi .90 .70
Nos. B230-B232 (3) 2.50 1.90

Surtax for Finnish Anti-Tuberculosis Assoc.

Globe Puzzle — SP125

Butterflies SP126

2m+40p, Symbolic world communication.

1984, May 28 Litho. ***Perf. 13***
B233 SP125 1.40m + 35p multi .85 .85
B234 SP125 2m + 40p multi 1.25 1.25

Surtax for Red Cross.

1986, May 22 Litho. ***Perf. 13***

#B235, Anthocharis cardamines. #B236, Nymphalis antiopa. #B237, Parnassius apollo.

B235 SP126 1.60m + 40p multi 1.10 .80
B236 SP126 2.10m + 45p multi 1.60 1.25
B237 SP126 5m + 50p multi 3.25 3.25
Nos. B235-B237 (3) 5.95 5.30

Surtax for Red Cross.

Festivals SP127

1988, Mar. 14 Litho. ***Perf. 13***
B238 SP127 1.40m +40p Christmas .85 .85
B239 SP127 1.80m +45p Easter 1.25 1.25
B240 SP127 2.40m +50p Midsummer 1.50 1.50
Nos. B238-B240 (3) 3.60 3.60

Surtax for the Red Cross.

Heodes virgaureae on Goldrod Plant SP128

Butterflies and plants: No. B242, *Agrodiaetus amandus* on meadow vetchling. No. B243, *Inachis io* on tufted vetch.

1990, Apr. 6 Photo. ***Perf. 12x11½***
B241 SP128 1.50m +40p multi 1.00 1.00
B242 SP128 2m +50p multi 1.25 1.25
B243 SP128 2.70m +60p multi 1.50 1.50
Nos. B241-B243 (3) 3.75 3.75

Surtax for the natl. Red Cross Soc.

Paintings by Helene Schjerfbeck — SP129

Designs: #B244a, The Little Convalescent, #B244b, Green Still-Life.

1991, Mar. 8 Litho. ***Perf. 13***
B244 SP129 Pair 3.00 3.00
a.-b. 2.10m +50p any single 1.50 1.50

Surtax for philately.

Butterflies SP130

#B245, Xestia brunneopicta. #B246, Acerbia alpina. #B247, Baptria tibiale.

Litho. & Embossed
1992, Apr. 22 ***Perf. 13***
B245 SP130 1.60m +40p multi 1.00 1.00
B246 SP130 2.10m +50p multi 1.25 1.25
B247 SP130 5m +60p multi 2.75 2.75
Nos. B245-B247 (3) 5.00 5.00

Surtax for Finnish Red Cross. Embossed "Arla 100" in braille for Arla Institute, training center for the blind, cent.

Autumn Landscape of Lake Pielisjarvi, by Eero Jarnefelt SP131

a, Tree-covered hill. b, Lake shoreline.

1993, Mar. 19 Litho. ***Perf. 13***
B248 SP131 2.30m + 70p Pair, #a.-b. 3.00 3.00

Surtax for philately.

Finnhorses SP132

1994, Mar. 11 Litho. ***Perf. 13***
B249 SP132 2m +40p Draft horses 1.25 1.25
B250 SP132 2.30m +50p Trotter 1.25 1.25
B251 SP132 4.20m +60p War horses, vert. 2.25 2.25
Nos. B249-B251 (3) 4.75 4.75

Surtax for Finnish Red Cross.

Paintings, by Albert Edelfelt (1854-1905) — SP133

#B252, Playing Boys on the Shore. #B253, Queen Blanche.

1995, Mar. 1 Litho. ***Perf. 13½***
B252 2.40m +60p multi 1.50 1.50

Size: 22x31mm

B253 2.40m +60p multi 1.50 1.50
a. SP133 Pair, #B252-B253 3.00 3.00

Surtax for philately.

Chickens SP134

1996, Mar. 18 Litho. ***Perf. 13***
B254 SP134 2.80m +60p Chicks 1.60 1.60
B255 SP134 3.20m +70p Hens 1.90 1.90
B256 SP134 3.40m +70p Rooster, vert. 2.00 2.00
Nos. B254-B256 (3) 5.50 5.50

Surtax for Finnish Red Cross.

The Aino Myth, by Akseli Gallen-Kallela (1865-1931)
SP135

Designs: No. B257, Väinämöinen proposing marriage to Aino in forest. No. B258, Aino jumping into water to escape Väinämöinen. No. B259, Aino at shore for bath.

1997, Sept. 5 Litho. *Perf. 13½x13*

Booklet Stamps

B257 SP135 2.80m +60p multi 1.60 1.60
B258 SP135 2.80m +60p multi 1.60 1.60
B259 SP135 2.80m +60p multi 1.60 1.60
a. Booklet pane, #B257-B259 5.00 5.00
Complete booklet, #B259a 5.00

No. B258 is 33x46mm.
Surtax for philately.

Pigs — SP136

2.80m+60p, Sow, piglets. 3.20m+70p, Three piglets. 3.40m+70p, Pig's head.

1998, Mar. 12 Litho. *Perf. 13*

B260 SP136 2.80m +60p multi 1.60 1.60
B261 SP136 3.20m +70p multi 1.90 1.90
B262 SP136 3.40m +70p multi 2.00 2.00
Nos. B260-B262 (3) 5.50 5.50

Surtax for Finnish Red Cross.

Paintings by Hugo Simberg (1873-1917)
SP137

a, Garden of Death. b, Wounded Angel.

Perf. 13¼x13¾

1999, Sept. 24 Litho.

B263 Booklet pane of 2 4.00 4.00
a.-b. SP137 3.50m +50p any single 1.90
Complete booklet, #B263 4.00

Surtax for philately.

Cow and Calf — SP138

Perf. 13¾x13¼

2000, Mar. 15 Litho.

B264 SP138 3.50m +70p Bull, vert. 2.00 2.00

Perf. 13¼x13¾

B265 SP138 4.80m +80p shown 2.75 2.75

Surtax for Finnish Red Cross.

AIR POST STAMPS

No. 178 Overprinted in Red

1930, Sept. 24 Unwmk. *Perf. 14*

C1 A28 10m gray lilac 140.00 *250.00*
Never hinged 225.00
a. 1830 for 1930 2,500. *3,750.*

Overprinted expressly for use on mail carried in "Graf Zeppelin" on return flight from Finland to Germany on Sept. 24, 1930, after which trip the stamps ceased to be valid for postage. Forgeries are almost always on No. 205, rather than No. 178.

Catalogue values for unused stamps in this section, from this point to the end of the section, are for Never Hinged items.

Douglas DC-2 — AP1

1944 Engr.

C2 AP1 3.50m dark brown .50 *.90*

Air Transport Service anniv, 1923-43.

Douglas DC-6 Over Winter Landscape — AP2

1950, Feb. 13

C3 AP2 300m blue 20.00 6.25

Available also for ordinary postage.

Redrawn

1958, Jan. 20 *Perf. 11½*

C4 AP2 300(m) blue 35.00 1.00

On No. C4 "mk" is omitted.
See Nos. C9-C9a.

Convair 440 over Lakes — AP3

1958, Oct. 31 Unwmk. *Perf. 11½*

C5 AP3 34m blue 1.25 .95

No. C5 Surcharged with New Value and Bars

1959, Apr. 5

C6 AP3 45m on 34m blue 2.25 2.25

1959, Nov. 2

C7 AP3 45m blue 2.00 .50

1963, Feb. 15

C8 AP3 45p blue 1.60 .55

On No. C7 the denomination is "45." On No. C8 it is "0.45."

DC-6 Type, Comma After "3"

Type I — 16 lines in "O"
Type II — 13 lines in "O"

1963, Oct. 10

C9 AP2 3m blue, Type II ('73) 2.00 .25
a. Type I 30.00 1.00

Convair Type of 1958

1970, July 15

C10 AP3 57p ultra 2.00 1.25

MILITARY STAMPS

Catalogue values for unused stamps in this section are for Never Hinged items.

M1

Unwmk.

1941, Nov. 1 Typo. *Imperf.*

M1 M1 (4m) blk, *dk org* .35 *.55*

#M1 has simulated roulette printed in black.

Type of 1930-46 Overprinted in Black

1943, Oct. 16 *Perf. 14*

M2 A26 2m deep orange .35 *.75*
M3 A26 3½m greenish blue .35 *.75*

Post Horn and Sword — M2

1943 Size: 29½x19½mm

M4 M2 (2m) green .20 *.35*
M5 M2 (3m) rose violet .20 *.35*

1944 Size: 20x16mm

M6 M2 (2m) green .20 .20
M7 M2 (3m) rose violet .20 .20

Post Horns and Arms of Finland — M3

1963, Sept. 26 Litho. *Perf. 14*

M8 M3 violet blue *160.00 160.00*

Used during maneuvers Sept. 30-Oct. 5, 1963. Valid from Sept. 26.

No. M8 Overprinted "1983"

1983, Apr. 20

M9 M3 violet blue *250.00 100.00*

Used during maneuvers Apr. 24-30.

PARCEL POST STAMPS

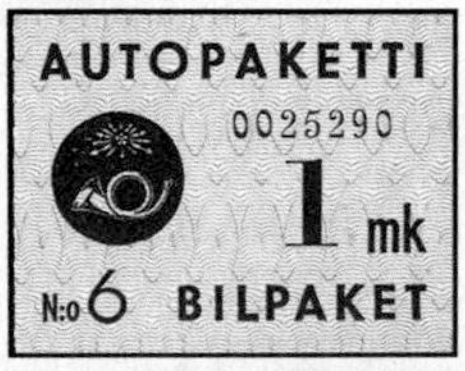

PP1

Wmk. Rose & Triangles Multiple

Rouletted 6 on 2 or 3 Sides

1949-50 Typo.

Q1 PP1 1m brt grn & blk 1.25 *4.50*
Q2 PP1 5m red & blk 10.50 *14.00*
Q3 PP1 20m org & blk 20.00 *22.50*
Q4 PP1 50m bl & blk ('50) 7.25 *11.00*
Q5 PP1 100m brn & blk ('50) 8.25 *11.00*
Nos. Q1-Q5 (5) 47.25 *63.00*
Set, never hinged 75.00

Catalogue values for unused stamps in this section, from this point to the end of the section, are for Never Hinged items.

Mail Bus — PP2

1952-58 Unwmk. Engr. *Perf. 14*

Q6 PP2 5m car rose 5.00 5.00
Q7 PP2 20m orange 12.50 8.50
Q8 PP2 50m blue ('54) 30.00 12.50
Q9 PP2 100m brn ('58) 37.50 18.00
Nos. Q6-Q9 (4) 85.00 44.00

Mail Bus — PP3

1963 *Perf. 12*

Q10 PP3 5p red & blk 4.00 4.00
Q11 PP3 20p org & blk 3.50 1.90
Q12 PP3 50p blue & blk 6.50 2.50
Q13 PP3 1m brn & blk 1.90 1.90
Nos. Q10-Q13 (4) 15.90 10.30

Nos. Q1-Q13 were issued only in booklets: panes of 6 for Nos. Q1-Q5, 10 for Nos. Q6-Q9 and 5 for Nos. Q10-Q13.

Used values are for regular postal or mail-bus cancels. Pen strokes, cutting or other cancels sell for half as much.

1981 SISU Bus — PP4

Photo. & Engr.

1981, Dec. 7 *Perf. 12 Horiz.*

Q14 PP4 50p dk bl & blk .60 *3.00*
Q15 PP4 1m dk brn & blk .90 *3.00*
Q16 PP4 5m grn & blk 3.50 *6.25*
Q17 PP4 10m red & blk 7.25 *12.50*
Nos. Q14-Q17 (4) 12.25 *24.75*

Parcel post stamps invalid after Jan. 9, 1985.

ALAND ISLANDS

LOCATION — A group of 6,554 islands at the mouth of the Gulf of Bothnia, between Finland and Sweden.
GOVT. — Province of Finland
AREA — 590 sq. mi.
POP. — 23,761
CAPITAL — Mariehamn

The province of Aland was awarded to Finland in 1921 by the League of Nations. The Swedish language is spoken and the province has a considerable amount of self-determination.

Catalogue values for unused stamps in this country are for Never Hinged items.

Gaff-rigged Sloop — A1

Aland Flag — A2

Midsummer Pole — A3

Landscapes — A4

Map of Scandinavia — A5

Seal of St. Olaf and Aland Province, 1326 — A6

Artifacts — A7

Sea Birds — A8

Gothic Tower, Jomala Church, 12th Cent. — A9

Mariehamn Town Hall, Designed by Architect Lars Sonck — A9a

Designs: 1.50m, Statue of Frans Petter von Knorring, vicar from 1834 to 1875, and St. Michael's Church, Finstrom, 12th cent. 1.60m, Burial site, clay hands. 1.70m, Somateria mollissima. 2.20m, Bronze Staff of Finby, apostolic decoration. 2.30m, Aythya fuligula. 5m, Outer Aland Archipelago. 8m, Farm and windmill. 12m, Melantha fusca. 20m, Ancient court site, contemporary monument.

1984-90 Engr. Unwmk. *Perf. 12*

1	A1	10p	magenta	.20	.20
2	A1	20p	brown olive	.20	.20
3	A1	50p	bright green	.20	.20
4	A1	1.10m	deep blue	.50	.35
5	A1	1.20m	black	.55	.45
6	A1	1.30m	dark green	.60	.45

Litho.

Perf. 14, 13x14 (#8)

7	A2	1.40m	multi	.75	.45
8	A9	1.40m	multi	1.50	1.50
9	A3	1.50m	multi, I	1.50	.45
9A	A3	1.50m	multi, II	.85	.45
10	A9	1.50m	multi	1.50	1.25

Perf. 13, 14 (#13)

11	A7	1.60m	multi, vert.	1.50	.50
12	A8	1.70m	multi	4.00	4.00
13	A9a	1.90m	multi	1.00	.70
14	A4	2m	multi	1.50	.60
15	A7	2.20m	multi, vert.	1.00	.75
16	A8	2.30m	multi	3.00	3.00
17	A5	3m	multi	2.00	2.00
18	A4	5m	multi, horiz.	2.50	1.75
19	A4	8m	multi, horiz.	4.00	3.00

Litho. & Engr.

20	A6	10m	multi	4.75	4.75

Litho.

21	A8	12m	multi	6.00	6.00
22	A7	20m	multi	9.75	9.75
			Nos. 1-22 (23)	49.35	42.75

On No. 9A (type II) "Aland" is 10½mm long, figure support is 2mm wide, pole supports are thinner, diagonal black highlighting lines in pole greenery and horizontal black line on support under the man removed.

Issued: #2-4, 7, 17, 20, 3/1/84; #1, 5, 6, 9, 1/2/85; #14, 18-19, 9/16/85; #11, 15, 22, 4/4/86; #12, 16, 21, 1/2/87; #8, 8/26/88; #13, 1/2/89; #10, 9/4/89; #9A, 5/21/90.

See Nos. 39-42, 87-92.

A10

A11

Bark Pommern and car ferries, Mariehamn West Harbor

1984, Mar. 1 Litho. *Perf. 14*

23	A10 2m multicolored		3.00	3.00

1986, Jan. 2 Litho. *Perf. 14*

24	A11 1.60m multicolored		1.90	1.90

1986 Nordic Orienteering Championships, Aug. 30-31.

Onningeby Artists' Colony, Cent. — A12

Design: Pallette, pen and ink drawing of Onningeby landscape, 1891, by Victor Westerholm (1860-1919), founder.

1986, Sept. 1 Litho.

25	A12 3.70m multicolored		1.75	1.75

Mariehamn Volunteer Fire Brigade, Cent. — A13

1987, Apr. 27 Litho. *Perf. 14*

26	A13 7m multicolored		6.00	6.00

Farjsund Bridge, 50th Anniv., Rebuilt in 1980 — A14

1987, Apr. 27 Engr. *Perf. 13x13½*

27	A14 1m greenish black		.50	.50

Municipal Meeting, Finstrom, 1917 — A15

1987, Aug. 20 Litho. *Perf. 14*

28	A15 1.70m multicolored		1.25	1.25

Movement for reunification with Sweden, 70th anniv.

Loading of Mail Barrels on Sailboat, Post Office, Eckero — A16

1988, Jan. 4 Litho. *Perf. 14*

29	A16 1.80m multicolored		2.25	2.00

Postal Service, 350th anniv. From Feb. I to May 31, Alanders were entitled to buy 20 stamps for 28m with a discount coupon.

New Aland Farm School, Horse-Drawn Plow — A17

1988, Mar. 29 Litho. *Perf. 14*

30	A17 2.20m multicolored		1.75	*2.25*

Haga Farm School, cent.; Aland Farm School, 75th anniv.; 50th anniv. of experimental farming on Aland.

Sailing Ships — A18

1988, June 4 Litho. *Perf. 13*

31	A18	1.80m Albanus, 1904, vert.	2.00	1.25
32	A18	2.40m Ingrid, c. 1900	3.00	2.50
33	A18	11m Pamir, c. 1900	9.50	8.00
		Nos. 31-33 (3)	14.50	11.75

Type of 1988 and

Orchids — A19

Fish A20

Handicrafts A21

Fresco, St. Anna's Church of Kumlinge A22

Mammals A23

Geological Formations A24 A25

Designs: 10p, Boulder field, Geta. #35, *Dactylorhiza sambucina*. #36, *Clupea harengus membras*. #37, *Erinaceus europauus*. #38, Drumlin, Finstrom. 1.70m, St. Andrew Church, Lumparland. #40, Vardo Church. #41, Hammarland Church. #42, Sottunga Church. #43, *Esox lucius*. #45, Diabase dike, Sottunga, Basskar. 2.10m, *Sciurus vulgaris*. 2.50m, *Cephalanthera longifolia*. #48, *Platichthys flesus*. #49, Pillow lava, Kumlinge, western Varpskar. #50, *Capreolus capreolus*. #51, Rouche Moutonne, Roda Kon, Lumparn. 6m, Folded gneiss, Sottunga, Gloskar. 13m, Tapestry, 1793. 14m, *Cypripedium calceolus*.

Perf. 13, 14 (#39-42, 44, 53), 15x14½ (10p, #38, 45, 49, 51-52)

1989-94 Litho.

34	A25	10p	multicolored	.20	.20
35	A19	1.50m	multicolored	2.75	2.25
36	A20	1.50m	multicolored	1.25	.75
37	A23	1.60m	multicolored	1.25	.60
38	A25	1.60m	multicolored	.90	.60
39	A9	1.70m	multicolored	1.25	1.10
40	A9	1.80m	multicolored	1.25	.95
41	A9	1.80m	multicolored	1.25	1.00
42	A9	1.80m	multicolored	1.00	1.00
43	A20	2m	multicolored	1.25	.85
44	A22	2m	multicolored	1.00	.85
45	A24	2m	multicolored	.85	.70
46	A23	2.10m	multicolored	1.50	.45
47	A19	2.50m	multicolored	3.25	2.50
48	A20	2.70m	multicolored	1.50	1.40
49	A24	2.70m	multicolored	1.25	.95
50	A23	2.90m	multicolored	1.50	1.50

51	A25	2.90m multicolored	1.25	1.10
52	A24	6m multicolored	2.50	2.50
53	A21	13m multicolored	6.50	5.75
54	A19	14m multicolored	9.50	9.00
		Nos. 34-54 (21)	42.95	36.00

Issued: 2.50m, 14m, #35, 4/10/89; 2.70m, #36, 43, 3/1/90; 13m, 4/19/90; 1.70m, #44, 9/10/90; 1.60m, 2.10m, #50, 3/3/91; #40, 10/9/91; #41 10/5/92; #45, 49, 52, 9/3/93; #42, 10/8/93; 10p, #38, 51, 2/1/94.

See Nos. 96, 102, 105.

Educational System of the Province, 350th Anniv. — A33

1989, May 31 Litho. *Perf. 14*

57	A33 1.90m multicolored	1.50	1.25

Souvenir Sheet

1991 Aland Island Games — A34

a, Volleyball. b, Shooting. c, Soccer. d, Running.

1991, Apr. 5 Litho. *Perf. 13x12½*

58	A34 2.10m Sheet of 4, #a.-d.	5.00	5.00

Autonomy of Aland, 70th Anniv. — A35

1991, June 4 *Perf. 13*

59	A35 16m multicolored	8.75	8.00

Kayaking A36

1991, June 4 *Perf. 14*

60	A36 2.10m shown	1.25	.75
61	A36 2.90m Cycling	1.75	1.25

Rev. Frans Peter Von Knorring (1792-1875), Educator — A37

Cape Horn Congress, Mariehamn, June 8-11 — A38

1992, Mar. 2 Litho. *Perf. 13*

62	A37 2 multicolored	1.25	1.25

Litho. & Engr.

Perf. 13½x14

63	A38 1 multicolored	1.75	1.75

No. 62 sold for 1.60m, No. 63 for 2.10m.

On stamps bearing the "denominations" "1" or "2," the number represents the class of mail.

Lighthouses A39

1992, May 8 Litho. *Perf. 13*

Booklet Stamps

64	A39 2.10m Ranno	5.25	4.00
65	A39 2.10m Salskar	5.25	4.00
66	A39 2.10m Lagskar	5.25	4.00
67	A39 2.10m Market	5.25	4.00
a.	Booklet pane of 4, #64-67	22.50	22.50

First Aland Provincial Parliament, 70th Anniv. — A40

1992, June 8 Litho. *Perf. 13*

68	A40 3.40m multicolored	1.75	1.75

Joel Pettersson (1892-1937), Painter — A41

1992, June 8

69	A41 2.90m Landscape from Lemland	1.50	1.50
70	A41 16m Self-Portrait	8.50	8.25

Arms of Aland — A42

1993, Mar. 1 Litho. *Perf. 14*

71	A42 1.60m gray, sepia & blue	1.00	1.00

Autonomy Act, Jan. 1.

Souvenir Sheet

Autonomous Postal Administration — A43

Designs: a, Inscriptions from old letter canceled in Kastelholm, vert. b, Mariehamn post office. c, Ferry, mail truck. d, New post office emblem, vert.

Perf. 12½x13, 14 (#b.-c.)

1993, Mar. 1 Litho., Engr. (#b.-c.)

72	A43 1.90m Sheet of 4, #a.-d.	3.75	3.75

Fiddler, Jan Karlsgarden Museum — A44

Folk Dresses — A45

2.30m, Boat Shed, Jan Karlsgarden Museum.

Perf. 13x12½, 12½x13

1993, May 7 Litho.

73	A44 2m multicolored	1.10	1.00
74	A44 2.30m multi, horiz.	1.40	1.25

1993, June 1 *Perf. 12½*

Clothing from: 1.90m, Saltvik. 3.50m, Brando, Eckero, Mariehamn. 17m, Finstrom.

75	A45 1.90m multicolored	1.25	1.00
76	A45 3.50m multicolored	1.75	1.50
77	A45 17m multicolored	9.00	8.50
	Nos. 75-77 (3)	12.00	11.00

Butterflies A46

A47

Perf. 14 on 3 Sides

1994, Mar. 1 Litho.

Booklet Stamps

78	A46 2.30m Melitaea cinxia	1.25	1.10
79	A46 2.30m Quercusia querqus	1.25	1.10
80	A46 2.30m Parnassius mnemosyne	1.25	1.10
81	A46 2.30m Hesperia comma	1.25	1.10
a.	Booklet pane, 2 each #78-81	10.00	*11.00*
	Nos. 78-81 (4)	5.00	4.40

1994, May 5 Litho. *Perf. 13*

Europa, Inventions and Discoveries: 2.30m, Diagram showing transmission of von Willebrand's Disease, discovered by E. A. von Willebrand. 2.90m, Purification of heparin, by Erik Jorpes.

82	A47 2.30m multicolored	*2.75*	*2.50*
83	A47 2.90m multicolored	*1.90*	*1.60*

Types of 1989-93 and:

Ice Age Survivors — A48

Fossils — A49

Sea Birds — A50

Bronze Age — A51

Stone Age — A52

Ships — A53

Lichens — A54

Primula Veris — A55

30p, Saduria entomon, mysis relicta. 40p, Trilobita asaphus. 1.80m, Sterna paradisaea. #87, Church of Mariehamn. #88, Church of Eckerö. #89, St. Bridget's Church, Lemland. #90, Church of St. John the Baptist, Sund. #91, St. George Church, Geta. #92, Church of Brando. #93, Bronze sword, bronze dagger. #94, Ship tumulus grave. #95, Larus canus. 2.30m, Pitcher of Kallskar. #97, Pottery. #98, Myoxocephalus quadricornis. 2.60m, Larus marinus. #100, Stone tools. #101, SS Thornbury. 3.40m, Erratic boulders. 3.50m, SS Osmo. 4.30m, Phoca hispida. 7m, Potholes. 9m, Gastropoda euomophalus. 18m, Settlement. 2, Hypogmnia physodes. 1, Xanthoria parietina.

Perf. 13 (A48, A50, A52), 15x14½, 14½x15, 14½ (40p, #88-89), 14 (#87, 90),

1994-2000 Engr.

84	A48	30p multi	.20	.20
85	A49	40p multi	.20	.20
86	A50	1.80m multi	.85	.85
87	A9	1.90m multi	.85	.85
88	A9	1.90m multi	.85	.85
89	A9	1.90m multi	.85	.85
90	A9	2m multi	.95	.70
91	A9	2m multi	.95	.95
92	A9	2m multi	.95	.95
93	A51	2m multi	.95	.95
94	A51	2.20m multi, vert.	1.10	1.10
95	A50	2.20m multi, vert.	1.10	1.10
96	A24	2.30m multi	1.10	1.00
97	A52	2.40m multi, vert.	1.25	1.10
98	A48	2.40m multi	1.25	1.10
99	A50	2.60m multi	1.25	1.10
100	A52	2.80m multi, vert.	1.50	.85
101	A53	2.80m multi	1.50	1.25
102	A24	3.40m multi, horiz.	1.75	1.50
103	A53	3.50m multi	1.75	1.50
104	A48	4.30m multi	2.25	1.90
105	A24	7m multi, horiz.	4.00	3.00
106	A49	9m multi	5.00	4.00
107	A52	18m multi	8.75	8.25

Perf. 13

107A	A54	2 multi	1.10	.95
107B	A54	1 multi	1.50	1.25

Self-Adhesive

Serpentine Die Cut Perf. 10

108	A55	2.40m multi	1.25	1.25
		Nos. 84-108 (27)	45.00	39.55

No. 108 was issued in sheets of 10.

Nos. 107A-107B sold for 2m and 2.40m, respectively, on day of issue.

Issued: #97, 100, 18m, 8/16/94; #90, 10/7/94; 2.30m, 3.40m, 7m, 1/2/95; #91, 9/15/95; 40p, #92, 9m, 10/9/96; 30p, #98, 4.30m, 2/3/97; #101, 103, 9/8/97; #87, 10/9/97; #88, 10/9/98; #93-94, 2/1/99; #108, 4/28/99; #107A-107B, 9/25/99; #89, 10/8/99; 1.80m, #95, 2.60m, 1/3/00.

Cargo Vessels — A58

Perf. 14 on 3 Sides

1995, Mar. 1 **Litho.**

Booklet Stamps

109 A58 2.30m Skuta	1.10	1.00
110 A58 2.30m Sump	1.10	1.00
111 A58 2.30m Storbat	1.10	1.00
112 A58 2.30m Jakt	1.10	1.00
a. Booklet pane, 2 each #109-112	9.00	*10.00*
Complete booklet, #112a	9.50	
Nos. 109-112 (4)	4.40	4.00

Entry into European Union — A59

1995, Mar. 1 **Litho.** ***Perf. 13x14***

113 A59 2.90m multicolored 1.50 *1.75*

Europa — A60

Tourism — A61

1995, May 5 **Litho.** ***Perf. 13x14***

114 A60 2.80m shown	*1.40*	*1.25*
115 A60 2.90m Dove, island in sea	*1.40*	*1.25*

1995, May 12

116 A61 2 Golf	1.25	1.00
117 A61 1 Fishing	1.50	1.00

Nos. 116-117 sold for value 2m and 2.30m, respectively.

Optimist Dinghy World Championships — A62

1995, June 2 **Litho.** ***Perf. 13½x14***

118 A62 3.40m multicolored 1.75 1.50

St. Olaf (995?-1030), Patron Saint of Aland — A63

Litho. & Engr.

1995, Sept. 15 ***Perf. 13½x13***

119 A63 4.30m multicolored 2.25 2.00

See Faroe Islands No. 289

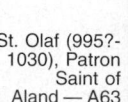

A64

A65

Greeting Stamps (stylized designs): No. 120, Fish with natl. flag, "Hälsningar fran Aland." No. 121, Yellow bird with flower, "Grattis."

1996, Feb. 14 **Litho.** ***Perf. 13x14***

120 A64 1 multicolored	1.25	.90
121 A64 1 multicolored	1.25	.90

Nos. 120-121 had a face value of 2.30m on day of issue.

1996, Mar. 1 ***Perf. 14 on 3 Sides***

Eagle owl (bubo bubo): No. 122, Landing on tree branch over lake. No. 123, Perched on branch over lake. No. 124, Male, darker feathers. No. 125, Female, lighter feathers.

Booklet Stamps

122 A65 2.40m multicolored	1.40	1.10
123 A65 2.40m multicolored	1.40	1.10
124 A65 2.40m multicolored	1.40	1.10
125 A65 2.40m multicolored	1.40	1.10
a. Booklet pane, 2 ea #122-125	11.50	11.50
Complete booklet, No. 125a	12.50	
Nos. 122-125 (4)	5.60	4.40

World Wildlife Fund.

Famous Women A66

Europa: 2.80m, Sally Salminen (1906-76), writer. 2.90m, Fanny Sundström (1883-1944), politician.

1996, May 6 **Litho.** ***Perf. 14x13***

126 A66 2.80m multicolored	*1.40*	*1.25*
127 A66 2.90m multicolored	*1.40*	*1.25*

A67

A68

1996, June 7 **Litho.** ***Perf. 13½x14***

128 A67 2.40m multicolored 1.25 1.10

Aland '96 Song and Music Festival.

1996, June 7 ***Perf. 13***

"Haircut," by Karl Emanuel Jansson (1846-74).

129 A68 18m multicolored 9.00 8.00

Spring Flowers — A69

Designs: No. 130, Tussilago farfara. No. 131, Hepatica nobilis. No. 132, Anemone nemorosa. No. 133, Anemone ranunculoides.

1997, Feb. 3 **Litho.** ***Perf. 14***

Booklet Stamps

130 A69 2.40m multicolored	1.10	1.10
131 A69 2.40m multicolored	1.10	1.10
132 A69 2.40m multicolored	1.10	1.10
133 A69 2.40m multicolored	1.10	1.10
a. Booklet pane, 2 each #130-133	9.00	*10.00*
Complete booklet, #133a	9.50	

A70

A71

1997, May 3 **Litho.** ***Perf. 14x13½***

134 A70 3.40m multicolored 1.60 1.60

1st Floorball World Championships, Aland.

1997, May 9 ***Perf. 13x14***

Devil's Dance with Clergyman's Wife.

135 A71 2.90m multicolored *1.40* *1.10*

Europa.

Kalmar Union, 600th Anniv. — A72

Design: Kastelholm Castle, arms of Lord High Chancellor Bo Jonsson Grip.

1997, May 30 **Litho.** ***Perf. 14x13***

136 A72 2.40m multicolored 1.25 1.10

Souvenir Sheet

Autonomy, 75th Anniv. — A73

Illustration reduced.

1997, June 9 ***Perf. 13***

137 A73 20m multicolored 10.00 10.00

No. 137 contains a holographic image. Soaking in water may affect the hologram.

Horticulture A74

1998, Feb. 2 **Litho.** ***Perf. 14½x15***

138 A74 2m Apples	.95	.95
139 A74 2.40m Cucumbers	1.10	1.10

Youth Activities A75

#140, Riding moped. #141, Computer. #142, Listening to music. #143, Aerobics.

1998, Mar. 28 ***Perf. 14 on 3 Sides***

Booklet Stamps

140 A75 2.40m multicolored	1.10	1.10
141 A75 2.40m multicolored	1.10	1.10
142 A75 2.40m multicolored	1.10	1.10
143 A75 2.40m multicolored	1.10	1.10
a. Booklet pane, 2 each #140-143	9.00	*10.00*
Complete booklet, #143a	9.50	

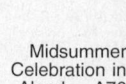

Midsummer Celebration in Aland — A76

1998, Apr. 27 **Litho.** ***Perf. 14***

144 A76 4.20m multicolored *2.00* *1.75*

Europa.

Passenger Ferry — A77

1998, May 8 ***Perf. 14½***

145 A77 2.40m multicolored 1.10 1.10

Intl. Year of the Ocean — A78

1998, May 8

146 A78 6.30m multicolored 3.00 3.00

ATP Senior Tour of Champions Tennis Tournament, Mariehamn A79

Serpentine Die Cut

1998, June 25 **Litho.**

Self-Adhesive

147 A79 2.40m multicolored 1.25 1.25

Issued in sheets of 10.

Scouting — A80

1998, Aug. 1 ***Perf. 14***

148 A80 2.80m multicolored 1.40 1.40

Foyers — A81

Homesteads: 1.60m, Seffers. 2m, Labbas. 2.90m, Abras.

1998, Sept. 11 **Litho.** ***Perf. 14½***

149 A81 1.60m multicolored	.75	.75
150 A81 2m multicolored	.95	.95
151 A81 2.90m multicolored	1.40	1.40
Nos. 149-151 (3)	3.10	3.10

18th Century Furniture Ornamentation A82

Perf. 14 on 3 Sides

1999, Feb. 1 Litho.

Booklet Stamps

152	A82 2.40m Wardrobe	1.10	1.10
153	A82 2.40m Distaff	1.10	1.10
154	A82 2.40m Chest	1.10	1.10
155	A82 2.40m Spinning wheel	1.10	1.10
a.	Booklet pane, 2 each #152-155	9.00	*10.00*
	Complete booklet, #155a	9.50	

Passage of Cape Horn by Grain Ships Pamir & Passat, 50th Anniv. A83

1999, Mar. 19 Litho. *Perf. 14½*

156 A83 3.40m multicolored 1.60 1.60

Beginning with No. 157, denominations are indicated on many stamps in both Markkas and Euros. The value shown is in Markkas.

Nature Reserve, Kökar — A84

1999, Apr. 28 Litho. *Perf. 13*

157 A84 2.90m multicolored *1.40 1.25*

Europa.

Match Sailboat Racing — A85

1999, Aug. 5 Litho. *Perf. 14½x15*

158 A85 2.70m multicolored 1.25 1.25

UPU, 125th Anniv. A86

1999, Sept. 25

159 A86 2.90m multicolored 1.40 1.40

Finnish Cross-Country Championships, Mariehamn — A87

1999, Oct. 9 Litho. *Perf. 14¾x14½*

160 A87 3.50m multicolored 1.75 1.75

Souvenir Sheet

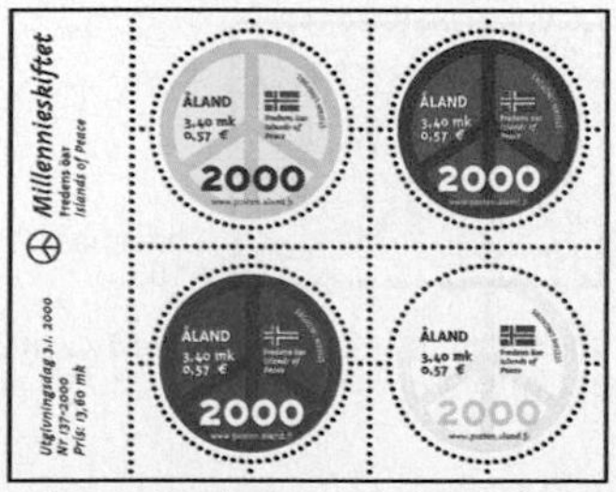

Peace Symbol, Aland Flag — A88

Background colors: a, Yellow. b, Red. c, Blue. d, White.

Litho. & Embossed

2000, Jan. 3 *Perf. 13*

161 A88 3.40m Sheet of 4, #a.-d. 6.50 6.50

Elk — A89

Elk in: No. 162, Spring. No. 163, Summer. No. 164, Autumn. No. 165, Winter.

Perf. 11¾on 3 sides

2000, Mar. 1 Litho.

Booklet Stamps

162	A89 2.60m multicolored	1.25	1.25
163	A89 2.60m multicolored	1.25	1.25
164	A89 2.60m multicolored	1.25	1.25
165	A89 2.60m multicolored	1.25	1.25
a.	Block of 4, #162-165	5.00	5.00
b.	Booklet pane, 2 #165a	10.00	*11.00*
	Complete booklet, #165b	10.50	

Europa, 2000

Common Design Type

2000, May 9 *Perf. 13*

166 CD17 3m multicolored *1.75 1.25*

A90

A91

2000, June 9 *Die Cut Perf. 13x13¼*

Self-Adhesive

Coil Stamp

167 A90 2.60m multicolored 1.25 1.25

Gymnastics Festival, Mariehamn.

2000, July 21 Litho. *Perf. 13½x13¼*

168 A91 3.40m multicolored 1.60 1.60

Cutty Sark Tall Ships race to Mariehamn.

Vikings From Aland — A92

2000, July 28

169 A92 4.50m multicolored 2.10 2.10

Recreation of Viking market, Saltvik.

Architecture by Hilda Hongell (1867-1952) A93

2000, Aug. 25 *Perf. 13¼x13¾*

170	A93 3.80m shown	1.75	1.75
171	A93 10m House, diff.	4.75	4.75

Christianity, 2000th Anniv. — A94

2000, Oct. 9 *Perf. 13*

172 A94 3m multicolored 1.40 1.25

Church Type of 1984-90 and:

Swamp Plants — A95

Swamp plants: 1.90m, Equisetum fluviatile. 2.80m, Lycopodium annotinum. 3.50m, Polypodium vulgare.

Churches: No. 179, Föglö Church, Föglö. 2m, Kökar Church, Kökar.

Perf. 13x13¼, 13 (#178)

2000-01 Litho.

177	A95 1.90m multicolored	.90	.85
178	A9 2m multicolored	.95	.90
179	A9 2m multi	.95	.90
180	A95 2.80m multicolored	1.40	1.40
182	A95 3.50m multicolored	1.75	1.75
	Nos. 177-182 (5)	5.95	5.80

These stamps are part of an ongoing definitive set. Numbers have been reserved for additional stamps.

Issued: 2m, 10/9; 1.90m, 2.80m, 3.50m, 1/2/01; No. 179, 10/9/01.

Worldwide Fund for Nature (WWF) — A100

Polysticta stelleri: a, Pair in flight. b, Pair on rock. c, Pair in water. d, Male in water.

Perf. 13¼ on 3 sides

2001, Jan. 2 Litho.

Booklet Stamps

185	A100 Block of 4	5.00	5.00
a.-d.	2.70m any single	1.25	1.10
e.	Booklet pane, 2 #185	10.00	*11.00*
	Booklet, #185e	11.00	

Valentine's Day — A101

2001, Feb. 14 *Perf. 14½x14¾*

186 A101 3.20m multicolored 1.50 1.50

Europa A102

2001, May 9 Litho. *Perf. 14½x14¾*

187 A102 3.20m multi *1.60 1.25*

Windmills A103

Windmill types: 3m, Archipelago. 7m, Timbered, horiz. 20m, Nest, horiz.

Perf. 13¾x14¼, 14¼x13¾

2001, June 8

188-190 A103 Set of 3 14.50 14.50

Puppies — A104

Designs: 2, Golden retriever. 1, Wire-haired dachshund.

2001, Sept. 3 *Perf. 13¼*

191-192 A104 Set of 2 2.75 2.75

Nos. 191-192 sold for 2.30m and 2.70m respectively on day of issue.

100 Cents = 1 Euro (€)

Church Type of 1998 with Euro Denominations and

Fauna — A105

Post Terminal — A106

Mushrooms A107

Designs: 5c, Coronella austriaca. 10c, Chanterelle mushroom. 35c, Saltviks Church. 40c, Kumlinge Church. 50c, King Bolete mushroom. 70c, Triturus cristatus. €1, Post Terminal. €2.50, Parasol mushroom.

Perf. 12½, 13 (#193, 196), 13¼ (#198), 14¾x14 (#195)

2002-03 Litho.

193	A105	5c multi	.20	.20
194	A107	10c multi	.30	.30
195	A9	35c multi	1.00	1.00
196	A9	40c multi	1.10	1.10
197	A107	50c multi	1.40	1.40
198	A105	70c multi	2.00	2.00
199	A106	€1 multi	3.00	2.75
200	A107	€2.50 multi	7.25	7.25
		Nos. 193-200 (8)	16.25	16.00

Issue dates: 5c, 70c, 1/2/02; €1, 2/28/02; 35c, 10/9/02; 10c, 50c, €2.50, 1/2/03. No. 196, 10/9/03.

This is an expanding set. Numbers may change.

Introduction of the Euro — A108

2002, Jan. 2 Litho. *Perf. 12½*

201 A108 60c multi 2.00 1.75

St. Canute's Day — A109

2002, Jan. 2

202 A109 €2 multi 5.75 5.75

Cuisine — A110

Flowers and: a, Gravlax, boiled potatoes. b, Fried herring, beets, mashed potatoes. c, Black bread, cheese, butter. d, Pancake with prune sauce and whipped cream, coffee.
Illustration reduced.

Perf. 13½x13¼ on 3 Sides

2002, Feb. 28 **Litho.**

203	A110	Block of 4	7.00	6.00
a.-d.		1 Any single	1.75	1.40
e.		Booklet pane, 2 #203	14.00	11.00
		Booklet, #203e	15.00	

Nos. 203a-203d each sold for 55c on day of issue.

Europa — A111

2002, May 3 ***Perf. 13¼***

204 A111 40c multi *1.25 1.00*

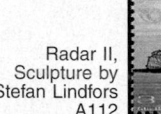

Radar II, Sculpture by Stefan Lindfors A112

2002, May 3 ***Perf. 13***

205 A112 €3 multi 8.75 8.50

"My Aland," by Lill Lindfors A113

2002, Aug. 12 **Litho.** ***Perf. 13¼***

206 A113 90c multi 2.50 2.50

Iron Age Artifacts — A114

Designs: No. 207, 2, Buckle found in Persby. No. 208, 1, Ornamental pin found in Syllöda.

2002, Sept. 2 ***Perf. 13x13¼***

207-208 A114 Set of 2 3.00 2.50

Nos. 207-208 sold for 45c and 55c respectively on day of issue.

Janne Holmén, Marathon Gold Medalist in European Track and Field Championships A115

2002, Nov. 1 ***Perf. 12½***

209 A115 1 multi 1.60 1.50

Sold for 55c on day of issue.

House Cats — A116

2003, Mar. 14 **Litho.** ***Perf. 13¼***

210 A116 2 Tovis 1.50 1.25
211 A116 1 Randi, horiz. 2.00 1.75

Nos. 210-211 sold for 45c and 55c respectively on day of issue.

Landscape in Summer, by Elin Danielson-Gambogi (1861-1919) — A117

No. 212: a, Woman at fence. b, Tree without leaves. c, Sun. d, Boat.
Illustration reduced.

2003, Mar. 28 ***Perf. 14 Vert.***

Booklet Stamps

212	A117	Horiz. strip of 4	6.25	6.25
a.-d.		1 Any single	1.50	1.25
e.		Booklet pane, 2 #212	12.50	12.50
		Complete booklet, #212e	13.00	

Nos. 212a-212d each sold for 55c on day of issue.

Europa — A118

2003, May 9 ***Perf. 13¼***

213 A118 45c multi *1.25 1.00*

Museum Ship "Pommern," Cent. A119

2003, June 6 ***Die Cut Perf. 9¼x9½***

Booklet Stamp

Self-Adhesive

214 A119 55c multi		1.60	1.60
a.	Booklet pane of 4	6.50	6.50
	Complete booklet, 2 #214a	13.00	

Mark and Stephen Levengood on Beach — A120

2003, June 18 ***Perf. 12½***

215 A120 55c multi 1.60 1.60

Aland Folk Music Association, 50th Anniv. — A121

2003, Aug. 1 ***Perf. 14¼***

216 A121 €1.10 buff & black 3.25 3.25

St. Lucia's Day Celebrations A122

2003, Oct. 9 **Litho.** ***Perf. 12½***

217 A122 60c multi 1.75 1.75

Mammals — A123

Designs: 20c, Mustela erminea. 60c, Vulpes vulpes. €3, Martes martes.

2004, Feb. 2 **Litho.** ***Perf. 14½x14¼***

218 A123 20c multi	.75	.50
219 A123 60c multi	1.75	1.50
220 A123 €3 multi	9.50	8.50
Nos. 218-220 (3)	12.00	10.50

Souvenir Sheet

Norse Gods Fenja and Menja — A124

2004, Mar. 26 ***Perf. 14¼x14¾***

221 A124 55c multi 1.60 1.60

Aland Flag, 50th Anniv. — A125

Serpentine Die Cut 12½

2004, Apr. 23

Booklet Stamp

Self-Adhesive

222 A125 1 multi		1.50	1.50
a.	Booklet pane of 4	6.00	5.75
	Complete booklet, 2 #222a	12.50	

No. 222a was reprinted in 2007 with a hole for a pegboard hook.

Finnish Pres. Mauno Koivisto and Guests on Boat — A126

2004, Apr. 23 ***Perf. 12½***

223 A126 90c multi 2.50 2.50

Europa — A127

2004, May 10 ***Perf. 13¾x14¼***

224 A127 75c multi *2.00 1.75*

Destruction of Bomarsund Fortress, 150th Anniv. — A128

No. 225: a, Fortress, six ships in harbor. b, Fortress, three ships in harbor. c, Three soldiers in foreground. d, Six soldiers in foreground.

2004, June 9 ***Perf. 13***

225	Booklet pane of 4	8.50	8.25
a.-d.	A128 75c Any single	2.10	2.10
	Complete booklet, 2 #225	17.00	

2004 Summer Olympics, Athens A183

2004, Aug. 13 **Litho.** ***Perf. 14¼***

226 A183 80c multi 2.25 2.25

Landscapes A184

Designs: 2, Storklynkan, Brändö. 1, Prästgardsnäset Nature Reserve, Finström.

2004, Aug. 13 ***Perf. 12½***

227-228 A184 Set of 2 3.25 3.00

Nos. 227-228 sold for 50c and 60c respectively on day of issue.

Christmas A185

2004, Oct. 8 ***Perf. 14½x14¾***

229 A185 45c multi 1.75 1.40

Birds — A186

Designs: 15c, Phalacrocorax carbo sinensis. 65c, Cygnus cygnus. €4, Ardea cinerea, vert.

2005, Jan. 14 Litho. ***Perf. 13¼***
230 A186 15c multi .45 .45
231 A186 65c multi 1.90 1.90
232 A186 €4 multi 11.50 11.50
Nos. 230-232 (3) 13.85 13.85

Automobiles — A187

No. 233: a, 1928 Oakland Sport Cabriolet. b, 1939 Ford V8. c, 1957 Buick Super 4D HT. d, 1964 Volkswagen 1200.

2005, Mar. 4 ***Perf. 13¼ Horiz.***
Booklet Stamps
233 Vert. strip of 4 7.00 7.00
a.-d. A187 1 Any single 1.75 1.75
e. Booklet pane, 2 #233 14.00 —
Complete booklet, #233e 14.00

Stamps sold for 60c each on day of issue.

Europa A188

2005, Apr. 29 ***Perf. 13¼***
234 A188 90c multi *2.50 2.10*

Walpurgis Night Bonfire A189

Serpentine Die Cut 12½
2005, Apr. 29
Self-Adhesive
Booklet Stamp
235 A189 2 multi 1.40 1.40
a. Booklet pane of 4 5.75
Complete booklet, 2 #235a 11.50

Stamp sold for 50c on day of issue.

Tennis Player Bjorn Borg — A190

2005, May 26 ***Perf. 12½***
236 A190 55c multi 1.60 1.60

Mr. Black and Mr. Smith at Bomarsund, by Fritz von Dardel A191

2005, Aug. 12 Litho. ***Perf. 13¾***
237 A191 €1.30 multi 3.75 3.75

Schooner Linden — A192

2005, Aug. 26 ***Perf. 13¼***
238 A192 60c multi 1.75 1.75

Landscapes Type of 2004

Designs: 70c, Pine tree on Sandö Island. 80c, Cliffs, Gröndal.

2005, Aug. 26 ***Perf. 12½***
239-240 A184 Set of 2 4.25 4.25

Christmas — A193

Litho. with Hologram Applied
2005, Oct. 10 ***Perf. 13***
241 A193 45c multi 1.25 1.25

Stars in hologram differ on each stamp.

Beetles A194

Designs: 40c, Potosia cuprea. 65c, Coccinella septempunctata. €2, Oryctes nasicornis.

Litho. & Embossed
2006, Jan. 2 ***Perf. 13½***
242 A194 40c multi 1.10 1.10
243 A194 65c multi 1.90 1.90
244 A194 €2 multi 5.75 5.75
Nos. 242-244 (3) 8.75 8.75

Woman Suffrage in Finland, Cent. — A195

2006, Mar. 8 Litho. ***Perf. 12½***
245 A195 85c multi 2.50 2.50

Demilitarization of Aland, 150th Anniv. — A196

2006, Mar. 29 ***Perf. 13¾***
246 A196 €1.50 multi 4.25 4.25

Souvenir Sheet

Lettesgubbe, Mythological Being — A197

2006, Mar. 29 ***Perf. 12½x13***
247 A197 85c multi 2.50 2.50

Europa — A198

2006, May 4
248 A198 €1.30 multi 3.75 3.75

A199

Serpentine Die Cut 10 Syncopated
2006, May 26
249 A199 1 multi 2.00 2.00
a. Booklet pane of 8 16.00

No. 249 sold for 65c on day of issue. Design portion of stamp could be personalized at €10.40 per booklet with a minimum purchase of three booklets. The label design shown is a generic vignette. Other generic vignettes were created for sale at stamp shows beginning in 2008.

Tattoos — A200

No. 250: a, Tribal tattoo on man's biceps. b, Sailor's tattoo on man's forearm. c, Flower tattoo, on woman's torso.

2006, Sept. 7 ***Perf. 14 Vert.***
Booklet Stamps
250 Horiz. strip of 3 5.75 5.75
a.-c. A200 65c Any single 1.90 1.90
d. Booklet pane, 3 #250 17.50
Complete booklet, #250d 17.50

Fishing Boat From Television Film Directed by Ake Lindman A201

2006, Aug. 4 Litho. ***Perf. 12½***
251 A201 75c multi 2.25 2.25

Landscapes Type of 2004

Designs: 55c, Foggy grove, windmill and houses, Söderby, Lemland. €1.20, Rocks, Norra Essvik, Sottunga.

2006, Aug. 4
252-253 A184 Set of 2 5.00 5.00

Christmas A202

Litho. With Holograms Affixed
2006, Oct. 9 ***Perf. 13***
254 A202 (50c) multi 1.40 1.40

Flowers A203

Designs: 80c, Tripolium vulgare. 90c, Lythrum salicaria. €5, Angelica archangelica.

2007, Feb. 1 Litho. ***Perf. 12½x13***
255 A203 80c multi 2.10 2.10
256 A203 90c multi 2.40 2.40
257 A203 €5 multi 13.00 13.00
Nos. 255-257 (3) 17.50 17.50

Mail Planes A204

Designs: 2, Junkers F13. 1, Saab 340.

2007, Mar. 1 ***Perf. 12½***
258-259 A204 Set of 2 3.25 3.25

No. 258 sold for 55c, and No. 259 sold for 70c on day of issue.

Landscapes Type of 2004

2007, Mar. 13
260 A194 2 Skaftö, Kumlinge 1.50 1.50

Sold for 55c on day of issue.

Untitled Painting by Tove Jansson A205

2007, Apr. 18 ***Perf. 13¼x13¾***
261 A205 85c multi 2.40 2.40

Europa — A206

2007, May 9 *Perf. 12½x13¼*

262 A206 70c multi 1.90 1.90

Scouting, cent.

Contemporary Crafts — A207

Designs: No. 263, Bridal crown, by Titti Sundblom. No. 264, Floral textile design, by Maria Korpi-Gordon and Adam Gordon. No. 265, Cups, bowl and plate, by Judy Kuyitunen.

2007, May 18 *Perf. 13 Horiz.*

Booklet Stamps

263	A207	1 multi	1.90	1.90
264	A207	1 multi	1.90	1.90
265	A207	1 multi	1.90	1.90
a.		Booklet pane, 3 each #263-265	17.50	—
		Complete booklet, #265a	17.50	

Nos. 263-265 each sold for 70c on day of issue.

A208

Serpentine Die Cut 10 Syncopated

2007, June 7

Booklet Stamp

Self-Adhesive

266	A208	1 multi	1.90	1.90
a.		Booklet pane of 8	15.50	

No. 266 sold for 70c on day of issue. Design portion of stamp could be personalized at €10.40 per booklet with a minimum purchase of three booklets.

Emigration to America A209

2007, Aug. 9 Litho. *Perf. 13¼x12½*

267 A209 75c multi 2.10 2.10

Kjusan, Hammarland A210

2007, Oct. 1 *Perf. 12½*

268 A210 1 multi 2.00 2.00

No. 268 sold for 70c on day of issue.

Christmas — A211

2007, Oct. 9 *Perf. 14*

269 A211 (50c) multi 1.50 1.50

Fish A212

Designs: 45c, Perca fluviatilis. €4.50, Sander lucioperca.

2008, Feb. 1 Litho. *Perf. 13¼x13*

270	A212	45c multi	1.40	1.40
271	A212	€4.50 multi	13.50	13.50

Souvenir Sheet

Mythical Princess Signhild at Drottningkleven — A213

Perf. 12½x13¼

2008, Mar. 27 **Litho.**

272 A213 (85c) multi 2.75 2.75

Badhusberget, Mariehamn — A214

Langvikshagen, Lumparland — A215

2008, Apr. 15 *Perf. 13x12½*

273	A214	(70c) multi	2.25	2.25
274	A215	(70c) multi	2.25	2.25

2008 Summer Olympics, Beijing A216

2008, May 9 *Perf. 13¾*

275 A216 (90c) multi 2.75 2.75

Europa A217

2008, May 9 *Perf. 13¼x13*

276 A217 €1 multi 3.25 3.25

Lighthouses A218

No. 277: a, Marhällan Lighthouse. b, Gustaf Dalén Lighthouse. c, Kökarsören Lighthouse. d, Bogskär Lighthouse.

Litho., Litho & Engr (#277c-277d)

2008, June 6 *Perf. 12¾ on 3 Sides*

Booklet Stamps

277		Block or strip of 4	9.75	9.75
a.-d.		A218 (75c) Any single	2.40	2.40
e.		Booklet pane, 2 #277	19.50	—
		Complete booklet, #277e	19.50	

Within the booklet pane, stamps in one row are tete-beche in relation to stamps in the adjacent row.

Gravel Road and Profiles of Marcus Grönholm, Rally Driver, and Christoph Treier, Trainer A219

2008, July 26 Litho. *Perf. 13½*

278 A219 (90c) multi 3.00 3.00

Particles of granite were applied to portions of the design using a thermographic process.

Aland Peasant Bride, by Karl Emanuel Jansson — A220

2008, Aug. 15 *Perf. 13x13¼*

279 A220 €1.50 multi 4.50 4.50

Christmas A221

Litho. With Hologram Applied

2008, Oct. 9 *Perf. 13¾x13¼*

280 A221 (55c) multi 1.50 1.50

Personalized Stamp — A222

Serpentine Die Cut 10 Syncopated

2008, Oct. 9 **Litho.**

Booklet Stamp

Self-Adhesive

281	A222	(75c) multi	2.00	2.00
a.		Booklet pane of 8	16.00	

The generic design portion of the stamp shown could be personalized.

1810 Boundary Post — A223

Litho. & Embossed With Foil Application

2009, Jan. 22 *Perf. 14¼*

282 A223 (80c) multi 2.25 2.25

Souvenir Sheet

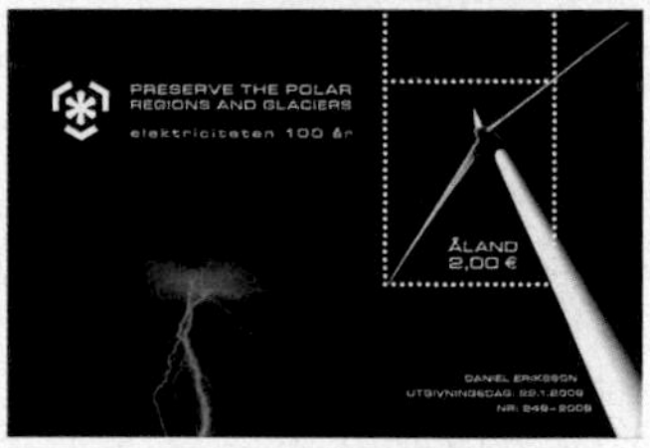

Electricity on Aland Islands, Cent. — A224

Litho. & Embossed

2009, Jan. 22 *Perf. 12½x13¼*

283 A224 €2 black 5.50 5.50

FIUME

'fyü-ˌmā

LOCATION — A city and surrounding territory on the Adriatic Sea
GOVT. — Formerly a part of Italy
AREA — 8 sq. mi.
POP. — 44,956 (estimated 1924)

Fiume was under Hapsburg rule after 1466 and was transferred to Hungarian control after 1870. Of mixed Italian and Croatian population and strategically important - it was Hungary's only international seaport - Fiume was disputed between Italy and the newly-created Kingdom of the Serbs, Croats and Slovenes (later Yugoslavia), following World War I. A force of Allied troops occupied the city in Nov. 1918, while its future status was negotiated at the Paris Peace Conference.

In Sept., 1919, the Italian nationalist poet Gabriele d'Annunzio organized his legionnaires and seized Fiume, together with the islands of Arbe, Carnaro and Veglia, in the name of Italy. D'Annunzio established an autonomous administration, which soon came into conflict with the Italian government. There followed several years of instability, with three Italian interventions after 1920. In Jan. 1924, the Treaty of Rome between Italy anf Yugoslavia established formal Italian sovereignty over Fiume, and Fiume stamps were replaced by those of Italy after March 31, 1924.

100 Filler = 1 Korona
100 Centesimi = 1 Corona (1919)
100 Centesimi = 1 Lira

See note on FIUME-KUPA Zone, Italian Occupation, after Yugoslavia No. NJ22.

The overprints on Nos. 1-23a have been extensively forged. Even the inexpensive values are difficult to find with genuine overprints. Forgeries of many later issues also exist, most created for the packet trade in the 1920s. Values are for genuine stamps. Collectors should be aware that stamps sold "as is" are likely to be forgeries, and unexpertized collections should be assumed to consist of mostly forged stamps. Education plus working with knowledgeable dealers is mandatory in this collecting area. More valuable stamps should be expertized.

Hungarian Stamps of 1916-18 Overprinted

1918, Dec. 2 Wmk. 137 Perf. 15

On Stamps of 1916

White Numerals

1a	A8	10f rose	100.00	45.00
2	A8	15f violet	40.00	28.00

Value for Nos. 1 is for handstamped overprint. Value for No. 2 is for typographed overprint.

On Stamps of 1916-18

Colored Numerals

3	A9	2f brown orange	3.25	1.60
4	A9	3f red violet	3.25	1.60
5	A9	5f green	3.25	1.60
6	A9	6f grnsh blue	3.25	1.60
7a	A9	10f rose red	*65.00*	*24.00*
8	A9	15f violet	3.25	1.60
9	A9	20f gray brown	3.25	1.60
10	A9	25f deep blue	12.00	2.00
11	A9	35f brown	6.50	3.25
12a	A9	40f olive green	95.00	40.00

White Numerals

13	A10	50f red vio & lil	4.00	2.40
14	A10	75f brt bl & pale bl	9.50	3.25
15	A10	80f grn & pale grn	9.50	2.40
16	A10	1k red brn & claret	32.50	8.00
17	A10	2k ol brn & bis	4.00	2.40
18	A10	3k dk vio & ind	40.00	20.00
19	A10	5k dk brn & lt brn	87.50	32.50
20a	A10	10k vio brn & vio	450.00	200.00

Inverted or double overprints exist on most of Nos. 4-15.

On Stamps of 1918

21	A11	10f scarlet	3.25	3.25
22	A11	20f dark brown	2.40	1.60
23a	A12	40f olive green	27.50	11.00

The overprint on Nos. 3-23a was applied by 2 printing plates and 6 handstamps. Values are for the less costly. Values of Nos. 7a, 12a, 20a and 23a are for handstamps. See the *Scott Specialized Catalogue of Stamps and Covers* for detailed listings.

Postage Due Stamps of Hungary, 1915-20 Ovptd. & Surcharged in Black

1919, Jan.

24	D1	45f on 6f green & red	13.00	*14.00*
25	D1	45f on 20f green & red	35.00	14.00
		Set, never hinged	120.00	

Hungarian Savings Bank Stamp Surcharged in Black — A2

1919, Jan. 29

26	A2	15f on 10f dk violet	17.50	16.00
		Never hinged	45.00	

"Italy" — A3

Italian Flag on Clock-Tower in Fiume — A4

"Revolution" A5

Sailor Raising Italian Flag at Fiume (1918) A6

Nos. 30-43 exist on three types of paper: (A) grayish, porous paper, printed in sheets of 70 stamps (Jan, Feb. printings); (B) translucent or semi-translucent good quality white paper, printed in sheets of 70 stamps (March printing); and (C) good quality medium white paper, plain and opaque, sometimes grayish or yellowish, printed in sheets of 100 (April printing). Values are for the least expensive variety. See the *Scott Specialized Catalogue of Stamps and Covers* for detailed listings.

1919 Unwmk. Litho. Perf. 11½

27	A3	2c dull blue (C)	1.60	1.60
28	A3	3c gray brown (C)	1.60	1.60
29	A3	5c yellow green (C)	1.60	1.60
30a	A4	10c rose (A)	24.00	12.00
31	A4	15c violet (C)	1.60	1.60
32a	A4	20c green (A)	3.25	2.40
33	A5	25c dark blue (C)	2.40	1.60
34	A6	30c deep violet (C)	2.40	1.60
35	A5	40c brown (C)	2.40	1.60
36	A5	45c orange (C)	2.40	2.40
37	A6	50c yellow green (C)	2.40	1.60
38	A6	60c claret (C)	2.40	1.60
39	A6	1cor brown orange (C)	4.00	2.40
40	A6	2cor brt blue (C)	4.00	2.40
41	A6	3cor orange red (C)	4.75	2.40
42	A6	5cor deep brown (C)	32.50	32.50
43a	A6	10cor olive green (A)	40.00	*65.00*
		Nos. 27-43a (17)	133.30	*135.90*

The earlier printings of Jan. and Feb. are on thin grayish paper, the Mar. printing is on semi-transparent white paper, all in sheets of 70. An Apr. printing is on white paper of medium thickness in sheets of 100. Part-perf. examples of most of this series are known.

For surcharges see Nos. 58, 60, 64, 66-69.

A7

A8

A9

A10

1919, July 28 Perf. 11½

46	A7	5c yellow green	1.60	.80
47	A8	10c rose	1.60	.80
48	A9	30c violet	6.50	2.40
49	A10	40c yellow brown	1.60	*1.60*
50	A10	45c orange	6.50	5.50
51	A9	50c yellow green	6.50	5.50
52	A9	60c claret	6.50	5.50
a.		Perf. 13x12½	175.00	—
		Never hinged	260.00	
b.		Perf. 10½	350.00	
		Never hinged	550.00	
53	A9	10cor olive green	6.50	*16.00*
a.		Perf. 13x12½	55.00	*95.00*
		Never hinged	85.00	
b.		Perf. 10½	350.00	350.00
		Never hinged	550.00	
		Nos. 46-53 (8)	37.30	38.10
		Set, never hinged	90.00	

Five other denominations (25c, 1cor, 2cor, 3cor and 5cor) were not officially issued. Some examples of the 25c are known canceled.

For surcharges see Nos. 59, 61-63, 65, 70.

Stamps of 1919 Handstamp Surcharged

1919-20

58	A4	5c on 20c green ('20)	1.60	1.60
59	A10	5c on 25c blue	1.60	1.60
60	A5	10c on 45c orange	1.60	1.60
61	A9	15c on 30c vio ('20)	1.60	1.60
62	A10	15c on 45c orange	1.60	1.60
63	A9	15c on 60c cl ('20)	1.60	1.60
64	A6	25c on 50c yel grn ('20)	14.50	*28.00*
65	A9	25c on 50c yel grn ('20)	1.60	1.60
66	A6	55c on 1cor brn org	35.00	32.50
67	A6	55c on 2cor brt bl	4.50	*8.00*
68	A6	55c on 3cor org red	4.50	7.00
69	A6	55c on 5cor dp brn	4.50	7.00
70	A9	55c on 10cor ol grn	28.00	32.50
		Nos. 58-70 (13)	102.20	*126.20*
		Set, never hinged	225.00	

Semi-Postal Stamps of 1919 Surcharged:

a

b

1919-20

73	SP6(a)	5c on 5c green	1.60	1.60
74	SP6(a)	10c on 10c rose	1.60	1.60
75	SP6(a)	15c on 15c gray	1.60	1.60
76	SP6(a)	20c on 20c org	1.60	1.60
77	SP9(a)	25c on 25c bl ('20)	1.60	1.60
78	SP7(b)	45c on 45c ol grn	2.40	2.40
79	SP7(b)	60c on 60c rose	2.40	2.40
80	SP7(b)	80c on 80c violet	1.60	1.60
81	SP7(b)	1cor on 1cor sl	2.40	2.40
82	SP8(a)	2cor on 2cor red brn	3.25	3.25
83	SP8(a)	3cor on 3cor blk brn	5.00	5.00
84	SP8(a)	5cor on 5cor yel brn	7.50	7.50
85	SP8(a)	10cor on 10cor dk vio ('20)	2.50	2.50
		Nos. 73-85 (13)	35.05	35.05
		Set, never hinged	75.00	

Double or inverted surcharges, or imperf. varieties, exist on most of Nos. 73-85.

There were three settings of the surcharges on Nos. 73-85 except No. 77 which is known only with one setting.

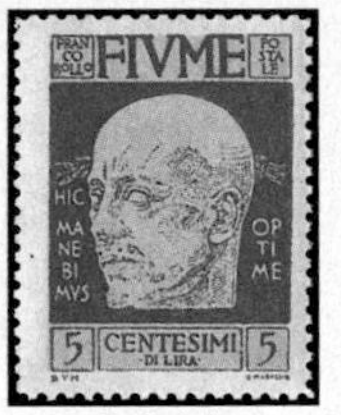

Gabriele d'Annunzio — A11

Severing the Gordian Knot — A12

1920, Sept. 12 Typo. Perf. 11½

Pale Buff Background

86	A11	5c green	1.60	1.60
87	A11	10c carmine	1.60	1.60
88	A11	15c dark gray	1.60	1.60
89	A11	20c orange	1.60	1.60
90	A11	25c dark blue	2.40	2.40
91	A11	30c red brown	2.40	2.40
92	A11	45c olive gray	3.25	3.25
93	A11	50c lilac	3.25	3.25
94	A11	55c bister	3.25	3.25
95	A11	1 l black	15.00	*22.50*
96	A11	2 l red violet	15.00	*22.50*
97	A11	3 l dark green	15.00	*22.50*
98	A11	5 l brown	75.00	42.50
99	A11	10 l gray violet	17.50	*27.50*
		Nos. 86-99 (14)	158.45	*158.45*
		Set, never hinged	350.00	

Counterfeits of Nos. 86 to 99 are plentiful.

For overprints see Nos. 134-148.

1920, Sept. 12

Designs: 10c, Ancient emblem of Fiume. 20c, Head of "Fiume." 25c, Hands holding daggers.

100	A12	5c green	57.50	32.50
101	A12	10c deep rose	30.00	25.00
102	A12	20c brown orange	57.50	25.00
103	A12	25c indigo	30.00	*55.00*
a.		25c blue	125.00	125.00
		Nos. 100-103 (4)	175.00	137.50
		Set, never hinged	425.00	

Anniv. of the occupation of Fiume by d'Annunzio. They were available for franking the correspondence of the legionnaires on the day of issue only, Sept. 12, 1920.

Counterfeits of Nos. 100-103 are plentiful.
For overprints and surcharges see Nos. 104-133, E4-E9.

Nos. 100-103 Overprinted or Surcharged in Black or Red and New Values

1920, Nov. 20

104	A12	1c on 5c green	1.60	1.60
105	A12	2c on 25c indigo (R)	1.60	1.60
a.		2c on 25c blue (R)	80.00	80.00
106	A12	5c green	20.00	1.75
107	A12	10c rose	20.00	1.75
108	A12	15c on 10c rose	1.75	1.75
109	A12	15c on 20c brn org	1.50	*1.75*
110	A12	15c on 25c ind (R)	1.75	*1.75*
a.		15c on 25c blue (R)	175.00	175.00
111	A12	20c brown orange	1.75	1.75
112	A12	25c indigo (R)	1.75	1.75
a.		25c blue (R)	7.50	7.50
113	A12	25c indigo (Bk)	175.00	175.00
a.		25c blue (Bk)	225.00	225.00
114	A12	25c on 10c rose	2.00	3.75
115	A12	50c on 20c brn org	5.00	2.00
116	A12	55c on 5c green	21.00	3.75
117	A12	1 l on 10c rose	40.00	28.00
118	A12	1 l on 25c ind (R)	100.00	100.00
a.		1 l on 25c blue (R)	600.00	600.00
119	A12	2 l on 5c green	40.00	32.50
120	A12	5 l on 10c rose	200.00	*225.00*
121	A12	10 l on 20c brn org	700.00	550.00
		Nos. 104-121 (18)	1,334.	1,135.
		Set, never hinged	3,000.	

The Fiume Legionnaires of d'Annunzio occupied the islands of Arbe and Veglia in the Gulf of Carnaro Nov. 13, 1920-Jan. 5, 1921.
Varieties of overprint or surcharge exist for most of Nos. 104-121.
#113, 117-121, 125, 131 have a backprint.

Nos. 106-107, 111, 113, 115-116 Overprinted or Surcharged at top

1920, Nov. 18

122	A12	5c green	24.00	19.50
123	A12	10c rose	32.50	*36.00*
124	A12	20c brown org	65.00	40.00
125	A12	25c deep blue	36.00	*40.00*
126	A12	50c on 20c brn org	67.50	40.00
127	A12	55c on 5c green	67.50	40.00
		Nos. 122-127 (6)	292.50	215.50
		Set, never hinged	700.00	

The overprint on Nos. 122-125 comes in two widths: 11mm and 14mm. Values are for the 11mm width.

Nos. 106-107, 111, 113, 115-116 Overprinted or Surcharged at top

1920, Nov. 18

128	A12	5c green	24.00	19.50
129	A12	10c rose	32.50	*36.00*
130	A12	20c brown orange	65.00	40.00
131	A12	25c deep blue	36.00	*40.00*
132	A12	50c on 20c brn org	67.50	40.00
133	A12	55c on 5c green	67.50	40.00
		Nos. 128-133 (6)	292.50	215.50
		Set, never hinged	700.00	

The overprint on Nos. 128-131 comes in two widths: 17mm and 19mm. Values are for the 17mm width.
Nos. 122-133 exist with double and inverted overprints.

Counterfeits of these overprints exist.

Nos. 86-99 Overprinted

1921, Feb. 2
Pale Buff Background

134	A11	5c green	1.60	1.60
135	A11	10c carmine	1.60	1.60
136	A11	15c dark gray	1.60	*1.60*
137	A11	20c orange	2.40	2.40
138	A11	25c dark blue	2.40	2.40
139	A11	30c red brown	2.40	2.40
140	A11	45c olive gray	1.75	1.75
141	A11	50c lilac	2.75	2.00
142	A11	55c bister	2.50	2.00
143	A11	1 l black	140.00	*145.00*
144	A11	2 l red violet	80.00	80.00
145	A11	3 l dark green	80.00	80.00
146	A11	5 l brown	80.00	80.00
147	A11	10 l gray violet	80.00	80.00

With Additional Surcharge

148	A11	1 l on 30c red brn	1.50	1.50
		Nos. 134-148 (15)	480.50	484.25
		Set, never hinged	1,100.	

Most of Nos. 134-143, 148 and E10-E11 exist with inverted or double overprint.
See Nos. E10-E11.

First Constituent Assembly

Nos. B4-B15 Overprinted

1921, Apr. 24

149	SP6	5c blue green	4.75	4.00
150	SP6	10c rose	4.75	4.00
151	SP6	15c gray	4.75	4.00
152	SP6	20c orange	4.75	4.00
153	SP7	45c olive green	14.50	9.50
154	SP7	60c car rose	14.50	9.50
155	SP7	80c brt violet	20.00	20.00

With Additional Overprint "L"

156	SP7	1 l on 1cor dk sl	24.00	24.00
157	SP8	2 l on 2cor red brn	95.00	3.25
158	SP8	3 l on 3cor blk brn	95.00	*105.00*
159	SP8	5 l on 5cor yel brn	95.00	4.00
160	SP8	10 l on 10cor dk vio	145.00	145.00
		Nos. 149-160 (12)	522.00	336.25
		Set, never hinged	1,200.	

The overprint exists inverted on several denominations.

Second Constituent Assembly
"Constitution" Issue of 1921 With Additional Overprint "1922"

1922

161	SP6	5c blue green	4.00	2.75
162	SP6	10c rose	1.60	*1.60*
163	SP6	15c gray	17.50	8.00
164	SP6	20c orange	1.75	1.75
165	SP7	45c olive grn	11.50	9.50
166	SP7	60c car rose	1.60	*2.75*
167	SP7	80c brt violet	1.60	*2.75*
168	SP7	1 l on 1cor dk slate	1.75	*2.25*
169	SP8	2 l on 2cor red brn	17.50	12.00
170	SP8	3 l on 3cor blk brn	1.75	*2.75*
171	SP8	5 l on 5cor yel brn	1.75	*2.75*
		Nos. 161-171 (11)	62.30	48.85
		Set, never hinged	140.00	

Nos. 161-171 have the overprint in heavier type than Nos. 149-160 and "IV" in Roman instead of sans-serif numerals.
The overprint exists inverted or double on almost all values.

Venetian Ship — A16

Roman Arch — A17

St. Vitus — A18

Rostral Column — A19

1923, Mar. 23 ***Perf. 11½***
Pale Buff Background

172	A16	5c blue green	1.60	1.60
173	A16	10c violet	1.60	1.60
174	A16	15c brown	1.60	1.60
175	A17	20c orange red	1.60	1.60
176	A17	25c dark gray	1.60	1.60
177	A17	30c dark green	1.60	1.60
178	A18	50c dull blue	1.60	1.60
179	A18	60c rose	2.50	*2.40*
180	A18	1 l dark blue	2.50	*2.50*
181	A19	2 l violet brown	55.00	11.00
182	A19	3 l olive bister	45.00	37.50
183	A19	5 l yellow brown	45.00	45.00
		Nos. 172-183 (12)	161.20	109.60
		Set, never hinged	360.00	

Nos. 172-183 Overprinted

1924, Feb. 22
Pale Buff Background

184	A16	5c blue green	1.60	*4.00*
185	A16	10c violet	1.60	*4.00*
186	A16	15c brown	1.60	*4.00*
187	A17	20c orange red	1.60	*4.00*
188	A17	25c dk gray	1.60	*4.00*
189	A17	30c dk green	1.60	*4.00*
190	A18	50c dull blue	1.60	*4.00*
191	A18	60c red	1.60	*4.00*
192	A18	1 l dark blue	1.60	*4.00*
193	A19	2 l violet brown	3.25	*13.00*
194	A19	3 l olive	6.00	*16.50*
195	A19	5 l yellow brown	6.00	*16.50*
		Nos. 184-195 (12)	29.65	*82.00*
		Set, never hinged	60.00	

The overprint exists inverted on almost all values.

Nos. 172-183 Overprinted

1924, Mar. 1
Pale Buff Background

196	A16	5c blue green	1.60	*2.40*
197	A16	10c violet	1.60	*2.40*
198	A16	15c brown	1.60	*2.40*
199	A17	20c orange red	1.60	*2.40*
200	A17	25c dark gray	1.60	*2.40*
201	A17	30c dark green	1.60	*2.40*
202	A18	50c dull blue	1.60	*2.40*
203	A18	60c red	1.60	*2.40*
204	A18	1 l dark blue	1.60	*2.40*
205	A19	2 l violet brown	2.40	*5.00*
206	A19	3 l olive	2.75	*5.00*
207	A19	5 l yellow brown	2.75	*5.00*
		Nos. 196-207 (12)	22.30	*36.60*
		Set, never hinged	40.00	

Postage stamps of Fiume were superseded by stamps of Italy.

SEMI-POSTAL STAMPS

Semi-Postal Stamps of Hungary, 1916-17 Overprinted

1918, Dec. 2 **Wmk. 137** ***Perf. 15***

B1	SP3	10f + 2f rose	6.50	5.50
a.		Inverted overprint	65.00	40.00
B2	SP4	15f + 2f dl vio	6.50	5.50
a.		Inverted overprint	125.00	40.00
B3	SP5	40f + 2f brn car	11.50	5.50
a.		Inverted overprint	67.50	37.50
		Nos. B1-B3 (3)	24.50	16.50
		Set, never hinged	60.00	

Examples of Nos. B1-B3 with overprint handstamped sell for higher prices.

Statue of Romulus and Remus Being Suckled by Wolf — SP6

Venetian Galley — SP7

Church of St. Mark's, Venice — SP8

Perf. 11½
1919, May 18 **Unwmk.** **Typo.**

B4	SP6	5c +5 l bl grn	28.00	17.50
B5	SP6	10c +5 l rose	28.00	17.50
B6	SP6	15c +5 l dk gray	28.00	17.50
B7	SP6	20c +5 l orange	28.00	17.50
B8	SP7	45c +5 l ol grn	28.00	17.50
B9	SP7	60c +5 l car rose	28.00	17.50
B10	SP7	80c +5 l lilac	28.00	17.50
B11	SP7	1cor +5 l dk slate	28.00	17.50
B12	SP8	2cor +5 l red brn	28.00	17.50
B13	SP8	3cor +5 l blk brn	28.00	17.50
B14	SP8	5cor +5 l yel brn	28.00	17.50
B15	SP8	10cor +5 l dk vio	28.00	17.50
		Nos. B4-B15 (12)	336.00	210.00
		Set, never hinged	800.00	

200th day of peace. The surtax aided Fiume students in Italy. "Posta di Fiume" is printed on the back of Nos. B4-B16.
The surtax is shown on the stamps as "LIRE 5" but actually was 5cor.
For surcharges and overprints see Nos. 73-85, 149-171, J15-J26.

Dr. Antonio Grossich — SP9

1919, Sept. 20
B16 SP9 25c + 2 l blue 3.00 3.00
Never hinged 7.25

Surtax for the Dr. Grossich Foundation.

SPECIAL DELIVERY STAMPS

Special Delivery Stamp of Hungary, 1916, Overprinted like Nos. 1-23

1918, Dec. 2 Wmk. 137 *Perf. 15*
E1 SD1 2f gray green & red 4.00 4.00
Never hinged 10.00

Handstamped overprints sell for more.

SD3

Perf. 11½
1920, Sept. 12 Unwmk. Typo.
E2 SD3 30c slate blue 25.00 25.00
E3 SD3 50c rose 25.00 25.00
Set, never hinged 120.00

For overprints see Nos. E10-E11.

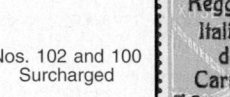

Nos. 102 and 100 Surcharged

1920, Nov.
E4 A12 30c on 20c brn org 150.00 127.50
E5 A12 50c on 5c green 210.00 95.00

Nos. E4-E5 have a backprint.

Same Surcharge as on Nos. 124, 122
E6 A12 30c on 20c brn org 225.00 145.00
E7 A12 50c on 5c green 175.00 145.00

Overprint on Nos. E6-E7 is 11mm wide.

Same Surcharge as on Nos. 130, 128
E8 A12 30c on 20c brn org 225.00 145.00
E9 A12 50c on 5c green 175.00 145.00
Nos. E4-E9 (6) 1,160. 802.50
Set, never hinged 2,900.

Overprint on Nos. E8-E9 is 17mm wide.

Nos. E2 and E3 Overprinted

1921, Feb. 2
E10 SD3 30c slate blue 10.00 12.00
E11 SD3 50c rose 15.00 12.00
Set, never hinged 60.00

Fiume in 16th Century SD4

1923, Mar. 23 *Perf. 11, 11½*
E12 SD4 60c rose & buff 20.00 13.50
E13 SD4 2 l dk bl & buff 20.00 15.00
Set, never hinged 85.00

Nos. E12-E13 Overprinted

1924, Feb. 22
E14 SD4 60c car & buff 2.25 *7.00*
E15 SD4 2 l dk bl & buff 2.25 *7.00*
Set, never hinged 9.00

Nos. E12-E13 Overprinted

1924, Mar. 1
E16 SD4 60c car & buff 2.75 *6.00*
E17 SD4 2 l dk bl & buff 2.75 *6.00*
Set, never hinged 10.00

POSTAGE DUE STAMPS

Postage Due Stamps of Hungary, 1915-1916, Overprinted

1918, Dec. Wmk. 137 *Perf. 15*
J1 D1 6f green & black 175.00 87.50
J2 D1 12f green & black 190.00 60.00
J3 D1 50f green & black 60.00 27.50
Set, never hinged 900.00

J4 D1 1f green & red 36.00 17.50
J5 D1 2f green & red 4.75 4.75
J6 D1 5f green & red 32.50 45.00
J7 D1 6f green & red 4.75 4.75
J8 D1 10f green & red 28.00 20.00
J9 D1 12f green & red 4.75 4.75
J10 D1 15f green & red 28.00 28.00
J11 D1 20f green & red 4.75 4.75
J12 D1 30f green & red 28.00 28.00
Nos. J4-J12 (9) 171.50 157.50
Set, never hinged 275.00

The overprint on Nos. J1-J12 was applied both by press and handstamp. Values are for the less costly. Inverted and double overprints exist. Excellent forgeries exist.

Eagle — D2

Perf. 11½
1919, July 28 Unwmk. Typo.
J13 D2 2c brown 1.75 1.60
J14 D2 5c brown 1.75 1.60
Set, never hinged 8.00

Semi-Postal Stamps of 1919 with Overprint "Valore Globale" Surcharged:

1921, Mar. 21
J15 SP6 2c on 15c gray 4.75 4.75
J16 SP6 4c on 10c rose 4.00 4.00
J17 SP9 5c on 25c blue 4.00 4.00
J18 SP6 6c on 20c orange 4.00 4.00
J19 SP6 10c on 20c orange 4.75 4.75

Surcharged:

J20 SP7 20c on 45c olive grn 2.00 *3.25*
J21 SP7 30c on 1cor dk slate 8.00 *8.00*
J22 SP7 40c on 80c violet 4.00 *4.00*
J23 SP7 50c on 60c carmine 4.00 *4.00*
J24 SP7 60c on 45c olive grn 2.00 *3.25*
J25 SP7 80c on 45c olive grn 2.00 *3.25*

Surcharged like Nos. J15-J19
J26 SP8 1 l on 2cor red brown 16.00 *16.00*
Nos. J15-J26 (12) 59.50 *63.25*
Set, never hinged 65.00

See note below No. 85 regarding settings of "Valore Globale" overprint.

NEWSPAPER STAMPS

Newspaper Stamp of Hungary, 1914, Overprinted like Nos. 1-23

1918, Dec. 2 Wmk. 137 *Imperf.*
P1 N5 (2f) orange 4.00 2.40
Never hinged 10.00

Handstamped overprints sell for more.

Eagle N1

1919 Unwmk. *Perf. 11½*
P2 N1 2c deep buff 7.00 *11.00*

Re-engraved
P3 N1 2c deep buff 7.00 *11.00*
Set, never hinged 35.00

In the re-engraved stamp the top of the "2" is rounder and broader, the feet of the eagle show clearly and the diamond at bottom has six lines instead of five.

Steamer — N2

1920, Sept. 12
P4 N2 1c gray green 2.75 1.75
Never hinged 6.00

No. P4 exists imperf.

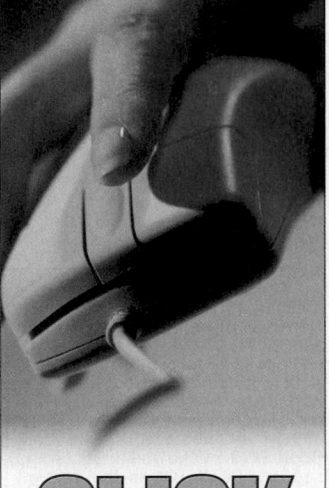

FRANCE

ˈfrants

LOCATION — Western Europe
GOVT. — Republic
AREA — 210,033 sq. mi.
POP. — 58,978,172 (1999 est.)
CAPITAL — Paris

100 Centimes = 1 Franc
100 Cents = 1 Euro (2002)

Catalogue values for unused stamps in this country are for Never Hinged items, beginning with Scott 299 in the regular postage section, Scott B42 in the semi-postal section, Scott C18 in the airpost section, Scott CB1 in the airpost semi-postal section, Scott J69 in the postage due section, Scott M10 in the military stamps section, Scott 1O1 in the section for official stamps for the Council of Europe, Scott 2O1 for the section for UNESCO, Scott S1 for franchise stamps, Scott N27 for occupation stamps, and Scott 2N1 for AMG stamps.

Ceres — A1

FORTY CENTIMES

4
Type I

4
Type II

1849-50 Typo. Unwmk. *Imperf.*

1	A1	10c bis, *yelsh* ('50)	*2,000.*	275.00
a.		10c dark bister, *yelsh*	2,300.	350.00
b.		10c greenish bister	2,750.	425.00
d.		Tête beche pair	*115,000.*	*18,500.*
2	A1	15c green, *grnsh* ('50)	*23,000.*	900.00
a.		15c yellow green, *grnsh*	*22,500.*	900.00
c.		Tête bêche pair		—
3	A1	20c blk, *yelsh*	400.00	45.00
a.		20c black	475.00	55.00
b.		20c black, *buff*	1,400.	225.00
c.		Tête bêche pair	*10,000.*	*6,600.*
4	A1	20c dark blue	*2,850.*	
a.		20c blue, *bluish*	*2,200.*	
b.		20c blue, *yelsh*	*3,500.*	
c.		Tête bêche pair	*70,000.*	
6	A1	25c lt bl, *bluish*	*6,750.*	40.00
a.		25c blue, *bluish* ('50)	*6,750.*	40.00
b.		25c blue, *yelsh*	*6,400.*	50.00
c.		Tête bêche pair	*185,000.*	*13,500.*
7	A1	40c org, *yelsh* (I) ('50)	*3,750.*	475.00
a.		40c org ver, *yelsh* (I)	*4,250.*	525.00
b.		40c orange, *yelsh* (II)	*25,000.*	*6,750.*
c.		Pair, types I and II	*40,000.*	*13,250.*
g.		Vertical half used as 20c on cover		*215,000.*
8	A1	1fr ver, *yelsh*	*100,000.*	*15,500.*
a.		1fr dull org red	*100,000.*	*19,500.*
b.		Tête bêche pair	*95,000.*	*172,500.*
c.		1fr pale ver ("Vervelle")	*26,500.*	
d.		As "c," tête bêche pair	*480,000.*	
9	A1	1fr light carmine	*11,000.*	800.00
a.		Tête bêche pair	*235,000.*	*23,500.*
b.		1fr brown carmine	*13,250.*	1,100.
c.		1fr dk car, *yelsh*	*11,500.*	825.00

No. 4, which lacks gum, was not issued due to a rate change to 25c after the stamps were prepared. An essay with a red "25" surcharge on No. 4 was rejected.

An ungummed sheet of No. 8c was found in 1895 among the effects of Anatole A. Hulot, the printer. It was sold to Ernest Vervelle, a Parisian dealer, by whose name the stamps are known.

See Nos. 329-329e, 612-613, 624.

Nos. 1, 4a, 6a, 7 and 13 are of similar designs and colors to French Colonies Nos. 9, 11, 12, 14, and 8. There are numerous shades of each. Identification by those who are not experts can be difficult, though cancellations can be used as a guide for used stamps. Because of the date of issue the Colonies stamps are similar in shades and papers to the perforated French stamps,

Nos. 23a, 54, 57-59, and are not as clearly printed. Except for No. 13, unused, the French Colonies stamps sell for much less than the values shown here for properly identified French versions.

Expertization of these stamps is recommended.

1862 Re-issue

1g	A1	10c bister	550.
2d	A1	15c yellow green	700.
3d	A1	20c black, *yellowish*	450.
4d	A1	20c blue	450.
6d	A1	25c blue	500.
7d	A1	40c orange (I)	700.
7e	A1	40c orange (II)	*11,500.*
h.		Pair, types I and II	*16,500.*
9d	A1	1fr pale lake	750.

The re-issues are fine impressions in lighter colors and on whiter paper than the originals. An official imitation of the essay, 25c on 20c blue, also in a lighter shade and on whiter paper, was made at the same time as the re-issues.

President Louis Napoleon — A2

Emperor Napoleon III — A3

1852

10	A2	10c pale bister, *yelsh*	*34,500.*	575.00
a.		10c dark bister, *yelsh*	*37,000.*	650.00
11	A2	25c blue, *bluish*	*2,900.*	40.00
b.		25c dark blue, *blush*	*3,500.*	70.00

1862 Re-issue

10b	A2	10c bister	700.00
11a	A2	25c blue	450.00

The re-issues are in lighter colors and on whiter paper than the originals.

1853-60 *Imperf.*

Die I. The curl above the forehead directly below "R" of "EMPIRE" is made up of two lines very close together, often appearing to form a single thick line. There is no shading across the neck.

Die II. The curl is made of two distinct, more widely separated lines. There are lines of shading across the upper neck.

12	A3	1c ol grn, *pale bl* ('60)	190.00	80.00
a.		1c bronze grn, *pale bluish*	200.00	95.00
13	A3	5c grn, *grnsh* (I) ('54)	800.00	85.00
14	A3	10c bis, *yelsh* (I)	425.00	9.00
a.		10c yellow, *yelsh* (I)	1,500.	37.50
b.		10c bister brn, *yelsh* (I)	550.00	25.00
c.		10c bis, *yelsh* (II) ('60)	550.00	22.50
15	A3	20c bl, *bluish* (I) ('54)	190.00	1.50
a.		20c dark bl, *bluish* (I)	250.00	2.00
b.		20c milky blue (I)	275.00	12.50
c.		20c blue, *lilac* (I)	4,500.	82.50
d.		20c bl, *bluish* (II) ('60)	325.00	4.75
e.		Half used as 10c on cover		*18,500.*
f.		Tête-bêche pair	*190,000.*	
16	A3	20c bl, *grnsh* (II)	*5,000.*	190.00
a.		20c blue, *greenish* (I)	*4,250.*	125.00
17	A3	25c bl, *bluish* (I)	2,300.	250.00
18	A3	40c org, *yelsh* (I)	2,250.	12.50
a.		40c org ver, *yellowish*	*2,750.*	20.00
b.		Half used as 20c on cover		*135,000.*
19	A3	80c lake, *yelsh* (I) ('54)	3,400.	82.50
a.		Tête bêche pair	*325,000.*	*17,500.*
b.		Half used as 40c on cover		*40,000.*
20	A3	80c rose, *pnksh* (I) ('60)	2,400.	47.50
a.		Tete bêche pair	*57,500.*	*13,000.*
21	A3	1fr lake, *yelsh* (I)	*8,000.*	*3,250.*
a.		Tête bêche pair	*310,000.*	*130,000.*

Most values of the 1853-60 issue are known privately rouletted, pin-perf., perf. 7 and percé en scie.

1862 Re-issue

17c	A3	25c blue (I)	425.
19c	A3	80c lake (I)	1,500.
21c	A3	1fr lake (I)	1,800.
d.		Tête bêche pair	*30,000.*

The re-issues are in lighter colors and on whiter paper than the originals.

1862-71 *Perf. 14x13½*

22	A3	1c ol grn, *pale bl* (II)	160.00	40.00
a.		1c bronze grn, *pale bl* (II)	160.00	40.00
23	A3	5c yel grn, *grnsh* (I)	375.00	20.00
a.		5c deep green, *grnsh* (I)	250.00	16.00
24	A3	5c grn, *pale bl* ('71) (I)	1,950.	100.00
25	A3	10c bis, *yelsh* (II)	1,450.	4.25
a.		10c yel brn, *yelsh* (II)	2,000.	10.50
26	A3	20c bl, *bluish* (II)	225.00	1.25
a.		Tête bêche pair (II)	4,000.	1,000.
27	A3	40c org, *yelsh* (I)	1,300.	7.50
28	A3	80c rose, *pnksh* (I)	1,200.	37.50
a.		80c brt rose, *pinkish* (I)	1,500.	57.50
c.		Tête bêche pair (I)	*20,500.*	*8,250.*

No. 26a imperf is from a trial printing.

A4

A5

Napoleon III — A6

1863-70 *Perf. 14x13½*

29	A4	1c brnz grn, *pale bl* ('70)	45.00	20.00
a.		1c olive green, *pale blue*	45.00	20.00
30	A4	2c red brn, *yelsh*	82.50	25.00
b.		Half used as 1c on cover		*42,500.*
31	A4	4c gray	200.00	52.50
a.		Tete beche pair	*20,000.*	*13,250.*
d.		Half used as 2c on cover		*60,000.*
32	A5	10c bis, *yelsh* ('67)	325.00	6.00
c.		Half used as 5c on cover with other stamps		*3,750.*
33	A5	20c bl, *bluish* ('67)	225.00	1.60
c.		Half used as 10c on cover		*52,500.*
34	A5	30c brn, *yelsh* ('67)	750.00	17.00
a.		30c dk brn, *yellowish*	1,225.	37.50
35	A5	40c pale org, *yellowish*	750.00	10.00
a.		40c org, *yelsh* ('68)	750.00	10.00
c.		Half used as 20c on cover		*42,500.*
36	A5	80c rose, *pnksh* ('68)	1,000.	24.00
a.		80c carmine, *yellowish*	1,400.	40.00
d.		Half used as 40c on cover		*50,000.*
e.		Quarter used as 20c on cover		*57,500.*
37	A6	5fr gray lil, *lav* ('69)	*6,000.*	825.00
a.		"5" and "F" omitted		*112,500.*
c.		5fr bluish gray, *lavender*	*6,500.*	1,000.
d.		As #37, "5" and "F" in light blue	*8,000.*	1,100.

No. 33 exists in two types, differing in the size of the dots at either side of POSTES.

On No. 37, the "5" and "F" vary in height from 3¾mm to 4½mm. These figures normally appear in gray but exist in blue or black.

All known examples of No. 37a are more or less damaged.

No. 29 was reprinted in 1887 by authority of Granet, Minister of Posts. The reprints show a yellowish shade under the ultraviolet lamp. Value $850.

For surcharge see No. 49.

Original Issue Imperfs

31c	A4	4c gray	400.	175.
32b	A5	10c bister, *yellowish*	450.	175.
33b	A5	20c blue, *bluish*	375.	160.
36c	A5	80c rose, *pinkish*		—
37b	A6	5fr gray lilac, *lavender*	*8,500.*	8,500.

Imperfs, "Rothschild" Re-issue

Paper Colors are the Same

29b	A4	1c olive green	1,200.
30a	A4	2c pale red brown	190.
31b	A4	4c pale gray	140.
32a	A5	10c pale bister	140.
33a	A5	20c pale blue	250.
34c	A5	30c pale brown	150.
35b	A5	40c pale orange	225.
36b	A5	80c rose	425.

The re-issues constitute the "Rothschild Issue." These stamps were authorized exclusively for the banker to use on his correspondence. Used copies exist.

Ceres

A7 A8

A9

A10

A11

Bordeaux Issue

On the lithographed stamps, except for type I of the 20c, the shading on the cheek and neck is in lines or dashes, not in dots. On the typographed stamps the shading is in dots. The 2c, 10c and 20c (types II and III) occur in two or more types. The most easily distinguishable are:

2c — Type A. To the left of and within the top of the left "2" are lines of shading composed of dots.

2c — Type B. These lines of dots are replaced by solid lines.

10c — Type A. The inner frame lines are of the same thickness as all other frame lines.

10c — Type B. The inner frame lines are much thicker than the others.

Three Types of the 20c.

A9 — The inscriptions in the upper and lower labels are small and there is quite a space between the upper label and the circle containing the head. There is also very little shading under the eye and in the neck.

A10 — The inscriptions in the labels are similar to those of the first type, the shading under the eye and in the neck is heavier and the upper label and circle almost touch.

A11 — The inscriptions in the labels are much larger than those of the two preceding types, and are similar to those of the other values of the same type in the set.

1870-71 Litho. *Imperf.*

38 A7 1c ol grn, *pale bl* 160.00 115.00
- *a.* 1c bronze grn, *pale blue* 200.00 *150.00*

39 A7 2c red brn, *yelsh* (B) 275.00 250.00
- *a.* 2c brick red, *yelsh* (B) 825.00 625.00
- *b.* 2c chestnut, *yelsh* (B) 1,500. 850.00
- *c.* 2c chocolate, *yelsh* (A) 825.00 725.00

40 A7 4c gray 275.00 225.00

41 A8 5c yel green, *greenish* 275.00 175.00
- *a.* 5c grn, *grnsh* 350.00 175.00
- *b.* 5c emerald, *greenish* 3,600. 1,250.

42 A8 10c bis, *yelsh* (A) 1,000. 60.00
- *a.* 10c bister, *yellowish* (B) 1,000. 90.00

43 A9 20c bl, *bluish* *22,000.* 575.00
- *a.* 20c dark blue, *bluish* *24,500.* 825.00

44 A10 20c bl, *bluish* 950.00 45.00
- *a.* 20c dark blue, *bluish* 1,250. 100.00
- *b.* 20c ultra, *bluish* *22,000.* *3,300.*

45 A11 20c bl, *bluish* ('71) 950.00 18.00
- *a.* 20c ultra, *bluish* 2,750. 1,250.

46 A8 30c brn, *yelsh* 375.00 225.00
- *a.* 30c blk brn, *yelsh* 2,000. 825.00

47 A8 40c org, *yelsh* 475.00 115.00
- *a.* 40c yel orange, *yelsh* 1,450. 250.00
- *b.* 40c red orange, *yelsh* 725.00 190.00
- *c.* 40c scarlet, *yelsh* *3,200.* *775.00*

48 A8 80c rose, *pinkish* 525.00 250.00
- *a.* 80c dull rose, *pinkish* 1,000. 275.00

All values of the 1870 issue are known privately rouletted, pin-perf. and perf. 14.

See Nos. 50-53.

A12

Dark Blue Surcharge

1871 Typo. *Perf. 14x13½*

49 A12 10c on 10c bister 1,900.
- *a.* Pale blue surcharge 1,900.

#49 was never placed in use. Counterfeits exist.

A13

A14

Two types of the 40c as in the 1849-50 issue.

1870-73 Typo. *Perf. 14x13½*

50 A7 1c ol grn, *pale bl* 45.00 13.00
- *a.* 1c bronze grn, *pale bl* ('72) 52.50 15.00

51 A7 2c red brn, *yelsh* ('70) 90.00 15.00

52 A7 4c gray ('70) 275.00 45.00

53 A7 5c yel grn, *pale bl* ('72) 175.00 8.25
- *a.* 5c green 175.00 8.25

54 A13 10c bis, *yelsh* 600.00 65.00
- *a.* Tête beche pair *6,250.* *2,600.*
- *b.* Half used as 5c on cover *5,000.*

55 A13 10c bis, *rose* ('73) 300.00 10.50
- *a.* Tête bêche pair 4,250. 2,000.

56 A13 15c bis, *yelsh* ('71) 350.00 5.00
- *a.* Tête bêche pair *42,500.* *13,500.*

57 A13 20c dl bl, *bluish* 250.00 7.50
- *a.* 20c bright blue, *bluish* 400.00 9.00
- *b.* Tête bêche pair 4,250. 1,650.
- *c.* Half used as 10c on cover *62,500.*
- *d.* Quarter used as 5c on cover *57,500.*

58 A13 25c bl, *bluish* ('71) 125.00 1.25
- *a.* 25c dk bl, *bluish* 150.00 1.25
- *b.* Tête bêche pair *7,500.* *3,500.*

59 A13 40c org, *yelsh* (I) 525.00 7.00
- *a.* 40c orange yel, *yelsh* (I) 650.00 10.00
- *b.* 40c orange, *yelsh* (II) 3,500. 150.00
- *c.* 40c orange yel, *yelsh* (II) 3,500. 150.00
- *d.* Pair, types I and II *7,250.* 575.00
- *f.* Half used as 20c on circular *25,000.*
- *g.* Half used as 20c on cover *50,000.*

No. 58 exists in three main plate varieties, differing in one or another of the flower-like corner ornaments.

Margins on this issue are extremely small.

Nos. 54, 57 and 58 were reprinted imperf. in 1887. See note after No. 37.

Imperf.

50b	A7	1c	300.00
51a	A7	2c	400.00
52a	A7	4c	500.00
53b	A7	5c yel grn, *pale bl*	325.00
55b	A13	10c	400.00
56b	A13	15c	425.00

1872-75 *Perf. 14x13½*

Larger Numerals

60 A14 10c bis, *rose* ('75) 375.00 12.00
- *a.* Cliché of 15c in plate of 10c *4,250.* *4,750.*
- *b.* Pair, #60, 60a *7,500.* *9,500.*

61 A14 15c bister ('73) 375.00 4.00

62 A14 30c brn, *yelsh* 650.00 6.50

63 A14 80c rose, *pnksh* 725.00 13.50

Nos. 60-63 (4) 2,125. 36.00

Imperf.

62a	A14	30c	575.00
63a	A14	80c	825.00

Peace and Commerce ("Type Sage") — A15

Type I. The "N" of "INV" is under the "B" of "REPUBLIQUE."

Type II. The "N" of "INV" is under the "U" of "REPUBLIQUE."

1876-78 *Perf. 14x13½*

Type I

64 A15 1c grn, *grnsh* 140.00 70.00

65 A15 2c grn, *grnsh* 1,450. 250.00

66 A15 4c grn, *grnsh* 160.00 55.00

67 A15 5c grn, *grnsh* 700.00 45.00

68 A15 10c grn, *grnsh* 825.00 22.50

69 A15 15c gray lil, *grysh* 825.00 18.00

70 A15 20c red brn, *straw* 600.00 18.00

71 A15 20c bl, *bluish* *32,500.*

72 A15 25c ultra, *bluish* *7,750.* 57.50

73 A15 30c brn, *yelsh* 425.00 8.25

74 A15 40c red, *straw* ('78) 600.00 35.00

75 A15 75c car, *rose* 950.00 13.50

76 A15 1fr brnz grn, *straw* 925.00 11.00

No. 71 was never put into use.

The reprints of No. 71 are type II. They are imperforate or with forged perforation.

For overprints and surcharges see Offices in China Nos. 1-17, J7-J10, J20-J22, Offices in Egypt, Alexandria 1-15, Port Said 1-17, Offices in Turkish Empire 1-7, Cavalle 1-8, Dedeagh 1-8, Port Lagos 1-5, Vathy 1-9, Offices in Zanzibar 1-33, 50-54, Offices in Morocco 1-8, and Madagascar 14-27.

Imperf.

64a	A15	1c	175.00
65a	A15	2c	1,100.
66a	A15	4c	190.00
67a	A15	5c	575.00
68a	A15	10c	650.00
69a	A15	15c	650.00
70a	A15	20c	425.00
73a	A15	30c	300.00
74a	A15	40c	275.00
75a	A15	75c	600.00
76a	A15	1fr	450.00

Beware of French Colonies #24-29.

1876-77 *Perf. 14x13½*

Type II

77 A15 2c grn, *grnsh* 115.00 19.00

78 A15 5c grn, *grnsh* 25.00 .60
- *a.* Imperf. 175.00

79 A15 10c grn, *grnsh* 1,100. 240.00

80 A15 15c gray lil, *grysh* 675.00 1.90

81 A15 25c ultra, *bluish* 425.00 1.00
- *a.* 25c blue, *bluish* 475.00 1.50
- *b.* Pair, types I & II *65,000.* *17,500.*
- *c.* Imperf. 325.00

82 A15 30c yel brn, *yelsh* 82.50 1.40
- *a.* 30c brown, *yellowish* 90.00 1.40
- *b.* Imperf. 525.00

83 A15 75c car, *rose* ('77) 1,775. 110.00

84 A15 1fr brnz grn, *straw* ('77) 150.00 7.50
- *a.* Imperf. 925.00

Beware of French Colonies #31, 35.

1877-80

86 A15 1c blk, *lil bl* 3.75 1.75
- *a.* 1c black, *gray blue* 3.75 1.75
- *b.* Imperf. 75.00

87 A15 1c blk, *Prus bl* ('80) *11,000.* *4,350.*

Values for No. 87 are for copies with the perfs touching the design on at least one side.

88 A15 2c brn, *straw* 4.50 1.90
- *a.* 2c brown, *yellow* 4.50 1.90
- *b.* Imperf. 200.00

89 A15 3c yel, *straw* ('78) 200.00 42.50
- *a.* Imperf. 150.00

90 A15 4c claret, *lav* 5.00 1.90
- *a.* 4c vio brown, *lavender* 8.25 4.50
- *b.* Imperf. 60.00

91 A15 10c blk, *lavender* 35.00 1.00
- *a.* 10c black, *rose lilac* 37.50 1.00
- *b.* 10c black, *lilac* 37.50 1.00
- *c.* Imperf. 70.00

92 A15 15c blue ('78) 22.50 .60
- *a.* Imperf. 95.00
- *b.* 15c blue, *bluish* 450.00 15.00

93 A15 25c blk, *red* ('78) 1,075. 25.00
- *a.* Imperf. 675.00

94 A15 35c blk, *yel* ('78) 525.00 35.00
- *a.* 35c blk, *yel org* 525.00 35.00
- *b.* Imperf. 250.00

95 A15 40c red, *straw* ('80) 90.00 2.10
- *a.* Imperf. 250.00

96 A15 5fr vio, *lav* 450.00 70.00
- *a.* As #96, imperf. 750.00
- *b.* 5fr red lilac, *lavender* 650.00 90.00

Beware of French Colonies #38-40, 42, 44.

1879-90

97 A15 3c gray, *grysh* ('80) 4.00 1.75
- *a.* Imperf. 65.00

98 A15 20c red, *yel grn* 37.50 4.25
- *a.* 20c red, *deep green* ('84) 70.00 5.75
- *b.* Imperf. 100.00

99 A15 25c yel, *straw* 325.00 5.00
- *a.* Imperf. 250.00

100 A15 25c blk, *pale rose* ('86) 70.00 1.00
- *a.* Imperf. 150.00

101 A15 50c rose, *rose* ('90) 200.00 2.75
- *a.* 50c carmine, *rose* 225.00 3.25

102 A15 75c dp vio, *org* ('90) 200.00 32.50
- *a.* 75c deep violet, *yellow* 275.00 45.00

Nos. 97-102 (6) 836.50 47.25

Beware of French Colonies #43.

1892

Quadrille Paper

103 A15 15c blue 12.50 .35
- *a.* Imperf. 175.00

1898-1900

Ordinary Paper

104 A15 5c yellow green 16.00 1.25
- *a.* Imperf. 82.50

Type I

105 A15 5c yellow green 14.00 1.25
- *a.* Imperf. 550.00

106 A15 10c blk, *lavender* 21.00 2.50
- *a.* Imperf. 250.00

107 A15 50c car, *rose* 200.00 30.00

108 A15 2fr brn, *azure* ('00) 110.00 40.00
- *b.* Imperf. *2,225.*

Nos. 104-108 (5) 361.00 75.00

See No. 226.

Reprints of A15, type II, were made in 1887 and left imperf. See note after No. 37. Value for set of 27, $3,300.

Liberty, Equality, Fraternity A16

"The Rights of Man" A17

Liberty and Peace A18

1900-29 *Perf. 14x13½*

No.	Type	Description	Unused	Used
109	A16	1c gray	.55	.40
110	A16	2c violet brn	.70	.25
111	A16	3c orange	.45	.45
a.		3c red	19.00	7.50
112	A16	4c yellow brn	3.25	1.60
113	A16	5c green	2.00	.35
b.		Booklet pane of 10	350.00	
114	A16	7½c lilac ('26)	.60	.40
115	A16	10c lilac ('29)	4.00	.60
116	A17	10c carmine	25.00	1.50
a.		Numerals printed separately	24.00	10.00
117	A17	15c orange	8.00	.60
118	A17	20c brown vio	55.00	9.00
119	A17	25c blue	125.00	1.75
a.		Numerals printed separately	115.00	9.00
120	A17	30c violet	70.00	5.75
121	A18	40c red & pale bl	15.00	.85
122	A18	45c green & bl ('06)	29.00	2.10
123	A18	50c bis brn & gray	100.00	1.65
124	A18	60c vio & ultra ('20)	1.00	1.25
125	A18	1fr claret & ol grn	26.50	.85
126	A18	2fr gray vio & yel	600.00	75.00
127	A18	2fr org & pale bl ('20)	42.50	.60
128	A18	3fr vio & bl ('25)	26.50	7.50
129	A18	3fr brt vio & rose ('27)	55.00	2.75
130	A18	5fr dk bl & buff	82.50	5.00
131	A18	10fr grn & red ('26)	125.00	16.50
132	A18	20fr mag & grn ('26)	200.00	37.50
		Nos. 109-132 (24)	1,597.	174.20

In the 10c and 25c values, the first printings show the numerals to have been impressed by a second operation, whereas, in later printings, the numerals were inserted in the plates. Two operations were used for all 20c and 30c, and one operation for the 15c.

No. 114 was issued precanceled only. Values for precanceled stamps in first column are for those which have not been through the post and have original gum. Values in the second column are for postally used, gumless stamps.

See Off. in China #34, 40-44, Off. in Crete 1-5, 10-15, Off. in Egypt, Alexandria 16-20, 26-30, 77, 84-86, Port Said 18-22, 28-32, 83, 90-92, Off. in Turkish Empire 21-26, 31-33, Cavalle 9, Dedeagh 9.

For overprints & surcharge see #197, 246, C1-C2, M1, P7. Off. in China 57, 62-65, 71, 73, 75, 83-85, J14, J27, Off. in Crete 17-20, Off. in Egypt, Alexandria 31-32, 34-35, 40-48, 57-64, 66, 71-73, Port Said 33, 35-40, 43, 46-57, 59, 65-71, 73, 78-80, Off. in Turkish Empire 35-38, 47-49, Cavalle 13-15, Dedeagh 16-18, Off. in Zanzibar 39, 45-49, 55, Off. in Morocco 11-15, 20-22, 26-29, 35-41, 49-54, 72-76, 84-85, 87-89, B6.

Imperf.

No.	Type	Description	Unused	Used
109a	A16	1c	62.50	
110a	A16	2c	75.00	60.00
111b	A16	3c	62.50	
112a	A16	4c	175.00	125.00
113a	A16	5c	82.50	
116b	A17	10c #116 or 116a	275.00	*140.00*
117a	A17	15c	200.00	*175.00*
119b	A17	25c #119 or 119a	550.00	
121a	A18	40c	225.00	160.00
122a	A18	45c	300.00	
123a	A18	50c	425.00	375.00
124a	A18	60c	575.00	
125a	A18	1fr	275.00	325.00
126a	A18	2fr	*1,450.*	
127a	A18	2fr	525.00	
128a	A18	3fr	800.00	500.00
129a	A18	3fr	475.00	
130a	A18	5fr	1,050.	

No. 126a is valued without gum.

Flat Plate & Rotary Press

The following stamps were printed by both flat plate and rotary press: Nos. 109-113, 144-146, 163, 166, 168, 170, 177-178, 185, 192 and P7.

A19

Sower A20

1902

No.	Type	Description	Unused	Used
133	A19	10c rose red	26.50	.90
134	A19	15c pale red	11.00	.60
135	A19	20c brown violet	82.50	14.00
136	A19	25c blue	100.00	2.25
137	A19	30c lilac	250.00	14.50
		Nos. 133-137 (5)	470.00	32.25

Imperf

No.	Type	Description	Unused	Used
133a	A19	10c rose red	450.00	275.00
134a	A19	15c pale red	450.00	325.00
135a	A19	20c brown violet	800.00	475.00
136a	A19	25c blue	950.00	625.00
137a	A19	30c lilac	1,100.	

See Off. in China #35-39, Off. in Crete 6-10, Off. in Egypt, Alexandria 21-25, 81-82, Port Said 23-27, 87-88, Off. in Turkish Empire 26-30, Cavalle 10-11, Dedeagh 10-11.

For overprints and surcharges see #M2, Off. in China 45, 58-61, 66-70, 76-82, J15-J16, J28-J30, Off. in Crete 16, Off. in Egypt, Alexandria 33, 36-39, 49-50, 52-56, 65, 67-70, B1-B4, Port Said 34, 41-42, 44-45, 57, 60-64, 77, 74-77, B1-B4, Off. in Turkish Empire 34, 39, Cavalle 12, Dedeagh 15, Off. in Zanzibar 40-44, 56-59, Off. in Morocco 16-19, 30-34, 42-48, 77-83, 86, B1-B5, B7, B9.

1903-38

No.	Type	Description	Unused	Used
138	A20	10c rose	8.00	.40
139	A20	15c slate grn	13.00	.25
b.		Booklet pane of 10	450.00	
140	A20	20c violet brn	67.50	1.90
141	A20	25c dull blue	75.00	1.40
142	A20	30c violet	175.00	5.25
143	A20	45c lt violet ('26)	6.00	1.90
144	A20	50c dull blue ('21)	27.50	1.40
145	A20	50c gray grn ('26)	6.25	1.25
146	A20	50c vermilion ('26)	1.25	.25
a.		Booklet pane of 10	40.00	
147	A20	50c grnsh bl ('38)	1.00	.35
148	A20	60c lt vio ('24)	6.25	2.10
149	A20	65c rose ('24)	3.00	1.75
150	A20	65c gray grn ('27)	6.50	2.10
151	A20	75c rose lil ('26)	5.25	.60
152	A20	80c ver ('25)	26.50	9.50
153	A20	85c ver ('24)	13.50	3.25
154	A20	1fr dull blue ('26)	6.00	.75
		Nos. 138-154 (17)	447.50	34.40
		Set, never hinged	940.00	

See Nos. 941, 942A. For surcharges and overprints see Nos. 229-230, 232-233, 236, 256, B25, B29, B32, B36, B40, M3-M4, M6, Offices in Turkish Empire 46, 54.

Imperf.

No.	Type	Description	Unused	Used
138a	A20	10c	175.00	
139a	A20	15c	140.00	55.00
140a	A20	20c	300.00	160.00
141a	A20	25c	350.00	
142a	A20	30c	625.00	
144a	A20	50c	140.00	
145a	A20	50c	125.00	
146b	A20	50c	70.00	
147a	A20	50c	67.50	
149a	A20	65c	300.00	
151a	A20	75c	450.00	
154a	A20	1fr	*1,000.*	

No. 146b is valued without gum.

Ground A21

No Ground A22

1906, Apr. 13

With Ground Under Feet of Figure

No.	Type	Description	Unused	Used
155	A21	10c red	2.50	1.75
a.		Imperf., pair, without gum	275.00	225.00
		As "a," with gum	450.00	

1906-37

TEN AND THIRTY-FIVE CENTIMES

Type I — Numerals and letters of the inscriptions thin.

Type II — Numerals and letters thicker.

No Ground Under the Feet

No.	Type	Description	Unused	Used
156	A22	1c olive bis ('33)	.20	.30
157	A22	2c dk green ('33)	.20	.30
158	A22	3c ver ('33)	.20	.30
159	A22	5c green ('07)	1.50	.25
a.		Imperf., pair	40.00	30.00
b.		Booklet pane of 10	100.00	
160	A22	5c orange ('21)	1.25	.30
a.		Booklet pane of 10	72.50	
161	A22	5c cerise ('34)	.20	.25
162	A22	10c red (II) ('07)	1.50	.25
a.		Imperf., pair	37.50	115.00
b.		10c red (I) ('06)	8.25	1.00
c.		As #162b, imperf., pair	37.50	115.00
d.		Booklet pane of 10 (I)	125.00	
e.		Booklet pane of 10 (II)	75.00	
f.		Booklet pane of 6 (II)	240.00	
163	A22	10c grn (II) ('21)	1.00	.55
a.		10c green (I) ('27)	32.50	37.50
b.		Booklet pane of 10 (II, "Phena")	350.00	
c.		Booklet pane of 10 (I, "Mineraline")	3,200.	
164	A22	10c ultra ('32)	1.40	.25
165	A22	15c red brn ('26)	.25	.20
a.		Booklet pane of 10	27.50	
166	A22	20c brown	3.00	.65
a.		Imperf., pair	82.50	100.00
b.		20c black brown	6.00	2.00
167	A22	20c red vio ('26)	.25	.25
a.		Booklet pane of 10	7.50	
168	A22	25c blue	2.40	.25
a.		Booklet pane of 10	37.50	
b.		Imperf., pair	45.00	60.00
169	A22	25c yel brown ('27)	.20	.20
a.		25c red brown	.30	.20
170	A22	30c orange	13.50	1.40
a.		Imperf., pair	200.00	175.00
171	A22	30c red ('21)	6.50	2.25
172	A22	30c cerise ('25)	1.25	.80
a.		Booklet pane of 10	13.50	
b.		Imperf, pair	575.00	
173	A22	30c lt blue ('25)	3.75	.60
a.		Booklet pane of 10	35.00	
b.		Imperf, pair	2,200.	
174	A22	30c cop red ('37)	.25	.30
a.		Booklet pane of 10	9.00	
175	A22	35c vio (II) ('26)	8.25	.90
a.		Imperf., pair	150.00	115.00
b.		35c violet (I) ('06)	150.00	7.50
c.		As "b," Imperf., pair, without gum	*575.00*	
176	A22	35c green ('37)	.50	.55
a.		Imperf, pair	750.00	
177	A22	40c olive ('25)	1.40	.55
b.		Booklet pane of 10	30.00	
178	A22	40c ver ('26)	2.50	.80
a.		Booklet pane of 10	25.00	
179	A22	40c violet ('27)	2.00	.90
180	A22	40c lt ultra ('28)	1.25	.50
181	A22	1.05fr ver ('25)	9.50	5.25
182	A22	1.10fr cerise ('27)	11.50	2.50
183	A22	1.40fr cerise ('26)	20.00	22.50
184	A22	2fr Prus grn ('31)	14.00	1.75
		Nos. 156-184 (29)	109.70	45.85
		Set, never hinged	225.00	

The 10c and 35c, type I, were slightly retouched by adding thin white outlines to the sack of grain, the underside of the right arm and the back of the skirt. It is difficult to distinguish the retouches except on clearly-printed copies. The white outlines were made stronger on the stamps of type II.

Stamps of types A16, A18, A20 and A22 were printed in 1916-20 on paper of poor quality, usually grayish and containing bits of fiber. This is called G. C. (Grande Consommation) paper.

#160, 162b, 163, 175b, 176 exist imperf.

See #241-241b. For surcharges & overprint see #227-228, 234, 238, 240, 400, B1, B24, B28, B31, B35, B37, B39, B41, M5, P8, Off. in Turkish Empire 40-45, 52, 55.

Louis Pasteur — A23

1923-26

No.	Type	Description	Unused	Used
185	A23	10c green	.55	.30
a.		Booklet pane of 10	15.00	
186	A23	15c green ('24)	1.40	.30
187	A23	20c green ('26)	2.75	.90
188	A23	30c red	.90	*1.50*
189	A23	30c green ('26)	.55	.50
190	A23	45c red ('24)	1.90	2.10
191	A23	50c blue	4.50	.50
192	A23	75c blue ('24)	3.75	1.00
a.		Imperf., pair	250.00	
193	A23	90c red ('26)	11.00	3.50
194	A23	1fr blue ('25)	21.00	.50
195	A23	1.25fr blue ('26)	25.00	8.00
196	A23	1.50fr blue ('26)	5.25	.50
		Nos. 185-196 (12)	78.55	19.60
		Set, never hinged	150.00	

Nos. 185, 188 and 191 were issued to commemorate the cent. of the birth of Pasteur.

For surcharges and overprint see Nos. 231, 235, 257, B26, B30, B33, C4.

No. 125 Overprinted in Blue

1923, June 15

No.	Type	Description	Unused	Used
197	A18	1fr claret & ol grn	400.00	440.00
		Never hinged	825.00	

Allegory of Olympic Games at Paris A24

The Trophy A25

Milo of Crotona — A26

Victorious Athlete — A27

1924, Apr. 1 *Perf. 14x13½, 13½x14*

No.	Type	Description	Unused	Used
198	A24	10c gray grn & yel grn	2.25	1.25
199	A25	25c rose & dk rose	3.00	.80
200	A26	30c brn red & blk	9.50	11.00
201	A27	50c ultra & dk bl	26.00	5.75
		Nos. 198-201 (4)	40.75	18.80
		Set, never hinged	125.00	

Imperf Singles

198a	A24	10c	1,000.	
199a	A25	25c	1,000.	*725.00*
200a	A26	30c	1,000.	*1,000.*
201a	A27	50c	1,000.	

8th Olympic Games, Paris.

Pierre de Ronsard (1524-85), Poet — A28

1924, Oct. 6 ***Perf. 14x13½***

219 A28 75c blue, *bluish*	1.90	1.40
Never hinged	2.75	

"Light and Liberty" Allegory A29

Majolica Vase — A30

Potter Decorating Vase — A31

Terrace of Château A32

1924-25 ***Perf. 14x13½, 13½x14***

220 A29 10c dk grn & yel ('25)	.55	.75
221 A30 15c ind & grn ('25)	.55	.85
a. Imperf.	375.00	
Never hinged	600.00	
222 A31 25c vio brn & garnet	.80	.50
223 A32 25c gray bl & vio ('25)	1.60	.65
a. Imperf.	425.00	150.00
Never hinged	700.00	
224 A31 75c indigo & ultra	3.50	2.25
225 A29 75c dk bl & lt bl ('25)	18.00	6.50
a. Imperf.	375.00	
Never hinged	600.00	
Nos. 220-225 (6)	25.00	11.50
Set, never hinged	52.50	

Intl. Exhibition of Decorative Modern Arts at Paris, 1925.

Philatelic Exhibition Issue
Souvenir Sheet

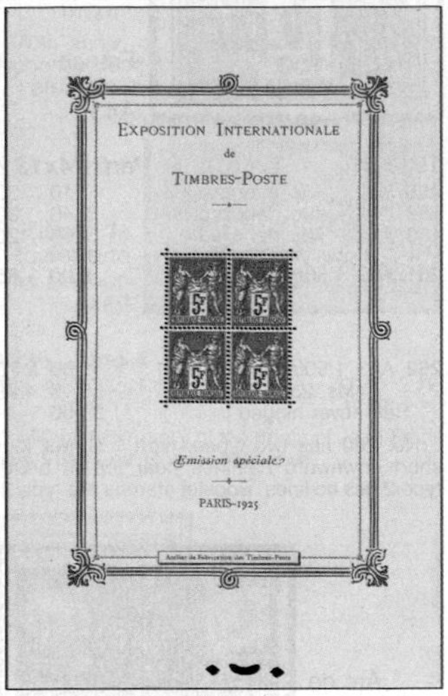

A32a

1925, May 2 ***Perf. 14x13½***

226 A32a Sheet of 4, A15 II	1,000.	850.00
Never hinged	2,850.	
a. Imperf. sheet	*5,000.*	1,750.
Never hinged	*7,750.*	
b. 5fr carmine, perf.	110.00	140.00
c. 5fr carmine, imperf.	900.00	
Never hinged	1,325.	

These were on sale only at the Intl. Phil. Exhib., Paris, May, 1925. Size: 140x220mm.

Nos. 148-149, 152-153, 173, 175, 181, 183, 192, 195 Surcharged

1926-27

227 A22 25c on 30c lt bl	.20	.50
228 A22 25c on 35c violet	.20	.50
a. Double surcharge	525.00	350.00
229 A20 50c on 60c lt vio ('27)	1.40	1.10
230 A20 50c on 65c rose ('27)	.75	.55
a. Inverted surcharge	*1,225.*	*1,400.*
231 A23 50c on 75c blue	3.25	1.50
232 A20 50c on 80c ver ('27)	1.25	1.10
233 A20 50c on 85c ver ('27)	2.25	1.00
234 A22 50c on 1.05fr ver	1.25	.75
235 A23 50c on 1.25fr blue	2.75	2.25
236 A20 55c on 60c lt vio	125.00	52.50
238 A22 90c on 1.05fr ver ('27)	2.25	2.75
240 A22 1.10fr on 1.40fr cer	1.00	1.10
Nos. 227-240 (12)	141.55	65.60
Set, never hinged	275.00	

Issue dates: Nos. 229-230, 232-234, 1927.

No. 236 is known only precanceled. See second note after No. 132.

Nos. 229, 230, 234, 238 and 240 have three bars instead of two. The 55c surcharge has thinner, larger numerals and a rounded "c." Width, including bars, is 17mm, instead of 13mm.

The 55c was used only precanceled at the Department stores of Louvre in Paris, August 1926.

Strasbourg Exhibition Issue
Souvenir Sheet

A32b

1927, June 4

241 A32b Sheet of 2	1,000.	1,000.
Never hinged	2,150.	
a. 5fr light ultra (A22)	180.00	225.00
Never hinged	300.00	225.00
b. 10fr carmine rose (A22)	190.00	225.00
Never hinged	300.00	225.00

Sold at the Strasbourg Philatelic Exhibition as souvenirs. Size: 111x140mm.

Marcelin Berthelot (1827-1907), Chemist and Statesman — A33

1927, Sept. 7

242 A33 90c dull rose	1.90	.60
Never hinged	3.00	

For surcharge see No. C3.

Lafayette, Washington, S. S. Paris and Airplane "Spirit of St. Louis" — A34

1927, Sept. 15

243 A34 90c dull red	1.25	1.75
a. Value omitted	2,000.	1,725.
244 A34 1.50fr deep blue	4.00	2.50
a. Value omitted	1,450.	
Set, never hinged	10.00	

Visit of American Legionnaires to France, September, 1927. Exist imperf.

Joan of Arc — A35

1929, Mar.

245 A35 50c dull blue	1.90	.20
Never hinged	2.75	
a. Booklet pane of 10	50.00	
b. Imperf.	140.00	

500th anniv. of the relief of Orleans by the French forces led by Joan of Arc.

Corvette "La Capricieuse" — A264

1955, July 9
773 A264 30fr aqua & dk blue 6.00 4.50

Centenary of the voyage of La Capricieuse to Canada.

Bordeaux
A265

Designs: 8fr, Marseille. 10fr, Nice. 12fr, Valentre bridge, Cahors. 18fr, Uzerche. 25fr, Fortifications, Brouage.

1955, Oct. 15

774	A265	6fr carmine lake	.20	.20
775	A265	8fr indigo	.45	.20
776	A265	10fr dp ultra	.20	.20
777	A265	12fr violet & brn	.20	.20
778	A265	18fr bluish grn & ind	.85	.20
779	A265	25fr org brn & red brn	1.25	.20
		Nos. 774-779 (6)	3.15	1.20

See Nos. 838-839. For surcharges see Reunion Nos. 312-317, 323.

Mount Pelée, Martinique
A266

1955, Nov. 1
780 A266 20fr dk & lt purple 3.50 .20

Gérard de Nerval — A267

1955, Nov. 11
781 A267 12fr lake & sepia .55 .35

Centenary of the death of Gérard de Nerval (Labrunie), author.

Arms Type of 1949

Arms of: 50c, County of Foix. 70c, Marche. 80c, Roussillon. 1fr, Comtat Venaissin.

Perf. 14x13½

1955, Nov. 19 Typo. Unwmk.

782	A182	50c multicolored	.20	.20
783	A182	70c red, blue & yel	.20	.20
784	A182	80c brown, yel & red	.20	.20
785	A182	1fr blue, red & yel	.20	.20
		Nos. 782-785 (4)	.80	.80

Concentration Camp Victim and Monument
A268

Belfry at Douai
A269

1956, Jan. 14 Engr. *Perf. 13*
786 A268 15fr brn blk & red brn .65 .50

Natl. memorial for Nazi deportation victims erected at the Natzwiller Struthof concentration camp in Alsace.

1956, Feb. 11
787 A269 15fr ultra & indigo .55 .55

Col. Emil Driant
A270

1956, Feb. 21
788 A270 15fr dark blue .40 .35

40th anniv. of the death of Col. Emil Driant during the battle of Verdun.

Trench Fighting — A271

1956, Mar. 3
789 A271 30fr indigo & dk olive 2.00 1.50

40th anniversary of Battle of Verdun.

Jean Henri Fabre, Entomology
A272

Scientists: 15fr, Charles Tellier, Refrigeration. 18fr, Camille Flammarion, Popular Astronomy. 30fr, Paul Sabatier, Catalytic Chemistry.

1956, Apr. 7

790	A272	12fr vio brn & org brn	1.00	.65
791	A272	15fr vio bl & int blk	1.00	.65
792	A272	18fr brt ultra	1.90	1.60
793	A272	30fr Prus grn & dk grn	4.75	2.90
		Nos. 790-793 (4)	8.65	5.80

Grand Trianon, Versailles
A273

1956, Apr. 14
794 A273 12fr vio brn & gray grn 1.50 1.00

Symbols of Latin American and French Culture
A274

1956, Apr. 21
795 A274 30fr brown & red brn 2.50 1.60

Issued in recognition of the friendship between France and Latin America.

"The Smile of Reims" and Botticelli's "Spring"
A275

1956, May 5
796 A275 12fr black & green .75 .55

Issued to emphasize the cultural and artistic kinship of Reims and Florence.

Leprosarium and Maltese Cross — A276

1956, May 12
797 A276 12fr sepia, red brn & red .40 .35

Issued in honor of the Knights of Malta.

St. Yves de Treguier
A277

1956, May 19
798 A277 15fr bluish gray & blk .35 .25

St. Yves, patron saint of lawyers.

Marshal Franchet d'Esperey
A278

Miners Monument
A279

1956, May 26
799 A278 30fr deep claret 2.75 1.90

Centenary of the birth of Marshal Louis Franchet d'Esperey.

1956, June 2
800 A279 12fr violet brown .45 .40

Town Montceau-les-Mines, 100th anniv.

Basketball
A280

"Rebuilding Europe"
A281

Sports: 40fr, Pelota (Jai alai). 50fr, Rugby. 75fr, Mountain climbing.

1956, July 7

801	A280	30fr gray vio & blk	1.50	.20
802	A280	40fr brown & vio brn	6.00	.30
803	A280	50fr rose vio & vio	2.00	.20
804	A280	75fr indigo, grn & bl	12.00	2.00
		Nos. 801-804 (4)	21.50	2.70

For surcharges see Reunion Nos. 318-321.

Europa Issue

Perf. 13½x14

1956, Sept. 15 Typo. Unwmk.
805 A281 15fr rose & rose lake *1.00* .25

Perf. 13

Engr.

806 A281 30fr lt blue & vio bl *6.00* .85

Issued to symbolize the cooperation among the six countries comprising the Coal and Steel Community.

No. 805 measures 21x35½mm, No. 806 measures 22x35½mm.

Dam at Donzère-Mondragon — A282

Cable Railway to Pic du Midi — A283

Rhine Port of Strasbourg
A284

1956, Oct. 6 Engr. *Perf. 13*

807	A282	12fr gray vio & vio brn	1.60	1.10
808	A283	18fr indigo	3.25	2.25
809	A284	30fr indigo & dk blue	14.00	6.25
		Nos. 807-809 (3)	18.85	9.60

French technical achievements.

Antoine-Augustin Parmentier — A285

1956, Oct. 27
810 A285 12fr brown red & brown .75 .65

Parmentier, nutrition chemist, who popularized the potato in France.

Petrarch — A286

Portraits: 12fr, J. B. Lully. 15fr, J. J. Rousseau. 18fr, Benjamin Franklin. 20fr, Frederic Chopin. 30fr, Vincent van Gogh.

1956, Nov. 10

811 A286 8fr green .85 .65
812 A286 12fr claret .85 .65
813 A286 15fr dark red 1.25 .65
814 A286 18fr ultra 2.75 2.25
815 A286 20fr brt violet 3.75 1.75
816 A286 30fr brt grnsh blue 5.75 3.00
Nos. 811-816 (6) 15.20 8.95

Famous men who lived in France.

Pierre de Coubertin and Olympic Stadium A287

1956, Nov. 24

817 A287 30fr dk blue gray & pur 2.00 1.25

Issued in honor of Baron Pierre de Coubertin, founder of the modern Olympic Games.

Homing Pigeon A288

1957, Jan. 12

818 A288 15fr dp ultra, ind & red brn .45 .25

Victor Schoelcher — A289

1957, Feb. 16 **Engr.**

819 A289 18fr lilac rose .65 .65

Issued in honor of Victor Schoelcher, who freed the slaves in the French Colonies.

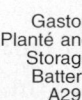

Sèvres Porcelain A290

1957, Mar. 23 **Unwmk.** ***Perf. 13***

820 A290 30fr ultra & vio blue .85 .40

Bicentenary of the porcelain works at Sèvres (in 1956).

Gaston Planté and Storage Battery A291

Designs: 12fr, Antoine Béclère and X-ray apparatus. 18fr, Octave Terrillon, autoclave, microscope and surgical instruments. 30fr, Etienne Oemichen and early helicopter.

1957, Apr. 13

821 A291 8fr gray blk & dp cl .50 .50
822 A291 12fr dk bl, blk & emer .55 .55
823 A291 18fr rose red & mag 1.40 1.40
824 A291 30fr green & slate grn 2.50 2.50
Nos. 821-824 (4) 4.95 4.95

Uzès Chateau A292

1957, Apr. 27

825 A292 12fr slate bl & bis brn .40 .40

Jean Moulin A293

Le Quesnoy A294

Portraits: 10fr, Honoré d'Estienne d'Orves. 12fr, Robert Keller. 18fr, Pierre Brossolette. 20fr, Jean-Baptiste Lebas.

1957, May 18

826 A293 8fr violet brown 1.00 .45
827 A293 10fr black & vio bl 1.00 .45
828 A293 12fr brown & sl grn 1.00 .80
829 A293 18fr purple & blk 1.60 1.25
830 A293 20fr Prus bl & dk bl 1.50 .90
Nos. 826-830 (5) 6.10 3.85

Issued in honor of the heroes of the French Underground of World War II.
See #879-882, 915-919, 959-963, 990-993.

1957, June 1

831 A294 8fr dk slate green .25 .20

See No. 837. For surcharge see Reunion No. 322.

Symbols of Justice A295

1957, June 1

832 A295 12fr sepia & ultra .25 .20

French Cour des Comptes, 150th anniv.

Farm Woman Type of 1954

1957-59 ***Perf. 14x13½***

833 A236 6fr orange .20 .20
833A A236 10fr brt green ('59) .75 .20
834 A236 12fr red lilac .25 .20
Nos. 833-834 (3) 1.20 .60

Nos. 833-834 issued without precancellation.

Symbols of Public Works A296

1957, June 20 **Engr.** ***Perf. 13***

835 A296 30fr sl grn, brn & ocher 1.90 1.10

Brest A297

1957, July 6

836 A297 12fr gray grn & brn ol 1.00 1.00

Scenic Types of 1955, 1957

Designs: 15fr, Le Quesnoy. 35fr, Bordeaux. 70fr, Valentre bridge, Cahors.

1957, July 19 **Unwmk.**

837 A294 15fr dk bl grn & sep .40 .20
838 A265 35fr dk bl grn & sl grn 3.25 1.10
839 A265 70fr black & dull grn 22.50 2.00
Nos. 837-839 (3) 26.15 3.30

Gallic Cock Type of 1954

1957 **Typo.** ***Perf. 14x13½***

840 A237 5fr olive bister .40 .20
841 A237 10fr bright blue 1.75 .35
842 A237 15fr plum 2.25 .75
843 A237 30fr bright red 10.00 3.00
844 A237 45fr green 21.00 12.50
Nos. 840-844 (5) 35.40 16.80

Nos. 840-844 are known only precanceled. See second note after No. 132.

Leo Lagrange and Stadium A298

1957, Aug. 31 **Engr.** ***Perf. 13***

845 A298 18fr lilac gray & blk .55 .55

Intl. University Games, Paris, 8/31-9/8.

"United Europe" — A299

Auguste Comte — A300

1957, Sept. 16

846 A299 20fr red brown & green *.40 .30*
847 A299 35fr dk brown & blue *1.00 .65*

A united Europe for peace and prosperity.

1957, Sept. 14

848 A300 35fr brown red & sepia .45 .35

Centenary of the death of Auguste Comte, mathematician and philosopher.

Roman Amphitheater, Lyon — A301

1957, Oct. 5 ***Perf. 13***

849 A301 20fr brn org & brn vio .45 .35

2,000th anniv. of the founding of Lyon.

Sens River, Guadeloupe A302

Beynac-Cazenac, Dordogne A303

Nicolaus Copernicus A304

Designs: 10fr, Elysee Palace. 25fr, Chateau de Valencay, Indre. 35fr, Rouen Cathedral. 50fr, Roman Ruins, Saint-Remy. 65fr, Evian-les-Bains.

1957, Oct. 19

850 A302 8fr green & lt brn .20 .20
851 A302 10fr dk ol bis & vio brn .20 .20
852 A303 18fr indigo & dk brn .20 .20
853 A302 25fr bl gray & vio brn .60 .20
854 A303 35fr car rose & lake .20 .20
855 A302 50fr ol grn & ol bister .50 .20
856 A302 65fr dk blue & indigo .65 .35
Nos. 850-856 (7) 2.55 1.55

See #907-909. For overprint and surcharges see #1O1, Reunion 325, 328-329, 332-334.

1957, Nov. 9 **Engr.** ***Perf. 13***

Portraits: 10fr, Michelangelo. 12fr, Miguel de Cervantes. 15fr, Rembrandt. 18fr, Isaac Newton. 25fr, Mozart. 35fr, Johann Wolfgang von Goethe.

857 A304 8fr dark brown .90 .65
858 A304 10fr dark green .90 .65
859 A304 12fr dark purple .90 .80
860 A304 15fr brown & org brn 1.10 .90
861 A304 18fr deep blue 1.60 1.00
862 A304 25fr lilac & claret 1.60 1.00
863 A304 35fr blue 1.90 1.10
Nos. 857-863 (7) 8.90 6.10

Louis Jacques Thénard A305

1957, Nov. 30 **Unwmk.**

864 A305 15fr ol bis & grnsh blk .40 .30

Centenary of the death of L. J. Thenard, chemist, and the founding of the Charitable Society of the Friends of Science.

Dr. Philippe Pinel A306

Joseph Louis Lagrange A307

French Physicians: 12fr, Fernand Widal. 15fr, Charles Nicolle. 35fr, René Leriche.

1958, Jan. 25

865 A306 8fr brown olive .90 .60
866 A306 12fr brt vio blue .90 .60
867 A306 15fr deep blue 1.40 .80
868 A306 35fr black 1.75 1.10
Nos. 865-868 (4) 4.95 3.10

1958, Feb. 15 ***Perf. 13***

French Scientists: 12fr, Urbain Jean Joseph Leverrier. 15fr, Jean Bernard Leon Foucault. 35fr, Claude Louis Berthollet.

869 A307 8fr blue grn & vio bl .90 .55
870 A307 12fr sepia & gray 1.00 .70
871 A307 15fr slate grn & grn 1.90 .95
872 A307 35fr maroon & cop red 2.40 1.25
Nos. 869-872 (4) 6.20, 3.45

Lourdes Type of 1954

1958

873 A241 20fr grnsh bl & ol .30 .20

Le Havre A308

Maubeuge — A309

Designs: 18fr, Saint-Die. 25fr, Sete.

1958, Mar. 29 Engr. *Perf. 13*

874 A308 12fr ol grn & car rose .65 .40
875 A309 15fr brt purple & brn .65 .40
876 A309 18fr ultra & indigo 1.00 .80
877 A308 25fr dk bl, bl grn & brn 1.25 .80
Nos. 874-877 (4) 3.55 2.40

Reconstruction of war-damaged cities.

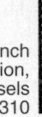

French Pavilion, Brussels A310

1958, Apr. 12

878 A310 35fr brn, dk grn & bl .30 .25

Issued for the Universal and International Exposition at Brussels.

Heroes Type of 1957

8fr, Jean Cavaillès. 12fr, Fred Scamaroni. 15fr, Simone Michel-Levy. 20fr, Jacques Bingen.

1958, Apr. 19

879 A293 8fr violet & black .65 .65
880 A293 12fr ultra & green .65 .65
881 A293 15fr brown & gray 1.60 .90
882 A293 20fr olive & ultra 1.25 1.00
Nos. 879-882 (4) 4.15 3.20

Issued in honor of the heroes of the French Underground in World War II.

Bowling A311

Sports: 15fr, Naval joust. 18fr, Archery, vert. 25fr, Breton wrestling, vert.

1958, Apr. 26

883 A311 12fr rose & brown .85 .75
884 A311 15fr bl, ol gray & grn 1.10 .85
885 A311 18fr green & brown 2.00 1.10
886 A311 25fr brown & indigo 2.90 1.75
Nos. 883-886 (4) 6.85 4.45

Senlis Cathedral — A312

1958, May 17

887 A312 15fr ultra & indigo .40 .40

Bayeux Tapestry Horsemen A313

1958, June 21

888 A313 15fr blue & carmine .35 .25

Common Design Types pictured following the introduction.

Europa Issue, 1958

Common Design Type

1958, Sept. 13 Engr. *Perf. 13*

Size: 22x36mm

889 CD1 20fr rose red *.40* .20
890 CD1 35fr ultra *1.25* *.30*

Foix Chateau A314

1958, Oct. 11

891 A314 15fr ultra, grn & ol brn .40 .30

City Halls, Paris and Rome A315

1958, Oct. 11

892 A315 35fr gray, grnsh bl & rose red .40 .30

Issued to publicize the cultural ties between Rome and Paris and the need for European unity.

UNESCO Building, Paris A316

Design: 35fr, Different view of building.

1958, Nov. 1 *Perf. 13*

893 A316 20fr grnsh blue & ol bis .20 .20
894 A316 35fr dk sl grn & red org .20 .20

UNESCO Headquarters in Paris opening, Nov. 3.

Soldier's Grave in Wheat Field A317

Arms of Marseille A318

1958, Nov. 11

895 A317 15fr dk green & ultra .30 .25

40th anniv. of the World War I armistice.

1958-59 Typo. *Perf. 14x13½*

Cities: 70c, Lyon. 80c, Toulouse. 1fr, Bordeaux. 2fr, Nice. 3fr, Nantes. 5fr, Lille. 15fr, Algiers.

896 A318 50c dk blue & ultra .20 .20
897 A318 70c multicolored .20 .20
898 A318 80c red, blue & yel .20 .20
899 A318 1fr dk bl, yel & red .20 .20
900 A318 2fr dk bl, red & grn .20 .20
901 A318 3fr multicolored .20 .20
902 A318 5fr dk brown & red .20 .20
903 A318 15fr multi ('59) .20 .20
Nos. 896-903 (8) 1.60 1.60

See Nos. 938, 940, 973, 1040-1042, 1091-1095, 1142-1144. For surcharges see Reunion Nos. 336, 345-346, 350-351, 353.

Arc de Triomphe and Flowers — A319

1959, Jan. 17 Engr. *Perf. 13*

904 A319 15fr brn, bl, grn, cl & red .45 .30

Paris Flower Festival.

Symbols of Learning and Medal A320

1959, Jan. 24 *Perf. 13*

905 A320 20fr lake, blk & vio .25 .20

Sesquicentennial of the Palm Leaf Medal of the French Academy.

Charles de Foucauld A321

1959, Jan. 31

906 A321 50fr dp brn, bl & mar .50 .35

Issued to honor Father Charles de Foucauld, explorer and missionary of the Sahara.

Type of 1957

Designs: 30fr, Elysee Palace. 85fr, Evian-les Bains. 100fr, Sens River, Guadeloupe.

1959, Feb. 10

907 A302 30fr dk slate green 2.25 .25
908 A302 85fr deep claret 3.25 .30
909 A302 100fr deep violet 27.50 .45
Nos. 907-909 (3) 33.00 1.00

Gallic Cock Type of 1954

1959 Typo. *Perf. 14x13½*

910 A237 8fr violet .55 .25
911 A237 20fr yellow grn 1.75 .65
912 A237 40fr henna brn 4.00 2.25
913 A237 55fr emerald 17.00 10.00
Nos. 910-913 (4) 23.30 13.15

Nos. 910-913 were issued with precancellation. See second note after No. 132. See Nos. 952-955.

Miners' Tools and School A322

1959, Apr. 11 Engr. *Perf. 13*

914 A322 20fr red, blk & blue .25 .20

175th anniv. of the National Mining School.

Heroes Type of 1957

Portraits: No. 915, The five martyrs of the Buffon school. No. 916, Yvonne Le Roux. No. 917, Médéric-Védy. No. 918, Louis Martin-Bret. 30fr, Gaston Moutardier.

1959, Apr. 25 Engr. *Perf. 13*

915 A293 15fr black & vio .40 .20
916 A293 15fr mag & rose vio .40 .40
917 A293 20fr green & grnsh bl .40 .40
918 A293 20fr org brn & brn .50 .50
919 A293 30fr magenta & vio .65 .50
Nos. 915-919 (5) 2.35 2.00

Dam at Foum el Gherza A323

Marcoule Atomic Center — A324

Designs: 30fr, Oil field at Hassi Messaoud, Sahara. 50fr, C. N. I. T. Building (Centre National des Industries et des Techniques).

1959, May 23

920 A323 15fr olive & grnsh bl .35 .20
921 A324 20fr brt car & red brn .50 .50
922 A324 30fr dk blue, brn & grn .50 .50
923 A323 50fr ol grn & sl blue .75 .55
Nos. 920-923 (4) 2.10 1.75

French technical achievements.

Marceline Desbordes-Valmore — A325

1959, June 20

924 A325 30fr blue, brn & grn .25 .20

Centenary of the death of Marceline Desbordes-Valmore, poet.

Pilots Goujon and Rozanoff A326

1959, June 13

925 A326 20fr lt blue & org brn .50 .40

Issued in honor of Charles Goujon and Col. Constantin Rozanoff, test pilots.

Tancarville Bridge A327

1959, Aug. 1 Engr. *Perf. 13*

926 A327 30fr dk blue, brn & ol .50 .20

Marianne and Ship of State A328

Jean Jaures A329

1959, July Typo. *Perf. 14x13½*

927 A328 25fr black & red .30 .20

See No. 942. For surcharge see No. B336.

1959, Sept. 12 Engr. *Perf. 13*

928 A329 50fr chocolate .40 .25

Jean Jaures, socialist leader, birth cent.

Europa Issue, 1959
Common Design Type

1959, Sept. 19

Size: 22x36mm

929 CD2 25fr bright green *.75 .35*
930 CD2 50fr bright violet *1.10 .55*

Blood Donors A330

1959, Oct. 17 **Engr.**
931 A330 20fr magenta & gray .25 .20

French-Spanish Handshake — A331

1959, Oct. 24 ***Perf. 13***
932 A331 50fr blue, rose car & org .55 .35

300th anniv. of the signing of the Treaty of the Pyrenees.

Polio Victim Holding Crutches A332

Henri Bergson A333

1959, Oct. 31
933 A332 20fr dark blue .25 .20

Vaccination against poliomyelitis.

1959, Nov. 7
934 A333 50fr lt red brown .40 .25

Henri Bergson, philosopher, birth cent.

Avesnes-sur-Helpe — A334

Design: 30fr, Perpignan.

1959, Nov. 14
935 A334 20fr sepia & blue .40 .20
936 A334 30fr brn, dp claret & bl .40 .20

New NATO Headquarters, Paris — A335

1959, Dec. 12
937 A335 50fr green, brn & ultra .60 .40

10th anniv. of the NATO.

Types of 1958-59 and

Farm Woman A336

Sower A337

Designs: 5c, Arms of Lille. 15c, Arms of Algiers. 25c, Marianne and Ship of State.

Perf. 14x13½

1960-61 **Unwmk.** **Typo.**
938 A318 5c dk brown & red 7.25 .20
939 A336 10c brt green .25 .20
940 A318 15c red, ultra, yel & grn .60 .20
941 A337 20c grnsh bl & car rose .20 .20
942 A328 25c ver & ultra 2.25 .20
b. Booklet pane of 8 27.50
c. Booklet pane of 10 32.50
942A A337 30c gray & ultra ('61) 2.00 .30
Nos. 938-942A (6) 12.55 1.30

See Nos. 707-708, 833-834 for the Farm Woman type (A336), but with no decimals in denominations.

For surcharges see Reunion Nos. 337-338, 341. For overprint see Algeria No. 286.

Laon Cathedral A338

Kerrata Gorge — A339

Designs: 30c, Fougères Chateau. 50c, Mosque, Tlemcen. 65c, Sioule Valley. 85c, Chaumont Viaduct. 1fr, Cilaos Church, Reunion.

1960, Jan. 16 **Engr.** ***Perf. 13***
943 A338 15c blue & indigo .40 .20
944 A338 30c blue, sepia & grn 3.75 .20
945 A339 45c brt vio & ol gray .85 .20
946 A339 50c sl grn & lt cl 2.50 .20
947 A338 65c sl grn, bl & blk brn 1.25 .20
948 A338 85c blue, sep & grn 3.00 .20
949 A339 1fr vio bl, bl & grn 3.00 .20
Nos. 943-949 (7) 14.75 1.40

For surcharges see Reunion Nos. 335, 340, 342. For overprint see Algeria Nos. 288-289.

Pierre de Nolhac A340

1960, Feb. 13
950 A340 20c black & gray .50 .35

Centenary of the birth of Pierre de Nolhac, curator of Versailles and historian.

Museum of Art and Industry, Saint-Etienne — A341

1960, Feb. 20
951 A341 30c brn, car & slate .60 .30

Gallic Cock Type of 1954

1960 **Typo.** ***Perf. 14x13½***
952 A237 8c violet .95 .20
953 A237 20c yellow grn 3.25 .30
954 A237 40c henna brn 9.00 2.00
955 A237 55c emerald 29.00 16.00
Nos. 952-955 (4) 42.20 18.50

Nos. 952-955 were issued only precanceled. See second note after No. 132. See Nos. 910-913.

View of Cannes A342

1960, Mar. 5 **Engr.** ***Perf. 13***
956 A342 50c red brn & lt grn .70 .50

Meeting of European municipal administrators, Cannes, Mar., 1960.

Woman of Savoy and Alps A343

Woman of Nice and Shore A344

1960 **Unwmk.** ***Perf. 13***
957 A343 30c slate green .65 .50
958 A344 50c brn, yel & rose .65 .40

Cent. of the annexation of Nice and Savoy.

Heroes Type of 1957

Portraits: No. 959, Edmund Debeaumarché. No. 960, Pierre Massé. No. 961, Maurice Ripoche. No. 962, Leonce Vieljeux. 50c, Abbé René Bonpain.

1960, Mar. 26
959 A293 20c bister & blk 2.50 1.50
960 A293 20c pink & rose cl 1.90 1.50
961 A293 30c vio & brt vio 1.90 1.50
962 A293 30c sl bl & brt bl 3.50 2.50
963 A293 50c sl grn & red brn 3.50 3.25
Nos. 959-963 (5) 13.30 10.25

Issued in honor of the heroes of the French Underground of World War II.

"Education" and Children A345

1960, May 21 **Engr.** ***Perf. 13***
964 A345 20c rose lilac, pur & blk .25 .20

1st secondary school in Strasbourg, 150th anniv.

Blois Chateau A346

View of La Bourboule A347

1960, May
965 A346 30c dk bl, sep & grn .85 .65
966 A347 50c ol brown, car & grn .65 .50

Lorraine Cross A348

Marianne A349

1960, June 18
967 A348 20c red brn, dk brn & yel grn .65 .25

20th anniv. of the French Resistance Movement in World War II.

1960, June 18 **Typo.** ***Perf. 14x13½***
968 A349 25c lake & gray .20 .20
a. Booklet pane of 8 4.50
b. Booklet pane of 10 3.50

For surcharge see Reunion No. 339. For overprint see Algeria No. 287.

Jean Bouin and Stadium A350

1960, July 9 **Engr.** ***Perf. 13***
969 A350 20c blue, mag & ol gray .35 .25

17th Olympic Games, Rome, 8/25-9/11.

Europa Issue, 1960
Common Design Type

1960, Sept. 17 ***Perf. 13***

Size: 36x22mm

970 CD3 25c green & bluish grn .20 .20
971 CD3 50c maroon & red lilac *.30* .20

Lisieux Basilica A351

1960, Sept. 24 ***Perf. 13***
972 A351 15c blue, gray & blk .25 .20

Arms Type of 1958-59

Design: Arms of Oran.

1960, Oct. 15 **Typo.** ***Perf. 14x13½***
973 A318 5c red, bl, yel & emer .20 .20

Madame de Stael by François Gerard — A352

1960, Oct. 22 **Engr.** ***Perf. 13***
974 A352 30c dull claret & brn .35 .25

Madame de Stael (1766-1817), writer.

Gen. J. B. E. Estienne A353

1960, Nov. 5
975 A353 15c lt lilac & black .25 .20

Centenary of the birth of Gen. Jean Baptiste Eugene Estienne.

Marc Sangnier and Youth Hostel at Bierville A354

1960, Nov. 5

976 A354 20c blue, blk & lilac .25 .20

Issued to honor Marc Sangnier, founder of the French League for Youth Hostels.

Badge of Order of Liberation — A355

1960, Nov. 14 Engr. *Perf. 13*

977 A355 20c black & brt green .40 .25

Order of Liberation, 20th anniversary.

Lapwings A356

Birds: 30c, Puffin. 45c, European teal. 50c, European bee-eaters.

1960, Nov. 12

978 A356 20c multicolored .30 .20
979 A356 30c multicolored .30 .25
980 A356 45c multicolored .95 .50
981 A356 50c multicolored .85 .25
Nos. 978-981 (4) 2.40 1.20

Issued to publicize wildlife protection.

André Honnorat A357

1960, Nov. 19

982 A357 30c blue, blk & green .30 .25

Honnorat, statesman, fighter against tuberculosis and founder of the University City of Paris, an intl. students' community.

St. Barbara and Medieval View of School A358

1960, Dec. 3 Engr.

983 A358 30c red, bl & ol brn .35 .30

St. Barbara School, Paris, 500th anniv.

"Mediterranean" by Aristide Maillol — A359

1961, Feb. 18 Unwmk. *Perf. 13*

984 A359 20c carmine & indigo .25 .20

Aristide Maillol, sculptor, birth cent.

Marianne by Cocteau — A360

1961, Feb. 23

985 A360 20c blue & carmine .25 .20

A second type has an extra inverted V-shaped mark (a blue flag top) at right of hair tip. Value unused $3.25, used 60 cents.

For surcharge see Reunion No. 357.

Paris Airport, Orly A361

1961, Feb. 25

986 A361 50c blk, dk bl, & bluish grn .45 .35

Inauguration of new facilities at Orly airport.

George Méliès and Motion Picture Screen A362

1961, Mar. 11

987 A362 50c pur, indigo & ol bis .60 .40

Cent. of the birth of George Méliès, motion picture pioneer.

Jean Baptiste Henri Lacordaire — A363

1961, Mar. 25 *Perf. 13*

988 A363 30c lt brown & black .30 .30

Cent. of the death of the Dominican monk Lacordaire, orator and liberal Catholic leader.

A364

1961, Mar. 25

989 A364 30c grn, red brn & red .30 .25

Introduction of tobacco use into France, fourth centenary. By error stamp portrays Jan Nicquet instead of Jean Nicot.

Heroes Type of 1957

Portraits: No. 990, Jacques Renouvin. No. 991, Lionel Dubray. No. 992, Paul Gateaud. No. 993, Mère Elisabeth.

1961, Apr. 22

990 A293 20c blue & lilac 1.00 .50
991 A293 20c gray grn & blue 1.00 .50
992 A293 30c brown org & blk 1.60 .90
993 A293 30c violet & blk 1.25 1.00
Nos. 990-993 (4) 4.85 2.90

Bagnoles-de-l'Orne — A365

1961, May 6

994 A365 20c olive, ocher, bl & grn .20 .20

Dove, Olive Branch and Federation Emblem — A366

1961, May 6

995 A366 50c brt bl, grn & mar .30 .20

World Federation of Ex-Service Men.

Deauville in 19th Century A367

1961, May 13 Engr.

996 A367 50c rose claret 1.90 1.20

Centenary of Deauville.

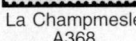

La Champmeslé A368

Mont-Dore, Snowflake and Cable Car A369

French actors: #998, Talma. #999, Rachel. #1000, Gérard Philipe. #1001, Raimu.

1961, June 10 Unwmk. *Perf. 13*

Dark Carmine Frame

997 A368 20c choc & yel grn 1.00 .40
998 A368 30c brown & crimson 1.00 .40
999 A368 30c yel grn & sl grn 1.00 .40
1000 A368 50c olive & choc 1.40 .60
1001 A368 50c bl grn & red brn 1.40 .60
Nos. 997-1001 (5) 5.80 2.40

Issued to honor great French actors and in connection with the Fifth World Congress of the International Federation of Actors.

1961, July 1

1002 A369 20c orange & rose lilac .20 .20

Pierre Fauchard A370

St. Theobald's Church, Thann A371

1961, July 1

1003 A370 50c dk green & blk .55 .30

Bicentenary of the death of Pierre Fauchard, 1st surgeon dentist.

1961, July 1

1004 A371 20c sl grn, vio & brn .65 .35

800th anniversary of Thann.

Europa Issue, 1961

Common Design Type

1961, Sept. 16 *Perf. 13*

Size: 35x22mm

1005 CD4 25c vermilion .20 .20
1006 CD4 50c ultramarine *.25 .25*

Beach and sailboats, Arcachon A372

15c, Saint-Paul, Maritime Alps. 45c, Sully-sur-Loire Chateau. 50c, View of Cognac. 65c, Rance Valley and Dinan. 85c, City hall and Rodin's Burghers, Calais. 1fr, Roman gates of Lodi, Medea, Algeria.

1961, Oct. 9 Engr. *Perf. 13*

1007 A372 15c blue & purple .20 .20
1008 A372 30c ultra, sl grn & lt brn .25 .20
1009 A372 45c vio bl, red brn & grn .25 .20
1010 A372 50c grn, Prus bl & sl 1.25 .20
1011 A372 65c red brn, sl grn & bl .50 .20
1012 A372 85c sl grn, sl & red brn .60 .25
1013 A372 1fr dk bl, sl & bis 5.00 .25
Nos. 1007-1013 (7) 8.05 1.50

For surcharges see Reunion Nos. 347-348. For overprint see Algeria No. 290.

Blue Nudes, by Matisse — A373

Paintings: 50c, "The Messenger," by Braque. 85c, "The Cardplayers," by Cézanne. 1fr, "The 14th July," by Roger de La Fresnaye.

1961, Nov. 10 *Perf. 13x12*

1014 A373 50c dk brn, bl, blk & gray 2.90 1.60
1015 A373 65c grn, vio, & ultra 5.00 2.50
1016 A373 85c blk, brn, red & ol 2.50 1.25
1017 A373 1fr multicolored 4.00 2.50
Nos. 1014-1017 (4) 14.40 7.85

Liner France A374

1962, Jan. 11 Engr. *Perf. 13*

1018 A374 30c dk blue, blk & car .60 .45

New French liner France.

Skier Going Downhill — A375

Maurice Bourdet — A376

1962, Jan. 27 *Perf. 13*
1019 A375 30c shown .20 .20
1020 A375 50c Slalom .40 .30

Issued to publicize the World Ski Championships, Chamonix, Feb. 1962.

1962, Feb. 17
1021 A376 30c slate .30 .20

60th anniv. of the birth of Maurice Bourdet, radio commentator and resistance hero.

Pierre-Fidele Bretonneau — A377

1962, Feb. 17
1022 A377 50c brt lilac & blue .35 .25

Centenary of the death of Pierre-Fidele Bretonneau, physician.

Chateau and Bridge, Laval, Mayenne A378

Gallic Cock A379

1962, Feb. 24
1023 A378 20c bis brn & slate grn .25 .20

1962-65 *Perf. 13*
1024 A379 25c ultra, car & brn .25 .20
a. Bklt. pane of 4 (horiz. strip) 2.50
1024B A379 30c gray grn, red & brn ('65) .85 .20
c. Booklet pane of 5 5.00
d. Booklet pane of 10 10.00

No. 1024 was also issued on experimental luminescent paper in 1963. Value $750.

Ramparts of Vannes A380

Dunkirk — A381

Paris Beach, Le Touquet A381a

1962 **Engr.** *Perf. 13*
1025 A380 30c dark blue .80 .50
1026 A381 95c grn, bis & red lil 1.60 .90
1027 A381a 1fr grn, red brn & bl .45 .20
Nos. 1025-1027 (3) 2.85 1.60

No. 1026 for the 300th anniv. of Dunkirk.

Stage Setting and Globe A382

1962, Mar. 24 **Unwmk.**
1028 A382 50c sl grn, ocher & mag .55 .30

International Day of the Theater, Mar. 27.

Memorial to Fighting France, Mont Valerien A383

Resistance Heroes' Monument, Vercors — A384

Design: 50c, Ile de Sein monument.

1962, Apr. 7
1029 A383 20c olive & slate grn .80 .50
1030 A384 30c bluish black .80 .50
1031 A384 50c blue & indigo 1.00 .80
Nos. 1029-1031 (3) 2.60 1.80

Issued to publicize memorials for the French Underground in World War II.

Malaria Eradication Emblem and Swamp — A385

Nurses with Child and Hospital — A386

1962, Apr. 14 **Engr.**
1032 A385 50c dk blue & dk red .35 .30

WHO drive to eradicate malaria.

1962, May 5 **Unwmk.** *Perf. 13*
1033 A386 30c bl grn, gray & red brn .35 .30

National Hospital Week, May 5-12.

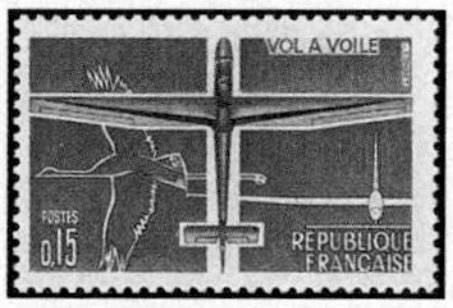

Glider A387

20c, Planes showing development of aviation.

1962, May 12
1034 A387 15c orange red & brn .30 .20
1035 A387 20c lil rose & rose cl .35 .25

Issued to publicize sports aviation.

School Emblem — A388

1962, May 19 **Engr.**
1036 A388 50c mar, ocher & dk vio .50 .30

Watchmaker's School at Besançon, cent.

Louis XIV and Workers Showing Modern Gobelin A389

1962, May 26 **Unwmk.** *Perf. 13*
1037 A389 50c ol, sl grn & car .50 .30

Gobelin tapestry works, Paris, 300th anniv.

Blaise Pascal A390

1962, May 26
1038 A390 50c slate grn & dp org .50 .30

Blaise Pascal (1623-1662), mathematician, scientist and philosopher.

Palace of Justice, Rennes A391

1962, June 12
1039 A391 30c blk, grysh bl & grn 1.40 .60

Arms Type of 1958-59

5c, Amiens. 10c, Troyes. 15c, Nevers.

1962-63 **Typo.** *Perf. 14x13½*
1040 A318 5c ver, ultra & yel .20 .20
1041 A318 10c red, ultra & yel ('63) .20 .20
1042 A318 15c ver, ultra & yel .20 .20
Nos. 1040-1042 (3) .60 .60

Phosphor Tagging

In 1970 France began to experiment with luminescence. Phosphor bands have been added to Nos. 1041, 1143, 1231, 1231C, 1292A-1294B, 1494-1498, 1560-1579B, etc.

Rose — A392

Design: 30c, Old-fashioned rose.

1962, Sept. 8 **Engr.** *Perf. 13*
1043 A392 20c ol, grn & brt car .65 .40
1044 A392 30c dk sl grn, ol & car .65 .40

Europa Issue, 1962

Common Design Type

1962, Sept. 15

Size: 36x22mm

1045 CD5 25c violet .20 .20
1046 CD5 50c henna brown .35 .20

Space Communications Center, Pleumeur-Bodou, France — A394

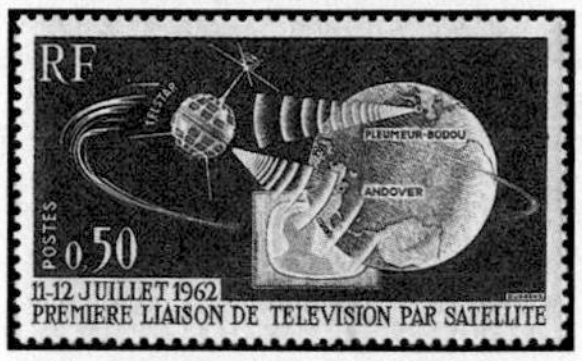

Telstar, Earth and Television Set — A395

1962, Sept. 29 **Engr.** *Perf. 13*
1047 A394 25c gray, yel & grn .25 .20
1048 A395 50c dk bl, grn & ultra .40 .30

1st television connection of the US and Europe through Telstar satellite, July 11-12.

For surcharges see Reunion Nos. 343-344.

"Bonjour Monsieur Courbet" by Gustave Courbet — A396

Paintings: 65c, "Madame Manet on Blue Sofa," by Edouard Manet. 1fr, "Guards officer on horseback," by Theodore Géricault, vert.

1962, Nov. 9 *Perf. 13x12, 12x13*
1049 A396 50c multicolored 3.25 2.50
1050 A396 65c multicolored 2.50 1.60
1051 A396 1fr multicolored 5.75 3.25
Nos. 1049-1051 (3) 11.50 7.35

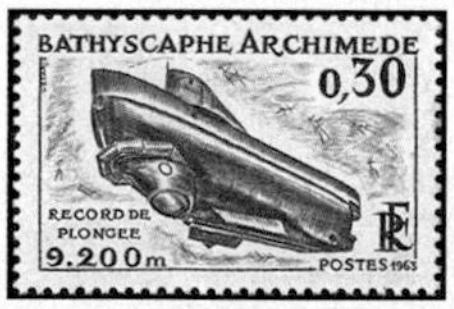

Bathyscaph "Archimede" — A397

1963, Jan. 26 **Unwmk.** *Perf. 13*
1052 A397 30c dk blue & blk .25 .20

French deep-sea explorations.

Flowers and Nantes Chateau A398

1963, Feb. 11
1053 A398 30c vio bl, car & sl grn .25 .20

Nantes flower festival.

St. Peter, Window at St. Foy de Conches A399

50c, Jacob Wrestling with the Angel, by Delacroix.

1963, Mar. 2 ***Perf. 12x13***
1054 A399 50c multicolored 3.00 1.50
1055 A399 1fr multicolored 4.00 2.50

See Nos. 1076-1077.

Hungry Woman and Wheat Emblem A400

1963, Mar. 21 **Engr.** ***Perf. 13***
1056 A400 50c slate grn & brn .30 .20

FAO "Freedom from Hunger" campaign.

Cemetery and Memorial, Glières — A401

Design: 50c, Memorial, Ile de la Cité, Paris.

1963, Mar. 23 **Unwmk.** ***Perf. 13***
1057 A401 30c dk brown & olive .55 .55
1058 A401 50c indigo .55 .55

Heroes of the resistance against the Nazis.

Beethoven, Birthplace at Bonn and Rhine A402

#1060, Emile Verhaeren, memorial at Roisin & residence. #1061, Giuseppe Mazzini, Marcus Aurelius statue & Via Appia, Rome. #1062, Emile Mayrisch, Colpach Chateau & blast furnace, Esch. #1063, Hugo de Groot, Palace of Peace, The Hague & St. Agatha Church, Delft.

1963, Apr. 27 **Unwmk.** ***Perf. 13***
1059 A402 20c ocher, sl & brt grn .35 .25
1060 A402 20c purple, blk & mar .35 .25
1061 A402 20c maroon, sl & ol .35 .25
1062 A402 20c mar, dk brn & ocher .35 .25
1063 A402 30c dk brn, vio & ocher .35 .25
Nos. 1059-1063 (5) 1.75 1.25

Issued to honor famous men of the European Common Market countries.

Hotel des Postes and Stagecoach, 1863 — A403

1963, May 4
1064 A403 50c grayish black .35 .25

1st Intl. Postal Conference, Paris, 1863.

Lycée Louis-le-Grand, Belvédère, Panthéon and St. Etienne du Mont Church — A404

1963, May 18
1065 A404 30c slate green .30 .25

400th anniversary of the Jesuit Clermont secondary school, named after Louis XIV.

St. Peter's Church and Ramparts, Caen A405

1963, June 1 **Unwmk.** ***Perf. 13***
1066 A405 30c gray blue & brn .25 .25

Radio Telescope, Nançay — A406

1963, June 8 **Engr.**
1067 A406 50c dk bl & dk brn .45 .35

Amboise Chateau A407

Saint-Flour — A408

Designs: 50c, Côte d'Azur Varoise. 85c, Vittel. 95c, Moissac.

1963, June 15
1068 A407 30c slate, grn & bis .25 .20
1069 A407 50c dk grn, dk bl & hn brn .40 .20
1070 A408 60c ultra, dk grn & hn brn .45 .20
1071 A407 85c dk grn, yel grn & brn 1.40 .30
1072 A408 95c dk brown & black .85 .25
Nos. 1068-1072 (5) 3.35 1.15

For surcharge see Reunion No. 355.

Water Skiing Slalom A409

1963, Aug. 31 **Unwmk.** ***Perf. 13***
1073 A409 30c sl grn, blk & car .30 .20

World Water Skiing Championships, Vichy.

Europa Issue, 1963
Common Design Type
1963, Sept. 14
Size: 36x22mm
1074 CD6 25c red brown *.25 .25*
1075 CD6 50c green *.35 .25*

Art Type of 1963

Designs: 85c, "The Married Couple of the Eiffel Tower," by Marc Chagall. 95c, "The Fur Merchants," window, Chartres Cathedral.

1963, Nov. 9 **Engr.** ***Perf. 12x13***
1076 A399 85c multicolored 1.75 1.25
1077 A399 95c multicolored .65 .65

Philatec Issue
Common Design Type
1963, Dec. 14 **Unwmk.** ***Perf. 13***
1078 CD118 25c dk gray, sl grn & dk car .20 .20

For surcharge see Reunion No. 349.

Radio and Television Center, Paris A411

1963, Dec. 15 **Engr.**
1079 A411 20c org brn, slate & ol .20 .20

Fire Brigade Insignia, Symbols of Fire, Water and Civilian Defense A412

1964, Feb. 8 **Engr.** ***Perf. 13***
1082 A412 30c blue, org & red .50 .25

Issued to honor the fire brigades and civilian defense corps.

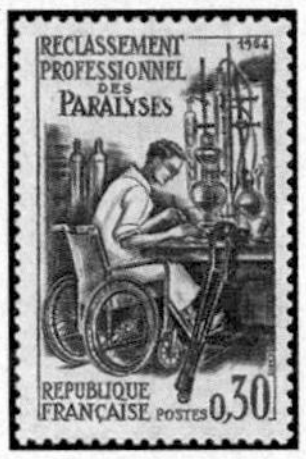

Handicapped Laboratory Technician — A413

1964, Feb. 22 **Unwmk.** ***Perf. 13***
1083 A413 30c grn, red brn & brn .25 .20

Rehabilitation of the handicapped.

John II the Good (1319-64) by Girard d'Orleans A414

1964, Apr. 25 ***Perf. 12x13***
1084 A414 1fr multicolored 1.60 1.10

Stamp of 1900 A415

Mechanized Mail Handling A416

Designs: No. 1086, Stamp of 1900, Type A17. No. 1088, Telecommunications.

1964, May 9 ***Perf. 13***
1085 A415 25c bister & dk car .30 .30
1086 A415 25c bister & blue .30 .30
1087 A416 30c blk, bl & org brn .30 .30
1088 A416 30c blk, car rose & bluish grn .30 .30
a. Strip of 4, #1085-1088 + label 1.25 1.25

Printed in sheets of 20 stamps, containing five No. 1088a. The label shows the Philatec emblem in green.

Type of Semi-Postal Issue
with "25e ANNIVERSAIRE" added
1964, May 9
1089 SP208 25c multicolored .25 .20

25th anniversary, night airmail service.

Madonna and Child from Rose Window of Notre Dame A417

1964, May 23 ***Perf. 12x13***
1090 A417 60c multicolored .55 .55

Notre Dame Cathedral, Paris, 800th anniv.

Arms Type of 1958-59

Arms: 1c, Niort. 2c, Guéret. 12c, Agen. 18c, Saint-Denis, Réunion. 30c, Paris.

1964-65 **Typo.** ***Perf. 14x13½***
1091 A318 1c vio blue & yel .20 .20
1092 A318 2c emer, vio bl & yel .20 .20
1093 A318 12c black, red & yel .20 .20
1094 A318 18c multicolored .40 .25
1095 A318 30c vio bl & red ('65) .50 .20
a. Booklet pane of 10 15.00
Nos. 1091-1095 (5) 1.50 1.05

Gallic Coin — A418

Perf. 13½x14
1964-66 **Typo.** **Unwmk.**
1096 A418 10c emer & bister .75 .20
1097 A418 15c org & bister ('66) .30 .20
1098 A418 25c lilac & brn .45 .20
1099 A418 50c brt blue & brn .85 .75
Nos. 1096-1099 (4) 2.35 1.35

Nos. 1096-1099 are known only precanceled. See second note after No. 132. See Nos. 1240-1242, 1315-1318, 1421-1424.

Postrider, Rocket and Radar Equipment — A419

1964, June 5 **Engr.** ***Perf. 13***
1100 A419 1fr brn, dk red & dk bl 25.00 20.00

Sold for 4fr, including 3fr admission to PHILATEC. Issued in sheets of 8 stamps and 8 labels (2x8 subjects with labels in horizontal rows 1, 4, 5, 8; stamps in rows 2, 3, 6, 7). Commemorative inscriptions on side margins. Value $200.

Caesar's Tower, Provins — A420

Chapel of Notre Dame du Haut, Ronchamp
A421

1964-65

1101 A421 40c sl grn, dk brn & brn ('65) .25 .20
1102 A420 70c slate, grn & car .35 .20
1103 A421 1.25fr brt bl, sl grn & ol .75 .30
Nos. 1101-1103 (3) 1.35 .70

The 40c was issued in vertical coils in 1971. Every 10th coil stamp has a red control number printed twice on the back.

For surcharges see Reunion Nos. 352, 361.

Mandel — A422 Judo — A423

1964, July 4 **Unwmk.** ***Perf. 13***

1104 A422 30c violet brown .25 .20

Georges Mandel (1885-1944), Cabinet minister, executed by the Nazis.

1964, July 4

1105 A423 50c dk blue & vio brn .25 .20

18th Olympic Games, Tokyo, 10/10-25/64.

Champlevé Enamel from Limoges, 12th Century
A424

Design: No. 1107, The Lady (Claude Le Viste?) with the Unicorn, 15th cent. tapestry.

1964 ***Perf. 12x13***

1106 A424 1fr multicolored 1.25 .80
1107 A424 1fr multicolored .65 .45

No. 1106 shows part of an enamel sepulchral plate portraying Geoffrey IV, Count of Anjou and Le Maine (1113-1151), who was called Geoffrey Plantagenet.

Issue dates: #1106, July 4. #1107, Oct. 31.

Paris Taxis Carrying Soldiers to Front, 1914
A425

1964, Sept. 5 **Unwmk.** ***Perf. 13***

1108 A425 30c black, blue & red .25 .20

50th anniversary of Battle of the Marne.

Europa Issue, 1964

Common Design Type

1964, Sept. 12 **Engr.**

Size: 22x36mm

1109 CD7 25c dk car, dp ocher & grn .20 .20
1110 CD7 50c vio, yel grn & dk car .25 .20

Cooperation Issue

Common Design Type

1964, Nov. 6 **Unwmk.** ***Perf. 13***

1111 CD119 25c red brn, dk brn & dk bl .25 .20

Joux Chateau — A427

1965, Feb. 6 **Engr.**

1112 A427 1.30fr redsh brn, brn red & dk brn 1.50 .35

"The English Girl from the Star" by Toulouse-Lautrec — A428

St. Paul on the Damascus Road, Window, Cathedral of Sens — A429

Leaving for the Hunt — A430

Apocalypse Tapestry, 14th Century
A431

"The Red Violin" by Raoul Dufy — A432

Designs: No. 1115, "August" miniature of Book of Hours of Jean de France, Duc de Berry ("Les Très Riches Heures du Duc de Berry"), painted by Flemish brothers, Pol, Hermant and Jannequin Limbourg, 1411-16. No. 1116, Scene from oldest existing set of French tapestries, showing the Winepress of the Wrath of God (Revelations 14: 19-20).

1965 ***Perf. 12x13, 13x12***

1113 A428 1fr multicolored .50 .40
1114 A429 1fr multicolored .50 .40
1115 A430 1fr multicolored .30 .30
1116 A431 1fr multicolored .30 .30
1117 A432 1fr blk, pink & car .30 .30
Nos. 1113-1117 (5) 1.90 1.70

No. 1114 issued to commemorate the 800th anniversary of the Cathedral of Sens.

Issued: #1113, 3/12; #1114, 6/5; #1115, 9/25; #1116, 10/30; #1117, 11/6.

Returning Deportees, 1945 — A433

1965, Apr. 1 **Unwmk.** ***Perf. 13***

1118 A433 40c Prussian green .50 .30

20th anniv. of the return of people deported during World War II.

House of Youth and Culture, Troyes
A434

1965, Apr. 10 **Engr.**

1119 A434 25c ind, brn & dk grn .25 .20

20th anniv. of the establishment of recreational cultural centers for young people.

Woman Carrying Flowers
A435

Flags of France, US, USSR and Great Britain Crushing Swastika
A436

1965, Apr. 24 **Unwmk.** ***Perf. 13***

1120 A435 60c dk grn, dp org & ver .35 .20

Tourist Campaign of Welcome & Amiability.

1965, May 8

1121 A436 40c black, car & ultra .40 .20

20th anniv. of victory in World War II.

Telegraph Key, Syncom Satellite and Pleumeur-Bodou Station — A437

1965, May 17

1122 A437 60c dk blue, brn & blk .50 .30

Centenary of the ITU.

Croix de Guerre — A438

1965, May 22 **Engr.**

1123 A438 40c red, brn & brt grn .55 .35

50th anniv. of the Croix de Guerre medal.

Cathedral of Bourges — A439

Moustiers-Sainte-Marie — A440

Views: 30c, Road and tunnel, Mont Blanc. 60c, Aix-les-Bains, sailboat. 75c, Tarn Gorge, Lozère mountains. 95c, Vendée River, man poling boat, and windmill. 1fr, Prehistoric stone monuments, Carnac.

1965

1124 A439 30c bl, vio bl & brn vio .25 .20
1125 A439 40c gray bl & redsh brn .40 .20
1126 A440 50c grn, bl gray & bis .40 .20
1127 A439 60c blue & red brn .85 .25
1128 A439 75c brown, bl & grn 1.25 .90
1129 A440 95c brown, grn & bl 5.75 .90
1130 A440 1fr gray, grn & brn 1.40 .25
Nos. 1124-1130 (7) 10.30 2.90

No. 1124 for the opening of the Mont Blanc Tunnel. No. 1125 (Bourges Cathedral) was issued in connection with the French Philatelic Societies Federation Congress, held at Bourges.

Issued: 40c, June 5; 50c, June 19; 30c, 60c, July 17; others, July 10.

For surcharges see Reunion #354, 362, 365.

Europa Issue, 1965

Common Design Type

1965, Sept. 25 ***Perf. 13***

Size: 36x22mm

1131 CD8 30c red *.25 .30*
1132 CD8 60c gray *.50 .50*

Planting Seedling A441

Etienne Régnault, "Le Taureau" and Coast of Reunion A442

1965, Oct. 2

1133 A441 25c slate grn, yel grn & red brn .20 .20

National reforestation campaign.

1965, Oct. 2

1134 A442 30c indigo & dk car .20 .20

Tercentenary of settlement of Reunion.

Atomic Reactor and Diagram, Symbols of Industry, Agriculture and Medicine — A443

1965, Oct. 9

1135 A443 60c brt blue & blk .50 .30

Atomic Energy Commission, 20th anniv.

Air Academy and Emblem A444

1965, Nov. 6 ***Perf. 13***

1136 A444 25c dk blue & green .35 .30

Air Academy, Salon-de-Provence, 50th anniv.

French Satellite A-1 Issue

Common Design Type

Design: 60c, A-1 satellite.

1965, Nov. 30 **Engr.** ***Perf. 13***

1137 CD121 30c Prus bl, brt bl & blk .25 .20

1138 CD121 60c blk, Prus bl & brt bl .40 .25

a. Strip of 2, #1137-1138 + label .65 .65

Launching of France's 1st satellite, 11/26/65.

For surcharges see Reunion Nos. 358-359.

Arms of Auch — A446

Cities: 20c, Saint-Lô. 25c, Mont-de-Marsan.

Typographed, Photogravure (20c)

1966 ***Perf. 14x13; 14 (20c)***

1142 A446 5c blue & red .20 .20

1143 A446 20c vio bl, sil, gold & red .20 .20

1144 A446 25c red brown & ultra .60 .20

Nos. 1142-1144 (3) 1.00 .60

The 5c and 20c were issued in sheets and in vertical coils. In the coils, every 10th stamp has a red control number on the back.

For surcharges see Reunion Nos. 360-360A.

French Satellite D-1 Issue

Common Design Type

1966, Feb. 18 **Engr.** ***Perf. 13***

1148 CD122 60c blue blk, grn & cl .25 .20

Horses from Bronze Vessel of Vix — A448

"The Newborn" by Georges de La Tour — A449

The Baptism of Judas (4th Century Bishop of Jerusalem) — A450

"The Moon and the Bull" Tapestry by Jean Lurçat A451

"Crispin and Scapin" by Honoré Daumier — A452

1966 ***Perf. 13x12, 12x13***

1149 A448 1fr multicolored .40 .35

1150 A449 1fr multicolored .40 .35

1151 A450 1fr multicolored .40 .35

1152 A451 1fr multicolored .40 .30

1153 A452 1fr multicolored .40 .30

Nos. 1149-1153 (5) 2.00 1.65

The design of No. 1149 is a detail from a 6th century B.C. vessel, found in 1953 in a grave near Vix, Cote d'Or.

The design of No. 1151 is from a stained glass window in the 13th century Sainte-Chapelle, Paris.

No. 1150 exists in an imperf, ungummed souv. sheet with 2 progressive die proofs, issued for benefit of the Postal Museum, and not postally valid. Value $2.

Issued: #1149, 3/26; #1150, 6/25; #1151, 10/22; #1152, 11/19; #1153, 12/10.

Chessboard, Knight, Emblems for King and Queen — A453

St. Michael Slaying the Dragon — A455

Rhone Bridge, Pont-Saint-Esprit — A454

1966, Apr. 2 **Engr.** ***Perf. 13***

1154 A453 60c sepia, gray & dk vio bl .60 .45

Issued to publicize the Chess Festival.

1966, Apr. 23 **Unwmk.** ***Perf. 13***

1155 A454 25c black & dull blue .20 .20

1966, Apr. 30 **Litho. & Engr.**

1156 A455 25c multicolored .20 .20

Millenium of Mont-Saint-Michel.

Stanislas Leszczynski, Lunéville Chateau — A456

1966, May 6 **Engr.**

1157 A456 25c slate, grn & brn .20 .20

200th anniv. of the reunion of Lorraine and Bar (Barrois) with France.

St. Andrew's and Sèvre River, Niort — A457

1966, May 28 **Engr.** ***Perf. 13***

1158 A457 40c brt bl, indigo & grn .30 .20

Bernard Le Bovier de Fontenelle and 1666 Meeting Room A458

1966, June 4

1159 A458 60c dk car rose & brn .30 .25

300th anniversary, Académie des Sciences.

William the Conqueror, Castle and Norman Ships — A459

1966, June 4

1160 A459 60c brown red & dp bl .40 .30

900th anniversary of Battle of Hastings.

Tracks, Globe and Eiffel Tower A460

1966, June 11

1161 A460 60c dk brn, car & dull bl .85 .45

19th International Railroad Congress.

Oléron Bridge A461

1966, June 20

1162 A461 25c Prus bl, brn & bl .20 .20

Issued to commemorate the opening of Oléron Bridge, connecting Oléron Island in the Bay of Biscay with the French mainland.

Europa Issue, 1966

Common Design Type

1966, Sept. 24 **Engr.** ***Perf. 13***

Size: 22x36mm

1163 CD9 30c Prussian blue *.25* *.25*

1164 CD9 60c red *.35* *.25*

Vercingetorix at Gergovie, 52 B.C. — A462

Bishop Remi Baptizing King Clovis, 496 A.D. — A463

Design: 60c, Charlemagne attending school (page holding book for crowned king).

1966, Nov. 5 ***Perf. 13***

1165 A462 40c choc, grn & gray bl .35 .30

1166 A463 40c dk red brn & blk .35 .30

1167 A463 60c pur, rose car & brn .35 .30

Nos. 1165-1167 (3) 1.05 .90

Map of Pneumatic Post and Tube A464

1966, Nov. 11
1168 A464 1.60fr maroon & indigo .75 .40

Centenary of Paris pneumatic post system.

Val Chateau — A465

1966, Nov. 19 **Engr.** ***Perf. 13***
1169 A465 2.30fr dk bl, sl grn & brn 2.00 .30

Rance Power Station A466

1966, Dec. 3
1170 A466 60c dk bl, sl grn & brn .45 .45

Tidal power station in the estuary of the Rance River on the English Channel.

European Broadcasting Union Emblem — A467

1967, Mar. 4 **Engr.** ***Perf. 13***
1171 A467 40c dk blue & rose brn .25 .20

3rd Intl. Congress of the European Broadcasting Union, Paris, Mar. 8-22.

Father Juniet's Gig by Henri Rousseau — A468

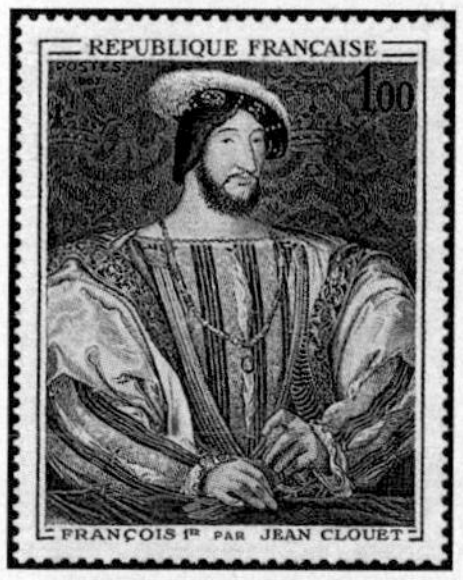

Francois I by Jean Clouet A469

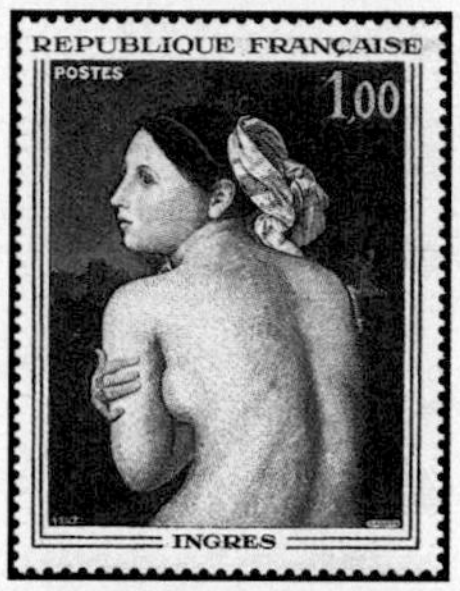

The Bather by Jean-Dominique Ingres — A470

St. Eloi, the Goldsmith, at Work — A471

1967 **Engr.** ***Perf. 13x12, 12x13***

1172	A468	1fr multicolored	.40	.40
1173	A469	1fr multicolored	.40	.40
1174	A470	1fr multicolored	.40	.35
1175	A471	1fr multicolored	.40	.35
		Nos. 1172-1175 (4)	1.60	1.50

The design of No. 1175 is from a 16th century stained glass window in the Church of Sainte Madeleine, Troyes.

Issued: #1172, 4/15; #1173, 7/1; #1174, 9/9; #1175, 10/7.

Snow Crystal and Olympic Rings — A472

1967, Apr. 22 **Photo.** ***Perf. 13***
1176 A472 60c brt & lt blue & red .40 .25

Issued to publicize the 10th Winter Olympic Games, Grenoble, Feb. 6-18, 1968.

French Pavilion, EXPO '67 — A473

1967, Apr. 22 **Engr.**
1177 A473 60c dull bl & bl grn .35 .30

Intl. Exhibition EXPO '67, Montreal, Apr. 28-Oct. 27, 1967.

For surcharge see Reunion No. 363.

Europa Issue, 1967

Common Design Type

1967, Apr. 29

Size: 22x36mm

1178	CD10	30c blue & gray	*.25*	*.25*
1179	CD10	60c brown & lt blue	*.55*	*.45*

Great Bridge, Bordeaux A474

1967, May 8
1180 A474 25c olive, blk & brn .25 .20

Nungesser, Coli and "L'Oiseau Blanc" A475

1967, May 8
1181 A475 40c slate, dk & lt brn .50 .35

40th anniv. of the attempted transatlantic flight of Charles Nungesser and François Coil, French aviators.

Goüin House, Tours — A476

1967, May 13 **Engr.** ***Perf. 13***
1182 A476 40c vio bl, red brn & red .55 .25

Congress of the Federation of French Philatelic Societies in Tours.

Ramon and Alfort Veterinary School A477

1967, May 27
1183 A477 25c brn, dp bl & yel grn .25 .20

200th anniv. of the Alfort Veterinary School and to honor Professor Gaston Ramon (1886-1963).

Robert Esnault-Pelterie, Diamant Rocket and A-1 Satellite — A478

1967, May 27
1184 A478 60c slate & vio blue .50 .30

Issued to honor Robert Esnault-Pelterie (1881-1957), aviation and space expert.

City Hall, Saint-Quentin A479

Saint-Germain-en-Laye — A480

Views: 60c, Clock Tower, Vire. 75c, Beach, La Baule, Brittany. 95c, Harbor, Boulogne-sur-Mer. 1fr, Rodez Cathedral. 1.50fr, Morlaix; old houses, grotesque carving, viaduct.

1967

1185	A479	50c bl, sl bl & brn	.40	.20
1186	A479	60c dp bl, sl bl & dk red brn	.60	.50
1187	A480	70c rose car, red brn & bl	.40	.20
1188	A480	75c multicolored	1.60	1.25
1189	A480	95c sky bl, lil & sl grn	1.25	1.10
1190	A479	1fr indigo & bl gray	.65	.20
1191	A479	1.50fr brt bl, brt grn & red brn	1.25	.30
		Nos. 1185-1191 (7)	6.15	3.75

Issued: 1fr, 1.50fr, June 10; 70c, June 17; 50c, 60c, 95c, July 8; 75c, July 24.

Orchids — A481

1967, July 29 **Engr.** ***Perf. 13***
1192 A481 40c dp car, brt pink & pur .90 .50

Orleans flower festival.

Scales of Justice, City and Harbor A482

1967, Sept. 4
1193 A483 60c dk plum, dl bl & ocher .50 .30

9th Intl. Accountancy Cong., Paris, 9/6-12.

Cross of Lorraine, Soldiers and Sailors — A483

1967, Oct. 7 **Engr.** ***Perf. 13***
1194 A482 25c brn, dp ultra & bl .20 .20

25th anniv. of the Battle of Bir Hacheim.

Marie Curie, Bowl Glowing with Radium A484

1967, Oct. 23 **Engr.** ***Perf. 13***
1195 A484 60c dk blue & ultra .40 .30

Marie Curie (1867-1934), scientist who discovered radium and polonium, Nobel prize winner for physics and chemistry.

Lions Emblem A485

Marianne (by Cheffer) — A486

1967, Oct. 28
1196 A485 40c dk car & vio bl 1.00 .50

50th anniversary of Lions International.

For surcharge see Reunion No. 364.

1967, Nov. 4 **Engr.**

1197 A486 25c dark blue .40 .20
1198 A486 30c bright lilac .45 .20
a. Booklet pane of 5 6.00
b. Booklet pane of 10 12.00

Coils (vertical) of Nos. 1197 and 1231 show a red number on the back of every 10th stamp.

See Nos. 1230-1231C. For surcharges see Reunion Nos. 367-368, 389.

King Philip II (Philip Augustus) at Battle of Bouvines A487

Designs: No. 1200, Election of Hugh Capet as King, horiz. 60c, King Louis IX (St. Louis) holding audience for the poor.

1967, Nov. 13 **Engr.** ***Perf. 13***

1199 A487 40c gray & black .40 .30
1200 A487 40c steel bl & ultra .40 .30
1201 A487 60c grn & dk red brn .50 .30
Nos. 1199-1201 (3) 1.30 .90

Commemorative Medal — A488

1968, Jan. 6 **Engr.** ***Perf. 13***

1202 A488 40c dk slate grn & bis .25 .20

50th anniversary of postal checking service.

Various Road Signs — A489

1968, Feb. 24

1203 A489 25c lil, red & dk bl grn .25 .20

Issued to publicize road safety.

Prehistoric Paintings, Lascaux Cave — A490

Arearea (Merriment) by Paul Gauguin — A491

The Dance by Emile Antoine Bourdelle A492

Portrait of the Model by Auguste Renoir A493

1968 **Engr.** ***Perf. 13x12, 12x13***

1204 A490 1fr multicolored .55 .40
1205 A491 1fr multicolored .65 .40
1206 A492 1fr car & gray olive .65 .40
1207 A493 1fr multicolored .65 .40
Nos. 1204-1207 (4) 2.50 1.60

Issue dates: #1204, Apr. 13; #1205, Sept. 21; #1206, Oct. 26; #1207, Nov. 9.

Audio-visual Institute, Royan — A494

1968, Apr. 13 ***Perf. 13***

1208 A494 40c slate grn, brn & Prus bl .25 .20

5th Conference for World Cooperation with the theme of teaching living languages by audio-visual means.

Europa Issue, 1968

Common Design Type

1968, Apr. 27

Size: 36x22mm

1209 CD11 30c brt red lil & ocher *.30* .20
1210 CD11 60c brown & lake *.60* *.30*

Alain René Le Sage — A495

1968, May 4

1211 A495 40c blue & rose vio .25 .20

Alain René Le Sage (1668-1747), novelist and playwright.

Chateau de Langeais A496

1968, May 4

1212 A496 60c slate bl, grn & red brn .50 .40

Pierre Larousse A497

1968, May 11 **Engr.** ***Perf. 13***

1213 A497 40c rose vio & brown .25 .20

Pierre Larousse (1817-75), grammarian, lexicographer and encyclopedist.

Gnarled Trunk and Fir Tree — A498

1968, May 18 **Engr.** ***Perf. 13***

1214 A498 25c grnsh bl, brn & grn .25 .20

Twinning of Rambouillet Forest in France and the Black Forest in Germany.

Map of Papal Enclave, Valréas, and John XXII Receiving Homage A499

1968, May 25

1215 A499 60c brn, bis brn & pur .55 .40

Papal enclave at Valréas, 650th anniv.

Louis XIV, Arms of France and Flanders A500

1968, June 29

1216 A500 40c rose car, gray & lemon .25 .20

300th anniv. of the Treaty of Aachen which reunited Flanders with France.

Martrou Bridge, Rochefort A501

1968, July 20

1217 A501 25c sky bl, blk & dk red brn .25 .20

Letord Lorraine Bimotor Plane over Map of France A502

1968, Aug. 17 **Engr.** ***Perf. 13***

1218 A502 25c brt blue, indigo & red .50 .30

1st regularly scheduled air mail route in France from Paris to St. Nazaire, 50th anniv.

Tower de Constance, Aigues-Mortes A503

1968, Aug. 31

1219 A503 25c red brn, sky bl & olive bister .25 .20

Bicentenary of the release of Huguenot prisoners from the Tower de Constance, Aigues-Mortes.

Cathedral and Pont Vieux, Beziers A504

1968, Sept. 7 **Engr.** ***Perf. 13***

1220 A504 40c ind, bis & grn .85 .50

"Victory" over White Tower of Salonika — A505

1968, Sept. 28

1221 A505 40c red lilac & plum .25 .20

50th anniv. of the armistice on the eastern front in World War I, Sept. 29, 1918.

Louis XV, Arms of France and Corsica A506

1968, Oct. 5 ***Perf. 13***

1222 A506 25c ultra, grn & blk .25 .20

Return of Corsica to France, 200th anniv.

Relay Race A507

1968, Oct. 12

1223 A507 40c ultra, brt grn & ol brn .50 .30

19th Olympic Games, Mexico City, 10/12-27.

Polar Camp with Helicopter, Plane and Snocat Tractor — A508

1968, Oct. 19

1224 A508 40c Prus bl, lt grnsh bl & brn red .35 .20

20 years of French Polar expeditions. For surcharge see Reunion No. 366.

Leon Bailby, Paris Opera Staircase and Hospital Beds — A509

"Victory" over Arc de Triomphe and Eternal Flame — A510

1968, Oct. 26

1225 A509 40c ocher & maroon .25 .20

50th anniv. of the "Little White Beds" children's hospital fund.

1968, Nov. 9 **Engr.** ***Perf. 13***

1226 A510 25c dk car rose & dp blue .25 .20

50th anniv. of the armistice which ended World War I.

Death of Bertrand Du Guesclin at Chateauneuf-de-Randon, 1380 — A511

#1228, King Philip IV (the Fair) and first States-General assembly, 1302, horiz. 60c, Joan of Arc leaving Vaucouleurs, 1429.

1968, Nov. 16

1227 A511 40c green, ultra & brn .40 .30
1228 A511 40c cop red, grn & gray .40 .30
1229 A511 60c vio bl, sl bl & bis .40 .30
Nos. 1227-1229 (3) 1.20 .90

See No. 1260.

Marianne Type of 1967

1969-70 **Engr.** ***Perf. 13***

1230 A486 30c green .35 .20
a. Booklet pane of 10 8.50
1231 A486 40c deep carmine .45 .20
a. Booklet pane of 5 (horiz. strip) 7.50
b. Booklet pane of 10 8.50
d. With label ('70) .50 .25

Typo. ***Perf. 14x13***

1231C A486 30c blue green .20 .20
Nos. 1230-1231C (3) 1.00 .60

No. 1231d was issued in sheets of 50 with alternating labels showing coat of arms of Perigueux, arranged checkerwise, to commemorate the inauguration of the Perigueux stamp printing plant.

The 40c coil is noted after No. 1198.

Church of Brou, Bourg-en-Bresse — A512

Views: 80c, Vouglans Dam, Jura. 85c, Chateau de Chantilly. 1.15fr, Sailboats in La Trinité-sur-Mer harbor.

1969 **Engr.** ***Perf. 13***

1232 A512 45c olive, bl & red brn .25 .20
1233 A512 80c ol bis, brn red & dk brn .45 .20
1234 A512 85c sl grn, dl bl & gray .90 .45
1235 A512 1.15fr brt bl, gray grn & brn .90 .40
Nos. 1232-1235 (4) 2.50 1.25

"February" Bas-relief from Amiens Cathedral A513

Philip the Good, by Roger van der Weyden A514

Sts. Savin and Cyprian before Ladicius, Mural, St. Savin, Vienne — A515

The Circus, by Georges Seurat A515a

1969 ***Perf. 12x13***

1236 A513 1fr dk green & brn .60 .45
1237 A514 1fr multicolored .60 .45
1238 A515 1fr multicolored .60 .45
1239 A515a 1fr multicolored .60 .45
Nos. 1236-1239 (4) 2.40 1.80

Issue dates: No. 1236, Feb. 22; No. 1237, May 3; No. 1238, June 28; No. 1239, Nov. 8.

Gallic Coin Type of 1964-66

1969 **Typo.** ***Perf. 13½x14***

1240 A418 22c brt green & vio .80 .20
1241 A418 35c red & ultra 1.65 .40
1242 A418 70c ultra & red brn 6.00 2.00
Nos. 1240-1242 (3) 8.45 2.60

Nos. 1240-1242 are known only precanceled. See note after No. 132.

Hautefort Chateau A516

1969, Apr. 5 **Engr.** ***Perf. 13***

1243 A516 70c blue, slate & bister .40 .30

Irises A517

1969, Apr. 12 **Photo.**

1244 A517 45c multicolored .40 .30

3rd Intl. Flower Show, Paris, 4/23-10/5.

Europa Issue, 1969

Common Design Type

1969, Apr. 26 **Engr.** ***Perf. 13***

Size: 36x22mm

1245 CD12 40c carmine rose *.20 .20*
1246 CD12 70c Prussian blue *.30 .25*

Albert Thomas and Thomas Memorial, Geneva A518

1969, May 10 **Engr.** ***Perf. 13***

1247 A518 70c brn, ol bis & ind .40 .30

ILO, 50th anniv., and honoring Thomas (1878-1932), director of the ILO (1920-32).

Garigliano Battle Scene, 1944 — A519

1969, May 10

1248 A519 45c black & violet .50 .50

25th anniv. of the Battle of the Garigliano against the Germans.

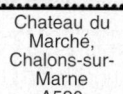

Chateau du Marché, Chalons-sur-Marne A520

Parachutists over Normandy Beach A521

1969, May 24

1249 A520 45c bis, dull bl & grn .50 .40

Federation of French Philatelic Societies, 42nd congress.

1969, May 31

1250 A521 45c dk blue & vio bl 1.25 .55

Landing of Special Air Service and Free French commandos in Normandy, June 6, 1944, 25th anniv.

Monument of the French Resistance, Mt. Mouchet — A522

1969, June 7

1251 A522 45c dk grn, slate & ind .90 .65

25th anniv. of the battle of Mt. Mouchet between French resistance fighters and the Germans, June 2 and 10, 1944.

French Troops Landing in Provence — A523

1969, Aug. 23 **Engr.** ***Perf. 13***

1252 A523 45c slate & blk brn 1.00 .65

25th anniv. of the landing of French and American forces in Provence, Aug. 15, 1944.

Russian and French Aviators — A524

1969, Oct. 18 **Engr.** ***Perf. 13***

1253 A524 45c slate, dp bl & car 1.00 .80

Issued to honor the French aviators of the Normandy-Neman Squadron who fought on the Russian Front, 1942-45.

Kayak on Isère River A525

1969, Aug. 2 **Engr.** ***Perf. 13***

1254 A525 70c org brn, ol & dk bl .45 .30

Intl. Canoe and Kayak Championships, Bourg-Saint-Maurice, Savoy, July 31-Aug. 6.

Napoleon as Young Officer and his Birthplace, Ajaccio — A526

1969, Aug. 16

1255 A526 70c brt grnsh bl, ol & rose vio .45 .30

Napoleon Bonaparte (1769-1821).

For surcharge see Reunion No. 370.

Drops of Water and Diamond
A527

Mediterranean Mouflon
A528

1969, Sept. 27

1256 A527 70c blk, dp bl & brt grn .50 .30

European Water Charter.

1969, Oct. 11

1257 A528 45c ol, blk & org brn *3.25 1.25*

Issued to publicize wildlife protection.

Central School of Arts and Crafts
A529

1969, Oct. 18

1258 A529 70c dk grn, yel grn & org .40 .30

Inauguration of the Central School of Arts and Crafts at Chatenay-Malabry.

Nuclear Submarine "Le Redoutable" — A530

1969, Oct. 25

1259 A530 70c dp bl, grn & sl grn .40 .30

Type of 1968 and

Henri IV and Edict of Nantes — A531

Designs: No. 1260, Pierre Terrail de Bayard wounded at Battle of Brescia (after a painting in Versailles). No. 1262, Louis XI, Charles the Bold and map of France.

1969, Nov. 8 Engr. *Perf. 13*

1260 A511 80c brn, bister & blk .50 .30
1261 A531 80c blk & vio bl .50 .30
1262 A531 80c ol, dp grn & dk red brn .50 .30
Nos. 1260-1262 (3) 1.50 .90

"Firecrest" and Alain Gerbault — A532

1970, Jan. 10 Engr. *Perf. 13*

1263 A532 70c ind, brt bl & gray .75 .50

Completion of Alain Gerbault's trip around the world aboard the "Firecrest," 1923-29, 40th anniv.

Gendarmery Emblem, Mountain Climber, Helicopter, Motorcyclists and Motorboat — A533

1970, Jan. 31

1264 A533 45c sl grn, dk bl & brn 1.25 .50

National Gendarmery, founded 1791.

Field Ball Player — A534

1970, Feb. 21 Engr. *Perf. 13*

1265 A534 80c slate green .50 .50

7th Intl. Field Ball Games, Feb. 26-Mar. 8.

Alphonse Juin and Church of the Invalides — A535

1970, Feb. 28

1266 A535 45c gray bl & dk brn .35 .20

Issued to honor Marshal Alphonse Pierre Juin (1888-1967), military leader.

Aerotrain
A536

1970, Mar. 7

1267 A536 80c purple & gray .65 .50

Introduction of the aerotrain, which reaches a speed of 320 miles per hour.

Pierre Joseph Pelletier, Joseph Bienaimé Caventou, Quinine Formula and Cell — A537

1970, Mar. 21 Engr. *Perf. 13*

1268 A537 50c slate grn, sky bl & dp car .35 .30

Discovery of quinine, 150th anniversary.

Pink Flamingos
A538

Diamant B Rocket and Radar
A539

1970, Mar. 21

1269 A538 45c olive, gray & pink .35 .25

European Nature Conservation Year, 1970.

1970, Mar. 28

1270 A539 45c bright green .65 .40

Space center in Guyana and the launching of the Diamant B rocket, Mar. 10, 1970.

Europa Issue, 1970

Common Design Type

1970, May 2 Engr. *Perf. 13*

Size: 36x22mm

1271 CD13 40c deep carmine *.25* .20
1272 CD13 80c sky blue *.50* .20

Annunication, by Primitive Painter of Savoy, 1480 — A540

The Triumph of Flora, by Jean Baptiste Carpeaux — A541

Diana Returning from the Hunt, by François Boucher — A542

Dancer with Bouquet, by Edgar Degas
A543

1970 ***Perf. 12x13, 13x12***

1273 A540 1fr multicolored .85 .45
1274 A541 1fr red brown .85 .45
1275 A542 1fr multicolored .85 .45
1276 A543 1fr multicolored .85 .45
Nos. 1273-1276 (4) 3.40 1.80

Issue dates: #1273, May 9; #1274, July 4; #1275, Oct. 10; #1276, Nov. 14.

Arms of Lens, Miner's Lamp and Pit Head
A544

1970, May 16 Engr. *Perf. 13*

1277 A544 40c scarlet .25 .20

43rd Natl. Congress of the Federation of French Philatelic Societies, Lens, May 14-21.

Diamond Rock, Martinique
A545

Haute Provence Observatory and Spiral Nebula — A546

Designs: 95c, Chancelade Abbey, Dordogne. 1fr, Gosier Islet, Guadeloupe.

1970, June 20 Engr. *Perf. 13*

1278 A545 50c sl grn, brt bl & plum .45 .20
1279 A545 95c lt ol, car & brn 1.25 1.00
1280 A545 1fr sl grn, brt bl & dk car rose .55 .20
1281 A546 1.30fr dk bl, vio bl & dk grn 1.90 1.00
Nos. 1278-1281 (4) 4.15 2.40

Hand Reaching for Freedom
A547

Handicapped Javelin Thrower
A548

1970, June 27

1282 A547 45c vio bl, bl & bister .40 .25

Liberation of concentration camps, 25th anniv.

1970, June 27

1283 A548 45c rose car, ultra & emer .40 .25

Issued to publicize the International Games of the Handicapped, St. Etienne, June 1970.

Pole Vault — A549

1970, Sept. 11 Engr. *Perf. 13*
1284 A549 45c car, bl & indigo .45 .25

First European Junior Athletic Championships, Colombes, Sept. 11-13.

Royal Salt Works, Arc-et-Senans — A550

1970, Sept. 26
1285 A550 80c bl, brn & dk grn 1.50 .65

Restoration of the 18th cent. Royal Salt Works buildings, by Claude Nicolas Ledoux (1736-1806) at Arc-et-Senans, for use as a center for studies of all aspects of future human life.

Armand Jean du Plessis, Duc de Richelieu — A551

Designs: No. 1287, Battle of Fontenoy, 1745. No. 1288, Louis XIV and Versailles.

1970, Oct. 17 Engr. *Perf. 13*
1286 A551 45c blk, sl & car rose .65 .35
1287 A551 45c org, brn & indigo .65 .35
1288 A551 45c sl grn, lem & org brn .65 .35
Nos. 1286-1288 (3) 1.95 1.05

UN Headquarters in New York and Geneva — A552

1970, Oct. 24 Engr. *Perf. 13*
1289 A552 80c ol, dp ultra & dk pur .55 .40

25th anniversary of the United Nations.

View of Bordeaux and France No. 43 — A553

1970, Nov. 7
1290 A553 80c vio bl & gray bl .55 .35

Centerary of the Bordeaux issue.

Col. Denfert-Rochereau and Lion of Belfort, by Frederic A. Bartholdi — A554

1970, Nov. 14
1291 A554 45c dk bl, ol & red brn .40 .25

Centenary of the siege of Belfort during Franco-Prussian War.

Marianne (by Bequet) — A555

1971-74 Typo. *Perf. 14x13*
1292 A555 45c sky blue .30 .20
1292A A555 60c green ('74) .90 .20

For surcharges see Reunion #371, 397-398.

Engr. *Perf. 13*
1293 A555 50c rose carmine .30 .20
a. Bklt. pane of 5 (horiz. strip) 5.00
b. Booklet pane of 10 10.00
1294 A555 60c green ('74) 5.00 .35
a. Booklet pane of 10 65.00
1294B A555 80c car rose ('74) .50 .20
c. Booklet pane of 5 9.00
d. Booklet pane of 10 12.00
Nos. 1293-1294B (3) 5.80 .75

Nos. 1294 and 1294B issued also in vertical coils with control number on back of every 10th stamp.

No. 1293 issued only in booklets and in vertical coils with red control number on back of every 10th stamp.

See Nos. 1494-1498.

St. Matthew, Sculpture from Strasbourg Cathedral A556

Winnower, by François Millet A557

The Dreamer, by Georges Rouault A558

1971 Engr. *Perf. 12x13*
1295 A556 1fr dark red brown .85 .50
1296 A557 1fr multicolored .85 .40
1297 A558 1fr multicolored .85 .40
Nos. 1295-1297 (3) 2.55 1.30

Issued: #1295, 1/23; #1296, 4/3; #1297, 6/5.

Figure Skating Pair A560

1971, Feb. 20 Engr. *Perf. 13*
1299 A560 80c vio bl, sl & aqua .55 .30

World Figure Skating Championships, Lyons, Feb. 23-28.

Underwater Exploration — A561

1971, Mar. 6
1300 A561 80c blue blk & bl grn .55 .30

International Exhibition of Ocean Exploration, Bordeaux, Mar. 9-14.

Cape Horn Clipper "Antoinette" and Solidor Castle, Saint-Malo — A562

1971, Apr. 10 Engr. *Perf. 13*
1301 A562 80c blue, pur & slate 1.25 .90

For surcharge see Reunion No. 372.

Pyrenean Chamois — A563

1971, Apr. 24 Engr. *Perf. 13*
1302 A563 65c bl, dk brn & brn ol .65 .30

National Park of Western Pyrenees.

Europa Issue, 1971
Common Design Type and

Santa Maria della Salute, Venice A564

1971, May 8 Engr. *Perf. 13*
1303 A564 50c blue gray & ol bis *.30 .25*

Size: 36x22mm
1304 CD14 80c rose lilac *.45 .40*

Cardinal, Nobleman and Lawyer — A565

Storming of the Bastille — A566

Design: No. 1306, Battle of Valmy.

1971
1305 A565 45c bl, rose red & pur .55 .40
1306 A565 45c bl, ol bis & brn red .65 .40
1307 A566 65c dk brn, gray bl & mag 1.00 .40
Nos. 1305-1307 (3) 2.20 1.20

No. 1305 commemorates the opening of the Estates General, May 5, 1789; No. 1306, Battle of Valmy (Sept. 20, 1792) between French and Prussian armies; 65c, Storming of the Bastille, Paris, July 14, 1789.

Issued: #1305, 5/8; #1306, 9/18; 65c, 7/10.

Grenoble A568

1971, May 29 Engr. *Perf. 13*
1308 A568 50c ocher, lil & rose red .35 .20

44th Natl. Cong. of the Federation of French Philatelic Societies, Grenoble, May 30-31.

"Rural Family Aid" Shedding Light on Village — A569

1971, June 5
1309 A569 40c vio, bl & grn .25 .20

Aid for rural families.
For surcharge see Reunion No. 373.

Chateau and Fort de Sedan A570

Pont d'Arc, Ardèche Gorge — A571

Views: 60c, Sainte Chapelle, Riom. 65c, Fountain and tower, Dole. 90c, Tower and street, Riquewihr.

1971 Engr. *Perf. 13*
1310 A571 60c black, grn & bl .25 .20
1311 A571 65c lil, ocher & blk .35 .20
1312 A571 90c grn, vio brn & red brn .50 .20

1313 A570 1.10fr sl grn, Prus bl & brn .60 .30
1314 A571 1.40fr sl grn, bl & dk brn .75 .20
Nos. 1310-1314 (5) 2.45 1.10

Issued: 60c, 6/19; 65c, 90c, 7/3; 1.10fr, 1.40fr, 6/12.
For surcharges see Reunion Nos. 374, 381.

Gallic Coin Type of 1964-66

1971, July 1 Typo. *Perf. 13½x14*

1315 A418 26c lilac & brn .50 .20
1316 A418 30c lt brown & brn .90 .20
1317 A418 45c dull green & brn 1.75 .30
1318 A418 90c red & brown 2.25 .50
Nos. 1315-1318 (4) 5.40 1.20

Nos. 1315-1318 are known only precanceled. See second paragraph after No. 132.

Bourbon Palace A572

1971, Aug. 28 Engr. *Perf. 13*

1319 A572 90c violet blue .75 .25

59th Conf. of the Interparliamentary Union.

Embroidery and Tool Making A573

1971, Oct. 16

1320 A573 90c brn red, brt lil & cl .50 .30

40th anniv. of the first assembly of presidents of artisans' guilds.
For surcharge see Reunion No. 375.

Reunion Chameleon A574

1971, Nov. 6 Photo. *Perf. 13*

1321 A574 60c brn, yel, grn & blk 1.10 .65

Nature protection.

De Gaulle Issue
Common Design Type and

De Gaulle in Brazzaville, 1944 — A576

Designs: No. 1324, De Gaulle entering Paris, 1944. No. 1325, Pres. de Gaulle, 1970.

1971, Nov. 9 Engr.

1322 CD134 50c black 1.10 .65
1323 A576 50c ultra 1.10 .65
1324 A576 50c rose red 1.10 .65
1325 CD134 50c black 1.10 .65
a. Strip of 4, #1322-1325 + label 4.50 4.00

1st anniv. of the death of Charles de Gaulle.
See Reunion Nos. 377, 380.

Antoine Portal and first Session of Academy — A577

1971, Nov. 13

1326 A577 45c dk purple & mag .35 .30

Sesquicentennial of the founding of the National Academy of Medicine; Baron Antoine Portal was first president.

L'Etude, by Jean Honoré Fragonard A578

Women in Garden, by Claude Monet A579

St. Peter Presenting Pierre de Bourbon, by Maitre de Moulins A580

Boats, by André Derain — A581

1972 Engr. *Perf. 12x13, 13x12*

1327 A578 1fr black & multi .90 .75
1328 A579 1fr slate grn & multi 1.75 .75
1329 A580 2fr dk brown & multi 2.50 1.25
1330 A581 2fr yellow & multi 3.50 1.50
Nos. 1327-1330 (4) 8.65 4.25

Issue dates: #1327, Jan. 22; #1328, June 17; #1329, Oct. 14; #1330, Dec. 16.

Map of South Indian Ocean, Penguin and Ships — A582

1972, Jan. 29 *Perf. 13*

1331 A582 90c black, bl & ocher .65 .40

Bicentenary of discovery of the Crozet and Kerguelen Islands.

Slalom and Olympic Emblems A583

1972, Feb. 7

1332 A583 90c dk olive & dp car .55 .35

11th Winter Olympic Games, Sapporo, Japan, Feb. 3-13.

Hearts, UN Emblem, Caduceus and Pacemaker A584

1972, Apr. 8 Engr. *Perf. 13*

1333 A584 45c dk car, org & gray .35 .25

"Your heart is your health," world health month.

Red Deer, Sologne Plateau — A585

Charlieu Abbey A585a

Bazoches-du-Morvand Chateau — A586

Saint-Just Cathedral, Narbonne A587

1972 *Perf. 13*

1334 A585 1fr ocher & red brn .65 .20
1335 A585a 1.20fr sl & dull brn .65 .20
1336 A586 2fr sl grn, blk & red brn 1.00 .20
1337 A587 3.50fr bl, gray ol & car rose 1.90 .55
Nos. 1334-1337 (4) 4.20 1.15

Issued: 1fr, 9/10; 1.20fr, 4/29; 2fr, 9/9; 3.50fr, 4/8.
For surcharge see Reunion No. 388.

Eagle Owl — A588

Nature protection: 60c, Salmon, horiz.

1972

1338 A588 60c grn, ind & brt bl 2.25 .60
1339 A588 65c sl, ol brn & sep 1.40 .30

Issue dates: 60c, May 27; 65c, Apr. 15.

Europa Issue 1972
Common Design Type and

Aix-la-Chapelle Cathedral — A589

1972, Apr. 22 Engr. *Perf. 13*

1340 A589 50c yel, vio brn & dk ol *.25 .25*

Photo.
Size: 22x36mm

1341 CD15 90c red org & multi *.50 .45*

Bouquet Made of Hearts and Blood Donors' Emblem A590

Newfoundlander "Côte d'Emeraude" A591

1972, May 5 Engr.

1342 A590 40c red .30 .20

20th anniv. of the Blood Donors Association of Post and Telecommunications Employees.
For surcharge see Reunion No. 383.

1972, May 6

1343 A591 90c org, vio bl & sl grn 1.00 .80

Cathedral, Saint-Brieuc A592

1972, May 20

1344 A592 50c lilac rose .30 .20

45th Congress of the Federation of French Philatelic Societies, Saint-Brieuc, May 21-22.

Hand Holding Symbol of Postal Code A593

1972, June 3 Typo. *Perf. 14x13*

1345 A593 30c green, blk & car .20 .20
1346 A593 50c car, blk & yel .30 .20

Introduction of postal code system.
For surcharges see Reunion Nos. 384-385.

Old and New Communications A594

1972, July 1 Engr. *Perf. 13*

1347 A594 45c slate & vio blue .40 .20

21st Intl. Congress of P.T.T. (Post, Telegraph & Telephone) Employees, Paris, 7/1-7.

Hurdler and Olympic Rings A595

1972, July 8

1348 A595 1fr deep olive .50 .20

20th Olympic Games, Munich, 8/26-9/11.

Hikers and Mt. Aigoual — A596

Bicyclist — A597

1972, July 15 Photo. *Perf. 13*

1349 A596 40c brt rose & multi 1.50 .60

Intl. Year of Tourism and 25th anniv. of the Natl. Hikers Association.

1972, July 22 Engr.

1350 A597 1fr gray, brn & lil 1.90 .60

World Bicycling Championships, Marseille, July 29-Aug. 2.

"Incroyables and Merveilleuses," 1794 — A598

French History: 60c, Bonaparte at the Arcole Bridge. 65c, Egyptian expedition (soldiers and scientists finding antiquities; pyramids in background).

1972 Engr. *Perf. 13*

1351 A598 45c ol, dk grn & car rose .40 .30
1352 A598 60c red, blk & ind .85 .40
1353 A598 65c ocher, ultra & choc .85 .40
Nos. 1351-1353 (3) 2.10 1.10

. Issued: 45c, Oct. 7; 60c, 65c, Nov. 11.

Champollion, Rosetta Stone with Key Inscription — A599

1972, Oct. 14

1354 A599 90c vio bl, brn red & blk .60 .30

Sesquicentennial of the deciphering of hieroglyphs by Jean-François Champollion.

St. Teresa, Portal of Notre Dame of Alençon A600

1973, Jan. 6 Engr. *Perf. 13*

1355 A600 1fr Prus blue & indigo .60 .45

Centenary of the birth of St. Teresa of Lisieux, the Little Flower (Thérèse Martin, 1873-1897), Carmelite nun.

Anthurium (Martinique) — A601

1973, Jan. 20 Photo.

1356 A601 50c gray & multi .40 .20

Colors of France and Germany Interlaced — A602

1973, Jan. 22

1357 A602 50c multicolored .40 .20

10th anniv. of the Franco-German Cooperation Treaty. See Germany No. 1101.

Polish Immigrants — A603

1973, Feb. 3 Engr. *Perf. 13*

1358 A603 40c slate grn, dp car & brn .25 .25

50th anniversary of Polish immigration into France, 1921-1923.

Last Supper, St. Austremoine Church, Issoire — A604

Kneeling Woman, by Charles Le Brun A605

Angel, Wood, Moutier-D'Ahun — A606

Lady Playing Archlute, by Antoine Watteau A607

1973 Engr. *Perf. 12x13*

1359 A604 2fr brown & multi 1.75 1.25
1360 A605 2fr dk red & yel 1.75 1.40
1361 A606 2fr ol brn & vio brn 1.75 1.25
1362 A607 2fr black & multi 1.75 1.25
Nos. 1359-1362 (4) 7.00 5.15

Issue dates: #1359, Feb. 10; #1360, Apr. 28; #1361, May 26; #1362, Sept. 22.

Tuileries Palace, Telephone Relays A608

Oil Tanker, Francis I Lock A609

Airbus A300-B A610

1973

1363 A608 45c ultra, sl grn & bis .30 .20
1364 A609 90c plum, blk & bl .55 .20
1365 A610 3fr dk brn, bl & blk 1.90 .80
Nos. 1363-1365 (3) 2.75 1.20

French technical achievements.
Issued: 45c, 5/15; 90c, 10/27; 3fr, 4/7.

Europa Issue 1973

Common Design Type and

City Hall, Brussels, CEPT Emblem — A611

1973, Apr. 14 Engr. *Perf. 13*

1366 A611 50c brt pink & choc *.45 .25*

Photo.

Size: 36x22mm

1367 CD16 90c slate grn & multi *1.60 .75*

Masonic Lodge Emblem A612

1973, May 12 Engr. *Perf. 13*

1368 A612 90c magenta & vio bl .55 .30

Bicentenary of the Free Masons of France.

Guadeloupe Raccoon A613

White Storks A614

1973

1369 A613 40c lilac, sepia & olive .35 .20
1370 A614 60c blk, aqua & org red .50 .25

Nature protection.
Issue dates: 40c, June 23; 60c, May 12.

Tourist Issue

Doubs Waterfall A615

Clos-Lucé, Amboise A617

Palace of Dukes of Burgundy, Dijon A616

Design: 90c, Gien Chateau.

1973 Engr. *Perf. 13*

1371 A615 60c multicolored .30 .20
1372 A616 65c red & purple .30 .20
1373 A616 90c Prus bl, ind & brn .35 .20
1374 A617 1fr ocher, bl & sl grn .35 .20
Nos. 1371-1374 (4) 1.30 .80

Issued: 60c, 9/8; 65c, 5/19; 90c, 8/18; 1fr, 6/23.
For surcharge see Reunion No. 387.

Academy Emblem — A618

1973, May 26
1375 A618 1fr lil, slate grn & red .50 .30

Academy of Overseas Sciences, 50th anniv.

Racing Car and Clocks A619

1973, June 2
1376 A619 60c dk brown & blue .65 .50

24-hour automobile race at Le Mans, 50th anniv.

Five-master France II — A620

1973, June 9
1377 A620 90c ultra, Prus bl & ind 1.25 .65

For surcharge see Reunion No. 386.

Tower and Square, Toulouse — A621

1973, June 9
1378 A621 50c purple & red brn .35 .20

46th Congress of the Federation of French Philatelic Societies, Toulouse, June 9-12.

Dr. Armauer G. Hansen — A622

Ducretet and his Transmission Diagram — A623

1973, Sept. 29 Engr. *Perf. 13*
1379 A622 45c grn, dk ol & ocher .30 .20

Centenary of the discovery of the Hansen bacillus, the cause of leprosy.

1973, Oct. 6
1380 A623 1fr yel grn & magenta .55 .40

75th anniversary of the first transmission of radio signals from the Eiffel Tower to the Pantheon by Eugene Ducretet (1844-1915).

Molière as Sganarelle — A624

1973, Oct. 20
1381 A624 1fr dk red & olive brn .55 .35

Moliere (Jean-Baptiste Poquelin; 1622-1673), playwright and actor.

Pierre Bourgoin and Philippe Kieffer A625

1973, Oct. 27
1382 A625 1fr red, rose cl & vio bl .50 .30

Pierre Bourgoin (1907-70), and Philippe Kieffer (1899-1963), heroes of the Free French forces in World War II.

Napoleon, Jean Portalis and Palace of Justice, Paris — A626

Exhibition Halls — A627

The Coronation of Napoleon, by Jean Louis David — A628

1973 Engr. *Perf. 13*

1383 A626 45c blue, choc & gray .55 .30
1384 A627 60c ol, sl grn & brn .55 .50
1385 A628 1fr sl grn, ol & claret .65 .55
Nos. 1383-1385 (3) 1.75 1.35

History of France. 45c, for the preparation of the Code Napoleon; 60c, Napoleon's encouragement of industry; 1fr, his coronation.
Issued: 45c, 11/3; 60c, 11/24; 1fr, 11/12.

Eternal Flame, Arc de Triomphe A629

Weather Vane A630

1973, Nov. 10
1386 A629 40c pur, vio bl & red .40 .30

50th anniv. of the Eternal Flame at the Arc de Triomphe, Paris.

1973, Dec. 1
1387 A630 65c ultra, blk & grn .40 .30

50th anniv. of the Dept. of Agriculture.

Human Rights Flame and Man — A631

Postal Museum — A632

1973, Dec. 8 Engr. *Perf. 13*
1388 A631 45c car, org & blk .30 .25

25th anniversary of the Universal Declaration of Human Rights.

1973, Dec. 19
1389 A632 50c maroon & bister .30 .25

Opening of new post and philately museum, Paris.

ARPHILA 75 Emblem A633

1974, Jan. 19 Engr. *Perf. 13*
1390 A633 50c brn, bl & brt lil .25 .20

ARPHILA 75 Philatelic Exhibition, Paris, June 1975.
For surcharge see Reunion No. 390.

Concorde over Charles de Gaulle Airport A634

Turbotrain T.G.V. 001 A635

Phenix Nuclear Power Station A636

1974 Engr. *Perf. 13*

1391 A634 60c pur & ol gray .40 .30
1392 A635 60c multicolored 1.10 .55
1393 A636 65c multicolored .40 .30
Nos. 1391-1393 (3) 1.90 1.15

French technical achievements.
Issued: #1391, 3/18; #1392, 8/31; 65c, 9/21.

Cardinal Richelieu, by Philippe de Champaigne — A637

Painting by Joan Miró A638

Canal du Loing, by Alfred Sisley — A639

"In Honor of Nicolas Fouquet," Tapestry by Georges Mathieu A640

Engr., Photo. (#1395, 1397)
1974 *Perf. 12x13, 13x12*

1394 A637 2fr multicolored 1.25 1.00
1395 A638 2fr multicolored 1.25 1.25
1396 A639 2fr multicolored 1.75 1.25
1397 A640 2fr multicolored 1.75 1.25
Nos. 1394-1397 (4) 6.00 4.75

Nos. 1394-1397 are printed in sheets of 25 with alternating labels publicizing "ARPHILA 75," Paris, June 6-16, 1975.
Issue dates: #1394, Mar. 23; #1395, Sept. 14; #1396, Nov. 9; #1397, Nov. 16.
For surcharges see Reunion Nos. 391-394.

French Alps and Gentian
A641

1974, Mar. 30 Engr. *Perf. 13*
1398 A641 65c vio blue & gray .40 .25

Centenary of the French Alpine Club.

Europa Issue 1974

"Age of Bronze," by Auguste Rodin — A642

"Air," by Aristide Maillol
A643

1974, Apr. 20 *Perf. 13*
1399 A642 50c brt rose lil & blk *.30 .25*
1400 A643 90c olive & brown *.90 .50*

Sea Rescue — A644

1974, Apr. 27
1401 A644 90c multicolored .50 .40

Reorganized sea rescue organization.
For surcharge see Reunion No. 395.

Council Building, View of Strasbourg and Emblem — A645

1974, May 4 Engr. *Perf. 13*
1402 A645 45c indigo, bister & bl .30 .25

25th anniversary of the Council of Europe.

Tourist Issue

View of Salers
A646

Basilica of St. Nicolas de Porte — A647

Seashell over Corsica — A648

Design: 1.10fr, View of Lot Valley.

1974 Engr. *Perf. 13*
1403 A646 65c yel grn & choc .25 .20
1404 A646 1.10fr choc & sl grn .45 .30
1405 A647 2fr gray & lilac .80 .30
1406 A648 3fr multicolored 1.00 .40
Nos. 1403-1406 (4) 2.50 1.20

Issued: 65c, 6/22; 1.10fr, 9/7; 2fr, 10/12; 3fr, 5/11.

Bison
A649

Giant Armadillo of Guyana
A650

1974
1407 A649 40c bis, choc & bl .35 .20
1408 A650 65c slate, olive & grn .35 .20

Nature protection.
Issued: #1407, May 25; #1408, Oct. 19.

Americans Landing in Normandy and Arms of Normandy — A651

General Marie-Pierre Koenig — A652

Order of the French Resistance — A653

1974
1409 A651 45c grn, rose & ind .80 .50
1410 A652 1fr multicolored .50 .35
1411 A653 1fr multicolored .65 .50
Nos. 1409-1411 (3) 1.95 1.35

30th anniversary of the liberation of France from the Nazis. Design of No. 1410 includes diagram of battle of Bir-Hakeim and Free French and Bir-Hakeim memorials.

Issued: 45c, 6/8; #1410, 5/25; #1411, 11/23.
See No. B478.

Pfister House, 16th Century, Colmar — A654

1974, June 1
1412 A654 50c multicolored .25 .20

47th Congress of the Federation of French Philatelic Societies, Colmar, May 30-June 4.

Chess
A655

1974, June 8
1413 A655 1fr dk brown & multi .60 .35

21st Chess Olympiad, Nice, June 6-30.

Facade with Statue of Louis XIV, and 1675 Medal — A656

1974, June 15
1414 A656 40c indigo, bl & brn .30 .20

300th anniversary of the founding of the Hotel des Invalides (Home for poor and sick officers and soldiers).

Peacocks Holding Letter, and Globe — A657

1974, Oct. 5 Engr. *Perf. 13*
1415 A657 1.20fr ultra, dp grn & dk car .50 .30

Centenary of Universal Postal Union.
For surcharge see Reunion No. 396.

Copernicus and Heliocentric System — A658

1974, Oct. 12
1416 A658 1.20fr multicolored .45 .30

500th anniversary of the birth of Nicolaus Copernicus (1473-1543), Polish astronomer.

Tourist Issue

Palace of Justice, Rouen
A659

Saint-Pol-de-Leon
A660

Chateau de Rochechouart — A661

1975 Engr. *Perf. 13*
1417 A659 85c multicolored .35 .30
1418 A660 1.20fr bl, bis & choc .40 .30
1419 A661 1.40fr brn, ind & grn .50 .30
Nos. 1417-1419 (3) 1.25 .90

Issued: 85c, 1/25; 1.20fr, 1/18; 1.40fr, 1/11.

Snowy Egret — A662

Gallic Coin — A663

1975, Feb. 15 Engr. *Perf. 13*
1420 A662 70c brt blue & bister .40 .30

Nature protection.

1975, Feb. 16 Typo. *Perf. 13½x14*
1421 A663 42c orange & mag 1.25 .50
1422 A663 48c lt bl & red brn 1.50 .80
1423 A663 70c brt pink & red 2.50 1.25
1424 A663 1.35fr lt green & brn 2.75 1.50
Nos. 1421-1424 (4) 8.00 4.05

Nos. 1421-1424 are known only precanceled. See second note after No. 132. See Nos. 1460-1463, 1487-1490.

The Eye — A664

Ionic Capital — A665

Graphic Art — A666

Ceres — A667

1975	**Engr.**	***Perf. 13***	
1425 A664	1fr red, pur & org	.45	.30
1426 A665	2fr grn, sl grn & mag	.80	.55
1427 A666	3fr dk car & ol grn	1.25	.90
1428 A667	4fr red, sl grn & bis	1.60	1.25
	Nos. 1425-1428 (4)	4.10	3.00

Souvenir Sheet

1429	Sheet of 4	7.50	7.50
a.	A664 2fr dp car & slate blue	1.00	1.00
b.	A665 3fr brt bl, sl bl & dp car	1.40	1.40
c.	A666 4fr slate blue, brt bl & plum	2.00	2.00
d.	A667 6fr brt bl, sl bl & plum	2.50	2.50

ARPHILA 75, Intl. Philatelic Exhibition, Paris, 6/6-16. Issued: 1fr, 3/1; 2fr, 3/22; 3fr, 4/19; 4fr, 5/17; #1429, 4/2.

Pres. Georges Pompidou A668

Paul as Harlequin, by Picasso A669

1975, Apr. 3	**Engr.**	***Perf. 13***	
1430 A668	80c black & gray	.30	.20

Georges Pompidou (1911-74), President of France, 1969-74.

1975, Apr. 26 Photo. *Perf. 13*

Europa; 1.20fr, Woman on Balcony, by Kees van Dongen

1431 A669	80c multi	*.45*	*.35*
1432 A669	1.20fr multi, horiz.	*.90*	*.70*

Machines, Globe, Emblem A670

1975, May 3		**Engr.**	
1433 A670	1.20fr blue, blk & red	.65	.30

World Machine Tool Exhib., Paris, 6/7-26.

Senate Assembly Hall A671

1975, May 24	**Engr.**	***Perf. 13***	
1434 A671	1.20fr olive & dk car	.65	.40

Centenary of the Senate of the Republic.

Meter Convention Document, Atom Diagram and Waves — A672

1975, May 31			
1435 A672	1fr multicolored	.55	.30

Cent. of Intl. Meter Convention, Paris, 1875.

Metro Regional Train A673

"Gazelle" Helicopter A674

1975			
1436 A673	1fr indigo & brt bl	.90	.30
1437 A674	1.30fr vio bl & grn	.65	.40

French technical achievements.
Issue dates: 1fr, June 21; 1.30fr, May 31.

Youth and Flasks, Symbols of Study and Growth — A675

1975, June 21			
1438 A675	70c red pur & blk	.30	.20

Student Health Foundation.

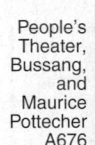

People's Theater, Bussang, and Maurice Pottecher A676

1975, Aug. 9	**Engr.**	***Perf. 13***	
1439 A676	85c multicolored	.30	.20

80th anniversary of the People's Theater at Bussang, founded by Maurice Pottecher.

Regions of France

Central France A677

Aquitaine A678

Limousin A679

Picardy A680

Burgundy A681

Loire A682

Guyana A683

Auvergne A684

Poitou-Charentes A685

Southern Pyrenees A686

Pas-de-Calais — A687

1975-76	**Engr.**	***Perf. 13***	
1440 A677	25c blue & yel grn	.25	.20
1441 A678	60c multicolored	.25	.20
1442 A679	70c multicolored	.50	.35
1443 A680	85c bl, grn & org	.70	.35
1444 A681	1fr red, yel & mar	.70	.35
1445 A682	1.15fr bl, bis & grn	.70	.35
1446 A683	1.25fr multicolored	.65	.50
1447 A684	1.30fr dk bl & red	.85	.50
1448 A685	1.90fr sl, ol & Prus bl	1.00	.50
1449 A686	2.20fr multicolored	1.10	1.00
1450 A687	2.80fr car, bl & blk	1.40	1.00
	Nos. 1440-1450 (11)	8.10	5.30

Issued: 85c, 11/15; 1fr, 10/25; 1.15fr, 9/6; 1.30fr, 10/4/75; 1.90fr, 12/6; 2.80fr, 12/13; 25c, 1/31/76; 2.20fr, 1/10/76; 60c, 5/22/76; 70c, 5/29/76; 1.25fr, 10/16/76.

A690

A691

French Flag, F.-H. Manhes, Jean Verneau, Pierre Kaan

1975, Sept. 27			
1453 A690	1fr multicolored	.50	.30

Liberation of concentration camps, 30th anniversary. F.-H. Manhes (1889-1959), Jean Verneau (1890-1944) and Pierre Kaan (1903-1945) were French resistance leaders, imprisoned in concentration camps.

1975, Oct. 11

Monument, by Joseph Riviere.

1454 A691	70c multicolored	.40	.30

Land Mine Demolition Service, 30th anniversary. Monument was erected in Alsace to honor land mine victims.

Symbols of Suburban Living A692

1975, Oct. 18			
1455 A692	1.70fr brown, bl & grn	.75	.50

Creation of new towns.

Women and Rainbow — A693

1975, Nov. 8		**Photo.**	
1456 A693	1.20fr silver & multi	.45	.40

International Women's Year 1975.

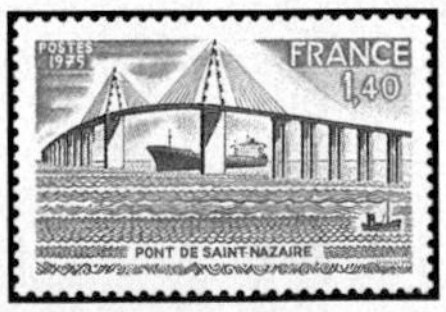

Saint-Nazaire Bridge — A694

1975, Nov. 8		**Engr.**	
1457 A694	1.40fr bl, ind & grn	.60	.30

French and Russian Flags — A695

Frigate Melpomene A696

1975, Nov. 22

1458 A695 1.20fr bl, red & ocher .50 .30

Franco-Soviet diplomatic relations, 50th anniv.

1975, Dec. 6

1459 A696 90c multicolored 1.25 .65

Gallic Coin Type of 1975

1976, Jan. 1 Typo. *Perf. 13½x14*

1460	A663	50c	lt green & brn	1.10	.70
1461	A663	60c	lilac & brn	1.75	1.00
1462	A663	90c	orange & brn	2.25	1.25
1463	A663	1.60fr	violet & brn	4.00	2.00
	Nos. 1460-1463 (4)			9.10	4.95

Nos. 1460-1463 are known only precanceled. See second note after No. 132.

Lintel, St. Genis des Fontaines Church A697

Venus of Brassempouy (Paleolithic) — A698

"The Joy of Life," by Robert Delaunay A699

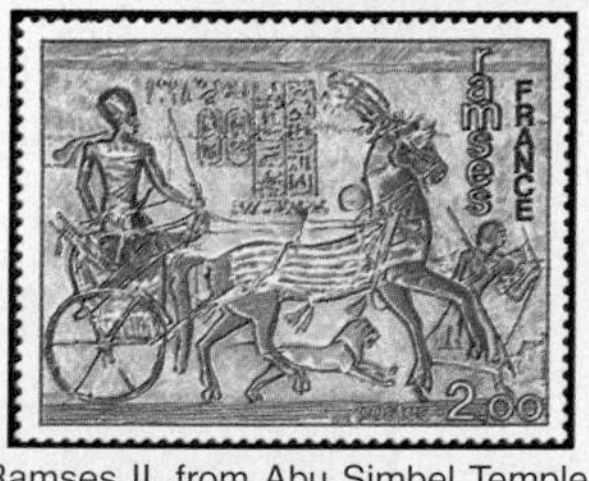

Ramses II, from Abu Simbel Temple, Egypt — A700

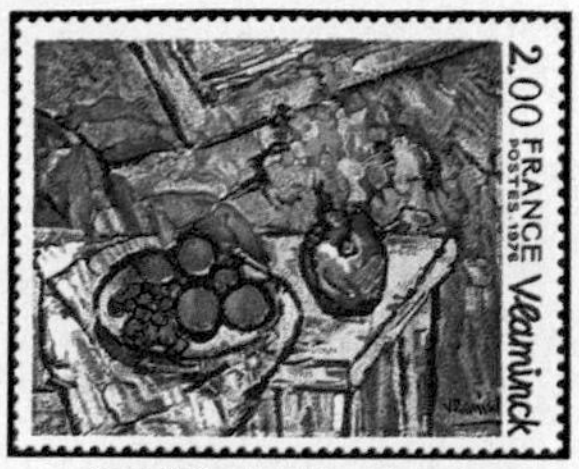

Still Life, by Maurice de Vlaminck — A701

1976 Engr. *Perf. 13*

1464	A697	2fr	blue & slate bl	1.25	.75
1465	A698	2fr	dk brn & yel	1.25	.60

Photo. *Perf. 12½x13*

1466 A699 2fr multicolored 1.25 .80

Engr. *Perf. 13x12½*

1467 A700 2fr multicolored .95 .75

Perf. 13

1468 A701 2fr multicolored .95 .60
Nos. 1464-1468 (5) 5.65 3.50

Issued: #1464, 1/24; #1465, 3/6; #1466, 7/24; #1467, 9/4; #1468, 12/18.

Tourist Issue

Chateau Fort de Bonaguil A702

Lodève Cathedral — A703

Biarritz A704

Thiers — A705

Ussel — A706

Chateau de Malmaison A707

1976 Engr. *Perf. 13*

1469	A702	1fr	multicolored	.35	.20
1470	A703	1.10fr	violet blue	.50	.35
1471	A704	1.40fr	multicolored	.65	.30
1472	A705	1.70fr	multicolored	.65	.25
1473	A706	2fr	multicolored	.90	.25
1474	A707	3fr	multicolored	1.10	.25
	Nos. 1469-1474 (6)			4.15	1.60

Issue dates: 1fr, 2fr, July 10; 1.10fr, Nov. 13; 1.40fr, Sept. 25; 1.70fr, Oct. 9; 3fr, Apr. 10.

Destroyers, Association Emblem A708

1976, Apr. 24

1475 A708 1fr vio bl, mag & lem .50 .30

Naval Reserve Officers Assoc., 50th anniv.

Gate, Rouen — A709

Young Person — A710

1976, Apr. 24

1476 A709 80c olive gray & sal .35 .20

49th Congress of the Federation of French Philatelic Societies, Rouen, Apr. 23-May 2.

1976, Apr. 27

1477 A710 60c bl grn, ind & car .35 .25

JUVAROUEN 76, International Youth Philatelic Exhibition, Rouen, Apr. 25-May 2.

Europa Issue 1976

Ceramic Pitcher, Strasbourg, 18th Century A711

1.20fr, Sevres porcelain plate & CEPT emblem.

1976, May 8 Photo. *Perf. 13*

1478	A711	80c	multicolored	*.30*	*.30*
1479	A711	1.20fr	multicolored	*.65*	*.55*

Count de Vergennes and Benjamin Franklin — A712

1976, May 15 Engr. *Perf. 13*

1480 A712 1.20fr multicolored .50 .30

American Bicentennial.

A713

A714

Battle of Verdun Memorial.

1976, June 12 Engr.

1481 A713 1fr multicolored .45 .20

Battle of Verdun, 60th anniversary.

1976, June 12 Photo.

1482 A714 1.20fr Communication .50 .40

Troncais Forest — A715

Cross of Lorraine — A716

1976, June 19 Engr.

1483 A715 70c green & multi .35 .20

Protection of the environment.

1976, June 19

1484 A716 1fr multicolored .60 .25

Association of Free French, 30th anniv.

Symphonie Communications Satellite — A717

1976, June 26 Photo.

1485 A717 1.40fr multicolored .65 .50

French technical achievements.

Gallic Coin Type of 1975

1976, July 1 Typo. *Perf. 13½x14*

1487	A663	52c	ver & dk brn	.65	.40
1488	A663	62c	vio & dk brn	1.25	.75
1489	A663	95c	tan & dk brn	1.65	1.00
1490	A663	1.70fr	dk bl & dk brn	3.00	1.50
	Nos. 1487-1490 (4)			6.55	3.65

Nos. 1487-1490 are known only precanceled. See second note after No. 132.

Paris Summer Festival — A719

1976, July 10 Engr.

1491 A719 1fr multicolored .65 .30

Summer festival in Tuileries Gardens, Paris.

Emblem and Soldiers A720

1976, July 8

1492 A720 1fr blk, dp bl & mag .50 .25

Officers Reserve Corps, centenary.

Sailing A721

1976, July 17

1493 A721 1.20fr blue, blk & vio .65 .35

21st Olympic Games, Montreal, Canada, July 17-Aug. 1.

Marianne Type of 1971-74

1976 Typo. *Perf. 14x13*

1494 A555 80c green .50 .20

Engr. ***Perf. 13***

1495 A555 80c green 1.25 .50
a. Booklet pane of 10 15.00
1496 A555 1fr carmine rose .55 .20
a. Booklet pane of 5 4.00
b. Booklet pane of 10 8.00
Nos. 1495-1496 (2) 1.80 .70

No. 1495 issued in booklets only. "POSTES" 6mm long on Nos. 1292A and 1494; 4mm on others.

#1494, 1496 were issued untagged in 1977.

Coil Stamps

1976, Aug. 1 Engr. ***Perf. 13 Horiz.***

1497 A555 80c green .65 .55
1498 A555 1fr carmine rose .65 .55

Red control number on back of every 10th stamp.

Woman's Head, by Jean Carzou — A722

1976, Sept. 18 Engr. ***Perf. 13x12½***

1499 A722 2fr multicolored .90 .65

Old and New Telephones A723

1976, Sept. 25 Engr. ***Perf. 13***

1500 A723 1fr multicolored .50 .25

Centenary of first telephone call by Alexander Graham Bell, Mar. 10, 1876.

Festival Emblem and Trophy, Pyrenees, Hercules and Pyrène — A724

Police Emblem — A725

1976, Oct. 2

1501 A724 1.40fr multicolored .65 .45

10th Intl. Tourist Film Festival, Tarbes, 10/4-10.

1976, Oct. 9 Engr. ***Perf. 13***

1502 A725 1.10fr ultra, red & ol .50 .30

National Police, help and protection.

Atomic Particle Accelerator, Diagram A726

1976, Oct. 22 Photo.

1503 A726 1.40fr multicolored .85 .55

European Center for Nuclear Research (CERN).

"Exhibitions" — A727

1976, Nov. 20 Engr. ***Perf. 13***

1504 A727 1.50fr multicolored .75 .50

Trade Fairs and Exhibitions.

Abstract Design A728

1976, Nov. 27 Photo.

1505 A728 1.10fr multicolored .50 .40

Customs Service.

Atlantic Museum, Port Louis — A729

1976, Dec. 4 Engr.

1506 A729 1.45fr grnsh bl & olive .65 .50

Regions of France

Réunion A730

Martinique A731

Franche-Comté A732

Brittany A733

Languedoc-Roussillon — A734

Rhône-Alps A735

Champagne-Ardennes A736

Alsace A737

Photo. (1.45fr, 1.50fr, 2.50fr); Engr.

1977 ***Perf. 13***

1507 A730 1.45fr grn & lil rose .65 .40
1508 A731 1.50fr multicolored .65 .60
1509 A732 2.10fr multicolored .90 .65
1510 A733 2.40fr multicolored 1.10 .35
1511 A734 2.50fr multicolored 1.10 .85
1512 A735 2.75fr Prus blue 1.50 .90
1513 A736 3.20fr multicolored 1.60 1.00
1514 A737 3.90fr multicolored 2.25 1.50
Nos. 1507-1514 (8) 9.75 6.25

Issued: 1.45fr, 2/5; 1.50fr, 1/29; 2.10fr, 1/8; 2.40fr, 2/19; 2.50fr, 1/15; 2.75fr, 1/22; 3.20fr, 4/16; 3.90fr, 2/26.

Pompidou Cultural Center — A738

1977, Feb. 5 Engr. ***Perf. 13***

1515 A738 1fr multicolored .35 .20

Inauguration of the Georges Pompidou National Center for Art and Culture, Paris.

Dunkirk Harbor A739

1977, Feb. 12

1516 A739 50c multicolored .25 .20

Expansion of Dunkirk harbor facilities.

Bridge at Mantes, by Corot — A740

Virgin and Child, by Rubens A741

Tridimensional Design, by Victor Vasarely — A742

Head and Eagle, by Pierre-Yves Tremois A743

1977 Engr. ***Perf. 13x12½***

1517 A740 2fr multicolored 1.10 .85

Perf. 12x13

1518 A741 2fr multicolored 1.25 .85

Perf. 12½x13

1519 A742 3fr ultra & sl grn 1.50 .85

Photo.

1520 A743 3fr dark red & blk 1.90 1.40
Nos. 1517-1520 (4) 5.75 3.95

Issue dates: No. 1517, Feb. 12; No. 1518, Nov. 5; No. 1519, Apr. 7; No. 1520, Sept. 17.

Hand Holding Torch and Sword — A744

Pisces — A745

1977, Mar. 5 Engr. ***Perf. 13***

1521 A744 80c ultra & multi .50 .30

"France remembers its dead."

1977-78 Engr. ***Perf. 13***

Zodiac Signs: 58c, Cancer. 61c, Sagittarius. 68c, Taurus. 73c, Aries. 78c, Libra. 1.05fr, Scorpio. 1.15fr, Capricorn. 1.25fr, Leo. 1.85fr, Aquarius. 2fr, Virgo. 2.10fr, Gemini.

1522 A745 54c violet blue .65 .30
1523 A745 58c emerald 1.00 .40
1524 A745 61c brt blue .55 .30
1525 A745 68c deep brown .85 .35
1526 A745 73c rose carmine 1.50 .80
1527 A745 78c vermilion .65 .35
1528 A745 1.05fr brt lilac 1.50 .75
1529 A745 1.15fr orange 2.25 1.40
1530 A745 1.25fr lt olive grn 1.25 .60
1531 A745 1.85fr slate grn 2.75 1.25
1532 A745 2fr blue green 3.00 1.75
1533 A745 2.10fr lilac rose 1.65 1.00
Nos. 1522-1533 (12) 17.60 9.25

Issued: 54c, 68c, 1.05fr, 1.85fr, 4/1/77; others, 1978.

Nos. 1522-1533 are known only precanceled. See second note after No. 132.

Village in Provence A746

Europa: 1.40fr, Brittany port.

1977, Apr. 23
1534 A746 1fr multicolored *.45* *.25*
1535 A746 1.40fr multicolored *1.00* *.35*

Flowers and Gardening A747

1977, Apr. 23 **Engr.** ***Perf. 13***
1536 A747 1.70fr multicolored .80 .50

National Horticulture Society, centenary.

Symbolic Flower A748

1977, May 7
1537 A748 1.40fr multicolored .65 .45

Intl. Flower Show, Nantes, May 12-23.

Battle of Cambray A749

1977, May 14
1538 A749 80c multicolored .40 .30

Capture of Cambray and the incorporation of Cambresis District into France, 300th anniv.

Carmes Church, School, Map of France A750

Modern Constructions A751

1977, May 14
1539 A750 1.10fr multicolored .50 .30

Catholic Institutes in France.

1977, May 21
1540 A751 1.10fr multicolored .55 .30

European Federation of the Construction Industry.

Annecy Castle A752

1977, May 28
1541 A752 1fr multicolored .60 .30

Congress of the Federation of French Philatelic Societies, Annecy, May 28-30.

Tourist Issue

Abbey, Pont-à-Mousson — A753

Abbey Tower, Saint-Amand-les-Eaux A754

Collegiate Church of Dorat A755

Fontenay Abbey A756

Bayeux Cathedral — A757

Chateau de Vitré A758

1977	**Engr.**	***Perf. 13***	
1542 A753	1.25fr multicolored	.60	.35
1543 A754	1.40fr multicolored	.65	.35
1544 A755	1.45fr multicolored	.75	.45
1545 A756	1.50fr multicolored	.75	.25
1546 A757	1.90fr black & yel	1.00	.35
1547 A758	2.40fr black & yel	1.10	.35
	Nos. 1542-1547 (6)	4.85	2.10

Issued: 1.25fr, 10/1; 1.40fr, 9/17; 1.45fr, 7/16; 1.50fr, 6/4; 1.90fr, 7/9; 2.40fr, 9/24.

Polytechnic School and "X" — A759

1977, June 4 **Engr.** ***Perf. 13***
1548 A759 1.70fr multicolored .75 .30

Relocation at Palaiseau of Polytechnic School, founded 1794.

Soccer and Cup — A760

1977, June 11
1549 A760 80c multicolored .90 .50

Soccer Cup of France, 60th anniversary.

De Gaulle Memorial — A761

Stylized Map of France — A762

Photo. & Embossed

1977, June 18
1550 A761 1fr gold & multi 1.00 .50

5th anniversary of dedication of De Gaulle memorial at Colombey-les-Deux-Eglises.

1977, June 18 **Engr.** ***Perf. 13***
1551 A762 1.10fr ultra & red .55 .30

French Junior Chamber of Commerce.

Battle of Nancy A763

Arms of Burgundy A764

1977, June 25
1552 A763 1.10fr blue & slate 1.10 .40

Battle of Nancy between the Dukes of Burgundy and Lorraine, 500th anniversary.

1977, July 2
1553 A764 1.25fr ol brn & slate grn .55 .25

Annexation of Burgundy by the French Crown, 500th anniversary.

Association Emblem A765

1977, July 8
1554 A765 1.40fr ultra, olive & red .55 .25

French-speaking Parliamentary Association.

Red Cicada — A766

1977, Sept. 10 **Photo.** ***Perf. 13***
1555 A766 80c multicolored .55 .30

Nature protection.

French Handicrafts A767

1977, Oct. 1 **Engr.** ***Perf. 13***
1556 A767 1.40fr multicolored .65 .45

French craftsmen.

Industry and Agriculture — A768

1977, Oct. 22
1557 A768 80c brown & olive .30 .25

Economic & Social Council, 30th anniv.

Table Tennis A769

1977, Dec. 17 **Engr.** ***Perf. 13***
1558 A769 1.10fr multicolored 3.25 1.00

French Table Tennis Federation, 50th anniv., and French team, gold medal winner, Birmingham.

Abstract, by Roger Excoffon — A770

1977, Dec. 17 ***Perf. 13x12½***
1559 A770 3fr multicolored 2.00 1.00

Sabine, after David — A771

1977-78	**Engr.**	***Perf. 13***	
1560 A771	1c slate	.20	.20
1561 A771	2c brt violet	.20	.20
1562 A771	5c slate green	.20	.20
1563 A771	10c red brown	.20	.20
1564 A771	15c Prus blue	.20	.20
1565 A771	20c brt green	.20	.20
1566 A771	30c orange	.20	.20
1567 A771	50c red lilac	.20	.20
1568 A771	80c green	1.10	.20
a.	Booklet pane of 10	11.00	
1569 A771	80c olive	.30	.20
1570 A771	1fr red	1.25	.20
a.	Booklet pane of 5	8.50	
b.	Booklet pane of 10	15.00	
1571 A771	1fr green	.55	.20
a.	Booklet pane of 10	5.50	
1572 A771	1.20fr red	.55	.20
a.	Booklet pane of 5	4.25	
b.	Booklet pane of 10	7.75	
1573 A771	1.40fr brt blue	2.00	.20
1574 A771	1.70fr grnsh blue	.70	.20
1575 A771	2fr emerald	.70	.20
1576 A771	2.10fr lilac rose	.75	.20
1577 A771	3fr dark brown	1.00	.30
	Nos. 1560-1577 (18)	10.50	3.70

Issued: #1560-1567, 1573, 1575, 1577, 4/3/78; #1568, 1570, 12/19/77; #1569, 1571, 1572, 1574, 1576, 6/5/78.

Coil Stamps

1978 *Perf. 13 Horiz.*

1578 A771 80c bright green 1.40 1.00
1579 A771 1fr bright green 1.10 1.00
1579A A771 1fr bright red 1.40 1.00
1579B A771 1.20fr bright red 1.10 1.00
Nos. 1578-1579B (4) 5.00 4.00

See Nos. 1658-1677.
For similar design inscribed "REPUBLIQUE FRANCAISE" see type A900.

Percheron, by Jacques Birr A772

Osprey — A773

1978 **Photo.** *Perf. 13*
1580 A772 1.70fr multicolored 1.00 .80

Engr.

1581 A773 1.80fr multicolored .90 .50

Nature protection.
Issue dates: 1.70fr, Jan. 7; 1.80fr, Oct. 14.

Tournament, 1662, Etching — A774

Institut de France and Pont des Arts, Paris, by Bernard Buffet — A776

Horses, by Yves Brayer — A777

1978 **Engr.** *Perf. 12x13*
1582 A774 2fr black 3.00 1.25

Perf. 13x12

1584 A776 3fr multicolored 2.75 1.40
1585 A777 3fr multicolored 2.00 1.20
Nos. 1582-1585 (3) 7.75 3.85

Issued: 2fr, 1/14; #1584, 2/4; #1585, 12/9.

Communications School and Tower — A778

1978, Jan. 19 **Engr.** *Perf. 13*
1586 A778 80c Prussian blue .30 .25

Natl. Telecommunications School, cent.

Swedish and French Flags, Map of Saint Barthelemy A779

1978, Jan. 19
1587 A779 1.10fr multicolored .45 .25

Centenary of the reunion with France of Saint Barthelemy Island, West Indies.

Regions of France

Ile de France — A780

Tanker, Refinery, Flower, Upper Normandy A781

Lower Normandy A782

1978 **Photo.** *Perf. 13*
1588 A780 1fr red, blue & blk .50 .20

Engr.

1589 A781 1.40fr multicolored .75 .35

Photo.

1590 A782 1.70fr multicolored 1.10 .50
Nos. 1588-1590 (3) 2.35 1.05

Issued: 1fr, 3/4; 1.40fr, 1/21; 1.70fr, 3/31.

Stylized Map of France A788

Young Stamp Collector A789

1978, Feb. 11 **Engr.** *Perf. 13*
1596 A788 1.10fr violet & green .45 .25

Program of administrative changes, 15th anniv.

1978, Feb. 25
1597 A789 80c multicolored .30 .25

JUVEXNIORT, Youth Philatelic Exhibition, Niort, Feb. 25-March 5.

Tourist Issue

Verdon Gorge — A790

Saint-Saturnin Church — A792

Pont Neuf, Paris A791

Our Lady of Bec-Hellouin Abbey — A793

Chateau D'Esquelbecq — A794

Aubazine Abbey A795

Fontevraud Abbey A796

1978 **Engr.** *Perf. 13*
1598 A790 50c multicolored .20 .20
1599 A791 80c multicolored .35 .25
1600 A792 1fr black .35 .25
1601 A793 1.10fr multicolored .50 .25
1602 A794 1.10fr multicolored .50 .20
1603 A795 1.25fr carmine & brn .85 .30
1604 A796 1.70fr multicolored .90 .40
Nos. 1598-1604 (7) 3.65 1.85

Issued: 1.25fr, 2/18; 50c, 3/6; #1601, 3/26; 80c, 5/27; 1fr, 6/10; 1.70fr, 6/3; #1602, 6/17.

Fish and Corals — A797

1978, Apr. 15 **Photo.** *Perf. 13*
1605 A797 1.25fr multicolored 1.00 .85

Port Cros National Park, 15th anniversary.

Flowers, Butterflies and Houses — A798

1978, Apr. 22 **Engr.** *Perf. 13*
1606 A798 1.70fr multicolored 2.75 .35

Beautification of France campaign, 50th anniv.

Hands Shielding Source of Heat and Light A799

1978, Apr. 22
1607 A799 1fr multicolored .60 .25

Energy conservation.

World War I Memorial near Lens — A800

Fountain of the Innocents, Paris — A801

1978, May 6
1608 A800 2fr lemon & magenta 1.00 .30

Colline Notre Dame de Lorette memorial of World War I.

1978, May 6

Europa: 1.40fr, Flower Park Fountain, Paris.

1609 A801 1fr multicolored *.40 .25*
1610 A801 1.40fr multicolored *.90 .50*

Maurois Palace, Troyes — A802

1978, May 13
1611 A802 1fr multicolored .55 .30

51st Congress of the Federation of French Philatelic Societies, Troyes, May 13-15.

Roland Garros Tennis Court and Player — A803

1978, May 27
1612 A803 1fr multicolored 2.50 .40

Roland Garros Tennis Court, 50th anniv.

Hand and Plant — A804

Printing Office Emblem — A805

1978, Sept. 9 Engr. *Perf. 13*
1613 A804 1.30fr brown, red & grn .60 .25

Encouragement of handicrafts.

1978, Sept. 23
1614 A805 1fr multicolored .50 .20

National Printing Office, established 1538.

Fortress, Besançon, and Collegiate Church, Dole — A806

Valenciennes and Maubeuge — A807

1978
1615 A806 1.20fr multicolored .55 .20
1616 A807 1.20fr multicolored .55 .20

Reunion of Franche-Comté and Valenciennes and Maubeuge with France, 300th anniversary.
Issued: #1615, Sept. 23; #1616, Sept. 30.

Sower Type of 1906-1937 and Academy Emblem — A808

Gymnasts, Strasbourg Cathedral, Storks — A809

1978, Oct. 7
1617 A808 1fr multicolored .45 .30

Academy of Philately, 50th anniversary.

1978, Oct. 21
1618 A809 1fr multicolored .70 .30

19th World Gymnastics Championships, Strasbourg, Oct. 23-26.

Various Sports A810

Polish Veterans' Monument A811

1978, Oct. 21
1619 A810 1fr multicolored 1.10 .40

Sports for all.

1978, Nov. 11
1620 A811 1.70fr multicolored .80 .50

Polish veterans of World War II.

Railroad Car and Monument, Compiègne Forest, Rethondes A812

1978, Nov. 11 Engr. *Perf. 13*
1621 A812 1.20fr indigo .75 .30

60th anniversary of World War I armistice.

Handicapped People — A813

1978, Nov. 18
1622 A813 1fr multicolored .45 .25

Rehabilitation of the handicapped.

Human Rights Emblem A814

1978, Dec. 9 Engr. *Perf. 13*
1623 A814 1.70fr dk brown & blue .80 .40

30th anniversary of Universal Declaration of Human Rights.

Child and IYC Emblem A815

1979, Jan. 6 Engr. *Perf. 13*
1624 A815 1.70fr multicolored 4.00 2.50

International Year of the Child.

"Music," 15th Century Miniature — A816

1979, Jan. 13 *Perf. 13x12½*
1625 A816 2fr multicolored 1.50 .90

Diana Taking a Bath, d'Ecouen Castle A817

Church at Auvers-on-Oise, by Vincent Van Gogh — A818

Head of Marianne, by Salvador Dali A819

Fire Dancer from The Magic Flute, by Chaplain Midy A820

1979 Photo. *Perf. 12½x13*
1626 A817 2fr multicolored 1.40 1.00
1627 A818 2fr multicolored 5.50 1.25
1628 A819 3fr multicolored 1.50 1.00
1629 A820 3fr multicolored 1.50 1.00
Nos. 1626-1629 (4) 9.90 4.25

Issue dates: #1626, Sept. 22; #1627, Oct. 27; #1628, Nov. 19; #1629, Nov. 26.

Orange Agaric — A821

Mushrooms: 83c, Death trumpet. 1.30fr, Olive wood pleurotus. 2.25fr, Cauliflower claveria.

1979, Jan. 15 Engr. *Perf. 13*
1630 A821 64c orange .50 .25
1631 A821 83c brown .50 .30
1632 A821 1.30fr yellow bister 1.00 .50
1633 A821 2.25fr brown purple 1.50 1.00
Nos. 1630-1633 (4) 3.50 2.05

Nos. 1630-1633 are known only precanceled. See second note after No. 132.

Victor Segalen A822

1979, Jan. 20
1634 A822 1.50fr multicolored .70 .30

Physician, explorer and writer (1878-1919).

Hibiscus and Palms — A823

1979, Feb. 3
1635 A823 35c multicolored .20 .20

International Flower Festival, Martinique.

Buddha, Stupas, Temple of Borobudur A824

1979, Feb. 24
1636 A824 1.80fr ol & slate grn .85 .40

Save the Temple of Borobudur, Java, campaign.

Boy, by Francisque Poulbot (1879-1946) A825

1979, Mar. 24 Photo.
1637 A825 1.30fr multicolored .60 .25

Tourist Issue

Chateau de Maisons, Laffitte A826

Bernay and St. Pierre sur Dives Abbeys — A827

View of Auray — A827a

Steenvorde Windmill — A828

Wall Painting, Niaux Cave A829

Royal Palace, Perpignan A830

1979 Engr. *Perf. 13*

1638	A826	45c	multicolored	.30	.20
1639	A827	1fr	multicolored	.45	.25
1640	A827a	1fr	multicolored	.45	.25
1641	A828	1.20fr	multicolored	.55	.25
1642	A829	1.50fr	multicolored	.70	.40
1643	A830	1.70fr	multicolored	.75	.60
			Nos. 1638-1643 (6)	3.20	1.95

Issued: 45c, 10/6; #1639, 6/16; #1640, 6/30; 1.20fr, 6/12; 1.50fr, 7/9; 1.70fr, 4/21.

Honey Bee A831

1979, Mar. 31 Engr. *Perf. 13*

1644 A831 1fr multicolored .85 .30

Nature protection.

St. Germain des Prés Abbey A832

1979, Apr. 21

1645 A832 1.40fr multicolored .65 .35

Simoun Mail Monoplanes, 1935, and Map of Mail Routes — A833

Europa: 1.70fr, Floating spheres used on Seine during siege of Paris, 1870.

1979, Apr. 28

1646	A833	1.20fr	multicolored	*.75*	*.35*
1647	A833	1.70fr	multicolored	*1.00*	*.50*

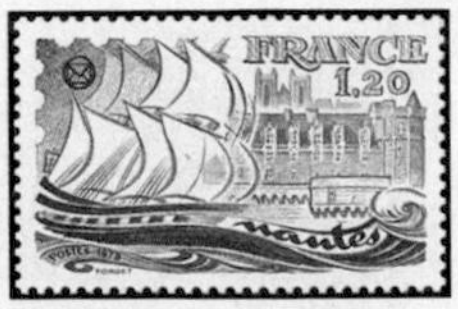

Ship and View of Nantes A834

1979, May 5 Engr. *Perf. 13*

1648 A834 1.20fr multicolored .55 .30

52nd National Congress of French Philatelic Societies, Nantes, May 5-7.

Royal Palace, 1789 — A835

1979, May 19

1649 A835 1fr car rose & pur .45 .25

European Elections A836

1979, May 19 Photo. *Perf. 13*

1650 A836 1.20fr multicolored .55 .25

European Parliament, 1st direct elections, June 10.

Joan of Arc Monument A837

1979, May 24 Engr.

1651 A837 1.70fr brt lilac rose .75 .40

Joan of Arc, the Maid of Orleans (1412-1431).

Felix Guyon and Catheters A840

1979, June 23

1652 A840 1.80fr sepia & blue .60 .20

Felix Guyon (1831-1920), urologist.

Lantern Tower, La Rochelle A841

Telecom '79 A842

Towers: 88c, Chartres Cathedral. 1.40fr, Bourges Cathedral. 2.35fr, Amiens Cathedral.

1979, Aug. 13 Engr. *Perf. 13*

1653	A841	68c	vio brn & blk	.30	.30
1654	A841	88c	ultra & blk	.40	.30
1655	A841	1.40fr	gray grn & blk	.65	.50
1656	A841	2.35fr	dull brn & blk	1.10	.60
			Nos. 1653-1656 (4)	2.45	1.70

Nos. 1653-1656 are known only precanceled. See second note after No. 132. See Nos. 1684-1687, 1719-1722, 1814-1817.

1979, Sept. 22

1657 A842 1.10fr multicolored .40 .20

3rd World Telecommunications Exhibition.

Sabine Type of 1977-78

1979-81 Engr. *Perf. 13*

1658	A771	40c	brown ('81)	.20	.20
1659	A771	60c	red brn ('81)	.25	.20
1660	A771	70c	violet blue	.30	.25
1661	A771	90c	brt lilac ('81)	.40	.30
1662	A771	1fr	gray olive	.45	.20
1663	A771	1.10fr	green	.70	.25
1664	A771	1.20fr	green ('80)	.55	.20
1665	A771	1.30fr	rose red	.70	.20
1666	A771	1.40fr	rose red ('80)	.65	.20
1667	A771	1.60fr	purple	1.00	.30
1668	A771	1.80fr	ocher	.85	.60
1669	A771	3.50fr	lt ol grn ('81)	1.60	.60
1670	A771	4fr	brt car ('81)	1.80	.40
1671	A771	5fr	brt grnsh bl ('81)	2.25	.30
			Nos. 1658-1671 (14)	11.70	4.20

Coil Stamps

1979-80 *Perf. 13 Horiz.*

1674	A771	1.10fr	green	1.75	.60
1675	A771	1.20fr	green ('80)	.65	.50
1676	A771	1.30fr	rose red	1.75	.60
1677	A771	1.40fr	rose red ('80)	.90	.40
			Nos. 1674-1677 (4)	5.05	2.10

Lorraine Region — A845

1979, Nov. 10

1678 A845 2.30fr multicolored 1.00 .30

Gears A847

1979, Nov. 17 *Perf. 13*

1680 A847 1.80fr multicolored .85 .40

Central Technical School of Paris, 150th anniv.

Judo Throw A848

1979, Nov. 24 Engr.

1681 A848 1.60fr multicolored .75 .40

World Judo Championships, Paris, Dec.

Violins — A849

1979, Dec. 10

1682 A849 1.30fr multicolored .60 .35

Eurovision A850

1980, Jan. 12 Engr. *Perf. 13x13½*

1683 A850 1.80fr multicolored 1.00 .70

Tower Type of 1979

Designs: 76c, Chateau d'Angers. 99c, Chateau de Kerjean. 1.60fr, Chateau de Pierrefonds. 2.65fr, Chateau de Tarascon.

1980, Jan. 21 Engr.

1684	A841	76c	grnsh bl & blk	.35	.30
1685	A841	99c	slate grn & blk	.45	.30
1686	A841	1.60fr	red & blk	.75	.55
1687	A841	2.65fr	brn org & blk	1.25	.65
			Nos. 1684-1687 (4)	2.80	1.80

Nos. 1684-1687 are known only precanceled. See second note after No. 132.

Self-portrait, by Albrecht Dürer, Philexfrance '82 Emblem — A851

Woman Holding Fan, by Ossip Zadkine A852

Abstract, by Raoul Ubak — A853

Hommage to J.S. Bach, by Jean Picart Le Doux — A854

Peasant, by Louis Le Nain
A855

Woman with Blue Eyes, by Modigliani
A856

Abstract, by Hans Hartung
A857

Engraved, Photogravure (#1691, 1694)

1980 ***Perf. 12½x13, 13x12½***

1688 A851 2fr multicolored 1.00 .90
1689 A852 3fr multicolored 1.50 1.00
1690 A853 3fr multicolored 1.50 1.00
1691 A854 3fr multicolored 1.50 1.00
1692 A855 3fr multicolored 1.50 1.00
1693 A856 4fr multicolored 3.00 1.25
1694 A857 4fr ultra & black 2.00 1.25
Nos. 1688-1694 (7) 12.00 7.40

Issued: #1688, 6/7; #1689, 1/19; #1690, 2/2; #1691, 9/20; #1693, 10/26; #1692, 11/10; #1694, 12/20.

Giants of the North Festival — A858

French Cuisine — A859

1980, Feb. 16 ***Perf. 13***
1695 A858 1.60fr multicolored .75 .35

1980, Feb. 23
1696 A859 90c red & lt brown .80 .40

Woman Embroidering
A860

Fight Against Cigarette Smoking
A861

Photogravure and Engraved

1980, Mar. 29 ***Perf. 13***
1697 A860 1.10fr multicolored .50 .30

1980, Apr. 5 **Photo.** ***Perf. 13***
1698 A861 1.30fr multicolored .60 .20

Aristide Briand — A862

Europa: 1.80fr, St. Benedict.

1980, Apr. 26 **Engr.** ***Perf. 13***
1699 A862 1.30fr multicolored .60 .30
1700 A862 1.80fr red & red brown .85 .50

Aristide Briand (1862-1932), prime minister, 1909-1911, 1921-1922; St. Benedict, patron saint of Europe.

Liancourt, College, Map of Northwestern France — A863

1980, May 19 **Engr.** ***Perf. 13***
1701 A863 2fr dk green & pur .90 .35

National College of Arts and Handicrafts (founded by Larochefoucauld Liancourt) bicentenary.

Cranes, Town Hall Tower, Dunkirk — A864

1980, May 24
1702 A864 1.30fr multicolored .60 .20

53rd Natl. Congress of French Federation of Philatelic Societies, Dunkirk, May 24-26.

Tourist Issue

Chateau de Maintenon
A866

Cordes
A865

Montauban
A867

St. Peter's Abbey, Solesmes
A868

Puy Cathedral
A869

1980 **Engr.** ***Perf. 13***
1703 A865 1.50fr multicolored .70 .30
1704 A866 2fr multicolored .90 .30
1705 A867 2.30fr multicolored 1.00 .30
1706 A868 2.50fr multicolored 1.10 .30
1707 A869 3.20fr multicolored 1.50 .55
Nos. 1703-1707 (5) 5.20 1.75

Issued: #1703, 4/5; #1704, 6/7; #1705, 5/7; #1706, 9/20; #1707, 5/12.

Graellsia Isabellae
A870

1980, May 31 **Photo.**
1708 A870 1.10fr multicolored .75 .35

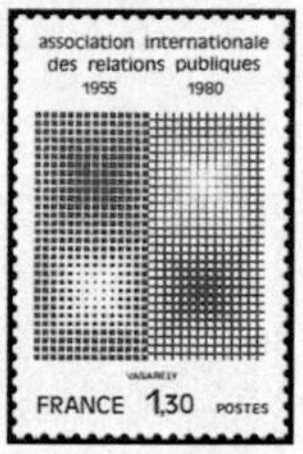

Association Emblem — A871

1980, June 10 **Photo.**
1709 A871 1.30fr red & blue .60 .25

Intl. Public Relations Assoc., 25th anniv.

Marianne, French Architecture
A872

1980, June 21 **Engr.**
1710 A872 1.50fr bluish & gray blk .70 .30

Heritage Year.

Earth Sciences
A873

1980, July 5
1711 A873 1.60fr dk brown & red .75 .50

International Geological Congress.

Rochambeau's Landing — A874

1980, July 15
1712 A874 2.50fr multicolored 1.10 .50

Rochambeau's landing at Newport, R.I. (American Revolution), bicentenary.

Message of Peace, by Yaacov Agam — A875

1980, Oct. 4 **Photo.** ***Perf. 11½x13***
1713 A875 4fr multicolored 3.50 1.00

French Golf Federation
A876

1980, Oct. 18 **Engr.**
1714 A876 1.40fr multicolored .65 .30

Comedie Francaise, 300th Anniversary
A877

1980, Oct. 18
1715 A877 2fr multicolored .90 .45

Charles de Gaulle — A878

1980, Nov. 10 **Photo.** ***Perf. 13***
1716 A878 1.40fr multicolored 1.00 .50

40th anniversary of De Gaulle's appeal of June 18, and 10th anniversary of his death.

Guardsman — A879

1980, Nov. 24 **Engr.** ***Perf. 13***
1717 A879 1.70fr multicolored .80 .45

Rambouillet Chateau
A880

1980, Dec. 6 **Engr.** ***Perf. 13***
1718 A880 2.20fr multicolored 1.00 .35

Tower Type of 1979

Designs: 88c, Imperial Chapel, Ajaccio. 1.14fr, Astronomical Clock, Besancon. 1.84fr, Coucy Castle ruins. 3.05fr, Font-de-Gaume cave drawing, Les Eyzies de Tayac.

1981, Jan. 11 **Engr.** ***Perf. 13***
1719 A841 88c dp mag & blk .40 .20
1720 A841 1.14fr ultra & blk .55 .30
1721 A841 1.84fr dk green & blk .85 .50
1722 A841 3.05fr brn red & blk 1.40 .80
Nos. 1719-1722 (4) 3.20 1.80

Nos. 1719-1722 are known only precanceled. See second note after No. 132.

Microelectronics — A881

1981 **Photo.**
1723 A881 1.20fr shown .75 .30
1724 A881 1.20fr Biology .55 .30
1725 A881 1.40fr Energy .65 .30
1726 A881 1.80fr Marine exploration .85 .50
1727 A881 2fr Telemetry .90 .65
Nos. 1723-1727 (5) 3.70 2.05

Issue dates: #1723, Feb. 5; others, Mar. 28.

Abstract, by Albert Gleizes
A882

1981, Feb. 28 ***Perf. 12½x13***
1728 A882 4fr multicolored 2.00 .90

The Footpath by Camille Pissaro — A883

1981, Apr. 18 **Engr.** ***Perf. 13x12½***
1729 A883 2fr multicolored 1.25 .90

Child Watering Smiling Map of France — A884

1981, Mar. 14 **Engr.** ***Perf. 13***
1730 A884 1.40fr multicolored .65 .25

Sully Chateau, Rosny-sur-Seine — A885

1981, Mar. 21
1731 A885 2.50fr multicolored 1.10 .40

Tourist Issue

Roman Temple, Nimes — A886

Church of St. Jean, Lyon — A887

St. Anne d'Auray Basilica — A888

Vaucelles Abbey
A889

Notre Dame of Louviers
A890

1981, Apr. 11 **Engr.** ***Perf. 13***
1732 A886 1.70fr multicolored .85 .30

1981
1733 A887 1.40fr dk red & dk brn .65 .30
1734 A888 2.20fr blue & black 1.00 .50

Issue dates: 1.40fr, May 30; 2.20fr, July 4.

1981
1735 A889 2fr red & black .90 .40
1736 A890 2.20fr red brn & dk brn 1.00 .50
Nos. 1732-1736 (5) 4.40 2.00

Issue dates: 2fr, Sept. 19; 2.20fr, Sept. 26.

Europa Issue 1981

Folkdances
A891

1981, May 4 ***Perf. 13***
1737 A891 1.40fr Bouree *.65 .25*
1738 A891 2fr Sardane *1.25 .40*

Bookbinding
A892

Cadets
A893

1981, Apr. 4 ***Perf. 13***
1739 A892 1.50fr olive & car rose .70 .40

1981, May 16
1740 A893 2.50fr multicolored 1.10 .30

Military College at St. Maixent centenary.

Man Drawing Geometric Diagram — A894

1981, May 23 **Photo.**
1741 A894 2fr shown 1.40 .90
1742 A894 2fr Faces 1.40 .90
a. Pair, #1741-1742 + label 3.50 3.00

PHILEXFRANCE '82 Stamp Exhibition, Paris, June 11-21, 1982.

Theophraste Renaudot and Emile de Girardin — A895

Public Gardens, Vichy — A896

1981, May 30 **Engr.**
1743 A895 2.20fr black & red 1.00 .40

350th anniversary of La Gazette (founded by Renaudot), and death centenary of founder of Le Journal (de Girardin).

1981, June 6
1744 A896 1.40fr multicolored .65 .30

54th National Congress of French Federation of Philatelic Societies, Vichy.

Higher National College for Commercial Studies Centenary
A897

1981, June 20 ***Perf. 13***
1745 A897 1.40fr multicolored .65 .30

Sea Shore Conservation — A898

1981, June 20
1746 A898 1.60fr multicolored .75 .55

World Fencing Championship, Clermont-Ferrand, July 2-13 — A899

1981, June 27
1747 A899 1.80fr multicolored .85 .45

Sabine, after David — A900

1981, Sept. 1 **Engr.**
1755 A900 1.40fr green .85 .20
1756 A900 1.60fr red 1.00 .25
1757 A900 2.30fr blue 1.40 .85
Nos. 1755-1757 (3) 3.25 1.30

Coil Stamps

1981 **Engr.** ***Perf. 13 Horiz.***
1758 A900 1.40fr green .75 .50
1759 A900 1.60fr red .75 .40

Highway Safety ("Drink or Drive") A901

1981, Sept. 5 ***Perf. 13***
1768 A901 1.60fr multicolored .75 .35

45th Intl. PEN Club Congress
A902

Jules Ferry, Statesman
A903

1981, Sept. 19 ***Perf. 13***
1769 A902 2fr multicolored .90 .35

1981, Sept. 26 ***Perf. 12½x13***
1770 A903 1.60fr multicolored .75 .35

Free compulsory public school centenary.

Natl. Savings Bank Centenary
A904

1981, Sept. 21 **Photo.** ***Perf. 13***
1771 A904 1.40fr multicolored .65 .20
1772 A904 1.60fr multicolored .75 .20

The Divers, by Edouard Pignon — A905

1981, Oct. 3 ***Perf. 13x12½***
1773 A905 4fr multicolored 1.90 .90

Alleluia, by Alfred Manessier
A906

1981, Dec. 19 Photo. *Perf. 12x13*
1774 A906 4fr multicolored 1.90 .90

Tourist Issue

Saint-Emilion — A907

Crest — A908

1981 Engr. *Perf. 13x12½*
1775 A907 2.60fr dk red & lt ol grn 1.20 .35

Perf. 13
1776 A908 2.90fr dk green 1.40 .25

Issued: #1775, Oct. 10; #1776, Nov. 28.

150th Anniv. of Naval Academy
A909

1981, Oct. 17 *Perf. 13*
1777 A909 1.40fr multicolored .65 .35

A910

A911

St. Hubert Kneeling before the Stag, 15th cent. sculpture.

1981, Oct. 24
1778 A910 1.60fr multicolored .75 .35

Museum of hunting and nature.

1981, Nov. 2

V. Schoelcher, J. Jaures, J. Moulin, the Pantheon.

1779 A911 1.60fr blue & dull pur .75 .30

Intl. Year of the Disabled
A912

1981, Nov. 7
1780 A912 1.60fr multicolored .75 .25

Men Leading Cattle, 2nd Cent. Roman Mosaic — A913

1981, Nov. 14 *Perf. 13x12*
1781 A913 2fr multicolored 1.10 .90

Virgil's birth bimillennium.

Martyrs of Chateaubriant
A914

1981, Dec. 12 Engr. *Perf. 13*
1782 A914 1.40fr multicolored .65 .25

Liberty, after Delacroix — A915

1982 Engr. *Perf. 13*
1783 A915 5c dk green .20 .20
1784 A915 10c dull red .20 .20
1785 A915 15c brt rose lilac .35 .35
1786 A915 20c brt green .20 .20
1787 A915 30c orange .20 .20
1788 A915 40c brown .20 .20
a. Bklt. pane of 5, 4 No. 1784, No. 1788 ('87) 1.00
1789 A915 50c lilac .25 .20
1790 A915 60c lt red brn .30 .20
1791 A915 70c ultra .30 .20
1792 A915 80c lt olive grn .35 .20
1793 A915 90c brt lilac .40 .20
1794 A915 1fr olive green .45 .20
1795 A915 1.40fr green .65 .20
1796 A915 1.60fr green .75 .20
1797 A915 1.60fr red .75 .20
1798 A915 1.80fr red .85 .20
1799 A915 2fr brt yel grn .90 .20
1800 A915 2.30fr blue 2.00 1.25
1801 A915 2.60fr blue 2.00 1.00
1802 A915 3fr chocolate 1.40 .30
1803 A915 4fr brt carmine 1.90 .30
1804 A915 5fr gray blue 2.25 .20
Nos. 1783-1804 (22) 16.85 6.60

Coil Stamps
Perf. 13 Horiz.

1805 A915 1.40fr green 1.25 .90
1806 A915 1.60fr red 1.25 .90
1807 A915 1.60fr green .85 .50
1807A A915 1.80fr red .90 .50
Nos. 1805-1807A (4) 4.25 2.80

Issued: 5c-50c, 1fr-1.40fr, 2fr, 2.30fr, 5fr, #1797, 1/2; 1.80fr, 2.60fr, #1796, 6/1; 60c-90c, 3fr, 4fr, 11/3.

See Nos. 1878-1897A, 2077-2080. For surcharge see No. 2115.

Tourist Issue

St. Pierre and Miquelon
A916

Corsica
A917

Renaissance Fountain, Aix-en Provence — A918

Collonges-la-Rouge — A919

Castle of Henry IV, Pau
A920

Lille — A921

Chateau Ripaille, Haute-Savoie — A921a

1982 Engr. *Perf. 12½*
1808 A916 1.60fr dk blue & blk .75 .25
1809 A917 1.90fr blue & red .90 .25

Perf. 13
1810 A918 2fr multicolored .90 .40
1811 A919 3fr multicolored 1.40 .30
1812 A920 3fr ultra & dk bl 1.40 .40

Issued: 1.60fr, 1.90fr, Jan. 9; 2fr, June 21, No. 1811, July 5, No. 1812, May 15.

1982 *Perf. 13x12½*
1813 A921 1.80fr dull red & ol .85 .25
1813A A921a 2.90fr multicolored 1.40 .80
Nos. 1808-1813A (7) 7.60 2.65

Issue dates: 1.80fr, Oct. 16; 2.90fr, Sept. 4.

Tower Type of 1979

97c, Tanlay Castle, Yonne. 1.25fr, Salses Fort, Pyrenees-Orientales. 2.03fr, Montlhery Tower, Essonne. 3.36fr, Chateau d'If Bouches-du-Rhone.

1982, Jan. 11 Engr. *Perf. 13*
1814 A841 97c olive grn & blk .45 .20
1815 A841 1.25fr red & blk .55 .25
1816 A841 2.03fr sepia & blk .95 .50
1817 A841 3.36fr ultra & blk 1.50 .80
Nos. 1814-1817 (4) 3.45 1.75

Nos. 1814-1817 are known only precanceled. See second note after No. 132.

800th Birth Anniv. of St. Francis of Assisi
A922

1982, Feb. 6 Photo. & Engr.
1818 A922 2fr black & blue .90 .50

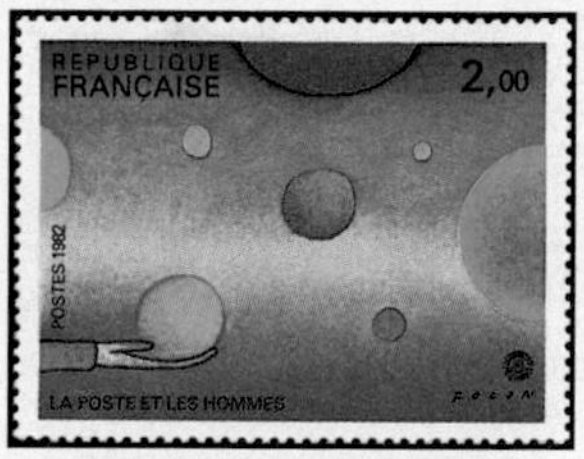

Posts and Mankind — A923

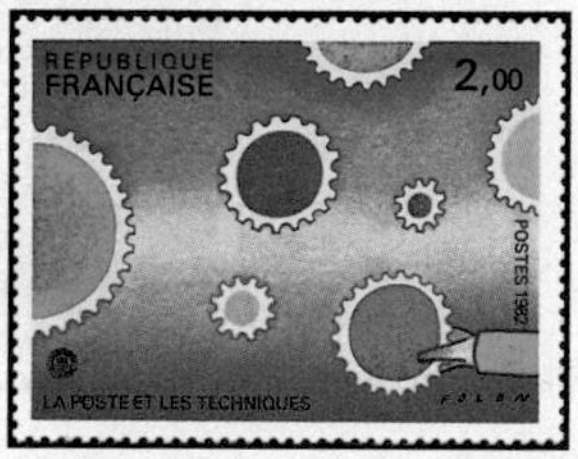

Posts and Technology — A924

Illustration reduced.

1982, Feb. 13 Photo.
1819 A923 2fr multicolored 3.50 2.00
1820 A924 2fr multicolored 3.50 2.00
a. Pair, #1819-1820 + label 9.00 6.50

PHILEXFRANCE '82 Stamp Exhibition, Paris, June 11-21.

Souvenir Sheet

Marianne, by Jean Cocteau — A925

1982, June 11
1821 A925 Sheet of 2 14.00 14.00
a. 4fr red & blue *6.00 6.00*
b. 6fr blue & red *6.00 6.00*

Sold only with 20fr show admission ticket.

Scouting Year
A926

1982, Feb. 20 Engr.
1822 A926 2.30fr yel grn & blk 1.00 .30

31st Natl. Census — A927

1982, Feb. 27 Photo.
1823 A927 1.60fr multicolored .75 .20

Bale-Mulhouse Airport Opening — A928

1982, Mar. 15 Engr. *Perf. 13*
1824 A928 1.90fr multicolored .90 .50

Fight Against Racism A929

1982, Mar. 20
1825 A929 2.30fr brn & red org 1.00 .50

Blacksmith — A930

1982, Apr. 17
1826 A930 1.40fr multicolored .65 .40

Europa 1982 A931

1982, Apr. 24
1827 A931 1.60fr Treaty of Rome, 1957 .75 .30
1828 A931 2.30fr Treaty of Verdun, 843 1.30 .40

1982 World Cup A932

1982, Apr. 28
1829 A932 1.80fr multicolored 1.60 .35

Young Greek Soldier, Hellenic Sculpture, Agude A933

1982, May 15 ***Perf. 12½x13***
1830 A933 4fr multicolored 1.90 1.00

Embarkation for Ostia, by Claude Gellee — A934

The Lacemaker, by Vermeer A935

Turkish Chamber, by Balthus — A936

1982 Photo. ***Perf. 13x12½, 12½x13***
1831 A934 4fr multicolored 1.90 1.00
1832 A935 4fr multicolored 1.90 1.00
1833 A936 4fr multicolored 1.90 1.00
Nos. 1831-1833 (3) 5.70 3.00

Issued: #1831, 6/19; #1832, 9/4; #1833, 11/6.

35th Intl. Film Festival, Cannes — A937

Natl. Space Studies Center, 20th Anniv. — A938

1982, May 15 Photo. ***Perf. 13***
1834 A937 2.30fr multicolored 1.00 .80

1982, May 15 Engr.
1835 A938 2.60fr multicolored 1.20 .50

A939

A940

1982, June 4 Photo.
1836 A939 2.60fr multicolored 1.20 .50

Industrialized Countries' Summit Meeting, Versailles, June 4-6.

1982, June 4 Engr. ***Perf. 13***
1837 A940 1.60fr ol grn & dk grn .75 .20

Jules Valles (1832-1885), writer.

Frederic and Irene Curie, Radiation Diagrams A941

1982, June 26
1838 A941 1.80fr multicolored .85 .35

Electric Street Lighting Centenary A942

1982, July 10
1839 A942 1.80fr dk blue & vio .85 .25

The Family, by Marc Boyan A943

Photogravure and Engraved

1982, Sept. 18 ***Perf. 12½x13***
1840 A943 4fr multicolored 2.00 1.00

Natl. Fed. of Firemen, Cent. A944

Marionettes A945

1982, Sept. 18 Engr. ***Perf. 13***
1841 A944 3.30fr red & sepia 1.75 .40

1982, Sept. 25
1842 A945 1.80fr multicolored .85 .35

Rugby A946

1982, Oct. 9
1843 A946 1.60fr multicolored 2.00 .35

Higher Education A947

1982, Oct. 16
1844 A947 1.80fr red & black .85 .35

TB Bacillus Centenary A948

1982, Nov. 13
1845 A948 2.60fr red & black 1.20 .40

St. Teresa of Avila (1515-82) A949

Leon Blum (1872-1950), Politician A950

1982, Nov. 20
1846 A949 2.10fr multicolored .95 .45

1982, Dec. 18 Engr. ***Perf. 13***
1847 A950 1.80fr dk brn & brn .85 .25

Cavelier de la Salle (1643-1687), Explorer — A951

1982, Dec. 18 ***Perf. 13x12½***
1848 A951 3.25fr multicolored 1.50 .50

Spring — A952

1983, Jan. 17 Engr. ***Perf. 13***
1849 A952 1.05fr shown .50 .40
1850 A952 1.35fr Summer .60 .50
1851 A952 2.19fr Autumn 1.00 .75
1852 A952 3.63fr Winter 1.60 1.25
Nos. 1849-1852 (4) 3.70 2.90

Nos. 1849-1852 known only precanceled. See second note after No. 132.

Provence-Alpes-Cote d'Azur — A953

Brantome (Perigord) A954

Concarneau — A955

Noirlac Abbey A956

Jarnac A957

Charleville-Mezieres — A958

Illustration A958 reduced.

1983 **Photo.** ***Perf. 13***
1853 A953 1fr multicolored .45 .25

Engr.

Perf. 13x12½

1854 A954 1.80fr multicolored .85 .20

Perf. 13

1855 A955 3fr multicolored 1.40 .60

Perf. 13x12½

1856 A956 3.60fr multicolored 1.60 .35

Issued: 1fr, 1/8; 1.80fr, 2/5; 3fr, 6/11; 3.60fr, 7/2.

1983 ***Perf. 13x12½***
1857 A957 2fr multicolored .90 .35
1858 A958 3.10fr multicolored 1.40 .85
Nos. 1853-1858 (6) 6.60 2.60

Issued: 2fr, Oct. 8; 3.10fr, Sept. 17.

Martin Luther (1483-1546) — A959

1983, Feb. 12 **Engr.** ***Perf. 13***
1859 A959 3.30fr dk brn & tan 1.50 .55

Alliance Francaise Centenary A960

1983, Feb. 19
1860 A960 1.80fr multicolored .85 .35

Danielle Casanova (d. 1942), Resistance Leader A961

1983, Mar. 8
1861 A961 3fr blk & red brn 1.40 .35

World Communications Year — A962

1983, Mar. 12 **Photo.**
1862 A962 2.60fr multicolored 1.20 .75

Manned Flight Bicentenary — A963

1983, Mar. 19 **Photo.** ***Perf. 13***
1863 2fr Hot air balloon .90 .65
1864 3fr Hydrogen balloon 1.40 .80
a. A963 Pair, #1863-1864 + label 2.50 2.50

Female Nude, by Raphael A964

Aurora-Set, by Dewasne — A965

1983 **Engr.** ***Perf. 13***
1865 A964 4fr multicolored 1.90 1.00

Photo.

1866 A965 4fr multicolored 1.90 1.00

Issue dates: #1866, Mar. 19; #1865, Apr. 9.

Illustration from Perrault's Folk Tales, by Gustave Dore A966

1983, June 18 **Engr.** ***Perf. 13***
1867 A966 4fr red & black 1.90 1.00

Homage to Jean Effel A967

1983, Oct. 15
1868 A967 4fr multicolored 1.90 1.00

Le Lapin Agile, by Utrillo — A968

1983, Dec. 3 ***Perf. 13x12½***
1869 A968 4fr multicolored 1.90 1.00

Thistle — A969

Europa 1983 — A970

1983, Apr. 23 **Engr.** ***Perf. 12½x12***
1870 A969 1fr shown .45 .30
1871 A969 2fr Martagon lily .90 .30
1872 A969 3fr Aster 1.40 .60
1873 A969 4fr Aconite 1.90 .60
Nos. 1870-1873 (4) 4.65 1.80

1983, Apr. 29 ***Perf. 13***
1874 A970 1.80fr Symbolic shutter *2.00* .50
1875 A970 2.60fr Lens-to-screen diagram *2.10* .75

Centenary of Paris Convention for the Protection of Industrial Property — A971

1983, May 14 **Photo.** ***Perf. 13***
1876 A971 2fr multicolored .90 .30

French Philatelic Societies Congress, Marseille A972

1983, May 21 **Engr.** ***Perf. 13***
1877 A972 1.80fr multicolored .85 .35

Liberty Type of 1982

1983-87 **Engr.** ***Perf. 13***
1878 A915 1.70fr green .75 .20
1879 A915 1.80fr green .80 .20
1880 A915 1.90fr green .85 .20
1881 A915 2fr red .90 .20
1882 A915 2fr green .90 .20
1883 A915 2.10fr red .95 .20
1884 A915 2.20fr red 1.00 .20
a. Booklet pane of 10 10.00
b. Bklt. pane, #1788, 4 #1884 5.00
c. With label ('87) 1.00 .20
1885 A915 2.80fr blue 1.25 .90
1886 A915 3fr blue 1.40 .50
1887 A915 3.20fr blue 1.50 .90
1888 A915 3.40fr blue 1.60 .75
1889 A915 3.60fr blue 1.60 .65
1890 A915 10fr purple 4.50 .20
1891 A915 (1.90fr) green .90 .20
1892 A915 (2fr) green .90 .20
Nos. 1878-1892 (15) 19.80 5.70

Coil Stamps

Engr. ***Perf. 13 Horiz.***
1893 A915 1.70fr green 1.00 .80
1894 A915 1.80fr green 1.00 .50
1895 A915 1.90fr green 1.25 .30
1896 A915 2fr red 1.00 .30
1897 A915 2.10fr red 1.10 .60
1897A A915 2.20fr red 1.00 .50
Nos. 1893-1897A (6) 6.35 3.00

#1891 is inscribed "A," #1892 "B."

No. 1884c was issued in sheets of 50 plus 50 alternating labels picturing the PHILEXFRANCE '89 emblem to publicize the international philatelic exhibition.

Issued: 2.80fr, 10fr, #1881, 6/1; 1.70fr, 2.10fr, 3fr, 7/1/84; 1.80fr, 2.20fr, 3.20fr, 8/1/85; 3.40fr, #1891, 8/1/86; 1.90fr, 9/13/86; #1882, 10/15/87; 3.60fr, #1892, 8/1/87.

For surcharge see No. 2115.

50th Anniv. of Air France A973

1983, June 18
1898 A973 3.45fr multicolored 1.60 .85

Treaties of Versailles and Paris Bicentenary — A974

1983, Sept. 2 ***Perf. 13x12½***
1899 A974 2.80fr multicolored 1.25 .60

Jewelry Making A975

1983, Sept. 10 **Photo.** ***Perf. 13***
1900 A975 2.20fr multicolored 1.00 .35

30th Anniv. of Customs Cooperation Council — A976

1983, Sept. 22 **Engr.** ***Perf. 13x12½***
1901 A976 2.30fr multicolored 1.00 .45

Michaux's Bicycle A977

1983, Oct. 1 **Engr.** ***Perf. 13***
1902 A977 1.60fr multicolored .75 .40

Natl. Weather Forecasting — A978

1983, Oct. 22 **Engr.** ***Perf. 12½x13***
1903 A978 1.50fr multicolored .70 .20

Berthie Albrecht (1893-1943) — A979

1983, Nov. 5
1904 A979 1.60fr dk brown & olive .75 .35
1905 A979 1.60fr Rene Levy (1906-1943) .75 .35

Resistance heroines.

A980

A981

1983, Dec. 16
1906 A980 2fr dk gray & red .90 .25

Pierre Mendes France (1907-1982), Premier.

1984, Mar. 22 ***Perf. 13***
1907 A981 3.60fr Union leader Waldeck-Rousseau 1.60 .35

Trade Union centenary.

Homage to the Cinema, by Cesar
A982

1984, Feb. 4 **Engr.** ***Perf. 12½x13***
1908 A982 4fr multicolored 2.00 1.00

Four Corners of the Sky, by Jean Messagier — A983

1984, Mar. 31 **Photo.** ***Perf. 13x12½***
1909 A983 4fr multicolored 2.00 1.00

Dining Room Corner, at Cannet, by Pierre Bonnard — A984

Photogravure and Engraved
1984, Apr. 14 ***Perf. 12½x12***
1910 A984 4fr multicolored 2.00 1.00

Pythia, by Andre Masson
A985

Painter at the Feet of His Model, by Helion
A986

1984 **Photo.** ***Perf. 12x13***
1911 A985 5fr multicolored 2.25 1.00
1912 A986 5fr multicolored 2.25 1.00

Issue dates: #1911, Oct. 13; #1912, Dec. 1.

Guadeloupe — A987

1984, Feb. 25 ***Perf. 13***
1913 A987 2.30fr Map, West Indian dancers 1.00 .35

Vauban Citadel, Belle Ile-en-Mer
A988

Cordouan Lighthouse — A989

La Grande Chartreuse Monastery, 900th Anniv.
A990

Palais Ideal, Hauterives-Drome — A991

Montsegur Chateau
A992

1984 **Engr.** ***Perf. 13***
1914 A988 2.50fr multicolored 1.10 .35
1915 A989 3.50fr multicolored 1.60 .40

Issued: #1914, 5/26; #1915, 6/23.

1984
1916 A990 1.70fr multicolored .80 .40
1917 A991 2.10fr multicolored .95 .30
1917A A992 3.70fr multicolored 1.75 .40
Nos. 1914-1917A (5) 6.20 1.85

Issued: 1.70fr, 7/7; 2.10fr, 6/30; 3.70fr, 9/15.

Flora Tristan (1803-44), Feminist
A992a

1984, Mar. 8
1918 A992a 2.80fr multicolored 1.25 .50

Playing Card Suits — A993

1984, Apr. 11 **Engr.**
1919 A993 1.14fr Hearts .55 .50
1920 A993 1.47fr Spades .70 .60
1921 A993 2.38fr Diamonds 1.10 .85
1922 A993 3.95fr Clubs 1.80 1.40
Nos. 1919-1922 (4) 4.15 3.35

Nos. 1919-1922 known only precanceled. See second note after No. 132.

450th Anniv. of Cartier's Landing in Quebec
A994

1984, Apr. 20 **Photo. & Engr.**
1923 A994 2fr multicolored .90 .25

See Canada No. 1011.

Philex '84, Dunkirk
A995

1984, Apr. 21 ***Perf. 13x12½***
1924 A995 1.60fr multicolored .75 .35

Europa (1959-84)
A996

1984, Apr. 28 **Engr.** ***Perf. 13***
1925 A996 2fr red brown *1.10 .35*
1926 A996 2.80fr blue *1.75 .60*

2nd European Parliament Election
A997

1984, Mar. 24 **Photo.** ***Perf. 13***
1927 A997 2fr multicolored .90 .25

Foreign Legion
A998

1984, Apr. 30 **Engr.** ***Perf. 13x12½***
1928 A998 3.10fr multicolored 1.40 .50

40th Anniv. of Liberation
A999

Photogravure and Engraved
1984, May 8 ***Perf. 12½x13***
1929 A999 2fr Resistance .90 .50
1930 A999 3fr Landing 1.40 .60
a. Pair, #1929-1930 + label 2.50 2.50

Olympic Events — A1000

Illustration reduced.

1984, June 1 ***Perf. 13***
1931 A1000 4fr multicolored 1.90 .80

Intl. Olympic Committee, 90th anniv. and 1984 Summer Olympics.

Engraving — A1001

1984, June 8 **Engr.**
1932 A1001 2fr multicolored .90 .25

Bordeaux
A1002

1984, June 9 ***Perf. 13x12½***
1933 A1002 2fr red .90 .25

French Philatelic Societies Congress, Bordeaux.

Natl. Telecommunications College, 40th Anniv. — A1003

1984, June 16 **Photo.** ***Perf. 13***
1934 A1003 3fr Satellite, phone, keyboard 1.40 .35

25th Intl. Geography Congress, Paris — A1004

Illustration reduced.

1984, Aug. 25 **Engr.** ***Perf. 13x12½***
1935 A1004 3fr Alps 1.40 .50

Telecom I Satellite
A1005

1984, Sept. 1 **Photo.** ***Perf. 13***
1936 A1005 3.20fr multicolored 1.50 .50

High-speed Train Mail Transport
A1006

1984, Sept. 8
1937 A1006 2.10fr Electric train, Paris-Lyon 1.00 .25

Local Birds A1007

Marx Dormoy (1888-1941) A1008

Photogravure and Engraved
1984, Sept. 22 ***Perf. 12½x12***
1938 A1007 1fr Gypaetus barbatus .45 .25
1939 A1007 2fr Circaetus gallicus .90 .25
1940 A1007 3fr Accipiter nisus 1.40 .75
1941 A1007 5fr Peregrine falcon 2.25 .55
Nos. 1938-1941 (4) 5.00 1.80

1984, Sept. 22 **Engr.** ***Perf. 13***
1942 A1008 2.40fr multicolored 1.10 .35

A1009

— A1010

1984, Oct. 6 **Engr.** ***Perf. 12½x13***
1943 A1009 3fr Automobile plans 1.40 .35

100th anniv. of the automobile.

1984, Nov. 3
1944 A1010 2.10fr multicolored .95 .25

Pres. Vincent Auriol (1884-1966).

9th 5-Year Plan A1011

1984, Dec. 8 **Photo.** ***Perf. 13***
1945 A1011 2.10fr dk blue & scar .95 .25

French Language Promotion — A1012

1985, Jan. 15 **Engr.** ***Perf. 12½x13***
1946 A1012 3fr multicolored 1.40 .35

Tourism Issue

View of Vienne A1013

Cathedral at Montpelier A1014

St. Michel de Cuxa (Codalet) Abbey — A1015

Talmont Church, Saintonge Romane A1016

Solutre A1017

1985 ***Perf. 13x12½***
1947 A1013 1.70fr ol blk & dk grn .75 .25
1948 A1014 2.10fr sepia & org .95 .25
1949 A1015 2.20fr multicolored 1.00 .35
1950 A1016 3fr multicolored 1.40 .55
1951 A1017 3.90fr multicolored 1.75 .40
Nos. 1947-1951 (5) 5.85 1.80

Issue dates: 1.70fr, Jan. 19; 2.10fr, Mar. 30; 2.20fr, July 6; 3fr, June 15; 3.90fr, Sept. 28.

French TV, 50th Anniv. A1018

1985, Jan. 26 **Photo.** ***Perf. 13***
1952 A1018 2.50fr multicolored 1.10 .50

Months of the Year — A1019

1985, Feb. 11 **Engr.**
1953 A1019 1.22fr January .65 .35
1954 A1019 1.57fr February .75 .50
1955 A1019 2.55fr March 1.25 1.00
1956 A1019 4.23fr April 2.25 1.50

1986, Feb. 10 **Engr.** ***Perf. 13***
1957 A1019 1.28fr May .65 .35
1958 A1019 1.65fr June .75 .50
1959 A1019 2.67fr July 1.25 1.10
1960 A1019 4.44fr August 2.25 1.60

1987, Feb. 16 **Engr.**
1961 A1019 1.31fr September .70 .35
1962 A1019 1.69fr October .90 .50
1963 A1019 2.74fr November 1.40 1.10
1964 A1019 4.56fr December 2.50 1.90
Nos. 1953-1964 (12) 15.30 10.75

Nos. 1953-1964 are known only precanceled. See second note after No. 132.

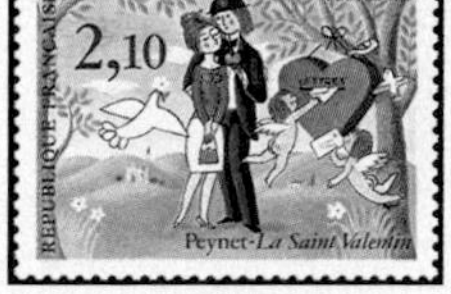

St. Valentine, by Raymond Peynet A1020

1985, Feb. 14 **Photo.** ***Perf. 13x12½***
1965 A1020 2.10fr multicolored .95 .25

Pauline Kergomard (1838-1925) A1021

1985, Mar. 8 **Engr.** ***Perf. 13x12½***
1966 A1021 1.70fr int bl & cop red .75 .25

Stained Glass Window, Strasbourg Cathedral A1022

Still-life with Candle, Nicolas de Stael — A1023

1985 **Engraved** ***Perf. 12x13***
1967 A1022 5fr multicolored 4.00 1.25

Photo.
Perf. 13x12
1968 A1023 5fr multicolored 3.00 1.00

Issue dates: #1967, Apr. 13; #1968, June 1.

Untitled Abstract by Jean Dubuffet — A1024

Octopus Overlaid on Manuscript, by Pierre Alechinsky — A1025

Photogravure; Engraved (#1970)
1985 ***Perf. 13x12½***
1969 A1024 5fr multicolored 2.50 1.25
1970 A1025 5fr multicolored 2.50 1.00

Issued: #1969, Sept. 14; #1970, Oct. 12.

The Dog, Abstract by Alberto Giacometti (1901-1966) — A1026

1985, Dec. 7 **Engr.** ***Perf. 13x12½***
1971 A1026 5fr grnsh blk & lt lem 2.50 1.00

Housing in Givors A1027

Contemporary architecture by Jean Renaude.

1985, Apr. 20 **Engr.** ***Perf. 13***
1972 A1027 2.40fr blk, yel org & ol grn 1.10 .50

Landevennec Abbey, 1500th Anniv. — A1028

1985, Apr. 20 ***Perf. 13x12½***
1973 A1028 1.70fr green & brn vio .60 .20

A1029

A1030

Europa: 2.10fr, Adam de la Halle (1240-1285), composer. 3fr, Darius Milhaud (1892-1974), composer.

1985, Apr. 27 ***Perf. 12½x13***
1974 A1029 2.10fr dr bl, blk, & brt bl 1.00 .40
1975 A1029 3fr dk bl, brt bl & blk 1.75 .65

1985, May 8 ***Perf. 13x12½***
1976 A1030 2fr Return of peace .80 .55
1977 A1030 3fr Return of liberty 1.40 .55
a. Pair, #1976-1977 + label 2.25 2.25

Liberation of France from German occupation forces, 40th anniv.

Natl. Philatelic Congress, Tours — A1031

1985, May 25 ***Perf. 12½x13***
1978 A1031 2.10fr Tours Cathedral .95 .35

Rabies Vaccine Cent. A1032

1985, June 1 *Perf. 13x12½*

1979 A1032 1.50fr Pasteur inoculating patient .70 .25

Mystere Falcon-900 A1033

1985, June 1 *Perf. 13*

1980 A1033 10fr blue 4.50 2.00

Lake Geneva Life-Saving Society Cent. A1034

1985, June 15

1981 A1034 2.50fr blk, red & brt ultra 1.10 .50

UN, 40th Anniv. — A1035

Huguenot Cross — A1036

1985, June 26 *Perf. 13x12½*

1982 A1035 3fr multicolored 1.40 .35

1985, Aug. 31 **Engr.** *Perf. 12½x13*

1983 A1036 2.50fr dp vio, dk red brn & dk red 1.10 .35

King Louis XIV revoked the Edict of Nantes on Oct. 18, 1685, dispossessing French Protestants of religious and civil liberty.

A1037

A1038

Trees, leaves and fruit of the beech, elm, oak and spruce varieties.

1985, Sept. 21 **Engr.** *Perf. 12½*

1984 A1037 1fr shown .45 .25
1985 A1037 2fr Ulmus montana .90 .25
1986 A1037 3fr Quercus pedunculata 1.40 .60
1987 A1037 5fr Picea abies 2.25 .35
Nos. 1984-1987 (4) 5.00 1.45

1985, Nov. 2 **Engr.** *Perf. 12½x13*

La France Mourning the Dead, Eternal Flame.

1988 A1038 1.80fr brn, org & lake .85 .25

Memorial Day.

A1039

A1040

1985, Nov. 9 **Engr.**

1989 A1039 3.20fr black & blue 1.50 .50

Charles Dullin, 1885-1949, impresario, theater.

1985, Nov. 16 **Engr.** *Perf. 13x12½*

1990 A1040 2.20fr red & black 1.00 .20

National information system.

Thai Ambassadors at the Court of King Louis XIV, Painting A1041

1986, Jan. 25 **Engr.** *Perf. 13*

1991 A1041 3.20fr rose lake & blk 1.50 .75

Normalization of diplomatic relations with Thailand, 300th anniv.

Leisure, by Fernand Leger A1042

1986, Feb. 1 **Photo.** *Perf. 13*

1992 A1042 2.20fr multicolored 1.00 .20

1936 Popular Front, 50th anniv.

Venice Carnival, Paris — A1043

1986, Feb. 12 *Perf. 12½x13*

1993 A1043 2.20fr multicolored 1.00 .20

La Marianne, Typograph by Raymond Gid A1044

Photogravure & Engraved

1986, Mar. 3 *Perf. 12½x13½*

1994 A1044 5fr black & dk red 2.25 1.00

Tourism Issue

Filitosa, South Corsica A1045

Loches Chateau A1046

Norman Manor, St. Germain de Livet A1047

Notre-Dame-en-Vaux Monastery, Marne — A1048

Market Square, Bastide de Monpazier, Dordogne — A1049

Illustration A1049 reduced.

1986 **Engr.** *Perf. 13*

1995 A1045 1.80fr multicolored .85 .25
1996 A1046 2fr int blue & blk .90 .50
1997 A1047 2.20fr grnsh bl, brn & grn 1.00 .35
1998 A1048 2.50fr henna brn & sepia 1.10 .40

Perf. 13x12½

1999 A1049 3.90fr blk & yel org 1.75 .90
Nos. 1995-1999 (5) 5.60 2.40

Issued: 2.20fr, 3/3; 2fr, 6/14; 2.50fr, 6/9; 1.80fr, 3.90fr, 7/5.

Louise Michel (1830-1905), Anarchist — A1050

1986, Mar. 10 **Engr.**

2000 A1050 1.80fr dk red & gray blk .80 .20

City of Science and Industry, La Villette — A1051

1986, Mar. 17

2001 A1051 3.90fr multicolored 1.75 .50

Center for Modern Asia-Africa Studies A1052

1986, Apr. 12 **Photo.** *Perf. 13*

2002 A1052 3.20fr Map 1.50 .30

Skibet, Abstract by Maurice Esteve — A1053

Virginia, Abstract by Alberto Magnelli — A1054

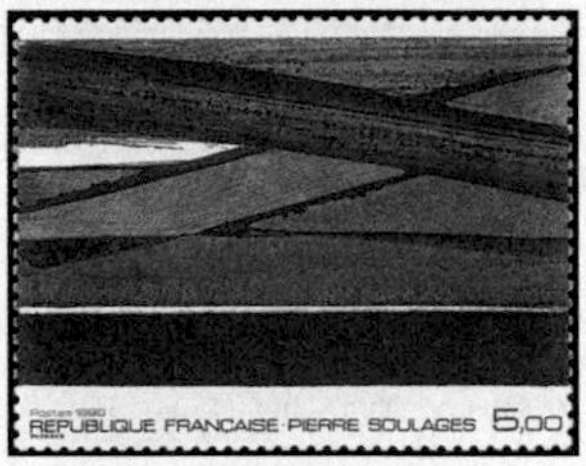

Abstract, by Pierre Soulages — A1055

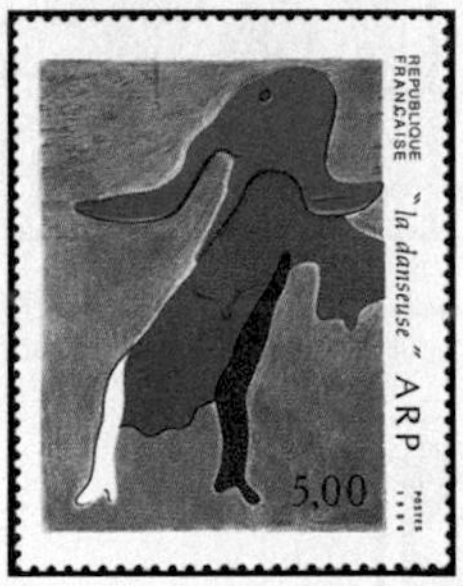

The Dancer, by Jean Arp A1056

Isabelle d'Este, by Leonardo da Vinci A1057

Perf. 12½x13, 13x12½ (#2005, 2006)

1986 **Photo., Engr. (#2005, 2007)**

2003 A1053 5fr multicolored 2.25 1.00
2004 A1054 5fr multicolored 2.25 1.00
2005 A1055 5fr brt vio, blk & brn gray 2.25 1.00
2006 A1056 5fr multicolored 2.25 1.00
2007 A1057 5fr blk, red brn & grnsh yel 2.25 1.00
Nos. 2003-2007 (5) 11.25 5.00

Issued: #2003, Apr. 14; #2004, June 25; #2005, Dec. 22; #2006, 2007, Nov. 10.

Victor Basch (1863-1944), IPY Emblem — A1058

1986, Apr. 28 Engr. *Perf. 13*
2008 A1058 2.50fr black & yel grn 1.10 .30

International Peace Year.

Europa 1986 A1059

1986, Apr. 28 *Perf. 13x12½*
2009 A1059 2.20fr Civet cat 1.00 .35
2010 A1059 3.20fr Bat 1.50 .65

St. Jean-Marie Vianney, Curé of Ars A1060

1986, May 3 Engr. *Perf. 13x12½*
2011 A1060 1.80fr sepia, brn org & brn .80 .25

Philatelic Societies Federation Congress, Nancy — A1061

1986, May 17 *Perf. 13*
2012 A1061 2.20fr Exposition Center 1.00 .25

Mens World Volleyball Championship A1062

Statue of Liberty, Cent. A1063

1986, May 24 Engr. *Perf. 13*
2013 A1062 2.20fr dk vio, brn vio & scar 1.00 .35

1986, July 4 *Perf. 13*
2014 A1063 2.20fr scar & dk blue 1.00 .25

See US No. 2224.

1st Ascent of Mt. Blanc, 1786 A1064

1986, Aug. 8 Engr. *Perf. 13x12½*
2015 A1064 2fr J. Balmat, M.G. Paccard .90 .50

Pierre-Louis Moreau de Maupertuis (1698-1759), La Condamine and Sextant — A1065

1986, Sept. 5
2016 A1065 3fr multicolored 1.40 .55

Lapland Expedition, 250th anniv., proved Earth's poles are flattened.
See Finland No. 741.

Marcassite A1066

1986, Sept. 13 *Perf. 12½*
2017 A1066 2fr shown .90 .25
2018 A1066 3fr Quartz 1.40 .25
2019 A1066 4fr Calcite 1.75 .70
2020 A1066 5fr Fluorite 2.25 .70
Nos. 2017-2020 (4) 6.30 1.90

Souvenir Sheet

Natl. Film Industry, 50th Anniv. A1067

Personalities and film scenes: a, Louis Feuillade, The Vampires. b, Max Linder. c, Sacha Guitry, Romance of the Trickster. d, Jean Renoir, The Grand Illusion. e, Marcel Pagnol, The Baker's Woman. f, Jean Epstein, The Three-Sided Mirror. g, Rene Clair, Women of the Night. h, Jean Gremillon, Talk of Love. i, Jacques Becker, Helmet of Gold. j, Francois Truffaut, The Young Savage.

1986, Sept. 20 Photo. *Perf. 13x12½*
2021 Sheet of 10 10.00 10.00
a.-j. A1067 2.20fr any single 1.00 1.00

Scene from Le Grand Meaulnes, by Henry Alain-Fournier (b. 1886), Novelist A1068

Professional Education, Cent. A1069

1986, Oct. 4 Engr. *Perf. 12½x13*
2022 A1068 2.20fr black & dk red 1.00 .25

1986, Oct. 4
2023 A1069 1.90fr brt vio & dp lil rose .85 .25

World Energy Conf., Cannes A1070

Mulhouse Technical Museum A1071

1986, Oct. 5 Photo. *Perf. 13*
2024 A1070 3.40fr multicolored 1.50 .50

1986, Dec. 1 Engr.
2025 A1071 2.20fr int blue, dk red & blk 1.00 .45

Museum at Orsay, Opening — A1072

1986, Dec. 10 Photo.
2026 A1072 3.70fr bluish blk & pck bl 1.75 .60

Fulgence Bienvenue (1852-1934), and the Metro — A1073

1987, Jan. 17 Engr. *Perf. 13*
2027 A1073 2.50fr vio brn, brn & dk grn 1.10 .35

A1074

A1075

1987, Jan. 24
2028 A1074 1.90fr grn & grnsh blk .85 .20

Raoul Follereau (1903-1977), care for lepers.

1987, Mar. 7 Engr. *Perf. 12½x13*
2029 A1075 1.90fr black & red .85 .20

Cutlery industry, Thiers.

Tourist Issue

Redon, Ille et Vilaine A1076

Azay-le-Rideau Chateau — A1077

Meuse District — A1078

De Gaulle's Home, Etretat A1079

Les Baux-de-Provence — A1080

Illustration A1078 reduced.

1987 Engr. *Perf. 13*
2030 A1076 2.20fr dp rose lil, blk & brn ol 1.10 .25
2031 A1077 2.50fr Prus blue & olive grn 1.25 .25

Perf. 12½
2032 A1078 3.70fr multicolored 1.75 .25

Photo. *Perf. 13*
2033 A1079 2.20fr multicolored 1.00 .25

Engr.
2034 A1080 3fr dk ol bis & dp vio 1.40 .90
Nos. 2030-2034 (5) 6.50 1.90

Issued: #2030, 3/7; #2033, 6/12; 2.50fr, 5/9; 3fr, 6/27; 3.70fr, 5/30.

Charles Edouard Jenneret (Le Corbusier) (1887-1965), Architect — A1081

1987, Apr. 11 Photo. *Perf. 13x12½*
2035 A1081 3.70fr Abstract 1.75 .50

Europa 1987 A1082

Modern architecture: 2.20fr, Metal factory at Boulogne-Billancourt, by architect Claude Vasconi. 3.40fr, Rue Mallet-Stevens housing, by Robert Mallet-Stevens.

1987, Apr. 25 Engr. *Perf. 13x12½*
2036 A1082 2.20fr dk blue & grn *1.25* .50
2037 A1082 3.40fr brn & dk grn *1.75* .65

Abstract Painting, by Bram van Velde — A1083

Woman under Parasol, by Eugene Boudin (1824-1898) — A1084

Precambrien, by Camille Bryen — A1085

World, Bronze Sculpture by Antoine Pevsner — A1086

Perf. 12½x13, 13x12½ (Nos. 2039, 2041)

Photo., Engr. (Nos. 2039, 2041)

1987

2038 A1083 5fr multicolored 2.25 1.00
2039 A1084 5fr multicolored 2.25 1.00
2040 A1085 5fr multicolored 2.25 1.00
2041 A1086 5fr bister & blk 2.25 1.00
Nos. 2038-2041 (4) 9.00 4.00

Issue dates: #2038, Apr. 25; #2039, May 23; #2040, Sept. 12; #2041, Nov. 14.

Gaspard de Montagnes, from a Manuscript Illustration — A1087

1987, May 9 Engr. *Perf. 13*
2042 A1087 1.90fr dp grn & sepia .85 .20

Henri Pourrat (1887-1959), novelist.

Natl. Philatelic Societies Congress, Lens A1088

1987, June 6 *Perf. 13x13½*
2043 A1088 2.20fr choc & red 1.00 .30

Involvement of U.S. Forces in WW I, 70th Anniv. A1089

Design: Stars and Stripes, troops, Gen. John J. Pershing (1860-1948), American army commander.

1987, June 13 *Perf. 13*
2044 A1089 3.40fr olive grn, saph & ver 1.50 .70

A1090

A1091

1987, June 17 Photo.
2045 A1090 2fr multicolored .90 .60

6th Intl. Cable Car Transport Congress, Grenoble.

1987, June 20 Litho.
2046 A1091 1.90fr pale chalky blue & blk .90 .55

Accession of Hugh Capet (c.938-996), 1st king of France, millenary.

A1092

A1093

1987, June 20 Engr. *Perf. 12½x13*
2047 A1092 2.20fr multicolored 1.00 .30

La Fleche Natl. Military School.

1987, June 27 Photo. *Perf. 13*
2048 A1093 1.90fr multicolored .90 .55

World Assembly of Expatriate Algerians, Nice.

World Wrestling Championships — A1094

1987, Aug. 21 Engr.
2049 A1094 3fr brt pur, vio gray & brt olive grn 1.40 .60

Mushrooms A1095

William the Conqueror (c. 1027-1087) A1096

1987, Sept. 5 *Perf. 12½*
2050 A1095 2fr Gyroporus cyanescens .90 .25
2051 A1095 3fr Gomphus clavatus 1.40 .35
2052 A1095 4fr Morchella conica 1.75 .60
2053 A1095 5fr Russula virescens 2.25 .60
Nos. 2050-2053 (4) 6.30 1.80

1987, Sept. 5 *Perf. 13*
2054 A1096 2fr Bayeux Tapestry detail .90 .35

Montbenoit Le Saugeais A1097

Design: Abbey of Medieval Knights, cloisters, winter scene.

1987, Sept. 19
2055 A1097 2.50fr saph, blk & scar 1.10 .55

Pasteur Institute, Cent. — A1098

1987, Oct. 3
2056 A1098 2.20fr dp blue & dk red 1.00 .20

Blaise Cendrars (1887-1961), Poet and Novelist — A1099

Treaty of Andelot, 1400th Anniv. — A1100

Pen and ink portrait by Modigliani.

1987, Nov. 6 *Perf. 12½*
2057 A1099 2fr brt grn, buff & blk .90 .35

1987, Nov. 28 *Perf. 12½x13*
2058 A1100 3.70fr multicolored 1.75 .55

Gen. Leclerc (1902-1947), Marshal of France — A1101

1987, Nov. 28 *Perf. 13x12½*
2059 A1101 2.20fr multicolored 1.00 .25

Liberty Type of 1982

1987-90 *Perf. 13*
2077 A915 3.70fr brt lilac rose 1.75 .35
2078 A915 (2.10fr) green ('90) .95 .20
2079 A915 (2.30fr) red ('90) 1.00 .20
Nos. 2077-2079 (3) 3.70 .75

Coil Stamp

Engr.

Perf. 13 Horiz.
2080 A915 2fr emerald green .90 .30

Issued: 2fr, 8/1; 3.70fr, 11/16; #2078-2079, 1/2.

Nos. 2078-2079 are inscribed "C."

Franco-German Cooperation Treaty, 25th Anniv. — A1102

1988, Jan. 15 *Perf. 13*
2086 A1102 2.20fr Adenauer, De Gaulle 1.00 .35

See Fed. Rep. of Germany No. 1546.

Marcel Dassault (1892-1986), Aircraft Designer — A1103

1988, Jan. 23 Photo.
2087 A1103 3.60fr brt ultra, gray blk & dk red 1.60 .70

Communications A1104

Great Synagogue, Rue Victoire, Paris A1105

Angouleme Festival prize-winning cartoons.

1988, Jan. 29 Photo. *Perf. 13½x13*

Booklet Stamps

2088 A1104 2.20fr Pellos 1.00 .50
2089 A1104 2.20fr Reiser 1.00 .50
2090 A1104 2.20fr Marijac 1.00 .50
2091 A1104 2.20fr Fred 1.00 .50
2092 A1104 2.20fr Moebius 1.00 .50
2093 A1104 2.20fr Gillon 1.00 .50
2094 A1104 2.20fr Bretecher 1.00 .50
2095 A1104 2.20fr Forest 1.00 .50
2096 A1104 2.20fr Mezieres 1.00 .50
2097 A1104 2.20fr Tardi 1.00 .50
2098 A1104 2.20fr Lob 1.00 .50
2099 A1104 2.20fr Bilal 1.00 .50
a. Bklt. pane of 12, #2088-2099 12.00

1988, Feb. 7 Litho. *Perf. 13*
2100 A1105 2fr black & gold .90 .25

The Four Elements — A1106

1988, Feb. 1 Engr. *Perf. 13*
2101 A1106 1.36fr Air .65 .40
2102 A1106 1.75fr Water .80 .40
2103 A1106 2.83fr Fire 1.25 1.00
2104 A1106 4.75fr Earth 2.25 1.75
Nos. 2101-2104 (4) 4.95 3.55

Nos. 2101-2104 known only precanceled. See second note after No. 132.

PHILEXFRANCE '89 — A1107

1988, Mar. 4
2105 A1107 2.20fr #1885, emblem 1.00 .20

Postal Training College, Cent. A1108

1988, Mar. 29
2106 A1108 3.60fr multicolored 1.60 .40

Philex-Jeunes '88, Youth Stamp Show — A1109

1988, Apr. 8 ***Perf. 13x12½***
2107 A1109 2fr multicolored .90 .25

Blood Donation — A1110

1988, Apr. 9 Photo. ***Perf. 13½x13***
2108 A1110 2.50fr multicolored 1.10 .40

Europa 1988 A1111

Communication and transportation.

1988, Apr. 30 Engr. ***Perf. 13***
2109 A1111 2.20fr Cables, satellites *1.75 .35*
2110 A1111 3.60fr Rail cars *2.50 .60*

Jean Monnet (1888-1979), Economist — A1112

1988, May 10 ***Perf. 12½x13***
2111 A1112 2.20fr black & brn ol 1.00 .25

Philatelic Congress, Valence A1113

1988, May 21 ***Perf. 13x12½***
2112 A1113 2.20fr multicolored 1.00 .35

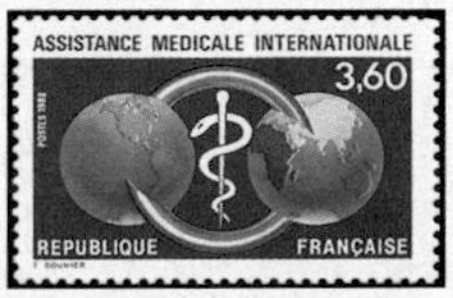

Intl. Medical Assistance A1114

1988, May 28 Photo. ***Perf. 13***
2113 A1114 3.60fr multicolored 1.60 .50

Aid to the Handicapped — A1115

1988, May 28
2114 A1115 3.70fr multicolored 1.75 .50

No. 1884 Surcharged in European Currency Units

1988, Apr. 16 **Engr.**
2115 A915 2.20fr red 1.00 .25

Tourist Issue

Hermes Dicephalus (Roman Empire), Frejus — A1116

Ship Museum, Douarnenez — A1117

Chateau Sedieres, Correze — A1118

Cirque de Gavarnie A1119

View of Perouges, Ain A1120

1988, June 12 Engr. ***Perf. 13x12½***
2116 A1116 3.70fr multicolored 1.75 .80

1988 ***Perf. 13, 12½x13 (#2118)***
2117 A1117 2fr multicolored .90 .25
2118 A1118 2.20fr multicolored 1.00 .35
2119 A1119 3fr multicolored 1.40 .40

Issued: 2.20fr, 7/2; 2fr, 7/4; 3fr, 7/23.

1988, Sept. 10 ***Perf. 13x12½***
2120 A1120 2.20fr multicolored 1.00 .25
Nos. 2116-2120 (5) 6.05 2.05

French Revolution, Bicent. — A1121

Designs: 3fr, Assembly of the Three Estates, Vizille. 4fr, Day of the Tiles (Barricades), Grenoble.

1988, June 18 **Engr.**
2121 A1121 3fr multicolored 1.40 1.00
2122 A1121 4fr multicolored 1.90 1.00
a. Pair, #2121-2122 + label 3.50 3.00

PHILEXFRANCE '89.

Buffon's Natural History — A1122

Alpine Troops, Cent. — A1123

1988, June 18 ***Perf. 12½***
2123 A1122 2fr Otters .90 .20
2124 A1122 3fr Stag 1.40 .30
2125 A1122 4fr Fox 1.90 .70
2126 A1122 5fr Badger 2.25 .60
Nos. 2123-2126 (4) 6.45 1.80

1988, June 25 ***Perf. 13***
2127 A1123 2.50fr multicolored 1.10 .65

Roland Garros (1888-1918), 1st Pilot to Fly Across the Mediterranean, Sept. 23, 1913 — A1124

1988, July 2 Engr. ***Perf. 13x12½***
2128 A1124 2fr brt grn bl & olive .90 .25

Nov. 11, 1918 Armistice Ending World War I, 70th Anniv. A1125

1988, Sept. 10 Engr. ***Perf. 13***
2129 A1125 2.20fr brt blue, gray & blk 1.00 .25

Homage to Leon Degand, Sculpture by Robert Jacobsen A1126

1988, Sept. 22 ***Perf. 12½x13***
2130 A1126 5fr blk & dp claret 2.25 1.00

French-Danish cultural exchange program, 10th anniv. See Denmark No. 860.

Strasbourg, 2000th Anniv. — A1127

1988, Sept. 24 ***Perf. 13***
2131 A1127 2.20fr Municipal arms 1.00 .25

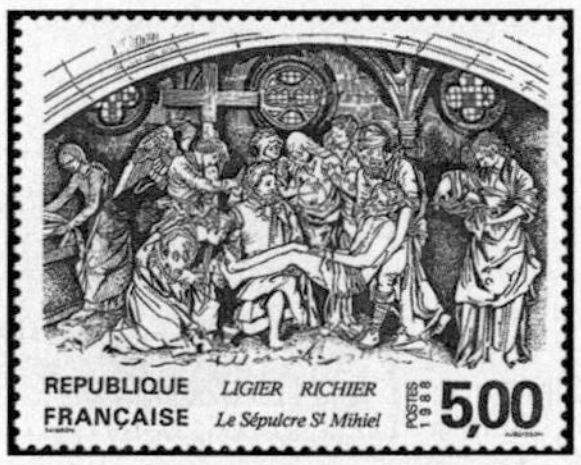

St. Mihiel Sepulcher, by Ligier Richier (c. 1500-1567), Sculptor — A1128

Composition, 1954, by Serge Poliakoff (1906-1969) — A1129

La Pieta de Villeneuve-les-Avignon, by Enguerrand Quarton (1444-1466) — A1130

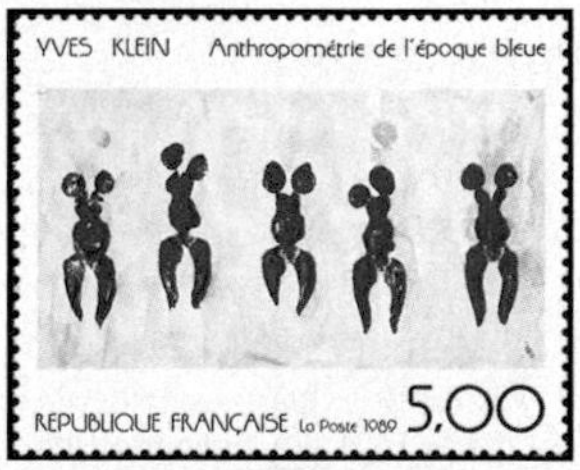

Anthropometry of the Blue Period, by Yves Klein — A1131

1988-89 Engr. ***Perf. 13x12½***
2132 A1128 5fr black brown 2.25 1.00

Photo.
2133 A1129 5fr multicolored 2.25 1.00
2134 A1130 5fr multicolored 2.25 1.00
2135 A1131 5fr multi ('89) 2.25 1.00
Nos. 2132-2135 (4) 9.00 4.00

Issue dates: #2132, Oct. 15; #2133, Oct. 22; #2134, Dec. 10; #2135, Jan. 21.

Thermal Springs A1132

1988, Nov. 21 Engr. ***Perf. 13x12½***
2136 A1132 2.20fr multicolored 1.00 .25

Metamecanique, by Jean Tinguely — A1133

1988, Nov. 25 Photo.
2137 A1133 5fr multicolored 3.00 1.00

See Switzerland No. 828.

UN Declaration of Human Rights, 40th Anniv. A1134

1988, Dec. 12 Litho. *Perf. 13*
2138 A1134 2.20fr dk bl & grnsh bl 1.00 .25

French Revolution, Bicent. — A1135

1989, Jan. 1 Photo. *Perf. 13x12½*
2139 A1135 2.20fr red & vio blue 1.00 .20

Valentin Hauy (1745-1822), Founder of the School for the Blind, Paris, 1791 — A1136

Photo. & Embossed

1989, Jan. 28
2140 A1136 2.20fr multicolored 1.00 .40

Estienne School, Cent. — A1137

1989, Feb. 4 Engr. *Perf. 12½*
2141 A1137 2.20fr gray, black & red 1.00 .25

European Parliament Elections A1138

1989, Mar. 4 Litho. *Perf. 13*
2142 A1138 2.20fr multicolored 1.00 .20

A1139

1989 Engr. *Perf. 12½x13*

2143	A1139	2.20fr Liberty	1.00	.25
2144	A1139	2.20fr Equality	1.00	.25
2145	A1139	2.20fr Fraternity	1.00	.25
a.		Strip of 3, #2143-2145 + label	3.00	2.50

Bicent. of the French revolution and the Declaration of Rights of Man and the Citizen. No. 2145a contains inscribed label picturing PHILEXFRANCE '89 emblem.

Issue dates: #2143, Mar. 18; #2144, Apr. 22; #2145, May 27; #2145a, July 14.

French-Soviet Joint Space Flight — A1140

1989, Mar. 4 Litho. *Perf. 13*
2146 A1140 3.60fr multicolored 1.60 .60

Historic Sights, Paris — A1141

Designs: No. 2147, Arche de la Defense. No. 2148, Eiffel Tower. No. 2149, Grand Louvre. No. 2150, Notre Dame Cathedral. No. 2151, Bastille Monument and Opera de la Bastille. #2151a has a continuous design.

1989, Apr. 21 Engr. *Perf. 13x12½*

2147	A1141	2.20fr multicolored	1.00	.85
2148	A1141	2.20fr multicolored	1.00	.85
2149	A1141	2.20fr multicolored	1.00	.85
2150	A1141	2.20fr multicolored	1.00	.85
2151	A1141	2.20fr multicolored	1.00	.85
a.		Strip of 5, #2147-2151	5.00	5.00

Europa 1989 A1142

Children's games.

1989, Apr. 29 *Perf. 13*

2152	A1142	2.20fr Hopscotch	*1.00*	*.30*
2153	A1142	3.60fr Catch (ball)	*2.50*	*.70*

ITU Plenipotentiaries Conference, Nice — A1143

1989, May 23 Litho.
2154 A1143 3.70fr dk bl, dl org & red 1.75 .40

Tourist Issue

Fontainebleau Forest — A1144

Vaux le Vicomte — A1145

La Brenne — A1146

Illustrations A1145-A1146 reduced.

1989, May 20 Engr. *Perf. 13*
2155 A1144 2.20fr multicolored 1.00 .30

Perf. 13x12½

2156	A1145	3.70fr ol bis & blk	1.75	.75
2157	A1146	4fr violet blue	1.90	.75
		Nos. 2155-2157 (3)	4.65	1.80

Issued: 2.20fr, 5/20; 3.70fr, 7/14; 4fr, 8/25.

World Cycling Championships, Chambery — A1147

1989, June 3 Litho. *Perf. 13*
2158 A1147 2.20fr multi 1.00 .25

Jehan de Malestroit, Dept. of Morbihan — A1148

1989, June 10 Engr. *Perf. 12½x13*
2159 A1148 3.70fr multicolored 1.75 .55

Preliminary Sketch (Detail) for *Oath of the Tennis Court,* by David — A1149

Regatta with Wind Astern, by Charles Lapicque A1150

1989, June 19 Photo. *Perf. 13x12½*
2160 A1149 5fr multicolored 2.25 1.00

Perf. 12½

2161 A1150 5fr multicolored 2.25 1.00

No. 2160 for French revolution bicent. Issued: #2160, 6/19; #2161, 9/23.

Souvenir Sheet

Revolution Bicentennial — A1151

Revolutionaries: a, Madame Roland (1754-1793). b, Camille Desmoulins (1760-1794). c, Condorcet (1743-1794). d, Kellermann (1735-1820).

1989, June 26 Engr. *Perf. 13*

2162	A1151	Sheet of 4	4.00	3.50
a.-d.		2.20fr any single	1.00	.75

15th Summit of the Arch Meeting of Leaders from Industrial Nations, July 14-16
A1152

1989, July 14 Photo.
2163 A1152 2.20fr multicolored 1.00 .35

Declaration of the Rights of Man and the Citizen, Versailles, Aug. 26, 1789 — A1153

Details of an anonymous 18th-19th cent. painting in Carnavalet Museum: No. 2168a, Preamble, Article I. No. 2168b, Articles VII-XI. No. 2168c, Articles II-VI. No. 2168d, Articles XII-XVII.

Litho. & Engr.

1989, Aug. 26 *Perf. 13x11½*

2164	A1153	2.50fr Preamble, Article I	1.00	.90
2165	A1153	2.50fr Art. II-VI	1.00	.90
2166	A1153	2.50fr Art. VII-XI	1.00	.90
2167	A1153	2.50fr Art. XII-XVII	1.00	.90
a.		Strip, #2164-2167 + label	4.00	3.50

Souvenir Sheet
Perf. 13x12½

2168 Sheet of 4 20.00 20.00
a.-d. A1153 5fr any single 5.00 5.00

No. 2168 contains 4 52x41mm stamps. Sold for 50fr, including admission fee to PHILEX-FRANCE '89.

Value of No. 2168 is for examples on plain paper. Examples on fluorescent paper seem to have been distributed in North America, and may not have been distributed widely or made available in Europe. Value $250.

Musical Instruments — A1154

1989 Litho. *Perf. 12x12½*

2169 A1154 1.39fr Harp .65 .40
2170 A1154 1.79fr Piano .80 .40
2171 A1154 2.90fr Trumpet 1.25 .90
2172 A1154 4.84fr Violin 2.25 1.75
Nos. 2169-2172 (4) 4.95 3.45

Nos. 2169-2172 are known only precanceled. See second note after No. 132.

See #2233-2239, 2273-2283, 2368-2371.

TGV Atlantic A1155

1989, Sept. 23 Photo. *Perf. 13*

2173 A1155 2.50fr dk bl, sil & red 1.10 .50

Clermont-Ferrand Tramway, Cent. — A1156

1989, Oct. 28 Engr.

2174 A1156 3.70fr blk & dk ol bis 1.75 .40

Villers-Cotterets Ordinance, 450th Anniv. — A1157

1989, Oct. 28 Engr.

2175 A1157 2.20fr blk, dp cl & red 1.00 .25

Baron Augustin-Louis Cauchy (1789-1857), Mathematician — A1158

1989, Nov. 10 *Perf. 13x12½*

2176 A1158 3.60fr red, blk & bl grn 1.60 .50

Marshal Jean de Lattre de Tassigny (1889-1952) — A1159

1989, Nov. 18 *Perf. 13*

2177 A1159 2.20fr bl, blk & red 1.00 .35

Harki Soldiers of France A1160

1989, Dec. 9 Photo.

2178 A1160 2.20fr multicolored 1.00 .35

Marianne — A1161

1990-92 Engr. *Perf. 13*

2179 A1161 10c brn blk .20 .20
a. Bklt. pane, #2180, 4 #2179 1.00
2180 A1161 20c lt green .20 .20
2181 A1161 50c brt violet .20 .20
2182 A1161 1fr orange .45 .20
2183 A1161 2fr apple grn .90 .20
2184 A1161 2.10fr dark grn .95 .20
2185 A1161 2.20fr dark grn 1.00 .20
2186 A1161 2.20fr emerald 1.00 .20
2187 A1161 2.30fr red 1.00 .20
a. Bklt. pane, #2180, 4 #2187 5.00
2188 A1161 2.50fr red 1.10 .20
2189 A1161 3.20fr blue 1.50 .75
2190 A1161 3.40fr blue 1.60 .40
2191 A1161 3.80fr lilac rose 1.75 .30
2192 A1161 4fr lilac rose 1.90 .20
2193 A1161 4.20fr lilac rose 1.90 .20
2194 A1161 5fr greenish blue 2.25 .20
2195 A1161 10fr violet 4.50 .25
2196 A1161 (2.20fr) dk grn 1.00 .20
2197 A1161 (2.50fr) red 1.10 .20
Nos. 2179-2197 (19) 24.50 4.70

Coil Stamps
Perf. 13 Horiz.

2198 A1161 2.10fr dk grn 1.00 .20
2199 A1161 2.20fr dk grn 1.00 .60
2200 A1161 2.30fr red 1.00 .20
2201 A1161 2.50fr red 1.10 .20
Nos. 2198-2201 (4) 4.10 1.20

Die Cut
Self-Adhesive

2202 A1161 2.30fr red 1.00 .20
a. Booklet pane of 10 10.00
2203 A1161 2.50fr red 1.10 .20
a. Booklet pane of 10 11.00
b. Booklet pane of 5 5.50
2204 A1161 (2.50fr) red 1.10 .20
a. Booklet pane of 10 11.00
Nos. 2202-2204 (3) 3.20 .60

Issued: #2187, 1/2; #2198, 1/1; 10c, 20c, 50c, 3.20fr, 3.80fr, 3/26; #2202, 1/29; #2182-2183, 2194-2195, 5/21; #2196-2197, 8/19/91; 2.20fr, 2.50fr, 3.40fr, 4fr, 9/30/91; #2179a, 2187a, 2199, 2201, 1991; 4.20fr, 9/24/92; #2203-2204, 1992; 2.10fr, 1993.

Peelable paper backing serves as booklet cover for Nos. 2202, 2203. No. 2203b has separate backing with no printing.

Nos. 2196-2197, 2204 inscribed "D."

See Nos. 2333-2348.

Lace Work A1162

1990, Feb. 3 Engr. *Perf. 13x12½*

2205 A1162 2.50fr red 1.10 .40

1992 Winter Olympics, Albertville — A1163

1990, Feb. 9 Photo. *Perf. 13*

2206 A1163 2.50fr multicolored 1.10 .20

Charles de Gaulle (1890-1970) A1164

Max Hymans (1900-1961), Planes and ACC Emblem A1165

1990, Feb. 24 Engr. *Perf. 12½x13*

2207 A1164 2.30fr brt vio, vio bl & blk 1.00 .25

1990, Mar. 3 *Perf. 13*

2208 A1165 2.30fr brt vio, brt bl & dk ol grn 1.00 .25

Profile of a Woman, by Odilon Redon A1166

Head of Christ, Wissembourg — A1167

Cambodian Dancer by Auguste Rodin — A1168

Jaune et Gris by Roger Bissiere A1169

1990 Litho. *Perf. 13½x14*

2209 A1166 5fr multicolored 2.25 1.00

Perf. 12½x13
Engr.

2210 A1167 5fr multicolored 2.25 1.00
2211 A1168 5fr multicolored 2.25 1.00

Photo.

2212 A1169 5fr multicolored 2.25 1.00
Nos. 2209-2212 (4) 9.00 4.00

Issue dates: No. 2209, Mar. 3; No. 2210, June 16; No. 2211, June 9; No. 2212, Dec. 8.

Jean Guehenno (1890-1978) A1170

Litho. & Engr.

1990, Mar. 24 *Perf. 13*

2213 A1170 3.20fr buff & red brn 1.50 .40

Tourism Series

Flaran Abbey, Gers A1171

Cluny A1172

Pont Canal de Briare A1173

Cap Canaille, Cassis A1174

1990, Apr. 21 Engr. *Perf. 13*

2214 A1171 3.80fr sepia & blk 1.75 .50

1990

2215 A1172 2.30fr multicolored 1.00 .25
2216 A1173 2.30fr multicolored 1.00 .25
2217 A1174 3.80fr multicolored 1.75 .50
Nos. 2215-2217 (3) 3.75 1.00

Issued: #2215, 6/23; #2216, 7/7; 3.80fr, 7/14.

Europa 1990 A1175

Post offices.

1990, Apr. 28 Engr. *Perf. 13*
2218 A1175 2.30fr Macon *1.50* *.50*
2219 A1175 3.20fr Cerizay *2.25* *.80*

Arab World Institute — A1176

1990, May 5 *Perf. 12½x13*
2220 A1176 3.80fr brt bl, dk red & dp bl 1.75 .45

Labor Day, Cent. A1177

1990, May 1 Photo. *Perf. 13*
2221 A1177 2.30fr multicolored 1.00 .25

Villefranche-sur-Saone — A1178

1990, June 2 Engr. *Perf. 13x12½*
2222 A1178 2.30fr multicolored 1.00 .25

National philatelic congress.

A1179

A1181

1990, June 6 *Perf. 13x12½*
2223 A1179 2.30fr La Poste 1.00 .25

Whitbread trans-global yacht race.

1990, June 17 *Perf. 12½x13*
2225 A1181 2.30fr multicolored 1.00 .25

De Gaulle's Call for French Resistance, 50th anniv.

Franco-Brazilian House, Rio de Janeiro — A1182

1990, July 14 *Perf. 13*
2226 A1182 3.20fr multicolored 1.50 .75

See Brazil No. 2255.

A1183

A1184

Designs: Fish.

1990, Oct. 6 Engr. *Perf. 12½*
2227 A1183 2fr Rutilus rutilus .90 .20
2228 A1183 3fr Perca fluviatilis 1.40 .25
2229 A1183 4fr Salmo salar 1.90 .50
2230 A1183 5fr Esox lucius 2.25 .50
Nos. 2227-2230 (4) 6.45 1.45

1990, Sept. 29 Photo. *Perf. 12½x13*
2231 A1184 2.30fr multicolored 1.00 .50

Natl. Institute of Geography, 50th anniv.

Souvenir Sheet

French Revolution, Bicentennial — A1185

Designs: a, Gaspard Monge. b, Abbe Gregoire. c, Creation of the Tricolor. d, Creation of the French departments.

1990, Oct. 15 Engr. *Perf. 13*
2232 A1185 Sheet of 4 4.50 4.50
a.-d. 2.50fr any single 1.10 1.10

Musical Instrument Type of 1989

1990, Sept. 1 Litho. *Perf. 13*
2233 A1154 1.46fr Accordion .65 .40
2234 A1154 1.89fr Breton bag-pipe .85 .60
2235 A1154 3.06fr Tambourin 1.75 1.50
2236 A1154 5.10fr Hurdy-gurdy 3.00 2.40
Nos. 2233-2236 (4) 6.25 4.90

1990, Nov. Litho. *Perf. 13*
2237 A1154 1.93fr like #2169 1.10 .75
2238 A1154 2.39fr like #2170 1.25 .90
2239 A1154 2.74fr like #2172 2.00 1.25
Nos. 2237-2239 (3) 4.35 2.90

Nos. 2233-2239 are known only precanceled. See second note after No. 132.

Maurice Genevoix (1890-1980), Novelist — A1186

1990, Nov. 12 Engr. *Perf. 13*
2240 A1186 2.30fr lt green & blk 1.00 .20

Organization for Economic Cooperation and Development, 30th Anniv. — A1187

1990, Dec. 15 Litho.
2241 A1187 3.20fr dk & lt blue 1.50 .75

"The Swing" by Auguste Renoir (1841-1919) — A1188

1991, Feb. 23 Engr. *Perf. 12½x13*
2242 A1188 5fr multicolored 2.25 1.00

Youth Philatelic Exhibition, Cholet A1189

1991, Mar. 30 Litho. *Perf. 13*
2243 A1189 2.50fr multicolored 1.10 .40

Art Series

Le Noeud Noir by Georges Seurat (1859-1891) — A1190

Apres Nous La Maternite, by Max Ernst (1891-1976) — A1191

Volte Faccia by Francois Rouan A1192

O Tableau Noir by Roberto Matta (b. 1911) — A1193

1991 Engr. *Perf. 12½x13*
2244 A1190 5fr pale yellow & blk 2.25 1.00

Photo. *Perf. 13*
2245 A1191 2.50fr multicolored 1.10 .80

Engr. *Perf. 12½x13*
2246 A1192 5fr black 2.25 1.00

Photo. *Perf. 13x12½*
2247 A1193 5fr multicolored 2.25 1.00
Nos. 2244-2247 (4) 7.85 3.80

Issued: #2244, 4/13: #2245, 10/10; #2246, 11/9; #2247, 11/30.

Wolfgang Amadeus Mozart (1756-1791), Composer — A1194

1991, Apr. 9 Photo. *Perf. 13*
2248 A1194 2.50fr bl, blk & red 1.10 .60

National Printing Office, 350th Anniv. — A1195

1991, Apr. 13
2249 A1195 4fr multicolored 1.90 .60

Tourism Series

Chevire Bridge, Nantes — A1196

Carennac Castle A1197

Pipe Organ, Wasquehal A1198

Valley of Munster A1199

1991 **Engr.** ***Perf. 13***
2250 A1196 2.50fr multicolored 1.10 .25

Perf. 12x13
2251 A1197 2.50fr multicolored 1.10 .30

Perf. 12
2252 A1198 4fr black & buff 1.90 .55

Perf. 13x12½
2253 A1199 4fr violet 1.90 .55
Nos. 2250-2253 (4) 6.00 1.65

Issue dates: No. 2250, Apr. 27; Nos. 2251, 2253, July 6; No. 2252, June 22.

Europa A1200

Concours Lepine, 90th Anniv. A1201

1991, Apr. 27 ***Perf. 12½x13***
2254 A1200 2.50fr Ariane launch site, French Guiana 1.10 .20
2255 A1200 3.50fr Television satellite 1.60 .55

Compare with No. 2483.

1991, Apr. 27 ***Perf. 13***
2256 A1201 4fr multicolored 1.90 .80

French Assoc. of Small Manufacturers and Inventors.

Philatelic Society Congress, Perpignan A1202

1991, May 18
2257 A1202 2.50fr multicolored 1.10 .25

French Open Tennis Championships, Cent. — A1203

1991, May 24 **Engr.** ***Perf. 13***
2258 A1203 3.50fr multicolored 1.60 .50

Souvenir Sheet

French Revolution, Bicent. — A1204

Designs: a, Theophile Malo Corret, La Tour d'Auvergne (1743-1800). b, Liberty Tree. c, National police, bicent. d, Louis Antoine-Leon de St. Just (1767-1794).

1991, June 1 **Engr.** ***Perf. 13***
2259 A1204 Sheet of 4 4.50 3.00
a.-d. 2.50fr any single 1.10 .75

A1205 A1206

1991, June 13 **Photo.** ***Perf. 13***
2260 A1205 2.50fr multicolored 1.10 .45

Gaston III de Foix (Febus) (1331-1391), general.

1991, Sept. 14 **Engr.** ***Perf. 12½***

Designs: Wildlife.

2261 A1206 2fr Ursus arctos .90 .30
2262 A1206 3fr Testudo hermanni 1.40 .30
2263 A1206 4fr Castor fiber 1.90 .75
2264 A1206 5fr Alcedo atthis 2.25 .75
Nos. 2261-2264 (4) 6.45 2.10

10th World Forestry Congress A1207

1991, Sept. 22 **Engr.** ***Perf. 13x12½***
2265 A1207 2.50fr multicolored 1.10 .25

School of Public Works, Cent. A1208

1991, Oct. 5 **Litho. & Engr.** ***Perf. 13***
2266 A1208 2.50fr multicolored 1.10 .35

Marcel Cerdan (1916-1949), Middleweight Boxing Champion — A1209

1991, Oct. 19 **Photo.** ***Perf. 13***
2267 A1209 2.50fr black & red 1.10 .35

Amnesty International, 30th Anniv. — A1210

1991, Oct. 19
2268 A1210 3.40fr multicolored 1.60 .60

A1211 A1212

1991, Nov. 14 **Engr.** ***Perf. 13***
2269 A1211 2.50fr Olympic flame 1.10 .25

1992 Winter Olympics, Albertville.

1991, Dec. 7 ***Perf. 13***
2270 A1212 2.50fr dk & lt blue 1.10 .30

Fifth Handicapped Olympics.

Voluntary Attachment of Mayotte to France, Sesquicentennial — A1213

1991, Dec. 21 **Engr.**
2271 A1213 2.50fr multicolored 1.10 .25

French Pavilion, Expo '92, Seville A1214

Litho. & Engr.

1992, Jan. 18 ***Perf. 13***
2272 A1214 2.50fr multicolored 1.10 .25

Musical Instruments Type of 1989

1992, Jan. 31 **Litho.** ***Perf. 13***
2273 A1154 1.60fr Guitar 45.00 25.00
2274 A1154 1.98fr like #2233 4.00 3.00
2275 A1154 2.08fr Saxophone 2.00 1.50
2276 A1154 2.46fr like #2234 2.00 1.50
2277 A1154 2.98fr Banjo 2.00 1.50
2278 A1154 3.08fr like #2235 6.00 4.00
2279 A1154 3.14fr like #2236 2.75 2.00
2280 A1154 3.19fr like #2169 7.00 4.00
2281 A1154 5.28fr Xylophone 5.50 3.50
2282 A1154 5.30fr like #2170 3.50 2.00
2283 A1154 5.32fr like #2172 3.50 2.50
Nos. 2273-2283 (11) 83.25 50.50

Perf. 12

2273a A1154 1.60fr Guitar 7.50 4.50
2274a A1154 1.98fr like #2233 150.00 140.00
2275a A1154 2.08fr Saxophone 40.00 30.00
2276a A1154 2.46fr like #2234 12.00 7.50
2278a A1154 3.08fr like #2235 12.00 7.50
2279a A1154 3.14fr like #2236 60.00 50.00
2280a A1154 3.19fr like #2169 8.00 5.00
2281a A1154 5.28fr Xylophone 30.00 20.00
2282a A1154 5.30fr like #2170 75.00 60.00
2283a A1154 5.32fr like #2172 25.00 20.00
Nos. 2273a-2283a (10) 419.50 344.50

Nos. 2273-2283 are known only precanceled. See 2nd note after No. 132. See Nos. 2303-2306.

1992 Summer Olympics, Barcelona A1215

1992, Apr. 3 **Photo.** ***Perf. 13***
2284 A1215 2.50fr multicolored 1.10 .25

See Greece No. 1730.

Marguerite d'Angouleme (1492-1549) A1216

1992, Apr. 11 **Litho.** ***Perf. 13***
2285 A1216 3.40fr multicolored 1.60 .90

Founding of Ajaccio, 500th Anniv. A1217

Virgin and Child Beneath a Garland by Botticelli.

1992, Apr. 30 **Photo.** ***Perf. 13***
2286 A1217 4fr multicolored 1.90 .60

A1218 A1219

Discovery of America, 500th Anniv.: 2.50fr, Map, navigation instruments. 3.40fr, Sailing ship, map.

1992, May 9 **Engr.** ***Perf. 13x12½***
2287 A1218 2.50fr multicolored *1.25 .30*
2288 A1218 3.40fr multicolored *2.00 .65*

Europa.

1992, May 30 **Litho.** ***Perf. 13***
2289 A1219 3.40fr multicolored 1.60 .80

Intl. Bread and Cereal Congress.

Tourism Series

Ourcq Canal A1220

Mt. Aiguille
A1221

Biron Castle
A1223

Lorient
A1222

1992, May 30 **Engr.** ***Perf. 13***

2290	A1220 4fr black, blue & grn	1.90	.50

1992, June 27 **Engr.** ***Perf. 13***

2291	A1221 3.40fr multicolored	1.60	.75

First ascension of Mt. Aiguille, 500th anniv.

1992, July 4 **Engr.** ***Perf. 13***

2292	A1222 4fr multicolored	1.90	.25

1992, July 4 ***Perf. 12½x13***

2293	A1223 2.50fr multicolored	1.10	.50

Natl. Philatelic Societies Congress, Niort
A1224

1992, June 6 **Photo.** ***Perf. 13***

2294	A1224 2.50fr multicolored	1.10	.25

Natl. Art Festival.

1992 Olympic Games, Albertville and Barcelona
A1225

1992, June 19 ***Perf. 12½x13½***

2295	A1225 2.50fr multicolored	1.10	.35

Tautavel Man
A1226

1992, June 20 **Photo.** ***Perf. 13***

2296	A1226 3.40fr multicolored	1.60	.60

Portrait of Jacques Callot (1592-1635), by Claude Deruet — A1227

1992, June 27 **Engr.** ***Perf. 12x13***

2297	A1227 5fr buff & brown	2.25	.75

Flowers — A1228

2fr, Pancratium maritimum. 3fr, Drosera rotundifolia. 4fr, Orchis palustris. 5fr, Nuphar luteum.

1992, Sept. 12 **Engr.** ***Perf. 12½***

2298	A1228 2fr multicolored	.90	.30
2299	A1228 3fr multicolored	1.40	.30
2300	A1228 4fr multicolored	1.90	.70
2301	A1228 5fr multicolored	2.25	.70
	Nos. 2298-2301 (4)	6.45	2.00

First French Republic, Bicent.
A1229

1992, Sept. 26 ***Perf. 13***

2302	A1229 2.50fr multicolored	1.10	.20

Musical Instruments Type of 1989

1992, Oct. **Litho.** ***Perf. 13***

2303	A1154 1.73fr like #2273	.80	.20
2304	A1154 2.25fr like #2275	1.00	.50
2305	A1154 3.51fr like #2277	1.60	1.00
2306	A1154 5.40fr like #2281	2.50	1.75
	Nos. 2303-2306 (4)	5.90	3.45

Nos. 2303-2306 are known only precanceled. See second note after No. 132.

Proclamation of First French Republic, Bicent. — A1230

Paintings or drawings by contemporary artists: No. 2307, Tree of Freedom, by Pierre Alechinsky. No. 2308, Portrait of a Young Man, by Martial Raysse. No. 2309, Marianne with Body and Head of Rooster, by Gerard Garouste. No. 2310, "Republique Francaise," by Jean-Charles Blais.

1992, Sept. 26 **Engr.** ***Perf. 13***

2307	A1230 2.50fr red	1.10	.20
2308	A1230 2.50fr red	1.10	.20
2309	A1230 2.50fr red	1.10	.20
2310	A1230 2.50fr red	1.10	.20
	Nos. 2307-2310 (4)	4.40	.80

Single European Market
A1231

1992, Nov. 6 **Photo.** ***Perf. 12½x13½***

2311	A1231 2.50fr multicolored	1.10	.35

First Mail Flight from Nancy to Luneville, 80th Anniv.
A1232

1992, Nov. 12 ***Perf. 13***

2312	A1232 2.50fr multicolored	1.10	.45

Marcel Paul (1900-1982), Minister of Industrial Production — A1233

1992, Nov. 13 **Engr.**

2313	A1233 4.20fr claret & blue	1.90	.55

Contemporary Art — A1234

#2314, Le Rendezvous d'Ephese, by Paul Delvaux, Belgium. #2315, Abstract painting, by Alberto Burri, Italy. #2316, Abstract painting, by Antoni Tapies, Spain. #2317, Portrait of John Edwards, by Francis Bacon, Great Britain.

1992 **Photo.** ***Perf. 13x12½***

2314	A1234 5fr multicolored	2.25	1.00
2315	A1234 5fr multicolored	2.25	1.00
2316	A1234 5fr multicolored	2.25	1.00
2317	A1234 5fr multicolored	2.25	1.00
	Nos. 2314-2317 (4)	9.00	4.00

Issued: #2314, 11/20; #2315-2317, 11/21.
See Nos. 2379-2390.

Gypsy Culture — A1235

1992, Dec. 5 **Photo.** ***Perf. 13***

2318	A1235 2.50fr multicolored	1.10	.30

Yacht "La Poste," Entrant in Whitbread Trans-Global Race — A1236

1993, Feb. 6 **Engr.** ***Perf. 12***

2319	A1236 2.50fr multicolored	1.10	.40

See No. 2375.

Water Birds — A1237

1993, Feb. 6 ***Perf. 12½x12***

2320	A1237 2fr Harle piette	.90	.30
2321	A1237 3fr Fuligule nyroca	1.40	.30
2322	A1237 4fr Tadorne de belon	1.90	.75
2323	A1237 5fr Harle huppe	2.25	.70
	Nos. 2320-2323 (4)	6.45	2.05

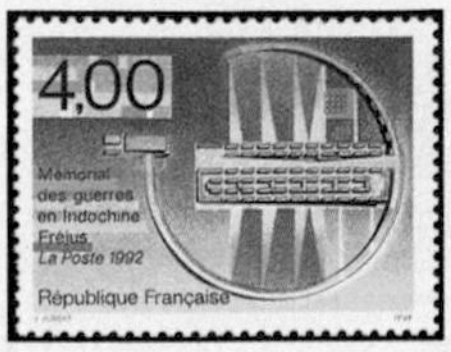

Memorial to Indochina War, Frejus
A1238

Litho. & Engr.

1993, Feb. 16 ***Perf. 13x13½***

2324	A1238 4fr multicolored	1.90	.60

Stamp Day — A1239

1993, Mar. 6 **Photo.** ***Perf. 13***

2325	A1239 2.50fr red & multi	1.75	1.00
2326	A1239 2.50fr +60c red & multi	1.40	.80
a.	Bklt. pane of 4 #2325, 3 #2326 + label	13.00	

Mediterranean Youth Games, Agde — A1240

1993, Mar. 13 **Photo.** ***Perf. 13***

2327	A1240 2.50fr multicolored	1.10	.20

Human Rights, Intl. Mixed Masonic Order, Cent. — A1241

1993, Apr. 3 **Engr.** ***Perf. 13***

2328	A1241 3.40fr blue & black	1.60	.50

Contemporary Art — A1242

Europa: 2.50fr, Painting, Rouge Rythme Bleu, by Olivier Debre. 3.40fr, Sculpture, Le Griffu, by Germaine Richier, vert.

Perf. 13x12½, 12½x13

1993, Apr. 17 **Litho.**

2329	A1242 2.50fr multicolored	1.10	.35
2330	A1242 3.40fr multicolored	1.60	.80

Marianne Type of 1990

1993-96 **Engr.** ***Perf. 13***

2333	A1161 2fr blue	1.75	.20
2334	A1161 2.40fr emerald	1.40	.20
2335	A1161 2.70fr emerald	1.60	.25
2336	A1161 3.50fr apple green	1.75	.30
2337	A1161 3.80fr blue	1.90	.50
2338	A1161 4.40fr blue	2.25	.40
2339	A1161 4.50fr mag	2.25	.40
2340	A1161 (2.50fr) red	1.25	.20
	Nos. 2333-2340 (8)	14.15	2.45

Perf. 13 Horiz.

Coil Stamps

2341	A1161	2.40fr emerald	1.40	.60
2342	A1161	2.70fr emerald	3.00	.20
2343	A1161	(2.80fr) red	1.75	.20

Self-Adhesive

Die Cut

2344	A1161	70c brown	13.00	12.00

Serpentine Die Cut Vert.

2345	A1161	70c brown	13.00	10.00
2346	A1161	1fr orange	7.00	2.50
a.		Booklet pane, 3 #2348, 1 #2346	9.00	
		Complete bklt., 2 #2346a	20.00	

Die Cut

2347	A1161	(2.50fr) red	1.50	.20
a.		Booklet pane of 10 (see footnote)	16.00	
b.		Bklt. pane of 4 + label	6.00	
c.		Booklet pane, #2344, 3 #2347 + label	30.00	
d.		Booklet pane of 10 (see footnote)	15.00	

Serpentine Die Cut Vert.

2348	A1161	(2.80fr) red	1.25	.20
a.		Bklt. pane of 4 + label	5.00	
b.		Booklet pane of 10 (see footnote)	13.00	
c.		Booklet pane, #2345, 3 #2348 + label	18.00	
d.		Booklet pane of 10 (see footnote)	13.00	
e.		Booklet pane of 10 (see footnote)	13.00	
f.		Booklet pane of 10 (see footnote)	—	

Nos. 2340, 2347 pay postage for the first class letter rate and sold for 2.50fr when first released. They have no denomination or letter inscription. Nos. 2343 and 2348 had a face value of 2.80fr when released.

No. 2347a has all stamps adjoining and has selvage covering backing paper (booklet cover), No. 2347d is comprised of two strips of 5 stamps each with yellow backing paper showing.

No. 2348b has the same format as No. 2347a. No. 2348d has a format similar to No. 2347d except there is a narrow selvage strip between the left six stamps and the right four stamps. No. 2348e is like No. 2348f but lacks the selvage strip. No. 2348f has a format similar to No. 2347a except it has a wide selvage strip between the left four stamps and the right six stamps.

Backing paper of Nos. 2347b and 2347c may have cuts along fold and were sold in a booklet for 20fr.

Issued: #2340, 2347, 4/19/93; 70c, July; 2fr, 7/31/94; #2341-2343, 4/1/94; #2345, 2348, 2/14/94; 1fr, 2.70fr, 3.80fr, 4.50fr, 3/18/96.

Tourism Series

Chinon — A1243

Illustration reduced.

Village of Minerve — A1244

Chaise-Dieu Abbey — A1245

Montbeliard — A1246

1993, Apr. 24	**Engr.**	*Perf. 13x12½*		
2355 A1243	4.20fr dk grn, ol grn & brn		2.00	.80

1993, July 17		*Perf. 13*		
2356 A1244	4.20fr red brown & yel grn		2.00	.50

1993

2357 A1245	2.80fr multicolored	1.25	.35
2358 A1246	4.40fr multicolored	2.00	.60
	Nos. 2355-2358 (4)	7.25	2.25

Issued: #2357, Sept. 4; #2358, Sept. 11.

Ninth European Conference on Protection of Human Rights — A1247

1993, May 8	**Engr.**	*Perf. 12½x13*	
2359 A1247	2.50fr multicolored	1.10	.30

Django Reinhardt (1910-1953), Musician — A1248

1993, May 14	**Litho.**	*Perf. 13*	
2360 A1248	4.20fr multicolored	1.90	.60

Louise Weiss (1893-1983), Suffragist — A1249

1993, May 15	**Engr.**	*Perf. 13x12½*	
2361 A1249	2.50fr blk, buff & red	1.10	.35

Philatelic Society Congress, Lille A1250

1993, May 29	**Engr.**	*Perf. 13x12½*	
2362 A1250	2.50fr bl, dk bl & lil	1.10	.45

Natural History Museum, Bicent. A1251

Litho. & Engr.

1993, June 5		*Perf. 13*	
2363 A1251	2.50fr multicolored	1.10	.30

Martyrs and Heroes of the Resistance — A1252

1993, June 18	**Photo.**	*Perf. 13*	
2364	2.50fr red, black & gray	1.10	.60
2365	4.20fr red, black & gray	1.90	1.00
a.	A1252 Pair, #2364-2365	3.00	2.50

A1254

A1255

1993, July 10	**Engr.**	*Perf. 13x12½*	
2366 A1254	2.50fr multicolored	1.10	.30

Claude Chappe's Semaphore Telegraph, bicent.

1993, July 10	**Engr.**	*Perf. 12½x13*	
2367 A1255	3.40fr bl, grn & red	1.60	.75

Train to Lake Artouste, Laruns, highest train ride in Europe.

Musical Instruments Type of 1989

1993, July 1	**Litho.**	*Perf. 13*		
2368 A1154	1.82fr	like #2171	.85	.40
2369 A1154	2.34fr	like #2235	1.10	.75
2370 A1154	3.86fr	like #2236	1.75	1.00
2371 A1154	5.93fr	like #2281	2.75	2.00
	Nos. 2368-2371 (4)		6.45	4.15

Nos. 2368-2371 are known only precanceled. See note after No. 132.

Liberation of Corsica, 50th Anniv. — A1256

1993, Sept. 9	**Engr.**	*Perf. 13*	
2372 A1256	2.80fr lake, bl & blk	1.25	.30

Saint Thomas, by Georges de la Tour (1593-1652) — A1257

1993, Sept. 9	**Photo.**	*Perf. 12½x13*	
2373 A1257	5fr multicolored	2.25	1.00

Service as Military Hospital of Val de Grace Monastery, Bicent. — A1258

1993, Sept. 25	**Engr.**	*Perf. 13*	
2374 A1258	3.70fr multicolored	1.75	.35

Whitbread Trans-Global Race Type

1993, Sept. 27	**Engr.**	*Perf. 12*	
2375 A1236	2.80fr multicolored	1.25	.40

The Muses, by Maurice Denis (1870-1943) — A1259

1993, Oct. 2	**Photo.**	*Perf. 12½x13*	
2376 A1259	5fr multicolored	2.25	1.00

The Clowns, by Albert Gleizes (1881-1953) A1260

1993, Oct. 2	**Photo.**	*Perf. 13½x12½*	
2377 A1260	2.80fr multicolored	1.25	.30

Natl. Circus Center, Chalons-sur-Marne.

Clock Tower Bellringer Statues of Lambesc — A1261

1993, Oct. 9	**Engr.**	*Perf. 13x12½*	
2378 A1261	4.40fr multicolored	2.00	.70

European Contemporary Art Type

Designs: No. 2379, Abstract, by Takis. No. 2380, Abstract, by Maria Helena Vieira da Silva. No. 2381, Abstract Squares, by Sean Scully. No. 2382, Abstract, by Georg Baselitz, Germany.

1993-94	**Photo.**	*Perf. 13x12½*		
2379 A1234	5fr	blk & ver	2.25	1.00
2380 A1234	5fr	multicolored	2.25	1.00
2381 A1234	6.70fr	multicolored	3.00	1.00

Perf. 13

2382 A1234	6.70fr	multicolored	3.00	1.00
	Nos. 2379-2382 (4)		10.50	4.00

Issued: #2379, 10/9/93; #2380, 12/11/93; #2381, 1/29/94; #2382, 11/19/94.

Greetings A1266

Greeting, artist: #2383, Happy Birthday, Claire Wendling. #2384, Happy Birthday, Bernard Olivie. #2385, Happy Anniversary, Stephane Colman. #2386, Happy Anniversary, Guillaune Sorel. #2387, With Love, Jean-Michel Thiriet. #2388, Please Write, Etienne Davodeau. #2389, Congratulations, Johan de Moor. #2390, Good luck, "Mezzo." #2391, Best Wishes, Nicolas de Crecy. #2392, Best Wishes, Florence Magnin. #2393, Merry Christmas, Thierry Robin. #2394, Merry Christmas, Patrick Prugne.

1993, Oct. 21	**Photo.**	*Perf. 13½x13*	

Booklet Stamps

2383 A1266	2.80fr multicolored	1.25	.30
2384 A1266	2.80fr multicolored	1.25	.30
2385 A1266	2.80fr multicolored	1.25	.30

2386 A1266 2.80fr multicolored 1.25 .30
2387 A1266 2.80fr multicolored 1.25 .30
2388 A1266 2.80fr multicolored 1.25 .30
2389 A1266 2.80fr multicolored 1.25 .30
2390 A1266 2.80fr multicolored 1.25 .30
2391 A1266 2.80fr multicolored 1.25 .30
2392 A1266 2.80fr multicolored 1.25 .30
2393 A1266 2.80fr multicolored 1.25 .30
2394 A1266 2.80fr multicolored 1.25 .30
a. Bklt. pane, #2383-2394 12.50

Perf. 12½

2383a A1266 2.80fr 1.25 .30
2384a A1266 2.80fr 1.25 .30
2385a A1266 2.80fr 1.25 .30
2386a A1266 2.80fr 1.25 .30
2387a A1266 2.80fr 1.25 .30
2388a A1266 2.80fr 1.25 .30
2389a A1266 2.80fr 1.25 .30
2390a A1266 2.80fr 1.25 .30
2391a A1266 2.80fr 1.25 .30
2392a A1266 2.80fr 1.25 .30
2393a A1266 2.80fr 1.25 .30
2394b A1266 2.80fr 1.25 .30
c. Booklet pane of 12, #2383a-2393a, 2394b 14.00

Souvenir Sheet

European Stamp Exhibition, Salon du Timbre A1267

a, Rhododendrons. b, Flowers in park, Paris.

1993, Nov. 10 ***Perf. 13***
2395 A1267 2.40fr #a.-b.+ 2 labels 16.00 16.00
Sold for 15fr.

Louvre Museum, Bicent. A1268

1993, Nov. 20
2396 A1268 2.80fr Louvre, 1793 1.25 1.00
2397 A1268 4.40fr Louvre, 1993 2.00 1.25
a. Pair, #2396-2397 3.50 2.50

Glassware, 1901 — A1269

Cast Iron, c. 1900 — A1270

Furniture, c. 1902 — A1271

Stoneware, c. 1898 — A1272

Decorative arts by: No. 2398, Emile Galle (1846-1904). No. 2399, Hector Guimard (1867-1942). No. 2400, Louis Majorelle (1859-1926). No. 2401, Pierre-Adrien Dalpayrat (1844-1910).

Perf. 13½x12½

1994. Jan. 22 **Photo.**
2398 A1269 2.80fr multicolored 1.25 .35
2399 A1270 2.80fr multicolored 1.25 .35
2400 A1271 4.40fr multicolored 2.00 .65
2401 A1272 4.40fr multicolored 2.00 .65
Nos. 2398-2401 (4) 6.50 2.00

Stained Glass Window, St. Julian's Cathedral, Le Mans A1273

1994, Feb. 12 **Engr.** ***Perf. 12½x13***
2402 A1273 6.70fr multicolored 3.00 1.00

City of Bastia — A1274

1994, Feb. 19 ***Perf. 13x12½***
2403 A1274 4.40fr blue & brown 2.00 .30

Tourism Series

Argentat A1275

1994, June 18 **Engr.** ***Perf. 12x12½***
2404 A1275 4.40fr red brown & rose carmine 2.00 .60

European Parliamentary Elections — A1276

1994, Feb. 26 **Litho.** ***Perf. 13***
2405 A1276 2.80fr multicolored 1.25 .25

Laurent Mourguet (1769-1844), Creator of Puppet, Guignol — A1277

1994, Mar. 4 **Photo.** ***Perf. 13***
2406 A1277 2.80fr multicolored 1.25 .35

French Polytechnic Institute, Bicent. A1277a

1994, Mar. 11
2407 A1277a 2.80fr multicolored 1.25 .35

Stamp Day A1278

1994, Mar. 12 **Engr.** ***Perf. 13***
2408 A1278 2.80fr blue & red *5.00 2.25*
2409 A1278 2.80fr +60c blue & red *1.40 1.25*
a. Booklet pane of 4 #2408, 3 #2409 + 1 label *25.00*

No. 2408 issued only in booklets.

Swedish Ballet Costume — A1279

Banquet for Gustavus III at the Trianon, 1784, by Lafrensen — A1280

French-Swedish cultural relations: No. 2411, Tuxedo costume for Swedish ballet. No. 2412, Viking ships. No. 2413, Viking ship. No. 2415, Swedish, French flags.

1994, Mar. 18 **Engr.** ***Perf. 13***
2410 A1279 2.80fr multicolored 3.50 1.25
2411 A1279 2.80fr multicolored 3.50 1.25
2412 A1279 2.80fr multicolored 3.50 1.25
2413 A1279 2.80fr multicolored 3.50 1.25
2414 A1280 3.70fr multicolored 4.00 2.00
2415 A1280 3.70fr multicolored 4.00 2.00
a. Booklet pane of #2410-2415 25.00

See Sweden Nos. 2065-2070.

Pres. Georges Pompidou (1911-1974) A1281

1994, Apr. 9 **Engr.** ***Perf. 13***
2416 A1281 2.80fr olive brown 1.25 .30

Resistance of the Maquis, 50th Anniv. A1282

1994, Apr. 9
2417 A1282 2.80fr multicolored 1.25 .30

Philexjeunes '94, Grenoble — A1283

1994, Apr. 22 **Photo.**
2418 A1283 2.80fr multicolored 1.25 .30

Europa A1284

Discoveries: 2.80fr, AIDS virus, by scientists of Pasteur Institute. 3.70fr, Formula for wave properties of matter, developed by Louis de Broglie.

1994, Apr. 30 **Photo. & Engr.**
2419 A1284 2.80fr multicolored 1.25 .30
a. With label 1.25 .75
2420 A1284 3.70fr multicolored 1.75 .85

No. 2419a issued Dec. 1, 1994.

Opening of Channel Tunnel — A1285

Designs: Nos. 2421, 2423, British lion, French rooster, meeting over Channel. Nos. 2422, 2424, Joined hands above speeding train.

1994, May 3 **Photo.** ***Perf. 13***
2421 A1285 2.80fr dk blue & multi 1.25 .30
2422 A1285 2.80fr dk blue & multi 1.25 .30
a. Pair, #2421-2422 2.75 1.50
2423 A1285 4.30fr lt blue & multi 2.00 .90
2424 A1285 4.30fr multicolored 2.00 .90
a. Pair, #2423-2424 4.50 2.25
Nos. 2421-2424 (4) 6.50 2.40

See Great Britain Nos. 1558-1561.

Asian Development Bank, Board of Governors Meeting, Nice — A1286

1994, May 3 **Photo.** ***Perf. 13***
2425 A1286 2.80fr multicolored 1.25 .30

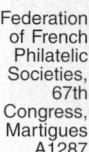

Federation of French Philatelic Societies, 67th Congress, Martigues A1287

1994, May 20 **Engr.** ***Perf. 12x12½***
2426 A1287 2.80fr multicolored 1.25 .30

Court of Cassation A1288

Litho. & Engr.

1994, June 3 ***Perf. 13***
2427 A1288 2.80fr multicolored 1.25 .30

D-Day, 50th Anniv. A1289

No. 2429, Tank, crowd waving Allied flags.

1994, June 4 **Engr.**
2428 A1289 4.30fr multicolored 2.00 .50
2429 A1289 4.30fr multicolored 2.00 .50

Liberation of Paris, 50th anniv. (#2429).

Mount St. Victoire, by Paul Cezanne (1839-1906) — A1290

1994, June 18 **Photo.** ***Perf. 13***
2430 A1290 2.80fr multicolored 1.25 .30

Intl. Olympic Committee, Cent. A1291

1994, June 23 **Litho.** ***Perf. 13***
2431 A1291 2.80fr multicolored 1.25 .25

Saulx River Bridge, Rupt aux Nonains A1292

1994, July 2 **Engr.**
2432 A1292 2.80fr blackish blue 1.25 .25

Organ, Poitiers Cathedral — A1293

1994, July 2 ***Perf. 13x12½***
2433 A1293 4.40fr multicolored 2.00 .55

Allied Landings in Provence, 50th Anniv. A1294

1994, Aug. 13 **Engr.** ***Perf. 13***
2434 A1294 2.80fr multicolored 1.25 .30

Moses and the Daughters of Jethro, by Nicolas Poussin (1594-1665) — A1295

Illustration reduced.

1994, Sept. 10
2435 A1295 4.40fr yel brn & blk 1.90 .90

Natl. Conservatory of Arts and Crafts, Bicent. — A1296

1994, Sept. 24 ***Perf. 13x12½***
2436 A1296 2.80fr Foucault's pendulum 1.25 .30

The Great Cascade, St. Cloud Park — A1297

1994, Sept. 24 ***Perf. 12½x13***
2437 A1297 3.70fr multicolored 1.75 .50

Leaves — A1298

1994 **Litho.** ***Perf. 13***
2438 A1298 1.91fr Oak .85 .40
2439 A1298 2.46fr Sycamore 1.10 .70
2440 A1298 4.24fr Chestnut 2.00 1.00
2441 A1298 6.51fr Holly 3.00 2.00
Nos. 2438-2441 (4) 6.95 4.10

Nos. 2438-2441 are known only precanceled. See second note after No. 132.
See Nos. 2517-2520.

Ecole Normale Superieure (Teachers' School), Bicent. — A1299

1994, Oct. 8 **Engr.** ***Perf. 13***
2442 A1299 2.80fr red & dk bl 1.25 .45

Georges Simenon (1903-89), Writer A1300

Litho. & Engr.

1994, Oct. 15 ***Perf. 13***
2443 A1300 2.80fr multicolored 1.25 .25

See Belgium No. 1567, Switzerland No. 948.

Souvenir Sheet

European Stamp Exhibition — A1301

a, Flowers in park, Paris. b, Dalhias, vert.

1994, Oct. 15 **Photo.** ***Perf. 13***
2444 A1301 2.80fr Sheet of 2, #a.-b. 15.00 15.00

No. 2444 sold for 16fr.

Natl. Drug Addiction Prevention Day — A1302

1994, Oct. 15
2445 A1302 2.80fr multicolored 1.25 .25

Grand Lodge of France, Cent. A1303

1994, Nov. 5 **Engr.**
2446 A1303 2.80fr multicolored 1.25 .25

Alain Colas (1943-78), Sailor A1304

1994, Nov. 19
2447 A1304 3.70fr green & black 1.75 .60

French Natl. Press Federation, 50th Anniv. A1305

1994, Dec. 9 **Photo.** ***Perf. 13***
2448 A1305 2.80fr multicolored 1.25 .30

Champs Elysees — A1306

Illustration reduced.

1994, Dec. 31
2449 A1306 4.40fr multicolored 2.00 .75

No. 2449 printed with se-tenant label.

Souvenir Sheet

Motion Pictures, Cent. — A1307

Faces on screen and: a, Projector at right. b, Projector facing away from screen. c, Projector facing screen. d, Reels of film.

1995, Jan. 14 **Photo.** ***Perf. 13***
2450 A1307 Sheet of 4 5.50 5.50
a.-d. 2.80fr any single 1.25 1.25

Normandy Bridge — A1308

Illustration reduced.

1995, Jan. 20 **Engr.** ***Perf. 13***
2451 A1308 4.40fr multicolored 2.00 .75

A1309

A1310

1995, Jan. 21 ***Perf. 13x12***
2452 A1309 2.80fr multicolored 1.25 .30

European Notaries Public.

1995, Feb. 18 **Photo.** ***Perf. 13***
2453 A1310 3.70fr multicolored 1.75 1.00

Louis Pasteur (1822-95).

Art Series

St. Taurin's Reliquary, Evreaux
A1311

Study for the Dream of Happiness, by Pierre Prud'hon (1758-1823) — A1312

Abstract, by Zao Wou-ki — A1313

Abstract, by Per Kirkeby, Denmark — A1314

1995 **Photo. & Engr.** ***Perf. 12x13***
2454 A1311 6.70fr multicolored 3.00 1.10

Engr.
Perf. 13x12
2455 A1312 6.70fr slate & blue 3.00 1.10

Litho.
Perf. 14
2456 A1313 6.70fr multicolored 3.00 1.10

Photo.
Perf. 13
2457 A1314 6.70fr multicolored 3.00 1.10
Nos. 2454-2457 (4) 12.00 4.40

Issued: #2454, 2/25/95; #2455, 5/12/95; #2456, 6/10/95; #2457, 9/23/95.

Tourism Series

Stenay Malt Works
A1315

Remiremont, Vosges — A1316

Nyons Bridge, Drome
A1317

Barbizon, Home of Landscape Artists
A1318

1995, Feb. 25 **Engr.** ***Perf. 13x12½***
2458 A1315 2.80fr ol & dk grn 1.25 .30
2459 A1316 2.80fr brn, grn & bl 1.25 .30

Perf. 12½x13
2460 A1317 4.40fr multicolored 2.00 .75

Photo.
Perf. 13½
2461 A1318 4.40fr multicolored 2.00 .75
Nos. 2458-2461 (4) 6.50 2.10

Issued: #2458, 2/25/95; #2459, 5/13/95; #2460, 5/20/95; #2461, 9/30/95.

A1319

John J. Audubon (1785-1851)
A1320

Designs: No. 2462, Snowy egret. No. 2463, Band-tailed pigeon. 4.30fr, Common tern. 4.40fr, Brown-colored rough-legged buzzard.

1995, Feb. 25 **Photo.** ***Perf. 12½x12***
2462 A1319 2.80fr multicolored 1.25 .40
2463 A1320 2.80fr multicolored 1.25 .40
2464 A1319 4.30fr multicolored 2.00 .75
2465 A1320 4.40fr multicolored 2.00 .75
a. Souvenir sheet of 4, #2462-2465, perf. 13 7.00 7.00
Nos. 2462-2465 (4) 6.50 2.30

Stamp Day
A1321

1995, Mar. 4 **Engr.** ***Perf. 13***
2466 A1321 2.80fr multicolored 6.00 3.00
2467 A1321 2.80fr +60c multi 1.60 1.40
a. Booklet pane, 4 #2466, 3 #2467+label 29.00
Complete booklet, #2467 30.00

No. 2466 issued only in booklets.

Work Councils, 50th Anniv. — A1322

1995, Mar. 7 **Engr.** ***Perf. 13***
2468 A1322 2.80fr dk bl, brn & sky bl 1.25 .30

Advanced Institute of Electricity, Cent.
A1323

1995, Mar. 11 **Photo.**
2469 A1323 3.70fr multicolored 1.75 .40

Institute of Oriental Languages, Bicent.
A1324

1995, Mar. 25 **Photo.** ***Perf. 13***
2470 A1324 2.80fr multicolored 1.25 .30

Jean Giono (1895-1970), Writer — A1325

1995, Mar. 25 **Engr.**
2471 A1325 3.70fr multicolored 1.75 1.00

Iron and Steel Industry in Lorraine — A1326

1995, Apr. 1 ***Perf. 13x12***
2472 A1326 2.80fr multicolored 1.25 .30

End of World War II, 50th Anniv.
A1327

Europa: 2.80fr, Barbed wire, laurel wreath. 3.70fr, Broken sword, emblem of European Union.

1995, Apr. 29 **Photo.** ***Perf. 13***
2473 A1327 2.80fr multicolored 1.25 .30
2474 A1327 3.70fr multicolored 1.75 .75

Forestry Profession, Ardennes — A1328

1995, May 2 **Engr.** ***Perf. 12½x13***
2475 A1328 4.40fr multicolored 2.00 .80

End of World War II, 50th Anniv.
A1329

1995, May 8 **Photo.** ***Perf. 13***
2476 A1329 2.80fr multicolored 1.25 .35

Natl. Assembly — A1330

1995, May 13 **Photo.** ***Perf. 13x12½***
2477 A1330 2.80fr multicolored 1.25 .60

French's People's Relief Assoc., 50th Anniv.
A1331

1995, May 20 **Engr.** ***Perf. 12½x13***
2478 A1331 2.80fr multicolored 1.25 .30

Scenes of France — A1332

#2479, Forest, Vosges. #2480, Massif, Brittany. #2481, Wetlands, cattle, Camargue. #2482, Volcanoes, Auvergne.

1995, May 27 ***Perf. 13***
2479 A1332 2.40fr green 1.10 .25
2480 A1332 2.40fr green 1.10 .25
2481 A1332 2.80fr red 1.25 .30
2482 A1332 2.80fr red 1.25 .30
Nos. 2479-2482 (4) 4.70 1.10

Ariane Rocket on Launch Pad, French Guiana — A1333

1995, June 1 **Engr.** ***Perf. 12½x13***
2483 A1333 2.80fr bl, grn & red 1.25 .30

Compare with No. 2254.

A1334

A1335

1995, June 2 **Engr.** ***Perf. 13***
2484 A1334 2.80fr multicolored 1.25 .30

68th Congress of French Federation of Philatelic Organizations, Orleans.

1995, June 3
2485 A1335 4.40fr Town of Correze 2.00 .75

A1336 A1337

Fables of Jean de la Fontaine (1621-95): No. 2486, The Grasshopper and The Ant. No. 2487, The Frog Who Could Make Himself Larger than an Ox. No. 2488, The Wolf and the Lamb. No. 2489, The Crow and the Fox. No. 2490, The Cat, the Weasel, and the Small Rabbit. No. 2491, The Tortoise and the Hare.

1995, June 24 Photo. *Perf. 13*

2486	A1336	2.80fr	multicolored	1.40	.75
2487	A1336	2.80fr	multicolored	1.40	.75
2488	A1336	2.80fr	multicolored	1.40	.75
2489	A1336	2.80fr	multicolored	1.40	.75
2490	A1336	2.80fr	multicolored	1.40	.75
2491	A1336	2.80fr	multicolored	1.40	.75
a.	Strip, #2486-2491 + 2 labels			9.00	8.00

1995, July 9 Photo. *Perf. 13*

2492 A1337 2.80fr multicolored 1.25 .30

Velodrome d'Hiver raid.

André Maginot (1877-1932), Creator of Maginot Line — A1338

1995, Sept. 9 Engr. *Perf. 13*

2493 A1338 2.80fr multicolored 1.25 .30

Women's Grand Masonic Lodge of France, 50th Anniv. — A1339

1995, Sept. 16 *Perf. 13x12½*

2494 A1339 2.80fr multicolored 1.25 .30

Hospital Pharmacies, 500th Anniv. — A1340

1995, Sept. 23 *Perf. 12½x13*

2495 A1340 2.80fr multicolored 1.25 .30

Natl. School of Administration, 50th Anniv. — A1341

1995, Oct. 5 Photo. *Perf. 13*

2496 A1341 2.80fr multicolored 1.25 .30

The Cradle, by Berthe Morisot (1841-95) A1342

1995, Oct. 7 Litho. *Perf. 13½x14*

2497 A1342 6.70fr multicolored 3.00 1.00

The French Institute, Bicent. — A1343

1995, Oct. 14 Engr. *Perf. 12½x13*

2498 A1343 2.80fr blk, grn & red 1.25 .30

Automobile Club of France, Cent. A1344

1995, Nov. 4 Engr. *Perf. 13x12½*

2499 A1344 4.40fr blk, bl & red 2.00 .60

UN, 50th Anniv. A1345

1995, Nov. 16 Photo. *Perf. 13*

2500 A1345 4.30fr multicolored 2.00 1.00

Francis Jammes (1868-1938), Poet — A1346

1995, Dec. 2 Engr. *Perf. 13*

2501 A1346 3.70fr black & blue 1.75 1.00

A1347

A1348

1995, Dec. 9 Litho. & Engr.

2502 A1347 2.80fr Evry Cathedral 1.25 .30

1995, Dec. 12 Photo. *Perf. 13*

2503 A1348 2.80fr multicolored 1.25 .30

1998 World Cup Soccer Championships, France.

Art Series

Abstract, by Lucien Wercollier — A1349

Design: No. 2505, The Netherlands (Horizon), abstract photograph, by Jan Dibbets.

1996 *Perf. 13x12½*

2504	A1349	6.70fr	multicolored	3.00	1.00
2505	A1349	6.70fr	multicolored	3.00	1.00

Issued: #2504, 1/20; #2505, 2/10.

Arawak Civilization, Saint Martin — A1350

Design: 2.80fr, Dog figurine, 550 B.C.

1996, Feb. 10 Engr. *Perf. 13*

2506 A1350 2.80fr multicolored 1.25 .40

The Augustus Bridge over the Nera River, by Camille Corot (1796-1875) — A1351

1996, Mar. 2 Litho. *Perf. 13*

2507 A1351 6.70fr multicolored 3.00 1.00

St. Patrick A1352

1996, Mar. 16 Photo. *Perf. 13*

2508 A1352 2.80fr multicolored 1.25 .50

The Sower, 1903 — A1353

1996, Mar. 16 Litho. & Engr.

2509	A1353	2.80fr	multicolored	6.00	5.00
2510	A1353	2.80fr +60c	multi	1.75	1.25
a.	Booklet pane, 4 #2509, 3 #2510 + label			30.00	
	Complete booklet, #2510a			32.50	

Stamp Day.

Jacques Rueff (1896-1978), Economist — A1354

1996, Mar. 23 Engr. *Perf. 13x12½*

2511 A1354 2.80fr multicolored 1.25 .50

René Descartes (1596-1650) A1355

1996, Mar. 30 Engr. *Perf. 12½x13*

2512 A1355 4.40fr red 2.00 1.00

Gas & Electric Industries, 50th Anniv. A1356

1996, Apr. 6 Photo. *Perf. 13*

2513 A1356 3fr multicolored 1.40 .35

Natl. Parks A1357

1996, Apr. 20

2514	A1357	3fr	Cévennes	1.40	.60
2515	A1357	4.40fr	Vanoise	2.00	1.00
2516	A1357	4.40fr	Mercantour	2.00	1.25
	Nos. 2514-2516 (3)			5.40	2.85

See Nos. 2569-2572.

Leaf Type of 1994

1996, Mar. Litho. *Perf. 13*

2517	A1298	1.87fr	Ash	.85	.30
2518	A1298	2.18fr	Beech	1.00	.65
2519	A1298	4.66fr	Walnut	2.10	1.25
2520	A1298	7.11fr	Elm	3.25	2.00
	Nos. 2517-2520 (4)			7.20	4.20

Nos. 2517-2520 are known only precanceled. Values for precanceled stamps in first column are for those which have not been through the post and have original gum. Values in second column are for postally used, gumless stamps.

Madame Marie de Sévigné (1626-96), Writer — A1358

1996, Apr. 27 **Photo.** ***Perf. 13***
2521 A1358 3fr multicolored 1.40 .65

Europa.

Natl. Institute of Agronomy Research, 50th Anniv. A1359

1996, May 4 **Photo.** ***Perf. 13***
2522 A1359 3.80fr multicolored 1.75 1.00

Joan of Arc's House, Domremy-La-Pucelle — A1360

1996, May 11
2523 A1360 4.50fr multicolored 2.10 .70

RAMOGE Agreement Between France, Italy, Monaco, 20th Anniv. A1361

1996, May 14 **Photo. & Engr.**
2524 A1361 3fr multicolored 1.40 .35

See Monaco No. 1998, Italy No. 2077.

69th Congress of Federation of Philatelic Assoc., Clermont-Ferrand — A1362

1996, May 24 **Engr.** ***Perf. 13***
2525 A1362 3fr brn, red & grn 1.40 .35

Tourism Series

Bitche, Moselle A1363

Iles Sanguinaires, Ajaccio, Southern Corsica — A1364

Thoronet Abbey, Var A1365

Chambéry Cathedral, Savoie A1366

1996 **Engr.** ***Perf. 12½x13***
2526 A1363 3fr multicolored 1.40 .35
2527 A1364 3fr multicolored 1.40 .35

Perf. 13x12½
2528 A1365 3.80fr brn & claret 1.75 .70

Photo.
Perf. 13
2529 A1366 4.50fr multicolored 2.10 .75

Issued: #2526, 5/25/96; #2527, 6/1/96; 3.80fr, 7/6/96; 4.50fr, 6/8/96.

1998 World Cup Soccer Championships, France — A1367

Various stylized soccer plays, name of host city in France.

1996, June 1 **Photo.** ***Perf. 13***
2530 A1367 3fr Lens 1.40 .35
2531 A1367 3fr Toulouse 1.40 .35
2532 A1367 3fr Saint-Etienne 1.40 .35
2533 A1367 3fr Montpellier 1.40 .35
Nos. 2530-2533 (4) 5.60 1.40

See Nos. 2584-2587, 2623-2624, sheet of 10, #2624a.

Art Series

Gallo-Roman Bronze Statue of Horse, Neuvy-en-Sullias, Loiret — A1368

Imprints of Cello Fragments, by Arman — A1369

1996 **Engr.** ***Perf. 13***
2534 A1368 6.70fr multicolored 3.00 1.00

Photo.
2535 A1369 6.70fr multicolored 3.00 1.00

Issued: #2534, 6/8/96; #2535, 9/21/96.

A1371

A1372

1996, June 15 **Photo.** ***Perf. 13***
2537 A1371 3fr multicolored 1.40 .50

Modern Olympic Games, cent.

1996, June 15 **Engr.** ***Perf. 12½x13***
2538 A1372 4.40fr deep purple 2.00 1.00

Jacques Marette (1922-84), Member of Parliament.

A1373

A1374

1996, June 29 **Photo.** ***Perf. 13***
2539 A1373 3fr multicolored 1.40 .35

Train between Ajaccio and Vizzavona, cent.

1996, Sept. 6 **Engr.** ***Perf. 13x12½***
2540 A1374 3fr dark blue & yel 1.40 .30

Notre Dame de Fourvière Basilica, Lyon, cent.

Baptism of Clovis, 1500th Anniv. A1375

1996, Sept. 14 ***Perf. 13***
2541 A1375 3fr multicolored 1.40 .30

Henri IV High School, Bicent. — A1376

1996, Oct. 12 **Engr.** ***Perf. 12½x13***
2542 A1376 4.50fr brown & blue 2.10 .80

UNICEF, 50th Anniv. A1377

1996, Oct. 19 **Photo.** ***Perf. 13***
2543 A1377 4.50fr multicolored 2.10 .80

Economic and Social Council, 50th Anniv. — A1378

1996, Oct. 26 **Engr.** ***Perf. 13***
2544 A1378 3fr red, black & blue 1.40 .30

UNESCO, 50th Anniv. A1379

1996, Nov. 2 **Litho.** ***Perf. 13***
2545 A1379 3.80fr multicolored 1.75 .75

A1380

A1381

1996, Nov. 7 **Photo.** ***Perf. 13***
2546 A1380 3fr multicolored 1.40 .30

Autumn Stamp Show, 50th anniv.

1996, Nov. 16
2547 A1381 3fr multicolored 1.40 .30

Creation of French Overseas Departments, 50th anniv.

André Malraux (1901-76), Writer A1382

1996, Nov. 23 **Engr.** ***Perf. 13***
2548 A1382 3fr deep green black 1.40 .30

French School in Athens, 150th Anniv. A1383

1996, Nov. 23 **Photo.**
2549 A1383 3fr multicolored 1.40 .30

Cannes Film Festival, 50th Anniv. A1384

1996, Nov. 30
2550 A1384 3fr multicolored 1.40 .30

New National Library of France A1385

1996, Dec. 14
2551 A1385 3fr multicolored 1.40 .30

A1386 A1387

1997, Jan. 4

2552	A1386	3fr	multicolored	1.40	.30

Francois Mitterrand (1916-96).

1997, Jan. 24 Photo. *Perf. 13*

2553	A1387	3fr	multicolored	1.40	.30

Participatory innovation.

Georges Pompidou Natl. Center of Art and Culture, 20th Anniv. A1388

1997, Jan. 31 Engr. *Perf. 12½x13*

2554	A1388	3fr	multicolored	1.40	.30

Happy Holiday A1389

1997, Feb. 8 Photo. *Perf. 13*

2555	A1389	3fr	shown	1.40	.30
2556	A1389	3fr	Happy birthday	1.40	.30

Natl. School of Bridges and Highways, 250th Anniv. A1390

Photo. & Engr.

1997, Feb. 14 *Perf. 12½x13*

2557	A1390	3fr	multicolored	1.40	.30

Saint-Laurent-du-Maroni, French Guiana — A1391

Photo. & Engr.

1997, Feb. 22 *Perf. 12½x13*

2558	A1391	3fr	multicolored	1.40	.30

Art Series

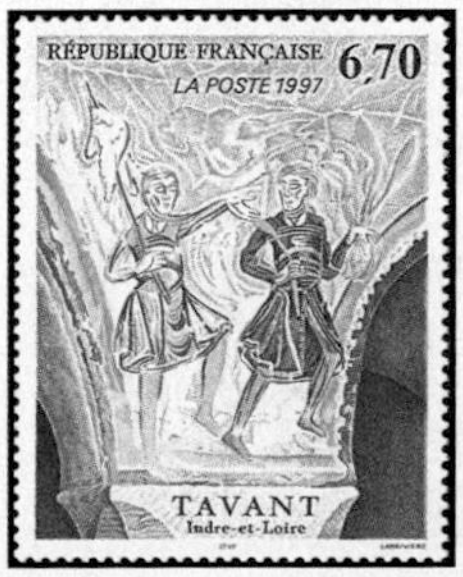

Church Fresco, Tavant A1392

Painting by Bernard Moninot — A1393

The Thumb, Polished Bronze, by César A1394

Grapes and Pomegranates, by Jean Baptiste Chardin — A1395

1997 Engr. *Perf. 13*

2559	A1392	6.70fr	multicolored	3.00	1.00

Photo.

2560	A1393	6.70fr	multicolored	3.00	1.00
2561	A1394	6.70fr	multicolored	3.00	1.00
2562	A1395	6.70fr	multicolored	3.00	1.00
	Nos. 2559-2562 (4)			12.00	4.00

Issued: #2559, 3/1; #2560, 3/29; #2561, 9/13; #2562, 9/27.

Tourism Series

Millau — A1396

Guimiliau Church Close — A1398

Fresco, Saint Eutrope des Salles-Lavauguyon — A1397

Sablé-Sur-Sarthe — A1399

1997 Engr. *Perf. 12½x13*

2563	A1396	3fr	grn & dk bl grn	1.40	.30

Perf. 13

2564	A1397	4.50fr	multicolored	2.10	.75
2565	A1398	3fr	multicolored	1.40	.30

Perf. 12½x13

2566	A1399	3fr	multicolored	1.40	.20
	Nos. 2563-2566 (4)			6.30	1.55

Issued: #2563, 3/15; #2564, 6/14; #2565, 7/12; #2566, 9/20.

Vignette of Type A17 — A1400

Litho. & Engr.

1997, Mar. 15 *Perf. 13½x13*

2567	A1400	3fr	multicolored	6.00	5.00
2568	A1400	3fr +60c	multi	2.50	2.00
a.			Booklet pane, 4 #2567, 3 #2568 + label	32.50	
			Complete booklet, #2568a	35.00	

Stamp Day.
No. 2567 issued only in booklets.

National Parks Type of 1996

1997, Apr. 12 Photo. *Perf. 13*

2569	A1357	3fr	Parc des Ecrins	1.40	.40
2570	A1357	3fr	Guadeloupe Park	1.40	.40
2571	A1357	4.50fr	Parc des Pyrénées	2.10	.90
2572	A1357	4.50fr	Port-Cros Park	2.10	.90
	Nos. 2569-2572 (4)			7.00	2.60

Puss-in-Boots A1401

1997, Apr. 26 Engr. *Perf. 13*

2573	A1401	3fr	blue	1.40	.30

Europa.

Philexjeunes '97, Nantes — A1402

1997, May 2 Litho. *Perf. 13*

2574	A1402	3fr	multicolored	1.40	.30

Cartoon Journey of a Letter A1403

"Envelope": No. 2575, Writing letter. No. 2576, Climbing ladder to go into letter box. No. 2577, On wheels. No. 2578, Following postman carrying another "Envelope." No. 2579, Held by girl. No. 2580, At feet of girl reading long letter.

1997, May 8 Photo. *Perf. 13*

2575	A1403	3fr	multicolored	2.50	1.00
2576	A1403	3fr	multicolored	2.50	1.00
2577	A1403	3fr	multicolored	2.50	1.00
2578	A1403	3fr	multicolored	2.50	1.00
2579	A1403	3fr	multicolored	2.50	1.00
2580	A1403	3fr	multicolored	2.50	1.00
a.			Strip of 6, #2575-2580 + label	18.00	12.00

Self-Adhesive

Serpentine Die Cut 11

2580B	A1403	3fr	like #2575	2.00	1.25
2580C	A1403	3fr	like #2576	2.00	1.25
2580D	A1403	3fr	like #2577	2.00	1.25
2580E	A1403	3fr	like #2578	2.00	1.25
2580F	A1403	3fr	like #2579	2.00	1.25
2580G	A1403	3fr	like #2580	2.00	1.25
h.			Booklet pane, 2 each #2580B-2580G	27.50	27.50

By its nature No. 2580h is a complete booklet. The peelable paper backing serves as a booklet cover.

See Nos. 2648-2659.

Honoring French Soldiers in North Africa (1952-62) A1404

1997, May 10 Litho. *Perf. 13*

2581	A1404	3fr	multicolored	1.40	.30

French Federation of Philatelic Associations, 70th Congress, Versailles — A1405

Illustration reduced.

1997, May 17 Photo. *Perf. 13*

2582	A1405	3fr	multicolored	1.40	.30

Printed with se-tenant label.

Château de Plessis-Bourré, Maine and Loire Rivers — A1406

1997, May 24 Litho. & Engr.

2583	A1406	4.40fr	multicolored	2.00	1.00

1998 World Cup Soccer Championships Type

Stylized action scenes, name of host city in France.

1997, May 31 Photo. *Perf. 13½*

2584	A1367	3fr	Lyon	1.40	.35
2585	A1367	3fr	Marseilles	1.40	.35
2586	A1367	3fr	Nantes	1.40	.35
2587	A1367	3fr	Paris	1.40	.35
	Nos. 2584-2587 (4)			5.60	1.40

Saint Martin of Tours (316-97) Apostle of the Gauls A1408

1997, July 5 Engr. *Perf. 13*

2588	A1408	4.50fr	multicolored	2.00	.65

Marianne — A1409

1997, July 14 Engr. *Perf. 13*

2589	A1409	10c	brown	.20	.20
2590	A1409	20c	brt blue grn	.20	.20
2591	A1409	50c	purple	.25	.20
2592	A1409	1fr	bright org	.45	.20
2593	A1409	2fr	bright blue	.90	.30
2594	A1409	2.70fr	bright grn	1.25	.20
2595	A1409	(3fr)	red	1.40	.25
2596	A1409	3.50fr	apple grn	1.60	.25
2597	A1409	3.80fr	blue	1.75	.25
2598	A1409	4.20fr	dark org	1.90	.30
2599	A1409	4.40fr	blue	2.00	.30
2600	A1409	4.50fr	bright pink	2.10	.30
2601	A1409	5fr	brt grn blue	5.25	.30

2602 A1409 6.70fr dark green 3.00 .30
 a. Souvenir sheet, #2594-2600, 2602 14.00 14.00
2603 A1409 10fr violet 4.50 .35
 a. Souvenir sheet, #2589-2593, 2601, 2603 12.00 12.00
Nos. 2589-2603 (15) 26.75 3.90

Self-Adhesive
Booklet Stamps
Die Cut x Serpentine Die Cut 7

2603B A1409 1fr brt org 2.25 .50
 c. Booklet pane, #2603B, 3 #2604 7.75
 Booklet, 2 #2603Bc 16.00
2604 A1409 (3fr) red 1.40 .25
 a. Booklet pane of 10 14.00

Coil Stamps
Perf. 13 Horiz.

2604B A1409 2.70fr bright grn 1.25 .50
2605 A1409 (3fr) red 1.40 .30

Nos. 2595, 2604-2605 were valued at 3fr on day of issue.

Issued: Nos. 2602a, 2603a, 11/12/01. No. 2603B, 9/1/97.

See Nos. 2835-2835C, 2921-2922.

1997 World Rowing Championships, Savoie — A1410

1997, Aug. 30 Engr. ***Perf. 13x12½***
2606 A1410 3fr blue & magenta 1.40 .30

Basque Corsairs A1411

1997, Sept. 13 ***Perf. 13***
2607 A1411 3fr multicolored 1.40 .30

Saint-Maurice Basilica, Epinal — A1412

1997, Sept. 20 ***Perf. 13x12½***
2608 A1412 3fr multicolored 1.40 .30

Fresh Fish Merchants, Port of Boulogne A1413

1997, Sept. 26 ***Perf. 13***
2609 A1413 3fr multicolored 1.40 .30

Japan Year — A1414

1997, Oct. 4 Engr. ***Perf. 13***
2610 A1414 4.90fr multicolored 2.25 1.25

1997 World Judo Championships — A1415

1997, Oct. 9 Photo. ***Perf. 13***
2611 A1415 3fr multicolored 1.40 .35

Sceaux Estate, Hauts-de-Seine — A1416

1997, Oct. 11
2612 A1416 3fr multicolored 1.40 .30

Saar-Lorraine-Luxembourg Summit — A1417

1997, Oct. 16 Photo. ***Perf. 13***
2613 A1417 3fr multicolored 1.40 .30

See Germany #1982, Luxembourg #972.

College of France A1418

1997, Oct. 18 Engr.
2614 A1418 4.40fr multicolored 2.00 .90

Quality — A1419

1997, Oct. 18 Photo.
2615 A1419 4.50fr multicolored 2.10 .60

A1420

Season's Greetings A1421

1997 Photo. ***Perf. 13***
2616 A1420 3fr Cat & mouse 1.40 .30

Photo. & Embossed
2617 A1421 3fr Mailman 1.40 .30

Issued: No. 2616, 11/8; No. 2617, 11/22.

Protection of Abused Children — A1422

1997, Nov. 20 Photo.
2618 A1422 3fr multicolored 1.40 .30

Marshal Jacques Leclerc (Philippe de Haute Cloque) (1902-47) A1423

1997, Nov. 28 Photo. ***Perf. 13***
2619 A1423 3fr multicolored 1.40 .30

Philexfrance '99, World Stamp Exposition — A1424

1997, Dec. 6 Engr.
2620 A1424 3fr red & blue 1.40 .30

Abbey of Moutier D'Ahun, Creuse A1425

1997, Dec. 13
2621 A1425 4.40fr multicolored 2.00 1.00

Michel Debré (1912-96), Politician A1426

1998, Jan. 15 Photo.
2622 A1426 3fr multicolored 1.40 .30

1998 World Cup Soccer Championships Type

Stylized action scenes, name of host city in France.

1998, Jan. 24 ***Perf. 13½***
2623 A1367 3fr Saint-Denis 1.40 .30
2624 A1367 3fr Bordeaux 1.40 .30
 a. Sheet of 10, #2530-2533, #2584-2587, #2623-2624 + label 14.00 14.00

National Assembly, Bicent. — A1427

1998, Jan. 24 ***Perf. 13***
2625 A1427 3fr multicolored 1.40 .30

Valentine's Day A1428

1998, Jan. 31
2626 A1428 3fr multicolored 1.40 .30

Office of Mediator of the Republic, 25th Anniv. A1429

1998, Feb. 5
2627 A1429 3fr multicolored 1.40 .30

A1430

1998, Feb. 28 Photo. ***Perf. 12½***
2628 A1430 3fr multicolored 1.40 .30

Self-Adhesive
Serpentine Die Cut

2629 A1430 3fr like #2628 1.40 .30
 a. Booklet pane of 10 14.00 14.00
 b. Sheet of 1 + 7 labels 14.00 14.00

1998 World Cup Soccer Championships, France.

The peelable paper backing of No. 2629a serves as a booklet cover.

See No. 2665.

A1431

1998, Feb. 21 Engr. ***Perf. 13½x13***
2630 A1431 3fr Detail of design A16 6.50 4.50
2631 A1431 3fr +60c like #2630 2.50 2.50
 a. Booklet pane, 4 #2630, 3 #2631 + label 34.00
 Complete booklet, #2631a 35.00

Stamp Day. No. 2630 issued only in booklets.

A1432

1998, Feb. 28 Engr. ***Perf. 13***
2632 A1432 4.50fr blue 2.10 .75

Father Franz Stock (1904-48), prison chaplain.

Happy Birthday A1433

1998, Mar. 13 Photo. ***Perf. 13x13½***
2633 A1433 3fr multicolored 1.40 .30

Union of Mulhouse with France, Bicent. A1434

1998, Mar. 14
2634 A1434 3fr multicolored 1.40 .30

Citeaux Abbey, 900th Anniv. A1435

1998, Mar. 14 **Engr.** ***Perf. 13***
2635 A1435 3fr multicolored 1.40 .30

Sous-Préfecture Hotel, Saint-Pierre, Réunion — A1436

1998, Apr. 4 **Engr.** ***Perf. 13***
2636 A1436 3fr multicolored 1.40 .30

Réunion's architectural heritage.

"The Return," by René Magritte — A1437

1998, Apr. 18 **Photo.**
2637 A1437 3fr multicolored 1.40 .50

See Belgium No. 1691.

Edict of Nantes, 400th Anniv. A1438

1998, Apr. 18 **Litho.**
2638 A1438 4.50fr Henry IV 2.10 .75

Art Series

Detail from "Entry of the Crusaders into Constantinople," by Delacroix (1798-1863) — A1439

Le Printemps, by Pablo Picasso (1881-1973) — A1440

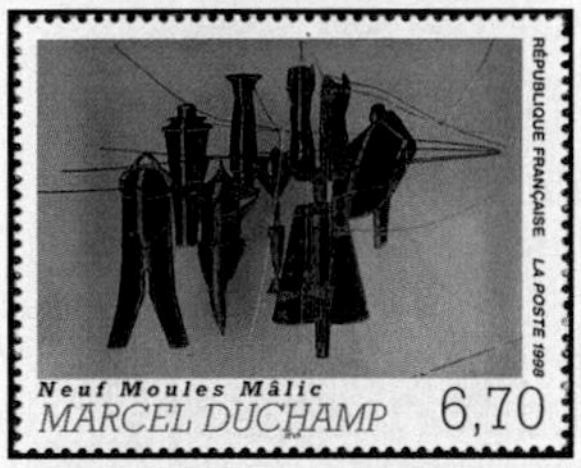

Neuf Moules Malic, by Marcel Duchamp (1887-1968) — A1441

Vision After the Sermon, by Paul Gauguin (1848-1903) — A1442

1998 **Engr.** ***Perf. 12x13***
2639 A1439 6.70fr multicolored 3.00 1.00

Litho.

Perf. 13

2640 A1440 6.70fr multicolored 3.00 1.00

Photo.

2641 A1441 6.70fr multicolored 3.00 1.00
2642 A1442 6.70fr multicolored 3.00 1.00

Issued: #2639, 4/25; #2640, 5/15; #2641, 10/17; #2642, 12/5.

Abolition of Slavery, 150th Anniv. A1443

1998, Apr. 25 **Litho.** ***Perf. 13***
2643 A1443 3fr multicolored 1.40 .30

Tourism Series

Le Gois Causeway, Island of Noirmoutier, Vendée — A1444

Bay of Somme, Picardy — A1445

Château de Crussol, Ardèche A1446

Collegiate Church of Mantes — A1447

1998, May 2 **Photo.**
2644 A1444 3fr multicolored 1.40 .30
2645 A1445 3fr multicolored 1.40 .30

Engr.

2646 A1446 3fr multicolored 1.40 .30
2647 A1447 4.40fr multicolored 2.00 1.00
Nos. 2644-2647 (4) 6.20 1.90

Issued: #2644, 5/2; #2645, 6/27; #2646, 7/4; #2647, 9/19.

Journey of a Letter Type

Historic "letters:" No. 2648, Dove carrying letter, Noah's Ark. No. 2649, Egyptian writing letter on papyrus. No. 2650, Soldier running to Athens with letter to victory at Marathon. No. 2651, Knight carrying letter on horseback. No. 2652, Writing letters with quill and ink. No. 2653, Astronaut carrrying letter in space from earth to the moon.

1998, May 9 **Photo.** ***Perf. 13x13½***

2648	A1403	3fr	multicolored	2.50	1.00
2649	A1403	3fr	multicolored	2.50	1.00
2650	A1403	3fr	multicolored	2.50	1.00
2651	A1403	3fr	multicolored	2.50	1.00
2652	A1403	3fr	multicolored	2.50	1.00
2653	A1403	3fr	multicolored	2.50	1.00
a.	Strip, #2648-2653 + label			16.00	10.00

Booklet Stamps

Self-Adhesive

Serpentine Die Cut 11

2654	A1403	3fr	like #2648	2.25	1.25
2655	A1403	3fr	like #2649	2.25	1.25
2656	A1403	3fr	like #2650	2.25	1.25
2657	A1403	3fr	like #2651	2.25	1.25
2658	A1403	3fr	like #2652	2.25	1.25
2659	A1403	3fr	like #2653	2.25	1.25
a.	Bklt. pane, 2 ea #2654-2659			27.50	27.50

By its nature No. 2659a is a complete booklet. The peelable paper backing serves as a booklet cover.

League of Human Rights, Cent. — A1448

1998, May 9 ***Perf. 13***
2660 A1448 4.40fr multicolored 2.00 1.00

Henri Collet (1885-1951), Composer — A1449

1998, May 15 **Engr.** ***Perf. 12x13***
2661 A1449 4.50fr black, gray & buff 2.10 .90

French Federation of Philatelic Assoc., 71st Congress, Dunkirk — A1450

Photo. & Engr.

1998, May 29 ***Perf. 13***
2662 A1450 3fr multicolored 1.40 .30

Mont-Saint-Michel — A1451

1998, June 6 **Photo.** ***Perf. 13***
2663 A1451 3fr multicolored 1.40 .30

Natl. Music Festival — A1452

1998, June 13
2664 A1452 3fr multicolored 1.40 .50

Europa.

1998 World Cup Soccer Championships Type with Added Inscription, "Champion du Monde"

1998, July 12 **Photo.** ***Perf. 12½***
2665 A1430 3fr multicolored 1.40 .30

Stéphane Mallarmé (1842-98), Poet A1453

Photo. & Engr.

1998, Sept. 5 ***Perf. 13***
2666 A1453 4.40fr multicolored 2.00 .90

Flowers — A1453a

1998, Sept. 9 **Litho.** ***Perf. 13***

2666A	A1453a	1.87fr	Liseron	.85	.30
2666B	A1453a	2.18fr	Coquelicot	1.00	.55
2666C	A1453a	4.66fr	Violette	2.10	1.25
2666D	A1453a	7.11fr	Bouton d'or	3.25	2.00
	Nos. 2666A-2666D (4)			7.20	4.10

Nos. 2666A-2666D are known only precanceled. See second note after #132.

A1454

A1455

1998, Sept. 12 **Photo.**
2667 A1454 3fr multicolored 1.40 .30

Aéro Club of France, cent.

1998, Oct. 23 **Photo.** ***Perf. 13***

"The Little Prince," by Antoine de Saint-Exupéry (1900-44): a, Standing in uniform with sword, horiz. b, Seated on wall. c, "The Little Prince on Asteroid B-612." d, Pouring water from sprinkling can. e, Walking along cliff, fox, horiz.

2668 Strip of 5 + 2 labels 7.00 6.00
a.-e. A1455 3fr any single 1.40 .60
f. Souv. sheet, #2668a-2668e 9.00 9.00

Philexfrance '99. No. 2668f was released 9/12 and sold for 25fr.

Hall of Heavenly Peace, Imperial Palace, Beijing, China A1456

1998, Sept. 12 **Photo.** ***Perf. 13x13½***
2669 A1456 3fr shown 1.40 .40
2670 A1456 4.90fr The Louvre, France 2.25 1.00

See China People's Republic #2895-2896.

Garnier Palace, Home of the Paris Opera — A1457

1998, Sept. 19 **Photo.** ***Perf. 13***
2671 A1457 4.50fr multicolored 2.10 .75

Horses A1458

1998, Sept. 27
2672 A1458 2.70fr Camargue 1.25 .30
2673 A1458 3fr Pottok 1.40 .50
2674 A1458 3fr French trotter 1.40 .50
2675 A1458 4.50fr Ardennais 2.10 .80
Nos. 2672-2675 (4) 6.15 2.10

Paris Auto Show, Cent. A1459

1998, Oct. 1 ***Perf. 12***
2676 A1459 3fr multicolored 1.40 .30

5th Republic, 40th Anniv. A1460

1998, Oct. 3 **Photo.** ***Perf. 13***
2677 A1460 3fr blue, gray & red 1.40 .30

Saint-Dié, Capital of Vosges Mountain Region — A1461

1998, Oct. 3 **Engr.** ***Perf. 13***
2678 A1461 3fr Tower of Liberty 1.40 .30

End of World War I, 80th Anniv. A1462

1998, Oct. 17 **Photo.** ***Perf. 13x13½***
2679 A1462 3fr multicolored 1.40 .40

Intl. Union for the Conservation of Nature and Natural Resources, 50th Anniv. — A1463

1998, Nov. 3 **Litho.**
2680 A1463 3fr multicolored 1.40 .40

New Year A1464

Christmas A1465

1998, Nov. 7 **Photo.** ***Perf. 13***

Background Colors

2681 A1464 3fr deep blue 1.40 .75
2682 A1465 3fr green 1.40 .75
2683 A1464 3fr yellow 1.40 .75
2684 A1465 3fr red 1.40 .75
2685 A1464 3fr green 1.40 .75
a. Strip of 5, #2681-2685 7.00 6.00

Issued in sheets of 10 stamps. Location of "Bonne Annee" and "Meilleurs Voeux" varies.

Doctors Without Borders A1466

1998, Nov. 21 ***Perf. 13x13½***
2686 A1466 3fr multicolored 1.40 .30

European Parliament, Strasbourg A1467

1998, Dec. 5 **Photo.** ***Perf. 13***
2687 A1467 3fr multicolored 1.40 .30

Universal Declaration of Human Rights, 50th Anniv. A1468

#2688, Faces of people of various races, globe. #2689, René Cassin (1887-1976), principal author of Declaration, Eleanor Roosevelt (1884-1962), Chaillot Palace, Paris.

1998, Dec. 10 **Litho.** ***Perf. 13***
2688 A1468 3fr multicolored 1.40 .30
2689 A1468 3fr multicolored 1.40 .30

Discovery of Radium, Cent., ZOE Reactor, 50th Anniv. A1469

1998, Dec. 15 **Photo.** ***Perf. 13***
2690 A1469 3fr multicolored 1.40 .40

Introduction of the Euro — A1470

1999 **Engr.** ***Perf. 13***
2691 A1470 3fr red & blue 1.40 .25

Booklet Stamps

Self-Adhesive

Die Cut x Serpentine Die Cut 7

2691A A1470 3fr red & blue 1.40 .25
b. Booklet pane of 10 14.00

Issued: No. 2691, 1/1/99. No. 2691A, 2/15/99. Values are shown in both Francs and Euros on Nos. 2691-2691A. No. 2691Ab is a complete booklet.

Euro currency did not circulate until 2002.

French Postage Stamps, 150th Anniv. A1471

1999, Jan. 1 **Photo.** ***Perf. 13***

Booklet Stamps

2692 A1471 3fr black & red 6.50 4.50
2693 A1471 3fr red & black 1.25 .75
a. Booklet pane, #2692, 4 #2693 + label 11.50
Complete booklet, #2693a 12.00

No. 2692 has black denomination; No. 2693 has red denomination.

Stamp Day.

Public Assistance Hospital, Paris, 150th Anniv. A1472

1999, Jan. 9
2694 A1472 3fr multicolored 1.40 .30

Diplomatic Relations with Israel, 50th Anniv. — A1473

1999, Jan. 24
2695 A1473 4.40fr multicolored 2.00 .75

Festival Stamps A1474

1999, Feb. 6 **Photo.** ***Perf. 13***
2696 A1474 3fr Stars, "Je t'aime" 1.40 .30
2697 A1474 3fr Rose 1.40 .30

Booklet Stamps

Self-Adhesive

Die Cut Perf. 10

2698 A1474 3fr like #2696 1.40 .30
2699 A1474 3fr like #2697 1.40 .30
a. Bklt. pane, 5 ea #2698-2699 14.00

No. 2699a is a complete booklet.

Art Series

St. Luke the Evangelist, Sculpture by Jean Goujon (1510-66) A1475

Painting, "Waterlillies in Moonlight," by Claude Monet (1840-1926) — A1476

Stained Glass, Cathedral of Auch, by Arnauld de Moles, 16th Cent. A1477

Charles I, King of England, by Sir Anthony Van Dyck
A1478

1999 Engr. *Perf. 13*

2700 A1475 6.70fr multicolored 3.00 1.00

Litho.

2701 A1476 6.70fr multicolored 3.00 1.00

Engr.

2702 A1477 6.70fr multicolored 3.00 1.00

Photo.

Perf. 13¼x13

2703 A1478 6.70fr multicolored 3.00 1.00
Nos. 2700-2703 (4) 12.00 4.00

Issued: #2700, 2/13; #2701, 5/29; #2702, 6/19; #2703, 11/11.

National Census — A1479

1999, Feb. 20 Photo. *Perf. 13½*

2704 A1479 3fr multicolored 1.40 .30

Cultural Heritage of Lebanon
A1480

Mosaic illustrating transformation of Zeus into bull, Natl. Museum of Beirut.

1999, Feb. 27 *Perf. 12½*

2705 A1480 4.40fr multicolored 2.00 .90

Asterix, by Albert Uderzo and Rene Goscinny
A1481

1999, Mar. 6 Photo. *Perf. 13¼*

2706 A1481 3fr multicolored 1.75 .50
a. Perf. 13¼x12¾ 1.75 .90

Booklet Stamp

Perf. 13¼x12¾

2707 A1481 3fr +60c like #2706 3.50 2.00
b. Booklet pane, 4 #2706a, 3 #2707 + label 15.00
Complete booklet, #2707b 16.00

Souvenir Sheet

2707A A1481 3fr +60c like #2706 3.00 2.50

Stamp Day. Stamp design in #2707A continues into the margins.

Council of Europe, 50th Anniv.
A1482

1999, Mar. 19

2708 A1482 3fr multicolored 1.40 .30

A1483

Announcements — A1483a

1999, Mar. 20 *Perf. 13*

2709 A1483 3fr Marriage (Oui) 1.40 .30
2710 A1483 3fr It's a boy (C'est un garcon) 1.40 .30
2711 A1483 3fr It's a girl(C'est une fille) 1.40 .30
2712 A1483a 3fr Thank you 1.40 .30
Nos. 2709-2712 (4) 5.60 1.20

See Nos. 2721-2722.

Souvenir Sheet

PhilexFrance '99 — A1484

Works of art: a, Venus de Milo. b, Mona Lisa, by Da Vinci. c, Liberty Guiding the People, by Delacroix.

Litho. & Engr.

1999, Mar. 26 *Perf. 13¼*

2713 A1484 Sheet of 3 50.00 50.00
a.-b. 5fr each 10.00 10.00
c. 10fr multicolored 20.00 20.00

No. 2713 sold for 50fr, with 30fr serving as a donation to the Assoc. for the Development of Philately.

Elections to the European Parliament
A1485

1999, Mar. 27 Photo. *Perf. 13*

2714 A1485 3fr multicolored 1.40 .30

Richard I, the Lion-Hearted (1157-1199), King of England — A1486

1999, Apr. 10 Engr. *Perf. 13x12½*

2715 A1486 3fr multicolored 1.40 .35

Tourism Series

Dieppe
A1487

Haut-Koenigsbourg Castle, Bas-Rhin — A1488

Birthpalce of Champollion, Figeac — A1489

Chateau, Arnac-Pompadour — A1490

Illustration reduced (A1488).

1999 Engr. *Perf. 13½*

2716 A1487 3fr multicolored 1.40 .30

Litho. & Engr.

Perf. 13

2717 A1488 3fr multicolored 1.40 .50
2718 A1489 3fr multicolored 1.40 .30

Engr.

2719 A1490 3fr multicolored 1.40 .30
Nos. 2716-2719 (4) 5.60 1.40

Issued: #2716, 4/17; #2717, 5/15; #2718, 6/26; #2719, 7/10.

The Camargue Nature Preserve
A1491

1999, Apr. 24 Photo. *Perf. 13x13½*

2720 A1491 3fr multicolored 1.40 .50

Europa.

Announcements Type of 1999 and

A1492

1999, May 13 Photo. *Perf. 13*

2721 A1483 3fr Nice Holiday (bonnes vacances) 1.40 .30
2722 A1483 3fr Happy Birthday (joyeux anniversaire) 1.40 .30
2723 A1492 3fr Long Live Vacations (Vive les vacances 1.40 .30
Nos. 2721-2723 (3) 4.20 .90

Saint Pierre, Martinique
A1493

1999, May 15

2724 A1493 3fr multicolored 1.10 .25

Detail of "Noctuelles" Dish, by Émile Gallé, School of Nancy Museum
A1494

1999, May 22

2725 A1494 3fr multicolored 1.40 .30

Souvenir Sheet

World Old Roses Competition, Lyon — A1495

a, 4.50fr, Mme. Caroline Testout. b, 3fr, Mme. Alfred Carrière. c, 4.50fr, La France.

1999, May 28 *Perf. 13½x13*

2726 A1495 Sheet of 3, #a.-c. 8.00 8.00

Court of Saint-Emilion, 800th Anniv. — A1496

1999, May 29 Engr. *Perf. 13¼x13*

2727 A1496 3.80fr multicolored 1.75 .90

Hotel de la Monnaie, French Mint Headquarters — A1497

1999, June 5 Engr. *Perf. 13*

2728 A1497 4.50fr brn org & bl 2.10 .75

A1498

A1499

1999, June 12 Photo. *Perf. 13¼*

2729 A1498 3fr multicolored 1.40 .40

Countess of Segur (1799-1874), children's storyteller.

1999, June 19 *Perf. 13*

2730 A1499 3fr Welcome 1.40 .30

René Caillié (1799-1838), Explorer of Africa — A1500

1999, June 26 Engr. *Perf. 13¼*
2731 A1500 4.50fr multicolored 2.10 .75

1st French Postage Stamps, 150th Anniv. A1501

1999, July 2 Photo. *Perf. 11¾x13*
2732 A1501 6.70fr multicolored 3.00 1.75

PhilexFrance '99, World Philatelic Exhibition.
No. 2732 was printed with a se-tenant label and contains a holographic image. Soaking in water may affect the hologram.

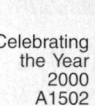

Celebrating the Year 2000 A1502

1999, July 5 Photo. *Perf. 13*
2733 A1502 3fr multicolored 1.40 .30

Year 2000 Stamp Design Contest Winner — A1503

1999, July 6
2734 A1503 3fr multicolored 1.40 .30

Total Solar Eclipse, Aug. 11, 1999 A1504

1999, July 8 *Perf. 12x12¼*
2735 A1504 3fr multicolored 1.40 .40

Gathering of Tall Ships, Rouen, July 9-18 A1505

Sailing ships: a, Simón Bolivar. b, Iskra. c, Statsraad Lehmkuhl. d, Asgard II. e, Belle Poule. f, Belem. g, Amerigo Vespucci. h, Sagres. i, Europa. j, Cuauhtemoc.

1999, July 10 Photo. *Perf. 13*
2736 1fr Sheet of 10 6.00 6.00
a.-j. A1505 any single .50 .50

1999 Rugby World Cup, Cardiff, Wales A1506

1999, Sept. 11 Photo. *Perf. 13¼*
2737 A1506 3fr multicolored 1.40 .40
a. Miniature sheet of 10 11.00

Value is for copy with surrounding selvage.
One stamp in No. 2737a has a missing "F" in the printer's mark.

Frédéric Ozanam (1813-53), Historian — A1507

1999, Sept. 11 Engr. *Perf. 13*
2738 A1507 4.50fr multicolored 2.10 .75

Emmaus Movement, 50th Anniv. A1508

1999, Sept. 26 Photo. *Perf. 13*
2739 A1508 3fr multicolored 1.40 .40

Cats and Dogs — A1509

1999, Oct. 2 Photo. *Perf. 13¼*
2740 A1509 2.70fr Chartreux cat 1.25 .30
2741 A1509 3fr European cat 1.40 .30
2742 A1509 3fr Pyrenean Mountain dog 1.40 .30
2743 A1509 4.50fr Brittany spaniel 2.10 .75
Nos. 2740-2743 (4) 6.15 1.65

Frédéric Chopin (1810-49), Composer A1510

1999, Oct. 17 Engr. *Perf. 13¼*
2744 A1510 3.80fr multicolored 1.75 .75

See Poland No. 3484.

A1511

Best Wishes for Year 2000 A1512

1999, Nov. 20 Photo. *Perf. 13x13¼*
2745 A1511 3fr multi 1.40 .30
2746 A1512 3fr multi 1.40 .30

No. 2746 was printed with se-tenant label.

Paris Metro, Cent. A1513

1999, Dec. 4 Photo. *Perf. 13*
2747 A1513 3fr multi 1.40 .30

Council of State, Bicent. — A1514

1999, Dec. 11
2748 A1514 3fr multi 1.40 .30

Reconstruction of Lighthouses — A1515

2000, Jan. 1 Photo. *Perf. 13x12¾*
2749 A1515 3fr multi 1.40 .30

Reconstruction of San Juan de Salvamento Lighthouse, Argentina and replication of its design at La Rochelle, France.

Hearts A1516

2000, Jan. 8 Photo. *Perf. 13*
2750 A1516 3fr Snakes 1.40 .30
2751 A1516 3fr Face 1.40 .30
a. Souvenir sheet, 3 #2750, 2 #2751 9.00 9.00

Self-Adhesive Booklet Stamps
Serpentine Die-Cut

2752 A1516 3fr Like #2750 1.40 .30
2753 A1516 3fr Like #2751 1.40 .30
a. Bklt. pane, 5 ea #2752-2753 14.00

Values for Nos. 2750-2751 are for copies with surrounding selvage. No. 2753a is a complete booklet.

Bank of France, Bicent. — A1517

Prefectorial Corps, Bicent. — A1518

2000, Jan. 15 Litho. *Perf. 13*
2754 A1517 3fr multi 1.40 .30

2000, Feb. 17 Photo. *Perf. 13x12¼*
2755 A1518 3fr multi 1.40 .30

Art Series

Venus and the Graces Offering Gifts to a Young Girl, by Sandro Botticelli (1445-1510) — A1519

The Waltz, by Camille Claudel A1520

Visage Rouge, by Gaston Chaissac A1521

Carolingian Mosaic, Germigny-des-Prés — A1522

2000 Photo. *Perf. 13¼x13*
2756 A1519 6.70fr multi 3.00 1.00
2757 A1520 6.70fr multi 3.00 1.00
2758 A1521 6.70fr multi 3.00 1.00
2759 A1522 6.70fr multi 3.00 1.00

Issued: #2756, 2/25; #2757, 4/8; #2758, 9/23; 10/21.

Tourism Series

Carcassonne — A1523

Saint-Guilhem-Le-Désert — A1524

Gérardmer A1525

Abbey Church of Ottmarsheim — A1526

Illustration A1523 reduced.

2000 Photo. *Perf. 13*
2760 A1523 3fr multi 1.40 .30

Engr.
Perf. 13¼
2761 A1524 3fr multi 1.40 .30
2762 A1525 3fr multi 1.40 .30

Perf. 12¼x13
2763 A1526 3fr multi 1.40 .30
Nos. 2760-2763 (4) 5.60 1.20

Issued: #2760, 3/3; #2761, 4/8; #2762, 4/17; #2763, 6/17.

Tintin — A1527

2000, Mar. 11 Photo. *Perf. 13¼*
2764 A1527 3fr multi 1.40 .50
a. Perf. 13½x13 2.00 .75

Perf. 13½x13
2765 A1527 3fr + 60c multi 4.00 2.00
a. Booklet pane, 4 #2764a, 3 #2765 + label 20.00
Complete booklet, #2765a 21.00
b. Souvenir sheet of 1 3.00 2.50

Stamp Day.

Bretagne Parliament Building Restoration — A1528

2000, Mar. 25 Photo. *Perf. 13¼*
2766 A1528 3fr multi 1.40 .30

Madagascar Periwinkles — A1529

2000, Mar. 25 Litho. *Perf. 13x13¼*
2767 A1529 4.50fr multi 2.10 .60

Felicitations A1530

2000, Apr. 7 Photo. *Perf. 13x13¼*
2768 A1530 3fr multi 1.40 .30

The 20th Century — A1531

No. 2769: a, France as World Cup soccer champions, 1998, vert. b, Marcel Cerdan wins middleweight boxing title, 1948. c, Charles Lindbergh flies solo across Atlantic, 1927. d, Jean-Claude Killy wins three Winter Olympics gold medals, 1968, vert. e, Carl Lewis wins four Olympic gold medals, 1984, vert.
Illustration reduced.

Perf. 13¼x13 (vert. stamps), 13x13¼
2000, Apr. 15
2769 A1531 Sheet, 2 ea #a-e 14.00 14.00
a.-e. 3fr any single 1.40 .75

Top part of No. 2769 contains Nos. 2769a-2769e and is separated from bottom part of sheet by a row of rouletting.
See No. 2787, 2804, 2837, 2881, 2915.

Automobiles — A1532

No. 2770: a, Bugatti 35. b, Citroen Traction. c, Renault 4CV. d, Simca Chambord. e, Hispano-Suiza K6. f, Volkswagen Beetle. g, 1962 Cadillac. h, Peugeot 203. i, Citroen DS19. j, Ferrari 250 GTO.
Illustration reduced.

2000, May 5 *Perf. 13¼x13*
2770 A1532 Sheet of 10, #a.-j. 7.50 7.50
a.-e. 1fr any single .45 .35
f.-j. 2fr any single .90 .60

Europa, 2000
Common Design Type

2000, May 9 Photo. *Perf. 13¼*
2771 CD17 3fr multi 1.40 .40

Henry-Louis Duhamel du Monceau (1700-82), Agronomist — A1533

2000, May 13 Engr. *Perf. 13*
2772 A1533 4.50fr multi 2.10 .65

French Federation of Philatelic Associations, 73rd Congress, Nevers — A1534

2000, May 19 Engr. *Perf. 13¼*
2773 A1534 3fr multi 1.40 .30

A1535

A1536

2000, June 1 Photo. *Perf. 13¼x13*
2774 A1535 3fr Happy Vacation 1.40 .30

2000, June 3 Engr. *Perf. 13x12¼*
2775 A1536 3fr multi 1.40 .30

First Ascent of Annapurna, 50th anniv.

Nature A1537

2.70fr, Agrias sardanapalus butterfly. #2777, Giraffe. #2778, Allosaurus. 4.50fr, Tulipa lutea.

2000, June 17 Photo. *Perf. 13¼*
2776 A1537 2.70fr multi 1.25 .50
2777 A1537 3fr multi, vert. 1.40 .50
2778 A1537 3fr multi 1.40 .50
2779 A1537 4.50fr multi, vert 2.10 .90
a. Souvenir sheet, #2776-2779 7.00 7.00
Nos. 2776-2779 (4) 6.15 2.40

Antoine de Saint-Exupéry (1900-44), Aviator, Writer — A1538

2000, June 24 Photo. *Perf. 13¼x13*
2780 A1538 3fr multi 1.40 .30

Yellow Train of Cerdagne, Cent. A1539

2000, July 14 *Perf. 13x13¼*
2781 A1539 3fr multi 1.40 .30

Folklore A1540

2000, Aug. 12 Photo. *Perf. 13*
2782 A1540 4.50fr multi 2.10 .65

2000 Summer Olympics, Sydney A1541

Designs: No. 2783, Cycling, fencing, relay racer. No. 2784, Relay racer, judo, diving.

2000, Sept. 9
2783 A1541 3fr multi 1.40 .50
2784 A1541 3fr multi 1.40 .50
a. Pair, #2783-2784 3.00 2.00
b. Sheet, 5 #2784a + label 15.00 15.00

Olymphilex 2000, Sydney (#2784b).

Brother Alfred Stanke (1904-75) A1542

2000, Sept. 23 Engr.
2785 A1542 4.40fr multi 2.00 .90

S.O.S. Amitié, 40th Anniv. A1543

2000, Sept. 30 Litho. *Perf. 13*
2786 A1543 3fr multi 1.40 .30

20th Century Type

No. 2787: a, Man on the Moon, 1969, vert. b, Paid vacations, 1936. c, Invention of washing machine, 1901, vert. d, Woman suffrage, 1944, vert. e, Universal Declaration of Human Rights, 1948.

Perf. 13¼x13 (vert. stamps), 13x13¼
2000, Sept. 30 Photo.
2787 A1531 Sheet, 2 each #a-e 14.00 14.00
a.-e. 3fr Any single 1.40 .50

The top and bottom parts of No. 2787 contains Nos. 2787a-2787e and are separated by a row of rouletting.

2001, Start of New Millennium
A1544

2000, Oct. 14 Litho. *Perf. 13*
2788 A1544 3fr multi 1.40 .30

The Lovers' Kiosk, by Peynet
A1545

2000, Nov. 4 Engr. *Perf. 13¼x13*
2789 A1545 3fr multi 1.40 .50

Endangered Birds — A1546

2000, Nov. 4 Photo. *Perf. 13¼*
2790 A1546 3fr Kiwi 1.40 .40
2791 A1546 5.20fr Falcon 2.50 1.50

See New Zealand Nos. 1688, 1694.

Start of the 3rd Millennium — A1547

Illustration reduced.

2000, Nov. 9 Photo. *Perf. 13x13¼*
2792 A1547 3fr multi + label 1.40 .30

Issued in sheets of 10 stamps + 10 labels, which could be personalized for an extra fee.

Holiday Greetings
A1548

2000, Nov. 11 *Perf. 12¼x13*
2793 A1548 3fr Meilleurs voeux 1.40 .30

Perf. 13¼
2794 A1548 3fr Bonne année 1.40 .30

Union of Metallurgical & Mining Industries, Cent. — A1549

Engr. with Foil Application
2000, Dec. 9 *Perf. 13x13¼*
2795 A1549 4.50fr multi 2.10 .90

World Handball Championships — A1550

2001, Jan. 20 Photo. *Perf. 13¼*
2796 A1550 3fr multi 1.40 .30

Heart
A1551

2001, Jan. 27
2797 A1551 3fr multi 1.40 .30
a. Souvenir sheet of 5 10.00 10.00

Value of No. 2797 is for copy with surrounding selvage.

Art Series

The Peasant Dance, by Pieter Breughel, the Elder — A1552

Hotel des Chevaliers de Saint-Jean-de-Jérusalem — A1553

Yvette Guilbert Singing "Linger, Longer, Loo," by Henri de Toulouse-Lautrec (1864-1901) — A1554

Honfleur at Low Tide, by Johan Barthold Jongkind — A1555

Engr., Photo (#2800), Litho (#2801)
2001 *Perf. 13x13¼, 13¼x13 (#2800)*
2798 A1552 6.70fr multi 3.00 1.00
2799 A1553 6.70fr multi 3.00 1.00
2800 A1554 6.70fr multi 3.00 1.00
2801 A1555 6.70fr multi 3.00 1.00
Nos. 2798-2801 (4) 12.00 4.00

Issued: No. 2798, 2/3; No. 2799, 4/21; No. 2800, 9/8; No. 2801, 10/27.

Gaston Lagaffe, by André Franquin
A1556

2001, Feb. 24 Photo. *Perf. 13¼*
2802 A1556 3fr multi 1.40 .50
a. Perf. 13¼x13 1.40 .65

Perf. 13¼x13
2803 A1556 3fr +60c multi 5.00 3.50
a. Souvenir sheet of 1 3.50 2.50
b. Booklet pane, 5 #2802a, 3 #2803 22.00
Booklet, #2803b 22.50

Stamp Day.

20th Century Type of 2000

No. 2804 — Communications: a, Television. b, Compact disc. c, Advertisements, vert. d, Radio, vert. e, Portable telephone, vert.

Perf. 13¼x13 (vert. stamps), 13x13¼
2001, Mar. 17 Photo.
2804 A1531 Sheet, 2 each #a-e 14.00 14.00
a.-e. 3fr Any single 1.40 .75

Top part of No. 2804 contains Nos. 2804a-2804e and is separated from bottom part by a row of rouletting.

Announcements — A1557

Designs: No. 2805, It's a girl. No. 2806, It's a boy. No. 2807, Thank you. 4.50fr, Yes (marriage).

2001 *Perf. 13*

Frame Color
2805 A1557 3fr brt pink 1.40 .30
a. Litho., stamp + label 6.50 6.50
2806 A1557 3fr brt blue 1.40 .30
a. Litho., stamp + label 6.50 6.50
2807 A1557 3fr brt yel grn 1.40 .30
a. Litho., stamp + label 6.50 6.50
2808 A1557 4.50fr orange 2.10 .75
Nos. 2805-2808 (4) 6.30 1.65

Issued: Nos. 2805-2808, 3/23; Nos. 2805a-2807a, 11/8.

Nos. 2805a-2807a were issued in sheets of 10 stamps and 10 labels that sold for 60fr on day of issue. The labels could be personalized. Frames on Nos. 2805 and 2806 look splotchy, while those on Nos. 2805a and 2806a have a distinct dot structure. The frame on No. 2807 has tightly spaced small dots, while on No. 2807a, the dots are more widely spaced.

Wildlife — A1558

2001, Apr. 21 Photo. *Perf. 13¼*
2809 A1558 2.70fr Squirrel 1.25 .40
2810 A1558 3fr Roe deer 1.40 .40
2811 A1558 3fr Hedgehog, horiz. 1.40 .40
2812 A1558 4.50fr Ermine 2.10 .75
a. Souvenir sheet, #2809-2812 7.00 6.50

Tourism Issue

Nogent-le-Rotrou
A1559

Besançon
A1560

Calais
A1561

Château de Grignan
A1562

Engr., Litho & Engr. (#2813)
2001 *Perf. 13¼x13 (#2813), 13*
2813 A1559 3fr multi 1.40 .40
2814 A1560 3fr multi 1.40 .30
2815 A1561 3fr multi 1.40 .30
2816 A1562 3fr multi 1.40 .30
Nos. 2813-2816 (4) 5.60 1.30

Issued: No. 2813, 4/28; No. 2814, 5/5; No. 2815, 6/16; No. 2816, 7/7.

Europa — A1563

2001, May 8 Photo. *Perf. 13*
2817 A1563 3fr multi 1.40 .35

Gardens of Versailles — A1564

Illustration reduced.

2001, May 12
2818 A1564 4.40fr multi 2.00 1.00

Singers — A1565

Designs: No. 2819, Claude François (1939-78). No. 2820, Léo Ferré (1916-93). No. 2821, Serge Gainsbourg (1928-91). No. 2822, Dalida (1933-87). No. 2823, Michel Berger (1947-92). No. 2824, Barbara (1930-97).

2001, May 19 Photo. *Perf. 13*
2819 A1565 3fr multi 1.40 .75
2820 A1565 3fr multi 1.40 .75
2821 A1565 3fr multi 1.40 .75
2822 A1565 3fr multi 1.40 .75
2823 A1565 3fr multi 1.40 .75
2824 A1565 3fr multi 1.40 .75
a. Souvenir sheet, #2819-2824 11.00 11.00
Nos. 2819-2824 (6) 8.40 4.50

No. 2824a sold for 28fr with the Red Cross receiving 10fr of that.

Old Lyon — A1566

2001, May 19 Engr. *Perf. 13¼*
2825 A1566 3fr multi 1.40 .30

French Federation of Philatelic Associations 74th Congress, Tours — A1567

2001, June 1
2826 A1567 3fr multi 1.40 .30

Jean Vilar (1912-71), Actor A1568

Litho. & Engr.
2001, June 7 *Perf. 13*
2827 A1568 3fr multi 1.40 .40

Vacation A1569

2001, June 10 Litho. *Perf. 13*
2828 A1569 3fr multi 1.40 .30

Booklet Stamp
Self-Adhesive

2829 A1569 3fr multi 1.40 .30
a. Booklet of 10 14.00

1 Euro Coin A1570

2001, June 23 Photo. *Perf. 12½*
2830 A1570 3fr multi 1.40 .30

Value is for copy with surrounding selvage.

Albert Caquot (1881-1976), Engineer — A1571

2001, June 30 Engr. *Perf. 13¼*
2831 A1571 4.50fr multi 2.00 .75

Law Guaranteeing Freedom of Association, Cent. — A1572

2001, July 1 Photo. *Perf. 13*
2832 A1572 3fr multi 1.40 .30

Trains — A1573

No. 2833: a, Eurostar. b, American 220. c, Crocodile. d, Crampton. e, Garratt 59. f, Pacific Chapelon. g, Mallard. h, Capitole. i, Autorail Panoramique. j, 230 Class P8.

2001, July 6 Photo. *Perf. 13¼*
2833 A1573 Sheet of 10 7.50 7.50
a.-j. 1.50fr Any single .75 .65

Geneva Convention on Refugees, UN High Commisioner for Refugees, 50th Anniv. — A1574

2001, July 28 *Perf. 13*
2834 A1574 4.50fr multi 2.00 .75

Marianne Type of 1997 Inscribed "RF" at Lower Left

2001 Engr. *Perf. 13*
2835 A1409 (3fr) red 1.40 .25
d. Sheet of 15 + 15 labels 60.00 —

Serpentine Die Cut 6¾ Vert.
Self-Adhesive
Booklet Stamp

2835A A1409 (3fr) red 1.40 .25
b. Booklet of 10 15.00

2001, Aug. 1 Engr. *Perf. 13 Horiz.*
Coil Stamp
Water-Activated Gum

2835C A1409 (3fr) red 1.40 .25

Issued: Nos. 2835, 2835C, 8/1; No. 2835A, 9/24.

No. 2835d sold for €10.03. Labels could be personalized for an additional price.

"La Poste" and engraver are at right.

Pierre de Fermat (1601-65), Mathematician — A1575

2001, Aug. 19 Engr. *Perf. 13¼x13*
2836 A1575 4.50fr multi 2.00 .75

20th Century Type of 2000

No. 2837 — Science: a, First man in space. b, DNA. c, Chip cards. d, Laser. e, Penicillin.

Perf. 13¼x13 (vert. stamps), 13
2001, Sept. 22 Photo.
2837 A1531 Sheet, 2 each #a-e 14.00 14.00
a.-e. 3fr Any single 1.40 .70

Top part of No. 2837 contains Nos. 2837a-2837e and is separated from bottom part of sheet by a row of rouletting.

Astrolabe Sculpture, Val-de-Reuil A1576

2001, Sept. 29 *Perf. 13*
2838 A1576 3fr multi 1.40 .30

Halloween A1577

2001, Oct. 20
2839 A1577 3fr multi 1.40 .30
a. Souvenir sheet of 5 + 4 labels 8.00 8.00

Jean Pierre-Bloch (1905-99), Human Rights Advocate — A1578

2001, Nov. 8 Engr. *Perf. 13*
2840 A1578 4.50fr multi 2.00 .75

Albert Decaris (1901-88), Artist A1579

2001, Nov. 9 Engr. *Perf. 13¼x13*
2841 A1579 3fr multi 1.40 .40

Jacques Chaban-Delmas (1915-2000), Politician — A1580

2001, Nov. 10 Engr. *Perf. 13x13¼*
2842 A1580 3fr multi 1.40 .40

Holiday Greetings A1581

Designs: Nos. 2843, 2845 Bonne Année (Happy New Year). Nos. 2844, 2846 Meilleurs Voeux (Best wishes).

2001, Nov. 9 Litho. *Perf. 13*
2843 A1581 3fr multi 1.40 .30
2844 A1581 3fr multi 1.40 .30

Serpentine Die Cut 11
Self-Adhesive
Booklet Stamps

2845 A1581 3fr multi 1.40 .30
2846 A1581 3fr multi 1.40 .30
a. Booklet, 5 each # 2845-2846 14.00

Fountains A1582

Designs: 3fr, Nejjarine Fountain, Fez, Morocco. 3.80fr, Wallace Fountain, Paris.

2001, Dec. 14 Photo. *Perf. 13¼*
2847 A1582 3fr multi 1.40 .40
2848 A1582 3.80fr multi 1.75 1.00

See Morocco Nos. 914-915.

100 Cents = 1 Euro (€)

Marianne (With Euro Denominations) A1583

Orchids A1584

2002, Jan. 1 Engr. *Perf. 13*
2849 A1583 1c yellow .20 .20
2850 A1583 2c brown .20 .20
2851 A1583 5c brt bl grn .20 .20
2852 A1583 10c purple .25 .20
2853 A1583 20c brt org .60 .30
2854 A1583 41c brt green 1.20 .20
2855 A1583 50c dk blue 1.50 .25
2856 A1583 53c apple grn 1.60 .40
2857 A1583 58c blue 1.75 .50
2858 A1583 64c dark org 1.90 .50
2859 A1583 67c brt blue 2.00 .50
a. deep blue 2.00 .50
2860 A1583 69c brt pink 2.10 .60
2861 A1583 €1 Prus blue 3.00 .80
2862 A1583 €1.02 dk green 3.00 .90
a. Souvenir sheet, #2835, 2854, 2856-2858, 2859a, 2860, 2862 15.00 15.00
2863 A1583 €2 violet 6.00 1.50
a. Souvenir sheet, #2849-2853, 2855, 2861, 2863 12.00 12.00
Nos. 2849-2863 (15) 25.50 7.25

Coil Stamp
Perf. 13 Horiz.

2864 A1583 41c brt green 1.25 .30

See Nos. 2952-2957, 3043,

2002, Jan. 2 Litho. *Perf. 13*

Designs: 29c, Orchis insularis. 33c, Ophrys fuciflora.

2865	A1584 29c multi	.80	.30
2866	A1584 33c multi	1.00	.40

Nos. 2865-2866 are known only precanceled. See second note after #132.

Heart of Voh, Photograph by Yann Arthurs-Bertrand — A1585

2002, Jan. 18 Photo. *Perf. 13¼*

2867	A1585 46c multi	1.40	.40
a.	Souvenir sheet of 5	7.00	7.00

Value of No. 2867 is for copy with surrounding selvage.

2002 Winter Olympics, Salt Lake City — A1586

2002, Jan. 26 *Perf. 13*

2868	A1586 46c multi	1.40	.30

Art Series

Sphere Concorde, by Jesús Rafael Soto A1587

The Kiss, by Gustav Klimt A1588

The Dancers, by Fernando Botero A1589

Self-Portrait, by Elisabeth Vigée-Lebrun — A1590

2002 Photo. *Perf. 13¼x13*

2869	A1587 75c multi	2.25	1.00
2870	A1588 €1.02 multi	3.00	1.00
2871	A1589 €1.02 multi	3.00	1.00

Engr.

2872	A1590 €1.02 multi	3.00	1.00
	Nos. 2869-2872 (4)	11.25	4.00

Issued: No. 2869, 11/11. No. 2870, 2/8; No. 2871, 4/27. No. 2872, 10/12.

Alain Bosquet (1919-98), Poet — A1591

2002, Feb. 16 Engr. *Perf. 13*

2873	A1591 58c multi	1.75	1.00

It's A Girl A1592

It's A Boy A1593

Yes A1594

2002, Feb. 23 Photo.

2874	A1592 46c multi	1.40	.30
2875	A1593 46c multi	1.40	.30
2876	A1594 69c multi	2.00	.30
	Nos. 2874-2876 (3)	4.80	.90

Europa — A1595

2002, Mar. 2 *Perf. 13¼*

2877	A1595 46c multi	1.40	.30

Boule and Bill, by Jean Roba — A1596

Designs: 46c, Boule, Bill, bird. 46c+9c, Boule, Bill, ball.

2002, Mar. 16 *Perf. 13¼*

2878	A1596 46c multi	1.40	.50
a.	Perf. 13¼x13	2.00	.60

Perf. 13¼x13

2879	A1596 46c +9c multi	4.00	3.00
a.	Souvenir sheet of 1	3.00	2.50
b.	Booklet pane, 5 #2878a, 3 #2879	22.00	—
	Booklet, #2879b	22.50	

Stamp Day. Stamp on No. 2879a has continuous design.

Nimes Amphitheater — A1597

Litho. & Engr.

2002, Mar. 22 *Perf. 13*

2880	A1597 46c multi	1.40	.30

20th Century Type of 2000

No. 2881 — Transportation: a, Concorde supersonic airplane. b, TGV train. c, Ocean liner France, vert. d, Mobylette motor scooter, vert. e, Citroen 2 CV automobile, vert.

Perf. 13, 13¼x13 (vert. stamps)

2002, Mar. 23 Photo.

2881	A1531 Sheet, 2 each #a-e	14.00	14.00
a.-e.	46c Any single	1.40	.75

Top part of No. 2881 contains Nos. 2881a-2881e and is separated from bottom part of sheet by a row of rouletting.

Encounter of Matthew Flinders and Nicolas Boudin, Bicent. A1598

Map of Australia, portrait and ship of: 46c, Flinders. 79c, Boudin.

2002, Apr. 4 *Perf. 13¼*

2882	A1598 46c multi	1.40	.40
2883	A1598 79c multi	2.25	1.25

See Australia Nos. 2053-2054.

Tourism Series

La Charité-sur-Loire — A1599

Collioure A1600

Locronan A1601

Neufchateau — A1602

Engraved (#2884, 2886), Photo. (#2885)

2002 *Perf. 13¼*

2884	A1599 46c multi	1.40	.30
2885	A1600 46c multi	1.40	.30
2886	A1601 46c multi	1.40	.30
2887	A1602 46c multi	1.40	.30
	Nos. 2884-2887 (4)	5.60	1.20

Issue dates: No. 2884, 4/6; No. 2885, 6/22; No. 2886, 7/13; No. 2887, 10/12/02.

Numbers have been reserved for additional stamps in this set.

Birthday Greetings A1603

Invitation A1604

2002, Apr. 6 Photo. *Perf. 13*

2888	A1603 46c multi	1.40	.30
a.	Litho., stamp + label	6.00	6.00
2889	A1604 46c multi	1.40	.30
a.	Litho., stamp + label	6.00	6.00

Issued: Nos. 2888a, 2889a, 11/7. Nos. 2888a and 2889a were issued in sheets of 10 stamps and 10 labels that sold for €6.19 on day of issue. The labels could be personalized.

No. 2888a has a duller blue in "Anniversaire" than No. 2888, but is otherwise quite similar in appearance. The gold ink on No. 2889a has a more coppery look than that on No. 2889.

100th Paris-Roubaix Bicycle Race — A1605

2002, Mar. 13

2890	A1605 46c multi	1.40	.30

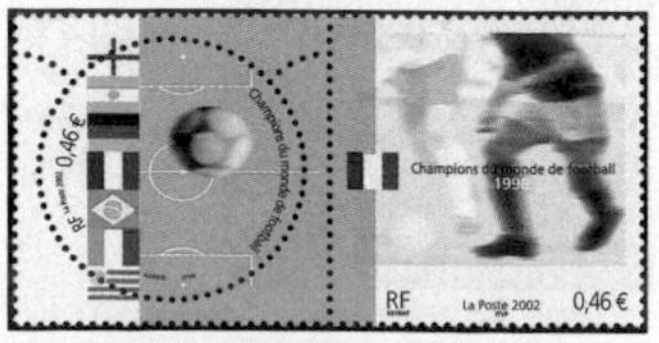

2002 World Cup Soccer Championships, Japan and Korea — A1606

No. 2891: a, Flags, soccer ball and field (32mm diameter). b, Soccer player, year of French championship.

Illustration reduced.

2002, Apr. 27 *Perf. 12¾*

2891 A1606	Horiz. pair	2.75	2.50
a.-b.	46c Any single	1.40	.30
c.	Sheet, 5 #2891	15.00	15.00

Issued: No. 2891c, 5/18.

See Argentina No. 2184, Brazil No. 2840, Germany No. 2163, Italy No. 2526 and Uruguay No. 1946.

Marine Life A1607

Designs: 41c, Sea turtle (tortue luth), vert. No. 2893, Killer whale (orque). No. 2894, Dolphin (grand dauphin). 69c, Seal (phoque veau marin).

2002, May 4 *Perf. 13¼*

2892 A1607	41c multi	1.25	.30
2893 A1607	46c multi	1.25	.30
2894 A1607	46c multi	1.25	.30
2895 A1607	69c multi	2.00	.75
a.	Souvenir sheet, #2892-2895	6.50	6.50
	Nos. 2892-2895 (4)	5.75	1.65

Worldwide Fund for Nature (#2895a).

French Federation of Philatelic Associations 75th Congress, Marseilles — A1608

Illustration reduced.

2002, May 17 **Engr.** *Perf. 13*

2896 A1608 46c multi 1.40 .30

Legion of Honor, Bicent. A1609

Rocamadour A1610

2002, May 18 **Photo.**

2897 A1609 46c multi 1.40 .30

2002, May 25 *Perf. 13¼*

2898 A1610 46c multi 1.40 .30

Louis Delgrés (1766-1802), Soldier — A1611

2002, May 25

2899 A1611 46c multi 1.40 .30

Vacation A1612

2002, June 8 **Litho.** *Perf. 13*

2900 A1612 46c multi 1.40 .30

Self-Adhesive

Serpentine Die Cut 11

2901 A1612	46c multi	1.40	.30
a.	Booklet pane of 10	14.00	

World Disabled Athletics Championships — A1613

2002, June 15 **Photo.** *Perf. 13¼*

2902 A1613 46c multi 1.40 .30

Saint-Ser Chapel — A1614

2002, June 22 **Engr.** *Perf. 13x13¼*

2903 A1614 46c multi 1.40 .30

Metz Cathedral Stained Glass A1615

2002, July 6 **Engr.** *Perf. 13¼x13*

2904 A1615 46c multi 1.40 .40

Jazz Musicians — A1616

Designs: No. 2905, Louis Armstrong (1901-71). No. 2906, Ella Fitzgerald (1918-96). No. 2907, Duke Ellington (1899-1974). No. 2908, Stéphane Grappelli (1908-97). No. 2909, Michel Petrucciani (1962-99), horiz. No. 2910, Sidney Bechet (1897-1959), horiz.

2002, July 13 **Photo.** *Perf. 13*

2905 A1616	46c multi	1.40	.75
2906 A1616	46c multi	1.40	.75
2907 A1616	46c multi	1.40	.75
2908 A1616	46c multi	1.40	.75
2909 A1616	46c multi	1.40	.75
2910 A1616	46c multi	1.40	.75
a.	Souvenir sheet, #2905-2910	12.00	12.00
	Nos. 2905-2910 (6)	8.40	4.50

No. 2910a sold for €4.36, with the Red Cross receiving €1.60 of that.

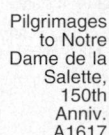

Pilgrimages to Notre Dame de la Salette, 150th Anniv. A1617

2002, Aug. 15 **Engr.** *Perf. 13¼x13*

2911 A1617 46c multi 1.40 .30

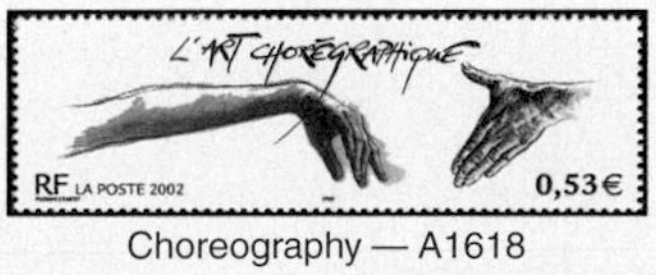

Choreography — A1618

Illustration reduced.

2002, Sept. 13 **Photo.** *Perf. 13x13¼*

2912 A1618 53c multi 1.50 .60

Motorcycles — A1619

No. 2913: a, Honda 750 four. b, Terrot 500 RGST. c, Majestic. d, Norton Commando 750. e, Voxan 1000 Café Racer. f, BMW R90S. g, Harley Davidson Hydra Glide. h, Triumph Bonneville 650. i, Ducati 916. j, Yamaha 500 XT.

2002, Sept. 14 *Perf. 13¼x13*

2913 A1619	Sheet of 10	12.00	12.00
a.-e.	16c any single	.75	.60
f.-j.	30c any single	.90	.75

Georges Perec (1936-82), Writer — A1620

2002, Sept. 21 **Engr.** *Perf. 13¼*

2914 A1620 46c multi 1.40 .30

20th Century Type of 2000

No. 2915 — Photographs of everyday life: a, Family on motor scooter, 1955, vert. b, Man, horse and wagon, 1947. c, Woman ironing, 1950. d, Boy at fountain, 1950, vert. e, Girl in classroom, 1965, vert.

Perf. 13¼x13 (vert. stamps), 13

2002, Sept. 28 **Photo.**

2915 A1531	Sheet, 2 each #a-e	14.00	14.00
a.-e.	46c Any single	1.40	.75

Top part of No. 2915 contains Nos. 2915a-2915e and is separated from bottom part of sheet by a row of rouletting.

Emile Zola (1840-1902), Novelist — A1621

2002, Oct. 5 *Perf. 13*

2916 A1621 46c multi 1.40 .30

Souvenir Sheet

European Capitals — A1622

Attractions in Rome: a, Trevi Fountain. b, Coliseum, horiz. c, Trinità de Monti Church and Spanish Steps. d, St. Peter's Basilica, horiz.

2002, Nov. 7 *Perf. 13¼x13, 13x13¼*

2917 A1622	Sheet of 4	6.00	6.00
a.-d.	46c Any single	1.40	.75

See Nos. 2985, 3052, 3138, 3223, 3340, 3535.

Globe and Microcircuits A1623

2002, Nov. 8 **Photo.** *Perf. 13*

2918 A1623	46c multi	1.40	.30
a.	Litho., stamp + label	6.00	6.00

Issued: No. 2918a, 11/7. No. 2918a was issued in sheets of 10 stamps and 10 labels that sold for €6.19 on day of issue. The labels could be personalized.

No. 2918a has a hairline at top, above "RF" that No. 2918 does not have, but is otherwise quite similar in appearance.

Holiday Greetings A1624

2002, Nov. 8 **Photo.** *Perf. 13*

2919 A1624	46c multi	1.40	.30
a.	Litho., stamp + label	6.00	6.00

Booklet Stamp

Self-Adhesive

Serpentine Die Cut 11

2920 A1624	46c multi	1.40	.30
a.	Booklet pane of 10	14.00	

Issued: No. 2919a, 11/7. No. 2919a was issued in sheets of 10 stamps and 10 labels that sold for €6.19 on day of issue. The labels could be personalized.

No. 2919a has a finer dot structure, which is most noticeable in the chimney smoke, than No. 2919.

Marianne Type of 1997 Inscribed "RF" at Lower Left

2002, Nov. 9 **Engr.** *Perf. 13*

2921 A1409 (41c) bright green 1.20 .25

Coil Stamp

Perf. 13 Horiz.

2922 A1409 (41c) bright green 1.20 .25

Alexandre Dumas (Father) (1802-70), Writer A1625

2002, Nov. 30 **Photo.** *Perf. 13*

2924 A1625 46c multi 1.40 .30

Léopold Sédar Senghor (1906-2001), President of Senegal, Poet — A1626

2002, Dec. 20

2925	A1626 46c multi	1.40	.30

Hearts A1627

2003, Jan. 11 *Perf. 13¼*

2926	A1627 46c Four hearts	1.40	.30
a.	Souvenir sheet of 5	7.00	7.00
2927	A1627 69c Roses	2.00	.60

Values for Nos. 2926-2927 are for copies with surrounding selvage.

Thank You A1628

Birth A1629

2003, Jan. 11 *Perf. 13*

2928	A1628 46c multi	1.40	.30
2929	A1629 46c brt org & brt bl	1.40	.30

Franco-German Cooperation Treaty, 40th Anniv. — A1630

2003, Jan. 16 *Perf. 13¼*

2930	A1630 46c multi	1.40	.40

Delegation for Land-use Planning and Regional Action, 40th Anniv. A1631

2003, Feb. 8 **Photo.** *Perf. 13*

2931	A1631 46c multi	1.40	.30

Geneviève de Gaulle Anthonioz (1920-2002), World War II Resistance Fighter — A1632

2003, Feb. 11

2932	A1632 46c blk & ol brn	1.40	.30

Paris Chamber of Commerce and Industry, Bicent. — A1633

2003, Feb. 22 *Perf. 13¼*

2933	A1633 46c multi	1.40	.30

Lucky Luke, by Morris (Maurice De Bevere) — A1634

Lucky Luke and Jolly Jumper: 46c, Skipping rope on ball on high wire. 46c+9c, Following dog, Rantanplan.

2003, Mar. 15 **Photo.** *Perf. 13¼*

2934	A1634 46c multi	1.40	.65
a.	Perf. 13¼x13	1.40	.65

Perf. 13¼x13

2935	A1634 46c +9c multi	3.50	2.00
a.	Souvenir sheet of 1	3.00	2.50
b.	Booklet pane, 5 #2934a, 3 #2935	17.50	—
	Complete booklet, #2935b	18.00	

Stamp Day.

Birds A1635

Designs: 41c, Colibri à tete bleue (Cyanophaia bicolor). No. 2937, Toucan ariel (Ramphastos vitellinus). No. 2938, Colibri grenat (Eulampis jugularis), vert. 69c, Terpsiphone de Bourbon (Terpsiphone bourbonnensis).

2003, Mar. 22 **Photo.** *Perf. 13¼*

2936	A1635 41c multi	1.20	.30
2937	A1635 46c multi	1.40	.30
2938	A1635 46c multi	1.40	.30
2939	A1635 69c multi	2.00	.75
a.	Souvenir sheet, #2936-2939	7.00	7.00
	Nos. 2936-2939 (4)	6.00	1.65

Nantes A1636

2003, Apr. 4 **Engr.**

2940	A1636 46c multi	1.40	.30

Pierre Bérégovoy (1925-93), Prime Minister — A1637

2003, Apr. 30 **Engr.** *Perf. 13x13¼*

2941	A1637 46c multi	1.40	.30

Milan Stefanik (1880-1919), Czechoslovakian General — A1638

2003, May 3 *Perf. 13¼*

2942	A1638 50c multi	1.50	.40

See Slovakia No. 428.

Europa — A1639

2003, May 8 **Photo.**

2943	A1639 50c multi	1.50	.40

Charter of Fundamental Rights of the European Union — A1640

2003, May 8

2944	A1640 50c multi	1.50	.30

Aircraft Carrier "Charles de Gaulle" A1641

2003, May 8 **Engr.**

2945	A1641 50c multi	1.50	.30

Aspects of Life in the French Regions A1642

No. 2946: a, Beach cabins. b, Fishing net. c, Vineyards of Champagne. d, Camembert cheese, vert. e, Foie gras, vert. f, Petanque. g, Puppet show (Guignol), vert. h, Crepe, vert. i, Cassoulet. j, Limoges porcelain.

2003, May 24 **Photo.** *Perf. 13*

2946	Sheet of 10	15.00	15.00
a.-j.	A1642 50c Any single	1.40	1.25

No. 2946 has three vertical rows of rouletting, separating sheet into quarters.

Nos. 2946a-2946j were also issued in large booklets containing panes of 1 of each stamp. The booklet sold for €19.

See Nos. 2978, 3007, 3047, 3106, 3139, 3192, 3234, 3299, 3300, 3357, 3427, 3505.

Art Series

"The Dying Slave" and "The Rebel Slave," by Michelangelo — A1643

The Red Buoy, by Paul Signac A1644

Untitled Abstract by Vassily Kandinsky A1645

Marilyn, by Andy Warhol A1646

2003 **Engr.** *Perf. 13¼x13*

2947	A1643 75c multi	2.25	1.00

Photo.

2948	A1644 75c multi	2.25	1.00

Litho.

2949	A1645 €1.11 multi	3.25	1.25
2950	A1646 €1.11 multi	3.25	1.40
	Nos. 2947-2950 (4)	11.00	4.65

Issued: No. 2947, 5/24. Nos. 2948, 2949, 7/5. No. 2950, 11/8.

A sheet containing 3 No. 2949 and 12 imperforate color progressive proofs was bound in a book that sold for €60.

Happy Birthday A1647

2003, May 31 **Photo.** *Perf. 13¼*

2951	A1647 50c multi	1.40	.35
a.	Souvenir sheet of 5	7.00	7.00
b.	Litho., stamp + label	1.75	1.75

Issued: No. 2951b, 2004. No. 2951b was issued in sheets of 10 stamps + 10 labels that sold for €6.67 on day of issue. The labels could be personalized. The background on

No. 2951 looks splotchy while that of No. 2951b has a dot structure.

Marianne With Euro Denominations Type of 2002

2003, June 1 Engr. *Perf. 13*

2952 A1583 58c apple grn 1.60 .40
2953 A1583 70c yellow grn 2.00 .50
2954 A1583 75c bright blue 2.25 .50
2955 A1583 90c dark blue 2.60 1.00
2956 A1583 €1.11 red lilac 3.25 1.00
2957 A1583 €1.90 violet brown 5.50 1.25
a. Souvenir sheet, #2835, 2921, 2952-2957 22.00 22.00
Nos. 2952-2957 (6) 17.20 4.65

No. 2957a issued 2/28/04.

Orchids Type of 2002

Designs: 30c, Platanthera chlorantha. 35c, Dactylorhiza savogiensis.

2003, June 1 Litho. *Perf. 13*

2958 A1584 30c multi .85 .30
2959 A1584 35c multi 1.00 .40

Nos. 2958-2959 are known only precanceled, See second note after #132.

French Federation of Philatelic Associations 76th Congress, Mulhouse A1648

2003, June 6 Engr. *Perf. 13¼*

2960 A1648 50c multi 1.50 .40

Vacation — A1649

Perf. 12¾x13¼

2003, June 14 Litho.

2961 A1649 50c multi 1.50 .30

Self-Adhesive
Booklet Stamp
Serpentine Die Cut 11

2962 A1649 50c multi 1.50 .30
a. Booklet pane of 10 15.00

Tourism Issue

Notre Dame de l'Epine Basilica — A1650

Tulle A1651

Arras — A1652

Pontarlier A1653

Perf. 13x13¼, 13 (#2965)

2003, June 21 Engr.

2963 A1650 50c multi 1.50 .30
2964 A1651 50c multi 1.50 .30
2965 A1652 50c multi 1.50 .40
2966 A1653 50c multi 1.50 .40
Nos. 2963-2966 (4) 6.00 1.40

Issued: Nos. 2963, 2964, 6/21. No. 2965, 9/20. No. 2966, 10/11.
No. 2965, illustration reduced.

French Freemasonry, 275th Anniv. — A1654

2003, June 28 Engr. *Perf. 13¼x13*

2967 A1654 50c multi 1.40 .30

Tour de France Bicycle Race, Cent. A1655

No. 2968: a, Maurice Garin, winner of 1903 race. b, Cyclist with arms raised.

2003, June 28 Photo. *Perf. 13*

2968 A1655 Vert. pair 3.00 2.00
a.-b. 50c Either single 1.50 .30

Values are for stamps with surrounding selvage.

Saint-Père Church, Yonne — A1656

2003, July 12 Engr. *Perf. 13¼*

2969 A1656 50c multi 1.50 .30

World Track and Field Championships, Paris — A1657

Illustration reduced.

2003, July 19 Photo. *Perf. 13*

2970 A1657 50c multi 1.50 .30

Characters From French Literature — A1658

Designs: No. 2971, Eugène-François Vidocq (1775-1857), convict and police official. No. 2972, Esmerelda, from *Notre-Dame de Paris,* by Victor Hugo. No. 2973, Claudine, from *Claudine* novels, by Colette. No. 2974, Nana, from *Rougon-Macquart,* by Emile Zola. No. 2975, La Comte de Monte-Cristo, from *La Comte de Monte-Cristo,* by Alexandre Dumas (pere). No. 2976, Gavroche, from *Les Miserables,* by Hugo.

2003, Aug. 30 Photo. *Perf. 13*

2971 A1658 50c multi 1.50 .75
2972 A1658 50c multi 1.50 .75
2973 A1658 50c multi 1.50 .75
2974 A1658 50c multi 1.50 .75
2975 A1658 50c multi 1.50 .75
2976 A1658 50c multi 1.50 .75
a. Souvenir sheet, #2971-2976 14.00 14.00
Nos. 2971-2976 (6) 9.00 4.50

No. 2976a sold for €4.60, with the Red Cross receiving €1.60 of that.

Ahmad Shah Massoud (1953-2001), Afghan Northern Alliance Leader — A1659

2003, Sept. 9

2977 A1659 50c multi 1.50 .30

Aspects of Life in French Regions Type of 2003

No. 2978: a, Chateau de Chenonceau. b, House, Alsace. c, Roof, Bourgogne. d, Genoese Tower, Corsica, vert. e, Arc de Triomphe, vert. f, Farm house, Provence. g, Pointe du Raz, vert. h, Mont Blanc, vert. i, Basque house. j, Pont du Gard.

2003, Sept. 20 Photo. *Perf. 13*

2978 Sheet of 10 15.00 15.00
a.-j. A1642 50c Any single 1.50 1.25

No. 2978 has three vertical rows of rouletting, separating sheet into quarters.
Nos. 2978a-2978j were also issued in large booklets containing panes of 1 of each stamp. The booklet sold for €19.

Gardens and Parks — A1660

No. 2979: a, Buttes-Chaumont Park. b, Jardin du Luxembourg.

2003, Sept. 27 *Perf. 13¼x13*

2979 Sheet of 2 11.00 11.00
a.-b. A1660 €1.90 Either single 5.50 5.50

Salon du Timbre 2004. No. 2979 has four vertical rows of rouletting, separating sheet into fifths, with the two stamps in the central fifth.
See Nos. 3029, 3118, 3201, 3316, 3429.

Motor Vehicles — A1661

No. 2980: a, 1954 Isobloc 648 DP 102 bus (Autocar). b, 1950 SFV 302 Tractor. c, 1938 Delahaye fire truck with mechanical aerial ladder. d, Renault Kangaroo Express postal van. e, 1932 Renault TN6 Paris city bus. f, 1910 Berliet 22hp Type M delivery truck. g, 1957 Berliet T100 heavy-duty truck. h, Citroen police van. i, Citroen DS ambulance. j, 1964 Hotchkiss fire truck.

2003, Oct. 24 Photo. *Perf. 13¼*

2980 A1661 Sheet of 10 9.00 9.00
a.-e. 20c Any single .55 .45
f.-j. 30c Any single .85 .65

Philexjeunes 2003 Philatelic Exhibition, Dunkerque.

A1662

Holiday Greetings A1663

2003, Nov. 6 Photo. *Perf. 13*

2981 A1662 50c multi 1.50 .35
a. Litho., stamp + label 6.00 6.00

Litho.

2982 A1663 50c multi 1.50 .35
a. Sheet of 10 + 10 labels 60.00 60.00

Booklet Stamp
Self-Adhesive
Serpentine Die Cut 11¼

2983 A1663 50c multi 1.50 .35
a. Booklet pane of 10 15.00

Nos. 2981a, 2982a, 2004. Nos. 2981a and 2982 were issued in sheets of 10 stamps + 10 labels that sold for €6.67 each on day of issue. The labels could be personalized. The background on No. 2981 looks splotchy while that of No. 2981a has a dot structure.

A souvenir sheet containing No. 2982 was sold for €6 by mail order only. It was not available through standing order subscriptions and was not offered in the philatelic bureau's sales catalog. 50,000 copies of this sheet were printed. Value $250.

Sower Type of 1903, Cent. — A1664

Serpentine Die Cut 6¾ Vert.

2003, Nov. 6 **Engr.**

Booklet Stamp

2984 A1664 50c red 3.50 3.00
a. Booklet pane, 5 each # 2984, 2835A 25.00

European Capitals Type of 2002

No. 2985 — Attractions in Luxembourg: a, Citadelle Saint-Esprit. b, Notre Dame Cathedral, horiz. c, Adolphe Bridge, horiz. d, Grand Duke's Palace.

Perf. 13¼x13, 13x13¼

2003, Nov. 7 **Photo.**

2985 A1622 Sheet of 4 7.50 7.50
a.-d. 50c Any single 1.50 1.00

Indian and French Artisan's Work A1665

Designs: 50c, Illumination depicting rooster, France, 15th cent. 90c, Jewelry design, India, 19th cent.

2003, Nov. 29 **Engr.** ***Perf. 13¼x13***

2986 A1665 50c multi 1.50 .40
2987 A1665 90c multi 2.60 1.50

See India No. 2040.

Launch of the Queen Mary 2 — A1666

2003, Dec. 12 **Photo.** ***Perf. 13¼***

2988 A1666 50c multi 1.40 .30

Greetings A1667

Holes punched through dots in "i's."

2004, Jan. 9 **Photo.** ***Perf. 13***

2989 A1667 50c shown 1.50 .30
2990 A1667 50c Un grand merci 1.50 .30

No Holes Punched Through Dots of "i's"

Stamp + Label

2991 A1667 50c Like No. 2989 6.00 6.00
2992 A1667 50c Like No. 2990 6.00 6.00

Nos. 2991-2992 were issued in sheets of 10 stamps + 10 labels that sold for €6.67 on day of issue. The labels could be personalized.

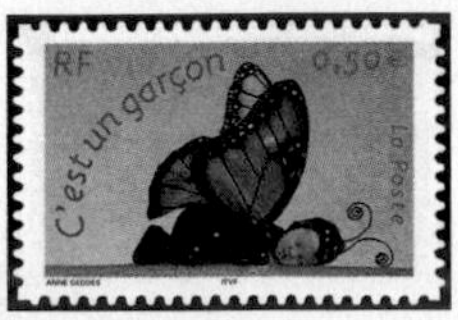

It's a Boy A1668

It's a Girl A1669

2004 **Litho.** ***Perf. 13***

Stamp + Label

2993 A1668 50c multi 6.00 6.00
2994 A1669 50c multi 6.00 6.00

Booklet Stamps

Self-Adhesive

Serpentine Die Cut 11

2995 A1668 50c multi 1.50 .35
a. Booklet pane of 10 15.00
2996 A1669 50c multi 1.50 .35
a. Booklet pane of 10 15.00

Nos. 2993-2994 were issued in sheets of 10 stamps + 10 labels that sold for €6.67 on day of issue. The labels could be personalized.
Nos. 2995-2996 issued 1/9/04.

Hearts A1670

Designs: 50c, Chanel No. 5 perfume bottle. 75c, Woman, Eiffel Tower.

2004, Jan. 9 **Photo.** ***Perf. 13***

2997 A1670 50c multi 1.50 .35
a. Souvenir sheet of 5 7.50 7.50
b. Litho., stamp + label, perf. 13¼ 6.00 6.00
2998 A1670 75c multi 2.25 .75
a. Litho., stamp + label, perf. 13¼ 6.00 6.00

Nos. 2997b and 2998a were each printed in sheets of 10 stamps + 10 labels that could be personalized and sold for €6.69 and €10 respectively. On No. 2997b, there are large brown dots arranged in circles in the shading on the green rectangles, while on No. 2997 the brown dots are small and arranged in rows. On No. 2998a, the dots in the sky are larger and father apart than the tiny dots found on No. 2998.
Values are for stamps with surrounding selvage.

Tourism Issue

Lille, 2004 European Cultural Capital A1671

2004, Jan. 10 **Photo.** ***Perf. 13***

2999 A1671 50c multi 1.50 .35

Art Series

Statue of Liberty, Sculpted by Frederic Auguste Bartholdi (1834-1904) — A1672

2004, Feb. 21 **Engr.** ***Perf. 13¼x13***

3000 A1672 90c multi 2.60 1.50

Queen Eleanor of Aquitaine (c. 1122-1204) A1673

2004, Feb. 28 ***Perf. 13x13¼***

3001 A1673 50c multi 1.50 .35

Stamp Day — A1674

Characters of Walt Disney: 45c, Donald Duck. 50c, Mickey Mouse. 75c, Minnie Mouse.

2004, Mar. 6 **Photo.** ***Perf. 13¼***

3002 A1674 50c multi 1.50 .35
a. Perf. 13¼x13 (from booklet pane) 1.50 .35

Booklet Stamps

Perf. 13¼x13

3003 A1674 45c multi 1.30 .30
3004 A1674 75c multi 2.25 .60
a. Booklet pane, 2 #3003, 4 each #3002a, 3004 17.50 —
Complete booklet, #3004a 18.00

Civil Code, Bicent. A1675

2004, Mar. 12 **Engr.** ***Perf. 13¼x13***

3005 A1675 50c multi 1.50 .35

George Sand (1804-76), Writer A1676

2004, Mar. 20 **Engr.** ***Perf. 13¼x13***

3006 A1676 50c multi 1.50 .35

Aspects of Life in French Regions Type of 2003

No. 3007: a, Cutlery. b, Produce of Provence, vert. c, Beaujolais grapes, vert. d, Bread. e, Woman wearing coif, vert. f, Oysters, vert. g, Quiche Lorraine. h, Bullfighting. i, Clafoutis. j, Bagpipers.

2004, Mar. 26 **Photo.** ***Perf. 13***

3007 Sheet of 10 15.00 15.00
a.-j. A1642 50c Any single 1.50 1.00

No. 3007 has three vertical rows of rouletting, separating sheet into quarters.

Clermont-Ferrand — A1677

2004, Mar. 26 **Engr.** ***Perf. 13¼***

3008 A1677 50c multi 1.50 .35

Entente Cordiale, Cent. — A1678

Designs: 50c, Coccinelle, by Sonia Delaunay. 75c, Lace 1 (trial proof) 1968, by Sir Terry Frost.

2004, Apr. 6 **Photo.** ***Perf. 13¼***

3009 A1678 50c multi 1.50 .35
3010 A1678 75c multi 2.25 .75

See Great Britain Nos. 2200-2201.

Road Safety — A1679

2004, Apr. 7

3011 A1679 50c multi 1.50 .35

See United Nations Offices in Geneva No. 424.

Art Series

La Méridienne d'Après Millet, by Vincent van Gogh — A1680

2004, July 2 **Photo.** ***Perf. 13x13¼***

3012 A1680 75c multi 2.25 .95

Art Series

Un Combat de Coqs, by Jean-Léon Gérôme — A1681

Galatée aux Sphères, by Salvador Dali A1682

2004 **Photo.** ***Perf. 13x13¼***

3013 A1681 €1.11 multi 3.25 1.40
3014 A1682 €1.11 multi 3.25 1.40

Issued: No. 3013, 4/17; No. 3014, 6/19.

Tourism Issue

Bordeaux — A1683

Vaux-sur-Mer — A1684

Notre Dame de l'Assomption Cathedral, Luçon — A1685

Illustration reduced.

2004 Litho. & Engr. *Perf. 13*

3015	A1683	50c multi		1.50	.35

Engr.

Perf. 13¼

3016	A1684	50c multi	1.50	.35
3017	A1685	50c multi	1.50	.35

Issued: No. 3015, 4/26; No. 3016, 7/17; No. 3017, 10/2.

Farm Animals A1686

2004, Apr. 26 Photo. *Perf. 13¼*

3018	A1686	45c Rabbit	1.25	.30
3019	A1686	50c Cow, vert.	1.50	.35
3020	A1686	50c Chicken	1.50	.35
3021	A1686	75c Burro, vert.	2.25	.60
a.		Souvenir sheet, #3018-3021	7.00	6.50

Expansion of the European Union A1687

2004, May 1 Photo. *Perf. 13¼*

3022	A1687	50c multi	1.50	.40

Battle of Dien Bien Phu, 50th Anniv. — A1688

2004, May 7 *Perf. 13¼x13*

3023	A1688	50c multi	1.50	.40

Europa A1689

2004 Photo. *Perf. 13x13¼*

3024	A1689	50c multi	1.50	.35

Litho.

Booklet Stamp

Self-Adhesive

Serpentine Die Cut 11

3025	A1689	50c multi	2.00	.35
a.		Booklet pane of 10	15.00	

Issued: No. 3024, 5/9; No. 3025, 6/4.

Blake and Mortimer, Comic Book Characters by Edgar P. Jacobs A1690

Blake and Mortimer and: 50c, Brick wall, vert. €1, Blue background.

2004, May 15 Photo. *Perf. 13¼*

3026	A1690	50c multi	1.50	.35
3027	A1690	€1 multi	3.00	1.25

See Belgium No. 2020.

FIFA (Fédération Internationale de Football Association), Cent. — A1691

2004, May 20 *Perf. 13¼x13*

3028	A1691	50c multi	1.50	.35

Gardens and Parks Type of 2003

No. 3029: a, Jardin des Tuileries. b, Parc Floral de Paris.

2004, June 4 *Perf. 13¼x13*

3029		Sheet of 2	11.50	11.50
a.-b.	A1660	€1.90 Either single	5.75	5.75
c.		Souvenir sheet, #2979a-2979b, 3029a-3029b	25.00	25.00

Salon du Timbre 2004. No. 3029 has four vertical rows of rouletting, separating sheet into fifths, with the two stamps in the central fifth.

D-Day Invasion of France, 60th Anniv. — A1692

2004, June 5 *Perf. 13*

3030	A1692	50c multi	1.50	.35

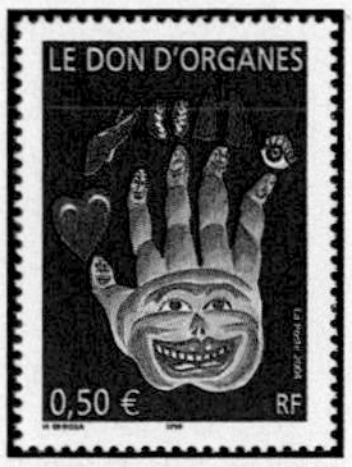

Organ Donation A1693

2004, June 22 *Perf. 13¼*

3031	A1693	50c multi	1.50	.35

Pierre Dugua de Mons, Leader of First French Settlement in Acadia, and Ship A1694

Litho. & Engr.

2004, June 26 *Perf. 13*

3032	A1694	90c multi	2.75	1.50

See Canada No. 2044.

Napoleon I and the Imperial Guard — A1695

Designs: No. 3033, Light cavalry (Chasseur à cheval). No. 3034, Artilleryman and cannon (Artilleur à pied), horiz. No. 3035, Dragoon. No. 3036, Mameluke. No. 3037, Napoleon I. No. 3038, Grenadier (Grenadier à pied).

2004, June 26 Photo.

3033	A1695	50c multi	1.50	.75
3034	A1695	50c multi	1.50	.75
3035	A1695	50c multi	1.50	.75
3036	A1695	50c multi	1.50	.75
3037	A1695	50c multi	1.50	.75
3038	A1695	50c multi	1.50	.75
a.		Souvenir sheet, #3033-3038	12.50	12.50
		Nos. 3033-3038 (6)	9.00	4.50

No. 3038a sold for €4.60, with the Red Cross receiving €1.60 of that.

French Federation of Philatelic Associations 77th Congress, Paris — A1696

Litho. & Engr.

2004, June 27 *Perf. 13¼x13*

3039	A1696	50c multi	1.50	.35

2004 Summer Olympics, Athens — A1697

2004, June 28 Photo. *Perf. 13¼*

3040		50c Modern athletes	1.50	.60
3041		50c Ancient athletes	1.50	.60
a.	A1697	Pair, #3040-3041	3.25	2.25

Printed in sheets containing five of each stamp.

A souvenir sheet containing No. 3041 was issued Aug. 2 and sold for €2.51. Value $20.

Happy Birthday A1698

2004, June 30 Photo. *Perf. 13¼*

3042	A1698	50c multi	1.50	.35
a.		Souvenir sheet of 5	7.50	7.50
b.		Litho. stamp + label	6.00	6.00

No. 3042b printed in sheets of 10 stamps + 10 labels that could be personalized that sold for €8. No. 3042b has a dark green inscription at left with a distinct dot pattern. No. 3042 has a lighter green inscription.

Marianne Type of 1997 Inscribed "RF" at Lower Left and Type of 2002 With Euro Denominations

2004 Litho. *Perf. 13*

3043		Sheet of 15 + 15 labels	50.00	50.00
a.	A1583	1c orange yellow	.20	.20
b.	A1583	2c brown	.20	.20
c.	A1583	5c brt bl green	.20	.20
d.	A1583	10c purple	.30	.30
e.	A1583	20c orange	.60	.60
f.	A1583	58c apple green	1.75	1.75
g.	A1583	70c olive	2.10	2.10
h.	A1583	75c sky blue	2.25	2.25
i.	A1583	90c dark blue	2.75	2.75
j.	A1583	€1 Prussian blue	3.00	3.00
k.	A1583	€1.11 red lilac	3.25	3.25
l.	A1583	€1.90 violet brown	5.75	5.75
m.	A1583	€2 violet	6.00	6.00
n.	A1409	(45c) green	1.40	1.40
o.	A1409	(50c) red	1.50	1.50

No. 3043 sold for €10.03. Stamps have a glossy varnish.

Marianne and Emblem of World Fund to Combat AIDS, Tuberculosis and Smoking — A1699

2004, July 1 Engr. *Perf. 13*

3044	A1699	(50c) red	1.50	.35

Extreme Sports — A1700

No. 3045: a, Skateboarding. b, Parachuting. c, Sailboarding. d, Surfing. e, Luge. f, BMX bicycling. g, Paragliding. h, Jetskiing. i, Snowboarding. j, Rollerblading.

2004, July 3 Photo. *Perf. 13¼x13*

3045 A1700 Sheet of 10 7.50 7.50
a.-e. 20c Any single .60 .50
f.-j. 30c Any single .90 .75

Orchid Type of 2002

Design: 39c, Orchis insularis.

2004, Sept. 1 Litho. *Perf. 13*

3046 A1584 39c multi 1.20 .75

No. 3046 known only precanceled. See second note after No. 132.

Aspects of Life in the French Regions Type of 2003

No. 3047: a, House, Normandy. b, Chambord Chateau. c, Gorges, Tarn, vert. d, Notre Dame Cathedral, Paris, vert. e, Windmill, vert. f, Cave dwellings. g, Creek, Cassis, vert. h, Cap-Ferret Lighthouse, vert. i, Castle ruins. j, Alpine chalet.

2004, Sept. 18 Photo. *Perf. 13*

3047 Sheet of 10 15.00 15.00
a.-j. A1642 50c Any single 1.50 1.25

No. 3047 has three vertical rows of rouletting separating sheet into quarters.
Each stamp exists in booklet pane of 1 from booklet that sold for €19.

Halloween
A1701

2004, Oct. 9 Litho. *Perf. 13*

3048 A1701 50c multi 1.50 .35

Félix Eboué (1884-1944), Colonial Governor — A1702

2004, Oct. 16 Photo.

3049 A1702 50c multi 1.50 .40

Ouistreham Lighthouse
A1703

2004, Oct. 30 *Perf. 13¼*

3050 A1703 50c multi 1.50 .40

Marianne — A1704

Serpentine Die Cut 6¾ Vert.

2004, Nov. 10 Engr.

Booklet Stamp
Self-Adhesive

3051 A1704 50c multi 2.50 2.00
a. Booklet pane, 5 each #2835A, 3051 20.00

European Capitals Type of 2002

No. 3052 — Attractions in Athens: a, Greek Academy. b, Parthenon. c, Odeon of Herodes Atticus. d, Church of the Holy Apostles, vert.

Perf. 13x13¼, 13¼x13

2004, Nov. 11 Photo.

3052 A1622 Sheet of 4 7.50 7.50
a.-d. 50c Any single 1.50 .90

A1705

A1706

A1707

A1708

A1709

Holiday Greetings
A1710

2004, Nov. 12 Photo. *Perf. 13*

3053 A1705 50c multi 1.50 .40

Litho.

3054 A1706 50c multi + label 6.00 6.00
3055 A1707 50c multi + label 6.00 6.00
3056 A1708 50c multi + label 6.00 6.00
3057 A1709 50c multi + label 6.00 6.00
3058 A1710 50c multi + label 6.00 6.00
a. Vert. strip of 5, #3054-3059 + 5 labels 30.00 30.00
Miniature sheet, 2 #3058a + 10 labels 60.00 60.00

Booklet Stamps
Self-Adhesive

Serpentine Die Cut 11¼x11

3059 A1706 50c multi 1.50 .40
3060 A1707 50c multi 1.50 .40
3061 A1708 50c multi 1.50 .40
3062 A1709 50c multi 1.50 .40
3063 A1710 50c multi 1.50 .40
a. Booklet pane, 2 each #3059-3063 15.00
Nos. 3053-3063 (11) 39.00 32.40

Miniature sheet containing Nos. 3054-3058 sold for €6.69. Labels could be personalized. No. 3055 exists in a souvenir sheet of 1 stamp without label that sold for €3. Value $35.

Henri Wallon (1812-1904), Historian and Politician — A1711

2004, Nov. 13 Photo. *Perf. 13*

3064 A1711 50c multi 1.50 .40

Opening of Millau Viaduct — A1712

Illustration reduced.

2004, Dec. 14 Photo. *Perf. 13*

3065 A1712 50c multi 1.50 .40

Marianne — A1713

Inscribed "ITVF" at Bottom

2005 Engr. *Perf. 13*

3066 A1713 1c yellow .20 .20
a. Inscribed "Phil@poste" at bottom .20 .20
3067 A1713 5c brown black .20 .20
a. Inscribed "Phil@poste" at bottom .20 .20
3068 A1713 10c violet .25 .20
3069 A1713 (45c) green 1.25 .25
a. Inscribed "Phil@poste" at bottom 1.25 .25
3070 A1713 (50c) red 1.50 .25
a. Sheet of 15 + 15 labels 60.00 60.00
b. Inscribed "Phil@poste" at bottom 1.40 .25
3071 A1713 55c dark blue 1.60 .50
3072 A1713 58c olive green 1.75 .40
3073 A1713 64c dark green 1.90 .40
3074 A1713 70c dark green 2.10 .50
3075 A1713 75c light blue 2.25 .40
3076 A1713 82c fawn 2.40 .45
3077 A1713 90c dark blue 2.75 .90
3078 A1713 €1 orange 3.00 1.00
a. Inscribed "Phil@poste" at bottom 2.60 .55
3079 A1713 €1.11 red violet 3.25 .80
3080 A1713 €1.22 red violet 3.50 .75
3081 A1713 €1.90 chocolate 5.75 1.20
3082 A1713 €1.98 chocolate 6.00 2.00
Nos. 3066-3082 (17) 39.65 10.40

Booklet Stamp
Self-Adhesive

Serpentine Die Cut 6¾ Vert.

3083 A1713 (50c) red 1.50 .20
a. Booklet pane of 10 (see footnote) 15.00
b. Booklet pane of 10 (see footnote) 15.00
c. Booklet pane of 20 30.00
d. As #3083, with "Phil@poste" inscription 1.50 .20
e. Booklet pane, 10 #3083d 15.00
f. Booklet pane of 12 #3083d 17.00

Coil Stamps

Perf. 13 Horiz.

3086 A1713 (45c) green 1.25 .30
a. "Inscribed "Phil@poste" at bottom 1.40 .25
3087 A1713 (50c) red 1.50 .25
3087A A1713 55c dark blue 1.60 .60
b. Inscribed "Phil@poste" at bottom 1.60 .25

Issued: Nos. 1c, 10c, (45c), (50c), 58c, 70c, 75c, 90c, €1, €1.11, €1.90, 1/8. 5c, No. 3071, 64c, 82c, €1.22, €1.98, 3/1. No. 3087A, 7/15. Nos. 3083d, 3083e, 10/1/06. Face values shown for Nos. 3069, 3070, 3083, 3086 and 3087 are those the stamps sold for on the day of issue. No. 3070a sold for €10.03 and the labels could be personalized for an additional fee. No. 3083a has a narrow strip of selvage separating the four stamps at left, from the six stamps, at right, and is on a white backing paper. No. 3083b is comprised of two horizontal strips of five stamps on a yellow backing paper. No. 3083d sold for 54c on day of issue.
Nos. 3066a, 3067a, 3069a, 3070b issued 2006. No. 3083f, Jan. 2007. On day of issue, No. 3069a sold for 49c; No. 3070b for 54c.
A sheet of 10 litho. stamps similar to No. 3068 + 10 labels exists, but was not sold.
No. 3086a was issued in 2008 and sold for 50c.
No. 3087b was issued in 2008 and sold for 55c.
See Nos. 3211, 3211N, 3212, 3247-3255D, 3302.

Rabbi Shlomo Yitshaqi (Rashi) (1040-1105) — A1714

2005, Jan. 16 Engr. *Perf. 13¼*

3088 A1714 50c multi 1.75 .40

Hearts
A1715

Designs: 53c, Polka dots. 82c, Bird and flowers.

2005, Jan. 29 Photo. *Perf. 13¼*

3089 A1715 53c multi 1.50 .40
a. Souvenir sheet of 5 7.50 7.50
b. Litho, stamp + label 5.00 5.00
3090 A1715 82c multi 2.50 1.00
a. Litho, stamp + label 6.00 6.00

Values are for stamps with surrounding selvage.
Sheets of 10 of No. 3089b sold for €6.86, and sheets of 10 of No. 3090a sold for €8.78. Labels could be personalized for an additional fee.
See Nos. 3134, 3136.

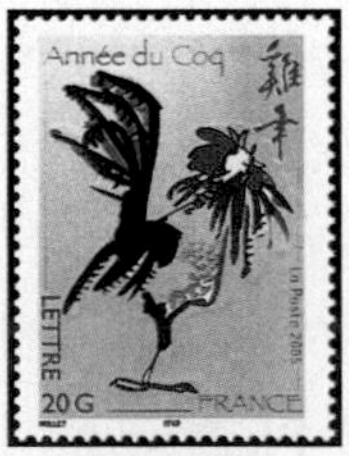

New Year 2005 (Year of the Rooster)
A1716

Photo. & Embossed

2005, Jan. 29 *Perf. 13½x13*

3091 A1716 (50c) multi 1.50 .40

Printed in sheets of 10.

Rotary International, Cent. — A1717

2005, Feb. 19 Photo. *Perf. 13¼*

3092 A1717 53c multi 1.50 .40

Titeuf — A1718

Nadia — A1719

Manu — A1720

2005, Feb. 28 Photo. *Perf. 13¼*

3093 A1718 (50c) red & multi 1.50 .40
 a. Perf. 13¼x13 (booklet stamp) 1.50 .40

Booklet Stamps

3094 A1719 (45c) green & multi 1.40 .35
3095 A1720 (90c) blue & multi 2.75 .70
 a. Booklet pane, 2 #3094, 4 each #3093a, 3095 20.00 —
 Complete booklet, #3095a 21.00

Characters from Titeuf, comic strip by Zep. Stamp Day.

Greetings Type of 2004 Inscribed "Lettre 20g"

Designs: Nos. 3096, 3097A, "Ceci est une invitation." Nos. 3097, 3097B, "Un grand merci."

No. 3097C, "Ceci est une invitation." No. 3097D, "Un grand merci."

2005-06 Photo. *Perf. 13*

Holes Punched Through Dots of "i's"

3096 A1667 (53c) brt lil rose & yel 1.50 .40
3097 A1667 (53c) brt yel grn & red lil 1.50 .40

Litho.

No Holes Punched Through Dots of "i's"

Stamp + Label

3097A A1667 (53c) brt lil rose & yel 4.50 4.50
3097B A1667 (53c) brt yel grn & red lil 4.50 4.50

Self-Adhesive

No Holes Punched Through Dots of "i's"

Serpentine Die Cut 11¼x11

Stamp + Label

3097C A1667 (53c) brt lil rose & yel 2.40 2.40
3097D A1667 (53c) brt yel grn & rrd lil 2.40 2.40

Nos. 3097A-3097B were issued in sheets of 10 stamps + 10 labels that sold for €8 on day of issue. The labels could be personalized.

Nos. 3097C-3097D were each issued in sheets of 10 stamps + 10 labels that sold for €8.61. Labels could be personalized.

Issued: Nos. 2096-3097B, 3/1/05. Nos. 3097C-3097D, 2006.

Art Series

The Guitarist, by Jean-Baptiste Greuze (1725-1805) — A1721

White Bear, Sculpture by François Pompon — A1722

Sicile, by Nicolas de Stael — A1723

2005 Photo. *Perf. 13x13¼*

3098 A1721 82c multi 2.40 1.00
3099 A1722 90c multi 2.75 1.50
3100 A1723 €1.22 multi 3.50 1.60

Issued: €1.22, 3/5. 90c, 7/2. 82c, 9/24.

Orchids — A1725

Designs: No. 3102, Cypripedium calceolus. No. 3103, Paphiopedilum Mabel Sanders. 55c, Oncidium papilio. 82c, Paphinia cristata, horiz.

2005, Mar. 11 Photo. *Perf. 13¼*

3102 A1725 53c multi 1.60 .40
3103 A1725 53c multi 1.60 .40
3104 A1725 55c multi 1.60 .45
3105 A1725 82c multi 2.40 1.00
 a. Souvenir sheet, #3102-3105 7.50 7.50
 Nos. 3102-3105 (4) 7.20 2.25

Aspects of Life in French Regions Type of 2003

No. 3106: a, Nautical jousting. b, Clocks of Franche-Comte, vert. c, Cantal cheese and bread, vert. d, Dancers and accordion player. e, Bouillabaisse. f, P'tit Quinquin statue, vert. g, Rillettes (chopped pork). h, Sauerkraut and sausage, beer stein. i, Pelota, vert. j, Sugar cane, vert.

2005, Mar. 19 Photo. *Perf. 13*

3106 Sheet of 10 16.00 16.00
 a.-j. A1642 53c Any single 1.50 1.25

No. 3106 has three vertical rows of rouletting, separating sheet into quarters.

Each stamp exists in a booklet pane of 1 from a booklet that sold for €19. Value $50.

Tourism Issue

Aix-en-Provence — A1726

Gulf of Morbihan — A1727

Villefranche-sur-Mer — A1728

La Roque-Gageac — A1729

Illustration A1727 is reduced.

2005 Engr. *Perf. 13¼, 13 (#3108)*

3107 A1726 53c multi 1.60 .40

Photo.

3108 A1727 53c multi 1.60 .40
3109 A1728 53c multi 1.60 .40

Engr.

3110 A1729 53c multi 1.60 .40

Issued: No. 3107, 4/1; No. 3108, 5/5; No. 3109, 6/4; No. 3110, 7/23.

Happy Birthday A1730

2005, Apr. 2 Photo. *Perf. 13*

3111 A1730 (53c) multi 1.60 .40
 a. Souvenir sheet of 5 8.00 8.00
 b. Litho., stamp + label 6.00 6.00

Sheets of 10 and 10 labels of No. 3111b sold for €6.86. Labels could be personalized for an additional fee.

Albert Einstein (1879-1955), Physicist — A1731

2005, Apr. 16 *Perf. 13¼*

3112 A1731 53c multi 1.60 .40

Alexis de Tocqueville (1805-59), Writer — A1732

2005, Apr. 23 Engr. *Perf. 13x13¼*

3113 A1732 90c multi 2.75 1.00

Liberation of Concentration Camp Internees, 60th Anniv. — A1733

2005, Apr. 24 Photo. *Perf. 13¼*

3114 A1733 53c multi 1.60 .40

Battle of Austerlitz, Bicent. A1734

Litho. & Engr.

2005, May 4 *Perf. 13¼*

3115 A1734 55c multi 1.60 .45

See Czech Republic No. 3273.

French Federation of Philatelic Associations, 78th Congress, Nancy — A1735

Illustration reduced.

2005, May 5 Engr. *Perf. 13*

3116 A1735 53c multi + label 1.60 .40

A souvenir sheet of one stamp without label exists. Value $12.

Europa — A1736

2005, May 8 Photo. *Perf. 13¼*

3117 A1736 53c multi 1.60 .50

Gardens and Parks Type of 2003
Souvenir Sheet

No. 3118 — Sculptures in Jardin de la Fontaine, Nimes: a, Denomination in green. b, Denomination in white.

2005, May 15 *Perf. 13¼x13*
3118 Sheet of 2 12.00 12.00
a.-b. A1660 €1.98 Either single 6.00 6.00

Salon du Timbre 2005. No. 3118 has four vertical rows of rouletting, separating sheet into fifths, with the two stamps in the central fifth.

Vacation A1737

Serpentine Die Cut 11
2005, May 23 **Litho.**
Booklet Stamp
Self-Adhesive
3119 A1737 (53c) multi 1.60 .40
a. Booklet pane of 10 16.00

Stories by Jules Verne (1828-1905) A1738

Designs: No. 3120, Five Weeks in a Balloon (Cinq Semaines en Ballon). No. 3121, From the Earth to the Moon (De la Terre à la Lune). No. 3122, Journey to the Center of the Earth (Voyage au Centre de la Terre), horiz. No. 3123, Michael Strogoff, horiz. No. 3124, Around the World in Eighty Days (Le Tour du Monde en Quatre-vingts Jours). No. 3125, 20,000 Leagues Under the Sea (Vingt Mille Lieues Sous les Mers).

2005, May 28 **Photo.** *Perf. 13*
3120 A1738 53c multi 1.60 .75
3121 A1738 53c multi 1.60 .75
3122 A1738 53c multi 1.60 .75
3123 A1738 53c multi 1.60 .75
3124 A1738 53c multi 1.60 .75
3125 A1738 53c multi 1.60 .75
a. Souvenir sheet, #3120-3125 12.00 12.00
Nos. 3120-3125 (6) 9.60 4.50

No. 3125a sold for €4.80 with the Red Cross receiving €1.62 of that.

Miniature Sheet

Gordon Bennett Cup, Cent. — A1739

No. 3126 — Inscriptions: a, La Coupe Gordon Bennett (Car No. 1 facing right). b, La Coupe Gordon Bennett (Car No. 1 facing left). c, La Formule 1, vert. d, Le Rallye-Raid, vert. e, Les Rallyes. f, La Course d'endurance.

2005, June 2 **Photo.** *Perf.*
3126 A1739 Sheet of 10, #a-b, 2 each #c-f 19.00 19.00
a.-f. 53c Any single 1.75 .85

A souvenir sheet containing No. 3126a sold for €3. Value $100.

Environmental Charter — A1740

Illustration reduced.

2005, June 5 **Litho.** *Perf. 13*
3127 A1740 53c multi, *lt green* 1.60 .40

Enactment of Handicapped Persons Rights Law — A1741

2005, June 18 **Photo.** *Perf. 13¼*
3128 A1741 53c multi 1.60 .35

It's a Boy A1742

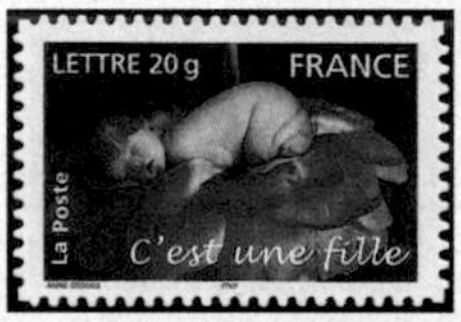

It's a Girl A1743

2005 **Litho.** *Perf. 13x13¼*
3129 A1742 (53c) multi + label 4.00 4.00
3130 A1743 (53c) multi + label 4.00 4.00

Booklet Stamps
Self-Adhesive
Serpentine Die Cut 11¼x11
3131 A1742 (53c) multi 1.60 .35
a. Booklet pane of 10 16.00
b. Sheet of 10 + 10 labels 23.00
3132 A1743 (53c) multi 1.60 .35
a. Booklet pane of 10 16.00
b. Sheet of 10 + 10 labels 23.00

Sheets of 10 stamps and 10 labels of Nos. 3129 and 3130 each sold for €6.86. Nos. 3131b and 3132b each sold for €8.61. Labels could be personalized for an additional fee.

Hearts Types of 2004-05
Serpentine Die Cut
2005, July 15 **Photo.**
Self-Adhesive
3133 A1670 50c Like #2997 5.00 3.50
3134 A1715 53c Like #3089 6.00 4.50
3135 A1670 75c Like #2998 6.00 4.50
3136 A1715 82c Like #3090 7.00 5.50
Nos. 3133-3136 (4) 24.00 18.00

Haras du Pin Natl. Stud Farm A1744

2005, July 16 *Perf. 13*
3137 A1744 53c multi 1.60 .40

European Capitals Type of 2002

No. 3138 — Attractions in Berlin: a, Brandenburg Gate. b, Kaiser Wilhelm Memorial Church, vert. c, Philharmonic Hall. d, Reichstag.

Perf. 13x13¼, 13¼x13
2005, Aug. 27 **Photo.**
3138 A1622 Sheet of 4 6.50 6.50
a.-d. 53c Any single 1.60 1.00

Aspects of Life in the French Regions Type of 2003

No. 3139: a, Lake Annecy. b, Etretat Cliffs, vert. c, Pigeon house, vert. d, Wash house (lavoir). e, Banks of the Seine. f, Carnac megaliths. g, House, Sologne. h, Pilat Sand Dune. i, Stiff Lighthouse, vert. j, Stone hut (borie), vert.

2005, Sept. 17 *Perf. 13*
3139 Sheet of 10 16.00 16.00
a.-j. A1642 53c Any single 1.60 1.25

No. 3139 has three vertical rows of rouletting, separating sheet into quarters.

Nos. 3139a-3139j were also issued in large booklets containing panes of 1 of each stamp. The booklet sold for €19. Value $60.

Art Series

Les Halles Centrales, Designed by Victor Baltard (1805-74) — A1745

2005, Sept. 17 **Engr.** *Perf. 13x13¼*
3140 A1745 €1.22 multi 3.50 1.25

Breast Cancer Awareness A1746

2005, Oct. 1 **Photo.** *Perf. 13¼*
3141 A1746 53c multi 1.60 .35

A1747

A1748

A1749

A1750

A1751

A1752

A1753

A1754

A1755

Cat, Comics by Philippe Geluck A1756

Serpentine Die Cut 11¼x11
2005, Oct. 1 **Litho.**
Booklet Stamps
Self-Adhesive
3142 A1747 (53c) multi 1.60 .35
3143 A1748 (53c) multi 1.60 .35
3144 A1749 (53c) multi 1.60 .35
3145 A1750 (53c) multi 1.60 .35
3146 A1751 (53c) multi 1.60 .35
3147 A1752 (53c) multi 1.60 .35
3148 A1753 (53c) multi 1.60 .35
3149 A1754 (53c) multi 1.60 .35
3150 A1755 (53c) multi 1.60 .35
3151 A1756 (53c) multi 1.60 .35
a. Booklet pane of 10, #3142-3151 16.00

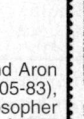

Raymond Aron (1905-83), Philosopher A1757

2005, Oct. 7 **Engr.** *Perf. 13¼x13*
3152 A1757 53c multi 1.60 .35

Souvenir Sheet

The Annunciation, by Raphael — A1758

No. 3153: a, Drawing of Angel, painting of Virgin Mary. b, Painting of Angel, drawing of Virgin Mary.

Litho. & Engr.
2005, Nov. 10 *Perf. 13x13¼*
3153 A1758 Sheet of 2 4.00 4.00
a. 53c multi 1.60 1.60
b. 55c multi 1.60 1.60

See Vatican City Nos. 1312-1314.

Marianne — A1759

Serpentine Die Cut 6¾ Vert.

2005, Nov. 11 **Engr.**

Booklet Stamp

Self-Adhesive

3154 A1759 53c red 3.00 2.50
a. Booklet pane, 5 each #3083, 3154 22.50

Video Game Characters — A1760

No. 3155: a, Link. b, Pac-Man. c, Prince of Persia. d, Spyro. e, Donkey Kong. f, Mario. g, Adibou. h, Rayman. i, Lara Croft. j, The Sims.

2005, Nov. 11 **Photo.** ***Perf. 13¼x13***

3155 A1760	Sheet of 10	9.00	9.00
a.-e.	20c Any single	.60	.50
f.-j.	33c Any single	1.00	.75

Avicenna (980-1037), Scientist — A1761

2005, Nov. 12 **Engr.** ***Perf. 13x13¼***

3156 A1761 53c multi 1.60 .35

Holiday Greetings A1762

Designs: Nos. 3157, 3162, Bear, three penguins and sled. Nos. 3158, 3163, Two penguins, reindeer and sled. Nos. 3159, 3164, Two penguins, bear and sled. Nos. 3160, 3165, Three penguins. Nos. 3161, 3166, Two penguins, reindeer and snowman.

2005, Nov. 12 **Litho.** ***Perf. 13***

3157 A1762 (53c) multi + label		6.00	4.00
3158 A1762 (53c) multi + label		6.00	4.00
3159 A1762 (53c) multi + label		6.00	4.00
3160 A1762 (53c) multi + label		6.00	4.00
3161 A1762 (53c) multi + label		6.00	4.00
a.	Vert. strip of 5, #3157-3161, + 5 labels	30.00	30.00
	Miniature sheet, 2 #3161a	60.00	60.00

Booklet Stamps

Self-Adhesive

Serpentine Die Cut 11¼x11

3162 A1762 (53c) multi		1.60	.35
3163 A1762 (53c) multi		1.60	.35
3164 A1762 (53c) multi		1.60	.35
3165 A1762 (53c) multi		1.60	.35
3166 A1762 (53c) multi		1.60	.35
a.	Booklet pane, 2 each #3162-3166	16.00	
	Nos. 3157-3166 (10)	38.00	21.75

Miniature sheet containing Nos. 3157-3161 sold for €6.86. Labels could be personalized.

No. 3161 exists in a souvenir sheet of one stamp without label, that sold for €3. Value $35.

Jacob Kaplan (1895-1994), Grand Rabbi of France — A1763

2005, Nov. 14 **Engr.** ***Perf. 13***

3167 A1763 53c multi 1.60 .35

Orchid Type of 2002

Design: Orchis insularis.

2005 **Litho.** ***Perf. 13***

3168 A1584 42c multi 1.25 .75

No. 3168 is known only precanceled. See second note after #132.

Law Separating Church and State, Cent. — A1764

2005, Dec. 3 **Photo.** ***Perf. 13¼x13***

3169 A1764 53c multi 1.60 .35

Hearts A1765

Designs: (53c), Hearts, octagons and diamonds. (82c), Heart and stripes.

2006, Jan. 7 **Photo.** ***Perf. 13¼***

3170 A1765 (53c) multi		1.60	.40
a.	Souvenir sheet of 5	8.00	8.00
b.	Litho., stamp + label	4.00	4.00
3171 A1765 (82c) multi		2.40	.70
a.	Litho., stamp + label	4.00	4.00

Self-Adhesive

Serpentine Die Cut

3172 A1765 (53c) Like #3170		3.00	1.50
a.	Sheet of 10 + 10 labels	23.00	
3173 A1765 (82c) Like #3171		4.00	3.00
a.	Sheet of 10 + 10 labels	30.00	

Values are for stamps with surrounding selvage. Sheets of 10 of No. 3170b sold for €6.86, and sheets of No. 3172a. No. 3172a sold for €8.61; No. 3173a for €11.54. Labels could be personalized for an additional fee.

New Year 2006 (Year of the Dog) — A1766

2006, Jan. 21 **Photo.** ***Perf. 13¼x13***

3174 A1766 (53c) multi 1.60 .40

A souvenir sheet containing No. 3174 sold for €3. Value $14.

Impressionist Paintings — A1767

Designs: Nos. 3175a, 3176, Portraits from the Country, by Gustave Caillebotte. Nos. 3175b, 3183, Dancers, by Edgar Degas. Nos. 3175c, 3181, Marguerite Gachet in the Garden, by Vincent van Gogh. Nos. 3175d, 3179, Two Young Girls at the Piano, by Auguste Renoir. Nos. 3175e, 3177, The Butterfly Hunt, by Berthe Morisot. Nos. 3175f, 3184, Luncheon on the Grass, by Edouard Manet. Nos. 3175g, 3182, Evening Air, by Henri-Edmond Cross. Nos. 3175h, 3180, The Shepherdess (Young Peasant Girl with a Stick), by Camille Pissarro. Nos. 3175i, 3178, Mother and Child, by Mary Cassatt. Nos. 3175j, 3185, Women of Tahiti on the Beach, by Paul Gauguin.

2006 **Litho.** ***Perf. 13¼***

3175	Sheet of 10 +10 labels	35.00	35.00
a.-j.	A1767 (53c) Any single + label	3.50	3.50

Booklet Stamps

Self-Adhesive

Serpentine Die Cut 11¼x11

3176 A1767 (53c) multi		1.60	.40
3177 A1767 (53c) multi		1.60	.40
3178 A1767 (53c) multi		1.60	.40
3179 A1767 (53c) multi		1.60	.40
3180 A1767 (53c) multi		1.60	.40
3181 A1767 (53c) multi		1.60	.40
3182 A1767 (53c) multi		1.60	.40
3183 A1767 (53c) multi		1.60	.40
3184 A1767 (53c) multi		1.60	.40
3185 A1767 (53c) multi		1.60	.40
a.	Booklet pane of 10, #3176-3185	16.00	
b.	Sheet of 10, #3176-3185, + 10 labels	*65.00*	

Issued: No. 3175, 6/1; Nos. 3176-3185, 1/21. No. 3175 sold for €6.86. No. 3185b sold for €8.61. Labels could be personalized.

2006 Winter Olympics, Turin — A1768

2006, Feb. 4 **Photo.** ***Perf. 13***

3186 A1768 53c multi 1.60 .35

Spirou — A1769

Fantasio, Spip and Spirou — A1770

Fantasio A1771

2006, Feb. 25 ***Perf. 13¼***

3187 A1769 (53c) multi		1.60	.40
a.	Perf. 13¼x13 (booklet stamp)	1.60	.40

Booklet Stamps

Perf. 13¼x13

3188 A1770 (48c) multi		1.40	.35
3189 A1771 (90c) multi		2.75	.65
a.	Booklet pane, 4 each #3187a, 3188, 2 #3189	17.50	—
	Complete booklet, #3189a	18.00	

Characters from Spirou, by Robert Velter. Stamp Day.

Courrières Coal Mine Disaster, Cent. — A1772

2006, Feb. 25 ***Perf. 13¼***

3190 A1772 53c multi 1.60 .40

Douaumont Ossuary — A1773

2006, Mar. 4 **Engr.**

3191 A1773 53c multi 1.60 .40

Aspects of Life in the French Regions Type of 2003

No. 3192: a, Yellow plums (mirabelle). b, Salt marsh (marais salants). c, Butter (beurre). d, Roquefort cheese, vert. e, Olive oil, vert. f, Carnival, vert. g, Grape harvests (vendanges), vert. h, Waiter at café, vert. i, Transhumance of livestock. j, Marshland gardens (hortillonages).

2006, Mar. 25 **Photo.** ***Perf. 13***

3192	Sheet of 10	16.00	16.00
a.-j.	A1642 53c Any single	1.60	1.25

No. 3192 has three vertical rows of rouletting, separating sheet into quarters.

Nos. 3192a-3192j were also issued in large booklets containing panes of 1 of each stamp. The booklet sold for €19. Value $42.50.

Tourism Issue

Yvoire A1774

Dijon A1775

Antibes Juan-les-Pins — A1776

Thionville A1777

2006 Photo. *Perf. 13*
3193 A1774 53c multi 1.60 .40

Engr.
Perf. 13¼
3194 A1775 53c multi 1.60 .40

Litho. & Engr.
Perf. 13x13¼
3195 A1776 53c multi 1.60 .40

Engraved
3196 A1777 54c multi 1.60 .40
Nos. 3193-3196 (4) 6.40 1.60

Issued: No. 3193, 3/25; No. 3194, 4/7. No. 3195, 7/15. No. 3196, 9/16.

Art Series

Prehistoric Drawings in Rouffignac Cave — A1778

Bathers, by Paul Cézanne — A1779

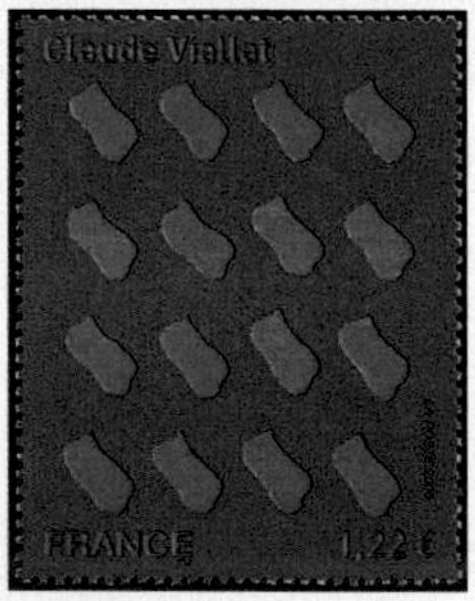

Untitled Painting by Claude Viallat A1780

Beggars Receiving Alms at the Door of a House, by Rembrandt A1781

Engr., Photo (#3198, 3199)
2006 *Perf. 13x13¼*
3197 A1778 55c multi 1.60 .75
3198 A1779 82c multi 2.40 .75

Perf. 13¼x13
3199 A1780 €1.22 brt pink & bl grn 3.50 1.00
3200 A1781 €1.30 multi 3.75 1.00
Nos. 3197-3200 (4) 11.25 3.50

Issued: 82c, 4/8; 55c, 5/27; No. 3199, 6/3. No. 3200, 11/10.

Gardens and Parks Type of 2003
Souvenir Sheet

No. 3201: a, Vallée-aux-Loups Park. b, Albert Kahn Gardens.

2006, Apr. 22 Photo. *Perf. 13¼x13*
3201 Sheet of 2 16.50 16.50
a.-b. A1660 €1.98 Either single 6.50 6.50
c. Souvenir sheet, #3118a, 3118b, 3201a, 3201b 34.00 34.00

Salon du Timbre 2006. No. 3201 has four vertical rows of rouletting, separating sheet into fifths, with the two stamps in the central fifth.

No. 3201c issued 6/16.

Young Animals A1782

Designs: No. 3202, Puppy. No. 3203, Kitten. 55c, Foal, horiz. 82c, Lamb, horiz..

2006, Apr. 22 *Perf. 13¼*
3202 A1782 53c multi 1.60 .40
3203 A1782 53c multi 1.60 .40
3204 A1782 55c multi 1.60 .40
3205 A1782 82c multi 2.40 .65
a. Souvenir sheet, #3202-3205 7.50 7.50
Nos. 3202-3205 (4) 7.20 1.85

Europa A1783

2006, Apr. 30
3206 A1783 53c multi 1.60 .40

Pierre Bayle (1647-1706), Philiosopher A1784

2006, May 2 Engr. *Perf. 13x13¼*
3207 A1784 53c blk & brn 1.60 .40

Remembrance of Slavery Day, 5th Anniv. — A1785

2006, May 10 Photo. *Perf. 13¼*
3208 A1785 53c multi 1.60 .40

Vacation A1786

Serpentine Die Cut 11¼x11
2006, May 27 Litho.
Booklet Stamp
Self-Adhesive
3209 A1786 (53c) multi 1.60 .40
a. Booklet pane of 10 16.00

Miniature Sheet

2006 World Cup Soccer Championships, Germany — A1787

No. 3210: a, Replacement players (39x25mm). b, Fans (39x25mm). c, Player with ball near chest (32mm diameter). d, Player kicking ball (32mm diameter). e, Goalie throwing ball (32mm diameter). f, Player making scissor kick (32mm diameter). g, Two players (32mm diameter). h, Referee (25x39mm). i, Coach (39x25mm). j, Cameramen (39x25mm).

2006, May 27 Photo. *Perf. 12¾*
3210 A1787 Sheet of 10 16.00 16.00
a.-j. 53c Any single 1.60 1.25

Marianne Type of 2005
2006 Litho. *Perf. 13*
3211 Sheet of 15, #a-k, 2 each #l-m, + 15 labels 50.00 50.00
a. A1713 1c yellow orange .20 .20
b. A1713 5c dark brown .20 .20
c. A1713 10c violet .40 .40
d. A1713 55c blue 2.00 2.00
e. A1713 64c olive green 2.25 2.25
f. A1713 75c light blue 2.50 2.50
g. A1713 82c fawn 3.00 3.00
h. A1713 90c dark blue 3.25 3.25
i. A1713 €1 dull orange 3.50 3.50
j. A1713 €1.22 red violet 4.25 4.25
k. A1713 €1.98 brown 6.75 6.75
l. A1713 (48c) green 1.75 1.75
m. A1713 (53c) red 1.90 1.90

Serpentine Die Cut 11¼
Self-Adhesive
3211N Sheet of 15, #3211No-3211Ny, 2 each #3211Nz, 3211Naa, + 15 labels *100.00*
o. A1713 1c yellow orange .30 .30
p. A1713 5c dark brown .30 .30
q. A1713 10c violet .50 .50
r. A1713 55c blue 2.75 2.75
s. A1713 64c olive green 3.00 3.00
t. A1713 75c light blue 3.50 3.50
u. A1713 82c fawn 3.75 3.75
v. A1713 90c dark blue 4.50 4.50
w. A1713 €1 dull orange 4.75 4.75
x. A1713 €1.22 red violet 6.00 6.00
y. A1713 €1.98 brown 8.00 8.00
z. A1713 (48c) green 2.25 2.25
aa. A1713 (53c) red 2.50 2.50

Etched on Foil
Die Cut Perf. 13
3212 A1713 €5 *silver* 18.50 18.50

Nos. 3211a-3211m, 3211No-3211Naa and 3212 have "Phil@poste" inscription at bottom. Nos. 3211 and 3211N have stamps with a glossy varnish. No. 3211 sold for €12.04 and labels could be personalized. No. 3211N sold for €15.05 and labels could be personalized. No. 3212 was sold in a protective package.

Costumes From Operas by Wolfgang Amadeus Mozart — A1788

Designs: No. 3213, The Magic Flute. No. 3214, Don Giovanni. No. 3215, The Marriage of Figaro. No. 3216, The Clemency of Titus. No. 3217, The Abduction from the Seraglio (L'enlèvement au Sérail). No. 3218, Cosi Fan Tutte.

2006, June 17 Photo. *Perf. 13*
3213 A1788 53c multi 1.60 .75
3214 A1788 53c multi 1.60 .75
3215 A1788 53c multi 1.60 .75
3216 A1788 53c multi 1.60 .75
3217 A1788 53c multi 1.60 .75
3218 A1788 53c multi 1.60 .75
a. Souvenir sheet, #3213-3218 12.00 12.00
Nos. 3213-3218 (6) 9.60 4.50

Nos. 3213-3218 were each printed in souvenir sheets containing one stamp that sold as a set for €15, and in booklet panes containing one stamp in a large book that sold for €19. Value: set of 6 sheets $40; set of 6 panes in book $50. No. 3218a sold for €4.80, with the Red Cross receiving €1.62 of that.

UNESCO World Heritage Sites A1789

Designs: 53c, Provins. 90c, Mont Saint-Michel.

2006, June 17 Photo. *Perf. 13¼*
3219 A1789 53c multi 1.60 .40
3220 A1789 90c multi 2.60 .70

See United Nations Offices in Geneva Nos. 459-461.

Garnier Opera House, Paris — A1790

2006, June 18 Engr. *Perf. 13x13¼*
3221 A1790 53c multi + label 1.60 .40

French Federation of Philatelic Associations 79th Congress, Paris. No. 3221 exists in a souvenir sheet of 1 (without label), issued in 2007 that sold for €3.

Happy Birthday A1791

2006, June 19 Photo. *Perf. 13*
3222 A1791 (53c) multi 1.60 .40
a. Souvenir sheet of 5 8.00 8.00
b. Litho. stamp + label 4.00 4.00

Serpentine Die Cut 11
Self-Adhesive
3222C A1791 (53c) multi + label 2.40 2.40

Sheets of 10 of No. 3222b sold for €6.86. No. 3222C was printed in sheets of 10 stamps + 10 labels that sold for €8.61. Labels could be personalized for an additional fee.

European Capitals Type of 2002
Souvenir Sheet

No. 3223 — Attractions in Nicosia, Cyprus: a, Chrysaliniotissa Church. b, Archaeological Museum. c, Famagusta Gate. d, Archbishop's residence (Archeveché).

2006, June 20 Photo. *Perf. 13x13¼*
3223 A1622 Sheet of 4 7.00 7.00
a.-d. 53c Any single 1.60 1.00

Tango Dancing
A1792

2006, June 21 Photo. *Perf. 12¼*

3224 A1792 53c Dancers 1.60 .40
3225 A1792 90c Musician 2.60 .70

See Argentina Nos. 2395-2396.

La Poste's Business Foundation, 10th Anniv. — A1793

2006, June 22 Litho. *Perf. 13*

3226 A1793 (53c) multi, *tan* 1.60 .40

French Open Golf Championship, Cent. — A1794

Photo. & Embossed

2006, June 24 *Perf. 13*

3227 A1794 53c multi 1.60 .40

A souvenir sheet containing No. 3227 sold for €3. Value $12.

Rotary International Type of 2005

Serpentine Die Cut 11

2006, July 1 Photo.

Self-Adhesive

3227A A1717 53c multi 1.60 .40

French Soccer Team's Second-Place Showing in 2006 World Cup — A1795

2006, July 5 Photo. *Perf. 13¼*

Size: 35x26mm

3228 A1795 53c multi 1.60 .40

Litho.

Size: 35x22mm

Perf. 13

3229 A1795 53c multi + label 5.00 4.00

Serpentine Die Cut 11¼x11

Self-Adhesive

3229A A1795 53c multi + label 10.00 5.00

No. 3229 was printed in sheets of 10 stamps and 10 labels that sold for €6.94. Value $55. No. 3229A was printed in sheets of 10 stamps + 10 labels that sold for €8.61. Value $140. Labels could be personalized.

Quai Branly Museum — A1796

Illustration reduced.

2006, July 8 Photo. *Perf. 13x13¼*

3230 A1796 53c multi 1.60 .40

Reinstatement of Capt. Alfred Dreyfus, Cent. — A1797

2006, July 12 Engr.

3231 A1797 53c multi 1.60 .40

Claude-Joseph Rouget de Lisle (1760-1836), Composer of "La Marseillaise" — A1798

2006, July 13 Photo. *Perf. 13¼*

3232 A1798 53c multi 1.60 .40

Pablo Casals (1876-1973), Cellist — A1799

2006, July 29

3233 A1799 53c multi 1.60 .40

Aspects of Life in French Regions Type of 2003

No. 3234: a, Catalan Towers. b, La Croisette, Cannes. c, Brocéliande Forest. d, Volcanic craters, Auvergne, vert. e, Les Invalides, Paris, vert. f, Chateau de Chaumont, Chaumont-sur-Loire. g, Ardèche Gorges, vert. h, Flour mill, Valmy, vert. i, Grotto of Messabielle, Lourdes. j, Calanches de Piana, Corsica.

2006, Sept. 2 Photo. *Perf. 13*

3234 Sheet of 10 16.00 16.00
a.-j. A1642 54c Any single 1.60 1.25

No. 3234 has three vertical rows of rouletting, separating sheet into quarters.

Nos. 3234a-3234j were also issued in large booklets containing panes of 1 of each stamp. The booklet sold for €19. Value $42.50.

A1800

A1801

A1802

A1803

A1804

A1805

A1806

A1807

A1808

Cubitus, Comics by Michel Rodrigue and Pierre Aucaigne
A1809

Serpentine Die Cut 11¼x11

2006, Sept. 20 Litho.

Self-Adhesive

Booklet Stamps

3235 A1800 (54c) multi 1.60 .40
3236 A1801 (54c) multi 1.60 .40
3237 A1802 (54c) multi 1.60 .40
3238 A1803 (54c) multi 1.60 .40
3239 A1804 (54c) multi 1.60 .40
3240 A1805 (54c) multi 1.60 .40
3241 A1806 (54c) multi 1.60 .40
3242 A1807 (54c) multi 1.60 .40
3243 A1808 (54c) multi 1.60 .40
3244 A1809 (54c) multi 1.60 .40
a. Booklet pane of 10, #3235-3244 16.00

Sculptures by Constantin Brancusi (1876-1957) — A1810

Designs: 54c, Sleeping Muse. 85c, Sleep.

2006, Sept. 25 Photo. *Perf. 13¼*

3245 A1810 54c multi 1.60 .40
3246 A1810 85c multi 2.50 .75

See Romania Nos. 4878-4879.

Marianne Type of 2005

2006, Oct. 1 Engr. *Perf. 13*

Inscribed "Phil@poste" at Bottom

3247 A1713 10c gray .50 .20
3248 A1713 60c dark blue 2.50 .40
3249 A1713 70c yel green 2.75 .40
3250 A1713 85c purple 4.00 .60
3251 A1713 86c fawn 4.00 .60
3252 A1713 €1.15 blue 5.00 1.00
3253 A1713 €1.30 red violet 5.50 1.00
3254 A1713 €2.11 chocolate 9.00 1.50
Nos. 3247-3254 (8) 33.25 5.70

Coil Stamp

Perf. 13 Horiz.

3255 A1713 60c dark blue 2.00 .50

Serpentine Die Cut 11¼

2006 Engr.

Self-Adhesive

3255A A1713 (54c) red + label 2.40 2.40
3255C A1713 60c dark blue + label 2.50 2.50
3255D A1713 86c fawn + label 3.00 3.00
Nos. 3255A-3255D (3) 7.90 7.90

A number has been reserved for an additional stamp. Nos. 3255A, 3255C and 3255D were printed in sheets of 15 stamps + 15 labels that could be personalized. Sheets of No. 3255A sold for €13.29; No. 3255C, €14.04; No. 3255D, €17.31.

Aviation Without Borders — A1811

2006, Oct. 7 Photo. *Perf. 13*

3256 A1811 54c multi 1.60 .40

Henri Moissan (1852-1907), 1906 Nobel Chemistry Laureate — A1812

2006, Oct. 14 Engr. *Perf. 13¼x13*

3257 A1812 54c multi 1.60 .40

"Shared Memories," Intl. Conference on Veterans, Paris — A1813

2006, Oct. 26 Photo. *Perf. 13¼*

3258 A1813 54c multi 1.60 .40

Marianne — A1814

Serpentine Die Cut 6¾ Vert.

2006, Nov. 8 Engr.

Self-Adhesive

Booklet Stamp

3259 A1814 54c red 3.00 2.50
a. Booklet pane, 5 each #3083d, 3259 22.50

Miniature Sheet

Flying Machines — A1815

No. 3260: a, Gustave Ponton d'Amécourt's helicopter. b, Alberto Santos-Dumont's monoplane, "Demoiselle," horiz. c, Jean Marie Le Bris's bird-shaped glider, horiz. d, Clément Ader's "Avion III," horiz. e, Henri Fabré's seaplane, horiz. f, Jean-Pierre Blanchard's balloon.

Litho. & Engr.

2006, Nov. 9 *Perf. 13*

3260 A1815 Sheet of 6 10.00 10.00
a.-f. 54c Any single 1.60 1.25

Inauguration of Aulnay-sous-Bois to Bondy Tram-Train Line — A1816

2006, Nov. 18 Photo. *Perf. 13x13¼*

3261 A1816 54c multi 1.60 .50

Holiday Greetings A1817

Designs: No. 3262, Reindeer, sleigh, four penguins. No. 3263, Reindeer with fishing pole, three penguins. No. 3264, Reindeer, Christmas tree, two penguins. No. 3265, Reindeer skating, three penguins. No. 3266, Reindeer with gift boxes, three penguins.

2006, Nov. 25 Litho. *Perf. 13¼*

3261A A1817 (54c) multi + label 1.90 1.90
3261B A1817 (54c) multi + label 1.90 1.90
3261C A1817 (54c) multi + label 1.90 1.90
3261D A1817 (54c) multi + label 1.90 1.90
3261E A1817 (54c) multi + label 1.90 1.90
f. Vert. strip of 5, #3261A-3261E, + 5 labels 12.00 12.00
Miniature sheet, 2 #3261Ef 30.00 30.00

Self-Adhesive

Booklet Stamps

Serpentine Die Cut 11¼x11

3262 A1817 (54c) multi 1.60 .50
3263 A1817 (54c) multi 1.60 .50
3264 A1817 (54c) multi 1.60 .50
3265 A1817 (54c) multi 1.60 .50
3266 A1817 (54c) multi 1.60 .50
a. Booklet pane, 2 each #3262-3266 16.00
Nos. 3262-3266 (5) 8.00 2.50

Miniature sheet containing Nos. 3261A-3261E sold for €6.94. Value $60. Labels could be personalized. Value $60.

A souvenir sheet containing a perf. 13 example of No. 3266 sold for €3. Value $17.50. A sheet containing 5 No. 3261A + 5 labels exists, but was not sold.

Grand Masonic Lodge of France A1818

2006, Dec. 1 Photo. *Perf. 13x13¼*

3267 A1818 54c multi 1.50 .50

Alain Poher (1909-96), Politician, and Senate Building A1819

2006, Dec. 2 Engr. *Perf. 13¼*

3268 A1819 54c multi 1.50 .50

Opening of New Paris Tramway A1820

2006, Dec. 16 Photo. *Perf. 13¼*

3269 A1820 54c multi 1.75 .75

Orchids Type of 2002

Designs: 31c, Platanthera chlorantha. 36c, Dactylorhiza savogiensis. 43c, Orchis insularis.

2007, Jan. 2 Litho. *Perf. 13*

3270 A1584 31c multi .80 .20
3271 A1584 36c multi .95 .20
3272 A1584 43c multi 1.10 .20
Nos. 3270-3272 (3) 2.85 .60

Nos. 3270-3272 are known only precanceled. See second note after #132.

Hearts A1821

"Givenchy" in: (54c), Black and white. (86c), Red.

2007, Jan. 6 Photo. *Perf. 13¼*

Inscribed "Lettre 20 g"

3273 A1821 (54c) red & black 1.40 .45
a. Souvenir sheet of 5 7.00 7.00

Inscribed "Lettre 50 g"

3274 A1821 (86c) black & red 2.25 .75

Values are for stamps with surrounding selvage.

Serpentine Die Cut

Self-Adhesive

3275 A1821 (54c) Like #3273 1.40 .45

Inscribed "Lettre 50 g"

3276 A1821 (86c) Like #3274 2.25 .75

New Year 2007 (Year of the Pig) — A1822

2007, Jan. 27 Photo. *Perf. 13¼x13*

3277 A1822 (54c) multi 1.40 .45
a. Litho., stamp + label 2.50 2.50

Serpentine Die Cut 11

Self-Adhesive

3277B A1822 (54c) multi + label 11.00 11.00

No. 3277 has a somewhat blurrier image than No. 3277a. Sheets of 5 #3277a + 5 labels sold for €3.51. Value $15. Labels could be personalized. No. 3277 exists in a souvenir sheet of 1 that sold for €3. Value $10.

No. 3277B was printed in sheets of 10 + 10 labels that sold for €8.86. Value $125. Labels could be personalized.

Egyptian Hippopotamus Figurine — A1823

Head of Aphrodite A1824

Winged Victory of Samothrace A1825

Fresco, Pompeii A1826

King Amenemhet III of Egypt A1827

Statue of Juno A1828

Egyptian Harpist A1829

Etruscan Sarcophagus of Husband and Wife — A1830

Egyptian Statue of Seated Scribe A1831

Head of Pericles A1832

Serpentine Die Cut 11¼x11

2007, Jan. 27 Litho.

Booklet Stamps

Self-Adhesive

3279 A1823 (54c) multi 1.50 .45
3280 A1824 (54c) multi 1.50 .45
3281 A1825 (54c) multi 1.50 .45
3282 A1826 (54c) multi 1.50 .45
3283 A1827 (54c) multi 1.50 .45
3284 A1828 (54c) multi 1.50 .45
3285 A1829 (54c) multi 1.50 .45
3286 A1830 (54c) multi 1.50 .45
3287 A1831 (54c) multi 1.50 .45
3288 A1832 (54c) multi 1.50 .45
a. Booklet pane of 10, #3279-3288 17.00

Tourism Issue

Valenciennes A1833

2007 Engr. *Perf. 13¼*

3289 A1833 54c red & blue 1.50 .50

Issued: No. 3289, 2/3.

Tourism Issue

Limoges A1834

2007 Engr. *Perf. 13¼*

3290 A1834 54c multi 1.50 .50

Issued: No. 3290, 3/23.

Tourism Issue

Arcachon A1835

2007, May 19 Photo. *Perf. 13¼*

3291 A1835 54c multi 1.50 .50

Tourism Issue

Castres A1836

2007, July 20 Engr. *Perf. 13¼*

3292 A1836 54c multi 1.50 .50

Tourism Issue

Firminy — A1837

2007, Sept. 15 Engr. *Perf. 13¼*

3293 A1837 54c multi 1.60 .55

Rights of France A1838

2007, Feb. 5 Photo. *Perf. 13¼*

3294 A1838 54c multi 1.50 .50

Art Issue

Book Illumination from Sélestat Library — A1839

Galerie des Glaces, Versailles Palace — A1840

La Barrière Fleurie, by Paul Sérusier A1841

Gallic Boar Ensign — A1842

Perf. 12¼x13, 13¼x13 (#3297), 13x13¼ (#3296, 3298)

Engraved, Photo. (#3296, 3297)

2007

3295	A1839	60c multi	1.60	.80
3296	A1840	85c multi	2.50	1.25
3297	A1841	86c multi	2.50	1.25
3298	A1842	€1.30 multi	3.50	1.75

Issued: No. 3295, 2/10. No. 3297, 10/13. No. 3298, 6/2. No. 3296, 11/10.

Aspects of Life in the French Regions Type of 2003

No. 3299: a, Baux-de-Provence. b, Banks of the Loire. c, Grande-Chartreuse Massif. d, Saint-Tropez. e, Doubs Waterfall, vert. f, Fontainebleau Forest, vert. g, Chantilly Castle. h, Saint-Malo. i, Ballon d'Alsace, vert. j, Midi Canal, vert.

2007, Feb. 24 Photo. _Perf. 13_

3299	Sheet of 10	15.00	15.00
a.-j.	A1642 54c Any single	1.50	.50

No. 3299 has three vertical rows of rouletting, separating sheet into quarters.

Nos. 3299a-3299j were also issued in large booklets containing panes of 1 of each stamp. The booklet sold for €19.

Aspects of Life in French Regions Type of 2003 Inscribed "Lettre Prioritaire 20g"

2007, Feb. Photo. _Perf. 13_

Stamp + Label

3300	A1642 (54c) Arc de Triomphe, vert.	4.00	4.00

No. 3300 was printed in sheets of 10 stamps + 10 different labels that sold for €6.85. Value $45.

Marianne Type of 2005

2007 Litho. _Perf. 13_

Stamps Inscribed "Phil@poste"

Without Varnish

3302	Sheet of 15, #a-k, 2 each #l-m, + 15 labels	60.00	60.00
a.	A1713 1c yellow orange	.30	.30
b.	A1713 5c brown	.40	.40
c.	A1713 10c gray	.75	.75
d.	A1713 60c blue	2.75	2.75
e.	A1713 70c lt yellow green	3.25	3.25
f.	A1713 85c purple	3.75	3.75
g.	A1713 86c pink	4.00	4.00
h.	A1713 €1 orange	5.00	5.00
i.	A1713 €1.15 light blue	5.50	5.50
j.	A1713 €1.30 red violet	6.00	6.00
k.	A1713 €2.11 maroon	9.00	9.00
l.	A1713 (49c) blue green	2.50	2.50
m.	A1713 (54c) red	2.75	2.75

No. 3302 sold for €14.40 and has personalizable labels.

Harry Potter — A1843

Designs: (49c), Hermione Granger. (85c), Ron Weasley.

2007, Mar. 12 Photo. _Perf. 13¼_

3303	A1843 (54c) red & multi	1.50	.50
a.	Souvenir sheet of 1	1.50	1.50
b.	Perf. 13¼x13 (booklet stamp)	1.75	.50

Booklet Stamps

Perf. 13¼x13

3304	A1843 (49c) blue & multi	1.50	.45
3305	A1843 (85c) grn & multi	2.50	.75
a.	Booklet pane of 10, 4 #3303b, 3 each #3304-3305	17.00	—
	Complete booklet, #3305a	17.00	

Stamp Day. Sheets of five serpentine die cut 11 self-adhesive stamps of each denomination and five labels that could not be personalized exist. Each sheet sold for €6.50. Value, set $70.

Albert Londres (1884-1932), Journalist — A1844

2007, Mar. 16 Engr. _Perf. 13x13¼_

3306	A1844 54c multi	1.50	.50

Six different souvenir sheets containing one No. 3306 exist. The set sold for €15. Value, set $45.

Audit Office, Bicent. A1845

2007 _Perf. 13¼x13_

3307	A1845 54c multi	1.50	.50
3307A	A1845 54c multi	1.50	.50

Issued: No. 3307, 3/17; No. 3307A, 7/20.

Treaty of Rome, 50th Anniv. A1846

2007, Mar. 23 Photo. _Perf. 13¼_

3308	A1846 54c multi	1.50	.50

Sébastaen Le Prestre de Vauban (1633-1707), Military Engineer — A1847

2007, Mar. 30 Engr.

3309	A1847 54c multi	1.50	.50

2007 Rugby World Cup A1848

2007, Apr. 14 Photo. _Perf. 13¼_

3310	A1848 54c multi	1.50	.50
a.	Perf. 13x13¼ + label	4.00	4.00

No. 3310a was printed in sheets of 5 stamps and 5 labels that could be personalized that sold for €4.20. Value $45.

Endangered Animals in Overseas Departments A1849

Designs: No. 3312, Antillean iguana. No. 3313, Raccoon, horiz. 60c, Jaguar, horiz. 86c, Barau's petrel, horiz..

2007, Apr. 28 Photo. _Perf. 13¼_

3312	A1849 54c multi	1.50	.50
3313	A1849 54c multi	1.50	.50
3314	A1849 60c multi	1.75	.60
3315	A1849 86c multi	2.40	.80
a.	Souvenir sheet, #3312-3315	7.25	7.25
	Nos. 3312-3315 (4)	7.15	2.40

Gardens and Parks Type of 2003

Souvenir Sheet

No. 3316 — Parc de la Tete d'Or, Lyon: a, Red flowers. b, White flowers.

2007, Apr. 28 _Perf. 13¼x13_

3316	Sheet of 2	11.50	11.50
a.-b.	A1660 €2.11 Either single	5.75	3.00

Salon du Timbre. No. 3316 has four vertical rows of rouletting, separating sheet into fifths, with the two stamps in the central fifth.

Vacations A1850

Designs: No. 3317, Wooden fence and red hollyhocks. No. 3318, Angelfish. No. 3319, Blue flowers. No. 3320, Blueberries. No. 3321, Canoes. No. 3322, Dyed wool hanging on rods. No. 3323, Glacier. No. 3324, Palm tree. No. 3325, Beach umbrellas and woman. No. 3326, Boxes of color pigments.

Serpentine Die Cut 11¼x11

2007, Apr. 28 Litho.

Booklet Stamps

Self-Adhesive

3317	A1850 (54c) multi	1.50	.50
3318	A1850 (54c) multi	1.50	.50
3319	A1850 (54c) multi	1.50	.50
3320	A1850 (54c) multi	1.50	.50
3321	A1850 (54c) multi	1.50	.50
3322	A1850 (54c) multi	1.50	.50
3323	A1850 (54c) multi	1.50	.50
3324	A1850 (54c) multi	1.50	.50
3325	A1850 (54c) multi	1.50	.50
3326	A1850 (54c) multi	1.50	.50
a.	Booklet pane of 10, #3317-3326	15.00	

Europa A1851

2007, May 1 Photo. _Perf. 13¼_

3327	A1851 60c multi	1.75	.60

Scouting, cent.

Intl. Sailing Federation, Cent. — A1852

Illustration reduced.

2007, May 4 _Perf. 13_

3328	A1852 85c multi	2.40	.80

A souvenir sheet containing No. 3328 sold for €3.

Tintin and Snowy — A1853

Characters from Tintin comic strips and books, by Hergé: No. 3330, Professor Calculus (Tournesol). No. 3331, Captain Haddock. No. 3332, Thomson and Thompson (Dupondt). No. 3333, Bianca Castafiore. No. 3334, Chang (Tchang).

2007, May 12

3329	A1853 54c multi	1.50	.50
3330	A1853 54c multi	1.50	.50
3331	A1853 54c multi	1.50	.50
3332	A1853 54c multi	1.50	.50
3333	A1853 54c multi	1.50	.50
3334	A1853 54c multi	1.50	.50
a.	Souvenir sheet, #3329-3334	13.50	13.50

No. 3334a sold for €5, with the Red Cross receiving €1.76 of that.

Religious Art — A1854

Designs: 54c, Nativity, 15th cent. miniature, from Armenia. 85c, The Smile of Reims.

2007, May 22 _Perf. 13¼_

3335	A1854 54c multi	1.50	.50
3336	A1854 85c multi	2.40	.80

See Armenia Nos. 749-750.

Inauguration of Eastern France TGV Train Service — A1855

2007, June 9 ***Perf. 13***

3337 A1855 54c multi 1.50 .50

French Federation of Philatelic Associations 80th Congress, Poitiers — A1856

Illustration reduced.

2007, June 15 Engr. ***Perf. 13x13¼***

3338 A1856 54c multi + label 1.50 .50

Miniature Sheet

2007 Rugby World Cup, France — A1857

No. 3339 — Inscriptions: a, Touche (Throw-in, 30x39mm elliptical). b, Melée (scrum). c, Attaque (player running with ball). d, Essai (try). e, Transformation (kick, 30x39mm elliptical). f, Passe (pass). g, Raffut (stiff-arm). h, Haka (dance). i, Plaquage (tackle). j, Supporteurs (fans).

2007, June 23 ***Perf. 13x13¼***

3339 A1857 Sheet of 10 15.00 15.00

a.-j. 54c Any single 1.50 .50

European Capitals Type of 2002

Souvenir Sheet

No. 3340 — Attractions in Brussels: a, Maison du Roi (Royal Palace). b, Hotel du Ville (City Hall), vert. c, Mannekin Pis, vert. d, Atomium.

Perf. 13x13¼, 13¼x13 (vert. stamps)

2007, June 30

3340 A1622 Sheet of 4 6.00 6.00

a.-d. 54c Any single 1.50 .50

Association of French Mayors, Cent. — A1858

2007, July 5 Photo. ***Perf. 13¼***

3341 A1858 54c multi 1.50 .50

Pierre Pfimlin (1907-2000), Mayor of Strasbourg A1859

2007, July 7 Photo. ***Perf. 13¼***

3342 A1859 60c multi 1.75 .60

2007 Rugby World Cup, France A1860

Litho. With Three-Dimensional Plastic Affixed

2007, Sept. 5 ***Serpentine Die Cut 11***

Self-Adhesive

3343 A1860 €3 multi 8.25 4.25

Happy Birthday A1861

2007, Sept. 8 Photo. ***Perf. 13x13¼***

3344 A1861 (54c) multi 1.60 .55

a. Litho., with attached label 2.40 2.40

No. 3344 was printed in a sheet of 5; No. 3344a was printed in a sheet of 5 + 5 labels that sold for €4.20.

Gift Boxes — A1862

Boxes and: Nos. 3345a, 3346, Butterflies. Nos. 3345b, 3348, Flowers. Nos. 3345c, 3347, Hearts. Nos. 3345d, 3350, Musical notes. Nos. 3345e, 3349, Bubbles.

2007, Sept. 8 Litho. ***Perf. 13¼***

3345 Sheet of 5 + 5 labels 12.00 12.00

a.-e. A1862 (54c) Any single + label 2.40 2.40

Self-Adhesive

Booklet Stamps

Serpentine Die Cut 11

3346 A1862 (54c) multi 1.60 .55

3347 A1862 (54c) multi 1.60 .55

3348 A1862 (54c) multi 1.60 .55

3349 A1862 (54c) multi 1.60 .55

3350 A1862 (54c) multi 1.60 .55

a. Booklet pane of 5 #3346-3350 8.00

No. 3345 sold for €4.20.

Sully Prudhomme (1839-1907), Poet — A1863

2007, Sept. 15 Engr. ***Perf. 13¼***

3351 A1863 €1.30 multi 3.75 1.25

A1864

A1865

A1866

A1867

Cows A1868

Serpentine Die Cut 11

2007, Sept. 20 Litho.

Self-Adhesive

Booklet Stamps

3352 A1864 (54c) multi 1.60 .55

3353 A1865 (54c) multi 1.60 .55

3354 A1866 (54c) multi 1.60 .55

3355 A1867 (54c) multi 1.60 .55

3356 A1868 (54c) multi 1.60 .55

a. Booklet pane, 2 each #3352-3356 16.00

Nos. 3352-3356 (5) 8.00 2.75

Aspects of Life in French Regions Type of 2003

No. 3357: a, Sèvres porcelain. b, Grasse perfume. c, Christmas market. d, Marseille soap. e, Giants, vert. f, Basque beret, vert. g, Aubusson tapestries. h, Lyonnaise tavern. i, Slipper, vert. j, Canteloupe, vert.

2007, Sept. 29 Photo. ***Perf. 13***

3357 Sheet of 10 16.00 16.00

a.-j. A1642 54c Any single 1.60 .55

No. 3357 has three vertical rows of rouletting separating sheet into quarters.

Nos. 3357a-3357j were also issued in large booklets containing panes of 1 of each stamp. The booklet sold for €19. Value $55.

Space Age, 50th Anniv. — A1869

2007, Oct. 4 ***Perf. 13x12½***

3358 A1869 85c multi 2.40 .80

Medical Research Foundation, 60th Anniv. — A1870

2007, Oct. 20 ***Perf. 13¼***

3359 A1870 54c multi 1.60 .55

Guy Moquet (1924-41), World War II Resistance Fighter — A1871

2007, Oct. 22 Engr.

3360 A1871 54c multi 1.60 .55

Dole A1872

2007, Nov. 2

3361 A1872 54c multi 1.60 .55

Personalized Stamp With Country Name on Short Side — A1873

Personalized Stamp With Country Name on Long Side A1874

Serpentine Die Cut 11¼ Syncopated

2007, Nov. Litho.

Self-Adhesive

Inscribed: "Lettre Prioritaire 20 g"

3362 A1873 (54c) multi 3.00 3.00

3363 A1874 (54c) multi 3.00 3.00

Inscribed: "Monde 20 g"

3364 A1873 (85c) multi 4.00 4.00

3365 A1874 (85c) multi 4.00 4.00

Inscribed: "Lettre Prioritaire 50 g"

3366 A1873 (86c) multi 4.00 4.00

3367 A1874 (86c) multi 4.00 4.00

Nos. 3362-3367 (6) 22.00 22.00

Nos. 3362-3367 were each printed in sheets of ten, having vignettes that could be personalized or chosen from a library of stock designs, two of which are shown on the illustrated stamps. Sheets of Nos. 3362 and 3363 each sold for €10.03, and sheets of Nos. 3364-3367 each sold for €13.38.

Jean-Baptiste Charcot (1867-1936), Polar Explorer
A1875

Ship Pourquoi-Pas? — A1876

2007, Nov. 8 Engr. *Perf. 13x12¾*

3368 A1875 54c multi 1.60 .55
3369 A1876 60c multi 1.75 .60
a. Horiz. pair, #3368-3369 3.50 1.25

See Greenland No. 505.

Marianne — A1877

Serpentine Die Cut 6¾ Vert.
2007, Nov. 8 Engr.
Self-Adhesive
Booklet Stamp

3370 A1877 54c red 1.60 .55
a. Booklet pane, 6 each #3083d, 3370 19.50

Miniature Sheet

Lighthouses — A1878

No. 3371: a, Cap Fréhel Lighthouse. b, Espiguette Lighthouse. c, D'ar-Men Lighthouse. d, Grand-Léjon Lighthouse. e, Porquerolles Lighthouse, horiz. f, Chassiron Lighthouse, horiz.

Litho. & Engr.
2007, Nov. 9 *Perf. 13*

3371 A1878 Sheet of 6 9.75 9.75
a.-f. 54c Any single 1.60 .55

2007 Women's World Handball Championships, France — A1879

2007, Nov. 10 Photo. *Perf. 13¼*

3372 A1879 54c multi 1.60 .55

Holiday Greetings
A1880

No. 3377: a, Squirrel with stocking cap. b, Bird with party hat. c, Hedgehog with party cap. d, Dog with stocking cap. e, Deer with stocking cap.

No. 3378, Squirrel with stocking cap. No. 3379, Bird with party hat. No. 3380, Deer with stocking cap. No. 3381, Hedgehog with party hat. No. 3382, Dog with stocking cap.

2007, Nov. 24 Litho. *Perf. 13¼*

3377 Sheet of 5 + 5 labels 12.50 12.50
a.-e. A1880 (54c) Any single + label 2.50 2.50

Booklet Stamps
Self-Adhesive
Serpentine Die Cut 11

3378 A1880 (54c) multi 1.60 .55
3379 A1880 (54c) multi 1.60 .55
3380 A1880 (54c) multi 1.60 .55
3381 A1880 (54c) multi 1.60 .55
3382 A1880 (54c) multi 1.60 .55
a. Booklet pane, 2 each #3378-3382 16.00

No. 3377 sold for €4.20 and had labels that could not be personalized.

A souvenir sheet of 1 of No. 3381 sold for €3.

Marianne Type of 2005

2008 Engr. *Perf. 13*

3383 A1713 (65c) dark blue 2.00 .40
3384 A1713 72c yel green 2.25 .45
3385 A1713 88c fawn 2.75 .55
3386 A1713 €1.25 blue 4.00 .80
3387 A1713 €1.33 red violet 4.25 .85
3388 A1713 €2.18 chocolate 6.75 1.40
Nos. 3383-3388 (6) 22.00 4.45

Coil Stamp
Perf. 13 Horiz.

3388A A1713 (65c) dark blue 2.00 .40

Issued: Nos. 3383-3388A, 3/1.

Marianne Type of 2005
Serpentine Die Cut 6¾ Vert.
2008 Engr.
Booklet Stamp
Self-Adhesive

3389 A1713 (60c) blue 1.90 .50
a. Booklet pane of 12 23.00

Issued: No. 3389, 1/2.

Hearts
A1881

Designs: (54c), Face. (86c), Plant with heart-shaped leaves.

2008, Jan. 5 Photo. *Perf. 13¼*

3390 A1881 (54c) multi 1.60 .55
a. Souvenir sheet of 5 8.00 8.00
3390b Sheet of 10 + 10 labels 20.00 —
3391 A1881 (86c) multi 2.60 .90

Self-Adhesive
Serpentine Die Cut

3392 A1881 (54c) multi 1.60 .55

Values are for stamps with surrounding selvage.

No. 3390b issued 1/5/08. It was sold for €6.86. Labels could not be personalized.

New Year 2008 (Year of the Rat) — A1882

2008, Jan. 26 Photo. *Perf. 13¼x13*

3393 A1882 (54c) multi 1.60 .55

Printed in sheets of 5.

Paintings
A1883

Designs: No. 3394, Legend of St. Francis: Sermon to the Birds, by Giotto di Bondone. No. 3395, Seaport at Sunset, by Claude Lorrain. No. 3396, The Birth of Venus, by Sandro Botticelli. No. 3397, Napoleon Bonaparte Crossing the Alps, by Jacques-Louis David. No. 3398, La Belle Jardinière (Madonna and Child with St. John the Baptist), by Raphael, vert. No. 3399, Head of a Girl in a Turban, by Jan Vermeer, vert. No. 3400, Summer, by Giuseppe Arcimboldo, vert. No. 3401, Mona Lisa, by Leonardo da Vinci, vert. No. 3402, Infant Maria Marguerita, by Diego Velásquez, vert. No. 3403, Money Changer with Wife, by Quentin Massys (Metsys), vert.

Serpentine Die Cut 11
2008, Jan. 26 Litho.
Booklet Stamps
Self-Adhesive

3394 A1883 (54c) multi 1.60 .55
3395 A1883 (54c) multi 1.60 .55
3396 A1883 (54c) multi 1.60 .55
3397 A1883 (54c) multi 1.60 .55
3398 A1883 (54c) multi 1.60 .55
3399 A1883 (54c) multi 1.60 .55
3400 A1883 (54c) multi 1.60 .55
3401 A1883 (54c) multi 1.60 .55
3402 A1883 (54c) multi 1.60 .55
3403 A1883 (54c) multi 1.60 .55
a. Booklet pane of 10, #3394-3403 16.00

France Stadium, 10th Anniv.
A1884

2008, Jan. 28 Photo. *Perf. 13¼*

3404 A1884 54c multi 1.60 .55

Tourism Issue

Vendôme
A1885

2008 Engr. *Perf. 13¼*

3405 A1885 54c multi 1.75 .60

Issued: No. 3405, 2/2.

Tourism Issue

La Rochelle — A1886

Toulon
A1887

Richelieu
A1888

Le Havre — A1889

Illustration A1886 reduced.

2008 Engr. *Perf. 13*

3406 A1886 55c multi 1.75 .60
3407 A1887 55c multi 1.75 .60
3408 A1888 55c multi 1.75 .60
3409 A1889 55c multi 1.50 .50
Nos. 3406-3409 (4) 6.75 2.30

Issued: No. 3406, 4/5; Nos. 3407-3408, 7/5; No. 3409, 9/13.

Art Issue

Globes of Vincenzo Coronelli
A1890

Young Girl Warming Her Hands at a Large Stove, by Jean-Jacues Henner — A1891

Untitled Work by Gérard Garouste
A1892

A Theater Box Office, by Honoré Daumier
A1893

2008 Litho. & Engr. *Perf. 13¼x13*

3410 A1890 85c multi 2.60 1.25
3411 A1891 88c multi 2.25 1.10
3412 A1892 €1.33 multi 4.25 2.10

3413 A1893 €1.33 choc & bl gray 3.50 1.75
Nos. 3410-3413 (4) 12.60 6.20

Issued: No. 3410, 2/; No. 3412, 6/19; No. 3411, 10/18; No. 3413, 11/7.

A souvenir sheet containing No. 3410 sold for €3.

Emir Abdelkader (1808-83), Algerian Leader — A1894

2008, Feb. 20 Engr. ***Perf. 13¼***
3414 A1894 54c multi 1.75 .60

Droopy Dog A1895

Red-haired Woman A1896

The Wolf A1897

Design: €2.18, Droopy Dog, diff.

2008, Mar. 1 Photo. ***Perf. 13¼***
3415 A1895 (55c) multi 1.75 .60
3416 A1896 (55c) multi 1.75 .60
3417 A1897 (55c) multi 1.75 .60
a. Strip of 3, #3415-3417 5.25 1.90

Souvenir Sheet

Perf. 13x13¼

3418 A1895 €2.18 multi 6.75 6.75

Booklet Stamps

Self-Adhesive

3419 A1895 (55c) multi 1.75 .60
3420 A1896 (55c) multi 1.75 .60
3421 A1897 (55c) multi 1.75 .60
a. Booklet pane of 10, 4 #3419, 3 each #3420-3421 17.50

Cartoon characters created by Tex Avery; Stamp Day. No. 3418 contains one 35x27mm stamp that has thermographic ink (on cartoon balloon) that when warmed, changes color allowing a message below the ink to appear.

Nos. 3419-3421 exist in three sheets, each containing 5 of each stamp + 5 non-personalizable labels. Each sheet sold for €6.50.

Sound Recording Libraries A1898

2008, Mar. 15 Photo. ***Perf. 13¼***
3422 A1898 55c multi 1.75 .60

Flowers — A1899

Designs: 37c, Aquilegia. 38c, Tulipa sp. 44c, Bellis perennis. 45c, Primula veris.

2008, Mar. 1 Litho. ***Perf. 13***
3423 A1899 37c multi 1.10 .25
3424 A1899 38c multi 1.25 .25
3425 A1899 44c multi 1.40 .30
3426 A1899 45c multi 1.40 .30
Nos. 3423-3426 (4) 5.15 1.10

Nos. 3423-3426 are known only precanceled. See second note after #132.

Aspects of Life in French Regions Type of 2003

No. 3427: a, Chateau d'Ussé, Rigny-Ussé. b, Vézelay. c, Place des Vosges, Le Marais district, Paris. d, Le Marais Poitevin (Poitevin Marsh). e, Cugarel Windmill, Castelnaudary, vert. f, Red granite coastal rocks, vert. g, Honfleur. h, La Petite France district, Strasbourg. i, La Boétie House, Sarlat-la-Canéda, vert. j, Marfate Cirque, Reunion, vert.

2008, Mar. 29 Photo. ***Perf. 13***
3427 Sheet of 10 17.50 17.50
a.-j. A1642 55c Any single 1.75 1.25

No. 3427 has three vertical rows of rouletting, separating sheet into quarters. Nos. 3427a-3427j were also issued in a large booklet containing panes of 1 of each stamp. The booklet sold for €19.

Lyon — A1900

Litho. & Engr.

2008, Apr. 4 ***Perf. 13***
3428 A1900 55c multi 1.75 .60

Gardens and Parks Type of 2003

No. 3429: a, Parc Longchamp, Marseille. b, Parc Borely, Marseille.

2008 Photo. ***Perf. 13¼x13***
3429 Sheet of 2 13.50 13.50
a.-b. A1660 €2.18 Either single 6.75 3.50
c. Miniature sheet of 4, #3316a, 3316b, 3429a, 3429b 27.50 27.50

Salon du Timbre. No. 3429 has four vertical rows of rouletting, separating sheet into fifths, with the two stamps in the central fifth.

Issued: No. 3429, 4/12; No. 3429c, 6/14.

Prehistoric Animals A1901

Designs: No. 3430, Phorusrhacos. No. 3431, Smilodon. 65c, Megaloceros, horiz. 88c, Mammoth, horiz.

2008, Apr. 19 ***Perf. 13¼***
3430 A1901 55c multi 1.75 .60
3431 A1901 55c multi 1.75 .60
3432 A1901 65c multi 2.00 .65
3433 A1901 88c multi 2.75 .90
a. Miniature sheet, #3430-3433 8.25 8.25
Nos. 3430-3433 (4) 8.25 2.75

First Heart Transplant in Europe, 40th Anniv. — A1902

2008, Apr. 24 ***Perf. 13¼x13***
3434 A1902 55c red & black 1.75 .60

Valentré Bridge, Cahors A1903

2008, Apr. 26 Engr. ***Perf. 13x13¼***
3435 A1903 55c multi 1.75 .60

Europa A1904

2008, May 4 Photo. ***Perf. 13x13¼***
3436 A1904 55c multi 1.75 .60

Quebec City, Canada, 400th Anniv. A1905

2008, May 16 Engr. ***Perf. 13***
3437 A1905 85c multi 2.75 .90

See Canada No. 2269.

A souvenir sheet containing No. 3437 and Canada No. 2269 sold for $4.99 in Canada and was sold in France for €15 as part of a set additionally containing six different souvenir sheets containing only No. 3437.

Happy Birthday A1906

2008, May 28 **Photo.**
3438 A1906 (55c) multi 1.75 .60

Printed in sheets of 5.

It's a Boy A1907

It's a Girl A1908

2008, May 28 ***Serpentine Die Cut 11***

Booklet Stamps

Self-Adhesive

3439 A1907 (55c) multi, unscratched panel 1.75 .60
a. Scratched panel .60
b. Booklet pane of 10 #3439 17.50
3440 A1908 (55c) multi, unscratched panel 1.75 .60
a. Scratched panel .60
b. Booklet pane of 10 #3440 17.50

Scratch-off panels on Nos. 3439-3440 cover pictures and text for baby boy and girl, respectively.

Vacations A1909

Designs: No. 3441, Ferns. No. 3442, Butterfly on leaf. No. 3443, Hands holding plant's leaves. No. 3444, Coconut palm tree. No. 3445, Path beside forest lake. No. 3446, Golf ball, putter and hole. No. 3447, Water lily and lily pads. No. 3448, Watering cans and foliage. No. 3449, Sliced kiwi fruit. No. 3450, Shelled and unshelled peas.

Serpentine Die Cut 11

2008, May 28 **Litho.**

Booklet Stamps

Self-Adhesive

3441 A1909 (55c) multi 1.75 .60
3442 A1909 (55c) multi 1.75 .60
3443 A1909 (55c) multi 1.75 .60
3444 A1909 (55c) multi 1.75 .60
3445 A1909 (55c) multi 1.75 .60
3446 A1909 (55c) multi 1.75 .60
3447 A1909 (55c) multi 1.75 .60
3448 A1909 (55c) multi 1.75 .60
3449 A1909 (55c) multi 1.75 .60
3450 A1909 (55c) multi 1.75 .60
a. Booklet pane of 10, #3441-3450 17.50

Evreux Belfry — A1910

2008, May 31 Engr. ***Perf. 13***
3451 A1910 55c multi 1.75 .60

French Federation of Philatelic Associations 81st Congress, Paris — A1911

Illustration reduced.

2008, June 14 ***Perf. 13x13¼***
3452 A1911 55c multi + label 1.75 .60

Marianne and Stars A1912

Hand Depositing Ballot A1913

Tree in Hand A1914

Dove A1915

2008 Engr. ***13, Die Cut Perf. 13***
3453 A1912 1c yellow .20 .20
3454 A1912 5c gray brown .20 .20
3455 A1912 10c gray .30 .20
3456 A1912 (50c) green 1.60 .25
3457 A1912 (55c) red 1.75 .40
3458 A1912 (65c) dark blue 2.10 .50
3459 A1912 72c olive green 2.25 .60
3460 A1912 85c purple 2.75 .70
3461 A1912 88c fawn 2.75 .70
3462 A1912 €1 orange 3.25 .80
3463 A1912 €1.25 blue 4.00 1.00

3464 A1912 €1.33 red violet 4.25 1.10
3465 A1912 €2.18 chocolate 7.00 2.40

Self-Adhesive
Etched on Foil

3466 A1912 *€5 silver* 16.00 16.00
Nos. 3453-3466 (14) 48.40 25.05

Litho.

3467 Sheet of 15, #3467a-3467k, 2 each #3467l-3467m, + 15 labels 40.00 40.00
a. A1912 1c yellow .20 .20
b. A1912 5c brown .20 .20
c. A1912 10c gray .35 .35
d. A1912 (65c) dark blue 2.40 2.40
e. A1912 72c olive green 2.60 2.60
f. A1912 85c purple 3.00 3.00
g. A1912 88c fawn 3.25 3.25
h. A1912 €1 orange 3.50 3.50
i. A1912 €1.25 blue 4.50 4.50
j. A1912 €1.33 red violet 4.75 4.75
k. A1912 €2.18 brn violet 7.75 7.75
l. A1912 (50c) green 1.75 1.75
m. A1912 (55c) red 2.00 2.00

Coil Stamps
Perf. 13 Horiz.
Engr.

3468 A1912 (50c) green 1.60 .25
3469 A1912 (55c) red 1.75 .40
3470 A1912 (65c) dark blue 2.10 .50

Booklet Stamps
Self-Adhesive
Serpentine Die Cut 6¾ Vert.

3471 A1912 (55c) red 1.75 .40
a. Booklet pane of 20 35.00
b. Booklet pane of 10 17.50
c. Booklet pane of 12 21.00
3472 A1913 55c red 1.75 .40
3473 A1914 55c red 1.75 .40
3474 A1915 55c red 1.75 .40
a. Booklet pane of 12, 6 #3471, 2 each #3472-3474 21.00
3475 A1912 (65c) dark blue 2.10 .50
3476 A1913 65c dark blue 2.10 .50
3477 A1914 65c dark blue 2.10 .50
3478 A1915 65c dark blue 2.10 .50
a. Booklet pane of 12, 6 #3475, 2 each #3476-3478 26.00
Nos. 3471-3478 (8) 15.40 3.60

Issued: No. 3457, 6/17; No. 3741c, 9/8; No. 3466, 7/1; others, 6/14. On day of issue, No. 3467 sold for €12.54. Labels on No. 3467 could not be personalized.

No. 3471b is comprised of two horizontal strips of five stamps on a yellow backing paper.

See Nos. 3532, 3564-3566.

Ecology A1916

Designs: No. 3479, Tree. No. 3480, Bicycle. No. 3481, World map. No. 3482, Computer. No. 3483, Water droplets. No. 3484, Sun. No. 3485, Two plastic bottles. No. 3486, Three plastic bottles. No. 3487, Apple core. No. 3488, Strawberry.

Serpentine Die Cut 11
2008, June 14 **Photo.**

Booklet Stamps
Self-Adhesive

3479 A1916 (55c) multi 1.75 .60
3480 A1916 (55c) multi 1.75 .60
3481 A1916 (55c) multi 1.75 .60
3482 A1916 (55c) multi 1.75 .60
3483 A1916 (55c) multi 1.75 .60
3484 A1916 (55c) multi 1.75 .60
3485 A1916 (55c) multi 1.75 .60
3486 A1916 (55c) multi 1.75 .60
3487 A1916 (55c) multi 1.75 .60
3488 A1916 (55c) multi 1.75 .60
a. Booklet pane of 10, #3479-3488 17.50

Trapeze Artist — A1917

Bareback Rider — A1918

Clown — A1919

Lion Tamer — A1920

Clown — A1921

Juggler — A1922

2008, June 15 **Photo.** ***Perf. 13***

3489 A1917 55c multi 1.75 .60
3490 A1918 55c multi 1.75 .60
3491 A1919 55c multi 1.75 .60
3492 A1920 55c multi 1.75 .60
3493 A1921 55c multi 1.75 .60
3494 A1922 55c multi 1.75 .60
a. Souvenir sheet, #3489-3494 16.50 16.50
Nos. 3489-3494 (6) 10.50 3.60

No. 3494a sold for €5.10, with the Red Cross receiving €1.80 of that.

2008 Summer Olympics, Beijing — A1923

Designs: No. 3495, Equestrian, cycling. No. 3496, Swimming, rowing, horiz. No. 3497, Judo, fencing, horiz. No. 3498, Tennis, running.

Perf. 13¼x13, 13x13¼
2008, June 16

3495 A1923 55c multi 1.75 .60
3496 A1923 55c multi 1.75 .60
3497 A1923 55c multi 1.75 .60
a. Pair, #3496-3497 3.50 1.75
3498 A1923 55c multi 1.75 .60
a. Vert. pair, #3495, 3498 3.50 1.75
Nos. 3495-3498 (4) 7.00 2.40

Nos. 3495-3498 were printed in a sheet of 10 containing 2 each #3495 and #3498 and 3 each #3496-3497.

Charles de Gaulle Memorial, Paris A1924

2008, June 18 **Engr.** ***Perf. 13¼***
3499 A1924 55c multi 1.75 .60

Miniature Sheet

European Projects — A1925

No. 3500: a, Map of Europe, 1-euro coin. b, Flags of France and European Union, horiz (French Presidency of European Union). c, Earth and Galileo probe, horiz. d, Students and flags (Erasmus higher education program).

2008, June 19 **Photo.** ***Perf. 13***
3500 A1925 Sheet of 4 7.00 7.00
a.-d. 55c Any single 1.75 .60

Miniature Sheet

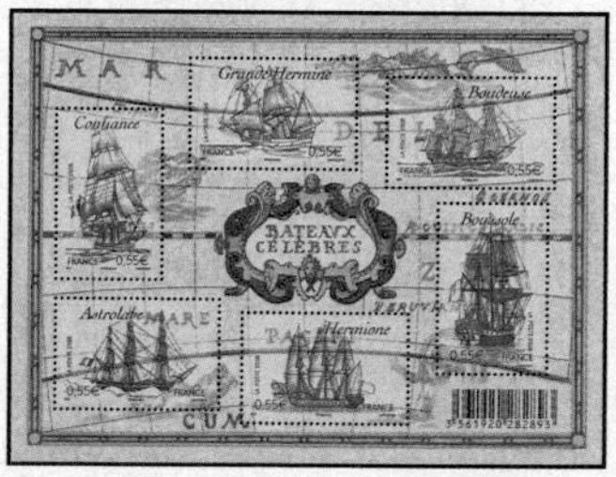

Famous Ships — A1926

No. 3501: a, Confiance. b, Grande Hermine, horiz. c, Boudeuse, horiz. d, Astrolabe, horiz. e, Hermione, horiz. f, Boussole.

2008, June 20
3501 A1926 Sheet of 6 10.50 10.50
a.-f. 55c Any single 1.75 .60

French and Brazilian Landscapes — A1927

Designs: 55c, Amazonian forest, Brazil. 85c, Glacier, France.

2008, July 13
3502 A1927 55c multi 1.75 .60
3503 A1927 85c multi 2.75 .90
a. Horiz. pair, #3502-3503 4.50 2.25

See Brazil No. 3052.

Mediterranean Summit, Paris — A1928

2008, July 13 ***Perf. 13¼***
3504 A1928 55c multi 1.75 .60

Aspects of Life in French Regions Type of 2003

No. 3505: a, Espadrilles. b, Stew (pot au feu). c, Chestnuts (chataigne). d, Fireworks (feu d'artifice). e, Epinal prints (l'image d'Epinal), vert. f, Lentils (lentille), vert. g, Reblochon cheese. h, Calissons (candy). i, Stilt walker (les échasses), vert. j, Mustard (moutarde), vert.

2008, Sept. 6 **Photo.** ***Perf. 13***
3505 Sheet of 10 15.00 15.00
a.-j. A1642 55c Any single 1.50 .50

No. 3505 has three vertical rows of rouletting, separating sheet into quarters.

Nos. 3505a-3505j also were issued in large booklets containing panes of 1 of each stamp. The booklet sold for €19.

Josselin A1929

2008, Sept. 20 **Engr.** ***Perf. 13¼***
3506 A1929 55c multi 1.50 .50

A1930

A1931

A1932

A1933

A1934

A1935

A1936

A1937

A1938

Garfield, Comic Strip by Jim Davis A1939

Serpentine Die Cut 11¼x11

2008, Sept. 18 **Photo.**

Booklet Stamps

Self-Adhesive

3507	A1930	(55c) multi		1.50	.50
3508	A1931	(55c) multi		1.50	.50
3509	A1932	(55c) multi		1.50	.50
3510	A1933	(55c) multi		1.50	.50
3511	A1934	(55c) multi		1.50	.50
3512	A1935	(55c) multi		1.50	.50
3513	A1936	(55c) multi		1.50	.50
3514	A1937	(55c) multi		1.50	.50
3515	A1938	(55c) multi		1.50	.50
3516	A1939	(55c) multi		1.50	.50
a.	Booklet pane of 10, #3507-3516			15.00	
	Nos. 3507-3516 (10)			15.00	5.00

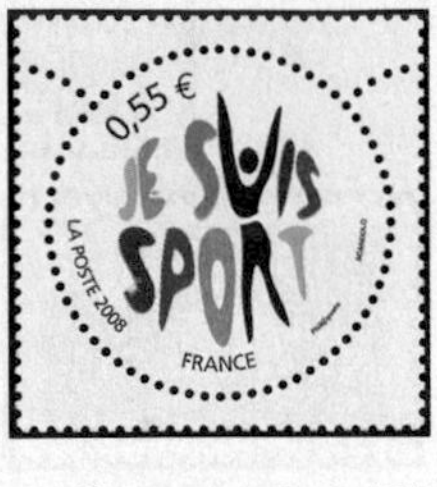

"I Am Sport" A1940

2008, Oct. 2 **Photo.** ***Perf. 12½***

3517	A1940	55c multi	1.50	.50

Values are for stamps with surrounding selvage.

Fifth Republic, 50th Anniv. A1941

2008. Oct. 4 ***Perf. 13¼***

3518	A1941	55c multi	1.50	.50

Seascapes of Viet Nam and France — A1942

Designs: 55c, Along Bay, Viet Nam. 85, Strait of Bonifacio, France.

2008, Oct. 15 **Photo.** ***Perf. 13x12¾***

3519	A1942	55c multi	1.40	.45
3520	A1942	85c multi	2.25	.75

See Viet Nam Nos. 3340-3341.

Types of 1959-2008

Serpentine Die Cut 6¾ Vert.

2008, Nov. 6 **Photo.**

Booklet Stamps

Self-Adhesive

3521	A328	55c multi	1.40	.45
3522	A349	55c multi	1.40	.45
3523	A360	55c multi	1.40	.45
3524	A379	55c multi	1.40	.45
3525	A486	55c dark red	1.40	.45
3526	A555	55c rose carmine	1.40	.45
3527	A771	55c bright red	1.40	.45
3528	A915	55c red	1.40	.45
3529	A1161	55c red	1.40	.45
3530	A1409	55c red	1.40	.45
3531	A1713	55c red	1.40	.45
3532	A1912	55c red	1.40	.45
a.	Booklet pane of 12, #3521-3532		17.00	
	Nos. 3521-3532 (12)		16.80	5.40

Landmarks of France and Israel — A1943

Airplane, stamped first flight cover and: 55c, Haifa waterfront, Israel. 85c, Eiffel Tower, Paris.

2008, Nov. 6 **Photo.** ***Perf. 13***

3533	A1943	55c multi	1.40	.45
3534	A1943	85c multi	2.25	.75

First flight between France and Israel, 60th anniv. See Israel Nos. 1750-1751.

European Capitals Type of 2002

No. 3535 — Attractions in Prague: a, Tour du Petit Coté (Charles Bridge and Tower), vert. b, Hotel de ville horloge astronomique et calandrier (City Hall astronomical clock), vert. c, Eglise Notre-Dame-de-Tyn (Tyn Cathedral), vert. d, Le Chateau (Hradcany Castle).

Perf. 13¼x13, 13x13¼ (#3535d)

2008, Nov. 7 **Photo.**

3535	A1622	Sheet of 4	5.75	5.75
a.-d.		55c Any single	1.40	.45

A1944

A1945

A1946

A1947

A1948

A1949

A1950

A1951

A1952

A1953

A1954

A1955

A1956

Happy Holidays — A1957

Serpentine Die Cut 11¼x11

2008, Nov. 8 **Photo.**

Booklet Stamps

Self-Adhesive

3536	A1944	(55c) multi	1.40	.45
3537	A1945	(55c) multi	1.40	.45
3538	A1946	(55c) multi	1.40	.45
3539	A1947	(55c) multi	1.40	.45
3540	A1948	(55c) multi	1.40	.45
3541	A1949	(55c) multi	1.40	.45

Serpentine Die Cut 11x11¼

3542	A1950	(55c) multi	1.40	.45
3543	A1951	(55c) multi	1.40	.45
3544	A1952	(55c) multi	1.40	.45
3545	A1953	(55c) multi	1.40	.45
3546	A1954	(55c) multi	1.40	.45
3547	A1955	(55c) multi	1.40	.45
3548	A1956	(55c) multi	1.40	.45
3549	A1957	(55c) multi	1.40	.45
a.	Booklet pane of 14, #3536-3549		20.00	
	Nos. 3536-3549 (14)		19.60	6.30

End of World War I, 90th Anniv. A1958

2008, Nov. 11 **Engr.** ***Perf. 13¼***

3550	A1958	55c multi	1.40	.45

Marianne and Stars Type of 2008

Serpentine Die Cut 6¾ Horiz.

2008 **Engr.**

Coil Stamps

Self-Adhesive

3564	A1912	(50c) green	1.40	1.40
3565	A1912	(55c) red	1.50	1.50
3566	A1912	(65c) dark blue	1.90	1.90
	Nos. 3564-3566 (3)		4.80	4.80

Flowers — A1959

Designs: 31c, Helianthus annuus. 33c, Magnolia.

2008, Nov. 12 **Litho.** ***Perf. 13***

3567	A1959	31c multi	.80	.25
3568	A1959	33c multi	.85	.25

Nos. 3567-3568 are known only precanceled. See note under #132.

Trees and Map of Mediterranean Area — A1960

2008, Nov. 20 **Photo.** ***Perf. 13x12¾***

3569	A1960	85c multi	2.25	.75

See Lebanon No. 645.

Subject Index of French Commemorative Issues

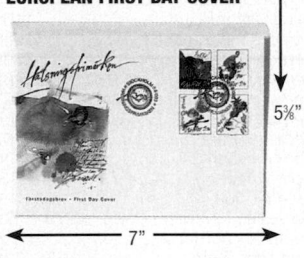

FRANCE

SEMI-POSTAL STAMPS

No. 162 Surcharged in Red and:

No. B1

SP2

1914 Unwmk. Typo. *Perf. 14x13½*

B1 A22 10c + 5c red 5.00 4.25
Never hinged 7.00
B2 SP2 10c + 5c red 32.50 3.25
Never hinged 70.00
a. Booklet pane of 10 600.00
Never hinged 800.00

Issue dates: #B1, Aug. 11; #B2, Sept. 10.
For overprint see Offices in Morocco #B8.

Widow at Grave SP3

War Orphans SP4

Woman Plowing — SP5

"Trench of Bayonets" SP6

Lion of Belfort SP7

"La Marseillaise" — SP8

1917-19

B3 SP3 2c + 3c vio brn 4.50 5.00
Never hinged 10.00
B4 SP4 5c + 5c grn ('19) 19.00 9.00
Never hinged 45.00
B5 SP5 15c + 10c gray grn 30.00 27.50
Never hinged 70.00
B6 SP5 25c + 15c dp bl 77.50 57.50
Never hinged 175.00
B7 SP6 35c + 25c sl & vio 135.00 125.00
Never hinged 350.00
B8 SP7 50c + 50c pale brn & dk brn 225.00 180.00
Never hinged 650.00
B9 SP8 1fr + 1fr cl & mar 425.00 400.00
Never hinged 1,100.
B10 SP8 5fr + 5fr dp bl & blk 1,550. 1,450.
Never hinged 3,500.
Nos. B3-B10 (8) 2,466. 2,254.

See #B20-B23. For surcharges see #B12-B19.

Hospital Ship and Field Hospital SP9

1918, Aug.

B11 SP9 15c + 5c sl & red 125.00 60.00
Never hinged 250.00

Semi-Postal Stamps of 1917-19 Surcharged

1922, Sept. 1

B12 SP3 2c + 1c violet brn .50 *.80*
Never hinged 1.00
B13 SP4 5c + 2½c green .80 *1.25*
Never hinged 1.50
B14 SP5 15c + 5c gray grn 1.25 *1.60*
Never hinged 2.60
B15 SP5 25c + 5c deep bl 2.30 *2.50*
Never hinged 4.75
B16 SP6 35c + 5c sl & vio 13.00 *15.00*
Never hinged 30.00
B17 SP7 50c + 10c pale brn & dk brn 19.00 *24.00*
Never hinged 39.00
a. Pair, one without surcharge
B18 SP8 1fr + 25c cl & mar 32.50 *37.50*
Never hinged 60.00
B19 SP8 5fr + 1fr bl & blk 150.00 *155.00*
Never hinged 275.00
Nos. B12-B19 (8) 219.35 237.65
Set, never hinged 415.00

Style and arrangement of surcharge differs for each denomination.

Types of 1917-19

1926-27

B20 SP3 2c + 1c violet brn 1.50 1.40
Never hinged 3.25
B21 SP7 50c + 10c ol brn & dk brn 20.00 12.50
Never hinged 50.00
B22 SP8 1fr + 25c dp rose & red brn 55.00 42.50
Never hinged 130.00
B23 SP8 5fr + 1fr sl bl & blk 105.00 100.00
Never hinged 240.00
Nos. B20-B23 (4) 181.50 156.40

Sinking Fund Issues

Types of Regular Issues of 1903-07 Surcharged in Red or Blue

1927, Sept. 26

B24 A22 40c + 10c lt blue (R) 5.75 5.75
Never hinged 10.50
B25 A20 50c + 25c green (Bl) 8.25 *9.00*
Never hinged 14.00

Surcharge on #B25 differs from illustration.

Type of Regular Issue of 1923 Surcharged in Black

B26 A23 1.50fr + 50c orange 14.50 14.00
Never hinged 37.50
Nos. B24-B26 (3) 28.50 28.75

See Nos. B28-B33, B35-B37, B39-B41.

Industry and Agriculture SP10

1928, May Engr. *Perf. 13½*

B27 SP10 1.50fr + 8.50fr dull blue 130.00 *150.00*
Never hinged 200.00
a. Blue green 500.00 *550.00*
Never hinged 725.00

Types of 1903-23 Issues Surcharged like Nos. B24-B26

1928, Oct. 1 *Perf. 14x13½*

B28 A22 40c + 10c gray lilac (R) 13.00 *14.00*
Never hinged 32.50
B29 A20 50c + 25c orange brn (Bl) 32.50 29.00
Never hinged 60.00
B30 A23 1.50fr + 50c rose lilac (Bk) 52.50 42.50
Never hinged 100.00
Nos. B28-B30 (3) 98.00 85.50

Types of 1903-23 Issues Surcharged like Nos. B24-B26

1929, Oct. 1

B31 A22 40c + 10c green 18.00 *19.00*
Never hinged 37.50
B32 A20 50c + 25c lil rose 30.00 30.00
Never hinged 60.00
B33 A23 1.50fr + 50c chestnut 60.00 *65.00*
Never hinged 130.00
Nos. B31-B33 (3) 108.00 114.00

"The Smile of Reims" SP11

1930, Mar. 15 Engr. *Perf. 13*

B34 SP11 1.50fr + 3.50fr red vio 75.00 *82.50*
Never hinged 130.00
a. Booklet pane of 4 300.00
Never hinged 525.00
b. Booklet pane of 8 600.00
Never hinged 1,050.
Complete booklet, #B34b 1,100.

Booklets containing No. B34 have two panes of 4 (#B34a) connected by a gutter, the complete piece constituting #B34b, which is stapled into the booklet through the gutter.

Types of 1903-07 Issues Surcharged like Nos. B24-B25

1930 Oct. 1 *Perf. 14x13½*

B35 A22 40c + 10c cerise 20.00 *21.00*
Never hinged 70.00
B36 A20 50c + 25c gray brown 37.50 *42.50*
Never hinged 120.00
B37 A22 1.50fr + 50c violet 65.00 *70.00*
Never hinged 190.00
Nos. B35-B37 (3) 122.50 133.50

Allegory, French Provinces SP12

1931, Mar. 1 *Perf. 13*

B38 SP12 1.50fr + 3.50fr grn 125.00 *140.00*
Never hinged 300.00

Types of 1903-07 Issues Surcharged like Nos. B24-B25

1931, Oct. 1 *Perf. 14x13½*

B39 A22 40c + 10c ol grn 40.00 *45.00*
Never hinged 90.00
B40 A20 50c + 25c gray vio 100.00 *110.00*
Never hinged 190.00
B41 A22 1.50fr + 50c deep red 100.00 *110.00*
Never hinged 175.00
Nos. B39-B41 (3) 240.00 265.00

Catalogue values for unused stamps in this section, from this point to the end of the section, are for Never Hinged items.

"France" Giving Aid to an Intellectual SP13

Symbolic of Music SP14

1935, Dec. 9 Engr. *Perf. 13*

B42 SP13 50c + 10c ultra 4.00 2.50
Hinged 2.50
B43 SP14 50c + 2fr dull red 125.00 45.00
Hinged 55.00

The surtax was for the aid of distressed and exiled intellectuals.
For surcharge see No. B47.

Statue of Liberty SP15

Children of the Unemployed SP16

1936-37

B44 SP15 50c + 25c dk blue ('37) 7.50 5.00
Hinged 4.00
B45 SP15 75c + 50c violet 20.00 10.00
Hinged 9.50

Surtax for the aid of political refugees.
For surcharge see No. B47.

1936, May

B46 SP16 50c + 10c copper red 7.50 5.00
Hinged 4.50

The surtax was for the aid of children of the unemployed.

No. B43 Surcharged in Black

1936, Nov.

B47 SP14 20c on 50c + 2fr dull red 4.00 3.00
Hinged 2.75

Jacques Callot SP17

Anatole France (Jacques Anatole Thibault) — SP18

Hector Berlioz SP19

Victor Hugo SP20

Auguste Rodin SP21

Louis Pasteur SP22

1936-37 **Engr.**

B48 SP17 20c + 10c brown car 4.50 2.50
Hinged 2.25
B49 SP18 30c + 10c emer ('37) 5.00 2.75
Hinged 2.25
B50 SP19 40c + 10c emer 4.50 2.75
Hinged 2.25
B51 SP20 50c + 10c copper red 6.50 3.75
Hinged 3.50
B52 SP21 90c + 10c rose red ('37) 13.00 6.50
Hinged 6.00
B53 SP22 1.50fr + 50c deep ultra 37.50 20.00
Hinged 20.00
Nos. B48-B53 (6) 71.00 38.25

The surtax was used for relief of unemployed intellectuals.

1938

B54 SP18 30c +10c brn car 3.00 1.75
Hinged 1.75
B55 SP17 35c +10c dull grn 3.50 2.40
Hinged 2.40
B56 SP19 55c +10c dull vio 10.00 4.00
Hinged 6.00
B57 SP20 65c +10c ultra 11.50 4.00
Hinged 6.00
B58 SP21 1fr +10c car lake 8.50 4.50
Hinged 4.75
B59 SP22 1.75fr + 25c dp blue 35.00 17.00
Hinged 17.00
Nos. B54-B59 (6) 71.50 33.65

Tug of War
SP23

Foot Race
SP24

Hiking — SP25

1937, June 16

B60 SP23 20c + 10c brown 3.00 2.25
Hinged 1.60
B61 SP24 40c + 10c red brown 3.00 2.25
Hinged 1.60
B62 SP25 50c + 10c black brn 3.00 2.25
Hinged 1.60
Nos. B60-B62 (3) 9.00 6.75

The surtax was for the Recreation Fund of the employees of the Post, Telephone and Telegraph.

Pierre Loti (Louis Marie Julien Viaud)
SP26

1937, Aug.

B63 SP26 50c + 20c rose car 7.50 5.00
Hinged 3.75

The surtax was for the Pierre Loti Monument Fund.

"France" and Infant
SP27

1937-39

B64 SP27 65c + 25c brown vio 5.25 2.75
Hinged 3.25
B65 SP27 90c + 30c pck bl ('39) 3.50 2.75
Hinged 2.10

The surtax was used for public health work.

Winged Victory of Samothrace
SP28

Jean Baptiste Charcot
SP29

1937, Aug.

B66 SP28 30c blue green 175.00 40.00
Hinged 65.00
B67 SP28 55c red 175.00 40.00
Hinged 65.00

On sale at the Louvre for 2.50fr. The surtax of 1.65fr was for the benefit of the Louvre Museum.

1938-39

B68 SP29 65c + 35c dk bl grn 3.25 3.25
Hinged 1.60
B69 SP29 90c + 35c brt red vio ('39) 37.50 19.00
Hinged 11.00

Surtax for the benefit of French seamen.

Palace of Versailles
SP30

1938, May 9

B70 SP30 1.75fr + 75c dp bl 37.50 19.00
Hinged 19.00

Natl. Exposition of Painting and Sculpture at Versailles.

The surtax was for the benefit of the Versailles Concert Society.

French Soldier
SP31

Monument
SP32

1938, May 16

B71 SP31 55c + 70c brown vio 8.50 5.25
Hinged 4.75
B72 SP31 65c + 1.10fr pck bl 8.50 5.25
Hinged 4.75

The surtax was for a fund to erect a monument to the glory of the French Infantrymen.

1938, May 25

B73 SP32 55c + 45c vermilion 22.50 12.50
Hinged 10.00

The surtax was for a fund to erect a monument in honor of the Army Medical Corps.

Reims Cathedral
SP33

"France" Welcoming Her Sons
SP34

1938, July 10

B74 SP33 65c + 35c ultra 17.50 10.50
Hinged 8.50

Completion of the reconstruction of Reims Cathedral, July 10, 1938.

1938, Aug. 8

B75 SP34 65c + 60c rose car 8.50 5.75
Hinged 4.00

The surtax was for the benefit of French volunteers repatriated from Spain.

Curie Issue
Common Design Type

1938, Sept. 1

B76 CD80 1.75fr + 50c dp ultra 21.00 12.50
Hinged 8.75

Victory Parade Passing Arc de Triomphe
SP36

1938, Oct. 8

B77 SP36 65c + 35c brown car 5.75 4.50
Hinged 3.25

20th anniversary of the Armistice.

Student and Nurse — SP37

1938, Dec. 1

B78 SP37 65c + 60c pck blue 15.00 8.25
Hinged 8.00

The surtax was for Student Relief.

Blind Man and Radio
SP38

1938, Dec.

B79 SP38 90c + 25c brown vio 15.00 9.00
Hinged 8.00

The surtax was used to help provide radios for the blind.

Civilian Facing Firing Squad — SP39

Red Cross Nurse — SP40

1939, Feb. 1

B80 SP39 90c + 35c black brn 17.00 10.50
Hinged 8.75

The surtax was used to erect a monument to civilian victims of World War I.

1939, Mar. 24

B81 SP40 90c + 35c dk sl grn, turq bl & red 13.00 8.25
Hinged 6.75

75th anniv. of the Intl. Red Cross Soc.

Army Engineer
SP41

1939, Apr. 3

B82 SP41 70c + 50c vermilion 12.50 8.25
Hinged 6.00

Army Engineering Corps. The surtax was used to erect a monument to those members who died in World War I.

Ministry of Post, Telegraph and Telephone
SP42

1939, Apr. 8

B83 SP42 90c + 35c turq blue 37.50 20.00
Hinged 19.00

The surtax was used to aid orphans of employees of the postal system. Opening of the new building for the Ministry of Post, Telegraph and Telephones.

Mother and Child — SP43

Eiffel Tower — SP44

1939, Apr. 24

B84 SP43 90c + 35c red 3.75 2.50
Hinged 2.40

The surtax was used to aid children of the unemployed.

1939, May 5

B85 SP44 90c + 50c red violet 15.00 9.00
Hinged 8.75

50th anniv. of the Eiffel Tower. The surtax was used for celebration festivities.

Puvis de Chavannes — SP45

Claude Debussy
SP46

Honoré de Balzac SP47

Claude Bernard SP48

1939-40

B86 SP45 40c + 10c ver 1.75 1.00
Hinged .80
B87 SP46 70c + 10c brn vio 8.25 2.50
Hinged 3.50
B87A SP46 80c + 10c brn vio ('40) 9.00 7.50
Hinged 4.25
B88 SP47 90c + 10c brt red vio 7.25 2.50
Hinged 3.25
B88A SP47 1fr + 10c brt red vio ('40) 9.00 7.50
Hinged 4.25
B89 SP48 2.25fr + 25c brt ultra 28.00 11.50
Hinged 14.50
B89A SP48 2.50fr + 25c brt ultra ('40) 9.00 7.50
Hinged 4.25
Nos. B86-B89A (7) 72.25 40.00

The surtax was used to aid unemployed intellectuals.

Mothers and Children
SP49 SP50

1939, June 15

B90 SP49 70c + 80c bl, grn & vio 5.25 4.50
Hinged 3.25
B91 SP50 90c + 60c dk brn, dl vio & brn 8.50 5.25
Hinged 4.75

The surtax was used to aid France's repopulation campaign.

"The Letter" by Jean Honoré Fragonard SP51

Statue of Widow and Children SP52

1939, July 6

B92 SP51 40c + 60c brn, sep & pur 4.25 2.75
Hinged 2.40

The surtax was used for the Postal Museum.

1939, July 20

B93 SP52 70c + 30c brown vio 25.00 12.00
Hinged 12.00

Surtax for the benefit of French seamen.

French Soldier SP53

Colonial Trooper SP54

1940, Feb. 15

B94 SP53 40c + 60c sepia 3.75 2.75
Hinged 2.00
B95 SP54 1fr + 50c turq blue 3.75 2.75
Hinged 2.00

The surtax was used to assist the families of mobilized men.

World Map Showing French Possessions — SP55

1940, Apr. 15

B96 SP55 1fr + 25c scarlet 2.75 2.75
Hinged 2.00

Marshal Joseph J. C. Joffre SP56

Marshal Ferdinand Foch — SP57

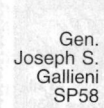

Gen. Joseph S. Gallieni SP58

Woman Plowing SP59

1940, May 1

B97 SP56 80c + 45c choc 8.25 6.00
Hinged 3.50
B98 SP57 1fr + 50c dk vio 7.50 6.00
Hinged 3.25
B99 SP58 1.50fr + 50c brn red 7.50 4.00
Hinged 3.25
B100 SP59 2.50fr + 50c indigo & dl bl 15.00 11.50
Hinged 7.50
Nos. B97-B100 (4) 38.25 27.50

The surtax was used for war charities.

Doctor, Nurse, Soldier and Family SP60

Nurse and Wounded Soldier SP61

1940, May 12

B101 SP60 80c + 1fr dk grn & red 8.25 6.00
Hinged 4.00
B102 SP61 1fr + 2fr sep & red 11.50 6.50
Hinged 5.25

The surtax was used for the Red Cross.

Nurse with Injured Children — SP62

1940, Nov. 12

B103 SP62 1fr + 2fr sepia 1.25 .80
Hinged .80

The surtax was used for victims of the war.

Wheat Harvest SP63

Sowing SP64

Picking Grapes SP65

Grazing Cattle SP66

1940, Dec. 2

B104 SP63 80c + 2fr brn blk 3.25 2.10
Hinged 1.60
B105 SP64 1fr + 2fr chest-nut 3.25 2.10
Hinged 1.60
B106 SP65 1.50fr + 2fr brt vio 3.25 2.10
Hinged 1.60
B107 SP66 2.50fr + 2fr dp grn 4.00 2.25
Hinged 1.60
Nos. B104-B107 (4) 13.75 8.55

The surtax was for national relief.

Prisoners of War
SP67 SP68

1941, Jan. 1

B108 SP67 80c + 5fr dark grn 1.60 1.50
B109 SP68 1fr + 5fr rose brn 1.75 1.60

The surtax was for prisoners of war.

Science Fighting Cancer SP69

1941, Feb. 20

B110 SP69 2.50fr + 50c slate blk & brn 1.60 1.40

Surtax used for the control of cancer.

Type of 1941 Surcharged "+10c" in Blue

1941, Mar. 4

B111 A109 1fr + 10c crimson .25 .20

Men Hauling Coal SP70

"France" Aiding Needy Man SP71

1941

B112 SP70 1fr + 2fr sepia 2.75 1.40
B113 SP71 2.50fr + 7.50fr dk bl 9.00 3.00

The surtax was for Marshal Pétain's National Relief Fund.

Liner Pasteur SP72

Red Surcharge

1941, July 17

B114 SP72 1fr + 1fr on 70c dk bl grn .40 .40

World Map, Mercator Projection SP73

1941

B115 SP73 1fr + 1fr multi .80 .50

Fisherman — SP74

1941, Oct. 23

B116 SP74 1fr + 9fr dk blue grn 1.00 .90

Surtax for benefit of French seamen.

Arms of Various Cities

Nancy SP75

Lille SP76

Rouen SP77

Bordeaux SP78

Blind Man and Beggar, Engraving by Jacques Callot — SP205

Design: 20fr+8fr, Women beggars.

1957, Dec. 7 **Engr.** ***Perf. 13***

B318 SP205 15fr + 7fr ultra & red 4.50 4.50

a. Bklt. pane, 4 ea, gutter btwn. 45.00 45.00

B319 SP205 20fr + 8fr dk vio brn & red 4.50 4.50

The surtax was for the Red Cross.

Motorized Mail Distribution SP206

1958, Mar. 15

B320 SP206 15fr + 5fr multi 1.90 1.50

Stamp Day, Mar. 15.

Portrait Type of 1955

Portraits: No. B321, Joachim du Bellay. No. B322, Jean Bart. No. B323, Denis Diderot. No. B324, Gustave Courbet. 20fr+8fr, J. B. Carpeaux. 35fr+15fr, Toulouse-Lautrec.

1958, June 7 **Engr.** ***Perf. 13***

B321 SP200 12fr + 4fr yel grn 1.75 1.75
B322 SP200 12fr + 4fr dk blue 1.75 1.75
B323 SP200 15fr + 5fr dull cl 2.00 2.00
B324 SP200 15fr + 5fr ultra 2.25 2.25
B325 SP200 20fr + 8fr brt red 2.25 2.25
B326 SP200 35fr + 15fr green 2.25 2.25
Nos. B321-B326 (6) 12.25 12.25

St. Vincent de Paul — SP207

Portrait: 20fr+8fr, J. H. Dunant.

1958, Dec. 6 **Unwmk.**

Cross in Carmine

B327 SP207 15fr + 7fr grayish grn 1.25 1.25

a. Bklt. pane, 4 each, gutter btwn. 20.00

B328 SP207 20fr + 8fr violet 1.25 1.25

The surtax was for the Red Cross.

Plane Landing at Night SP208

1959, Mar. 21

B329 SP208 20fr + 5fr sl grn, blk & rose .50 .50

Issued for Stamp Day, Mar. 21, and to publicize night air mail service.

The surtax was for the Red Cross.

See No. 1089.

Geoffroi de Villehardouin and Ships — SP209

Designs: No. B331, André Le Nôtre and formal garden. No. B332, Jean Le Rond d'Alembert, books and wheel. No. B333, David d'Angers, statue and building. No. B334, M. F. X. Bichat and torch. No. B335, Frédéric Auguste Bartholdi, Statue of Liberty and Lion of Belfort.

1959, June 13 **Engr.** ***Perf. 13***

B330 SP209 15fr + 5fr vio blue 1.25 1.25
B331 SP209 15fr + 5fr dk sl grn 1.25 1.25
B332 SP209 20fr + 10fr olive bis 1.25 1.25
B333 SP209 20fr + 10fr dk gray 1.25 1.25
B334 SP209 30fr + 10fr dk car rose 1.75 1.75
B335 SP209 30fr + 10fr org brn 1.75 1.75
Nos. B330-B335 (6) 8.50 8.50

The surtax was for the Red Cross.

No. 927 Surcharged

1959, Dec. **Typo.** ***Perf. 14x13½***

B336 A328 25fr + 5fr black & red .30 .30

Surtax for the flood victims at Frejus.

Charles Michel de l'Épée — SP210

Design: 25fr+10fr, Valentin Hauy.

1959, Dec. 5 **Engr.** ***Perf. 13***

Cross in Carmine

B337 SP210 20fr + 10fr blk & cl 2.00 2.00

a. Bklt. pane, 4 each, gutter btwn. 30.00

B338 SP210 25fr + 10fr dk blue & blk 2.50 2.50

The surtax was for the Red Cross.

Ship Laying Underwater Cable SP211

1960, Mar. 12

B339 SP211 20c + 5c grnsh bl & dk bl 1.50 1.50

Issued for the Day of the Stamp. The surtax went to the Red Cross.

Refugee Girl Amid Ruins — SP212

1960, Apr. 7

B340 SP212 25c + 10c grn, brn & ind .30 .25

World Refugee Year, July 1, 1959-June 30, 1960. The surtax was for aid to refugees.

Michel de L'Hospital SP213

#B342, Henri de la Tour D'Auvergne, Viscount of Turenne. #B343, Nicolas Boileau (Despreaux). #B344, Jean-Martin Charcot, M.D. #B345, Georges Bizet. 50c+15c, Edgar Degás.

1960, June 11 **Engr.** ***Perf. 13***

B341 SP213 10c + 5c pur & rose car 2.50 2.50
B342 SP213 20c + 10c ol & vio brn 3.25 3.25
B343 SP213 20c + 10c Prus grn & dp yel grn 3.25 3.25
B344 SP213 30c + 10c rose car & rose red 5.00 5.00
B345 SP213 30c + 10c dk bl & vio bl 5.00 5.00
B346 SP213 50c + 15c sl bl & gray 5.50 5.50
Nos. B341-B346 (6) 24.50 24.50

The surtax was for the Red Cross.

See Nos. B350-B355.

Staff of the Brotherhood of St. Martin — SP214

Letter Carrier, Paris 1760 — SP215

25c+10c, St. Martin, 16th cent. wood sculpture.

1960, Dec. 3 **Unwmk.** ***Perf. 13***

B347 SP214 20c + 10c rose cl & red 3.25 3.25

a. Bklt. pane, 4 each, gutter btwn. 32.50

B348 SP214 25c + 10c lt ultra & red 3.25 3.25

The surtax was for the Red Cross.

1961, Mar. 18 ***Perf. 13***

B349 SP215 20c + 5c sl grn, brn & red .75 .75

Stamp Day. Surtax for Red Cross.

Famous Men Type of 1960

Designs: 15c+5c, Bertrand Du Guesclin. B351, Pierre Puget. #B352, Charles Coulomb. 30c+10c, Antoine Drouot. 45c+10c, Honoré Daumier. 50c+15c, Guillaume Apollinaire.

1961, May 20 **Engr.**

B350 SP213 15c + 5c red brn & blk 2.50 2.50
B351 SP213 20c + 10c dk grn & lt bl 2.50 2.50
B352 SP213 20c + 10c ver & rose car 2.50 2.50
B353 SP213 30c + 10c blk & brn org 3.50 3.50
B354 SP213 45c + 10c choc & dk grn 3.50 3.50
B355 SP213 50c + 15c dk car rose & vio 4.00 4.00
Nos. B350-B355 (6) 18.50 18.50

"Love" by Rouault SP216

Medieval Royal Messenger SP217

Designs from "Miserere" by Georges Rouault: 25c+10c, "The Blind Consoles the Seeing."

1961, Dec. 2 ***Perf. 13***

B356 SP216 20c + 10c brn, blk & red 2.50 2.50

a. Bklt. pane, 4 each, gutter btwn. 30.00

B357 SP216 25c + 10c brn, blk & red 2.50 2.50

The surtax was for the Red Cross.

1962, Mar. 17

B358 SP217 20c + 5c rose red, bl & sepia .80 .80

Stamp Day. Surtax for Red Cross.

Denis Papin, Scientist SP218

Rosalie Fragonard by Fragonard SP219

Portraits: No. B360, Edme Bouchardon, sculptor. No. B361, Joseph Lakanal, educator. 30c+10c, Gustave Charpentier, composer. 45c+15c, Edouard Estaunié, writer. 50c+20c, Hyacinthe Vincent, physician and bacteriologist.

1962, June 2 **Engr.**

B359 SP218 15c + 5c bluish grn & dk gray 2.25 2.25
B360 SP218 20c + 10c cl brn 2.25 2.25
B361 SP218 20c + 10c gray & sl 2.50 2.50
B362 SP218 30c + 10c brt bl & ind 3.00 3.00
B363 SP218 45c + 15c org brn & choc 3.00 3.00
B364 SP218 50c + 20c grnsh bl & blk 3.50 3.50
Nos. B359-B364 (6) 16.50 16.50

The surtax was for the Red Cross.

1962, Dec. 8

Design: 25c+10c, Child dressed as Pierrot.

Cross in Red

B365 SP219 20c + 10c redsh brown 1.75 1.75

a. Bklt. pane, 4 ea, gutter btwn. 32.00

B366 SP219 25c + 10c dull grn 2.25 2.25

The surtax was for the Red Cross.

For surcharges see Reunion Nos. B16-B17.

Jacques Amyot, Classical Scholar SP220

30c+10c, Pierre de Marivaux, playwright. 50c+20c, Jacques Daviel, surgeon.

1963, Feb. 23 **Unwmk.** ***Perf. 13***

B367 SP220 20c + 10c mar, gray & pur 1.25 1.25
B368 SP220 30c + 10c Prus grn & mar 1.25 1.25
B369 SP220 50c + 20c ultra, ocher & ol 1.50 1.50
Nos. B367-B369 (3) 4.00 4.00

The surtax was for the Red Cross.

Roman Chariot SP221

1963, Mar. 16 **Engr.**

B370 SP221 20c + 5c brn org & vio brn .25 .25

Stamp Day. Surtax for Red Cross.

Étienne Méhul, Composer SP222

Designs: 30c+10c, Nicolas-Louis Vauquelin, chemist. 50c+20c, Alfred de Vigny, poet.

1963, May 25 **Unwmk.** ***Perf. 13***

B371 SP222 20c + 10c dp bl, dk brn & dp org 1.25 1.25
B372 SP222 30c + 10c mag, gray ol & blk 1.25 1.25
B373 SP222 50c + 20c sl, blk & brn 1.50 1.50
Nos. B371-B373 (3) 4.00 4.00

The surtax was for the Red Cross.

"Child with Grapes" by David d'Angers and Centenary Emblem — SP223

25c+10c, "The Fifer," by Edouard Manet.

1963, Dec. 9 **Unwmk.** ***Perf. 13***

B374 SP223 20c + 10c black & red .75 .75
a. Bklt. pane, 4 each, gutter btwn. 9.00 9.00
B375 SP223 25c + 10c sl grn & red .75 .75

Cent. of the Intl. and French Red Cross. Surtax for the Red Cross.
For surcharges see Reunion Nos. B18-B19.

Post Rider, 18th Century SP224

1964, Mar. 14 **Engr.**

B376 SP224 20c + 5c Prus green .30 .30

Issued for Stamp Day.

Resistance Memorial by Watkin, Luxembourg Gardens — SP225

De Gaulle's 1940 Poster "A Tous les Francais" SP226

Street Fighting in Paris and Strasbourg. SP227

Designs: 20c+5c, "Deportation," concentration camp with watchtower and barbed wire. No. B381, Allied troops landing in Normandy and Provence.

1964 **Engr.** ***Perf. 13***

B377 SP225 20c + 5c slate blk .50 .50

Perf. 12x13

B378 SP226 25c + 5c dk red, bl, red & blk .65 .65

Perf. 13

B379 SP227 30c + 5c blk, bl & org brn .75 .75
B380 SP227 30c + 5c org brn, cl & blk .75 .75
B381 SP225 50c + 5c dk grn .90 .90
Nos. B377-B381 (5) 3.55 3.55

20th anniv. of liberation from the Nazis.
Issue dates: #B377, B381, Mar. 21; #B378, June 18; #B379, June 6; #B380, Aug. 22.

President René Coty SP229

Jean Nicolas Corvisart SP230

Portraits: No. B383, John Calvin. No. B384, Pope Sylvester II (Gerbert).

1964 **Unwmk.** ***Perf. 13***

B382 SP229 30c + 10c dp cl & blk .25 .25
B383 SP229 30c + 10c dk grn, blk & brn .25 .25
B384 SP229 30c + 10c slate & cl .25 .25
Nos. B382-B384 (3) .75 .75

The surtax was for the Red Cross.
Issued: #B382, 4/25; #B383, 5/25; #B384, 6/1.

1964, Dec. 12 **Engr.**

Portrait: 25c+10c, Dominique Larrey.

Cross in Carmine

B385 SP230 20c + 10c black .35 .35
a. Bklt. pane, 4 ea, gutter btwn. 3.50
B386 SP230 25c + 10c black .35 .35

Jean Nicolas Corvisart (1755-1821), physician of Napoleon I, and Dominique Larrey (1766-1842), Chief Surgeon of the Imperial Armies. The surtax was for the Red Cross.
For surcharges see Reunion Nos. B20-B21.

Paul Dukas, Composer — SP231

#B387, Duke François de La Rochefoucauld, writer. #B388, Nicolas Poussin, painter. #B389, Duke Charles of Orléans, poet.

1965, Feb. **Engr.** ***Perf. 13***

B387 SP231 30c + 10c org brn & dk bl .40 .40
B388 SP231 30c + 10c car & dk red brn .40 .40
B389 SP231 40c + 10c dk red brn, dk red & Prus bl .50 .50
B390 SP231 40c + 10c dk brn & sl bl .50 .50
Nos. B387-B390 (4) 1.80 1.80

The surtax was for the Red Cross.
Issued: #B387, B390 2/13; #B388-B389 2/20.

Packet "La Guienne" SP232

1965, Mar. 29 **Unwmk.** ***Perf. 13***

B391 SP232 25c + 10c multi .75 .50

Issued for Stamp Day, 1965. "La Guienne" was used for transatlantic mail service. Surtax was for the Red Cross.

Infant with Spoon by Auguste Renoir — SP233

Design: 30c+10c, Coco Writing (Renoir's daughter Claude).

1965, Dec. 11 **Engr.** ***Perf. 13***

Cross in Carmine

B392 SP233 25c + 10c slate .30 .30
a. Bklt. pane, 4 ea, gutter btwn. 2.75
B393 SP233 30c + 10c dull red brn .30 .30

The surtax was for the Red Cross.
For surcharges see Reunion Nos. B22-B23.

Francois Mansart and Carnavalet Palace, Paris SP234

#B395, St. Pierre Fourier and Basilica of St. Pierre Fourier, Mirecourt. #B396, Marcel Proust and St. Hilaire Bridge, Illiers. #B397, Gabriel Fauré, monument and score of "Penelope." #B398, Elie Metchnikoff, microscope and Pasteur Institute. #B399, Hippolyte Taine and birthplace.

1966 **Engr.** ***Perf. 13***

B394 SP234 30c + 10c dk red brn & grn .35 .35
B395 SP234 30c + 10c blk & gray grn .35 .35
B396 SP234 30c + 10c ind, sep & grn .35 .35
B397 SP234 30c + 10c bis brn & ind .35 .35
B398 SP234 30c + 10c blk & dl brn .35 .35
B399 SP234 30c + 10c grn & ol brn .35 .35
Nos. B394-B399 (6) 2.10 2.10

The surtax was for the Red Cross.
Issued: #B394-B396, 2/12; others, 6/25.

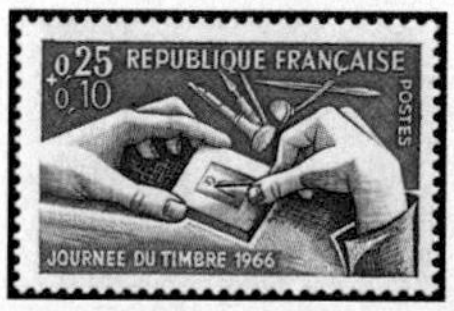

Engraver Cutting Die and Tools SP235

1966, Mar. 19 **Engr.** ***Perf. 13***

B400 SP235 25c + 10c slate, dk brn & dp org .30 .30

Stamp Day. Surtax for Red Cross.

Angel of Victory, Verdun Fortress, Marching Troops — SP236

First Aid on Battlefield, 1859 — SP237

1966, May 28 ***Perf. 13***

B401 SP236 30c + 5c Prus bl, ultra & dk bl .20 .20

Victory of Verdun, 50th anniversary.

1966, Dec. 10 **Engr.** ***Perf. 13***

#B403, Nurse giving first aid to child, 1966.

Cross in Carmine

B402 SP237 25c + 10c green .35 .35
a. Bklt. pane, 4 ea, gutter btwn. 3.50
B403 SP237 30c + 10c slate .40 .40

The surtax was for the Red Cross.
For surcharges see Reunion Nos. B24-B25.

Emile Zola — SP238

Letter Carrier, 1865 — SP239

No. B405, Beaumarchais (pen name of Pierre Augustin Caron). No. B406, St. Francois de Sales (1567-1622). No. B407, Albert Camus (1913-1960).

1967 **Engr.** ***Perf. 13***

B404 SP238 30c + 10c sl bl & bl .35 .35
B405 SP238 30c + 10c rose brn & lil .35 .35
B406 SP238 30c + 10c dl vio & pur .35 .35
B407 SP238 30c + 10c brn & dl cl .35 .35
Nos. B404-B407 (4) 1.40 1.40

The surtax was for the Red Cross.
Issued: #B404-B405, 2/4; others, 6/24.

1967, Apr. 8

B408 SP239 25c + 10c indigo, grn & red .30 .25

Issued for Stamp Day.

Ivory Flute Player — SP240

Ski Jump and Long Distance Skiing — SP241

30c+10c, Violin player, ivory carving.

1967, Dec. 16 **Engr.** ***Perf. 13***

Cross in Carmine

B409 SP240 25c + 10c dl vio & lt brn .40 .40
a. Bklt. pane, 4 ea, gutter btwn. 3.50
B410 SP240 30c + 10c grn & lt brn .40 .40

The surtax was for the Red Cross.
For surcharges see Reunion Nos. B26-B27.

1968, Jan. 27

Designs: 40c+10c, Ice hockey. 60c+20c, Olympic flame and snowflakes. 75c+25c, Woman figure skater. 95c+35c, Slalom.

B411 SP241 30c + 10c ver, gray & brn .35 .35
B412 SP241 40c + 10c lil, lem & brt mag .35 .35
B413 SP241 60c + 20c dk grn, org & brt vio .50 .50
B414 SP241 75c + 25c brt pink, yel grn & blk .60 .60
B415 SP241 95c + 35c bl, brt pink & red brn .60 .60
Nos. B411-B415 (5) 2.40 2.40

Issued for the 10th Winter Olympic Games, Grenoble, Feb. 6-18.

Rural Mailman, 1830 — SP242

1968, Mar. 16 **Engr.** *Perf. 13*
B416 SP242 25c + 10c multi .25 .25

Issued for Stamp Day.

François Couperin, Composer, and Instruments SP243

Portraits: No. B418, Gen. Louis Desaix de Veygoux (1768-1800) and scene showing his death at the Battle of Marengo, Italy. No. B419, Saint-Pol-Roux (pen name of Paul-Pierre Roux, 1861-1940), Christ on the Cross and ruins of Camaret-sur-Mer. No. B420, Paul Claudel (poet and diplomat, 1868-1955) and Joan of Arc at the stake.

1968 **Engr.** *Perf. 13*
B417 SP243 30c + 10c pur & rose lil .25 .25
B418 SP243 30c + 10c dk grn & brn .25 .25
B419 SP243 30c + 10c cop red & ol bis .25 .25
B420 SP243 30c + 10c dk brn & lil .25 .25
Nos. B417-B420 (4) 1.00 1.00

Issue dates: Nos. B417-B418, Mar. 23; Nos. B419-B420, July 6.

Spring, by Nicolas Mignard — SP244

Paintings by Nicolas Mignard; 30c+10c, Fall. No. B423, Summer. No. B424, Winter.

1968-69 **Engr.** *Perf. 13*
Cross in Carmine
B421 SP244 25c + 10c pur & sl bl .30 .30
a. Bklt. pane, 4 ea #B421-B422 with gutter btwn.) 3.00
B422 SP244 30c + 10c brn & rose car .30 .30
B423 SP244 40c + 15c dk brn & brn ('69) .50 .50
a. Bklt. pane, 4 ea #B423, B424 with gutter btwn.) 3.50
B424 SP244 40c + 15c pur & Prus bl ('69) .50 .50
Nos. B421-B424 (4) 1.60 1.60

The surtax was for the Red Cross.
For surcharges see Reunion Nos. B28-B31.

Mailmen's Omnibus, 1881 SP245

1969, Mar. 15 **Engr.** *Perf. 13*
B425 SP245 30c + 10c brn, grn & blk .25 .25

Issued for Stamp Day.
For surcharge see Reunion No. B32.

Gen. Francois Marceau — SP246

Portraits: No. B427, Charles Augustin Sainte-Beuve (1804-1869), writer. No. B428, Albert Roussel (1869-1937), musician. No. B429, Marshal Jean Lannes (1769-1809). No. B430, Georges Cuvier (1769-1832), naturalist. No. B431, André Gide, (1869-1951), writer.

1969
B426 SP246 50c + 10c brn red .50 .50
B427 SP246 50c + 10c slate bl .50 .50
B428 SP246 50c + 10c dp vio bl .50 .50
B429 SP246 50c + 10c choc .50 .50
B430 SP246 50c + 10c dp plum .50 .50
B431 SP246 50c + 10c blue grn .50 .50
Nos. B426-B431 (6) 3.00 3.00

The surtax was for the Red Cross.
Issued: Nos. B426-B428, Mar. 24; No. B429, May 10; Nos. B430-B431, May 17.

Gen. Jacques Leclerc, La Madeleine and Battle — SP247

1969, Aug. 23 **Engr.** *Perf. 13*
B432 SP247 45c + 10c slate & ol 1.00 1.00

Liberation of Paris, 8/25/44, 25th anniv.

Same Inscribed "Liberation de Strasbourg"

1969, Nov. 22 **Engr.** *Perf. 13*
B433 SP247 70c + 10c brn, choc & olive 3.50 3.50

25th anniv. of the liberation of Strasbourg.

Philibert Delorme, Architect, and Chateau d'Anet SP248

Designs: No. B435, Louis Le Vau (1612-1670), architect, and Vaux-le-Vicomte Chateau, Paris. No. B436, Prosper Merimée (1803-1870), writer, and Carmen. No. B437, Alexandre Dumas (1802-1870), writer, and Three Musketeers. No. B438, Edouard Branly (1844-1940), physicist, electric circuit and convent of the Carmes, Paris. No. B439, Maurice de Broglie (1875-1960), physicist, and X-ray spectrograph.

1970 **Engr.** *Perf. 13*
B434 SP248 40c + 10c slate grn .50 .50
B435 SP248 40c + 10c dk car .50 .50
B436 SP248 40c + 10c Prus blue .50 .50
B437 SP248 40c + 10c violet bl .50 .50
B438 SP248 40c + 10c dp brown .50 .50
B439 SP248 40c + 10c dk gray .50 .50
Nos. B434-B439 (6) 3.00 3.00

The surtax was for the Red Cross.
Issued: #B434-B436, 2/14; others, 4/11.

City Mailman, 1830 — SP249

"Life and Death" — SP250

1970, Mar. 14
B440 SP249 40c + 10c blk, ultra & dk car rose .40 .40

Issued for Stamp Day.
For surcharge see Reunion No. B33.

1970, Apr. 4
B441 SP250 40c + 10c brt bl, ol & car rose .25 .25

Issued to publicize the fight against cancer in connection with Health Day, Apr. 7.

Marshal de Lattre de Tassigny — SP251

1970, May 8 **Engr.** *Perf. 13*
B442 SP251 40c + 10c slate & vio bl .50 .50

25th anniv. of the entry into Berlin of French troops under Marshal Jean de Lattre de Tassigny, May 8, 1945.

Lord and Lady, Dissay Chapel Fresco — SP252

#B444, Angel holding whips, from fresco in Dissay Castle Chapel, Vienne, c. 1500.

1970, Dec. 12 **Engr.** *Perf. 13*
Cross in Carmine
B443 SP252 40c + 15c green .55 .55
a. Bklt. pane, 4 ea, gutter btwn. 12.50
B444 SP252 40c + 15c cop red .55 .55

The surtax was for the Red Cross.
For surcharges see Reunion Nos. B34-B35.

Daniel-Francois Auber and "Fra Diavolo" Music — SP253

#B446, Gen. Charles Diego Brosset (1898-1944), Basilica of Fourvière. #B447, Victor Grignard (1871-1935), chemist, Nobel Prize medal. #B448, Henri Farman (1874-1958), plane. #B449, Gen. Charles Georges Delestraint (1879-1945), scroll. #B450, Jean Eugène Robert-Houdin (1805-71), magician's act.

1971 **Engr.** *Perf. 13*
B445 SP253 50c + 10c brn vio & brn .75 .75
B446 SP253 50c + 10c dk sl grn & ol gray .75 .75
B447 SP253 50c + 10c brn red & olive .75 .75
B448 SP253 50c + 10c vio bl & vio .75 .75
B449 SP253 50c + 10c pur & cl .85 .85
B450 SP253 50c + 10c sl grn & bl grn .85 .85
Nos. B445-B450 (6) 4.70 4.70

The surtax was for the Red Cross.
Issued: #B445-B446, 3/6; #B447, 5/8; #B448, 5/29; #B449-B450, 10/16.

Army Post Office, 1914-1918 SP254

1971, Mar. 27 **Engr.** *Perf. 13*
B451 SP254 50c + 10c ol, brn & bl .45 .45

Stamp Day, 1971.
For surcharge see Reunion No. B36.

Girl with Dog, by Greuze SP255

Aristide Bergès (1833-1904) SP256

Design: 50c+10c, "The Dead Bird," by Jean-Baptiste Greuze (1725-1805).

1971, Dec. 11
Cross in Carmine
B452 SP255 30c + 10c violet bl .70 .70
a. Bklt. pane, 4 each, gutter btwn. 6.00
B453 SP255 50c + 10c dp car .70 .70

The surtax was for the Red Cross.
For surcharges see Reunion Nos. B37-B38.

1972 **Engr.** *Perf. 13*

#B455, Paul de Chomedey (1612-76), founder of Montreal, and arms of Neuville-sur-Vanne. #B456, Edouard Belin (1876-1963), inventor. #B457, Louis Blériot (1872-1936), aviation pioneer. #B458, Adm. François Joseph, Count de Grasse (1722-88), hero of the American Revolution. #B459, Théophile Gautier (1811-72), writer.

B454 SP256 50c + 10c blk & grn .75 .75
B455 SP256 50c + 10c blk & bl .75 .75
B456 SP256 50c + 10c blk & lil rose .75 .75
B457 SP256 50c + 10c red & blk .75 .75
B458 SP256 50c + 10c org & blk 1.00 1.00
B459 SP256 50c + 10c blk & brn 1.00 1.00
Nos. B454-B459 (6) 5.00 5.00

The surtax was for the Red Cross.
Issued: #B454-B455, Feb. 19; #B456, June 24; #B457, July 1; #B458-B459, Sept. 9.

Rural Mailman, 1894 SP257

Nicolas Desgenettes SP258

1972, Mar. 18 **Engr.** *Perf. 13*
B460 SP257 50c + 10c bl, yel & ol gray 1.00 .75

Stamp Day 1972.
For surcharge see Reunion No. B39.

1972, Dec. 16 **Engr.** *Perf. 13*

Designs: 30c+10c, René Nicolas Dufriche, Baron Desgenettes, M.D. (1762-1837).

50c+10c, François Joseph Broussais, M.D. (1772-1838).

B461 SP258 30c + 10c sl grn & red .65 .50
a. Bklt. pane, 4 ea, gutter btwn. 7.00
B462 SP258 50c + 10c red .65 .50

The surtax was for the Red Cross.
For surcharges see Reunion Nos. B40-B41.

Tony Garnier (1869-1948), architect — SP259

#B463, Gaspard de Coligny (1519-1572), admiral and Huguenot leader. #B464, Ernest Renan (1823-1892), philologist and historian. #B465, Alberto Santos Dumont (1873-1932), Brazilian aviator. #B466, Gabrielle-Sidonie Colette (1873-1954), writer. #B467, René Duguay-Trouin (1673-1736), naval commander. #B468, Louis Pasteur (1822-1895), chemist, bacteriologist. #B469, Tony Garnier (1869-1948), architect.

1973 Engr. *Perf. 13*

B463 SP259 50c + 10c multi .85 .85
B464 SP259 50c + 10c multi .85 .85
B465 SP259 50c + 10c multi .85 .85
B466 SP259 50c + 10c multi .85 .85
B467 SP259 50c + 10c multi .85 .85
B468 SP259 50c + 10c multi .85 .85
B469 SP259 50c + 10c multi .85 .85
Nos. B463-B469 (7) 5.95 5.95

Issued: #B463, 2/17; #B464, 4/28; #B465, 5/26; #B466, 6/2; #B467, 6/9; #B468, 10/6; #B469, 11/17.

Mail Coach, 1835 SP260

1973, Mar. 24 Engr. *Perf. 13*

B470 SP260 50c + 10c grnsh blue .35 .35

Stamp Day, 1973.
For surcharge see Reunion No. B42.

Mary Magdalene SP261

St. Louis-Marie de Montfort SP262

50c+10c, Mourning woman. Designs are from 15th cent. Tomb of Tonnerre.

1973, Dec. 1

B471 SP261 30c + 10c sl grn & red .55 .55
a. Bklt. pane, 4 each, gutter btwn. 6.00
B472 SP261 50c + 10c dk gray & red .55 .55

Surtax was for the Red Cross.
For surcharges see Reunion Nos. B43-B44.

1974, Feb. 23 Engr. *Perf. 13*

Portraits: No. B474, Francis Poulenc (1899-1963), composer. No. B475, Jules Barbey d'Aurevilly (1808-1889), writer. No. B476, Jean Giraudoux (1882-1944), writer.

B473 SP262 50c + 10c multi 1.10 1.10
B474 SP262 50c + 10c multi .70 .70
B475 SP262 80c + 15c multi .80 .80
B476 SP262 80c + 15c multi .80 .80
Nos. B473-B476 (4) 3.40 3.40

Issue dates: No. B473, Mar. 9; No. B474, July 20; Nos. B475-B476, Nov. 16.

Automatically Sorted Letters — SP263

1974, Mar. 9 Engr. *Perf. 13*

B477 SP263 50c + 10c multi .30 .25

Stamp Day 1974. Automatic letter sorting center, Orleans-la-Source, opened 1/30/73.
For surcharge see Reunion No. B45.

Order of Liberation and 5 Honored Cities — SP264

1974, June 15 Engr. *Perf. 13*

B478 SP264 1fr + 10c multi .75 .40

30th anniv. of liberation from the Nazis.

"Summer" SP265

"Winter" SP266

Designs: B481, "Spring" (girl on swing). B482, "Fall" (umbrella and rabbits).

1974, Nov. 30 Engr. *Perf. 13*

B479 SP265 60c + 15c multi .60 .60
a. Bklt. pane, 4 ea, gutter btwn. 6.00
B480 SP266 80c + 15c multi .60 .60

For surcharges see Reunion Nos. B46-B47.

1975, Nov. 29

B481 SP265 60c + 15c multi .50 .50
a. Bklt. pane, 4 ea, gutter btwn. 4.75
B482 SP266 80c + 20c multi .50 .50

Surtax was for the Red Cross.

Dr. Albert Schweitzer SP267

Edmond Michelet SP268

André Siegfried and Map SP269

#B483, Albert Schweitzer (1875-1965), medical missionary. #B484, Edmond Michelet (1899-1970), Resistance hero, statesman. #B485, Robert Schuman (1886-1963), promoter of United Europe. #B486, Eugene Thomas (1903-69), minister of PTT. #B487, André Siegfried (1875-1959), political science professor, writer.

1975 Engr. *Perf. 13*

B483 SP267 80c + 20c multi .50 .50
B484 SP268 80c + 20c bl & ind .50 .50
B485 SP268 80c + 20c blk & ind .50 .50
B486 SP268 80c + 20c blk & sl .50 .50
B487 SP269 80c + 20c blk & bl .50 .50
Nos. B483-B487 (5) 2.50 2.50

Issued: #B483, 1/11; #B484, 2/22; #B485, 5/10; #B486, 6/28; #B487, 11/15.

Second Republic Mailman's Badge — SP270

1975, Mar. 8 Photo.

B488 SP270 80c + 20c multi .50 .40

Stamp Day.

"Sage" Type of 1876 SP271

Marshal A. J. de Moncey SP272

1976, Mar. 13 Engr. *Perf. 13*

B489 SP271 80c + 20c blk & lil .45 .45

Stamp Day 1976.

1976 Engr. *Perf. 13*

#B491, Max Jacob (1876-1944), Dadaist writer, by Picasso. #B492, Jean Mounet-Sully (1841-1916), actor. #B493, Gen. Pierre Daumesnil (1776-1832). #B494, Eugène Fromentin (1820-1876), painter.

B490 SP272 80c + 20c multi .50 .50
B491 SP272 80c + 20c red brn & ol .50 .50
B492 SP272 80c + 20c multi .50 .50
B493 SP272 1fr + 20c multi .50 .50
B494 SP272 1fr + 20c multi .50 .50
Nos. B490-B494 (5) 2.50 2.50

Issued: #B490, 5/22; #B491, 7/22; #B492, 8/28; #B493, 9/4; #B494, 9/25.

Anna de Noailles SP273

St. Barbara SP274

1976, Nov. 6 Engr. *Perf. 13*

B495 SP273 1fr + 20c multi .60 .60

Anna de Noailles (1876-1933), writer & poet.

1976, Nov. 20

Design: 1fr+25c, Cimmerian Sibyl. Sculptures from Brou Cathedral.

Cross in Carmine

B496 SP274 80c + 20c violet .60 .60
a. Bklt. pane, 4 ea, gutter btwn. 6.00
B497 SP274 1fr + 25c dk brown .80 .80

Surtax was for the Red Cross.

Marckolsheim Relay Station Sign — SP275

1977, Mar. 26 Engr. *Perf. 13*

B498 SP275 1fr + 20c multi .40 .40

Stamp Day.

Edouard Herriot, Statesman and Writer SP276

Christmas Figurine, Provence SP277

Designs: No. B500, Abbé Breuil (1877-1961), archaeologist. No. B501, Guillaume de Machault (1305-1377), poet and composer. No. B502, Charles Cross (1842-1888).

1977 Engr. *Perf. 13*

B499 SP276 1fr + 20c multi .60 .60
B500 SP276 1fr + 20c multi .60 .60
B501 SP276 1fr + 20c multi .60 .60
B502 SP276 1fr + 20c multi .60 .60
Nos. B499-B502 (4) 2.40 2.40

Issued: #B499, Oct. 8; #B500, Oct. 15; #B501, Nov. 12; #B502, Dec. 3.

1977, Nov. 26

1fr+25c, Christmas figurine (woman), Provence.

B503 SP277 80c + 20c red & ind .45 .45
a. Bklt. pane, 4 ea, gutter btwn. 4.50
B504 SP277 1fr + 25c red & sl grn .55 .55

Surtax was for the Red Cross.

Marie Noel, Writer — SP278

Mail Collection, 1900 — SP279

#B506, Georges Bernanos (1888-1948), writer. #B507, Leo Tolstoi (1828-1910), Russian writer. #B508, Charles Marie Leconte de Lisle (1818-1894), poet. #B509, Voltaire (1694-1778) and Jean Jacques Rousseau (1712-1778). #B510, Claude Bernard (1813-1878), physiologist.

1978 Engr. *Perf. 13*

B505 SP278 1fr + 20c multi .55 .55
B506 SP278 1fr + 20c multi .55 .55
B507 SP278 1fr + 20c multi .55 .55
B508 SP278 1fr + 20c multi .55 .55
B509 SP278 1fr + 20c multi .55 .55
B510 SP278 1fr + 20c multi .55 .55
Nos. B505-B510 (6) 3.30 3.30

Issued: #B505, 2/11; #B506, 2/18; #B507, 4/15; #B508, 3/26; #B509, 7/1; #B510, 9/16.

1978, Apr. 8 Engr. *Perf. 13*

B511 SP279 1fr + 20c multi .50 .40

Stamp Day 1978.

SP280

SP281

1fr+25c, The Hare & the Tortoise. 1.20fr+30c, The City Mouse & the Country Mouse.

1978, Dec. 2 **Engr.** ***Perf. 13***

B512 SP280 1fr + 25c multi .75 .65
a. Bklt. pane, 4 ea, gutter btwn. 6.00
B513 SP280 1.20fr + 30c multi .75 .65

Surtax was for the Red Cross.

1979 **Engr.** ***Perf. 13***

#B514, Ladislas Marshal de Berchény (1689-1778). #B515, Leon Jouhaux (1879-1954), labor leader. #B516, Peter Abelard (1079-1142), theologian and writer. #B517, Georges Courteline (1860-1929), humorist. #B518, Simone Weil (1909-1943), social philosopher. #B519, André Malraux (1901-1976), novelist.

B514 SP281 1.20fr + 30c multi .60 .60
B515 SP281 1.20fr + 30c multi .60 .60
B516 SP281 1.20fr + 30c multi .60 .60
B517 SP281 1.20fr + 30c multi .60 .60
B518 SP281 1.30fr + 30c multi .60 .60
B519 SP281 1.30fr + 30c multi .60 .60
Nos. B514-B519 (6) 3.60 3.60

Issued: #B514, 1/13; #B515, 5/12; #B516, 6/9; #B517, 6/25; #B518, 11/12; #B519, 11/26.

General Post Office, from 1908 Post Card SP282

1979, Mar. 10 **Engr.** ***Perf. 13***

B520 SP282 1.20fr + 30c multi .60 .40

Stamp Day 1979.

Woman, Stained-Glass Window — SP283

Stained-glass windows, Church of St. Joan of Arc, Rouen: 1.30fr+30c, Simon the Magician.

1979, Dec. 1 ***Perf. 13***

B521 SP283 1.10fr + 30c multi .50 .40
B522 SP283 1.30fr + 30c multi .60 .45
a. Bklt. pane, 4 each #521-522, with gutter btwn., perf. 12½x13 6.00

Surtax was for the Red Cross.

Eugene Viollet le Duc (1814-1879), Architect — SP284

Jean-Marie de Le Mennais (1780-1860), Priest and Educator — SP285

#B524, Jean Monnet (1888-1979), economist and diplomat. #B525, Viollet le Duc (1814-1879), architect and writer. #B526, Frederic Mistral (1830-1914), poet. #B527, Saint-John Perse (Alexis Leger, 1887-1975), poet and diplomat. #B528, Pierre Paul de Riquet (1604-1680), canal builder.

1980 **Engr.** ***Perf. 13***

B523 SP284 1.30fr + 30c multi .70 .70
B524 SP285 1.30fr + 30c multi .70 .70
B525 SP285 1.40fr + 30c blue .70 .70
B526 SP285 1.40fr + 30c black .70 .70
B527 SP285 1.40fr + 30c multi .70 .70
B528 SP284 1.40fr + 30c multi .70 .70
Nos. B523-B528 (6) 4.20 4.20

Issued: #B523, Feb. 16; #B524-B526, Sept. 6; #B527-B528, Oct. 11.

The Letter to Melie, by Avati, Stamp Day, 1980 — SP286

1980, Mar. 8 **Photo.**

B529 SP286 1.30fr + 30c multi .60 .45

Filling the Granaries, Choir Stall Detail, Amiens Cathedral — SP287

#B531, Grapes from the Promised Land.

1980, Dec. 6 **Engr.** ***Perf. 13***

B530 SP287 1.20fr + 30c red & dk red brn .70 .70
B531 SP287 1.40fr + 30c red & dk red brn .80 .80
a. Bklt. pane, 4 #B530-B531, with gutter btwn., perf. 12½x13 6.50

Sister Anne-Marie Javouhey (1779-1851), Founded Congregation of St. Joseph of Cluny — SP288

#B532, Louis Armand (1905-71), railway engineer. #B533, Louis Jouvet (1887-1951), theater director. #B534, Marc Boegner (1881-1970), peace worker. #B536, Jacques Offenbach (1819-80), composer. #B537, Pierre Teilhard de Chardin (1881-1955), philosopher. Nos. B532-B533, B537 vert.

1981 **Engr.** ***Perf. 13***

B532 SP288 1.20 + 30c multi .65 .65
B533 SP288 1.20 + 30c multi .65 .65
B534 SP288 1.40 + 30c multi .65 .65
B535 SP288 1.40 + 30c multi .65 .65
B536 SP288 1.40 + 30c multi .65 .65
B537 SP288 1.40 + 30c multi .65 .65
Nos. B532-B537 (6) 3.90 3.90

Issued: #B532, 5/23; #B533, 6/13; #B534, 11/14; #B535, 2/7; #B536, 2/14; #B537, 5/23.

The Love Letter, by Goya — SP289

1981, Mar. 7 ***Perf. 13x12½***

B538 SP289 1.40 + 30c multi 1.00 .90

Stamp Day 1981.

Scourges of the Passion SP290

Guillaume Postel (1510-1581), Theologian — SP291

Stained-glass Windows, Church of the Sacred Heart, Audincourt: 1.60fr+30c, "Peace."

1981, Dec. 5 **Photo.** ***Perf. 13***

B539 SP290 1.40 + 30c multi .75 .65
B540 SP290 1.60 + 30c multi .70 .45
a. Bklt. pane, 4 ea, gutter btwn. 6.00

1982 **Engr.** ***Perf. 13***

#B542, Henri Mondor (1885-1962), physician. #B543, Andre Chantemesse (1851-1919), Scientist. #B544, Louis Pergaud (1882-1915), writer. #B545, Robert Debre (1882-1978), writer. #B546, Gustave Eiffel (1832-1923), engineer.

B541 SP291 1.40 + 30c multi .65 .45
B542 SP291 1.40 + 30c dk brn & dk bl .65 .40
B543 SP291 1.60 + 30c multi .70 .70
B544 SP291 1.60 + 40c multi .70 .70
B545 SP291 1.60 + 40c dk blue .90 .70
B546 SP291 1.80 + 40c sepia .90 .70
Nos. B541-B546 (6) 4.50 3.65

Woman Reading, by Picasso — SP292

1982, Mar. 27 ***Perf. 13x12½***

B547 SP292 1.60 + 40c multi 1.00 .75

Stamp Day.

SP293

SP294

Jules Verne books: 1.60fr+30c, Five Weeks in a Balloon. 1.80fr+40c, 20,000 Leagues under the Sea.

1982, Nov. 20 ***Perf. 13***

B548 SP293 1.60 + 30c multi .75 .65
B549 SP293 1.80 + 40c multi .75 .65
a. Bklt. pane, 4 each #B548-B549, with gutter btwn., perf. 12½x13 8.00

Surtax was for Red Cross.

1983 **Engr.** ***Perf. 12½x13***

#B550, Andre Messager (1853-1929). #B551, J.A. Gabriel (1698-1782), architect. #B552, Hector Berlioz (1803-69), composer. #B553, Max Fouchet (1913-80). #B554, Rene Cassin (1887-1976). #B555, Stendhal (Marie Henri Beyle, 1783-1842).

B550 SP294 1.60 + 30c multi .65 .65
B551 SP294 1.60 + 30c multi .65 .65
B552 SP294 1.80 + 40c dp lil & blk .75 .75
B553 SP294 1.80 + 40c multi .75 .75
B554 SP294 2fr + 40c multi .80 .80
B555 SP294 2fr + 40c multi .80 .80
Nos. B550-B555 (6) 4.40 4.40

Issued: #B550, 1/15; #B551, 4/16; #B552, 1/22; #B553, 4/30; #B554, 6/25; #B555, 11/12.

Man Dictating a Letter, by Rembrandt — SP295

Photo. & Engr.

1983, Feb. 26 ***Perf. 13X12½***

B556 SP295 1.80 + 40c multi 1.20 .75

Stamp Day.

Virgin with Child, Baillon, 14th Cent. — SP296

Design: No. B558, Virgin with Child, Genainville, 16th Cent.

1983, Nov. 26 **Engr.** ***Perf. 13***

B557 SP296 1.60 + 40c shown .65 .45
B558 SP296 2fr + 40c multi .85 .55
a. Bklt. pane, 4 #B557-B558, with gutter btwn., perf. 12½x13 6.50

Emile Littre (1801-1881), Physician — SP297

#B560, Jean Zay (1904-44). #B561, Pierre Corneille (1606-1684. #B562, Gaston Bachelard (1884-1962). #B563, Jean Paulhan (1884-1968). #B564, Evariste Galois (1811-1832).

1984 **Engr.** ***Perf. 13***

B559 SP297 1.60fr + 40c plum & blk .85 .85
B560 SP297 1.60fr + 40c dk grn & blk .85 .85
B561 SP297 1.70fr + 40c dp vio & blk .85 .85
B562 SP297 2fr + 40c gray & blk .85 .85
B563 SP297 2.10fr + 40c dk brn & blk .90 .80
B564 SP297 2.10fr + 40c ultra & blk .90 .80
Nos. B559-B564 (6) 5.20 5.00

SP298

SP299

Diderot Holding a Letter, by L.M. Van Loo.

1984, Mar. 17 Engr. *Perf. 12½x13*
B565 SP298 2fr + 40c multi 1.25 .90

1984, Nov. 24 Photo. *Perf. 12½x13*

The Rose Basket, by Caly.

B566 SP299 2.10fr + 50c pnksh (basket) & multi 1.10 .90
a. Salmon (basket) & multi, perf. 13½x13 1.10 .90
b. As "a," bklt. pane of 10 + 2 labels 11.00

Surtax was for the Red Cross.

Jules Romains (1885-1972) — SP300

Authors: No. B568, Jean-Paul Sartre (1905-1980). No. B569, Romain Rolland (1866-1944). No. B570, Roland Dorgeles (1885-1973). No. B571, Victor Hugo (1802-1885). No. B572, Francois Mauriac (1885-1970).

1985, Feb. 23 Engr. *Perf. 13*
B567 SP300 1.70fr + 40c *3.25 3.25*
B568 SP300 1.70fr + 40c *3.25 3.25*
B569 SP300 1.70fr + 40c *3.25 3.25*
B570 SP300 2.10fr + 50c *3.75 3.75*
B571 SP300 2.10fr + 50c *3.75 3.75*
B572 SP300 2.10fr + 50c *3.75 3.75*
a. Bklt. pane, 1 each + 2 labels, perf. 15x14½ *32.50*
Nos. B567-B572 (6) *21.00 21.00*

SP301

SP302

Stamp Day: Canceling apparatus invented by Eugene Daguin (1849-1888).

1985, Mar. 16 Engr. *Perf. 12½x13*
B573 SP301 2.10fr + 50c brn blk & bluish gray 1.00 .85

1985, Nov. 23 Photo.

Issenheim Altarpiece retable.

B574 SP302 2.20fr + 50c multi 1.00 .85
a. As "b," bklt. pane of 10 10.00
b. Perf. 13½x13 1.00 .85

Surtax for the Red Cross.

SP303

SP304

Famous men: No. B575, Francois Arago (1786-1853), physician, politician. No. B576, Henri Moissan (1852-1907), chemist. No. B577, Henri Fabre (1882-1984), engineer. No. B578, Marc Seguin (1786-1875), engineer. No. B579, Paul Herault (1863-1914), chemist.

1986, Feb. 22 Engr. *Perf. 13*
B575 SP303 1.80fr + 40c multi .95 .95
B576 SP303 1.80fr + 40c multi .95 .95
B577 SP303 1.80fr + 40c multi .95 .95
B578 SP303 2.20fr + 50c multi 1.10 1.10
B579 SP303 2.20fr + 50c multi 1.10 1.10
a. Bklt. pane of 5, #B575-B579, + 3 labels 8.00
Nos. B575-B579 (5) 5.05 5.05

1986, Mar. 1 Engr. *Perf. 13x12½*
B580 SP304 2.20fr + 50c brn blk *6.00 6.00*

Pierre Cot (1895-1977).

Mail Britzska SP305

1986, Apr. 5 *Perf. 13*
B581 SP305 2.20fr + 60c pale tan & dk vio brn 1.10 1.00

Booklet Stamp

B582 SP305 2.20fr + 60c buff & blk 1.20 1.00
a. Bklt. pane of 6 + 2 labels 7.50

Stamp Day. See Nos. B590-B591, B599-B600, B608-B609.

Stained Glass Window (detail), by Vieira da Silva, St. Jacques of Reims Church, Marne — SP306

1986, Nov. 24 Photo. *Perf. 12½x13*
B583 SP306 2.20fr + 60c multi 1.20 .95
a. As "b," bklt. pane of 10 12.00
b. Perf. 13½x13 1.20 .95

Surtaxed to benefit the natl. Red Cross.

Physicians and Biologists SP307

#B584, Charles Richet (1850-1935). #B585, Eugene Jamot (1879-1937). #B586, Bernard Halpern (1904-1978). #B587, Alexandre Yersin (1863-1943). #B588, Jean Rostand (1894-1977). #B589, Jacques Monod (1910-1976).

1987, Feb. 21 Engr. *Perf. 13*
B584 SP307 1.90fr + 50c deep ultra .95 .95
B585 SP307 1.90fr + 50c dull lil .95 .95
B586 SP307 1.90fr + 50c grnish gray .95 .95
B587 SP307 2.20fr + 50c grnish gray 1.10 1.10
B588 SP307 2.20fr + 50c deep ultra 1.10 1.10
B589 SP307 2.20fr + 50c dull lil 1.10 1.10
a. Bklt. pane of 6, #B584-B589 *6.50*
Nos. B584-B589 (6) 6.15 6.15

Stamp Day Type of 1986

Stamp Day 1987: Berline carriage.

1987, Mar. 14 Engr.
B590 SP305 2.20fr + 60c buff & sepia 1.10 .95

Booklet Stamp

B591 SP305 2.20fr + 60c pale & dk bl 1.25 .95
a. Bklt. pane of 6 + 2 labels 8.00

Flight Into Egypt, Retable by Melchior Broederlam SP308

1987, Nov. 21 Photo. *Perf. 12½x13*
B592 SP308 2.20fr +60c multi 1.10 .95
a. As "b," bklt. pane of 10 + 2 labels 11.00
b. Perf. 13½x13 1.10 .95

Surtaxed to benefit the Red Cross.

Explorers SP309

Profiles & maps: #B593, Marquis Abraham Duquesne (1610-1688), naval commander. #B594, Pierre Andre de Suffren (1729-1788). #B595, Jean-Francois de La Perouse (1741-1788). #B596, Mahe de La Bourdonnais (1699-1753). #B597, Louis-Antoine de Bougainville (1729-1811). #B598, Jules Dumont d'Urville (1790-1842).

1988, Feb. 20 Engr. *Perf. 13*
B593 SP309 2fr + 50c multi .90 .80
B594 SP309 2fr + 50c multi .90 .80
B595 SP309 2fr + 50c multi .90 .80
B596 SP309 2.20fr + 50c multi 1.00 .85
B597 SP309 2.20fr + 50c multi 1.00 .85
B598 SP309 2.20fr + 50c multi 1.00 .85
a. Bklt. pane of 6, #B593-B598 6.00

Stamp Day Type of 1986

Stamp Day 1988: Postal coach.

1988, Mar. 29 Engr.
B599 SP305 2.20fr +60c dk lilac 1.10 1.00

Booklet Stamp

B600 SP305 2.20fr +60c sepia 1.10 1.00
a. Bklt. pane of 6 + 2 labels 6.50

Intl. Red Cross, 125th Anniv. — SP310

1988, Nov. 19 Engr. *Perf. 12½x13*
B601 SP310 2.20fr +60c multi 1.10 1.00
a. As "b," bklt. pane of 10+2 labels 11.00
b. Perf. 13½x13 1.10 1.00

Revolution Leaders and Heroes SP311

#B602, Emmanuel Joseph Sieyes (1748-1836). #B603, Honore Gabriel Riqueti, Comte de Mirabeau (1749-91). #B604, Louis Marie de Noailles (1756-1804). #B605, Lafayette. #B606, Antoine Pierre Joseph Marie Barnave (1761-93). #B607, Jean Baptiste Drouet (1763-1824).

1989, Feb. 25 Engr. *Perf. 13*
B602 SP311 2.20fr +50c multi 1.10 .90
B603 SP311 2.20fr +50c multi 1.10 .90
B604 SP311 2.20fr +50c multi 1.10 .90
B605 SP311 2.20fr +50c multi 1.10 .90
B606 SP311 2.20fr +50c multi 1.10 .90
B607 SP311 2.20fr +50c multi 1.10 .90
a. Bklt. pane, 1 each + 2 labels 6.60

French Revolution, bicent.

Stamp Day Type of 1986

Design: Paris-Lyon stagecoach.

1989, Apr. 15 Engr. *Perf. 13*
B608 SP305 2.20fr +60c pale bl & dk bl 1.10 .95

Booklet Stamp

B609 SP305 2.20fr +60c pale lil & pur 1.00 .95
a. Bklt. pane of 6 + 2 labels 8.00

Stamp Day 1989.

Bird From a Silk Tapestry, Lyon, 18th Cent. — SP312

1989, Nov. 18 Photo. *Perf. 12½x13*
B610 SP312 2.20fr +60c multi 1.10 .90
a. As "b," bklt. pane of 10 12.00
b. Perf. 13½x13 1.10 .90

Surtax for the natl. Red Cross.

1992 Winter Olympics, Albertville SP313

1990, Feb. 9 Engr. *Perf. 13*
B611 SP313 2.30fr +20c red, bl & blk 1.10 .85

See Nos. B621-B627, B636-B637, B639.

Stamp Day SP314

1990, Mar. 17 Photo.
B612 SP314 2.30fr +60c ultra, bl & brt yel 1.20 1.00

Booklet Stamp

B613 SP314 2.30fr +60c ultra, grn, yel & brt grn 1.20 1.00
a. Bklt. pane of 6 + 2 labels 8.00

SP315

SP316

Quimper or Brittany Ware Faience plate.

1990, May 5 Photo. *Perf. 12½x13*
B614 SP315 2.30fr +60c multi 1.10 1.00
a. As "b," bklt. pane of 10+2 labels 12.00
b. Perf. 13½x13 1.20 1.00

Surcharge benefited the Red Cross.

1990, June 16 Photo. *Perf. 13*

#B615, Aristide Bruant. #B616, Maurice Chevalier. #B617, Tino Rossi. #B618, Edith Piaf. #B619, Jacques Brel. #B620, Georges Brassens.

B615 SP316 2.30fr +50c multi 1.00 1.00
B616 SP316 2.30fr +50c multi 1.00 1.00
B617 SP316 2.30fr +50c multi 1.00 1.00
B618 SP316 2.30fr +50c multi 1.00 1.00

B619 SP316 2.30fr +50c multi 1.00 1.00
B620 SP316 2.30fr +50c multi 1.00 1.00
a. Bklt. pane, 1 each +2 labels 6.00

Albertville Olympic Type

Designs: No. B621, Ski jumping. No. B622, Speed skiing. No. B623, Slalom skiing. No. B624, Cross-country skiing. No. B625, Ice hockey. No. B626, Luge. No. B627, Curling.

1990-91 Engr. *Perf. 13*

B621 SP313 2.30fr +20c multi 1.00 .95
B622 SP313 2.30fr +20c multi 1.00 .95
B623 SP313 2.30fr +20c multi 1.00 .95
B624 SP313 2.30fr +20c multi 1.00 .95
B625 SP313 2.30fr +20c multi 1.00 .95
B626 SP313 2.50fr +20c multi 1.10 1.10
B627 SP313 2.50fr +20c multi 1.10 1.10
Nos. B621-B627 (7) 7.20 6.95

Issued: #B621, 12/22/90; #B622, 12/29/90; #B623, 1/19/91; #B624, 2/2/91; #B625, 2/9/91; #B626, 3/2/91; #B627, 4/20/91.
No. B624 inscribed "La Poste 1992."

Paul Eluard (1895-1952) — SP317

Poets: No. B629, Andre Breton (1896-1966). No. B630, Louis Aragon (1897-1982). No. B631, Francis Ponge (1899-1988). No. B632, Jacques Prevert (1900-1977). No. B633, Rene Char (1907-1988).

1991, Feb. 23 Engr. *Perf. 12½x13*

B628 SP317 2.50fr +50c multi 1.10 1.10
B629 SP317 2.50fr +50c multi 1.10 1.10
B630 SP317 2.50fr +50c multi 1.10 1.10
B631 SP317 2.50fr +50c multi 1.10 1.10
B632 SP317 2.50fr +50c multi 1.10 1.10
B633 SP317 2.50fr +50c multi 1.10 1.10
a. Bklt. pane, 1 each +2 labels, perf. 13 7.50

Stamp Day SP318

1991, Mar. 16 Photo. *Perf. 13*

B634 SP318 2.50fr +60c blue machine 1.25 1.25
B635 SP318 2.50fr +60c purple machine 1.25 1.25
a. Bklt. pane of 6 + 2 labels 8.50

Winter Olympics Type of 1990

#B636, Acrobatic skiing. #B637, Alpine skiing.

1991 Engr. *Perf. 13*

B636 SP313 2.50fr +20c multi 1.10 .95
B637 SP313 2.50fr +20c multi 1.10 .95

Issued: #B636, Aug. 3; #B637, Aug. 17.
Nos. B636-B637 inscribed "La Poste 1992."

The Harbor of Toulon by Francois Nardi SP319

1991, Dec. 2 Photo. *Perf. 13x12½*

B638 SP319 2.50fr +60c multi 1.20 1.10
a. Perf. 13x13½ 1.20 1.10
b. As "a," bklt. pane of 10 + 2 labels 12.00

Surtax for the Red Cross.

Winter Olympics Type of 1990
Miniature Sheet

a, like #B611. b, like #B621. c, like #B622. d, like #B623. e, like #B624. f, like #B625.

1992, Feb. 8 Engr. *Perf. 13*

B639 Sheet of 10 + label 18.00 18.00
a.-f. SP313 2.50fr +20c multi 1.75 1.75

No. B639 contains one each B626-B627, B636-B637, B639a-B639f. Central label is litho.

Stamp Day SP320

1992, Mar. 7 Litho. *Perf. 13*

B640 SP320 2.50fr +60c gray people 1.10 1.10

Booklet Stamp
Photo.

B641 SP320 2.50fr +60c red people 1.25 1.10
a. Bklt. pane of 6 + 2 labels 8.00

SP321

SP322

Composers: No. B642, Cesar Franck (1822-1890). No. B643, Erik Satie (1866-1925). No. B644, Florent Schmitt (1870-1958). No. B645, Arthur Honegger (1892-1955). No. B646, Georges Auric (1899-1983). No. B647, Germaine Tailleferre (1892-1983).

1992, Apr. 11 Photo. *Perf. 13*

B642 SP321 2.50fr +50c multi 1.10 1.10
B643 SP321 2.50fr +50c multi 1.10 1.10
B644 SP321 2.50fr +50c multi 1.10 1.10
B645 SP321 2.50fr +50c multi 1.10 1.10
B646 SP321 2.50fr +50c multi 1.10 1.10
B647 SP321 2.50fr +50c multi 1.10 1.10
a. Bklt. pane of 6, #B642-B647 8.00

1992, Nov. 28 Photo. *Perf. 13½x13*

B648 SP322 2.50fr +60c multi 1.20 1.10
a. Bklt. pane of 10 + 2 labels 12.00

Mutual Aid, Strasbourg. Surtax for the Red Cross.

Writers SP323

#B649, Guy de Maupassant (1850-93). #B650, Alain (Emile Chartier) (1868-1951). #B651, Jean Cocteau (1889-1963). #B652, Marcel Pagnol (1895-1974). #B653, Andre Chamson (1900-83). #B654, Marguerite Yourcenar (1903-87).

1993, Apr. 24 Engr. *Perf. 13*

B649 SP323 2.50fr +50c multi 1.10 1.10
B650 SP323 2.50fr +50c multi 1.10 1.10
B651 SP323 2.50fr +50c multi 1.10 1.10
B652 SP323 2.50fr +50c multi 1.10 1.10
B653 SP323 2.50fr +50c multi 1.10 1.10
B654 SP323 2.50fr +50c multi 1.10 1.10
a. Bklt. pane of 6, #B649-B654 + 2 labels 8.00

When Nos. B650-B654 are normally centered, inscriptions at base of the lower panel are not parallel to the perforations at bottom. On all six stamps the lower panel is not centered between the side perforations.

SP324

SP325

St. Nicolas, Image of Metz.

1993, Nov. 27 Engr. *Perf. 12½x13*

B655 SP324 2.80fr +60c multi 1.25 1.10
a. Perf. 13½x13 1.25 1.10
b. As "a," Bklt. pane of 10 +2 labels 15.00

Surtax for Red Cross.

1994, Sept. 17 Photo. *Perf. 13*

Stage and Screen Personalities: No. B656, Yvonne Printemps (1894-1977). No. B657, Fernandel (1903-71). No. B658, Josephine Baker (1906-75). No. B659, Bourvil (1917-70). No. B660, Yves Montand (1921-91). No. B661, Coluche (1944-86).

B656 SP325 2.80fr +60c multi 1.25 1.25
B657 SP325 2.80fr +60c multi 1.25 1.25
B658 SP325 2.80fr +60c multi 1.25 1.25
B659 SP325 2.80fr +60c multi 1.25 1.25
B660 SP325 2.80fr +60c multi 1.25 1.25
B661 SP325 2.80fr +60c multi 1.25 1.25
a. Bklt. pane, #B656-B661 + 2 labels 8.00

SP326

SP327

Designs: #B662, St. Vaast, Arras Tapestry. #B663, Brussels tapestry from Reydams workshop, Horse Museum, Saumur.

1994-95 Photo. *Perf. 12½x13*

B662 SP326 2.80fr +60c multi 1.50 1.40
a. Perf. 13½x13 1.50 1.40
b. Bklt. pane, 10 #B662a + 2 labels 15.00
Complete booklet, #B662b 16.00
B663 SP326 2.80fr +60c multi 1.50 1.50
a. Perf. 13½x13 1.50 1.50
b. Bklt. pane, 10 #B663a + 2 labels 15.00
Complete booklet, #B663b 15.00

Surtax for Red Cross.
Issued: #B662, 11/26/94; #B663, 5/13/95.

1995, Nov. 25 Engr. *Perf. 13*

Provencal Nativity Figures: No. B664, The Shepherd. No. B665, The Miller. No. B666, The Simpleton and the Tambour Player. No. B667, The Fishmonger. No. B668, The Scissor Grinder. No. B669, The Elders.

B664 SP327 2.80fr +60c multi 1.40 1.40
B665 SP327 2.80fr +60c multi 1.40 1.40
B666 SP327 2.80fr +60c multi 1.40 1.40
B667 SP327 2.80fr +60c multi 1.40 1.40
B668 SP327 2.80fr +60c multi 1.40 1.40
B669 SP327 2.80fr +60c multi 1.40 1.40
a. Booklet pane, Nos. B664-B669 + 2 labels 10.00
Complete booklet, No. B669a 11.00

SP328

Famous Fictional Detectives and Criminals: #B670, Rocambole. #B671, Arsène Lupin. #B672, Joseph Rouletabille. #B673, Fantômas. #B674, Commissioner Maigret. #B675, Nestor Burma.

1996, Oct. 5 Photo. *Perf. 13*

B670 SP328 3fr +60c multi 1.40 1.40
B671 SP328 3fr +60c multi 1.40 1.40
B672 SP328 3fr +60c multi 1.40 1.40
B673 SP328 3fr +60c multi 1.40 1.40
B674 SP328 3fr +60c multi 1.40 1.40
B675 SP328 3fr +60c multi 1.40 1.40
a. Booklet pane, #B670-B675 + 2 labels 9.00
Complete booklet, #B675a 11.00

Christmas SP329

1996, Nov. 16 Photo. *Perf. 12¾x13*

B676 SP329 3fr +60c multi 1.45 1.45
a. Perf. 13¼x13 1.50 1.50
b. Booklet pane, 10 #B676a + 2 labels 15.00 —
Complete booklet, #B676b 15.00

Surtax for Red Cross.

Adventure Heroes SP330

1997, Oct. 25 Photo. *Perf. 13*

B677 SP330 3fr +60c Sir Lancelot 1.40 1.40
B678 SP330 3fr +60c Pardaillan 1.40 1.40
B679 SP330 3fr +60c D'Artagnan 1.40 1.40
B680 SP330 3fr +60c Cyrano de Bergerac 1.40 1.40
B681 SP330 3fr +60c Captain Fracasse 1.40 1.40
B682 SP330 3fr +60c Le Bossu 1.40 1.40
a. Booklet pane, #B677-B682 + 2 labels 9.00
Complete booklet, #682a 9.00

Christmas, New Year — SP331

1997, Nov. 6 Photo. *Perf. 12¾x13*

B683 SP331 3fr +60c multi 1.40 1.25
a. Perf. 13¼x13 1.40 1.25
b. Booklet pane, 10 #B683a + 2 labels 14.00 —
Complete booklet, #B683b 15.00

Surtax for the Red Cross.

SP332

Actors of the French Cinema: #B684, Romy Schneider (1938-82). #B685, Simone Signoret (1921-85). #B686, Jean Gabin (1904-76). #B687, Louis de Funés (1914-83). #B688, Bernard Blier (1916-89). #B689, Lino Ventura (1919-87).

1998, Oct. 3 Photo. *Perf. 13*

B684 SP332 3fr +60c multi 1.40 1.40
B685 SP332 3fr +60c multi 1.40 1.40
B686 SP332 3fr +60c multi 1.40 1.40
B687 SP332 3fr +60c multi 1.40 1.40
B688 SP332 3fr +60c multi 1.40 1.40
B689 SP332 3fr +60c multi 1.40 1.40
a. Booklet pane, #B684-B689 + label 9.50
Complete booklet, #B689a 10.00

Christmas SP333

1998, Nov. 5 Photo. *Perf. 12½x13*

B690 SP333 3fr +60c multi 1.40 1.40
a. Perf. 13½x13 1.40 1.40
b. Booklet pane, 10 #B690a + 2 labels 14.00
Complete booklet, #B690b 15.00

Surtax for Red Cross.

Famous Photographers — SP334

Photographs by: #B691, Robert Doisneau (1912-94). #B692, Brassai (Gyula Halasz) (1899-1984). #B693, Jacques Lartigue (1894-1986). #B694, Henri Cartier-Bresson (b. 1908). #B695, Eugene Atget (1857-1927). #B696, Felix Nadar (1820-1910).

1999, July 10 Photo. *Perf. 13*

B691 SP334 3fr +60c multi 1.40 1.40
B692 SP334 3fr +60c multi 1.40 1.40
B693 SP334 3fr +60c multi 1.40 1.40
B694 SP334 3fr +60c multi 1.40 1.40
B695 SP334 3fr +60c multi 1.40 1.40
B696 SP334 3fr +60c multi 1.40 1.40
a. Booklet pane, #B691-B696 8.50
Complete booklet, #B696a 9.00

New Year 2000 — SP335

1999, Nov. 10 Photo. *Perf. 12¾x13*

B697 SP335 3fr +60c multi 1.40 1.40
a. Perf. 13½x13 1.40 1.40
b. Booklet pane, 10 #B697a + 2 labels 14.00
Complete booklet, #B697b 14.00

Surtax for Red Cross.

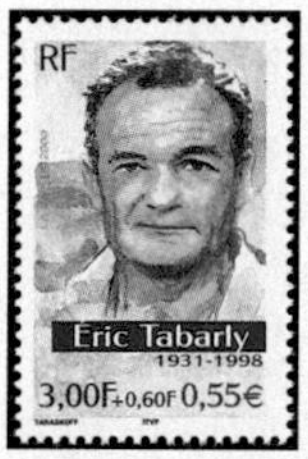

Adventurers SP336

#B698, Eric Tabarly (1931-98), sailor. #B699, Alexandra David-Néel (1868-1969), opera singer, Asian traveler. #B700, Haroun Tazieff (1914-98), vulcanologist. #B701, Paul-Emile Victor (1907-55), ethnologist, polar explorer. #B702, Jacques-Yves Cousteau (1910-97), oceanographer. #B703, Norbert Casteret (1897-1987), speleologist.

2000, Sept. 16 Photo. *Perf. 13¼x13*

B698 SP336 3fr +60c multi 1.40 1.40
B699 SP336 3fr +60c multi 1.40 1.40
B700 SP336 3fr +60c multi 1.40 1.40
B701 SP336 3fr +60c multi 1.40 1.40
B702 SP336 3fr +60c multi 1.40 1.40
B703 SP336 3fr +60c multi 1.40 1.40
a. Booklet pane, #B698-B703 8.50
Booklet, #B703a 8.50

Toy Airplane — SP337

2000, Nov. 9 Photo. *Perf. 13¼x13*

B704 SP337 3fr +60c multi 1.40 1.40
a. Booklet pane of 10 + 2 labels 14.00
Booklet, #B704a 15.00

Surtax for Red Cross.

Santa Claus and Tree Ornaments SP338

2001, Nov. 8 Photo. *Perf. 12¾x13*

B705 SP338 3fr +60c multi 1.40 1.40
a. Perf 13½x13 1.40 1.40
b. Booklet pane of 10 14.00 —
Booklet, #B705a 14.00

Surtax for Red Cross.

Infant Jesus Asleep, by Giovanni Battista Salvi — SP339

2002, Nov. 7 Photo. *Perf. 12¾x13*

B706 SP339 46c +9c multi 1.40 1.40
a. Perf. 13½x13 1.40 1.40
b. As "a," booklet pane of 10 14.00 —
Booklet, #B706b 14.00

Surtax for Red Cross.

Virgin with Grapes, by Pierre Mignard — SP340

2003, Nov. 6 Photo. *Perf. 13¼x13*

Booklet Stamp

B707 SP340 50c +(16c) multi 1.50 1.50
a. Booklet pane of 10 15.00 —
Complete booklet, #B707a 15.00

Surtax for Red Cross.

Virgin With Child, Attributed to Cretan School — SP341

2004, Nov. 10 Photo. *Perf. 13¼x13*

Booklet Stamp

B708 SP341 50c +(16c) multi 1.75 1.75
a. Booklet pane of 10 + 2 labels 17.50 —
Complete booklet, #B708a 17.50

Surtax for Red Cross.

Dec. 26, 2004 Tsunami Victim Relief SP342

2005, Jan. 13 Engr. *Perf. 13*

B709 SP342 (50c) +20c red 1.90 1.90

Virgin and Child, by Hans Memling SP343

2005, Nov. 10 Photo. *Perf. 13½x13*

Booklet Stamp

B710 SP343 53c +(17c) multi 1.75 1.75
a. Booklet pane of 10 + 2 labels 17.50 —
Complete booklet, #B710a 17.50

Surtax for Red Cross.

SP344

Children's Art — SP345

2006, Nov. 25 Photo. *Perf. 13½x13*

Booklet Stamps

B711 SP344 (54c) +(17c) multi 1.90 1.90
B712 SP345 (54c) +(17c) multi 1.90 1.90
a. Booklet pane, 5 each #B711-B712, + 2 labels 19.00 —
Complete booklet, #B712a 19.00

Surtax for Red Cross.

Red Cross
SP346 SP347

Serpentine Die Cut 11

2007, Nov. 24 Photo.

Self-Adhesive

Booklet Stamps

B713 SP346 (54c) +(17c) multi 2.10 2.10
B714 SP347 (54c) +(17c) multi 2.10 2.10
a. Booklet pane, 5 each #B713-B714 21.00

Surtax for Red Cross.

Red Cross
SP348 SP349

Serpentine Die Cut 11x11¼

2008, Nov. 8 Photo.

Booklet Stamps

Self-Adhesive

B715 SP348 (55c) +(18c) multi 1.90 1.90
B716 SP349 (55c) +(18c) multi 1.90 1.90
a. Booklet pane of 10, 2 each #B715-B716 19.00

Surtax for Red Cross.

AIR POST STAMPS

Nos. 127, 130 Overprinted in Dark Blue or Black

Perf. 14x13½

1927, June 25 Unwmk.

C1 A18 2fr org & bl (DB) 200.00 225.00
Never hinged 400.00
C2 A18 5fr dk bl & buff 200.00 225.00
Never hinged 400.00

On sale only at the Intl. Aviation Exhib. at Marseilles, June, 1927. One set could be purchased by each holder of an admission ticket. Excellent counterfeits exist.

Nos. 242, 196 Surcharged

1928, Aug. 23

C3 A33 10fr on 90c 1,800. 1,800.
Never hinged 2,500.
a. Inverted surcharge 16,500. 16,500.
Never hinged 25,000.
b. Space between "10" and bars 6½mm 3,100. 3,100.
Never hinged 5,100.
C4 A23 10fr on 1.50fr 8,250. 8,250.
Never hinged 12,500.
a. Space between "10" and bars 6½mm 10,750. 10,750.
Never hinged 16,500.

Nos. C3-C4 received their surcharge in New York by order of the French consul general. They were for use in paying the 10fr fee for letters leaving the liner Ile de France on a catapulted hydroplane when the ship was one day off the coast of France on its eastward voyage.

The normal space between "10" and bars is 4½mm, but on 10 stamps in each pane of 50 the space is 6½mm. Counterfeits exist.

View of Marseille, Church of Notre Dame at Left — AP1

1930-31 Engr. *Perf. 13*

C5 AP1 1.50fr dp carmine 21.00 4.00
Never hinged 40.00
C6 AP1 1.50fr dk bl ('31) 19.00 2.25
Never hinged 35.00
a. 1.50fr ultramarine 50.00 21.00
Never hinged 90.00
b. As "a," with perf. initials "E.I.P.A.30" 450.00 350.00
Never hinged 700.00

No. C6a was sold at the Intl. Air Post Exhib., Paris, Nov. 6-20, 1930, at face value plus 5fr, the price of admission.

Forgeries abound of No. C6b. Certificates from recognized authorities are recommended.

Blériot's Monoplane AP2

1934, Sept. 1 *Perf. 13*

C7 AP2 2.25fr violet 24.00 6.00
Never hinged 32.50

1st flight across the English Channel, by Louis Blériot.

Plane over Paris AP3

1936

C8 AP3 85c dp green 2.25 2.25
Never hinged 5.00
C9 AP3 1.50fr blue 10.50 5.50
Never hinged 18.00
C10 AP3 2.25fr violet 18.00 7.00
Never hinged 35.00
C11 AP3 2.50fr rose 32.50 8.25
Never hinged 45.00
C12 AP3 3fr ultra 26.00 2.50
Never hinged 37.50
C13 AP3 3.50fr orange brn 62.50 24.00
Never hinged 105.00
C14 AP3 50fr emerald 825.00 325.00
Never hinged 1,450.
a. 50fr deep green 1,000. 525.00
Never hinged 1,650.
Nos. C8-C14 (7) 976.75 374.50

Monoplane over Paris — AP4

Paper with Red Network Overprint

1936, July 10 ***Perf. 12½***

C15 AP4 50fr ultra 575.00 310.00
Never hinged 1,150.

Airplane and Galleon — AP5

Airplane and Globe AP6

1936, Aug. 17 ***Perf. 13***

C16 AP5 1.50fr dk ultra 17.50 5.25
Never hinged 35.00
C17 AP6 10fr Prus green 290.00 130.00
Never hinged 700.00

100th air mail flight across the South Atlantic.

Catalogue values for unused stamps in this section, from this point to the end of the section, are for Never Hinged items.

Centaur and Plane — AP7

Iris — AP8

Zeus Carrying Hebe AP9

Chariot of the Sun AP10

1946-47 **Engr.** **Unwmk.**

C18 AP7 40fr dk green .65 .20
C19 AP8 50fr rose pink .65 .20
C20 AP9 100fr dk blue ('47) 7.00 4.00
C21 AP10 200fr red 6.00 1.50
Nos. C18-C21 (4) 14.30 5.90

Issued: 50fr, 200fr, 5/27; 40fr, 7/1; 100fr, Jan.

For surcharges see Reunion Nos. C35-C38.

Ile de la Cité, Paris, and Gull — AP11

1947, May 7

C22 AP11 500fr dk Prus grn 50.00 45.00

UPU 12th Cong., Paris, May 7-July 7.

View of Lille AP12

Air View of Paris — AP13

200fr, Bordeaux. 300fr, Lyon. 500fr, Marseille.

1949-50 **Unwmk.** ***Perf. 13***

C23 AP12 100fr sepia 1.40 .40
C24 AP12 200fr dk bl grn 12.50 .75
C25 AP12 300fr purple 15.00 10.00
C26 AP12 500fr brt red 57.50 5.75
C27 AP13 1000fr sep & blk, *bl* ('50) 150.00 27.50
Nos. C23-C27 (5) 236.40 44.40

For surcharges see Reunion Nos. C39-C41.

Alexander III Bridge and Petit Palais, Paris — AP14

1949, June 13

C28 AP14 100fr brown car 7.50 5.75

International Telegraph and Telephone Conference, Paris, May-July 1949.

Jet Plane, Mystère IV — AP15

Planes: 200fr, Noratlas. 500fr, Miles Magister. 1000fr, Provence.

1954, Jan. 16

C29 AP15 100fr red brn & bl 3.00 .20
C30 AP15 200fr blk brn & vio bl 11.00 .25
C31 AP15 500fr car & org 200.00 12.50
C32 AP15 1000fr vio brn, bl grn & ind 110.00 16.00
Nos. C29-C32 (4) 324.00 28.95

See No. C37. For surcharges see Reunion Nos. C42-C45, C48.

Maryse Bastié and Plane AP16

1955, June 4 **Unwmk.** ***Perf. 13***

C33 AP16 50fr dp plum & rose pink 6.50 4.00

Issued to honor Maryse Bastié, 1898-1952.

Morane Saulnier 760 Paris AP17

Designs: 300fr, Morane Saulnier 760 "Paris." 1000fr, Alouette helicopter.

1957-59 **Engr.** ***Perf. 13***

C34 AP17 300fr sl grn, grnsh bl & sep ('59) 5.00 3.00
C35 AP17 500fr dp ultra & blk 30.00 3.75
C36 AP17 1000fr lil, ol blk & blk ('58) 52.50 19.00
Nos. C34-C36 (3) 87.50 25.75

See Nos. C38-C41. For surcharges see Reunion Nos. C46-C47, C49-C51.

Types of 1954-59

Planes: 2fr, Noratlas. 3fr, MS760, Paris. 5fr, Caravelle. 10fr, Alouette helicopter.

1960, Jan. 11

C37 AP15 2fr vio bl & ultra 1.60 .20
a. 2fr ultramarine 3.25 .40
C38 AP17 3fr sl grn, grnsh bl & sep 1.60 .20
C39 AP17 5fr dp ultra & blk 3.25 .75
C40 AP17 10fr lil, ol blk & blk 13.00 2.00
Nos. C37-C40 (4) 19.45 3.15

Type of 1957-59

Design: 2fr, Jet plane, Mystère 20.

1965, June 12 **Engr.** ***Perf. 13***

C41 AP17 2fr slate bl & indigo .85 .20

Concorde Issue

Common Design Type

1969, Mar. 2 **Engr.** ***Perf. 13***

C42 CD129 1fr indigo & brt bl 1.00 .35

The 0.95fr stamp in this design was prepared but not issued. Value $30,000.

Jean Mermoz, Antoine de Saint-Exupéry and Concorde — AP19

1970, Sept. 19 **Engr.** ***Perf. 13***

C43 AP19 20fr blue & indigo 9.00 .60

Jean Mermoz (1901-36) and writer Antoine de Saint-Exupéry (1900-44), aviators and air mail pioneers.

Balloon, Gare d'Austerlitz, Paris — AP20

1971, Jan. 16 **Engr.** ***Perf. 13***

C44 AP20 95c bl, vio bl, org & sl grn .90 .55

Centenary of the balloon post from besieged Paris, 1870-71.

Didier Daurat, Raymond Vanier and Plane Landing at Night — AP21

1971, Apr. 17 **Engr.** ***Perf. 13***

C45 AP21 5fr Prus bl, blk & lt grn 2.00 .20

Didier Daurat (1891-1969) and Raymond Vanier (1895-1965), aviation pioneers.

For surcharge see Reunion No. C52.

Hélène Boucher, Maryse Hilsz and Caudron-Renault and Moth-Morane Planes — AP22

Design: 15fr, Henri Guillaumet, Paul Codos, Latécoère 521, Guillaumet's crashed plane in Andes, skyscrapers.

1972-73 **Engr.** ***Perf. 13***

C46 AP22 10fr plum, red & sl 4.50 .40
C47 AP22 15fr dp car, gray & brn ('73) 6.50 .65

Hélène Boucher (1908-34), Maryse Hilsz (1901-46), Henri Guillaumet (1902-40) and Paul Codos (1896-1960), aviation pioneers.

Issue dates: 10fr, June 10; 15fr, Feb. 24.

Concorde AP23

1976, Jan. 10 **Engr.** ***Perf. 13***

C48 AP23 1.70fr brt bl, red & blk 1.00 .50

First flight of supersonic jet Concorde from Paris to Rio de Janeiro, Jan. 21.

Planes over the Atlantic, New York-Paris — AP24

1977, June 4 **Engr.** ***Perf. 13***

C49 AP24 1.90fr multicolored .90 .50

1st transatlantic flight by Lindbergh from NY to Paris, 50th anniv., and 1st attempted westbound flight by French aviators Charles Nungesser and Francois Coli.

Plane over Flight Route AP25

1978, Oct. 14 Engr. *Perf. 13*

C50 AP25 1.50fr multicolored .90 .35

75th anniversary of first airmail route from Villacoublay to Pauillac, Gironde.

Rocket, Concorde, Exhibition Hall — AP26

1979, June 9 Engr. *Perf. 13*

C51 AP26 1.70fr ultra, org & brn 1.25 .80

33rd International Aerospace and Space Show, Le Bourget, June 11-15.

First Nonstop Transatlantic Flight, Paris-New York — AP27

1980, Aug. 30 Engr. *Perf. 13*

C52 AP27 2.50fr vio brn & ultra 1.00 .40

34th Intl. Space and Aeronautics Exhibition, June 5-14 AP28

1981, June 6 Engr. *Perf. 13*

C53 AP28 2fr multicolored 2.00 .50

Dieudonné Costes and Joseph Le Brix and their Breguet Bi-plane — AP29

1981, Sept. 12 Engr.

C54 AP29 10fr dk brown & red 4.50 .40

1st So. Atlantic crossing, Oct. 14-15, 1927.

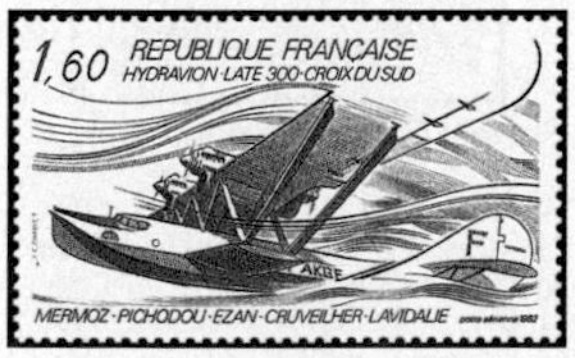

Seaplane Late-300 — AP30

1982, Dec. 4 Engr.

C55 AP30 1.60fr multicolored .80 .60

Farman F-60 Goliath — AP31

Planes: 20fr, CAMS-53 seaplane. 30fr, Wibault 283 Monoplane. 50fr, Dewoitine 338.

1984-87 Engr.

C56	AP31	15fr dark blue	5.00	.60
C57	AP31	20fr dp org ('85)	7.50	.60
C58	AP31	30fr brt vio ('86)	10.00	1.50
C59	AP31	50fr green ('87)	15.00	4.50
		Nos. C55-C59 (5)	38.30	7.80

Issued: 15fr, 3/3; 20fr, 3/2; 30fr, 10/11; 50fr, 4/11.

Breguet XIV — AP32

1997, Nov. 15 Photo. *Perf. 13x13¼*

C60	AP32 20fr shown		10.00	4.00
	a.	Perf. 13x12½	9.00	1.75
C61	AP32 30fr Potez 25		15.00	4.00
	a.	Perf. 13x12½	14.00	2.50

Issued: No. C60 11/15/97; No. C60a, 7/13/98; 30fr, 7/13/98.

Nos. C60 and C61 were issued in panes of 40 (5x8), Nos. C60a and C61a in panes of 10 (2x5).

Airbus A300-B4 — AP33

1999, Apr. 10 Photo. *Perf. 13x13¼*

C62	AP33 15fr multicolored		12.00	4.00
	a.	Perf. 13x12½	7.00	1.25

No. C62 was issued in panes of 40 (5x8), No. C62a in panes of 10 (2x5).

Couzinet 70 — AP34

2000, Feb. 12 *Perf. 13¼x13¼*

C63	AP34 50fr multi		22.50	9.00
	a.	Perf. 13x12½	22.50	6.00

No. C63 was issued in panes of 40 (5x8), No. C63a in panes of 10 (2x5).

First Flight of Airbus A300, 30th Anniv. — AP35

2002, Oct. 26 Photo. *Perf. 13x13¼*

C64 AP35 €3 multi 9.00 1.75

No. C64 was issued both in panes of 40 and 10, same perforation.

Jacqueline Auriol (1917-2000), Pilot, and Jet — AP36

Litho. & Engr.

2003, June 21 *Perf. 13*

C65	AP36 €4 multi		12.00	2.50
	a.	Miniature sheet of 10	120.00	—

Marie Marvingt (1875-1963), Pilot — AP37

Litho. & Engr.

2004, June 29 *Perf. 13¼x13*

C66	AP37 €5 multi		15.00	3.00
	a.	Sheet of 10	150.00	—

Adrienne Bolland (1895-1975), Pilot — AP38

Litho. & Engr.

2005, Oct. 22 *Perf. 13*

C67	AP38 €2 multi		6.00	1.50
	a.	Miniature sheet of 10	60.00	—

Airbus A380 — AP39

2006, June 23 Photo. *Perf. 13x13¼*

C68	AP39 €3 multi		9.00	1.75
	a.	Miniature sheet of 10	90.00	—

Helicopters, Cent. — AP40

2007, Feb. 19 Photo. *Perf. 13x12½*

C69	AP40 €3 multi		8.00	1.60
	a.	Perf. 13x13¼	8.00	1.60

No. C69 was issued in panes of 40; No. C69a in panes of 10.

French Acrobatic Patrol — AP41

Litho. & Engr.

2008, Sept. 13 *Perf. 13*

C70 AP41 €3 multi 8.25 1.75

AIR POST SEMI-POSTAL STAMPS

Catalogue values for unused stamps in this section are for Never Hinged items.

Antoine de Saint-Exupéry — SPAP1

Col. Jean Dagnaux SPAP2

1948 Unwmk. Engr. *Perf. 13*

CB1	SPAP1	50fr + 30fr vio brn	2.75	1.60
CB2	SPAP2	100fr + 70fr dk blue	3.75	2.25

Modern Plane and Ader's "Eole" SPAP3

1948, Feb.

CB3 SPAP3 40fr + 10fr dk blue 1.60 1.50

50th anniv. of the flight of Clément Ader's plane, the Eole, in 1897.

POSTAGE DUE STAMPS

D1

D2

1859-70 Unwmk. Litho. *Imperf.*

J1	D1	10c black	26,000.	240.00
J2	D1	15c black ('70)	130.00	*250.00*

In the lithographed stamps the central bar of the "E" of "CENTIMES" is very short, and the accent on "a" slants at an angle of 30 degree, for the 10c and 17 degree for the 15c, while on the typographed the central bar of the "E" is almost as wide as the top and bottom bars and the accent on the "a" slants at an angle of 47 degree.

No. J2 is known rouletted unofficially.

1859-78 Typo.

J3	D1	10c black	30.00	17.50
J4	D1	15c black ('63)	35.00	15.00
J5	D1	20c black ('77)	4,100.	
J6	D1	25c black ('71)	150.00	50.00
J7	D1	30c black ('78)	225.00	125.00
J8	D1	40c blue ('71)	325.00	*425.00*
	a.	40c ultramarine	6,500.	5,700.
	b.	40c Prussian blue	2,600.	
J9	D1	60c yellow ('71)	475.00	*1,050.*
J10	D1	60c blue ('78)	60.00	*110.00*
	a.	60c dark blue	600.00	*725.00*
J10B	D1	60c black	2,700.	

The 20c & 60c black were not put into use.

Nos. J3, J4, J6, J8 and J9 are known rouletted unofficially and Nos. J4, J6, J7 and J10 pin-perf. unofficially.

1882-92 *Perf. 14x13½*

J11	D2	1c black	2.50	2.50
J12	D2	2c black	30.00	26.00
J13	D2	3c black	30.00	25.00
J14	D2	4c black	60.00	40.00
J15	D2	5c black	130.00	32.50
J16	D2	10c black	110.00	2.50
J17	D2	15c black	77.50	10.50

J18 D2 20c black 350.00 140.00
J19 D2 30c black 210.00 2.50
J20 D2 40c black 140.00 60.00
J21 D2 50c blk ('92) 600.00 175.00
J22 D2 60c blk ('84) 600.00 57.50
J23 D2 1fr black 750.00 350.00
J24 D2 2fr blk ('84) 1,400. 825.00
J25 D2 5fr blk ('84) 3,000. 1,600.

Excellent counterfeits exist of Nos. J23-J25.

See Nos. J26-J45A. For overprints and surcharges see Offices in China Nos. J1-J6, J33-J40, Offices in Egypt, Alexandria J1-J5, Port Said J1-J8, Offices in Zanzibar 60-62, J1-J5, Offices in Morocco 9-10, 24-25, J1-J5, J10-J12, J17-J22, J35-J41.

1884

J26 D2 1fr brown 400.00 90.00
J27 D2 2fr brown 190.00 130.00
J28 D2 5fr brown 450.00 325.00

1893-1941

J29 D2 5c blue ('94) .25 .30
J30 D2 10c brown .25 .30
J31 D2 15c lt grn ('94) 28.00 1.40
J32 D2 20c ol grn ('06) 6.50 .65
J33 D2 25c rose ('23) 6.50 3.75
J34 D2 30c red ('94) .25 .20
J35 D2 30c org red ('94) 475.00 85.00
J36 D2 40c rose ('25) 11.50 4.50
J37 D2 45c grn ('24) 9.00 5.25
J38 D2 50c brn vio ('95) .50 .30
a. 50c lilac .50 .30
J39 D2 60c bl grn ('25) 1.00 .55
J40 D2 1fr rose, *straw* ('96) 475.00 375.00
J41 D2 1fr red brn, *straw* ('20) 9.50 .30
J42 D2 1fr red brn ('35) 1.25 .40
J43 D2 2fr red org ('10) 225.00 65.00
J44 D2 2fr brt vio ('26) .65 *.75*
J45 D2 3fr magenta ('26) .65 *.75*
J45A D2 5fr red org ('41) 1.40 *2.25*

D3

D4

1908-25

J46 D3 1c olive grn 1.00 *1.25*
J47 D3 10c violet 1.10 .30
a. Imperf., pair 175.00
J48 D3 20c bister ('19) 40.00 1.25
J49 D3 30c bister ('09) 14.00 .40
J50 D3 50c red ('09) 275.00 60.00
J51 D3 60c red ('25) 2.75 *3.75*
Nos. J46-J51 (6) 333.85 66.95

"Recouvrements" stamps were used to recover charges due on undelivered or refused mail which was returned to the sender.

For surcharges see Offices in Morocco Nos. J6-J9, J13-J16, J23-J26, J42-J45.

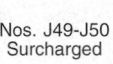

Nos. J49-J50 Surcharged

1917

J52 D3 20c on 30c bister 20.00 4.00
J53 D3 40c on 50c red 10.50 4.00
a. Double surcharge 475.00

In Jan. 1917 several values of the current issue of postage stamps were handstamped "T" in a triangle and used as postage due stamps.

Recouvrements Stamps of 1908-25 Surcharged

1926

J54 D3 50c on 10c lilac 3.50 3.25
J55 D3 60c on 1c ol grn 7.00 5.00
J56 D3 1fr on 60c red 18.00 10.00
J57 D3 2fr on 60c red 18.00 10.50
Nos. J54-J57 (4) 46.50 28.75

1927-31

J58 D4 1c olive grn ('28) 1.00 1.00
J59 D4 10c rose ('31) 1.90 1.40
J60 D4 30c bister 4.50 .50
J61 D4 60c red 4.50 .50
J62 D4 1fr violet 14.00 3.25
J63 D4 1fr Prus grn ('31) 17.00 .55
J64 D4 2fr blue 80.00 42.50
J65 D4 2fr olive brn ('31) 150.00 26.00
Nos. J58-J65 (8) 272.90 75.70

Nos. J62 to J65 have the numerals of value double-lined.

Nos. J64, J62 Surcharged in Red or Black

1929

J66 D4 1.20fr on 2fr blue 42.50 11.00
J67 D4 5fr on 1fr vio (Bk) 65.00 15.00
Set, never hinged 250.00

No. J61 Surcharged

1931

J68 D4 1fr on 60c red 30.00 2.75
Never hinged 60.00

Catalogue values for unused stamps in this section, from this point to the end of the section, are for Never Hinged items.

Sheaves of Wheat
D5 D6

Perf. 14x13½

1943-46 Unwmk. Typo.

J69 D5 10c sepia .20 .20
J70 D5 30c brt red vio .20 .20
J71 D5 50c blue grn .20 .20
J72 D5 1fr brt ultra .20 .20
J73 D5 1.50fr rose red .45 .40
J74 D5 2fr turq blue .45 .40
J75 D5 3fr brn org .45 .40
J76 D5 4fr dp vio ('45) 5.50 3.00
J77 D5 5fr brt pink .60 .40
J78 D5 10fr red org ('45) 3.50 .40
J79 D5 20fr ol bis ('46) 10.00 2.75
Nos. J69-J79 (11) 21.75 8.55

Type of 1943
Inscribed "Timbre Taxe"

1946-53

J80 D5 10c sepia ('47) 1.25 1.25
J81 D5 30c brt red vio ('47) 1.25 1.25
J82 D5 50c blue grn ('47) 25.00 9.50
J83 D5 1fr brt ultra ('47) .25 .25
J85 D5 2fr turq blue .25 .25
J86 D5 3fr brown org .25 .25
J87 D5 4fr deep violet .25 .25
J88 D5 5fr brt pink ('47) .25 .25
J89 D5 10fr red org ('47) .25 .25
J90 D5 20fr olive bis ('47) 2.00 .45
J91 D5 50fr dk green ('50) 25.00 1.40
J92 D5 100fr dp green ('53) 77.50 6.75
Nos. J80-J92 (12) 133.50 22.10

For surcharges see Reunion Nos. J36-J44.

1960 Typo. *Perf. 14x13½*

J93 D6 5c bright pink 3.25 .40
J94 D6 10c red orange 5.00 .30
J95 D6 20c olive bister 4.00 .30
J96 D6 50c dark green 12.50 1.25
J97 D6 1fr deep green 50.00 2.00
Nos. J93-J97 (5) 74.75 4.25

For surcharges see Reunion Nos. J46-J48. For overprints see Algeria Nos. J49-J53.

D7

D8

Flowers: 5c, Centaury. 10c, Gentian. 15c, Corn poppy. 20c, Violets. 30c, Forget-me-not. 40c, Columbine. 50c, Clover. 1fr, Soldanel.

1964-71 Typo. *Perf. 14x13½*

J98 D7 5c car rose, red & grn ('65) .20 .20
J99 D7 10c car rose, brt bl & grn ('65) .20 .20
J100 D7 15c brn, grn & red .20 .20
J101 D7 20c dk grn, grn & vio ('71) .20 .20
J102 D7 30c brn, ultra & grn .20 .20
J103 D7 40c dk grn, scar & yel ('71) .25 .20
J104 D7 50c vio bl, car & grn ('65) .25 .20
J105 D7 1fr vio bl, lil & grn ('65) .40 .20
Nos. J98-J105 (8) 1.90 1.60

For surcharges see Reunion Nos. J49-J55.

1982-83 Engr. *Perf. 13*

J106 D8 10c Ampedus Cinnabarinus .20 .20
J107 D8 20c Dorcadion fuliginator .20 .20
J108 D8 30c Leptura cordigera .20 .20
J109 D8 40c Paederus littoralis .20 .20
J110 D8 50c Pyrochroa coccinea .20 .20
J111 D8 1fr Scarites laevigatus .30 .20
J112 D8 2fr Trichius gallicus .55 .20
J113 D8 3fr Adalia alpina .90 .20
J114 D8 4fr Apoderus coryli 1.20 .20
J115 D8 5fr Trichodes alvearius 1.50 .20
Nos. J106-J115 (10) 5.45 2.00

Issued: 30c, 40c, 3fr, 5fr, 1/3/83; others, 1/4/82.

MILITARY STAMPS

Regular Issue Overprinted in Black or Red

1901-39 Unwmk. *Perf. 14x13½*

M1 A17 15c orange ('01) 65.00 6.00
a. Inverted overprint 300.00 150.00
b. Imperf., pair 425.00
M2 A19 15c pale red ('03) 65.00 6.00
M3 A20 15c slate grn ('04) 52.50 6.00
a. No period after "M" 110.00 57.50
b. Imperf., pair 290.00
M4 A20 10c rose ('06) 30.00 8.25
a. No period after "M" 82.50 45.00
b. Imperf., pair 350.00
M5 A22 10c red ('07) 1.75 1.00
a. Inverted overprint 105.00 65.00
b. Imperf., pair 190.00
M6 A20 50c vermilion ('29) 4.75 1.00
a. No period after "M" 32.50 18.00
b. Period in front of F 32.50 18.00
M7 A45 50c rose red ('34) 2.75 .55
a. No period after "M" 29.00 16.00
b. Inverted overprint 150.00 110.00
M8 A45 65c brt ultra (R) ('38) .30 .30
a. No period after "M" 29.00 16.00
M9 A45 90c ultra (R) ('39) .40 .35
Nos. M1-M9 (9) 222.45 29.45

"F. M." are initials of Franchise Militaire (Military Frank). See No. S1.

Catalogue values for unused stamps in this section, from this point to the end of the section, are for Never Hinged items.

M1

Flag — M2

1946-47 Typo.

M10 M1 dark green 1.75 .65
M11 M1 rose red ('47) .30 .20

Nos. M10-M11 were valid also in the French colonies.

1964, July 20 *Perf. 13x14*

M12 M2 multicolored .30 .35

OFFICIAL STAMPS

FOR THE COUNCIL OF EUROPE

For use only on mail posted in the post office in the Council of Europe Building, Strasbourg.

Catalogue values for unused stamps in this section are for Never Hinged items.

For French stamp inscribed "Conseil de l'Europe" see No. 679.

France No. 854 Overprinted: "CONSEIL DE L'EUROPE"

Unwmk.

1958, Jan. 14 Engr. *Perf. 13*

1O1 A303 35fr car rose & lake 1.25 *2.25*

Council of Europe Flag — O1

1958-59

Flag in Ultramarine

1O2 O1 8fr red org & brn vio .25 .25
1O3 O1 20fr yel & lt brn .35 .35
1O4 O1 25fr lil rose & sl grn ('59) 1.10 1.10
1O5 O1 35fr red .55 .55
1O6 O1 50fr lilac rose ('59) 2.25 2.25
Nos. 1O2-1O6 (5) 4.50 4.50

1963, Jan. 3

Flag in Ultramarine

1O7 O1 20c yel & lt brn 1.25 1.25
1O8 O1 25c lil rose & sl grn 2.00 2.00
1O9 O1 50c lilac rose 2.50 2.50
Nos. 1O7-1O9 (3) 5.75 5.75

Centime value stamps shown the denomination as "0,20," etc.

1965-71

Flag in Ultramarine & Yellow

1O10 O1 25c ver, yel & sl grn 1.10 1.10
1O11 O1 30c ver & yel 1.10 1.10
1O12 O1 40c ver, yel & gray 1.75 1.75
1O13 O1 50c red, yel & grn 2.25 2.25
1O14 O1 60c ver, yel & vio 1.50 1.50
1O15 O1 70c ver, yel & dk brn 5.50 5.50
Nos. 1O10-1O15 (6) 13.20 13.20

Issue dates: 25c, 30c, 60c, Jan. 16, 1965; 50c, Feb. 20, 1971; others, Mar. 24, 1969.

Type of 1958 Inscribed "FRANCE"

1975-76 Engr. *Perf. 13*

Flag in Ultramarine & Yellow

1O16 O1 60c org, yel & emer .85 .85
1O17 O1 80c yel & mag 1.25 1.25
1O18 O1 1fr car, yel & gray ol ('76) 5.50 5.50
1O19 O1 1.20fr org, yel & bl 4.50 4.50
Nos. 1O16-1O19 (4) 12.10 12.10

Issue dates: 1fr, Oct. 16; others, Nov. 22.

New Council Headquarters, Strasbourg — O2

1977, Jan. 22 Engr. *Perf. 13*

1O20 O2 80c car & multi 1.00 .50
1O21 O2 1fr brown & multi 1.00 .50
1O22 O2 1.40fr gray & multi 2.00 1.00
Nos. 1O20-1O22 (3) 4.00 2.00

Human Rights Emblem in Upper Left Corner

1978, Oct. 14

1O23 O2 1.20fr red lilac & multi .45 .40
1O24 O2 1.70fr blue & multi .75 .55

30th anniversary of the Universal Declaration of Human Rights.

Council Headquarters Type of 1977

1980, Nov. 24 Engr. *Perf. 13*

1O25	O2	1.40fr olive	.50	.50
1O26	O2	2fr blue gray	.90	.90

New Council Headquarters, Strasbourg — O3

1981-84 Engr.

1O27	O3	1.40fr multicolored	.50	.50
1O28	O3	1.60fr multicolored	.50	.40
1O29	O3	1.70fr emerald	.75	.75
1O30	O3	1.80fr multicolored	.70	.70
1O31	O3	2fr multicolored	.90	.90
1O32	O3	2.10fr red	1.00	1.00
1O33	O3	2.30fr multicolored	1.00	1.00
1O34	O3	2.60fr multicolored	1.00	1.00
1O35	O3	2.80fr multicolored	1.00	1.00
1O36	O3	3fr brt blue	1.25	1.25
		Nos. 1O27-1O36 (10)	8.60	8.50

Issued: 1.40, 1.60, 2.30fr, 11/21; 1.80, 2.60fr, 11/13/82; 2, 2.80fr, 11/21/83; 1.70, 2.10, 3fr, 11/5/84.

Youth's Leg, Sneaker, Shattered Eggshell O4

1985, Aug. 31 Engr. *Perf. 13*

1O37	O4	1.80fr brt green	.90	.90
1O38	O4	2.20fr vermilion	.90	.90
1O39	O4	3.20fr brt blue	1.40	1.40
		Nos. 1O37-1O39 (3)	3.20	3.20

New Council Headquarters, Strasbourg — O5

1986-87 Engr. *Perf. 13*

1O40	O5	1.90fr green	.90	.90
1O41	O5	2fr brt yel grn	1.10	1.10
1O42	O5	2.20fr red	.90	.90
1O43	O5	3.40fr blue	1.75	1.75
1O44	O5	3.60fr brt blue	2.25	2.25
		Nos. 1O40-1O44 (5)	6.90	6.90

Issued: 1.90, 2.20, 3.40fr, 12/13; 2, 3.60fr, 10/10/87.

Council of Europe, 40th Anniv. O6

1989, Feb. 4 Litho. & Engr.

1O45	O6	2.20fr multicolored	1.40	1.40
1O46	O6	3.60fr multicolored	2.25	2.25

Denominations also inscribed in European Currency Units (ECUs).

Map of Europe O7

1990-91 Litho. *Perf. 13*

1O47	O7	2.30fr multicolored	1.00	1.00
1O48	O7	2.50fr multicolored	1.00	1.00
1O49	O7	3.20fr multicolored	1.60	1.60
1O50	O7	3.40fr multicolored	1.60	1.60
		Nos. 1O47-1O50 (4)	5.20	5.20

Issued: 2.30fr, 3.20fr, 5/26/90; 2.50fr, 3.40fr, 11/23/91.

36 Heads, by Hundertwasser O8

1994, Jan. 15 Litho. *Perf. 13*

1O51	O8	2.80fr multicolored	1.40	1.40
1O52	O8	3.70fr multicolored	1.75	1.75

Palace of Human Rights, Strasbourg O9

1996, June 1 Litho. *Perf. 13*

1O53	O9	3fr multicolored	.90	.90
1O54	O9	3.80fr multicolored	1.60	1.60

Charioteer of Delphi — O10

1999, Sept. 18 Photo. *Perf. 13*

1O55	O10	3fr shown	1.40	1.40
1O56	O10	3.80fr Nike	1.75	1.75

Girl, Penguin and Boy — O11

2001, Dec. 1 Litho. *Perf. 13*

1O57	O11	3fr red & multi	.90	.90
1O58	O11	3.80fr grn & multi	1.40	1.40

Hiker on Stars — O12

2003, Oct. 18 Litho. *Perf. 13*

1O59	O12	50c Hiker facing left	1.25	1.25
1O60	O12	75c Hiker facing right	1.75	1.75

O13

O14

2005, Sept. 18 Litho. *Perf. 13*

1O61	O13	55c multi	1.40	1.40
1O62	O14	75c multi	1.90	1.90

Map of Europe O15

Sculpture by Mariano González Beltrán O16

2007, June 23 Litho. *Perf. 13*

1O63	O15	60c multi	1.75	1.75
1O64	O16	85c multi	2.40	2.40

FOR THE UNITED NATIONS EDUCATIONAL, SCIENTIFIC AND CULTURAL ORGANIZATION

For use only on mail posted in the post office in the UNESCO Building, Paris.

Catalogue values for unused stamps in this section are for Never Hinged items.

For French stamps inscribed "UNESCO" see Nos. 572, 893-894, 2545.

Khmer Buddha and Hermes by Praxiteles O1

1961-65 Unwmk. Engr. *Perf. 13*

2O1	O1	20c dk gray, ol bis & bl	.25	*.55*
2O2	O1	25c blk, lake & grn	.40	*.90*
2O3	O1	30c choc & bis brn ('65)	.60	*.60*
2O4	O1	50c blk, red & vio bl	1.50	*1.75*
2O5	O1	60c grnsh bl, red brn & rose lil ('65)	1.40	1.40
		Nos. 2O1-2O5 (5)	4.15	5.20

Book and Globe — O2

1966, Dec. 17

2O6	O2	25c gray	.50	.50
2O7	O2	30c dark red	.65	.65
2O8	O2	60c green	1.10	1.10
		Nos. 2O6-2O8 (3)	2.25	2.25

20th anniversary of UNESCO.

Human Rights Flame — O3

1969-71 Engr. *Perf. 13*

2O9	O3	30c sl grn, red & dp brn	.60	.60
2O10	O3	40c dk car rose, red & dp brn	.95	.95
2O11	O3	50c ultra, car & brn ('71)	2.00	2.00
2O12	O3	70c pur, red & sl	3.00	3.00
		Nos. 2O9-2O12 (4)	6.55	6.55

Universal Declaration of Human Rights.

Type of 1969 Inscribed "FRANCE"

1975, Nov. 15 Engr. *Perf. 13*

2O13	O3	60c grn, red & dk brn	1.10	1.10
2O14	O3	80c ocher, red & red brn	1.65	1.65
2O15	O3	1.20fr ind, red & brn	4.25	4.25
		Nos. 2O13-2O15 (3)	7.00	7.00

O4

1976-78 Engr. *Perf. 13*

2O16	O4	80c multi	.85	.85
2O17	O4	1fr multi	.85	.85
2O18	O4	1.20fr multi	.50	.50
2O19	O4	1.40fr multi	2.25	1.25
2O20	O4	1.70fr multi	.75	.75
		Nos. 2O16-2O20 (5)	5.20	4.20

Issued: 1.20, 1.70fr, 10/14/78; others, 10/23/76.

Slave Quarters, Senegal O5

Designs: 1.40fr, Mohenjo-Daro excavations, Pakistan. 2fr, Sans-Souci Palace, Haiti.

1980, Nov. 17 Engr. *Perf. 13*

2O21	O5	1.20fr multi	.45	.45
2O22	O5	1.40fr multi	.50	.50
2O23	O5	2fr multi	.65	.65
		Nos. 2O21-2O23 (3)	1.60	1.60

Hue, Vietnam — O7

Designs: 1.40fr, Building, Fez, Morocco. 1.60fr, Seated deity, Sukhotai, Thailand. 2.30fr, Fort St. Elmo, Malta, horiz. 2.60fr, St. Michael Church ruins, Brazil.

1981-82

2O24	O7	1.40fr multi	.60	.60
2O25	O7	1.60fr multi	.60	.60
2O26	O7	1.80fr shown	.70	.70
2O27	O7	2.30fr multi	.80	.80
2O28	O7	2.60fr multi	.90	.90
		Nos. 2O24-2O28 (5)	3.60	3.60

Issued: 1.80fr, 2.60fr, 10/23/82; others, 12/12/81.

Mosque, Chinguetti, Mauritania O8

Roman Theater and female standing sculpture, Carthage, Tunisia — O8a

Architecture: 1.70fr, Church, Lalibela, Ethiopia. 2.10fr, San'a, Yemen. 2.20fr, Old Town Square and wrought iron latticework, Havana. 2.80fr, Enclosure wall interior, Istanbul. 3fr, Church, Kotor, Yugoslavia. 3.20fr, Temple of Anuradhapura and bas-relief of two women, Sri Lanka.

1983-85 **Engr.**

2O29	O8	1.70fr	multi	.70	.70
2O30	O8a	1.80fr	multi	.80	.80
2O31	O8	2fr	multi	.75	.75
2O32	O8	2.10fr	multi	.80	.80
2O33	O8a	2.20fr	multi	.90	.90
2O34	O8	2.80fr	multi	1.00	1.00
2O35	O8	3fr	multi	1.10	1.10
2O36	O8a	3.20fr	multi	1.50	1.50
	Nos. 2O29-2O36 (8)			7.55	7.55

Issued: 2fr, 2.80fr, 10/10; 1.70fr, 2.10fr, 3fr, 10/22/84; 1.80fr, 2.20fr, 3.20fr, 10/26/85.

Tikal Temple, Guatemala — O9

1986, Dec. 6 **Engr.** ***Perf. 13***

2O37	O9	1.90fr	shown	1.00	1.00
2O38	O9	3.40fr	Bagerhat Mosque, Bangladesh	1.75	1.75

The Parthenon, Athens O10

1987, Dec. 5 **Engr.** ***Perf. 13x12½***

2O39	O10	2fr	shown	.90	.90
2O40	O10	3.60fr	Temple of Philae, Egypt	1.60	1.60

Shibam, Yemen People's Democratic Republic O11

Perf. 13x12½, 12½x13

1990, Apr. 7 **Engr.**

2O41	O11	2.30fr	San Francisco de Lima, Peru, vert.	1.10	1.10
2O42	O11	3.20fr	shown	1.50	1.50

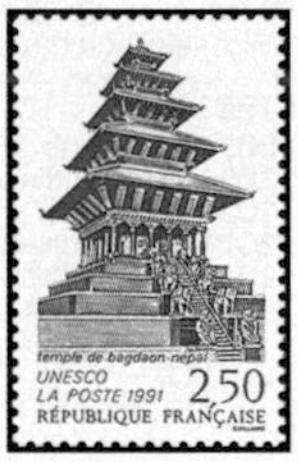

Bagdaon Temple, Nepal — O12

3.40fr, Citadel of Harat, Afghanistan, horiz.

1991, Nov. 23

2O43	O12	2.50fr	choc & dk red	1.25	1.25
2O44	O12	3.40fr	grn, brn & ol	1.50	1.50

Tassili N'Ajjer Natl. Park, Algeria O13

Design: 2.80fr, Angkor Wat Archaeological Park, Cambodia, vert.

1993, Oct. 23 **Litho.** ***Perf. 13***

2O45	O13	2.80fr	multicolored	1.25	1.25
2O46	O13	3.70fr	multicolored	2.00	2.00

UNESCO, 50th Anniv. O14

Designs: 3fr, Uluru Natl. Park, Australia. 3.80fr, Los Glaciares Natl. Park, Argentina.

1996, June 1 **Litho.** ***Perf. 13***

2O47	O14	3fr	multicolored	1.50	1.50
2O48	O14	3.80fr	multicolored	2.00	2.00

Detail of Dionysus Fresco, Pompeii — O15

Moai Statues, Easter Island O16

1998, Oct. 24 **Litho.** ***Perf. 13***

2O49	O15	3fr	multicolored	1.50	1.50
2O50	O16	3.80fr	multicolored	1.90	1.90

Sphinx and Pyramids, Egypt O17

Komodo Dragon, Komodo Natl. Park, Indonesia O18

2001, Dec. 1 **Litho.** ***Perf. 13***

2O51	O17	3fr	multi	1.60	1.60
2O52	O18	3.80fr	multi	2.00	2.00

Reindeer, Lapland O19

Church of the Resurrection, St. Petersburg, Russia — O20

2003, Dec. 6 **Litho.** ***Perf. 13***

2O53	O19	50c	multi	1.40	1.40
2O54	O20	75c	multi	2.00	2.00

Bison in Bialowieza Forest, Poland — O21

Petra, Jordan O22

2005, Nov. 26 **Litho.** ***Perf. 13***

2O55	O21	55c	multi	1.50	1.50
2O56	O22	90c	multi	2.25	2.25

Siberian Tiger — O23

Luang Prabang, Laos O24

2006, Dec. 7 **Litho.** ***Perf. 13***

2O57	O23	60c	multi	1.60	.40
2O58	O24	85c	multi	2.25	.60

Ksar d'Ait-Ben-Haddou, Morocco — O25

Koala, Australia — O26

2007, Dec. 13 **Litho.** ***Perf. 13***

2O59	O25	60c	multi	1.75	1.75
2O60	O26	85c	multi	2.50	2.50

NEWSPAPER STAMPS

Coat of Arms — N1

1868 **Unwmk.** **Typo.** ***Imperf.***

P1	N1	2c	lilac	300.00	65.00
P2	N1	2c (+ 2c)	blue	600.00	275.00

Perf. 12½

P3	N1	2c	lilac	52.50	25.00
P4	N1	2c (+ 4c)	rose	250.00	100.00
P5	N1	2c (+ 2c)	blue	75.00	35.00
P6	N1	5c	lilac	1,250.	550.00

Nos. P2, P4, and P5 were sold for face plus an added fiscal charge indicated in parenthesis. Nos. P1, P3 and P6 were used simply as fiscals.

The 2c rose and 5c lilac imperforate and the 5c rose and 5c blue, both imperforate and perforated, were never put into use.

Nos. P1-P6 were reprinted for the 1913 Ghent Exhibition and the 1937 Paris Exhibition (PEXIP).

No. 109 Surcharged in Red

1919 ***Perf. 14x13½***

P7	A16	½c on 1c gray	.30	.30
a.		Inverted surcharge	1,200.	1,150.

No. 156 Surcharged

1933

P8	A22	½c on 1c olive bister	.30	.30

PARCEL POST STAMPS

Inscribed "I APPORT A LA GARE" — PP1

Perfs As Noted

1892 **Unwmk.** **Typo.**

Q1	PP1	25c brown, *yel,* perf 13½	825.00	290.00
		Never hinged	1,500.	
Q2	PP1	25c brown, *yel,* perf 11	30.00	24.00
		Never hinged	45.00	
a.		Printed on both sides	400.00	
		Never hinged	650.00	

Inscribed "II VALEUR DECLAREE" — PP2

Q3	PP2	10c red, perf 13½	1,000.	275.00
		Never hinged	1,750.	
Q4	PP2	10c red, perf 10x13½	875.00	325.00
		Never hinged	1,600.	
Q5	PP2	10c org red, perf 11	30.00	14.00
		Never hinged	42.50	
Q6	PP2	10c red, imperf	22.50	16.50
		Never hinged	32.50	

Inscribed "III LIVRAISON PAR EXPRESS" — PP3

Q7	PP3	25c green, perf 13½	57.50	32.50
		Never hinged	115.00	
Q8	PP3	25c green, perf 11	45.00	24.00
		Never hinged	70.00	

See Nos. Q22-Q26.

Locomotive — PP4

A set of six stamps, in the design above, was prepared in 1901 as postal tax stamps for expedited parcels but were not issued. All are perf 14x13½. Values: 5c gray, $3, never hinged $4; 10c gray, $3, never hinged $5; 20c rose, $20, never hinged $29; 50c blue, $7, never hinged $11.50; 1fr brown, $8, never hinged $12; 2fr brown red, $37.50, never hinged $57.50.

PP5

1918 ***Perf. 11***

Type I: Large Trefoil Under "N" of "MAJORATION"

Q9 PP5 5c black 1.25 .85
Never hinged 2.00
Q10 PP5 15c brn lilac 1.25 .85
Never hinged 2.00

Imperforate

Q11 PP5 5c black 3.25 2.50
Never hinged 6.25
Q12 PP5 15c brn lilac 9.00 4.25
Never hinged 14.00
Nos. Q9-Q12 (4) 14.75 8.45

40c values, perforated 11 and imperf, in orange, were prepared but not issued. Value, perf or imperf, $375.

Type II: Small Trefoil Under "O" of "MAJORATION"
Perf. 11

Q13 PP5 5c black 140.00 45.00
Never hinged 275.00
Q14 PP5 35c red 3.75 2.50
Never hinged 5.00
Q15 PP5 50c vio blue 4.50 1.60
Never hinged 7.00
Q16 PP5 1fr yellow 4.25 1.60
Never hinged 7.00

Imperforate

Q17 PP5 5c black 130.00 45.00
Never hinged 260.00
Q18 PP5 15c brn lilac 30.00 16.50
Never hinged 50.00
Q19 PP5 35c red 3.25 2.50
Never hinged 6.75
Q20 PP5 50c vio blue 24.00 14.00
Never hinged 40.00
Q21 PP5 1fr yellow 18.50 12.50
Never hinged 30.00
Nos. Q13-Q21 (9) 358.25 141.20

See Nos. Q41-Q44, Q143-Q145.
For surcharges, see Nos. Q28-Q40.

Type of 1892

1918-23 ***Perf. 10½x11***

Q22 PP1 30c brn, *yel* 37.50 16.50
Never hinged 55.00
a. Imperf 200.00
Never hinged 290.00
Q23 PP1 60c brn, *straw* ('23) 47.50 30.00
Never hinged 70.00
a. Imperf 190.00
Never hinged 275.00
Q24 PP2 15c vermilion ('22) 16.00 11.00
Never hinged 23.00
Q25 PP3 30c green 40.00 21.00
Never hinged 57.50
a. Imperf 240.00
Never hinged 325.00
Q26 PP3 60c green ('23) 75.00 50.00
Never hinged 110.00
Nos. Q22-Q26 (5) 216.00 128.50

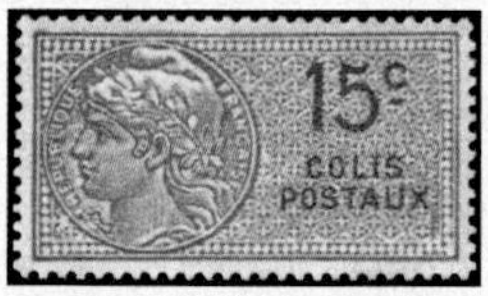

PP6

1924, Oct. ***Perf. 14***

Q27 PP6 15c rose & blue 4.00 3.75
Never hinged 5.00
a. Imperf 550.00
Never hinged 750.00

No. Q27 is a postal tax stamp, issued to show the collection of a new 15c excise fee on rail parcels. On July 3, 1925, its use was extended to all fiscal categories.

Surcharged in Black or Red (R) on Nos. Q9//Q16 and Types of 1918

1926 ***Perf. 13***

Q28 PP5 20c on 2fr rose 1.90 1.10
Never hinged 2.75
Q29 PP5 30c on 2fr yellow 1.90 1.10
Never hinged 2.75
a. "0f30" omitted 190.00
Never hinged 250.00
Q30 PP5 40c on 3fr gray 1.90 1.40
Never hinged 2.75
Q31 PP5 45c on 3fr orange 1.90 1.40
Never hinged 2.75
a. Period after "f" omitted 19.00 19.00
Never hinged 30.00
Q32 PP5 95c on 1fr yel 8.00 2.75
Never hinged 12.50
a. Imperf 90.00
Never hinged 150.00
Q33 PP5 1.35fr on 3fr vio 10.50 4.50
Never hinged 14.00
a. Imperf 150.00
Never hinged 225.00
Q34 PP5 1.45fr on 5fr black (R) 1.90 1.00
Never hinged 2.75
Q35 PP5 1.75fr on 2fr blue 10.50 4.50
Never hinged 14.00
Q36 PP5 1.85fr on 10c orange 1.90 1.20
Never hinged 2.75
Q37 PP5 1.95fr on 15c lilac ben 2.50 1.75
Never hinged 3.50
a. Imperf 110.00
Never hinged 175.00
Q38 PP5 2.35fr on 25c green 1.90 1.00
Never hinged 2.75
a. Imperf 110.00
Never hinged 175.00
Q39 PP5 2.90fr on 35c red 2.50 1.00
Never hinged 3.50
a. Dots before and after "f" 140.00
Never hinged 200.00
b. Imperf 125.00
Never hinged 190.00
Q40 PP5 3.30fr on 50c blue violet (R) 2.50 1.25
Never hinged 3.50
a. Double surcharge 250.00
Never hinged 375.00
b. Imperf 90.00
Never hinged 140.00
Nos. Q28-Q40 (13) 49.80 23.95

Type of 1918

1926 ***Perf. 11***

Q41 PP5 10c orange 2.00 1.25
Never hinged 3.75
a. Imperf 4.00
Never hinged 6.50
Q42 PP5 25c pale green 2.00 1.25
Never hinged 3.75
a. Imperf 4.00
Never hinged 6.50
Q43 PP5 2fr pale blue 25.00 14.50
Never hinged 42.50
a. Imperf 50.00
Never hinged 80.00
Q44 PP5 3fr violet 110.00 67.50
Never hinged 190.00
a. Imperf 225.00
Never hinged 360.00
Nos. Q41-Q44 (4) 139.00 84.50

Inscribed "APPORT A LA GARE" — PP7

1926

Q45 PP7 1fr on 60c brown, *yellow* 13.50 10.50
Never hinged 24.00
a. Imperf 190.00
Never hinged 300.00
Q46 PP7 1fr brown, *yellow* 17.50 13.00
Never hinged 30.00
Q47 PP7 1.30fr on 1fr brown, *yellow* 17.50 12.50
Never hinged 30.00
Q48 PP7 1.50fr brown, *yellow* 20.00 11.50
Never hinged 32.50
Q49 PP7 1.65fr brown, *yellow* 15.00 12.50
Never hinged 24.00
Q50 PP7 1.90fr on 1fr brown, *yellow* 17.50 12.50
Never hinged 30.00
Q51 PP7 2.10fr on 1.65fr brown, *yellow* 17.50 12.50
Never hinged 30.00
Nos. Q45-Q51 (6) 101.00 72.50

See Nos. Q91-Q95, footnote following No. Q102, Q143-Q145.
For overprints and surcharges, see Nos. Q76-Q78, Q83-Q86, Q91-Q92, boxed note following Q95, Q96-Q99, Q107-QQ109, boxed note following Q159.

PP8

Type I Type II Type III

1926-38

Q52 PP8 15c brown, *yel*, type I 7.50 3.00
Never hinged 11.00
a. Imperf 180.00
Never hinged 275.00
Q53 PP8 15c brown, *yel*, type II ('32) 8.00 4.25
Never hinged 11.50
a. Type III ('38) 210.00
Never hinged 275.00
b. As "a," imperf 240.00
Never hinged 300.00

Nos. Q52-Q53a were issued for use in Paris only. No. Q53a was prepared but not issued.

Inscribed "VALEUR DECLAREE" — PP9

The additional numerals overprinted on Nos. Q56-Q63 and on Nos. Q72-Q75 indicate the weight category of the parcels being sent.

1926

Q54 PP9 50c on 15c red 3.00 1.60
Never hinged 5.00
a. Imperf 180.00
Never hinged 275.00
Q55 PP9 50c red 750.00 750.00
Never hinged 1,200.
a. Imperf 1,200.
Never hinged 1,650.
Q56 PP9 50c red, ovptd. "1" 4.50 2.00
Never hinged 7.00
a. Imperf 200.00
Never hinged 300.00
b. Double overprint "1" 300.00
Never hinged 400.00
Q57 PP9 55c on 15c red, ovptd. "1" 6.75 5.00
Never hinged 11.50
a. Imperf 190.00
Never hinged —
Q58 PP9 55c on 50c red, ovptd. "1" 6.75 5.00
Never hinged 11.50
Q59 PP9 65c on 50c red 2.50 2.50
Never hinged 4.25
Q60 PP9 65c on 50c red, ovptd. "1" 15.00 8.25
Never hinged 27.50
Q61 PP9 1.50fr on 50c red, ovptd. "3" 7.00 5.00
Never hinged 12.00
a. Imperf 275.00
Never hinged 375.00
Q62 PP9 2.00fr on 50c red, ovptd. "4" 8.25 3.75
Never hinged 14.00
Q63 PP9 2.50fr on 50c red, ovptd. "5" 15.00 8.25
Never hinged 26.50
Nos. Q54-Q63 (9) 803.75 783.10

See Nos. Q79, Q93, Q150-Q152.
For overprints and surcharges, see No. Q87, boxed note following No. Q95, Q100, Q110, Q123-Q124, Q138.

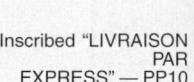

Inscribed "LIVRAISON PAR EXPRESS" — PP10

Q64 PP10 1.00fr on 60c grn 13.50 10.50
Never hinged 24.00
a. Imperf 225.00
Never hinged 325.00
Q65 PP10 1.00fr green 125.00 75.00
Never hinged 250.00
Q66 PP10 1.30fr on 1fr grn 16.50 12.50
Never hinged 29.00
Q67 PP10 1.50fr green 16.50 15.00
Never hinged 32.50
Q68 PP10 1.65fr green 16.50 15.00
Never hinged 32.50
Q69 PP10 1.90fr on 1.50fr grn 16.50 12.50
Never hinged 30.00
Q70 PP10 2.10fr on 1.65fr grn 30.00 14.00
Never hinged 50.00
Nos. Q64-Q70 (7) 234.50 154.50

For overprints and surcharges, see Nos. Q80-Q82, Q88-Q90, Q94, boxed note following Q95, Q101-Q105, Q111-Q113, Q125-Q132, Q139-Q141, Q146-Q149.

Inscribed "INTERETS A LA LIVRAISON" — PP11

Q71 PP11 50c lilac 3.00 1.60
Never hinged 5.00
a. Imperf 225.00 190.00
Never hinged 325.00
Q72 PP11 50c lilac, ovptd. "1" 6.75 4.25
Never hinged 10.00
a. Imperf 200.00
Never hinged 300.00
Q73 PP11 1.50fr on 50c lilac, ovptd. "3" 7.50 5.00
Never hinged 11.50
a. Imperf 200.00
Never hinged 300.00
Q74 PP11 2.00fr on 50c lilac, ovptd. "4" 10.00 7.00
Never hinged 16.00
Q75 PP11 2.50fr on 50c lilac, ovptd. "5" 10.00 7.00
Never hinged 16.50
a. Imperf 210.00
Never hinged 310.00
Nos. Q71-Q75 (4) 27.25 17.85

1926 Issues Overprinted

1928

Inscribed "APPORT A LA GARE"

Q76 PP7 1.00fr brn, *yel* 16.50 14.00
Never hinged 25.00
a. Imperf 190.00 190.00
Never hinged 300.00
Q77 PP7 1.50fr brn, *yel* 16.50 13.00
Never hinged 25.00
Q78 PP7 1.65fr brn, *yel* 16.50 13.00
Never hinged 25.00

Inscribed "VALEUR DECLAREE"

Q79 PP9 50c red 5.75 4.25
Never hinged 8.25
a. Imperf 190.00 190.00
Never hinged 300.00
b. Inverted overprint 210.00
Never hinged 310.00

Inscribed "LIVRAISON PAR EXPRESS"

Q80 PP10 1.00fr green 17.00 13.50
Never hinged 26.00
Q81 PP10 1.50fr green 17.00 13.50
Never hinged 26.00
Q82 PP10 1.65fr green 17.00 13.50
Never hinged 27.50
Nos. Q76-Q82 (7) 106.25 84.75

1926 Issues Surcharged

1928

Inscribed "APPORT A LA GARE"

Q83 PP7 1.45fr on 60c brn, *yel* 7.00 6.75
Never hinged 10.00
Q84 PP7 1.45fr on 1fr brn, *yel* 40.00 32.50
Never hinged 70.00
Q85 PP7 2.15fr on 1.50fr brn, *yel* 62.50 42.50
Never hinged 105.00
Q86 PP7 2.35fr on 1.65fr brn, *yel* 62.50 42.50
Never hinged 105.00

Inscribed "VALEUR DECLAREE"

Q87 PP9 75c on 50c red 2.10 1.60
Never hinged 3.25
a. Imperf 210.00
Never hinged 400.00

Inscribed "LIVRAISON PAR EXPRESS"

Q88 PP10 1.45fr on 1fr green 62.50 42.50
Never hinged 105.00
Q89 PP10 2.15fr on 1.50fr green 62.50 42.50
Never hinged 105.00
Q90 PP10 2.35fr on 1.65fr green 62.50 42.50
Never hinged 105.00
Nos. Q83-Q90 (8) 361.60 253.35

Types of 1926 and

PP12

1933-34

Inscribed "APPORT A LA GARE"

Q91 PP7 1.45fr brn, *yel* 55.00 25.00
Never hinged 82.50
Q92 PP7 2.35fr brn, *yel* 1,400.
Never hinged 1,900.

A 2.15fr value, brown on yellow paper, was prepared but not issued without overprint or surcharge.

For overprints and surcharges, see Nos. Q96, Q98, Q99, Q107-Q109, Q115, Q116, Q118, Q120-Q122, Q135-Q137.

Inscribed "VALEUR DECLAREE"

Q93 PP9 75c red 18.00 3.25
Never hinged 22.50
a. Imperf 180.00

For overprints and surcharges on No. Q93, see Nos. Q110, Q123, Q124, Q138.

A 1.15fr black in this design, imperf, was prepared but not issued. Value, $400.

Inscribed "LIVRAISON PAR EXPRESS"

Q94 PP10 1.45fr yel grn 450.00 300.00
Never hinged 675.00

Two other values, 2.15fr and 2.35fr were prepared but not issued without overprint or surcharge.

For overprints and surcharges, see Nos. Q101, Q103, Q105, Q111-Q113, Q125, Q126, Q128, Q130-Q132. Q139-Q141.

Inscribed "COLIS ENCOMBRANT"

Q95 PP12 2fr blue ('34) 45.00 21.00
Never hinged 70.00

For overprints and surcharges, see Nos. Q106, Q114, Q133, Q134, Q142.

Nos. Q46, Q48, Q49, Q55, Q65, Q67 and Q68 overprinted "B" were not issued. Values: 1fr (#Q46), $95; never hinged $130; 1.50fr (#Q48), $95, never hinged $130; 1.65fr (#Q49), $95, never hinged $130; 50c (#Q55), $95, never hinged $130; 1fr (#Q65), $92.50, never hinged $140; 1.50fr (#Q67), $92.50, never hinged $140; 1.65fr (#Q68), $92.50, never hinged $140.

Stamps and Types of 1926-34 Overprinted

1937

Inscribed "APPORT A LA GARE"

Q96 PP7 1.45fr brn, *yel* 6.75 6.75
Never hinged 10.00
Q97 PP7 1.45fr brn, *yel* 37.50 31.00
Never hinged 57.50
Q98 PP7 1.45fr brn, *yel* 25.00 19.00
Never hinged 37.50
Q99 PP7 1.45fr brn, *yel* 25.00 19.00
Never hinged 37.50

Inscribed "VALEUR DECLAREE"

Q100 PP9 50c red 17.50 16.50
Never hinged 25.00
a. Imperf 225.00
Never hinged 325.00

Inscribed "LIVRAISON PAR EXPRESS"

Q101 PP10 1.45fr green 17.50 16.50
Never hinged 25.00
Q102 PP10 2.15fr on 1.50fr green 17.50 16.50
Never hinged 25.00
Q103 PP10 2.15fr green 42.50 30.00
Never hinged 67.50
a. Imperf 210.00
Never hinged 315.00
Q104 PP10 2.65fr on 1.65fr green 250.00 110.00
Never hinged 350.00
Q105 PP10 2.35fr green 17.50 12.50
Never hinged 26.00

Inscribed "COLIS ENCOMBRANT"

Q106 PP12 2fr blue 37.50 35.00
Never hinged 57.50
Nos. Q96-Q106 (11) 494.25 312.75

For overprints and surcharges, see Nos. Q146-Q149.

Types of 1933-34 Surcharged

1937

Inscribed "APPORT A LA GARE"

Q107 PP7 1.85fr on 1.45fr brown, *yellow* 15.00 12.50
Never hinged 26.00
Q108 PP7 2.75fr on 2.15fr brown, *yellow* 15.00 12.50
Never hinged 45.00
Q109 PP7 3.05fr on 2.55fr brown, *yellow* 50.00 26.00
Never hinged 90.00

Inscribed VALEUR DECLAREE

Q110 PP9 .95fr on 75c red 42.50 25.00
Never hinged 67.50

Inscribed LIVRAISON PAR EXPRESS

Q111 PP10 1.85fr on 1.45fr green 70.00 45.00
Never hinged 115.00
Q112 PP10 2.75fr on 2.15fr green 50.00 45.00
Never hinged 115.00
Q113 PP10 3.05fr on 2.35fr green 50.00 45.00
Never hinged 115.00

Inscribed COLIS ENCOMBRANT

Q114 PP12 2.60fr on 2fr blue 17.50 17.50
Never hinged 26.00
Nos. Q107-Q114 (7) 292.50 211.00

Stamps and Types of 1926-34 Overprinted

1937

Inscribed "APPORT A LA GARE"

Q115 PP7 1.45fr brn, *yel* 3.00 2.50
Never hinged 4.50
Q116 PP7 1.85fr on 1.45fr brown, *yellow* 3.00 2.50
Never hinged 4.50
Q117 PP7 2.15fr on 1.50fr brown, *yellow* 2.50 2.50
Never hinged 4.25
Q118 PP7 2.15fr brn, *yel* 42.50 35.00
Never hinged 62.50
Q119 PP7 2.35fr on 1.65fr brown, *yellow* 575.00 475.00
Never hinged 800.00
Q120 PP7 2.35fr brn, *yel* 3.00 2.50
Never hinged 4.50
Q121 PP7 2.75fr on 2.15fr brown, *yellow* 3.25 2.50
Never hinged 5.75
Q122 PP7 3.05fr on 2.35fr brown, *yellow* 6.50 6.25
Never hinged 10.00

Inscribed VALEUR DECLAREE

Q123 PP9 75c red 3.75 3.50
Never hinged 5.50
a. Pair, one without overprint 195.00
Never hinged 300.00
Q124 PP9 95c on 75c red 3.00 3.00
Never hinged 3.75

Inscribed LIVRAISON PAR EXPRESS

Q125 PP10 1.45fr green 4.25 3.25
Never hinged 6.25
Q126 PP10 1.85fr on 1.45fr brn, *yel* 5.75 4.25
Never hinged 8.25
Q127 PP10 2.15fr on 1.50fr green 375.00 325.00
Never hinged 500.00
Q128 PP10 2.15fr green 18.50 16.50
Never hinged 27.50
Q129 PP10 2.35fr on 1.65fr green 675.00 725.00
Never hinged 1,100.
Q130 PP10 2.35fr green 11.00 10.50
Never hinged 15.00
Q131 PP10 2.75fr on 2.15fr green 29.00 32.50
Never hinged 45.00
Q132 PP10 3.05fr on 2.35fr green 29.00 32.50
Never hinged 45.00

Inscribed COLIS ENCOMBRANT

Q133 PP12 2fr blue 3.00 2.10
Never hinged 4.50
a. Pair, imperf between 130.00
Never hinged 210.00
Q134 PP12 2.60fr on 2fr blue 3.25 2.50
Never hinged 5.50
Nos. Q115-Q134 (19) 1,796. 1,686.

For additional surcharges, see Nos. Q146-Q149.

Stamps and Types of 1933-34 Surcharged

1938

Inscribed "APPORT A LA GARE"

Q135 PP7 2.30fr on 1.45fr brown, *yellow* 3.75 3.00
Never hinged 5.50
Q136 PP7 3.45fr on 2.15fr brown, *yellow* 3.75 3.00
Never hinged 5.50
Q137 PP7 3.85fr on 1.45fr brown, *yellow* 3.75 3.00
Never hinged 5.50

Inscribed VALEUR DECLAREE

Q138 PP9 1.15fr on 75c red 1.60 1.60
Never hinged 2.50

Inscribed LIVRAISON PAR EXPRESS

Q139 PP10 2.30fr on 1.45fr green 3.75 3.00
Never hinged 5.50
Q140 PP10 3.45fr on 2.15fr green 3.75 3.00
Never hinged 5.50
Q141 PP10 3.85fr on 2.35fr green 3.75 3.00
Never hinged 5.50

Inscribed COLIS ENCOMBRANT

Q142 PP12 3.25fr on 2fr blue 1.60 1.60
Never hinged 2.50
Nos. Q135-Q142 (7) 24.10 19.60

For Nos. Q135-Q138, Q140-Q142 overprinted "E," see second editor's note following No. Q159.

Type of 1918

1938 ***11, Imperf (#Q161)***

Q143 PP5 10c gray black 17.50 16.00
Never hinged 26.00
a. Imperf 26.00
Never hinged 42.50
Q144 PP5 20c brown lilac 17.50 16.00
Never hinged 26.00
a. Imperf 42.50
Never hinged 62.50
Q145 PP5 25c green, imperf *50.00* *20.00*
Never hinged *80.00*
Nos. Q143-Q145 (3) 85.00 52.00

Two additional values,a 10c rose lilac and a 15c ultramarine, were prepare with this set but not issued. Values, each stamp: $90, never hinged $150. Both stamps also exist imperf. Values, each: $82.50; never hinged $150.

Nos. Q103, Q105, Q112, Q113 Overprinted

1938 ***Perf. 11***

Q146 PP10 2.30fr on 2.15fr green 62.50 62.50
Never hinged 80.00
Q147 PP10 2.30fr on 2.35fr green 62.50 62.50
Never hinged 80.00
Q148 PP10 2.30fr on 2.75fr on 2.15fr green 140.00 100.00
Never hinged 200.00
Q149 PP10 2.30fr on 3.05fr on 2.35fr green 140.00 100.00
Never hinged 200.00
Nos. Q146-Q149 (4) 405.00 325.00

Types of 1926 and

PP13

PP14

PP15

PP16

1938-39

Inscribed VALEUR DECLAREE

Q150 PP9 1fr red ('39) 2.50 2.50
Never hinged 4.00
Q151 PP9 1.15fr red 1.25 1.25
Never hinged 2.10
Imperf 140.00
Never hinged 225.00
Q152 PP9 5fr red ('39) 2.50 *2.75*
Never hinged 4.00

Inscribed AU DESSUS DE 10

Q153 PP13 2.40fr brown, *yellow* 2.50 *2.75*
Never hinged 4.00
Q154 PP13 3.50fr brown, *yellow* 2.50 *2.75*
Never hinged 4.00
Q155 PP13 3.80fr brown, *yellow* 2.50 *2.75*
Never hinged 4.00
Imperf 125.00
Never hinged 190.00

Inscribed REMBOURSEMENT

Q156 PP14 2.50fr yel grn ('39) 2.50 2.25
Never hinged 4.00
Q157 PP14 7.50fr yel grn ('39) 2.75 2.50
Never hinged 4.25

Inscribed INTERET A LA LIVRAISON

Q158 PP15 1fr lilac ('39) 9.50 6.75
Never hinged 14.00

Inscribed ENCOMBRANT

Q159 PP16 3.20fr blue 11.00 7.50
Never hinged 16.00
Nos. Q150-Q159 (10) 39.50 33.75

Two additional values, 3.45fr and 3.85fr, type PP7, brown on yellow paper, imperforate, were prepared but not issued. Values, each: $140; never hinged, $225.

Nos. Nos. Q135-Q138, Q140-Q142 were overprinted "E" in 1939, in anticipation of new rates to take effect April 1, but were not issued. Values: 2.30fr on 1.45fr, $525, never hinged $800; 3.45fr on 2.15fr, $675, never hinged $1,050; 3.85fr on 2.35fr, $675, never hinged $1050; 1.15fr on 75c, $275, never hinged $425; 3.45fr on 2.15fr, $1,850, never hinged $3,000; 3.85fr on 2.35fr, $1,850, never hinged $3,000; 3.25fr on 2fr, $575, never hinged $825.

In 1941, two sets were prepared in anticipation of new rate increases on April 1. They were not issued.

Six stamps in a new design, consisting of a 10c greenish gray, 30c blue, 50c brown, 1fr blue violet, 2fr orange and 5fr red. Values: 10c $185, never hinged $275; 30c $240, never hinged $325; 50c $240, never hinged $325; 1fr $185, never hinged $275; 2fr $185, never hinged $275; 5fr $185, never hinged $275;

Nos. Q93, Q153-Q155 and Q159 overprinted "E." Values: 75c -; other values $575, never hinged $875.

PP17

PP18

1941 *Perf. 12½*

Without Denominations

Q160	PP17 (2.70fr) brown	5.50	4.50
	Never hinged	9.00	
Q161	PP17 (3.90fr) blue	5.50	4.50
	Never hinged	9.00	
Q162	PP17 (4.20fr) green	5.50	4.50
	Never hinged	9.00	
Q163	PP18 (3.50fr) blue	10.50	9.50
	Never hinged	14.00	
	Nos. Q160-Q163 (4)	27.00	23.00

Five stamps in the designs of PP20-PP22 below, but with blank value tablets, were prepared with Nos. Q160-Q163 but were not issued. Values: (1fr) brown, (5fr) red and (2.50fr) blue, each $67.50, never hinged $90; (7.50fr) green, $290, never hinged $400; (1fr) violet, $120, never hinged $180.

See Nos. Q178-Q181, Q200-Q206.

"Domicile"
PP19

"Valeur Declaree"
PP20

"Remboursement"
PP21

"Interet A La Livraison"
PP22

"Encombrant" — PP23

1941 *Perf. 12½, 13 (#Q167-171)*

Q164	PP19 2.70fr brown	6.75	5.50
	Never hinged	11.00	
Q165	PP19 3.90fr blue	6.75	5.50
	Never hinged	11.00	
Q166	PP19 4.20fr green	6.75	5.50
	Never hinged	11.00	
Q167	PP20 1fr brown	2.75	1.25
	Never hinged	4.25	
Q168	PP20 5fr red	1.50	*1.75*
	Never hinged	2.25	
Q169	PP21 2.50fr blue	1.50	*1.75*
	Never hinged	2.25	
Q170	PP21 7.50fr green	3.75	3.50
	Never hinged	6.00	
Q171	PP22 1fr violet	1.00	1.00
	Never hinged	1.75	
Q172	PP23 3.50fr blue	37.50	16.50
	Never hinged	52.50	
	Nos. Q164-Q172 (9)	68.25	42.25

See Nos. Q173-Q177, Q186-Q194, Q200-Q206.

For surcharges, see footnote following No. Q177, Nos. Q182-Q185, Q207-Q210.

Types of 1941 with Bold Numerals

1942, Feb. *Perf. 13*

Q173	PP20 1fr brown	2.75	1.25
	Never hinged	4.25	
Q174	PP20 5fr red	1.50	*1.75*
	Never hinged	2.25	
Q175	PP21 2.50fr blue	1.50	1.25
	Never hinged	2.25	
Q176	PP21 7.50fr green	6.75	*7.00*
	Never hinged	11.00	
Q177	PP22 1fr violet	67.50	1.00
	Never hinged	100.00	
	Nos. Q173-Q177 (5)	80.00	12.25

See Nos. Q173-Q177, Q186-Q194, Q200-Q206. See No. Q194.

Nine stamps from the 1941-42 issues were surcharged "+3F / C.N.S. / Cheminots" to raise funds for a philatelic exhibition organized by railroad employees, which took place in Paris on Dec. 26 and 27, 1942. They were not valid for postage. Value, set: $110; never hinged $160.

Type of 1941 Inscribed "F" in Value Tablets

1943 *Perf. 12½*

Q178	PP17 (3fr) brown	3.00	3.00
	Never hinged	4.25	
Q179	PP17 (4.30fr) blue	3.00	3.00
	Never hinged	4.25	
Q180	PP17 (4.70fr) green	3.00	3.00
	Never hinged	4.25	
Q181	PP18 (3.50fr) blue	7.00	7.00
	Never hinged	14.00	
	Nos. Q178-Q181 (4)	16.00	16.00

Stamps of 1941 Surcharged in Black or Red

1943

Q182	PP19 3fr on 2.70fr brn	11.00	11.00
	Never hinged	16.00	
Q183	PP19 4.5fr on 3.90fr blue (R)	2.50	*3.00*
	Never hinged	4.50	
Q184	PP19 4.7fr on 4.20fr green (R)	3.50	3.00
	Never hinged	5.00	
Q185	PP23 3.9fr on 3.50fr blue (R)	3.50	3.50
	Never hinged	5.00	
	Nos. Q182-Q185 (4)	20.50	20.50

Denominations in Black or Red

1943 **Unwmk.**

Q186	PP19 3fr brn	3.75	*4.25*
	Never hinged	5.50	
Q187	PP19 4.3fr blue (R)	10.00	5.75
	Never hinged	12.50	
Q188	PP19 4.7fr green (R)	11.50	2.50
	Never hinged	15.00	
Q189	PP23 3.9fr blue (R)	70.00	60.00
	Never hinged	110.00	
	Nos. Q186-Q189 (4)	95.25	72.50

1943 **Wmk. 407**

Q190	PP19 3fr brn	12.50	11.00
	Never hinged	21.00	
Q191	PP19 4.3fr blue	20.00	13.00
	Never hinged	32.50	
Q192	PP19 4.7fr green	21.00	13.50
	Never hinged	32.50	
Q193	PP23 3.9fr blue	12.50	12.50
	Never hinged	110.00	
	Nos. Q190-Q193 (4)	66.00	50.00

1944

Q194	PP21 20fr orange	5.00	*6.75*
	Never hinged	6.75	

Hydroelectric Dam — PP24

Electric Train — PP25

Power Line — PP26

1944 *Perf. 12½, 13 (#Q167-171)*

Q195	PP24 1fr violet	6.75	6.75
	Never hinged	9.00	
Q196	PP24 5fr red brn	6.75	6.75
	Never hinged	9.00	
Q197	PP25 2.5fr blue	6.75	6.75
	Never hinged	9.00	
Q198	PP25 7.5fr green	6.75	6.75
	Never hinged	9.00	
Q199	PP26 1fr vio blue	6.75	6.75
	Never hinged	9.00	
	Nos. Q195-Q199 (5)	33.75	33.75

A 20fr orange, design PP25, was prepared but not issued. Values: $1,150; never hinged, $1,650.

Nos. Q195-Q199 exist unwatermarked, but were not issued in this form Values, each: $275; never hinged $425.

Types of 1941 Inscribed "G" in Value Tablets

1945 **Unwmk.**

Q200	PP17 (5fr) brown	5.50	*6.00*
	Never hinged	7.00	
Q201	PP17 (7.20fr) blue	5.50	*6.00*
	Never hinged	7.00	
Q202	PP17 (7.60fr) green	5.50	*6.00*
	Never hinged	7.00	
Q203	PP18 (6.60fr) blue	6.25	*6.75*
	Never hinged	8.75	
	Nos. Q200-Q203 (4)	22.75	*24.75*

Wmk. 407

Q204	PP17 (5fr) brown	16.50	16.50
	Never hinged	24.00	
Q205	PP17 (7.20fr) blue	12.50	*12.50*
	Never hinged	18.00	
Q206	PP17 (7.60fr) green	12.50	*12.50*
	Never hinged	18.00	
	Nos. Q204-Q206 (3)	41.50	41.50

Nos. Q190-Q193 Surcharged

1945 **Wmk. 407**

Q207	PP19 5fr on 3fr brown	6.25	6.25
	Never hinged	8.75	
Q208	PP19 7.2fr on 4fr blue	6.25	6.25
	Never hinged	8.75	
Q209	PP19 7.8fr on 4.70fr green	6.25	6.25
	Never hinged	8.75	
Q210	PP23 6.65fr on 3.90fr blue	7.50	7.50
	Never hinged	11.50	
	Nos. Q207-Q210 (4)	26.25	26.25

Nos. Q186-Q189 were also surcharged but were not issued. Values, each: $45; never hinged $72.50.

Electric Train — PP27

Transformer PP28

Denominations in Black

1945

Q211	PP27 5fr brown	16.00	16.00
	Never hinged	22.50	
Q212	PP27 7.2fr blue	15.00	15.00
	Never hinged	22.50	
Q213	PP27 7.8fr green	15.00	15.00
	Never hinged	22.50	
Q214	PP28 3.95fr blue	6.75	6.75
	Never hinged	9.00	
	Nos. Q211-Q214 (4)	52.75	52.75

Nos. Q211-Q213 without watermark were not issued. Value, set: $50; never hinged, $80.

A set of ten stamps in the design above were prepared in 1945, but were not issued. Value, each: $300; never hinged, $450.

Four stamps of Types PP27-PP28, inscribed "H" in the value tablet, were also prepared by not issued. Value, set: $2,400; never hinged, $3,750.

Locomotive — PP29

1944 Wmk. 407 *Perf. 13*

Q215	PP29	1fr deep green	4.25	1.25
		Never hinged	8.25	
Q216	PP29	2fr gray brown	5.75	1.60
		Never hinged	12.50	
Q217	PP29	5fr ultramarine	27.50	1.60
		Never hinged	35.00	
Q218	PP29	10fr red	13.50	1.60
		Never hinged	22.50	
Q219	PP29	20fr olive green	11.50	1.60
		Never hinged	17.50	
Q220	PP29	50fr red orange	21.00	1.60
		Never hinged	30.00	
Q221	PP29	100fr gray black	37.50	1.60
		Never hinged	57.50	
		Nos. Q215-Q221 (7)	121.00	10.85

Unwmk.

Q222	PP29	1fr deep green	11.00	5.50
		Never hinged	16.50	
Q223	PP29	2fr gray brown	14.00	5.50
		Never hinged	21.00	
Q224	PP29	5fr ultramarine	45.00	5.50
		Never hinged	70.00	
Q225	PP29	10fr red	29.00	5.50
		Never hinged	42.50	
Q226	PP29	20fr olive green	21.00	5.50
		Never hinged	32.50	
Q227	PP29	50fr red orange	42.50	5.50
		Never hinged	62.50	
Q228	PP29	100fr gray black	75.00	6.00
		Never hinged	110.00	
		Nos. Q222-Q228 (7)	237.50	39.00

Nos. Q215-Q234 were issued for use on small packets. Effective January 1, 1946, the parcel and small packet services were unified, and all issued thereafter were valid for both servives.

See Nos. Q229-Q254.

1944-45 Wmk. 407

Q229	PP29	3fr gray	6.75	1.60
		Never hinged	12.50	
Q230	PP29	4fr black	11.00	2.50
		Never hinged	16.50	
Q231	PP29	7fr violet	70.00	3.00
		Never hinged	110.00	
Q232	PP29	8fr yel grn	20.00	2.50
		Never hinged	32.50	
Q233	PP29	9fr dk blue	32.50	5.00
		Never hinged	55.00	
Q234	PP29	30fr red brn	90.00	1.60
		Never hinged	140.00	
		Nos. Q229-Q234 (6)	230.25	16.20

1946

Q235	PP29	6fr claret	17.50	1.60
		Never hinged	26.00	
Q236	PP29	40fr yel brn	27.50	1.60
		Never hinged	40.00	
Q237	PP29	60fr lake red	29.00	1.60
		Never hinged	42.50	
Q238	PP29	70fr violet	200.00	30.00
		Never hinged	275.00	
Q239	PP29	80fr yel grn	27.50	2.50
		Never hinged	40.00	
Q240	PP29	90fr dk blue	150.00	27.50
		Never hinged	240.00	
Q241	PP29	200fr emer grn	32.50	2.50
		Never hinged	55.00	
		Nos. Q235-Q241 (7)	484.00	67.30

1947

Q242	PP29	5fr pale blue	21.00	2.25
		Never hinged	32.50	
Q243	PP29	7fr pale vio	275.00	18.50
		Never hinged	425.00	
Q244	PP29	9fr pale grn	200.00	16.50
		Never hinged	300.00	
Q245	PP29	30fr pale gray brn	75.00	2.25
		Never hinged	110.00	
Q246	PP29	70fr pale viol	200.00	7.50
		Never hinged	300.00	
Q247	PP29	90fr pale ultra	140.00	2.50
		Never hinged	225.00	
Q248	PP29	100fr yellow	400.00	3.00
		Never hinged	550.00	
		Nos. Q242-Q248 (7)	1,311.	52.50

1948

Q249	PP29	500fr yel	87.50	2.50
		Never hinged	140.00	
Q250	PP29	1000fr yel	325.00	17.50
		Never hinged	500.00	

1951-52

Q251	PP29	10fr grn	57.50	8.25
		Never hinged	90.00	
Q252	PP29	20fr vio	57.50	15.00
		Never hinged	90.00	
Q253	PP29	50fr blue	70.00	10.00
		Never hinged	110.00	
Q254	PP29	100fr rose ver	21.00	1.75
		Never hinged	30.00	
		Nos. Q251-Q254 (4)	206.00	35.00

Electric Train — PP30

1960

Q255	PP30	5c orange	11.50	2.10
		Never hinged	17.50	
Q256	PP30	10c red	10.50	8.25
		Never hinged	16.00	
Q257	PP30	20c dp red	8.75	3.75
		Never hinged	13.50	
Q258	PP30	30c dp red	8.75	3.75
		Never hinged	13.50	
Q259	PP30	40c dp red	8.75	7.50
		Never hinged	13.50	
Q260	PP30	50c dp red	8.75	4.25
		Never hinged	13.50	
Q261	PP30	60c dp red	7.50	4.25
		Never hinged	11.00	
Q262	PP30	70c dp red	7.50	4.25
		Never hinged	11.00	
Q263	PP30	80c dp red	11.50	4.25
		Never hinged	17.50	
Q264	PP30	90c dp red	11.50	4.25
		Never hinged	17.50	
Q265	PP30	1fr blue	13.00	2.25
		Never hinged	20.00	
Q266	PP30	2fr blue	13.00	2.25
		Never hinged	20.00	
Q267	PP30	3fr blue	13.00	2.25
		Never hinged	20.00	
Q268	PP30	4fr blue	13.00	2.25
		Never hinged	20.00	
Q269	PP30	5fr blue	13.00	2.25
		Never hinged	20.00	
Q270	PP30	10fr yellow	15.00	2.50
		Never hinged	22.50	
Q271	PP30	20fr dp grn	20.00	16.00
		Never hinged	30.00	
		Nos. Q255-Q271 (17)	195.00	76.35

1960 Unwmk.

Q272	PP30	5c orange	14.00	6.25
		Never hinged	32.50	
Q273	PP30	20c dp red	210.00	55.00
		Never hinged	325.00	
Q274	PP30	30c dp red	150.00	55.00
		Never hinged	325.00	
Q275	PP30	40c dp red	110.00	30.00
		Never hinged	160.00	
Q276	PP30	70c dp red	22.50	7.50
		Never hinged	32.50	
Q277	PP30	80c dp red	22.50	6.50
		Never hinged	32.50	
Q278	PP30	90c dp red	22.50	6.50
		Never hinged	32.50	
Q279	PP30	1fr blue	20.00	3.75
		Never hinged	30.00	
Q280	PP30	2fr blue	20.00	3.75
		Never hinged	30.00	
Q281	PP30	3fr blue	20.00	3.75
		Never hinged	30.00	
Q282	PP30	4fr blue	20.00	3.75
		Never hinged	30.00	
Q283	PP30	5fr blue	20.00	3.75
		Never hinged	30.00	
Q284	PP30	10fr yellow	25.00	6.25
		Never hinged	37.50	
Q285	PP30	20fr dp grn	30.00	21.00
		Never hinged	45.00	
		Nos. Q272-Q285 (14)	706.50	212.75

FRANCHISE STAMP

No. 276 Overprinted "F"

1939 Unwmk. *Perf. 14x13½*

S1	A45	90c ultramarine	1.90	*2.50*
		Never hinged	2.75	
	a.	Period following "F"	20.00	20.00
		Never hinged	29.00	

No. S1 was for the use of Spanish refugees in France. "F" stands for "Franchise."

OCCUPATION STAMPS

Issued under German Occupation (Alsace and Lorraine)

OS1

1870 Typo. Unwmk. *Perf. 13½x14*

Network with Points Up

N1	OS1	1c bronze grn	100.00	*110.00*
	a.	1c olive green	100.00	*110.00*
N2	OS1	2c dark brown	190.00	190.00
	a.	2c red brown	190.00	190.00
N3	OS1	4c gray	200.00	115.00
N4	OS1	5c yel grn	200.00	15.00
N5	OS1	10c yel bister brn	155.00	6.50
	a.	10c yel brown	170.00	7.00
	b.	Network lemon yellow	200.00	10.00
N6	OS1	20c ultra	190.00	17.50
N7	OS1	25c brown	210.00	110.00
	a.	25c blk brown	160.00	80.00

There are three varieties of the 4c and two of the 10c, differing in the position of the figures of value, and several other setting varieties.

Network with Points Down

N8	OS1	1c olive grn	525.00	*725.00*
N9	OS1	2c red brn	265.00	*625.00*
N10	OS1	4c gray	265.00	225.00
N11	OS1	5c yel grn	6,500.	650.00
N12	OS1	10c bister	265.00	21.50
	a.	Network lemon yellow	325.00	57.50
N13	OS1	20c ultra	340.00	100.00
N14	OS1	25c brown	725.00	325.00

Official imitations have the network with points downward. The "P" of "Postes" is 2½mm from the border in the imitations and 3mm in the originals.

The word "Postes" measures 12¾ to 13mm on the imitations, and from 11 to 12½mm on the originals.

The imitations are perf. 13½x14½; originals, perf. 13½x14¼.

The stamps for Alsace and Lorraine were replaced by stamps of the German Empire on Jan. 1, 1872.

German Stamps of 1905-16 Surcharged:

1916 Wmk. 125 *Perf. 14, 14½*

N15	A16	3c on 3pf brown	1.25	1.25
N16	A16	5c on 5pf green	1.25	1.25
N17	A22	8c on 7½pf org	2.00	2.00
N18	A16	10c on 10pf car	2.00	2.00
N19	A22	15c on 15pf yel brn	1.25	1.25
N20	A16	25c on 20pf blue	1.25	1.25
	a.	25c on 20pf ultramarine	2.00	2.00
N21	A16	40c on 30pf org & blk, *buff*	2.90	2.75
N22	A16	50c on 40pf lake & blk	2.90	2.75
N23	A16	75c on 60pf mag	12.50	12.50
N24	A16	1fr on 80pf lake & blk, *rose*	12.50	12.50

N25	A17	1fr25c on 1m car	47.50	47.50
	a.	Double surcharge	—	
N26	A21	2fr50c on 2m gray bl	47.50	47.50
	a.	Double surcharge	—	
		Nos. N15-N26 (12)	134.80	134.50

These stamps were also used in parts of Belgium occupied by the German forces.

Catalogue values for unused stamps in this section, from this point to the end of the section, are for Never Hinged items.

Alsace
Issued under German Occupation

Stamps of Germany 1933-36 Overprinted in Black

1940 Wmk. 237 *Perf. 14*

N27	A64	3pf olive bister	.80	.55
N28	A64	4pf dull blue	.80	.55
N29	A64	5pf brt green	.80	.55
N30	A64	6pf dark green	.80	.55
N31	A64	8pf vermilion	.80	.55
N32	A64	10pf chocolate	.80	.55
N33	A64	12pf dp carmine	1.00	.55
N34	A64	15pf maroon	1.00	.55
N35	A64	20pf brt blue	1.65	.75
N36	A64	25pf ultra	1.65	.75
N37	A64	30pf olive grn	1.65	.75
N38	A64	40pf red violet	2.90	1.00
N39	A64	50pf dk grn & blk	7.00	3.25
N40	A64	60pf claret & blk	7.00	3.25
N41	A64	80pf dk blue & blk	17.50	7.00
N42	A64	100pf orange & blk	17.50	7.00
		Nos. N27-N42 (16)	63.65	28.15

Lorraine
Issued under German Occupation

Stamps of Germany 1933-36 Overprinted in Black

1940 Wmk. 237 *Perf. 14*

N43	A64	3pf olive bister	1.00	.75
N44	A64	4pf dull blue	1.00	.75
N45	A64	5pf brt green	1.00	*4.00*
N46	A64	6pf dark green	1.00	.75
N47	A64	8pf vermilion	1.00	*.75*
N48	A64	10pf chocolate	1.50	.85
N49	A64	12pf deep carmine	1.50	.85
N50	A64	15pf maroon	1.50	.75
	a.	Inverted surcharge	—	
N51	A64	20pf brt blue	1.65	1.00
N52	A64	25pf ultra	1.40	1.00
N53	A64	30pf olive grn	2.10	1.00
N54	A64	40pf red violet	2.50	1.25
N55	A64	50pf dk grn & blk	6.00	3.00
N56	A64	60pf claret & blk	6.00	3.00
N57	A64	80pf dk blue & blk	18.00	7.50
N58	A64	100pf orange & blk	18.00	7.50
		Nos. N43-N58 (16)	65.15	*34.70*

Besetztes Gebiet Nordfrankreich

These three words, in a rectangular frame covering two stamps, were handstamped in black on Nos. 267, 367 and 369 and used in the Dunkerque region in July-August, 1940. The German political officer of Dunkerque authorized the overprint. The prevalence of forgeries and later favor overprints makes expertization mandatory.

ALLIED MILITARY GOVERNMENT

Stamps formerly listed in this section as Nos. 2N1-2N20 are now listed with regular stamps of France as Nos. 475-476H and 523A-523J.

FRENCH OFFICES ABROAD

Prior to 1923 several of the world powers maintained their own post offices in China for the purpose of sending and receiving overseas mail. French offices were maintained in Canton, Hoi Hao (Hoihow), Kwangchowan (Kouang-tchéou-wan), Mongtseu (Mong-tseu), Packhoi (Paknoi), Tong King (Tchongking), Yunnan Fou (Yunnanfu).

100 Centimes = 1 Franc
100 Cents = 1 Piaster
100 Cents = 1 Dollar

OFFICES IN CHINA

Peace and Commerce Stamps of France Overprinted in Red or Black

1894-1900 Unwmk. *Perf. 14x13½*

1 A15 5c grn, *grnsh* (R) 2.90 2.50
2 A15 5c yel grn, I (R) ('00) 2.90 2.50
a. Type II 45.00 29.00
3 A1510c blk, *lav*, I (R) 8.25 2.50
a. Type II 25.00 16.50
4 A1515c bl (R) 11.50 4.00
5 A1520c red, *grn* 7.00 4.50
6 A1525c blk, *rose* (R) 8.25 2.50
a. Double overprint 200.00
b. Pair, one without overprint 500.00
7 A1530c brn, *bis* 8.25 5.25
8 A1540c red, *straw* 9.00 6.50
9 A1550c car, *rose*, I 25.00 15.00
a. Red overprint 57.50
b. Type II (Bk) 15.00 8.25
10 A1575c dp vio, *org* (R) 75.00 52.50
11 A15 1fr brnz grn, *straw* 15.00 6.50
a. Double overprint 375.00 *400.00*
12 A15 2fr brn, *az* ('00) 30.00 29.00
12A A15 5fr red lil, *lav* 70.00 55.00
b. Red overprint 475.00
Nos. 1-12A (13) 273.05 188.25

For surcharges and overprints see Nos. 13-17, J7-J10, J20-J23.

No. 11 Surcharged in Black **25**

13 A1525c on 1fr brnz grn, *straw* 125.00 75.00

No. 6 Surcharged in Red

1901

14 A15 2c on 25c blk, *rose* 1,000. 325.00
15 A15 4c on 25c blk, *rose* 1,250. 450.00
16 A15 6c on 25c blk, *rose* 1,000. 375.00
17 A15 16c on 25c blk, *rose* 300.00 190.00
a. Black surcharge *6,750.*
Nos. 14-17 (4) 3,550. 1,340.

Stamps of Indo-China Surcharged in Black

1902-04

18a A3 1c blk, *lil bl* ('04) 2.50 2.50
19 A3 2c brn, *buff* 3.75 3.75
20a A3 4c claret, *lav* ('04) 3.75 2.90
21a A3 5c yellow grn ('04) 4.50 2.90
22 A3 10c red 5.75 5.00
23 A3 15c gray 6.50 5.75
24a A3 20c red, *grn* ('04) 8.25 7.50
25a A3 25c blk, *rose* ('04) 11.00 11.00
26 A3 25c blue ('04) 9.00 7.50
27a A3 30c brn, *bis* ('04) 8.25 7.50
28a A3 40c red, *straw* ('04) 24.00 18.00
29 A3 50c car, *rose* 62.50 62.50
30 A3 50c brn, *azure* ('04) 9.00 8.25
31a A3 75c vio, *org* ('04) 30.00 25.00
32a A3 1fr brnz grn, *straw* ('04) 40.00 40.00
33a A3 5fr red lil, *lavender* ('04) 82.50 80.00
Nos. 18a-33a (16) 311.25 290.05

The Chinese characters surcharged on Nos. 18-33 are the Chinese equivalents of the French values and therefore differ on each denomination. Two printings exist, differing slightly in the size of "CHINE." Values above are for the less expensive variety. See the *Scott Classic Specialized Catalogue of Stamps and Covers* for detailed listings. Many varieties of surcharge exist.

Liberty, Equality and Fraternity
A3

"Rights of Man"
A4

A5

1902-03 Typo.

34 A3 5c green 5.00 3.25
35 A4 10c rose red ('03) 2.50 1.90
36 A4 15c pale red 2.50 1.90
37 A4 20c brn vio ('03) 7.50 6.50
38 A4 25c blue ('03) 5.75 3.00
39 A4 30c lilac ('03) 8.25 7.00
40 A5 40c red & pale bl 16.50 14.50
41 A5 50c bis brn & lav 22.50 16.00
42 A5 1fr claret & ol grn 29.00 16.50
43 A5 2fr gray vio & yel 57.50 45.00
44 A5 5fr dk bl & buff 82.50 70.00
Nos. 34-44 (11) 239.50 185.55

For surcharges and overprints see Nos. 45, 57-85, J14-J16, J27-J30.

Surcharged in Black

1903

45 A4 5c on 15c pale red 16.50 16.50
a. Inverted surcharge 125.00 75.00

Stamps of Indo-China, 1904-06, Surcharged as Nos. 18-33 in Black

1904-05

46 A4 1c olive grn 2.00 2.00
47 A4 2c vio brn, *buff* 2.00 2.00
47A A4 4c cl, *bluish* 900.00 750.00
48 A4 5c deep grn 2.00 2.00
49 A4 10c carmine 2.90 2.90
50 A4 15c org brn, *bl* 2.90 2.90
51 A4 20c red, *grn* 11.00 11.00
52 A4 25c deep blue 10.00 5.75
53 A4 40c blk, *bluish* 8.25 5.75
54 A4 1fr pale grn 325.00 275.00
55 A4 2fr brn, *org* 37.50 32.50
56 A4 10fr org brn, *grn* 145.00 135.00
Nos. 46-56 (12) 1,448. 1,226.

Many varieties of the surcharge exist.

Stamps of 1902-03 Surcharged in Black

1907

57 A3 2c on 5c green 2.50 1.65
58 A4 4c on 10c rose red 1.80 1.50
a. Pair, one without surcharge —
59 A4 6c on 15c pale red 2.75 2.25
60 A4 8c on 20c brn vio 5.00 5.00
a. "8" inverted 65.00 67.50
61 A4 10c on 25c blue 1.65 1.25
62 A5 20c on 50c bis brn & lav 5.25 3.25
a. Double surcharge
b. Triple surcharge 425.00 425.00
63 A5 40c on 1fr claret & ol grn 21.00 13.50
64 A5 2pi on 5fr dk bl & buff 21.00 13.50
a. Double surcharge *2,100.* *1,650.*
Nos. 57-64 (8) 60.95 41.90

Stamps of 1902-03 Surcharged in Black

1911-22

65 A3 2c on 5c green 1.80 1.40
66 A4 4c on 10c rose red 1.90 1.50
67 A4 6c on 15c org 4.50 1.80
68 A4 8c on 20c brn vio 2.00 1.80
69 A4 10c on 25c bl ('21) 3.75 1.90
70 A4 20c on 50c bl ('22) 50.00 55.00
71 A5 40c on 1fr cl & ol grn 6.50 4.25

No. 44 Surcharged

73 A5 $2 on 5fr bl & buff ('22) 165.00 *190.00*
Nos. 65-73 (8) 235.45 257.65

Types of 1902-03 Surcharged like Nos. 65-71

1922

75 A3 1c on 5c org 5.00 5.25
76 A4 2c on 10c grn 5.75 6.25
77 A4 3c on 15c org 8.25 9.00
78 A4 4c on 20c red brn 10.00 12.00
79 A4 5c on 25c dk vio 5.00 4.50
80 A4 6c on 30c red 11.00 9.00
82 A4 10c on 50c blue 13.00 9.00
83 A5 20c on 1fr claret & ol grn 32.50 *40.00*
84 A5 40c on 2fr org & pale bl 42.50 *50.00*
85 A5 $1 on 5fr dk bl & buff 135.00 *145.00*
Nos. 75-85 (10) 268.00 290.00

POSTAGE DUE STAMPS

Postage Due Stamps of France Handstamped in Red or Black

1901-07 Unwmk. *Perf. 14x13½*

J1 D2 5c lt bl (R) 6.50 3.75
J2 D2 10c choc (R) 10.00 5.25
J3 D2 15c lt grn (R) 10.00 6.50
J4 D2 20c ol grn (R) ('07) 11.50 10.00
J5 D2 30c carmine 16.00 11.00
J6 D2 50c lilac 16.00 11.00
Nos. J1-J6 (6) 70.00 47.50

Stamps of 1894-1900 Handstamped in Carmine **A PERCEVOIR**

1903

J7 A15 5c yel grn — 2,250.
a. Purple handstamp —
b. 5c green, *greenish* —
J8 A15 10c blk, *lavender* — —
a. Purple handstamp —
J9 A15 15c blue — 1,250.
a. Purple handstamp —
J10 A15 30c brn, *bister* — 350.
a. Purple handstamp —

Same Handstamp on Stamps of 1902-03 in Carmine

1903

J14 A3 5c green — 2,000.
a. Purple handstamp —
J15 A4 10c rose red — 425.
a. Purple handstamp —
J16 A4 15c pale red — 325.
a. Purple handstamp —

Stamps of 1894-1900 Handstamped in Carmine

1903

J20 A15 5c yellow green — 1,100.
a. Purple handstamp —
b. 5c green, *greenish* —
J21 A15 10c blk, *lavender* — —
a. Purple handstamp —
J22 A15 15c blue — 350.
a. Purple handstamp —
J23 A15 30c brn, *bister* — 325.
a. Purple handstamp —

Same Handstamp on Stamps of 1902-03 in Carmine or Purple

1903

J27 A3 5c green (C) — 1,750.
a. Purple handstamp —
J28 A4 10c rose red (C) — 225.00
a. Purple handstamp —
J29 A4 15c pale red (C) — 225.00
a. Purple handstamp —
J30 A4 30c lilac (P) —

The handstamps on Nos. J7-J30 are found inverted, double, etc.

The cancellations on these stamps should have dates between Sept. 1, and Nov. 30, 1903, to be genuine.

Postage Due Stamps of France, 1893-1910 Surcharged like Nos. 65-71

1911

J33 D2 2c on 5c blue 2.50 2.10
a. Double surcharge 125.00 —
J34 D2 4c on 10c choc 2.50 2.10
a. Double surcharge 125.00 —
J35 D2 8c on 20c ol grn 2.90 2.50
a. Double surcharge 125.00 —
J36 D2 20c on 50c lilac 2.90 2.50
Nos. J33-J36 (4) 10.80 9.20

1922

J37 D2 1c on 5c blue 82.50 *95.00*
J38 D2 2c on 10c brn 145.00 *165.00*
J39 D2 4c on 20c ol grn 145.00 *165.00*
J40 D2 10c on 50c brn vio 125.00 *185.00*
Nos. J37-J40 (4) 497.50 610.00

CANTON

Stamps of Indo-China, 1892-1900, Overprinted in Red

1901 Unwmk. *Perf. 14x13½*

1 A3 1c blk, *lil bl* 1.75 1.75
1A A3 2c brn, *buff* 2.25 2.25
2 A3 4c claret, *lav* 3.75 3.75
2A A3 5c grn, *grnsh* 575.00 575.00
3 A3 5c yel grn 2.60 2.60
4 A3 10c blk, *lavender* 6.50 6.50
5 A3 15c blue, quadrille paper 5.25 5.25
6 A3 15c gray 6.25 6.25
a. Double overprint 19.00
7 A3 20c red, *grn* 20.00 20.00
8 A3 25c blk, *rose* 11.50 11.50
9 A3 30c brn, *bister* 28.00 28.00
10 A3 40c red, *straw* 28.00 28.00
11 A3 50c car, *rose* 32.50 32.50
12 A3 75c dp vio, *org* 32.50 32.50
13 A3 1fr brnz grn, *straw* 40.00 40.00
14 A3 5fr red lil, *lav* 225.00 225.00
Nos. 1-14 (16) 1,020. 1,020.

The Chinese characters in the overprint on Nos. 1-14 read "Canton." On Nos. 15-64, they restate the denomination of the basic stamp.

Surcharged in Black

1903-04

15 A3 1c blk, *lil bl* 3.75 3.25
16 A3 2c brn, *buff* 3.75 3.25
17 A3 4c claret, *lav* 3.75 3.25
18 A3 5c yellow green 3.90 3.40
19 A3 10c rose red 3.90 3.40
20 A3 15c gray 3.90 3.40

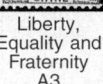

21	A3	20c red, *grn*	17.50	15.00
22	A3	25c blue	6.00	6.00
23	A3	25c blk, *rose* ('04)	9.50	6.50
24	A3	30c brn, *bister*	24.00	16.00
25	A3	40c red, *straw*	60.00	47.50
26	A3	50c car, *rose*	310.00	280.00
27	A3	50c brn, *az* ('04)	67.50	60.00
28	A3	75c dp vio, *org*	60.00	55.00
a.		"INDO-CHINE" inverted	*47,500.*	
29	A3	1fr brnz grn, *straw*	60.00	55.00
30	A3	5fr red lil, *lav*	60.00	55.00
		Nos. 15-30 (16)	697.45	615.95

Many varieties of the surcharge exist on #15-30.

Stamps of Indo-China, 1892-1906, Surcharged in Red or Black

A second printing of the 1906 surcharges of Canton, Hoi Hao, Kwangchowan, Mongtseu, Packhoi, Tong King and Yunnan Fou was made in 1908. The inks are grayish instead of full black and vermilion instead of carmine. Values are for the cheaper variety which usually is the second printing.

The 4c and 50c of the 1892 issue of Indo-China are known with this surcharge and similarly surcharged for other cities in China. The surcharges on these two stamps are always inverted. It is stated that they were irregularly produced and never issued.

1906

31	A4	1c ol grn (R)	2.00	2.00
32	A4	2c vio brn, *buff*	2.00	2.00
33	A4	4c cl, *bluish* (R)	2.00	2.00
34	A4	5c dp grn (R)	1.75	1.75
35	A4	10c carmine	2.60	2.60
36	A4	15c org brn, *bl*	20.00	20.00
37	A4	20c red, *grn*	11.00	11.00
38	A4	25c deep blue	4.75	4.75
39	A4	30c pale brn	16.00	16.00
40	A4	35c blk, *yel* (R)	12.00	12.00
41	A4	40c blk, *bluish* (R)	20.00	20.00
42	A4	50c bister brn	13.00	13.00
43	A3	75c dp vio, *org* (R)	60.00	60.00
44	A4	1fr pale grn	24.00	24.00
45	A4	2fr brn, *org* (R)	35.00	35.00
46	A3	5fr red lil, *lav*	80.00	80.00
47	A4	10fr org brn, *grn*	72.50	72.50
		Nos. 31-47 (17)	378.60	378.60

Surcharge exists inverted on 1c, 25c & 1fr.

Stamps of Indo-China, 1907, Surcharged "CANTON", and Chinese Characters, in Red or Blue

1908

48	A5	1c ol brn & blk	.95	.95
49	A5	2c brn & blk	1.00	1.00
50	A5	4c bl & blk	2.00	1.20
51	A5	5c grn & blk	2.00	1.60
52	A5	10c red & blk (Bl)	2.40	2.00
53	A5	15c vio & blk	3.25	2.75
54	A6	20c vio & blk	4.50	3.50
55	A6	25c bl & blk	4.50	3.50
56	A6	30c brn & blk	7.25	6.75
57	A6	35c ol grn & blk	7.50	6.75
58	A6	40c brn & blk	9.50	6.75
59	A6	50c car & blk (Bl)	9.50	6.75
60	A7	75c ver & blk (Bl)	9.50	8.75
61	A8	1fr car & blk (Bl)	16.00	12.00
62	A9	2fr grn & blk	40.00	35.50
63	A10	5fr bl & blk	55.00	47.50
64	A11	10fr pur & blk	80.00	80.00
		Nos. 48-64 (17)	254.85	227.25

Nos. 48-64 Surcharged with New Values in Cents or Piasters in Black, Red or Blue

1919

65	A5	2/5c on 1c	1.00	.95
66	A5	4/5c on 2c	1.00	.95
67	A5	1 3/5c on 4c (R)	1.00	.95
68	A5	2c on 5c	1.40	1.40
69	A5	4c on 10c (Bl)	1.60	1.60
a.		Chinese "2" instead of "4"	30.00	30.00
70	A5	6c on 15c	2.00	1.60
71	A6	8c on 20c	3.50	1.60
72	A6	10c on 25c	4.50	1.60
73	A6	12c on 30c	1.75	1.75
a.		Double surcharge	120.00	120.00
74	A6	14c on 35c	1.75	1.60
a.		Closed "4"	8.75	8.75
75	A6	16c on 40c	1.75	1.60
76	A6	20c on 50c (Bl)	2.10	1.60
77	A7	30c on 75c (Bl)	2.10	1.60
78	A8	40c on 1fr (Bl)	11.00	6.50
79	A9	80c on 2fr (R)	17.00	8.50
80	A10	2pi on 5fr (R)	29.00	29.00
81	A11	4pi on 10fr (R)	29.00	29.00
		Nos. 65-81 (17)	111.45	91.80

HOI HAO

Stamps of Indo-China Overprinted in Red

1901 Unwmk. *Perf. 14x13½*

1	A3	1c blk, *lil bl*	3.25	3.25
2	A3	2c brn, *buff*	4.00	4.00
3	A3	4c claret, *lav*	4.00	4.00
4	A3	5c yel grn	4.00	4.00
5	A3	10c blk, *lavender*	12.00	9.50
6	A3	15c blue	1,700.	725.00
7	A3	15c gray	6.40	4.00
8	A3	20c red, *grn*	27.50	22.50
9	A3	25c blk, *rose*	16.00	12.00
10	A3	30c brn, *bister*	60.00	60.00
11	A3	40c red, *straw*	60.00	60.00
12	A3	50c car, *rose*	60.00	60.00
13	A3	75c dp vio, *org*	225.00	195.00
14	A3	1fr brnz grn, *straw*	725.00	675.00
15	A3	5fr red lil, *lav*	725.00	650.00
		Nos. 1-15 (15)	3,632.	2,488.

The Chinese characters in the overprint on Nos. 1-15 read "Hoi Hao." On Nos. 16-66, they restate the denomination of the basic stamp.

Surcharged in Black

1903-04

16	A3	1c blk, *lil bl*	1.75	1.75
17	A3	2c brn, *buff*	1.80	1.80
18	A3	4c claret, *lav*	2.90	2.90
19	A3	5c yel grn	3.00	3.00
20	A3	10c red	3.40	3.40
21	A3	15c gray	3.75	3.75
22	A3	20c red, *grn*	7.25	7.25
23	A3	25c blue	5.00	5.00
24	A3	25c blk, *rose* ('04)	7.25	7.25
25	A3	30c brn, *bister*	5.50	5.50
26	A3	40c red, *straw*	32.50	32.50
27	A3	50c car, *rose*	28.00	28.00
28	A3	50c brn, *az* ('04)	130.00	130.00
29	A3	75c dp vio, *org*	42.50	42.50
a.		"INDO-CHINE" inverted	*42,500.*	
30	A3	1fr brnz grn, *straw*	62.50	62.50
31	A3	5fr red lil, *lav*	200.00	200.00
		Nos. 16-31 (16)	537.10	537.10

Many varieties of the surcharge exist on #1-31.

Stamps of Indo-China, 1892-1906, Surcharged in Red or Black

1906

32	A4	1c ol grn (R)	8.00	8.00
33	A4	2c vio brn, *buff*	8.00	8.00
34	A4	4c cl, *bluish* (R)	8.00	8.00
35	A4	5c dp grn (R)	8.00	8.00
36	A4	10c carmine	8.00	8.00
37	A4	15c org brn, *bl*	30.00	30.00
38	A4	20c red, *grn*	12.00	12.00
39	A4	25c deep blue	9.50	9.50
40	A4	30c pale brn	12.00	12.00
41	A4	35c blk, *yel* (R)	20.00	20.00
42	A4	40c blk, *bluish* (R)	20.00	20.00
43	A4	50c gray brn	20.00	20.00
44	A3	75c dp vio, *org* (R)	60.00	60.00
45	A4	1fr pale grn	60.00	60.00
46	A4	2fr brn, *org* (R)	60.00	60.00
47	A3	5fr red lil, *lav*	120.00	120.00
48	A4	10fr org brn, *grn*	140.00	140.00
		Nos. 32-48 (17)	603.50	603.50

Stamps of Indo-China, 1907, Surcharged "HOI HAO" and Chinese Characters, in Red or Blue

1908

49	A5	1c ol brn & blk	1.35	1.35
50	A5	2c brn & blk	1.40	1.40
51	A5	4c bl & blk	1.60	1.60
52	A5	5c grn & blk	2.40	2.40
53	A5	10c red & blk (Bl)	2.40	2.40
54	A5	15c vio & blk	6.50	6.50
55	A6	20c vio & blk	6.50	6.50
56	A6	25c bl & blk	6.50	6.50
57	A6	30c brn & blk	6.50	6.50
58	A6	35c ol grn & blk	6.50	6.50
59	A6	40c brn & blk	7.25	7.25
61	A6	50c car & blk (Bl)	9.25	9.25
62	A7	75c ver & blk (Bl)	8.75	8.75
63	A8	1fr car & blk (Bl)	26.00	26.00
64	A9	2fr grn & blk	40.00	40.00
65	A10	5fr bl & blk	67.50	67.50
66	A11	10fr pur & blk	100.00	*100.00*
		Nos. 49-66 (17)	300.40	300.40

Nos. 49-66 Surcharged with New Values in Cents or Piasters in Black, Red or Blue

1919

67	A5	2/5c on 1c	1.20	1.20
68	A5	4/5c on 2c	1.20	1.20
69	A5	1 3/5c on 4c (R)	1.60	1.60
70	A5	2c on 5c	2.00	2.00
71	A5	4c on 10c (Bl)	2.40	2.40
a.		Chinese "2" instead of "4"	8.75	8.75
72	A5	6c on 15c	2.00	2.00
73	A6	8c on 20c	4.00	4.00
a.		"S" of "CENTS" omitted	110.00	110.00
74	A6	10c on 25c	5.50	5.50
75	A6	12c on 30c	4.00	4.00
76	A6	14c on 35c	3.25	3.25
a.		Closed "4"	40.00	40.00
77	A6	16c on 40c	4.00	4.00
79	A6	20c on 50c (Bl)	3.25	3.25
80	A7	30c on 75c (Bl)	9.50	9.50
81	A8	40c on 1fr (Bl)	20.00	20.00
82	A9	80c on 2fr (R)	55.00	55.00
83	A10	2pi on 5fr (R)	80.00	80.00
a.		Triple surch. of new value	675.00	*675.00*
84	A11	4pi on 10fr (R)	200.00	200.00
		Nos. 67-84 (17)	398.90	398.90

KWANGCHOWAN

A Chinese Territory leased to France, 1898 to 1945.

Stamps of Indo-China, 1892-1906, Surcharged in Red or Black

1906 Unwmk. *Perf. 14x13½*

1	A4	1c ol grn (R)	8.00	8.00
2	A4	2c vio brn, *buff*	8.00	8.00
3	A4	4c cl, *bluish* (R)	8.00	8.00
4	A4	5c dp grn (R)	8.00	8.00
5	A4	10c carmine	8.00	8.00
6	A4	15c org brn, *bl*	30.00	30.00
7	A4	20c red, *grn*	12.00	12.00
8	A4	25c deep blue	9.50	9.50
9	A4	30c pale brn	12.00	12.00
10	A4	35c blk, *yel* (R)	20.00	20.00
11	A4	40c blk, *bluish* (R)	20.00	20.00
12	A4	50c bister brn	20.00	20.00
13	A3	75c dp vio, *org* (R)	60.00	60.00
14	A4	1fr pale grn	40.00	40.00
15	A4	2fr brn, *org* (R)	52.50	52.50
16	A3	5fr red lil, *lav*	190.00	190.00
17	A4	10fr org brn, *grn*	240.00	240.00
		Nos. 1-17 (17)	746.00	746.00

Various varieties of the surcharge exist on Nos. 2-10.

Stamps of Indo-China, 1907, Surcharged "KOUANG-TCHEOU" and Value in Chinese in Red or Blue

1908

18	A5	1c ol brn & blk	1.35	1.35
19	A5	2c brn & blk	1.35	1.35
20	A5	4c bl & blk	1.35	1.35
21	A5	5c grn & blk	1.40	1.40
22	A5	10c red & blk (Bl)	1.40	1.40
23	A5	15c vio & blk	3.00	3.00
24	A6	20c vio & blk	5.50	5.50
25	A6	25c bl & blk	6.00	6.00
26	A6	30c brn & blk	8.75	8.75
27	A6	35c ol grn & blk	12.00	12.00
28	A6	40c brn & blk	12.00	12.00
30	A6	50c car & blk (Bl)	13.50	13.50
31	A7	75c ver & blk (Bl)	13.50	13.50
32	A8	1fr car & blk (Bl)	20.00	20.00
33	A9	2fr grn & blk	30.00	30.00
34	A10	5fr bl & blk	65.00	65.00
35	A11	10fr pur & blk	92.50	92.50
a.		Double surcharge	800.00	
b.		Triple surcharge	800.00	
		Nos. 18-35 (17)	288.60	288.60

The Chinese characters overprinted on Nos. 1 to 35 repeat the denomination of the basic stamp.

Nos. 18-35 Surcharged with New Values in Cents or Piasters in Black, Red or Blue

1919

36	A5	2/5c on 1c	.95	.80
37	A5	4/5c on 2c	.95	.80
38	A5	1 3/5c on 4c (R)	.95	.80
39	A5	2c on 5c	1.40	.80
a.		"2 CENTS" inverted	80.00	
40	A5	4c on 10c (Bl)	3.00	2.50
41	A5	6c on 15c	1.60	1.60
42	A6	8c on 20c	4.00	4.00
43	A6	10c on 25c	12.00	12.00
44	A6	12c on 30c	2.75	2.75
45	A6	14c on 35c	2.75	2.75
a.		Closed "4"	40.00	32.50
46	A6	16c on 40c	2.00	2.00
48	A6	20c on 50c (Bl)	2.00	2.00
49	A7	30c on 75c (Bl)	9.50	9.50
50	A8	40c on 1fr (Bl)	9.50	9.50
a.		"40 CENTS" inverted	9.50	9.50
51	A9	80c on 2fr (R)	16.00	16.00
52	A10	2pi on 5fr (R)	160.00	150.00
53	A11	4pi on 10fr (R)	30.00	30.00
		Nos. 36-53 (17)	259.35	247.80

Stamps of Indo-China, 1922-23, Overprinted in Black, Red or Blue

1923

54	A12	1/10c blk & sal (Bl)	.30	.30
55	A12	1/5c dp bl & blk (R)	.30	.30
a.		Black overprint	120.00	
56	A12	2/5c ol brn & blk (R)	.30	.30
57	A12	4/5c brt rose & blk	.45	.45
58	A12	1c yel brn & blk (Bl)	.45	.45
59	A12	2c gray grn & blk (R)	.80	.80
60	A12	3c vio & blk (R)	.80	.80
61	A12	4c org & blk	.95	.95
62	A12	5c car & blk	.95	.95
63	A13	6c dl red & blk	.95	.95
64	A13	7c ol grn & blk	1.35	1.35
65	A13	8c black (R)	2.00	2.00
66	A13	9c yel & blk	2.00	2.00
67	A13	10c bl & blk	1.75	1.75
68	A13	11c vio & blk	1.90	1.90
69	A13	12c brn & blk	1.90	1.90
70	A13	15c org & blk	2.25	2.25
71	A13	20c bl & blk, *straw* (R)	2.25	2.25
72	A13	40c ver & blk, *bluish* (Bl)	2.75	2.75
73	A13	1pi bl grn & blk, *grnsh*	6.50	6.50
74	A13	2pi vio brn & blk, *pnksh* (Bl)	14.00	14.00
		Nos. 54-74 (21)	44.90	44.90

Indo-China Stamps of 1927 Overprinted in Black or Red

1927

75	A14	1/10c lt ol grn (R)	.30	.30
76	A14	1/5c yellow	.30	.30
77	A14	2/5c lt blue (R)	.45	.45
78	A14	4/5c dp brown	.45	.45
79	A14	1c orange	.65	.65
80	A14	2c blue grn (R)	.95	.95
81	A14	3c indigo (R)	.95	.95
82	A14	4c lilac rose	.95	.95
83	A14	5c deep violet	.95	.95
84	A15	6c deep red	.95	.95
85	A15	7c lt brown	.95	.95
86	A15	8c gray grn (R)	1.10	1.10
87	A15	9c red violet	1.25	1.25
88	A15	10c lt bl (R)	1.25	1.25
89	A15	11c orange	1.25	1.25
90	A15	12c myr grn (R)	1.25	1.25
91	A16	15c dl rose & ol brn	2.40	2.40
92	A16	20c vio & sl (R)	2.10	2.10
93	A17	25c org brn & lil rose	2.10	2.10
94	A17	30c dp bl & ol gray (R)	1.35	1.35
95	A18	40c ver & lt bl	1.35	1.35
96	A18	50c lt grn & sl (R)	2.10	2.10
97	A19	1pi dk bl, blk & yel (R)	3.50	3.50
98	A19	2pi red, dp bl & org (R)	4.25	4.25
a.		Double overprint	130.00	
		Nos. 75-98 (24)	33.10	33.10

Stamps of Indo-China, 1931-41, Overprinted in Black or Red

1937-41 *Perf. 13, 13½*

99	A20	1/10c Prus blue	.25	.25
100	A20	1/5c lake	.25	.25
101	A20	2/5c orange red	.40	.40
102	A20	1/2c red brown	.30	.30
103	A20	4/5c dk violet	.30	.30
104	A20	1c black brown	.30	.30
105	A20	2c dk green	.30	.30
a.		Inverted overprint	120.00	

106 A21 3c dk green .75 .75
107 A21 3c yel brn ('41) .30 .30
108 A21 4c dk blue (R) .95 .95
109 A21 4c dk green ('41) .30 .30
110 A21 4c yel org ('41) 2.10 2.10
111 A21 5c dp violet .85 .85
112 A21 5c dp green ('41) .45 .45
113 A21 6c orange red .65 .65
114 A21 7c black (R) ('41) .65 .65
115 A21 8c rose lake ('41) .65 .65
116 A21 9c blk, *yel* (R) ('41) .85 .85
d. Black overprint 8.75 8.75
117 A22 10c dk blue (R) 1.00 1.00
118 A22 10c ultra, *pink* (R) ('41) .75 .75
119 A22 15c dk bl (R) .75 .75
120 A22 18c bl (R) ('41) .45 .45
121 A22 20c rose .75 .75
122 A22 21c olive grn .75 .75
123 A22 22c green ('41) .55 .55
124 A22 25c dp violet 2.75 2.75
125 A22 25c dk bl (R) ('41) .75 .75
126 A22 30c orange brn .75 .75
127 A23 50c dk brown .95 .95
128 A23 60c dl violet .95 .95
129 A23 70c lt bl (R) ('41) .75 .75
130 A23 1pi yel green 1.90 1.90
131 A23 2pi red 2.10 2.10
Nos. 99-131 (33) 26.50 26.50

For types A20-A23 without "RF," see Nos. 137-153.

Common Design Types pictured following the introduction.

Colonial Arts Exhibition Issue
Common Design Type
Souvenir Sheet

1937 Engr. *Imperf.*
132 CD79 30c green & sepia 8.75 10.00

New York World's Fair Issue
Common Design Type

1939 Unwmk. *Perf. 12½x12*
133 CD82 13c carmine lake 1.00 1.00
134 CD82 23c ultramarine 1.00 1.00

Petain Issue
Indo-China Nos. 209-209A Overprinted "KOUANG TCHEOU" in Blue or Red

1941 Engr. *Perf. 12½x12*
135 A27a 10c car lake (B) .65
136 A27a 25c blue (R) .65

Nos. 135-136 were issued by the Vichy government in France, but were not placed on sale in Kwangchowan.

For surcharges, see Nos. B9-B10.

Indo-China Types of 1937-41 without "RF" Overprinted "KOUANG TCHEOU" in Blue or Red

1942-44
137 A20 ⅖c orange red .25
138 A20 ⅓c red brown .25
139 A20 1c black brown .30
140 A20 2c dark green .65
141 A21 3c yellow brown .65
142 A21 4c yellow orange .30
143 A21 5c deep green .45
144 A21 9c black, *yellow* .30
145 A22 10c ultramarine, *pink* (R) .55
146 A22 18c blue (R) 160.00
147 A22 22c green .55
148 A22 30c orange brown .65
149 A23 50c dark brown .55
150 A23 60c dull violet .55
151 A23 70c light blue (R) .75
152 A23 1pi yellow green 1.20
153 A23 2pi red 1.25
Nos. 137-153 (17) 169.20

Nos. 137-153 were issued by the Vichy government in France, but were not placed on sale in Kwangchowan.

SEMI-POSTAL STAMPS

French Revolution Issue
Common Design Type

1939 Unwmk. Photo. *Perf. 13*
Name and Value typo. in Black
B1 CD83 6c + 2c green 8.75 8.75
B2 CD83 7c + 3c brown 8.75 8.75
B3 CD83 9c + 4c red org 8.75 8.75
B4 CD83 13c + 10c rose pink 8.75 8.75
B5 CD83 23c + 20c blue 8.75 8.75
Nos. B1-B5 (5) 43.75 43.75

Indo-China Nos. B19A and B19C Overprinted "KOUANG-TCHEOU" in Blue or Red, and Common Design Type

1941 Photo. *Perf. 13½*
B6 SP1 10c + 10c red (B) .65
B7 CD86 15c + 30c mar & car .85
B8 SP2 25c + 10c blue (R) .65
Nos. B6-B8 (3) 2.15

Nos. B6-B8 were issued by the Vichy government in France, but were not placed on sale in Kwangchowan.

Indo-China Nos. B21A-B21B Overprinted "KOUANG-TCHEOU" in Blue or Red

1944 Engr. *Perf. 12½x12*
B9 A27a 5c + 15c on 25c deep blue (R) .75
B10 A27a + 25c on 10c car lake .75

Colonial Development Fund.

Nos. B9-B10 were issued by the Vichy government in France, but were not placed on sale in Kwangchowan.

AIR POST SEMI-POSTAL STAMPS

Indo-China Nos. CB2-CB4 Overprinted "KOUANG-TCHEOU" in Blue or Red
Methods and Perfs as Before

1942, June 22
CB1 SPAP1 15c + 35c green .85
CB2 SPAP2 20c + 60c brown .85
CB3 SPAP3 30c + 90c car red .85
Nos. CB1-CB3 (3) 2.55

Native children's welfare fund.

Nos. CB1-CB3 were issued by the Vichy government in France, but were not placed on sale in Kwangchowan.

Colonial Education Fund
Indo-China No. CB5 Overprinted "KOUANG-TCHEOU" in Blue or Red
Perf. 12½x13½

1942, June 22 Engr.
CB4 CD86a 12c + 18c blue & red .85

No. CB4 was issued by the Vichy government in France, but was not placed on sale in Kwangchowan.

MONGTSEU (MENGTSZ)

Stamps of Indo-China Surcharged in Black

1903-04 Unwmk. *Perf. 14x13½*
1 A3 1c blk, *lil bl* 7.25 7.25
2 A3 2c brn, *buff* 6.50 6.50
3 A3 4c claret, *lav* 8.00 8.00
4 A3 5c yel grn 5.50 5.50
5 A3 10c red 8.00 8.00
6 A3 15c gray 9.50 9.50
7 A3 20c red, *grn* 11.00 11.00
7C A3 25c blk, *rose* 650.00 650.00
8 A3 25c blue 11.00 11.00
9 A3 30c brn, *bister* 9.00 9.00
10 A3 40c red, *straw* 67.50 67.50
11 A3 50c car, *rose* 400.00 400.00
12 A3 50c brn, *az* ('04) 110.00 110.00
13 A3 75c dp vio, *org* 87.50 87.50
a. "INDO-CHINE" inverted 60,000.
14 A3 1fr brnz grn, *straw* 95.00 95.00
15 A3 5fr red lil, *lav* 100.00 100.00
Nos. 1-15 (16) 1,585. 1,585.

Many Surcharge varieties exist on #1-15.

Stamps of Indo-China, 1892-1906, Surcharged in Red or Black

1906
16 A4 1c ol grn (R) 4.75 4.75
17 A4 2c vio brn, *buff* 4.75 4.75
18 A4 4c cl, *bluish* (R) 4.75 4.75
19 A4 5c dp grn (R) 5.50 5.50
20 A4 10c carmine 4.75 4.75
21 A4 15c org brn, *bl* 30.00 30.00
22 A4 20c red, *grn* 12.00 12.00
23 A4 25c deep blue 9.50 9.50
24 A4 30c pale brn 12.00 12.00
25 A4 35c blk, *yel* (R) 11.00 11.00
26 A4 40c blk, *bluish* (R) 16.00 16.00
27 A4 50c bister brn 20.00 20.00
28 A3 75c dp vio, *org* (R) 60.00 60.00
a. "INDO-CHINE" inverted 60,000.
29 A4 1fr pale grn 40.00 40.00
30 A4 2fr brn, *org* (R) 52.50 52.50
31 A3 5fr red lil, *lav* 120.00 120.00
32 A4 10fr org brn, *grn* 140.00 140.00
a. Chinese characters inverted 1,600. *1,850.*
Nos. 16-32 (17) 547.50 547.50

Inverted varieties of the surcharge exist on Nos. 19, 22 and 32.

Stamps of Indo-China, 1907, Surcharged "MONGTSEU" and Value in Chinese in Red or Blue

1908
33 A5 1c ol brn & blk .95 .95
34 A5 2c brn & blk 1.00 1.00
35 A5 4c bl & blk 1.00 1.00
36 A5 5c grn & blk 1.00 1.00
37 A5 10c red & blk (Bl) 2.40 2.40
38 A5 15c vio & blk 2.40 2.40
39 A6 20c vio & blk 4.75 4.75
40 A6 25c bl & blk 14.00 14.00
41 A6 30c brn & blk 5.50 5.50
42 A6 35c ol grn & blk 6.50 6.50
43 A6 40c brn & blk 4.25 4.25
45 A6 50c car & blk (Bl) 5.50 5.50
46 A7 75c ver & blk (Bl) 12.50 12.50
47 A8 1fr car & blk (Bl) 12.00 12.00
48 A9 2fr grn & blk 17.50 17.50
49 A10 5fr bl & blk 92.50 92.50
50 A11 10fr pur & blk 110.00 110.00
Nos. 33-50 (17) 293.75 293.75

The Chinese characters overprinted on Nos. 1 to 50 repeat the denomination of the basic stamp.

Nos. 33-50 Surcharged with New Values in Cents or Piasters in Black, Red or Blue

1919
51 A5 ⅖c on 1c 1.35 1.35
52 A5 ⅘c on 2c 1.45 1.45
53 A5 1⅗c on 4c 1.60 1.60
54 A5 2c on 5c 1.35 1.35
55 A5 4c on 10c (Bl) 2.40 2.40
56 A5 6c on 15c 2.60 2.60
57 A6 8c on 20c 5.50 5.50
58 A6 10c on 25c 4.50 4.50
59 A6 12c on 30c 4.50 4.50
60 A6 14c on 35c 2.75 2.75
a. Closed "4" 16.00 16.00
61 A6 16c on 40c 3.75 3.75
63 A6 20c on 50c (Bl) 4.25 4.25
64 A7 30c on 75c (Bl) 8.00 8.00
65 A8 40c on 1fr (Bl) 8.00 8.00
66 A9 80c on 2fr (R) 8.00 8.00
a. Triple surch., one inverted 475.00 475.00
67 A10 2pi on 5fr (R) 160.00 160.00
a. Triple surch., one inverted 475.00 475.00
b. Double surcharge 800.00 800.00
68 A11 4pi on 10fr (R) 27.50 27.50
Nos. 51-68 (17) 247.50 247.50

PAKHOI

Stamps of Indo-China Surcharged in Black

1903-04 Unwmk. *Perf. 14x13½*
1 A3 1c blk, *lil bl* 6.00 6.00
2 A3 2c brn, *buff* 5.25 5.25
3 A3 4c claret, *lav* 5.25 5.25
4 A3 5c yel grn 4.00 4.00
5 A3 10c red 4.50 4.50
6 A3 15c gray 4.50 4.50
7 A3 20c red, *grn* 9.50 9.50
8 A3 25c blue 7.50 7.50
9 A3 25c blk, *rose*('04) 6.00 6.00
10 A3 30c brn, *bister* 7.25 7.25
11 A3 40c red, *straw* 50.00 50.00
12 A3 50c car, *rose* 310.00 310.00
13 A3 50c brn, *az* ('04) 45.00 45.00
14 A3 75c dp vio, *org* 60.00 60.00
a. "INDO-CHINE" inverted 45,000.
15 A3 1fr brnz grn, *straw* 60.00 60.00
16 A3 5fr red lil, *lav* 120.00 120.00
Nos. 1-16 (16) 704.75 704.75

Many varieties of the surcharge exist.

Stamps of Indo-China 1892-1906, Surcharged in Red or Black

1906
17 A4 1c ol grn (R) 8.00 8.00
18 A4 2c vio brn, *buff* 8.00 8.00
19 A4 4c cl, *bluish* (R) 8.00 8.00
20 A4 5c dp grn (R) 8.00 8.00
21 A4 10c carmine 8.00 8.00
22 A4 15c org brn,*bl* 30.00 30.00
23 A4 20c red, *grn* 12.00 12.00
24 A4 25c deep blue 9.50 9.50
25 A4 30c pale brn 12.00 12.00
26 A4 35c blk, *yel* (R) 20.00 20.00
27 A4 40c blk, *bluish*(R) 20.00 20.00
28 A4 50c bister brn 20.00 20.00
29 A3 75c dp vio, *org* (R) 60.00 60.00
30 A4 1fr pale grn 40.00 40.00
31 A4 2fr brn, *org*(R) 52.50 52.50
32 A3 5fr red lil, *lav* 120.00 120.00
33 A4 10fr org brn, *grn* 140.00 140.00
Nos. 17-33 (17) 576.00 576.00

Various surcharge varieties exist on #17-24.

Stamps of Indo-China, 1907, Surcharged "PAKHOI" and Value in Chinese in Red or Blue

1908
34 A5 1c ol brn & blk .80 .80
35 A5 2c brn & blk .80 .80
36 A5 4c bl & blk .80 .80
37 A5 5c grn & blk 1.25 1.25
38 A5 10c red & blk (Bl) 1.25 1.25
39 A5 15c vio & blk 1.75 1.75
40 A6 20c vio & blk 1.75 1.75
41 A6 25c bl & blk 2.40 2.40
42 A6 30c brn & blk 3.00 3.00
43 A6 35c ol grn & blk 3.00 3.00
44 A6 40c brn & blk 3.00 3.00
46 A6 50c car & blk (Bl) 3.00 3.00
47 A7 75c ver & blk (Bl) 5.40 5.40
48 A8 1fr car & blk (Bl) 6.75 6.75
49 A9 2fr grn & blk 15.00 15.00
50 A10 5fr bl & blk 75.00 75.00
51 A11 10fr pur & blk 130.00 130.00
Nos. 34-51 (17) 254.95 254.95

The Chinese characters overprinted on Nos. 1 to 51 repeat the denomination of the basic stamps.

Nos. 34-51 Surcharged with New Values in Cents or Piasters in Black, Red or Blue

1919
52 A5 ⅖c on 1c .80 .80
a. "PAK-HOI" and Chinese double 150.00
53 A5 ⅘c on 2c .80 .80
54 A5 1⅗c on 4c (R) .80 .80
55 A5 2c on 5c 2.00 2.00
56 A5 4c on 10c (Bl) 3.00 3.00
57 A5 6c on 15c 1.35 1.35
58 A6 8c on 20c 3.00 3.00
59 A6 10c on 25c 3.75 3.75
60 A6 12c on 30c 1.35 1.35
a. "12 CENTS" double 550.00
61 A6 14c on 35c .95 .95
a. Closed "4" 12.00 12.00
62 A6 16c on 40c 2.40 2.40
64 A6 20c on 50c (Bl) 1.80 1.80
65 A7 30c on 75c (Bl) 8.00 8.00
66 A8 40c on 1fr (Bl) 10.00 10.00
67 A9 80c on 2fr (R) 9.25 9.25
68 A10 2pi on 5fr (R) 14.00 14.00
69 A11 4pi on 10fr (R) 32.50 32.50
Nos. 52-69 (17) 95.75 95.75

TCHONGKING (CHUNGKING)

Stamps of Indo-China Surcharged in Black

1903-04 Unwmk. *Perf. 14x13½*
1 A3 1c blk, *lil bl* 4.00 4.00
2 A3 2c brn, *buff* 4.00 4.00
3 A3 4c claret, *lav* 4.75 4.75
4 A3 5c yel grn 4.75 4.75
5 A3 10c red 4.75 4.75
6 A3 15c gray 4.75 4.75
7 A3 20c red, *grn* 7.25 7.25
8 A3 25c blue 47.50 47.50
9 A3 25c blk, *rose* ('04) 8.75 8.75
10 A3 30c brn, *bister* 12.50 12.50
11 A3 40c red, *straw* 52.50 52.50
12 A3 50c car, *rose* 200.00 200.00
13 A3 50c brn, *az* ('04) 110.00 110.00

14	A3	75c vio, *org*	40.00	40.00
15	A3	1fr brnz grn, *straw*	52.50	52.50
16	A3	5fr red lil, *lav*	92.50	92.50
		Nos. 1-16 (16)	650.50	650.50

Many surcharge varieties exist on #1-14.

Stamps of Indo-China and French China, issued in 1902 with similar overprint, but without Chinese characters, were not officially authorized.

Stamps of Indo-China, 1892-1906, Surcharged in Red or Black

1906

17	A4	1c ol grn (R)	8.00	8.00
18	A4	2c vio brn, *buff*	8.00	8.00
19	A4	4c cl, *bluish* (R)	8.00	8.00
20	A4	5c dp grn (R)	8.00	8.00
21	A4	10c carmine	8.00	8.00
22	A4	15c org brn, *bl*	30.00	30.00
23	A4	20c red, *grn*	12.00	12.00
24	A4	25c deep blue	9.50	9.50
25	A4	30c pale brn	12.00	12.00
26	A4	35c blk, *yellow* (R)	20.00	20.00
27	A4	40c blk, *bluish* (R)	20.00	20.00
28	A4	50c bis brn	20.00	20.00
29	A3	75c dp vio, *org* (R)	60.00	60.00
30	A4	1fr pale grn	40.00	40.00
31	A4	2fr brn, *org* (R)	52.50	52.50
32	A3	5fr red lil, *lav*	120.00	120.00
33	A4	10fr org brn, *grn*	140.00	140.00
		Nos. 17-33 (17)	576.00	576.00

Variety "T" omitted in surcharge occurs once in each sheet of Nos. 17-33. Other surcharge varieties exist, such as inverted surcharge on 1c and 2c.

Stamps of Indo-China, 1907, Surcharged "TCHONGKING" and Value in Chinese in Red or Blue

1908

34	A5	1c ol brn & blk	.55	.55
35	A5	2c brn & blk	.80	.80
36	A5	4c bl & blk	1.00	1.00
37	A5	5c grn & blk	1.60	1.60
38	A5	10c red & blk (Bl)	1.60	1.60
39	A5	15c vio & blk	2.40	2.40
40	A6	20c vio & blk	2.40	2.40
41	A6	25c bl & blk	4.50	4.50
42	A6	30c brn & blk	2.75	2.75
43	A6	35c ol grn & blk	6.50	6.50
44	A6	40c brn & blk	12.00	12.00
45	A6	50c car & blk (Bl)	9.50	9.50
46	A7	75c ver & blk (Bl)	8.00	8.00
47	A8	1fr car & blk (Bl)	12.00	12.00
48	A9	2fr grn & blk	80.00	80.00
49	A10	5fr bl & blk	35.00	35.00
50	A11	10fr pur & blk	200.00	200.00
		Nos. 34-50 (17)	380.60	380.60

The Chinese characters overprinted on Nos. 1 to 50 repeat the denomination of the basic stamp.

Nos. 34-50 Surcharged with New Values in Cents or Piasters in Black, Red or Blue

1919

51	A5	2/5c on 1c	1.00	.95
52	A5	4/5c on 2c	1.00	.95
53	A5	1 3/5c on 4c (R)	1.00	.95
54	A5	2c on 5c	1.35	1.35
55	A5	4c on 10c (Bl)	1.00	.95
56	A5	6c on 15c	1.25	1.20
57	A6	8c on 20c	2.50	.95
58	A6	10c on 25c	7.25	6.50
59	A6	12c on 30c	2.40	1.20
60	A6	14c on 35c	1.60	1.60
a.		Closed "4"	27.50	27.50
61	A6	16c on 40c	1.80	1.80
a.		"16 CENTS" double	110.00	110.00
62	A6	20c on 50c (Bl)	9.50	8.00
63	A7	30c on 75c (Bl)	8.00	5.75
64	A8	40c on 1fr (Bl)	8.00	6.00
65	A9	80c on 2fr (R)	8.00	5.50
66	A10	2pi on 5fr (R)	8.00	8.00
67	A11	4pi on 10fr (R)	16.00	16.00
		Nos. 51-67 (17)	79.65	67.65

YUNNAN FOU

(Formerly Yunnan Sen, later known as Kunming)

Stamps of Indo-China Surcharged in Black

1903-04		Unwmk.	*Perf. 14x13½*	
1	A3	1c blk, *lil bl*	6.00	6.00
2	A3	2c brn, *buff*	6.00	6.00
3	A3	4c claret, *lav*	6.75	6.75
4	A3	5c yel green	6.00	6.00
5	A3	10c red	6.75	6.75
6	A3	15c gray	6.75	6.75
7	A3	20c red, *grn*	10.00	10.00
8	A3	25c blue	6.00	6.00
9	A3	30c brn, *bister*	10.00	10.00
10	A3	40c red, *straw*	70.00	50.00
11	A3	50c car, *rose*	330.00	320.00
12	A3	50c brn, *az* ('04)	160.00	160.00
13	A3	75c dp vio, *org*	55.00	52.50
a.		"INDO-CHINE" inverted	*45,000.*	
14	A3	1fr brnz grn, *straw*	55.00	52.50
15	A3	5fr red lil, *lav*	110.00	110.00
		Nos. 1-15 (15)	844.25	809.25

The Chinese characters overprinted on Nos. 1 to 15 repeat the denomination of the basic stamp.

Many varieties of the surcharge exist.

Stamps of Indo-China, 1892-1906, Surcharged in Red or Black

1906		Unwmk.	*Perf. 14x13½*	
17	A4	1c ol grn (R)	4.75	4.75
18	A4	2c vio brn, *buff*	4.75	4.75
19	A4	4c cl, *bluish* (R)	4.75	4.75
20	A4	5c dp grn (R)	4.75	4.75
21	A4	10c carmine	4.75	4.75
22	A4	15c org brn, *bl*	30.00	30.00
23	A4	20c red, *grn*	12.00	12.00
24	A4	25c deep blue	9.50	9.50
25	A4	30c pale brn	12.00	12.00
26	A4	35c blk, *yel* (R)	16.00	16.00
27	A4	40c blk, *bluish* (R)	16.00	16.00
28	A4	50c bister brn	16.00	16.00
29	A3	75c dp vio, *org* (R)	60.00	60.00
30	A4	1fr pale grn	40.00	40.00
31	A4	2fr brn, *org* (R)	52.50	52.50
32	A3	5fr red lil, *lav*	120.00	120.00
33	A4	10fr org brn, *grn*	140.00	140.00
		Nos. 17-33 (17)	547.75	547.75

Various varieties of the surcharge exist on Nos. 18, 20, 21 and 27.

Stamps of Indo-China, 1907, Surcharged "YUNNANFOU," and Value in Chinese in Red or Blue

1908

34	A5	1c ol brn & blk	.95	.95
35	A5	2c brn & blk	1.20	1.20
36	A5	4c bl & blk	1.40	1.40
37	A5	5c grn & blk	2.40	2.40
38	A5	10c red & blk (Bl)	2.40	2.40
39	A5	15c vio & blk	5.50	5.50
40	A6	20c vio & blk	5.25	5.25
41	A6	25c bl & blk	8.00	8.00
42	A6	30c brn & blk	6.50	6.50
43	A6	35c ol grn & blk	6.50	6.50
44	A6	40c brn & blk	7.25	7.25
45	A6	50c car & blk (Bl)	8.00	8.00
46	A7	75c ver & blk (Bl)	8.75	8.75
47	A8	1fr car & blk (Bl)	13.50	13.50
48	A9	2fr grn & blk	22.50	22.50
a.		"YUNANNFOU"	2,200.	2,200.
49	A10	5fr bl & blk	52.50	52.50
a.		"YUNANNFOU"	2,200.	2,200.
50	A11	10fr pur & blk	100.00	100.00
a.		"YUNANNFOU"	2,200.	2,200.
		Nos. 34-50 (17)	252.60	252.60

The Chinese characters overprinted on Nos. 17-50 repeat the denomination of the basic stamp.

Nos. 34-50 Surcharged with New Values in Cents or Piasters in Black, Red or Blue

1919

51	A5	2/5c on 1c	.95	.95
a.		New value double	120.00	
52	A5	4/5c on 2c	1.20	1.20
53	A5	1 3/5c on 4c (R)	1.20	1.20
54	A5	2c on 5c	1.75	1.75
a.		Triple surcharge	180.00	
55	A5	4c on 10c (Bl)	1.25	1.25
56	A5	6c on 15c	2.40	2.40
57	A6	8c on 20c	1.60	1.60
58	A6	10c on 25c	3.25	3.25
59	A6	12c on 30c	8.00	8.00
60	A6	14c on 35c	12.50	12.50
a.		Closed "4"	120.00	120.00
61	A6	16c on 40c	8.00	8.00
62	A6	20c on 50c (Bl)	1.60	1.60
63	A7	30c on 75c (Bl)	8.00	8.00
64	A8	40c on 1fr (Bl)	32.50	32.50
65	A9	80c on 2fr (R)	12.00	12.00
a.		Triple surch., one inverted	225.00	
66	A10	2pi on 5fr (R)	60.00	60.00
67	A11	4pi on 10fr (R)	32.50	32.50
		Nos. 51-67 (17)	188.70	188.70

OFFICES IN CRETE

Austria, France, Italy and Great Britain maintained their own post offices in Crete during the period when that country was an autonomous state.

100 Centimes = 1 Franc

Liberty, Equality and Fraternity
A1

"Rights of Man"
A2

Liberty and Peace (Symbolized by Olive Branch)
A3

Perf. 14x13½

1902-03		Unwmk.		Typo.
1	A1	1c gray	2.00	2.00
2	A1	2c violet brown	2.00	2.00
3	A1	3c red orange	2.00	2.00
4	A1	4c yellow brown	2.00	2.00
5	A1	5c green	2.00	2.00
6	A2	10c rose red	2.40	2.00
7	A2	15c pale red ('03)	3.25	2.40
8	A2	20c brown vio ('03)	4.00	3.25
9	A2	25c blue ('03)	5.50	3.25
10	A2	30c lilac ('03)	5.50	3.25
11	A3	40c red & pale bl	11.00	9.50
12	A3	50c bis brn & lav	16.00	11.00
13	A3	1fr claret & ol grn	20.00	18.00
14	A3	2fr gray vio & yel	32.50	27.50
15	A3	5fr dk blue & buff	52.50	47.50
		Nos. 1-15 (15)	162.65	137.65

A4

A5

Black Surcharge

1903

16	A4	1pi on 25c blue	47.50	40.00
17	A5	2pi on 50c bis brn & lav	67.50	52.50
18	A5	4pi on 1fr claret & ol grn	105.00	92.50
19	A5	8pi on 2fr gray vio & yel	120.00	120.00
20	A5	20pi on 5fr dk bl & buff	200.00	195.00
		Nos. 16-20 (5)	540.00	500.00

OFFICES IN EGYPT

French post offices formerly maintained in Alexandria and Port Said.

100 Centimes = 1 Franc

ALEXANDRIA

Stamps of France Overprinted in Red, Blue or Black

1899-1900		Unwmk.	*Perf. 14x13½*	
1	A15	1c blk, *lil bl* (R)	2.00	2.00
a.		Double overprint	140.00	
b.		Triple overprint	160.00	
2	A15	2c brn, *buff* (Bl)	2.75	2.40
3	A15	3c gray, *grysh* (Bl)	2.75	2.40
4	A15	4c cl, *lav* (Bl)	3.25	2.75
5	A15	5c yel grn, (I) (R)	5.50	3.25
a.		Type II (R)	140.00	92.50
6	A15	10c blk, *lav*, (I) (R)	8.00	6.50
a.		Type II (R)	55.00	32.50
7	A15	15c blue (R)	8.00	3.50
8	A15	20c red, *grn*	13.00	7.25
a.		Double overprint		
9	A15	25c blk, *rose* (R)	6.50	3.50
a.		Inverted overprint	87.50	
b.		Double ovpt., one invtd.	140.00	
10	A15	30c brn, *bis*	14.00	10.00
11	A15	40c red, *straw*	12.00	12.00
12	A15	50c car, *rose* (II)	30.00	16.00
a.		Type I	140.00	24.00
13	A15	1fr brnz grn, *straw*	29.00	21.00
14	A15	2fr brn, *az* ('00)	75.00	75.00
15	A15	5fr red lil, *lav*	110.00	100.00
		Nos. 1-15 (15)	321.75	267.55

A2

A3

A4

1902-03

16	A2	1c gray	.65	.40
17	A2	2c violet brn	.65	.55
18	A2	3c red orange	.65	.55
19	A2	4c yellow brn	.90	.80
20	A2	5c green	4.00	3.75
21	A3	10c rose red	1.25	.75
22	A3	15c orange	1.50	1.00
a.		15c pale red ('03)	3.90	1.20
23	A3	20c brn vio ('03)	2.40	1.40
24	A3	25c blue ('03)	1.40	.65
25	A3	30c violet ('03)	6.50	4.00
26	A4	40c red & pale bl	4.25	2.00
27	A4	50c bis brn & lav	8.75	2.50
28	A4	1fr cl & ol grn	8.00	3.50
29	A4	2fr gray vio & yel	20.00	10.00
30	A4	5fr dk bl & buff	24.00	15.00
		Nos. 16-30 (15)	84.90	46.85

The 2c, 5c, 10c, 20c and 25c exist imperf. Value, each $45.

See #77-86. For surcharges see #31-73, B1-B4.

Stamps of 1902-03 Surcharged Locally in Black

1921

31	A2	2m on 5c green	6.50	4.00
32	A2	3m on 3c red org	12.00	9.50
a.		Larger numeral	120.00	100.00
33	A3	4m on 10c rose	5.50	4.75
34	A2	5m on 1c dk gray	12.00	9.50
35	A2	5m on 4c yel brn	16.00	11.00
36	A3	6m on 15c orange	5.50	4.75
a.		Larger numeral	100.00	100.00
37	A3	8m on 20c brn vio	6.50	4.75
a.		Larger numeral	72.50	52.50
38	A3	10m on 25c blue	4.00	4.00
a.		Inverted surcharge	40.00	40.00
b.		Double surcharge	40.00	40.00
39	A3	12m on 30c vio	14.00	14.00
40	A2	15m on 2c vio brn	12.00	12.00

Nos. 26-30 Surcharged

41	A4	15m on 40c	20.00	16.00
42	A4	15m on 50c	9.50	8.75
43	A4	30m on 1fr	140.00	140.00
44	A4	60m on 2fr	225.00	225.00
a.		Larger numeral	800.00	800.00
45	A4	150m on 5fr	300.00	300.00

Port Said Nos. 20 and 19 Surcharged like Nos. 32 and 40

45A	A2	3m on 3c red org	125.00	125.00
46	A2	15m on 2c vio brn	125.00	125.00
		Nos. 31-46 (17)	1,038.	1,018.

Alexandria No. 28 Surcharged with Two New Values

1921
46A A4 30m on 15m on 1fr 1,100. *1,200.*

The surcharge "15 Mill." was made in error and is canceled by a bar.
The surcharges were lithographed on Nos. 31, 33, 38, 39 and 42 and typographed on the other stamps of the 1921 issue. Nos. 34, 36 and 37 were surcharged by both methods.

Alexandria Stamps of 1902-03 Surcharged in Paris

1921-23
47 A2 1m on 1c gray 2.75 2.10
48 A2 2m on 5c green 2.10 1.75
49 A3 4m on 10c rose 2.75 2.40
50 A3 4m on 10c green ('23) 2.00 2.00
51 A2 5m on 3c red org ('23) 6.00 4.25
52 A3 6m on 15c orange 1.80 1.50
53 A3 8m on 20c brn vio 2.00 .95
54 A3 10m on 25c blue 1.20 1.10
55 A3 10m on 30c vio 3.25 2.75
56 A3 15m on 50c bl ('23) 2.75 2.75

Nos. 27-30 and Type of 1902 Surcharged

57 A4 15m on 50c 4.50 2.75
58 A4 30m on 1fr 3.50 2.25
59 A4 60m on 2fr *2,000.* *2,200.*
60 A4 60m on 2fr org & pale bl ('23) 10.00 10.00
61 A4 150m on 5fr 12.00 8.00
Nos. 47-58,60-61 (14) 56.60 44.55

Stamps and Types of 1902-03 Surcharged with New Values and Bars in Black

1925
62 A2 1m on 1c gray 1.00 1.00
63 A2 2m on 5c orange 1.00 1.00
64 A2 2m on 5c green 1.30 1.30
65 A3 4m on 10c green .95 .80
66 A2 5m on 3c red org 1.25 1.00
67 A3 6m on 15c orange 1.10 .95
68 A3 8m on 20c brn vio 1.40 1.20
69 A3 10m on 25c blue .85 .75
70 A3 15m on 50c blue 1.90 1.20
71 A4 30m on 1fr cl & ol grn 3.00 2.40
72 A4 60m on 2fr org & pale bl 3.50 3.25
73 A4 150m on 5fr dk bl & buff 5.00 4.00
Nos. 62-73 (12) 22.25 18.85

Types of 1902-03 Issue

1927-28
77 A2 3m orange ('28) 2.00 1.60
81 A3 15m slate blue 2.00 1.60
82 A3 20m rose lil ('28) 5.50 4.00
84 A4 50m org & blue 9.50 8.00
85 A4 100m sl bl & buff 12.00 10.00
86 A4 250m gray grn & red 21.00 14.00
Nos. 77-86 (6) 52.00 39.20

SEMI-POSTAL STAMPS

Regular Issue of 1902-03 Surcharged in Carmine

1915 **Unwmk.** ***Perf. 14x13½***
B1 A3 10c + 5c rose 1.10 1.10

Sinking Fund Issue

Type of 1902-03 Issue Surcharged in Blue or Black

1927-30
B2 A3 15m + 5m deep org 4.75 4.75
B3 A3 15m + 5m red vio ('28) 8.00 8.00
a. 15m + 5m violet ('30) 12.00 12.00

Type of 1902-03 Issue Surcharged as in 1927-28

1929
B4 A3 15m + 5m fawn 9.50 9.50

POSTAGE DUE STAMPS

Postage Due Stamps of France, 1893-1920, Surcharged in Paris in Black

1922 **Unwmk.** ***Perf. 14x13½***
J1 D2 2m on 5c blue 2.00 2.00
J2 D2 4m on 10c brown 2.00 2.00
J3 D2 10m on 30c rose red 2.40 2.40
J4 D2 15m on 50c brn vio 2.75 2.75
J5 D2 30m on 1fr red brn, *straw* 4.00 4.00
Nos. J1-J5 (5) 13.15 13.15

D3

1928 **Typo.**
J6 D3 1m slate 1.60 1.60
J7 D3 2m light blue 1.00 1.00
J8 D3 4m lilac rose 1.60 1.60
J9 D3 5m gray green 1.75 1.75
J10 D3 10m light red 2.10 2.10
J11 D3 20m violet brn 1.90 1.90
J12 D3 30m green 4.50 4.50
J13 D3 40m lt violet 4.75 4.75
Nos. J6-J13 (8) 19.20 19.20

#J6-J13 were also available for use in Port Said.

PORT SAID

Stamps of France Overprinted in Red, Blue or Black

1899-1900 **Unwmk.** ***Perf. 14x13½***
1 A15 1c blk, *lil bl* (R) 1.60 1.10
2 A15 2c brn, *buff* (bl) 1.60 1.25
3 A15 3c gray, *grysh* (Bl) 1.60 1.60
4 A15 4c claret, *lav* (Bl) 1.60 1.60
5 A15 5c yel grn (I) (R) 8.00 4.00
a. Type II (R) 45.00 14.00
6 A15 10c blk, *lav* (I) (R) 12.00 12.00
a. Type II (R) 60.00 47.50
7 A15 15c blue (R) 12.00 8.00
8 A15 20c red, *grn* 13.50 10.00
9 A15 25c blk, *rose* (R) 12.00 4.00
a. Double overprint 240.00
b. Inverted overprint 240.00
10 A15 30c brn, *bister* 13.50 12.00
a. Inverted overprint 240.00
11 A15 40c red, *straw* 12.00 12.00
12 A15 50c car, *rose* (II) 18.00 12.00
a. Type I 280.00 100.00
b. Double overprint (II) 340.00
13 A15 1fr brnz grn, *straw* 27.50 16.00
14 A15 2fr brn, *az* ('00) 67.50 60.00
15 A15 5fr red lil, *lav* 110.00 87.50
Nos. 1-15 (15) 312.40 243.05

Regular Issue Surcharged in Red

1899
16 A15 25c on 10c blk, *lav* 120.00 27.50
a. Inverted surcharge 225.00

With Additional Surcharge "25" in Red

17 A15 25c on 10c blk, *lav* 440.00 160.00
a. "25" inverted 1,400. 1,200.
b. "25" in black 2,400.
c. As "b," "VINGT CINQ" inverted 3,000.
d. As "b," "25" vertical 3,000.
e. As "c" and "d" 3,000.

A2

A3

A4

1902-03 **Typo.**
18a A2 1c gray .65 .65
19 A2 2c violet brn .65 .65
20 A2 3c red orange .75 .65
21 A2 4c yellow brown 1.00 .80
22 A2 5c blue green 1.10 .80
a. 5c yellow green 4.00 2.75
23 A3 10c rose red 1.50 1.10
24 A3 15c pale red ('03) 2.75 1.80
a. 15c orange 4.00 2.40
25 A3 20c brn vio ('03) 2.75 2.00
26 A3 25c blue ('03) 2.25 1.40
27 A3 30c violet ('03) 5.50 4.50
28 A4 40c red & pale bl 5.25 3.50
29 A4 50c bis brn & lav 8.00 6.50
30 A4 1fr claret & ol grn 10.00 8.25
31 A4 2fr gray vio & yel 13.50 13.50
32 A4 5fr dk bl & buff 32.50 27.50
Nos. 18a-32 (15) 88.15 73.60

See #83-92. For surcharges see #33-80, B1-B4.

Stamps of 1902-03 Surcharged Locally

1921
33 A2 2m on 5c green 8.00 8.00
a. Inverted surcharge 40.00 40.00
34 A3 4m on 10c rose 7.25 7.25
a. Inverted surcharge 40.00 40.00
35 A2 5m on 1c 9.50 9.50
a. Inverted surcharge 65.00 65.00
c. Surcharged "2 Milliemes" 47.50 47.50
36 A2 5m on 2c 15.00 15.00
a. Surcharged "2 Milliemes" 60.00 60.00
b. As "a," inverted 140.00 140.00
37 A2 5m on 3c 12.50 12.50
a. Inverted surcharge 47.50 47.50
b. On Alexandria #18 340.00 340.00
38 A2 5m on 4c 8.75 8.75
a. Inverted surcharge 65.00 65.00
39 A2 10m on 2c 15.00 15.00
40 A2 10m on 4c 27.50 27.50
a. Inverted surcharge 80.00 80.00
41 A3 10m on 25c 7.25 7.25
a. Inverted surcharge 60.00 60.00
42 A3 12m on 30c 32.50 32.50
43 A2 15m on 4c 8.00 8.00
a. Inverted surcharge 67.50 67.50
44 A3 15m on 15c pale red 47.50 47.50
a. Inverted surcharge 120.00 120.00
45 A3 15m on 20c 47.50 47.50
a. Inverted surcharge 120.00 120.00
46 A4 30m on 50c 260.00 260.00
47 A4 60m on 50c 300.00 300.00
48 A4 150m on 50c 340.00 340.00

Nos. 46, 47 and 48 have a bar between the numerals and "Millièmes," which is in capital letters.

Same Surcharge on Stamps of French Offices in Turkey, 1902-03

49 A2 2m on 2c vio brn 140.00 140.00
50 A2 5m on 1c gray 120.00 120.00
a. "5" inverted 6,750.
Nos. 33-50 (18) 1,406. 1,406.

Nos. 28-32 Surcharged

51 A4 15m on 40c 52.50 52.50
52 A4 15m on 50c 72.50 72.50
b. Bar below 15 45.00 45.00
53 A4 30m on 1fr 250.00 250.00
54 A4 60m on 2fr 67.50 67.50
55 A4 150m on 5fr 225.00 225.00
Nos. 51-55 (5) 667.50 667.50

Overprinted "MILLtEMES"

51a A4 15m on 40c 350.00 350.00
52a A4 15m on 50c 400.00 400.00
53a A4 30m on 1fr 1,200. 1,200.
54a A4 60m on 2fr 340.00 340.00
55a A4 150m on 5fr 925.00 925.00
Nos. 51a-55a (5) 3,215. 3,215.

Stamps of 1902-03 Surcharged in Paris

1921-23
56 A2 1m on 1c gray 1.10 1.10
57 A2 2m on 5c green 1.10 1.10
58 A3 4m on 10c rose 2.10 2.10
59 A2 5m on 3c red org 7.50 7.50
60 A3 6m on 15c orange 3.25 3.25
a. 6m on 15c pale red 12.00 12.00
61 A3 8m on 20c brn vio 4.00 4.00
62 A3 10m on 25c blue 2.40 2.40
63 A3 10m on 30c violet 6.50 6.50
64 A3 15m on 50c blue 5.50 5.50

Nos. 29-32 and Type of 1902 Surcharged

65 A4 15m on 50c 5.00 5.00
66 A4 30m on 1fr 8.00 8.00
67 A4 60m on 2fr 120.00 120.00
68 A4 60m on 2fr org & pale blue 11.00 11.00
69 A4 150m on 5fr 16.00 16.00
Nos. 56-69 (14) 193.45 193.45

Stamps and Types of 1902-03 Surcharged with New Values and Bars

1925
70 A2 1m on 1c gray .75 .75
71 A2 2m on 5c green 1.00 1.00
72 A3 4m on 10c rose red .85 .85
73 A2 5m on 3c red org 1.00 1.00
74 A3 6m on 15c orange 1.00 1.00
75 A3 8m on 20c brn vio .95 .95
76 A3 10m on 25c blue 1.40 1.40
77 A3 15m on 50c blue 1.60 1.60
78 A4 30m on 1fr cl & ol grn 2.50 2.50
79 A4 60m on 2fr org & pale blue 2.25 2.25
80 A4 150m on 5fr dk bl & buff 3.00 3.00
Nos. 70-80 (11) 16.30 16.30

Types of 1902-03 Issue

1927-28
83 A2 3m orange ('28) 1.50 1.50
87 A3 15m slate bl 1.80 1.80
88 A3 20m rose lil ('28) 2.25 2.25
90 A4 50m org & blue 4.00 4.00
91 A4 100m slate bl & buff 4.75 4.75
92 A4 250m gray grn & red 8.00 8.00
Nos. 83-92 (6) 22.30 22.30

SEMI-POSTAL STAMPS

Regular Issue of 1902-03 Surcharged in Carmine

1915 **Unwmk.** ***Perf. 14x13½***
B1 A3 10c + 5c rose 1.20 1.20

Sinking Fund Issue

Type of 1902-03 Issue Surcharged like Alexandria Nos. B2-B3 in Blue or Black

1927-30

B2	A3	15m + 5m dp org (Bl)	4.75	4.75
B3	A3	15m + 5m red vio ('28)	8.00	8.00
a.		15m + 5m violet ('30)	12.00	12.00
B4	A3	15m + 5m fawn ('29)	9.50	9.50
		Nos. B2-B4 (3)	22.25	22.25

POSTAGE DUE STAMPS

Postage Due Stamps of France, 1893-1906, Surcharged Locally in Black

15

Millièmes

1921 Unwmk. *Perf. 14x13½*

J1	D2	12m on 10c brown	52.50	55.00
J2	D2	15m on 5c blue	80.00	87.50
J3	D2	30m on 20c ol grn	80.00	87.50
a.		Inverted surcharge	1,000.	1,000.
J4	D2	30m on 50c red vio	3,000.	3,400.

Same Surcharged in Red or Blue

1921

J5	D2	2m on 5c bl (R)	47.50	52.50
a.		Blue surcharge	275.00	275.00
J6	D2	4m on 10c brn (Bl)	47.50	52.50
a.		Surcharged "15 Milliemes"	650.00	650.00
J7	D2	10m on 30c red (Bl)	47.50	52.50
a.		Inverted surcharge	140.00	140.00
J8	D2	15m on 50c brn vio (Bl)	60.00	65.00
a.		Inverted surcharge	140.00	140.00
		Nos. J5-J8 (4)	8.20	8.20

Nos. J5-J8 exist with second "M" in "Milliemes" inverted, also with final "S" omitted. Value, each $150-$175.

Alexandria Nos. J6-J13 were also available for use in Port Said.

OFFICES IN TURKEY

Various powers maintained post offices in the Turkish Empire before World War I by authority of treaties which ended with the signing of the Treaty of Lausanne in 1923. The foreign post offices were closed Oct. 27, 1923.

100 Centimes = 1 Franc

25 Centimes = 40 Paras = 1 Piaster

2ovpt

Stamps of France Surcharged in Black or Red

1885-1901 Unwmk. *Perf. 14x13½*

1	A15	1pi on 25c yel, *straw*	460.00	12.00
a.		Inverted surcharge	2,250.	2,100.
2	A15	1pi on 25c blk, *rose* (R) ('86)	3.50	.95
a.		Inverted surcharge	350.00	300.00
3	A15	2pi on 50c car, *rose* (II) ('90)	16.00	2.40
a.		Type I ('01)	325.00	45.00
4	A15	3pi on 75c car, *rose*	24.00	12.00
5	A1	4pi on 1fr brnz grn, *straw*	24.00	12.00
6	A15	8pi on 2fr brn, *az* ('00)	32.50	20.00
7	A15	20pi on 5fr red lil, *lav* ('90)	95.00	52.50
		Nos. 1-7 (7)	655.00	111.85

A2

A3

A4

A5

A6

1902-07 Typo. *Perf. 14x13½*

21	A2	1c gray	.65	.65
22	A2	2c vio brn	.65	.65
23	A2	3c red org	.65	.65
24	A2	4c yel brn	2.40	1.00
a.		Imperf., pair	80.00	
25	A2	5c grn ('06)	.95	.65
26	A3	10c rose red	.95	.65
27	A3	15c pale red ('03)	2.40	1.20
28	A3	20c brn vio ('03)	3.00	1.90
29	A3	25c blue ('07)	40.00	*47.50*
a.		Imperf., pair	360.00	
30	A3	30c lilac ('03)	4.75	2.40
31	A4	40c red & pale bl	4.75	2.60
32	A4	50c bis brn & lav ('07)	175.00	*200.00*
a.		Imperf., pair	800.00	
33	A4	1fr claret & ol grn ('07)	375.00	*400.00*
a.		Imperf., pair	950.00	

Black Surcharge

34	A5	1pi on 25c bl ('03)	.95	.65
a.		Second "I" omitted	27.50	20.00
b.		Double surcharge	65.00	52.50
35	A6	2pi on 50c bis brn & lavender	3.50	1.20
36	A6	4pi on 1fr cl & ol grn	4.00	1.60
a.		Imperf., pair	650.00	
37	A6	8pi on 2fr gray vio & yel	17.50	12.00
38	A6	20pi on 5fr dk bl & buff	8.00	4.00
		Nos. 21-38 (18)	645.10	679.30

Nos. 29, 32-33 were used during the early part of 1907 in the French Offices at Harar and Diredawa, Ethiopia. Djibouti and Port Said stamps were also used.

No. 27 Surcharged in Green

1 Piastre

Beyrouth

1905

39	A3	1pi on 15c pale red	1,900.	300.
a.		"Piastte"	5,750.	1,300.

Stamps of France 1900-21 Surcharged:

On A22

On A20

On A18

1921-22

40	A22	30pa on 5c grn	.80	.80
41	A22	30pa on 5c org	.80	.80
42	A22	1pi20pa on 10c red	.80	.80
43	A22	1pi20pa on 10c grn	1.00	.80
44	A22	3pi30pa on 25c bl	1.35	.80
45	A22	4pi20pa on 30c org	1.40	.95
a.		"4" omitted	875.00	
46	A20	7pi20pa on 50c bl	1.40	.95
47	A18	15pi on 1fr car & ol grn	2.10	1.60
48	A18	30pi on 2fr org & pale bl	10.00	8.00
49	A18	75pi on 5fr dk bl & buff	9.50	6.00
		Nos. 40-49 (10)	29.15	21.50

Stamps of France, 1903-07, Handstamped

1923

52	A22	1pi20pa on 10c red	52.50	50.00
54	A20	3pi30pa on 15c gray grn	20.00	20.00
55	A22	7pi20pa on 35c vio	24.00	24.00
a.		1pi20pa on 35c violet	1,200.	1,200.
		Nos. 52-55 (3)	96.50	94.00

CAVALLE (CAVALLA)

Stamps of France Overprinted or Surcharged in Red, Blue or Black

1893-1900 Unwmk. *Perf. 14x13½*

1	A15	5c grn, *grnsh* (R)	20.00	16.00
2	A15	5c yel grn (I) ('00) (R)	21.00	20.00
3	A15	10c blk, *lav* (II)	40.00	21.00
a.		10c black, *lavender* (I)	150.00	120.00
4	A15	15c blue (R)	40.00	21.00
5	A15	1pi on 25c blk, *rose*	26.00	18.00
6	A15	2pi on 50c car, *rose*	80.00	60.00
7	A15	4pi on 1fr brnz grn, *straw* (R)	100.00	90.00
8	A15	8pi on 2fr brn, *az* ('00) (Bk)	110.00	110.00
		Nos. 1-8 (8)	437.00	356.00

A3

A4

A5

A6

1902-03

9	A3	5c green	2.00	1.60
10	A4	10c rose red ('03)	2.00	1.60
11	A4	15c orange	2.40	1.60
a.		15c pale red ('03)	9.50	9.50

Surcharged in Black

12	A5	1pi on 25c bl	3.50	2.40
13	A6	2pi on 50c bis brn & lav	10.00	6.50
14	A6	4pi on 1fr cl & ol grn	12.50	8.75
15	A6	8pi on 2fr gray vio & yel	16.00	13.50
		Nos. 9-15 (7)	48.40	35.95

DEDEAGH (DEDEAGATCH)

Stamps of France Overprinted or Surcharged in Red, Blue or Black

1893-1900 Unwmk. *Perf. 14x13½*

1	A15	5c grn, *grnsh* (II) (R)	13.50	12.00
2	A15	5c yel grn (I) ('00) (R)	12.00	11.00
3	A15	10c blk, *lav* (II)	22.50	16.00
a.		Type I	35.00	27.50
4	A15	15c blue (R)	27.50	24.00
5	A15	1pi on 25c blk, *rose*	32.50	27.50
6	A15	2pi on 50c car, *rose*	52.50	40.00
7	A15	4pi on 1fr brnz grn, *straw* (R)	67.50	55.00
8	A15	8pi on 2fr brn, *az* ('00) (Bk)	100.00	80.00
		Nos. 1-8 (8)	328.00	265.50

A3

A4

A5

A6

1902-03

9	A3	5c green	2.40	2.00
10	A4	10c rose red ('03)	2.40	2.00
11	A4	15c orange	5.25	4.00

Black Surcharge

15	A5	1pi on 25c bl ('03)	2.75	2.40
16	A6	2pi on 50c bis brn & lav	9.50	8.00
a.		Double surcharge	240.00	
17	A6	4pi on 1fr cl & ol grn	16.00	13.50
18	A6	8pi on 2fr gray vio & yel	25.00	24.00
		Nos. 9-18 (7)	63.30	55.90

PORT LAGOS

Stamps of France Overprinted or Surcharged in Red or Blue

1893 Unwmk. *Perf. 14x13½*

1	A15	5c grn, *grnsh* (R)	24.00	24.00
2	A15	10c blk, *lav*	47.50	40.00
3	A15	15c blue (R)	72.50	55.00
4	A15	1pi on 25c blk, *rose*	60.00	47.50
5	A15	2pi on 50c car, *rose*	160.00	80.00
6	A15	4pi on 1fr brnz grn, *straw* (R)	100.00	80.00
		Nos. 1-6 (6)	464.00	326.50

VATHY (SAMOS)

Stamps of France Overprinted or Surcharged in Red, Blue or Black

1894-1900 Unwmk. *Perf. 14x13½*

1	A15	5c grn, *grnsh* (R)	7.25	6.50
2	A15	5c yel grn (I) ('00) (R)	7.25	6.50
a.		Type II	70.00	70.00
3	A15	10c blk, *lav* (I)	14.00	12.00
a.		Type II	45.00	35.00
4	A15	15c blue (R)	12.50	12.50
5	A15	1pi on 25c blk, *rose*	16.00	8.00
6	A15	2pi on 50c car, *rose*	25.00	20.00
7	A15	4pi on 1fr brnz grn, *straw* (R)	30.00	27.50
8	A15	8pi on 2fr brn, *az* ('00) (Bk)	65.00	65.00
9	A15	20pi on 5fr lil, *lav* ('00) (Bk)	87.50	87.50
		Nos. 1-9 (9)	264.50	245.50

OFFICES IN ZANZIBAR

Until 1906 France maintained post offices in the Sultanate of Zanzibar, but in that year Great Britain assumed direct control over this protectorate and the French withdrew their postal system.

16 Annas = 1 Rupee

A1

A2

Stamps of France Surcharged in Red, Blue or Black

1894-96 Unwmk. *Perf. 14x13½*

1	A15	½a on 5c grn, *grnsh*	9.50	7.25
2	A15	1a on 10c blk, *lav* (Bl)	14.00	12.00
3	A15	1½a on 15c bl ('96)	21.00	20.00
a.		"ANNAS"	100.00	87.50
4	A15	2a on 20c red, *grn* ('96) (Bk)	18.00	14.00
a.		"ANNA"	2,200.	2,200.
5	A15	2½a on 25c blk, *rose* (Bl)	12.00	8.75
a.		Double surcharge	240.00	240.00
6	A15	3a on 30c brn, *bis* ('96) (Bk)	20.00	17.50
7	A15	4a on 40c red, *straw* ('96) (Bk)	27.50	24.00
8	A15	5a on 50c car, *rose* (Bl)	35.00	32.50
9	A15	7½a on 75c vio, *org* ('96)	475.00	390.00
10	A15	10a on 1fr brnz grn, *straw*	65.00	52.50
11	A15	50a on 5fr red lil, *lav* ('96) (Bk)	300.00	250.00
		Nos. 1-11 (11)	997.00	828.50

1894

12	A15	½a & 5c on 1c blk, *lil bl* (R)	190.00	*210.00*
13	A15	1a & 10c on 3c gray, *grysh* (R)	175.00	*190.00*
14	A15	2½a & 25c on 4c cl, *lav* (Bk)	225.00	*260.00*
15	A15	5a & 50c on 20c red, *grn* (Bk)	240.00	*265.00*
16	A15	10a & 1fr on 40c red, *straw* (Bk)	460.00	*500.00*
		Nos. 12-16 (5)	1,290.	1,425.

There are two distinct types of the figures 5c, four of the 25c and three of each of the others of this series.

Stamps of France Surcharged in Red, Blue or Black

1896-1900

17a	A15	½a on 5c grn, *grnsh* (C)	10.00	8.00
18	A15	½a on 5c yel grn (I) (R)	7.25	6.50
a.		Type II	8.75	7.25
19	A15	1a on 10c blk, *lav* (II) (Bl)	8.75	7.25
a.		Type I	21.00	18.00
20	A15	1½a on 15c bl (R)	10.00	8.75
a.		Carmine surcharge	10.00	8.75
21	A15	2a on 20c red, *grn*	8.75	8.75
a.		"ZANZIBAR" double	200.00	200.00
b.		"ZANZIBAR" triple	200.00	200.00
22	A15	2½a on 25c blk, *rose* (Bl)	10.00	8.75
a.		Inverted surcharge	260.00	200.00
23	A15	3a on 30c brn, *bis*	10.00	8.75
24	A15	4a on 40c red, *straw*	12.50	9.50
25	A15	5a on 50c rose, *rose* (II) (Bl)	45.00	32.50
a.		Type I	120.00	100.00
26	A15	10a on 1fr brnz grn, *straw* (R)	27.50	24.00
27	A15	20a on 2fr brn, *az*	35.00	27.50
a.		"ZANZIBAS"	640.00	725.00
b.		"ZANZIBAR" triple		1,600.
28	A15	50a on 5fr lil, *lav*	65.00	60.00
a.		"ZANZIBAS"	8,750.	
		Nos. 17a-28 (12)	249.75	210.25

For surcharges see Nos. 50-54.

A4

A5

1897

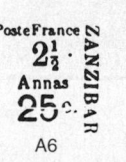

29	A4	2½a & 25c on ½a on 5c grn, *grnsh*	1,100.	150.
30	A4	2½a & 25c on 1a on 10c *lav*	*3,600.*	800.
31	A4	2½a & 25c on 1½a on 15c blue	*3,600.*	675.
32	A5	5a & 50c on 3a on 30c brn, *bis*	*3,600.*	600.
33	A5	5a & 50c on 4a on 40c red, *straw*	*3,600.*	800.

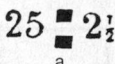

PosteFrance 2½ Annas 25c ZANZIBAR

A6

PosteFrance 5 Annas 50c ZANZIBAR

A7

Printed on the Margins of Sheets of French Stamps

Perf. 14x13½ on one or more sides

1897

34	A6	2½a & 25c grn, *grnsh*	*1,050.*
35	A6	2½a & 25c blk, *lav*	*3,250.*
36	A6	2½a & 25c blue	*2,600.*
37	A7	5a & 50c brn, *bis*	*2,750.*
38	A7	5a & 50c red, *straw*	*3,250.*

There are 5 varieties of figures in the above surcharges.

A8

A9

A10

Surcharged in Red or Black

1902-03 *Perf. 14x13½*

39	A8	½a on 5c grn (R)	6.50	5.50
40	A9	1a on 10c rose red ('03)	7.25	7.25
41	A9	1½a on 15c pale red ('03)	14.00	13.50
42	A9	2a on 20c brn vio ('03)	17.50	14.00
43	A9	2½a on 25c bl ('03)	17.50	14.00
44	A9	3a on 30c lil ('03)	12.50	12.50
a.		5a on 30c (error)	325.00	*360.00*
45	A10	4a on 40c red & pale bl	27.50	24.00
46	A10	5a on 50c bis brn & lav	24.00	20.00
47	A10	10a on 1fr cl & ol grn	32.50	27.50
48	A10	20a on 2fr gray vio & yel	80.00	72.50
49	A10	50a on 5fr dk bl & buff	100.00	87.50
		Nos. 39-49 (11)	339.25	298.25

For see Reunion Nos. 55-59.

Nos. 23-24 Surcharged in Black:

25 2½

a

50 5

b

c

1904

50	A15	25c & 2½a on 4a on 40c		1,000.
51	A15	50c & 5a on 3a on 30c		1,200.
52	A15	50c & 5a on 4a on 40c	6,500.	1,200.
53	A15	1fr & 10a on 3a on 30c		1,900.
54	A15	1fr & 10a on 4a on 40c		1,900.

Nos. 39-40, 44 Surcharged in Red or Black:

2 25

d

e

50c cinq

f

1 fr dix

g

55	A8	25c & 2a on ½a on 5c (R)	3,000.	130.00
56	A9	25c & 2½a on 1a on 10c	6,500.	150.00
a.		Inverted surcharge		1,500.
57	A9	25c & 2½a on 3a on 30c		2,250.
a.		Inverted surcharge		3,900.
b.		Double surch., both invtd.		2,600.
58	A9	50c & 5a on 3a on 30c		1,200.
59	A9	1fr & 10a on 3a on 30c		1,900.

No. J1-J3 With Various Surcharges Overprinted:

"Timbre" in Red

60	D1	½a on 5c blue	425.00

Overprinted "Affrancht" in Black

61	D1	1a on 10c brown	425.00

With Red Bars Across "CHIFFRE" and "TAXE"

62	D1	1½a on 15c green	1,000.

The illustrations are not exact reproductions of the new surcharges but are merely intended to show their relative positions and general styles.

POSTAGE DUE STAMPS

Postage Due Stamps of France Surcharged in Red, Blue or Black Like Nos. 17-28

1897 Unwmk. *Perf. 14x13½*

J1	D2	½a on 5c blue (R)	20.00	12.00
J2	D2	1a on 10c brn (Bl)	20.00	12.00
a.		Inverted surcharge	160.00	*180.00*
J3	D2	1½a on 15c grn (R)	32.50	12.00
J4	D2	3a on 30c car (Bk)	27.50	20.00
J5	D2	5a on 50c lil (Bl)	32.50	24.00
a.		2½a on 50c lilac (Bl)	1,400.	1,250.
		Nos. J1-J5 (5)	132.50	80.00

For overprints see Nos. 60-62.

REUNION

LOCATION — An island in the Indian Ocean about 400 miles east of Madagascar
GOVT. — Department of France
AREA — 970 sq. mi.
POP. — 490,000 (est. 1974)
CAPITAL — St. Denis

The colony of Réunion became an integral part of the Republic, acquiring the same status as the departments in metropolitan France, under a law effective Jan. 1, 1947.

On Jan. 1, 1975, stamps of France replaced those inscribed or overprinted "CFA."

100 Centimes = 1 Franc

Catalogue values for unused stamps in this country are for Never Hinged items, beginning with Scott 224 in the regular postage section, Scott B15 in the semi-postal section, Scott C18 in the airpost section, and Scott J26 in the postage due section.

For French stamps inscribed "Reunion" see Nos. 949, 1507.

A1

A2

1852 Unwmk. Typo. *Imperf.*

1 A1 15c black, *blue* *36,000.* *22,500.*
2 A2 30c black, *blue* *36,000.* *22,500.*

Four varieties of each value.

The reprints are printed on a more bluish paper than the originals. They have a frame of a thick and a thin line, instead of one thick and two thin lines. Value, $45 each.

Stamps of French Colonies Surcharged or Overprinted in Black:

a

b

1885

3 A1(a) 5c on 40c org, *yelsh* 375.00 340.00
a. Inverted surcharge 1,750. 1,750.
4 A1(a) 25c on 40c org, *yelsh* 65.00 52.50
a. Inverted surcharge 875.00 800.00
b. Double surcharge 875.00 800.00
5 A5(a) 5c on 30c brn, *yelsh* 65.00 52.50
a. "5" inverted 3,000. 3,000.
b. Double surcharge 875.00 875.00
6 A4(a) 5c on 40c org, *yelsh* (I) 55.00 45.00
a. 5c on 40c org, *yelsh* (II) 2,500. 2,500.
b. Inverted surcharge (I) 875.00 875.00
c. Double surcharge (I) 875.00 875.00
7 A8(a) 5c on 30c brn, *yelsh* 20.00 14.00
8 A8(a) 5c on 40c ver, *straw* 125.00 100.00
a. Inverted surcharge 875.00 800.00
b. Double surcharge 875.00 800.00
9 A8(a) 10c on 40c ver, *straw* 24.00 20.00
a. Inverted surcharge 875.00 800.00
b. Double surcharge 875.00 800.00
10 A8(a) 20c on 30c brn, *yelsh* 80.00 72.50

Overprint Type "b"
With or Without Accent on "E"

1891

11 A4 40c org, *yelsh* (I) 550.00 540.00
a. 40c orange, *yelsh* (II) *6,500.* *6,500.*
12 A7 80c car, *pnksh* 72.50 60.00
13 A8 30c brn, *yelsh* 47.50 47.50
14 A8 40c ver, *straw* 35.00 35.00
15 A8 75c car, *rose* 425.00 425.00
16 A8 1fr brnz grn, *straw* 52.50 45.00

Perf. 14x13½

17 A9 1c blk, *lil bl* 4.75 4.00
a. Inverted overprint 60.00 60.00
b. Double overprint 52.50 52.50
18 A9 2c brn, *buff* 6.50 4.75
a. Inverted overprint 40.00 40.00
19 A9 4c claret, *lav* 9.50 8.00
a. Inverted overprint 72.50 72.50
20 A9 5c grn, *grnsh* 11.00 8.75
a. Inverted overprint 60.00 60.00
b. Double overprint 60.00 55.00
21 A9 10c blk, *lav* 35.00 8.00
a. Inverted overprint 87.50 80.00
b. Double overprint 100.00 80.00
22 A9 15c blue 52.50 8.75
a. Inverted overprint 120.00 105.00
23 A9 20c red, *grn* 40.00 30.00
a. Inverted overprint 150.00 130.00
b. Double overprint 130.00 120.00
24 A9 25c blk, *rose* 45.00 7.25
a. Inverted overprint 125.00 120.00
25 A9 35c dp vio, *yel* 40.00 32.50
b. Inverted overprint 125.00 175.00
26 A9 40c red, *straw* 67.50 60.00
a. Inverted overprint 240.00 225.00
27 A9 75c car, *rose* 600.00 525.00
a. Inverted overprint 1,600. 1,400.
28 A9 1fr brnz grn, *straw* 525.00 400.00
a. Inverted overprint 1,600. 1,500.
b. Double overprint 1,500. 1,400.

The varieties "RUNION," "RUENION," "REUNIONR," "ERUNION," "EUNION," "REUNIN," "REUNIOU" and "REUNOIN" are found on most stamps of this group. See *Scott Classic Specialized Catalogue of Stamps and Covers* for detailed listings. There are also many broken letters.

For surcharges see Nos. 29-33, 53-55.

No. 23 with Additional Surcharge in Black:

c

d

e

f

1891

29 A9(c) 02c on 20c red, *grn* 14.00 14.00
a. Inverted surcharge 67.50 67.50
30 A9(c) 15c on 20c red, *grn* 17.50 17.50
a. Inverted surcharge 67.50 67.50
31 A9(d) 2c on 20c red, *grn* 4.75 4.75
32 A9(e) 2c on 20c red, *grn* 5.50 5.50
33 A9(f) 2c on 20c red, *grn* 8.75 8.75
Nos. 29-33 (5) 50.50 50.50

Navigation and Commerce — A14

1892-1905 Typo. *Perf. 14x13½*
Name of Colony in Blue or Carmine

34 A14 1c blk, *lil bl* 2.00 1.20
35 A14 2c brn, *buff* 2.00 1.20
36 A14 4c claret, *lav* 2.75 2.00
37 A14 5c grn, *grnsh* 6.75 2.00
38 A14 5c yel grn ('00) 1.40 1.40
39 A14 10c blk, *lav* 8.75 2.75
40 A14 10c red ('00) 3.25 2.50
41 A14 15c bl, quadrille paper 30.00 3.25
42 A14 15c gray ('00) 8.75 3.25
43 A14 20c red, *grn* 20.00 8.75
44 A14 25c blk, *rose* 21.00 3.50
a. "Reunion" double 400.00 *425.00*
45 A14 25c blue ('00) 26.00 25.00
46 A14 30c brn, *bis* 23.00 12.00
47 A14 40c red, *straw* 30.00 19.00
48 A14 50c car, *rose* 72.50 40.00
a. "Reunion" in red and blue 500.00 500.00
49 A14 50c brn, *az* ("Reunion" in car) ('00) 52.50 47.50
50 A14 50c brn, *az* ("Reunion" in bl) ('05) 52.50 47.50
51 A14 75c dp vio, *org* 60.00 45.00
a. "Reunion" double 350.00 350.00
52 A14 1fr brnz grn, *straw* 47.50 35.00
a. "Reunion" double 350.00 *360.00*
Nos. 34-52 (19) 470.65 302.80

Perf. 13½x14 stamps are counterfeits.

For surcharges and overprint see Nos. 56-59, 99-106, Q1.

French Colonies No. 52 Surcharged in Black:

g

h

j

1893

53 A9(g) 2c on 20c red, *grn* 3.25 3.25
54 A9(h) 2c on 20c red, *grn* 5.50 5.50
55 A9(j) 2c on 20c red, *grn* 21.00 21.00
Nos. 53-55 (3) 29.75 29.75

Reunion Nos. 47-48, 51-52 Surcharged in Black

1901

56 A14 5c on 40c red, *straw* 6.50 6.50
a. Inverted surcharge 45.00 45.00
b. No bar 240.00 240.00
c. Thin "5" — —
d. "5" inverted 1,400. 1,200.
57 A14 5c on 50c car, *rose* 7.25 7.25
a. Inverted surcharge 45.00 45.00
b. No bar 240.00 240.00
c. Thin "5" —
58 A14 15c on 75c vio, *org* 20.00 20.00
a. Inverted surcharge 55.00 55.00
b. No bar 240.00 240.00
c. Thin "5" and small "1" 45.00 45.00
d. As "c," inverted 800.00 800.00
59 A14 15c on 1fr brnz grn, *straw* 18.00 18.00
a. Inverted surcharge 55.00 55.00
b. No bar 240.00 240.00
c. Thin "5" and small "1" 40.00 40.00
d. As "c," inverted
Nos. 56-59 (4) 51.75 51.75

Map of Réunion A19

Coat of Arms and View of St. Denis A20

View of St. Pierre — A21

1907-30 Typo.

60 A19 1c vio & car rose .30 .30
61 A19 2c brn & ultra .30 .30
62 A19 4c ol grn & red .40 .40
63 A19 5c grn & red 1.25 .40
64 A19 5c org & vio ('22) .30 .30
65 A19 10c car & grn 2.50 .40
66 A19 10c grn ('22) .30 .30
67 A19 10c brn red & org red, *bluish* ('26) .70 .70
68 A19 15c blk & ultra .55 .40
69 A19 15c gray grn & bl grn ('26) .40 .40
70 A19 15c bl & lt red ('28) .55 .45
71 A20 20c gray grn & bl grn .45 .45
72 A20 25c dp bl & vio brn 6.50 3.25
73 A20 25c lt brn & bl ('22) .55 .55
74 A20 30c yel brn & grn 1.40 .85
75 A20 30c rose & pale rose ('22) 1.40 1.40
76 A20 30c gray & car rose ('26) .55 .55
77 A20 30c dp grn & yel grn ('28) 1.20 1.10
78 A20 35c ol grn & bl 1.60 1.00
79 A20 40c gray grn & brn ('25) .70 .70
80 A20 45c vio & car rose 1.75 1.00
81 A20 45c red brn & ver ('26) .85 .85
82 A20 45c vio & red org ('28) 2.75 2.50
83 A20 50c red brn & ultra 4.50 1.50
84 A20 50c bl & ultra ('22) 1.40 1.40
85 A20 50c yel & vio ('26) 1.10 1.10
86 A20 60c dk bl & yel brn ('26) 1.00 1.00
87 A20 65c vio & lt bl ('28) 1.50 1.40
88 A20 75c red & car rose .80 .70
89 A20 75c ol brn & red vio ('28) 2.25 2.10
90 A20 90c brn red & brt red ('30) 8.00 7.25
91 A21 1fr ol grn & bl 1.40 1.25
92 A21 1fr blue ('26) .95 .95
93 A21 1fr yel brn & lav ('28) 1.50 .70
94 A21 1.10fr org brn & rose lil ('28) 1.40 1.25
95 A21 1.50fr dk bl & ultra ('30) 12.50 12.50
96 A21 2fr red & grn 4.75 3.25
97 A21 3fr red vio ('30) 12.00 8.75
98 A21 5fr car & vio brn 9.50 5.50
Nos. 60-98 (39) 91.80 69.15

For surcharges see #107-121, 178-180, B1-B3.

Stamps of 1892-1900 Surcharged in Black or Carmine

1912

99 A14 5c on 2c brn, *buff* 1.40 1.40
100 A14 5c on 15c gray (C) 1.40 1.40
a. Inverted surcharge 210.00 210.00
101 A14 5c on 20c red, *grn* 2.40 2.40
102 A14 5c on 25c blk, *rose* (C) 1.60 1.60
103 A14 5c on 30c brn, *bis* (C) 1.40 1.40
104 A14 10c on 40c red, *straw* 1.40 1.40
105 A14 10c on 50c brn, *az* (C) 5.50 5.50
106 A14 10c on 75c dp vio, *org* 8.75 8.75
Nos. 99-106 (8) 23.85 23.85

Two spacings between the surcharged numerals are found on Nos. 99 to 106. For detailed listings, see the *Scott Classic Specialized Catalogue of Stamps and Covers.*

No. 62 Surcharged

1917

107 A19 1c on 4c ol grn & red 1.75 1.75
a. Inverted surcharge 80.00 80.00
b. Double surcharge 60.00 60.00

Stamps and Types of 1907-30 Surcharged in Black or Red

1922-33

108 A20 40c on 20c grn & yel .80 .80
109 A20 50c on 45c red brn & ver ('33) 1.20 1.20
109A A20 50c on 45c vio & red org ('33) 325.00 275.00
b. Double surcharge 1,750.

No.	Type	Description	Unused	Used
110	A20	50c on 65c vio & lt bl ('33)	1.20	1.20
111	A20	60c on 75c red & rose	.85	.85
112	A19	65c on 15c blk & ultra (R) ('25)	1.90	1.90
113	A19	85c on 15c blk & ultra (R) ('25)	1.90	1.90
114	A20	85c on 75c red & cer ('25)	2.10	2.10
115	A20	90c on 75 brn red & rose red ('27)	2.10	2.10
		Nos. 108-109,110-115 (8)	12.05	12.05

Stamps and Type of 1907-30 Surcharged with New Value and Bars in Black or Red

1924-27

No.	Type	Description	Unused	Used
116	A21	25c on 5fr car & brn	1.00	1.00
a.		Double surcharge	110.00	
117	A21	1.25fr on 1fr bl (R) ('26)	1.00	.95
a.		Double surcharge	125.00	
118	A21	1.50fr on 1fr ind & ultra, *bluish* ('27)	1.40	1.40
a.		Double surcharge	140.00	
119	A21	3fr on 5fr dl red & lt bl ('27)	3.50	3.00
120	A21	10fr on 5fr bl grn & brn red ('27)	16.00	14.00
121	A21	20fr on 5fr blk brn & rose ('27)	20.00	16.00
		Nos. 116-121 (6)	42.90	36.35

Common Design Types pictured following the introduction.

Colonial Exposition Issue

Common Design Types

1931 Engr. *Perf. 12½*

Name of Country Typo. in Black

No.	Type	Description	Unused	Used
122	CD70	40c dp green	5.25	5.25
123	CD71	50c violet	5.25	5.25
124	CD72	90c red orange	5.25	5.25
125	CD73	1.50fr dull blue	5.25	5.25
		Nos. 122-125 (4)	21.00	21.00

Cascade of Salazie — A22

Waterfowl Lake and Anchain Peak — A23

Léon Dierx Museum, St. Denis — A24

Perf. 12, 12½ and Compound

1933-40 Engr.

No.	Type	Description	Unused	Used
126	A22	1c violet	.25	.25
127	A22	2c dark brown	.25	.25
128	A22	3c rose vio ('40)	.25	.25
129	A22	4c olive green	.25	.25
130	A22	5c red orange	.25	.25
131	A22	10c ultramarine	.25	.25
132	A22	15c black	.25	.25
133	A22	20c indigo	.30	.25
134	A22	25c red brown	.40	.30
135	A22	30c dark green	.40	.40
136	A23	35c green ('38)	.55	.55
137	A23	40c ultramarine	.55	.55
138	A23	40c brn blk ('40)	.40	.40
139	A23	45c red violet	.85	.85
140	A23	45c green ('40)	.45	.45
141	A23	50c red	.30	.25
142	A23	55c brn org ('38)	1.25	1.00
143	A23	60c dull bl ('40)	.45	.45
144	A23	65c olive green	.95	.80
145	A23	70c ol grn ('40)	.65	.65
146	A23	75c dark brown	4.50	3.75
147	A23	80c black ('38)	.85	.80
148	A23	90c carmine	2.25	2.00
149	A23	90c dl rose vio ('39)	.85	.85
150	A23	1fr green	1.75	.70
151	A23	1fr dk car ('38)	2.25	.70
152	A23	1fr black ('40)	.70	.70
153	A24	1.25fr orange brown	.70	.55
154	A24	1.25fr brt car rose ('39)	.85	.85
155	A22	1.40fr pck bl ('40)	.85	.85
156	A24	1.50fr ultramarine	.40	.40
157	A22	1.60fr dk car rose ('40)	1.25	1.25
158	A24	1.75fr olive green	.85	.65
159	A22	1.75fr dk bl ('38)	1.40	.85
160	A24	2fr vermilion	.55	.55
161	A22	2.25fr brt ultra ('39)	1.75	1.75
162	A22	2.50fr chnt ('40)	1.25	1.25
163	A24	3fr purple	.55	.55
164	A24	5fr magenta	.55	.55
165	A24	10fr dark blue	.95	.95
166	A24	20fr red brown	1.50	1.50
		Nos. 126-166 (41)	35.80	30.65

For overprints and surcharges see Nos. 177A, 181-220, 223, C1.

60c, 1fr without "RF," see Nos. 237A-237B.

Paris International Exposition Issue

Common Design Types

1937 *Perf. 13*

No.	Type	Description	Unused	Used
167	CD74	20c dp vio	2.25	2.25
168	CD75	30c dk grn	2.25	2.25
169	CD76	40c car rose	2.25	2.25
170	CD77	50c dk brn & blk	2.10	2.10
171	CD78	90c red	2.10	2.10
172	CD79	1.50fr ultra	2.25	2.25
		Nos. 167-172 (6)	13.20	13.20
		Set, never hinged	20.00	

Colonial Arts Exhibition Issue

Souvenir Sheet

Common Design Type

1937 *Imperf.*

No.	Type	Description	Unused	Used
173	CD74	3fr ultra	8.50	*10.00*
		Never hinged	16.00	

New York World's Fair Issue

Common Design Type

1939 Engr. *Perf. 12½x12*

No.	Type	Description	Unused	Used
174	CD82	1.25fr car lake	1.40	1.40
175	CD82	2.25fr ultra	1.40	1.40
		Set, never hinged	4.50	

For overprints see Nos. 221-222.

St. Denis Roadstead and Marshal Pétain A25

1941 Unwmk. *Perf. 11½x12*

No.	Type	Description	Unused	Used
176	A25	1fr brown	.80	
177	A25	2.50fr blue	.80	
		Set, never hinged	2.00	

Nos. 176-177 were issued by the Vichy government in France, but were not placed on sale in Réunion.

For surcharges, see Nos. B13-B14.

No. 144 Surcharged in Carmine

1943

No.	Type	Description	Unused	Used
177A		1fr on 65c olive grn	1.10	.65
		Never hinged	1.60	

De Pronis Landing on Reunion — A25a

1943 *Perf. 12½x12*

No.	Type	Description	Unused	Used
177B	A25a	60c blk brn & red	.55	
177C	A25a	80c green & blue	.40	
177D	A25a	1.50fr dk brn red	.35	
177E	A25a	4fr ultra & red	.35	
177F	A25a	5fr red brn & black	.55	
177G	A25a	10fr violet & green	.65	
		Nos. 177B-177G,C13A-C13F (12)	5.70	
		Set, never hinged	8.00	

300th Ann. of French settlement on Réunion.

Nos. 177B-177G were issued by the Vichy government in France, but were not placed on sale in Réunion.

Stamps of 1907 Overprinted in Blue Violet

q

1943 Unwmk. *Perf. 14x13½*

No.	Type	Description	Unused	Used
178	A19(q)	4c ol gray & pale red	5.00	5.00
179	A20(q)	75c red & lil rose	1.60	1.60
180	A21(q)	5fr car & vio brn	60.00	60.00

Stamps of 1933-40 Overprinted in Carmine, Black or Blue Violet

No.	Type	Description	Unused	Used
181	A22(r)	1c rose vio (C)	.90	.90
182	A22(r)	2c blk brn (C)	.90	.90
183	A22(r)	3c rose vio (C)	.90	.90
184	A22(r)	4c ol yel (C)	.90	.90
185	A22(r)	5c red org	.90	.90
186	A22(r)	10c ultra (C)	.90	.90
187	A22(r)	15c blk (C)	.90	.90
188	A22(r)	20c ind (C)	.90	.90
189	A22(r)	25c red brn (BlV)	1.10	1.10
190	A22(r)	30c dk grn (C)	1.25	1.25
191	A23(q)	35c green	.75	.75
192	A23(q)	40c dl ultra (C)	.75	.75
193	A23(q)	40c brn blk (C)	.75	.75
194	A23(q)	45c red vio	.75	.75
195	A23(q)	45c green	.75	.75
196	A23(q)	50c org red	.75	.75
197	A23(q)	55c brn org	.75	.75
198	A23(q)	60c dl bl (C)	3.00	3.00
199	A23(q)	65c ol grn	.75	.75
200	A23(q)	70c ol grn (C)	2.10	2.10
201	A23(q)	75c dk brn (C)	4.75	4.75
202	A23(q)	80c blk (C)	.90	.90
203	A23(q)	90c dl rose vio	.90	.90
204	A23(q)	1fr green	.90	.90
205	A23(q)	1fr dk car	.90	.90
206	A23(q)	1fr blk (C)	2.50	2.50
207	A24(q)	1.25fr org brn (BlV)	.90	.90
208	A24(q)	1.25fr brt car rose	2.75	2.75
209	A22(r)	1.40fr pck bl (C)	1.90	1.90
210	A24(q)	1.50fr ultra (C)	.90	.90
211	A22(r)	1.60fr dk car rose	2.10	2.10
212	A24(q)	1.75fr ol grn (C)	2.40	2.40
213	A22(r)	1.75fr dk bl (C)	4.25	4.25
214	A24(q)	2fr vermilion	.90	.90
215	A22(r)	2.25fr brt ultra (C)	4.25	4.25
216	A22(r)	2.50fr chnt (BlV)	6.50	6.50
217	A24(q)	3fr pur (C)	.90	.90
218	A24(q)	5fr brn lake (BlV)	2.00	2.00
219	A24(q)	10fr dk bl (C)	7.75	7.75
220	A24(q)	20fr red brn (BlV)	11.00	11.00

New York World's Fair Issue Overprinted in Black or Carmine

No.	Type	Description	Unused	Used
221	CD82(q)	1.25fr car lake	3.50	3.50
222	CD82(q)	2.25fr ultra (C)	3.50	3.50
		Nos. 178-222 (45)	153.60	153.60
		Set, never hinged	235.00	

No. 177A Overprinted Type "q"

1943 *Perf. 12½*

No.	Type	Description	Unused	Used
223	A23	1fr on 65c ol grn	.65	.65
		Never hinged	1.00	

Catalogue values for unused stamps in this section, from this point to the end of the section, are for Never Hinged items.

Produce of Réunion A26

1943 Photo. *Perf. 14½x14*

No.	Type	Description	Unused	Used
224	A26	5c dull brown	.20	.20
225	A26	10c dk blue	.20	.20
226	A26	25c emerald	.20	.20
227	A26	30c dp orange	.20	.20
228	A26	40c dk slate grn	.20	.20
229	A26	80c rose violet	.65	.50
230	A26	1fr red brown	.20	.20
231	A26	1.50fr crimson	.65	.50
232	A26	2fr black	.65	.50
233	A26	2.50fr ultra	.95	.70
234	A26	4fr dk violet	1.25	.90
235	A26	5fr bister	1.25	.90
236	A26	10fr dark brown	1.75	1.40
237	A26	20fr dark green	2.50	1.75
		Nos. 224-237 (14)	10.85	8.35

For surcharges see Nos. 240-247.

Type of 1933-40 without "RF"

1944 Engr. *Perf. 12½*

No.	Type	Description	Unused	Used
237A	A23	60c dull blue	1.40	1.00
237B	A23	1fr black & blue	1.40	1.00

Nos. 237A-237B were issued by the Vichy government in France, but were not placed on sale in Réunion.

Eboue Issue

Common Design Type

1945 Engr. *Perf. 13*

No.	Type	Description	Unused	Used
238	CD91	2fr black	1.00	1.00
239	CD91	25fr Prussian green	1.40	1.00

Nos. 224, 226 and 233 Surcharged with New Values and Bars in Carmine or Black

1945 *Perf. 14½x14*

No.	Type	Description	Unused	Used
240	A26	50c on 5c dl brn (C)	.20	.20
241	A26	60c on 5c dl brn (C)	.20	.20
242	A26	70c on 5c dl brn (C)	.20	.20
243	A26	1.20fr on 5c dl brn (C)	.70	.50
244	A26	2.40fr on 25c emer	.70	.50
245	A26	3fr on 25c emer	1.25	.90
246	A26	4.50fr on 25c emer	1.25	.90
247	A26	15fr on 2.50fr ultra (C)	1.50	1.10
		Nos. 240-247 (8)	6.00	4.50

Cliff — A27

Cutting Sugar Cane — A28

Cascade A29

Banana Tree A30

Mountain Scene A31

Ship Approaching Réunion — A32

1947 Unwmk. Photo. *Perf. 13½*

249 A27 10c org & grnsh blk .20 .20
250 A27 30c org & brt bl .20 .20
251 A27 40c org & brn .20 .20
252 A28 50c bl grn & brn .20 .20
253 A28 60c dk bl & brn .20 .20
254 A28 80c brn & ol brn .55 .45
255 A29 1fr dl bl & vio brn .55 .45
256 A29 1.20fr bl grn & gray .80 .65
257 A29 1.50fr org & vio brn .80 .65
258 A30 2fr gray bl & bl grn .80 .65
259 A30 3fr vio brn & bl grn .80 .65
260 A30 3.60fr dl red & rose red .90 .70
261 A30 4fr gray bl & buff .80 .65
262 A31 5fr rose lil & brn 1.10 .65
263 A31 6fr bl & brn 1.25 .70
264 A31 10fr org & ultra 3.00 1.40
265 A32 15fr gray bl & vio brn 4.25 2.50
266 A32 20fr bl & org 6.00 3.75
267 A32 25fr rose lil & brn 7.00 4.00
Nos. 249-267 (19) 29.60 18.85

Stamps of France, 1945-49, Surcharged type "a" or "b" in Black or Carmine

On A147

Others

1949 Unwmk. *Perf. 14x13½, 13*

268 A153 10c on 30c .20 .20
269 A153 30c on 50c .55 .20
270 A146 50c on 1fr 1.25 .90
271 A146 60c on 2fr 7.25 1.40
272 A147 1fr on 3fr 1.75 .70
273 A147 2fr on 4fr 6.75 1.60
274 A147 2.50fr on 5fr 18.00 10.50
275 A147 3fr on 6fr 2.10 1.40
276 A147 4fr on 10fr 1.90 1.60
277 A162 5fr on 20fr (C) 9.25 1.40
278 A147 6fr on 12fr 27.50 2.25
279 A160 7fr on 12fr 8.50 3.00
280 A165 8fr on 25fr (C) 35.00 3.25
281 A165 10fr on 25fr (C) 2.50 1.40
282 A174 11fr on 18fr (C) 16.00 2.10
Nos. 268-282 (15) 138.50 31.90

The letters "C. F. A." are the initials of "Colonies Francaises d'Afrique," referring to the currency which is expressed in French Africa francs.

The surcharge on Nos. 277, 279, 282 includes two bars.

1950 *Perf. 14x13½*

283 A182 10c on 50c bl, red & yel .55 .55
284 A182 1fr on 2fr grn, yel & red (#619) 9.50 3.50
285 A147 2fr on 5fr lt grn 16.00 4.25
Nos. 283-285 (3) 26.05 8.30

Surcharged Type "a" and Bars

1950-51 *Perf. 13*

286 A188 5fr on 20fr dk red 9.25 1.75
287 A185 8fr on 25fr dp ultra ('51) 9.25 1.75

Stamps of France, 1951-52, Surcharged in Black or Red

1951-52 *Perf. 14x13½, 13*

288 A182 50c on 1fr bl, red & yel .65 .70
289 A182 1fr on 2fr vio bl, red & yel (#662) .65 .70
290 A147 2fr on 5fr dl vio 4.00 1.90
291 A147 3fr on 6fr grn 7.75 1.60
292 A220 5fr on 20fr dk pur (R; '52) 2.75 1.60
293 A147 6fr on 12fr red org ('52) 8.50 2.00
294 A215 8fr on 40fr vio (R) ('52) 6.00 .70
295 A147 9fr on 18fr cerise 19.00 4.25
296 A208 15fr on 30fr ind (R) 10.00 2.25
Nos. 288-296 (9) 59.30 15.70

The surcharge on Nos. 292, 294 and 296 include two bars.

France No. 697 Surcharged Type "a" in Black

1953 *Perf. 14x13½*

297 A182 50c on 1fr blk, red & yel .35 .20

France No. 688 Surcharged type "c" in Black

Perf. 13

298 A230 3fr on 6fr dp plum & car 1.10 .80

France Nos. 703 and 705 Surcharged Type "a" in Red or Blue

1954

299 A235 8fr on 40fr (R) 32.50 7.50
300 A235 20fr on 75fr 72.50 32.50

France Nos. 698, 721, 713, and 715 Surcharged Type "a" in Black

Perf. 14x13½, 13

301 A182 1fr on 2fr 4.25 2.00
302 A241 4fr on 10fr 4.00 1.25
303 A238 8fr on 40fr 9.25 1.60
304 A238 20fr on 75fr 12.00 1.60

The surcharge on Nos. 303 and 304 includes two bars.

France Nos. 737, 719 and 722-724 Surcharged in Black or Red

305 A182(b) 1fr on 2fr .50 .50
306 A241(a) 2fr on 6fr (R) .80 .50
307 A242(a) 6fr on 12fr 8.50 1.60
308 A241(b) 9fr on 18fr 9.50 4.50
309 A241(a) 10fr on 20fr 6.75 1.40
Nos. 299-309 (11) 160.55 54.95

The surcharge on Nos. 306-308 includes two bars; on No. 309 three bars.

France No. 720 Surcharged Type "c" in Red, Bars at Lower Left

1955 *Perf. 13*

310 A241 3fr on 8fr brt bl & dk grn 1.25 1.10

France Nos. 785, 774-779 Surcharged Type "a" in Black or Red

Perf. 14x13½, 13

1955-56 Typo., Engr.

311 A182 50c on 1fr .30 .30
312 A265 2fr on 6fr ('56) 1.10 .70
313 A265 3fr on 8fr .95 .50
314 A265 4fr on 10fr 1.10 .50
315 A265 5fr on 12fr (R) 1.10 .50
316 A265 6fr on 18fr (R) .95 .50
317 A265 10fr on 25fr 1.40 .50
Nos. 311-317 (7) 6.90 3.50

The surcharge on Nos. 312-317 includes two bars.

France Nos. 801-804 Surcharged Type "a" or "b" in Black or Red

1956 Engr. *Perf. 13*

318 A280(a) 8fr on 30fr (R) 4.75 1.10
319 A280(b) 9fr on 40fr 7.00 2.75
320 A280(a) 15fr on 50fr 8.75 1.60
321 A280(a) 20fr on 75fr (R) 8.50 2.10
Nos. 318-321 (4) 29.00 7.55

The surcharge on Nos. 318, 319 and 321 includes two bars.

France Nos. 837 and 839 Surcharged Type "a" in Red

1957 *Perf. 13*

322 A294 7fr on 15fr 1.10 .50
323 A265 17fr on 70fr 5.75 2.10

The surcharge on Nos. 322-323 includes two bars.

No. 322 has three types of "7" in the sheet of 50. There are 34 of the "normal" 7; 10 of a slightly thinner 7, and 6 of a slightly thicker 7.

France Nos. 755-756, 833-834, 851-855, 908, 949 Surcharged in Black or Red Type "a", "b" or

d

Typographed, Engraved

1957-60 *Perf. 14x13½, 13*

324 A236(b) 2fr on 6fr .30 .30
325 A302(b) 3fr on 10fr ('58) .50 .50
326 A236(b) 4fr on 12fr 3.25 .75
327 A236(b) 5fr on 10fr 2.00 1.00
328 A303(b) 6fr on 18fr 1.10 .50
329 A302(a) 9fr on 25fr (R) ('58) 1.10 .65
330 A252(a) 10fr on 20fr (R) 1.60 .30
331 A252(a) 12fr on 25fr 5.75 .50
332 A303(a) 17fr on 35fr 2.50 1.60
333 A302(a) 20fr on 50fr 1.60 .80
334 A302(a) 25fr on 85fr 3.50 1.60
335 A339(d) 50fr on 1fr ('60) 2.75 .80
Nos. 324-335 (12) 25.95 9.30

The surcharge includes two bars on Nos. 324, 326-327, 329-331, 333 and 335.

France Nos. 973, 939 and 968 Surcharged

e

f

1961-63 Typo. *Perf. 14x13½*

336 A318(e) 2fr on 5c multi .30 .20
337 A336(e) 5fr on 10c brt grn 1.25 .50
338 A336(b) 5fr on 10c brt grn ('63) 1.40 .75
339 A349(f) 12fr on 25c lake & gray .30 .30
Nos. 336-339 (4) 3.25 1.75

The surcharge on No. 337 includes three bars. No. 338 has "b" surcharge and two bars.

France Nos. 943, 941 and 946 Surcharged "CFA" and New Value in Two Lines in Black or Red

Engraved, Typographed

1961 Unwmk. *Perf. 13, 14x13½*

340 A338 7fr on 15c 1.00 .80
341 A337 10fr on 20c .30 .30
342 A339 20fr on 50c (R) 16.00 4.50
Nos. 340-342 (3) 17.30 5.60

Surcharge on No. 342 includes 3 bars.

France Nos. 1047-1048 Surcharged with New Value, "CFA" and Two Bars

1963, Jan. 2 Engr. *Perf. 13*

343 A394 12fr on 25c .90 .90
344 A395 25fr on 50c .90 .90

1st television connection of the US and Europe through the Telstar satellite, July 11-12, 1962.

France Nos. 1040-1041, 1007 and 1009 Surcharged Similarly to Type "e"

Typographed, Engraved

1963 *Perf. 14x13½, 13*

345 A318 2fr on 5c .30 .30
346 A318 5fr on 10c .25 .20
347 A372 7fr on 15c .60 .50
348 A372 20fr on 45c 1.25 .75
Nos. 345-348 (4) 2.40 1.75

Two-line surcharge on No. 345; No. 347 has currency expressed in capital "F" and two heavy bars through old value; two thin bars on No. 348.

France No. 1078 Surcharged Type "e" in Two Lines in Dark Blue

1964, Feb. 8 Engr. *Perf. 13*

349 CD118 12fr on 25c 1.25 1.25

"PHILATEC," Intl. Philatelic and Postal Techniques Exhib., Paris, June 5-21, 1964.

France Nos. 1092, 1094 and 1102 Surcharged with New Value and "CFA"

Typographed, Engraved

1964 *Perf. 14x13½, 13*

350 A318 1fr on 2c .25 .20
351 A318 6fr on 18c .30 .30
352 A420 35fr on 70c 1.40 .90
Nos. 350-352 (3) 1.95 1.40

Surcharge on No. 352 includes two bars.

France Nos. 1095, 1126, 1070 Surcharged with New Value and "CFA"

1965

353 A318 15fr on 30c .50 .30
354 A440 25fr on 50c .95 .90
355 A408 30fr on 60c 1.40 .95
Nos. 353-355 (3) 2.85 2.15

Two bars obliterate old denomination on Nos. 354-355.

Etienne Regnault, "Le Taureau" and Coast of Reunion — A33

1965, Oct. 3 Engr. *Perf. 13*

356 A33 15fr bluish blk & dk car .90 .65

Tercentenary of settlement of Reunion.

France No. 985 Surcharged with New Value, Two Bars and "CFA"

1966, Feb. 13 Engr. *Perf. 13*

357 A360 10fr on 20c bl & car 1.25 .70

French Satellite A-1 Issue

France Nos. 1137-1138 Surcharged with New Value, Two Bars and "CFA" and Red

1966, Mar. 27 Engr. *Perf. 13*

358 CD121 15fr on 30c 1.10 1.00
359 CD121 30fr on 60c 1.25 1.10
a. Strip of 2 + label 3.25 3.00

France Nos. 1142, 1143, 1101 and 1127 Surcharged with New Value, "CFA" and Two Bars

1967-69 Typo. *Perf. 14x13*

360 A446 2fr on 5c bl & red .30 .30

Photo. *Perf. 13*

360A A446 10fr on 20c multi ('69) .30 .30

Engr.

361 A421 20fr on 40c multi .90 .70
362 A439 30fr on 60c bl & red brn 1.90 1.25

EXPO '67 Issue

France No. 1177 Surcharged with New Value, "CFA" and Two Bars

1967, June 12 Engr. *Perf. 13*

363 A473 30fr on 60c dl bl & bl grn 2.25 1.60

EXPO '67, Montreal, Apr. 28-Oct. 27.

Lions Issue

France No. 1196 Surcharged in Violet Blue with New Value, "CFA" and Two Bars

1967, Oct. 29 Engr. *Perf. 13*

364 A485 20fr on 40c 2.50 1.10

50th anniversary of Lions International.

France No. 1130 Surcharged in Violet Blue with New Value, "CFA" and Two Bars

1968, Feb. 26 Engr. *Perf. 13*

365 A440 50fr on 1fr 2.40 1.50

France No. 1224 Surcharged with New Value, "CFA" and Two Bars

1968, Oct. 21 Engr. *Perf. 13*

366 A508 20fr on 40c multi 1.25 .90

20 years of French Polar expeditions.

France Nos. 1230-1231 Surcharged with New Value, "CFA" and Two Bars

1969, Apr. 13 Engr. *Perf. 13*
367 A486 15fr on 30c green .65 .50
368 A486 20fr on 40c dp car .70 .30

France No. 1255 Surcharged with New Value, "CFA" and Two Bars

1969, Aug. 18 Engr. *Perf. 13*
370 A526 35fr on 70c multi 1.40 1.25

Napoleon Bonaparte (1769-1821).

France No. 1293 Surcharged with New Value and "CFA"

1971, Jan. 16 Engr. *Perf. 13*
371 A555 25fr on 50c rose car .70 .30

France No. 1301 Surcharged with New Value and "CFA"

1971, Apr. 13 Engr. *Perf. 13*
372 A562 40fr on 80c multi 1.75 1.25

France No. 1309 Surcharged with New Value, "CFA" and 2 Bars

1971, June 5 Engr. *Perf. 13*
373 A569 15fr on 40c multi .90 .70

Aid for rural families.

France No. 1312 Surcharged with New Value and "CFA"

1971, Aug. 30 Engr. *Perf. 13*
374 A571 45fr on 90c multi 1.10 .90

France No. 1320 Surcharged with New Value and "CFA"

1971, Oct. 18
375 A573 45fr on 90c multi 1.25 .95

40th anniversary of the first assembly of presidents of artisans' guilds.

Réunion Chameleon A34

1971, Nov. 8 Photo. *Perf. 13*
376 A34 25fr multi 1.40 .90

Nature protection.

Common Design Type and

De Gaulle in Brazzaville, 1944 — A35

Designs: No. 377, Gen. de Gaulle, 1940. No. 379, de Gaulle entering Paris, 1944. No. 380, Pres. de Gaulle, 1970.

1971, Nov. 9 Engr.
377 CD134 25fr black 1.60 1.60
378 A35 25fr ultra 1.60 1.60
379 A35 25fr rose red 1.60 1.60
380 CD134 25fr black 1.60 1.60
a. Strip of 4 + label 8.75 8.00

Charles de Gaulle (1890-1970), president of France. Nos. 377-380 printed se-tenant in sheets of 20 containing 5 strips of 4 plus labels with Cross of Lorraine and inscription.

France No. 1313 Surcharged with New Value and "CFA"

1972, Jan. 17 Engr. *Perf. 13*
381 A570 50fr on 1.10fr multi 1.25 1.10

Map of South Indian Ocean, Penguin and Ships — A36

1972, Jan. 31 Engr. *Perf. 13*
382 A36 45fr blk, bl & ocher 2.10 2.10

Bicentenary of the discovery of the Crozet and Kerguelen Islands.

France No. 1342 Surcharged with New New Value, "CFA" and 2 Bars in Red

1972, May. 8 Engr. *Perf. 13*
383 A590 15fr on 40c red .90 .90

20th anniv. of Blood Donors' Assoc. of Post and Telecommunications Employees.

France Nos. 1345-1346 Surcharged with New Value, "CFA" and 2 Bars

1972, June 5 Typo. *Perf. 14x13*
384 A593 15fr on 30c multi .45 .45
385 A593 25fr on 50c multi .75 .65

Introduction of postal code system.

France No. 1377 Surcharged with New Value, "CFA" and 2 Bars in Ultramarine

1973, June 12 Engr. *Perf. 13*
386 A620 45fr on 90c multi 1.75 1.25

France Nos. 1374, 1336 Surcharged with New Value and "CFA" in Ultramarine or Red

1973 Engr. *Perf. 13*
387 A617 50fr on 1fr multi (U) 1.10 .95
388 A586 100fr on 2fr multi (R) 1.75 1.10

On No. 388, two bars cover "2.00".
Issue dates: 50fr, June 24; 100fr, Oct. 13.

France No. 1231C Surcharged with New Value, "CFA" and 2 Bars

1973, Nov. Typo. *Perf. 14x13*
389 A486 15fr on 30c bl grn 4.50 .70

France No. 1390 Surcharged with New Value, "CFA" and 2 Bars in Red

1974, Jan. 20 Engr. *Perf. 13*
390 A633 25fr on 50c multi .70 .70

ARPHILA 75 Phil. Exhib., Paris, June 1975.

France Nos. 1394-1397 Surcharged "100 FCFA" in Black, Ultramarine or Brown

Engr. (#391, 393), Photo. (#392, 394)
1974 *Perf. 12x13, 13x12*
391 A637 100fr on 2fr (Bk) 2.40 2.40
392 A638 100fr on 2fr (U) 2.75 2.25
393 A639 100fr on 2fr (Br) 2.75 2.25
394 A640 100fr on 2fr (U) 2.75 2.25
Nos. 391-394 (4) 10.65 9.15

Nos. 391-394 printed in sheets of 25 with alternating labels publicizing "ARPHILA 75," Paris June 6-16, 1975.
Two bars obliterate original denomination on Nos. 391-393.

France No. 1401 Surcharged "45 FCFA" and 2 Bars in Red

1974, Apr. 29 Engr. *Perf. 13*
395 A644 45fr on 90c multi 1.75 1.25

Reorganized sea rescue organization.

France No. 1415 Surcharged with New Value, 2 Bars and "FCFA" in Ultramarine

1974, Oct. 6 Engr. *Perf. 13*
396 A657 60fr on 1.20fr multi 1.40 1.25

Centenary of Universal Postal Union.

France Nos. 1292A and 1294B Surcharged with New Value and "FCFA" in Ultramarine

1974, Oct. 19 Typo. *Perf. 14x13*
397 A555 30fr on 60c grn 1.75 1.60

Engr.
Perf. 13
398 A555 40fr on 80c car rose 2.10 1.75

SEMI-POSTAL STAMPS

No. 65 Surcharged in Black or Red

1915 Unwmk. *Perf. 14x13½*
B1 A19 10c + 5c (Bk) 160.00 120.00
a. Inverted surcharge 400.00 350.00
B2 A19 10c + 5c (R) 1.60 1.60
a. Inverted surcharge 72.50 72.50

No. 65 Surcharged in Red

1916
B3 A19 10c + 5c 1.90 1.90

Curie Issue
Common Design Type

1938 *Perf. 13*
B4 CD80 1.75fr + 50c brt ultra 13.50 13.50
Never hinged 22.50

French Revolution Issue
Common Design Type

1939 Photo. Unwmk.
Name and Value Typo. in Black
B5 CD83 45c + 25c grn 12.50 12.50
B6 CD83 70c + 30c brn 12.50 12.50
B7 CD83 90c + 35c red org 12.50 12.50
B8 CD83 1.25fr + 1fr rose pink 12.50 12.50
B9 CD83 2.25fr + 2fr blue 12.50 12.50
Nos. B5-B9 (5) 62.50 62.50
Set, never hinged 105.00

See CB1.

Common Design Type and

Artillery Colonel — SP1

Colonial Infantry SP2

1941 Unwmk. *Perf. 13½*
B10 SP1 1fr + 1fr red 1.60
B11 CD86 1.50fr + 3fr claret 1.60
B12 SP2 2.50fr + 1fr blue 1.60
Nos. B10-B12 (3) 4.80
Set, never hinged 6.00

Nos. B10-B12 were issued by the Vichy government in France, but were not placed on sale in Reunion.

Nos. 176-177 Surcharged in Black or Red

1944 Engr. *Perf. 12½x12*
B13 50c + 1.50fr on 2.50fr deep blue (R) .80
B14 + 2.50fr on 1fr yel brn .80
Set, never hinged 2.00

Colonial Development Fund.
Nos. B13-B14 were issued by the Vichy government in France, but were not placed on sale in Réunion.

Catalogue values for unused stamps in this section, from this point to the end of the section, are for Never Hinged items.

Red Cross Issue
Common Design Type

1944 *Perf. 14½x14*
B15 CD90 5fr + 20fr black 1.60 1.10

The surtax was for the French Red Cross and national relief.

France Nos. B365-B366 Surcharged with New Value, "CFA" and Two Bars

1962, Dec. 10 Engr. *Perf. 13*
B16 SP219 10 + 5fr on 20 + 10c 2.10 2.10
B17 SP219 12 + 5fr on 25 + 10c 2.40 2.40

The surtax was for the Red Cross.

France Nos. B374-B375 Surcharged with New Value, "CFA" and Two Bars in Red

1963, Dec. 9
B18 SP223 10 + 5fr on 20 + 10c 2.75 2.75
B19 SP223 12 + 5fr on 25 + 10c 2.75 2.75

Centenary of the Intl. Red Cross. The surtax was for the Red Cross.

France Nos. B385-B386 Surcharged with New Value, "CFA" and Two Bars in Dark Blue

1964, Dec. 13 Unwmk. *Perf. 13*
B20 SP230 10 + 5fr on 20 + 10c 1.60 1.60
B21 SP230 12 + 5fr on 25 + 10c 1.90 1.90

Jean Nicolas Corvisart (1755-1821) and Dominique Larrey (1766-1842), physicians. The surtax was for the Red Cross.

France Nos. B392-B393 Surcharged with New Value, "CFA" and Two Bars

1965, Dec. 12 Engr. *Perf. 13*
B22 SP233 12 + 5fr on 25 + 10c 1.40 1.40
B23 SP233 15 + 5fr on 30 + 10c 1.50 1.50

The surtax was for the Red Cross.

France Nos. B402-B403 Surcharged with New Value, "CFA" and Two Bars

1966, Dec. 11 Engr. *Perf. 13*
B24 SP237 12 + 5fr on 25 + 10c 1.40 1.40
B25 SP237 15 + 5fr on 30 + 10c 1.40 1.40

The surtax was for the Red Cross.

France Nos. B409-B410 Surcharged with New Value, "CFA" and Two Bars

1967, Dec. 17 Engr. *Perf. 13*
B26 SP240 12 + 5fr on 25 + 10c 2.75 2.75
B27 SP240 15 + 5fr on 30 + 10c 3.50 3.50

Surtax for the Red Cross.

France Nos. B421-B424 Surcharged with New Value, "CFA" and Two Bars

1968-69 Engr. *Perf. 13*
B28 SP244 12 + 5fr on 25 + 10c 1.60 1.40
B29 SP244 15 + 5fr on 30 + 10c 1.75 1.40
B30 SP244 20 + 7fr on 40 + 15c ('69) 1.40 1.40
B31 SP244 20 + 7fr on 40 + 15c ('69) 1.40 1.40
Nos. B28-B31 (4) 6.15 5.60

The surtax was for the Red Cross.

France No. B425 Surcharged with New Value, "CFA" and Two Bars

1969, Mar. 17 Engr. *Perf. 13*
B32 SP245 15fr + 5fr on 30c + 10c 1.40 1.40

Stamp Day.

France No. B440 Surcharged with New Value, "CFA" and Two Bars

1970, Mar. 16 Engr. *Perf. 13*
B33 SP249 20fr + 5fr on 40c + 10c 1.10 .95

Stamp day.

France Nos. B443-B444 Surcharged with New Value "CFA" and Two Bars

1970, Dec. 14 Engr. *Perf. 13*

B34 SP252 20 + 7fr on 40 + 15c 2.40 2.00
B35 SP252 20 + 7fr on 40 + 15c 2.40 2.40

The surtax was for the Red Cross.

France No. B451 Surcharged with New Value, "CFA" and Two Bars

1971, Mar. 29 Engr. *Perf. 13*

B36 SP254 25fr + 5fr on 50c + 10c 1.10 .90

Stamp Day.

France Nos. B452-B453 Surcharged with New Value, "CFA" and Two Bars

1971, Dec. 13

B37 SP255 15fr + 5fr on 30c + 10c 1.25 1.25
B38 SP255 25fr + 5fr on 50c + 10c 1.25 1.25

The surtax was for the Red Cross.

France No. B460 Surcharged with New Value and "CFA"

1972, Mar. 20 Engr. *Perf. 13*

B39 SP257 25fr + 5fr on 50c + 10c 1.10 1.10

Stamp Day.

France Nos. B461-B462 Surcharged with New Value, "CFA" and Two Bars in Red or Green

1972, Dec. 16 Engr. *Perf. 13*

B40 SP258 15 + 5fr on 30 + 10c 1.10 1.10
B41 SP258 25 + 5fr on 50 + 10c (G) 1.25 1.25

Surtax was for the Red Cross.

France No. B470 Surcharged with New Value, "CFA" and Two Bars in Red

1973, Mar. 26 Engr. *Perf. 13*

B42 SP260 25fr +5fr on 50c +10c 1.25 1.25

Stamp Day.

France Nos. B471-B472 Surcharged with New Value, "CFA" and Two Bars in Red

1973, Dec. 3 Engr. *Perf. 13*

B43 SP261 15 +5fr on 30c +10c 1.25 1.25
B44 SP261 25 +5fr on 50c +10c 1.25 1.25

Surtax was for the Red Cross.

France No. B477 Surcharged "25 + 5 FCFA"

1974, Mar. 11 Engr. *Perf. 13*

B45 SP263 25fr + 5fr on 50c + 10c .95 .95

Stamp Day.

France Nos. B479-B480 Surcharged with New Value, "FCFA" and Two Bars in Green or Red

1974, Nov. 30 Engr. *Perf. 13*

B46 SP265 30 + 7fr on 60 + 15c (G) 1.25 1.25
B47 SP266 40 + 7fr on 80 + 15c (R) 1.25 1.25

Surtax was for the Red Cross.

AIR POST STAMPS

No. 141 Overprinted in Blue

1937, Jan. 23 Unwmk. *Perf. 12½*

C1 A23 50c red 290.00 250.00
Never hinged 500.00
a. Vert. pair, one without overprint 1,800. 1,800.
b. Inverted overprint 6,000.

Flight of the "Roland Garros" from Reunion to France by aviators Laurent, Lenier and Touge in Jan.-Feb., 1937.

Airplane and Landscape — AP2

1938, Mar. 1 Engr. *Perf. 12½*

C2 AP2 3.65fr slate blue & car .95 .85
C3 AP2 6.65fr brown & org red .95 .85
C4 AP2 9.65fr car & ultra .95 .85
C5 AP2 12.65fr brown & green 1.90 1.40
Nos. C2-C5 (4) 4.75 3.95
Set, never hinged 7.50

For overprints see Nos. C14-C17.

Plane and Bridge over East River AP3

Plane and Landscape AP4

1942, Oct. 19 *Perf. 12x12½*

C6 AP3 50c olive & pur .35
C7 AP3 1fr dk bl & scar .35
C8 AP3 2fr brn & blk .60
C9 AP3 3fr rose lil & grn 1.10
C10 AP3 5fr red org & red brn 1.10

Frame Engr., Center Photo.

C11 AP4 10fr dk grn, red org & vio 1.10
C12 AP4 20fr dk bl, brn vio & red 1.10
C13 AP4 50fr brn car, Prus grn & bl 1.50
Nos. C6-C13 (8) 7.20
Set, never hinged 9.50

Nos. C6-C13 were issued by the Vichy government in France, but were not placed on sale in Réunion.

De Poivre AP4a

1943 *Perf. 12½x12*

C13A AP4a 1fr sepia & red .25
C13B AP4a 2fr green & blue .35
C13C AP4a 3fr dk brown red .40
C13D AP4a 5fr ultramarine & red .55
C13E AP4a 10fr red brown & black .55
C13F AP4a 20fr violet & green .75
Nos. C13A-C13F (6) 2.85
Set, never hinged 4.00

300th Ann. of French settlement on Réunion.

Nos. C13A-C13F were issued by the Vichy government in France, but were not placed on sale in Réunion.

Nos. C2-C5 Overprinted in Black or Carmine

1943 Unwmk. *Perf. 12½*

C14 AP2 3.65fr sl bl & car 5.25 5.25
C15 AP2 6.65fr brn & org red 5.25 5.25
C16 AP2 9.65fr car & ultra (C) 5.25 5.25
C17 AP2 12.65fr brn & grn 5.25 5.25
Nos. C14-C17 (4) 21.00 21.00
Set, never hinged 30.00

Catalogue values for unused stamps in this section, from this point to the end of the section, are for Never Hinged items.

Common Design Type

1944 Photo. *Perf. 14½x14*

C18 CD87 1fr dk org .45 .30
C19 CD87 1.50fr brt red .45 .30
C20 CD87 5fr brn red .60 .45
C21 CD87 10fr black 1.10 .80
C22 CD87 25fr ultra 1.25 .95
C23 CD87 50fr dk grn 1.25 .95
C24 CD87 100fr plum 1.75 1.25
Nos. C18-C24 (7) 6.85 5.00

Victory Issue
Common Design Type

1946, May 8 Engr. *Perf. 12½*

C25 CD92 8fr olive gray 1.10 .90

European victory of the Allied Nations in WWII.

Chad to Rhine Issue
Common Design Types

1946, June 6

C26 CD93 5fr orange 1.25 .85
C27 CD94 10fr sepia 1.25 .85
C28 CD95 15fr grnsh blk 1.25 .85
C29 CD96 20fr lilac rose 1.75 1.25
C30 CD97 25fr greenish blue 1.75 1.25
C31 CD98 50fr green 2.00 1.50
Nos. C26-C31 (6) 9.25 6.55

Shadow of Plane — AP5

Plane over Réunion — AP6

Air View of Réunion and Shadow of Plane — AP7

Perf. 13x12½

1947, Mar. 24 Photo. Unwmk.

C32 AP5 50fr ol grn & bl gray 10.50 8.00
C33 AP6 100fr dk brn & org 16.00 16.00
C34 AP7 200fr dk bl & org 20.00 13.00
Nos. C32-C34 (3) 46.50 37.00

France, Nos. C18-C21 Surcharged and Bars, in Carmine or Black

c

1949 Unwmk. *Perf. 13*

C35 AP7 20fr on 40fr (C) 3.50 1.25
C36 AP8 25fr on 50fr 4.25 1.40
C37 AP9 50fr on 100fr (C) 10.00 4.25
C38 AP10 100fr on 200fr 52.50 21.00
Nos. C35-C38 (4) 70.25 27.90

France Nos. C24, C26 and C27 Surcharged Type "c" and Bars in Black

1949-51

C39 AP12 100fr on 200fr ('51) 125.00 26.50
C40 AP12 200fr on 500fr 52.50 21.00
C41 AP13 500fr on 1000fr ('51) 315.00 210.00
Nos. C39-C41 (3) 492.50 257.50

France Nos. C29-C32 Surcharged "CFA," New Value and Bars in Blue or Red

1954, Feb. 10

C42 AP15(c) 50fr on 100fr 2.50 1.25
C43 AP15 100fr on 200fr (R) 5.00 1.40
C44 AP15(c) 200fr on 500fr 40.00 12.50
C45 AP15 500fr on 1000fr 35.00 12.50
Nos. C42-C45 (4) 82.50 27.65

France Nos. C35-C36 Surcharged "CFA," New Values and Bars in Red or Black

1957-58 Engr. *Perf. 13*

C46 AP17 200fr on 500fr (R) 24.00 6.75
C47 AP17 500fr on 1000fr ('58) 24.00 13.00

France Nos. C37, C39-C40 Surcharged "CFA," New Value and Bars in Red or Black

1961-64

C48 AP15 100fr on 2fr 6.25 1.25
C49 AP17 200fr on 5fr 6.25 3.00
C50 AP17 500fr on 10fr (B;'64) 14.00 6.25
Nos. C48-C50 (3) 26.50 10.50

France No. C41 Surcharged "CFA," New Value and Two Bars in Red

1967, Jan. 27 Engr. *Perf. 13*

C51 AP17 100fr on 2fr sl bl & ind 2.00 .80

France No. C45 Surcharged in Red with "CFA," New Value and Two Bars in Red

1972, May 14 Engr. *Perf. 13*

C52 AP21 200fr on 5fr multi 4.50 1.75

AIR POST SEMI-POSTAL STAMPS

French Revolution Issue
Common Design Type

1939 Unwmk. *Perf. 13*

Name and Value Typo. in Orange

CB1 CD83 3.65fr + 4fr brn blk 24.00 24.00
Never hinged 35.00

Felix Guyon Hospital, St. Denis — SPAP1

Perf. 13½x12½

1942, June 22 **Engr.**

CB2	SPAP1	1.50fr + 3.50fr lt green	1.00	
CB3	SPAP1	2fr + 6fr yellow brown	1.00	
		Set, never hinged	2.50	

Native children's welfare fund.

Nos. CB2-CB3 were issued by the Vichy government in France, but were not placed on sale in Réunion.

Colonial Education Fund

Common Design Type

1942, June 22

CB4	CD86a	1.20fr + 1.80fr blue & red	.90	
		Never hinged	1.25	

No. CB4 was issued by the Vichy government in France, but was not placed on sale in Réunion.

POSTAGE DUE STAMPS

D1

D2

1889-92 **Unwmk.** **Type-set** ***Imperf.***
Without Gum

J1	D1	5c black	27.50	13.50
J2	D1	10c black	32.50	13.50
J3	D1	15c black ('92)	65.00	40.00
J4	D1	20c black	47.50	26.00
J5	D1	30c black	45.00	26.00
		Nos. J1-J5 (5)	217.50	119.00

Ten varieties of each value.

Nos. J1-J2, J4-J5 issued on yellowish paper in 1889; Nos. J1-J3, J5 on bluish white paper in 1892.

Nos. J1-J5 exist with double impression. Values $125-$190.

1907 **Typo.** ***Perf. 14x13½***

J6	D2	5c carmine, *yel*	.85	.85
J7	D2	10c blue, *bl*	.85	.85
J8	D2	15c black, *bluish*	1.40	1.40
J9	D2	20c carmine	1.40	1.40
J10	D2	30c green, *grnsh*	2.10	2.10
J11	D2	50c red, *green*	2.50	2.50
J12	D2	60c carmine, *bl*	2.50	2.50
J13	D2	1fr violet	2.75	2.75
		Nos. J6-J13 (8)	14.35	14.35
		Set, never hinged	25.00	

Type of 1907 Issue Surcharged

1927

J14	D2	2fr on 1fr org red	12.00	12.00
J15	D2	3fr on 1fr org brn	12.00	12.00
		Set, never hinged	37.50	

Arms of Réunion
D3

Numeral
D4

1933 **Engr.** ***Perf. 13x13½***

J16	D3	5c deep violet	.20	.20
J17	D3	10c dark green	.20	.20
J18	D3	15c orange brown	.20	.20
J19	D3	20c light red	.35	.35
J20	D3	30c olive green	.35	.35
J21	D3	50c ultramarine	.80	.80
J22	D3	60c black brown	.80	.80
J23	D3	1fr light violet	.80	.80
J24	D3	2fr deep blue	.80	.80
J25	D3	3fr carmine	1.00	1.00
		Nos. J16-J25 (10)	5.50	5.50
		Set, never hinged	9.00	

Catalogue values for unused stamps in this section, from this point to the end of the section, are for Never Hinged items.

1947 **Unwmk.** **Photo.** ***Perf. 13***

J26	D4	10c dark violet	.20	.20
J27	D4	30c brown	.20	.20
J28	D4	50c blue green	.20	.20
J29	D4	1fr orange	.55	.45
J30	D4	2fr red violet	.55	.45
J31	D4	3fr red brown	.80	.65
J32	D4	4fr blue	1.40	1.10
J33	D4	5fr henna brown	1.75	1.40
J34	D4	10fr slate green	1.75	1.40
J35	D4	20fr violet blue	1.75	.90
		Nos. J26-J35 (10)	9.15	6.95

France, Nos. J83-J92 Surcharged in Black

1949-53

J36	D5	10c on 1fr brt ultra	.20	.20
J37	D5	50c on 2fr turq bl	.40	.35
J38	D5	1fr on 3fr brn org	.55	.35
J39	D5	2fr on 4fr dp vio	.55	.35
J40	D5	3fr on 5fr brt pink	6.00	2.50
J41	D5	5fr on 10fr red org	.95	.70
J42	D5	10fr on 20fr ol bis	1.90	1.90
J43	D5	20fr on 50fr dk grn ('50)	12.00	5.25
J44	D5	50fr on 100fr dp grn ('53)	29.00	13.00
		Nos. J36-J44 (9)	51.55	24.60

Same Surcharge on France Nos. J93, J95-J96

1962-63 **Typo.** ***Perf. 14x13½***

J46	D6	1fr on 5c brt pink ('63)	2.75	1.10
J47	D6	10fr on 20c ol bis ('63)	5.25	2.50
J48	D6	20fr on 50c dk grn	20.00	12.00
		Nos. J46-J48 (3)	28.00	15.60

France Nos. J98-J102, J104-J105 Surcharged with New Value and "CFA"

1964-71 **Unwmk.** ***Perf. 14x13½***

J49	D7	1fr on 5c	.20	.20
J50	D7	5fr on 10c	.30	.20
J51	D7	7fr on 15c	.50	.45
J52	D7	10fr on 20c ('71)	1.40	.55
J53	D7	15fr on 30c	.65	.45
J54	D7	20fr on 50c	.80	.55
J55	D7	50fr on 1fr	1.40	1.25
		Nos. J49-J55 (7)	5.25	3.65

PARCEL POST STAMP

No. 40 Overprinted

1906 **Unwmk.** ***Perf. 14x13½***

Q1	A14	10c red	21.00	21.00

FRENCH COLONIES

ˈfrench ˈkä-lə-nēz

From 1859 to 1906 and from 1943 to 1945 special stamps were issued for use in all French Colonies which did not have stamps of their own.

100 Centimes = 1 Franc

Catalogue values for unused stamps in this country are for Never Hinged items, beginning with Scott B1 in the semi-postal section and Scott J23 in the postage due section.

Perforations: Nos. 1-45 are known variously perforated privately.

Gum: Many of Nos. 1-45 were issued without gum. Some were gummed locally.

Reprints: Nos. 1-7, 9-12, 24, 26-42, 44 and 45 were reprinted officially in 1887. These reprints are ungummed and the colors of both design and paper are deeper or brighter than the originals. Value for Nos. 1-6, $20 each.

Eagle and Crown — A1

1859-65 **Unwmk.** **Typo.** ***Imperf.***

1	A1	1c ol grn, *pale bl* ('62)	24.00	*27.50*
2	A1	5c yel grn, *grnsh* ('62)	24.00	16.00
3	A1	10c bister, *yel*	32.50	8.00
a.		Pair, one sideways	1,000.	525.00
4	A1	20c bl, *bluish* ('65)	35.00	13.50
5	A1	40c org, *yelsh*	27.50	13.50
6	A1	80c car rose, *pnksh* ('65)	110.00	60.00
		Nos. 1-6 (6)	253.00	138.50

For surcharges see Reunion Nos. 3-4.

Napoleon III
A2 A3

Ceres
A4

Napoleon III
A5

1871-72 ***Imperf.***

7	A2	1c ol grn, *pale bl* ('72)	80.00	80.00
8	A3	5c yel grn, *grnsh* ('72)	1,000.	400.00
9	A4	10c bis, *yelsh*	375.00	130.00
a.		Tête bêche pair	*55,000.*	*22,500.*
10	A4	15c bis, *yelsh* ('72)	325.00	13.00
11	A4	20c blue, *bluish*	525.00	125.00
a.		Tête bêche pair		*18,000.*
12	A4	25c bl, *bluish* ('72)	175.00	13.00
13	A5	30c brn, *yelsh*	175.00	60.00
14	A4	40c org, *yelsh* (I)	250.00	13.00
a.		Type II	*3,500.*	*650.00*
b.		Pair, types I & II	*7,250.*	*1,750.*
15	A5	80c rose, *pnksh*	1,100.	115.00
		Nos. 7-15 (9)	4,005.	949.00

For 40c types I-II see illustrations over France #1.

For surcharges see Reunion Nos. 5-6.

See note after France No. 9 for additional information on Nos. 8-9, 11-12, 14.

Ceres
A6 A7

1872-77 ***Imperf.***

16	A6	1c ol grn, *pale bl* ('73)	13.00	*14.50*
17	A6	2c red brn, *yelsh* ('76)	475.00	750.00
18	A6	4c gray ('76)	*11,000.*	475.00
19	A6	5c grn, *pale bl*	17.50	9.50
20	A7	10c bis, *rose* ('76)	240.00	13.00
21	A7	15c bister ('77)	525.00	100.00
22	A7	30c brn, *yelsh*	130.00	21.00
23	A7	80c rose, *pnksh* ('73)	625.00	140.00

No. 17 was used only in Cochin China, 1876-77. Excellent forgeries of Nos. 17 and 18 exist.

With reference to the stamps of France and French Colonies in the same designs and colors see the note after France No. 9.

Peace and Commerce
A8

Commerce
A9

1877-78 **Type I** ***Imperf.***

24	A8	1c grn, *grnsh*	35.00	*45.00*
25	A8	4c grn, *grnsh*	24.00	14.50
26	A8	30c brn, *yelsh* ('78)	52.50	52.50
27	A8	40c ver, *straw*	35.00	21.00
28	A8	75c rose, *rose* ('78)	75.00	*100.00*
29	A8	1fr brnz grn, *straw*	60.00	*67.50*
		Nos. 24-29 (6)	281.50	300.50

Type II

30	A8	2c grn, *grnsh*	17.50	11.00
31	A8	5c grn, *grnsh*	24.00	5.50
32	A8	10c grn, *grnsh*	125.00	24.00
33	A8	15c gray, *grnsh*	250.00	72.50
34	A8	20c red brn, *straw*	52.50	9.50
35	A8	25c ultra *bluish*	52.50	8.75
a.		25c blue, *bluish* ('78)	*4,250.*	175.00
36	A8	35c vio blk, *org* ('78)	67.50	32.50
		Nos. 30-36 (7)	589.00	163.75
		Nos. 24-36 (13)	870.50	464.25

1878-80

Type II

38	A8	1c blk, *lil bl*	21.00	21.00
39	A8	2c brn, *buff*	21.00	*24.00*
40	A8	4c claret, *lav*	32.50	*45.00*
41	A8	10c blk, *lav* ('79)	120.00	27.50
42	A8	15c blue ('79)	35.00	17.50
43	A8	20c red, *grn* ('79)	87.50	17.50
44	A8	25c blk, *red* ('79)	600.00	275.00
45	A8	25c yel, *straw* ('80)	725.00	32.50
		Nos. 38-45 (8)	1,642.	460.00

No. 44 was used only in Mayotte, Nossi-Be and New Caledonia. Forgeries exist.

The 3c yellow, 3c gray, 15c yellow, 20c blue, 25c rose and 5fr lilac were printed together with the reprints, and were never issued.

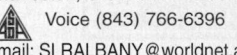

1881-86 *Perf. 14x13½*

46	A9	1c blk, *lil bl*	5.50	4.75
47	A9	2c brn, *buff*	5.50	4.75
48	A9	4c claret, *lav*	5.50	5.50
49	A9	5c grn, *grnsh*	6.50	3.25
50	A9	10c blk, *lavender*	11.00	4.75
51	A9	15c blue	16.00	3.25
52	A9	20c red, *yel grn*	52.50	18.00
53	A9	25c yel, *straw*	17.50	5.50
54	A9	25c blk, *rose* ('86)	24.00	3.25
55	A9	30c brn, *bis*	45.00	21.00
56	A9	35c vio blk, *yel org*	40.00	30.00
a.		35c violet black, *yellow*	100.00	52.50
57	A9	40c ver, *straw*	45.00	27.50
58	A9	75c car, *rose*	120.00	60.00
59	A9	1fr brnz grn, *straw*	80.00	45.00
		Nos. 46-59 (14)	474.00	236.50

Nos. 46-59 exist imperforate. They are proofs and were not used for postage, except the 10c.

For stamps of type A9 surcharged with numerals see: Cochin China, Diego Suarez, Gabon, Malagasy (Madagascar), Nossi-Be, New Caledonia, Reunion, Senegal, Tahiti.

SEMI-POSTAL STAMPS

Catalogue values for unused stamps in this section are for Never Hinged items.

Resistance Fighters — SP1

1943 **Unwmk.** **Litho.** *Rouletted*

B1	SP1	1.50fr + 98.50fr ind & gray	47.50	*65.00*
		Without label	21.00	*35.00*

The surtax was for the benefit of patriots and the French Committee of Liberation.

No. B1 was printed in sheets of 10 (5x2) with adjoining labels showing the Lorraine cross.

Colonies Offering Aid to France SP2

1943 *Perf. 12*

B2	SP2	9fr + 41fr red violet	3.50	10.50

Surtax for the benefit of French patriots.

Patriots and Map of France SP3

1943

B3	SP3	50c + 4.50fr yel grn	1.25	*10.50*
B4	SP3	1.50fr + 8.50fr cerise	1.25	*10.50*
B5	SP3	3fr + 12fr grnsh bl	1.25	*10.50*
B6	SP3	5fr + 15fr olive gray	1.25	*1.50*
		Nos. B3-B6 (4)	5.00	33.00

Surtax for the aid of combatants and patriots.

Refugee Family SP4

1943

B7	SP4	10fr + 40fr dull blue	5.25	*12.50*

The surtax was for refugee relief work.

Woman and Child with Wing — SP5

1944

B8	SP5	10fr + 40fr grnsh blk	6.75	*21.00*

Surtax for the benefit of aviation.

Nos. B1-B8 were prepared for use in the French Colonies, but after the landing of Free French troops in Corsica they were used there and later also in Southern France. They became valid throughout France in Nov. 1944.

POSTAGE DUE STAMPS

D1

1884-85 **Unwmk.** **Typo.** *Imperf.*

J1	D1	1c black	4.00	4.00
J2	D1	2c black	4.00	4.00
J3	D1	3c black	4.00	4.00
J4	D1	4c black	4.75	4.00
J5	D1	5c black	6.50	3.25
J6	D1	10c black	8.75	6.50
J7	D1	15c black	13.00	10.50
J8	D1	20c black	16.00	10.50
J9	D1	30c black	17.50	8.75
J10	D1	40c black	21.00	8.75
J11	D1	60c black	27.50	16.00
J12	D1	1fr brown	35.00	27.50
a.		1fr black	300.00	
J13	D1	2fr brown	35.00	27.50
a.		2fr black	300.00	*325.00*
J14	D1	5fr brown	110.00	67.50
a.		5fr black	425.00	*450.00*

Nos. J12a, J13a and J14a were not regularly issued.

1894-1906

J15	D1	5c pale blue	1.60	1.60
J16	D1	10c gray brown	1.60	1.60
J17	D1	15c pale green	1.60	1.60
J18	D1	20c olive grn ('06)	1.60	1.60
J19	D1	30c carmine	2.75	1.60
J20	D1	50c lilac	2.75	1.60
J21	D1	60c brown, *buff*	4.50	2.75
a.		60c dark violet, *buff*	4.75	2.75
J22	D1	1fr red, *buff*	7.50	4.50
a.		1fr rose, *buff*	27.50	19.00
		Nos. J15-J22 (8)	23.90	16.85

For overprints see New Caledonia Nos. J1-J8.

Catalogue values for unused stamps in this section, from this point to the end of the section, are for Never Hinged items.

D2

1945 **Litho.** *Perf. 12*

J23	D2	10c slate blue	.45	*16.00*
J24	D2	15c yel green	.45	*16.00*
J25	D2	25c deep orange	.45	*16.00*
J26	D2	50c greenish blk	1.00	*16.00*
J27	D2	60c copper brn	1.00	*16.00*
J28	D2	1fr deep red lil	1.00	*16.00*
J29	D2	2fr red	1.00	*16.00*
J30	D2	4fr slate gray	4.50	*20.00*
J31	D2	5fr brt ultra	4.50	*20.00*
J32	D2	10fr purple	22.50	*52.50*
J33	D2	20fr dull brown	4.00	*20.00*
J34	D2	50fr deep green	7.25	*27.50*
		Nos. J23-J34 (12)	48.10	252.00

FRENCH CONGO

'french 'käŋ-ˌgō

LOCATION — Central Africa
GOVT. — French possession

French Congo was originally a separate colony, but was joined in 1888 to Gabon and placed under one commissioner-general with a lieutenant-governor presiding in Gabon and another in French Congo. In 1894 the military holdings in Ubangi were attached to French Congo, and in 1900 the Chad military protectorate was added. Postal service was not established in Ubangi or Chad, however, at that time. In 1906 Gabon and Middle Congo were separated and French Congo ceased to exist as such. Chad and Ubangi remained attached to Middle Congo as the joint dependency of "Ubangi-Chari-Chad," and Middle Congo stamps were used there.

Issues of the Republic of the Congo are listed under Congo People's Republic (ex-French).

100 Centimes = 1 Franc

Watermarks

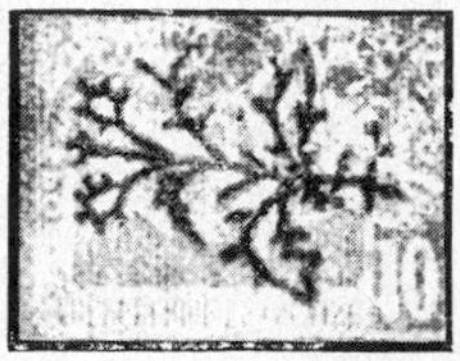

Wmk. 122 — Thistle Branch

Wmk. 123 — Rose Branch

Wmk. 124 — Olive Branch

Stamps of French Colonies Surcharged Horizontally in Red or Black

1891 **Unwmk.** *Perf. 14x13½*

1	A9	5c on 1c blk, *lil bl* (R)	*6,250.*	*4,400.*
2	A9	5c on 1c blk, *lil bl*	175.00	100.00
a.		Double surcharge	625.00	425.00
3	A9	5c on 15c blue	275.00	150.00
a.		Double surcharge	650.00	325.00
5	A9	5c on 25c blk, *rose*	110.00	80.00
a.		Inverted surcharge		

First "O" of "Congo" is a Capital, "Francais" with Capital "F"

1891-92

6	A9	5c on 20c red, *grn*	1,200.	425.00
7	A9	5c on 25c blk, *rose*	175.00	80.00
a.		Surcharge vertical	240.00	92.50
8	A9	10c on 25c blk, *rose*	225.00	60.00
a.		Inverted surcharge	400.00	150.00
b.		Surcharge vertical	200.00	100.00
d.		Double surcharge	390.00	190.00
9	A9	10c on 40c red, *straw*	2,400.	350.00
10	A9	15c on 25c blk, *rose*	200.00	45.00
a.		Surcharge vertical	240.00	80.00
c.		Double surcharge	350.00	175.00

First "O" of Congo small
Surcharge Vert., Down or Up
No period

11	A9	5c on 25c blk, *rose*	250.00	120.00
12	A9	10c on 25c blk, *rose*		—
13	A9	15c on 25c blk, *rose*	400.00	160.00

Postage Due Stamps of French Colonies Surcharged in Red or Black Reading Down or Up

1892 *Imperf.*

14	D1	5c on 5c blk (R)	160.00	130.00
15	D1	5c on 20c blk (R)	160.00	130.00
16	D1	5c on 30c blk (R)	210.00	150.00
17	D1	10c on 1fr brown	175.00	125.00
a.		Double surcharge	4,000.	
b.		Surcharge horiz.		*2,250.*
		Nos. 14-17 (4)	705.00	535.00

Excellent counterfeits of Nos. 1-17 exist.

Navigation and Commerce — A3

1892-1900 **Typo.** *Perf. 14x13½*

Colony Name in Blue or Carmine

18	A3	1c blk, *lil bl*	1.60	1.60
19	A3	2c brn, *buff*	3.00	3.00
a.		Name double	175.00	175.00
20	A3	4c claret, *lav*	3.00	3.00
a.		Name in blk and in blue	175.00	175.00
21	A3	5c grn, *grnsh*	6.00	6.00
22	A3	10c blk, *lavender*	19.00	19.00
a.		Name double	800.00	550.00
23	A3	10c red ('00)	2.75	2.00
24	A3	15c blue, quadrille paper	52.50	17.00
25	A3	15c gray ('00)	9.25	6.75
26	A3	20c red, *grn*	19.00	17.00
27	A3	25c blk, *rose*	24.00	16.00
28	A3	25c blue ('00)	10.50	10.50
29	A3	30c brn, *bis*	27.50	20.00
30	A3	40c red, *straw*	52.50	32.50
31	A3	50c car, *rose*	47.50	32.50
32	A3	50c brn, *az* ('00)	13.50	12.50
a.		Name double	750.00	750.00
33	A3	75c dp vio, *org*	40.00	32.50
34	A3	1fr brnz grn, *straw*	55.00	32.50
		Nos. 18-34 (17)	386.60	264.35

Perf. 13½x14 stamps are counterfeits.
For surcharges see Nos. 50-51.

Leopard — A4

Bakalois Woman — A5

Coconut Grove — A6

1900 **Wmk. 122** *Perf. 11*

35	A4	1c brn vio & gray lilac	.80	.80
a.		Background inverted	72.50	72.50
36	A4	2c brn & org	.80	.80
a.		2c dark red & red	160.00	*250.00*
b.		Imperf., pair	87.50	*100.00*

37 A4 4c scar & gray bl 1.60 1.20
a. 4c dark red & red 700.00
b. Background inverted 87.50 80.00
38 A4 5c grn & gray grn 2.40 1.20
a. Imperf., pair 140.00 140.00
39 A4 10c dk red & red 7.25 2.75
a. Imperf., pair 140.00 140.00
40 A4 15c dl vio & ol grn 2.40 1.20
a. Imperf. pair 105.00

Wmk. 123

41 A5 20c yel grn & org 2.40 2.00
42 A5 25c bl & pale bl 3.25 2.00
44 A5 40c org brn & brt grn 5.25 2.40
a. Imperf., pair 105.00 105.00
b. Center inverted 190.00 160.00
45 A5 50c gray vio & lil 6.75 6.00
46 A5 75c red vio & org 15.00 10.00
a. Imperf., pair 105.00 105.00

Wmk. 124

47 A6 1fr gray lil & ol 24.00 17.50
a. Center inverted 275.00 275.00
b. Imperf., pair 140.00 140.00
48 A6 2fr car & brn 40.00 30.00
a. Imperf., pair 275.00 275.00
49 A6 5fr brn org & gray 85.00 72.50
a. 5fr ocher & gray 750.00 *950.00*
b. Center inverted 425.00 425.00
c. Wmk. 123 500.00 500.00
d. Imperf., pair 750.00 750.00
Nos. 35-49 (14) 196.90 150.35

For surcharges see Nos. 52-53.

Nos. 26 and 29 Surcharged in Black

Valeur
15

1900 **Unwmk.** ***Perf. 14x13½***
50 A3 5c on 20c red, *grn* *26,000.* *6,000.*
a. Double surcharge *18,000.*
51 A3 15c on 30c brn, *bis* *20,000.* *2,600.*
a. Double surcharge *6,000.*

Nos. 43 and 48 Surcharged in Black:

a

0,10

b

1903 **Wmk. 123** ***Perf. 11***
52 A5 5c on 30c 300.00 150.00
a. Inverted surcharge *2,700.*

Wmk. 124

53 A6 10c on 2fr 350.00 140.00
a. Inverted surcharge *2,700.*
b. Double surcharge *3,100.*

Counterfeits of the preceding surcharges are known.

FRENCH EQUATORIAL AFRICA

'french ˌē-kwə-'tōr-ē-əl 'a-fri-kə

LOCATION — North of Belgian Congo and south of Libya
GOVT. — French Colony
AREA — 959,256 square miles
POP. — 4,491,785
CAPITAL — Brazzaville

In 1910 Gabon and Middle Congo, with its military dependencies, were politically united as French Equatorial Africa. The component colonies were granted administrative autonomy. In 1915 Ubangi-Chari-Chad was made an autonomous civilian colony and in 1920 Chad was made a civil colony. In 1934 the four colonies were administratively united as one colony, but this federation was not completed until 1936. Each colony had its own postal administration until 1936. The postal issues of the former colonial subdivisions are listed under the names of those colonies.

In 1958, French Equatorial Africa was divided into four republics: Chad, Congo, Gabon and Central African Republic (formerly Ubangi-Chari).

Stamps other than Nos. 189-192 are inscribed with "Afrique Equatoriale Francaise" or "AEF" and the name of one of the component colonies are listed under those colonies.

100 Centimes = 1 Franc

Catalogue values for unused stamps in this country are for Never Hinged items, beginning with Scott 142 in the regular postage section, Scott B8A in the semi-postal section, Scott C17 in the airpost section, and Scott J12 in the postage due section.

Stamps of Gabon, 1932, Overprinted "Afrique Equatoriale Francaise" and Bars Similar to "a" and "b" in Black

Perf. 13x13½, 13½x13

1936 **Unwmk.**
1 A16 1c brown violet .30 .40
2 A16 2c black, *rose* .55 .65
3 A16 4c green 1.10 1.25
4 A16 5c grnsh blue 1.10 1.25
5 A16 10c red, *yel* 1.00 1.25
6 A17 40c brown violet 3.00 2.40
7 A17 50c red brown 2.40 1.90
8 A17 1fr yel grn, *bl* 27.50 12.50
9 A18 1.50fr dull blue 8.00 2.10
10 A18 2fr brown red 16.00 9.50
Nos. 1-10 (10) 60.95 33.20

Stamps of Middle Congo, 1933 Overprinted in Black:

a

b

c

1936
11 A4 (b) 1c lt brown .25 .30
12 A4 (b) 2c dull blue .30 .40
13 A4 (b) 4c olive green 1.40 1.50
14 A4 (b) 5c red violet .80 .90
15 A4 (b) 10c slate 1.40 1.10
16 A4 (b) 15c dk violet 1.90 1.60
17 A4 (b) 20c red, *pink* 1.90 1.40
18 A4 (b) 25c orange 2.90 2.10
19 A5 (a) 40c orange brn 3.90 2.50
20 A5 (c) 50c black violet 3.90 2.40
21 A5 (c) 75c black, *pink* 4.75 4.00
22 A5 (a) 90c carmine 4.75 3.50
23 A5 (c) 1.50fr dark blue 3.25 2.00
24 A6 (a) 5fr slate blue 52.50 32.50
25 A6 (a) 10fr black 32.50 24.00
26 A6 (a) 20fr dark brown 32.50 32.50
Nos. 11-26 (16) 148.90 112.70

Common Design Types pictured following the introduction.

Paris International Exposition Issue
Common Design Types

1937, Apr. 15 **Engr.** ***Perf. 13***
27 CD74 20c dark violet 2.10 2.10
28 CD75 30c dark green 2.10 2.10
29 CD76 40c carmine rose 2.10 2.10
30 CD77 50c dk brn & bl 2.10 2.10
31 CD78 90c red 2.25 2.25
32 CD79 1.50fr ultra 2.25 2.25
Nos. 27-32 (6) 12.90 12.90

Logging on Loéme River — A1

People of Chad — A2

Pierre Savorgnan de Brazza A3

Emile Gentil — A4

Paul Crampel A5

Governor Victor Liotard A6

Two types of 25c:
Type I — Wide numerals (4mm).
Type II — Narrow numerals (3½mm).

1937-40 **Photo.** ***Perf. 13½x13***
33 A1 1c brown & yel .25 .25
34 A1 2c violet & grn .25 .25
35 A1 3c blue & yel ('40) .25 .30
36 A1 4c magenta & bl .30 .30
37 A1 5c dk & lt green .50 .30
38 A2 10c magenta & blue .30 .30
39 A2 15c blue & buff .30 .30
40 A2 20c brown & yellow .30 *.30*
41 A2 25c cop red & bl (I) .75 .30
a. Type II 2.75 2.00
42 A3 30c gray grn & grn .80 .55
43 A3 30c chlky bl, ind & buff ('40) .40 .50
44 A2 35c dp grn & yel ('38) .95 .80
45 A3 40c cop red & bl .40 .30
46 A3 45c dk bl & lt grn 4.50 3.50
47 A3 45c dp grn & yel grn ('40) .55 .65
48 A3 50c brown & yellow .40 .25
49 A3 55c pur & bl ('38) .80 .75
50 A3 60c mar & gray bl ('40) .65 .75
51 A4 65c dk bl & lt grn .80 .40
52 A4 70c dp vio & buff ('40) .75 .80
53 A4 75c ol blk & dl yel 5.25 4.50
54 A4 80c brn & yel ('38) .55 .55
55 A4 90c copper red & buff .55 .40
56 A4 1fr dk vio & lt grn 2.10 1.10
57 A3 1fr cer & dl org ('38) 3.00 1.25
58 A4 1fr bl grn & sl grn ('40) .55 .55
59 A5 1.25fr cop red & buff 1.25 .90
60 A5 1.40fr dk brn & pale grn ('40) 1.00 1.25
61 A5 1.50fr dk & lt blue 1.50 .75
62 A5 1.60fr dp vio & buff ('40) 1.00 1.25
63 A5 1.75fr brn & yel 1.75 .90
64 A4 1.75fr bl & lt bl ('38) .75 .65
65 A5 2fr dk & lt green .95 .75
66 A6 2.15fr brn, vio & yel ('38) 1.00 .80
67 A6 2.25fr bl & lt bl ('39) 1.60 1.60
68 A6 2.50fr rose lake & buff ('40) 1.25 1.25
69 A6 3fr dk blue & buff .75 .40
70 A6 5fr dk & lt green 1.40 .95
71 A6 10fr dk violet & bl 3.25 2.50
72 A6 20fr ol blk & dl yel 3.50 3.50
Nos. 33-72 (40) 47.15 37.65

For overprints and surcharges see Nos. 80-127, 129-141, B2-B3, B10-B13, B22-B23.

Colonial Arts Exhibition Issue
Souvenir Sheet
Common Design Type

1937 ***Imperf.***
73 CD79 3fr red brown 11.00 *12.00*
Never hinged 15.00

Count Louis Edouard Bouet-Willaumez and His Ship "La Malouine" — A7

1938, Dec. 5 ***Perf. 13½***
74 A7 65c gray brown 1.10 1.10
75 A7 1fr deep rose 1.20 1.20
76 A7 1.75fr blue 1.50 1.50
77 A7 2fr dull violet 2.10 2.10
Nos. 74-77 (4) 5.90 5.90
Set, never hinged 11.50

Centenary of Gabon.

New York World's Fair Issue
Common Design Type

1939, May 10 **Engr.** ***Perf. 12½x12***
78 CD82 1.25fr carmine lake 1.60 1.60
79 CD82 2.25fr ultra 1.60 1.60
Set, never hinged 4.25

Libreville View and Marshal Petain A7a

1941 **Engr.** ***Perf. 12½x12***
79A A7a 1fr bluish green 1.20
79B A7a 2.50fr blue 1.20
Set, never hinged 3.00

Nos. 79A-79B were issued by the Vichy government in France, but were not placed on sale in French Equatorial Africa.
For surcharges, see Nos. B36-B37.

Stamps of 1936-40, Overprinted in Carmine or Black:

Nos. 80-82, 84-88, 93

Nos. 83, 89-92, 94-125

1940-41 ***Perf. 13½x13***
80 A1 1c brn & yel (C) 2.00 2.00
81 A1 2c vio & grn (C) 2.00 2.00
82 A1 3c blue & yel (C) 2.00 2.00
83 A4 4c ol grn (No. 13) 13.50 11.00
b. Inverted overprint 110.00 *130.00*
84 A1 5c dk grn & lt grn (C) 2.00 2.00
85 A2 10c magenta & bl 2.40 2.40
86 A2 15c blue & buff (C) 2.00 2.00
87 A2 20c brn & yel (C) 2.00 2.00
88 A2 25c cop red & bl 9.50 9.50
89 A3 30c gray grn & grn (C) 17.50 12.50
90 A3 30c gray grn & grn ('41) 3.25 3.25
91 A3 30c chlky bl, ind & buff (C) ('41) 8.75 8.00
92 A3 30c chlky bl, ind & buff ('41) 12.50 11.00
93 A2 35c dp grn & yel (C) 2.40 2.40
94 A3 40c cop red & bl 1.60 1.60
b. Inverted overprint *92.50*
95 A3 45c dp grn & yel grn (C) 1.60 1.20

96 A3 45c dp grn & yel grn ('41) 2.00 2.00
97 A3 50c brn & yel (C) 6.75 6.00
98 A3 50c brn & yel ('41) 6.50 5.50
99 A3 55c pur & bl (C) 1.60 1.20
100 A3 55c pur & bl ('41) 2.00 2.00
101 A3 60c mar & gray bl 1.60 1.60
102 A4 65c dk bl & lt grn 1.60 1.60
103 A4 70c dp vio & buff 1.60 1.60
104 A4 75c ol blk & dl yel 65.00 65.00
105 A4 80c brown & yellow 1.60 1.60
106 A4 90c cop red & buff 1.60 1.60
107 A4 1fr bl grn & sl grn 9.50 8.75
108 A4 1fr bl grn & sl grn (C) ('41) 7.25 6.75
109 A3 1fr cer & dl org 2.40 2.40
110 A5 1.40fr dk brn & pale grn 1.60 1.60
111 A5 1.50fr dk bl & lt bl 1.60 1.60
112 A5 1.60fr dp vio & buff 1.60 1.60
113 A5 1.75fr brown & yel 2.00 2.00
114 A6 2.15fr brn, vio & yel 2.00 2.00
115 A6 2.25fr bl & lt bl (C) 1.60 1.60
116 A6 2.25fr bl & lt bl ('41) 4.00 4.00
117 A6 2.50fr rose lake & buff 1.60 1.60
118 A6 3fr dk bl & buff (C) 1.60 1.60
119 A6 3fr dk bl & buff ('41) 4.00 4.00
120 A6 5fr dk grn & lt grn (C) 4.00 4.00
121 A6 5fr dk grn & lt grn ('41) 110.00 65.00
122 A6 10fr dk vio & bl (C) 2.75 2.75
123 A6 10fr dk vio & bl ('41) 110.00 65.00
124 A6 20fr ol blk & dl yel (C) 2.40 2.40
125 A6 20fr ol blk & dl yel ('41) 16.00 13.50
Nos. 80-125 (46) 462.75 356.70

For overprints and surcharges see Nos. 129-132, B12-B13, B22-B23.

For types of Nos. 38//61 without "RF," see Nos. 155A-155B.

Double Overprint

80a	A1	1c	300.00	190.00
81a	A1	2c	25.00	
82a	A1	3c	25.00	
83a	A4	4c	72.50	
84a	A1	5c	25.00	
85a	A2	10c	25.00	
86a	A2	15c	25.00	
87a	A2	20c	25.00	
88a	A2	25c	45.00	
89a	A3	30c		92.50
90a	A3	30c	52.50	
91a	A3	30c	40.00	40.00
93a	A2	35c	225.00	
94a	A3	40c	40.00	
96a	A3	45c	40.00	*60.00*
98a	A3	50c	45.00	
100a	A3	55c	40.00	
102a	A4	65c	40.00	
103a	A4	70c	45.00	
105a	A4	80c	45.00	
106a	A4	90c	40.00	
b.		one inverted	110.00	
109a	A4	1fr One inverted	110.00	
110a	A5	1.40fr	45.00	
111a	A5	1.50fr	45.00	
114a	A6	2.15fr	35.00	
115a	A6	2.25fr	45.00	
116a	A6	2.25fr	40.00	
117a	A6	2.50fr	45.00	
119a	A6	3fr	40.00	
123a	A6	10fr	45.00	*47.50*
124a	A6	20fr	45.00	
Nos. 96a-124a (17)			790.00	

Nos. 48, 51 Surcharged in Black or Carmine

1940
126 A3 75c on 50c .75 .75
a. Double surcharge 35.00
127 A4 1fr on 65c (C) .75 .75
a. Double surcharge 27.50
Set, never hinged 5.00

Middle Congo No. 67 Overprinted in Carmine like No. 80
Perf. 13½
128 A4 4c olive green 62.50 52.50

Stamps of 1940 With Additional Overprint in Black

1940 ***Perf. 13½x13***
129 A4 80c brown & yel 17.00 12.50
a. Overprint without "2" 130.00
130 A4 1fr bl grn & sl grn 18.00 13.50
131 A3 1fr cer & dull org 22.50 17.50
132 A5 1.50fr dk bl & lt bl 15.00 12.00
Nos. 129-132 (4) 72.50 55.50

Arrival of General de Gaulle in Brazzaville, capital of Free France, Oct. 24, 1940.

These stamps were sold affixed to post cards and at a slight increase over face value to cover the cost of the cards.

For surcharges see #B12-B13, B22-B23.

Stamps of 1937-40 Overprinted in Black

1941
133 A1 1c brown & yel 2.40 2.40
134 A1 2c violet & grn 2.40 2.40
135 A1 3c blue & yel 2.40 2.40
136 A1 5c dk & lt green 2.40 2.40
137 A2 10c magenta & bl 2.40 2.40
138 A2 15c blue & buff 2.40 2.40
139 A2 20c brown & yel 2.40 2.40
140 A2 25c copper red & bl 5.50 5.50
141 A2 35c dp grn & yel 5.50 5.50
a. Double overprint 100.00
Nos. 133-141 (9) 27.80 27.80
Set, never hinged 45.00

There are 2 settings of the overprint on Nos. 133-141 & C10. The 1st has 1mm between lines of the overprint, the 2nd has 2mm.

Catalogue values for unused stamps in this section, from this point to the end of the section, are for Never Hinged items.

Phoenix — A8

1941 **Photo.** ***Perf. 14x14½***
142 A8 5c brown .30 .25
143 A8 10c dark blue .30 .25
144 A8 25c emerald .30 .25
145 A8 30c deep orange .30 .25
146 A8 40c dk slate grn .55 .30
147 A8 80c red brown .55 .30
148 A8 1fr deep red lilac .55 .30
149 A8 1.50fr brt red .75 .40
150 A8 2fr gray .75 .40
151 A8 2.50fr brt ultra .80 .65
152 A8 4fr dull violet .80 .65
153 A8 5fr yellow bister .80 .65
154 A8 10fr deep brown 1.25 .95
155 A8 20fr deep green 1.50 1.20
Nos. 142-155 (14) 9.50 6.80

For surcharges see #158-165, B14-B21, B24-B35.

Types of 1937-40 without "RF"

1944 ***Perf. 13½***
155A A2 10c magenta & blue .90
155B A2 15c blue & buff 1.20
155C A3 60c maroon & gray blue 1.50
155D A5 1.50fr dk & lt blue 2.00
Nos. 155A-155D (4) 5.60

Nos. 155A-155D were issued by the Vichy government in France, but were not sold in French Equatorial Africa.

Eboue Issue
Common Design Type

1945 **Unwmk.** **Engr.** ***Perf. 13***
156 CD91 2fr black .55 .40
157 CD91 25fr Prussian green 1.90 1.40

Nos. 156 and 157 exist imperforate.

Nos. 142, 144 and 151 Surcharged with New Values and Bars in Red, Carmine or Black

1946 ***Perf. 14x14½***
158 A8 50c on 5c (R) .80 .65
159 A8 60c on 5c (R) .80 .65
160 A8 70c on 5c (R) .80 .65
161 A8 1.20fr on 5c (C) .80 .65
162 A8 2.40fr on 25c 1.40 1.00
163 A8 3fr on 25c 1.40 1.00
164 A8 4.50fr on 25c 1.75 1.20
165 A8 15fr on 2.50fr (C) 1.90 1.40
Nos. 158-165 (8) 9.65 7.20

Black Rhinoceros and Rock Python A9

Jungle Scene — A10

Mountainous Shore Line — A11

Gabon Forest — A12

Niger Boatman — A13

Young Bacongo Woman — A14

1946 **Unwmk.** **Engr.** ***Perf. 12½***
166 A9 10c deep blue .30 .25
167 A9 30c violet blk .30 .25
168 A9 40c dp orange .30 .25
169 A10 50c violet bl .65 .50
170 A10 60c dk carmine .65 .50
171 A10 80c dk ol grn .65 .50
172 A11 1fr dp orange .95 .30
173 A11 1.20fr dp claret .95 .65
174 A11 1.50fr dk green 1.40 .95
175 A12 2fr dk vio brn .55 .25
176 A12 3fr rose carmine .80 .50
177 A12 3.60fr red brown 3.50 2.50
178 A12 4fr deep blue .80 .30
179 A13 5fr dk brown 1.00 .25
180 A13 6fr deep blue 1.00 .30
181 A13 10fr black 2.10 .75
182 A14 15fr brown 2.10 .75
183 A14 20fr dp claret 2.10 .80
184 A14 25fr black 2.60 .80
Nos. 166-184 (19) 22.70 11.35

Imperforates

Most French Equatorial Africa stamps from 1951 onward exist imperforate in issued and trial colors, and also in small presentation sheets in issued colors.

Pierre Savorgnan de Brazza — A15

1951, Nov. 5 ***Perf. 13***
185 A15 10fr indigo & dk grn 1.20 .40

Cent. of the birth of Pierre Savorgnan de Brazza, explorer.

Military Medal Issue
Common Design Type
Engraved and Typographed

1952, Dec. 1 ***Perf. 13***
186 CD101 15fr multicolored 7.25 5.50

Lt. Gov. Adolphe L. Cureau A16

1954, Sept. 20 **Engr.**
187 A16 15fr ol grn & red brn 1.60 .55

Savannah Monitor A17

1955, May 2 **Unwmk.**
188 A17 8fr dk grn & claret 2.25 .95

International Exhibition for Wildlife Protection, Paris, May 1955.

FIDES Issue
Common Design Type

Designs: 5fr, Boali Waterfall and Power Plant, Ubangi-Chari. 10fr, Cotton, Chad. 15fr, Brazzaville Hospital, Middle Congo. 20fr, Libreville Harbor, Gabon.

1956, Apr. 25 ***Perf. 13x12½***
189 CD103 5fr dk brn & claret .65 .30
190 CD103 10fr blk & bluish grn .80 .40
191 CD103 15fr ind & gray vio .80 .40
192 CD103 20fr dk red & red org 1.10 .65
Nos. 189-192 (4) 3.35 1.75

Coffee Issue

Coffee A19

1956, Oct. **Engr.** ***Perf. 13***
193 A19 10fr brn vio & vio bl 1.10 .40

Leprosarium at Mayumba and Maltese Cross — A20

1957, Mar. 11
194 A20 15fr grn, bl grn & red 1.90 .80

Issued in honor of the Knights of Malta.

Giant Eland A21

1957, Nov. 4
195 A21 1fr shown .75 .40
196 A21 2fr Lions .75 .40
197 A21 3fr Elephant, vert. .90 .40
198 A21 4fr Greater kudu, vert. .90 .40
Nos. 195-198 (4) 3.30 1.60

WHO Building, Brazzaville
A22

1958, May 19 Engr. *Perf. 13*

199 A22 20fr dk green & org brn 1.20 .65

10th anniv. of WHO.

Flower Issue

Common Design Type

1958, July 7 Photo. *Perf. 12x12½*

200	CD104	10fr Euadania	1.40	.50
201	CD104	25fr Spathodea	1.90	.75

Human Rights Issue

Common Design Type

1958, Dec. 10 Engr. *Perf. 13*

202 CD105 20fr Prus grn & dk bl 2.25 1.00

SEMI-POSTAL STAMPS

Common Design Type

1938, Oct. 24 Engr.

B1 CD80 1.75fr + 50c brt ultra 21.00 21.00
Never hinged 32.50

Nos. 51, 64 Surcharged in Black or Red

1938, Nov. 7 *Perf. 13x13½*

B2	A4	65c + 35c dk bl & lt grn (R)	2.40	2.40
B3	A4	1.75fr + 50c bl & lt bl	2.40	2.40
		Set, never hinged	7.00	

The surtax was for welfare.

French Revolution Issue

Common Design Type

Name and Value Typo. in Black

1939, July 5 Photo.

B4	CD83	45c + 25c green	14.50	14.50
B5	CD83	70c + 30c brown	14.50	14.50
B6	CD83	90c + 35c red org	14.50	14.50
B7	CD83	1.25fr + 1fr rose pink	14.50	14.50
B8	CD83	2.25fr + 2fr blue	14.50	14.50
		Nos. B4-B8 (5)	72.50	72.50
		Set, never hinged	110.00	

Surtax used for the defense of the colonies.

Catalogue values for unused stamps in this section, from this point to the end of the section, are for Never Hinged items.

Common Design Type and

Native Artilleryman
SP1

Gabon Infantryman
SP2

1941 Photo. *Perf. 13½*

B8A	SP1	1fr + 1fr red	3.50
B8B	CD86	1.50fr + 3fr maroon	3.50
B8C	SP2	2.50fr + 1fr blue	3.50
		Nos. 8A-8C (3)	10.50

Nos. B8A-B8C were issued by the Vichy government in France, but were not placed on sale in French Equatorial Africa.

Brazza and Stanley Pool
SP3

1941 Photo. *Perf. 14½x14*

B9 SP3 1fr + 2fr dk brn & red 1.60 1.20

The surtax was for a monument to Pierre Savorgnan de Brazza.

Nos. 67, 71 Surcharged in Red

1943, June 28 *Perf. 13½x13*

B10	A6	2.25fr + 50fr	24.00	14.50
B11	A6	10fr + 100fr	87.50	52.50

Nos. 129 and 132 with additional Surcharge in Carmine

1944

B12	A4	80c + 10fr	42.50	27.50
B13	A5	1.50fr + 15fr	42.50	27.50

Same surcharge printed Vertically on Nos. 142-146, 148, 150-151

Perf. 14x14½

B14	A8	5c + 10fr brown	13.50	8.75
B15	A8	10c + 10fr dk bl	13.50	8.75
B16	A8	25c + 10fr emer	13.50	8.75
B17	A8	30c + 10fr dp org	13.50	8.75
B18	A8	40c + 10fr dk sl grn	13.50	8.75
B19	A8	1fr + 10fr dp red lil	13.50	8.75
B20	A8	2fr + 20fr gray	13.50	8.75
B21	A8	2.50fr + 25fr brt ultra	13.50	8.75
		Nos. B12-B21 (10)	193.00	125.00

Nos. 129 and 132 with additional Surcharge in Carmine

1944 *Perf. 13½x13*

B22	A4	80c + 10fr	42.50	26.00
B23	A5	1.50fr + 15fr	42.50	26.00

Same Surcharge printed Vertically on Nos. 142-146, 148, 150-155

Perf. 14x14½

B24	A8	5c + 10fr brn	13.50	8.75
B25	A8	10c + 10fr dk bl	13.50	8.75
B26	A8	25c + 10fr emer	13.50	8.75
B27	A8	30c + 10fr dp org	13.50	8.75
B28	A8	40c + 10fr dk sl grn	13.50	8.75
B29	A8	1fr + 10fr dp red lil	13.50	8.75
B30	A8	2fr + 20fr gray	13.50	8.75
B31	A8	2.50fr + 25fr brt ultra	13.50	8.75
B32	A8	4fr + 40fr dl vio	13.50	8.75
B33	A8	5fr + 50fr yel bis	13.50	8.75
B34	A8	10fr + 100fr dp brn	13.50	8.75
B35	A8	20fr + 200fr dp grn	13.50	8.75
		Nos. B22-B35 (14)	247.00	157.00

Nos. B12 to B35 were issued to raise funds for the Committee to Aid the Fighting Men and Patriots of France.

Nos. 79A-79B Surcharged in Black or Red

1944 Engr. *Perf. 12½x12*

B36		50c + 1.50fr on 2.50fr deep blue (R)	1.40
B37		+ 2.50fr on 1fr green	1.40

Colonial Development Fund.

Nos. B36-B37 were issued by the Vichy government in France, but were not placed on sale in French Equatorial Africa.

Red Cross Issue

Common Design Type

1944 Photo. *Perf. 14½x14*

B38 CD90 5fr + 20fr royal blue 1.50 1.10

The surtax was for the French Red Cross and national relief.

Tropical Medicine Issue

Common Design Type

1950, May 15 Engr. *Perf. 13*

B39 CD100 10fr + 2fr dk bl grn & vio brn 7.25 5.50

The surtax was for charitable work.

AIR POST STAMPS

Hydroplane over Pointe-Noire — AP1

Trimotor over Stanley Pool — AP2

1937 Unwmk. Photo. *Perf. 13½*

C1	AP1	1.50fr ol blk & yel	.30	.30
C2	AP1	2fr mag & blue	.50	.50
C3	AP1	2.50fr grn & buff	.50	.50
C4	AP1	3.75fr brn & lt grn	.80	.80
C5	AP2	4.50fr cop red & bl	.80	.80
C6	AP2	6.50fr bl & lt grn	1.40	1.40
C7	AP2	8.50fr red brn & yel	1.60	1.60
C8	AP2	10.75fr vio & lt grn	1.60	1.60
		Nos. C1-C8 (8)	7.50	7.50

For overprints and surcharges see #C9-C16, CB2.

For types AP1, AP2 without "RF," see Nos. C23A-C23L.

Nos. C1, C3-C7 Overprinted in Black like Nos. 133-141

1940-41

C9	AP1	1.50fr ('41)	240.00	240.00
C10	AP1	2.50fr	2.40	2.40
a.		Double overprint	240.00	240.00
b.		Inverted overprint	240.00	240.00
C11	AP1	3.75fr ('41)	240.00	240.00
C12	AP2	4.50fr	2.75	2.75
a.		Double overprint	240.00	240.00
C13	AP2	6.50fr	3.50	3.50
a.		Double overprint	120.00	120.00
C14	AP2	8.50fr	2.40	2.40

No. C8 Surcharged in Carmine

C15 AP2 50fr on 10.75fr 9.50 9.50

No. C3 Surcharged in Black

C16	AP1	10fr on 2.50fr ('41)	95.00	95.00
		Nos. C9-C16 (8)	595.55	595.55

Counterfeits of Nos. C9 and C11 exist. See note following No. 141.

Catalogue values for unused stamps in this section, from this point to the end of the section, are for Never Hinged items.

Common Design Type

1941 Photo. *Perf. 14½x14*

C17	CD87	1fr dark orange	.95	.35
C18	CD87	1.50fr brt red	.95	.50
C19	CD87	5fr brown red	1.60	.80
C20	CD87	10fr black	1.75	.95
C21	CD87	25fr ultra	1.60	1.10
C22	CD87	50fr dark green	1.60	1.10
C23	CD87	100fr plum	2.25	1.20
		Nos. C17-C23 (7)	10.70	6.00

Types of 1937 without "RF" and

Sikorsky 5.43 Seaplane and Canoe — AP2a

Perf. 13½, 13 (#C23M)

1943, Oct. 18-1944 Unwmk.

C23A	AP1	1.50fr ol blk & yel	.40
C23B	AP1	2fr mag & blue	.40
C23C	AP1	2.50fr grn & buff	.40
C23D	AP1	3.75fr brn & lt grn	.65
C23E	AP2	4.50fr cop red & bl	.65
C23F	AP2	5fr green	1.00
C23G	AP2	6.50fr bl & lt grn	.95
C23H	AP2	8.50fr red brn & yel	.80
C23I	AP2	10fr gray & brn ('44)	.95
C23J	AP2	10.75fr vio & lt grn	1.00
C23K	AP2	20fr yel & brn red ('44)	1.00
C23L	AP2	50fr gray grn & blk ('44)	1.60
C23M	AP2a	100fr red brown ('44)	1.20
		Nos. C23A-C23M (13)	11.00

Issue dates: Nos. C23I, C23K-L, 4/3/44; C23M, 6/26/44.

Nos. C23A-C23M were issued by the Vichy government in France, but were not sold in French Equatorial Africa.

Victory Issue

Common Design Type

Perf. 12½

1946, May 8 Unwmk. Engr.

C24 CD92 8fr lilac rose 1.10 .90

Chad to Rhine Issue

Common Design Types

1946, June 6

C25	CD93	5fr dk violet	1.40	1.00
C26	CD94	10fr slate green	1.40	1.10
C27	CD95	15fr deep blue	2.40	1.75
C28	CD96	20fr red orange	2.40	1.75
C29	CD97	25fr sepia	2.40	1.75
C30	CD98	50fr brown carmine	2.75	2.10
		Nos. C25-C30 (6)	12.75	9.45

Palms and Village — AP3

Village and Waterfront — AP4

Bearers in Jungle — AP5

1946 Engr. *Perf. 13*
C31 AP3 50fr red brn 3.25 .80
C32 AP4 100fr grnsh blk 4.75 1.00
C33 AP5 200fr deep blue 11.00 1.75
Nos. C31-C33 (3) 19.00 3.55

UPU Issue
Common Design Type

1949, July 4
C34 CD99 25fr green 14.50 11.00

Brazza Holding Map — AP6

1951, Nov. 5
C35 AP6 15fr brn, indigo & red 2.10 1.40

Cent. of the birth of Pierre Savorgnan de Brazza, explorer.

Archbishop Augouard and St. Anne Cathedral, Brazzaville — AP7

1952, Dec. 1
C36 AP7 15fr ol grn, dk brn & vio brn 6.50 2.40

Cent. of the birth of Archbishop Philippe-Prosper Augouard.

Anhingas — AP8

1953, Feb. 16
C37 AP8 500fr grnsh blk, blk & slate 45.00 7.25

Liberation Issue
Common Design Type

1954, June 6
C38 CD102 15fr vio & vio brn 9.50 7.25

Log Rafts — AP9

Designs: 100fr, Fishing boats and nets, Lake Chad. 200fr, Age of mechanization.

1955, Jan. 24 Engr.
C39 AP9 50fr ind, brn & dk grn 2.40 .75
C40 AP9 100fr aqua, dk grn & blk brn 7.25 1.25
C41 AP9 200fr red & deep plum 12.00 2.40
Nos. C39-C41 (3) 21.65 4.40

Gov. Gen. Félix Eboué, View of Brazzaville and the Pantheon — AP10

1955, Apr. 30 Unwmk. *Perf. 13*
C42 AP10 15fr sep, brn & slate bl 6.00 2.10

Gen. Louis Faidherbé and African Sharpshooter AP11

1957, July 20
C43 AP11 15fr sepia & org ver 3.50 1.90

Centenary of French African Troops.

AIR POST SEMI-POSTAL STAMPS

French Revolution Issue
Common Design Type

1939 Unwmk. Photo. *Perf. 13*
Name and Value Typo. in Orange
CB1 CD83 4.50fr + 4fr brn blk 35.00 35.00

SPAP1

SPAP2

SPAP3

Unwmk.
1942, June 22 Engr. *Perf. 13*
CB2 SPAP1 1.50fr + 3.50fr green 1.40
CB3 SPAP2 2fr + 6fr brown 1.40
CB4 SPAP3 3fr + 9fr carmine 1.40
Nos. CB2-CB4 (3) 4.20

Native children's welfare fund.

Nos. CB2-CB4 were issued by the Vichy government in France, but were not placed on sale in French Equatorial Africa.

Colonial Education Fund
Common Design Type

1942, June 22
CB5 CD86a 1.20fr + 1.80fr bl & red 1.40

No. CB5 was issued by the Vichy government in France, but was not placed on sale in French Equatorial Africa.

#C8 Surcharged in Red like #B10-B11

1943, June 28 *Perf. 13½*
CB6 AP2 10.75fr + 200fr 190.00 190.00

Counterfeits exist.

POSTAGE DUE STAMPS

Numeral of Value on Equatorial Butterfly — D1

1937 Unwmk. Photo. *Perf. 13*

J1	D1	5c redsh pur & lt bl	.25	.25
J2	D1	10c cop red & buff	.25	.25
J3	D1	20c dk grn & grn	.30	.30
J4	D1	25c red brn & buff	.30	.30
J5	D1	30c cop red & lt bl	.50	.50
J6	D1	45c mag & yel grn	.75	.75
J7	D1	50c dk ol grn & buff	.80	.80
J8	D1	60c redsh pur & yel	.95	.95
J9	D1	1fr brown & yel	1.00	1.00
J10	D1	2fr dk bl & buff	1.40	1.40
J11	D1	3fr red brn & lt grn	1.50	1.50
		Nos. J1-J11 (11)	8.00	8.00
		Set, never hinged	11.00	

Catalogue values for unused stamps in this section, from this point to the end of the section, are for Never Hinged items.

D2

1947 Engr.

J12	D2	10c red	.40	.25
J13	D2	30c dp org	.40	.25
J14	D2	50c greenish bl	.40	.25
J15	D2	1fr carmine	.50	.30
J16	D2	2fr emerald	.65	.40
J17	D2	3fr dp red lil	.65	.40
J18	D2	4fr dp ultra	1.40	1.00
J19	D2	5fr red brown	1.40	1.00
J20	D2	10fr peacock blue	1.60	1.40
J21	D2	20fr sepia	2.10	1.50
		Nos. J12-J21 (10)	9.50	6.75

FRENCH GUIANA

ˈfrench gē-ˈa-nə

LOCATION — On the northeast coast of South America bordering on the Atlantic Ocean.
GOVT. — French colony
AREA — 34,740 sq. mi.
POP. — 28,537 (1946)
CAPITAL — Cayenne

French Guiana became an overseas department of France in 1946.

100 Centimes = 1 Franc

Catalogue values for unused stamps in this country are for Never Hinged items, beginning with Scott 171 in the regular postage section, Scott B12 in the semi-postal section, Scott C9 in the air-post section, and Scott J22 in the postage due section.

See France No. 1446 for French stamp inscribed "Guyane."

Stamps of French Colonies Surcharged in Black

1886, Dec. Unwmk. *Imperf.*
1 A8 5c on 2c grn, *grnsh*, srchg 12mm high 675.00 600.00
a. Double surcharge 1,700. 1,700.
b. Surcharge 10½mm high 875.00 825.00
c. No "f" after "O" 725.00 675.00

Perf. 14x13½
2 A9 5c on 2c brn, *buff*, srchg 12mm high 560.00 525.00
a. No "f" after "O" 490.00 425.00
b. As "a," double surcharge 1,500. 1,500.

Nos. 1-2 unused are valued without gum.

Avril 1887.
—
GUY FRANÇ
0f 20

"Av" of Date Line Inverted-Reversed

1887, Apr. *Imperf.*
4 A8 20c on 35c blk, *org* 60.00 50.00
a. Double surcharge 200.00 200.00
b. No "f" after "O" 130.00 130.00

Date Line Reads "Avril 1887"
5 A8 5c on 2c grn, *grnsh* 150.00 120.00
a. Double surcharge 750.00 750.00
b. No "f" after "O" 340.00 340.00
c. Pair, one stamp without surcharge 1,350.
6 A8 20c on 35c blk, *org* 325.00 290.00
a. Double surcharge 1,050. 1,050.
b. No "f" after "O" 725.00 725.00
c. Vertical pair, #6 + #4 1,900.
7 A7 25c on 30c brn, *yelsh* 50.00 40.00
On cover 2,500.
a. Double surcharge 750.00 750.00
b. No "f" after "O" 210.00 210.00

Nos. 4-7 unused are valued without gum.

French Colonies Nos. 22 & 26 Surcharged

8 A7 5c on 30c brn, *yelsh* 140.00 120.00
a. Double surcharge 725.00 725.00
b. Inverted surcharge 1,050. 1,050.
c. Pair, one without surcharge 1,600.
9 A8 5c on 30c brn, *yelsh* 1,450. 1,450.

Nos. 8-9 unused are valued without gum.

French Colonies Nos. 22 and 28 Surcharged:

1888

10 A7 5c on 30c brn, *yelsh* 150.00 125.00
b. Double surcharge 450.00 450.00
c. Inverted surcharge 575.00 525.00
11 A8 10c on 75c car, *rose* 375.00 290.00
No gum 290.00
a. Double surcharge 1,000. 1,000.
b. Pair, one stamp without surcharge 2,250.

No. 10 unused is valued without gum.

Stamps of French Colonies Overprinted in Black

1892, Feb. 20 ***Imperf.***

12 A8 2c grn, *grnsh* 750.00 750.00
a. Inverted overprint 2,900. 2,900.
13 A7 30c brn, *yelsh* 140.00 140.00
a. Inverted overprint 525.00 525.00
14 A8 35c blk, *orange* *2,500.* *2,750.*
15 A8 40c red, *straw* 175.00 130.00
16 A8 75c car, *rose* 180.00 130.00
a. Inverted overprint 625.00 500.00
17 A8 1fr brnz grn, *straw* 210.00 160.00
a. Inverted overprint 675.00 675.00
b. Double overprint 675.00 675.00
c. Triple overprint 1,600. 1,600.

Nos. 12-14 unused are valued without gum.

1892 ***Perf. 14x13½***

18 A9 1c blk, *lil bl* 45.00 30.00
19 A9 2c brn, *buff* 45.00 35.00
20 A9 4c claret, *lav* 37.50 35.00
21 A9 5c grn, *grnsh* 45.00 35.00
a. Inverted overprint 130.00 130.00
b. Double overprint 130.00 130.00
22 A9 10c blk, *lavender* 60.00 37.50
a. Inverted overprint 190.00 190.00
b. Double overprint 260.00 260.00
23 A9 15c blue 60.00 45.00
a. Double overprint 260.00 260.00
24 A9 20c red, *grn* 52.50 37.50
25 A9 25c blk, *rose* 72.50 35.00
a. Double overprint 225.00 260.00
b. Triple overprint 225.00 260.00
26 A9 30c brn, *bis* 45.00 37.50
27 A9 35c blk, *orange* 225.00 225.00
a. Inverted overprint 560.00 560.00
28 A9 40c red, *straw* 130.00 120.00
a. Inverted overprint 260.00 260.00
29 A9 75c car, *rose* 140.00 110.00
30 A9 1fr brnz grn, *straw* 350.00 310.00
a. Double overprint 350.00
Nos. 18-30 (13) 1,307. 1,092.

French Colonies No. 51 Surcharged

1892, Dec.

31 A9 5c on 15c blue 60.00 45.00
a. Double surcharge 300.00 275.00
b. No "f" after "O" 150.00 130.00
c. Pair, one stamp without surcharge 1,500. 1,500.

Navigation and Commerce — A12

1892-1904 Typo. ***Perf. 14x13½***
Name of Colony in Blue or Carmine

32 A12 1c blk, *lil bl* 1.75 1.75
33 A12 2c brn, *buff* 1.25 1.25
34 A12 4c claret, *lav* 1.75 1.75
a. "GUYANE" double 260.00
35 A12 5c grn, *grnsh* 11.00 10.00
36 A12 5c yel grn ('04) 1.75 1.50
37 A12 10c blk, *lavender* 12.00 7.25
38 A12 10c red ('00) 4.50 1.50
39 A12 15c blue, quadrille paper 40.00 4.00
40 A12 15c gray, *lt gray* ('00) 120.00 100.00
41 A12 20c red, *grn* 24.00 17.50
42 A12 25c blk, *rose* 20.00 5.50
43 A12 25c blue ('00) 19.00 *22.50*
44 A12 30c brn, *bis* 21.00 16.00
45 A12 40c red, *straw* 22.50 16.00
46 A12 50c car, *rose* 32.50 18.00
47 A12 50c brn, *az* ('00) 26.00 26.00
48 A12 75c dp vio, *org* 32.50 26.00
49 A12 1fr brn grn, *straw* 16.00 14.00
50 A12 2fr vio, *rose* ('02) 160.00 16.00
Nos. 32-50 (19) 567.50 306.50

Perf. 13½x14 stamps are counterfeits.
For surcharges see Nos. 87-93.

Great Anteater — A13

Washing Gold — A14

Palm Grove at Cayenne A15

1905-28

51 A13 1c black .40 .40
52 A13 2c blue .40 .40
a. Imperf 55.00
53 A13 4c red brn .40 .40
54 A13 5c green 1.20 1.00
55 A13 5c org ('22) .40 *.45*
56 A13 10c rose 1.25 1.10
57 A13 10c grn ('22) .65 .40
58 A13 10c red, *bluish* ('25) .45 .45
59 A13 15c violet 1.50 1.25
60 A14 20c red brn .65 .65
61 A14 25c blue 2.50 1.60
62 A14 25c vio ('22) .60 .50
63 A14 30c black 1.50 1.00
64 A14 30c rose ('22) .50 *.60*
65 A14 30c red org ('25) .45 .45
66 A14 30c dk grn, *grnsh* ('28) 1.10 1.10
67 A14 35c blk, *yel* ('06) .65 .65
68 A14 40c rose .85 .85
69 A14 40c black ('22) .40 *.45*
70 A14 45c olive ('07) .95 .95
71 A14 50c violet 3.50 3.00
72 A14 50c blue ('22) .55 *.65*
73 A14 50c gray ('25) .80 .80
74 A14 60c lil, *rose* ('25) .65 .65
75 A14 65c myr grn ('26) .80 .80
76 A14 75c green 1.40 1.40
77 A14 85c magenta ('26) .80 .80
78 A15 1fr rose .85 .85
a. Imperf 80.00
79 A15 1fr bl, *bluish* ('25) .80 .80
80 A15 1fr bl, *yel grn* ('28) 2.25 2.25
81 A15 1.10fr lt red ('28) 1.40 1.40
82 A15 2fr blue 1.00 1.00
83 A15 2fr org red, *yel* ('26) 2.40 2.40
84 A15 5fr black 6.75 6.00
a. Imperf 80.00
85 A15 10fr grn, *yel* ('24) 12.00 *13.50*
a. Printed on both sides 130.00
86 A15 20fr brn lake ('24) 14.50 16.00
Nos. 51-86 (36) 67.25 66.95

For surcharges see Nos. 94-108, B1-B2.

Issue of 1892 Surcharged in Black or Carmine

1912

87 A12 5c on 2c brn, *buff* 1.60 *2.00*
88 A12 5c on 4c cl, *lav* (C) 1.20 *1.60*
89 A12 5c on 20c red, *grn* 1.40 *1.90*
90 A12 5c on 25c blk, *rose* (C) 4.00 4.75
91 A12 5c on 30c brn, *bis* (C) 1.40 *1.90*
92 A12 10c on 40c red, *straw* 1.40 *1.90*
93 A12 10c on 50c car, *rose* 4.00 *5.25*
a. Double surcharge 525.00
Nos. 87-93 (7) 15.00 19.30

Two spacings between the surcharged numerals are found on Nos. 87 to 93. For detailed listings, see the *Scott Classic Specialized Catalogue of Stamps and Covers.*

No. 59 Surcharged in Various Colors

1922

94 A13 1c on 15c vio (Bk) .65 *.75*
a. Double surcharge 87.50
95 A13 2c on 15c vio (Bl) .65 *.75*
a. Inverted surcharge 95.00
b. In pair with unovptd. stamp 240.00
c. No. 95a, in pair with unovptd. stamp 800.00
96 A13 4c on 15c vio (G) .65 *.75*
a. Double surcharge 87.50
b. In pair with unovptd. stamp 275.00
97 A13 5c on 15c vio (R) .65 *.75*
Nos. 94-97 (4) 2.60 3.00

Type of 1905-28 Surcharged in Blue

1923

98 A15 10fr on 1fr grn, *yel* 21.00 *24.00*
99 A15 20fr on 5fr lilac, *rose* 21.00 *24.00*

Stamps and Types of 1905-28 Surcharged with New Value and Bars in Black or Red

1924-27

100 A13 25c on 15c vio ('25) .70 *.80*
a. Triple surcharge 120.00 110.00
b. In pair with unovptd. stamp 240.00
101 A15 25c on 2fr bl ('24) .80 *.90*
a. Double surcharge 140.00
b. Triple surcharge 150.00
102 A14 65c on 45c ol (R) ('25) 1.60 *1.75*
103 A14 85c on 45c ol (R) ('25) 1.60 *1.75*
104 A14 90c on 75c red ('27) 1.25 1.40
105 A15 1.05fr on 2fr lt yel brn ('27) 1.25 1.40
106 A15 1.25fr on 1fr ultra (R) ('26) 1.40 *1.60*
107 A15 1.50fr on 1fr lt bl ('27) 1.40 *1.60*
108 A15 3fr on 5fr vio ('27) 1.60 *1.80*
a. No period after "F" 12.00 12.00
Nos. 100-108 (9) 11.60 13.00

Carib Archer — A16

Shooting Rapids, Maroni River A17

Government Building, Cayenne — A18

1929-40 ***Perf. 13½x14***

109 A16 1c gray lil & grnsh bl .25 .25
a. Imperf 32.50
110 A16 2c dk red & bl grn .25 .25
a. Imperf 32.50
111 A16 3c gray lil & grnsh bl ('40) .30 .30
112 A16 4c ol brn & red vio .30 .30
113 A16 5c Prus bl & red org .30 .30
114 A16 10c mag & brn .30 .30
115 A16 15c yel brn & red org .30 .30
a. Imperf 32.50
116 A16 20c dk bl & ol grn .30 .30
117 A16 25c dk red & dk brn .45 .45

Perf. 14x13½

118 A17 30c dl & lt grn .65 .65
119 A17 30c grn & brn ('40) .45 .45
120 A17 35c Prus grn & ol grn ('38) .95 .95
121 A17 40c org brn & ol gray .30 .30
122 A17 45c grn & dk brn .90 .90
123 A17 45c ol grn & lt grn ('40) .70 .70
124 A17 50c dk bl & ol gray .40 .40
a. Imperf 32.50
125 A17 55c vio bl & car ('38) 1.40 1.40
126 A17 60c sal & grn ('40) .70 .70
a. Imperf 47.50
127 A17 65c sal & grn .90 .90
128 A17 70c ind & sl bl ('40) 1.20 1.20
129 A17 75c ind & sl bl .95 .95
130 A17 80c blk & vio bl ('38) .80 .80
131 A17 90c dk red & ver .90 .90
132 A17 90c red vio & brn ('39) 1.10 1.10
133 A17 1fr lt vio & brn .65 .65
134 A17 1fr car & lt red ('38) 1.90 1.90
135 A17 1fr blk & vio bl ('40) .80 .80
136 A18 1.05fr ver & olivine 4.75 4.75
137 A18 1.10fr ol brn & red vio 6.50 5.50
138 A18 1.25fr blk brn & bl grn ('33) .80 .80
139 A18 1.25fr rose & lt red ('39) .95 .95
140 A18 1.40fr ol brn & red vio ('40) 1.10 1.10
141 A18 1.50fr dk bl & lt bl .40 .40
142 A18 1.60fr ol brn & bl grn ('40) 1.10 1.10
143 A18 1.75fr brn red & blk brn ('33) 2.00 2.00
144 A18 1.75fr vio bl ('38) 1.40 1.40
145 A18 2fr dk grn & rose red .65 .65
146 A18 2.25fr vio bl ('39) 1.10 1.10
147 A18 2.50fr cop red & brn ('40) 1.10 1.10
148 A18 3fr brn red & red vio .70 .70
149 A18 5fr dl vio & yel grn 1.00 1.00
150 A18 10fr ol gray & dp ultra 1.25 1.25
151 A18 20fr indigo & ver 2.25 2.25
Nos. 109-151 (43) 45.45 44.45

For types A16-A18 without "RF," see Nos. 170C-170E.

Common Design Types pictured following the introduction.

Colonial Exposition Issue
Common Design Types

1931 Engr. ***Perf. 12½***
Name of Country in Black

152 CD70 40c dp green 5.25 5.25
153 CD71 50c violet 5.25 5.25
154 CD72 90c red orange 5.25 5.25
155 CD73 1.50fr dull blue 5.25 5.25
Nos. 152-155 (4) 21.00 21.00

Recapture of Cayenne by d'Estrées, 1676 — A19

Products of French Guiana A20

1935, Oct. 21 ***Perf. 13***

156 A19 40c gray brn 5.25 5.25
157 A19 50c dull red 9.50 8.00
158 A19 1.50fr ultra 5.25 5.25
159 A20 1.75fr lilac rose 12.00 11.00
160 A20 5fr brown 9.50 8.75
161 A20 10fr blue green 10.50 9.50
Nos. 156-161 (6) 52.00 47.75

Tercentenary of the founding of French possessions in the West Indies.

Paris International Exposition Issue
Common Design Types

1937, Apr. 15

162 CD74 20c deep violet 1.60 1.60
163 CD75 30c dark green 1.60 1.60
164 CD76 40c carmine rose 1.60 1.60
165 CD77 50c dark brown 1.40 1.40
166 CD78 90c red 1.40 1.40
167 CD79 1.50fr ultra 1.60 1.60
Nos. 162-167 (6) 9.20 9.20

Colonial Arts Exhibition Issue
Souvenir Sheet
Common Design Type

1937 ***Imperf.***

168 CD75 3fr violet 10.50 *13.50*

New York World's Fair Issue
Common Design Type

1939, May 10 Engr. ***Perf. 12½x12***

169	CD82	1.25fr car lake	1.20	1.20
170	CD82	2.25fr ultra	1.20	1.20

View of Cayenne and Marshal Petain
A21a

1941 Engr. ***Perf. 12½x12***

170A	A21a	1fr deep lilac	.80	.80
170B	A21a	2.50fr blue	.80	.80

For surcharges, see Nos. B11A-B11B.

Types of 1929-40 without "RF"

1944 ***Methods and Perfs as Before***

170C	A16	15c yel brn & red org	1.10	
170D	A17	1fr black & vio blue	1.10	
170E	A18	1.50fr dk blue & lt blue	1.40	
		Nos. 170C-170E (3)	3.60	

Nos. 170C-170E were issued by the Vichy government in France, but were not issued in French Guiana.

Catalogue values for unused stamps in this section, from this point to the end of the section, are for Never Hinged items.

Eboue Issue
Common Design Type

1945 Engr. ***Perf. 13***

171	CD91	2fr black	.95	.80
172	CD91	25fr Prussian green	1.40	1.20

This issue exists imperforate.

Arms of Cayenne
A22

1945 Litho. ***Perf. 12***

173	A22	10c dp gray violet	.30	.25
174	A22	30c brown org	.30	.25
175	A22	40c lt blue	.30	.25
176	A22	50c violet brn	.70	.55
177	A22	60c orange yel	.70	.55
178	A22	70c pale brown	.70	.55
179	A22	80c lt green	.70	.55
180	A22	1fr blue	.30	.25
181	A22	1.20fr brt violet	.70	.55
182	A22	1.50fr dp orange	.95	.70
183	A22	2fr black	1.00	.80
184	A22	2.40fr red	1.00	.80
185	A22	3fr pink	1.00	.80
186	A22	4fr dp ultra	1.25	.95
187	A22	4.50fr dp yel grn	1.25	.95
188	A22	5fr orange brn	1.25	.95
189	A22	10fr dk violet	1.25	.95
190	A22	15fr rose carmine	1.25	.95
191	A22	20fr olive green	1.40	1.10
		Nos. 173-191 (19)	16.30	12.70

Hammock
A23

Guiana Girl
A26

Maroni River Bank
A24

Inini Scene
A25

Toucans
A27

Parrots
A28

Perf. 13.

1947, June 2 Unwmk. Engr.

192	A23	10c dk blue grn	.30	.25
193	A23	30c brt red	.30	.25
194	A23	50c dk vio brn	.30	.25
195	A24	60c grnsh blk	.55	.40
196	A24	1fr red brn	.80	.55
197	A24	1.50fr black brn	.80	.55
198	A25	2fr dp yel grn	1.00	.70
199	A25	2.50fr dp ultra	1.00	.70
200	A25	3fr red brn	.80	.65
201	A26	4fr black brn	2.00	1.20
202	A26	5fr deep blue	1.60	1.00
203	A26	6fr red brown	1.60	1.00
204	A27	10fr deep ultra	6.75	4.50
205	A27	15fr black brn	6.75	4.75
206	A27	20fr red brn	8.75	4.75
207	A28	25fr brt bl grn	12.00	7.25
208	A28	40fr black brn	10.50	7.25
		Nos. 192-208 (17)	55.80	36.00

SEMI-POSTAL STAMPS

Regular Issue of 1905-28 Surcharged in Red

1915 Unwmk. ***Perf. 13½x14***

B1	A13	10c + 5c rose	15.00	*18.00*
a.		Inverted surcharge	240.00	240.00
b.		Double surcharge	240.00	240.00

Regular Issue of 1905-28 Surcharged in Rose

B2	A13	10c + 5c rose	1.60	1.60

Curie Issue
Common Design Type

1938 ***Perf. 13***

B3	CD80	1.75fr + 50c brt ultra	12.50	12.50

French Revolution Issue
Common Design Type

1939 Photo.

Name and Value in Black

B4	CD83	45c + 25c green	11.00	11.00
B5	CD83	70c + 30c brown	11.00	11.00
B6	CD83	90c + 35c red org	11.00	11.00
B7	CD83	1.25fr + 1fr rose pink	11.00	11.00
B8	CD83	2.25fr + 2fr blue	11.00	11.00
		Nos. B4-B8 (5)	55.00	55.00

Common Design Type and

Colonial Infantryman — SP1

Colonial Policeman
SP2

1941 Photo. ***Perf. 13½***

B9	SP1	1fr + 1fr red	1.25
B10	CD86	1.50fr + 3fr maroon	1.40
B11	SP2	2.50fr + 1fr blue	1.25
		Nos. B9-B11 (3)	3.90

Nos. B9-B11 were issued by the Vichy government in France, but were not placed on sale in French Guiana.

Nos. 170A-170B Surcharged in Black or Red

1944 Engr. ***Perf. 12½x12***

B11A	50c + 1.50fr on 2.50fr deep blue (R)	.80
B11B	+ 2.50fr on 1fr dp lilac	.80

Colonial Development Fund.

Nos. B11A-B11B were issued by the Vichy government in France, but were not placed on sale in French Guiana.

Catalogue values for unused stamps in this section, from this point to the end of the section, are for Never Hinged items.

Red Cross Issue
Common Design Type

1944 ***Perf. 14½x14***

B12	CD90	5fr + 20fr dk copper brn	1.60	1.20

The surtax was for the French Red Cross and national relief.

AIR POST STAMPS

Cayenne
AP1

Perf. 13½

1933, Nov. 20 Unwmk. Photo.

C1	AP1	50c orange brn	.30	.30
C2	AP1	1fr yellow grn	.45	.45
C3	AP1	1.50fr dk blue	.65	.65
C4	AP1	2fr orange	.65	.65
C5	AP1	3fr black	.80	.80
C6	AP1	5fr violet	.80	.80
C7	AP1	10fr olive grn	.80	.80
C8	AP1	20fr scarlet	1.10	1.10
		Nos. C1-C8 (8)	5.55	5.55

For No. C1 without "RF," see No. C8A.

Catalogue values for unused stamps in this section, from this point to the end of the section, are for Never Hinged items.

Type of 1933 without "RF" and

AP1a

AP1b

Perf. 13½, 13 (#C8C)

1941-44 Photo, Engr. (#C8C)

C8A	AP1	50c orange brn	1.00
C8B	AP1a	50f bl grn & red brown ('42)	1.40
C8C	AP1b	100f dk blue ('44)	1.60
		Nos. C8A-C8C (3)	4.00

Nos. C8A-C8C were issued by the Vichy government in France, but were not placed on sale in French Guiana.

Common Design Type

1945 Photo. ***Perf. 14½x14***

C9	CD87	50fr dark green	1.25	.95
C10	CD87	100fr plum	2.25	1.80

Victory Issue
Common Design Type

1946, May 8 Engr. ***Perf. 12½***

C11	CD92	8fr black	1.60	1.20

Chad to Rhine Issue
Common Design Types

1946, June 6

C12	CD93	5fr dk slate bl	1.60	1.40
C13	CD94	10fr lilac rose	1.60	1.40
C14	CD95	15fr dk vio brn	1.60	1.40
C15	CD96	20fr dk slate grn	1.90	1.50
C16	CD97	25fr vio brown	2.25	1.80
C17	CD98	50fr bright lilac	2.75	2.10
		Nos. C12-C17 (6)	11.70	9.60

Eagles — AP2

Tapir — AP3

Toucans — AP4

1947, June 2 Engr. ***Perf. 13***

C18	AP2	50fr deep green	21.00	17.00
C19	AP3	100fr red brown	14.50	12.00
C20	AP4	200fr dk gray bl	29.00	22.50
		Nos. C18-C20 (3)	64.50	51.50

AIR POST SEMI-POSTAL STAMPS

French Revolution Issue
Common Design Type

Unwmk.

1939, July 5 Photo. ***Perf. 13***

Name & Value Typo. in Orange

CB1	CD83	5fr + 4fr brn blk	20.00	20.00

Nurse with Mother & Child — SPAP1

Unwmk.

1942, June 22 Engr. *Perf. 13*

CB2	SPAP1	1.50fr + 50c green	1.00	
CB3	SPAP1	2fr + 6fr brn & red	1.00	

Native children's welfare fund.

Nos. CB2-CB3 were issued by the Vichy government in France, but were not placed on sale in French Guiana.

Colonial Education Fund
Common Design Type

1942, June 22

CB4	CD86a	1.20fr + 1.80fr blue & red	1.10	

No. CB4 was issued by the Vichy government in France, but was not placed on sale in French Guiana.

POSTAGE DUE STAMPS

Postage Due Stamps of France, 1893-1926, Overprinted

1925-27 Unwmk. *Perf. 14x13½*

J1	D2	5c light blue	.65	*.70*
a.		In pair with unovptd. stamp	350.00	
J2	D2	10c brown	.85	*1.00*
J3	D2	20c olive green	1.00	*1.20*
J4	D2	50c violet brown	1.40	*1.60*
J5	D2	3fr magenta ('27)	7.75	*7.75*

Surcharged in Black

J6	D2	15c on 20c ol grn	.95	*1.10*
a.		Blue surcharge	65.00	
J7	D2	25c on 5c lt bl	1.25	*1.40*
a.		In pair with unovptd. stamp	350.00	
J8	D2	30c on 20c ol grn	1.40	*1.60*
J9	D2	45c on 10c brn	1.40	*1.60*
J10	D2	60c on 5c lt bl	1.40	*1.60*
J11	D2	1fr on 20c ol grn	1.90	*2.10*
J12	D2	2fr on 50c vio brn	1.90	*2.25*
		Nos. J1-J12 (12)	21.85	*23.90*

Royal Palms — D3

Guiana Girl — D4

1929, Oct. 14 Typo. *Perf. 13½x14*

J13	D3	5c indigo & Prus bl	.40	*.50*
J14	D3	10c bis brn & Prus grn	.40	*.50*
J15	D3	20c grn & rose red	.40	*.50*
J16	D3	30c ol brn & rose red	.40	*.50*
J17	D3	50c vio & ol brn	.90	*1.00*
J18	D3	60c brn red & ol brn	1.25	*1.40*
J19	D4	1fr dp bl & org brn	1.60	*1.90*
J20	D4	2fr brn red & bluish grn	1.90	*2.10*
J21	D4	3fr violet & blk	4.00	*4.50*
		Nos. J13-J21 (9)	11.25	*12.90*

Catalogue values for unused stamps in this section, from this point to the end of the section, are for Never Hinged items.

D5

1947, June 2 Engr. *Perf. 14x13*

J22	D5	10c dk car rose	.30	.30
J23	D5	30c dull green	.40	.40
J24	D5	50c black	.40	.40
J25	D5	1fr brt ultra	.50	.50
J26	D5	2fr dk brown red	.50	.50
J27	D5	3fr deep violet	.90	.70
J28	D5	4fr red	1.25	1.00
J29	D5	5fr brown violet	1.40	1.10
J30	D5	10fr blue green	2.10	1.75
J31	D5	20fr lilac rose	2.75	2.10
		Nos. J22-J31 (10)	10.50	8.75

FRENCH GUINEA

ˈfrench ˈgi-nē

LOCATION — On the coast of West Africa, between Portuguese Guinea and Sierra Leone.
GOVT. — French colony
AREA — 89,436 sq. mi.
POP. — 2,058,442 (est. 1941)
CAPITAL — Conakry

French Guinea stamps were replaced by those of French West Africa around 1944-45. French Guinea became the Republic of Guinea Oct. 2, 1958. See "Guinea" for issues of the republic.

100 Centimes = 1 Franc

See French West Africa No. 66 for additional stamp inscribed "Guinee" and "Afrique Occidentale Francaise."

Navigation and Commerce A1

Fulah Shepherd A2

Perf. 14x13½

1892-1900 Typo. Unwmk.

Name of Colony in Blue or Carmine

1	A1	1c black, *lilac bl*	1.40	1.40
2	A1	2c brown, *buff*	1.90	1.90
3	A1	4c claret, *lav*	2.40	2.00
4	A1	5c green, *grnsh*	8.00	4.75
5	A1	10c blk, *lavender*	7.25	4.75
6	A1	10c red ('00)	45.00	40.00
7	A1	15c blue, quadrille paper	13.50	6.75
8	A1	15c gray, *lt gray* ('00)	100.00	87.50
9	A1	20c red, *grn*	20.00	12.50
10	A1	25c black, *rose*	13.50	8.00
11	A1	25c blue ('00)	24.00	24.00
12	A1	30c brown, *bis*	35.00	30.00
13	A1	40c red, *straw*	35.00	30.00
a.		"GUINEE FRANCAISE" double	450.00	450.00
14	A1	50c car, *rose*	40.00	35.00
15	A1	50c brown, *az* ('00)	40.00	40.00
16	A1	75c dp vio, *org*	55.00	47.50
17	A1	1fr brnz grn, *straw*	47.50	40.00
		Nos. 1-17 (17)	489.45	416.05

Perf. 13½x14 stamps are counterfeits.
For surcharges see Nos. 48-54.

1904

18	A2	1c black, *yel grn*	1.00	1.00
19	A2	2c vio brn, *buff*	1.10	1.10
20	A2	4c carmine, *bl*	1.50	1.50
21	A2	5c green, *grnsh*	1.50	1.50
22	A2	10c carmine	3.25	2.00
23	A2	15c violet, *rose*	9.25	4.75
24	A2	20c carmine, *grn*	12.00	12.00
25	A2	25c blue	15.00	10.50
26	A2	30c brown	19.00	19.00
27	A2	40c red, *straw*	27.50	22.50
28	A2	50c brown, *az*	27.50	24.00
29	A2	75c green, *org*	27.50	27.50
30	A2	1fr brnz grn, *straw*	45.00	45.00
31	A2	2fr red, *org*	85.00	85.00
32	A2	5fr green, *yel grn*	100.00	100.00
		Nos. 18-32 (15)	376.10	357.35

For surcharges see Nos. 55-62.

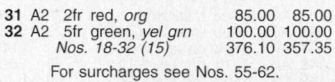

Gen. Louis Faidherbé A3

Oil Palm — A4

Dr. Noel Eugène Ballay A5

1906-07

Name of Colony in Red or Blue

33	A3	1c gray	.80	.80
34	A3	2c brown	1.10	1.00
35	A3	4c brown, *bl*	1.40	1.40
36	A3	5c green	3.00	1.90
37	A3	10c carmine (B)	24.00	1.60
38	A4	20c black, *blue*	5.50	3.50
39	A4	25c blue, *pnksh*	5.50	5.50
40	A4	30c brown, *pnksh*	7.25	4.00
41	A4	35c black, *yellow*	4.75	2.40
42	A4	45c choc, *grnsh gray*	5.50	4.00
43	A4	50c dp violet	12.00	9.50
44	A4	75c blue, *org*	8.75	4.00
45	A5	1fr black, *az*	20.00	20.00
46	A5	2fr blue, *pink*	40.00	*45.00*
47	A5	5fr car, *straw* (B)	60.00	*65.00*
		Nos. 33-47 (15)	199.55	*169.60*

Regular Issues Surcharged in Black or Carmine

1912

On Issue of 1892-1900

48	A1	5c on 2c brown, *buff*	1.40	*1.60*
49	A1	5c on 4c cl, *lav* (C)	.95	*1.10*
50	A1	5c on 15c blue (C)	1.00	*1.25*
51	A1	5c on 20c red, *grn*	4.00	*4.50*
52	A1	5c on 30c brn, *bis* (C)	4.75	*5.25*
53	A1	10c on 40c red, *straw*	2.25	*2.40*
54	A1	10c on 75c dp vio, *org*	7.25	*8.00*
a.		Double surcharge, inverted	275.00	

On Issue of 1904

55	A2	5c on 2c vio brn, *buff*	1.00	1.00
a.		Pair, one without surcharge	600.00	
56	A2	5c on 4c car, *blue*	1.10	1.10
57	A2	5c on 15c violet, *rose*	1.10	1.10
58	A2	5c on 20c car, *grn*	1.40	1.40
59	A2	5c on 25c blue (C)	1.50	1.50
60	A2	5c on 30c brown (C)	1.90	2.00
61	A2	10c on 40c red, *straw*	1.90	2.00
62	A2	10c on 50c brn, *az* (C)	4.50	5.00
		Nos. 48-62 (15)	36.00	*39.20*

Two spacings between the surcharged numerals are found on Nos. 48 to 62. For detailed listings, see the *Scott Classic Specialized Catalogue of Stamps and Covers.*

Ford at Kitim — A6

1913-33 *Perf. 13½x14*

63	A6	1c violet & bl	.25	.25
64	A6	2c brn & vio brn	.25	.25
65	A6	4c gray & black	.25	.25
66	A6	5c yel grn & bl grn	1.00	.40
a.		Booklet pane of 4		—
		Complete booklet, 10 #66a	175.00	
67	A6	5c brn vio & grn ('22)	.25	.25
68	A6	10c red org & rose	.90	.40
a.		Booklet pane of 4		—
		Complete booklet, 10 #68a	325.00	
69	A6	10c yel grn & bl grn ('22)	.30	.25
70	A6	10c vio & ver ('25)	.50	.25
71	A6	15c vio brn & rose ('16)	.50	.30
a.		Booklet pane of 4		—
		Complete booklet, 10 #71a	725.00	
72	A6	15c gray grn & yel grn ('25)	.30	.25
73	A6	15c red brn & rose lil ('27)	.30	.30
74	A6	20c brown & violet	.40	.30
75	A6	20c grn & bl grn ('26)	.80	.65
76	A6	20c brn red & brn ('27)	.80	.40
77	A6	25c ultra & blue	2.40	1.40
78	A6	25c black & vio ('22)	.65	.65
79	A6	30c vio brn & grn	1.40	1.00
80	A6	30c red org & rose ('22)	1.00	.90
81	A6	30c rose red & grn ('25)	.30	.30
82	A6	30c dl grn & bl grn ('28)	1.40	1.00
83	A6	35c blue & rose	.55	.50
84	A6	40c green & gray	.95	.80
85	A6	45c brown & red	1.00	.95
86	A6	50c ultra & black	6.00	4.50
87	A6	50c ultra & bl ('22)	1.00	.75
88	A6	50c yel brn & ol ('25)	.55	.50
89	A6	60c vio, *pnksh* ('25)	.65	.50
90	A6	65c yel brn & sl bl ('26)	1.75	1.10
91	A6	75c red & ultra	1.25	1.25
92	A6	75c indigo & dl bl ('25)	1.25	1.00
93	A6	75c mag & yel grn ('27)	1.40	1.00
94	A6	85c ol grn & red brn ('26)	1.10	1.00
95	A6	90c brn red & rose ('30)	5.50	4.50
96	A6	1fr violet & black	1.40	1.40
97	A6	1.10fr vio & ol brn ('28)	8.25	6.50
98	A6	1.25fr vio & yel brn ('33)	2.00	1.25
99	A6	1.50fr dk bl & lt bl ('30)	5.25	2.40
100	A6	1.75fr ol brn & vio ('33)	1.60	1.50
101	A6	2fr orange & vio brn	3.25	2.10
102	A6	3fr red violet ('30)	7.50	5.25
103	A6	5fr black & vio	12.50	12.50
104	A6	5fr dl bl & blk ('22)	2.40	2.10
		Nos. 63-104 (42)	81.05	63.10

Nos. 66 and 68 exist on both ordinary and chalky paper, No. 71 on chalky paper only.

For surcharges see Nos. 105-115, B1.

Nos. 66, 68 and 77 pasted on colored cardboard and overprinted "VALEUR D'ECHANGE" were used as emergency currency in 1920.

Type of 1913-33 Surcharged

1922

105	A6	60c on 75c violet, *pnksh*	.65	.65

Stamps and Type of 1913-33 Surcharged with New Value and Bars

1924-27

106	A6	25c on 2fr org & brn (R)	.50	.50
107	A6	25c on 5fr dull bl & blk	.50	.50
108	A6	65c on 75c rose & ultra ('25)	1.25	1.25
109	A6	85c on 75c rose & ultra ('25)	1.75	1.75
110	A6	90c on 75c brn red & cer ('27)	2.25	2.25
111	A6	1.25fr on 1fr dk bl & ultra ('26)	1.10	1.00

112 A6 1.50fr on 1fr dp bl & lt bl ('27) 1.75 1.75
113 A6 3fr on 5fr mag & sl ('27) 4.00 4.00
114 A6 10fr on 5fr bl & bl grn, *bluish* ('27) 8.00 8.00
115 A6 20fr on 5fr rose lil & brn ol, *pnksh* ('27) 18.00 18.00
Nos. 106-115 (10) 39.10 39.00

Common Design Types pictured following the introduction.

Colonial Exposition Issue
Common Design Types

1931 Engr. *Perf. 12½*
Name of Country in Black

116 CD70 40c deep green 4.50 4.50
a. "GUINÉE FRANCAISE" omitted 52.50 *60.00*
117 CD71 50c violet 4.50 4.50
118 CD72 90c red orange 4.50 4.50
a. "GUINÉE FRANCAISE" omitted 52.50 *60.00*
119 CD73 1.50fr dull blue 4.50 4.50
a. "GUINÉE FRANCAISE" omitted 40.00 *40.00*
Nos. 116-119 (4) 18.00 18.00
Set, never hinged 29.25

Paris International Exposition Issue
Common Design Types

1937 *Perf. 13*

120 CD74 20c deep violet 1.60 1.60
121 CD75 30c dark green 1.60 1.60
122 CD76 40c carmine rose 1.60 1.60
123 CD77 50c dark brown 1.60 1.60
124 CD78 90c red 1.75 1.75
125 CD79 1.50fr ultra 1.90 1.90
Nos. 120-125 (6) 10.05 10.05
Set, never hinged 16.00

Colonial Arts Exhibition Issue
Souvenir Sheet
Common Design Type

1937 *Imperf.*

126 CD76 3fr Prussian green 8.00 *9.50*
Never hinged 12.00

Guinea Village A7

Hausa Basket Workers A8

Forest Waterfall A9

Guinea Women — A10

1938-40 *Perf. 13*

128 A7 2c vermilion .25 .25
129 A7 3c ultra .25 .25
130 A7 4c green .25 .25
131 A7 5c rose car .25 .25
132 A7 10c peacock blue .25 .25
133 A7 15c violet brown .25 .25
134 A8 20c dk carmine .30 .25
135 A8 25c pck blue .40 .25
136 A8 30c ultra .40 .25
137 A8 35c green .55 .50
138 A8 40c blk brn ('40) .30 .30
139 A8 45c dk green ('40) .30 .30
140 A8 50c red brown .55 .50
141 A9 55c dk ultra 1.00 .80
142 A9 60c dk ultra ('40) .80 .80
143 A9 65c green 1.25 .80
144 A9 70c green ('40) 1.25 1.25
145 A9 80c rose violet .75 .55
146 A9 90c rose vio ('39) 1.25 1.25
147 A9 1fr orange red 2.50 1.80
148 A9 1fr brn blk ('40) .50 .50
149 A9 1.25fr org red ('39) 1.40 1.40
150 A9 1.40fr brown ('40) 1.25 1.25
151 A9 1.50fr violet 2.40 1.90
152 A10 1.60fr org red ('40) 1.40 1.40
153 A10 1.75fr ultra .80 .75
154 A10 2fr magenta .95 .65
155 A10 2.25fr brt ultra ('39) 1.75 1.75
156 A10 2.50fr brn blk ('40) 1.40 1.40
157 A10 3fr peacock blue .90 .40
158 A10 5fr rose violet .90 .75
159 A10 10fr slate green 1.25 1.10
160 A10 20fr chocolate 2.50 1.90
Nos. 128-160 (33) 30.50 26.25
Set, never hinged 42.50

For surcharges see Nos. B8-B11.
For types A7-A10 without "RF," see Nos. 168-174.

Caillié Issue
Common Design Type

1939 Engr. *Perf. 12½x12*

161 CD81 90c org brn & org .90 .90
162 CD81 2fr brt violet 1.00 1.00
163 CD81 2.25fr ultra & dk bl 1.00 1.00
Nos. 161-163 (3) 2.90 2.90

René Caillié, French explorer, death cent.

New York World's Fair Issue
Common Design Type

1939

164 CD82 1.25fr carmine lake 1.25 1.25
165 CD82 2.25fr ultra 1.25 1.25

Ford at Kitim and Marshal Petain — A11

1941 *Perf. 12x12½*

166 A11 1fr green .75 —
167 A11 2.50fr deep blue .80 —

For surcharges, see Nos. B15-B16.

Types of 1933-40 without "RF"

1943-44 *Perf. 13*

168 A7 10c peacock blue .50
169 A8 20c dk carmine .75
170 A8 30c ultramarine .75
171 A8 40c black brown 1.10
172 A9 60c dk ultramarine 1.25
173 A9 1.50fr violet 1.40
174 A10 2fr magenta 1.50
Nos. 168-174 (7) 7.25

Nos. 168-174 were issued by the Vichy government in France, but were not placed on sale in French Guinea.

SEMI-POSTAL STAMPS

Regular Issue of 1913 Surcharged in Red

1915 Unwmk. *Perf. 13½x14*

B1 A6 10c + 5c org & rose 1.60 1.20

Exists on both ordinary and chalky paper.

Curie Issue
Common Design Type

1938 Engr. *Perf. 13*

B2 CD80 1.75fr + 50c brt ultra 9.00 9.00

French Revolution Issue
Common Design Type

1939 Photo.
Name and Value Typo. in Black

B3 CD83 45c + 25c green 9.00 9.00
B4 CD83 70c + 30c brown 9.00 9.00
B5 CD83 90c + 35c red org 9.00 9.00
B6 CD83 1.25fr + 1fr rose pink 9.00 9.00
B7 CD83 2.25fr + 2fr blue 9.00 9.00
Nos. B3-B7 (5) 45.00 45.00
Set, never hinged 72.50

Stamps of 1938, Surcharged in Black

1941 Unwmk. *Perf. 13*

B8 A8 50c + 1fr red brn 2.40 2.40
B9 A9 80c + 2fr rose vio 6.50 6.50
B10 A9 1.50fr + 2fr brn 6.50 6.50
B11 A10 2fr + 3fr magenta 6.50 6.50
Nos. B8-B11 (4) 21.90 21.90

Common Design Type and

Senegalese Soldier SP1

Colonial Infantryman SP2

1941 Unwmk. *Perf. 13*

B12 SP1 1fr + 1fr red 1.25
B13 CD86 1.50fr + 3fr maroon 1.25
B14 SP2 2.50fr + 1fr blue 1.25
Nos. B12-B14 (3) 3.75

Nos. B12-B14 were issued by the Vichy government in France, but were not placed on sale in the French Guinea.

Nos. 166-167 Surcharged in Black or Red

1944 Engr. *Perf. 12½x12*

B15 50c + 1.50fr on 2.50fr deep blue (R) .80
B16 + 2.50fr on 1fr green .80

Colonial Development Fund.
Nos. B15-B16 were issued by the Vichy government in France, but were not placed on sale in French Guinea.

AIR POST STAMPS

Common Design Type

1940 Unwmk. Engr. *Perf. 12½x12*

C1 CD85 1.90fr ultra .55 .55
C2 CD85 2.90fr dark red .65 .65
C3 CD85 4.50fr dk gray grn .80 .80
C4 CD85 4.90fr yellow bis .80 .80
C5 CD85 6.90fr dp orange 1.20 1.20
Nos. C1-C5 (5) 4.00 4.00

Common Design Types

1942 Engr.

C6 CD88 50c car & blue .25
C7 CD88 1fr brown & blk .30
C8 CD88 2fr dk grn & red brn .30
C9 CD88 3fr dk bl & scar .50
C10 CD88 5fr vio & brn red .80

Frame Engraved, Center Typographed

C11 CD89 10fr multicolored .80
C12 CD89 20fr multicolored .95
C13 CD89 50fr multicolored 1.25 —
Nos. C6-C13 (8) 5.15

There is doubt whether Nos. C6-C12 were officially placed in use.

AIR POST SEMI-POSTAL STAMPS

Dahomey types SPAP1-SPAP3 inscribed "Guinée Frcaise" or "Guinée"

Perf. 13½x12½, 13 (#CB3)
Photo, Engr. (#CB3)

1942, June 22

CB1 SPAP1 1.50fr + 3.50fr green .80 *5.25*
CB2 SPAP2 2fr + 6fr brown .80 *5.25*
CB3 SPAP3 3fr + 9fr car red .80 *5.25*
Nos. CB1-CB3 (3) 2.40 *15.75*

Native children's welfare fund.

Colonial Education Fund
Common Design Type

Perf. 12½x13½

1942, June 22 Engr.

CB4 CD86a 1.20fr + 1.80fr blue & red .80 *5.25*

POSTAGE DUE STAMPS

Fulah Woman D1

Heads and Coast D2

1905 Unwmk. Typo. *Perf. 14x13½*

J1 D1 5c blue 1.75 1.75
J2 D1 10c brown 1.90 1.90
J3 D1 15c green 5.50 3.50
J4 D1 30c rose 5.50 3.50
J5 D1 50c black 9.25 9.25
J6 D1 60c dull orange 12.50 12.00
J7 D1 1fr violet 40.00 40.00
Nos. J1-J7 (7) 76.40 71.90

"Guinèe" in Red or Blue

1906-08

J8 D2 5c grn, *grnsh* ('08) 20.00 12.50
J9 D2 10c violet brn ('08) 5.50 5.50
J10 D2 15c dk blue ('08) 5.50 5.50
J11 D2 20c blk, *yellow* 5.50 5.50
J12 D2 30c red, *straw* ('08) 27.50 26.00
J13 D2 50c violet ('08) 24.00 24.00
J14 D2 60c blk, *buff* ('08) 22.50 22.50
J15 D2 1fr blk, *pnksh* ('08) 13.50 13.50
Nos. J8-J15 (8) 124.00 115.00

D3

D4

1914

J16 D3 5c green .40 .40
J17 D3 10c rose .40 .40
J18 D3 15c gray .55 .55
J19 D3 20c brown .75 .75
J20 D3 30c blue .75 .75
J21 D3 50c black .95 .95
J22 D3 60c orange 1.90 1.90
J23 D3 1fr violet 1.90 1.90
Nos. J16-J23 (8) 7.60 7.60

Type of 1914 Issue Surcharged

1927

J24 D3 2fr on 1fr lil rose 7.25 7.25
J25 D3 3fr on 1fr org brn 7.25 7.25

1938 **Engr.**

J26	D4	5c dk violet	.25	.25
J27	D4	10c carmine	.25	.25
J28	D4	15c green	.25	.25
J29	D4	20c red brown	.30	.30
J30	D4	30c rose violet	.30	.30
J31	D4	50c chocolate	.65	.65
J32	D4	60c peacock blue	.95	.95
J33	D4	1fr vermilion	.95	.95
J34	D4	2fr ultra	.95	.95
J35	D4	3fr black	1.50	1.50
		Nos. J26-J35 (10)	6.35	6.35

For No. J27 without "RF," see No. J36.

Type of 1938 without "RF"

1944

J36	D4	10c carmine	.50

No. J36 was issued by the Vichy government in France, but was not placed on sale in French Guinea.

FRENCH INDIA

'french 'in-dē-ə

LOCATION — East coast of India bordering on Bay of Bengal.
GOVT. — French Territory
AREA — 196 sq. mi.
POP. — 323,295 (1941)
CAPITAL — Pondichéry

French India was an administrative unit comprising the five settlements of Chandernagor, Karikal, Mahé, Pondichéry and Yanaon. These united with India in 1949 and 1954.

100 Centimes = 1 Franc
24 Caches = 1 Fanon (1923)
8 Fanons = 1 Rupie

Catalogue values for unused stamps in this country are for Never Hinged items, beginning with Scott 210 in the regular postage section, Scott B14 in the semi-postal section, and Scott C7 in the airpost section.

Navigation and Commerce — A1

A2

Perf. 14x13½

1892-1907 **Typo.** **Unwmk.**

Colony Name in Blue or Carmine

1	A1	1c blk, *lil bl*	1.40	1.00
2	A1	2c brn, *buff*	2.25	1.50
3	A1	4c claret, *lav*	2.75	2.25
4	A1	5c grn, *grnsh*	5.50	3.50
5	A1	10c blk, *lavender*	12.00	2.75
6	A1	10c red ('00)	4.75	2.40
7	A1	15c bl, quadrille paper	13.50	5.25
8	A1	15c gray, *lt gray* ('00)	30.00	27.50
9	A1	20c red, *grn*	7.25	5.25
10	A1	25c blk, *rose*	4.75	2.40
11	A1	25c blue ('00)	18.00	12.00
12	A1	30c brn, *bis*	52.50	47.50
13	A1	35c blk, *yel* ('06)	19.00	8.00
14	A1	40c red, *straw*	7.25	6.50
15	A1	45c blk, *gray grn* ('07)	4.75	*5.50*
16	A1	50c car, *rose*	6.50	6.50
17	A1	50c brn, *az* ('00)	15.00	*17.50*
18	A1	75c dp vio, *org*	8.75	*9.50*
19	A1	1fr brnz grn, *straw*	12.00	*13.50*
		Nos. 1-19 (19)	227.90	180.30

Perf. 13½x14 stamps are counterfeits.

Nos. 10 and 16 Surcharged in Carmine or Black

1903

20	A1	5c on 25c blk, *rose*	350.00	225.00
21	A1	10c on 25c blk, *rose*	350.00	225.00
22	A1	15c on 25c blk, *rose*	125.00	110.00
23	A1	40c on 50c car, *rose* (Bk)	475.00	400.00
		Nos. 20-23 (4)	1,300.	960.00

Counterfeits of Nos. 20-23 abound.

1903

Revenue Stamp Surcharged in Black

24	A2	5c gray blue	27.50	27.50

The bottom of the revenue stamps were cut off.

Brahma — A5

Kali Temple near Pondichéry A6

1914-22 ***Perf. 13½x14, 14x13½***

25	A5	1c gray & blk	.30	.30
26	A5	2c brn vio & blk	.30	.30
27	A5	2c grn & brn vio ('22)	.40	.40
28	A5	3c brown & blk	.40	.40
29	A5	4c orange & blk	.40	.40
30	A5	5c bl grn & blk	.65	.65
31	A5	5c vio brn & blk ('22)	.40	.40
32	A5	10c dp rose & blk	1.25	1.25
33	A5	10c grn & blk ('22)	.80	.80
34	A5	15c vio & blk	1.00	1.00
35	A5	20c org red & blk	1.60	1.60
36	A5	25c blue & blk	1.60	1.60
37	A5	25c ultra & fawn ('22)	1.25	1.25
38	A5	30c ultra & blk	3.00	3.00
39	A5	30c rose & blk ('22)	1.25	1.25
40	A6	35c choc & blk	1.75	1.75
41	A6	40c org red & blk	1.75	1.75
42	A6	45c bl grn & blk	1.75	1.75
43	A6	50c dp rose & blk	1.75	1.75
44	A6	50c ultra & bl ('22)	1.90	1.90
45	A6	75c blue & blk	3.50	3.50
46	A6	1fr yellow & blk	3.50	3.50
47	A6	2fr violet & blk	5.25	5.25
48	A6	5fr ultra & blk	2.75	2.75
49	A6	5fr rose & blk ('22)	4.00	4.00
		Nos. 25-49 (25)	42.50	42.50

For surcharges see Nos. 50-79, 113-116, 156A, B1-B5.

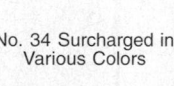

No. 34 Surcharged in Various Colors

1922

50	A5	1c on 15c (Bk)	.80	.80
51	A5	2c on 15c (Bl)	.80	.80
53	A5	5c on 15c (R)	.80	.80
		Nos. 50-53 (3)	2.40	2.40

Stamps and Types of 1914-22 Surcharged with New Values in Caches, Fanons and Rupies in Black, Red or Blue:

1923-28

54	A5	1ca on 1c gray & blk (R)	.30	.30
55	A5	2ca on 5c vio brn & blk	.50	.50
a.		Horizontal pair, imperf. between		—
56	A5	3ca on 3c brn & blk	.55	.55
57	A5	4ca on 4c org & blk	.80	.80
58	A5	6ca on 10c grn & blk	.95	.95
59	A6	6ca on 45c bl grn & blk (R)	.95	.95
60	A5	10ca on 20c dp red & bl grn ('28)	2.50	2.50
61	A5	12ca on 15c vio & blk	.95	.95
62	A5	15ca on 20c org & blk	1.40	1.40
63	A6	16ca on 35c lt bl & yel brn ('28)	2.50	2.50
64	A5	18ca on 30c rose & blk	2.10	2.10
65	A6	20ca on 45c grn & dl red ('28)	1.75	1.40
66	A5	1fa on 25c dp grn & rose red ('28)	3.25	3.25
67	A6	1fa3ca on 35c choc & blk (Bl)	1.10	1.10
68	A6	1fa6ca on 40c org & blk (R)	1.40	1.10
69	A6	1fa12ca on 50c ultra & bl (Bl)	1.60	1.50
70	A6	1fa12ca on 75c bl & blk (Bl)	1.25	1.25
a.		Double surcharge	140.00	
71	A6	1fa16ca on 75c brn red & grn ('28)	3.00	2.50
72	A5	2fa9ca on 25c ultra & fawn (Bl)	1.40	1.10
73	A6	2fa12ca on 1fr vio & dk brn ('28)	2.75	2.75
74	A6	3fa3ca on 1fr yel & blk (R)	1.60	1.40
a.		Double surcharge	140.00	
75	A6	6fa6ca on 2fr vio & blk (Bl)	4.75	4.00
76	A6	1r on 1fr grn & dp bl (R) ('26)	8.00	7.25
77	A6	2r on 5fr rose & blk (R)	7.25	6.50
a.		Double surcharge	140.00	
78	A6	3r on 2fr gray & bl vio (R) ('26)	19.00	17.50
79	A6	5r on 5fr rose & blk, *grnsh* ('26)	24.00	21.00
		Nos. 54-79 (26)	95.60	87.10

Nos. 60, 63, 66 and 73 have the original value obliterated by bars.

A7

A8

1929

80	A7	1ca dk gray & blk	.25	.25
81	A7	2ca vio brn & blk	.25	.25
82	A7	3ca brn & blk	.25	.25
83	A7	4ca org & blk	.30	.30
84	A7	6ca gray grn & grn	.30	.30
85	A7	10ca brn, red & grn	.30	.30
86	A8	12ca grn & lt grn	.70	.65
87	A7	16ca brt bl & blk	.90	.90
88	A7	18ca brn red & ver	.90	.90
89	A7	20ca dk bl & grn, *bluish*	.70	.70
90	A8	1fa gray grn & rose red	.70	.65
91	A8	1fa6ca red org & blk	.70	.65
92	A8	1fa12ca dp bl & ultra	.70	.65
93	A8	1fa16ca rose red & grn	.90	.90
94	A8	2fa12ca brt vio & brn	1.10	.95
95	A8	6fa6ca dl vio & blk	1.25	.95
96	A8	1r gray grn & dp bl	1.10	.95
97	A8	2r rose & blk	1.50	1.10
98	A8	3r lt gray & gray lil	2.75	2.10
99	A8	5r rose & blk, *grnsh*	2.75	2.25
		Nos. 80-99 (20)	18.30	15.95

For overprints and surcharges see Nos. 117-134, 157-176, 184-209G.

Common Design Types pictured following the introduction.

Colonial Exposition Issue
Common Design Types

1931 **Engr.** ***Perf. 12½***

100	CD70	10ca deep green	4.00	4.00
101	CD71	12ca violet	4.00	4.00
102	CD72	18ca red orange	4.00	4.00
103	CD73	1fa12ca dull blue	4.00	4.00
		Nos. 100-103 (4)	16.00	16.00

Paris International Exposition Issue
Common Design Types

1937 ***Perf. 13***

104	CD74	8ca dp violet	2.00	2.00
105	CD75	12ca dk green	2.25	2.25
106	CD76	16ca car rose	2.25	2.25
107	CD77	20ca dk brown	1.40	1.40
108	CD78	1fa12ca red	1.75	1.75
109	CD79	2fa12ca ultra	2.25	2.25
		Nos. 104-109 (6)	11.90	11.90

For overprints see Nos. 135-139, 177-181.

Colonial Arts Exhibition Issue
Souvenir Sheet
Common Design Type

1937 ***Imperf.***

110	CD79	5fa red violet	8.75	*12.00*

For overprint see No. 140.

New York World's Fair Issue
Common Design Type

1939 **Engr.** ***Perf. 12½x12***

111	CD82	1fa12ca car lake	1.25	1.25
112	CD82	2fa12ca ultra	1.60	1.60

For overprints see Nos. 141-142, 182-183.

Temple near Pondichéry and Marshal Petain A9

1941 Engr. *Perf. 12½x12*

112A	A9	1fa16ca car & red	.80	
112B	A9	4fa4ca blue	.80	

Nos. 112A-112B were issued by the Vichy government in France, but were not placed on sale in French India.

For surcharges, see Nos. B13B-B13C.

Nos. 62, 64, 67, 72 Overprinted in Carmine or Blue (#116):

a

FRANCE LIBRE
b

1941 Unwmk. *Perf. 13½x14*

113	A5 (a)	15ca on 20c	80.00	80.00
114	A5 (a)	18ca on 30c	15.00	15.00
115	A6 (a)	1fa3ca on 35c	125.00	125.00
a.		Horiz. overprint	125.00	125.00
116	A5 (b)	2fa9ca on 25c	1,400.	1,000.
a.		Overprint "a" (Bl)	1,300.	1,000.
b.		Overprint "b" (C)	*2,000.*	*2,000.*

Nos. 81-99 Overprinted Type "a" in Carmine or Blue

1941

117	A7	2ca (C)	12.00	12.00
118	A7	3ca (C)	4.75	4.75
119	A7	4ca (C)	13.50	13.50
120	A7	6ca (C)	4.75	4.75
121	A7	10ca (Bl)	6.50	6.50
122	A8	12ca (C)	4.75	4.75
123	A7	16ca (C)	4.75	4.75
123A	A7	18ca (Bl)	600.00	600.00
124	A7	20ca (C)	4.75	4.75
125	A8	1fa (Bl)	4.75	4.75
126	A8	1fa6ca (C)	4.75	4.75
127	A8	1fa12ca (C)	6.50	6.50
128	A8	1fa16ca (C)	4.75	4.75
129	A8	2fa12ca (C)	4.75	4.75
130	A8	6fa6ca (C)	4.75	4.75
131	A8	1r (C)	4.75	4.75
132	A8	2r (C)	4.75	4.75
133	A8	3r (C)	6.50	6.50
134	A8	5r (C)	10.50	10.50
		Nos. 117-123,124-134 (18)	112.50	112.50

Same Overprints on Paris Exposition Issue of 1937

1941 *Perf. 13*

135	CD74 (b)	8ca (C)	8.75	8.75
135A	CD74 (b)	8ca (Bl)	240.00	240.00
135B	CD74 (a)	8ca (C)	175.00	175.00
135C	CD74 (a)	8ca (Bl)	225.00	225.00
136	CD75 (a)	12ca (C)	6.00	6.00
137	CD76 (a)	16ca (Bl)	6.00	6.00
138	CD78 (a)	1fa12ca (Bl)	6.00	6.00
139	CD79 (a)	2fa12ca (C)	6.00	6.00
		Nos. 135-139 (8)	672.75	672.75

Inverted overprints exist.

Souvenir Sheet

No. 110 Overprinted "FRANCE LIBRE" Diagonally in Blue Violet

Two types of overprint:
I — Overprint 37mm. With serifs.
II — Overprint 24mm, as type "a" shown above No. 113. No serifs.

1941 Unwmk. *Imperf.*

140	CD79	5fa red vio (I)	725.00	650.00
a.		Type II	875.00	875.00

Overprinted on New York World's Fair Issue, 1939

Perf. 12½x12

141	CD82 (a)	1fa12ca (Bl)	4.75	4.75
142	CD82 (a)	2fa12ca (C)	4.75	4.75

Lotus Flowers — A10

1942 Unwmk. Photo. *Perf. 14x14½*

143	A10	2ca brown	.30	.30
144	A10	3ca dk blue	.30	.30
145	A10	4ca emerald	.30	.30
146	A10	6ca dk orange	.30	.30
147	A10	12ca grnsh blk	.30	.30
148	A10	16ca rose violet	.30	.30
149	A10	20ca dk red brn	.65	.65
150	A10	1fa brt red	.70	.65
151	A10	1fa18ca slate blk	.90	.80
152	A10	6fa6ca brt ultra	1.50	1.40
153	A10	1r dull violet	1.25	1.25
154	A10	2r bister	1.50	1.25
155	A10	3r chocolate	1.50	1.40
156	A10	5r dk green	2.00	1.90
		Nos. 143-156 (14)	11.80	11.10

Stamps of 1923-39 Overprinted in Blue or Carmine

c

d

1942-43 *Perf. 13½x14, 14x13½*

Overprinted on No. 64

156A	A5 (c)	18ca on 30c (B)	275.00	225.00

Overprinted on #81-82, 84, 86-99

157	A7 (c)	2ca (C)	3.25	3.25
a.		"FRANCE LIBRE" in black	225.00	175.00
158	A7 (c)	3ca (C)	2.40	2.40
159	A7 (c)	6ca (Bl)	3.25	3.25
160	A8 (d)	12ca (Bl)	3.25	3.25
161	A7 (c)	16ca (C)	3.25	3.25
162	A7 (c)	18ca (Bl)	2.40	2.40
163	A7 (c)	20ca (Bl) ('43)	7.25	5.50
164	A7 (c)	20ca (C)	2.40	2.40
165	A8 (d)	1fa (Bl)	2.40	2.40
166	A8 (d)	1fa6ca (C)	3.25	3.25
167	A8 (d)	1fa12ca (C)	3.25	3.25
168	A8 (d)	1fa16ca (Bl)	3.25	3.25
169	A8 (d)	2fa12ca (Bl)	80.00	80.00
170	A8 (d)	2fa12ca (C)	3.25	3.25
171	A8 (d)	6fa6ca (C)	4.00	4.00
172	A8 (d)	1r (C)	7.25	7.25
173	A8 (d)	2r (C)	7.25	7.25
174	A8 (d)	3r (C)	7.25	7.25
175	A8 (d)	3r (Bl) ('43)	175.00	175.00
176	A8 (d)	5r (C)	7.25	7.25
		Nos. 156A-176 (21)	605.85	554.10

Same Overprints on Paris International Exposition Issue of 1937

Perf. 13

177	CD74 (c)	8ca (Bl)	7.25	7.25
178	CD75 (d)	12ca (Bl)	7.25	7.25
179	CD76 (d)	16ca (Bl)	1,300.	1,300.
180	CD78 (d)	1fa12ca (Bl)	7.25	7.25
181	CD79 (d)	2fa12ca (C)	7.25	7.25

Same Overprint on New York World's Fair Issue, 1939

Perf. 12½x12

182	CD82 (d)	1fa12ca (Bl)	7.25	7.25
183	CD82 (d)	2fa12ca (C)	7.25	7.25

No. 87 Surcharged in Carmine

1942-43 *Perf. 13½x14*

184	A7	1ca on 16ca	72.50	45.00
185	A7	4ca on 16ca ('43)	72.50	45.00
186	A7	10ca on 16ca	55.00	35.00
187	A7	15ca on 16ca	55.00	35.00
188	A7	1fa3ca on 16ca ('43)	72.50	45.00
189	A7	2fa9ca on 16ca ('43)	72.50	45.00
190	A7	3fa3ca on 16ca ('43)	55.00	35.00
		Nos. 184-190 (7)	455.00	285.00

Nos. 95-99 Surcharged in Carmine

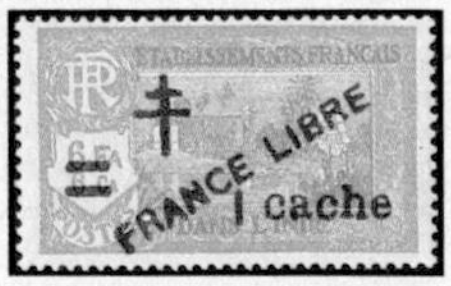

1943 *Perf. 14x13½*

191	A8	1ca on 6fa6ca	11.00	11.00
192	A8	4ca on 6fa6ca	11.00	11.00
193	A8	10ca on 6fa6ca	11.00	11.00
194	A8	15ca on 6fa6ca	11.00	11.00
195	A8	1fa3ca on 6fa6ca	11.00	11.00
196	A8	2fa9ca on 6fa6ca	12.00	12.00
197	A8	3fa3ca on 6fa6ca	12.00	12.00
198	A8	1ca on 1r	4.50	4.50
199	A8	2ca on 1r	1.60	1.60
200	A8	4ca on 1r	1.60	1.60
201	A8	6ca on 2r	1.60	1.60
202	A8	10ca on 2r	1.60	1.60
203	A8	12ca on 2r	1.60	1.60
204	A8	15ca on 3r	1.60	1.60
205	A8	16ca on 3r	1.60	1.60
206	A8	1fa3ca on 3r	1.60	1.60
207	A8	1fa6ca on 5r	2.00	2.00
208	A8	1fa12ca on 5r	2.40	2.40
209	A8	1fa16ca on 5r	2.40	2.40
		Nos. 191-209 (19)	103.10	103.10

In 1943, 200 each of 27 stamps were overprinted in red or dark blue, "FRANCE TOUJOURS" and a Lorraine Cross within a circle measuring 17½mm in diameter. Overprinted were Nos. 81-99, 104-109, 111-112.

No. 95 Surcharged in Carmine with New Value and Bars

1943 Unwmk. *Perf. 14x13½*

209A	A8	1ca on 6fa6ca	35.00	27.50
209B	A8	4ca on 6fa6ca	35.00	27.50
209C	A8	10ca on 6fa6ca	24.00	16.00
209D	A8	15ca on 6fa6ca	24.00	16.00
209E	A8	1fa3ca on 6fa6ca	32.50	27.50
209F	A8	2fa9ca on 6fa6ca	32.50	27.50
209G	A8	3fa3ca on 6fa6ca	35.00	27.50
		Nos. 209A-209G (7)	218.00	169.50

Catalogue values for unused stamps in this section, from this point to the end of the section, are for Never Hinged items.

Eboue Issue

Common Design Type

1945 Engr. *Perf. 13*

210	CD91	3fa8ca black	.70	.70
211	CD91	5r1fa16ca Prus grn	1.25	1.25

Nos. 210 and 211 exist imperforate.

Apsaras — A11

Brahman Ascetic — A12

Designs: 6ca, 8ca, 10ca, Dvarabalagar. 12ca, 15ca, 1fa, Vishnu. 1fa6ca, 2fa, 2fa2ca, Dvarabalagar (foot raised). 2fa12ca, 3fa, 5fa, Temple Guardian. 7fa12ca, 1r2fa, 1r4fa12ca, Tigoupalagar.

1948 Photo. *Perf. 13x13½*

212	A11	1ca dk ol grn	.25	.25
213	A11	2ca orange brn	.25	.25
214	A11	4ca vio, *cr*	.30	.30
215	A11	6ca yellow org	1.00	.65
216	A11	8ca gray blk	1.00	1.00
217	A11	10ca dl yel grn, *pale grn*	1.00	1.00
218	A11	12ca violet brn	.70	.65
219	A11	15ca Prus grn	.70	.65
220	A11	1fa vio, *pale rose*	1.00	.80
221	A11	1fa6ca brown red	1.00	.80
222	A11	2fa dk green	1.00	.80
223	A11	2fa2ca blue, *cr*	1.25	1.00
224	A11	2fa12ca brown	1.25	1.00
225	A11	3fa dp orange	2.40	1.00
226	A11	5fa red vio, *rose*	2.10	1.25
227	A11	7fa12ca dk brown	2.40	1.25
228	A11	1r2fa brown blk	4.25	4.25
229	A11	1r4fa12ca olive grn	4.25	4.25
		Nos. 212-229 (18)	26.10	21.15

1952

230	A12	18ca rose red	1.75	1.75
231	A12	1fa15ca vio blue	2.40	2.40
232	A12	4fa olive grn	3.00	3.00
		Nos. 230-232 (3)	7.15	7.15

Military Medal Issue

Common Design Type

1952 Engr. and Typo. *Perf. 13*

233	CD101	1fa multi	4.75	4.75

SEMI-POSTAL STAMPS

Regular Issue of 1914 Surcharged in Red

1915 Unwmk. *Perf. 14x13½*

B1	A5	10c + 5c rose & blk	2.10	2.10
a.		Inverted surcharge	200.00	200.00

There were two printings of this surcharge; in the first it was placed at the bottom of the stamp, in the second it was near the top.

Regular Issue of 1914 Surcharged in Red

1916

B2	A5	10c + 5c rose & blk	21.00	21.00
a.		Inverted surcharge	200.00	200.00
b.		Double surcharge	200.00	200.00

Surcharged

B3	A5	10c + 5c rose & blk	3.25	3.25

Surcharged

B4	A5	10c + 5c rose & blk	1.60	1.60

Surcharged

B5 A5 10c + 5c rose & blk 2.25 2.25

Curie Issue
Common Design Type

1938 **Engr.** ***Perf. 13***

B6 CD80 2fa12ca + 20ca brt ultra 8.75 8.75

French Revolution Issue
Common Design Type

1939 **Photo.**

Name and Value Typo. in Black

B7	CD83	18ca + 10ca grn	8.75	8.75
B8	CD83	1fa6ca + 12ca brn	8.75	8.75
B9	CD83	1fa12ca + 16ca red org	8.75	8.75
B10	CD83	1fa16ca + 1fa16ca rose pink	8.75	8.75
B11	CD83	2fa12ca + 3fa blue	8.75	8.75
		Nos. B7-B11 (5)	43.75	43.75

Common Design Type and

Non-Commissioned Officer, Native Guard — SP1

Sepoy SP2

1941 **Photo.** ***Perf. 13½***

B12	SP1	1fa16ca + 1fa16ca red	1.25
B13	CD86	2fa12ca + 5fa mar	1.25
B13A	SP2	4fa4ca + 1fa16ca bl	1.25
		Nos. B12-B13A (3)	3.75

Nos. B12-B13A were issued by the Vichy government in France, but were not placed on sale in French India.

Nos. 112A-112B Surcharged in Black or Red

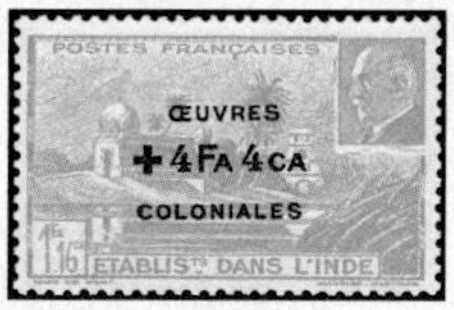

1944 **Engr.** ***Perf. 12½x12***

B13B	20ca + 2fa12ca on 4fa4ca deep blue (R)	1.00
B13C	+ 4fa4ca on 1fa16ca car & red	1.00

Colonial Development Fund.

Nos. B13B-B13C were issued by the Vichy government in France, but were not placed on sale in French India.

Catalogue values for unused stamps in this section, from this point to the end of the section, are for Never Hinged items.

Red Cross Issue
Common Design Type

1944 **Photo.** ***Perf. 14½x14***

B14 CD90 3fa + 1r4fa dk ol brn 1.25 1.25

The surtax was for the French Red Cross and national relief.

Tropical Medicine Issue
Common Design Type

1950 **Engr.** ***Perf. 13***

B15 CD100 1fa + 10ca ind & dp bl 4.00 4.00

The surtax was for charitable work.

AIR POST STAMPS

Common Design Type

1942 Unwmk. Photo. ***Perf. 14½x14***

C1	CD87	4fa dark orange	.90	.90
C2	CD87	1r bright red	.90	.90
C3	CD87	2r brown red	1.40	1.40
C4	CD87	5r black	1.40	1.40
C5	CD87	8r ultra	2.10	2.10
C6	CD87	10r dark green	2.10	2.10
		Nos. C1-C6 (6)	8.80	8.80

Catalogue values for unused stamps in this section, from this point to the end of the section, are for Never Hinged items.

Victory Issue
Common Design Type

1946 **Engr.** ***Perf. 12½***

C7 CD92 4fa dk blue green .95 .95

Chad to Rhine Issue
Common Design Types

1946, June 6

C8	CD93	2fa12ca olive bis	.95	.95
C9	CD94	5fa dark blue	.95	.95
C10	CD95	7fa12ca dk purple	1.50	1.50
C11	CD96	1r2fa green	1.50	1.50
C12	CD97	1r4fa12ca dk car	1.90	1.90
C13	CD98	3r1fa violet brn	2.40	2.40
		Nos. C8-C13 (6)	9.20	9.20

A 3r ultramarine and red, picturing the Temple of Chindambaram, was sold at Paris June 7 to July 8, 1948, but not placed on sale in the colony. Value $5.75.

Bas-relief Figure of Goddess — AP1

Wing and Temple — AP2

Bird over Palms — AP3

Perf. 12x13, 13x12

1949 **Photo.** **Unwmk.**

C14	AP1	1r yellow & plum	4.75	3.50
C15	AP2	2r green & dk grn	4.75	4.50
C16	AP3	5r lt bl & vio brn	21.00	16.00
		Nos. C14-C16 (3)	30.50	24.00

UPU Issue
Common Design Type

1949 **Engr.** ***Perf. 13***

C17 CD99 6fa lilac rose 8.75 8.75

Universal Postal Union, 75th anniv.

Liberation Issue
Common Design Type

1954, June 6

C18 CD102 1fa sepia & vio brn 8.00 8.00

AIR POST SEMI-POSTAL STAMPS

Girl's School SPAP1

Perf. 12½x13½

1942, June 22 **Unwmk.** **Photo.**

CB1	SPAP1	2fa12ca + 5fa20ca green	.95
CB2	SPAP1	3fa8ca + 1r2fa yel brn	.95

Native children's welfare fund.

Nos. CB1-CB2 were issued by the Vichy government in France, but were not placed on sale in French India.

Colonial Education Fund
Common Design Type

1942, June 22

CB3 CD86a 2fa + 3fa blue & red .90

No. CB3 was issued by the Vichy government in France, but was not placed on sale in French India.

POSTAGE DUE STAMPS

Postage Due Stamps of France Surcharged like Nos. 54-75 in Black, Blue or Red

1923 **Unwmk.** ***Perf. 14x13½***

J1	D2	6ca on 10c brn	1.25	1.25
J2	D2	12ca on 25c rose (Bk)	1.25	1.25
J3	D2	15ca on 20c ol grn (R)	1.60	1.60
J4	D2	1fa6ca on 30c red	1.60	1.60
J5	D2	1fa12a on 50c brn vio	2.75	2.75
J6	D2	1fa15ca on 5c bl (Bk)	2.75	2.75
J7	D2	3fa3ca on 1fr red brn, *straw*	3.25	3.25
		Nos. J1-J7 (7)	14.45	14.45

Types of Postage Due Stamps of French Colonies, 1884-85, Surcharged with New Values as in 1923 in Red or Black Bars over Original Values

1928

J8	D1	4ca on 20c gray lil	1.60	1.60
J9	D1	1fa on 30c orange	3.00	3.00
J10	D1	1fa16ca on 5c bl blk (R)	3.00	3.00
J11	D1	3fa on 1fr lt grn	3.50	3.50
		Nos. J8-J11 (4)	11.10	11.10

D3

1929 **Typo.**

J12	D3	4ca deep red	.50	.50
J13	D3	6ca blue	.65	.65
J14	D3	12ca green	.65	.65
J15	D3	1fa brown	1.25	1.25
J16	D3	1fa12ca lilac gray	1.25	1.25
J17	D3	1fa16ca buff	1.75	1.75
J18	D3	3fa lilac	2.10	2.10
		Nos. J12-J18 (7)	8.15	8.15

D4

1948 Unwmk. Photo. ***Perf. 13x13½***

J19	D4	1ca dk violet	.30	.30
J20	D4	2ca dk brown	.50	.50
J21	D4	6ca blue green	.50	.50
J22	D4	12ca dp orange	.70	.70
J23	D4	1fa dk car rose	.80	.80
J24	D4	1fa12ca brown	.80	.80
J25	D4	2fa dk slate bl	1.25	1.25
J26	D4	2fa12ca henna brn	1.60	1.60
J27	D4	5fa dk olive grn	2.10	2.10
J28	D4	1r dk blue vio	2.75	2.75
		Nos. J19-J28 (10)	11.30	11.30

FRENCH MOROCCO

'french mə-'rä-ˌkō

LOCATION — Northwest coast of Africa
GOVT. — French Protectorate
AREA — 153,870 sq. mi.
POP. — 8,340,000 (estimated 1954)
CAPITAL — Rabat

French Morocco was a French Protectorate from 1912 until 1956 when it, along with the Spanish and Tangier zones of Morocco, became the independent country, Morocco.

Stamps inscribed "Tanger" were for use in the international zone of Tangier in northern Morocco.

100 Centimos = 1 Peseta
100 Centimes = 1 franc (1917)

Catalogue values for unused stamps in this country are for Never Hinged items, beginning with Scott 177 in the regular postage section, Scott B26 in the semi-postal section, Scott C27 in the airpost section, Scott CB23A in the airpost semi-postal section, and Scott J46 in the postage due section.

French Offices in Morocco

A1

A2

Stamps of France Surcharged in Red or Black

1891-1900 Unwmk. ***Perf. 14x13½***

1 A1 5c on 5c grn, *grnsh* (R) 12.00 3.50
a. Imperf., pair 150.00
2 A1 5c on 5c yel grn (II) (R) ('99) 30.00 27.50
a. Type I 30.00 24.00
3 A1 10c on 10c blk, *lav* (II) (R) 30.00 3.25
a. Type I 37.50 20.00
b. 10c on 25c black, *rose* 775.00
4 A1 20c on 20c red, *grn* 32.50 25.00
5 A1 25c on 25c blk, *rose* (R) 27.50 3.50
a. Double surcharge 200.00
b. Imperf., pair 160.00
6 A1 50c on 50c car, *rose* (II) 92.50 40.00
a. Type I 350.00 250.00
7 A1 1p on 1fr brnz grn, *straw* 105.00 67.50
8 A1 2p on 2fr brn, *az* (Bk) ('00) 240.00 225.00
Nos. 1-8 (8) 569.50 395.25

No. 3b was never sent to Morocco.

France Nos. J15-J16 Overprinted in Carmine

1893

9 A2 5c black 2,500. 1,100.
10 A2 10c black 2,100. 725.

Counterfeits exist.

A3

18srch

A5

Surcharged in Red or Black

1902-10

11 A3 1c on 1c gray (R) ('08) 2.25 1.20
12 A3 2c on 2c vio brn ('08) 2.25 1.20
13 A3 3c on 3c red org ('08) 2.75 1.20
14 A3 4c on 4c yel brn ('08) 10.00 6.75
15 A3 5c on 5c grn (R) 8.00 3.50
a. Double surcharge 325.00
16 A4 10c on 10c rose red ('03) 6.50 2.50
a. Surcharge omitted 200.00
17 A4 20c on 20c brn vio ('03) 29.00 18.00
18 A4 25c on 25c bl ('03) 29.00 2.40
19 A4 35c on 35c vio ('10) 37.50 21.00
20 A5 50c on 50c bis brn & lav ('03) 52.50 13.00
21 A5 1p on 1fr cl & ol grn ('03) 105.00 65.00
22 A5 2p on 2fr gray vio & yel ('03) 130.00 87.50
Nos. 11-22 (12) 414.75 223.25

Nos. 11-14 exist spelled CFNTIMOS or GENTIMOS.

The 25c on 25c with surcharge omitted is listed as No. 81a.

For overprints and surcharges see Nos. 26-37, 72-79, B1, B3.

Postage Due Stamps Nos. J1-J2 Handstamped

1903

24 D2 5c on 5c light blue 1,400. 1,400.
25 D2 10c on 10c choc 2,600. 2,600.

Nos. 24 and 25 were used only on Oct. 10, 1903. Used copies were not canceled, the overprint serving as a cancellation.

Counterfeits exist.

Types of 1902-10 Issue Surcharged in Red or Blue

1911-17

26 A3 1c on 1c gray (R) .80 .75
27 A3 2c on 2c vio brn .80 .75
28 A3 3c on 3c orange .80 .75
29 A3 5c on 5c green (R) .95 .55
30 A4 10c on 10c rose .95 .55
a. Imperf., pair 250.00
31 A4 15c on 15c org ('17) 3.00 2.10
32 A4 20c on 20c brn vio 4.25 3.00
33 A4 25c on 25c blue (R) 2.10 1.60
34 A4 35c on 35c violet (R) 8.50 3.50
35 A5 40c on 40c red & pale bl ('17) 7.50 5.00
36 A5 50c on 50c bis brn & lav (R) 23.00 13.00
37 A5 1p on 1fr cl & ol grn 17.50 8.75
Nos. 26-37 (12) 70.15 40.30

For surcharges see Nos. B1, B3.

Stamps of this design were issued by the Cherifien posts in 1912-13. The Administration Cherifinne des Postes, Telegraphes et Telephones was formed in 1911 under French guidance. See Morocco in Vol. 4 for listings.

French Protectorate

A6

A7

A8

Issue of 1911-17 Overprinted "Protectorat Francais"

1914-21

38 A6 1c on 1c gray .55 .40
39 A6 2c on 2c vio brn .55 .40
40 A6 3c on 3c orange .95 .50
41 A6 5c on 5c green .75 .50
a. New value omitted 250.00 250.00
42 A7 10c on 10c rose .55 .30
a. New value omitted 500.00 500.00
43 A7 15c on 15c org ('17) .65 .50
a. New value omitted 100.00 100.00
44 A7 20c on 20c brn vio 4.00 3.50
a. "Protectorat Francais" double 275.00 275.00
45 A7 25c on 25c blue 1.90 .50
a. New value omitted 300.00 300.00
46 A7 25c on 25c violet ('21) 1.20 .30
a. "Protectorat Francais" omitted 72.50 72.50
b. "Protectorat Francais" dbl. 160.00 160.00
c. "Protectorat Francais" dbl. (R + Bk) 160.00 160.00
47 A7 30c on 30c vio ('21) 16.00 8.00
48 A7 35c on 35c violet 4.75 1.60
49 A8 40c on 40c red & pale bl 16.00 7.50
a. New value omitted 350.00 350.00
50 A8 45c on 45c grn & bl ('21) 45.00 35.00
51 A8 50c on 50c bis brn & lav 1.40 .55
a. "Protectorat Francais" invtd. 190.00 190.00
b. "Protectorat Francais" dbl. 400.00 400.00
52 A8 1p on 1fr cl & ol grn 2.75 .75
a. "Protectorat Francais" invtd. 300.00 300.00
b. New value double 180.00 180.00
c. New value dbl., one invtd. 190.00 190.00
53 A8 2p on 2fr gray vio & yel 5.25 1.40
a. New value omitted 160.00 160.00
b. "Protectorat Francais" omitted 95.00 95.00
c. New value double *200.00*
d. New value dbl., one invtd.
54 A8 5p on 5fr dk bl & buff 14.00 4.50
Nos. 38-54 (17) 116.25 66.20

For surcharges see Nos. B2, B4-B5.

Tower of Hassan, Rabat — A9

Mosque of the Andalusians, Fez — A10

City Gate Chella A11

Koutoubiah, Marrakesh A12

Bab Mansour, Meknes A13

Roman Ruins, Volubilis A14

1917 Engr. ***Perf. 13½x14, 14x13½***

55 A9 1c grnsh gray .50 .50
56 A9 2c brown lilac .65 .50
57 A9 3c orange brn .65 .50
a. Imperf., pair 87.50
58 A10 5c yellow grn .65 .40
59 A10 10c rose red .65 .40
60 A10 15c dark gray .65 .50
a. Imperf., pair 65.00
61 A11 20c red brown 3.00 2.10
62 A11 25c dull blue 3.25 .90
63 A11 30c gray violet 4.00 2.50
64 A12 35c orange 4.00 2.50
65 A12 40c ultra 1.40 .90
66 A12 45c gray green 27.50 12.50
67 A13 50c dk brown 4.50 2.60
a. Imperf., pair 65.00
68 A13 1fr slate 12.00 3.50
a. Imperf., pair 65.00
69 A14 2fr black brown 160.00 85.00
70 A14 5fr dk gray grn 40.00 35.00
71 A14 10fr black 40.00 35.00
Nos. 55-71 (17) 303.40 185.30

See note following #115. See #93-105. For surcharges see #120-121.

Types of the 1902-10 Issue Overprinted

1918-24 ***Perf. 14x13½***

72 A3 1c gray .50 .50
73 A3 2c violet brn .50 .50
74 A3 3c red orange .80 .80
75 A3 5c green .80 .80
76 A3 5c orange ('23) 1.75 1.75
77 A4 10c rose 1.60 1.20
78 A4 10c green ('24) 1.40 1.10
79 A4 15c orange 1.40 .90
80 A4 20c violet brn 2.25 1.75
81 A4 25c blue 2.10 1.75
a. "TANGER" omitted 400.00 400.00
82 A4 30c red org ('24) 2.50 2.40
83 A4 35c violet 2.90 2.10
84 A5 40c red & pale bl 3.00 2.00
85 A5 50c bis brn & lav 25.00 14.00
86 A4 50c blue 16.00 11.00
87 A5 1fr claret & ol grn 13.50 5.75
88 A5 2fr org & pale bl ('24) 72.50 67.50
89 A5 5fr dk bl & buff ('24) 62.50 60.00
Nos. 72-89 (18) 211.00 175.80

Types of 1917 and

Tower of Hassan, Rabat — A15

Bab Mansour, Meknes A16

Roman Ruins, Volubilis A17

1923-27 Photo. ***Perf. 13½***

90 A15 1c olive green .25 .25
91 A15 2c brown vio .25 .25
92 A15 3c yellow brn .25 .25
93 A10 5c orange .25 .25
94 A10 10c yellow grn .25 .25
95 A10 15c dk gray .25 .25
96 A11 20c red brown .25 .25
97 A11 20c red vio ('27) .50 .50
98 A11 25c ultra .30 .30
99 A11 30c deep red .30 .30
100 A11 30c turq bl ('27) .95 .75
101 A12 35c violet .90 .65

102 A12	40c	orange red	.25	.25
103 A12	45c	deep green	.30	.30
104 A16	50c	dull turq	.50	.30
105 A12	50c	olive grn ('27)	.65	.30
106 A16	60c	lilac	.90	.30
107 A16	75c	red vio ('27)	.70	.50
108 A16	1fr	deep brown	.65	.50
109 A16	1.05fr	red brn ('27)	1.40	.80
110 A16	1.40fr	dull rose ('27)	.80	.75
111 A16	1.50fr	turq bl ('27)	1.20	.30
112 A17	2fr	olive brn	1.25	.90
113 A17	3fr	dp red ('27)	1.50	.95
114 A17	5fr	dk gray grn	3.00	2.25
115 A17	10fr	black	8.50	4.25
		Nos. 90-115 (26)	26.30	16.90

Nos. 90-110, 112-115 exist imperf. The stamps of 1917 were line engraved. Those of 1923-27 were printed by photogravure and have in the margin at lower right the imprint "Helio Vaugirard."

See #B36. For surcharges see #122-123.

No. 102 Surcharged in Black

1930

120 A12 15c on 40c orange red 1.40 1.40

Nos. 100, 106 and 110 Surcharged in Blue Similarly to No. 176

1931

121 A11 25c on 30c turq blue		2.25	2.00
a.	Inverted surcharge	110.00	110.00
122 A16 50c on 60c lilac		.95	.30
a.	Inverted surcharge	140.00	140.00
b.	Double surcharge	140.00	140.00
123 A16 1fr on 1.40fr rose		3.00	1.50
a.	Inverted surcharge	140.00	140.00
	Nos. 121-123 (3)	6.20	3.80

Old Treasure House and Tribunal, Tangier A18

Roadstead at Agadir A19

Post Office at Casablanca A20

Moulay Idriss of the Zehroun A21

Kasbah of the Oudayas, Rabat A22

Court of the Medersa el Attarine at Fez A23

Saadiens' Tombs at Marrakesh A25

Kasbah of Si Madani el Glaoui at Ouarzazat A24

1933-34 Engr. *Perf. 13*

124 A18	1c	olive blk	.25	.25
125 A18	2c	red violet	.25	.25
126 A19	3c	dark brown	.25	.25
127 A19	5c	brown red	.25	.25
128 A20	10c	blue green	.30	.30
129 A20	15c	black	.30	.30
130 A20	20c	red brown	.30	.30
131 A21	25c	dark blue	.30	.30
132 A21	30c	emerald	.50	.30
133 A21	40c	black brn	.50	.30
134 A22	45c	brown vio	.75	.65
135 A22	50c	dk blue grn	.75	.30
a.		Booklet pane of 10	—	
b.		Booklet pane of 20	—	
		Complete booklet, #135b	1,400.	
136 A22	65c	brown red	.30	.30
a.		Booklet pane of 10	—	
b.		Booklet pane of 20	—	
		Complete booklet, #135b	55.00	
137 A23	75c	red violet	.75	.30
138 A23	90c	orange red	.50	.30
139 A23	1fr	deep brown	1.00	.50
140 A23	1.25fr	black ('34)	1.40	.95
141 A24	1.50fr	ultra	.50	.30
142 A24	1.75fr	myr grn ('34)	.75	.30
143 A24	2fr	yellow brn	4.25	.80
144 A24	3fr	car rose	55.00	6.50
145 A25	5fr	red brown	11.00	2.40
146 A25	10fr	black	8.75	6.50
147 A25	20fr	bluish gray	8.00	6.50
		Nos. 124-147 (24)	96.90	29.40

Booklets containing Nos. 135 and 136 each have two panes of 10 (#135a, 136a) connected by a gutter, the complete piece constituting No. 135b or 136b, which is stapled into the booklet through the gutter.

For surcharges see #148, 176, B13-B20.

No. 135 Surcharged in Red

1939

148 A22 40c on 50c dk bl grn .75 .30

Mosque of Salé — A26

Sefrou — A27

Cedars — A28

Goatherd A29

Ramparts of Salé — A30

Scimitar-horned Oryxes — A31

Fez — A33

Valley of Draa A32

1939-42

149 A26	1c	rose violet	.25	.25
150 A27	2c	emerald	.25	.25
151 A27	3c	ultra	.25	.25
152 A26	5c	dk bl grn	.25	.25
153 A27	10c	brt red vio	.25	.25
154 A28	15c	dk green	.25	.25
155 A28	20c	black grn	.25	.25
156 A29	30c	deep blue	.25	.25
157 A29	40c	chocolate	.25	.25
158 A29	45c	Prus green	.55	.55
159 A30	50c	rose red	1.50	.90
159A A30	50c	Prus grn ('40)	.30	.25
160 A30	60c	turq blue	1.25	.75
160A A30	60c	choc ('40)	.30	.25
161 A31	70c	dk violet	.25	.25
162 A32	75c	grnsh blk	.50	.50
163 A32	80c	pck bl ('40)	.30	.25
163A A32	80c	dk grn ('42)	.30	.25
164 A30	90c	ultra	.30	.25
165 A28	1fr	chocolate	.30	.25
165A A32	1.20fr	rose vio ('42)	.65	.30
166 A32	1.25fr	henna brn	1.10	.65
167 A32	1.40fr	rose violet	.65	.30
168 A30	1.50fr	cop red ('40)	.30	.25
168A A30	1.50fr	rose ('42)	.25	.25
169 A33	2fr	Prus green	.25	.25
170 A33	2.25fr	dark blue	.65	.50
170A A26	2.40fr	red ('42)	.30	.30
171 A26	2.50fr	scarlet	1.00	.65
171A A26	2.50fr	dp blue ('40)	.95	.65
172 A33	3fr	black brown	.50	.30
172A A26	4fr	dp ultra ('42)	.30	.30
172B A32	4.50fr	grnsh blk ('42)	.65	.55
173 A31	5fr	dark blue	.65	.50
174 A31	10fr	red	1.20	.90
174A A31	15fr	Prus grn ('42)	4.25	3.50
175 A31	20fr	dk vio brn	2.00	1.75
		Nos. 149-175 (37)	23.75	18.60
		Set, never hinged	30.00	

See Nos. 197-219. For surcharges see Nos. 244, 261-262, B21-B24, B26, B28, B32.

No. 136 Surcharged in Black

1940

176 A22 35c on 65c brown red	1.75	.90
a. Pair, one without surcharge	3.00	2.25

The surcharge was applied on alternate rows in the sheet, making No. 176a. This was done to make a pair equal 1fr, the new rate.

Catalogue values for unused stamps in this section, from this point to the end of the section, are for Never Hinged items.

One Aim Alone-Victory A34

Tower of Hassan, Rabat A35

1943 Litho. *Perf. 12*

177 A34 1.50fr deep blue .30 .25

1943

178 A35	10c	rose lilac	.40	.25
179 A35	30c	blue	.40	.25
180 A35	40c	lake	.40	.25
181 A35	50c	blue green	.40	.25
182 A35	60c	dk vio brn	.40	.25
183 A35	70c	rose violet	.40	.25
184 A35	80c	gray green	.40	.25
185 A35	1fr	car lake	.40	.25
186 A35	1.20fr	violet	.40	.25
187 A35	1.50fr	red	.40	.25
188 A35	2fr	lt bl grn	.40	.25
189 A35	2.40fr	car rose	.40	.25
190 A35	3fr	olive brn	.40	.25
191 A35	4fr	dk ultra	.40	.25
192 A35	4.50fr	slate blk	.40	.25
193 A35	5fr	dull blue	.55	.25
194 A35	10fr	orange brn	.55	.40
195 A35	15fr	slate grn	1.40	.55
196 A35	20fr	deep plum	2.25	.80
		Nos. 178-196 (19)	10.75	5.75

Types of 1939-42

Perf. 13½x14, 14x13½

1945-47 Typo. Unwmk.

197 A27	10c	red violet	.30	.25
199 A29	40c	chocolate	.30	.25
200 A30	50c	Prus grn	.30	.25
203 A28	1fr	choc ('46)	.30	.25
204 A32	1.20fr	vio brn ('46)	.40	.25
205 A27	1.30fr	blue ('47)	.65	.30
206 A30	1.50fr	deep red	.30	.25
207 A33	2fr	Prus grn	.30	.25
209 A33	3fr	black brn	.30	.25
210 A29	3.50fr	dk red ('47)	.90	.55
212 A31	4.50fr	magenta ('47)	.40	.30
214 A31	5fr	indigo	.95	.50
215 A32	6fr	chlky bl ('46)	.55	.30
216 A31	10fr	red	1.90	.75
217 A31	15fr	Prus grn	2.10	.75
218 A31	20fr	dk vio brn	3.00	1.25
219 A31	25fr	black brn	2.90	2.00
		Nos. 197-219 (17)	15.85	8.70

For surcharges see #261-263, B26, B28, B32.

The Terraces — A37

Mountain District — A39

Fortress A38

Marrakesh A40

Gardens of Fez — A41

Ouarzazat District — A42

1947 Engr. Unwmk. *Perf. 13*

221	A37	10c black brn	.30	.25
222	A37	30c brt red	.40	.25
223	A37	50c brt grnsh bl	.30	.25
224	A37	60c brt red vio	.30	.25
225	A38	1fr black	.30	.25
226	A38	1.50fr blue	.40	.25
227	A39	2fr brt green	.55	.30
228	A39	3fr brown red	.30	.25
229	A40	4fr dk bl vio	.40	.25
230	A41	5fr dk green	.80	.50
231	A40	6fr crimson	.30	.25
232	A41	10fr dp blue	.80	.30
233	A42	15fr dk grn	1.40	1.00
234	A42	20fr henna brn	1.10	.55
235	A42	25fr purple	1.90	1.10
		Nos. 221-235 (15)	9.55	6.00

1948-49

236	A37	30c purple	.30	.25
237	A38	2fr vio brn ('49)	.55	.30
238	A40	4fr green	.65	.30
239	A41	8fr org ('49)	1.40	.80
240	A41	10fr blue	.90	.30
241	A42	10fr car rose	.75	.55
242	A38	12fr red	1.00	.65
243	A42	18fr deep blue	2.00	1.10
		Nos. 236-243 (8)	7.55	4.25

For surcharges see Nos. 263, 293-294.

No. 175 Surcharged with New Value and Wavy Lines in Carmine

1948

244	A31	8fr on 20fr dk vio brn	1.00	.65

Fortified Oasis A43

Walled City — A44

1949

245	A43	5fr blue green	.90	.40
246	A44	15fr red	1.25	.50
247	A44	25fr ultra	1.50	.55
		Nos. 245-247 (3)	3.65	1.45

See No. 300.

Detail, Gate of Oudayas, Rabat — A45

Nejjarine Fountain, Fez — A46

Garden, Meknes — A47

1949 *Perf. 14x13*

248	A45	10c black	.30	.25
249	A45	50c rose brn	.30	.25
250	A45	1fr blue vio	.30	.25
251	A46	2fr dk car rose	.30	.25
252	A46	3fr dark blue	.50	.25
253	A46	5fr brt green	.95	.25
254	A47	8fr dk bl grn	1.25	.50
255	A47	10fr brt red	1.25	.50
		Nos. 248-255 (8)	5.15	2.50

Postal Administration Building, Meknes — A48

1949, Oct. *Perf. 13*

256	A48	5fr dark green	2.25	1.75
257	A48	15fr deep carmine	2.40	1.90
258	A48	25fr deep blue	2.75	2.10
		Nos. 256-258 (3)	7.40	5.75

75th anniv. of the UPU.

Todra Valley A49

1950

259	A49	35fr red brown	1.20	.30
260	A49	50fr indigo	1.20	.30

See No. 270.

Nos. 204 and 205 Surcharged in Black or Blue

1950 *Perf. 14x13½, 13½x14*

261	A32	1fr on 1.20fr vio brn (Bk)	.40	.30
262	A27	1fr on 1.30fr blue (Bl)	.30	.25

The surcharge is transposed and spaced to fit the design on No. 262.

No. 231 Surcharged with New Value and Wavy Lines in Black

1951 *Perf. 13*

263	A40	5fr on 6fr crimson	.40	.25

Statue of Gen. Jacques Leclerc — A50

1951, Apr. 28 Engr.

264	A50	10fr blue green	2.00	1.60
265	A50	15fr deep carmine	2.50	2.00
266	A50	25fr indigo	2.50	2.00
		Nos. 264-266 (3)	7.00	5.60

Unveiling of a monument to Gen. Leclerc at Casablanca, Apr. 28, 1951. See No. C39.

Loustau Hospital, Oujda A51

Designs: 15fr, New Hospital, Meknes. 25fr, New Hospital, Rabat.

1951

267	A51	10fr indigo & pur	2.10	1.60
268	A51	15fr Prus grn & red brn	2.10	1.60
269	A51	25fr dk brn & ind	2.40	1.90
		Nos. 267-269 (3)	6.60	5.10

Todra Valley Type of 1950

1951

270	A49	30fr ultramarine	1.25	.30

Pigeons at Fountain A52

Karaouine Mosque, Fez A53

Patio, Oudayas A54

Oudayas Point, Rabat A55

Patio of Old House — A56

Type I (No. 275)

Type II (No. 276)

Perf. 14x13, 13

1951-53 Engr. Unwmk.

271	A52	5fr magenta ('52)	.30	.25
272	A53	6fr bl grn ('52)	.45	.30
273	A52	8fr brown ('52)	.45	.30
273A	A53	10fr rose red ('53)	.45	.30
274	A53	12fr dp ultra ('52)	.75	.30
275	A54	15fr red brn (I)	3.50	.25
276	A54	15fr red brn (II)	1.25	.25
277	A55	15fr pur ('52)	1.25	.25
278	A55	18fr red ('52)	2.00	.75
279	A56	20fr dp grnsh bl ('52)	2.00	.50
		Nos. 271-279 (10)	12.40	3.45

See Nos. 297-299.

8th-10th Cent. Capital A57

Casablanca Monument A58

Capitals: 20fr, 12th Cent. 25fr, 13th-14th Cent. 50fr, 17th Cent.

1952, Apr. 5 *Perf. 13*

280	A57	15fr deep blue	3.00	2.40
281	A57	20fr red	3.00	2.40
282	A57	25fr purple	3.00	2.40
283	A57	50fr deep green	3.00	2.40
		Nos. 280-283 (4)	12.00	9.60

1952 Sept. 22 Engr. & Typo.

284	A58	15fr multicolored	3.50	2.50

Creation of the French Military Medal, cent.

Daggers of South Morocco A59

Post Rider and Public Letter-writer A60

Designs: 20fr and 25fr, Antique brooches.

1953, Mar. 27 Engr.

285	A59	15fr dk car rose	3.50	2.75
286	A59	20fr violet brn	3.50	2.75
287	A59	25fr dark blue	3.50	2.75
		Nos. 285-287 (3)	10.50	8.25

See No. C46.

1953, May 16

288	A60	15fr violet brown	1.75	1.40

Stamp Day, May 16, 1953.

Bine el Ouidane Dam — A61

1953, Nov. 3 *Perf. 13*

290	A61	15fr indigo	1.90	1.50

See No. 295.

Mogador Fortress — A62

Design: 30fr, Moorish knights.

1953, Dec. 4

291	A62	15fr green	2.25	1.50
292	A62	30fr red brown	2.25	1.50

Issued to aid Army Welfare Work.

Nos. 226 and 243 Surcharged with New Value and Wavy Lines in Black

1954

293	A38	1fr on 1.50fr blue	.30	.25
294	A42	15fr on 18fr dp bl	.90	.75

Dam Type of 1953

1954, Mar. 8

295	A61	15fr red brn & indigo	1.20	.95

Station of Rural Automobile Post — A63

1954, Apr. 10

296	A63	15fr dk blue grn	1.20	.80

Stamp Day, April 10, 1954.

Types of 1951-53

1954 Engr. *Perf. 14x13*

297	A52	15fr dk blue green	.90	.25

Typo.

298	A52	5fr magenta	.90	.30
299	A55	15fr rose violet	1.25	.30
		Nos. 297-299 (3)	3.05	.85

Walled City Type of 1949

1954 Engr. *Perf. 13*

300	A44	25fr purple	1.75	.50

Marshal Lyautey at Rabat A64

Lyautey, Builder of Cities — A65

Designs: 15fr, Marshal Lyautey at Khenifra. 50fr, Hubert Lyautey, Marshal of France.

1954, Nov. 17

301	A64	5fr indigo	2.40	2.00
302	A64	15fr dark green	2.60	2.10
303	A65	30fr rose brown	3.75	3.00
304	A65	50fr dk red brn	3.75	3.00
		Nos. 301-304 (4)	12.50	10.10

Marshal Hubert Lyautey, birth cent.

Franco-Moslem Education — A66

Moslem Student at Blackboard — A67

Designs: 30fr, Moslem school at Camp Boulhaut. 50fr, Moulay Idriss College at Fez.

1955, Apr. 16 Unwmk. *Perf. 13*

305	A66	5fr indigo	1.90	1.50
306	A67	15fr rose lake	2.00	1.60
307	A66	30fr chocolate	2.10	1.90
308	A67	50fr dk blue grn	2.75	2.10
		Nos. 305-308 (4)	8.75	7.10

Franco-Moslem solidarity.

Map and Rotary Emblem A68

1955, June 11

309	A68	15fr bl & org brn	1.60	.95

Rotary Intl., 59th anniv.

Post Office, Mazagan A69

1955, May 24

310	A69	15fr red	1.10	.65

Stamp Day.

Bab el Chorfa, Fez A70

Mahakma (Courthouse), Casablanca A71

Fortress, Safi — A72

Designs: 50c, 1fr, 2fr, 3fr, Mrissa Gate, Salé. 10fr, 12fr, 15fr, Minaret at Rabat. 30fr, Menara Garden Marrakesh. 40fr, Tafraout Village. 50fr, Portuguese cistern, Mazagan. 75fr, Garden of Oudaya, Rabat.

1955 *Perf. 13½x13, 13x13½, 13*

311	A70	50c brn vio	.30	.25
312	A70	1fr blue	.30	.25
313	A70	2fr red lilac	.30	.25
314	A70	3fr bluish blk	.40	.25
315	A70	5fr vermilion	1.25	.30
316	A70	6fr green	.75	.30
317	A70	8fr orange brn	1.20	.50
318	A70	10fr violet brn	1.60	.30
319	A70	12fr greenish bl	.80	.50
320	A70	15fr magenta	1.10	.25
321	A71	18fr dk green	1.60	.75
322	A71	20fr brown lake	.95	.30
323	A72	25fr brt ultra	2.50	.30
324	A72	30fr green	2.25	.50
325	A72	40fr orange red	2.25	.30
326	A72	50fr black brn	6.00	.55
327	A71	75fr greenish bl	2.95	.95
		Nos. 311-327 (17)	26.50	6.80

Succeeding issues, released under the Kingdom, are listed under Morocco in Vol. 4.

SEMI-POSTAL STAMPS

French Protectorate

No. 30 Surcharged in Red ✚ 5c

1914 Unwmk. *Perf. 14x13½*

B1	A4	10c + 5c on 10c	*22,500.*	*26,000.*

Known only with inverted red surcharge.

Same Surcharge on No. 42 with "Protectorat Francais"

B2	A7	10c + 5c on 10c rose	5.50	5.50
a.		Double surcharge	160.00	160.00
b.		Inverted surcharge	190.00	190.00
c.		"c" omitted	100.00	100.00

On Nos. B1 and B2 the cross is set up from pieces of metal (quads), the horizontal bar being made from two long pieces, the vertical bar from two short pieces. Each cross in the setting of twenty-five differs from the others.

No. 30 Handstamp Surcharged in Red ✚ 5c

B3	A4	10c + 5c on 10c rose	*1,500.*	*1,200.*

No. B3 was issued at Oujda. The surcharge ink is water-soluble.

No. 42 Surcharged in Vermilion or Carmine

B4	A7	10c + 5c on 10c (V)	21.00	21.00
a.		Double surcharge	225.00	225.00
b.		Inverted surcharge	225.00	225.00
c.		Double surch., one invtd.	175.00	175.00
B5	A7	10c +5c on 10c (C)	450.00	475.00
a.		Inverted surcharge	1,300.	1,300.

On #B4-B5 the horizontal bar of the cross is single and not as thick as on #B1-B2.

No. B5 was sold largely at Casablanca.

SP1

SP2

Carmine Surcharge

1915

B6	SP1	5c + 5c green	3.25	2.40
a.		Inverted surcharge	300.00	300.00
B7	SP2	10c + 5c rose	4.00	4.00

No. B6 was not issued without the Red Cross surcharge. No. B7 was also used in Tangier.

SP3

SP4

France No. B2 Overprinted in Black

B8	SP3	10c + 5c red	6.75	6.75

Carmine Surcharge

1917

B9	SP4	10c + 5c on 10c rose	2.75	2.75

On No. B9 the horizontal bar of the cross is made from a single, thick piece of metal.

Marshal Hubert Lyautey — SP5

1935, May 15 Photo. *Perf. 13x13½*

B10	SP5	50c + 50c red	9.50	9.50
B11	SP5	1fr + 1fr dk grn	10.50	10.50
B12	SP5	5fr + 5fr blk brn	45.00	45.00
		Nos. B10-B12 (3)	65.00	65.00
		Set, never hinged	95.00	

Stamps of 1933-34 Surcharged in Blue or Red

1938 *Perf. 13*

B13	A18	2c + 2c red vio	4.75	4.75
B14	A19	3c + 3c dk brn	4.75	4.75
B15	A20	20c + 20c red brn	4.75	4.75
B16	A21	40c + 40c blk brn (R)	4.75	4.75
B17	A22	65c + 65c brn red	5.25	5.25
B18	A23	1.25fr + 1.25fr blk (R)	5.25	5.25
B19	A24	2fr + 2fr yel brn	5.25	5.25
B20	A25	5fr + 5fr red brn	5.25	5.25
		Nos. B13-B20 (8)	40.00	40.00
		Set, never hinged	60.00	

Stamps of 1939 Surcharged in Black

1942

B21	A29	45c + 2fr Prus grn	4.75	4.75
B22	A30	90c + 4fr ultra	4.75	4.75
B23	A32	1.25fr + 6fr henna brn	4.75	4.75
B24	A26	2.50fr + 8fr scarlet	4.75	4.75
		Nos. B21-B24 (4)	19.00	19.00
		Set, never hinged	27.00	

The arrangement of the surcharge differs slightly on each denomination.

Catalogue values for unused stamps in this section, from this point to the end of the section, are for Never Hinged items.

No. 207 Surcharged in Black

1945 Unwmk. *Perf. 13½x14*

B26	A33	2fr + 1fr Prus green	.65	.50

For surcharge see No. B28.

Mausoleum of Marshal Lyautey — SP7

Statue of Marshal Lyautey — SP8

1945 Litho. *Perf. 11½*

B27	SP7	2fr + 3fr dark blue	.65	.30

The surtax was for French works of solidarity.

No. B26 Surcharged in Red

1946 *Perf. 13½x14*

B28	A33	3fr (+ 1fr) on 2fr + 1fr	.40	.25

Perf. 13½x14, 13

1946, Dec. 16 Engr.

B29	SP8	2fr + 10fr black	1.60	1.40
B30	SP8	3fr + 15fr cop red	1.75	1.40
B31	SP8	10fr + 20fr brt bl	2.50	2.00
		Nos. B29-B31 (3)	5.85	4.80

The surtax was for works of solidarity.

No. 212 Surcharged in Rose Violet

1947, Mar. 15 *Perf. 13½x14*

B32	A31	4.50fr + 5.50fr magenta	2.50	1.50

Stamp Day, 1947.

Map and Symbols of Prosperity from Phosphates SP9

1947 *Perf. 13*

B33	SP9	4.50fr + 5.50fr green	1.40	.90

25th anniv. of the exploitations of the Cherifien Office of Phosphates.

Power — SP10

Health — SP11

1948, Feb. 9
B34 SP10 6fr + 9fr red brn 2.75 2.25
B35 SP11 10fr + 20fr dp ultra 2.75 2.25

The surtax was for combined works of Franco-Moroccan solidarity.

Type of Regular Issue of 1923, Inscribed: "Journee du Timbre 1948"

1948, Mar. 6
B36 A16 6fr + 4fr red brown 1.20 .90

Stamp Day, Mar. 6, 1948.

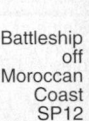

Battleship off Moroccan Coast SP12

1948, Aug.
B37 SP12 6fr + 9fr purple 2.00 1.40

The surtax was for naval charities.

Wheat Field near Meknes SP13

Designs: 2fr+5fr, Olive grove, Taroudant. 3fr+7fr, Net and coastal view. 5fr+10fr, Aguedal Gardens, Marrakesh.

1949, Apr. 12 Engr. Unwmk.
Inscribed: "SOLIDARITÉ 1948"
B38 SP13 1fr + 2fr orange 1.90 1.40
B39 SP13 2fr + 5fr car 1.90 1.50
B40 SP13 3fr + 7fr pck bl 1.90 1.50
B41 SP13 5fr + 10fr dk brn vio 1.90 1.50
a. Sheet of 4, #B38-B41 22.50 17.50
Nos. B38-B41,CB31-CB34 (8) 16.30 13.20

Gazelle Hunter, from 1899 Local Stamp SP14

1949, May 1
B42 SP14 10fr + 5fr choc & car rose 1.75 1.40

Stamp Day and 50th anniversary of Mazagan-Marrakesh local postage stamp.

Moroccan Soldiers, Flag SP15

Rug Weaving SP16

1949
B43 SP15 10fr + 10fr bright red 1.50 1.25

The surtax was for Army Welfare Work.

1950, Apr. 11

Designs: 2fr+5fr, Pottery making, 3fr+7fr, Bookbinding. 5fr+10fr, Copper work.

Inscribed: "SOLIDARITE 1949"
B44 SP16 1fr + 2fr dp car 2.10 1.75
B45 SP16 2fr + 5fr dk brnsh bl 2.10 1.75
B46 SP16 3fr + 7fr dk pur 2.25 1.90
B47 SP16 5fr + 10fr red brn 2.25 1.90
a. Sheet of 4, #B44-B47 25.00 20.00
Nos. B44-B47,CB36-CB39 (8) 19.40 16.00

Ruins of Sala Colonia at Chella SP17

1950, Sept. 25 Engr. *Perf. 13*
B48 SP17 10fr + 10fr dp magenta 1.75 1.75
B49 SP17 15fr + 15fr indigo 1.75 1.75

The surtax was for Army Welfare Work.

AIR POST STAMPS

French Protectorate

Biplane over Casablanca AP1

1922-27 Photo. Unwmk. *Perf. 13½*
C1 AP1 5c dp orange ('27) .50 .50
C2 AP1 25c dp ultra 1.10 .95
C3 AP1 50c grnsh blue 1.25 .90
C4 AP1 75c dp blue 80.00 12.50
C5 AP1 75c dp green 1.00 .50
C6 AP1 80c vio brn ('27) 1.75 .55
C7 AP1 1fr vermilion 1.00 .50
C8 AP1 1.40fr brn lake ('27) 2.40 1.25
C9 AP1 1.90fr dp blue ('27) 2.50 1.60
C10 AP1 2fr black vio 2.25 1.10
a. 2fr deep violet 2.25 1.40
C11 AP1 3fr gray blk 2.50 1.60
Nos. C1-C11 (11) 96.25 21.95

The 25c, 50c, 75c deep green and 1fr each were printed in two of three types, differing in frameline thickness, or hyphen in "Helio-Vaugirard" imprint.

Imperf., Pairs

C1a AP1 5c 55.00
C2a AP1 25c 65.00
C3a AP1 50c 55.00
C4a AP1 75c 550.00
C5a AP1 75c 72.50
C6a AP1 80c 55.00
C7a AP1 1fr 72.50
C10b AP1 2fr 210.00

Nos. C8-C9 Surcharged in Blue or Black

1931, Apr. 10
C12 AP1 1fr on 1.40fr (B) 1.75 1.75
a. Inverted surcharge 290.00 290.00
C13 AP1 1.50fr on 1.90fr (Bk) 1.90 1.90

Rabat and Tower of Hassan AP2

Casablanca AP3

1933, Jan. Engr.
C14 AP2 50c dark blue .80 .75
C15 AP2 80c orange brn .80 .65
C16 AP2 1.50fr brown red .80 .75
C17 AP3 2.50fr carmine rose 5.50 1.10
C18 AP3 5fr violet 3.00 1.60
C19 AP3 10fr blue green 1.10 1.10
Nos. C14-C19 (6) 12.00 5.95

For surcharges see Nos. CB22-CB23.

Storks and Minaret, Chella — AP4

Plane and Map of Morocco AP5

1939-40 *Perf. 13*
C20 AP4 80c Prus green .25 .25
C21 AP4 1fr dk red .25 .25
C22 AP5 1.90fr ultra .40 .30
C23 AP5 2fr red vio ('40) .40 .25
C24 AP5 3fr chocolate .40 .25
C25 AP4 5fr violet 1.25 .75
C26 AP5 10fr turq blue 1.20 .50
Nos. C20-C26 (7) 4.15 2.55

Catalogue values for unused stamps in this section, from this point to the end of the section, are for Never Hinged items.

Plane over Oasis — AP6

1944 Litho. *Perf. 11½*
C27 AP6 50c Prus grn .50 .30
C28 AP6 2fr ultra .50 .30
C29 AP6 5fr scarlet .50 .30
C30 AP6 10fr violet 1.25 1.00
C31 AP6 50fr black 1.90 1.50
C32 AP6 100fr dp bl & red 3.00 3.00
Nos. C27-C32 (6) 7.65 6.40

For surcharge see No. CB24.

Plane AP7

1945 Engr. *Perf. 13*
C33 AP7 50fr sepia 1.20 .95

Moulay Idriss — AP8

La Medina AP9

1947-48
C34 AP8 9fr dk rose car .40 .30
C35 AP8 40fr dark blue .90 .50
C36 AP8 50fr dp claret ('47) 1.25 .30
C37 AP9 100fr dp grnsh bl 3.25 .95
C38 AP9 200fr henna brn 6.50 1.50
Nos. C34-C38 (5) 12.30 3.55

Leclerc Type of Regular Issue

1951, Apr. 28
C39 A50 50fr purple 3.00 2.50

Unveiling of a monument to Gen. Leclerc at Casablanca, Apr. 28, 1951.

Kasbah of the Oudayas, Rabat AP11

1951, May 22
C40 AP11 300fr purple 22.50 10.00

Ben Smine Sanatorium AP12

1951, June 4
C41 AP12 50fr pur & Prus grn 3.25 2.50

Fortifications, Chella — AP13

Plane Near Marrakesh AP14

Fort, Anti-Atlas Mountains AP15

View of Fez AP16

1952, Apr. 19 Unwmk. *Perf. 13*
C42 AP13 10fr blue green 1.00 .50
C43 AP14 40fr red 1.75 .50
C44 AP15 100fr brown 4.00 1.00
C45 AP16 200fr purple 10.00 4.25
Nos. C42-C45 (4) 16.75 6.25

Antique Brooches — AP17

1953, Mar. 27

C46	AP17	50fr dark green	3.50	2.75

"City" of the Agdal, Meknes AP18

20fr, Yakoub el Mansour, Rabat. 40fr, Ainchock, Casablanca. 50fr, El Aliya, Fedala.

1954, Mar. 8

C47	AP18	10fr olive brown	3.25	2.50
C48	AP18	20fr purple	3.25	2.50
C49	AP18	40fr red brown	3.25	2.50
C50	AP18	50fr deep green	3.25	2.50
		Nos. C47-C50 (4)	13.00	10.00

Franco-Moroccan solidarity.

Naval Vessel and Sailboat AP19

Village in the Anti-Atlas AP20

"Ksar es Souk," Rabat and Plane AP21

1954, Oct. 18

C51	AP19	15fr dk blue green	2.10	1.60
C52	AP19	30fr violet blue	2.40	1.90

1955, July 25 **Engr.** ***Perf. 13***

200fr, Estuary of Bou Regreg, Rabat and Plane.

C53	AP20	100fr brt violet	2.75	.50
C54	AP20	200fr brt carmine	6.00	.95
C55	AP21	500fr grnsh blue	13.00	3.25
		Nos. C53-C55 (3)	21.75	4.70

AIR POST SEMI-POSTAL STAMPS

French Protectorate

Moorish Tribesmen SPAP1

Designs: 25c, Moor plowing with camel and burro. 50c, Caravan nearing Saffi. 75c, Walls, Marrakesh. 80c, Sheep grazing at Azrou. 1fr, Gate at Fez. 1.50fr, Aerial view of Tangier. 2fr, Aerial view of Casablanca. 3fr, Storks on old wall, Rabat. 5fr, Moorish fete.

Perf. 13½

1928, July 26 **Photo.** **Unwmk.**

CB1	SPAP1	5c	dp blue	4.75	4.75
CB2	SPAP1	25c	brn org	4.75	4.75
CB3	SPAP1	50c	red	4.75	4.75
CB4	SPAP1	75c	org brn	4.75	4.75
CB5	SPAP1	80c	olive grn	4.75	4.75
CB6	SPAP1	1fr	orange	4.75	4.75
CB7	SPAP1	1.50fr	Prus bl	4.75	4.75
CB8	SPAP1	2fr	dp brown	4.75	4.75
CB9	SPAP1	3fr	dp violet	4.75	4.75
CB10	SPAP1	5fr	brown blk	4.75	4.75
			Nos. CB1-CB10 (10)	47.50	47.50

These stamps were sold in sets only and at double their face value. The money received for the surtax was divided among charitable and social organizations. The stamps were not sold at post offices but solely by subscription to the Moroccan Postal Administration.

Overprinted in Red or Blue (25c, 50c, 75c, 1fr)

1929, Feb. 1

CB11	SPAP1	5c	dp blue	4.75	4.75
CB12	SPAP1	25c	brown org	4.75	4.75
CB13	SPAP1	50c	red	4.75	4.75
CB14	SPAP1	75c	org brn	4.75	4.75
CB15	SPAP1	80c	olive grn	4.75	4.75
CB16	SPAP1	1fr	orange	4.75	4.75
CB17	SPAP1	1.50fr	Prus bl	4.75	4.75
CB18	SPAP1	2fr	dp brown	4.75	4.75
CB19	SPAP1	3fr	dp violet	4.75	4.75
CB20	SPAP1	5fr	brown blk	4.75	4.75
			Nos. CB11-CB20 (10)	47.50	47.50

These stamps were sold at double their face values and only in Tangier. The surtax benefited various charities.

Marshal Hubert Lyautey SPAP10

1935, May 15 ***Perf. 13½***

CB21	SPAP10	1.50fr + 1.50fr blue	20.00	20.00

Nos. C14, C19 Surcharged in Red

1938 ***Perf. 13***

CB22	AP2	50c + 50c dk bl	6.00	6.00
CB23	AP3	10fr + 10fr bl grn	6.00	6.00

Catalogue values for unused stamps in this section, from this point to the end of the section, are for Never Hinged items.

Plane over Oasis SPAP11

Statue of Marshal Lyautey SPAP12

1944 **Litho.** ***Perf. 11½***

CB23A	SPAP11	1.50fr + 98.50fr	2.25	1.50

The surtax was for charity among the liberated French.

No. C29 Surcharged in Black

1946, June 18 ***Perf. 11***

CB24	AP6	5fr + 5fr scarlet	1.25	.90

6th anniv. of the appeal made by Gen. Charles de Gaulle, June 18, 1940. The surtax was for the Free French Association of Morocco.

1946, Dec. **Engr.** ***Perf. 13***

CB25	SPAP12	10fr +30fr dk grn	2.50	1.90

The surtax was for works of solidarity.

Replenishing Stocks of Food — SPAP13

Agriculture SPAP14

1948, Feb. 9 **Unwmk.**

CB26	SPAP13	9fr +26fr dp grn	2.00	1.50
CB27	SPAP14	20fr +35fr brown	2.00	1.50

The surtax was for combined works of Franco-Moroccan solidarity.

Tomb of Marshal Hubert Lyautey — SPAP15

1948, May 18 ***Perf. 13***

CB28	SPAP15	10fr +25fr dk grn	1.40	1.10

Lyautey Exposition, Paris, June, 1948.

P.T.T. Clubhouse SPAP16

1948, June 7 **Engr.**

CB29	SPAP16	6fr + 34fr dk grn	2.10	1.75
CB30	SPAP16	9fr + 51fr red brn	2.10	1.75

The surtax was used for the Moroccan P.T.T. employees vacation colony at Ifrane.

View of Agadir SPAP17

Plane over Globe SPAP18

Designs: 6fr+9fr, Fez. 9fr+16fr, Atlas Mountains. 15fr+25fr, Valley of Draa.

1949, Apr. 12 ***Perf. 13***

Inscribed: "SOLIDARITÉ 1948"

CB31	SPAP17	5fr +5fr dk grn	2.10	1.75
CB32	SPAP17	6fr +9fr org red	2.10	1.75
CB33	SPAP17	9fr +16fr blk brn	2.25	1.90
CB34	SPAP17	15fr +25fr ind	2.25	1.90
a.		Sheet of 4, #CB31-CB34	25.00	20.00
		Nos. CB31-CB34 (4)	8.70	7.30

1950, Mar. 11 **Engr. & Typo.**

CB35	SPAP18	15fr + 10fr bl grn & car	1.40	1.10

Day of the Stamp, Mar. 11-12, 1950, and 25th anniv. of the 1st post link between Casablanca and Dakar.

Scenes and Map: Northwest Corner SPAP19

Designs (quarters of map): 6fr+9fr, NE, 9fr+16fr, SW. 15fr+25fr, SE.

1950, Apr. 11 **Engr.**

Inscribed: "SOLIDARITE 1949"

CB36	SPAP19	5fr +5fr dp ultra	2.60	2.10
CB37	SPAP19	6fr +9fr Prus grn	2.60	2.10
CB38	SPAP19	9fr +16fr dk brn	2.75	2.25
CB39	SPAP19	15fr +25fr brn red	2.75	2.25
a.		Sheet of 4, #CB36-CB39	22.50	17.50
		Nos. CB36-CB39 (4)	10.70	8.70

Arch of Triumph of Caracalla at Volubilis SPAP20

1950, Sept. 25 **Unwmk.**

CB40	SPAP20	10fr + 10fr sepia	1.75	1.40
CB41	SPAP20	15fr + 15fr bl grn	1.75	1.40

The surtax was for Army Welfare Work.

Casablanca Post Office and First Air Post Stamp SPAP21

1952, Mar. 8 ***Perf. 13***

CB42	SPAP21	15fr + 5fr red brn & dp grn	4.50	4.00

Day of the Stamp, Mar. 8, 1952, and 30th anniv. of French Morocco's 1st air post stamp.

POSTAGE DUE STAMPS

French Offices in Morocco

Postage Due Stamps and Types of France Surcharged in Red or Black

1896 **Unwmk.** ***Perf. 14x13½***

On Stamps of 1891-93

J1	D2	5c on 5c lt bl (R)	7.25	4.75
J2	D2	10c on 10c choc (R)	12.00	5.50
J3	D2	30c on 30c car	27.50	21.00
a.		Pair, one without surcharge		
J4	D2	50c on 50c lilac	29.00	21.00
a.		"S" of "CENTIMOS" omitted	325.00	240.00
J5	D2	1p on 1fr lil brn	340.00	325.00

1909-10 On Stamps of 1908-10

J6	D3	1c on 1c ol grn (R)	2.40	2.40
J7	D3	10c on 10c violet	32.50	30.00
J8	D3	30c on 30c bister	40.00	35.00
J9	D3	50c on 50c red	65.00	65.00
		Nos. J6-J9 (4)	139.90	132.40

Postage Due Stamps of France Surcharged in Red or Blue

1911 On Stamps of 1893-96

J10	D2	5c on 5c blue (R)	4.00	4.00
J11	D2	10c on 10c choc (R)	14.50	14.50
a.		Double surcharge	210.00	*240.00*
J12	D2	50c on 50c lil (Bl)	17.50	17.50

On Stamps of 1908-10

J13	D3	1c on 1c ol grn (R)	2.40	2.40
J14	D3	10c on 10c vio (R)	6.75	6.75
J15	D3	30c on 30c bis (R)	8.00	8.00
J16	D3	50c on 50c red (Bl)	15.00	15.00
		Nos. J10-J16 (7)	68.15	68.15

For surcharges see Nos. JN23-J26.

French Protectorate

D4

D5

Type of 1911 Issue Overprinted "Protectorat Francais"

1915-17

J17	D4	1c on 1c black	.55	.55
a.		New value double	160.00	
J18	D4	5c on 5c blue	2.10	1.50
J19	D4	10c on 10c choc	2.60	1.75
J20	D4	20c on 20c ol grn	2.60	1.75
J21	D4	30c on 30c rose red	6.00	5.25
J22	D4	50c on 50c vio brn	8.50	6.00
		Nos. J17-J22 (6)	22.35	16.80

Nos. J13 to J16 With Additional Overprint "Protectorat Francais"

1915

J23	D3	1c on 1c ol grn	1.25	1.25
J24	D3	10c on 10c violet	2.50	2.25
J25	D3	30c on 30c bister	2.90	2.60
J26	D3	50c on 50c red	2.90	2.60
		Nos. J23-J26 (4)	9.55	8.70

1917-26 Typo.

J27	D5	1c black	.25	.25
J28	D5	5c deep blue	.30	.25
J29	D5	10c brown	.55	.30
J30	D5	20c olive green	2.10	1.25
J31	D5	30c rose	.30	.30
J32	D5	50c lilac brown	.55	.25
J33	D5	1fr red brn, *straw* ('26)	.95	.65
J34	D5	2fr violet ('26)	1.75	1.10
		Nos. J27-J34 (8)	6.75	4.35

See #J49-J56, Morocco #J1-J4. For surcharges see #J46-J48.

Postage Due Stamps of France, 1882-1906 Overprinted

1918

J35	D2	1c black	.80	.80
J36	D2	5c blue	1.60	1.60
J37	D2	10c chocolate	1.60	1.60
J38	D2	15c green	3.50	3.50
J39	D2	20c olive green	5.25	5.25
J40	D2	30c rose red	12.00	12.00
J41	D2	50c violet brown	19.00	19.00
		Nos. J35-J41 (7)	43.75	43.75

Postage Due Stamps of France, 1908-19 Overprinted

1918

J42	D3	1c olive green	.80	.80
J43	D3	10c violet	2.40	2.40
J44	D3	20c bister	7.25	7.25
J45	D3	40c red	17.50	17.50
		Nos. J42-J45 (4)	27.95	27.95

Catalogue values for unused stamps in this section, from this point to the end of the section, are for Never Hinged items.

Nos. J31 and J29 Surcharged

1944 Unwmk. *Perf. 14x13½*

J46	D5	50c on 30c rose	3.00	2.50
J47	D5	1fr on 10c brown	5.25	3.75
J48	D5	3fr on 10c brown	12.50	9.50
		Nos. J46-J48 (3)	20.75	15.75

Type of 1917-1926

1945-52 Typo.

J49	D5	1fr brn lake ('47)	.95	.75
J50	D5	2fr rose lake ('47)	1.20	.80
J51	D5	3fr ultra	.65	.40
J52	D5	4fr red orange	.75	.30
J53	D5	5fr green	1.40	.50
J54	D5	10fr yellow brn	1.60	.50
J55	D5	20fr carmine ('50)	1.60	1.00
J56	D5	30fr dull brn ('52)	2.50	1.60
		Nos. J49-J56 (8)	10.65	5.85

PARCEL POST STAMPS

French Protectorate

PP1

1917 Unwmk. *Perf. 13½x14*

Q1	PP1	5c green	.95	.65
Q2	PP1	10c carmine	.95	.65
Q3	PP1	20c lilac brown	.95	.65
Q4	PP1	25c blue	1.60	.80
Q5	PP1	40c dark brown	2.40	1.20
Q6	PP1	50c red orange	2.75	.80
Q7	PP1	75c pale slate	3.50	2.40
Q8	PP1	1fr ultra	4.75	.80
Q9	PP1	2fr gray	7.25	1.40
Q10	PP1	5fr violet	10.50	1.40
Q11	PP1	10fr black	16.00	1.50
		Nos. Q1-Q11 (11)	51.60	12.25

FRENCH POLYNESIA

ˈfrench ˌpä-lə-ˈnē-zhə

(French Oceania)

LOCATION — South Pacific Ocean
GOVT. — French Overseas Territory
AREA — 1,522 sq. mi.
POP. — 242,073 (1999 est.)
CAPITAL — Papeete

In 1903 various French Establishments in the South Pacific were united to form a single colony. Most important of the island groups are the Society Islands, Marquesas Islands, the Tuamotu group and the Gambier, Austral, and Rapa Islands. Tahiti, largest of the Society group, ranks first in importance.

100 Centimes = 1 Franc

Catalogue values for unused stamps in this country are for Never Hinged items, beginning with Scott 136 in the regular postage section, Scott B11 in the semi-postal section, Scott C2 in the airpost section, Scott CB1 in the airpost semi-postal section, Scott J18 in the postage due section, and Scott O1 in the officials section.

Navigation and Commerce — A1

Perf. 14x13½

1892-1907 Typo. Unwmk.

Name of Colony in Blue or Carmine

1	A1	1c black, *lil bl*	1.60	1.60
2	A1	2c brown, *buff*	2.40	2.40
3	A1	4c claret, *lav*	4.00	3.75
4	A1	5c green, *grnsh*	12.00	9.25
5	A1	5c yellow grn ('06)	4.00	2.40
6	A1	10c blk, *lavender*	27.50	12.50
7	A1	10c red ('00)	4.00	2.40
8	A1	15c blue, quadrille paper	32.50	12.00
9	A1	15c gray, *lt gray* ('00)	8.00	7.25
10	A1	20c red, *grn*	17.50	14.50
11	A1	25c black, *rose*	55.00	27.50
12	A1	25c blue ('00)	27.50	16.00
13	A1	30c brown, *bis*	16.00	13.50
14	A1	35c black, *yel* ('06)	9.50	9.50
15	A1	40c red, *straw*	132.50	80.00
16	A1	45c blk, *gray grn* ('07)	6.50	*6.50*
17	A1	50c car, *rose*	9.00	9.00
18	A1	50c brown, *az* ('00)	250.00	200.00
19	A1	75c dp vio, *org*	12.00	12.00
20	A1	1fr brnz grn, *straw*	13.50	13.50
		Nos. 1-20 (20)	645.00	455.55

Perf. 13½x14 stamps are counterfeits.
For overprint and surcharge see #55, B1.

Tahitian Girl — A2

Kanakas — A3

Fautaua Valley — A4

1913-30

21	A2	1c violet & brn	.25	.25
22	A2	2c brown & blk	.25	.25
23	A2	4c orange & bl	.35	.35
24	A2	5c grn & yel grn	1.25	.80
25	A2	5c bl & blk ('22)	.50	.50
26	A2	10c rose & org	1.90	1.25
27	A2	10c bl grn & yel grn ('22)	1.25	1.25
28	A2	10c org red & brn red, *bluish* ('26)	1.40	1.40
29	A2	15c org & blk ('15)	.80	.65
a.		Imperf., pair	175.00	
30	A2	20c black & vio	1.10	1.00
a.		Imperf., pair	175.00	
31	A2	20c grn & bl grn ('26)	1.00	1.00
32	A2	20c brn red & dk brn ('27)	1.60	1.60
33	A3	25c ultra & blue	1.50	1.00
34	A3	25c vio & rose ('22)	.75	.75
35	A3	30c gray & brown	4.00	3.25
a.		Imperf., pair	325.00	
36	A3	30c rose & red org ('22)	2.75	2.75
37	A3	30c blk & red org ('26)	.75	.75
38	A3	30c slate bl & bl grn ('27)	1.75	1.75
39	A3	35c green & rose	1.25	1.25
40	A3	40c black & green	1.10	1.10
41	A3	45c orange & red	1.10	1.10
42	A3	50c dk brown & blk	15.00	13.00
43	A3	50c ultra & bl ('22)	1.25	1.25
44	A3	50c gray & bl vio ('26)	.90	.90
45	A3	60c green & blk ('25)	1.25	1.25
46	A3	65c ol brn & red vio ('27)	3.00	3.00
47	A3	75c vio brn & vio	2.25	2.25
48	A3	90c brn red & rose ('30)	14.50	14.50
49	A4	1fr rose & black	5.25	3.50
50	A4	1.10fr vio & dk brn ('28)	1.60	1.60
51	A4	1.40fr bis brn & vio ('29)	4.00	4.00
52	A4	1.50fr ind & bl ('30)	15.00	15.00
53	A4	2fr dk brown & grn	5.25	3.50
54	A4	5fr violet & bl	10.50	10.50
		Nos. 21-54 (34)	106.35	98.25

For surcharges see Nos. 56-71, B2-B4.

No. 7 Overprinted

1915

55	A1	10c red	5.50	5.50
a.		Inverted overprint	200.00	200.00

For surcharge see No. B1.

No. 29 Surcharged

1916

56	A2	10c on 15c org & blk	2.75	2.75

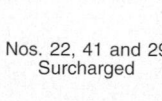

Nos. 22, 41 and 29 Surcharged

1921

57	A2	5c on 2c brn & blk	36.00	36.00
58	A3	10c on 45c org & red	36.00	36.00
59	A2	25c on 15c org & blk	7.25	7.25
		Nos. 57-59 (3)	79.25	79.25

On No. 58 the new value and date are set wide apart and without bar.

Types of 1913-30 Issue Surcharged in Black or Red

1923-27

60	A3	60c on 75c bl & brn	.55	.55
61	A4	65c on 1fr dk bl & ol (R) ('25)	1.75	1.75
62	A4	85c on 1fr dk bl & ol (R) ('25)	1.90	1.90
63	A3	90c on 75c brn red & cer ('27)	2.60	2.60
		Nos. 60-63 (4)	6.80	6.80

No. 26 Surcharged

1924

64	A2	45c on 10c rose & org	2.75	2.75
a.		Inverted surcharge	2,400.	2,400.

Stamps and Type of 1913-30 Surcharged with New Value and Bars in Black or Red

1924-27

65	A4	25c on 2fr dk brn & grn	1.10	1.10
66	A4	25c on 5fr vio & bl	1.10	1.10
67	A4	1.25fr on 1fr dk bl & ultra (R) ('26)	1.10	1.10
68	A4	1.50fr on 1fr dk bl & lt bl ('27)	3.50	3.50
69	A4	20fr on 5fr org & brt vio ('27)	32.50	26.00
		Nos. 65-69 (5)	39.30	32.80

Surcharged in Black or Red

1926

70	A4	3fr on 5fr gray & blue	3.25	2.50
71	A4	10fr on 5fr grn & blk (R)	6.75	6.75

Papetoai Bay, Moorea A5

1929, Mar. 25

72	A5	3fr green & dk brn	8.00	8.00
73	A5	5fr lt blue & dk brn	14.50	14.50
74	A5	10fr lt red & dk brn	42.50	42.50
75	A5	20fr lilac & dk brn	47.50	47.50
		Nos. 72-75 (4)	112.50	112.50

For overprints see Nos. 128, 130, 132, 134.

Common Design Types pictured following the introduction.

Colonial Exposition Issue

Common Design Types

1931, Apr. 13 Engr. *Perf. 12½*

Name of Country Printed in Black

76	CD70	40c deep green	7.25	7.25
77	CD71	50c violet	7.25	7.25
78	CD72	90c red orange	7.25	7.25
79	CD73	1.50fr dull blue	7.25	7.25
		Nos. 76-79 (4)	29.00	29.00

Spear Fishing A12

Tahitian Girl — A13

Idols A14

1934-40 Photo. *Perf. 13½, 13½x13*

80	A12	1c gray black	.25	.25
81	A12	2c claret	.25	.25
82	A12	3c lt blue ('40)	.25	.25
83	A12	4c orange	.50	.50
84	A12	5c violet	.80	.80
85	A12	10c dark brown	.30	.30
86	A12	15c green	.50	.50
87	A12	20c red	.50	.50
88	A13	25c gray blue	.80	.80
89	A13	30c yellow green	1.10	1.10
90	A13	30c org brn ('40)	.65	.65
91	A14	35c dp green ('38)	3.50	3.50
92	A13	40c red violet	.50	.50
93	A13	45c brown orange	8.75	8.75
94	A13	45c dk green ('39)	1.50	1.50
95	A13	50c violet	.50	.50
96	A13	55c blue ('38)	6.50	6.50
97	A13	60c black ('39)	.75	.75
98	A13	65c brown	3.25	3.25
99	A13	70c brt pink ('39)	1.40	1.40
100	A13	75c olive green	8.00	8.00
101	A13	80c violet brn ('38)	2.00	2.00
102	A13	90c rose red	.75	.75
103	A14	1fr red brown	.75	.75
104	A14	1.25fr brown violet	6.75	6.75
105	A14	1.25fr rose red ('39)	1.25	1.25
106	A14	1.40fr org yel ('39)	1.10	1.10
107	A14	1.50fr blue	.75	.75
108	A14	1.60fr dull vio ('39)	1.25	1.25
109	A14	1.75fr olive	6.50	6.50
110	A14	2fr red	1.10	1.10
111	A14	2.25fr deep blue ('39)	1.25	1.25
112	A14	2.50fr black ('39)	1.25	1.25
113	A14	3fr brown org ('39)	1.50	1.50
114	A14	5fr red violet ('39)	1.00	1.00
115	A14	10fr dk grn ('39)	3.00	3.00
116	A14	20fr dk brn ('39)	3.50	3.50
		Nos. 80-116 (37)	74.25	74.25

For overprints see #126-127, 129, 131, 133, 135.

For types A12-A14 without "RF," see Nos. 135A-135E.

Paris International Exposition Issue

Common Design Types

1937 Engr. *Perf. 13*

117	CD74	20c deep violet	3.25	3.25
118	CD75	30c dark green	3.25	3.25
119	CD76	40c carmine rose	3.25	3.25
120	CD77	50c dk brn & bl	4.00	4.00
121	CD78	90c red	4.00	4.00
122	CD79	1.50fr ultra	4.75	4.75
		Nos. 117-122 (6)	22.50	22.50

Colonial Arts Exhibition Issue

Souvenir Sheet

Common Design Type

1937 *Imperf.*

123	CD78	3fr emerald	36.00	*52.50*
		Never hinged	55.00	

New York World's Fair Issue

Common Design Type

1939, May 10 Engr. *Perf. 12½x12*

124	CD82	1.25fr carmine lake	2.25	2.25
125	CD82	2.25fr ultra	2.25	2.25
		Set, never hinged	7.50	

Fautaua Valley and Marshal Petain A15

1941 Engr. *Perf. 12½x12*

125A	A15	1fr bluish green	1.00	
125B	A15	2.50fr deep blue	1.25	
		Set, never hinged	3.25	

Nos. 125A-125B were issued by the Vichy government in France, but were not placed on sale in the French Polynesia.

For surcharges, see Nos. B12B-B12C.

Stamps of 1929-39 Overprinted in Black or Red

1941 *Perf. 14x13½, 13½x13*

126	A14	1fr red brown (Bk)	4.75	*6.50*
127	A14	2.50fr black	7.25	*9.50*
128	A5	3fr grn & dk brn	7.25	7.25
129	A14	3fr brn org (Bk)	8.00	10.50
130	A5	5fr lt bl & dk brn	7.25	7.25
131	A14	5fr red vio (Bk)	8.00	10.50
132	A5	10fr lt red & dk brn	21.50	*25.00*
133	A14	10fr dark green	80.00	*100.00*
134	A5	20fr lil & dk brn	120.00	120.00
135	A14	20fr dark brown	72.50	*92.50*
		Nos. 126-135 (10)	336.50	
		Set, never hinged	480.00	

Types of 1934-39 without "RF"

1942-44 Photo. *Perf. 13½*

135A	A12	10c dark brown	.55
135B	A13	30c orange brown	.75
135C	A14	1.50fr blue	.95
135D	A14	10fr dark green	1.50
135E	A14	20fr dark brown	2.40
		Nos. 135A-135E (5)	6.15

Nos. 135A-135E were issued by the Vichy government in France, but were not placed on sale in French Polynesia.

Catalogue values for unused stamps in this section, from this point to the end of the section, are for Never Hinged items.

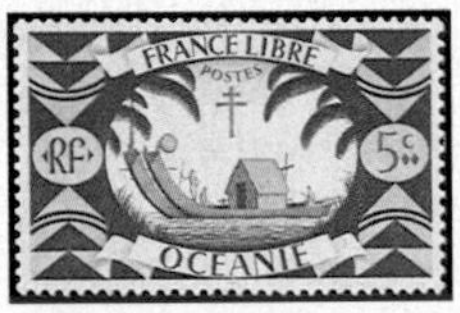

Ancient Double Canoe A16

1942 Photo. *Perf. 14½x14*

136	A16	5c dark brown	.40	.20
137	A16	10c dk gray bl	.40	.20
138	A16	25c emerald	.40	.20
139	A16	30c red orange	.40	.20
140	A16	40c dk slate grn	.40	.20
141	A16	80c red brown	.40	.20
142	A16	1fr rose violet	.50	.35
143	A16	1.50fr brt red	.65	.50
144	A16	2fr gray black	1.00	.75
145	A16	2.50fr brt ultra	2.50	1.75
146	A16	4fr dull violet	1.75	1.25
147	A16	5fr bister	1.75	1.25
148	A16	10fr deep brown	2.50	1.90
149	A16	20fr deep green	3.00	2.10
		Nos. 136-149 (14)	16.05	11.05

For surcharges see Nos. 152-159.

Eboue Issue

Common Design Type

1945 Engr. *Perf. 13*

150	CD91	2fr black	1.00	.75
151	CD91	25fr Prus green	2.60	2.10

Nos. 150 and 151 exist imperforate.

Nos. 136, 138 and 145 Surcharged with New Values and Bars in Carmine or Black

1946 *Perf. 14½x14*

152	A16	50c on 5c (C)	.60	.50
153	A16	60c on 5c (C)	.60	.50
154	A16	70c on 5c (C)	.60	.50
155	A16	1.20fr on 5c (C)	.80	.65
156	A16	2.40fr on 25c (Bk)	1.60	1.25
157	A16	3fr on 25c (Bk)	1.00	.75
158	A16	4.50fr on 25c (Bk)	2.00	1.50
159	A16	15fr on 2.50fr (C)	2.40	1.75
		Nos. 152-159 (8)	9.60	7.40

Coast of Mooréa A17

Fisherman and Catch — A18

Tahitian Girl — A20

House at Faa — A19

Island of Borabora A21

Island Women A22

1948 Unwmk. Engr. *Perf. 13*

160	A17	10c brown	.50	.35
161	A17	30c blue green	.50	.35
162	A17	40c deep blue	.50	.35
163	A18	50c red brown	.50	.35
164	A18	60c dk brown ol	.65	.50
165	A18	80c brt blue	.65	.50
166	A19	1fr red brown	.65	.35
167	A19	1.20fr slate	.65	.50
168	A19	1.50fr deep ultra	.65	.50
169	A20	2fr sepia	1.10	.75
170	A20	2.40fr red brown	1.25	1.00
171	A20	3fr purple	11.50	2.50
172	A20	4fr blue black	2.40	1.40
173	A21	5fr sepia	3.75	1.60
174	A21	6fr steel blue	3.75	2.10
175	A21	10fr dk brown ol	4.75	1.75
176	A22	15fr vermilion	7.25	2.75
177	A22	20fr slate	7.25	3.25
178	A22	25fr sepia	9.00	5.00
		Nos. 160-178 (19)	57.25	25.85

Imperforates

Most French Polynesia stamps from 1948 onward exist imperforate in issued and trial colors, and also in small presentation sheets in issued colors.

Military Medal Issue

Common Design Type

1952, Dec. 1 Engr. & Typo.

179	CD101	3fr multicolored	13.50	10.00

Girl of Borabora — A23

Girl Playing Guitar — A24

1955, Sept. 26 Engr.

180	A23	9fr dk brn, blk & red	11.00	7.25

FIDES Issue

Common Design Type

Design: 3fr, Dry dock at Papeete.

1956, Oct. 22 Engr. *Perf. 13x12½*

181	CD103	3fr grnsh blue	4.00	2.00

1958, Nov. 3 Unwmk. *Perf. 13*

Designs: 4fr, 7fr, 9fr, Man with headdress. 10fr, 20fr, Girl with shells on beach.

182	A24	10c grn & redsh brn	.70	.60
183	A24	25c slate grn, cl & car	.85	.65
184	A24	1fr brt bl, brn & red org	1.10	.70
185	A24	2fr brn, vio brn & vio	1.25	.70
186	A24	4fr sl grn & org yel	1.60	1.10
187	A24	7fr red brn, grn & org	3.25	1.75
188	A24	9fr vio brn, grn & org	5.75	2.50
189	A24	10fr dk bl, brn & car	5.25	2.50
190	A24	20fr pur, rose red & brn	9.50	5.50
		Nos. 182-190 (9)	29.25	16.00

See Nos. 304-306.

Human Rights Issue

Common Design Type

1958, Dec. 10

191	CD105	7fr dk gray & dk bl	13.00	8.75

Flower Issue

Common Design Type

1959, Jan. 3 Photo. *Perf. 12½x12*

192	CD104	4fr Breadfruit	6.50	4.00

Spear Fishing — A25

Tahitian Dancers A26

1960, May 16 Engr. *Perf. 13*

193	A25	5fr green, brn & lil	1.40	1.10
194	A26	17fr ultra, brt grn & red brn	6.25	2.75

Post Office, Papeete A27

1960, Nov. 19 Unwmk. *Perf. 13*

195	A27	16fr green, bl & claret	6.00	3.50

Saraca Indica — A28

1962, July 12 Photo. *Perf. 13*

196	A28	15fr shown	16.00	14.00
197	A28	25fr Hibiscus	24.00	16.00

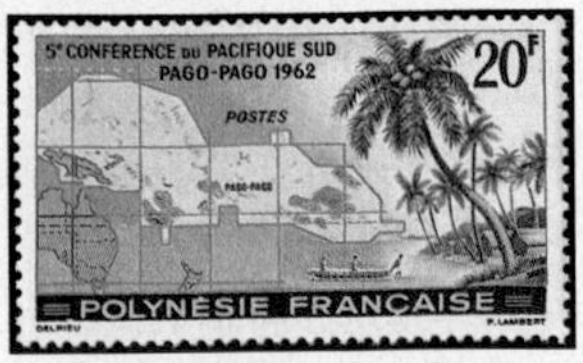

Map of Australia and South Pacific — A29

1962, July 18 *Perf. 13x12*

198	A29	20fr multicolored	18.00	8.00

5th South Pacific Conf., Pago Pago, July 1962.

Spined Squirrelfish A30

Fish: 10fr, One-spot butterflyfish. 30fr, Radiate lionfish. 40fr, Horned boxfish.

1962, Dec. 15 Engr. *Perf. 13*

199	A30	5fr black, mag & bis	4.50	2.00
200	A30	10fr multicolored	6.50	3.00
201	A30	30fr multicolored	13.00	8.00
202	A30	40fr multicolored	16.00	12.00
		Nos. 199-202 (4)	40.00	25.00

Soccer — A30a

Design: 50fr, Throwing the javelin.

1963, Aug. 29 Photo. *Perf. 12½*

203	A30a	20fr brt ultra & brn	9.50	6.50
204	A30a	50fr brt car rose & ultra	17.00	9.50

South Pacific Games, Suva, 8/29-9/7.

Red Cross Centenary Issue

Common Design Type

1963, Sept. 2 Engr. *Perf. 13*

205	CD113	15fr vio brn, gray & car	14.50	11.50

Human Rights Issue

Common Design Type

1963, Dec. 10 Unwmk. *Perf. 13*

206	CD117	7fr green & vio bl	14.50	9.50

Philatec Issue

Common Design Type

1964, Apr. 9 Unwmk. *Perf. 13*

207	CD118	25fr grn, dk sl grn & red	17.00	12.00

Tahitian Dancer A31

1964, May 14 Engr. *Perf. 13*

208	A31	1fr multicolored	.45	.45
209	A31	3fr dp claret, blk & org	1.00	1.00

Soldiers, Truck and Battle Flag — A32

1964, July 10 Photo. *Perf. 12½*

210 A32 5fr multicolored 12.00 4.50

Issued to honor the Tahitian Volunteers of the Pacific Battalion. See No. C31.

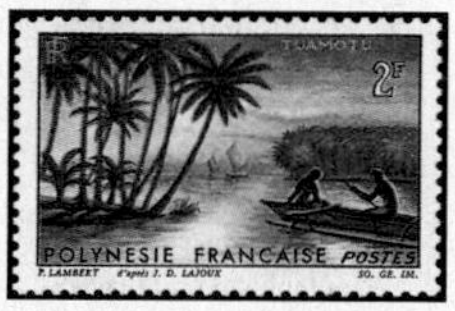

Tuamotu Scene A33

Views: 4fr, Borabora. 7fr, Papeete Harbor. 8fr, Paul Gauguin's tomb, Marquesas. 20fr, Mangareva, Gambier Islands.

1964, Dec. 1 Litho. *Perf. 12½x13*

211 A33 2fr multicolored .95 .55
212 A33 4fr multicolored 1.60 .55
213 A33 7fr multicolored 3.25 1.40
214 A33 8fr multicolored 4.25 2.00
215 A33 20fr multicolored 10.00 3.25
Nos. 211-215,C32 (6) 30.55 11.75

Painting from a School Dining Room — A34

1965, Nov. 29 Engr. *Perf. 13*

216 A34 20fr dk brn, sl grn & dk car 21.00 12.50

Publicizing the School Canteen Program. See #C38.

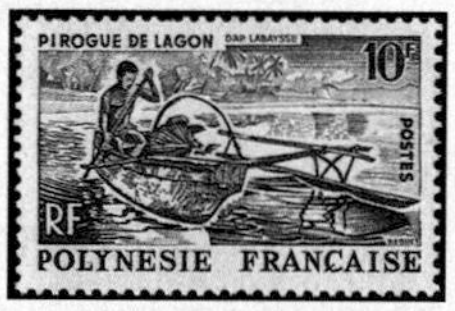

Outrigger Canoe on Lagoon A35

Ships: 11fr, Large cruising yacht, vert. 12fr, Motorboat for sport fishing. 14fr, Outrigger canoes with sails. 19fr, Schooner, vert. 22fr, Modern coaster "Oiseau des Isles II."

1966, Aug. 30 Engr. *Perf. 13*

217 A35 10fr brt ultra, emer & mar 3.00 .95
218 A35 11fr mar, dk bl & sl grn 3.00 1.75
219 A35 12fr emer, dk bl & red lil 4.00 1.90
220 A35 14fr brn, bl & slate grn 6.00 2.10
221 A35 19fr scar, sl grn & dp bl 7.00 2.25
222 A35 22fr multicolored 10.00 4.25
Nos. 217-222 (6) 33.00 13.20

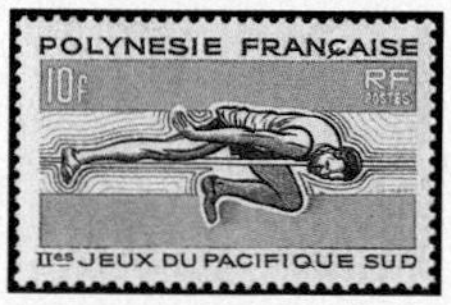

High Jump A36

Designs: 20fr, Pole vault, vert. 40fr, Women's basketball, vert. 60fr, Hurdling.

1966, Dec. 15 Engr. *Perf. 13*

223 A36 10fr dk red, lem & blk 2.40 1.60
224 A36 20fr blue, emer & blk 5.50 2.10
225 A36 40fr emer, brt pink & blk 10.50 5.25
226 A36 60fr dull yel, bl & blk 17.50 9.00
Nos. 223-226 (4) 35.90 17.95

2nd South Pacific Games, Nouméa, New Caledonia, Dec. 8-18.

Poi Pounder — A37

Javelin Throwing — A38

1967, June 15 Engr. *Perf. 13*

227 A37 50fr orange & blk 17.50 10.50

Society for Oceanic Studies, 50th anniv.

1967, July 11

5fr, Spring dance. 15fr, Horse race. 16fr, Fruit carriers' race. 21fr, Canoe race.

228 A38 5fr multi, horiz. 1.25 .95
229 A38 13fr multi 4.75 1.60
230 A38 15fr multi, horiz. 4.75 1.75
231 A38 16fr multi 4.75 3.00
232 A38 21fr multi, horiz. 10.00 5.25
Nos. 228-232 (5) 25.50 12.55

Issued to publicize the July Festival.

Earring — A39

Art of the Marquesas Islands: 10fr, Carved mother-of-pearl. 15fr, Decorated canoe paddle. 23fr, Oil vessel. 25fr, Carved stilt stirrups. 30fr, Fan handles. 35fr, Tattooed man. 50fr, Tikis.

1967-68 Engr. *Perf. 13*

233 A39 10fr dp cl, dl red & ultra 2.50 .70
234 A39 15fr black & emerald 3.25 1.50
235 A39 20fr ol gray, dk car & lt bl 5.50 2.25
236 A39 23fr dk brn, ocher & bl 7.00 4.25
237 A39 25fr dk brn, dk bl & lil 7.00 4.00
238 A39 30fr brown & red lilac 8.75 4.25
239 A39 35fr ultra & dk brn 14.50 6.50
240 A39 50fr brn, sl grn & lt bl 15.50 7.50
Nos. 233-240 (8) 64.00 30.95

Issued: 20fr, 25fr, 30fr, 50fr, 12/19/67; others 2/28/68.

WHO Anniversary Issue
Common Design Type

1968, May 4 Engr. *Perf. 13*

241 CD126 15fr bl grn, mar & dp vio 10.50 4.50
242 CD126 16fr org, lil & bl grn 10.50 7.50

Human Rights Year Issue
Common Design Type

1968, Aug. 10 Engr. *Perf. 13*

243 CD127 15fr blue, red & brn 11.50 5.75
244 CD127 16fr brn, brt pink & ultra 11.50 7.50

Tiare Apetahi A40

Flower: 17fr, Tiare Tahiti.

1969, Mar. 27 Photo. *Perf. 12½x13*

245 A40 9fr multicolored 2.25 1.25
246 A40 17fr multicolored 4.50 2.25

3rd South Pacific Games, Port Moresby, Papua and New Guinea, Aug. 13-23 — A41

1969, Aug. 13 Engr. *Perf. 13*

247 A41 9fr Boxer, horiz 3.50 1.40
248 A41 17fr High jump 7.50 2.25
249 A41 18fr Runner 9.50 3.75
250 A41 22fr Long jump 12.50 7.50
Nos. 247-250 (4) 33.00 14.90

ILO Issue
Common Design Type

1969, Nov. 24 Engr. *Perf. 13*

251 CD131 17fr org, emer & ol 11.00 5.50
252 CD131 18fr org, dk brn & vio bl 11.00 6.50

Territorial Assembly A42

Buildings: 14fr, Governor's Residence. 17fr, House of Tourism. 18fr, Maeva Hotel. 24fr, Taharaa Hotel.

1969, Dec. 22 Photo. *Perf. 12½x12*

253 A42 13fr black & multi 3.00 1.40
254 A42 14fr black & multi 4.50 1.75
255 A42 17fr black & multi 7.25 3.75
256 A42 18fr black & multi 8.00 4.25
257 A42 24fr black & multi 13.75 7.50
Nos. 253-257 (5) 36.50 18.65

Stone Figure with Globe — A43

Designs: 40fr, Globe, plane, map of Polynesia and men holding "PATA" sign, horiz. 60fr, Polynesian carrying globe.

1970, Apr. 7 Engr. *Perf. 13*

258 A43 20fr deep plum, gray & bl 7.00 3.50
259 A43 40fr emer, rose lil & ultra 11.50 5.50
260 A43 60fr red brn, bl & dk brn 19.50 10.50
Nos. 258-260 (3) 38.00 19.50

Issued to publicize the 1970 Pacific Area Travel Association Congress (PATA).

UPU Headquarters Issue
Common Design Type

1970, May 20 Engr. *Perf. 13*

261 CD133 18fr maroon, pur & brn 10.50 5.00
262 CD133 20fr lilac rose, ol & ind 10.50 5.50

Night Fishing — A44

1971, May 11 Photo. *Perf. 13*

263 A44 10fr multicolored 12.50 5.25
Nos. 263,C71-C73 (4) 39.75 19.75

Flowers — A45

Designs: Various flowers. 12fr is horiz.

Perf. 12½x13, 13x12½

1971, Aug. 27

264 A45 8fr multicolored 2.25 1.10
265 A45 12fr multicolored 3.75 1.90
266 A45 22fr multicolored 6.00 3.00
Nos. 264-266 (3) 12.00 6.00

Day of a Thousand Flowers.

Water-skiing Slalom — A46

Designs: 20fr, Water-skiing, jump, vert. 40fr, Figure water-skiing.

1971, Oct. 11 Engr. *Perf. 13*

267 A46 10fr grnsh bl, dk red & brn 6.50 2.25
268 A46 20fr car, emer & brn 9.50 4.25
269 A46 40fr brn, grn & lil 21.00 13.00
Nos. 267-269 (3) 37.00 19.50

World water-skiing championships, Oct. 1971.

De Gaulle Issue
Common Design Type

30fr, As general, 1940. 50fr, As president, 1970.

1971, Nov. 9 Engr. *Perf. 13*

270 CD134 30fr red lilac & blk 20.00 10.50
271 CD134 50fr red lilac & blk 27.50 17.50

Map of Tahiti and Jerusalem Cross A47

1971, Dec. 18 Photo. *Perf. 13x12½*

272 A47 28fr lt blue & multi 14.50 9.00

2nd rally of French Boy Scouts and Guides, Taravao, French Polynesia.

"Alcoholism" A48

Mother and Child A49

1972, Mar. 24 Photo. *Perf. 13*

273 A48 20fr brown & multi 12.00 6.00

Fight against alcoholism.

1973, Sept. 26 Photo. *Perf. 12½x13*

274 A49 28fr pale yellow & multi 10.00 5.25

Day nursery.

Polynesian Golfer — A50

Design: 24fr, Atimaono Golf Course.

1974, Feb. 27 Photo. *Perf. 13*

275 A50 16fr multicolored	8.75	3.50
276 A50 24fr multicolored	11.00	5.50

Atimaono Golf Course.

Hand Throwing Life Preserver to Puppy — A51

1974, May 9 Photo. *Perf. 13*

277 A51 21fr brt blue & multi	12.50	5.25

Society for the Protection of Animals.

Around a Fire, on the Beach A52

Polynesian Views: 2fr, Lagoons and mountains. 6fr, Pebble divers. 10fr, Lonely Mountain and flowers, vert. 15fr, Sailing ship at sunset. 20fr, Lagoon and mountain.

1974, May 22

278 A52 2fr multicolored	.90	.60
279 A52 5fr multicolored	1.10	.90
280 A52 6fr multicolored	1.90	1.10
281 A52 10fr multicolored	2.10	1.25
282 A52 15fr multicolored	4.25	1.75
283 A52 20fr multicolored	7.00	2.10
Nos. 278-283 (6)	17.25	7.70

Polynesian Woman and UPU Emblem — A53

Lion, Sun and Emblem — A54

1974, Oct. 9 Engr. *Perf. 13*

284 A53 65fr multicolored	12.50	8.00

Centenary of Universal Postal Union.

1975, June 17 Photo.

285 A54 26fr multicolored	12.50	5.25

15th anniv. of Lions Intl. in Tahiti.

Fish and Leaf A55

1975, July 9 Litho. *Perf. 12*

286 A55 19fr dp ultra & green	11.00	4.50

Polynesian Association for the Protection of Nature.

Georges Pompidou, Pres. of France — A55a

1976, Feb. 16 Engr. *Perf. 13*

287 A55a 49fr dk violet & black	12.00	7.25

See France No. 1430.

Alain Gerbault and Sailboat A56

1976, May 25 Photo. *Perf. 13*

288 A56 90fr multicolored	14.50	9.50

Alain Gerbault's arrival in Bora Bora, 50th anniv.

Turtle — A57

Design: 42fr, Hand protecting bird.

1976, June 24 Litho. *Perf. 12½*

289 A57 18fr multicolored	15.00	4.50
290 A57 42fr multicolored	21.00	11.50

World Ecology Day.

A. G. Bell, Telephone, Radar and Satellite — A58

1976, Sept. 15 Engr. *Perf. 13*

291 A58 37fr multicolored	11.00	5.25

Centenary of first telephone call by Alexander Graham Bell, Mar. 10, 1876.

Dugout Canoes — A59

1976, Dec. 16 Litho. *Perf. 13x12½*

292 A59 25fr Marquesas	4.00	3.00
293 A59 30fr Raiatea	5.00	4.00
294 A59 75fr Tahiti	10.00	6.00
295 A59 100fr Tuamotu	12.50	7.50
Nos. 292-295 (4)	31.50	20.50

Sailing Ship — A60

Designs: Various sailing vessels.

1977, Dec. 22 Litho. *Perf. 13*

296 A60 20fr multicolored	6.50	2.10
297 A60 50fr multicolored	7.50	2.40
298 A60 85fr multicolored	9.50	4.00
299 A60 120fr multicolored	16.00	6.00
Nos. 296-299 (4)	39.50	14.50

Hibiscus — A61

Girl with Shells on Beach — A62

Designs: 10fr, Vanda orchids. 16fr, Pua (fagraea berteriana). 22fr, Gardenia.

1978-79 Photo. *Perf. 12½x13*

300 A61 10fr multicolored	1.25	.50
301 A61 13fr multicolored	2.75	1.25
302 A61 16fr multicolored	3.00	2.00
303 A61 22fr multicolored	2.00	1.25
Nos. 300-303 (4)	9.00	5.00

Issued: 13fr, 16fr, 8/23; 10fr, 22fr, 1/25/79.

1978, Nov. 3 Engr. *Perf. 13*

Design A24 with "1958 1978" added: 28fr, Man with headdress. 36fr, Girl playing guitar.

304 A62 20fr multicolored	3.25	.80
305 A62 28fr multicolored	4.00	1.75
306 A62 36fr multicolored	6.00	2.75
a. Souvenir sheet of 3	30.00	30.00
Nos. 304-306 (3)	13.25	5.30

20th anniv. of stamps inscribed: Polynesie Francaise. #306a contains #304-306 in changed colors.

Ships — A63

1978, Dec. 29 Litho. *Perf. 13x12½*

307 A63 15fr Tahiti	1.75	.85
308 A63 30fr Monowai	3.00	1.40
309 A63 75fr Tahitien	4.75	3.50
310 A63 100fr Mariposa	9.00	3.50
Nos. 307-310 (4)	18.50	9.25

Porites Coral A64

Design: 37fr, Montipora coral.

1979, Feb. 15 *Perf. 13x12½*

311 A64 32fr multicolored	2.75	1.40
312 A64 37fr multicolored	4.00	2.25

Raiatea A65

Landscapes: 1fr, Moon over Bora Bora. 2fr, Mountain peaks, Ua Pou. 3fr, Sunset over Motu Tapu. 5fr, Motu. 6fr, Palm and hut, Tuamotu.

1979, Mar. 8 Photo. *Perf. 13x13½*

313 A65 1fr multicolored	.20	.20
314 A65 2fr multicolored	.20	.20
315 A65 3fr multicolored	.35	.20
316 A65 4fr multicolored	.50	.20
317 A65 5fr multicolored	.85	.40
318 A65 6fr multicolored	1.00	.65
Nos. 313-318 (6)	3.10	1.85

See Nos. 438-443 for redrawn designs.

Dance Costumes A66

1979, July 14 Litho. *Perf. 12½*

319 A66 45fr Fetia	2.00	1.10
320 A66 51fr Teanuanua	3.00	1.40
321 A66 74fr Temaeva	4.00	2.50
Nos. 319-321 (3)	9.00	5.00

Hill, Great Britain No. 53, Tahiti No. 28 — A67

1979, Aug. 1 Engr. *Perf. 13*

322 A67 100fr multicolored 5.25 3.25

Sir Rowland Hill (1795-1879), originator of penny postage.

Hastula Strigilata — A68

Statue Holding Rotary Emblem — A69

Shells: 28fr, Scabricola variegata. 35fr, Fusinus undatus.

1979, Aug. 22 Litho. *Perf. 12½*

323 A68 20fr multicolored 2.00 .80
324 A68 28fr multicolored 2.75 .90
325 A68 35fr multicolored 3.75 2.50
Nos. 323-325 (3) 8.50 4.20

1979, Nov. 30 Litho. *Perf. 13*

326 A69 47fr multicolored 3.50 2.10

Rotary International, 75th anniversary; Papeete Rotary Club, 20th anniversary.
For overprint see No. 330.

Myripristis Murdjan A70

Fish: 8fr, Napoleon. 12fr, Emperor.

1980, Jan. 21 Litho. *Perf. 12½*

327 A70 7fr multicolored 2.00 .55
328 A70 8fr multicolored 2.00 .70
329 A70 12fr multicolored 2.50 1.00
Nos. 327-329 (3) 6.50 2.25

No. 326 Overprinted and Surcharged in Gold: "75eme / ANNIVERSAIRE / 1905-1980"

1980, Feb. 23 Litho. *Perf. 13*

330 A69 77fr on 47fr multi 6.50 3.50

Rotary International, 75th anniversary.

CNEXO Fish Hatchery A71

1980, Mar. 17 Photo. *Perf. 13x13½*

331 A71 15fr shown 1.50 1.00
332 A71 22fr Crayfish 1.50 1.00

Papeete Post Office Building Opening A72

1980, Apr. 30 Photo. *Perf. 13x12½*

333 A72 50fr multicolored 3.00 1.75

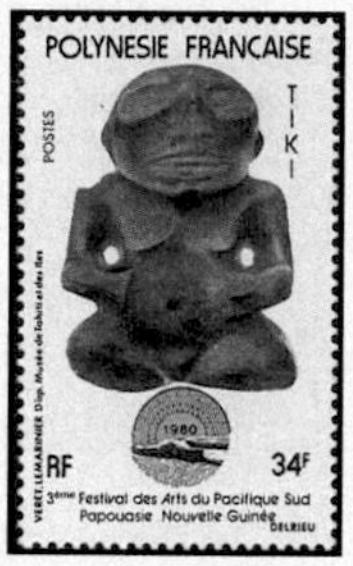

Tiki and Festival Emblem — A73

1980, June 30 Photo. *Perf. 13½*

334 A73 34fr shown 1.50 1.00
335 A73 39fr Drum (pahu) 2.25 1.40
336 A73 49fr Ax (to'i) 3.00 2.00
a. Souv. sheet of 3, #334-336 13.50 13.00
Nos. 334-336 (3) 6.75 4.40

South Pacific Arts Festival, Port Moresby, Papua New Guinea.

Titmouse Henparrot — A74

Charles de Gaulle — A75

Perf. 13x12½, 12½x13

1980, Oct. 20 Photo.

337 A74 25fr White sea-swallow, horiz. 2.50 .75
338 A74 35fr shown 3.00 1.00
339 A74 45fr Minor frigate bird, horiz. 4.00 1.25
Nos. 337-339 (3) 9.50 3.00

1980, Nov. 9 Engr. *Perf. 12½x13*

340 A75 100fr multicolored 5.50 3.25

Naso Vlamingi (Karaua) A76

1981, Feb. 5 Litho. *Perf. 12½*

341 A76 13fr shown 2.25 .50
342 A76 16fr Lutjanus vaigensis (toau) 2.25 .60
343 A76 24fr Plectropomus leopardus (tonu) 3.00 .75
Nos. 341-343 (3) 7.50 1.85

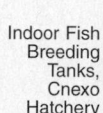

Indoor Fish Breeding Tanks, Cnexo Hatchery A77

1981, May 14 Photo. *Perf. 13x13½*

344 A77 23fr shown 1.25 .80
345 A77 41fr Mussels 2.00 1.10

Folk Dancers A78

Perf. 13x13½, 13½x13

1981, July 10 Litho.

346 A78 26fr shown 1.40 .65
347 A78 28fr Dancer 1.40 1.10
348 A78 44fr Dancers, vert. 2.40 1.50
Nos. 346-348 (3) 5.20 3.25

Sterna Bergii — A79

1981, Sept. 24 Litho. *Perf. 13*

349 A79 47fr shown 1.50 .90
350 A79 53fr Ptilinopus purpuratus, vert. 1.50 1.10
351 A79 65fr Estrilda astrild, vert. 2.00 1.50
Nos. 349-351 (3) 5.00 3.50

See Nos. 370-372.

Huahine Island A80

1981, Oct. 22 Litho. *Perf. 12½*

352 A80 34fr shown 1.50 .80
353 A80 134fr Maupiti 3.50 2.10
354 A80 136fr Bora-Bora 3.50 2.10
Nos. 352-354 (3) 8.50 5.00

A81

1982, Feb. 4 Photo. *Perf. 13x13½*

355 A81 30fr Parrotfish 1.10 .80
356 A81 31fr Regal angel 1.50 .80
357 A81 45fr Spotted bass 1.60 1.25
Nos. 355-357 (3) 4.20 2.85

Pearl Industry A82

1982, Apr. 22 Photo. *Perf. 13x13½*

358 A82 7fr Pearl beds 1.25 .35
359 A82 8fr Extracting pearls 1.50 .35
360 A82 10fr Pearls 2.00 .50
Nos. 358-360 (3) 4.75 1.20

Tahiti "No. 1A," Emblem — A83

1982, May 12 Engr. *Perf. 13*

361 A83 150fr multicolored 5.00 3.50
a. Souvenir sheet 17.50 17.50

PHILEXFRANCE Stamp Exhibition, Paris, June 11-21. No. 361a contains No. 361 in changed colors.

King Holding Carved Scepter — A84

Designs: Coronation ceremony.

1982, July 12 Photo. *Perf. 13½x13*

362 A84 12fr shown .50 .20
363 A84 13fr King, priest .50 .20
364 A84 17fr Procession 1.00 .50
Nos. 362-364 (3) 2.00 .90

Championship Emblem — A85

1982, Aug. 13 *Perf. 13*

365 A85 90fr multicolored 3.00 2.10

4th Hobie-Cat 16 World Catamaran Sailing Championship, Tahiti, Aug. 15-21.

First Colloquium on New Energy Sources — A86

1982, Sept. 29 Litho.

366 A86 46fr multicolored 2.75 .90

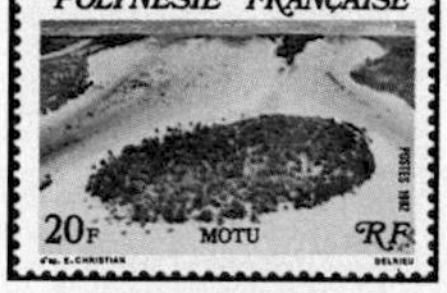

Motu, Tuamotu Islet — A87

1982, Oct. 12 Litho. *Perf. 13*

367 A87 20fr shown .75 .35
368 A87 33fr Tupai Atoll 1.00 .50
369 A87 35fr Gambier Islds. 1.50 .60
Nos. 367-369 (3) 3.25 1.45

Bird Type of 1981

1982, Nov. 17 Litho. *Perf. 13*

370 A79 37fr Sacred egret 2.25 .60
371 A79 39fr Pluvialis dominica, vert. 2.25 .70

372 A79 42fr Lonchura castane-othorax 4.50 .95
Nos. 370-372 (3) 9.00 2.25

Fish — A88

1983, Feb. 9 Litho. *Perf. 13x13½*
373 A88 8fr Acanthurus lineatus .75 .35
374 A88 10fr Caranx me-lampygus 1.00 .35
375 A88 12fr Carcharhinus mela-nopterus 1.50 .50
Nos. 373-375 (3) 3.25 1.20

The Way of the Cross, Sculpture by Damien Haturau — A89

1983, Mar. 9 Litho. *Perf. 13*
376 A89 7fr shown 1.00 .25
377 A89 21fr Virgin and Child 1.50 .50
378 A89 23fr Christ 1.75 .35
Nos. 376-378 (3) 4.25 1.10

Traditional Hats — A90

1983, May 24 Litho. *Perf. 13x12½*
379 A90 11fr Acacia .75 .35
380 A90 13fr Niau .75 .35
381 A90 25fr Ofe 1.00 .50
382 A90 35fr Ofe, diff. 1.25 .50
Nos. 379-382 (4) 3.75 1.70

See Nos. 393-396.

Chieftain in Traditional Costume, Sainte-Christine Isld. — A91

Traditional Costumes, Marquesas Islds.

1983, July 12 Photo. *Perf. 13*
383 A91 15fr shown .75 .50
384 A91 17fr Man 1.00 .50
385 A91 28fr Woman 1.25 .50
Nos. 383-385 (3) 3.00 1.50

See Nos. 397-399, 419-421.

Polynesian Crowns — A92

Various flower garlands.

1983, Oct. 19 Litho. *Perf. 13*
386 A92 41fr multicolored 1.40 .60
387 A92 44fr multicolored 1.60 .60
388 A92 45fr multicolored 2.00 .80
Nos. 386-388 (3) 5.00 2.00

See Nos. 400-402.

Martin Luther (1483-1546) A93

Tiki Carvings — A94

1983, Nov. 10 Engr. *Perf. 13*
389 A93 90fr black, brn & lil gray 2.50 1.25

1984, Feb. 8 Litho. *Perf. 12½x13*

Various carvings.

390 A94 14fr multicolored .80 .25
391 A94 16fr multicolored 1.00 .50
392 A94 19fr multicolored 1.25 .40
Nos. 390-392 (3) 3.05 1.15

Hat Type of 1983

1984, June 20 Litho. *Perf. 13x12½*
393 A90 20fr Aeho ope .50 .35
394 A90 24fr Paeore .60 .35
395 A90 26fr Ofe fei .75 .50
396 A90 33fr Hua .80 .50
Nos. 393-396 (4) 2.65 1.70

Costume Type of 1983

1984, July 11 Litho. *Perf. 13*
397 A91 34fr Tahitian playing nose flute .75 .50
398 A91 35fr Priest, Oei-eitia .90 .50
399 A91 39fr Tahitian adult and child .90 .50
Nos. 397-399 (3) 2.55 1.50

Garland Type of 1983

1984, Oct. 24 Litho. *Perf. 13x12½*
400 A92 46fr Moto'i Lei .90 .50
401 A92 47fr Pitate Lei 1.00 .60
402 A92 53fr Bougainvillea Lei 1.25 .80
Nos. 400-402 (3) 3.15 1.90

4th Pacific Arts Festival, Noumea, New Caledonia, Dec. 8-22 — A95

1984, Nov. 20 Litho. *Perf. 13*
403 A95 150fr Statue, head-dress 3.50 2.25

See No. C213.

Paysage D'Anaa, by Jean Masson — A96

Paintings: 50fr, Sortie Du Culte, by Jacques Boulaire. 75fr, La Fete, by Robert Tatin. 85fr, Tahitiennes Sur La Plage, by Pierre Heyman.

Perf. 12½x13, 13x12½

1984, Dec. 12 Litho.
404 A96 50fr multi, vert. 1.25 .60
405 A96 65fr multicolored 1.40 .75
406 A96 75fr multicolored 1.90 .90
407 A96 85fr multicolored 2.25 1.50
Nos. 404-407 (4) 6.80 3.75

Tiki Carvings — A97

Polynesian Faces — A98

1985, Jan. 23 Litho. *Perf. 13½*
408 A97 30fr multicolored .60 .35
409 A97 36fr multicolored .80 .45
410 A97 40fr multicolored .90 .75
Nos. 408-410 (3) 2.30 1.55

1985, Feb. 20 Photo. *Perf. 12½x13*
411 A98 22fr multicolored .45 .35
412 A98 39fr multicolored .80 .45
413 A98 44fr multicolored 1.00 .75
Nos. 411-413 (3) 2.25 1.55

Early Tahiti — A99

Perf. 13x12½, 12½x13

1985, Apr. 24 Litho.
414 A99 42fr Entrance to Papee-te 1.00 .60
415 A99 45fr Girls, vert. 1.40 .80
416 A99 48fr Papeete market 1.50 .90
Nos. 414-416 (3) 3.90 2.30

5th Intl. Congress on Coral Reefs, Tahiti A100

1985, May 28 Litho. *Perf. 13½*
417 A100 140fr Local reef for-mation 3.00 2.00

Printed se-tenant with label picturing congress emblem.

National Flag A101

1985, June 28
418 A101 9fr Flag, natl. arms 1.50 1.00

Costume Type of 1983

18th-19th Cent. Prints, Beslu Collection.

1985, July 17 *Perf. 13*
419 A91 38fr Tahitian dancer 1.25 .50
420 A91 55fr Man and woman from Otahiti, 1806 1.75 .75
421 A91 70fr Traditional chief 2.50 .90
Nos. 419-421 (3) 5.50 2.15

Local Foods — A103

1985-86 Litho. *Perf. 13*
422 A103 25fr Roasted pig 1.00 .40
423 A103 35fr Pit fire 1.50 .60
423A A103 80fr Fish in coco-nut milk 2.00 1.40
423B A103 110fr Fafaru 2.50 1.75
Nos. 422-423B (4) 7.00 4.15

Issued: 25fr, 35fr, 11/14; 80fr, 110fr, 5/20/86.

See Nos. 458-459, 474-475.

Catholic Churches — A104

1985, Dec. 11 Litho. *Perf. 13*
424 A104 90fr St. Anne's, Otepipi 1.90 1.10
425 A104 100fr St. Michael's Cathedral, Rik-itea 2.00 1.10
426 A104 120fr Cathedral, exte-rior 2.40 1.60
Nos. 424-426 (3) 6.30 3.80

Nos. 424-426 printed se-tenant with labels picturing local religious art.

Crabs A105

1986, Jan. 22 *Perf. 13½*
427 A105 18fr Fiddler .50 .35
428 A105 29fr Hermit .75 .35
429 A105 31fr Coconut 1.25 .50
Nos. 427-429 (3) 2.50 1.20

Faces of Polynesia A106

1986, Feb. 19 *Perf. 12½x13, 13x12½*
430 A106 43fr Boy, fish 1.00 .50
431 A106 49fr Boy, coral 1.25 .50
432 A106 51fr Boy, turtle, vert. 1.40 .60
Nos. 430-432 (3) 3.65 1.60

Old Tahiti — A107

1986, Mar. 18 *Perf. 13x12½*
433 A107 52fr Papeete 1.10 .60
434 A107 56fr Harpoon fishing 1.25 .60
435 A107 57fr Royal Palace, Papeete 1.40 .75
Nos. 433-435 (3) 3.75 1.95

Tiki Rock Carvings — A108

1986, Apr. 16
436 A108 58fr Atuona, Hiva Oa 1.75 .70
437 A108 59fr Ua Huka Hill, Hane Valley 1.75 .70

Landscapes Type Redrawn

1986-88 **Litho.** *Perf. 13½*
438 A65 1fr multi, type 2 ('88) 2.00 .35
  a. Type 1 ('86) 4.25 1.00
  b. Type 3 ('91) 15.00 4.00
439 A65 2fr multicolored .40 .20
440 A65 3fr multicolored .45 .20
441 A65 4fr multicolored ('87) .75 .30
442 A65 5fr multicolored .75 .30
443 A65 6fr multicolored .65 .30
Nos. 438-443 (6) 5.00 1.65

Nos. 438-443 printed in sharper detail, and box containing island name is taller. Nos. 439-443 margin is inscribed "CARTOR" instead of "DELRIEU."

No. 438 has three types of inscription below design: type 1, photographer's name at left, no inscription at right; type 2, photographer's name at left 9.5mm long, printer's name (Cartor) at right; type 3, photographer's name at left 12.5mm long, Cartor at right.

Traditional Crafts A109

Perf. 13x12½, 12½x13
1986, July 17 **Litho.**
444 A109 8fr Quilting, vert. .25 .20
445 A109 10fr Baskets, hats .25 .25
446 A109 12fr Grass skirts .85 .30
Nos. 444-446 (3) 1.35 .75

Building a Pirogue (Canoe) A110

1986, Oct. 21 **Litho.** *Perf. 13½*
447 A110 46fr Boat-builders 1.25 .60
448 A110 50fr Close-up 1.50 .80

Medicinal Plants — A111

Polynesians A112

1986, Nov. 19 *Perf. 13*
449 A111 40fr Phymatosorus .80 .50
450 A111 41fr Barringtonia asiatica .90 .50
451 A111 60fr Ocimum bacilicum 1.50 .90
Nos. 449-451 (3) 3.20 1.90

See Nos. 495-497.

1987, Jan. 21 **Litho.** *Perf. 13½*
452 A112 28fr Old man .60 .35
453 A112 30fr Mother and child .75 .50
454 A112 37fr Old woman 1.00 .60
Nos. 452-454 (3) 2.35 1.45

Crustaceans — A113

1987, Feb. 18 *Perf. 12½x13*
455 A113 34fr Carpilius maculatus 1.00 .50
456 A113 35fr Parribacus antarticus 1.00 .50
457 A113 39fr Justitia longimana 1.25 .50
Nos. 455-457 (3) 3.25 1.50

Local Foods Type of 1985

1987, Mar. 19 **Litho.** *Perf. 13*
458 A103 33fr Papaya poe 2.00 .60
459 A103 65fr Chicken fafa 3.00 .90

Polynesian Petroglyphs A114

1987, May 13 *Perf. 12½*
460 A114 13fr Tipaerui, Tahiti .35 .20
461 A114 21fr Turtle, Raiatea Is. .60 .35

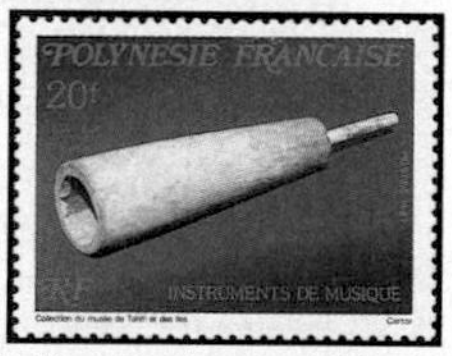

Calling Devices and Musical Instruments, Museum of Tahiti and the Isles — A115

1987, July 1 *Perf. 13½*
462 A115 20fr Wood horn .80 .20
463 A115 26fr Triton's conch .80 .50
464 A115 33fr Nose flutes 1.00 .60
Nos. 462-464 (3) 2.60 1.30

Medicinal Plants — A116

1987, Sept. 16 *Perf. 12½x13*
465 A116 46fr Thespesia populnea 1.00 .60
466 A116 53fr Ophioglossum reticulatum 1.40 .60
467 A116 54fr Dicrocephala latifolia 1.40 .60
Nos. 465-467 (3) 3.80 1.80

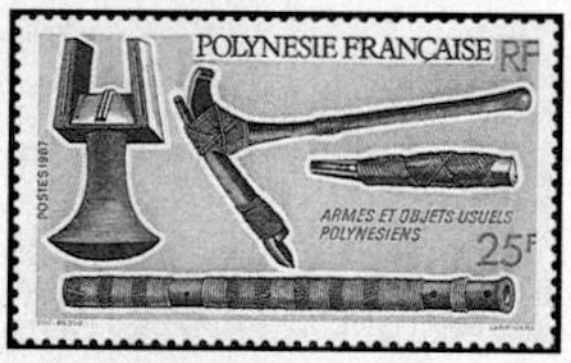

Ancient Weapons and Tools — A117

Designs: 25fr, Adze, war club, chisel, flute. 27fr, War clubs, tatooing comb, mallet. 32fr, Headdress, necklaces, nose flute.

1987, Oct. 14 **Engr.** *Perf. 13*
468 A117 25fr lt olive grn & blk .60 .40
469 A117 27fr Prus grn & int blue .75 .45
470 A117 32fr brt olive bis & brn blk .80 .55
Nos. 468-470 (3) 2.15 1.40

Catholic Missionaries — A118

Monsignors: 95fr, Rene Ildefonse Dordillon (1808-1888), bishop of the Marquesas Isls. 105fr, Tepano Jaussen (1815-1891), first bishop of Polynesia. 115fr, Paul Laurent Maze (1885-1976), archbishop of Papeete.

1987, Dec. 9 **Litho.**
471 A118 95fr multicolored 2.00 1.50
472 A118 105fr multicolored 2.25 1.75
473 A118 115fr multicolored 2.50 1.90
Nos. 471-473 (3) 6.75 5.15

Local Foods Type of 1985

1988, Jan. 12 **Litho.** *Perf. 13*
474 A103 40fr Crayfish (varo) 2.00 .60
475 A103 75fr Bananas in coconut milk 3.00 1.25

Nos. 474-475 are vert.

Authors — A119

62fr, James Norman Hall (1887-1951). 85fr, Charles Bernard Nordhoff (1887-1947).

1988, Feb. 10
476 A119 62fr multicolored 1.50 .80
477 A119 85fr multicolored 2.00 .90

Traditional Housing — A120

11fr, Taranpoo Opoa Is., Raiatea. 15fr, Tahaa Village. 17fr, Community meeting house, Tahiti.

1988, Mar. 16 **Litho.** *Perf. 13x12½*
478 A120 11fr multicolored 1.00 .30
479 A120 15fr multicolored 1.00 .30
480 A120 17fr multicolored 1.50 .30
Nos. 478-480 (3) 3.50 .90

Point Venus Lighthouse, 120th Anniv. — A121

1988, Apr. 21 **Litho.** *Perf. 13*
481 A121 400fr multicolored 9.00 6.00

Tapa-cloth Paintings by Paul Engdahl A122

1988, May 20
482 A122 52fr multicolored 1.40 .80
483 A122 54fr multicolored 1.50 .90
484 A122 64fr multicolored 1.60 1.25
Nos. 482-484 (3) 4.50 2.95

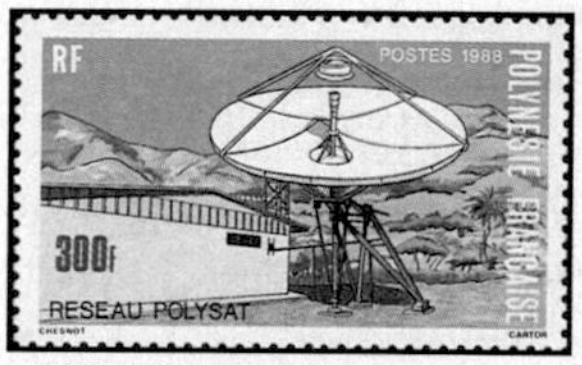

POLYSAT (Domestic Communications Network) — A123

1988, June 15 **Litho.** *Perf. 12½x12*
485 A123 300fr multicolored 6.00 4.75

Tahitian Dolls — A124

Designs: 42fr, Wearing grass skirt and headdress. 45fr, Wearing print dress and straw hat, holding guitar. 48fr, Wearing print dress and straw hat, holding straw bag.

1988, June 27 *Perf. 13x12½*
486 A124 42fr multicolored 1.00 .60
487 A124 45fr multicolored 1.25 .60
488 A124 48fr multicolored 1.50 .75
Nos. 486-488 (3) 3.75 1.95

Visiting a Marae at Nuku Hiva, Engraving by J. & E. Verreaux A125

1988, Aug. 1 Engr. *Perf. 13*
489 A125 68fr black brown 2.00 1.25

Size: 143x101mm

490 A125 145fr violet brn & grn 5.25 4.00

SYDPEX '88, July 30-Aug. 7, Australia. No. 490 pictures a Russian navy officer (probably Krusenstern) visiting the Marquesas Islanders; denomination LR.

Map Linking South America and South Pacific Islands — A126

1988, Aug. 30 Engr.
491 A126 350fr multicolored 7.50 4.50

Eric de Bisschop (1890-1958), explorer who tried to prove that there was an exchange of peoples between the South Pacific islands and So. America, rather than that the island populations originated from So. America.

Seashells A127

1988, Sept. 21 Litho. *Perf. 13½*
492 A127 24fr Kermia barnardi .60 .35
493 A127 35fr Vexillum suavis 1.00 .50
494 A127 44fr Berthelinia 1.40 .75
Nos. 492-494 (3) 3.00 1.60

Medicinal Plants Type of 1986

1988, Oct. 18 Engr. *Perf. 13*
495 A111 23fr Davallia solida .75 .35
496 A111 36fr Rorippa sarmentosa 1.10 .50
497 A111 49fr Lindernia crustacea 1.40 .75
Nos. 495-497 (3) 3.25 1.60

Protestant Missionaries — A128

1988, Dec. 7 Litho.
498 A128 80fr Henry Nott (1774-1844) 1.50 .90
499 A128 90fr Papeiha (1800-40) 2.00 1.25
500 A128 100fr Samuel Raapoto (1921-76) 2.25 1.40
Nos. 498-500 (3) 5.75 3.55

Tahiti Post Office A129

1989, Jan. 12 Engr.
501 A129 30fr P.O., 1875 .75 .40
502 A129 40fr P.O., 1915 1.00 .55

Center for Arts and Crafts A130

1989, Feb. 15 Litho. *Perf. 12½*
503 A130 29fr Marquesas Is. lidded bowl .85 .40
504 A130 31fr Mother-of-pearl pendant .95 .45

Copra Industry

Extracting Coconut Meat From Shell — A131a

Drying Coconut Meat in Sun — A131

1989, Mar. 16 Litho. *Perf. 13*
505 A131a 55fr multicolored *75.00 75.00*
506 A131 70fr multicolored *2.50 2.50*

Tapa Art — A132

43fr, Wood statue (pole), Marquesas Islands, vert. 51fr, Hand-painted bark tapestry, Society Is. 56fr, Concentric circles, Tubuai, Austral Islands.

1989, Apr. 18 Litho. *Perf. 13½*
507 A132 43fr multicolored .90 .60
508 A132 51fr shown 1.25 .75
509 A132 56fr multicolored 1.50 .90
Nos. 507-509 (3) 3.65 2.25

Polynesian Environment A133

1989, May 17 Litho. *Perf. 13x12½*
510 A133 120fr shown 3.00 1.60
511 A133 140fr Diving for seashells 3.50 1.90

Polynesian Folklore A134

Perf. 13x12½, 12½x13

1989, June 28 Litho.
512 A134 47fr Stone-lifting contest, vert. 1.25 .60
513 A134 61fr Dancer, vert. 1.50 .75
514 A134 67fr Folk singers 1.90 .80
Nos. 512-514 (3) 4.65 2.15

Bounty Castaways, from an Etching by Robert Dodd — A135

1989, July 7 Engr. *Perf. 13*
515 A135 100fr dp blue & bl grn 2.50 1.60

Souvenir Sheet

Imperf

516 A135 200fr dk ol grn & dk brn *12.50* 12.50

PHILEXFRANCE '89 and 200th annivs. of the mutiny on the *Bounty* and the French revolution.

No. 515 printed se-tenant with label picturing exhibition emblem.

Reverend-Father Patrick O'Reilly (1900-1988) A136

1989, Aug. 7 Engr. *Perf. 13x13½*
517 A136 52fr yel brn & myrtle grn 1.40 .75

Miniature Sheet

Messages A137

a, Get well soon. b, Good luck. c, Happy birthday. d, Keep in touch. e, Congratulations.

1989, Sept. 27 Litho. *Perf. 12½*
518 A137 42fr Sheet of 5, #a.-e. 7.50 7.50

Sea Shells A138

1989, Oct. 12 Litho. *Perf. 13½*
523 A138 60fr Triphoridae 1.60 .80
524 A138 69fr Muricidae favartia 1.75 .90
525 A138 73fr Muricidae morula 2.00 1.00
Nos. 523-525 (3) 5.35 2.70

Te Faaturama, c. 1892, by Gauguin A139

1989, Nov. 19 Litho. *Perf. 12½x13*
526 A139 1000fr multicolored 22.50 13.00

Legends — A140

Designs: 66fr, Maui, birth of the islands, vert. 82fr, Mt. Rotui, the pierced mountain. 88fr, Princess Hina and the eel King of Lake Vaihiria.

1989, Dec. 6 Litho. *Perf. 13*
527 A140 66fr olive brn & blk 1.25 .90
528 A140 82fr buff & blk 1.75 1.10
529 A140 88fr cream & blk 1.90 1.15
Nos. 527-529 (3) 4.90 3.15

Vanilla Orchid — A141

1990, Jan. 11 Litho.
530 A141 34fr Flower 1.40 .60
531 A141 35fr Bean pods 1.75 .60

Marine Life A142

1990, Feb. 9 Litho. *Perf. 13½*
532 A142 40fr *Kuhlia marginata* 1.40 .60
533 A142 50fr *Macrobrachium* 1.60 .75

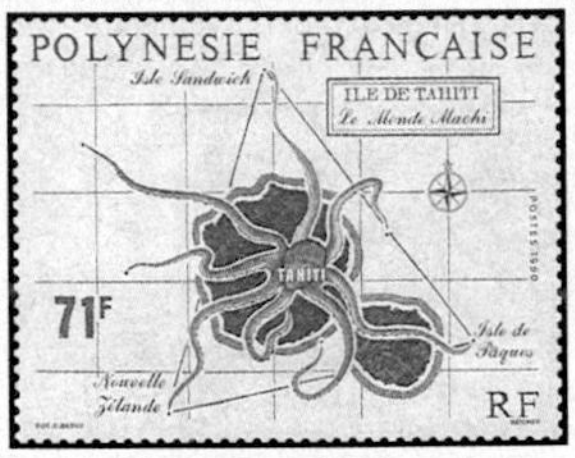

Tahiti, Center of Polynesian Triangle — A143

Maohi settlers and maps of island settlements: 58fr, Hawaiian Islands. 59fr, Easter Island. 63fr, New Zealand.

1990, Mar. 14 Engr. *Perf. 13*
534 A143 58fr black 1.75 .85
535 A143 59fr bluish gray *47.50* 22.50
536 A143 63fr olive green 2.25 .95
537 A143 71fr Prussian blue 2.50 1.10
Nos. 534-537 (4) *54.00* 25.40

See Nos. 544-545.

Papeete Village, Cent. — A144

1990, May 16 Litho.
538 A144 150fr New City Hall 3.50 2.00
539 A144 250fr Old Town Hall 5.00 3.25

A145

A146

Designs: Endangered birds.

1990, June 5 *Perf. 13½*
540 A145 13fr Porzana tabuensis .75 .20
541 A145 20fr Vini ultramarina 1.75 .35

1990, July 10 *Perf. 13*
542 A146 39fr multicolored 1.00 .60

Lions Club in Papeete, 30th anniv.

Gen. Charles de Gaulle, Birth Cent. — A147

1990, Sept. 2 **Litho.**
543 A147 200fr multi 4.00 3.00

No. 536 with Different Colors and Inscriptions

1990, Aug. 24 **Engr.** *Perf. 13*
544 A143 125fr Man, map 3.00 2.00

Souvenir Sheet

Imperf

545 A143 230fr like No. 544 6.00 6.00

New Zealand 1990.

Intl. Tourism Day — A148

1990, Sept. 27 **Litho.** *Perf. 12½*
546 A148 8f red & yellow pareo 1.00 .35
547 A148 10fr yellow pareo 1.00 .35
548 A148 12fr blue pareo 1.00 .75
Nos. 546-548 (3) 3.00 1.45

Polynesian Legends — A149

170fr, Legend of the Uru. 290fr, Pipiri-ma, vert. 375fr, Hiro, God of Thieves, vert.

1990, Nov. 7 **Litho.** *Perf. 13*
549 A149 170fr multicolored 4.00 2.50
550 A149 290fr multicolored 7.50 4.50
551 A149 375fr multicolored 11.00 5.75
Nos. 549-551 (3) 22.50 12.75

Tiare Flower — A150

Pineapple A151

Designs: 28fr, Flower crown, lei. 30fr, Flowers in bloom. 37fr, Lei.

1990, Dec. 5 *Perf. 12½*
552 A150 28fr multicolored .75 .45
553 A150 30fr multicolored 1.00 .50
554 A150 37fr multicolored 1.25 .60
Nos. 552-554 (3) 3.00 1.55

1991, Jan. 9 ***Die Cut***

Self-adhesive

555 A151 42fr shown 1.10 .90
556 A151 44fr Pineapple field 1.40 1.10

#555-556 are on paper backing perf. 12½.

Marine Life A152

1991, Feb. 7 *Perf. 12½*
557 A152 7fr Nudibranch .50 .20
558 A152 9fr Galaxaura tenera .75 .20
559 A152 11fr Adusta cumingii .75 .20
Nos. 557-559 (3) 2.00 .60

Maohi Islands — A153

18th Century scenes of: 68fr, Woman of Easter Island, vert. 84fr, Twin-hulled canoe, Hawaii. 94fr, Maori village, New Zealand.

1991, Mar. 13 **Engr.** *Perf. 13*
560 A153 68fr olive 47.50 32.50
561 A153 84fr black 2.50 1.75
562 A153 94fr brown 3.00 1.75
Nos. 560-562 (3) 53.00 36.00

Basketball, Cent. — A154

1991, May 15 **Litho.** *Perf. 13*
563 A154 80fr multicolored 1.75 1.25

Birds — A155

1991, June 5 *Perf. 13½*
564 A155 17fr Halcyon gambieri .60 .25
565 A155 21fr Vini kuhlii .90 .35

Still Life with Oranges in Tahiti by Paul Gauguin — A156

1991, June 9 **Litho.** *Perf. 13*
566 A156 700fr multicolored 17.50 12.00

Sculptures of the Marquesas Islands — A157

56fr, White Tiki with Club, vert. 102fr, Warriors Carrying Tired Man, vert. 110fr, Native Canoe.

1991, July 17 **Litho.** *Perf. 13*
567 A157 56fr multicolored 1.25 .85
568 A157 102fr multicolored 2.25 1.50
569 A157 110fr multicolored 2.50 1.75
Nos. 567-569 (3) 6.00 4.10

Wolfgang Amadeus Mozart, Death Bicent. — A158

1991, Aug. 28 **Engr.** *Perf. 13x12½*
570 A158 100fr multicolored 3.50 1.75

Stone Fishing — A159

1991, Oct. 9 **Litho.** *Perf. 13*
571 A159 25fr Fishing boats, vert. .60 .40
572 A159 57fr Man hurling stone, vert. 1.25 .90
573 A159 62fr Trapped fish 1.50 1.25
Nos. 571-573 (3) 3.35 2.55

Phila Nippon '91 A160

Designs: 50fr, Drawings of marine life by Jules-Louis Lejeune, vert. 70fr, Sailing ship, La Coquille. 250fr, Contains designs from Nos. 574-575.

Perf. 12½x13, 13x12½

1991, Nov. 16 **Engr.**
574 A160 50fr multicolored 1.25 .60
575 A160 70fr multicolored 1.75 1.00

Size: 100x75mm

Imperf

576 A160 250fr multicolored 6.00 6.00
Nos. 574-576 (3) 9.00 7.60

Central Bank for Economic Co-operation, 50th Anniv. — A161

1991, Dec. 2 **Litho.** *Perf. 13x12½*
577 A161 307fr multicolored 7.00 4.50

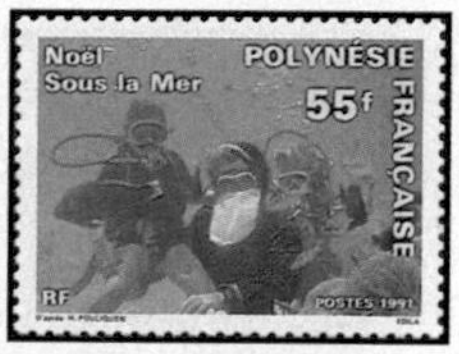

Christmas A162

Perf. 12½x13, 13x12½

1991, Dec. 11 **Litho.**
578 A162 55fr Scuba divers 1.25 .75
579 A162 83fr Underwater scene 1.75 1.35
580 A162 86fr Nativity, vert. 1.75 1.35
Nos. 578-580 (3) 4.75 3.45

Tourism — A163

1992, Feb. 12 *Perf. 13*
581 A163 1fr shown .20 .20
582 A163 2fr Horses, beach .35 .25
583 A163 3fr Girl holding fish .50 .30
584 A163 4fr Waterfalls, vert. .60 .35
585 A163 5fr Sailing .75 .40
586 A163 6fr Waterfalls, helicopter, vert. 1.00 .45
Nos. 581-586 (6) 3.40 1.95

Views from Space — A164

1992, Mar. 18 Litho. *Perf. 13x12½*

587 A164 46fr Tahiti 1.10 .90
588 A164 72fr Mataiva 1.60 1.40
589 A164 76fr Bora Bora 1.75 1.50

Size: 130x100mm

Imperf

590 A164 230fr Satellite imaging system 5.75 5.75
Nos. 587-590 (4) 10.20 9.55

International Space Year.

World Health Day A165

1992, Apr. 7 *Perf. 13½*

591 A165 136fr multicolored 3.00 2.25

Discovery of America, 500th Anniv. — A166

1992, May 22 *Perf. 13*

592 A166 130fr multicolored 3.00 2.25

Size: 140x100mm

Imperf

593 A166 250fr multicolored 6.00 6.00

World Columbian Stamp Expo '92, Chicago.

Traditional Dances — A167

Dance from: 95fr, Tahiti. 105fr, Hawaii. 115fr, Tonga.

1992, June 17 Engr. *Perf. 13*

594 A167 95fr brown black 2.25 1.65
595 A167 105fr olive brown 2.50 1.85
596 A167 115fr red brn & olive grn 2.75 2.00
Nos. 594-596 (3) 7.50 5.50

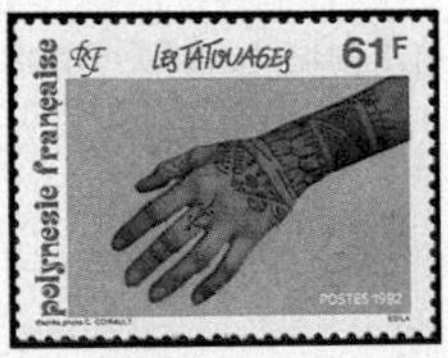

Tattoos A168

1992, July 8 Litho. *Perf. 12½*

597 A168 61fr Hand 1.75 1.00
598 A168 64fr Man, vert. 1.75 1.00

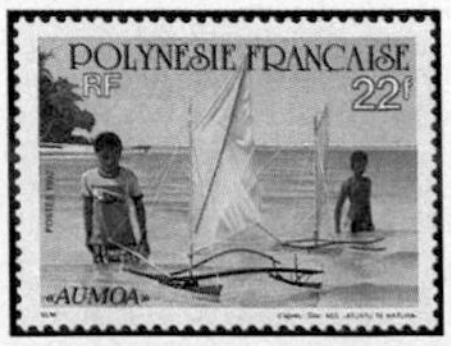

Children's Games A169

1992, Aug. 5 *Perf. 13½*

599 A169 22fr Outrigger canoe models .50 .35
600 A169 31fr String game .75 .45
601 A169 45fr Stilt game, vert. 1.25 .70
Nos. 599-601 (3) 2.50 1.50

Herman Melville, 150th Anniv. of Arrival in French Polynesia — A170

1992, Sept. 16 *Perf. 12½*

602 A170 78fr multicolored 4.50 1.25

6th Festival of Pacific Arts, Rarotonga — A171

40fr, Men on raft. 65fr, Pirogues, Tahiti.

1992, Oct. 16 Engr. *Perf. 13*

603 A171 40fr lake 1.00 .60
604 A171 65fr blue 1.75 1.00

First French Polynesian Postage Stamps, Cent. — A172

1992, Nov. 18 Photo. *Perf. 13*

605 A172 200fr multicolored 4.75 3.25

Paintings A173

55fr, Two Women Talking, by Erhard Lux. 60fr, Bouquet of Flowers, by Uschi. 75fr, Spearfisherman, by Pierre Kienlen. 85fr, Mother Nursing Child, by Octave Morillot.

1992, Dec. 9 *Perf. 12½x13*

606 A173 55fr multicolored 1.50 .75
607 A173 60fr multicolored 1.75 1.40
608 A173 75fr multicolored 1.90 1.50
609 A173 85fr multicolored 2.50 1.60
Nos. 606-609 (4) 7.65 5.25

Net Thrower A174

Bonito Fishing A175

1993, Feb. 10 Litho. *Die Cut*

Self-Adhesive

Size: 26x36mm

610 A174 46fr blue & multi 1.50 1.00

Size: 17x23mm

611 A174 46fr green & multi 1.50 1.00
a. Booklet pane of 10 15.00

1993, Mar. 10 *Perf. 13½*

612 A175 68fr Line & hook 1.60 1.25
613 A175 84fr Boat, horiz. 1.90 1.50
614 A175 86fr Drying catch 2.10 1.50
Nos. 612-614 (3) 5.60 4.25

Allied Airfield on Bora Bora, 50th Anniv. — A176

1993, Apr. 5 *Perf. 13*

615 A176 120fr multicolored 3.00 2.25

Jacques Boullaire, Artist, Birth Cent. — A177

Various scenes depicting life on: 32fr, Moorea. 36fr, Tuamotu. 39fr, Rurutu. 51fr, Nuku Hiva.

1993, May 6 Engr.

616 A177 32fr brown black .75 .60
617 A177 36fr brick red .85 .65
618 A177 39fr violet 1.00 .75
619 A177 51fr light brown 1.40 1.00
Nos. 616-619 (4) 4.00 3.00

Sports Festival — A178

1993, May 15 Litho. *Perf. 12½*

620 A178 30fr multicolored .75 .60

Australian Mathematics Competition, 15th Anniv. — A179

1993, July 1 Litho. *Perf. 13½*

621 A179 70fr multicolored 1.60 1.10

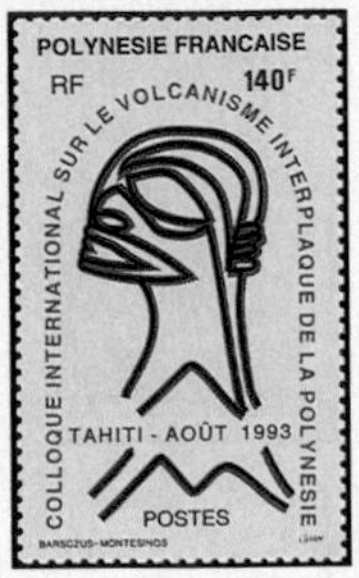

Intl. Symposium on Inter-Plate Volcanism, French University of the Pacific, Punaauia A180

1993, Aug. 2 Litho. *Perf. 13*

622 A180 140fr tan, blk & brn 3.50 2.50

Taipei '93 — A181

Tourism — A182

1993, Aug. 14 Litho. *Perf. 13½*

623 A181 46fr multicolored 2.50 .85

Exists without the Cartor imprint. Value, unused $15.

1993, Sept. 27

14fr, Boat tour. 20fr, Groom preparing for traditional wedding. 29fr, Beachside brunch.

624 A182 14fr multi, horiz. .60 .35
625 A182 20fr multi .65 .35
626 A182 29fr multi, horiz. .75 .45
Nos. 624-626 (3) 2.00 1.15

Exist without the Cartor imprint. Value, set unused $20.

Arrival of First French Gendarme in Tahiti, 150th Anniv. — A183

1993, Oct. 14 *Perf. 13*

627 A183 100fr multicolored 2.50 1.60

Exists without the Cartor imprint. Value, unused $15.

Alain Gerbault (1893-1941), Sailor — A184

1993, Nov. 17 Engr. *Perf. 13*

628 A184 150fr red, green & blue 4.00 2.75

Paintings — A185

Artists: 40fr, Vaea Sylvain. 70fr, A. Marere, vert. 80fr, J. Shelsher. 90fr, P.E. Victor, vert.

1993, Dec. 3 Photo. *Perf. 13*
629 A185 40fr multicolored 1.00 .70
630 A185 70fr multicolored 1.75 1.25
631 A185 80fr multicolored 1.90 1.25
632 A185 90fr multicolored 2.25 1.50
Nos. 629-632 (4) 6.90 4.70

French School of the Pacific, 30th Anniv. A186

1993, Dec. 7 Litho. *Perf. 12½*
633 A186 200fr multicolored 5.00 3.50

Whales and Dolphins A187

1994, Jan. 12 Litho. *Perf. 13½*
634 A187 25fr Whale breeching .75 .45
635 A187 68fr Dolphins 1.75 1.10
636 A187 72fr Humpback whales, vert. 2.00 1.25
Nos. 634-636 (3) 4.50 2.80

A188

A189

1994, Feb. 18 Litho. *Perf. 13½*
637 A188 51fr multicolored 2.00 .95

Hong Kong '94. New Year 1994 (Year of the Dog).

1994, Mar. 16
638 A189 180fr Sister Germaine Bruel 4.00 3.00

Arrival of Nuns from St. Joseph of Cluny, 150th anniv.

Church of Jesus Christ of Latter-day Saints in French Polynesia, 150th Anniv. A190

1994, Apr. 30 Litho. *Perf. 13½*
639 A190 154fr Tahiti temple 3.50 2.75

Conservatory of Arts and Crafts, Bicent. — A191

1994, May 25 Photo. *Perf. 13*
640 A191 316fr multicolored 7.50 5.50

Regional Associated Center of Papeete, 15th anniv.

Internal Self-Government, 10th Anniv. — A192

1994, June 29 Litho. *Perf. 13*
641 A192 500fr multicolored 12.00 7.50

Tahitian Academy, 20th Anniv. — A193

1994, July 2 Engr. *Perf. 13*
642 A193 136fr multicolored 3.00 2.00

Scenes of Old Tahiti — A194

1994, Aug. 10 Litho. *Perf. 13*
643 A194 22fr Papara .75 .40
644 A194 26fr Mataiea .85 .45
645 A194 51fr Taravao, vert. 1.60 .95
Nos. 643-645 (3) 3.20 1.80

See Nos. 673-675.

Faaturuma, by Paul Gauguin (1848-1903) A195

1994, Sept. 14 Litho. *Perf. 13*
646 A195 1000fr multicolored 22.50 15.00

Epiphyllum Oxypetalum A196

1994, Oct. 15 Litho. *Perf. 13½*
647 A196 51fr multicolored 1.75 .95

Hawaiki Nui Va'a '94 (Canoe Race) A197

Designs: a, 52fr, Yellow canoe, bow paddler. b, 76fr, Paddlers. c, 80fr, Paddlers, blue canoe. d, 94fr, Stern paddler, yellow canoe.

1994, Nov. 10 Litho. *Perf. 13½x13*
648 A197 Strip of 4, #a.-d. 8.00 4.75

No. 648 is a continuous design.

Paintings of French Polynesia — A198

62fr, Young girl, by Michelle Villemin. 78fr, Ocean tide, fish, by Michele Dallet. 102fr, Native carrying bundles of fruit, by Johel Blanchard. 110fr, View of coastline, by Pierre Lacouture.

1994, Dec. 19 Litho. *Perf. 13*
649 A198 62fr multi, vert. 1.60 .95
650 A198 78fr multi, vert. 1.90 1.25
651 A198 102fr multi, vert. 2.10 1.60
652 A198 110fr multi 2.40 1.75
Nos. 649-652 (4) 8.00 5.55

Don Domingo de Boenechea's Tautira Expedition, 220th Anniv. — A199

1995, Jan. 1
653 A199 92fr multicolored 2.75 1.40

South Pacific Tourism Year — A200

1995, Jan. 11 Litho. *Perf. 13½*
654 A200 92fr multicolored 2.25 1.40

New Year 1995 (Year of the Boar) A201

1995, Feb. 1 Litho.
655 A201 51fr multicolored 1.75 .80

Portions of the design on No. 655 were applied by a thermographic process producing a shiny, raised effect.

Exists without the Cartor imprint. Value, unused $9.

University Teacher's Training Institute of the Pacific — A202

1995, Mar. 8 Litho. *Perf. 13½*
656 A202 59fr multicolored 1.50 .95

Nature Protection A203

1995, May 4 Litho. *Perf. 13*
657 Strip of 3 + 2 labels 4.25 4.25
a. A203 22fr Head of turtle .75 .35
b. A203 29fr Turtle swimming 1.00 .50
c. A203 91fr Black coral 2.50 1.50

Louis Pasteur (1822-95) — A204

1995, May 8
658 A204 290fr dk blue & blue 7.25 5.00

Loti's Marriage, Novel by Julien Viaud (1850-1923) — A205

1995, May 19 Photo. *Perf. 13*
659 A205 66fr multicolored 1.75 1.10

A206

Birds — A207

1995, May 24 Litho. *Perf. 13½*
660 A206 150fr multicolored 3.50 2.25

Tahitian Monoi beauty aid.

1995, June 7
661 A207 22fr Ptilinopus huttoni .55 .35
662 A207 44fr Ducula galeata 1.10 .75

Tahitian Pearls A208

1995, June 14
663 A208 66fr shown 1.60 1.10
664 A208 84fr Eight pearls 2.10 1.40

On Nos. 663-664 portions of the design were applied by a thermographic process producing a shiny, raised effect.

Discovery of Marquesas Islands, 400th Anniv. — A209

a, Alvaro de Mendana de Neira, sailing ships. b, Pedro Fernandez de Quiros, map of islands.

1995, July 21 Litho. *Perf. 13*
665 Pair + label 8.00 6.00
a. A209 161fr multicolored 3.50 2.75
b. A209 195fr multicolored 4.50 3.25

A210

A211

1995, Aug. 12 Litho. *Perf. 13*
666 A210 83fr multicolored 2.00 1.40

10th South Pacific Games, Tahiti.

1995, Sept. 1 *Perf. 13½x13*

Pandanus plant: No. 667a, Entire plant. b, Flower. c, Fruit. d, Using dry leaves for weaving.

667 Strip of 4 8.50 6.00
a.-d. A211 91fr any single 2.00 1.50

Singapore '95.

UN, 50th Anniv. — A212

1995, Oct. 24 Litho. *Perf. 13*
668 A212 420fr multicolored 9.50 6.00

Paintings — A213

Designs: 57fr, The Paddler with the Yellow Dog, by Philippe Dubois, vert. 76fr, An Afternoon in Vaitape, by Maui Seaman, vert. 79fr, The Mama with the White Hat, by Simone Testeguide. 100fr, In Front of the Kellum House in Moorea, by Christian Deloffre.

1995, Dec. 6 Photo. *Perf. 13*
669 A213 57fr multicolored 1.25 .90
670 A213 76fr multicolored 1.60 1.25
671 A213 79fr multicolored 1.75 1.25
672 A213 100fr multicolored 2.25 1.60
Nos. 669-672 (4) 6.85 5.00

Scenes of Old Tahiti Type

1996, Jan. 17 Litho. *Perf. 13*
673 A194 18fr Fautaua .55 .30
674 A194 30fr District of Punaauia .85 .50
675 A194 35fr Tautira 1.10 .60
Nos. 673-675 (3) 2.50 1.40

New Year 1996 (Year of the Rat) — A214

1996, Feb. 19 Photo. *Perf. 13*
676 A214 51fr multicolored 1.75 .80

Portions of the design on No. 676 were applied by a thermographic process producing a shiny, raised effect.

Paul-Emile Victor (1907-95), Explorer, Writer — A215

1996, Mar. 7 Litho.
677 A215 500fr multicolored 12.00 8.00

Queen Pomare IV — A216

1996, Mar. 1 Litho. *Perf. 13*
678 A216 (51fr) multicolored 1.50 .80

Serpentine Die Cut 7 Vert.

Self-Adhesive

Size: 17x24mm

678A A216 (51fr) multicolored 2.00 1.15
b. Booklet pane of 5 10.00
Complete booklet, 2 #678b 20.00

Sea Shells A217

10fr, Conus pertusus. 15fr, Cypraea alisonae. 25fr, Vexillum roseotinctum.

1996, Apr. 10 Photo. *Perf. 13½x13*
679 A217 10fr multicolored .40 .20
680 A217 15fr multicolored .45 .25
681 A217 25fr multicolored .90 .40
Nos. 679-681 (3) 1.75 .85

Portions of the designs on Nos. 679-681 were applied by a thermographic process producing a shiny, raised effect.

Return of the Pacific Battalion, 50th Anniv. — A218

1996, May 5 Litho. *Perf. 13*
682 A218 100fr multicolored 3.00 1.60

CHINA '96, 9th Asian Intl. Philatelic Exhibition A219

Design: 200fr, Chinese School, Tahiti, 1940. Illustration reduced.

1996, May 18 *Perf. 13x13½*
683 A219 50fr multicolored 1.25 .80

Souvenir Sheet

Imperf

684 A219 200fr multicolored 4.50 3.40

Birds A220

1996, June 12 Litho. *Perf. 13x13½*
685 A220 66fr Sula sula 1.50 1.10
686 A220 79fr Fregata minor 2.00 1.25
687 A220 84fr Anous stolidus 2.00 1.40
Nos. 685-687 (3) 5.50 3.75

Musical Instruments A221

1996, July 10 *Perf. 13x13½*
688 A221 5fr Pahu, ukulele, toere .30 .20
689 A221 9fr Toere .40 .20
690 A221 14fr Pu, vivo .50 .20
Nos. 688-690 (3) 1.20 .60

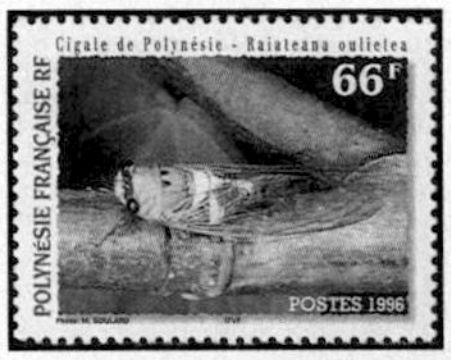

Raiateana Oulietea A222

1996, Aug. 7 Litho. *Perf. 13x13½*
691 A222 66fr multicolored 1.75 1.10

A223

A224

1996, Sept. 9 Litho. *Perf. 13*
692 A223 70fr Ruahatu, God of the Ocean 1.75 1.10

7th Pacific Arts Festival.

1996, Oct. 16 Engr. *Perf. 13*

Stamp Day: Young Tahitian girl (Type A2), Noho Mercier, taken from photo by Henry Lemasson (1870-1956), postal administrator.

693 A224 92fr black, red & blue 2.50 1.50

First Representative Assembly, 50th Anniv. — A225

1996, Nov. 7 Litho. *Perf. 13*

694 A225 85fr multicolored	2.25	.90

Paintings of Tahitian Women — A226

Designs: 70fr, Woman lounging on Bora Bora Beach, by Titi Bécaud. 85fr, "Woman with Crown of Auti leaves," by Maryse Noguier, vert. 92fr, "Dreamy Woman," by Christine de Dinechin, vert. 96fr, Two working women, by Andrée Lang, vert.

1996, Dec. 4 Litho. *Perf. 13*

695 A226 70fr multicolored	1.75	.75
696 A226 85fr multicolored	1.90	.90
697 A226 92fr multicolored	2.25	1.00
698 A226 96fr multicolored	2.50	1.00
Nos. 695-698 (4)	8.40	3.65

A227

A228

1997, Jan. 2 Litho. *Perf. 13*

699 A227 55fr brown	1.25	.55

Society of South Sea Studies, 80th anniv.

1997, Feb. 7 Photo. *Perf. 13½x13*

700 A228 13fr multicolored	.75	.20

New Year 1997 (Year of the Ox). Portions of the design were applied by a thermographic process producing a shiny, raised effect.

Arrival of Evangelists in Tahiti, Bicent. — A229

Designs: a, Sailing ship, "Duff." b, Painting, "Transfer of the Matavai District to the L.M.S. Missionaries," by Robert Smirke.

1997, Mar. 5 Litho. *Perf. 13*

701 A229 43fr Pair, #a.-b. + label	3.00	.85

Tifaifai (Tahitian Bedspread) A230

Various leaf and floral patterns.

1997, Apr. 16

702 A230 1fr multicolored	.20	.20
703 A230 5fr multicolored	.20	.20
704 A230 70fr multicolored	1.60	.70
Nos. 702-704 (3)	2.00	1.10

PACIFIC 97 — A231

Sailing ships carrying mail, passengers between Tahiti and San Francisco: No. 705, Tropic Bird, 1897. No. 706, Papeete/Zélee, 1892.

1997, May 29 Litho. *Perf. 13*

705 A231 92fr multicolored	2.25	.90
706 A231 92fr multicolored	2.25	.90
a. Pair, #705-706	5.25	5.25
b. Souvenir sheet, #705-706	65.00	65.00

No. 706b sold for 400fr.

Island Scenes A232

#707, Flower. #708, Rowing canoe, sun behind mountain. #709, Throwing spears. #710. Aerial view of island. #711, Fish. #712, Women walking on beach. #713, Holding oyster shell with pearls. #714, Boat with sail down, sunset across water. #715, Snorkeling, sting ray. #716, Bananas, pineapples. #717, Palm tree, beach. #718, Women dancers in costume.

1997, June 25 Litho. *Perf. 13*

Booklet Stamps

707 A232 85fr multicolored	10.00	9.00
708 A232 85fr multicolored	10.00	9.00
709 A232 85fr multicolored	10.00	9.00
710 A232 85fr multicolored	10.00	9.00
711 A232 85fr multicolored	10.00	9.00
712 A232 85fr multicolored	10.00	9.00
a. Bklt. pane of 6, #707-712	60.00	
713 A232 85fr multicolored	10.00	9.00
714 A232 85fr multicolored	10.00	9.00
715 A232 85fr multicolored	10.00	9.00
716 A232 85fr multicolored	10.00	9.00
717 A232 85fr multicolored	10.00	9.00
718 A232 85fr multicolored	10.00	9.00
a. Bklt. pane of 6, #713-718	60.00	
Complete booklet, 2 each #712a, #718a	240.00	

Traditional Dance Costumes A233

Designs: 4fr, Warrior's costume. 9fr, Women's costume. 11fr, Couple.

1997, July 10 Litho. *Perf. 13½x13*

719 A233 4fr multicolored	.40	.20
720 A233 9fr multicolored	.50	.20
721 A233 11fr multicolored	.75	.20
Nos. 719-721 (3)	1.65	.60

Kon-Tiki Expedition, 50th Anniv. — A234

1997, Aug. 7 Litho. *Perf. 13*

722 A234 88fr multicolored	2.25	.80

Artists in Tahiti — A235

Designs: 85fr, Painting, "The Fruit Carrier," by Monique "Mono" Garnier-Bissol. 96fr, "Revival of Our Resources," mother of pearl painting, by Camélia Maraea. 110fr, "Tahitian Spirit," pottery, by Peter Owen, vert. 126fr, "Monoi," surrealist painting, by Elisabeth Stefanovitch.

1997, Oct. 15 Litho. *Perf. 13*

723 A235 85fr multicolored	1.90	.80
724 A235 96fr multicolored	2.00	.90
725 A235 110fr multicolored	2.50	1.00
726 A235 126fr multicolored	3.00	1.10
Nos. 723-726 (4)	9.40	3.80

Te Arii Vahine, by Paul Gauguin (1848-1903) — A236

1997, Nov. 6 Litho. *Perf. 13*

727 A236 600fr multicolored	15.00	5.75

Christmas A237

1997, Dec. 3 Litho. *Perf. 13*

728 A237 118fr multicolored	3.00	1.10

New Year 1998 (Year of the Tiger) A238

1998, Jan. 28 Photo. *Perf. 13*

729 A238 96fr multicolored	2.50	.90

Portions of the design on No. 729 were applied by a thermographic process producing a shiny, raised effect.

Domestic Airline Network — A239

Designs: a, 70fr, Grumman Widgeon, 1950. b, 85fr, DHC 6 Twin-Otter, 1968. c, 70fr, Fairchild FH 227, 1980. d, 85fr, ATR 42-500, 1998.

1998, Apr. 16 Photo. *Perf. 13*

730 A239 Strip of 4, #a.-d. + label	6.50	2.90

Orchids A240

5fr, Dendrobium "Royal King." 20fr, Oncidium "Ramsey." 50fr, Ascodenca "Laksi." 100fr, Cattleya "hybride."

1998, May 14 Photo. *Perf. 13*

731 A240 5fr multi	.25	.20
732 A240 20fr multi, vert.	.50	.20
733 A240 50fr multi, vert.	1.25	.45
734 A240 100fr multi	2.25	.95
Nos. 731-734 (4)	4.25	1.80

On Nos. 731-734 portions of the design were applied by a thermographic process producing a shiny, raised effect.

The Lovers, by Paul Gauguin (1848-1903) — A241

1998, June 7 Photo. *Perf. 13x12½*

735 A241 1000fr multicolored	22.50	9.00

Printed se-tenant with label.

1998 World Cup Soccer Championships, France — A242

1998, June 10

736 A242 85fr multicolored	2.00	.75

For overprint see No. 742.

Tahiti Festival of Flower and Shell Garlands — A243

Women wearing various garlands of flowers or shells.

1998, July 16 Photo. *Perf. 13½*

737 A243 55fr multicolored	1.25	.50
738 A243 65fr multicolored	1.60	.60
739 A243 70fr multicolored	1.75	.65
740 A243 80fr multicolored	2.00	.75
Nos. 737-740 (4)	6.60	2.50

Painting, "Underwater World of Polynesia," by Stanley Haumani
A244

1998, Sept. 10 Photo. *Perf. 12½x13*

741	A244 200fr multicolored	4.25	2.00

No. 736 Ovptd. in Blue & Black "France / Championne / du Munde"

1998, Oct. 28 Photo. *Perf. 13½*

742	A242 85fr multicolored	2.00	.80

Autumn Philatelic Fair, Paris — A246

Watercolor paintings of Papeete Bay, by René Gillotin (1814-61), 250fr each: a, Beach at left, people. b, Beach at right, people.

1998, Nov. 5 *Perf. 13*

743	A246 Pair, #a.-b. + label	12.00	5.00
c.	Souvenir sheet, #a.-b., imperf.	12.00	5.00

Life in Tahiti and the Islands
A247

Paintings by André Deymonaz: 70fr, Return to the Market, vert. 100fr, Bonito Fish Stalls, vert. 102fr, Going Fishing. 110fr, Discussion after Church Services.

1998, Dec. 10 Photo. *Perf. 13*

744	A247 70fr multicolored	1.60	.70
745	A247 100fr multicolored	2.50	1.00
746	A247 102fr multicolored	2.50	1.00
747	A247 110fr multicolored	2.75	1.10
	Nos. 744-747 (4)	9.35	3.80

St. Valentine's Day — A248

1999, Feb. 11 Litho. *Perf. 13*

748	A248 96fr multicolored	2.50	.90

New Year 1999 (Year of the Rabbit)
A249

1999, Feb. 16

749	A249 118fr Rabbits, flowers	2.50	1.10

Portions of the design of No. 749 were applied by a thermographic process producing a shiny, raised effect.

Marine Life
A250

Designs: 70fr, Ptérois volitans. 85fr, Hippocampus histrix. 90fr, Antennarius pictus. 120fr, Taenianotus triacanthus.

1999, Mar. 18 Photo. *Perf. 13*

750	A250 70fr multicolored	1.50	.65
751	A250 85fr multicolored	1.90	.80
752	A250 90fr multicolored	2.00	.80
753	A250 120fr multicolored	2.75	1.10
	Nos. 750-753 (4)	8.15	3.35

Portions of the designs on Nos. 750-753 were applied by a thermographic process producing a shiny, raised effect.

IBRA '99, World Philatelic Exhibition, Nuremberg
A251

Tatooed men of Marquesas Islands, 1804: 90fr, Holding staff, fan. 120fr, Wearing blue cape.

Photo. & Engr.

1999, Apr. 27 *Perf. 13¼*

754	A251 90fr multicolored	2.00	.90
755	A251 120fr multicolored	2.75	1.25

Mother's Day
A252

1999, May 27 Litho. *Perf. 13¼*

756	A252 85fr Children, vert.	1.90	.75
757	A252 120fr shown	2.75	1.00

A253

Island Fruits
A254

#758, Breadfruit, vert. 120fr, Coconut.

#760: a, Papaya. b, Guava (goyave). c, Mombin. d, Rambutan. e, Star apple (pomme-etoile). f, Otaheite gooseberry (seurette). g, Rose apple. h, Star fruit (carambole). i, Spanish lime (quenette). j, Sweetsop (pomme-cannelle). k, Cashew (pomme de cajou). l, Passion fruit.

1999 Litho. *Perf. 13½x13, 13x13½*

758	A253 85fr multicolored	1.90	.75
759	A253 120fr multicolored	2.75	1.10

Souvenir Booklet

760	Complete bklt.	30.00	
a.-l.	A254 85fr Any single	2.00	1.40

Issued: #758, 120fr, 7/21; #760, 7/21.

No. 760 sold for 1200fr, and contains two booklet panes, containing Nos. 760a-760f, and Nos. 760g-760l.

No. 720, 1856 Letter, 1864 Postmark — A255

1999, July 2 Litho. *Perf. 13*

761	A255 180fr multicolored	4.00	2.25
a.	Souvenir sheet of 1	12.00	12.00

150th anniv. of French postage stamps, PhilexFrance 99.

No. 761 issued se-tenant with label. No. 761a sold for 500fr.

Frédéric Chopin (1810-49), Composer — A256

1999, July 2 Litho. *Perf. 13*

762	A256 250fr multicolored	5.50	2.50

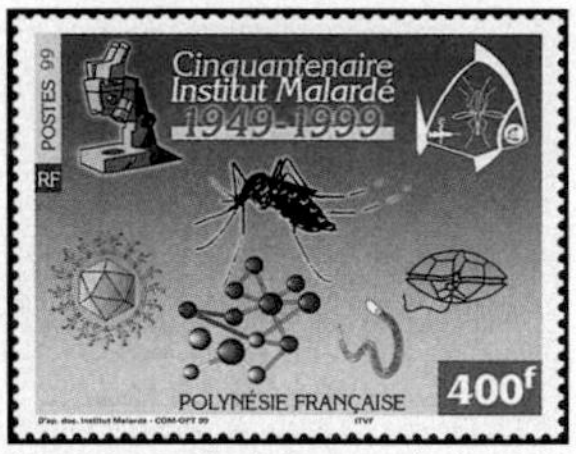

Malardé Medical Research Institute, 50th Anniv. — A257

1999, Sept. 27

763	A257 400fr multicolored	8.75	3.75

Nudes
A258

Paintings by: 85fr, J. Sorgniard. 120fr, J. Dubrusk. 180fr, C. Deloffre. 250fr, J. Gandouin.

1999, Oct. 14 Litho. *Perf. 13*

764	A258 85fr multi	2.00	.75
765	A258 120fr multi	3.00	1.10
766	A258 180fr multi	4.25	1.60
767	A258 250fr multi	5.75	2.25
	Nos. 764-767 (4)	15.00	5.70

Tahiti on the Eve of the Year 2000
A259

1999, Nov. 10 Litho. *Perf. 13*

768	A259 85fr multi	2.25	.75

5th Marquesas Islands Arts Festival
A260

1999, Dec. 10

769	A260 90fr multi	2.00	.80

Year 2000 — A261

85fr, Hands of adult and infant. 120fr, Eye.

2000, Jan. 3 *Perf. 13¼x13, 13x13¼*

770	A261 85fr multi, vert.	1.90	.75
771	A261 120fr multi	2.75	1.10

New Year 2000 (Year of the Dragon)
A262

2000, Feb. 5 Litho. *Perf. 13x13¼*

772	A262 180fr multi	4.00	1.50

Portions of the design were applied by a thermographic process producing a shiny, raised effect.

Postal Service Emblem and Stamps
A263

2000, Mar. 15 Litho. *Perf. 13x13¼*

773	A263 90fr multi	2.00	.75

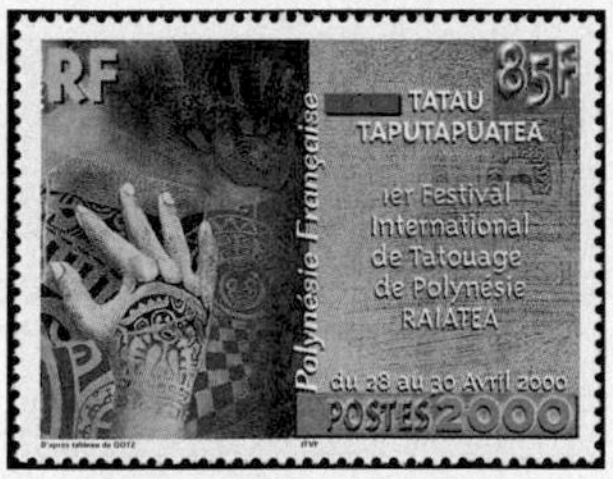

First Intl. Tattoo Festival, Raiatea — A264

Various tattoos.

2000, Apr. 28 ***Perf. 13***

774 A264 85fr multi 1.90 .70
775 A264 120fr multi 2.75 .95
776 A264 130fr multi 2.90 1.00
777 A264 160fr multi 3.50 1.25
Nos. 774-777 (4) 11.05 3.90

Beautiful Women of French Polynesia — A265

2000, May 30

778 A265 300fr multi 6.75 3.00
a. Souvenir sheet of 1 12.00 11.50

No. 778a sold for 500fr.

Traditional Dresses — A266

Denominations: 85fr, 120fr, 160fr, 250fr.

2000, June 21 Litho. ***Perf. 13¼x13***

779-782 A266 Set of 4 13.50 6.00

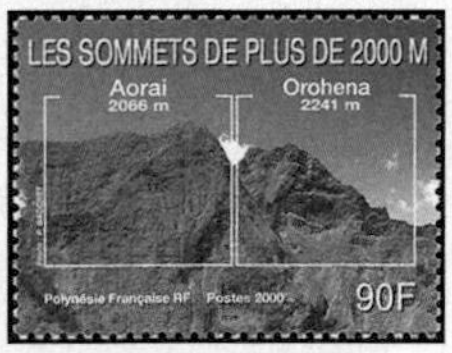

Mountains A267

Designs: 90fr, Mts. Aorai and Orohena. 180fr, Mts. Orohena and Aorai.

2000, July 10 ***Perf. 13x13¼***

783-784 A267 Set of 2 6.00 2.60

Traditional Sports A268

120fr, Fruit carrying. 250fr, Stone lifting, vert.

Perf. 13x13¼, 13¼x13

2000, Sept. 15

785-786 A268 Set of 2 8.25 3.50

Native Woven Crafts A269

No. 787, Fans. No. 788, Hat.

2000, Oct. 3 Litho. ***Perf. 13x13¼***

787-788 A269 85fr Set of 2 3.75 1.75

Year of Ancient Tahitian Language Reo Ma'ohi A270

2000, Nov. 9 Litho. ***Perf. 13x13¼***

789 A270 120fr multi 2.75 1.20

Portions of the design were applied by a thermographic process producing a shiny, raised effect.

Advent of New Millennium — A271

2000, Dec. 28

790 A271 85fr multi 1.90 .90

Central School, Cent. — A272

Designs: No. 791, 85fr, Central School. No. 792, 85fr, Paul Gauguin High School.

2001, Jan. 16

791-792 A272 Set of 2 3.75 1.75

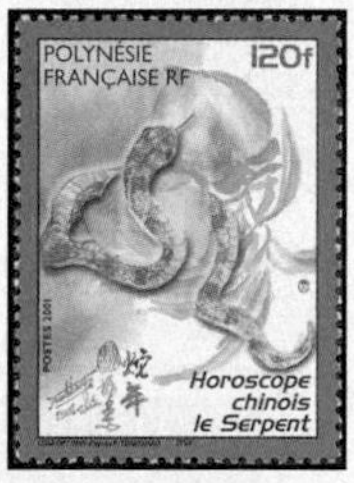

New Year 2001 (Year of the Snake) — A273

2001, Jan. 24 ***Perf. 13¼x13***

793 A273 120fr multi 2.75 1.20

Portions of the design were applied by a thermographic process producing a shiny, raised effect.

Landscapes A274

Designs: 35fr, Vaiharuru Waterfall. 50fr, Vahiria Lake, horiz. 90fr, Hakaui Valley.

Perf. 13¼x13, 13x13¼

2001, Feb. 26 **Litho.**

794-796 A274 Set of 3 4.00 1.75

Year of the Polynesian Child — A275

2001, Mar. 28 Litho. ***Perf. 13x13¼***

797 A275 55fr multi 1.25 .55

Polynesian Singers — A276

Designs: 85fr, Eddie Lund. 120fr, Charley Mauu. 130fr, Bimbo. 180fr, Marie Mariteragi and Emma Terangi, horiz.

2001, Apr. 12 ***Perf. 13¼x13, 13x13¼***

798-801 A276 Set of 4 11.50 5.00

Volunteers of the Pacific Batallion, 60th Anniv. A277

2001, Apr. 21 ***Perf. 13x13¼***

802 A277 85fr multi 1.90 .90

Surfing Waves of Teahupoo A278

2001, May 4

803 A278 120fr multi 2.75 1.20

Internal Autonomy, 17th Anniv. A279

2001, June 29 Litho. ***Perf. 13***

804 A279 250fr multi 5.50 2.50
a. Souvenir sheet of 1 11.00 11.00

No. 804a sold for 500fr.

Pirogue Racing — A280

Designs: 85fr, Male racers. 120fr, Female racers.

2001, July 12 ***Perf. 13¼x13***

805-806 A280 Set of 2 4.50 2.00
a. Souvenir sheet, #805-806, imperf. 5.50 5.50

No. 806a sold for 250fr.

Hardwood Trees A281

Designs: 90fr, Tou. 130fr, Ati. 180fr, Miro.

2001, Oct. 23 Litho. ***Perf. 13x13½***

807-809 A281 Set of 3 9.00 8.00

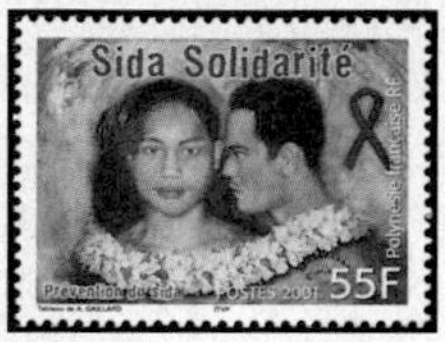

AIDS Prevention A282

2001, Sept. 20 Litho. ***Perf. 13x13¼***

810 A282 55fr multi 2.50 1.10

Year of Dialogue Among Civilizations A283

2001, Oct. 9 ***Perf. 13***

811 A283 500fr multi 11.50 10.00

Perfume Flowers — A284

Designs: 35fr, Gardenia tahitensis. 50fr, Fagraea berteriana. 85fr, Gardenia jasminoides.

2001, Nov. 8 ***Perf. 13¼x13***

812-814 A284 Set of 3 4.25 3.50

Portions of the designs were applied by a thermographic process producing a shiny, raised effect.

Christmas A285

2001, Dec. 6 ***Perf. 13x13¼***

815 A285 120fr multi 2.75 2.40

New Year 2002 (Year of the Horse) A286

2002, Feb. 12 Litho. ***Perf. 13x13¼***

816 A286 130fr multi 2.90 2.60

Portions of the design were applied by a thermographic process producing a shiny, raised effect.

Happy Holidays A287

Greetings A288

2002, Feb. 28 Background Colors

817	A287	55fr red	1.25	1.10
818	A288	55fr blue	1.25	1.10
819	A287	85fr blue	1.90	1.75
820	A288	85fr green	1.90	1.75
		Nos. 817-820 (4)	6.30	5.70

10th World Outrigger Canoe Championships — A289

Canoe rowers and emblems: 120fr, 180fr.

2002, Mar. 9 Photo. ***Perf. 13¼***

821-822 A289 Set of 2 6.75 6.25

Sea Urchins A290

Designs: 35fr, Echinometra sp. 50fr, Heterocentrotus trigonarius. 90fr, Echinothrix calamaris. 120fr, Toxopneustes sp.

2002, Apr. 18 Litho. ***Perf. 13x13¼***

823-826 A290 Set of 4 6.50 6.25

Blood Donation — A291

2002, May 3 Litho. ***Perf. 13¼x13***

827 A291 130fr multi 3.25 3.25

2002 World Cup Soccer Championships, Japan and Korea — A292

2002, May 30

828 A292 85fr multi 1.90 1.75

Traditional Sports — A293

Designs: 85fr, Coconut husking. 120fr, Fruit carrying. 250fr, Javelin throwing.

2002, June 27

829-831 A293 Set of 3 10.00 9.00

House of James Norman Hall — A294

2002, July 4 ***Perf. 13x13¼***

832 A294 90fr multi 2.00 1.90

Papeete Market — A295

2002, Aug. 30 Litho. ***Perf. 13***

833 A295 400fr multi 8.75 8.00

a. Souvenir sheet of 1 11.00 11.00

Amphilex 2002 Stamp Exhibition, Amsterdam (#833a). No. 833a sold for 500fr.

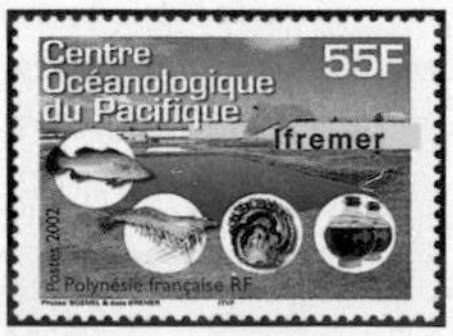

Pacific Oceanology Center, Vairoa A296

Designs: 55fr, Research pond, fish, shrimp, oyster, and flasks. 90fr, Aeriel view of center, fish, shrimp and oyster.

2002, Sept. 26 Photo. ***Perf. 13¼***

834-835 A296 Set of 2 3.50 2.40

Taapuna Master 2002 Surfing Competition A297

2002, Oct. 21 Litho. ***Perf. 13x13¼***

836 A297 120fr multi 2.75 2.00

Halophilic Flowers A298

Designs: 85fr, Hibiscus tiliaceus. 130fr, Scaveola sericea. 180fr, Guettarda speciosa.

2002, Nov. 7

837-839 A298 Set of 3 8.75 6.75

Polynesians at Festivals A299

Designs: 55fr, Dancers and bus. 120fr, Musicians, vert.

2002, Dec. 5 ***Perf. 13x13¼, 13¼x13***

840-841 A299 Set of 2 3.75 3.00

New Year 2003 (Year of the Ram) — A300

2003, Feb. 1 Litho. ***Perf. 13¼x13***

842 A300 120fr multi 2.75 2.25

Portions of the design was applied by a thermographic process producing a shiny, raised effect.

Polynesian Women — A301

2003, Mar. 8 Litho. ***Perf. 13¼x13***

843 A301 55fr multi 1.25 1.00

Waterfalls — A302

2003, Apr. 10 ***Perf. 13***

844 A302 330fr multi 7.25 6.00

Old Papeete A303

Designs: 55fr, Automobiles and buildings, vert. 85fr, Ship in harbor. 90fr, People with bicycles in front of buildings (50x28mm). 120fr, Tree-lined street (50x28mm).

Perf. 13¼x13, 13x13¼, 13

2003, May 15

845-848 A303 Set of 4 7.75 7.00

848a Souvenir sheet, #845-848 12.00 12.00

No. 848a sold for 550fr.

Fish — A304

2003, June 12 Litho. ***Perf. 13***

849 A304 460fr multi 9.00 9.00

Portions of the design were applied by a thermographic process producing a shiny, raised effect.

Outrigger Canoes A305

Designs: No. 850, 85fr, shown. No. 851, 85fr, Three sailors on canoe at sea. No. 852, 85fr, Three sailors on canoe, vert. No. 853, 85fr, Sailor sitting on outrigger, vert.

Perf. 13x13¼, 13¼x13

2003, July 11 **Litho.**

850-853 A305 Set of 4 7.50 6.50

Firewalkers A306

Orange-banded Cowrie — A307

2003, Aug. 14 Photo. ***Perf. 13¼***

854 A306 130fr multi 2.50 2.50

Perf. 13x13¼

855 A307 420fr multi 8.50 8.50

Are You Jealous? by Paul Gauguin (1848-1903) — A308

2003, Sept. 11 ***Perf. 13x12¼***

856 A308 250fr multi 5.00 5.00

Office of Posts and Telecommunications Emblem — A308a

Type I: "Postes 2003" at right.
Type II: "Postes" only at right.

Serpentine Die Cut 6½ Vert.

2003, Oct. 1 **Engr.**

Booklet Stamp
Self-Adhesive

856A A308a (60fr) blue (type II, *2006*   *1.25 1.25*
- *b.* Booklet pane of 10   *12.50*
- *c.* Type I   *25.00 25.00*
- *d.* As "c," booklet pane of 10   *250.00*
- *e.* As #856A, inscribed "Phil@poste"   1.40 1.40
- *f.* Booklet pane of 10 #856Ae   14.00

Issued: No. 856Ac, 10/1/03. No. 856A, 2006. No. 856Ae, 2007 (?).
See No. 869.

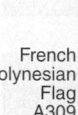

French Polynesian Flag A309

2003, Oct. 1 **Litho.** ***Perf. 13x13¼***
857 A309 (60fr) multi   1.25 1.25

Tiki — A310

2003, Oct. 1 ***Perf. 13¼x13***
858 A310 100fr multi   2.00 2.00

Reissued in 2006 on shiny paper with much deeper colors. Values the same.

Flowers A311

Designs: 90fr, Orchid. 130fr, Rose de porcelain (torch ginger).

2003, Oct. 4 **Litho.** ***Perf. 13x13¼***
859-860 A311 Set of 2   4.50 4.50

Portions of the designs were applied by a thermographic process producing a shiny, raised effect.

Bora Bora A312

Designs: No. 861, 60fr, Painting of Bora Bora by A. Van Der Heyde. No. 862, 60fr, Aerial photograph of Bora Bora.

2003, Nov. 6 **Litho.** ***Perf. 13x13¼***
861-862 A312 Set of 2   2.75 2.75

Tiki — A313

2003, Dec. 6 ***Perf. 13***
863 A313 190fr multi   4.00 4.00

Buildings and Palm Trees A314

2003, Dec. 19 ***Perf. 13x13¼***
864 A314 90fr multi   1.90 1.90

New Year 2004 (Year of the Monkey) — A315

2004, Jan. 22 **Litho.** ***Perf. 13¼x13***
865 A315 130fr multi   3.50 3.50

A portion of the design was applied by a thermographic process producing a shiny, raised effect.

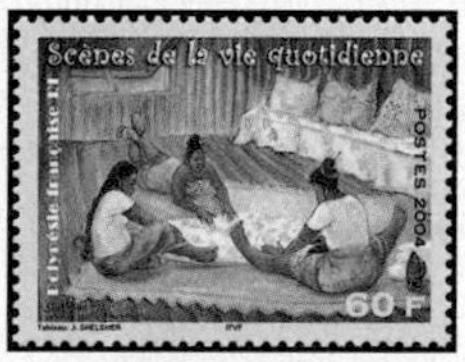

Scenes From Everyday Life A316

Designs: 60fr, Women working with cloth. 90fr, Street scene, vert.

Perf. 13x13¼, 13¼x13

2004, Feb. 13 **Litho.**
866-867 A316 Set of 2   3.25 3.25

Polynesian Woman — A317

2004, Mar. 8 ***Perf. 13¼x13***
868 A317 90fr multi   2.00 1.90

Post Emblem Type of 2003

Serpentine Die Cut 6½ Vert.

2004, Apr. 22 **Engr.**

Booklet Stamp
Self-Adhesive

869 A308a (90fr) red   *7.50 2.00*
- *a.* Booklet pane of 10   *75.00*

No. 869 lacks year date.

Polynesian Economic Development — A318

2004, Apr. 23 **Litho.** ***Perf. 13x12¾***
870 A318 500fr multi   11.00 10.00

Arahurahu Marae, Paea — A319

2004, Apr. 23
871 A319 500fr multi   11.00 10.00

Vanilla — A320

2004, May 14 ***Perf. 13¼x13***
872 A320 90fr multi   1.90 1.90

No. 872 is impregnated with a vanilla scent.

Mobile Snack Bars — A321

2004, May 28 ***Perf. 13x12¾***
873 A321 300fr multi   6.50 6.25

Handicrafts A322

Designs: No. 874, 60fr, Artisan braiding fibers. No. 875, 60fr, Mother-of-pearl carving. No. 876, 90fr, Artisan carving statue. No. 877, 90fr, Hat.

2004, June 26 ***Perf. 13x13¼***
874-877 A322 Set of 4   7.00 6.25

Portion of the designs were applied by a thermographic process producing a shiny, raised effect.

Involvement in South Pacific Area of Office of Posts and Telecommunications — A323

Designs: 100fr, Earth, Sun on horizon. 130fr, Satellite dish, building.

2004, July 23 **Photo.** ***Perf. 13¼***
878-879 A323 Set of 2   5.00 4.75

Information Technology and Communications A324

Designs: No. 880, 190fr, Computer keyboard, "@." No. 881, 190fr, Satellite, satellite dish.

2004, Sept. 23 **Litho.** ***Perf. 13¼x13***
880-881 A324 Set of 2   8.00 8.00

Omai, Polynesian Capt. James Cook Brought to England — A325

2004, Oct. 14 ***Perf. 13***
882 A325 250fr multi   5.25 5.25

Shell Collectors A326

2004, Nov. 10 **Photo.** ***Perf. 13¼***
883 A326 60fr multi   1.40 1.40

A souvenir sheet of one sold for 250fr.

Adenium Obesum A327

Alpinia Purpurata A328

Ixora Chinensis A329

Gardenia Taitensis A330

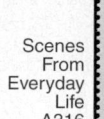

Heliconia Psittacorum — A331

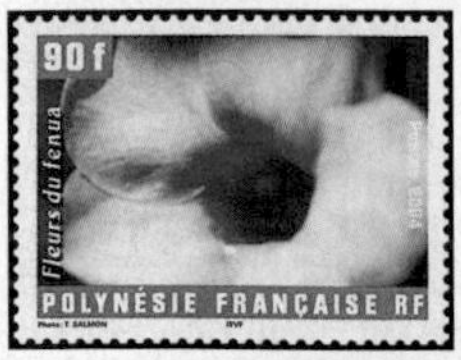

Allamanda Blanchetii A332

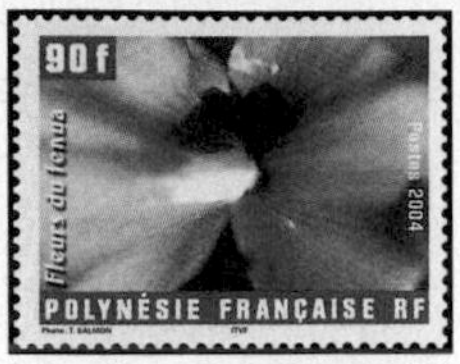

Otacanthus Caeruleus — A333

Hibiscus Rosa-sinensis — A334

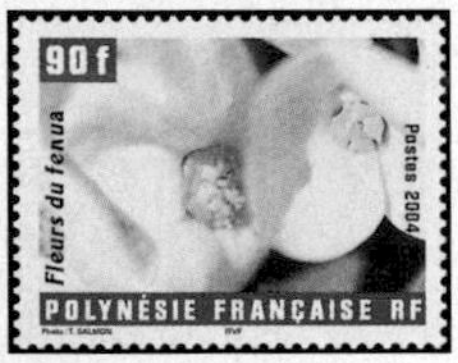

Euphorba Milii A335

Asocenda Hybrid of Vanda x Ascocentrum — A336

Mussaenda Erythrophylia — A337

Bougainvillea Glabra — A338

2004, Nov. 10 Litho. *Perf. 13x13¼*

884	Booklet pane of 6	15.00	—
a.	A327 90fr multi	2.50	2.50
b.	A328 90fr multi	2.50	2.50
c.	A329 90fr multi	2.50	2.50
d.	A330 90fr multi	2.50	2.50
e.	A331 90fr multi	2.50	2.50
f.	A332 90fr multi	2.50	2.50
885	Booklet pane of 6	15.00	—
a.	A333 90fr multi	2.50	2.50
b.	A334 90fr multi	2.50	2.50
c.	A335 90fr multi	2.50	2.50
d.	A336 90fr multi	2.50	2.50
e.	A337 90fr multi	2.50	2.50
f.	A338 90fr multi	2.50	2.50
	Complete booklet, #884-885	30.00	

Complete booklet sold for 1200fr.

Christmas A339

2004, Dec. 17
886 A339 60fr multi 1.40 1.40

A portion of the design was applied by a thermographic process producing a shiny, raised effect.

Bamboo — A340

2005, Feb. 9 *Perf. 13¼x13*
887 A340 130fr multi 3.00 3.00

New Year 2005. A portion of the design was applied by a thermographic process producing a shiny, raised effect.

People and Hut A341

2005, Feb. 25 *Perf. 13x13¼*
888 A341 90fr multi 2.00 2.00

Polynesian Women — A342

Designs: 60fr, Woman wearing lei. 90fr, Woman wearing flower garland on head and robe.

2005, Mar. 8 *Perf. 13¼x13*
889-890 A342 Set of 2 3.50 3.50

Woman Making Tapa Cloth — A343

2005, Apr. 22 *Perf. 13*
891 A343 250fr multi 5.50 5.50

Tifaifai A344

2005, Mar. 23 Litho. *Perf. 13x13¼*
892 A344 5fr multi .25 .20

Angelfish A345

Designs: No. 893, 90fr, Centropyge bispinosa. No. 894, 90fr, Centropyge loricula. No. 895, 130fr, Centropyge heraldi. No. 896, 130fr, Centropyge flavissima.

2005, May 27 Litho. *Perf. 13x13¼*
893-896 A345 Set of 4 9.00 9.00
896a Souvenir sheet, #893-896 9.00 9.00

Portions of the designs were applied by a thermographic process producing a shiny, raised effect.

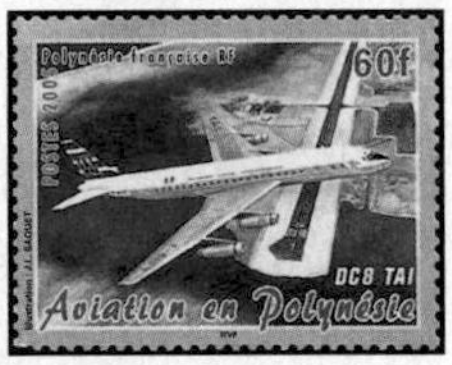

Historic Airplanes A346

Designs: No. 897, 60fr, TAI DC-8, first jet in Tahiti, 1961. No. 898, 60fr, Pan American Boeing 707, first foreign flight, 1963. No. 899, 100fr, Air France Boeing 707, first Air France flight to Tahiti, 1973. No. 900, 100fr, Air Tahiti Nui Airbus A340-300, first Tahitian airline, 2000.

2005, June 24
897-900 A346 Set of 4 6.50 6.50

Musical Instruments A347

Designs: No. 901, 130fr, Drum. No. 902, 130fr, Nose flutes, horiz.

2005, July 22 *Perf. 13¼x13, 13x13¼*
901-902 A347 Set of 2 5.50 5.50

Polynesian Landscapes — A348

2005, Aug. 26 *Perf. 13*
903 A348 300fr multi 6.25 6.25

Pineapples A349

Designs: 90fr, Close-up of spines. 130fr, Entire fruit.

2005, Sept. 23 Litho. *Perf. 13¼x13*
904-905 A349 Set of 2 4.50 4.50

Nos. 904-905 are impregnated with pineapple scent.

Marae — A350

Marquesan Tohua — A351

2005, Oct. 21 *Perf. 13*
906 A350 500fr multi 10.00 10.00
907 A351 500fr multi 10.00 10.00

Autonomy, 20th Anniv. (in 2004) — A352

2005, Nov. 10 *Perf. 13¼x13*
908 A352 60fr multi 1.75 1.75

No. 908 was printed in France and distributed there in June 2004 but was not sold in French Polynesia until 2005, where it was available from the philatelic bureau upon request, and not through standing orders.

O'Parrey Harbor, Tahiti A353

2005, Nov. 10 Engr. *Perf. 13x12½*
909 A353 100fr multi 2.00 2.00

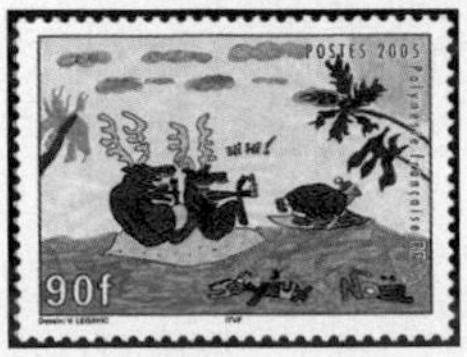

Christmas A354

2005, Dec. 16 Litho. *Perf. 13x13¼*
910 A354 90fr multi 2.00 2.00

Lotus Flower A355

Litho. & Silk-screened

2006, Jan. 30 *Perf. 13x13¼*
911 A355 130fr multi 2.60 2.60

A356

Hearts A357

2006, Feb. 14 Photo. *Perf. 13*
912 A356 60fr multi 1.25 1.25
913 A357 90fr multi 1.90 1.90

Values are for stamps with surrounding selvage.

Polynesian Women — A358

Woman: 60fr, At water's edge. 90fr, With oil lamp.

2006, Mar. 8 Litho. *Perf. 13¼x13*
914-915 A358 Set of 2 3.25 3.25

Maupiti — A359

2006, Apr. 26 Engr. *Perf. 13x13¼*
916 A359 500fr multi 11.00 11.00

History of the Marquesas (Washington) Islands — A360

Designs: 60fr, Native man and woman. 130fr, Ships.

2006, May 27 Litho. *Perf. 13¼x13*
917-918 A360 Set of 2 4.00 4.00
918a Souvenir sheet, #917-918 4.00 4.00

Diners and Musicians — A361

2006, June 6 *Perf. 13*
919 A361 300fr multi 6.50 6.50

Polynesian Ground Dove A362

Tuamotu Sandpiper A363

2006, June 21 *Perf. 13x13¼*
920 A362 250fr multi 5.25 5.25
921 A363 250fr multi 5.25 5.25

Heiva — A364

Designs: 90fr, Canoe race. 130fr, Stone lifting. 190fr, Dancer.

2006, July 19 *Perf. 13¼x13*
922-924 A364 Set of 3 8.75 8.75

Frangipani Flowers A365

2006, Aug. 23 Litho. *Perf. 13x13½*
925 A365 90fr multi 1.90 1.90

No. 925 is impregnated with frangipani scent.

A366

World Tourism Day A367

Designs: 40fr, Ruins. No. 927, 90fr, Waterfall, woman and child. 130fr, Clothing at open-air market.

No. 929: a, Dancers with yellow skirts. b, Surfer. c, House and palm tree. d, Pearls. e, Fish and coral. f, Islanders in outrigger canoes.

No. 930: a, Woman in hammock. b, Stilt houses. c, Tower and boats. d, Horses and riders. e, Aerial view of island. f, Diver and sting ray.

2006, Sept. 22 *Perf. 13¼x13*
926-928 A366 Set of 3 5.50 5.50

Booklet Stamps

Perf. 13x13¼

929 Booklet pane of 6 12.50 —
a.-f. A367 90fr Any single 2.00 2.00
930 Booklet pane of 6 12.50 —
a.-f. A367 90fr Any single 2.00 2.00
Complete booklet, #929-930 25.00

Complete booklet sold for 1200fr.

Paintings A368

Designs: 60fr, Javelin Throwing, by Monique Garnier Bissol. 90fr, Market Life, by Albert Luzuy, horiz. 100fr, Island Quay, by Gilbert Chaussoy, horiz. 190fr, Vahine, by Olivier Louzé.

2006, Oct. 25 *Perf. 13*
931-934 A368 Set of 4 9.50 9.50

Engravings by Paul Gauguin (1848-1903) — A369

Engravings depicting: 60fr, Women. 130fr, Cow and man carrying items on stick.

2006, Nov. 8 Engr. *Perf. 13¼*
935-936 A369 Set of 2 4.25 4.25

Children's Art A370

2006, Dec. 13 Litho. *Perf. 13x13¼*
937 A370 90fr multi 2.00 2.00

Beach Gear — A371

Designs: 60fr, Flip-flops. 90fr, Surfboards.

Serpentine Die Cut 11x11¼

2007 Photo.

Self-Adhesive

938 A371 60fr multicolored 1.25 1.25
a. Blue tips of die cutting along left side 1.25 1.25
939 A371 90fr multicolored 2.00 2.00
a. Light blue tips of die cutting along bottom 2.00 2.00

Issued: Nos. 938a, 939a, 1/24; Nos. 938-939, Feb. Nos. 938a and 939a are from the original printing, and are from sheets having adjacent stamps and die cutting that does not extend through the backing paper. Nos. 938-939, which were distributed to the philatelic trade, are from sheets with selvage around each stamp, and with rouletting that extends through the backing paper that allows the stamps to be removed from the sheet more easily.

New Year 2007 (Year of the Pig) A372

2007, Feb. 19 Litho. *Perf. 13x13¼*
940 A372 130fr multi 3.00 3.00

Portions of the design were applied by a thermographic process producing a shiny, raised effect.

Painting of Polynesian Woman by Mathius — A373

Photograph of Polynesian Woman by John Stember — A374

2007, Mar. 8 Litho. *Perf. 13¼x13*
941 A373 60fr multi 1.40 1.40

Perf. 13x13¼

942 A374 90fr multi 2.00 2.00

Audit Office, Bicent. A375

2007, Mar. 17 Engr. *Perf. 13¼x13*
943 A375 90fr multi 2.00 2.00

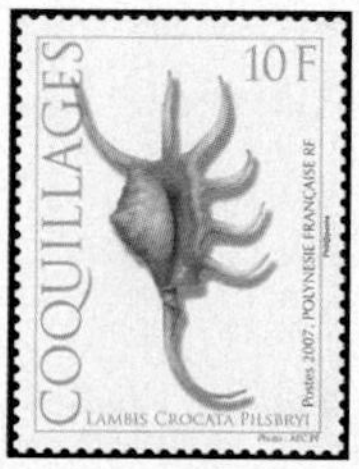

Shells — A376

Designs: 10fr, Lambis crocata pilsbryi. 60fr, Cypraea thomasi. 90fr, Cyrtulus serotinus. 130fr, Chicoreus laqueatus.

2007, Apr. 25 Litho.
944-947 A376 Set of 4 6.75 6.75
947a Souvenir sheet, #944-947 6.75 6.75

Coconut A377

2007, May 23 ***Perf. 13x13¼***
948 A377 90fr multi 2.00 2.00

No. 948 is impregnated with a coconut scent.

Ships — A378

Designs: No. 949, 250fr, Gunboat Zélée. No. 950, 250fr, Passenger and cargo liner Sagittaire.

2007, June 22 ***Perf. 13***
949-950 A378 Set of 2 11.50 11.50

Heiva Festival — A379

Various women dancers: 65fr, 100fr, 140fr.

2007, July 4 ***Perf. 13¼x13***
951-953 A379 Set of 3 7.00 7.00

Arrival of Kon-Tiki Expedition in Polynesia, 60th Anniv. — A380

Litho. & Silk-screened

2007, Aug. 7 ***Perf. 13***
954 A380 300fr multi 7.00 7.00

Arrival of Ship at Papeete Dock — A381

2007, Aug. 29 **Litho.** ***Perf. 13***
955 A381 190fr multi 4.50 4.50

Old and Modern Photos of Papeete — A382

Designs: 65fr, Rue Gauguin, 2007. 100fr, Rue de la Petite-Pologne (now Rue Gauguin), 1907.

2007, Sept. 26
956-957 A382 Set of 2 4.00 4.00

Old Franc and Centime Notes — A383

Designs: 65fr, 1919 2-franc Chamber of Commerce note. 140fr, 1942 2-franc note. 500fr, 1943 50-centime note.

2007, Oct. 26 **Engr.** ***Perf. 13***
958-960 A383 Set of 3 17.00 17.00

Flowers A384

Designs: 100fr, Hibiscus. 140fr, Bird-of-paradise (Oiseaux de paradis).

Litho. & Silk-screened

2007, Nov. 8 ***Perf. 13x13¼***
961-962 A384 Set of 2 6.00 6.00

Christmas A385

2007, Dec. 6 **Litho.** ***Perf. 13x13¼***
963 A385 100fr multi 2.50 2.50

Marine Life A386

Designs: 10fr, Himantura fai. 20fr, Tursiops truncatus. 40fr, Megaptera novaeangliae. 65fr, Negaprion acutidens.

2008, Jan. 10
964-967 A386 Set of 4 3.50 3.50

New Year 2008 (Year of the Rat) — A387

2008, Feb. 7 **Photo.** ***Perf. 13¼x13***
968 A387 140fr multi 3.75 3.75

Paintings of Women by Bénilde Menghini — A388

Designs: 65fr, Woman picking mangos. 100fr, Women scaling fish.

2008, Mar. 7 **Litho.**
969-970 A388 Set of 2 4.25 4.25

Paintings by Polynesian Artists A389

Unnamed paintings depicting: No. 971, 100fr, Boat and reef, by Torea Chan. No. 972, 100fr, Polynesian man, by Raymond Vigor. No. 973, 100fr, Fruit bowl, by Teurarea Prokop, horiz.

2008, Apr. 10 ***Perf. 13x13¼, 13¼x13***
971-973 A389 Set of 3 8.00 8.00

Pouvanaa a Oopa (1895-1977), Politician — A390

2008, May 20 **Litho.** ***Perf. 13***
974 A390 500fr multi 13.00 13.00

Island Touring Vehicles — A391

Designs: 65fr, Motor scooter. 100fr, Bus, horiz.

Serpentine Die Cut 11

2008, June 12 **Photo.**

Self-Adhesive

975-976 A391 Set of 2 4.25 4.25

Heiva Festival A392

Designs: 65fr, Woman with floral headdress. 140fr, Tattooed man. 190fr, Girl dancing.

2008, July 16 **Litho.** ***Perf. 13***
977-979 A392 Set of 3 10.00 10.00

Sports — A393

Designs: No. 980, 140fr, Table tennis. No. 981, 140fr, Weight lifting.

2008, Aug. 8 **Litho.** ***Perf. 13¼x13***
980-981 A393 Set of 2 7.00 7.00

End of Tahiti Nui Expedition, 50th Anniv. — A394

2008, Aug. 29 **Litho.** ***Perf. 13***
982 A394 190fr multi 4.50 4.50

Eric de Bisschop (1890-1958), expedition leader.

Polynesian Scenes A395

No. 983: a, Woman crouching. b, Woman under shelter. c, Boat in bay near cliffs. d, Orange flowers. e, Red hibiscus flower. f, Island. g, Woman with headdress. h, White flower. i, Woman with headdress and flower garland. j, Pink flower. k, Islands. l, Bay near mountains.

Serpentine Die Cut 11¼x11

2008, Sept. 8

Self-Adhesive

983 Booklet pane of 12 29.00
a.-d. A395 65fr Any single 1.50 1.50
e.-h. A395 100fr Any single 2.40 2.40
i.-l. A395 140fr Any single 3.25 3.25

Gardenia Taitensis in Bottle of Monoi Oil — A396

2008, Sept. 17 ***Perf. 13¼x13***
984 A396 100fr multi 2.40 2.40

No. 984 is impregnated with a gardenia scent.

Aviation Anniversaries — A397

Designs: No. 985, 250fr, Air service between France and French Polynesia, 50th anniv. No. 986, 250fr, Air Tahiti Nui, 10th anniv.

2008, Oct. 15 Litho. *Perf. 13*
985-986 A397 Set of 2 11.00 11.00

French Polynesia Postage Stamps, 50th Anniv. — A398

Designs: 65fr, French Polynesia #185. 100fr, Vignette of French Polynesia #C24. 140fr, French Polynesia #J29.

2008, Nov. 6 Engr. *Perf. 13*
987-989 A398 Set of 3 6.75 6.75

SEMI-POSTAL STAMPS

Nos. 55 and 26 Surcharged in Red

1915 Unwmk. *Perf. 14x13½*
B1 A1 10c + 5c red 22.50 22.50
a. "e" instead of "c" 57.50 57.50
b. Inverted surcharge 160.00 160.00
B2 A2 10c + 5c rose & org 7.50 7.50
a. "e" instead of "c" 40.00 40.00
b. "c" inverted 47.50 47.50
c. Inverted surcharge 225.00 225.00

Surcharged in Carmine

B3 A2 10c + 5c rose & org 3.25 3.25
a. "e" instead of "c" 25.00 25.00
b. Inverted surcharge 150.00 150.00

Surcharged in Carmine

1916
B4 A2 10c + 5c rose & org 3.25 3.25

Curie Issue
Common Design Type

1938 Engr. *Perf. 13*
B5 CD80 1.75fr + 50c brt ultra 14.00 14.00

French Revolution Issue
Common Design Type

1939 Photo.
Name and Value Typo. in Black
B6 CD83 45c + 25c grn 14.00 14.00
B7 CD83 70c + 30c brn 14.00 14.00
B8 CD83 90c + 35c red org 14.00 14.00
B9 CD83 1.25fr + 1fr rose pink 14.00 14.00
B10 CD83 2.25fr + 2fr blue 14.00 14.00
Nos. B6-B10 (5) 70.00 70.00
Set, never hinged 120.00

Catalogue values for unused stamps in this section, from this point to the end of the section, are for Never Hinged items.

Common Design Type and

Marine Officer — SP1

"L'Astrolabe" — SP2

1941 Photo. *Perf. 13½*
B11 SP1 1fr + 1fr red 2.50
B12 CD86 1.50fr + 3fr maroon 2.50
B12A SP2 2.50fr + 1fr blue 2.50
Nos. B11-B12A (3) 7.50

Nos. B11-B12A were issued by the Vichy government in France, and were not placed on sale in French Polynesia.

Nos. 125A-125B Surcharged in Black or Red

1944 Engr. *Perf. 12½x12*
B12B 50c + 1.50fr on 2.50fr deep blue (R) 1.25
B12C + 2.50fr on 1fr green 1.50

Colonial Development Fund.

Nos. B12B-B12C were issued by the Vichy government in France, but were not placed on sale in French Polynesia.

Red Cross Issue
Common Design Type

1944 Photo. *Perf. 14½x14*
B13 CD90 5fr + 20fr peacock blue 1.60 1.10

The surtax was for the French Red Cross and national relief.

Tropical Medicine Issue
Common Design Type

1950, July 17 Engr. *Perf. 13*
B14 CD100 10fr + 2fr dk bl grn & dk grn 9.00 5.75

The surtax was for charitable work.

AIR POST STAMPS

Seaplane in Flight AP1

Perf. 13½
1934, Nov. 5 Unwmk. Photo.
C1 AP1 5fr green .75 .75

For overprint see No. C2.
For Type AP1 without "RF," see Nos. C1A-C1D.

Type of 1934 without "RF" and

Beach Scene — AP1a

Perf. 13½, 13 (#C1E)
1944 Photo, Engr. (#C1E)
C1A AP1 5fr green .60
C1B AP1 10fr black .90
C1C AP1 20fr orange .95
C1D AP1 50fr gray blue 1.25
C1E AP1a 100fr turquoise blue 3.00
Nos. C1A-C1E (5) 6.70

Nos. C1A-C1E were issued by the Vichy government in France, but were not placed on sale in French Polynesia.

Catalogue values for unused stamps in this section, from this point to the end of the section, are for Never Hinged items.

No. C1 Overprinted in Red

1941
C2 AP1 5fr green 3.75 3.00

Common Design Type

1942 *Perf. 14½x14*
C3 CD87 1fr dark orange .75 .50
C4 CD87 1.50fr bright red .75 .60
C5 CD87 5fr brown red 1.00 .80
C6 CD87 10fr black 1.50 1.10
C7 CD87 25fr ultra 2.25 1.60
C8 CD87 50fr dark green 2.25 1.60
C9 CD87 100fr plum 2.25 1.60
Nos. C3-C9 (7) 10.75 7.80

Victory Issue
Common Design Type

1946, May 8 Engr. *Perf. 12½*
C10 CD92 8fr dark green 2.25 1.60

Chad to Rhine Issue
Common Design Types

1946, June 6
C11 CD93 5fr red orange 1.75 1.50
C12 CD94 10fr dk olive bis 1.75 1.50
C13 CD95 15fr dk yellow grn 1.75 1.50
C14 CD96 20fr carmine 2.25 1.75
C15 CD97 25fr dk rose violet 3.00 2.50
C16 CD98 50fr black 3.50 3.00
Nos. C11-C16 (6) 14.00 11.75

Shearwater and Moorea Landscape — AP2

Fishermen — AP3

Shearwater over Maupiti Shoreline — AP4

1948, Mar. 1 Unwmk. *Perf. 13*
C17 AP2 50fr red brown 21.00 8.75
C18 AP3 100fr purple 17.50 5.75
C19 AP4 200fr blue green 37.50 15.00
Nos. C17-C19 (3) 76.00 29.50

UPU Issue
Common Design Type

1949
C20 CD99 10fr deep blue 14.50 11.50

Gauguin's "Nafea faaipoipo" — AP5

1953, Sept. 24
C21 AP5 14fr dk brn, dk gray grn & red 62.50 50.00

50th anniv. of the death of Paul Gauguin.

Liberation Issue
Common Design Type

1954, June 6
C22 CD102 3fr dk grnsh bl & bl grn 7.50 5.75

Bahia Peak, Borabora — AP6

1955, Sept. 26 Unwmk. *Perf. 13*
C23 AP6 13fr indigo & blue 8.00 4.00

Mother-of-Pearl Artist — AP7

Designs: 50fr, "Women of Tahiti," Gauguin, horiz. 100fr, "The White Horse," Gauguin. 200fr, Night fishing at Moorea, horiz.

1958, Nov. 3 Engr. *Perf. 13*
C24 AP7 13fr multicolored 14.00 4.00
C25 AP7 50fr multicolored 13.50 4.00
C26 AP7 100fr multicolored 22.50 6.75
C27 AP7 200fr lilac & slate 45.00 21.00
Nos. C24-C27 (4) 95.00 35.75

Airport, Papeete — AP8

1960, Nov. 19
C28 AP8 13fr rose lil, vio, & yel grn 3.50 2.40

Telstar Issue
Common Design Type

1962, Dec. 5 *Perf. 13*
C29 CD111 50fr red lil, mar & vio bl 12.50 8.00

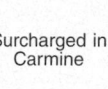

Tahitian Dancer — AP10

1964, May 14 Photo. *Perf. 13*

C30 AP10 15fr multicolored 5.25 2.00

Map of Tahiti and Free French Emblems — AP11

1964, July 10 Unwmk.

C31 AP11 16fr multicolored 17.50 9.00

Issued to commemorate the rallying of French Polynesia to the Free French cause.

Moorea Scene — AP12

1964, Dec. 1 Litho. *Perf. 13*

C32 AP12 23fr multicolored 10.50 4.00

ITU Issue

Common Design Type

1965, May 17 Engr. *Perf. 13*

C33 CD120 50fr vio, red brn & bl 100.00 52.50

Paul Gauguin — AP13

Design: 25fr, Gauguin Museum (stylized). 40fr, Primitive statues at Gauguin Museum.

1965 Engr. *Perf. 13*

C34 AP13 25fr olive green 8.75 4.50
C35 AP13 40fr blue green 17.00 8.00
C36 AP13 75fr brt red brown 25.00 15.00
Nos. C34-C36 (3) 50.75 27.50

Opening of Gauguin Museum, Papeete. Issued: 25fr, 75fr, 6/13. 40fr, 11/7.

Skin Diver with Spear Gun — AP14

1965, Sept. 1 Engr. *Perf. 13*

C37 AP14 50fr red brn, dl bl & dk grn 100.00 55.00

World Championships in Underwater Fishing, Tuamotu Archipelago, Sept. 1965.

Painting from a School Dining Room — AP15

Radio Tower, Globe and Palm — AP16

1965, Nov. 29

C38 AP15 80fr brn, bl, dl bl & red 25.00 17.50

School Canteen Program.

1965, Dec. 29 Engr. *Perf. 13*

C39 AP16 60fr org, grn & dk brn 21.00 15.00

50th anniversary of the first radio link between Tahiti and France.

French Satellite A-1 Issue

Common Design Type

Designs: 7fr, Diamant Rocket and launching installations. 10fr, A-1 satellite.

1966, Feb. 7

C40 CD121 7fr choc, dp grn & lil 6.75 6.00
C41 CD121 10fr lil, dp grn & dk brn 6.75 6.00
a. Pair, #C40-C41 + label 16.00 16.00

French Satellite D-1 Issue

Common Design Type

1966, May 10 Engr. *Perf. 13*

C42 CD122 20fr multicolored 8.00 5.00

Papeete Harbor — AP17

1966, June 30 Photo. *Perf. 13*

C43 AP17 50fr multicolored 17.50 11.00

"Vive Tahiti" by A. Benichou — AP18

1966, Nov. 28 Photo. *Perf. 13*

C44 AP18 13fr multicolored 12.50 6.50

Explorer's Ship and Canoe — AP19

Designs: 60fr, Polynesian costume and ship. 80fr, Louis Antoine de Bougainville, vert.

1968, Apr. 6 Engr. *Perf. 13*

C45 AP19 40fr multicolored 8.75 3.25
C46 AP19 60fr multicolored 11.50 6.50
C47 AP19 80fr multicolored 14.50 8.75
a. Souv. sheet, #C45-C47 160.00 160.00
Nos. C45-C47 (3) 34.75 18.50

200th anniv. of the discovery of Tahiti by Louis Antoine de Bougainville. Issued: 40fr, 4/6/68.

The Meal, by Paul Gauguin — AP20

1968, July 30 Photo. *Perf. 12x12½*

C48 AP20 200fr multicolored 45.00 32.50

See #C63-C67, C78-C82, C89-C93, C98.

Shot Put — AP21

PATA 1970 Poster — AP22

1968, Oct. 12 Engr. *Perf. 13*

C49 AP21 35fr dk car rose & brt grn 18.00 9.00

19th Olympic Games, Mexico City, 10/12-27.

Concorde Issue

Common Design Type

1969, Apr. 17

C50 CD129 40fr red brn & car rose 55.00 35.00

1969, July 9 Photo. *Perf. 12½x13*

C51 AP22 25fr blue & multi 21.00 7.25

Issued to publicize PATA 1970 (Pacific Area Travel Association Congress), Tahiti.

Underwater Fishing — AP23

52fr, Hand holding fish made up of flags, vert.

1969, Aug. 5 Photo. *Perf. 13*

C52 AP23 48fr blk, grnsh bl & red lil 42.50 13.50
C53 AP23 52fr bl, blk & red 47.50 22.50

Issued to publicize the World Underwater Fishing Championships.

Gen. Bonaparte as Commander of the Army in Italy, by Jean Sebastien Rouillard — AP24

1969, Oct. 15 Photo. *Perf. 12½x12*

C54 AP24 100fr car & multi 87.50 67.50

Bicentenary of the birth of Napoleon Bonaparte (1769-1821).

Eiffel Tower, Torii and EXPO Emblem — AP25

Pearl Diver Descending, and Basket — AP26

Design: 30fr, Mount Fuji, Tower of the Sun and EXPO emblem, horiz.

1970, Sept. 15 Photo. *Perf. 13*

C55 AP25 30fr multicolored 22.50 8.00
C56 AP25 50fr multicolored 32.50 12.00

EXPO '70 International Exposition, Osaka, Japan, Mar. 15-Sept. 13.

1970, Sept. 30 Engr. *Perf. 13*

Designs: 5fr, Diver collecting oysters. 18fr, Implantation into oyster, horiz. 27fr, Open oyster with pearl. 50fr, Woman with mother of pearl jewelry.

C57 AP26 2fr slate, grnsh bl & red brn 1.50 .90
C58 AP26 5fr grnsh blue, ultra & org 2.75 1.50
C59 AP26 18fr sl, mag & org 3.75 2.75
C60 AP26 27fr brt pink, brn & dl lil 9.25 4.75

C61 AP26 50fr gray, red brn & org 16.00 7.50
Nos. C57-C61 (5) 33.25 17.40

Pearl industry of French Polynesia.

The Thinker, by Auguste Rodin and Education Year Emblem — AP27

1970, Oct. 15 Engr. *Perf. 13*
C62 AP27 50fr bl, ind & fawn 19.00 10.50

International Education Year.

Painting Type of 1968

Paintings by Artists Living in Polynesia: 20fr, Woman on the Beach, by Yves de Saint-Front. 40fr, Abstract, by Frank Fay. 60fr, Woman and Shells, by Jean Guillois. 80fr, Hut under Palms, by Jean Masson. 100fr, Polynesian Girl, by Jean-Charles Bouloc, vert.

Perf. 12x12½, 12½x12

1970, Dec. 14 Photo.
C63 AP20 20fr brn & multi 9.00 4.00
C64 AP20 40fr brn & multi 13.50 7.50
C65 AP20 60fr brn & multi 18.00 11.00
C66 AP20 80fr brn & multi 22.50 16.00
C67 AP20 100fr brn & multi 30.00 22.50
Nos. C63-C67 (5) 93.00 61.00

South Pacific Games Emblem — AP28

1971, Jan. 26 *Perf. 12½*
C68 AP28 20fr ultra & multi 9.00 5.00

Publicity for 4th South Pacific Games, held in Papeete, Sept. 8-19, 1971.

Memorial Flame — AP29

1971, Mar. 19 Photo. *Perf. 12½*
C69 AP29 5fr multicolored 9.50 5.00

In memory of Charles de Gaulle.

Soldier and Badge — AP30

1971, Apr. 21
C70 AP30 25fr multicolored 12.00 6.75

30th anniversary of departure of Tahitian volunteers to serve in World War II.

Water Sports Type

Designs: 15fr, Surfing, vert. 16fr, Skin diving, vert. 20fr, Water-skiing with kite.

1971, May 11 Photo. *Perf. 13*
C71 A44 15fr multicolored 7.00 3.50
C72 A44 16fr multicolored 8.25 3.25
C73 A44 20fr multicolored 12.00 7.75
Nos. C71-C73 (3) 27.25 14.50

Sailing AP31

1971, Sept. 8 *Perf. 12½*
C74 AP31 15fr shown 7.00 3.50
C75 AP31 18fr Golf 8.75 4.75
C76 AP31 27fr Archery 13.50 7.25
C77 AP31 53fr Tennis 22.50 13.50
a. Souv. sheet, #C74-C77 200.00 200.00
Nos. C74-C77 (4) 51.75 29.00

4th So. Pacific Games, Papeete, Sept. 8-19.

Painting Type of 1968

Paintings by Artists Living in Polynesia: 20fr, Hut and Palms, by Isabelle Wolf. 40fr, Palms on Shore, by André Dobrowolski. 60fr, Polynesian Woman, by Françoise Séli, vert. 80fr, Holy Family, by Pierre Heymann, vert. 100fr, Crowd, by Nicolai Michoutouchkine.

1971, Dec. 15 Photo. *Perf. 13*
C78 AP20 20fr multicolored 8.00 4.50
C79 AP20 40fr multicolored 12.50 7.50
C80 AP20 60fr multicolored 15.00 10.00
C81 AP20 80fr multicolored 21.00 12.50
C82 AP20 100fr multicolored 35.00 22.50
Nos. C78-C82 (5) 91.50 57.00

Papeete Harbor — AP32

1972, Jan. 13
C83 AP32 28fr violet & multi 13.50 8.00

Free port of Papeete, 10th anniversary.

Figure Skating and Dragon AP33

1972, Jan. 25 Engr. *Perf. 13*
C84 AP33 20fr ultra, lake & brt grn 11.00 7.00

11th Winter Olympic Games, Sapporo, Japan, Feb. 3-13.

South Pacific Commission Headquarters, Noumea — AP34

1972, Feb. 5 Photo. *Perf. 13*
C85 AP34 21fr blue & multi 13.50 5.25

South Pacific Commission, 25th anniv.

Festival Emblem — AP35

1972, May 9 Engr. *Perf. 13*
C86 AP35 36fr orange, bl & grn 9.00 5.25

So. Pacific Festival of Arts, Fiji, May 6-20.

Kon Tiki and Route, Callao to Tahiti — AP36

1972, Aug. 18 Photo. *Perf. 13*
C87 AP36 16fr dk & lt bl, blk & org 12.00 6.50

25th anniversary of the arrival of the raft Kon Tiki in Tahiti.

Charles de Gaulle and Memorial — AP37

1972, Dec. 9 Engr. *Perf. 13*
C88 AP37 100fr slate 67.50 42.50

Painting Type of 1968

Paintings by Artists Living in Polynesia: 20fr, Horses, by Georges Bovy. 40fr, Sailboats, by Ruy Juventin, vert. 60fr, Harbor, by André Brooke. 80fr, Farmers, by Daniel Adam, vert. 100fr, Dancers, by Aloysius Pilioko, vert.

1972, Dec. 14 Photo.
C89 AP20 20fr gold & multi 9.75 4.25
C90 AP20 40fr gold & multi 12.00 6.75
C91 AP20 60fr gold & multi 21.00 9.50
C92 AP20 80fr dk grn, buff & dk brn 27.50 13.00
C93 AP20 100fr gold & multi 32.50 25.00
Nos. C89-C93 (5) 102.75 58.50

St. Teresa and Lisieux Basilica AP38

1973, Jan. 23 Engr. *Perf. 13*
C94 AP38 85fr multicolored 27.50 17.50

Centenary of the birth of St. Teresa of Lisieux (1873-1897), Carmelite nun.

Nicolaus Copernicus — AP39

1973, Mar. 7 Engr. *Perf. 13*
C95 AP39 100fr brn, vio bl & red lil 35.00 17.50

Copernicus (1473-1543), Polish astronomer.

Plane over Tahiti — AP40

1973, Apr. 3 Photo. *Perf. 13*
C96 AP40 80fr ultra, gold & lt grn 25.00 16.00

Air France's World Tour via Tahiti.

DC-10 at Papeete Airport — AP41

1973, May 18 Engr. *Perf. 13*
C97 AP41 20fr bl, ultra & sl grn 18.50 9.00

Start of DC-10 service.

Painting Type of 1968

Design: 200fr, "Ta Matete" (seated women), by Paul Gauguin.

1973, June 7 Photo. *Perf. 13*
C98 AP20 200fr multicolored 27.50 20.00

Paul Gauguin (1848-1903), painter.

Pierre Loti and Characters from his Books — AP42

1973, July 4 Engr. *Perf. 13*
C99 AP42 60fr multicolored 40.00 20.00

Pierre Loti (1850-1923), French naval officer and writer.

Woman with Flowers, by Eliane de Gennes AP43

Paintings by Artists Living in Polynesia: 20fr, Sun, by Jean Francois Favre. 60fr, Seascape, by Alain Sidet. 80fr, Crowded Bus, by Francois

Ravello. 100fr, Stylized Boats, by Jackie Bourdin, horiz.

1973, Dec. 13 Photo. *Perf. 13*

C100 AP43 20fr gold & multi 9.00 2.75
C101 AP43 40fr gold & multi 13.00 6.00
C102 AP43 60fr gold & multi 19.00 10.50
C103 AP43 80fr gold & multi 25.00 17.00
C104 AP43 100fr gold & multi 30.00 20.00
Nos. C100-C104 (5) 96.00 56.25

Bird, Fish, Flower and Water — AP44

Catamaran under Sail — AP45

1974, June 12 Photo. *Perf. 13*

C105 AP44 12fr blue & multi 7.50 5.25

Nature protection.

1974, July 22 Engr. *Perf. 13*

C106 AP45 100fr multicolored 27.50 16.00

2nd Catamaran World Championships.

Still-life, by Rosine Temarui-Masson — AP46

Paintings by Artists Living in Polynesia: 40fr, Palms and House on Beach, by Marcel Chardon. 60fr, Man, by Marie-Françoise Avril. 80fr, Polynesian Woman, by Henriette Robin. 100fr, Lagoon by Moon-light, by David Farsi, horiz.

1974, Dec. 12 Photo. *Perf. 13*

C107 AP46 20fr gold & multi 18.00 8.50
C108 AP46 40fr gold & multi 27.50 9.50
C109 AP46 60fr gold & multi 32.50 12.00
C110 AP46 80fr gold & multi 45.00 16.50
C111 AP46 100fr gold & multi 65.00 27.50
Nos. C107-C111 (5) 188.00 74.00

See Nos. C122-C126.

Polynesian Gods of Travel — AP47

Designs: 75fr, Tourville hydroplane, 1929. 100fr, Passengers leaving plane.

1975, Feb. 7 Engr. *Perf. 13*

C112 AP47 50fr sep, pur & brn 12.00 6.00
C113 AP47 75fr grn, bl & red 18.00 8.00
C114 AP47 100fr grn, sep & car 27.50 15.00
Nos. C112-C114 (3) 57.50 29.00

Fifty years of Tahitian aviation.

French Ceres Stamp and Woman — AP48

1975, May 29 Engr. *Perf. 13*

C115 AP48 32fr ver, brn & blk 10.00 5.00

ARPHILA 75 International Philatelic Exhibition, Paris, June 6-16.

Shot Put and Games' Emblem AP50

1975, Aug. 1 Photo. *Perf. 13*

C117 AP50 25fr shown 4.75 3.00
C118 AP50 30fr Volleyball 7.00 3.75
C119 AP50 40fr Women's swimming 9.25 5.25
Nos. C117-C119 (3) 21.00 12.00

5th South Pacific Games, Guam, Aug. 1-10.

Flowers, Athlete, View of Montreal — AP51

1975, Oct. 15 Engr. *Perf. 13*

C120 AP51 44fr brt bl, ver & blk 12.00 6.50

Pre-Olympic Year 1975.

UPU Emblem, Jet and Letters — AP52

1975, Nov. 5 Engr. *Perf. 13*

C121 AP52 100fr brn, bl & ol 25.00 13.00

World Universal Postal Union Day.

Paintings Type of 1974

Paintings by Artists Living in Polynesia: 20fr, Beach Scene, by R. Marcel Marius, horiz. 40fr, Roofs with TV antennas, by M. Anglade, horiz. 60fr, Street scene with bus, by J. Day, horiz. 80fr, Tropical waters (fish), by J. Steimetz. 100fr, Women, by A. van der Heyde.

1975, Dec. 17 Litho. *Perf. 13*

C122 AP46 20fr gold & multi 3.50 1.75
C123 AP46 40fr gold & multi 6.50 3.00
C124 AP46 60fr gold & multi 10.00 4.50
C125 AP46 80fr gold & multi 13.00 7.50
C126 AP46 100fr gold & multi 16.00 12.00
Nos. C122-C126 (5) 49.00 28.75

Concorde — AP53

1976, Jan. 21 Engr. *Perf. 13*

C127 AP53 100fr car, bl & ind 19.00 13.00

First commercial flight of supersonic jet Concorde from Paris to Rio, Jan. 21.

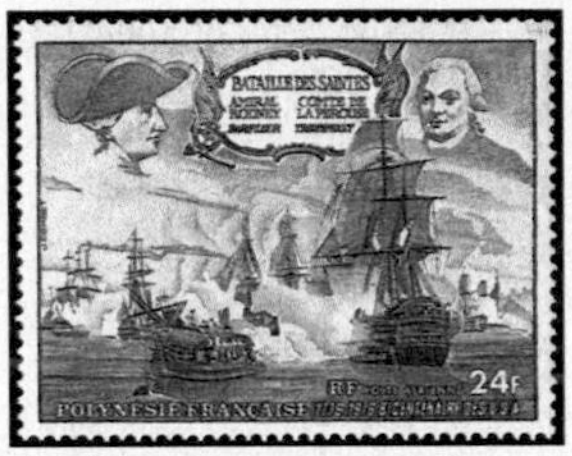

Adm. Rodney, Count de la Perouse, "Barfleur" and "Triomphant" in Battle — AP54

31fr, Count de Grasse and Lord Graves, "Ville de Paris" & "Le Terible" in Chesapeake Bay Battle.

1976, Apr. 15 Engr. *Perf. 13*

C128 AP54 24fr grnsh bl, lt brn & blk 5.00 2.50
C129 AP54 31fr mag, red & lt brn 5.75 3.50

American Bicentennial.

King Pomaré I — AP55

Portraits: 21fr, King Pomaré II. 26fr, Queen Pomaré IV. 30fr, King Pomaré V.

1976, Apr. 28 Litho. *Perf. 12½*

C130 AP55 18fr olive & multi 1.75 .75
C131 AP55 21fr multicolored 2.00 1.10
C132 AP55 26fr gray & multi 2.75 1.25
C133 AP55 30fr plum & multi 3.00 1.90
Nos. C130-C133 (4) 9.50 5.00

Pomaré Dynasty. See Nos. C141-C144.

Running and Maple Leaf — AP56

Designs: 34fr, Long jump, vert. 50fr, Olympic flame and flowers.

1976, July 19 Engr. *Perf. 13*

C134 AP56 26fr ultra & multi 4.25 2.10
C135 AP56 34fr ultra & multi 6.00 2.75
C136 AP56 50fr ultra & multi 11.50 5.00
a. Min. sheet, #C134-C136 95.00 95.00
Nos. C134-C136 (3) 21.75 9.85

21st Olympic Games, Montreal, Canada, July 17-Aug. 1.

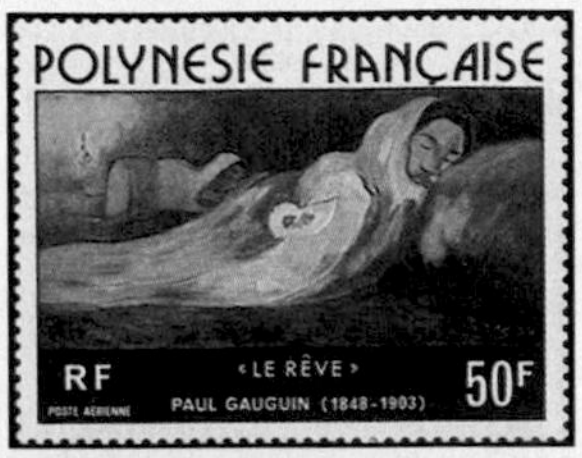

The Dream, by Paul Gauguin — AP57

1976, Oct. 17 Photo. *Perf. 13*

C137 AP57 50fr multicolored 11.00 7.25

Murex Steeriae — AP58

Pocillopora AP59

Sea Shells: 27fr, Conus Gauguini. 35fr, Conus marchionatus.

1977, Mar. 14 Photo. *Perf. 12½x13*

C138 AP58 25fr vio bl & multi 4.25 1.25
C139 AP58 27fr ultra & multi 4.25 1.50
C140 AP58 35fr blue & multi 5.00 2.00
Nos. C138-C140 (3) 13.50 4.75

See Nos. C156-C158.

Royalty Type of 1976

19fr, King Maputeoa, Mangareva. 33fr, King Camatoa V, Raiatea. 39fr, Queen Vaekehu, Marquesas. 43fr, King Teurarii III, Rurutu.

1977, Apr. 19 Litho. *Perf. 12½*

C141 AP55 19fr dull red & multi 1.25 .95
C142 AP55 33fr dk blue & multi 1.90 1.25
C143 AP55 39fr ultra & multi 1.90 1.25
C144 AP55 43fr green & multi 2.75 1.90
Nos. C141-C144 (4) 7.80 5.35

Polynesian rulers.

Perf. 13x12½, 12½x13

1977, May 23 Photo.

Design: 25fr, Acropora, horiz.

C145 AP59 25fr multicolored 1.90 1.10
C146 AP59 33fr multicolored 2.75 1.90

3rd Symposium on Coral Reefs, Miami, Fla. See Nos. C162-C163.

De Gaulle Memorial — AP60

Tahitian Dancer — AP61

Photogravure and Embossed

1977, June 18 ***Perf. 13***
C147 AP60 40fr gold & multi 8.00 5.00

5th anniversary of dedication of De Gaulle memorial at Colombey-les-Deux-Eglises.

1977, July 14 Litho. ***Perf. 12½***
C148 AP61 27fr multicolored 5.00 2.50

Charles A. Lindbergh and Spirit of St. Louis — AP62

1977, Aug. 18 Litho. ***Perf. 12½***
C149 AP62 28fr multicolored 8.00 3.50

Lindbergh's solo transatlantic flight from New York to Paris, 50th anniv.

Mahoe — AP63

Palms on Shore — AP64

1977, Sept. 15 Photo. ***Perf. 12½x13***
C150 AP63 8fr shown 1.40 .80
C151 AP63 12fr Frangipani 1.75 1.25

1977, Nov. 8 Photo. ***Perf. 12½x13***
C152 AP64 32fr multicolored 10.00 4.50

Ecology, protection of trees.

Rubens' Son Albert AP65

1977, Nov. 28 Engr. ***Perf. 13***
C153 AP65 100fr grnsh blk & rose cl 12.00 8.00

Peter Paul Rubens (1577-1640), painter, 400th birth anniversary.

Capt. Cook and "Discovery" — AP66

Design: 39fr, Capt. Cook and "Resolution."

1978, Jan. 20 Engr. ***Perf. 13***
C154 AP66 33fr multicolored 2.50 3.00
C155 AP66 39fr multicolored 3.00 3.50

Bicentenary of Capt. James Cook's arrival in Hawaii.

For overprints see Nos. C166-C167.

Shell Type of 1977

Sea Shells: 22fr, Erosaria obvelata. 24fr, Cypraea ventriculus. 31fr, Lambis robusta.

1978, Apr. 13 Photo. ***Perf. 13½x13***
C156 AP58 22fr brt blue & multi 2.50 1.25
C157 AP58 24fr brt blue & multi 2.50 1.50
C158 AP58 31fr brt blue & multi 4.00 2.50
Nos. C156-C158 (3) 9.00 5.25

Tahitian Woman and Boy, by Gauguin AP67

1978, May 7 ***Perf. 13***
C159 AP67 50fr multicolored 14.00 9.00

Paul Gauguin (1848-1903).

Antenna and ITU Emblem AP68

1978, May 17 Litho. ***Perf. 13***
C160 AP68 80fr gray & multi 6.00 3.25

10th World Telecommunications Day.

Soccer and Argentina '78 Emblem — AP69

1978, June 1
C161 AP69 28fr multicolored 6.00 3.00

11th World Cup Soccer Championship, Argentina, June 1-25.

Coral Type of 1977

Designs: 26fr, Fungia, horiz. 34fr, Millepora.

Perf. 13x12½, 12½x13
1978, July 13 **Photo.**
C162 AP59 26fr multicolored 3.00 2.00
C163 AP59 34fr multicolored 4.00 3.00

Radar Antenna, Polynesian Woman — AP70

1978, Sept. 5 Engr. ***Perf. 13***
C164 AP70 50fr blue & black 3.00 1.75

Papenoo earth station.

Bird and Rainbow over Island — AP71

1978, Oct. 5 **Photo.**
C165 AP71 23fr multicolored 6.00 1.75

Nature protection.

Nos. C154-C155 Overprinted in Black or Violet Blue: "1779-1979 / BICENTENAIRE / DE LA / MORT DE"

1979, Feb. 14 Engr. ***Perf. 13***
C166 AP66 33fr multi 4.00 2.50
C167 AP66 39fr multi (VBl) 5.00 3.50

Bicentenary of Capt. Cook's death. On No. C167 date is last line of overprint.

Children, Toys and IYC Emblem — AP72

1979, May 3 Engr. ***Perf. 13***
C168 AP72 150fr multicolored 15.00 7.00

International Year of the Child.

"Do you expect a letter?" by Paul Gauguin — AP73

1979, May 20 Photo. ***Perf. 13***
C169 AP73 200fr multicolored 17.50 8.00

Shell and Carved Head — AP74

1979, June 30 Engr. ***Perf. 13***
C170 AP74 44fr multicolored 3.50 2.00

Museum of Tahiti and the Islands.

Conference Emblem over Island AP75

1979, Oct. 6 Photo. ***Perf. 13***
C171 AP75 23fr multicolored 2.25 1.10

19th South Pacific Conf., Tahiti, Oct. 6-12.

Flying Boat "Bermuda" — AP76

Planes Used in Polynesia: 40fr, DC-4 over Papeete. 60fr, Britten-Norman "Islander." 80fr, Fairchild F-27A. 120fr, DC-8 over Tahiti.

1979, Dec. 19 Litho. ***Perf. 13***
C172 AP76 24fr multicolored 1.00 .50
C173 AP76 40fr multicolored 1.75 1.00
C174 AP76 60fr multicolored 2.75 1.50
C175 AP76 80fr multicolored 3.50 2.25
C176 AP76 120fr multicolored 6.00 3.00
Nos. C172-C176 (5) 15.00 8.25

See Nos. C180-C183.

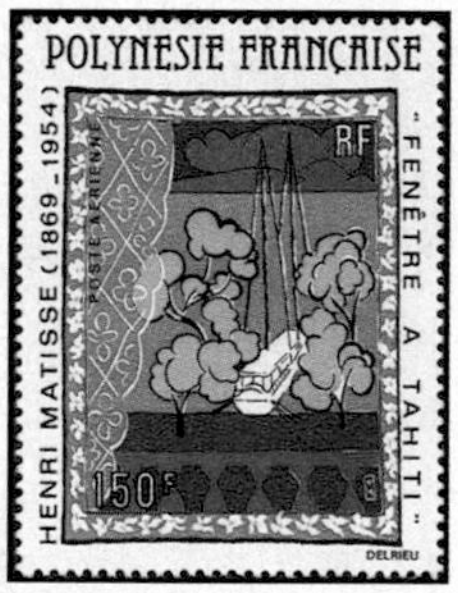

Window on Tahiti, by Henri Matisse AP77

1980, Feb. 18 **Photo.**
C177 AP77 150fr multicolored 8.00 5.00

Marshi Metua No Tehamana, by Gauguin AP78

1980, Aug. 24 Photo. ***Perf. 13***
C178 AP78 500fr multicolored 16.00 11.00

Sydpex '80, Philatelic Exhibition, Sydney Town Hall — AP79

1980, Sept. 29 Photo. ***Perf. 13***
C179 AP79 70fr multicolored 7.00 4.50

Aviation Type of 1979

1980, Dec. 15 Litho. *Perf. 13*

C180	AP76	15fr Catalina	1.25	.75
C181	AP76	26fr Twin Otter	2.50	1.00
C182	AP76	30fr CAMS 55	3.00	1.25
C183	AP76	50fr DC-6	4.50	1.75
		Nos. C180-C183 (4)	11.25	4.75

And The Gold of their Bodies, by Gauguin — AP80

1981, Mar. 15 Photo. *Perf. 13*

C184	AP80	100fr multicolored	7.50	3.00

20th Anniv. of Manned Space Flight AP81

1981, June 15 Litho. *Perf. 12½*

C185	AP81	300fr multicolored	7.50	5.00

First Intl. Pirogue (6-man Canoe) Championship — AP82

1981, July 25 Litho. *Perf. 13x12½*

C186	AP82	200fr multicolored	5.00	4.00

Matavai Bay, by William Hodges — AP83

Paintings: 60fr, Poedea, by John Weber, vert. 80fr, Omai, by Joshua Reynolds, vert. 120fr, Point Venus, by George Tobin.

1981, Dec. 10 Photo. *Perf. 13*

C187	AP83	40fr multicolored	1.10	.90
C188	AP83	60fr multicolored	1.75	1.25
C189	AP83	80fr multicolored	2.75	1.75
C190	AP83	120fr multicolored	3.50	2.40
		Nos. C187-C190 (4)	9.10	6.30

See Nos. C194-C197, C202-C205.

TB Bacillus Centenary — AP84

1982, Mar. 24 Engr. *Perf. 13*

C191	AP84	200fr multicolored	5.00	3.00

1982 World Cup — AP85

1982, May 18 Litho. *Perf. 13*

C192	AP85	250fr multicolored	5.75	4.00

French Overseas Possessions' Week, Sept. 18-25 — AP86

1982, Sept. 17 Engr.

C193	AP86	110fr multicolored	2.75	1.65

Painting Type of 1981

Designs: 50fr, The Tahitian, by M. Radiguet, vert. 70fr, Souvenir of Tahiti, by C. Giraud. 100fr, Beating Cloth Lengths, by Atlas JL the Younger. 160fr, Papeete Harbor, by C.F. Gordon Cumming.

1982, Dec. 15 Photo. *Perf. 13*

C194	AP83	50fr multicolored	2.00	.75
C195	AP83	70fr multicolored	2.50	1.10
C196	AP83	100fr multicolored	3.00	1.60
C197	AP83	160fr multicolored	5.00	3.25
		Nos. C194-C197 (4)	12.50	6.70

Wood Cutter, by Gauguin AP87

Photo. & Engr.

1983, May 8 *Perf. 12½x13*

C198	AP87	600fr multicolored	16.00	8.00

Voyage of Capt. Bligh — AP88

1983, June 9 Litho. *Perf. 13*

C199	AP88	200fr Map, fruit	6.00	3.00

BRASILIANA '83 Intl. Stamp Exhibition, Rio de Janeiro, July 29-Aug. 7 — AP89

1983, July 29 Litho. *Perf. 13x12½*

C200	AP89	100fr multicolored	2.50	1.75
a.		Souvenir sheet	6.00	6.00

1983, Aug. 4 Litho. *Perf. 13x12½*

C201	AP89	110fr Bangkok '83	3.00	2.00
a.		Souvenir sheet	7.50	7.50

Painting Type of 1981

20th Cent. Paintings: 40fr, View of Moorea, by William Alister MacDonald (1861-1956). 60fr, The Fruit Carrier, by Adrian Herman Gouwe (1875-1965). 80fr, Arrival of the Destroyer Escort, by Nicolas Mordvinoff (1911-1977). 100fr, Women on a Veranda, by Charles Alfred Le Moine (1872-1918).

1983, Dec. 22 Photo. *Perf. 13*

C202	AP83	40fr multi	1.00	.75
C203	AP83	60fr multi, vert.	1.50	1.00
C204	AP83	80fr multi, vert.	1.60	1.25
C205	AP83	100fr multi	2.00	1.60
		Nos. C202-C205 (4)	6.10	4.60

ESPANA '84 — AP90

Design: Maori canoers.

1984, Apr. 27 Engr. *Perf. 13*

C206	AP90	80fr brn red & dk bl	2.25	1.50

Souvenir Sheet

C207	AP90	200fr dk bl & dk red	12.00	12.00

Woman with Mango, by Gauguin AP91

Photo. & Engr.

1984, May 27 *Perf. 12½x13*

C208	AP91	400fr multicolored	11.00	6.00

Ausipex '84 — AP92

Details from Human Sacrifice of the Maori in Tahiti, 18th cent. engraving.

1984, Sept. 5 Litho. *Perf. 13x12½*

C209	AP92	120fr Worshippers	3.00	2.25
C210	AP92	120fr Preparation	3.00	2.25
a.		Pair, #C209-C210 + label	7.50	7.50

Souvenir Sheet

C211	AP92	200fr Entire	9.50	9.50

Painting by Gaugin (1848-1903) — AP93

Design: Where have we come from? What are we? Where are we going?

Illustration reduced.

1985, Mar. 17 Litho. *Perf. 13½x13*

C212	AP93	550fr multi	14.00	7.50

4th Pacific Arts Festival Type

1985, July 3 Litho. *Perf. 13*

C213	A95	200fr Islander, tiki, artifacts	4.50	3.00

Intl. Youth Year — AP95

1985, Sept. 18 Litho.

C214	AP95	250fr Island youths, frigate bird	5.50	3.25

ITALIA '85 — AP96

Designs: Ship sailing into Papeete Harbor, 19th century print.

1985, Oct. 22 Engr.

C215	AP96	130fr multicolored	2.75	2.50

Souvenir Sheet

C216	AP96	240fr multicolored	7.50	7.50

1st Intl. Marlin Fishing Contest, Feb. 27-Mar. 5 — AP97

1986, Feb. 27 Litho. *Perf. 12½*

C217	AP97	300fr multicolored	6.50	4.00

Arrival of a Boat, c.1880 — AP98

1986, June 24 Engr. *Perf. 13*
C218 AP98 400fr intense blue 8.75 5.25

STOCKHOLMIA '86 — AP99

Design: Dr. Karl Solander and Anders Sparrmann, Swedish scientists who accompanied Capt. Cook, and map of Tahiti.

1986, Aug. 28 Engr. *Perf. 13*
C219 AP99 150fr multicolored 3.25 2.25

Souvenir Sheet

C220 AP99 210fr multicolored 4.75 4.75

Protestant Churches — AP100

1986, Dec. 17 Litho. *Perf. 13*
C221 AP100 80fr Tiva, 1955 1.75 .90
C222 AP100 200fr Avera, 1880 4.50 2.10
C223 AP100 300fr Papetoai, 1822 6.50 3.25
Nos. C221-C223 (3) 12.75 6.25

Broche Barracks, 120th Anniv. — AP101

1987, Apr. 21 Litho. *Perf. 12½x12*
C224 AP101 350fr multicolored 7.75 5.00

CAPEX '87 — AP102

Design: George Vancouver (1757-1798), English navigator and cartographer, chart and excerpt from ship's log.

1987, June 15 Engr. *Perf. 13*
C225 AP102 130fr multi 2.90 2.25

Imperf

Size: 143x100mm

C226 AP102 260fr multicolored 5.75 5.75

Soyez Mysterieuses, from a 5-Panel Sculpture by Paul Gauguin, Gauguin Museum — AP103

Illustration reduced.

1987, Nov. 15 *Perf. 13*
C227 AP103 600fr multicolored 14.00 9.50

AIR POST SEMI-POSTAL STAMPS

Catalogue values for unused stamps in this section are for Never Hinged items.

French Revolution Issue
Common Design Type
Unwmk.

1939, July 5 Photo. *Perf. 13*
Name and Value Typo. in Orange
CB1 CD83 5fr + 4fr brn blk 52.50 29.00

Mother & Children on Beach — SPAP1

Perf. 12½x13½
1942, June 22 Engr.
CB2 SPAP1 1.50fr + 3.50fr green 1.50
CB3 SPAP1 2fr + 6fr yellow brown 1.50

Native children's welfare fund.

Nos. CB2-CB3 were issued by the Vichy government in France, but were not placed on sale in French Polynesia.

Colonial Education Fund
Common Design Type

1942, June 22
CB4 CD86a 1.20fr + 1.80fr blue & red 1.50

No. CB4 was issued by the Vichy government in France, but was not placed on sale in French Polynesia.

POSTAGE DUE STAMPS

Postage Due Stamps of French Colonies, 1894-1906, Overprinted

1926-27 Unwmk. *Perf. 14x13½*
J1 D1 5c light blue .60 .60
J2 D1 10c brown .60 .60
J3 D1 20c olive green .95 .95
J4 D1 30c dull red 1.00 1.00
J5 D1 40c rose 2.25 2.25
J6 D1 60c blue green 2.25 2.25
J7 D1 1fr red brown, *straw* 2.25 2.25
J8 D1 3fr magenta ('27) 9.50 9.50

With Additional Surcharge of New Value

J9 D1 2fr on 1fr orange red 2.75 2.75
Nos. J1-J9 (9) 22.15 22.15

Fautaua Falls, Tahiti — D2

Tahitian Youth — D3

1929 Typo. *Perf. 13½x14*
J10 D2 5c lt blue & dk brn .50 .50
J11 D2 10c vermilion & grn .60 .60
J12 D2 30c dk brn & dk red 1.25 1.25
J13 D2 50c yel grn & dk brn 1.00 1.00
J14 D2 60c dl vio & yel grn 2.75 2.75
J15 D3 1fr Prus bl & red vio 2.25 2.25
J16 D3 2fr brn red & dk brn 1.50 1.50
J17 D3 3fr bl vio & bl grn 1.50 1.50
Nos. J10-J17 (8) 11.35 11.35

Catalogue values for unused stamps in this section, from this point to the end of the section, are for Never Hinged items.

D4

Polynesian Club — D5

1948 Engr. *Perf. 14x13*
J18 D4 10c brt blue grn .30 .20
J19 D4 30c black brown .30 .20
J20 D4 50c dk car rose .40 .25
J21 D4 1fr ultra .55 .45
J22 D4 2fr dk blue green .75 .60
J23 D4 3fr red 1.50 1.25
J24 D4 4fr violet 1.60 1.40
J25 D4 5fr lilac rose 2.40 1.90
J26 D4 10fr slate 3.25 2.25
J27 D4 20fr red brown 4.50 3.75
Nos. J18-J27 (10) 15.55 12.25

1958 Unwmk. *Perf. 14x13*
J28 D5 1fr dk brn & grn .55 .50
J29 D5 3fr bluish blk & hn brn .75 .75
J30 D5 5fr brown & ultra .90 .90
Nos. J28-J30 (3) 2.20 2.15

Tahitian Bowl — D6

1984-87 Litho. *Perf. 13*
J31 D6 1fr Mother-of-pearl fish hook, vert. .25 .25
J32 D6 3fr shown .25 .25
J33 D6 5fr Marquesan fan .25 .25
J34 D6 10fr Lamp stand, vert. .40 .40
J35 D6 20fr Wood headrest ('87) .55 .55
J36 D6 50fr Wood scoop ('87) 1.25 1.25
Nos. J31-J36 (6) 2.95 2.95

Issued: #J31-34, 3/15; #J35-J36, 8/18.

OFFICIAL STAMPS

Catalogue values for unused stamps in this section are for Never Hinged items.

Breadfruit O1

Polynesian Fruits: 2fr, 3fr, 5fr, like 1fr. 7fr, 8fr, 10fr, 15fr, "Vi Tahiti." 19fr, 20fr, 25fr, 35fr, Avocados. 50fr, 100fr, 200fr, Mangos.

1977, June 9 Litho. *Perf. 12½*
O1 O1 1fr ultra & multi .25 .25
O2 O1 2fr ultra & multi .25 .25
O3 O1 3fr ultra & multi .25 .25
O4 O1 5fr ultra & multi .25 .25
O5 O1 7fr red & multi .50 .50
O6 O1 8fr red & multi .55 .55
O7 O1 10fr red & multi .60 .60
O8 O1 15fr red & multi 1.00 1.00
O9 O1 19fr black & multi 1.25 1.25
O10 O1 20fr black & multi 1.50 1.50
O11 O1 25fr black & multi 1.75 1.75
O12 O1 35fr black & multi 2.25 2.25
O13 O1 50fr black & multi 2.50 2.50
O14 O1 100fr red & multi 4.50 4.50
O15 O1 200fr ultra & multi 8.00 8.00
Nos. O1-O15 (15) 25.40 25.40

1982-86 *Perf. 13*
O1a O1 1fr ultra & multi .45 .45
O2a O1 2fr ultra & multi .45 .45
O3a O1 3fr ultra & multi .65 .65
O4a O1 5fr ultra & multi 1.25 1.25
O5a O1 7fr red & multi 1.50 1.50
O6a O1 8fr red & multi 2.00 2.00
O7a O1 10fr red & multi 2.00 2.00
O8a O1 15fr red & multi ('84) 2.00 2.00
O10a O1 20fr black & multi 2.00 2.00
O11a O1 25fr black & multi ('84) 2.00 2.00
O12a O1 35fr black & multi ('84) 4.75 4.75
O13a O1 50fr black & multi ('84) 12.00 12.00
O14a O1 100fr red & multi ('86) 24.00 24.00
O15a O1 200fr ultra & multi ('86) 26.00 26.00
Nos. O1a-O15a (14) 81.05 81.05

Nos. O1-O15 have dull finish (matte) gum. Nos. O1a-O15a have shiny gum.

Stamps and Postmarks — O2

1fr, French Colonies #5. 2fr, French Colonies #27, #12. 3fr, French Colonies #29, 1884 Papeete postmark. 5fr, Newspaper franked with surcharge of Tahiti #2, 1884 Papeete postmark. 9fr, #176. 10fr, #4, 1894 octagonal postmark. 20fr, #6, #8. 46fr, #48. 51fr, #147-148, Vaitepaua-Makatea Island postmark. 70fr, Visit Tahiti postmark on postal card piece. 85fr, #59 with 1921 manuscript cancel, vert. 100fr, #181. 200fr, #C21, 1st day cancel.

Perf. 13¼, 13¼x13 (#O26), 13x13¼ (#O27)

1993-99 Litho.
O16 O2 1fr multicolored .20 .20
O17 O2 2fr multicolored .20 .20
O18 O2 3fr multicolored .20 .20
O19 O2 5fr multicolored .20 .20
O20 O2 9fr multicolored .75 .75
O21 O2 10fr multicolored .20 .20
O22 O2 20fr multicolored .50 .50
O23 O2 46fr multicolored 1.10 1.10
O24 O2 51fr multicolored 1.90 1.90
O25 O2 70fr multicolored 1.75 1.75
O26 O2 85fr multicolored 1.90 1.90
O27 O2 100fr multicolored 2.25 2.25
O28 O2 200fr multicolored 3.50 3.50
Nos. O16-O28 (13) 14.65 14.65

Issued: 51fr, 4/6/94; 9fr, 85fr, 4/21/97; others, 1/13/93.

1997-98 Litho. *Perf. 13¼x13,*
O16a O2 1fr multicolored .50 .50
O17a O2 2fr multicolored .50 .50
O18a O2 3fr multicolored .50 .50
O19a O2 5fr multicolored .75 .75
O20a O2 10fr multicolored .75 .75
O21a O2 20fr multicolored .75 .75
O23a O2 70fr multicolored 1.50 1.50
O24a O2 100fr multicolored 1.90 1.90
O25a O2 200fr multicolored 4.50 4.50

Issued: Nos. O17a, O19a, O23a, O25a, 1997; Nos. O16a, O18a, 1998. Nos. O20a, O21a, O24a, 1999.

FRENCH SOUTHERN AND ANTARCTIC TERRITORIES

'french 'sə-thərn and
ˌant-ärk-tik 'ter-ə-'tōr-ēs

POP. — 130 staff

Formerly dependencies of Madagascar, these areas, comprising the Kerguelen Archipelago; St. Paul, Amsterdam and Crozet Islands and Adelle Land in Antarctica achieved territorial status on August 6, 1955.

100 Centimes = 1 Franc
100 Cents = 1 Euro (2002)

Catalogue values for all unused stamps in this country are for Never Hinged items.

Madagascar No. 289 Overprinted in Red:

Unwmk.

1955, Oct. 28 Engr. *Perf. 13*
1 A25 15f dk grn & dp ultra 14.50 *29.00*

Rockhopper Penguins, Crozet Archipelago — A1

New Amsterdam A2

Design: 10fr, 15fr, Elephant seal.

1956, Apr. 25 Engr. *Perf. 13*
2 A1 50c dk blue, sepia & yel .45 *.75*
3 A1 1fr ultra, org & gray .45 *.75*
4 A2 5fr blue & dp ultra 3.00 *3.25*
5 A2 8fr gray vio & dk brn 18.00 *21.00*
6 A2 10fr indigo 6.50 6.25
7 A2 15fr indigo & brn vio 8.00 7.50
Nos. 2-7 (6) 36.40 39.50

Polar Observation A3

1957, Oct. 11
8 A3 5fr black & violet 3.50 *5.00*
9 A3 10fr rose red 4.75 *5.75*
10 A3 15fr dark blue 5.75 *7.50*
Nos. 8-10 (3) 14.00 18.25

International Geophysical Year, 1957-58.

Imperforates

Most stamps of this French possession exist imperforate in issued and trial colors, and also in small presentation sheets in issued colors.

Flower Issue
Common Design Type

Design: Pringlea, horiz.

1959 Photo. *Perf. 12½x12*
11 CD104 10fr sal, grn & yel 10.00 8.00

Common Design Types pictured following the introduction.

Light-mantled Sooty Albatross — A4

Coat of Arms — A5

Designs: 40c, Skua, horiz. 12fr, King shag.

1959, Sept. 14 Engr. *Perf. 13*
12 A4 30c blue, grn & red brn .50 *.75*
13 A4 40c blk, dl red brn & bl .50 *.75*
14 A4 12fr lt blue & blk 13.50 8.75
Nos. 12-14 (3) 14.50 10.25

1959, Sept. 14 Typo. *Perf. 13x14*
15 A5 20fr ultra, lt bl & yel 21.00 11.50

Sheathbills — A6

4fr, Sea leopard, horiz. 25fr, Weddell seal at Kerguélen, horiz. 85fr, King penguin.

1960, Dec. 15 Engr. *Perf. 13*
16 A6 2fr grnsh bl, gray & choc 1.75 *2.25*
17 A6 4fr bl, dk brn & dk grn 9.50 7.50
18 A6 25fr sl grn, bis brn & blk 100.00 42.50
19 A6 85fr grnsh bl, org & blk 22.50 14.50
Nos. 16-19 (4) 133.75 66.75

Yves-Joseph de Kerguélen-Trémarec — A7

1960, Nov. 22
20 A7 25fr red org, dk bl & brn 29.00 22.50

Yves-Joseph de Kerguélen-Trémarec, discoverer of the Kerguélen Archipelago.

Charcot, Compass Rose and "Pourquoi-pas?" — A8

1961, Dec. 26 Unwmk. *Perf. 13*
21 A8 25fr brn, grn & red 29.00 22.50

25th anniv. of the death of Commander Jean Charcot (1867-1936), Antarctic explorer.

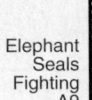

Elephant Seals Fighting A9

1963, Feb. 11 Engr. *Perf. 13*
22 A9 8fr dk blue, blk & claret 12.00 7.50

See No. C4.

Penguins and Camp on Crozet Island A10

20fr, Research station & IQSY emblem.

1963, Dec. 16 Unwmk. *Perf. 13*
23 A10 5fr blk, red brn & Prus bl 65.00 35.00
24 A10 20fr vio, sl & red brn 80.00 55.00

Intl. Quiet Sun Year, 1964-65. See #C6.

Great Blue Whale A11

Black-browed Albatross — A12

Aurora Australis, Map of Antarctica and Rocket — A13

10fr, Cape pigeons. 12fr, Phylica trees, Amsterdam Island. 15fr, Killer whale (orca).

1966-69 Engr. *Perf. 13*
25 A11 5fr brt bl & indigo 21.00 11.50
26 A12 10fr sl, ind & ol brn 32.50 25.00
27 A11 12fr brt bl, sl grn & lemon 22.50 14.00
27A A11 15fr ol, dk bl & ind 12.00 7.25
28 A12 20fr slate, ol & org 400.00 225.00
Nos. 25-28 (5) 488.00 282.75

Issued: 5fr, 12/12; 20fr, 1/3/68; 10fr, 12fr, 1/6/69; 15fr, 12/21/69.

1967, Mar. 4 Engr. *Perf. 13*
29 A13 20fr mag, blue & blk 29.00 22.50

Launching of the 1st space rocket from Adelie Land, Jan., 1967.

Dumont d'Urville A14

1968, Jan. 20
30 A14 30fr lt ultra, dk bl & dk brn 140.00 80.00

Jules Sébastien César Dumont D'Urville (1790-1842), French naval commander and South Seas explorer.

WHO Anniversary Issue
Common Design Type

1968, May 4 Engr. *Perf. 13*
31 CD126 30fr red, yel & bl 65.00 45.00

Human Rights Year Issue
Common Design Type

1968, Aug. 10 Engr. *Perf. 13*
32 CD127 30fr grnsh bl, red & brn 60.00 45.00

Polar Camp with Helicopter, Plane and Snocat Tractor — A15

1969, Mar. 17 Engr. *Perf. 13*
33 A15 25fr Prus bl, lt grnsh bl & brn red 25.00 15.00

20 years of French Polar expeditions.

ILO Issue
Common Design Type

1970, Jan. 1 Engr. *Perf. 13*
35 CD131 20fr org, dk bl & brn 18.50 11.00

UPU Headquarters Issue
Common Design Type

1970, May 20 Engr. *Perf. 13*
36 CD133 50fr blue, plum & ol bis 45.00 29.00

Ice Fish A16

Fish: Nos. 38-43, Antarctic cods, various species. 135fr, Zanchlorhynchus spinifer.

1971 Engr. *Perf. 13*
37 A16 5fr brt grn, ind & org 1.75 .85
38 A16 10fr redsh brn & dp vio 2.00 .95
39 A16 20fr dp cl, brt grn & org 4.25 2.10
40 A16 22fr pur, brn ol & mag 4.00 3.25
41 A16 25fr grn, ind & org 6.00 2.75
42 A16 30fr sep, gray & bl vio 7.50 4.25
43 A16 35fr sl grn, dk brn & ocher 6.50 3.25
44 A16 135fr Prus bl, dp org & ol grn 11.00 5.25
Nos. 37-44 (8) 43.00 22.65

Issued: #37-39, 41-42, 1/1; #40, 43-44, 12/22.

Map of Antarctica A17

Microzetia Mirabilis A18

1971, Dec. 22
45 A17 75fr red 27.50 25.00

Antarctic Treaty pledging peaceful uses of and scientific cooperation in Antarctica, 10th anniv.

1972

Insects: 15fr, Christiansenia dreuxi. 22f, Phtirocoris antarcticus. 30fr, Antarctophytosus atriceps. 40fr, Paractora drenxi. 140fr, Pringleophaga Kerguelenensis.

46 A18 15fr cl, org & brn 10.00 6.00
47 A18 22fr vio bl, sl grn & yel 14.50 9.25
48 A18 25fr grn, rose lil & pur 5.75 4.75
49 A18 30fr blue & multi 18.00 10.00

50	A18	40fr dk brn, ocher & blk	8.75	4.75
51	A18	140fr bl, emer & brn	12.50	8.75
		Nos. 46-51 (6)	69.50	43.50

Issued: #48, 50-51, 1/3; #46-47, 49, 12/16.

De Gaulle Issue
Common Design Type

Designs: 50fr, Gen. de Gaulle, 1940. 100fr, Pres. de Gaulle, 1970.

1972, Feb. 1 Engr. *Perf. 13*

52	CD134	50fr brt grn & blk	21.00	13.50
53	CD134	100fr brt grn & blk	26.00	20.00

Kerguelen Cabbage — A19

Designs: 61fr, Azorella selago, horiz. 87fr, Acaena ascendens, horiz.

1972-73

54	A19	45fr multicolored	10.00	5.00
55	A19	61fr multicolored	3.50	2.75
56	A19	87fr multicolored	5.75	4.00
		Nos. 54-56 (3)	19.25	11.75

Issued: 45fr, 12/18; others, 12/13/73.

Mailship Sapmer and Map of Amsterdam Island — A20

1974, Dec. 31 Engr. *Perf. 13*

57	A20	75fr bl, blk & dk brn	7.25	5.25

25th anniversary of postal service.

Antarctic Tern — A21

Designs: 50c, Antarctic petrel. 90c, Sea lioness. 1fr, Weddell seal. 1.20fr, Kerguelen cormorant, vert. 1.40fr, Gentoo penguin, vert.

1976, Jan. Engr. *Perf. 13*

58	A21	40c multicolored	4.75	3.00
59	A21	50c multicolored	4.75	3.00
60	A21	90c multicolored	7.50	4.00
61	A21	1fr multicolored	12.00	9.25
62	A21	1.20fr multicolored	15.00	11.00
63	A21	1.40fr multicolored	14.00	11.50
		Nos. 58-63 (6)	58.00	41.75

James Clark Ross — A22

James Cook — A23

Design: 30c, Climbing Mount Ross.

1976, Dec. 16 Engr. *Perf. 13*

64	A22	30c multicolored	4.50	3.00
65	A22	3fr multicolored	4.50	3.00

First climbing of Mount Ross, Kerguelen Island, Jan. 5, 1975.

1976, Dec. 16

66	A23	70c multicolored	13.50	10.00

Bicentenary of Capt. Cook's voyage past Kerguelen Island. See No. C46.

Commerson's Dolphins — A24

1977, Feb. 1 Engr. *Perf. 13*

67	A24	1.10fr Blue whale	5.75	3.25
68	A24	1.50fr shown	5.75	4.00

Macrocystis Algae — A25

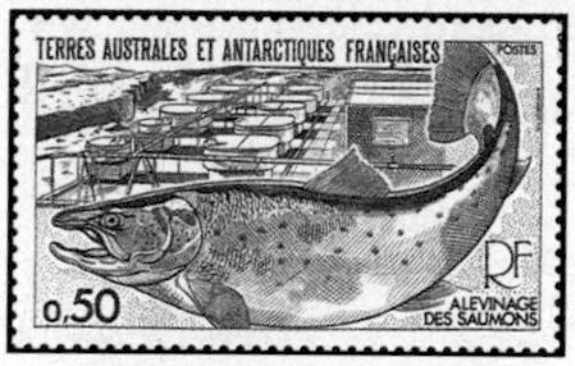
Salmon Hatchery — A26

Magga Dan — A27

Designs: 70c, Durvillea algae. 90c, Albatross. 1fr, Underwater sampling and scientists, vert. 1.40fr, Thala Dan and penguins.

1977, Dec. 20 Engr. *Perf. 13*

69	A25	40c ol brn & bis	1.10	.70
70	A26	50c dk bl & pur	1.40	1.00
71	A25	70c blk, grn & brn	1.60	1.00
72	A26	90c grn, brt bl & brn	1.60	1.00
73	A27	1fr slate	1.40	1.00
74	A27	1.20fr multi	3.25	1.60
75	A27	1.40fr multi	2.00	1.60
		Nos. 69-75 (7)	12.35	7.90

See Nos. 77-79.

A28

A29

Explorer with French and Expedition Flags.

1977, Dec. 24

76	A28	1.90fr multicolored	7.75	5.00

French Polar expeditions, 1947-48.

Types of 1977

40c, Forbin, destroyer. 50c Jeanne d'Arc, helicopter carrier. 1.40fr, Kerguelen cormorant.

1979, Jan. 1 Engr. *Perf. 13*

77	A27	40c black & blue	1.40	1.10
78	A27	50c black & blue	1.60	1.10
79	A26	1.40fr multicolored	1.60	1.10
		Nos. 77-79 (3)	4.60	3.30

1979, Jan. 1

80	A29	1.20fr citron & indigo	1.40	1.10

R. Rallier du Baty. See Nos. 97, 100, 111, 117, 129, 135, 188.

French Navigators Monument, Hobart — A30

1979, Jan. 1

81	A30	1fr multicolored	.90	.80

French navigators and explorers.

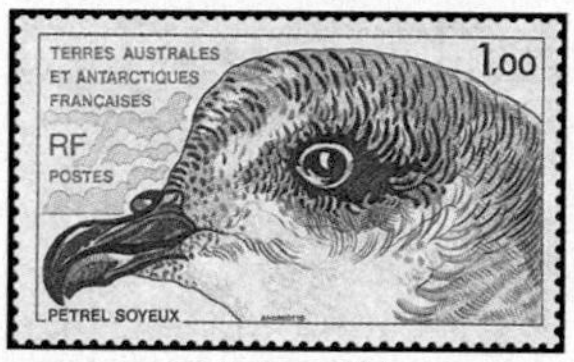
Petrel — A31

1979 Engr. *Perf. 13*

82	A31	70c Rockhopper penguins, vert.	1.25	1.00
83	A31	1fr shown	1.50	1.25

Commandant Bourdais — A32

1979

84	A32	1.10fr *Doudart de Lagree,* vert.	1.25	1.00
85	A32	1.50fr shown	1.50	1.25

Adm. Antoine d'Entrecasteaux A33

Sebastian de el Cano A34

1979

86	A33	1.20fr multicolored	1.40	1.10

1979

Discovery of Amsterdam Island, 1522: 4fr, Victoria, horiz.

87	A34	1.40fr multicolored	1.10	.80
88	A34	4fr multicolored	2.00	1.60

Adelie Penguins — A35

Adelie Penguin — A36

Sea Leopard A37

1980, Dec. 15 Engr. *Perf. 13*

89	A35	50c rose violet	1.40	1.25
90	A36	60c multicolored	1.40	.90
91	A35	1.20fr multicolored	2.00	1.10
92	A37	1.30fr multicolored	1.40	1.25
93	A37	1.80fr multicolored	1.40	1.25
		Nos. 89-93 (5)	7.60	5.75

20th Anniv. of Antarctic Treaty — A38

1981, June 23 Engr. *Perf. 13*
94 A38 1.80fr multicolored 4.50 4.50

Alouette II — A39

1981-82 Engr. *Perf. 13*
95 A39 55c brown & multi .55 .45
96 A39 65c blue & multi .55 .45

Explorer Type of 1979

1981
97 A29 1.40fr Jean Loranchet .80 .55

Landing Ship Le Gros Ventre, Kerguelen — A41

1983, Jan. 3 Engr. *Perf. 13*
98 A41 55c multicolored .90 .65

Our Lady of the Winds Statue and Church, Kerguelen — A42

1983, Jan. 3
99 A42 1.40fr multicolored .90 .90

Explorer Type of 1979

Design: Martin de Vivies, Navigator.

1983, Jan. 3
100 A29 1.60fr multicolored .90 .75

Eaton's Ducks A44

1983, Jan. 3
101 A44 1.50fr multicolored .90 .60
102 A44 1.80fr multicolored .90 .75

Trawler Austral — A45

1983, Jan. 3
103 A45 2.30fr multicolored 1.40 1.10

Freighter Lady Franklin — A46

1983, Aug. 4 Engr. *Perf. 13*
104 A46 5fr multicolored 4.00 3.00

Glaciology — A47

Design: Scientists examining glacier, base.

1984, Jan. 1 Engr. *Perf. 13*
105 A47 15c multicolored .35 .30
106 A47 1.70fr multicolored .80 .55

Crab-eating Seal — A48

Penguins — A49

1984, Jan. 1
107 A48 60c multicolored .55 .45
108 A49 70c multicolored .45 .45
109 A49 2fr multicolored 1.25 1.00
110 A48 5.90fr multicolored 2.00 1.75
Nos. 107-110 (4) 4.25 3.65

Explorer Type of 1979

1984, Jan. 1
111 A29 1.80fr Alfred Faure .90 .70

Biomass — A51

1985, Jan. 1 Engr. *Perf. 13*
112 A51 1.80fr multicolored .80 .55
113 A51 5.20fr multicolored 2.00 1.75

Emperor Penguins — A52

Snowy Petrel — A53

1985, Jan. 1 Engr. *Perf. 13*
114 A52 1.70fr multicolored 1.00 .80
115 A53 2.80fr multicolored 1.25 1.10

Port Martin — A54

1985, Jan. 1 Engr. *Perf. 13*
116 A54 2.20fr multicolored 1.25 .80

Explorer Type of 1979

1985, Jan. 1 Engr. *Perf. 13*
117 A29 2fr Andre-Frank Liotard .90 .70

Antarctic Fulmar — A56

1986, Jan. 1 Engr. *Perf. 13*
118 A56 1fr shown .55 .45
119 A56 1.70fr Giant petrels .80 .75
Nos. 118-119,C91 (3) 3.35 2.95

Echinoderms — A57

1986, Jan. 1
120 A57 1.90fr shown .90 .75

Cotula Plumosa — A58

Shipping — A59

1986, Jan. 1
121 A58 2.30fr shown .90 .75
122 A58 6.20fr Lycopodium. saururus 2.50 1.90

1986, Jan. 1
123 A59 2.10fr Var research ship .90 .85
124 A59 3fr Polarbjorn support ship 1.25 1.25

Marine Life — A60

1987, Jan. 1 Engr. *Perf. 13½x13*
125 A60 50c dk blue & org .50 .50

Flora — A61

1987, Jan. 1
126 A61 1.80fr Poa cookii .70 .50
127 A61 6.50fr Lichen, Neuropogon taylori 2.00 1.90

Marret Base, Adelie Land — A62

1987, Jan. 1
128 A62 2fr yel brn, dk ultra & lake .90 .70

Explorer Type of 1979

1987, Jan. 1
129 A29 2.20fr Adm. Mouchez 1.00 .75

Reindeer — A64

1987, Jan. 1
130 A64 2.50fr black 1.25 .80

Transport Ship Eure — A65

1987, Jan. 1
131 A65 3.20fr dk ultra, Prus grn & dk grn 1.25 1.00

Macaroni Penguins — A66

1987, Jan. 1 ***Perf. 13x12½***
132 A66 4.80fr multicolored 2.50 1.90

Elephant Grass — A67

1988, Jan. 1 **Engr.** ***Perf. 13***
133 A67 1.70fr Prus grn, emer & olive .75 .65

Rev.-Father Lejay, Explorer — A68

1988, Jan. 1
134 A68 2.20fr vio, ultra & blk .90 .80

Explorer Type of 1979

Design: Robert Gessain (1907-86).

1988, Jan. 1
135 A29 3.40fr gray, dk red & blk 1.40 1.10

Le Gros Ventre, 18th Cent. — A70

1988, Jan. 1
136 A70 3.50fr dp ultra, bl grn & brn 1.25 1.25

Mermaid and B.A.P. Jules Verne, Research Vessel — A71

1988, Jan. 1
137 A71 4.90fr gray & dk blue 2.50 1.75

La Fortune, Early 19th Cent. — A72

1988, Jan. 1
138 A72 5fr blk & dull bl grn 2.25 1.75

Wilson's Petrel — A73

1988, Jan. 1
139 A73 6.80fr blk, sepia & dl bl grn 2.75 2.25

See Nos. 143-144.

Mt. Ross Campaign (in 1987) — A74

1988, Jan. 1 ***Perf. 13x12½***
140 A74 2.20fr Volcanic rock cross-sections 1.00 1.00
141 A74 15.10fr Kerguelen Is. 5.50 5.50
a. Pair, #140-141 + label 7.50 7.50

Darrieus System Wind Vane Electric Generator — A75

1988, Jan. 1 **Engr.** ***Perf. 13***
142 A75 1fr dark blue & blue .50 .35

Fauna Type of 1988

1989, Jan. 1 **Engr.**
143 A73 1.10fr Lithodes .40 .40
144 A73 3.60fr Blue petrel 1.40 .75

Fern A76

1989, Jan. 1
145 A76 2.80fr *Blechnum penna Marina* 1.00 .90

Minerals A77

1989, Jan. 1
146 A77 5.10fr Mesotype 2.00 2.00
147 A77 7.30fr Analcime 3.00 3.00

Henri and Rene Bossiere, Pioneers of the Kerguelen Isls. — A78

1989, Jan. 1
148 A78 2.20fr multicolored 1.10 .75

Kerguelen Is. Sheep — A79

1989, Jan. 1 ***Perf. 13½x13***
149 A79 2fr multicolored .75 .65

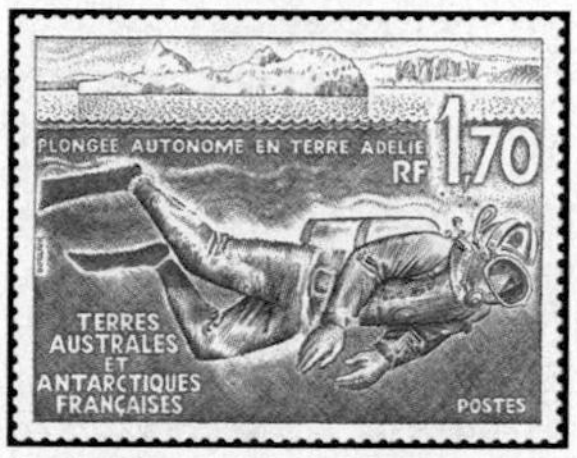

Scuba Diver, Adelie Coast — A80

1989, Jan. 1
150 A80 1.70fr dk olive bis, blue & dk grn .75 .60

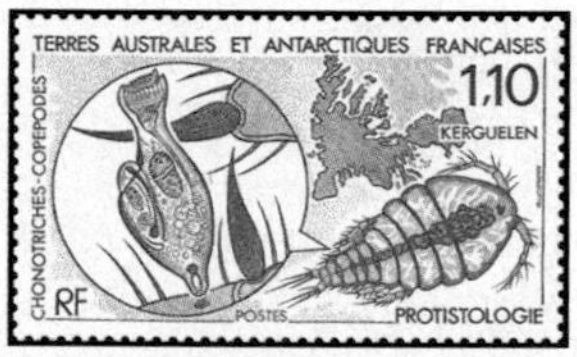

Map of Kerguelen Island, Protozoa and Copepod — A81

1990, Jan. 1 **Engr.** ***Perf. 13***
151 A81 1.10fr blk, brt blue & red brn .75 .40

Study of protista, Kerguelan Is.

Cattle on Farm, Sea Birds — A82

1990, Jan. 1
152 A82 1.70fr Prus blue, grn & brn blk .75 .60

Rehabilitation of the environment, Amsterdam Is.

Quoy and *Copendium decollata* — A83

Dumont d'Urville (1790-1842), Explorer — A84

1990, Jan. 1 ***Perf. 13½x13***
153 A83 2.20fr brt blue, blk & red brn .85 .75

Jean Rene C. Quoy (1790-1869), naturalist, navigator.

1990, Jan. 1
154 A84 3.60fr ultra & blk 1.50 1.10

Yellow-billed Albatross — A85

1990, Jan. 1 ***Perf. 13x12½***
155 A85 2.80fr multicolored 1.75 .90

Aragonite A86

1990, Jan. 1
156 A86 5.10fr deep ultra & dark yel grn 2.50 1.75

Ranunculus pseudo trullifolius — A87

1990, Jan. 1 *Perf. 13*
157 A87 8.40fr dp bl, org & emer grn 3.00 2.75

Penguin Type of Airpost 1974

1991, Jan. 1
158 AP18 50c blue grn, bl & blk .75 .20

Postal Service at Crozet Island, 30th anniv.

Moss — A88

1991, Jan. 1 *Perf. 13x12½*
159 A88 1.70fr gray, brn & blk .80 .65

Adm. Max Douguet (1903-1989) A89

1991, Jan. 1
160 A89 2.30fr org brn, blk & bl 1.25 .90

Lighter L'Aventure — A90

1991, Jan. 1 **Engr.** *Perf. 13*
161 A90 3.20fr brn, grn & bl 1.50 1.25

Sea Lions — A91

1991, Jan. 1 *Perf. 13*
162 A91 3.60fr blue & ol brn 2.25 1.40

Mordenite — A92

1991, Jan. 1
163 A92 5.20fr blk, grn bl & grn 2.75 2.00

Champsocephalus Gunnari — A93

1991, Jan. 1
164 A93 7.80fr blue & green 3.00 3.00

A94 A95

1991, Jan. 1
165 A94 9.30fr ol grn & rose red 4.00 3.50

Antarctic Treaty, 30th anniv.

1992, Jan. 1 **Engr.** *Perf. 13*

Design: Colobanthus Kerguelensis.

166 A95 1fr bl grn, grn & brn .85 .45

Globe Challenge Yacht Race — A96

1992, Jan. 1 **Litho.**
167 A96 2.20fr multicolored 1.25 1.00

Dissostichus Eleginoides — A97

1992, Jan. 1 **Engr.**
168 A97 2.30fr blue, ol grn & red brn 1.40 1.00

Paul Tchernia A98

1992, Jan. 1 **Engr.** *Perf. 13*
169 A98 2.50fr brown & green 1.00 1.00

Capt. Marion Dufresne (1724-1772) — A99

1992, Jan. 1 **Engr.** *Perf. 13*
170 A99 3.70fr red, blk & bl 1.50 1.50

Supply Ship Tottan, 1951 — A100

1992, Jan. 1 **Engr.** *Perf. 13*
171 A100 14fr blue grn, brn & bl 5.75 5.75

WOCE Program — A101

1992, Jan. 1
172 A101 25.40fr multi 12.00 10.50

Coat of Arms — A102

1992-95 **Engr.** *Perf. 13*
173 A102 10c black .25 .20
174 A102 20c greenish blue .25 .20
175 A102 30c red .25 .20
176 A102 40c green .40 .20
177 A102 50c orange .40 .20
Nos. 173-177 (5) 1.55 1.00

Issued: 10c, 1/1/92; 20c, 30c, 1/1/93; 40c, 1/1/94; 50c, 1/2/95.

See Nos. 295-299.

Garnet A103

1993, Jan. 1 **Engr.** *Perf. 13*
183 A103 1fr multicolored 1.25 .30

See Nos. 194, 203, 212, 222, 235, 244, 259, 279, 300, 330.

Research Ship Marion Dufresne, 20th Anniv. — A104

Lyallia Kerguelensis A105

1993, Jan. 1
184 A104 2.20fr multicolored 1.25 .60

1993, Jan. 1
185 A105 2.30fr blue & green 1.25 .60

A106

A107

1993, Jan. 1
186 A106 2.50fr Killer whale 1.50 .70
187 A107 2.50fr Skua 7.00 .70

Explorer Type of 1979 and

Weather station, Adelie Land A108

Design: 2.50fr, Andre Prudhomme (1930-1959), Meteorologist.

1993, Jan. 1 *Perf. 12½x13*
188 A29 2.50fr blue, blk & org 1.00 .65
189 A108 22fr org, blk & bl 8.50 6.00
a. Pair, #188-189 + label 11.00 11.00

Centriscops Obliquus — A109

1993, Jan. 1 *Perf. 13*
190 A109 3.40fr multicolored 1.50 .90

Freighter Italo Marsano — A110

1993, Jan. 1
191 A110 3.70fr multicolored 1.75 1.00

ECOPHY Program A111

1993, Jan. 1
192 A111 14fr black, blue & brn 6.50 4.25

L'Astrolabe on Northeast Route, 1991 A112

1993, Jan. 1
193 A112 22fr multicolored 9.25 5.75

Mineral Type of 1993

1994, Jan. 1 Engr. *Perf. 13*
194 A103 1fr Cordierite .75 .35

Felis Catus — A113

1994, Jan. 1
195 A113 2fr green & black 3.50 1.25

A114

1994, Jan. 1 Engr. *Perf. 13*
196 A114 2.40fr dk brn, blk & bl 1.50 .65

A115

1994, Jan. 1
197 A115 2.80fr slate blue 1.25 .70

Robert Pommier (1919-61) A116

1994, Jan. 1
198 A116 2.80fr multicolored 1.25 .70

A117

Designs: 2.80fr, C.A. Vincendon Dumoulin (1811-58), hydrographer. 23fr, Measuring Earth's magnetic field.

1994, Jan. 1 *Perf. 12½x13*
199 2.80fr black & blue 1.40 .70
200 23fr blue & black 8.75 5.75
a. A118 Pair, #199-200 + label 11.00 11.00

Rascasse — A119

1994, Jan. 1 *Perf. 13*
201 A119 3.70fr bl grn & red brn 1.50 .95

Kerguelen of Tremarec — A120

1994, Jan. 1
202 A120 4.30fr multicolored 1.75 1.10

Mineral Type of 1993

1995, Jan. 2 Engr. *Perf. 13*
203 A103 1fr Olivine 1.25 .30

Mancoglosse Antarctique — A121

1995, Jan. 2
204 A121 2.40fr ol brn, vio & bl grn 1.50 .95

Andree (1903-90) and Edgar de la Rue (1901-91) A122

1995, Jan. 2
205 A122 2.80fr bl, red brn & mag 1.50 .85

SODAR Station — A123

1995, Jan. 2
206 A123 2.80fr vio, mag & red brn 1.25 .85

Mont D'Alsace — A124

1995, Jan. 2
207 A124 3.70fr dk bl, vio, red brn 1.75 1.10

Balaenoptera Acutorostrata — A125

1995, Jan. 2
208 A125 23fr blue, claret & ind 10.00 6.50

Sailing Ship Tamaris A126

1995, Jan. 2
209 A126 25.80fr multicolored 11.00 7.50

L'Heroine, Crozet Islands Mission, 1837 — A127

1995, Jan. 2
210 A127 27.30fr blue 11.50 7.75

Creation of the Territories, 40th Anniv. — A128

Illustration reduced.

1995, Aug. 7 Litho. *Imperf.*
Size: 143x84mm
211 A128 30fr multicolored 14.00 14.00

Mineral Type of 1993

1996, Jan. 1 Engr. *Perf. 13*
212 A103 1fr Amazonite 1.00 .30

White-chinned Petrel — A129

1996, Jan. 1
213 A129 2.40fr blue black 1.25 .70

Expedition Ship Yves de Kerguelen — A130

1996, Jan. 1
214 A130 2.80fr multicolored 1.50 .80

Benedict Point Scientific Research Station, Amsterdam Island — A131

1996, Jan. 1
215 A131 2.80fr multicolored 1.50 .80

Paul-Emile Victor (1907-1995), Polar Explorer — A132

Designs: 2.80fr, Victor crossing Greenland with sled dogs, 1936. 23fr, Victor, penguins, Dumont d'Urville Base, Adélie Land.

1996, Jan. 1
216 A132 2.80fr multicolored 1.50 .90
217 A132 23fr multicolored 12.00 8.00
a. Pair, #216-217 + label 14.00 14.00

Admiral Jacquinot (1796-1879), Antarctic Explorer — A133

1996, Jan. 1
218 A133 3.70fr dark blue & blue 1.75 1.10

Trawler Austral — A134

1996, Jan. 1 **Photo. & Engr.**
219 A134 4.30fr multicolored 2.25 1.40

Lycopodium Magellanicum — A135

1996, Jan. 1 **Engr.**
220 A135 7.70fr multicolored 3.00 2.25

Search for Micrometeorites, Cape Prudhomme — A136

1996, Jan. 1
221 A136 15fr vio, blk & grn bl 8.00 5.00

Mineral Type of 1993

1997, Jan. 1 **Engr.** ***Perf. 13x12½***
222 A103 1fr Amethyst 1.25 .40

Storm Petrel — A137

1997, Jan. 1 ***Perf. 13***
223 A137 2.70fr blue & indigo 1.50 .90

Rene Garcia (1915-95), Windmill A138

1997, Jan. 1
224 A138 3fr multicolored 1.50 1.00

Research Ship Marion Dufresne — A139

Illustration reduced.

Photo. & Engr.

1997, Jan. 1 ***Perf. 13x12½***
225 A139 3fr multicolored 1.75 1.00

A140

A141

1997, Jan. 1 **Engr.** ***Perf. 13***
226 A140 4fr black & brown 1.75 1.25

Jean Turquet (1867-1945).

1997, Jan. 1
227 A141 5.20fr multicolored 2.25 1.60

Church of Our Lady of Birds, Crozet Island.

A142

A143

1997, Jan. 1
228 A142 8fr multicolored 4.00 2.60

Army Health Service.

1997, Jan. 1
229 A143 29.20fr Poa Kerguelensis 12.50 9.25

French Polar Expeditions, 50th Anniv. — A144

Designs: No. 230, Greenland Expedition. No. 231, Port Martin, 1950-51, Marret Base, 1952, Adélie Land. No. 232, Dumont D'Urville, 1956, Charcot Station, Magnetic Pole, 1957.

Photo. & Engr.

1997, Feb. 28 ***Perf. 13x12½***
230 A144 1fr multicolored .75 .30
231 A144 1fr multicolored .75 .30
232 A144 1fr multicolored .75 .30
a. Strip of 3, #230-232 4.00 2.00

Yves-Joseph de Kerguelen Trémarec (1734-97) — A145

3fr, Portrait. 24fr, Cook's landing at Kerguelen Island, Dec. 1776.

1997, Mar. 3 **Engr.** ***Perf. 13***
233 3fr multicolored 1.25 .90
234 24fr multicolored 9.75 7.25
a. A145 Pair, #233-234 + label 14.00 10.00

No. 234 is 37x37mm.

Mineral Type of 1993

1998, Jan. 2 **Engr.** ***Perf. 13***
235 A103 1fr Rock crystal 1.00 .30

Fisheries Management — A146

Designs: No. 236, Fishing boats. No. 237, Examining fish, performing research.

1998, Jan. 2
236 A146 2.60fr multicolored 1.50 .75
237 A146 2.60fr multicolored 1.50 .75
a. Pair, #236-237 + label 4.00 4.00

Gray-headed Albatross — A147

1998, Jan. 2
238 A147 2.70fr multicolored 1.75 .75

Ecology of St. Paul Island — A148

1998, Jan. 2
239 A148 3fr bl, brn & grn 1.75 .85

A149

A150

1998, Jan. 2 ***Perf. 13x13½***
240 A149 3fr lilac, blue & black 1.60 .85

Etienne Peau, Antarctic explorer.

1998, Jan. 2
241 A150 4fr lt org, blk & red brn 1.75 1.10

Georges Laclavere (1906-94), geographer.

Mole Shark — A151

1998, Jan. 2 ***Perf. 13***
242 A151 27fr multicolored 11.00 7.25

"Le Cancalais" — A152

1998, Jan. 2
243 A152 29.20fr multicolored 12.00 7.75

Mineral Type of 1993

1999, Jan. 1 **Engr.** ***Perf. 13***
244 A103 1fr Epidote, vert. 1.00 .30

Chinstrap Penguin — A153

1999, Jan. 1
245 A153 2.70fr brn, blk & bl 1.50 .85

Pierre Sicaud (1911-98), Antarctic Explorer, Commander of Outpost at Kerguelen Islands — A154

1999, Jan. 1
246 A154 3fr black & green 1.40 .95

Penguins of Crozet Islands — A155

Illustration reduced.

1999, Jan. 1
247 A155 3fr multicolored 2.00 .85

Jacques-André Martin (1911-49) — A156

1999, Jan. 1
248 A156 4fr multicolored 1.60 1.10

Ray — A157

1999, Jan. 1 ***Perf. 12½***
249 A157 5.20fr mag, bl & brn 2.50 1.50

Value is for stamp with surrounding rectangular selvage.

F.S. Floreal — A158

1999, Jan. 1 Photo. *Perf. 13*

250 A158 5.20fr multicolored 2.50 1.40

No. 250 was printed se-tenant with label. Value is for stamp with label attached.

"Pop Cat" Program, Kerguelen Islands — A159

1999, Jan. 1 Engr.

251 A159 8fr multicolored 4.25 2.75

Study of Albatrosses on Artificial Nests A160

1999, Jan. 1

252 A160 16fr olive, grn & blk 7.00 4.50

Amsterdam Base, Kerguelen Base, 50th Anniv. — A161

1999, Jan. 1

253 A161 3fr Amsterdam Base 6.00 .85

254 A161 24fr Kerguelen Base 10.50 6.50

a. Pair, #253-254 + label 18.00 15.00

Festuca Contracta A162

1999, Jan. 1

255 A162 24fr dk grn, ol & bl grn 10.50 6.50

Geoleta Program — A163

1999, Jan. 1 *Perf. 13x12½*

256 A163 29.20fr blk, bl & red brn 13.00 7.75

Voyage of Marion Dufresne II — A164

a, Docked, Reunion. b, Passengers in dining salon. c, Penguins, Crozet Island. d, Postal manager of Alfred Faure, Crozet Island, vert. e, Port of France, Kerguelen Island. f, Port Couvreux, Kerguelen Island. g, Offloading stores, Port of France, Kerguelen Island. h, Port Jeanne d'arc, Kerguelen Island. i, St. Paul Island. j, Ruins of lobster cannery, St. Paul Island. k, Martin de Vivies Base, Amsterdam Island. l, Offloading cargo, Amsterdam Island.

1999, May 1 Litho. *Perf. 13*

257 A164 Souv. bklt., #a.-l. 77.50

Nos. 257a-257l are all non-denominated. Stamps are valid for 20 gram international letter rate. Each stamp appears on a separate booklet pane showing an enlarged design of the stamp. Booklet sold for 100fr.

See Nos. 294, 329, 359, 390.

Souvenir Sheet

PhilexFrance '99, World Philatelic Exhibition — A165

Antarctic postmarks on stamps: a, Malagasy Republic #280. b, Malagasy Republic #282. c, Malagasy Republic #C42. d, #21.

1999, July 2 Litho. & Engr. *Perf. 13*

258 A165 5.20fr Sheet of 4, #a.-d. 11.50 7.00

Nos. 258b-258c are each 40x52mm.

Mineral Type of 1993

2000, Jan. Engr. *Perf. 12¾x13*

259 A103 1fr Mica, *vert.* .75 .25

Puffin — A166

2000, Jan. *Perf. 13x12¾*

260 A166 2.70fr multi 1.75 .80

André Beaugé (1913-97) A167

2000, Jan. *Perf. 12¾x13*

261 A167 3fr multi 1.40 .70

Abby Jane Morrell — A168

Sled Dog Hobbs — A170

Oceanographic Survey — A169

2000, Jan. *Perf. 13¼x13*

262 A168 4fr multi 1.75 .95

2000, Jan. *Perf. 13x12½*

263 A169 4.40fr multi 1.90 1.00

2000, Jan. *Perf. 12¾x13*

264 A170 5.20fr multi 2.25 1.25

Sleep Study — A171

Illustration reduced

2000, Jan. Photo. *Perf. 13x12½*

265 A171 8fr multi + label 3.50 1.90

Ship "La Perouse" — A172

2000, Jan. Engr. *Perf. 13x12½*

266 A172 16fr multi 7.00 3.75

Lantern Fish — A173

2000, Jan.

267 A173 24fr multi 10.50 5.50

Larose Bay — A174

2000, Jan.

268 A174 27fr multi 12.00 6.25

Explorers A175

#269, Yves Joseph de Kerguelen-Trémarec (1734-97). #270, Jules Sébastien César Dumont D'Urville (1790-1842). #271, Raymond Rallier du Baty (1881-1978). #272, Edgar Aubert de La Rüe (1901-91). #273, Paul-Emile Victor (1907-95).

2000, Jan. *Perf. 13*

Booklet Stamps

269 A175 3fr multi 1.50 .70

270 A175 3fr multi 1.50 .70

271 A175 3fr multi 1.50 .70

272 A175 3fr multi 1.50 .70

273 A175 3fr multi 1.50 .70

a. Bklt. pane, #269-273 + 2 labels 8.00

Complete booklet, #273a 9.50

Souvenir Sheet

The Third Millennium — A176

No. 274: a, Penguins, Crozet Islands. b, Seals, Kerguelen Islands. c, Crustacean, Saint-Paul and Amsterdam Islands. d, Hovering vehicle, Adelie Land.

2000, Jan. Photo. *Perf. 13*

274 A176 3fr Sheet of 4, #a.-d. 6.00 4.75

Bird Demographic Studies — A177

Designs: 5.20fr, Bird banding. 8fr, Albatross, graph. 16fr, Emperor penguins, graph.

2000, Jan. *Perf. 13x13¼*

275 A177 5.20fr multi 2.25 1.25

Size: 50x28mm

276 A177 8fr multi 3.50 1.90

277 A177 16fr multi 7.00 3.75

a. Horiz. strip, #275-277 14.00 14.00

Relocation of Headquarters to Reunion — A178

2000, Aug. 6 Litho. *Perf. 13*

278 A178 27fr multi 12.00 5.50

Mineral Type of 1993

2001, Jan. 1 Engr. *Perf. 13x12¾*

279 A103 1fr Magnetite 1.00 .30

Diving Petrel — A179

2001, Jan. 1 ***Perf. 13x13¼***
280 A179 2.70fr multi 1.50 .60

High Mountain Military Group A180

2001, Jan. 1 ***Perf. 13¼x13***
281 A180 3fr multi 1.40 .65

Kerguelen Arch — A181

2001, Jan. 1 ***Perf. 13***
282 A181 3fr blue gray 2.00 .70

Xavier-Charles Richert (1913-92) A182

Jean Coulomb A183

2001, Jan. 1
283 A182 3fr multi 1.40 .65

2001, Jan. 1
284 A183 4fr multi 1.75 .85

Memorial to 1874 Astronomical Observation, St. Paul Island — A184

2001, Jan. 1
285 A184 8fr brn & blk 3.50 1.75

Frigate La Fayette — A185

2001, Jan. 1 ***Perf. 13x13¼***
286 A185 16fr multi 7.00 3.50

Squid — A186

2001, Jan. 1
287 A186 24fr multi 10.50 5.00

Amateur Radio Link Between Space Station Mir and Crozet Island — A187

2001, Jan. 1 **Litho.** ***Perf. 13***
288 A187 27fr multi 12.00 5.50

Bryum Laevigatum — A188

2001, Jan. 1 **Engr.** ***Perf. 13x12½***
289 A188 29.20fr multi 13.00 6.00

Souvenir Sheet

Ships — A189

No. 290: a, Carmen. b, Austral. c, Ramuntcho. d, Samper 1.

2001, Jan. 1 ***Perf. 13x13½***
290 A189 5.20fr Sheet of 4, #a-d 9.00 4.50

Souvenir Sheet

Wildlife — A190

No. 291: a, Albatrosses. b, Emperor penguins, horiz. c, Sea lions, horiz. d, Whales.

2001, Jan. 1 **Litho.** ***Perf. 13***
291 A190 3fr Sheet of 4, #a-d 9.00 5.00

Antarctic Treaty, 40th Anniv. — A191

2001, June 23 **Engr.** ***Perf. 13x12¾***
292 A191 5.20fr dark & sky blue 3.25 1.00

Commission for the Conservation of Antarctic Marine Living Resources, 20th Anniv. — A192

2001, Oct. 22 **Litho.** ***Perf. 13***
293 A192 5.20fr multi 4.50 2.00

Voyage Booklet Type of 1999

Adélie Land: a, Boat in pack ice. b, Dumont d'Urville Base. c, Adélie penguin rookery. d, L'Astrolabe Glacier. e, Pointe Géologie Archipelago. f, Release of meteorological balloon. g, Equipment convoy. h, Helicopter transport of fresh supplies. i, Arrival of emperor penguins. j, Telecommunications center. k, Looking towards the Antarctic. l, Cape Prud'homme. m, Ship L'Astrolabe anchored. n, Dispatch of mail.

2001, Oct. 29 ***Perf. 13***
294 A164 Souvenir booklet, 2 each #a-n 95.00

Nos. 294a-294n are all non-denominated. Stamps are valid for 20 gram international letter rate. Each stamp appears ofn a separate booklet pane showing an enlarged design of the stamp and on one pane with all of the stamps and four labels found at the center of the booklet. the booklet sold for 196.78fr.

100 Cents = 1 Euro (€)

Arms Type of 1992-95 with Euro Denominations

2002, Jan. 2 **Engr.** ***Perf. 13***

295	A102	1c black	.20	.20
296	A102	2c greenish blue	.25	.20
297	A102	5c red	.30	.20
298	A102	10c green	.40	.20
299	A102	20c orange	.70	.20
		Nos. 295-299 (5)	1.85	1.00

Mineral Type of 1993 with Euro Denomination

2002, Jan. 2 **Engr.** ***Perf. 12¾x13***
300 A103 15c Nepheline, vert. .75 .20

Albatross A193

2002, Jan. 2 ***Perf. 13¼x13***
301 A193 41c multi 2.00 .75

Ship "Marion Dufresne" — A194

2002, Jan. 2 ***Perf. 13x13¼***
302 A194 46c multi 1.40 .60

1963-83 Telegraph Station, Crozet Island A195

2002, Jan. 2 **Litho.** ***Perf. 13***
303 A195 46c multi 1.50 .60

Jacques Dubois (1920-2000) A196

2002, Jan. 2 **Engr.**
304 A196 61c multi 1.90 .90

Engraved Rock, Saint Paul Island — A197

2002, Jan. 2 ***Perf. 13x13¼***
305 A197 79c multi 2.40 1.25

Kerguelen Cabbage A198

2002, Jan. 2 ***Perf. 12¼***
306 A198 €1.22 multi 3.50 1.75

Passage of the Ship "Gauss," Cent. — A199

2002, Jan. 2 ***Perf. 13x12¼***
307 A199 €2.44 multi 7.25 3.50

Crab — A200

2002, Jan. 2 *Perf. 13x13¼*
308 A200 €3.66 multi 11.00 5.25

Pack Ice Diatoms — A201

2002, Jan. 2 **Litho.** *Perf. 13*
309 A201 €4.12 multi 12.50 6.00

French Geographic Society Building, Paris — A202

2002, Jan. 2 **Engr.** *Perf. 13¼x13*
310 A202 €4.45 multi + label 13.50 8.00

Cartoker Program — A203

No. 311: a, 46c, Diagram of plate tectonics. b, €3.66, Geological map of Kerguelen Island. Illustration reduced.

2002, Jan. 2 *Perf. 13x12¼*
311 A203 Horiz. pair, #a-b, + central label 12.50 12.50

Souvenir Sheet

Olympic Games for Antarctic Animals — A204

No. 312: a, Albatrosses flying marathon. b, Langoustines diving, vert. c, Penguins riding bobsled course, vert. d, Killer whales performing synchronized swimming, vert.

2002, Jan. 2 **Litho.** *Perf. 13*
312 A204 46c Sheet of 4, #a-d 5.50 5.50

Souvenir Sheet

Animals and Their Young — A205

No. 313: a, Penguins. b, Sea lions. c, Albatrosses. d, Elephant seals.

2002, Jan. 2
313 A205 79c Sheet of 4, #a-d 9.50 9.50

Introduction of the Euro A206

2002, Feb. 17
314 A206 46c blue & black 3.00 .60

Mineral Type of 1993

2003, Jan. **Engr.** *Perf. 13¼*
315 A103 15c Apatite, vert. 1.00 .30

Lobster Processing Plant, Saint-Paul — A207

2003, Jan. *Perf. 13x13¼*
316 A207 41c multi 1.20 .65

Luc Marie Bayle (1914-2000), Painter — A208

2003, Jan. **Litho.** *Perf. 13*
317 A208 46c multi 1.50 .70

Emperor Penguins — A209

2003, Jan.
318 A209 46c multi 2.00 .80

Otice Hydroacoustic Station — A210

2003, Jan. **Engr.** *Perf. 13x13¼*
319 A210 61c multi 1.90 1.00

Restoration of Port Jeanne d'Arc — A211

2003, Jan. *Perf. 13x12¼*
320 A211 79c multi 2.40 1.25

Phylica — A212

2003, Jan. *Perf. 13x13¼*
321 A212 €1.22 multi 3.75 2.25

Ship "Bougainville" A213

2003, Jan. *Perf. 13¼x13*
322 A213 €2.44 multi 7.25 4.25

Chub — A214

2003, Jan. **Engr.** *Perf. 13x13¼*
323 A214 €3.66 multi 11.00 6.50

Ile aux Pingouins — A215

2003, Jan. *Perf. 13x12¼*
324 A215 €3.66 black 11.00 6.50

Super Darn Antenna Array — A216

Illustration reduced.

2003, Jan. *Perf. 13*
325 A216 €4.12 multi 12.50 7.00

Souvenir Sheet

Paintings Revised to Reflect a Less Southerly Antarctica — A217

No. 326: a, Triumph of Venus with fish and lobsters. b, King Louis XV and wife with penguins, vert. c, Jules Dumont d'Urville and wife in a grassy Adélie Land. d, Chevalier Yves de Kerguelin under umbrella, seal in pool, vert.

2003, Jan. **Litho.**
326 A217 46c Sheet of 4, #a-d 6.50 6.50

Protective Clothing — A218

Cold-weather outerwear from: a, 1898. b, 1912. c, 2002. d, 1980, e, 1996.

2003, Jan. **Photo.** *Perf. 13¼x13*
327 Booklet pane of 5 12.00 —
a.-e. A218 79c Any single 2.40 1.25
Booklet, #327 12.00

Voyage of the Ship "Français," Cent. — A219

2003, Aug. 31 Engr. *Perf. 13x13¼*

328	Horiz. strip of 3	13.50	13.50
a.	A219 79c Capt. J.-B. Charcot	2.40	1.25
b.	A219 €1.22 Ship in ice, horiz.	3.50	2.00
c.	A219 €2.44 Ship in harbor, horiz.	7.25	4.25

Stamp size: Nos. 328b-328c, 49x29mm.

Voyage Booklet Type of 1999

Recipes: a, Truite aus deux citrons (trout and waterfall). b, Veau d'Amsterdam à la savoyarde (cattle). c, Lapin "Volage" à la cannelle (rabbits, penguins). d, Rôti de légine de l'île de l'est (fish). e, Civet de renne "Volcan du diable," (reindeer). f, Iles antarctiques flottantes. g, Langouste à la mode de Saint-Paul (lobster). h, Gigot de mouflon aux 5 épices et aux pommes (sheep). i, Cabot tropical (fish, ship). j, Tagine d'agneau aux épices de la Réunion (sheep). k, Moules au pastis (mussels). l, Glace à la menthe sauvage d'Amsterdam (mint plant).

2003, Nov. 6 Litho. *Perf. 13*

329 A164 Souvenir booklet, #a-l 55.00

Nos. 329a-329l are all non-denominated. Stamps are valid for 20 gram international letter rate. Each stamp appears on a separate booklet pane showing an enlarged design of the stamp. The booklet sold for €17.

Mineral Type of 1993

2004, Jan. 1 Engr. *Perf. 13¼*

330 A103 15c Chalcedony, vert. 1.25 .40

A220

A221

2004, Jan. 1 Engr. *Perf. 13x13¼*

331 A220 45c multi 1.40 .85

Mario Marret, director of film "Terre Adélie."

2004, Jan. 1

332 A221 50c multi 1.75 .95

Col. Robert Genty (1910-2001).

Albert Faure Base, Crozet Island, 40th Anniv. — A222

Illustration reduced.

2004, Jan. 1 Litho. & Engr.

333 A222 50c multi 1.50 .95

Péron's Dolphins — A223

2004, Jan. 1 Litho. *Perf. 13*

334 A223 75c multi 2.50 1.50

Twin Otter Flights A224

2004, Jan. 1 Photo. *Perf. 12¾*

335 A224 90c multi 2.75 1.75

Values are for stamps with surrounding selvage.

Iceberg — A225

2004, Jan. 1 Engr. *Perf. 13x13¼*

336 A225 €1.30 multi 4.00 2.40

Grave of Sailors from the Volage — A226

2004, Jan. 1 *Perf. 13¼x13*

337 A226 €2.50 multi 7.50 5.00

Krill — A227

2004, Jan. 1 *Perf. 13x13¼*

338 A227 €4 multi 12.00 8.00

Ship "Dives" — A228

2004, Jan. 1

339 A228 €4.50 multi 13.50 9.25

Souvenir Sheet

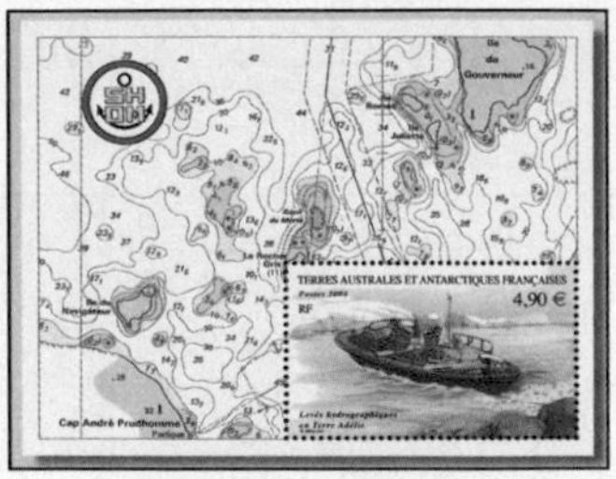

Hydrological Surveys, Adélie Land — A229

2004, Jan. 1 Litho. *Perf. 13*

340 A229 €4.90 multi 15.00 10.50

Souvenir Sheet

Imaginary "TAAFland" Theme Park — A230

No. 341: a, Whale statue, pyramidal entrance structure. b, Showgirls, seals, vert. c, Boy and girl with ice cream cones, vert. d, Woman in swimsuit, penguins.

2004, Jan. 1

341 A230 50c Sheet of 4, #a-d 6.00 3.75

Souvenir Sheet

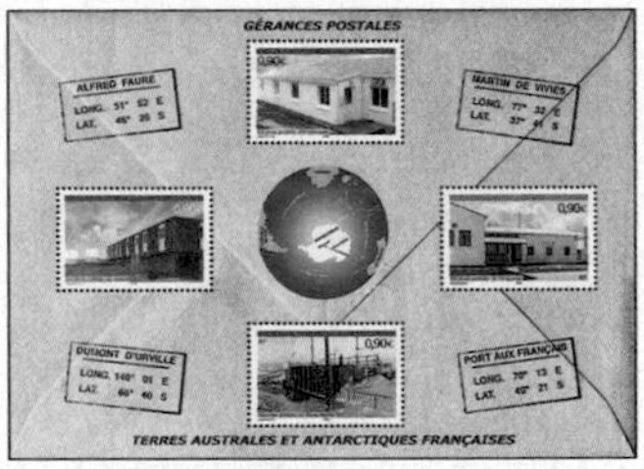

Post Offices — A231

No. 342: a, Amsterdam Island. b, Crozet Island. c, Kerguelen Island. d, Adélie Land.

2004, Jan. 1

342 A231 90c Sheet of 4, #a-d 11.00 7.25

Penguin and Liberty Cap — A232

2004, June 26 Engr. *Perf. 13¼x13*

343 A232 €4.50 multi 14.50 12.00

Mineral Type of 1993

2005, Jan. 1 Engr. *Perf. 13¼*

344 A103 15c Agate .50 .50

Albert Bauer (1916-2003), Glaciologist — A233

2005, Jan. 1 *Perf. 13x13¼*

345 A233 45c multi 1.75 1.75

Roger Barberot (1915-2002), Administrator A234

2005, Jan. 1

346 A234 50c multi 1.75 1.75

Ship "Cap Horn" — A235

2005, Jan. 1

347 A235 50c multi 1.75 1.75

Seal Pot A236

2005, Jan. 1 Litho. *Perf. 13*

348 A236 50c multi 2.00 2.00

Macgillivray's Prion — A237

2005, Jan. 1 Engr. *Perf. 13x13¼*

349 A237 75c multi 2.25 2.25

Studer Valley — A238

2005, Jan. 1 *Perf. 13x12½*

350 A238 90c multi 2.75 2.75

Peigne des Néréides A239

2005, Jan. 1 *Perf. 12¼*
351 A239 €2.50 multi 7.50 7.50

Harpovoluta Charcoti — A240

2005, Jan. 1 *Perf. 13x12½*
352 A240 €4 multi 13.50 13.50

Murray's Ray — A241

2005, Jan. 1 Litho. *Perf. 13*
353 A241 €4.50 multi 13.50 13.50

Elephant Seal and Oceanographic Chart — A242

Illustration reduced.

2005, Jan. 1 Engr.
354 A242 €4.90 multi 15.00 15.00

Concordia Station — A243

Illustration reduced.

2005, Jan. 3 Litho. *Perf. 13*
355 A243 50c multi 1.50 1.50

Return of the Ship "Français," Cent. — A244

Illustration reduced.

2005, Mar. 4 Engr. *Perf. 13x13¼*
356 A244 €4.50 multi + label 14.00 14.00

Disappearance of Paul-Emile Victor, 10th Anniv. — A245

2005, Mar. 7 Litho. *Perf. 13*
357 A245 50c multi 1.75 1.75

50th Anniversary Coat of Arms — A246

2005, Aug. 6
358 A246 (90c) multi 2.75 2.75
a. Booklet pane of 1 4.00 —

No. 358a is found in No. 359.

Voyage Booklet Type of 1999

History: a, Discovery of Amsterdam Island, 1522. b, Discovery of Crozet Island, 1772. c, Discovery of Kerguelen Island, 1772, vert. d, Discovery of Adélie Land, 1840. e, Astronomers viewing 1874 transit of Venus on St. Paul Island. f, Wreck of the Strathmore, 1875. g, Port Jeanne d'Arc, 1908. h, Port-Couvreux, 1925. i, Building of Port-Martin, 1950. j, Antarctic Treaty, 1959. k, Building of fourth base, 1963-64.

2005, Aug. 6 Litho. *Perf. 13*
359 A164 Souvenir booklet, #a-k, 358a 50.00

Nos. 359a-359k are all non-denominated. Stamps are valid for 90c, the 20 gram international letter rate. Each stamp appears on a separate booklet pane showing an enlarged design of the stamp. The booklet sold for €18.

Penguins and No. 1 — A247

2005, Nov. 2
360 A247 90c multi 3.00 3.00

French Southern & Antarctic Territories, 50th anniv.

Souvenir Sheet

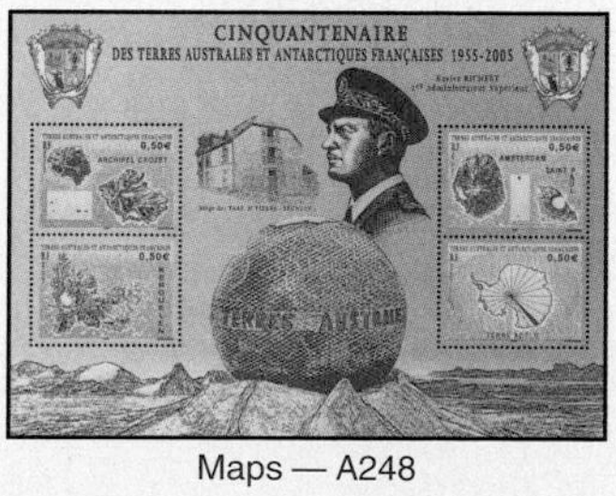

Maps — A248

Maps of: a, Crozet Archipelago. b, Amsterdam and St. Paul Islands. c, Kerguelen Island. d, Adélie Land.

Litho. & Engr.
2005, Nov. 10 *Perf. 13x13¼*
361 A248 50c Sheet of 4, #a-d 6.00 6.00

French Southern & Antarctic Territories, 50th anniv.

Rutile A249

2006, Jan. 1 Engr. *Perf. 13x12½*
362 A249 15c multi .60 .60

A250

A251

2006, Jan. 1 *Perf. 13x13¼*
363 A250 48c pur & red 1.50 1.50

Charles Vélain (1845-1925), geologist.

2006, Jan. 1
364 A251 53c multi 1.60 1.60

Albert Seyrolle (1887-1919), mariner.

Amsterdam Island Garden — A252

2006, Jan. 1 Litho. *Perf. 13*
365 A252 53c multi 1.60 1.60

Ship "Osiris" — A253

2006, Jan. 1 Photo. *Perf. 13x13¼*
366 A253 90c multi 2.75 2.75

Dumont d'Urville Base, 50th Anniv. — A254

Illustration reduced.

2006, Jan. 1 Engr. *Perf. 13x12½*
367 A254 90c multi 2.75 2.75

Virgin of the Seal Hunters — A255

2006, Jan. 1 *Perf. 12½x13*
368 A255 €2.50 multi 7.50 7.50

Lagenorhynchus Cruciger — A256

2006, Jan. 1 *Perf. 13x13¼*
369 A256 €4 multi 12.00 12.00

Keguelen Hake — A257

2006, Jan. 1
370 A257 €4.53 multi 13.50 13.50

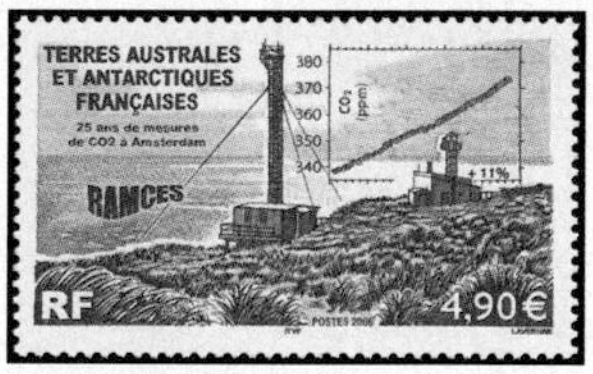

Amsterdam Island Carbon Dioxide Measurements, 25th Anniv. — A258

2006, Jan. 1
371 A258 €4.90 multi 15.00 15.00

Miniature Sheet

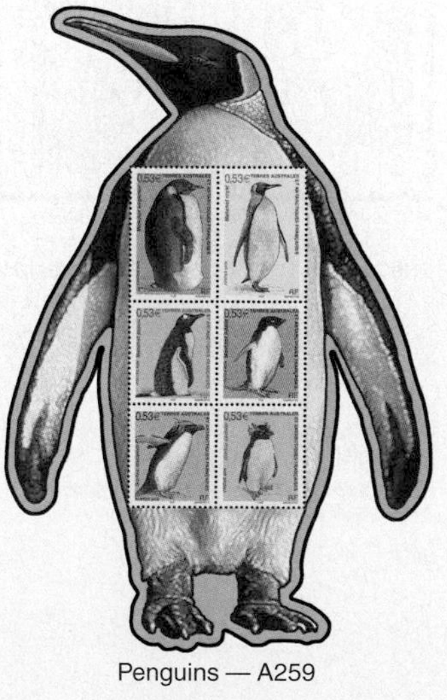

Penguins — A259

No. 372 — Penguin (background color): a, Emperor penguin (lilac, 22x36mm). b, King penguin (pale yellow green, 22x36mm). c, Gentoo penguin (green, 22x27mm). d, Adélie penguin (pink, 22x27mm). e, Macaroni penguin (orange, 22x27mm). f, Rockhopper penguin (blue, 22x27mm).

Litho. & Engr.

2006, Jan. 1 *Perf. 13*
372 A259 53c Sheet of 6, #a-f 11.00 11.00

Souvenir Sheet

Albatross — A260

Litho. & Engr.

2006, June 1 *Perf. 13*
373 A260 €4.53 multi 14.50 14.50

Souvenir Sheet

Albatross — A261

Litho. & Engr.

2006, Nov. 8 *Perf. 13*
374 A261 90c multi 3.00 3.00

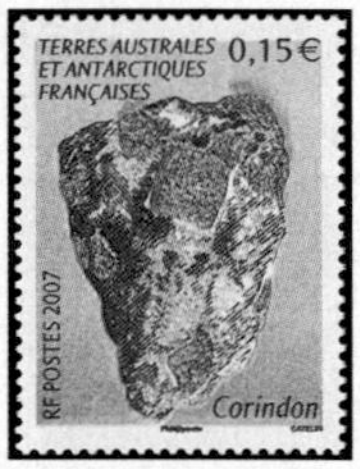

Corundum A262

2007, Jan. 1 **Engr.** *Perf. 13¼*
375 A262 15c multi 1.25 1.25

A263 A264

2007, Jan. 1 *Perf. 13x13¼*
376 A263 49c multi 1.50 1.50

Louis-Francois Aleno de Saint Aloüarn (1738-72), explorer who claimed Australia for France.

2007, Jan. 1
377 A264 54c multi 1.60 1.60

Marthe Emmanuel (1901-97), assistant to explorer Jean Charcot.

Cattle, Amsterdam Island — A265

2007, Jan. 1 *Perf. 13x12½*
378 A265 54c multi 1.50 1.50

Ship Tonkinois — A266

2007, Jan. 1 *Perf. 13x13¼*
379 A266 90c multi 2.50 2.50

Ile de la Baleine — A267

2007, Jan. 1 *Perf. 13x12½*
380 A267 90c multi 2.50 2.50

Archaeology on Saint Paul Island — A268

2007, Jan. 1 *Perf. 12½x13*
381 A268 €2.50 multi 7.00 7.00

Lampris Immaculatus — A269

2007, Jan. 1 *Perf. 13x12½*
382 A269 €4 multi 11.00 11.00

Astonomy at Concordia — A270

Litho. & Engr.

2007, Jan. 1 *Perf. 13*
383 A270 €4.90 multi 14.00 14.00

French Polar Expeditions, 60th Anniv. — A271

No. 384: a, Expedition headquarters, Paris, men shaking hands over globe. b, Expedition headquarters.

2007, Jan. 1 **Engr.** *Perf. 13x13¼*
384 Horiz. pair + central label 13.50 13.50
a. A271 54c multi 1.75 1.75
b. A271 €4 multi 11.00 11.00

Miniature Sheet

Albatrosses — A272

No. 385: a, Amsterdam albatross. b, Great albatross (Grand albatros). c, Black-browed albatross (Albatros à sourcils noir). d, Yellow-beaked albatross (Albatros à bec jaune). e, Sooty albatross (Albatros fuligineux).

Litho. & Engr.

2007, Jan. 1 *Perf. 13*
385 A272 54c Sheet of 5, #a-e 7.50 7.50

Intl. Polar Year — A273

No. 386: a, Penguins. b, Map of Antarctica, French Southern & Antarctic Territories #9.

2007, Mar. 1 **Litho.** *Perf. 13*
386 Horiz. pair + central label 15.00 15.00
a. A273 90c multi 2.75 2.75
b. A273 €4 multi 12.00 12.00

Audit Office, Bicent. A274

2007 Mar. 19 **Engr.** *Perf. 13¼*
387 A274 90c multi 4.50 4.50

Miniature Sheet

Indian Ocean Islands — A275

No. 388: a, Ile Tromelin. b, Iles Glorieuses. c, Ile Juan de Nova. d, Ile Bassas da India. e, Ile Europa.

2007, May 10 **Photo.** *Perf. 13x13¼*
388 A275 54c Sheet of 5, #a-e 9.00 9.00

Path of Sun on June 21 Over Dumont d'Urville Base — A276

Illustration reduced.

2007, June 21
389 A276 90c multi 3.00 3.00

Voyage Booklet Type of 1999

No. 390 — Photographs of land features: a, Apostle Island, Crozet Archipelago. b, Chamonix Lake, Kerguelen Island. c, Phylicia forest, Amsterdam Island. d, Gulf of Morbihan, Kerguelen Islands. e, Mount Cook, Chamonix Lake and glacier, Kerguelen Islands. f, Tourbiéres Plateau, Amsterdam Island. g, Nuageuses Islands, Kerguelen Islands. h, Caldera, Amsterdam Island. i, Mount Cook, Kerguelen Island. j, Central Plateau, Kerguelen Island. k, Isle of Penguins, Crozet Archipelago. l, Antonelli Crater, Amsterdam Island. m, Lake on Possession Island, Crozet Archipelago. n, Rocks off Apostle Island, Crozet Archipelago. o, Geographic Society Peninsula, Kerguelen Island. p, Ronarch Peninsula, Kerguelen Island.

2007, Nov. 8 **Litho.** *Perf. 13*
390 A164 (90c) Souvenir booklet, #a-p 60.00

No. 390 sold for €20, and contains four panes, consisting of a block of four stamps of Nos. 390a-390d, 390e-390h, 390i-390l, and 390m-390p.

French Southern and Antarctic Territories Flag — A277

2008, Jan. 1 **Litho.** *Perf. 13*

Background Color

391 A277 1c black .20 .20
392 A277 2c blue .20 .20
393 A277 5c red .20 .20
394 A277 10c green .30 .30
395 A277 20c brn orange .60 .60
Nos. 391-395 (5) 1.50 1.50

Spinel — A278

2008, Jan. 1 Engr. *Perf. 13¼*
396 A278 15c multi .45 .45

Samivel (1907-92), Writer — A279

St. Paul Island — A280

2008, Jan. 1 *Perf. 13x13¼*
397 A279 54c grn & brown 1.60 1.60

2008, Jan. 1
398 A280 54c blue & dk blue 1.60 1.60

Construction of Port Jeanne d'Arc, Cent. — A281

Illustration reduced.

2008, Jan. 1 *Perf. 13x12¾*
399 A281 90c multi 2.75 2.75

Rockhopper Penguins — A282

2008, Jan. 1 *Perf. 13x12½*
400 A282 90c multi 2.75 2.75

Shipwreck of L'Esperance — A283

2008, Jan. 1 Litho. *Perf. 13x12¾*
401 A283 90c multi 2.75 2.75

Macrourus Carinatus — A284

2008, Jan. 1 Engr. *Perf. 13x12½*
402 A284 €4 multi 12.00 12.00

Galium Antarcticum A285

2008, Jan. 1 *Perf. 12½x13*
403 A285 €4.54 multi 13.50 13.50

Adélie Land Coastal Ichthyology Program A286

2008, Jan. 1 Litho. *Perf. 13*
404 A286 €4.90 multi 14.50 14.50

Souvenir Sheet

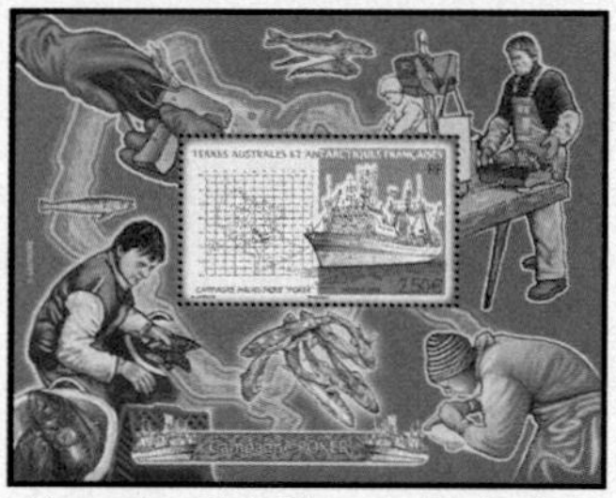

Kerguelen Fish Biomass Evaluation Project (POKER) — A287

2008, Jan. 1 Litho. & Engr.
405 A287 €2.50 multi 7.50 7.50

Souvenir Sheet

Elephant Seals — A288

No. 406: a, Head of adult female. b, Seals initiating combat. c, Juvenile seal. d, Head of adult male.

2008, Jan. 1
406 A288 54c Sheet of 4, #a-d 6.50 6.50

Gérard Mégie (1946-2004), Ozone Researcher — A289

2008, Feb. 15 Engr. *Perf. 13x13¼*
407 A289 54c multi 1.75 1.75

Miniature Sheet

Birds — A290

No. 408: a, Sooty tern (Sterne fulgineuse). b, Red-footed booby (Fou a pieds rouges), vert. c, Masked booby (Fou masque), vert. d, Great frigatebird (Fregate du Pacifique), vert. e, Tropicbird (Paille en queue).

Perf. 13¼x13 (#408a, 408e), 13x13¼
2008, June 1 Litho. & Engr.
408 A290 54c Sheet of 5, #a-e 8.50 8.50

Earth and Birds — A291

Illustration reduced.

2008, June 14 Photo. *Perf. 13*
409 A291 €4.54 multi 14.50 14.50

AIR POST STAMPS

Emperor Penguins and Map of Antarctica — AP1

Unwmk.
1956, Apr. 25 Engr. *Perf. 13*
C1 AP1 50fr lt ol grn & dk grn 42.50 29.00
C2 AP1 100fr dl bl & indigo 35.00 25.00

Wandering Albatross — AP2

1959, Sept. 14
C3 AP2 200fr brn red, bl & blk 40.00 27.50

Adélie Penguins — AP3

1963, Feb. 11 Unwmk. *Perf. 13*
C4 AP3 50fr blk, dk bl & dp cl 42.50 32.50

Telstar Issue
Common Design Type

1963, Feb. 11
C5 CD111 50fr dp bl, ol & grn 29.00 21.00

Radio Towers, Adelie Penguins and IQSY Emblem — AP4

1963, Dec. 16 Engr.
C6 AP4 100fr bl, ver & blk 110.00 87.50

International Quiet Sun Year, 1964-65.

Discovery of Adelie Land — AP5

1965, Jan. 20 Engr. *Perf. 13*
C7 AP5 50fr blue & indigo 125.00 87.50

125th anniversary of the discovery of Adelie Land by Dumont d'Urville.

ITU Issue
Common Design Type

1965, May 17 Unwmk. *Perf. 13*
C8 CD120 30fr multi 200.00 160.00

French Satellite A-1 Issue
Common Design Type

Designs: 25fr, Diamant rocket and launching installations. 30fr, A-1 satellite.

1966, Mar. 2 Engr. *Perf. 13*
C9 CD121 25fr dk grn, choc & sl 13.50 10.00
C10 CD121 30fr choc, sl & dk grn 13.50 10.00
a. Pair, #C9-C10 + label 29.00 24.00

French Satellite D-1 Issue
Common Design Type

1966, Mar. 27
C11 CD122 50fr dk pur, lil & org 57.50 40.00

Ionospheric Research Pylon, Adelie Land — AP6

1966, Dec. 12
C12 AP6 25fr plum, bl & dk brn 32.50 17.50

Port aux Français, Emperor Penguin and Explorer — AP7

40fr, Aerial view of Saint Paul Island.

1968-69 **Engr.** ***Perf. 13***
C13 AP7 40fr brt bl & dk gray 42.50 27.50
C14 AP7 50fr lt ultra, dk grn & blk 175.00 110.00

Issue dates: 50fr, Jan. 21; 40fr, Jan. 5, 1969.

Kerguelen Island and Rocket — AP8

Design: 30fr, Adelie Land.

1968, Apr. 22 **Engr.** ***Perf. 13***
C15 AP8 25fr sl grn, dk brn & Prus bl 19.00 14.00
C16 AP8 30fr dk brn, sl grn & Prus bl 19.00 14.00
a. Pair, #C15-C16 + label 40.00 30.00

Space explorations with Dragon rockets, 1967-68.

Eiffel Tower, Antarctic Research Station, Ship from Paris Arms and Albatross AP9

1969, Jan. 13
C17 AP9 50fr bright blue 45.00 35.00

5th Consultative Meeting of the Antarctic Treaty Powers, Paris, Nov. 18, 1968.

Concorde Issue
Common Design Type

1969, Apr. 17
C18 CD129 85fr indigo & blue 55.00 37.50

Prepared but not issued with 87fr denomination. Value $6,000.

Map of Amsterdam Island AP10

Map of Kerguelen Island — AP11

Coat of Arms AP12

Designs: 50fr, Possession Island. 200fr, Point Geology Archipelago.

1969-71 **Engr.** ***Perf. 13***
C19 AP10 30fr brown 19.00 12.50
C20 AP11 50fr sl grn, bl & dk red 21.00 14.00
C21 AP11 100fr blue & blk 85.00 40.00
C22 AP10 200fr sl grn, brn & Prus bl 70.00 42.50
C23 AP12 500fr peacock blue 20.00 15.00
Nos. C19-C23 (5) 215.00 124.00

30fr for the 20th anniv. of the Amsterdam Island Meteorological Station.
Issued: 100fr, 500fr, 12/21; 30fr, 3/27/70; 50fr, 12/22/70; 200fr, 1/1/71.

Port-aux-Français, 1970 — AP13

Design: 40fr, Port-aux-Français, 1950.

1971, Mar. 9 **Engr.** ***Perf. 13***
C24 AP13 40fr bl, ocher & sl grn 19.00 12.00
C25 AP13 50fr bl, grn ol & sl grn 19.00 12.00
a. Pair, #C24-C25 + label 40.00 27.50

20th anniversary of Port-aux-Français on Kerguelen Island.

Marquis de Castries Taking Possession of Crozet Island, 1772 — AP14

250fr, Fleur-de-lis flag raising on Kerguelen Is.

1972 **Engr.** ***Perf. 13***
C26 AP14 100fr black 45.00 29.00
C27 AP14 250fr black & dk brn 100.00 45.00

Bicentenary of the discovery of the Crozet and Kerguelen Islands.
Issue dates: 100fr, Jan. 24; 250fr, Feb. 23.

M. S. Galliéni — AP15

1973, Jan. 25 **Engr.** ***Perf. 13***
C28 AP15 100fr black & blue 25.00 17.50

Exploration voyages of the Galliéni.

"Le Mascarin," 1772 — AP16

Sailing Ships: 145fr, "L'Astrolabe," 1840. 150fr, "Le Rolland," 1774. 185fr, "La Victoire," 1522.

1973, Dec. 13 **Engr.** ***Perf. 13***
C29 AP16 120fr brown olive 6.00 4.00
C30 AP16 145fr brt ultra 6.00 4.00
C31 AP16 150fr slate 7.50 5.00
C32 AP16 185fr ocher 9.50 6.00
Nos. C29-C32 (4) 29.00 19.00

Ships used in exploring Antarctica.
See Nos. C37-C38.

Alfred Faure Base — AP17

Design: Nos. C33-C35 show panoramic view of Alfred Faure Base.

1974, Jan. 7 **Engr.** ***Perf. 13***
C33 AP17 75fr Prus bl, ultra & brn 8.00 5.25
C34 AP17 110fr Prus bl, ultra & brn 11.00 8.00
C35 AP17 150fr Prus bl, ultra & brn 14.00 8.00
a. Triptych, Nos. C33-C35 37.50 30.00

Alfred Faure Antarctic Base, 10th anniv.

Penguin, Map of Antarctica, Letters — AP18

1974, Oct. 9 **Engr.** ***Perf. 13***
C36 AP18 150fr multicolored 7.00 5.50

Centenary of Universal Postal Union.

Ship Type of 1973

100fr, "Le Français." 200fr, "Pourquoi-pas?"

1974, Dec. 16 **Engr.** ***Perf. 13***
C37 AP16 100fr brt blue 5.50 3.00
C38 AP16 200fr dk car rose 9.00 4.50

Ships used in exploring Antarctica.

Rockets over Kerguelen Islands — AP19

Design: 90fr, Northern lights over map of northern coast of Russia.

1975, Jan. 26 **Engr.** ***Perf. 13***
C39 AP19 45fr purple & multi 7.00 4.00
C40 AP19 90fr purple & multi 9.00 5.25
a. Pair, #C39-C40 + label 19.00 13.00

Franco-Soviet magnetosphere research.

"La Curieuse" — AP20

Ships: 2.70fr, Commandant Charcot. 4fr, Marion-Dufresne.

1976, Jan. **Engr.** ***Perf. 13***
C41 AP20 1.90fr multicolored 3.25 2.00
C42 AP20 2.70fr multicolored 5.00 3.25
C43 AP20 4fr red & multi 9.00 4.25
Nos. C41-C43 (3) 17.25 9.50

Dumont d'Urville Base, 1956 — AP21

4fr, Dumont d'Urville Base, 1976, Adelie Land.

1976, Jan.
C44 AP21 1.20fr multicolored 9.00 4.00
C45 AP21 4fr multicolored 11.00 7.25
a. Pair, #C44-C45 + label 24.00 16.00

Dumont d'Urville Antarctic Base, 20th anniv.

Capt. Cook's Ships Passing Kerguelen Island — AP22

1976, Dec. 31 **Engr.** ***Perf. 13***
C46 AP22 3.50fr slate & blue 13.00 8.00

Bicentenary of Capt. Cook's voyage past Kerguelen Island.

Sea Lion and Cub AP23

1977-79 **Engr.** ***Perf. 13***
C47 AP23 4fr dk blue grn ('79) 3.00 2.50
C48 AP23 10fr multicolored 10.00 9.00

Satellite Survey, Kerguelen — AP24

Designs: 70c, Geophysical laboratory. 1.90fr, Satellite and Kerguelen tracking station. 3fr, Satellites, Adelie Land.

1977-79 **Engr.** ***Perf. 13***
C49 AP24 50c multi ('79) .90 .70
C50 AP24 70c multi ('79) .90 .70
C51 AP24 1.90fr multi ('79) 1.60 1.40
C52 AP24 2.70fr multi ('78) 2.75 2.00
C53 AP24 3fr multicolored 4.25 3.25
Nos. C49-C53 (5) 10.40 8.05

Elephant Seals — AP25

1979, Jan. 1
C54 AP25 10fr multicolored 5.50 4.50

Challenger — AP26

1979, Jan. 1
C55 AP26 2.70fr black & blue 2.00 1.75

Antarctic expeditions to Crozet and Kerguelen Islands, 1872-1876.

La Recherche and L'Esperance — AP27

1979
C56 AP27 1.90fr deep blue 1.25 1.10

Arrival of d'Entrecasteaux and Kermadec at Amsterdam Island, Mar. 28, 1792.

Lion Rock — AP28

1979
C57 AP28 90c multicolored .90 .70

Natural Arch, Kerguelen Island, 1840 — AP29

1979
C58 AP29 2.70fr multicolored 1.25 1.10

Phylica Nitida, Amsterdam Island — AP30

1979
C59 AP30 10fr multicolored 4.00 3.25

Charles de Gaulle, 10th Anniversary of Death AP31

1980, Nov. 9 **Engr.** ***Perf. 13***
C60 AP31 5.40fr multicolored 11.00 8.00

HB-40 Castor Truck and Trailer — AP32

1980, Dec. 15
C61 AP32 2.40fr multicolored 1.25 1.00

Supply Ship Saint Marcouf — AP33

1980, Dec. 15
C62 AP33 3.50fr shown 1.60 1.10
C63 AP33 7.30fr Icebreaker Norsel 2.50 2.00

Glacial Landscape, Dumont d'Urville Sea — AP34

Chionis — AP35

Adele Dumont d'Urville (1798-1842) — AP36

Arcad III — AP37

25th Anniv. of Charcot Station — AP38

Antares — AP39

1981 **Engr.** ***Perf. 13, 12½x13 (2fr)***
C64 AP34 1.30fr multicolored .70 .45
C65 AP35 1.50fr black .70 .50
C66 AP36 2fr black & lt brn .90 .85
C67 AP37 3.85fr multicolored 1.60 1.25
C68 AP38 5fr multicolored 1.75 1.50
C69 AP39 8.40fr multicolored 2.75 2.25
Nos. C64-C69 (6) 8.40 6.80

PHILEXFRANCE '82 Stamp Exhibition, Paris, June 11-21 — AP40

1982, June 11 **Engr.** ***Perf. 13***
C70 AP40 8fr multicolored 5.25 5.25

French Overseas Possessions Week, Sept. 18-25 — AP41

1982, Sept. 17 **Engr.** ***Perf. 13***
C71 AP41 5fr Commandant Charcot 1.75 1.75

Apostle Islands — AP42

1983, Jan. 3 **Engr.** ***Perf. 13***
C72 AP42 65c multicolored .55 .35

Sputnik I, 25th Anniv. of Intl. Geophysical Year — AP43

Orange Bay Base, Cape Horn, 1883, Cent. — AP44

5.20fr, Scoresby Sound Base, Greenland, 50th anniv.

1983, Jan. 3
C73 AP43 1.50fr multicolored .60 .60
C74 AP44 3.30fr multicolored 1.75 1.75
C75 AP44 5.20fr multicolored 2.00 2.00
a. Strip of 3, #C73-C75 4.50 4.50

AP45

1983, Jan. 3
C76 AP45 4.55fr dark blue 3.75 3.00

Abstract, by G. Mathieu — AP46

Illustration reduced.

1983, Jan. 3 **Photo.** ***Perf. 13x13½***
C77 AP46 25fr multicolored 10.00 8.00

Erebus off Antarctic Ice Cap, 1842 — AP47

Port of Joan of Arc, 1930 — AP48

1984, Jan. 1 Engr. *Perf. 13*
C78 AP47 2.60fr ultra & dk blue 1.10 1.00
C79 AP48 4.70fr multicolored 1.75 1.75

Aurora Polaris — AP49

1984, Jan. 1 Photo.
C80 AP49 3.50fr multicolored 2.00 1.25

Manned Flight Bicentenary (1983) — AP50

Various balloons and airships.

1984, Jan. 1 Engr.
C81 AP50 3.50fr multicolored 1.75 1.75
C82 AP50 7.80fr multicolored 2.75 2.75
a. Pair, #C81-C82 + label 5.00 5.00

Patrol Boat Albatros — AP51

1984, July 2 Engr. *Perf. 13*
C83 AP51 11.30fr multi 4.25 4.25

NORDPOSTA Exhibition — AP52

1984, Nov. 3 Engr. *Perf. 13*
C84 AP52 9fr Scientific Vessel Gauss 4.50 3.50

Issued se-tenant with label.

Corsican Sheep — AP53

Amsterdam Albatross AP54

1985, Jan. 1 Engr. *Perf. 13*
C85 AP53 70c Mouflons .50 .35
C86 AP54 3.90fr Diomedia amsterdamensis 1.50 1.25

La Novara, Frigate AP55

1985, Jan. 1 Engr. *Perf. 13*
C87 AP55 12.80fr La Novara at St. Paul 5.00 4.50

Explorer and Seal, by Tremois — AP56

Design: Explorer, seal, names of territories. Illustration reduced.

1985, Jan. 1 Photo. *Perf. 13x12½*
C88 AP56 30fr + label 11.00 8.50

Sailing Ships, Ropes, Flora & Fauna — AP57

1985, Aug. 6 Engr. *Perf. 13*
C89 AP57 2fr blk, brt bl & ol grn .70 .55
C90 AP57 12.80fr blk, ol grn & brt bl 3.75 3.75
a. Pair, #C89-C90 + label 5.50 5.50

French Southern & Antarctic Territories, 30th anniv. No. C90a has continuous design with center label.

Bird Type of 1986

1986, Jan. 1 Engr. *Perf. 13½x13*
C91 A56 4.60fr Sea Gulls 2.00 1.75

Antarctic Atmospheric Research, 10th Anniv. — AP58

1986, Jan. 1
C92 AP58 14fr blk, dk red & brt org 5.00 4.00

Jean Charcot (1867-1936), Explorer — AP59

1986, Jan. 1
C93 AP59 2.10fr Ship Pourquoi Pas .90 .60
C94 AP59 14fr Ship in storm 4.50 4.25
a. Pair, #C93-C94 + label 6.00 6.00

SPOT Satellite over the Antarctic — AP60

1986, May 26 Engr. *Perf. 13*
C95 AP60 8fr dp ultra, sep & dk ol grn 3.25 2.50

J.B. Charcot — AP61

1987, Jan. 1 Engr. *Perf. 13x13½*
C96 AP61 14.60fr multi 5.00 4.50

Ocean Drilling Program — AP62

1987, Jan. 1 *Perf. 13½x13*
C97 AP62 16.80fr lem, dk ultra & bluish blk 5.50 4.50

INMARSAT — AP63

1987, Mar. 2 Engr. *Perf. 13*
C98 AP63 16.80fr multi 8.00 7.50

French Polar Expeditions, 40th Anniv. — AP64

1988, Jan. 1
C99 AP64 20fr lake, ol grn & plum 8.00 6.75

Views of Penguin Is. — AP65

1988, Jan. 1
C100 AP65 3.90fr dk bl & sep 1.75 1.50
C101 AP65 15.10fr dp grn, choc brn & dk bl 5.50 5.00

See Nos. C103, C109.

Founding of Permanent Settlements in the Territories, 40th Anniv. — AP66

1989, Jan. 1 Engr. *Perf. 13½x13*
C102 AP66 15.50fr black 5.00 4.75

Island View Type

1989, Jan. 1
C103 AP65 8.40fr Apostle Islands 2.75 2.50

La Curieuse — AP68

1989, Jan. 1 *Perf. 13x12½*
C104 AP68 2.20fr multicolored .80 .70
C105 AP68 15.50fr multi, diff. 5.00 5.00
a. Pair, #C104-C105 + label 6.00 6.00

No. C105a label continues the design.

French Revolution, Bicent. — AP69

1989, July 14 Engr. *Perf. 13x12½*
C106 AP69 5fr pink, dark olive grn & dark blue 5.00 5.00

Souvenir Sheet
Perf. 13

C107 Sheet of 4 9.75 9.75
a. AP69 5fr Prus green, brt ultra & dark red 2.40 2.40

No. C107 for PHILEXFRANCE '89.

15th Antarctic Treaty Summit Conference — AP70

1989, Oct. 9 Engr. *Perf. 13*
C108 AP70 17.70fr multicolored 6.00 5.75

Island View Type

1990, Jan. 1 Engr. *Perf. 13*
C109 AP65 7.30fr Isle of Pigs, Crozet Isls. 3.00 2.40

L'Astrolabe, Expedition Team — AP72

1990, Jan. 1
C110 AP72 15.50fr dk red vio & blk 5.00 5.00

Discovery of Adelie Land by Dumont D'Urville, 150th anniv.

L'Astrolabe, Commanded by Dumont D'Urville, 1840 — AP73

1990, Jan. 1
C111 AP73 2.20fr *L'Astrolabe,* 1988 .80 .75
C112 AP73 15.50fr shown 5.00 5.00
a. Pair, #C111-C112 + label 6.50 6.50

Bird, by Folon — AP74

Illustration reduced.

1990, Jan. 1 Litho. *Perf. 12½x13*
C113 AP74 30fr multicolored 10.00 9.50

Albatross, Argos Satellite AP75

1991, Jan. 1
C114 AP75 2.10fr red brn, bl & brn 1.25 .80

Climatological Research — AP76

1991, Jan. 1 Engr. *Perf. 13*
C115 AP76 3.60fr Weather balloons, instruments 1.40 1.40
C116 AP76 20fr Research ship 7.75 7.75
a. Pair, #C115-C116 + label 10.00 10.00

Charles de Gaulle (1890-1970) — AP77

1991, Jan. 1
C117 AP77 18.80fr blk, red & bl 7.25 7.25

Cape Petrel — AP78

1992, Jan. 1 Engr. *Perf. 13*
C118 AP78 3.40fr multicolored 2.00 1.40

French Institute of Polar Research and Technology — AP79

#C120, Polar bear with man offering flowers.

1991, Dec. 16 Engr. *Perf. 13x12*
C119 AP79 15fr multicolored 5.75 5.75
C120 AP79 15fr multicolored 5.75 5.75
a. Strip, #C119-C120 + label 12.00 12.00

Christopher Columbus and Discovery of America — AP80

1992, Jan. 1 *Perf. 13*
C121 AP80 22fr multicolored 9.75 9.75

Mapping Satellite Poseidon — AP81

1992, Jan. 1 Engr. *Perf. 13*
C122 AP81 24.50fr multi 11.00 10.50

Dumont d'Urville Base, Adelie Land — AP82

Illustration reduced.

1992, Jan. 1 Litho. *Perf. 13x12½*
C123 AP82 25.70fr multi 12.00 10.50

Amateur Radio — AP83

1993, Jan. 1 Engr. *Perf. 13*
C124 AP83 2fr multicolored 2.00 .75

New Animal Biology Laboratory, Adelie Land — AP84

1993, Jan. 1
C125 AP84 25.40fr multicolored 11.00 6.75

Support Base D10 — AP85

1993, Jan. 1
C126 AP85 25.70fr ol, red & bl 11.00 7.00

Opening of Adelie Land Airfield — AP86

1993, Jan. 1
C127 AP86 30fr multicolored 13.00 8.75

Krill — AP87

1994, Jan. 1 Engr. *Perf. 13*
C128 AP87 15fr black 6.50 4.00

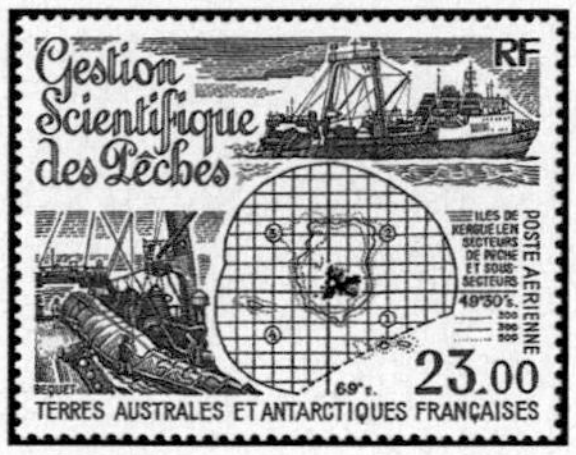

Fishery Management — AP88

1994, Jan. 1
C129 AP88 23fr multicolored 10.00 6.00

Satellite, Ground Station — AP89

Design: 27.30fr, Lidar Station.

1994, Jan. 1
C130 AP89 26.70fr multicolored 12.00 7.00
C131 AP89 27.30fr multicolored 12.00 7.25

Arrival of Emperor Penguins — AP90

Illustration reduced.

1994, Jan. 1 *Perf. 13x12½*
C132 AP90 28fr blue & black 12.00 7.50

Erebus Mission — AP91

1995, Jan. 2 Engr. *Perf. 13*
C133 AP91 4.30fr bl, vio & slate 2.25 1.50

Moving of Winter Station, Charcot — AP92

1995, Jan. 2 **Litho.**
C134 AP92 15fr multicolored 6.50 4.25

G. Lesquin (1803-30) — AP93

Illustration reduced.

1995, Jan. 2
C135 AP93 28fr multicolored 12.00 8.00

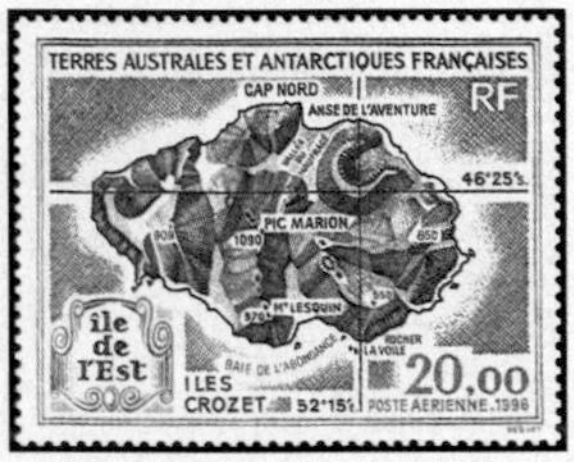

Map of East Island — AP94

1996, Jan. 1 **Engr.** ***Perf. 13***
C136 AP94 20fr multicolored 8.50 6.00

Expedition to Dome/C — AP95

1996, Jan. 1
C137 AP95 23fr dark blue 10.00 7.00

Blue Whale, Southern Whale Sanctuary — AP96

1996, Jan. 1
C138 AP96 26.70fr multicolored 12.00 8.00

Port-Couvreux — AP97

1996, Jan. 1
C139 AP97 27.30fr multicolored 12.00 8.50

Jasus Paulensis AP98

1997, Jan. 1 **Engr.** ***Perf. 12½x13***
C140 AP98 5.20fr multicolored 2.75 1.75

Racing Yacht Charentes 2 — AP99

1997, Jan. 1 **Litho.** ***Perf. 13***
C141 AP99 16fr multicolored 7.50 5.50

John Nunn, Shipwrecked 1825-29, Hope Cottage — AP100

1997, Jan. 1 **Engr.**
C142 AP100 20fr multicolored 8.75 6.25

ICOTA Program — AP101

1997, Jan. 1
C143 AP101 24fr multicolored 10.50 7.50

Harpagifer Spinosus — AP102

1997, Jan. 1
C144 AP102 27fr multicolored 12.00 8.50

EPICA Program — AP103

1998, Jan. 2 **Engr.** ***Perf. 13***
C145 AP103 5.20fr dk brn & lil 2.50 1.40

First Radio Meteorological Station, Port Aux Francais — AP104

1998, Jan. 2
C146 AP104 8fr black, blue & red 3.75 2.25

King Penguin, Argos Satellite AP105

1998, Jan. 2 ***Perf. 12½x13***
C147 AP105 16fr multicolored 7.00 4.75

Ranunculas Moseleyi AP106

1998, Jan. 2
C148 AP106 24fr multicolored 10.50 6.50

Intl. Geophysical Year, 40th Anniv. — AP107

Illustration reduced.

1998, Oct. **Engr.** ***Perf. 13x12½***
C149 AP107 5.20fr dk bl, blk & brick red 2.50 1.40

FRENCH SUDAN

'french sü-'dan

LOCATION — In northwest Africa, north of French Guinea and Ivory Coast
GOVT. — French Colony
AREA — 590,966 sq. mi.
POP. — 3,794,270 (1941)
CAPITAL — Bamako

In 1899 French Sudan was abolished as a separate colony and was divided among Dahomey, French Guinea, Ivory Coast, Senegal and Senegambia and Niger. Issues for French Sudan were resumed in 1921.

From 1906 to 1921 a part of this territory was known as Upper Senegal and Niger. A part of Upper Volta was added in 1933. See Mali.

100 Centimes = 1 Franc

See French West Africa No. 70 for stamp inscribed "Soudan Francais" and "Afrique Occidentale Francaise."

Navigation and Commerce
A1 A2
Stamps of French Colonies, Surcharged in Black

Perf. 14x13½

1894, Apr. 12 **Unwmk.**

1	A1	15c on 75c car, *rose*	*4,500.*	*2,250.*
2	A1	25c on 1fr brnz grn, *straw*	*4,750.*	*1,600.*

The imperforate stamp like No. 1 was made privately in Paris from a fragment of the lithographic stone which had been used in the Colony for surcharging No. 1.

Counterfeit surcharges exist.

1894-1900 **Typo.** ***Perf. 14x13½***
Name of colony in Blue or Carmine

3	A2	1c blk, *lil bl*	1.40	1.40
4	A2	2c brn, *buff*	2.10	2.10
5	A2	4c claret, *lav*	5.25	5.25
6	A2	5c grn, *grnsh*	8.75	8.75
7	A2	10c blk, *lav*	20.00	20.00
8	A2	10c red ('00)	6.50	6.50
9	A2	15c blue, quadrille paper	6.50	6.50
10	A2	15c gray, *lt gray* ('00)	6.75	6.75
11	A2	20c red, *grn*	27.50	27.50
12	A2	25c blk, *rose*	25.00	25.00
13	A2	25c blue ('00)	7.25	7.25
14	A2	30c brn, *bister*	40.00	40.00
15	A2	40c red, *straw*	32.50	32.50
16	A2	50c car, *rose*	52.50	52.50
17	A2	50c brn, *az* ('00)	11.50	11.50
18	A2	75c dp vio, *org*	47.50	47.50
19	A2	1fr brnz grn, *straw*	10.50	10.50
		Nos. 3-19 (17)	311.50	311.50

Perf. 13½x14 stamps are counterfeits.

Nos. 8, 10, 13, 17 were issued in error. They were accepted for use in the other colonies.

Camel and Rider — A3

Stamps of Upper Senegal and Niger Overprinted in Black

1921-30 ***Perf. 13½x14***

21	A3	1c brn vio & vio	.25	.30
22	A3	2c dk gray & dl vio	.25	.30
23	A3	4c blk & blue	.25	.30
24	A3	5c ol brn & dk brn	.25	.30
25	A3	10c yel grn & bl grn	.80	.50
26	A3	10c red vio & bl ('25)	.30	.30
27	A3	15c red brn & org	.30	.40
28	A3	15c yel grn & dp grn ('25)	.30	.30
29	A3	15c org brn & vio ('27)	1.40	1.40
30	A3	20c brn vio & blk	.30	.40
31	A3	25c blk & bl grn	.95	.75
a.		Booklet pane of 4		—
		Complete booklet, 5 #31a	525.00	
32	A3	30c red org & rose	1.40	1.20
33	A3	30c bl grn & blk ('26)	.65	.55
34	A3	30c dl grn & bl grn ('28)	1.75	1.75
35	A3	35c rose & vio	.40	.50
36	A3	40c gray & rose	1.00	.90
37	A3	45c bl & ol brn	.90	.90
38	A3	50c ultra & bl	1.40	1.10
39	A3	50c red org & bl ('26)	1.20	1.10
40	A3	60c vio, *pnksh* ('26)	1.10	.90
41	A3	65c bis & pale bl ('28)	1.50	1.50
42	A3	75c org & ol brn	1.25	1.20
43	A3	90c brn red & pink ('30)	5.50	5.50
44	A3	1fr dk brn & dl vio	1.40	1.40
45	A3	1.10fr gray lil & red vio ('28)	2.90	3.25
46	A3	1.50fr dp bl & bl ('30)	5.50	5.50
47	A3	2fr green & blue	2.10	2.00
48	A3	3fr red vio ('30)	11.00	11.00
a.		Double overprint	180.00	
49	A3	5fr violet & blk	6.00	6.00
		Nos. 21-49 (29)	52.30	51.50

Type of 1921 Surcharged

1922, Sept. 28

50 A3 60c on 75c vio, *pnksh* .50 .50

Stamps and Type of 1921-30 Surcharged with New Values and Bars

1925-27

51 A3 25c on 45c .65 .65
52 A3 65c on 75c 1.60 1.60
53 A3 85c on 2fr 1.60 1.60
54 A3 85c on 5fr 1.90 1.90
55 A3 90c on 75c brn red & sal pink ('27) 2.10 2.00
56 A3 1.25fr on 1fr dp bl & lt bl (R) ('26) 1.20 1.20
57 A3 1.50fr on 1fr dp bl & ultra ('27) 1.20 1.20
58 A3 3fr on 5fr dl red & brn org ('27) 6.00 5.25
59 A3 10fr on 5fr brn red & bl grn ('27) 22.50 19.00
60 A3 20fr on 5fr vio & ver ('27) 29.00 29.00
Nos. 51-60 (10) 67.75 63.40

Sudanese Woman — A4

Entrance to the Residency at Djenné — A5

Sudanese Boatman — A6

1931-40 Typo. *Perf. 13x14*

61 A4 1c dk red & blk .25 .25
62 A4 2c dp bl & org .25 .25
63 A4 3c dk red & blk ('40) .25 .25
64 A4 4c gray lil & rose .25 .25
65 A4 5c ind & grn .25 .25
66 A4 10c ol grn & rose .25 .25
67 A4 15c blk & brt vio .30 .30
68 A4 20c hn brn & lt bl .30 .30
69 A4 25c red vio & lt red .30 .30
70 A5 30c grn & lt grn .75 .50
71 A5 30c dk bl & red org ('40) .30 .30
72 A5 35c ol grn & grn ('38) .50 .50
73 A5 40c ol grn & pink .30 .30
74 A5 45c dk bl & red org .95 .65
75 A5 45c ol grn & grn ('40) .50 .50
76 A5 50c red & blk .30 .30
77 A5 55c ultra & car ('38) .50 .50
78 A5 60c brt bl & brn ('40) 1.00 1.00
79 A5 65c brt vio & blk .65 .50
80 A5 70c vio bl & car rose ('40) .80 .80
81 A5 75c brt bl & ol brn 2.25 1.75
82 A5 80c car & brn ('38) .50 .50
83 A5 90c dp red & red org 1.50 .75
84 A5 90c brt vio & sl blk ('39) .80 .90
85 A5 1fr indigo & grn 6.75 1.75
86 A5 1fr rose red ('38) 4.25 4.25
87 A5 1fr car & brn ('40) .80 .80
88 A6 1.25fr vio & dl vio ('33) .75 .75
89 A6 1.25fr red ('39) .80 .90
90 A6 1.40fr brt vio & blk ('40) 1.25 .90
91 A6 1.50fr dk bl & ultra .65 .50
92 A6 1.60fr brn & dp bl ('40) .80 .80
93 A6 1.75fr dk brn & dp bl ('33) .80 .80
94 A6 1.75fr vio bl ('38) .75 .75
95 A6 2fr org brn & grn .75 .50
96 A6 2.25fr vio bl & ultra ('39) .95 1.00
97 A6 2.50fr lt brn ('40) 1.40 1.40
98 A6 3fr Prus grn & brn .75 .30
99 A6 5fr red & blk 1.90 1.20
100 A6 10fr dl bl & grn 2.00 1.90
101 A6 20fr red vio & brn 2.75 2.25
Nos. 61-101 (41) 42.10 32.90

For surcharges see Nos. B7-B10.
For 10c and 30c, without "RF," see Nos. 120-121.

For surcharges see Nos. B7-B10.
Common Design Types pictured following the introduction.

Colonial Exposition Issue
Common Design Types

1931, Apr. 13 Engr. *Perf. 12½*
Name of Country Printed in Black

102 CD70 40c deep green 3.50 3.50
103 CD71 50c violet 3.50 3.50
104 CD72 90c red orange 3.50 3.50
105 CD73 1.50fr dull blue 3.50 3.50
Nos. 102-105 (4) 14.00 14.00

Paris International Exposition Issue
Common Design Types

1937, Apr. 15 *Perf. 13*

106 CD74 20c dp violet 1.75 1.75
107 CD75 30c dk green 1.75 1.75
108 CD76 40c carmine rose 1.75 1.75
109 CD77 50c dk brown 1.40 1.40
110 CD78 90c red 1.40 1.40
111 CD79 1.50fr ultra 1.90 1.90
Nos. 106-111 (6) 9.95 9.95

Colonial Arts Exhibition Issue
Souvenir Sheet
Common Design Type

1937 Engr. *Imperf.*

112 CD77 3fr magenta & blk 8.00 *9.50*

Caillie Issue
Common Design Type

1939, Apr. 5 *Perf. 12½x12*

113 CD81 90c org brn & org .90 .90
114 CD81 2fr brt violet .95 .95
115 CD81 2.25fr ultra & dk bl .95 .95
Nos. 113-115 (3) 2.80 2.80

New York World's Fair Issue
Common Design Type

1939, May 10

116 CD82 1.25fr carmine lake 1.00 1.00
117 CD82 2.25fr ultra 1.00 1.00

Entrance to the Residency at Djenné and Marshal Pétain — A7

1941 Engr. *Perf. 12x12½*

118 A7 1fr green .75 —
119 A7 2.50fr blue .75 —

For surcharges, see Nos. B14-B15.

Types of 1931-40 without "RF"

1943-44 Typo. *Perf. 13½x14*

120 A4 10c ol green & rose .50
121 A5 30c dk bl & red org .75

Nos. 120-121 were issued by the Vichy government in France, but were not placed on sale in French Sudan.

Stamps of French Sudan were superseded by those of French West Africa.

SEMI-POSTAL STAMPS

Curie Issue
Common Design Type
Unwmk.

1938, Oct. 24 Engr. *Perf. 13*

B1 CD80 1.75fr + 50c brt ultra 12.50 12.50

French Revolution Issue
Common Design Type

1939, July 5 Photo.
Name and Value Typo. in Black

B2 CD83 45c + 25c green 10.00 10.00
B3 CD83 70c + 30c brown 10.00 10.00
B4 CD83 90c + 35c red orange 10.00 10.00
B5 CD83 1.25fr + 1fr rose pink 10.00 10.00
B6 CD83 2.25fr + 2fr blue 10.00 10.00
Nos. B2-B6 (5) 50.00 50.00

Stamps of 1931-40, Surcharged in Black or Red

1941 *Perf. 13x14*

B7 A5 50c + 1fr red & blk (R) 2.40 2.40
B8 A5 80c + 2fr car & brn 7.25 7.25
B9 A6 1.50fr + 2fr dk bl & ultra 7.25 7.25
B10 A6 2fr + 3fr org brn & grn 7.25 7.25
Nos. B7-B10 (4) 24.15 24.15

Common Design Type and

Native Officer — SP1

Aviation Officer — SP2

1941 Photo. *Perf. 13½*

B11 SP1 1fr + 1fr red 1.20
B12 CD86 1.50fr + 3fr claret 1.20
B13 SP2 2.50fr + 1fr blue 1.20
Nos. B11-B13 (3) 3.60

Surtax for the defense of the colonies.
Issued by the Vichy government in France, but not placed on sale in French Sudan.

Petain Type of 1941 Surcharged in Black or Red

1944 Engr. *Perf. 12x12½*

B14 50c + 1.50fr on 2.50fr deep blue (R) .75
B15 + 2.50fr on 1fr green .75

Colonial Development Fund.
Nos. B14-B15 were issued by the Vichy government in France, but were not placed on sale in French Sudan.

AIR POST STAMPS

Common Design Type
Perf. 12½x12

1940, Feb. 8 Unwmk. Engr.

C1 CD85 1.90fr ultra .40 .40
C2 CD85 2.90fr dark red .55 .55
C3 CD85 4.50fr dk grn green .95 .95
C4 CD85 4.90fr yellow bister .95 .95
C5 CD85 6.90fr deep orange 1.10 1.10
Nos. C1-C5 (5) 3.95 3.95

Common Design Types

1942, Oct. 19

C6 CD88 50c carmine & bl .25 —
C7 CD88 1fr brown & blk .30
C8 CD88 2fr dk grn & red brn .50
C9 CD88 3fr dk blue & scar .65
C10 CD88 5fr vio & brn red .65

Frame Engr., Center Typo.

C11 CD89 10fr ultra, ind & gray blk .95
C12 CD89 20fr rose car, mag & lt vio 1.10
C13 CD89 50fr yel grn, dl grn & dl bl 2.00 —
Nos. C6-C13 (8) 6.40

There is doubt whether Nos. C7-C12 were officially placed in use.

AIR POST SEMI-POSTAL STAMPS

Types of Dahomey Air Post Semi-Postal Issue

Perf. 13½x12½, 13 (#CB3)
Photo, Engr. (#CB3)

1942, June 22

CB1 SPAP1 1.50fr + 3.50fr green .75 *5.00*
CB2 SPAP2 2fr + 6fr brown .75 *5.00*
CB3 SPAP2 3fr + 9fr car red .75 *5.00*
Nos. CB1-CB3 (3) 2.25 *15.00*

Native children's welfare fund.

Colonial Education Fund
Common Design Type
Perf. 12½x13½

1942, June 22 Engr.

CB4 CD86a 1.20fr + 1.80fr blue & red .75 *5.00*

POSTAGE DUE STAMPS

D1

D2

Postage Due Stamps of Upper Senegal and Niger Overprinted

Perf. 14x13½

1921, Dec. Unwmk. Typo.

J1 D1 5c green .50 .50
J2 D1 10c rose .65 .65
J3 D1 15c gray .80 .80
J4 D1 20c brown 1.00 1.10
J5 D1 30c blue 1.00 1.10
J6 D1 50c black 1.75 1.90
J7 D1 60c orange 1.90 2.10
J8 D1 1fr violet 2.40 2.60
Nos. J1-J8 (8) 10.00 10.75

Type of 1921 Issue Surcharged

1927, Oct. 10

J9 D1 2fr on 1fr lilac rose 6.50 6.50
J10 D1 3fr on 1fr org brown 6.50 6.50

1931, Mar. 9

J11 D2 5c green .25 .25
J12 D2 10c rose .25 .25
J13 D2 15c gray .30 .30
J14 D2 20c dark brown .30 .30
J15 D2 30c dark blue .50 .50
J16 D2 50c black .55 .55
J17 D2 60c deep orange 1.10 1.10
J18 D2 1fr violet 1.40 1.40
J19 D2 2fr lilac rose 1.50 1.50
J20 D2 3fr red brown 1.50 1.50
Nos. J11-J20 (10) 7.65 7.65

FRENCH WEST AFRICA

ˈfrench ˈwest ˈa-fri-kə

LOCATION — Northwestern Africa
GOVT. — French colonial administrative unit
AREA — 1,821,768 sq. mi.
POP. — 18,777,163 (est.)
CAPITAL — Dakar

French West Africa comprised the former colonies of Senegal, French Guinea, Ivory Coast, Dahomey, French Sudan, Mauritania, Niger and Upper Volta.

In 1958, these former colonies became republics, eventually issuing their own stamps. Until the republic issues appeared, stamps of French West Africa continued in use. The Senegal and Sudanese Republics issued stamps jointly as the Federation of Mali, starting in 1959.

Catalogue values for all unused stamps in this country are for Never Hinged items.

Many stamps other than Nos. 65-72 and 77 are inscribed "Afrique Occidentale Francaise" and the name of one of the former colonies. See listings in these colonies for such stamps.

Senegal No. 156 Surcharged in Red

1943 Unwmk. *Perf. 12½x12*

1 A30	1.50fr on 65c dk vio	.90	.75
2 A30	5.50fr on 65c dk vio	1.20	.80
3 A30	50fr on 65c dk vio	3.50	1.60

Mauritania No. 91 Surcharged in Red

1943 *Perf. 13*

4 A7	3.50fr on 65c dp grn	.75	.55
5 A7	4fr on 65c dp grn	.75	.55
6 A7	5fr on 65c dp grn	1.25	1.10
7 A7	10fr on 65c dp grn	1.25	1.10
	Nos. 1-7 (7)	9.60	6.45

Senegal No. 143, 148 and 188 Surcharged with New Values in Black and Orange

1944 *Perf. 12½x12*

8 A29	1.50fr on 15c blk (O)	.65	.50
9 A29	4.50fr on 15c blk (O)	.90	.75
10 A29	5.50fr on 2c brn	2.25	1.50
11 A29	10fr on 15c blk (O)	3.25	1.60
12 CD81	20fr on 90c org brn & org	2.10	1.60
13 CD81	50fr on 90c org brn & org	5.25	2.75

Mauritania No. 109 Surcharged in Black

14 CD81	15fr on 90c org brn & org	2.00	1.60
	Nos. 8-14 (7)	16.40	10.30

Common Design Types pictured following the introduction.

Eboue Issue
Common Design Type

1945 Engr. *Perf. 13*

15 CD91	2fr black	.90	.65
16 CD91	25fr Prussian green	2.25	1.60

Nos. 15 and 16 exist imperforate.

Colonial Soldier — A1

1945 Litho. *Perf. 12½x12, 12*

17 A1	10c indigo & buff	.40	.25
18 A1	30c olive & yel	.40	.25
19 A1	40c blue & buff	.65	.50
20 A1	50c red org & gray	.65	.50
21 A1	60c ol brn & bl	.65	.50
22 A1	70c mag & cit	.65	.50
23 A1	80c bl grn & pale lem	.65	.50
24 A1	1fr brn vio & cit	.75	.55
25 A1	1.20fr gray brn & cit	4.25	2.25
26 A1	1.50fr choc & pink	.75	.50
27 A1	2fr ocher and gray	.90	.50
28 A1	2.40fr red & gray	1.25	.95
29 A1	3fr brn red & yelsh	.75	.40
30 A1	4fr ultra & pink	.75	.40
31 A1	4.50fr org brn & yelsh	.75	.40
32 A1	5fr dk pur & yelsh	.75	.40
33 A1	10fr ol grn & pink	1.40	.95
34 A1	15fr orange & yel	2.50	1.40
35 A1	20fr sl grn & grnsh	2.90	1.60
	Nos. 17-35 (19)	21.75	13.30

Rifle Dance, Mauritania — A2

Shelling Coconuts, Togo — A6

Bamako Dike, French Sudan — A3

Trading Canoe, Niger River — A4

Oasis of Bilma, Niger — A5

Kouandé Weaving, Dahomey A7

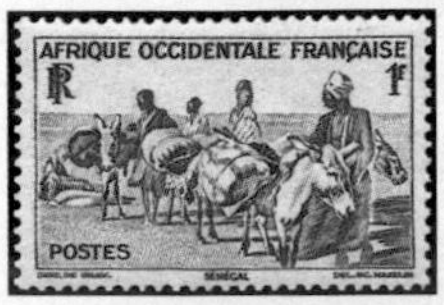

Donkey Caravan, Senegal A8

Crocodile and Hippopotamus, Ivory Coast — A9

Gathering Coconuts, French Guinea — A10

Peul Woman of Dienné — A12

Bamako Fountain, French Sudan A11

Bamako Market — A13

Dahomey Laborer — A14

Woman of Mauritania A15

Fula Woman, French Guinea A16

Djenné Mosque, French Sudan A17

Monorail Train, Senegal A18

Agni Woman, Ivory Coast — A19

Azwa Women at Niger River — A20

1947 Engr. Unwmk. *Perf. 12½*

36 A2	10c blue	.40	.25
37 A3	30c red brn	.40	.25
38 A4	40c gray grn	.65	.25
39 A5	50c red brn	.50	.25
40 A6	60c gray blk	.90	.50
41 A7	80c brown vio	.90	.50
42 A8	1fr maroon	.65	.30
43 A9	1.20fr dk blue grn	1.90	1.40
44 A10	1.50fr ultra	1.90	1.10
45 A11	2fr red orange	.90	.25
46 A12	3fr chocolate	.90	.30
47 A13	3.60fr brown red	1.75	1.40
48 A14	4fr deep blue	.65	.30
49 A15	5fr gray green	.65	.25
50 A16	6fr dark blue	.90	.30
51 A17	10fr brn red	1.40	.25
52 A18	15fr sepia	2.60	.30
53 A19	20fr chocolate	1.60	.30
54 A20	25fr grnsh blk	3.00	.50
	Nos. 36-54 (19)	22.55	8.95

Types of 1947

1948 Re-engraved

55 A6	60c brown olive	.95	.65
56 A12	3fr chocolate	.95	.50

Nos. 40 and 46 are inscribed "TOGO" in lower margin. Inscription omitted on Nos. 55 and 56.

Imperforates

Most stamps of French West Africa from 1949 onward exist imperforate in issued and trial colors, and also in small presentation sheets in issued colors.

Military Medal Issue
Common Design Type
Engraved and Typographed

1952, Dec. 1 *Perf. 13*

57 CD101	15fr multicolored	8.75	6.50

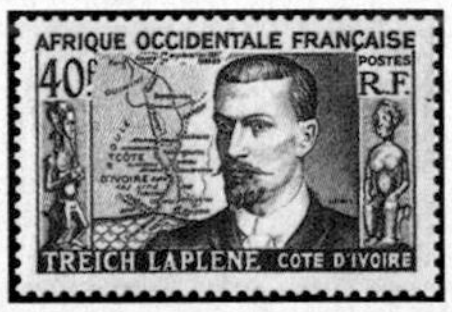

Treich Laplène and Map — A21

1952, Dec. 1 Engr.

58 A21	40fr brown lake	2.40	.40

Marcel Treich Laplène, a leading contributor to the development of Ivory Coast.

Medical Laboratory A22

1953, Nov. 18

59 A22	15fr brn, dk bl grn & blk brn	1.40	.25

Couple Feeding Antelopes A23

1954, Sept. 20

60 A23	25fr multicolored	1.90	.30

Gov. Noel Eugène Ballay A24

1954, Nov. 29

61 A24	8fr indigo & brown	2.00	.75

Chimpanzee — A25

Giant Pangolin A26

1955, May 2 Unwmk. *Perf. 13*
62 A25 5fr gray & dk brn 1.90 .65
63 A26 8fr brn & bl grn 1.90 .75

International Exhibition for Wildlife Protection, Paris, May 1955.

Map, Symbols of Industry, Rotary Emblem A27

1955, July 4
64 A27 15fr dark blue 2.00 .65

50th anniv. of the founding of Rotary Intl.

FIDES Issue
Common Design Type

Designs: 1fr, Date grove, Mauritania. 2fr, Milo Bridge, French Guinea. 3fr, Mossi Railroad, Upper Volta. 4fr, Cattle raising, Niger. 15fr, Farm machinery and landscape, Senegal. 17fr, Woman and Niger River, French Sudan. 20fr, Palm oil production, Dahomey. 30fr, Road construction, Ivory Coast.

1956 Engr. *Perf. 13x12½*
65 CD103 1fr dk grn & dk bl grn 1.00 .65
66 CD103 2fr dk bl grn & bl 1.40 .65
67 CD103 3fr dk brn & red brn 1.60 1.00
68 CD103 4fr dk car rose 1.75 1.10
69 CD103 15fr ind & ultra 1.50 .55
70 CD103 17fr dk bl & ind 1.75 .75
71 CD103 20fr rose lake 1.90 .65
72 CD103 30fr dk pur & claret 1.90 1.00
Nos. 65-72 (8) 12.80 6.35

Coffee A28a

1956, Oct. 22 *Perf. 13*
73 A28a 15fr dk blue green 1.00 .75

Mobile Leprosy Clinic and Maltese Cross A29

1957, Mar. 11
74 A29 15fr dk red brn, pur & red 2.00 .75

Issued in honor of the Knights of Malta.

Map of Africa — A30

1958, Feb. Unwmk. *Perf. 13*
75 A30 20fr multicolored 1.60 .75

6h Intl.Cong. for African Tourism at Dakar.

"Africa" and Communications Symbols — A31

1958, Mar. 15 Engr.
76 A31 15fr org, ultra & choc 1.75 .65

Stamp Day. See No. 86.

Abidjan Bridge A32

1958, Mar. 15
77 A32 20fr dk sl grn & grnsh bl 1.75 .75

Bananas A33

1958, May 19 *Perf. 13*
78 A33 20fr rose lil, dk grn & olive 1.60 .30

Flower Issue
Common Design Type

10fr, Gloriosa. 25fr, Adenopus. 30fr, Cyrtosperma. 40fr, Cistanche. 65fr, Crinum Moorei.

1958-59 Photo. *Perf. 12x12½*
79 CD104 10fr multicolored .95 .40
80 CD104 25fr red, yel & grn 1.50 .75
81 CD104 30fr multicolored 1.75 1.00
82 CD104 40fr blk brn, grn & yel 2.25 1.40
83 CD104 65fr multicolored 2.40 1.20
Nos. 79-83 (5) 8.85 4.75

Issued: 25fr, 40fr, 1/5/59; others, 7/7/58.

Moro Naba Sagha and Map — A34

1958, Nov. 1 Engr. *Perf. 13*
84 A34 20fr ol brn, car & vio 1.40 .65

10th anniv. of the reestablishment of the Upper Volta territory.

Human Rights Issue
Common Design Type

1958, Dec. 10
85 CD105 20fr maroon & dk bl 2.25 1.75

Type of 1958 Redrawn

1959, Mar. 21 Engr. *Perf. 13*
86 A31 20fr red, grnsh bl & sl grn 3.25 3.25

Name of country omitted on No. 86; "RF" replaced by "CF," inscribed "Dakar-Abidjan." Stamp Day.

SEMI-POSTAL STAMPS

Red Cross Issue
Common Design Type
Perf. 14½x14

1944, Dec. Photo. Unwmk.
B1 CD90 5fr + 20fr plum 6.50 4.75

The surtax was for the French Red Cross and national relief.

Type of France, 1945, Overprinted in Black

1945, Oct. 13 Engr. *Perf. 13*
B2 SP150 2fr + 3fr orange red 1.10 .80

Tropical Medicine Issue
Common Design Type

1950, May 15 *Perf. 13*
B3 CD100 10fr +2fr red brn & sep 9.50 7.25

The surtax was for charitable work.

AIR POST STAMPS

Common Design Type

1945 Photo. Unwmk. *Perf. 14½x14*
C1 CD87 5.50fr ultra 2.00 .95
C2 CD87 50fr dark green 3.50 1.25
C3 CD87 100fr plum 4.00 1.40
Nos. C1-C3 (3) 9.50 3.60

Victory Issue
Common Design Type

1946, May 8 Engr. *Perf. 12½*
C4 CD92 8fr violet 1.60 .95

Chad to Rhine Issue
Common Design Types

1946, June 6
C5 CD93 5fr brown car 1.90 1.40
C6 CD94 10fr deep blue 1.90 1.40
C7 CD95 15fr brt violet 2.10 1.60
C8 CD96 20fr dk slate grn 2.40 1.90
C9 CD97 25fr olive brn 2.60 2.25
C10 CD98 50fr brown 3.50 2.75
Nos. C5-C10 (6) 14.40 11.30

Antoine de Saint-Exupéry, Map and Natives — AP1

Plane over Dakar — AP2

Great White Egrets in Flight — AP3

Natives and Phantom Plane — AP4

1947, Mar. 24 Engr.
C11 AP1 8fr red brown 1.25 .55
C12 AP2 50fr rose violet 3.50 1.00
C13 AP3 100fr ultra 15.00 4.75
C14 AP4 200fr slate gray 12.50 4.75
Nos. C11-C14 (4) 32.25 11.05

UPU Issue
Common Design Type

1949, July 4 *Perf. 13*
C15 CD99 25fr multicolored 12.50 8.75

Vridi Canal, Abidjan — AP5

1951, Nov. 5 Unwmk. *Perf. 13*
C16 AP5 500fr red org, bl grn & dp ultra 32.50 4.75

Liberation Issue
Common Design Type

1954, June 6
C17 CD102 15fr indigo & ultra 9.50 5.50

Logging — AP6

Designs: 100fr, Radiotelephone exchange. 200fr, Baobab trees.

1954, Sept. 20
C18 AP6 50fr ol grn & org brn 3.50 .80
C19 AP6 100fr ind, dk brn & dk grn 5.50 1.20
C20 AP6 200fr bl grn, grnsh blk & brn lake 17.00 2.75
Nos. C18-C20 (3) 26.00 4.75

Gen. Louis Faidherbé and African Sharpshooter AP7

1957, July 20 Unwmk. *Perf. 13*
C21 AP7 15fr indigo & blue 1.75 1.40

Centenary of French African troops.

Gorée Island and Woman — AP8

Designs: 20fr, Map with planes and ships. 25fr, Village and modern city. 40fr, Seat of Council of French West Africa. 50fr, Worker, ship and peanut plant. 100fr, Bay of N'Gor.

1958, Mar. 15 Engr.
C22 AP8 15fr blk brn, grn & vio 1.40 .80
C23 AP8 20fr blk brn, dk bl & red brn 1.40 .80
C24 AP8 25fr blk vio, bis & grn 1.40 1.00
C25 AP8 40fr dk bl, brn & grn 1.60 1.00
C26 AP8 50fr violet, brn & grn 2.50 1.40
C27 AP8 100fr brown, bl & grn 6.75 2.10
a. Souvenir sheet of 6, #C22-C27 17.50 13.50
Nos. C22-C27 (6) 15.05 7.10

Centenary of Dakar.

Woman Playing Native Harp — AP9

1958, Dec. 1 Unwmk. *Perf. 13*
C28 AP9 20fr red brn, blk & gray 1.60 .75

Inauguration of Nouakchott as capital of Mauritania.

POSTAGE DUE STAMPS

D1

1947 Engr. Unwmk. *Perf. 13*

J1 D1 10c red .40 .25
J2 D1 30c deep orange .40 .25
J3 D1 50c greenish blk .40 .25
J4 D1 1fr carmine .40 .25
J5 D1 2fr emerald .50 .30
J6 D1 3fr red lilac .90 .65
J7 D1 4fr deep ultra 1.10 .80
J8 D1 5fr red brown 2.25 1.60
J9 D1 10fr peacock blue 2.90 2.25
J10 D1 20fr sepia 5.25 3.75
Nos. J1-J10 (10) 14.50 10.35

OFFICIAL STAMPS

Mask — O1

Designs: Various masks.

Perf. 14x13

1958, June 2 Typo. Unwmk.

O1 O1 1fr dk brn red .90 .75
O2 O1 3fr brt green .65 .55
O3 O1 5fr crim rose .65 .40
O4 O1 10fr light ultra .65 .40
O5 O1 20fr bright red 1.40 .65
O6 O1 25fr purple 1.10 .65
O7 O1 30fr green 2.25 1.10
O8 O1 45fr gray black 3.00 1.40
O9 O1 50fr dark red 3.25 1.00
O10 O1 65fr brt ultra 4.25 1.20
O11 O1 100fr olive bister 9.50 1.60
O12 O1 200fr deep green 20.00 4.00
Nos. O1-O12 (12) 47.60 13.70

FUJEIRA

fü-'jī-rə

LOCATION — Oman Peninsula, Arabia, on Persian Gulf
GOVT. — Sheikdom under British protection

Fujeira is one of six Persian Gulf sheikdoms to join the United Arab Emirates which proclaimed independence Dec. 2, 1971. See United Arab Emirates.

100 Naye Paise = 1 Rupee

Catalogue values for all unused stamps in this country are for Never Hinged items.

Sheik Hamad bin Mohammed al Sharqi and Grebe — A1

Sheik and: 2np, 50np, Arabian oryx. 3np, 70np, Hoopoe. 4np, 1r, Wild ass. 5np, 1.50r, Herons in flight. 10np, 2r, Arabian horses. 15np, 3r, Leopard. 20np, 5r, Camels. 30np, 10r, Hawks.

Photo. & Litho.

1964 Unwmk. *Perf. 14*

Size: 36x24mm

1 A1 1np gold & multi .20 .20
2 A1 2np gold & multi .20 .20
3 A1 3np gold & multi .20 .20
4 A1 4np gold & multi .20 .20
5 A1 5np gold & multi .20 .20
6 A1 10np gold & multi .20 .20
7 A1 15np gold & multi .20 .20
8 A1 20np gold & multi .20 .20
9 A1 30np gold & multi .20 .20

Size: 43x28mm

10 A1 40np gold & multi .30 .20
11 A1 50np gold & multi .30 .20
12 A1 70np gold & multi .35 .20
13 A1 1r gold & multi .50 .20
14 A1 1.50r gold & multi .75 .20
15 A1 2r gold & multi 1.00 .20

Size: 53½x35mm

16 A1 3r gold & multi 1.50 .25
17 A1 5r gold & multi 2.00 .35
18 A1 10r gold & multi 4.75 .50
Nos. 1-18 (18) 13.25 4.10

Issued: 20np, 30np, 70np, 1.50r, 3r, 10r, Nov. 14; others, Sept. 22.
Exist imperf. Value, set $16.

Sheik Hamad and Shot Put A2

1964, Dec. 6 *Perf. 14*

Size: 43x28mm

19 A2 25np shown .20 .20
20 A2 50np Discus .20 .20
21 A2 75np Fencing .25 .25
22 A2 1r Boxing .30 .30
23 A2 1.50r Relay race .40 .35
24 A2 2r Soccer .50 .40

Size: 53½x35mm

25 A2 3r Pole vaulting .90 .50
26 A2 5r Hurdling 2.25 .75
27 A2 7.50r Equestrian 3.50 .90
Nos. 19-27 (9) 8.50 3.85

18th Olympic Games, Tokyo, 10/10-25/64.
Exist imperf. Value, set $12.

John F. Kennedy — A3

Kennedy: 10np, As sailor in the Pacific. 15np, As naval lieutenant. 20np, On speaker's rostrum. 25np, Sailing with family. 50np, With crowd of people. 1r, With Mrs. Kennedy, Lyndon B. Johnson. 2r, With Eisenhower on White House porch. 3r, With Mrs. Kennedy & Caroline. 5r, Portrait.

1965, Feb. 23 Photo. *Perf. 13½*

Size: 29x44mm

Black Design with Gold Inscriptions

28 A3 5np pale gray .20 .20
29 A3 10np pale yellow .20 .20
30 A3 15np pink .20 .20
31 A3 20np pale greenish gray .20 .20
32 A3 25np pale blue .25 .20
33 A3 50np pale rose .30 .20

Size: 33x51mm

34 A3 1r pale gray .75 .30
35 A3 2r pale green 1.25 .40
36 A3 3r pale gray 2.00 .50
37 A3 5r pale yellow 2.75 .80
Nos. 28-37 (10) 8.10 3.20

Pres. John F. Kennedy (1917-1963). A souvenir sheet contains 2 29x44mm stamps similar to Nos. 36-37 with pale blue (3r) and pale rose (5r) backgrounds. Value (unused): perf $7; imperf $9.
Nos. 28-37 exist imperf. Value $14.

AIR POST STAMPS

Arabian Oryx — AP1

Photo. & Litho.

1965, Aug. 16 Unwmk. *Perf. 13½*

Size: 43x28mm

C1 AP1 15np Grebe .25 .20
C2 AP1 25np shown .25 .20
C3 AP1 35np Hoopoe .35 .20
C4 AP1 50np Wild ass .40 .20
C5 AP1 75np Herons in flight .45 .20
C6 AP1 1r Arabian horses .50 .20

Size: 53½x35mm

C7 AP1 2r Leopard 1.00 .20
C8 AP1 3r Camels 1.75 .25
C9 AP1 5r Hawks 3.75 .50
Nos. C1-C9 (9) 8.70 2.15

Exist imperf. Value, set $10.

AIR POST OFFICIAL STAMPS

Type of Air Post Issue, 1965

Photo. & Litho.

1965, Nov. 10 Unwmk. *Perf. 13½*

Size: 43x28mm

CO1 AP1 75np Arabian horses .50 .25

Perf. 13

Size: 53½x35mm

CO2 AP1 2r Leopard 1.25 .40
CO3 AP1 3r Camels 2.00 .60
CO4 AP1 5r Hawks 3.75 1.00
Nos. CO1-CO4 (4) 7.50 2.25

Exist imperf. Values same as perf.

OFFICIAL STAMPS

Type of Air Post Issue, 1965

Photo. & Litho.

1965, Oct. 14 Unwmk. *Perf. 13½*

Size: 43x28mm

O1 AP1 25np Grebe .20 .20
O2 AP1 40np Arabian oryx .20 .20
O3 AP1 50np Hoopoe .25 .20
O4 AP1 75np Wild ass .40 .20
O5 AP1 1r Herons in flight .75 .20
Nos. O1-O5 (5) 1.80 1.00

Exist imperf. Values same as perf.

FUNCHAL

fün-'shäl

LOCATION — A city and administrative district in the Madeira island group in the Atlantic Ocean northwest of Africa
GOVT. — A part of the Republic of Portugal
POP. — 150,574 (1900)

Postage stamps of Funchal were superseded by those of Portugal.

1000 Reis = 1 Milreis

King Carlos
A1 A2

Perf. 11½, 12½, 13½

1892-93 Typo. Unwmk.

1 A1 5r yellow 3.00 1.50
a. Diagonal half used as 2½r on entire newspaper 5.00
b. Perf. 11½ 4.00 2.75
2 A1 10r red violet 2.50 1.50
3 A1 15r chocolate 3.25 2.50
4 A1 20r lavender 3.75 2.10
a. Perf. 13½ 8.75 6.25
5a A1 25r dark green 4.75 1.00
6 A1 50r ultra 4.75 2.10
a. Perf. 13½ 8.75 5.50
7 A1 75r carmine 7.00 5.50
8 A1 80r yel green 14.00 9.50
a. Perf. 13½ 17.50 12.00
9 A1 100r brn, *yel* ('93) 9.00 4.00
a. Diagonal half used as 50r on cover 100.00
10 A1 150r car, *rose* ('93) 52.50 26.00
11 A1 200r dk bl, *bl* ('93) 60.00 37.50
12 A1 300r dk bl, *sal* ('93) 60.00 47.50
Nos. 1-12 (12) 224.50 140.70

Nos. 1-12 were printed on both enamel-surfaced and chalky papers. Values are for the most common varieties. For detailed listings, see the *Scott Classic Specialized Catalogue.*

The reprints of this issue have shiny white gum and clean-cut perforation 13½. The shades differ from those of the originals and the uncolored paper is thin.

1897-1905 *Perf. 12*

Name and Value in Black except Nos. 25 and 34

13 A2 2½r gray .50 .35
14 A2 5r orange .50 .35
15 A2 10r light green .50 .35
16 A2 15r brown 5.00 3.00
17 A2 15r gray grn ('99) 3.25 2.25
18 A2 20r gray vio 1.40 .75
19 A2 25r sea green 2.75 .75
20 A2 25r car rose ('99) 1.40 .55
a. Booklet pane of 6 —
21 A2 50r dark blue 6.00 4.00
a. Perf. 12½ 18.00 7.25
22 A2 50r ultra ('05) 1.50 .90
23 A2 65r slate blue ('98) 1.25 .90
24 A2 75r rose 1.40 .95
25 A2 75r brn & red, *yel* ('05) 4.00 1.40
26 A2 80r violet 1.40 1.10
27 A2 100r dark blue, *blue* 1.40 1.10
a. Diagonal half used as 50r on cover —
28 A2 115r org brn, *pink* ('98) 2.25 1.40
29 A2 130r gray brown, *buff* ('98) 2.25 1.40
30 A2 150r lt brn, *buff* 2.75 1.25
31 A2 180r sl, *pnksh* ('98) 2.25 1.40
32 A2 200r red vio, *pale lil* 3.00 2.10
33 A2 300r blue, *rose* 3.00 2.10
34 A2 500r blk & red, *bl* 5.00 2.40
a. Perf. 12½ 15.00 7.75
Nos. 13-34 (22) 52.75 30.75

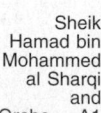

Tughra (similar tughras can be found on stamps of Turkey in Asia, Afghanistan and Saudi Arabia)

Mohammed V

Mustafa Kemal

Plane, Star and Crescent

TURKEY IN ASIA

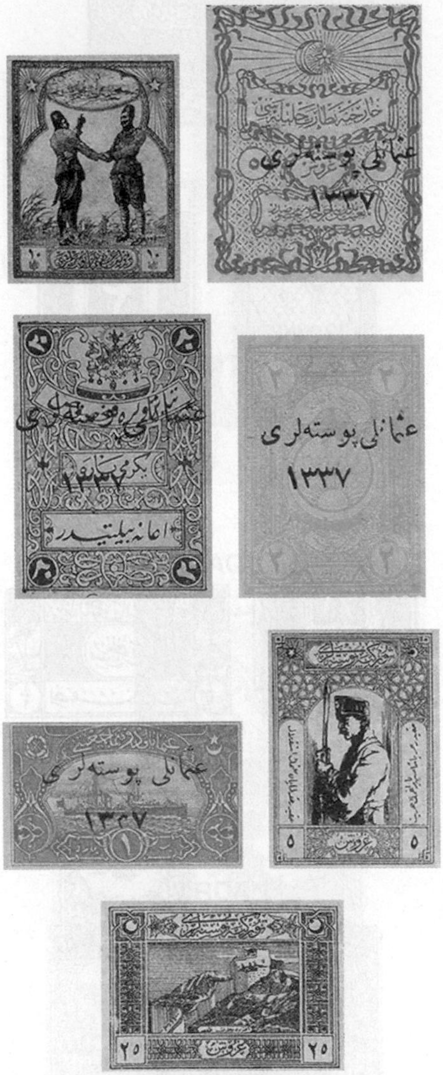

Other Turkey in Asia pictorials show star & crescent.
Other stamps show tughra shown under Turkey.

6. GREEK INSCRIPTIONS

GREECE

Country Name in various styles
(Some Crete stamps overprinted with the Greece country name are listed in Crete.)

Lepta

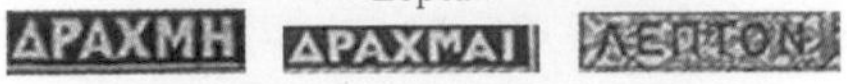

Drachma Drachmas Lepton

Abbreviated Country Name 

Other forms of Country Name

No country name

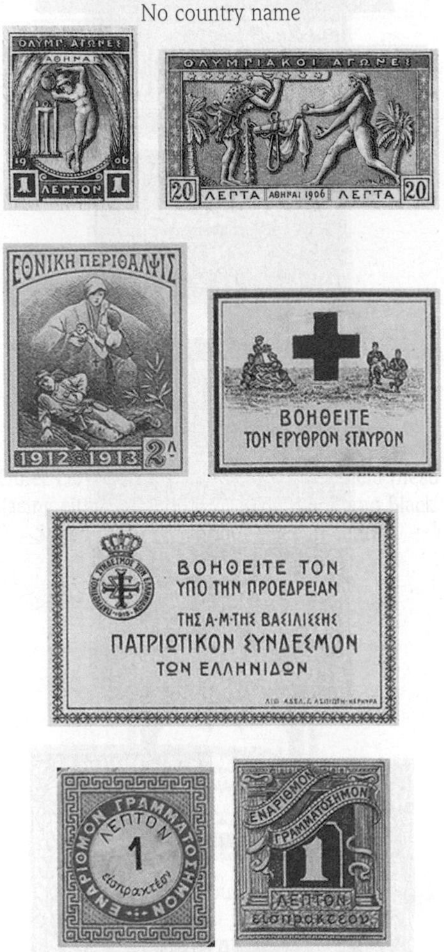

CRETE

Country Name

These words are on other stamps

Grosion

Crete stamps with a surcharge that have the year "1922" are listed under Greece.

EPIRUS **IONIAN IS.**

Country Name

7. CYRILLIC INSCRIPTIONS

RUSSIA

Postage Stamp

Imperial Eagle

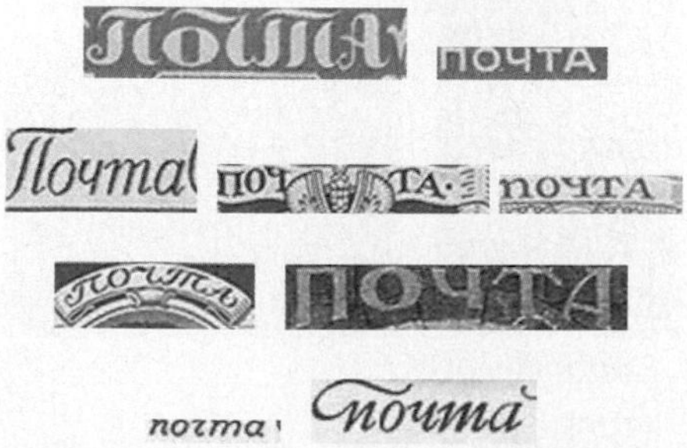

Postage in various styles

Abbreviation for Kopeck

Abbreviation for Ruble

Russian

Abbreviation for Russian Soviet Federated Socialist Republic

RSFSR stamps were overprinted (see below)

Abbreviation for Union of Soviet Socialist Republics

This item is footnoted in Latvia

RUSSIA - Army of the North

"OKCA"

RUSSIA - Wenden

RUSSIAN OFFICES IN THE TURKISH EMPIRE

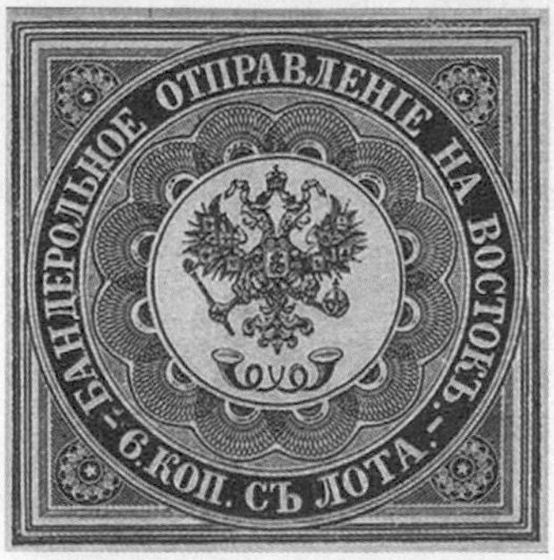

These letters appear on other stamps of the Russian offices.

The unoverprinted version of this stamp and a similar stamp were overprinted by various countries (see below).

ARMENIA

BELARUS

FAR EASTERN REPUBLIC

Country Name

SOUTH RUSSIA

Country Name

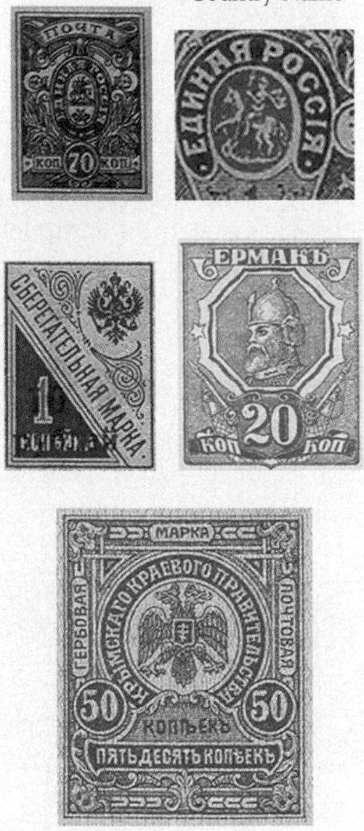

FINLAND

Circles and Dots on stamps similar to Imperial Russia issues

BATUM

Forms of Country Name

TRANSCAUCASIAN FEDERATED REPUBLICS

Abbreviation for Country Name

KAZAKHSTAN

Country Name

KYRGYZSTAN

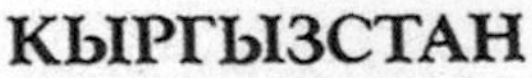

Country Name

ROMANIA

TADJIKISTAN

Country Name & Abbreviation

UKRAINE

Country Name in various forms

The trident appears on many stamps, usually as an overprint.

Abbreviation for Ukrainian Soviet Socialist Republic

WESTERN UKRAINE

Abbreviation for Country Name

AZERBAIJAN

Country Name

А.С.С.Р.

Abbreviation for Azerbaijan Soviet Socialist Republic

MONTENEGRO

ЦРНЕГОРЕ

ЦРНА ГОРА

Country Name in various forms

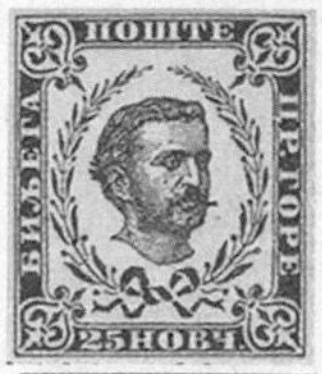

ЦР. ГОРЕ

Abbreviation for country name

No country name (A similar Montenegro stamp without country name has same vignette.)

SERBIA

СРПСКА СРБИЈА

Country Name in various forms

СРП. К. С.

Abbreviation for country name

No country name

SERBIA & MONTENEGRO

YUGOSLAVIA

ЈУГОСЛАВИЈА

Showing country name

No Country Name

MACEDONIA

МАКЕДОНИЈА

МАКЕДОНИЈА

Country Name

МАКЕДОНСКИ

Different form of Country Name

BOSNIA & HERZEGOVINA (Serb Administration)

РЕПУБЛИКА СРПСКА

Country Name

РЕПУБЛИКЕ СРПСКЕ

Different form of Country Name

No Country Name

BULGARIA

Country Name Postage

Stotinka

Stotinki (plural) Abbreviation for Stotinki

Country Name in various forms and styles

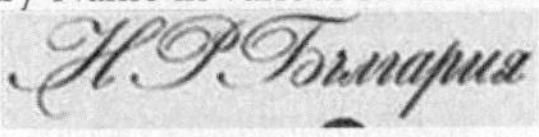

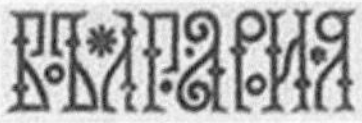

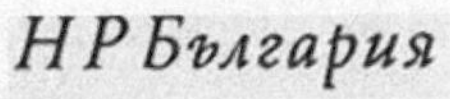

No country name

Abbreviation for Lev, leva

MONGOLIA

Country name in one word Tugrik in Cyrillic

Country name in two words Mung in Cyrillic

Mung in Mongolian

Tugrik in Mongolian

Arms

No Country Name

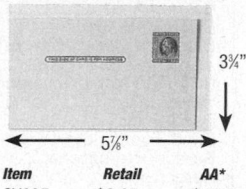

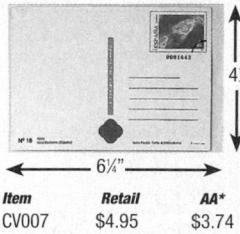

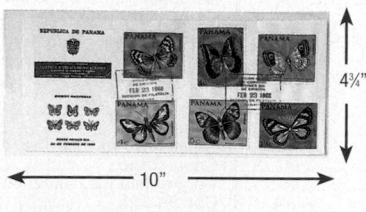

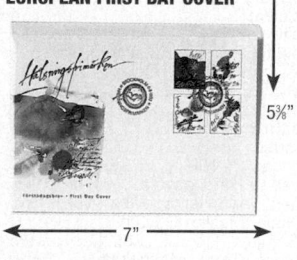

INDEX AND IDENTIFIER

All page numbers shown are those in this Volume 2.

Postage stamps that do not have English words on them are shown in the Identifier which begins on page 1400.

INDEX TO ADVERTISERS
2010 VOLUME 2

2010
VOLUME 2
DEALER DIRECTORY
YELLOW PAGE LISTINGS

This section of your Scott Catalogue contains advertisements to help you conveniently find what you need, when you need it...!

Accessories

BROOKLYN GALLERY COIN & STAMP, INC.
8725 4th Ave.
Brooklyn, NY 11209
PH: 718-745-5701
FAX: 718-745-2775
info@brooklyngallery.com
www.brooklyngallery.com

Aerophilately

HENRY GITNER PHILATELISTS, INC.
PO Box 3077-S
Middletown, NY 10940
PH: 845-343-5151
PH: 800-947-8267
FAX: 845-343-0068
hgitner@hgitner.com
www.hgitner.com

Appraisals

HERITAGE AUCTION GALLERIES
3500 Maple Ave, 17th Floor
Dallas, TX 75219
PH: 800-872-6467
FAX: 214-409-1425
Stamps@HA.com
HA.com

PHILIP WEISS AUCTIONS
1 Neil Ct.
Oceanside, NY 11572
PH: 516-594-0731
FAX: 516-594-9414

Asia

MICHAEL ROGERS, INC.
415 S. Orlando Ave.
Winter Park, FL 32789-3683
PH: 407-644-2290
PH: 800-843-3751
FAX: 407-645-4434
Stamps@michaelrogersinc.com
www.michaelrogersinc.com

THE STAMP ACT
PO Box 1136
Belmont, CA 94002
PH: 650-703-2342
PH: 650-592-3315
FAX: 650-508-8104
thestampact@sbcglobal.net
www.thestampact.com

Auctions

DANIEL F. KELLEHER CO., INC.
20 Walnut St.
Suite 213
Wellesley, MA 02481
PH: 781-235-0990
FAX: 781-235-0945

JACQUES C. SCHIFF, JR., INC.
195 Main St.
Ridgefield Park, NJ 07660
PH: 201-641-5566
FAX: 201-641-5705

Auctions

MICHAEL ROGERS, INC.
415 S. Orlando Ave.
Winter Park, FL 32789-3683
PH: 407-644-2290
PH: 800-843-3751
FAX: 407-645-4434
Stamps@michaelrogersinc.com
www.michaelrogersinc.com

PHILIP WEISS AUCTIONS
1 Neil Ct.
Oceanside, NY 11572
PH: 516-594-0731
FAX: 516-594-9414

R. MARESCH & SON LTD.
5th Floor - 6075 Yonge St.
Toronto, ON M2M 3W2
CANADA
PH: 416-363-7777
FAX: 416-363-6511
www.maresch.com

THE STAMP CENTER DUTCH COUNTRY AUCTIONS
4115 Concord Pike
Wilmington, DE 19803
PH: 302-478-8740
FAX: 302-478-8779
auctions@thestampcenter.com
www.thestampcenter.com

Auctions - Public

ALAN BLAIR STAMPS/ AUCTIONS
5405 Lakeside Ave.
Suite 1
Richmond, VA 23228
PH: 800-689-5602
FAX: 804-262-9307
alanblair@verizon.net
www.alanblairstamps.com

HERITAGE AUCTION GALLERIES
3500 Maple Ave, 17th Floor
Dallas, TX 75219
PH: 800-872-6467
FAX: 214-409-1425
Stamps@HA.com
HA.com

British Commonwealth

ARON R. HALBERSTAM PHILATELISTS, LTD.
PO Box 150168
Van Brunt Station
Brooklyn, NY 11215-0168
PH: 718-788-3978
FAX: 718-965-3099
arh@arhstamps.com
www.arhstamps.com

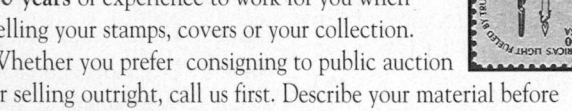

Auctions

British Commonwealth

Cameroons (Brit. & Ger.)

COLONIAL STAMP COMPANY
5757 Wilshire Blvd. PH #8
Los Angeles, CA 90036
PH: 323-933-9435
FAX: 323-939-9930
Toll Free in North America
PH: 877-272-6693
FAX: 877-272-6694
info@colonialstampcompany.com
www.colonialstampcompany.com

Canada

COLONIAL STAMP COMPANY
5757 Wilshire Blvd. PH #8
Los Angeles, CA 90036
PH: 323-933-9435
FAX: 323-939-9930
Toll Free in North America
PH: 877-272-6693
FAX: 877-272-6694
info@colonialstampcompany.com
www.colonialstampcompany.com

Cape of Good Hope

COLONIAL STAMP COMPANY
5757 Wilshire Blvd. PH #8
Los Angeles, CA 90036
PH: 323-933-9435
FAX: 323-939-9930
Toll Free in North America
PH: 877-272-6693
FAX: 877-272-6694
info@colonialstampcompany.com
www.colonialstampcompany.com

Caroline Islands (Ger.)

COLONIAL STAMP COMPANY
5757 Wilshire Blvd. PH #8
Los Angeles, CA 90036
PH: 323-933-9435
FAX: 323-939-9930
Toll Free in North America
PH: 877-272-6693
FAX: 877-272-6694
info@colonialstampcompany.com
www.colonialstampcompany.com

Cayman Islands

COLONIAL STAMP COMPANY
5757 Wilshire Blvd. PH #8
Los Angeles, CA 90036
PH: 323-933-9435
FAX: 323-939-9930
Toll Free in North America
PH: 877-272-6693
FAX: 877-272-6694
info@colonialstampcompany.com
www.colonialstampcompany.com

Central America

GUY SHAW
PO Box 27138
San Diego, CA 92198
PH/FAX: 858-485-8269
guyshaw@guyshaw.com
www.guyshaw.com

China

MICHAEL ROGERS, INC.
415 S. Orlando Ave.
Winter Park, FL 32789-3683
PH: 407-644-2290
PH: 800-843-3751
FAX: 407-645-4434
Stamps@michaelrogersinc.com
www.michaelrogersinc.com

THE STAMP ACT
PO Box 1136
Belmont, CA 94002
PH: 650-703-2342
PH: 650-592-3315
FAX: 650-508-8104
thestampact@sbcglobal.net
www.thestampact.com

TILL NEUMANN CLASSIC PHILATELY
PO Box 10 29 40
28029 Bremen, GERMANY
PH: +49.421.79 40 260
FAX: +49.421.79 40 261
tn@klassische-philatelie.de
www.klassische-philatelie.de

British Commonwealth

Chi PRC

MR. GUANLUN HONG
Jade Crown International Stamp Company
PO Box 118
Blaine, WA 98231 USA
PH: 1-604-288-8815
PH: 1-888-482-6586
FAX: 1-604-288-8815
guanlun@hotmail.com
guanlun@shaw.ca
haitaohong@hotmail.com

THE STAMP ACT
PO Box 1136
Belmont, CA 94002
PH: 650-703-2342
PH: 650-592-3315
FAX: 650-508-8104
thestampact@sbcglobal.net
www.thestampact.com

Cyprus

COLONIAL STAMP COMPANY
5757 Wilshire Blvd. PH #8
Los Angeles, CA 90036
PH: 323-933-9435
FAX: 323-939-9930
Toll Free in North America
PH: 877-272-6693
FAX: 877-272-6694
info@colonialstampcompany.com
www.colonialstampcompany.com

Ducks

MICHAEL JAFFE
PO Box 61484
Vancouver, WA 98666
PH: 360-695-6161
PH: 800-782-6770
FAX: 360-695-1616
mjaffe@brookmanstamps.com
www.brookmanstamps.com

Egypt

KAMAL SHALABY
3, Aly Basha Fahmy St.
8th Floor, Gleem
Alexandria, EGYPT
PH/FAX: +203-5840254
Cell: +2-0105838213
alexstamplover@yahoo.com
www.stampsofegypt.com

Falkland Islands

ARON R. HALBERSTAM PHILATELISTS, LTD.
PO Box 150168
Van Brunt Station
Brooklyn, NY 11215-0168
PH: 718-788-3978
FAX: 718-965-3099
arh@arhstamps.com
www.arhstamps.com

COLONIAL STAMP COMPANY
5757 Wilshire Blvd. PH #8
Los Angeles, CA 90036
PH: 323-933-9435
FAX: 323-939-9930
Toll Free in North America
PH: 877-272-6693
FAX: 877-272-6694
info@colonialstampcompany.com
www.colonialstampcompany.com

Fiji

WWW.WORLDSTAMPS.COM
242 W. Saddle River Rd.
Suite C
Upper Saddle River, NJ 07458
PH: 201-236-8122
FAX: 201-236-8133
by mail:
Frank Geiger Philatelists
info@WorldStamps.com
www.WorldStamps.com

France & Colonies

E. JOSEPH MCCONNELL
PO Box 683
Monroe, NY 10949
PH: 845-783-9791
FAX: 845-782-0347
ejstamps@gmail.com
www.EJMcConnell.com

TILL NEUMANN CLASSIC PHILATELY
PO Box 10 29 40
28029 Bremen, GERMANY
PH: +49.421.79 40 260
FAX: +49.421.79 40 261
tn@klassische-philatelie.de
www.klassische-philatelie.de

WULFF'S STAMPS
PO Box 661746
Sacramento, CA 95866
PH/FAX: 800-884-0656
PH/FAX: 916-489-0656
service@wulffstamps.com
www.wulffstamps.com

French S. Antarcti

E. JOSEPH MCCONNELL
PO Box 683
Monroe, NY 10949
PH: 845-783-9791
FAX: 845-782-0347
ejstamps@gmail.com
www.EJMcConnell.com

German Colonies

COLONIAL STAMP COMPANY
5757 Wilshire Blvd. PH #8
Los Angeles, CA 90036
PH: 323-933-9435
FAX: 323-939-9930
Toll Free in North America
PH: 877-272-6693
FAX: 877-272-6694
info@colonialstampcompany.com
www.colonialstampcompany.com

Great Britain-Pricelis

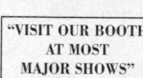

COLONIAL STAMP COMPANY
5757 Wilshire Blvd. PH #8
Los Angeles, CA 90036
PH: 323-933-9435
FAX: 323-939-9930
Toll Free in North America
PH: 877-272-6693
FAX: 877-272-6694
info@colonialstampcompany.com
www.colonialstampcompany.com

Japan

MICHAEL ROGERS, INC.
415 S. Orlando Ave.
Winter Park, FL 32789-3683
PH: 407-644-2290
PH: 800-843-3751
FAX: 407-645-4434
Stamps@michaelrogersinc.com
www.michaelrogersinc.com

Korea

MICHAEL ROGERS, INC.
415 S. Orlando Ave.
Winter Park, FL 32789-3683
PH: 407-644-2290
PH: 800-843-3751
FAX: 407-645-4434
Stamps@michaelrogersinc.com
www.michaelrogersinc.com

Latin America

GUY SHAW
PO Box 27138
San Diego, CA 92198
PH/FAX: 858-485-8269
guyshaw@guyshaw.com
www.guyshaw.com

Manchukuo

MICHAEL ROGERS, INC.
415 S. Orlando Ave.
Winter Park, FL 32789-3683
PH: 407-644-2290
PH: 800-843-3751
FAX: 407-645-4434
Stamps@michaelrogersinc.com
www.michaelrogersinc.com

Middle East-Arab

MICHAEL ROGERS, INC.
415 S. Orlando Ave.
Winter Park, FL 32789-3683
PH: 407-644-2290
PH: 800-843-3751
FAX: 407-645-4434
Stamps@michaelrogersinc.com
www.michaelrogersinc.com

New Issues

DAVIDSON'S STAMP SERVICE
PO Box 36355
Indianapolis, IN 46236-0355
PH: 317-826-2620
ed-davidson@earthlink.net
www.newstampissues.com

WWW.WORLDSTAMPS.COM
242 W. Saddle River Rd.
Suite C
Upper Saddle River, NJ 07458
PH: 201-236-8122
FAX: 201-236-8133
by mail:
Frank Geiger Philatelists
info@WorldStamps.com
www.WorldStamps.com

New Issues - Retail

BOMBAY PHILATELIC INC.
PO Box 90937
Raleigh, NC 27675
PH: 561-499-7990
FAX: 561-499-7553
sales@bombaystamps.com
www.bombaystamps.com

Postal History

TILL NEUMANN CLASSIC PHILATELY
PO Box 10 29 40
28029 Bremen, GERMANY
PH: +49.421.79 40 260
FAX: +49.421.79 40 261
tn@klassische-philatelie.de
www.klassische-philatelie.de

Proofs & Essays

HENRY GITNER PHILATELISTS, INC.
PO Box 3077-S
Middletown, NY 10940
PH: 845-343-5151
PH: 800-947-8267
FAX: 845-343-0068
hgitner@hgitner.com
www.hgitner.com

South America

GUY SHAW
PO Box 27138
San Diego, CA 92198
PH/FAX: 858-485-8269
guyshaw@guyshaw.com
www.guyshaw.com

STAMP STORES

California

BROSIUS STAMP, COIN & SUPPLIES
2105 Main St.
Santa Monica, CA 90405
PH: 310-396-7480
FAX: 310-396-7455

COLONIAL STAMP CO./ BRITISH EMPIRE SPECIALIST
5757 Wilshire Blvd. PH #8
(by appt.)
Los Angeles, CA 90036
PH: 323-933-9435
FAX: 323-939-9930
Toll Free in North America
PH: 877-272-6693
FAX: 877-272-6694
info@colonialstampcompany.com
www.colonialstampcompany.com

FISCHER-WOLK PHILATELICS
22762 Aspan St.
Suite 211
Lake Forest, CA 92630
PH: 949-837-2932
fw@occoxmail.com

NATICK STAMPS & HOBBIES
411 E. Huntington Dr.
Suite 209
Arcadia, CA 91006
PH: 626-445-2185
natickco@att.net

Colorado

SHOWCASE STAMPS
3865 Wadsworth
Wheat Ridge, CO 80033
PH: 303-425-9252
kbeiner@colbi.net
www.showcasestamps.com

Connecticut

SILVER CITY COIN & STAMP
41 Colony St.
Meriden, CT 06451
PH: 203-235-7634
FAX: 203-237-4915

Georgia

STAMPS UNLIMITED OF GEORGIA, INC.
100 Peachtree St.
Suite 1460
Atlanta, GA 30303
PH: 404-688-9161
tonyroozen@yahoo.com

Illinois

DR. ROBERT FRIEDMAN & SONS
2029 W. 75th St.
Woodridge, IL 60517
PH: 800-588-8100
FAX: 630-985-1588
drbobstamps@yahoo.com
www.drbobfriedmanstamps.com

SIDMORE STAMPS
145 E. Lincoln Hwy.
DeKalb, IL 60115
PH: 815-787-7000
sidmorestamps@verizon.net
www.sidmorestamps.net
Authorized APS Dealer

Indiana

KNIGHT STAMP & COIN CO.
237 Main St.
Hobart, IN 46342
PH: 219-942-4341
PH: 800-634-2646
knight@knightcoin.com
www.knightcoin.com

Massachusetts

KAPPY'S COINS & STAMPS
534 Washington St.
Norwood, MA 02062
PH: 781-762-5552
kappyscoins@aol.com

New Jersey

BERGEN STAMPS & COLLECTIBLES
306 Queen Anne Rd.
Teaneck, NJ 07666
PH: 201-836-8987

New Issues

Stamp Shows

STAMP STORES

New Jersey

PHILLY STAMP & COIN CO., INC.
683 Haddon Ave.
Collingswood, NJ 08108
PH: 856-854-5333
FAX: 856-854-5377
phillysc@verizon.net
www.phillystampandcoin.com

TRENTON STAMP & COIN CO.
Thomas DeLuca
Store: Forest Glen Plaza
1804 Route 33
Hamilton Square, NJ 08690
Mail: PO Box 8574
Trenton, NJ 08650
PH: 800-446-8664
PH: 609-584-8100
FAX: 609-587-8664
TOMD4TSC@aol.com

New York

CHAMPION STAMP CO., INC.
432 W. 54th St.
New York, NY 10019
PH: 212-489-8130
FAX: 212-581-8130
championstamp@aol.com
www.championstamp.com

Ohio

HILLTOP STAMP SERVICE
Richard A. Peterson
PO Box 626
Wooster, OH 44691
PH: 330-262-8907
PH: 330-262-5378
hilltop@bright.net

THE LINK STAMP CO.
3461 E. Livingston Ave.
Columbus, OH 43227
PH/FAX: 614-237-4125
PH/FAX: 800-546-5726

Texas

HERITAGE AUCTION GALLERIES
3500 Maple Ave, 17th Floor
Dallas, TX 75219
PH: 800-872-6467
FAX: 214-409-1425
Stamps@HA.com
HA.com

Virginia

KENNEDY'S STAMPS & COINS, INC.
7059 Brookfield Plaza
Springfield, VA 22150
PH: 703-569-7300
FAX: 703-569-7644
j.w.kennedy@verizon.net

LATHEROW & CO., INC.
5054 Lee Hwy.
Arlington, VA 22207
PH: 703-538-2727
PH: 800-647-4624
FAX: 703-538-5210
latherow@filatco.com

Topicals

E. JOSEPH MCCONNELL
PO Box 683
Monroe, NY 10949
PH: 845-783-9791
FAX: 845-782-0347
ejstamps@gmail.com
www.EJMcConnell.com

Topicals-Columbus

MR. COLUMBUS
PO Box 1492
Fennville, MI 49408
PH: 269-543-4755
columbus@accn.org

Topicals-Miscellaneous

HENRY GITNER PHILATELISTS, INC.
PO Box 3077-S
Middletown, NY 10940
PH: 845-343-5151
PH: 800-947-8267
FAX: 845-343-0068
hgitner@hgitner.com
www.hgitner.com

United States

ACS STAMP COMPANY
10831 Chambers Way
Commerce City, CO 80022
PH: 303-841-8666
ACS@ACSStamp.com
www.acsstamp.com

BROOKMAN STAMP CO.
PO Box 90
Vancouver, WA 98666
PH: 360-695-1391
PH: 800-545-4871
FAX: 360-695-1616
larry@brookmanstamps.com
www.brookmanstamps.com

U.S.-Collections Wanted

DR. ROBERT FRIEDMAN & SONS
2029 W. 75th St.
Woodridge, IL 60517
PH: 800-588-8100
FAX: 630-985-1588
drbobstamps@yahoo.com
www.drbobfriedmanstamps.com

U.S.-Rare Stamps

HERITAGE AUCTION GALLERIES
3500 Maple Ave, 17th Floor
Dallas, TX 75219
PH: 800-872-6467
FAX: 214-409-1425
Stamps@HA.com
HA.com

Want Lists

CHARLES P. SCHWARTZ
PO Box 165
Mora, MN 55051
PH: 320-679-4705
charlesp@ecenet.com

Want Lists-British Empire 1840-1935 German Cols./Offices

COLONIAL STAMP COMPANY
5757 Wilshire Blvd. PH #8
Los Angeles, CA 90036
PH: 323-933-9435
FAX: 323-939-9930
Toll Free in North America
PH: 877-272-6693
FAX: 877-272-6694
info@colonialstampcompany.com
www.colonialstampcompany.com

Wanted-Estates

HERITAGE AUCTION GALLERIES
3500 Maple Ave, 17th Floor
Dallas, TX 75219
PH: 800-872-6467
FAX: 214-409-1425
Stamps@HA.com
HA.com

Wanted to Buy

HERITAGE AUCTION GALLERIES
3500 Maple Ave, 17th Floor
Dallas, TX 75219
PH: 800-872-6467
FAX: 214-409-1425
Stamps@HA.com
HA.com

Wanted-U.S.

HERITAGE AUCTION GALLERIES
3500 Maple Ave, 17th Floor
Dallas, TX 75219
PH: 800-872-6467
FAX: 214-409-1425
Stamps@HA.com
HA.com

Wanted-U.S. Collections

BROOKMAN STAMP CO.
PO Box 90
Vancouver, WA 98666
PH: 360-695-1391
PH: 800-545-4871
FAX: 360-695-1616
larry@brookmanstamps.com
www.brookmanstamps.com

Wanted-Worldwide Collections

DR. ROBERT FRIEDMAN & SONS
2029 W. 75th St.
Woodridge, IL 60517
PH: 800-588-8100
FAX: 630-985-1588
drbobstamps@yahoo.com
www.drbobfriedmanstamps.com

THE STAMP CENTER DUTCH COUNTRY AUCTIONS
4115 Concord Pike
Wilmington, DE 19803
PH: 302-478-8740
FAX: 302-478-8779
auctions@thestampcenter.com
www.thestampcenter.com

Websites

ACS STAMP COMPANY
10831 Chambers Way
Commerce City, CO 80022
PH: 303-841-8666
ACS@ACSStamp.com
www.acsstamp.com

HERITAGE AUCTION GALLERIES
3500 Maple Ave, 17th Floor
Dallas, TX 75219
PH: 800-872-6467
FAX: 214-409-1425
Stamps@HA.com
HA.com

Wholesale

HENRY GITNER PHILATELISTS, INC.
PO Box 3077-S
Middletown, NY 10940
PH: 845-343-5151
PH: 800-947-8267
FAX: 845-343-0068
hgitner@hgitner.com
www.hgitner.com

Worldwide Stamps

WWW.WORLDSTAMPS.COM
242 W. Saddle River Rd.
Suite C
Upper Saddle River, NJ 07458
PH: 201-236-8122
FAX: 201-236-8133
by mail:
Frank Geiger Philatelists
info@WorldStamps.com
www.WorldStamps.com

Worldwide